Children's Books in Print

1991-1992

Subject Guide

A Subject Index to Children's Books

This edition of SUBJECT GUIDE TO CHILDREN'S
BOOKS IN PRINT
is prepared by R. R. Bowker's
Database Publishing Group in collaboration
with the Publication Systems Department.

Staff of the Database Publishing Group includes:
Peter Simon, Vice President, Database Publishing Group;
Brenda A. McElroy, Senior Managing Editor;
Michael Olenick, Managing Editor;
Angela Barrett, Barbara Holton, Associate Editors;
Marilyn Fay, Kate Magrath, Joseph V. Tondi,
Ann Zimmer, Assistant Editors.

Max Kobrinsky, Data Processing Operations Manager;
Jack Murphy, Operations Supervisor.

Children's Books in Print

1991-1992

Subject Guide

A Subject Index to Children's Books

R. R. BOWKER
New Providence, New Jersey

Published by R. R. Bowker, Division of Reed Publishing USA
121 Chanlon Road, New Providence, NJ 07974.
Copyright © 1991 by Reed Publishing USA, Inc.
All rights reserved.

International Standard Book Number 0-8352-3047-3
International Standard Serial Number 0000-0167
Library of Congress Catalog Number 70-101705
Printed and bound in the United States of America

ISBN 0-8352-3047-3

9 780835 230476

FOREWORD

STARTING FROM THE SUBJECT

Patrons in bookstores and libraries serving children often begin their requests by referring to the subject of the book they seek rather than its title or author, optimistic that the staff can supply from the subject clue the finding or ordering essentials. But knowledgeable staff with a children's book specialty have always been in far shorter supply than the demand, and such requests have produced more quandaries than complete patron satisfaction. Booksellers could rely only on highly trained memories and selfmade lists; librarians could turn only to what was listed in their catalogs, part of their own selective collections. *Subject Guide to Children's Books in Print* is now the starting point for answers to such stumping requests as, "How many books are there on bionics for kids?" or "Can I get a children's book on the care and training of elephants?"

Subject Guide to Children's Books in Print is a cross-referenced subject arrangement of the 73,051 children's books listed in the 1991-1992 edition of its companion volume, the author, title, illustrator index *Children's Books in Print*. Both of these bibliographies are scheduled for annual correction, expansion and general revision and both are part of R. R. Bowker's continuing effort to expand its essential *In Print* services, *Books in Print* and *Subject Guide to Books in Print*.

Children's Books in Print and its separate *Subject Guide* are the result of planning that began in the Spring of 1965, when The Children's Book Council, Inc., through its joint committee with the American Library Association, formally proposed that R. R. Bowker undertake to publish a subject guide to the available children's books. R. R. Bowker promised to publish this bibliography as soon as data could be collected that would allow us to produce as nearly a complete *In Print* bibliography as possible. At that time, Bowker was in the first stages of planning the transfer to computer storage of all of its bibliographic data, so it was 1969 before the first step in fulfilling the promise was achieved. The first step was the first edition of *Children's Books in Print* because, logically, its *Subject Guide* could not be produced until we had obtained the necessary information on as many of the available children's books as possible for subject classification.

Subject Guide to Children's Books in Print is compiled by Bowker's Database Publishing Group based upon information supplied by the juvenile book publishers. Our subject headings are those normally employed for library catalogs, drawn from the fourteenth edition of *Sears List of Subject Headings* and the thirteenth edition of *Library of Congress Subject Headings*. Because fiction and picture books make up a major part of the books published for children, their main subject headings presented a major problem. It was finally decided that formal library subject headings, as many as reasonable for each title, would be employed, rather than attempt full thematic groupings of books.

Subject Guide to Children's Books in Print is designed as an aid, not a replacement, for the children's book specialists who can read any number of thematic overtones into the fiction and picture books published for children. It is intended as the bibliography from which to start, but only knowledgeable, well-read personnel can follow through on the sensitive, always challenging, task of finding the right books at the right time for the children who want them.

Lillian N. Gerhardt
Editor-in-Chief
SCHOOL LIBRARY JOURNAL

How to Use
SUBJECT GUIDE
TO CHILDREN'S
BOOKS IN PRINT

This twenty-second edition of *Subject Guide to Children's Books in Print* was produced from records stored on magnetic tape, edited by computer programs, and set in type by computer-controlled photo-composition. This volume includes the titles listed in *Children's Books in Print*. In *Subject Guide* some 60,975 titles appear 63,792 times under 6,630 subject categories. These titles are available from 4,528 United States publishers and distributors. A Key to Publishers' and Distributors' Abbreviations appears at the end of the book.

NEW FEATURE: PUBLISHER PROVIDED ANNOTATIONS

Appearing for the first time this year are annotated entries, using information provided by participating publishers. This feature allows publishers to purchase space to highlight and describe their titles, and provides the reader with extra book information which he or she will find valuable for reference and acquisition decisions. If you wish to participate in this program, please contact Bowker at 908-464-6800.

HOW THE SUBJECT HEADINGS WERE ASSIGNED

Subject Guide to Children's Books in Print 1991-1992 is based primarily on the fourteenth edition of *Sears List of Subject Headings*. When appropriate subject headings were unavailable in the Sears List, subject headings were chosen from the thirteenth edition of *Library of Congress Subject Headings*. The Sears listing does not include headings for persons and places. These headings were derived from the official LC cataloging information, where available, or from official bibliographic tools. Many headings were consolidated where they seemed too cumbersome for the needs of this *Subject Guide*. Wherever cataloging information was unavailable headings were assigned from the Sears or LC listings by a trained cataloger. Some books have been assigned to a single category, while other books have been assigned two, three or more headings.

ALPHABETICAL ARRANGEMENT OF SUBJECT CATEGORIES

Headings are filed alphabetically with the following conditions and variations. First, punctuation is not considered:

ART, ANCIENT
ART—FICTION
ART, GREEK

Second, proper nouns precede improper nouns and names of people precede geographical names:

CLAY, HENRY
CLAY, MISSOURI
CLAY

Third, when personal names appear as headings, those without surnames appear first and religious titles precede royal titles:

JOHN, POPE
JOHN, ST.
JOHN 2ND, KING OF ENGLAND
JOHN, ROBERT

ALPHABETICAL ARRANGEMENT OF TITLES WITHIN THE SUBJECT CATEGORIES

Under each subject heading entries are filed *alphabetically by word*, with the following exceptions:

Initial articles of titles in English, French, German, Italian and Spanish are deleted from both author and title entries.

M', Mc and *Mac* are filed as if they were written *Mac* and are interfiled with other names beginning with *Mac;* for example, Macan, McAnally, Macardle, McAree, McArthur, Macarthur, Macartney, M'Aulay, Macaulay, McAuley. Within a specific name grouping *Mc* and *Mac* are interfiled according to the given name of the author; for example, Macdonald, Agnes; MacDonald, Alexander; McDonald, Annie L.; MacDonald, Austin F.; MacDonald, Betty. Compound names are listed under the first part of the name, and cross-references appear under the last part of the name.

Entries beginning with initial letters (whether authors' given names, or titles) are filed first, e.g., Smith, H.C., comes before Smith, Harold A.; B is for Betsy comes before Baba, Babar, etc.

Numerals, including year dates, are written out in most cases and are filed alphabetically.

U.S., UN, Dr., Mr., and St. are filed as though they were spelled out.

SPECIAL NOTE
ON HOW TO FIND AN
AUTHOR'S COMPLETE LISTING

When sorting author listings by computer it is not possible to group the entire listing for an individual together under one heading unless a standard spelling and format for each name is used. The information in *Subject Guide to Children's Books in Print 1991-1992* comes from data received from the publishers. If a name appears in various forms in this data, the listings in the index may be divided into several groups.

INFORMATION INCLUDED IN ENTRIES

Entries include the following bibliographic information, when available: author, co-author, editor, co-editor, translator, co-translator, illustrator, co-illustrator, photographer, co-photographer, title, number of volumes, edition, Library of Congress number, series information, language if other than English, whether or not illustrated, grade range, year of publication, type of binding if other than cloth over boards, price, International Standard Book Number, publisher's order number, imprint and publisher abbreviation. When an entry includes the prices for both hardcover and paperback editions, the publication date within the entry refers to the hardcover binding; however, when the paperback binding is the only one included in the entry, the publication date is the paperback publication date. (Information on the International Standard Book Numbering System is available from R. R. Bowker.)

The prices cited are those provided by the publisher and generally refer to either the trade edition or the Publisher's Library Bound edition (PLB). The abbreviation PLB is used whenever the price cited is for a publisher's library bound edition.

Since some trade editions are bound to the same standards as some library editions, the symbol "g" is used *after* a price to indicate that the edition is guaranteed by the publisher to give satisfaction in normal library use.

If the price is merely tentatively suggested, a lower case "t" follows the anticipated price, e.g., 3.87t; "x" indicates a short discount—20%, or less. Short discount (20% or less) information is generally supplied by publishers to Bowker for each publication. However, all publishers do not uniformly supply this information, and Bowker can only make its best efforts to transmit this information when it is provided. PLB indicates a publishers' library binding.

The symbol "a" after a price indicates that a library binding is available at a special price.

An "i" following the price indicates an invoice price. Specific policies for such titles should be obtained from individual publishers.

KEY TO PUBLISHERS' AND DISTRIBUTORS' ABBREVIATIONS

Publishers' and distributors' names are abbreviated in the listings of *Subject Guide to Children's Books in Print*. A key to these abbreviations will be found in *Key to Publishers' & Distributors' Abbreviations* at the end of this volume. Entries in this "Key" are arranged alphabetically by the abbreviations used in the bibliographic entries. The full name, ISBN prefix, editorial address, telephone number, ordering address (if different from the editorial address), and imprints follow the abbreviation. SAN (Standard Address Number) is a unique identification code for each address of each organization in or served by the book industry.

For example:

Bowker, (Bowker, R. R., 0-8352), Div. of Reed Publishing U.S.A., 121 Chanlon Rd., New Providence, NJ 07974 (SAN 214-1191). Tel 908-464-6800; Toll free: 800-521-8110, 800-537-8416 (in Canada).

If an entry contains a "Pub. by" note after the price the title should be ordered from the distributor whose abbreviation appears at the end of the entry. Entries which include the note "Dist. by" should also be ordered from the distributor, not the publisher.

The information in this bibliography has been obtained from publishers' catalogs and from other information submitted by publishers for *Books in Print 1991-92*.

LIST OF ABBREVIATIONS

a	after price, specially priced library edition available	k	kindergarten audience level
abr.	abridged	l.p.	long playing
adpt.	adapted	ltd. ed.	limited edition
Amer.	American	lab.	laboratory
annot.	annotation(s), annotated	lang(s).	language(s)
ans.	answer(s)	LAT	Latin
app.	appendix	lea.	leather
approx.	approximately	lib.	library
assn.	association	lit.	literature, literary
auth.	author	math.	mathematics
bd.	bound	mod.	modern
bdg.	binding	mor.	morocco
bds.	boards	MS, MSS	manuscript, manuscripts
bibl(s).	bibliography(ies)	natl.	national
bk(s).	book, books	no., nos.	number, numbers
bklet(s)	booklets	o.p.	out of print
Bro.	Brother	orig.	original text, not a reprint
coll.	college	o.s.i.	out of stock indefinitely
comm.	commission, committee	pap.	paper
co.	company	photos	photographs, photographer
cond.	condensed	PLB	publisher's library binding
comp(s).	compiler(s)	POL	Polish
corp.	corporation	pop. ed.	popular edition
dept.	department	POR	Portuguese
diag(s).	diagram(s)	prep.	preparation
dir.	director	probs.	problems
disk	software disk or diskette	prog. bk.	programmed book
dist.	distributed	ps	preschool audience level
Div.	Division	pseud.	pseudonym
doz.	dozen	pt(s).	part, parts
ea.	each	pub.	published, publisher, publishing
ed.	editor, edited, edition	pubn.	publication
eds.	editions, editors	ref(s).	reference(s)
educ.	education	repr.	reprint
elem.	elementary	reprod(s).	reproduction(s)
ency.	encyclopedia	rev.	revised
ENG	English	rpm.	revolution per minute (phono records)
enl.	enlarged	RUS	Russian
exp.	expurgated	SAN	Standard Address Number
fac.	facsimile	S&L	Signed and Limited
fasc.	fascicule	s.p.	school price
fict.	fiction	scp	single copy Direct to the **Consumer Price**
fig(s).	figure(s)	sec.	section
for.	foreign	sel.	selected
FRE	French	ser.	series
frwd.	foreword	Soc.	Society
g	after price, guaranteed juvenile binding	sols.	solutions
gen.	general	SPA	Spanish
GER	German	Sr. (after given name)	Senior
GRE	Greek	Sr. (before given name)	Sister
gr.	grade, grades	St.	Saint
hdbk.	handbook	subs.	subsidiary
HEB	Hebrew	subsc.	subscription
i	invoice price—see publisher for specific pricing policies	suppl.	supplement
ISBN	International Standard Book Number	t	after price, tentative price
i.t.a.	initial teaching alphabet	tech.	technical
Illus.	illustrated, illustration(s), illustrator(s)	text ed.	text edition
in prep.	in preparation	tr.	translator, translated, translation
incl.	includes, including	univ.	university
inst.	institute	vol(s).	volume, volumes
intro.	introduction	wkbk.	workbook
ITA	Italian	x	after price, short discount (20% or less)
Jr.	Junior	YA	young adult audience level
jt. auth.	joint author	yrbk.	yearbook
jt. ed.	joint editor		

INTERNATIONAL STANDARD
BOOK NUMBER

The 1991-1992 SUBJECT GUIDE TO CHILDREN'S BOOKS IN PRINT lists each title or edition of a title in the book indexes with an ISBN. All publishers were notified and requested to submit a valid ISBN for their titles.

During the past decade, the majority of the publishers complied with requirements of the standard and implemented the ISBN. At present, approximately 97% of all new titles and all new editions are submitted for listing with a valid ISBN.

To fulfill the responsibility of accomplishing total book numbering, the ISBN Agency allocated the ISBN prefixes 0-317, 0-318, 0-685 and 0-686 to number their titles in the BOOKS IN PRINT database without an ISBN. Titles not having an ISBN at the closing date of this publication were assigned an ISBN with one of these prefixes by the International Standard Book Numbering Agency.

Titles numbered within the prefixes 0-317, 0-318, 0-685 and 0-686 are:
—Publishers who did not assign ISBNs to their titles.
—Distributors with titles published and imported from countries not in the ISBN system, or not receiving the ISBN from the originating publisher.
—Errors from transposition and transcription which occurred in transmitting the ISBN to the BOOKS IN PRINT database.

All the ISBNs listed in BOOKS IN PRINT are validated by using the check digit control, and only valid ISBNs are listed in the BIP database.

All publishers participating in the ISBN system having titles numbered within the prefixes 0-317, 0-318, 0-685 and 0-686 will receive a computer printout, requesting them to submit the correct ISBN.

Publishers not participating in the ISBN system may request from the ISBN Agency the assignment of an ISBN Publisher Prefix, and start numbering their titles.

The Book Industry System Advisory Committee (BISAC) has developed a standard format for data transmission, and many companies are already accepting orders transmitted on magnetic tape using the ISBN.

BISAC has also developed several other formats, also using the ISBN, including the title status format from which it is possible to update bibliographic information by magnetic tape exchange. Books in Print has been participating in such an exchange with many publishers, and welcomes inquiries from prospective participants.

The ISBN Agency and the Database Publishing Group of R.R. Bowker wish to express their appreciation to all publishers who collaborated in making the ISBN system the standard of the publishing industry.

SAN, an acronym of Standard Address Number, is a unique identification code for each address of each organization in or served by the book industry.

SANs are assigned to publishers, distributors, wholesalers, associations, software producers and manufacturers in the U.S.

The SAN itself merely defines an address. It becomes functional only in its application to activities such as purchasing, invoicing, billing, shipping, receiving, paying, crediting and refunding.

For additional information related to the ISBN total numbering, please refer to Emery Koltay, Director of the ISBN/SAN Agency, c/o R.R. Bowker.

SUBJECT GUIDE TO CHILDREN'S BOOKS IN PRINT 1991-1992

A

A B C BOOKS
see Alphabet Books
A. D. C.
see Child Welfare
ABACUS
Cotter, Joan A. Worksheets for the Abacus, Vol. 2. (Illus.). 122p. (gr. 3-4). 1988. 16.95 (ISBN 0-9609636-5-0). Activities Learning.
Dilson, Jesse. Abacus. Pozzi, Angela, illus. (gr. 5-8). 1975. pap. 6.95 (ISBN 0-312-00140-1). St Martin.
ABANDONED TOWNS
see Cities and Towns, Ruined, Extinct, etc.
ABDUL-JABBAR, KAREEM, 1947-
Carpenter, Jerry & Dimeglio, Steve. Kareem Abdul-Jabbar. Deegan, Paul, ed. (Illus.). 32p. (gr. 4). 1988. PLB 11.90 (ISBN 0-939179-36-9). Abdo & Dghtrs.
ABNORMAL PSYCHOLOGY
see Psychology, Pathological
ABOLITION OF SLAVERY
see Abolitionists
ABOLITIONISTS
Ferris, Jeri. Walking the Road to Freedom: A Story about Sojourner Truth. Hanson, Peter E., illus. 64p. (gr. 3-6). 1989. pap. 4.95 (ISBN 0-685-25646-4, First Ave Edns). Lerner Pubns.
McKissack, Patricia & McKissack, Fredrick. Frederick Douglass: The Black Lion. LC 86-32695. (Illus.). 136p. (gr. 4 up). 1987. PLB 17.27 (ISBN 0-516-03221-6); pap. 5.95 (ISBN 0-516-43221-4). Childrens.
Taylor-Boyd, Susan. Sojourner Truth: The Courageous Former Slave Whose Eloquence Helped Promote Human Equality. LC 89-4345. (Illus.). 68p. (gr. 5-6). 1990. PLB 12.95 (ISBN 0-8368-0101-6). Gareth Stevens Inc.
ABORTION
Flanders, Carl N. Library in a Book: Abortion. 256p. (gr. 9-12). 1990. 22.95 (ISBN 0-8160-1908-8). Facts on File.
Wharton, Mandy. Abortion. LC 89-31782. (Illus.). 64p. (gr. 7-10). 1989. PLB 11.90 (ISBN 0-531-17189-2). Watts.
ABORTION-FICTION
Beckman, Gunnel. Mia Alone. Tate, Joan, tr. 112p. (gr. 7 up). 1978. pap. 1.25 (ISBN 0-440-95586-6, LFL). Dell.
Minshull, Evelyn W. But I Thought You Really Loved Me. LC 76-14992. 150p. (gr. 7 up). 1976. 7.25 (ISBN 0-664-32600-5, Westminster). Westminster John Knox.
ABRAHAM, THE PATRIARCH
Abraham. (Illus.). (gr. 2-4). 3.50 (ISBN 0-7214-1110-X). Ladybird Bks.
Barrett, Ethel. Abraham: God's Faithful Pilgrim. LC 82-12330. 128p. (Orig.). (gr. 3 up). 1982. pap. 3.95 (ISBN 0-8307-0769-7, 5810906). Regal.
Caffrey, Stephanie & Kenslea, Timothy. The Family That Wanted a Home. (Orig.). (gr. 3-5). 1978. pap. 1.95 (ISBN 0-8192-1235-0). Morehouse Pub.
Golann, Cecil P. Mission on a Mountain: The Story of Abraham & Isaac. Hechtkopf, H., illus. LC 73-7498. 32p. (gr. k-5). 1975. PLB 6.95 (ISBN 0-8225-0363-8). Lerner Pubns.
Rives, Elsie. Abraham: Man of Faith. (Illus.). (gr. 1-6). 1976. 5.95 (ISBN 0-8054-4223-5, 4242-23). Broadman.

Zlotowitz, Bernard M. & Maiben, Dina. Abraham's Great Discovery. Sweeny, Raquel, illus. 32p. 1991. 12.95t (ISBN 0-911389-04-0). NightinGale Res.
ABSENCE FROM SCHOOL
see School Attendance
ACADIANS
Amoss, Berthe. The Loup Garou. Amoss, Berthe, illus. LC 79-20536. 48p. (ps-4). 1979. 8.95 (ISBN 0-88289-189-8). Pelican.
Longfellow, Henry Wadsworth. Evangeline & Other Poems. Bennet, C. L., intro. by. (gr. 7 up). pap. 1.95 (ISBN 0-8049-0094-9, CL-94). Airmont.
ACCIDENTS-FICTION
see also Aeronautics–Accidents; Disasters; Fires; First Aid; Traffic Accidents–Fiction
Byars, Betsy C. The Eighteenth Emergency. Grossman, Robert, illus. (gr. 4-6). 1981. pap. 3.95 (ISBN 0-14-031451-2, Puffin). Puffin Bks.
Carrick, Carol. The Accident. Carrick, Donald, illus. LC 76-3532. 32p. (ps-3). 1979. 13.95 (ISBN 0-395-28774-X, Clarion); pap. 4.95 (ISBN 0-89919-041-3). HM.
Durham, Jamie A. Little Airplane. Pittman, Dockery, illus. 32p. (ps). Date not set. write for info. Magpie AL.
Forman, James D. The Big Bang. LC 89-31252. 160p. (gr. 7 up). 1989. 12.95 (ISBN 0-684-19004-4, Scribners Young Read). Macmillan Child Grp.
Lester, Helen. It Wasn't My Fault. Munsinger, Lynn, illus. LC 84-19212. 32p. (gr. k-3). 1985. 13.95 (ISBN 0-395-35629-6). HM.
Strasser, Todd. The Accident. LC 87-37411. 192p. (gr. 7 up). 1988. 14.95 (ISBN 0-440-50061-3). Delacorte.
—The Accident. (gr. k up). 1990. pap. 3.25 (ISBN 0-440-20635-9, LFL). Dell.
Tricker, Andy. Accidents Will Happen. 196p. (gr. 7-9). 1989. pap. 9.95 (ISBN 0-233-98095-4, Pub. by A Deutsch England). Trafalgar Sq.
ACCIDENTS-PREVENTION
see also Safety Education
Berry, Joy W. What to Do When Your Mom or Dad Says "Be Prepared" Bartholomew, illus. Berry, Joy W., intro. by. LC 81-83790. (Illus.). 48p. (gr. 3-7). 1982. 4.98 (ISBN 0-941510-02-6). Living Skills.
Kyte, Kathy S. Play It Safe: The Kids' Guide to Personal Safety & Crime Prevention. LC 83-6086. (Illus.). 128p. (gr. 5 up). 1983. Knopf.
Safety. (Illus.). 48p. (gr. 6-12). 1986. pap. 1.85 (ISBN 0-8395-3347-0, 3347). BSA.
ACCLIMATIZATION
see Adaptation (Biology); Man–Influence of Environment
ACCOUNTING
Halbur, Donna K. Accountants Visit School. Kearney, Paul, illus. 24p. (gr. 3-5). 1979. pap. 3.00 (ISBN 0-686-25249-7). Halbur.
ACCOUNTING MACHINES
see Calculating Machines
ACID RAIN
Acid Rain Foundation, Inc. Staff, compiled by. Acid Rain Curriculum: Grades 6-12. (Illus.). (gr. 6-12). 1986. 59.95 (ISBN 0-935577-03-3). Acid Rain Found.
Bright, Michael. Acid Rain. (Illus.). 32p. (gr. 2-4). 1991. PLB 11.90 (ISBN 0-531-17303-8, Gloucester Pr). Watts.
Hessler, Edward W. & Stubbs, Harriett. Acid Rain Science Projects. 20p. (Orig.). (gr. 5-12). 1987. pap. 9.95 (ISBN 0-935577-09-2). Acid Rain Found.

Hocking, Colin, et al. Acid Rain. Bergman, Lincoln & Fairwell, Kay, eds. Bavilacqua, Carol & Craig, Rose, illus. Hoyt, Richard & Bergman, Lincoln, photos by. 168p. (gr. 6-10). 1990. pap. 11.00 (ISBN 0-912511-74-5). Lawrence Science.
McCormick, John. Acid Rain. (Illus.). 32p. (gr. 5-8). 1991. PLB 11.90 (ISBN 0-531-17358-5, Gloucester Pr). Watts.
Neal, Philip. Acid Rain. (Illus.). 48p. (gr. 7-12). 1986. 19.95 (ISBN 0-85219-623-7, Pub. by Batsford England). Trafalgar Sq.
Snodgrass, M. E. Environmental Awareness: Acid Rain. James, Jody, ed. Vista Three Design Staff, illus. LC 90-26255. 48p. (gr. 4 up). 1991. lib. bdg. 14.95 (ISBN 0-944280-30-7). BSP Pub Inc.
Stubbs, Harriett, et al. Acid Rain Curriculum. Flor, Dick, illus. (Orig.). (gr. 4-8). 1985. tchrs' ed. 19.95 (ISBN 0-935577-00-9). Acid Rain Found.
Stubbs, Harriett S., et al. Acid Rain Reader. Eclov, Homer, illus. 20p. (Orig.). (gr. 4-8). 1989. pap. 5.95 (ISBN 0-935577-12-2); pap. 2.50 (ISBN 0-685-17881-1). Acid Rain Found.
Turck, Mary. Acid Rain. LC 90-35495. (Illus.). 48p. (gr. 5-6). 1990. RSBE 10.95 (ISBN 0-89686-547-9, Crestwood Hse). Macmillan Child Grp.
Tyson, Peter. Acid Rain. (Illus.). (gr. 5 up). 1992. PLB 19.95 (ISBN 0-7910-1577-7). Chelsea Hse.
ACOUSTICS
see Hearing; Music–Acoustics and Physics; Sound
ACQUIRED IMMUNE DEFICIENCY SYNDROME
see Aids (Disease)
ACTING
see also Actors and Actresses; Pageants; Theater
Foley, Kathryn, et al. The Good Apple Guide to Creative Drama. 128p. (gr. 2-6). 1981. 9.95 (ISBN 0-86653-030-4, GA 258). Good Apple.
Roddy, Ruth M. Monologues for Kids. 64p. (Orig.). (gr. 1-3). 1987. pap. 5.95 (ISBN 0-940669-02-1). Dramaline Pubns.
Stuntmen & Special Effects. (Illus.). (gr. 8-12). 1982. 7.95 (ISBN 0-698-20564-2, Coward). Putnam Pub Group.
ACTING-FICTION
Anderson, Mary. Tune in Tomorrow. 192p. (gr. 7 up). 1985. pap. 2.50 (ISBN 0-380-69870-6, Flare). Avon.
Ashley, Ellen. Lights, Camera, Action. 160p. 1991. pap. 3.50 (ISBN 0-449-14586-7, Pub. by Girls Only). Fawcett.
—Understudy. 176p. 1990. pap. 3.50 (ISBN 0-449-14585-9, Pub. by Girls Only). Fawcett.
Dreiser, Theodore. Sister Carrie. Simpson, Claude, ed. LC 59-1819. (gr. 9 up). 1972. pap. 8.36 (ISBN 0-395-05134-7, RivEd). HM.
Goffstein, Brooke. An Actor. Goffstein, Brooke, illus. LC 87-165. 32p. (ps up). 1987. 12.95 (ISBN 0-06-022168-2); PLB 12.89 (ISBN 0-06-022169-0). HarpC Child Bks.
Greydanus, Rose. Let's Pretend. Winborn, Marsha, illus. LC 81-2357. 32p. (gr. k-2). 1981. PLB 10.89 (ISBN 0-89375-545-1); pap. text ed. 2.95 (ISBN 0-89375-546-X). Troll Assocs.
Hickman, Martha W. When Can Daddy Come Home? Livingston, Francis, illus. 48p. (gr. 1-3). 1983. 1.00 (ISBN 0-687-44969-3). Abingdon.
Hughes, Dean. Nutty, the Movie Star. 144p. (gr. 3-7). 1991. pap. 3.95 (ISBN 0-689-71524-2, Aladdin). Macmillan Child Grp.
Kaplan, Marcia P. & Kaplan, David E. Happiness. Mendez, Phil, et al, illus. 96p. (Orig.). (gr. 1 up). 1986. 5.95 (ISBN 0-9617744-3-6). Cheers.

Koehler-Pentacoff, Elizabeth. Curtain Call. (Illus.). 80p. (gr. k-6). 1989. pap. text ed. 7.95 (ISBN 0-86530-065-8, IP 166-4). Incentive Pubns.

Martin, Ann M. Stage Fright. Sims, Blanche, illus. LC 84-47834. 144p. (gr. 3-7). 1984. 13.95 (ISBN 0-8234-0541-9). Holiday.

—Stage Fright. Sims, Blanche, illus. 144p. (gr. 4-6). 1986. pap. 2.50 (ISBN 0-590-40874-7, Apple Paperbacks). Scholastic Inc.

Nixon, Joan L. Caught in the Act. (gr. 7 up). 1989. pap. 3.50 (ISBN 0-553-27912-2, Starfire). Bantam.

Park, Barbara. Almost Starring Skinnybones. LC 87-28752. 112p. (gr. 3-7). 1989. pap. 2.95 (ISBN 0-394-82591-8, Bullseye Bks). Knopf.

Pfeffer, Susan B. Starring Peter & Leigh. LC 78-72855. 1978. 7.95 (ISBN 0-440-08226-9). Delacorte.

Rosofsky, Iris. My Aunt Ruth. LC 90-4940. 224p. (gr. 7 up). 1991. 13.95 (ISBN 0-06-025087-9); PLB 13.89 (ISBN 0-06-025088-7). HarpC Child Bks.

Sansevere, Carol Q. Screen Test. 160p. (Orig.). (gr. 5-9). Date not set. pap. 2.95 (ISBN 1-55802-203-1). Lynx Bks.

Walker, Paul R. Method. 1990. 14.95 (ISBN 0-15-200528-5). HarbraceJ.

ACTING–VOCATIONAL GUIDANCE

Rawson, Ruth. Acting. Matthau, W., intro. by. LC 68-21664. (Illus.). (gr. 7 up). 1970. PLB 14.95 (ISBN 0-8239-0151-3). Rosen Group.

Williamson, Walter. Early Stages: The Professional Theater & the Young Actor. LC 85-26467. (Illus.). 128p. (gr. 6 up). 1986. 12.95 (ISBN 0-8027-6624-2); lib. bdg. 12.85 (ISBN 0-8027-6630-7). Walker & Co.

ACTORS AND ACTRESSES

see also Acting; Acting–Vocational Guidance; Black Actors; Motion Pictures–Biography; Theater

Axiom Informaton Resources Staff. Star Guide 1992-1993: Where to Contact over 3200 Movie Stars, TV Stars, Rock Stars, Sports Stars, & Other Famous Celebrities. rev. ed. Robinson, Terry, ed. 200p. 1992. pap. 12.95 (ISBN 0-943213-04-5). Axiom Info Res.

Beaton, Margaret. Oprah Winfrey: TV Talk Show Host. LC 90-2150. (Illus.). (gr. 4 up). 1990. PLB 17.27 (ISBN 0-516-03270-4). Childrens.

Bergman, Carol. Mae West. Horner, Matina. (Illus.). 112p. (gr. 5 up). 1988. lib. bdg. 17.95 (ISBN 1-55546-681-8). Chelsea Hse.

Catalano, Grace. Alyssa Milano: She's the Boss. (gr. 7 up). 1989. pap. 2.95 (ISBN 0-318-41642-5, Starfire). Bantam.

—Alyssa Milano: She's the Boss. (gr. 6-9). 1989. pap. 2.75 (ISBN 0-553-28158-5). Bantam.

—River Phoenix: Hero & Heartthrob. (gr. 7 up). 1988. pap. 2.75 (ISBN 0-553-27728-6, Starfire). Bantam.

Collins, Tom. Jane Fonda: An American Original. 1990. 12.95 (ISBN 0-531-15149-2). Watts.

—Jane Fonda: An American Original. (gr. 4-7). 1990. PLB 13.90 (ISBN 0-531-10929-1). Watts.

Fiori, Carlo. The Story of Shirley Temple Black: Biography, No. 16. (gr. k-6). 1990. pap. 2.95 (ISBN 0-440-40284-0, YB). Dell.

Grace Kelly. 48p. (gr. 5-6). 1989. PLB 10.95 (ISBN 0-685-26350-9). Capstone Pr.

Green, Carl R. & Sanford, William R. Michael J. Fox. LC 86-16623. (Illus.). 32p. (gr. 4-5). PLB 9.95 (ISBN 0-89686-298-4, Crestwood Hse). Macmillan Child Grp.

Greenberg, Keith E. Michael J. Fox. (Illus.). 32p. (gr. 4-9). 1986. PLB 9.95 (ISBN 0-8225-1611-X). Lerner Pubns.

—Ralph Macchio. (Illus.). 40p. (gr. 4-9). 1987. PLB 9.95 (ISBN 0-8225-1616-0). Lerner Pubns.

Greene, Constance C. Star Shine. LC 85-40458. 144p. (gr. 5-9). 1985. pap. 11.95 (ISBN 0-670-80772-9). Viking Child Bks.

—Star Shine. (gr. k-6). 1987. pap. 2.75 (ISBN 0-440-47920-7, YB). Dell.

Haskins, James S. Shirley Temple Black: Actress to Ambassador. Ruff, Donna, illus. 64p. (gr. 2-5). 1989. pap. 3.95 (ISBN 0-14-032491-7, Puffin). Puffin Bks.

Haskins, Jim. Bill Cosby: America's Most Famous Father. 128p. (gr. 7-9). 1988. 13.95 (ISBN 0-8027-6785-0); PLB 14.85 (ISBN 0-8027-6786-9). Walker & Co.

Hewett, Joan. On Camera: The Story of a Child Actor. Hewett, Richard, illus. LC 87-5125. 64p. (gr. 2-5). 1987. 13.95 (ISBN 0-89919-469-9, Pub. by Clarion). Ticknor & Fields.

John Wayne. 48p. (gr. 5-6). 1989. PLB 10.95 (ISBN 0-685-26355-X). Capstone Pr.

Koenig, Teresa & Bell, Rivian. Eddie Murphy. (Illus.). 48p. (gr. 4-9). 1985. PLB 8.95 (ISBN 0-8225-1602-0). Lerner Pubns.

Latham, Caroline. Katherine Hepburn. Horner, Matina, intro. by. (Illus.). 112p. (gr. 5 up). 1989. 17.95 (ISBN 1-55546-658-3); pap. 9.95 (ISBN 0-7910-0416-3). Chelsea Hse.

Marilyn Monroe. 48p. (gr. 5-6). 1989. PLB 10.95 (ISBN 0-685-26351-7). Capstone Pr.

Micklos, John, Jr. Leonard Nimoy: A Stars Trek. LC 87-32457. (Illus.). 64p. (gr. 3 up). 1988. PLB 10.95 (ISBN 0-87518-376-X, Dillon). Macmillan Child Grp.

Perl, Lila. Molly Picon: A Gift of Laughter. Ruff, Donna, illus. 64p. (gr. 4-7). 1990. 12.95 (ISBN 0-8276-0336-3). JPS Phila.

Petrucelli. Cher, Reading Level 2. (Illus.). 24p. (gr. 1-4). Date not set. PLB 12.33 (ISBN 0-86592-432-5). Rourke Corp.

Schneck, Paul D. Mork & Mindy. 32p. (gr. 4 up). 1980. PLB 8.95s.p. (ISBN 0-87191-754-8); PLB 12.80 (ISBN 0-685-01261-1). Creative Ed.

Shorto, Russell. Jane Fonda: Political Activism. (Illus.). 104p. (gr. 7 up). 1991. PLB 19.95 (ISBN 1-56294-045-7). Millbrook Pr.

Smith, Betsy C. A Day in the Life of an Actress. Buckley, F. Reid, Jr., illus. LC 84-8678. 32p. (gr. 4-8). 1985. PLB 11.79 (ISBN 0-8167-0105-9); pap. text ed. 2.95 (ISBN 0-8167-0106-7); cassettes avail. Troll Assocs.

ADAGES

see Proverbs

ADAM (BIBLICAL CHARACTER)

Adam & Eve. (ps-2). 1989. text ed. 3.95 cased (ISBN 0-7214-5259-0). Ladybird Bks.

Storr, Catherine, retold by. Adam & Eve. Russell, Jim, illus. LC 82-23060. 32p. (gr. k-4). 1983. PLB 14.65 (ISBN 0-8172-1981-1). Raintree Pubs.

When God Made Adam & Eve. (Illus.). (gr. 2-4). 3.50 (ISBN 0-7214-0985-7). Ladybird Bks.

ADAMS, ABIGAIL (SMITH) 1744-1818

Fradin, Dennis B. Abigail Adams: Adviser to a President. LC 88-31331. (Illus.). 48p. (gr. 3-6). 1989. PLB 14.95 (ISBN 0-89490-228-8). Enslow Pubs.

Osborne, Angela. Abigail Adams. Horner, Matina S., intro. by. (Illus.). 112p. (gr. 5 up). 1989. 17.95 (ISBN 1-55546-635-4); pap. 9.95 (ISBN 0-7910-0405-8). Chelsea Hse.

Peterson, Helen S. Abigail Adams: Dear Partner. Fraser, Betty, illus. 80p. (gr. 2-6). 1991. Repr. of 1967 ed. PLB 12.95 (ISBN 0-7910-1402-9). Chelsea Hse.

Waldrop, Ruth. Abigail Adams. LC 88-6137. (Illus.). 109p. (gr. 3 up). 1988. PLB 10.95 (ISBN 0-9616894-2-0); pap. 6.95 (ISBN 0-9616894-1-2). Rusk Inc.

Witter, Evelyn. Abigail Adams: First Lady of Faith & Courage. Hanzel, Linda & Hanzel, Linda, illus. LC 76-2416. (gr. 3-6). 1976. pap. 6.95 (ISBN 0-915134-94-2). Mott Media.

ADAMS, JOHN, PRESIDENT U. S. 1735-1826

Brill, Marlene T. John Adams. (Illus.). 100p. (gr. 3 up). 1989. PLB 17.27 (ISBN 0-516-41384-8); pap. 6.95 (ISBN 0-318-41758-8). Childrens.

Dwyer, Frank. John Adams. (Illus.). (gr. 5 up). 1989. 17.95 (ISBN 1-55546-801-2). Chelsea Hse.

Santrey, Laurence. John Adams, Brave Patriot. Smolinski, Dick, illus. LC 85-1095. 48p. (gr. 4-6). 1986. lib. bdg. 10.79 (ISBN 0-8167-0559-3); pap. text ed. 2.95 (ISBN 0-8167-0560-7). Troll Assocs.

Stefoff, Rebecca. John Adams: 2nd President of the United States. Young, Richard G., ed. LC 87-32752. (Illus.). (gr. 5-9). 1988. PLB 17.26 (ISBN 0-944483-10-0). Garrett Ed Corp.

ADAMS, JOHN QUINCY, PRESIDENT U. S. 1767-1848

Greenblatt, Miriam. John Quincy Adams: Sixth President of the United States. Young, Richard G., ed. LC 89-39950. (Illus.). 128p. (gr. 5-9). 1990. PLB 17.26 (ISBN 0-944483-21-6). Garrett Ed Corp.

Jones, K. V., ed. John Quincy Adams, Seventeen Sixty-Seven to Eighteen Forty-Eight: Chronology, Documents, Bibliographical Aids. LC 71-111216. 80p. (gr. 9 up). 1970. PLB 10.00 (ISBN 0-379-12073-9). Oceana.

Kent, Zachary. John Quincy Adams. LC 86-31022. (Illus.). 100p. (gr. 3 up). 1987. PLB 17.27 (ISBN 0-516-01386-6); pap. 6.95 (ISBN 0-516-41386-4). Childrens.

ADAMS, SAMUEL, 1722-1803

Fritz, Jean. Why Don't You Get a Horse, Sam Adams? Hyman, Trina S., illus. 48p. (gr. 2-6). 1982. 9.95 (ISBN 0-698-20292-9, Coward); pap. 5.95 (ISBN 0-698-20545-6, Coward). Putnam Pub Group.

ADAPTATION (BIOLOGY)

see also Man–Influence of Environment

Cochrane, Jennifer. Nature. (Illus.). 48p. (gr. 5-8). 1991. PLB 13.90 (ISBN 0-531-19143-5, Warwick). Watts.

Maynard, Thane. Animal Inventors. (Illus.). 64p. (gr. 5-8). 1991. PLB 11.90 (ISBN 0-531-20051-5). Watts.

ADDAMS, JANE, 1860-1935

Gleiter, Jan & Thompson, Kathleen. Jane Addams. (Illus.). 32p. (Orig.). (gr. 2-5). 1987. PLB 16.67 (ISBN 0-8172-2662-1); pap. text ed. 9.27 (ISBN 0-8172-2666-4). Raintree Pubs.

Klingel, Cynthia & Zadra, Dan. Jane Addams. (Illus.). 32p. 1987. 16.45 (ISBN 0-88682-165-7); PLB 11.50s.p. (ISBN 0-685-23217-4). Creative Ed.

Mitchard, Jacquelyn. Jane Addams: Pioneer in Social Reform & Activist for World Peace. LC 89-49624. (Illus.). 64p. (gr. 5-6). 1991. PLB 12.95 (ISBN 0-8368-0144-X). Gareth Stevens Inc.

Wheeler, Leslie A. Jane Addams. Gallin, Richard, ed. (Illus.). 144p. (gr. 5-9). 1990. lib. bdg. 13.98 (ISBN 0-382-09962-1); pap. 7.95 (ISBN 0-382-09968-0). Silver Burdett Pr.

ADDING MACHINES

see Calculating Machines

ADENAUER, KONRAD, 1876-1967

Finke, Blythe F. Konrad Adenauer: Architect of the New Germany. Rahmas, D. Steve, ed. LC 79-190241. 32p. (Orig.). (gr. 7-12). 1972. lib. bdg. 4.20 incl. catalog cards (ISBN 0-87157-523-X); pap. 2.95 vinyl laminated covers (ISBN 0-87157-023-8). SamHar Pr.

ADIRONDACK MOUNTAINS

Steinberg, Michael. Our Wilderness: How the People of New York Found, Changed & Preserved the Adirondacks. LC 91-16550. (Illus.). 112p. (gr. 4-8). 1991. 14.95 (ISBN 0-935272-56-9); 18.95 (ISBN 0-685-35784-8). ADK Mtn Club.

A history of the 6-million-acre Adirondack Park of New York State, which includes towns & farms, businesses & timberlands as well as 1.2 million acres of wilderness. Written for ages 10 & up (Gr. 4-8). Historic photographs by Stoddard & Apperson. Publication coincides with the 1992 Centennial of the Adirondack Park. Book carries conservationist message. *Publisher Provided Annotation.*

Vesty, John. Adirontreks: Places & People in the Adirondacks. LC 90-82523. (Illus.). 268p. (Orig.). (gr. 8). Date not set. pap. 19.95 (ISBN 0-9626876-0-X). J Vesty Co.

ADJUSTMENT, SOCIAL

see Social Adjustment

ADMINISTRATION

see Political Science

see names of countries, cities, etc. with the subdivision Politics and Government, e.g. U. S.–Politics and Government; etc.

ADMINISTRATION OF JUSTICE

see Justice, Administration of

ADOLESCENCE

Callister, Joann I. Teenagers in Crisis: Not Alone. LC 90-23970. 96p. (Orig.). 1991. pap. 8.95 (ISBN 0-931832-80-2). Fithian Pr.

Coombs, H. Samm. Teenage Survival Manual: How to Reach '20' in One Piece (And Enjoy Every Step of the Journey) 4th, rev. ed. Lipney, Stephanie & Moore, Dick, illus. 240p. (gr. 9-12). 1989. pap. 9.95 (ISBN 0-925258-08-3). DB Inc CA.

Crawford, Kenneth & Simmons, Paul. Growing up with Sex. 80p. (gr. 7-9). 1973. pap. 6.95 (ISBN 0-8054-5312-1). Broadman.

Cruz, Nicky & Buckingham, Jamie. Run Baby Run. (gr. 9-12). 1984. pap. 3.50 (ISBN 0-515-09105-7). Jove Pubns.

D, Lisa, ed. Stepping Stones to Recovery for Young People. LC 91-8676. 240p. (Orig.). (gr. 9-12). 1991. pap. 6.95 (ISBN 0-934125-19-8). Glen Abbey Bks.

Daniels, Rebecca. Hallelujah! I'm Special. McClure, Nancee, illus. 48p. (gr. k-3). 1985. wkbk. 6.95 (ISBN 0-86653-174-2, SS 816). Good Apple.

Dockrey, Karen. What's Your Problem? 96p. (gr. 7 up). 1987. pap. 12.99 (ISBN 0-89693-381-4); pap. 2.50 student bk. (ISBN 0-317-60085-0). Victor Bks.

Eagan, Andrea B. Why Am I So Miserable If These Are the Best Years of My Life? Frankfort, Ellen, intro. by. LC 75-43726. 240p. (gr. 8 up). 1976. 12.95 (ISBN 0-397-31655-0, Lipp Jr Bks). HarpC Child Bks.

Eager, George B. Teen Talk. 48p. (Orig.). (gr. 7-12). 1981. pap. 1.00 (ISBN 0-9603752-1-X). Mailbox.

Edens, David. The Changing Me. 48p. (gr. 4-6). 1991. pap. 9.95 (ISBN 0-8054-4411-4). Broadman.

Espeland, Pamela & Wallner, Rosemary. Making the Most of Today: Daily Readings for Young People on Self-Awareness, Creativity & Self-Esteem. 380p. (Orig.). (gr. 6 up). 1991. pap. 8.95 (ISBN 0-915793-33-4). Free Spirit Pub.

Gilbert, Sara. Go for It: Get Organized. LC 89-13765. 144p. (gr. 7 up). 1990. 12.95 (ISBN 0-688-08852-X); pap. 6.95 (ISBN 0-688-09619-0, Pub. by Beech Tree Bks). Morrow Jr Bks.

Go Ask Alice. 192p. (gr. 7 up). 1976. pap. 3.50 (ISBN 0-380-00523-9, Flare). Avon.

Hartley, Fred. Growing Pains: First Aid for Teenagers. 160p. (Orig.). (gr. 7-12). 1981. pap. 6.95 (ISBN 0-8007-5067-5, Power Bks). Revell.

Johnson, Eric W. How to Live with Parents & Teachers. LC 86-9273. 156p. (gr. 5-10). 1986. 12.95 (ISBN 0-664-21273-5, Westminster). Westminster John Knox.

Mayle, Peter. What's Happening to Me? Walter, Paul & Robins, Arthur, illus. LC 75-14410. 56p. (gr. 3 up). 1975. 12.00 (ISBN 0-8184-0221-0); pap. 6.95 (ISBN 0-8184-0312-8). Carol Pub Group.

Miller, Alice. Young Girl's Diary. 1991. pap. 10.95 (ISBN 0-385-41596-6, Anchor Pr). Doubleday.

Packer, Kenneth L. Puberty: The Story of Growth & Change. Green, Anne C., illus. LC 89-5665. 109p. (gr. 6-9). 1989. PLB 12.40 (ISBN 0-531-10810-4). Watts.

Parramon, J. M., et al. Teenagers. 32p. (gr. 3-5). Eng. ed. pap. 3.95 (ISBN 0-8120-3851-7); Span. ed.: Los Jovenes. pap. 4.95 (ISBN 0-8120-3855-X). Barron.

Powledge, Fred. You'll Survive: Late Blooming, Early Blooming, Loneliness, Klutziness, & Other Problems of Adolescence, & How to Live Through Them. LC 85-43351. 144p. (gr. 6-8). 1986. 12.95 (ISBN 0-684-18632-2, Scribners Young Read). Macmillan Child Grp.

Roberts, Gail C. & Guttormson, Lorraine. You & School: A Survival Guide for Adolescence. Wallner, Rosemary, ed. 112p. (Orig.). (gr. 6 up). 1990. pap. 8.95 (ISBN 0-915793-25-3). Free Spirit Pub.

—You & Stress: A Survival Guide for Adolescence. Wallner, Rosemary, ed. 112p. (Orig.). (gr. 6 up). 1990. pap. 8.95 (ISBN 0-915793-26-1). Free Spirit Pub Co.

—You & Your Family: A Survival Guide for Adolescence. Wallner, Rosemary, ed. 112p. (Orig.). (gr. 6 up). 1990. pap. 8.95 (ISBN 0-915793-24-5). Free Spirit Pub.
Rosenberg, Ellen. Growing up Feeling Good: A Growing up Handbook Especially for Kids. 1989. pap. 10.95 (ISBN 0-14-034264-8, Puffin). Puffin Bks.
Sheffield, Margaret. Life Blood. Bewley, Sheila, illus. LC 87-46237. (gr. k-3). 1989. 14.95 (ISBN 0-394-57065-0). Knopf.
Sheperd, Scott. What Do You Think of You? A Teen's Guide to Finding Self-Esteem. Hesse, Bonnie, ed. (Illus.). 100p. (Orig.). 1990. 6.95 (ISBN 0-89638-220-6, 04119). CompCare.
Smith, Lucinda I. Growing up Female: New Challenges, New Choices. LC 86-31261. 160p. (gr. 7 up). 1987. lib. bdg. 12.98 (ISBN 0-671-63445-3). Messner.
Smith, Michael W. & Ridenour, Fritz. Old Enough to Know. large type ed. 111p. 1989. pap. write for info. (ISBN 0-8499-3163-0). Word Bks.
Stephens, Andrea. Stressed-Out but Hanging Tough. 160p. (gr. 8-12). 1989. pap. 6.95 (ISBN 0-8007-5326-7, Power Bks). Revell.
Stewart, Gail. Peer Pressure. LC 89-31258. (Illus.). 48p. (gr. 4 up). 1989. 10.95 (ISBN 0-89686-444-8, Crestwood Hse). Macmillan Child Grp.
Wallace, Carol M. Should You Shut Your Eyes When You Kiss? Or, How to Survive "The Best Years of Your Life" Weston, Martha, illus. LC 83-5458. 112p. (gr. 7 up). 1983. 13.45i (ISBN 0-316-91998-5). Little.
Wilson, Olga E. Coming to Terms. LC 89-90272. (Orig.). (gr. 9 up). 1989. pap. 7.95 (ISBN 0-9623513-0-X). O E Wilson.
Wingerd, William N. Understanding & Enjoying Adolescence. 1988. pap. text ed. 17.40 (ISBN 0-8013-0215-3, 75873). Longman.

ADOLESCENCE–FICTION

Baer, Judy. Broken Promises. 128p. (Orig.). (gr. 7 up). 1989. pap. 3.95 (ISBN 1-55661-087-4). Bethany Hse.
Bawden, Nina. Henry. Powzyk, Joyce, illus. LC 87-29339. (gr. 3 up). 1988. PLB 13.95 (ISBN 0-688-07894-X). Lothrop.
Blume, Judy. Are You There, God? It's Me, Margaret. LC 79-122741. 160p. (gr. 4-6). 1982. 12.95 (ISBN 0-02-710990-9, Bradbury Pr). Macmillan Child Grp.
—La Ballena. Ada, Alma F., tr. LC 83-2731. (SPA.). 160p. (gr. 4-6). 1983. 12.95 (ISBN 0-02-710940-2, Bradbury Pr). Macmillan Child Grp.
—Estas Ahi, Dios? Soy Yo, Margaret. Ada, Alma F., tr. LC 83-2730. (SPA.). 160p. (gr. 5-7). 1983. 12.95 (ISBN 0-02-710950-X, Bradbury Pr). Macmillan Child Grp.
Brooks, Robert F. Children's Stories for Teenage Adults. rev. ed. (Illus.). 32p. (Orig.). (gr. 5-9). pap. 3.00 (ISBN 0-936868-05-8). Freeland Pubns.
Byars, Betsy C. Bingo Brown & the Language of Love. 160p. (gr. 3-7). 1989. 12.95 (ISBN 0-670-82791-6). Viking Child Bks.
Calhoun, Mary. Honestly, Katie John. Frame, Paul, illus. LC 63-8473. 224p. (gr. 4-7). 1963. PLB 12.89 (ISBN 0-06-020936-4). HarpC Child Bks.
—Katie John. LC 60-5775. (Illus.). 128p. (gr. 3-6). 1972. pap. 3.50 (ISBN 0-06-440028-X, Trophy). HarpC Child Bks.
Callan, Jamie. Over the Hill at Fourteen. 176p. (gr. 7 up). pap. 1.95 (ISBN 0-451-13090-1, Sig Vista). NAL-Dutton.
Cleary, Beverly. Fifteen. Krush, Joe & Krush, Beth, illus. LC 56-7509. 256p. (gr. 6-9). 1956. 12.95 (ISBN 0-688-21285-9); PLB 12.88 (ISBN 0-688-31285-3, Morrow Jr Bks). Morrow Jr Bks.
Cleaver, Vera & Cleaver, Bill. Me Too. 160p. (gr. 7-9). 1973. 13.95 (ISBN 0-397-31485-X, Lipp Jr Bks). HarpC Child Bks.
Clements, Bruce. Anywhere Else but Here. LC 80-11345. 208p. (gr. 7 up). 1980. 11.95 (ISBN 0-374-30371-1). FS&G.
Close, Jessie. The Warping of Al. LC 90-4058. 288p. (gr. 7 up). 1990. 15.95 (ISBN 0-06-021280-2); PLB 15.89 (ISBN 0-06-021281-0). HarpC Child Bks.
Collier, James L. The Winchesters. 176p. (gr. 4). 1989. pap. 2.95 (ISBN 0-380-70808-6, Flare). Avon.
Danziger, Paula. The Pistachio Prescription. LC 77-86330. 168p. (gr. 7 up). 1978. pap. 12.95 (ISBN 0-385-28784-4). Delacorte.
DeClements, Barthe. Seventeen & In-Between. 166p. (Orig.). (gr. 7 up). 1985. pap. 2.50 (ISBN 0-590-41115-2, Point). Scholastic Inc.
Edwards, Archibald C. Charlotte. Musser, Rebecca F., illus. LC 90-63680. 112p. (Orig.). (gr. 7 up). 1990. pap. 11.95 (ISBN 0-9626413-0-8). Rosedale Pr.
Ellis, Jana. Hometown Hero. LC 89-34374. 160p. (gr. 7 up). 1989. pap. text ed. 2.50 (ISBN 0-8167-1609-9). Troll Assocs.
—Slave for a Day. LC 89-34375. 160p. (gr. 7 up). 1989. pap. text ed. 2.50 (ISBN 0-8167-1610-2). Troll Assocs.
Eyerly, Jeannette. If I Loved You Wednesday. LC 80-7772. 128p. (gr. 7up). 1980. PLB 12.89 (ISBN 0-397-31914-2, Lipp Jr Bks). HarpC Child Bks.
Fitzhugh, Louise. The Long Secret. 240p. (gr. 3-7). 1980. pap. 3.50 (ISBN 0-440-44977-4, YB). Dell.
Fitzpatrick, Regina D. It Wasn't the Truth They Told. Graves, Helen, ed. LC 88-50112. 80p. (gr. 4-8). 1988. 6.95 (ISBN 1-55523-142-X). Winston-Derek.
Gold, Robert S. Point of Departure. (gr. 7-12). 1981. pap. 2.75 (ISBN 0-685-01409-6, LE). Dell.
Graber, Richard. Black Cow Summer. LC 80-7767. 224p. (gr. 7 up). 1980. PLB 9.89 (ISBN 0-06-022119-4). HarpC Child Bks.
Greene, Bette. Philip Hall Likes Me. I Reckon Maybe. Lilly, Charles, illus. LC 74-2887. 160p. (gr. 3-6). 1974. 13.95 (ISBN 0-8037-6098-1); PLB 13.89 (ISBN 0-8037-6096-5). Dial Bks Young.
Greene, Constance C. Just Plain Al. LC 86-5516. 144p. (gr. 5-9). 1986. pap. 12.95 (ISBN 0-670-81250-1). Viking Child Bks.
—Your Old Pal, Al. LC 79-12350. (gr. 5-9). 1979. pap. 13.95 (ISBN 0-670-79575-5). Viking Child Bks.
Griffith, Helen V. Journal of a Teenage Genius. (gr. 3-7). 1987. 11.75 (ISBN 0-688-07226-7). Greenwillow.
—Journal of a Teenage Genius. 128p. (gr. 7 up). pap. 2.50 (ISBN 0-8167-1325-1). Troll Assocs.
Hamilton, Morse. Effie's House. LC 89-11918. 224p. (gr. 7 up). 1990. 13.95 (ISBN 0-688-09307-8). Greenwillow.
Hautzig, Deborah. Hey, Dollface. LC 78-54685. 160p. (gr. 7-9). 1978. PLB 11.88 (ISBN 0-688-84170-8). Greenwillow.
Holman, Felice. Slake's Limbo. LC 74-11675. 126p. (gr. 4-8). 1974. 12.95 (ISBN 0-684-13926-X, Scribners Young Read). Macmillan Child Grp.
Joosse, Barbara M. Pieces of the Picture. LC 88-28151. 144p. (gr. 5-7). 1989. 12.95 (ISBN 0-397-32342-5, Lipp Jr Bks); PLB 12.89 (ISBN 0-397-32343-3, Lipp Jr Bks). HarpC Child Bks.
Judy Blume. Incl. Are You There, God? It's Me, Margaret; Blubber; Otherwise Known As Sheila the Great; Superfudge; Tales of a Fourth Grade Nothing. 1983. pap. 13.00 boxed set (ISBN 0-440-44348-2). Dell.
Kaplow, Robert. Alessandra in Love. LC 88-23141. 160p. (gr. 7 up). 1989. 11.95 (ISBN 0-397-32281-X, Lipp Jr Bks); PLB 12.89 (ISBN 0-397-32282-8, Lipp Jr Bks). HarpC Child Bks.
Kaufman, Stephen. Does Anyone Here Know the Way to Thirteen? 157p. (gr. 5 up). 1985. 11.95 (ISBN 0-395-35974-0). HM.
Kerr, M. E. Dinky Hocker Shoots Smack! LC 72-80366. 204p. (gr. 7 up). 1972. PLB 12.89 (ISBN 0-06-023151-3). HarpC Child Bks.
—I'll Love You When You're More Like Me. LC 76-58709. 192p. (gr. 7 up). 1989. pap. 3.50 (ISBN 0-06-447004-0, Trophy). HarpC Child Bks.
Knowles, John. Separate Peace. (gr. 7 up). 1985. pap. 3.95 (ISBN 0-553-28041-4). Bantam.
Koertge, Ron. Where the Kissing Never Stops. LC 86-10947. 224p. (gr. 7 up). 1986. 14.95 (ISBN 0-316-50096-8). Little.
Koff, Richard M. Christopher. Kelly, Orly, ed. Reinertson, Barbara, illus. LC 81-65885. 128p. (gr. 7 up). 1981. 8.95 (ISBN 0-89742-050-0). Celestial Arts.
Konigsburg, E. L. Throwing Shadows. 168p. (gr. 7 up). 1988. pap. 3.95 (ISBN 0-02-044140-1, Collier Young Ad). Macmillan Child Grp.
Larimer, Tamela. Buck. LC 86-90774. 176p. (Orig.). (gr. 7 up). 1986. pap. 2.50 (ISBN 0-380-75172-0, Flare). Avon.
Lee, Joanna. I Want to Keep My Baby! 176p. (Orig.). (gr. 9-12). 1977. pap. 3.50 (ISBN 0-451-15733-8, Sig). NAL-Dutton.
Le Guin, Ursula K. Very Far Away from Anywhere Else. LC 76-4472. 96p. (gr. 6-9). 1976. 12.95 (ISBN 0-689-30525-7, Atheneum Child Bk). Macmillan Child Grp.
L'Engle, Madeleine. A Wind in the Door. LC 73-75176. 224p. (gr. 7 up). 1973. 15.95 (ISBN 0-374-38443-6). FS&G.
McCullers, Carson. Heart Is a Lonely Hunter. LC 83-61845. (gr. 10-12). 1970. pap. 3.95 (ISBN 0-553-25481-2). Bantam.
McDonnell, Christine. Friends First. 176p. (gr. 4 up). 1990. pap. 11.95 (ISBN 0-670-81923-9). Viking Child Bks.
McManus, Dorothy. Song of Sirius. Myhre, M., ed. McManus, Michael, illus. 155p. (Orig.). 1990. pap. 8.00 (ISBN 0-929686-01-2). Temple Golden Pubns.
Madison, Winifred. A Portrait of Myself. LC 78-13897. (Illus.). 1979. (Random Juv); lib. bdg. 7.99 (ISBN 0-394-94021-0). Random.
Major, Kevin. Far from Shore: A Novel. LC 81-65495. 192p. (gr. 7 up). 1981. 12.95 (ISBN 0-385-28266-4). Delacorte.
Naughton, Jim. My Brother Stealing Second. LC 88-22035. 224p. (gr. 7 up). 1989. PLB 13.89 (ISBN 0-06-024375-9). HarpC Child Bks.
Neff, Carolyn & Verett, Dotty. Blue Jean Days. Bachelis, Faren, ed. Franklin, Jean, illus. 32p. (gr. 4-6). 1982. wkbk 5.00 (ISBN 0-931724-20-1). Dandy Lion.
Neufeld, John. Lisa, Bright & Dark. (gr. 7 up). 1969. 18.95 (ISBN 0-87599-153-X). S G Phillips.
Neville, Emily C. It's Like This, Cat. Weiss, Emil, illus. LC 62-21292. 192p. (gr. 5-9). 1975. pap. 2.95 (ISBN 0-06-440073-5, Trophy). HarpC Child Bks.
O'Donnell, Thomas. The Journal of Malt Witty. 1989. 10.00 (ISBN 0-533-08038-X). Vantage.
Oneal, Zibby. Language of Goldfish. 1990. pap. 3.95 (ISBN 0-14-034540-X, Puffin). Puffin Bks.
Pfeffer, Susan B. Turning Thirteen. LC 88-11347. 144p. (gr. 6-8). 1988. pap. 12.95 (ISBN 0-590-40764-3, Scholastic Hardcover). Scholastic Inc.
Pike, Christopher. Gimme a Kiss. 160p. (gr. 8 up). 1988. pap. 3.50 (ISBN 0-671-73682-5, Archway). PB.
Posner, Richard. Goodnight, Cinderella. LC 89-17091. 242p. 1989. 13.95 (ISBN 0-87131-587-4). M Evans.
Ransom, Candice F. Thirteen. 192p. (Orig.). (gr. 6 up). 1986. pap. 2.50 (ISBN 0-590-40192-0, Apple Paperbacks). Scholastic Inc.
Rockwell, Thomas. Hey, Lover Boy. LC 80-68739. 160p. (gr. 8-12). 1981. 8.95 (ISBN 0-440-03583-X). Delacorte.
Ruckman, Ivy. No Way Out. LC 87-47817. 224p. (gr. 7 up). 1989. pap. 3.50 (ISBN 0-06-447003-2, Trophy). HarpC Child Bks.
Schwartz, Joel L. The Diary of a Teenage Health Freak. (gr. k-12). 1990. pap. text ed. 3.50 (ISBN 0-440-20636-7, LFL). Dell.
Schwartz, Sheila. Growing up Guilty. LC 78-3284. 1978. Pantheon.
Scoppettone, Sandra. Happy Endings Are All Alike. LC 78-2976. (gr. 7 up). 1978. 16.95i (ISBN 0-06-025239-1). HarpC Child Bks.
Shannon, Jacqueline. Faking It. 176p. (Orig.). 1989. pap. 2.95 (ISBN 0-380-75601-3, Flare). Avon.
Shles, Larry. Aliens in My Nest: Squib Meets the Teen Creature. Winch, Bradley L., ed. Shles, Larry, illus. LC 88-80770. 80p. (Orig.). (gr. k up). 1988. pap. 7.95 (ISBN 0-915190-49-4, JP9049-4). Jalmar Pr.
Smith, Doris B. Last Was Lloyd. 144p. (gr. 3-7). 1981. pap. 12.95 (ISBN 0-670-41921-4). Viking Child Bks.
Stewart, A. C. Dark Dove. LC 74-14814. 192p. (gr. 6-9). 1974. 18.95 (ISBN 0-87599-203-X). S G Phillips.
Van Leeuwen, Jean. Dear Mom, You're Ruining My Life. LC 88-3705. (Illus.). 160p. (gr. 4-7). 1989. 13.95 (ISBN 0-8037-0572-7); PLB 13.89 (ISBN 0-8037-0573-5). Dial Bks Young.
Wardlaw, Lee. Corey's Fire. 160p. (gr. 5). 1990. pap. 2.95 (ISBN 0-380-75791-5, Flare). Avon.
Weber, Lenora M. How Long Is Always? LC 75-1937. 226p. (gr. 7 up). 1970. 14.95 (ISBN 0-690-40680-0, Crowell Jr Bks). HarpC Child Bks.
Wersba, Barbara. Just Be Gorgeous. LC 87-45858. 160p. (gr. 7 up). 1988. 11.95 (ISBN 0-06-026359-8); PLB 11.89 (ISBN 0-06-026360-1). HarpC Child Bks.
—Wonderful Me. LC 88-21166. 160p. (gr. 7 up). 1989. 12.95 (ISBN 0-06-026361-X); PLB 12.89 (ISBN 0-06-026362-8). HarpC Child Bks.
Wilder, Laura I. First Four Years. Williams, Garth, illus. Macbride, R. L., intro. by. LC 76-135774. (Illus.). (gr. 5-9). 1971. 14.95 (ISBN 0-06-026426-8); PLB 14.89 (ISBN 0-06-026427-6). HarpC Child Bks.
Willey, Margaret. If Not for You. LC 88-3343. 160p. (gr. 7 up). 1988. 11.95 (ISBN 0-06-026494-2); PLB 11.89 (ISBN 0-06-026499-3). HarpC Child Bks.
Windsor, Patricia. The Hero. (gr. k-12). 1990. pap. 3.25 (ISBN 0-440-20638-3, LFL). Dell.
Wolitzer, Hilma. Out of Love. LC 76-40983. (Illus.). 160p. (gr. 5 up). 1976. 11.95 (ISBN 0-374-35675-0). FS&G.
Wyss, Thelma H. Here at the Scenic-Vu Motel. LC 87-45308. 160p. (gr. 7 up). 1989. pap. 3.50 (ISBN 0-06-447001-6, Trophy). HarpC Child Bks.
Zach, Cheryl. Tug of War. 144p. (Orig.). 1988. pap. 2.95 (ISBN 1-55802-073-X). Lynx Bks.
Zindel, Paul. I Never Loved Your Mind. LC 73-105476. 192p. (gr. 7 up). 1970. PLB 12.89 (ISBN 0-06-026822-0). HarpC Child Bks.
—Pardon Me, You're Stepping on My Eyeball. LC 75-25410. 272p. (gr. 7 up). 1976. PLB 12.89 (ISBN 0-06-026838-7). HarpC Child Bks.

ADOPTION

Bunin, Sherry & Bunin, Catherine. Is That Your Sister? LC 76-60. (Illus.). 1976. Pantheon.
Cohen, Shari. Coping with Being Adopted. Rosen, Ruth, ed. 132p. (gr. 7 up). 1988. lib. bdg. 12.95 (ISBN 0-8239-0770-8). Rosen Group.
Crook, Marion. Teenagers Talk about Adoption. 116p. (Orig.). (gr. 6 up). 1990. pap. 10.95 (ISBN 1-55021-047-5, Pub. by NC Pr Canada). Seven Hills Bk Dists.
Dellinger, Annetta E. Adopted & Loved Forever. (Illus.). (ps-2). 1987. 5.95 (ISBN 0-570-04167-8, 56-1624). Concordia.
DuPrau, Jeanne. Adoption: The Facts, Feelings & Issues of a Double Heritage. rev. ed. Steltenpohl, Jane, ed. 128p. (gr. 7 up). 1990. PLB 12.98 (ISBN 0-671-69328-X); pap. 4.95 (ISBN 0-671-69329-8). Messner.
Fairbank, Anna. Lucky Me! An Adoption Story. Weston, Martha, illus. LC 88-60649. 32p. (Orig.). (ps-1). 1988. pap. 8.95 (ISBN 0-945436-01-7). Mariah Pr.
Fisher, Iris L. Katie-Bo: An Adoption Story. Schaer, Miriam, illus. (ps-3). 1988. 9.95 (ISBN 0-915361-91-4, Dist. by Watts). Adama Pubs Inc.

Gabel, Susan. Filling in the Blanks: A Guided Look at Growing up Adopted. Seregny, Julie, illus. 160p. (gr. 5-10). 1988. pap. 16.95 (ISBN 0-9609504-8-6). Perspect Indiana.
A lifebook/workbook for 10 to 14-year-old adoptees designed to be completed with an adult helper. A removable guide to usage for adults is included. Through a step-by-step process, older children may seek answers to questions about their families, & the self esteem & identity issues common to all young people. Designed to be used by children

adopted in infancy or at an older age, domestically or internationally, from agencies or independently, into single or two parent homes. Other adoption related children's books for Perspective Press include Jane Schnitter's WILLIAM IS MY BROTHER (family built by birth & adoption), Janice Koch's OUR BABY: A BIRTH & ADOPTION STORY (sex education), Anne Brodzinsky's THE MULBERRY BIRD (a birthmother's viewpoint), Ann Angel's REAL FOR SURE SISTER (transracial adoption); & Susan Gabel's WHERE THE SUN KISSES THE SEA. Distributed by Ingram, Baker & Taylor or contact the publisher at (317) 872-3055.
Publisher Provided Annotation.

Gay, Kathlyn. Adoption & Foster Care. 128p. (gr. 6 up). 1990. 17.95 (ISBN 0-89490-239-3). Enslow Pubs.

Girard, Linda W. Adoption Is for Always. Levine, Abby, ed. LC 86-15843. (Illus.). 32p. (gr. 2-5). 1986. 10.95 (ISBN 0-8075-0185-9). A Whitman. STARRED, SCHOOL LIBRARY JOURNAL. "Celia (who appears to be five or six years old) has always known that she was adopted, but she is just beginning to understand the significance of the word. Although her parents deal with her questions with honesty & love, Celia experiences a confused mixture of fear & anger.... This well-written book succeeds as a story as well as bibliotherapy. Information a young child can understand about adoption is skillfully integrated into the text. Expressive pencil drawings within colored borders enhance the story. One of the best titles about adoption available for young children. "This is attractive & absorbing-- a very good source for adults looking for ways to deal with children's feelings about adoption."-- BOOKLIST.
Publisher Provided Annotation.

Glotzbach, Gerri. Adoption. (Illus.). 64p. (gr. 7 up). 1990. lib. bdg. 15.93 (ISBN 0-86593-078-3); lib. bdg. 11.95s.p. (ISBN 0-685-36294-9). Rourke Corp.
Hess, Edith & Blass, Jacqueline. Peter & Susie Find a Family. (Illus.). 28p. (gr. 2-4). 1985. Repr. of 1981 ed. 1.00 (ISBN 0-687-30848-8). Abingdon.

**Koch, Janice. Our Baby: A Birth & Adoption Story. Goldberg, Pat, illus. LC 85-6392. 27p. (ps-2). 1985. 10.95 (ISBN 0-9609504-3-5). Perspect Indiana.
A sex education book designed specifically for children who were adopted as babies into two parent families. Using correct anatomical terminology, the author, a science educator & adoptive parent, introduces the very young adoptee to the idea that there are two ways for grown ups to become parents: by birth & by adoption. In a format designed to be personalized with snapshots & words for an individual child it is explained that he was conceived by & born to birthparents & then adopted into a loving family who anticipated his arrival with excitement. Well reviewed in all adoption periodicals as well as by PARENT'S magazine & Planned Parenthood. Other adoption related children's books from Perspectives**

Press include Jane Schnitter's WILLIAM IS MY BROTHER (family built by birth & adoption), Anne Brodzinsky's THE MULBERRY BIRD (a birthmother's viewpoint), Ann Angel's REAL FOR SURE SISTER (transracial adoption), Susan Gabel's WHERE THE SUN KISSES THE SEA (international placement), & Susan Gabel's FILLING IN THE BLANKS: A GUIDED LOOK AT GROWING UP ADOPTED (adolescence). Distributed by Ingram, Baker & Taylor or contact the publisher at (317) 872-3055.
Publisher Provided Annotation.

Landau, Elaine. Black Market Adoption & the Sale of Children. (gr. 4-7). 1990. PLB 12.90 (ISBN 0-531-10914-3). Watts.
Lindsay, Jeanne W. Pregnant Too Soon: Adoption Is an Option. rev. ed. Morford, Pam P., illus. Monserrat, Catherine, frwd. by. (Illus.). 224p. (gr. 7-12). 1987. pap. 9.95 (ISBN 0-930934-25-3); tchr's. guide 2.50 (ISBN 0-930934-27-X). Morning Glory.
Lowe, Darla. Story of Adoption: Why Do I Look Different? Carney, Christina S., illus. LC 87-46273. (Orig.). (gr. 3-6). 1987. pap. 5.95 (ISBN 0-9606090-2-4). EastWest Pr.
Nickman, Steven L. The Adoption Experiences. LC 85-8957. 192p. (gr. 7 up). 1985. lib. bdg. 13.98 (ISBN 0-671-50817-2). Messner.
Peebles, Catherine & Edge, Denzil. A Natural Curiosity: Taffy's Search for Self. LC 87-36882. (Illus., Orig.). 1988. pap. 6.95 (ISBN 0-939991-01-2). Learning KY.
Powledge, Fred. So You're Adopted. LC 81-23278. 112p. (gr. 5 up). 1982. 12.95 (ISBN 0-684-17347-6, Scribners Young Read). Macmillan Child Grp.
Pursell, Margaret S. A Look at Adoption. LC 17-13080. (Illus.). 36p. (gr. 3-6). 1977. PLB 6.95 (ISBN 0-8225-1310-2). Lerner Pubns.
Rosenberg, Maxine B. Being Adopted. Ancona, George, photos by. LC 83-17522. (Illus.). 48p. (gr. 1-4). 1984. 13.95 (ISBN 0-688-02672-9); lib. bdg. 13.88 (ISBN 0-688-02673-7). Lothrop.
—Growing up Adopted. LC 89-9899. 128p. (gr. 4 up). 1989. 12.95 (ISBN 0-02-777912-2, Bradbury Pr). Macmillan Child Grp.
—Talking about Stepfamilies. Visher, Emily, afterword by. LC 90-33540. (Illus.). 160p. (gr. 4 up). 1990. 13.95 (ISBN 0-02-777913-0, Bradbury Pr). Macmillan Child Grp.
Sanford, Doris. Brian Was Adopted. Davis, Deena, ed. Evans, Graci, illus. LC 89-31410. 28p. (gr. k-4). 1989. 6.95 (ISBN 0-88070-300-8). Multnomah.
Scott, Elaine. Adoption. LC 80-14848. (Illus.). (gr. 4 up). 1980. 9.90 (ISBN 0-531-02937-9). Watts.
Stein, Sara B. The Adopted One. Stone, Erika, illus. (gr. k-6). 1979. 12.95 (ISBN 0-8027-6346-4); pap. 7.95 (ISBN 0-8027-7224-2). Walker & Co.
Stewart, Gail B. Adoption. LC 89-1525. (Illus.). 47p. (gr. 4 up). 1989. 10.95 (ISBN 0-89686-443-X, Crestwood Hse). Macmillan Child Grp.
ADOPTION–FICTION
see also Foster Home Care–Fiction

**Angel, Ann. Real for Sure Sister. LC 87-29217. (Illus.). 72p. (gr. 3-6). 1988. 12.95 (ISBN 0-9609504-7-8). Perspect Indiana.
Youngsters will readily identify with Amanda, the oldest in a family of soon-to-be four children, all of whom were adopted. Only as they await the arrival of a new biracial baby sister (yuck! it's been nice to be the only girl!) does Amanda become aware of the adoption issues around her-the social worker, the judges & their power; the neighbors, perfect strangers & their odd comments--& begin to deal with her own feelings about being adopted & being part of a multiracial family as well as about sibling rivalry. Whimsical illustrations add fun to this chapter book. Other adoption related children's books from Perspectives Press include Jane Schnitter's WILLIAM IS MY BROTHER (family built by adoption), Janice Koch's OUR BABY: A BIRTH & ADOPTION STORY (sex education), Anne Brodzinsky's THE MULBERRY BIRD (a birthmother's**

viewpoint), Susan Gabel's WHERE THE SUN KISSES THE SEA (international placement), & Susan Gabel's FILLING IN THE BLANKS: A GUIDED LOOK AT GROWING UP ADOPTED (adolescence). Distributed by Ingram, Baker & Taylor or contact the publisher at (317) 872-3055.
Publisher Provided Annotation.

Auch, Mary J. A Sudden Change of Family. LC 90-55100. 112p. (gr. 3-7). 1990. 13.95 (ISBN 0-8234-0842-6). Holiday.
Blomquist, Geraldine M. & Blomquist, Paul B. Zachary's New Home: A Story for Foster & Adopted Children. Lemieux, Margo, illus. 32p. (ps-2). 1990. 16.95 (ISBN 0-945354-28-2); pap. 5.95 (ISBN 0-945354-27-4). Magination Pr.
Bloom, Suzanne. A Family for Jamie: An Adoption Story. Bloom, Suzanne, illus. LC 90-42589. 24p. (ps-1). 1991. 12.95 (ISBN 0-517-57492-6, C N Potter Bks); PLB 13.99 (ISBN 0-517-57493-4, C N Potter Bks). Crown.
Boyd, Lizi. The Not-So-Wicked Stepmother. (Illus.). 32p. (ps-3). 1989. pap. 3.95 (ISBN 0-14-050720-5, Puffin). Puffin Bks.

**—The Mulberry Bird: Story of an Adoption. LC 86-2460. (Illus.). 48p. (gr. k-5). 1986. 9.95 (ISBN 0-9609504-5-1). Perspect Indiana.
This award winning (Catholic Adoptive Parents Association) book uses the story of a mother bird & her much loved baby to explore why a birthparent might make an adoption plan-an area which rarely receives much attention in adoption literature, but the issue which is of the greatest concern to children who were adopted. The author was part of a Rutgers University team which has conducted a longitudinal study of what children understand & when. Well reviewed in adoption periodicals, Small Press Book Review, School Library Journal, etc., this is the best selling children's book from a publisher focusing exclusively on adoption issues. Other adoption related children's books from Perspectives Press include Jane Schnitter's WILLIAM IS MY BROTHER (family built by birth & adoption), Janice Koch's OUR BABY: A BIRTH & ADOPTION STORY (sex education), Ann Angel's REAL FOR SURE SISTER (transracial adoption); Susan Gabel's WHERE THE SUN KISSES THE SEA (international placement), & Susan Gabel's FILLING IN THE BLANKS: A GUIDED LOOK AT GROWING UP ADOPTED (adolescence). Distributed by Ingram, Baker & Taylor or contact the publisher at (317) 872-3055.**

Callen, Larry. The Just-Right Family. McQueen, Lucinda, illus. 40p. 1984. 5.95 (ISBN 0-910313-26-1). Parker Bros.

Cleaver, Vera & Cleaver, Bill. Trial Valley. LC 76-54303. 192p. (gr. 7 up). 1991. pap. 3.50 (ISBN 0-06-447076-8, Trophy). HarpC Child Bks.

Gabel, Susan L. Where the Sun Kisses the Sea. Bowring, Joanne, illus. LC 89-16296. 32p. (ps-5). 1989. 15.95 (ISBN 0-944934-00-5). Perspect Indiana.
Gorgeous full color water color illustrations illuminate the poetry-tinged language of this story for all ages of a young boy's journey home. Though his caregivers in the orphanage in a far away land have been kind & his life secure & comfortable, the boy dreams of a smaller house, with only a few children, where everyone shares the same family name. As he flies across the sea, we share his fears & apprehensions as well as his ultimate joy in a forever family. Appropriate for children adopted at an older age either in the U.S. or internationally. Well reviewed by every adoption-related periodical & School Library Journal. Other adoption related children's books from Perspectives Press include Jane Schnitter's WILLIAM IS MY BROTHER (family built by birth & adoption), Janice Koch's OUR BABY: A BIRTH & ADOPTION STORY (sex education), Anne Brodzinsky's THE MULBERRY BIRD (a birthmother's viewpoint), Ann Angel's REAL FOR SURE SISTER (transracial adoption); & Susan Gabel's FILLING IN THE BLANKS: A GUIDED LOOK AT GROWING UP ADOPTED (adolescence). Distributed by Ingram, Baker & Taylor or contact the publisher at (317) 872-3055.
Publisher Provided Annotation.

George, Jean C. Shark Beneath the Reef. LC 88-25194. 192p. (gr. 7 up). 1991. pap. 3.50 (ISBN 0-06-440308-4, Trophy). HarpC Child Bks.

Gordon, Shirley. The Boy Who Wanted a Family. Robinson, Charles, illus. LC 79-2003. 96p. (gr. 1-4). 1980. PLB 12.89 (ISBN 0-06-022052-X). HarpC Child Bks.

Haywood, Carolyn. Penny & Peter. rev. ed. Haywood, Carolyn & Yakovetic, Joe, illus. LC 46-21128. 170p. (gr. 1-4). 1986. pap. 4.95 (ISBN 0-15-260467-7, VoyB). HarBraceJ.

Holland, Isabelle. House in the Woods. 1991. 15.95 (ISBN 0-316-37178-5). Little.

Howard, Ellen. Her Own Song. LC 88-3393. 176p. (gr. 3-7). 1988. 13.95 (ISBN 0-689-31444-2, Atheneum Child Bk). Macmillan Child Grp.

Keller, Holly. Horace. LC 90-30750. (Illus.). 32p. (ps up). 1991. 13.95 (ISBN 0-688-09831-2); PLB 13.88 (ISBN 0-688-09832-0). Greenwillow.

Koehler, Phoebe. The Day We Met You. LC 89-35344. 48p. (ps-k). 1990. 12.95 (ISBN 0-02-750901-X, Bradbury Pr). Macmillan Child Grp.

Kropp, Paul. Jo's Search. Collins, Heather, illus. LC 88-14082. 96p. (Orig.). (gr. 7 up). 1989. pap. 2.95 (ISBN 0-02-041794-2, Collier Young Ad). Macmillan Child Grp.

Magorian, Michelle. Good Night, Mr. Tom. LC 80-8444. 336p. (gr. 7 up). 1982. 13.95 (ISBN 0-06-024078-4); PLB 13.89 (ISBN 0-06-024079-2). HarpC Child Bks.

Mills, Claudia. Boardwalk with Hotel. 144p. (gr. 7-12). 1986. pap. 2.50 (ISBN 0-553-15397-8, Skylark). Bantam.

Morris, Winifred. The Jell-O Syndrome. LC 90-1437. 176p. (gr. 7 up). 1990. pap. 3.95 (ISBN 0-02-044712-4, Collier Young Ad). Macmillan Child Grp.

Neufeld, John. Edgar Allan. Dunlap, Loren, illus. LC 68-31175. (gr. 5-8). 1968. 18.95 (ISBN 0-87599-149-1). S G Phillips.

Okimoto, Jean. Molly By Any Other Name. (gr. 9-12). 1990. 13.95 (ISBN 0-590-42993-0). Scholastic Inc.

Schnitter, Jane. William Is My Brother. LC 90-21364. (Illus.). 32p. (ps-3). 1991. 10.95 (ISBN 0-944934-03-X). Perspect Indiana.
Families expanded by both birth & adoption will enjoy this illustrated story of two brothers--one born to their parents & the other adopted. William & Tony discover that they are alike in many ways & different in many ways, like all brothers, & that what makes each special is his unique qualities, not the way he joined the family. A noted adoption therapist wrote "This book is superb. It addresses all of the information I believe is important. It helps children understand they are born & adopted. It addresses being different & being special, & includes those positive emotions about the process of adopting, stressing the love, excitement & happiness." Warm brown illustrations depict a racially ambiguous family. Other adoption related children's books from Perspectives Press include Janice Koch's OUR BABY: A BIRTH & ADOPTION STORY (sex education), Anne Brodzinsky's THE MULBERRY BIRD (a birthmother's viewpoint), Ann Angel's REAL FOR SURE SISTER (transracial adoption); Susan Gabel's WHERE THE SUN KISSES THE SEA (international placement), & Susan Gabel's FILLING IN THE BLANKS: A GUIDED LOOK AT GROWING UP ADOPTED (adolescence). Distributed by Ingram, Baker & Taylor, or contact the Publisher at (317) 872-3055.
Publisher Provided Annotation.

Stahl, Hilda. Kayla O'Brian: Trouble at Bitter Creek Ranch. 128p. (Orig.). (gr. 4-7). 1991. pap. 4.95 (ISBN 0-89107-611-5). Good News.

Swartley, David W. My Friend, My Brother. Converse, James, illus. LC 79-26273. 104p. (gr. 6 up). 1980. pap. 3.95 (ISBN 0-8361-1916-9). Herald Pr.

Turner, Ann. Through Moon & Stars & Night Skies. Hale, James G., illus. LC 87-35044. 32p. (ps-3). 1990. 12.95 (ISBN 0-06-026189-7); PLB 12.89 (ISBN 0-06-026190-0). HarpC Child Bks.

Viglucci, Pat C. Cassandra Robbins, Esq. 176p. (Orig.). (gr. 8-12). 1987. pap. 4.95 (ISBN 0-938961-01-2, Stamp Out Sheep Pr). Sq One Pubs.

Wasson, Valentina P. The Chosen Baby. 3rd ed. LC 76-41391. (gr. k-3). 1977. 14.95 (ISBN 0-397-31738-7, Lipp Jr Bks). HarpC Child Bks.

ADULTHOOD

Doolittle, Hilda. The Hedgehog. Schaffner, Perdita, intro. by. Plank, George, illus. LC 88-3927. 96p. 1988. 12.95 (ISBN 0-8112-1069-3). New Directions.

ADVENTURE AND ADVENTURERS
see also Discoveries (In Geography); Escapes; Explorers; Frontier and Pioneer Life; Heroes; Sea Stories; Seafaring Life; Shipwrecks; Underwater Exploration; Voyages and Travels

Allan, Mabel E. The Horns of Danger. 192p. (gr. 7-11). 1981. 8.95 (ISBN 0-396-07987-3, Putnam). Putnam Pub Group.

Armstrong, Beverly. Pirates, Explorers, Tailblazers. 112p. (gr. 4-6). 1987. 9.95 (ISBN 0-88160-152-7, LW 908). Learning Wks.

Birenbaum, Barbara. The Gooblins Night. Birenbaum, Barbara, illus. LC 85-62585. 44p. (gr. 2-5). 1985. pap. 5.95 (ISBN 0-935343-31-8). Peartree.

Blotnick, Elihu. Glimmins: Children of the Western Woods. Blotnick, Elihu, illus. 72p. (gr. 1 up). pap. 11.95 (ISBN 0-915090-18-X). Calif Street.

Cone, Molly. The Big Squeeze. 160p. (gr. 5-9). 1984. 11.95 (ISBN 0-395-36262-8). HM.

Curtis, Philip. Invasion of the Comet People: A Capers Book. Ross, Tony, illus. LC 82-9923. 128p. (gr. 3-5). 1983. lib. bdg. 5.99 (ISBN 0-394-95490-4). Knopf.

Cutting, Edith. Zillah-Abidan. Grossman, Dan, illus. 48p. (gr. 2-7). 1985. wkbk. 2.48 (ISBN 0-86653-306-0). Good Apple.

Danielson, Peter. The Golden Pharoah. 416p. (Orig.). 1986. pap. 4.95 (ISBN 0-553-26885-6). Bantam.

Defoe, Daniel. Robinson Crusoe. Iljinski, Igor, illus. 192p. (gr. 4 up). 1989. 14.95 (ISBN 0-8120-5967-0). Barron.

Donev, Stef. Adventures. Hughes, Mark, illus. 48p. (gr. 5-9). 1985. PLB 10.69 (ISBN 0-87617-023-8, Pub. by C Hayes Pr). Penworthy Pub.

—Amazing Adventures. Hughes, Mark, illus. 48p. (gr. 5-9). 1985. pap. 5.95 (ISBN 0-88625-093-5). Durkin Hayes Pub.

Duggleby, John. Doomed Expeditions. LC 89-25459. (Illus.). 48p. (gr. 5 up). 1990. 10.95 (ISBN 0-89686-506-1, Crestwood Hse). Macmillan Child Grp.

—Impossible Quests. LC 89-28988. (Illus.). 48p. (gr. 5 up). 1990. 10.95 (ISBN 0-89686-509-6, Crestwood Hse). Macmillan Child Grp.

Dumas, Alexandre. The Three Musketeers. unabridged ed. Bair, Lowell, tr. from FRE. 560p. 1984. pap. 5.95 (ISBN 0-553-21337-7, Bantam Classics). Bantam.

Estes, James L. Alabama's Youngest Admirals. Krauel, Mary E., ed. Christian, Releta, illus. 32p. (Orig.). (gr. 4-12). 1991. pap. 8.95 (ISBN 0-9628634-0-8). J L Estes.

Field, Rachael. Calico Bush. (gr. 4-8). 1988. pap. 3.25 (ISBN 0-440-40100-3, YB). Dell.

Forsse, Ken. Teddy Ruxpin & the Mudblups. High, David, et al, illus. 26p. (ps). 1985. incl. audio-cassette 9.95 (ISBN 0-934323-03-8). Alchemy Comms.

—Tweeg & the Bounders. High, David, et al, illus. 26p. (ps). 1985. incl. audio-cassette 9.95 (ISBN 0-934323-10-0). Alchemy Comms.

Goold, I. The Rutan Voyager. (Illus.). 32p. (gr. 4 up). Date not set. PLB 14.00 (ISBN 0-86592-869-X). Rourke Corp.

Guillot, Rene. Wind of Chance. Dale, Norman, tr. Collot, Pierre, illus. (gr. 6-9). 1958. 18.95 (ISBN 0-87599-048-7). S G Phillips.

Johnson, Annabel & Johnson, Edgar. The Grizzly. Riswold, Gilbert, illus. LC 64-11831. 194p. (gr. 5-9). 1973. pap. 3.50 (ISBN 0-06-440036-0, Trophy). HarpC Child Bks.

Kauffmann, Joel. Wolf Hunter. 112p. (Orig.). (gr. 1-7). 1986. pap. 0.20 (ISBN 0-687-45890-0). Abingdon.

Kelly, Terry, et al. Daring Deeds. Gagne, Dennis, illus. 48p. (gr. 5-9). 1985. pap. 5.95 (ISBN 0-88625-092-7). Durkin Hayes Pub.

McCaughren, Tom. Run to Earth. (Illus.). 144p. (ps-8). 1984. pap. 7.95 (ISBN 0-86327-116-2, Pub. by Wolfhound Press Eire). Dufour.

McClung, Robert M. The True Adventures of Grizzly Adams. LC 85-8886. (Illus.). 208p. (gr. 5 up). 1985. 11.95 (ISBN 0-688-05794-2). Morrow Jr Bks.

Melanos, Jack. Sinbad & the Evil Genii. (Orig.). (gr. k up). 1985. pap. 4.50 (ISBN 0-87602-251-4). Anchorage.

Monro, Louise. Forest of Fear. Packard, Edward, created by. 128p. (Orig.). (gr. 4). 1986. pap. 2.25 (ISBN 0-553-25490-1). Bantam.

Morey, Walt. Angry Waters. Spillman, Fredicka, illus. (Orig.). (gr. 5-9). 1990. Repr. 6.95 (ISBN 0-936085-10-X). Blue Heron OR.

Nordhoff, Charles & Hall, James N. The Bounty Trilogy. (Illus.). (gr. 9 up). 1982. 29.95 (ISBN 0-316-61161-1, Pub. by Atlantic Monthly Pr). Little.

Paulsen, Gary. Sentries. LC 85-26978. 160p. (gr. 7 up). 1986. 13.95 (ISBN 0-02-770100-X, Bradbury Pr). Macmillan Child Grp.

Rappaport, Doreen. Living Dangerously: American Women Who Risked Their Lives for Adventure. LC 90-28915. (Illus.). 96p. (gr. 4-7). 1991. 13.95 (ISBN 0-06-025108-5); PLB 13.89 (ISBN 0-06-025109-3). HarpC Child Bks.

Rardin, Susan L. Captives in a Foreign Land. 224p. (gr. 5 up). 1984. 12.95 (ISBN 0-395-36216-4). HM.

Rathert, Donna. Advent Is for Waiting. (Illus.). 24p. (ps). 1987. pap. 2.95 (ISBN 0-317-60419-8, 56-1569). Concordia.

Rawlinson, J. Space to Seabed. (Illus.). 32p. (gr. 4 up). Date not set. PLB 14.00 (ISBN 0-86592-872-X). Rourke Corp.

Razzi, Jim, adapted by. The Jungle Book. 48p. (Orig.). (gr. 4). 1986. pap. 4.95 (ISBN 0-553-05409-0). Bantam.

Roddy, Lee. Secret of the Shark Pit: A Ladd Family Adventure. Christian, S. Rickly, ed. 136p. (Orig.). (gr. 3-6). 1988. pap. 4.99 (ISBN 0-929608-14-3). Focus Family.

Rudig, Doug. Big Bend Adventure Guide. Pearson, John R. & Deckert, Frank J., eds. (Illus.). 32p. (Orig.). (gr. k-6). 1983. pap. 2.00 (ISBN 0-912001-10-0). Big Bend.

Sharp, Margery. The Rescuers. (gr. 3-6). 15.00 (ISBN 0-8446-6412-X). Peter Smith.

Sofer, Barbara. Holiday Adventures of Achbar. Gaelen, Nina, illus. LC 82-23398. 64p. (gr. k-5). 1983. pap. 3.95 (ISBN 0-930494-22-9). Kar Ben.

Sonnleitner, A. T. Cave Children. Bell, Anthea, tr. from GER. LC 70-120785. (Illus.). (gr. 8 up). 1971. 18.95 (ISBN 0-87599-169-6). S G Phillips.

Stevenson, Robert Louis. Treasure Island. 1991. pap. 3.75 (ISBN 0-425-12335-9). Berkley Pub.

Sweetgall, Robert & Peleg, Dorith E. Road Scholars: The Story of Twenty-Eight Kids Who Decided to Take a Hike for Their Health. (Illus.). 64p. (Orig.). 1989. pap. 20.00 (ISBN 0-939041-07-3). Creative Walking.

Thompson, Jonathon. Air Raiders. (Illus.). 75p. (gr. 6-12). 4.50 (ISBN 0-933479-02-6). Thompson.

—Superflyer: Captain John Champion Flyer. 40p. (gr. 3-6). 3.95 (ISBN 0-933479-08-5). Thompson.

Treasure Island. (ps-6). 1988. pap. 4.87 (ISBN 0-582-54163-8, 74270). Longman.

Twain, Mark. Adventures of Tom Sawyer. 1986. 2.98 (ISBN 0-671-08315-5). S&S Trade.

Verne, Jules. Flight to France. (gr. 5 up). 4.95 (ISBN 0-685-28715-7). Assoc Bk.

Wulffson, Don L. Incredible True Adventures. (Illus.). 112p. (gr. 9-12). 1986. 8.95 (ISBN 0-396-08799-X, Putnam). Putnam Pub Group.

ADVENTURE AND ADVENTURERS–FICTION

Aber, Linda. Lost Girls Adrift. 176p. (gr. 3-7). 1991. pap. 2.75 (ISBN 0-590-43536-1, Apple Paperbacks). Scholastic Inc.

—Lost Girls Alone. 176p. (gr. 3-7). 1991. pap. 2.75 (ISBN 0-590-43535-3, Apple Paperbacks). Scholastic Inc.

Adler, C. S. The Silver Coach. 112p. (gr. 3-7). 1988. pap. 2.50 (ISBN 0-380-75498-3, Camelot). Avon.

Adler, David A. Cam Jansen & the Mystery of the Gold Coins. Natti, Susanna, illus. 64p. (gr. k-6). 1984. pap. 2.75 (ISBN 0-440-40996-9, YB). Dell.

The Adventures of Jason Ashley. (gr. 4-6). 1990. 1.55 (ISBN 0-89636-119-5). Accent Bks.

Affabee, Eric. G. I. Joe & the Everglades Swamp Terror. (Orig.). (gr. 5 up). 1987. pap. 2.50 (ISBN 0-345-34628-9). Ballantine.

Agee, Jon. Ellsworth. (Illus.). (gr. 4-7). 1983. 10.95 (ISBN 0-394-85995-2). Random.

Ahern, Jerry & Ahern, Sharon. The Defender, No. 3. (Orig.). 1988. pap. 3.50 (ISBN 0-318-33285-X). Dell.

Ahlberg, Allan. The Mighty Slide. Voake, Charlotte, illus. 96p. (gr. 1-6). 1988. pap. 10.95 (ISBN 0-670-81677-9). Viking Child Bks.

Aiken, Joan. Bridle the Wind. LC 83-5355. 224p. (gr. 7 up). 1983. 14.95 (ISBN 0-385-29301-1). Delacorte.

—The Teeth of the Gale. LC 87-35050. 320p. (gr. 7 up). 1988. PLB 14.89 (ISBN 0-06-020045-6). HarpC Child Bks.

Albertson, Jon. Falklands Fiasco. Hooper, Anne, ed. Pheris, William E., IV, illus. 284p. (gr. 12). 1989. 16.95 (ISBN 0-9621448-1-9). Aeolus Bks.

—Valley of the Condor. Hooper, Anne, ed. 300p. (gr. 12). 1990. write for info. (ISBN 0-9621448-3-5). Aeolus Bks.

Alcock, Vivien. The Steonwalkers. (gr. k-6). 1990. pap. 2.95 (ISBN 0-440-40300-6, Pub. by Yearling Classics). Dell.

Alexander, Lloyd. The Drackenberg Adventure. (gr. k-6). 1990. pap. 3.50 (ISBN 0-440-40296-4, Pub. by Yearling Classics). Dell.

—The Drackenburg Adventure. LC 87-36881. 160p. (gr. 5-9). 1988. 12.95 (ISBN 0-525-44389-4, 01258-370, DCB). Dutton Child Bks.

—The El Dorado Adventure. LC 86-29157. (gr. 5-9). 1987. 13.95 (ISBN 0-525-44313-4, DCB). Dutton Child Bks.

—The Illyrian Adventure. LC 85-30762. (Illus.). 160p. (gr. 5-9). 1986. 13.95 (ISBN 0-525-44250-2, DCB). Dutton Child Bks.

—The Illyrian Adventure. (gr. k-12). 1987. pap. 2.75 (ISBN 0-440-94018-4, LFL). Dell.

—The Jedera Adventure. 160p. (gr. 5-9). 1989. 13.95 (ISBN 0-525-44481-5, DCB). Dutton Child Bks.

—The Jedera Adventure. 1990. pap. 3.50 (ISBN 0-440-40295-6, YB). Dell.

—Marvelous Misadventures of Sebastian. LC 70-166879. (gr. 4 up). 1973. 14.95 (ISBN 0-525-34739-9, DCB); (DCB). Dutton Child Bks.

—The Philadelphia Adventure. (gr. 5-9). 1990. 13.95 (ISBN 0-525-44564-1, DCB). Dutton Child Bks.

—The Remarkable Journey of Prince Jen. 224p. (gr. 5 up). 1991. 13.95 (ISBN 0-525-44826-8, DCB). Dutton Child Bks.

Allard, Harry. Bumps in the Night. Marshall, James, illus. 48p. (gr. 1-4). 1984. pap. 2.25 (ISBN 0-553-15284-X, Skylark). Bantam.

Allen, Pamela. Hidden Treasure. Allen, Pamela, illus. 32p. (gr. k-3). 1987. 13.95 (ISBN 0-399-21427-5, Putnam). Putnam Pub Group.

Allston, Aaron. Mythic Greece: Age of Heroes. Charlton, Coleman, ed. Loubet, Dennis, illus. 160p. (Orig.). (gr. 10-12). 1988. pap. 12.00 (ISBN 1-55806-002-2, 1020). Iron Crown Ent Inc.

Altsheler, Joseph A. After the Battle. rev. ed. (gr. 9-12). 1989. Repr. of 1905 ed. multi-media kit 35.00 (ISBN 0-685-31125-2). Balance Pub.

—The Forest Runners. 300p. Date not set. 13.95 (ISBN 0-929146-04-2). Voyageur Pub.

Amthor, Terry K. Action on Akaisha Outstation. 32p. (gr. 10-12). 1985. 6.00 (ISBN 0-915795-46-9, 9101). Iron Crown Ent Inc.

Ansell, Rod & Percy, Rachel. To Fight the Wild. LC 85-22023. (Illus.). 156p. (gr. 7-8). 1986. 12.95 (ISBN 0-15-289068-8, HJ). Harbracej.

Apple, Victor, II. Tom Swift the Astral Fortress. (gr. 5-6). 15.95 (ISBN 0-88411-461-9, Pub. by Aeonian Pr). Amereon Ltd.

Appleton, Victor. The Invisible Force. Barish, Wendy, ed. 192p. (Orig.). (gr. 3-8). 1983. 8.50 (ISBN 0-671-43958-8, Little Simon); pap. 3.40 (ISBN 0-671-43959-6). S&S Trade.

—Tom Swift: Gateway to Doom. Barish, Wendy, ed. 192p. (gr. 8-10). 1983. 8.95 (ISBN 0-671-43956-1, Little Simon); pap. 3.95 (ISBN 0-671-43957-X). S&S Trade.

—The Tom Swift Gift Set, 3 vols. Boxed Set. pap. 7.95 (ISBN 0-317-12430-7, Little Simon). S&S Trade.

Appleton, Victor, II. Tom Swift & His Electronic Electroscope. (gr. 5-6). 15.95 (ISBN 0-88411-462-7, Pub. by Aeonian Pr). Amereon Ltd.

—Tom Swift & His Space Solatron. (gr. 5-6). 15.95 (ISBN 0-88411-457-0, Pub. by Aeonian Pr). Amereon Ltd.

—Tom Swift & His Triphibian Atomicar. (gr. 5-6). 14.95 (ISBN 0-88411-459-7, Pub. by Aeonian Pr). Amereon Ltd.

—Tom Swift Terror on the Moons of Jupiter. (gr. 5-6). 15.95 (ISBN 0-88411-460-0, Pub. by Aeonian Pr). Amereon Ltd.

—Tom Swift the Alien Probe. (gr. 5-6). 15.95 (ISBN 0-88411-464-3, Pub. by Aeonian Pr). Amereon Ltd.

—Tom Swift the City in the Stars. (gr. 5-6). 15.95 (ISBN 0-88411-463-5, Pub. by Aeonian Pr). Amereon Ltd.

—Tom Swift the Rescue Mission. (gr. 5-6). 15.95 (ISBN 0-88411-458-9, Pub. by Aeonian Pr). Amereon Ltd.

—Tom Swift the Water in Outer Space. (gr. 5-6). 14.95 (ISBN 0-88411-465-1, Pub. by Aeonian Pr). Amereon Ltd.

Aragones, Sergio & Zone, Ray. Aragones 3-D. Aragones, Sergio, illus. 64p. (Orig.). (gr. 9-12). 1989. pap. 4.95 (ISBN 0-317-93126-1). Three-D Zone.

Ardizzone, Edward. The Little Tim & Brave Sea Captain. (Illus.). 48p. (ps-3). 1983. pap. 3.95 (ISBN 0-14-050175-4, Puffin). Puffin Bks.

Around the World in Eighty Days. (Illus.). (gr. 3-5). 3.50 (ISBN 0-7214-0721-8). Ladybird Bks.

Arrick, Fran. God's Radar. 224p. (gr. 6-12). 1986. pap. 2.95 (ISBN 0-440-92960-1, LFL). Dell.

Asch, Frank. Skyfire. Asch, Frank, illus. LC 88-3193. 32p. (ps-2). 1988. 12.95 (ISBN 0-671-66692-4); pap. 4.95 (ISBN 0-671-66861-7). S&S Trade.

Ashwill, Beverley. The Blue-Eyed Ninja Warrior. Ashwill, Betty J., illus. LC 90-83313. 43p. (gr. 3-9). 1990. pap. 5.98 (ISBN 0-941381-05-6). BJO Enterprises.

Avi. Shadrach's Crossing. LC 82-19008. 192p. (gr. 5 up). 1983. 10.95 (ISBN 0-394-85816-6); lib. bdg. 10.99 o.p (ISBN 0-394-95816-0). Pantheon.

Babbitt, Natalie. The Eyes of the Amaryllis. 128p. (gr. 3 up). 1986. pap. 3.50 (ISBN 0-374-42238-9). FS&G.

Bach, Jennifer & Brost, Amy. The Great Zopper Toothpaste Treasure. 64p. (Orig.). (gr. 5 up). 1988. pap. 2.50 (ISBN 0-553-15583-0, Skylark). Bantam.

Baker, Michael K. The Sword. LC 84-90678. 303p. (gr. 5up). 1985. text ed. 8.00 (ISBN 0-932543-01-4); pap. 8.00 (ISBN 0-932543-00-6). M B Pub.

Ballantyne, Robert M. The Coral Island. (gr. 4-6). 1986. pap. 2.25 (ISBN 0-14-035040-3, Puffin). Puffin Bks.

Bang, Molly. Yellow Ball. Bang, Molly, illus. LC 90-46077. 24p. (ps up). 1991. 12.95 (ISBN 0-688-06314-4); PLB 12.88 (ISBN 0-688-06315-2, Morrow Jr Bks). Morrow Jr Bks.

Bannister, Ned. Code Name: North Star. (gr. 4 up). 1989. pap. 2.95 (ISBN 0-345-35921-6). Ballantine.

Baroness Orczy. The Scarlet Pimpernel. (gr. k-6). 1989. pap. 3.50 (ISBN 0-440-40220-4, YB). Dell.

Bashful Bard. Search for Rainbow's End. Bashful Bard, illus. LC 89-84962. 28p. (Orig.). (ps-1). 1989. pap. 2.95 (ISBN 1-877906-01-8). Kenney Pubns.

Baum, L. Frank. Sky Island. Neill, John R., illus. 288p. (gr. 3 up). 1988. 17.95 (ISBN 0-929605-02-0); pap. 9.95 (ISBN 0-929605-01-2). Books Wonder.

Bawden, Nina. The Finding. (gr. k-6). 1988. pap. 2.95 (ISBN 0-440-40004-X). Dell.

Bell, Clare. Ratha's Creature. (gr. k-12). 1987. pap. 2.95 (ISBN 0-440-97298-1, LFL). Dell.

—Tomorrow's Sphinx. LC 86-8479. 312p. (gr. 7 up). 1986. 15.95 (ISBN 0-689-50402-0, M K McElderry). Macmillan Child Grp.

—Tomorrow's Sphinx. (gr. k-12). 1988. pap. 3.25 (ISBN 0-440-20124-1, LFL). Dell.

Bell, William. Crabbe's Journey. (gr. 7 up). 1987. 12.95 (ISBN 0-316-08837-4). Little.

Bellairs, John. The Lamp from the Warlock's Tomb. LC 87-21404. 176p. (gr. 5 up). 1988. 12.95 (ISBN 0-8037-0512-3); PLB 12.89 (ISBN 0-8037-0535-2). Dial Bks Young.

Benedict, Rex. Run for Your Sweet Life. Christiana, David, illus. LC 86-45507. 128p. (gr. 5 up). 1986. 11.95 (ISBN 0-374-36359-5). FS&G.

Berends, Polly. Ozma & the Wayward Wand. Rose, David, illus. LC 84-17972. 80p. (gr. 2-6). 1985. (Random Juv); pap. 1.95 (ISBN 0-394-87068-9). Random.

Bicknell, Arthur. Scavenger's Hunt. (Orig.). (gr. k-12). 1987. pap. 2.95 (ISBN 0-440-97672-3, LFL). Dell.

Billac, Pete. The Annihilator: All Must Die. Davis, Sharon K., ed. LC 80-85318. 176p. (Orig.). (gr. 12 up). 1987. pap. 1.95 (ISBN 0-317-67266-5). Swan Pub.

Blair, Cynthia. Apple Pie Adventure. (gr. 4 up). 1989. pap. 2.95 (ISBN 0-449-70308-8, Juniper). Fawcett.

Bly, Stephen A. The President Is Stuck in the Mud. (Orig.). (gr. 3-8). 1982. pap. 3.95 (ISBN 0-89191-661-X, 55614). Cook.

Bodie, Idella. The Mystery of the Pirate's Treasure. Yancey, Louise, illus. LC 72-94930. 136p. (gr. 5-9). 1984. pap. 6.95 (ISBN 0-87844-059-3). Sandlapper Pub Co.

—Stranded! Sookikian, Charles J., illus. LC 84-14098. 132p. (Orig.). (gr. 5-9). 1984. pap. 6.95 (ISBN 0-87844-060-7). Sandlapper Pub Co.

Bohl, Al. Zaanan: The Dream of Delasor. (Illus.). 224p. (gr. 3 up). 1990. pap. 2.50 (ISBN 1-55748-124-5). Barbour & Co.

Bond, Nancy. A String on the Harp. (gr. 5-9). 1987. pap. 5.95 (ISBN 0-14-032376-7, Puffin). Puffin Bks.

Bond, Ruskin. The Hidden Pool. Das, Arup, illus. 64p. (Orig.). (gr. k-3). 1980. pap. 2.75 (ISBN 0-89744-211-3, Pub. by Children's Bk Trust India). Auromere.

Bosse, Malcolm. Captives of Time. LC 86-32943. 256p. (gr. 7 up). 1987. pap. 14.95 (ISBN 0-385-29583-9). Delacorte.

—Captives of Time. (gr. k-12). 1989. pap. 3.50 (ISBN 0-440-20311-2, LFL). Dell.

Bowkett, Stephen. Dualists. (gr. 5-8). 1990. pap. 17.95 (ISBN 0-575-04106-4, Pub. by Gollancz UK). Trafalgar Sq.

Boyd, John R. & Boyd, Mary A. Input - Output. (Illus.). 272p. (Orig.). (gr. 7-12). 1989. pap. 8.95 (ISBN 0-933759-14-2); 4.95 (ISBN 0-933759-15-0); cassette tape set 29.95 (ISBN 0-933759-16-9). Abaca Bks.

Bradman, Tony. The Bluebeards: Adventure on Skull Island. Murphy, Rowan B., illus. 64p. (gr. 3-6). 1990. pap. 2.95 (ISBN 0-8120-4421-5). Barron.

Bradshaw, Gillian. The Dragon & the Thief. LC 90-48259. (Illus.). (gr. 5 up). 1991. 13.95 (ISBN 0-688-10575-0). Greenwillow.

Brancato, Robin F. Sweet Bells Jangled out of Tune. 182p. (gr. 7 up). 1983. pap. 2.50 (ISBN 0-590-40459-8, Point). Scholastic Inc.

Brandenberg, Franz. Leo & Emily's Big Idea. (gr. k-6). 1990. pap. 2.95 (ISBN 0-440-40302-2, Pub. by Yearling Classics). Dell.

Branscum, Robbie. The Adventures of Johnny May. Howland, Deborah, illus. LC 83-49464. 128p. (gr. 4-7). 1984. PLB 12.89. (ISBN 0-06-020615-2). HarpC Child Bks.

Bray, Marian F. Springtime of Khan. LC 88-19917. (gr. 7-9). 1988. pap. 3.95 (ISBN 1-55513-123-9, Chariot Bks). Cook.

Brenford, Dana. Tiger on the Loose. LC 88-22845. (Illus.). 64p. (gr. 5-6). 1988. PLB 10.95 (ISBN 0-89686-424-3, Crestwood Hse). Macmillan Child Grp.

—Tracks in the North Woods. Schaeppi, Kristi, illus. LC 88-21963. 64p. (gr. 5-6). 1988. PLB 10.95 (ISBN 0-89686-420-0, Crestwood Hse). Macmillan Child Grp.

—A Whale of a Rescue. Schaeppi, Kristi, illus. LC 88-22854. 64p. (gr. 5-6). 1988. PLB 10.95 (ISBN 0-89686-422-7, Crestwood Hse). Macmillan Child Grp.

Brennan, J. H. The Gateway of Doom. (Orig.). (gr. k-12). 1987. pap. 2.50 (ISBN 0-440-92800-1, LFL). Dell.

—Realm of Chaos. (Orig.). (gr. k-12). 1987. pap. 2.50 (ISBN 0-440-97325-2, LFL). Dell.

Brewton, Sara, et al, eds. My Tang's Tungled & Other Ridiculous Situations. Booth, Graham, illus. LC 73-254. 128p. (gr. 5 up). 1989. PLB 12.89 (ISBN 0-690-04778-9, Crowell Jr Bks). HarpC Child Bks.

Brightfield, Richard. The Deadly Shadow. 128p. (Orig.). (gr. 4 up). 1985. pap. 2.25 (ISBN 0-553-25498-7). Bantam.

—The Dragon's Den. (Illus.). 128p. (gr. 5-9). 1984. pap. 2.25 (ISBN 0-553-25918-0). Bantam.

—Escape. (ps-7). 1987. pap. 1.95 (ISBN 0-553-23294-0). Bantam.

—Escape from the Kingdom of Frome, No. 3: The Caverns of Mornas. 144p. (Orig.). (gr. 7-12). 1987. pap. 2.50 (ISBN 0-553-26200-9). Bantam.

—Hijacked. (gr. 9-12). 1990. pap. 2.99 (ISBN 0-553-28635-8). Bantam.

—Hyperspace. (ps-7). 1987. pap. 2.25 (ISBN 0-553-26371-4). Bantam.

—Planet of the Dragons. (gr. 5 up). 1988. pap. 2.50 (ISBN 0-553-26887-2). Bantam.

—Secret of the Pyramids. (ps-7). 1987. pap. 2.25 (ISBN 0-553-25761-7). Bantam.

—The Secret Treasure of Tibet. 128p. (Orig.). (gr. 4). 1984. pap. 2.25 (ISBN 0-553-25501-0). Bantam.

Brown, Marc. Arthur's Tooth: An Arthur Adventure. Kroupa, Melanie, ed. Brown, Marc, illus. LC 85-72092. 32p. (gr. 1-3). 1985. PLB 13.95 (ISBN 0-87113-006-8); pap. 3.95 (ISBN 0-685-10321-8). Atlantic Monthly.

Brown, Margaret W. Willie's Adventures. LC 84-43141. 72p. (ps-3). 1988. PLB 11.89 (ISBN 0-06-020769-8). HarpC Child Bks.

Brown, Rose M. The PMS Zone. Skeeter, illus. 80p. (Orig.). 1988. pap. 7.95 (ISBN 0-9622109-0-0). Skeetoonies.
Budbill, David. Snowshoe Trek to Otter River. (Illus.). 96p. (gr. 4-6). 1984. pap. 2.50 (ISBN 0-553-15469-9, Skylark). Bantam.
Buehrer, Ruth. Escape from Sugarloaf Mine. Bee, Marty, illus. LC 87-83575. 102p. (Orig.). (gr. k-7). 1987. pap. 6.00 incl. parents-teacher manual (ISBN 0-945072-00-7, Gldn Apple Bks). NACE.
The Burning Land. (gr. 7 up). 1987. pap. 2.50 (ISBN 0-671-55007-1, Archway). PB.
Burningham, John. Would You Rather... Burningham, John, illus. LC 78-7088. 32p. (ps-2). 1978. 13.95 (ISBN 0-690-03917-4, Crowell Jr Bks). HarpC Child Bks.
Byars, Betsy C. Cracker Jackson. LC 84-24684. 168p. (gr. 5-7). 1985. pap. 12.95 (ISBN 0-670-80546-7). Viking Child Bks.
Cairis, Nicholas T. Island of the Titans. Mather, Pamela, ed. (Illus.). 90p. (Orig.). 1989. pap. 4.95 (ISBN 0-929624-02-5). Pegasus Bks.
The Canada Day Adventure. (gr. k-3). 1981. Incl. 1 bk. & 1 cass. 10.95 (ISBN 0-89290-160-8, BC18-6); Incl. 6 bks. & 1 cass. 29.95 (ISBN 0-685-30797-2, BC18-6). Soc for Visual.
Cannon, A. E. Cal Cameron by Day, Spider-Man by Night. LC 87-24655. 160p. (gr. 7 up). 1988. pap. 13.95 (ISBN 0-385-29635-5). Delacorte.
—Cal Cameron by Day, Spiderman by Night. (gr. k-12). 1989. pap. 3.25 (ISBN 0-440-20313-9, LFL). Dell.
Carlson, Natalie S. The Happy Orpheline. (gr. k-6). 1987. pap. 2.75 (ISBN 0-440-43455-6, YB). Dell.
Carpenter. The Captain Hook Affair. write for info. HM.
Carr, Jan. Lookout's Big Adventure. Hudson, Carol, illus. 32p. (gr. k-3). 1988. pap. 2.50 (ISBN 0-590-42114-X). Scholastic Inc.
Carrick, Carol. Aladdin & the Wonderful Lamp. Carrick, Donald, illus. 1992. pap. 3.95 (ISBN 0-590-41680-4). Scholastic Inc.
Carrie, Christopher. Quest for the Jungle City. (Illus.). 40p. (gr. k up). 1990. 1.59 (ISBN 0-86696-245-X). Binney & Smith.
Carrol, Jed L. The Adventures of Buffalo Barney: A Romp Through the Middle Atlantic States, Vol. 1. Gillen, Charles J., illus. 96p. (Orig.). 1989. write for info. Explore Your World Pubns.
Carter, Alden R. The Shoshoni. (Illus.). 64p. (gr. 3 up). 1991. pap. 4.95 (ISBN 0-531-15605-2). Watts.
—Up Country. 224p. (gr. 7 up). 1989. 14.95 (ISBN 0-399-21583-2, Putnam). Putnam Pub Group.
Cartwright, Pauline. Arthur & the Dragon. LC 90-10091. (Illus.). 32p. (gr. 1-4). 1990. PLB 17.28 (ISBN 0-8114-2689-0). Steck-V.
Cate, Dick. Twisters. Binch, Caroline, illus. 160p. (gr. 5-8). 1989. 17.95 (ISBN 0-575-04099-8, Pub. by Gollancz England). Trafalgar Sq.
Chambers, Aidan. Seal Secret. LC 80-8456. 128p. (gr. 5 up). 1981. 8.95 (ISBN 0-06-021258-6). HarpC Child Bks.
Chant, Barry. Spindles & the Giant Eagle Rescue. 1991. PLB 3.95 (ISBN 0-8423-6214-2). Tyndale.
Chartier, Normand. Over the River & Thro' the Woods. (Illus.). 24p. (ps-3). 1990. 5.95 (ISBN 0-671-64150-6, Little Simon); pap. 2.25 (ISBN 0-671-72337-5). S&S Trade.
Cheatham, Ann. Black Harvest. (Orig.). (gr. k-12). 1987. pap. 2.50 (ISBN 0-440-91039-0, LFL). Dell.
Choose Your Own Adventure, 5 vols, No. 1. (gr. 4). Boxed Set. pap. 9.75 (ISBN 0-553-30307-4, Skylark). Bantam.
Choose Your Own Adventure, 5 vols, No. 2. (gr. 4). Boxed Set. pap. 9.75 (ISBN 0-553-30308-2, Skylark). Bantam.
Choose Your Own Adventure, 5 vols, No. 3. Boxed Set. pap. 9.75 (ISBN 0-553-30310-4, Skylark). Bantam.
Choose Your Own Adventure, 5 vols, No. 4. (gr. 4). Boxed Set. pap. 9.75 (ISBN 0-553-30434-8). Bantam.
Christelow, Eileen. Henry & the Red Stripes. Christelow, Eileen, illus. 32p. (ps-3). 1982. 10.50 (ISBN 0-89919-118-5, Clarion). HM.
Christopher, John. Beyond the Burning Lands. 1974. pap. 3.95 (ISBN 0-02-042380-2). Macmillan Child Grp.
—Beyond the Burning Lands. (gr. 5-9). 1991. 15.75 (ISBN 0-8446-6447-2). Peter Smith.
Christopher, Matt. Hard Drive to Short. (gr. 4-7). 1991. pap. 3.95 (ISBN 0-316-14071-6). Little.
—Too Hot to Handle. (gr. 4-7). 1991. pap. 3.95 (ISBN 0-316-14074-0). Little.
Clark, Margaret G. Freedom Crossing. 192p. (gr. 4-7). 1989. pap. 2.50 (ISBN 0-590-42418-1, Apple Paperbacks). Scholastic Inc.
Cleary, Beverly. Henry Huggins. Darling, Louis, illus. Palacios, Argentina, tr. LC 82-25889. (SPA., Illus.). (gr. 3-7). 1983. 12.95 (ISBN 0-688-02014-3). Morrow.
—Ramona the Brave. Tiegreen, Alan, illus. 192p. (gr. k-6). 1984. pap. 3.25 (ISBN 0-440-47351-9, YB). Dell.
—The Real Hole. (gr. k-6). 1987. pap. 3.95 (ISBN 0-440-47521-X, YB). Dell.
Cleaver, Vera & Cleaver, Bill. Delpha Green & Company. LC 79-172141. 144p. (gr. 6 up). 1972. (Junior Bks); pap. 2.95 (ISBN 0-397-31344-6, LSC-8). HarperCollins.
Clifford, Eth. Just Tell Me When We're Dead! Hughes, George, illus. LC 83-10865. 144p. (gr. 2-5). 1983. 11.95 (ISBN 0-395-33071-8). HM.
Cohen, Miriam. See You in Second Grade. (gr. k-6). 1990. pap. 2.95 (ISBN 0-440-40303-0, Pub. by Yearling Classics). Dell.
Collier, James L. & Collier, Christopher. Jump Ship to Freedom. (gr. k-6). 1987. pap. 3.50 (ISBN 0-440-44323-7, Yearling). Dell.
Compton, Sara. Amazon: Where Do Fish Swim Through the Treetops? LC 88-16919. 112p. 1989. pap. text ed. 3.95 (ISBN 0-07-047994-1). McGraw.
—Venice: Who Are the Three? 112p. (gr. 4-6). 1989. pap. text ed. 3.95 (ISBN 0-07-047997-6). McGraw.
Conaway, Judith, adapted by. Twenty-Thousand Leagues under the Sea. D'Achille, Gino, illus. 96p. (gr. 2-5). 1983. 2.95 (ISBN 0-394-85333-4); lib. bdg. 4.99 (ISBN 0-394-95333-9). Random.
Cone, Molly. Mishmash & The Big Fat Problem. Shortall, Leonard, illus. (gr. 2-5). 1982. 13.95 (ISBN 0-395-32078-X). HM.
Conley, Pauline C. The Code Breaker. (Orig.). (gr. 4 up). 1983. pap. 4.50 (ISBN 0-87602-241-7). Anchorage.
Cool, Joyce. The Kidnapping of Courtney Van Allen & What's-Her-Name. 176p. 1988. pap. 2.75 (ISBN 0-553-15597-0, Starfire). Bantam.
Cooney, Caroline B. The Fire. 1990. pap. 2.95 (ISBN 0-590-41641-3). Scholastic Inc.
Coontz, Otto. The Night Walkers. LC 82-6161. (gr. 5 up). 1982. 9.95 (ISBN 0-395-32557-9). HM.
Cooper, Kay. Who Put the Cannon in the Courthouse Square? 128p. 1991. pap. 2.95 (ISBN 0-380-71298-9, Camelot). Avon.
Cooper, Susan. Over Sea, under Stone. 256p. (gr. 5 up). 1989. pap. 3.50 (ISBN 0-02-042785-9, Collier Young Ad). Macmillan Child Grp.
Corbett, Scott. The Hangman's Ghost Trick. Galdone, Paul, illus. 96p. (gr. 4-6). 1983. pap. 2.25 (ISBN 0-590-40126-2, Apple Paperbacks). Scholastic Inc.
Corby, Ellen. The Pebble of Gibraltar. 1988. 13.95 (ISBN 0-533-07623-4). Vantage.
Cossi, Olga. The Great Getaway. LC 89-42637. 32p. (gr. 1-2). 1990. PLB 12.95 (ISBN 0-8368-0107-5). Gareth Stevens Inc.
Cresswell, Helen. Bagthorpes Abroad: Being the Fifth Part of The Bagthorpe Saga. LC 84-7125. 180p. (gr. 5-9). 1984. 13.95 (ISBN 0-02-725390-2, Mcmillan Child Bk). Macmillan Child Grp.
—Bagthorpes Liberated. LC 89-2434. 192p. (gr. 5 up). 1989. 13.95 (ISBN 0-02-725441-0, Mcmillan Child Bk). Macmillan Child Grp.
Cross, Gillian. Born of the Sun. (gr. k-12). 1987. pap. 2.95 (ISBN 0-440-90710-1, LFL). Dell.
—A Map of Nowhere. LC 88-24559. 160p. (gr. 4-7). 1989. 13.95 (ISBN 0-8234-0741-1). Holiday.
Crutcher, Chris. Running Loose. (gr. 7 up). 1986. pap. 3.25 (ISBN 0-440-97570-0, LFL). Dell.
—Stonan! (gr. k-12). 1988. pap. 3.25 (ISBN 0-440-20080-6, LFL). Dell.
Crutchfield, Charles. Brigands of Mirkwood. Fenlon, Peter C., ed. McBride, Angus, illus. 32p. (Orig.). (gr. 10-12). 1987. pap. 7.00 (ISBN 0-915795-85-X, 8090). Iron Crown Ent Inc.
—Far Harad, the Scorched Land. Charlton, Coleman, ed. McBride, Angus, illus. 64p. (gr. 10-12). 1988. pap. 12.00 (ISBN 1-55806-007-3, 3800). Iron Crown Ent Inc.
Curry, Jane L. The Daybreakers. Robinson, Charles, illus. (gr. 3-7). 1991. 20.50 (ISBN 0-8446-6474-X). Peter Smith.
Curtis, Philip. Invasion of the Brain Sharpeners. Sims, Blanche, illus. LC 80-21434. 128p. (gr. 3-6). 1981. Knopf.
Cutting, Edith. Esli-Malcah. Grossman, Dan, illus. 48p. (gr. 2-7). 1985. wkbk. 2.48 (ISBN 0-86653-307-9). Good Apple.
—Hannah-Arod. Grossman, Dan, illus. 48p. (gr. 2-7). 1985. wkbk. 2.48 (ISBN 0-86653-304-4). Good Apple.
Dahl, Roald. Charlie y la Fabrica de Chocolate. (SPA.). 7.95 (ISBN 0-685-31016-7). Santillana.
—Going Solo. (Illus.). 208p. (gr. 8 up). 1986. 14.95 (ISBN 0-374-16503-3). FS&G.
Dale, Penny. Bet You Can't. Dale, Penny, illus. LC 87-3780. 32p. (ps-1). 1988. 12.95 (ISBN 0-397-32235-6, Lipp Jr Bks); PLB 12.89 (ISBN 0-397-32256-9). HarpC Child Bks.
Dann, Colin. The Ram of Sweetriver. 160p. (gr. 3-5). 1987. 15.95 (ISBN 0-09-165070-4, Pub. by Hutchinson UK). Trafalgar Sq.
Davis, Jim. Garfield Goes Underground. LC 83-60600. (Illus.). 32p. (gr. k-5). 1983. pap. 1.25 (ISBN 0-394-86121-3). Random.
Davoll, Barbara. A Load of Trouble. Hockerman, David, illus. 24p. 1988. pap. 5.99 (ISBN 0-89693-407-1); cassette 8.99 (ISBN 0-89693-618-X). Victor Bks.
—Rainy Day Rescue. Hockerman, Dennis, illus. 24p. 1988. 5.99 (ISBN 0-89693-408-X); cassette 8.99 (ISBN 0-89693-619-8). Victor Bks.
—Saved by the Bell. Hockerman, Dennis, illus. 24p. 1988. text ed. 5.99 (ISBN 0-89693-403-9); cassette 8.99 (ISBN 0-89693-614-7). Victor Bks.
Day, Edward C. John Tabor's Ride. Zimmer, Dirk, illus. LC 88-9065. 40p. (ps-3). 1989. 12.95 (ISBN 0-394-88577-5); lib. bdg. 13.99 (ISBN 0-394-98577-X). Knopf.
De Brunhoff, Jean & De Brunhoff, Laurent. Babar's Anniversary Album. De Brunhoff, Jean & De Brunhoff, Laurent, illus. Sendak, Maurice, intro. by. LC 81-5182. 144p. (ps-3). 1981. 16.95 (ISBN 0-394-84813-6); lib. bdg. 16.99 (ISBN 0-394-94813-0). Random.
Dee, M. M. Adventures of Dusty. LC 84-81557. (Illus.). 48p. (gr. k-4). 1985. 9.95 (ISBN 0-937460-14-1). Hendrick-Long.
DeFord, Deborah H. & Stout, Harry S. An Enemy among Them. 208p. (gr. 5-9). 1987. 13.95 (ISBN 0-395-44239-7). HM.
De Goscinny, Rene. Asterix Chez les Helvetes. (FRE., Illus.). (gr. 7-9). 19.95 (ISBN 0-685-28427-1, FC889). French & Eur.
—Asterix en Hispanie. (FRE., Illus.). (gr. 7-9). 19.95 (ISBN 0-685-28428-X, FC887). French & Eur.
—Asterix et le Chaudron. (FRE., Illus.). (gr. 7-9). 19.95 (ISBN 0-685-28429-8, FC885). French & Eur.
—Asterix la Zizanie. (FRE., Illus.). (gr. 7-9). 19.95 (ISBN 0-685-28426-3, FC888). French & Eur.
De Goscinny, Rene & Uderzo, M. Domaine des Dieux. (FRE., Illus.). (gr. 7-9). 19.95 (ISBN 0-685-28430-1, FC886). French & Eur.
Delporte, pseud. Romeo & Smurfette & Twelve Other Smurfy Stories. Peyo, illus. LC 82-60258. 48p. (gr. 4-7). 1983. 2.95 (ISBN 0-394-85618-X). Random.
Delton, Judy. Back Yard Angel. Morrill, Leslie, illus. 112p. (gr. k up). 1990. pap. 2.95 (ISBN 0-440-40445-2, YB). Dell.
Demarest, Chris L. The Lunatic Adventure of Kitman & Willy. Demarest, Chris L., illus. LC 87-32354. 32p. (ps-3). 1988. pap. 12.95 (ISBN 0-671-65695-3). S&S Trade.
Dengler, Sandy. Three in One Pioneer Family Adventure Series. (gr. 6). 1985. pap. 5.95 (ISBN 0-8024-6365-7). Moody.
De Pauw, Linda G. Seafaring Women. (gr. 7 up). 1982. 13.95 (ISBN 0-395-32434-3). HM.
Derwent, Lavinia. Return to Sula. 128p. (gr. 5-8). 1989. pap. 5.95 (ISBN 0-86241-073-8, Pub. by Cnngt Pub Ltd). Trafalgar Sq.
Dever, Joe. California Countdown. 1990. pap. 3.95 (ISBN 0-425-12311-1). Berkley Pub.
—Emerald Enchanter. Cige, Hillary, ed. (gr. 12 up). 1988. pap. 3.95 (ISBN 0-425-10696-9, Pub. by Berkley-Pacer). Berkley Pub.
Dewey, Ariane. Gib Morgan, Oilman. Dewey, Ariane, illus. LC 86-284. 48p. (gr. 1-3). 1987. 11.75 (ISBN 0-688-06566-X); PLB 11.88 (ISBN 0-688-06567-8). Greenwillow.
—Pecos Bill. LC 82-9229. (Illus.). 56p. (gr. k-3). 1983. 14.95 (ISBN 0-688-01410-0). Greenwillow.
Dickinson, Mary. Alex's Outing. Firmin, Charlotte, illus. 32p. (ps-2). 1983. 9.95 (ISBN 0-233-97558-6). Andre Deutsch.
Dicks, Terrance. Goliath at the Dog Show. Littlewood, Valerie, illus. 64p. (gr. k-4). 1987. 7.95 (ISBN 0-8120-5821-6); pap. 2.95 (ISBN 0-8120-3818-5). Barron.
—Goliath on Vacation. Littlewood, Valerie, illus. 64p. (gr. k-4). 1987. 7.95 (ISBN 0-8120-5824-0); pap. 2.95 (ISBN 0-8120-3821-5). Barron.
DiGirolamo, Vincent. Whispers under the Wharf. LC 90-331073. 144p. (Orig.). 1990. pap. 8.95 (ISBN 0-931832-52-7). Fithian Pr.
Dixon. Ice Age Explorer. (ps-7). 1987. pap. 2.50 (ISBN 0-553-27049-4). Bantam.
Dodson, Susan. The Eye of the Storm. (gr. 7 up). pap. 2.25 (ISBN 0-317-62893-3). S&S Trade.
Dolb, K. Danger at Demon's Cove. (Illus.). 48p. (gr. 4-9). 1988. PLB 10.96 (ISBN 0-88110-333-0); pap. 4.50 (ISBN 0-7460-0179-7). EDC.
Doty, Randall. Ents of Fangorn. Fenlon, Peter C., ed. McBride, Angus, illus. 60p. (Orig.). (gr. 10-12). 1987. pap. 12.00 (ISBN 0-915795-84-1, 3500). Iron Crown Ent Inc.
Downing, Peggy. Help! I'm Shrinking! LC 86-6841. 144p. (gr. 4-6). 1986. pap. 3.95 (ISBN 1-55513-032-1). Cook.
Doyle, Arthur Conan. The Lost World. (Illus.). 272p. (gr. 5 up). 1991. pap. 2.95 (ISBN 0-14-035013-6, Puffin). Puffin Bks.
Dragonwagon, Crescent & Zindel, Paul. To Take a Dare. 240p. (gr. 7-12). 1984. pap. 2.95 (ISBN 0-553-26601-2). Bantam.
Duncan, Lois. Locked in Time. 240p. (gr. 7 up). 1985. 12.95 (ISBN 0-316-19555-3). Little.
Dygard, Thomas J. The Rookie Arrives. 176p. (gr. 5-9). 1989. pap. 3.95 (ISBN 0-14-034112-9, Puffin). Puffin Bks.
Edler, Timothy J. T-Boy & the Trial for Life. (Illus.). 36p. (gr. k-8). 1978. pap. 6.00 (ISBN 0-931108-02-0). Little Cajun Bks.
Edmonds, Walter. Matchlock Gun. 50p. (gr. 3-6). 1991. pap. 4.95 (ISBN 0-8167-2367-2). Troll Assocs.
Edwards, Michelle. Misha the Minstrel. LC 84-62336. (Illus.). 32p. (gr. 3-7). 1985. 8.95 (ISBN 0-930100-19-0). Holy Cow.
Elbl, Martin. Tales of the Amazon. Neubacher, Gerda, illus. 32p. (gr. k-3). 1985. 10.95 (ISBN 0-88625-127-3). Durkin Hayes Pub.
Elford, George R. Recall to Inferno: Devil's Guard Two. (Orig.). 1988. pap. 3.95 (ISBN 0-440-20199-3). Dell.
Ellenby, Jean. The Tudor Household. (Illus.). 32p. (gr. 2-8). 1985. pap. 3.95 (ISBN 0-521-27899-6). Cambridge U Pr.
Elliott, Dan. The Adventures of Ernie & Bert in Twiddlebug Land. LC 83-61719. (Illus.). 32p. (ps-3). 1984. pap. 1.25 (ISBN 0-394-85925-1, Random Juv). Random.
Ellis, Terry. The Invasion of Willow Wood Springs. LC 85-63826. (Illus.). 168p. (Orig.). (gr. 4 up). 1989. pap. 3.75 (ISBN 0-915677-32-6). Roundtable Pub.

Estes, Rose. Children of the Dragon. Lundgren, Carl, illus. LC 84-22318. 224p. (gr. 4-9). 1985. (Random Juv); pap. 2.95 (ISBN 0-394-86433-6). Random.

Evans, Shirlee. Tree Tall & the Whiteskins. LC 85-13952. (Illus.). 112p. (gr. 9 up). 1985. pap. 3.95 (ISBN 0-8361-3402-8). Herald Pr.

Evslin, Bernard. Adventures of Ulysses. 1989. pap. 2.75 (ISBN 0-590-42599-4). Scholastic Inc.

The Fantastic Four in the Island of Danger. 32p. 1988. pap. 1.50 (ISBN 0-517-55633-2). Crown.

Farrell, Simon & Sutherland, Jon. Last Invasion. (gr. 7 up). 1988. pap. 2.75 (ISBN 0-425-10835-X, Pub. by Berkley-Pacer). Berkley Pub.

Fasco, Rudolph. In Quest of the Zohar. Frades, Ernesto, ed. Pereira, Ernesto, illus. 275p. (Orig.). 1990. pap. write for info. (ISBN 0-9624929-0-6). Little Great Whale.

Fidler, Kathleen. The Desperate Journey. (Illus.). 158p. (gr. 5-8). 1989. pap. 5.95 (ISBN 0-86241-056-8, Pub. by Cnngt Pub Ltd). Trafalgar Sq.

Field, Arthur W. Cisco & the Twin Foals. Cosgrove, Colleen B., illus. LC 83-61713. 160p. (gr. 8 up). 1983. 12.00 (ISBN 0-935356-06-1). Mills Pub Co.

Field, Eugene. Wynken, Blyken & Nod. 1989. pap. 2.95 (ISBN 0-590-42422-X). Scholastic Inc.

Fleischman, Sid. Humbug Mountain. Von Schmidt, Eric, illus. LC 78-9419. (gr. 4-6). 1978. 14.95i (ISBN 0-316-28569-2, Pub. by Atlantic Monthly Pr). Little.

—Jingo Django. Von Schmidt, Eric, illus. 172p. (gr. 3-7). 1988. pap. 4.95 (ISBN 0-316-28554-4). Little.

—The Whipping Boy. Sis, Peter, illus. LC 85-17555. 96p. (gr. 2-6). 1986. PLB 13.95 (ISBN 0-688-06216-4). Greenwillow.

Flory, Jane. The Great Bamboozlement. Flory, Jane, illus. 160p. (gr. 5-9). 1982. 13.95 (ISBN 0-395-31859-9). HM.

Foley, Louise. Australia: Find the Flying Foxes. LC 88-16911. 112p. 1988. pap. text ed. 3.95 (ISBN 0-07-047996-8). McGraw.

Foley, Louise M. Danger at Anchor Mine. 128p. (gr. 4). 1985. pap. 2.25 (ISBN 0-553-25496-0). Bantam.

Foley, Tod. Beyond the Core: Frontier Zone 5. Amthor, Terry K., ed. 64p. (Orig.). (gr. 10-12). 1987. pap. 12. 00 (ISBN 0-915795-83-3, 9600, Dist. by Berkley Pub Group). Iron Crown Ent Inc.

—Tales from Deep Space. Amthor, Terry K., ed. McKie, Angus, illus. 32p. (Orig.). (gr. 10-12). 1988. pap. 6.00 (ISBN 1-55806-006-5, 9103). Iron Crown Ent Inc.

Follow the Drinking Gourd. LC 88-9661. 48p. (gr. 1-4). 1988. 15.95 (ISBN 0-394-89694-7). Knopf.

Forsse, Ken. The Airship. High, David, et al, illus. 26p. (ps). 1985. incl. audio-cassette 9.95 (ISBN 0-934323-00-3). Alchemy Comms.

—All about Bears. High, David, et al, illus. 26p. (ps). 1985. incl. audio-cassette 9.95 (ISBN 0-934323-09-7). Alchemy Comms.

—Grubby's Romance. High, David, et al, illus. 26p. (ps). 1985. incl. audio-cassette 9.95 (ISBN 0-934323-04-6). Alchemy Comms.

—Grunge Music. High, David, et al, illus. 26p. (ps). 1985. incl. audio-cassette 9.95 (ISBN 0-934323-06-2). Alchemy Comms.

—The Missing Princess. High, David & Hicks, Russell, illus. 26p. (ps). 1985. incl. audio-cassette 9.95 (ISBN 0-934323-11-9). Alchemy Comms.

—The Story of Faded Fobs. High, David, et al, illus. 26p. (ps). 1985. incl. audio-cassette 9.95 (ISBN 0-934323-02-X). Alchemy Comms.

—Take a Good Look. High, David, et al, illus. 26p. (ps). 1985. incl. audio-cassette 9.95 (ISBN 0-934323-08-9). Alchemy Comms.

—Teddy Ruxpin's Lullabies. High, David, et al, illus. 26p. (ps). 1985. incl. audio-cassette 9.95 (ISBN 0-934323-01-1). Alchemy Comms.

Foster, Janet. Journey to the Top of the World. Foster, Janet, photos by. (Illus.). (gr. 3-7). 1988. 14.95 (ISBN 0-13-511445-4). P-H.

Fradon, Dana. Sir Dana - A Knight: As Told by His Trusty Armor. Fradon, Dana, illus. LC 88-3968. 32p. (gr. 3-7). 1988. 13.95 (ISBN 0-525-44424-6, DCB). Dutton Child Bks.

French, Michael. Circle of Revenge. LC 88-19340. 160p. (gr. 6 up). 1988. 13.95 (ISBN 0-553-05495-3, Starfire). Bantam.

—Pursuit. 192p. (gr. 9 up). 1983. pap. 2.95 (ISBN 0-440-96665-5, LFL). Dell.

French, Michael, adapted by. Indiana Jones & the Temple of Doom: The Storybook Based on the Movie. LC 84-1980. (Illus.). 64p. (gr. 3-7). 1984. (Random Juv); lib. bdg. 7.99 (ISBN 0-394-96387-3). Random.

Friedman, Joy T. Away We Go. (Illus.). 24p. (ps-3). 1978. 2.50 (ISBN 0-448-46517-5, G&D). Putnam Pub Group.

Friedman, Judith & Sonnenblick, Carol. Attack Pack. 128p. (gr. 4-12). 1982. write for info. (ISBN 0-9609616-0-7). New Dir Pr.

Fritz, Jean. Stonewall. Gammell, Stephen, illus. 160p. (gr. 5-9). 1989. pap. 3.95 (ISBN 0-14-032937-4, Puffin). Puffin Bks.

Froehlich, Margaret W. Hide Crawford Quick. LC 82-21184. 176p. (gr. 5 up). 1983. 9.95 (ISBN 0-395-33884-0). HM.

Frost, Erica. Jonathan's Amazing Adventure. Hall, Susan, illus. LC 85-14129. 48p. (Orig.). (gr. 1-3). 1986. PLB 9.89 (ISBN 0-8167-0662-X); pap. text ed. 2.95 (ISBN 0-8167-0663-8). Troll Assocs.

Fujikawa, Gyo. Jenny & Jupie to the Rescue. Fujikawa, Gyo, illus. LC 82-80870. 32p. (gr. k-2). 1982. 3.95 (ISBN 0-448-11754-1, G&D). Putnam Pub Group.

Furman, Abraham L., ed. Everygirls Adventure Stories. (Illus.). (gr. 6-10). PLB 6.70 (ISBN 0-8313-0053-1). Lantern.

Gackenbach, Dick. The Dog & the Deep Dark Woods. LC 83-47694. (Illus.). 32p. (ps-3). 1984. PLB 11.89 (ISBN 0-06-021978-5). HarpC Child Bks.

Garcia, Vince. Quest of the Ancients. Cabuco, et al, illus. 224p. (Orig.). (gr. 9-12). 1990. pap. 23.00 (ISBN 0-9628003-0-9). Unicorn Game Pubns.

Gardiner, John R. Top Secret. Simont, Marc, illus. 129p. (gr. 3-7). 1985. 14.95 (ISBN 0-316-30368-2). Little.

Garner, Alan. The Stone Book Quartet. (gr. k-12). 1988. pap. 4.95 (ISBN 0-440-40049-X, Pub by Yearning Classics). Dell.

Gaspar, Tomas R. La Aventura de Yolanda; Yolanda's Hike. (ENG & SPA., Illus.). (ps-3). 1974. 5.95 (ISBN 0-938678-03-5). New Seed.

Gasperini, Jim. Secrets of the Knights. (ps-7). 1984. pap. 2.50 (ISBN 0-553-26960-7). Bantam.

Gates, Doris. A Fair Wind for Troy. Mikolayack, Charles, illus. 96p. (gr. 4-6). 1984. pap. 4.95 (ISBN 0-14-031718-X, Puffin). Puffin Bks.

Geller, Norman. Unto Dust You Shall Return. Grant, Larry & Jalbert, Marc, illus. 16p. (gr. 6-10). 1986. pap. 4.95 (ISBN 0-915753-11-1). N Geller Pub.

Gilden, Mel. Pokey to the Rescue. Couman, Carol & Codor, Dick, illus. (gr. k-3). 1988. pap. 2.25 (ISBN 0-671-63900-5, Little Simon). S&S Trade.

—RV & the Haunted Garage. Bouman, Carol & Codor, Dick, illus. (gr. k-3). 1988. pap. 2.25 (ISBN 0-671-63901-3, Little Simon). S&S Trade.

Gilliam, Terry & McKeown, Charles. The Adventures of Baron Munchausen: The Novel. Gilliam, Terry, illus. 175p. (Orig.). 1989. pap. 12.95 (ISBN 1-55783-039-8). Applause Theatre Bk Pubs.

Gilligan, Alison. The Treasure of the Onyx. 1990. pap. 2.95 (ISBN 0-553-28610-2). Bantam.

Gilligan, Shannon. The Case of the Silk King. large type ed. Bolle, Frank, illus. 114p. (gr. 3-7). 1987. Repr. of 1986 ed. 8.95 (ISBN 0-942545-14-1); PLB 9.95 (ISBN 0-942545-19-2, Dist. by Grolier). Grey Castle.

—Case of the Silk King. (gr. 5-12). 1986. pap. 2.75 (ISBN 0-553-25489-8). Bantam.

—The Fairy Kidnap. 64p. (Orig.). (gr. 2 up). 1985. pap. 2.25 (ISBN 0-553-15488-5). Bantam.

—The Three Wishes. 64p. (Orig.). (gr. 1-3). 1984. pap. text ed. 2.25 (ISBN 0-553-15444-3, Skylark). Bantam.

Gire, Ken. Adventures in the Big Thicket. Kobobel, Janet, ed. (Illus.). 112p. (gr. k-5). 1990. 17.99 (ISBN 0-929608-72-0). Focus Family.

Gold, Avner. The Dream. Reinman, Y. Y., ed. Hinlicky, G., illus. 112p. (gr. 7-11). 1983. pap. 7.95 (ISBN 0-935063-01-3). CIS Comm.

—The Promised Child. Reinman, Y. Y., ed. Hinlicky, G., illus. LC 85-72493. 128p. (gr. 7-11). 1985. 9.95 (ISBN 0-935063-10-2); pap. 7.95 (ISBN 0-935063-00-5). CIS Comm.

—Twilight. Reinman, Y. Y., ed. Hinklicky, G., illus. LC 85-72404. 128p. (gr. 7-11). 1985. 9.95 (ISBN 0-935063-11-0); pap. 7.95 (ISBN 0-935063-03-X). CIS Comm.

—The Year of the Sword. Reinman, Y. Y., ed. Hinlicky, G., illus. 112p. (gr. 5 up). 1984. pap. 7.95 (ISBN 0-935063-02-1). CIS Comm.

Goodall, John S. Creepy Castle. LC 74-16836. (Illus.). 60p. 1975. 12.95 (ISBN 0-689-50027-0, M K McElderry). Macmillan Child Grp.

—The Story of a Castle. Goodall, John S., illus. LC 86-70130. 60p. 1986. 14.95 (ISBN 0-689-50405-5, M K McElderry). Macmillan Child Grp.

Goodman, Deborah L. The Trumpet of Terror. 128p. (Orig.). (gr. 4). 1986. pap. 2.25 (ISBN 0-553-25491-X). Bantam.

—Vanished! 128p. (Orig.). (gr. 4). 1986. pap. 2.25 (ISBN 0-553-25941-5). Bantam.

Goodman, Julius. The Magic Path. 64p. (Orig.). (gr. 2). 1985. pap. 2.25 (ISBN 0-553-15482-6). Bantam.

Gorog, Judith. Winning Scheherazade. LC 90-1134. 112p. (gr. 5 up). 1991. SBE 11.95 (ISBN 0-689-31648-8, Atheneum Child Bk). Macmillan Child Grp.

Goscinny, Rene de. Asterix et la Serpe d'or. (FRE., Illus.). (gr. 3-8). 15.95 (ISBN 0-685-28431-X). French & Eur.

Gould, Toni. The Adventures of Mel & Tess. (Illus.). (gr. 1-3). 1984. PLB 12.85 (ISBN 0-8027-9188-3); pap. text ed. 9.50 (ISBN 0-8027-9189-1). Walker & Co.

Graham, Bob. Crusher is Coming! (ps-3). 1988. pap. 12. 95 (ISBN 0-670-82081-4). Viking Child Bks.

Grahame, Kenneth. Adventures in the Wild Wood. Palazzo-Craig, Janet, adapted by. Baer, Mary A., illus. LC 81-16417. 32p. (gr. 2-5). 1982. PLB 10.79 (ISBN 0-89375-638-5); pap. text ed. 2.95 (ISBN 0-89375-639-3). Troll Assocs.

Grant, Myrna. Ivan & the Daring Escape. LC 89-80820. (Illus.). 167p. (gr. 1-8). 1989. pap. 4.95 (ISBN 0-88419-257-1, Creation Hse). Strang Comms Co.

—Ivan & the Informer. LC 89-80819. (Illus.). 108p. (gr. 1-8). 1989. pap. 4.95 (ISBN 0-88419-256-3, Creation Hse). Strang Comms Co.

Graver, Fred. The Journey to Stonehenge. (gr. 4 up). 1984. pap. 2.25 (ISBN 0-553-25961-X). Bantam.

Greenwald, Sheila. Mat Pit & the Tunnel Tenants. Greenwald, Sheila, illus. 128p. (gr. k-6). 1989. pap. 2.75 (ISBN 0-440-40155-0, YB). Dell.

Griffin, Judith B. Phoebe the Spy. (gr. 4-6). 1979. pap. 1.50 (ISBN 0-590-05758-8). Scholastic Inc.

Grove, Vicki. Junglerama. 160p. (gr. 5 up). 1989. 13.95 (ISBN 0-399-21624-3, Putnam). Putnam Pub Group.

Haas, Dorothy. Dorothy & the Seven-Leaf Clover. Rose, David, illus. LC 84-16080. 64p. (gr. 2-6). 1985. lib. bdg. 4.99 (ISBN 0-394-97037-3, Random Juv). Random.

—The Secret Life of Dilly McBean. 208p. (gr. 3-7). 1988. pap. 2.95 (ISBN 0-590-43138-2). Scholastic Inc.

—Tink in a Tangle. Tucker, Kathleen, ed. Apple, Margot, illus. LC 83-16654. 128p. (gr. 2-5). 1984. PLB 9.95 (ISBN 0-8075-7952-1). A Whitman.

Haggard, H. Rider. Allan Quartermain. (Illus.). 288p. (gr. 5 up). 1991. pap. 2.95 (ISBN 0-14-035117-5, Puffin). Puffin Bks.

—King Solomon's Mines. 256p. (gr. 3-7). 1983. pap. 2.25 (ISBN 0-14-035014-4, Puffin). Puffin Bks.

Hahn, Mary D. Tallahassee Higgins. LC 86-17513. 192p. (gr. 5-7). 1987. 13.95 (ISBN 0-89919-495-8, Pub. by Clarion). Ticknor & Fields.

Haley, Patrick. Wildflower & the Big Voice in the Sky. Kool, Jonna, illus. LC 82-82990. 44p. (gr. 3-4). 1982. 9.00 (ISBN 0-9605738-1-X). East Eagle.

Hamerstrom, Frances. Adventure of the Stone Man. (gr. 4-7). 1990. pap. 10.95 (ISBN 1-55821-084-9). Lyons & Burford.

Hamilton, Virginia. The Magical Adventures of the Pretty Pearl. LC 84-48344. 320p. (gr. 6 up). 1986. pap. 5.50 (ISBN 0-06-440178-2, Trophy). HarpC Child Bks.

Handford, Martin. Find Waldo Now. Handford, Martin, illus. (ps up). 1988. 12.95 (ISBN 0-316-34292-0). Little.

Hannan, Peter. Escape from Camp Wannabarf. Hannan, Peter, illus. LC 90-33203. 32p. (Orig.). (ps-2). 1991. PLB 8.99 (ISBN 0-679-90287-2); pap. 3.95 (ISBN 0-679-80287-8). Knopf.

Hansjurgen Press & Littlewood, Barbara S. The Adventures of the Black Hand Gang. Littlewood, Barbara S., illus. 128p. (gr. 3-7). 1983. pap. 6.95 (ISBN 0-13-013938-6, Pub. by Treehouse); pap. 4.95 (ISBN 0-13-014035-X). P-H.

Hardcastle, Michael. Quake. 128p. (gr. 7 up). 1988. 10.95 (ISBN 0-317-69550-9). Faber & Faber.

Hargreaves, Roger. Mr. Lazy. 32p. (ps-k). 1980. 1.25 (ISBN 0-8431-0806-1). Price Stern.

—Mr. Lazy. 32p. (ps up). 1976. PLB 8.70s.p. (ISBN 0-87191-761-0); PLB 12.45 (ISBN 0-685-09331-X). Creative Ed.

Harris, Geraldine. The Seventh Gate, No. 4. (gr. k-12). 1987. pap. 2.95 (ISBN 0-440-97747-9, LFL). Dell.

Hastings. Rufus & Christopher in the Land of Lies. LC 70-190271. (Illus.). 32p. (gr. 2-4). 1972. PLB 9.95 (ISBN 0-87783-061-4); pap. 3.94 deluxe ed. (ISBN 0-87783-107-6); cassette 7.94x (ISBN 0-87783-198-X). Oddo.

Hauser, Hillary. Call to Adventure. Hauser, Hillary, photos by. LC 87-70932. (Illus.). 240p. (Orig.). (gr. 6 up). 1987. pap. 14.95 (ISBN 0-917665-18-X). Bookmakers Guild.

Hayes, Frederick & Hayes, Jean. The Adventures of Pinto Bean & Chapulin. Kiefer, Jill, illus. 20p. (Orig.). (gr. 1-8). 1988. pap. text ed. 6.95 (ISBN 0-317-93098-2). Pinto Pub.

Hayes, Geoffrey. The Treasure of the Lost Lagoon: A Step Three Book. Hayes, Geoffrey, illus. LC 90-40118. 48p. (Orig.). (gr. 2-3). 1991. 2.95 (ISBN 0-679-81484-1, Random Juv); lib. bdg. 6.99 (ISBN 0-679-91484-6). Random.

Haynes, Betsy. In Trouble. (gr. 3-6). 1990. pap. 2.95 (ISBN 0-553-15814-7). Bantam.

—Taffy Sinclair Strikes Again. 128p. (gr. 4-6). 1991. pap. 2.99 (ISBN 0-553-15645-4, Skylark). Bantam.

—Teen Taxi. (gr. 4-7). 1990. pap. 2.75 (ISBN 0-553-15794-9). Bantam.

Haywood, Carolyn. Hello, Star. Durrell, Julie, illus. LC 87-11204. 64p. (gr. k-2). 1987. 12.95 (ISBN 0-688-06650-X, Morrow Junior Books); lib. bdg. 12.88 (ISBN 0-688-06651-8, Morrow Junior Books). Morrow.

Heide, Florence P. The Adventures of Treehorn. Gorey, Edward, illus. 128p. (gr. k-3). 1983. pap. 1.95 (ISBN 0-440-40045-7, YB). Dell.

Helfer, Andrew. Batman: The Purrfect Crime. (Illus.). (ps-3). 1991. pap. write for info. (ISBN 0-307-12621-8, Golden Pr). Western Pub.

Helfer, Andy. Indiana Jones & the Cup of the Vampire. LC 84-91043. (gr. 5 up). 1986. pap. 2.95 (ISBN 0-345-33829-4). Ballantine.

Heller, Nicholas. An Adventure at Sea. LC 87-25525. (Illus.). 24p. (ps-3). 1988. 11.95 (ISBN 0-688-07846-X); PLB 11.88 (ISBN 0-688-07847-8). Greenwillow.

Hendry, Frances. Quest for a Kelpie. LC 87-19666. 160p. (gr. 4-7). 1988. 12.95 (ISBN 0-8234-0680-6). Holiday.

Herge. Der Arumbaya-Fetisch. (GER., Illus.). 62p. pap. 19.95 (ISBN 0-686-54309-2). French & Eur.

—El Asunto Tornasol. (SPA., Illus.). 62p. 19.95 (ISBN 0-686-54344-0). French & Eur.

—Aterrizaje en la Luna. (SPA., Illus.). 62p. 19.95 (ISBN 0-686-54343-2). French & Eur.

—The Black Island. (Illus.). 62p. 19.95 (ISBN 0-416-92640-1). French & Eur.

—The Black Island. LC 74-21624. (gr. k up). 1975. pap. 6.95 (ISBN 0-316-35835-5, Joy St Bks). Little.

—Der Blaue Lotos. (GER., Illus.). 62p. pap. 19.95 (ISBN 0-686-54308-4). French & Eur.

—The Calculus Affair. (Illus.). 62p. 19.95 (ISBN 0-416-60560-5); pap. 4.95 (ISBN 0-416-77390-7). French & Eur.
—El Cangrejo Pinzas Oro. (SPA., Illus.). 62p. 19.95 (ISBN 0-686-54335-1). French & Eur.
—The Castafiore Emerald. (Illus.). 62p. (Also avail. in FR. & Span.). 19.95 (ISBN 0-416-92630-4); pap. 4.95 (ISBN 0-416-77400-8). French & Eur.
—El Cetro de Ottokar. (SPA., Illus.). 62p. 19.95 (ISBN 0-686-54334-3). French & Eur.
—Les Cigares du Pharaon. (FRE.). (gr. 7-9). looseleaf bdg. 19.95 (ISBN 0-685-23409-6). French & Eur.
—Los Cigarros del Faraon. (SPA., Illus.). 62p. 19.95 (ISBN 0-686-54330-0). French & Eur.
—Les Cigars du Pharon. (FRE., Illus.). 62p. 19.95 (ISBN 0-686-54288-6). French & Eur.
—Cigars of the Pharaoh. (Illus.). 62p. 19.95 (ISBN 0-416-08830-9). French & Eur.
—Cigars of the Pharoah. LC 74-21620. (gr. k up). 1975. pap. 6.95 (ISBN 0-316-35836-3, Joy St Bks). Little.
—The Crab with the Golden Claws. (Illus.). 62p. (gr. 3-8). 19.95 (ISBN 0-416-60500-1). French & Eur.
—Crabe aux d'or. (FRE., Illus.). 62p. 19.95 (ISBN 0-686-54292-4). French & Eur.
—Crabe aux pinces d'or. (FRE., Illus.). (gr. 7-9). looseleaf bdg. 19.95 (ISBN 0-685-28408-5). French & Eur.
—Destination Moon. (gr. 3-8). looseleaf bdg. 19.95 (ISBN 0-685-23515-7). French & Eur.
—Destination Moon. (Illus.). 62p. 19.95 (ISBN 0-416-92550-2). French & Eur.
—Il Drago Blu. (ITA., Illus.). 62p. pap. 19.95 (ISBN 0-686-54352-1). French & Eur.
—La Estrella Misteriosa. (SPA., Illus.). 62p. 19.95 (ISBN 0-686-54336-X). French & Eur.
—Explorers of the Moon. (Illus.). 62p. 19.95 (ISBN 0-416-92560-X). French & Eur.
—Explorers on the Moon. (gr. 3-8). looseleaf bdg. 19.95 (ISBN 0-685-23411-8). French & Eur.
—Der Fall Bienlein. (GER., Illus.). 62p. pap. 19.95 (ISBN 0-686-54321-1). French & Eur.
—Flight Seven-Fourteen. (Illus.). 62p. 19.95 (ISBN 0-416-92650-9). French & Eur.
—Flight Seven-Fourteen. LC 74-21623. (gr. k up). 1975. pap. 7.95 (ISBN 0-316-35837-1, Joy St Bks). Little.
—Flug 714 nach Sydney. (GER., Illus.). 62p. pap. 19.95 (ISBN 0-686-54325-4). French & Eur.
—Das Geheimnis der "Einhorn" (GER., Illus.). 62p. pap. 19.95 (ISBN 0-686-54314-9). French & Eur.
—Der Geheimnisvolle Stern. (GER., Illus.). 62p. pap. 19.95 (ISBN 0-686-54313-0). French & Eur.
—Il Granchio d'Oro. (ITA., Illus.). 62p. pap. 19.95 (ISBN 0-686-54354-8). French & Eur.
—Im Reiche des Schwarzen Goldes. (GER., Illus.). 62p. pap. 19.95 (ISBN 0-686-54318-1). French & Eur.
—La Isla Negra. (SPA., Illus.). 62p. 19.95 (ISBN 0-686-54333-5). French & Eur.
—Las Joyas de la Castafiore. (SPA., Illus.). 62p. 19.95 (ISBN 0-686-54347-5). French & Eur.
—Die Juwelen der Sangerin. (GER., Illus.). 62p. pap. 19.95 (ISBN 0-686-54324-6). French & Eur.
—King Ottokar's Sceptre. (Illus.). 62p. 19.95 (ISBN 0-416-60510-9). French & Eur.
—Kohle an Bord. (GER., Illus.). 62p. pap. 19.95 (ISBN 0-686-54322-X). French & Eur.
—Konig Ottokars Zepter. (GER., Illus.). 62p. pap. 19.95 (ISBN 0-686-54311-4). French & Eur.
—Die Krabbe mit den Goldenen Scheren. (GER., Illus.). 62p. pap. 19.95 (ISBN 0-686-54312-2). French & Eur.
—Land of Black Gold. (Illus.). 62p. 19.95 (ISBN 0-416-08840-6). French & Eur.
—El Loto Azul. (SPA., Illus.). 62p. 19.95 (ISBN 0-686-54331-9). French & Eur.
—Le Lotus Bleu. (FRE.). (gr. 2-9). looseleaf bdg. 19.95 (ISBN 0-685-23413-4). French & Eur.
—Objetivo: la Luna. (SPA., Illus.). 62p. 19.95 (ISBN 0-686-54342-4). French & Eur.
—L' Oreille Cassee. (FRE., Illus.). 62p. 19.95 (ISBN 0-686-54290-8). French & Eur.
—La Oreja Rota. (SPA., Illus.). 62p. 19.95 (ISBN 0-686-54332-7). French & Eur.
—Prisoners of the Sun. (Illus.). 62p. 19.95 (ISBN 0-416-92620-7); pap. 4.95 (ISBN 0-416-77410-5). French & Eur.
—Red Rackham's Treasure. (Illus.). 62p. 19.95 (ISBN 0-416-92540-5). French & Eur.
—The Red Sea Sharks. (Illus., J). (gr. 3-8). 19.95 (ISBN 0-685-23417-7). French & Eur.
—Reiseziel Mond. (GER., Illus.). 62p. pap. 19.95 (ISBN 0-686-54319-X). French & Eur.
—Sceptre D'ottokar. (FRE., Illus.). (gr. 7-9). looseleaf bdg. 19.95 (ISBN 0-685-28411-5). French & Eur.
—Lo Scettro di Ottokar. (ITA., Illus.). 62p. pap. 19.95 (ISBN 0-686-54353-X). French & Eur.
—Der Schatz Rackhams des Roten. (GER., Illus.). 62p. pap. 19.95 (ISBN 0-686-54315-7). French & Eur.
—Schritte auf dem Mond. (GER., Illus.). 62p. pap. 19.95 (ISBN 0-686-54320-3). French & Eur.
—Die Schwarze Insel. (GER., Illus.). 62p. pap. 19.95 (ISBN 0-686-54310-6). French & Eur.
—Secret de la Licorne. (FRE., Illus.). (gr. 7-9). 19.95 (ISBN 0-685-28414-X). French & Eur.
—The Secret of the Unicorn. (Illus.). 62p. 19.95 (ISBN 0-416-92530-8). French & Eur.
—El Secreto del Unicornio. (SPA., Illus.). 62p. 19.95 (ISBN 0-686-54337-8). French & Eur.
—Il Segreto del Liocorno. (ITA., Illus.). 62p. pap. 19.95 (ISBN 0-686-54355-6). French & Eur.
—Le Sette Sfere di Cristallo. (ITA., Illus.). 62p. pap. 19.95 (ISBN 0-686-54357-2). French & Eur.
—The Seven Crystal Balls. (Illus.). 62p. (gr. 3-8). 19.95 (ISBN 0-416-92610-X). French & Eur.
—Shooting Star. (Illus.). (gr. 3-8). looseleaf bdg. 19.95 (ISBN 0-685-23419-3). French & Eur.
—Die Sieben Kristallkugeln. (GER., Illus.). 62p. pap. 19.95 (ISBN 0-686-54316-5). French & Eur.
—Las Siete Bolas de Cristal. (SPA., Illus.). 62p. 19.95 (ISBN 0-686-54339-4). French & Eur.
—I Sigari del Faraone. (ITA., Illus.). 62p. pap. 19.95 (ISBN 0-686-54351-3). French & Eur.
—Der Sonnentempel. (GER., Illus.). 62p. pap. 19.95 (ISBN 0-686-54317-3). French & Eur.
—Stock de Coque. (SPA., Illus.). 62p. 19.95 (ISBN 0-686-54345-9). French & Eur.
—Temple du Soleil. (FRE., Illus.). (gr. 7-9). 19.95 (ISBN 0-685-28412-3). French & Eur.
—El Templo del Sol. (SPA., Illus.). 62p. 19.95 (ISBN 0-686-54340-8). French & Eur.
—Il Templo del Sol. (ITA., Illus.). 62p. pap. 19.95 (ISBN 0-686-54358-0). French & Eur.
—El Tesoro de Rackham. (SPA., Illus.). 62p. 19.95 (ISBN 0-686-54338-6). French & Eur.
—Il Tesoro di Rakam. (ITA., Illus.). 62p. pap. 19.95 (ISBN 0-686-54356-4). French & Eur.
—Tim in Tibet. (GER., Illus.). 62p. pap. 19.95 (ISBN 0-686-54323-8). French & Eur.
—Tim und der Haifschsee. (GER., Illus.). 62p. pap. 19.95 (ISBN 0-686-54326-2). French & Eur.
—Tim und die Picaros. (GER., Illus.). 62p. pap. 19.95 (ISBN 0-686-54327-0). French & Eur.
—Tintin & the Broken Ear. (Illus.). 62p. 19.95 (ISBN 0-416-83450-7). French & Eur.
—Tintin & the Golden Fleece. (gr. 3-8). 19.95 (ISBN 0-685-11599-2). French & Eur.
—Tintin & the Lake of Sharks. (Illus.). 62p. 19.95 (ISBN 0-416-78950-1). French & Eur.
—Tintin & the Picaros. (Illus.). 62p. 19.95 (ISBN 0-416-85170-3). French & Eur.
—Tintin au Congo. (FRE., Illus.). (gr. 7-9). 19.95 (ISBN 0-685-28415-8). French & Eur.
—Tintin au Pays de L'or Noir. (FRE.). (gr. 7-9). 19.95 (ISBN 0-685-23420-7). French & Eur.
—Tintin Au Tibet. (gr. 7-9). looseleaf bdg. 19.95 (ISBN 0-685-23422-3). French & Eur.
—Tintin en America. (SPA., Illus.). 62p. 19.95 (ISBN 0-686-54329-7). French & Eur.
—Tintin en Amerique. (FRE., Illus.). 62p. 19.95 (ISBN 0-686-54287-8). French & Eur.
—Tintin en el Congo. (SPA., Illus.). 62p. 19.95 (ISBN 0-686-54328-9). French & Eur.
—Tintin en el Pais del Oro Negro. (SPA., Illus.). 62p. 19.95 (ISBN 0-686-54341-6). French & Eur.
—Tintin en el Tibet. (SPA., Illus.). 62p. 19.95 (ISBN 0-686-54346-7). French & Eur.
—Tintin et les Picaros. (FRE., Illus.). 62p. 19.95 (ISBN 0-686-54304-1). French & Eur.
—Tintin im Amerika. (GER., Illus.). 62p. pap. 19.95 (ISBN 0-686-54306-8). French & Eur.
—Tintin im Kongo. (GER., Illus.). 62p. pap. 19.95 (ISBN 0-686-54305-X). French & Eur.
—Tintin in America. (Illus.). 62p. 19.95 (ISBN 0-416-86120-2). French & Eur.
—Tintin in Tibet. (Illus.). 62p. 19.95 (ISBN 0-416-92600-2). French & Eur.
—Tintin in Tibet. LC 74-21621. (gr. k up). 1975. pap. 6.95 (ISBN 0-316-35839-8, Joy St Bks). Little.
—Tintin y los Picaros. (SPA., Illus.). 62p. 19.95 (ISBN 0-686-54349-1). French & Eur.
—Tresor De Rackham le Rouge. (FRE., Illus.). 62p. (gr. 7-9). 19.95 (ISBN 0-685-28413-1). French & Eur.
—Vuelo 714 para Sidney. (SPA., Illus.). 62p. 19.95 (ISBN 0-686-54348-3). French & Eur.
—Y las Naranjas Azules. (SPA., Illus.). 62p. 19.95 (ISBN 0-685-01781-8). French & Eur.
—Die Zigarren des Pharaos. (GER., Illus.). 62p. pap. 19.95 (ISBN 0-686-54307-6). French & Eur.
Herman, Charlotte. Millie Cooper, Take a Chance. Cogancherry, Helen, illus. 112p. 1985. 11.95 (ISBN 0-525-44157-3, DCB). Dutton Child Bks.
Herzig, Alison C. Boonsville Bombers. (gr. 4-7). 1991. 11.95 (ISBN 0-670-83595-1). Viking Child Bks.
Hezlep, William. Cayman Duppy. (gr. 5 up). 1984. pap. text ed. 5.00 (ISBN 0-88734-403-8). Players Pr.
Higgins, Betty. The Knight Riders. Sun Star Publications Staff, ed. (Illus.). 32p. (gr. 3-8). 1986. pap. 2.95 (ISBN 0-937787-17-5). Sun Star Pubns.
—Passing Through. Sun Star Publications Staff, ed. (Illus.). 26p. (gr. 3-8). 1986. pap. 2.95 (ISBN 0-937787-03-5). Sun Star Pubns.
Highwater, Jamake. Legend Days. LC 82-48852. 160p. (gr. 7 up). 1984. 12.95 (ISBN 0-06-022303-0); PLB 12.89 (ISBN 0-06-022304-9). HarpC Child Bks.
Hildick, E. W. The Ghost Squad & the Halloween Conspiracy. 176p. 1986. pap. 1.95 (ISBN 0-8125-6852-4, Dist. by Warner Publisher Services & St. Martin's Press). Tor Bks.
—The Ghost Squad Breaks Through. 144p. 1986. pap. 1.95 (ISBN 0-8125-6850-8, Dist. by Warner Pub. Services & St. Martin's Press). Tor Bks.
Hill, Douglas. Day of the Starwind. (Orig.). (gr. k-12). 1987. pap. 2.50 (ISBN 0-440-91762-X, LFL). Dell.
—Deathwing over Veynaa. (Orig.). (gr. k-12). 1987. pap. 2.50 (ISBN 0-440-91743-3, LFL). Dell.
—Planet of the Warlord. (gr. 7 up). 1987. pap. 2.50 (ISBN 0-440-97126-8). Dell.
—Young Legionary. (gr. k-12). 1987. pap. 2.50 (ISBN 0-440-99910-3, LFL). Dell.
Hilliard, Susan. City of Gold. Ostendorf, Ned, illus. 144p. (gr. 5-7). 1989. pap. 3.95 (ISBN 0-87403-584-8, 3984). Standard Pub.
—The Giant Killer & the Jealous King. Ostendorf, Ned, illus. 143p. 1989. pap. 3.95 (ISBN 0-87403-582-1, 3982). Standard Pub.
—Out of the Wilderness. Ostendorf, Ned, illus. 144p. (gr. 5-7). 1989. pap. 3.95 (ISBN 0-87403-581-3, 3981). Standard Pub.
Hilts, Len. Quanah Parker: Warrior for Freedom, Ambassador for Peace. LC 87-8488. 160p. (gr. 2-7). 1987. 12.95 (ISBN 0-15-200565-X, Gulliver Bks). HarBraceJ.
Himmelman, John. Montigue on the High Seas. LC 87-32615. (Illus.). 32p. (ps-3). 1988. pap. 12.95 (ISBN 0-670-81861-5). Viking Child Bks.
Holl, Kristi. Danger at Hanging Rock. (gr. 7-9). 1989. pap. 3.95 (ISBN 1-55513-067-4, Chariot Bks). Cook.
Holman, Felice. Escape of the Giant Hogstalk. (gr. 4-7). 1990. pap. 3.95 (ISBN 0-689-71397-5, Aladdin). Macmillan Child Grp.
Holyer, Erna M. Reservoir Road Adventure. (Orig.). (gr. 5-8). 1982. pap. 3.95 (ISBN 0-8010-4261-5). Baker Bk.
Hooks, William J. Pioneer Cat. Robinson, Charles, illus. LC 88-4708. 64p. (Orig.). (gr. 2-4). 1988. lib. bdg. 6.99 (ISBN 0-394-92038-4, Random Juv); pap. 2.50 (ISBN 0-394-82038-X, Random Juv). Random.
Hope, Anthony. Prisoner of Zenda. Teitel, N. R., intro. by. (Illus.). (gr. 8 up). pap. 1.25 (ISBN 0-8049-0139-2, CL-139). Airmont.
—Prisoner of Zenda. 176p. (gr. 4-6). 1984. pap. 2.25 (ISBN 0-14-035032-2, Puffin). Puffin Bks.
Hope, Laura L. Adventure in the Country. Gonzalez, Pepe, illus. 120p. (gr. 2-5). 1989. 5.95 (ISBN 0-448-09072-4, G&D). Putnam Pub Group.
Horie, Michiaki & Horie, Hildegard. Lost Identity. Huff, Dawn, tr. from GER. 96p. (Orig.). (gr. 7 up). 1987. pap. 5.95 (ISBN 0-939925-09-5). R C Law & Co.
The Horror of High Ridge. (gr. 4). 1983. pap. 2.25 (ISBN 0-553-26309-9). Bantam.
Hostetler, Kay. Lost. Pressler, Cecil, illus. 51p. (gr. k-3). 1989. 12.99. Spec Creations.
Howard, Milly. Brave the Wild Trail. (Illus.). 129p. (Orig.). (gr. 4-6). 1987. pap. 4.95 (ISBN 0-89084-384-8). Bob Jones Univ Pr.
Howe, James. Mister Tinker in Oz. Rose, David, illus. LC 84-16105. 64p. (gr. 2-6). 1985. (Random Juv); pap. 1.95 (ISBN 0-394-87038-7). Random.
Huckleberry Finn. (gr. 4 up). 1988. Incl. 26 cards. 22.00 (ISBN 0-8172-2179-4). Raintree Pubs.
Hunt, Irene. Up the Road Slowly. (gr. 4-9). 1988. pap. 2.50 (ISBN 0-318-37118-9). Scholastic Inc.
Hunter, Mollie. A Pistol in Greenyards. 192p. (gr. 5-8). 1990. pap. 5.95 (ISBN 0-86241-175-0, Pub. by Cnngt UK). Trafalgar Sq.
—A Sound of Chariots. LC 72-76523. 256p. (gr. 5-9). 1988. pap. 3.95 (ISBN 0-06-440235-5, Trophy). HarpC Child Bks.
Hurwitz, Johanna. The Adventures of Ali Baba Bernstein. LC 84-27387. (Illus.). 96p. (gr. 2-5). 1985. 12.95 (ISBN 0-688-04161-2); PLB 12.88 (ISBN 0-688-04345-3, Morrow Jr Bks). Morrow Jr Bks.
—The Adventures of Ali Baba Bernstein. Owens, Gail, illus. 96p. (gr. 2-5). 1987. pap. 2.50 (ISBN 0-590-42011-9, Lucky Star). Scholastic Inc.
—The Adventures of Ali Baba Bernstein. 96p. (gr. 2-5). 1987. pap. 2.50 (ISBN 0-590-42922-1). Scholastic Inc.
Hutchens, Paul. The Killer Bear. rev. ed. 1989. pap. 3.95 (ISBN 0-8024-6957-4). Moody.
—The Lost Campers. rev. ed. 1989. pap. 3.95 (ISBN 0-8024-6959-0). Moody.
—Lost in the Blizzard. (gr. 3-7). 1970. pap. 3.50 (ISBN 0-8024-4817-8). Moody.
—The Mystery Cave. rev. ed. 1989. pap. 3.95 (ISBN 0-8024-6961-2). Moody.
—The Secret Hideout. rev. ed. 1989. pap. 3.95 (ISBN 0-8024-6960-4). Moody.
—The Sugar Creek Gang & Blue Cow. (Illus.). 128p. (gr. 3-7). 1971. pap. 3.50 (ISBN 0-8024-4822-4). Moody.
—Sugar Creek Gang & Screams in the Night. (gr. 3-7). 1967. pap. 3.50 (ISBN 0-8024-4812-7). Moody.
—Sugar Creek Gang & the Chicago Adventure & One Stormy Day. (gr. 3-7). 1968. pap. 5.95 (ISBN 0-8024-1237-8). Moody.
—Sugar Creek Gang & the Colorado Kidnapping. (gr. 3-7). 1970. pap. 3.50 (ISBN 0-8024-4827-5). Moody.
—Sugar Creek Gang & the Ghost Dog. (gr. 3-7). 1968. pap. 3.50 (ISBN 0-8024-4832-1). Moody.
—Sugar Creek Gang & the Indian Cemetary. (gr. 3-7). 1970. pap. 3.50 (ISBN 0-8024-4813-5). Moody.
—The Sugar Creek Gang & the Killer Bear. (gr. 3-7). pap. 3.50 (ISBN 0-8024-4802-X). Moody.
—Sugar Creek Gang & the Killer Cat. (gr. 3-7). 1966. pap. 3.50 (ISBN 0-8024-4825-9). Moody.
—Sugar Creek Gang & the Lost Campers. (gr. 3-7). 1968. pap. 3.50 (ISBN 0-8024-4804-6). Moody.
—Sugar Creek Gang & the Mystery Cave. (gr. 3-7). 1966. pap. 3.50 (ISBN 0-8024-4807-0). Moody.
—Sugar Creek Gang & the Palm Tree Manhunt. (gr. 3-7). 1969. pap. 3.50 (ISBN 0-8024-4808-9). Moody.
—Sugar Creek Gang & the Secret Hideout. (gr. 3-7). 1968. pap. 3.50 (ISBN 0-8024-4806-2). Moody.
—The Swamp Robber. (gr. 3-7). 1966. pap. 3.50 (ISBN 0-8024-4801-1). Moody.

—The Swamp Robber. rev. ed. 1989. pap. 3.95 (ISBN 0-8024-6956-6). Moody.
—The Teacher Trouble. (gr. 3-7). 1970. pap. 3.50 (ISBN 0-8024-4811-9). Moody.
—The Thousand Dollar Fish. (gr. 3-7). 1966. pap. 3.50 (ISBN 0-8024-4815-1). Moody.
—The Treasure Hunt. (gr. 3-7). 1967. pap. 3.50 (ISBN 0-8024-4814-3). Moody.
—The Watermelon Mystery. (Illus.). 128p. (gr. 3-7). 1971. pap. 3.50 (ISBN 0-8024-4826-7). Moody.
—The Western Adventure. (gr. 3-7). 1966. pap. 3.50 (ISBN 0-8024-4824-0). Moody.
—The White Boat Rescue. (gr. 3-7). 1970. pap. 3.50 (ISBN 0-8024-4833-X). Moody.
—The Winter Rescue. (gr. 3-7). 1970. pap. 3.50 (ISBN 0-8024-4803-8). Moody.
—The Winter Rescue. rev. ed. 1989. pap. 3.95 (ISBN 0-8024-6958-2). Moody.
Ingle, Annie, adapted by. Robin Hood. D'Andrea, Domenick, illus. LC 90-23078. 96p. (Orig.). (gr. 2-7). 1991. lib. bdg. 5.99 (ISBN 0-679-91045-X, Random Juv); pap. 2.95 (ISBN 0-679-81045-5). Random.
It's Your Adventure, Unit 11. (gr. 3). 1991. 5-pack 21.25 (ISBN 0-88106-791-1). Charlesbridge Pub.
Jackson, Steve & Livingstone, Ian. Seas of Blood. (Orig.). (gr. 5 up). 1986. pap. 2.50 (ISBN 0-440-97708-8, LFL). Dell.
Jacques, Brian. Redwall. LC 86-25467. (gr. k up). 1987. 15.95 (ISBN 0-399-21424-0, Philomel). Putnam Pub Group.
Jacques, Chester & Siembieda, Kevin. Ghost Ship. Marciniszyn, Alex, ed. Cowan, Denys & Burke, Jeff, illus. 48p. (Orig.). (gr. 7 up). 1988. pap. 7.95 (ISBN 0-916211-29-0, 554). Palladium Bks.
James L. & Collier, Christopher. War Comes to Willy Freeman. (gr. k-6). 1987. pap. 3.50 (ISBN 0-440-49504-0, YB). Dell.
Jeffries, Roderic. Trapped. LC 79-182580. 160p. (gr. 4-6). 1973. pap. 3.50 (ISBN 0-06-440035-2, Trophy). HarpC Child Bks.
Joachim, Mary J. Captain & Joey & the Tumbled down Cabin. Decker, Tim, illus. LC 89-81198. 47p. (Orig.). 1990. pap. 4.95 (ISBN 0-916383-99-7). Aegina Pr.
Johnson, Annabel & Johnson, Edgar. The Danger Quotient. LC 83-48439. 224p. (gr. 7 up). 1984. PLB 13.89. (ISBN 0-06-022853-9). HarpC Child Bks.
Johnson, Crockett. Harold's Circus. LC 59-5318. (ps-3). 1959. PLB 11.89 (ISBN 0-06-022966-7). HarpC Child Bks.
Johnson, Lois W. The Disappearing Stranger. 144p. (Orig.). (gr. 3-5). 1990. pap. 4.95 (ISBN 1-55661-100-5). Bethany Hse.
—The Hidden Message. LC 89-78390. 144p. (Orig.). (gr. 3-8). 1990. pap. 4.95 (ISBN 1-55661-101-3). Bethany Hse.
Johnson, Neil. Born to Run. (ps-4). 1989. pap. 3.95 (ISBN 0-590-42836-5). Scholastic Inc.
Johnson, Oliver. The Lord of Shadow Keep. 160p. (gr. 12 up). 1986. pap. 2.95 (ISBN 0-425-08861-8, Pub. by Berkley-Pacer). Berkley Pub.
Johnson, Tara. Huckleberry Fun. LC 89-51090. 44p. (gr. k-3). 1990. 5.95 (ISBN 1-55523-248-5). Winston-Derek.
Johnston, Tony. The Adventures of Mole & Troll. (gr. k-6). 1989. pap. 2.95 (ISBN 0-440-40218-2, YB). Dell.
Jonas, Ann. The Trek. Jonas, Ann, illus. LC 84-25962. 32p. (gr. k-3). 1985. 14.95 (ISBN 0-688-04799-8); lib. bdg. 14.88 (ISBN 0-688-04800-5). Greenwillow.
Jones, Marvin E. Danger in the Big Thicket: The Adventures of Sassy & Rowdy Krackers, Bk. 3. Czarnecki, Tim, illus. 176p. (gr. 4-7). 9.95 (ISBN 0-89015-752-9); pap. 4.95 (ISBN 0-89015-779-0). Eakin Pr.
Joyce, James. The Boarding House. (Illus.). 1982. 15.65 (ISBN 0-87191-895-1); PLB 10.95s.p. (ISBN 0-685-23241-7). Creative Ed.
Judson, William. Cold River. 192p. (gr. 9-12). Date not set. pap. 2.95 (ISBN 0-451-15254-9, Sig). NAL-Dutton.
Karlin, Bernie & Karlin, Mati. Night Ride. Karlin, Bernie, illus. (ps-2). 1988. pap. 12.95 (ISBN 0-671-66733-5). S&S Trade.
Kaye, Marilyn. Gonzo the Great. Attinello, Lauren, illus. 32p. (gr. 1-3). 1989. pap. 2.50 (ISBN 0-590-40706-6). Scholastic Inc.
Keene, Carolyn. The Sign of the Twisted Candle. (Illus.). 196p. (gr. 3-9). 4.50 (ISBN 0-448-09509-2, G&D). Putnam Pub Group.
Kellogg, Steven. Ralph's Secret Weapon. Kellogg, Steven, illus. LC 82-22115. (ps-3). 1983. 13.95 (ISBN 0-8037-7086-3); PLB 13.89 (ISBN 0-8037-7087-1); pap. 3.95 (ISBN 0-8037-0307-4). Dial Bks Young.
Kellogg, Steven, adapted by. & illus. Paul Bunyan. LC 83-26684. 40p. (ps-3). 1984. 15.95 (ISBN 0-688-03849-2); PLB 15.88 (ISBN 0-688-03850-6, Morrow Jr Bks); pap. 5.95 (ISBN 0-688-05800-0, Mulberry Bks). Morrow Jr Bks.
Kendall, Sarita. The Bell Reef. Hudson, Mark, illus. 144p. (gr. 5-9). 1990. 13.95 (ISBN 0-395-53354-6). HM.
Kennaway, James. Tunes of Glory. 192p. 1989. pap. 9.95 (ISBN 0-86241-223-4, Pub. by Cnngt Pub Ltd). Trafalgar Sq.
Kennedy, Richard. Amy's Eyes. Egielski, Richard, illus. LC 82-48841. 448p. (ps up). 1985.. 14.95 (ISBN 0-06-023219-6). HarpC Child Bks.
Kessler, Leonard. The Big Mile Race. Kessler, Leonard, illus. LC 82-9274. 48p. (gr. 1-3). 1983. 9.00 (ISBN 0-688-01420-8). Greenwillow.
Key, Alexander. Escape to Witch Mountain. 1979. pap. 1.75 (ISBN 0-671-56044-1). S&S Trade.
Kherdian, David. Bridger: The Story of Mountain Man. LC 86-7558. 160p. (gr. 7 up). 1987. 11.75 (ISBN 0-688-06510-4). Greenwillow.
Kidd, Ronald. Sizzle & Splat. (gr. 5-8). 1986. pap. 2.95 (ISBN 0-440-47970-3, YB). Dell.
Kidnapped. (Illus.). (gr. 3-5). 3.50 (ISBN 0-7214-0862-1). Ladybird Bks.
Kindell, Roy. Night Sky Star Lore. (Illus.). 52p. (Orig.). (gr. 7 up). 1989. pap. 5.95 (ISBN 0-9625388-0-9). Ursa Major Corp.
King, Vivienne, et al. Let's Go on Safari. O'Halloran, Tim, illus. 32p. (ps-3). 1985. pap. 3.95 (ISBN 0-88625-107-9). Durkin Hayes Pub.
King-Smith, Dick. The Fox Busters. (gr. k-6). 1990. pap. 2.95 (ISBN 0-440-40288-3, Pub. by Yearling Classics). Dell.
—Magnus Powermouse. Rayner, Mary, illus. LC 83-48435. 128p. (gr. 5 up). 1984. PLB 11.89 (ISBN 0-06-023232-3). HarpC Child Bks.
Kipling, Rudyard. Captains Courageous. (gr. 4-7). 1990. pap. 2.95 (ISBN 0-590-44724-6). Scholastic Inc.
—Gunga Din. Parker, Robert A., illus. LC 86-19388. 32p. (gr. 1 up). 1987. 12.95 (ISBN 0-15-200456-4, Gulliver Bks). HarBraceJ.
—Just So Stories. Salter, Safaya, illus. LC 86-46271. 96p. (gr. 4-6). 1987. 16.95 (ISBN 0-8050-0439-4). H Holt & Co.
—Kim. (gr. 8 up). pap. 1.95 (ISBN 0-8049-0075-2). Airmont.
—Puck of Pook's Hill. 1987. pap. 2.25 (ISBN 0-14-035077-2, Puffin). Puffin Bks.
Kirchoff, Mary L. Kendermore. LC 88-51719. (Illus.). 352p. (Orig.). 1989. pap. 3.95 (ISBN 0-88038-754-8). TSR Inc.
Klein, Suzy. Orp. 96p. (gr. 3-7). 1989. 12.95 (ISBN 0-399-21639-1, Putnam). Putnam Pub Group.
Knudson, R. R. Sanboomer. 192p. (gr. 6 up). 1980. pap. 1.95 (ISBN 0-440-99908-1, LFL). Dell.
Koike, Kazuo. Crying Freeman, Vol. 1. Horibuchi, Seiji, ed. Fujii, Satoru, et al, trs. from JPN. Ikegami, Ryoichi, illus. 64p. (Orig.). (gr. 12 up). 1989. pap. text ed. 3.50 (ISBN 0-929279-50-6). Viz Commns Inc.
—Crying Freeman, Vol. 2. Horibuchi, Seiji, ed. Fujii, Satoru, et al, trs. from JPN. Ikegami, Ryoichi, illus. 64p. (Orig.). (gr. 12 up). 1989. pap. text ed. 3.50 (ISBN 0-929279-51-4). Viz Commns Inc.
—Crying Freeman, Vol. 3. Horibuchi, Seiji, ed. Fujii, Satoru, et al, trs. from JPN. Ikegami, Ryoichi, illus. 64p. (Orig.). (gr. 12 up). 1989. pap. text ed. 3.50 (ISBN 0-929279-52-2). Viz Commns Inc.
—Crying Freeman, Vol. 4. Horibuchi, Seiji, ed. Fujii, Satoru, et al, trs. from JPN. Ikegami, Ryoichi, illus. 64p. (Orig.). (gr. 12 up). 1990. pap. text ed. 3.50 (ISBN 0-929279-53-0). Viz Commns Inc.
—Crying Freeman, Vol. 5. Horibuchi, Seiji, ed. Fujii, Satoru, et al, trs. from JPN. Ikegami, Ryoichi, illus. 64p. (Orig.). (gr. 12 up). 1990. pap. text ed. 3.50 (ISBN 0-929279-54-9). Viz Commns Inc.
—Crying Freeman, Vol. 6. Horibuchi, Seiji, ed. Fujii, Satoru, et al, trs. from JPN. Ikegami, Ryoichi, illus. 64p. (Orig.). (gr. 12 up). 1990. pap. text ed. 3.50 (ISBN 0-929279-55-7). Viz Commns Inc.
—Crying Freeman, Vol. 8. Horibuchi, Seiji, ed. Fugii, Satoru, et al, trs. from JPN. Ikegami, Ryoichi, illus. 64p. (Orig.). (gr. 12 up). 1990. pap. text ed. 3.50 (ISBN 0-929279-57-3). Viz Commns Inc.
Koike, Kazyo. Crying Freeman, Vol. 7. Horibuchi, Seiji, ed. Fujii, Satoru, et al, trs. from JPN. Ikegami, Ryoichi, illus. 64p. (Orig.). (gr. 12 up). 1990. pap. text ed. 3.50 (ISBN 0-929279-56-5). Viz Commns Inc.
Koltz, Tony. Terror Island. 128p. (gr. 4). 1986. pap. 2.25 (ISBN 0-553-25885-0). Bantam.
Konigsburg, E. L. Up from Jericho Tel. (gr. k-6). 1987. pap. 2.95 (ISBN 0-440-49142-8, YB). Dell.
Korman, Gordon. This Can't Be Happening at Macdonald Hall. 128p. (gr. 4-6). 1979. pap. 2.50 (ISBN 0-590-40534-9, Apple Paperbacks). Scholastic Inc.
Kotzwinkle, William. E. T. The Extraterrestrial Storybook. (gr. 2-6). 1988. pap. 3.50 (ISBN 0-318-37397-1, Pub. by Berkley-Pacer). Berkley Pub.
Kumin, Maxine. The Long Approach. 112p. 1985. pap. 14.95 (ISBN 0-670-80429-0). Viking Penguin.
Kushner, Ellen. Enchanted Kindom. (ps-7). 1986. pap. 2.25 (ISBN 0-553-25861-3). Bantam.
—The Knights of the Round Table. 128p. (gr. 4). 1988. pap. 2.50 (ISBN 0-318-37113-8). Bantam.
—Mystery of the Secret Room. (gr. 5-12). 1987. pap. 2.25 (ISBN 0-553-26270-X). Bantam.
—Outlaws of Sherwood Forest. 128p. (Orig.). (gr. 5 up). 1985. pap. 2.25 (ISBN 0-553-26388-9). Bantam.
—Statue of Liberty Adventure. (ps-7). 1986. pap. 2.25 (ISBN 0-553-25813-3). Bantam.
Lam, Roger. The Cuckoo Clock Adventure. Gibb, George, ed. Sweetman, Daniel, illus. LC 82-99848. (Orig.). (gr. 5-12). 1983. pap. 2.25 (ISBN 0-943310-01-6). Six Pr.
Landis, Mary M. Trouble at Windy Acres. (gr. 5-10). 1976. 6.95 (ISBN 0-686-15486-X). Rod & Staff.
Larrick, Nancy, intro. by. Piping Down the Valleys Wild. Raskin, Ellen, illus. LC 68-27742. 256p. (ps-3). 1985. 14.95 (ISBN 0-385-29429-8). Delacorte.
Larsen, Anita. Lost & Never Found. (gr. 4-7). 1991. pap. 2.75 (ISBN 0-590-44447-6). Scholastic Inc.
—Lost & Never Found Two. (gr. 4-7). 1991. pap. 2.75 (ISBN 0-590-43878-6). Scholastic Inc.
Lasky, Kathryn. Beyond the Divide. (gr. 7 up). 1986. pap. 3.25 (ISBN 0-440-91021-8, LFL). Dell.
—The Bone Wars. LC 88-13426. 378p. (gr. 7 up). 1988. 12.95 (ISBN 0-688-07433-2, Morrow Junior Books). Morrow.
Laughlin, Rosemary M. Trouble on the Shoshone. LC 88-50762. 94p. (gr. 5-8). 1989. pap. 5.95 (ISBN 1-55523-154-3). Winston-Derek.
Laury, Jean R. No Dragons On My Quilt. 1990. 12.95 (ISBN 0-89145-967-7). Collector Bks.
Lavender, David. The Trail to Santa Fe. rev. ed. Eggenhoffer, Nicholas, illus. LC 58-9634. 112p. (gr. 4-8). pap. 8.95 (ISBN 0-939729-15-6). Trails West Pub.
Lawrence, Edith. The Wayfaring Princes: A Tale of Questing & Adventure. Keltz, Martha, illus. 136p. (Orig.). (gr. 4-7). 1987. pap. 8.00 (ISBN 0-936132-86-8). Merc Pr NY.
Lawrence, Louise. The Warriors of Taan. LC 87-45291. 224p. (gr. 7 up). 1988. 12.95 (ISBN 0-06-023736-8); PLB 12.89 (ISBN 0-06-023737-6). HarpC Child Bks.
Lawson, Robert. The Fabulous Flight. (Illus.). 152p. (gr. 4-8). 1984. pap. 5.95 (ISBN 0-316-51731-3). Little.
Learngis. Amazing Ben Franklin. 80p. (Orig.). 1987. pap. 2.50 (ISBN 0-553-15504-0). Bantam.
Lee, Jeanne M. Ba-Nam. Lee, Jeanne M., illus. LC 86-27127. 32p. (gr. k-2). 1987. 13.95 (ISBN 0-8050-0169-7). H Holt & Co.
Leedy, Loreen. A Dragon Christmas: Things to Make & Do. Leedy, Loreen, illus. LC 88-4635. 32p. (gr. k-3). 1988. reinforced bdg. 13.95 (ISBN 0-8234-0716-0). Holiday.
Leeson, Muriel. The Bedford Adventure. Ponter, James, illus. LC 87-11943. 136p. (Orig.). (gr. 4-9). 1987. pap. 4.50 (ISBN 0-8361-3448-6). Herald Pr.
Le Guin, Ursula K. The Farthest Shore. rev. ed. Garraty, Gail, illus. LC 72-75273. 240p. (gr. 6 up). 1990. 16.95 (ISBN 0-689-31683-6, Atheneum Child Bk). Macmillan Child Grp.
—The Tombs of Atuan. large type ed. 216p. (gr. 5 up). 1988. lib. bdg. 13.95x (ISBN 0-8161-4430-3, Large Print Bks). G K Hall.
Lehner, Devony. Tinker's Journey Home. Maloney, P. Dennis, ed. Adamson, Charlotte, illus. 34p. (ps-6). 12.95 (ISBN 0-940305-00-3). P D Maloney.
Leibold, Jay. Beyond the Great Wall. (gr. 5 up). 1987. pap. 2.50 (ISBN 0-553-26725-6). Bantam.
—Grand Canyon Odyssey. 128p. (Orig.). (gr. 5). 1985. pap. 2.25 (ISBN 0-553-26522-9). Bantam.
Leonard, Larry. Far Walker. Gustavson, Susan, illus. LC 88-12290. 120p. (gr. 1 up). 1988. 12.95 (ISBN 0-932576-60-5). Breitenbush Bks.
Leonard, Laura. Finding Papa. LC 90-23742. 192p. (gr. 3-7). 1991. 13.95 (ISBN 0-689-31526-0, Atheneum Child Bk). Macmillan Child Grp.
Leonard, Marcia. Your First Adventure: Little Goat's Big Brother, No. 12. Santoro, Chris, illus. 24p. (Orig.). 1987. pap. 2.50 (ISBN 0-553-15503-2). Bantam.
Lessac, Frane. My Little Island. Lessac, Frane, illus. LC 84-48355. 48p. (gr. 1-4). 1985. 12.95 (ISBN 0-397-32114-7, Lipp Jr Bks); PLB 12.89 (ISBN 0-397-32115-5). HarpC Child Bks.
Levitin, Sonia. Incident at Loring Groves. LC 87-24591. 192p. (gr. 7 up). 1988. 14.95 (ISBN 0-8037-0455-0). Dial Bks Young.
—The Mark of Conte. 240p. (gr. 7 up). 1987. pap. 3.95 (ISBN 0-02-044191-6, Collier Young Ad). Macmillan Child Grp.
Lewis, C. S. The Lion, the Witch & the Wardrobe: Gift Edition. Hague, Michael, illus. LC 83-61572. 192p. (gr. 3 up). 1983. 21.50 (ISBN 0-02-758200-0, Mcmillan Child Bk). Macmillan Child Grp.
Lindbergh, Anne M. The Prisoner of Pineapple Place. LC 87-28815. 160p. (gr. 3-7). 1988. 13.95 (ISBN 0-15-263559-9, HJ). HarBraceJ.
Lindgren, Astrid. The New Adventures of Pippi Longstocking. (Illus.). 1988. pap. 7.95 (ISBN 0-670-82260-4). Viking Child Bks.
—Pippi Goes on Board. 172p. 1980. PLB 12.95x (ISBN 0-89967-014-8). Harmony Raine.
—Pippi Longstocking. 175p. 1980. Repr. PLB 12.95x (ISBN 0-89967-013-X). Harmony Raine.
—The Runaway Sleigh Ride. Wikland, Ilon, illus. LC 83-23347. 32p. (ps-3). 1984. pap. 11.95 (ISBN 0-670-40454-3). Viking Child Bks.
Lionni, Leo. Tico & the Golden Wings. LC 64-18321. (Illus.). 32p. (ps-6). 1975. pap. 3.95 (ISBN 0-394-83078-4). Knopf.
Lipsyte, Robert. The Contender. LC 67-19623. 190p. (gr. 7-9). 1967. PLB 12.89 (ISBN 0-06-023920-4). HarpC Child Bks.
Lister, Robin. The Odyssey. Baker, Alan, illus. LC 87-19055. 96p. (gr. 3 up). 1988. 15.95 (ISBN 0-385-24280-8). Doubleday.
Litowinsky, Olga. High Voyage: The Final Crossing of Christopher Columbus. (gr. 9-12). 1991. 14.95 (ISBN 0-385-30304-1). Delacorte.
Little, Jean & De Vries, Maggie. Once upon a Golden Apple. Gilman, Phoebe, illus. 32p. (ps-3). 1991. 12.95 (ISBN 0-670-82963-3). Viking Child Bks.
Littlefoot's Adventures. 24p. (gr. k-3). 1989. pap. 2.25 (ISBN 0-448-09354-5, G&D). Putnam Pub Group.
Lofting, Hugh. Travels of Doctor Dolittle. reissued ed. Perkins, Al, adapted by. LC 67-25853. (Illus.). 64p. (ps-2). 1967. 6.95 (ISBN 0-394-80048-6); PLB 7.99 (ISBN 0-394-90048-0). Random.
London, Jack. Call of the Wild. (gr. 9-12). 1987. pap. 2.95 (ISBN 0-590-44001-2, NAL). Scholastic Inc.

—Call of the Wild. 128p. (gr. 9-12). 1990. pap. 2.50 (ISBN 0-8125-0432-1). Tor Bks.
—Jack London's Stories of the North. 256p. (gr. 4 up). 1989. pap. 2.50 (ISBN 0-590-42272-3, Apple Paperbacks). Scholastic Inc.
—Jack London's Stories of the North. 256p. (gr. 4 up). 1989. pap. 2.95 (ISBN 0-590-44229-5). Scholastic Inc.
—White Fang: Illustrated Classics. Arneson, D. J., ed. Walker, Karen, illus. 128p. (Orig.). 1990. pap. 1.95 (ISBN 0-942025-84-9). Kidsbks.
London, Jack & Conrad, Joseph. Reader's Digest Best Loved Books for Young Readers: The Call of the Wild & Typhoon. Ogburn, Jackie, ed. Schoenherr, John & Mullins, Frank, illus. 136p. (gr. 4-12). 1989. 3.99 (ISBN 0-945260-28-8). Choice Pub NY.
Lost on the Amazon. (Illus.). (gr. 4). 1983. pap. 2.25 (ISBN 0-553-25795-1). Bantam.
Lowry, Lois. Anastasia at Your Service. 160p. (gr. 3-6). 1984. pap. 2.95 (ISBN 0-440-40290-5, YB). Dell.
Lykken, Laurie. Little Room of Terror: Adventure Novel. 160p. (Orig.). (gr. 4-8). 1990. pap. 2.95 (ISBN 0-87406-538-0). Willowisp Pr.
Lynn, Claire. A Cave Is a Deep Dark Hole. 48p. (gr. 1-4). 1978. pap. 1.95 (ISBN 0-89323-012-X, 100). Bible Memory.
Macaulay, David. Unbuilding. Macaulay, David, illus. LC 80-15491. 128p. (gr. 5 up). 1987. pap. 6.95 (ISBN 0-395-45360-7). HM.
McCaughrean, Geraldine. Saint George & the Dragon. Palin, Nicki, illus. 32p. (ps-3). 1989. 13.95 (ISBN 0-385-26528-X, Zephyr-BFYR); PLB 14.99 (ISBN 0-385-26529-8, Zephyr-BFYR). Doubleday.
McCay, William. Young Indiana Jones & the Circle of Death, Bk. 3. LC 89-43390. 112p. (Orig.). (gr. 3-7). 1990. PLB 6.99 (ISBN 0-679-90578-2); pap. 2.95 (ISBN 0-679-80578-8). Random.
—Young Indiana Jones & the Curse of the Ruby Cross, Bk. 8. LC 90-53242. 128p. (Orig.). (gr. 3-7). 1991. PLB 6.99 (ISBN 0-679-91181-2); pap. 2.95 (ISBN 0-679-81181-8). Random.
—Young Indiana Jones & the Ghostly Riders, Bk. 7. LC 90-53241. 128p. (Orig.). (gr. 3-7). 1991. PLB 6.99 (ISBN 0-679-91180-4); pap. 2.95 (ISBN 0-679-81180-X). Random.
—Young Indiana Jones & the Plantation Treasure, Bk. 1. LC 89-43388. 112p. (Orig.). (gr. 3-7). 1990. PLB 6.99 (ISBN 0-679-90579-0); pap. 2.95 (ISBN 0-679-80579-6). Random.
MacDonald, George. Sir Gibbie. Lindskoog, Kathryn, ed. Demlow, Durand, illus. 200p. (Orig.). (gr. 3-7). 1992. pap. 6.99 (ISBN 0-88070-414-4). Multnomah.
MacDonald, Golden. The Little Island. Weisgard, Leonard, illus. (gr. 1-4). 1990. pap. 3.95 (ISBN 0-590-41096-2, Blue Ribbon Bks); incl. cassette 6.95 (ISBN 0-590-63536-0). Scholastic Inc.
McDonough, Barbara. Meet Me at the Fair: A "Choose Your Own Adventure" that lets You Explore the Exciting Treasures of the 1904 St. Louis World's Fair. Wissmann, Joyce, illus. 64p. (Orig.). (gr. 4-6). 1988. pap. 4.50 (ISBN 0-931821-43-6). Info Res Cons.
McGovern, Ann. Robin Hood of Sherwood Forest. 128p. (gr. 3-7). 1985. pap. 2.75 (ISBN 0-590-43615-5). Scholastic Inc.
McGuire, Catherine. Captive Planet. LC 83-91425. 160p. (gr. 5 up). 1984. pap. 2.25 (ISBN 0-394-72730-4). Random.
Mack, Jacqueline. Tales about Tails. Halloway, Jan, illus. 24p. (ps-k). 1985. 10.95 (ISBN 0-88625-089-7). Durkin Hayes Pub.
McKeage, Jeff. Raiders of Cardolan. Charlton, Coleman, ed. Horne, Daniel, illus. 32p. (Orig.). (gr. 10-12). 1988. pap. 6.00 (ISBN 1-55806-005-7, 8108). Iron Crown Ent Inc.
Mackenzie, Jake. The Haunted City of Gold: The Secret Files of Dakota King, No. 2. (Illus.). 96p. (Orig.). (gr. 4-6). 1987. pap. 2.50 (ISBN 0-590-40750-3). Scholastic Inc.
McKinley, Robin. Outlaws of Sherwood. LC 88-45227. 256p. (gr. 7 up). 1988. 11.95 (ISBN 0-688-07178-3). Greenwillow.
McKinney, Jack. Death Dance. (gr. 10 up). 1988. pap. 4.95 (ISBN 0-345-35302-1, Del Rey). Ballantine.
McKinstry, Anne P. Can You Come with Me? McKinstry-Peterson, Laurel, illus. 44p. (gr. 4-8). 1986. 5.95 (ISBN 1-55523-034-2). Winston-Derek.
MacLachlan, Patricia. Unclaimed Treasures. LC 83-47714. 128p. (gr. 5-7). 1984. 11.95 (ISBN 0-06-024093-8); PLB 12.89 (ISBN 0-06-024094-6). HarpC Child Bks.
McLaughlin, Frank. Yukon Journey. 1991. pap. 2.95 (ISBN 0-590-43538-8). Scholastic Inc.
McQueen, Lucinda, illus. Xavier's Fantastic Discovery. LC 83-20446. 1984. incl. cassette 7.95 (ISBN 0-910313-60-1); 5.95 (ISBN 0-910313-25-3). Parker Bros.
McSwigan, Marie. Snow Treasure. 160p. (gr. 3-7). 1986. pap. 2.75 (ISBN 0-590-42537-4). Scholastic Inc.
Mahy, Margaret. The Blood-&-Thunder Adventure on Hurricane Peak. Smith, Wendy, illus. LC 89-8098. 144p. (gr. 4-7). 1989. 12.95 (ISBN 0-689-50488-8, M K McElderry). Macmillan Child Grp.
Major, Kevin. Thirty-Six Exposures. (gr. k-12). 1988. pap. 3.25 (ISBN 0-440-20163-2, LFL). Dell.
Maloney, Ray. Impact Zone. LC 85-16156. 256p. (gr. 7 up). 1986. 14.95 (ISBN 0-385-29447-6). Delacorte.
Mann, Roland. Cat & Mouse Collection. Ulm, Chris, ed. Byrd, Mitch & Butler, Steven, illus. 140p. 1991. pap. 9.95 (ISBN 0-944735-70-3). Malibu Graphics.
Mark, Jan. Fun. Foreman, Michael, illus. 32p. (ps-5). 1988. pap. 11.95 (ISBN 0-670-82457-7). Viking Child Bks.
Marrone, Russell. The Wizard's Quest. Marrone, Russell, illus. LC 87-50268. 102p. (gr. 3-5). 1987. 7.95 (ISBN 1-55523-078-4). Winston-Derek.
Marshall, Anthony. George's Story. LC 89-50143. (gr. 6-12). 1989. 9.95 (ISBN 0-932433-58-8). Windswept Hse.
Marshall, James. Taking Care of Carruthers. (Illus.). (gr. 4-6). 1981. 9.95 (ISBN 0-395-28593-3). HM.
—Yummers! (Illus.). (gr. 4-8). 1986. pap. 4.95 (ISBN 0-395-39590-9, Sandpiper). HM.
Martin, Ann M. Baby-Sitters Little Sister. (ps-1). 1989. pap. 2.50 (ISBN 0-590-41784-3, #03). Scholastic Inc.
Martin, Bill, Jr. & Archambault, John. White Dynamite & Curly Kidd. Rand, Ted, illus. LC 85-27214. 32p. (gr. k-3). 1986. 12.95 (ISBN 0-8050-0658-3). H Holt & Co.
Martin, Les. Indiana Jones & the Last Crusade. LC 89-3609. (Illus.). 128p. (gr. 5-9). 1989. PLB 5.99 (ISBN 0-394-94594-8). Random.
—Young Indiana Jones & the Gypsy Revenge, Bk. 6. LC 90-52818. 128p. (Orig.). (gr. 3-7). 1991. PLB 6.99 (ISBN 0-679-91179-0); pap. 2.95 (ISBN 0-679-81179-6). Random.
—Young Indiana Jones & the Princess of Peril, Bk. 5. LC 90-52817. 128p. (Orig.). (gr. 3-7). 1991. PLB 6.99 (ISBN 0-679-91178-2); pap. 2.95 (ISBN 0-679-81178-8). Random.
—Young Indiana Jones & the Secret City, Bk. 4. LC 89-43391. 112p. (Orig.). (gr. 3-7). 1990. PLB 6.99 (ISBN 0-679-90580-4); pap. 2.95 (ISBN 0-679-80580-X). Random.
—Young Indiana Jones & the Tomb of Terror, Bk. 2. LC 89-43389. 112p. (Orig.). (gr. 3-7). 1990. PLB 6.99 (ISBN 0-679-90581-2); pap. 2.95 (ISBN 0-679-80581-8). Random.
Masefield, John. The Midnight Folk. (gr. k-6). 1985. pap. 4.95 (ISBN 0-440-45631-2, Pub. by Yearling Classics). Dell.
Masse, Stephen V. Shadow Stealer. LC 87-32459. 127p. (gr. 4 up). 1988. 9.95 (ISBN 0-87518-379-4, Dillon). Macmillan Child Grp.
Matalon, David. Target: Hero. Bell, Robert, ed. Lyle, Tom, illus. 32p. (Orig.). (gr. 10-12). 1988. pap. 6.00 (ISBN 1-55806-004-9, 34). Iron Crown Ent Inc.
Mathieson, David. Trial by Wilderness. LC 84-27766. 176p. (gr. 7 up). 1985. 11.95 (ISBN 0-395-37697-1). HM.
Matthews, Morgan. Brave Sir Laughalot. Baer, Mary A., illus. LC 85-14010. 48p. (Orig.). (gr. 1-3). 1986. PLB 9.89 (ISBN 0-8167-0594-1); pap. text ed. 2.95 (ISBN 0-8167-0595-X). Troll Assocs.
Maxwell, Arthur. Uncle Arthur's Storytime: Children's True Adventures, 3 vols. (Illus.). 1989. Set. 29.95 (ISBN 0-685-37412-2); 12.95 ea. (ISBN 0-943497-71-X). Vol. 1 (ISBN 0-943497-72-8). Vol. 2 (ISBN 0-943497-73-6). Vol. 3. Wolgemuth & Hyatt.
Mayne, William. Gideon Ahoy. large type ed. 178p. (gr. 3-8). 1989. Repr. of 1987 ed. PLB 14.95 (ISBN 1-85089-967-3, Pub. by Clio Pr England). ABC-CLIO.
Mejo, Oscar de. The Forty-Niner. Mejo, Oscar de, illus. LC 84-48340. 48p. (gr. k-3). 1985. PLB 11.89 (ISBN 0-06-021578-X). HarpC Child Bks.
Meyer, Rich. Thieves of Tharbad. (Illus.). 36p. (gr. 10-12). 1985. 7.00 (ISBN 0-915795-35-3, 8050). Iron Crown Ent Inc.
Micro Adventure Series. Incl. Jungle Quest. Stine, Megan & Stine, H. William. (ISBN 0-317-33166-3); Million Dollar Gamble. West, Chassie (ISBN 0-317-33167-1); Time Trap. Favors, Jean (ISBN 0-317-33168-X). 128p. (gr. 4 up). 1984. pap. 1.95 ea. Scholastic Inc.
Miller, Marvin & Robinson, Nancy K. TACK Against Time. Tiegreen, Alan, illus. 128p. (gr. 2-5). 1986. pap. 2.25 (ISBN 0-590-33668-1, Lucky Star). Scholastic Inc.
—TACK into Danger. Tiegreen, Alan, illus. 128p. (gr. 3-4). 1986. pap. 2.25 (ISBN 0-590-33667-3, Lucky Star). Scholastic Inc.
Miller, Timothy B. Just in the Nick of Time. LC 87-72303. 90p. (Orig.). (gr. 5 up). 1989. pap. 6.00 (ISBN 0-916383-48-2). Aegina Pr.
Miskin, Richard. The Cross & the Ring. 125p. 1987. pap. 3.95 (ISBN 0-310-55362-8, 19038P). Zondervan.
Mitchell, Adrian. The Baron Rides Out: A Baron Munchausen Tall Tale. Benson, Patrick, illus. LC 85-3715. 24p. (gr. 3 up). 1985. 11.95 (ISBN 0-399-21280-9, Philomel). Putnam Pub Group.
Montgomery. Help! You're Shrinking. (gr. 2-4). 1987. pap. 2.25 (ISBN 0-553-15532-6, Skylark). Dell.
—Indian Trail. (gr. 2-4). 1987. pap. 2.25 (ISBN 0-553-15496-6, Skylark). Dell.
Montgomery, R. A. Abominable Snowman. (ps-7). 1987. pap. 2.25 (ISBN 0-553-25965-2). Bantam.
—Dream Trips. (gr. 2-4). 1987. pap. 2.25 (ISBN 0-553-15506-7, Skylark). Bantam.
—Genie in the Bottle. (gr. 2-4). 1987. pap. 2.25 (ISBN 0-553-15495-8, Skylark). Bantam.
—Inside UFO 54-40. (ps-7). 1987. pap. 2.25 (ISBN 0-553-25987-3). Bantam.
—The Race Forever. (ps-7). 1987. pap. 2.25 (ISBN 0-553-25988-1). Bantam.
—Secret of the Ninja. (ps-7). 1987. pap. 2.25 (ISBN 0-553-26484-2). Bantam.
—Smoke Jumper. 1991. pap. 2.95 (ISBN 0-553-28861-X). Bantam.
—Survival at Sea. (ps-7). 1987. pap. 2.25 (ISBN 0-553-26560-1). Bantam.
Montgomery, Raymond A. The Abominable Snowman. large type ed. Granger, Paul, illus. 116p. (gr. 2-7). 1987. 8.95 (ISBN 0-942545-02-8); PLB 9.95 (ISBN 0-942545-08-7, Dist. by Grolier). Grey Castle.
—Beyond Escape. 128p. (gr. 4). 1986. pap. 2.25 (ISBN 0-553-26169-X). Bantam.
—Caravan. 64p. (Orig.). (gr. 4). 1987. pap. 2.25 (ISBN 0-553-15477-X, Skylark). Bantam.
—Danger Zones. 176p. (Orig.). (gr. 4). 1987. pap. 2.95 (ISBN 0-553-26791-4). Bantam.
—Fire. 64p. (Orig.). (gr. 2 up). 1985. pap. 2.25 (ISBN 0-553-15462-1). Bantam.
—Home in Time for Christmas. 64p. (gr. 1-4). 1987. pap. 2.25 (ISBN 0-553-15553-9, Skylark). Bantam.
—Lost Dog! 64p. (Orig.). 1985. pap. 2.25 (ISBN 0-553-15508-3). Bantam.
—The Owl Tree. 64p. (Orig.). (gr. 4). 1986. pap. 2.25 (ISBN 0-553-15449-4). Bantam.
—Prisoner of the Ant People. Reese, Ralph, illus. 115p. (gr. 4). 1983. pap. 2.25 (ISBN 0-553-25763-3). Bantam.
—The Race Forever. large type ed. 116p. (gr. 3-7). 1987. Repr. of 1983 ed. 8.95 (ISBN 0-942545-12-5); PLB 9.95 (ISBN 0-942545-17-6, Dist. by Grolier). Grey Castle.
—Return to Atlantis, No. 78. 176p. (Orig.). (gr. 5 up). 1988. pap. 2.75 (ISBN 0-553-27123-7). Bantam.
—Sand Castle. 64p. (Orig.). (gr. 4). 1986. pap. 2.25 (ISBN 0-553-15458-3). Bantam.
—Spooky Thanksgiving. 64p. (gr. 2). 1988. pap. 2.75 (ISBN 0-553-15672-1, Skylark). Bantam.
—Track of the Bear. 64p. (gr. 2). 1988. pap. 2.50 (ISBN 0-553-27533-X). Bantam.
—Trouble on Planet Earth. Reese, Ralph, illus. (Orig.). (gr. 4). 1984. pap. text ed. 2.25 (ISBN 0-553-26308-0). Bantam.
—War with the Evil Power Master. 128p. (Orig.). (gr. 4). 1984. pap. 2.25 (ISBN 0-553-25778-1). Bantam.
Moon, Sheila. Hunt down the Prize. Renfrew, Susan, illus. LC 86-19576. 245p. (gr. 8-12). 1986. pap. 8.95 (ISBN 0-917479-09-2). Guild Psy.
Morey, Walt. Death Walk. Spillman, Fredrika, illus. (gr. 5-12). 1991. 13.95 (ISBN 0-936085-18-5). Blue Heron OR.
—Deep Trouble. Spillman, Fredrika, contrib. by. (gr. 4-9). pap. 6.95 (ISBN 0-936085-15-0). Blue Heron OR.
—Home Is the North. Spillman, Fredrika, contrib. by. (gr. 4-9). pap. 6.95 (ISBN 0-936085-11-8). Blue Heron OR.
—Run Far, Run Fast. Spillman, Fredrika, contrib. by. (gr. 4-9). pap. 6.95 (ISBN 0-936085-16-9). Blue Heron OR.
Morpurgo, Michael. King of the Cloud Forests. (gr. 10 up). 1988. pap. 12.95 (ISBN 0-670-82069-5). Viking Child Bks.
Morris, Gilbert. The Saintly Buccaneer. LC 88-33337. 288p. (Orig.). (gr. 11 up). 1989. pap. 6.95 (ISBN 1-55661-048-3). Bethany Hse.
Mosley, Francis. Jason & the Golden Fleece. (Illus.). 32p. (gr. 1-4). 1989. 11.95 (ISBN 0-233-98325-2). Andre Deutsch.

Mullin, Penn. High-Five Series: Whale Summer, Spirits of the Canyon & Trail to Danger, 3 bks. (Orig.). (gr. 7 up). 1991. Set, 64p. ea. pap. text ed. 12.50 ea. (ISBN 0-87879-913-3, High Noon Books). Acad Therapy.
The High Five Series is a set of 3 high interest (for ages 12-16)/low level (3rd grade readability) novels for youngsters who enjoy outdoor adventures based on real-life settings. Each short novel describes a vivid "close call" that rivets & holds the reader's attention. The central characters (brothers Mark & Jason Conway) are capable youngsters who use their heads in the crises that occur. Their reactions are neither too heroic nor unbelievable, & the real life facts included in each story add a ring of authenticity. Spirits of the Canyon: The world of Navajo secrets & legends about ancient spirits unfolds as the brothers explore Canyon de Chelly in the Southwest. Trail to Danger: The trail to Sky Lake leads to danger for Mark & Jason & a group of youngsters venturing into the mountains for a weekend backpacking trip. Whale Summer: A summer job at Sea Center holds excitement & surprises as Mark & Jason learn what goes on behind the scenes at the killer whale show. Each softcover novel is 64

pages & features 5 pen & ink illustrations & a 4-color cover. *Publisher Provided Annotation.*

Murrow, Lisa K. West Against the Wind. 240p. (gr. 7 up). pap. 2.50 (ISBN 0-8167-1324-3). Troll Assocs.

Myers, Walter D. The Legend of Tarik. 192p. (gr. 7 up). 1982. pap. 2.50 (ISBN 0-590-41211-6, Point); tchr's. guide 1.25 (ISBN 0-590-40673-6). Scholastic Inc.

—The Legend of Tarik. 180p. (gr. 7 up). 1991. pap. 2.95 (ISBN 0-590-44426-3). Scholastic Inc.

Naylor, Phyllis R. The Dark of the Tunnel. LC 84-20441. 216p. (gr. 8 up). 1985. 14.95 (ISBN 0-689-31098-6, Atheneum Child Bk). Macmillan Child Grp.

Nelson, Ray, Jr. Incredible Adventures of Donovan Willoughby. (Illus.). (ps-7). 1990. 12.95 (ISBN 0-89802-551-6). Beautiful Am.

Nelson, Theresa. The Twenty-Five Cent Miracle. LC 85-17061. 224p. (gr. 7 up). 1986. 14.95 (ISBN 0-02-724370-2, Bradbury Pr). Macmillan Child Grp.

Nesbit, Edith. Cockatoucan. Hughes, Elroy, illus. LC 87-8925. 32p. (gr. 1 up). 1988. 10.95 (ISBN 0-8037-0474-7). Dial Bks Young.

—The Ice Dragon. Grey, Carole, illus. LC 87-8963. 32p. (gr. 1 up). 1988. 10.95 (ISBN 0-8037-0475-5). Dial Bks Young.

—New Treasure Seekers. (gr. 5-8). 1988. 14.25 (ISBN 0-8446-6348-4). Peter Smith.

—The Railway Children. 240p. (gr. 3-7). 1983. pap. 2.25 (ISBN 0-14-035005-5, Puffin). Puffin Bks.

—Story of the Amulet. 1986. pap. 2.25 (ISBN 0-14-035063-2, Puffin). Puffin Bks.

Neubacher, Gerda. Tales from the Beechy Woods: Fluff's Birthday. Neubacher, Gerda, illus. 32p. (ps-k). 1983. 10.95 (ISBN 0-88625-044-7). Durkin Hayes Pub.

Newman, Marc. Longhorn Territory. 128p. (Orig.). (gr. 4). 1987. pap. 2.50 (ISBN 0-553-26904-6). Bantam.

Newman, Matt H., ed. Rumpelstiltskin. LC 66-3460. (Illus.). (gr. k-3). 1980. 6 bks. & 1 cass. 29.95 (ISBN 0-89290-086-5, BC13-3); 1 bk. & 1 cass. 10.95 (ISBN 0-318-42850-4). Soc for Visual.

Newth, Philip. Roly Goes Exploring. LC 81-5899. (ps-1). 1987. PLB 13.95 (ISBN 0-399-61217-3, Philomel). Putnam Pub Group.

Ney, John. Ox & the Prime-Time Kid. LC 85-19116. 224p. (gr. 8-12). 1985. 10.95 (ISBN 0-910923-23-X). Pineapple Pr.

Ngugi wa Thiong'o. Njamba Nene & the Flying Bus. Wangui wa Goro, tr. Kariuki, Emmanuel, illus. LC 88-70433. 34p. (gr. 2-7). 1990. 12.95 (ISBN 0-86543-079-9); pap. 5.95 (ISBN 0-86543-080-2). Africa World.

—Njamba Nene's Pistol. Wangui wa Goro, tr. Kariuki, Emmanuel, illus. LC 88-70432. 32p. (gr. 2-7). 1990. 12.95 (ISBN 0-86543-081-0); pap. 5.95 (ISBN 0-86543-082-9). Africa World.

Nichols, Paul. Captains. (gr. 4 up). 1989. pap. 2.95 (ISBN 0-345-35917-8). Ballantine.

Nicieza, Mariano. Space: 34-24-34: The Exciting Adventures of the Nova Girls. O'Connor, Thom, et al, illus. 64p. (Orig.). (gr. 9). 1989. write for info. MN DPPD Inc.

Nine, F. X. Mega Man. 1990. pap. 2.95 (ISBN 0-590-43772-0). Scholastic Inc.

—Worlds of Power, No. 5. 1990. pap. 2.95 (ISBN 0-590-43769-0). Scholastic Inc.

Nixon, Joan L. The Stalker. (gr. 7 up). 1987. pap. 3.50 (ISBN 0-440-97753-3, LFL). Dell.

Noll, Sally. Off & Counting. LC 84-17943. (Illus.). 32p. (ps). 1985. pap. 3.95 (ISBN 0-14-050502-4, Puffin). Puffin Bks.

Norton, Mary. The Borrowers Avenged. (gr. 3-6). 1988. 17.25 (ISBN 0-8446-6358-1). Peter Smith.

O'Brien, Robert C. The Secret of NIMH. (Illus.). 264p. (gr. 4-6). 1982. pap. 2.25 (ISBN 0-590-33894-3, Apple Paperbacks). Scholastic Inc.

—Secret of Nimh. 1988. pap. 2.75 (ISBN 0-590-41708-8). Scholastic Inc.

O'Byrne-Pelham, Fran & Balcer, Bernadette. The Search for the Atocha Treasure. LC 88-20201. (Illus.). 128p. (gr. 4 up). 1989. PLB 12.95 (ISBN 0-87518-399-9, Dillon). Macmillan Child Grp.

O'Connor, Jane. Sir Small & the Dragonfly. O'Brien, John, illus. LC 87-35309. 32p. (Orig.). (ps-1). 1988. lib. bdg. 6.99 (ISBN 0-394-99625-9, Random Juv); pap. 2.95 (ISBN 0-394-89625-4, Random Juv). Random.

O'Dell, Scott. Sing Down the Moon. LC 71-98513. (gr. 5 up). 1970. 13.95 (ISBN 0-395-10919-1). HM.

—Zia. Lewin, Ted, illus. LC 75-44156. 224p. (gr. 4-8). 1976. 14.95 (ISBN 0-395-24393-9). HM.

O'Donohoe, Nick. Too, Too Solid Flesh. LC 88-51731. 352p. (Orig.). 1989. pap. 3.95 (ISBN 0-88038-767-X). TSR Inc.

O'Hara, Mary. Thunderhead. LC 87-45653. 320p. (gr. 7 up). 1988. pap. 3.95 (ISBN 0-06-080903-5, P-903, PL). HarperCollins.

Oliver, M. Agent Arthur's Arctic Adventure. (Illus.). 48p. 1990. lib. bdg. 10.96 (ISBN 0-88110-408-6); pap. 4.50 (ISBN 0-7460-0145-2). EDC.

Ollivant, Alfred. Bob, Son of Battle. Hinkle, Don, ed. Riccio, Frank, illus. LC 87-15477. 48p. (gr. 3-6). 1988. PLB 12.89 (ISBN 0-8167-1211-5); pap. text ed. 3.95 (ISBN 0-8167-1212-3). Troll Assocs.

Olsen, Tillie. Yonnondio: From the Thirties. 144p. (gr. 9 up). 1975. pap. 1.95 (ISBN 0-440-39881-9, LE). Dell.

Orczy, Emmuska. The Scarlet Pimpernel. 256p. (gr. 5 up). 1989. pap. 2.95 (ISBN 0-14-035056-X, Puffin). Puffin Bks.

Packard, Edward. The Castle of Frome. 144p. (Orig.). (gr. 7-12). 1986. pap. 2.50 (ISBN 0-553-26089-8). Bantam.

—The Cave of Time. large type ed. (Illus.). 115p. (gr. 3-7). 1987. 8.95 (ISBN 0-942545-01-X); PLB 9.95 (ISBN 0-942545-07-9, Dist. by Grolier). Grey Castle.

—Ghost Hunter. 128p. (Orig.). (gr. 4). 1986. pap. 2.99 (ISBN 0-553-26983-6). Bantam.

—The Great Easter Bunny Adventure. 64p. (Orig.). (gr. 4). 1987. pap. 2.50 (ISBN 0-553-15492-3, Skylark). Bantam.

—Journey to the Year Three Thousand: Cyoa Superadventure. (Orig.). (gr. 4). 1987. pap. 2.95 (ISBN 0-553-26157-6). Bantam.

—Mountain Survival. 128p. (gr. 4-6). pap. text ed. 2.25 (ISBN 0-553-26252-1). Bantam.

—Secret of the Sun God. (ps-7). 1987. pap. 2.25 (ISBN 0-553-26529-6). Bantam.

—Skateboard Champion. 1991. pap. 2.95 (ISBN 0-553-28898-9). Bantam.

—Sugarcane Island. 128p. (gr. 4). 1986. pap. 2.25 (ISBN 0-553-26040-5). Bantam.

—Supercomputer. 128p. (Orig.). (gr. 4). 1984. pap. 2.25 (ISBN 0-553-25818-4). Bantam.

—Underground Kingdom. (ps-7). 1983. pap. 2.25 (ISBN 0-553-25989-X). Bantam.

—You Are a Shark. (gr. 5-12). 1985. pap. 2.25 (ISBN 0-553-26386-2). Bantam.

—Your Code Name Is Jonah. large type ed. Granger, Paul, illus. 114p. (gr. 3-7). 1987. Repr. of 1979 ed. 8.95 (ISBN 0-942545-15-X); PLB 9.95 (ISBN 0-942545-20-6, Dist. by Grolier). Grey Castle.

Parish, Peggy. Pirate Island Adventure. (gr. 3-6). 1991. 15.00 (ISBN 0-8446-6453-7). Peter Smith.

Parkin, Geo, et al, illus. This Weekend: We Took the Robots to the Zoo; The Monsters Came to Stay; We Got a Puppy; I Had Measles; I Got Lost & We Went to the Pond, 6 bks. 96p. (gr. k-1). Set. pap. text ed. 28.90 (ISBN 1-55624-251-4). Wright Group.

Paterson, Katherine. The Sign of the Chrysanthemum. Landa, Peter, illus. LC 72-7553. 128p. (gr. 6 up). 1988. pap. 3.50 (ISBN 0-06-440232-0, Trophy). HarpC Child Bks.

Patience, John. Adventures in Fern Hollow. (Illus.). 64p. (ps-1). 1985. 2.98 (ISBN 0-517-45856-X). Outlet Bk Co.

Paton-Walsh, Jill. Fireweed. LC 73-109554. 144p. (gr. 6 up). 1970. 14.95 (ISBN 0-374-32310-0, Sunburst). FS&G.

Paulsen, Gary. The Crossing. LC 87-7738. 128p. (gr. 6-8). 1987. 11.95 (ISBN 0-531-05709-7); PLB 11.99 (ISBN 0-531-08309-8). Orchard Bks Watts.

—The Foxman. 128p. (gr. 4 up). 1990. pap. 11.95 (ISBN 0-670-83360-6). Viking Child Bks.

—Sentries. (gr. 5-9). pap. 3.95 (ISBN 0-317-62279-X, Puffin). Puffin Bks.

—Tracker. (gr. 5-9). pap. 3.95 (ISBN 0-317-62280-3, Puffin). Puffin Bks.

Payne, Bernal C., Jr. Experiment in Terror. 224p. (gr. 5-9). 1987. 13.95 (ISBN 0-395-44260-5). HM.

Pckard, Edward. The Power Dome. (gr. 9-12). 1991. pap. 2.95 (ISBN 0-553-28837-7). Bantam.

Pels, Richard & Pels, Winslow. The Doorknob of Destiny. (Illus.). 64p. (gr. 3-5). 1989. 14.95 (ISBN 0-8092-4401-2, Calico Bks). Contemp Bks.

Peretti, Frank. The Tombs of Anak. LC 86-73183. 144p. (Orig.). (gr. 5-8). 1987. pap. 4.95 (ISBN 0-89107-442-2, Crossway Bks). Good News.

Peretti, Frank E. Escape from the Island of Aquarius. LC 85-72915. (gr. 5-8). 1986. pap. 4.95 (ISBN 0-89107-384-1, Crossway Bks). Good News.

—Trapped at the Bottom of the Sea. LC 87-71893. (gr. 5-8). 1988. pap. 4.95 (ISBN 0-89107-467-8, Crossway Bks). Good News.

Perlman, Dory. The Secret of the Unicorn Queen: Final Test. 128p. 1988. pap. 3.95 (ISBN 0-449-90298-6, Columbine). Fawcett.

Perrin, Steve. Voice of Doom. 32p. (Orig.). (gr. 10-12). 1987. pap. 6.00 (ISBN 0-915795-80-9, 38). Iron Crown Ent Inc.

Peterson, John. The Littles & the Big Storm. Clark, Robert C., illus. (gr. 4-6). 1979. pap. 2.25 (ISBN 0-590-32010-6). Scholastic Inc.

—The Littles to the Rescue. Clark, Robert C., illus. (gr. 4-6). 1971. pap. 2.50 (ISBN 0-590-40137-8). Scholastic Inc.

—The Littles to the Rescue. (gr. 2-5). 1988. 14.75 (ISBN 0-8446-6352-2). Peter Smith.

Pfeffer, Susan B. Courage, Dana. 160p. (gr. k-6). 1984. pap. 2.75 (ISBN 0-440-41541-1, YB). Dell.

—Kid Power Strikes Back. Grant, Leigh, illus. 128p. (gr. 4-6). 1987. pap. 2.50 (ISBN 0-590-33468-9, Apple Paperbacks). Scholastic Inc.

—Truth or Dare. 176p. (gr. 5-8). 1986. pap. 2.50 (ISBN 0-590-41104-7, Apple Paperbacks). Scholastic Inc.

Phillips, Tony. Turbo Cowboys: Jump Start, No. 1. (gr. 3 up). 1988. pap. 2.95 (ISBN 0-345-35121-5). Ballantine.

Pierce, Tamora. Alanna: The First Adventure, Bk. One. LC 83-2595. 252p. (gr. 6 up). 1983. 14.95 (ISBN 0-689-30994-5, Atheneum Child Bk). Macmillan Child Grp.

Pingry, Patricia. Joshua & the Bugles of Jericho. Spence, James, illus. 24p. (Orig.). (ps-3). 1988. pap. 3.95 (ISBN 0-8249-8178-2). Ideals.

Pini, Wendy & Pini, Richard. Elfquest: The Cry from Beyond. (Illus.). 160p. (Orig.). (gr. 4 up). 1990. pap. 16.95 (ISBN 0-936861-23-1, Father Tree Pr). WARP Graphics.

Preiss, Byron. Time Traveler. 80p. 1987. pap. 2.50 (ISBN 0-553-15483-4, Skylark). Bantam.

Pullein-Thompson, Christine. A Home for Jessie. (Illus.). 144p. (gr. 3-6). 1988. 2.50 (ISBN 0-87406-335-3, 33-17187-9). Willowisp Pr.

Pullman, Philip. The Ruby in the Smoke. Foster, Frances, ed. Greenstein, Mina, designed by. LC 86-20983. 208p. (gr. 7 up). 1987. 11.95 (ISBN 0-394-88826-X); lib. bdg. 11.99 (ISBN 0-394-98826-4). Knopf.

—Shadow in the North. LC 87-29846. 320p. (gr. 7 up). 1988. 12.95 (ISBN 0-394-89453-7); lib. bdg. 13.99 (ISBN 0-394-99453-1). Knopf.

Pyle, Howard. Otto of the Silver Hand. Pyle, Howard, illus. xv, 173p. (gr. 5-9). 1967. pap. 5.95 (ISBN 0-486-21784-1). Dover.

—Reader's Digest Best Loved Books for Young Readers: The Merry Adventures of Robin Hood. Ogburn, Jackie, ed. Huens, Jean L., illus. 136p. (gr. 4-12). 1989. 3.99 (ISBN 0-945260-20-2). Choice Pub NY.

Quinn, Kaye. Call of the Jungle. (Illus.). 48p. (Orig.). (gr. k-3). 1989. pap. 2.95 (ISBN 0-8431-2705-8). Price Stern.

—Dolphin's Cave. (Illus.). 48p. (Orig.). (gr. k-3). 1989. pap. 2.95 (ISBN 0-8431-2707-4). Price Stern.

—Secret of Ghost Mountain. (Illus.). 48p. (Orig.). (gr. k-3). 1989. pap. 2.95 (ISBN 0-8431-2706-6). Price Stern.

Radin, Ruth Y. Tac's Island. 80p. (gr. 2-9). pap. 2.95 (ISBN 0-8167-1320-0). Troll Assocs.

—Tac's Turn. 80p. (gr. 2-9). pap. 2.95 (ISBN 0-8167-1319-7). Troll Assocs.

Razzi, Jim. The Flying Carpet. 64p. (Orig.). (gr. 2). 1985. pap. 1.95 (ISBN 0-553-15306-4). Bantam.

Razzi, Jim, adapted by. Disney CYOA. 48p. (Orig.). 1986. pap. 4.95 (ISBN 0-553-05419-8). Bantam.

Reese, Bob. The Critter Race. LC 81-3874. (Illus.). 24p. (ps-2). 1981. PLB 11.27 (ISBN 0-516-02302-0); pap. 2.95 (ISBN 0-516-42302-9). Childrens.

—Huzzard Buzzard. LC 81-6118. (Illus.). 24p. (ps-2). 1981. PLB 11.27 (ISBN 0-516-02303-9); pap. 2.95 (ISBN 0-516-42303-7). Childrens.

—Tweedle-De-Dee Tumbleweed. LC 81-6155. (Illus.). 24p. (ps-2). 1981. PLB 11.27 (ISBN 0-516-02307-1); pap. 2.95 (ISBN 0-516-42307-X). Childrens.

Reeves, Adrienne E. Willie & the Number Three Door & Other Adventures. Hosack, Leona H., illus. 120p. (Orig.). (gr. 1-3). 1991. pap. 8.95 (ISBN 0-87743-703-3). Baha'i.

Regan, Peter. Touchstone. Leonard, Pamela, illus. 208p. (gr. 4-7). 1989. 13.95 (ISBN 0-947962-44-1, Pub. by Childrens Pr). Irish Bks Media.

Richardson, Dawn. Smoke. 112p. (gr. 9-12). 1985. 7.95 (ISBN 0-920806-73-2, Pub. by Penumbra Pr CN). U of Toronto Pr.

Roberts, Rachel S. Crisis at Pemberton Dike. Converse, James, illus. LC 83-18664. 152p. (gr. 7-10). 1984. pap. 4.95 (ISBN 0-8361-3350-1). Herald Pr.

Robinson, Andrew. Wrath of the Seven Horsemen. MacDonald, George & Charlton, S. Coleman, eds. 32p. (Orig.). (gr. 10-12). 1987. pap. 6.00 (ISBN 0-915795-86-8, 31). Iron Crown Ent Inc.

Robinson Crusoe. (Illus.). 224p. (gr. 3 up). 1990. pap. 2.50 (ISBN 1-55748-118-0). Barbour & Co.

Robinson Crusoe. 352p. 1989. pap. 2.50 (ISBN 0-8125-0482-8). Tor Bks.

Roche, P. K. Webster & Arnold & the Giant Box. Roche, P. K., illus. LC 80-11595. 56p. (ps-3). 1980. PLB 5.89 (ISBN 0-8037-9436-3). Dial Bks Young.

Roddy, Lee. D. J. Dillon & Dooger, the Grasshopper Hound. 144p. (gr. 3-7). 1985. pap. 4.99 (ISBN 0-88207-497-0). Victor Bks.

—D. J. Dillon & the City Bear's Adventures. 144p. (gr. 3-7). 1985. pap. 4.99 (ISBN 0-88207-496-2). Victor Bks.

—D. J. Dillon & the Ghost Dog of Stoney Ridge. 144p. (gr. 3-7). 1985. pap. 4.99 (ISBN 0-88207-498-9). Victor Bks.

—D. J. Dillon & the Hair-Pulling Bear Dog. 144p. (gr. 3-7). 1985. pap. 4.99 (ISBN 0-88207-499-7). Victor Bks.

—Danger on Thunder Mountain. 176p. (Orig.). (gr. 3 up). 1989. pap. 4.95 (ISBN 1-55661-028-9). Bethany Hse.

—The Flaming Trap. 176p. (Orig.). (gr. 4-8). 1990. pap. 4.95 (ISBN 1-55661-095-5). Bethany Hse.

—The Overland Escape. LC 88-63471. 160p. (gr. 2-6). 1989. pap. text ed. 4.95 (ISBN 1-55661-026-2). Bethany Hse.

—The Secret of the Howling Cave. 192p. (Orig.). (gr. 4-10). 1990. pap. 4.95 (ISBN 1-55661-094-7). Bethany Hse.

Rodgers, Raboo. Rainbow Factor. LC 84-22567. 178p. (gr. 5 up). 1985. 11.95 (ISBN 0-395-35643-1). HM.

Rogers, Barbara. God Rescues His People Activity Book. 72p. (Orig.). (ps-1). 1983. pap. 3.00 (ISBN 0-8361-3338-2). Herald Pr.

Ross, Tony. Treasure of Cozy Cove. (ps-3). 1990. 12.95 (ISBN 0-374-37744-8). FS&G.

Rotsler, William. The A-Team, No. 2: The Danger Maze. Arico, Diane, ed. 128p. (Orig.). (gr. 8-12). 1984. pap. 3.95 (ISBN 0-671-52761-4, Little Simon). S&S Trade.

—Plot-It-Yourself Adventure: Goonies Cavern of Horror. Arico, Diane, ed. 128p. (Orig.). (gr. 3-7). 1985. pap. 3.95 (ISBN 0-671-60135-0, Little Simon). S&S Trade.

Ruckman, Ivy. Night of the Twisters. LC 83-46168. 160p. (gr. 3-6). 1986. pap. 3.50 (ISBN 0-06-440176-6, Trophy). HarpC Child Bks.

Ryder, Joanne. The Night Flight. Schwartz, Amy, illus. LC 85-4482. 32p. (gr. k-3). 1985. 12.95 (ISBN 0-02-778020-1, Four Winds). Macmillan Child Grp.

Rylant, Cynthia. A Fine White Dust. (gr. k-6). 1987. pap. 2.95 (ISBN 0-440-42499-2, YB). Dell.

—Henry & Mudge in Puddle Trouble. LC 89-39810. 48p. (gr. 1-3). 1990. pap. 3.95 (ISBN 0-689-71400-9, Aladdin). Macmillan Child Grp.

—Henry & Mudge: The First Book. Stevenson, Sucie, illus. 48p. (gr. 1-3). 1990. pap. 3.95 (ISBN 0-689-71399-1, Aladdin). Macmillan Child Grp.

Saban, Vera. Johnny Egan of the Paintrock. Saban, Sonja, illus. LC 85-30958. 130p. (Orig.). (gr. 4-8). 1986. pap. 7.95x (ISBN 0-914565-13-3). Capstan Pubns.
Ten-year-old Johnny lives on a cattle ranch in the Big Horn Basin of Wyoming, where he is joined by his 14-year-old cousin. They live the life of typical boys: with the same joys & sadness, hopes & fears that youngsters are familiar with today. There is adventure & some mystery. There are problems & there are some decisions to be made. Young people reading this book will readily identify with all the situations & be inspired & encouraged with the working out of the lives of these two boys. The family travels in a horse-drawn wagon, but there are such things as automobiles & telephones, too. It's an interesting era for the reader to become acquainted with, & particularly in this part of America, one of our newest frontiers. The illustrations by Sonja Bernard, from suggestions by fourth-grade readers of the manuscript, add even more interest to the book. To order this book & for additional information on other TimberTrails Books, call (307) 568-2604.
Publisher Provided Annotation.

—Test of the Tenderfoot. Elliot, Tony, illus. LC 89-9729. 147p. (gr. 5-8). 1989. 7.95 (ISBN 0-914565-35-4). Capstan Pubns.
Modern-day fiction, set in the West. Two young teen-aged boys experience an adventure in the western mountains that helps them see more clearly their own strengths & weaknesses & to face the realities of their lives. Lanny Curtis, a boy from the East, has entered Junior High School in a small western town. He is eager to make friends but, small for his age & very near-sighted, he lacks self-confidence. When Steven Harper invites him to spend the weekend at his ranch home, Lanny is pleased & excited, for he is a lover of nature. Since the Harper ranch is at the foot of the mountains, Lanny hopes to have the opportunity to visit those high places. Steve, aggressive & often boastful, makes that visit possible. Their trip into those mountains becomes a frightening experience, one that is a test of each boy's strength & wisdom. This story, a TimberTrails Book, has adventure & suspense & will be enjoyed by Junior High School Students. The illustrations by Tony Elliot, an authority on Western settings, add interest to the book. To order this book & for additional information on other TimberTrails Books, call (307) 568-2604.
Publisher Provided Annotation.

Saccoman, Patty. The Adventures of Studley. 26p. (gr. 4-7). 1988. 7.95 (ISBN 0-533-07074-0). Vantage.

Sallis, Susan. Secret Places of the Stairs. LC 83-48442. 160p. (gr. 7 up). 1984. PLB 12.89 (ISBN 0-06-025147-6). HarpC Child Bks.

Saltzman, Mark. The Adventures of Milo & Otis. LC 88-33011. (Illus.). 40p. 1989. 14.95 (ISBN 0-688-08808-2); lib. bdg. 14.88 (ISBN 0-688-08216-5, Morrow Jr Bks). Morrow Jr Bks.

Sandberg, Inger. Dusty Wants to Help. Mauver, Judy A., tr. from SWE. Sandberg, Lasse, illus. 32p. (ps up). 1987. 6.95 (ISBN 9-12-958336-5, Pub. by R & S Bks). FS&G.

Sargent, Pamela. Eye of the Comet. LC 83-47696. 288p. (gr. 6-9). 1984. pap. 8.95 (ISBN 0-06-025196-4). HarpC Child Bks.

Saunders, Susan. Blizzard at Black Swan Inn. 64p. (Orig.). (gr. 4). 1986. pap. 2.25 (ISBN 0-553-15379-X). Bantam.

—Dorothy & the Magic Belt. Rose, David, illus. LC 84-17946. 64p. (gr. 2-6). 1985. (Random Juv); pap. 1.95 (ISBN 0-394-87067-0). Random.

—Haunted Halloween Party. 64p. (Orig.). (gr. 4). 1986. pap. 2.50 (ISBN 0-553-15453-2). Bantam.

—Miss Liberty Caper. (gr. 2-4). 1986. pap. 2.25 (ISBN 0-553-15416-8, Skylark). Bantam.

—The Movie Mystery. (gr. 2-4). 1987. pap. 2.25 (ISBN 0-553-15509-1, Skylark). Bantam.

Saunders, Susan & Packard, Edward. Ice Cave. (gr. 2-4). 1987. pap. 2.25 (ISBN 0-553-15467-2, Skylark). Bantam.

Savage, Cindy. The Curse of Blood Swamp. 112p. (Orig.). (gr. 4-6). 1990. pap. text ed. 2.95 (ISBN 0-87406-466-X). Willowisp Pr.

Scariano, Margaret, et al. High Adventures, 2 sets. (Illus.). 1984. pap. 15.00 ea. (High Noon Books). Set 1, 48p (ISBN 0-87879-404-2, High Noon Books). Set 2, 48p (ISBN 0-87879-410-7, High Noon Books). Acad Therapy.

Schantz, Daniel. Wheeler's Big Break. Ostendorf, Ned, illus. 96p. (Orig.). (gr. 3-6). 1988. pap. 3.95 (ISBN 0-87403-451-5, 24-02911). Standard Pub.

—Wheeler's Big Move. Ostendorf, Ned, illus. 96p. (gr. 3-6). 1989. pap. 3.95 (ISBN 0-87403-574-0, 3954). Standard Pub.

—Wheeler's Freedom. Ostendorf, Ned, illus. 96p. (Orig.). (gr. 3-6). 1988. pap. 3.95 (ISBN 0-87403-453-1, 24-02913). Standard Pub.

—Wheeler's Special Gift. Ostendorf, Ned, illus. 96p. (Orig.). (gr. 3-6). 1989. pap. 3.95 (ISBN 0-87403-572-4, 3952). Standard Pub.

—Wheeler's Treasure. Ostendorf, Ned, illus. 96p. (gr. 3-6). 1989. pap. 3.95 (ISBN 0-87403-571-6, 3951). Standard Pub.

—Wheeler's Vacation. Ostendorf, Ned, illus. 96p. (Orig.). (gr. 3-6). 1988. pap. 3.95 (ISBN 0-87403-452-3, 24-02912). Standard Pub.

Schultz, Irene. The Woodland Gang & the Missing Will. (Illus.). 128p. (gr. 3 up). 1984. pap. 4.95 (ISBN 0-201-50073-6). Addison-Wesley.

—The Woodland Gang & the Old Gold Coins. (Illus.). 128p. (gr. 3 up). 1984. pap. 4.95 (ISBN 0-201-50075-2). Addison-Wesley.

—The Woodland Gang & the Stolen Animals. (Illus.). 128p. (gr. 3 up). 1984. pap. 4.95 (ISBN 0-201-50074-4). Addison-Wesley.

—The Woodland Gang & the Two Lost Boys. (Illus.). 128p. (gr. 3 up). 1984. pap. 4.95 (ISBN 0-201-50072-8). Addison-Wesley.

Scieszka, Jon. The Not-So-Jolly-Roger. Smith, Lane, illus. 64p. (gr. 3-7). 1991. 10.95 (ISBN 0-670-83754-7). Viking Child Bks.

Scott, Gini G. The Shaman Warrior. Hyatt, Christopher S. & Alli, Anterofrwd. by. LC 87-83637. 250p. (Orig.). 1988. pap. text ed. 12.95 (ISBN 0-941404-67-6). New Falcon Pubns.

Scullard, Sue. Miss Fanshawe & the Great Dragon Adventure. Scullard, Sue, illus. 32p. (ps-4). 1987. 9.95 (ISBN 0-312-00510-5). St Martin.

Seale, Jan E. The Ballad of the Men at Mier: The Black Bean Expedition. Coleman, Bernice, illus. 46p. (gr. 4-8). 1986. lib. bdg. 10.95 (ISBN 0-936927-14-3); pap. 7.95 (ISBN 0-936927-15-1). Knowing Pr.

The Second Conquest. 96p. (gr. 6-9). 1985. pap. 4.95 (ISBN 0-521-31705-3). Cambridge U Pr.

Selfish Giant. LC 65-2063. (Illus.). (gr. k-3). 1980. 6 bks. & 1 cass. 29.95 (ISBN 0-89290-088-1, BC16-1); 1 bk. & 1 cass. 10.95 (ISBN 0-318-42854-7). Soc for Visual.

Serraillier, Ian. Escape from Warsaw. 1990. pap. 2.95 (ISBN 0-590-43715-1). Scholastic Inc.

Severance, Charles L. Tales of the Thumb. 2nd ed. LC 72-86863. (Illus.). (gr. 3-6). pap. 4.75 (ISBN 0-932411-00-2). Pub Div JCS.

Seymour, Peter. What's in the Cave? Carter, David, illus. LC 84-81820. 18p. (ps-k). 1985. 7.95 (ISBN 0-03-002554-0). H Holt & Co.

Shadow over the Marsh. 96p. (gr. 6-9). 1985. pap. 4.95 (ISBN 0-521-31704-5). Cambridge U Pr.

Shane, Harold G. Robin Hood & Allan-A-Dale. Clark, William, ed. LC 68-3588. (Illus.). (gr. 3-5). 1980. 6 bks. & 1 cass. 29.95 (ISBN 0-89290-081-4, BC15-4); 1 bk. & 1 cass. 10.95 (ISBN 0-318-42852-0). Soc for Visual.

—Ulysses & Circe. Clark, William, ed. LC 68-3549. (Illus.). (gr. 4-8). 1980. 6 bks. & 1 cass. 29.95 (ISBN 0-89290-082-2, BC15-5); 1 bk. & 1 cass. 10.95 (ISBN 0-318-42853-9). Soc for Visual.

Sharmat, Marjorie W. Nate the Great & the Snowy Trail. Simont, Marc, illus. 48p. (gr. k-6). 1984. pap. 2.75 (ISBN 0-440-46276-2, YB). Dell.

—Nate the Great Stalks Stupidweed. Simont, Marc, illus. 48p. (gr. 9-12). 1989. pap. 2.95 (ISBN 0-440-40150-X, YB). Dell.

Sheldon, Ann. Anything for Kelly. 128p. (gr. 3-7). 1989. pap. 2.75 (ISBN 0-671-67474-9, Minstrel Bks). PB.

—The Golden Secret. Irvin, Trevor, illus. (gr. 2-4). 1988. pap. 2.75 (ISBN 0-671-64034-8, Minstrel Bks). PB.

—Kathy in Charge. 128p. 1990. pap. 2.75 (ISBN 0-671-67476-5, Minstrel Bks). PB.

—The Ride to Gold Canyon. (Orig.). (gr. 3-6). 1989. pap. 2.75 (ISBN 0-671-64039-9, Minstrel Bks). PB.

—A Star for Linda. (gr. 3-6). 1988. pap. 2.75 (ISBN 0-671-64035-6, Minstrel Bks). PB.

Shemin, Margaretha. The Little Riders. Spier, Peter, illus. 80p. (gr. 3-7). 1988. 12.95 (ISBN 0-399-21462-3, Putnam). Putnam Pub Group.

Shipwrecked: Based on the Exciting New Movie from Walt Disney Pictures. 120p. (gr. 3up). 1991. pap. 2.95 (ISBN 0-590-44775-0, Point). Scholastic Inc.

Shreve, Susan. The Masquerade. LC 79-20073. 224p. 1980. lib. bdg. 7.99 (ISBN 0-394-94142-X). Knopf.

Shulevitz, Uri. The Strange & Exciting Adventures of Jeramiah Hush. (Illus.). 96p. (gr. 2-5). 1986. 11.95 (ISBN 0-374-33656-3). FS&G.

Siegel, Barbara & Siegel, Scott. Operation Deathstone. (Orig.). (gr. 6 up). 1986. pap. 1.95 (ISBN 0-345-32936-8). Ballantine.

Siegman, Meryl. Volcano. 128p. (Orig.). (gr. 4). 1987. pap. 2.25 (ISBN 0-553-26197-5). Bantam.

Simmons, Herbert R. & Boyice, Lester L. Star Patrol: The Adventures Begin. Peck, Bill, illus. 56p. (ps-7). 1987. lib. bdg. 8.95 (ISBN 0-930355-05-9). ELRAMCO Enter.

Simons-Ailes, Sandra. Roundup. (Illus.). 34p. (Orig.). (ps-7). 1981. pap. 3.75 (ISBN 0-915347-04-0). Pueblo Acoma Pr.

Skittles in Action. (ps). 1976. 2.00 (ISBN 0-904494-35-7, Brimax Bks). Borden.

Slote, Alfred. The Trouble on Janus. Watts, James, illus. LC 85-40099. 192p. (gr. 3-6). 1985. PLB 13.89 (ISBN 0-397-32159-7, Lipp Jr Bks). HarpC Child Bks.

—The Trouble on Janus. Watts, James, illus. LC 85-40099. 192p. (gr. 3-6). 1988. pap. 3.50 (ISBN 0-06-440216-9, Trophy). HarpC Child Bks.

Smith, Alison. Trap of Gold. (gr. 8-12). 1985. 10.95 (ISBN 0-396-08721-3, Putnam). Putnam Pub Group.

Smith, Doris B. Return to Bitter Creek. 176p. (gr. 3-7). 1988. pap. 3.95 (ISBN 0-14-032223-X, Puffin). Puffin Bks.

Smith, Mark & Thomson, Jamie. Inferno. (gr. 7 up). 1988. pap. 3.50 (ISBN 0-425-11396-5, Pub. by Berkley-Pacer). Berkley Pub.

—Overlord. (gr. 7 up). 1988. pap. 3.50 (ISBN 0-425-11262-4, Pub. by Berkley-Pacer). Berkley Pub.

—Warbringer! (gr. 7 up). 1988. pap. 3.50 (ISBN 0-425-11311-6, Pub. by Berkley-Pacer). Berkley Pub.

Snyder, Zilpha K. Song of the Gargoyle. 1991. 14.95 (ISBN 0-385-30301-7). Delacorte.

Sobel, Barbara. Papa, Molly & the Great Prairie. LC 87-81236. (gr. 3-6). 1987. 7.59 (ISBN 0-87386-045-4); bk. & cassette 16.99 (ISBN 0-317-55334-8); pap. 1.95 (ISBN 0-87386-044-6). Jan Prods.

Sochard, Ruth. Pirates of Pelargir. Fenlon, Peter, ed. McBride, Angus, illus. 32p. (Orig.). (gr. 10-12). 1987. pap. 6.00 (ISBN 0-915795-44-2, 8104). Iron Crown Ent Inc.

Spremich, Andrew. The Flight of the Dragon. Kratoville, Betty L., ed. Lucey, Jack, illus. 64p. (gr. 3-9). 1989. lib. bdg. 4.95 (ISBN 0-87879-619-3, High Noon Books). Acad Therapy.

Springstubb, Tricia. Which Way to the Nearest Wilderness? (gr. k-12). 1987. pap. 2.75 (ISBN 0-440-99554-X, LFL). Dell.

Stahl, Hilda. Kayla O'Brian & the Dangerous Journey. LC 90-80618. 128p. (Orig.). (gr. 4-7). 1990. pap. 4.95 (ISBN 0-89107-577-1, Crossway Bks). Good News.

—Teddy Jo & the Kidnapped Heir. 128p. (gr. 2-7). 1984. pap. 2.95 (ISBN 0-8423-6951-1). Tyndale.

—Teddy Jo & the Ragged Beggars. 128p. (gr. 6-8). 1984. pap. 2.95 (ISBN 0-8423-6950-3). Tyndale.

Standish, Burt L. Frank Merriwell's Chums. Rudman, Jack, ed. (gr. 9 up). 9.95 (ISBN 0-8373-9302-7); pap. 3.95 (ISBN 0-8373-9002-8). F Merriwell.

—Frank Merriwell's Foes. Rudman, Jack, ed. (gr. 9 up). 9.95 (ISBN 0-8373-9303-5); pap. 3.95 (ISBN 0-8373-9003-6). F Merriwell.

—Frank Merriwell's Trip West. Rudman, Jack, ed. (gr. 9 up). Date not set. 9.95 (ISBN 0-8373-9304-3); pap. 3.95 (ISBN 0-8373-9004-4). F Merriwell.

Staplehurst, Graham. Gates of Mordor. Fenlon, Peter, ed. McBride, Angus, illus. 32p. (Orig.). (gr. 10-12). 1987. pap. 6.00 (ISBN 0-915795-81-7, 8105, Dist. by Berkley Pub Group). Iron Crown Ent Inc.

—Robin Hood. Fenlon, Peter & Charlton, S. Coleman, eds. McBride, Angus, illus. 160p. (Orig.). (gr. 10-12). 1987. pap. 15.00 (ISBN 0-915795-28-0, 1010). Iron Crown Ent Inc.

Steele, Jason. Ship of Terror: Adventure Novel. 96p. (Orig.). (gr. 4-8). 1990. pap. 2.95 (ISBN 0-87406-526-7). Willowisp Pr.

Steele, Mary Q. Journey Outside. Negri, Rocco, illus. (gr. 3-7). 1979. pap. 3.95 (ISBN 0-14-030588-2, Puffin). Puffin Bks.
Stehr, Frederic. Gulliver. (Illus.). 28p. (gr. 3 up). 1988. 10.95 (ISBN 0-374-30865-9). FS&G.
Steig, William. La Isla de Abel. (SPA.). 14.95 (ISBN 0-685-31021-3). Santillana.
—Spinky Sulks. LC 88-81292. (Illus.). 32p. (ps up). 1988. 13.95 (ISBN 0-374-38321-9). FS&G.
—The Zabajaba Jungle. Steig, William, illus. LC 87-17690. (ps-4). 1987. 13.95 (ISBN 0-374-38790-7). FS&G.
Stein, Kevin. Brothers Majere. LC 88-51720. (Illus.). 352p. (Orig.). 1990. pap. 4.95 (ISBN 0-88038-776-9). TSR Inc.
Steiner, Barbara. Oliver Dibbs to the Rescue! Christelow, Eileen, illus. LC 85-42801. 96p. (gr. 3-5). 1985. 11.95 (ISBN 0-02-787890-2, Four Winds). Macmillan Child Grp.
Stevenson. Sword of Caesar. (ps-7). 1987. pap. 2.50 (ISBN 0-553-26531-8). Bantam.
Stevenson, James. Higher on the Door. LC 86-14925. (Illus.). 32p. (gr. k-3). 1987. 11.75 (ISBN 0-688-06636-4); PLB 11.88 (ISBN 0-688-06637-2). Greenwillow.
Stevenson, Robert Louis. Black Arrow. (gr. 4 up). 1990. pap. 3.50 (ISBN 0-440-40359-6). Dell.
—The Body Snatcher. Gibson, Gerald, illus. (gr. 7 up). 1989. 12.95 (ISBN 0-318-41647-6). P Bedrick Bks.
—Kidnapped. (gr. 8 up). 1964. pap. 1.95 (ISBN 0-8049-0010-8, CL-10). Airmont.
—Kidnapped. Ward, Lynd, illus. LC 99-933315. (gr. 4-6). companion lib. ed. o.p. 2.95 (ISBN 0-448-05474-4, G&D); il. jr. lib. o.p. 5.95 (ISBN 0-448-05815-4); deluxe ed. 11.95 (ISBN 0-448-06015-9). Putnam Pub Group.
—Kidnapped. Gianni, Gary, illus. 296p. (Orig.). 1988. pap. 7.95 (ISBN 0-8092-4486-1, Calico Bks). Contemp Bks.
—Kidnapped. (gr. 5-6). 1988. pap. 3.95 (ISBN 0-582-01383-6). Dearborn Trade.
—Kidnapped: Children's Classic. 1989. 9.99 (ISBN 0-517-68783-6). Outlet Bk Co.
—Treasure Island. (Illus.). (gr. 1-9). 1947. deluxe ed. 10.95 (ISBN 0-448-06025-6, G&D). Putnam Pub Group.
—Treasure Island. Letley, Emma, ed. (gr. 7-12). 1985. pap. 2.25 (ISBN 0-19-281681-0). Oxford U Pr.
—Treasure Island. (Illus.). (gr. 7-12). 1982. pap. 4.25 (ISBN 0-19-581379-0). Oxford U Pr.
—Treasure Island. (gr. 7 up). 1965. pap. 1.75 (ISBN 0-451-51917-5, Sig Classics). NAL-Dutton.
—Treasure Island. 224p. (Orig.). (gr. 4-7). 1988. pap. 2.50 (ISBN 0-590-41617-0, Pub. by Apple Classics). Scholastic Inc.
—Treasure Island. Hitchner, Earle, ed. De John, Marie, illus. LC 89-20561. 48p. (gr. 3-6). 1989. lib. bdg. 12.89 (ISBN 0-8167-1877-6); pap. text ed. 3.95 (ISBN 0-8167-1878-4). Troll Assocs.
—Treasure Island. abridged ed. Norby, Lisa, adapted by. Fernandez, Fernando, illus. LC 89-70039. 96p. (Orig.). (gr. 2-6). 1990. PLB 5.99 (ISBN 0-679-90402-6); pap. 2.95 (ISBN 0-679-80402-1). Random.
—Treasure Island. 272p. 1990. pap. 2.50 (ISBN 0-8125-0508-5). Tor Bks.
Stickland, Paul. Special Engines. Stickland, Paul, illus. 16p. (ps-1). 1988. 3.95 (ISBN 0-8249-8257-6). Ideals.
Stine, R. L. Twisted. 1987. pap. 2.75 (ISBN 0-590-43139-0). Scholastic Inc.
Stockton, Frank R. The Griffin & the Minor Canon. Sendak, Maurice, illus. LC 85-45827. 56p. (ps up). 1986. Repr. of 1964 ed. 13.95 (ISBN 0-06-025816-0); PLB 13.89 (ISBN 0-06-025817-9). HarpC Child Bks.
Stoneley, Jack. Scruffy. LC 78-20723. (gr. 3-7). 1988. pap. 2.95 (ISBN 0-394-82039-8, Bullseye Bks). Knopf.
Storr, Catherine, ed. Odysseus & the Enchanters. (Illus.). 32p. (gr. k-5). 1985. PLB 16.67 (ISBN 0-8172-2502-1); pap. 9.27 (ISBN 0-8172-2510-2). Raintree Pubs.
Strasser, Todd. Beyond the Reef. 1991. pap. 3.50 (ISBN 0-440-20881-5). Dell.
—Wildlife. (gr. k-12). 1988. pap. 2.95 (ISBN 0-440-20151-9, LE). Dell.
Stroh, R. W. Adventure in the Lost World. Mulkey, Kim, illus. LC 85-2530. 96p. (gr. 3-6). 1985. lib. bdg. 9.49 (ISBN 0-8167-0535-6); pap. text ed. 2.95 (ISBN 0-8167-0536-4). Troll Assocs.
Survivors. (gr. 7 up). 1987. pap. 2.50 (ISBN 0-671-55733-5, Archway). PB.
Sutton, Larry. Taildraggers High. LC 85-47592. 161p. (gr. 5 up). 1985. 11.95 (ISBN 0-374-37372-8). FS&G.
Sweeney. Disaster. 1980. 8.95 (ISBN 0-679-20954-9). McKay.
Sweeny, Joyce. Center Line. 256p. (gr. k-12). 1985. pap. 2.95 (ISBN 0-440-91127-3, LFL). Dell.
Swift, Jonathan. Gulliver's Stories. 1989. pap. 2.75 (ISBN 0-590-41842-4). Scholastic Inc.
Swiss Family Robinson. (ps-6). 1988. pap. 4.87 (ISBN 0-582-54157-3, 74264). Longman.
Swoboda, Dana. Mr. Man in the Skies. LC 88-35619. (Orig.). (gr. 5-9). 1991. pap. 4.00 (ISBN 0-915541-89-0). Star Bks Inc.
Tafuri, Nancy. Junglewalk. LC 87-8558. (Illus.). 32p. (ps-3). 1988. 14.95 (ISBN 0-688-07182-1); lib. bdg. 14.88 (ISBN 0-688-07183-X). Greenwillow.
Teets, Cathy. The Adventures of Goba & Willie. Teets, Bob, ed. Murphy, Kim, illus. 100p. (Orig.). (gr. 6). Date not set. pap. write for info. Headline Bks.
Teichman, Avigail. The Captive Sultan. Reinman, Y. Y., ed. Hinklicky, G., illus. LC 85-72403. 128p. (gr. 7-11). 1985. 7.95 (ISBN 0-935063-12-9); pap. 5.95 (ISBN 0-935063-04-8). CIS Comm.
Tejima, Keizaburo. Owl Lake. Tejima, Keizaburo, illus. (ps-1). 1987. 13.95 (ISBN 0-399-21426-7, Philomel). Putnam Pub Group.
Templeton, Larry D. The Stars of Childsland. Templeton, Larry D., illus. 22p. (gr. k-3). 1982. pap. 1.98 (ISBN 0-9608914-0-4). Templeton.
Terman, Douglas. Space & Beyond. (ps-7). 1987. pap. 2.25 (ISBN 0-553-25921-0). Bantam.
Testa, Fulvio. If You Seek Adventure. Testa, Fulvio, illus. LC 83-20920. 32p. (ps-2). 1984. 10.95 (ISBN 0-8037-0073-3). Dial Bks Young.
Thomas, Joyce C. Journey. (gr. 7 up). 1988. pap. 12.95 (ISBN 0-590-40627-2, Scholastic Hardcover). Scholastic Inc.
—Journey. 1990. pap. 2.75 (ISBN 0-590-40628-0). Scholastic Inc.
Thompson, Jonathan, Jr. Air Raiders Five. 50p. (gr. 7-12). 5.00 (ISBN 0-933479-09-3). Thompson.
—Air Raiders Four. (Illus.). 65p. (gr. 7-12). 4.35 (ISBN 0-933479-07-7). Thompson.
—Air Raiders Six. (Illus.). (gr. 7-12). write for info. (ISBN 0-933479-17-4). Thompson.
—Air Raiders Three. (Illus.). 85p. (gr. 7-12). 5.25 (ISBN 0-933479-06-9). Thompson.
—Semantography. (Illus.). 60p. (gr. 7-12). write for info. (ISBN 0-933479-13-1). Thompson.
Thompson, Jonathon, Jr. Air Raiders Two. (Illus.). 70p. (gr. 7-12). 1987. 4.60 (ISBN 0-933479-10-7). Thompson.
Thompson, Julian F. The Taking of Mariasburg. (gr. 8 up). 1989. pap. 2.95 (ISBN 0-590-41246-9). Scholastic Inc.
Thompson, Paul B. & Carter, Tonya R. Darkness & Light. LC 88-51718. (Illus.). 352p. (Orig.). 1989. pap. 4.95 (ISBN 0-88038-722-X). TSR Inc.
Thomsen, Paul. Mountain of Fire. 64p. (ps-7). 1990. pap. 6.95 (ISBN 1-56121-025-0). Wolgemuth & Hyatt.
—Operation Rawhide. 64p. (gr. 4-7). 1990. pap. 6.95 (ISBN 1-56121-015-3). Wolgemuth & Hyatt.
Thomson, Pat. One of Those Days. (gr. k-6). 1987. pap. 2.50 (ISBN 0-440-46646-6, YB). Dell.
Tjepkema, Edith R. Alaskan Paradise. 115p. (Orig.). (gr. 8 up). 1989. pap. 4.50 (ISBN 0-9620280-1-0). Northland Pr.
—North to Paradise. 103p. (Orig.). (gr. 8-12). 1987. pap. 4.50 (ISBN 0-9620280-0-2). Northland Pr.
Tolan, Stephanie S. The Great Skinner Homestead. LC 88-3970. 160p. (gr. 7 up). 1988. 13.95 (ISBN 0-02-789362-6, Four Winds). Macmillan Child Grp.
Townsend, John R. The Fortunate Isles. LC 88-35690. 256p. (gr. 7 up). 1989. 13.95 (ISBN 0-397-32365-4, Lipp Jr Bks); PLB 13.89 (ISBN 0-397-32366-2, Lipp Jr Bks). HarpC Child Bks.
Treasure Island. (Illus.). (gr. 3-5). 3.50 (ISBN 0-7214-0597-5). Ladybird Bks.
Troll. Legend of Sleepy Hollow Activity Book. 64p. (gr. 3-6). 1991. pap. 1.95 (ISBN 0-8167-2284-6). Troll Assocs.
Turner, Ann. Dakota Dugout. Himler, Ronald, illus. LC 85-3084. 32p. (gr. k-3). 1985. 12.95 (ISBN 0-02-789700-1, Mcmillan Child Bk). Macmillan Child Grp.
Twain, Mark. Adventures of Huckleberry Finn. LC 85-9576. 187p. (gr. 4-6). 1983. Repr. PLB 15.95x (ISBN 0-89966-468-7). Buccaneer Bks.
—Adventures of Tom Sawyer. LC 62-19420. 167p. (gr. 4-6). 1983. Repr. PLB 15.95x (ISBN 0-89966-467-9). Buccaneer Bks.
—The Adventures of Tom Sawyer. Moser, Barry, illus. Glassman, Peter, afterword by. LC 89-60838. (Illus.). 272p. (ps up). 1989. 21.95 (ISBN 0-688-07510-X). Morrow Jr Bks.
—Huckleberry Finn & Tom Sawyer among the Indians: And Other Unfinished Stories. 1989. pap. 8.95 (ISBN 0-520-05110-6). U of Cal Pr.
—The Man That Corrupted Hadleyburg: A Classic Story of Honesty. (Illus.). 72p. (gr. 6 up). 1986. PLB 10.95s.p. (ISBN 0-88682-006-5); 15.65. Creative Ed.
—Tom Sawyer. Edwards, June, adapted by. Naprstek, Joel, illus. LC 80-22095. 48p. (gr. 4 up). 1983. PLB 17.32 (ISBN 0-8172-1665-0); pap. 9.27 (ISBN 0-8172-2025-9). Raintree Pubs.
—Tom Sawyer & Buried Treasure. Richardson, I. M., adapted by. Dodson, Bert, illus. LC 83-18049. 32p. (gr. 3-6). 1984. PLB 10.79 (ISBN 0-8167-0063-X); pap. text ed. 2.95 (ISBN 0-8167-0064-8); cassette avail. Troll Assocs.
—Tom Sawyer Becomes a Pirate. Dodson, Bert, illus. Richardson, I. M., adapted by. LC 83-18037. (Illus.). 32p. (gr. 3-6). 1984. PLB 10.79 (ISBN 0-8167-0061-3); pap. text ed. 2.95 (ISBN 0-8167-0062-1); cassette avail. Troll Assocs.
—Tom Sawyer: Danger in the Graveyard. Dodson, Bert, illus. Richardson, I. M., adapted by. LC 83-18036. (Illus.). 32p. (gr. 3-6). 1984. PLB 10.79 (ISBN 0-8167-0059-1); pap. text ed. 2.95 (ISBN 0-8167-0060-5). Troll Assocs.
—Tom Sawyer Lost in a Cave. Dodson, Bert, illus. Richardson, I. M., adapted by. LC 83-18043. (Illus.). 32p. (gr. 3-6). 1984. PLB 10.79 (ISBN 0-8167-0065-6); pap. text ed. 2.95 (ISBN 0-8167-0066-4); cassette avail. Troll Assocs.
Two Oars Power. Date not set. write for info. Songbird & Seabird.
Tyler, Jenny & Round, Graham. Escape from Blood Castle. (Illus.). 48p. (gr. 4-9). 1986. PLB 10.96 (ISBN 0-88110-388-8); pap. 4.50 (ISBN 0-86020-950-4). EDC.
Valloglise, P. Luc. The Search for the Rabbit. 138p. (gr. 7 up). 1988. pap. 8.00 (ISBN 0-934852-55-3). Lorien Hse.
Van Allsburg, Chris. The Wreck of the Zephyr. Van Allsburg, Chris, illus. LC 82-23371. 32p. (ps up). 1983. 15.95 (ISBN 0-395-33075-0). HM.
Vardeman, Robert E. Road to the Stars. LC 87-45307. 224p. (gr. 7 up). 1988. 13.95 (ISBN 0-06-026288-5); PLB 13.89 (ISBN 0-06-026289-3). HarpC Child Bks.
Verne, Jules. Around the World in Eighty Days. 253p. (gr. 5 up). 1964. pap. 2.95 (ISBN 0-440-90285-1, LFL). Dell.
—Around the World in Eighty Days. Moser, Barry, illus. LC 87-62829. 256p. (gr. 5 up). 1988. 19.95 (ISBN 0-688-07508-8); signed ltd. ed. 175.00 (ISBN 0-688-08257-2, Morrow Jr Bks). Morrow Jr Bks.
—Around the World in Eighty Days. 224p. (gr. 9-12). 1990. pap. 2.50 (ISBN 0-8125-0430-5). Tor Bks.
—Around the World in Eighty Days. 1990. pap. 2.25 (ISBN 0-14-035114-0, Puffin). Puffin Bks.
—The Mysterious Island. reissued ed. Wyeth, N. C., illus. LC 88-3167. 512p. 1988. 24.95 (ISBN 0-684-18957-7, Scribners Young Read); deluxe ed. 100.00 limited ed. (ISBN 0-684-18991-7, Scribner). Macmillan Child Grp.
Vickery, Eugene L. Enchanted Hike: Children's Adventure Story in Verse. Meet Magical Rabbit in California. St. George, Adrianne B., illus. 20p. (Orig.). (gr. 1-8). 1987. pap. 3.95 (ISBN 0-937775-04-5). Stonehaven Pubs.
Vinge, Joan D. Tarzan, King of the Apes. LC 83-42826. (Illus.). 128p. (gr. 5-9). 1983. lib. bdg. 4.99 (ISBN 0-394-96212-5). Random.
Vinge, Joan D., adapted by. Return of the Jedi. LC 82-20538. (Illus.). 64p. (gr. 3-8). 1983. lib. bdg. 7.99 (ISBN 0-394-95624-9). Random.
Vogel, Ilse-Margret. Tikhon. LC 84-48443. (Illus.). 128p. (gr. 3-7). 1984. PLB 11.89 (ISBN 0-06-026329-6). HarpC Child Bks.
Voigt, Cynthia. On Fortune's Wheel. LC 89-39010. 288p. (gr. 6 up). 1990. 14.95 (ISBN 0-689-31636-4, Atheneum Child Bk). Macmillan Child Grp.
Waddell, Martin. Going West. Dupasquier, Philippe, illus. LC 83-48650. 32p. (gr. 1-4). 1984. HarpC Child Bks.
Wallace. Rock & Roll Mystery, No. 69. 1987. pap. 2.25 (ISBN 0-553-26653-5). Bantam.
Wallace, Bill. Danger in Quicksand Swamp. LC 89-83485. 196p. (gr. 3-7). 1989. 14.95 (ISBN 0-8234-0786-1). Holiday.
—Shadow on the Snow. LC 84-48743. 160p. (gr. 4-7). 1985. 13.95 (ISBN 0-8234-0557-5). Holiday.
Wallerstein, James S. Adventure: Five Plays for Youth. Goodwin, Chester, illus. Incl. Windigo Island; Bobby & the Time Machine; The Cactus Wild-Cat; Johnny Aladdin; Raymond & the Monster. (gr. 5 up). 1971. 5.95 (ISBN 0-912388-01-3). Aurelon.
Walt Disney Choose Your Own Adventure. (ps-1). 1985. write for info. Bantam.
The Washington's Birthday Surprise. (gr. k-3). 1981. Incl. 1 bk. & 1 cass. 10.95 (ISBN 0-89290-159-4, BC18-5); Incl. 6 bks. & 1 cass. 29.95 (ISBN 0-685-30796-4, BC18-5). Soc for Visual.
Watson, James. Make Your Move. 160p. (gr. 6-10). 1991. 17.95 (ISBN 0-575-04397-0, Pub. by Gollancz UK). Trafalgar Sq.
—Talking in Whispers. LC 83-17595. 144p. (gr. 7-12). 1984. Knopf.
Watts, Bernadette. Tattercoats. Watts, Bernadette, illus. LC 87-30198. 32p. (gr. k-3). 1989. 13.95 (ISBN 1-55858-002-6). North-South Bks NYC.
Weil, Ann. Red Sails to Capri. 160p. (gr. 5-9). 1988. pap. 3.95 (ISBN 0-14-032858-0, Puffin). Puffin Bks.
Weingardt, Richard. Sound the Charge. Mayabb, Darrell, illus. LC 78-59321. 184p. (gr. 6-12). 9.95 (ISBN 0-932446-00-0); pap. 4.95 (ISBN 0-932446-01-9). Jacqueline Enter.
Wells, Rosemary. Through the Hidden Door. (gr. 7 up). 1989. pap. 2.75 (ISBN 0-590-41786-X, Point). Scholastic Inc.
Werlin, Marvin & Werlin, Mark. The Savior. 480p. (gr. 9 up). 1979. pap. 2.75 (ISBN 0-440-17748-0, LFL). Dell.
Westcott, C. T. Silver Wings & Leather Jackets. (Orig.). 1989. pap. 3.50 (ISBN 0-440-20239-6). Dell.
White, Ellen E. Long Live the Queen. (gr. 7 up). 1989. pap. 13.95 (ISBN 0-590-40850-X). Scholastic Inc.
White, Theodore H. The Sword in the Stone. 288p. (gr. 7 up). 1978. pap. 3.50 (ISBN 0-440-98445-9, LE). Dell.
Williams, Barbara. Mitzi & Frederick the Great. (gr. k-6). 1987. pap. 2.50 (ISBN 0-440-45867-6, YB). Dell.
Williams, Geoffrey T. Saber Tooth: A Dinosaur World Adventure. Cremins, Robert, illus. 32p. (gr. 1-5). 1988. pap. 2.95 (ISBN 0-8431-2308-7); pap. 8.95 bk. & cass. (ISBN 0-8431-2319-2). Price Stern.
Willner, Carl. Havens of Gondor, Land of Belfalas. Fenlon, Peter, ed. McBride, Angus, illus. 64p. (Orig.). (gr. 10-12). 1987. pap. 12.00 (ISBN 0-915795-25-6, 3300). Iron Crown Ent Inc.
Wiseman, David. Blodwen & the Guardians. LC 83-8500. 176p. (gr. 5up). 1983. 6.95 (ISBN 0-395-33892-1). HM.
Withey, Barbara H. The Serpent Ring. LC 87-32458. (Illus.). 192p. (gr. 5 up). 1988. 10.95 (ISBN 0-87518-378-6, Dillon). Macmillan Child Grp.

Wofford, Roberta A. Sidney & Sally: The Danger of Strangers. Wofford, Roberta A., illus. 38p. (gr. k-4). 1987. pap. text ed. 1.85 (ISBN 0-9616198-0-5). Pt Orchard Spec.

Wojciechowski, Susan. And the Other, Gold. LC 87-5797. 160p. (gr. 5 up). 1987. 12.95 (ISBN 0-531-05702-X); PLB 12.99 (ISBN 0-531-08302-0). Orchard Bks Watts.

Wolverton, Linda. Running Before the Wind. (gr. 6 up). 1987. 12.95 (ISBN 0-395-42116-0). HM.

Woods, Harold & Woods, Geraldine. Tarzan of the Apes. Gaydos, Tim, illus. LC 81-19873. 96p. (gr. 2-5). 1991. lib. bdg. 5.99 (ISBN 0-394-95089-5, Random Juv); pap. 2.95 (ISBN 0-394-85089-0, Random Juv). Random.

World's Great Adventure Stories. facsimile ed. LC 79-163049. (gr. 7 up). Repr. of 1929 ed. 38.50 (ISBN 0-8369-3963-8). Ayer Co Pubs.

Worley, Daryl. Billy & the Attic Adventure. Daab, John, illus. (ps). 1989. 9.95 (ISBN 0-924067-00-4). Tyke Corp.

Wren, Percival C. Reader's Digest Best Loved Books for Young Readers: Beau Geste. Ogburn, Jackie, ed. Galli, Stan, illus. 160p. (gr. 4-12). 1989. 3.99 (ISBN 0-945260-33-4). Choice Pub NY.

Wright, Betty R. The Pike River Phantom. LC 88-45276. 160p. (gr. 4-7). 1988. 13.95 (ISBN 0-8234-0721-7). Holiday.

Wright, Bob. The Red Hot Rod. bilingual ed. Bourne, Phyllis & Tusquets, Eugenia, trs. from ENG. Heidinger, Herb, illus. (SPA & ENG.). 96p. (gr. 1-5). 1989. pap. text ed. 4.95 (ISBN 0-87879-661-4, High Noon Books). Acad Therapy.

Wright, David, tr. Beowulf. (Orig.). (gr. 9 up). 1957. pap. 2.50 (ISBN 0-14-044070-4, Penguin Classics). Viking Penguin.

Wyss, Johann. The Swiss Family Robinson. (Illus.). 96p. (gr. 2-6). 1989. pap. 2.95 (ISBN 0-448-11078-4, G&D). Putnam Pub Group.

—Swiss Family Robinson. (gr. 4-7). 1991. pap. 3.50 (ISBN 0-440-40430-4, Pub. by Yearling Classics). Dell.

Wyss, Johann D. Swiss Family Robinson. (gr. 4-7). 1991. pap. 3.25 (ISBN 0-590-44014-4). Scholastic Inc.

Yep, Laurence. Mountain Light. LC 85-42643. 256p. (gr. 7 up). 1985. PLB 12.89 (ISBN 0-06-026759-3). HarpC Child Bks.

Yorinks, Arthur. It Happened in Pinsk. (Illus.). (ps up). 1987. pap. 3.95 (ISBN 0-374-43649-5). FS&G.

Young, Alida E. Return of the Tomb of Death. 122p. (Orig.). (gr. 4-6). 1990. pap. text ed. 2.50 (ISBN 0-87406-455-4). Willowisp Pr.

Yue, David & Yue, Charlotte. The Pueblo. (Illus.). (gr. 8-11). 1986. 12.95 (ISBN 0-395-38350-1). HM.

Yvart, Jacques. The Rising of the Wind: Adventures along the Beaufort Scale. Lazorthes, Jean, tr. from FRE. Forgeot, Claire, illus. LC 83-83203. 48p. (Orig.). (gr. 7 up). 1984. 15.95 (ISBN 0-88138-031-8). Green Tiger Pr.

Zaring, Jane. Sharkes in the North Woods. (gr. 5-8). 1982. 9.95 (ISBN 0-395-32271-5). HM.

Zeder, Suzan. Wiley & the Hairy-Man. (gr. k up). 1978. 4.50 (ISBN 0-87602-219-0). Anchorage.

Zindel, Paul. The Amazing & Death-Defying Diary of Eugene Dingman. (gr. 7 up). 1989. pap. 2.95 (ISBN 0-553-27768-5, Starfire). Bantam.

ADVERTISING

see also Marketing; Posters; Salesmen and Salesmanship; Signs and Signboards

Frisch, C. Advertising. (Illus.). 48p. (gr. 4-8). 1989. lib. bdg. 14.00 (ISBN 0-86592-078-8). Rourke Corp.

Lusted, David. Advertising. LC 88-29288. (Illus.). 48p. (gr. 6-12). 1989. PLB 12.95 (ISBN 0-86307-976-8). Marshall Cavendish.

Wake, Susan. Advertising. Stefoff, Rebecca, ed. LC 90-3895. (Illus.). 32p. (gr. 4-8). 1991. PLB 17.26 (ISBN 0-944483-95-X). Garrett Ed Corp.

ADVERTISING, PICTORIAL

see Posters

ADVERTISING AS A PROFESSION

Storms, Laura. Careers with an Advertising Agency. Blumenfeld, Milton J., illus. LC 83-24401. 36p. (gr. 2-5). 1984. lib. bdg. 7.95 (ISBN 0-8225-0339-5). Lerner Pubns.

AENEAS

Virgil. Virgil's Aeneid. Dryden, John, tr. Andrews, C. A., intro. by. (gr. 11 up). 1968. pap. 1.95 (ISBN 0-8049-0177-5, CL-177). Airmont.

AERIAL ROCKETS

see Rockets (Aeronautics)

AERODYNAMICS

see also Aeronautics

AERONAUTICAL INSTRUMENTS

see also names of specific instruments, e.g. Gyroscope, etc.

AERONAUTICAL SPORTS

see also names of specific sports, e.g. Airplane Racing; Skydiving; etc.

AERONAUTICS

see also Airplanes; Airships; Astronautics; Balloons; Flight; Flying Saucers; Helicopters; Kites; Rocketry; Rockets (Aeronautics)

Aviation. (Illus.). 72p. (gr. 6-12). 1968. pap. 1.85 (ISBN 0-8395-3293-8, 3293). BSA.

Berger, Gilda. Aviation. (Illus.). 96p. (gr. 4up). PLB 9.90 (ISBN 0-531-04645-1). Watts.

Berliner, Don. Distance Flights. (Illus.). 72p. (gr. 5 up). 1990. 15.95 (ISBN 0-8225-1589-X). Lerner Pubns.

—Record Breaking Airplanes. (Illus.). 48p. (gr. 4-9). 1985. PLB 9.95 (ISBN 0-8225-0429-4). Lerner Pubns.

Carter, Sharon. Careers in Aviation. Rosen, Ruth, ed. (gr. 7-12). 1989. PLB 12.95 (ISBN 0-8239-0965-4). Rosen Group.

Cohen, Lynn. Air & Space. 64p. (ps-2). 1988. 6.95 (ISBN 0-912107-80-4, MM984). Monday Morning Bks.

Crisfield, Deborah. An Air Show Adventure. Emmerich, Donald, illus. LC 89-34372. 32p. (gr. 3-6). 1990. PLB 10.79 (ISBN 0-8167-1735-4); pap. text ed. 2.95 (ISBN 0-8167-1736-2). Troll Assocs.

Croome, Angela. Hovercraft. Wilkinson, Gerald, illus. (gr. 5 up). 1962. 14.95 (ISBN 0-8392-3008-7). Astor-Honor.

Hoare, Robert. Story of Aircraft & Travel by Air. (Illus.). (gr. 7 up). 1982. Repr. 14.95 (ISBN 0-7136-0115-9). Dufour.

Ingoglia, Gina. Airplanes & Things That Fly. (Illus.). 24p. (ps-k). 1989. pap. write for info. (ISBN 0-307-11807-X, Pub. by Golden Bks). Western Pub.

—The Big Book of Real Airplanes. Guzzi, George, illus. (gr. 1-4). 1987. 7.95 (ISBN 0-448-19179-2, G&D). Putnam Pub Group.

Jacobs, Lou, Jr. Highways in the Sky: The Story of Air Traffic Control. LC 74-17687. (Illus.). 128p. (gr. 4-6). 1975. 5.95 (ISBN 0-672-52075-3, Bobbs). Macmillan.

Jefferis, David. Supersonic Flight. (Illus.). 32p. (gr. 4-6). 1989. PLB 11.90 (ISBN 0-531-10637-3). Watts.

Mackie, Dan. Flight. Shulist, Steve, illus. 32p. (gr. 5-9). 1985. pap. 4.95 (ISBN 0-88625-112-5). Durkin Hayes Pub.

Moulton, Robert R. First to Fly. LC 83-11971. (Illus.). 120p. (gr. 5 up). 1983. PLB 12.95 (ISBN 0-8225-1576-8). Lerner Pubns.

Sabin, Louis. Wilbur & Orville Wright: The Flight to Adventure. Lawn, John, illus. LC 82-15879. 48p. (gr. 4-6). 1983. PLB 10.79 (ISBN 0-89375-851-5); pap. text ed. 2.95 (ISBN 0-89375-852-3). Troll Assocs.

Stoff, Joshua. Dirigible. LC 85-7461. (Illus.). 112p. (gr. 3 up). 1985. 12.95 (ISBN 0-689-31084-6, Atheneum Child Bk). Macmillan Child Grp.

Tunney, Christopher. Aircraft. LC 79-64384. (Illus.). 36p. (gr. 3-6). 1980. PLB 9.95 (ISBN 0-8225-1176-2). Lerner Pubns.

Williams, Brian. Pioneers of Flight. LC 90-9470. (Illus.). 48p. (gr. 4-8). 1990. PLB 18.60 (ISBN 0-8114-2755-2). Steck-V.

Zisfein, Melvin B. Flight: A Panorama of Aviation. Parker, Robert A., illus. (gr. 4 up). 1981. Knopf.

AERONAUTICS–ACCIDENTS

see also Survival (After Airplane Accidents, Shipwrecks, Etc.)

Barrett, Norman. Picture World of Airport Rescue. LC 90-31221. (Illus.). 32p. (gr. k-4). 1991. PLB 11.40 (ISBN 0-531-14088-1). Watts.

Day, James. The Hindenburg Tragedy. Spender, Nick, illus. LC 88-19879. 32p. (gr. 3-6). 1989. PLB 10.90 (ISBN 0-531-18238-X, Pub. by Bookwright Pr). Watts.

Lightner, Robert. Triumph Through Tragedy. 70p. (Orig.). (gr. 7 up). 1980. pap. 2.50 (ISBN 0-89323-008-1, 330). Bible Memory.

Terror in the Skies: The Inside Story of the World's Worst Air Crashes. (Illus.). 256p. 1988. 16.95 (ISBN 0-8065-1091-9, Citadel Pr). Carol Pub Group.

AERONAUTICS–BIOGRAPHY

see also Air Pilots; Women in Aeronautics

Jefferis, David. The First Flyers: Pioneers of Aviation. FS-Ltd Staff, ed. (Illus.). 32p. (gr. 4-9). 1988. PLB 11.90 (ISBN 0-531-10563-6). Watts.

AERONAUTICS, COMMERCIAL

see also Air Lines

Jacobs, Lou, Jr. Jumbo Jets. LC 73-78280. (Illus.). (gr. 5-9). 1969. 7.50 (ISBN 0-672-52280-2, Bobbs). Macmillan.

Jefferis, David. Giants of the Air: The Story of Commercial Aviation. FS Staff, ed. (Illus.). 32p. (gr. 4-9). 1988. PLB 11.90 (ISBN 0-531-10564-4). Watts.

AERONAUTICS–FICTION

Bachman-Heinz, Margaret I. Andy's Love for Dottie & Derry. Decareau, John, illus. 1990. 6.95 (ISBN 0-533-08988-3). Vantage.

Hallam, Leslie T. Andy's Headache. 1990. 6.95 (ISBN 0-533-08821-6). Vantage.

Horgan, Dorothy. Then the Zeppelins Came. 112p. (gr. 6 up). 1990. jacketed 14.95 (ISBN 0-19-271598-4). Oxford U Pr.

AERONAUTICS–FLIGHTS

see also Space Flight

Jefferis, David. Epic Flights. Franklin Watts Ltd., ed. (Illus.). 32p. (gr. 7-9). 1988. PLB 11.90 (ISBN 0-531-10507-5). Watts.

Kaufmann, John. Voyager: Flight Around the World. LC 88-6879. 64p. (gr. 5-10). 1989. lib. bdg. 15.95 (ISBN 0-89490-185-0). Enslow Pubs.

AERONAUTICS–HISTORY

Berliner, Don. Before the Wright Brothers. (Illus.). 72p. (gr. 5 up). 1990. 14.95 (ISBN 0-8225-1588-1). Lerner Pubns.

Gibbons, Gail. Flying. Gibbons, Gail, illus. LC 85-22027. 32p. (ps-3). 1985. 14.95g (ISBN 0-8234-0599-0). Holiday.

Radford, Don. Looking at Flight. (Illus.). 72p. (gr. 7-12). 1984. 18.95 (ISBN 0-7134-4257-3, Pub. by Batsford England). Trafalgar Sq.

Stoff, Joshua. From Airship to Spaceship: Long Island Aviation & Spaceflight. LC 90-47647. (Illus.). 96p. (gr. 4-10). 1991. 15.00 (ISBN 1-55787-074-8, NY71060, Empire State Bks); pap. 7.95 (ISBN 1-55787-075-6, NY71059, Empire State Bks). Heart of the Lakes.

AERONAUTICS, MILITARY

see also Aircraft Carriers; Airplanes, Military

also names of wars with the subdivision Aerial Operations

Baker, David. Airborne Early Warning. (Illus.). 48p. (gr. 3-8). 1989. lib. bdg. 18.60 (ISBN 0-86592-533-X). Rourke Corp.

—Airlift. (Illus.). 48p. (gr. 3-8). 1989. lib. bdg. 18.60 (ISBN 0-86592-531-3). Rourke Corp.

—Anti-Submarine Warfare. 48p. (gr. 3-8). 1989. lib. bdg. 18.60 (ISBN 0-86592-532-1). Rourke Corp.

—Future Fighters. (Illus.). 48p. (gr. 3-8). 1989. lib. bdg. 18.60 (ISBN 0-86592-535-6). Rourke Corp.

—Ground Attack Planes. 48p. (gr. 3-8). 1989. lib. bdg. 18.60 (ISBN 0-86592-536-4). Rourke Corp.

—Navy Strike Planes. (Illus.). 48p. (gr. 3-8). 1989. lib. bdg. 18.60 (ISBN 0-86592-534-8). Rourke Corp.

Nicholaus, J. Air Defence Weapons. (Illus.). 48p. (gr. 3-8). 1989. lib. bdg. 18.60 (ISBN 0-86592-423-6). Rourke Corp.

—Army Air Support. (Illus.). 48p. (gr. 3-8). 1989. lib. bdg. 18.60 (ISBN 0-86592-421-X). Rourke Corp.

Watry, Charles A. & Hall, Duane L. Aerial Gunners: The Unknown Aces of World War II. LC 85-91368. (Illus.). 256p. (Orig.). 1986. pap. 12.95 (ISBN 0-914379-01-1). Cal Aero Pr.

AERONAUTICS, NAVAL

see Aeronautics, Military

AERONAUTICS–PILOTING

see Airplanes–Piloting

AERONAUTICS–SAFETY MEASURES

Hawkes, Nigel. Safety in the Sky. 1990. PLB 8.90 (ISBN 0-531-17207-4). Watts.

AERONAUTICS–VOCATIONAL GUIDANCE

Ayres, Carter M. Pilots & Aviation. (Illus.). 72p. (gr. 5 up). 1990. PLB 15.95 (ISBN 0-8225-1590-3). Lerner Pubns.

AERONAUTICS–VOYAGES

see Aeronautics–Flights

AEROSPACE MEDICINE

see Space Medicine

AFFECTION

see Friendship; Love

AFGHANISTAN

Afghanistan. LC 80-18356. (gr. 4 up). 1980. PLB 10.40 (ISBN 0-531-04157-3). Watts.

Clifford, Mary L. The Land & People of Afghanistan. LC 88-21419. (Illus.). 240p. (gr. 6 up). 1989. 14.95 (ISBN 0-397-32338-7, Lipp Jr Bks); PLB 14.89 (ISBN 0-397-32339-5, Lipp Jr Bks). HarpC Child Bks.

Griffiths, J. Conflict in Afghanistan. (Illus.). 80p. (gr. 7 up). Date not set. PLB 17.26 (ISBN 0-86592-039-7). Rourke Corp.

Herda, D. J. Afghan Rebels. (ps-3). 1990. PLB 12.90 (ISBN 0-531-10897-X). Watts.

Howarth, Michael. Afghanistan. (Illus.). (gr. 5 up). 1988. 14.95 (ISBN 0-7910-0100-8). Chelsea Hse.

Knowledge Unlimited Staff. Afghanistan: The Long Fight for Freedom. (Illus.). 22p. (gr. 4-12). 1983. incl. filmstrip, cass., guide 28.00 (ISBN 0-915291-00-2). Know Unltd.

Lerner Publications, Department of Geography Staff, ed. Afghanistan in Pictures. (Illus.). 64p. (gr. 5 up). 1989. 12.95 (ISBN 0-8225-1849-X). Lerner Pubns.

Shokla, Surinder K. Afghanistan. (Illus.). 110p. (gr. 9 up). 1989. text ed. 22.50x (ISBN 0-685-21870-8, Pub. by Sterling Pubs India). Apt Bks.

AFRICA

Barnes-Svarney, Patricia. Zimbabwe. (Illus.). 96p. (gr. 5 up). 1989. 14.95 (ISBN 1-55546-799-7). Chelsea Hse.

Baynham, Simon. Africa. (Illus.). 64p. (gr. 4 up). 1987. PLB 10.29 (ISBN 0-531-10319-6). Watts.

Benoit, Marie. Mauritius. (Illus.). (gr. 5 up). 1989. 14.95 (ISBN 0-7910-0126-1). Chelsea Hse.

Berger, Gilda. U. S. A. for Africa, Rock Aid in the Eighties. LC 86-24718. (Illus.). 96p. (gr. 7-12). 1987. lib. bdg. 12.90 (ISBN 0-531-10299-8). Watts.

Browder, Atlantis T. & Browder, Anthony T. My First Trip to Africa. Browder, Anne, ed. Aaron, Malcolm, illus. LC 91-70328. 38p. (Orig.). 1991. 16.95 (ISBN 0-924944-02-1); pap. 8.95 (ISBN 0-924944-01-3). Inst Karmic. Approved for use in New York City's School System two months after publication, MY FIRST TRIP TO AFRICA is the collaborative effort of 8-year-old Atlantis & her father Anthony Browder, author of "From The Browder File, 22 Essays on the African American Experience." MY FIRST TRIP TO AFRICA chronicles the experience of then 7-year-old Atlantis during a 13-day study tour to Egypt in November, 1989. It contains a Parent/Teacher Guide, 27 photographs,

15 illustrations, 3 maps & a 42 word glossary. The Parent/Teacher Guide is an aid providing topics of discussion for children in the classroom, at the dinner table or at bedtime; including activities designed to stimulate a better understanding of all the topics referenced in the narrative. This narrative written specifically for children, will assist them in understanding aspects of personal, world & African history. MY FIRST TRIP TO AFRICA makes good reading for children & adults alike. "Uniquely written from a child's perspective, encompassing historical facts/information every African American of any age should know."--The Capitol Spotlight. "Atlantis's reflections were teamed with photographs taken by Atlantis, her father & her grandmother."--The Washington Post. "...filled with pictures of the historical legacy of Kemet, along with American edifices reminiscent of Ancient Egyptian architecture."--Washington Afro-American.
Publisher Provided Annotation.

Cameroon. (Illus.). (gr. 5 up). 1990. 14.95 (ISBN 0-7910-0144-X). Chelsea Hse.
Carrick, Noel. New Guinea. (Illus.). 96p. (gr. 5 up). 1989. 14.95 (ISBN 0-222-00916-0). Chelsea Hse.
Chad. (Illus.). (gr. 5 up). 1989. 14.95 (ISBN 0-7910-0147-4). Chelsea Hse.
Cheney, Patricia. The Land & People of Zimbabwe. LC 89-36244. (Illus.). 256p. (gr. 6 up). 1990. 15.95 (ISBN 0-397-32392-1, Lipp Jr Bks); PLB 15.89 (ISBN 0-397-32393-X, Lipp Jr Bks). HarpC Child Bks.
Chiasson, John. African Journey. Chiasson, John, photos by. LC 86-8233. (Illus.). 64p. (gr. 3-6). 1987. 16.95 (ISBN 0-02-718530-3, Bradbury Pr). Macmillan Child Grp.
Chijioke, F. A. Ancient Africa. LC 75-80850. (Illus.). 48p. (gr. 5-8). 1969. pap. 5.50 (ISBN 0-8419-0013-2, Africana). Holmes & Meier.
Clark, Leon E. Through African Eyes, Vol. 2: The Present: Tradition & Change. (Illus.). 292p. (Orig.). (gr. 9-12). 1992. 28.95x (ISBN 0-938960-36-9); pap. text ed. 19.95x (ISBN 0-938960-28-8). CITE.
Conway, Mike. Swaziland. (Illus.). (gr. 5 up). 1989. 14.95 (ISBN 0-7910-0131-8). Chelsea Hse.
Department of Geography, Lerner Publications. Zimbabwe in Pictures. (Illus.). 64p. (gr. 5 up). 1988. 12.95 (ISBN 0-8225-1825-2). Lerner Pubns.
Eko, Paul M. Cry Cry My Beloved People. Scalist, Paula, ed. 286p. 1990. 18.95x (ISBN 0-685-28130-2). Backwards & Backwards.
—Water Finds Its Own Level. Scalist, Paula, ed. 105p. 1990. pap. 8.95 (ISBN 0-685-28132-9). Backwards & Backwards.
Ellis, Veronica F. Afro-Bets Activity & Enrichment Guide: First Book about Africa. (gr. 1-4). Date not set. pap. 7.95 (ISBN 0-940975-07-6). Just Us Bks.
—Afro-Bets First Book about Africa. Ford, George, illus. LC 89-85157. 32p. (Orig.). (gr. 1-4). 1990. PLB 13.95 (ISBN 0-940975-12-2); pap. 6.95 (ISBN 0-940975-03-3). Just Us Bks.
Equatorial Guinea. (Illus.). (gr. 5 up). 1989. 13.95 (ISBN 0-7910-0121-0). Chelsea Hse.
Fairfield, Sheila. People & Nations of Africa. LC 88-42922. (Illus.). 64p. (gr. 5-6). 1988. PLB 13.95 (ISBN 1-55532-903-9). Gareth Stevens Inc.
Georges, D. V. Africa. LC 86-9586. (Illus.). 48p. (gr. k-4). 1986. PLB 14.60 (ISBN 0-516-01287-8); pap. 4.95 (ISBN 0-516-41287-6). Childrens.
Gess, Denise. Togo. (Illus.). 96p. (gr. 5 up). 1988. lib. bdg. 14.95x (ISBN 1-55546-190-5). Chelsea Hse.
Greenfield, Eloise. Africa Dream. Byard, Carole, illus. LC 77-5080. 32p. (ps-3). 1989. PLB 13.89 (ISBN 0-690-04776-2, Crowell Jr Bks). HarpC Child Bks.
Haskins, Jim. Count Your Way Through Africa. Knutson, Barbara, illus. 24p. (gr. 1-4). 1989. 11.95 (ISBN 0-87614-347-8); pap. 4.95 (ISBN 0-87614-514-4). Carolrhoda Bks.
Head, Bessie. When Rain Clouds Gather. 188p. (Orig.). 1987. pap. 7.95 (ISBN 0-435-90726-3, 90726). Heinemann Ed.
Henry-Biabaud, Chantal. Living in the Heart of Africa. Bogard, Vicki, tr. from FRE. Poissenot, Jean-Marie, illus. LC 90-50774. 38p. (gr. k-5). 1991. 4.95 (ISBN 0-944589-29-4, 294). Young Discovery Lib.
James, R. S. Mozambique. (Illus.). 104p. (gr. 5 up). 1988. lib. bdg. 14.95 (ISBN 1-55546-194-8). Chelsea Hse.
Kamba, Polo. Why Do Africans Hate Cats. Scalist, Paula, ed. (Illus.). 98p. 1990. pap. 7.95x (ISBN 0-685-28131-0). Backwards & Backwards.
Kerina, Jane. African Crafts. Feelings, Tom, illus. LC 69-18916. (gr. 2-6). 1970. PLB 12.95 (ISBN 0-87460-084-7). Lion Bks.
Laure, Jason. Angola. LC 90-2143. (Illus.). 128p. (gr. 5-9). 1990. PLB 25.27 (ISBN 0-516-02721-2). Childrens.
Law, Kevin. Rwanda. (Illus.). 96p. (gr. 5 up). 1988. lib. bdg. 14.95 (ISBN 1-55546-783-0). Chelsea Hse.
Lerner Publications, Department of Geography Staff. Botswana in Pictures. (Illus.). 64p. (gr. 5 up). 1990. PLB 12.95 (ISBN 0-8225-1856-2). Lerner Pubns.
Levine, Bobbie & Lichter, Carolyn. A Child's Walk Through Africa. (Illus.). 38p. (gr. 3-6). 1987. spiral bdg. 1.50 (ISBN 0-912303-38-7). Michigan Mus.
Lye, Keith. Africa. Ron Hayward Associates, illus. 40p. (gr. 4-9). 1987. PLB 12.40 (ISBN 0-531-17065-9, Gloucester Pr). Watts.
Murphy, E. Jefferson. Understanding Africa. rev. ed. Jefferson, Louise E., illus. LC 77-11560. (gr. 7 up). 1978. (Crowell Jr Bks). HarpC Child Bks.
Murray, Jocelyn. Africa. 96p. 1990. 17.95 (ISBN 0-8160-2209-7). Facts on File.
Musgrove, Margaret W. Ashanti to Zulu: African Traditions. Dillon, Leo & Dillon, Diane, illus. LC 76-6610. 32p. (gr. k up). 1980. pap. 4.95 (ISBN 0-8037-0308-2). Dial Bks Young.
Sabin, Francene. Africa. Eitzen, Allan, illus. LC 84-10560. 32p. (gr. 3-6). 1985. PLB 9.49 (ISBN 0-8167-0236-5); pap. text ed. 2.95 (ISBN 0-8167-0237-3). Troll Assocs.
Stark, Al. Zimbabwe: A Treasure of Africa. LC 85-6944. (Illus.). 160p. (gr. 5 up). 1986. PLB 14.95 (ISBN 0-87518-308-5, Dillon). Macmillan Child Grp.
Steyn. The Bushman of the Kalahari, Reading Level 5. (Illus.). 48p. (gr. 4-8). Date not set. PLB 15.33 (ISBN 0-86625-267-3). Rourke Corp.
Timberlake, Lloyd. Famine in Africa. LC 85-81982. (Illus.). 32p. (gr. 4-8). 1986. PLB 8.90 (ISBN 0-531-17017-9, Gloucester Pr). Watts.
Zareef, Linda. Africa: A Glance at an Amazing Continent. (Illus.). (ps-6). 1989. write for info. (ISBN 0-9625787-0-3). An Awareness.

AFRICA–BIOGRAPHY

Bentley, Judith. Archbishop Tutu of South Africa. LC 88-410. 96p. (gr. 5-10). 1988. lib. bdg. 16.95 (ISBN 0-89490-180-X). Enslow Pubs.
Greene, Carol. Desmond Tutu: Bishop of Peace. LC 86-9582. (Illus.). 32p. (gr. 2-5). 1986. PLB 13.27 (ISBN 0-516-03634-3); pap. 3.95 (ISBN 0-516-43634-1). Childrens.
Griffin, Michael. A Family in Kenya. (Illus.). 32p. (gr. 2-5). 1988. lib. bdg. 9.95 (ISBN 0-8225-1680-2). Lerner Pubns.
Meltzer, Milton. Winnie Mandela: The Soul of South Africa. Marchesi, Stephen, illus. (gr. 2-6). 1987. pap. 3.95 (ISBN 0-14-032181-0, Puffin). Puffin Bks.

AFRICA, CENTRAL

Central African Republic. (Illus.). (gr. 5 up). 1989. 14.95 (ISBN 0-7910-0146-6). Chelsea Hse.
Lerner Publications, Department of Geography Staff, ed. Cameroon in Pictures. (Illus.). 64p. (gr. 5 up). 1989. PLB 12.95 (ISBN 0-8225-1857-0). Lerner Pubns.
—Central African Republic in Pictures. (Illus.). 64p. (gr. 5 up). 1989. 12.95 (ISBN 0-8225-1858-9). Lerner Pubns.

AFRICA, EAST

Dichmann, Kurt. Operations East Africa. Brown, Bill, ed. (Illus.). 96p. (Orig.). (gr. 9-12). 1989. pap. write for info. Ceise Corp.
Hallett, Bill & Hallett, Jane. Look up Look down Look All Around East African Safari. Jackson, Lori, illus. 32p. (Orig.). (gr. 3-8). 1990. pap. 2.95 activity bk. (ISBN 1-877827-01-0). Look & See.
Kaufmann, Herbert. Lost Freedom. (Illus.). (gr. 7 up). 1969. 12.95 (ISBN 0-8392-3083-4). Astor-Honor.
McKinzie, Harry & Tindimwebwa, Issy. Names from East Africa. Campbell, Elisabeth, ed. 42p. (Orig.). 1980. pap. 4.95 (ISBN 0-86626-007-2). McKinzie Pub.
Niger. (Illus.). (gr. 5 up). 1990. 14.95 (ISBN 0-7910-0129-6). Chelsea Hse.
Rosenthal, R. The Sign of the Ivory Horn: Eastern African Civilizations. LC 70-132279. (gr. 9 up). 1971. PLB 17.50 (ISBN 0-379-00449-6). Oceana.
Stelson, Caren B. Safari. Stelson, Kim A., illus. 40p. (gr. k-4). 1989. pap. 5.95 (ISBN 0-685-25642-1, First Ave Edns). Lerner Pubns.
Time-Life Books Editors. East Africa. LC 87-10222. (Illus.). 160p. 1987. 14.95 (ISBN 0-8094-5193-X); lib. bdg. write for info. (ISBN 0-8094-5194-8). Time-Life.

AFRICA–FICTION

Aardema, Verna. Bringing the Rain to Kapiti Plain. Vidal, Beatriz, illus. LC 80-25886. 32p. (ps). 1981. 14.95 (ISBN 0-8037-0809-2); PLB 13.89 (ISBN 0-8037-0807-6). Dial Bks Young.
Alcock, Gudrun. Dooley's Lion: A Junior Novel. Brittenham, Paul, illus. LC 85-9957. 112p. (gr. 3-7). 1985. 11.95 (ISBN 0-88045-066-5). Stemmer Hse.
Bess, Clayton. Story for a Black Night. LC 81-13396. (gr. 7 up). 1982. 12.95 (ISBN 0-395-31857-2). HM.
Cheney-Coker, Syl. The Last Harmattan of Alusine Dunbar: A Novel of Magical Vision. 398p. (Orig.). (gr. 9-12). 1990. pap. text ed. 9.95x (ISBN 0-435-90572-4, 90572). Heinemann Ed.
Emecheta, Buchi. The Joys of Motherhood. 224p. (Orig.). 1989. pap. 7.95 (ISBN 0-435-90684-4, 90684). Heinemann Ed.
Frost, T. Olly on Safari. (Illus.). 32p. (ps-3). 1987. PLB 14.65 (ISBN 0-88625-189-3); pap. 2.95 (ISBN 0-88625-187-7). Durkin Hayes Pub.
Guy, Rosa. Mother Crocodile: An Uncle Amadou Tale from Senegal. Steptoe, John, illus. LC 80-393. 32p. (ps-3). 1982. 8.89 (ISBN 0-385-28455-1); pap. 8.95 (ISBN 0-385-28454-3). Delacorte.
Lewin, Hugh. Jafta. Kopper, Lisa, illus. LC 82-12847. 24p. (ps-3). 1983. PLB 9.95 (ISBN 0-87614-207-2); pap. 3.95 (ISBN 0-87614-494-6). Carolrhoda Bks.
—Jafta & the Wedding. Kopper, Lisa, illus. LC 82-12836. 24p. (ps-3). 1983. PLB 9.95 (ISBN 0-87614-210-2); pap. 3.95 (ISBN 0-87614-497-0). Carolrhoda Bks.
—Jafta's Father. Kopper, Lisa, illus. LC 82-12837. 24p. (ps-3). 1983. PLB 9.95 (ISBN 0-87614-209-9); pap. 3.95 (ISBN 0-87614-496-2). Carolrhoda Bks.
McDowell, Robert E. & Lavitt, Edward, eds. Third World Voices for Children. Isaac, Barbara K., illus. LC 71-169091. 156p. (gr. 5-9). 1971. 5.95 (ISBN 0-89388-020-5, Odarkai). Okpaku Communications.
McKissack, Patricia. Who Is Coming? Martin, Clovis, illus. LC 86-11805. 32p. (ps-2). 1986. PLB 11.93 (ISBN 0-516-02073-0); pap. 2.95 (ISBN 0-516-42073-9). Childrens.
Njoku, Scholastica I. Dog What? Fergurson, Meg, illus. 49p. (gr. k up). 1989. perfect bdg. 6.95x (ISBN 0-9617833-1-1). S I NJOKU.
Packard, Edward. Africa: Where Do Elephants Live Underground. 112p. (gr. 4-6). 1989. pap. text ed. 3.95 (ISBN 0-07-047998-4). McGraw.
Poland, Marguerite. The Wood-Ash Stars. Altshuler, Shanne, illus. 64p. 1990. pap. 5.95 (ISBN 0-86486-089-7, Pub. by D Philip South Africa). Interlink Pub.
Sackett, Elisabeth. Danger on the African Grassland. (ps-3). 1991. 12.95 (ISBN 0-316-76596-1). Little.
Silver, Norman. No Tigers in Africa. (Illus.). 100p. (gr. 7 up). 1991. 13.95 (ISBN 0-525-44733-4, DCB). Dutton Child Bks.
Stevenson, William. The Bushbabies. Ambrus, Victor, illus. (gr. 5-9). 1984. 16.00 (ISBN 0-8446-6167-8). Peter Smith.
Walter, Mildred P. Brother to the Wind. Dillon, Diane & Dillon, Leo, illus. LC 83-26800. 32p. (ps-2). 1985. PLB 14.88 (ISBN 0-688-03812-3). Lothrop.
Weerusinghe, Christabel. Happy New Year in Sri Lanka. Deepa, illus. 52p. (Orig.). (gr. 2 up). 1986. pap. 6.50 (ISBN 0-941402-05-3). Devon Pub.
Williams, Karen L. When Africa Was Home. Cooper, Floyd, illus. LC 90-7684. 32p. (ps-1). 1991. 14.95 (ISBN 0-531-05925-1); PLB 14.99 (ISBN 0-531-08525-2). Orchard Bks Watts.
Zimelman, Nathan. Treed by a Pride of Irate Lions. Goffe, Toni, illus. LC 89-30344. (gr. k-3). 1990. 14.95 (ISBN 0-316-98802-2). Little.

AFRICA–HISTORY

Across Africa & Arabia. (Illus.). 128p. 1990. 17.95x (ISBN 0-8160-1878-2). Facts on File.
Africa & the Origin of Humans. (Illus.). 80p. (gr. 4 up). 1988. PLB 22.00 (ISBN 0-8172-3301-6). Raintree Pubs.
Chu, Daniel & Skinner, Eliott. A Glorious Age in Africa: The Story of Three Great African Empires. Barnett, Moneta, illus. LC 90-80150. 124p. (gr. 6-12). 1990. 19.95 (ISBN 0-86543-166-3); pap. 7.95 (ISBN 0-86543-167-1). Africa World.
Cosgrove, Stephen. Bangalee. (gr. 1-6). 1976. pap. 2.95 (ISBN 0-8431-0550-X). Price Stern.
Frazee, Charles & Yopp, Hallie K. The Ancient World. Frazee, Kathleen & Lumba, Eric, illus. (gr. 6). 1990. text ed. 21.08 (ISBN 1-878-47351-4); tchr's. ed. 27.08 (ISBN 1-878473-54-9); wkbk. 5.50 (ISBN 1-878473-55-7). Delos Pubns.
—Medieval & Early Modern Times. Frazee, Kathleen & Lumba, Eric, illus. (gr. 7). 1990. pap. text ed. 24.77 (ISBN 1-878473-56-5); tchr's. ed. 30.77 (ISBN 1-878473-58-1). Delos Pubns.
Rosenthal, R. The Sign of the Ivory Horn: Eastern African Civilizations. LC 70-132279. (gr. 9 up). 1971. PLB 17.50 (ISBN 0-379-00449-6). Oceana.
Rowell, Trevor. The Scramble for Africa. (Illus.). 72p. (gr. 7-12). 1987. 19.95 (ISBN 0-7134-5200-5, Pub. by Batsford England). Trafalgar Sq.

AFRICA–NATIVE RACES

African Islamic Mission Staff. One Hundred Amazing Facts about the Nubian Man & Woman. Obaba, Al I., ed. (Illus.). 124p. (Orig.). Date not set. pap. text ed. 8.95 (ISBN 0-916157-87-3). African Islam Miss Pubns.
Stevens, Rita. Venda. (Illus.). 96p. (gr. 7 up). 1989. lib. bdg. 14.95 (ISBN 1-55546-788-1). Chelsea Hse.

AFRICA–SOCIAL LIFE AND CUSTOMS

Musgrove, Margaret W. Ashanti to Zulu: African Traditions. Dillon, Diane & Dillon, Leo, illus. LC 76-6610. (gr. k-4). 1976. 16.95 (ISBN 0-8037-0357-0); PLB 15.89 (ISBN 0-8037-0358-9). Dial Bks Young.
Westbrook, Henry S. Burned at the Stake. Obaba, Al I., ed. 124p. (Orig.). Date not set. pap. text ed. 9.95 (ISBN 0-916157-88-1). African Islam Miss Pubns.

AFRICA, SOUTH

Bigelow, William. Strangers in Their Own Country: A Curriculum Guide on South Africa. Brutus, Dennis, frwd. by. LC 85-71369. (Illus.). 104p. (Orig.). (gr. 8 up). 1987. pap. 12.95 (ISBN 0-86543-010-1). Africa World.
Brickhill, Joan. South Africa: The End of Apartheid? (Illus.). 40p. (gr. 5-9). 1991. PLB 11.90 (ISBN 0-531-17283-X, Gloucester Pr). Watts.
Department of Geography, Lerner Publications. South Africa in Pictures. (Illus.). 64p. (gr. 5 up). 1988. PLB 12.95 (ISBN 0-8225-1835-X). Lerner Pubns.

Gould, Dennis E. Botswana. (Illus.). (gr. 5 up). 1988. 14.95 (ISBN 0-222-01101-7). Chelsea Hse.
Harris, Sarah. Timeline: South Africa. (Illus.). 64p. (gr. 7-9). 1988. 19.95 (ISBN 0-85219-724-1, Pub. by Batsford England). Trafalgar Sq.
Rogers, Barbara R. South Africa. Rogers, Stillman, illus. LC 89-43188. 64p. (gr. 5-6). 1991. PLB 12.95 (ISBN 0-8368-0247-0). Gareth Stevens Inc.
Stein, R. Conrad. South Africa. LC 86-9651. (Illus.). 128p. (gr. 5-9). 1986. PLB 25.27 (ISBN 0-516-02784-0). Childrens.
Tonsing-Carter, Betty. Lesotho. (Illus.). (gr. 5 up). 1988. 14.95 (ISBN 0-7910-0097-4). Chelsea Hse.

AFRICA, SOUTH–BIOGRAPHY

Denenberg, Barry. Nelson Mandela: "No Easy Walk to Freedom" 160p. (gr. 3-9). 1991. 13.95 (ISBN 0-590-44163-9, Scholastic Hardcover). Scholastic Inc.
First, Ruth. One Hundred Seventeen Days. Sachs, Albie & Lodge, Tomfrwd. by. 192p. (gr. 11-12). 1989. 24.00 (ISBN 0-85345-789-1); pap. 9.00 (ISBN 0-85345-790-5). Monthly Rev.
Hargrove, J. Nelson Mandela: South Africa's Silent Voice of Protest. (Illus.). (gr. 4 up). 1989. 17.27 (ISBN 0-516-03266-6); pap. 5.95 (ISBN 0-516-43266-4). Childrens.
Haskins, James. Winnie Mandela: Life of Struggle. (Illus.). 192p. (gr. 6 up). 1988. 14.95 (ISBN 0-399-21515-8, Putnam). Putnam Pub Group.
Hoobler, Dorothy & Hoobler, Thomas. Nelson & Winnie Mandela. LC 86-26631. (Illus.). 112p. (gr. 7-12). 1987. PLB 13.90 (ISBN 0-531-10332-3). Watts.
Kumalo, Alf. Mandela Echoes of Era. Es'Kia Mphahlele & Sisulu, Waltertext by. 176p. (ps-3). 1990. pap. 16.95 (ISBN 0-14-014316-5, Penguin Bks). Viking Penguin.
Lantier, Patricia. Desmond Tutu: Religious Leader Devoted to Freedom. LC 90-10044. (Illus.). 64p. (gr. 3-4). 1991. lib. bdg. 12.95 (ISBN 0-685-38446-2). Gareth Stevens Inc.
Meyer, Carolyn. Voices of South Africa: Growing up in a Troubled Land. LC 86-45059. 224p. (gr. 7 up). 1986. 16.95 (ISBN 0-15-200637-0). HarBraceJ.
Pround, Benjamin. Nelson Mandela: Strength & Spirit of a Free South Africa. LC 90-24026. (Illus.). 68p. (gr. 5-6). 1991. PLB 13.95 (ISBN 0-8368-0357-4). Gareth Stevens Inc.
Vail, John. Nelson & Winnie Mandela. Schlesinger, Arthur M. (Illus.). 112p. (gr. 5 up). 1989. lib. bdg. 17.95 (ISBN 1-55546-841-1). Chelsea Hse.
Wimer, David. Desmond TuTu: Religious Leader Devoted to Freedom. Lantier, Patricia, adapted by. LC 90-10044. (Illus.). 64p. (gr. 3-4). 1991. PLB 12.95 (ISBN 0-8368-0459-7). Gareth Stevens Inc.
Winner, David. Desmond Tutu: The Courageous & Eloquent Archbishop Struggling Against Apartheid in South Africa. Sherwood, Rhoda, ed. LC 88-4883. (Illus.). 68p. (gr. 5-6). 1989. PLB 12.95 (ISBN 1-55532-822-9). Gareth Stevens Inc.

AFRICA, SOUTH–FICTION

Haggard, H. Rider. King Solomon's Mines. 256p. (gr. 3-7). 1983. pap. 2.25 (ISBN 0-14-035014-4, Puffin). Puffin Bks.
Komai, Felicia, ed. Cry, the Beloved Country. (gr. 9 up). 1954. pap. 1.35 (ISBN 0-377-80501-7). Friendship Pr.
Naidoo, Beverley. Journey to Jo'burg: A South African Story. Velasquez, Eric, illus. LC 85-45508. 96p. (gr. 4-7). 1988. pap. 3.50 (ISBN 0-06-440237-1, Trophy). HarpC Child Bks.
Naidoo, Beverly. Journey to Jo'burg: A South African Story. Velasquez, Eric, illus. LC 85-45508. 96p. (gr. 4-7). 1986. 11.95 (ISBN 0-397-32168-6, Lipp Jr Bks); PLB 13.89 (ISBN 0-397-32169-4, Lipp Jr Bks). HarpC Child Bks.
Paton, Alan. Cry, the Beloved Country. 1977. 35.00x (ISBN 0-684-15559-1, Scribner); pap. 9.95 (ISBN 0-684-71863-4, Scribner); pap. text ed. 11.25 (ISBN 0-684-51544-X, Scribner). Macmillan.
—Tales from a Troubled Land. 1977. 20.00 (ISBN 0-684-15135-9, Scribner); (Scribner). Macmillan.

AFRICA, SOUTH–HISTORY

Hayward, Jean. South Africa since Nineteen Forty-Eight. LC 89-7619. (Illus.). 63p. (gr. 6 up). 1989. PLB 12.90 (ISBN 0-531-18262-2). Watts.
Stewart, Gail B. South Africa. LC 90-36292. (Illus.). 48p. (gr. 5-6). 1990. RSBE 10.95 (ISBN 0-89686-539-8, Crestwood Hse). Macmillan Child Grp.

AFRICA, SOUTH–RACE RELATIONS

Bower, Paula R. Apartheid Is Wrong: A Curriculum for Young People. (Illus.). 280p. (gr. 1-12). 1989. 3-ring hard cover notebook 15.00 (ISBN 1-878537-00-8). Educ Racism & Apart.
Evans, Mike. South Africa. (Illus.). 32p. (gr. 4-9). 1991. PLB 8.90 (ISBN 0-531-17056-X, Gloucester Pr). Watts.
Leas, Allan. Apartheid. (Illus.). 72p. (gr. 7-11). 1991. 19.95 (ISBN 0-7134-6499-2, Pub. by Batsford UK). Trafalgar Sq.
Tessendorf, K. C. Along the Road to Soweto: A Racial History of South Africa. LC 88-30535. (Illus.). 160p. (gr. 6 up). 1989. 14.95 (ISBN 0-689-31401-9, Atheneum Child Bk). Macmillan Child Grp.

AFRICA, SOUTHWEST

Angola. (Illus.). (gr. 5 up). 1988. 14.95 (ISBN 0-7910-0142-3). Chelsea Hse.
Gould, D. E. Namibia. (Illus.). (gr. 5 up). 1990. 14.95 (ISBN 0-7910-0107-5). Chelsea Hse.

AFRICA, SUB-SAHARAN

Chan, Stephen. Southern Africa. (Illus.). 48p. (gr. 5 up). 1989. PLB 16.98 (ISBN 0-382-09737-8). Silver Burdett Pr.
Roddis, Ingrid. Sudan. (Illus.). (gr. 5 up). 1988. 14.95 (ISBN 0-222-00964-0). Chelsea Hse.

AFRICA, WEST

Cote D'Ivoire (Ivory Coast) in Pictures. (Illus.). 64p. (gr. 5 up). 1988. 12.95 (ISBN 0-8225-1828-7). Lerner Pubns.
Jacobsen, Peter & Kristensen, Preben. A Family in West Africa. LC 84-73577. (Illus.). 32p. (gr. 1-6). 1985. PLB 11.90 (ISBN 0-531-18000-X, Pub. by Bookwright Pr). Watts.
Laure, Jason. Zambia. LC 89-34281. 128p. (gr. 5-9). 1989. PLB 25.27 (ISBN 0-516-02716-6). Childrens.
Lerner Publications, Department of Geography Staff, ed. Mali in Pictures. (Illus.). 64p. (gr. 5 up). 1990. PLB 12.95 (ISBN 0-8225-1869-4). Lerner Pubns.
Naylor, Kim. Mali. (Illus.). (gr. 5 up). 1988. 14.95 (ISBN 1-55546-181-6). Chelsea Hse.
Perryman, Andrew. Gabon. (Illus.). (gr. 5 up). 1988. 14.95 (ISBN 0-7910-0122-9). Chelsea Hse.
Preston, Edna M. Squawk to the Moon, Little Goose. Cooney, Barbara, illus. LC 84-22296. 32p. (ps-1). 1985. pap. 3.95 (ISBN 0-14-050546-6, Puffin). Puffin Bks.
Schwartz, L. Ride & Seek. 1987. 5.95 (ISBN 0-88160-159-4, LW 103). Learning Wks.
Wilkins, Frances. Gambia. (Illus.). (gr. 5 up). 1988. 14.95 (ISBN 0-222-01129-7). Chelsea Hse.

AFRICA, WEST–FICTION

Herge. Tintin au Congo. (FRE., Illus.). (gr. 7-9). 19.95 (ISBN 0-685-28415-8). French & Eur.

AFRICAN-AMERICANS

see Blacks

AFRICAN LANGUAGES

Feelings, Muriel. Jambo Means Hello: Swahili Alphabet Book. Feelings, Tom, illus. LC 73-15441. 56p. (gr. k-3). 1985. Repr. of 1974 ed. 13.95 (ISBN 0-8037-4346-7); PLB 13.89 (ISBN 0-8037-4350-5). Dial Bks Young.

AFRO-AMERICANS

see Blacks

AGE

Edelson, Edward. Aging. (Illus.). (gr. 6-12). 1991. 18.95 (ISBN 0-7910-0035-4). Chelsea Hse.
Klein, Leonore. Old, Older, Oldest. Kessler, Leonard, illus. 48p. (ps-3). 1983. 9.95 (ISBN 0-8038-5396-3). Hastings.

AGED

Langone, John. Growing Older. (gr. 9-12). 1991. 14.95 (ISBN 0-316-51459-4). Little.
Leiner, Katherine. Between Old Friends. Arthur, Michael H., photos by. (Illus.). 32p. (gr. 4-6). 1987. lib. bdg. 9.90 (ISBN 0-531-10291-2). Watts.
Swisher, Karin & Deal, Tara, eds. The Elderly: Opposing Viewpoints. LC 89-25950. (Illus.). 264p. (gr. 10 up). 1990. lib. bdg. 15.95 (ISBN 0-89908-475-3); pap. text ed. 8.95 (ISBN 0-89908-450-8). Greenhaven.
Van Zwanenberg, Fiona. Caring for the Aged. LC 89-31783. (Illus.). 64p. (gr. 7-10). 1989. PLB 11.90 (ISBN 0-531-17190-6). Watts.
Whitelaw, Nancy. A Beautiful Pearl. Tucker, Kathleen, ed. Friedman, Judith, illus. 32p. (gr. 2-5). 1991. 12.95 (ISBN 0-8075-0599-4). A Whitman.

AGED–FICTION

Albright, Nancy T., illus. I Know an Old Lady Who Swallowed a Fly. (Orig.). (ps-6). 1985. pap. 3.50 (ISBN 0-913545-10-4). Moonlight FL.
Bulla, Clyde R. The Stubborn Old Woman. Rockwell, Anne, illus. LC 78-22506. 48p. (gr. 1-4). 1980. 11.95i (ISBN 0-690-03945-X, Crowell Jr Bks). HarpC Child Bks.
Clifford, Eth. The Rocking Chair Rebellion. (gr. 5-9). 1978. 13.95 (ISBN 0-395-27163-0). HM.
French, Dorothy K. I Don't Belong Here. LC 79-26905. 104p. (gr. 7-10). 1980. 8.95 (ISBN 0-664-32664-1, Westminster). Westminster John Knox.
Galdone, Paul. The Greedy Old Fat Man. LC 83-2057. (Illus.). 32p. (ps-3). 1983. 13.95 (ISBN 0-89919-188-6, Clarion). HM.
Goudge, Eileen. Old Enough: Super Seniors, No. 1. (gr. 6 up). 1986. pap. 2.95 (ISBN 0-440-96118-1, LFL). Dell.
Green, Wendy. Grandma's Grave. (ps-3). 1989. pap. 1.95 (ISBN 0-7459-1738-0). Lion USA.
Greene, Carol. The Old Ladies Who Liked Cats. Krupinski, Loretta, illus. LC 90-4443. 32p. (gr. k-3). 1991. 14.95 (ISBN 0-06-022104-6); PLB 14.89 (ISBN 0-06-022105-4). HarpC Child Bks.
Hughes, Shirley. The Snow Lady. 32p. 1990. 13.95 (ISBN 0-688-09874-6); PLB 13.88 (ISBN 0-688-09875-4). Lothrop.
Johnson, Angela. When I Am Old with You. Soman, David, illus. LC 89-70928. 32p. (ps-2). 1990. 14.95 (ISBN 0-531-05884-0); PLB 14.99 (ISBN 0-531-08484-1). Orchard Bks Watts.
Palmer, Michele. Zoup Soup. Gugler, Janine, illus. LC 78-66342. (ps-1). 1978. pap. 1.95 (ISBN 0-932306-00-4). Rocking Horse.
Ruby, Lois. This Old Man. LC 84-14258. 192p. (gr. 7 up). 1984. 11.95 (ISBN 0-395-36563-5). HM.
Skorpen, Liesel M. Grace. LC 83-49472. 128p. (gr. 5 up). 1984. HarpC Child Bks.
Stobbs, William. I Know an Old Lady Who Swallowed a Fly. (Illus.). 26p. (ps-1). 1987. 12.95 (ISBN 0-19-279837-5). Oxford U Pr.

Wakeman, Cheryl A. Johnnie Ollie Carri III & His Friend. Womack, Fred, illus. 32p. (ps-3). 1985. 5.95 (ISBN 0-9614819-0-0). R E Moen.
JOHNNIE OLLIE CARRI III & HIS FRIEND is more than just an enjoyable children's book. It teaches a valuable lesson to children of all ages concerning the vital contributions of the elderly & the physically handicapped make to society. Johnnie Ollie walks home through the park each day, just so he can share his school day's activities with his special friend, Mister. The beautiful friendship is obvious to the reader as Johnnie shares happenings from a "typical school day" with which all children can identify. The reader never realizes until the very end that the elderly man has been deaf from birth & that he cannot hear a word Johnnie speaks--but that is not an obstacle in their wonderful relationship. Schools in California, Minnesota & Wisconsin have used this book to supplement units dealing with the elderly, the handicapped & sensitivity to others. Illustrated by noted children's illustrator FRED WOMACK. Full color throughout & printed on durable, high quality color-text paper.
Publisher Provided Annotation.

AGENTS

see Salesmen and Salesmanship

AGGREGATES (MATHEMATICS)

see Set Theory

AGNEW, SPIRO T., 1918-

Kurland, Gerald. Spiro Agnew: Controversial Vice-President of the Nixon Administration. Rahmas, D. Steve, ed. LC 72-190234. 32p. (Orig.). (gr. 7-12). 1972. PLB 4.20 incl. catalog cards (ISBN 0-87157-516-7). SamHar Pr.

AGRICULTURAL BANKS

see Banks and Banking

AGRICULTURAL BOTANY

see Botany, Economic

AGRICULTURAL CHEMISTRY

see also Soils

AGRICULTURAL MACHINERY

Boy Scouts of America. Farm Mechanics. (Illus.). 64p. (gr. 6-12). 1984. pap. 1.85 (ISBN 0-8395-3346-2, 3346). BSA.
Bushey, Jerry. Farming the Land: Modern Farmers & Their Machines. (Illus.). (gr. k-4). 1987. pap. 4.95 (ISBN 0-685-25637-5, First Ave Edns). Lerner Pubns.

Kalman, Bobbie. The Gristmill. (Illus.). 32p. (gr. 3-4). 1990. lib. bdg. 14.95 (ISBN 0-86505-486-X); pap. 7.95 (ISBN 0-86505-506-8). Crabtree Pub Co.
THE GRISTMILL takes a step-by-step look at how a simple water-powered gristmill grinds grain. Detailed diagrams show how the waterwheel, gears, & millstones worked. The book also looks at the role of the miller in the community, the dangers of milling, & the parts of grain that make up wholewheat flour. THE GRISTMILL is part of THE HISTORIC COMMUNITIES SERIES, fun-to-read books that provides a wealth of information for young readers. The series introduces children to the concept of earlier times in history & looks at community life. THE HISTORIC COMMUNITIES SERIES is beautifully designed, presenting information in two-page spreads through lively text, a multitude of color photographs, & detailed sketches. The books provide a close-up look at each topic, with step-by-step

explanations of how tools & processes work. They are excellent for preparing young children for visits to historic sites & provide good follow-up material.
Publisher Provided Annotation.

Marston, Hope I. Machines on the Farm. (Illus.). 64p. (gr. k-3). 1982. 8.95 (ISBN 0-396-08070-7, Putnam). Putnam Pub Group.
Olney, Ross R. The Farm Combine. LC 84-5288. (Illus.). 64p. (gr. 4 up). 1984. PLB 10.85 (ISBN 0-8027-6568-8). Walker & Co.
Stephen, R. J. Farm Machinery. LC 85-52092. (Illus.). 32p. (gr. k-6). 1987. PLB 11.40 (ISBN 0-531-10186-X). Watts.

AGRICULTURAL PRODUCTS
see Farm Produce

AGRICULTURAL TOOLS
see Agricultural Machinery

AGRICULTURE
see also Botany, Economic; Dairying; Domestic Animals; Farms; Forests and Forestry; Fruit Culture; Gardening; Land; Livestock; Soils
also names of agricultural products e.g. Corn; etc.; and headings beginning with the words Agricultural and Farm

Becklake, John & Becklake, Sue. Food & Farming. (Illus.). 40p. (gr. 6-9). 1991. PLB 11.90 (ISBN 0-531-17288-0, Gloucester Pr). Watts.
Bellville, Cheryl W. Farming Today Yesterday's Way. LC 84-3215. (Illus.). 32p. (gr. k-4). 1984. PLB 9.95 (ISBN 0-87614-220-X). Carolrhoda Bks.
Boy Scouts of America. Agribusiness. (Illus.). 72p. (Orig.). (gr. 6-12). 1987. pap. 1.85 (ISBN 0-317-66865-X, 3272). BSA.
Fun to Make Farm. 1989. pap. 3.99 (ISBN 0-517-68794-1). Outlet Bk Co.
Gibbons, Gail. Farming. Gibbons, Gail, illus. LC 87-21254. 32p. (ps-3). 1988. PLB 14.95 (ISBN 0-8234-0682-2); pap. 5.95 (ISBN 0-8234-0797-7). Holiday.
Gorman, Carol. America's Farm Crisis. (Illus.). 128p. (gr. 7-12). 1987. lib. bdg. 12.90 (ISBN 0-531-10408-7). Watts.
Huggett, Frank. Farming in Great Britain. (Illus.). 64p. (gr. 7 up). 1970. 14.95 (ISBN 0-7136-1527-3). Dufour.
Imershein, Betsy. Farmer. Steltenpohl, Jane, ed. (Illus.). 32p. (gr. k-3). 1990. PLB 9.98 (ISBN 0-671-68185-0); pap. 4.95 (ISBN 0-671-68188-5). Messner.
Kennedy, Elba H. How Would You Like to Be a Farmer? (Illus.). 80p. (gr. k-3). 1988. pap. 6.95 (ISBN 0-8059-3112-0). Dorrance.
Kerr, James. Egyptian Farmers. (Illus.). 24p. (gr. 2-5). 1991. PLB 10.40 (ISBN 0-531-18374-2, Pub. by Bookwright Pr). Watts.
Kushner, Jill M. The Farming Industry. (Illus.). 72p. (gr. 4-8). lib. bdg. 10.40 (ISBN 0-531-04822-5). Watts.
Lambert, Mark. Farming & the Environment. LC 90-45614. (Illus.). 48p. (gr. 4-9). 1990. PLB 18.60 (ISBN 0-8114-2392-1). Steck-V.
McConnell, Em. The Great Farm Adventure. Moser, Jeanie W., illus. (gr. k-3). Bk. & cassette 4.95 (ISBN 0-932715-07-9). Evans FL.
Murphy, Wendy. Future World of Agriculture. LC 84-12807. (Illus.). 112p. (gr. k-8). 1984. lib. bdg. 12.90 (ISBN 0-531-04880-2). Watts.
Sabin, Louis. Agriculture. Veno, Joseph, illus. LC 84-2710. 32p. (gr. 3-6). 1985. PLB 9.49 (ISBN 0-8167-0204-7); pap. text ed. 2.95 (ISBN 0-8167-0205-5). Troll Assocs.
Sully, Nina. Looking at Food. (Illus.). 72p. (gr. 7-12). 1984. 18.95 (ISBN 0-7134-3536-4, Pub. by Batsford England). Trafalgar Sq.

AGRICULTURE–FICTION

Hale, Kathleen. Orlando Buys a Farm. 32p. (gr. 3-6). 1990. 15.95 (ISBN 0-7232-3649-6). Warne.
Hines, Anna G. Come to the Meadow. Hines, Anna G., illus. LC 83-14408. 32p. (ps-3). 1984. 12.95 (ISBN 0-89919-227-0, Clarion). Hm.
Selden, George. The Old Meadow. Williams, Garth, illus. 192p. (gr. 3-7). 1987. 12.95 (ISBN 0-374-35616-5). FS&G.

AGRICULTURE–VOCATIONAL GUIDANCE

Stone, Archie A., et al. Careers in Agribusiness & Industry. 4th ed. LC 76-106341. (Illus.). 368p. (gr. 9-12). 1991. 31.95 (ISBN 0-8134-2898-X); text ed. 23. 95. Inter Print Pubs.

AGRONOMY
see Agriculture

AIDS (DISEASE)

AIDS: Answers for Everyone. 96p. (Orig.). (gr. 6-12). 1989. pap. text ed. 9.95 (ISBN 0-929496-01-9). Treehaus Comns.
Armstrong, Ewan. Impact of AIDS. (ps-3). 1990. PLB 11. 90 (ISBN 0-531-17225-2). Watts.
Bartel, Nettie R., et al. SIDA: Lo Que Todos Debemos Saber: Cuaderno del Estudiante. Rojas, Miriam M., tr. from ENG. (SPA., Illus.). (gr. 7-12). 1989. Level I, 96 p. wkbk. 8.00 (ISBN 0-929853-00-8); Level II, 112 p. wkbk. 9.00 (ISBN 0-929853-01-6); parents hdbk. 3.00 (ISBN 0-929853-02-4). Condor Pubns Inc.
Beshara, Raymond, et al. What You Should Know about AIDS. (Illus.). 72p. (gr. 6-10). 1989. pap. text ed. 9.85 (ISBN 0-9623161-2-1); tchr's. ed. 3.00 (ISBN 0-9623161-3-X). ERN Inc.
Bevan, Nicholas. AIDS & Drugs. FS-Aladdin Staff, ed. (Illus.). 64p. (gr. 6 up). 1988. PLB 11.90 (ISBN 0-531-10625-X). Watts.
Check, William A. AIDS. (Illus.). 124p. (gr. 6-12). 1988. lib. bdg. 18.95 (ISBN 0-7910-0054-0); pap. 9.95 (ISBN 0-7910-0481-3). Chelsea Hse.
Consumer Reports Books Editors, et al. AIDS: Trading Fears for Facts. 176p. (Orig.). (gr. 8 up). 1989. pap. 3.95 (ISBN 0-89043-269-4). Consumer Reports.
Eagles, Douglas. The Menace of AIDS: A Shadow on Our Land. Solomon, Maury, ed. (Illus.). 72p. (gr. 5 up). 1988. PLB 10.40 (ISBN 0-531-10567-9). Watts.
Fassler, David & McQueen, Kelly. Que Es Un Virus? Un Libro Para Ninos Sobre el SIDA. Quinones, Wanda M., tr. from ENG. LC 90-24631. (Illus.). 70p. (Orig.). (ps-5). 1991. pap. 8.95 (ISBN 0-914525-17-4); pap. text ed. 8.95 (ISBN 0-685-39483-2); pap. 12.95 plastic comb. (ISBN 0-914525-16-6); 8.95 (ISBN 0-685-39484-0). Waterfront Bks.
—What's a Virus, Anyway? The Kids' Book about AIDS. LC 89-40719. (Illus.). 85p. (Orig.). (ps-6). 1990. plastic comb spiral 10.95 (ISBN 0-914525-14-X); pap. 8.95 (ISBN 0-914525-15-8). Waterfront Bks.
Flanders, Stephen. Library in a Book: AIDS. 240p. (gr. 9-12). 1990. 22.95x (ISBN 0-8160-1910-X). Facts on File.
Girard, Linda W. Alex, the Kid with AIDS. Levine, Abby, ed. Sims, Blanche, illus. 32p. (gr. 2-5). 1990. PLB 12.95 (ISBN 0-8075-0245-6). A Whitman.
Hausherr, Rosmarie. Children & the AIDS Virus: A Book for Children, Parents, & Teachers. Hausherr, Rosmarie, illus. (ps up). 1989. 13.95 (ISBN 0-89919-834-1, Pub. by Clarion); pap. 4.95 (ISBN 0-318-41625-5, Pub. by Clarion). Ticknor & Fields.
Hyde, Margaret O. AIDS: What Does It Mean to You? rev. ed. 128p. (gr. 7 up). 1987. 12.95 (ISBN 0-8027-6699-4); lib. bdg. 13.85 (ISBN 0-8027-6705-2); pap. 6.95 (ISBN 0-8027-6747-8). Walker & Co.
Hyde, Margaret O. & Forsyth, Elizabeth. AIDS: What Does It Mean to You? 3rd, rev. ed. 124p. (gr. 7 up). 1990. 13.95 (ISBN 0-8027-6897-0); lib. bdg. 14.85 (ISBN 0-8027-6898-9). Walker & Co.
—Know about AIDS. rev. ed. Weber, Deborah, illus. 102p. (gr. 3-7). 1990. 12.95 (ISBN 0-8027-6920-9); lib. bdg. 13.85 (ISBN 0-8027-6921-7). Walker & Co.
Jackson, Tim. AIDS: Just the Facts Jack. Jackson, Tim, illus. (Orig.). (gr. 5 up). 1988. pap. 1.95 (ISBN 0-942675-06-1, 6). Creative License.
—What Are Friends For? HIV Safe Coloring Book. Jackson, Tim, illus. 32p. (Orig.). (gr. 3-6). 1990. pap. write for info. (ISBN 0-942675-08-8, 0942675088). Creative License.
Kellogg, Nancy R. AIDS: Elementary-Intermediate Curriculum. (gr. 5-7). 1990. tchr's. ed. 8.95 (ISBN 0-944584-11-X). Sopris.
Kerrins, Joseph & Jacobs, George W. The AIDS File. 2nd ed. Doohan, Julie, ed. (Illus.). 160p. (gr. 8 up). 1989. cloth 14.95 (ISBN 0-9618059-2-7). Cromlech Bks.
Kuklin, Susan. Fighting Back: What Some People Are Doing about AIDS. (Illus.). 144p. (gr. 8 up). 1989. 13. 95 (ISBN 0-399-21621-9, Putnam). Putnam Pub Group.
Kurland, Morton L. Coping with AIDS: Facts & Fears. rev. & updated ed. (gr. 7-12). 1990. lib. bdg. 12.95 (ISBN 0-8239-1148-9). Rosen Group.
Landau, Elaine. We Have AIDS. 1990. 11.95 (ISBN 0-531-15152-2). Watts.
—We Have AIDS. LC 89-24801. 126p. (gr. 7 up). 1990. PLB 12.90 (ISBN 0-531-10898-8). Watts.
Lerner, Ethan A. Comprendiendo el SIDA. Wilken, Mark, illus. (SPA.). 64p. (gr. 3-6). 1988. 11.95 (ISBN 0-8225-2000-1). Lerner Pubns.
—Understanding AIDS. (Illus.). 70p. (gr. 3-6). 1987. PLB 11.95 (ISBN 0-8225-0024-8). Lerner Pubns.
LeVert, Suzanne. AIDS: In Search of a Killer. LC 86-33218. (Illus.). 128p. (gr. 6 up). 1986. lib. bdg. 12.98 (ISBN 0-671-62840-2); pap. 5.95 (ISBN 0-671-65662-7). Messner.
Lord, John. Infection, the Immune System, & AIDS. (Illus.). 56p. (Orig.). (gr. 11-12). 1989. pap. 4.95x (ISBN 0-934653-18-6). Enterprise Educ.

Mozeleski, Peter A. & Mozeleski, Paul M. The Rubber Bros Comics. Wilda, Fred, illus. 192p. (gr. 6-12). 1990. pap. write for info (ISBN 1-880058-00-6). Rubbers Bros Comics.
This is an AIDS education & prevention publication in a comic non-violent format. The projected 48 issues come in Vols. 1-4, Nos. 1-12. Vol. 1, No.1 is completed in English (ISBN 1-880058-01-4) & Spanish (ISBN 1-880058-13-8). Vol. 1, No. 2 will also be available in English (ISBN 1-880058-02-2) & Spanish (ISBN 1-880058-14-6) by September, 1991. Not only is the comic geared for 6th to 12th grade levels, it will also find appeal among college students & professors, & parents should utilize it as a teaching aid. Tests can be easily made up. This comic is direct enough to allow instructors to become creative & work closely with their students. Its main objective, AIDS prevention, is carried out through the use of condom characters fighting the evils of A-Man, the AIDS Man. This form of comic entertainment will make everyone realize that if they use condoms in their relationships, they will contribute immensely to the prevention of AIDS, the killer virus. This is a unique concept in educating school age children up through adults about the dangers & prevention of the disease. In upcoming issues, the latest factual information from the CDC is included, done in such a way so the reader does not get bogged down with numbers, but instead, will be informed about the alarming statistics. The comic also includes a page promoting nutrition, an activity page, & 3 ad pages.
Publisher Provided Annotation.

Nourse, Alan E. AIDS. LC 86-15743. (Illus.). 128p. (gr. 7-12). 1986. PLB 12.90 (ISBN 0-531-10235-1). Watts.
—Teen Guide to AIDS Prevention. (Illus.). 64p. (gr. 9-12). 1990. PLB 12.40 (ISBN 0-531-10966-6). Watts.
Opheim, Teresa. AIDS: Distinguishing Between Fact & Opinion. (Illus.). 32p. (gr. 3-6). 1990. PLB 8.95 (ISBN 0-89908-633-0). Greenhaven.
Quackenbush, Marcia & Villarreal, Sylvia. Does AIDS Hurt? Educating Young Children about AIDS. Nelson, Mary, ed. 148p. (Orig.). (ps-6). 1988. pap. 14.95 (ISBN 0-941816-52-4). Network Pubns.
Sanford, Doris. David Has AIDS. Davis, Deena, ed. Evans, Graci, illus. LC 89-3162. 29p. (gr. k-4). 1989. 6.95 (ISBN 0-88070-299-0). Multnomah.
Schwartz, L. AIDS Answers for Teens. 32p. (gr. 7-12). 1987. 4.95 (ISBN 0-685-30889-8, LW 273). Learning Wks.

Schwartz, Linda. AIDS Answers for Teens. rev. ed. (Illus.). 32p. (Orig.). (gr. 7-12). 1990. pap. 4.95 (ISBN 0-88160-155-1). Learning Wks.

—AIDS Questions & Answers for Kids. rev. ed. (Illus.). 24p. 1990. 3.95 (ISBN 0-88160-154-3, LW272). Learning Wks.
Silverstein, Alvin & Silverstein, Virginia B. AIDS: Deadly Threat. LC 85-23393. (Illus.). 96p. (gr. 6-12). 1986. PLB 16.95 (ISBN 0-89490-128-1). Enslow Pubs.
Silverstein, Alvin & Silverstein, Virginia. Learning about AIDS. LC 87-24373. 64p. (gr. 4-6). 1989. lib. bdg. 15. 95 (ISBN 0-89490-176-1). Enslow Pubs.
Sroka, Stephen R. Guia Para Educadores Sobre el SIDA y Otras ETS. Urizar, Hugo, tr. from ENG. (SPA., Illus.). 105p. (gr. 5-12). 1991. tchr's. ed. 25.00 (ISBN 0-9622034-1-6). Hlth Educ Consults.
Taylor, Barbara. Everything You Need to Know about AIDS. Rosen, Ruth, ed. Glassman, Richard, photos by. (Illus.). 64p. (gr. 7 up). 1988. PLB 12.95 (ISBN 0-8239-0809-7). Rosen Group.
Turck, Mary. AIDS. LC 88-20259. (Illus.). 48p. (gr. 5-6). 1988. PLB 10.95 (ISBN 0-89686-412-X, Crestwood Hse). Macmillan Child Grp.
Wilson, Jonnie. AIDS. (Illus.). 96p. (gr. 5 up). 1989. PLB 11.95 (ISBN 1-56006-105-7). Lucent Bks.

AIR
Here are entered works treating of air as an element and of its chemical and physical properties. Works treating of the body of air surrounding the earth are entered under Atmosphere.
see also Atmosphere

Air. (Illus.). (gr. 3-5). 3.50 (ISBN 0-7214-0658-0). Ladybird Bks.
Ardley, Neil. The Science Book of Air. Van Doren, Liz, ed. (Illus.). 28p. (gr. 2-5). 1991. 9.95 (Gulliver Bks). HarBraceJ.
—Science Book of Air. (gr. 4-7). 1991. 9.95 (ISBN 0-15-200578-1). HarBraceJ.
Brandt, Keith. Air. Burns, Raymond, illus. LC 84-2608. 32p. (gr. 3-6). 1985. PLB 9.49 (ISBN 0-8167-0130-X); pap. text ed. 2.95 (ISBN 0-8167-0131-8). Troll Assocs.
Branley, Franklyn M. Air Is All Around You. Rev. ed. Keller, Holly, illus. LC 85-47884. 32p. (gr. k-3). 1986. 13.95 (ISBN 0-690-04502-6, Crowell Jr Bks); PLB 13. 89 (ISBN 0-690-04503-4). HarpC Child Bks.
Dolan, Edward F., Jr. Great Mysteries of the Air. (Illus.). 128p. (gr. 9-12). 1983. 8.95 (ISBN 0-396-08185-1, Putnam). Putnam Pub Group.
Heslewood, Juliet. Earth, Air, Fire & Water. Lydbury, Jane, et al, illus. 182p. (gr. 4-8). 1989. jacketed 15.95 (ISBN 0-19-278107-3). Oxford U Pr.

Jefferies, Lawrence. Air, Air, Air. Johnson, Lewis, illus. LC 82-15808. 32p. (gr. 3-6). 1983. PLB 10.59 (ISBN 0-89375-880-9); pap. text ed. 2.95 (ISBN 0-89375-881-7). Troll Assocs.

Johnston, Tom. Air, Air Everywhere. Pooley, Sarah, illus. LC 87-42752. 32p. (gr. 4-6). 1988. PLB 10.95 (ISBN 1-55532-406-1). Gareth Stevens Inc.

Llewellyn, Claire. First Look in the Air. (Illus.). 32p. (gr. 1-2). 1991. PLB 10.95 (ISBN 0-8368-0701-4). Gareth Stevens Inc.

Parramon, J. M., et al. Air. 32p. (ps). 1985. pap. 3.95 (ISBN 0-8120-3597-6). Barron.

—El Aire. (SPA.). 32p. (ps). 1985. pap. 3.95 (ISBN 0-8120-3620-4). Barron.

Smith, Henry. Amazing Air. Firth, Barbara, et al, illus. LC 82-80991. 48p. (gr. 3-6). 1983. PLB 11.88 (ISBN 0-688-00973-5). Lothrop.

Swallow, Su. Air. LC 90-31033. (Illus.). 32p. (gr. k-4). 1991. PLB 11.90 (ISBN 0-531-14097-0). Watts.

Taylor, Barbara. Air & Flight. (Illus.). 40p. (gr. k-4). 1991. PLB 11.90 (ISBN 0-531-19129-X, Warwick). Watts.

—Air & Flying. (Illus.). 32p. (gr. 5-8). 1991. PLB 11.40 (ISBN 0-531-14183-7). Watts.

Webb, Angela. Air. (Illus.). 32p. (gr. k-3). 1987. PLB 10.90 (ISBN 0-531-10369-2). Watts.

Wilkins, Mary-Jane. Air, Light & Water. Bull, Peter, illus. LC 90-42620. 40p. (Orig.). (gr. 2-5). 1991. pap. 3.95 (ISBN 0-679-80859-0). Random.

AIR–POLLUTION

Bailey, Donna. What We Can Do about Noise & Fumes. (Illus.). 32p. (gr. k-4). 1991. PLB 11.40 (ISBN 0-531-11018-4). Watts.

Becklake, John. Pollution. (Illus.). 40p. (gr. 5-8). 1990. PLB 11.90 (ISBN 0-531-17233-3). Watts.

Breiter, Herta S. Pollution. LC 87-23233. (Illus.). 48p. (Orig.). (gr. 2-6). 1987. PLB 17.32 (ISBN 0-8172-3259-1); pap. 9.27 (ISBN 0-8172-3284-2). Raintree Pubs.

Bright, Michael. Traffic Pollution. (Illus.). 32p. (gr. k-4). 1991. PLB 11.40 (ISBN 0-531-17349-6, Gloucester Pr). Watts.

Dolan, Edward F. Our Poisoned Sky. (Illus.). 144p. (gr. 7 up). 1991. 14.95 (ISBN 0-525-65056-3, Cobblehill Bks). Dutton Child Bks.

Gay, Kathlyn. Air Pollution. (Illus.). 144p. (gr. 9-12). 1991. PLB 12.90 (ISBN 0-531-13002-9). Watts.

Gold, Susan D. Toxic Waste. LC 90-36295. (Illus.). 48p. (gr. 5-6). 1990. RSBE 10.95 (ISBN 0-89686-542-8, Crestwood Hse). Macmillan Child Grp.

Greene, Carol. Caring for Our Air. (Illus.). 32p. (gr. 1-4). 1991. PLB 12.95 (ISBN 0-89490-351-9). Enslow Pubs.

Gutnik, Martin J. The Challenge of Clean Air. 64p. (gr. 6 up). 1990. 15.95 (ISBN 0-89490-272-5). Enslow Pubs.

—Experiments That Explore the Greenhouse Effect. (Illus.). 72p. (gr. 5-8). 1991. PLB 13.90 (ISBN 1-56294-012-0). Millbrook Pr.

Jennings, Terry. Air. LC 89-453. (Illus.). 32p. (gr. 3-6). 1989. 14.60 (ISBN 0-516-08435-6); pap. 4.95 (ISBN 0-516-48435-4). Childrens.

Kiefer, Irene. Poisoned Land: The Problems of Hazardous Waste. LC 80-22120. (Illus.). 96p. (gr. 6-9). 1981. 13.95 (ISBN 0-689-30837-X, Atheneum Child Bk). Macmillan Child Grp.

Lambert, David. Pollution & Conservation. (Illus.). 32p. (gr. 1-6). 1986. PLB 8.99 (ISBN 0-531-18060-3, Pub. by Bookwright). Watts.

Lee, Sally. The Throwaway Society. (Illus.). 128p. (gr. 9-12). 1990. PLB 12.90 (ISBN 0-531-10947-X). Watts.

Lo Pinto, Richard W. Pollution. Head, J. J., ed. Steffen, Ann T., illus. LC 86-72203. 16p. (Orig.). (gr. 10 up). 1987. pap. text ed. 2.15 (ISBN 0-89278-392-3, 45-9792). Carolina Biological.

Miller, Christina G. & Berry, Louise A. Acid Rain. LC 86-8605. (Illus.). 128p. (gr. 7 up). 1986. lib. bdg. 12.98 (ISBN 0-671-60177-6). Messner.

O'Neill, Mary. Air Scare. Bindon, John, illus. LC 89-49626. 32p. (gr. 3-6). 1991. lib. bdg. 12.89 (ISBN 0-8167-2082-7); pap. text ed. 3.95 (ISBN 0-8167-2083-5). Troll Assocs.

Sandak, Cass R. A Reference Guide to Clean Air. 128p. 1990. 17.95 (ISBN 0-89490-261-X). Enslow Pubs.

Snodgrass, M. E. Environmental Awareness: Air Pollution. James, Jody, ed. Vista Three Design Staff, illus. LC 90-25726. 48p. (gr. 4 up). 1991. lib. bdg. 14.95 (ISBN 0-944280-31-5). BSP Pub Inc.

Snow, Ted. Global Change. LC 90-37680. (Illus.). 48p. (gr. k-4). 1990. PLB 14.60 (ISBN 0-516-01105-7); pap. 4.95 (ISBN 0-516-41105-5). Childrens.

Stille, Darlene. The Greenhouse Effect. LC 90-2147. (Illus.). 48p. (gr. k-4). 1990. PLB 14.60 (ISBN 0-516-01106-5); pap. 4.95 (ISBN 0-516-41106-3). Childrens.

Taylor, Ron. Facts on Radon & Asbestos. (ps-3). 1990. PLB 11.90 (ISBN 0-531-10920-8). Watts.

Woods, Geraldine & Woods, Harold. Pollution. LC 84-20982. (Illus.). 72p. (gr. 4 up). 1985. PLB 10.40 (ISBN 0-531-04916-7). Watts.

AIR CARGO

see Aeronautics, Commercial

AIR CRASHES

see Aeronautics–Accidents

AIR FREIGHT

see Aeronautics, Commercial

AIR LINES

Barrett, Norman S. Airliners. LC 84-50697. 32p. (gr. 3-6). 1989. pap. 3.95 (ISBN 0-531-15137-9). Watts.

Rogers, Fred. Going on an Airplane. Judkis, Jim, photos by. (Illus.). 32p. (ps-2). 1989. pap. 5.95 (ISBN 0-399-21633-2, Putnam); 12.95 (ISBN 0-399-21635-9). Putnam Pub Group.

AIR PILOTS

see also Astronauts; Women in Aeronautics

Ayres, Carter M. Chuck Yeager: Fighter Pilot. (Illus.). 48p. (gr. 4 up). 1988. PLB 9.95 (ISBN 0-8225-0483-9). Lerner Pubns.

Bauer, Judith. What's It Like to Be an Airline Pilot. Iosa, Ann W., illus. LC 89-34397. 32p. (gr. k-3). 1990. PLB 10.89 (ISBN 0-8167-1791-5); pap. text ed. 2.50 (ISBN 0-8167-1792-3). Troll Assocs.

Gaffney, Timothy R. Chuck Yeager: First Man to Fly Faster than Sound. LC 86-9555. (Illus.). 128p. (gr. 4 up). 1986. PLB 17.27 (ISBN 0-516-03223-2). Childrens.

Gething, M. The Test Pilot. (Illus.). 32p. (gr. 4 up). Date not set. PLB 14.00 (ISBN 0-86592-414-7). Rourke Corp.

Harris, Jack. Test Pilots. LC 89-31126. (Illus.). 48p. (gr. 4-5). 1989. 10.95 (ISBN 0-89686-429-4, Crestwood Hse). Macmillan Child Grp.

Jaspersohn, William. A Week in the Life of an Airline Pilot. (gr. 4-7). 1991. 14.95 (ISBN 0-316-45822-8). Little.

Levinson, Nancy S. Chuck Yeager the Man Who Broke the Sound Barrier. LC 87-25431. 133p. (gr. 5 up). 1988. 13.95 (ISBN 0-8027-6781-8); PLB 14.85 (ISBN 0-8027-6799-0). Walker & Co.

Tessendorf, K. C. Barnstormers & Daredevils. LC 87-15194. (Illus.). 96p. (gr. 4 up). 1988. 13.95 (ISBN 0-689-31346-2, Atheneum Child Bk). Macmillan Child Grp.

Worthington, George. In Search of World Records. LC 80-82032. (gr. 10-12). 1980. 18.95 (ISBN 0-938282-01-8). Hang Gliding.

AIR POLLUTION

see Air–Pollution

AIR RAIDS–PROTECTIVE MEASURES

see Aeronautics, Military

AIR TRANSPORT

see Aeronautics, Commercial

AIR WARFARE

see Aeronautics, Military; Airplanes, Military;
see names of wars with the subdivision Aerial Operations, e.g. World War, 1939-1945–Aerial Operations; etc.

AIRCRAFT

see Airplanes; Airships; Helicopters

Coombs, Charles I. Ultralights: The Flying Featherweights. LC 83-17411. (Illus.). 160p. (gr. 5 up). 1984. 12.95 (ISBN 0-688-02775-X). Morrow Jr Bks.

AIRCRAFT CARRIERS

Norman, C. J. Aircraft Carriers. LC 85-51452. 32p. (gr. 3-6). 1989. pap. 3.95 (ISBN 0-531-15136-0). Watts.

—Aircraft Carriers. LC 85-51452. (Illus.). 32p. (gr. 1-6). 1986. PLB 11.40 (ISBN 0-531-10088-X). Watts.

Preston, Anthony. Aircraft Carriers. Gibbons, Tony, et al, illus. LC 84-9669. 48p. (gr. 5 up). 1985. PLB 9.95 (ISBN 0-8225-1377-3, First Ave Edns); pap. 4.95 (ISBN 0-8225-9504-4, First Ave Edns). Lerner Pubns.

Rawlinson, J. Nuclear Carriers. (Illus.). 48p. (gr. 3-8). 1989. lib. bdg. 18.60 (ISBN 0-86625-084-0). Rourke Corp.

Stephen, R. J. Picture World of Aircraft Carriers. 1990. PLB 11.40 (ISBN 0-531-14008-3). Watts.

AIRPLANE ACCIDENTS

see Aeronautics–Accidents

AIRPLANE CARRIERS

see Aircraft Carriers

AIRPLANE RACING

Berliner, Don. Airplane Racing. LC 79-4491. (Illus.). 52p. (gr. 4-9). 1979. PLB 9.95 (ISBN 0-8225-0432-4). Lerner Pubns.

AIRPLANES

see also Aeronautics
also types of airplanes, e.g. Bombers; Vertically Rising Airplanes; etc.

Aircraft. (Illus.). 32p. (ps-6). 1983. pap. 2.95 (ISBN 0-87474-825-9, AICBP). Smithsonian.

The Aircraft Encyclopedia. (gr. 3 up). 1985. pap. 6.95 (ISBN 0-671-55337-2, Little Simon). S&S Trade.

Althea. Man Flies On. (Illus.). 32p. (gr. 5-7). 1983. pap. 2.95 (ISBN 0-521-27173-8). Cambridge U Pr.

—Man in the Sky. (Illus.). 32p. (gr. 5-7). 1983. pap. 2.95 (ISBN 0-521-27172-X). Cambridge U Pr.

Barton, Byron. Airplanes. LC 85-47899. (Illus.). 32p. (ps-k). 1986. 6.95 (ISBN 0-694-00060-4, Crowell Jr Bks); PLB 11.89 (ISBN 0-690-04532-8). HarpC Child Bks.

Berliner, Don. Home-Built Airplanes. LC 79-1460. (Illus.). 48p. (gr. 4-9). 1979. PLB 9.95 (ISBN 0-8225-0433-2). Lerner Pubns.

—Personal Airplanes. LC 81-15658. (Illus.). 56p. (gr. 4-9). 1982. PLB 9.95 (ISBN 0-8225-0447-2). Lerner Pubns.

—Record Breaking Airplanes. (Illus.). 48p. (gr. 4-9). 1985. PLB 9.95 (ISBN 0-8225-0429-4). Lerner Pubns.

—Unusual Airplanes. (Illus.). 48p. (gr. 4-9). 1985. lib. bdg. 9.95 (ISBN 0-8225-0431-6). Lerner Pubns.

—Yesterday's Airplanes. LC 80-10915. (Illus.). 48p. (gr. 4-9). 1980. PLB 9.95 (ISBN 0-8225-0444-8). Lerner Pubns.

Cawthorne, Nigel. Airliners. Franklin Watts Ltd., ed. Shone, Rob, illus. 32p. (gr. 7-9). 1988. PLB 8.90 (ISBN 0-531-17073-X, Gloucester Pr). Watts.

Curry, Barbara. Model Historical Aircraft. LC 82-4779. (Illus.). 32p. (gr. 4 up). 1982. PLB 10.40 (ISBN 0-531-04465-3). Watts.

Emert, Phyllis. Special Task Aircraft. (Illus.). 64p. (gr. 5-9). 1990. lib. bdg. 12.98 (ISBN 0-671-68963-0); pap. 5.95 (ISBN 0-671-68968-1). Messner.

—Transports & Bombers. (Illus.). 64p. (gr. 5-9). 1990. lib. bdg. 12.98 (ISBN 0-671-68961-4); pap. 5.95 (ISBN 0-671-68966-5). Messner.

Emert, Phyllis R. Mysteries of Ships & Planes. 1990. pap. 2.50 (ISBN 0-8125-9427-4). Tor Bks.

Grimm, Rosemary. Stunt Planes. LC 87-29020. (Illus.). 48p. (gr. 5-6). 1988. PLB 10.95 (ISBN 0-89686-363-8, Crestwood Hse). Macmillan Child Grp.

Hewish, Mark. Jets. (gr. 5-9). 1976. pap. 6.95 (ISBN 0-86020-051-5, Usborne-Hayes). EDC.

Jacobs, Lou, Jr. Jumbo Jets. LC 73-78280. (Illus.). (gr. 5-9). 1969. 7.50 (ISBN 0-672-52280-2, Bobbs). Macmillan.

Jefferis, David. Flight: Fliers & Flying Machines. (Illus.). 48p. (gr. 5-8). 1991. 13.95 (ISBN 0-531-15233-2); PLB 13.90 (ISBN 0-531-11093-1). Watts.

Jets & Bombers. (Illus.). 32p. (gr. 1-6). 1987. 2.50 (ISBN 0-87406-272-1, 46-15095-4). Willowisp Pr.

Johnstone, Hugh. Aircraft & Rockets. (Illus.). 40p. (gr. 5-9). 1989. PLB 12.40 (ISBN 0-531-17185-X). Watts.

Lenga. Amazing Fact Book of Planes. (Illus.). 32p. (gr. 4-8). 1987. PLB 11.95 (ISBN 0-87191-848-X). Creative Ed.

Lenski, Lois. Little Airplane. Lenski, Lois, illus. LC 59-12487. (gr. k-3). 1980. 5.25 (ISBN 0-8098-1004-2). McKay.

Little, Karen E. & Thomas, A. Finding Out about Things that Fly. (Illus.). 24p. (gr. 2-4). 1987. PLB 11.96 (ISBN 0-88110-306-3); pap. 3.95 (ISBN 0-7460-0104-5). EDC.

Moxon, Julian. How Jet Engines Are Made. LC 85-21049. (Illus.). 32p. (gr. 7 up). 12.95 (ISBN 0-8160-0037-9). Facts on File.

Nahum, Andrew. Flying Machine. King, Dave, et al, photos by. LC 90-4007. (Illus.). 64p. (gr. 5 up). 1990. 13.95 (ISBN 0-679-80744-6); PLB 14.99 (ISBN 0-679-90744-0). Crown.

Peterson, David. Airplanes. LC 81-7671. (Illus.). 48p. (gr. k-4). 1981. PLB 14.60 (ISBN 0-516-01606-7); pap. 4.95 (ISBN 0-516-41606-5). Childrens.

Petty, Kate. On a Plane. Riquier, Aline, illus. 32p. (ps-3). 1984. 10.90 (ISBN 0-531-04716-4). Watts.

Pleasance, G., illus. Airplanes. 16p. (ps-3). 1989. pap. 2.95 (ISBN 0-8249-8314-9). Ideals.

Potter, Tony. See How It Works: Planes. Lawrie, Robin, illus. 28p. (ps-3). 1989. pap. 7.95 (ISBN 0-689-71304-5, Aladdin). Macmillan Child Grp.

Rockwell, Anne. Planes. Rockwell, Anne, illus. LC 84-13732. 24p. (ps-1). 1985. 12.95 (ISBN 0-525-44159-X, DCB). Dutton Child Bks.

—Planes. (Illus.). (ps-1). 1989. pap. 3.95 (ISBN 0-525-44540-4, DCB). Dutton Child Bks.

Schleier, Curt. The Team Behind Your Airline Flight. LC 80-27174. 94p. (gr. 5-8). 1981. 9.95 (ISBN 0-664-32678-1, Westminster). Westminster John Knox.

Schulz, Charles M. Snoopy's Facts & Fun Book about Planes. Schulz, Charles M., illus. LC 79-674. (ps-1). 1979. (Random Juv); PLB 3.99 (ISBN 0-685-04263-4). Random.

Space, Peggy. A Trip on a Jet Plane: Photos & Fun for Boys & Girls. Space, Peggy & Scarpace, Frank, illus. 32p. (gr. 3-7). 1981. pap. 2.50 (ISBN 0-942772-00-8). Image Pubns.

Spizzirri Publishing Co. Staff. Aircraft: An Educational Coloring Book. Spizzirri, Linda, ed. Fuller, Glenn & Spizzirri, Peter M., illus. 32p. (gr. 1-8). 1981. pap. 1.95 (ISBN 0-86545-033-1). Spizzirri.

Stacey, Tom. Airplanes: The Lure of Flight. LC 90-6471. (Illus.). 96p. (gr. 5-8). 1990. PLB 15.95 (ISBN 1-56006-203-7). Lucent Bks.

Steele, Philip. Planes. LC 90-41181. (Illus.). 32p. (gr. 5-6). 1991. SBE 9.95 (ISBN 0-89686-524-X, Crestwood Hse). Macmillan Child Grp.

Stein, R. Conrad. The Story of the Flight at Kitty Hawk. LC 81-1634. (Illus.). 32p. (gr. 3-6). 1981. PLB 13.27 (ISBN 0-516-04614-4). Childrens.

Stephen, R. J. The Picture World of Airliners. (Illus.). 32p. (gr. k-4). 1989. PLB 11.40 (ISBN 0-531-10724-8). Watts.

Tunney, Christopher. Aircraft. LC 79-64384. (Illus.). 36p. (gr. 3-6). 1980. PLB 9.95 (ISBN 0-8225-1176-2). Lerner Pubns.

AIRPLANES–ACCIDENTS

see Aeronautics–Accidents

AIRPLANES–FICTION

Cotler, Joanna. Sky Above Earth Below. Cotler, Joanna, illus. LC 89-26743. 32p. (ps-k). 1990. 14.95 (ISBN 0-06-021365-5); PLB 14.89 (ISBN 0-06-021366-3). HarpC Child Bks.

Durham, Jamie A. Little Airplane. Pittman, Dockery, illus. 32p. (ps). Date not set. write for info. Magpie AL.

Florian, Douglas. Airplane Ride. LC 83-45048. (Illus.). 32p. (ps-2). 1984. 10.53i (ISBN 0-690-04364-3, Crowell Jr Bks). HarpC Child Bks.

Hildick, E. W. The Ghost Squad Flies Concorde. LC 84-1487. (gr. 5-9). 1985. 10.95 (ISBN 0-525-44191-3, 01063-320, DCB). Dutton Child Bks.

Munsch, Robert. Angela's Airplane. Martchenko, Michael, illus. 24p. (gr. k-3). 1988. 12.95 (ISBN 1-550370-27-8); pap. 4.95 (ISBN 1-550370-26-X). Firefly Bks Ltd.

Oechsli, Helen & Oechsli, Kelly. Fly Away! Oechsli, Kelly, illus. LC 88-4295. 32p. (ps-1). 1988. 12.95 (ISBN 0-02-768520-9, Mcmillan Child Bk). Macmillan Child Grp.
Owen, Annie. Annie's One to Ten. Owen, Annie, illus. LC 88-13370. 32p. 1989. 8.95 (ISBN 0-394-82791-0); lib. bdg. 9.99 (ISBN 0-394-92791-5). Knopf.
Sheridan, John. Eric & the Lost Planes. Livingstone, Malcolm, illus. LC 79-7321. (gr. 5-8). 1979. PLB 8.95 (ISBN 0-672-52612-3, Bobbs). Macmillan.
Spier, Peter. Bored, Nothing to Do. Spier, Peter, illus. LC 77-20726. 48p. (gr. 1-3). 1978. 11.95 (ISBN 0-385-13177-1). Doubleday.
Testa, Fulvio. The Paper Airplane. LC 81-8358. (Illus.). 32p. (gr. k-3). 1988. 12.95 (ISBN 1-55858-060-3); pap. 4.95 (ISBN 1-55858-061-1). North-South Bks NYC.
Tubby, I. M. I'm a Little Airplane. Kraus, Robert, ed. (Illus.). 10p. (ps). 1982. pap. 2.95 (ISBN 0-671-45565-6, Little Simon). S&S Trade.
Yep, Laurence. Dragonwings. LC 74-2625. 256p. (gr. 6 up). 1977. pap. 3.50 (ISBN 0-06-440085-9, Trophy). HarpC Child Bks.

AIRPLANES–FLIGHT TESTING
see Airplanes–Testing

AIRPLANES, JET PROPELLED
see Jet Planes

AIRPLANES, MILITARY
see also types of military airplanes, e.g. Bombers

Baker, David. Bombers. (Illus.). 48p. (gr. 3-8). 1987. PLB 18.60 (ISBN 0-86592-355-8). Rourke Corp.
—Land-Based Fighters. (Illus.). 48p. (gr. 3-8). 1987. PLB 18.60 (ISBN 0-86592-351-5). Rourke Corp.
—Military Aircraft Library, 6 bks, Set II, Reading Level 5. (Illus.). 288p. (gr. 3-8). Date not set. Set. PLB 111.60 (ISBN 0-86592-530-5). Rourke Corp.
—Navy Fighters. (Illus.). 48p. (gr. 3-8). 1987. PLB 18.60 (ISBN 0-86592-352-3). Rourke Corp.
—Research Planes. (Illus.). 48p. (gr. 3-8). 1987. PLB 18.60 (ISBN 0-86592-354-X). Rourke Corp.
—Spy Planes. (Illus.). 48p. (gr. 3-8). 1987. PLB 18.60 (ISBN 0-317-60507-0). Rourke Corp.
Begarnie, Luke. Fighters, Choppers & Bombers. (Illus.). 32p. 1987. pap. 3.95 (ISBN 0-590-40738-4). Scholastic Inc.
Norman, C. J. Combat Aircraft. LC 85-51453. (Illus.). 32p. (gr. 1-6). 1986. PLB 11.40 (ISBN 0-531-10089-8). Watts.
—Combat Aircraft. 1989. pap. 3.95 (ISBN 0-531-15139-5). Watts.
Stephen, R. J. Picture World of Combat Aircraft. 1990. PLB 11.40 (ISBN 0-531-14009-1). Watts.
Sullivan, George. Famous Air Force Bombers. (Illus.). 64p. (gr. 3-7). 1985. 9.95 (ISBN 0-396-08621-7, Putnam). Putnam Pub Group.
—Famous Navy Attack Planes. (Illus.). 64p. (gr. 3-7). 1986. 10.95 (ISBN 0-396-08770-1, Putnam). Putnam Pub Group.
—Famous Navy Fighter Planes. (Illus.). 64p. (gr. 3-7). 1986. 11.99 (ISBN 0-399-61230-0, Putnam). Putnam Pub Group.
—Famous U. S. Spy Planes. (Illus.). 64p. (gr. 9-12). 1987. 11.99 (ISBN 0-399-61229-7, Putnam). Putnam Pub Group.
Thum, Marcella & Thum, Gladys. Airlift: The Story of the Military Airlift Command. 144p. (gr. 7-11). 1986. 12.95 (ISBN 0-396-08529-6, Putnam). Putnam Pub Group.

AIRPLANES–MODELS

Arceneaux, Marc. Paper Airplanes. (Illus.). 32p. 1974. pap. 4.50 (ISBN 0-8431-1703-6). Price Stern.
Barrett, N. S. Airliners. Bryan, Tony, illus. LC 84-50697. 32p. (gr. k-3). 1985. PLB 10.90 (ISBN 0-531-03720-7). Watts.
Lord, Suzanne. Radio Controlled Model Airplanes. LC 88-7109. (Illus.). 48p. (gr. 5-6). 1988. PLB 10.95 (ISBN 0-89686-378-6, Crestwood Hse). Macmillan Child Grp.
McNeil, M. J. The KnowHow Book of Flying Models: Lots of Models That Really Fly from Paper & Card. (Illus.). 32p. (gr. 3-6). 1977. pap. 5.95 (ISBN 0-86020-007-8). EDC.
Step by Step Airplanes That Really Fly. (ps up). 1990. PLB 5.98 (ISBN 0-7924-5020-5, Mallard Pr). BDD Promo Bk.

AIRPLANES, NAVAL
see Airplanes, Military

AIRPLANES–OPERATION
see Airplanes–Piloting

AIRPLANES–PILOTING

Berliner, Don. The World Aerobatics Championships. (Illus.). 64p. (gr. 5 up). 1989. 12.95 (ISBN 0-8225-0531-2). Lerner Pubns.

AIRPLANES–PILOTS
see Air Pilots

AIRPLANES–RACING
see Airplane Racing

AIRPLANES–TESTING

Berliner, Don. Research Airplanes: Testing the Boundaries of Flight. (Illus.). 64p. (gr. 5 up). 1988. PLB 15.95 (ISBN 0-8225-1582-2). Lerner Pubns.

AIRPORTS

Barton, Byron. Airport. Barton, Byron, illus. LC 79-7816. 32p. (ps-k). 1982. 14.95 (ISBN 0-690-04168-3, Crowell Jr Bks); PLB 14.89 (ISBN 0-690-04169-1). HarpC Child Bks.
—Airport. Barton, Byron, illus. LC 79-7816. 32p. (ps-1). 1987. pap. 4.95 (ISBN 0-06-443145-2, Trophy). HarpC Child Bks.
Butler, Daphne. First Look at the Airports. LC 90-10266. (Illus.). 32p. (gr. 1-2). 1991. lib. bdg. 10.95 (ISBN 0-8368-0501-1). Gareth Stevens Inc.
Davies, Mark. Inside the Airport. Geary, Rick, illus. 32p. 1990. 12.95 (ISBN 0-8092-4274-5, Calico Bks). Contemp Bks.
Dupasquier, Philippe. The Airport. Dupasquier, Philippe, illus. 24p. (gr. k-1). 1984. pap. 3.95 (ISBN 0-448-21503-9, G&D). Putnam Pub Group.
Jay, Michael & Hewish, Mark. Airports. LC 81-70048. 32p. (gr. 2-4). 1982. PLB 7.99 (ISBN 0-531-04370-3). Watts.
Langley, Andrew. Airports. rev. ed. Franklin Watts Ltd., ed. (Illus.). 32p. (ps-6). 1988. PLB 10.90 (ISBN 0-531-10445-1). Watts.
Peterson, David. Airports. LC 81-7736. (Illus.). 48p. (gr. k-4). 1981. PLB 14.60 (ISBN 0-516-01607-5). Childrens.

AIRSHIPS
see also Aeronautics; Balloons

Sullivan, George. Famous Blimps & Airships. (Illus.). 64p. (gr. 5-9). 1988. 11.95 (ISBN 0-396-09119-9, Putnam). Putnam Pub Group.

ALABAMA

Carole Marsh Alabama Books, 31 bks. Set. 638.45 (ISBN 0-7933-1274-4). Gallopade Pub Group.
Carpenter, Allan. Alabama. LC 77-13920. (Illus.). 96p. (gr. 4 up). 1978. PLB 19.93 (ISBN 0-516-04101-0). Childrens.
Estes, James L. Alabama's Youngest Admirals. Krauel, Mary E., ed. Christian, Releta, illus. 132p. (Orig.). (gr. 4-12). 1991. pap. 8.95 (ISBN 0-9628634-0-8). J L Estes.
Fradin, Dennis. Alabama: In Words & Pictures. Wahl, Richard, illus. LC 80-15135. 48p. (gr. 2-5). 1980. PLB 15.93 (ISBN 0-516-03901-6). Childrens.
McNair, Sylvia. Alabama. LC 88-11744. (Illus.). 144p. (gr. 4 up). 1988. PLB 25.27 (ISBN 0-516-00447-6). Childrens.
Marks, Henry S. Who Was Who in Alabama. LC 74-188627. (gr. 9-12). 1972. 14.95 (ISBN 0-87397-017-9). Strode.
Marsh, Carole. Alabama & Other State Greats (Biographies) (Illus.). (gr. 3-12). 1990. PLB 19.95 (ISBN 1-55609-469-8); pap. 14.95 (ISBN 1-55609-468-X); computer disk 29.95 (ISBN 0-7933-1338-4). Gallopade Pub Group.
—Alabama Bandits, Bushwackers, Outlaws, Crooks, Devils, Ghosts, Desperadoes & Other Assorted & Sundry Characters! (Illus.). (gr. 3-12). 1990. PLB 19.95 (ISBN 0-7933-0041-X); pap. 14.95 (ISBN 0-7933-0040-1); computer disk 29.95 (ISBN 0-7933-0042-8). Gallopade Pub Group.
—Alabama Classic Christmas Trivia: Stories, Recipes, Activities, Legends, Lore & More! (Illus.). (gr. 3-12). 1990. PLB 19.95 (ISBN 0-7933-0044-4); pap. 14.95 (ISBN 0-7933-0043-6); computer disk 29.95 (ISBN 0-7933-0045-2). Gallopade Pub Group.
—Alabama Coastales. (Illus.). (gr. 3-12). 1990. PLB 19.95 (ISBN 1-55609-465-5); pap. 14.95 (ISBN 1-55609-120-6); computer disk 29.95 (ISBN 0-7933-1334-1). Gallopade Pub Group.
—The Alabama Hot Air Balloon Mystery. (Illus.). (gr. 2-9). 1990. 19.95 (ISBN 0-7933-2318-5); pap. 14.95 (ISBN 0-7933-2319-3); computer disk 29.95 (ISBN 0-7933-2320-7). Gallopade Pub Group.
—Alabama "Jography" A Fun Run Thru Our State! (Illus.). (gr. 3-12). 1990. PLB 19.95 (ISBN 1-55609-461-2); pap. 14.95 (ISBN 1-55609-092-7); computer disk 29.95 (ISBN 0-7933-1327-9). Gallopade Pub Group.
—Alabama Kid's Cookbook: Recipes, How-to, History, Lore & More! (Illus.). (gr. 3-12). 1990. PLB 19.95 (ISBN 0-7933-0082-7); pap. 14.95 (ISBN 0-7933-0081-9); computer disk 29.95 (ISBN 0-7933-0083-5). Gallopade Pub Group.
—Alabama Quiz Bowl Crash Course! (Illus.). (gr. 3-12). 1990. PLB 19.95 (ISBN 1-55609-467-1); pap. 14.95 (ISBN 1-55609-466-3); computer disk 29.95 (ISBN 0-7933-1333-3). Gallopade Pub Group.
—Alabama School Trivia: An Amazing & Fascinating Look at Our State's Teachers, Schools & Students! (Illus.). (gr. 3-12). 1990. PLB 19.95 (ISBN 0-7933-0079-7); pap. 14.95 (ISBN 0-7933-0049-5); computer disk 29.95 (ISBN 0-7933-0080-0). Gallopade Pub Group.
—Alabama Silly Basketball Sportsmysteries, Vol. I. (Illus.). (gr. 3-12). 1990. PLB 19.95 (ISBN 0-7933-0047-9); pap. 14.95 (ISBN 0-7933-0046-0); computer disk 29.95 (ISBN 0-7933-0048-7). Gallopade Pub Group.
—Alabama Silly Basketball Sportsmysteries, Vol. II. (Illus.). (gr. 3-12). 1990. PLB 19.95 (ISBN 0-7933-1562-X); pap. 14.95 (ISBN 0-7933-1563-8); computer disk 29.95 (ISBN 0-7933-1564-6). Gallopade Pub Group.
—Alabama Silly Football Sportsmysteries, Vol. I. (Illus.). (gr. 3-12). 1990. PLB 19.95 (ISBN 1-55609-464-7); pap. 14.95 (ISBN 1-55609-463-9); computer disk 29.95 (ISBN 0-7933-1329-5). Gallopade Pub Group.
—Alabama Silly Football Sportsmysteries, Vol. II. (Illus.). (gr. 3-12). 1990. PLB 19.95 (ISBN 0-7933-1339-2); pap. 14.95 (ISBN 0-7933-1340-6); computer disk 29.95 (ISBN 0-7933-1341-4). Gallopade Pub Group.
—Alabama Silly Trivia! (Illus.). (gr. 3-12). 1990. PLB 19.95 (ISBN 1-55609-460-4); pap. 14.95 (ISBN 1-55609-038-2); computer disk 29.95 (ISBN 0-7933-1326-0). Gallopade Pub Group.
—Alabama's (Most Devastating!) Disasters & (Most Calamitous!) Catastrophies! (Illus.). (gr. 3-12). 1990. PLB 19.95 (ISBN 0-7933-0038-X); pap. 14.95 (ISBN 0-7933-0037-1); computer disk 29.95 (ISBN 0-7933-0039-8). Gallopade Pub Group.
—Avast, Ye Slobs! Alabama Pirate Trivia. (Illus.). (gr. 3-12). 1990. PLB 19.95 (ISBN 0-7933-0088-6); pap. 14.95 (ISBN 0-7933-0087-8); computer disk 29.95 (ISBN 0-7933-0089-4). Gallopade Pub Group.
—The Beast of the Alabama Bed & Breakfast. (Illus.). (gr. 3-12). 1990. PLB 19.95 (ISBN 0-7933-1332-5); pap. 14.95 (ISBN 0-7933-1331-7); computer disk 29.95 (ISBN 0-7933-1330-9). Gallopade Pub Group.
—The Hard-to-Believe-But-True! Book of Alabama History, Mystery, Trivia, Legend, Lore, Humor & More. (Illus.). (gr. 3-12). 1990. PLB 19.95 (ISBN 0-7933-0085-1); pap. 14.95 (ISBN 0-7933-0084-3); computer disk 29.95 (ISBN 0-7933-0086-X). Gallopade Pub Group.
—If My Alabama Mama Ran the World! (Illus.). (gr. 3-12). 1990. PLB 19.95 (ISBN 0-7933-1335-X); pap. 14.95 (ISBN 0-7933-1336-8); computer disk 29.95 (ISBN 0-7933-1337-6). Gallopade Pub Group.
—Let's Quilt Alabama & Stuff It Topographically! (Illus.). (gr. 3-12). 1990. PLB 19.95 (ISBN 1-55609-462-0); pap. 14.95 (ISBN 1-55609-073-0); computer disk 29.95 (ISBN 0-7933-1328-7). Gallopade Pub Group.
Penner, Lucille R. The Honey Book. new ed. LC 80-249. (Illus.). 160p. (gr. 7 up). 1980. 10.95 (ISBN 0-8038-3054-8). Hastings.
Swindler, William F. & Trover, Ellen L., eds. Chronology & Documentary Handbook of the State of Alabama, No. 3. LC 72-51. 142p. (gr. 9-12). 1972. PLB 8.50 (ISBN 0-379-16126-5). Oceana.
Thompson, Kathleen. Alabama. LC 87-26486. 48p. (gr. 3 up). 1988. 17.32 (ISBN 0-86514-461-3). Raintree Pubs.
Townsend, Sandra S. The Old Jail Remembers Tuscaloosa. (Illus.). 44p. (Orig.). (gr. 5-12). 1987. pap. 4.50 (ISBN 0-943487-03-X). Sevgo Pr.
Walter, Eugene. Mobile Mardi Gras Annual 1948, Vol. 1, No. 2. Plummer, Cameron, ed. Walter, Eugene, illus. 32p. (gr. 7 up). 1948. pap. 7.00 (ISBN 0-940882-05-1). HB Pubns.

ALABAMA–FICTION

Brown, Faye. Chinch Bugs, Chinky Pins, & Chinie-Berry Beads. Brown, Trillie, illus. 191p. (Orig.). 1990. pap. 7.95 (ISBN 0-943487-24-2). Sevgo Pr.
Cole, Brenda. Alabama Night. 157p. (gr. 9-12). 1988. pap. 2.25 (ISBN 0-373-88037-5). Harlequin Bks.

ALAMO–SEIGE, 1836

Carter, Alden R. Last Stand at the Alamo. (ps-3). 1990. PLB 11.90 (ISBN 0-531-10888-0). Watts.
Fisher, Leonard E. The Alamo. Fisher, Leonard E., illus. LC 86-46204. 64p. (gr. 3-7). 1987. reinforced bdg. 13.95 (ISBN 0-8234-0646-6). Holiday.
Lawson, Don. The United States in the Mexican War. McCullough, Robert, illus. LC 76-11022. 160p. (gr. 7 up). 1988. PLB 12.89 (ISBN 0-690-04723-1, Crowell Jr Bks). HarpC Child Bks.
Richards, Norman. The Story of the Alamo. LC 70-100698. (Illus.). 32p. (gr. 4-8). 1970. 13.27 (ISBN 0-516-04601-2); pap. 3.95 (ISBN 0-516-44601-0). Childrens.
Warren, Robert Penn. Remember the Alamo! (Illus.). (gr. 4-6). 1963. Random.

ALAMO–SEIGE, 1836–FICTION

Cousins, Margaret. The Boy in the Alamo. Eggenhofer, Nicholas, illus. LC 83-72585. 180p. (gr. 5-7). 1983. pap. 5.95 (ISBN 0-931722-26-8). Corona Pub.
Jakes, John. Susanna of the Alamo: A True Story. Bacon, Paul, illus. LC 85-27143. 32p. (gr. 1-5). 1986. 13.95 (ISBN 0-15-200592-7, Gulliver Bks). HarBraceJ.
Rice, James. Texas Jack at the Alamo. Rice, James, illus. 40p. 1989. 11.95 (ISBN 0-88289-725-X). Pelican.
Wheatly, Mark. Build the Alamo. Eakin, Ed, ed. (Illus.). 32p. (gr. 4-5). 1989. 10.95 (ISBN 0-89015-721-9). Eakin Pr.

ALASKA

Carole Marsh Alaska Books, 31 bks. Set. 638.45 (ISBN 0-7933-1275-2). Gallopade Pub Group.
Carpenter, Allan. Alaska. LC 78-12419. (Illus.). 96p. (gr. 4 up). 1979. PLB 19.93 (ISBN 0-516-04102-9). Childrens.
Cheney. Alaska: Indians, Eskimos, Russians & the Rest. 1980. 8.95 (ISBN 0-396-07792-7, Putnam). Putnam Pub Group.
Cobb, Vicki. This Place Is Cold. Lavallee, Barbara, illus. (gr. 2-4). 1989. 13.95 (ISBN 0-8027-6852-0); PLB 13.85 (ISBN 0-8027-6853-9). Walker & Co.
—This Place Is Cold. Lavallee, Barbara, illus. 32p. (gr. 2-5). 1990. pap. 7.95 (ISBN 0-8027-7340-0). Walker & Co.
Dunmire, Marj. National Parks of Alaska. (Illus.). 48p. (gr. 2-8). 1991. pap. 4.95 (ISBN 0-942559-07-X). Pegasus Graphics.
Dunnakoo, Terry. Alaska. (Illus.). 72p. (gr. 4-9). PLB 10.40 (ISBN 0-531-10375-7). Watts.
Fradin, Dennis. Alaska: In Words & Pictures. Ulm, Robert, illus. LC 77-4353. 48p. (gr. 2-5). 1977. PLB 15.93 (ISBN 0-516-03902-4). Childrens.
Gill, Shelley R. Thunderfeet, Alaska's Dinosaurs & Other Prehistoric Critters. (Illus.). 36p. (Orig.). (gr. k-4). 1988. pap. 11.95 incl. cass. (ISBN 0-934007-03-9). Paws Four Pub.
Heinrichs, Ann. Alaska. LC 90-33847. (Illus.). 144p. (gr. 4 up). 1990. PLB 25.27 (ISBN 0-516-00448-4). Childrens.

Hiscock, Bruce. Tundra: The Arctic Land. Hiscock, Bruce, illus. LC 85-28769. 144p. (gr. 3 up). 1986. 13. 95 (ISBN 0-689-31219-9, Atheneum Child Bk). Macmillan Child Grp.

Holen, Susan D. Alaska Wildlife: A Coloring Book. Holen, Anne M., ed. Holen, Betsy L., illus. 44p. (gr. 3-8). 1989. pap. 4.95 (ISBN 0-922127-00-X). Paisley Pub.

—Alaska's Wild Coast. Holen, Anne M., ed. Holen, Betsy L., illus. 48p. (Orig.). (gr. 3-8). Date not set. pap. write for info. Paisley Pub.

Madison, Kathy. Fun Guide to Anchorage. Lauzen, Elizabeth, ed. Burrus, Sue, illus. 32p. (Orig.). (gr. 1-6). 1987. pap. 3.50 incl. wkbk. (ISBN 0-942553-00-4). Madison Aves.

Marsh, Carole. Alaska & Other State Greats (Biographies) (Illus.). (gr. 3-12). 1990. PLB 19.95 (ISBN 1-55609-483-3); pap. 14.95 (ISBN 1-55609-482-5); computer disk 29.95 (ISBN 0-7933-1354-6). Gallopade Pub Group.

—Alaska Bandits, Bushwackers, Outlaws, Crooks, Devils, Ghosts, Desperadoes & Other Assorted & Sundry Characters! (Illus.). (gr. 3-12). 1990. PLB 19.95 (ISBN 0-7933-0094-0); pap. 14.95 (ISBN 0-7933-0093-2); computer disk 29.95 (ISBN 0-7933-0095-9). Gallopade Pub Group.

—Alaska Classic Christmas Trivia: Stories, Recipes, Activities, Legends, Lore & More! (Illus.). (gr. 3-12). 1990. PLB 19.95 (ISBN 0-7933-0097-5); pap. 14.95 (ISBN 0-7933-0096-7); computer disk 29.95 (ISBN 0-7933-0098-3). Gallopade Pub Group.

—Alaska Coastales. (Illus.). (gr. 3-12). 1990. PLB 19.95 (ISBN 1-55609-479-5); pap. 14.95 (ISBN 1-55609-478-7); computer disk 29.95 (ISBN 0-7933-1353-8). Gallopade Pub Group.

—The Alaska Hot Air Balloon Mystery. (Illus.). (gr. 2-9). 1990. 19.95 (ISBN 0-7933-2327-4); pap. 14.95 (ISBN 0-7933-2328-2); computer disk 29.95 (ISBN 0-7933-2329-0). Gallopade Pub Group.

—Alaska "Jography" A Fun Run Thru Our State! (Illus.). (gr. 3-12). 1990. PLB 19.95 (ISBN 1-55609-473-6); pap. 14.95 (ISBN 1-55609-472-8); computer disk 29. 95 (ISBN 0-7933-1343-0). Gallopade Pub Group.

—Alaska Kid's Cookbook: Recipes, How-to, History, Lore & More! (Illus.). (gr. 3-12). 1990. PLB 19.95 (ISBN 0-7933-0106-8); pap. 14.95 (ISBN 0-7933-0105-X); computer disk 29.95 (ISBN 0-7933-0107-6). Gallopade Pub Group.

—Alaska Quiz Bowl Crash Course! (Illus.). (gr. 3-12). 1990. PLB 19.95 (ISBN 1-55609-481-7); pap. 14.95 (ISBN 1-55609-480-9); computer disk 29.95 (ISBN 0-7933-1352-X). Gallopade Pub Group.

—Alaska School Trivia: An Amazing & Fascinating Look at Our State's Teachers, Schools & Students! (Illus.). (gr. 3-12). 1990. PLB 19.95 (ISBN 0-7933-0103-3); pap. 14.95 (ISBN 0-7933-0102-5); computer disk 29. 95 (ISBN 0-7933-0104-1). Gallopade Pub Group.

—Alaska Silly Basketball Sportsmysteries, Vol. I. (Illus.). (gr. 3-12). 1990. PLB 19.95 (ISBN 0-7933-0100-9); pap. 14.95 (ISBN 0-7933-0099-1); computer disk 29. 95 (ISBN 0-7933-0101-7). Gallopade Pub Group.

—Alaska Silly Basketball Sportsmysteries, Vol. II. (Illus.). (gr. 3-12). 1990. PLB 19.95 (ISBN 0-7933-1565-4); pap. 14.95 (ISBN 0-7933-1566-2); computer disk 29. 95 (ISBN 0-7933-1567-0). Gallopade Pub Group.

—Alaska Silly Football Sportsmysteries, Vol. I. (Illus.). (gr. 3-12). 1990. PLB 19.95 (ISBN 1-55609-477-9); pap. 14.95 (ISBN 1-55609-476-0); computer disk 29. 95 (ISBN 0-7933-1345-7). Gallopade Pub Group.

—Alaska Silly Football Sportsmysteries, Vol. II. (Illus.). (gr. 3-12). 1990. PLB 19.95 (ISBN 0-7933-1346-5); pap. 14.95 (ISBN 0-7933-1347-3); computer disk 29. 95 (ISBN 0-7933-1348-1). Gallopade Pub Group.

—Alaska Silly Trivia! (Illus.). (gr. 3-12). 1990. PLB 19.95 (ISBN 1-55609-471-X); pap. 14.95 (ISBN 1-55609-470-1); computer disk 29.95 (ISBN 0-7933-1342-2). Gallopade Pub Group.

—Alaska's (Most Devastating!) Disasters & (Most Calamitous!) Catastrophies! (Illus.). (gr. 3-12). 1990. PLB 19.95 (ISBN 0-7933-0091-6); pap. 14.95 (ISBN 0-7933-0090-8); computer disk 29.95 (ISBN 0-7933-0092-4). Gallopade Pub Group.

—Avast, Ye Slobs! Alaska Pirate Trivia. (Illus.). (gr. 3-12). 1990. PLB 19.95 (ISBN 0-7933-0112-2); pap. 14. 95 (ISBN 0-7933-0111-4); computer disk 29.95 (ISBN 0-7933-0113-0). Gallopade Pub Group.

—The Best of the Alaska Bed & Breakfast. (Illus.). (gr. 3-12). 1990. PLB 19.95 (ISBN 0-7933-1349-X); pap. 14. 95 (ISBN 0-7933-1350-3); computer disk 29.95 (ISBN 0-7933-1351-1). Gallopade Pub Group.

—The Hard-to-Believe-But-True! Book of Alaska History, Mystery, Trivia, Legend, Lore, Humor & More. (Illus.). (gr. 3-12). 1990. PLB 19.95 (ISBN 0-7933-0109-2); pap. 14.95 (ISBN 0-7933-0108-4); computer disk 29.95 (ISBN 0-7933-0110-6). Gallopade Pub Group.

—If My Alaska Mama Ran the World! (Illus.). (gr. 3-12). 1990. PLB 19.95 (ISBN 0-7933-1355-4); pap. 14.95 (ISBN 0-7933-1356-2); computer disk 29.95 (ISBN 0-7933-1357-0). Gallopade Pub Group.

—Let's Quilt Alaska & Stuff It Topographically! (Illus.). (gr. 3-12). 1990. PLB 19.95 (ISBN 1-55609-475-2); pap. 14.95 (ISBN 1-55609-094-3); computer disk 29. 95 (ISBN 0-7933-1344-9). Gallopade Pub Group.

Nault, Andy. Staying Alive in Alaska's Wild. Loftin, Tee, ed. (Illus.). 224p. (Orig.). (gr. 5 up). 1980. pap. 8.95 (ISBN 0-934812-01-2). Tee Loftin.

Oberle, Joseph G. Anchorage. LC 89-26068. (Illus.). 60p. (gr. 3 up). 1990. PLB 12.95 (ISBN 0-87518-420-0, Dillon). Macmillan Child Grp.

Postell, Alice E. Where Did the Reindeer Come From? Alaska Experience the First Fifty Years. York, Susan P., ed. DeArmond, Robert N., frwd. by. LC 90-146. (Illus.). 144p. (gr. 9 up). 1990. write for info. (ISBN 0-9626090-0-5). Amaknak Pr.
The beginning of the domestic reindeer industry in Alaska reads like a story. The Reverend Sheldon Jackson, a Presbyterian Missionary, became the first Government Agent for Education in Alaska, & while on this assignment he learned of the near-starvation among Eskimos. White men had hunted, & driven off, their source of wildlife & seafood. The account of bringing reindeer from Siberia, & his efforts to prepare Alaska Natives to meet the influx of "outsiders" is filled with frustrations, excitement & intrigue. Cultural conflicts, tradition & superstitions were ever present. The endless Arctic nights & brief bug-infested summers added problems. Whaling ships frozen in Arctic ice demanded sacrifice of reindeer herds for relief. Reindeer Fairs were held to stimulate interest & competition among the herders. Epidemics of measles & smallpox decimated the Eskimo leadership that was developing. The Nome gold-rush added endless complications. The first 50 years of Reindeer Industry reached a milestone when the Reindeer Act of 1937 mandated that all reindeer be returned to Alaska Natives, for whom they were intended from the beginning. 15 boxed stories give details of leading characters as well as other interesting facts. 48 historic photos have informative captions. Map of Alaska, index & bibliography. This is exciting reading for all ages.
Publisher Provided Annotation.

Puhalo, Lazar. Innokenty of Alaska. Novakshonoff, V., illus. 86p. (Orig.). (gr. 8 up). 1986. pap. 5.00 (ISBN 0-913026-86-7). Synaxis Pr.

Standiford, Natalie. The Bravest Dog Ever: The True Story of Balto. Cook, Donald, tr. LC 89-3465. (Illus.). 47p. (Orig.). (gr. 1-3). 1989. PLB 6.99 (ISBN 0-394-99695-X, Random Juv); pap. 2.95 (ISBN 0-394-89695-5). Random.

Thompson, Kathleen. Alaska. LC 87-26487. 48p. (gr. 3 up). 1988. 17.32 (ISBN 0-86514-471-0). Raintree Pubs.

Warbelow, Willy L. Empire on Ice. Clark, Marvin, ed. (Illus.). 256p. (Orig.). (gr. 9 up). 1990. 32.50 (ISBN 0-937708-22-4); pap. 19.95 (ISBN 0-937708-21-6). Great Northwest.

ALASKA–FICTION

Arnold, Marti. Alaska, Uncle Jim & Me. Lesko, Marian, ed. Dessereau, April & Present, David, illus. 146p. (Orig.). (gr. 6 up). 1983. pap. 5.95 (ISBN 0-912683-00-7). Fireweed.

Harms, Valerie. Frolic's Dance. Buzzanco, Eileen M., illus. LC 88-64155. 32p. (gr. k-4). 1989. 11.95 (ISBN 0-924483-01-6); bk. & cassette 14.95 (ISBN 0-924483-04-0); bk., cassette & toy 41.95 (ISBN 0-924483-07-5); write for info. cassette (ISBN 0-924483-10-5). Soundprints.

London, Jack. Call of the Wild. (gr. 6 up). 1964. pap. 2.50 (ISBN 0-8049-0030-2, CL-30). Airmont.

—The Call of the Wild. Kezer, Karel, illus. LC 63-14831. 144p. (gr. 6 up). 1970. 12.95 (ISBN 0-02-759510-2, Mcmillan Child Bk). Macmillan Child Grp.

—The Call of the Wild. Doctorow, E. L., intro. by. LC 90-50182. 1990. pap. 8.50 (ISBN 0-679-72535-0, Vin). Random.

—White Fang. (gr. 6 up). 1964. pap. 2.50 (ISBN 0-8049-0036-1, CL-36). Airmont.

Morey, Walt. Gentle Ben. Schoenherr, John, illus. (gr. 4 up). 1965. 12.95 (ISBN 0-525-30429-0, DCB). Dutton Child Bks.

—Kavik, the Wolf Dog. Parnall, Peter, illus. LC 68-24727. (gr. 5-9). 1977. 12.95 (ISBN 0-525-33093-3, DCB); (DCB). Dutton Child Bks.

—Kavik, the Wolf Dog. 1989. pap. 2.75 (ISBN 0-590-40937-9). Scholastic Inc.

Reiser, Joanne. Hannah's Alaska. Downing, Julie, illus. LC 83-8668. 32p. (gr. 3-6). 1983. PLB 14.65 (ISBN 0-940742-23-3). Raintree Pubs.

Ritchie, Jo-An. Jonie in Alaska. Wheeler, Gerald, ed. 128p. (Orig.). (gr. 8 up). 1985. pap. 5.50 (ISBN 0-8280-0250-9). Review & Herald.

Roe, JoAnn. Marco the Manx Series, 3 bks. Runestrand, Meredith & Mayo, Steve, illus. (gr. k-5). Date not set. Fisherman Cat. PLB 10.95 (ISBN 0-931551-02-1); Alaska Cat. PLB 10.95 (ISBN 0-931551-05-6); Castaway Cat. pap. 5.95 (ISBN 0-931551-03-X); Fisherman Cat. pap. 6.95 (ISBN 0-931551-01-3); Alaska Cat. pap. 6.95 (ISBN 0-931551-04-8). Montevista Pr.
"Marco the Manx Series": Each book is a complete story. (1) Castaway Cat, 56 pp, B/W watercolors, color cover, paper only $5.95 (ISBN 0-931551-03-X, 2nd printing). A Manx "city cat," falls off a sailboat, has to survive on an island for the winter. Ocean lore, raccoon fights, eagles. (2) Fisherman Cat, 64 pp, color watercolors, paper $6. 95 (ISBN 0-931551-01-3), library binding $10.95 (ISBN 0-931551-02-1). Marco the Manx goes aboard a disabled fishing boat, is trapped below, goes off toward Alaskan fishing grounds. Salmon life cycle, fishing lore. (3) Alaska Cat, 64 pp, color watercolors, paper $6.95 (ISBN 0-931551-04-8); library binding $10.95 (ISBN 0-931551-05-6). Marco's boat is shipwrecked off Sitka, Alaska. Once ashore he encounters bears, is rescued by native children. Totems, etc. Castaway Cat won a national first prize for excellence. Was used in school reading test. Distributors: Pacific Pipeline, 19215 - 66th Avenue South, Kent WA 98032-1171. (206) 872-5523. Alaska News Agency, 325 Potter Street, Anchorage AK 99518. (907) 563-3251. Baker & Taylor, Reno, Momence, etc.
Publisher Provided Annotation.

Schurfranz, Vivian. Megan, No. 16. 224p. (Orig.). (gr. 7 up). 1986. pap. 2.75 (ISBN 0-590-41468-2, Sunfire). Scholastic Inc.

TallMountain, Mary. Green March Moons. Senungetuk, Joseph E., illus. LC 87-6018. 32p. (Orig.). (gr. 6 up). 1987. pap. 7.95 (ISBN 0-938678-10-8). New Seed.

Tjepkema, Edith R. Alaskan Paradise. 115p. (Orig.). (gr. 8 up). 1989. pap. 4.50 (ISBN 0-9620280-1-0). Northland Pr.

Wittanen, Etolin. Auke Lake Tales. Alenov, Nick & Alenov, Lydia, illus. 53p. (Orig.). (gr. 3-6). 1986. pap. 5.00 (ISBN 0-911523-05-7). Synaxis Pr.

ALASKA–HISTORY

Bowkett, Gerald E. Reaching for a Star: The Final Campaign for Alaska Statehood. Matson, Sue, ed. Stevens, Ted, intro. by. (Illus.). 162p. (Orig.). (gr. 9-12). 1989. 22.95 (ISBN 0-945397-04-6); pap. 14.95 (ISBN 0-945397-05-4). Epicenter Pr.

Calvin, Margaret. An Alaskan A B C Coloring Book. Griffith, Sandy, illus. 32p. (Orig.). (ps-4). 1986. pap. 3.95 (ISBN 0-9615529-3-X). Old Harbor Pr.

Clinton, Susan. The Story of Seward's Folly. Neely, Keith, illus. LC 86-30947. 32p. (gr. 3-6). 1987. PLB 13.27 (ISBN 0-516-04727-2). Childrens.

Hedrick, Basil & Savage, Susan. Steamboats on the Chena: The Founding & Development of Fairbanks, Alaska. (Orig.). (gr. 9-12). 1988. pap. 9.95 (ISBN 0-945397-00-3). Epicenter Pr.

Madison, Curt & Yarber, Yvonne Y. Edgar Kallands-A Biography: Kaltag. 64p. (Orig.). 1983. pap. 6.95 (ISBN 0-910871-00-0). Spirit Mount Pr.

Swindler, William F. & Trover, Ellen L., eds. Chronology & Documentary Handbook of the State of Alaska, No. 2. LC 72-2484. 112p. (gr. 9-12). 1972. PLB 8.50 (ISBN 0-379-16127-3). Oceana.

ALBERTA–FICTION

London, Jack. The Call of the Wild. new ed. Platt, Kin, ed. Carrillo, Fred, illus. LC 73-75461. 64p. (Orig.). (gr. 5-10). 1973. pap. 2.95 (ISBN 0-88301-095-X). Pendulum Pr.

—The Call of the Wild. Nordlicht, Lillian, adapted by. & adapted by. LC 79-24464. (Illus.). 48p. (gr. 4 up). Pub. 1980. PLB 17.32 (ISBN 0-8172-1656-1). Raintree Pubs.

—The Call of the Wild. Nordlicht, Lillian, adapted by. & adapted by. LC 79-24464. (Illus.). 48p. (gr. 4 up). Pub. 1980. PLB 17.32 (ISBN 0-8172-1656-1). Raintree Pubs.

—The Call of the Wild. 176p. (gr. 6 up). 1987. pap. 2.50 (ISBN 0-590-40594-2, Apple Paperbacks). Scholastic Inc.

Sohl, Marcia & Dackerman, Gerald. The Call of the Wild Student Activity Book. (Illus.). 16p. (gr. 4-10). 1976. pap. 1.25 (ISBN 0-88301-182-4). Pendulum Pr.

ALCINDOR, LEW, 1947-

see Abdul-Jabbar, Kareem, 1947-

ALCOHOLICS

see Alcoholism

ALCOHOLISM

Abbey, Nancy & Wagman, Ellen. Saying No to Alcohol. Nelson, Mary, ed. (Illus.). 72p. 1987. tchrs. ed. 11.95 (ISBN 0-941816-37-0). Network Pubns.

Alahow-to-Parent. The ALAHOW-to-Parent Group Manual. LC 89-81350. 172p. (Orig.). (gr. 8-12). 1989. pap. text ed. write for info. Alahow to Parent.

Anderson, Peggy K. Coming Home: Children's Stories for Adult Children of Alcoholics. Detterbeck, Nancy, illus. LC 87-73388. 160p. (Orig.). (gr. 5-10). 1988. pap. 7.95 (ISBN 0-934125-06-6). Glen Abbey Bks.

Bollendorf, Robert. Sober Spring. (ps-3). 1991. pap. 5.95 (ISBN 0-8066-2539-2). Augsburg Fortress.

Booher, Albert R. Alcohol. 11p. (gr. 5-9). 1988. pap. text ed. 5.95 (ISBN 0-685-28977-X). Madonna Edu Syst.

—Drug & Alcohol Review. 13p. (gr. 5-9). 1988. pap. text ed. 5.95 (ISBN 0-685-28970-2). Madonna Edu Syst.

—Drug & Alcohol Terms. 9p. (gr. 5-9). 1988. pap. text ed. 5.95 (ISBN 0-685-28975-3). Madonna Edu Syst.

Brooks, Cathleen. The Secret Everyone Knows. 40p. (gr. 5-10). 1989. pap. 1.95 (ISBN 0-685-26029-1, 5165B). Hazelden.

Chemically Dependent Anonymous. LC 90-81598. 344p. (Orig.). (gr. 9 up). 1990. pap. 10.00 (ISBN 0-9626438-0-7). CDA Commns.

Claypool, Jane. Alcohol & You. rev. ed. Greenberg, Lorna, ed. LC 88-10258. (Illus.). 112p. 1988. PLB 12.90 (ISBN 0-531-10566-0). Watts.

Coffey, Wayne. Straight Talk about Drinking: Teenagers Speak Out about Alcohol. LC 87-32446. 256p. (gr. 7 up). 1988. pap. 8.95 (ISBN 0-452-26061-2, Plume). NAL-Dutton.

Cohen, Daniel & Cohen, Susan. A Six-Pack & a Fake I.D. Teens Look at the Drinking Question. LC 85-25337. 156p. (gr. 7 up). 1985. 13.95 (ISBN 0-87131-459-2). M Evans.

Curtis, Robert H. Questions & Answers about Alcoholism. LC 76-7560. (Illus.). 1976. 10.95 (ISBN 0-13-748459-3). P-H.

Drugs & Drinking. 48p. (gr. 6-8). 1990. pap. 6.95 (ISBN 1-55945-118-1). Group Pub.

Duggan, Maureen H. Mommy Doesn't Live Here Anymore. Liberman, Jane, illus. 48p. (Orig.). (ps-7). 1987. pap. 8.95 (ISBN 0-944453-01-5). B Brae. "Mommy Doesn't Live Here Anymore" - a sensitive chronicle of a mother's alcoholism & how it affected her children. It has successfully captured the essence of life within an alcoholic family: the stresses, tensions, pressures & pains. Most importantly, it has done so from the vantage point of the child, as the child reflects upon the total experience. No other work has presented such a realistic portrayal of the magnitude of suffering, emotional pain & psychic turmoil of young children within alcoholic families. It reveals the thoughts, reasoning, feelings & behaviors of children in alcoholic homes, & yet, accomplishes such spirit of understanding & sympathy within an overall message of hope & help for our children. "Mommy Doesn't Live Here Anymore" is an inspirational work, revealing that the tragedies of familial alcoholism & tragic consequences for our youth need to be dealt with in a personal & delicate manner." Maureen Duggan has always been regarded highly for her thoughtful & gentle manner, compassionate understanding, & her acute sensitivity towards alcoholics & family needs. Her own serenity & spirituality are guides for many seeking their own honesty & fulfillment."--Nelson C. Acquilano, Executive Director, Council on Alcoholism of The Finger Lakes, N.Y. *Publisher Provided Annotation.*

Englebardt, Stanley L. Kids & Alcohol, the Deadliest Drug. LC 75-20327. 64p. (gr. 5 up). 1975. PLB 12.88 (ISBN 0-688-51717-X). Lothrop.

Fitzmahan, Don. The Roller Coaster: A Story of Alcoholism & the Family. Cocklin-Ray, Christine, illus. Black, Claudia, intro. by. LC 88-63798. (Illus.). 36p. (Orig.). (gr. 6). 1986. pap. 5.95 (ISBN 0-935529-11-X). Comprehen Health Educ.

Graeber, Laurel. Are You Dying for a Drink? Teenagers & Alcohol Abuse. LC 85-8880. (Illus.). 128p. (gr. 7 up). 1986. lib. bdg. 12.98 (ISBN 0-671-50818-0); lib. bdg. 4.95 (ISBN 0-671-63180-2). Messner.

Grosshandler, Janet. Coping with Drinking & Driving. Rosen, Ruth, ed. (gr. 7-12). 1990. lib. bdg. 12.95 (ISBN 0-8239-1156-X). Rosen Group.

Gunn, Jeffrey. Pen Pals, Vol. 11: Facts about Alcohol. Wolfe, Debra, illus. (Orig.). (gr. 3). 1990. pap. write for info. (ISBN 1-879146-11-8). Knowldg Pub.

Hablemos Francamente de las Drogas y el Alcohol. (SPA.). 160p. 1990. 15.95 (ISBN 0-8160-2496-0). Facts on File.

Hall, Lindsey & Cohn, Leigh. Dear Kids of Alcoholics. Lingenfelter, Rosemary E., illus. 96p. (gr. 3-10). 1988. pap. 6.95 (ISBN 0-936077-18-2). Gurze Bks.

Hamilton, Dorothy. Mari's Mountain. Graber, Esther R., illus. LC 78-10620. 120p. (gr. 7-10). 1978. pap. 3.95 (ISBN 0-8361-1869-3). Herald Pr.

Hastings, Jill M. & Typpo, Marion H. Elephant in the Living Room: The Children's Book. Noland, Mimi, illus. LC 84-70189. 88p. (Orig.). (gr. 3-8). 1984. wkbk. 7.00 (ISBN 0-89638-071-8, 03319). CompCare.

Hjelmeland, Andy. Drinking & Driving. LC 89-25406. (Illus.). 48p. (gr. 4 up). 1990. 10.95 (ISBN 0-89686-496-0, Crestwood Hse). Macmillan Child Grp.

Hyde, Margaret O. Alcohol: Uses & Abuses. LC 87-12161. (Illus.). 96p. (gr. 6-12). 1988. lib. bdg. 16.95 (ISBN 0-89490-155-9). Enslow Pubs.

Jones, Michael P., ed. What Getting Drunk Doesn't Make You. (Illus.). 20p. 1984. text ed. 5.00 (ISBN 0-89904-027-6); pap. text ed. 2.00 (ISBN 0-89904-197-3). Crumb Elbow Pub.

Jones, Ralph E. Straight Talk: Answers to Questions Young People Ask about Alcohol. Joiner, Lee M., ed. 64p. (Orig.). (gr. 10 up). 1988. pap. 4.95 (ISBN 0-943519-08-X, B1908). Human Servs Inst.

—Straight Talk: Answers to Questions Young People Ask about Alcohol. 1989. No. 70005. pap. 4.95 (ISBN 0-8306-9005-0). TAB Bks.

Langone, John. Bombed, Buzzed, Smashed, or...Sober: A Book about Alcohol. (gr. 7 up). 1976. 14.95 (ISBN 0-316-51424-1). Little.

Larsen, Kent P. I Wasn't Born Drunk. (Orig.). Date not set. pap. write for info. K P Larsen Inc.

Lutes, Chris. What Teenagers Are Saying about Drugs & Alcohol. 1990. pap. 7.95 (ISBN 0-310-71051-0, Campus Life). Zondervan.

Milgram, Gail G. Coping with Alcohol. rev. ed. (Illus.). (gr. 7-12). 1987. PLB 12.95 (ISBN 0-8239-0747-3). Rosen Group.

Morreim, Dennis C. Changed Lives: The Story of Alcoholics Anonymous. (ps-3). 1991. pap. 8.95 (ISBN 0-8066-2548-1). Augsburg Fortress.

Newman, Susan. You Can Say No to a Drink or a Drug: What Every Kid Should Know. (Illus.). 1986. pap. 8.95 (ISBN 0-399-51228-4, Perigee Bks). Putnam Pub Group.

Newton, David E. Particle Accelerations. (Illus.). 128p. (gr. 10-12). 1990. 12.40 (ISBN 0-531-10671-3). Watts.

Nielsen, Nancy. Teen Alcoholism. LC 90-66. (Illus.). 96p. (gr. 5-8). 1990. PLB 11.95 (ISBN 1-56006-121-9). Lucent Bks.

O'Neill, Catherine. Focus on Alcohol. Neuahaus, David, illus. 56p. (gr. 3-7). 1990. PLB 14.95 (ISBN 0-941477-96-7). TFC Bks MD.

O'Sullivan, Carol. Alcohol: Understanding Words in Context. (Illus.). 32p. (gr. 3-6). 1990. PLB 8.95 (ISBN 0-89908-634-9). Greenhaven.

Porterfield, Kay M. Coping with an Alcoholic Parent. rev. ed. (gr. 7-12). 1990. 12.95 (ISBN 0-8239-1143-8). Rosen Group.

Rosenberg, Maxine B. Not My Family: Sharing the Truth about Alcoholism. LC 88-10468. 112p. (gr. 4-7). 1988. 12.95 (ISBN 0-02-777911-4, Bradbury Pr). Macmillan Child Grp.

Ross, Ron. When I Grow Up I Want to Be an Adult: Christ-Centered Recovery Workbook for Adult Children. Halvorson, Ronald S. & Deilgat, Valerie B., eds. LC 90-60660. 205p. (Orig.). (gr. 12). 1990. wkbk. 12.95 (ISBN 0-941405-15-X). Recovery SD.

Ryan, Elizabeth A. Straight Talk about Drugs & Alcohol. 160p. 1989. 16.95x (ISBN 0-8160-1525-2). Facts on File.

Seixas, Judith S. Alcohol-What It Is, What It Does. Huffman, Tom, illus. LC 76-43344. 56p. (gr. 1-4). 1977. o.s.i 8.50 (ISBN 0-688-80080-7, Mulberry); PLB 11.88 (ISBN 0-688-84080-9, Mulberry). Morrow.

—Living with a Parent Who Drinks Too Much. LC 78-11108. 128p. (gr. 3-6). 1979. 11.95 (ISBN 0-688-80196-X); PLB 11.88 (ISBN 0-688-84196-1). Greenwillow.

Shuker, Nancy. Everything You Need to Know about an Alcoholic Parent. Rosen, Ruth, ed. (gr. 7-12). 1989. PLB 12.95 (ISBN 0-8239-1011-3). Rosen Group.

Silverstein, Alvin & Silverstein, Virginia B. Alcoholism. LC 75-17938. 128p. (gr. 5-8). 1975. PLB 12.89 (ISBN 0-397-31648-8, Lipp Jr Bks); pap. 3.50 o. p. (ISBN 0-397-31649-6, JBL-J, Lipp Jr Bks). HarpC Child Bks.

Silverstein, Herma. Alcoholism. (Illus.). 96p. (gr. 9-12). 1990. PLB 12.40 (ISBN 0-531-10879-1). Watts.

Snyder, Anne. Kids & Drinking. Harlan, Susan, illus. 47p. (gr. 3-7). 1977. pap. 4.95 (ISBN 0-89638-010-6, 03061). CompCare.

Stronck, David. Alcohol-The Real Story. Nelson, Mary & Clark, Kay, eds. Ransom, Robert D., illus. 30p. (gr. 5-8). 1987. pap. text ed. 2.95 (ISBN 0-941816-35-4). Network Pubns.

Taylor, Barbara. Everything You Need to Know about Alcohol. Glassman, Richard, photos by. (Illus.). 64p. (gr. 7-12). 1989. 12.95 (ISBN 0-8239-0813-5). Rosen Group.

Turck, Mary. Alcohol & Tobacco. LC 88-20253. (Illus.). 48p. (gr. 5-6). 1988. PLB 10.95 (ISBN 0-89686-411-1, Crestwood Hse). Macmillan Child Grp.

Twist, Clint. Facts on Alcohol. (Illus.). 32p. (gr. 5-6). 1989. PLB 11.90 (ISBN 0-531-10821-X). Watts.

Vigna, Judith. I Wish Daddy Didn't Drink So Much. Fay, Ann, ed. (Illus.). 40p. (ps-3). 1988. PLB 12.95 (ISBN 0-8075-3523-0). A Whitman.

Ward, Brian R. Alcohol Abuse. Franklin Watts Ltd., ed. (Illus.). 32p. (gr. 7-12). 1988. PLB 12.40 (ISBN 0-531-10359-5). Watts.

What's "Drunk," Mama? (Illus.). 30p. (ps-5). 1988. 1.25 (ISBN 0-910034-64-8); cassette avail. (ISBN 0-910034-65-6); booklet & cassette pkg. 5.00. Al-Anon.

Wilson, Cliff. Excerpts of Sobriety: An Alcoholismistic Expression - Special Adolescent Edition. Wilson, Pamela & Hubel, Gordon, eds. Wilson, Jerry, illus. LC 87-90540. 45p. (gr. 4-12). 1987. pap. 4.95x (ISBN 0-939847-06-X). Sobriety Pr.

ALCOHOLISM–FICTION

Bauer, Marion D. Shelter from the Wind. LC 75-28184. 112p. (gr. 6 up). 1979. 13.95 (ISBN 0-395-28890-8, Clarion). HM.

Brooks, Bruce. No Kidding. LC 88-22057. 224p. (gr. 7 up). 1989. 13.95 (ISBN 0-06-020722-1); PLB 13.89 (ISBN 0-06-020723-X). HarpC Child Bks.

Kenny, Kevin & Krull, Helen. Sometimes My Mom Drinks Too Much. Cogancherry, Helen, illus. Neidengard, Ted, intro. by. LC 80-14515. (Illus.). 32p. (gr. k-6). 1980. PLB 16.67 (ISBN 0-8172-1366-X). Raintree Pubs.

Nickerson, Sara. Peter Parrot, Private Eye. Bagley, Michael, illus. Counts, Sandra J., frwd. by. LC 88-63800. (Illus.). 43p. (Orig.). (gr. 2-6). 1988. pap. 5.95 (ISBN 0-935529-07-1). Comprehen Health Educ.

Tapp, Kathy K. Smoke from the Chimney. 180p. (gr. 4-7). 1989. pap. 3.95 (ISBN 0-689-71323-1, Aladdin). Macmillan Child Grp.

Woodson, Jacqueline. Dear One. (gr. 4-7). 1991. 14.00 (ISBN 0-385-30416-1). Delacorte.

ALCOTT, LOUISA MAY, 1832-1888

Alcott, Louisa May. Louisa's Wonder Book: An Unknown Alcott Juvenile. Stern, Madeline B., ed. LC 76-358119. (Illus.). 1975. Repr. of 1870 ed. 7.50 (ISBN 0-916699-08-0). CMU Clarke Hist Lib.

Burke, Kathleen. Louisa May Alcott. Horner, Matina, intro. by. (Illus.). 112p. (gr. 5 up). 1988. lib. bdg. 17.95 (ISBN 1-55546-637-0). Chelsea Hse.

Greene, Carol. Louisa May Alcott: Author, Nurse, Suffragette. LC 84-5902. (Illus.). 112p. (gr. 4 up). 1984. lib. bdg. 17.27 (ISBN 0-516-03208-9). Childrens.

Johnston, Norma. Louisa May: The World & Works of Louisa May Alcott. LC 91-7896. (Illus.). 224p. (gr. 6 up). 1991. 15.95 (ISBN 0-02-747705-3, Four Winds). Macmillan Child Grp.

Mcgill, Marcy. Louisa May Alcott. (Orig.). (gr. k-6). 1988. pap. 2.95 (ISBN 0-440-40022-8, YB). Dell.

Meigs, Cornelia. Invincible Louisa. LC 68-21174. (Illus.). (gr. 7 up). 1968. 16.95 (ISBN 0-316-56590-3). Little.

—Invincible Louisa: The Story of Louisa May Alcott. 256p. 1987. pap. 2.50 (ISBN 0-590-41937-4). Scholastic Inc.

Santrey, Laurence. Louisa May Alcott, Young Writer. Speidel, Sandra, illus. LC 85-1086. 48p. (gr. 4-6). 1986. lib. bdg. 10.79 (ISBN 0-8167-0563-1); pap. text ed. 2.95 (ISBN 0-8167-0564-X). Troll Assocs.

ALEUTIAN ISLANDS–FICTION

Taylor, John. Volcano in Our Yard. (Illus.). (gr. 2-5). 1975. 4.95 (ISBN 0-686-11663-1). Thompson's.

ALEXANDER THE GREAT, 356-323 B.C.

Alexander, the Great: In Arabic. (Illus.). (gr. 8-12). 3.50x (ISBN 0-86685-183-6). Intl Bk Ctr.

Harris, Nathaniel. Alexander the Great & the Greeks. LC 85-71725. (Illus.). 64p. (gr. k-3). 1986. PLB 12.40 (ISBN 0-531-18030-1, Pub. by Bookwright Pr). Watts.

Lasker, Joe. The Great Alexander the Great. (ps-3). 1990. pap. 3.95 (ISBN 0-14-054318-X, Puffin). Puffin Bks.

ALEXANDRA, CONSORT OF NICHOLAS 2ND, EMPEROR OF RUSSIA, 1872-1918

Massie, Robert K. Nicholas & Alexandra. LC 67-24627. (gr. 7 up). 1972. 29.95 (ISBN 0-689-10177-5, Atheneum). Macmillan.

ALGAE

Greenaway, Theresa. First Plants. LC 90-10003. (Illus.). 48p. (gr. 5-9). 1990. PLB 18.60 (ISBN 0-8114-2734-X). Steck-V.

Kavaler, Lucy E. Green Magic: Algae Rediscovered. Helmer, Jean C., illus. LC 81-43872. 128p. (gr. 5 up). 1983. 12.95 (ISBN 0-690-04221-3, Crowell Jr Bks). HarpC Child Bks.

ALGEBRA

see also Numbers Theory

Bureloff, Morris. Algebra Acrobatic Puzzles. (Illus.). (gr. 7-12). 1988. pap. 6.95 (ISBN 0-918932-93-9). Activity Resources.

Churchill, Eric R. Algebra Flipper. 49p. (gr. 5 up). 1989. Repr. of 1987 ed. trade edition 5.95 (ISBN 1-878383-03-5). C Lee Pubns.

CMSP Projects. Prealgebra. rev. ed. (Illus.). 101p. pap. text ed. write for info. (ISBN 0-942851-00-5). CMSP Projects.

Edmondson, Amy. Success Through Algebra. (gr. 8-12). 1989. 24.95 (ISBN 0-945525-12-5). Supercamp.

Laycock, Mary & Schadler, Reuben. Algebra in Concrete. (gr. 6-10). 1973. pap. 6.95 (ISBN 0-918932-00-9). Activity Resources.

McCabe, J. L. Everyday Algebra. 133p. (Orig.). 1987. pap. text ed. 13.95 (ISBN 0-942465-07-5, 2 212 939). Everyday Bks.

Radvany, Ruth, et al. Intermediate Algebra Study Aid. 1974. pap. 2.50 (ISBN 0-87738-038-4). Youth Ed.

Stallings, Pat. Puzzling Your Way into Algebra. new ed. Stallings, Pat, illus. (gr. 7-10). 1978. pap. text ed. 6.95 (ISBN 0-918932-58-0). Activity Resources.

Wohlberg, Myrna F., et al. Elementary Algebra Study Aid. 1980. pap. 2.50 (ISBN 0-87738-037-6). Youth Ed.

ALGERIA

Hostetler, Marian. Fear in Algeria. Converse, James, illus. LC 79-18132. 128p. (gr. 5-10). 1979. pap. 3.95 (ISBN 0-8361-1905-3). Herald Pr.

McDowall, David. Algeria. (Illus.). (gr. 5 up). 1988. 14.95 (ISBN 0-222-00963-2). Chelsea Hse.

ALIENS

see also Citizenship

Crosby, Nina E. & Marten, Elizabeth H. Don't Teach Let Me Learn about Presidents, of the U. S. People, Genealogy, Immigrants. (Illus.). 80p. (Orig.). (gr. 3-9). 1979. pap. 8.95 tchr's. enrichment manual (ISBN 0-914634-67-4, 7912). DOK Pubs.

Freedman, Russell. Immigrant Kids. LC 79-20060. 64p. (gr. 3-7). 1980. 13.95 (ISBN 0-525-32538-7, DCB). Dutton Child Bks.

Hartmann, Edward G. American Immigration. LC 79-12998. (Illus.). 120p. (gr. 5 up). 1979. PLB 11.95 (ISBN 0-8225-0232-1); pap. 3.95 (ISBN 0-8225-1030-8). Lerner Pubns.

Kurelek, William & Engelhart, Margaret S. They Sought a New World: The Story of European Immigration to North America. (Illus.). 48p. (gr. 4 up). 1985. 14.95 (ISBN 0-88776-172-0, Dist. by U of Toronto Pr); pap. 7.95 (ISBN 0-88776-213-1). Tundra Bks.

Mizumura, Kazue. If I Were a Cricket... Mizumura, Kazue, illus. LC 73-3495. 32p. (ps-3). 1973. PLB 13.89 (ISBN 0-690-00076-6, Crowell Jr Bks). HarpC Child Bks.

Perrin, Linda. Immigrants from the Far East. LC 80-65840. 192p. 1980. 12.95 (ISBN 0-385-28115-3). Delacorte.

Robbins, Albert. Immigrants from Northern Europe. LC 80-68741. 224p. 1982. 9.95 (ISBN 0-385-28138-2). Delacorte.

ALIENS–FICTION

Buss, Fran L. Journey of the Sparrows. 160p. (gr. 5-9). 1991. 14.95 (ISBN 0-525-67362-8, Lodestar Bks). Dutton Child Bks.

Garehime, Ed. Mr. Jelly Bean, No. 1. 2nd ed. American Red Cross Staff, tr. Garehime, Marianne, illus. LC 77-82261. 64p. (ps-4). 1979. 9.95 (ISBN 0-918822-01-7). Deem Corp.

ALL FOOLS' DAY

see April Fools' Day

ALL HALLOWS' EVE

see Halloween

ALLEGORIES

see also Fables; Parables

Bunting, Eve. Terrible Things: An Allegory of the Holocaust. rev. ed. Gammell, Stephen, illus. 24p. (gr. 1-4). 1989. Repr. of 1980 ed. 10.95 (ISBN 0-8276-0325-8). JPS Phila.

Bunyan, John. Pilgrim's Progress. (gr. 9 up). 1968. pap. 1.95 (ISBN 0-8049-0183-X, CL-183). Airmont.

Butler, Samuel. Erewhon. Threapleton, M. M., intro. by. (gr. 11 up). pap. 1.25 (ISBN 0-8049-0130-9, CL-130). Airmont.

Wagener, Gerda. Leo the Lion. Ignatowicz, Nina, tr. from GER. Michl, Reinhard, illus. LC 90-46272. 32p. (gr. k-3). 1991. 14.95 (ISBN 0-06-021656-5); PLB 14.89 (ISBN 0-06-021657-3). HarpC Child Bks.

ALLERGY

Dees, Susan C. Allergy. Head, J. J., ed. Imrick, Ann T., illus. LC 86-72199. 16p. (Orig.). (gr. 10 up). 1988. pap. text ed. 2.15 (ISBN 0-89278-169-6, 45-9769). Carolina Biological.

Frazier, Claude A. Sniff, Sniff Al-er-gee. new ed. Carlson, Paul H., illus. LC 76-27985. (gr. k-3). 1978. 6.75 (ISBN 0-910812-19-5); pap. 3.25 (ISBN 0-910812-24-1). Johnny Reads.

Seixas, Judith. Allergies--What They Are, What They Do. Huffman, Tom, illus. LC 90-30753. 56p. (gr. 1 up). 1991. 12.95 (ISBN 0-688-09638-7); PLB 12.88 (ISBN 0-688-08877-5). Greenwillow.

Silverstein, Alvin & Silverstein, Virginia B. Allergies. Cohen, Sheldon, intro. by. LC 77-1284. (gr. 6-9). 1977. 12.95 (ISBN 0-397-31758-1, Lipp Jr Bks). HarpC Child Bks.

ALLIGATORS

Aliki. Use Your Head, Dear. Aliki, illus. LC 82-11911. 48p. (gr. k-3). 1983. 13.95 (ISBN 0-688-01811-4); PLB 13.88 (ISBN 0-688-01812-2). Greenwillow.

Barrett, Norman. Cocodrilos y Caimanes. LC 88-51517. (SPA., Illus.). 32p. (gr. k-4). 1991. PLB 11.40 (ISBN 0-531-07919-8). Watts.

—Crocodiles & Alligators. (Illus.). 32p. (gr. k-6). 1990. 11.40 (ISBN 0-531-10705-1). Watts.

Bender, Lionel. Crocodiles & Alligators. FS-Aladdin Staff, ed. LC 88-50513. (Illus.). 32p. (gr. 1-6). 1988. PLB 11.90 (ISBN 0-531-17100-0, Gloucester Pr). Watts.

—First Sight: Crocodiles & Alligators. 1990. pap. 3.95 (ISBN 0-531-17258-9). Watts.

Bright, Michael. Alligators & Crocodiles. (Illus.). 32p. (gr. 5-8). 1990. PLB 11.90 (ISBN 0-531-17245-7). Watts.

Butterworth, Christine. Alligators. LC 90-9927. (Illus.). 32p. (gr. 1-4). 1990. PLB 14.64 (ISBN 0-8114-2639-4). Steck-V.

Dow, Lesley. Alligators & Crocodiles. 72p. 1990. 17.95x (ISBN 0-8160-2273-9). Facts on File.

Farre, Marie. Crocodiles & Alligators. Matthews, Sarah, tr. from FRE. Wallis, Diz, illus. LC 87-31804. 38p. (gr. k-5). 1988. 4.95 (ISBN 0-944589-01-4, 014). Young Discovery Lib.

Knight, David. I Can Read About Alligators & Crocodiles. LC 78-73733. (Illus.). (gr. 2-4). 1979. pap. 1.95 (ISBN 0-89375-200-2). Troll Assocs.

Martin, L. Alligators. (Illus.). 24p. (gr. k-5). 1989. lib. bdg. 11.93 (ISBN 0-86592-579-8). Rourke Corp.

Morrison, Susan D. The Alligator. LC 83-21034. (Illus.). 48p. (gr. 4-5). 1984. PLB 10.95 (ISBN 0-89686-242-9, Crestwood Hse). Macmillan Child Grp.

Petty, Kate. Crocodiles & Alligators. Johnson, Karen, illus. 1990. pap. 2.95 (ISBN 0-531-15153-0). Watts.

Rothaus, Jim. Alligators & Crocodiles. 24p. (gr. 3). 1988. 11.95 (ISBN 0-88682-220-3). Creative Ed.

Serventy, Vincent. Crocodile & Alligator. LC 84-15890. (Illus.). 24p. (gr. k-5). 1985. PLB 13.32 (ISBN 0-8172-2404-1). Raintree Pubs.

Shaw, Evelyn. Alligator. Zweifel, Frances, illus. LC 70-183157. 64p. (gr. k-3). 1972. 11.95 (ISBN 0-06-025556-0). HarpC Child Bks.

Stone, Lynn M. Alligators & Crocodiles. LC 89-9985. 48p. (gr. k-4). 1989. PLB 14.60 (ISBN 0-516-01170-7); pap. 4.95 (ISBN 0-516-41170-5). Childrens.

Taylor, Dave. The Alligator & the Everglades. (Illus.). 32p. (gr. 3-4). 1990. lib. bdg. 14.95 (ISBN 0-86505-367-7); pap. 7.95 (ISBN 0-86505-397-9). Crabtree Pub Co.

Wildlife Education, Ltd. Staff. Alligators & Crocodiles. Hoopes, Barbara, illus. 20p. (Orig.). (gr. 5 up). 1984. pap. 2.25 (ISBN 0-937934-25-9). Wildlife Educ.

ALLIGATORS–FICTION

Dorros, Arthur. Alligator Shoes. Dorros, Arthur, illus. LC 82-2409. (ps-k). 1982. 3.95 (ISBN 0-525-44001-1, Dutton). NAL-Dutton.

Eastman, Philip D. Flap Your Wings. Eastman, Philip D., illus. (ps-2). 1969. (Random Juv). Random.

Kinnell, Galway. How the Alligator Missed Breakfast. Munsinger, Lynn, illus. 32p. (gr. k-3). 1982. 8.95 (ISBN 0-395-32436-X). HM.

Kraus, Robert. Miss Gator's School House, 6 bks. Kraus, Robert, illus. (gr. k-3). 1989. Set, 48p. ea. lib. bdg. 53.88 (ISBN 0-671-94105-4); Set, 48p. ea. pap. 21.00 (ISBN 0-671-94106-2). Messner.

Mayer, Mercer. There's an Alligator under My Bed. LC 86-19944. (Illus.). 32p. (ps-3). 1987. 13.95 (ISBN 0-8037-0374-0); PLB 11.89 (ISBN 0-8037-0375-9). Dial Bks Young.

Minarik, Else H. No Fighting, No Biting! Sendak, Maurice, illus. LC 58-5293. 64p. (gr. k-3). 1958. 11.95 (ISBN 0-06-024290-6); PLB 11.89 (ISBN 0-06-024291-4). HarpC Child Bks.

Mozelle, Shirley. Zack's Alligator. Watts, James, illus. LC 88-32069. 64p. (gr. k-3). 1989. 11.95 (ISBN 0-06-024309-0); PLB 11.89 (ISBN 0-06-024310-4). HarpC Child Bks.

Nickl, Peter. Crocodile, Crocodile. Schroeder, Binnette, illus. Cutler, Ebbitt, tr. (Illus.). 32p. 1989. 11.95 (ISBN 0-940793-33-4, Pub. by Crocodile Bks); pap. 6.95 (ISBN 0-940793-32-6, Pub. by Crocodile Bks). Interlink Pub.

Olson, Margaret J. Aloysious Alligator. 2nd ed. Olson, Margaret J., illus. (gr. k-2). 1980. pap. 3.00 (ISBN 0-934876-14-2). Creative Storytime.

Rice, James. Gaston Goes to Nashville. Rice, James, illus. 32p. (gr. k-6). 1985. 11.95 (ISBN 0-88289-477-3). Pelican.

—Gaston Goes to Texas. Rice, James, illus. LC 78-12490. 32p. (ps-6). 1978. 11.95 (ISBN 0-88289-204-5). Pelican.

—Gaston Lays an Offshore Pipeline. LC 79-20335. (Illus.). (gr. 1-6). 1979. 11.95 (ISBN 0-88289-177-4). Pelican.

—Gaston the Green-Nosed Alligator. (Illus.). 40p. (gr. 1-6). 1974. 11.95 (ISBN 0-88289-049-2). Pelican.

Roberts, Jo-Anna. Alligator & the Toothfairy. Kinnell, Shannon, illus. 56p. (ps-2). 1991. 11.50g (ISBN 1-879212-00-5). Desert Star Intl.

Scott, Jack D. Alligator. Sweet, Ozzie, photos by. (Illus.). 64p. (gr. 4 up). 1984. 12.95 (ISBN 0-399-21011-3, Putnam). Putnam Pub Group.

Searcy, Margaret Z. Alli Gator Gets a Bump on His Nose. Wise, Lu Celia, illus. LC 78-61369. (gr. 2-4). 1978. 7.50 (ISBN 0-916620-20-4). Portals Pr.

Stevenson, James. Monty. Stevenson, James, illus. LC 78-11409. 32p. (gr. k-3). 1979. PLB 12.88 (ISBN 0-688-84209-7). Greenwillow.

Stone, Kazuko G. Goodnight Twinklegator. (ps-3). 1990. pap. 12.95 (ISBN 0-590-43183-8). Scholastic Inc.

Van Caster, Nancy. An Alligator Lives in Benjamin's House. Gottlieb, Dale, illus. 32p. (ps-2). 1990. 13.95 (ISBN 0-399-21489-5, Philomel Bks). Putnam Pub Group.

Waber, Bernard. Lyle & the Birthday Party. (Illus.). 48p. (gr. k-3). 1973. pap. 4.95 (ISBN 0-395-17451-1, 4-97508, Sandpiper). HM.

Wiles, Mary J. The Alligator with a Toothache. (ps-3). 1978. pap. 1.75 (ISBN 0-8198-0355-3). Dghtrs St Paul.

ALLOYS

see also Metallurgy

ALMANACS

see also Calendars; Yearbooks

Anthony, Susan C. Facts Plus: An Almanac of Essential Information. LC 91-70863. (Illus.). 250p. (Orig.). (gr. 4-8). 1991. pap. 15.95 (ISBN 1-879478-00-5); 3 wire bound 16.95 (ISBN 1-879478-01-3). Instr Res Co.
FACTS PLUS: AN ALMANAC OF ESSENTIAL INFORMATION is a concise, authoritative, user-friendly reference book compiled with students & classroom teachers in mind. Its clear, easy-to-read format, large type & 3,876 word index facilitate the learning of skills for information literacy. Included are sections on Time & Space; Science & Health; The Earth & Its People; The United States; Maps (a short atlas); Libraries & Books; The English Language; Writing; Music & Art; Math & Numbers; a Handbook of how-to information & a section of sources & notes with additional information. FACTS PLUS would be especially useful for educators emphasizing geography, integrating whole language across the curriculum, or utilizing real statistics to teach math problem solving. The Handbook includes guidelines for etiquette, interviewing, writing research reports, making speeches, & taking tests. This book is recommended for classrooms & libraries, for children in grades 4-8, for adults learning English or basic skills, or for anyone needing a source of quick, up-to-date reference information. FACTS PLUS would be an excellent gift from parents or grandparents to their school-aged children. Quantity discounts are available to educational institutions for classroom sets.
Reviewed in June 1, 1991 BOOKLIST/REFERENCE BOOKS BULLETIN.
Publisher Provided Annotation.

Aylesworth, Thomas G. Kids' World Almanac of the United States. 288p. (gr. 3-7). 1990. 14.95 (ISBN 0-88687-479-3); pap. 6.95 (ISBN 0-88687-478-5). Pharos Bks NY.

Elwood, Ann & Madigan, Carol O. The Macmillan Book of Fascinating Facts: An Almanac for Kids. Martin, Dick, illus. LC 88-22844. 448p. (gr. 4 up). 1989. 16.95 (ISBN 0-02-733461-9, Mcmillan Child Bk). Macmillan Child Grp.

Elwood, Ann, et al. Macmillan Illustrated Almanac for Kids. Barrett, Lindsey, illus. LC 81-82099. 400p. (gr. 4 up). 1984. (Mcmillan Child Bk); pap. 7.95 (ISBN 0-02-043040-X). Macmillan Child Grp.

—Macmillan Illustrated Almanac for Kids. Barrett, Lindsey, illus. 448p. (gr. 4 up). 1986. pap. 10.95 (ISBN 0-02-043100-7, Aladdin). Macmillan Child Grp.

Facts & Lists. 192p. (gr. 3-7). 1988. pap. 12.95 (ISBN 0-7460-0026-X). EDC.

Franklin, Benjamin. Poor Richard's Almanack. (gr. 7 up). dust jacket 9.95 (ISBN 0-88088-918-7). Peter Pauper.

Grisewood, John. The Doubleday Children's Almanac. Beal, George, ed. LC 85-16263. (Illus.). 320p. (gr. 3 up). 1986. 17.95 (ISBN 0-385-23408-2). Doubleday.

Lipkind, William. Days to Remember. Snyder, Jerome, illus. (gr. 3 up). 1961. 10.95 (ISBN 0-8392-3006-0). Astor-Honor.

McLoone-Basta, Margo & Siegel, Alice. The Second Kids' World Almanac of Records & Facts. World Almanac Staff, ed. 288p. (gr. 3-9). 1987. 14.95 (ISBN 0-88687-397-5); pap. 6.95 (ISBN 0-88687-317-7). Pharos Bks NY.

Siegel, Alice & McLoone, Margo. Kids' World Almanac of Records & Facts. (gr. 3-7). 1986. pap. 6.95 (ISBN 0-88687-319-3). Pharos Bks NY.

Zimmerman. Book of Records. (Illus.). 48p. (gr. 1-7). 1978. 5.95 (ISBN 0-448-47626-6, G&D); PLB 5.99 (ISBN 0-448-13026-2). Putnam Pub Group.

ALPHABET

see also Writing

Amery. Alphabet Book. (gr. k-2). 1979. (Usborne-Hayes); PLB 11.96 (ISBN 0-88110-065-X); pap. 2.95 (ISBN 0-86020-358-1). EDC.

Beller, Janet. A-B-C-ing: An Action Alphabet. Beller, Janet, illus. LC 83-23925. 32p. (ps-1). 1984. pap. text ed. 8.95 (ISBN 0-517-55208-6). Crown.

Blankholm, Robert F. Twenty-Six Friends: The Shape of the Alphabet Letters. 2nd ed. LC 90-71355. (Illus.). 64p. 1990. pap. 7.95 (ISBN 0-933499-02-7). Stagecoach Rd Pr.

Borba, Michele & Ungaro, Dan. The Complete Letter Book. 112p. (gr-3). 1980. 9.95 (ISBN 0-916456-80-3, GA 182). Good Apple.

Bumgardner, Joyce C. My Writing Book. 1989. pap. 2.50 (ISBN 0-590-41785-1). Scholastic Inc.

Crowther, Robert. The Most Amazing Hide-&-Seek Alphabet Book. LC 77-79334. (Illus.). (ps-1). 1978. pap. 13.95 (ISBN 0-670-48996-4). Viking Child Bks.

Domanska, Janina. A Was an Angler. LC 88-35589. (Illus.). 32p. (ps up) 1991. 13.95 (ISBN 0-688-06990-8); PLB 13.88 (ISBN 0-688-06991-6). Greenwillow.

Dowdell, D. Secrets of the ABCs. LC 65-22301. (Illus.). 64p. (gr. 2 up). 1968. PLB 10.95 (ISBN 0-87783-035-5). Oddo.

Edens, Cooper. The Glorious ABC. LC 90-30566. (Illus.). 40p. 1990. 14.95 (ISBN 0-689-31605-4, Atheneum Child Bk). Macmillan Child Grp.

Everything from A to Z: Learning about Letters & Sounds. (ps-3). pap. write for info. incl. cassette (ISBN 0-307-13801-1, Golden Bks). Western Pub.

Fisher, Leonard E. Alphabet Art: Thirteen ABCs from Around the World. LC 84-28752. (Illus.). 64p. (gr. 3-7). 1984. Repr. of 1978 ed. 14.95 (ISBN 0-02-735230-7, Four Winds). Macmillan Child Grp.

Fitzgerald, Phyllis. Alphabets. LC 87-51494. (Illus.). 30p. (gr. k-2). 1988. 6.95 (ISBN 1-55523-130-6). Winston-Derek.

Geringer, Laura. The Cow Is Mooing Anyhow. Zimmer, Dirk, illus. LC 85-45251. 40p. (ps-4). 1991. 14.95 (ISBN 0-06-021986-6); PLB 14.89 (ISBN 0-06-021987-4). HarpC Child Bks.

Gregorich, Barbara. Capital Letters. Pape, Richard, illus. 24p. (gr. 3-4). 1980. wkbk. 2.95 (ISBN 0-89403-604-1). EDC.

Hawkins, Colin & Hawkins, Jacqui. Busy ABC. (ps-1). 1987. pap. 8.95 (ISBN 0-670-81153-X). Viking Child Bks.

Hoban, Tana. Twenty-Six Letters & Ninety-Nine Cents. LC 86-11993. (Illus.). 32p. (ps-3). 1987. 14.95 (ISBN 0-688-06361-6); PLB 14.88 (ISBN 0-688-06362-4). Greenwillow.

Isadora, Rachel. City Seen from A to Z. Isadora, Rachel, illus LC 82-11966. 32p. (gr. k-3). 1983. PLB 11.88 (ISBN 0-688-01803-3). Greenwillow.

Johnson, Laura R. The Teddy Bear ABC. Sanford, Margaret L., illus. LC 84-144481. 60p. (ps-2). 1982. pap. 7.95 (ISBN 0-914676-86-5). Green Tiger Pr.

Kaye, Catherine B. Word Works: Why the Alphabet Is a Kid's Best Friend. Weston, Martha, illus. 128p. (gr. 4 up). 1985. 14.95 (ISBN 0-316-48376-1); pap. 7.95 (ISBN 0-316-48375-3). Little.

Lear, Edward. An Edward Lear Alphabet. Newsom, Carol, illus. LC 82-10037. (ps-3). 1986. 3.95 (ISBN 0-688-06523-6, Mulberry). Morrow.

Lewis, Shari & Martin, Norman. Shari Lewis' Lamb Chop in the Land of No Letters. 3.50 (ISBN 1-55802-292-9). Lynx Bks.

Lionni, Leo. Letters. LC 84-10084. (Illus.). 12p. (ps). 1985. 3.95 (ISBN 0-394-87001-8, Pant Bks Young). Pantheon.

Lobel, Arnold. On Market Street. Lobel, Anita, illus. LC 80-21418. 40p. (gr. k-3). 1981. 13.95 (ISBN 0-688-80309-1); PLB 13.88 (ISBN 0-688-84309-3). Greenwillow.

Mahiri, Jabari. The Day They Stole the Letter J. Carter, Dorothy, illus. (Orig.). (gr. 3-5). 1981. pap. 3.95 (ISBN 0-88378-084-4). Third World.

Patton, Sally. Alphabetics: A History of Our Alphabet. rev. ed. 96p. (gr. 2-8). 1989. pap. text ed. 14.95 (ISBN 0-913705-40-3, ZS06-V). Zephyr Pr AZ.

Potter, Beatrix. Peter Rabbit's ABC. Potter, Beatrix, illus. 48p. (ps-2). 1987. 6.95 (ISBN 0-7232-3423-X). Warne.

Rice, James. Cajun Alphabet: Full-Color Edition. (Illus.). 64p. (ps-8). 1991. 16.95 (ISBN 0-88289-822-1). Pelican.

—Texas Alphabet. Rice, James, illus. 132p. (gr. k-5). 1988. 12.95 (ISBN 0-88289-692-X). Pelican.

Taulbee, Annette. Alphabet. (Illus.). 24p. (ps-k). 1986. 3.98 (ISBN 0-86734-059-2, FS-3051). Schaffer Pubns.

—Alphabet Dot-to-Dot. (Illus.). 24p. (ps-k). 1986. 3.98 (ISBN 0-86734-062-2, FS-3054). Schaffer Pubns.

Time-Life Books Editors. The Great ABC Treasure Hunt: A Hidden Picture Alphabet Book. (Illus.). 56p. (ps-2). 1991. write for info. (ISBN 0-8094-9254-7); lib. bdg. write for info. (ISBN 0-8094-9255-5). Time-Life.

Warren, Jean, et al, eds. Alphabet Theme-a-Saurus: The Great Big Book of Letter Recognition. Mohrmann, Gary, illus. LC 90-71272. 280p. 1991. pap. text ed. 19.95 (ISBN 0-911019-38-3). Warren Pub Hse.

Wheeler, Sharon, ed. Alphabet. Koeller, Neena C., illus. (ps). 1984. wkbk 1.95 (ISBN 0-916119-02-5). Creat Teach Pr.

ALPHABET BOOKS

Here are entered A B C books.

A B C Board Book. (ps). 1958. bds. 3.95 (ISBN 0-448-03075-6, G&D). Putnam Pub Group.

ABC. 32p. (ps-k). 1986. write for info. (ISBN 0-307-05160-9, Pub. by Golden Bks). Western Pub.

ABC. (Illus.). (ps-k). bds. 3.50 (ISBN 0-7214-9582-6). Ladybird Bks.

ABC. (Illus.). (ps-2). 1.95 (ISBN 0-7214-5182-9). Ladybird Bks.

ABC. (Illus.). (ps-k). 3.50 (ISBN 0-7214-1114-2). Ladybird Bks.

ABC. (Illus.). (ps-2). 3.50 (ISBN 0-7214-0513-4). Ladybird Bks.

ABC. (Illus.). (ps). 1992. 3.50 (ISBN 0-7214-5206-X). Ladybird Bks.

ABC. (Illus.). (ps). pap. 1.25 (ISBN 0-7214-9553-2). Ladybird Bks.

ABC & You. (ps-k). 1990. text ed. 3.95 cased (ISBN 0-7214-5274-4). Ladybird Bks.

ABC Pack, No. 476. (Illus.). (ps-k). incl. chart, activity bk. 6.95 (ISBN 0-7214-5165-9). Ladybird Bks.

ABC's in Arabic. (Illus.). (ps-3). 3.50x (ISBN 0-86685-180-1). Intl Bk Ctr.

Abranson, Lillian. Hanukkah ABC. (Illus.). (gr. 3-7). 1968. pap. 5.00 (ISBN 0-914080-60-1). Shulsinger Sales.

Adams, Pam, illus. I-Spy ABC. 16p. (ps-2). 1978. 8.00 (ISBN 0-85953-066-3, Pub. by Child's Play England). Childs Play.

Agard, John. The Calypso Alphabet. Bent, Jennifer, illus. 32p. (ps-2). 1989. 13.95 (ISBN 0-8050-1177-3). H Holt & Co.

Allington, Richard L. Letters. Garcia, Tom, illus. LC 82-9785. 32p. (gr. k-3). 1985. PLB 15.33 (ISBN 0-8172-1384-8); pap. 9.27 (ISBN 0-8172-2480-7). Raintree Pubs.

Anglund, Joan W. In a Pumpkin Shell. Anglund, Joan W., illus. LC 60-10243. (ps-2). 1977. pap. 3.95 (ISBN 0-15-644425-9, VoyB). HarBraceJ.

—In a Pumpkin Shell: A Mother Goose ABC. Anglund, Joan W., illus. LC 60-10243. (gr. k-3). 1960. 10.95 (ISBN 0-15-238269-0, HJ). HarBraceJ.

Animal Alphabet. (Illus.). (ps-2). 3.50 (ISBN 0-7214-0993-8). Ladybird Bks.

Animal Alphabet Book. (Illus.). (gr. k-3). 3.95 (ISBN 0-7214-9532-X). Ladybird Bks.

Anno, Mitsumasa. Anno's Alphabet: An Adventure in Imagination. Anno, Mitsumasa, illus. LC 73-21652. 64p. (gr. k up). 1975. 15.95 (ISBN 0-690-00540-7, Crowell Jr Bks); PLB 15.89 (ISBN 0-690-00541-5). HarpC Child Bks.

Auerbach, Stevanne. The Alphabet Tree. Patch, Lila, illus. LC 85-51922. 58p. (gr. k-2). 1986. pap. 4.95 (ISBN 0-932433-15-4). Windswept Hse.

Azarian, Mary. A Farmer's Alphabet. LC 80-84938. 56p. (ps-2). 1981. 14.95 (ISBN 0-87923-394-X); pap. 12.95 (ISBN 0-87923-397-4). Godine.

—Farmers Alphabet Junior. LC 80-84938. 64p. 1985. pap. 7.95 (ISBN 0-87923-589-6). Godine.

Baby's First ABC. 12p. (ps). 1978. 3.95 (ISBN 0-448-40864-3, G&D). Putnam Pub Group.

Banner, Angela. Ant & Bee & Kind Dog. Ward, Bryan, illus. 96p. (ps-1). 5.95 (ISBN 0-434-92960-3, Pub. by W Heinemann Ltd). Trafalgar Sq.

Barr, Marilyn. ABC Puppets. (Illus.). 64p. (ps-1). 1989. 6.95 (ISBN 0-912107-95-2, MM1912). Monday Morning Bks.

Barr, Marilynn. ABC Art. (Illus.). 64p. (ps-1). 1989. 6.95 (ISBN 0-912107-97-9, MM1914). Monday Morning Bks.

Bassett, Scott & Bassett, Tammy. Artemus & the Alphabet. Bassett, Scott, illus. 32p. (ps-k). 1980. 6.95x (ISBN 0-9605548-0-7); PLB 6.95x (ISBN 0-9605548-1-5). Bassett & Brush.

Beidwell, Norman. Clifford's ABC. (ps-3). 1986. pap. 2.25 (ISBN 0-590-44286-4). Scholastic Inc.

Benji's Book of ABC. (ps). 1976. bds. 5.50 (ISBN 0-904494-12-8, Brimax Bks). Borden.

Berenstain, Stan & Berenstain, Janice. The B Book. (Illus.). (ps-1). 1971. lib. bdg. 7.99 (ISBN 0-394-92324-3, Random Juv); PLB 6.99 (ISBN 0-685-04254-5). Random.

—C Is for Clown. (Illus.). (ps-1). 1972. (Random Juv); lib. bdg. 6.99 (ISBN 0-394-92492-4). Random.

Berger, Terry. Ben's ABC Day. Kandell, Alice, illus. LC 81-13754. 32p. (gr. k-3). 1982. PLB 14.88 (ISBN 0-688-00882-8). Lothrop.

Big ABC & Counting Book. (Illus.). (ps-k). 8.95 (ISBN 0-7214-7506-X). Ladybird Bks.

Blake, Quentin. Quentin Blake's ABC. Blake, Quentin, illus. LC 88-26621. 40p. (ps-1). 1989. 11.95 (ISBN 0-394-84149-2); PLB 12.99 (ISBN 0-394-94149-7). Knopf.

Bliss, Richard B., ed. Dinosaur ABC's Activity Book. rev. ed. Schmitt, Doug, illus. 32p. (gr. k-3). 1986. pap. 3.95 (ISBN 0-89051-113-6). Master Bks.

Bond, Susan. Ride with Me Through ABC. Lemke, Horst, illus. LC 67-19376. 32p. (ps-k). 6.95 (ISBN 0-87592-043-8). Scroll Pr.

Boynton, Sandra. Moo Baa La La La. Klimo, Kate, ed. Boynton, Sandra, illus. 14p. 1982. 3.95 (ISBN 0-671-44901-X, Little Simon). S&S Trade.

Bridwell, Norman. Clifford's ABC. Bridwell, Norman, illus. 32p. (ps-k). 1986. pap. 1.95 (ISBN 0-590-40453-9). Scholastic Inc.

Broomfield, Robert. Baby Animal ABC. (Orig.). (ps-k). 1968. pap. 3.50 (ISBN 0-14-050006-5, Penguin Bks). Viking Penguin.

Brown, Mik. Mik Brown's ABC. (Illus.). 32p. (ps-k). 1989. pap. 2.95 (ISBN 0-8249-8375-0). Ideals.

Brown, Ruth. Alphabet Times Four: An International ABC. 32p. 1991. 13.95 (ISBN 0-525-44831-4, SDCB). Dutton Child Bks.

Bustard, Anne. T Is for Texas. LC 89-35633. (Illus.). 32p. (ps-2). 1989. 12.95 (ISBN 0-89658-113-6). Voyageur Pr.

Carson, Patti & Dellosa, Janet. Alphabet Sounds & Pictures. Carson, Patti & Dellosa, Janet, illus. 32p. (ps-1). 1983. pap. 1.98 (ISBN 0-88724-003-8, CD-7004). Carson-Dellos.

—Letters & the Sounds They Make. Carson, Patti & Dellosa, Janet, illus. 21p. (gr. k-1). 1984. pap. 1.98 (ISBN 0-88724-074-7, CD-7017). CArson-Dellos.

Carson, Patti, et al. A to Z Alphabet Kids. (Illus.). 32p. (ps-1). 1984. pap. 1.98 (ISBN 0-88724-090-9, CD-7029). Carson-Dellos.

Chouinard, Roger & Chouinard, Mariko. Amazing Animal Alphabet Book. Chouinard, Roger, illus. LC 87-13692. 32p. (ps-3). 1988. 12.95 (ISBN 0-385-24029-5); pap. 13.99 (ISBN 0-385-24030-9). Doubleday.

Conran, Sebastian. My First ABC Book. Conran, Sebastian, illus. LC 87-14562. 64p. (ps-1). 1988. bds. 6.95 (ISBN 0-689-71198-0, Aladdin). Macmillan Child Grp.

Cook, Lynn. A Canadian ABC: An Alphabet Book for Kids. MacDonald, Thoreau, illus. 60p. 1990. pap. 8.95 (ISBN 0-921254-24-5, Pub. by Penumbra Pr CN). U of Toronto Pr.

---

well as to various colonial activities such as a fair, a ride in an oxcart, children's games, & a visit to Tarpley's Store. The inviting illustrations colorfully re-create authentic colonial clothing, architecture, agriculture, & animal husbandry. To order: Colonial Williamsburg Wholesale Sales, PO Box C, Williamsburg, VA 23187, (804) 220-7178.
Publisher Provided Annotation.

Coudron, Jill M. Alphabet Activities. (ps-3). 1982. pap. 10.95 (ISBN 0-8224-0297-1). Fearon Teach Aids.
—Alphabet Stories. (ps-3). 1982. pap. 10.95 (ISBN 0-8224-0299-8). Fearon Teach Aids.
Crews, Donald. We Read: A to Z. Crews, Donald, illus. LC 83-25453. 64p. (ps-1). 1984. 14.95 (ISBN 0-688-03843-3); PLB 14.88 (ISBN 0-688-03844-1). Greenwillow.
Crowther, Robert. The Most Amazing Hide-&-Seek Alphabet Book. LC 77-79334. (Illus.). (ps-1). 1978. pap. 13.95 (ISBN 0-670-48996-4). Viking Child Bks.
Daniel, Becky. Animals Love Their Alphabet. 32p. (ps-k). 1991. 7.95 (ISBN 0-86653-579-9). Good Apple.
Darling, Kathy. ABC Animal Crafts. 64p. (ps-2). 1988. 6.95 (ISBN 0-912107-77-4, MM940). Monday Morning Bks.
—Alphabet Crafts. 64p. (gr. k-2). 1985. 6.95 (ISBN 0-912107-32-4). Monday Morning Bks.
Davis, Jim. Garfield A to Z Zoo. Fentz, Mike & Kuhn, Dave, illus. LC 83-17697. 24p. (ps-5). 1984. pap. 1.25 (ISBN 0-394-86483-2, Random Juv). Random.
De Brunhoff, Laurent. Babar's ABC. LC 83-2987. (Illus.). 36p. (gr. k-1). 1983. PLB 10.99 (ISBN 0-394-95920-5); pap. 8.95 (ISBN 0-394-85920-0). Random.
Dellosa, Janet & Carson, Patti. The Letters A-Z. (Illus.). 32p. (ps-1). 1984. pap. 1.98 (ISBN 0-88724-093-3, CD-7032). Carson-Dellos.
Doolittle, Eileen. The Ark in the Attic: An Alphabet Adventure. Ockenga, Starr, photos by. LC 86-45534. (ps up). 1987. 19.95 (ISBN 0-87923-684-1). Godine.
Downie, Jill. Alphabet Puzzle. Downie, Jill, illus. LC 88-80278. 64p. (ps-1). 1988. 16.00 (ISBN 0-688-08044-8). Lothrop.
Dr. Seuss. Dr. Seuss's ABC. Dr. Seuss, illus. LC 63-9810. 72p. (gr. k-3). 1960. 6.95 (ISBN 0-394-80030-3); lib. bdg. 7.99 (ISBN 0-394-90030-8). Beginner.
—Dr. Seuss's ABC. (Illus.). 64p. (ps-1). 1988. pap. 6.95 bk. & cassette pkg. (ISBN 0-394-89784-6, Random Juv). Random.
Duke, Kate. The Guinea Pig ABC. Duke, Kate, illus. LC 83-1410. 32p. (ps-1). 1983. 12.95 (ISBN 0-525-44058-5, DCB). Dutton Child Bks.
—The Guinea Pig ABC. Duke, Kate, illus. 32p. (ps-1). 1986. pap. 3.95 (ISBN 0-525-44274-X, DCB). Dutton Child Bks.
Dulac, Glen J. The Color Coded Alphabet, an Alphabet for Easy Reading: The Alphabet as It Has Never Been Seen Before. Dulac, Glen J. & Dulac, John J., illus. (ps-2). 1990. 49.50 (ISBN 0-9628227-2-8). Desert Bks.
Eastman, Philip D. The Alphabet Book. Eastman, Philip D., illus. LC 73-16859. 32p. (ps-3). 1974. pap. 2.25 (ISBN 0-394-82818-6, Random Juv). Random.
Edades, Jean. An Animal ABC. Garibay, U. N., illus. (gr. 3-5). 1979. pap. 3.50 (ISBN 0-686-25221-7, Pub. by New Day Pub Philippines). Cellar.
Egermeier, Elsie E. Picture Story Bible ABC Book. rev. ed. (Illus.). (ps-1). 1963. 5.95 (ISBN 0-87162-262-9, D1703). Warner Pr.
Ehrlich, Doris. Animal Alphabet. 2nd ed. O'Rourke, Dawn M., illus. 36p. (ps-k). 1988. pap. text ed. 80.00 classroom pack (ISBN 0-932957-90-0); tchr's. ed. 4.50 (ISBN 0-932957-91-9); wkbk. 3.90 (ISBN 0-932957-89-7); wall posters 17.50 (ISBN 0-932957-96-X). Natl School.
Eichenberg, Fritz. Ape in a Cape: An Alphabet of Odd Animals. Eichenberg, Fritz, illus. LC 52-6908. (ps-3). 1952. 12.95 (ISBN 0-15-203722-5, HJ). HarBraceJ.
Emberley, Ed E. Ed Emberley's A. B. C. (Illus.). 56p. (gr. k-2). 1978. lib. bdg. 15.95 (ISBN 0-316-23408-7). Little.
Epstin, Vivian S. The ABCs of What a Girl Can Be. (Illus.). 32p. (ps-3). 1980. 5.95 (ISBN 0-9601002-2-9). V S Epstein.
Erickson, Gina C. Alphabet Tails. Foster, Kelli C., ed. Russell, Kerri G., illus. 73p. (gr. k-4). 1989. pap. 6.95 (ISBN 0-927971-00-3). OnTrack Inc.
F. J. Strauss Co., Inc. Staff. Alphabet. F. J. Strauss Co., Inc. Staff, illus. 10p. (ps). Date not set. write for info. vinyl (ISBN 0-945987-08-0). F J Strauss.
Ferguson, Dwayne. Afro-Bets A B C Coloring & Activity Book. (ps-3). 1989. pap. 3.95 (ISBN 0-940975-13-0). Just Us Bks.
Fisher, Leonard E. The ABC Exhibit. LC 90-6639. (Illus.). 32p. 1991. 15.95 (ISBN 0-02-735251-X, Mcmillan Child Bk). Macmillan Child Grp.
Fletcher, Cynthia H. My Jesus Pocketbook of ABC's. Sherman, Erin, illus. LC 81-80218. 32p. (Orig.). (ps-3). 1981. pap. 0.69 (ISBN 0-937420-01-8). Stirrup Assoc.
Foltzer, Monica. Alphabet Picture Key Word Cards. Hoffman, Jo-Ann, illus. 38p. 1987. 38 cards 4.60 (ISBN 0-9607918-5-X, A 505419). St Ursula.
Fortey, Richard. Dinosaur's Alphabet. (gr. 4-8). 1990. 14.95 (ISBN 0-8120-6202-7). Barron.
Friskey, Margaret. Indian Two Feet & the ABC Moose Hunt. Hawkinson, John, illus. LC 77-4467. 32p. (gr. k-2). 1977. PLB 14.60 (ISBN 0-516-03500-2). Childrens.
Fujikawa, Gyo, illus. Gyo Fujikawa's A to Z Picture Book. LC 73-16655. 80p. (gr. k-3). 1974. 9.95 (ISBN 0-448-11741-X, G&D). Putnam Pub Group.
Gag, Wanda. ABC Bunny. Gag, Wanda, illus. LC 33-27359. (gr. k-2). 1978. 8.95 (ISBN 0-698-20000-4, Coward); 6.99g (ISBN 0-698-30000-9, Coward); pap. 4.95 (ISBN 0-698-20465-4, Coward). Putnam Pub Group.
Gamec, Hazel S. The Disappearing ABC Game Book. Gamec, Hazel S., illus. 12p. write for info. (ISBN 0-938042-02-5). Printek.
Garcia, Mary H. & Gonzalez-Mena, Janet. The Big E: Learning Package One. Ragan, Lise B., ed. LC 75-27579. (Prog. Bk.). (gr. 1-2). 1976. tchr's program 12.95 (ISBN 0-8325-0464-5); student workbook 3.95 (ISBN 0-8325-0465-3). program package 49.95 (ISBN 0-685-02500-4). Natl Textbk.
Geisert, Arthur. Alphabet Book. (ps-1). 1985. write for info. HM.
Gould, Ellen. The Red Letter Alphabet Book. Kelley, Cathy, illus. 29p. (gr. k up). 1983. pap. 7.00 (ISBN 0-938017-00-4). Learn Tools.
Gregorich, Barbara. El Alfabeto: Minusculas: Alphabet: Lowercase. Hoffman, Joan, ed. Shepherd-Bartram, tr. from ENG. Pape, Richard, illus. (SPA.). 32p. (Orig.). (ps). 1987. wkbk. 1.99 (ISBN 0-938256-76-9). Sch Zone Pub Co.
—Alphabet Avalanche. Hoffman, Joan, ed. Alexander, Barbara, et al, illus. 32p. (Orig.). (ps-1). wkbk. 1.99 (ISBN 0-88743-128-3). Sch Zone Pub Co.
—Alphabet Skills: Kindergarten. Hoffman, Joan, ed. Koontz, Robin M., illus. 32p. (gr. k). 1990. wkbk. 3.49 (ISBN 0-88743-177-1). Sch Zone Pub Co.
—El Alfabeto: Mayusculas: Alphabet: Uppercase. Hoffman, Joan, ed. Shepherd-Bartram, tr. from ENG. Pape, Richard, illus. (SPA.). 32p. (Orig.). (ps). 1987. wkbk. 1.99 (ISBN 0-938256-75-0). Sch Zone Pub Co.
Gregory, Elizabeth. Alfred's Alphabet Antics. (Illus.). 1981. 6.95 (ISBN 0-933184-07-7); pap. 4.95 (ISBN 0-933184-08-5). Flame Intl.
Gundersheimer, Karen. ABC Say with Me. 1985. 3.95 (ISBN 0-694-00104-X, Carousel Bks). HarperCollins.
Hague, Kathleen. Alphabears. Hague, Michael, illus. (ps-2). 1985. PLB incl. cassette 19.95 (ISBN 0-941078-99-X). Live Oak Media.
—Alphabears: An ABC Book. 1984. 10.95 (ISBN 0-03-062543-2). HR&W.
Hall, Mahji. T Is for "Terrific", Mahji's ABC's. Hall, Mahji, illus. LC 88-62371. 32p. (Orig.). (ps-3). 1989. PLB 9.95 (ISBN 0-940880-21-0); pap. text ed. 4.95 (ISBN 0-940880-22-9). Open Hand.
Hammond, Arissa, et al. My Friends ABC Book. LC 88-70949. (Illus.). 32p. (gr. 2 up). 1988. 10.00 (ISBN 0-9605968-4-4). Bright Bks.
Harada, Joyce, illus. It's the A.B.C. Book. 32p. (ps). 1982. limp 7.95 (ISBN 0-89346-157-1). Heian Intl.
Harrison, Ted. A Northern Alphabet. Harrison, Ted, illus. LC 82-50244. 32p. (ps-1). 1989. 14.95 (ISBN 0-88776-209-3); pap. 6.95 (ISBN 0-88776-233-6). Tundra Bks.
Henry Hound's ABC. (ps-k). 1990. bds. 3.95 (ISBN 0-7214-9123-5). Ladybird Bks.
Henson, Jim. Bean Bunny's ABC Book. (ps). 1991. 6.95 (ISBN 1-56282-027-3). W Disney Pub.
Hoban, Tana. A, B, See! LC 81-6890. (Illus.). 32p. (gr. k-3). 1982. PLB 13.88 (ISBN 0-688-00833-X). Greenwillow.
Holt, Virginia. A, My Name Is Alice: A Sesame Street Alphabet Book. Mathieu, Joe, illus. LC 88-18520. 32p. (Orig.). (ps). 1989. lib. bdg. 5.99 (ISBN 0-394-92241-7); pap. 2.25 (ISBN 0-394-82241-2). Random.
Hubbard, Woodleigh. C Is for Curious: An ABC of Feelings. Hubbard, Woodleigh, illus. 40p. (ps-1). 1990. 12.95 (ISBN 0-87701-679-8). Chronicle Bks.
I Know Letters. (Illus.). 32p. (ps). 1985. pap. write for info. (ISBN 0-307-03584-0, Pub. by Golden Bks). Western Pub.
Jeffares, Jeanne. An Around-the-World Alphabet. Jeffares, Jeanne, illus. LC 89-32135. 36p. 1989. 14.95 (ISBN 0-87226-324-X). P Bedrick Bks.
Jefferds, Vince. Disney's Elegant ABC Book. Klimo, Kate, ed. Disney, Walt. Walt Disney Studios, illus. 96p. 1985. pap. 14.95 (ISBN 0-671-45571-0, Little Simon); coloring bk. 2.95 (ISBN 0-671-55434-4). S&S Trade.
Johnson, Audean, illus. A to Z: Look & See. 32p. (Orig.). 1989. pap. 1.95 (ISBN 0-394-86127-2). Random.
Johnson, Crockett. Harold's ABC. Johnson, Crockett, illus. LC 63-14444. 64p. (ps-3). 1981. pap. 3.95 (ISBN 0-06-443023-5, Trophy). HarpC Child Bks.
Kahn, Peggy. The Care Bears' Book of ABC's. Bracken, Carolyn, illus. LC 82-18538. 40p. (ps-2). 1983. lib. bdg. 4.99 (ISBN 0-394-95808-X). Random.
King, Tony. The Moving Alphabet Book. (Illus.). 14p. 1982. 9.95 (ISBN 0-399-20923-9, Putnam). Putnam Pub Group.
Kishta, Leila. ABC Rhymes for Young Muslims. Quinlan, Hamid, ed. Ali, Abdullah, illus. LC 83-70183. 32p. (gr. 1-6). 1983. pap. 3.00 (ISBN 0-89259-044-0). Am Trust Pubns.
Kitamura, Satoshi. What's Inside: The Alphabet Book. Kitamura, Satoshi, illus. LC 84-73117. 32p. (ps up). 1985. 12.95 (ISBN 0-374-38306-5). FS&G.
Kitchen, Bert. Animal Alphabet. Kitchen, Bert, illus. LC 83-23929. 32p. (ps up). 1984. 13.95 (ISBN 0-8037-0117-9). Dial Bks Young.
—Animal Alphabet. Kitchen, Bert, illus. LC 83-23929. 32p. (Orig.). (ps up). 1988. pap. 4.95 (ISBN 0-8037-0431-3). Dial Bks Young.
Korn, Barbara. Down Alphabet Trail with Hank the Pig. 1991. 6.95 (ISBN 0-8062-4108-X). Carlton.
Kraus, Robert, et al. The Old-Fashioned Raggedy Ann & Andy ABC Book. Kraus, Pam, ed. Gruelle, Johnny, illus. 32p. (ps-2). 1980. 5.95 (ISBN 0-671-42552-8, Little Simon). S&S Trade.
Kreeger, Charlene. The Alaska ABC Book. (Illus.). 36p. (Orig.). (gr. k-1). 1978. pap. 6.95 (ISBN 0-933914-01-6). Paws Four Pub.
Laird. The Alphabet Zoo. LC 74-190264. (Illus.). 32p. (ps-2). 1972. PLB 9.95 (ISBN 0-87783-053-3); pap. 3.94 deluxe ed. o.s.i (ISBN 0-87783-079-7). Oddo.
Larsen, Rayola C. Alphabet Talk: Gospel Rhymes for Each Letter of the Alphabet. Perry, Lucille R., illus. LC 89-83429. 32p. (Orig.). (gr. k-3). 1989. pap. 3.95 (ISBN 0-88290-147-8). Horizon Utah.
Lear, Edward. An Edward Lear Alphabet. Newsom, Carol, illus. LC 82-10037. 32p. (gr. k-3). 1983. PLB 11.88 (ISBN 0-688-00965-4). Lothrop.
Leonard, Marcia. Alphabet Bandits: An ABC Book. Cocca-Leffler, Maryann, illus. LC 89-4933. 24p. (gr. k-2). 1990. PLB 8.79 (ISBN 0-8167-1718-4); pap. text ed. 1.95 (ISBN 0-8167-1719-2). Troll Assocs.
Let's Learn Set. Incl. Positions (7008); Alphabet Sounds & Pictures (7004); Capital & Lower Case Letters (7005); Numbers, Number Words, & Sets (7006); Shapes (7007); Consonants (7009); Color Words (7002); Fun with Numbers (7018); Letters & the Sounds They Make (7017); All about Me (7010); Pre-School & Kindergarten Skills (7015); Printing Practice (7014). 32p. 1984. pap. 285.12 set- 12 each of 12 different "Let's Learn" titles: 144 bks (ISBN 0-88724-099-2). Carson-Dellos.
Lichtner, Schomer. Alphabet Drawings. Lichtner, Schomer, illus. 88p. (Orig.). (gr. k up). 1973. pap. 4.50 (ISBN 0-686-97176-0). Lichtner.
Lieberman, Lillian. ABC Consonants. 64p. (gr. k-2). 1985. 6.95 (ISBN 0-912107-29-4). Monday Morning Bks.
—ABC Letters. 64p. (gr. k-2). 1984. 6.95 (ISBN 0-912107-10-3). Monday Morning Bks.
—ABC Order. 64p. (gr. k-3). 1984. 6.95 (ISBN 0-912107-12-X). Monday Morning Bks.
—ABC Rhymes. 64p. (gr. k-3). 1985. 6.95 (ISBN 0-912107-28-6). Monday Morning Bks.
—ABC Vowels. 64p. (gr. k-2). 1985. 6.95 (ISBN 0-912107-30-8). Monday Morning Bks.
Linden, Elizabeth. America's Big Cities' ABC's. Linden, Elizabeth, illus. 54p. (Orig.). (ps-2). 1990. pap. 0.50 (ISBN 0-9625072-2-9). B G Keogh.
A Little ABC Book. 16p. (ps-k). 1980. bds. 2.95 (ISBN 0-671-41342-2, Little). S&S Trade.
Lucero, Faustina H. Little Indians' ABC. LC 73-87800. (Illus.). 32p. (gr. k-2). 1974. PLB 9.95 (ISBN 0-87783-129-7); pap. 3.94 deluxe ed. (ISBN 0-87783-130-0). Oddo.
Lundell, Margo. Disney Babies A to Z. (Illus.). 14p. (ps-k). 1989. write for info. (ISBN 0-307-12317-0, Pub. by Golden Bks). Western Pub.
McConnell, Keith. The SeAlphabet Encyclopedia. McConnell, Keith, illus. 48p. (gr. 4 up). 1982. pap. 5.95 (ISBN 0-88045-016-9). Stemmer Hse.
McCord, Cindy & Ross, Shirley. Animal Rhythms Alphabet. 64p. (ps-2). 1988. 6.95 (ISBN 0-912107-69-3, MM976). Monday Morning Bks.
—Animal Rhythms Consonants. 64p. (ps-2). 1988. 6.95 (ISBN 0-912107-70-7, MM977). Monday Morning Bks.
—Animal Rhythms Vowels. 64p. (ps-2). 1988. 6.95 (ISBN 0-912107-71-5, MM978). Monday Morning Bks.
Mack, Stan. The King's Cat Is Coming. Mack, Stan, illus. (ps-1). 1976. lib. bdg. 4.99 (ISBN 0-394-93302-8). Pantheon.
McKie, Roy. The Alphabet Block Book. McKie, Roy, illus. LC 79-63611. (ps-1). 1979. 3.95 (ISBN 0-394-84269-3, Random Juv). Random.
McKissack, Patricia & McKissack, Fredrick. Big Bug Book of the Alphabet. Bartholomew, illus. LC 87-61653. 24p. (Orig.). (gr. k-1). 1987. spiral bdg. 14.95 (ISBN 0-88335-764-X); pap. text ed. 4.95 (ISBN 0-88335-774-7). Milliken Pub Co.
McMillan, Mary. God's ABC Zoo. Grossman, Dan, illus. 48p. (ps-1). 1987. pap. 6.95 (ISBN 0-86653-405-9, SS1802). Good Apple.
Magee, Doug. All Aboard ABC. (ps). 1990. 13.95 (ISBN 0-525-65036-9, Cobblehill Bks). Dutton Child Bks.
Magel, John. Dr. Moggle's Alphabet Challenge. Delcol, Claudia, illus. 32p. (ps up). 1985. write for info. (ISBN 0-528-82165-2). Macmillan.
Mayer, Marianna. The Unicorn Alphabet. Hague, Michael, illus. 32p. (gr. 1 up). 1989. 14.95 (ISBN 0-8037-0372-4); PLB 14.89 (ISBN 0-8037-0373-2). Dial Bks Young.
Mazzarella, Mimi. Alphabatty Animals & Funny Foods. Mazzarella, Mimi & Mazzarella, James, illus. LC 83-81449. 96p. (Orig.). (gr. k-3). 1984. pap. 5.95 (ISBN 0-89709-045-4). Liberty Pub.

Mendoza, George. Alphabet Sheep. Reidy, Kathleen, illus. LC 81-81046. 48p. (gr. k-2). 1982. 5.95 (ISBN 0-448-12220-0, G&D). Putnam Pub Group.

Miller, Jane. The Farm Alphabet Book. Miller, Jane, illus. 32p. (ps-2). 1987. pap. 2.50 (ISBN 0-590-31991-4). Scholastic Inc.

Mr. Lion's I-Spy ABC. 16p. (Orig.). (ps-2). 1975. pap. 5.00 (ISBN 0-85953-065-5, Pub. by Child's Play England). Childs Play.

Mister Tom. Queen Fussy. Spivey, Elvera, illus. 48p. (gr. 2-4). 1973. Cassette. write for info. Oddo.

Moak, Allen. A Big City ABC. (Illus.). 32p. (ps up). 1989. text ed. 14.95 (ISBN 0-88776-161-5, Dist. by U of Toronto Pr); pap. 6.95 (ISBN 0-88776-238-7). Tundra Bks.

Moddy, Marlys. ABC Book of Feelings. (Illus.). 32p. (ps-3). 1991. 7.95 (ISBN 0-570-04190-2, 56-1649). Concordia. The ABC Book of Feelings is a fun, new way to learn the ABC's--& all about feelings at the same time! Journey through the alphabet with a delightful mouse who experiences all kinds of emotions, starting with "A" for "afraid" & ending with "Z" for "zany." Children ages 4 to 8 learn the ABC's & how to express their God-given emotions, realizing that Jesus loves them always & helps them understand their feelings...even when they feel "Y" for "yucky." Award-winning illustrator Joe Buddy's whimsical, colorful illustrations capture children's attention. The charming drawings help children understand what the "feeling" words mean. A wonderful book for parents who want to explain to their children that God has given all people emotions; & assist parents in helping their children express their feelings. 32pp. Hardback. $7.95 Concordia Publishing House. Item no. 56-1649 ISBN 0-570-04190-2 To order--Call toll free 1-800-325-3040.
Publisher Provided Annotation.

Moncure, Jane B. Magic Monsters Act the Alphabet. Endres, Helen, illus. LC 79-23841. (ps-3). 1980. PLB 11.97 (ISBN 0-89565-116-5). Childs World.

—My "b" Sound Box. Sommers, Linda, illus. LC 77-23588. (ps-2). 1977. 11.97 (ISBN 0-913778-92-3); pap. 6.96 (ISBN 0-89565-182-3). Childs World.

—My "d" Sound Box. Sommers, Linda, illus. LC 78-8450. (ps-2). 1978. PLB 11.97 (ISBN 0-89565-044-4); pap. 6.96 (ISBN 0-89565-186-6). Childs World.

—My "f" Sound Box. Sommers, Linda, illus. LC 77-9377. (ps-2). 1977. PLB 11.97 (ISBN 0-913778-93-1); pap. 6.96 (ISBN 0-89565-185-8). Childs World.

—My "h" Sound Box. Sommers, Linda, illus. LC 77-8977. (ps-2). 1977. PLB 11.97 (ISBN 0-913778-94-X); pap. 6.96 (ISBN 0-89565-184-X). Childs World.

—My "l" Sound Box. Sommers, Linda, illus. LC 78-8373. (ps-2). 1978. PLB 11.97 (ISBN 0-89565-045-2); pap. 6.96 (ISBN 0-89565-189-0). Childs World.

—My "p" Sound Box. Sommers, Linda, illus. LC 78-7841. (ps-2). 1978. PLB 11.97 (ISBN 0-89565-047-9); pap. 6.96 (ISBN 0-89565-187-4). Childs World.

—My "r" Sound Box. Sommers, Linda, illus. LC 78-7842. (ps-2). 1978. PLB 11.97 (ISBN 0-89565-048-7); pap. 6.96 (ISBN 0-89565-190-4). Childs World.

—My "s" Sound Box. Sommers, Linda, illus. LC 77-8970. (ps-2). 1977. PLB 11.97 (ISBN 0-913778-95-8); pap. 6.96 (ISBN 0-89565-181-5). Childs World.

—My "t" Sound Box. Sommers, Linda, illus. LC 77-23587. (ps-2). 1977. PLB 11.97 (ISBN 0-913778-96-6); pap. 6.96 (ISBN 0-89565-183-1). Childs World.

—My "w" Sound Box. Sommers, Linda, illus. LC 78-8614. (ps-2). 1978. PLB 11.97 (ISBN 0-89565-046-0); pap. 6.96 (ISBN 0-89565-188-2). Childs World.

The Muppet Babies' ABC. LC 83-62170. 28p. (ps). 1984. boards 2.95 (ISBN 0-394-86363-1, Random Juv). Random.

My First ABC. (Illus.). 32p. (ps). 1985. 3.95 (ISBN 0-394-87698-9). Random.

Name Game Staff. Hanukkah Alphabet. (Illus.). (ps-5). 1977. pap. 2.50 (ISBN 0-914080-63-6). Shulsinger Sales.

Nedobeck, Don. Nedobeck's Alphabet Book. (Illus.). 26p. (gr. 1-8). 1988. 9.95 (ISBN 0-944314-00-7). New Wrinkle.

Neumeier, Marty & Glaser, Byron. Action Alphabet. Neumeier, Marty & Glaser, Byron, illus. LC 84-25322. 56p. (ps-1). 1985. 12.95 (ISBN 0-688-05703-9); lib. bdg. 12.88 (ISBN 0-688-05704-7). Greenwillow.

Newberry, Clare T. The Kittens' ABC. LC 64-19712. 32p. (ps-3). 1965. Repr. 14.95; PLB 14.89. HarpC Child Bks.

Owens, Mary B. A Caribou Alphabet. McCollough, Mark, contrib. by. (Illus.). 40p. (ps-3). 1990. pap. 4.95 (ISBN 0-374-41043-7, Sunburst). FS&G.

Oxenbury, Helen. Helen Oxenbury's ABC of Things. Oxenbury, Helen, illus. LC 83-5263. 56p. (ps-3). 1983. PLB 13.95 (ISBN 0-385-29291-0); pap. 12.95 (ISBN 0-385-29290-2). Delacorte.

Pajot-Smith, Jean. Li'l Tuffy & His ABC's. Smith, Jean P., illus. 64p. (ps-4). pap. 5.00 (ISBN 0-87485-063-0). Johnson Chi.

Pallotta, Jerry. The Flower Alphabet Book. Evans, Leslie, illus. 32p. (ps-3). 1989. 11.95 (ISBN 0-88106-459-9); pap. 6.95 (ISBN 0-88106-453-X). Charlesbridge Pub.

—The Frog Alphabet Book. Masiello, Ralph, illus. 32p. (Orig.). (ps-4). 1990. 11.95 (ISBN 0-88106-463-7); pap. 6.95 (ISBN 0-88106-462-9). Charlesbridge Pub.

—The Furry Alphabet Book. Stuart, Edgar, illus. 32p. (Orig.). (ps-4). 1990. 11.95 (ISBN 0-88106-465-3); pap. 6.95 (ISBN 0-88106-464-5). Charlesbridge Pub.

—Going Lobstering. Bolster, Rob, illus. 32p. (Orig.). (ps-4). 1990. 14.95 (ISBN 0-88106-475-0); pap. 7.95 (ISBN 0-88106-474-2). Charlesbridge Pub.

—The Ocean Alphabet Book. Mazzola, Frank, Jr., illus. 32p. (ps-3). 1989. 11.95 (ISBN 0-88106-458-0); pap. 6.95 (ISBN 0-88106-452-1). Charlesbridge Pub.

—The Underwater Alphabet Book. (Illus.). 32p. (ps-8). 1991. 14.95 (ISBN 0-88106-461-0); pap. 6.95 (ISBN 0-88106-455-6). Charlesbridge Pub.

—Yucky Reptile Alphabet Book. (ps-3). 1990. 11.95 (ISBN 0-88106-460-2); pap. 6.95 (ISBN 0-88106-454-8). Charlesbridge Pub.

Palotta, Jerry. The Icky Bug Alphabet Book. Masiello, Ralph, illus. 32p. (ps-3). 1989. 14.95 (ISBN 0-88106-456-4); pap. 6.95 (ISBN 0-88106-450-5). Charlesbridge Pub.

Pare, Roger. A, B, C...Play with Me! (ps-1). 1988. Incl. one bk., one game, & two puzzles. pap. 12.95 (ISBN 0-88166-121-X, Dist. by Simon & Schuster). Meadowbrook.

—A, B, C...Play with Me! 1988. 12.95 (ISBN 0-671-67103-0). S&S Trade.

—L' Alphabet: A Child's Introduction to the Letters & Sounds of French. Pare, Roger, illus. 32p. 1990. 7.95 (ISBN 0-8442-1395-0). Natl Textbk.

Paul, Ann W. Eight Hands Round: A Patchwork Alphabet. Winter, Jeanette, illus. LC 88-745. 32p. (gr. 3 up). 1991. 14.95 (ISBN 0-06-024689-8); PLB 14.89 (ISBN 0-06-024704-5). HarpC Child Bks.

Pavao, John. Understanding Book. Perle, Ruth L., ed. Abisch, Roz & Kaplan, Boche, illus. (gr. 1). 1977. pap. text ed. 1.75 (ISBN 0-89796-863-8). New Dimens Educ.

Peek-a-Boo ABC. LC 82-60108. (ps). 1982. bds. 5.95 (ISBN 0-394-85418-7). Random.

Pessin, Deborah. Aleph-Bet Story Book. (Illus.). (gr. 1-3). 1946. 10.95 (ISBN 0-685-02702-3). JPS Phila.

Peter Rabbit's ABC Frieze. 1987. 5.00 (ISBN 0-7232-5637-3). Warne.

Peyo. The Smurf ABC Book. LC 83-3298. (Illus.). 32p. (ps-1). 1983. lib. bdg. 4.99 (ISBN 0-394-96073-4). Random.

Pienkowski, Jan. ABC. Pienkowski, Jan, illus. (ps). 1989. 2.95 (ISBN 0-671-68133-8). S&S Trade.

Piers, Helen. Puppy's ABC. (Illus.). 32p. (ps-k). 1987. 9.95 (ISBN 0-19-520606-1). Oxford U Pr.

Poltarnees, Welleran, et al, eds. A. B. C. of Fashionable Animals. Neilson, Harry B., et al, illus. 64p. 1989. 12. 95 (ISBN 0-88138-122-5). Green Tiger Pr.

Portugal, Jan. ABC Sillies. Portugal, Jan, illus. LC 83-10291. 56p. (Orig.). (ps-1). 1983. pap. 3.00 (ISBN 0-937148-13-X). Wild Horses.

Postman, Frederica. Yiddish Alphabet Book. Stone, Bonnie, illus. 1988. 12.95 (ISBN 1-55774-029-1, Dist. by Watts). Adama Pubs Inc.

Pragoff, Fiona. Alphabet. LC 87-635. (Illus.). (ps-k). 1987. pap. 6.95 (ISBN 0-385-24171-2). Doubleday.

Red Hawk, Richard. A,B,C's the American Indian Way. (Illus.). 55p. (Orig.). (ps-8). 1988. pap. 6.95 (ISBN 0-940113-15-5). Sierra Oaks Pub.

Rey, H. A. Curious George Learns the Alphabet. (Illus.). 72p. (gr. k-3). 1963. 12.95 (ISBN 0-395-16031-6). HM.

Rice, James, illus. Cowboy Alphabet. (gr. k-4). 1983. 9.95 (ISBN 0-88289-427-7). Pelican.

Rich, Beatrice. ABCDEFGHIJKLMNOPQRSTUVWXYZ in English & French. LC 81-20838. (Illus.). 64p. (gr. k-2). 1983. PLB 12.95 (ISBN 0-87460-353-6). Lion Bks.

Rockwell, Anne. Albert B. Cub & Zebra: An Alphabet Storybook. Reissue. ed. Rockwell, Anne, illus. LC 76-54224. 32p. (ps-1). 1977. 13.95 (ISBN 0-690-01350-7, Crowell Jr Bks). HarpC Child Bks.

Roe, Richard, illus. Animal ABC. LC 84-6828. 24p. (ps-1). 1984. (Pub. by BYR). Random.

Rosario, Idalia. Idalia's Project ABC-Proyecto ABC: An Urban Alphabet Book in English & Spanish. Idalia, Rosario, illus. LC 80-21013. (gr. k-3). 1987. pap. 3.95 (ISBN 0-8050-0296-0). H Holt & Co.

Ross, Harry. Fraggles Alphabet Pie. 1988. write for info. (ISBN 0-02-689115-8). Checkerboard Pr.

Rosser, J. K. Teenage Mutant Ninja Turtles ABC's for a Better Planet. GEE Studio Staff, illus. LC 90-53247. 32p. (Orig.). (ps-3). 1991. PLB 5.99 (ISBN 0-679-91383-1); pap. 2.25 (ISBN 0-679-81383-7). Random.

Roziere, Gael. Artist's Alphabet: A Child's Activity Book for Language, Movement & Painting. 28p. (ps-4). 1988. pap. 5.95 wkbk. (ISBN 0-9619004-2-3). M Press CA.

Rubin, Cynthia E., selected by. ABC Americana from the National Gallery of Art. (Illus.). 32p. (ps up). 1989. 11.95 (ISBN 0-15-200660-5, Gulliver Bks). HarBraceJ.

Salinas-Norman, Bobbi. Salinas-Norman's ABC's. Rodriguez-Nieto, Catherine & Rodriguez-Nieto, Alcides, eds. (Illus.). 80p. (ps-6). 1986. wkbk. 7.95 (ISBN 0-934925-02-X); tchr's guide, 150 p. 13.95 (ISBN 0-934925-01-1). Pinata Pubns.

Salyers, Gary C. ABC's Fun for Everyone. Pickett, Sophia, illus. 54p. (ps-3). 1991. PLB write for info. (ISBN 0-9629632-1-6); pap. 11.95 (ISBN 0-9629632-0-8). Sugar Plum Pr. "I found ABC'S FUN FOR EVERYONE to be spellbinding for our kindergarten kids. The rhymes relate to things which children readily identify. Making learning a positive experience at an early age is crucial to the continued academic development of America's youth. ABC'S FUN FOR EVERYONE ignites the spark of enthusiasm in young minds & the twinkle of recognition in young eyes. The illustrations are simply wonderful.. .with bright, fresh characters whose gentle smiles draw your attention to each page. I loved it...you'll love it... but, most importantly, your kids will read it again & again," Ms. Nancy Wade, Kindergarten Teacher.
Publisher Provided Annotation.

Scarry, Richard. Richard Scarry's ABC Word Book. (Illus.). (ps-2). 1971. 9.95 (ISBN 0-394-82339-7, Random Juv); lib. bdg. 5.99 (ISBN 0-394-92339-1). Random.

—Richard Scarry's Find Your ABC's. (Illus.). (ps-1). 1973. pap. 2.25 (ISBN 0-394-82683-3). Random.

Schaffer, Frank, PUblications Staff. The Alphabet. (Illus.). 24p. (ps-2). 1978. wkbk. 3.98 (ISBN 0-86734-001-0, FS 3002). Schaffer Pubns.

—Beginning Activities with the Alphabet. (Illus.). 24p. (ps-k). 1980. 3.98 (ISBN 0-86734-015-0, FS 3028). Schaffer Pubns.

—Printing with Peter Possum. (Illus.). 24p. (gr. k-2). 1978. wkbk. 3.98 (ISBN 0-86734-006-1, FS 3007). Schaffer Pubns.

Schmid-Belk, Donna D. The Arizona Alphabet Book. Belk, Gordon G., ed. Ives, Michael, illus. 32p. (Orig.). (ps-8). 1989. pap. text ed. 7.95 (ISBN 0-685-28841-2). Donna Dee Bks.

Sendak, Maurice. Alligators All Around. Sendak, Maurice, illus. 32p. (ps-3). 1962. PLB 12.89 (ISBN 0-06-025530-7). HarpC Child Bks.

—Alligators All Around: An Alphabet. Sendak, Maurice, illus. LC 62-13315. 32p. (ps-3). 1991. pap. 2.95 (ISBN 0-06-443254-8, Trophy). HarpC Child Bks.

Sesame Street Editors. The Sesame Street ABC Book of Words. McNaught, Harry, illus. LC 86-62405. 48p. (ps-k). 1988. (Random Juv); pap. 10.95 (ISBN 0-394-88880-4). Random.

Sesame Street Staff, et al. The Sesame Street ABC Storybook. LC 74-5522. (Illus.). 72p. (gr. k-3). 1974. 5.95 (ISBN 0-394-82921-2, Random Juv); lib. bdg. 5.99 (ISBN 0-394-92921-7). Random.

Shirley, Gayle. A Is for Animals. Bergum, Connie, illus. 56p. (ps-3). 1990. pap. 8.95 (ISBN 1-56044-025-2). Falcon Pr MT.

Shroyer, Susan P. & Kimmel, Joan G. ABC - Sign with Me. Kimmel, Joan G., illus. 32p. (Orig.). (ps-2). 1987. pap. 4.95 (ISBN 0-939849-00-3). Sugar Sign Pr.

Shumsky, Adaia & Shumsky, Abraham. The Alef-Bet Primer Reading Practice Book. Bass, Marilyn, illus. 80p. (gr. k-3). 1984. pap. text ed. 5.00 (ISBN 0-8074-0257-5, 405315). UAHC.

Silbert, Linda P. & Silbert, Alvin J. Make My Own Book Kit Alphabet. (ps-2). 1984. wkbk. 5.98 (ISBN 0-89544-319-8). Silbert Bress.

Sloane, Eric. ABC Book of Early Americana. LC 89-24603. (Illus.). 64p. 1990. 16.95 (ISBN 0-8050-1294-X). H Holt & Co.

Smalley, Guy, illus. My Very Own Book of ABCs. 32p. (ps-2). 1989. 9.95 (ISBN 0-929793-02-1). Camex Bks Inc.

Smiles & Frowns - Ups & Downs with the Alphabet Pals: Rainy Days & Rainbows. LC 89-51291. (Illus.). 20p. (ps). 1989. lib. bdg. write for info. (ISBN 0-7166-1903-2). World Bk.

Spizman, Robyn. Bulletin Boards: For Reading, Spelling & Language Skills. Pesiri, Evelyn, illus. 64p. (gr. k-6). 1984. wkbk. 6.95 (ISBN 0-86653-210-2, GA 574). Good Apple.

Stifle, J. M. Set of ABC Books, 2 bks. 1981. pap. 6.25 (ISBN 0-570-04055-8, 56-1716). Concordia.

Stockham, Peter, ed. The Mother's Picture Alphabet. Anelay, Henry, illus. 64p. (ps-3). 1975. pap. 4.50 (ISBN 0-486-23089-9). Dover.

Szekeres, Cyndy. ABC. Szekeres, Cyndy, illus. LC 82-839989. 22p. (ps up). 1983. write for info. (ISBN 0-307-12120-8, 12120, Golden Bks). Western Pub.

Tallarico, Tony, illus. A B C. 28p. (ps). 1988. 2.95 (ISBN 0-89828-064-8, 80648). Tuffy Bks.

—Alphabet. 12p. (ps). 1987. bds. 3.95 (ISBN 0-89828-317-5, 04010). Tuffy Bks.

Taylor, Kenneth N. Big Thoughts for Little People. (ps-3). 1983. 10.95 (ISBN 0-8423-0164-X). Tyndale.

Thomson, Ruth. All about ABC. King, Pauline, illus. LC 87-42592. 32p. (gr. 1-2). 1987. PLB 10.95 (ISBN 1-55532-311-1). Gareth Stevens Inc.

Thornhill, Jan. Wildlife ABC: A Nature Alphabet Book. (ps-3). 1990. pap. 14.95 (ISBN 0-671-67925-2). S&S Trade.

Tinies ABC Pop-Up Book. (Illus.). (ps-1). 1.49 (ISBN 0-517-43893-3). Outlet Bk Co.

Torrence, Susan. The California Alphabet Book. Torrence, Charles, ed. Torrence, Susan, illus. LC 86-51505. 32p. (gr. k-3). 1987. pap. 6.95 (ISBN 0-914281-48-8). Torrence Pubns.

Torrence, Susan & Polansky, Leslie. The Oregon Alphabet Book. 2nd ed. Torrence, Susan, illus. 32p. (ps-6). 1983. 5.95 (ISBN 0-914281-00-3). Torrence Pubns.

Travers, Pamela L. Mary Poppins from A to Z. Shepard, Mary, illus. LC 62-15629. (gr. 1-3). 1962. 10.95 (ISBN 0-15-252590-4, HJ). HarBraceJ.

Tudor, Tasha. A Is for Annabelle. Tudor, Tasha, illus. LC 60-15911. (ps-1). 1988. pap. 4.95 (ISBN 0-02-688534-4, Aladdin). Macmillan Child Grp.

Twinn, Colin. Bunnykins ABC. (Illus.). 23p. (ps-1). 1989. 4.95 (ISBN 0-7232-3604-6). Warne.

Tyler, J. & Cartwright, S. Alphabet Book. (Illus.). 32p. (ps). 1991. 8.95 (ISBN 0-7460-0434-6, Usborne); lib. bdg. 13.96 (ISBN 0-88110-446-9, Usborne). EDC.

Walsh, Abigail M. The A to Z Book. Stearns, Helen M., ed. Urbahn, Clara, illus. 32p. (ps-5). 1988. 10.95 (ISBN 0-9614281-4-7). Cricketfield Pr.

Watson, Clyde. Applebet: An ABC. Watson, Wendy, illus. LC 81-19399. 32p. (ps-3). 1982. 12.95 (ISBN 0-374-30384-3). FS&G.

—Applebet: An ABC. Watson, Wendy, illus. 32p. (ps up). 1987. pap. 3.95 (ISBN 0-374-40427-5). FS&G.

Which One Doesn't Belong - ABC's. (ps-k). 1989. pap. write for info. (ISBN 0-307-04726-1). Western Pub.

Whitehead, Patricia. Arnold Plays Baseball. Karas, Brian, illus. LC 84-8827. 32p. (gr. k-2). 1985. PLB 10.89 (ISBN 0-8167-0367-1); pap. text ed. 2.95 (ISBN 0-8167-0368-X). Troll Assocs.

—Best Halloween Book. Britt, Stephanie, illus. LC 84-8828. 32p. (gr. k-2). 1985. PLB 10.89 (ISBN 0-8167-0373-6); pap. text ed. 2.95 (ISBN 0-8167-0374-4). Troll Assocs.

—Best Thanksgiving Book. Hall, Susan T., illus. LC 84-8831. 32p. (gr. k-2). 1985. PLB 10.89 (ISBN 0-8167-0371-X); pap. text ed. 2.95 (ISBN 0-8167-0372-8). Troll Assocs.

—Best Valentine Book. Harvy, Paul, illus. LC 84-8829. 32p. (gr. k-2). 1985. PLB 10.89 (ISBN 0-8167-0369-8); pap. text ed. 2.95 (ISBN 0-8167-0370-1). Troll Assocs.

—Dinosaur Alphabet Book. Snyder, Joel, illus. LC 84-8839. 32p. (gr. k-2). 1985. PLB 10.89 (ISBN 0-8167-0363-9); pap. text ed. 2.95 (ISBN 0-8167-0364-7). Troll Assocs.

Wildsmith. Brian Wildsmith's ABC's. 1962. 12.95 (ISBN 0-531-01525-4). Watts.

Wiskur, Darrell. Silver Dollar City's ABC Words & Rhymes. Silver Dollar City, Inc. Staff, ed. Wiskur, Darrell, illus. (ps-1). 1977. 1.99g (ISBN 0-686-19127-7). Silver Dollar.

Wynne, Patricia, illus. The Animal ABC. LC 77-74470. 14p. (ps-k). 1977. bds. 3.95 (ISBN 0-394-83589-1, Random Juv). Random.

Zitlaw, JoAnn B. & Frank, Cheryl S. Alpha-Pets. Zitlaw, JoAnn B. & Frank, Cheryl S., illus. 200p. (ps-2). 1985. wkbk. 12.95 (ISBN 0-86653-292-7, GA 645). Good Apple.

ALPS–FICTION

Courage Mountain: The Further Adventures of Heidi. 168p. 1989. pap. 3.95 (ISBN 0-14-034354-7, Puffin). Puffin Bks.

Spyri, Johanna. Heidi. LC 85-13292. (gr. 5 up). 1964. pap. 1.95 (ISBN 0-8049-0018-3, CL-18). Airmont.

—Heidi. LC 85-13292. (Illus.). (gr. 4-6). 1988. pap. 2.95 (ISBN 0-590-42046-1). Scholastic Inc.

—Heidi. 128p. (gr. 2-6). 1989. pap. 2.95 (ISBN 0-448-11076-8, G&D). Putnam Pub Group.

Ullman, James R. Banner in the Sky. LC 54-7296. 256p. (gr. 7 up). 1988. 12.95 (ISBN 0-397-32141-4, Lipp Jr Bks); PLB 12.89 (ISBN 0-397-30264-9, Lipp Jr Bks). HarpC Child Bks.

ALTITUDE, INFLUENCE OF

see Man–Influence of Environment

AMATEUR THEATRICALS

see also Acting; Make-Up, Theatrical; One-Act Plays; Shadow Pantomimes and Plays; Theater–Production and Direction

Liggett, Clayton E. Concert Theatre. LC 72-104705. (Illus.). (gr. 9 up). 1970. PLB 11.95 (ISBN 0-8239-0194-7). Rosen Group.

AMATEUR THEATRICALS–FICTION

Ryan, Mary C. Who Says I Can't? The Secret Life of Walter Mitty. 160p. (gr. 12 up). 1988. 12.95 (ISBN 0-316-76374-8). Little.

AMAZON RIVER

Cheney. The Amazon. (Illus.). 72p. (gr. 4-8). lib. bdg. 10.40 (ISBN 0-531-04818-7). Watts.

Huntley, Beth. Amazon Adventure. LC 88-42908. (Illus.). 32p. (gr. 4-5). 1989. PLB 10.95 (ISBN 1-55532-917-9). Gareth Stevens Inc.

AMAZON RIVER–FICTION

Elbl, Martin. Tales from the Amazon. Neubacher, Gerda, illus. 32p. (gr. k-3). 1986. PLB 11.66 (ISBN 0-87617-032-7, Pub. by C Hayes Pr). Penworthy Pub.

AMAZON VALLEY

Cobb, Vicki. This Place Is Wet. Lavallee, Barbara, illus. 32p. (gr. 2-4). 1989. 12.95 (ISBN 0-8027-6880-6); PLB 13.85 (ISBN 0-8027-6881-4). Walker & Co.

AMERICA

see also Central America; Latin America; North America; South America

Aten, Jerry. Americans, Too! 80p. (gr. 4 up). 1982. 7.95 (ISBN 0-86653-099-1, GA 444). Good Apple.

Fairfield, Sheila. People & Nations of the Americas. LC 88-42921. (Illus.). 64p. (gr. 5-6). 1988. PLB 13.95 (ISBN 1-55532-904-7). Gareth Stevens Inc.

Frazee, Charles & Yopp, Hallie K. Medieval & Early Modern Times. Frazee, Kathleen & Lumba, Eric, illus. (gr. 7). 1990. pap. text ed. 24.77 (ISBN 1-878473-56-5); tchr's. ed. 30.77 (ISBN 1-878473-58-1). Delos Pubns.

Lye, Keith. The Americas. Ron Hayward Associates, illus. 40p. (gr. 4-9). 1987. PLB 12.40 (ISBN 0-531-17066-7, Gloucester Pr). Watts.

The Southern World. (Illus.). 128p. 1990. 17.95x (ISBN 0-8160-1881-2). Facts on File.

AMERICA–ANTIQUITIES

Civilizations of the Americas. (Illus.). 80p. (gr. 4 up). 1988. PLB 22.00 (ISBN 0-8172-3306-7). Raintree Pubs.

AMERICA–DISCOVERY AND EXPLORATION

see also Explorers; Northwest Passage

Asimov, Isaac. Christopher Columbus. LC 90-25836. (Illus.). 64p. (gr. 3-4). 1991. PLB 14.95 (ISBN 0-8368-0556-9). Gareth Stevens Inc.

Barden, Renardo. The Discovery of America: Opposing Viewpoints. LC 89-11709. (Illus.). 112p. (gr. 3-10). 1989. PLB 12.95 (ISBN 0-89908-071-5). Greenhaven.

De Kay, James T. Meet Christopher Columbus. Mays, Victor, illus. LC 68-23104. (gr. 2-6). 1968. 3.95 (ISBN 0-394-80071-0, Random Juv); lib. bdg. 8.99 (ISBN 0-394-90071-5). Random.

Fritz, Jean. Where Do You Think You're Going, Christopher Columbus? Tomes, Margot, illus. 80p. (gr. 3-7). 1981. 13.95 (ISBN 0-399-20723-6, Putnam); pap. 7.95 (ISBN 0-399-20734-1, Putnam). Putnam Pub Group.

Gaffron, Norma. El Dorado, Land of Gold: Opposing Viewpoints. LC 90-3838. (Illus.). 112p. (gr. 3-8). 1990. PLB 13.95 (ISBN 0-89908-086-3). Greenhaven.

Irwin, Constance. Strange Footprints on the Land. LC 78-19519. (Illus.). 192p. (gr. 7 up). 1980. 10.95 (ISBN 0-06-022772-9). HarpC Child Bks.

Johnson, Spencer. The Value of Curiosity: The Story of Christopher Columbus. Pileggi, Stephen, illus. LC 77-11032. (gr. k-6). 9.95 (ISBN 0-916392-13-9, Pub. by Value Communications). Oak Tree Pubns.

Krensky, Stephen. Who Really Discovered America? Donnelly, Judy, ed. Sullivan, Steve, illus. 64p. (gr. 3-7). 1991. Repr. of 1987 ed. 12.95 (ISBN 0-8038-9306-X). Hastings.

Las Casas, Bartholomew. The Log of Christopher Columbus' First Voyage to America: In the Year 1492, As Copied Out in Brief by Bartholomew Las Casas. LC 88-32567. (Illus.). 84p. (gr. 3 up). 1989. Repr. of 1938 ed. lib. bdg. 17.00 (ISBN 0-208-02247-3, Pub. by Linnet). Shoe String.

Leon, George D. Explorers of the Americas Before Columbus. (Illus.). 64p. (gr. 7-9). 1990. 12.90 (ISBN 0-531-10667-5). Watts.

Morison, Samuel E. Christopher Columbus, Mariner. (Illus.). 192p. (gr. 9-12). 1983. pap. 8.95 (ISBN 0-452-00992-8, Mer). NAL-Dutton.

Parker, Margot. What Is Columbus Day? Bates, Matt, illus. LC 85-12748. 46p. (gr. k-2). 1985. PLB 14.60 (ISBN 0-516-03781-1). Childrens.

Roop, Peter & Roop, Connie, eds. I, Columbus: My Journal - 1492. Hanson, Peter, illus. 57p. (gr. 4-7). 1990. 13.95 (ISBN 0-8027-6977-2); lib. bdg. 14.85 (ISBN 0-8027-6978-0). Walker & Co.

Smith, Carter, ed. Explorers & Settlers: A Sourcebook on Colonial America. (Illus.). 96p. (gr. 5 up). 1991. PLB 19.95 (ISBN 1-56294-035-X); pap. write for info. (ISBN 1-878841-64-5). Millbrook Pr.

AMERICA–DISCOVERY AND EXPLORATION–FICTION

Litowinsky, Olga. High Voyage: The Final Crossing of Christopher Columbus. (gr. 9-12). 1991. 14.95 (ISBN 0-385-30304-1). Delacorte.

O'Dell, Scott. King's Fifth. Bryant, Samuel, illus. (gr. 7-10). 1966. 14.95 (ISBN 0-395-06963-7). HM.

AMERICAN ABORIGINES

see Indians of North America; Indians of South America

AMERICAN ARTISTS

see Artists, American

AMERICAN AUTHORS

see Authors, American

AMERICAN BISON

see Bison

AMERICAN CIVIL WAR

see U. S.–History–Civil War

AMERICAN CIVILIZATION

see U. S.–Civilization

AMERICAN COLONIES

see U. S.–History–Colonial Period

AMERICAN ESSAYS

Paget, Stephen. I Wonder: Essays for the Young People. facs. ed. LC 68-54365. (gr. 7 up). 1968. Repr. of 1911 ed. 14.00 (ISBN 0-8369-0765-5). Ayer Co Pubs.

AMERICAN FURNITURE

see Furniture, American

AMERICAN INDIANS

see Indians; Indians of North America; Indians of South America

AMERICAN LITERATURE

Cooper, James Fenimore. The Two Admirals: A Tale. LC 88-12190. 511p. (Orig.). (gr. 9-12). 1990. 49.50x (ISBN 0-88706-905-3); pap. 16.95x (ISBN 0-88706-907-X). State U NY Pr.

Faulkner, William. Portable Faulkner. rev. ed. Cowley, Malcolm, ed. (gr. 10 up). 1977. pap. 9.95 (ISBN 0-14-015018-6, Penguin Bks). Viking Penguin.

Holmes, Oliver W. Autocrat of the Breakfast-Table. Andrews, C. A., intro. by. (gr. 11 up). pap. 1.95 (ISBN 0-8049-0159-7, CL-159). Airmont.

Thoreau, Henry David. Walden. Langmack, F., intro. by. Bd. with On Civil Disobedience. (gr. 10up). pap. 1.50 (ISBN 0-8049-0083-3, CL-83). Airmont.

—Walden. Sherman, Paul, ed. Bd. with Civil Disobedience. LC 60-16148. (gr. 9 up). 1960. pap. 8.76 (ISBN 0-395-05113-4, RivEd). HM.

AMERICAN LITERATURE–BIBLIOGRAPHY

Kellman, Steven G. The Modern American Novel: An Annotated Bibliography. 200p. 1991. PLB 40.00x (ISBN 0-89356-664-0, Magill Bks). Salem Pr.

AMERICAN LITERATURE–BIOGRAPHY

see Authors, American

AMERICAN LITERATURE–COLLECTIONS

Wolfe, Thomas, et al. A Southern Appalachian Reader. McNeil, Nellie, et al, eds. (Illus.). 500p. (gr. 10-12). 1988. pap. text ed. 14.95 (ISBN 0-913239-50-X). Appalach Consortium.

AMERICAN MUSIC

see Music, American

AMERICAN MUSICIANS

see Musicians, American

AMERICAN PAINTERS

see Painters, American

AMERICAN POETRY

see also Black Poetry

Adoff, Arnold. Eats: Poems. Russo, Susan, illus. LC 79-11300. (gr. 4 up). 1979. 13.95 (ISBN 0-688-41901-1); PLB 12.88 (ISBN 0-688-51901-6). Lothrop.

Dickinson, Emily. I'm Nobody! Who Are You? Poems of Emily Dickinson for Children. Schneider, Rex, illus. Sewall, Richard, intro. by. LC 78-6828. (Illus.). 96p. (gr. 1 up). 1978. 21.95 (ISBN 0-916144-21-6); pap. 14.95 (ISBN 0-916144-22-4). Stemmer Hse.

Frost, Robert. Stopping by Woods on a Snowy Evening. Jeffers, Susan, illus. LC 78-8134. (ps up). 1978. 12.95 (ISBN 0-525-40115-6, 01063-320, DCB). Dutton Child Bks.

Hearne, Betsy. Polaroid: And Other Poems of View. LC 90-45577. (Illus.). 80p. (gr. 7 up). 1991. SBE 12.95 (ISBN 0-689-50530-2, M K McElderry). Macmillan Child Grp.

Hoberman, Mary Ann. A Fine Fat Pig: And Other Animal Poems. Zeldis, Malcah, illus. LC 90-37403. 32p. (ps-2). 1991. 14.95 (ISBN 0-06-022425-8); PLB 14.89 (ISBN 0-06-022426-6). HarpC Child Bks.

Lewis, Claudia. Up in the Mountains: And Other Poems of Long Ago. Fontaine, Joel, illus. LC 90-4439. 64p. (gr. 3-7). 1991. 13.95 (ISBN 0-06-023810-0); PLB 13.89 (ISBN 0-06-023812-7). HarpC Child Bks.

Longfellow, Henry Wadsworth. Children's Own Longfellow. (Illus.). 109p. (gr. 4-6). 1908. 16.95 (ISBN 0-395-06889-4). HM.

—Paul Revere's Ride. Rand, Ted, illus. 1990. 14.95 (ISBN 0-525-44610-9, DCB). Dutton Child Bks.

McCord, David. For Me to Say. Kane, Henry B., illus. (gr. 5 up). 1970. 12.95 (ISBN 0-316-55511-8). Little.

Moss, Elaine. From Morn to Midnight. Ichikawa, Satomi, illus. LC 77-2548. (gr. k-3). 1977. (Crowell Jr Bks); PLB 8.79 (ISBN 0-685-85787-5). HarpC Child Bks.

O'Donnell, Elizabeth L. The Twelve Days of Summer. Schmidt, Karen L., illus. LC 89-35161. 32p. (ps up). 1991. 13.95 (ISBN 0-688-08202-5); PLB 13.88 (ISBN 0-688-08203-3, Morrow Jr Bks). Morrow Jr Bks.

Poe, Edgar Allan. Edgar Allan Poe, Stories & Poems. (gr. 9 up). pap. 3.25 (ISBN 0-8049-0008-6, CL-8). Airmont.

Prelutsky, Jack. The Baby Uggs Are Hatching! Stevenson, James, illus. LC 81-7266. 32p. (gr. k-3). 1982. 13.95 (ISBN 0-688-00922-0); PLB 13.88 (ISBN 0-688-00923-9). Greenwillow.

—It's Snowing! It's Snowing! Titherington, Jeanne, illus. LC 83-16583. 48p. (gr. 1-3). 1984. 12.95 (ISBN 0-688-01512-3); PLB 12.88 (ISBN 0-688-01513-1). Greenwillow.

—It's Thanksgiving. Hafner, Marylin, illus. LC 81-1929. 48p. (gr. 1-3). 1982. 12.95 (ISBN 0-688-00441-5); lib. bdg. 12.88 (ISBN 0-688-00442-3). Greenwillow.

Roche, P. K. Jump All the Morning: A Child's Day in Verse. LC 83-17006. (Illus.). 32p. (gr. k-1). 1984. pap. 11.95 (ISBN 0-670-41057-8). Viking Child Bks.

Whitman, Walt. Leaves of Grass. Gemme, F. R., intro. by. (gr. 11 up). pap. 3.50 (ISBN 0-8049-0091-4, CL-91). Airmont.

Zolotow, Charlotte. Wake up & Goodnight. Weisgard, Leonard, illus. LC 75-135187. (ps-3). 1971. 8.61i (ISBN 0-06-027041-1). HarpC Child Bks.

AMERICAN POETRY–COLLECTIONS

Elledge, Scott, ed. Wider Than the Sky: Poems to Grow up With. LC 90-4135. 368p. (gr. 5 up). 1990. 19.95 (ISBN 0-06-021786-3); PLB 19.89 (ISBN 0-06-021787-1). HarpC Child Bks.

Field, Eugene. Wynken, Blynken & Nod. Jeffers, Susan, illus. LC 82-2434. 32p. (ps-1). 1982. 11.95 (ISBN 0-525-44022-4, DCB). Dutton Child Bks.

Josefowitz, Natasha. A Hundred Scoops of Ice Cream. 60p. 1989. pap. 3.95 (ISBN 0-88166-157-0, Dist. by Simon & Schuster). Meadowbrook.

Madgett, Naomi L., intro. by. Adam of Ife: Black Women in Praise of Black Men. LC 91-61410. (Illus., Orig.). 1991. pap. 15.00 (ISBN 0-916418-80-4). Lotus.

Ross, H. K., ed. Great American Story Poems-Collection. 160p. (gr. 5-12). 1991. pap. 8.95 (ISBN 0-87460-385-4). Lion Bks.

AMERICAN WIT AND HUMOR

Bonham, Tal D. The Treasury of Clean Teenage Jokes. LC 85-4134. (gr. 7 up). 1985. pap. 3.95 (ISBN 0-8054-5713-5, 4257-13). Broadman.

Corbett, Scott. Jokes to Read in the Dark. Gusman, Annie, illus. LC 79-23129. 80p. (gr. 5-9). 1980. 12.95 (ISBN 0-525-32796-7, 01063-320, DCB); (DCB). Dutton Child Bks.

Dr. Seuss. I Had Trouble in Getting to Solla Sollew. Dr. Seuss, illus. LC 65-23994. 64p. (gr. k-3). 1980. pap. 3.95 (ISBN 0-394-84542-0, Random Juv). Random.

Fleischman, Sid. McBroom's Almanac. Lorraine, Walter H., illus. (gr. 3-7). 1984. 14.95 (ISBN 0-316-26009-6, Joy St Bks). Little.

Frascino, Edward. King Henry the Ape: Animal Jokes. Frascino, Edward & Frascino, Edward, illus. 40p. (gr. 2-5). 1990. PLB 11.95 (ISBN 0-945912-08-0). Pippin Pr.

Keane, Bil. Wanna Be Smiled At? (Illus.). 128p. (gr. 4 up). 1985. pap. 3.50 (ISBN 0-449-12816-4, GM). Fawcett.

Lobel, Arnold. On the Day Peter Stuyvesant Sailed into Town. Lobel, Arnold, illus. LC 75-148420. 48p. (ps-3). 1971. PLB 13.89 (ISBN 0-06-023972-7). HarpC Child Bks.

McKie, Roy. The Joke Book. McKie, Roy, illus. LC 78-62699. (ps-2). 1979. lib. bdg. 5.99 (ISBN 0-394-94077-6, Random Juv); pap. 2.25 (ISBN 0-394-84077-1). Random.

Masin, Herman L. The Funniest Moments in Sports. Callahan, Kevin, illus. LC 73-86219. 128p. (gr. 4 up). 1973. 5.95 (ISBN 0-87131-133-X). M Evans.

Riley, James W. The Gobble-Uns'll Git You Ef You Don't Watch Out! Schick, Joel, illus. LC 74-23110. (gr. 2-5). 1975. 13.95 (ISBN 0-397-31621-6, Lipp Jr Bks). HarpC Child Bks.

Schwartz, Alvin. Witcracks: Jokes & Jests from American Folklore. (Illus.). 128p. (gr. 4 up). 1973. PLB 12.89 (ISBN 0-685-31435-9, Lipp Jr Bks). HarpC Child Bks.

Weber, Bruce. The Funniest Moments in School. Callahan, Kevin, illus. LC 73-88721. 128p. (gr. 4 up). 1973. pap. 2.95 (ISBN 0-87131-153-4). M Evans.

AMERICAN WIT AND HUMOR, PICTORIAL

Ketcham, Hank. Dennis the Menace: The Short Swinger. (Illus.). 1981. pap. 1.50 (ISBN 0-449-13641-8, GM). Fawcett.

Loveland, Nicole. Boogins' Rainy Day. Stebbins, Pat, illus. (ps-3). 1985. PLB 5.95 (ISBN 0-917107-02-0). Cat-Tales Pr.

Roop, Peter. Go Hog Wild! (ps-3). 1990. pap. 2.95 (ISBN 0-8225-9555-9). Lerner Pubns.

Roop, Peter & Roop, Connie. Out to Lunch: Jokes about Food. Hanson, Joan, illus. LC 84-4416. 32p. (gr. 1-4). 1984. PLB 7.95 (ISBN 0-8225-0983-0, First Ave Edns); pap. 2.95 (ISBN 0-8225-9552-4, First Ave Edns). Lerner Pubns.

Roop, Peter, et al. Go Hog Wild: Jokes from down on the Farm. Hanson, Joan, illus. LC 84-5662. 32p. (gr. 1-4). 1984. PLB 8.95 (ISBN 0-8225-0982-2). Lerner Pubns.

—Space Out: Jokes about Outer Space. Hanson, Joan, illus. LC 84-5650. 32p. (gr. 1-4). 1984. PLB 8.95 (ISBN 0-8225-0984-9). Lerner Pubns.

Williams, C. Fred. Adventure Tales of Arkansas: A Cartoon History of a Spirited People. Lisenby, Foy & Poole, Jerry D., illus. Clinton, Bill & Jonsson, Phillip R.intro. by. x, 38p. (Orig.). (gr. 5-7). 1986. pap. 5.95 (ISBN 0-9616677-0-2); tchr's. ed. 3.50 (ISBN 0-9616677-1-0). Signal Media.

AMERICANISMS

Guralnik, David B., ed. Webster's New World Dictionary: Basic School Edition. 1976. 15.00 (ISBN 0-13-944652-4). P-H.

AMPHIBIANS

see also names of amphibians, e.g. Frogs; Salamanders; etc.

Berkowitz, Henry. Amphibians & Reptiles. Berkowitz, Henry, illus. 32p. (Orig.). (gr. 1-9). 1985. pap. 2.50 (ISBN 0-317-66182-5). Banyan Bks.

Caitlin, Stephen. Discovering Reptiles & Amphibians. Johnson, Pamela, illus. LC 89-4972. 32p. (gr. 2-4). 1990. PLB 10.89 (ISBN 0-8167-1753-2); pap. text ed. 2.95 (ISBN 0-8167-1754-0). Troll Assocs.

Losito, Linda, et al. Reptiles & Amphibians. (Illus.). 96p. 1989. 17.95x (ISBN 0-8160-1965-7). Facts on File.

Parker, Nancy W. Frogs, Toads, Lizards & Salamanders. Wright, Joan R., illus. (gr. 1 up). 1990. 13.95 (ISBN 0-688-08680-2); PLB 13.88 (ISBN 0-688-08681-0). Greenwillow.

Sabin, Louis. Reptiles & Amphibians. Zink-White, Nancy, illus. LC 84-8445. 32p. (gr. 3-6). 1985. PLB 9.49 (ISBN 0-8167-0294-2); pap. text ed. 2.95 (ISBN 0-8167-0295-0). Troll Assocs.

Wiessinger, John. Fish, Frogs & Snakes - Right Before Your Eyes. LC 89-1511. (Illus.). 64p. (gr. 4-10). 1989. PLB 15.95 (ISBN 0-89490-265-2). Enslow Pubs.

Wrigley, Robert E. Reptiles & Amphibians. Dahl, K. & Doran, J., illus. 40p. (Orig.). (gr. 2-6). 1990. pap. 4.95 (ISBN 0-920534-53-8, Pub. by Hyperion Pr Ltd CN). Sterling.

Zappler, George & Zappler, Lisbeth. Amphibians As Pets. LC 72-92252. 160p. (gr. 3-9). 1973. pap. 5.95 (ISBN 0-385-08581-8). Doubleday.

AMUNDSEN, ROALD ENGELBREGHT GRAVNING, 1872-1928

Mason, Theodore K. Two Against the Ice, Amundsen & Ellsworth. 1982. 13.95 (ISBN 0-396-08092-8, Putnam). Putnam Pub Group.

AMUNDSEN-SCOTT SOUTH POLE STATION

Sipiera, Paul. Roald Amundsen & Robert Scott: Race for the South Pole. LC 90-2178. (Illus.). 128p. (gr. 3 up). 1990. PLB 25.27 (ISBN 0-516-03056-6). Childrens.

AMUSEMENTS

see also Amateur Theatricals; Circus; Dancing; Entertaining; Fortune Telling; Games; Hobbies; Magic; Mathematical Recreations; Play; Puzzles; Recreation; Riddles; Scientific Recreations; Sports; Theater; Toys; Ventriloquism

Armstrong, Bev. Have Fun Following Directions. Armstrong, Bev, illus. 32p. (gr. k-3). 1979. wkbk. 3.95 (ISBN 0-88160-077-6, LW 810). Learning Wks.

Beard, Daniel C. American Boys Handy Book: What to Do & How to Do It. facs. ed. LC 66-15858. (Illus.). (gr. 4 up). 1966. 14.95 (ISBN 0-8048-0006-5). C E Tuttle.

Betts, Keith & McCollam, Dan. Junior High Game Nights: Wild & Crazy Outreach Events for Junior High Ministry. 96p. 1991. pap. 9.95 (ISBN 0-310-53811-4, Pub. by Youth Spec). Zondervan.

Bony Skeleton's Cut-Out Fun Book. 24p. (Orig.). (ps-k). 1991. pap. 3.95 (ISBN 0-8249-8347-5). Ideals.

Burns, Marilyn. The Book of Think: Or How to Solve Problems Twice Your Size. Weston, Martha, illus. (gr. 5 up). 1976. 14.95 (ISBN 0-316-11742-0); pap. 8.95 (ISBN 0-316-11743-9). Little.

Butterfield, S. Borders & Beyond. (gr. 1-6). 1985. 5.95 (ISBN 0-88160-118-7, LW250). Learning Wks.

Caney, Steven. Steve Caney's Toybook. LC 75-8814. (Illus.). 176p. (ps-5). 1972. pap. 7.95 (ISBN 0-911104-17-8, 023). Workman Pub.

—Steven Caney's Playbook. LC 75-9816. (Illus.). 240p. (ps-5). 1975. pap. 8.95 (ISBN 0-911104-38-0, 050). Workman Pub.

Carlson, Nancy. Harriet & the Roller Coaster. Carlson, Nancy, illus. (gr. k-3). 1985. bk. & cassette 19.95 (ISBN 0-941078-56-6); pap. 12.95 bk. & cassette (ISBN 0-941078-54-X); cassette, 4 paperbacks & guide 27.95 (ISBN 0-941078-55-8). Live Oak Media.

Carson, Patti & Dellosa, Janet. Doggone Good Fun Book. Carson, Patti & Dellosa, Janet, illus. 32p. (ps-1). 1982. pap. 1.59 (ISBN 0-88724-055-0, CD-8010). Carson-Dellos.

Cassidy, John & Stillinger, Scott. The Official Koosh Book: Thirty-Three Kooshy Activities. Taber, Ed, illus. 70p. (Orig.). (gr. 1). 1989. pap. 9.95 incl. koosh ball (ISBN 0-932592-23-6). Klutz Pr.

Colby, Sas & Shirkus, Lorraine. The Pocket Book: A Child's Activity Book. Shirkus, Lorraine, illus. 10p. (ps-k). Date not set. 39.95 (ISBN 0-922656-00-2). Design Matters Inc.

Conaway, Judith. Happy Day! Things to Make & Do. Barto, Renzo, illus. LC 86-7131. 48p. (gr. 1-5). 1987. PLB 11.89 (ISBN 0-8167-0842-8); pap. text ed. 2.95 (ISBN 0-8167-0843-6). Troll Assocs.

—Springtime Surprises: Things to Make & Do. Barto, Renzo, illus. LC 85-16497. 48p. (gr. 1-5). 1986. PLB 11.89 (ISBN 0-8167-0670-0); pap. text ed. 2.95 (ISBN 0-8167-0671-9). Troll Assocs.

—Things That Go! How to Make Toy Boats, Cars, & Planes. Barto, Renzo, illus. LC 86-7130. 48p. (gr. 1-5). 1987. PLB 11.89 (ISBN 0-8167-0838-X); pap. text ed. 2.95 (ISBN 0-8167-0839-8). Troll Assocs.

Crooks, Linda H., et al. Kindergang Kindergarten Skills Booklets, 5 vols. 2nd ed. Crooks, Linda H., illus. (gr. k). 1988. Repr. of 1985 ed. Set. write for info. tchr's. ed. (ISBN 1-877594-00-8); wkbk. avail. I Can.

Davies, Kate. Play Mask Book - Wizard of Oz. 12p. (ps-3). 1991. pap. 5.95 (ISBN 0-8167-2373-7). Troll Assocs.

Davis, Duane. Listen & Play with My Friends & Me Activity Manual. rev. ed. (ps-k). 1988. wkbk. 24.00 (ISBN 0-88671-331-5). Am Guidance.

Draze, Dianne. Pot Pourri. (Illus.). (gr. 3-8). 1978. pap. 7.00 (ISBN 0-931724-01-5). Dandy Lion.

Draze, Dianne L. The Last Word Book. Werth, Debbie & Jones, Liza, illus. (gr. 4-7). 1978. pap. 6.00 (ISBN 0-931724-00-7). Dandy Lion.

Falk, Cathy. Year-Round Preschool Activity Patterns. 48p. (Orig.). (ps-k). 1983. pap. 5.95 (ISBN 0-87239-680-0, 2141). Standard Pub.

Feinman, Jeffry & Schwartz, Betty. Freebies for Kids. Rev. Updated ed. 208p. (gr. 3-6). 1983. pap. 4.95 (ISBN 0-671-42657-5, Little Simon). S&S Trade.

Ferguson-Florissant Early Education Teachers Staff. Home Activities for Fours. Wilson, Marion M., ed. (Illus.). 110p. (Orig.). (ps). 1990. pap. text ed. 15.00 (ISBN 0-939418-60-6). Ferguson-Florissant.

Filkins, Vanessa. Early Learning Bulletin Boards. 144p. (ps-2). 1990. 10.95 (ISBN 0-86653-529-2, GA1141). Good Apple.

Find a Way Back Activity Book. (gr. 2). 1991. 3.90 (ISBN 0-88106-748-2). Charlesbridge Pub.

Find a Way Back Activity Book (EV) (gr. 2). 1991. 3.90 (ISBN 0-88106-747-4). Charlesbridge Pub.

Fujikawa, Gyo. Let's Play. (ps-1). 1975. 3.50 (ISBN 0-448-11958-7, G&D). Putnam Pub Group.

Fun & Games. (Illus.). (ps-5). 3.50 (ISBN 0-7214-0543-6). Ladybird Bks.

Fun & Games Sticker Book: At the Zoo. 1990. 2.98 (ISBN 0-8317-3657-7). Smithmark.

Fun & Games Sticker Book: Castles. 1990. 2.98 (ISBN 0-8317-3654-2). Smithmark.

Fun & Games Sticker Book: Doll's House. 1990. 2.98 (ISBN 0-8317-3656-9). Smithmark.

Fun & Games Sticker Book: Under the Sea. 1990. 2.98 (ISBN 0-8317-3655-0). Smithmark.

Furetig, Mary & Kreisberg, Darlene. Rainbow Writing: An Activity Journal for Young Writers & Artists. Bacchini, Lisa, illus. (Orig.). (gr. 1-3). 1990. pap. 9.95 (ISBN 0-9628216-0-8). Dream Tree Pr.

Games We Like. (Illus.). (ps-5). 3.50 (ISBN 0-7214-0555-X); Series S05, Set 1. flash cards 4.75; Series S05, Set 2. flash cards 4.75. Ladybird Bks.

Gamiello, Elvira. Monster Activity & Game Book. (Illus., Orig.). (gr. 4-6). 1988. pap. 1.95 (ISBN 0-942025-28-8). Kidsbks.

Gastman, J. Weil. Creatrivia. 112p. (gr. 4-8). 1989. 9.95 (ISBN 0-86653-482-2, GA1087). Good Apple.

Gerver, Jane, ed. The Storytime Activity Book. McCarthy, Kathleen, illus. 32p. (gr. 1-3). 1986. wkbk. 3.95 (ISBN 0-394-88168-0). Random.

Gleason, Karan. Factivities. 144p. (gr. k-5). 1991. 11.95 (ISBN 0-86653-601-9, GA1320). Good Apple.

—Sunny Day Fun. Hyndman, Kathryn, illus. 112p. (gr. k-5). 1989. wkbk. 9.95 (ISBN 0-86653-463-6, GA1068). Good Apple.

Glovach, Linda & Glovach, Linda. The Little Witch's Dinosaur Book. (Illus.). 48p. (gr. 1-4). 1984. 8.95 (ISBN 0-13-537739-0). P-H.

Glover, S. & Grewe, G. Bulletin Board Smorgasbord. (gr. 2-6). 1982. 9.95 (ISBN 0-88160-091-1, LW 233). Learning Wks.

Going to Playgroup. (Illus.). (ps). 3.50 (ISBN 0-7214-0851-6). Ladybird Bks.

Green Tiger Press Staff, ed. Bubbles & Bubble Blowers. (Illus.). 12p. (gr. 7-9). 1982. pap. 2.50 (ISBN 0-88138-000-8). Green Tiger Pr.

Highlights for Children Staff. Activity Books. Highlights for Children Staff, illus. 32p. (gr. 1-6). 1989. pap. 2.95 (ISBN 0-87534-381-3). Highlights.

—Activity Books. Highlights for Children Staff, illus. 32p. (gr. 1-6). 1989. pap. 2.95 (ISBN 0-87534-382-1). Highlights.

—Activity Books. Highlights for Children Staff, illus. 32p. (gr. 1-6). 1989. pap. 2.95 (ISBN 0-87534-383-X). Highlights.

—Activity Books. Highlights for Children Staff, illus. 32p. (gr. 1-6). 1989. pap. 2.95 (ISBN 0-87534-384-8). Highlights.

—Activity Books. Highlights for Children Staff, illus. 32p. (gr. 1-6). 1989. pap. 2.95 (ISBN 0-87534-385-6). Highlights.

—Activity Books. Highlights for Children Staff, illus. 32p. (gr. 1-6). 1989. pap. 2.95 (ISBN 0-87534-386-4). Highlights.

—Activity Books. Highlights for Children Staff, illus. 32p. (gr. 1-6). 1989. pap. 2.95 (ISBN 0-87534-387-2). Highlights.

—Activity Books. Highlights for Children Staff, illus. 32p. (gr. 1-6). 1989. pap. 2.95 (ISBN 0-87534-388-0). Highlights.

—Activity Books. Highlights for Children Staff, illus. 32p. (gr. 1-6). 1989. pap. 2.95 (ISBN 0-87534-389-9). Highlights.

—Activity Books. Highlights for Children Staff, illus. 32p. (gr. 1-6). 1989. pap. 2.95 (ISBN 0-87534-390-2). Highlights.

—What's Wrong & Other Mixed-up Fun. Highlights for Children Staff, illus. 32p. (gr. k-6). 1990. pap. 2.95 (ISBN 0-87534-464-X). Highlights.

—What's Wrong & Other Mixed-up Fun. Highlights for Children Staff, illus. 32p. (gr. k-6). 1990. pap. 2.95 (ISBN 0-87534-444-5). Highlights.

—What's Wrong & Other Mixed-up Fun. Highlights for Children Staff, illus. 32p. (gr. k-6). 1990. pap. 2.95 (ISBN 0-87534-449-6). Highlights.

—What's Wrong & Other Mixed-up Fun. Highlights for Children Staff, illus. 32p. (gr. k-6). 1990. pap. 2.95 (ISBN 0-87534-455-0). Highlights.

—What's Wrong & Other Mixed-up Fun. Highlights for Children Staff, illus. 32p. (gr. k-6). 1990. pap. 2.95 (ISBN 0-87534-463-1). Highlights.

—Winter Sports. Highlights for Children Staff, illus. 48p. (gr. 3-7). 1990. pap. 2.95 (ISBN 0-87534-351-1). Highlights.

Hogrogian, Nonny. Handmade Secret Hiding Places. LC 75-4379. (Illus.). 48p. (ps-5). 1990. pap. 7.95 (ISBN 0-685-29752-7); deluxe ed. 4.95 (ISBN 0-87951-376-4). Overlook Pr.

Hudson, Cheryl W. Afro-Bets 1 2 3 Coloring & Activity Book. Date not set. pap. 2.95 (ISBN 0-940975-09-2). Just Us Bks.

Hyndman, Kathryn. Hidden Picture Fun. 112p. (ps-2). 1991. 9.95 (ISBN 0-86653-614-0, GA1333). Good Apple.

Jenkins, Sheila, et al. Polka Dotted Pals, Pt. 1. 100p. (gr. k-1). 1980. pap. 8.95 (ISBN 0-932970-13-3). Prinit Pr.

Kalman, Bobbie. All about Me Activity Guide. (Illus.). 96p. (gr. k-2). 1985. pap. 14.95 (ISBN 0-86505-066-X). Crabtree Pub Co.

Karabatsos, Lewis T., ed. Bricks & Brackets: A Lowell Activity Book. 19p. (Orig.). (gr. 1-6). 1981. pap. 0.95 (ISBN 0-942472-04-7). Lowell Museum.

Leos, Frances. I Am Curious about Reading: A Curious George Activity Book. Campana, Manny, illus. 48p. (Orig.). (ps-2). 1987. pap. 1.95 wkbk. (ISBN 0-590-41045-8). Scholastic Inc.

Levy, Nathan. Stories with Holes, Vols. 1-8. 20p. 1990. pap. 5.00 ea. (ISBN 1-878347-11-X). NL Assocs.
"Stories With Holes" is the result of several years' accumulation, by the author & others, of puzzling stories that lend themselves to what I call thinking games. The games have become the means for hundreds of teachers to carry on a totally enjoyable process of training students in critical & imaginative thinking.
Publisher Provided Annotation.

Lewis, Shari. Shari Lewis Presents One Hundred & One Things for Kids to Do. Buller, Jon, illus. LC 86-43065. 96p. (gr. 1-5). 1987. lib. bdg. 9.99 (ISBN 0-394-98966-X, Random Juv); pap. 7.95 (ISBN 0-394-88966-5). Random.

McClure, Nancee. Clip & Copy Art: Creative Curriculum Cutouts. (Illus.). (gr. k-8). 1989. 11.95 (ISBN 0-86653-487-3, GA1086). Good Apple.

—Clip & Copy Art: Holidays, Seasons & Events. (Illus.). (gr. k-8). 1989. 11.95 (ISBN 0-86653-486-5, GA1085). Good Apple.

McCully, Emily A. Picnic. LC 83-47913. (Illus.). 32p. (ps-1). 1984. PLB 13.89 (ISBN 0-06-024100-4). HarpC Child Bks.

McKissack, Patricia & McKissack, Fredrick. Big Bug Book of Things to Do. Bartholomew, illus. LC 87-61651. 24p. (Orig.). (gr. k-1). 1987. spiral bdg. 14.95 (ISBN 0-88335-766-6); pap. text ed. 4.95 (ISBN 0-88335-776-3). Milliken Pub co.

McMillan, Mary. Christian Parties for Autumn & Winter. 96p. (ps-3). 1989. 9.95 (ISBN 0-86653-497-0, SS1815). Good Apple.

The Magician's Activity Book. (Illus.). (ps-2). 1.95 (ISBN 0-7214-3096-1). Ladybird Bks.

Marsh, Carole. Thirty Days Has September: Calendar Trivia & Activities for Kids. (gr. 3-9). 1990. 19.95 (ISBN 0-7933-0015-0); pap. 14.95 (ISBN 0-7933-0016-9); computer disk 29.95 (ISBN 0-7933-0017-7). Gallopade Pub Group.

—Worlds Fair Kit S. P. A. R. K. (Illus., Orig.). (gr. 3-12). 1986. pap. 24.95 (ISBN 0-935326-85-5). Gallopade Pub Group.

Morgridge, Tashia. Award-Winning Activities for All Curriculum Areas. (gr. 1-6). 1990. pap. 12.95 (ISBN 0-8224-7336-4). Fearon Teach Aids.

Orleans, Jacob S. Great Big Book of Pencil Puzzles. pap. 5.95 (ISBN 0-399-50942-9, Perigee Bks). Putnam Pub Group.

Outdoor Fun: A-Z Activity Book. 1989. 3.50 (ISBN 0-517-68797-6, Chatham River Pr). Outlet Bk Co.

Packard, Mary. Fun Factory. Barish, Wendy, ed. 64p. (Orig.). (gr. 3-8). 1984. pap. 2.95 (ISBN 0-671-47729-3, Little Simon). S&S Trade.

—Mickey's Riddles, Codes, & Games Book. Barish, Wendy, ed. 64p. (gr. 7 up). 1984. pap. 2.95 (ISBN 0-671-47731-5, Little Simon). S&S Trade.

Palumbo, Thomas J. Tuesday Timely Teasers. Hyndman, Kathryn, illus. 64p. (gr. 3-8). 1985. wkbk. 6.95 (ISBN 0-86653-309-5, GA 648). Good Apple.

Patrick, Sally, et al. The Month by Month Treasure Box. LC 86-82599. (Illus.). 80p. (Orig.). (ps-1). 1988. 7.95 (ISBN 0-86530-124-7, IP 130-1). Incentive Pubns.

Pendergast, Kathleen. Say Another One about Playing. LC 83-62129. (Illus.). 54p. (gr. k-6). 1983. pap. 6.95 (ISBN 0-942178-02-5). Madison Park Pr.

Pitcher, Caroline. Space & Spacecraft. Nevett, Louise, illus. 32p. (gr. k-3). PLB 11.90 (ISBN 0-531-04659-1). Watts.

Pre-School Activities. (Illus.). 24p. (ps-k). 1986. 3.98 (ISBN 0-86734-064-9, FS-3056). Schaffer Pubns.

Rogulic-Newsome, Lisa. Theme of the Week. 208p. (gr. 1-5). 1991. 13.95 (ISBN 0-86653-602-7, GA1321). Good Apple.

Schaffer, Frank, Publications Staff. Beginning Activities with Numbers. (Illus.). 24p. (ps-k). 1980. 3.98 (ISBN 0-86734-014-2, FS 3027). Schaffer Pubns.

—Beginning Activities with Pencil & Paper. (Illus.). 24p. (ps-k). 1980. 3.98 (ISBN 0-86734-017-7, FS 3030). Schaffer Pubns.

—Beginning Activities with Shapes. (Illus.). 24p. (ps-k). 1980. 3.98 (ISBN 0-86734-013-4, FS 3026). Schaffer Pubns.

—Beginning Activities with the Alphabet. (Illus.). 24p. (ps-k). 1980. 3.98 (ISBN 0-86734-015-0, FS 3028). Schaffer Pubns.

—Following Directions. (Illus.). 24p. (gr. 2-4). 1978. wkbk. 3.98 (ISBN 0-86734-008-8, FS 3009). Schaffer Pubns.

—Getting Ready for Kindergarten. (Illus.). 24p. (ps-k). 1978. wkbk. 3.98 (ISBN 0-86734-000-2, FS 3001). Schaffer Pubns.

Schwartz, L. Creative Capers. (gr. 4-6). 1985. 5.95 (ISBN 0-88160-117-9, LW 251). Learning Wks.

—Flip Kit. (gr. 1-6). 1989. 4.95 (ISBN 0-88160-183-7, LW 146). Learning Wks.

—Flip Kit Refills - Ten. (gr. 1-6). 1989. 29.95 (ISBN 0-88160-180-2, LW 145). Learning Wks.

Silverstein, Herma. Scream Machines: Roller Coasters Past, Present & Future. (Illus.). 128p. (gr. 3 up). 1986. 13.95 (ISBN 0-8027-6618-8); lib. bdg. 13.85 (ISBN 0-8027-6619-6). Walker & Co.

The Snowman Christmas Book. (Illus.). (ps-2). 1990. 1.95 (ISBN 0-7214-3202-6). Ladybird Bks.

Sohl, Marcia & Dackerman, Gerald. Me Time Machine: Student Activity Book. (Illus.). 16p. (gr. 4-10). 1976. pap. 1.25 (ISBN 0-88301-186-7). Pendulum Pr.

Spizman, Robyn. Bulletin Boards Plus. 112p. (gr. k-6). 1989. 9.95 (ISBN 0-86653-510-1, GA1080). Good Apple.

Stanish, Bob. The Ambidextrous Mind Book. 144p. (gr. 2-8). 1989. 11.95 (ISBN 0-86653-502-0, GA1092). Good Apple.

—Creative Activity Cards. 96p. (gr. 3-8). 1991. 10.95 (ISBN 0-86653-613-2, GA1332). Good Apple.

Stewart, Margaret A. The Best Book a Mother Ever Had. Imholte, Max, illus. 146p. (ps-3). 1985. pap. 12.95 spiral bdg. (ISBN 0-931047-00-5). KinderPr.
AS SWEET AS APPLE PIE! A double-ringed spiral bound illustrated collection of all those traditional songs, fingerplays, games, & crafts for babies & young children which you may think you know, but discover you have forgotten over the years. Included with the collection is a "baby memories" section which provides a special memorabilia area for recording family data, baby "firsts", & children's pictures for up to four children. Throughout the book are black & white illustrations for your children to color or just enjoy with the songs. Over one hundred songs include such titles as "Here Comes Peter Cottontail", "Frosty the Snowman", "Rudolph the Red-nosed Reindeer", "Here Comes Santa Claus", & "This Land Is Your Land", in addition to traditional lullabies, nursery rhymes, holiday, Bible, patriotic & favorite childhood songs. Favorite games for parties, jumprope rhymes, & craft ideas, methods, & recipes round out this book to make it a must for every new mother, father, grandparent, or newborn to primary teacher & daycare operator. Recommended for all those who take delight in children from newborn through age eight.
Publisher Provided Annotation.

Sugimura, et al. American-Japanese Coloring & Talking Books, Bks. 6-10. (gr. k-4). pap. 1.95 ea.; Bk. 6, Customs. (ISBN 0-8048-0012-X); Bk. 7, Dressing. (ISBN 0-8048-0013-8); Bk. 8, Riding. (ISBN 0-8048-0017-0). Vk. 9, Houses. (ISBN 0-8048-0016-2); Bk. 10, Story Book Heroes. (ISBN 0-8048-0019-7). C E Tuttle.

Tallarico, Anthony. Detect Donald. (Illus.). 24p. (Orig.). pap. 2.95 (ISBN 0-942025-79-2). Kidsbks.

—Detect Donald. (Illus.). 24p. 1990. 9.95 (ISBN 0-942025-99-7). Kidsbks.

—Find Frankie. (Illus., Orig.). pap. 2.95 (ISBN 0-942025-76-8). Kidsbks.

—Find Frankie. (Illus.). 24p. 1990. 9.95 (ISBN 0-942025-82-2). Kidsbks.

—Find Freddie. (Illus.). 24p. 1990. 9.95 (ISBN 0-942025-13-X). Kidsbks.

—Hunt for Hector. (Illus.). 24p. 1990. 9.95 (ISBN 0-942025-27-X). Kidsbks.

—Look for Laura. (Illus.). 24p. (Orig.). pap. 2.95 (ISBN 0-942025-77-6). Kidsbks.

—Look for Laura. (Illus.). 24p. 1990. 9.95 (ISBN 0-942025-89-X). Kidsbks.

—Look for Lisa. (Illus.). 24p. 1990. 9.95 (ISBN 0-942025-61-X). Kidsbks.

—Search for Sam. (Illus.). 24p. 1990. 9.95 (ISBN 0-942025-58-X). Kidsbks.

—Search for Santa. (Illus.). 32p. (Orig.). 1990. 10.95 (ISBN 0-942025-71-7); pap. 3.95 (ISBN 0-942025-72-5). Kidsbks.

—Search for Susie. (Illus.). 24p. (Orig.). pap. 2.95 (ISBN 0-942025-78-4). Kidsbks.

—Search for Susie. (Illus.). 24p. 1990. 9.95 (ISBN 0-942025-97-0). Kidsbks.

—What's Wrong Here, No. 2. (Illus.). 64p. (Orig.). 1990. pap. 1.95 (ISBN 0-942025-92-X). Kidsbks.

Teacher Planning Guide, Units 1 & 2. (gr. 1). 1991. 27.50 (ISBN 0-88106-702-4). Charlesbridge Pub.

Teacher Planning Guide, Units 3 & 4. (gr. 1). 1991. 27.50 (ISBN 0-88106-719-9). Charlesbridge Pub.

Teacher Planning Guide, Units 5 & 6. (gr. 2). 1991. 27.50 (ISBN 0-88106-740-7). Charlesbridge Pub.

Teacher Planning Guide, Units 7 & 8. (gr. 2). 1991. 27.50 (ISBN 0-88106-754-7). Charlesbridge Pub.

Teacher Planning Guide, Units 9 & 10. (gr. 3). 1991. 27. 50 (ISBN 0-88106-771-7). Charlesbridge Pub.

Van Steenwyk, Elizabeth. Behind the Scenes at the Amusement Park. Tucker, Kathleen, ed. LC 83-1307. (Illus.). 48p. (gr. 4 up). 1983. PLB 12.95 (ISBN 0-8075-0605-2). A Whitman.

Walker, Karen, illus. Make-a-Face: Monster Faces. 24p. (Orig.). 1990. pap. 1.95 (ISBN 0-942025-98-9). Kidsbks.

Wathen, Judy & Sussman, Ellen. Teach Me Fun & Games. Burris, Priscilla, illus. 40p. (Orig.). (ps-k). 1989. pap. 4.95 (ISBN 0-933606-76-1); tchr's. guide avail. Monkey Sisters.

Wayman & Plum. Secrets & Surprises. 96p. (gr. k-8). 1977. 9.95 (ISBN 0-916456-13-7, GA70). Good Apple.

Webster, Harriet. Winter Book. Trivas, Irene, illus. LC 88-1662. 128p. (Orig.). (gr. 3-7). 1988. pap. 4.95 (ISBN 0-689-71235-9, Aladdin). Macmillan Child Grp.

Wilkes, Angela. My First Activity Book. (Illus.). (gr. 1-5). 1990. write for info. Knopf.

Wolff, Margaret. Kid's After School Activity Book. (Illus.). (gr. 1-5). 1985. pap. 6.95 (ISBN 0-8224-4228-0). Fearon Teach Aids.

Yolen, Jane, compiled by. The Lap-Time Song & Play Book. Tomes, Margot, illus. Stemple, Adam, contrib. by. (Illus.). (ps up). 1989. 15.95 (ISBN 0-15-243588-3). HarBraceJ.

Zubrowski, Bernie. A Children's Museum Activity Book: Bubbles. Drescher, Joan, illus. LC 78-27497. (gr. 5-7). 1979. pap. 6.95 (ISBN 0-316-98881-2). Little.

ANALYSIS, MICROSCOPIC
see Microscope and Microscopy

ANATOMY
Here are entered general treatises and works on human anatomy. General works on animal anatomy are entered under Anatomy, Comparative.
see also Anatomy, Comparative; Bones; Nervous System; Physiology;
also subjects with the subdivision Anatomy, e.g. Birds–Anatomy; Botany–Anatomy; etc.; and names of organs and regions of the body, e.g. Heart

Allison, Linda. Blood & Guts. (Illus.). (gr. 5-12). 1976. 14.95 (ISBN 0-316-03442-8); pap. 8.95 (ISBN 0-316-03443-6). Little.

Ask about the Human Body. 64p. (gr. 4-5). 1987. PLB 18.25 (ISBN 0-8172-2884-5); pap. 13.27 (ISBN 0-8172-2896-9). Raintree Pubs.

Avraham, Regina. The Circulatory System. Koop, C. Everett, intro. by. (Illus.). 112p. (gr. 5-12). 1989. 18.95 (ISBN 0-7910-0013-3). Chelsea Hse.

—The Reproductive System. (Illus.). (gr. 5-12). 1991. 18. 95 (ISBN 0-7910-0025-7). Chelsea Hse.

Bassett, Kerry. My Very Own Special Body Book. 4th ed. McDaniel, Diane, illus. Wooley, Marilyn J., intro. by. (Illus.). 18p. (ps-2). 1987. pap. 3.25 (ISBN 0-9620154-0-7). Hawthorne Pr.

Bender, Lionel. The Body. (Illus.). 32p. (gr. 5-6). 1989. PLB 11.90 (ISBN 0-531-17183-3). Watts.

Berger, Gilda. The Human Body. May, Darcy, illus. 1989. 9.95 (ISBN 0-385-24278-6); PLB 10.99 (ISBN 0-385-24279-4). Doubleday.

Berger, Melvin. Why I Cough, Sneeze, Shiver, Hiccup, & Yawn. Keller, Holly, illus. LC 82-45587. 40p. (gr. k-3). 1983. PLB 13.89 (ISBN 0-690-04254-X, Crowell Jr Bks). HarpC Child Bks.

Berry, Joy W. Teach Me about My Body. Dickey, Kate, ed. LC 85-45092. (Illus.). 36p. (ps). 1986. 4.98 (ISBN 0-685-10730-2). Grolier Inc.

The Body. (Illus.). 112p. (gr. 4-9). Date not set. 19.95x (ISBN 1-85435-071-4). Marshall Cavendish.

Bogot, Howard & Syme, Daniel. My Body Is Something Special. (Illus.). (ps). 1982. pap. 4.00 (ISBN 0-8074-0152-8, 101715). UAHC.

Boynton, Sandra. The Going to Bed Book. Klimo, Kate, ed. Boynton, Sandra, illus. 14p. (ps-k). 1982. 3.95 (ISBN 0-671-44902-8, Little Simon). S&S Trade.

Braithwaite, Althea. How My Body Works. Cony, Frances, illus. 24p. (ps-2). 1990. 1.95 (ISBN 1-878624-22-9, 1553800022). McClanahan Bk.

Brenner, Barbara. Bodies. Ancona, George, illus. (ps-3). 1973. 13.95 (ISBN 0-525-26770-0, DCB). Dutton Child Bks.

Bruun, Ruth D. & Bruun, Bertel. The Human Body. Wynne, Patricia, illus. LC 82-5210. 96p. (gr. 5 up). 1982. lib. bdg. 11.99 (ISBN 0-394-94424-0); pap. 11. 95 smythe-sewn (ISBN 0-394-84424-6). Random.

Buxbaum, Susan K. & Gelman, Rita G. Body Noises: Where They Come from, Why They Happen. Lloyd, Angie, illus. LC 83-320. 72p. (gr. 3-7). 1983. 8.95 (ISBN 0-394-85771-2). Knopf.

Carratello, Patty. Body Basics. Wright, Theresa, illus. 48p. (gr. 1-5). 1987. wkbk. 5.95 (ISBN 1-55734-220-2). Tchr Create Mat.

Caselli, Giovanni. The Human Body & How It Works. (Illus.). 64p. (gr. 2-6). 1987. 14.95 (ISBN 0-448-18997-6, G&D). Putnam Pub Group.

Cassin, Sue. Fascinating Facts about Your Body. 1990. 9.95 (ISBN 1-55782-328-6). Warner Bks.

Cobb, Vicki. For Your Own Protection: Stories Science Photos Tell. LC 89-2342. (Illus.). 32p. (gr. 3-6). 1989. 14.95 (ISBN 0-688-08787-6); PLB 14.88 (ISBN 0-688-08788-4). Lothrop.

Cole, Joanna. The Human Body: How We Evolved. Gaffney-Kessell, Walter, illus. LC 86-23679. 64p. (ps-3). 1987. 12.95 (ISBN 0-688-06719-0); lib. bdg. 12.88 (ISBN 0-688-06720-4, Morrow Jr Bks). Morrow Jr Bks.

—The Magic School Bus Inside the Human Body. Deger, Bruce, illus. (ps-3). 1990. pap. 3.95 (ISBN 0-590-41427-5). Scholastic Inc.

Cole, Joanna & Degen, Bruce. The Magic School Bus Inside the Body. 1989. pap. 13.95 (ISBN 0-590-41426-7, Scholastic Hardcovers). Scholastic Inc.

Conway, Lorraine. Body Systems. Atkins, Linda, illus. 64p. (gr. 5 up). 1984. wkbk. 6.95 (ISBN 0-86653-153-X, GA 552). Good Apple.

—The Human Body. 64p. (gr. 5 up). 1980. 6.95 (ISBN 0-916456-67-6, GA 178). Good Apple.

Crump, Donald J., ed. Your Wonderful Body. LC 81-47892. 104p. (gr. 4-8). 1982. 6.95 (ISBN 0-87044-423-9); PLB 8.50 (ISBN 0-87044-428-X). Natl Geog.

Dubov, Christine. Aleksandra, Where Is Your Nose. Schneider, Josef, photos by. (Illus.). 12p. (ps). 1986. 3.95 (ISBN 0-312-01719-7). St Martin.

Eastman, David. I Can Read About My Own Body. LC 72-96958. (Illus.). (gr. 2-4). 1973. pap. 1.95 (ISBN 0-89375-057-3). Troll Assocs.

Edelson, Edward. The Immune System. (Illus.). (gr. 5-12). 1990. 18.95 (ISBN 0-7910-0021-4). Chelsea Hse.

—The Neurological System. (Illus.). (gr. 7-12). 1989. 18. 95 (ISBN 0-7910-0023-0). Chelsea Hse.

Elting, Mary. The Answer Book about You. Barnes-Murphy, Rowan, illus. (gr. 3-7). 1984. pap. 2.95 (ISBN 0-448-13800-X, G&D). Putnam Pub Group.

—The Macmillan Book of the Human Body. Moldoff, Kirk, illus. LC 85-24204. 80p. (gr. 3-7). 1986. pap. 8.95 (ISBN 0-02-043080-9, Aladdin). Macmillan Child Grp.

—Macmillan Book of the Human Body. LC 85-24204. (Illus.). 80p. (gr. 3-7). 1986. 15.95 (ISBN 0-02-733440-6, Mcmillan Child Bk). Macmillan Child Grp.

Faulkner, Keith. This Is Me. Lambert, Jonathan, illus. 10p. (ps-k). 1987. 5.95 (ISBN 0-312-00967-4). St Martin.

Freeman, Lory. Mi Cuerpo Es Mio. Dunn, Lois, tr. from ENG. Deach, Carol, illus. LC 85-62435. (SPA.). 32p. (Orig.). (ps). 1985. pap. 3.95 (ISBN 0-943990-19-X). Parenting Pr.

Gamlin, Linda. The Human Body. FS-Aladdin Staff, ed. Hayward, Ron, illus. 40p. (gr. 4-9). 1988. PLB 12.40 (ISBN 0-531-17117-5, Gloucester Pr). Watts.

Goldman, Meredith & Lissauer, T. Human Body. Ashman, Iain, illus. 32p. (gr. 6 up). 1983. lib. bdg. 13. 96 (ISBN 0-88110-150-8); pap. 6.95 (ISBN 0-86020-747-1). EDC.

Goldsmith, Ilse. Human Anatomy for Children. Krause, William, illus. (gr. 5-8). 1969. pap. 2.95 (ISBN 0-486-22355-8). Dover.

Hindley & Rawson. How Your Body Works. (gr. 2-5). 1975. (Usborne-Hayes); PLB 13.96 (ISBN 0-88110-113-3); pap. 6.95 (ISBN 0-86020-198-8). EDC.

The How & Why Activity Wonder Book of the Human Body. (Illus.). (gr. k-9). 1988. pap. 1.95 (ISBN 0-318-36493-X). Scholastic Inc.

Human Body. (Illus.). 32p. (ps up). 1986. 2.95 (ISBN 0-8431-4281-2). Price Stern.

The Human Body. 48p. (gr. 5-6). 1989. PLB 10.95 (ISBN 0-685-26337-1). Capstone Pr.

Human Body. LC 90-34570. (Illus.). 64p. (gr. 4-6). 1990. PLB 12.95 (ISBN 0-8368-0055-9). Gareth Stevens Inc.

Jennings, Terry. The Human Body. LC 88-22859. (Illus.). 32p. (gr. 3-6). 1989. PLB 14.60 (ISBN 0-516-08404-6); pap. 4.95 (ISBN 0-516-48404-4). Childrens.

Johnson, John E. The Me Book. Johnson, John E., illus. LC 79-62042. (ps). 1979. 2.95 (ISBN 0-394-84243-X, Random Juv). Random.

Kalman, Bobbie. My Busy Body. (Illus.). 32p. (gr. k-2). 1985. 14.95 (ISBN 0-86505-065-1); pap. 6.95 (ISBN 0-86505-089-9). Crabtree Pub Co.

Kaufman, Joe. Joe Kaufman's Big Book About the Human Body. (Illus.). 96p. (gr. 1-7). 1987. write for info. (ISBN 0-307-16843-3, Pub. by Golden Bks). Western Pub.

Keen, Martin L. The Human Body. (gr. 4-6). pap. 2.95 (ISBN 0-8431-4261-8). Price Stern.

Kile, Marilyn & Baird, Kristin. My Body Belongs to Me. (gr. k-2). 1986. text ed. 17.95 (ISBN 0-88671-173-8, 7202). Am Guidance.

—What Would You Do If...? 1986. pap. text ed. 10.50 (ISBN 0-88671-172-X, 7205). Am Guidance.

Kingston, Arlene. I'm Small Thats All. (Illus.). (ps up). 1989. pap. write for info. (ISBN 0-929934-02-4). Child Time Pubs.

Kittredge, Mary. The Human Body: An Overview. (Illus.). (gr. 5-12). 1990. 18.95 (ISBN 0-7910-0019-2). Chelsea Hse.

Lauber, Patricia. Your Body & How It Works. (Illus.). (gr. 3-5). 1966. (Random Juv); PLB 10.99 (ISBN 0-394-90125-8). Random.

Llewellyn, Claire. First Look at Keeping Warm. LC 91-9423. (Illus.). 32p. (gr. 1-2). 1991. PLB 10.95 (ISBN 0-8368-0704-9). Gareth Stevens Inc.

Markle, Sandra. Outside & Inside You. Kuklin, Susan, illus. LC 90-37791. 40p. (ps-3). 1991. RSBE 14.95 (ISBN 0-02-762311-4, Bradbury Pr). Macmillan Child Grp.

Our Bodies. LC 90-36755. (Illus.). 64p. (gr. 2-3). 1990. PLB 12.95 (ISBN 0-8368-0080-X). Gareth Stevens Inc.

Oxenbury, Helen. Merry Mix-ups. Oxenbury, Helen, illus. LC 79-2980. 9p. (ps-3). 1985. 4.95 (ISBN 0-694-00034-5). HarpC Child Bks.

Packard, Mary, text by. From Head to Toes: How Your Body Works. Leder, Dora, illus. (ps up). 1985. pap. 8.95 (ISBN 0-671-49772-3, Little Simon). S&S Trade.

Penn, Linda. The Human Body. 32p. (gr. k-3). 1986. wkbk. 4.95 (ISBN 0-86653-352-4, GA 686). Good Apple.

Quinn, Kaye. The Human Body. (Illus.). 80p. (Orig.). (gr. 2-4). 1989. pap. 2.50 (ISBN 0-8431-2378-8). Price Stern.

Rosenfeld, Dina. All about Us. Zelcer, Amir, illus. 32p. (ps). 1988. write for info. Hachai Pubns.

Royston, Angela. The Human Body & How It Works. Shone, Rob, illus. 40p. (gr. 4-5). 1991. PLB 11.40 (ISBN 0-531-19102-8). Watts.

—The Human Body & How It Works. Stone, Rob, illus. LC 90-42978. 40p. (Orig.). (gr. 2-5). 1991. pap. 3.95 (ISBN 0-679-80860-4). Random.

Sabin, Francene. Human Body. Sibley, Don, illus. LC 84-2591. 32p. (gr. 3-6). 1985. PLB 9.49 (ISBN 0-8167-0170-9); pap. text ed. 2.95 (ISBN 0-8167-0171-7). Troll Assocs.

Schlossberg, Leon. The Johns Hopkins Human Anatomy Series. (Illus.). (gr. 8 up). 1986. markable ed. 36.95 (ISBN 0-9603730-2-0). Anatomical Chart.

Schoen, Mark. Bellybuttons Are Navels. Quay, M. J., illus. Calderone, Mary, intro. by. (Illus.). 40p. (ps-3). 1990. Repr. 15.95 (ISBN 0-87975-585-7). Prometheus Bks.

The Simon & Schuster Pocket Book of the Human Body. (gr. 3 up). 1987. pap. 6.95 (ISBN 0-671-62973-5, Little Simon). S&S Trade.

Sproule, Anna. Body Watch: Know Your Insides. LC 87-80100. (Illus.). 48p. (gr. 1-4). 1987. 12.95x (ISBN 0-8160-1782-4). Facts on File.

Stark, Fred. Start Exploring Gray's Anatomy: A Fact-Filled Coloring Book. (Illus.). 128p. (Orig.). (gr. 2 up). 1991. pap. 7.95 (ISBN 0-89471-863-0). Running Pr.

Thomson, Arthur. Handbook of Anatomy for Art Students. 5th ed. (Illus.). (gr. 9-12). 1929. pap. text ed. 9.95 (ISBN 0-486-21163-0). Dover.

Townsend, Anne. Marvelous Me: All about the Human Body. (Illus.). 48p. (ps-1). 1985. 13.95 (ISBN 0-85648-577-2). Lion USA.

Wells, Donna K. Your Body: Treasures Inside. Endres, Helen, illus. LC 90-30632. 32p. (ps-2). 1990. lib. bdg. 11.97 (ISBN 0-89565-576-4). Childs World.

Western, Joan & Wilson, Ron. The Human Body. Atkinson, Mike, illus. LC 90-38929. 96p. (gr. 3-6). 1991. PLB 14.89 (ISBN 0-8167-2234-X); pap. text ed. 6.95 (ISBN 0-8167-2235-8). Troll Assocs.

What's Inside My Body? (Illus.). 24p. (ps-3). 1991. 8.95 (ISBN 1-879431-07-6); PLB 9.99 (ISBN 1-879431-22-X). Dorling Kindersley.
Designed to satisfy a child's natural curiosity, the WHAT'S INSIDE? series gives a fascinating behind-the-scenes look at an array of subjects. Each book features bright, full color photography & overlay illustrations that show the inner workings of an object, from a shell to a teddy bear to a goldfish. Short, easy-to-read labels & leader lines make this a terrific series for beginning readers, & are great for reading aloud, too. The perfect answer to one of the questions children ask most often: WHAT'S INSIDE? Taken together, Dorling Kindersley's WHAT'S INSIDE? series serves as a valuable reference tool for home, school, & library.
Publisher Provided Annotation.

Wong, Ovid. Your Body & How It Works. Donahoe, Lindaanne, illus. LC 86-9686. 128p. (gr. 5 up). 1986. PLB 17.27 (ISBN 0-516-00534-0). Childrens.

ANATOMY, ARTISTIC

Brenner, Barbara. Faces. Ancona, George, illus. (ps-1). 1970. 13.95 (ISBN 0-525-29518-6, DCB). Dutton Child Bks.

Zaidenberg, Arthur. How to Draw Heads & Faces. Zaidenberg, Arthur, illus. LC 66-10314. 64p. (gr. 5-10). 1966. PLB 12.89 (ISBN 0-200-03893-1, Crowell Jr Bks). HarpC Child Bks.

ANATOMY, COMPARATIVE

see also Man–Origin and Antiquity

Cooper, Gail. Inside Animals. Cooper, Gail, illus. LC 87-4526. 64p. (gr. 4-8). 1987. Repr. PLB 9.95 (ISBN 0-915391-23-6, Pub. by Mad Hatter Bks). Slawson Comm.

Goor, Ron & Goor, Nancy. Heads. Goor, Ron, illus. LC 87-30262. 64p. (gr. 2-6). 1988. 13.95 (ISBN 0-689-31400-0, Atheneum Child Bk). Macmillan Child Grp.

Perkins, Al. Nose Book. McKie, Roy, illus. LC 71-117540. (ps-1). 1970. 6.95 (ISBN 0-394-80623-9, Random Juv); lib. bdg. 7.99 (ISBN 0-394-90623-3). Random.

Wenster, David. Dissection Projects. Jackman, Antoinette, illus. Rasof, Henry, ed. (Illus.). 96p. (gr. 5-8). 1988. 10.40 (ISBN 0-531-10474-5). Watts.

ANATOMY, DENTAL

see Teeth

ANCIENT ART

see Art, Ancient

ANCIENT CIVILIZATION

see Civilization, Ancient

ANCIENT HISTORY

see History, Ancient

ANDERSEN, HANS CHRISTIAN, 1805-1875

Cote. Hans Christian Andersen, Reading Level 2. (Illus.). 24p. (gr. 1-4). Date not set. PLB 12.33 (ISBN 0-86592-430-9). Rourke Corp.

Greene, Carol. Hans Christian Andersen: Teller of Tales. LC 85-27991. (Illus.). 128p. (gr. 4-7). 1986. PLB 17.27 (ISBN 0-516-03216-X). Childrens.

Johnson, Spencer. The Value of Fantasy: The Story of Hans Christian Andersen. LC 79-18237. (Illus.). (gr. k-6). 1979. 9.95 (ISBN 0-916392-43-0, Pub. by Value Communications). Oak Tree Pubns.

ANDERSON, MARIAN, 1902-

McKissack, Patricia & McKissack, Fredrick. Marian Anderson: A Great Singer. Ostendorf, Ned, illus. LC 90-19163. 32p. (gr. 1-4). 1991. PLB 12.95 (ISBN 0-89490-303-9). Enslow Pubs.

Tedards, Anne. Marian Anderson. Horner, Matina, intro. by. (Illus.). 112p. (Orig.). (gr. 5 up). 1988. 17.95 (ISBN 1-55546-638-9); pap. 9.95 (ISBN 0-7910-0216-0). Chelsea Hse.

ANDES MOUNTAINS

Cobb, Vicki. This Place Is High. Lavallee, Barbara, illus. 32p. (gr. 2-4). 1989. 12.95 (ISBN 0-8027-6882-2); PLB 13.85 (ISBN 0-8027-6883-0). Walker & Co.

ANECDOTES

Gauch, Patricia L. Christina Katerina & the Box. Burn, Doris, illus. 48p. 1980. pap. 2.95 (ISBN 0-698-20524-3, Coward). Putnam Pub Group.

ANGELS–FICTION

Bartone, Elisa. The Angel Who Forgot. Cline, Paul, illus. 48p. (Orig.). (ps up). 1986. pap. 5.95 (ISBN 0-88138-072-5). Green Tiger Pr.

Carney, Mary L. Too Tough to Hurt. 128p. 1991. pap. 5.95 (ISBN 0-310-28621-2, Youth Bks). Zondervan.

Ching Yee, Janice. God's Meekest Angels. (Illus.). (gr. k-6). 1981. pap. 3.00 (ISBN 0-931420-10-5). Pi Pr.

Collington, Peter. The Angel & the Soldier Boy. Collington, Peter, illus. LC 86-20169. 32p. (ps-2). 1988. pap. 4.95 (ISBN 0-394-81967-5). Knopf.

Cummings, Pat. C.L.O.U.D.S. LC 85-9719. (Illus.). 32p. (ps-3). 1986. 12.95 (ISBN 0-688-04682-7); PLB 12.88 (ISBN 0-688-04683-5). Lothrop.

Dellinger, Annetta E. Angels Are My Friends. LC 85-7858. 32p. (gr. 5-9). 1985. 5.95 (ISBN 0-570-04120-1, 56-1531). Concordia.

Delton, Judy. Back Yard Angel. Morrill, Leslie, illus. 112p. (gr. 2-5). 1983. 13.95 (ISBN 0-395-33883-2). HM.

Ebisch, Glen. Angel in the Snow. (gr. 7 up). 1988. pap. 2.25 (ISBN 0-317-69513-4). S&S Trade.

Eliason, Peter. The Comeuppance of Dipsey Dolan. 162p. (Orig.). (gr. 2-10). 1984. pap. 5.95 (ISBN 0-916777-34-0). W P Allen.

Elwood, Roger. Angelwalk. LC 87-70456. 192p. (Orig.). 1988. pap. 7.95 (ISBN 0-89107-440-6, Crossway Bks). Good News.

Fontenot, Mary A. Star Seed. Cregan, Nannette, illus. 32p. (gr. k-4). 1986. Repr. 6.95 (ISBN 0-88289-628-8). Pelican.

Hamilton, Jamar W. Julie's Angel. (gr. 4-7). 1990. pap. 5.95 (ISBN 0-925928-06-2). Tiny Thought.

Kavanaugh, James. The Crooked Angel. 2nd ed. Havelock, Elaine, illus. 64p. (ps-3). 1990. pap. 9.95 (ISBN 1-878995-02-2). S J Nash Pub.

Messmer, Barbara A. The Starshiners & the Gloomies. 1991. 7.95 (ISBN 0-533-08634-5). Vantage.

Peckinpah, Sandra L. Rosey...the Imperfect Angel. Moore, Trisha, illus. LC 90-63058. 32p. (ps-4). 1991. 15.95 (ISBN 0-9627806-0-X). Dasan Prodns.

Tazewell, Charles. Littlest Angel. Leone, S., illus. 32p. (gr. k-6). 1946. PLB 14.60 (ISBN 0-516-03533-9). Childrens.

Thomas, Kathy. The Angel's Quest. Seitz, Jacqueline, illus. 32p. (gr. 2-6). 1983. casebound 9.95 (ISBN 0-914544-99-3). Living Flame Pr.
Zimelman, Nathan. The Star of Melvin. Dunrea, Olivier, illus. LC 86-171. 32p. (ps-2). 1987. 12.95 (ISBN 0-02-793750-X, Mcmillan Child Bk). Macmillan Child Grp.

ANGINA PECTORIS
see Heart–Diseases

ANGLING
see Fishing

ANGLO-SAXONS
Ellenby, J. Anglo-Saxon Household. (Illus.). 32p. (gr. 1-5). 1986. 6.95 (ISBN 0-521-30379-6); pap. 3.95 (ISBN 0-521-31676-6). Cambridge U Pr.

ANIMAL BABIES
see Animals–Infancy

ANIMAL BEHAVIOR
see Animals–Habits and Behavior

ANIMAL COLORATION
see Color of Animals

ANIMAL COMMUNICATION
Battaglia, Aurelius, illus. Animal Sounds. 22p. (ps). 1981. write for info. (ISBN 0-307-12122-4, Golden Bks). Western Pub.
Cole, Jacci. Animal Communication: Opposing Viewpoints. LC 88-24401. (Illus.). 112p. (gr. 3-8). 1988. PLB 13.95 (ISBN 0-89908-062-6). Greenhaven.
Flegg, Jim. Animal Communication. (Illus.). 32p. (gr. 4-6). 1991. PLB 11.90 (ISBN 1-878137-23-9). Newington.
Gans, Roma. Bird Talk. Polseno, Jo, illus. LC 71-132298. 40p. (gr. k-3). 1971. 13.95 (ISBN 0-690-14592-6, Crowell Jr Bks). HarpC Child Bks.
Johnson, Rebecca L. The Secret Language: Pheromones in the Animal World. (Illus.). 64p. (gr. 5 up). 1989. 15. 95 (ISBN 0-8225-1586-5). Lerner Pubns.
McDonnell, Janet. Animal Communication. LC 88-36643. (Illus.). 48p. (gr. 2-6). 1989. PLB 10.95 (ISBN 0-89565-513-6); pap. 6.96 (ISBN 0-89565-531-4). Childs World.
—Animal Talk: Barks, Growls, Hisses, Howls. Ching, illus. LC 89-23990. 32p. (ps-2). 1990. lib. bdg. 11.97 (ISBN 0-89565-558-6). Childs World.
Mcnulty, Faith. With Love from Koko. (gr. k up). 1990. pap. 12.95 (ISBN 0-590-42774-1). Scholastic Inc.
Pluckrose, Henry. Whoops, Words & Whistles. (Illus.). 32p. (gr. k-4). 1990. PLB 10.40 (ISBN 0-531-14047-4). Watts.

ANIMAL DRAWING
see Animal Painting and Illustration

ANIMAL HOMES
see Animals–Habitations

ANIMAL INDUSTRY
see Domestic Animals; Livestock

ANIMAL INTELLIGENCE
see also Animals–Habits and Behavior
Hinde, R. A. & Hinde, J. S. Instinct & Intelligence. 3rd ed. Head, J. J., ed. LC 87-70404. (Illus.). 16p. (gr. 10 up). 1987. pap. 2.15 (ISBN 0-89278-063-0, 45-9663). Carolina Biological.
Sattler, Helen R. Fish Facts & Bird Brains: Animal Intelligence. Maestro, Giulio, illus. LC 83-20805. 128p. (gr. 5-9). 1984. 13.95 (ISBN 0-525-66915-9, Lodestar Bks). Dutton Child Bks.

ANIMAL KINGDOM
see Zoology

ANIMAL LANGUAGE
see Animal Communication

ANIMAL LIGHT
see Bioluminescence

ANIMAL LORE
see Animals, Mythical; Natural History

ANIMAL MAGNETISM
see Hypnotism

ANIMAL MIGRATION
see Animals–Migration

ANIMAL PAINTING AND ILLUSTRATION
see also Animals in Art; Photography of Animals
Arnosky, Jim. Near the Sea. 32p. 1990. 13.95 (ISBN 0-688-08164-9); PLB 13.88 (ISBN 0-688-09327-2). Lothrop.
Baby Animals. (Illus.). 32p. (gr. 1-6). 1987. 1.00 (ISBN 0-87406-270-5, 46-15096-5). Willowisp Pr.
Davidow-Goodman, Ann. Let's Draw Animals. (Illus.). (gr. 1-5). 1960. 2.95 (ISBN 0-448-02917-0, G&D); PLB 5.99 (ISBN 0-448-03326-7). Putnam Pub Group.
Fun to Draw Teddy Bears. (Illus.). 32p. (gr. 1-6). 1989. 2.50 (ISBN 0-87406-353-1, 46-17358-6). Willowisp Pr.
Hamm, Jack. How to Draw Animals. Hamm, Jack, illus. (gr. 7 up). 1969. pap. 6.95 (ISBN 0-399-50802-3, G&D). Putnam Pub Group.
Hart, Tony. Animals & Figures. (Illus.). 32p. (gr. 1-4). 1984. 5.95 (ISBN 0-7182-2950-9, Pub. by W Heinemann Ltd). Trafalgar Sq.
Laidman, Hugh. Animals: How to Draw Them. LC 75-11930. (Illus.). 160p. (gr. 7 up). 1979. pap. 12.95 (Dutton). NAL-Dutton.
Pinkus, Sue. Let's All Draw Cats, Dogs & Other Animals. 1991. pap. 16.95 (ISBN 0-8230-2705-8). Watson-Guptill.
—Let's All Draw Dinosaurs, Pterodactyls & Other Prehistoric Creatures. 1991. pap. 16.95 (ISBN 0-8230-2706-6). Watson-Guptill.
Sperling, Anita. Funny Animals Tracing Fun. 1989. pap. 1.95 (ISBN 0-590-42197-2). Scholastic Inc.
Wildsmith, Brian. Animal Shapes. Wildsmith, Brian, illus. (ps-3). 1981. 9.95 (ISBN 0-19-279733-6). Oxford U Pr.
Zaidenberg, Arthur. How to Draw Dogs, Cats & Horses. Zaidenberg, Arthur, illus. LC 59-5390. (gr. 5-10). 1959. PLB 12.89 (ISBN 0-200-71811-8, B37171, Crowell Jr Books). HarpC Child Bks.
—How to Draw Wild Animals. Zaidenberg, Arthur, illus. LC 57-12534. (gr. 5-10). 1958. PLB 12.89 (ISBN 0-200-71141-5, Crowell Jr Books). HarpC Child Bks.

ANIMAL PHOTOGRAPHY
see Photography of Animals

ANIMAL PHYSIOLOGY
see Zoology

ANIMAL PRODUCTS
see names of special products, e.g. Hides and Skins; Ivory; etc

ANIMAL PSYCHOLOGY
see Animal Intelligence

ANIMALS
see also Color of Animals; Desert Animals; Domestic Animals; Fresh-Water Animals; Geographical Distribution of Animals and Plants; Marine Animals; Natural History; Pets; Zoological Gardens; Zoology also names of orders and classes of the animal kingdom (e.g. Birds; Insects; etc.); and names of animals, e.g. Dogs; Bears; etc.
Aaseng, Nathan. Animal Specialists. Dornisch, Alcuin C., illus. 48p. (gr. k-3). 1987. PLB 7.95 (ISBN 0-8225-1120-7). Lerner Pubns.
—Horned Animals. Dornisch, Alcuin C., illus. 48p. (gr. k-3). 1987. PLB 6.95 (ISBN 0-8225-1119-3). Lerner Pubns.
—Meat-Eating Animals. Dornisch, Alcuin C., illus. 48p. (gr. k-3). 1987. PLB 6.95 (ISBN 0-8225-1118-5). Lerner Pubns.
—Prey Animals. Dornisch, Alcuin, illus. 48p. (gr. k-3). 1987. PLB 6.95 (ISBN 0-8225-1121-5). Lerner Pubns.
Alborough, Jez. Beaky. Alborough, Jez, illus. 32p. (ps-3). 1990. 13.95 (ISBN 0-395-53348-1). HM.
Alday, Gretchen P. Devoted Friends: Amazing True Stories about Animals Who Cared. LC 89-29937. 144p. (Orig.). (gr. 5 up). 1990. pap. 6.95 (ISBN 1-55870-151-6, Shoe Tree Pr). Betterway Pubns.
Alexander, R. McNeill. Animal Movement. Head, J. J., ed. Botzis, Ka, illus. LC 84-45834. 16p. (Orig.). (gr. 10 up). 1985. pap. text ed. 2.15 (ISBN 0-89278-364-8, 45-9764). Carolina Biological.
All about Animals. (Illus.). (ps-7). 1987. 5.95 (ISBN 0-553-05413-9). Bantam.
Allen, Robert. A Child's Book of Animals. Sahula, Peter, photos by. (Illus.). 64p. (ps-1). 1981. 3.95 (ISBN 0-448-41056-7, G&D). Putnam Pub Group.
Altman, Joyce & Goldberg, Sue. Dear Bronx Zoo. Falk, Douglas, frwd. by. LC 89-28226. (Illus.). 160p. (gr. 3 up). 1990. 13.95 (ISBN 0-02-700640-9, Mcmillan Child Bk). Macmillan Child Grp.
Animal Follies. (ps up). 1990. PLB 5.98 (ISBN 0-7924-5156-2, Mallard Pr). BDD Promo Bk.
Animal Masks: Tiger & Bear. (ps up). 1990. pap. 4.98 (ISBN 0-8317-0357-1). Smithmark.
The Animal Storybook. (Illus.). (gr. 1-7). 1978. (G&D); PLB 5.99 (ISBN 0-448-13028-9, G&D). Putnam Pub Group.
Animals. 96p. (gr. 3-8). 1987. PLB 240.00 set (ISBN 0-685-18918-X). Raintree Pubs.
Animals. (Illus.). (gr. k-3). 3.95 (ISBN 0-7214-5215-9). Ladybird Bks.
Animals. (Illus.). (ps-k). 3.95 (ISBN 0-7214-5158-6). Ladybird Bks.
Animals. (Illus.). (ps). 3.50 (ISBN 0-7214-1096-0). Ladybird Bks.
Animals. (Illus.). (ps). 3.50 (ISBN 0-7214-9087-5). Ladybird Bks.
Animals. (Illus.). (ps). 2.50 (ISBN 0-7214-9090-5). Ladybird Bks.
Animals. (gr. 1-4). 1991. pap. 3.95 (ISBN 0-7214-5323-6). Ladybird Bks.
Animals, Birds & Fish. (Illus.). (ps-5). 3.50 (ISBN 0-7214-8003-9); wkbk. B 1.95. Ladybird Bks.
Animals, Birds, Bees, & Flowers. Date not set. 5.98 (ISBN 0-517-68230-3). Outlet Bk Co.
Animals in Action. (Illus.). 88p. (ps-3). 1989. 15.93 (ISBN 0-8094-4869-6); lib. bdg. 21.27 (ISBN 0-8094-4870-X). Time-Life.
Argent, Kerry. Animal Capers. 1990. 11.95 (ISBN 0-8037-0718-5); PLB 11.89 (ISBN 0-8037-0752-5). Dial Bks Young.
Arnosky, Jim. Deer at the Brook. LC 84-12239. (Illus.). 32p. (ps-3). 1986. 13.95 (ISBN 0-688-04099-3); PLB 13.88 (ISBN 0-688-04100-0). Lothrop.
Ask about Wild Animals. 64p. (gr. 4-5). 1987. PLB 18.25 (ISBN 0-8172-2880-2); pap. 13.27 (ISBN 0-8172-2892-6). Raintree Pubs.
Baby Animals. 12p. (ps). 1978. 2.95 (ISBN 0-448-40870-8, G&D). Putnam Pub Group.
Baby Animals. 1990. 2.98 (ISBN 0-8317-7252-2). Smithmark.
Baby's First Book. 12p. (ps). 1978. 3.95 (ISBN 0-448-40861-9, G&D). Putnam Pub Group.
Bailey, Jill & Seddon, Tony. Animal Movement. (Illus.). 64p. 1988. 14.95x (ISBN 0-8160-1656-9). Facts on File.
—Animal Vision. (Illus.). 64p. 1988. 14.95x (ISBN 0-8160-1652-6). Facts on File.
Bailey, Vanessa. Animal Opposites. (ps). 1991. 5.95 (ISBN 0-8120-6244-2). Barron.
Bank Street College of Education Editors. Animals, Animals, Animals: At Home - In the Circus - At the Zoo. (Illus.). 64p. (ps-k). 1985. pap. 2.95 (ISBN 0-8120-3610-7). Barron.
Barr, Marilyn. Fearon's Animal Theme Activity Sheets. (ps-1). 1989. pap. 5.95 (ISBN 0-8224-0501-6). Fearon Teach Aids.
Barrett, N. S. Polar Animals. FS Staff, ed. (Illus.). 32p. (gr. 1-6). 1988. PLB 11.40 (ISBN 0-531-10531-8). Watts.
Barrett, Norman. Animales Polares. LC 87-50851. (SPA., Illus.). 32p. (gr. k-4). 1990. PLB 11.40 (ISBN 0-531-07900-7). Watts.
—Picture Library: Polar Animals. 1990. pap. 3.95 (ISBN 0-531-15207-3). Watts.
Baskin-Salzberg, Anita & Salzberg, Allen. Predators! (Illus.). 64p. (gr. 3-5). 1991. PLB 11.90 (ISBN 0-531-20009-4). Watts.
Beach, Stewart. Good Morning-Sun's Up. Sugita, Yataka, illus. LC 79-108178. 32p. (ps-3). 8.95 (ISBN 0-87592-021-7). Scroll Pr.
Bender, Lionel. Animals of the Night. (Illus.). 32p. (gr. k-6). 1989. PLB 11.90 (ISBN 0-531-17161-2). Watts.
—First Sight: Animals of the Night. 1990. pap. 3.95 (ISBN 0-531-17257-0). Watts.
Big & Little Animals. (Illus.). 32p. (ps-1). 1986. pap. 1.25 (ISBN 0-8431-1522-X). Price Stern.
Bishop, Dorothy S. The Lion & the Mouse. (FRE & ENG., Illus.). 72p. 1989. pap. 4.95 (ISBN 0-8442-1084-6, Passport Bks). Natl Textbk.
Blackmore, Michael. Your Book of Watching Wildlife. (gr. 7 up). 1972. 7.95 (ISBN 0-571-08347-1). Transatl Arts.
Blocksma, Mary. Amazing Mouths & Menus. Ames, Lee J., illus. 64p. (gr. 2-6). 1986. 12.95 (ISBN 0-13-023854-6). P-H.
Boney, Lesley, illus. Wild Animals. 48p. (gr. k-5). 1988. pap. 2.95 (ISBN 0-8431-2246-3). Price Stern.
Booth, Eugene. In the Jungle. LC 77-7947. (Illus.). 24p. (gr. k-3). 1977. PLB 13.32 (ISBN 0-8393-0104-9). Raintree Pubs.
—Under the Ground. LC 77-8037. (Illus.). (gr. k-3). 1977. PLB 13.32 (ISBN 0-8393-0110-3). Raintree Pubs.
Borden, Beatrice B. Wild Animals of Africa. (Illus.). 48p. (ps-2). 1982. lib. bdg. 6.99 (ISBN 0-394-95306-1). Random.
Brigandi, Pat. Animals! Animals! Animals! A Feely Sticker Fun Kit. Duell, Nancy, illus. 24p. (Orig.). (gr. k-3). 1987. pap. 3.95 (ISBN 0-590-40550-0). Scholastic Inc.
Broekel, Ray. Animal Observations. LC 89-25363. (Illus.). 48p. (gr. k-4). 1990. PLB 14.60 (ISBN 0-516-01182-0); pap. 4.95 (ISBN 0-516-41182-9). Childrens.
Brooks, F. Protecting Endangered Species. (Illus.). 24p. (gr. 2-5). 1991. lib. bdg. 11.96 (ISBN 0-88110-500-7, Usborne); pap. 4.50 (ISBN 0-7460-0608-X, Usborne). EDC.
Brown, Richard, illus. Muchas Palabras Sobre Animals. (SPA.). 32p. (ps-1). 1989. pap. 3.95 (ISBN 0-15-200531-5). HarBraceJ.
—One Hundred Words about Animals. (ps-1). 1989. pap. 4.95 (ISBN 0-15-200554-4, Voy B). HarBraceJ.
Burgener, Melinda B. Sierra Club WILDCARDS: Record-Setting Animals. Burgener, Melinda B., illus. 24p. (ps up). 1989. pap. 7.95 (ISBN 0-316-11618-1). Little.
Burton, Jane. Animal Activities, 4 vols. Burton, Jane & Taylor, Kim, illus. 128p. (gr. 2-3). 1989. Set. PLB 43. 80 (ISBN 0-8368-0184-9). Gareth Stevens Inc.
—Animals Keeping Clean. LC 88-43144. (Illus.). 24p. (Orig.). (ps-3). 1989. lib. bdg. 5.99 (ISBN 0-394-92261-1). Random.
—Animals Keeping Cool. LC 88-43143. (Illus.). 24p. (Orig.). (ps-3). 1989. lib. bdg. 5.99 (ISBN 0-394-92260-3). Random.
—Animals Keeping Safe. LC 88-43152. (Illus.). 24p. (Orig.). (ps-3). 1989. lib. bdg. 5.99 (ISBN 0-394-92263-8). Random.
—Animals Keeping Warm. LC 88-43147. (Illus.). 24p. (Orig.). (ps-3). 1989. PLB 5.99 (ISBN 0-394-92262-X). Random.
—Keeping Safe. Burton, Jane & Taylor, Kim, photos by. LC 89-11416. (Illus.). 32p. (gr. 2-3). 1989. PLB 10.95 (ISBN 0-8368-0186-5). Gareth Stevens INc.
Burton, Jane, ed. & photos by Keeping Warm. LC 89-11411. (Illus.). 32p. (gr. 2-3). 1989. PLB 10.95 (ISBN 0-8368-0185-7). Gareth Stevens Inc.
Burton, Maurice. Warm-Blooded Animals. (Illus.). 64p. (gr. 4-7). 1985. 15.95 (ISBN 0-8160-1059-5). Facts on File.
Burton, Robert. Arctic. (Illus.). 24p. (gr. k-4). 1991. PLB 13.25 (ISBN 1-878137-16-6). Newington.
—Desert. (Illus.). 24p. (gr. k-4). 1991. PLB 13.25 (ISBN 1-878137-17-4). Newington.
Carratello, John & Carratello, Patty. Hands on Science: Animals. Wright, Terry, illus. 32p. (gr. 2-5). 1988. wkbk. 4.95 (ISBN 1-55734-225-3). Tchr Create Mat.
Carrie, Christopher. Playful Jungle Friends. (Illus.). 32p. (Orig.). (ps-k). 1990. 1.99 (ISBN 0-86696-238-7). Binney & Smith.
Cartwright, Pauline. All Creatures. LC 90-10021. (Illus.). 16p. (gr. 1-4). 1990. PLB 14.64 (ISBN 0-8114-2695-5). Steck-V.
Carwardine, Mark. The Illustrated World of Animals. (Illus.). (gr. 3-7). 1988. pap. 12.95 (ISBN 0-671-66563-4). S&S Trade.
—Illustrated World of Wild Animals. (gr. 4-7). 1990. pap. 7.95 (ISBN 0-671-66564-2). S&S Trade.
Cassin, Sue. Fascinating Facts about Animals. 1990. 9.95 (ISBN 1-55782-329-4). Warner Bks.

Cecotti, Loralie. Washington Wildlife. Hamer, Bonnie, illus. 24p. (Orig.). (gr. k-5). 1984. pap. text ed. 2.75 (ISBN 0-318-04105-7). Coffee Break.
Chesney, Sandy. The Zapped Tadpole & More. 93p. 1991. pap. 6.95 (ISBN 0-8163-1029-7). Pacific Pr Pub Assn.
Civardi & Kilpatrick. How Animals Live. (gr. 4-6). 1981. (Usborne-Hayes); PLB 13.96 (ISBN 0-88110-081-1); pap. 6.95 (ISBN 0-86020-196-1). EDC.
Cold-Blooded Animals. LC 80-24150. (Illus.). 80p. (gr. k-6). 1986. pap. 13.27 (ISBN 0-8172-2584-6). Raintree Pubs.
Colors, Shapes, Words, & Numbers. Date not set. 5.98 (ISBN 0-517-68231-1). Outlet Bk Co.
Conforth, Kellie. A Picture Book of Arctic Animals. Conforth, Kellie, illus. LC 90-44896. 24p. (gr. 1-4). 1991. lib. bdg. 9.59 (ISBN 0-8167-2144-0); pap. text ed. 2.50 (ISBN 0-8167-2145-9). Troll Assocs.
Conway, Lorraine. Animals. 64p. (gr. 5 up). 1980. 6.95 (ISBN 0-916456-68-4, GA 177). Good Apple.
—Plants & Animals in Nature. Akins, Linda, illus. 64p. (gr. 5 up). 1986. wkbk. 6.95 (ISBN 0-86653-356-7, GA 797). Good Apple.
Cook, David. Land Animals. Cook, David, illus. LC 84-12072. 32p. (gr. 3-7). 1985. bds. 5.95 (ISBN 0-517-55430-5). Crown.
Cork. Wild Animals. (gr. 2-5). 1982. (Usborne-Hayes); PLB 11.96 (ISBN 0-88110-077-3); pap. 3.95 (ISBN 0-86020-628-9). EDC.
Cortright, Sandy. Zoo Animals. Carroll, Marilee, illus. 80p. (ps). 1990. pap. 6.95 (ISBN 0-8120-4436-3). Barron.
Costa de Beauregard, Diane. Animals in Jeopardy. Bogard, Vicki, tr. from FRE. De Hugo, Pierre, illus. LC 90-50779. 38p. (gr. k-5). 1991. 4.95 (ISBN 0-944589-37-5, 375). Young Discovery Lib.
Cousins, Lucy. Country Animals. Cousins, Lucy, illus. LC 90-35894. (ps). 1991. bds. 3.95 (ISBN 0-688-10070-8, Tambourine Bks). Morrow.
—Garden Animals. Cousins, Lucy, illus. LC 90-36259. (ps). 1991. bds. 3.95 (ISBN 0-688-10072-4, Tambourine Bks). Morrow.
Cox. Understanding Zoo Animals. (gr. 3-6). 1980. (Usborne-Hayes); PLB 13.96 (ISBN 0-88110-092-7); pap. 5.95 (ISBN 0-86020-251-8). EDC.
Crump, Donald J., ed. Animal Families. (Illus.). (gr. k-4). 1990. Set. 13.95 (ISBN 0-87044-819-6); lib. bdg. write for info. (ISBN 0-87044-824-2). Natl Geog.
Cutts, David. I Can Read About Creatures of the Night. LC 78-68468. (Illus.). (gr. 2-5). 1979. pap. 1.95 (ISBN 0-89375-202-9). Troll Assocs.
Davidson, Margaret. Wild Animal Families. new ed. Stiles, Fran, illus. 64p. (gr. 2-5). 1980. 8.95 (ISBN 0-8038-8098-7). Hastings.
DeBruin, Jerry. Young Scientists Explore: Animals, Bk. 2. 32p. (gr. 4 up). 1982. 4.95 (ISBN 0-86653-073-8, GA 406). Good Apple.
De la Sota, Ann. Amazing Animals. (Illus.). 32p. (gr. 3 up). 1986. incl. hand held Decoder 5.95 (ISBN 0-88679-457-9). Educ Insights.
Demi. Demi's Opposites: An Animal Game Book. Demi, illus. (ps-2). 1990. 10.95 (ISBN 0-448-18995-X, G&D). Putnam Pub Group.
De Paola, Tomie. Fin M'Coul, the Giant of Knockmany Hill. LC 80-2254. (Illus.). 32p. (gr. k-3). 1981. reinforced bdg. 14.95 (ISBN 0-8234-0384-X); pap. 5.95 (ISBN 0-8234-0385-8). Holiday.
De Sairigne, Catherine. Animals in Winter. Matthews, Sarah, tr. from FRE. Mathieu, Agnes, illus. LC 87-34086. 38p. (gr. k-5). 1988. 4.95 (ISBN 0-944589-05-7, 057). Young Discovery Lib.
Dikis, Eloise. The Twelve Powers of Animals. Wortman, Mary, ed. Ford, Phyllis, illus. 44p. (ps-5). 1989. comb bdg. 7.95 (ISBN 0-939339-06-4). AFCOM Pub.
Dreyer, Ellen. Wild Animals. Hall, Douglas & Dennison, Graham, illus. LC 90-11163. 96p. (gr. 2-5). 1991. PLB 14.89 (ISBN 0-8167-2242-0); pap. text ed. 6.95 (ISBN 0-8167-2243-9). Troll Assocs.
Dudley, Lynn. Farm Animals. (gr. 4-7). 1990. pap. 5.95 (ISBN 0-8167-2087-8). Troll Assocs.
—Forest Animals. (gr. 4-7). 1990. pap. 5.95 (ISBN 0-8167-2084-3). Troll Assocs.
Dunmire, Marj. Mountain Wildlife. Dunmire, Marj, illus. 48p. (Orig.). (gr. 2 up). 1986. pap. 3.95 (ISBN 0-942559-03-7). Pegasus Graphics.
Dunn, Phoebe. Animal Friends. Dunn, Phoebe, illus. LC 85-2254. 24p. (ps-1). 1985. (Random Juv). Random.
D'yley, Enid F. Animal Fables & Other Tales Retold: Africa in the New World. LC 87-73226. 40p. (Orig.). (gr. 1-7). 1989. 12.95 (ISBN 0-86543-075-6); pap. 5.95 (ISBN 0-86543-076-4). Africa World.
Earthbooks, Inc. Staff. National Wildlife Federation's Book of Endangered Species. Maestis, Ken, illus. 64p. (Orig.). (gr. 4-6). 1991. pap. 5.95 (ISBN 1-877731-17-X). Earthbooks Inc.
Elliott, Tony. High Country Wildlife. Elliott, Tony, illus. LC 86-2218. 64p. (Orig.). (gr. 1-6). 1988. pap. 2.50 (ISBN 0-914565-20-6, 20-6). Capstan Pubns.
Elting, Mary. The Answer Book about Animals. Barnes-Murphy, Rowan, illus. (gr. 3-7). 1984. pap. 2.95 (ISBN 0-448-13801-8, G&D). Putnam Pub Group.
Emberley, Ed E. Drawing Book of Animals. (Illus.). 32p. (gr. 1-3). 1973. lib. bdg. 12.95 (ISBN 0-316-23597-0). Little.
Exotic Animals. (Illus.). 20p. (gr. k up). 1990. laminated, wipe clean surface 3.95 (ISBN 0-88679-588-5). Educ Insights.
Farm Animals. 7p. (ps-1). 1973. 2.50 (ISBN 0-448-09730-3, G&D). Putnam Pub Group.
Felder, Deborah G. The Kids' World Almanac of Animals & Pets. Lane, John, illus. 1990. 14.95 (ISBN 0-88687-556-0); pap. 6.95 (ISBN 0-88687-555-2). Pharos Bks NY.
Fichter, George S. Poisonous Animals. (Illus.). 64p. (gr. 5-8). 1991. PLB 11.90 (ISBN 0-531-20050-7). Watts.
Fisher, Ronald M. Animals in Winter. Crump, Donald J., ed. LC 82-47859. 32p. (gr. 3-8). 1982. 10.95 set (ISBN 0-87044-453-0); lib. bdg. 12.95 library binding (ISBN 0-685-05546-9). Natl Geog.
Flegg, Jim. Animal Builders. (Illus.). 32p. (gr. 4-6). 1991. PLB 11.90 (ISBN 1-878137-05-0). Newington.
—Animal Helpers. (Illus.). 32p. (gr. 4-6). 1991. PLB 11.90 (ISBN 1-878137-06-9). Newington.
—Animal Hunters. (Illus.). 32p. (gr. 4-6). 1991. PLB 11.90 (ISBN 1-878137-04-2). Newington.
—Animal Senses. (Illus.). 32p. (gr. 4-6). 1991. PLB 11.90 (ISBN 1-878137-21-2). Newington.
Forest Babies. (Illus.). 1990. 4.98 (ISBN 0-8317-6851-7). Smithmark.
Forsyth, Adrian. Architecture of Animals. 72p. (gr. 8 up). 1989. 15.95 (ISBN 0-920656-16-1); pap. 9.95 (ISBN 0-920656-08-0). Firefly Bks Ltd.
Fortson, Walter. Amazing Animal Facts. Starver, Randy, et al, illus. LC 89-80109. 128p. (Orig.). (gr. 5). 1989. pap. 6.95 (ISBN 0-685-29400-5). Fortson Pubs.
Frith, Michael. Some of Us Walk, Some Fly, Some Swim. LC 73-158391. (Illus.). (gr. k-6). 1971. PLB 4.95 (ISBN 0-394-82325-7). Beginner.
Fujikawa, Gyo. Baby Animals. (Illus.). 14p. (ps). 1978. bds. 2.50 (ISBN 0-448-16281-4, G&D). Putnam Pub Group.
Gabb, Michael. Creatures Great & Small. LC 79-64386. (Illus.). 36p. (gr. 3-6). 1980. PLB 8.95 (ISBN 0-8225-1178-9, First Ave Edns); pap. 4.95 (ISBN 0-8225-9540-0, First Ave Edns). Lerner Pubns.
Ganeri, A. Animal Facts: Records-Lists-Facts-Comparisons. (Illus.). 48p. (gr. 3-7). 1988. PLB 12.96 (ISBN 0-88110-317-9); pap. 5.95 (ISBN 0-86020-971-7). EDC.
Ganeri, Anita. Animal Babies. Taylor, Kate, illus. 32p. (ps-1). Date not set. 6.95 (ISBN 0-8120-6241-8). Barron.
—Animal Camouflage. Taylor, Kate, illus. 32p. (ps-1). Date not set. 6.95 (ISBN 0-8120-6236-1). Barron.
—Animal Movements. Taylor, Kate, illus. 32p. (ps-1). Date not set. 6.95 (ISBN 0-8120-6238-8). Barron.
—Animal Talk. Taylor, Kate, illus. 32p. (ps-1). Date not set. 6.95 (ISBN 0-8120-6239-6). Barron.
Gise, Joanne. A Picture Book of Desert Animals. Pistolesi, Roseanna, illus. LC 90-40436. 24p. (gr. 1-4). 1991. lib. bdg. 9.59 (ISBN 0-8167-2148-3); pap. text ed. 2.50 (ISBN 0-8167-2149-1). Troll Assocs.
—A Picture Book of Wild Animals. Pistolesi, Roseanna, illus. LC 89-37334. 24p. (gr. 1-4). 1990. lib. bdg. 9.59 (ISBN 0-8167-1908-X); pap. text ed. 2.50 (ISBN 0-8167-1909-8). Troll Assocs.
Glass, Marvin. Animal Band. Glass, Marvin, illus. 12p. (gr. 2-4). 1990. bds. 3.95 (ISBN 1-878624-02-4). McClanahan Bk.
—Creatures' Features. Glass, Marvin, illus. 12p. (gr. 2-4). 1990. bds. 3.95 (ISBN 1-878624-03-2). McClanahan Bk.
—Go Like a Turtle. Glass, Marvin, illus. 12p. (gr. 2-4). 1990. bds. 3.95 (ISBN 1-878624-04-0). McClanahan Bk.
Goin, Kenn, et al. Bugs to Bunnies: Hands-on Animal Science Activities for Young Children. (Illus.). 192p. (Orig.). (gr. k-2). 1989. pap. text ed. 14.95 (ISBN 0-943129-03-6). Chatterbox Pr.
Gould, G. Animals in Danger, 5 bks, Reading Level 5. (Illus.). 160p. (gr. 3-6). Date not set. Set. PLB 66.33. Rourke Corp.
—Asia, Reading Level 5. (Illus.). 32p. (gr. 3-6). Date not set. PLB 13.26. Rourke Corp.
—Europe, Reading Level 5. (Illus.). 32p. (gr. 3-6). Date not set. Set. PLB 66.33; PLB 13.26 ea. Rourke Corp.
—North America, Reading Level 5. (Illus.). 32p. (gr. 3-6). Date not set. PLB 13.26. Rourke Corp.
Greeley, Valerie, illus. Field Animals. LC 83-22507. 12p. (ps). 1984. bds. 3.95 (ISBN 0-911745-23-8, Bedrick Blackie). P Bedrick Bks.
—Zoo Animals. LC 83-22513. 12p. (ps). 1984. bds. 3.95 (ISBN 0-911745-24-6, Bedrick Blackie). P Bedrick Bks.
Greene, Carol. Caring for Our Animals. (Illus.). 32p. (gr. 1-4). 1991. PLB 12.95 (ISBN 0-89490-352-7). Enslow Pubs.
Gutfreund, Geraldine M. Animals Have Cousins Too: Five Surprising Relatives of Animals You Know. (Illus.). 64p. (gr. 5-8). 1990. PLB 11.90 (ISBN 0-531-10861-9). Watts.
Hale, Yvonne. Creatures Featured. 1988. 5.95 (ISBN 0-533-07542-4). Vantage.
Hanak, Mirko, illus. Animals We Love, Bks. 1 & 2. LC 72-89571. 32p. (gr. k-4). 1973. 9.95 ea. Bk. 1 (ISBN 0-87592-005-5). Bk. 2 (ISBN 0-87592-006-3). Scroll Pr.
Harrison, Virginia & Losito, Linda. The World of Ants. LC 89-4466. (Illus.). 32p. (gr. 2-3). 1989. PLB 10.95 (ISBN 0-8368-0136-9). Gareth Stevens Inc.
Harrison, Virginia & Pollack, Steve. The World of Animals. LC 89-11357. (Illus.). 64p. (gr. 2-3). 1989. PLB 12.95 (ISBN 0-8368-0028-1). Gareth Stevens Inc.
Hegeman, Kathryn T. The Animal Kingdom. Hegeman, Mark, et al, illus. (gr. k-3). 1982. tchr's. manual 10.00 (ISBN 0-89824-031-X); wkbk. 4.99 (ISBN 0-89824-030-1). Trillium Pr.
Herbst, Judith. Animal Amazing: A Casebook of Unsolved Zoological Mysteries. LC 90-62. 192p. (gr. 5 up). 1991. SBE 13.95 (ISBN 0-689-31556-2, Atheneum Child Bk). Macmillan Child Grp.
Hirschi, Ron. Loon Lake. Cox, Daniel J., photos by. LC 90-34396. (Illus.). 32p. (ps-3). 1991. 13.95 (ISBN 0-525-65046-6, Cobblehill Bks). Dutton Child Bks.
Hoffman, Mary. Wild Cat. LC 86-10007. (Illus.). 24p. (gr. k-5). 1986. PLB 13.32 (ISBN 0-8172-2399-1). Raintree Pubs.
Holmes, Martha. Deadly Animals. Vaughan, Mike, illus. LC 90-26903. (ps-3). 1991. 12.95 (ISBN 0-689-31737-9, Atheneum Child Bk). Macmillan Child Grp.
Humphreys, Dena. Animals Every Child Should Know. Freund, Rudolph, illus. 32p. (gr. k-3). 1982. 3.95 (ISBN 0-448-04245-2, G&D). Putnam Pub Group.
Ingram, Victoria. Animals. 64p. (gr. k-3). 1987. 6.95 (ISBN 0-912107-61-8). Monday Morning Bks.
Insects & Small Animals. (Illus.). (gr. 4 up). 3.50 (ISBN 0-7214-0320-4). Ladybird Bks.
Jacka, Martin. Waiting for Billy. LC 90-7957. (Illus.). 32p. (ps-2). 1991. 13.95 (ISBN 0-531-05933-2); PLB 13.99 (ISBN 0-531-08533-3). Orchard Bks Watts.
Jambert, Mark & Williams, John. Animal Ecology. Caulkins, Janet, ed. (Illus.). 48p. (gr. 4-9). 1987. 12.40 (ISBN 0-531-18155-3, Pub. by Bookwright Pr). Watts.
Jarrell, Randall. The Animal Family. facsimile ed. Sendak, Maurice, illus. LC 65-20659. 200p. (gr. 1 up). 1985. 12.95 (ISBN 0-685-10494-X, Pant Bks Young). Pantheon.
—La Familia Animal. (SPA.). 4.95 (ISBN 0-685-31019-1). Santillana.
Jefferies, Lawrence. Amazing World of Animals. D'Adamo, Anthony, illus. LC 82-20061. 32p. (gr. 3-6). 1983. PLB 10.59 (ISBN 0-89375-898-1); pap. text ed. 2.95 (ISBN 0-89375-899-X). Troll Assocs.
Jennings, Terry. Small Garden Animals. LC 88-36216. (Illus.). 32p. (gr. 3-6). 1989. PLB 14.60 (ISBN 0-516-08442-9); pap. 4.95 (ISBN 0-516-48442-7). Childrens.
Johnston, Ginny & Cutchins, Judy. Windows on Wildlife. LC 89-34487. (Illus.). 48p. (gr. 2 up). 1990. 13.95 (ISBN 0-688-07872-9); PLB 13.88 (ISBN 0-688-07873-7, Morrow Jr Bks). Morrow Jr Bks.
Kalman, Bobbie. Animal Worlds. (Illus.). 32p. (gr. 2-3). 1986. 6.95 (ISBN 0-86505-071-6); pap. 5.95 (ISBN 0-86505-093-7). Crabtree Pub Co.

—Arctic Animals. (Illus.). 56p. (gr. 3-4). 1988. 15.95 (ISBN 0-86505-145-3); pap. 7.95 (ISBN 0-86505-155-0). Crabtree Pub Co.
ARCTIC ANIMALS portrays the fascinating land & sea mammals, birds, insects, & fish that live in the Arctic. The lives of these creatures are a struggle for survival, even though their bodies are ingeniously adapted to withstand this unforgiving environment. ARCTIC ANIMALS belongs to the Arctic World Series. The four, large, full-color books explore the wildlife & wild landscape of the north & the communities & customs of the people. Hundreds of breathtaking photographs show the exciting life that flourishes in this beautiful, yet forbidding land.
Publisher Provided Annotation.

Kinghorn, Harriet & Morberg, Mary. Research Shapes: Animals. (Illus.). 64p. (gr. 2-5). 1989. 6.95 (ISBN 1-878279-02-5, MM1919). Monday Morning Bks.
Kitchen, Bert. Animal Alphabet. Kitchen, Bert, illus. LC 83-23929. 32p. (ps up). 1984. 13.95 (ISBN 0-8037-0117-9). Dial Bks Young.
Kudlinski, Kathleen V. Animal Tracks & Traces. Morgan, Mary, illus. 48p. 1991. 13.90t (ISBN 0-531-15219-7); PLB 12.90 (ISBN 0-531-10742-6). Watts.
LaBonte, Gail. Leeches, Lampreys, & Other Cold-Blooded Bloodsuckers. (Illus.). 64p. (gr. 5-8). 1991. PLB 11.90 (ISBN 0-531-20027-2). Watts.
Lauber, Patricia. What Big Teeth You Have! Weston, Martha, illus. LC 85-47902. 64p. (gr. 2-6). 1986. 11.95 (ISBN 0-690-04506-9, Crowell Jr Bks); PLB 11.89 (ISBN 0-690-04507-7, Crowell Jr Bks). HarpC Child Bks.
Lavies, Bianca. Tree Trunk Traffic. Lavies, Bianca, photos by. (Illus.). 32p. (ps-2). 1989. 13.95 (ISBN 0-525-44495-5, DCB). Dutton Child Bks.
Little People Big Book about Amazing Animals. 64p. (ps-1). 1990. write for info. (ISBN 0-8094-7487-5); PLB write for info. (ISBN 0-8094-7488-3). Time-Life.
Little People Big Book About Animals. 64p. (ps-1). 1989. write for info. (ISBN 0-8094-7450-6); PLB write for info. (ISBN 0-8094-7451-4). Time-Life.

Living Planet Press Staff. Sharing the Planet with Animals: An Endangered Wildlife Coloring Book. (Illus.). 48p. (ps-3). 1991. pap. 4.95 (ISBN 1-879326-08-6). Living Planet Pr.

Lopshire, Robert. The Biggest, Smallest, Fastest, Tallest Things You've Ever Heard of. Lopshire, Robert, illus. LC 79-7824. 64p. (gr. 1-4). 1980. 11.95 (ISBN 0-690-04013-X, Crowell Jr Bks); PLB 11.89 (ISBN 0-690-04014-8). HarpC Child Bks.

Lumley, Kathryn W. Work Animals. LC 83-7511. (Illus.). 48p. (gr. k-4). 1983. 14.60 (ISBN 0-516-01711-X). Childrens.

MacCarthy, Patricia. Animals Galore. 1989. 11.95 (ISBN 0-8037-0721-5). Dial Bks Young.

McCay, William. Animals in Danger: A Pop-up Book. Mosley, Keith, illus. 12p. (gr. 1-7). 1990. pap. 12.95 (ISBN 0-689-71408-4, Aladdin). Macmillan Child Grp.

McClung, Robert M. Gorilla. Brady, Irene, illus. LC 84-718. 96p. (gr. 3-7). 1984. 11.00 (ISBN 0-688-03875-1). Morrow Jr Bks.

McDonnell, Janet. Animal Builders. LC 88-36641. (Illus.). 48p. (gr. 2-6). 1989. PLB 10.95 (ISBN 0-89565-511-X); pap. 6.96 (ISBN 0-89565-529-2). Childs World.

Machines, Cars, Boats, & Airplanes. Date not set. 5.98 (ISBN 0-517-68232-X). Outlet Bk Co.

McKean, Barb. Wild Animals. Rowden, Rick & Winik, J. T., illus. 32p. (gr. 3-7). 1985. pap. 3.50 (ISBN 0-88625-117-6). Durkin Hayes Pub.

McKowen, K. D. Wildlife Activity & Coloring Book. rev. ed. McKowen, K. D., illus. 32p. (gr. 2-6). 1987. workbook 1.50 (ISBN 0-913635-02-2). Aspen Prods.

Mcphail, David. Animals A to Z. 1989. pap. 2.50 (ISBN 0-590-40347-8). Scholastic Inc.

McPhail, David, illus. David McPhail's Animals A to Z. (ps-1). 1988. pap. 12.95 (ISBN 0-590-40715-5). Scholastic Inc.

Marshall, James. What's the Matter with Carruthers? Marshall, James, illus. LC 72-75607. 32p. (gr. k-3). 1972. 14.95 (ISBN 0-395-13895-7). HM.

Mason, George F. Animal Tracks. LC 87-31124. (Illus.). 95p. (gr. 4-11). 1988. Repr. of 1943 ed. lib. bdg. 14.50 (ISBN 0-208-02213-9, Linnet). Shoe String.

Maynard, Thane. Animal Inventors. (Illus.). 64p. (gr. 5-8). 1991. PLB 11.90 (ISBN 0-531-20051-5). Watts.

Merriam, Eve. Where Is Everybody? DeGroat, Diane, illus. (ps-1). 1989. pap. 14.95 (ISBN 0-671-64964-7). S&S Trade.

Miller, J. P. Farmer John's Animals. Miller, J. P., illus. LC 79-63900. (ps-1). 1979. 3.95 (ISBN 0-394-84270-7, Random Juv). Random.

Miller, J. P., illus. The Cow Says Moo. (ps). 1979. 3.50 (ISBN 0-394-84131-X, Random Juv). Random.

Moncure, Jane B. Kinds of Animals: Flyers, Leapers, Crawlers, Creepers. Hohag, Linda, illus. LC 89-71172. 32p. (ps-2). 1990. lib. bdg. 11.97 (ISBN 0-89565-567-5). Childs World.

Morris, Dean. Animals That Burrow. rev. ed. LC 87-16694. (Illus.). 48p. (gr. 2-6). 1987. PLB 17.32 (ISBN 0-8172-3201-X). Raintree Pubs.

—Animals That Live in Shells. rev. ed. LC 87-20556. (Illus.). 48p. (gr. 2-6). 1987. PLB 17.32 (ISBN 0-8172-3202-8). Raintree Pubs.

—Endangered Animals. (ps-3). 1990. pap. 11.99 (ISBN 0-8172-3232-X). Raintree Pubs.

My Book of Baby Forest Animals. (ps-2). 3.95 (ISBN 0-7214-5150-0). Ladybird Bks.

My Book of Baby Zoo Animals. (ps-2). 3.95 (ISBN 0-7214-5149-7). Ladybird Bks.

Nakatani, Chiyoko, ed. Animal Opposites. (Illus.). 22p. (ps-1). 1981. 3.50 (ISBN 0-89346-194-6). Heian Intl.

Nash, Bartleby. Mother Nature's Greatest Hits: The Top 40 Wonders of the Animal World. (Illus.). 144p. (Orig.). 1991. pap. 5.95 (ISBN 0-9626072-7-4). Living Planet Pr.

Our Animals. (ps). 1982. 3.95 (ISBN 0-685-05830-1). Borden.

Palazzo, Tony. The Biggest & the Littlest Animals. Palazzo, Tony, illus. LC 77-112374. 40p. (gr. k-3). 1973. PLB 11.95 (ISBN 0-87460-225-4). Lion Bks.

Parr, John. Baby Animals. Parr, John, illus. LC 79-62943. (ps). 1979. 3.50 (ISBN 0-394-84244-8). Random.

Parsons, Alexandra. Amazing Poisonous Animals. Young, Jerry, photos by. LC 90-31883. 32p. (Orig.). (gr. 1-5). 1991. lib. bdg. 9.99 (ISBN 0-679-90699-1); pap. 6.95 (ISBN 0-679-80699-7). Knopf.

Patent, Hinshaw Dorothy. How Smart Are Animals? (gr. 8-12). 1990. 17.95 (ISBN 0-15-236770-5). HarbraceJ.

Paterson, Bettina. My First Animals. Paterson, Bettina, illus. LC 89-17275. 32p. (ps-k). 1990. 8.95 (ISBN 0-690-04775-4, Crowell Jr Bks); PLB 9.89 (ISBN 0-690-04777-0, Crowell Jr Bks). HarpC Child Bks.

—My First Wild Animals. Paterson, Bettina, illus. LC 89-17305. 32p. (ps-k). 1991. 8.95 (ISBN 0-690-04771-1, Crowell Jr Bks); PLB 9.89 (ISBN 0-690-04773-8, Crowell Jr Bks). HarpC Child Bks.

Pearce, Q. L. Armadillos & Other Unusual Animals. Steltenpohl, Jane, ed. Fraser, Mary A., illus. 64p. (gr. 4-6). 1989. PLB 12.98 (ISBN 0-671-68528-7); pap. 5.95 (ISBN 0-671-68645-3). Messner.

Peet, Bill. The Ant & the Elephant. Peet, Bill, illus. LC 74-179918. 48p. (gr. k-3). 1980. 13.95 (ISBN 0-395-16963-1); pap. 3.95 (ISBN 0-395-29205-0). HM.

Penguins: Animal Information Ser. 32p. (ps-1). 1986. pap. 1.25 (ISBN 0-8431-1524-6). Price Stern.

Penn, Linda. Wild Plants & Animals. Weiser, Liz, illus. 32p. (gr. k-3). 1986. wkbk. 4.95 (ISBN 0-86653-351-6, GA 687). Good Apple.

—Young Scientists Explore: Animal Friends. Scott, Elaine, illus. 32p. (gr. k-3). 1983. wkbk. 4.95 (ISBN 0-86653-124-6, GA 454). Good Apple.

Perenyi, Constance. Growing Wild: Inviting Wildlife into Your Yard. Perenyi, Constance, illus. 40p. (gr. 1-3). 1991. 14.95 (ISBN 0-941831-60-4); pap. 9.95 (ISBN 0-941831-63-9). Beyond Words Pub.

Peters, David. Giants of Land, Sea & Air - Past & Present: A Sierra Club Book Series. Peters, David, illus. LC 86-2719. 64p. (gr. 3 up). 1986. 15.95 (ISBN 0-394-87805-1); lib. bdg. 15.99 (ISBN 0-394-97805-6). Knopf.

Pollack, Steve. Animal Life. LC 89-11367. (Illus.). 64p. (gr. 4-6). 1989. 12.95 (ISBN 0-8368-0003-6). Gareth Stevens Inc.

Porter, Keith. Looking at Animals. LC 87-80094. (Illus.). 48p. (gr. 1-4). 1987. 12.95x (ISBN 0-8160-1784-0). Facts on File.

Priestley, Anne. Big Animals. Jackson, Ian, illus. LC 87-4621. 32p. (ps-1). 1987. 3.95 (ISBN 0-394-89188-0, Random Juv); lib. bdg. 7.99 (ISBN 0-394-99188-5, BYR). Random.

Propper, et al. World Animal Library, 17 bks, Reading Level 3-4. (Illus.). 476p. (gr. 2-5). Date not set. Set. PLB 248.20 (ISBN 0-86592-850-9). Rourke Corp.

Purcell, John W. African Animals. LC 82-9541. (Illus.). (gr. k-4). 1982. 14.60 (ISBN 0-516-01665-2); pap. 4.95 (ISBN 0-516-41665-0). Childrens.

Quinn, Kaye. Zoo Animals. (gr. 4-7). 1991. pap. 2.95 (ISBN 0-8431-2720-1). Price Stern.

Rahn, Joan E. Animals That Changed History. Rahn, Joan E., illus. LC 86-3635. 128p. (gr. 4-8). 1986. 12.95 (ISBN 0-689-31137-0, Atheneum Child Bk). Macmillan Child Grp.

Raintree Publishers Staff. Animals. LC 87-28712. (Illus.). 64p. (Orig.). (gr. 5-9). 1988. PLB 19.99 (ISBN 0-8172-3083-1). Raintree Pubs.

—Animals at the Water's Edge. LC 87-20687. (Illus.). 48p. (gr. k-6). 1987. PLB 15.99 (ISBN 0-8172-3115-3). Raintree Pubs.

—Animals in Cities & Parks. LC 87-20684. (gr. k-6). 1987. 15.99 (ISBN 0-8172-3116-1). Raintree Pubs.

—Animals in Houses & Gardens. LC 87-20775. (Illus.). (gr. k-6). 1987. PLB 15.99 (ISBN 0-8172-3114-5). Raintree Pubs.

—Animals in Rivers & Ponds. LC 87-20685. (Illus.). 48p. (gr. k-6). 1987. PLB 15.99 (ISBN 0-8172-3113-7). Raintree Pubs.

—Animals in the Forest. LC 87-20689. (Illus.). 48p. (gr. k-6). 1987. PLB 15.99 (ISBN 0-8172-3111-0). Raintree Pubs.

—Animals in the Mountains. LC 87-20688. (Illus.). 48p. (gr. k-6). 1987. PLB 15.99 (ISBN 0-8172-3112-9). Raintree Pubs.

Read a Picture: Animals. 1991. 4.98 (ISBN 0-8317-7351-0). Smithmark.

Riha, Susanne. Animals in Winter. (Illus.). 32p. (gr. 1-5). 1989. PLB 14.95 (ISBN 0-87614-355-9). Carolrhoda Bks.

River, Chatham. Animal Fun: A-Z Activity Books. 1989. 3.50 (ISBN 0-517-68796-8). Outlet Bk Co.

Roe, Richard. Baby Animals. Roe, Richard, illus. LC 85-2223. 24p. (ps-1). 1985. 3.95 (ISBN 0-394-86956-7, Random Juv). Random.

Roots, Clive. Vanishing Animals of the World. Krsten, Peter, illus. 40p. (Orig.). (gr. 3-9). 1990. pap. 4.95 (ISBN 0-920534-66-X, Pub. by Hyperion Pr Ltd CN). Sterling.

—Venomous Animals of the World. Karsten, Peter, illus. 40p. (gr. 3-9). 1990. pap. 4.95 (ISBN 0-920534-88-0, Pub. by Hyperion Pr Ltd CN). Sterling.

Royston, Angela. Hedgehog. Pledger, Maurice, illus. 24p. (gr. k-3). 1989. pap. 2.95 (ISBN 0-8249-8371-8). Ideals.

Ruffault, Charlotte. Animals Underground. Matthews, Sarah, tr. from FRE. Underhill, Graham, illus. LC 87-34616. 38p. (gr. k-5). 1988. 4.95 (ISBN 0-944589-03-0, 030). Young Discovery Lib.

Ryden, Hope. Wild Animals of Africa ABC. LC 89-2529. (Illus.). 32p. (ps-3). 1989. 12.95 (ISBN 0-525-67290-7, Lodestar Bks). Dutton Child Bks.

Sargent, William. Night Reef: Dusk to Dawn on a Coral Reef. (Illus.). 40p. (gr. 5-8). 1991. 13.95; PLB 13.90 (ISBN 0-531-11073-7). Watts.

Schulz, Charles M. Charlie Brown's Super Book of Questions & Answers: About All Kinds of Animals from Snails to People. LC 75-39340. (Illus.). (gr. 3-6). 1976. 10.95 (ISBN 0-394-83249-3, Random Juv). Random.

Schwartz, L. Trivia Trackdown - Animals & Science. (gr. 4-6). 1985. 3.95 (ISBN 0-88160-119-5, LW 252). Learning Wks.

Selsam, Millicent E. & Hunt, Joyce. A First Look at Animals That Eat Other Animals. Springer, Harriet, illus. 64p. (gr. 5 up). 1990. 11.95 (ISBN 0-8027-6895-4); PLB 12.85 (ISBN 0-8027-6896-2). Walker & Co.

Serventy, Vincent. Kookaburra. LC 84-17969. (Illus.). 24p. (gr. k-5). 1985. PLB 13.32 (ISBN 0-8172-2417-3). Raintree Pubs.

Settel, Joanne & Baggett, Nancy. Why Do Cats' Eyes Glow in the Dark? And Other Questions Kids Ask About Animals. Tunney, Linda, illus. LC 87-13708. 112p. (gr. 3-7). 1988. 12.95 (ISBN 0-689-31267-9, Atheneum Child Bk). Macmillan Child Grp.

Simon, Seymour. Animal Fact: Animal Fable. De Groat, Diane, illus. LC 78-14866. (gr. k-3). 1988. pap. 4.95 (ISBN 0-517-53794-X). Crown.

—Little Giants. Carroll, Pamela, illus. LC 82-14139. 48p. (gr. k-5). 1983. PLB 14.88 (ISBN 0-688-01731-2). Morrow Jr Bks.

—One Hundred & One Questions & Answers about Dangerous Animals. Friedman, Ellen, illus. LC 84-42975. 96p. (gr. 3-7). 1985. 12.95 (ISBN 0-02-782710-0, Mcmillan Child Bk). Macmillan Child Grp.

Singer, Arthur. Wild Animals from Alligator to Zebra. (ps-1). 1973. pap. 1.95 (ISBN 0-394-82701-5, Random Juv). Random.

Slier, Debby. Little Animals. 12p. (ps). 1989. 2.95 (ISBN 1-56288-147-7). Checkerboard Pr.

Smalley, Guy, illus. My Very Own Book of Mother Goose Animals. 24p. (ps-2). 1989. 9.95 (ISBN 0-929793-01-3). Camex Bks Inc.

Smith, William J. Birds & Beasts. Hnizdovsky, Jacques, illus. (gr. k up). 1990. 18.95 (ISBN 0-87923-865-8). Godine.

Spectacular Animals & Fascinating Animals. (Illus.). (gr. 1-7). 1990. 15.95 ea., 192pgs. ea. Spectacular Animals (ISBN 0-87449-817-1). Fascinating Animals (ISBN 0-87449-818-X). Modern Pub NYC.

Spencer, Eve. Animal Babies One Two Three. David, Susan, illus. 24p. (ps-2). 1990. PLB 12.33 (ISBN 0-8172-3581-7). Raintree Pubs.

Spizzirri Publishing Co. Staff & Spizzirri, Linda. Animal Family Calendar: An Educational Coloring Book. (Illus.). 32p. (gr. k-5). 1983. pap. 1.95 (ISBN 0-86545-048-X). Spizzirri.

—Animal Giants: An Educational Coloring Book. (Illus.). 32p. (gr. k-5). 1985. pap. 1.95 (ISBN 0-86545-066-8). Spizzirri.

Stacy, Tom. The World of Animals. Robson, Eric, illus. 40p. (gr. 4-5). 1991. PLB 11.40 (ISBN 0-531-19103-6). Watts.

Staple, Michele & Gamlin, Linda. The Random House Book of One Thousand One Questions & Answers about Animals. LC 90-30716. (Illus.). 160p. (Orig.). (gr. 3-7). 1990. lib. bdg. 10.95 (ISBN 0-679-80731-4); pap. 12.99 (ISBN 0-679-90731-9). Random.

Stewart, Frances T. & Stewart, Charles P. Animals & Their Environments. Barrett, Robert, illus. LC 86-46116. 10p. (ps). 1987. sticker book 7.95 (ISBN 0-694-00179-1). HarpC Child Bks.

Stewart, K. K. God Made Me Special. LC 82-62731. (Illus.). 24p. (ps-2). 1983. 1.99 (ISBN 0-87239-635-5, 3555). Standard Pub.

Stone, Lynn. African Animals Discovery Library, 6 bks. (Illus.). 144p. (gr. k-5). 1990. Set. lib. bdg. 71.60 (ISBN 0-86593-047-3); Set. lib. bdg. 53.70s.p. (ISBN 0-685-36343-0). Rourke Corp.

—Australian Animals Discovery Library, 6 bks. (Illus.). 144p. (gr. k-5). 1990. Set. lib. bdg. 71.60 (ISBN 0-86593-054-6); Set. lib. bdg. 53.70s.p. (ISBN 0-685-36368-6). Rourke Corp.

—North American Animal Discovery Library, 6 bks. (Illus.). 144p. (gr. k-5). 1990. Set. lib. bdg. 71.60 (ISBN 0-86593-040-6); Set. lib. bdg. 53.70s.p. (ISBN 0-685-36336-8). Rourke Corp.

Sussman, Susan & James, Robert. Lies (People Believe) about Animals. Tucker, Kathleen, ed. Leavitt, Fred, illus. LC 86-15949. 47p. (gr. 2-7). 1987. PLB 10.95 (ISBN 0-8075-4530-9). A Whitman.

Swartzentruber. God Made the Animals. (gr. 1 up). 1976. 2.45 (ISBN 0-686-18185-9). Rod & Staff.

Talkabout Animals. (ARA., Illus.). (gr. 1-3). 3.50x (ISBN 0-86685-231-X). Intl Bk Ctr.

Tallarico, Anthony. Endangered Animals Activity Book. (Illus.). 64p. (Orig.). 1990. pap. 1.95 (ISBN 0-942025-12-1). Kidsbks.

Taylor, Barbara. Ready Set Go: Animals Everywhere. 1991. 4.98 (ISBN 0-8317-7355-3). Smithmark.

Taylor, David. Animal Magicians. (Illus.). 48p. (gr. 4 up). 1989. 12.95 (ISBN 0-8225-2175-X). Lerner Pubns.

—Animal Olympians. (Illus.). 48p. (gr. 4 up). 1989. 12.95 (ISBN 0-8225-2177-6). Lerner Pubns.

—Animal Olympians: Sporting Champions of the Animal World. (Illus.). 48p. (gr. 4 up). Repr. of 1989 ed. 5.95g (ISBN 0-8225-9576-1). Lerner Pubns.

Taylor, Kim. Hidden by Darkness. (gr. 4-7). 1990. 9.95 (ISBN 0-385-30178-2). Delacorte.

—Hidden Inside. (gr. 4-7). 1990. 9.95 (ISBN 0-385-30182-0). Delacorte.

Tomkins, Jasper. The Catalog. LC 84-144717. (Illus.). 56p. (gr. k up). 1981. pap. 5.95 (ISBN 0-914676-54-7, Star & Elephant Bks.). Green Tiger Pr.

Tunney, Christopher. Midnight Animals. Atkinson, Mike & Francis, John, illus. LC 87-4792. 24p. (gr. 2-5). 1987. lib. bdg. 5.99 (ISBN 0-394-99213-X, Random Juv); pap. 2.95 (ISBN 0-394-89213-5, Random Juv). Random.

Turner, F. Bernadette. Faith of Little Creatures. (gr. 1-3). pap. 2.50 (ISBN 0-8315-0138-3). Speller.

Tyler, J. Animal Words. (gr. 3 up). 1989. 6.96 (ISBN 0-88110-343-8). EDC.

Urquhart, Jennifer C. Animals That Travel. Crump, Donald J., ed. LC 82-47856. 32p. (ps-3). 1982. PLB 10.95 set (ISBN 0-685-05548-5); lib. bdg. 12.95 (ISBN 0-87044-450-6). Natl Geog.

Van Der Meer, Ron. Amazing Animal Senses. (gr. 9-12). 1990. 10.95 (ISBN 0-316-89624-1, Joy St Bks). Little.

Waldrop, Victor H., et al. The Unhuggables: The Truth about Snakes, Slugs, Skunks, Spiders, & Other Animals That Are Hard to Love. Pidgeon, Jean, illus. LC 88-19531. 96p. (gr. 2-7). 1988. 14.95 (ISBN 0-912186-91-7, 19419); PLB 17.95 (ISBN 0-912186-96-8, 19419). Natl Wildlife.

Watson. Animal Legends. (gr. k-4). 1982. 6.95 (ISBN 0-86020-673-4, Usborne-Hayes); PLB 11.96 (ISBN 0-88110-094-3); pap. 3.95 (ISBN 0-86020-672-6). EDC.

Watson, Carol. Magical Animals. Price, Nick, illus. (gr. k-4). 1982. 6.95 (ISBN 0-86020-671-8, Usborne-Hayes); PLB 11.96 (ISBN 0-88110-095-1); pap. 3.95 (ISBN 0-86020-670-X). EDC.

Wexo, John B. Endangered Animals. 24p. (gr. 4). 1989. 11.95s.p. (ISBN 0-88682-269-6); 17.10 (ISBN 0-685-28185-X). Creative Ed.

Whyte, Malcolm. Zoo Animals. (Illus.). 32p. (Orig.). (gr. 1-4). pap. 3.50 (ISBN 0-8431-1961-6). Price Stern.

Wild Animals. 32p. (Orig.). (ps-1). 1984. pap. 1.25 (ISBN 0-8431-1514-9). Price Stern.

Wild Animals. (Illus.). 32p. (ps up). 1986. 2.95 (ISBN 0-8431-4284-7). Price Stern.

Wild Animals. (Illus.). (gr. k-9). 1988. pap. 1.25 (ISBN 0-318-37126-X). Scholastic Inc.

Wild Animals. (Illus.). 88p. (ps-3). 1989. 15.93 (ISBN 0-8094-4877-7); lib. bdg. 21.27 (ISBN 0-8094-4878-5). Time-Life.

Wild Animals. (Illus.). 20p. (gr. k up). 1990. laminated, wipe clean surface 3.95 (ISBN 0-88679-822-1). Educ Insights.

Wild Animals. (Illus.). 16p. (gr. k up). 1990. 9.95 (ISBN 0-88679-660-1). Educ Insights.

Wild Animals of North America. (Illus.). 32p. (gr. 1-4). 1987. pap. 2.95 (ISBN 0-8431-4295-2). Price Stern.

Wild, Anne. Animal Mobiles. (Illus.). 28p. (Orig.). (gr. 4 up). 1985. pap. 4.95 (ISBN 0-317-14829-X). Parkwest Pubns.

Wildlife Education, Ltd. Staff. Gorillas. Orr, Richard, et al, illus. 20p. (Orig.). (gr. 1-8). 1984. pap. 2.25 (ISBN 0-937934-28-3). WildLife Educ.

—Rhinos. Woods, Michael, et al, illus. 20p. (Orig.). (gr. 1-8). 1985. pap. 2.25 (ISBN 0-937934-29-1). Wildlife Educ.

Wildsmith, Brian. Animal Games. Wildsmith, Brian, illus. (ps-3). 1980. 9.95 (ISBN 0-19-279731-X). Oxford U Pr.

—Animal Homes. Wildsmith, Brian, illus. (ps-3). 1980. 9.95 (ISBN 0-19-279732-8). Oxford U Pr.

—Animal Homes. (Illus.). 32p. (ps up). 1991. pap. 4.95 (ISBN 0-19-272176-3, 12407). Oxford U Pr.

—Animal Tricks. (Illus.). 32p. (ps up). 1991. pap. 4.95 (ISBN 0-19-272173-9, 12408). Oxford U Pr.

Williams, Brenda & Williams, Brian. The World of Animals. Robson, Eric, illus. LC 90-42619. 40p. (Orig.). (gr. 2-5). 1991. pap. 3.95 (ISBN 0-679-80864-7). Random.

Wolff, Robert. Animals of Europe. Dallet, Robert, illus. LC 77-78379. 160p. (gr. 3-9). 1969. PLB 29.95 (ISBN 0-87460-092-8). Lion Bks.

—Animals of the Americas. Dallet, Robert, illus. LC 73-78378. (gr. 3-9). 1969. PLB 29.95 (ISBN 0-87460-093-6). Lion Bks.

—Animals of the Americas. Dallet, Robert, illus. LC 73-78378. (gr. 3-9). 1969. PLB 29.95 (ISBN 0-87460-093-6). Lion Bks.

Wood, Robert W. Thirty-Nine Easy Animal Biology Experiments. (Illus.). 160p. (gr. 3-8). 1991. 16.95 (ISBN 0-8306-6594-3, 3594); pap. 9.95 (ISBN 0-8306-3594-7). TAB Bks.

Yolen, Jane. The Acorn Quest. Natti, Susanna, illus. LC 80-2755. 64p. (gr. 3-6). 1981. PLB 12.89 (ISBN 0-690-04107-1, Crowell Jr Bks). HarpC Child Bks.

Zeff. Animal Word Book. (gr. 1-9). 1980. 11.95 (ISBN 0-86020-555-X, Usborne-Hayes); French ed. 11.95 (ISBN 0-86020-556-8). EDC.

Zokeisha. A Little Book of Baby Animals. Klimo, Kate, ed. Zokeisha, illus. 16p. 1982. 2.95 (ISBN 0-671-44840-4, Little Simon). S&S Trade.

Zoo Animals. LC 90-48751. 24p. (ps-k). 1991. pap. 6.95 (ISBN 0-689-71406-8, Aladdin). Macmillan Child Grp.

ANIMALS–ANATOMY

see Anatomy, Comparative

ANIMALS–COLOR

see Color of Animals

ANIMALS–DICTIONARIES

Brown, Richard. One Hundred Words about Animals. Brown, Richard, illus. (gr. k-2). 1990. incl. cass. 19.95 (ISBN 0-87488-183-8); pap. 12.95 incl. cass. (ISBN 0-87499-182-X); Set; incl. 4 bks., cass., & guide. pap. 27. 95 (ISBN 0-87499-184-6). Live Oak Media.

The Eyewitness Visual Dictionary of Animals. (Illus.). 64p. (gr. 6 up). 1991. 14.95 (ISBN 1-879431-19-X); PLB 15.99 (ISBN 1-879431-34-3). Dorling Kindersley.

Scarry. Dictionnaire Animaux. (FRE.). (gr. 3-8). 24.95 (ISBN 0-685-28442-5). French & Eur.

Tison, Annette. Big Book of Animal Records. Tison, Annette & Taylor, Talus, illus. LC 84-81434. 96p. (gr. 2-6). 1985. 9.95 (ISBN 0-448-18968-2, G&D). Putnam Pub Group.

ANIMALS–DISEASES

see Veterinary Medicine

ANIMALS–FICTION

see also Animals–Habits and Behavior; Fables

Aardema, Verna. Princess Gorilla & a New Kind of Water. Chase, Victoria, illus. LC 86-32888. 32p. (ps-3). 1988. 10.95 (ISBN 0-8037-0412-7); PLB 10.89 (ISBN 0-8037-0413-5). Dial Bks Young.

Adams, Georgie & Axworthy, Anni. The Cat Sat on the Rat. (Illus.). 24p. (ps-1). 1989. 5.95 (ISBN 0-8120-6148-9). Barron.

Aesop. Aesop for Children. Winter, Milo, illus. LC 86-73175. 96p. (gr. 2 up). 1984. Repr. of 1919 ed. 12.95 (ISBN 1-56288-039-X). Checkerboard Pr.

—The Hare & the Tortoise. Friedman, Arthur, illus. LC 80-28162. 32p. (gr. k-3). 1981. PLB 9.79 (ISBN 0-89375-468-4); pap. text ed. 1.95 (ISBN 0-89375-469-2). Troll Assocs.

—The Lion & the Mouse. Dole, Bob, illus. LC 80-28154. 32p. (gr. k-3). 1981. PLB 9.79 (ISBN 0-89375-466-8); pap. text ed. 1.95 (ISBN 0-89375-467-6). Troll Assocs.

Alexander, Martha. Even That Moose Won't Listen to Me. Alexander, Martha, illus. 32p. (ps-k). 1988. 11.95 (ISBN 0-8037-0187-X); PLB 9.89 (ISBN 0-8037-0188-8). Dial Bks Young.

Allan, Ted. Willie the Squowse. Blake, Quentin, illus. (gr. 2 up). 1978. 8.95 (ISBN 0-8038-8086-3). Hastings.

Allen, Jeffrey. Mary Alice, Operator Number Nine. Marshall, James, illus. 32p. (gr. 1-3). 1975. lib. bdg. 14.95i (ISBN 0-316-03425-8). Little.

Anders, Rebecca. Dolly the Donkey. Hammarberg, Dyan, tr. LC 76-1283. (Illus.). 24p. (gr. k-4). 1976. PLB 6.95 (ISBN 0-87614-062-2). Carolrhoda Bks.

Anholt, Catherine. Chaos at Cold Custard Farm. (Illus.). 32p. (ps up). 1988. 13.95 (ISBN 0-19-520645-2). Oxford U Pr.

—Truffles in Trouble. Anholt, Catherine, illus. LC 86-47830. (ps-3). 1987. 9.95 (ISBN 0-316-04260-9). Little.

—Truffles Is Sick. Anholt, Catherine, illus. LC 86-47831. (ps-3). 1987. 9.95 (ISBN 0-316-04259-5). Little.

Argent, Kerry & Trinca, Rod. One Woolly Wombat. Argent, Kerry, illus. 32p. (ps-1). 1987. pap. 6.95 (ISBN 0-916291-10-3). Kane-Miller Bk.

Aruego, Jose & Dewey, Ariane. We Hide, You Seek. LC 78-13638. (Illus.). 32p. (gr. k-3). 1979. 13.95 (ISBN 0-688-80201-X); PLB 13.88 (ISBN 0-688-84201-1). Greenwillow.

Asuka, Ken. Toto Visits Mystic Mountain. Young, Richard Y., ed. Kaisei-sha, tr. Asuka, Ken, illus. LC 89-11754. 32p. (gr. 1-3). 1989. PLB 13.26 (ISBN 0-944483-46-1). Garrett Ed Corp.

Aych, Mary J. Pick of the Litter. (gr. 4-7). 1990. pap. 2.95 (ISBN 0-553-15808-2). Bantam.

Baby Animals. (ARA., Illus.). (gr. 1-3). 3.50x (ISBN 0-86685-186-0). Intl Bk Ctr.

Bains, Rae. Hiccups, Hiccups. Coontz, Otto, illus. LC 81-4638. 32p. (gr. k-2). 1981. PLB 10.89 (ISBN 0-89375-537-0); pap. text ed. 2.95 (ISBN 0-89375-538-9). Troll Assocs.

Bakko, Darlene. Unusual Animals A to Z. Davenport, May, illus. LC 82-71047. 26p. (Orig.). (gr. k-5). 1982. color bk., spiral bdg. 1.50x (ISBN 0-943864-30-5). Davenport.

Barberis, France. Would You Like a Parrot? Barberis, Franco, illus. LC 67-28671. 32p. (ps-k). 8.95 (ISBN 0-87592-060-8). Scroll Pr.

Barnes, Jill & Asuka, Ken. Smile for Toto. Rubin, Caroline, ed. Japan Foreign Rights Centre Staff, tr. from JPN. Asuka, Ken, illus. LC 90-37747. 32p. (gr. k-4). 1990. PLB 15.93 (ISBN 0-944483-87-9). Garrett Ed Corp.

—Toto in Trouble. Rubin, Caroline, ed. Japan Foreign Rights Centre Staff, tr. from JPN. Asuka, Ken, illus. LC 90-37749. 32p. (gr. k-4). 1990. PLB 15.93 (ISBN 0-944483-86-0). Garrett Ed Corp.

Barnes, Jill & Ishinabe, Fusako. Spring Snowman. Rubin, Caroline, ed. Japan Foreign Rights Centre Staff, tr. from JPN. Ishinabe, Fusako, illus. LC 90-37748. 32p. (gr. k-3). 1990. PLB 15.93 (ISBN 0-944483-83-6). Garrett Ed Corp.

Barnes, Joyce B. Patches, the Blessed Beast of Burden. Ramirez-Walker, Linda J., illus. 36p. 1990. 15.00 (ISBN 0-9628493-0-8). J B Barnes.

Barrett, John. The Littlest Mule. Silver Dollar City, Inc. Staff, ed. Baer, Jane & Baer, Dale, illus. (ps-5). 1977. 2.99g (ISBN 0-686-19125-0). Silver Dollar.

Barrett, Judith. Animals Should Definitely Not Act Like People. Barrett, Ron, illus. LC 80-13364. 32p. (ps-2). 1980. 13.95 (ISBN 0-689-30768-3, Atheneum Child Bk). Macmillan Child Grp.

—Animals Should Definitely Not Wear Clothing. Barrett, Ron, illus. LC 70-115078. 32p. (ps-2). 1970. 13.95 (ISBN 0-689-20592-9, Atheneum Child Bk). Macmillan Child Grp.

—Animals Should Definitely Not Wear Clothing. Barrett, Ron, illus. (ps-2). 1974. pap. 3.95 (ISBN 0-689-70412-7, Aladdin). Macmillan Child Grp.

Baumann, Hans. Chip Has Many Brothers. Carle, Eric, illus. LC 85-3671. 26p. (gr. 1-5). 1985. 11.95 (ISBN 0-399-21283-3, Philomel). Putnam Pub Group.

Beatty, Patricia. Eight Mules from Monterey. LC 81-22284. 224p. (gr. 4-6). 1982. 12.95 (ISBN 0-688-01047-4). Morrow.

Bell, Anthea. Animal Antics. Janosch, illus. 128p. (gr. k-2). 1987. 17.95 (ISBN 0-86264-033-4, Pub. by Anderson Pr UK). Trafalgar Sq.

Bennett, David. One Cow Moo Moo. Cooke, Andy, illus. 32p. (ps). 1990. 11.95 (ISBN 0-8050-1416-0). H Holt & Co.

Bennett, Jill. Animal Fair. (ps-3). 1990. 12.95 (ISBN 0-670-82691-X). Viking Child Bks.

Berends, Polly B. Ladybug & Dog & the Night Walk. Szekeres, Cyndy, illus. LC 79-20692. 32p. (ps). 1980. (Random Juv). Random.

Berenstain, Stan & Berenstain, Janice. After the Dinosaurs. Berenstain, Stan & Berenstain, Janice, illus. LC 88-42588. 32p. (Orig.). (gr. k-3). 1988. lib. bdg. 5.99 (ISBN 0-394-90518-0, Random Juv); pap. 2.25 (ISBN 0-394-80518-6, Random Juv). Random.

Blassingame, Wyatt. The Strange Armadillo. (gr. 2-5). 1983. 8.95 (ISBN 0-396-08180-0, Putnam). Putnam Pub Group.

Blocksma, Mary. The Pup Went Up. Kalthoff, Sandra C., illus. LC 82-19862. 24p. (ps-2). 1983. PLB 12.33 (ISBN 0-516-01583-4); pap. 3.95 (ISBN 0-516-41583-2). Childrens.

Bonsall, Crosby N. Who's a Pest? Bonsall, Crosby N., illus. LC 62-13310. 64p. (gr. k-3). 1962. PLB 11.89 (ISBN 0-06-020621-7). HarpC Child Bks.

Boon, Emilie. One, Two, Three, How Many Animals Can You See? Boon, Emilie, illus. LC 87-61302. 32p. (ps-2). 1987. 12.95 (ISBN 0-531-05701-1); PLB 12.99 (ISBN 0-531-08301-2). Orchard Bks Watts.

Boyd, Patricia R. The Furry Wind. Spring, Grace J., illus. 28p. (gr. 2-3). 1982. pap. 2.25 (ISBN 0-9603840-4-9). Andrew Mtn Pr.

Boynton, Sandra. A to Z. Boynton, Sandra, illus. 7p. (ps). 1990. bds. 3.95 (ISBN 0-671-49317-5, Little Simon). S&S Trade.

Brennan, J. H. The Den of Dragons. 192p. (gr. 6 up). 1986. pap. 2.50 (ISBN 0-440-91873-1, LFL). Dell.

Brett, Jan. Annie & the Wild Animals. Brett, Jan, illus. LC 84-19818. 32p. (gr. k-3). 1990. 13.95 (ISBN 0-395-37800-1); pap. write for info. (ISBN 0-395-53962-5). HM.

—Annie & the Wild Animals. Brett, Jan, illus. (ps-3). 1989. pap. 3.95 (ISBN 0-395-51006-6, Sandpiper). HM.

Brooke, L. Leslie. Stories from the Golden Goose Book. (ps-3). 1987. 4.95 (ISBN 0-7232-3530-9). Warne.

Broomfield, Robert. Baby Animal ABC. (Orig.). (ps-k). 1968. pap. 3.50 (ISBN 0-14-050006-5, Penguin Bks). Viking Penguin.

Brown, Bob. The Turtle's Darshan for All the Animals. (Illus.). 32p. (gr. 2 up). 1973. pap. 2.00 (ISBN 0-913078-17-4). Sheriar Pr.

Brown, Craig. My Barn. LC 90-41758. (Illus.). 24p. (ps up). 1991. 13.95 (ISBN 0-688-08785-X); PLB 13.88 (ISBN 0-688-08786-8). Greenwillow.

Brown, Jerome C. Paper Menagerie. (Illus.). (gr. 3-12). 1984. pap. 4.95 (ISBN 0-8224-5191-3). Fearon Teach Aids.

Brown, Marc. Arthur Goes to Camp. Brown, Marc, illus. LC 81-15588. 32p. (ps-3). 1984. 14.95 (ISBN 0-316-11218-6, Joy St Bks); pap. 4.95 (ISBN 0-316-11058-2, Joy St Bks). Little.

—Arthur's Nose. Brown, Marc, illus. 32p. (ps-3). 1986. lib. bdg. 14.95 (ISBN 0-316-11193-7, Joy St Bks); pap. 4.95 (ISBN 0-316-11070-1, Joy St Bks). Little.

—Arthur's Teacher Trouble. Brown, Marc, illus. 32p. (ps-3). 1989. 13.95 (ISBN 0-316-11244-5, Joy St Bks); pap. 4.95 (ISBN 0-316-11186-4, Joy St Bks). Little.

—Arthur's Tooth. Brown, Marc, illus. 32p. (ps-3). 1985. 14.95 (ISBN 0-316-11245-3, Joy St Bks). Little.

—D. W. All Wet. Brown, Marc, illus. (ps-3). 1988. 10.95 (ISBN 0-316-11077-9, Joy St Bks). Little.

Brown, Marcia. Once a Mouse. Brown, Marcia, illus. LC 61-14769. 32p. (ps-3). 1972. 13.95 (ISBN 0-684-12662-1, Scribners Young Read). Macmillan Child Grp.

Brown, Margaret W. Four Fur Feet. Charlip, Remy, illus. 48p. (gr. 1-3). 1989. Repr. of 1961 ed. 13.95 (ISBN 0-929077-03-2, Hopscotch Bks); PLB 12.95 (ISBN 0-317-92548-2, Hopscotch Bks). Watermark Inc.

—Fox Eyes. Williams, Garth, illus. LC 76-43086. (ps-3). 1977. Pantheon.

Bullock, Kathleen. It Changed to Rain. Bullock, Kathleen, illus. (ps-1). 1989. pap. 13.95 (ISBN 0-671-66005-5). S&S Trade.

Burgess, Thonrton W. The Adventures of Johnny Chuck. (gr. 5-6). 15.95 (ISBN 0-88411-787-1, Pub. by Aeonian Pr). Amereon Ltd.

Burgess, Thornton. Old Mother West Wind. Hague, Michael, illus. LC 89-20088. 96p. (gr. k-4). 1990. 18. 95 (ISBN 0-8050-1005-X). H Holt & Co.

Burgess, Thornton W. The Adventures of Grandfather Frog. (gr. 5-6). 15.95 (ISBN 0-88411-777-4, Pub. by Aeonian Pr). Amereon Ltd.

—The Adventures of Jerry Muskrat. (gr. 5-6). 13.95 (ISBN 0-88411-782-0, Pub. by Aeonian Pr). Amereon Ltd.

—The Adventures of Ol' Mistah Buzzard. (gr. 5-6). 15.95 (ISBN 0-88411-784-7, Pub. by Aeonian Pr). Amereon Ltd.

—The Adventures of Old Man Coyote. (gr. 5-6). 15.95 (ISBN 0-88411-781-2, Pub. by Aeonian Pr). Amereon Ltd.

—The Adventures of Old Mr. Toad. (gr. 5-6). 15.95 (ISBN 0-88411-785-5, Pub. by Aeonian Pr). Amereon Ltd.

—The Adventures of Poor Mrs. Quack. (gr. 5-6). 15.95 (ISBN 0-88411-775-8, Pub. by Aeonian Pr). Amereon Ltd.

—The Adventures of Prickly Porky. (gr. 5-6). 15.95 (ISBN 0-88411-783-9, Pub. by Aeonian Pr). Amereon Ltd.

—Adventures of Whitefoot the Woodmouse. Cady, Harrison & Kerr, George, illus. (gr. k-3). 1944. (G&D). Putnam Pub Group.

—Animal Tales: A Platt & Munk Classic. Cady, Harrison, illus. LC 89-80884. 96p. (ps up). 1990. 9.95 (ISBN 0-448-47286-4, G&D). Putnam Pub Group.

—Mother West Wind's Neighbors. Cady, Harrison, illus. LC 68-21862. (gr. 1 up). 1985. pap. 5.95 (ISBN 0-316-11656-4). Little.
—Old Mother West Wind. golden anniversary ed. Cady, Harrison, illus. (gr. 1 up). 1985. 14.95 (ISBN 0-316-11648-3); pap. 6.95 (ISBN 0-316-11655-6). Little.
Burman, Ben L. Thunderbolt at Catfish Bend. Caddy, Alic, illus. 114p. (gr. 5 up). 1984. 10.95 (ISBN 0-685-08084-6); 10.95 (ISBN 0-943436-03-6). Wieser & Wieser.
Burnford, Sheila. The Incredible Journey. (gr. 6-8). 1977. pap. 2.95 (ISBN 0-553-26218-1). Bantam.
—The Incredible Journey. (gr. 6-8). 13.95 (ISBN 0-88411-099-0, Pub. by Aeonian Pr). Amereon Ltd.
—The Incredible Journey. large type ed. (gr. 6-8). Repr. of 1960 ed. write for info. (ISBN 0-89064-027-0). NAVH.
Burningham, John. Mr. Gumpy's Outing. LC 77-159507. (Illus.). 32p. (ps). 1971. 14.95 (ISBN 0-8050-0708-3). H Holt & Co.
Buskohl, Esther E. Honey: Story of a Little Brown Mule. Buskohl, Esther E., illus. LC 85-80216. 80p. (Orig.). (gr. 3-5). 1985. 9.95 (ISBN 0-9614991-0-9); pap. 4.95 (ISBN 0-9614991-1-7). EEBART.
Bussard, Paula J. Rascal Says, "I'm Sorry" Wigginton, Shirley, ed. Goodridge, Lawrence, illus. 30p. (gr. k-4). 1987. 1.39 (ISBN 0-87403-253-9, 3453). Standard Pub.
Butler, M. Christina. Picnic Pandemonium. Rutherford, Meg, illus. LC 90-10148. 28p. (gr. 1-2). 1991. PLB 10.95 (ISBN 0-8368-0433-3). Gareth Stevens Inc.
Byars, Betsy. The Animal, the Vegetable, & John D. Jones. Sanderson, Ruth, illus. 160p. (gr. 5 up). 1983. pap. 2.95 (ISBN 0-440-40356-1, YB). Dell.
Byars, Betsy C. The House of Wings. Schwartz, Daniel, illus. 160p. (gr. 4-6). 1972. pap. 13.95 (ISBN 0-670-38025-3). Viking Child Bks.
Carey, Mary. Scuffy's Underground Adventure. (Illus.). 24p. (ps-2). 1989. write for info. (ISBN 0-307-12058-9, Pub. by Golden Bks). Western Pub.
Carle, Eric. Catch the Ball. 10p. 1982. 4.95 (ISBN 0-399-20885-2, Philomel). Putnam Pub Group.
Carpenter. The Wind in the Willows. write for info. HM.
Carratello, Patty. Duke the Blue Mule. Spivak, Darlene, ed. Smythe, Linda, illus. 16p. (gr. k-2). 1988. wkbk. 1.95 (ISBN 1-55734-384-5). Tchr Create Mat.
Carris, Joan. Hedgehogs in the Closet. Newsom, Carol, illus. LC 87-45309. 160p. (gr. 5 up). 1988. (Lipp Jr Bks); PLB 13.89 (ISBN 0-397-32234-8, Lipp Jr Bks). HarpC Child Bks.
Carter, Anne. Ruff Leaves Home. Butler, John, illus. LC 85-17519. 32p. (gr. k-3). 1987. bds. 5.95 (ISBN 0-517-56068-2). Crown.
Casad, Mary B. Bluebonnet at Dinosaur Valley State Park. Vincent, Benjamin, illus. LC 90-7338. 32p. (gr. k-3). 1990. 11.95 (ISBN 0-88289-776-4). Pelican.
Causley, Charles. Quack! Said the Billy-Goat. Firth, Barbara, illus. LC 85-23856. 24p. (ps-2). 1986. PLB 11.89 (ISBN 0-397-32192-9, Lipp Jr Bks). HarpC Child Bks.
Cavanna, Betty. Petey. Krush, Beth & Krush, Jo, illus. LC 73-4351. 144p. (gr. 3-6). 1973. 5.50 (ISBN 0-664-32532-7, Westminster). Westminster John Knox.
Cazet, Denys. Lucky Me. Cazet, Denys, illus. LC 81-7711. 32p. (ps-2). 1983. 12.96 (ISBN 0-02-717870-6, Bradbury Pr). Macmillan Child Grp.
—Mother Night. LC 88-36439. (Illus.). 32p. (ps-1). 1989. 14.95 (ISBN 0-531-05830-1); PLB 14.99 (ISBN 0-531-08430-2). Orchard Bks Watts.
Cleaver, Vera. Sweetly Sings the Donkey. LC 85-40098. 160p. (gr. 5-9). 1988. pap. 2.95 (ISBN 0-06-440233-9, Trophy). HarpC Child Bks.
Clifford, Eth. The Wild One. Stewart, Arvis, illus. LC 74-8899. 208p. (gr. 5-9). 1974. 5.95 (ISBN 0-395-19491-1). HM.
Coats, Laura J. Ten Little Animals. Coats, Laura J., illus. LC 89-36778. 32p. (ps-1). 1990. 11.95 (ISBN 0-02-719054-4, Mcmillan Child Bk). Macmillan Child Grp.
Cole, Joanna. Animal Sleepyheads: One to Ten. Bassett, Jeni, illus. LC 87-9813. 32p. (gr. k-3). 1988. pap. 10.95 (ISBN 0-590-40919-0, Scholastic Hardcover). Scholastic Inc.
Cole, Michael. Head in the Sand. Clifford, Rowan, illus. LC 90-30086. 24p. (ps-3). 1990. PLB 12.95 (ISBN 0-87614-435-0). Carolrhoda Bks.
Coleman, William L. If Animals Could Talk. LC 87-7141. (Illus.). 144p. (Orig.). (gr. 2-6). 1987. pap. 5.95 (ISBN 0-87123-961-2). Bethany Hse.
Collins, Pat L. Tomorrow, up & Away. Munsinger, Lynn, illus. 32p. (gr. k-3). 1990. 13.95 (ISBN 0-395-51524-6). HM.
Corddry, Thomas. Kibby & the Red Elephant. Kock, Carl, illus. LC 72-13771. (gr. 3-6). 1973. 6.95 (ISBN 0-87955-106-2). O'Hara.
Cosgrove, Stephen. Catundra. James, Robin, illus. 32p. (gr. 1-4). 1978. pap. 2.95 (ISBN 0-8431-0571-2). Price Stern.
—Kyomi. James, Robin, illus. (Orig.). (gr. k-4). 1984. pap. 2.95 (ISBN 0-8431-1164-X). Price Stern.
—Minikin. James, Robin, illus. (Orig.). (gr. k-4). 1984. pap. 2.95 (ISBN 0-8431-1163-1). Price Stern.
Cowley, Joy. The Poor, Sore Paw, 6 bks. Kincaid, Eric, illus. 16p. (Orig.). (gr. k-2). 1987. Set. pap. text ed. 19.80 (ISBN 1-55624-739-7). Wright Group.
—The Poor, Sore Paw. Kincaid, Eric, illus. 16p. (Orig.). (gr. k-2). 1987. pap. text ed. 23.00 (ISBN 1-55624-162-3). Wright Group.
Croser, Nigel. Help! Alder, George, illus. LC 89-35648. 28p. (gr. 1-2). 1989. PLB 10.95 (ISBN 0-8368-0223-3). Gareth Stevens Inc.
Crowe, Robert L. Tyler Toad & the Thunder. Chorao, Kay, illus. LC 80-347. 32p. (ps-1). 1980. 9.95 (ISBN 0-525-41795-8, DCB). Dutton Child Bks.
Crutcher, Chris. Running Loose. (gr. 7 up). 1986. pap. 3.25 (ISBN 0-440-97570-0, LFL). Dell.
Currie, Quinn. Beautiful Joe. rev. & abr. ed. Heinonen, Susan, illus. Amory, Cleveland, intro. by. (Illus.). 72p. (gr. k-8). 1990. pap. 8.95 (ISBN 0-9623072-1-1). S Ink WA.
Cutler, Ivor. Herbert: Five Stories. Benson, Patrick, illus. LC 88-2918. 48p. (ps-2). 1988. 13.00 (ISBN 0-688-08147-9); PLB 12.88 (ISBN 0-688-08148-7). Lothrop.
Cuyler, Margery. That's Good! That's Bad! Catrow, David, illus. LC 90-49353. 32p. (ps-2). 1991. 15.95 (ISBN 0-8050-1535-3). H Holt & Co.
Dahl, Roald. Dirty Beasts. Fawcett, Rosemary, illus. LC 85-594. 32p. (gr. 1 up). 1984. 12.95 (ISBN 0-374-31790-9). FS&G.
—The Wonderful Story of Henry Sugar & Six More. LC 77-5354. 32p. (gr. 5 up). 1991. 15.00 (ISBN 0-394-83604-9). Knopf.
Dalgliesh, Alice. Fourth of July Story. Nonnast, Marie, illus. LC 56-6138. 32p. (ps-3). 1972. 13.95 (ISBN 0-684-13164-1, Scribners Young Read); (Scribner). Macmillan Child Grp.
Danziger, Paula. It's an Aardvark-Eat-Turtle World. (gr. 5 up). 1986. pap. 3.25 (ISBN 0-440-94028-1, LFL). Dell.
Davidson, Alice J. Beware When Elephants Sneeze. (Illus.). 1986. 4.95 (ISBN 0-8378-5086-X). Gibson.
—Monkeys Never Say Please. (Illus.). 1986. 4.95 (ISBN 0-8378-5085-1). Gibson.
Davidson, Jill A. And That's What Happened to Little Lucy: Just Right for 3's & 4's. Meisel, Paul, illus. LC 88-22687. 32p. (ps). 1989. 4.95 (ISBN 0-394-89945-8, Random Juv). Random.
Davis, Jim. Garfield A to Z Zoo. Fentz, Mike & Kuhn, Dave, illus. LC 83-17697. 24p. (ps-5). 1984. pap. 1.25 (ISBN 0-394-86483-2, Random Juv). Random.
Day, Alexandra. Frank & Ernest. Day, Alexandra, illus. 40p. (gr. k-3). 1988. 12.95 (ISBN 0-590-41557-3, Pub. by Scholastic Hardcover). Scholastic Inc.
DeGroat, Florence. Animal Stories. Wilson, Patricia, illus. 88p. (gr. 2-6). 1983. pap. 2.95 (ISBN 0-87516-509-5). DeVorss.
Demers, Paul. Oliver & Ophelia: A Tale of Opossums. Delaney, Jacqueline K., illus. LC 85-6020. 20p. (Orig.). (gr. 1-6). 1986. pap. 2.95 (ISBN 0-916897-04-4). Andrew Mtn Pr.
Demi. Demi's Find the Animal ABC. Demi, illus. LC 85-70285. 48p. (ps up). 1985. 9.95 (ISBN 0-448-18970-4, G&D). Putnam Pub Group.
—Find Demi's Baby Animals. LC 89-82234. (Illus.). 48p. 1990. 13.95 (ISBN 0-448-19169-5, G&D). Putnam Pub Group.
Despain, Goldie B. Tiny Ant Who Scared a Horned Toad. Petie, Haris, illus. (ps-3). 1970. write for info. (ISBN 0-8313-0029-9); PLB 6.70 (ISBN 0-685-02940-9). Lantern.
Diestel-Feddersen, Mary. Try Again, Sally Jane. Ashley, Yvonne, illus. LC 86-42810. 30p. (gr. 2-3). 1987. PLB 12.95 (ISBN 1-55532-150-X). Gareth Stevens Inc.
Disney, Walt, Productions Staff. Walt Disney Productions Presents Tod & Copper from The Fox & the Hound. LC 81-2619. (Illus.). 48p. (ps-3). 1981. 4.95 (ISBN 0-394-84819-5). Random.
—Walt Disney Productions Presents Tod & Vixey from The Fox & the Hound. LC 81-5209. (Illus.). 48p. (ps-3). 1981. 4.95 (ISBN 0-394-84904-3). Random.
—Walt Disney's the Adventures of Mr. Toad Adapted from the Wind in the Willows. LC 81-2783. (Illus.). 48p. (ps-3). 1981. 4.95 (ISBN 0-394-84818-7). Random.
Doney, Meryl. The Ninety-Ninth Sheep. (Illus.). 1991. 8.95 (ISBN 0-8423-4740-2). Tyndale.
Downing, Julie. White Snow-Blue Feather. Downing, Julie, illus. LC 89-815. 32p. (ps-1). 1989. 13.95 (ISBN 0-02-732530-X, Bradbury Pr). Macmillan Child Grp.
Dummer, H. Boylston. Adventures of the Animal Town Aviators, Bk. I. Dummer, H. Boylston, illus. 118p. (ps-3). 1989. 17.95 (ISBN 0-87510-198-4, Bks from the Christ Sci Monitor). Chr Science.
—Adventures of the Animal Town Aviators, Bk. II. Dummer, H. Boylston, illus. 118p. (ps-3). 1989. 17.95 (ISBN 0-87510-199-2, Bks from the Christ Sci Monitor). Chr Science.
Duncan, Riana. A Nutcracker in a Tree: A Book of Riddles. Duncan, Riana, illus. LC 80-67492. 32p. (gr. k-3). 1981. PLB 8.95 (ISBN 0-385-28733-X); pap. 8.95 (ISBN 0-385-28732-1). Delacorte.
Dunn, Phoebe & Dunn, Judy. The Animals of Buttercup Farm. Dunn, Phoebe, photos by. LC 81-4892. (Illus.). 48p. (ps-1). 1981. 8.95 (ISBN 0-394-84798-9). Random.
Duvoisin, Roger. Our Veronica Goes to Petunia's Farm. Duvoisin, Roger, illus. (gr. k-3). 1962. lib. bdg. 6.99 (ISBN 0-394-91469-4). Knopf.
Eckert, Allan W. Incident at Hawk's Hill. Schoenherr, John, illus. 173p. (gr. 7 up). 1971. 14.95 (ISBN 0-316-20866-3). Little.
Economos, Chris. Let's Take the Bus. (Illus.). 32p. (gr. 1-4). 1989. PLB 13.32 (ISBN 0-8172-3500-0). Raintree Pubs.
Edington, Andy. Monkeying with the Flood. Eakin, Ed, ed. Messina, Linda, illus. 32p. (gr. 1-2). 1989. 10.95 (ISBN 0-89015-736-7, Pub. by Panda Bks). Eakin Pr.
Elliott, Joey. Beezle's Bravery. Buzzanco, Eileen M., illus. 32p. (gr. k-4). 1989. 11.95 (ISBN 0-924483-17-2); book & audiocassette 14.95 (ISBN 0-924483-15-6); book, audiocassette & toy 36.95 (ISBN 0-924483-13-X); Narration of the story by Tom Chapin. write for info. audiocassette (ISBN 0-924483-19-9). Soundprints.
—Scamp's New Home. Buzzanco, Eileen M., illus. 32p. (gr. k-4). 1989. 11.95 (ISBN 0-924483-16-4); book & audiocassette 14.95 (ISBN 0-924483-14-8); book, audiocassette & toy 41.95 (ISBN 0-924483-12-1); Narration of the story by Tom Chapin. write for info. audiocassette (ISBN 0-924483-18-0). Soundprints.
Enns, Peter & Forsberg, Glen. Six Stories of Jesus. Friesen, John H., illus. 24p. (ps-5). 1985. 4.95 (ISBN 0-936215-05-4); cassette incl. STL Intl.
Erickson, Phoebe. Black Penny. Erickson, Phoebe, illus. (gr. 3-6). 1982. pap. 5.50 (ISBN 0-317-13562-7). P Erickson.
Erickson, Russell. A Toad for Tuesday. Di Fiori, Lawrence, illus. LC 73-19900. 64p. (gr. k-4). 1974. PLB 12.88 (ISBN 0-688-51569-X). Lothrop.
Ets, Marie H. Play with Me. Ets, Marie H., illus. (ps-1). 1955. pap. 13.95 (ISBN 0-670-55977-6). Viking Child Bks.
Farris, Mary H. Ms. Felicity Ferret Visits Mongoose Hill. (gr. 1-3). 1987. 4.95 (ISBN 0-533-07017-1). Vantage.
Favorite Mother Goose & Animal Tales. (Illus.). 72p. (ps-1). 1989. write for info. (ISBN 0-307-15822-5, Pub. by Golden Bks). Western Pub.
Feldman, Eve. Get Set & Go! (Illus.). 32p. (gr. 1-4). 1989. PLB 13.32 (ISBN 0-8172-3501-9). Raintree Pubs.
Ferns, Ronald. Osbert & Lucy. Ferns, Ronald, illus. LC 88-21359. 32p. (gr. k-3). 1989. 13.95 (ISBN 0-06-021835-5); PLB 13.89 (ISBN 0-06-021836-3). HarpC Child Bks.
Finzel, Julia. Large As Life. LC 90-49816. (Illus.). 32p. (ps up). 1991. 14.95 (ISBN 0-688-10652-8); PLB 14.88 (ISBN 0-688-10653-6). Lothrop.
Fischetto, Laura. Inside Noah's Ark. Galli, Letizia, illus. 32p. (ps-3). 1989. pap. 13.95 (ISBN 0-670-83028-3). Viking Child Bks.
Fisher, Barbara. Big Harold & Tiny Enid. (Illus.). 26p. (Orig.). (gr. 1-3). 1975. pap. 2.00 (ISBN 0-934830-01-0). Ten Penny.
Flack, Marjorie. Angus Lost. (ps-k). 1989. PLB 12.95 (ISBN 0-385-07214-7); pap. 13.99 (ISBN 0-385-07601-0). Doubleday.
—Ask Mr. Bear. Flack, Marjorie, illus. LC 58-8370. 32p. (ps-1). 1971. pap. 3.95 (ISBN 0-02-043090-6, Aladdin). Macmillan Child Grp.
Fontenot, Mary A. Clovis Crawfish & Bertile's Bon Voyage. Blazek, Scott R., illus. 32p. (ps-8). 1991. 11.95 (ISBN 0-88289-825-6). Pelican.
—Clovis Crawfish & Michelle Mantis. Blazek, Scott R., illus. 32p. 1989. 11.95 (ISBN 0-88289-730-6). Pelican.
—Clovis Crawfish & Petit Papillon. Graves, Keith, illus. LC 83-27325. 52p. (gr. k-5). 1985. Repr. 11.95 (ISBN 0-88289-448-X). Pelican.
—Clovis Crawfish & the Orphan Zo Zo. Vincent, Eric, illus. LC 81-17740. 32p. (gr. k-2). 1983. 11.95 (ISBN 0-88289-312-2). Pelican.
—Clovis Crawfish & the Singing Cigales. Vincent, Eric, illus. LC 81-5608. 32p. (ps-4). 1981. 11.95 (ISBN 0-88289-270-3). Pelican.
Forrester, Victoria. The Magnificent Moo. LC 82-13781. (Illus.). 40p. (gr. k-1). 1983. 10.95 (ISBN 0-689-30954-6, Atheneum Childrens Bks). Macmillan Child Grp.
Frederick, Ruth. A Surprise for Miss Van. O'Connell, Ruth A., illus. 32p. (gr. 1-2). 1991. pap. 3.99 (ISBN 0-87403-805-7, 24-03895). Standard Pub.
Frith, Michael. Some of Us Walk, Some Fly, Some Swim. LC 73-158391. (Illus.). (gr. k-6). 1971. PLB 4.95 (ISBN 0-394-82325-7). Beginner.
Gackenbach, Dick. Hound & Bear. Gackenbach, Dick, illus. LC 76-3525. 32p. (ps-3). 1979. 14.95 (ISBN 0-395-28796-0, Clarion). HM.
Galdone, Paul. The Little Red Hen. LC 72-97770. (Illus.). 32p. (ps-2). 1979. 13.95 (ISBN 0-395-28803-7, Clarion). HM.
—The Turtle & the Monkey. (Illus.). 32p. (ps-3). 1983. 13.95 (ISBN 0-89919-145-2, Clarion). HM.
Galdone, Paul, retold by. & illus. The Three Billy Goats Gruff. LC 72-85338. 32p. (ps-3). 1979. 13.95 (ISBN 0-395-28812-6, Clarion). HM.
Gammell, Stephen. Once upon MacDonald's Farm. Gammell, Stephen, illus. LC 84-29356. 32p. (gr. k-3). 1984. Repr. of 1981 ed. 12.95 (ISBN 0-02-737210-3, Four Winds). Macmillan Child Grp.
Garis, Howard R. Uncle Wiggily & His Friends. (Illus.). 98p. (ps-3). 1978. 7.95 (ISBN 0-448-40504-0, G&D); PLB 3.79 (ISBN 0-448-13023-8). Putnam Pub Group.
—Uncle Wiggily's Storybook. (Illus.). 260p. (ps-4). 1987. pap. 9.95 (ISBN 0-448-40090-1, G&D). Putnam Pub Group.
Garrick, Carol. Big Old Bones: A Dinosaur Tale. Garrick, Donald, illus. 32p. (gr. k-2). 1989. 13.95 (ISBN 0-89919-734-5, Pub. by Clarion). Ticknor & Fields.
Garside, Alice H. The Man, the Fox & the Skunk. 24p. (Orig.). (gr. k-2). 1989. pap. text ed. 2.00 (ISBN 1-882063-06-6). Cottage Pr MA.
Gee, John. Timbertoes. (Illus.). 32p. (gr. k-2). 1967. pap. 2.95 (ISBN 0-87534-133-0). Highlights.

George, Gail. The Popples & the Puppy. Henry, Barb, illus. LC 85-63821. 32p. (ps-3). 1986. pap. 1.25 (ISBN 0-394-88304-7, Random Juv). Random.

George, William T. & George, Lindsay B. Fishing at Long Pond. LC 89-77514. (Illus.). 24p. (ps up). 1991. 13.95 (ISBN 0-688-09401-5); PLB 13.88 (ISBN 0-688-09402-3). Greenwillow.

Geringer, Laura. The Cow Is Mooing Anyhow. Zimmer, Dirk, illus. LC 85-45251. 40p. (ps-4). 1991. 14.95 (ISBN 0-06-021986-6); PLB 14.89 (ISBN 0-06-021987-4). HarpC Child Bks.

Gerver, Michael. The Popples & the Kitchen Caper. Fahrion, Michael, illus. LC 85-63793. 32p. (ps-3). 1986. pap. 1.25 (ISBN 0-394-88351-9, Random Juv). Random.

Gibbons, Gail. Prehistoric Animals. Gibbons, Gail, illus. LC 88-4661. 32p. (ps-3). 1988. reinforced bdg. 14.95 (ISBN 0-8234-0707-1). Holiday.

Giff, Patricia R. Lazy Lions, Lucky Lambs. Sims, Blanche, illus. 80p. (gr. k-6). 1985. pap. 2.99 (ISBN 0-440-44640-6, YB). Dell.

Ginsburg, Mirra. Across the Stream. Tafuri, Nancy, illus. LC 81-20306. 24p. (ps-1). 1982. 13.95 (ISBN 0-688-01204-3); PLB 13.88 (ISBN 0-688-01206-X). Greenwillow.

—Mushroom in the Rain. Aruego, Jose & Dewey, Ariane, illus. LC 72-92438. 32p. (ps-1). 1987. 13.95 (ISBN 0-02-736241-8, Mcmillan Child Bk). Macmillan Child Grp.

—Mushroom in the Rain. Ginsburg, Mirra, illus. LC 90-31814. 32p. (ps-1). 1990. pap. 3.95 (ISBN 0-689-71441-6, Aladdin). Macmillan Child Grp.

Gipson, Morrell & Mangold, Paul. Whose Tracks Are These? Stefoff, Rebecca, ed. LC 90-13798. (Illus.). 24p. (gr. k-3). 1990. PLB 13.26 (ISBN 0-944483-93-3). Garrett Ed Corp.

Glaser, Michael. Does Anyone Know Where a Hermit Crab Goes? Glaser, Michael, illus. LC 82-84341. 32p. (Orig.). (ps-3). 1983. pap. 3.95 (ISBN 0-911635-00-9). Knickerbocker.

Goldsborough, June. What's in the Woods? LC 76-10271. (Illus.). 32p. 1981. pap. 2.95 (ISBN 0-13-955047-X). P-H.

Gomi, Taro. My Friends. LC 89-23940. (Illus.). 32p. (ps-1). 1990. 9.95 (ISBN 0-87701-688-7). Chronicle Bks.

Goodrich, Beatrice. Happy Hollow Stories, Bk. 1. LC 86-51204. (Illus.). 54p. (gr. k-6). 1987. pap. 5.95 (ISBN 0-932433-20-0). Windswept Hse.

Graham. Wind in the Willows. 1988. pap. 2.25 (ISBN 0-14-035087-X, Puffin). Puffin Bks.

Graham, John. I Love You, Mouse. De Paola, Tomie, illus. LC 76-8022. (gr. k-2). 1976. 12.95 (ISBN 0-15-238005-1, HJ). HarBraceJ.

Grahame, Kenneth. The Adventures of Mole, Rat & Toad. Palazzo-Craig, Janet, adapted by. Baer, Mary A., illus. LC 81-16422. 32p. (gr. 2-5). 1982. PLB 10.79 (ISBN 0-89375-636-9); pap. text ed. 2.95 (ISBN 0-89375-637-7). Troll Assocs.

—The Adventures of Toad. Shepard, Ernest, illus. LC 90-45374. 48p. (ps-3). 1991. pap. 4.95 POB (ISBN 0-689-71498-X, Aladdin). Macmillan Child Grp.

—The Battle at Toad Hall. Palazzo-Craig, Janet, adapted by. Baer, Mary A., illus. LC 81-16407. 32p. (gr. 2-5). 1982. PLB 10.79 (ISBN 0-89375-642-3); pap. text ed. 2.95 (ISBN 0-89375-643-1). Troll Assocs.

—More Adventures with Mr. Toad. Palazzo-Craig, Janet, adapted by. Baer, Mary A., illus. LC 81-16412. 32p. (gr. 2-5). 1982. PLB 10.79 (ISBN 0-89375-640-7); pap. text ed. 2.95 (ISBN 0-89375-641-5). Troll Assocs.

—Open Road. 1987. pap. 2.25 (ISBN 0-671-63626-X, Little Simon). S&S Trade.

—The Return of the Hero. Shepard, Ernest, illus. LC 90-1286. 48p. (ps-3). 1991. pap. 4.95 POB (ISBN 0-689-71497-1, Aladdin). Macmillan Child Grp.

—River Bank. 1987. pap. 2.25 (ISBN 0-671-63627-8, Little Simon). S&S Trade.

—The River Bank & the Open Road. Shepard, Ernest, illus. LC 90-45376. 48p. (ps-3). 1991. pap. 4.95 POB (ISBN 0-689-71496-3, Aladdin). Macmillan Child Grp.

—El Viento en los Sauces I & II. (SPA.). 4.95 ea. Santillana.

—The Wild Wood. (Illus.). 1987. pap. 2.25 (ISBN 0-671-63628-6, Little Simon). S&S Trade.

—The Wild Wood & Mole's Christmas. Shepard, Ernest, illus. LC 90-45375. 48p. (ps-3). 1991. pap. 4.95 POB (ISBN 0-689-71495-5, Aladdin). Macmillan Child Grp.

—The Wind in the Willlows. LC 80-12509. (ps up). 1986. 19.95 (ISBN 0-8050-0213-8). H Holt & Co.

—Wind in the Willows. (gr. 4 up). pap. 2.75 (ISBN 0-8049-0105-8, CL-105). Airmont.

—The Wind in the Willows. 253p. (gr. 5-6). Repr. of 1908 ed. lib. bdg. 17.95x (ISBN 0-88411-877-0, Pub. by Aeonian Pr). Amereon Ltd.

—Wind in the Willows. 234p. 1981. Repr. lib. bdg. 14.95x (ISBN 0-89966-305-2). Buccaneer Bks.

—Wind in the Willows. (Illus.). (gr. 3-9). deluxe ed. 11.95 (ISBN 0-448-06028-0, G&D); Companion lib. ed. o.p. 2.95 (ISBN 0-448-05481-7). Putnam Pub Group.

—The Wind in the Willows. Morrill, Les, illus. Sale, Roger, intro. by. (Illus.). 256p. (gr. 4-12). 1983. pap. 1.95 (ISBN 0-553-21129-3, Bantam Classics). Bantam.

—The Wind in the Willows. Burningham, John, illus. 240p. (gr. 1 up). 1983. 15.75 (ISBN 0-670-77120-1). Viking Penguin.

—The Wind in the Willows. Green, Peter, ed. (gr. 5 up). 1983. pap. 2.95 (ISBN 0-19-281640-3). Oxford U Pr.

—The Wind in the Willows. 75th Anniversary ed. Shepard, Ernest H., illus. Hodges, Margaret, pref. by. LC 83-11573. (Illus.). 256p. (gr. 3 up). 1983. 18.95 (ISBN 0-684-17957-1, Scribners Young Read). Macmillan Child Grp.

—The Wind in the Willows. Burningham, John, illus. 240p. (gr. 4-6). 1984. pap. 2.95 (ISBN 0-14-031544-6, Penguin Bks). Viking Penguin.

—The Wind in the Willows. Flax, Zena, illus. LC 85-13538. 224p. (gr. 2 up). 1985. 12.95 (ISBN 0-915361-32-9, Dist. by Watts). Adama Pubs Inc.

—The Wind in the Willows. Lee, Robert J., illus. 256p. (gr. 1 up). 1969. pap. 3.25 (ISBN 0-440-49555-5, YB). Dell.

—The Wind in the Willows. Smallman, Steven, illus. 208p. (Orig.). (gr. 4-6). 1988. pap. 2.50 (ISBN 0-590-41294-9, Apple Classics). Scholastic Inc.

—The Wind in the Willows. Suydam, Arthur, illus. 196p. (Orig.). 1988. pap. 7.95 (ISBN 0-8092-4489-6, Calico Bks). Contemp Bks.

—The Wind in the Willows. Shepard, Ernest H., illus. 272p. (ps up). 1989. pap. 4.95 (ISBN 0-689-71310-X, Aladdin). Macmillan Child Grp.

—The Wind in the Willows. Morrill, Les, illus. Sale, Roger, intro. by. (Illus.). 256p. 1983. pap. 2.95 (ISBN 0-553-21368-7, Bantam Classics Spectra). Bantam.

—The Wind in the Willows. 208p. (gr. 4-7). 1988. pap. 2.75 (ISBN 0-590-43404-7). Scholastic Inc.

—Wind in the Willows. 1987. 3.98 (ISBN 0-671-08895-5). S&S Trade.

—Wind in the Willows. 224p. 1990. pap. 2.50 (ISBN 0-8125-0510-7). Tor Bks.

—Wind in the Willows, Vol. 1. 1972. 12.95 (ISBN 0-684-12819-5, Scribners Young Read). Macmillan Child Grp.

Greeley, Valerie. White Is the Moon. Greeley, Valerie, illus. LC 90-40522. 24p. (ps-1). 1991. 12.95 (ISBN 0-02-736915-3, Mcmillan Child Bk). Macmillan Child Grp.

Green, Carl R. & Sanford, William R. The Porcupine. LC 85-7899. (Illus.). 48p. (gr. 5-6). 1985. 10.95 (ISBN 0-89686-280-1, Crestwood Hse). Macmillan Child Grp.

Gregorich, Barbara. Nine Men Chase a Hen. Hoffman, Joan, ed. Sandford, John, illus. 16p. (Orig.). (gr. k-2). 1984. pap. 1.95 (ISBN 0-88743-009-0, 06009). Sch Zone Pub Co.

Grey, J. The Turtle Who Wanted to Run. LC 68-56813. (Illus.). 32p. (gr. 1-3). 1968. PLB 9.95 (ISBN 0-87783-045-2). Oddo.

Gross, Ruth B., retold by. The Bremen Town Musicians. Kent, Jack, illus. 32p. (gr. k-3). 1975. pap. 2.50 (ISBN 0-685-04527-7); record incl. Scholastic Inc.

Grosset & Dunlap Staff. Who Says Quack? (Illus.). 18p. (ps). 1991. bds. 2.95 (ISBN 0-448-40123-1, G&D). Putnam Pub Group.

Grossman, Bill. Donna O'Neeshuck Was Chased by Some Cows. Truesdell, Sue, illus. LC 85-45823. 40p. (gr. k-3). 1988. 12.95 (ISBN 0-06-022158-5); PLB 12.89 (ISBN 0-06-022159-3). HarpC Child Bks.

Gullikson, Sandy. Trouble For Breakfast. LC 89-38539. (Illus.). 32p. (ps-3). 1990. 11.95 (ISBN 0-8037-0775-4); PLB 11.89 (ISBN 0-8037-0776-2). Dial Bks Young.

Gurney, Nancy & Gurney, Eric. King, the Mice & the Cheese. Vallier, Jean, illus. LC 89-8463. 72p. (gr. k-3). 1965. 6.95 (ISBN 0-394-80039-7); lib. bdg. 7.99 (ISBN 0-394-90039-1). Random.

Gustafson, Scott. Alphabet Soup: A Feast of Letters. (Illus.). 48p. 1990. 14.95 (ISBN 0-8092-4299-0). Contemp Bks.

—Animal Orchestra: A Book of Numbers. Gustafson, Scott, illus. 32p. 1988. pap. 13.95 (ISBN 0-8092-4483-7, Calico Bks). Contemp Bks.

Haas, Jessie. The Sixth Sense & Other Stories. LC 88-45226. 192p. (gr. 1-5). 1988. 11.95 (ISBN 0-688-08129-0). Greenwillow.

Hader, Berta & Hader, Elmer. The Big Snow. 2nd ed. Hader, Berta & Hader, Elmer, illus. LC 87-38488. 48p. (gr. k-4). 1988. pap. 4.95 (ISBN 0-689-71260-X, Aladdin). Macmillan Child Grp.

Hadithi, Mwenye. Lazy Lion. (ps-4). 1990. 14.95 (ISBN 0-316-33725-0). Little.

Haley, Gail E. A Story, A Story. Haley, Gail E., illus. LC 69-18961. 36p. (ps-3). 1970. 14.95 (ISBN 0-689-20511-2, Atheneum Child Bk). Macmillan Child Grp.

Hall, Willis. The Return of the Antelope. large type ed. 256p. (gr. 3-7). 1990. lib. bdg. 17.95x (ISBN 0-7451-1103-3, Lythway Large Print). G K Hall.

Hamlyn, J. Sheba Learns the Great Outdoors. 65p. (gr. 1-4). Date not set. pap. 5.25 (ISBN 1-878950-00-2). Sheba Bks Intl.

Hammer, Charles. Me, the Beef, & the Bum. LC 83-25521. 181p. (gr. 5 up). 1984. 12.95 (ISBN 0-374-34903-7). FS&G.

Harris, Joel C. Complete Tales of Uncle Remus. Chase, Richard, ed. (Illus.). 832p. (gr. 7 up). 1955. 35.00 (ISBN 0-395-06799-5). HM.

—Favorite Uncle Remus. Van Santvoord, George & Coolidge, Archibald C., eds. Van Santvoord, George & Coolidge, Archibald C., illus. 320p. (gr. 4-8). 1973. 17.95 (ISBN 0-395-06800-2). HM.

—Uncle Remus. Frost, A. B., illus. LC 65-14828. (gr. 3 up). 1987. Schocken.

—Walt Disney's Uncle Remus Stories. Palmer, Marion, ed. Dempster, Al & Justice, Bill, illus. (gr. 3-5). 1964. write for info. (ISBN 0-307-15551-X, Golden Bks). Western Pub.

Harris, Joel C. & Metaxas, Eric, eds. Brer Rabbit & the Wonderful Tar Baby. Drescher, Henrik, illus. LC 90-7166. 32p. (gr. k up). 1990. 14.95 (ISBN 0-88708-144-4, Rabbit Ears); incl. cass. 19.95 (ISBN 0-88708-145-2). Picture Bk Studio.

Harris, Rosemary. The Shadow on the Sun. 192p. (gr. 2-6). 1991. pap. 4.95 (ISBN 0-571-14185-4). Faber & Faber.

Hart, Sharon M. Animal Rescue Farm, No. 4. 1989. pap. 2.50 (ISBN 0-590-41504-2). Scholastic Inc.

Hartman, Gail. As the Crow Flies: A First Book of Maps. Stevenson, Harvey, illus. (ps-1). 1991. 12.95 (ISBN 0-02-743005-7, Bradbury Pr). Macmillan Child Grp.

Hayes, Joe. No Way, Jose! De Ninguna Manera, Jose! Jelinek, Lucy, illus. 32p. (Orig.). (ps-3). 1986. pap. 3.95 (ISBN 0-939729-00-8); cassette & bk. pkg. 7.95 (ISBN 0-939729-01-6). Trails West Pub.

Hayward, Linda. All Stuck Up. Chartier, Normand, illus. LC 89-34675. 32p. (Orig.). (ps-1). 1990. PLB 6.99 (ISBN 0-679-90216-3); pap. 2.95 (ISBN 0-679-80216-9). McKay.

Hazen, Barbara S. Wally the Worry-Warthog. Stevens, Janet, illus. 32p. (ps-3). 1990. 13.95 (ISBN 0-89919-896-1, Clarion Bks). HM.

Heine, Helme. Friends. Heine, Helme, illus. LC 82-49350. 32p. (ps-2). 1982. 13.95 (ISBN 0-689-50256-7, M K McElderry). Macmillan Child Grp.

—Friends. Heine, Helme, illus. LC 86-3379. 32p. (ps-3). 1986. pap. 3.95 (ISBN 0-689-71083-6, Aladdin). Macmillan Child Grp.

Heller, Ruth. Animals Born Alive & Well. Heller, Ruth, illus. LC 82-80872. 48p. (gr. k-2). 1982. 8.95 (ISBN 0-448-01822-5, G&D). Putnam Pub Group.

Helmrath, M. O. & Bartlett, J. L. Bobby Bear in the Spring. LC 68-56810. (Illus.). 32p. (ps-1). 1968. PLB 12.35 prebound (ISBN 0-87783-007-X); cassette 7.94x (ISBN 0-87783-180-7). Oddo.

Hennessy, B. G. Eeney Meeney Miney Mo. LC 90-31535. (ps-3). 1990. 13.95 (ISBN 0-670-82864-5). Viking Child Bks.

Henry, Marguerite. Brighty of the Grand Canyon. Dennis, Wesley, illus. LC 53-7233. (gr. 2-9). 1991. 12.95 (ISBN 0-02-743664-0, Mcmillan Child Bk). Macmillan Child Grp.

Higgins, Kitty. Andy McClark the Aardvark. James, Robin, illus. 24p. 1990. 5.95 (ISBN 0-8431-2742-2). Price Stern.

—Polly Porter the Platypus: Lemon Rhyme Readers Ser. James, Robin, illus. 24p. (ps-1). 1990. pap. 5.95 (ISBN 0-8431-2744-9). Price Stern.

Hill, Eric. Spot's Birthday Party. (Illus.). (ps-k). 1982. 10.95 (ISBN 0-399-20903-4, Putnam). Putnam Pub Group.

Hoban, Lillian. Silly Tilly's Thanksgiving Dinner. Hoban, Lillian, illus. LC 89-29287. 64p. (gr. k-3). 1990. 11.95 (ISBN 0-06-022422-3); PLB 11.89 (ISBN 0-06-022423-1). HarpC Child Bks.

—The Sugar Snow Spring. Hoban, Lillian, illus. LC 72-9866. 48p. (ps-3). 1973. PLB 11.89 (ISBN 0-06-022334-0). HarpC Child Bks.

Hoff, Syd. Albert the Albatross. Hoff, Syd, illus. LC 61-5767. 32p. (gr. k-3). 1961. PLB 10.89 (ISBN 0-06-022446-0). HarpC Child Bks.

Holl, Adelaide. Have You Seen My Puppy. Veno, Joe, illus. (ps-1). 1968. (Random Juv). Random.

—Rain Puddle. Duvoisin, Roger, illus. LC 65-22026. 32p. (gr. k-3). 1965. PLB 14.88 (ISBN 0-688-51096-5). Lothrop.

Holt, Virginia. One More Popple. Kolding, Richard M., illus. LC 85-63429. (ps-1). 1986. 3.95 (ISBN 0-394-88258-X, Random Juv). Random.

Hood, Thomas. Before I Go to Sleep. Begin-Callanan, Maryjane, illus. 32p. (ps-3). 1990. 14.95 (ISBN 0-399-21638-3, Putnam). Putnam Pub Group.

Hooper, Patrica. A Bundle of Beasts. Steele, Mark, illus. LC 86-34413. 64p. (gr. 3-7). 1987. 12.95 (ISBN 0-395-44259-1). HM.

Hopkins, Lee B., ed. Creatures. Ormai, Stella, illus. LC 84-15698. 32p. (ps-3). 1985. 14.95 (ISBN 0-15-220875-5, HJ). HarBraceJ.

Howe, James. Morgan's Zoo. (Illus.). 192p. (gr. 3-7). 1986. pap. 3.50 (ISBN 0-380-69994-X, Camelot). Avon.

Howker, Janni. The Nature of the Beast. LC 84-25328. 137p. (gr. 7-9). 1985. reinforced bdg. 10.25 (ISBN 0-688-04233-3). Greenwillow.

Hubner, Carol K. The Whispering Mezuzah. Kramer, Devorah, illus. (gr. 3-9). 1979. 6.95 (ISBN 0-910818-18-5). Judaica Pr.

Hunt, Robert. Coco & Chacha: The Coatis. Dunnington, Tom, illus. LC 74-735893. (gr. 2-5). 1978. 6 bks. & 1 cass. 29.95 (ISBN 0-89290-034-2); 1 bk. & 1 cass. 10.95 (ISBN 0-685-04635-4). Soc for Visual.

Hurd, Edith T. Come & Have Fun. Hurd, Clement, illus. LC 62-13324. 32p. (gr. k-3). 1962. PLB 10.89 (ISBN 0-06-022681-1). HarpC Child Bks.

—Day the Sun Danced. Hurd, Clement, illus. LC 64-16641. 32p. (gr. k-3). 1966. PLB 13.89 (ISBN 0-06-022692-7). HarpC Child Bks.

—Last One Home Is a Green Pig. Hurd, Clement, illus. LC 59-8972. 64p. (gr. k-3). 1959. PLB 11.89 (ISBN 0-06-022716-8). HarpC Child Bks.

Ingoglia, Gina. Nature Babies. (Illus.). 24p. (ps-k). 1989. pap. write for info. (ISBN 0-307-11716-2, Pub. by Golden Bks). Western Pub.
Ipcar, Dahlov. Flood of Creatures. (gr. 2-5). 1985. pap. 6.95 (ISBN 0-930096-73-8). G Gannett.
James, Christopher. Bump & the Bucket. (Illus.). 24p. (ps-3). 1990. 7.50 (ISBN 0-88625-279-2). Durkin Hayes Pub.
—Bump the Builder. (Illus.). 24p. (ps-3). 1990. pap. 7.50 (ISBN 0-88625-278-4). Durkin Hayes Pub.
James, D. H. Sheba Consumes Whatever She Can. 98p. 1990. 19.95 (ISBN 1-878950-01-0). Sheba Bks Intl.
Janice. Little Bear's Thanksgiving. Mariana, illus. LC 67-22593. 32p. (gr. k-3). 1967. PLB 12.88 (ISBN 0-688-51078-7). Lothrop.
Janosch. I'll Make You Well, Tiger, Said the Bear. Janosch, illus. LC 86-11274. 48p. (ps up). 1987. 9.95 (ISBN 0-915361-42-6, Dist. by Watts). Adama Pubs Inc.
Jarrell, Randall. Animal Family. Sendak, Maurice, illus. LC 65-20659. (gr. 3 up). 1985. 16.95 (ISBN 0-394-81043-0). Pantheon.
Jefferies, Richard. Wood Magic. LC 74-82725. 1974. 8.95 (ISBN 0-89388-177-5). Okpaku Communications.
Johnson, Annabel. I Am Leaper. (gr. 4-7). 1990. 11.95 (ISBN 0-590-43400-4). Scholastic Inc.
Johnston, Tony. Yonder. Bloom, Lloyd, illus. LC 86-11549. 32p. (ps-3). 1988. 12.95 (ISBN 0-8037-0277-9); PLB 12.89 (ISBN 0-8037-0278-7). Dial Bks Young.
Jones, Marvin E. The Enchanted Valley: The Adventures of Sassy & Rowdy Krackers, Bk. I. Seidl, Tony, ed. Czarnecki, Tim, illus. 176p. (gr. 4-7). 1990. 9.95 (ISBN 0-89015-750-2); pap. 4.95 (ISBN 0-89015-777-4). Eakin Pr.
—Gory Gary Strikes Back: The Adventures of Sassy & Rowdy Krackers, Bk. 2. Seidl, Tony, ed. Czarnecki, Tim, illus. 176p. (gr. 4-7). pap. 9.95 (ISBN 0-89015-751-0); pap. 4.95 (ISBN 0-89015-778-2). Eakin Pr.
Jordan, Tom. The Lady of the Frogs: An Afternoon's Adventure for Trisand & Panda With. 2nd ed. Jordan, Tom, illus. LC 90-80793. 64p. (gr. 4-5). 1990. pap. 2.95 (ISBN 0-9626442-9-3). Didymus Pub.
The Jungle Book. Date not set. 9.98 (ISBN 0-517-67902-7). Outlet Bk Co.
Jwing-Ming, Yang. The Fox Borrows the Tiger's Awe. Dougall, Alan, ed. Xieu-Lin, Li, illus. 54p. (gr. 4 up). 1990. 9.95 (ISBN 0-940871-12-2). Yangs Martial Arts.
Kahng, David & Kahng, Kim, eds. The Loathsome Dragon. (Illus.). (gr. k-4). 1987. 13.95 (ISBN 0-399-21407-0, Putnam). Putnam Pub Group.
Kaplan, Carol B. Animal Tales Big Book Package, 6 bks. Bolinske, Janet L., ed. Quenell, Midge, illus. 144p. (ps-k). 1988. Set of 6 bks., 24 pgs. ea. bk. 100.00 (ISBN 0-88335-759-3). Milliken Pub Co.
—Wicker's Wishes. Bolinske, Janet L., ed. Quenell, Midge, illus. LC 87-63001. 24p. (Orig.). (ps-k). 1988. 17.95 (ISBN 0-88335-757-7); pap. 4.95 (ISBN 0-88335-075-0). Milliken Pub Co.
Keats, Ezra J. Kitten for a Day. Keats, Ezra J., illus. LC 81-69518. 32p. (ps-3). 1984. 12.95 (ISBN 0-02-749630-9, Four Winds). Macmillan Child Grp.
Keller, Beverly. Fowl Play, Desdemona. LC 88-9481. 176p. (gr. 4-7). 1989. 11.95 (ISBN 0-688-06920-7). Lothrop.
—No Beasts! No Children! LC 87-45288. 128p. (gr. 3-7). 1988. pap. 3.50 (ISBN 0-06-440225-8, Trophy). HarpC Child Bks.
Kemp, Gene. Just Ferret. 128p. (gr. 3-7). 1990. bds. 10.95 laminated (ISBN 0-571-14286-9). Faber & Faber.
Kennaway, Mwalimu & Kennaway, Adrienne. Awful Aardvark. Kennaway, Mwalimu & Kennaway, Adrienne, illus. LC 89-80028. (ps-2). 1989. 14.95 (ISBN 0-316-59218-8). Little.
Kerven, Rosalind. King Leopard's Gift: And Other Legends of the Animal World. Waldman, Bryna, illus. 32p. 1990. 12.95 (ISBN 0-521-36180-X). Cambridge U Pr.
—Legends of the Animal World. (Illus.). 32p. (gr. 3-7). 1986. 11.95 (ISBN 0-521-30576-4). Cambridge U Pr.
Kessler, Leonard. Old Turtle's Baseball Stories. Kessler, Leonard, illus. LC 81-6390. 56p. (gr. 1-3). 1982. 13.95 (ISBN 0-688-00723-6); PLB 13.88 (ISBN 0-688-00724-4). Greenwillow.
Kherdian, David. The Animal. Hogrogian, Nonny, illus. LC 83-22268. 40p. (gr. k up). 1984. Knopf.
King, Loretta M. The Purple Sea Horse & Other Stories. LC 79-56712. (Illus., Orig.). (gr. k-3). 1979. pap. 4.95 (ISBN 0-934104-02-6). Woodland.
Kipling, Rudyard. The Beginning of the Armadillos. Cauley, Lorinda B., illus. LC 85-5444. 48p. (gr. 4-8). 1985. 14.95 (ISBN 0-15-206380-3, Pub. by HJ). HarBraceJ.
—Beginning of the Armadillos. 1990. pap. 3.95 (ISBN 0-15-206381-1, VoyB). HarbraceJ.
—Elephants Child. 1989. 9.99 (ISBN 0-85953-275-5). Childs Play.
—How the Camel Got His Hump. Turska, Krystyna, illus. (ps-3). 1988. 4.95 (ISBN 0-7232-3450-7). Warne.
—How the Camel Got His Hump: Just So Stories. Langley, Jonathan, illus. LC 87-29156. 24p. (ps-3). 1988. 5.95 (ISBN 0-399-21553-0, Philomel Bks). Putnam Pub Group.
—Jungle Book. Eichenberg, Fritz, illus. (gr. 4-6). 1950. deluxe ed. 11.95 (ISBN 0-448-06014-0, G&D); pap. 7.95 (ISBN 0-448-11014-8, G&D); (G&D). Putnam Pub Group.
—The Jungle Book. Foreman, Michael, illus. (gr. 5-9). 13. 95 (ISBN 0-317-62543-8). Viking Child Bks.
—The Jungle Book. Robson, Wallace, intro. by. 320p. 1987. pap. 4.95 (ISBN 0-19-281650-0). Oxford U Pr.
—The Jungle Book. 1987. pap. 2.25 (ISBN 0-14-035074-8, Puffin). Puffin Bks.
—The Jungle Book. 1987. 14.95 (ISBN 0-670-80241-7). Viking Child Bks.
—Jungle Books. (gr. 5 up). pap. 1.95 (ISBN 0-8049-0109-0, CL-109). Airmont.
—Just So Stories. (gr. 3 up). pap. 1.75 (ISBN 0-8049-0123-6, CL-123). Airmont.
—Just So Stories. (Illus.). 64p. (gr. 4 up). 1982. write for info. (ISBN 0-528-82422-8); PLB write for info. (ISBN 0-528-80077-9). Checkerboard Pr.
—Just So Stories. (Illus.). (gr. 2-9). 1979. 3.98 (ISBN 0-517-26655-5). Outlet Bk Co.
—Just So Stories. (gr. 2-9). 8.98 (ISBN 0-517-63177-6). Outlet Bk Co.
—Just So Stories. Foreman, Michael, illus. (ps up). 12.95 (ISBN 0-317-62525-X). Viking Child Bks.
—Just So Stories. 1987. pap. 2.25 (ISBN 0-14-035075-6, Puffin). Puffin Bks.
—Just So Stories. Frampton, David, illus. LC 90-19429. 128p. (gr. 3-7). 1991. 19.95 (ISBN 0-06-023294-3); PLB 19.89 (ISBN 0-06-023296-X). HarpC Child Bks.
—New Illustrated Just So Stories. Nicholas, illus. (gr. 1-7). 1952. 13.95 (ISBN 0-385-02129-1). Doubleday.
—Newly Illustrated Just So Stories. Nicolas, illus. 1989. pap. 8.95 (ISBN 0-385-26133-0). Doubleday.
—Reader's Digest Best Loved Books for Young Readers: The Jungle Books. Ogburn, Jackie, ed. Jouve, Paul, illus. 160p. (gr. 4-12). 1989. 3.99 (ISBN 0-945260-26-1). Choice Pub NY.
—The Second Jungle Book. 1987. pap. 2.25 (ISBN 0-14-035079-9, Puffin). Puffin Bks.
—Stalky & Company. 1988. pap. 2.95 (ISBN 0-14-035080-2, Puffin). Puffin Bks.
Koch, Michelle. Hoot, Howl, Hiss. LC 90-38484. (Illus.). 24p. (ps up). 1991. 13.95 (ISBN 0-688-09651-4); PLB 13.88 (ISBN 0-688-09652-2). Greenwillow.
Koopmans, Loek. The Woodcutter's Mitten: An Old Tale. Koopmans, Loek, illus. LC 90-2545. 32p. (ps-2). 1990. 13.95 (ISBN 0-940793-67-9, Crocodile Bks). Interlink Pub.
Kraus, Robert & Brook, Bonnie. Squirmy's Big Secret. Kraus, Robert, illus. 48p. (ps-3). 1990. lib. bdg. 8.98 (ISBN 0-671-70851-1); pap. 3.50 (ISBN 0-671-70852-X). Silver Pr.
Krauss, Ruth. The Happy Day. Simont, Marc, illus. LC 49-10568. 30p. (ps-3). 1949. 11.95 (ISBN 0-06-023395-8); PLB 11.89 (ISBN 0-06-023396-6). HarpC Child Bks.
Krulik, Nancy E. Animals on the Job. 1990. pap. 2.50 (ISBN 0-590-42986-8). Scholastic Inc.
Kurtycz, Marcos & Kobeh, Ana G. Tigers & Opossums: Animal Legends. Kurtycz, Marcos & Kobeh, Ana G., illus. LC 82-17949. (gr. k-3). 1984. 12.95 (ISBN 0-316-50718-0). Little.
Kuskin, Karla. Roar & More. rev. ed. Kuskin, Karla, illus. LC 89-15650. 48p. (ps-1). 1990. PLB 13.89 (ISBN 0-06-023619-1, Trophy). HarpC Child Bks.
Laird, Donivee M. Will Wai Kula & the Three Mongooses. Jossem, Carol, illus. LC 83-8805. 44p. (gr. k-3). 1983. 7.95x (ISBN 0-940350-13-0). Barnaby Bks.
Lawson, Robert. Rabbit Hill. Lawson, Robert, illus. (gr. 4-6). 1944. pap. 12.95 (ISBN 0-670-58675-7). Viking Child Bks.
Leaf, Munro. El Cuento de Ferdinando. Belpre, Pura, tr. Lawson, Robert, illus. (SPA.). 72p. (ps-3). 1962. pap. 11.95 (ISBN 0-670-25065-1). Viking Child Bks.
—El Cuento de Ferdinando: The Story of Ferdinand. Lawson, Robert, illus. Belpre, Pura, tr. (SPA., Illus.). 72p. (ps-3). 1990. pap. 3.95 (ISBN 0-14-054253-1, Puffin). Puffin Bks.
Lear, Edward. The Owl & the Pussycat. West, Colin, illus. (ps-3). 1988. 4.95 (ISBN 0-7232-3541-4). Warne.
Learner, Vickie M., illus. Willoughby Wallaby. 1987. pap. 5.95 incl. audiocassette (ISBN 0-553-45903-1). Bantam.
Leedy, Loreen. The Great Trash Bash. Leedy, Loreen, illus. LC 90-46554. 32p. (ps-3). 1991. PLB 14.95 (ISBN 0-8234-0869-8). Holiday.
Lehn, Cornelia. The Sun & the Wind. Regier, Robert, illus. 32p. (gr. k-5). 1983. 7.95 (ISBN 0-87303-072-9). Faith & Life.
L'Engle, Madeleine. Dance in the Desert. Shimin, Symeon, illus. LC 68-29465. 64p. (ps up). 1969. 14.95 (ISBN 0-374-31684-8). FS&G.
Leslie, Amanda. Hidden Animals. Leslie, Amanda, illus. LC 88-4099. 32p. (ps-1). 1989. 6.95 (ISBN 0-8037-0567-0). Dial Bks Young.
Leslie-Melville, Betty. Walter Warthog: The Warthog That Moved In. (Illus.). 48p. (ps-3). 1989. 12.95 (ISBN 0-385-26378-3, Zephyr-BFYR); PLB 13.99 (ISBN 0-385-26379-1, Zephyr-BFYR). Doubleday.
Lester, Alison. Imagine. Lester, Alison, illus. 32p. (gr. k-3). 1990. 13.95 (ISBN 0-395-53753-3). HM.
Lester, Helen. It Wasn't My Fault. Munsinger, Lynn, illus. (ps-3). 1989. pap. 5.95 (ISBN 0-395-51007-4, Sandpiper). HM.
Lester, Julius, as told by. More Tales of Uncle Remus: Further Adventures of Brer Rabbit, His Friends, Enemies & Others. Pinkney, Jerry, illus. LC 86-32890. 160p. (ps up). 1988. 15.00 (ISBN 0-8037-0419-4); PLB 15.89 (ISBN 0-8037-0420-8). Dial Bks Young.
Lester, Julius & Fogelman, Phyllis J., eds. Further Tales of Uncle Remus: The Misadventures of Brer Rabbit, Brer Fox, Brer Wolf, the Doodang, & All the Other Creatures. Pinkney, Jerry, illus. LC 88-20223. 160p. (ps up). 1990. 15.00 (ISBN 0-8037-0610-3); PLB 14. 89 (ISBN 0-8037-0611-1). Dial Bks Young.
Lewis, C. S. The Magician's Nephew. Baynes, Pauline, illus. LC 55-14869. 176p. (gr. 4 up). 1988. 12.95 (ISBN 0-02-758340-6, Mcmillan Child Bk). Macmillan Child Grp.
—Prince Caspian. Baynes, Pauline, illus. LC 51-12799. 192p. (gr. 4 up). 1988. 12.95 (ISBN 0-02-758580-8, Mcmillan Child Bk). Macmillan Child Grp.
Lewis, Naomi. Cry Wolf & Other Aesop Fables. Castle, Barry, illus. 32p. (ps up). 1988. 16.95 (ISBN 0-19-520710-6). Oxford U Pr.
—Hare & Badger Go to Town. Ross, Tony, illus. 32p. (ps-1). 1987. 9.95 (ISBN 0-905478-94-0, Pub. by Century UK). Trafalgar Sq.
Lewis, R. Aunt Armadillo. (Illus.). 24p. (ps-8). 1985. 12. 95 (ISBN 0-920303-38-2); pap. 4.95 (ISBN 0-920303-39-0). Firefly Bks Ltd.
Lewis, Shari. Baby Lamb Chop Loves Animals. Beylon, Cathy, illus. 12p. (ps-k). 1991. bds. 3.95 (ISBN 0-679-81723-9). Random.
Lionni, Leo. A Color of His Own. Lionni, Leo, illus. LC 75-28456. 36p. (gr. k-3). 1976. PLB 14.99 (ISBN 0-394-93231-5). Pantheon.
Littke, Lael. The Day Woodchuck Would Chuck Wood at Peanut Butter Pond. Britt, Stephanie M., illus. 36p. (ps-1). 1990. pap. 15.95 incl. audiocassette (ISBN 1-55999-124-0). LinguiSystems.
Lloyd, David. Hello, Goodbye. Voce, Louise, illus. LC 87-17110. (ps-1). 1988. 12.95 (ISBN 0-688-07698-X); lib. bdg. 12.88 (ISBN 0-688-07699-8). Lothrop.
Lobel, Arnold. Fables. Lobel, Arnold, illus. LC 79-2004. 48p. (gr. 1-4). 1980. 14.95 (ISBN 0-06-023973-5); PLB 14.89 (ISBN 0-06-023974-3). HarpC Child Bks.
—Grasshopper on the Road. Lobel, Arnold, illus. LC 77-25653. 64p. (gr. k-3). 1978. 11.95 (ISBN 0-06-023961-1); PLB 11.89 (ISBN 0-06-023962-X). HarpC Child Bks.
—Mouse Tales. Lobel, Arnold, illus. LC 66-18654. 64p. (gr. k-3). 1972. 11.95 (ISBN 0-06-023941-7); PLB 11. 89 (ISBN 0-06-023942-5). HarpC Child Bks.
Lockwood, Barbara & McAuley, Marilyn. God Keeps Them Safe. 1988. bds. 4.95 (ISBN 1-55513-518-8, Chariot Bks). Cook.
—God Made Little & Big. LC 87-62019. 1988. bds. 4.95 (ISBN 1-55513-517-X, Chariot Bks). Cook.
Lofting, Hugh. Doctor Dolittle: A Treasury. 1990. Repr. lib. bdg. 25.95x (ISBN 0-89966-674-4). Buccaneer Bks.
—Dr. Dolittle & the Green Canary. (gr. k-6). 1988. pap. 3.50 (ISBN 0-440-40079-1, YB). Dell.
—Doctor Dolittle's Bag of Books. (gr. 4-7). 1988. pap. 13. 45 (ISBN 0-440-36000-5). Dell.
—Doctor Dolittle's Caravan. Lofting, Hugh, illus. 1989. 14.95 (ISBN 0-440-50117-2). Delacorte.
—Doctor Dolittle's Circus. Lofting, Hugh, illus. 240p. (gr. 4-7). 1988. 14.95 (ISBN 0-440-50056-7). Delacorte.
—Dr. Doolittle's Post Office. (gr. k-6). 1988. pap. 3.50 (ISBN 0-440-40096-1, YB). Dell.
—The Story of Doctor Dolittle. (gr. k-6). 1988. pap. 2.95 (ISBN 0-685-18953-8). Dell.
—The Story of Doctor Dolittle. centenary ed. Lofting, Christopher, afterword by. (Illus.). 144p. (gr. 4-6). 1988. pap. 13.95 (ISBN 0-385-29662-2). Delacorte.
—Travels of Doctor Dolittle. reissued ed. Perkins, Al, adapted by. LC 67-25853. (Illus.). 64p. (ps-2). 1967. 6.95 (ISBN 0-394-80048-6); PLB 7.99 (ISBN 0-394-90048-0). Random.
—The Voyage of Doctor Dolittle. (gr. 4-7). 1988. pap. 3.50 (ISBN 0-440-40002-3, YB). Dell.
Logan, Dick, et al. Thunder & the Circus. LC 77-74689. 32p. (ps-7). 1987. PLB 10.45s.p. (ISBN 0-87191-790-4); PLB 14.95s.p. (ISBN 0-685-09307-7). Creative Ed.
—Thunder & the Dinosaur Puppet. LC 77-74688. 32p. (ps-7). 1987. PLB 10.45s.p. (ISBN 0-87191-789-0); PLB 14.95s.p. (ISBN 0-685-09308-5). Creative Ed.
—Thunder Comes to the Rescue. LC 77-74685. 32p. (ps-7). 1987. PLB 10.45s.p. (ISBN 0-87191-786-6); PLB 14.95 (ISBN 0-685-09309-3). Creative Ed.
—Thunder Disappears. LC 77-74686. 32p. (ps-7). 1987. PLB 10.45s.p. (ISBN 0-87191-787-4); PLB 14.95 (ISBN 0-685-09310-7). Creative Ed.
—Thunder Eats a Haystack. LC 77-74680. 32p. (ps-7). 1987. PLB 10.45s.p. (ISBN 0-87191-782-3); PLB 14. 95 (ISBN 0-685-09311-5). Creative Ed.
—Thunder Gets a House. LC 77-74681. 32p. (ps-7). 1987. PLB 10.45s.p. (ISBN 0-87191-783-1); PLB 14. 95 (ISBN 0-685-09312-3). Creative Ed.
—Thunder Goes for a Walk. LC 77-74683. 32p. (ps-7). 1987. PLB 10.45s.p. (ISBN 0-87191-785-8); PLB 14. 95 (ISBN 0-685-09314-X). Creative Ed.
—Thunder Goes to a Party. LC 77-74682. 32p. (ps-7). 1987. PLB 10.45s.p. (ISBN 0-87191-784-X); PLB 14. 95 (ISBN 0-685-09313-1). Creative Ed.
—Thunder Makes a Sandcastle. LC 77-74687. 32p. (ps-7). 1987. PLB 10.45s.p. (ISBN 0-87191-788-2); PLB 14.95 (ISBN 0-685-09315-8). Creative Ed.
Lopshire, Robert. I Want to Be Somebody New. Lopshire, Robert, illus. LC 85-43098. 48p. (gr. k-3). 1986. 6.95 (ISBN 0-394-87616-4); lib. bdg. 7.99 (ISBN 0-394-97616-9). Beginner.
Luna, C. J. Armil's Armor. (gr. 1-3). 1989. 4.95 (ISBN 0-533-08065-7). Vantage.

Lunn, Carolyn. Bobby's Zoo. Dunnington, Tom, illus. LC 88-36865. 32p. (ps-2). 1989. PLB 11.93 (ISBN 0-516-02089-7); pap. 2.95 (ISBN 0-516-42089-5). Childrens.

Lurie, Alison. Fabulous Beasts. Beisner, Monika, illus. LC 81-12546. 32p. (ps-3). 1981. 12.95 (ISBN 0-374-32242-2). FS&G.

Luton, Mildred. Little Chicks' Mothers & All the Others. Rae, Mary M., illus. LC 82-6880. 32p. (ps-k). 1985. pap. 3.95 (ISBN 0-14-050468-0, Puffin). Puffin Bks.

Luttrell, Ida. Three Good Blankets. McDermott, Michael, illus. LC 89-36353. 32p. (ps-2). 1990. 13.95 (ISBN 0-689-31586-4, Atheneum Child Bk). Macmillan Child Grp.

Lyon, George E. A Regular Rolling Noah. Gammell, Stephen, illus. 32p. (gr. k-3). 1991. pap. 4.95 (ISBN 0-689-71449-1, Aladdin). Macmillan Child Grp.

McBarnet, Gill. The Pink Parrot. McBarnett, Gill, illus. 40p. (gr. k-2). 1986. 7.95 (ISBN 0-9615102-1-8). Ruwanga Trad.

McDowell, Mildred. The Squirrel & the Frog. Brennan, Nancy, illus. Harman, Sandra L., intro. by. LC 76-133256. (Illus.). 44p. (gr. 1-2). 1971. 2.50 (ISBN 0-87884-007-9). Unicorn Ent.

Machlis, Nancy. Koalaroo Finds a Friend. Niemetz, Catherine, illus. LC 88-82283. 50p. (ps-2). Date not set. write for info. Koalaroo Enter.

McNally, Darcie, adapted by. In a Cabin in a Wood. Koontz, Robin M., illus. LC 89-25192. 32p. (ps-3). 1991. 12.95 (ISBN 0-525-65035-0, Cobblehill Bks). Dutton Child Bks.

McPhail, David. The Bear's Toothache. McPhail, David, illus. (ps-3). 1988. pap. 4.95 (ISBN 0-316-56325-0, Joy St Bks). Little.

—The Party. (ps-4). 1990. 14.95 (ISBN 0-316-56330-7, Joy St Bks). Little.

—Those Terrible Toy-Breakers. McPhail, David, illus. LC 80-10450. 48p. (ps-3). 1980. 5.95 (ISBN 0-8193-1019-0); PLB 5.95 (ISBN 0-8193-1020-4). Parents.

Mann, Marek. The Animals' Christmas Surprise. Young, Richard G., ed. Mann, Marek, illus. LC 89-11896. 24p. (gr. 1-3). 1989. PLB 13.26 (ISBN 0-944483-51-8). Garrett Ed Corp.

Mariotti, Mario & Marchiori, Roberto, illus. Hanimals. LC 84-144738. 40p. (Orig.). (gr. 4 up). 1982. pap. 7.95 (ISBN 0-914676-90-3, Star & Elephant Bks.). Green Tiger Pr.

Maris, Ron. Bernard's Boring Day. 1990. 12.95 (ISBN 0-385-29948-6). Doubleday.

Marshall, James. Rats on the Roof: And Other Stories. Marshall, James, illus. LC 90-44084. 80p. (gr. 1-5). 1991. 12.95 (ISBN 0-8037-0834-3); lib. bdg. 12.89 (ISBN 0-8037-0835-1). Dial Bks Young.

—Willis. Marshall, James, illus. (ps-3). 1989. pap. 4.95 (ISBN 0-395-51008-2, Sandpiper). HM.

—Wings: A Tale of Two Chickens. Marshall, James, illus. LC 85-40953. 32p. (ps-3). 1986. pap. 12.95 (ISBN 0-670-80961-6). Viking Child Bks.

Martin, David. Gator & Mary's Traveling Band. Getz, Arthur, illus. LC 80-20965. 32p. (ps-3). 1981. 9.95 (ISBN 0-8037-4556-7). Dial Bks Young.

Marzollo, Jean. Pretend You're a Cat. Fogelman, Phyllis J., ed. Pinkney, Jerry, illus. LC 89-34546. 32p. (ps-3). 1990. 12.95 (ISBN 0-8037-0773-8); PLB 12.89 (ISBN 0-8037-0774-6). Dial Bks Young.

Mason, Judy S. Mr. Farmer & His Animals. Scoggan, Nita, ed. Wilson, Krista, illus. Shaw, Gwen, intro. by. (Illus.). 52p. (Orig.). (gr. 3 up). 1987. pap. 3.95 (ISBN 0-910487-11-1). Royalty Pub.

Mathiesen, Egon. Jungle in the Wheat Field. (Illus.). (gr. k-3). 1960. 9.95 (ISBN 0-8392-3014-1). Astor-Honor.

Matthews, Morgan. The Big Race. Schindler, S. D., illus. LC 88-1287. 48p. (Orig.). (gr. 1-4). 1989. PLB 9.89 (ISBN 0-8167-1329-4); pap. text ed. 2.95 (ISBN 0-8167-1330-8). Troll Assocs.

Mayer, Mercer. Little Critter's: This Is My School. (ps-3). 1990. write for info. (ISBN 0-307-11589-5). Western Pub.

—Two-Minute Little Critter Stories. (ps). 1990. write for info. (ISBN 0-307-12192-5). Western Pub.

—What Do You Do with a Kangaroo? Mayer, Mercer, illus. 48p. (gr. k-3). 1987. pap. 3.95 (ISBN 0-590-41436-4). Scholastic Inc.

Mazer, Anne. The Salamander Room. Johnson, Steve, illus. LC 90-33301. 32p. (ps-3). 1991. 14.00 (ISBN 0-394-82945-X); PLB 14.99 (ISBN 0-394-92945-4). Knopf.

Mellecker, Judith. The Fox & the Kingfisher. Parker, Robert A., illus. LC 89-27180. 48p. (gr. k-4). 1990. 14.95 (ISBN 0-679-80539-7); lib. bdg. 15.99 (ISBN 0-679-90539-1). Knopf.

Meyer, Carolyn & Gallenkamp, Charles. The Mystery of the Ancient Maya. LC 84-24209. (Illus.). 160p. (gr. 7 up). 1985. 13.95 (ISBN 0-689-50319-9, M K McElderry). Macmillan Child Grp.

Miles, John C., ed. Treasury of Animal Stories. Oak-Rhind, Mary & Dennison, Graham, illus. LC 90-11158. 96p. (gr. 2-5). 1991. lib. bdg. 14.89 (ISBN 0-8167-2240-4); pap. text ed. 6.95 (ISBN 0-8167-2241-2). Troll Assocs.

Milne, A. A. Pooh's Birthday Book. Shepard, Ernest H., illus. 160p. (gr. 1-3). 1991. pap. 3.50 (ISBN 0-440-46934-1, YB). Dell.

—When We Were Very Young. Shepard, Ernest H., illus. 112p. (gr. 2-5). 1970. pap. 3.25 (ISBN 0-440-49485-0, YB). Dell.

Milne, A. A. & Shepard. Pooh's Bedtime Book. (Illus.). 48p. (ps-3). 1980. 9.95 (ISBN 0-525-37373-X, DCB). Dutton Child Bks.

Minarik, Else H. Cat & Dog. Siebel, Fritz, illus. LC 60-14998. 32p. (gr. k-2). 1960. PLB 10.89 (ISBN 0-06-024221-3). HarpC Child Bks.

—Kiss for Little Bear. Sendak, Maurice, illus. LC 57-9263. 32p. (gr. k-3). 1968. 10.95 (ISBN 0-06-024298-1); PLB 10.89 (ISBN 0-06-024299-X). HarpC Child Bks.

—The Little Girl & the Dragon. Gourlault, Martine, illus. LC 90-38495. 24p. (ps up). 1991. 13.95 (ISBN 0-688-09913-0); PLB 13.88 (ISBN 0-688-09914-9). Greenwillow.

Moncure, Jane B. How Many Ways Can You Cut a Pie? Hohag, Linda, illus. LC 87-15807. 32p. (ps-2). 1987. PLB 11.97 (ISBN 0-89565-408-3); pap. 6.96 (ISBN 0-89565-439-3). Childs World.

—Nanny Goat's Boat. Friedman, Joy, illus. LC 87-12839. 32p. (ps-2). 1987. PLB 11.97 (ISBN 0-89565-404-0); pap. 6.96 (ISBN 0-89565-445-8). Childs World.

Montgomery, Rutherford. Rufus. Nenninger, J. D., illus. LC 78-150819. (Orig.). (gr. 4-8). 1973. 4.95 (ISBN 0-87004-227-0). Caxton.

Montgomery, Rutherford G. Carcajou. Cram, L. D., illus. LC 36-6665. (gr. 6-8). 1936. 4.95 (ISBN 0-87004-105-3). Caxton.

Moser, Erwin. The Crow in the Snow & Other Bedtime Stories. Agee, Joel, tr. from GER. Moser, Erwin, illus. LC 86-10740. 48p. (ps up). 1986. 10.95 (ISBN 0-915361-49-3, Dist. by Watts). Adama Pubs Inc.

Nakosteen, Mehdi. Mulla's Donkey & Other Friends. LC 74-620109. (Illus.). 150p. 1988. 20.00 (ISBN 0-317-90546-5); pap. 8.50 (ISBN 0-317-90547-3). Iran Bks.

Nash, Ogden. The Animal Garden. Knight, Hilary, illus. LC 65-21772. 48p. (gr. 10 up). 1988. pap. 5.95 (ISBN 0-87131-568-8). M Evans.

Ned the Lonely Donkey. (ARA., Illus.). (gr. 3-5). 3.50x (ISBN 0-86685-211-5). Intl Bk Ctr.

Nister, Ernest. Animal Tales. Nister, Ernest, illus. 1981. 9.95 (ISBN 0-399-20801-1, Philomel). Putnam Pub Group.

—The Animals' Picnic. (Illus.). 20p. 1988. 13.95 (ISBN 0-399-21579-4, Philomel Bks). Putnam Pub Group.

Nockels, David. Animal Marvels. Nockels, David, illus. LC 80-25443. 12p. (ps-3). 1981. 3.50 (ISBN 0-8037-0085-7). Dial Bks Young.

Nodset, Joan L. Who Took the Farmer's Hat? Siebel, Fritz, illus. LC 62-17964. 32p. (gr. k-3). 1963. PLB 12.89 (ISBN 0-06-024566-2). HarpC Child Bks.

Novak, Matt. Mr. Floop's Lunch. LC 89-22963. (Illus.). 32p. (ps-1). 1990. 12.95 (ISBN 0-531-05826-3); PLB 12.99 (ISBN 0-531-08426-4). Orchard Bks Watts.

Oetting, Rae. Timmy Tiger to the Rescue. LC 70-108733. (Illus.). 32p. (ps-4). 1970. PLB 9.95x (ISBN 0-87783-043-6); pap. 3.94x deluxe ed (ISBN 0-87783-112-2); cassette 7.94x (ISBN 0-87783-229-3). Oddo.

—Timmy Tiger's New Coat. LC 74-108734. (Illus.). 32p. (ps-2). 1970. PLB 9.95 (ISBN 0-87783-044-4); pap. 3.94 deluxe ed (ISBN 0-87783-113-0); cassette 7.94x (ISBN 0-87783-230-7). Oddo.

—Timmy Tiger's New Friend. LC 77-108732. (Illus.). (ps-2). 1970. PLB 9.95 (ISBN 0-87783-042-8); pap. 3.94 deluxe ed (ISBN 0-87783-114-9); cassette 7.94x (ISBN 0-87783-231-5). Oddo.

Ormerod, Jan. Our Ollie. LC 85-17133. (Illus.). 24p. (ps). 1986. 4.95 (ISBN 0-688-04208-2). Lothrop.

—Young Joe. LC 85-17128. (Illus.). 24p. (ps). 1985. 4.95 (ISBN 0-688-04210-4). Lothrop.

Osborne, Mary P. Mo & His Friends. DiSalvo-Ryan, DyAnne, illus. LC 87-15655. 48p. (ps-3). 1989. 9.95 (ISBN 0-8037-0504-2); 9.89 (ISBN 0-8037-0505-0). Dial Bks Young.

O'Toole, Donna. Aarvy Aardvark Finds Hope: A Read-Aloud Story for People of All Ages. McWhirter, Mary Lou, illus. 80p. (Orig.). (ps up). 1989. pap. 9.95 (ISBN 1-878321-25-0, Mntn Rainbow); tchr's. guide 6.95 (ISBN 1-878321-26-9, Mntn Rainbow); audio tape 9.95 (ISBN 0-685-20985-7, Mntn Rainbow). Rainbow NC.
"Aarvy Aardvark Finds Hope" by Donna O'Toole. This read-aloud story for people of all ages is about loving & losing friendship & hope. Through it readers will learn how healing & growing through even the most devastating losses is possible. "Seldom does a book come along that has unique appeal & offers something meaningful for all ages. AARVY AARDVARK FINDS HOPE is such a book."--The Grief Support & Education Center, Canton, Ohio. "This is the most wonderful book I have seen - & I have been doing 'death & dying' work for over 15 years."--Helen Fitzgerald, Fairfax, Virginia. "This story has strength, wisdom & beauty. It shows how long it can take to "be yourself" after you've lost so much of importance. Yet it is hopeful - permission giving to open to one's imagination - to once again play in a world so charged by life!"--John Schneider, Ph.D. Dept. of Psychiatry, M.S.U. "A fine book. It belongs in every home, classroom & library."--Ann Isaacs, Publisher The Creative Child & Adult Quarterly. "I love Aarvy Aardvark Finds Hope!"--Elizabeth Kuebler Ross.
Publisher Provided Annotation.

Oxenbury, Helen. Curious Creatures. Oxenbury, Helen, illus. LC 79-2980. 9p. (ps-3). 1985. 4.95 (ISBN 0-694-00033-7). HarpC Child Bks.

Packard, Edward. Jungle Safari. Tomei, Lorna, illus. 51p. (gr. 4). 1983. pap. 2.25 (ISBN 0-553-15403-6). Bantam.

Pagnucci, Franco & Susan. Story Start Animals. (gr. 2-5). 1990. pap. 7.95 (ISBN 0-8224-6398-9). Fearon Teach Aids.

Pantell, Dora. Miss Pickerell & the Last World. Geer, Charles, illus. LC 86-13353. 160p. (gr. 1-6). 1986. PLB 12.90 (ISBN 0-531-10229-7). Watts.

Parnall, Peter. Winter Barn. Parnall, Peter, illus. LC 86-23898. 32p. (gr. k-3). 1986. 13.95 (ISBN 0-02-770170-0, Mcmillan Child Bk). Macmillan Child Grp.

Paterson, Cynthia & Paterson, Brian. The Foxwood Treasure. (Illus.). 32p. (ps-3). 1985. 6.95 (ISBN 0-8120-5664-7). Barron.

—Robbery at Foxwood. (Illus.). 32p. (ps-3). 1985. 6.95 (ISBN 0-8120-5665-5). Barron.

Patterson, Geoffrey. Lion & the Gyspy. (ps-3). 1991. 14.95 (ISBN 0-385-41536-2). Doubleday.

Paxton, Tom. Belling the Cat: And Other Aesop's Fables. Rayevsky, Robert, illus. LC 89-39851. 40p. (ps up). 1990. 13.95 (ISBN 0-688-08158-4); PLB 13.88 (ISBN 0-688-08159-2, Morrow Jr Bks). Morrow Jr Bks.

Peck. Grumpalump. (ps-3). 1991. 14.95 (ISBN 0-89919-871-6, Clarion Bks). HM.

Peek, Merle. Mary Wore Her Red Dress, & Henry Wore His Green Sneakers. Peek, Merle, illus. LC 84-12733. 32p. (ps-2). 1985. 13.95 (ISBN 0-89919-324-2, Clarion). Ticknor & Fields.

Peet, Bill. Farewell to Shady Glade. (Illus.). 48p. (gr. k-3). 1966. 13.95 (ISBN 0-395-18975-6); pap. 4.95 (ISBN 0-395-31128-4). HM.

—Jethro & Joel Were a Troll. LC 86-20879. (Illus.). 32p. (gr. k-3). 1990. 12.95 (ISBN 0-395-43081-X); pap. 4.95 (ISBN 0-395-53968-4). HM.

—No Such Things. Peet, Bill, illus. LC 82-23234. 32p. (gr. k-3). 1985. 13.95 (ISBN 0-395-33888-3); pap. 3.95 (ISBN 0-395-39594-1). HM.

—Smokey. Peet, Bill, illus. 48p. (gr. k-3). 1983. pap. 3.95 (ISBN 0-395-34924-9). HM.

Petersham, Maud & Petersham, Miska. The Box with Red Wheels. reissued ed. Petersham, Maud & Petersham, Miska, illus. LC 49-11325. 32p. (ps-1). 1986. 12.95 (ISBN 0-02-771350-4, Mcmillan Child Bk). Macmillan Child Grp.

Pilling, Ann. Donkey's Day Out. (ps-3). 1990. 11.95 (ISBN 0-7459-1618-X). Lion USA.

Poe, Edgar Allan. The Fall of the House of Usher. Cutts, David E., adapted by. Crowell, James, illus. LC 81-15958. 32p. (gr. 5-10). 1982. PLB 10.79 (ISBN 0-89375-624-5); pap. text ed. 2.95 (ISBN 0-89375-625-3). Troll Assocs.

Poltarnees, Welleran. Amy & Nathaniel. Cline, Paul, illus. 32p. 1989. 11.95 (ISBN 0-88138-118-7). Green Tiger Pr.

Poole, Valerie. Obadiah Coffee & the Music Contest. Poole, Valerie, illus. LC 89-49548. 32p. (ps-3). 1991. 14.95 (ISBN 0-06-021619-0); PLB 14.89 (ISBN 0-06-021620-4). HarpC Child Bks.

Potter, Beatrix. Animal Homes. 12p. 1991. bds. 3.50 (ISBN 0-7232-3782-4). Warne.

—Beatrix Potter Collection, 3 vols. (ps-3). 1987. Set. write for info. (ISBN 0-317-52263-9); Collection #1. 18.95 (ISBN 0-7232-5163-0); Collection #2. 18.95 (ISBN 0-7232-5164-9); Collection #3. 18.95 (ISBN 0-7232-5165-7). Warne.

—Beatrix Potter Mask Book. (ps-3). 1990. pap. 9.95 (ISBN 0-7232-3619-4). Warne.

—Beatrix Potter's Derwentwater. Bartlett, Wynne & Whalley, Joyce I., eds. 144p. (ps up). 1988. pap. 10.95 (ISBN 0-7232-3312-8). Warne.

—Beatrix Potter's Farmhouse Box. (Illus.). (ps-3). 1989. Set of 6. 28.95 (ISBN 0-7232-5169-X). Warne.

—Country Tales. Baynes, Pauline, illus. (ps-3). 1987. 4.95 (ISBN 0-7232-3447-7). Warne.

—Dinner Time. 12p. 1991. bds. 3.50 (ISBN 0-7232-3781-6). Warne.

—Further Tales from Beatrix Potter. (Illus.). 112p. (ps-3). 1987. 7.95 (ISBN 0-7232-3509-0). Warne.

—Ginger & Pickles. LC 85-13641. (Illus.). 64p. (gr. 2 up). 1985. pap. 1.75 (ISBN 0-486-24969-7). Dover.

—Happy Families. 12p. 1991. bds. 3.50 (ISBN 0-7232-3783-2). Warne.

—Hill Top Tales. (Illus.). 128p. (ps up). 1989. 8.95 (ISBN 0-7232-3548-1). Warne.

—More Tales from Beatrix Potter. (ps-3). 1988. 8.95 (ISBN 0-7232-3366-7). Warne.
—Peter Rabbit & Other Stories. 1989. 4.98 (ISBN 0-89009-187-0). Bk Sales Inc.
—The Pie & the Patty-Pan. (Illus.). 46p. 1976. pap. 1.75 (ISBN 0-486-23383-9). Dover.
—The Stories of Beatrix Potter, Vol. 1. Potter, Beatrix, illus. 96p. (ps-2). Date not set. 4 bks. & 2 audio cassettes 14.98 (ISBN 1-55886-063-0). Smarty Pants.
—The Stories of Beatrix Potter, Vol. 2. Potter, Beatrix, illus. 96p. (ps-2). Date not set. 4 bks. & 2 audio cassettes 14.98 (ISBN 1-55886-067-3). Smarty Pants.
—The Tale of Mr. Jeremy Fisher. Horden, Michael, read by. (ps-3). 1989. pap. 6.95 bk. & tape (ISBN 0-7232-3669-0). Warne.
—The Tale of Mrs. Tiggy-Winkle. Atkinson, Allen, illus. 1984. pap. 2.25 (ISBN 0-553-15204-1). Bantam.
—The Tale of Peter Rabbit. (Illus.). 60p. (gr. 1-5). 1972. pap. 1.75 (ISBN 0-486-22827-4). Dover.
—Tale of Peter Rabbit. new ed. Apple, Margot, illus. LC 78-18071. 32p. (gr. k-3). 1979. PLB 9.79 (ISBN 0-89375-124-3); pap. 1.95 (ISBN 0-89375-102-2). Troll Assocs.
—The Tale of Peter Rabbit. Atkinson, Allen, illus. 64p. (Orig.). 1984. pap. 2.50 (ISBN 0-553-15470-2). Bantam.
—Tale of Peter Rabbit & Other Stories. Delacre, Lulu, illus. 1985. 6.95 (ISBN 0-685-10253-X, Little Simon). S&S Trade.
—The Tale of Peter Rabbit & Other Stories. Delacre, Lulu, illus. 1985. pap. 6.95 (ISBN 0-671-52403-8, Little Simon). S&S Trade.
—Tales from Beatrix Potter. Potter, Beatrix, illus. 228p. (ps-3). 1986. 7.95 (ISBN 0-7232-3971-1). Warne.
—Wag-by-Wall. Baynes, Pauline, illus. (ps-3). 1987. 4.95 (ISBN 0-7232-3448-5). Warne.
Pratt, Davis. Magic Animals of Japan. Kula, Elsa, illus. LC 67-17483. (gr. 1-4). 1967. (Pub. by Parnassus); PLB 5.88 (ISBN 0-87466-020-3). HM.
Preston, Edna M. & Bennett, Rainey. The Temper Tantrum Book. (Illus.). (ps-3). 1976. pap. 4.95 (ISBN 0-14-050181-9, Puffin). Puffin Bks.
Price & Watson. Animal Stories. (gr. k-4). 1982. 10.95 (ISBN 0-86020-666-1, Usborne-Hayes). EDC.
Provensen, Alice & Provensen, Martin. An Owl & Three Pussycats. Provensen, Alice & Provensen, Martin, illus. LC 81-2855. 32p. (ps-2). 1981. (Atheneum Childrens Bks). Macmillan Child Grp.
Quackenbush, Robert. The Beagle & Mr. Fly Catcher: A Story of Charles Darwin. LC 83-8721. (Illus.). 40p. (gr. 4-6). 1983. 8.95 (ISBN 0-13-071290-6). P-H.
—Sheriff Sally Gopher & the Thanksgiving Caper. Quackenbush, Robert, illus. LC 82-135. 32p. (gr. 1-3). 1982. PLB 13.88 (ISBN 0-688-01293-0). Lothrop.
Radley, Gail. Special Strengths. Boddy, Joe, illus. 64p. (gr. 2-6). 1984. pap. 6.95 (ISBN 0-87743-702-5, Pub. by Bellwood Pr). Baha'i.
Reese, Bob. Rapid Robert & Hiss the Snake. LC 83-7622. (Illus.). 32p. (ps-2). 1983. PLB 11.93 (ISBN 0-516-02322-5). Childrens.
Reichert, John J. Color the Creatures. (Illus.). (gr. 4-12). 1979. pap. 1.50 (ISBN 0-930504-03-8). Polaris Pr.
Rey, H. A. Feed the Animals. (Illus.). 24p. (gr. k-3). 1944. pap. 2.25 (ISBN 0-395-07063-5, Sandpiper). HM.
—Where's My Baby? (Illus.). (gr. k-3). 1943. pap. 2.25 (ISBN 0-395-07069-4, Sandpiper). HM.
Rice, Eve. Sam Who Never Forgets. LC 76-30370. 32p. (ps-3). 1977. PLB 11.88 (ISBN 0-688-84088-4). Greenwillow.
Robertson, Graeme. The Battle of Bongerhoohoo. Szmid, Gordon, illus. LC 79-11855. (gr. 3-7). 1979. PLB 8.95 (ISBN 0-672-52592-5, Bobbs). Macmillan.
Rockwell, Anne. Big Boss. (Illus.). 64p. (gr. 1-3). 1987. pap. 3.95 (ISBN 0-689-71125-5, Aladdin). Macmillan Child Grp.
Rose, Gerald. Trouble in the Ark. LC 89-37270. (ps-1). 1989. 10.95 (ISBN 0-8192-1511-2). Morehouse Pub.
Rosenberg, Amye. Two-Minute Animal Stories. 1990. pap. write for info. (ISBN 0-307-12190-9, Golden Pr). Western Pub.
Ross, Tony. Hugo & the Ministry of Holidays. (Illus.). 28p. (gr. k-2). 1987. 11.95 (ISBN 0-905478-86-X, Pub. by Hutchinson UK). Trafalgar Sq.
Royds, Caroline, selected by. The Animal Tale Treasury. Spenceley, Annabel, illus. LC 86-5010. 96p. (ps up). 1986. 12.95 (ISBN 0-399-21335-X, Putnam). Putnam Pub Group.
Ryder, Joanne. Fog in the Meadow. Owens, Gail, illus. LC 77-25650. (ps-3). 1979. 9.57i (ISBN 0-06-025148-4). HarpC Child Bks.

Ryder, Virginia P. Three Monkey Saves the Day. Kilgore, Julia, illus. 21p. (Orig.). (gr. k-12). 1991. pap. 8.95 (ISBN 0-935098-04-6). Amigo Pr. An imaginative story drawn from animal myths of the ancient Mexican codices. Ideal for ethnic studies as Latinos find magic & pride in their Pre-Columbian heritage. All the children will love the antics of Mexico's typical animals; the Mexican hairless dog, the ocelot & the howler monkey. The story illustrates contemporary ways of thinking about & protecting wild animals. The title of the story is based on the Aztec calendar. The calendar-stone, as well as the gold, carnelian & jade gifts can be viewed today at one of the world's greatest archaeological museums which is in Mexico City. The peoples of meso-America believed that the world came to an end every 52 years. Tzintzin, the priest in the story, helps to save the world by capturing a new day. He performs his secret priestly duties with his helpers, Oco, a howling monkey, Chichi, a blue Mexican hairless dog & the eagle. The priest recalls how he found & captured his animal friends in the jungle. Children will love coloring the large line drawings of each of the animals. A favorite picture is of the priest when he finds the old ocelot asleep in the tall grasses. He cares for the ocelot until it dies a natural death from old age. The ocelot wills the priest his fur coat to use as a rug when he no longer needs it. The story is a little sad but quite beautiful. Each of the incidents of the story can promote lively discussions on ethnicity, environmental literacy, archaeology, geography, & many other topics.
Publisher Provided Annotation.

Rylant, Cynthia. Every Living Thing. Schindler, S. D., illus. LC 88-19359. 96p. (gr. 5 up). 1988. pap. 3.50 (ISBN 0-689-71263-4, Aladdin). Macmillan Child Grp.
Sadler, Marilyn. It's Not Easy Being a Bunny. Bollen, Roger, illus. LC 83-2680. 48p. (gr. k-3). 1983. 6.95 (ISBN 0-394-86102-7); lib. bdg. 6.99 (ISBN 0-394-96102-1). Beginner.
Samit & the Dragon. 36p. (ps-4). 1985. 8.95 (ISBN 0-88684-177-1); cassette tape avail. Listen USA.
Samton, Sheila W. Beside the Bay. (ps-1). 1987. 12.95 (ISBN 0-399-21420-8, Philomel Bks). Putnam Pub Group.
Say, Allen. The Bicycle Man. Say, Allen, illus. (ps-3). 1989. pap. 4.95 (ISBN 0-395-50652-2, Sandpiper). HM.
Scarry, Richard. Richard Scarry's ABC Word Book. (Illus.). (ps-2). 1971. 9.95 (ISBN 0-394-82339-7, Random Juv); lib. bdg. 5.99 (ISBN 0-394-92339-1). Random.
—Richard Scarry's Animal Nursery Tales. (Illus.). (ps-1). 1975. write for info. (ISBN 0-307-16810-7, Golden Bks). Western Pub.
Schaffer, Libor. Arthur Sets Sail. Mathieu, Agnes, illus. LC 87-1594. 32p. (gr. k-3). 1987. 13.95 (ISBN 1-55858-059-X). North-South Bks NYC.
Scheidl, Gerda M. The Little Donkey. Watts, Bernadette, illus. LC 87-73271. 32p. (gr. k-3). 1988. 12.95 (ISBN 1-55858-026-3). North-South Bks NYC.
Schenk de Regniers, Beatrice. Going for a Walk. LC 81-48065. (Illus.). 32p. (ps-1). 1982. Repr. of 1961 ed. PLB 12.89 (ISBN 0-06-024852-1). HarpC Child Bks.
Schick, Joel & Schick, Alice. Santaberry & the Snard. (gr. 4). 1976. 12.00 (ISBN 0-912846-23-2). Bookstore Pr.
Scott, Dixon. A Fresh Wind in the Willows. (gr. k-6). 1987. pap. 2.50 (ISBN 0-440-42741-X, YB). Dell.
Sears, Jeanne. Danger-Watch Out! Cohen, Dorothy P., illus. 12p. (ps-3). 1988. pap. 1.95 (ISBN 0-9621086-0-X). J Sears.
Selden, George. The Cricket in Times Square. Williams, Garth, illus. LC 60-12640. 160p. (gr. 4 up). 1960. 13.95 (ISBN 0-374-31650-3). FS&G.
—Tucker's Countryside. Williams, Garth, illus. LC 69-14975. 176p. (gr. 3 up). 1969. 12.95 (ISBN 0-374-37854-1). FS&G.
Sendak, Maurice. Higglety Pigglety Pop: Or, There Must Be More to Life. Sendak, Maurice, illus. LC 67-18553. 80p. (gr. k-3). 1967. 14.95 (ISBN 0-06-025487-4). HarpC Child Bks.
Sesame Street Staff. In & Out, Up & Down. Smollin, Michael J., illus. LC 81-83697. 28p. (ps). 1982. bds. 2.95 (ISBN 0-394-85151-X). Random.
Seton, Ernest T. Animal Heroes. rev. ed. Seton, Ernest T., illus. LC 87-71143. 368p. (gr. 5 up). 1987. pap. 9.95 (ISBN 0-88739-055-2). Creative Arts Bk.
—Wild Animals I Have Known. rev. ed. Seton, Ernest T., illus. LC 87-71147. 368p. (gr. 5 up). 1987. pap. 9.95 (ISBN 0-88739-053-6). Creative Arts Bk.
Shannon, George. Dance Away! Aruego, Jose & Dewey, Ariane, illus. LC 81-6391. 32p. (gr. k-3). 1982. 13.95 (ISBN 0-688-00838-0); PLB 13.88 (ISBN 0-688-00839-9). Greenwillow.
Sharmat, Marjorie W. Hooray for Father's Day. Wallner, John, illus. LC 86-15037. 32p. (gr. k-3). 1987. 14.95g (ISBN 0-8234-0637-7). Holiday.
—I'm Terrific. Chorao, Kay, illus. LC 76-9094. 32p. (gr. k-3). 1977. reinforced bdg. 13.95 (ISBN 0-8234-0282-7). Holiday.
Shivkumar. Stories from Panchatantra: Book I. Biswas, Pulak, illus. (gr. 1-9). 1979. 4.50 (ISBN 0-89744-162-1). Auromere.
—Stories from Panchatantra: Book II. Bhusan, Reboti, illus. (gr. 1-9). 1979. 4.50 (ISBN 0-89744-163-X). Auromere.
—Stories from Panchatantra: Book III. Mukerji, Debrabrata, illus. (gr. 1-9). 1979. 4.50 (ISBN 0-89744-164-8). Auromere.
—Stories from Panchatantra: Book IV. Biswas, Pulak, illus. (gr. 1-9). 1979. 4.50 (ISBN 0-89744-165-6); pap. write for info. Auromere.
Silverstein, Shel. Giraffe & a Half. Silverstein, Shel, illus. LC 64-19709. 48p. (gr. k-3). 1964. 12.95 (ISBN 0-06-025655-9); PLB 12.89 (ISBN 0-06-025656-7). HarpC Child Bks.
Singer, Bill. The Fox with Cold Feet. Kendrick, Dennis, illus. LC 80-10288. 48p. (ps-3). 1980. 5.95 (ISBN 0-8193-1021-2); PLB 5.95 (ISBN 0-8193-1022-0). Parents.
Singer, Marilyn. Tarantulas on the Brain. Grant, Leigh, illus. LC 81-48659. 192p. (gr. 4-7). 1982. HarpC Child Bks.
Siracusa, Catherine. No Mail for Mitchell: A Step 1 Book - Preschool-Gr. 1. Siracusa, Catherine, illus. LC 89-70010. 32p. (Orig.). (ps-1). 1990. lib. bdg. 6.99 (ISBN 0-679-90476-X); pap. 2.95 (ISBN 0-679-80476-5). Random.
Slate, Joseph. The Star Rocker. Zimmer, Dirk, illus. LC 81-47854. 32p. (ps-1). 1982. 7.64i (ISBN 0-06-025748-2). HarpC Child Bks.
Sly Fox & the Little Red Hen in Arabic. (Illus.). (gr. 4-6). 3.50x (ISBN 0-86685-224-7). Intl Bk Ctr.
Smith, Elizabeth S. A Dolphin Goes to School: The Story of Squirt, a Trained Dolphin. LC 85-28407. (Illus.). 96p. (gr. 2-5). 1986. 12.95 (ISBN 0-688-04815-3); lib. bdg. 12.88 (ISBN 0-688-04816-1, Morrow Jr Bks). Morrow Jr Bks.
Smith, Emma. Emily the Traveling Guinea Pig. (gr. 1-5). 1960. 10.95 (ISBN 0-8392-3007-9). Astor-Honor.
Solotareff, Gregoire. Never Trust an Ogre! LC 87-30239. (Illus.). 32p. (ps-2). 1988. Repr. of 1986 ed. 11.95 (ISBN 0-688-07740-4); lib. bdg. 11.88 (ISBN 0-688-07741-2). Greenwillow.
Spier, Peter. Gobble, Growl, Grunt. Spier, Peter, illus. LC 79-14430. 24p. (ps-1). 1988. 6.95 (ISBN 0-385-24094-5). Doubleday.
—Peter Spier's Little Animal Books, 4 bks. Spier, Peter, illus. (ps). 1987. Boxed Set. bds. 10.00 laminated (ISBN 0-385-19715-2). Doubleday.
Stadler, John. Animal Cafe. LC 85-26789. (Illus.). 32p. (ps-2). 1986. pap. 3.95 (ISBN 0-689-71063-1, Aladdin). Macmillan Child Grp.
—Cat is Back at Bat. Stadler, John, illus. 32p. (ps-2). 1991. 10.95 (ISBN 0-525-44762-8, DCB). Dutton Child Bks.
Stanish, Bob. Hippogriff Feathers. (gr. 3-12). 1981. 9.95 (ISBN 0-86653-009-6, GA 237). Good Apple.
—I Believe in Unicorns. (gr. 3-8). 1979. 8.95 (ISBN 0-916456-51-X, GA107). Good Apple.
Stefanec-Ogren, Cathy. Sly, P. I. The Case of the Missing Shoes. Circolo, Priscilla P., illus. LC 87-29352. 48p. (gr. 1-4). 1989. 10.95 (ISBN 0-06-024631-6); PLB 10.89 (ISBN 0-06-024632-4). HarpC Child Bks.
Steig, William. The Amazing Bone. Steig, William, illus. 32p. (gr. 1-3). 1977. pap. 3.95 (ISBN 0-14-050247-5, Puffin). Puffin Bks.
—Amos & Boris. (Illus.). (gr. 1-3). 1977. pap. 3.95 (ISBN 0-14-050229-7, Puffin). Puffin Bks.
—The Real Thief. Steig, William, illus. LC 73-77910. 64p. (ps up). 1976. pap. 2.95 (ISBN 0-374-46208-9, Sunburst). FS&G.
—Sylvester & the Magic Pebble. LC 80-12314. (Illus.). 32p. (gr. k-4). 1988. PLB 12.95 (ISBN 0-671-66154-X); pap. 5.95 (ISBN 0-671-66269-4). S&S Trade.
Stevenson, James. Here Comes Herb's Hurricane! Reissue. Stevenson, James, illus. LC 73-7138. 160p. (gr. 4-6). 1973. PLB 12.89 (ISBN 0-06-025783-0). HarpC Child Bks.
—Oh No, It's Waylon's Birthday! LC 88-4574. (Illus.). 48p. (gr. 1 up). 1989. 11.95 (ISBN 0-688-08235-1); PLB 11.88 (ISBN 0-688-08236-X). Greenwillow.
Streiber, William R. & Rizzoto, Flora M. Popo: The Adventures of a Mexican Donkey. Ely, Gladys, illus. LC 70-146604. (gr. 1-4). 1971. 3.75 (ISBN 0-8356-0420-9, Quest). Theos Pub Hse.
Streit, Jacob. Animal Stories. Piening, Jacob, tr. from GER. 36p. (gr. 3-5). 1974. pap. 10.95 (ISBN 0-88010-035-4, Pub. by Verlag Walter Keller Switzerland). Anthroposophic.
Summers, Joan. God's Little Animals: Easy Illustrations & Bible Parallels. (Illus.). 32p. (gr. k-4). 1969. pap. 1.95 (ISBN 0-88243-718-6, 02-0718). Gospel Pub.
Tafuri, Nancy. Where We Sleep. LC 86-27115. (Illus.). (ps). pap. 3.95 (ISBN 0-688-07189-9). Greenwillow.
Tales from the Jungle Book. (Illus.). (gr. 3-5). 3.50 (ISBN 0-7214-0997-0). Ladybird Bks.

Tallarico, Tony. Animals. (Illus.). 12p. (gr. 3-8). 1982. pap. 3.95 (ISBN 0-89828-300-0). Tuffy Bks.

Thaler, Mike. Come & Play, Hippo. Chambliss, Maxie, illus. LC 87-33489. 64p. (gr. k-3). 1991. 11.95 (ISBN 0-06-026176-5); PLB 11.89 (ISBN 0-06-026177-3). HarpC Child Bks.

Thomas, Gail F. Lucky the Alligator. 1992. 7.95 (ISBN 0-8062-4117-9). Carlton.

Tripp, Valerie. Happy, Happy Mother's Day! Martin, Sandra K., illus. LC 89-35757. 24p. (ps-2). 1989. PLB 12.33 (ISBN 0-516-01521-4); pap. 3.95 (ISBN 0-516-41521-2). Childrens.

Troughton, Joanna. Mouse-Deer's Market: A Folk Tale from Borneo. Troughton, Joanna, illus. LC 84-11049. 28p. (ps-3). 1984. 14.95 (ISBN 0-911745-63-7, Bedrick Blackie). P Bedrick Bks.

Truelson, Thomas. Travels with Tiny Teddy: Cape Cod: The Great Escape. Burke, Kerry, illus. 40p. (Orig.). (gr. 1-3). 1988. pap. 3.95 (ISBN 0-685-19995-9). Lighthse Bks MA.

Twinn, Michael. Lady Who Loved Animals. Adams, Pam, illus. 32p. (ps-2). 1981. 5.50 (ISBN 0-85953-121-X, Pub. by Child's Play England). Childs Play.

Tyler, J. Animal Words. 1989. 2.95 (ISBN 0-7460-0252-1, Usborne). EDC.

Ungerer, Tomi. The Beast of Monsieur Racine. (Illus.). 32p. (ps up). 1986. pap. 4.95 (ISBN 0-374-40570-0). FS&G.

Uttley, Alison. The May Queen. Percy, Graham, illus. 32p. (ps-2). 1989. bds. 4.95 laminated (ISBN 0-571-15296-1). Faber & Faber.

Vail, Virginia. All the Way Home. 128p. (Orig.). (gr. 4-6). 1987. pap. 2.50 (ISBN 0-590-40186-6, Apple Paperbacks). Scholastic Inc.

—A Kid's Best Friend. 112p. (Orig.). (gr. 5-7). 1986. pap. 2.50 (ISBN 0-590-40182-3, Apple Paperbacks). Scholastic Inc.

—Pets Are For Keeps. 128p. (Orig.). (gr. 3-6). 1986. pap. 2.50 (ISBN 0-590-40181-5, Apple Paperbacks). Scholastic Inc.

Van der Meer, Ron & Van der Meer, Atie. Fun with Animals. (ps-3). 1990. 5.95 (ISBN 0-399-21789-4, Putnam). Putnam Pub Group.

Velthuijs, Max. Frog & the Birdsong. (ps-3). 1991. bds. 13.95 jacketed (ISBN 0-374-32467-0). FS&G.

Vermeylen, Terry J. I Am Juma, Manatee. 88p. (gr. 4 up). 1987. pap. 6.95 (ISBN 0-8059-3055-8). Dorrance.

Vincent, Gabrielle. Bravo, Ernest & Celestine! Vincent, Gabrielle, illus. LC 81-6423. 24p. (gr. k-3). 1982. 10.75 (ISBN 0-688-00857-7); PLB 10.88 (ISBN 0-688-00858-5). Greenwillow.

—Ernest & Celestine's Picnic. Vincent, Gabrielle, illus. LC 82-2909. 24p. (gr. k-3). 1982. 10.75 (ISBN 0-688-01250-7); PLB 10.88 (ISBN 0-688-01252-3). Greenwillow.

Waber, Bernard. Anteater Named Arthur. Waber, Bernard, illus. LC 67-20374. 48p. (gr. k-3). 1977. 13.95 (ISBN 0-395-20336-8); pap. 4.95 (ISBN 0-395-25936-3). HM.

—Lyle Finds His Mother. Waber, Bernard, illus. (gr. k-3). 1978. pap. 4.95 (ISBN 0-395-27398-6). HM.

—You Look Ridiculous Said the Rhinoceros to the Hippopotamus. (Illus.). (gr. k-3). 1979. pap. 4.95 (ISBN 0-395-28007-9). HM.

Wadsworth, Olivia A. & Rae, Mary M. Over in the Meadow: A Counting-Out Rhyme. LC 84-19653. 32p. 1985. pap. 10.95 (ISBN 0-670-53276-2). Viking Child Bks.

Wahl, Jan. Pleasant Fieldmouse. Sendak, Maurice, illus. LC 64-14684. 80p. (gr. k-3). 1964. PLB 11.89 (ISBN 0-06-026331-8). HarpC Child Bks.

Wales, Prince of. The Old Man of Lochnagar. Casson, Hugh, illus. LC 80-24716. 48p. (ps-3). 1980. 11.95 (ISBN 0-374-35613-0). FS&G.

Wallner, S. J. Friendly Little Hobo. LC 68-56814. (Illus.). 48p. (gr. 2-4). 1968. PLB 10.95 (ISBN 0-87783-013-4); pap. 3.94 deluxe ed. (ISBN 0-87783-092-4). Oddo.

Walt Disney's the Jungle Book. (ps-3). 1990. write for info. (ISBN 0-307-12107-0). Western Pub.

Warburg, Sandol S. Growing Time. Weisgard, Leonard, illus. (ps-3). 1989. pap. 4.95 (ISBN 0-395-51009-0, Sandpiper). HM.

The Water Babies. (gr. k-6). 1986. 8.98 (ISBN 0-517-61817-6). Outlet Bk Co.

Watkins, Dawn L. A King for Brass Cobweb. Smith, Anne, ed. Hannon, Holly, illus. (Orig.). (gr. k-1). 1990. pap. write for info. (ISBN 0-89084-505-0). Bob Jones Univ Pr.

Watson, Nancy D. The Birthday Goat. Watson, Wendy, illus. LC 73-3389. 40p. (ps-3). 1974. 6.95i (ISBN 0-690-00145-2, Crowell Jr Bks). HarpC Child Bks.

Weiss, Nicki. Where Does the Brown Bear Go? (ps). 1990. pap. 3.95 (ISBN 0-14-054181-0, Puffin). Puffin Bks.

Wells, Rosemary. Peabody. LC 83-7207. (Illus.). 32p. (ps-2). 1983. 13.95 (ISBN 0-8037-0004-0); PLB 13.89 (ISBN 0-8037-0005-9). Dial Bks Young.

Wheeler, Cindy. Marmalade's Nap. LC 81-20868. (Illus.). 24p. (ps-1). 1983. lib. bdg. 9.99 (ISBN 0-394-95022-4). Knopf.

White, E. B. Charlotte's Web. LC 52-9760. (Illus.). 1974. pap. 3.50 (ISBN 0-06-440055-7, Trophy). HarpC Child Bks.

—E. B. White Boxed Set. Incl. Charlotte's Web; The Trumpet of the Swan; Stuart Little. (Illus.). (gr. 3 up). 27.60i (ISBN 0-686-77171-0). HarpC Child Bks.

Wickum, Mabel. The Egg. LC 88-51385. (Illus.). 44p. (gr. k-2). 1989. pap. 4.95 (ISBN 1-55523-199-3). Winston-Derek.

Wildsmith, Brian. The Miller, the Boy & the Donkey. Wildsmith, Brian, illus. 32p. (ps-1). 1987. 12.95 (ISBN 0-19-279652-6); pap. 6.95 (ISBN 0-19-272114-3). Oxford U Pr.

—Professor Noah's Spaceship. Wildsmith, Brian, illus. 32p. (ps-3). 1980. 14.95 (ISBN 0-19-279741-7); pap. 5.95 (ISBN 0-19-272149-6). Oxford U Pr.

—Seasons. Wildsmith, Brian, illus. (ps-3). 1980. 9.95 (ISBN 0-19-279730-1). Oxford U Pr.

—Wild Animals. (Illus.). (ps). 1976. pap. 6.95 (ISBN 0-19-272103-8). Oxford U Pr.

Williams, Barbara. A Valentine for Cousin Archie. Chorao, Kay, illus. LC 80-181. 32p. (gr. k-3). 1981. 8.95 (ISBN 0-525-41930-6, DCB). Dutton Child Bks.

Williams, H. Lickety Split, Adventure Through Time. (Illus.). 32p. (gr. 1-4). 1988. pap. 2.95 (ISBN 0-88625-173-7). Durkin Hayes Pub.

—Lickety Split, Lost Your Marbles. (Illus.). 32p. (gr. 1-4). 1988. pap. 2.95 (ISBN 0-88625-178-8). Durkin Hayes Pub.

—Lickety Split, Meets Fire Puffin. (Illus.). 32p. (gr. 1-4). 1988. pap. 2.95 (ISBN 0-88625-175-3). Durkin Hayes Pub.

—Lickety Split, Who Are You? (Illus.). 32p. (gr. 1-4). 1988. pap. 2.95 (ISBN 0-88625-181-8). Durkin Hayes Pub.

Williams, Letty. Little Red Hen: La Pequena Gallina Roja. Williams, Herb, illus. LC 78-75684. (ENG & SPA.). (ps-3). 1969. (Pub. by Treehouse); pap. 3.95 (ISBN 0-13-537894-X). P-H.

Williams, Sue. I Went Walking. Vivas, Julie, illus. (ps-3). 1990. 13.95 (ISBN 0-15-200471-8, Gulliver Bks). HarbraceJ.

—I Went Walking. Vivas, Julie, illus. 32p. (ps-2). Date not set. pap. write for info. (ISBN 0-15-238010-8). HarBraceJ.

Wilson, Sarah. Beware the Dragons! Wilson, Sarah, illus. LC 85-42614. 32p. (gr. k-3). 1985. 12.95 (ISBN 0-06-026508-6); PLB 12.89 (ISBN 0-06-026509-4). HarpC Child Bks.

Winch, Madeleine. Come by Chance. Winch, Madeleine, illus. LC 89-22157. 32p. (ps-2). 1990. 11.95 (ISBN 0-517-57666-X); PLB 11.99 (ISBN 0-517-57667-8). Crown.

Wind in the Willows. (Illus.). 224p. (gr. 3-9). 1985. 15.95 (ISBN 0-399-20944-1, Putnam); pap. 6.95 (ISBN 0-448-11028-8, Putnam). Putnam Pub Group.

The Wind in the Willows. (gr. 4 up). 1988. pap. 4.87 (ISBN 0-318-32663-9, 74252). Longman.

The Wind in the Willows. (Illus.). (gr. 3-5). 3.50 (ISBN 0-7214-0757-9). Ladybird Bks.

Winteringham, Victoria. Penguin Day. Winteringham, Victoria, illus. LC 81-47112. 32p. (gr. k-3). 1982. 7.64i (ISBN 0-06-026513-2). HarpC Child Bks.

Wittman, Sally. Pelly & Peak. LC 77-11833. (Illus.). (ps-3). 1978. PLB 11.89 (ISBN 0-06-026560-4). HarpC Child Bks.

Wojciechowska, Maia. Shadow of a Bull. LC 64-12563. (Illus.). 176p. (gr. 5 up). 1972. 13.95 (ISBN 0-689-30042-5, Atheneum Child Bk). Macmillan Child Grp.

Wood, Audrey. The Napping House. Wood, Don, illus. 32p. (ps-2). Date not set. pap. write for info. (ISBN 0-15-256711-9). HarBraceJ.

Wood, Jenny. My First Book of Animals. 1990. 9.95 (ISBN 1-55782-330-8). Warner Bks.

Wood, Leslie. Dig Dig. (Illus.). 16p. (ps up). 1988. pap. 2.95 (ISBN 0-19-272185-2). Oxford U Pr.

Woolf, Virginia. Nurse Lugton's Curtain. Van Doren, Liz, ed. Vivas, Julie, illus. 32p. (gr. 2 up). 1991. 14.95 (ISBN 0-15-200545-5, Gulliver Bks). HarBraceJ.

Wrightson, Patricia. Moon-Dark. Young, Noela, illus. LC 87-3903. 176p. (gr. 4-7). 1988. Repr. of 1987 ed. 13.95 (ISBN 0-689-50451-9, M K McElderry). Macmillan Child Grp.

Yabuuchi, Masayuki. Whose Footprints? LC 84-1087. (Illus.). 32p. (gr. k-1). 1985. 8.95 (ISBN 0-399-21209-4, Philomel). Putnam Pub Group.

Yolen, Jane. Baby Bear's Bedtime Book. LC 89-2161. (gr. k-3). 1990. 13.95 (ISBN 0-15-205120-1). HarbraceJ.

—A Sending of Dragons. McKeveny, Tom, illus. LC 87-6689. 240p. (gr. 7 up). 1987. pap. 14.95 (ISBN 0-385-29587-1). Delacorte.

Zadra, Dan. Just Keep on Keepin' On. (Illus.). 32p. (gr. 6 up). 1986. PLB 10.95s.p. (ISBN 0-88682-020-0); 15.65. Creative Ed.

Zahava, Irene, ed. Through Other Eyes: Animal Stories by Women. 200p. (Orig.). 1988. lib. bdg. 23.95 (ISBN 0-89594-315-8); pap. 8.95 (ISBN 0-89594-314-X). Crossing Pr.

Zimmerman, Andrea G. Riddle Zoo. 64p. (gr. 3-7). 1981. 9.25 (ISBN 0-525-38300-X, Dutton). NAL-Dutton.

Zindel, Paul. The Pigman's Legacy. 128p. (gr. 12 up). 1984. pap. 3.50 (ISBN 0-553-26599-7). Bantam.

ANIMALS–GEOGRAPHICAL DISTRIBUTION

see Geographical Distribution of Animals and Plants

ANIMALS–HABITATIONS

Animal Habitats, 24 vols. (Illus.). 768p. (gr. 4-6). 1987. Set. PLB 262.80 (ISBN 0-8368-0262-4). Gareth Stevens Inc.

Animal Homes. (gr. 3-5). 1981. incl. cass. & tchr's. guide 28.95 (ISBN 0-686-73888-8, 04919). Natl Geog.

Animal Homes. (Illus.). (gr. k-3). 3.95 (ISBN 0-7214-5216-7). Ladybird Bks.

Baby Animals in the Wild. (Illus.). (ps-k). bds. 3.50 (ISBN 0-7214-9535-4). Ladybird Bks.

Bailey, Jill & Seddon, Tony. Animal Parenting. (Illus.). 64p. 1989. 14.95x (ISBN 0-8160-1654-2). Facts on File.

—Anticipating the Seasons. (Illus.). 64p. 1988. 14.95x (ISBN 0-8160-1653-4). Facts on File.

Burton, Robert. Towns. (Illus.). 24p. (gr. 2-4). 1991. PLB 13.25 (ISBN 1-878137-18-2). Newington.

Chastain, Frances. Animals of Ancient China. (Illus.). 34p. (ps-2). 1986. text ed. 5.95 (ISBN 0-8351-1790-1). China Bks.

Coldrey, Jennifer. Chicken on the Farm. LC 86-5716. (Illus.). 32p. (gr. 4-6). 1986. 10.95 (ISBN 1-55532-067-8). Gareth Stevens Inc.

—The Crab on the Seashore. LC 85-30293. (Illus.). 32p. (gr. 4-6). 1987. 10.95 (ISBN 1-55532-060-0). Gareth Stevens Inc.

—Frog in the Pond. LC 85-30300. (Illus.). 32p. (gr. 4-6). 1987. 10.95 (ISBN 1-55532-059-7). Gareth Stevens Inc.

—The Rabbit in the Fields. LC 85-30298. (Illus.). 32p. (gr. 4-6). 1987. 10.95 (ISBN 1-55532-061-9). Gareth Stevens Inc.

—The Squirrel in the Trees. LC 85-30292. (Illus.). 32p. (gr. 4-6). 1986. 10.95 (ISBN 1-55532-062-7). Gareth Stevens Inc.

—The Swan on the Lake. LC 86-5719. (Illus.). 32p. (gr. 4-6). 1987. 10.95 (ISBN 1-55532-066-X). Gareth Stevens Inc.

—The World of Chickens. LC 86-5718. (Illus.). 32p. (gr. 2-3). 1986. 10.95 (ISBN 1-55532-071-6). Gareth Stevens Inc.

—The World of Crabs. LC 85-30294. (Illus.). 32p. (gr. 2-3). 1986. 10.95 (ISBN 1-55532-063-5). Gareth Stevens Inc.

—The World of Frogs. LC 85-30297. (Illus.). 32p. (gr. 2-3). 1987. 10.95 (ISBN 1-55532-024-4). Gareth Stevens Inc.

—The World of Rabbits. LC 85-28988. (Illus.). 32p. (gr. 2-3). 1986. 10.95 (ISBN 1-55532-064-3). Gareth Stevens Inc.

—The World of Squirrels. LC 85-30296. (Illus.). 32p. (gr. 2-3). 1987. 10.95 (ISBN 1-55532-065-1). Gareth Stevens Inc.

—The World of Swans. LC 86-5721. (Illus.). 32p. (gr. 2-3). 1987. 10.95 (ISBN 1-55532-070-8). Gareth Stevens Inc.

Cranfield, Ingrid. Animal World. (Illus.). 64p. (gr. 4-6). 1991. PLB 13.90 (ISBN 1-56294-008-2). Millbrook Pr.

Crump, Donald J., ed. Animal Homes, No. 1. (Illus.). (ps-3). 1989. 19.95 (ISBN 0-87044-758-0). Natl Geog.

Dewey, Jennifer O. Animal Architecture. LC 90-43010. (Illus.). 72p. (gr. 3-6). 1991. 14.95 (ISBN 0-531-05930-8); PLB 14.99 (ISBN 0-531-08530-9). Orchard Bks Watts.

Feltwell, John. Animals & Where They Live. (Illus.). 64p. (gr. 2-6). 1988. 7.95 (ISBN 0-448-19218-7, G&D). Putnam Pub Group.

Gamlin, Linda. The Deer in the Forest. Oxford Scientific Film Staff, illus. LC 87-9916. 32p. (gr. 4-6). 1987. PLB 10.95 (ISBN 1-55532-273-5). Gareth Stevens Inc.

George, Jean C. One Day in the Prairie. Marstall, Bob, illus. LC 85-48254. 48p. (gr. 5-7). 1986. PLB 12.89 (ISBN 0-690-04566-2, Crowell Jr Bks). HarpC Child Bks.

Greenway, Shirley. Burrows. (Illus.). 24p. (gr. k-4). 1991. PLB 13.25 (ISBN 1-878137-11-5). Newington.

—Forests. (Illus.). 24p. (gr. k-4). 1991. PLB 13.25 (ISBN 1-878137-08-5). Newington.

—Jungles. (Illus.). 24p. (gr. k-4). 1991. PLB 13.25 (ISBN 1-878137-09-3). Newington.

—Water. (Illus.). 24p. (gr. k-4). 1991. PLB 13.25 (ISBN 1-878137-10-7). Newington.

Harrison, Virginia & Banks, Martin. The World of Polar Bears. LC 89-4470. (Illus.). 32p. (gr. 2-3). 1989. PLB 10.95 (ISBN 0-8368-0139-3). Gareth Stevens Inc.

Kohl, Judith & Kohl, Herbert. Pack, Band & Colony: The World of Social Animals. La Farge, Margaret, illus. LC 82-20951. 114p. (gr. 6 up). 1983. 13.95 (ISBN 0-374-35694-7). FS&G.

Moncure, Jane B. What Does Word Bird See? Gohman, Vera, illus. LC 81-21594. (ps-2). 1982. lib. bdg. 11.97 (ISBN 0-89565-220-X). Childs World.

Mora, Emma. Animals of the Forest. (Illus.). 30p. (ps-1). 1986. 3.95 (ISBN 0-8120-5722-8). Barron.

Nelson, JoAnne. A Home in a Tree. Cogbill, Mary, illus. 16p. (Orig.). (gr. k-2). 1990. pap. 3.95 (ISBN 1-878624-11-3). McClanahan Bk.

Nussbaum, Hedda. Animals Build Amazing Homes. Santoro, Christopher, illus. LC 79-11326. (gr. 2-5). 1979. 7.95 (ISBN 0-394-83850-5, Random Juv). Random.

Parnall, Peter. Woodpile. Parnall, Peter, illus. LC 89-29322. 32p. (gr. k-3). 1990. 14.95 (ISBN 0-02-770155-7, Mcmillan Child Bk). Macmillan Child Grp.

Parramon, J. M. & Rius, Maria. Life in the Air. 32p. (gr. 3-5). 1987. pap. 3.95 ea. Eng. ed (ISBN 0-8120-3863-0). Span. ed.: La Vida en el Aire (ISBN 0-8120-3867-3). Barron.

Pemberton, Nancy. Animal Habitats: The Best Home of All. Dunnington, Tom, illus. LC 90-30633. 32p. (ps-2). 1990. lib. bdg. 11.97 (ISBN 0-89565-578-0). Childs World.

Pezzoli, F. & Mora, E. Animals of the Wild. (Illus.). 30p. (ps-1). 1986. 3.95 (ISBN 0-8120-5721-X). Barron.

—Farm Animals. (Illus.). 30p. (ps-1). 1986. 3.95 (ISBN 0-8120-5723-6). Barron.

Pluckrose, Henry. Homes, Holes & Hives. (Illus.). 32p. (gr. k-4). 1990. PLB 10.40 (ISBN 0-531-14046-6). Watts.

Podendorf, Illa. Animal Homes. LC 82-4466. (Illus.). 48p. (gr. k-4). 1982. PLB 14.60 (ISBN 0-516-01666-0). Childrens.

Pringle, Laurence. Home: How Animals Find Comfort & Safety. LC 87-13119. (Illus.). 64p. (gr. 3-7). 1987. 12.95 (ISBN 0-684-18526-1, Scribners Young Read). Macmillan Child Grp.

Reid, Struan. Bird World. (Illus.). 64p. (gr. 4-6). 1991. PLB 13.90 (ISBN 1-56294-009-0). Millbrook Pr.

Robson, Denny. Animal Homes. (ps). 1991. 5.95 (ISBN 0-8120-6242-6). Barron.

Rojankovsky, Feodor. Animals on the Farm. Rojankovsky, Feodor, illus. LC 67-18586. (gr. k-3). 1967. lib. bdg. 14.99 (ISBN 0-394-91875-4). Knopf.

Saintsing, David. The World of Butterflies. LC 86-5706. (Illus.). 32p. (gr. 2-3). 1986. 10.95 (ISBN 1-55532-072-4). Gareth Stevens Inc.

Shale, David & Coldrey, Jennifer. Man-of-War at Sea. LC 86-5703. (Illus.). 32p. (gr. 4-6). 1987. 10.95 (ISBN 1-55532-069-4). Gareth Stevens Inc.

—The World of a Jellyfish. LC 86-5704. (Illus.). 32p. (gr. 2-3). 1986. 10.95 (ISBN 1-55532-073-2). Gareth Stevens Inc.

Taylor, Kim. Hidden Underneath. (gr. 4-7). 1990. 9.95 (ISBN 0-385-30180-4). Delacorte.

Whalley, Mary & Whalley, Paul. Butterfly in the Garden. LC 86-5705. (Illus.). 32p. (gr. 4-6). 1986. 10.95 (ISBN 1-55532-068-6). Gareth Stevens Inc.

Where Animals Live, 24 vols. (Illus.). (gr. 2-3). 1988. Set. 238.80 (ISBN 0-8368-0263-2). Gareth Stevens Inc.

ANIMALS–HABITS AND BEHAVIOR

Here are entered factual books whose aim is to describe and instruct. Fictional or legendary tales about animals are entered under Animals–Stories.

see also Animal Intelligence; Animals–Fiction; Animals–Migration; Nature Study; Tracking and Trailing; also names of animals with the subdivision Habits and Behavior, e.g. Birds–Habits and Behavior; etc.

Adrian, Mary. Wildlife on the Watch. Zallinger, Jean, illus. 64p. (gr. 2-6). 1974. PLB 6.95 (ISBN 0-8038-1553-0). Hastings.

Allen, Pamela. Fancy That! LC 88-1642. (Illus.). 32p. (ps-2). 1988. 12.95 (ISBN 0-531-05763-1); PLB 12.99 (ISBN 0-531-08363-2). Orchard Bks Watts.

Animal Science. (Illus.). 96p. (gr. 6-12). 1984. pap. 1.85 (ISBN 0-8395-3395-0, 3395). BSA.

Animals & Their Homes Series. (Illus.). (gr. k-6). 1987. Set of 6 titles, 48 pp. ea. PLB 95.94 (ISBN 0-8172-3110-2); Set. 15.99 ea. Raintree Pubs.

Animals in the Wild. (Illus.). (gr. k-5). 1987. Set of 26 titles, 24 pp. ea. PLB 241.56 (ISBN 0-8172-2422-X); 13.32 ea. Raintree Pubs.

Baby Animals: Animal Information Learn & Color Kits. 30p. incl. poster, 6 markers 5.00 (ISBN 0-8431-6250-3). Price Stern.

Baby Animals in the Wild. (Illus.). (ps-k). bds. 3.50 (ISBN 0-7214-9535-4). Ladybird Bks.

Baby Zoo Animals: Animal Information Learn & Color Kits. 30p. 1989. incl. poster, 6 markers 5.00 (ISBN 0-8431-6251-1). Price Stern.

Bailey, Jill. Mouths. LC 83-13840. (Illus.). 14p. (gr. k). 1984. 3.95 (ISBN 0-399-21028-8, Putnam). Putnam Pub Group.

—Noses. LC 83-13694. (Illus.). 14p. (gr. k-1). 1984. 3.95 (ISBN 0-399-21027-X, Putnam). Putnam Pub Group.

Bailey, Jill & Seddon, Tony. Animal Movement. (Illus.). 64p. 1988. 14.95x (ISBN 0-8160-1656-9). Facts on File.

Banks, Merry. Animals of the Night. Himler, Ronald, illus. LC 89-6194. 32p. (ps-k). 1990. 13.95 (ISBN 0-684-19093-1, Scribners Young Read). Macmillan Child Grp.

Barrett, Judith. Animals Should Definitely Not Act Like People. Barrett, Ron, illus. LC 80-13364. 32p. (ps-2). 1985. pap. 3.95 (ISBN 0-689-71033-X, A-147, Aladdin). Macmillan Child Grp.

Barrett, Katharine. Animals in Action. Bergman, Lincoln & Fairwell, Kay, eds. Baker, Lisa H., illus. Barrett, Reginald & Craig, Rose, photos by. (Illus.). 44p. (Orig.). (gr. 6-9). 1986. pap. 7.50 (ISBN 0-912511-10-9). Lawrence Science.

—Mapping Animal Movements. Bergman, Lincoln & Fairwell, Kay, eds. Baker, Lisa H. & Bevilacqua, Carol, illus. Barrett, Reginald, et al, photos by. 41p. (Orig.). (gr. 5-9). 1987. pap. 6.50 (ISBN 0-912511-60-5). Lawrence Science.

Bevington, Jeff. Animals on the Move, 6 bks. Holmes, Stephen, illus. 16p. (Orig.). (gr. 2-4). 1986. Set. pap. text ed. 23.30 incl. tchr's. notes (ISBN 1-55624-008-2). Wright Group.

Braithwaite, Althea. Gorillas. (ps-6). 1988. PLB 7.95 (ISBN 0-88462-170-7); pap. 2.95 (ISBN 0-88462-171-5). Dearborn Finan.

Browne, Anthony. Gorilla. Browne, Anthony, illus. LC 85-13. 32p. (ps-3). 1985. 8.95 (ISBN 0-394-87525-7); lib. bdg. 13.99 (ISBN 0-394-97525-1). Knopf.

Burton, Jane. Animals at Home. (Illus.). 24p. (gr. k-4). 1991. PLB 13.25 (ISBN 1-878137-12-3). Newington.

—Animals at Night. (Illus.). 24p. (gr. k-4). 1991. PLB 13.25 (ISBN 1-878137-13-1). Newington.

—Animals at Work. (Illus.). 24p. (gr. k-4). 1991. PLB 13.25 (ISBN 1-878137-15-8). Newington.

—Animals Eating. (Illus.). 24p. (gr. k-4). 1991. PLB 13.25 (ISBN 1-878137-00-X). Newington.

—Animals Fighting. (Illus.). 24p. (gr. k-4). 1991. PLB 13.25 (ISBN 1-878137-03-4). Newington.

—Animals Learning. (Illus.). 24p. (gr. k-4). 1991. PLB 13.25 (ISBN 1-878137-01-8). Newington.

—Animals Talking. (Illus.). 24p. (gr. k-4). 1991. PLB 13.25 (ISBN 1-878137-02-6). Newington.

—Keeping Clean. Burton, Jane & Taylor, Kim, photos by. LC 89-11557. (Illus.). 32p. (gr. 2-3). 1989. PLB 10.95 (ISBN 0-8368-0187-3). Gareth Stevens Inc.

—Keeping Cool. Burton, Jane & Taylor, Kim, photos by. LC 89-11412. (Illus.). 32p. (gr. 2-3). 1989. PLB 10.95 (ISBN 0-8368-0188-1). Gareth Stevens Inc.

Carwardine, Mark. Animals in the Cold. Young, Richard G., ed. Channell, Jim, illus. LC 89-32827. 45p. (gr. 3-5). 1989. PLB 13.26 (ISBN 0-944483-26-7). Garrett Ed Corp.

—Animals on the Move. Young, Richard G., ed. Francis, John, illus. LC 89-32809. 45p. (gr. 3-5). 1989. PLB 13.26 (ISBN 0-944483-27-5). Garrett Ed Corp.

—Nibblers & Gnawers. Young, Richard G., ed. Twinney, Dick, illus. LC 89-32807. 45p. (gr. 3-5). 1989. PLB 13.26 (ISBN 0-944483-29-1). Garrett Ed Corp.

—Night Animals. Young, Richard G., ed. Camm, Martin, illus. LC 89-7880. 45p. (gr. 3-5). 1989. PLB 13.26 (ISBN 0-944483-30-5). Garrett Ed Corp.

Chald, Dorothy. Animals Can be Special Friends. Halverson, Lydia, illus. LC 84-23300. 32p. (ps-2). 1985. lib. bdg. 13.27 (ISBN 0-516-01978-3); pap. 4.60 (ISBN 0-516-41978-1). Childrens.

Chen, Tony, illus. Animals Showing Off, No. 1. (gr. k-3). 1989. 19.95 (ISBN 0-87044-724-6). Natl Geog.

Chicago Zoological Society Staff, ed. Animal Families. (Orig.). (gr. k-2). 1986. pap. text ed. 30.00 (ISBN 0-913934-04-6). Chicago Zoo.

—Creature Features. (Orig.). (gr. 2-3). 1986. pap. text ed. 30.00 (ISBN 0-913934-05-4). Chicago Zoo.

Cole, Joanna. Daytime Animals. Lilly, Kenneth, illus. LC 85-4301. 32p. (ps-2). 1985. 9.95 (ISBN 0-394-87188-X); lib. bdg. 12.99 (ISBN 0-394-97188-4). Knopf.

Craig, Janet. Amazing World of Night Creatures. Helmer, Jean, illus. LC 89-5002. 32p. (gr. 2-4). 1990. PLB 10.89 (ISBN 0-8167-1749-4); pap. text ed. 2.95 (ISBN 0-8167-1750-8). Troll Assocs.

Crump, Donald J., ed. Amazing Things Animals Do. (gr. 3-8). 1989. 6.95 (ISBN 0-87044-709-2); PLB 8.50 (ISBN 0-87044-704-1). Natl Geog.

—Animal Architects. LC 87-12198. (Illus.). 104p. (gr. 3-8). 1987. 6.95 (ISBN 0-87044-612-6); PLB 8.50 (ISBN 0-87044-617-7). Natl Geog.

—Animals at Play. (Illus.). (gr. k-4). 1988. Set. 10.95 (ISBN 0-685-31763-3); Set. PLB 12.95 (ISBN 0-685-31764-1). Natl Geog.

—Animals in Summer. (Illus.). (gr. k-4). 1988. Set. 10.95 (ISBN 0-685-31761-7); Set. PLB 12.95 (ISBN 0-685-31762-5). Natl Geog.

—Books for Young Explorers, 4 vols, Set 13. Incl. Baby Bears & How They Grow. Buxton, Jane H; Saving Our Animal Friends. McGrath, Susan; Animals That Live in Trees. McCauley, Jane R; Animals & Their Hiding Places. McCauley, Jane R. 1986. Set. 10.95 (ISBN 0-87044-638-X); Set. PLB 12.95 (ISBN 0-87044-643-6). Natl Geog.

—How Animals Behave. LC 84-989. (Illus.). 104p. (gr. 3-8). 1984. 6.95 (ISBN 0-87044-500-6); PLB 8.50 (ISBN 0-87044-505-7). Natl Geog.

—Secrets of Animal Survival. LC 81-47895. (Illus.). 104p. (gr. 3 up). 1983. 6.95 (ISBN 0-87044-426-3); PLB 8.50 (ISBN 0-87044-431-X). Natl Geog.

Danziger, Paula. It's an Aardvark-Eat-Turtle World. LC 84-17645. 144p. (gr. 7 up). 1985. pap. 12.95 (ISBN 0-385-29371-2). Delacorte.

Darling, David. Could You Ever Speak Chimpanzee? (Illus.). (gr. 4 up). 1990. 14.95 (ISBN 0-87518-448-0, Dillon). Macmillan Child Grp.

Dorros, Arthur. Yum, Yum. Dorros, Arthur, illus. LC 87-47542. 12p. (ps-1). 1987. 2.95 (ISBN 0-694-00187-2, Crowell Jr Bks). HarpC Child Bks.

Dubov, Christine S. Oink! & Other Sounds. Hathon, Elizabeth, photos by. LC 90-47303. (Illus.). 12p. (ps). 1991. bds. 3.95 (ISBN 0-688-10102-X, Tambourine Bks). Morrow.

Echols, Jean C. Animal Defenses. Bergman, Lincoln & Fairwell, Kay, eds. Bevilacqua, Carol, illus. Barrett, Reginald & Craig, Rose, photos by. (Illus.). 27p. (Orig.). (ps-k). 1987. pap. 6.50 (ISBN 0-912511-09-5). Lawrence Science.

Epstein, Sam & Epstein, Beryl. Bugs for Dinner? Gaffney-Kessell, Walter, illus. LC 88-26654. 48p. (gr. 1-5). 1989. 12.95 (ISBN 0-02-733501-1, Mcmillan Child Bk). Macmillan Child Grp.

Flegg, Jim. Animal Movement. (Illus.). 32p. (gr. 4-6). 1991. PLB 11.90 (ISBN 1-878137-22-0). Newington.

Fortman, Jan. Creatures of Mystery. LC 77-24705. (Illus.). 48p. (gr. 4 up). 1983. PLB 17.32 (ISBN 0-8172-1063-6); pap. 9.27 (ISBN 0-8172-2157-3). Raintree Pubs.

Foster, Susan Q. The Humming Bird among the Flowers. Oxford Scientific Films Ser., photos by. LC 89-31912. (Illus.). 32p. (gr. 4-6). 1989. PLB 10.95 (ISBN 0-8368-0115-6). Gareth Stevens Inc.

Freedman, Russell. Animal Superstars: Biggest, Strongest, Fastest, Smartest. (Illus.). 112p. (gr. 5 up). 1984. pap. 5.95 (ISBN 0-13-037615-9). P-H.

—Can Bears Predict Earthquakes? Unsolved Mysteries of Animal Behavior. (Illus.). 96p. (gr. 5 up). 1982. 10.95 (ISBN 0-13-114009-4). P-H.

—When Winter Comes. Johnson, Pamela, illus. LC 80-22831. (gr. 1-3). 1981. 10.95 (ISBN 0-525-42583-7, DCB). Dutton Child Bks.

Gattis, L. S., III. Animal Tracking for Pathfinders: A Basic Youth Enrichment Skill Honor Packet. (Illus.). 26p. (Orig.). (gr. 5 up). 1989. pap. 5.00 tchr's. ed. (ISBN 0-936241-48-9). Cheetah Pub.

Getting to Know Animals. 24p. (Orig.). (ps). pap. 3.95 (ISBN 0-8431-3138-1); Little Q Answer Wand 7.00 (ISBN 0-318-39951-2). Price Stern.

Glass, Marvin. All Kinds of Weather. Glass, Marvin, illus. 12p. (gr. 2-4). 1990. bds. 3.95 (ISBN 1-878624-01-6). McClanahan Bk.

Goaman. Animal World. Quinn, David, illus. 32p. (gr. 6up). 1984. 13.96 (ISBN 0-88110-168-0); PLB 5.95 (ISBN 0-86020-751-X). EDC.

Green, Carl R. & Sanford, William R. The Badger. LC 85-19486. (Illus.). 48p. (gr. 4-5). 1986. PLB 10.95 (ISBN 0-89686-290-9, Crestwood Hse). Macmillan Child Grp.

—The Hyena. LC 88-5876. (Illus.). 48p. (gr. 5-6). 1988. PLB 10.95 (ISBN 0-89686-384-0, Crestwood Hse). Macmillan Child Grp.

Hamsa, Bobbie. Animal Babies. Dunnington, Tom, illus. LC 84-27459. 32p. (ps-2). 1985. lib. bdg. 11.93 (ISBN 0-516-02066-8); pap. 2.95 (ISBN 0-516-42066-6). Childrens.

Harrar, George & Harrar, Linda. Signs of the Apes, Songs of the Whales. (Illus.). (gr. 3 up). 1989. pap. 14.95 (ISBN 0-671-67748-9); pap. 5.95 (ISBN 0-671-67767-5). S&S Trade.

Harrison, Virginia. The World of Humming Birds. Oxford Scientific Films Staff, photos by. LC 89-31913. (Illus.). 32p. (gr. 2-3). 1989. PLB 10.95 (ISBN 0-8368-0140-7). Gareth Stevens Inc.

—The World of Snakes. Oxford Scientific Films Staff, photos by. LC 89-4634. (Illus.). 32p. (gr. 2-3). 1989. PLB 10.95 (ISBN 0-8368-0143-1). Gareth Stevens Inc.

Henry, Marguerite. Marguerite Henry's All About Horses. Osborne, M., illus. (gr. 4-8). 1967. (Random Juv). Random.

Herberman, Ethan. The City Kid's Field Guide. (gr. 3 up). 1989. pap. 14.95 (ISBN 0-671-67749-7); pap. 5.95 (ISBN 0-671-67746-2). S&S Trade.

Hess, Lilo. Time for Ferrets. LC 87-9765. (Illus.). 48p. (gr. 3-6). 1987. 12.95 (ISBN 0-684-18788-4, Scribners Young Read). Macmillan Child Grp.

Hirschland, Roger. How Animals Care for Their Babies. Crump, Donald J., ed. (Illus.). 32p. (ps-3). 1987. Set. 10.95 (ISBN 0-87044-678-9); Set. lib. bdg. 12.95 (ISBN 0-685-17641-X). Natl Geog.

Hornblow, Leonora & Hornblow, Arthur. Animals Do the Strangest Things. Frith, Michael K., illus. (gr. 2-6). 1965. 5.95 (ISBN 0-394-80056-7, Random Juv); lib. bdg. 8.99 (ISBN 0-394-90056-1). Random.

—Animals Do the Strangest Things. Kohler, Keith, illus. LC 88-37710. 64p. (gr. 2-4). 1990. lib. bdg. 6.99 (ISBN 0-394-94308-2); pap. 3.95 (ISBN 0-394-84308-8). Random.

Horton, et al. Amazing Fact Book of Animals. (Illus.). 32p. 1987. 11.95 (ISBN 0-685-23221-2) (ISBN 0-685-23222-0). Creative Ed.

Jarrell, Randall. The Animal Family. Sendak, Maurice, illus. LC 65-20659. 192p. (gr. 1 up). 1987. 12.95 (ISBN 0-685-17591-X); pap. 5.95 (ISBN 0-394-88964-9). Knopf.

Kipling, Rudyard. How the Leopard Got His Spots. Loestoeter, Lori, illus. LC 89-31374. (ps up). 1989. 14.95 (ISBN 0-88708-111-8, Rabbit Ears); book & cassette package 19.95 (ISBN 0-88708-112-6). Picture Bk Studio.

Koebner, Linda. For Kids Who Love Animals: A Guide to Sharing the Planet. (Illus.). 150p. (Orig.). (gr. 2-7). 1991. pap. 6.95 (ISBN 1-879326-03-5). Living Planet Pr.

Kohl, Judith & Kohl, Herbert. The View from the Oak. Bayless, Roger, illus. 112p. (gr. 5 up). 1988. 13.95 (ISBN 0-316-50137-9). Little.

Kostyal, Karen. Raccoons. Crump, Donald J., ed. (Illus.). 32p. (ps-3). 1987. Set. 10.95 (ISBN 0-87044-677-0); Set. lib. bdg. 12.95 (ISBN 0-87044-682-7). Natl Geog.

Kudlinski, Kathleen V. Animal Tracks & Traces. Morgan, Mary, illus. 32p. (gr. 1 up). 1991. 12.95 (ISBN 0-531-15185-9). Watts.

Kuskin, Karla. Roar & More. LC 56-8138. (Illus.). 32p. (ps-3). 1977. pap. 1.95 (ISBN 0-06-443019-7, Trophy). HarpC Child Bks.

Lavine, Sigmund A. Wonders of Badgers. 1985. 10.95 (ISBN 0-396-08581-4, Putnam). Putnam Pub Group.

Lesser, Carolyn. The Goodnight Circle. Cauley, Lorinda B., illus. LC 84-4501. (ps-3). 1984. 14.95 (ISBN 0-15-232158-6, HJ). HarBraceJ.

Linley, Mike. The Snake in the Grass. Oxford Scientific Films Staff, photos by. LC 89-4621. (Illus.). 32p. (gr. 4-6). 1989. PLB 10.95 (ISBN 0-8368-0118-0). Gareth Stevens Inc.

Linsenmaier, Walter. Wonders of Nature. Linsenmaier, Walter, illus. LC 78-62133. 32p. (ps-3). 1980. (Random Juv). Random.

McCauley, Jane. Africa's Animal Giants. Crump, Donald J., ed. (Illus.). 32p. (ps-3). 1987. Set 10.95 (ISBN 0-87044-680-0); lib. bdg. 12.95 Set (ISBN 0-87044-685-1). Natl Geog.

McCauley, Jane R. Ways Animals Sleep, 4 vols. LC 83-13189. 32p. (ps-3). 1983. Set. 10.95 (ISBN 0-87044-489-1); PLB 12.95 (ISBN 0-87044-494-8). Natl Geog.

McClung, Robert M. All about Animals & Their Young. (Illus.). (gr. 4-6). 1964. (Random Juv). Random.

McGrath, Susan. How Animals Talk, 4 vols, No. 3. Crump, Donald J., ed. (Illus.). 32p. (ps-3). 1987. Set. 10.95 (ISBN 0-87044-679-7); Set. lib. bdg. 12.95 (ISBN 0-685-17642-8). Natl Geog.

Mattioli, Massimo, illus. Animalisms One. 96p. (ps-2). 1976. pap. 2.50 (ISBN 0-85953-059-0, Pub. by Child's Play England). Childs Play.

Mimicry & Camouflage. 64p. (gr. 5 up). 1988. 14.95 (ISBN 0-8160-1657-7). Facts On File.

Moncure, Jane B. Night Animals: Wake-Up, Little Owl! Halverson, Lydia, illus. LC 89-71173. 32p. (ps-2). 1990. lib. bdg. 11.97 (ISBN 0-89565-568-3). Childs World.

Morris, Dean. Dinosaurs & Other First Animal. (ps-3). 1990. pap. 11.99 (ISBN 0-8172-3231-1). Raintree Pubs.

—Dinosaurs & Other First Animals. LC 87-16670. (Illus.). 48p. (gr. 2-6). 1987. PLB 17.32 (ISBN 0-8172-3206-0). Raintree Pubs.

—Endangered Animals. rev. ed. LC 87-20459. (Illus.). 48p. (gr. 2-6). 1987. PLB 17.32 (ISBN 0-8172-3207-9). Raintree Pubs.

Palazzo, Tony & Fox, Robin. Passel of Possums. Palazzo, Tony, illus. (gr. k-3). 1968. PLB 11.95 (ISBN 0-87460-099-5). Lion Bks.

Parker, Steve. Camouflage. (Illus.). 32p. (gr. 5-8). 1991. PLB 11.90 (ISBN 0-531-17313-5, Gloucester Pr). Watts.

Pearce, Q. L. Animal Footnotes. Bettoli, Delana, illus. 40p. (gr. k-3). 1991. lib. bdg. 12.98 (ISBN 0-671-69116-3); pap. 8.95 (ISBN 0-671-69117-1). Silver Pr.

Peters, Sharon. Animals at Night. Harvey, Paul, illus. LC 82-19226. 32p. (gr. k-2). 1982. lib. bdg. 10.89 (ISBN 0-89375-903-1); pap. 2.95 (ISBN 0-8167-1477-0). Troll Assocs.

Pope, Joyce. Do Animals Dream? Children's Questions about Animals Most Often Asked of the Natural History Museum. LC 86-40029. (Illus.). 96p. 1986. pap. 16.95 (ISBN 0-670-81233-1). Viking Child Bks.

—Kenneth Lilly's Animals. Lilly, Kenneth, illus. LC 87-31147. 96p. (gr. 3 up). 1988. 16.95 (ISBN 0-688-07696-3). Lothrop.

Powzyk, Joyce. Animal Camouflage: A Closer Look. Powzyk, Joyce, illus. LC 89-9848. (gr. 2-9). 1990. 15.95 (ISBN 0-02-774980-0, Bradbury Pr). Macmillan Child Grp.

Pragoff, Fiona. What Color? LC 87-645. (Illus.). 20p. (gr. k-3). 1987. pap. 6.95 (ISBN 0-385-24173-9). Doubleday.

Pringle, Laurence. Animals at Play. LC 85-901. (Illus.). 80p. (gr. 3-7). 1985. 17.95 (ISBN 0-15-203554-0, HJ). HarBraceJ.

Quiri, Patricia R. Metamorphosis. (Illus.). 64p. (gr. 5-8). 1991. PLB 11.90 (ISBN 0-531-20042-6). Watts.

Redmond, Ian. The Elephant in the Bush. Oxford Scientific Films Staff, photos by. LC 89-11297. (Illus.). 32p. (gr. 4-6). 1989. PLB 10.95 (ISBN 0-8368-0116-4). Gareth Stevens Inc.

Rosenthal, Mark. Predators. LC 83-7512. (Illus.). 48p. (gr. k-4). 1983. PLB 14.60 (ISBN 0-516-01707-1). Childrens.

Rowland-Entwistle, Theodore. Animal Homes. Allen, Graham, et al, illus. LC 86-26145. 24p. (gr. 2-5). 1987. lib. bdg. 5.99 (ISBN 0-394-98974-0, Random Juv); (BYR). Random.

—Animal Journeys. Allen, Graham, illus. LC 87-4789. 24p. (gr. 2-5). 1987. lib. bdg. 5.99 (ISBN 0-394-99212-1, Random Juv); pap. 2.95 (ISBN 0-394-89212-7, Random Juv). Random.

Schmid, Eleonore. Farm Animals. Schmid, Eleonore, illus. LC 85-63302. 12p. (ps-k). 1986. 3.95 (ISBN 1-55858-045-X). North-South Bks NYC.

Selsam, Millicent E. Hidden Animals. LC 72-85020. (Illus.). 64p. (gr. k-3). 1969. PLB 9.89 (ISBN 0-06-025282-0). HarpC Child Bks.

—How to Be a Nature Detective. Keats, Ezra J., illus. LC 66-15947. 48p. (gr. 1-5). 1966. PLB 13.89 (ISBN 0-06-025301-0). HarpC Child Bks.

—Toda Clase de Bebes. De Kohen, Clara I., tr. Shimin, Symeon, illus. (SPA.). 40p. (gr. k-3). 1980. pap. 1.95 (ISBN 0-590-31214-6). Scholastic Inc.

Selsam, Millicent E. & Hunt, Joyce. A First Look at Seals, Sea Lions, & Walruses. Springer, Harriett, illus. LC 87-29491. 36p. (ps-3). 1988. pap. 10.95 (ISBN 0-8027-6787-7); pap. text ed. 11.85 (ISBN 0-8027-6788-5). Walker & Co.

Seuling, Barbara. Elephants Can't Jump: And Other Freaky Facts about Animals. LC 84-10219. (Illus.). 96p. (gr. 3-7). 1985. 11.95 (ISBN 0-525-67155-2, Lodestar Bks). Dutton Child Bks.

Seymour, Simon. Strange Creatures. LC 81-4433. (Illus.). 48p. (gr. 3-7). 1984. 11.95 (ISBN 0-02-782860-3, Four Winds). Macmillan Child Grp.

Silver, Donald M. The Animal World: From Single-Cell Creatures to Giants of the Land & Sea. Wynne, Patricia, illus. LC 86-3894. 112p. (gr. 5 up). 1987. lib. bdg. 9.99 (ISBN 0-394-96650-3, Random Juv); pap. 8.95 (ISBN 0-394-86650-9, BYR). Random.

Taylor, Kim. Too Clever to See. (gr. 2-5). 1991. 9.95 (ISBN 0-385-30216-9); PLB 10.99 (ISBN 0-385-30217-7). Delacorte.

Tee-Van, Helen D. Small Mammals Are Where You Find Them. (Illus.). (gr. 3-7). 1967. lib. bdg. 5.99 (ISBN 0-394-91643-3). Knopf.

Tison, Annette & Taylor, Talus. Amazing Animal Builders. Tison, Annette & Taylor, Talus, illus. 40p. (Orig.). (gr. 2-6). 1989. pap. 5.95 (ISBN 0-448-21551-9, G&D). Putnam Pub Group.

—Animals Large & Small. Tison, Annette & Taylor, Talus, illus. 40p. (Orig.). (gr. 2-6). 1989. pap. 5.95 (ISBN 0-448-21552-7, G&D). Putnam Pub Group.

—The Big Book of Amazing Animal Behavior. Tison, Annette & Taylor, Talus, illus. 96p. (gr. 2-5). 1987. 9.95 (ISBN 0-448-18998-4, G&D). Putnam Pub Group.

Tomb, Howard. Living Monsters: The World's Most Dangerous Animals. Marchesi, Stephen, illus. 48p. (gr. 3-7). 1990. PLB 9.95 (ISBN 0-671-69017-5). S&S Trade.

Venino, Suzanne. Animals Helping People. Crump, Donald J., ed. LC 83-13184. 32p. (ps-3). 1983. 10.95 set (ISBN 0-87044-488-3); lib. bdg. 12.95 (ISBN 0-87044-493-X). Natl Geog.

Waldrop, Victor H., ed. Endangered Animals. Langford, Alton, illus. LC 89-12099. 96p. (gr. 2-7). 1989. 14.95 (ISBN 0-945051-09-3, 19421); PLB 17.95 (ISBN 0-945051-11-5, 19422). Natl Wildlife.

—What Do Animals See, Hear, Smell, & Feel? Pidgeon, Jean, illus. Hair, Jay D., intro. by. LC 90-6171. (Illus.). 96p. (gr. 2-7). 1990. 14.95 (ISBN 0-945051-23-9, 19425); PLB 17.95 (ISBN 0-945051-24-7, 19426). Natl Wildlife.

Wildlife Education, Ltd. Staff. Night Animals. Stuart, Walter, illus. 20p. (Orig.). (gr. 5 up). 1984. pap. 2.25 (ISBN 0-937934-26-7). Wildlife Educ.

Zapun, Simone. Wonderful Wild Animals. Hildebrandt, Greg & Hildebrandt, Tim, illus. 64p. (ps-3). 1989. 9.95 (ISBN 0-448-09078-3, G&D). Putnam Pub Group.

Ziefert, Harriet. Dark Night, Sleepy Night. Baruffi, Andrea, illus. LC 87-25759. 32p. (Orig.). (ps-3). 1988. pap. 3.50 (ISBN 0-14-050812-0, Puffin). Puffin Bks.

ANIMALS–HIBERNATION

Bird, E. J. How Do Bears Sleep? Bird, E. J., illus. 32p. (ps-3). pap. 5.95 (ISBN 0-87614-522-5). Carolrhoda Bks.

Brimner, Larry D. Animals That Hibernate. (Illus.). 64p. (gr. 3-6). 1991. PLB 11.90 (ISBN 0-531-20018-3). Watts.

Facklam, Margery. Do Not Disturb: The Mysteries of Animal Hibernation & Sleep. Johnson, Pamela, illus. LC 88-10921. 48p. (gr. 3-6). 1989. 12.95 (ISBN 0-316-27379-1). Little.

Stidworthy, John. Hibernation. (Illus.). 32p. (gr. 5-8). 1991. PLB 11.90 (ISBN 0-531-17309-7, Gloucester Pr). Watts.

ANIMALS–INFANCY

Baby Animals. (Illus.). (ps-1). 1971. bds. 2.50 (ISBN 0-448-02682-1, G&D). Putnam Pub Group.

Baby Animals. 32p. (Orig.). 1984. pap. 1.25 (ISBN 0-8431-1512-2). Price Stern.

Baby Animals. (Illus.). (gr. 1-4). 3.50 (ISBN 0-7214-0378-6). Ladybird Bks.

Baby Animals & Their Mothers. 1987. 1.95 (ISBN 0-8351-1707-3). China Bks.

Baby Animals at Home. (Illus.). (ps-k). bds. 3.50 (ISBN 0-7214-9533-8). Ladybird Bks.

Baby Farm Animals. (Illus.). (ps). pap. 1.25 (ISBN 0-7214-9548-6). Ladybird Bks.

Baby Zoo Animals. (Illus.). 32p. (ps-1). 1986. pap. 1.25 (ISBN 0-8431-1521-1). Price Stern.

Brown, Margaret W. Baby Animals. LC 88-18481. (Illus.). 32p. (ps-1). 1989. Repr. of 1941 ed. 10.95 (ISBN 0-394-82040-1); lib. bdg. 11.99 (ISBN 0-394-92040-6). Random.

Burton, Jane. Baby Animals Growing Up, 12 vols. Burton, Jane, illus. 384p. (gr. 2-3). 1989. Set. PLB 131.40 (ISBN 0-8368-0201-2). Gareth Stevens Inc.

Dickinson, Rebecca. Animal Babies. Bonforte, Lisa, illus. LC 87-81765. 22p. (ps). 1988. write for info. (ISBN 0-307-12116-X, Pub. by Golden Bks). Western Pub.

Freedman, Russell. Farm Babies. LC 81-2898. (Illus.). 40p. (gr. k-3). 1981. reinforced bdg. 12.95 (ISBN 0-8234-0426-9). Holiday.

Freschet, Berniece. Racoon Baby. Arnosky, James, illus. LC 83-4634. 48p. (gr. 1-8). 1984. PLB 6.99 (ISBN 0-399-61149-5, Putnam). Putnam Pub Group.

—Wood Duck Baby. Arnosky, James, illus. 48p. (gr. 1-3). 1983. pap. 6.99 (ISBN 0-399-61191-6, Putnam). Putnam Pub Group.

Fujikawa, Gyo, illus. Baby Animals. (ps). 1963. bds. 3.95 (ISBN 0-448-03083-7, G&D). Putnam Pub Group.

Hirschland, Roger. How Animals Care for Their Babies. Crump, Donald J., ed. (Illus.). 32p. (ps-3). 1987. Set. 10.95 (ISBN 0-87044-678-9); Set. lib. bdg. 12.95 (ISBN 0-685-17641-X). Natl Geog.

Kalman, Bobbie. Animal Babies. (Illus.). 56p. (gr. 3-4). 1987. 15.95 (ISBN 0-86505-166-6); pap. 7.95 (ISBN 0-86505-186-0). Crabtree Pub Co.
ANIMAL BABIES, one of the four superbly illustrated books in the NORTH AMERICAN WILDLIFE SERIES is a favorite with all children. ANIMAL BABIES shows, from birth, the amazing struggle of animal young to escape their predators & survive in their changing environment. This book explores characteristics common to all mammal babies in their stages of life. The other books in the series are FOREST MAMMALS, OWLS, & BIRDS AT MY FEEDER. These big, beautiful, full-color books feature the art of internationally famous wildlife artist Glen Loates. The superb illustrations delight children while the engaging text encourages them to discover a new understanding of the exciting world of wildlife.
Publisher Provided Annotation.

Kuchalla, Susan. Baby Animals. Snyder, Joel, illus. LC 81-11434. 32p. (gr. k-2). 1982. lib. bdg. 10.89 (ISBN 0-89375-666-0); pap. 2.95 (ISBN 0-89375-667-9). Troll Assocs.

McDonnell, Janet. Baby Animals: Safe & Sound. Hohag, Linda, illus. LC 89-23978. 32p. (ps-2). 1990. lib. bdg. 11.97 (ISBN 0-89565-554-3). Childs World.

McNaught, Harry. Baby Animals. McNaught, Harry, illus. LC 75-36462. 14p. (ps-1). 1976. Repr. of 1976 ed. bds. 3.95 (ISBN 0-394-83241-8, Random Juv). Random.

Michel, Anna. Little Wild Chimpanzee. Parnall, Peter & Parnall, Virginia, illus. LC 77-20986. (gr. 1-4). 1978. lib. bdg. 7.99 (ISBN 0-394-93716-3). Pantheon.

Penny, Malcolm. Animals & Their Young. (Illus.). 32p. (gr. 1-6). 1987. lib. bdg. 8.99 (ISBN 0-531-18124-3, Pub. by Bookwright Pr). Watts.

Podendorf, Illa. Baby Animals. LC 81-9938. (Illus.). 48p. (gr. k-4). 1981. PLB 14.60 (ISBN 0-516-01605-9); pap. 4.95 (ISBN 0-516-41605-7). Childrens.

Roe, Richard. Baby Animals. Roe, Richard, illus. LC 85-2223. 24p. (ps-1). 1985. 3.95 (ISBN 0-394-86956-7, Random Juv). Random.

Warren, Elizabeth. I Can Read About Baby Animals. LC 74-24879. (Illus.). (gr. 1-2). 1975. pap. 1.95 (ISBN 0-89375-060-3). Troll Assocs.

Wildlife Education, Ltd. Staff. Baby Animals. (Illus.). 20p. (Orig.). (gr. 5 up). 1981. pap. 2.25 (ISBN 0-937934-06-2). Wildlife Educ.

ANIMALS–LANGUAGE

see Animal Communication

ANIMALS–LEGENDS

see Animals–Fiction

ANIMALS–MIGRATION

see also names of animals with the subdivision Migration, e.g. Birds–Migration

Flegg, Jim. Animal Travelers. (Illus.). 32p. (gr. 4-6). 1991. PLB 11.90 (ISBN 1-878137-07-7). Newington.

McDonnell, Janet. Animal Migration. LC 88-36640. (Illus.). 48p. (gr. 2-6). 1989. PLB 10.95 (ISBN 0-89565-514-4); pap. 6.96 (ISBN 0-89565-532-2). Childs World.

Nielsen, Nancy J. Animal Migration. (Illus.). 64p. (gr. 5-8). 1991. PLB 11.90 (ISBN 0-531-20044-2). Watts.

Sanders, John. All about Animal Migrations. Burns, Ray, illus. LC 83-6630. 32p. (gr. 3-6). 1984. PLB 10.59 (ISBN 0-89375-977-5); pap. text ed. 2.95 (ISBN 0-89375-978-3). Troll Assocs.

ANIMALS–PHOTOGRAPHY

see Photography of Animals

ANIMALS–PICTURES, ILLUSTRATIONS, ETC.

Animal Shape Board Book: The Circus Clown. 1988. 1.98 (ISBN 0-671-09437-8). S&S Trade.

Babson, Jane F. Babson's Bestiary. Babson, Jane F., illus. LC 90-71155. 32p. (ps-4). 1991. casebound 10.95g (ISBN 0-940787-02-4). Winstead Pr.
Second in a learning to read series for children & adults. Illustrated with original art, writing designed to stimulate interest, curiosity & intellectual skills. Thought-provoking. Acid-free paper, Special discounts to libraries, literacy programs. "The art book offers a superior presentation... includes some fun animal rhymes within the alphabet form... intriguing, unusual art. --THE MIDWEST BOOK REVIEW. "Attractive alphabet primer with its well-executed illustrations, a fun & funny book about animals." --THE BLOOMSBURY REVIEW.
Publisher Provided Annotation.

Baby Animals. (Illus.). (gr. 1-4). 3.50 (ISBN 0-7214-0378-6). Ladybird Bks.

Baby Animals at Home. (Illus.). (ps-k). bds. 3.50 (ISBN 0-7214-9533-8). Ladybird Bks.

Barrett, Judi. Animals Should Definitely Not Wear Clothing. Barrett, Ron, illus. 32p. (gr. k-3). 1990. incl. cass. 19.95 (ISBN 0-87499-147-1); pap. 12.95 incl. cass. (ISBN 0-87488-146-3); Set; incl. 4 bks., cass., & guide. pap. 27.95 (ISBN 0-87499-148-X). Live Oak Media.

Burton, Marilee R. Tail Toes Eyes Ears Nose. Burton, Marilee R., illus. LC 87-33276. 32p. (ps-1). 1988. 11. 95 (ISBN 0-06-020873-2); PLB 11.89 (ISBN 0-06-020874-0). HarpC Child Bks.

Ching, Patrick. Exotic Animals in Hawaii. Ching, Patrick, illus. 32p. (Orig.). (ps-6). 1988. pap. 3.95 (ISBN 0-935848-56-8). Bess Pr.

—Native Animals of Hawaii. Ching, Patrick, illus. 32p. (Orig.). (ps-6). 1988. pap. 3.95 (ISBN 0-935848-55-X). Bess Pr.

Cober, Alan E. Cober's Choice. LC 79-11882. (ps up). 1979. 10.95 (ISBN 0-525-28065-0, DCB). Dutton Child Bks.

Cole, Joanna. Large As Life Animals in Beautiful Life-Size Paintings. Lilly, Kenneth, illus. LC 89-15391. 56p. (ps-5). 1990. 14.95 (ISBN 0-679-80459-5). Knopf.

Crump, Donald J., ed. Animals Showing Off. (Illus.). (ps-5). 1988. Set. 19.95 (ISBN 0-685-31760-9). Natl Geog.

Day, O. M. ABC's of Bugs & Beasts. Day, O. M., illus. 31p. (Orig.). (gr. 3-12). 1991. pap. 11.95 (ISBN 0-9629795-1-1). Klar-Iden Pub.
ABC's of Bugs & Beasts is primarily a picture book with colorful & comical illustrations of insects & animals. Critics have called O. M. Day's book a work of art with depth & value above mere "read-to-me" entertainment. The book is meant to instill in children the concern for an interest in all living creatures, & to stimulate a desire for reading. O. M. Day specifically chose the insect to show that even they have a design in nature's plan, be it for good or for bad. Although focused to the younger child, older children also should have an interest. Various zoos find this publication appealing as well & are ordering. With the combination of the amusing illustrations & alphabet limericks, ABC's of Bugs & Beasts informs & entertains children. Klar-Iden, the publisher of ABC's of Bugs & Beasts is committed to publish only a small number of books each year, because it is their desire to produce quality rather than quantity. O. M. Day's book met their criteria. To order please contact Klar-Iden Publishing, 6963 Douglas Boulevard, Box #115, Granite Bay, CA 95661 or call (415) 856-1059.
Publisher Provided Annotation.

Eichenberg, Fritz. Ape in a Cape: An Alphabet of Odd Animals. Eichenberg, Fritz, illus. LC 52-6908. (ps-3). 1952. 12.95 (ISBN 0-15-203722-5, HJ). HarBraceJ.

Fisher, Esther. Animals A to Z: The Perfect Book for Children. (Illus.). 48p. 1989. 7.95 (ISBN 0-8062-3588-8). Carlton.

Gardner, Beau. Guess What? LC 85-242. (Illus.). 48p. (ps-3). 1985. 13.95 (ISBN 0-688-04982-6); PLB 13.88 (ISBN 0-688-04983-4). Lothrop.

Kuzmier, Kerrie & McCann, Jennifer. Manatees & Dugongs: A Coloring Book in English & Spanish. Inchaustequi, Sixto, tr. Beath, Mary, illus. (ENG & SPA.). 28p. (Orig.). (gr. 3-6). 1991. pap. text ed. 4.00 (ISBN 0-685-39509-X). Ctr Marine Cnsrv.

Looking at Animals. (Illus.). (ps). 3.50 (ISBN 0-7214-0787-0). Ladybird Bks.

McCay, William. Animals in Danger: A Pop-up Book. Mosley, Keith, illus. 12p. (gr. 1-7). 1990. pap. 12.95 (ISBN 0-689-71408-4, Aladdin). Macmillan Child Grp.

McMillan, Mary. God's ABC Zoo. Grossman, Dan, illus. 48p. (ps-1). 1987. pap. 6.95 (ISBN 0-86653-405-9, SS1802). Good Apple.

My First Book of Animals. (Illus.). 32p. (ps). 1985. 3.95 (ISBN 0-394-87688-1). Random.

Picture Book of Animals. (Illus.). (ps). 3.50 (ISBN 0-7214-0751-X). Ladybird Bks.

San Diego Zoological Society Staff, illus. Families. 12p. (ps-2). 1983. board 3.50 (ISBN 0-89346-218-7). Heian Intl.

—Mothers & Babies. 12p. (ps-2). 1983. board 3.50 (ISBN 0-89346-216-0). Heian Intl.

—Piggyback & Peek-a-Boo. 12p. (ps-2). 1983. board 3.50 (ISBN 0-89346-217-9). Heian Intl.

—A Visit to the Zoo. 12p. (ps-2). 1983. board 3.50 (ISBN 0-89346-219-5). Heian Intl.

Sterne, Noelle. Tyrannosaurus Wrecks. Chess, Victoria, illus. LC 78-22499. 32p. (gr. 1-4). 1983. pap. 4.95 (ISBN 0-06-443043-X, Trophy). HarpC Child Bks.

Teddies & Friends. (Illus.). 32p. (gr. 1-6). 1987. 2.50 (ISBN 0-87406-415-5, 46-19146-4). Willowisp Pr.

Truitt, Gloria A. Animals. Creative Co., illus. 16p. (Orig.). (ps-4). 1982. pap. 0.98 (ISBN 0-87239-597-9, 2384). Standard Pub.

Wild, Anne. Animal Mobiles. (Illus.). 28p. (Orig.). (gr. 4 up). 1985. pap. 4.95 (ISBN 0-317-14829-X). Parkwest Pubns.

—Dinosaur Mobiles. (Illus.). 28p. (Orig.). (gr. 4 up). 1985. pap. 4.95 (ISBN 0-906212-18-9). Parkwest Pubns.

—Dragon Mobiles. (Illus.). 28p. (Orig.). (gr. 4 up). 1985. pap. 4.95 (ISBN 0-906212-10-3). Parkwest Pubns.

Wildsmith, Brian. Animal Tricks. Wildsmith, Brian, illus. (ps-3). 1981. 9.95 (ISBN 0-19-279743-3). Oxford U Pr.

Woggon, Guillermo. Animales Que Dios Creo. Cranberry, Nola, tr. from ENG. (SPA., Illus.). 16p. (gr. 1-3). 1987. pap. 1.40 (ISBN 0-311-38560-5). Casa Bautista.

ANIMALS–POETRY

Amery, H., compiled by. The Usborne Book of Animal Poems. (Illus.). 32p. (gr. 2-6). 1990. lib. bdg. 13.96 (ISBN 0-88110-445-0, Usborne); pap. 5.95 (ISBN 0-7460-0442-7, Usborne). EDC.

Babson, Jane F. Babson's Bestiary. Babson, Jane F., illus. LC 90-71155. 32p. (ps-4). 1991. casebound 10.95g (ISBN 0-940787-02-4). Winstead Pr.
Second in a learning to read series for children & adults. Illustrated with original art, writing designed to stimulate interest, curiosity & intellectual skills. Thought-provoking. Acid-free paper, Special discounts to libraries, literacy programs. "The art book offers a superior presentation... includes some fun animal rhymes within the alphabet form... intriguing, unusual art. --THE MIDWEST BOOK REVIEW. "Attractive alphabet primer with its well-executed illustrations, a fun & funny book about animals." -- THE BLOOMSBURY REVIEW.
Publisher Provided Annotation.

Boden, Arthur & Woodside, John. Boden's Beasts. Boden, Art, illus. (gr. 1-5). 1964. 8.95 (ISBN 0-8392-3045-1). Astor-Honor.

Clark, Emma C. Never Saw a Purple Cow. (ps-3). 1991. 18.95 (ISBN 0-316-14500-9). Little.

Cole, William E., ed. An Arkful of Animals: Poems for the Very Young. Munsinger, Lynn, illus. 128p. (gr. 3-7). 1978. 13.95 (ISBN 0-395-27205-X). HM.

Gerry the Giraffe. (Illus.). (ps). 3.50 (ISBN 0-7214-0754-4). Ladybird Bks.

Gill, Shelley R. Alaska Mother Goose. Cartwright, Shannon, illus. 36p. (Orig.). (gr. k-6). 1987. pap. 7.95 (ISBN 0-934007-02-0). Paws Four Pub.

Hoberman, Mary Ann. A Fine Fat Pig: And Other Animal Poems. Zeldis, Malcah, illus. LC 90-37403. 32p. (ps-2). 1991. 14.95 (ISBN 0-06-022425-8); PLB 14.89 (ISBN 0-06-022426-6). HarpC Child Bks.

Kitchen, Bert. Gorilla-Chinchilla: And Other Animal Rhymes. Fogelman, Phyllis J., ed. Kitchen, Bert, illus. LC 89-16851. 32p. (ps up). 1990. 13.95 (ISBN 0-8037-0770-3); PLB 13.89 (ISBN 0-8037-0771-1). Dial Bks Young.

Lear, Edward. The Owl & the Pussy-Cat. Voce, Louise, illus. LC 90-39673. 32p. (ps up). 1991. 13.95 (ISBN 0-688-09536-4); PLB 13.88 (ISBN 0-688-09537-2). Lothrop.

Lewis, Patrick. A Hippopotamusn't: And Other Animal Verses. Fogelman, Phyllis J., ed. Chess, Victoria, illus. LC 87-24579. 40p. (ps-3). 1990. 12.95 (ISBN 0-8037-0518-2); PLB 12.89 (ISBN 0-8037-0519-0). Dial Bks Young.

Marsh, James. Bizarre Birds & Beasts: Animal Verses. 1991. 12.95 (ISBN 0-8037-1046-1). Dial Bks Young.

Nister, Ernest. Animal Playmates. (Illus.). 10p. 1990. 5.95 (ISBN 0-399-21957-9, Philomel Bks). Putnam Pub Group.

Prelutsky, Jack. Zoo Doings: Animal Poems. Zelinsky, Paul O., illus. LC 82-11996. 80p. (gr. 1-3). 1983. 11. 95 (ISBN 0-688-01782-7); PLB 11.88 (ISBN 0-688-01784-3). Greenwillow.

Rosenberg, Amye & Chamberlain, Margaret, illus. My Book of Animal Rhymes. (ps-2). 3.95 (ISBN 0-7214-5106-3). Ladybird Bks.

Ryder, Joanne. Mockingbird Morning. Nolan, Dennis, illus. LC 88-21305. 32p. (gr. k-3). 1989. 13.95 (ISBN 0-02-777961-0, Four Winds). Macmillan Child Grp.

Yolen, Jane. Ring of Earth: A Child's Book of Seasons. Wallner, John, illus. LC 86-4800. 32p. (ps-3). 1986. 14.95 (ISBN 0-15-267140-4, HJ). HarBraceJ.

ANIMALS–PROTECTION

see Animals–Treatment

ANIMALS–SONGS AND MUSIC

Langstaff, John & Rojankovsky, Feodor. Frog Went A-Courtin' Rojankovsky, Feodor, illus. LC 55-5237. (gr. k-3). 1955. 14.95 (ISBN 0-15-230214-X, HJ). HarBraceJ.

—Over in the Meadow. Rojankovsky, Feodor, illus. LC 57-8587. (gr. k-3). 1957. 14.95 (ISBN 0-15-258854-X, HJ). HarBraceJ.

Young, Roger & Caggiano, Rosemary. The Safari. 48p. (gr. k-8). 1979. pap. 10.95 (ISBN 0-86704-006-8). Clarus Music.

ANIMALS–TRAINING

see also names of animals with the subdivision Training, e.g., Dogs–Training; Horses–Training; etc.

Duden, Jane. Animal Handlers & Trainers. LC 89-31125. (Illus.). 48p. (gr. 4 up). 1989. 10.95 (ISBN 0-89686-427-8, Crestwood Hse). Macmillan Child Grp.

ANIMALS–TREATMENT

Amaral, Anthony. Movie Horses: Their Treatment & Training. (gr. 5-7). 5.50 (ISBN 0-672-50388-3, Bobbs). Macmillan.

Barton, Miles. Animal Rights. (Illus.). 32p. (gr. 7-9). 1987. PLB 11.90 (ISBN 0-531-17045-4, Gloucester Pr). Watts.

Dolan, Edward F., Jr. Animal Rights. 144p. (gr. 7-12). 1986. PLB 12.90 (ISBN 0-531-10247-5). Watts.

Guernsey, JoAnn B. Animal Rights. LC 90-33664. (Illus.). 48p. (gr. 5-6). 1990. RSBE 10.95 (ISBN 0-89686-534-7, Crestwood Hse). Macmillan Child Grp.

Rohr, Janelle, ed. Animal Rights: Opposing Viewpoints. LC 89-2227. (Illus.). 235p. (gr. 10 up). 1989. PLB 15. 95 (ISBN 0-89908-440-0); pap. 8.95 (ISBN 0-89908-415-X). Greenhaven.

Scott, Elaine. Safe in the Spotlight: The Dawn Animal Agency & the Sanctuary for Animals. Miller, Margaret, photos by. LC 90-49677. (Illus.). 80p. (gr. 3 up). 1991. 12.95 (ISBN 0-688-08177-0); PLB 12.88 (ISBN 0-688-08178-9, Morrow Jr Bks). Morrow Jr Bks.

Steffens, Bradley. Animal Rights: Distinguishing Between Fact & Opinion. (Illus.). 32p. (gr. 3-6). 1990. PLB 8.95 (ISBN 0-89908-635-7). Greenhaven.

Watson, Mary G. Beds & Bedding. Vincer, Carole, illus. 24p. (Orig.). (gr. 3 up). 1988. pap. 7.95 (ISBN 0-901366-27-7, Pub. by Threshold Bks). Half Halt Pr.

ANIMALS, AQUATIC

see Fresh-Water Animals; Marine Animals

ANIMALS, CRUELTY TO

see Animals–Treatment

ANIMALS, DOMESTIC

see Domestic Animals

ANIMALS, EXTINCT

see Extinct Animals

ANIMALS, FICTITIOUS

see Animals, Mythical

ANIMALS, FOSSIL

see Fossils

ANIMALS, FRESH-WATER

see Fresh-Water Animals

ANIMALS, IMAGINARY

see Animals, Mythical

ANIMALS, MARINE

see Marine Animals

ANIMALS, MYTHICAL

see also names of mythical animals, e.g. Unicorn, etc.

Baskin, Leonard & Baskin, Hosie. A Book of Dragons. Baskin, Leonard, illus. LC 85-6581. 48p. (gr. 4-6). 1985. 12.95 (ISBN 0-394-86298-8). Knopf.

Bennett, Jack. The Voyage of the Lucky Dragons. 156p. (gr. 5 up). 1985. pap. 5.95 (ISBN 0-13-944158-1). P-H.

Blythe, Richard. Dragons & Other Fabulous Beasts. French, Fiona & Troughton, Joann, illus. LC 79-51211. (gr. 3-7). 1980. 5.95 (ISBN 0-448-16561-9, G&D). Putnam Pub Group.

Burgess, Thornton W. Mother West Wind's Neighbors. (gr. 5-6). 16.95 (ISBN 0-88411-786-3, Pub. by Aeonian Pr). Amereon Ltd.

Cosgrove, Stephen. Muffin Muncher. James, Robin, illus. 32p. (gr. 1-6). 1975. pap. 2.95 (ISBN 0-8431-0561-5). Price Stern.

De Goscinny, Rene. La Serpe d'Or. (gr. 7-9). 19.95 (ISBN 0-685-33971-8, FC874). French & Eur.

Fletcher, Susan. Dragon's Milk. LC 88-35059. 224p. (gr. 5 up). 1989. 14.95 (ISBN 0-689-31579-1, Atheneum Child Bk). Macmillan Child Grp.

Gaffron, Norma. Unicorns: Opposing Viewpoints. LC 89-11660. (Illus.). 112p. (gr. 3-10). 1989. PLB 13.95 (ISBN 0-89908-063-4). Greenhaven.

Gag, Wanda. The Funny Thing. Gag, Wanda, illus. (gr. 1-3). 1960. PLB 6.99 (ISBN 0-698-30097-1, Coward). Putnam Pub Group.

Gannett, Ruth S. My Father's Dragon. gift edition ed. Gannett, Ruth S., illus. LC 48-6527. 88p. (gr. 2-5). 1986. 14.95 (ISBN 0-394-88460-4, Random Juv); PLB 14.99 (ISBN 0-394-91438-4). Random.

Grahame, Kenneth. Reluctant Dragon. Shepard, Ernest H., illus. 58p. (gr. 3-6). 1953. 8.95 (ISBN 0-8234-0093-X); pap. 4.95 (ISBN 0-8234-0755-1). Holiday.

—The Reluctant Dragon. Hague, Michael, illus. LC 83-209. 48p. (gr. 4-6). 1983. 14.95 (ISBN 0-8050-1112-9). H Holt & Co.

—The Reluctant Dragon. Richardson, I. M., ed. Ekman, Marlene, illus. LC 87-10906. 32p. (gr. k-4). 1987. lib. bdg. 9.79 (ISBN 0-8167-1059-7); pap. text ed. 1.95 (ISBN 0-8167-1060-0). Troll Assocs.

Green, Michael. Unicornis: On the History & Truth of the Unicorn. 2nd ed. Green, Michael, illus. LC 87-12676. 112p. (gr. 9 up). 1988. 19.95 (ISBN 0-89471-570-4); pap. 12.95 (ISBN 0-89471-550-X). Running Pr.

Himmel, Roger J. Care of Property. new ed. Manoni, Mary H., ed. Peters, Luther J. & Ross, Connie, illus. (gr. k-3). 1978. pap. text ed. 29.95 6 bks. & 1 cass. (ISBN 0-89290-046-6); pap. text ed. 10.95 1 bk. & 1 cass. (ISBN 0-685-04634-6). Soc for Visual.

Himmel, Roger J. & Manoni, Mary H. The Big Easter Egg Hunt. Peters, Luther J. & Ross, Connie, illus. LC 72-739482. (gr. k-3). 1978. pap. text ed. 29.95 6 bks. & 1 cass. (ISBN 0-89290-039-3); pap. text ed. 10.95 1 bk. & 1 cass. (ISBN 0-685-04629-X). Soc for Visual.

Hjelm, J. Thaddeus Jones & the Dragon. LC 68-56830. (Illus.). 64p. (gr. 2-5). 1968. PLB 10.95 (ISBN 0-87783-039-8); pap. 3.94 deluxe ed. (ISBN 0-87783-110-6). Oddo.

Kelley, True. Buggly Bear's Hiccup Cure. LC 81-16903. (Illus.). 48p. (ps-3). 1982. 5.95 (ISBN 0-8193-1081-6); PLB 5.95 (ISBN 0-8193-1082-4). Parents.

Kerven, Rosalind. The Slaying of the Dragon: Tales of the Hindu Gods. (Illus.). 100p. (gr. 4 up). 1988. 10.95 (ISBN 0-233-98037-7). Andre Deutsch.

Lathrop, Dorothy B. Animals of the Bible. Fish, Helen D., selected by. Lathrop, Dorothy, illus. LC 86-46118. 68p. (ps up). 1937. 15.95 (ISBN 0-397-31536-8, Lipp Jr Bks); PLB 15.89 (ISBN 0-397-30047-6). HarpC Child Bks.

Leaf, Margaret. Eyes of the Dragon. Young, Ed, illus. LC 85-11670. 32p. (ps-2). 1987. 14.95 (ISBN 0-688-06155-9); PLB 14.88 (ISBN 0-688-06156-7). Lothrop.

Lear, Edward & Nash, Ogden. Scroobious Pip. Burkert, Nancy E., illus. LC 68-10373. (gr. 3 up). 1968. 14.95 (ISBN 0-06-023764-3); PLB 14.89 (ISBN 0-06-023765-1). HarpC Child Bks.

Leedy, Loreen. A Number of Dragons. Leedy, Loreen, illus. LC 85-730. 32p. (ps-1). 1985. 14.95g (ISBN 0-8234-0568-0). Holiday.

McHargue, Georgess. Beasts of Never. Bozzo, Frank, illus. LC 67-18651. (gr. 8 up). 1968. 5.95 (ISBN 0-672-50217-8, Bobbs). Macmillan.

Marx, Doug. Mythical Beasts. 48p. (gr. 3-4). 1991. PLB 11.95 (ISBN 1-56065-046-X). Capstone Pr.

Mayer, Mercer. Whinnie the Lovesick Dragon. Hearn, Diane D., illus. LC 85-18886. 32p. (gr. k-3). 1986. 13.95 (ISBN 0-02-765180-0, Mcmillan Child Bk). Macmillan Child Grp.

Nesbit, Edith. The Book of Dragons. (gr. 4-6). 1986. pap. 4.95 (ISBN 0-440-40696-X, Pub. by Yearling Classics). Dell.

Peet, Bill. Cyrus the Unsinkable Sea Serpent. LC 74-20646. (Illus.). 48p. (gr. k-3). 1982. 13.95 (ISBN 0-395-20272-8); pap. 4.95 (ISBN 0-395-31389-X). HM.

—How Droofus the Dragon Lost His Head. Peet, Bill, illus. LC 75-135136. 48p. (gr. k-3). 1983. 13.95 (ISBN 0-395-15085-X); pap. 4.95 (ISBN 0-395-34066-7). HM.

Rice, James. Lyn & the Fuzzy. Rice, James, illus. LC 75-19096. 40p. (gr. 2-6). 1975. 11.95 (ISBN 0-88289-087-5). Pelican.

Selsam, Millicent E. & Hunt, Joyce. A First Look at Animals with Horns. Springer, Harriett, illus. (gr. 1 up). 1989. 10.95 (ISBN 0-8027-6871-7); PLB 11.85 (ISBN 0-8027-6872-5). Walker & Co.

Sendak, Maurice. Where the Wild Things Are. 25th anniversary ed. Sendak, Maurice, illus. LC 63-21253. 48p. (ps up). 1988. 13.95 (ISBN 0-06-025492-0); PLB 13.89 (ISBN 0-06-025493-9). HarpC Child Bks.

Shute, Linda. Clever Tom & the Leprechaun. 1990. pap. 3.95 (ISBN 0-590-43170-6). Scholastic Inc.

Snyder, Zilpha K. The Egypt Game. LC 67-2717. (gr. 4-6). 1986. pap. 3.50 (ISBN 0-440-42225-6, YB). Dell.

Sobol, Donald J. Encyclopedia Brown's Book of Wacky Animals. Enik, Ted, illus. LC 84-22608. 128p. (gr. 3-7). 1985. 11.95 (ISBN 0-688-04152-3). Morrow Jr Bks.

Sutcliff, Rosemary. Dragon Slayer. (gr. 4-6). 1976. pap. 3.95 (ISBN 0-14-030254-9, Puffin). Puffin Bks.

Voigt, Cynthia. Jackaroo. LC 85-7954. 320p. (gr. 8 up). 1985. 14.95 (ISBN 0-689-31123-0, Atheneum Child Bk). Macmillan Child Grp.

Walton, Robert. The Dragon & The Lemon Tree. Allen, Ginny, illus. LC 89-92122. 86p. (gr. 3-7). 1989. write for info. (ISBN 0-9623802-0-2). Pisces Pr CA.

Wild, Anne. Dragon Mobiles. (Illus.). 28p. (Orig.). (gr. 4 up). 1985. pap. 4.95 (ISBN 0-906212-10-3). Parkwest Pubns.

ANIMALS, PREHISTORIC

see Fossils

ANIMALS, SEA

see Marine Animals

ANIMALS AND CIVILIZATION

Arnosky, Jim. A Kettle of Hawks. Arnosky, Jim, illus. LC 89-12459. 32p. (gr. k-4). 1990. 13.95 (ISBN 0-688-09279-9); lib. bdg. 13.88 (ISBN 0-688-09280-2). Lothrop.

Curtis, Patricia. Animal Partners: Training Animals to Help People. (Illus.). 128p. (gr. 7 up). 1982. 10.95 (ISBN 0-525-66791-1, 01063-320, Lodestar Bks). Dutton Child Bks.

Lampton, Christopher. Endangered Species. Kline, M., ed. (Illus.). 128p. (gr. 7-12). 1988. PLB 12.90 (ISBN 0-531-10510-5). Watts.

ANIMALS IN ART

see also Animal Painting and Illustration

Haldane, Suzanne. The See-Through Zoo: How Glass Animals Are Made. Haldane, Suzanne, photos by. LC 83-13122. (Illus.). 48p. (gr. 2-6). 1984. (Pant Bks Young). Pantheon.

ANNIVERSARIES

see Holidays;

see names of special days, e.g. Fourth of July; etc.

ANNULMENT OF MARRIAGE

see Divorce

ANSWERS TO QUESTIONS

see Questions and Answers

ANT

see Ants

ANTARCTIC EXPEDITIONS

see Antarctic Regions

ANTARCTIC REGIONS

see also Scientific Expeditions; South Pole

Antarctica. 1991. pap. 14.95 (ISBN 0-671-73850-X). S&S Trade.

Asimov, Isaac. How Did We Find Out about Antarctica? Wool, David, illus. (gr. 5-8). 1979. PLB 11.85 (ISBN 0-8027-6371-5). Walker & Co.

Cowcher, Helen. Antarctica. Cowcher, Helen, illus. 32p. (ps-3). 1990. incl. audiocassette 17.95 (ISBN 0-924483-24-5). Soundprints.

Dewey, Jennifer O. The Wandering Albatross. Dewey, Jennifer O., illus. LC 88-31419. 48p. (gr. 3-6). 1989. 15.95 (ISBN 0-316-18209-5). Little.

Gilbreath, Alice. The Arctic & Antarctica: Roof & Floor of the World. LC 87-32448. (Illus.). (gr. 4 up). 1988. PLB 11.95 (ISBN 0-87518-373-5, Dillon). Macmillan Child Grp.

Hackwell, W. John. Desert of Ice: Life & Work in Antarctica. LC 89-35002. (Illus.). 48p. (gr. 5 up). 1991. SBE 14.95 (ISBN 0-684-19085-0, Scribners Young Read). Macmillan Child Grp.

Lye, Keith. Take a Trip to Antartica. LC 83-50997. (Illus.). 32p. (gr. 2-4). 1984. PLB 7.99 (ISBN 0-531-04514-5). Watts.

Sabin, Francene. Arctic & Antarctic Regions. Eitzen, Allan, illus. LC 84-2730. 32p. (gr. 3-6). 1985. PLB 9.49 (ISBN 0-8167-0234-9); pap. text ed. 2.95 (ISBN 0-8167-0235-7). Troll Assocs.

Seth, Roland. Antarctica. (Illus.). (gr. 5 up). 1988. 14.95 (ISBN 0-222-00866-0). Chelsea Hse.

Swan, Robert. Destination: Antarctica. Mear, Roger & Ward, Rebecca, photos by. (Illus.). 48p. (gr. 2-7). 1989. pap. 4.95 (ISBN 0-590-41286-8). Scholastic Inc.

ANTELOPES

Ahlstrom, Mark. The Pronghorn. LC 85-28054. (Illus.). 48p. (gr. 5-6). 1986. PLB 10.95 (ISBN 0-89686-292-5, Crestwood Hse). Macmillan Child Grp.

Hoffman, Mary. Antelope. LC 86-17715. (Illus.). 24p. (gr. k-5). 1987. PLB 13.32 (ISBN 0-8172-2703-2). Raintree Pubs.

Stone, Lynn. Antelopes. (Illus.). 24p. (gr. k-5). 1990. lib. bdg. 11.93 (ISBN 0-86593-053-8); lib. bdg. 8.95s.p. (ISBN 0-685-36345-7). Rourke Corp.

ANTHONY, SUSAN BROWNELL, 1820-1906

Clinton, Susan. The Story of Susan B. Anthony. Canaday, Ralph, illus. LC 86-9613. 32p. (gr. 3-6). 1986. PLB 13.27 (ISBN 0-516-04705-1); pap. 3.95 (ISBN 0-516-44705-X). Childrens.

Klingel, Cynthia & Zadra, Dan. Susan B. Anthony. (Illus.). 32p. 1987. 16.45 (ISBN 0-88682-164-9); PLB 11.50s.p. (ISBN 0-685-23216-6). Creative Ed.

Monsell, Helen A. Susan B. Anthony: Champion of Women's Rights. Fiorentino, Al, illus. LC 86-10716. 192p. (gr. 2-6). 1986. pap. 3.95 (ISBN 0-02-041800-0, Aladdin). Macmillan Child Grp.

ANTHONY OF PADUA, SAINT, 1195-1231

Windeatt, Mary F. St. Anthony of Padua. Harmon, Gedge, illus. 32p. (gr. 1-5). 1989. Repr. of 1954 ed. wkbk. 3.00 (ISBN 0-89555-369-4). TAN Bks Pubs.

ANTHROPOGEOGRAPHY

see also Man–Influence of Environment

ANTHROPOLOGY

see also Archeology; Civilization; Color of Man; Ethnology; Language and Languages; Man; Social Change also names of races and tribes

Aliki. Dinosaur Bones. Aliki, illus. LC 85-48246. 32p. (ps-3). 1988. 13.95 (ISBN 0-690-04549-2, Crowell Jr Bks); PLB 13.89 (ISBN 0-690-04550-6). HarpC Child Bks.

Bell, Neill. Only Human: Why We Are the Way We Are. Clifford, Sandy, illus. LC 83-9826. 128p. (gr. 4 up). 1983. 14.95 (ISBN 0-316-08816-1); pap. 8.95 (ISBN 0-316-08818-8). Little.

Diagram Group Staff & Lambert, David. The Field Guide to Early Man. (Illus.). 256p. (gr. 8-12). 1988. 21.95 (ISBN 0-8160-1517-1). Facts on File.

Gallagher, I. J. The Case of the Ancient Astronauts. LC 77-10822. (Illus.). 48p. (gr. 4 up). 1977. PLB 17.32 (ISBN 0-8172-1059-8); pap. 9.27 (ISBN 0-8172-2156-5). Raintree Pubs.

Gamlin, Linda. The Human Race. FS-Aladdin Staff, ed. Hayward, Ron, illus. 40p. (gr. 1-6). 1988. PLB 12.40 (ISBN 0-531-17118-3, Gloucester Pr). Watts.

Snedden, Genevra S. Mountain Cattle & Frontier People. 2nd ed. (Illus.). 160p. (gr. 6). 1989. pap. 16.00 (ISBN 0-685-32946-1). Intervale Pub Co.

Wong, Ovid. Prehistoric People. (Illus.). 48p. (gr. k-4). 1988. PLB 14.60 (ISBN 0-516-01217-7); pap. 4.95 (ISBN 0-516-41217-5). Childrens.

ANTIBIOTICS

see also names of specific antibiotics, e.g. Penicillin; etc.

ANTIDOTES

see Poisons

ANTIPATHIES

see Prejudices and Antipathies

ANTIQUES

see also Collectors and Collecting

Dunnan, Nancy. Collectibles. Raston, Emily, ed. (Illus.). 128p. (gr. 7 up). 1990. PLB 14.98 (ISBN 0-382-09918-4); PLB 11.24s.p.; pap. 7.95 (ISBN 0-382-24029-4); pap. 5.96s.p. Silver Burdett Pr.

Smith, Brad R. Country Antiques: A Child's Guide. Sagendorf, Kit, illus. 64p. (Orig.). (gr. 1-3). 1987. pap. 11.95 (ISBN 0-9618645-0-8). Sanford Hse Pr.

ANTIQUITIES

see Archeology; Indians of North America–Antiquities; Man–Origin and Antiquity; Man, Prehistoric

see names of countries, cities, etc. with the subdivision Antiquities, e.g. U. S.–Antiquities; etc

ANTI-REFORMATION

see Reformation

ANTISLAVERY

see Slavery in the U. S.

ANTS

Ant Rancher's Handbook. 64p. (gr. 4 up). 1990. pap. 7.95 (ISBN 0-89471-827-4); pap. 12.95 incl. ant colony (ISBN 0-685-31009-4). Running Pr.

Ants & Insects. (ARA., Illus.). (gr. 8-12). 3.50x (ISBN 0-86685-185-2). Intl Bk Ctr.

Dorros, Arthur. Ant Cities. Dorros, Arthur, illus. LC 85-48244. 32p. (ps-3). 1987. 13.95 (ISBN 0-690-04568-9, Crowell Jr Bks); PLB 13.89 (ISBN 0-690-04570-0, Crowell Jr Bks). HarpC Child Bks.

—Ant Cities. Dorros, Arthur, illus. LC 85-48244. 32p. (gr. k-3). 1988. pap. 4.50 (ISBN 0-06-445079-1, Trophy). HarpC Child Bks.

Fischer-Nagel, Heiderose & Fischer-Nagel, Andreas. An Ant Colony. Fischer-Nagel, Andreas & Fischer-Nagel, Heiderose, illus. 48p. (gr. 2-5). 1989. PLB 12.95 (ISBN 0-87614-333-8); pap. 6.95 (ISBN 0-87614-519-5). Carolrhoda Bks.

Lisker, Tom. Terror in the Tropics: The Army Ants. LC 77-10765. (Illus.). 48p. (gr. 4 up). 1983. PLB 17.32 (ISBN 0-8172-1060-1); pap. 9.27 (ISBN 0-8172-2168-9). Raintree Pubs.

Losito, Linda. The Ant on the Ground. Oxford Scientific Films Staff, photos by. LC 89-4460. (Illus.). 32p. (gr. 4-6). 1989. PLB 10.95 (ISBN 0-8368-0111-3). Gareth Stevens Inc.

Nanao, Jun. Life of the Ant. Pohl, Kathy, ed. LC 85-28198. (Illus.). 32p. (gr. 3-7). 1986. PLB 16.67 (ISBN 0-8172-2539-0); pap. text ed. 9.27 (ISBN 0-8172-2564-1). Raintree Pubs.

O'Toole, Christopher. Discovering Ants. LC 85-73663. (Illus.). 48p. (gr. 4-9). 1986. PLB 11.90 (ISBN 0-531-18056-5, Pub. by Bookwright). Watts.

Otoole, Christopher. Discovering Ants. 1990. pap. 4.95 (ISBN 0-531-18361-0). Watts.

Overbeck, Cynthia. Ants. LC 81-17216. (Illus.). 48p. (gr. 4 up). 1982. PLB 14.95 (ISBN 0-8225-1468-0, First Ave Edns); pap. 5.95 (ISBN 0-8225-9525-7, First Ave Edns). Lerner Pubns.

Patent, Dorothy H. Looking at Ants. Patent, Dorothy H., illus. LC 89-1943. 48p. (gr. 1-4). 1989. reinforced 12.95 (ISBN 0-8234-0771-3). Holiday.

Poole, Lynn & Poole, Gray. Weird & Wonderful Ants. Petersen, R. F., illus. (gr. 5 up). 1961. 8.95 (ISBN 0-8392-3041-9). Astor-Honor.

Sabin, Francene. Amazing World of Ants. Conner, Eulala, illus. LC 81-7492. 32p. (gr. 2-4). 1982. PLB 10.89 (ISBN 0-89375-558-3); pap. text ed. 2.95 (ISBN 0-89375-559-1). Troll Assocs.

Watts, Barrie. Ants. Watts, Barrie, photos by. (Illus.). 32p. (gr. k-4). 1990. PLB 10.40 (ISBN 0-531-14042-3); pap. 3.95 (ISBN 0-531-15615-X). Watts.

ANTS–FICTION

Barrett, Ethel. Puff the Uppity Ant. Blankenbaker, Frances, ed. Gaddy, David, illus. LC 89-37543. 24p. (gr. 3-7). 1989. 4.95 (ISBN 0-8307-1381-6, 5111872). Regal.

Clements, Jehan. Alfred the Ant: The First Storytelling "Flip Over" Picture Book. Clements, Jehan, illus. LC 89-61138. 48p. (gr. k-3). 1991. 20.00 (ISBN 0-9622500-0-7). Strytllr Co. The Storyteller Company presents a new concept in storytelling & story reading in the classroom. The unique format of the First Storytelling "Flip Over" Picture Book, is especially designed for elementary school teachers to use in the classroom. The children will just flip over The Very First Storytelling "Flip Over" Picture Book. ALFRED THE ANT, an ant who lives in Central Park, will be The First Storytelling "Flip Over" Picture Book.

This Pre-Bound Teacher's Edition contains 48 9" X 12" "Flip Over" pages, including a Teacher's Guide for grades K-3. Part I: The Storytelling version of ALFRED THE ANT, as told by Jehan Clements, also has suggested follow up activities for the children. Part II: The Illustrated Version of ALFRED THE ANT has 13 full color, full sized illustrations for the children. There are 13 full color reduced size illustrations, with large text type, for the teachers. There are also two master copies of the classroom activity pages & authors notes.
Publisher Provided Annotation.

Despain, Goldie B. Tiny Ant Who Scared a Horned Toad. Petie, Haris, illus. (ps-3). 1970. write for info. (ISBN 0-8313-0029-9); PLB 6.70 (ISBN 0-685-02940-9). Lantern.

Lehman, James H. The Saga of Shakespeare Pintlewood & the Great Silver Fountain Pen. Raschka, Christopher, illus. LC 90-82303. 32p. (gr. k-3). 1990. PLB 13.95 (ISBN 1-878925-00-8). Brotherstone Pubs. Shakespeare Pintlewood is an ant. Because he is small, he sees things as children do. After a heroic struggle to write with his large silver pen, he becomes a great literary ant. But he still doesn't know any children. So he shoulders his pen & sets out to find them. Lehman's wry, gentle story & Raschka's warm, delicately humorous illustrations, full of inviting detail, give an ant's eye (Child's eye) view of the hard work & pleasure of writing, of the deep satisfaction stories produce when they bring people together. Readers of all ages are charmed by Shakey & his quest to know & love children. "This is a good book. I liked it when Shakey slid across the spilled ink & when he rode on the little chair. Other kids would like Shakey."--Jennifer, age 5. "All the kids liked it. They wanted to know what happened to the pen. They really listened intently. It really grabbed their interest."--elementary special education teacher. "My daughter loves it. She took it to school & had her teacher read it in class."--mother of 7-year-old. "This book has good values--creativity, persistence, love & loyalty. Raschka's illustrations are inventive, bright, & detailed."--Ann Arbor News.
Publisher Provided Annotation.

Pellowski, Michael J. Who Can't Follow an Ant? Swan, Susan, illus. LC 85-14009. 48p. (Orig.). (gr. 1-3). 1986. PLB 9.89 (ISBN 0-8167-0592-5); pap. text ed. 2.95 (ISBN 0-8167-0593-3). Troll Assocs.

Sushiela. The Ant & the Grasshopper: A Love Story. Sushiela, illus. LC 89-92067. 129p. (Orig.). (gr. 5 up). 1990. pap. 15.95 (ISBN 0-9623363-1-9). Running Water.

Wilson, Frank. Twissington Ant's Great Discovery. 16p. (gr. 7-10). 1986. 15.00X (ISBN 0-7223-2042-6, Pub. by A H Stockwell England). State Mutual Bk.

ANXIETY
see Fear

APARTMENT HOUSES
see also Housing

APARTMENT HOUSES–FICTION

Alexander, Sue. Lila on the Landing. Eagle, Ellen, illus. LC 87-301. 64p. (gr. 2-5). 1987. 13.95 (ISBN 0-89919-340-4, Pub. by Clarion). Ticknor & Fields.

Herman, Charlotte. Millie Cooper, Take a Chance. Cogancherry, Helen, illus. 112p. (gr. 3 up). 1990. pap. 3.95 (ISBN 0-14-034119-6, Puffin). Puffin Bks.

Hest, Amy. Pete & Lily. LC 85-13992. 120p. (gr. 4-7). 1986. 11.95 (ISBN 0-89919-354-4, Pub. by Clarion). Ticknor & Fields.

Hurwitz, Johanna. Busybody Nora. Hoban, Lillian, illus. 64p. (gr. 2-5). 1991. pap. 3.95 (ISBN 0-14-034592-2, Puffin). Puffin Bks.

—Superduper Teddy. Hoban, Lillian, illus. 80p. (gr. 2-5). 1991. pap. 3.95 (ISBN 0-14-034593-0, Puffin). Puffin Bks.

Knox-Wagner, Elaine. An Apartment's No Place for a Kid. Tucker, Kathleen, ed. (Illus.). 32p. (ps-1). 1985. 10.95 (ISBN 0-8075-0373-8). A Whitman.

Roberts, Willo D. The Pet-Sitting Peril. LC 82-13757. 192p. (gr. 4-6). 1983. 13.95 (ISBN 0-689-30963-5, Atheneum Child Bk). Macmillan Child Grp.

APES
see also Chimpanzees

Animal Masks: Gorilla & Hippo. (ps up). 1990. pap. 4.98 (ISBN 0-8317-0358-X). Smithmark.

Barrett, Norman. Monos y Simios. LC 87-50849. (SPA., Illus.). 32p. (gr. k-4). 1991. PLB 11.40 (ISBN 0-531-07918-X). Watts.

—Picture Library: Monkey & Apes. 1990. pap. 3.95 (ISBN 0-531-15205-7). Watts.

Carwardine, Mark. Monkeys & Apes. Young, Richard G., ed. Camm, Martin, illus. LC 89-32808. 45p. (gr. 3-5). 1989. PLB 13.26 (ISBN 0-944483-28-3). Garrett Ed Corp.

Fitzpatrick, Michael. A Closer Look at Apes. rev. ed. (Illus.). 32p. (gr. 4-7). 1987. PLB 5.99 (ISBN 0-531-17038-1, Gloucester Pr). Watts.

Green, Carl R. & Sanford, William R. The Gorilla. LC 85-9991. (Illus.). 48p. (gr. 5-6). 1986. PLB 10.95 (ISBN 0-89686-269-0, Crestwood Hse). Macmillan Child Grp.

Hogan, Paula Z. The Gorilla. LC 79-13602. (Illus.). 32p. (gr. 1-4). 1979. PLB 16.67 (ISBN 0-8172-1501-8). Raintree Pubs.

Irvine, Georgeanne. Raising Gordy Gorilla at the San Diego Zoo. (Illus.). 48p. (gr. 3-7). 1990. PLB 14.95 (ISBN 0-671-68775-1). S&S Trade.

Lumley, Kathryn W. Monkeys & Apes. LC 82-12779. (Illus.). (gr. k-4). 1982. PLB 14.60 (ISBN 0-516-01633-4); pap. 4.95 (ISBN 0-516-41633-2). Childrens.

McDearmon, Kay. Orangutans: The Red Apes. (gr. 2-5). 1983. 8.95 (ISBN 0-396-08182-7, Putnam). Putnam Pub Group.

Morris, Dean. Monkeys & Apes. rev. ed. LC 87-16688. (Illus.). 48p. (gr. 3). 1987. PLB 15.99 (ISBN 0-8172-3211-7). Raintree Pubs.

—Monkeys & Apes. (gr. 2-6). 1990. pap. 17.32 (ISBN 0-8172-3236-2). Raintree Pubs.

Stone, Lynn. Gorillas. (Illus.). 24p. (gr. k-5). 1990. lib. bdg. 11.93 (ISBN 0-86593-063-5); lib. bdg. 11.93 (ISBN 0-685-36318-X). Rourke Corp.

Wexo, John B. Apes. 24p. (gr. 4). 1989. 11.95 (ISBN 0-88682-265-3). Creative Ed.

—Baby Animals. 24p. (gr. 4). 1989. 11.95 (ISBN 0-88682-270-X). Creative Ed.

Whitehead, Patricia. Monkeys. Dodson, Bert, illus. LC 81-11439. 32p. (gr. k-2). 1982. PLB 10.89 (ISBN 0-89375-670-9); pap. text ed. 2.95 (ISBN 0-89375-671-7). Troll Assocs.

Wildlife Education, Ltd. Staff. Apes. Hynes, Robert, et al, illus. 20p. (Orig.). (gr. 5 up). 1981. pap. 2.25 (ISBN 0-937934-03-8). Wildlife Educ.

—Orangutans. Meltzer, Dave, illus. 20p. (Orig.). (gr. 5 up). 1980. pap. 2.25 (ISBN 0-937934-02-X). Wildlife Educ.

APES–FICTION

Donovan, John. Family. LC 75-37409. 148p. (gr. 7 up). 1976. PLB 12.89 (ISBN 0-06-021722-7). HarpC Child Bks.

Eichenberg, Fritz. Ape in a Cape: An Alphabet of Odd Animals. Eichenberg, Fritz, illus. LC 52-6908. 32p. (ps-3). 1988. pap. 3.95 (ISBN 0-15-607830-9, VoyB). HarBraceJ.

Knight, Hilary. Where's Wallace? LC 64-19717. (ps-3). 1964. 14.95 (ISBN 0-06-023170-X); PLB 14.89 (ISBN 0-06-023171-8). HarpC Child Bks.

APICULTURE
see Bees

APOLLO PROJECT
see also headings beginning with Lunar and Moon

Furniss, Tim. The First Men on the Moon. Bull, Peter, illus. LC 88-24166. 32p. (gr. 4-6). 1989. PLB 11.40 (ISBN 0-531-18240-1). Watts.

Muirden, James. Going to the Moon. Code, Nigel, illus. LC 87-4560. 32p. (ps-1). 1987. 3.95 (ISBN 0-394-89186-4, Random Juv); lib. bdg. 7.99 (ISBN 0-394-99186-9). Random.

Stein, R. Conrad. The Story of Apollo II. Catrow, David J., III, illus. LC 85-10974. 31p. (gr. 3-4). 1985. PLB 13.27 (ISBN 0-516-04692-6). Childrens.

Vogt, Gregory. Apollo & the Moon Landing. (Illus.). 112p. (gr. 4-6). 1991. PLB 19.00 (ISBN 1-878841-31-9); pap. 4.95 (ISBN 1-878841-37-8). Millbrook Pr.

APOSTLES

Daughters of St. Paul. The Fisher Prince. (gr. 3-7). 3.00 (ISBN 0-8198-0233-6); pap. 2.00 (ISBN 0-685-01442-8). Dghtrs St Paul.

Hodges. Stephen, the First Martyr. 24p. (Orig.). (gr. k-4). 1985. pap. 1.39 (ISBN 0-570-06194-6, 59-1295). Concordia.

Rowell, Edmon L., Jr. Apostles: Jesus' Special Helpers. Padgett, James, illus. (gr. 1-6). 1979. 5.95 (ISBN 0-8054-4246-4, 4242-46). Broadman.

APPALACHIAN MOUNTAINS–FICTION

Cleaver, Vera & Cleaver, Bill. Where the Lilies Bloom. LC 75-82402. (Illus.). 176p. (gr. 4-9). 1969. 14.95 (ISBN 0-397-31111-7, Lipp Jr Bks). HarpC Child Bks.

Cutlip, Ralph V. Mountain Massacres & Other Stories of Appalachia. Hallinan, Brenda C., illus. 167p. (Orig.). (gr. 8 up). 1986. pap. 6.50 (ISBN 0-317-47675-0). B Cutlip.

Hamilton, Virginia. M. C. Higgins, the Great. LC 72-92439. 288p. (gr. 7 up). 1974. 14.95 (ISBN 0-02-742480-4, Mcmillan Child Bk). Macmillan Child Grp.

Miller, Jim W. Newfound. LC 89-42540. 256p. (gr. 7 up). 1989. 13.95 (ISBN 0-531-05845-X); PLB 13.99 (ISBN 0-531-08445-0). Orchard Bks Watts.

APPALACHIAN MOUNTAINS–SOCIAL LIFE AND CUSTOMS

Anderson, Joan W. Pioneer Children of Appalachia. (gr. 4-7). 1990. pap. 5.95 (ISBN 0-395-54792-X, Clarion Bks). HM.

Rylant, Cynthia. Appalachia: The Voices of Sleeping Birds. (ps). 1991. 14.95 (ISBN 0-15-201605-8). HarBraceJ.

APPARITIONS
see also Ghosts

Warner, John & Walker, Margaret. Apparitions. (Illus.). 160p. (gr. 6 up). 1987. pap. text ed. 7.50 (ISBN 0-89061-465-2). Jamestown Pubs.

APPLE

Eberle, Bob. Apple Shines. Weber, June K., illus. 96p. (gr. 4-8). 1983. wkbk. 8.95 (ISBN 0-86653-130-0, GA 471). Good Apple.

Johnson, Sylvia A. Apple Trees. Koike, Hiro, illus. LC 83-16230. 48p. (gr. 4 up). 1983. PLB 14.95 (ISBN 0-8225-1479-6). Lerner Pubns.

McMillan, Bruce. Apples, How They Grow. (Illus.). 48p. (ps-3). 1979. 14.95 (ISBN 0-395-27806-6). HM.

Patent, Dorothy H. An Apple a Day: From Orchard to You. Munoz, William, photos by. LC 89-33504. (Illus.). 64p. (gr. 3-7). 1990. 13.95 (ISBN 0-525-65020-2, Cobblehill Bks). Dutton Child Bks.

Watts, Barrie. Apple Tree. (Illus.). 24p. (gr. 2-5). 1987. 6.95 (ISBN 0-382-09440-9); 9.98 (ISBN 0-382-09436-0). Silver Burdett Pr.

APPLE II (COMPUTER)

Schiller, David. My First Computer Book: Apple II Series. LC 90-50367. 64p. (ps-2). 1991. pap. 17.95 (ISBN 0-89480-368-9, 1368). Workman Pub.

Vernier, David L., ed. Chaos in the Laboratory & Thirteen Other Science Projects Using the Apple II. LC 91-90900. (Illus.). 288p. (Orig.). (gr. 9 up). 1991. pap. 25.95 (ISBN 0-918731-46-1). Vernier Soft.

APPLE COMPUTERS

Kemnitz, Thomas M. & Mass, Lynne. Kids Working with Computers: The Apple BASIC Manual. Schlendorf, Lori, illus. 42p. (gr. 4-7). 1983. pap. 4.99 (ISBN 0-89824-092-1). Trillium Pr.

Luehrmann, Arthur & Peckham, Herbert. Appleworks Date Bases: A Hands-On Guide. (Illus.). 168p. (Orig.). (gr. 7-12). 1987. pap. text ed. 9.25 (ISBN 0-941681-03-3); tchr's. set 18.50 (ISBN 0-941681-11-4). Computer Lit Pr.

—Appleworks Spreadsheets: A Hands-On Guide. (Illus.). 160p. (Orig.). (gr. 7-12). 1987. pap. text ed. 9.25 (ISBN 0-941681-05-X); tchr's. set 18.50 (ISBN 0-941681-12-2). Computer Lit Pr.

—Hands-on Appleworks: A Guide to Word Processing, Data Bases & Spreadsheets. LC 87-836. (Illus.). 478p. (Orig.). (gr. 7-12). 1987. pap. text ed. 19.95 (ISBN 0-941681-07-6); tchr's. set 29.95 (ISBN 0-941681-13-0). Computer Lit Pr.

Pitter, Keiko. Using Apple Works: With Intro to Basic. (gr. 7-12). 1986. pap. text ed. 21.08 (ISBN 0-07-554148-3). McGraw.

Taitt, Kathy. Apple, Vol. 1. 59p. (gr. 4-12). 1983. pap. text ed. 11.95 (ISBN 0-88193-001-6). Create Learn.

—Apple, Vol. 2. 61p. (gr. 4-12). 1983. pap. text ed. 11.95 (ISBN 0-88193-002-4). Create Learn.

—Apple, Vol. 3. 55p. (gr. 5-12). 1983. pap. text ed. 11.95 (ISBN 0-88193-003-2). Create Learn.

—Apple, Vol. 4. 57p. (gr. 5-12). 1983. pap. text ed. 11.95 (ISBN 0-88193-004-0). Create Learn.

—Apple, Vol. 5. 57p. (gr. 6-12). 1983. pap. text ed. 11.95 (ISBN 0-88193-005-9). Create Learn.

—Apple, Vol. 6. 68p. (gr. 6-12). 1984. pap. text ed. 11.95 (ISBN 0-88193-006-7). Create Learn.

APPLIED PSYCHOLOGY
see Psychology, Applied

APPLIED SCIENCE
see Technology

APPRAISAL OF BOOKS
see Book Reviews; Books and Reading; Books and Reading–Best Books; Criticism; Literature–History and Criticism

APPRECIATION OF MUSIC
see Music–Analysis, Appreciation

APRIL FOOLS' DAY

Baker, James W. April Fools' Day Magic. Overlie, George, illus. 48p. (gr. 2-5). 1989. 7.95 (ISBN 0-8225-2230-6). Lerner Pubns.

Kelley, Emily. April Fool's Day. Nobens, Cheryl A., illus. LC 82-23559. 48p. (gr. k-4). 1983. PLB 9.95 (ISBN 0-87614-218-8); pap. 3.95 (ISBN 0-87614-481-4). Carolrhoda Bks.

Thayer, Marjorie. The April Foolers. Freeman, Don, illus. LC 77-15958. 32p. (gr. k-4). 1978. PLB 15.93 (ISBN 0-516-08883-1, Golden Gate). Childrens.

AQUARIUMS
see also Fish Culture; Goldfish

Barrie, Anmarie. A Step-by-Step Book about Our First Aquarium. (Illus.). 64p. 1987. 3.95 (ISBN 0-86622-454-8, SK003); lib. bdg. 9.95 (ISBN 0-86622-923-X, SK-003X). TFH Pubns.

Boyd, Kevin W. The Complete Aquarium Problem Solver. (Illus.). 32p. (gr. 10). 1989. pap. write for info. Boylen.
Broekel, Ray. Aquariums & Terrariums. LC 82-4428. (gr. k-4). 1982. 14.60 (ISBN 0-516-01660-1). Childrens.
—Tropical Fish. LC 82-19738. (Illus.). 48p. (gr. k-4). 1983. PLB 14.60 (ISBN 0-516-01687-3); pap. 4.95 (ISBN 0-516-41687-1). Childrens.
Field, Nancy & Machlis, Sally. Discovery Book for the Seattle Aquarium. rev. & abr. ed. Machlis, Sally, illus. 32p. (gr. 1-6). 1987. pap. 3.50 (ISBN 0-941042-07-3). Dog Eared Pubns.
Gilbert, Mariana. Your First Goldfish. (Illus.). 36p. (Orig.). 1991. pap. 1.95 (ISBN 0-86622-065-8, YF-108). TFH Pubns.
Paige, David. Behind the Scenes at the Aquarium. LC 77-24670. (Illus.). (gr. 4 up). 1977. PLB 12.95 (ISBN 0-8075-0607-9). A Whitman.
Palmer, Joan. Aquarium Fish. (Illus.). 48p. (gr. 7-9). 1990. 11.90 (ISBN 0-531-18250-9). Watts.
Parramon, J. M. My First Visit to the Aquarium. Sales, G., illus. 32p. (ps). 1990. pap. 4.95 (ISBN 0-8120-4304-9). Barron.
Quinn, Kaye. Aquarium Creatures. (gr. 4-7). 1991. pap. 2.95 (ISBN 0-8431-2719-8). Price Stern.
Thomas, Charles B. Water Gardens for Plants & Fish. (Illus.). 189p. (gr. 7 up). 1988. PLB 19.95 (ISBN 0-86622-942-6, TS-102). TFH Pubns.

AQUATIC ANIMALS
see Fresh-Water Animals; Marine Animals

AQUATIC PLANTS
see Marine Plants

ARAB COUNTRIES
Department of Geography, Lerner Publications. Sudan in Pictures. (Illus.). 64p. (gr. 5 up). 1988. PLB 12.95 (ISBN 0-8225-1839-2). Lerner Pubns.
Dutton, Roderic. An Arab Family. LC 85-10272. (Illus.). 32p. (gr. 2-5). 1985. PLB 9.95 (ISBN 0-8225-1660-8). Lerner Pubns.
Haskins, Jim. Count Your Way Through the Arab World. (Illus.). 24p. (gr. 1-4). 1987. lib. bdg. 11.95 (ISBN 0-87614-304-4); pap. 4.95 (ISBN 0-685-13264-1). Carolrhoda Bks.

ARAB-ISRAEL WAR, 1967
see Israel-Arab War, 1967-

ARAB-JEWISH RELATIONS
see Jewish-Arab Relations

ARABIA–FICTION
Riordan, James. Tales from the Arabian Nights. Ambrus, Victor G., illus. LC 84-62456. 128p. (gr. 4 up). 1985. 11.95 (ISBN 0-528-82672-7). Checkerboard Pr.

ARABIC LANGUAGE
First English & Arabic Picture Dictionary. (Illus.). (gr. 1-4). 3.50x (ISBN 0-86685-202-6). Intl Bk Ctr.
Giblin, James C. The Riddle of the Rosetta Stone: Key to Ancient Egypt. LC 89-29289. (Illus.). 96p. (gr. 3-7). 1990. 13.95 (ISBN 0-690-04797-5, Crowell Jr Bks); PLB 13.89 (ISBN 0-690-04799-1, Crowell Jr Bks). HarpC Child Bks.
Girgis, Nazih. The Arabic Alphabet. Lowry-Elks, C., illus. (ENG & ARA.). 57p. (gr. k-12). pap. 15.00 incl. cass. (ISBN 0-86685-340-5). Intl Bk Ctr.
Sheheen, Dennis, illus. A Child's Picture English-Arabic Dictionary. LC 85-15658. (gr. k-2). 1985. 9.95 (ISBN 0-915361-30-2, Dist. by Watts). Adama Pubs Inc.

ARBORICULTURE
see Forests and Forestry; Fruit Culture; Trees

ARABS
Alotaibi. Bedouin - Nomads of the Desert, Reading Level 5. (Illus.). 48p. (gr. 4-8). Date not set. PLB 15.33 (ISBN 0-86625-265-7). Rourke Corp.
Ashabranner, Brent. An Ancient Heritage: The Arab-American Minority. Conklin, Paul, illus. LC 90-30641. 160p. (gr. 3-7). 1991. 14.95 (ISBN 0-06-020048-0); PLB 14.89 (ISBN 0-06-020049-9). HarpC Child Bks.
Naff, Alixa. The Arab Americans. Moynihan, Daniel P., intro. by. (Illus.). 112p. (gr. 5 up). 1988. lib. bdg. 17.95 (ISBN 0-87754-861-7). Chelsea Hse.

ARABS–FICTION
Alexander, Sue. Nadia the Willful. Bloom, Lloyd, illus. LC 82-12602. 48p. (gr. k-3). 1983. lib. bdg. 12.99 (ISBN 0-394-95265-0). Pantheon.

ARBOR DAY
Burns, Diane L. Arbor Day. Rogers, Kathy, illus. 48p. (gr. k-4). 1989. 9.95 (ISBN 0-87614-346-X). Carolrhoda Bks.

ARCHEOLOGISTS
Williams, Barbara. Breakthrough: Women in Archaeology. LC 80-7687. (Illus.). 174p. 1981. 9.95 (ISBN 0-8027-6406-1). Walker & Co.

ARCHAEOLOGY
see Archeology

ARCHEOLOGY
see also Arms and Armor; Christian Art and Symbolism; Cities and Towns, Ruined, Extinct, etc.; Cliff Dwellers and Cliff Dwellings; Ethnology; Funeral Rites and Ceremonies; Gems; Heraldry; Indians of North America–Antiquities; Man, Prehistoric; Mounds and Mound Builders; Mummies; Numismatics; Pottery; Pyramids; Stone Age
also names of countries, cities, etc. with the subdivision Antiquities, e.g. U. S.–Antiquities
Anderson, Joan. From Map to Museum: Uncovering Mysteries of the Past. Ancona, George, photos by. LC 87-31307. (Illus.). 64p. (gr. 3-7). 1988. 12.95 (ISBN 0-688-06914-2); PLB 12.88 (ISBN 0-688-06915-0, Morrow Jr Bks). Morrow Jr Bks.
Branigan, Keith. Prehistory. Salariya, David & Willis, Shirley, illus. LC 84-50696. 40p. (gr. 4-9). 1986. lib. bdg. 12.40 (ISBN 0-531-03745-2). Watts.
Cork, Barbara. Archaeology. McEwan, Joe, illus. 32p. (gr. 5-8). 1985. PLB 13.96 (ISBN 0-88110-220-2, Pub. by Usborne); pap. 6.95 (ISBN 0-86020-865-6). EDC.
Fradin, Dennis B. Archaeology. LC 83-7309. 48p. (gr. k-4). 1983. PLB 14.60 (ISBN 0-516-01691-1); pap. 4.95 (ISBN 0-516-41691-X). Childrens.
Hackwell, W. John. Digging to the Past: Excavations in Ancient Lands. LC 86-13115. (Illus.). 64p. (gr. 3-7). 1986. 14.95 (ISBN 0-684-18692-6, Scribners Young Read). Macmillan Child Grp.
Johnson, Eileen, ed. An Ancient Watering Hole: The Lubbock Lake Landmark Story. Dean, David & Cokendolpher, Jean, illus. LC 90-90258. 32p. (Orig.). (gr. 2-5). 1990. pap. 3.00 (ISBN 0-89672-218-X). Tex Tech Univ Pr.
Leroi-Gourhan, Andre. The Hunters of Prehistory. Jacobson, Claire, tr. from FRE. LC 88-8121. (Illus.). 160p. (gr. 6 up). 1989. 12.95 (ISBN 0-689-31293-8, Atheneum Child Bk). Macmillan Child Grp.
Marston, Elsa. Mysteries in American Archaeology. LC 85-20259. (Illus.). 115p. (gr. 7 up). 1986. 13.95 (ISBN 0-8027-6608-0); lib. bdg. 13.85 (ISBN 0-8027-6627-7). Walker & Co.
Nichols, Peter & Nichols, Belia. Archaeology: A Study of the Past. Roberts, Melissa, ed. (Illus.). 48p. (gr. 2-4). 1988. 10.95 (ISBN 0-89015-606-9, Pub. by Panda Bks). Eakin Pr.
Place, Robin. Search for the Past, 6 bks. Rothmayr, Yvonne, illus. (Orig.). (gr. 2-4). 1986. Set. pap. text ed. 23.30 incl. tchr's. notes (ISBN 1-55624-010-4). Wright Group.
Prehistoric Encyclopedia. (Illus.). 144p. (gr. 4 up). 1989. Repr. 14.95 (ISBN 0-02-688539-5). Checkerboard Pr.
Raintree Publishers Staff. Archaeology. LC 87-28634. (Illus.). 64p. (Orig.). (gr. 5-9). 1988. PLB 19.99 (ISBN 0-8172-3077-7). Raintree Pubs.
Rhodes, Frank H., et al. Fossils. Perlman, Raymond, illus. (gr. 6 up). 1962. PLB write for info. (ISBN 0-307-63515-5); pap. write for info. (ISBN 0-307-24411-3, Golden Pr). Western Pub.
Snyder, Thomas F. Archeology Search Book. O'Neill, Martha, ed. Cullinan, Dorothy K. & Podgorski, Mary E., illus. 32p. (gr. 4-12). 1982. pap. text ed. 8.08 (ISBN 0-07-059467-8). McGraw.
Stuart, Gene S. Secrets from the Past. Crump, Donald J., ed. LC 79-1790. (Illus.). 104p. (gr. 3-8). 1979. 6.95 (ISBN 0-87044-316-X); PLB 8.50 (ISBN 0-87044-321-6). Natl Geog.
Sylvester, Diane & Wiemann, Mary. Mythology, Archeology, Architecture. 112p. (gr. 4-6). 1982. 9.95 (ISBN 0-88160-081-4, LW 901). Learning Wks.
Trease, Geoffrey. Hidden Treasure. Molan, Chris, illus. LC 88-21699. 48p. (gr. 4-6). 1989. 14.95 (ISBN 0-525-67270-2, Lodestar Bks). Dutton Child Bks.

ARCHEOLOGY–FICTION
Davis, Emmett. Clues in the Desert. Downing, Julie, illus. LC 83-8626. 32p. (gr. 3-6). 1983. PLB 14.65 (ISBN 0-940742-29-2). Raintree Pubs.
James, Carollyn. Digging up the Past: The Story of an Archaeological Adventure. Schindler, S. D., illus. 64p. (gr. 5-8). 1990. PLB 11.90 (ISBN 0-531-10878-3). Watts.
Peretti, Frank E. The Door in the Dragon's Throat. LC 85-70469. 128p. (gr. 5-8). 1985. pap. 4.95 (ISBN 0-89107-370-1, Crossway Bks). Good News.

ARCHERY
Boy Scouts of America. Archery. (Illus.). 56p. (gr. 6-12). 1986. pap. 1.85 (ISBN 0-8395-3381-0, 3381). BSA.

ARCHIMEDES, 287-212 B.C.
Ipsen, D. C. ARCHIMEDES: Greatest Scientist of the Ancient World. 64p. (gr. 6-10). 1989. lib. bdg. 15.95 (ISBN 0-89490-161-3). Enslow Pubs.

ARCHITECTS
Dolan, Edward F., Jr. Famous Builders of California. (Illus.). 128p. (gr. 9-12). 1987. 10.95 (ISBN 0-396-08847-3, Putnam). Putnam Pub Group.
Wadsworth, Ginger. Julia Morgan: Architect of Dreams. (Illus.). 128p. (gr. 5 up). 1990. PLB 15.95 (ISBN 0-8225-4903-4). Lerner Pubns.

ARCHITECTURAL ENGINEERING
see Building

ARCHITECTURE
see also Building; Castles; Cathedrals; Monuments; Palaces; Skyscrapers; Synagogues
also headings beginning with the word Architectural
Boy Scouts of America. Architecture. (Illus.). 46p. (gr. 6-12). 1966. pap. 1.85 (ISBN 0-8395-3321-7, 3321). BSA.
D'Alelio, Jane. I Know That Building! Discovering Architecture with Activities & Games. (Illus.). 88p. (gr. 3-6). 1989. pap. 14.95 (ISBN 0-89133-133-6). Preservation Pr.
Jann, Gayle. A Day in the Life of a Construction Foreman. Jann, Gayle, illus. LC 87-13761. 32p. (gr. 4-8). 1988. PLB 11.79 (ISBN 0-8167-1121-6); pap. text ed. 2.95 (ISBN 0-8167-1122-4). Troll Assocs.
Mandell, Myles K. Micromodels: Make Your Own Kremlin. (gr. 2 up). 1983. 4.95 (ISBN 0-399-50852-X, Perigee Bks). Putnam Pub Group.
Munro, Roxie, illus. Architects Make Zigzags: Looking at Architecture from A to Z. Maddex, Diane, contrib. by. LC 84-9679. (Illus.). 64p. (Orig.). (gr. 3 up). 1986. pap. 8.95 (ISBN 0-89133-121-2). Preservation Pr.
Patton, Sally & Maxon, Dianne. Architexture: A Shelter Word. rev. ed. 54p. (gr. 2-6). 1989. pap. text ed. 11.95 (ISBN 0-913705-38-1, ZS04). Zephyr Pr AZ.
Schulz, Charles M. Snoopy's Facts & Fun Book about Houses. Schulz, Charles M., illus. LC 79-676. 1979. (Random Juv). Random.
Shemie, Bonnie. Houses of Snow, Skin & Bones: Native Dwellings: The Far North. LC 89-50778. (Illus.). 24p. (gr. 3-7). 1989. 12.95 (ISBN 0-88776-240-9). Tundra Bks.
Stewart, G. In the Future. (Illus.). 32p. (gr. 3-8). 1989. lib. bdg. 13.26 (ISBN 0-86592-115-6). Rourke Corp.
Sylvester, Diane & Wiemann, Mary. Mythology, Archeology, Architecture. 112p. (gr. 4-6). 1982. 9.95 (ISBN 0-88160-081-4, LW 901). Learning Wks.
Weiss, Harvey. Model Buildings & How to Make Them. Weiss, Harvey, illus. LC 77-26597. (gr. 5 up). 1979. 13.95 (ISBN 0-685-02099-1, Crowell Jr Bks). HarpC Child Bks.
Wilson, Forrest. What It Feels Like to Be a Building. rev. ed. Wilson, Forrest, illus. LC 88-22382. 80p. (gr. 2 up). 1988. pap. 10.95 (ISBN 0-89133-147-6). Preservation Pr.
Young, C. Castles, Pyramids & Palaces. (Illus.). 48p. (ps-8). 1990. lib. bdg. 13.96 (ISBN 0-88110-411-6, Usborne); pap. 7.95 (ISBN 0-7460-0463-X, Usborne). EDC.

ARCHITECTURE, DOMESTIC
see also Houses
Buchanan, Ken. This House Is Made of Mud. Tracy, Libba, illus. LC 90-53589. 32p. (ps-3). 1991. 14.95 (ISBN 0-87358-518-6). Northland AZ.
Edom, H. Houses & Homes. (Illus.). 24p. (gr. 2-4). 1989. lib. bdg. 11.96 (ISBN 0-88110-398-5, Usborne); pap. 3.95 (ISBN 0-7460-0450-8, Usborne). EDC.
Marsh, Carole. The Boy-Is-This-Place-Big Biltmore House Spark Kit. (Illus., Orig.). (gr. 3-12). 1986. PLB 24.95 (ISBN 0-935326-22-7). Gallopade Pub Group.
Stewart, Gail. Living Spaces, 6 bks, Reading Level 4. (Illus.). 192p. (gr. 3-8). Date not set. Set. PLB 79.60 (ISBN 0-86592-105-9). Rourke Corp.

ARCHITECTURE–FICTION
Denslow, Sharon P. At Taylor's Place. Carpenter, Nancy, illus. LC 89-23898. 32p. (ps-2). 1990. 13.95 (ISBN 0-02-728685-1, Bradbury Pr). Macmillan Child Grp.
Radford, Derek. Harry Builds a House. Radford, Derek, illus. LC 90-187. 32p. (gr. k-3). 1990. pap. 10.95 (ISBN 0-689-71439-4, Aladdin). Macmillan Child Grp.

ARCHITECTURE–HISTORY
Giblin, James C. Let There Be Light: A Book about Windows. LC 87-35052. (Illus.). 176p. (gr. 3-7). 1988. 15.95 (ISBN 0-690-04693-6, Crowell Jr Bks); PLB 15.89 (ISBN 0-690-04695-2, Crowell Jr Bks). HarpC Child Bks.
Huntington, Lee P. Americans at Home: Four Hundred Years of American Houses. (Illus.). (gr. 6 up). 1980. 9.95 (ISBN 0-698-20530-8, Coward). Putnam Pub Group.
Ventura, Piero & Ceserani, Gian P. Grand Constructions. (Illus.). 108p. (gr. 5 up). 1983. pap. 19.95 (ISBN 0-399-20942-5, Putnam). Putnam Pub Group.

ARCHITECTURE, NAVAL
see Shipbuilding

ARCHITECTURE, RURAL
see Architecture, Domestic

ARCHITECTURE–VOCATIONAL GUIDANCE
Clinton, Susan. I Can Be an Architect. LC 85-28004. (Illus.). 32p. (gr. k-3). 1986. PLB 13.73 (ISBN 0-516-01890-6); pap. 3.95 (ISBN 0-516-41890-4). Childrens.

ARCTIC EXPEDITIONS
see Arctic Regions

ARCTIC REGIONS
see also Northwest Passage; Scientific Expeditions
Barrett, N. S. Polar Animals. FS Staff, ed. (Illus.). 32p. (gr. 1-6). 1988. PLB 11.40 (ISBN 0-531-10531-8). Watts.
Burton, Robert. Arctic. (Illus.). 24p. (gr. k-4). 1991. PLB 13.25 (ISBN 1-878137-16-6). Newington.
Hughes, Jill. Arctic Lands. Coombs, R. & Cordery, D., illus. (gr. 4-8). 1987. PLB 5.99 (ISBN 0-531-17036-5, Gloucester Pr). Watts.

Kalman, Bobbie. Arctic Animals. (Illus.). 56p. (gr. 3-4). 1988. 15.95 (ISBN 0-86505-145-3); pap. 7.95 (ISBN 0-86505-155-0). Crabtree Pub Co.
ARCTIC ANIMALS portrays the fascinating land & sea mammals, birds, insects, & fish that live in the Arctic. The lives of these creatures are a struggle for survival, even though their bodies are ingeniously adapted to withstand this unforgiving environment. ARCTIC ANIMALS belongs to the Arctic World Series. The four, large, full-color books explore the wildlife & wild landscape of the north & the communities & customs of the people. Hundreds of breathtaking photographs show the exciting life that flourishes in

this beautiful, yet forbidding land.
Publisher Provided Annotation.

—The Arctic Land. (Illus.). 56p. (gr. 3-4). 1988. 15.95 (ISBN 0-86505-144-5); pap. 7.95 (ISBN 0-86505-154-2). Crabtree Pub Co.
THE ARCTIC LAND is an exciting book on the physical world of the Arctic exploring such topics as weather patterns & sea formations, arctic resources & the dangers of pollution. Breathtaking photographs show the wonder of this pristine, beautiful land. Children will love this fascinating journey around the top of the world, from Canada, across Greenland, Lapland, & Siberia to Alaska. To eliminate stereotypes, these outstanding books were written with the assistance of native peoples. THE ARCTIC LAND belongs to the Arctic World Series. The four, large, full-color books explore the wildlife & wild landscape of the north & the communities & customs of the people. Hundreds of breathtaking photographs show the exciting life that flourishes in this beautiful, yet forbidding land.
Publisher Provided Annotation.

Kalman, Bobbie & Belsey, William. An Arctic Community. (Illus.). 56p. (gr. 3-4). 1988. 15.95 (ISBN 0-86505-147-X); pap. 7.95 (ISBN 0-86505-157-7). Crabtree Pub Co.
Sabin, Francene. Arctic & Antarctic Regions. Eitzen, Allan, illus. LC 84-2730. 32p. (gr. 3-6). 1985. PLB 9.49 (ISBN 0-8167-0234-9); pap. text ed. 2.95 (ISBN 0-8167-0235-7). Troll Assocs.
Salisbury, Mike. Arctic Expedition. LC 88-42905. 32p. (gr. 4-5). 1989. PLB 10.95 (ISBN 1-55532-920-9). Gareth Stevens Inc.
Stone, Lynn M. The Arctic. LC 84-23248. (Illus.). 48p. (gr. k-4). 1985. lib. bdg. 14.60 (ISBN 0-516-01935-X). Childrens.

ARCTIC REGIONS–FICTION
Houston, James. Frozen Fire: A Tale of Courage. Houston, James, illus. LC 77-6366. 160p. (gr. 7 up). 1977. 13.95 (ISBN 0-689-50083-1, M K McElderry). Macmillan Child Grp.
Miller, Sherry C. Snowharry Takes a Vacation (with Arctic Friends) Martinez, Jesse, illus. 32p. (gr. k-5). 1985. pap. write for info. saddle-stitched (ISBN 0-913379-03-4). Double M Pub.
Roth, Arthur. Iceberg Hermit. 224p. (gr. 7-12). 1976. pap. 2.25 (ISBN 0-590-01582-6). Scholastic Inc.

ARDENNES, BATTLE OF THE, 1944-1945
Stein, R. Conrad. The Story of the Battle of the Bulge. Aronson, Lou, illus. LC 77-5431. 32p. (gr. 3-5). 1977. PLB 13.27 (ISBN 0-516-04608-X). Childrens.
Toland, John. The Battle of the Bulge. (Illus.). (gr. 5-9). 1966. Random.

ARGENTINE REPUBLIC
Fox, Geoffrey. The Land & People of Argentina. LC 89-37811. (Illus.). 256p. (gr. 6 up). 1990. 16.95 (ISBN 0-397-32380-8, Lipp Jr Bks); PLB 16.89 (ISBN 0-397-32381-6, Lipp Jr Bks). HarpC Child Bks.
Hintz, Martin. Argentina. LC 85-2638. (Illus.). 127p. (gr. 4-6). 1985. PLB 25.27 (ISBN 0-516-02752-2). Childrens.
Jacobsen, Karen. Argentina. LC 90-36526. (Illus.). 48p. (gr. k-4). 1990. PLB 14.60 (ISBN 0-516-01101-4); pap. 4.95 (ISBN 0-516-41101-2). Childrens.
Lerner Publications, Department of Geography Staff, ed. Argentina in Pictures. (Illus.). 64p. (gr. 5 up). 1988. PLB 12.95 (ISBN 0-8225-1807-4). Lerner Pubns.
Liebowitz, Sol. Argentina. (Illus.). (gr. 5 up). 1990. 14.95 (ISBN 0-7910-1106-2). Chelsea Hse.
Lye, Keith. Take a Trip to Argentina. LC 86-50018. (Illus.). 32p. (gr. 1-6). 1986. PLB 7.99 (ISBN 0-531-10194-0). Watts.
Morrison, Marion. Argentina. (Illus.). 48p. (gr. 4-8). 1989. lib. bdg. 14.98 (ISBN 0-382-09793-9). Silver Burdett Pr.
Peterson, Marge & Peterson, Rob. Argentina: A Wild West Heritage. LC 89-11707. (Illus.). 128p. (gr. 5 up). 1989. PLB 14.95 (ISBN 0-87518-413-8, Dillon). Macmillan Child Grp.

ARGUMENTATION
see Debates and Debating; Logic
ARISTOCRACY
see also Democracy
ARITHMETIC
Addition Wipe-off Book. 24p. (Orig.). (gr. 1 up). 1987. pap. 1.95 (ISBN 0-590-40763-5). Scholastic Inc.
Addition Wipe-off Book. 24p. (Orig.). (gr. 1 up). 1988. pap. 1.95 (ISBN 0-590-42012-7). Scholastic Inc.

Allington, Richard L. Numbers. Garcia, Tom, illus. LC 79-19200. 32p. (gr. k-3). 1985. pap. 15.33 (ISBN 0-8172-1278-7); pap. 9.27 (ISBN 0-8172-2483-1). Raintree Pubs.
Amir-Moez, Ali R. & Menzel, Donald H. Fun with Numbers, Lines & Angles. 32p. (gr. 3-6). 1981. pap. 2.95 (ISBN 0-87534-179-9). Highlights.
Anno, Mitsumasa. Anno's Mysterious Multiplying Jar. Anno, Mitsumasa, illus. LC 82-22413. 48p. (gr. 3 up). 1983. pap. 14.95 (ISBN 0-399-20951-4, Philomel). Putnam Pub Group.
Beginning to Add. 32p. (gr. k-1). 1986. write for info. wkbk. (ISBN 0-307-03590-5, Pub. by Golden Bks). Western Pub.
Beginning to Count: Learning about Counting to 10. (ps-3). pap. write for info. incl. cassette (ISBN 0-307-13800-3, Golden Bks). Western Pub.
Beginning to Subtract. 32p. (gr. k-1). 1986. write for info. wkbk. (ISBN 0-307-03591-3, Pub. by Golden Bks). Western Pub.
Brazile, Lionel J., Jr. Arithmetic Summary Booklet. (Illus.). 16p. (Orig.). (gr. 1-9). 1990. pap. 12.95 (ISBN 0-9624016-0-9). Scholar Pub Co.
Buschemeyer, Robin Q. Number Pal. Launching Pad Studios, Inc. Staff, illus. 40p. (Orig.). (ps-3). 1986. pap. 2.99 (ISBN 0-935609-02-4). Eduplay.
Carson, Patti & Dellosa, Janet. Numbers, Number Words & Sets. Carson, Patti & Dellosa, Janet, illus. 32p. (ps-1). 1983. pap. 1.98 (ISBN 0-88724-005-4, CD-7006). Carson-Dellos.
—Subtraction Facts: Differences to Ten. Carson, Patti & Dellosa, Janet, illus. 32p. (gr. 1-2). 1984. pap. 1.98 (ISBN 0-88724-078-X, CD-7021). Carson-Dellos.
Daniel, Becky. Hooray for Addition Facts! (Illus.). 80p. (gr. 1-3). 1990. 9.95 (ISBN 0-86653-517-9, GA1133). Good Apple.
—Hooray for Division Facts! (Illus.). 80p. (gr. 2-4). 1990. 9.95 (ISBN 0-86653-520-9, GA1135). Good Apple.
—Hooray for Multiplication Facts! (Illus.). 80p. (gr. 2-4). 1990. 9.95 (ISBN 0-86653-519-5, GA1136). Good Apple.
—Hooray for Subtraction Facts! (Illus.). 80p. (gr. 1-3). 1990. 9.95 (ISBN 0-86653-518-7, GA1134). Good Apple.
Daniel, Becky & Daniel, Charlie. Arithmetrix. 64p. (gr. 5-8). 1980. 6.95 (ISBN 0-916456-75-7, GA 188). Good Apple.
Dellosa, Janet & Carson, Patti. Addition Facts: Sums to Ten. Dellosa, Janet & Carson, PAtti, illus. 32p. (gr. 1-2). 1984. pap. 1.98 (ISBN 0-88724-076-3, CD-7019). Carson-Dellos.
Dellosa, Janet, et al. Positions: Under, on, Beside, in, Behind. Dellosa, Janet & Carson, Patti, illus. 32p. (ps-1). 1983. pap. 1.98 (ISBN 0-88724-007-0, CD-7008). Carson-Dellos.
Gerver, Jane, ed. My First Book of Subtraction. McCarthy, Kathleen, illus. 32p. (gr. 1-3). 1986. wkbk. 3.95 (ISBN 0-394-88172-9). Random.
Get Ready for Math. 32p. (ps-1). 1986. write for info. wkbk. (ISBN 0-307-05164-1, Pub. by Golden Bks). Western Pub.
Gregorich, Barbara. Addition & Subtraction. Hoffman, Joan, ed. Koontz, Robin M., illus. 32p. (gr. 1). 1988. wkbk. 1.49 (ISBN 0-88743-163-1). Sch Zone Pub Co.
—Addition & Subtraction. Hoffman, Joan, ed. Koontz, Robin M., illus. 32p. (gr. 2). 1988. wkbk. 1.49 (ISBN 0-88743-169-0). Sch Zone Pub Co.
—Addition & Subtraction: First Grade. Hoffman, Joan, ed. Koontz, Robin M., illus. 32p. (gr. 1). 1990. wkbk. 3.49 (ISBN 0-88743-182-8). Sch Zone Pub Co.
—Addition & Subtraction: Second Grade. Hoffman, Joan, ed. Koontz, Robin M., illus. 32p. (gr. 2). 1990. wkbk. 3.49 (ISBN 0-88743-188-7). Sch Zone Pub Co.
—Number Skills One to Ten: Kindergarten. Hoffman, Joan, ed. Koontz, Robin M., illus. 32p. (gr. k). 1990. wkbk. 3.49 (ISBN 0-88743-175-5). Sch Zone Pub Co.
Gurau, Peter K. & Lieberthal, Edwin M. Fingermath. Gafney, Leo, ed. 192p. (gr. 3-8). 1980. text ed. 6.56 (ISBN 0-07-025223-8). McGraw.
—Fingermath, Bk. 2. Gafney, Leo, ed. (Illus.). (gr. 2-6). 1980. text ed. 6.56 (ISBN 0-07-025222-X). McGraw.
Harbin, Carey E. Fay, Jay & Adding Numbers. (Illus.). 29p. (Orig.). (ps-1). 1990. pap. text ed. 2.95 (ISBN 0-918995-04-3). Voc-Offers.
Hewavisenti, Latshmi. Measuring. (Illus.). 32p. (gr. k-4). 1991. PLB 11.40 (ISBN 0-531-17319-4, Gloucester Pr). Watts.
Jenkins, Lee. Coin Stamp Mathematics. Merrick, Paul, illus. (Orig.). (gr. k-4). 1977. pap. 6.95 (ISBN 0-918932-05-X). Activity Resources.
Kiso, Hideo. Ten Little Friends. (Illus.). 22p. (ps-1). 1981. 3.50 (ISBN 0-89346-199-7). Heian Intl.
Laycock, Mary, et al. Skateboard Practice: Addition & Subtraction. new ed. Kyzer, Martha, illus. (gr. 1-2). 1978. pap. text ed. 6.95 (ISBN 0-918932-55-6). Activity Resources.
Let's Add: Understanding Addition. (ps-3). pap. write for info. incl. cassette (ISBN 0-307-13803-8, Golden Bks). Western Pub.
Lund, Charles. Tricks of the Trade with Cards. new ed. Laycock, Mary, ed. (gr. 2-9). 1978. pap. text ed. 6.95 (ISBN 0-918932-57-2). Activity Resources.
Mitchell, Kimberly. Addition Facts: Sums to Eighteen. King, Jerry, illus. 32p. (gr. 2-3). 1984. pap. 1.98 (ISBN 0-88724-077-1, CD-7020). Carson-Dellos.
—Multiplication Facts. King, Jerry, illus. 32p. (gr. 3-4). 1984. pap. 1.98 (ISBN 0-88724-080-1, CD-7023). Carson-Dellos.

—Subtraction Facts: Differences to Eighteen. King, Jerry, illus. 32p. (gr. 2-3). 1984. pap. 1.98 (ISBN 0-88724-079-8, CD-7022). Carson-Dellos.
More Getting Ready for Reading & Math. (Illus.). 32p. (gr. k). 1986. write for info. wkbk. (ISBN 0-307-03594-8, Pub. by Golden Bks). Western Pub.
More Math 1. (Illus.). 32p. (gr. 1-2). 1986. write for info. wkbk. (ISBN 0-307-03595-6, Pub. by Golden Bks). Western Pub.
More or Less: Beginning to Add & Subtract. (ps-3). pap. write for info. incl. cassette (ISBN 0-307-13793-7, Golden Bks). Western Pub.
Ockenga, Earl & Rucker, Walt. Subtracting from Eighteen or Less. Dawson, Dave, illus. 16p. (gr. 1). 1990. pap. text ed. 1.25 (ISBN 1-56281-135-5, M135). Extra Eds.
—Subtracting from Ten or Less. Dawson, Dave, illus. 16p. (gr. 1). 1990. pap. text ed. 1.25 (ISBN 1-56281-110-X, M110). Extra Eds.
—Sums Through Eighteen. Dawson, Dave, illus. 16p. (gr. 1). 1990. pap. text ed. 1.25 (ISBN 1-56281-130-4, M130). Extra Eds.
—Sums Through Ten. Dawson, Dave, illus. 16p. (gr. 1). 1990. pap. text ed. 1.25 (ISBN 1-56281-105-3, M105). Extra Eds.
—Telling Time. Dawson, Dave, illus. 16p. (gr. 1). 1990. pap. text ed. 1.25 (ISBN 1-56281-120-7, M120). Extra Eds.
Pare, Roger. One, Two, Three... Play with Me! (ps-1). 1988. Incl. one bk., four games & ten mini-puzzles. 12.95 (ISBN 0-88166-120-1, Dist. by Simon & Schuster). Meadowbrook.
Paris, Pat. Tillie Tiger's Times Tables. (Illus.). 10p. (gr. 1-3). 1990. 11.95 (ISBN 0-8120-6110-1). Barron.
Petty, Kate. Numbers. LC 85-70952. (Illus.). 32p. (gr. k-6). 1986. lib. bdg. 10.40 (ISBN 0-531-17009-8, Gloucester Pr). Watts.
Rasmussen. Key to Percents, Bk. 1. 48p. (gr. 4-12). 1988. pap. text ed. 1.95 (ISBN 0-913684-57-0). Key Curr Pr.
—Key to Percents, Bk. 2. 48p. (gr. 4-12). 1988. pap. text ed. 1.95 (ISBN 0-913684-58-9). Key Curr Pr.
—Key to Percents, Bk. 3. 48p. (gr. 4-12). 1988. pap. text ed. 1.95 (ISBN 0-913684-59-7). Key Curr Pr.
—Key to Percents: Answers & Notes for Books 1-3. 48p. (gr. 4-12). 1988. pap. text ed. 1.95 (ISBN 0-913684-61-9). Key Curr Pr.
Reading, Writing & Arithmetic: Grade 2. 160p. 1973. pap. 1.95 (ISBN 0-448-02912-X, G&D). Putnam Pub Group.

Salant, Michael A. Arithmetic Is Fun: The Arithmetic Example Handbook of Grade-School Math. (Illus.). 96p. (Orig.). (gr. 1-6). 1991. 12.95x (ISBN 0-9609288-5-5); pap. 7.95x glow in the dark spiral bdg. (ISBN 0-9609288-4-7). M A Salant.
For Kids, Parents, Teachers, & Tutors. What to do & when. How to do it & why. Step-by-step examples, fully worked out. Whole numbers, fractions, decimals, percents, measurement, & more. Plus the old standbys: carrying, borrowing, reducing, cancelling, & more. Plus: Short-cuts, hints, tips, & useful techniques. Not a schoolbook for a particular grade or age, but an easy-to-use "at home" reference, covering many topics, that your child can refer to year after year. Less 20% discount to wholesalers, distributors, & jobbers: $1.59 for paper & $2.59 for hardcover. Plus 6% sales tax for D.C. residents only: 48 cents for paper & 78 cents for hardcover. Plus $2 ($3 foreign) for surface postage & handling. Please Note: Prepayment required (check with order). No returns. Order from your supplier or: Michael A. Salant, P.O. Box 33421, Farragut Station, Washington, D.C. 20033-0421.
Publisher Provided Annotation.

Schaffer, Frank, Publications Staff. Addition. (Illus.). 24p. (gr. 1-3). 1978. wkbk. 3.98 (ISBN 0-86734-007-X, FS 3008). Schaffer Pubns.
Smart, Margaret. Focus on Decimals, 2 vols. (Illus.). (gr. 7-9). 1977. pap. text ed. 6.50 ea.; Vol. 1. (ISBN 0-918932-12-2); Vol. 2. (ISBN 0-918932-13-0). Activity Resources.
The Subtraction Wipe-Off Book. 24p. (gr. 1 up). 1988. pap. 1.95 (ISBN 0-590-42042-9). Scholastic Inc.
ARITHMETIC–STUDY AND TEACHING
see also Counting Books
Johnson, Merideth. When I Learn to Add. 1990. 3.98 (ISBN 0-8317-9373-2). Smithmark.

—When I Learn to Count. 1990. 3.98 (ISBN 0-8317-9372-4). Smithmark.

ARIZONA

Adventures in Arizona: An Illustrated History. Caillou, Aliza, ed. Carlson, Diane, illus. 48p. (Orig.). (gr. 4 up). 1991. pap. 6.95 (ISBN 0-9628329-3-6). Thorne Enterprises.
A comprehensive historical chronicle for ages 10 years & up, fully illustrated with original black & white drawings by artist Diane Carlson. The book begins in prehistoric times showing flora, fauna, dinosaurs & early man in Arizona & includes descriptions of how the Grand Canyon was formed. Two main characters, a little girl & a little boy walk in & out of the story, commenting on its various aspects. The second section describes the three main original native language groups of Indian people living in Arizona (Yuman, Uto-Aztecan & Athapascan), where these people came from, how they are alike & different, (including home styles, food, arts, ceremonies & clothing) & what tribes we know them as today. The Early Explorers (from the Spanish to the Geological surveyors) follows, then there is a section on Civilization (Miners, homesteaders, etc.) & finally Modern Times which shows state industry & largest cities. The four-color front cover of the book illustrates the state flag & state symbols. The back cover includes a map of historic sites in Arizona.
Publisher Provided Annotation.

Arizona Adventure: History for Boys & Girls. (gr. 4-9). 1972. text ed. 6.00 (ISBN 0-910152-00-4). AZ Hist Foun.

Aylesworth, Thomas G. & Aylesworth, Virginia L. The West (Arizona, Nevada, Utah) (Illus.). 64p. (gr. 3 up). 1992. PLB 16.95 (ISBN 0-7910-1049-X). Chelsea Hse.

Carole Marsh Arizona Books, 31 bks. Set. 638.45 (ISBN 0-7933-1276-0). Gallopade Pub Group.

Carpenter, Allan. Arizona. LC 79-11802. (Illus.). 96p. (gr. 4 up). 1979. PLB 19.93 (ISBN 0-516-04103-7). Childrens.

Cobb, Vicki. This Place Is Dry. Lavallee, Barbara, illus. (gr. 2-4). 1989. 12.95 (ISBN 0-8027-6854-7); PLB 13.85 (ISBN 0-8027-6855-5). Walker & Co.

Filbin, Dan. Arizona. (Illus.). 72p. (gr. 3-6). 1990. PLB 12.95 (ISBN 0-8225-2705-7). Lerner Pubns.

Fradin, Dennis. Arizona: In Words & Pictures. LC 79-21480. (Illus.). 48p. (gr. 2-5). 1980. PLB 15.93 (ISBN 0-516-03903-2); pap. 4.95 (ISBN 0-516-43903-0). Childrens.

McCool, Grace. Gunsmoke; the True Story of Old Tombstone. 150p. 1990. pap. 6.95 (ISBN 0-918080-52-5). Treasure Chest.

Mackler, Carole B. & Holmgren, Renee. Sedona Coloring Book. (Illus., Orig.). (gr. k-8). 1989. pap. 6.95 (ISBN 0-317-94104-6). SSGI Pr.

Marsh, Carole. Arizona & Other State Greats (Biographies) (Illus.). (gr. 3-12). 1990. PLB 19.95 (ISBN 1-55609-507-4); pap. 14.95 (ISBN 1-55609-506-6); computer disk 29.95 (ISBN 0-7933-1373-2). Gallopade Pub Group.

—Arizona Bandits, Bushwackers, Outlaws, Crooks, Devils, Ghosts, Desperadoes & Other Assorted & Sundry Characters! (Illus.). (gr. 3-12). 1990. PLB 19.95 (ISBN 0-7933-0118-1); pap. 14.95 (ISBN 0-7933-0117-3); computer disk 29.95 (ISBN 0-7933-0119-X). Gallopade Pub Group.

—Arizona Classic Christmas Trivia: Stories, Recipes, Activities, Legends, Lore & More! (Illus.). (gr. 3-12). 1990. PLB 19.95 (ISBN 0-7933-0121-1); pap. 14.95 (ISBN 0-7933-0120-3); computer disk 29.95 (ISBN 0-7933-0122-X). Gallopade Pub Group.

—Arizona Coastales. (Illus.). (gr. 3-12). 1990. PLB 19.95 (ISBN 1-55609-503-1); pap. 14.95 (ISBN 1-55609-502-3); computer disk 29.95 (ISBN 0-7933-1369-4). Gallopade Pub Group.

—The Arizona Hot Air Balloon Mystery. (Illus.). (gr. 2-9). 1990. 19.95 (ISBN 0-7933-2336-3); pap. 14.95 (ISBN 0-7933-2337-1); computer disk 29.95 (ISBN 0-7933-2338-X). Gallopade Pub Group.

—Arizona "Jography" A Fun Run Thru Our State! (Illus.). (gr. 3-12). 1990. PLB 19.95 (ISBN 1-55609-498-1); pap. 14.95 (ISBN 1-55609-497-3); computer disk 29.95 (ISBN 0-7933-1359-7). Gallopade Pub Group.

—Arizona Kid's Cookbook: Recipes, How-to, History, Lore & More! (Illus.). (gr. 3-12). 1990. PLB 19.95 (ISBN 0-7933-0130-0); pap. 14.95 (ISBN 0-7933-0129-7); computer disk 29.95 (ISBN 0-7933-0131-9). Gallopade Pub Group.

—Arizona Quiz Bowl Crash Course! (Illus.). (gr. 3-12). 1990. PLB 19.95 (ISBN 1-55609-505-8); pap. 14.95 (ISBN 1-55609-504-X); computer disk 29.95 (ISBN 0-7933-1368-6). Gallopade Pub Group.

—Arizona School Trivia: An Amazing & Fascinating Look at Our State's Teachers, Schools & Students! (Illus.). (gr. 3-12). 1990. PLB 19.95 (ISBN 0-7933-0127-0); pap. 14.95 (ISBN 0-7933-0126-2); computer disk 29.95. Gallopade Pub Group.

—Arizona Silly Basketball Sportsmysteries, Vol. I. (Illus.). (gr. 3-12). 1990. PLB 19.95 (ISBN 0-7933-0124-6); pap. 14.95 (ISBN 0-7933-0123-8); computer disk 29.95 (ISBN 0-7933-0125-4). Gallopade Pub Group.

—Arizona Silly Basketball Sportsmysteries, Vol. II. (Illus.). (gr. 3-12). 1990. PLB 19.95 (ISBN 0-7933-1568-9); pap. 14.95 (ISBN 0-7933-1569-7); computer disk 29.95 (ISBN 0-7933-1570-0). Gallopade Pub Group.

—Arizona Silly Football Sportsmysteries, Vol. I. (Illus.). (gr. 3-12). 1990. PLB 19.95 (ISBN 1-55609-501-5); pap. 14.95 (ISBN 1-55609-500-7); computer disk 29.95 (ISBN 0-7933-1361-9). Gallopade Pub Group.

—Arizona Silly Football Sportsmysteries, Vol. II. (Illus.). (gr. 3-12). 1990. PLB 19.95 (ISBN 0-7933-1362-7); pap. 14.95 (ISBN 0-7933-1363-5); computer disk 29.95 (ISBN 0-7933-1364-3). Gallopade Pub Group.

—Arizona Silly Trivia! (Illus.). (gr. 3-12). 1990. PLB 19.95 (ISBN 1-55609-496-5); pap. 14.95 (ISBN 1-55609-495-7); computer disk 29.95 (ISBN 0-7933-1358-9). Gallopade Pub Group.

—Arizona's (Most Devastating!) Disasters & (Most Calamitous!) Catastrophies! (Illus.). (gr. 3-12). 1990. PLB 19.95 (ISBN 0-7933-0115-7); pap. 14.95 (ISBN 0-7933-0114-9); computer disk 29.95 (ISBN 0-7933-0116-5). Gallopade Pub Group.

—Avast, Ye Slobs! Arizona Pirate Trivia. (Illus.). (gr. 3-12). 1990. PLB 19.95 (ISBN 0-7933-0136-X); pap. 14.95 (ISBN 0-7933-0135-1); computer disk 29.95 (ISBN 0-7933-0137-8). Gallopade Pub Group.

—The Beast of the Arizona Bed & Breakfast. (Illus.). (gr. 3-12). 1990. PLB 19.95 (ISBN 0-7933-1365-1); pap. 14.95 (ISBN 0-7933-1366-X); computer disk 29.95 (ISBN 0-7933-1367-8). Gallopade Pub Group.

—The Hard-to-Believe-But-True! Book of Arizona History, Mystery, Trivia, Legend, Lore, Humor & More. (Illus.). (gr. 3-12). 1990. PLB 19.95 (ISBN 0-7933-0133-5); pap. 14.95 (ISBN 0-7933-0132-7); computer disk 29.95 (ISBN 0-7933-0134-3). Gallopade Pub Group.

—If My Arizona Mama Ran the World! (Illus.). (gr. 3-12). 1990. PLB 19.95 (ISBN 0-7933-1370-8); pap. 14.95 (ISBN 0-7933-1371-6); computer disk 29.95 (ISBN 0-7933-1372-4). Gallopade Pub Group.

—Let's Quilt Arizona & Stuff It Topographically! (Illus.). (gr. 3-12). 1990. PLB 19.95 (ISBN 1-55609-499-X); pap. 14.95 (ISBN 1-55609-128-1); computer disk 29.95 (ISBN 0-7933-1360-0). Gallopade Pub Group.

Salts, Roberta. Arizona Is for Kids. Fischer, Bruce, illus. 32p. (gr. 1-4). 1988. pap. 2.95 (ISBN 0-685-21928-3). Double B Pubns.

Swindler, William F. & Trover, Ellen L., eds. Chronology & Documentary Handbook of the State of Arizona. LC 72-5199. 128p. (gr. 9-12). 1972. PLB 8.50 (ISBN 0-379-16128-1). Oceana.

Tegeler, Dorothy. Hello Arizona: The Arizona Activity Book. Hicks, Mark, illus. 32p. (Orig.). 1987. pap. 3.50 (ISBN 0-943169-07-0). Fiesta Bks Inc.

Trimble, Marshall. Arizona: A Panoramic History of a Frontier State. LC 76-45265. 1977. pap. 14.95 (ISBN 0-385-12806-1). Doubleday.

Turner Program Services, Inc. Staff & Clark, James I. Arizona. LC 85-9978. (gr. 3 up). 1985. PLB 17.32 (ISBN 0-86514-425-7); cancelled Beta video (ISBN 0-86514-050-2); cancelled VHS video (ISBN 0-86514-125-8); cancelled 3/4" video (ISBN 0-86514-200-9); cancelled tchr's. guide (ISBN 0-86514-275-0); cancelled student activity bk. (ISBN 0-86514-350-1); cancelled index. Raintree Pubs.

Wagoner, Jay J. Arizona's Heritage. LC 77-10778. (Illus.). 496p. (gr. 8-12). 1983. text ed. 21.00x (ISBN 0-87905-028-4, Peregrine Smith). Gibbs Smith Pub.

ARIZONA–FICTION

Armer, Laura A. Waterless Mountain. Armer, Laura A., illus. (gr. 5-8). 1931. 11.95 (ISBN 0-679-20233-1). McKay.

Johnston, Annie F. The Little Colonel in Arizona. (gr. 5 up). 13.95 (ISBN 0-89201-033-9). Zenger Pub.

ARKANSAS

Aylesworth, Thomas G. & Aylesworth, Virginia L. South Central (Louisiana, Arkansas, Missouri, Kansas, Oklahoma) (Illus.). 64p. (gr. 3 up). 1992. PLB 16.95 (ISBN 0-7910-1047-3). Chelsea Hse.

Baker, Harri T. & Browning, Jane. An Arkansas History for Young People. (gr. 8). 1991. student wkbk. 28.00 (ISBN 1-55728-083-5); write for info. tchr's. manual (ISBN 1-55728-201-3). U of Ark Pr.

Carole Marsh Arkansas Books, 31 bks. Set. 638.45 (ISBN 0-7933-1277-9). Gallopade Pub Group.

Carpenter, Allan. Arkansas. LC 78-3786. (Illus.). 96p. (gr. 4 up). 1978. PLB 19.93 (ISBN 0-516-04104-5). Childrens.

Fradin, Dennis. Arkansas: In Words & Pictures. Wahl, Richard, illus. LC 80-11995. 48p. (gr. 2-5). 1980. PLB 15.93 (ISBN 0-516-03904-0). Childrens.

Heinrichs, Ann. Arkansas. LC 88-38529. (Illus.). 144p. (gr. 4 up). 1989. lib. bdg. 25.27 (ISBN 0-516-00450-6). Childrens.

Marsh, Carole. Arkansas & Other State Greats (Biographies) (Illus.). (gr. 3-12). 1990. PLB 19.95 (ISBN 1-55609-494-9); pap. 14.95 (ISBN 1-55609-493-0); computer disk 29.95 (ISBN 0-7933-1389-9). Gallopade Pub Group.

—Arkansas Bandits, Bushwackers, Outlaws, Crooks, Devils, Ghosts, Desperadoes & Other Assorted & Sundry Characters! (Illus.). (gr. 3-12). 1990. PLB 19.95 (ISBN 0-7933-0142-4); pap. 14.95 (ISBN 0-7933-0141-6); computer disk 29.95 (ISBN 0-7933-0143-2). Gallopade Pub Group.

—Arkansas Classic Christmas Trivia: Stories, Recipes, Activities, Legends, Lore & More! (Illus.). (gr. 3-12). 1990. PLB 19.95 (ISBN 0-7933-0145-9); pap. 14.95 (ISBN 0-7933-0144-0); computer disk 29.95 (ISBN 0-7933-0146-7). Gallopade Pub Group.

—Arkansas Coastales. (Illus.). (gr. 3-12). 1990. PLB 19.95 (ISBN 1-55609-490-6); pap. 14.95 (ISBN 1-55609-489-2); computer disk 29.95 (ISBN 0-7933-1385-6). Gallopade Pub Group.

—The Arkansas Hot Air Balloon Mystery. (Illus.). (gr. 2-9). 1990. 19.95 (ISBN 0-7933-2345-2); pap. 14.95 (ISBN 0-7933-2346-0); computer disk 29.95 (ISBN 0-7933-2347-9). Gallopade Pub Group.

—Arkansas "Jography" A Fun Run Thru Our State! (Illus.). (gr. 3-12). 1990. PLB 19.95 (ISBN 1-55609-485-X); pap. 14.95 (ISBN 1-55609-088-9); computer disk 29.95 (ISBN 0-7933-1375-9). Gallopade Pub Group.

—Arkansas Kid's Cookbook: Recipes, How-to, History, Lore & More! (Illus.). (gr. 3-12). 1990. PLB 19.95 (ISBN 0-7933-0154-8); pap. 14.95 (ISBN 0-7933-0153-X); computer disk 29.95 (ISBN 0-7933-0155-6). Gallopade Pub Group.

—Arkansas Quiz Bowl Crash Course! (Illus.). (gr. 3-12). 1990. PLB 19.95 (ISBN 1-55609-492-2); pap. 14.95 (ISBN 1-55609-491-4); computer disk 29.95 (ISBN 0-7933-1384-8). Gallopade Pub Group.

—Arkansas School Trivia: An Amazing & Fascinating Look at Our State's Teachers, Schools & Students! (Illus.). (gr. 3-12). 1990. PLB 19.95 (ISBN 0-7933-0151-3); pap. 14.95 (ISBN 0-7933-0150-5); computer disk 29.95 (ISBN 0-7933-0152-1). Gallopade Pub Group.

—Arkansas Silly Basketball Sportsmysteries, Vol. I. (Illus.). (gr. 3-12). 1990. PLB 19.95 (ISBN 0-7933-0149-1); pap. 14.95 (ISBN 0-7933-0147-5); computer disk 29.95. Gallopade Pub Group.

—Arkansas Silly Basketball Sportsmysteries, Vol. II. (Illus.). (gr. 3-12). 1990. PLB 19.95 (ISBN 0-7933-1571-9); pap. 14.95; computer disk 29.95 (ISBN 0-7933-1573-5). Gallopade Pub Group.

—Arkansas Silly Football Sportsmysteries, Vol. I. (Illus.). (gr. 3-12). 1990. PLB 19.95 (ISBN 1-55609-488-4); pap. 14.95 (ISBN 1-55609-487-6); computer disk 29.95 (ISBN 0-7933-1377-5). Gallopade Pub Group.

—Arkansas Silly Football Sportsmysteries, Vol. II. (Illus.). (gr. 3-12). 1990. PLB 19.95 (ISBN 0-7933-1378-3); pap. 14.95 (ISBN 0-7933-1379-1); computer disk 29.95 (ISBN 0-7933-1380-5). Gallopade Pub Group.

—Arkansas Silly Trivia! (Illus.). (gr. 3-12). 1990. PLB 19.95 (ISBN 1-55609-484-1); pap. 14.95 (ISBN 1-55609-083-8); computer disk 29.95 (ISBN 0-7933-1374-0). Gallopade Pub Group.

—Arkansas's (Most Devastating!) Disasters & (Most Calamitous!) Catastrophies! (Illus.). (gr. 3-12). 1990. PLB 19.95 (ISBN 0-7933-0139-4); pap. 14.95 (ISBN 0-7933-0138-6); computer disk 29.95 (ISBN 0-7933-0140-8). Gallopade Pub Group.

—Avast, Ye Slobs! Arkansas Pirate Trivia. (Illus.). (gr. 3-12). 1990. PLB 19.95 (ISBN 0-7933-0160-2); pap. 14.95 (ISBN 0-7933-0159-9); computer disk 29.95 (ISBN 0-7933-0161-0). Gallopade Pub Group.

—The Beast of the Arkansas Bed & Breakfast. (Illus.). (gr. 3-12). 1990. PLB 19.95 (ISBN 0-7933-1381-3); pap. 14.95 (ISBN 0-7933-1382-1); computer disk 29.95 (ISBN 0-7933-1383-X). Gallopade Pub Group.

—The Hard-to-Believe-But-True! Book of Arkansas History, Mystery, Trivia, Legend, Lore, Humor & More. (Illus.). (gr. 3-12). 1990. PLB 19.95 (ISBN 0-7933-0157-2); pap. 14.95 (ISBN 0-7933-0156-4); computer disk 29.95 (ISBN 0-7933-0158-0). Gallopade Pub Group.

—If My Arkansas Mama Ran the World! (Illus.). (gr. 3-12). 1990. PLB 19.95 (ISBN 0-7933-1386-4); pap. 14.95 (ISBN 0-7933-1387-2); computer disk 29.95 (ISBN 0-7933-1388-0). Gallopade Pub Group.

—Let's Quilt Arkansas & Stuff It Topographically! (Illus.). (gr. 3-12). 1990. PLB 19.95 (ISBN 1-55609-486-8); pap. 14.95 (ISBN 1-55609-078-1); computer disk 29.95 (ISBN 0-7933-1376-7). Gallopade Pub Group.

Swindler, William F. & Trover, Ellen L., eds. Chronology & Documentary Handbook of the State of Arkansas, No. 4. LC 72-5331. 141p. (gr. 9-12). 1972. PLB 8.50 (ISBN 0-379-16129-X). Oceana.

Thompson, Kathleen. Arkansas. LC 87-16372. 48p. (gr. 3 up). 1987. 17.32 (ISBN 0-86514-449-4); cancelled tchr's. study guide (ISBN 0-86514-600-4); cancelled Beta video (ISBN 0-86514-074-X); cancelled VHS video (ISBN 0-86514-149-5); cancelled 3/4" video (ISBN 0-317-67067-0). Raintree Pubs.

Zodrow, Brenda. Arkansas Coloring Book. (Illus.). 54p. (gr. k-4). 1990. 4.50 (ISBN 1-55728-179-3). U of Ark Pr.

ARKANSAS–FICTION

Crofford, Emily. A Matter of Pride. LaMarche, Jim, illus. LC 81-387. 48p. (gr. 2-6). 1991. Repr. of 1981 ed. PLB 11.95 (ISBN 0-87614-171-8, AACR2). Carolrhoda Bks.

Greene, Bette. Philip Hall Likes Me. I Reckon Maybe. Lilly, Charles, illus. LC 74-2887. 160p. (gr. 3-6). 1974. 13.95 (ISBN 0-8037-6098-1); PLB 13.89 (ISBN 0-8037-6096-5). Dial Bks Young.

Harris, Kathleen M. The Wonderful Hay Tumble. Gackenbach, Dick, illus. LC 87-12305. 32p. (ps-2). 1988. 12.95 (ISBN 0-688-07151-1); PLB 12.88 (ISBN 0-688-07152-X, Morrow Jr Bks). Morrow Jr Bks.

Medearis, Mary. Big Doc's Girl. LC 84-45641. 142p. (gr. 7-12). 1985. pap. 7.95 (ISBN 0-87483-105-9). August Hse.

ARMADA, 1588

Connatty, Mary. The Armada. Warwick Press, ed. (Illus.). 48p. (gr. 4-9). 1988. PLB 11.90 (ISBN 0-531-19030-7, Warwick). Watts.

McDowall, David. The Spanish Armada. (Illus.). 68p. (gr. 7-9). 1988. 19.95 (ISBN 0-7134-5671-X, Pub. by Batsford England). Trafalgar Sq.

The Spanish Armada. (Illus.). (gr. 5 up). 3.50 (ISBN 0-7214-1093-6). Ladybird Bks.

ARMADILLOS

Kipling, Rudyard. The Beginning of the Armadilloes: A Just So Story. Keeping, Charles, illus. LC 83-71481. 28p. (gr. 1-5). 1983. PLB 10.95 (ISBN 0-911745-03-3). P Bedrick Bks.

Lavies, Bianca. It's an Armadillo! 1989. 13.95 (ISBN 0-525-44523-4, DCB). Dutton Child Bks.

ARMAMENTS

see Disarmament

ARMED FORCES

see Soldiers

see names of countries and international organizations with the subdivision Armed Forces, e.g. U. S.–Armed Forces; etc.

ARMIES

see also Disarmament; Military Art and Science; Soldiers; War

also names of countries with the subhead Army (e.g. U. S. army; etc.); and headings beginning with the word Military

ARMORED CARS (TANKS)

see Tanks (Military Science)

ARMS, COATS OF

see Heraldry

ARMS AND ARMOR

see also Firearms

Armor. (Illus.). 64p. (gr. 3-9). 1990. PLB 16.95 (ISBN 1-85435-089-7). Marshall Cavendish.

Byam, Michele. Arms & Armor. King, Dave, photos by. LC 87-26449. (Illus.). 64p. (gr. 5 up). 1988. 15.00 (ISBN 0-394-89622-X); lib. bdg. 15.99 (ISBN 0-394-99622-4). Knopf.

Colby, C. B. Arms of Our Fighting Men: Personnel Weapons, Bazookas, Big Guns. rev. ed. (Illus.). (gr. 4-7). 1972. PLB 6.99 (ISBN 0-698-30432-2, Coward). Putnam Pub Group.

Harbor, B. Arms Trade. (Illus.). 48p. (gr. 5 up). Date not set. PLB 18.00 (ISBN 0-86592-283-7). Rourke Corp.

Hofsinde, Robert. Indian Warriors & Their Weapons. Hofsinde, Robert, illus. LC 65-11041. (gr. 4-7). 1965. PLB 11.88 (ISBN 0-688-31613-1, Morrow Junior Books). Morrow.

Hogg, Ian. Missiles & Artillery. (Illus.). 48p. (gr. 6 up). 1984. lib. bdg. 12.90 (ISBN 0-531-04934-5). Watts.

Tunis, Edwin. Weapons. LC 76-29699. (Illus.). 160p. (gr. 6 up). 1977. 24.95 (ISBN 0-690-01285-3, Crowell Jr Bks). HarpC Child Bks.

Wilkinson, Frederick. Arms & Armor. (Illus.). 32p. (gr. 2-4). 1984. PLB 7.99 (ISBN 0-531-03772-X). Watts.

ARMS CONTROL

see Disarmament

ARMSTRONG, DANIEL LOUIS, 1900-1971

Collier, James L. Louis Armstrong: An American Success Story. LC 84-42982. (Illus.). 176p. (gr. 5-9). 1985. 13.95 (ISBN 0-02-722830-4, Mcmillan Child Bk). Macmillan Child Grp.

Iverson, Genie. Louis Armstrong. Brooks, Kevin, illus. LC 76-4975. 40p. (gr. 1-4). 1976. PLB 14.89 (ISBN 0-690-01127-X, Crowell Jr Bks). HarpC Child Bks.

McKissack, Patricia & McKissack, Fredrick. Louis Armstrong: Jazz Musician. Ostendorf, Ned, illus. 32p. (gr. 1-4). 1991. PLB 12.95 (ISBN 0-89490-307-1). Enslow Pubs.

ARMY

see Military Art and Science

ARMY LIFE

see Soldiers

ARMY SCHOOLS

see Military Education

ARMY VEHICLES

see Vehicles, Military

ARNOLD, BENEDICT, 1741-1801

Fritz, Jean. Traitor: The Case of Benedict Arnold. Andre, John, illus. (gr. 3-7). 1981. 9.95 (ISBN 0-399-20834-8, Putnam). Putnam Pub Group.

—Traitor: The Case of Benedict Arnold. 192p. (gr. 5-9). 1989. pap. 3.95 (ISBN 0-14-032940-4, Puffin). Puffin Bks.

ART

see also Anatomy, Artistic; Animals in Art; Archeology; Architecture; Arts and Crafts; Blacks in Literature and Art; Christian Art and Symbolism; Collage; Collectors and Collecting; Design, Decorative; Drawing; Folk Art; Forgery of Works of Art; Gems; Graphic Arts; Illustration of Books; Painting; Photography, Artistic; Pictures; Portraits; Sculpture; Symbolism

Allen, Dorothy S. Plaster & Bisque Art: Special Finishes. Cole, Tom, ed. LC 80-70317. (Illus.). 44p. (gr. 4 up). 1981. pap. 2.95 (ISBN 0-9605204-4-9). Dots Pubns.

—Plaster & Bisque Art: The Soft Touch Technique. Cole, Tom, ed. LC 80-70317. (Illus.). 47p. (gr. 4 up). 1981. pap. 2.95 (ISBN 0-9605204-6-5). Dots Pubns.

—Plaster & Bisque Art: With Transparent Watercolor. Cole, Tom, ed. LC 80-70317. (Illus.). 57p. (gr. 4 up). 1981. pap. 1.95 (ISBN 0-9605204-5-7). Dots Pubns.

Allen, Dorothy S. & Cole, Tom. Plaster & Bisque Art: Mist, Museum Bronze, Pastel Chalk, Pearl & Suede Finishes. LC 80-70317. (Illus.). 52p. (gr. 4 up). 1981. pap. 2.95 (ISBN 0-9605204-3-0). Dots Pubns.

Amery, H. & Civardi, A. The KnowHow Book of Print & Paint: Lots of Ways to Make Pictures & Patterns. (Illus.). 32p. (gr. 3-6). 1977. pap. 5.95 (ISBN 0-86020-011-6). EDC.

Armstrong, B. Build a Doodle, No. 1. 32p. (gr. k-4). 1985. 2.95 (ISBN 0-88160-124-1, LW 133). Learning Wks.

—Build a Doodle, No. 2. 32p. (gr. k-4). 1985. 2.95 (ISBN 0-88160-125-X, LW 134). Learning Wks.

Arts & Entertainment. 96p. (gr. 3-8). 1987. PLB 240.00 set (ISBN 0-685-18919-8); pap. 13.27 (ISBN 0-8172-3060-2). Raintree Pubs.

Aydelott, Jimmie. Art & Math Throughout the Year. (gr. 1-6). 1989. pap. 6.95 (ISBN 0-8224-0104-5). Fearon Teach Aids.

Blansett, Mary L. & Schimminger, Lorraine. Put a Frog in Your Pocket. (Illus.). 112p. (gr. 3-6). 1985. guide 8.95 (ISBN 0-86530-085-2, IP 85-2). Incentive Pubns.

Brisson, Lynn. Three-D Art Projects That Teach. (Illus.). 80p. (gr. k-6). 1989. pap. text ed. 7.95 (ISBN 0-86530-084-4, IP 166-1). Incentive Pubns.

Brown, Charlene & Davis, Carolyn. Fabric Art Fun. Davis, Carolyn, illus. 64p. (Orig.). 1990. pap. text ed. 5.95 (ISBN 1-56010-059-1, BA11). W Foster Pub.

Chacon, Rick. Big & Easy Art. Chacon, Rick, illus. 32p. (ps). 1986. wkbk. 5.95 (ISBN 1-55734-074-9). Tchr Create Mat.

—Grocery Bag Art: Careers. Chacon, Rick, illus. 48p. (ps-3). 1986. wkbk. 5.95 (ISBN 1-55734-072-2). Tchr Create Mat.

—Grocery Bag Art: Circus. Chacon, Rick, illus. 48p. (ps-3). 1986. wkbk. 5.95 (ISBN 1-55734-070-6). Tchr Create Mat.

—Grocery Bag Art: Farm. Chacon, Rick, illus. 48p. (ps-3). 1986. wkbk. 5.95 (ISBN 1-55734-071-4). Tchr Create Mat.

—Grocery Bag Art: Holidays. Chacon, Rick, illus. 48p. (ps-3). 1986. wkbk. 5.95 (ISBN 1-55734-073-0). Tchr Create Mat.

Cincerelli, Carol J. Opening Six: Art for Grade Six. LC 79-3013. 192p. (gr. 6). 1980. pap. text ed. 10.25 (ISBN 0-934902-11-9). Learn Concepts OH.

—Opening VII: Art for Grade Seven. LC 79-3013. (gr. 7). 1980. pap. text ed. 10.25 (ISBN 0-934902-12-7). Learn Concepts OH.

—Opening VIII: Art for Grade Eight. LC 79-3013. (gr. 8). 1979. pap. text ed. 10.25 (ISBN 0-934902-13-5). Learn Concepts OH.

Climo, Lindee. Clyde. (Illus.). 24p. (gr. 1-4). 1986. text ed. 11.95 (ISBN 0-88776-185-2, Dist. by Univ. of Toronto Pr). Tundra Bks.

Cracchiolo, Rachelle & Smith, Mary D. Quick Fun Art. (Illus.). 54p. (gr. k-3). Date not set. wkbk. 5.95 (ISBN 1-55734-001-3). Tchr Create Mat.

—Saint Patrick's Day & Easter Activities. Crachiolo, Rachelle & Smith, Mary D., illus. 32p. (gr. 1-3). 1980. wkbk. 4.95 (ISBN 1-55734-016-1). Tchr Create Mat.

Cvach, Milos, text by. Robert Delaunay: The Eiffel Tower: An Art Play Book. Curtil, Sophie. (Illus.). 32p. (gr. 2 up). 1988. 17.95 (ISBN 0-8109-1141-8). Abrams.

Daugherty, Franklin. Postmodern Times. LC 87-71793. 280p. 1988. 14.95 (ISBN 0-944284-00-0). T C DeLeon.

Forte, Nancy. Warrior in Art. LC 65-29039. (Illus.). (gr. 5 up). 1966. PLB 5.95 (ISBN 0-8225-0162-7). Lerner Pubns.

Foster, Tom. Color to Read, Vol. Aleph. LuBin, L., ed. Foster, Tom, illus. 72p. (ps-1). 1990. lib. bdg. write for info.; pap. write for info.; write for info. tchr's. ed. Lubin Pr.

Freeberg, Dolores. Graph Paper Art. Freeberg, Dolores, illus. 48p. (gr. 2-6). 1986. wkbk. 5.95 (ISBN 1-55734-052-8). Tchr Create Mat.

Freeberg, Erling & Freeberg, Dolores. Challenging Graph Art. Freeberg, Erling & Freeberg, Dolores, illus. 48p. (gr. 2-6). 1987. wkbk. 5.95 (ISBN 1-55734-096-X). Tchr Create Mat.

—Holiday Graph Art. Freeberg, Erling & Freeberg, Dolores, illus. 48p. (gr. 2-6). 1987. wkbk. 5.95 (ISBN 1-55734-093-5). Tchr Create Mat.

—Patriotic Graph Art. Freeberg, Erling & Freeberg, Dolores, illus. 48p. (gr. 2-6). 1987. wkbk. 5.95 (ISBN 1-55734-094-3). Tchr Create Mat.

—Simple Graph Art. Freeberg, Erling & Freeberg, Dolores, illus. 48p. (gr. k-1). 1987. wkbk. 5.95 (ISBN 1-55734-095-1). Tchr Create Mat.

Frost, Joan. Art, Books & Children: Art Activities Based on Children's Literature. (Illus.). 88p. (gr. 1-6). 1984. spiral bdg. 12.95 (ISBN 0-938594-03-6). Spec Lit Pr.

Gabet, Marcia. Bulletin Boards for Holidays & Everyday. Gabet, Marcia, illus. 64p. (gr. k-6). 1985. wkbk. 6.95 (ISBN 1-55734-060-9). Tchr Create Mat.

Goffstein, M. B. An Artists Album. Goffstein, M. B., illus. LC 85-42612. 48p. (ps up). 1985. 12.95 (ISBN 0-06-021994-7); PLB 12.89 (ISBN 0-06-021995-5). HarpC Child Bks.

Gregson, Bob. Take Part Art. (gr. 3-6). 1990. pap. 13.95 (ISBN 0-8224-6781-X). Fearon Teach Aids.

Hodgson, Harriet. Artworks. Savage, Beth, illus. 64p. (gr. k-3). 1986. 6.95 (ISBN 0-912107-42-1, Dist. by Good Apple). Monday Morning Bks.

Hoeft, Pam. Holiday Art a la Carte. 112p. (gr. 4-8). 1982. 9.95 (ISBN 0-88160-049-0, LW 235). Learning Wks.

Hunt, Lynn B. An Artist Game Bag. 2nd ed. Hunt, Lynn B., illus. 106p. (gr. 10 up). 1990. Repr. of 1936 ed. 39.95 (ISBN 0-381-20045-0). Derrydale Pr.

Jones, Mary L. Woody Watches the Masters: Four Great Artists, Bk. 1. (Illus.). 36p. (gr. 3-7). 1985. 4.95 (ISBN 0-533-05814-7). Vantage.

Kamiya, Artie & Kamiya, Elizabeth. Mobiles, Banners & Chariots. McClure, Nancee, illus. 48p. (gr. k-6). 1984. wkbk. 6.95 (ISBN 0-86653-184-X, SS 815). Good Apple.

Kehl, Richard. Silver Departures. LC 84-144823. 96p. (Orig.). (gr. 9-12). pap. 5.95 (ISBN 0-88138-014-8). Green Tiger Pr.

Keightley, Moy. Investigating Art: A Practical Guide for Young People. (Illus.). 160p. (gr. 7 up). 17.95 (ISBN 0-87196-973-4). Facts on File.

Kropa, Susie. Faces, Legs, & Belly Buttons. Kropa, Susie, illus. 80p. (ps). 1984. wkbk. 7.95 (ISBN 0-86653-239-0, GA 564). Good Apple.

Laycock, Mary. Bucky for Beginners. Kyzer, Martha, illus. 64p. (Orig.). (gr. 4-12). 1984. pap. text ed. 6.95 (ISBN 0-918932-82-3). Activity Resources.

Li'l' Angelo Coloring Book. (Orig.). (gr. 1-2). 1989. pap. 2.00 (ISBN 1-55794-124-6). Eternal Wrd TV.

Moon, Marjorie, ed. A Is for Art. (Illus., Orig.). (ps-2). 1988. pap. 10.95 (ISBN 0-317-91187-2). M Moon.

Neal, Judith. Fun Projects for Kids: A Teacher's Guide to Classroom Art. Bellew, Mike, illus. LC 83-7657. 136p. (gr. k-6). 1983. PLB 21.27 (ISBN 0-516-00821-8). Childrens.

Nowlin, Susan & Sterling, Mary E. Think & Do Bulletin Boards. Wright, Terry, illus. 96p. (gr. k-4). 1988. wkbk. 9.95 (ISBN 1-55734-063-3). Tchr Create Mat.

Pierce, Brenda H. Creative Art Picture Starters: General Subjects - Level II. Pierce, Brenda H., illus. 32p. (gr. 4-6). 1988. tchr's. ed. 3.95 (ISBN 0-922694-03-6). Moons Creat Prods.

Raboff, Ernest. Marc Chagall. LC 87-45297. (Illus.). 32p. (gr. 1 up). 1988. pap. 5.95 (ISBN 0-06-446066-5, Trophy). HarpC Child Bks.

—Michelangelo Buonarroti. LC 87-45298. (Illus.). 32p. (gr. 1 up). 1988. pap. 7.95 (ISBN 0-06-446074-6, Trophy). HarpC Child Bks.

—Raphael Sanzio. Raboff, Ernest, illus. LC 87-45299. 32p. (gr. 1 up). 1988. pap. 5.95 (ISBN 0-06-446075-4, Trophy). HarpC Child Bks.

Roehrig, Catherine. Fun with Hieroglyphs: From the Metropolitan Museum of Art. 1990. 19.95 (ISBN 0-670-83576-5). Viking Child Bks.

Schnell, Louise. Seasonal Art. Evans, Carol, ed. Schnell, Louise, illus. 52p. (ps-3). 1988. wkbk. 5.95 (ISBN 0-915505-01-0). Tchr Tested-Child.

Sefkow, Paula & Berger, Helen. All Children Create: Levels Four to Six, an Elementary Art Curriculum, Vol. II. Gutek, Rob, illus. LC 80-82018. 204p. (Orig.). (gr. 4-6). 1981. pap. 24.95x (ISBN 0-918452-25-2). Learning Pubns.

Simon & Schuster Staff. S&S Coloring Book: Illustrated Questions & Answers. 1989. pap. 17.95 (ISBN 0-671-68354-3). S&S Trade.

Smith, Mary & Robison, Phyllis. Easy Art. Astrom, Lena, illus. 48p. (gr. k-3). 1982. wkbk. 5.95 (ISBN 1-55734-004-8). Tchr Create Mat.

Spencer, Pat. Bulletin Boards Through the Year. Spencer, Pat, illus. 96p. (gr. k-4). 1988. wkbk. 9.95 (ISBN 1-55734-062-5). Tchr Create Mat.

Spivak, Darlene. Hidden Pictures. Smythe, Linda, illus. 32p. (gr. k-2). 1988. wkbk. 4.95 (ISBN 1-55734-120-6). Tchr Create Mat.

Spivak, Darlene E. Graph Art Puzzles. Wright, Theresa N., illus. 48p. (gr. 2-5). 1987. wkbk. 5.95 (ISBN 1-55734-068-4). Tchr Create Mat.

Striker, Susan. Anti-Coloring Book of Masterpieces. (Illus.). 96p. (Orig.). (gr. 2 up). 1982. pap. 6.95 (ISBN 0-03-057874-4, Owl Bks). H Holt & Co.

—Build a Better Mousetrap. Striker, Susan, illus. 64p. (gr. 2 up). 1983. pap. 4.95 (ISBN 0-03-057876-0). H Holt & Co.

Sullivan, Dainna J. Big & Easy Community Helpers. Adkins, Lynda, illus. 48p. (ps-2). 1988. wkbk. 5.95 (ISBN 1-55734-106-0). Tchr Create Mat.

Sullivan, Dianna J. Big & Easy Art for Fall. Ecker, Beverly, illus. 48p. (ps-2). 1987. wkbk. 5.95 (ISBN 1-55734-082-X). Tchr Create Mat.
—Big & Easy Art for Patriotic Holidays. Adkins, Lynda, illus. 48p. (ps-2). 1987. wkbk. 5.95 (ISBN 1-55734-085-4). Tchr Create Mat.
—Big & Easy Art for Spring & Summer. Ecker, Beverly, illus. 64p. (ps-2). 1987. wkbk 6.95 (ISBN 1-55734-084-6). Tchr Create Mat.
—Big & Easy Art for Winter. Ecker, Beverly, illus. 48p. (ps-2). 1987. wkbk. 5.95 (ISBN 1-55734-083-8). Tchr Create Mat.
—Box Art Projects. Adkins, Lynda, illus. 32p. (gr. 1-4). 1988. wkbk. 4.95 (ISBN 1-55734-097-8). Tchr Create Mat.
—Container Art Projects. Adkins, Lynda, illus. 32p. (gr. 1-4). 1988. wkbk. 4.95 (ISBN 1-55734-098-6). Tchr Create Mat.
—Decorations & Clip Art for Holidays & Everyday. Ecker, Beverly, illus. 96p. (gr. k-4). 1987. wkbk. 9.95 (ISBN 1-55734-092-7). Tchr Create Mat.
—Holiday Art. Sullivan, Dianna J., illus. 48p. (gr. k-3). 1985. wkbk. 5.95 (ISBN 1-55734-007-2). Tchr Create Mat.
—Milk Carton Art Projects. Adkins, Lynda, illus. 32p. (gr. 1-4). 1988. wkbk. 4.95 (ISBN 1-55734-099-4). Tchr Create Mat.
Sullivan, Dianna J. & Walhood, Darlene. Seasonal Teacher Clip Art. Sullivan, Dianna J. & Walhood, Darlene, illus. 48p. (ps-8). 1986. wkbk. 5.95 (ISBN 1-55734-065-X). Tchr Create Mat.
Taylor, Anne. Math in Art. Taylor, Anne, illus. (Orig.). (gr. 1-9). 1974. pap. 6.95 (ISBN 0-918932-28-9). Activity Resources.
Tekerian, Irisa & Watrous, Merrill. Art & Writing Throughout the Year. (gr. 1-6). 1988. pap. 14.95 (ISBN 0-8224-0499-0). Fearon Teach Aids.
Triado, Juan-Ramon. The Key to Baroque Art. (Illus.). 80p. (gr. 8 up). 1990. PLB 15.95 (ISBN 0-8225-2056-7). Lerner Pubns.
West-Naus, Roberta. Art Aardvark. (Illus.). 72p. (gr. k-8). 1981. 7.95 (ISBN 0-88160-041-5, LW 226). Learning Wks.
Wickham, Geoffrey. Rapid Perspective. (gr. 10 up). 9.95 (ISBN 0-85458-050-6); pap. 7.95 (ISBN 0-85458-051-4). Transatl Arts.
Yenawine, Philip. Colors. (Illus.). (gr. 2-5). 1991. 14.00 (ISBN 0-385-30254-1); PLB 14.99 (ISBN 0-385-30314-9). Delacorte.

ART–ANALYSIS, INTERPRETATION, APPRECIATION
see Art–Study and Teaching

ART, ANCIENT
Prudhomme, Frances & Sternberg, Susan T. The Gift of the Greeks: Art & Civilization of Ancient Greece. 24p. (Orig.). (gr. 4-7). 1982. pap. 5.00 (ISBN 0-935213-04-X). A M Huntington Art.

ART, APPLIED
see Art Industries and Trade

ART, CHRISTIAN
see Christian Art and Symbolism

ART, CLASSICAL
see Art, Greek

ART–CRITICISM
see Art Criticism

ART, DECORATIVE
Here are entered general works on the decoration and use of artistic objects. Works limited to the external ornamentation of objects are entered under Design, Decorative.
see also Decoration and Ornament; Design, Decorative; Enamel and Enameling; Furniture; Illustration of Books; Needlework; Pottery

ART, ECCLESIASTICAL
see Christian Art and Symbolism

ART–EDUCATION
see Art–Study and Teaching

ART–FICTION
Agee, Jon. The Incredible Painting of Felix Clousseau. (Illus.). 32p. (ps up). 1988. 13.95 (ISBN 0-374-33633-4). FS&G.
Blos, Sarah I. & Davis, Julie N. Katsu & the Kite. (Illus.). 14p. 1988. pap. 0.96 (ISBN 0-912303-43-3). Michigan Mus.
Carrick, Donald. Morgan & the Artist. LC 84-14267. (Illus.). 32p. (ps-4). 1985. 12.95 (ISBN 0-89919-300-5, Clarion). HM.
Cohen, Miriam. No Good in Art. (gr. k-6). 1986. pap. 2.95 (ISBN 0-440-46389-0, YB). Dell.
Goffstein, Brooke. Artists' Helpers Enjoy the Evenings. Goffstein, M. B., illus. LC 86-45771. 32p. (ps up). 1987. 13.95 (ISBN 0-06-022181-X); PLB 13.89 (ISBN 0-06-022182-8). HarpC Child Bks.
Locker, Thomas. The Young Artist. (Illus.). 32p. (ps up). 1989. 15.95 (ISBN 0-8037-0625-1); PLB 15.89 (ISBN 0-8037-0627-8). Dial Bks Young.
Mayhew, James. Katie's Picture Show. (ps-3). 1989. 12.95 (ISBN 0-553-05846-0). Bantam.
Rylant, Cynthia. All I See. Catalanotto, Peter, illus. LC 88-42547. 32p. (gr. k-2). 1988. 15.95 (ISBN 0-531-05777-1); PLB 15.99 (ISBN 0-531-08377-2). Orchard Bks Watts.
Sandford, John. Slappy Hooper: The World's Greatest Sign Painter. 1990. 9.95 (ISBN 1-55782-359-6). Warner Bks.
Schick, Eleanor. Art Lessons. LC 86-243. (Illus.). 48p. (gr. k-3). 1987. 11.75 (ISBN 0-688-05120-0); lib. bdg. 11.88 (ISBN 0-688-05121-9). Greenwillow.
Stolz, Mary. Zekmet the Stone Carver: A Tale of Ancient Egypt. Lattimore, Deborah N., illus. LC 86-22931. 32p. (gr. 2-5). 1988. 13.95 (ISBN 0-15-299961-2). HarBraceJ.

ART–FORGERIES
see Forgery of Works of Art

ART–GALLERIES AND MUSEUMS
Mayers, Florence C. ABC: The Alef-Bet Book: The Israel Museum, Jerusalem. LC 88-27501. (Illus.). 32p. (gr. k up). 1989. 12.95 (ISBN 0-8109-1885-4). Abrams.

ART, GRAPHIC
see Graphic Arts

ART, GREEK
Prudhomme, Frances & Sternberg, Susan T. The Gift of the Greeks: Art & Civilization of Ancient Greece. 24p. (Orig.). (gr. 4-7). 1982. pap. 5.00 (ISBN 0-935213-04-X). A M Huntington Art.

ART–HISTORY
Belves, Pierre & Mathey, Francois. Enjoying the World of Art. (Illus.). (gr. 6 up). 1966. PLB 29.95 (ISBN 0-87460-100-2). Lion Bks.
Bracons, Jose. The Key to Gothic Art. (Illus.). 80p. (gr. 8 up). 1990. PLB 15.95 (ISBN 0-8225-2051-6). Lerner Pubns.
Cirlot, Lourdes. Modern Art of the Early 20th Century. (Illus.). 80p. (gr. 8 up). 1990. PLB 15.95 (ISBN 0-8225-2052-4). Lerner Pubns.
Raboff, Ernest. Diego Rodriguez de Silva y Velasquez. LC 87-16915. (Illus.). 32p. (gr. 1 up). 1988. Repr. of 1971 ed. 11.95 (ISBN 0-397-32219-4, Lipp Jr Bks). HarpC Child Bks.
—Diego Rodriguez de Silva y Velasquez. LC 87-17697. (Illus.). 32p. (gr. 1 up). 1988. pap. 5.95 (ISBN 0-06-446073-8, Trophy). HarpC Child Bks.
—Henri Rousseau. LC 87-16862. (Illus.). 32p. (gr. 1 up). 1988. Repr. of 1970 ed. 11.95 (ISBN 0-397-32221-6, Lipp Jr Bks). HarpC Child Bks.
—Henri Rousseau. LC 87-17700. (Illus.). 32p. (gr. 1 up). 1988. pap. 5.95 (ISBN 0-06-446069-X, Trophy). HarpC Child Bks.
—Paul Gauguin. LC 87-16914. (Illus.). 32p. (gr. 1 up). 1988. Repr. of 1975 ed. 11.95 (ISBN 0-397-32225-9, Lipp Jr Bks). HarpC Child Bks.
—Paul Gauguin. LC 87-17696. (Illus.). 32p. (gr. 1 up). 1988. pap. 5.95 (ISBN 0-06-446078-9, Trophy). HarpC Child Bks.
—Paul Klee. LC 87-16864. (Illus.). 32p. (gr. 1 up). 1988. Repr. of 1968 ed. 11.95 (ISBN 0-397-32226-7, Lipp Jr Bks). HarpC Child Bks.
—Paul Klee. LC 87-17699. (Illus.). 32p. (gr. 1 up). 1988. pap. 5.95 (ISBN 0-06-446065-7, Trophy). HarpC Child Bks.

ART, INDIAN
see Indians of North America–Art

ART, PRIMITIVE
see also Folk Art; Indians of North America–Art
also names of countries, cities, etc. with the subdivision Antiquities, e.g. U. S.–Antiquities; etc.

ART–PSYCHOLOGY
Brommer, Gerald F. & Horn, George F. Art in Your World. 2nd ed. LC 84-73493. (Illus.). 256p. (gr. 7-8). 1985. text ed. 26.95 (ISBN 0-87192-168-5, 168-5); tchr's. guide 10.95 (ISBN 0-685-01368-5, 168-5G). Davis Mass.

ART, RENAISSANCE
Arenas, Jose F. The Key to Renaissance Art. (Illus.). 80p. (gr. 8 up). 1990. PLB 15.95 (ISBN 0-8225-2057-5). Lerner Pubns.

ART–STUDY AND TEACHING
Atherton, Mary K., et al. Touch with Your Eyes! Frank, Phil, illus. 48p. (Orig.). (gr. k-8). 1982. pap. 4.50 (ISBN 0-9613069-0-4). Orinda Art Coun.
Barry, Jan. Draw, Design & Paint. (Illus.). 144p. (gr. 2-6). 1990. 10.95 (ISBN 0-86653-536-5, GA1142). Good Apple.
Cincerelli, Carol J. Opening Five: Art for Grade Five. LC 79-3013. 192p. (gr. 5). 1980. pap. text ed. 10.25 (ISBN 0-934902-10-0). Learn Concepts OH.
—Opening One: Art for Grade One. LC 79-3013. 174p. (gr. 1). 1979. pap. text ed. 9.75 (ISBN 0-934902-07-0). Learn Concepts OH.
—Opening Three: Art for Grade Three. LC 79-3013. 195p. (gr. 3). 1980. pap. text ed. 9.75 (ISBN 0-934902-09-7). Learn Concepts OH.
—Opening-Two: Art for Grade Two. LC 79-3013. (gr. 2). 1979. pap. text ed. 9.75 (ISBN 0-934902-06-2). Learn Concepts OH.
Coen, Rena N. Medicine in Art. LC 79-84408. (Illus.). 64p. (gr. 5 up). 1970. PLB 5.95 (ISBN 0-8225-0166-X). Lerner Pubns.
Hollingsworth, Patricia & Hollingsworth, Stephen. Smart Art: Learning to Classify & Critique Art. (Illus.). 112p. (Orig.). (gr. 3-8). 1989. pap. text ed. 12.95 (ISBN 0-913705-31-4, ZB09). Zephyr Pr AZ.
Hoover, F. L. Art Activities for the Very Young. LC 61-11263. (Illus.). (gr. k-3). 1961. pap. 7.95 (ISBN 0-87192-000-X). Davis Mass.
Katz, Phyllis. Exploring Science Through Art. (ps-3). 1990. PLB 11.90 (ISBN 0-531-10890-2). Watts.
Maid, Amy. Mindscapes. LC 82-9904. 67p. (gr. 3-8). 1983. pap. 11.95x (ISBN 0-8290-1001-7). Irvington.
Molyneux, Lynn & Bucur, Mike. Your Own Thing: Individual Art Projects for Primary Grades. Bucur, Mike, illus. 160p. (gr. k-6). 1983. perfect bdg. 9.95 (ISBN 0-685-29140-5). Trellis Bks Inc.
Savage, Stephen. Ancient Greek Monuments to Make: The Parthenon & the Theatre of Dionysos. Savage, Stephen, illus. Moon, Warren G., intro. by. (Illus.). 48p. (Orig.). (gr. 7 up). 1990. pap. 7.95 (ISBN 0-88045-096-7). Stemmer Hse.
Yenawine, Philip. Lines. (Illus.). (gr. 2-5). 1991. 14.00 (ISBN 0-385-30253-3); PLB 14.99 (ISBN 0-385-30313-0). Delacorte.
—Shapes. (Illus.). (gr. 2-5). 1991. 14.00 (ISBN 0-385-30255-X); PLB 14.99 (ISBN 0-385-30315-7). Delacorte.
—Stories. (Illus.). (gr. 2-5). 1991. 14.00 (ISBN 0-385-30256-8); PLB 14.99 (ISBN 0-385-30316-5). Delacorte.

ART–VOCATIONAL GUIDANCE
Henderson, Kathy. Market Guide for Young Artists & Photographers. LC 90-39084. (Illus.). 176p. (Orig.). (gr. 3 up). 1990. pap. 10.95 (ISBN 1-55870-176-1, Shoe Tree Pr). Betterway Pubns.

ART ANATOMY
see Anatomy, Artistic

ART APPRECIATION
see Art–Study and Teaching; Art Criticism; Painting; Pictures

ART CRITICISM
Hollingsworth, Patricia & Hollingsworth, Stephen. Smart Art: Learning to Classify & Critique Art. (Illus.). 112p. (Orig.). (gr. 3-8). 1989. pap. text ed. 12.95 (ISBN 0-913705-31-4, ZB09). Zephyr Pr AZ.
Judson, Bay, et al. Art Ventures: A Guide for Families to Ten Works of Art in the Carnegie Museum of Art. Koren, Edward, illus. LC 87-858. 24p. (Orig.). (gr. 4-6). 1987. pap. text ed. 5.95 (ISBN 0-88039-014-X). Mus Art Carnegie.

ART EDUCATION
see Art–Study and Teaching

ART FOGERIES
see Forgery of Works of Art

ART GALLERIES
see Art–Galleries and Museums

ART INDUSTRIES AND TRADE
see also Arts and Crafts; Folk Art
also special industries, trades, etc., e.g. Glass painting and staining; Leather Work
St. Tamara. Asian Crafts. St. Tamara, illus. LC 71-86983. (gr. 2-6). 1972. PLB 12.95 (ISBN 0-87460-148-7). Lion Bks.

ART MUSEUMS
see Art–Galleries and Museums

ART OBJECTS
see also classes of art objects, e.g. Furniture; pottery; etc.

ART OBJECTS, FORGERY OF
see Forgery of Works of Art

ART SCHOOLS
see Art–Study and Teaching

ARTHUR, KING
see also Grail
Andronik, Catherine M. Quest for a King: Searching for the Real King Arthur. LC 88-7381. (Illus.). 160p. (gr. 5 up). 1989. 12.95 (ISBN 0-689-31411-6, Atheneum Child Bk). Macmillan Child Grp.
Brim, C. Arthur: Tales of the Young King. (Illus.). 32p. (gr. 2-6). 1989. 10.95 (ISBN 0-88625-236-9). Durkin Hayes Pub.
Children's Treasury: King Arthur & His Knights. 1990. 7.98 (ISBN 0-8317-1357-7). Smithmark.
The Fall of Camelot. (Illus.). 144p. (gr. 7 up). 1986. 19.93 (ISBN 0-8094-5257-X); lib. bdg. 25.93 (ISBN 0-8094-5258-8). Time-Life.
Green, Roger L. King Arthur & His Knights of the Round Table. (Orig.). (gr. 5-7). 1974. pap. 2.95 (ISBN 0-14-030073-2, Penguin Bks). Viking Penguin.
Hastings, Selina. Sir Gawain & the Green Knight. Wijngaard, Juan, illus. LC 80-85379. 32p. (gr. 3-7). 1981. 12.95 (ISBN 0-688-00592-6). Lothrop.
Hodges, Margaret. Knight Prisoner: The Tale of Sir Thomas Malory & His King Arthur. LC 76-26693. (Illus.). 208p. (gr. 7 up). 1976. 10.95 (ISBN 0-374-34269-5). FS&G.
King Arthur. (Illus.). (gr. 3-7). 3.50 (ISBN 0-7214-0886-9). Ladybird Bks.
Lang, Andrew, ed. King Arthur: Tales of the Round Table. Ford, H. J., illus. LC 67-26996. (gr. 5 up). 1987. pap. 7.95 (ISBN 0-8052-0196-3). Schocken.
Lanier, Sidney. The Boy's King Arthur. reissued ed. Wyeth, N. C., illus. LC 73-13451. 336p. 1989. 24.95 (ISBN 0-684-19111-3, Scribners Young Read); deluxe ed. 75.00 (ISBN 0-684-19118-0, Scribner). Macmillan Child Grp.
Mallory, Thomas. King Arthur & His Knights of the Round Table. Lanier, Sidney & Pyle, Howard, eds. Florian, illus. 288p. (gr. 4-6). 1950. (G&D); 11.95 (ISBN 0-448-06016-7, G&D). Putnam Pub Group.
Mockler, Anthony. King Arthur & His Knights. Harris, Nick, illus. 308p. 1987. jacketed 18.95 (ISBN 0-19-274531-X). Oxford U Pr.
O'Neill, Catherine. Let's Visit a Chocolate Factory. Parker, James W., illus. LC 87-3460. 32p. (gr. 2-4). 1988. PLB 10.79 (ISBN 0-8167-1161-5); pap. text ed. 2.95 (ISBN 0-8167-1162-3). Troll Assocs.
Pyle, Howard. King Arthur. Hinkle, Don, ed. Tirtitilli, Jerry, illus. LC 87-15461. 48p. (gr. 3-6). 1988. PLB 12.89 (ISBN 0-8167-1213-1); pap. 3.95 (ISBN 0-8167-1214-X). Troll Assocs.
—Reader's Digest Best Loved Books for Young Readers: The Story of King Arthur & His Knights. Ogburn, Jackie, ed. Sweet, Darrell, illus. 208p. (gr. 4-12). 1989. 3.99 (ISBN 0-945260-31-8). Choice Pub NY.

—The Story of King Arthur & His Knights. Pyle, Howard, illus. xviii, 313p. (gr. 7 up). pap. 6.95 (ISBN 0-486-21445-1). Dover.

—The Story of Sir Lancelot & His Companions. (Illus.). 360p. (gr. 5 up). 1985. 18.95 (ISBN 0-684-18313-7, Scribners Young Read). Macmillan Child Grp.

—The Story of the Champions of the Round Table. Pyle, Howard, illus. xviii, 329p. (ps-4). 1968. pap. 7.95 (ISBN 0-486-21883-X). Dover.

—The Story of the Champions of the Round Table. LC 84-13881. (Illus.). 348p. (gr. 7 up). 1984. 18.95 (ISBN 0-684-18171-1, Scribners Young Read). Macmillan Child Grp.

—The Story of the Grail & the Passing of Arthur. Pyle, Howard, illus. LC 85-40302. 340p. (gr. 7 up). 1985. Repr. 18.95 (ISBN 0-684-18483-4, Scribners Young Read). Macmillan Child Grp.

Storr, Catherine. The Sword in the Stone. Hunter, Susan, illus. LC 84-18293. 32p. (gr. 2-5). 1985. PLB 16.67 (ISBN 0-8172-2113-1); pap. 9.27 (ISBN 0-8172-2256-1). Raintree Pubs.

Tennyson, Alfred. Idylls of the King. (gr. 10 up). 1968. pap. 2.75 (ISBN 0-8049-0180-5, CL-180). Airmont.

Twain, Mark. Connecticut Yankee in King Arthur's Court. LC 83-9162. (gr. 5 up). 1964. pap. 3.25 (ISBN 0-8049-0029-9, CL-29). Airmont.

—A Connecticut Yankee in King Arthur's Court. new & abr. ed. Fago, John N., ed. Redondo, Francisco, illus. LC 83-9162. (gr. 4-12). 1977. pap. text ed. 2.95 (ISBN 0-88301-263-4). Pendulum Pr.

—A Connecticut Yankee in King Arthur's Court. Hyman, Trina S., illus. LC 87-62879. 384p. (gr. 5 up). 1988. 19.95 (ISBN 0-688-06346-2); signed ltd. ed. 100.00 (ISBN 0-688-08258-0, Morrow Jr Bks). Morrow Jr Bks.

Winder, Blanche, ed. Stories of King Arthur. Gotlieb, Jules, illus. (gr. 4 up). pap. 1.95 (ISBN 0-8049-0167-8, CL-167). Airmont.

ARTHUR, KING–POETRY

Knowles, James, compiled by. King Arthur & His Knights. 1986. 8.98 (ISBN 0-517-61885-0). Outlet Bk Co.

Riordan, James. Tales of King Arthur. Ambrus, Victor G., illus. LC 81-86152. 128p. (gr. 4-7). 1982. 11.95 (ISBN 0-528-82383-3). Checkerboard Pr.

ARTHURIAN ROMANCES

see Arthur, King

ARTIFICIAL INTELLIGENCE

Belgum, Erik. Artificial Intelligence: Opposing Viewpoints. LC 90-3519. (Illus.). 112p. (gr. 3-8). 1990. PLB 13.95 (ISBN 0-89908-085-5). Greenhaven.

D'Ignazio, Fred & Wold, Allen L. The Science of Artificial Intelligence. 96p. (gr. 5 up). 1984. lib. bdg. 10.40 (ISBN 0-531-04703-2). Watts.

Holbrook, Sabra. Fighting Back: The Struggle for Gay Rights. LC 86-19755. 128p. (gr. 7 up). 1987. 13.95 (ISBN 0-525-67187-0, Lodestar Bks). Dutton Child Bks.

Hyde, Margaret O. Artificial Intelligence. rev. ed. LC 85-20573. (Illus.). 128p. (gr. 5-12). 1986. PLB 17.95 (ISBN 0-89490-124-9). Enslow Pubs.

ARTIFICIAL SATELLITES

see also Space Vehicles

Baker, David. Earth Watch. (Illus.). 48p. (gr. 3-8). 1989. lib. bdg. 18.60 (ISBN 0-86592-372-8). Rourke Corp.

Barrett, Norman. The Picture World of Rockets & Satellites. (Illus.). 32p. (gr. k-4). 1990. PLB 11.40 (ISBN 0-531-14055-5). Watts.

Bendick, Jeanne. Artificial Satellites: Helpers in Space. (Illus.). 32p. (gr. k-2). 1991. PLB 11.90 (ISBN 1-56294-002-3); pap. 3.95 (ISBN 1-878841-56-4). Millbrook Pr.

Couper, Heather & Henbest, Nigel. Spaceprobes & Satellites. (Illus.). 32p. (gr. 4-6). 1987. PLB 8.99 (ISBN 0-531-10360-9). Watts.

Herda, D. J. Operation Rescue: Satellite Maintenance & Repair. (Illus.). 64p. (gr. 5-8). 1990. PLB 11.90 (ISBN 0-531-10873-2). Watts.

Jefferis, David. Satellites. (Illus.). 32p. (gr. k-3). 1987. PLB 7.99 (ISBN 0-531-10348-X). Watts.

Long, Mark. The DBS Satellite Handbook. (Illus.). 356p. (gr. 12). 1991. 19.95 (ISBN 0-685-32641-1). MLE Inc.

Richards, Gregory B. Satellites. LC 83-7434. (Illus.). 48p. (gr. k-4). 1983. lib. bdg. 14.60 (ISBN 0-516-01708-X). Childrens.

Sabin, Francene. Rockets & Satellites. Maccabe, Richard, illus. LC 84-2738. 32p. (gr. 3-6). 1985. PLB 9.49 (ISBN 0-8167-0288-8); pap. text ed. 2.95 (ISBN 0-8167-0289-6). Troll Assocs.

Satellites & Space Stations: What They Can Do & How They Work. 48p. (gr. 6 up). 1986. PLB 13.96 (ISBN 0-88110-223-7); pap. 6.95 (ISBN 0-86020-937-7). EDC.

Spizzirri Publishing Co. Staff. Satellites: An Educational Coloring Book. Spizzirri, Linda, ed. (Illus.). 32p. (gr. 1-8). 1986. pap. 1.95 (ISBN 0-86545-074-9). Spizzirri.

Vogt, Gregory. Space Satellites. (Illus.). 32p. (gr. 4-9). 1987. PLB 11.90 (ISBN 0-531-10141-X). Watts.

ARTIFICIAL SATELLITES IN TELECOMMUNICATION

Herda, D. J. Communication Satellites. Kline, M., ed. (Illus.). 72p. (gr. 4-9). 1988. 10.40 (ISBN 0-531-10473-7). Watts.

Irvine, Mat. Telesatellite. (Illus.). 32p. (gr. 5-9). 1989. PLB 8.90 (ISBN 0-531-17157-4). Watts.

Long, Mark. The Satellite TV Answer Book. (Illus.). 224p. (gr. 12). 1989. 14.95 (ISBN 0-685-32640-3). MLE Inc.

ARTIFICIAL WEATHER CONTROL

see Weather Control

ARTILLERY

Nicholaus, J. Artillery. (Illus.). 48p. (gr. 3-8). 1989. lib. bdg. 18.60 (ISBN 0-86592-419-8). Rourke Corp.

ARTISTIC ANATOMY

see Anatomy, Artistic

ARTISTIC PHOTOGRAPHY

see Photography, Artistic

ARTISTS

see also Architects; Art–Vocational Guidance; Black Artists; Painters; Sculptors; Women As Artists

Balsamo, Kathy. Exploring the Lives of Gifted People-The Arts. Johnson, Phyllis, illus. 80p. (gr. 4 up). 1987. pap. 7.95 (ISBN 0-86653-406-7, GA1037). Good Apple.

Brommer, Gerald F. & Horn, George F. Art in Your World. 2nd ed. LC 84-73493. (Illus.). 256p. (gr. 7-8). 1985. text ed. 26.95 (ISBN 0-87192-168-5, 168-5); tchr's. guide 10.95 (ISBN 0-685-01368-5, 168-5G). Davis Mass.

Genius! The Artist & the Process, 6 bks. (Illus.). (gr. 7-9). 1990. 89.70 (ISBN 0-382-24030-8); lib. bdg. 107.88 (ISBN 0-382-09902-8). Silver Burdett Pr.

Goffstein, M. B. An Artist. Goffstein, M. B., illus. LC 79-2663. 32p. (ps-3). 1980. 12.95 (ISBN 0-06-022012-0). HarpC Child Bks.

—Lives of the Artists. LC 81-68932. (Illus.). 48p. (ps-3). 1981. 10.95 (ISBN 0-374-34628-3). FS&G.

Hutchinson, Duane. Grotto Father: Artist-Priest of the West Bend Grotto. LC 89-39029. 66p. 1989. pap. 4.95 (ISBN 0-934988-20-X). Foun Bks.

Hyman, Trina S. Self-Portrait: Trina Schart Hyman. Hyman, Trina S., illus. LC 80-26662. 32p. (gr. 4-7). 1989. PLB 14.89 (ISBN 0-06-022766-4). HarpC Child Bks.

Kurtzman, Harvey. My Life As a Cartoonist. (Illus.). 1988. pap. 2.75 (ISBN 0-671-63453-4, Minstrel Bks). PB.

Lipman, Jean & Aspinwall, Margaret. Alexander Calder & His Magical Mobiles. LC 81-1811. (Illus.). 96p. (ps up). 1981. 15.00 (ISBN 0-933920-17-2, Dist. by Rizzoli). Hudson Hills.

Muller, Gerald. Gentle Giants. (Illus.). (gr. 6-9). 1988. pap. 7.95 (ISBN 0-8198-3045-3). Dghtrs St Paul.

Raboff, Ernest. Marc Chagall. LC 87-45312. (Illus.). 32p. (gr. 1 up). 1988. Repr. of 1968 ed. 11.95 (ISBN 0-397-32222-4, Lipp Jr Bks). HarpC Child Bks.

—Michelangelo Buonarroti. LC 87-45313. (Illus.). 32p. (gr. 1 up). 1988. Repr. of 1971 ed. 11.95 (ISBN 0-397-32223-2, Lipp Jr Bks). HarpC Child Bks.

—Raphael Sanzio. LC 87-45314. (Illus.). 32p. (gr. 1 up). 1988. Repr. of 1971 ed. 11.95 (ISBN 0-397-32227-5, Lipp Jr Bks). HarpC Child Bks.

—Vincent Van Gogh. LC 87-45315. (Illus.). 32p. (gr. 1 up). 1988. Repr. of 1973 ed. 11.95 (ISBN 0-397-32230-5, Lipp Jr Bks). HarpC Child Bks.

Reef, Pat D. Dahlov Ipcar, Artist. (Illus.). 48p. (gr. 3-7). 1987. pap. 12.95 (ISBN 0-933858-20-5). Kennebec River.

Rowley, Patric. Artists: A Kansas Collection. Harper, Steve, photos by. (Illus.). 108p. (gr. 7-12). 1989. 34.95 (ISBN 0-9623079-0-4). Artists Registry.

Tudor, Tasha. The Springs of Joy. Tudor, Tasha, illus. LC 79-66708. 64p. (ps up). 1988. 12.95 (ISBN 0-02-689092-5). Checkerboard Pr.

Venezia, Mike. Van Gogh. Venezia, Mike, illus. LC 88-11842. 32p. (ps-4). 1988. PLB 14.60 (ISBN 0-516-02274-1); pap. 4.95 (ISBN 0-516-42274-X). Childrens.

ARTISTS, AMERICAN

Berry, Michael. Georgia O'Keeffe. Horner, Matina, intro. by. (Illus.). 112p. (Orig.). (gr. 5 up). 1989. 17.95 (ISBN 1-55546-673-7); pap. 9.95 (ISBN 0-7910-0420-1). Chelsea Hse.

Bockris, Victor. Life & Death of Andy Warhol. (ps-3). 1990. pap. 14.95 (ISBN 0-553-34929-5). Bantam.

Laing, Martha. Grandma Moses: The Grand Old Lady of American Art. Rahmas, D. Steve, ed. LC 71-190231. 32p. (Orig.). (gr. 7-9). 1972. lib. bdg. 4.20 incl. catalog cards (ISBN 0-87157-513-2); pap. 2.95 vinyl laminated covers (ISBN 0-87157-013-0). SamHar Pr.

O'Neal, Zibby. Grandma Moses: Painter of Rural America. Ruff, Donna, illus. (gr. 2-6). pap. 3.50 (ISBN 0-317-62289-7, Puffin). Puffin Bks.

ARTISTS, BLACK

see Black Artists

ARTISTS–FICTION

Auch, Mary J. Glass Slippers Give You Blisters. LC 88-45865. 176p. (gr. 3-7). 1989. 13.95 (ISBN 0-8234-0752-7). Holiday.

Goodman, Robert B. & Spicer, Robert A. The Magic Brush. Tabrah, Ruth, ed. Mui, Y. T., illus. LC 74-80513. (gr. 1-7). 1974. 5.95 (ISBN 0-89610-007-3). Island Heritage.

Nunes, Lygia B. My Friend the Painter. Pontiero, Giovanni, tr. from POR. 80p. (gr. 4-8). 1991. 13.95 (ISBN 0-15-256340-7). HarBraceJ.

Stewart, Celeste. Merry Berry. Weinberger, Jane & Black, Albert, eds. DeVito, Pamela, illus. LC 88-51280. 88p. (gr. 4-8). 1990. pap. 5.00 (ISBN 0-932433-53-7). Windswept Hse.

Turner, Ann. Time of the Bison. Peck, Beth, illus. LC 86-23476. 64p. (gr. 2-6). 1987. 12.95 (ISBN 0-02-789300-6, Mcmillan Child Bk). Macmillan Child Grp.

ARTISTS, NEGRO

see Black Artists

ARTISTS, SPANISH

Diego Rivera. (Illus.). 32p. (gr. 3-6). 1988. PLB 16.67 (ISBN 0-8172-2908-6). Raintree Pubs.

ARTISTS' MATERIALS

Sattler, Helen R. Recipes for Art & Craft Materials. rev. ed. Shohet, Marti, illus. LC 86-34271. 128p. (gr. 6 up). 1987. 13.95 (ISBN 0-688-07374-3). Lothrop.

ARTS, GRAPHIC

see Graphic Arts

ARTS, USEFUL

see Technology

ARTS AND CRAFTS

see also Basket Making; Bookbinding; Decoration and Ornament; Design, Decorative; Enamel and Enameling; Folk Art; Glass Painting and Staining; Handicraft; Jewelry; Leather Work; Metalwork; Modeling; Needlework; Pottery; Weaving; Wood Carving

Aulson, Pam. Crafty Ideas with Placemats. (Illus.). 24p. (gr. 6 up). 1979. pap. 3.00 (ISBN 0-9601896-3-7). Patch As Patch.

Ball, W. W. Fun with String Figures. LC 76-173664. (Illus.). 89p. (gr. k-3). 1971. pap. 2.95 (ISBN 0-486-22809-6). Dover.

Bonica, Diane. Writing & Art Go Hand in Hand. 80p. (gr. 2-6). 1988. pap. text ed. 7.95 (ISBN 0-86530-068-2, IP 13-2). Incentive Pubns.

Brommer, Gerald F. Wire Sculpture & Other Three Dimensional Construction. LC 68-19999. (Illus.). (gr. 5-12). 1968. 14.95 (ISBN 0-87192-025-5). Davis Mass.

Christmas Crib. (Illus.). (ps-2). 7.95 (ISBN 0-7214-3078-3). Ladybird Bks.

Forte, Imogene. Arts & Crafts: From Things Around the House. LC 83-80961. (Illus.). 80p. (gr. k-6). 1983. pap. text ed. 3.95 (ISBN 0-86530-090-9, IP909). Incentive Pubns.

—Nature Crafts. LC 84-62931. (Illus.). 80p. (gr. k-6). 1985. 3.95 (ISBN 0-86530-098-4, IP 91-2). Incentive Pubns.

Gleason, Karan. Rainy Day Fun. Filkins, Vanessa, illus. 112p. (gr. k-4). 1987. pap. 9.95 (ISBN 0-86653-408-3, GA1002). Good Apple.

Gregorich, Barbara. Chicken Scratch. Hoffman, Joan, ed. Alexander, Barbara, et al, illus. 32p. (Orig.). (ps-1). 1986. wkbk. 1.99 (ISBN 0-88743-127-5). Sch Zone Pub Co.

Hart, Tony. Making Treasure. (Illus.). 32p. (gr. 1-4). 1984. 5.95 (ISBN 0-7182-2955-X, Pub. by W Heinemann). Trafalgar Sq.

—Wool 'n' Things. (Illus.). 32p. (gr. 1-4). 1984. 5.95 (ISBN 0-7182-2954-1, Pub. by W Heinemann Ltd). Trafalgar Sq.

Highlights Editors. Party Ideas with Crafts Kids Can Make. (Illus.). 48p. (Orig.). (gr. 1-6). 1981. pap. 2.95 (ISBN 0-87534-310-4). Highlights.

Hyland, Anne M. Manual: School Library-Media Skills Test. LC 86-7249. 50p. (gr. 4 up). 1986. pap. text ed. 6.50 (ISBN 0-87287-524-5). Libs Unl.

Kerina, Jane. African Crafts. Feelings, Tom, illus. LC 69-18916. (gr. 2-6). 1970. PLB 12.95 (ISBN 0-87460-084-7). Lion Bks.

MacKenzie, Joy. The Big Book of Bible Crafts & Projects. Flint, Russ, illus. 212p. (Orig.). (ps-4). 1981. pap. 12.95 (ISBN 0-310-70151-1, 14019P). Zondervan.

More Super Search-a-Words. (gr. 2-5). 1987. pap. 1.49 (ISBN 0-671-64358-4, Little Simon). S&S Trade.

Perplexing Hidden Pictures. (Illus.). (gr. 2-5). 1987. pap. 1.49 (ISBN 0-671-64355-X, Little Simon). S&S Trade.

Ruschen, Gaye. Let's Learn about Arts & Crafts. Foster, Tom, illus. 64p. (ps-2). 1987. pap. 6.95 (ISBN 0-86653-389-3, GA1012). Good Apple.

Silbert, Linda P. & Silbert, Alvin J. Make My Own Book Kit Animals. (ps-2). 1984. wkbk. 5.98 (ISBN 0-89544-316-3). Silbert Bress.

—Make My Own Book Kit Numbers. (ps-2). 1984. wkbk. 5.98 (ISBN 0-89544-318-X). Silbert Bress.

—Make My Own Book Kit Shapes. (ps-2). 1984. wkbk. 5.98 (ISBN 0-89544-317-1). Silbert Bress.

Simon, Seymour. The Paper Airplane Book. Byron, Barton, illus. (gr. 4-6). 1971. pap. 11.95 (ISBN 0-670-53797-7). Viking Child Bks.

Zechlin, Katharina. Creative Enameling & Jewelry-Making. Kuttner, Paul, tr. LC 65-20877. (gr. 10 up). 1965. 6.95 (ISBN 0-8069-5062-5); PLB 6.69 (ISBN 0-8069-5063-3). Sterling.

Zubrowski, Bernie. Messing Around with Water Pumps & Siphons: A Children's Museum Activity Book. Lindblom, Steve, illus. 64p. (gr. 3-7). 1981. pap. 7.95 (ISBN 0-316-98877-4). Little.

ASHANTIS

McDermott, Gerald, retold by. & illus. Anansi the Spider: A Tale from the Ashanti. LC 76-150028. 40p. (gr. k-2). 1972. reinforced bdg. 14.95 (ISBN 0-8050-0310-X); pap. 5.95 (ISBN 0-8050-0311-8). H Holt & Co.

ASHE, ARTHUR, 1943-

Weissberg, Ed. Arthur Ashe. King, Coretta Scott, intro. by. (Illus.). 112p. (gr. 5 up). 1991. PLB 17.95 (ISBN 0-7910-1115-1). Chelsea Hse.

ASIA

see also Asia, Southeastern

Civilizations of Asia. (Illus.). 80p. (gr. 4 up). 1988. PLB 22.00 (ISBN 0-8172-3302-4). Raintree Pubs.

Coblence, Jean-Michel. Asian Civilizations. Lamb, Jane C., tr. from FRE. Ageorges, Veronique, illus. 77p. (gr. 7 up). 1988. 15.96 (ISBN 0-382-09483-2); 10.37s.p. (ISBN 0-685-18822-1). Silver Burdett Pr.

Fairfield, Sheila. People & Nations of Asia. LC 88-42920. (Illus.). 64p. (gr. 5-6). 1988. PLB 13.95 (ISBN 1-55532-905-5). Gareth Stevens Inc.

Foster, Leila M. Bhutan. LC 88-37375. (Illus.). 128p. (gr. 5-9). 1989. PLB 25.27 (ISBN 0-516-02709-3). Childrens.

Fyson, Nance L. People at Work in Sri Lanka. (gr. 6 up). 1988. 19.95 (ISBN 0-7134-5479-2, Pub. by Batsford England). Trafalgar Sq.

Georges, D. V. Asia. LC 86-9631. (Illus.). 48p. (gr. k-4). 1986. PLB 14.60 (ISBN 0-516-01288-6); pap. 4.95 (ISBN 0-516-41288-4). Childrens.

Lye, Keith. Asia & Australia. Ron Hayward Associates, illus. 40p. (gr. 4-9). 1987. PLB 12.40 (ISBN 0-531-17067-5, Gloucester Pr). Watts.

Major, John S. The Land & People of Mongolia. LC 89-37790. (Illus.). 224p. (gr. 6 up). 1990. 15.95 (ISBN 0-397-32386-7, Lipp Jr Bks); PLB 15.89 (ISBN 0-397-32387-5, Lipp Jr Bks). HarpC Child Bks.

Ryabko, E. We Live in the Asian U. S. S. R. (Illus.). 64p. (gr. 4-8). 1984. PLB 9.49 (ISBN 0-531-03831-9). Watts.

Sabin, Louis. Asia. Eitzen, Allan, illus. LC 84-10559. 32p. (gr. 3-6). 1985. PLB 9.49 (ISBN 0-8167-0274-8); pap. text ed. 2.95 (ISBN 0-8167-0275-6). Troll Assocs.

ASIA–DESCRIPTION AND TRAVEL

Levine, Bobbie & Lichter, Carolyn. A Child's Walk Through Asia. Wu, Marshall, illus. 25p. (gr. 2-6). 1984. spiral bdg. 1.50 (ISBN 0-912303-31-X). Michigan Mus.

ASIA–HISTORY

Across Asia by Land. (Illus.). 128p. 1990. 17.95x (ISBN 0-8160-1874-X). Facts on File.

Civilizations of the Middle East. (Illus.). 80p. (gr. 4 up). 1988. PLB 22.00 (ISBN 0-8172-3303-2). Raintree Pubs.

Frazee, Charles & Yopp, Hallie K. The Ancient World. Frazee, Kathleen & Lumba, Eric, illus. (gr. 6). 1990. text ed. 21.08 (ISBN 1-878-47351-4); tchr's. ed. 27.08 (ISBN 1-878473-54-9); wkbk. 5.50 (ISBN 1-878473-55-7). Delos Pubns.

—Medieval & Early Modern Times. Frazee, Kathleen & Lumba, Eric, illus. (gr. 7). 1990. pap. text ed. 24.77 (ISBN 1-878473-56-5); tchr's. ed. 30.77 (ISBN 1-878473-58-1). Delos Pubns.

ASIA, SOUTHEASTERN

Beckett, Ian. Southeast Asia From 1945. (Illus.). 64p. (gr. 4-12). 1987. lib. bdg. 10.29 (ISBN 0-531-10322-6). Watts.

McGuire, William. Southeast Asians. (Illus.). (gr. 5-10). 1991. PLB 12.40 (ISBN 0-531-11108-3). Watts.

Mason, Antony. Southeast Asia. (Illus.). 48p. (gr. 4-8). 1989. lib. bdg. 14.98 (ISBN 0-382-09796-3). Silver Burdett Pr.

San Suu Kyi Sung. Bhutan. (Illus.). (gr. 5 up). 1988. 14.95 (ISBN 0-222-01099-1). Chelsea Hse.

Time-Life Books Editors. Southeast Asia. (Illus.). 160p. (gr. 7 up). 1987. lib. bdg. 25.93 (ISBN 0-8094-5318-5). Time-Life.

ASIMOV, ISAAC, 1920-

Erlanger, Ellen. Isaac Asimov: Scientist & Storyteller. LC 86-10675. (Illus.). 56p. (gr. 4 up). 1986. PLB 9.95 (ISBN 0-8225-0482-0). Lerner Pubns.

ASSASSINATION

see also names of persons and groups of persons with the subdivision Assassination, e.g. Presidents–U. S. –Assassination

ASSES AND MULES–FICTION

Aspinall, Anthony. Misadventures of an Aging Mule. 400p. 1990. 34.95 (ISBN 0-233-98439-9, Pub. by A Deutsch UK). Trafalgar Sq.

Baily, Jane B. Dottie, the Unfoolish Mule. Parker, Carolyn, illus. LC 90-93258. 32p. (Orig.). (gr. k-3). 1990. pap. 6.95 (ISBN 0-9626642-1-9). J B Baily.

Brittain, Bill. Devil's Donkey. Glass, Andrew, illus. LC 80-7907. 128p. (gr. 3-7). 1982. pap. 3.50 (ISBN 0-06-440129-4, Trophy). HarpC Child Bks.

Carroll, John. Donkey Nina & the Giant. Chamberlain, Sarah, illus. LC 88-33552. (gr. k-3). 1989. 12.95 (ISBN 0-525-44478-5, DCB). Dutton Child Bks.

Cheadle, J. A. A Donkey's Life: A Story for Children. Thomas, Toni, illus. LC 80-123421. iii, 88p. (Orig.). (gr. 2-6). 1979. pap. 3.50 (ISBN 0-9604244-0-7). Heahstan Pr.

The story follows Don Quixotito, a donkey of principle, across the American continent, with stops in North Carolina, Mississippi, Texas, Colorado, & California. Six songs, chiefly regional, which the donkey hears along the way, are included. After being almost successfully captured by rustlers in Texas, he leaves, this song echoing in his ears: "I'm departin' from this state; the Rangers nearly cornered me..." "Once upon a time a book brought children love. It is a children's story about an adventuresome little donkey named Don Quixotito whose travels take him to many exciting places. I read the book at least ten times--in the bathtub, while eating breakfast, & while everyone else watched the New Year's Day parade on T.V."--Peggy Drapo in the Denton Record-Chronicle. "This charming little book is not only a delightful story of the adventures of a cunning little donkey. It can be a very pleasant lesson in geography for a grown person as well as a child. There is also a touch of the lore of Texas & Texans in his Travels."--Carl Warlaw, Texas writer.

Publisher Provided Annotation.

Hammond, Jane. Debra the Donkey. (ps-k). 1983. pap. 1.50 (ISBN 0-87162-288-2, D5602). Warner Pr.

Harwood, Pearl A. Mr. Bumba's Four-Legged Company. Folger, Joseph, illus. LC 65-27996. 32p. (gr. k-3). 1966. PLB 4.95 (ISBN 0-8225-0108-2). Lerner Pubns.

Jafa, Manorama. The Donkey on the Bridge. Bhusan, Rboti, illus. 24p. (Orig.). (gr. k-3). 1980. pap. 2.50 (ISBN 0-89744-209-1, Pub. by Children's Bk Trust India). Auromere.

Lynch, Patricia. Turf Cutter's Donkey. 243p. (ps-8). 1988. pap. 6.95 (ISBN 1-85371-016-4, Pub. by Poolbeg Press Ltd Eire). Dufour.

Pio, Adam. Magic Donkey. (Illus.). 32p. 1989. PLB 27.99 (ISBN 0-8172-2461-0); pap. 16.67 (ISBN 0-8172-2777-6). Raintree Pubs.

Scheidl, Gerda M. The Little Donkey. Watts, Bernadette, illus. 32p. (gr. k-3). 1989. pap. 1.95 (ISBN 1-55858-031-X). North-South Bks NYC.

Weber, Kathryn. Molly Moonshine & Timothy. Downey, Jane, illus. 44p. (gr. 2-4). 1990. pap. 2.95 (ISBN 1-878438-01-8). Ranch House Pr.

ASSISTANCE TO DEVELOPING AREAS

see Economic Assistance

ASTROLOGY

see also Occult Sciences

Branley, Franklyn M. Age of Aquarius: You & Astrology. Kessler, Leonard, illus. LC 78-22511. 80p. (gr. 5 up). 1979. PLB 12.89 (ISBN 0-690-03988-3, Crowell Jr Bks). HarpC Child Bks.

Cowger, Barry D. Family Dynamics & Astrology. Green, Jeff, intro. by. (Illus.). 175p. (Orig.). (gr. 12). 1990. pap. 9.95 (ISBN 0-685-29119-7). Envision Pub.

Daniels, Gail, ed. Cancer, the Moon Child. 160p. (Orig.). (gr. 7 up). 1985. pap. 1.95 (ISBN 0-448-47741-6). Putnam Pub Group.

Gibson, Paul. How to Be Your Own Astrologer. (Illus.). 28p. (gr. 7 up). 1987. pap. text ed. 13.20 (ISBN 0-9619757-0-9). Astor Pubns.

Goodman, Linda. Linda Goodman's Sun Signs. LC 68-31737. (gr. 9-12). 1968. 24.95 (ISBN 0-8008-4900-0). Taplinger.

Harris, Paula. Pisces. 40p. (gr. 4). 1989. 10.95s.p. (ISBN 0-88682-254-8); 15.65 (ISBN 0-685-28170-1). Creative Ed.

—Scorpio. 40p. (gr. 4). 1989. 10.95s.p. (ISBN 0-88682-260-2); 15.65 (ISBN 0-685-28176-0). Creative Ed.

Lely, James A. Aquarius. 40p. (gr. 4). 1989. 10.95 (ISBN 0-88682-258-0). Creative Ed.

—Libra. 40p. (gr. 4). 1989. 10.95s.p. (ISBN 0-88682-262-9); 15.65 (ISBN 0-685-28178-7). Creative Ed.

—Virgo. 40p. (gr. 4). 1989. 10.95s.p. (ISBN 0-88682-259-9); 15.65 (ISBN 0-685-28175-2). Creative Ed.

Paul, Kathleen. Aries. 40p. (gr. 4). 1989. 10.95 (ISBN 0-88682-255-6). Creative Ed.

—Taurus. 40p. (gr. 4). 1989. 10.95s.p. (ISBN 0-88682-257-2); 15.65 (ISBN 0-685-28173-6). Creative Ed.

Schwartz, Alvin. Telling Fortunes: Love Magic, Dream Signs, & Other Ways to Learn the Future. Cameron, Tracey, illus. LC 85-45174. 128p. (gr. 4 up). 1987. 12.95 (ISBN 0-397-32132-5, Lipp Jr Bks); PLB 12.89 (ISBN 0-397-32133-3, Lipp Jr Bks). HarpC Child Bks.

Swainson, Esme. Children: The Adventures of Rex & Zendah in the Zodiac. Rosicrucian Fellowship Staff, ed. (Illus.). 112p. (ps-8). 1981. pap. text ed. 4.95 (ISBN 0-911274-61-8). Rosicrucian.

Taylor, Paula. Cancer. 40p. (gr. 4). 1989. 10.95s.p. (ISBN 0-88682-261-0); 15.65 (ISBN 0-685-28177-9). Creative Ed.

—Capricorn. 40p. (gr. 4). 1989. 10.95s.p. (ISBN 0-88682-256-4); 15.65 (ISBN 0-685-28172-8). Creative Ed.

—Gemini. 40p. (gr. 4). 1989. 10.95s.p. (ISBN 0-88682-252-1); 15.65 (ISBN 0-685-28168-X). Creative Ed.

—Leo. 40p. (gr. 4). 1989. 10.95s.p. (ISBN 0-88682-253-X); 15.65 (ISBN 0-685-28169-8). Creative Ed.

—Sagittarius. 40p. (gr. 4). 1989. 10.95s.p. (ISBN 0-88682-251-3); 15.65 (ISBN 0-685-28167-1). Creative Ed.

Weber, Peter J. Zodiac Degrees. (Illus.). 128p. (Orig.). 1989. 14.95 (ISBN 0-940649-06-3); pap. 9.95 (ISBN 0-940649-05-5). Parnell Pub.

ASTRONAUTICS

see also Artificial Satellites; Interplanetary Voyages; Manned Space Flight; Outer Space; Rocketry; Space Flight; Space Flight to the Moon; Space Sciences; Space Vehicles

Alexander, Kent. The Kid's Book of Space Flight & Space Stations: With Air Links Modular Flight System. (Illus.). 64p. (gr. 5 up). 1990. 16.95 (ISBN 0-89471-878-9). Running Pr.

Alston, Edith. Let's Visit a Space Camp. Plunkett, Michael, illus. LC 89-34373. 32p. (gr. 2-4). 1990. lib. bdg. 10.79 (ISBN 0-8167-1743-5); pap. text ed. 2.95 (ISBN 0-8167-1744-3). Troll Assocs.

Arceneaux, Marc. Space Base Vehicles. Arceneaux, Marc, illus. (gr. 1-4). 1983. pap. 2.50 (ISBN 0-448-11052-0, G&D). Putnam Pub Group.

Asimov, Isaac. The World's Space Program. LC 89-43134. (Illus.). 32p. (gr. 3-4). 1990. PLB 11.95 (ISBN 1-55532-374-X). Gareth Stevens Inc.

Baker, D. Weightlessness, Reading Level 3. (Illus.). 32p. (gr. 2-6). Date not set. PLB 13.20 (ISBN 0-86592-970-X). Rourke Corp.

Barrett, Norman. The Picture World of Astronauts. (Illus.). 32p. (gr. k-4). 1990. PLB 11.40 (ISBN 0-531-14053-9). Watts.

Dewaard, John. History of NASA: America's Voyage to the Stars. 1984. 12.98 (ISBN 0-671-06983-7). S&S Trade.

Embury, Barbara & Crouch, Tom D. The Dream Is Alive: A Flight of Discovery Aboard the Space Shuttle. LC 90-55194. (Illus.). 64p. (gr. 3-7). 1990. 14.95 (ISBN 0-06-021813-4); PLB 14.89 (ISBN 0-06-021814-2). HarpC Child Bks.

Greene, Carol. Astronauts. LC 83-23142. (Illus.). 48p. (gr. k-4). 1984. lib. bdg. 14.60 (ISBN 0-516-01722-5); pap. 4.95 (ISBN 0-516-41722-3). Childrens.

Kent, Zachary. The Story of the Challenger Disaster. LC 86-6822. (Illus.). 32p. (gr. 3-6). 1986. PLB 13.27 (ISBN 0-516-04673-X); pap. 3.95 (ISBN 0-516-44673-8). Childrens.

Long, Kim. Astronaut Training Book for Kids. (gr. 5up). 1990. 15.95 (ISBN 0-525-67296-6, Lodestar Bks). Dutton Child Bks.

McKay, David. Space Scientist's Projects for Young Scientists. 1989. pap. 5.95 (ISBN 0-531-15134-4). Watts.

Mandell, Myles K. Micromodels: Make Your Own Stephenson's Rocket. (gr. 2 up). 1983. pap. 4.95 (ISBN 0-399-50854-6, Perigee Bks). Putnam Pub Group.

Mason, John. Spacecraft Technology. 1990. PLB 12.40 (ISBN 0-531-18328-9). Watts.

Satellites & Space Stations: What They Can Do & How They Work. 48p. (gr. 6 up). 1986. PLB 13.96 (ISBN 0-88110-223-7); pap. 6.95 (ISBN 0-86020-937-7). EDC.

Simon, Seymour. How to Be a Space Scientist in Your Own Home. Morrison, Bill, illus. LC 81-47759. (gr. 4-7). 1982. (Lipp Jr Bks); PLB 13.89 (ISBN 0-397-31991-6, Lipp Jr Bks). HarpC Child Bks.

Williams, Brian. Pioneers of Flight. LC 90-9470. (Illus.). 48p. (gr. 4-8). 1990. PLB 18.60 (ISBN 0-8114-2755-2). Steck-V.

ASTRONAUTICS–BIOGRAPHY

Behrens, June. Sally Ride, Astronaut: An American First. LC 83-23173. (Illus.). 32p. (gr. 2-5). 1984. lib. bdg. 13.27 (ISBN 0-516-03606-8); pap. 3.95 (ISBN 0-516-43606-6). Childrens.

Blacknall, Carolyn. Sally Ride: America's First Woman in Space. LC 84-12671. (Illus.). 80p. (gr. 3 up). 1984. lib. bdg. 10.95 (ISBN 0-87518-260-7, Dillon). Macmillan Child Grp.

ASTRONAUTS

Armbruster, Ann & Taylor, Elizabeth A. Astronaut Training. (Illus.). 64p. (gr. 5-8). 1990. PLB 11.90 (ISBN 0-531-10862-7). Watts.

Barrett, Norman. Astronauts. Saunders, Mike, illus. LC 85-50156. 32p. (gr. k-6). 1986. lib. bdg. 11.40 (ISBN 0-531-10002-2). Watts.

—The Picture World of Astronauts. (Illus.). 32p. (gr. k-4). 1990. PLB 11.40 (ISBN 0-531-14053-9). Watts.

Barton, Byron. I Want to Be an Astronaut. Barton, Byron, illus. LC 87-24311. 32p. (ps-1). 1988. 7.95 (ISBN 0-694-00261-5, Crowell Jr Bks); PLB 12.89 (ISBN 0-690-04744-4). HarpC Child Bks.

Behrens, June. I Can Be an Astronaut. LC 84-7601. (Illus.). 32p. (gr. k-3). 1984. lib. bdg. 13.93 (ISBN 0-516-01837-X); pap. 3.95 (ISBN 0-516-41837-8). Childrens.

—Puedo Ser un Astronauta. Kratky, Lada, tr. from ENG. LC 84-7601. (SPA., Illus.). 32p. (gr. k-3). 1984. lib. bdg. 13.93 (ISBN 0-516-31837-3); pap. 3.95 (ISBN 0-516-51837-2). Childrens.

Bernstein, Joanne E. & Blue, Rose. Judith Resnik: Challenger Astronaut. Gerber, Alan J., contrib. by. (Illus.). 144p. (gr. 5-9). 1990. 14.95 (ISBN 0-525-67305-9, Lodestar Bks). Dutton Child Bks.

Billings, Charlene. Christa McAuliffe: Pioneer Space Teacher. LC 86-13453. (Illus.). 64p. (gr. 5-10). 1986. PLB 15.95 (ISBN 0-89490-148-6). Enslow Pubs.

Briggs, Carole S. Women in Space: Reaching the Last Frontier. (Illus.). 80p. (gr. 5 up). 1988. PLB 15.95 (ISBN 0-8225-1581-4, First Ave Edns); pap. 5.95 (ISBN 0-8225-9547-8, First Ave Edns). Lerner Pubns.

Collins, Michael. Flying to the Moon & Other Strange Places. LC 76-25496. (Illus.). 192p. (gr. 4 up). 1976. pap. 3.45 (ISBN 0-374-42355-5). FS&G.

Crocker, Chris. Great American Astronauts. IRosoff, T., ed. (Illus.). 128p. (gr. 7 up). 1988. PLB 12.90 (ISBN 0-531-10500-8). Watts.

Fox, Mary V. Women Astronauts: Aboard the Space Shuttle. rev. ed. LC 87-10814. (Illus.). 144p. (gr. 7 up). 1987. lib. bdg. 13.98 (ISBN 0-671-64840-3); pap. 5.95 (ISBN 0-671-64841-1). Messner.

Goodman, Mike. Astronauts. LC 89-31222. (Illus.). 48p. (gr. 4-5). 1989. PLB 10.95 (ISBN 0-89686-430-8, Crestwood Hse). Macmillan Child Grp.

Haskins, James & Benson, Kathleen. Space Challenger: The Story of Guion Bluford. LC 84-4251. (Illus.). 64p. (gr. 3-6). 1984. PLB 11.95 (ISBN 0-87614-259-5). Carolrhoda Bks.

Hopkins, Lila. Eating Crow. Sloan, Frank, ed. 144p. (ps-6). 1988. PLB 12.90 (ISBN 0-531-10499-0). Watts.

Martin, Patricia S. Christine McAuliffe: Reach for the Stars. (Illus.). 24p. (gr. 1-4). 1987. PLB 12.33 (ISBN 0-86592-172-5). Set. Rourke Corp.

Moche, Dinah. The Astronauts. LC 78-54955. (Illus.). (ps-3). 1979. 4.99 (ISBN 0-394-93901-8, Random Juv); pap. 2.25 (ISBN 0-394-83901-3). Random.

Naden, Corinne. Ronald McNair. King, Coretta Scott, intro. by. (Illus.). 112p. (gr. 5 up). 1991. PLB 17.95 (ISBN 0-7910-1133-X). Chelsea Hse.

Naden, Corinne J. & Blue, Rose. Christa McAuliffe: Teacher in Space. (Illus.). 48p. (gr. 2-4). 1991. PLB 11.90 (ISBN 1-56294-046-5). Millbrook Pr.

O'Connor, Karen. Sally Ride & the New Astronauts. LC 82-21844. (Illus.). 96p. (gr. 5 up). 1983. PLB 11.90 (ISBN 0-531-04602-8). Watts.

Poskanzer, Susan C. What's It Like to Be an Astronaut. Eitzen, Allan, illus. LC 89-34393. 32p. (gr. k-3). 1990. PLB 10.89 (ISBN 0-8167-1793-1); pap. text ed. 2.50 (ISBN 0-8167-1794-X). Troll Assocs.

Schloss, Muriel. Mary Cleave, Astronaut. (gr. 5 up). 1990. write for info. (ISBN 0-9621820-2-8). Teachers Lab.

Spangenburg, Ray & Moser, Diane. Space People from A to Z. 136p. 1990. 22.95x (ISBN 0-8160-1851-0). Facts on File.

Stott, Carole. Into the Unknown. (Illus.). 48p. (gr. 5-7). 1989. PLB 8.99 (ISBN 0-531-19513-9). Watts.

Westman, Paul. Neil Armstrong: Space Pioneer. LC 80-10832. (Illus.). 64p. (gr. 4 up). 1980. PLB 9.95 (ISBN 0-8225-0479-0). Lerner Pubns.

ASTRONAUTS–FICTION

Eco, Umberto. The Three Astronauts. Carmi, Eugenio, illus. (gr. 1 up). 1989. 12.95 (ISBN 0-15-286383-4, HJ). HarBraceJ.

Johnson, Larry D. & Mills, Jane L. Arnie the Astronaut. Hebert, Kim T., illus. LC 86-60353. 22p. (Orig.). (ps-1). 1986. pap. 4.50 (ISBN 0-938155-02-4); pap. 12.00 set of 3 bks. (ISBN 0-685-13517-9). Read A Bol.

Moche, Dinah. If You Were an Astronaut. (Illus.). 24p. (ps-3). 1985. pap. write for info. (ISBN 0-307-11896-7, Pub. by Golden Bks). Western Pub.

Murphy, Elspeth C. Pug McConnell. LC 85-26922. 107p. (gr. 3-7). 1986. 3.95 (ISBN 0-89191-728-4, Chariot Bks). Cook.

North, Rick. Young Astronauts, No. 2. 1990. pap. 2.95 (ISBN 0-8217-3173-4). Zebra.

ASTRONOMICAL INSTRUMENTS

see also Telescope

ASTRONOMICAL OBSERVATORIES

Fradin, Dennis. Space Telescope. (Illus.). (gr. k-4). 1987. PLB 14.60 (ISBN 0-516-01239-8). Childrens.

ASTRONOMY

see also Almanacs; Astrology; Life on Other Planets; Meteorites; Meteors; Moon; Outer Space; Planets; Quasars; Seasons; Solar System; Space Sciences; Stars; Sun; Tides

Adler, David A. Hyperspace! Facts & Fun from All Over the Universe. Winkowski, Fred, illus. LC 81-70404. 80p. (gr. 3-7). 1982. Viking Penguin.

Apfel, Necia. Astronomy & Plantology: Projects for Young Scientists. (Illus.). 128p. (gr. 9up). PLB 12.90 (ISBN 0-531-04668-0). Watts.

Apfel, Necia H. Astronomy Projects for Young Scientists. LC 84-6454. (Illus.). 128p. (gr. 10 up). 1984. pap. 7.95 (ISBN 0-668-06006-9, 6006-9). Prentice Hall Pr.

—Nebulae. LC 86-33765. (Illus.). 48p. (gr. 3-6). 1988. 13.95 (ISBN 0-688-07228-3); PLB 13.88 (ISBN 0-688-07229-1). Lothrop.

Asimov, Isaac. Ancient Astronomy. LC 88-17564. (Illus.). 32p. (gr. 3-4). 1988. PLB 11.95 (ISBN 1-55532-368-5). Gareth Stevens Inc.

—Ancient Astronomy. (gr. 4-7). 1991. pap. 4.95 (ISBN 0-440-40387-1). Dell.

—The Asteroids. LC 87-42598. (Illus.). (gr. 3-4). 1988. PLB 11.95 (ISBN 1-55532-353-7). Gareth Stevens Inc.

—Astronomy Today. LC 89-4631. (Illus.). 32p. (gr. 3-4). 1989. PLB 11.95 (ISBN 1-55532-402-9). Gareth Stevens Inc.

—Earth: Our Home Base. LC 87-42607. (Illus.). 32p. (gr. 3-4). 1988. PLB 11.95 (ISBN 1-55532-362-6). Gareth Stevens Inc.

—The Earth's Moon. LC 87-42601. (Illus.). 32p. (gr. 3-4). 1988. PLB 11.95 (ISBN 1-55532-357-X). Gareth Stevens Inc.

—How Did We Find Out about Black Holes? Wool, David, illus. LC 73-4320. (gr. 5 up). 1978. PLB 12.85 reinforced (ISBN 0-8027-6337-5). Walker & Co.

—Index. LC 89-43142. (Illus.). 32p. (gr. 3-4). 1990. PLB 11.95 (ISBN 1-55532-900-4). Gareth Stevens Inc.

—Projects in Astronomy. LC 89-43133. (Illus.). 32p. (gr. 3-4). 1990. PLB 11.95 (ISBN 1-55532-401-0). Gareth Stevens Inc.

—Space Garbage. LC 88-42894. (Illus.). 32p. (gr. 3-4). 1989. PLB 11.95 (ISBN 1-55532-370-7). Gareth Stevens Inc.

Astronomy. LC 84-60400. (Illus.). 144p. (gr. 4 up). write for info. (ISBN 0-528-82394-9). Checkerboard Pr.

Astronomy Encyclopedia. (Illus.). 144p. (gr. 4 up). 1989. Repr. 14.95 (ISBN 0-02-688538-7). Checkerboard Pr.

Baker, D. Eyes in the Sky, Reading Level 3. (Illus.). 32p. (gr. 2-6). Date not set. PLB 13.20 (ISBN 0-86592-973-4). Rourke Corp.

Barrett, Norman. Night Sky. LC 85-50158. (Illus.). 32p. (gr. k-6). 1986. lib. bdg. 11.40 (ISBN 0-531-10004-9). Watts.

Bendick, Jeanne. Artificial Satellites: Helpers in Space. (Illus.). 32p. (gr. k-2). 1991. PLB 11.90 (ISBN 1-56294-002-3); pap. 3.95 (ISBN 1-878841-56-4). Millbrook Pr.

—Comets & Meteors: Visitors from Space. (Illus.). 32p. (gr. k-2). 1991. PLB 11.90 (ISBN 1-56294-001-5); pap. 3.95 (ISBN 1-878841-55-6). Millbrook Pr.

Berger, Melvin. Bright Stars, Red Giants & White Dwarfs. LC 82-23052. (Illus.). 64p. (gr. 5-9). 1983. 12.99 (ISBN 0-399-61209-2, Putnam). Putnam Pub Group.

—Planets, Stars & Galaxies. LC 78-16688. (Illus.). (gr. 6-8). 1978. PLB 7.99 (ISBN 0-399-61104-5, Putnam). Putnam Pub Group.

—Star Gazing, Comet Tracking & Sky Mapping. LC 84-8302. (Illus.). 64p. (gr. 5 up). 1984. 10.99 (ISBN 0-399-61211-4, Putnam). Putnam Pub Group.

Boy Scouts of America. Astronomy. (Illus.). 80p. (gr. 6-12). 1983. pap. 1.85 (ISBN 0-8395-3303-9, 3303). BSA.

Branley, Franklyn M. The Big Dipper. rev. ed. Coxe, Molly, illus. LC 90-31199. 32p. (ps-1). 1991. 13.95 (ISBN 0-06-020511-3); PLB 13.89 (ISBN 0-06-020512-1). HarpC Child Bks.

—The Sky Is Full of Stars. Bond, Felicia, illus. LC 81-43037. 40p. (gr. k-3). 1983. pap. 4.50 (ISBN 0-06-445002-3, Trophy). HarpC Child Bks.

—Star Guide. Eagle, Ellen, illus. LC 82-45928. 64p. (gr. 3-6). 1987. 11.95 (ISBN 0-690-04350-3, Crowell Jr Bks); PLB 11.89 (ISBN 0-690-04351-1, Crowell Jr Bks). HarpC Child Bks.

—Sun Dogs & Shooting Stars: A Skywatcher's Calendar. (Illus.). (gr. 5 up). 1980. 14.95 (ISBN 0-395-29520-3). HM.

—Superstar: The Supernova of Nineteen Eighty-Seven. Kelley, True, illus. LC 89-71164. 64p. (gr. 3-6). 1990. 13.95 (ISBN 0-690-04839-4, Crowell Jr Bks); PLB 13.89 (ISBN 0-690-04841-6, Crowell Jr Bks). HarpC Child Bks.

Brown, Robert & Jones, Brian. Exploring Space. LC 89-11278. (Illus.). 64p. (gr. 2-3). 1989. PLB 12.95 (ISBN 0-8368-0029-X). Gareth stevens Inc.

Caveney, Sylvia & Giesen, Rosemary. Where Am I? Stern, Simon, illus. LC 76-22476. 24p. (gr. k-3). 1977. PLB 5.95 (ISBN 0-8225-1365-X). Lerner Pubns.

Darling, David J. Comets, Meteors & Asteroids: Rocks in Space. LC 84-14275. (Illus.). 64p. (gr. 4 up). 1984. PLB 10.95 (ISBN 0-87518-264-X, Dillon). Macmillan Child Grp.

—The New Astronomy: An Ever-Changing Universe. Swofford, Jeanette, illus. LC 84-23083. 64p. (gr. 4 up). 1985. PLB 10.95 (ISBN 0-87518-288-7, Dillon). Macmillan Child Grp.

—The Stars: From Birth to Black Hole. Swofford, Jeanette, illus. LC 84-23067. 64p. (gr. 4 up). 1985. PLB 10.95 (ISBN 0-87518-284-4, Dillon). Macmillan Child Grp.

—Where Are We Going in Space? LC 84-12672. (Illus.). 64p. (gr. 4 up). 1984. PLB 10.95 (ISBN 0-87518-265-8, Dillon). Macmillan Child Grp.

Definitely from out of Town. 48p. (gr. 4-5). 1989. PLB 10.95 (ISBN 0-685-26417-3). Capstone Pr.

Dickinson, Terence. Exploring the Night Sky: The Equinox Astronomy Guide for Beginners. Bianchi, John, illus. 72p. (Orig.). (gr. 5 up). 1989. 15.95 (ISBN 0-920656-64-1); pap. 9.95 (ISBN 0-920656-66-8). Camden Hse Pub.

The New York Academy of Sciences judged EXPLORING THE NIGHT SKY to be the best book on science for older children published in 1987. The award recognized high-quality children's books about science to promote a greater understanding of the role science plays in today's world. In review, SCIENTIFIC AMERICAN magazine called "this admirable work.. .a beginner's bargain that is hard to beat, well suited for readers in the middle grades on up (& their elders too)." "...unusually realistic help, fulfilling the book's claim that it is an 'astronomy guide for beginners'". EXPLORING THE NIGHT SKY is an essential reference for homes, schools & libraries, & a perfect companion to the new EXPLORING THE SKY BY DAY.

Publisher Provided Annotation.

D'Ignazio, Fred. The New Astronomy: Probing the Secrets of Space. (Illus.). 72p. (gr. 4 up). 1982. PLB 10.40 (ISBN 0-531-04386-X). Watts.

The Emperor of Time. 48p. (gr. 4-5). 1989. PLB 10.95 (ISBN 0-685-26418-1). Capstone Pr.

Fradin, Dennis B. Astronomy. LC 82-19722. (Illus.). 48p. (gr. k-4). 1983. PLB 14.60 (ISBN 0-516-01673-3); pap. 4.95 (ISBN 0-516-41673-1). Childrens.

—Astronomy. LC 86-13671. (Illus.). 288p. (gr. 4 up). 1987. 38.60 (ISBN 0-516-00533-2). Childrens.

Gallant, Roy A. The Macmillan Book of Astronomy. Miller, Ron, et al, illus. LC 86-24158. 80p. (gr. 3-7). 1986. pap. 8.95 (ISBN 0-02-043230-5, Aladdin). Macmillan Child Grp.

Graham, Ian. Astronomer. (Illus.). 32p. (gr. 5-8). 1991. PLB 11.90 (ISBN 0-531-17314-3, Gloucester Pr). Watts.

Hamer, Martyn. Night Sky. (Illus.). (gr. k-3). 1983. PLB 7.99 (ISBN 0-531-04619-2). Watts.

Harris, Richard. I Can Read About the Sun & Other Stars. Krasnoborski, William, illus. LC 76-54577. (gr. 2-4). 1977. pap. 1.95 (ISBN 0-89375-044-1). Troll Assocs.

Heller, Robert, et al. Earth Science. 2nd ed. (Illus.). 1978. text ed. 32.24 (ISBN 0-07-028037-1). McGraw.

Herbst, Judith. Sky Above & Worlds Beyond. Rosenblum, Richard & Lovi, George, illus. LC 82-13749. 224p. (gr. 5 up). 1983. 14.95 (ISBN 0-689-30974-0, Atheneum Child Bk). Macmillan Child Grp.

Hirst, Robin & Hirst, Sally. My Place in Space. Harvey, Roland & Levine, Joe, illus. LC 89-37893. 40p. (ps-2). 1990. 13.95 (ISBN 0-531-05859-X); PLB 13.99 (ISBN 0-531-08459-0). Orchard Bks Watts.

How Do You Know That? 48p. (gr. 4-5). 1989. PLB 10.95 (ISBN 0-685-26419-X). Capstone Pr.

Hunig, Klaus. Astro-Dome Book: 3-D Map of the Night Sky. Solensten, Lori, ed. Zerner, Amy & Drake, Charles, illus. Himelfarb, Donna, intro. by. 68p. (Orig.). (gr. 4 up). 1983. pap. 9.95 incl. Constellation Handbook (ISBN 0-913319-00-7). Sunstone Pubns.

Jacobs, Francine. Cosmic Countdown: What Astronomers Have Learned about the Life of the Universe. Jastrow, Robert, frwd. by. LC 83-5535. (Illus.). 160p. (gr. 7 up). 1983. 9.95 (ISBN 0-87131-404-5). M Evans.

Jenkins, Gerald & Bear, Magdalen. The Tarquin Star Globe: To Cut Out & Make Yourself. (Illus.). 32p. (gr. 4 up). 1988. pap. 6.95 (ISBN 0-906212-60-X, Tarquin). Parkwest Pubns.

Jobb, Jamie. The Night Sky Book. (gr. 5 up). 1977. 14.95 (ISBN 0-316-46551-8); pap. 8.95 (ISBN 0-316-46552-6). Little.

Kelch, Joseph W. Small Worlds: Sixty Moons of Our Solar System. Steltenpohl, Jane, ed. (Illus.). 128p. (gr. 6-8). 1990. 13.95 (ISBN 0-671-70014-6); PLB 16.98 (ISBN 0-671-70013-8). Messner.

Kelsey, Larry & Hoff, Darrel. Recent Revolutions in Astronomy. LC 86-23340. (Illus.). 128p. (gr. 7-12). 1987. PLB 12.90 (ISBN 0-531-10340-4). Watts.

Lampton, Christopher. Astronomy: From Copernicus to the Space Telescope. LC 86-23436. (Illus.). 96p. (gr. 4-8). 1987. PLB 10.40 (ISBN 0-531-10300-5). Watts.

—Supernova! Solomon, Maury, ed. (Illus.). 128p. (gr. 7 up). 1988. PLB 12.90 (ISBN 0-531-10602-0). Watts.

Levinson, Riki. Mira Como Salen Las Estrellas. Goode, Diane, illus. (SPA.). (gr. 1-6). 14.95 (ISBN 84-372-6607-6). Santillana.

Lewellen, John. Moon, Sun & Stars. LC 81-7749. (Illus.). 48p. (gr. k-4). 1981. PLB 13.27 (ISBN 0-516-01637-7); pap. 4.95 (ISBN 0-516-41637-5). Childrens.

Lifestyles of the Big & Powerful. 48p. (gr. 4-5). 1989. PLB 10.95 (ISBN 0-685-26395-9). Capstone Pr.

Liptak, Karen. Astronomy Basics. (Illus.). 48p. (gr. 3-7). 1986. 10.95 (ISBN 0-13-049966-8). P-H.

Little People Big Book about Space. 64p. (ps-1). 1990. write for info. (ISBN 0-8094-7500-6); lib. bdg. write for info. (ISBN 0-8094-7501-4). Time-Life.

Looking for Little Green Men. 48p. (gr. 4-5). 1989. PLB 10.95 (ISBN 0-685-26396-7). Capstone Pr.

McGowen, Tom. Album of Astronomy. Ruth, Rod, illus. LC 79-9485. (gr. 4-10). 1979. write for info. (ISBN 0-528-82048-6). Checkerboard Pr.

—Album of Astronomy. Ruth, Rod, illus. 64p. (gr. 3-7). 1987. pap. 4.95 (ISBN 0-02-688501-8). Checkerboard Pr.

Mackie, Dan. Planets & Galaxies. Bastien, Charles & Livingston, Richard, illus. 32p. (gr. 5-9). 1985. pap. 4.95 (ISBN 0-88625-102-8). Durkin Hayes Pub.

—Space Tour. Hughes, Mark, illus. 32p. (gr. 5-9). 1985. pap. 4.95 (ISBN 0-88625-103-6). Durkin Hayes Pub.

Mammana, Dennis. The Night Sky: A Guide for the Young Astronomer. (Illus.). 96p. (Orig.). 1989. pap. 9.95 (ISBN 0-89471-764-2); bk. & telescope pkg. 14.95 (ISBN 0-89471-765-0). Running Pr.

Marsh, Carole. Astronomy for Kids: Milky Way & Mars Bars. (Illus.). 1990. 19.95 (ISBN 0-7933-0012-6); pap. 14.95 (ISBN 0-7933-0013-4); computer disk 29.95 (ISBN 0-7933-0014-2). Gallopade Pub Group.

Maurer, Richard. Junk in Space. (gr. 3 up). 1989. pap. 14.95 (ISBN 0-671-67768-3); pap. 5.95 (ISBN 0-671-67747-0). S&S Trade.

Mayall, R. Newton, et al. Sky Observer's Guide. rev. ed. Polgreen, John, illus. (gr. 9 up). 1985. pap. write for info. (ISBN 0-307-24009-6, Golden Pr). Western Pub.
Mayes, S. Why Is Night Dark? (Illus.). 24p. (gr. 1-4). 1990. lib. bdg. 11.96 (ISBN 0-88110-442-6, Usborne); pap. 3.95 (ISBN 0-7460-0428-1, Usborne). EDC.
Moche, Dinah. Amazing Space Facts. Alley, R. W., illus. & photos by LC 87-82370. 24p. (ps-3). 1988. pap. write for info. (ISBN 0-307-11815-0, Pub. by Golden Bks). Western Pub.
—Astronomy Today: Planets, Stars, Space Exploration. McNaught, Harry, illus. LC 82-5211. 96p. (gr. 5 up). 1982. lib. bdg. 11.99 (ISBN 0-394-94423-2); pap. 10. 95 (ISBN 0-394-84423-8). Random.
Moeschl, Richard. Exploring the Sky: 100 Projects for Beginning Astronomers. LC 88-21485. (Illus.). (gr. 7-10). 1988. pap. 14.95 (ISBN 1-55652-039-5). Chicago Review.
Myring, Lynn. Sun, Moon & Planets. (gr. 2-5). 1982. (Usborne-Hayes); PLB 11.96 (ISBN 0-88110-018-8); pap. 3.95 (ISBN 0-86020-580-0). EDC.
Not Quite Planets. 48p. (gr. 4-5). 1989. PLB 10.95 (ISBN 0-685-26330-4). Capstone Pr.
Penn, Linda. Young Scientist Explore: The Sun, Moon & Stars. Scott, Elaine, illus. 32p. (gr. k-3). 1985. wkbk. 4.95 (ISBN 0-86653-314-1, GA 653). Good Apple.
Raintree Publishers Staff. Astronomy. LC 87-28780. (Illus.). 64p. (Orig.). (gr. 5-9). 1988. PLB 19.99 (ISBN 0-8172-3080-7). Raintree Pubs.
Reigot, Betty P. A Book about Planets & Stars. (Illus.). 48p. (gr. 2-5). 1988. pap. 3.95 (ISBN 0-590-40593-4). Scholastic Inc.
Rey, H. A. The Stars: A New Way to See Them. 3rd ed. (Illus.). (gr. 8 up). 1973. 16.95 (ISBN 0-395-08121-1). HM.
Ridpath, Ian. Space. (Illus.). 48p. (gr. 5-8). 1991. PLB 13. 90 (ISBN 0-531-19144-3, Warwick). Watts.
Riley, Peter D. The Earth & Space. (Illus.). 48p. (gr. 4-6). 1986. 17.95 (ISBN 0-85219-598-2, Pub. by Batsford England). Trafalgar Sq.
Simon, Seymour. Galaxies. LC 87-23967. (Illus.). (ps-3). 1988. 14.95 (ISBN 0-688-08002-2); PLB 14.88 (ISBN 0-688-08004-9, Morrow Jr Bks). Morrow Jr Bks.
—Look to the Night Sky: An Introduction to Star Watching. (Illus.). (gr. 5-12). 1979. pap. 5.95 (ISBN 0-14-049185-6, Puffin). Puffin Bks.
Sipiera, Paul. I Can Be an Astronomer. LC 86-9629. (Illus.). 32p. (gr. k-3). 1986. PLB 13.93 (ISBN 0-516-01883-3). Childrens.
Snowden, S. The Young Astronomer. (Illus.). 32p. (gr. 5-10). 1983. PLB 13.96 (ISBN 0-88110-028-5); pap. 6.95 (ISBN 0-86020-651-3). EDC.
Sonneborn, Ruth A. The Star Wars Question & Answer Book of Space. (Illus.). (gr. k-3). 1979. (Random Juv). Random.
Stacy, Tom. The Sun, Stars & Planets. Bull, Peter & Quigley, Sebastian, illus. 40p. (gr. 4-5). 1991. PLB 11. 40 (ISBN 0-531-19107-9). Watts.
Thompson, C. E. Glow-in-the-Dark Constellations: A Field Guide for Young Stargazers. Chewning, Randy, illus. 32p. (gr. 1-5). 1989. 11.95 (ISBN 0-448-09070-8, G&D). Putnam Pub Group.
Van Cleave, Janice. Janice Van Cleave's Astronomy for Every Kid: 101 Easy Experiments That Really Work. 1991. pap. text ed. 10.95 (ISBN 0-471-53573-7). Wiley.
—Janice Van Cleave's Astronomy for Every Kid: 101 Easy Experiments That Really Work. 1991. text ed. 19.89 (ISBN 0-471-54285-7). Wiley.
Vbrova, Zuza. Space & Astronomy. LC 88-83111. (Illus.). 36p. (gr. 5-8). 1989. PLB 12.40 (ISBN 0-531-17143-4, Glouster Pr). Watts.
Weiss, Malcolm E. Sky Watchers of Ages Past. McFadden, Eliza, illus. (gr. 5-9). 1982. 7.95 (ISBN 0-395-29525-4). HM.
West, Robin. Far Out: How to Create Your Own Star World. Wolfe, Bob, photos by. (Illus.). 72p. (gr. k-4). 1987. lib. bdg. 14.95 (ISBN 0-87614-279-X); pap. 5.95 (ISBN 0-87614-463-6). Carolrhoda Bks.
Williams, Brenda & Williams, Brian. Sun, Stars & Planets. Bull, Peter, illus. LC 90-42979. 40p. (Orig.). (gr. 2-5). 1991. pap. 3.95 (ISBN 0-679-80862-0). Random.
Wolf, Donald D. & Wolf, Margot L. Stars, Moons & Planets. LC 82-80878. (Illus.). 64p. (gr. 3-8). 1982. pap. 3.95 (ISBN 0-448-04089-1, G&D). Putnam Pub Group.
Wood, Robert W. Thirty-Nine Easy Astronomy Experiments. (Illus.). 160p. 1991. 16.95 (ISBN 0-8306-7597-3, 3597); pap. 9.95 (ISBN 0-8306-3597-1). TAB Bks.
Wyler, Rose. The Starry Sky. Steltenpohl, Jane, ed. Petruccio, Steven, illus. 32p. (gr. k-2). 1989. lib. bdg. 11.98 (ISBN 0-671-66345-3); pap. 4.95 (ISBN 0-671-66349-6). Messner.
Zim, Herbert S. & Baker, Robert H. Stars. rev. ed. Irving, James G., illus. (gr. 6 up). 1985. pap. write for info. (ISBN 0-307-24493-8, Golden Pr). Western Pub.

ATHENS

Davis, William S. Day in Old Athens. LC 60-16707. (Illus.). (gr. 7 up). 20.00 (ISBN 0-8196-0111-X). Biblo.
Hughes, Richard. Adventure in Athens. Wheeler, Jill, ed. Lowery, Carol, illus. 48p. (gr. 4). 1989. lib. bdg. 10.95 (ISBN 0-939179-46-6). Abdo & Dghtrs.

ATHLETES

see also Black Athletes

Aaseng, Nathan. Carl Lewis: Legend Chaser. LC 84-23348. (Illus.). 56p. (gr. 4-9). 1985. PLB 8.95 (ISBN 0-8225-0496-0). Lerner Pubns.
—Superstars Stopped Short. LC 81-12431. (Illus.). 80p. (gr. 4 up). 1982. PLB 7.95 (ISBN 0-8225-1326-9). Lerner Pubns.
Cohen, Daniel & Cohen, Susan. Young & Famous: Sports Newest Superstars. (gr. 4 up). 1989. pap. 2.50 (ISBN 0-671-68725-5, Archway). PB.
Connolly, Pat. Coaching Evelyn: Fast, Faster, Fastest Woman in the World. LC 90-4835. (Illus.). 224p. (gr. 7 up). 1991. 15.95 (ISBN 0-06-021282-9); PLB 15.89 (ISBN 0-06-021283-7). HarpC Child Bks.
Corrigan, Robert J. Tracking Heroes: Thirteen Track & Field Champions. LC 89-51039. 163p. (gr. 4-9). 1990. 8.95 (ISBN 1-55523-236-1). Winston-Derek.
Frontier Press Company Staff. Lincoln Library of Sports Champions, 20 vols. 5th ed. LC 88-82571. (Illus.). 2560p. (gr. 4 up). 1989. Set. 439.00 (ISBN 0-912168-13-7). Frontier Pr Co.
Green, Carl R. & Sanford, William R. Hulk Hogan. LC 86-13381. (Illus.). 32p. (gr. 4-5). PLB 9.95 (ISBN 0-89686-299-2, Crestwood Hse). Macmillan Child Grp.
Hamill, Dorothy & Clairmont, Elva. Dorothy Hamill on & off the Ice. LC 83-6170. (Illus.). 192p. (gr. 8-12). 1983. lib. bdg. 10.99 (ISBN 0-394-95610-9). Knopf.
Harris, Jonathan. Drugged Athletes: The Crisis in American Sports. LC 86-29396. 204p. (gr. 5-9). 1987. 14.95 (ISBN 0-02-742740-4, Four Winds). Macmillan Child Grp.
Haskins, James. The Sports Great Magic Johnson. 64p. (gr. 4-12). 1989. lib. bdg. 15.95 (ISBN 0-89490-160-5). Enslow Pubs.
—Sugar Ray Leonard. LC 82-15227. (Illus.). 160p. (gr. 4 up). 1982. 14.95 (ISBN 0-688-01436-4). Lothrop.
Hill, Randall C. Superstars in Action: Courage & Daring. (Illus.). 108p. (gr. 5-12). 1990. PLB 6.00 (ISBN 0-8114-1598-8). Steck-V.
Jennings, Jay. Moments of Courage. (Illus.). 64p. (gr. 5-7). 1991. PLB 14.98 (ISBN 0-382-24108-8); PLB 11. 24s.p.; pap. 8.95 (ISBN 0-382-24114-2); pap. 6.71s.p. Silver Burdett Pr.
Knudson, R. R. Babe Didrikson: Athlete of the Century. Lewin, Ted, illus. 64p. (gr. 2-6). 1986. pap. 3.95 (ISBN 0-14-032095-4, Puffin). Puffin Bks.
Lundgren, Hal. Mary Lou Retton: Gold Medal Gymnast. LC 84-29313. (Illus.). 48p. (gr. 3 up). 1985. 13.27 (ISBN 0-516-04346-3); pap. 3.95 (ISBN 0-516-44346-1). Childrens.
McLeninghan, Valjean. Diana: Alone Against the Sea. Blair, Jay, illus. LC 79-21518. 48p. (gr. 4 up). 1980. PLB 15.99 (ISBN 0-8172-1557-3). Raintree Pubs.

Maitland, William J. Weight Training for Gifted Athletes. Mollen, Art, intro. by. LC 89-90833. (Illus.). 147p. (Orig.). (gr. 8 up). 1990. pap. 17.95 (ISBN 0-936759-01-1). Maitland Enter. Co-educational training & nutrition information for recreational through professional athletes ages 14 through adult. Endorsed by Dr. Art Mollen. Has easy-to-read large print with explicit photos for each exercise. Text is block paragraphs & non-technical language allowing quick sight reading. In-season - off-season schedules are discussed using psycho-physiological & plyometric disciplines. Warm-ups - warm-downs with proper & improper stretching are discussed fully. Development of the human body from childhood to maturation with muscle-skeletal diagrams. Charts for record of progress & alternate advanced exercises. Table of contents-bibliography. Author has trained & coached athletes in all sports for thirty years including recreational training activities for fitness. "Makes good sense for improving skills"--Dr. Art Mollen. "...I found your book. Used it - our game has improved immensely"--John Barclay, Hockey Coach, Phoenix, Arizona. "Taught me a great deal about training young athletes"--Michael Johnson, YMCA Coach, N.J. "Finally the answers I've been seeking in language I can understand"--Cara Schappat, Bangor, Maine. Also see BEGINNING WEIGHT TRAINING FOR YOUNG ATHLETES - AGES 12 THROUGH ADULT by same author.
Publisher Provided Annotation.

Martin, Patricia S. Dale Murphy: Baseball's Gentle Giant. (Illus.). 24p. (gr. 1-4). 1987. PLB 12.33 (ISBN 0-86592-167-9). Rourke Corp.
Newman, Matthew. Mary Decker Slaney. LC 86-16525. (Illus.). 48p. (gr. 5-6). PLB 10.95 (ISBN 0-89686-319-0, Crestwood Hse). Macmillan Child Grp.
Oana, Katherine. The Sporting Way to Reading Comprehension. Cooper, William H., ed. Shuster, Dorarhye, illus. LC 84-51195. 68p. (Orig.). (gr. 3-8). 1984. 5.27 (ISBN 0-914127-17-9). Univ Class.
Orr, Jack. Black Athlete: His Story in American History. Robinson, Jackie, intro. by. (gr. 6 up). 1969. PLB 14. 95 (ISBN 0-87460-104-5). Lion Bks.
Solomon, Abbot N. Secrets of the Super Athletes: Tip for Fans & Players-Football. (Illus., Orig.). (gr. 7 up). 1982. pap. 1.95 (ISBN 0-440-97979-X, LFL). Dell.
Sullivan, George. Great Lives: Sports. LC 88-15673. (Illus.). 288p. (gr. 4-6). 1988. 22.95 (ISBN 0-684-18510-5, Scribners Young Read). Macmillan Child Grp.
White, Ellen E. Bo Jackson: Playing the Games. (Illus.). 96p. (Orig.). (gr. 3-7). 1990. pap. 2.95 (ISBN 0-590-44075-6). Scholastic Inc.

ATHLETICS

see also Coaching (Athletics); Gymnastics; Olympic Games; Physical Education and Training; Sports; Track Athletics;
also names of specific athletic activities, e.g. Boxing; Rowing; etc.

Athletics. (Illus.). 22p. (gr. 6-12). 1964. pap. 1.85 (ISBN 0-8395-3324-1, 3324). BSA.
Brunner, Rick, et al. Soviet Training & Recovery Methods: For Competitive Athletes. LC 90-62005. (Illus.). 200p. (Orig.). (gr. 10 up). 1990. pap. 18.95 (ISBN 0-9622039-2-0). Sports Focus Pub.
Buchanan, David. Greek Athletics. McLeish, Kenneth & McLeish, Valerie, eds. (Illus.). 48p. (gr. 7-12). 1976. pap. text ed. 9.00 (ISBN 0-582-20059-8, 70659). Longman.
Gardner, Robert. The Young Athlete's Manual. LC 85-8864. (Illus.). 160p. (gr. 5 up). 1985. lib. bdg. 9.97 (ISBN 0-671-49369-8). Messner.
Morton, Miriam. Making of Champions: Soviet Sports for Children & Teenagers. LC 73-76326. (Illus.). 144p. (gr. 4-6). 1974. 6.25 (ISBN 0-689-30142-1, Atheneum). Macmillan Child Grp.
Shapiro, Harry. Facts on Drugs in Sports. (Illus.). 32p. (gr. 5-6). 1989. PLB 11.90 (ISBN 0-531-10823-6). Watts.
Sullivan, George. Modern Olympic Superstars. (Illus.). 112p. (gr. 9-12). 1979. 8.95 (ISBN 0-396-07651-3, Putnam). Putnam Pub Group.
Washington, Rosemary G. Mary Lou Retton: Power Gymnast. (Illus.). 56p. (gr. 4-9). 1985. PLB 8.95 (ISBN 0-8225-0497-9). Lerner Pubns.

ATHLETICS–FICTION

Brown, F. K. Last Hurdle. Spier, Peter, illus. LC 87-29761. 202p. (gr. 3-9). 1988. Repr. of 1953 ed. 17.50 (ISBN 0-208-02212-0, Linnet). Shoe String.
Cloverdale Press Editors. Out of Bounds. 160p. (gr. 6 up). 1987. pap. 2.50 (ISBN 0-553-26338-2, Starfire). Bantam.
Cloverdale Press, Inc. Editors, ed. Varsity Takedown Coach, No. 2. 128p. 1987. pap. 2.50 (ISBN 0-553-26209-2). Bantam.
Haigh, Sheila. The Little Gymnast. 144p. (gr. 3-7). 1987. pap. 2.50 (ISBN 0-590-40494-6, Apple Paperbacks). Scholastic Inc.
Hallowell, Tommy. Varsity Coach. 128p. (Orig.). 1986. pap. 2.50 (ISBN 0-553-26033-2, Starfire). Bantam.
Hargreaves, Roger. Mr. Strong. (Illus.). 32p. (ps-3). 1982. pap. 1.25 (ISBN 0-8431-0877-0). Price Stern.
Ibbitson, John. The Wimp & the Jock. Collins, Heather, illus. LC 88-14078. 96p. (Orig.). (gr. 7 up). 1989. pap. 2.95 (ISBN 0-02-041792-6, Collier Young Ad). Macmillan Child Grp.
Knudson, R. R. Rinehart Lifts. LC 80-66825. 192p. (gr. 4 up). 1980. 10.95 (ISBN 0-374-36294-7). FS&G.
—Zan Hagan's Marathon. LC 84-47843. 176p. (gr. 5 up). 1984. 12.95 (ISBN 0-374-38811-3). FS&G.
Levy, Elizabeth. The Beginners. (gr. 1-4). 1988. pap. 2. 50x (ISBN 0-590-41562-X, Apple Paperbacks). Scholastic Inc.
—First Meet. 128p. (gr. 3-7). 1988. pap. 2.50 (ISBN 0-590-41563-8, Apple Paperbacks). Scholastic Inc.
—The New Coach? 128p. (gr. 3-7). 1991. pap. 2.75 (ISBN 0-590-44695-9). Scholastic Inc.
—The Winner. 128p. (gr. 3-6). 1989. pap. 2.50 (ISBN 0-590-41565-4, Apple Paperbacks). Scholastic Inc.
Spinelli, Jerry. Maniac Magee. (gr. 4-7). 1990. 13.95 (ISBN 0-316-80722-2, Joy St Bks). Little.
Teague, Sam. The King of Hearts' Heart. 192p. (gr. 3-7). 1987. 13.95 (ISBN 0-316-83427-0). Little.
White, Terence. What Happened to Sherlock Holmes? as Set to Rest In... The Legend of Wilson-The Amazing Athlete. Blackburn, Francis, et al, eds. Meade, Javier & Jamieson, Lindsey, illus. Barton, Hill, intro. by. LC 83-51870. 102p. 1984. 9.95 (ISBN 0-9612698-0-4). Seagull Pub Co.

ATLANTIC CABLE

see Cables, Submarine

ATLANTIC STATES

Aylesworth, Thomas G. & Aylesworth, Virginia L. Atlantic: Virginia, W. Virginia, District of Columbia. (Illus.). 64p. (gr. 4-6). 1991. PLB 16.95 (ISBN 0-7910-1041-4). Chelsea Hse.

—The Mid-Atlantic (Pennsylvania, Delaware, Maryland) (Illus.). 66p. (Orig.). (gr. 3 up). 1988. 16.95 (ISBN 1-55546-554-4); pap. 6.95 (ISBN 0-7910-0537-2). Chelsea Hse.

Gilfond, Henry. The Northeast States. 96p. (gr. 4 up). 1984. lib. bdg. 10.40 (ISBN 0-531-04732-6). Watts.

ATLANTIS

Abels, Harriette S. Lost City of Atlantis. LC 87-13440. (Illus.). 48p. (gr. 5-6). 1987. PLB 10.95 (ISBN 0-89686-344-1, Crestwood Hse). Macmillan Child Grp.

Braymer, Marjorie. Atlantis: The Biography of a Legend. LC 82-16727. (Illus.). 256p. (gr. 7 up). 1983. 13.95 (ISBN 0-689-50264-8, M K McElderry). Macmillan Child Grp.

McCullough, Duane K. Spirit of Atlantis, Version 1-E: The Treasure Adventure, 4 vols. LC 88-92585. (Illus.). 100p. (Orig.). (ps-12). 1989. pap. text ed. write for info. (ISBN 0-9621605-2-0). D K McCullough.

McMullen, David. Atlantis: The Missing Continent. LC 77-22138. (Illus.). 48p. (gr. 4 up). 1983. PLB 17.32 (ISBN 0-8172-1047-4); pap. 9.27 (ISBN 0-8172-2152-2). Raintree Pubs.

Stein, Wendy. Atlantis: Opposing Viewpoints. LC 88-24470. (Illus.). 112p. (gr. 3-8). 1988. PLB 12.95 (ISBN 0-89908-056-1). Greenhaven.

ATLASES

American Map Corp. Staff, ed. Atlas Mundial. (Illus.). (gr. 7-12). 1990. pap. 2.75 (ISBN 0-8416-9555-5); Span. lang. ed. pap. write for info. Am Map.

Attmore, Stephen. Children's Atlas of the World. Fryer, George, illus. 32p. (gr. 1-4). 1991. pap. 4.95 (ISBN 0-8249-8507-9). Ideals.

Children's Atlas of the United States. (gr. 5-9). 1989. 14.95 (ISBN 0-528-83362-6). Rand McNally.

Children's First Atlas. (Illus.). (gr. 2-6). 1985. 2.98 (ISBN 0-517-47997-4). Outlet Bk Co.

Children's World Atlas. (Illus.). 96p. (gr. 5-9). 1989. 12.95 (ISBN 0-528-83348-0). Rand McNally.

Dicks, Brian, ed. Courage Children's Illustrated World Atlas. rev. ed. LC 88-43388. (Illus.). 128p. (gr. 1 up). 1989. Repr. of 1982 ed. 12.98 (ISBN 0-89471-703-0, Courage Bks). Running Pr.

Hammond Incorporated Staff. The World Atlas. LC 82-675036. (Illus.). 112p. (gr. 5 up). 1982. lib. bdg. 11.99 (ISBN 0-394-94663-4); pap. 12.95 smyth-sewn (ISBN 0-394-84663-X). Random.

Madden, James F. Understanding Maps. LC 79-67346. (Illus.). 64p. (gr. 3-6). 1984. pap. 6.20 (ISBN 0-8437-7400-2). Hammond Inc.

Middleton, Nick. Atlas of World Issues. (Illus.). 64p. (gr. 6 up). 1989. 16.95x (ISBN 0-8160-2022-1). Facts on File.

Morris, Neil. The Children's Illustrated Activity Atlas. LC 88-42913. (Illus.). 48p. (gr. 3-5). 1989. PLB 12.95 (ISBN 1-55532-927-6). Gareth Stevens Inc.

Olliver, Jane, ed. Doubleday Children's Atlas. LC 86-67523. (Illus.). 96p. (gr. k-6). 1987. pap. 12.95 (ISBN 0-385-23760-X). Doubleday.

Rand McNally Staff. Children's Atlas of Earth Through Time. Fagan, Elizabeth, ed. (Illus.). 80p. 1990. 14.95 (ISBN 0-528-83415-0). Rand McNally.

—Children's Atlas of the Universe. (Illus.). (gr. 3-7). 1990. 14.95 (ISBN 0-528-83408-8). Rand McNally.

—Children's Atlas of World Wildlife. Fagan, Elizabeth, ed. Willis, Jan, illus. 96p. (gr. 3-7). 1990. 14.95 (ISBN 0-528-83409-6). Rand McNally.

Rowland-Entwistle, Theodore. The Pop-Up Atlas of the World. Jacobs, Philip & Peterkin, Mike, illus. 18p. (gr. 3 up). 1988. pap. 12.95 (ISBN 0-671-65898-0, Little Simon). S&S Trade.

Sandford, Herbert. First Picture Atlas. 1989. 6.98 (ISBN 0-8317-3361-6). Smithmark.

Snow, Alan. My First Atlas. 1991. 5.98 (ISBN 0-8317-0226-5). Smithmark.

Snow, Jon. Atlas of Today. (Illus.). 64p. (gr. 7-12). 1987. PLB 15.90 (ISBN 0-531-19028-5, Pub. by Warwick Pr). Watts.

Tivers, Jacqueline & Day, Michael. The Viking Children's World Atlas: An Introductory Atlas for Young People. LC 83-675053. (Illus.). 48p. (gr. 4-6). 1983. pap. 9.95 (ISBN 0-670-21791-3). Viking Child Bks.

Tyler, J. Picture Atlas. (Illus.). 32p. (gr. 3-7). 1976. pap. 6.95 (ISBN 0-685-38857-3, Usborne). EDC.

World Atlas: A Resource for Students. (gr. 5-9). 1990. pap. 3.95 (ISBN 0-88463-480-9). Nystrom.

Wright, David & Wright, Jill. Facts on File Children's Atlas. updated ed. (Illus.). 96p. (gr. 6-10). 1991. 14.95 (ISBN 0-8160-2703-X). Facts on File.

Wright, Jill & Wright, David. Illustrated World Atlas. Warwick Press, ed. Streek, Tony, illus. 64p. (gr. 4-9). 1988. PLB 14.90 (ISBN 0-531-19033-1, Warwick). Watts.

—The Simon & Schuster Young Readers' Atlas. Barish, Wendy, ed. Saunders, Mike & Wright, David, illus. 192p. 1984. pap. 9.79 (ISBN 0-671-50657-9, Little Simon). S&S Trade.

ATLASES, HISTORICAL

Children's Atlas of World History. (Illus.). 96p. (gr. 4-8). 1989. 12.95 (ISBN 0-528-83349-9). Rand McNally.

Corbishley, Mike. Ancient Rome. Evans, Gillian, ed. (Illus.). 96p. 1989. 17.95 (ISBN 0-8160-1970-3). Facts on File.

Olliver, Jane. The Warwick Atlas of World History. JV-Warwick Press Staff, ed. LC 87-51627. (Illus.). 96p. (gr. 4-9). 1988. PLB 15.90 (ISBN 0-531-19037-4, Warwick). Watts.

Powell, Anton. Ancient Greece. (Illus.). 96p. 1989. 17.95 (ISBN 0-8160-1972-X). Facts on File.

ATMOSPHERE

Here are entered works treating the body of air surrounding the earth as distinguished from the upper rarefied air. Works dealing with air as an element and of its chemical and physical properties are entered under Air.

see also Air; Meteorology

Asimov, Isaac. How Did We Find Out about the Atmosphere? LC 84-27125. 64p. (gr. 5-9). 1985. 9.95 (ISBN 0-8027-6588-2); PLB 12.85 (ISBN 0-8027-6580-7). Walker & Co.

Behm, Barbara J., ed. Ask about the Earth & the Sky. (Illus.). 64p. (gr. 4-5). 1987. PLB 18.25 (ISBN 0-8172-2876-4); pap. 13.27 (ISBN 0-8172-2888-8). Raintree Pubs.

Bilger, Burkhard. Global Warming. (Illus.). (gr. 5 up). 1992. PLB 19.95 (ISBN 0-7910-1575-0). Chelsea Hse.

Branley, Franklyn M. Air Is All Around You. Keller, Holly, illus. LC 85-45405. 32p. (gr. k-3). 1986. incl. cassette 7.95 (ISBN 0-694-00202-X, Trophy); pap. 4.50 (ISBN 0-06-445048-1, Trophy). HarpC Child Bks.

—Oxygen Keeps You Alive. Madden, Don, illus. LC 73-139093. 40p. (gr. k-3). 1985. pap. 4.50 (ISBN 0-06-445021-X, Trophy). HarpC Child Bks.

Fisher, Marshall J. The Ozone Layer. (Illus.). (gr. 5 up). 1992. PLB 19.95 (ISBN 0-7910-1576-9). Chelsea Hse.

Gallant, Roy A. Rainbows, Mirages & Sundogs. LC 86-23728. (Illus.). 112p. (gr. 3-7). 1987. 13.95 (ISBN 0-02-737010-0, Mcmillan Child Bk). Macmillan Child Grp.

Gay, Kathlyn. The Greenhouse Effect. LC 85-26486. 128p. (gr. 7-12). 1986. PLB 12.90 (ISBN 0-531-10154-1). Watts.

Hocking, Colin, et al. Global Warming & the Greenhouse Effect. Bergman, Lincoln & Fairwell, Kay, eds. Klofkorn, Lisa & Craig, Rose, illus. Hoyt, Richard, photos by. 168p. (gr. 7-10). 1990. pap. 11.00 (ISBN 0-912511-75-3). Lawrence Science.

Margulis, Lynn & Sagan, Dorion. Biospheres from Earth to Space. 96p. (gr. 6-10). 1989. lib. bdg. 16.95 (ISBN 0-89490-188-5). Enslow Pubs.

Maury, Jean-Pierre. The Atmosphere. 80p. (gr. 8 up). 1989. pap. 4.95 (ISBN 0-8120-4213-1). Barron.

Neal, Philip. The Greenhouse Effect. (Illus.). 64p. (gr. 7-10). 1989. 19.95 (ISBN 0-85219-822-1, Pub. by Batsford England). Trafalgar Sq.

Pearce, Q. L. Lightning & Other Wonders of the Sky. Steltenpohl, Jane, ed. Fraser, Mary A., illus. 64p. (gr. 4-6). 1989. PLB 12.98 (ISBN 0-671-68534-1); pap. 5.95 (ISBN 0-671-68648-8). Messner.

Sky & Earth. (Illus.). 88p. (ps-3). 1990. 15.93 (ISBN 0-8094-4837-8); lib. bdg. 21.27 (ISBN 0-8094-4838-6). Time-Life.

Stefoff, Rebecca. Extinction. (Illus.). (gr. 5 up). 1992. PLB 19.95 (ISBN 0-7910-1578-5). Chelsea Hse.

Tivers, Jacqueline & Day, Michael. The Viking Children's World Atlas. LC 84-675391. (Illus.). (ps-7). 1985. pap. 5.95 (ISBN 0-14-031874-7, Puffin). Puffin Bks.

Verdat, Jean-Pierre. The Sky: Stars & Night. Bogard, Vicki, tr. from FRE. Broutin, Christian, illus. LC 90-50776. 38p. (gr. k-5). 1991. 4.95 (ISBN 0-944589-32-4, 324). Young Discovery Lib.

ATMOSPHERE-POLLUTION

see Air–Pollution

ATMOSPHERE, UPPER

Duden, Jane. The Ozone Layer. LC 90-36297. (Illus.). 48p. (gr. 5-6). 1990. RSBE 10.95 (ISBN 0-89686-546-0, Crestwood Hse). Macmillan Child Grp.

Hare, Tony. Ozone Layer. 1990. PLB 11.90 (ISBN 0-531-17218-X). Watts.

ATOLLS

see Coral Reefs and Islands

ATOMIC BOMB

Beyer, Don E. The Manhattan Project: America Makes the First Atomic Bomb. (Illus.). 128p. (gr. 7-12). 1991. PLB 12.90 (ISBN 0-531-11008-7). Watts.

Farris, John. Hiroshima. McGovern, Brian, illus. LC 90-34064. 64p. (gr. 5-8). 1990. PLB 11.95 (ISBN 1-56006-015-8). Lucent Bks.

Larsen, Rebecca. Oppenheimer & the Atomic Bomb. FS Staff, ed. (Illus.). 192p. (gr. 6-12). 1988. PLB 13.90 (ISBN 0-531-10607-1). Watts.

O'Neal, Michael. President Truman & the Atomic Bomb: Opposing Viewpoints. LC 90-35611. (Illus.). 112p. (gr. 3-8). 1990. PLB 13.95 (ISBN 0-89908-079-0). Greenhaven.

ATOMIC BOMB-FICTION

Miklowitz, Gloria D. After the Bomb. 156p. (gr. 7 up). 1987. pap. 2.50 (ISBN 0-590-40568-3); tchr's. guide 1.25 (ISBN 0-590-40664-7). Scholastic Inc.

ATOMIC NUCLEI

see Nuclear Physics

ATOMIC POWER

see Nuclear Power

ATOMS

see also Nuclear Physics

Ardley, Neil. The World of the Atom. (Illus.). 40p. (gr. 7-9). 1990. 12.40 (ISBN 0-531-17145-0). Watts.

Asimov, Isaac. How Did We Find Out about Atoms. LC 75-3910. 64p. (gr. 5-8). 1976. PLB 12.85 (ISBN 0-8027-6248-4). Walker & Co.

Averous, Pierre. The Atom. (gr. 6 up). 1988. 4.95 (ISBN 0-8120-3837-1). Barron.

Bains, Rae. Molecules & Atoms. Harriton, Chuck, illus. LC 84-2712. 32p. (gr. 3-6). 1985. PLB 9.49 (ISBN 0-8167-0284-5); pap. text ed. 2.95 (ISBN 0-8167-0285-3). Troll Assocs.

Berger, Melvin. Atoms, Molecules & Quarks. LC 86-636. (Illus.). 80p. (gr. 5 up). 1986. 11.99 (ISBN 0-399-61213-0, Putnam). Putnam Pub Group.

Bronowsky, J. & Selsam, Millicent E. Biography of an Atom. Reissued ed. Pursell, Weimer, illus. LC 64-19708. 48p. (gr. 4-7). 1965. PLB 12.89 (ISBN 0-06-020641-1). HarpC Child Bks.

Mebane, Robert C. & Rybolt, Thomas R. Adventures with Atoms & Molecules Bk. II: More Chemistry Experiments for Young People. Perkins, Ronald I., intro. by. LC 85-10177. (Illus.). 96p. (gr. 4-9). 1987. lib. bdg. 16.95 (ISBN 0-89490-164-8). Enslow Pubs.

ATTENDANCE, SCHOOL

see School Attendance

ATTILA, 406?-453

Vardy, Steven B. Attila. (Illus.). (gr. 5 up). 1991. 17.95 (ISBN 1-55546-803-9). Chelsea Hse.

ATTITUDE (PSYCHOLOGY)

see also Public Opinion

Simon, Norma. I Know What I Like. Leder, Dora, illus. LC 76-165822. (ps-2). 1971. PLB 10.95 (ISBN 0-8075-3507-9). A Whitman.

ATTORNEYS

see Lawyers

AUDIO-VISUAL EDUCATION

Black, Kaye. Kidvid: Fun-damentals of Video Education. Newcomer, Susan, ed. Murray, Joe, illus. 112p. (Orig.). (gr. 4-8). 1989. pap. write for info. (ISBN 0-913705-44-6). Zephyr Pr AZ.

AUDUBON, JOHN JAMES, 1785-1851

Gleiter, Jan & Thompson, Kathleen. John J. Audubon. (Illus.). 32p. (gr. 2-5). 1987. PLB 16.67 (ISBN 0-8172-2675-3); pap. text ed. 9.27 (ISBN 0-8172-2679-6). Raintree Pubs.

AUDUBON, JOHN JAMES, 1785-1851–FICTION

Brenner, Barbara. On the Frontier with Mr. Audubon. (Illus.). (gr. 3-6). 1977. 8.95 (ISBN 0-698-20385-2, Coward). Putnam Pub Group.

AUSTIN, STEPHEN FULLER, 1793-1836

McCall, Edith. Stalwart Men of Early Texas. Aronson, Lou, illus. LC 78-101296. 128p. (gr. 3-10). 1980. PLB 14.60 (ISBN 0-516-03371-9). Childrens.

AUSTRALIA

Arnold, Caroline. Australia Today. (Illus.). 96p. (gr. 4-9). 1987. PLB 10.40 (ISBN 0-531-10377-3). Watts.

Australian External Territories. (Illus.). (gr. 5 up). 1989. 13.95 (ISBN 0-7910-0133-4). Chelsea Hse.

Browne, Rollo. A Family in Australia. (Illus.). 32p. (gr. 2-5). 1987. PLB 9.95 (ISBN 0-8225-1671-3). Lerner Pubns.

Cranshaw, Peter. Australia. LC 88-18426. (Illus.). 48p. (gr. 4-8). 1988. PLB 14.98 (ISBN 0-382-09511-1). Silver Burdett Pr.

Crump, Donald J., ed. Surprising Lands Down Under. (Illus.). 1989. 7.95 (ISBN 0-318-42774-5); lib. bdg. 9.50 (ISBN 0-87044-714-9). Natl Geog.

Dolce, Laura. Australia. (Illus.). (gr. 5 up). 1990. 14.95 (ISBN 0-7910-1105-4). Chelsea Hse.

Georges, D. V. Australia. LC 86-9587. (Illus.). 48p. (gr. k-4). 1986. PLB 14.60 (ISBN 0-516-01290-8); pap. 4.95 (ISBN 0-516-41290-6). Childrens.

Gunner, Emily & McConky, Shirley. A Family in Australia. (Illus.). 32p. (gr. k-6). 1984. lib. bdg. 11.90 (ISBN 0-531-03824-6). Watts.

James, Ian. Australia. (Illus.). 32p. (gr. k-6). 1989. PLB 11.90 (ISBN 0-531-10759-0). Watts.

Kelly, Andrew. Australia. Bowden, David, photos by. Walker, Malcolm, illus. LC 87-34112. 48p. (gr. 5-8). 1989. PLB 12.40 (ISBN 0-531-18184-7, Pub. by Bookwright Pr). Watts.

—Australia. LC 90-38123. (Illus.). 32p. (gr. k-3). 1991. PLB 11.90 (ISBN 0-531-18381-5, Pub. by Bookwright Pr). Watts.

Lepthien, Emilie U. Australia. LC 82-4541. (Illus.). (gr. 5-9). 1982. PLB 25.27 (ISBN 0-516-02751-4). Childrens.

Lye, Keith. Asia & Australia. Ron Hayward Associates, illus. 40p. (gr. 4-9). 1987. PLB 12.40 (ISBN 0-531-17067-5, Gloucester Pr). Watts.

Nabhan, Martin. Australia. (Illus.). 64p. (gr. 7 up). 1990. lib. bdg. 15.93 (ISBN 0-86593-088-0); lib. bdg. 11.95s.p. (ISBN 0-685-36362-7). Rourke Corp.

Pepper, Susan. Passport to Australia. LC 86-50570. (Illus.). 48p. (gr. 4-8). 1987. PLB 12.90 (ISBN 0-531-10270-X). Watts.

Powzyk, Joyce. Wallaby Creek. LC 84-29757. (Illus.). 32p. (gr. 1-4). 1985. 12.95 (ISBN 0-688-05692-X); PLB 12.88 (ISBN 0-688-05693-8). Lothrop.

Rau, Margaret. Red Earth, Blue Sky: The Australian Outback. Rau, Margaret, photos by. LC 80-2457. 128p. (gr. 5 up). 1981. 12.95 (ISBN 0-690-04080-6, Crowell Jr Bks). HarpC Child Bks.

Santrey, Laurence. Australia. Eitzen, Allan, illus. LC 84-2636. 32p. (gr. 3-6). 1985. PLB 9.49 (ISBN 0-8167-0124-5); pap. text ed. 2.95 (ISBN 0-8167-0125-3). Troll Assocs.

Stanley-Baker, Penny. Australia: On the Other Side of the World. Valat, Pierre-Marie, illus. LC 87-34523. 38p. (gr. k-5). 1988. 4.95 (ISBN 0-944589-15-4, 154). Young Discovery Lib.

Stark, Al. Australia: A Lucky Land. LC 87-13424. (Illus.). 152p. (gr. 5 up). 1987. PLB 14.95 (ISBN 0-87518-365-4, Dillon). Macmillan Child Grp.

Truby, David. Take a Trip to Australia. LC 80-52721. (gr. 1-3). 1981. PLB 7.99 (ISBN 0-531-00988-2). Watts.

Wilson, Barbara K. Acacia Terrace. 1990. pap. 13.95 (ISBN 0-590-42885-3). Scholastic Inc.

AUSTRALIA–FICTION

Bound for Australia, No. 20. 144p. (Orig.). (gr. 7-12). 1987. pap. 2.50 (ISBN 0-553-26793-0). Bantam.

Clarke, J. Al Capsella & the Watchdogs. 144p. (gr. 7 up). 1991. 14.95 (ISBN 0-8050-1598-1). H Holt & Co.

—The Heroic Life of Al Capsella. LC 89-24629. 160p. (gr. 7 up). 1990. 14.95 (ISBN 0-8050-1310-5). H Holt & Co.

Foley, Louise. Australia: Find the Flying Foxes. LC 88-16911. 112p. 1988. pap. text ed. 3.95 (ISBN 0-07-047996-8). McGraw.

Pershall, Mary K. Hello, Barney! Wilson, Mark, illus. 32p. (ps-3). 1989. pap. 11.95 (ISBN 0-670-82406-2). Viking Child Bks.

Phipson, Joan. Hit & Run. 132p. (gr. 7 up). 1989. pap. 3.95 (ISBN 0-02-044665-9, Collier Young Ad). Macmillan Child Grp.

Pople, Maureen. A Nugget of Gold. 192p. (gr. 9 up). 1989. 13.95 (ISBN 0-8050-0984-1). H Holt & Co.

Thiele, Colin. The Hammerhead Light. LC 76-24311. (gr. 5 up). 1977. PLB 6.89 (ISBN 0-06-026117-X). HarpC Child Bks.

—Rotten Egg Paterson to the Rescue. Ritz, Karen, illus. LC 90-36189. 144p. (gr. 4-7). 1991. 13.95 (ISBN 0-06-026104-8); PLB 13.89 (ISBN 0-06-026105-6). HarpC Child Bks.

Tulloch, Richard. The Strongest Man in Gundiwallanup. O'Loughlin, Sue, illus. 32p. 1990. 9.95 (ISBN 0-521-36651-8). Cambridge U Pr.

Wrightson, Patricia. Balyet. 144p. (gr. 5-8). 1989. 12.95 (ISBN 0-689-50468-3, M K McElderry). Macmillan Child Grp.

AUSTRALIA–NATIVE RACES

Browne, Rollo. An Aboriginal Family. LC 84-19447. (Illus.). 32p. (gr. 2-5). 1985. PLB 9.95 (ISBN 0-8225-1655-1). Lerner Pubns.

Trezise, Percy. The Peopling of Australia. Keller, Kathy, intro. by. Trezise, Percy, illus. LC 88-20124. 32p. (gr. 2-3). 1988. PLB 12.95 (ISBN 1-55532-950-0). Gareth Stevens Inc.

AUSTRIA

Boluch, Kathleen A. Julia's World, Pt. 1: Better Times. Christiansen, Lee & Selwyn, Paul, illus. 58p. 1990. 14.95 (ISBN 0-9626365-0-9). Swarovski Amer Ltd.

Greene, Carol. Austria. LC 85-27994. (Illus.). 126p. (gr. 5-6). 1986. PLB 25.27 (ISBN 0-516-02756-5). Childrens.

AUSTRIA–FICTION

Orgel, Doris. The Devil in Vienna. LC 78-51319. (gr. 7 up). 1978. 8.95 (ISBN 0-8037-1920-5). Dial Bks Young.

AUTHORITARIANISM

see Totalitarianism

AUTHORS

see also Black Authors

also classes of writers (e.g. Novelists; Poets; etc.); and names of individual authors

Campbell, Patricia. Presenting Robert Cormier. 1990. pap. 4.95 (ISBN 0-440-20544-1, LFL). Dell.

Collins, David R. To the Point: A Story about E. B. White. Johnson, Amy, illus. 56p. (gr. 3-6). 1989. 9.95 (ISBN 0-87614-345-1); pap. 4.95 (ISBN 0-87614-508-X). Carolrhoda Bks.

Commire, Anne, ed. Something about the Author: Facts & Pictures about Contemporary Authors & Illustrators of Books for Young People. Incl. Vol. 1. 1971. 76.00 (ISBN 0-8103-0050-8); Vol. 2. 1972. 76.00 (ISBN 0-8103-0052-4); Vol. 3. 1972. 76.00 (ISBN 0-8103-0054-0); Vol. 4. 1973. 76.00 (ISBN 0-8103-0056-7); Vol. 5. 1974. 76.00 (ISBN 0-8103-0058-3); Vol. 6. 1974. 76.00 (ISBN 0-8103-0060-5); Vol. 7. 1975. 76.00 (ISBN 0-8103-0062-1); Vol. 8. 1976. 76.00 (ISBN 0-8103-0064-8); Vol. 9. 1976. 76.00 (ISBN 0-8103-0066-4); Vol. 10. 1976. 76.00 (ISBN 0-8103-0068-0); Vol. 11. 1977. 76.00 (ISBN 0-8103-0070-2); Vol. 12. 1977. 76.00 (ISBN 0-8103-0072-9); Vol. 13. 1978. 76.00 (ISBN 0-8103-0094-X); Vol. 14. 1978. 76.00 (ISBN 0-8103-0095-8); Vol. 15. 1979. 76.00 (ISBN 0-8103-0096-6); Vol. 16. 1979. 76.00 (ISBN 0-8103-0097-4); Vol. 17. 1979. 76.00 (ISBN 0-8103-0098-2); Vol. 18. 1980. 76.00 (ISBN 0-8103-0099-0); Vol. 19. 1980. 76.00 (ISBN 0-8103-0051-6); Vol. 20. 1980. 76.00 (ISBN 0-8103-0053-2); Vol. 21. 1981. 76.00 (ISBN 0-8103-0093-1); Vol. 22. 1981. 76.00 (ISBN 0-8103-0085-0); Vol. 23. 1981. 76.00 (ISBN 0-8103-0086-9); Vol. 24. 1981. 76.00 (ISBN 0-8103-0087-7); Vol. 25. 1981. 76.00 (ISBN 0-8103-0084-2); Vol. 26. 1982. 76.00 (ISBN 0-8103-0089-3); Vol. 27. 1982. 76.00 (ISBN 0-8103-0083-4); Vol. 28. 296p. 1982. 76.00 (ISBN 0-8103-0082-6); Vol. 29. 328p. 1982. 76.00 (ISBN 0-8103-0081-8). LC 72-27107. (gr. 7-12). 74.00x ea. Gale.

—Something about the Author: Facts & Pictures about Contemporary Authors & Illustrators of Books for Young People, Vol. 30. (Illus.). 304p. (gr. 9-12). 1983. 76.00x (ISBN 0-8103-0055-9). Gale.

—Something about the Author: Facts & Pictures about Contemporary Authors & Illustrators of Books for Young People, Vol. 34. (Illus.). 224p. (gr. 9-12). 1984. 76.00x (ISBN 0-8103-0063-X). Gale.

—Something about the Author: Facts & Pictures about Contemporary Authors & Illutrators of Books for Young People, Vol. 44. 300p. (gr. 9-12). 1986. 76.00x (ISBN 0-8103-2254-4). Gale.

—Yesterday's Authors of Books for Children: Facts & Pictures about Authors & Illustrators of Books for Young People, 2 vols. LC 76-17501. (Illus.). (gr. 7-12). 1978. 78.00x ea.; Vol. 1, 1977. 82.00 (ISBN 0-8103-0073-7); Vol. 2 1978. 82.00 (ISBN 0-8103-0090-7). Gale.

Fleissner, Else M. Herman N. Hesse: Modern German Poet & Writer. Rahmas, D. Steve, ed. LC 70-190244. 32p. (Orig.). (gr. 7-12). 1972. lib. bdg. 4.20 incl. catalog cards (ISBN 0-87157-526-4); pap. 2.95 vinyl laminated covers (ISBN 0-87157-026-2). SamHar Pr.

Goffstein, M. B. A Writer. LC 83-49488. (Illus.). 32p. (ps up). 1984. 12.95 (ISBN 0-06-022142-9); PLB 12.89 (ISBN 0-06-022143-7). HarpC Child Bks.

Hurwitz, Johanna. Astrid Lindgren: Storyteller to the World. Dooling, Michael, illus. 64p. (gr. 2-6). 1989. pap. 10.95 (ISBN 0-670-82207-8). Viking Child Bks.

James, Alan. Austria. (Illus.). 96p. (gr. 5 up). 1988. 14.95 (ISBN 0-222-00940-3). Chelsea Hse.

Konigsburg, E. L., et al. In My Own Words Series, 4 vols. (Illus.). 512p. (gr. 5-7). 1991. Set. 51.80 (ISBN 0-382-24097-9); Set. 38.85s.p.; Set. PLB 59.92 (ISBN 0-382-24089-8); Set. PLB 44.94s.p. Silver Burdett Pr.

Kresh, Paul. Isaac Bashevis Singer: The Story of a Storyteller. Scofield, Penrod, illus. LC 84-10271. 192p. (gr. 5 up). 1984. 13.95 (ISBN 0-525-67156-0, Lodestar Bks). Dutton Child Bks.

Magill, Frank N., ed. Cyclopedia of World Authors, No. II. 1640p. (gr. 9-12). 1989. lib. bdg. 300.00x (ISBN 0-89356-512-1, Magill Bks). Salem Pr.

Meltzer, Milton. Starting from Home: A Writer's Beginnings. 144p. (gr. 7 up). 1988. pap. 13.95 (ISBN 0-670-81604-3). Viking Child Bks.

Phillimore, J. Mansfield. (Illus.). 112p. (gr. 7 up). 1990. lib. bdg. 18.60 (ISBN 0-86593-020-1); lib. bdg. 13.95s.p. Rourke Corp.

Pryor, LaRita B. The African-American Writer's Survival Handbook: How & Where to Get Published. 250p. (gr. 9-12). 1990. text ed. 30.00 (ISBN 0-89341-649-5); pap. text ed. 17.50 (ISBN 0-89341-650-9). Longwood Pr.

Quackenbush, Robert. Once upon a Time! A Story of the Brothers Grimm. LC 85-9410. (Illus.). 40p. (gr. 2-6). 1986. PLB 11.95 (ISBN 0-671-66296-1). S&S Trade.

AUTHORS, AMERICAN

Ashabranner, Brent. The Times of My Life: A Memoir. (gr. 4-7). 1990. 14.95 (ISBN 0-525-65047-4, Cobblehill Bks). Dutton Child Bks.

Blair, Gwenda. Laura Ingalls Wilder. Allen, Thomas B., illus. 64p. (gr. 1-4). 1981. lib. bdg. 6.99 (ISBN 0-399-61139-8, Putnam); pap. 5.95 (ISBN 0-399-20953-0). Putnam Pub Group.

Crews, Donald. Bigmama's. LC 90-33142. (Illus.). 32p. (ps up). 1991. 13.95 (ISBN 0-688-09950-5); PLB 13.88 (ISBN 0-688-09951-3). Greenwillow.

Daly, John. Presenting S. E. Hinton. 1989. pap. 3.95 (ISBN 0-440-20482-8, LFL). Dell.

Ferrell, Keith. John Steinbeck: The Voice of the Land. LC 86-19623. 180p. (gr. 6 up). 1986. 11.95 (ISBN 0-87131-480-0). M Evans.

Gallo, Donald. Presenting Richard Peck. LC 89-32346. 176p. (gr. 8 up). 1989. lib. bdg. 19.95x (ISBN 0-8057-8209-5, Twayne). G K Hall.

Kane, Harnett T. Young Mark Twain & the Mississippi. Bjorklund, L., illus. LC 87-4531. 176p. (gr. 5-9). 1987. lib. bdg. 8.99 (ISBN 0-394-90413-3, Random Juv); pap. 2.95 (ISBN 0-394-89182-1). Random.

Meigs, Cornelia. Invincible Louisa. LC 68-21174. (Illus.). (gr. 7 up). 1968. 16.95 (ISBN 0-316-56590-3). Little.

Meltzer, Milton. Starting from Home: A Writer's Beginnings. (Illus.). 160p. (gr. 7 up). 1991. pap. 3.95 (ISBN 0-14-032299-X, Puffin). Puffin Bks.

Schoen, Celin V. Pearl Buck: Famed American Author of Oriental Stories. Rahmas, D. Steve, ed. LC 70-190247. 32p. (Orig.). (gr. 7-12). 1972. lib. bdg. 4.20 incl. catalog cards (ISBN 0-87157-530-2). SamHar Pr.

Stevenson, James. July. Stevenson, James, illus. LC 88-37584. (gr. k up). 1990. 12.95 (ISBN 0-688-08822-8); PLB 12.88 (ISBN 0-688-08823-6). Greenwillow.

Yates, Elizabeth. My Widening World: The Continuing Diary of Elizabeth Yates. LC 82-23713. (Illus.). 120p. (gr. 7 up). 1983. 12.95 (ISBN 0-664-32702-8, Westminster). Westminster John Knox.

AUTHORS, ENGLISH

Asbee, Sue. Woolf. (Illus.). 112p. (gr. 7 up). 1990. lib. bdg. 18.60 (ISBN 0-86593-019-8); lib. bdg. 13.95s.p. Rourke Corp.

Ferrell, Keith. George Orwell: The Political Pen. LC 84-25932. 192p. (gr. 7 up). 1984. 11.95 (ISBN 0-87131-444-4). M Evans.

AUTHORS–FICTION

Greenwald, Sheila. Write on, Rosy! A Young Author in Crisis. Greenwald, Sheila, illus. 128p. (gr. 3-6). 1988. 12.95 (ISBN 0-316-32705-0, Joy St Bks). Little.

Nixon, Joan L. If You Were a Writer. Degen, Bruce, illus. LC 88-402. 32p. (gr. k-3). 1988. 13.95 (ISBN 0-02-768210-2, Four Winds). Macmillan Child Grp.

Van Raven, Pieter. The Great Man's Secret. LC 88-29204. 176p. (gr. 7 up). 1989. 13.95 (ISBN 0-684-19041-9, Scribners Young Read). Macmillan Child Grp.

Williams, Barbara. Author & Squinty Gritt. (gr. 4-7). 1990. 12.95 (ISBN 0-525-44655-9, DCB). Dutton Child Bks.

AUTHORS, LATIN AMERICAN

Pablo Neruda. (Illus.). (gr. 5 up). 1992. PLB 17.95 (ISBN 0-7910-1248-4). Chelsea Hse.

Samuels, Steven. Jorge Luis Borges. (Illus.). (gr. 5 up). 1992. PLB 17.95 (ISBN 0-7910-1236-0). Chelsea Hse.

AUTHORSHIP

see also Drama–Technique; Fiction–Technique; Journalism; Versification

Aardema, Verna. Write a Folktale. (Illus.). 32p. (gr. 3-7). 1986. pap. 4.95 (ISBN 0-913839-59-0). Bk Lures.

Benjamin, Carol L. Writing for Kids. Benjamin, Carol L., illus. LC 85-42831. 80p. (gr. 3-8). 1985. pap. 4.95 (ISBN 0-06-446012-6, Trophy). HarpC Child Bks.

Brandt, Sue R. How to Write a Report. rev. ed. Green, Anne C., illus. LC 86-9056. 96p. (gr. 4-9). 1986. PLB 10.40 (ISBN 0-531-10216-5). Watts.

Broekel, Ray. I Can Be an Author. LC 85-28050. (Illus.). 32p. (gr. k-3). 1986. PLB 13.93 (ISBN 0-516-01891-4); pap. 3.95 (ISBN 0-516-41891-2). Childrens.

Buhay, Debra. Black & White of Writing. 30p. (gr. 12). Date not set. pap. 2.00 (ISBN 0-685-37411-4). D Hockenberry.

Cook, Shirley & Carl, Kathy. Linking Literature & Writing. (Illus.). 240p. (gr. k-3). 1989. pap. text ed. 14.95 (ISBN 0-86530-064-X, IP 166-5). Incentive Pubns.

Corbett, Paula. Fantasy Fling. 56p. (gr. 4-6). 1984. 7.95 (ISBN 0-88160-112-8, LW 247). Learning Wks.

Cotter, Paulette & Johansen, Carol. Dream Scenes. 48p. (gr. 3-6). 1983. 5.95 (ISBN 0-88160-100-4, LW 241). Learning Wks.

Daniel, Becky & Daniel, Charlie. Strain Your Brain. 48p. (gr. 4-6). 1980. 5.95 (ISBN 0-88160-032-6, LW 217). Learning Wks.

Dickinson, Dof. Write from the Start. (Illus.). 136p. (Orig.). (gr. 3 up). 1988. pap. 19.95 (ISBN 0-333-47822-3). Players Pr.

Dubrovin, Vivian. Write Your Own Story. 72p. (gr. 4-8). 1984. lib. bdg. 10.40 (ISBN 0-531-04739-3). Watts.

Dunbar, Robert E. Making Your Point. 1990. PLB 12.90 (ISBN 0-531-10905-4). Watts.

Ehrenhaft, George. The Writer's Survival Guide. 124p. (Orig.). (gr. 9-12). 1988. pap. text ed. 14.99, 8.99 per book for classroom sets (ISBN 0-87438-047-2); tchr's. ed. 14.99 (ISBN 0-87438-048-0). Media Basics.

Everhart, Nancy. So You Have to Write a Term Paper! LC 87-8251. (Illus.). 128p. (gr. 7-12). 1987. PLB 12.90 (ISBN 0-531-10427-3). Watts.

Fearn, Leif. Developmental Writing & the Writing Kabyn. 70p. (gr. 2-9). 1981. 1.00 (ISBN 0-940444-07-0). Kabyn.

Goldman, Elizabeth & Farnan, Nancy J. Developing Writers in Grades 7-12. 294p. (gr. 7-12). 1985. 44.90 (ISBN 0-940444-23-2). Kabyn.

Hamilton, Sally. Spin Your Wheels. 48p. (gr. 4-6). 1982. 5.95 (ISBN 0-88160-051-2, LW 237). Learning Wks.

Harner, David L. How to Publish a Tabloid Shopper. (Illus.). 248p. (Orig.). (gr. 12). 1989. pap. 22.95 (ISBN 0-685-26080-1). Harner Pubns.

Henderson, Kathy. Market Guide for Young Writers. 3rd ed. LC 90-38770. (Illus.). 176p. (gr. 3 up). 1990. pap. 10.95 (ISBN 1-55870-175-3, Shoe Tree Pr). Betterway Pubns.

How to Write & Sell. 4th ed. 122p. (Orig.). (gr. 6-12). 1983. pap. 7.95 (ISBN 0-317-92526-1). Raconteurs.

Joy, Flora. Shortcuts for Teaching Writing. 144p. (gr. 3-6). 1991. 10.95 (ISBN 0-86653-590-X). Good Apple.

Lauritzen, Cyndi. Create & Write. 48p. (gr. 4-6). 1982. 5.95 (ISBN 0-88160-052-0, LW 238). Learning Wks.

Lee, Betsy. Judy Blume's Story. LC 81-12494. (Illus.). 112p. (gr. 5 up). 1981. PLB 8.95 (ISBN 0-87518-209-7, Dillon). Macmillan Child Grp.

Livingston, Myra C. Poem-Making: Ways to Begin Writing Poetry. LC 90-5012. 176p. (gr. 4-8). 1991. 15.95 (ISBN 0-06-024019-9); PLB 15.89 (ISBN 0-06-024020-2). HarpC Child Bks.

McCabe, Robert E. & Goldman, Elizabeth. Getting Started in Developmental Writing. 100p. (gr. 2-9). 1982. 7.60 (ISBN 0-940444-17-8). Kabyn.

Marsh, Carole. Write Your Own Sports Mystery Kit. (Illus., Orig.). (gr. 3-12). 1986. pap. 24.00 (ISBN 0-935326-11-1). Gallopade Pub Group.

Meltzer, Milton. Starting from Home: A Writer's Beginnings. (Illus.). 160p. (gr. 7 up). 1991. pap. 3.95 (ISBN 0-14-032299-X, Puffin). Puffin Bks.

Murtha, Philly. Writing: You Can Be an Author. Redpath, Ann, ed. 32p. (gr. 4 up). 1984. 14.25 (ISBN 0-87191-998-2); PLB 9.95s.p. (ISBN 0-685-10404-4). Creative Ed.

Naylor, Phyllis R. How I Came to Be a Writer. LC 86-32283. (Illus.). 144p. (gr. 4). 1987. pap. 4.95 (ISBN 0-689-71129-8, Aladdin). Macmillan Child Grp.

Peck, Richard. Write a Tale of Terror. (Illus.). 32p. (gr. 5-10). 1987. pap. 4.95 (ISBN 0-913839-60-4). Bk Lures.

Polette, Nancy. The Best Ever Writing Models. (Illus.). 124p. (gr. 4-9). 1989. pap. 12.95 (ISBN 0-913839-78-7). Bk Lures.

—Write Your Own Fairy Tale. (Illus.). 32p. (gr. 3-7). 1986. pap. 4.95 (ISBN 0-913839-53-1). Bk Lures.

Polon, Linda. Stir up a Story. 48p. (gr. 4-6). 1981. 5.95 (ISBN 0-88160-037-7, LW 222). Learning Wks.

Rothstein, Evelyn, et al. Editing Writes, Blue Edition. Gompper, Gail, illus. (gr. 3-4). 1990. pap. 7.95 25 or more copies (ISBN 0-913935-46-8). ERA-CCR.

—Editing Writes, Green Edition. Gompper, Gail, illus. (gr. 5-7). 1990. pap. 7.95 (ISBN 0-913935-47-6). ERA-CCR.

—Editing Writes, Orange Edition. Gompper, Gail, illus. (gr. 2-8). 1990. pap. 7.95 25 or more copies (ISBN 0-913935-48-4). ERA-CCR.

—Creative Writes, Bk. B. 34p. (gr. 5-12). 1984. pap. 14. 95 (ISBN 0-913935-26-3). ERA-CCR.

Rubins, Diane T. The A-Plus Guide to Good Writing. 144p. (gr. 7 up). 1984. pap. 2.25 (ISBN 0-590-33315-1). Scholastic Inc.

Schwartz, Linda. Creative Writing Rocket. 48p. (gr. 1-4). 1976. 5.95 (ISBN 0-88160-003-2, LW 104). Learning Wks.

—The Creative Writing Roundup. 48p. (gr. 4-7). 1976. 5.95 (ISBN 0-88160-017-2, LW 201). Learning Wks.

Sebranek, Patrick, et al. The Write Source: A Student Handbook. Krenzke, Chris, illus. 304p. (gr. 4-8). 1987. 8.95 (ISBN 0-939045-02-8); text ed. 8.95 (ISBN 0-685-18820-5); pap. text ed. 5.95 (ISBN 0-939045-03-6). Write Source.

Shaw, Sally. Composition Capers. 48p. (gr. 4-6). 1982. 5.95 (ISBN 0-88160-044-X, LW 229). Learning Wks.

Spirack, Doris. Creative Writing Carousel. 48p. (gr. 4-6). 1982. 7.95 (ISBN 0-88160-086-5, LW 239). Learning Wks.

Tchudi, Susan. The Young Writer's Handbook. LC 84-5312. 160p. (gr. 5 up). 1984. 13.95 (ISBN 0-684-18090-1, Scribners Young Read). Macmillan Child Grp.

AUTHORSHIP–FICTION

Chambers, Aidan. Breaktime. LC 78-19472. 192p. (gr. 7 up). 1979. 13.95 (ISBN 0-06-021256-X). HarpC Child Bks.

Hunter, Mollie. Hold on to Love. LC 83-47695. 288p. (gr. 7 up). 1984. 12.95 (ISBN 0-06-022687-0); PLB 12.89 (ISBN 0-06-022688-9). HarpC Child Bks.

Suki: A Novel for Young People. 153p. (gr. 7-9). 6.50 (ISBN 0-686-74923-5). ADL.

Williams, Barbara. Author & Squinty Gritt. (gr. 4-7). 1990. 12.95 (ISBN 0-525-44655-9, DCB). Dutton Child Bks.

AUTOBIOGRAPHIES

Borg, Mary. Writing Your Life: Autobiographical Writing Activities for Young People. Blackstone, Ann, illus. 47p. (gr. 5-12). 1989. pap. text ed. 14.95 (ISBN 1-877673-09-9). Cottonwood Pr.

Ephron, Delia. My Life: A Personal & Private Fill-in-the-Blanks Record Book. Badger, Lorraine, designed by. (Illus.). 96p. (Orig.). (gr. 3-6). 1991. pap. 10.95 (ISBN 0-89471-986-6). Running Pr.

Hanna, Ken. My Life & Times: For Whatever They're Worth. LC 88-51575. 128p. 1989. pap. 6.95 (ISBN 1-55523-211-6). Winston-Derek.

Konopka, Gisela. Courage & Love. (Orig.). (gr. 7 up). 1988. pap. 10.95 (ISBN 0-9621328-0-2). G Konopka.

Little, Jean. Little by Little: A Writer's Education. (Illus.). 240p. (gr. 5-9). 1991. pap. 3.95 (ISBN 0-14-032325-2, Puffin). Puffin Bks.

My Diary. (Illus.). 128p. (gr. 3-8). 1987. 2.50 (ISBN 0-87406-145-8, 41-12220-1). Willowisp Pr.

Myers, Bernice. My Diary. (gr. 7-12). pap. 1.95 (ISBN 0-590-32409-8). Scholastic Inc.

Oke, Janette. Spunky's Diary. 99p. (gr. 5-12). 1982. pap. 4.95 (ISBN 0-934998-11-6). Bethel Pub.

Running Press Staff, ed. The Diarist's Journal. (Illus.). 192p. (gr. 7 up). 1988. 14.95 (ISBN 0-89471-635-2). Running Pr.

Schomburg, Kim. Your Very Own Baby-Sitting Diary. (Illus.). 64p. (gr. 4-8). 1988. 2.25 (ISBN 0-87406-364-7, 57-18088-1). Willowisp Pr.

Tolles, Martha. Who's Reading Darci's Diary? 128p. (gr. 4-6). 1985. pap. 2.50 (ISBN 0-590-41224-8, Apple Paperbacks). Scholastic Inc.

AUTOGRAPHS

Owens, Tom. Collecting Sports Autographs: Fun & Profit from This Easy-to-Learn Hobby. 128p. (Orig.). (gr. 7 up). 1989. pap. 6.95 (ISBN 0-933893-79-5). Bonus Books.

AUTOGRAPHS–COLLECTIONS

Frith, Michael. Autographs! I Collect Them! Frith, Michael, illus. LC 89-63064. 48p. (gr. 1-5). 1990. pap. 4.95 (ISBN 0-679-80691-1). McKay.

AUTOMATIC COMPUTERS

see Computers

AUTOMATIC CONTROL

see Automation

AUTOMATIC DATA PROCESSING

see Electronic Data Processing

AUTOMATIC INFORMATION RETRIEVAL

see Information Storage and Retrieval Systems

AUTOMATION

Asimov, Isaac. How Did We Find Out about Robots? Wool, David, illus. 64p. (gr. 4-7). 1984. PLB 10.85 (ISBN 0-8027-6563-7). Walker & Co.

Hellman, Hal. Computer Basics. Tvaryanas, Alphonse, illus. LC 82-21483. 48p. (gr. 3-7). 1983. 9.95 (ISBN 0-13-164574-9). P-H.

AUTOMOBILE ACCIDENTS

see Traffic Accidents

AUTOMOBILE DRIVERS

American Automobile Association Staff. Sportsmanlike Driving. 9th ed. 352p. (gr. 9-12). 1987. text ed. 22.16 (ISBN 0-07-001338-1); pap. text ed. 14.48 (ISBN 0-07-001339-X). McGraw.

AUTOMOBILE DRIVERS–FICTION

Gackenbach, Dick. Binky Gets a Car. (Illus.). 32p. (ps-2). 1983. 13.95 (ISBN 0-89919-144-4, Clarion). HM.

Road Aces, 5 novels in ea. set, Sets 1 & 2. (Illus.). 1985. Set. pap. 15.00 (ISBN 0-685-31193-7, High Noon Books). Set 1, 48p (ISBN 0-87879-490-5). Set 2, 48p (ISBN 0-87879-496-4). Acad Therapy.

AUTOMOBILE DRIVING

see Automobile Drivers

AUTOMOBILE ENGINES

see Automobiles–Engines

AUTOMOBILE RACING

see also Karts and Karting

Ayres, Carter M. Soaring. LC 85-23667. (Illus.). 40p. (gr. 4-9). 1985. PLB 9.95 (ISBN 0-8225-0442-1). Lerner Pubns.

Barrett, Norman. Carros de Carrera. (SPA., Illus.). 32p. (gr. k-4). 1990. PLB 11.40 (ISBN 0-531-07905-8). Watts.

—Dragsters. (Illus.). 32p. (gr. k-3). 1990. PLB 11.40 (ISBN 0-531-10274-2); pap. 3.95 (ISBN 0-531-15176-X). Watts.

—Race Cars. (Illus.). 32p. (gr. 2 up). 1991. pap. 3.95 (ISBN 0-531-15175-1). Watts.

—Racing Cars. (Illus.). 32p. (gr. 2 up). 1991. pap. 3.95 (ISBN 0-531-15143-3). Watts.

Cave, Ron & Cave, Joyce. What about-Racing Cars? West, David, illus. LC 82-81166. 32p. (gr. k-3). 1982. PLB 10.90 (ISBN 0-531-03464-X). Watts.

Chirinian, Alain. Race Cars. (Illus.). 64p. (gr. 5-9). 1989. PLB 10.98 (ISBN 0-671-68030-7); PLB 8.24s.p.; pap. 4.95 (ISBN 0-671-68035-8); pap. 3.71s.p. Messner.

—Tough Wheels Series, 4 vols. (Illus.). 256p. (gr. 5-9). 1989. Set. PLB 43.92 (ISBN 0-671-94096-1); Set. PLB 32.94s.p.; Set. pap. 19.80 (ISBN 0-671-93115-6); Set. pap. 14.85s.p. Messner.

Denan, Jay. Burnout: Funny Car Races. LC 79-64700. (Illus.). 32p. (gr. 4-9). 1980. PLB 10.79 (ISBN 0-89375-256-8); pap. 2.95 (ISBN 0-89375-257-6). Troll Assocs.

—The Glory Ride, Road Racing. LC 79-52179. (Illus.). 32p. (gr. 4-9). 1980. PLB 10.79 (ISBN 0-89375-254-1); pap. 2.95 (ISBN 0-89375-255-X). Troll Assocs.

—Hot on Wheels: The Rally Scene. LC 79-64701. (Illus.). 32p. (gr. 4-9). 1980. PLB 10.79 (ISBN 0-89375-258-4); pap. 2.95 (ISBN 0-89375-259-2). Troll Assocs.

—Start Your Engines: Racing the Championship Trail. LC 79-64702. (Illus.). 32p. (gr. 4-9). 1980. PLB 10.79 (ISBN 0-89375-260-6); pap. 2.95 (ISBN 0-89375-261-4). Troll Assocs.

Edmonds, I. G. Drag Racing for Beginners. LC 72-75894. (gr. 6-10). 6.50 (ISBN 0-672-51596-2, Bobbs). Macmillan.

Famous Sports Cars. (ps up). 1990. pap. 2.25 (ISBN 0-89954-061-9). Antioch Pub Co.

Flint, Russ. All about Racecars. LC 90-9844. (Illus.). 16p. (ps-2). 1990. PLB 9.95 (ISBN 0-8368-0426-0). Gareth Stevens Inc.

Gregory, Stephen. Racing to Win: The Salt Flats. new ed. LC 75-21845. (Illus.). (gr. 5-10). 1976. PLB 10.79 (ISBN 0-89375-010-7); pap. 2.95 (ISBN 0-89375-026-3). Troll Assocs.

Harmer, P. Racing Cars. (Illus.). 48p. (gr. 3-8). Date not set. PLB 18.60 (ISBN 0-86592-455-4). Rourke Corp.

Hill, Randal C. Superstars in Action: Auto Racing. 108p. (gr. 5-12). 1990. PLB 6.00 (ISBN 0-8114-1597-X). Steck-V.

Jefferis, David & Lafferty, Peter. Checkered Flag! The History of the Racing Car. LC 90-32128. (Illus.). 32p. (gr. 5-8). 1991. PLB 11.90 (ISBN 0-531-14122-5). Watts.

Knudson, Richard L. Land Speed Record Breakers. LC 80-17506. (Illus.). 48p. (gr. 4-9). 1981. PLB 9.95 (ISBN 0-8225-0438-3). Lerner Pubns.

—Racing Yesterday's Cars. (Illus.). 48p. (gr. 4-9). 1985. PLB 9.95 (ISBN 0-8225-0512-6). Lerner Pubns.

Krishef, Robert K. Indianapolis Five Hundred. LC 73-22152. (Illus.). 52p. (gr. 4-9). 1978. PLB 9.95 (ISBN 0-8225-0412-X). Lerner Pubns.

Lerner, Mark. Careers in Auto Racing. LC 80-12047. (Illus.). 36p. (gr. 2-5). 1980. PLB 7.95 (ISBN 0-8225-0343-3). Lerner Pubns.

—Quarter-Midget Racing Is for Me. Wolfe, Robert L., illus. LC 81-41. 48p. (gr. 2-5). 1981. PLB 8.95 (ISBN 0-8225-1125-8). Lerner Pubns.

Naden, C. J. I Can Read About Racing Cars. LC 78-74658. (Illus.). (gr. 3-6). 1979. pap. 1.95 (ISBN 0-89375-216-9). Troll Assocs.

Norman, C. J. The Picture World of Racing Cars. (Illus.). 32p. (gr. k-4). 1989. PLB 11.40 (ISBN 0-531-10728-0). Watts.

Olney, Ross R. Super-Champions of Auto Racing. LC 83-14407. (Illus.). 128p. (Orig.). (gr. 6up). 1984. 11.95 (ISBN 0-89919-259-9, Clarion). HM.

Orr, Frank. Great Moments in Auto Racing. LC 73-18087. (Illus.). 160p. 1974. lib. bdg. 3.69 (ISBN 0-394-92763-X). Random.

Puleo, Nicole. Drag Racing. LC 72-5420. (Illus.). 48p. (gr. 4-9). 1973. PLB 9.95 (ISBN 0-8225-0406-5). Lerner Pubns.

Race Cars. 48p. (gr. 3-4). 1989. PLB 10.95 (ISBN 0-685-26380-0). Capstone Pr.

St. John, Jetty. Monaco Grand Prix. (Illus.). 64p. (gr. 5 up). 1989. 12.95 (ISBN 0-8225-0530-4). Lerner Pubns.

Slater, Teddy. The Big Book of Real Race Cars & Race Car Driving. Courtney, Richard, illus. 48p. (gr. 1-4). 1989. PLB 7.95 (ISBN 0-448-19187-3, G&D). Putnam Pub Group.

Sosa, Maria. Dragsters. LC 87-15568. (Illus.). 48p. (gr. 5-6). 1987. PLB 10.95 (ISBN 0-89686-350-6, Crestwood Hse). Macmillan Child Grp.

Sullivan, George. Great Racing Cars. (gr. 5-9). 1987. 12. 95 (ISBN 0-396-08911-9, Putnam). Putnam Pub Group.

Walt Disney Staff. Cars! Cars! Cars! Featuring "The Love Bug" & Other Fun on Wheels. LC 77-74465. (Illus.). (gr. 2-6). 1977. (Random Juv); lib. bdg. 4.99 (ISBN 0-394-93598-5). Random.

Wilkinson, Sylvia. I Can Be a Race Car Driver. LC 86-9639. (Illus.). 32p. (gr. k-3). 1986. PLB 13.93 (ISBN 0-516-01898-1). Childrens.

AUTOMOBILE RACING–BIOGRAPHY

Dragsters. 48p. (gr. 3-4). 1989. PLB 10.95 (ISBN 0-685-26371-1). Capstone Pr.

Garlits, Don & Yates, Brock. Big Daddy: The Autobiography of Don Garlits. 2nd, rev., enl. & updated ed. Smith, Donna G., ed. (Illus.). 354p. 1990. 50.00 (ISBN 0-685-35751-1); pap. 9.95 (ISBN 0-9626565-0-X). D Garlits.

Wood, Tim. Motor Racing. Fairclough, Chris, photos by. LC 89-50201. (Illus.). 32p. (gr. k-3). 1989. PLB 10.40 (ISBN 0-531-10828-7). Watts.

AUTOMOBILE RACING–FICTION

Bumble, William. Speedy Wheels. 32p. (gr. 4up). 1988. pap. 3.95 (ISBN 0-590-41996-X). Scholastic Inc.

Carlson, Nancy. Loudmouth George & the Big Race. LC 83-5191. (Illus.). 32p. (ps-3). 1983. PLB 9.95 (ISBN 0-87614-215-3). Carolrhoda Bks.

Christopher, Matt. Drag Strip Racer. 180p. (gr. 4-6). 1982. 12.95 (ISBN 0-316-13904-1). Little.

Felsen, Henry G. Crash Club. 208p. (gr. 9-12). 1990. pap. 25.00 slipcase, ltd. ed. (ISBN 0-917473-06-X). G P Pub.

—Fever Heat. 224p. (gr. 9-12). 1990. pap. 25.00 slipcase, ltd. ed. (ISBN 0-917473-09-4). G P Pub.

—Hot Rod. 160p. (gr. 9-12). 1990. pap. 25.00 slipcase, ltd. ed. (ISBN 0-917473-11-6). G P Pub.

—Rag Top. 160p. (gr. 9-12). 1990. pap. 25.00 slipcase, ltd. ed. (ISBN 0-917473-08-6). G P Pub.

—Road Rocket. 216p. (gr. 9-12). 1990. pap. 25.00 slipcase, ltd. ed. (ISBN 0-917473-07-8). G P Pub.

—Street Rod. 160p. (gr. 9-12). 1990. pap. 25.00 slipcase, ltd. ed. (ISBN 0-917473-10-8). G P Pub.

Seablom, Seth H. The Great Mukilteo to Friday Harbor Auto Race. Seablom, Seth H., illus. LC 75-38037. (gr. 1-3). 1976. pap. 2.00 (ISBN 0-918800-00-5). Seablom.

AUTOMOBILE TOURING

see Automobiles–Touring

AUTOMOBILE TRUCKS

see Trucks

AUTOMOBILES

see also Trucks

also names of automobiles, e.g. Ford Automobile

Andersen, T. J. Baja Cars. LC 87-29022. (Illus.). 48p. (gr. 5-6). 1988. PLB 10.95 (ISBN 0-89686-357-3, Crestwood Hse). Macmillan Child Grp.

Arceneaux, Marc. Cars. Arceneaux, Marc, illus. (gr. 1-4). 1983. pap. 2.50 (ISBN 0-448-11056-3, G&D). Putnam Pub Group.

—City Vehicles. Arceneaux, Marc, illus. (gr. 1-4). 1983. pap. 2.50 (ISBN 0-448-11054-7, G&D). Putnam Pub Group.

—Country Vehicles. Arceneaux, Marc, illus. (gr. 1-4). 1983. pap. 2.50 (ISBN 0-448-11055-5, G&D). Putnam Pub Group.

—Trucks & Trailers. (gr. 1-4). 1983. pap. 2.50 (ISBN 0-448-11053-9, G&D). Putnam Pub Group.

Atkinson, Elizabeth. Monster Vehicles. 48p. (gr. 3-4). 1991. PLB 11.95 (ISBN 1-56065-077-X). Capstone Pr.

Barrett, Norman. Custom Cars. (Illus.). 32p. (gr. k-3). 1990. PLB 11.40 (ISBN 0-531-10273-4); pap. 3.95 (ISBN 0-531-15177-8). Watts.

Bendick, Jeanne. Automobiles. rev. ed. (Illus.). 72p. (gr. 4-8). lib. bdg. 10.40 (ISBN 0-531-04821-7). Watts.

Bouquet, Jeff S. Young Man's Guide to Autos: Basics, Operation, Safety & Maintenance. Kimmel, Nita, illus. 80p. 1991. 39.95x (ISBN 1-56216-017-6); pap. 25.00x (ISBN 1-56216-018-4). Systems Co.

Butler, Daphne. First Look at Cars. LC 90-10265. (Illus.). 32p. (gr. 1-2). 1991. lib. bdg. 10.95 (ISBN 0-8368-0503-8). Gareth Stevens Inc.

Cars, Trucks & Other Wheels. (Illus.). 32p. (gr. 1-6). 1987. 0.50 (ISBN 0-87406-044-3, 46-09430-8). Willowisp Pr.

Chirinian, Alain. Muscle Cars. Steltenpohl, Jane, ed. (Illus.). 64p. (gr. 5-9). 1989. PLB 10.98 (ISBN 0-671-68028-5); PLB 8.24s.p.; pap. 4.95 (ISBN 0-671-68033-1); pap. 3.71s.p. Messner.

—Weird Wheels. Steltenpohl, Jane, ed. (Illus.). 64p. (gr. 5-9). 1989. PLB 10.98 (ISBN 0-671-68031-5); PLB 8. 24s.p.; pap. 4.95 (ISBN 0-671-68036-6); pap. 3.71s.p. Messner.

Chlad, Dorothy. When I Ride in a Car. LC 83-7382. (Illus.). 32p. (ps-2). 1983. lib. bdg. 14.60 (ISBN 0-516-01987-2); pap. 3.95 (ISBN 0-516-41987-0). Childrens.

Cole, Joanna. Cars & How They Go. Gibbons, Gail, illus. LC 82-45575. 32p. (gr. 2-6). 1983. 12.95 (ISBN 0-690-04261-2, Crowell Jr Bks); PLB 12.89 (ISBN 0-690-04262-0, Crowell Jr Bks). HarpC Child Bks.

—Cars & How They Go. Gibbons, Gail, illus. LC 82-45575. 32p. (gr. 2-6). 1986. pap. 4.95 (ISBN 0-06-446052-5, Trophy). HarpC Child Bks.

Coleman, John. Your Book of Vintage Cars. Tucker, Harry, illus. (gr. 7 up). 1969. 7.95 (ISBN 0-571-08276-9). Transatl Arts.

Creighton, Susan. Funny Cars. LC 87-29016. (Illus.). 48p. (gr. 5-6). 1988. PLB 10.95 (ISBN 0-89686-362-X, Crestwood Hse). Macmillan Child Grp.

Dixon, Malcolm. Land Transportation. (Illus.). 48p. (gr. 5-8). 1991. RLB 12.40 (ISBN 0-531-18412-9, Pub. by Boatwright Pr). Watts.

Doerken, Nan. The First Family Car. 59p. (gr. 1-4). 1986. pap. 3.95 (ISBN 0-919797-53-9). Kindred Pr.

Estrem, Paul. Rocket-Powered Cars. LC 87-22374. (Illus.). 48p. (gr. 5-6). 1987. PLB 10.95 (ISBN 0-89686-352-2, Crestwood Hse). Macmillan Child Grp.

Ford, Barbara. The Automobile: Inventions That Changed Our Lives. (gr. 3-7). 1987. 10.95 (ISBN 0-8027-6724-9); PLB 11.85 (ISBN 0-8027-6725-7). Walker & Co.

Gerber, D. M. Power Cars. (Illus.). 24p. (gr. 1-8). 1990. 2.95 (ISBN 0-87406-461-9, 52-19490-1). Willowisp Pr.

Gibbons, Gail. Fill It Up! LC 84-45345. (Illus.). 32p. (gr. k-4). 1986. pap. 4.95 (ISBN 0-06-446051-7, Trophy). HarpC Child Bks.

Grebel, E. & Pogrund, P. Caring for Your Car. (Illus.). 64p. (gr. 9 up). 1981. pap. text ed. 3.95 (ISBN 0-915510-59-6). Janus Bks.

Gunning, Thomas G. Dream Cars. LC 89-11738. (Illus.). 72p. (gr. 3 up). 1989. PLB 12.95 (ISBN 0-87518-419-7, Dillon). Macmillan Child Grp.

Harris, Jack C. Dream Cars. LC 88-1827. (Illus.). 48p. (gr. 5-6). 1988. PLB 10.95 (ISBN 0-89686-376-X, Crestwood Hse). Macmillan Child Grp.

Jacobs, David. American Tow Trucks. (Illus.). 128p. (Orig.). (gr. 3-5). 1986. pap. 4.95 (ISBN 0-85045-692-4, Pub by Osprey England). Motorbooks Intl.

Kanetzke, Howard W. The Story of Cars. rev. ed. LC 87-23231. (Illus.). 48p. (gr. 2-6). 1987. PLB 17.32 (ISBN 0-8172-3261-3); pap. 9.27 (ISBN 0-8172-3286-9). Raintree Pubs.

Keatley, Lu. Automobiles. LC 76-50372. (Illus.). (gr. 4-7). 1977. pap. text ed. 4.91 (ISBN 0-89445-010-7). Specialty Bks Intl.

Knudson, Richard L. Restoring Yesterday's Cars. LC 82-24966. (Illus.). 48p. (gr. 4-9). 1983. PLB 9.95 (ISBN 0-8225-0440-5). Lerner Pubns.

Lambert, Mark. Car Technology. (ps-3). 1990. PLB 12.40 (ISBN 0-531-18329-7). Watts.

Langley, Andrew. Cars. rev. ed. Franklin Watts Ltd., ed. (Illus.). 32p. (ps-6). 1988. PLB 10.90 (ISBN 0-531-10450-8). Watts.

Leder, Jane M. Exotic Cars. LC 87-15572. (Illus.). 48p. (gr. 5-6). 1987. PLB 10.95 (ISBN 0-89686-351-4, Crestwood Hse). Macmillan Child Grp.

Lenski, Lois. Little Auto. Lenski, Lois, illus. LC 58-14239. (gr. k-3). 1980. 5.25 (ISBN 0-8098-1001-8). McKay.

Marshall, Ray & Bradley, John. The Car: Watch It Work by Operating the Moving Diagrams! Marshall, Ray & Bradley, John, illus. LC 83-40569. 10p. 1984. pap. 13.95 (ISBN 0-670-20371-8). Viking Child Bks.

The Motor Car. (ARA., Illus.). (gr. 5-12). 3.50x (ISBN 0-86685-209-3). Intl Bk Ctr.

Olney, Ross R. Internal Combustion Engine. LC 81-48604. (Illus.). 48p. (gr. 3-5). 1982. (Lipp Jr Bks). HarpC Child Bks.

Olson, Norman. I Can Read About Trucks & Cars. LC 72-96957. (Illus.). (gr. 2-4). 1973. pap. 1.95 (ISBN 0-89375-055-7). Troll Assocs.

Pinkus, Sue. Let's All Draw Cars, Trucks & Other Vehicles. 1991. pap. 16.95 (ISBN 0-8230-2704-X). Watson-Guptill.

Pizer, Vernon. The Irrepressible Automobile. 128p. (gr. 7-11). 1986. 10.95 (ISBN 0-396-08580-6, Putnam). Putnam Pub Group.

Potter, Tony. See How It Works: Cars. Lawrie, Robin, illus. 28p. (ps-3). 1989. pap. 7.95 (ISBN 0-689-71303-7, Aladdin). Macmillan Child Grp.

Price, Stern & Sloan Staff. Automobiles. (Illus.). 32p. (gr. 7-12). 1987. pap. 2.95 (ISBN 0-8431-4288-X). Price Stern.

Robinson, Scott. Indy Cars. LC 87-30509. (Illus.). 48p. (gr. 5-6). 1988. PLB 10.95 (ISBN 0-89686-356-5, Crestwood Hse). Macmillan Child Grp.

Rockwell, Anne. Cars. Rockwell, Anne, illus. LC 83-14080. (ps-1). 1984. 12.95 (ISBN 0-525-44079-8, DCB). Dutton Child Bks.

—Cars. Rockwell, Anne, illus. LC 83-14080. (ps-1). 1986. pap. 3.95 (ISBN 0-525-44241-3, DCB). Dutton Child Bks.

Rutland. Supercars. rev. ed. (gr. 4-6). 1984. (Usborne-Hayes); PLB 12.96 (ISBN 0-88110-126-5); pap. 5.95 (ISBN 0-86020-181-3). EDC.

Rutland, Jonathan. Amazing Fact Book of Cars. (Illus.). 32p. (gr. 4-8). 1987. PLB 11.95 (ISBN 0-87191-843-9). Creative Ed.

Scarry, Richard. Richard Scarry's Cars & Trucks & Things That Go. (Illus.). (ps-2). 1974. write for info. (ISBN 0-307-15785-7, Golden Bks). Western Pub.

Sobol, Donald J. Encyclopedia Brown's Book of Wacky Cars. Enik, Ted, illus. LC 86-23556. 128p. (gr. 3-7). 1987. 11.95 (ISBN 0-688-06222-9). Morrow Jr Bks.

Spizzirri Publishing Co. Staff. Automobiles: An Educational Coloring Book. Spizzirri, Linda, ed. Fuller, Glenn, et al, illus. 32p. (gr. 1-8). 1981. pap. 1.95 (ISBN 0-86545-032-3). Spizzirri.

Sports Cars. 48p. (gr. 3-4). 1989. PLB 10.95 (ISBN 0-685-26381-9). Capstone Pr.

Squire, David. Wheels. LC 79-5064. (Illus.). 36p. (gr. 3-6). 1980. PLB 9.95 (ISBN 0-8225-1186-X). Lerner Pubns.

Steele, Philip. Cars & Trucks. LC 90-41180. (Illus.). 32p. (gr. 5-6). 1991. SBE 9.95 (ISBN 0-89686-521-5, Crestwood Hse). Macmillan Child Grp.

Trier, Mike. Super Car. FS-Aladdin Staff, ed. Shone, Rob, illus. 32p. (gr. 4-9). 1988. PLB 11.90 (ISBN 0-531-17098-5, Gloucester Pr). Watts.

Walker, Sloan & Vasey, Andrew. The Only Other Crazy Car Book. LC 83-6546. (Illus.). 48p. (gr. 4 up). 1984. 10.95 (ISBN 0-8027-6504-1); PLB 11.85 (ISBN 0-8027-6517-3). Walker & Co.

Wilkinson, Sylvia. Automobiles. LC 82-4441. (Illus.). (gr. k-4). 1982. PLB 14.60 (ISBN 0-516-01608-3). Childrens.

AUTOMOBILES–ACCIDENTS

see Traffic Accidents

AUTOMOBILES–DESIGN AND CONSTRUCTION

The Motor Car. (Illus.). (gr. 4-5). 3.50 (ISBN 0-7214-0744-7). Ladybird Bks.

Schaefer, Margaret A. Let's Build a Car. McRae, Patrick, illus. 32p. (gr. 1-4). 1990. 11.95 (ISBN 0-8249-8431-5). Ideals.

Taylor, John. How Cars Are Made. LC 86-32878. (Illus.). 32p. (gr. 5-12). 1987. 12.95x (ISBN 0-8160-1689-5). Facts on File.

Walt Disney Staff. Cars! Cars! Cars! Featuring "The Love Bug" & Other Fun on Wheels. LC 77-74465. (Illus.). (gr. 2-6). 1977. (Random Juv); lib. bdg. 4.99 (ISBN 0-394-93598-5). Random.

AUTOMOBILES–DRIVING

see Automobile Drivers

AUTOMOBILES–ENGINES

Carroll, Bill. Ford V8 Performance Guide. (Illus., Orig.). (gr. 7 up). 1972. 7.95 (ISBN 0-910390-17-7). Auto Bk.

AUTOMOBILES–FICTION

Burningham, John. Mr. Gumpy's Motor Car. Burningham, John, illus. LC 75-4582. 48p. (gr. k-3). 1976. PLB 13.89 (ISBN 0-690-00799-X, Crowell Jr Bks). HarpC Child Bks.

Chorao, Kay. Kate's Car. Chorao, Kay, illus. LC 82-2393. 24p. (ps). 1982. 3.95 (ISBN 0-525-44011-9, DCB). Dutton Child Bks.

Collis, Len. My Little Car Book. Reeves, Eira, illus. 24p. (ps-3). 1988. 3.50 (ISBN 0-8120-5917-4). Barron.

Feder, Paula K. Did You Lose the Car Again? 1990. 10.95 (ISBN 0-525-44514-5, DCB). Dutton Child Bks.

Felsen, Henry G. Boy Gets Car. (Illus.). (gr. 7-11). 1968. lib. bdg. 5.39 (ISBN 0-394-90976-3, Random Juv). Random.

Fisher, Barbara. Car Boy. Fisher, Barbara, illus. 29p. (Orig.). (gr. k-2). 1977. pap. 2.00 (ISBN 0-934830-02-9). Ten Penny.

Fleming, Ian. Chitty-Chitty-Bang-Bang. Burningham, John, illus. LC 64-21282. 112p. (gr. 3-7). 1989. pap. 2.95 (ISBN 0-394-81948-9). Knopf.

Fowler, Richard. Mr. Little's Noisy Car. Fowler, Richard, illus. LC 85-80381. 20p. (ps-1). 1986. 9.95 (ISBN 0-448-18977-1, G&D). Putnam Pub Group.

Garage Song. 1991. pap. 13.95 (ISBN 0-671-73565-9). S&S Trade.

Goor, Ron & Goor, Nancy. In the Driver's Seat. LC 81-43885. (Illus.). (gr. 1-4). 1982. PLB 12.89 (ISBN 0-690-04177-2, Crowell Jr Bks). HarpC Child Bks.

Greenblat, Rodney A. Uncle Wizzmo's New Used Car. Greenblat, Rodney A., illus. LC 89-36577. 32p. (ps-3). 1990. 13.95 (ISBN 0-06-022097-X); PLB 13.89 (ISBN 0-06-022098-8). HarpC Child Bks.

—Uncle Wizzmo's New Used Car. Greenblat, Rodney A., illus. LC 89-36577. 32p. (ps-3). 1990. 13.95 (ISBN 0-06-022097-X); PLB 13.89 (ISBN 0-06-022098-8). HarpC Child Bks.

Gregorich, Barbara. Beep, Beep. Hoffman, Joan, ed. Taber, Ed, illus. 16p. (Orig.). (gr. k-2). 1984. pap. 1.95 (ISBN 0-88743-007-4, 06007). Sch Zone Pub Co.

Kraus, Robert. Bumpy the Car. Kraus, Robert, illus. 18p. (ps). 1985. 3.50 (ISBN 0-448-10221-8, G&D). Putnam Pub Group.

Lewis, Marjorie. Ernie & the Mile-Long Muffler. (Illus.). 40p. (gr. 6-9). 1982. 9.95 (ISBN 0-698-20557-X, Coward). Putnam Pub Group.

Little Car. (ps-1). 2.49 (ISBN 0-517-48302-5); pap. 2.49 (ISBN 0-517-46819-0). Outlet Bk Co.

The Little Red Car. (Illus.). 24p. (ps-3). 1978. 2.50 (ISBN 0-448-46527-2, G&D); PLB 3.59 (ISBN 0-448-13073-4). Putnam Pub Group.

Lovik, Craig. Andy & the Tire. Weatherby, Mark, illus. 32p. (Orig.). (ps-3). 1988. pap. 2.50 (ISBN 0-590-41323-6). Scholastic Inc.

Mones, illus. Safe Racing. (ps-2). 1987. 3.95 (ISBN 0-448-09885-7, G&D). Putnam Pub Group.

Osborne, Victor. Rex, the Most Special Car in the World. Anderson, Scoular, illus. 24p. (ps-3). 1989. PLB 12.95 (ISBN 0-87614-357-5). Carolrhoda Bks.

Owen, Annie. Bumper to Bumper. Owen, Annie, illus. LC 90-61964. 32p. (ps-1). 1991. 12.95 (ISBN 0-679-81448-5); PLB 13.99 (ISBN 0-679-91448-X). Knopf.

Oxenbury, Helen. The Car Trip. Oxenbury, Helen, illus. 24p. (ps-1). 1983. 3.95 (ISBN 0-8037-0009-1, 0383-120). Dial Bks Young.

Peppe, Rodney. Huxley Pig's Model Car. 1991. pap. 8.95 (ISBN 0-385-30238-X). Doubleday.

Roberts, Tony, illus. The Race. (ps-2). 1987. 3.95 (ISBN 0-448-09886-5, G&D). Putnam Pub Group.

—Race Cars. (ps-2). 1987. 3.95 (ISBN 0-448-09887-3, G&D). Putnam Pub Group.

Robertson, Keith. Henry Reed's Journey. McCloskey, Robert, illus. LC 63-8522. (gr. 4-6). 1963. pap. 13.95 (ISBN 0-670-36854-7). Viking Child Bks.

Ross, K. K. The Little Red Car. Alley, R. W., illus. LC 88-63930. 28p. (ps). 1990. 2.95 (ISBN 0-394-85376-8). Random.

Spier, Peter. Tin Lizzie. Spier, Peter, illus. LC 74-1510. 48p. (gr. 3-5). 1990. 5.95 (ISBN 0-385-13342-1); pap. 8.95 (ISBN 0-385-09470-1). Doubleday.

Spurr, Elizabeth. Mrs. Minetta's Car Pool. Sims, Blanche, illus. LC 84-20483. 32p. (ps-3). 1985. 12.95 (ISBN 0-689-31103-6, Atheneum Child Bk). Macmillan Child Grp.

Williams, Barbara. Author & Squinty Gritt. (gr. 4-7). 1990. 12.95 (ISBN 0-525-44655-9, DCB). Dutton Child Bks.

AUTOMOBILES–HISTORY

Coleman, John. Your Book of Veteran & Edwardian Cars. (gr. 7 up). 1972. 7.95 (ISBN 0-571-09375-2). Transatl Arts.

Evans, Arthur N. The Automobile. (Illus.). 52p. (gr. 5 up). 1985. PLB 9.95 (ISBN 0-8225-1232-7). Lerner Pubns.

—The Motor Car. LC 82-9713. (Illus.). 48p. (gr. 7 up). 1983. pap. 5.95 (ISBN 0-521-28416-3). Cambridge U pr.

Lafferty, Peter & Jefferis, David. Top Gear: The History of Automobiles. (Illus.). 32p. (gr. 5-8). 1990. PLB 11.90 (ISBN 0-531-14038-5). Watts.

Struthers, John. Dinosaur Cars. LC 77-6202. (Illus.). 56p. (gr. 4-9). 1977. PLB 9.95 (ISBN 0-8225-0416-2). Lerner Pubns.

AUTOMOBILES–LAWS AND REGULATIONS

see also Traffic Regulations

AUTOMOBILES–MODELS

Earl. Model Cars. 32p. (gr. 4 up). 1980. PLB 13.96 (ISBN 0-88110-130-3); pap. 5.95 (ISBN 0-86020-538-X). EDC.

Knudson, Richard L. Model Cars. LC 80-17153. (Illus.). 40p. (gr. 4-9). 1981. PLB 9.95 (ISBN 0-8225-0437-5). Lerner Pubns.

Sobol, Donald J. Encyclopedia Brown's Book of Wacky Cars. Enik, Ted, illus. 128p. (gr. 3-7). 1987. pap. 2.75 (ISBN 0-553-15512-1, Skylark). Bantam.

Viemeister, Peter. Microcars. LC 82-90754. (Illus.). 136p. (Orig.). (gr. 5 up). 1982. pap. 10.95 (ISBN 0-9608598-0-2). Hamiltons.

Weiss, Harvey. Model Cars & Trucks & How to Build Them. Weiss, Harvey, illus. LC 74-7403. 80p. (gr. 4-7). 1989. PLB 13.89 (ISBN 0-690-04842-4, Crowell Jr Bks). HarpC Child Bks.

AUTOMOBILES–MOTORS

see Automobiles–Engines

AUTOMOBILES–RACING

see Automobile Racing

AUTOMOBILES–REPAIRING

Florian, Douglas. An Auto Mechanic. LC 90-48809. (Illus.). 24p. (ps up). 1991. 13.95 (ISBN 0-688-10635-8); PLB 13.88 (ISBN 0-688-10636-6). Greenwillow.

Imershein, Betsy. Auto Mechanic. Steltenpohl, Jane, ed. Imershein, Betsy, illus. 32p. (gr. k-3). 1989. lib. bdg. 9.98 (ISBN 0-671-68184-2); pap. 4.95 (ISBN 0-671-68187-7). Messner.

Karwatka, Dennis, et al. Introductory Auto Mechanics. 608p. (gr. 9-12). 1986. text ed. 21.95 (ISBN 0-8219-0182-6, 80452); wkbk. 5.95 (ISBN 0-8219-0183-4, 80652); tchr's. guide 28.00 (ISBN 0-8219-0184-2, 80902); transparency masters 89.00 (ISBN 0-8219-0489-2, 80980). EMC.

AUTOMOBILES–SERVICE STATIONS

Dupasquier, Philippe. The Service Station. Dupasquier, Philippe, illus. 24p. (gr. k-1). 1984. pap. 3.95 (ISBN 0-448-21501-2, G&D). Putnam Pub Group.

AUTOMOBILES–TOURING

Bingham, Mindy. Berta Benz & the Motorwagen. Nolt, Christine, ed. (Illus.). 48p. (gr. 1-6). 1989. 14.95 (ISBN 0-911655-38-7). Advocacy Pr.

AUTOSUGGESTION

see Hypnotism

AUTUMN

Allington, Richard L. & Krull, Kathleen. Autumn. Bond, Bruce, illus. LC 80-25190. 32p. (gr. k-3). 1985. PLB 15.33 (ISBN 0-8172-1343-0); pap. text ed. 9.27 (ISBN 0-8172-2476-9). Raintree Pubs.

Carson, Patti & Dellosa, Janet. Fall Reading Activity Book. (Illus.). 32p. (ps-k). 1983. pap. 1.98 (ISBN 0-88724-035-6, CD-8026). Carson-Dellos.

—March Primary Reading & Art Activities. Carson, Patti & Dellosa, Janet, illus. 32p. (gr. 1-3). 1984. pap. 1.98 (ISBN 0-88724-024-0, CD-8039). Carson-Dellos.

Chupick, Carol O. Celebrate Autumn. Grossman, Dan, illus. 144p. (gr. k-3). 1985. wkbk. 10.95 (ISBN 0-86653-264-1, SS 838). Good Apple.

Glover, Susanne & Grewe, Georgeann. A Splash of Fall. Grewe, Georhgeann, illus. 128p. (gr. 2-5). 1987. pap. 9.95 (ISBN 0-86653-410-5). Good Apple.

Maass, Robert. When Autumn Comes. Maass, Robert, photos by. (Illus.). 32p. (gr. 1-3). 1990. 15.95 (ISBN 0-8050-1259-1). H Holt & Co.

Moncure, Jane B. Fall Is Here! Hook, Frances, illus. LC 75-14019. (ps-2). 1975. 8.95 (ISBN 0-913778-13-3). Childs World.

—Step into Fall: A New Season. Lexa-Senning, Susan, illus. LC 90-30637. 32p. (ps-2). 1990. lib. bdg. 11.97 (ISBN 0-89565-573-X). Childs World.

Santrey, Louis. Autumn. Sabin, Francene, illus. LC 82-19396. 32p. (gr. 4-7). 1983. lib. bdg. 10.79 (ISBN 0-89375-905-8); pap. text ed. 2.95 (ISBN 0-89375-906-6). Troll Assocs.

Tresselt, Alvin R. Autumn Harvest. Duvoisin, Roger, illus. LC 51-8824. 32p. (gr. k-3). 1951. PLB 15.88 (ISBN 0-688-51155-4). Lothrop.

Venino, Suzanne. What Happens in the Autumn? Crump, Donald J., ed. LC 82-47858. (ps-3). 1982. 10.95 set (ISBN 0-87044-452-2); lib. bdg. 12.95 (ISBN 0-685-05547-7). Natl Geog.

Webster, David. Fall. Steltenpohl, Jane, ed. Steadman, Barbara, illus. 48p. (gr. 2-4). 1989. lib. bdg. 10.98 (ISBN 0-671-65860-3); pap. 4.95 (ISBN 0-671-65985-5). Messner.
Whitlock, Ralph. Autumn. (Illus.). 48p. (gr. 1-6). 1987. lib. bdg. 12.90 (ISBN 0-531-18140-5, Pub. by Bookwright Pr). Watts.
Zinkgraf, June & Bauman, Toni. Fall Fantasies. 240p. (gr. k-6). 1980. 14.95 (ISBN 0-916456-61-7, GA 167). Good Apple.

AVALANCHES

Facklam, Howard & Facklam, Margery. Avalanche! LC 90-45622. (Illus.). 48p. (gr. 5-6). 1991. RSBE 10.95 (ISBN 0-89686-598-3, Crestwood Hse). Macmillan Child Grp.

AVIATION

see Aeronautics

AVIATORS

see Air Pilots

AZTECS

see Indians of Mexico–Aztecs

B

BABIES

see Infants

BABOONS

Stone, Lynn. Baboons. (Illus.). 24p. (gr. k-5). 1990. lib. bdg. 11.93 (ISBN 0-86593-067-8); lib. bdg. 8.95s.p. (ISBN 0-685-36315-5). Rourke Corp.

BABY ANIMALS

see Animals–Infancy

BABY SITTERS

Anderson, Stephen E. Wee-Sitt Babysitting Guide. Trost, Ed, ed. Anderson, Stephen E., illus. (Orig.). (gr. 6-9). 1989. pap. 4.95 (ISBN 0-685-29145-6). Chimurenga.
—Wee-Sitt Guide to Babysitting. Trost, Ed, ed. (Illus.). 21p. (Orig.). 1989. pap. text ed. 4.95 (ISBN 0-9624153-0-8). Chimurenga.
Dayee, Frances S. Babysitting. (gr. 4-7). 1990. PLB 12.40 (ISBN 0-531-10908-9). Watts.
Herzig, Alison C. & Mali, Jane L. Ten-Speed Babysitter. 144p. (gr. 2-9). pap. 2.95 (ISBN 0-8167-1368-5). Troll Assocs.
Lansky, Vicki. Dear Babysitter Handbook. (gr. 7 up). 1990. pap. 3.95 (ISBN 0-916773-16-7). Book Peddlers.
Lowry, Lois. Taking Care of Terrific. LC 82-23331. 160p. (gr. 5 up). 1983. 13.95 (ISBN 0-395-34070-5). HM.
Salk, Lee & Litvin, Jay. How to Be a Super Sitter. 128p. 1990. pap. 7.95 (ISBN 0-8442-8547-1). Natl Textbk.
Saunders, Rubie. Baby Sitting for Fun & Profit. 128p. (gr. 7-9). 1988. pap. 2.50 (ISBN 0-671-66706-8, Archway). PB.
Schneider, M. E. The Babysitter's Guide. (Orig.). (gr. 7-12). 1990. pap. 11.95 (ISBN 0-685-30792-1). Marlin Pub.

BABY SITTERS–FICTION

Black, Sonia & Brigandi, Pat. Baby-Sitters Club Notebook. (Illus.). (gr. 5 up). 1991. pap. 2.50 (ISBN 0-590-45074-3). Scholastic Inc.
Bradford, Jan. Caroline Zucker Meets Her Match. Ramsey, Marcy D., illus. LC 90-10813. 96p. (gr. 2-5). 1990. lib. bdg. 9.89 (ISBN 0-8167-2017-7); pap. text ed. 2.95 (ISBN 0-8167-2018-5). Troll Assocs.
Brandenberg, Franz. Leo & Emily & the Dragon. Aliki, illus. LC 83-14091. 56p. (gr. 1-3). 1984. 12.95 (ISBN 0-688-02531-5); PLB 12.88 (ISBN 0-688-02532-3). Greenwillow.
Brown, Fern. Baby-Sitter on Horseback. (gr. 5 up). 1988. pap. 2.95 (ISBN 0-449-70283-9, Juniper). Fawcett.
Christelow, Eileen. Jerome the Babysitter. Christelow, Eileen, illus. LC 84-12738. 32p. (ps-2). 1985. 12.95 (ISBN 0-89919-331-5, Clarion). HM.
—Jerome the Babysitter. Christelow, Eileen, illus. LC 84-12738. 32p. (ps-3). 1987. pap. 4.95 (ISBN 0-89919-520-2, Pub. by Clarion). Ticknor & Fields.
Dickinson, Mary. Alex & the Baby. (Illus.). 32p. (ps-1). 1983. 9.95 (ISBN 0-233-97465-2). Andre Deutsch.
Faucher, Elizabeth. Charles in Charge. 128p. (Orig.). (gr. 7 up). 1984. pap. 2.25 (ISBN 0-590-33550-2, Point). Scholastic Inc.
Green, Phyllis. Eating Ice Cream with a Werewolf. Stern, Patti, illus. LC 82-47727. 128p. (gr. 3-7). 1983. PLB 11.89 (ISBN 0-06-022141-0). HarpC Child Bks.
Greenberg, Barbara. Bravest Babysitter. Paterson, Diane, illus. LC 77-71516. 32p. (ps-3). 1986. pap. 3.95 (ISBN 0-8037-0309-0, 0383-120). Dial Bks Young.
Herzig, Alison C. & Mali, Jane L. The Ten Speed Babysitter. LC 87-13425. 144p. (gr. 4-7). 1987. 11.95 (ISBN 0-525-44340-1, 01160-350, DCB). Dutton Child Bks.
Hughes, Shirley. An Evening at Alfie's. Hughes, Shirley, illus. LC 84-11297. 32p. (ps-1). 1985. 14.95 (ISBN 0-688-04122-1); PLB 14.88 (ISBN 0-688-04123-X). Lothrop.
Kraus, Robert. Spider's Baby-Sitting Job. 1990. pap. 2.50 (ISBN 0-590-42445-9). Scholastic Inc.
Martin, Ann M. Baby-Sitter's Club. 1989. Set no. 5. pap. 11.00 (ISBN 0-590-63344-9, SCHOLASTIC). Scholastic Inc.
—Baby-Sitters Club, Bks. 5-8. (gr. 4-7). 1990. pap. 11.80 boxed set (ISBN 0-590-63672-3). Scholastic Inc.
—The Baby-Sitters Club, Bks. 9-12. (gr. 3-7). 1991. pap. 11.80 boxed set (ISBN 0-590-63701-0). Scholastic Inc.
—The Baby-Sitters Club, Bks. 13-16. (gr. 3-7). 1991. pap. 11.80 boxed set (ISBN 0-590-63705-3). Scholastic Inc.
—The Baby-Sitters Club, Bks. 17-20. (gr. 3-7). 1991. pap. 11.80 boxed set (ISBN 0-590-63704-5). Scholastic Inc.
—The Baby-Sitters Club, Bks. 21-24. (gr. 3-7). 1991. pap. 11.80 boxed set (ISBN 0-590-63703-7). Scholastic Inc.
—The Baby-Sitters Club, Bks. 25-28. (gr. 3-7). 1991. pap. 11.80 boxed set (ISBN 0-590-63702-9). Scholastic Inc.
—Baby-Sitters Club, Bks. 29-32. (gr. 4-7). 1990. pap. 11. 80 boxed set (ISBN 0-590-63583-2). Scholastic Inc.
—Baby-Sitters Club, 4 vols, Bks. 33-36. (gr. 4-7). 1990. Boxed set. pap. 11.80 (ISBN 0-590-63669-3). Scholastic Inc.
—Baby Sitter's Club: Claudia & New Girl, No. 12. (gr. 4-7). 1988. pap. 2.95 (ISBN 0-590-43721-6). Scholastic Inc.
—Baby-Sitter's Club: Little Sister. 1989. pap. 10.00 (ISBN 0-590-63403-8). Scholastic Inc.
—Baby-Sitter's Club, No. 31: Dawn's Wicked Stepsister. 1990. pap. 2.95 (ISBN 0-590-42497-1). Scholastic Inc.
—Baby-Sitter's Club Set, No. 6. 1989. pap. 11.00 (ISBN 0-590-63404-6). Scholastic Inc.
—The Baby-Sitters Club Super Summer Special, Bks. 1-3. (gr. 3-7). 1991. pap. 10.50 boxed set (ISBN 0-590-63714-2). Scholastic Inc.
—The Baby-Sitters Little Sister, Bks. 5-8. (gr. 2-4). 1990. pap. 10.00 boxed set (ISBN 0-590-63593-X). Scholastic Inc.
—The Baby-Sitters Little Sister, Bks. 9-12. (gr. 2-4). 1990. pap. 10.00 boxed set (ISBN 0-590-63668-5). Scholastic Inc.
—Baby-Sitters on Board! (gr. 3-6). pap. 2.95 (ISBN 0-318-37373-4). Scholastic Inc.
—Baby-Sitters' Winter Carnival. (gr. 4-6). 1989. pap. 3.50 (ISBN 0-590-42499-8, Apple Paperbacks). Scholastic Inc.
—Boy-Crazy Stacey. 160p. (Orig.). (gr. 4-6). 1987. pap. 2.50 (ISBN 0-590-41040-7, Apple Paperbacks). Scholastic Inc.
—Claudia & Mean Janine. 160p. (Orig.). (gr. 4-6). 1987. pap. 2.75 (ISBN 0-590-41041-5, Apple Paperbacks). Scholastic Inc.
—Claudia & Mean Janine. 1987. pap. 2.95 (ISBN 0-590-43719-4). Scholastic Inc.
—Claudia & the Bad Joke. 160p. (gr. 3-7). 1988. pap. 2.75 (ISBN 0-590-41583-2). Scholastic Inc.
—Claudia & the Phantom Phone Calls. 160p. (Orig.). (gr. 3-7). 1986. pap. 2.75 (ISBN 0-590-41986-2). Scholastic Inc.
—Claudia: The Genius of Elm Street. 1991. pap. 3.25 (ISBN 0-590-44970-2). Scholastic Inc.
—Dawn on the Coast. 1989. pap. 2.75 (ISBN 0-590-42007-0). Scholastic Inc.
—Jessi's Baby Sitter. (gr. 4-7). 1990. pap. 2.95 (ISBN 0-590-43565-5). Scholastic Inc.
—Jessi's Secret Language. 160p. (gr. 3-7). 1988. pap. 2.75 (ISBN 0-590-41586-7, Apple Paperbacks). Scholastic Inc.
—Karen's Little Sister. (gr. 2-3). 1989. pap. 2.50 (ISBN 0-590-42692-3, Apple Paperbacks). Scholastic Inc.
—Karen's Prize. 1990. pap. 2.50 (ISBN 0-590-43650-3). Scholastic Inc.
—Karen's Witch. 112p. (Orig.). (gr. 2-4). 1988. pap. 2.50 (ISBN 0-590-41783-5). Scholastic Inc.
—Kristy & the Baby Parade. 160p. (gr. 3-7). 1991. pap. 3.25 (ISBN 0-590-43574-4). Scholastic Inc.
—Kristy's Mystery Admirer. (gr. 4-7). 1990. pap. 2.95 (ISBN 0-590-43567-1). Scholastic Inc.
—Little Miss Stoneybrook & Dawn. 160p. (gr. 3-7). 1988. pap. 2.75 (ISBN 0-590-41587-5). Scholastic Inc.
—Logan Likes Maryanne. 160p. (Orig.). (gr. 4-6). 1988. pap. 2.75 (ISBN 0-590-41124-1, Apple Paperbacks). Scholastic Inc.
—Mallory & the Secret Diary. (gr. 5 up). 1989. pap. 2.95 (ISBN 0-590-42500-5, Apple Paperbacks). Scholastic Inc.
—Mallory & the Trouble with Twins. 160p. (gr. 3-7). 1989. pap. 2.75 (ISBN 0-590-42005-4, Apple Paperbacks). Scholastic Inc.
—Mary Anne Saves the Day. 176p. (Orig.). (gr. 3-7). 1987. pap. 2.75 (ISBN 0-590-42123-9, Apple Paperback). Scholastic Inc.
—Stacey & the Mystery of Stoneybrook. 1990. pap. 2.95. Scholastic Inc.
—The Truth about Stacey. 144p. (Orig.). (gr. 3-7). 1986. pap. 2.75 (ISBN 0-590-42124-7, Apple Paperbacks). Scholastic Inc.
—Welcome Back, Stacey. (gr. 5 up). 1989. pap. 2.95 (ISBN 0-590-42501-3, Apple Paperbacks). Scholastic Inc.
Orgel, Doris. My War with Mrs. Galloway. Newsom, Carol, illus. LC 84-19553. 80p. (gr. 4-6). 1985. pap. 9.95 (ISBN 0-670-50217-0). Viking Child Bks.
—My War with Mrs. Galloway. Newsom, Carol, illus. 80p. (gr. 2-5). 1986. pap. 3.95 (ISBN 0-14-032171-3, Puffin). Puffin Bks.
Parish, Peggy. Teach Us, Amelia Bedelia. Sweat, Lynn, illus. 64p. (gr. k-3). 1987. pap. 2.50 (ISBN 0-590-40940-9, Hello Reader). Scholastic Inc.
Pascal, Francine. Jessica the Babysitter. (gr. 4-7). 1991. pap. 2.75 (ISBN 0-553-15838-4). Bantam.
Pryor, Bonnie & Baird, Anne. Jenny's New Baby Sitter. Bracken, Carolyn & Fernandes, Eugenie, illus. (ps). 1987. 3.95 (ISBN 0-671-63758-4, Little Simon). S&S Trade.
Quackenbush, Robert. Henry Babysits. Quackenbush, Robert, illus. 48p. (ps-2). 1990. pap. 2.95 (ISBN 0-448-04338-6, G&D). Putnam Pub Group.
Roberts, Willo D. Baby-Sitting Is a Dangerous Job. LC 84-20445. 192p. (gr. 4-6). 1985. SBE 13.95 (ISBN 0-689-31100-1, Atheneum Child Bk). Macmillan Child Grp.
—Baby-Sitting Is a Dangerous Job. 144p. 1987. pap. 3.50 (ISBN 0-449-70177-8, Juniper). Fawcett.
Robertson, Keith. Henry Reed's Baby-Sitting Service. McCloskey, Robert, illus. (gr. 5-8). 1966. pap. 14.95 (ISBN 0-670-36825-3). Viking Child Bks.
Ross, Pat. M & M & the Bad News Babies. Hafner, Marylin, illus. LC 81-18714. 48p. (gr. 6-9). 1983. Knopf.
—M & M & the Bad News Babies. Hafner, Marylin, illus. 48p. (ps-3). 1985. pap. 2.95 (ISBN 0-14-031851-8, Puffin). Puffin Bks.
Rubel, Nicole. Uncle Henry & Aunt Henrietta's Honeymoon. Rubel, Nicole, illus. LC 85-15944. 32p. (ps-2). 1986. 10.95 (ISBN 0-8037-0246-9); PLB 10.89 (ISBN 0-8037-0247-7). Dial Bks Young.
Saunders, Susan. Patti's New Look. 80p. (Orig.). (gr. 4-6). 1988. pap. 2.50 (ISBN 0-590-40644-2, Apple Paperbacks). Scholastic Inc.
Shahan, Sherry. Baby-Sitting Crack-Up. Hickman, Estella, illus. 112p. (Orig.). (gr. 3-6). 1988. pap. 1.00 (ISBN 0-87406-326-4). Willowisp Pr.
Shreve, Susan. The Revolution of Mary Leary. LC 82-185. 192p. (gr. 5-9). 1982. Knopf.
Smith, Susan. Monster-Sitter. (gr. 5 up). 1987. pap. 2.50 (ISBN 0-671-63713-4, Archway). PB.
Steel, Danielle. Max & the Baby-Sitter. Rogers, Jacqueline, illus. (ps-2). 1989. 8.95 (ISBN 0-385-29796-3). Delacorte.
Stevens, Kathleen. The Beast & the Babysitter. Bowler, Ray, illus. LC 88-42917. 32p. (gr. 2-3). 1989. PLB 12. 95 (ISBN 1-55532-929-2). Gareth Stevens Inc.
Stine, R. L. The Baby-Sitter. 176p. (Orig.). (gr. 7 up). 1989. pap. 2.95 (ISBN 0-590-44236-8). Scholastic Inc.
Tolles, Martha. Katie's Baby-Sitting Job. 128p. (Orig.). (gr. 4-7). 1985. pap. 2.50 (ISBN 0-590-40724-4, Apple Paperbacks). Scholastic Inc.
—Katie's Baby-Sitting Job. 128p. (Orig.). (gr. 3-7). 1985. pap. 2.75 (ISBN 0-590-42608-7). Scholastic Inc.
Weyn, Suzanne. Checking In. LC 89-49703. 128p. (gr. 4-8). 1990. lib. bdg. 9.89 (ISBN 0-8167-2003-7); pap. text ed. 2.95 (ISBN 0-8167-2004-5). Troll Assocs.
—Liza's Lucky Break. LC 89-77117. 128p. (gr. 4-8). 1990. lib. bdg. 9.89 (ISBN 0-8167-2007-X); pap. text ed. 2.95 (ISBN 0-8167-2008-8). Troll Assocs.
—True Blue. LC 90-10830. 128p. (gr. 4-8). 1990. PLB 9.89 (ISBN 0-8167-2005-3); pap. text ed. 2.95 (ISBN 0-8167-2006-1). Troll Assocs.

BABYLONIA–FICTION

Walsh, Jill P. Babylon. (Illus.). 32p. (gr. k-3). 1982. 9.95 (ISBN 0-233-97362-1). Andre Deutsch.

BACH, JOHANN SEBASTIAN, 1685-1750

Great Composers, Bk. 1: Bach, Mozart, Beethoven. (Illus.). (gr. 5 up). 3.50 (ISBN 0-7214-0230-5). Ladybird Bks.
Patton, Barbara W. Introducing Johann Sebastian Bach. rev. ed. (Illus.). 48p. (Orig.). (gr. 3-9). 1992. pap. 6. 95x (ISBN 1-878636-01-4). Soundboard Bks.

BACILLI

see Bacteriology

BACKPACKING

Foster, Lynne. Take a Hike! The Sierra Club Beginner's Guide to Hiking & Backpacking. Weston, Martha, illus. (gr. 4-7). 1990. write for info. Sierra.
Petersen, P. J. Nobody Else Can Walk It for You. LC 81-69669. 224p. (gr. 7 up). 1982. 12.95 (ISBN 0-385-28730-5). Delacorte.
Randolph, John. Backpacking Basics. (Illus.). 48p. (gr. 3-7). 1982. 9.95 (ISBN 0-13-055798-6). P-H.
Zeleznak, Shirley. Backpacking. LC 79-27800. (Illus.). 32p. (gr. 5-6). 1980. lib. bdg. 9.95 (ISBN 0-89686-069-8, Crestwood Hse). Macmillan Child Grp.

BACTERIA

see Bacteriology

BACTERIOLOGY

see also Immunity; Microorganisms

Asimov, Isaac. How Did We Find Out about Germs. Wool, David, illus. LC 73-81402. 64p. (gr. 5-8). 1973. PLB 10.85 (ISBN 0-8027-6166-6). Walker & Co.
Berger, Melvin. Germs Make Me Sick! Hafner, Marilyn, illus. LC 84-45334. 32p. (ps-3). 1985. 13.95 (ISBN 0-690-04428-3, Crowell Jr Bks); PLB 13.89 (ISBN 0-690-04429-1). HarpC Child Bks.
—Germs Make Me Sick! Hafner, Marylin, illus. LC 84-45334. 32p. (ps-3). 1987. incl. cassette 7.95 (ISBN 0-694-00198-8, Trophy); pap. 4.50 (ISBN 0-06-445053-8, Trophy). HarpC Child Bks.
LeMaster, Leslie J. Bacteria & Viruses. LC 84-27414. (Illus.). 48p. (gr. k-4). 1985. lib. bdg. 14.60 (ISBN 0-516-01937-6). Childrens.
Rice, Judith A. Those Mean Nasty Dirty Downright Disgusting but...Invisible Germs. Merrill, Reed, illus. Gwaltney, Jack M., Jr. LC 89-34409. (Illus.). 32p. (Orig.). (ps-3). 1989. pap. 7.95 (ISBN 0-934140-46-4). Redleaf Pr.
Sabin, Francene. Microbes & Bacteria. Acosta, Andres, illus. LC 84-2749. 32p. (gr. 3-6). 1985. PLB 9.49 (ISBN 0-8167-0232-2); pap. text ed. 2.95 (ISBN 0-8167-0233-0). Troll Assocs.

BACTERIOLOGY–HISTORY

Asimov, Isaac. How Did We Find Out about Germs. Wool, David, illus. LC 73-81402. 64p. (gr. 5-8). 1973. PLB 10.85 (ISBN 0-8027-6166-6). Walker & Co.

BADEN-POWELL OF GILWELL, ROBERT STEPHENSON SMYTH BADEN-POWELL, 1ST BARON, 1857-1941

Brower, Pauline. Baden-Powell: Founder of the Boy Scouts. LC 89-33750. 32p. (gr. 2-5). 1989. PLB 13.27 (ISBN 0-516-04173-8). Childrens.

BADGES OF HONOR

see Decorations of Honor

BADGERS–FICTION

Banks, Martin. Discovering Badgers. Caulkins, Janet, ed. (Illus.). 48p. (gr. 1-6). 1988. PLB 11.90 (ISBN 0-531-18225-8, Pub. by Bookwright Pr). Watts.

Hoban, Russell. Baby Sister for Frances. Hoban, Lillian, illus. LC 64-15154. 32p. (gr. k-3). 1964. 12.95 (ISBN 0-06-022335-9); PLB 12.89 (ISBN 0-06-022336-7). HarpC Child Bks.

—A Bargain for Frances. Hoban, Lillian, illus. LC 70-80533. (gr. k-3). 1978. pap. 3.50 (ISBN 0-06-444001-X, Trophy). HarpC Child Bks.

—Bedtime for Frances. Williams, Garth, illus. LC 60-8347. 32p. (gr. k-3). 1960. 12.95 (ISBN 0-06-022350-2); PLB 12.89 (ISBN 0-06-022351-0). HarpC Child Bks.

—Best Friends for Frances. Hoban, Lillian, illus. LC 71-77935. 32p. (ps-3). 1969. 12.95 (ISBN 0-06-022327-8); PLB 13.89 (ISBN 0-06-022328-6). HarpC Child Bks.

—Birthday for Frances. Hoban, Lillian, illus. LC 68-24321. 32p. (gr. k-3). 1968. 13.95 (ISBN 0-06-022338-3); PLB 13.89 (ISBN 0-06-022339-1). HarpC Child Bks.

—Bread & Jam for Frances. Hoban, Lillian, illus. LC 64-19605. 32p. (gr. k-3). 1965. 13.95 (ISBN 0-06-022359-6); PLB 13.89 (ISBN 0-06-022360-X). HarpC Child Bks.

—Bread & Jam for Frances. Hoban, Lillian, illus. LC 64-19605. 32p. (ps-3). 1986. pap. 4.95 (ISBN 0-06-443096-0, Trophy). HarpC Child Bks.

Howker, Janni. Badger on the Barge & Other Stories. (gr. 5-9). 1987. pap. 4.95 (ISBN 0-14-032253-1, Puffin). Puffin Bks.

Lewis, Naomi. Hare & Badger Go to Town. Ross, Tony, illus. 32p. (ps-1). 1987. 9.95 (ISBN 0-905478-94-0, Pub. by Century UK). Trafalgar Sq.

MacDonald, Elizabeth. Mr. Badger's Birthday Pie. Smith, Claire, illus. LC 88-3852. 32p. (ps-2). 1989. 8.95 (ISBN 0-8037-0579-4). Dial Bks Young.

Minta, Kathryn A. The Digging Badger. (Illus.). 64p. (gr. 2-5). 1985. 9.95 (ISBN 0-396-08654-3, Putnam). Putnam Pub Group.

BAHAISM

Baha'u'llah. Blessed Is the Spot. Stevenson, Anna, illus. LC 58-8815. (gr. k-2). 1958. 14.50 (ISBN 0-87743-014-4, 352-040). Baha'i.

Garst, Hitjo. From Mountain to Mountain: Stories about Baha'u'llah. McKinley, Olive, tr. from DUT. Parsons, Brian, illus. 138p. (gr. 3-4). 1988. 19.95 (ISBN 0-85398-265-1). G Ronald Pub.

Heller, Wendy. My Name Is Nabil. (Illus.). 48p. (gr. 3-6). 1981. 5.95 (ISBN 0-933770-17-0). Kalimat.

Lee, Anthony A. The Cornerstone: A Story About 'Abdu'l-Baha in America. Irvine, Rex J., illus. 24p. (Orig.). (gr. k-5). 1979. pap. 3.00 (ISBN 0-933770-01-4). Kalimat.

—The Scottish Visitors: A Story about 'Abdu'l-Baha in Britain. Irving, Rex J., illus. 24p. (Orig.). (gr. k-5). 1981. pap. 3.00 (ISBN 0-933770-05-7). Kalimat.

—The Unfriendly Governor. Irvine, Rex John, illus. 24p. (gr. k-5). 1980. pap. 3.00 (ISBN 0-933770-02-2). Kalimat.

Weinberg, Robert, compiled by. & intro. by. Your True Brother. (Illus.). 24p. (Orig.). (gr. 8-10). 1991. pap. 6.50 (ISBN 0-85398-324-0). G Ronald Pub.

BAHAMAS

Greenfield, Eloise. Under the Sunday Tree. Ferguson, Amos, illus. LC 87-29373. 48p. (ps-1). 1988. 12.95 (ISBN 0-06-022254-9); PLB 12.89 (ISBN 0-06-022257-3). HarpC Child Bks.

McCulla, Patricia E. Bahamas. (Illus.). 104p. (gr. 5 up). 1988. lib. bdg. 14.95 (ISBN 1-55546-191-3). Chelsea Hse.

BAHAMAS–FICTION

Noronha, Francis P. The Magic Tree House. LC 85-91383. 42p. (gr. 3-5). 1986. 4.95 (ISBN 0-533-06888-6). Vantage.

BAKERS AND BAKERIES

Allard, Harry. The Cactus Flower Bakery. Delaney, Ned, illus. LC 90-36565. 32p. (ps-3). 1991. 14.95 (ISBN 0-06-020046-4); PLB 14.89 (ISBN 0-06-020047-2). HarpC Child Bks.

Jenness, Aylette. The Bakery Factory. LC 77-8094. (Illus.). (gr. 3-7). 1978. 8.95 (ISBN 0-690-03805-4, Crowell Jr Bks). HarpC Child Bks.

Moncure, Jane B. What Was It Before It Was Bread? Hygaard, Elizabeth, illus. LC 85-11402. 32p. (ps-2). 1985. PLB 11.97 (ISBN 0-89565-323-0). Childs World.

Whitmore, Arvella. Bread Winner. (gr. 4-7). 1990. 13.95 (ISBN 0-395-53705-3). HM.

Ziegler, Sandra. A Visit to the Bakery. Pilot Productions Staff, photos by. LC 86-32647. (Illus.). 32p. (gr. k-3). 1987. PLB 14.60 (ISBN 0-516-01495-1). Childrens.

BAKERS AND BAKERIES–VOCATIONAL GUIDANCE

Lillegard, Dee. I Can Be a Baker. LC 85-27976. (Illus.). 32p. (gr. k-3). 1986. PLB 13.93 (ISBN 0-516-01892-2). Childrens.

BAKING

see also Bread; Cake

Carlson, Anna L. & Wynne, Diana. My Brother & I Like Cookies. 2nd. ed. Wynne, Diana, illus. LC 80-81624. 96p. (Orig.). (gr. 1-7). 1983. pap. 4.95 (ISBN 0-939938-00-6). Karwyn Ent.

Carlson, Faith. A Cookie Christmas. Carlson, Faith, illus. 28p. (Orig.). (ps-2). 1986. pap. 5.00 (ISBN 0-932591-05-1). Baggeboda Pr.

Coyle, Rena. My First Baking Book. Arnold, Tedd, illus. LC 87-40646. 144p. (gr. 1-5). 1988. pap. 9.95 (ISBN 0-89480-579-7, 1579). Workman Pub.

Drew, Helen. My First Baking Book. LC 91-10239. (Illus.). 48p. (gr. 2-6). 1991. 12.00 (ISBN 0-679-81545-7); lib. bdg. 13.99 (ISBN 0-679-91545-1). Knopf.

Oppenneer, Betsy. Betsy's Breads. rev. ed. (Illus.). 40p. (gr. 8 up). 1991. pap. 7.95 (ISBN 0-9627665-2-6). Breadworks.

Stephens, Fran. Baking Projects for Children: Fun Foods to Make with Children from 4 to 10. Macdonald, Roland B. & Gray, Dan, illus. 128p. (gr. k-5). 1991. pap. 9.95 (ISBN 1-878767-10-0). Murdoch Bks.
Some of childhood's happiest memories are made in the kitchen along with the cookies & bread. Most of us remember getting to lick the bowl or sneaking a chocolate chip before they all went into the cookie batter. And we all remember the wonderful smells! BAKING PROJECTS FOR CHILDREN is not really a cookbook--there are recipes, but most projects take advantage of mixes, refrigerator & frozen doughs & other convenience products. We hope to get you & your child together in the kitchen having fun, because a child who thinks baking is fun will want to learn more about other sorts of cooking. The book includes a wide range of projects so that young children who are just learning to stir without sloshing all the flour out of the bowl will find fun things they can make--while children who have been making cookies for years will find some challenging new ideas to try. In the course of making gingerbread houses & Hand Sandwiches the parent & child learn a lot about making wonderful things in the kitchen & about each other. Even if the cookies burn, the Coca-Cola Cake collapses, the Flaming Cake sets off the smoke detector & the Red Velvet Cake turns out blue, you & your child will have a magical, memorable time together.
Publisher Provided Annotation.

BAKING–FICTION

Addison-Wesley Staff. The Gingerbread Man Little Book. (Illus.). 16p. (gr. k-3). 1989. pap. text ed. 4.50 (ISBN 0-201-19054-0). Addison-Wesley.

Chalmers, Mary. Take a Nap, Harry. Chalmers, Mary, illus. LC 89-77655. 32p. (ps-2). 1991. 13.95 (ISBN 0-06-021243-8); PLB 13.89 (ISBN 0-06-021244-6). HarpC Child Bks.

Elish, Dan. The Worldwide Dessert Contest. Gurney, John, illus. LC 87-24694. 208p. (gr. 4-6). 1988. 13.95 (ISBN 0-531-05752-6); PLB 13.99 (ISBN 0-531-08352-7). Orchard Bks Watts.

Gilson, Jamie. Can't Catch Me, I'm the Gingerbread Man. LC 80-39748. 192p. (gr. 5-9). 1981. 12.95 (ISBN 0-688-00435-0); PLB 12.88 (ISBN 0-688-00436-9). Lothrop.

MacDonald, Elizabeth. Miss Poppy & the Honey Cake. Smith, Claire, illus. LC 88-3851. 32p. (ps-2). 1989. 8.95 (ISBN 0-8037-0578-6). Dial Bks Young.

McGuire, Leslie. Miss Mopp's Lucky Day. Silver, Jody, illus. LC 81-4879. 48p. (ps-3). 1982. 5.95 (ISBN 0-8193-1061-1); PLB 5.95 (ISBN 0-8193-1062-X). Parents.

Mayer, Marianna. Marcel the Pastry Chef. McDermott, Gerald, illus. 32p. (ps-3). 1991. 14.95 (ISBN 0-553-05192-X). Bantam.

Spohn, Kate. Ruth's Bake Shop. Spohn, Kate, illus. LC 89-70930. 32p. (ps-2). 1990. 13.95 (ISBN 0-531-05889-1); PLB 13.99 (ISBN 0-531-08489-2). Orchard Bks Watts.

BALANCE OF NATURE

see Ecology

BALL GAMES

see names of games, e.g. baseball; soccer

BALLADS

see also Folk Songs

Tate, Carole. Rhymes & Ballads of London. LC 72-90691. (Illus.). 32p. (gr. k-4). 1973. 6.95 (ISBN 0-87592-042-X). Scroll Pr.

BALLET

Ballet. (Illus.). (gr. 5 up). 3.50 (ISBN 0-7214-0234-8). Ladybird Bks.

Berger, Gilda. Magic Slippers: Stories from the Ballet. 1990. 15.95 (ISBN 0-385-24935-7). Doubleday.

Briffa, Merice. A Ballet Lesson. 64p. 1985. pap. 9.95 (ISBN 0-908175-98-1, Pub. by Boolarong Pubns AT). Intl Spec Bk.

Butler, Joan & Walker, Katherine S. Ballet for Boys & Girls. (Illus.). (gr. 3-7). 1980. 9.95x (ISBN 0-13-055574-6). P-H.

Craig, Janet. Ballet Dancer. Todd, Barbara, illus. LC 88-10043. 32p. (gr. k-2). 1989. PLB 10.89 (ISBN 0-8167-1434-7); pap. text ed. 2.50 (ISBN 0-8167-1435-5). Troll Assocs.

French, Vivian. One Ballerina Two. Ormerod, Jan, illus. LC 90-45969. 32p. (ps up). 1991. 13.95 (ISBN 0-688-10333-2); PLB 13.88 (ISBN 0-688-10334-0). Lothrop.

Frost, Erica. I Can Read about Ballet. LC 74-24927. (Illus.). (gr. 2-4). 1975. pap. 1.95 (ISBN 0-89375-063-8). Troll Assocs.

Glassman, Bruce S. Mikhail Baryshnikov. (Illus.). 128p. (gr. 7-9). 1990. 14.98 (ISBN 0-382-24035-9); 11. 21s.p.; PLB 17.98; PLB 17.98 (ISBN 0-382-09907-9). Silver Burdett Pr.

Goodale, Katherine D. Pas de Trois, Fun with Ballet Words. Goodale, Kit, illus. Houlton, Loyce, intro. by. (Illus.). 25p. (Orig.). (gr. k-7). 1982. pap. 5.95 (ISBN 0-9609662-0-X). Goodale Pub.

Gregory, Cynthia. Cynthia Gregory Dances Swan Lake. Swope, Martha, illus. 48p. (gr. 3-7). 1990. PLB 14.95 (ISBN 0-671-68786-7). S&S Trade.

Grigorovich, Yuri & Vanslow, Victor. The Authorized Bolshoi Ballet Book of Raymonda. (Illus.). 107p. (gr. 3 up). 1988. 19.95 (ISBN 0-86622-642-7, Z104). TFH Pubns.

Grogorovich, Yuri & Demidov, Alexander. The Authorized Bolshoi Ballet Book of Ivan the Terrible. (Illus.). 109p. (gr. 3 up). 1988. 19.95 (ISBN 0-86622-643-5, Z105). TFH Pubns.

Gross. If You Were a Ballet Dancer. (gr. 3). 1979. pap. 1.95 (ISBN 0-590-05746-4). Scholastic Inc.

Harrison, Mary K. How to Dress Dancers: Costuming Techniques for Dance. LC 88-60948. (Illus.). 144p. (gr. 9-12). 1988. pap. 12.95 (ISBN 0-916622-73-8). Princeton Bk Co.

Jessel, Camilla. Life at the Royal Ballet School. Jessel, Camilla, illus. LC 79-12162. 143p. (gr. 4 up). 1979. 15.95 (ISBN 0-416-30191-6, NO. 0137). Routledge Chapman & Hall.

Kuklin, Susan. Reaching for Dreams: A Ballet from Rehearsal to Opening Night. Kuklin, Susan, illus. LC 86-15356. (gr. 4-9). 1987. 12.95 (ISBN 0-688-06316-0). Lothrop.

Looking at Ballet. 48p. (gr. 4-8). 1990. 13.95 (ISBN 1-85435-105-2). Marshall Cavendish.

Menning, Viiu. Great Dancers. Conkle, Nancy & Neary, D., illus. (Orig.). (gr. 8). pap. 3.50 (ISBN 0-88388-065-2). Bellerophon Bks.

Royal Academy of Dancing Staff. Ballet Class. Fonteyn de Arias, Margot, frwd. by. (Illus.). 144p. (gr. 4 up). 1985. 16.95 (ISBN 0-668-06427-7). Prentice Hall Pr.

Sanchez, Sharon S. About Ballet Performance. Bower, Adele, illus. 32p. (ps up). 1990. pap. 5.95 (ISBN 0-9626651-1-8). Dance Data.

Sanchez, Sharon S., ed. About Ballet Class. Bower, Adele, illus. 32p. (Orig.). (ps up). 1990. pap. 5.95 (ISBN 0-9626651-0-X). Dance Data.

Simon, Charnan. Evelyn Cisneros: Prima Ballerina. LC 90-40104. (Illus.). 32p. (gr. 2-5). 1990. PLB 13.27 (ISBN 0-516-04276-9). Childrens.

Sorine, Stephanie R. Our Ballet Class. Sorine, Daniel S., illus. LC 80-28927. 48p. (gr. k-3). 1981. lib. bdg. 8.99 (ISBN 0-394-94821-1). Knopf.

Switzer, Ellen. The Nutcracker: A Story & A Ballet. Cara, Costas & Cara, Stephen, photos by. LC 85-7463. (Illus.). 112p. (gr. 4-6). 1985. 16.95 (ISBN 0-689-31061-7, Atheneum Child Bk). Macmillan Child Grp.

Thomas, A. Ballet. (Illus.). 48p. (gr. 5 up). 1987. PLB 13.95 (ISBN 0-88110-244-X); pap. 6.95 (ISBN 0-7460-0085-5). EDC.

Thomas, A., et al. Ballet & Dance. (Illus.). 96p. (gr. 5 up). 1987. pap. 10.95 (ISBN 0-7460-0201-7). EDC.

Tichenor, Kay. Ballet Color & Story Album. (Illus.). 32p. 1976. pap. 4.50 (ISBN 0-8431-1718-4). Price Stern.

Tobias, Tobi. Arthur Mitchell. LC 74-13730. (Illus.). 40p. (gr. 1-5). 1975. PLB 12.89 (ISBN 0-690-00662-4, Crowell Jr Bks). HarpC Child Bks.

Winter, Ginny L. Ballet Book. Winter, Ginny L., illus. (gr. 1-5). 1962. 8.95 (ISBN 0-8392-3001-X). Astor-Honor.

BALLET–FICTION

Andersen, Hans Christian. The Red Shoes. Iwasaki, Chihiro, illus. LC 82-61836. 36p. (gr. 3 up). 1983. 15.95 (ISBN 0-907234-26-7). Picture Bk Studio.

Anderson, Marcie. Ballet Kitty. (Illus.). 24p. (ps-3). 1987. 1.95 (ISBN 0-87406-176-8). Willowisp Pr.

Asher, Sandy. Ballet, No. 3: Pat's Promise. 1990. pap. 2.50 (ISBN 0-590-41844-0). Scholastic Inc.

—Can David Do It? 80p. (gr. 2-4). 1991. pap. 2.50 (ISBN 0-590-43837-9). Scholastic Inc.

—Just Like Jenny. LC 82-70315. 160p. (gr. 5-9). 1986. pap. 2.50 (ISBN 0-440-94289-6). Dell.
—Just Like Jenny. LC 82-70315. (gr. 4-6). 1982. pap. 12.95 (ISBN 0-385-28496-9). Delacorte.
Bottner, Barbara. Dumb Old Casey Is a Fat Tree. LC 78-19474. (Illus.). 48p. (gr. 1-4). 1979. 11.89 (ISBN 0-06-020616-0). HarpC Child Bks.
Carlson, Nancy. Harriet's Recital. (Illus.). 32p. (ps-3). 1985. pap. 3.95 (ISBN 0-14-050464-8, Puffin). Puffin Bks.
Estoril, Jean. Ballet for Drina. 176p. (gr. 3-7). 1988. pap. 2.75 (ISBN 0-590-42190-5). Scholastic Inc.

Farrar, Susan C. Emily & Her Cavalier. Weinberger, Jane & Little, Carl, eds. LC 90-71373. (Illus.). 124p. 1991. 12.95g (ISBN 0-932433-76-6); pap. 9.95 (ISBN 0-932433-77-4). Windswept Hse.

—Samantha on Stage. Sanderson, Ruth, illus. 164p. (gr. 3 up). 1990. pap. 3.95 (ISBN 0-14-034328-8, Puffin). Puffin Bks.
Holabird, Katharine. Angelina Ballerina. Craig, Helen, illus. LC 83-8233. (ps-2). 1988. pap. 13.00 (ISBN 0-517-55083-0, C N Potter Bks). Crown.
Isadora, Rachel. My Ballet Class. LC 79-16297. (Illus.). 32p. (gr. k-3). 1980. 12.95 (ISBN 0-688-80253-2). Greenwillow.
Lichtner, Schomer. Ballerina's Holiday. (Illus.). 76p. (Orig.). (gr. 5 up). 1979. pap. 4.95 (ISBN 0-941074-04-8). Lichtner.
Malcolm, Jahnna N. Bad News Ballet, No. 2: Battle of the Bunheads. 1989. pap. 2.50 (ISBN 0-590-41916-1). Scholastic Inc.
—Bad News Ballet, No. 3: Stupid Cupid. 1989. pap. 2.75 (ISBN 0-590-42474-2). Scholastic Inc.
—Bad News Ballet, No. 4: Who Framed. 1989. pap. 2.75 (ISBN 0-590-42472-6). Scholastic Inc.
—Bad News Ballet, No. 5: Blubberina. 1989. pap. 2.75 (ISBN 0-590-42888-8). Scholastic Inc.
—Bad News Ballet, No. 7: The King & Us. 1990. pap. 2.75 (ISBN 0-590-43395-4). Scholastic Inc.
—Boo Who. (gr. 4-7). 1990. pap. 2.75 (ISBN 0-590-43397-0). Scholastic Inc.
Mallett, Jerry & Bartch, Marian. Bellyful of Ballet. Smith, Mark D., illus. 56p. (gr. 2-5). 1986. PLB 7.05 (ISBN 0-8479-9926-2, 027155). Perma Bound.
Oxenbury, Helen. The Dancing Class. Oxenbury, Helen, illus. LC 82-19791. 24p. (ps-1). 1983. 5.95 (ISBN 0-8037-1651-6, 0383-120). Dial Bks Young.
Smath, Jerry. Up Goes Mr. Downs. LC 84-1199. (Illus.). 48p. (ps-3). 1985. 5.95 (ISBN 0-8193-1137-5). Parents.
Streatfield, Noel. Ballet Shoes. (gr. 4-7). 16.25 (ISBN 0-8446-6241-0). Peter Smith.
Ure, Jean. What If They Saw Me Now? LC 83-14981. 160p. (gr. 7 up). 1984. 13.95 (ISBN 0-385-29317-8). Delacorte.
Utz. A Delightful Day with Bella Ballet. LC 75-190267. (Illus.). 32p. (gr. 2-3). 1972. PLB 9.95 (ISBN 0-87783-056-8); pap. 3.94 deluxe ed. (ISBN 0-87783-089-4). Oddo.
Weyn, Suzanne. Emma's Turn. Iskowitz, Joel, illus. LC 89-31348. 96p. (gr. 3-5). 1989. lib. bdg. 9.89 (ISBN 0-8167-1623-4); pap. text ed. 2.95 (ISBN 0-8167-1624-2). Troll Assocs.
—Stage Fright. Iskowitz, Joel, illus. LC 89-31349. 96p. (gr. 3-5). 1989. lib. bdg. 9.89 (ISBN 0-8167-1651-X); pap. text ed. 2.95 (ISBN 0-8167-1652-8). Troll Assocs.
—Three for the Show. Iskowitz, Joel, illus. LC 89-34547. 96p. (gr. 3-5). 1989. PLB 9.89 (ISBN 0-8167-1655-2); pap. text ed. 2.95 (ISBN 0-8167-1656-0). Troll Assocs.

BALLET–HISTORY

Golovkina, Sophia N. The Bolshoi Ballet School. Coey, Nigel T., tr. from RUS. Pcholkin, Vladimir, illus. 77p. (gr. 3 up). 1987. Repr. 19.95 (ISBN 0-86622-497-1, Z-112). TFH Pubns.

BALLETS–STORIES, PLOTS, ETC.

Hautzig, Deborah. The Story of the Nutcracker Ballet. Goode, Diane, illus. 32p. (ps-1). 1986. pap. 5.95 (ISBN 0-394-88296-2, Random Juv). Random.
—The Story of the Nutcracker Ballet. Goode, Diane, illus. LC 85-30149. 32p. (gr. 3-6). 1986. (Random Juv); pap. 2.25 (ISBN 0-394-88178-8, Random Juv). Random.
Hodges, M. Constance. Alice in Danceland. Hodges, Del & Mavity, Dennis, photos by. Troxel, Rose, illus. (Orig.). (gr. 3-8). 1979. PLB 5.95 (ISBN 0-934856-00-1). Delcon.
Marcus, Leonard S. Petrouchka: A Ballet Cut-Out Book. Kendall, Jane F., illus. 16p. (gr. 3-6). 1983. pap. 12.95 cutout bk. (ISBN 0-87923-469-5). Godine.
Riordan, James. Favorite Stories of the Ballet. Ambrus, Victor G., illus. Nureyev, Rudolf, frwd. by. LC 84-42778. (Illus.). (gr. 4 up). write for info. (ISBN 0-528-82178-4). Checkerboard Pr.
Rosenberg, Jane. Dance Me a Story: Twelve Tales from the Classic Ballets. Ashley, Merrill, intro. by. LC 84-51701. (Illus.). (gr. 1-4). 1985. 19.95 (ISBN 0-500-01359-4). Thames Hudson.

BALLOONS

see also Aeronautics

Adler, Irene. Ballooning: High & Wild. LC 75-23406. (Illus.). 32p. (gr. 5-10). 1976. PLB 10.79 (ISBN 0-89375-001-8); pap. 2.95 (ISBN 0-89375-017-4). Troll Assocs.
Balloons. (Illus.). 32p. (ps-6). 1983. pap. 2.95 (ISBN 0-87474-333-8, BACBP). Smithsonian.
Briggs, Carole S. Ballooning. LC 86-7365. (Illus.). 48p. (gr. 4-9). 1985. PLB 9.95 (ISBN 0-8225-0441-3). Lerner Pubns.
Cottrell, Leonard. Up in a Balloon. LC 69-17423. (Illus.). (gr. 8 up). 1970. 21.95 (ISBN 0-87599-142-4). S G Phillips.
Davies, Kay. My Balloon. (ps-3). 1990. 6.95 (ISBN 0-385-41131-6); PLB 7.99 (ISBN 0-385-41199-5). Doubleday.
Hall, Andy. Famous Balloon Mobiles. (Illus.). 28p. (Orig.). (gr. 6-7). 1985. pap. 4.95 (ISBN 0-317-14845-1). Parkwest Pubns.
Johnson, Neil. Fire & Silk: Flying in a Hot Air Balloon. (ps-3). 1991. 15.95 (ISBN 0-316-46959-9). Little.
Kaner, Etta. Balloon Science. (gr. 4-7). 1990. pap. 8.61 (ISBN 0-201-52378-7). Addison-Wesley.
Marriott. Amazing Fact Book of Balloons. (Illus.). 32p. (gr. 4-8). 1987. PLB 11.95 (ISBN 0-87191-841-2). Creative Ed.
Saunders, R. Balloon Voyager. (Illus.). 32p. (gr. 4 up). Date not set. PLB 14.00 (ISBN 0-86592-870-3). Rourke Corp.
Scarry, Huck. Balloon Trip: A Sketchbook. Scarry, Huck, illus. LC 82-23002. 68p. (gr. 3-7). 1983. 10.95 (ISBN 0-13-055939-3). P-H.
Senum, Marilyn. Hot Air Ballooning Color & Story Album. (gr. 2 up). pap. 3.95 (ISBN 0-8431-1723-0). Price Stern.

BALLOONS, DIRIGIBLE

see Airships

BALLOONS–FICTION

Bashful Bard. The Great Balloon Adventure. Bashful Bard, illus. LC 89-84961. 24p. (Orig.). (ps-1). 1989. pap. 2.99 (ISBN 1-877906-03-4). Kenney Pubns.
Birchman, David F. Victorious Paints the Great Ballooon. LC 90-1746. 64p. (gr. 2-6). 1991. 13.95 (ISBN 0-02-710111-8, Bradbury Pr). Macmillan Child Grp.
Bonsall, Crosby N. Mine's the Best. Bonsall, Crosby, illus. LC 72-9863. 32p. (ps-2). 1973. PLB 10.89 (ISBN 0-06-020578-4). HarpC Child Bks.
Coerr, Eleanor. The Big Balloon Race. Croll, Carolyn, illus. LC 80-8368. 64p. (gr. k-3). 1981. PLB 10.89 (ISBN 0-685-02057-6). HarpC Child Bks.
Darling, Benjamin. Robert & the Balloon Machine. Solliday, Tim, illus. 32p. 1989. 11.95 (ISBN 0-88138-120-9). Green Tiger Pr.
Du Bois, William P. The Twenty-One Balloons. Du Bois, William P., illus. 184p. (gr. 5-9). 1986. pap. 3.95 (ISBN 0-14-032097-0, Puffin). Puffin Bks.
Glennon, Karen M. Miss Eva & the Red Balloon. Poppel, Hans, illus. LC 89-32515. 32p. (ps-3). 1990. PLB 13.95 (ISBN 0-671-68854-5). S&S Trade.
Lamorisse, Albert. Red Balloon. Lamorisse, Albert, photos by. LC 57-9229. (Illus.). 45p. (gr. 3-7). 1967. 13.95 (ISBN 0-685-01494-0). Doubleday.
—The Red Balloon. LC 57-9229. (Illus.). 45p. (ps-3). 1978. 13.95 (ISBN 0-385-00343-9, Zephyr-BFYR); pap. 6.95 (ISBN 0-385-14297-8, Zephyr-BFYR). Doubleday.
Landis, James D. The Sisters Impossible. LC 78-32148. (gr. 4-7). 1979. Knopf.
Matthias, Catherine. Demasiados Globos (Too Many Balloons) Sharp, Gene, illus. LC 81-15520. (SPA.). 32p. (ps-2). 1990. PLB 11.93 (ISBN 0-516-33633-9); pap. 2.95 (ISBN 0-516-53633-8). Childrens.
—Too Many Balloons. Sharp, Gene, illus. LC 81-15520. 32p. (ps-2). 1982. PLB 11.93 (ISBN 0-516-03633-5); pap. text ed. 2.95 (ISBN 0-516-43633-3). Childrens.
Mott, Evelyn C. Balloon Ride. Mott, Evelyn C., illus. 32p. (ps-1). 1991. 12.95 (ISBN 0-8027-8124-1); PLB 13.85 (ISBN 0-8027-8126-8). Walker & Co.
Peck. Grumpalump. (ps-3). 1991. 14.95 (ISBN 0-89919-871-6, Clarion Bks). HM.
Pene Du Bois, William. Twenty-One Balloons. Pene Du Bois, William, illus. 192p. (gr. 4-8). 1982. pap. 2.75 (ISBN 0-440-49183-5, YB). Dell.
—The Twenty-One Balloons. Pene Du Bois, William, illus. (gr. 5-9). 1947. pap. 13.95 (ISBN 0-670-73441-1). Viking Child Bks.
Roberts, Thom. Atlantic Free Balloon Race. (gr. 3-7). 1986. pap. 2.50 (ISBN 0-380-89868-3, Camelot). Avon.
Scullard, Sue. The Great Round-the-World Balloon Race. Scullard, Sue, illus. 32p. (gr. 4-7). 1991. 12.95 (ISBN 0-525-44692-3, DCB). Dutton Child Bks.
Shaffer, Dianna. The Man Who Loved Balloons. Shaffer, Dianna, illus. 32p. (ps-8). Date not set. pap. text ed. 4.95 (ISBN 1-877995-02-9). Koala Pub Co.
Southall, Ivan. Let the Balloon Go. Weiman, Jon, illus. LC 84-5984. 144p. (gr. 4-6). 1985. 12.95 (ISBN 0-02-786220-8, Bradbury Pr). Macmillan Child Grp.
Verne, Jules. Around the World in Eighty Days. 1990. pap. 2.75 (ISBN 0-590-43053-X). Scholastic Inc.
—Round the World in Eighty Days. (gr. 9-12). 1991. pap. text ed. 4.87 (ISBN 0-582-01817-X, 78331). Longman.
Wade, Alan. I'm Flying! Mathers, Petra, illus. LC 88-31360. 40p. (gr. k-4). 1990. 13.95 (ISBN 0-394-84510-2); lib. bdg. 14.99 (ISBN 0-394-94510-7). Knopf.
Willard, Nancy. The Well-Mannered Balloon. D'Andrade, Diane, ed. Shekerjian, Hiag & Shekerjian, Regina, illus. 32p. (Orig.). (gr. k-3). 1991. pap. 3.95 (ISBN 0-15-294986-0, HJ). HarBraceJ.
Wood, Audrey. Balloonia. Wood, Audrey, illus. 32p. (ps-2). 1981. 5.50 (ISBN 0-85953-122-8, Pub. by Child's Play England). Childs Play.

BALLOT

see Elections

BALTIMORE–FICTION

Eichelberger, Rosa K. Big Fire in Baltimore. LC 78-31311. (Illus.). (gr. 3 up). 1979. pap. 7.95 (ISBN 0-916144-37-2). Stemmer Hse.

BANDITS

see Robbers and Outlaws

BANDS (MUSIC)

Kuribayashi, Pam. A Summer Madness. 79p. (Orig.). (gr. 10-12). 1988. pap. 5.95 (ISBN 0-685-22514-3). Prairie Shark Pr.

BANDS (MUSIC)–FICTION

Bowles, Brad. Grandma's Band. Chan, Anthony, illus. 48p. (gr. k-4). 1989. PLB 14.95 (ISBN 0-88045-112-2). Stemmer Hse.
Crocodile Rhythm Block. 1990. 9.98 (ISBN 0-8317-6172-5). Smithmark.
Kingsland, Robin. Bus Stop Bop. Ayliffe, Alex, illus. 32p. (ps-3). 1991. 14.95 (ISBN 0-670-83919-1). Viking Child Bks.
Parsley, Reed. Meet the Shrews. Fox, Sparky, illus. 48p. (gr. 2 up). 1991. bds. 14.00 (ISBN 0-671-74862-9, Green Tiger). S&S Trade.

BANGLADESH

Bailey, Donna & Sproule, Anna. Bangladesh. LC 90-9652. (Illus.). 32p. (gr. 2-5). 1990. PLB 14.64 (ISBN 0-8114-2559-2). Steck-V.
McClure, Vimala. Bangladesh: Rivers in a Crowded Land. LC 88-35911. (Illus.). 128p. (gr. 5 up). 1989. lib. bdg. 14.95 (ISBN 0-87518-404-9, Dillon). Macmillan Child Grp.
Wright, R. E. Bangladesh. (Illus.). (gr. 5 up). 1988. 14.95 (ISBN 0-7910-0098-2). Chelsea Hse.

BANKING

see Banks and Banking

BANKS AND BANKING

see also Credit; Investments; Money

Adler, David. Banks: Where the Money Is. Huffman, Tom, illus. LC 85-8848. 32p. (gr. 2-4). 1985. PLB 9.90 (ISBN 0-531-04878-0). Watts.
Dunnan, Nancy. Banking. Easton, Emily, ed. (Illus.). 128p. (gr. 12 up). 1990. lib. bdg. 14.98 (ISBN 0-382-09917-6); pap. 7.95 (ISBN 0-382-24028-6). Silver Burdett Pr.
Spiselman, David. A Teenagers Guide to Money, Banking & Finance. LC 87-11059. 128p. (gr. 6 up). 1989. lib. bdg. 11.29 (ISBN 0-671-64345-2); pap. 5.95 (ISBN 0-671-65979-0). Messner.

BANKS AND BANKING–VOCATIONAL GUIDANCE

Haddock, Patricia. Careers in Banking & Finance. Rosen, Ruth, ed. (gr. 7-12). 1989. PLB 12.95 (ISBN 0-8239-0962-X). Rosen Group.

BANNEKER, BENJAMIN, 1731-1806

Ferris, Jeri. What Are You Figuring Now? A Story about Benjamin Banneker. Johnson, Amy, illus. LC 88-7267. 56p. (gr. 3-6). 1988. PLB 9.95 (ISBN 0-87614-331-1); pap. 4.95 (ISBN 0-685-19616-X). Carolrhoda Bks.

BANNERS

see Flags

BAPTISM

Bothwell, H. Roger. My First Book about Baptism. (Illus.). (ps). 1978. pap. 1.95 (ISBN 0-8127-0179-8). Review & Herald.
Clawson, Jan. Baptism My Promise to Jesus. Fletcher, Amy, illus. 24p. (Orig.). (gr. 1-3). 1988. pap. 3.95 (ISBN 0-88290-298-9). Horizon Utah.
Davis, Susan. A Way to Remember. Davis, Tom, ed. 32p. (ps up). 1980. pap. 2.95 (ISBN 0-8280-0023-9). Review & Herald.
England, Kathleen. Why We Are Baptized. LC 78-19180. (Illus.). (gr. 2-5). 1978. pap. 5.95 (ISBN 0-87747-893-7). Deseret Bk.
Eynon, Dana. My New Life with Christ: Baptismal Certificate. Gehring, Jack, illus. 16p. (gr. 3-9). 1982. pap. 0.95 self-cover (ISBN 0-87239-529-4, 1177). Standard Pub.
Fogle, Jeanne S. Signs of God's Love: Baptism & Communion. Duckert, Mary J. & Lane, W. Ben, eds. Weidner, Bea, illus. 32p. (Orig.). (gr. 3-8). 1984. pap. 6.95 (ISBN 0-664-24636-2, Geneva Pr). Westminster John Knox.
Halverson, Sandy. Preparing for Baptism. 48p. (gr. 1-3). 1983. pap. 4.95 (ISBN 0-88290-233-4). Horizon-Utah.
Merrell, Karen D. Baptism. 24p. (ps-2). 1975. pap. 4.95 (ISBN 0-87747-559-8). Deseret Bk.
Todd, Richard E., ed. Baptism. Kellner, Ron, illus. 16p. (Orig.). (gr. 1-6). 1980. pap. 0.50 (ISBN 0-9605324-0-4). R E Todd.
Wittenback, Janet. God Makes Me His Child in Baptism. LC 85-7689. 24p. (gr. 2-5). 1985. pap. 2.95 (ISBN 0-570-04126-0, 56-1537). Concordia.

BAPTISTS

see also Mennonites

Jackson, Mark. Ready Set Grow! A Faith & Practice Primer for Regular Baptists. LC 89-38819. (Illus.). 112p. (Orig.). 1989. pap. text ed. 3.95 (ISBN 0-87227-138-2). Reg Baptist.

BAR

see Lawyers

BARBARY CORSAIRS

see Pirates

BARBECUE COOKING

see Outdoor Cookery

BARNUM, PHINEAS TAYLOR, 1810-1891
Tompert, Ann. The Greatest Show on Earth: A Biography of P. T. Barnum. LC 87-13600. (Illus.). 120p. (gr. 6 up). 1987. PLB 12.95 (ISBN 0-87518-370-0, Dillon). Macmillan Child Grp.
BARRISTERS
see Lawyers
BARROWS
see also Mounds and Mound Builders
BARS AND RESTAURANTS
see Restaurants, Bars, etc.
BARTON, CLARA HARLOWE, 1821-1912
Bains, Rae. Clara Barton: Angel of the Battlefield. LC 81-23123. (Illus.). 48p. (gr. 4-6). 1982. PLB 10.79 (ISBN 0-89375-752-7); pap. text ed. 2.95 (ISBN 0-89375-753-5). Troll Assocs.
Boylston, Helen D. Clara Barton, Founder of American Red Cross. (Illus.). (gr. 4-6). 1963. lib. bdg. 11.99 (ISBN 0-394-90358-7, Random Juv). Random.
Dubowski, Cathy E. Clara Barton: Healing the Wounds. (Illus.). 160p. (gr. 5 up). 1990. lib. bdg. 16.98 (ISBN 0-382-09940-0); pap. 8.95 (ISBN 0-382-24049-9). Silver Burdett Pr.
Kent, Zachary. The Story of Clara Barton. Canaday, Ralph, illus. LC 86-29899. 32p. (gr. 3-6). 1987. PLB 13.27 (ISBN 0-516-04725-6); pap. 3.95 (ISBN 0-516-44725-4). Childrens.
Klingel, Cynthia & Zadra, Dan. Clara Barton. (Illus.). 32p. 1987. 16.45 (ISBN 0-88682-168-1); PLB 11. 50s.p. (ISBN 0-685-23215-8). Creative Ed.
Rose, Mary C. Clara Barton: Soldier of Mercy. Johnson, E. Harper, illus. 80p. (gr. 2-6). 1991. Repr. of 1960 ed. PLB 12.95 (ISBN 0-7910-1403-7). Chelsea Hse.
Sonneborn, Liz. Clara Barton. (Illus.). (gr. 3-5). 1991. PLB 12.95 (ISBN 0-7910-1565-3). Chelsea Hse.
Stevenson, Augusta. Clara Barton: Founder of the American Red Cross. Giacoia, Frank, illus. LC 86-10750. 192p. (gr. 2-6). 1986. pap. 3.95 (ISBN 0-02-041820-5, Aladdin). Macmillan Child Grp.
BARUCH, BERNARD MANNES, 1870-1965
Finke, Blythe F. Bernard M. Baruch: Speculator & Statesman. Rahmas, D. Steve, ed. LC 78-190249. 32p. (Orig.). (gr. 7-12). 1972. lib. bdg. 4.20 incl. catalog cards (ISBN 0-87157-532-9); pap. 2.95 vinyl laminated covers (ISBN 0-87157-032-7). SamHar Pr.
BASEBALL
see also Little League Baseball; Softball
Aaseng, Nathan. Baseball: It's Your Team. (Illus.). 104p. (gr. 4 up). 1985. PLB 8.95 (ISBN 0-8225-1558-X). Lerner Pubns.
—Baseball: You Are the Manager. LC 82-268. (Illus.). 104p. (gr. 4up). 1983. PLB 8.95 (ISBN 0-8225-1552-0). Lerner Pubns.
—Baseball's Ace Relief Pitchers. LC 83-17585. (Illus.). 80p. (gr. 4up). 1984. PLB 7.95 (ISBN 0-8225-1334-X). Lerner Pubns.
—Baseball's Power Hitters. LC 83-1025. (Illus.). 80p. (gr. 4up). 1983. PLB 7.95 (ISBN 0-8225-1332-3). Lerner Pubns.
—Steve Carlton: Baseball's Silent Strongman. LC 83-17516. (Illus.). 64p. (gr. 4-9). 1984. PLB 8.95 (ISBN 0-8225-0491-X). Lerner Pubns.
—You Are the Manager: Baseball. 112p. (gr. 5 up). 1984. pap. 1.95 (ISBN 0-440-99829-8, LFL). Dell.
Alvarez, Mark. The Official Baseball Hall of Fame Answer Book. (gr. 3 up). 1989. pap. 6.95 (ISBN 0-671-67377-7, Little Simon). S&S Trade.
Appel, Marty. The First Book of Baseball. rev. ed. (Illus.). (gr. 2 up). 1988. 3.95 (ISBN 0-517-57264-8). Crown.
Arnow, Jan. Louisville Slugger: The Making of a Baseball Bat. Arnow, Jan, photos by. LC 84-7049. (Illus.). 48p. (gr. 3-7). 1984. 11.95 (ISBN 0-394-86297-X, Pant Bks Young); lib. bdg. 12.99 (ISBN 0-394-96297-4). Pantheon.
Ashburn, Richie & Lewis, Allen. Richie Ashburn's Phillies Trivia. LC 83-3335. (Illus.). 128p. (Orig.). (gr. 5 up). 1983. lib. bdg. 15.90 (ISBN 0-89471-220-9); pap. 7.95 (ISBN 0-89471-219-5). Running Pr.
Aylesworth, Thomas G. The Kids' World Almanac of Baseball. Lane, John, illus. Hershiser, Orel, intro. by. (Illus.). 288p. 1990. text ed. 14.95 (ISBN 0-88687-463-7); pap. 6.95 (ISBN 0-88687-563-3). Pharos Bks NY.
Baseball Card Collecting Kit. (Illus., Orig.). (gr. 5-9). 1991. pap. 4.95 (ISBN 0-942025-53-9). Kidsbks.
Benagh, Jim. Baseball: The Startling Stories Behind the Records. LC 86-30137. (Illus.). 128p. 1987. 12.95 (ISBN 0-8069-6402-2); lib. bdg. 15.69 (ISBN 0-8069-6403-0). Sterling.
Bloom, Marc. Baseball. (Illus.). 64p. (gr. 3-7). 1991. pap. 2.95 (ISBN 0-590-43314-8). Scholastic Inc.
Broekel, Ray. Baseball. LC 81-38480. (Illus.). 48p. (gr. k-4). 1982. PLB 14.60 (ISBN 0-516-01616-4); pap. 4.95 (ISBN 0-516-41616-2). Childrens.
Burchard, S. H. Sports Star: Fernando Valenzuela. LC 82-47932. (Illus.). 64p. (ps-3). 1982. 8.95 (ISBN 0-15-278044-0, HJ). HarBraceJ.
Campanis, Al. Play Ball with Roger the Dodger. Hoff, Syd, illus. 80p. (gr. 1-5). 1980. pap. 3.95 (ISBN 0-399-20711-2, Putnam). Putnam Pub Group.
Carroll, Bob. The Major League Way to Play Baseball. (Illus.). 96p. (gr. 3 up). 1991. bds. 12.95 (ISBN 0-671-73316-8, Little Simon); pap. 5.95 (ISBN 0-671-70441-9, Little Simon). S&S Trade.
—The Official Baseball Hall of Fame Fun & Fact Sticker Book. Carroll, Bob, illus. (gr. 3 up). 1989. pap. 7.95 (ISBN 0-671-67378-5, Little Simon). S&S Trade.
—Official Baseball Hall of Fame Sticker Book of Records. 1990. pap. 7.95 (ISBN 0-671-69091-4). S&S Trade.
—This Year in Baseball - 1991. (Illus.). 160p. (gr. 3 up). 1991. pap. 3.95 (ISBN 0-671-70439-7, Little Simon). S&S Trade.
Cawley, Sherry. Braves Fun Book I. 80p. (Orig.). 1986. pap. 3.95 (ISBN 0-937511-00-5). Fun Bk Enter.
Cebulash, Mel. Baseball Players Do Amazing Things. (Illus.). (gr. 2-5). 1973. 7.95 (ISBN 0-394-82611-6, Random Juv). Random.
Childress, Casey & McKenzie, Linda. A Beginner's Guide to Baseball Card Collecting: A Step-by-Step Guide for the Young Collector. LC 88-90757. (Illus.). 46p. (Orig.). (gr. 4-8). 1990. Repr. of 1988 ed. vinyl covers 7.95 (ISBN 0-9620167-0-5). C Mack Pub.
Cohen, Eliot. My Greatest Day in Baseball. (Illus.). 160p. (gr. 3 up). 1991. bds. 11.95 (ISBN 0-671-73319-2, Little Simon); pap. 3.95 (ISBN 0-671-70440-0, Little Simon). S&S Trade.
Cohen, Neil. The Official Baseball Hall of Fame Scorebook. (gr. 3 up). 1989. pap. 4.95 (ISBN 0-671-67380-7, Little Simon). S&S Trade.
Crose, Mark. Make the Team: Baseball. (gr. 4-7). 1991. pap. 5.95 (ISBN 0-316-16207-8). Little.
Dagavarian, Debra A., ed. A Century of Children's Baseball Stories, No. 2. 190p. (Orig.). (gr. 5 up). 1991. pap. 7.95 (ISBN 0-9625132-2-9). Meckler Corp.
Downing, Joan. Baseball Is Our Game. LC 82-4418. (Illus.). (gr. k-3). 1982. PLB 15.93 (ISBN 0-516-03402-2); pap. 3.95 (ISBN 0-516-43402-0). Childrens.
Feldman, Jay. Hitting. (Illus.). 96p. (gr. 5 up). 1991. bds. 12.95 (ISBN 0-671-73318-4, Little Simon); pap. 5.95 (ISBN 0-671-70442-7, Little Simon). S&S Trade.
Ferroli, Stephen J. Disciple of a Master (How to Hit a Baseball to Your Potential) Dickenson, Ken, illus. 200p. (Orig.). (gr. 7-12). 1986. pap. 9.95 (ISBN 0-939905-00-0). Line Drive.
Fertig, Dennis. Take Me Out to the Ball Game. Fay, Ann, ed. McMahon, William F., illus. 40p. (ps-3). 1987. PLB 10.95 (ISBN 0-8075-7735-9). A Whitman.
Foley, Red. Red Foley's Best Baseball Book Ever. Lieman, Jane, illus. 96p. (gr. 1 up). 1987. pap. 6.95 (ISBN 0-317-53000-3, Little Simon). S&S Trade.
—Red Foley's Best Baseball Book Ever. 5th, rev. & updated ed. (Illus.). 96p. (gr. 1 up). 1991. pap. 7.95 incl. stickers (ISBN 0-671-72723-0, Little Simon). S&S Trade.
Freeman, Mark. Squeeze Play. 144p. (gr. 7-9). 1989. pap. 2.95 (ISBN 0-345-35903-8). Ballantine.
Gelman, Mitch. World Series Pressure. Fiorentino, Al, illus. 128p. (Orig.). (gr. 4 up). 1984. pap. 1.95 (ISBN 0-671-47577-0, Archway). PB.
Gerberg, Mort. Bear-ly Bear-able Baseball Riddles, Jokes, & Knock-Knocks. 32p. (Orig.). (gr. 1-3). 1989. pap. 2.50 (ISBN 0-590-42583-8). Scholastic Inc.
Greene, Carol. I Can Be a Baseball Player. LC 84-23222. (Illus.). 32p. (gr. k-3). 1985. lib. bdg. 13.93 (ISBN 0-516-01845-0); pap. 3.95 (ISBN 0-516-41845-9). Childrens.
—Puedo Ser Jugador de Beisbol. Kratky, Lada, tr. LC 86-996. (SPA., Illus.). 32p. (gr. k-3). 1986. PLB 13.93 (ISBN 0-516-31845-4); pap. 3.95 (ISBN 0-516-51845-3). Childrens.
Gutelle, Andrew. Baseball's Best: Five True Stories. Spohn, Cliff, illus. LC 89-35413. 48p. (Orig.). (gr. 2-4). 1990. lib. bdg. 6.99 (ISBN 0-394-90983-6); pap. 2.95 (ISBN 0-394-80983-1). Random.
Gutman, Bill. Go for It: Baseball. Brown, Ben, illus. 64p. (gr. 4 up). 1989. PLB 16.50 (ISBN 0-942545-84-2). Grey Castle.
—Sports Illustrated Strange & Amazing Baseball Stories. 128p. (gr. 5 up). 1990. pap. 2.75 (ISBN 0-671-70120-7, Archway). PB.
Hale, Creighton H. Official Little League Baseball Rules in Pictures. (Illus.). 80p. (gr. 3-7). 1981. pap. 4.95 (ISBN 0-399-50824-4, Perigee Bks). Putnam Pub Group.
Hall, Katy & Eisenberg, Lisa. Baseball Bloopers. Callen, Liz, illus. LC 89-62210. 96p. (Orig.). (gr. 2-6). 1991. pap. 2.95 (ISBN 0-679-80335-1). Random.
—Oddball Baseball. Callen, Liz, illus. LC 89-62206. 96p. (Orig.). (gr. 2-6). 1991. pap. 2.95 (ISBN 0-679-80336-X). Random.
Highlights for Children Staff. Baseball. Highlights for Children Staff, illus. 48p. (gr. 3-7). 1990. pap. 2.95 (ISBN 0-87534-350-3). Highlights.
Horenstein, Henry. Spring Training. LC 87-34842. 48p. (gr. 3 up). 1988. 15.95 (ISBN 0-02-744440-6, Mcmillan Child Bk). Macmillan Child Grp.
Jarrett, William. Timetables of Sports History: Baseball. (Illus.). 96p. (gr. 6 up). 1989. 17.95 (ISBN 0-8160-1918-5). Facts on File.
Kalb, Jonah. The Easy Baseball Book. Kossin, Sandy, illus. LC 75-44085. 64p. (gr. 2-5). 1976. 14.95 (ISBN 0-395-24385-8). HM.
Kaplan, Jim. The Official Baseball Hall of Fame Book of Super Stars. (gr. 3 up). 1989. pap. 4.95 (ISBN 0-671-67379-3, Little Simon). S&S Trade.
Koosman, Jerry. Jerry Koosman's Guide for Young Pitchers. Meyers, Susan, ed. Oster, Don, et al. (Illus., Orig.). (gr. 2-6). pap. 5.95 (ISBN 0-9618437-0-5). Young Creations.
LaZebnik, Ken & Lehman, Steve. A Is for At Bat: A Baseball Primer. Nelson, Andy, illus. 32p. (ps-1). 1988. 8.95 (ISBN 0-929636-00-7). Culpepper Pr.

Maitland, William J. Young Ball Player's Guide to Safe Pitching: Ages Eight Thru Adult. (Illus.). 140p. (gr. 3 up). 1991. pap. 14.95 (ISBN 0-936759-14-3). Maitland Enter.
YOUNG BALL PLAYER'S GUIDE TO SAFE PITCHING - AGES EIGHT THRU ADULT shows safe methods of throwing the baseball with power & accuracy. Conditioning & strength training to develop the power throw & prevent injury to the developing arm of the young athlete. Black & white photos show methods of training the entire body to deliver the pitch, thus preventing injury to the crucial growth plates of the elbow. Action photos on the mound show the importance of the legs in power delivery for pitching or just throwing. Photos show the finger control possible when threads of the ball are positioned differently. This method teaches a safer method of pitching negating the use of the curveball at the arm's crucial stages of development. The end result will be a longer, injury-free baseball development. Author coached-trained young players thirty years (some now in minor leagues or received college scholarships for baseball). "I feel Maitland's books are well researched deserving the consideration of trainers, coaches, teachers, students & parents who must present a clear, concise & effective program. I highly recommend his works."--Dr. Art Mollen. Ben Franklin Book Award Nominee. Discounts 20%-40% to retailers, wholesalers to be set.
Publisher Provided Annotation.

—Young Ballplayers Guide to Safe Pitching - Ages 8 through Adult. Barclay, John, ed. Molen, Art, intro. by. (Illus.). 150p. (gr. 4 up). 1991. pap. write for info. (ISBN 0-936759-02-X). Maitland Enter.
Nuwer, Hank. Strategies of the Great Baseball Managers. Solomon, Maury, ed. (Illus.). 160p. (gr. 7 up). 1988. PLB 13.90 (ISBN 0-531-10601-2). Watts.
Palmer, Pete & Thom, John, eds. The Baseball Record Book. (Illus.). 96p. (gr. 3 up). 1991. pap. 5.95 (ISBN 0-671-70444-3, Little Simon). S&S Trade.
Plaut, David. Start Collecting Baseball Cards. LC 89-43016. (Illus.). 96p. (Orig.). (gr. 4 up). 1989. pap. 9.95 (ISBN 0-89471-762-6). Running Pr.
Playbook! Baseball: You Are the Manager, You Call the Shots. (gr. 3-7). 1990. pap. 4.95 (ISBN 0-316-83624-9). Little.
Red Foley's Best Baseball Book Ever. 3rd ed. (gr. 1 up). 1989. pap. 7.95 (ISBN 0-671-67376-9, Little Simon). S&S Trade.
Reiter. Rainy Day Baseball Games. 1991. pap. 2.95 (ISBN 0-8431-2812-7). Price Stern.
Rosenblum, Richard. Brooklyn Dodger Days. Rosenblum, Richard, illus. LC 90-36691. 32p. (gr. 1-5). 1991. SBE 12.95 (ISBN 0-689-31512-0, Atheneum Child Bk). Macmillan Child Grp.
Schlossberg, Dan. Pitching. (Illus.). 96p. (gr. 5 up). 1991. bds. 12.95 (ISBN 0-671-73317-6, Little Simon); pap. 5.95 (ISBN 0-671-70443-5, Little Simon). S&S Trade.
Shirts, Morris A. Warm up for Little League Baseball. rev. ed. (Illus.). (gr. 3-6). 1990. pap. 2.75 (ISBN 0-671-70119-3, Archway). PB.
Solomon, Chuck. Major-League Batboy. Solomon, Chuck, photos by. LC 90-43275. (Illus.). 32p. (gr. 2-5). 1991. 11.95 (ISBN 0-517-58244-9); PLB 12.99 (ISBN 0-517-58245-7). Crown.
Sporting News Staff. The Sporting News Baseball Guide for Kids: 1990. (Illus.). 96p. (gr. 7-12). 1990. pap. 5.95 (ISBN 0-89204-348-2). Sporting News.
Sullivan, George. The Art of Base-Stealing. (Illus.). 128p. (gr. 7-11). 1982. 11.95 (ISBN 0-396-08040-5, Putnam). Putnam Pub Group.
—Baseball Kids. LC 89-29102. (Illus.). 64p. (gr. 5 up). 1990. 13.95 (ISBN 0-525-65023-7, Cobblehill Bks). Dutton Child Bks.
—Better Baseball for Boys. (Illus.). 64p. (gr. 3-7). 1981. 10.99 (ISBN 0-685-25369-4, Putnam); pap. 2.95 (ISBN 0-396-08288-2, Putnam). Putnam Pub Group.
—Big League Spring Training. LC 88-28423. (Illus.). 128p. (gr. 4-8). 1989. 14.95 (ISBN 0-8050-0838-1). H Holt & Co.
—Pitcher. Madden, Don, illus. LC 85-47939. 64p. (gr. 4-7). 1986. PLB 10.89 (ISBN 0-690-04539-5, Crowell Jr Bks). HarpC Child Bks.

Supraner, Robyn. I Can Read About Baseball. LC 74-24926. (Illus.). (gr. 2-4). 1975. pap. 1.95 (ISBN 0-89375-062-X). Troll Assocs.
Weber, Bruce. Bruce Weber: Inside Baseball 1989. 1989. pap. 2.25 (ISBN 0-590-42449-1). Scholastic Inc.
—Bruce Weber: Inside Baseball 1990. 1990. pap. 2.25 (ISBN 0-590-43463-2). Scholastic Inc.
—Bruce Weber's Inside Baseball 1986. (Illus.). 112p. (Orig.). (gr. 7 up). 1986. pap. 1.95 (ISBN 0-590-40271-4). Scholastic Inc.
—Bruce Weber's Inside Baseball, 1988. (Illus.). 112p. (gr. 4 up). 1988. pap. 2.25 (ISBN 0-590-41716-9). Scholastic Inc.
—Inside Baseball, 1991. (gr. 4-7). 1991. pap. 2.25 (ISBN 0-590-44708-4). Scholastic Inc.
Weiner, Eric. The Kids Complete Baseball Catalogue. (Illus.). 256p. (gr. 5 up). 1991. lib. bdg. 15.98 (ISBN 0-671-70196-7); pap. 12.95 (ISBN 0-671-70197-5). Messner.

BASEBALL–BIOGRAPHY

Aaseng, Nathan. Baseball: It's Your Team. (gr. k-12). 1987. pap. 2.50 (ISBN 0-440-90507-9, LFL). Dell.
—Baseball's Finest Pitchers. LC 80-12275. (Illus.). 72p. (gr. 4 up). 1980. PLB 7.95 (ISBN 0-8225-1061-8). Lerner Pubns.
—Dwight Gooden: Strikeout King. (Illus.). 56p. (gr. 4-9). 1988. PLB 8.95 (ISBN 0-8225-0478-2, First Ave Edns); pap. 3.95 (ISBN 0-8225-9549-4, First Ave Edns). Lerner Pubns.
—Jose Canseco: Baseball's Forty-Forty Man. (Illus.). 56p. (gr. 4-9). 1989. PLB 8.95 (ISBN 0-8225-0493-6). Lerner Pubns.
—Pete Rose: Baseball's Charlie Hustle. LC 79-27377. (Illus.). 48p. (gr. 4-9). 1981. PLB 8.95 (ISBN 0-8225-0480-4). Lerner Pubns.
Aces of the Mound. (Illus.). 24p. (gr. 1 up). 1991. pap. 3.95 incl. stickers (ISBN 0-671-73635-3, Little Simon). S&S Trade.
Balzar, Howard. Baseball Super Stars. Allison, B., intro. by. (Illus.). 23p. (Orig.). (gr. 1-8). 1990. pap. 2.50 (ISBN 0-943409-14-4). Marketcom.
—Baseball Superstars. Allison, B., intro. by. 29p. (Orig.). Date not set. pap. 4.95 (ISBN 0-943409-18-7). Marketcom.
Buck, Ray. Cal Ripken, Jr. All Star Shortstop. LC 85-485. (Illus.). 41p. (gr. 2-8). 1985. lib. bdg. 13.27 (ISBN 0-516-04343-9). Childrens.
Clark, Steve. Wade Boggs: Baseball's Star Hitter. LC 87-33292. (Illus.). 64p. (gr. 3 up). 1988. PLB 10.95 (ISBN 0-87518-377-8, Dillon). Macmillan Child Grp.
Curato, Guy, pseud. Batting One Thousand - Baseball's Leading Hitters: A Tribute to Lou Gehrig. LC 88-82916. 124p. (Orig.). (gr. 9). 1989. pap. write for info. (ISBN 0-9621591-0-7). T Assicurato.
Devaney, John. Bo Jackson: A Star for All Seasons. (gr. 7 up). 1988. 13.95 (ISBN 0-8027-6818-0); PLB 14.85 (ISBN 0-8027-6819-9). Walker & Co.
—Sports Great Roger Clemens. 64p. (gr. 4-10). 1990. 15.95 (ISBN 0-89490-284-9). Enslow Pubs.
Frommer, Harvey. Baseball's Hall of Fame. LC 85-5337. (Illus.). 66p. (gr. 3-6). 1985. PLB 10.40 (ISBN 0-531-04904-3). Watts.
—Jackie Robinson. 128p. (gr. 7-12). 1984. lib. bdg. 12.90 (ISBN 0-531-04858-6). Watts.
Gilbert, Tom. Roberto Clemente. (Illus.). 112p. (gr. 5 up). 1991. PLB 17.95 (ISBN 0-7910-1240-9). Chelsea Hse.
Gloeckner, Carolyn. Fernando Valenzuela. (Illus.). 48p. (gr. 5-6). 1985. PLB 10.95 (ISBN 0-89686-256-9, Crestwood Hse). Macmillan Child Grp.
Gutman, Bill. Baseball's Hot New Stars. (Orig.). (gr. 5 up). 1989. pap. 2.75 (ISBN 0-671-68724-7, Archway). PB.
Hit Men. (Illus.). 24p. (gr. 1 up). 1991. pap. 3.95 incl. stickers (ISBN 0-671-73637-X, Little Simon). S&S Trade.
Home Run Kings. (Illus.). 24p. (gr. 1 up). 1991. pap. 3.95 incl. stickers (ISBN 0-671-73636-1, Little Simon). S&S Trade.
Humphrey, Kathryn L. Satchel Paige. Sloan, Frank, ed. (Illus.). 128p. (gr. 7-12). 1988. PLB 13.90 (ISBN 0-531-10513-X). Watts.
Johnson, Rick. Jim Abbott. (Illus.). 64p. (gr. 3 up). 1991. PLB 10.95 (ISBN 0-87518-459-6, Dillon). Macmillan Child Grp.
Johnstone, Jay & Talley, Rick. Some of My Best Friends Are Crazy: Baseball's Favorite Lunatic Goes in Search of His Peers. (Illus.). 228p. 1990. 18.95 (ISBN 0-02-559560-1). Macmillan.
Kaplan, Jim. Book of Superstars. 2nd ed. (gr. 4-7). 1990. pap. 4.95 (ISBN 0-671-69092-2, Little Simon). S&S Trade.
Kavanagh, Jack. Rogers Hornsby. Murray, Jim, intro. by. (Illus.). 64p. (gr. 3 up). 1991. PLB 14.95 (ISBN 0-7910-1178-X). Chelsea Hse.
—Walter Johnson. (Illus.). 64p. (gr. 3 up). 1992. PLB 14.95 (ISBN 0-7910-1179-8). Chelsea Hse.
Klein, Dave. Stars of the Major Leagues. LC 73-18739. (Illus.). 160p. (gr. 7-12). 1974. lib. bdg. 3.69 (ISBN 0-394-92762-1, Random Juv). Random.
Littwin, Mike. Fernando Valenzuela: The Screwball Artist. LC 82-23611. (Illus.). 48p. (gr. 2-8). 1983. PLB 13.27 (ISBN 0-516-04331-5); pap. 3.95 (ISBN 0-516-44331-3). Childrens.
Lundgren, Hal. Ryne Sandberg: The Triple Threat. LC 85-29895. (Illus.). 48p. (gr. 2-8). 1986. PLB 13.27 (ISBN 0-516-04357-9); pap. 3.95 (ISBN 0-516-44357-7). Childrens.
Macht, Norm. Jimmie Foxx. Murray, Jim, intro. by. (Illus.). 64p. (gr. 3 up). 1991. PLB 14.95 (ISBN 0-7910-1175-5). Chelsea Hse.
Macht, Norman L. Cy Young. (Illus.). 64p. (gr. 3 up). 1992. PLB 14.95 (ISBN 0-7910-1196-8). Chelsea Hse.
Martin, Patricia S. Dale Murphy: Baseball's Gentle Giant. (Illus.). 24p. (gr. 1-4). 1987. PLB 12.33 (ISBN 0-86592-167-9). Rourke Corp.
Modern Pub. NYC Staff. New Kids on the Block. (Illus.). 64p. (gr. 2-6). 1990. pap. 2.50 (ISBN 0-87449-823-6). Modern Pub NYC.
Monroe, Judy. Dave Winfield. LC 87-30503. (Illus.). 48p. (gr. 5-6). 1988. PLB 10.95 (ISBN 0-89686-370-0, Crestwood Hse). Macmillan Child Grp.
Motomora, Mitchell. Specs: The True Story of Baseball Player George Toporcer. Barbaresi, Nina, illus. 24p. (ps-2). 1990. 12.33 (ISBN 0-8172-3585-X); PLB 9.25. Raintree Pubs.
Murphy, Jim. Baseball's All-Time All-Stars. LC 83-14977. (Illus.). 128p. (gr. 4 up). 1984. 13.95 (ISBN 0-89919-229-7, Clarion). HM.
Nash, Bruce. Little Big Leaguers: Amazing Boyhood Stories of Today's Baseball Stars. (gr. 4-7). 1990. pap. 7.95 (ISBN 0-671-69360-3). S&S Trade.
Nash, Bruce & Zullo, Allan. More Little Big Leaguers: Amazing Boyhood Stories of Today's Baseball Stars. (Illus.). 96p. (gr. 1 up). 1991. pap. 7.95 incl. baseball cards (ISBN 0-671-73394-X, Little Simon). S&S Trade.
Newman, Matthew. Dwight Gooden. LC 86-16527. (Illus.). 48p. (gr. 5-6). PLB 10.95 (ISBN 0-89686-317-4, Crestwood Hse). Macmillan Child Grp.
Record Breakers. (Illus.). 24p. (gr. 1 up). 1991. pap. 3.95 (ISBN 0-671-73634-5, Little Simon). S&S Trade.
Rolfe, John. Bo Jackson. (gr. 4-7). 1991. pap. 4.95 (ISBN 0-316-75457-9). Little.
—Jim Abbott: Sports Illustrated Kids. (gr. 4-7). 1991. pap. 4.95 (ISBN 0-316-75459-5). Little.
Rosenthal, Bert. Dwight Gooden: King of the Ks. LC 85-11687. (Illus.). 48p. (gr. 2-5). 1985. PLB 13.27 (ISBN 0-516-04348-X); pap. 3.95 (ISBN 0-516-44348-8). Childrens.
Shannon, Mike. Willie Stargell. (Illus.). 64p. (gr. 3 up). 1992. PLB 14.95 (ISBN 0-7910-1192-5). Chelsea Hse.
Sloate, Susan. Hotshots: Baseball. (gr. 4-7). 1991. 17.95 (ISBN 0-316-79853-3). Little.
Stocker, Fern N. Billy Sunday: Baseball Preacher. (Orig.). (gr. 6). 1985. pap. text ed. 3.95 (ISBN 0-8024-0442-1). Moody.
Torres, J. A. & Sullivan, M. J. Sports Great Darryl Strawberry. 64p. (gr. 4-10). 1990. 15.95 (ISBN 0-89490-291-1). Enslow Pubs.
Walker, Paul R. Pride of Puerto Rico: The Life of Roberto Clemente. 144p. (gr. 8-12). 1988. 11.95 (ISBN 0-15-200562-5, Gulliver Bks). HarBraceJ.
Weber, Bruce. Sparky Anderson. LC 88-14985. (Illus.). 48p. (gr. 5-6). 1988. PLB 10.95 (ISBN 0-89686-379-4, Crestwood Hse). Macmillan Child Grp.

BASEBALL–DICTIONARIES

Hollander, Zander & Hollander, Phyllis. The Baseball Book: A Complete A to Z Encyclopedia of Baseball. LC 81-14384. (Illus.). 160p. (gr. 5 up). 1982. pap. 6.95 (ISBN 0-394-84296-0). Random.
Hollander, Zander, ed. The Baseball Book. rev. ed. LC 90-38060. (Illus.). 192p. (gr. 5 up). 1991. PLB 13.99 (ISBN 0-679-91055-7); pap. 9.95 (ISBN 0-679-81055-2). Random.
Walker, Henry. Illustrated Baseball Dictionary for Young People. Kessler, Leonard, illus. (gr. 4 up). 1978. pap. 2.50 (ISBN 0-13-450924-2, Pub. by Treehouse). P-H.

BASEBALL–FICTION

Aaseng, Nathan. Winning Season for the Braves. LC 82-72711. 1988. pap. 4.49 (ISBN 1-55513-950-7, Chariot Bks). Cook.
Adler, David A. Cam Jansen & the Mystery of the Babe Ruth Baseball. Natti, Susanna, illus. (gr. 1-4). 1984. pap. 2.75 (ISBN 0-440-41020-7, YB). Dell.
—Jeffrey's Ghost & the Leftover Baseball Team. Jenkins, Jean, illus. LC 83-22662. 64p. (gr. 2-4). 1984. 8.95 (ISBN 0-03-069282-2). H Holt & Co.
Aiello, Barbara & Shulman, Jeffrey. It's Your Turn at Bat: Featuring Mark Riley. Barr, Loel, illus. 48p. (gr. 3-6). 1988. PLB 12.95 (ISBN 0-941477-02-9). TFC Bks MD.
Bee, Clair. Dugout Jinx. (Illus.). 208p. 1990. Repr. lib. bdg. 16.95x (ISBN 0-89966-741-4). Buccaneer Bks.
Bonner. Two-Way Pitcher. (gr. 7 up). PLB 6.70 (ISBN 0-8313-0008-6). Lantern.
Bowen, Robert S. Infield Flash. LC 69-14320. (gr. 7-12). 1969. PLB 11.88 (ISBN 0-688-51007-8). Lothrop.
Cebulash, Mel. Ruth Marini: Dodger Ace. LC 82-20383. 144p. (gr. 4up). 1983. PLB 8.95 (ISBN 0-8225-0726-9). Lerner Pubns.
—Ruth Marini: World Series Star. 144p. (gr. 4 up). 1985. 8.95 (ISBN 0-8225-0727-7). Lerner Pubns.
Christopher, Matt. Baseball Pals. Henneberger, Robert, illus. (gr. 4-6). 1990. lib. bdg. 12.95 (ISBN 0-316-13950-5); pap. 3.95 (ISBN 0-316-14005-8). Little.
—Catcher with a Glass Arm. Caddell, Foster, illus. (gr. 4-6). 1985. pap. 3.95 (ISBN 0-316-13985-8). Little.
—The Dog That Pitched a No-Hitter. Vasconcellos, Daniel, illus. (gr. 1-3). 1988. 11.95 (ISBN 0-316-14057-0). Little.
—The Hit-Away Kid. (gr. 2-4). 1988. 9.95 (ISBN 0-316-13995-5). Little.
—Johnny No Hit. Burns, Raymond, illus. LC 77-5488. (gr. 1-3). 1977. 12.95 (ISBN 0-316-13974-2). Little.
—The Kid Who Only Hit Homers. Kidder, Harvey, illus. (gr. 4-6). 1972. lib. bdg. 13.95 (ISBN 0-316-13918-1). Little.
—The Kid Who Only Hit Homers. Kidder, Harvey, illus. 160p. (gr. 4 up). 1986. pap. 3.95 (ISBN 0-316-13987-4). Little.
—Look Who's Playing First Base. Kidder, Harvey, illus. (gr. 4-6). 1987. lib. bdg. 13.95 (ISBN 0-316-13933-5); pap. 3.95 (ISBN 0-316-13989-0). Little.
—Lucky Baseball Bat. (ps-3). 1991. 10.95 (ISBN 0-316-14073-2). Little.
—The Spy on Third Base. Ulrich, George, illus. LC 88-8914. (gr. 2-4). 1988. 10.95 (ISBN 0-316-13996-3). Little.
—Spy on Third Base, Vol. 1. (ps-3). 1990. pap. 2.95 (ISBN 0-316-14008-2). Little.
—The Year Mom Won the Pennant. LC 68-11110. (Illus.). (gr. 4-6). 1973. lib. bdg. 12.95 (ISBN 0-316-13954-8). Little.
—The Year Mom Won the Pennant. Caddell, Foster, illus. 160p. (gr. 4 up). 1986. pap. 3.95 (ISBN 0-316-13988-2). Little.
Cohen, Barbara. Thank You, Jackie Robinson. Cuffari, Richard, illus. LC 87-29341. (gr. 3-6). 1988. PLB 13.95 (ISBN 0-688-07909-1). Lothrop.
Cohen, Dan. The Case of the Battling Ball Clubs. Overlie, George, illus. LC 79-84356. 32p. (gr. 1-4). 1979. PLB 5.95 (ISBN 0-87614-101-7). Carolrhoda Bks.
Cooper, John R. Mel Martin: First Base Jinx. 208p. (gr. 3-7). 1982. 8.95 (ISBN 0-671-44539-1, Little Simon); pap. 2.95 (ISBN 0-671-44548-0). S&S Trade.
Cornwell, Anita. The Girls of Summer. Caines, Kelly, illus. LC 88-64051. 100p. (Orig.). (gr. 6 up). 1989. pap. 12.95 (ISBN 0-938678-11-6). New Seed.
Curtis, Gavin. Grandma's Baseball. Curtis, Gavin, illus. LC 89-22227. 32p. (ps-2). 1990. 12.95 (ISBN 0-517-57389-X); PLB 13.99 (ISBN 0-517-57390-3). Crown.
Dagavarian, Debra. Century of Children's Baseball Stories. (gr. 4-7). 1990. pap. 7.95 (ISBN 0-9625132-0-2). Stadium Bks.
Dixon, Michael B., et al. Striking Out! (Orig.). (gr. k up). 1984. pap. 4.50 (ISBN 0-87602-252-2). Anchorage.
Dolan, Ellen M. & Bolinske, Janet L., eds. Casey at the Bat. LC 87-61667. (Illus.). 32p. (Orig.). (gr. 1-3). 1987. text ed. 8.95 (ISBN 0-88335-558-2); pap. text ed. 4.95 (ISBN 0-88335-578-7). Milliken Pub Co.
Downing, Joan. El Beisbol Es Nuestro Juego. Kratky, Lada, tr. from ENG. Freeman, Tony, illus. LC 82-4418. (SPA.). 32p. (gr. k-3). 1984. lib. bdg. 15.93 (ISBN 0-516-33402-6); pap. 3.95 (ISBN 0-516-53402-5). Childrens.
Dygard, Thomas J. The Rookie Arrives. LC 87-26238. 208p. (gr. 7 up). 1988. 12.95 (ISBN 0-688-07598-3). Morrow Jr Bks.
Economos, Chris. The New Kid. (Illus.). 32p. (gr. 1-4). 1989. PLB 13.32 (ISBN 0-8172-3512-4). Raintree Pubs.
Ellis, Lucy. Pink Parrots - The Girls Strike Back: The Making of the Pink Parrots. (gr. 4-7). 1990. pap. 3.50 (ISBN 0-316-71967-6). Little.
Ethridge, Kenneth E. Viola, Furgy, Bobbi & Me. LC 88-28429. 168p. 1989. 13.95 (ISBN 0-8234-0746-2). Holiday.
Franklin, Lance. Double Play. 144p. (gr. 6 up). 1987. pap. 2.50 (ISBN 0-553-26526-1, Starfire). Bantam.
Freeman, Mark. Big League Break. 144p. (gr. 4 up). 1989. pap. 2.95 (ISBN 0-345-35904-6). Ballantine.
—Play Ball. 144p. (gr. 4 up). 1989. pap. 2.95 (ISBN 0-345-35902-X). Ballantine.
Gallina, Michael & Gallina, Jill. The Inside Pitch. Singer's ed. (gr. k-6). 1989. 2.95 (ISBN 0-931205-47-6); tchr's. ed. 14.95 (ISBN 0-931205-46-8). Jenson Pubns.
Giff, Patricia R. Left-Handed Shortstop. Morrill, Leslie, illus. 128p. (gr. k-6). 1989. pap. 2.95 (ISBN 0-440-44672-4, YB). Dell.
—Left-Handed Shortstop. Morrill, Leslie, illus. (gr. 4-6). 1980. pap. 11.95 (ISBN 0-385-28533-7); pap. 11.95 (ISBN 0-385-28534-5). Delacorte.
—Ronald Morgan Goes to Bat. Natti, Susanna, illus. 32p. (gr. k-4). 1988. pap. 10.95 (ISBN 0-670-81457-1). Viking Child Bks.
—Ronald Morgan Goes to Bat. Natti, Susanna, illus. 32p. (ps-3). 1990. pap. 3.95 (ISBN 0-14-050669-1, Puffin). Puffin Bks.
Gordon, Sharon. Play Ball, Kate! Page, Don, illus. LC 81-4855. 32p. (gr. k-2). 1981. pap. text ed. 10.89 (ISBN 0-89375-525-7); pap. 2.95 (ISBN 0-89375-526-5). Troll Assocs.
Grosser, Morton. The Fabulous Fifty. LC 89-77999. 240p. (gr. 7 up). 1990. 14.95 (ISBN 0-689-31656-9, Atheneum Child Bk). Macmillan Child Grp.
Halecroft, David. Wild Pitch. (Illus.). 128p. (gr. 3-7). 1991. pap. 2.95 (ISBN 0-14-034548-5, Puffin). Puffin Bks.
Hallowell, Tommy. Duel on the Diamond. 128p. (gr. 3 up). 1990. pap. 2.95 (ISBN 0-14-032910-2, Puffin). Puffin Bks.
—Duel on the Diamond. 1991. pap. 12.95 (ISBN 0-670-83729-6). Viking Child Bks.
Haynes, Mary. The Great Pretenders. LC 90-32162. 144p. (gr. 4-7). 1990. 12.95 (ISBN 0-02-743452-4, Bradbury Pr). Macmillan Child Grp.
Heller, Pete. Peppy Learns to Play Baseball. Kinsey, Thomas D., ed. Schaeffer, Bob, illus. 32p. (gr. k-5). pap. 3.95 (ISBN 0-932423-00-0). Summa Pub.

Hughes, Dean. All Together Now, Bk. 14. Lyall, Dennis, illus. LC 90-49458. 112p. (Orig.). (gr. 2-6). 1991. PLB 6.99 (ISBN 0-679-91541-9, Bullseye Bks); pap. 2.95 (ISBN 0-679-81541-4, Bullseye Bks). Knopf.
—Big Base Hit. Lyall, Dennis, illus. LC 89-37875. 96p. (Orig.). (gr. 2-6). 1990. PLB 6.99 (ISBN 0-679-90427-1); pap. 2.95 (ISBN 0-679-80427-7). McKay.
—Championship Game. (Illus.). 96p. (gr. 2-4). 1990. PLB 6.99 (ISBN 0-679-90433-6, Bullseye Bks); pap. 2.95 (ISBN 0-679-80433-1, Bullseye Bks). Knopf.
—Line Drive. Lyall, Dennis, illus. LC 90-1609. 96p. (Orig.). (gr. 2-6). 1990. lib. bdg. 6.99 (ISBN 0-679-90432-8, Bullseye Bks); pap. 2.95 (ISBN 0-679-80432-3, Bullseye Bks). Knopf.
—Making the Team. Lyall, Dennis, illus. LC 89-37926. 96p. (Orig.). (gr. 2-6). 1990. lib. bdg. 6.99 (ISBN 0-679-90426-3, Bullseye Bks); pap. 2.95 (ISBN 0-679-80426-9, Bullseye Bks). Knopf.
—Making the Team. Lyall, Dennis, illus. LC 89-37926. 96p. (Orig.). (gr. 2-6). 1990. lib. bdg. 6.99 (ISBN 0-679-90426-3, Bullseye Bks); pap. 2.95 (ISBN 0-679-80426-9, Bullseye Bks). Knopf.
—Play-Off, Bk. 13. Lyall, Dennis, illus. LC 90-49765. 112p. (Orig.). (gr. 2-6). 1991. PLB 6.99 (ISBN 0-679-91540-0, Bullseye Bks); pap. 2.95 (ISBN 0-679-81540-6, Bullseye Bks). Knopf.
—Rookie Star. Lyall, Dennis, illus. LC 89-28877. 96p. (gr. 2-6). 1990. PLB 6.99 (ISBN 0-679-90430-1, Bullseye Bks); pap. 2.95 (ISBN 0-679-80430-7, Bullseye Bks). Knopf.
—Safe at First, Bk. 11. Lyall, Dennis, illus. 96p. (Orig.). (gr. 2-6). 1991. PLB 6.99 (ISBN 0-679-91538-9, Bullseye Bks); pap. 2.95 (ISBN 0-679-81538-4, Bullseye Bks). Knopf.
—Stroke of Luck, Bk. 10. Lyall, Dennis, illus. LC 90-53313. 96p. (Orig.). (gr. 2-6). 1991. lib. bdg. 6.99 (ISBN 0-679-91537-0, Bullseye Bks); pap. 2.95 (ISBN 0-679-81537-6, Bullseye Bks). Knopf.
—Superstar Team, Bk. 9. Lyall, Dennis, illus. LC 90-53314. 96p. (Orig.). (gr. 2-6). 1991. lib. bdg. 6.99 (ISBN 0-679-91536-2, Bullseye Bks); pap. 2.95 (ISBN 0-679-81536-8, Bullseye Bks.). Knopf.
—Up to Bat, Bk. 12. Lyall, Dennis, illus. LC 90-49583. 112p. (Orig.). (gr. 2-6). 1991. PLB 6.99 (ISBN 0-679-91539-7, Bullseye Bks); pap. 2.95 (ISBN 0-679-81539-2, Bullseye Bks). Knopf.
—What a Catch! Lyall, Dennis, illus. LC 89-28876. 96p. (Orig.). (gr. 2-6). 1990. PLB 6.99 (ISBN 0-679-90429-8, Bullseye Bks); pap. 2.95 (ISBN 0-679-80429-3, Bullseye bks). Knopf.
Hurwitz, Johanna. Baseball Fever. Cruz, Ray, illus. LC 81-5633. 128p. (gr. 4-6). 1981. 12.95 (ISBN 0-688-00710-4); PLB 12.88 (ISBN 0-688-00711-2, Morrow Jr Bks). Morrow Jr Bks.
—Baseball Fever. 128p. (gr. 4-7). 1983. pap. 2.95 (ISBN 0-440-40311-1, YB). Dell.
Isadora, Rachel. Max. Isadora, Rachel, illus. LC 76-9088. 32p. (gr. k-3). 1976. 12.95 (ISBN 0-02-747450-X, Mcmillan Child Bk). Macmillan Child Grp.
Jenkins, Jerry. The Secret Baseball Challenge. (Orig.). (gr. 9-12). 1986. pap. text ed. 3.95 (ISBN 0-8024-8232-5). Moody.
Jenkins, Jerry B. Mystery At the Ballpark. (gr. 4-7). 1990. pap. 4.50 (ISBN 0-8024-0811-7). Moody.
Johnson, Neil. Batter Up. 1990. pap. 12.95 (ISBN 0-590-42729-6). Scholastic Inc.
Kalb, Jonah. The Goof That Won the Pennant. (Illus.). 112p. (gr. 3-7). 1976. 13.95 (ISBN 0-395-24834-5). HM.
Kelly, Jeffrey. The Basement Baseball Club. LC 86-27545. 160p. (gr. 3-5). 1987. 13.95 (ISBN 0-395-40774-5). HM.
Kessler, Leonard. Aqui Viene el Ponchado. Belpre, Pura, tr. Kessler, Leonard, illus. LC 69-14451. (SPA.). 64p. (gr. k-3). 1969. PLB 11.89 (ISBN 0-06-023154-8). HarpC Child Bks.
—Here Comes the Strikeout. Kessler, Leonard, illus. LC 65-10728. 64p. (gr. k-3). 1965. 11.95 (ISBN 0-06-023155-6); PLB 11.89 (ISBN 0-06-023156-4). HarpC Child Bks.
—Here Comes the Strikeout. Kessler, Leonard, illus. LC 65-10728. 64p. (ps-3). 1978. pap. 3.50 (ISBN 0-06-444011-7, Trophy). HarpC Child Bks.
—Old Turtle's Baseball Stories. Kessler, Leonard, illus. LC 81-6390. 56p. (gr. 1-3). 1982. 13.95 (ISBN 0-688-00723-6); PLB 13.88 (ISBN 0-688-00724-4). Greenwillow.
—Old Turtle's Baseball Stories. (gr. k-6). 1990. pap. 2.95 (ISBN 0-440-40277-8, YB). Dell.
Kline, Suzy. Herbie Jones & the Monster Ball. Williams, Richard, illus. 112p. (gr. 2-6). 1988. 12.95 (ISBN 0-399-21569-7, Putnam). Putnam Pub Group.
—Herbie Jones & the Monster Ball. Williams, Richard, illus. 128p. (gr. 3 up). 1990. pap. 3.95 (ISBN 0-14-034170-6, Puffin). Puffin Bks.
Kraus, Robert. How Spider Saved the Baseball Game. (ps-2). 1989. pap. 2.50 (ISBN 0-590-41791-6). Scholastic Inc.
Latimer, Jim. Fox under First Base. McCue, Lisa, illus. LC 89-27576. 32p. (gr. k-2). 1991. SBE 13.95 (ISBN 0-684-19053-2, Scribners Young Read). Macmillan Child Grp.
Lewis, Marjorie. Wrongway Applebaum. Apple, Margot, illus. LC 84-3242. 64p. (gr. 3-6). 1984. 9.95 (ISBN 0-698-20610-X, Coward). Putnam Pub Group.
Lord, Betty B. In the Year of the Boar & Jackie Robinson. Simont, Marc, illus. LC 83-48440. 176p. (gr. 3-7). 1986. pap. 3.50 (ISBN 0-06-440175-8, Trophy). HarpC Child Bks.
McGee & Me! No. 8: Take Me Out of the Ball Game. 92p. pap. 3.95 (ISBN 0-8423-4113-7). Tyndale.
Marzollo, Jean. The Pizza Pie Slugger. Sims, Blanche, illus. LC 88-33379. 64p. (Orig.). (gr. 2-4). 1989. PLB 6.99 (ISBN 0-394-92881-4); pap. 1.95 (ISBN 0-394-82881-X). Random.
Michaels, Ski. The Baseball Bat. Guzzi, George, illus. LC 85-14065. 48p. (Orig.). (gr. 1-3). 1986. PLB 9.89 (ISBN 0-8167-0596-8); pap. text ed. 2.95 (ISBN 0-8167-0597-6). Troll Assocs.
Montgomery, Robert. Grand Slam. Reese, Ralph, illus. LC 89-5198. 176p. (gr. 5-8). 1991. PLB 9.89 (ISBN 0-8167-1988-8); pap. text ed. 2.95 (ISBN 0-8167-1989-6). Troll Assocs.
—Home Run! Reese, Ralph, illus. LC 89-5190. 176p. (gr. 5-8). 1991. PLB 9.89 (ISBN 0-8167-1986-1); pap. text ed. 2.95 (ISBN 0-8167-1987-X). Troll Assocs.
—The Show! Reese, Ralph, illus. LC 89-20586. 176p. (gr. 5-8). 1989. PLB 9.89 (ISBN 0-8167-1984-5); pap. text ed. 2.95 (ISBN 0-8167-1985-3). Troll Assocs.
Myers, Walter D. Me, Mop, & the Moondance Kid. Pate, Rodney, illus. LC 88-6503. 128p. (gr. 3-7). 1988. 13.95 (ISBN 0-440-50065-6). Delacorte.
Nesbit, Jeffrey A. Absolutely Perfect Summer. 211p. (Orig.). (gr. 9-12). 1990. pap. 6.95 (ISBN 0-87788-005-0). Shaw Pubs.
Parish, Peggy. Play Ball, Amelia Bedelia. Tripp, Wallace, illus. LC 71-85028. 64p. (gr. k-3). 1972. 11.95 (ISBN 0-06-024655-3); PLB 11.89 (ISBN 0-06-024656-1). HarpC Child Bks.
Plantos, T. Heather Hits Her First Home Run. (Illus.). 24p. (ps-8). 1989. pap. 4.95 (ISBN 0-88753-185-7). Firefly Bks Ltd.
Real, Rory. A Baseball Dream. (Illus.). 32p. (ps-3). 1990. pap. 3.95 (ISBN 0-8120-4395-2). Barron.
Sachs, Marilyn. Matt's Mitt & Fleet-Footed Florence. 80p. 1991. pap. 2.95 (ISBN 0-380-70963-5, Camelot Young). Avon.
Schulz, Charles M. It's Arbor Day, Charlie Brown. Schulz, Charles M., illus. LC 76-40450. (gr. 3-5). 1977. 4.95 (ISBN 0-394-83447-X, Random Juv); lib. bdg. 4.99 (ISBN 0-394-93447-4). Random.
Sharp, Paul. Paul the Pitcher. LC 84-7011. (Illus.). 32p. (ps-2). 1984. lib. bdg. 11.93 (ISBN 0-516-02064-1); pap. 2.95 (ISBN 0-516-42064-X). Childrens.
—Ramon, el Lanzador (Paul the Pitcher) Sharp, Paul, illus. LC 84-7071. (SPA.). 32p. (ps-2). 1990. PLB 11.93 (ISBN 0-516-32064-5); pap. 2.95 (ISBN 0-516-52064-4). Childrens.
Slote, Alfred. Finding Buck McHenry. LC 90-39190. 256p. (gr. 3-7). 1991. 13.95 (ISBN 0-06-021652-2); PLB 13.89 (ISBN 0-06-021653-0). HarpC Child Bks.
—Hang Tough, Paul Mather. LC 72-11531. 160p. (gr. 4-7). 1973. 12.95 (ISBN 0-397-31451-5, Lipp Jr Bks). HarpC Child Bks.
—Make-Believe Ball Player. Newsom, Tom, illus. LC 89-30598. 112p. (gr. 2-5). 1989. 12.95 (ISBN 0-397-32285-2, Lipp Jr Bks); PLB 12.89 (ISBN 0-397-32286-0, Lipp Jr Bks). HarpC Child Bks.
—Rabbit Ears. LC 81-47760. 128p. (gr. 4-7). 1983. pap. 3.50 (ISBN 0-06-440134-0, Trophy). HarpC Child Bks.
Smith, Carole. The Hit & Run Connection. Fuhs, Pat, ed. DeJohn, Marie, illus. LC 81-12920. 128p. (gr. 4-9). 1981. PLB 9.95 (ISBN 0-8075-3317-3). A Whitman.
Smith, Robert K. Bobby Baseball. Tiegreen, Alan, illus. (gr. 3-7). 1989. 13.95 (ISBN 0-385-29807-2). Delacorte.
—Bobby Baseball. (gr. 4-7). 1991. pap. 3.25 (ISBN 0-440-40417-7). Dell.
Springstubb, Tricia. With a Name Like Lulu, Who Needs More Trouble? Kastner, Jill, illus. (gr. 5-9). 1989. 14.95 (ISBN 0-385-29823-4). Delacorte.
Stadler, John. Hooray for Snail! Stadler, John, illus. LC 83-46164. 32p. (ps-2). 1985. pap. 4.95 (ISBN 0-06-443075-8, Trophy). HarpC Child Bks.
Tunis, John R. Rookie of the Year. Brooks, Bruce & Bacom, Paulintro. by. 240p. (gr. 3-7). 1990. pap. 3.95 (ISBN 0-15-268880-3). HarbraceJ.
Williams, Karen L. Baseball & Butterflies. 80p. 1990. 12.95 (ISBN 0-688-09489-9). Lothrop.
Ziefert, Harriet. Strike Four! Smith, Mavis, illus. LC 87-25779. 32p. (Orig.). (ps-3). 1988. pap. 3.50 (ISBN 0-14-050811-2, Puffin). Puffin Bks.
Zirpoli, Jane. Roots in the Outfield. LC 87-33900. (gr. 3-7). 1988. 13.95 (ISBN 0-395-45184-1). HM.

BASEBALL–HISTORY

Aaseng, Nathan. Baseball's Greatest Teams. (Illus.). 80p. (gr. 4 up). 1985. PLB 9.95 (ISBN 0-8225-1526-1). Lerner Pubns.
Berler, Ron. Super Book of Baseball. (gr. 4-7). 1991. 19.95 (ISBN 0-316-09240-1). Little.
Cornwell, Anita. The Girls of Summer. Caines, Kelly, illus. LC 88-64051. 100p. (Orig.). (gr. 6 up). 1989. pap. 12.95 (ISBN 0-938678-11-6). New Seed.
Durant, John. The Story of Baseball. rev. 3rd ed. (Illus.). 302p. (gr. 6 up). 1973. 10.95 (ISBN 0-8038-6715-8). Hastings.
Foley, Red. Red Foley's Best Baseball Book Ever - 1988 Edition. (Orig.). (gr. 1 up). 1988. pap. 7.95 (ISBN 0-671-65725-9, Little Simon). S&S Trade.
Frommer, Harvey. A Hundred & Fiftieth Anniversary Album of Baseball. Solomon, Maury, ed. (Illus.). 96p. (gr. 7 up). 1988. PLB 13.90 (ISBN 0-531-10588-1). Watts.
Gutman, Bill. Sports Illustrated Great Moments in Baseball. (gr. 5 up). 1989. pap. 2.75 (ISBN 0-671-67914-7, Archway). PB.
Riley, James A., ed. Black Baseball Journal, Vol. 1, No. 1. (Illus.). 64p. (Orig.). 1990. pap. 6.95 (ISBN 0-9614023-5-0). TK Pubs.
Ritter, Lawrence S. The Story of Baseball. rev. ed. LC 89-48952. (Illus.). 224p. (gr. 5 up). 1990. 15.95 (ISBN 0-688-09056-7); pap. 9.95 (ISBN 0-688-09057-5, Pub. by Beech Tree Bks). Morrow Jr Bks.
Santos, Harry G. Town Team: The Folklore of Town Team Baseball. (Illus.). 120p. (Orig.). Date not set. pap. 12.95 (ISBN 0-940151-09-X). Statesman Exam.

BASEBALL–POETRY

Sullivan, George. All about Baseball. (Illus.). 128p. (gr. 3 up). 1989. 12.99 (ISBN 0-399-61226-2, Putnam); pap. 6.95 (ISBN 0-399-21734-7, Putnam). Putnam Pub Group.
Thayer, Ernest L. Casey at the Bat. Hull, Jim, illus. Gardner, Martin, intro. by. (Illus.). 17.00 (ISBN 0-8446-5613-5). Peter Smith.
—Casey at the Bat. LC 84-9891. (Illus.). (gr. 2-5). 1984. PLB 27.99 incl. cassette (ISBN 0-8172-2243-X); PLB 16.67 (ISBN 0-8172-2121-2); pap. 23.95 incl. cassette (ISBN 0-685-09508-8). Raintree Pubs.
—Casey at the Bat: A Ballad of the Republic, Sung in the Year 1888. Tripp, Wallace, illus. LC 77-21199. (gr. k-5). 1980. 13.95 (ISBN 0-399-21585-9, Putnam); pap. 1.95 (ISBN 0-698-20486-7, Putnam). Putnam Pub Group.
—Casey at the Bat: A Centennial Edition. Moser, Barry, illus. Hall, Donald, afterword by. LC 88-45285. (Illus.). 32p. (gr. 1 up). 1988. 14.95 (ISBN 0-87923-722-8). Godine.

BASEBALL CLUBS

Rothaus, James R. Atlanta Braves. 48p. (gr. 4-10). 1987. PLB 12.95s.p. (ISBN 0-88682-128-2). Creative Ed.
—Baltimore Orioles. 48p. (gr. 4-10). 1987. PLB 11.95 (ISBN 0-88682-129-0). Creative Ed.
—Boston Red Sox. 48p. (gr. 4-10). 1987. PLB 12.95s.p. (ISBN 0-88682-130-4); 18.50 (ISBN 0-685-19531-7). Creative Ed.
—California Angels. 48p. (gr. 4-10). 1987. PLB 12.95 (ISBN 0-88682-131-2). Creative Ed.
—Chicago Cubs. 48p. (gr. 4-10). 1987. PLB 11.95s.p. (ISBN 0-88682-132-0); 17.10 (ISBN 0-685-19534-1). Creative Ed.
—Chicago White Sox. 48p. (gr. 4-10). 1987. PLB 12.95s.p. (ISBN 0-88682-133-9); 18.50 (ISBN 0-685-19535-X). Creative Ed.
—Cincinnati Reds. 48p. (gr. 4-10). 1987. PLB 12.95s.p. (ISBN 0-88682-134-7); 18.50 (ISBN 0-685-19536-8). Creative Ed.
—Cleveland Indians. 48p. (gr. 4-10). 1987. PLB 12.95s.p. (ISBN 0-88682-135-5); 18.50 (ISBN 0-685-19539-2). Creative Ed.
—Detroit Tigers. 48p. (gr. 4-10). 1987. PLB 12.95 (ISBN 0-88682-136-3); 18.50 (ISBN 0-685-19541-4). Creative Ed.
—Houston Astros. (gr. 4-10). 1987. 18.50 (ISBN 0-88682-137-1); PLB 12.95 (ISBN 0-685-19548-1). Creative Ed.
—Kansas City Royals. 48p. (gr. 4-10). 1987. PLB 12.95s.p. (ISBN 0-88682-138-X); 18.50 (ISBN 0-685-19550-3). Creative Ed.
—Los Angeles Dodgers. 48p. (gr. 4-10). 1987. PLB 12.95s.p. (ISBN 0-88682-139-8); 18.50 (ISBN 0-685-19552-X). Creative Ed.
—Milwaukee Brewers. 48p. (gr. 4-10). 1987. PLB 12.95s.p. (ISBN 0-88682-140-1); 18.50 (ISBN 0-685-19553-8). Creative Ed.
—Minnesota Twins. 48p. (gr. 4-10). 1987. PLB 12.95s.p. (ISBN 0-88682-141-X); 18.50 (ISBN 0-685-19555-4). Creative Ed.
—Montreal Expos. 48p. (gr. 4-10). 1987. PLB 11.95s.p. (ISBN 0-88682-142-8); PLB 17.10 (ISBN 0-685-19556-2). Creative Ed.
—New York Mets. 48p. (gr. 4-10). 1987. PLB 12.95s.p. (ISBN 0-88682-143-6); PLB 18.50 (ISBN 0-685-19557-0). Creative Ed.
—New York Yankees. 48p. (gr. 4-10). 1987. PLB 12.95s.p. (ISBN 0-88682-144-4); PLB 18.50 (ISBN 0-318-32440-7). Creative Ed.
—Oakland A's. 48p. (gr. 4-10). 1987. PLB 12.95s.p. (ISBN 0-88682-145-2); PLB 18.50 (ISBN 0-318-32441-5). Creative Ed.
—Philadelphia Phillies. 48p. (gr. 4-10). 1987. PLB 12.95s.p. (ISBN 0-88682-146-0); PLB 18.50 (ISBN 0-318-32443-1). Creative Ed.
—Pittsburgh Pirates. 48p. (gr. 4-10). 1987. PLB 12.95s.p. (ISBN 0-88682-147-9); PLB 18.50 (ISBN 0-318-32444-X). Creative Ed.
—St. Louis Cardinals. 48p. (gr. 4-10). 1987. PLB 12.95s.p. (ISBN 0-88682-148-7); PLB 18.50 (ISBN 0-318-32446-6). Creative Ed.
—San Diego Padres. 48p. (gr. 4-10). 1987. PLB 12.95s.p. (ISBN 0-88682-149-5); PLB 18.50 (ISBN 0-318-32447-4). Creative Ed.
—San Francisco Giants. 48p. (gr. 4-10). 1987. PLB 12.95s.p. (ISBN 0-88682-150-9); PLB 18.50 (ISBN 0-318-32448-2). Creative Ed.
—Seattle Mariners. 48p. (gr. 4-10). 1987. PLB 12.95s.p. (ISBN 0-88682-151-7); PLB 18.50 (ISBN 0-318-32449-0). Creative Ed.

—Texas Rangers. 48p. (gr. 4-10). 1987. PLB 12.95s.p. (ISBN 0-88682-152-5); PLB 18.50 (ISBN 0-318-32452-0). Creative Ed.

—Toronto Blue Jays. 48p. (gr. 4-10). 1987. PLB 12.95s.p. (ISBN 0-88682-153-3); PLB 18.50 (ISBN 0-318-32453-9). Creative Ed.

BASIC (COMPUTER PROGRAM LANGUAGE)

Ault, Rosalie S. BASIC Programming for Kids. LC 83-12773. (Illus.). 192p. (gr. 5 up). 1983. 10.95 (ISBN 0-685-06975-3); pap. 9.95 (ISBN 0-395-34920-6). HM.

BASIC for Elementary Grades. (gr. 4 up). 1982. write for info. tchr's. guide (ISBN 0-89525-273-2); write for info. 5 filmstrips; Incl. filmstrips & 5 cassettes. tchr's. guide 149.00 (ISBN 0-685-08664-X). Ed Activities.

Brenan, Kathleen M. & Mandell, Steven L. Introduction to Computers & Basic Programming. 2nd ed. 564p. (gr. 9-12). 1987. text ed. 31.00 (ISBN 0-314-32166-7); Tchr's. manual. 15.95 (ISBN 0-314-43635-9); wkbk. 9.50 (ISBN 0-314-36064-6). West Pub.

Churchill, Eric R. BASIC Programming Flipper. 49p. (gr. 5 up). 1989. trade edition 5.95 (ISBN 1-878383-10-8). C Lee Pubns.

Cutler, C. Practice Your BASIC. Reed, Naomi, illus. 48p. (gr. 6 up). 1983. PLB 10.96 (ISBN 0-88110-142-7); pap. 3.95 (ISBN 0-86020-743-9). EDC.

Davies, H. & Whaton, M. Better BASIC. (Illus.). 48p. (gr. 6 up). 1983. lib. bdg. 10.96 (ISBN 0-88110-139-7); pap. 3.95 (ISBN 0-86020-733-1). EDC.

Feeman, Jeff & Feeman, Maryellen. Beginning with BASIC: Beginning Computer Skills. Fowler, Christopher, illus. 64p. (gr. 4-6). 1984. wkbk. 6.95 (ISBN 0-88724-028-3, CD-9040). Carson-Dellos.

—Problem Solving with BASIC. Fowler, Christopher & Rittenour, Gary, illus. 32p. (gr. 5 up). 1984. pap. 1.98 (ISBN 0-88724-105-0, CD-9048). Carson-Dellos.

Feeman, Maryellen & Feeman, Jeff. BASIC Programming I. Fowler, Christopher & Rittenour, Gary, illus. 32p. (gr. 2 up). 1984. pap. 1.98 (ISBN 0-88724-106-9, CD-9049). Carson Dellos.

—BASIC Programming II. Fowler, Christopher & Rittenour, Gary, illus. 32p. (gr. 2 up). 1984. pap. 1.98 (ISBN 0-88724-107-7, CD-9050). Carson-Dellos.

—BASIC Programming III. Rittenour, Gary, illus. 32p. (gr. 3 up). 1984. pap. 1.98 (ISBN 0-88724-108-5, CD-9051). Carson-Dellos.

Galanter, Eugene. Elementary Programming for Kids in BASIC. (Illus.). 192p. (Orig.). (gr. 3 up). 1983. 15.95 (ISBN 0-399-50938-0, G&D); pap. 7.95 (ISBN 0-399-50867-8). Putnam Pub Group.

Hurley, L. ZX-81 TS-1000: Programming for Young Programmers. (Illus.). 96p. (gr. 9up). 1983. pap. text ed. 9.95 (ISBN 0-07-031449-7, BYTE Bks). McGraw.

Kallas, John L. BASIC. 252p. (Orig.). (gr. 8-12). 1985. pap. text ed. 14.99 (ISBN 0-89824-145-6); 14.99 (ISBN 0-89824-167-7). Trillium Pr.

Kemnitz, T. M. & Mass, Lynne. Kids Working with Computers: Acorn BASIC. (gr. 2-6). 1984. 4.99 (ISBN 0-89824-086-7). Trillium Pr.

Kemnitz, Thomas M. & Mass, Lynne. Kids Working with Computers: The Apple BASIC Manual. Schlendorf, Lori, illus. 42p. (gr. 4-7). 1983. pap. 4.99 (ISBN 0-89824-092-1). Trillium Pr.

—Kids Working with Computers: The Atari BASIC Manual. Schlendorf, Lori, illus. 48p. (gr. 4-7). 1983. pap. 4.99 (ISBN 0-89824-062-X). Trillium Pr.

—Kids Working with Computers: The Texas Instruments BASIC Manual. Schlendorf, Lori, illus. 48p. (gr. 4-7). 1983. pap. 4.99 (ISBN 0-89824-059-X). Trillium Pr.

—Kids Working with Computers: The Timex-Sinclair BASIC Manual. Schlendorf, Lori, illus. 48p. (gr. 4-7). 1983. pap. 4.99 (ISBN 0-89824-058-1). Trillium Pr.

—Kids Working with Computers: TRS-80 BASIC Manual. Schlendorf, Lori, illus. 44p. (gr. 4-7). 1983. pap. 4.99 (ISBN 0-89824-050-6). Trillium Pr.

Kressen, David P. Teach Your Computer to Think in BASIC. Jacobs, Russell, ed. (Illus.). 88p. (gr. 5 up). 1983. pap. text ed. 7.50 (ISBN 0-918272-10-6). Jacobs.

Mackie, Dean & Mackie, David. BASIC. Migliore, Ron, illus. 48p. (gr. 1-5). 1985. pap. 3.95 (ISBN 0-88625-085-4). Durkin Hayes Pub.

Martin, Dianne & Heller, Rachelle. Bible Basic: Beginner. Ostendorf, Ned, illus. 64p. (gr. 5 up). 1986. 5.95 (ISBN 0-87403-051-X, 3191). Standard Pub.

Pitter, Keiko. Using Apple Works: With Intro to Basic. (gr. 7-12). 1986. pap. text ed. 21.08 (ISBN 0-07-554148-3). McGraw.

Simon, Seymour. The BASIC Book. Emberley, Barbara & Emberley, Ed E., illus. LC 85-47532. 32p. (gr. k-4). 1985. 13.95 (ISBN 0-690-04472-0, Crowell Jr Bks). HarpC Child Bks.

—The BASIC Book. Emberley, Barbara & Emberley, Ed E., illus. LC 85-42736. 32p. (gr. k-4). 1985. pap. 4.50 (ISBN 0-06-445015-5, Trophy). HarpC Child Bks.

Spencer, Donald D. BASIC Programming. LC 82-17689. 224p. (gr. 8 up). 1983. 7.95 (ISBN 0-89218-062-5, NO. 1133). Camelot Pub.

—Problem Solving with BASIC. LC 82-17875. 160p. (gr. 8 up). 1983. pap. 3.95x (ISBN 0-89218-075-7, NO. 1135). Camelot Pub.

Stedman, Robert E. & Cosgrove, R. Commodore 64 BASIC for Kids. (Illus.). 352p. (gr. 5-8). 1984. pap. 12.95 (ISBN 0-89303-378-2). Brady Bks.

Watson, Nancy R. Taking off with BASIC on the Commodore 64. (Illus.). 208p. (gr. 5 up). 1984. pap. 12.95 (ISBN 0-89303-868-7). Brady Bks.

BASKET MAKING

Boy Scouts of America. Basketry. (Illus.). 32p. (gr. 6-12). 1986. pap. 1.85 (ISBN 0-8395-3313-6, 3313). BSA.

Cary, Mara. Basic Baskets. LC 75-14222. 127p. 1975. HM.

BASKETBALL

Aaseng, Nathan. Basketball: You Are the Coach. LC 82-17261. (Illus.). 104p. (gr. 4up). 1983. PLB 8.95 (ISBN 0-8225-1553-9). Lerner Pubns.

—Basketball's High Flyers. Aaseng, Nathan, photos by. LC 79-17137. (Illus.). 80p. (gr. 4 up). 1980. PLB 7.95 (ISBN 0-8225-1058-8). Lerner Pubns.

—Basketball's Playmakers. LC 83-1041. (Illus.). 80p. (gr. 4up). 1983. PLB 7.95 (ISBN 0-8225-1330-7). Lerner Pubns.

—College Basketball: You Are the Coach. LC 83-19996. (Illus.). 104p. (gr. 4 up). 1984. lib. bdg. 8.95 (ISBN 0-8225-1555-5). Lerner Pubns.

Anderson, Dave. The Story of Basketball. Erving, Julius, intro. by. LC 88-6842. (Illus.). 192p. (gr. 5 up). 1988. 12.95 (ISBN 0-688-06748-4); pap. 8.95 (ISBN 0-688-06749-2, Pub. by Beech Tree Bks). Morrow Jr Bks.

Antonacci, Robert J. Basketball for Young Champions. 2nd ed. LC 78-8029. (Illus.). (gr. 4-6). 1979. text ed. 10.95 (ISBN 0-07-002141-4). McGraw.

Baize, Timothy. Broc: The Littlest Champion. LC 89-92510. (Illus.). 185p. (Orig.). (gr. 6-12). 1989. pap. 9.95 (ISBN 0-9625193-0-8). T Baize.

Barnett, Dick. Inside Basketball. (Illus.). 87p. 1971. pap. 6.95 (ISBN 0-8092-8860-5). Contemp Bks.

Bloom, Marc. Basketball. (gr. 4-7). 1991. pap. 2.95 (ISBN 0-590-43313-X). Scholastic Inc.

Bonvicini, Joan. Women's Basketball Drills: Offensive Drills. (Orig.). (gr. 7 up). 1988. pap. 6.25 (ISBN 0-932741-59-2). Championship Bks & Vid Prodns.

Cebulash, Mel. Basketball Players Do Amazing Things. LC 76-8127. (Illus.). (gr. 2-3). 1976. (Random Juv); lib. bdg. 8.99 (ISBN 0-394-93184-X). Random.

Clark, Steve. Illustrated Basketball Dictionary for Young People. Baginski, Frank, illus. (gr. 4 up). 1978. pap. 2.50 (ISBN 0-13-450940-4, Pub. by Treehouse). P-H.

Gutman, Bill. Go for It: Basketball. Brown, Ben, illus. 64p. (gr. 3-7). 1989. PLB 16.50 (ISBN 0-942545-92-3). Grey Castle.

Harris, Richard. I Can Read About Basketball. Milligan, John, illus. LC 76-54397. (gr. 2-5). 1977. pap. 1.95 (ISBN 0-89375-032-8). Troll Assocs.

Highlights for Children Staff. Basketball. Highlights for Children Staff, illus. 48p. (gr. 3-7). 1990. pap. 2.95 (ISBN 0-87534-353-8). Highlights.

Jarrett, William. TimeTables of Sports History: Basketball. (Illus.). 96p. 1990. 17.95x (ISBN 0-8160-1920-7). Facts on File.

Klein, Monica. The Backyard Basketball Superstar. Langner, Nolan, illus. LC 80-22113. 48p. (gr. 1-4). 1981. Knopf.

Levin, Robert, ed. Y Basketball Dribblers Manual: For 5th-6th Grade Players. Barrett, Jerry, illus. 40p. (gr. 5-6). 1984. pap. text ed. 4.00 (ISBN 0-931250-84-6, LYMC4666, Pub. by YMCA USA). Human Kinetics.

—Y Basketball Passers Manual: For 3rd-4th Grade Players. Barrett, Jery, illus. 36p. (gr. 3-4). 1984. pap. 4.00x (ISBN 0-931250-83-8, LYMC4665, Pub. by YMCA USA). Human Kinetics.

Morris, Greggory. Basketball Basics. Engelland, Tim, illus. LC 75-34142. (gr. 2-6). 1979. 6.95 (ISBN 0-13-072256-1, Pub. by Treehouse). P-H.

Rainbolt, Richard. Basketball's Big Men. LC 74-27471. (Illus.). 80p. (gr. 4 up). 1975. PLB 7.95 (ISBN 0-8225-1054-5). Lerner Pubns.

Rosenthal, Bert. Basketball. LC 82-19745. (Illus.). 48p. (gr. k-4). 1983. PLB 14.60 (ISBN 0-516-01674-1); pap. 4.95 (ISBN 0-516-41674-X). Childrens.

Ryan, Deborah. Women's Basketball Drills: Conditioning Drills. (Orig.). (gr. 7 up). 1988. pap. 6.25 (ISBN 0-932741-58-4). Championship Bks & Vid Prodns.

Sakurai, Jennifer. Rules of the Game: Basketball. 48p. 1990. pap. 3.95 (ISBN 0-8431-2432-6). Price Stern.

Smith, Alias & Pelkowski, Robert. Basketball: Rodney Rebound & Willie Dribble & DeeDee Dribble in The Runaway Basketball. 32p. (ps-3). 1989. pap. 3.95 (ISBN 0-8120-4241-7). Barron.

Sullivan, George. Better Basketball for Boys. (Illus.). 64p. (gr. 3-7). 1980. 9.95 (ISBN 0-396-07857-5, Putnam); (Putnam). Putnam Pub Group.

—Better Basketball for Girls. (Illus.). 64p. (gr. 3-7). 1978. 9.95 (ISBN 0-396-07580-0, Putnam); (Putnam). Putnam Pub Group.

Summitt, Pat. Women's Basketball Drills: General Drills. (Orig.). (gr. 7 up). 1988. pap. 6.25 (ISBN 0-932741-57-6). Championship Bks & Vid Prodns.

Webb, Equilla A. An Amateur's Guide to Basketball Recruiting. 60p. (Orig.). (gr. 9-12). 1989. pap. text ed. 9.95 (ISBN 0-9624771-0-9). Equilla Enterprises.

Woodard, Lynette & Cook, Kevin. Shoot for the Stars Basketball Handbook, Vol. 1. Bunch, Lewis & Washington, Marian, eds. Hankins, Rod & Ray, Dan, illus. 60p. (gr. 9-12). 1989. text ed. write for info. Worldwide Sports.

YMCA of the U. S. A. Staff. Y Basketball Shooters Manual. 44p. (gr. 7-9). 1985. pap. 4.00x (ISBN 0-931250-85-4, LYMC4667, Pub. by YMCA USA). Human Kinetics.

BASKETBALL–BIOGRAPHY

Balzar, Howard. Basketball Super Stars. Allison, B., intro. by. (Illus.). 23p. (Orig.). (gr. 1-8). 1990. pap. 2.50 (ISBN 0-943409-15-2). Marketcom.

Carpenter, Jerry & Dimeglio, Steve. Pat Riley. Deegan, Paul, ed. (Illus.). 32p. (gr. 4). 1990. PLB 9.95 (ISBN 0-939179-38-5). Abdo & Dghtrs.

Goodman, Michael E. Magic Johnson. LC 88-20982. (Illus.). 48p. (gr. 5-6). 1988. PLB 10.95 (ISBN 0-89686-382-4, Crestwood Hse). Macmillan Child Grp.

Herbert, Michael. Michael Jordan: The Bull's Air Power. LC 87-20868. 48p. (gr. 2 up). 1987. PLB 13.27 (ISBN 0-516-04362-5); pap. 3.95 (ISBN 0-516-44362-3). Childrens.

Jordan, Michael. Sports Illustrated For Kids Biography. (Illus.). (gr. 4-7). 1990. pap. 4.95 (ISBN 0-316-09229-0). Little.

Lazenby, Roland. Georgetown, the Championships & Thompson. Blatty, William P., intro. by. (Illus.). 128p. (gr. 4-12). 1985. 19.95 (ISBN 0-913767-08-5). Full Court VA.

Levin, Rich. Magic Johnson: Court Magician. LC 80-25814. (Illus.). 48p. (gr. 2-8). 1981. PLB 13.27 (ISBN 0-516-04313-7); pap. 3.95 (ISBN 0-516-44313-5). Childrens.

Libman. Moses Malone. (Illus.). 32p. (gr. 4 up). 1985. PLB 8.95. Creative Ed.

McCune, Dan. Michael Jordan. LC 87-29021. (Illus.). 48p. (gr. 5-6). 1988. PLB 10.95 (ISBN 0-89686-364-6, Crestwood Hse). Macmillan Child Grp.

Make the Team: Basketball - A Slammin', Jammin' Guide to Super Hoops. (gr. 3-7). 1990. 13.95 (ISBN 0-316-10748-4); pap. 5.95 (ISBN 0-316-10749-2). Little.

Miller, Dawn. David Robinson: Backboard Admiral. (Illus.). 64p. (gr. 4-9). 1991. PLB 8.95 (ISBN 0-8225-0494-4). Lerner Pubns.

Newman, Matthew. Larry Bird. LC 86-16524. (Illus.). 48p. (gr. 5-6). PLB 10.95 (ISBN 0-89686-314-X, Crestwood Hse). Macmillan Child Grp.

—Lynette Woodard. LC 86-19737. (Illus.). 48p. (gr. 5-6). PLB 10.95 (ISBN 0-89686-316-6, Crestwood Hse). Macmillan Child Grp.

—Patrick Ewing. LC 86-16522. (Illus.). 48p. (gr. 5-6). PLB 10.95 (ISBN 0-89686-315-8, Crestwood Hse). Macmillan Child Grp.

Paige, David. A Day in the Life of a School Basketball Coach. Smith, Bill, photos by. LC 80-54101. (Illus.). 32p. (gr. 4-8). 1981. PLB 11.79 (ISBN 0-89375-452-8); pap. 2.95 (ISBN 0-89375-453-6); cassettes avail. Troll Assocs.

Petrucelli. Michael Jordan, Reading Level 2. (Illus.). 24p. (gr. 1-4). Date not set. PLB 12.33 (ISBN 0-86592-428-7). Rourke Corp.

Rosenthal, Bert. Larry Bird: Cool Man on the Court. LC 80-27094. (Illus.). 48p. (gr. 2-8). 1981. PLB 13.27 (ISBN 0-516-04312-9); pap. 3.95 (ISBN 0-516-44312-7). Childrens.

Sealy, Adrienne V. Little Tommy & the Basketball. Walker, Walt, illus. (gr. 2-6). 1980. 3.50x (ISBN 0-9602670-4-2). Assn Family Living.

BASKETBALL–FICTION

Bassoff, Bruce. Supercharged: The Powers of Jon Bass. LC 89-18667. 128p. (gr. 4-8). 1990. 14.95 (ISBN 0-917665-38-4); pap. 9.95 (ISBN 0-917665-39-2). Bookmakers Guild.

Christopher, Matt. Johnny Long Legs. Kidder, Harvey, illus. 144p. (gr. 3-6). 1988. pap. 3.95 (ISBN 0-316-14065-1). Little.

—No Arm in Left Field. Goto, Byron, illus. (gr. 4-6). 1987. lib. bdg. 13.95 (ISBN 0-316-13964-5); pap. 3.95 (ISBN 0-316-13990-4). Little.

Cooper, Ilene. Choosing Sides. (Illus.). 218p. (gr. 3-7). 1991. pap. 3.95 (ISBN 0-14-034566-3, Puffin). Puffin Bks.

Cossi, Olga. The Magic Box. 192p. (gr. 12). 1990. 10.95 (ISBN 0-88289-748-9). Pelican.

Deuker, Carl. On the Devil's Court. 208p. (gr. 7 up). 1989. 13.95 (ISBN 0-316-18147-1, Joy St Bks). Little.

Dickmeyer, Lowell A. Basketball Is for Me. Oddie, Alan, photos by. LC 79-16954. (Illus.). 48p. (gr. 2-5). 1980. PLB 8.95 (ISBN 0-8225-1089-8). Lerner Pubns.

Dygard, Thomas J. Outside Shooter. (Illus.). 192p. (gr. 5 up). 1991. pap. 3.95 (ISBN 0-14-034671-6, Puffin). Puffin Bks.

—Rebound Caper. LC 82-18821. 176p. (gr. 7 up). 1983. 12.95 (ISBN 0-688-01707-X). Morrow Jr Bks.

—Tournament Upstart. LC 83-25039. 208p. (gr. 7 up). 1984. 9.50 (ISBN 0-688-02761-X). Morrow Jr Bks.

Elish, Dan. Jason & the Baseball Bear. Stadler, John, illus. LC 89-23102. 160p. (gr. 3-5). 1990. 13.95 (ISBN 0-531-05868-9); PLB 13.99 (ISBN 0-531-08468-X). Orchard Bks Watts.

Freeman, Mark. Halfcourt Hero. 1989. 2.95 (ISBN 0-345-35911-9). Ballantine.

Gault, Clare & Gault, Frank. Norman Plays Basketball. Myers, Bernice, illus. (gr. k-3). 1978. pap. 1.50 (ISBN 0-590-05394-9). Scholastic Inc.

Gorman, S. S. High-Fives: Slam Dunk. MacDonald, Patricia, ed. 128p. (Orig.). (gr. 3-6). 1990. pap. 2.95 (ISBN 0-671-70381-1, Minstrel Bks). PB.

Hallowell, Tommy. Jester in the Backcourt. 128p. (gr. 3 up). 1990. pap. 2.95 (ISBN 0-14-032911-0, Puffin). Puffin Bks.

—Jester in the Backcourt. (gr. 4-7). 1991. 12.95 (ISBN 0-670-83732-6). Viking Child Bks.

Jackson, Alison. Crane's Rebound. Hearn, Diane D., illus. 128p. (gr. 3-7). 1991. 12.95 (ISBN 0-525-44722-9, DCB). Dutton Child Bks.

—My Brother, the Star. 1990. 12.95 (ISBN 0-525-44512-9, DCB). Dutton Child Bks.

Jackson, C. Paul. Beginner under the Backboards. Butterfield, Ned, illus. LC 74-13428. 128p. (gr. 4-7). 1974. 8.95g (ISBN 0-8038-0762-7). Hastings.
Jenkins, Jerry. The Scary Basketball Player. (Orig.). (gr. 9-12). 1986. pap. text ed. 3.95 (ISBN 0-8024-8233-3). Moody.
Jones, Ron. B-Ball: The Team that Never Lost a Game. (gr. 5 up). 1990. 14.95 (ISBN 0-553-05867-3). Bantam.
Jorgensen, Dan. Andrea's Best Shot. LC 87-33760. 1988. pap. 4.49 (ISBN 1-55513-860-8, Chariot Bks). Cook.
Knudson, R. R. Zanbanger. LC 75-25416. 176p. (gr. 7 up). 1977. PLB 12.89 (ISBN 0-06-023214-5). HarpC Child Bks.
Mallett, Jerry & Bartch, Marian. Clearly Old Ernie. 151p. (gr. 4-7). 1989. PLB 7.85 (ISBN 0-8000-3303-5, 055786). Perma Bound.
Marshall, Kirk. Fast Breaks. (gr. 4 up). 1989. pap. 2.95 (ISBN 0-345-35908-9). Ballantine.
—Longshot Center. (gr. 4 up). 1989. pap. 2.95 (ISBN 0-345-35909-7). Ballantine.
—Pressure Play. (gr. 6-10). 1989. pap. 2.95 (ISBN 0-345-35913-5). Ballantine.
Myers, Walter D. Hoops. LC 81-65497. 224p. (gr. 7 up). 1981. 13.95 (ISBN 0-385-28142-0). Delacorte.
Peck, Robert N. Soup's Hoop. 1990. 13.95 (ISBN 0-385-29808-0). Doubleday.
Provost, Gary. Good If It Goes. (gr. 4-7). 1990. pap. 3.95 (ISBN 0-689-71381-9, Aladdin). Macmillan Child Grp.
Soto, G. Taking Sides. 1991. 15.95 (ISBN 0-15-284076-1, HJ). HarBraceJ.
Stine, Megan & Stine, H. William. Long Shot. LC 89-43395. (Orig.). (gr. 5 up). 1990. pap. 2.95 (ISBN 0-679-80526-5, Borzoi Sprinters). Knopf.
—Long Shot, Bk. 10. LC 89-24355. 144p. (gr. 5 up). 1990. lib. bdg. 7.99 (ISBN 0-679-90526-X). Random.
Tunis, John R. Yea! Wildcats. 1989. pap. 3.95 (ISBN 0-15-299718-0). HarbraceJ.
Weesner, Theodore. Winning the City. 1990. 17.45 (ISBN 0-671-64241-3). S&S Trade.

BASKETBALL–HISTORY

Anderson, Dave. The Story of Basketball. Erving, Julius, intro. by. LC 88-6842. (Illus.). 192p. (gr. 5 up). 1988. 12.95 (ISBN 0-688-06748-4); pap. 8.95 (ISBN 0-688-06749-2, Pub. by Beech Tree Bks). Morrow Jr Bks.
The NBA Finals. 32p. (gr. 4). 1990. 12.95s.p. (ISBN 0-88682-314-5); 18.50 (ISBN 0-685-28229-5). Creative Ed.
Packer, Billy & Lazenby, Roland. The Sporting News College Basketball's 25 Great Teams. (Illus.). 256p. (gr. 7-12). 1989. 19.95 (ISBN 0-89204-314-8). Sporting News.
Rice, Russell. Big Blue Machine: Kentucky Basketball. rev. ed. (Illus.). 492p. (gr. 6-12). 1988. 18.95 (ISBN 0-87397-306-2). Strode.

BASKETBALL CLUBS

Boyd, Brendan, text by. Hoops: Behind the Scenes with the Boston Celtics. Horenstein, Henry, photos by. (Illus.). 128p. (gr. 3-7). 1989. 15.95 (ISBN 0-316-37319-2); pap. 8.95 (ISBN 0-316-37309-5). Little.
The Final Four (NCAA Basketball) 32p. (gr. 4). 1990. 12.95s.p. (ISBN 0-88682-310-2); 18.50 (ISBN 0-685-28225-2). Creative Ed.
Zadra, Dan. Atlanta Hawks. rev. ed. (Illus.). 32p. (gr. 4 up). 1989. 12.95 (ISBN 0-88682-197-5). Creative Ed.
—Boston Celtics. rev. ed. (Illus.). 32p. (gr. 4 up). 1989. PLB 12.95 (ISBN 0-88682-198-3); 18.50 (ISBN 0-685-24576-4). Creative Ed.
—Chicago Bulls. rev. ed. (Illus.). 32p. (gr. 4 up). 1989. PLB 12.95 (ISBN 0-88682-199-1); 18.50 (ISBN 0-685-24577-2). Creative Ed.
—Cleveland Cavaliers. rev. ed. (Illus.). 32p. (gr. 4 up). 1989. PLB 12.95 (ISBN 0-88682-200-9); 18.50 (ISBN 0-685-24578-0). Creative Ed.
—Dallas Mavericks. (Illus.). 32p. (gr. 4 up). 1989. PLB 12.95 (ISBN 0-88682-201-7); 18.50 (ISBN 0-685-24579-9). Creative Ed.
—Denver Nuggets. rev. ed. (Illus.). 32p. (gr. 4 up). 1989. 18.50 (ISBN 0-685-24580-2); PLB 12.95 (ISBN 0-88682-202-5). Creative Ed.
—Detroit Pistons. rev. ed. (Illus.). 32p. (gr. 4 up). 1989. PLB 12.95 (ISBN 0-88682-203-3); 18.50 (ISBN 0-685-24581-0). Creative Ed.
—Golden State Warriors. rev. ed. (Illus.). 32p. (gr. 4 up). 1989. PLB 12.95 (ISBN 0-88682-204-1); 18.50 (ISBN 0-685-24582-9). Creative Ed.
—Houston Rockets. 32p. (gr. 4). 1989. 18.50 (ISBN 0-88682-205-X); PLB 12.95s.p. (ISBN 0-318-37909-0). Creative Ed.
—Indiana Pacers. (Illus.). 32p. (gr. 4 up). 1989. PLB 12.95 (ISBN 0-88682-206-8); 18.50 (ISBN 0-685-24583-7). Creative Ed.
—Los Angeles Clippers. rev. ed. (Illus.). 32p. (gr. 4 up). 1989. PLB 12.95 (ISBN 0-88682-216-5); 18.50 (ISBN 0-685-24591-8). Creative Ed.
—Los Angeles Lakers. rev. ed. (Illus.). 32p. (gr. 4 up). 1989. PLB 12.95s.p. (ISBN 0-88682-208-4); 18.50 (ISBN 0-685-24585-3). Creative Ed.
—Milwaukee Bucks. (Illus.). 32p. (gr. 4 up). 1989. PLB 12.95 (ISBN 0-88682-209-2); 18.50 (ISBN 0-685-24586-1). Creative Ed.
—New York Knicks. (Illus.). 32p. (gr. 4 up). 1989. PLB 12.95s.p. (ISBN 0-88682-211-4); PLB 18.50 (ISBN 0-685-24587-X). Creative Ed.
—Philadelphia 76ers. rev. ed. (Illus.). 32p. (gr. 4 up). 1989. PLB 12.95s.p. (ISBN 0-88682-212-2); PLB 18.50 (ISBN 0-685-24588-8). Creative Ed.
—Phoenix Suns. rev. ed. (Illus.). 32p. (gr. 4 up). 1989. PLB 12.95s.p. (ISBN 0-88682-213-0); PLB 18.50 (ISBN 0-685-24589-6). Creative Ed.
—Portland Trailblazers. (Illus.). 38p. (gr. 4 up). 1989. PLB 12.95s.p. (ISBN 0-88682-214-9); PLB 18.50 (ISBN 0-685-24590-X). Creative Ed.
—Sacramento Kings. (Illus.). 32p. (gr. 4 up). 1989. PLB 12.95 (ISBN 0-88682-207-6); PLB 18.50 (ISBN 0-685-24584-5). Creative Ed.
—Seattle Supersonics. rev. ed. (Illus.). 32p. (gr. 4 up). 1989. PLB 12.95s.p. (ISBN 0-88682-217-3); PLB 18.50 (ISBN 0-685-24592-6). Creative Ed.
—Utah Jazz. 32p. (gr. 4). 1989. 18.50 (ISBN 0-88682-218-1); PLB 12.95 (ISBN 0-318-37914-7). Creative Ed.
—Washington Bullets. 32p. (gr. 4). 1989. PLB 18.50 (ISBN 0-88682-219-X); PLB 12.95s.p. (ISBN 0-318-37915-5). Creative Ed.

BAT

see Bats

BATON TWIRLING

see Drum Majors

BATS

Braithwaite, Althea. Bats. (ps-6). 1988. PLB 7.95 (ISBN 0-88462-176-6); pap. 2.95 (ISBN 0-88462-177-4). Dearborn Finan.
Green, Carl R. & Sanford, William R. The Little Brown Bat. LC 85-22345. (Illus.). 48p. (gr. 4-5). 1986. PLB 10.95 (ISBN 0-89686-267-4, Crestwood Hse). Macmillan Child Grp.
Greenaway, Frank. Amazing Bats. Young, Jerry & Greenaway, Frank, photos by. LC 91-6517. (Illus.). 32p. (Orig.). (gr. 1-5). 1991. lib. bdg. 9.99 (ISBN 0-679-91518-4); pap. 7.00 (ISBN 0-679-81518-X). Knopf.
Halton, Cheryl M. Those Amazing Bats. (Illus.). 96p. (gr. 4 up). 1991. 12.95 (ISBN 0-87518-458-8, Dillon). Macmillan Child Grp.
Harrison, Virginia & Riley, Helen. The World of Bats. LC 89-4471. (Illus.). 32p. (gr. 2-3). 1989. PLB 10.95 (ISBN 0-8368-0137-7). Gareth Stevens Inc.
Hopf, Alice L. Bats. (Illus.). 64p. (gr. 7-10). 1985. 9.95 (ISBN 0-396-08502-4, Putnam). Putnam Pub Group.
Johnson, Sylvia A. Bats. Masuda, Modoki, illus. LC 85-15999. 48p. (gr. 4 up). 1985. PLB 14.95 (ISBN 0-8225-1461-3, First Ave Edns); pap. 5.95 (ISBN 0-8225-9500-1, First Ave Edns). Lerner Pubns.
Lovett, Sarah, text by. Extremely Weird Bats. (Illus.). 48p. (gr. 3 up). 1991. 9.95 (ISBN 1-56261-008-2). John Muir.
Pringle, Laurence. Batman: Exploring the World of Bats. Tuttle, Merlin D., illus. LC 90-8679. 48p. (gr. 4-6). 1991. SBE 13.95 (ISBN 0-684-19232-2, Scribners Young Read). Macmillan Child Grp.
Riley, Helen. The Bat in the Cave. Oxford Scientific Films Staff, photos by. LC 89-4469. (Illus.). 32p. (gr. 4-6). 1989. PLB 10.95 (ISBN 0-8368-0112-1). Gareth Stevens Inc.
Schlein, Miriam. Billions of Bats. Kessell, Walter, illus. 64p. (gr. 3-6). 1982. PLB 12.89 (ISBN 0-397-31985-1, Lipp Jr Bks). HarpC Child Bks.
Shebar, Sharon S. & Shebar, Susan E. Bats. (Illus.). 64p. (gr. 5-8). 1990. PLB 11.90 (ISBN 0-531-10863-5). Watts.
Tuttle, Merlin D. America's Neighborhood Bats: Understanding & Learning to Live in Harmony with Them. (Illus.). 104p. (gr. 10-12). 1988. 19.95 (ISBN 0-292-70403-8); pap. 9.95 (ISBN 0-292-70406-2). U of Tex Pr.
Warren, Elizabeth. I Can Read About Bats. LC 74-24928. (Illus.). (gr. 2-4). 1975. pap. 1.95 (ISBN 0-89375-064-6). Troll Assocs.
Wiessinger, John. Cats, Bats, & Bears - Right Before Your Eyes. Wiessinger, John, illus. LC 89-1411. 64p. (gr. 4-10). 1989. PLB 15.95 (ISBN 0-89490-266-0). Enslow Pubs.

BATS–FICTION

Carlson, Natalie S. Spooky & the Wizard's Bats. Glass, Andrew, illus. LC 85-18020. 32p. (ps-1). 1986. 12.95 (ISBN 0-688-06280-6); PLB 12.88 (ISBN 0-688-06281-4). Lothrop.
Danziger, Paula. There's a Bat in Bunk Five. 160p. (gr. 5-9). 1988. pap. 2.95 (ISBN 0-440-40098-8, LE). Dell.
Freeman, Don. Hattie the Backstage Bat. (Illus.). 32p. (Orig.). (ps-3). 1988. pap. 3.95 (ISBN 0-14-050893-7, Puffin). Puffin Bks.
Freeman, Lydia & Freeman, Don. Pet of the Met. (Illus.). 64p. (Orig.). (ps-3). 1988. pap. 4.95 (ISBN 0-14-050892-9, Puffin). Puffin Bks.
Jarrell, Randall. Bat-Poet. Sendak, Maurice, illus. LC 64-16812. 44p. (gr. 3-6). 1967. 13.95 (ISBN 0-02-747640-5, Mcmillan Child Bk). Macmillan Child Grp.
—The Bat-Poet. LC 76-17823. (Illus.). 44p. (gr. 3-6). 1977. pap. 4.95 (ISBN 0-02-043910-5, Aladdin). Macmillan Child Grp.
Johnson, Norma. Bats on the Bedstead. LC 86-27823. 128p. (gr. 3-7). 1987. 12.95 (ISBN 0-395-43022-4). HM.
Johnson, Norma T. Bats on the Bedstead. 128p. 1988. pap. 2.95 (ISBN 0-380-70540-0, Camelot). Avon.
Lent, Blair. Bayberry Bluff. (ps-3). 1987. 13.95 (ISBN 0-395-35384-X). HM.
Searcy, Margaret Z. Tiny Bat & the Ball Game. Wise, Lu Celia, illus. LC 78-61367. (gr. 2-4). 1978. 7.50 (ISBN 0-916620-19-0). Portals Pr.

BATTLE SHIPS

see Warships

BATTLES

Bogart, Bonnie. The Ewoks Join the Fight. De Groat, Diane, illus. LC 82-62834. 32p. (ps-4). 1983. Random.
Isaaman. Computer Battlegames. (gr. 5-9). 1983. 10.96 (ISBN 0-88110-132-X, 24052); pap. 3.95 (ISBN 0-86020-685-8). EDC.

BATTLESHIPS

see Warships

BAY OF PIGS

see Cuba–History

BAZAARS

see Fairs

BEACHES

see Seashore

BEAGLE EXPEDITION, 1831-1836

Hyndley, Kate. The Voyage of the Beagle. Bull, Peter, illus. LC 88-28695. 32p. (gr. 5-9). 1989. PLB 11.40 (ISBN 0-531-18272-X, Pub. by Bookwright Pr). Watts.

BEARS

Ahlstrom, Mark. The Polar Bear. LC 85-30900. (Illus.). 48p. (gr. 4-5). 1986. PLB 10.95 (ISBN 0-89686-268-2, Crestwood Hse). Macmillan Child Grp.
Ahlstrom, Mark E. The Black Bear. LC 85-22872. (Illus.). 48p. (gr. 4-5). 1985. 10.95 (ISBN 0-89686-276-3, Crestwood Hse). Macmillan Child Grp.
Bailey, Jill. Polar Bear Rescue. Green, John, illus. LC 90-4490. 48p. (gr. 3-7). 1991. PLB 17.28 (ISBN 0-8114-2708-0). Steck-V.
Baker, Lucy. Polar Bears. (Illus.). 32p. (gr. 2-6). 1990. pap. 4.95 (ISBN 0-14-034435-7, Puffin). Puffin Bks.
Banks, Martin. The Polar Bear on the Ice. Oxford Scientific Films Staff, photos by. LC 89-4472. (Illus.). 32p. (gr. 4-6). 1989. PLB 10.95 (ISBN 0-8368-0114-8). Gareth Stevens Inc.
Barrett, N. S. Bears. FS Staff, ed. 32p. (Orig.). (gr. 1-6). 1988. PLB 11.40 (ISBN 0-531-10526-1). Watts.
Bear. 1990. 2.95 (ISBN 0-8378-2055-3). Gibson.
The Bear Family. Date not set. 5.50 (ISBN 0-317-93752-9). W J Fantasy.
Bears. 32p. (Orig.). (ps-1). 1984. pap. 1.25 (ISBN 0-8431-1510-6). Price Stern.
Bears & Pandas. (Illus.). (gr. 1-4). 3.50 (ISBN 0-7214-0489-8). Ladybird Bks.
Bird, E. J. How Do Bears Sleep? Bird, E. J., illus. 32p. (ps-3). pap. 5.95 (ISBN 0-87614-522-5). Carolrhoda Bks.
Brenner, Barbara & Garelick, May. Two Orphan Cubs. Kors, Erika, illus. (ps-1). 1989. 12.95 (ISBN 0-8027-6868-7); PLB 13.85 (ISBN 0-8027-6869-5). Walker & Co.
Bright, Michael. Polar Bear. LC 89-50446. (Illus.). 32p. (gr. 5-7). 1989. PLB 11.90 (ISBN 0-531-17180-9). Watts.
Calabro, Marian. Operation Grizzly Bear. Craighead, John, et al, illus. LC 88-37497. 112p. (gr. 5 up). 1989. 12.95 (ISBN 0-02-716241-9, Four Winds). Macmillan Child Grp.
Dodd, Lynley. Wake Up Bear. Dodd, Lynley, illus. LC 86-42798. 32p. (gr. 1-2). 1988. PLB 10.95 (ISBN 1-55532-124-0). Gareth Stevens Inc.
Ford, Barbara. Black Bear: The Spirit of the Wilderness. 1990. pap. 4.95 (ISBN 0-395-56152-3). HM.
Galdone, Paul, ed. & illus. The Three Bears. LC 78-158833. 32p. (ps-3). 1979. 12.95 (ISBN 0-395-28811-8, Clarion). HM.
Geriner, Laura. Seven True Bear Stories. Maisto, Carol, illus. (gr. 2-5). 1979. 8.95 (ISBN 0-8038-6747-6). Hastings.
Graham, Ada & Graham, Frank. Bears in the Wild. Tyler, D. D., illus. LC 80-68732. 128p. (gr. 4-7). 1981. 8.95 (ISBN 0-440-00532-9); PLB 8.44 (ISBN 0-440-00538-8). Delacorte.
Hall, Katy. Grizzly Riddles. LC 86-29275. 1989. 9.95 (ISBN 0-8037-0376-7); PLB 9.89 (ISBN 0-8037-0377-5). Dial Bks Young.
Hanks, Jacqueline. The Loneliest Teddy Bear: Picture Book. (Illus.). 24p. (Orig.). (ps-3). 1990. pap. 1.95 (ISBN 0-87406-531-3). Willowisp Pr.
Harrison, Virginia & Banks, Martin. The World of Polar Bears. LC 89-4470. (Illus.). 32p. (gr. 2-3). 1989. PLB 10.95 (ISBN 0-8368-0139-3). Gareth Stevens Inc.
Hoffman, Mary. Bear. LC 86-6775. (Illus.). 24p. (gr. k-5). 1986. PLB 13.32 (ISBN 0-8172-2396-7). Raintree Pubs.
Johnston, Ginny & Cutchins, Judy. Andy Bear: A Polar Cub Grows Up at the Zoo. Noble, Constance, illus. LC 85-3095. 64p. (gr. 2-5). 1985. 13.00 (ISBN 0-688-05627-X); lib. bdg. 12.88 (ISBN 0-688-05628-8, Morrow Jr Bks). Morrow Jr Bks.
Kalas, Sybille. Polar Bear Family Book. (ps-3). 1990. 15.95 (ISBN 0-88708-157-6). Picture Bk Studio.
Koch, Thomas J. The Year of the Polar Bear. LC 74-17660. (Illus.). 224p. (gr. 3-5). 1975. 8.95 (ISBN 0-672-52062-1, Bobbs). Macmillan.
Kuchalla, Susan. Bears. Kelleher, Kathie, illus. LC 81-11368. 32p. (gr. k-2). 1982. lib. bdg. 10.89 (ISBN 0-89375-674-1); pap. 2.95 (ISBN 0-89375-675-X). Troll Assocs.
Nentl, Jerolyn. The Grizzly. LC 83-22354. (Illus.). 48p. (gr. 5-6). 1984. PLB 10.95 (ISBN 0-89686-245-3, Crestwood Hse). Macmillan Child Grp.
Palmer, S. Polar Bears. (Illus.). 24p. (gr. k-5). 1989. lib. bdg. 11.93 (ISBN 0-86592-360-4). Rourke Corp.
Penny, Malcolm. Bears. LC 90-35063. (Illus.). 32p. (gr. 2-4). 1991. PLB 11.90 (ISBN 0-531-18368-8, Pub. by Bookwright Pr). Watts.
—Let's Look At Bears. (ps-3). 1990. PLB 8.90 (ISBN 0-531-18321-1). Watts.

Petty, Kate. Bears. (Illus.). 24p. (gr. k-3). 1991. PLB 10. 40 (ISBN 0-531-17286-4, Gloucester Pr). Watts.

Pfeffer, Pierre. Bears, Big & Little. Bogard, Vicki, tr. from FRE. Stephan, Franck, illus. LC 89-8883. 38p. (gr. k-5). 1989. 4.95 (ISBN 0-944589-23-5, 023). Young Discovery Lib.

Pinkwater, Daniel. Bear's Picture. Pinkwater, Daniel, illus. (ps-3). 1984. 11.95 (ISBN 0-525-44102-6, DCB). Dutton Child Bks.

Pringle, Laurence. Bearman: Exploring the World of Black Bears. Rogers, Lynn, illus. LC 89-5890. 48p. (gr. 5-7). 1989. 13.95 (ISBN 0-684-19094-X, Scribners Young Read). Macmillan Child Grp.

Robinson, Sandra C. The Everywhere Bear. (Illus.). 64p. (gr. 4-6). 1992. pap. 6.95 (ISBN 1-879373-07-6). R Rinehart Inc.

Rosenthal, Mark. Bears. LC 82-17910. (Illus.). 48p. (gr. k-4). 1983. PLB 14.60 (ISBN 0-516-01675-X); pap. 4.95 (ISBN 0-516-41675-8). Childrens.

Schmidt, Annemarie & Schmidt, Christian R. Bears. (Illus.). 32p. (gr. 4-6). 1991. PLB 11.95 (ISBN 0-8368-0684-0). Gareth Stevens Inc.

Schneider, Jeff. My Friend the Polar Bear: An Ocean Magic Book. Spoon, Wilfred, illus. LC 90-61579. 12p. (ps). 1991. 4.95g (ISBN 1-877779-12-1). Schneider Educational.

Seymour, Peter. Busy Bears. Paris, Pat, illus. 22p. (ps-1). 1981. 5.95 (ISBN 0-8431-0640-9). Price Stern.

Simons, Jeff. Teddy Bears Care Enough. Kinarney, Tom, illus. 24p. (gr. 1-6). 1984. pap. 1.95 (ISBN 0-89954-283-2). Antioch Pub Co.

Stevenson, James. The Bear Who Had No Place to Go. Stevenson, James, illus. LC 70-186775. 48p. (ps-3). 1972. PLB 13.89 (ISBN 0-06-025781-4). HarpC Child Bks.

Stone, Lynn. Bears. (Illus.). 24p. (gr. k-5). 1990. lib. bdg. 11.93 (ISBN 0-86593-042-2); lib. bdg. 8.95s.p. Rourke Corp.

Whittaker, Bibby. A Closer Look at Bears & Pandas. rev. ed. (Illus.). (gr. 4-9). 1986. PLB 5.99 (ISBN 0-531-17026-8, Pub. by Gloucester). Watts.

Wiessinger, John. Cats, Bats, & Bears - Right Before Your Eyes. Wiessinger, John, illus. LC 89-1411. 64p. (gr. 4-10). 1989. PLB 15.95 (ISBN 0-89490-266-0). Enslow Pubs.

Wildlife Education, Ltd. Staff. Polar Bears. Espinoza, Rauol, et al, illus. 20p. (Orig.). (gr. k-12). 1985. pap. 2.25 (ISBN 0-937934-36-4). Wildlife Educ.

Ziefert, Harriet. Bear All Year. Lobel, Arnold, illus. LC 85-45339. 16p. (ps). 1986. 4.95 (ISBN 0-694-00087-6). HarpC Child Bks.

BEARS–FICTION

Adamson, Douglas. Charles Bear & the Mystery of the Forest, Bk. 1. 1975. pap. 20.00 (ISBN 0-686-15459-2). D Adamson.

Alborough, Jez. Running Bear. Alborough, Jez, illus. LC 85-12681. 32p. (ps-3). 1986. Knopf.

Alexander, Martha. And My Mean Old Mother Will Be Sorry, Blackboard Bear. Alexander, Martha, illus. LC 72-707. 32p. (ps-2). 1985. PLB 10.89 (ISBN 0-8037-0593-X). Dial Bks Young.

—Blackboard Bear. Alexander, Martha, illus. (Orig.). (ps-2). 1988. pap. 3.50 (ISBN 0-8037-0629-4). Dial Bks Young.

—I Sure Am Glad to See You, Blackboard Bear. LC 76-2280. (Illus.). (ps-3). 1979. 7.95 (ISBN 0-8037-4002-6); PLB 9.89 (ISBN 0-8037-4003-4). Dial Bks Young.

—I Sure Am Glad to See You, Blackboard Bear. (Illus.). (ps-3). 1979. pap. 3.50 (ISBN 0-8037-4008-5, Dial Pied Piper). Puffin Bks.

—We're in Big Trouble, Blackboard Bear. Alexander, Martha, illus. 32p. (ps-2). 1982. pap. 3.50 (ISBN 0-8037-9583-1). Dial Bks Young.

Allen, Pamela. Bertie & the Bear. Allen, Pamela, illus. 32p. (gr. k-3). 1984. 10.95 (ISBN 0-698-20600-2, Coward); pap. 4.95 (ISBN 0-698-20607-X, Coward). Putnam Pub Group.

Allred, Gordon. Old Crackfoot. Brown, Margery, illus. (gr. 5 up). 1965. 8.95 (ISBN 0-8392-3051-6). Astor-Honor.

Amery, H. Goldilocks & the Three Bears. Cartwright, Stephen, illus. 16p. (ps-2). 1988. 2.95 (ISBN 0-7460-0190-8); PLB 6.96 (ISBN 0-88110-318-7). EDC.

Anderson, Marcie. Teddy Finds a Home. (Illus.). 24p. (gr. k-2). 1988. 1.95 (ISBN 0-87406-271-3, 14-15391-3). Willowisp Pr.

Asch, Frank. Bear Shadow. Asch, Frank, illus. LC 82-18250. 32p. (ps-2). 1988. 12.95 (ISBN 0-671-66279-1); pap. 4.95 (ISBN 0-671-66866-8). S&S Trade.

—Bear's Bargain. Asch, Frank, illus. LC 85-6355. (ps-2). 1989. 12.95 (ISBN 0-671-66690-8); pap. 4.95 (ISBN 0-671-67838-8). S&S Trade.

—Milk & Cookies. LC 82-7962. (Illus.). 48p. (ps-3). 1982. 5.95 (ISBN 0-8193-1087-5); PLB 5.95 (ISBN 0-8193-1088-3). Parents.

—Popcorn. Asch, Frank, illus. LC 79-216. 48p. (ps-3). 1979. 5.95 (ISBN 0-8193-1001-8); lib. bdg. 5.95 (ISBN 0-8193-1002-6). Parents.

—Sand Cake. Asch, Frank, illus. LC 78-11183. 48p. (ps-3). 1979. 5.95 (ISBN 0-8193-0985-0); lib. bdg. 5.95 (ISBN 0-8193-0986-9). Parents.

Ash, Russell & Bond, Michael. The Life & Times of Paddington Bear. LC 88-62808. 160p. 1989. pap. 24. 95 (ISBN 1-851-45286-9). Viking Penguin.

Bach, Alice. Grouchy Uncle Otto. Kellogg, Steven, illus. LC 76-24304. 48p. (gr. k-4). 1977. 8.89 (ISBN 0-06-020344-7). HarpC Child Bks.

—The Most Delicious Camping Trip Ever. Kellogg, Steven, illus. LC 76-2956. 48p. (gr. k-3). 1976. HarpC Child Bks.

—The Smartest Bear & His Brother Oliver. Kellogg, Steven, illus. LC 74-29348. 48p. (gr. k-4). 1975. 5.95 (ISBN 0-06-020334-X). HarpC Child Bks.

Ballet Bears Getting in Shape. (ps-3). 1987. pap. 1.95 (ISBN 0-89954-729-X). Antioch Pub Co.

Barnes, Jill & Sueyoshi, Akiko. Great Day for Bears. Rubin, Caroline, ed. Japan Foreign Rights Centre Staff, tr. from JPN. Fujita, Miho, illus. LC 90-37753. 32p. (gr. k-3). 1990. PLB 15.93 (ISBN 0-944483-84-4). Garrett Ed Corp.

Baron, Michelle. The Sign of a Friend. Forsse, Ken & Becker, Mary, eds. High, David, et al, illus. 26p. (ps). 1986. 9.95 (ISBN 0-934323-37-2); pre-programmed audio cass. tape incl. Alchemy Comms.

Baron, Phil. The Do-Along Songbook. Forse, Ken, ed. High, David, et al, illus. 26p. (ps). 1986. 9.95 (ISBN 0-934323-34-8); pre-programmed audio cass. tape incl. Alchemy Comms.

—The Mushroom Forest. Forsse, Ken & Becker, Mary, eds. Conley-Gorniak, Allyn & Armstrong, Julie A., illus. 26p. (ps). 1986. 9.95 (ISBN 0-934323-36-4); pre-programmed audio cass. tape incl. Alchemy Comms.

Barton, Byron, retold by. & illus. The Three Bears. LC 90-43151. 32p. (ps-1). 1991. 11.95 (ISBN 0-06-020423-0); PLB 11.89 (ISBN 0-06-020424-9). HarpC Child Bks.

Baumann, Hans. Mischa & His Brothers. Neumeyer, Peter, tr. from GER. Michl, Reinhard, illus. 32p. (gr. 1 up). 1985. 12.95 (ISBN 0-88138-051-2). Green Tiger Pr.

Beck, Martine. Rescue of Brown Bear & White Bear. (ps-3). 1991. 14.95 (ISBN 0-316-08654-1). Little.

—Wedding of Brown Bear & White Bear, Vol. 1. (ps-3). 1990. 12.95 (ISBN 0-316-08652-5). Little.

Beck, Sara. Fanshen the Magic Bear. (Illus.). (gr. 1-5). 1973. 4.95 (ISBN 0-938678-01-9). New Seed.

Bellows, Cathy. The Grizzly Sisters. LC 90-38787. (Illus.). 32p. (ps-3). 1991. 14.95 (ISBN 0-02-709032-9, Mcmillan Child Bk). Macmillan Child Grp.

Bennett, David. The Lost Teddy. (Illus.). 24p. (ps-1). 1989. 5.95 (ISBN 0-8120-5913-1). Barron.

The Berenstain Bears' Trouble at School. (Illus.). (gr. k-9). 1988. pap. 1.95 (ISBN 0-318-36461-1). Scholastic Inc.

Berenstain, Janice & Berenstain, Stan. The Berenstain Bears Get in a Fight. Berenstain, Janice & Berenstain, Stan, illus. LC 81-15866. 32p. (ps-1). 1982. lib. bdg. 5.99 (ISBN 0-394-95132-8); pap. 2.25 (ISBN 0-394-85132-3). Random.

—The Berenstain Bears Go to Camp. Berenstain, Janice & Berenstain, Stan, illus. LC 81-15864. 32p. (ps-1). 1982. pap. 2.25 (ISBN 0-394-85131-5). Random.

Berenstain, Stan & Berenstain, Jan. The Berenstain Bears & the Prize Pumpkin. Berenstain, Stan & Berenstain, Jan, illus. LC 90-32865. 32p. (Orig.). (ps-1). 1990. lib. bdg. 5.99 (ISBN 0-679-90847-1); pap. 2.25 (ISBN 0-679-80847-7). Random.

—The Berenstain Bears & the Slumber Party. Berenstain, Stan & Berenstain, Jan, illus. LC 89-35223. 32p. (Orig.). 1990. PLB 5.99 (ISBN 0-679-90419-0); pap. 2.25 (ISBN 0-679-80419-6). McKay.

—The Berenstain Bears & Too Much Vacation. Berenstain, Stan & Berenstain, Jan, illus. LC 88-32094. 32p. (ps-1). 1990. pap. 5.95 (ISBN 0-679-80311-4); cass. incl. McKay.

—The Berenstain Bears Are a Family. Berenstain, Stan & Berenstain, Jan, illus. LC 90-63082. 24p. (Orig.). (ps). 1991. pap. 2.95 (ISBN 0-679-80746-2). Random.

—The Berenstain Bears at the Super-Duper Market. Berenstain, Stan & Berenstain, Jan, illus. LC 90-63080. 24p. (Orig.). (ps). 1991. pap. 2.95 (ISBN 0-679-80748-9). Random.

—The Berenstain Bears Don't Pollute Anymore. Berenstain, Stan & Berenstain, Jan, illus. LC 91-9147. 32p. (Orig.). (ps-1). 1991. lib. bdg. 5.99 (ISBN 0-679-92351-9, Random Juv); pap. 2.25 (ISBN 0-679-82351-4). Random.

—The Berenstain Bears' Four Seasons. Berenstain, Stan & Berenstain, Jan, illus. LC 90-63079. 24p. (Orig.). (ps). 1991. pap. 2.95 (ISBN 0-679-80749-7). Random.

—The Berenstain Bears Get the Gimmies. Berenstain, Stan & Berenstain, Jan, illus. LC 88-42587. 32p. (ps-1). 1990. pap. 5.95 (ISBN 0-679-80313-0); cass. incl. McKay.

—The Berenstain Bears Go Out for the Team. reissued ed. Berenstain, Stan & Berenstain, Jan, illus. LC 85-30164. 32p. (ps-1). 1991. pap. 5.95 incls. cassette (ISBN 0-679-81495-7). Random.

—The Berenstain Bears Say Good Night. Berenstain, Stan & Berenstain, Jan, illus. LC 90-63081. 24p. (Orig.). (ps). 1991. pap. 2.95 (ISBN 0-679-80747-0). Random.

—The Berenstain Bears' Trouble with Pets. Berenstain, Stan & Berenstain, Jan, illus. LC 90-32956. 32p. (Orig.). (ps-1). 1990. lib. bdg. 5.99 (ISBN 0-679-90848-X); pap. 2.25 (ISBN 0-679-80848-5). Random.

Berenstain, Stan & Berenstain, Janice. The Bear Detectives. Berenstain, Stan & Berenstain, Janice, illus. LC 75-1603. 48p. (gr. k-3). 1975. 6.95 (ISBN 0-394-83127-6); lib. bdg. 7.99 (ISBN 0-394-93127-0). Beginner.

—The Bear Detectives. Berenstain, Stan & Berenstain, Janice, illus. 48p. (ps-1). 1988. pap. 5.95 bk. & cassette pkg. (ISBN 0-394-80499-6, B Y R). Random.

—Bear Scouts. Berenstain, Stan & Berenstain, Janice, illus. LC 67-21919. 72p. (gr. k-3). 1967. 6.95 (ISBN 0-394-80046-X); lib. bdg. 7.99 (ISBN 0-394-90046-4). Beginner.

—Bears' Christmas. LC 79-117542. (Illus.). 72p. (gr. k-3). 1970. 5.95 (ISBN 0-394-80090-7); lib. bdg. 6.99 (ISBN 0-394-90090-1). Beginner.

—The Bears' Christmas. Berenstain, Stan & Berenstain, Janice, illus. 64p. (ps-1). 1988. pap. 6.95 bk. & cassette pkg. (ISBN 0-394-89835-4, Random Juv). Random.

—Bears in the Night. (Illus.). (ps-1). 1971. 6.95 (ISBN 0-394-82286-2, Random Juv); lib. bdg. 7.99 (ISBN 0-394-92286-7). Random.

—Bears on Wheels. LC 72-77840. (Illus.). (ps-1). 1969. 6.95 (ISBN 0-394-80967-X, Random Juv); lib. bdg. 7.99 (ISBN 0-394-90967-4). Random.

—Bears' Picnic. LC 66-10156. (Illus.). 72p. (gr. k-3). 1966. 6.95 (ISBN 0-394-80041-9); lib. bdg. 7.99 (ISBN 0-394-90041-3). Beginner.

—Bears' Vacation. Berenstain, Stan & Berenstain, Janice, illus. LC 68-28460. 72p. (gr. k-3). 1968. 6.95 (ISBN 0-394-80052-4); lib. bdg. 7.99 (ISBN 0-394-90052-9). Beginner.

—The Bears' Vacation. Berenstain, Stan & Berenstain, Janice, illus. 64p. (ps-1). 1987. pap. 5.95 incl. cassette (ISBN 0-394-88848-0, Random Juv). Random.

—The Berenstain Bears' Almanac. Berenstain, Stan, illus. LC 73-2298. 72p. (ps-4). 1984. pap. 4.95 (ISBN 0-394-86601-0, Random Juv). Random.

—The Berenstain Bears & Mama's New Job. Berenstain, Stan & Berenstain, Jan, illus. LC 84-4787. 32p. (ps-1). 1984. lib. bdg. 5.99 (ISBN 0-394-96881-6, Random Juv); pap. 2.25 (ISBN 0-394-86881-1). Random.

—The Berenstain Bears & the Bad Dream. Berenstain, Stan & Berenstain, Janice, illus. LC 87-27295. 32p. (ps-1). 1988. lib. bdg. 5.99 (ISBN 0-394-97341-0, Random Juv); pap. 2.25 (ISBN 0-394-87341-6). Random.

—The Berenstain Bears & the Bad Habit. Berenstain, Stan & Berenstain, Janice, illus. LC 86-3205. 32p. (ps-1). 1987. lib. bdg. 5.99 (ISBN 0-394-97340-2, Random Juv); pap. 2.25 (ISBN 0-394-87340-8, Random Juv). Random.

—The Berenstain Bears & the Bad Habit. (Illus.). (gr. k-9). 1988. pap. 1.95 (ISBN 0-318-36460-3). Scholastic Inc.

—The Berenstain Bears & the Big Election. Berenstain, Stan & Berenstain, Janice, illus. LC 83-62399. 32p. (ps-3). 1984. pap. 1.25 (ISBN 0-394-86542-1, Random Juv). Random.

—The Berenstain Bears & the Big Road Race. Berenstain, Stan & Berenstain, Janice, illus. LC 87-4581. 32p. (gr. k-3). 1987. lib. bdg. 5.99 (ISBN 0-394-99134-6, Random Juv); pap. 2.25 (ISBN 0-394-89134-1, Random Juv). Random.

—The Berenstain Bears & the Dinosaurs. Berenstain, Stan & Berenstain, Janice, illus. LC 84-60384. 32p. (ps-3). 1984. pap. 1.50 (ISBN 0-394-86883-8, Random Juv). Random.

—The Berenstain Bears & the Double Dare. Berenstain, Stan & Berenstain, Janice, illus. LC 87-27296. 32p. (ps-1). 1988. lib. bdg. 5.99 (ISBN 0-394-99748-4, Random Juv); pap. 2.25 (ISBN 0-394-89748-X). Random.

—The Berenstain Bears & the Ghost of the Forest. Berenstain, Stan & Berenstain, Janice, illus. LC 88-42586. 32p. (Orig.). (gr. k-3). 1988. lib. bdg. 5.99 (ISBN 0-394-90565-2, Random Juv); pap. 2.25 (ISBN 0-394-80565-8, Random Juv). Random.

—The Berenstain Bears & the Messy Room. Berenstain, Janice & Berenstain, Stan, illus. Lerner, Sharon, ed. 32p. (ps-2). 1983. lib. bdg. 5.99 (ISBN 0-394-95639-7); pap. 2.25 (ISBN 0-394-85639-2). Random.

—The Berenstain Bears & the Messy Room. Berenstain, Stan & Berenstain, Janice, illus. 32p. (ps-1). 1987. pap. 3.50 (ISBN 0-394-88892-8, Random Juv). Random.

—The Berenstain Bears & the Missing Dinosaur Bone. Berenstain, Stan & Berenstain, Janice, illus. LC 79-3458. 48p. (ps-3). 1980. 6.95 (ISBN 0-394-84447-5); lib. bdg. 7.99 (ISBN 0-394-94447-X). Beginner.

—The Berenstain Bears & the Missing Honey. Berenstain, Stan & Berenstain, Janice, illus. LC 87-4549. 32p. (ps-3). 1987. lib. bdg. 5.99 (ISBN 0-394-99133-8, Random Juv); pap. 2.25 (ISBN 0-394-89133-3, Random Juv). Random.

—The Berenstain Bears & the Sitter. Berenstain, Stan & Berenstain, Janice, illus. LC 81-50046. 32p. (ps-1). 1981. lib. bdg. 5.99 (ISBN 0-394-94837-8); pap. 1.95 (ISBN 0-394-84837-3). Random.

—The Berenstain Bears & the Sitter. Berenstain, Stan & Berenstain, Janice, illus. 32p. (ps-1). 1987. pap. 2.95 (ISBN 0-394-88890-1, Random Juv). Random.

—The Berenstain Bears & the Spooky Old Tree. LC 77-93771. (Illus.). (ps-2). 1978. 5.95 (ISBN 0-394-83910-2, Random Juv); lib. bdg. 7.99 (ISBN 0-394-93910-7). Random.

—The Berenstain Bears & the Trouble with Friends. Berenstain, Stan & Berenstain, Janice, illus. LC 85-30165. 32p. (ps-1). 1987. lib. bdg. 5.99 (ISBN 0-394-97339-9, Random Juv); pap. 3.50 (ISBN 0-394-88893-6, BYR). Random.

—The Berenstain Bears & the Truth. LC 83-3304. (Illus.). 32p. (ps-k). 1983. lib. bdg. 5.99 (ISBN 0-394-95640-0); pap. 1.95 (ISBN 0-394-85640-6). Random.

—The Berenstain Bears & the Truth. Berenstain, Stan & Berenstain, Janice, illus. LC 83-3304. 32p. (ps-1). 1988. pap. 3.50 (ISBN 0-394-89794-3, Random Juv); pap. 4.95 bk. & cassette pkg. (ISBN 0-394-89771-4). Random.
—The Berenstain Bears & the Week at Grandma's. Berenstain, Stan & Berenstain, Janice, illus. LC 85-25743. (ps-1). 1986. lib. bdg. 5.99 (ISBN 0-394-97335-6, Random Juv); pap. 2.25 (ISBN 0-394-87335-1, Random Juv). Random.
—The Berenstain Bears & the Wild, Wild Honey. LC 83-60057. (Illus.). 32p. (ps). 1983. pap. 1.25 (ISBN 0-394-85924-3). Random.
—The Berenstain Bears & Too Much Birthday. Berenstain, Stan & Berenstain, Janice, illus. LC 85-14529. 32p. (ps-1). 1986. lib. bdg. 5.99 (ISBN 0-394-97332-1); pap. 2.25 (ISBN 0-394-87332-7). Random.
—The Berenstain Bears & Too Much Junk Food. Berenstain, Stan & Berenstain, Janice, illus. Lerner, Sharon, ed. LC 84-40393. 32p. (ps-2). 1985. lib. bdg. 5.99 (ISBN 0-394-97217-1, Random Juv); pap. 2.25 (ISBN 0-394-87217-7). Random.
—The Berenstain Bears & Too Much TV. Berenstain, Stan & Berenstain, Jan, illus. LC 83-22887. (gr. 3-6). 1984. lib. bdg. 5.99 (ISBN 0-394-96570-1, Random Juv); pap. 2.25 (ISBN 0-394-86570-7, Random Juv). Random.
—The Berenstain Bears & Too Much TV. Berenstain, Stan & Berenstain, Janice, illus. (ps-1). 1989. bk. & cassette 5.95 (ISBN 0-394-82894-1). Random.
—The Berenstain Bears' Bath Book. Berenstain, Stan & Berenstain, Jan, illus. 10p. (ps). 1985. vinyl 2.95 (ISBN 0-394-87116-2, Random Juv). Random.
—The Berenstain Bears Blaze a Trail. Berenstain, Stan & Berenstain, Janice, illus. LC 87-4552. 32p. (ps-1). 1987. lib. bdg. 5.99 (ISBN 0-394-99132-X, Random Juv); pap. 2.25 (ISBN 0-394-89132-5, Random Juv). Random.
—The Berenstain Bears' Christmas Tree. LC 80-5087. (Illus.). 72p. (ps-3). 1980. 10.95 (ISBN 0-394-84566-8); lib. bdg. 9.99 (ISBN 0-394-94566-2). Random.
—Berenstain Bears Forget Their Manners. Berenstain, Stan & Berenstain, Janice, illus. LC 84-43156. 32p. (gr. k-3). 1985. lib. bdg. 5.99 (ISBN 0-394-97333-X); pap. 1.95 (ISBN 0-394-87333-5). Random.
—The Berenstain Bears Forget Their Manners. Berenstain, Stan & Berenstain, Janice, illus. 32p. (ps-1). 1986. pap. 5.95 with cassette (ISBN 0-394-88343-8, Random Juv). Random.
—Berenstain Bears Forget Their Manners. Berenstain, Stan & Berenstain, Janice, illus. LC 84-43156. 32p. (ps-1). 1988. pap. 3.50 (ISBN 0-394-89798-6, Random Juv). Random.
—The Berenstain Bears Get in a Fight. Berenstain, Stan & Berenstain, Janice, illus. 32p. (ps-1). 1987. pap. 2.95 (ISBN 0-685-17582-0, Random Juv). Random.
—The Berenstain Bears Get in a Fight. Berenstain, Stan & Berenstain, Janice, illus. 32p. (ps-1). 1988. pap. 4.95 bk. & cassette pkg. (ISBN 0-394-89778-1, Random Juv). Random.
—The Berenstain Bears Get Stage Fright. Berenstain, Stan & Berenstain, Janice, illus. LC 85-25716. 32p. (gr. 3-6). 1986. lib. bdg. 5.99 (ISBN 0-394-97337-2, Random Juv); pap. 1.95 (ISBN 0-394-87337-8, Random Juv). Random.
—The Berenstain Bears Get the Gimmies. Berenstain, Stan & Berenstain, Janice, illus. LC 88-42587. 32p. (Orig.). (ps-1). 1988. lib. bdg. 5.99 (ISBN 0-394-90566-0, Random Juv); pap. 2.25 (ISBN 0-394-80566-6, Random Juv). Random.
—The Berenstain Bears Go Fly a Kite. LC 83-60056. (Illus.). 32p. (ps-2). 1983. pap. 1.50 (ISBN 0-394-85921-9). Random.
—The Berenstain Bears Go to Camp. Berenstain, Stan & Berenstain, Janice, illus. (ps-1). 1989. 4.95 (ISBN 0-394-82896-8). Random.
—The Berenstain Bears Go to School. LC 77-79853. (Illus.). (ps-2). 1978. lib. bdg. 5.99 (ISBN 0-394-93736-8, Random Juv); pap. 2.25 (ISBN 0-394-83736-3). Random.
—The Berenstain Bears Go to the Doctor. Berenstain, Stan & Berenstain, Janice, illus. LC 81-50043. 32p. (ps-1). 1981. lib. bdg. 5.99 (ISBN 0-394-94835-1); pap. 2.25 (ISBN 0-394-84835-7). Random.
—The Berenstain Bears Go to the Doctor. Berenstain, Stan & Berenstain, Janice, illus. 32p. (ps-1). 1987. pap. 2.95 (ISBN 0-394-88889-8, Random Juv). Random.
—The Berenstain Bears in the Dark. LC 82-5395. 32p. (ps-1). 1982. pap. 2.25 saddle-stitched (ISBN 0-394-85443-8). Random.
—Berenstain Bears Learn about Strangers. Berenstain, Stan & Berenstain, Jan, illus. LC 84-43157. 32p. (ps-1). 1985. lib. bdg. 5.99 (ISBN 0-394-97334-8); pap. 2.25 (ISBN 0-394-87334-3). Random.
—The Berenstain Bears Learn about Strangers. (Illus.). 32p. (ps-1). 1986. pap. 4.95 (ISBN 0-394-88346-2, Random Juv). Random.
—The Berenstain Bears Meet Santa Bear. Berenstain, Stan & Berenstain, Janice, illus. LC 84-4829. 32p. (ps-1). 1988. pap. 2.95 book & puppet pkg. (ISBN 0-394-89797-8, Random Juv). Random.
—The Berenstain Bears Meet Santa Bear. Berenstain, Stan & Berenstain, Janice, illus. LC 84-4829. 32p. (ps-1). 1989. pap. 5.95 incl. cassette (ISBN 0-394-85228-1). Random.
—The Berenstain Bears' Moving Day. Berenstain, Stan & Berenstain, Janice, illus. LC 81-50044. 32p. (ps-1). 1981. lib. bdg. 5.99 (ISBN 0-394-94838-6); pap. 2.25 (ISBN 0-394-84838-1). Random.
—The Berenstain Bears' Nature Guide. Berenstain, Stan & Berenstain, Jan, illus. LC 75-8070. 72p. (ps-4). 1984. pap. 7.95 (ISBN 0-394-86602-9, Random Juv). Random.
—The Berenstain Bears' New Baby. Berenstain, Stan & Berenstain, Janice, illus. 32p. (gr. 1-3). 1985. pap. 5.95 (ISBN 0-394-87661-X, Random Juv). Random.
—The Berenstain Bears' Nursery Tales. (Illus.). (ps-1). 1973. pap. 2.25 (ISBN 0-394-82665-5, Random Juv). Random.
—The Berenstain Bears on the Job. Berenstain, Stan & Berenstain, Janice, illus. LC 87-9739. 32p. (gr. k-3). 1987. lib. bdg. 5.99 (ISBN 0-394-99131-1, Random Juv); pap. 2.25 (ISBN 0-394-89131-7, Random Juv). Random.
—The Berenstain Bears on the Moon. Berenstain, Stan & Berenstain, Janice, illus. LC 84-20428. 48p. (ps-3). 1985. 6.95 (ISBN 0-394-87180-4, Random Juv); lib. bdg. 6.99 (ISBN 0-394-97180-9). Random.
—The Berenstain Bears Ready, Set, Go! Berenstain, Stan & Berenstain, Janice, illus. LC 88-42589. 32p. (Orig.). (gr. k-3). 1988. lib. bdg. 5.99 (ISBN 0-394-90564-4, Random Juv); pap. 2.25 (ISBN 0-394-80564-X, Random Juv). Random.
—The Berenstain Bears' Science Fair. Berenstain, Stan & Berenstain, Janice, illus. LC 76-8121. 72p. (ps-4). 1984. pap. 6.95 (ISBN 0-394-86603-7, Random Juv). Random.
—The Berenstain Bears Shoot the Rapids. Berenstain, Stan & Berenstain, Janice, illus. LC 83-62400. 32p. (ps-3). 1984. pap. 1.50 (ISBN 0-394-86543-X, Random Juv). Random.
—The Berenstain Bears' Take-Along Library. Berenstain, Stan & Berenstain, Janice, illus. Incl. The Berenstain Bears Visit the Dentist. 32p; The Berenstain Bears & Too Much TV. 32p; The Berenstain Bears & the Sitter. 32p; The Berenstain Bears in the Dark. 32p; The Berenstain Bears & the Messy Room. 32p. (ps-3). 1985. 11.50 (ISBN 0-394-87615-6, Random Juv). Random.
—The Berenstain Bears to the Rescue. LC 83-60058. (Illus.). 32p. (ps-2). 1983. pap. 1.25 (ISBN 0-394-85923-5). Random.
—The Berenstain Bears' Toy Time. (Illus.). 12p. (ps). 1985. 2.95 (ISBN 0-394-87449-8, Random Juv). Random.
—The Berenstain Bears Trick or Treat. Berenstain, Stan & Berenstain, Janice, illus. LC 89-30884. 32p. (Orig.). (ps-1). 1989. PLB 5.99 (ISBN 0-679-90091-8, Random Juv); pap. 2.25 (ISBN 0-679-80091-3, Random Juv). Random.
—The Berenstain Bears' Trouble at School. Berenstain, Stan & Berenstain, Janice, illus. LC 86-4999. 32p. (ps-1). 1987. lib. bdg. 5.99 (ISBN 0-394-97336-4, Random Juv); pap. 2.25 (ISBN 0-394-87336-X, Random Juv). Random.
—The Berenstain Bears' Trouble with Money. LC 83-3305. (Illus.). 32p. (ps-k). 1983. lib. bdg. 5.99 (ISBN 0-394-95917-5); pap. 1.95 (ISBN 0-394-85917-0). Random.
—The Berenstain Bears Visit the Dentist. Berenstain, Stan & Berenstain, Janice, illus. LC 81-50045. 32p. (ps-1). 1981. lib. bdg. 5.99 (ISBN 0-394-94836-X); pap. 2.25 (ISBN 0-394-84836-5). Random.
—The Berenstain Bears Visit the Dentist. Berenstain, Stan & Berenstain, Janice, illus. 32p. (ps-1). 1987. pap. 2.95 (ISBN 0-394-88894-4, Random Juv). Random.
—Big Honey Hunt. LC 62-15115. (Illus.). 64p. (gr. 1-2). 1962. 6.95 (ISBN 0-394-80028-1); lib. bdg. 7.99 (ISBN 0-394-90028-6). Beginner.
—He Bear, She Bear. Berenstain, Stan & Berenstain, Janice, illus. LC 74-5518. 48p. (ps-1). 1974. 6.95 (ISBN 0-394-82997-2, Random Juv); lib. bdg. 7.99 (ISBN 0-394-92997-7). Random.
—Inside, Outside, Upside Down. LC 68-28465. (Illus.). (ps-1). 1968. 6.95 (ISBN 0-394-81142-9, Random Juv); lib. bdg. 7.99 (ISBN 0-394-91142-3). Random.
Bernier, Evariste. Baxter Bear & Moses Moose. Peterson, Dawn, illus. LC 90-61408. 48p. (gr. 1-4). 1990. 12.95 (ISBN 0-89272-287-8). Down East.
Big Ride for Little Bear. (ps-3). 1988. pap. 2.50 (ISBN 0-318-36463-8). Scholastic Inc.
Blanchard, Arlene. The Bear & Henry. Claverie, Jean, illus. 28p. (ps-1). 1987. 9.95 (ISBN 0-8120-5869-0). Barron.
Blocksma, Mary. The Best-Dressed Bear. Kalthoff, Sandra C., illus. LC 84-9565. 24p. (ps-2). 1984. lib. bdg. 12.33 (ISBN 0-516-01585-0); pap. text ed. 3.95 (ISBN 0-516-41585-9). Childrens.
Bolliger, Max. Three Little Bears. Wilkon, Jozef, illus. (ps-3). 1987. 12.95 (ISBN 1-55774-006-2, Dist. by Watts). Adama Pubs Inc.
Bond, Michael. Bear Called Paddington. Fortnum, Peggy, illus. LC 60-9096. 128p. (gr. 3-7). 1968. pap. 3.25 (ISBN 0-440-40483-5, YB). Dell.
—Bear Called Paddington. Fortnum, Peggy, illus. 128p. (gr. 1-5). 1960. 12.95 (ISBN 0-395-06636-0). HM.
—Great Big Paddington Book. 1988. 9.98 (ISBN 0-8317-4007-8). Smithmark.
—The Hilarious Adventures of Paddington, 5 bks. Incl. A Bear Called Paddington; More about Paddington; Paddington at Large; Paddington at Work; Paddington Helps Out. (Illus.). 1986. Boxed set. pap. 14.75 (ISBN 0-440-43668-0). Dell.
—More about Paddington. Fortnum, Peggy, illus. (gr. 4-6). 1962. 13.95 (ISBN 0-395-06640-9). HM.
—Paddington Abroad. Fortnum, Peggy, illus. 128p. (gr. 2-6). 1974. pap. 0.95 (ISBN 0-440-47352-7, YB). Dell.
—Paddington Abroad. Fortnum, Peggy, illus. LC 72-2753. 128p. (gr. 1-5). 1973. 13.95 (ISBN 0-395-14331-4). HM.
—Paddington at Large. (Illus.). (gr. 1-5). 1963. 13.95 (ISBN 0-395-06641-7). HM.
—Paddington at the Fair. McKee, David, illus. LC 85-5683. 32p. (ps-2). 1986. 5.95 (ISBN 0-399-21271-X, Putnam). Putnam Pub Group.
—Paddington at the Palace. McKee, David, illus. 32p. (ps-3). 1986. 5.95 (ISBN 0-399-21340-6, Putnam). Putnam Pub Group.
—Paddington at the Seaside. Banbery, Fred, illus. LC 77-90190. (ps-3). 1978. (Random Juv); lib. bdg. 4.99 (ISBN 0-394-93801-1). Random.
—Paddington at the Tower. Banbery, Fred, illus. LC 77-90189. (ps-3). 1978. (Random Juv); lib. bdg. 5.99 (ISBN 0-394-93802-X). Random.
—Paddington at the Zoo. Mckee, David, illus. 32p. (gr. k-2). 1985. 5.95 (ISBN 0-399-21201-9, Putnam). Putnam Pub Group.
—Paddington at Work. Fortnum, Peggy, illus. LC 67-20372. (gr. 1-5). 1967. 13.95 (ISBN 0-395-06637-9). HM.
—Paddington Bear. (Illus.). (ps-2). 1973. 5.95 (ISBN 0-394-82642-6, Random Juv); lib. bdg. 5.99 (ISBN 0-394-92642-0). Random.
—Paddington Cleans Up. McKee, David, illus. 32p. (ps-3). 1986. 5.95 (ISBN 0-399-21339-2, Putnam). Putnam Pub Group.
—Paddington Goes to Town. 128p. (gr. 2-5). 1972. pap. 2.75 (ISBN 0-440-46793-4, YB). Dell.
—Paddington Goes to Town. Fortnum, Peggy, illus. LC 68-28043. (gr. 1-5). 1977. 13.95 (ISBN 0-395-06635-2). HM.
—Paddington Helps Out. Fortnum, Peggy, illus. 128p. (gr. 3-7). 1982. pap. 2.95 (ISBN 0-440-46802-7, YB). Dell.
—Paddington Helps Out. Fortnum, Peggy, illus. (gr. 4-6). 1973. 13.95 (ISBN 0-395-06639-5). HM.
—Paddington Marches On. (Illus.). (gr. 4-6). 1965. 12.95 (ISBN 0-395-06642-5). HM.
—Paddington on Top. Fortnum, Peggy, illus. 128p. (gr. 1-5). 1975. 13.95 (ISBN 0-395-21897-7). HM.
—Paddington Takes the Air. Fortnum, Peggy, illus. LC 78-147902. (gr. 3-7). 1971. 14.95 (ISBN 0-395-10909-4). HM.
—Paddington Takes the Test. 128p. (gr. k-6). 1982. pap. 1.95 (ISBN 0-440-47021-8, YB). Dell.
—Paddington Works Hard. 1989. 2.98 (ISBN 0-8317-6803-7). Smithmark.
—Paddington's Art Exhibition. McKee, David, illus. 32p. (ps-2). 1986. 5.95 (ISBN 0-399-21270-1, Putnam). Putnam Pub Group.
—Paddington's Lucky Day. Banbery, Fred, illus. LC 74-5007. 36p. (ps-2). 1974. (Random Juv); lib. bdg. 4.99 (ISBN 0-394-92919-5). Random.
Bonners, Susan. Panda. LC 78-50404. (Illus.). 32p. (ps-3). 1978. pap. 6.95 (ISBN 0-385-28772-0); pap. 6.46 (ISBN 0-385-28775-5). Delacorte.
Bornstein, Harry, et al. Don't Be a Grumpy Bear: A Coloring Book about Manners in Signed English. Miller, Ralph R., illus. 32p. (ps-2). 1986. pap. 3.95 (ISBN 0-930323-26-2, Pub. by K Green Pubns). Gallaudet Univ Pr.
Bowden, Miriam. Paz the Wandering Bear in the Land of Numbers. Magellan, Mauro, illus. 32p. 1991. 12.95 (ISBN 0-89334-150-9). Humanics Ltd.
Bracken, Carolyn. Little Teddy Bear. McClain, Mary, illus. 12p. (ps-2). 1982. board 4.95 (ISBN 0-671-42550-1, Little Simon). S&S Trade.
Bracken, Carolyn, illus. Teddy Bear's Pockets. 8p. (ps). 1983. pap. 3.95 washable (ISBN 0-671-46448-5, Little Simon). S&S Trade.
Brett, Jan. Goldilocks & the Three Bears. (Illus.). 32p. (ps-3). 1990. pap. 5.95 (ISBN 0-399-22004-6, Sandcastle Bks). Putnam Pub Group.
Brimner, Larry D. Country Bear's Surprise. Councell, Ruth T., illus. LC 90-7717. 32p. (ps-2). 1991. 12.95 (ISBN 0-531-05811-5); PLB 12.99 (ISBN 0-531-08411-6). Orchard Bks Watts.
Brown, Ruth. The Grizzly Revenge. Brown, Ruth, illus. 32p. (gr. 3-6). 1987. 15.95 (ISBN 0-86264-024-5, Pub. by Anderson Pr UK). Trafalgar Sq.
Browne, Anthony. Bear Goes to Town. (ps-1). 1989. PLB 10.95 (ISBN 0-385-26524-7); pap. 11.99 (ISBN 0-385-26525-5). Doubleday.
—Bear Hunt. (ps-3). 1990. 11.95 (ISBN 0-385-41568-0); PLB 12.99 (ISBN 0-385-41569-9). Doubleday.
—The Little Bear Book. Browne, Anthony, illus. (ps-k). 1989. 5.95 (ISBN 0-385-26006-7, Zephyr-BFYR). Doubleday.
Bucknall, Caroline. One Bear All Alone. Bucknall, Caroline, illus. LC 85-6968. 32p. (ps-2). 1989. 13.95 (ISBN 0-8037-0238-8); pap. 4.95 (ISBN 0-8037-0645-6). Dial Bks Young.
Bunting, Eve. The Valentine Bears. Brett, Jan, illus. 32p. (gr. 3). 1985. 13.95 (ISBN 0-89919-138-X, Clarion); pap. 4.95 (ISBN 0-89919-313-7, Clarion). HM.
Burgess, Thornton. The Adventures of Buster Bear. 1986. Repr. lib. bdg. 17.95 (ISBN 0-89966-525-X). Buccaneer Bks.
Burt, Denise. I'm Not a Bear. Ryan, Ron, photos by. (Illus.). 32p. (gr. k-5). 1987. pap. 5.95 (ISBN 0-944176-00-3). Terra Nova.

Butler, Dorothy. My Brown Bear Barney. Fuller, Elizabeth, illus. LC 88-21199. 24p. (ps up). 1989. 13.95 (ISBN 0-688-08567-9); PLB 13.88 (ISBN 0-688-08568-7). Greenwillow.
The Care Bear Movie Book. (ps-3). 1985. 5.95 (ISBN 0-910313-99-7). Parker Bros.
Carle, Eric. The Honeybee & the Robber: A Moving Picture Book. Carle, Eric, illus. 16p. (gr. 4-8). 1981. 10.95 (ISBN 0-399-20767-8, Philomel). Putnam Pub Group.
Carlson, Anna L. Homer Bear's Secret. 1st. ed. Wynne, Dianna, illus. 24p. (Orig.). (gr. k-4). 1983. pap. 1.95 (ISBN 0-939938-05-7). Karwyn Ent.
Carlstrom, Nancy W. Better Not Get Wet, Jesse Bear. Degen, Bruce, illus. LC 87-10810. 32p. (ps-1). 1988. 13.95 (ISBN 0-02-717280-5, Mcmillan Child Bk). Macmillan Child Grp.
—It's About Time, Jesse Bear: And Other Rhymes. Degen, Bruce, illus. LC 88-8511. 32p. (ps-1). 1990. 13.95 (ISBN 0-02-717351-8, Mcmillan Child Bk). Macmillan Child Grp.
Cartlidge, Michelle. Bear's Room: No Peeking. (Illus.). 24p. (gr. k-2). 1986. 3.95 (ISBN 0-87406-124-5, 15-11820-5). Willowisp Pr.
Casterline, Charlotte L. The Asthma Attack by Bo B. Bear. Brunza-Horn, Nanette, illus. (Orig.). (ps-6). 1988. pap. 5.95 (ISBN 0-9617218-2-0). Info All Bk.
Cauley, Lorinda B., retold by. & illus. Goldilocks & the Three Bears. 32p. (ps-2). 1981. 14.95 (ISBN 0-399-20794-5, Putnam); pap. 5.95 (ISBN 0-399-20795-3). Putnam Pub Group.
Chevalier, Christa. The Little Bear Who Forgot. Tucker, Kathleen, ed. Chevalier, Christa, illus. LC 83-26083. 32p. (ps-3). 1984. PLB 11.50 (ISBN 0-8075-4571-6). A Whitman.
Christian, Mary B. Penrod's Party. Schindler, S. D., illus. LC 89-37203. 48p. (gr. 1-4). 1990. 11.95 (ISBN 0-02-718525-7, Mcmillan Child Bk). Macmillan Child Grp.
Coco, Eugene B. Baby Brown Bear's Big Bellyache. (Illus.). 24p. (ps-4). 1989. pap. write for info. (ISBN 0-307-14026-1). Western Pub.
—Baby Brown Bear's Big Bellyache. (Illus.). 24p. (ps-2). 1989. write for info. (ISBN 0-307-12088-0, Pub. by Golden Bks). Western Pub.
Cosgrove, Stephen. Buttermilk Bear. (Illus.). 32p. (gr. k-4). 1987. PLB 12.66 (ISBN 0-317-60471-6). Rourke Corp.
—Jingle Bear. James, Robin, illus. 32p. (Orig.). (gr. 1-4). 1985. pap. 2.95 (ISBN 0-8431-1440-1). Price Stern.
Cosgrove, Stephen E. Fiddler. Edelson, Wendy, illus. 32p. (ps-3). 1990. lib. bdg. 12.96 (ISBN 0-89565-665-5). Childs World.
Cowley, Joy. Old Grizzly, 6 bks. Van der Voo, Jan, illus. 16p. (Orig.). (gr. k-2). 1987. Set. pap. text ed. 19.80 (ISBN 1-55624-738-9). Wright Group.
—Old Grizzly. Van der Voo, Jan, illus. 16p. (Orig.). (gr. k-2). 1987. pap. text ed. 23.00 (ISBN 1-55624-161-5). Wright Group.
Craft, Ruth. The Winter Bear. LC 74-18178. (Illus.). 32p. (ps-2). 1979. pap. 2.50 (ISBN 0-689-70456-9, Aladdin). Macmillan Child Grp.
Crooks, Linda H., et al. Kindergang Kindergarten Skills Booklets, Featuring Busy Bear, Booklet 3. 2nd ed. Crooks, Linda H., illus. (gr. k). 1988. Repr. of 1985 ed. tchr's. ed. 9.19 (ISBN 1-877594-03-2); wkbk. 1.59 (ISBN 0-317-93575-5). I Can.
—Kindergang Kindergarten Skills Booklets, Featuring Lucky Lion, Booklet 1. 2nd ed. Crooks, Linda H., illus. (gr. k). 1988. Repr. of 1985 ed. tchr's. ed. 9.19 (ISBN 1-877594-01-6); wkbk. 1.59 (ISBN 0-317-93571-2). I Can.
Crozat, Francois. I Am a Little Bear-Mini. 1990. 2.95 (ISBN 0-8120-6191-8). Barron.
Czernecki, Stefan. Bear in the Sky. LC 90-30224. (Illus.). 64p. (gr. 2-7). 1990. 14.95 (ISBN 0-920534-63-5, Pub. by Hyperion Pr Ltd CN). Sterling.
Dabcovich, Lydia. Sleepy Bear. Dabcovich, Lydia, illus. 32p. (ps-2). 1982. 12.95 (ISBN 0-525-39465-6, DCB). Dutton Child Bks.
—Sleepy Bear. Dabcovich, Lydia, illus. 32p. (ps-2). 1985. pap. 4.95 (ISBN 0-525-44196-4, DCB). Dutton Child Bks.
Dalgliesh, Alice. The Bears on Hemlock Mountain. Sewell, Helen, illus. LC 89-27651. 64p. (gr. 1-4). 1990. Repr. of 1952 ed. 12.95 (ISBN 0-684-19169-5, Scribners Young Read). Macmillan Child Grp.
Daly, Niki. Teddy's Ear. (Illus.). 24p. (ps-1). 1985. pap. 4.95 (ISBN 0-670-80808-3). Viking Child Bks.
Damon, Laura. Birthday Buddies. Aiello, Laurel, illus. LC 87-10866. 32p. (gr. k-2). 1988. PLB 10.89 (ISBN 0-8167-1091-0); pap. text ed. 2.95 (ISBN 0-8167-1092-9). Troll Assocs.
—Fun in the Snow. Paterson, Diane, illus. LC 87-10843. 32p. (gr. k-2). 1988. PLB 10.89 (ISBN 0-8167-1081-3); pap. text ed. 2.95 (ISBN 0-8167-1082-1). Troll Assocs.

Davies, Leah. Kelly Bear Beginnings, 3 bks. Davies, Joy, illus. 96p. (ps-3). 1991. Set incl. Kelly Bear Feelings; Kelly Bear Behavior; Kelly Bear Health. pap. 13.50 (ISBN 0-9621054-3-0). Kelly Bear Bks.
The "KELLY BEAR" books teach children important life skills such as coping positively with emotions, learning appropriate behavior, making wholesome choices & accepting responsibility for their feelings, actions & bodies. Children identify with the green bear who is a positive role model. The INTERACTION books are to be read by an adult (teacher, librarian, counselor, parent) with a child or children. Throughout the books Kelly Bear asks questions that encourage children to share their thoughts & feelings, as Kelly Bear does. When adults listen with regard, children perceive themselves as valued & their self-esteem thrives. According to Dr. Kevin Swick, Univ. of South Carolina, the KELLY BEAR books have "exemplary situations"... which "have been used successfully with parents & children from every background & cultural orientation." Pam Kent, a teacher, Auburn, Alabama, states, "The books provide invaluable insights...a wonderful teaching tool." The acclaimed series is being used effectively with classrooms of children, in small groups, & with individuals, including high-risk & special education students. The KELLY BEAR books are the mainstay of an eight-week Drug Abuse Prevention Program (D.A.P.P.) $195.00. Kelly Bear Books, Route 3, Box 99, Lafayette, Alabama, (205) 864-8991.
Publisher Provided Annotation.

Davies, Leah G. Kelly Bear Behavior. Davies, Joy D., illus. LC 88-82603. 28p. (Orig.). (ps-3). 1988. pap. 4.50 (ISBN 0-9621054-1-4). Kelly Bear Bks.
—Kelly Bear Feelings. rev. ed. Davies, Joy D., illus. LC 88-82577. 28p. (ps-3). 1988. pap. 4.50 (ISBN 0-9621054-0-6). Kelly Bear Bks.
De Beer, Hans. Ahoy There, Little Polar Bear. De Beer, Hans, illus. LC 88-42533. 32p. (gr. k-3). 1988. 13.95 (ISBN 1-55858-028-X). North-South Bks NYC.
—Little Polar Bear. De Beer, Hans, illus. LC 86-33208. 32p. (gr. k-3). 1989. 13.95 (ISBN 1-55858-024-7); pap. 1.95 (ISBN 1-55858-030-1). North-South Bks NYC.
—Little Polar Bear Address Book. De Beer, Hans, illus. 128p. 1990. 7.95 (ISBN 1-55858-080-8). North-South Bks NYC.
De Brunhoff, Laurent. Babar Learns to Cook. De Brunhoff, Laurent, illus. LC 78-11769. (ps-3). 1979. lib. bdg. 5.99 (ISBN 0-394-94108-X); pap. 2.25 (ISBN 0-394-84108-5). Random.
Decker, Dorothy. Stripe Presents the ABC's. Decker, Dorothy, illus. LC 84-12180. 64p. (gr. k-3). 1984. PLB 10.95 (ISBN 0-87518-266-6, Dillon). Macmillan Child Grp.
—Stripe Visits New York. Decker, Dorothy, illus. LC 85-6768. 48p. (gr. k-3). 1986. PLB 10.95 (ISBN 0-87518-267-4, Dillon). Macmillan Child Grp.
Deihl, Edna G. The Teddy Bear That Prowled at Night. Russell, Mary L., illus. 24p. (gr. k-3). 1986. pap. 7.95 (ISBN 0-88138-079-2). Green Tiger Pr.
Dengler, Sandy. Smokey, a Simple Country Bear Who Made Good. Dengler, Sandy, illus. 31p. (gr. 3-5). 1987. pap. text ed. 3.00 (ISBN 0-914019-15-5). Pacif NW Natl Pks.
Dicks, Terrance. Enter T. R. Hellard, Susan, illus. 56p. (gr. 2-4). 1988. pap. 2.95 (ISBN 0-8120-4105-4). Barron.
—T. R's Day Out. Hellard, Susan, illus. 56p. (gr. 2-4). 1988. pap. 2.95 (ISBN 0-8120-4107-0). Barron.
—T. R's Halloween. Hellard, Susan, illus. 56p. (gr. 2-4). 1988. pap. 2.95 (ISBN 0-8120-4108-9). Barron.
Disney, Walt. New Adventure of Winnie the Pooh: Caws & Effect. 1991. 5.98 (ISBN 0-7924-5471-5). BDD Promo Bk.
—New Adventure of Winnie the Pooh: Eeyore's Tail Tale. 1991. 15.98 (ISBN 0-7924-5470-7). BDD Promo Bk.
—New Adventure of Winnie the Pooh: Fast Friends. 1991. 5.95 (ISBN 0-7924-5473-1). BDD Promo Bk.
—New Adventures of Winnie the Pooh: Rabbit Marks the Spot. 1991. 5.98 (ISBN 0-7924-5472-3). BDD Promo Bk.
Disney, Walt, Productions Staff. How Do You Do? I'm Winnie the Pooh. Disney, Walt, Productions Staff, tr. (Illus.). 10p. (ps). 1985. vinyl 3.95 (ISBN 0-394-87029-8, Random Juv). Random.
—Walt Disney's Winnie the Pooh & Tigger Too. LC 75-20349. (Illus.). 48p. (ps-3). 1976. 6.95 (ISBN 0-394-82569-1, Random Juv); lib. bdg. 4.99 (ISBN 0-394-92569-6). Random.
Doerksen, Nan. Bears for Breakfast: The Thiessen Family Adventures. Penner, Kathy, illus. 34p. (ps-k). 1983. pap. 2.50 (ISBN 0-919797-07-5). Kindred Pr.
Donnely, Marcus. Guffy the Bear. (Illus.). 32p. (ps). 1986. 4.50 (ISBN 0-938715-00-3). Toy Works Pr.
Douglass, Barbara. Good As New. Brewster, Patience, illus. LC 80-21406. 32p. (ps-1). 1982. 13.00 (ISBN 0-688-41983-6); PLB 12.88 (ISBN 0-688-51983-0). Lothrop.
Dyer, Jane, illus. Goldilocks & the Three Bears. 16p. (ps). 1984. 3.95 (ISBN 0-448-10213-7, G&D). Putnam Pub Group.
Eaton, Seymour. The Roosevelt Bears Go to Washington. Campbell, V. Floyd & Culver, R. K., illus. 192p. (gr. 6 up). 1981. pap. 4.50 (ISBN 0-486-24163-7). Dover.
—The Roosevelt Bears: Their Travels & Adventures. Campbell, V. Floyd, illus. 192p. (gr. 1 up). 1979. pap. 5.95 (ISBN 0-486-23819-9). Dover.
Fast, Suellen M. Golden-Brown Baby Bear & the Three Sisters. Serman, Gina L., ed. 30p. (Orig.). (ps up). pap. 4.00 (ISBN 0-935281-11-8). Daughter Cult.
Firmin, Peter. Boastful Mr. Bear. 1990. pap. 2.95 (ISBN 0-440-40371-5, YB). Dell.
Flack, Marjorie. Ask Mr. Bear. Flack, Marjorie, illus. (ps-3). 1990. incl. cass. 19.95 (ISBN 0-87499-044-0); pap. 12.95 incl. cass. (ISBN 0-87499-043-2); Set; incl. 4 bks., cass., & guide. pap. 27.95 (ISBN 0-87499-045-9). Live Oak Media.
Forsse, Ken. Teddy Ruxpin's Birthday. (Illus.). 26p. (ps). 1985. incl. audio-cassette 9.95 (ISBN 0-934323-13-5). Alchemy Comms.
—Teddy's Winter Adventure. (Illus.). 26p. (ps). 1985. incl. audio-cassette 9.95 (ISBN 0-934323-12-7). Alchemy Comms.
—The Wooly What's-It. High, David, et al, illus. 26p. (ps). 1985. incl. audio-cassette 9.95 (ISBN 0-934323-05-4). Alchemy Comms.
Freeman, Don. Beady Bear. (Illus.). (gr. 3-6). 1977. pap. 3.95 (ISBN 0-14-050197-5, Puffin). Puffin Bks.
—Bearymore. (Illus.). (ps-3). 1979. pap. 3.95 (ISBN 0-14-050279-3, Puffin). Puffin Bks.
—Bearymore. LC 76-94. (Illus.). 40p. (gr. k-3). 1976. 14.95 (ISBN 0-670-15174-2). Viking Child Bks.
—Corduroy. (Illus.). (gr. k-1). 1976. pap. 3.95 incl. cassette (ISBN 0-14-050173-8, Puffin). Puffin Bks.
Freeman, Don, illus. A Pocket for Corduroy. (ps). 1980. pap. 3.95 (ISBN 0-14-050352-8, Puffin). Puffin Bks.
Friskey, Margaret. Indian Two Feet & the Grizzly Bear. Hawkinson, John, illus. LC 74-7481. 32p. (gr. k-2). 1974. PLB 14.60 (ISBN 0-516-03508-8). Childrens.
Fujikawa, Gyo. Betty Bear's Birthday. (Illus.). (ps-2). 1977. 3.50 (ISBN 0-448-14369-0, G&D). Putnam Pub Group.
Gage, Wilson. Cully Cully & the Bear. Stevenson, James, illus. LC 82-11715. (ps-3). 1988. pap. 7.95 incl. cassette (ISBN 0-688-08401-X, Mulberry). Morrow.
—Cully Cully & the Bear. LC 82-11715. (Illus.). (ps-3). 1983. PLB 11.88 (ISBN 0-688-01769-X); pap. 3.95 (ISBN 0-688-07043-4). Greenwillow.
Galdone, Paul. The Three Bears. Galdone, Paul, illus. LC 78-158833. 32p. (ps-3). 1985. pap. 4.95 (ISBN 0-89919-401-X, Pub. by Clarion). Ticknor & Fields.
Gantschev, Ivan. Otto the Bear. Gantschev, Ivan, illus. 32p. (gr. k-3). 1986. 13.95 (ISBN 0-316-30348-8). Little.
George, Jean C. The Grizzly Bear with the Golden Ears. Schoenherr, John, illus. LC 80-7908. 32p. (ps-3). 1982. PLB 12.89 (ISBN 0-06-021966-1). HarpC Child Bks.
Gerstein, Mordicai. Anytime Mapleson & the Hungry Bears. Harris, Susan Y., illus. LC 89-34473. 32p. (ps-3). 1990. 13.95 (ISBN 0-06-022414-2); PLB 13.89 (ISBN 0-06-022415-0). HarpC Child Bks.
Ginsburg, Mirra. Two Greedy Bears. (Illus.). 32p. (ps-3). 1990. pap. 3.95 (ISBN 0-689-71392-4, Aladdin). Macmillan Child Grp.
—Two Greedy Bears: Adapted from a Hungarian Folk Tale. Aruego, Jose & Dewey, Ariane, illus. LC 76-8819. 32p. (ps-2). 1976. 13.95 (ISBN 0-02-736450-X, Mcmillan Child Bk). Macmillan Child Grp.
Girst, Jack A. Every Bunny Needs a Bear Friend. Girst, Jack A., illus. 32p. (gr. k-2). 1989. pap. 1.95 (ISBN 0-87403-634-8, 3973). Standard Pub.
Goldilocks & the Three Bears. (Illus.). 64p. (ps-3). 1991. 11.95 (ISBN 0-916410-55-2). A D Bragdon.
Goldman, Dara. There's No Such Thing! (Illus.). 32p. (ps-1). 1990. 12.95 (ISBN 0-399-22193-X, Putnam). Putnam Pub Group.
Goldstein, Bobbye. Bear in Mind: A Book of Bear Poems. DuBois, William P., illus. 32p. (ps-3). 1989. 11.95 (ISBN 0-670-81907-7). Viking Child Bks.
Graham, Ada & Graham, Frank. Bears in the Wild. Tyler, D. D., illus. 176p. (gr. 4-8). 1983. pap. 2.25 (ISBN 0-440-40897-0, YB). Dell.
Graham, Thomas. Mr. Bear's Boat. Graham, Thomas, illus. LC 87-24466. 32p. (ps-2). 1988. 11.95 (ISBN 0-525-44375-4, 01160-350, DCB). Dutton Child Bks.
—Mr. Bear's Chair. Graham, Thomas, illus. LC 86-19920. 32p. (ps-2). 1990. 10.95 (ISBN 0-525-44302-2, DCB); pap. 3.95 (ISBN 0-525-44651-6, DCB). Dutton Child Bks.
Grandma Marian, pseud. Mrs. Pam Polar Bear. Sullo, Lorraine T., illus. 32p. (gr. k-2). 1989. 7.95 (ISBN 0-9614989-9-4). Banmar Inc.

Green, Cecile. The Tale of Theodore Bear. Lysaker, Gene, illus. (gr. 1-2). 1978. pap. 1.25 (ISBN 0-89508-060-5). Rainbow Bks.

Gretz, Susanna. I'm Not Sleepy. Gretz, Susanna, illus. LC 85-13001. 10p. (ps-k). 1986. PLB 2.95 (ISBN 0-02-737470-X, Four Winds). Macmillan Child Grp.

—Teddy Bears Cure a Cold. Sage, Alison, illus. LC 84-4015. 40p. (gr. k-3). 1985. 13.95 (ISBN 0-02-736960-9, Four Winds). Macmillan Child Grp.

—Teddy Bears Cure a Cold. Sage, Alison, illus. 32p. (ps-2). 1986. pap. 3.95 (ISBN 0-590-43495-0). Scholastic Inc.

—Teddy Bears' Moving Day. Gretz, Susanna, illus. LC 88-10365. 32p. (gr. k-3). 1988. pap. 3.95 (ISBN 0-689-71269-3, Aladdin). Macmillan Child Grp.

—Teddy Bears Take the Train. Gretz, Susanna, illus. LC 87-8572. 32p. (gr. k-3). 1988. 13.95 (ISBN 0-02-738170-6, Four Winds). Macmillan Child Grp.

Greydanus, Rose. Bedtime Story. Cushman, Doug, illus. LC 86-30858. 32p. (gr. k-2). 1988. PLB 7.06 (ISBN 0-8167-0996-3); pap. text ed. 1.95 (ISBN 0-8167-0997-1). Troll Assocs.

Gruber, Suzanne. Monster under My Bed. Britt, Stephanie, illus. LC 84-45687. 32p. (gr. k-2). 1985. PLB 10.89 (ISBN 0-8167-0456-2); pap. text ed. 2.95 (ISBN 0-8167-0457-0). Troll Assocs.

Haas, Dorothy. Bears Upstairs. 1989. pap. 2.75 (ISBN 0-590-42561-7). Scholastic Inc.

Hader, Bertha. Three Bears. 1990. 3.98 (ISBN 0-8317-4272-0). Smithmark.

Hague, Kathleen. Alphabears: An ABC Book. Hague, Michael, illus. LC 83-26476. (gr. k-2). 1984. 12.95 (ISBN 0-8050-0841-1). H Holt & Co.

—Numbears: A Counting Book. Hague, Michael, illus. LC 85-27006. 32p. (gr. k-2). 1986. 11.95 (ISBN 0-8050-0309-6). H Holt & Co.

—Out of the Nursery, into the Night. Hague, Michael, illus. LC 86-14270. 32p. (gr. k-2). 1986. 13.95 (ISBN 0-8050-0088-7). H Holt & Co.

Hammond, Jane. Bradley the Bear. (ps-k). 1984. pap. 1.50 (ISBN 0-87162-393-5, D5606). Warner Pr.

Harrison, Susan J. Christmas with the Bears. Harrison, Susan J., illus. 24p. (ps up). 1987. PLB 9.95 (ISBN 0-525-44329-0, 0966-290, DCB). Dutton Child Bks.

Hasenau, F. A. Benjamin Visits the Jungle. LC 82-81827. (Illus.). (gr. k-2). 1982. 6.00 (ISBN 0-913042-14-5). Holland Hse Pr.

Hayes, Geoffrey. Christmas in Puttyville. Hayes, Geoffrey, illus. LC 85-2009. 40p. (ps-3). 1985. (Random Juv); lib. bdg. 5.99 (ISBN 0-394-97286-4). Random.

Hefter, Richard. Babysitter Bears. Hefter, Richard, illus. LC 83-8205. (gr. 3-6). 1983. 5.95 (ISBN 0-911787-08-9). Optimum Res Inc.

—Bears Away from Home. Hefter, Richard, illus. LC 83-4149. (gr. 3-6). 1983. 5.95 (ISBN 0-911787-05-4). Optimum Res Inc.

—Fast Food. Hefter, Richard, illus. LC 83-6734. (gr. 3-6). 1983. 5.95 (ISBN 0-911787-09-7). Optimum Res Inc.

—Neat Feet. Hefter, Richard, illus. LC 83-8035. (gr. 3-6). 1983. 5.95 (ISBN 0-911787-07-0). Optimum Res Inc.

—The Stickybear's Scary Night. (Illus.). 29p. (ps-1). 1984. 1.95 (ISBN 0-911787-41-0). Optimum Res Inc.

—Where Is the Bear? Hefter, Richard, illus. LC 83-6296. 32p. (gr. 3-6). 1983. 5.95 (ISBN 0-911787-06-2). Optimum Res Inc.

Hellard, Terrance. T. R. Goes to School. Hellard, Susan, illus. 56p. (gr. 2-4). 1988. pap. 2.95 (ISBN 0-8120-4106-2). Barron.

Heller, Nicholas. Mathilda the Dream Bear. LC 88-3830. (Illus.). 32p. (ps up). 1989. 12.95 (ISBN 0-688-08238-6); PLB 12.88 (ISBN 0-688-08239-4). Greenwillow.

Helmrath, M. O. & Bartlett, J. L. Bobby Bear & the Bees. LC 68-56806. (Illus.). 32p. (ps-1). 1968. PLB 12.35 prebound (ISBN 0-87783-003-7); cassette 7.94x (ISBN 0-87783-177-7). Oddo.

—Bobby Bear Finds Maple Sugar. LC 68-56805. (Illus.). 32p. (ps-1). 1968. PLB 12.35 prebound (ISBN 0-87783-005-3). cassette 7.94x (ISBN 0-87783-178-5). Oddo.

—Bobby Bear Goes Fishing. LC 68-56807. (Illus.). 32p. (ps-1). 1968. pap. 12.35 prebound (ISBN 0-87783-006-1); cassette 7.94x (ISBN 0-87783-179-3). Oddo.

—Bobby Bear in the Spring. LC 68-56810. (Illus.). 32p. (ps-1). 1968. PLB 12.35 prebound (ISBN 0-87783-007-X); cassette 7.94x (ISBN 0-87783-180-7). Oddo.

—Bobby Bear Series, 18 bks. (Illus.). (ps-1). Set. PLB 189.60 set (ISBN 0-87783-163-7). 8 cassettes 63.52x (ISBN 0-87783-181-5). Oddo.

—Bobby Bear's Halloween. LC 68-56808. (Illus.). 32p. (ps-1). 1968. PLB 9.95 (ISBN 0-87783-004-5); cassette 7.94x (ISBN 0-87783-183-1). Oddo.

—Bobby Bear's Rocket Ride. LC 68-56809. (Illus.). 32p. (ps-1). 1968. PLB 12.35 prebound (ISBN 0-87783-008-8); cassette 7.94x (ISBN 0-87783-186-6). Oddo.

Heymann, Daniele. The Bear: The Storybook of the Film by Jean-Jacques Annaud. (Illus.). 64p. 1989. bds. 9.95x (ISBN 0-312-03020-7). St Martin.

Hill, Eric. Baby Bear's Bedtime. Hill, Eric, illus. LC 83-43133. 24p. (ps-1). 1984. (Random Juv); PLB 4.99 (ISBN 0-685-07903-1). Random.

—Good Morning, Baby Bear. Hill, Eric, illus. LC 83-43135. 24p. (gr. k-1). 1984. 3.95 (ISBN 0-394-86571-5, Random Juv); pap. 3.95 (ISBN 0-685-07904-X). Random.

—Spot's Baby Sister: A Lift-the-Flap Book. Hill, Eric, illus. 22p. (ps-k). 1989. 10.95 (ISBN 0-399-21640-5, Putnam). Putnam Pub Group.

Hissey, Jane. Little Bear's Trousers. (ps-2). 1987. 13.95 (ISBN 0-399-21493-3, Philomel Bks). Putnam Pub Group.

—Little Bear's Trousers: An Old Bear Story. (Illus.). 32p. (ps-3). 1990. pap. 5.95 (ISBN 0-399-22016-X, Philomel Bks). Putnam Pub Group.

—Old Bear. Hissey, Jane, illus. 32p. (ps-3). 1989. pap. 5.95 (ISBN 0-399-22015-1, Philomel, Sandcastle Bks). Putnam Pub Group.

—Old Bear Tales. Hissey, Jane, illus. LC 88-14155. 80p. 1988. 16.95 (ISBN 0-399-21642-1, Philomel Bks). Putnam Pub Group.

Hoff, Syd. Grizzwold. Hoff, Syd, illus. LC 64-14366. 64p. (gr. k-3). 1963. PLB 11.89 (ISBN 0-06-022481-9). HarpC Child Bks.

Horejs, Vit. Pig & Bear. Henstra, Friso, illus. LC 88-21304. 48p. (gr. 2-4). 1989. 11.95 (ISBN 0-02-744421-X, Four Winds). Macmillan Child Grp.

Horn, Suzanne. How Many Bones in a Bear. (Illus.). 32p. (gr. 2-4). 1984. pap. 4.95 (ISBN 0-913839-41-8). Bk Lures.

Hubert, Amelia. Sweet Dreams for Sally. Cooke, Tom, illus. 40p. (ps-3). 1983. 5.95 (ISBN 0-910313-01-6, 7002). Parker Bros.

Hughes, Margaret A. Teddy Ruxpin Summertime. Hicks, Russell, et al, illus. 26p. (ps). 1987. incl. pre-programmed cass. 14.50 (ISBN 0-934323-55-0). Alchemy Comms.

Ingoglia, Gina. Three Bears. (ps-3). 1990. write for info. (ISBN 0-307-11594-1). Western Pub.

Ingpen, Robert. The Age of Acorns. Ingpen, Robert, illus. LC 90-433. 28p. (ps). 1990. 14.95 (ISBN 0-87226-436-X). P Bedrick Bks.

—The Idle Bear. Ingpen, Robert, illus. LC 87-1187. 26p. (ps up). 1987. 12.95 (ISBN 0-87226-159-X, Bedrick Blackie). P Bedrick Bks.

—The Miniature Idle Bear. LC 87-1187. (Illus.). 32p. (gr. 1 up). 1989. 4.95 (ISBN 0-87226-418-1, Bedrick Blackie). P Bedrick Bks.

Isenberg. Adventures of Albert: The Running Bear. (ps-3). 1982. 13.95 (ISBN 0-89919-113-4). Ticknor & Fields.

Isenberg, Barbara & Wolf, Susan. The Adventures of Albert, the Running Bear. Gackenbach, Dick, illus. (gr. k-3). 1985. pap. 12.95 incl. cassette (ISBN 0-941078-88-4); pap. 27.95 incl. cassette, 4 paperbacks guide (ISBN 0-941078-89-2); PLB incl. cassette 19.95 (ISBN 0-941078-90-6). Live Oak Media.

—The Adventures of Albert the Running Bear. Gachenbach, Dick, illus. LC 82-1311. 32p. (ps-3). 1987. 11.95 (ISBN 0-317-60202-0, Pub. by Clarion); pap. 4.95 (ISBN 0-685-18672-5). Ticknor & Fields.

—The Adventures of Albert, the Running Bear. Gackenbach, Dick, illus. 1988. pap. 6.95 incl. cass. (ISBN 0-89919-839-2, Clarion Bks). HM.

—Albert the Running Bear Gets the Jitters. De Groat, Diane, illus. 40p. (gr. k-4). 1987. 13.95 (ISBN 0-89919-517-2, Pub. by Clarion); pap. 4.95 (ISBN 0-89919-532-6). Ticknor & Fields.

James, Thomas. Harry Helps Out. (Illus.). (gr. 1-2). 1972. pap. 1.95 (ISBN 0-89375-048-4). Troll Assocs.

Janice. Little Bear Marches in the Saint Patrick's Day Parade. Mariana, illus. LC 67-15712. 40p. (gr. k-3). PLB 11.88 (ISBN 0-688-51075-2). Lothrop.

—Little Bear's Christmas. Mariana, illus. LC 64-21191. (gr. k-3). 1964. PLB 12.88 (ISBN 0-688-51076-0). Lothrop.

Jarman, Cin & Rose, September. Sherwood. 96p. 1989. 7.95 (ISBN 0-8062-3464-4). Carlton.

Jensen, Helen Z. When Panda Came to Our House. Jensen, Helen Z., illus. LC 85-4589. 32p. (ps-3). 1985. 11.95 (ISBN 0-8037-0236-1, 01160-350). Dial Bks Young.

Johnson, Mary E. The Adventures of Maggie & Her Teddy Bear. Johnson, Margie, illus. (ps). 1984. 4.95 (ISBN 0-318-01304-5). Animal Cracker.

Jonas, Ann. Two Bear Cubs. Jonas, Ann, illus. LC 82-2860. 24p. (gr. k-3). 1982. PLB 11.88 (ISBN 0-688-01408-9). Greenwillow.

Jones, Donna J. Barnabas Bear. Grove, Jason, illus. 32p. (gr. k-5). 1987. pap. 3.50 (ISBN 0-9617382-1-9). Glacier Pub.

Kahn, Peggy. The Care Bears' Book of ABC's. Bracken, Carolyn, illus. LC 82-18538. 40p. (ps-2). 1983. lib. bdg. 4.99 (ISBN 0-394-95808-X). Random.

—The Care Bears: Try, Try Again! Fahrion, Michael, illus. LC 85-2152. 40p. (ps-3). 1985. (Random Juv); lib. bdg. 4.99 (ISBN 0-394-97503-0). Random.

—The Care Bears' Up & Down. Katz, Bobbi, ed. Bracken, Carolyn, illus. LC 83-62100. 14p. (ps). 1984. pap. 1.95 (ISBN 0-394-86445-X, Random Juv). Random.

Katz, Bobbi. The Care Bears & the Big Clean-Up. Kolding, Richard, illus. LC 91-52705. 40p. (ps-4). 1991. 4.99 (ISBN 0-679-82367-0, Random Juv). Random.

—Play with the Care Bears. Katz, Bobbi, illus. LC 84-61375. 14p. (ps). 1985. pap. 4.95 (ISBN 0-394-87098-0, Random Juv). Random.

Kennedy, Jimmy. The Miniature Teddy Bear's Picnic. Theobalds, Prue, illus. LC 86-32111. 32p. 1989. 4.95 (ISBN 0-87226-417-3, Bedrick Blackie). P Bedrick Bks.

—The Teddy Bears' Picnic. Day, Alexandra, illus. LC 84-145012. 40p. (ps-2). 1989. 15.95 (ISBN 0-88138-010-5); incl. cass. tape 19.95 (ISBN 0-88138-126-8). Green Tiger Pr.

—The Teddy Bears' Picnic. Theobalds, Prue, illus. LC 86-32111. 32p. (ps-2). 1987. 14.95 (ISBN 0-87226-153-0, Bedrick Blackie). P Bedrick Bks.

—The Teddy Bears' Picnic. Theobalds, Prue, illus. LC 86-32111. 32p. 1990. pap. 6.95 (ISBN 0-87226-424-6). P Bedrick Bks.

Kesey, Ken. Little Tricker the Squirrel Meets Big Double the Bear. Moser, Barry, illus. 1990. 14.95 (ISBN 0-670-81136-X). Viking Child Bks.

Kletter, Lenore. Santabear's High Flying Adventure. (Illus.). 32p. (gr. 1-3). 1987. 12.99 (ISBN 0-9619204-0-8). Santabear Bks.

Kozikowski, Renate. Teddy Bears Picnic. 32p. (ps-2). 1990. 10.95 (ISBN 0-689-71362-2, Aladdin). Macmillan Child Grp.

—Titus Bear's Summer. Kozikowski, Renate, illus. LC 85-45685. 14p. (ps). 1987. 3.50 (ISBN 0-694-00070-1). HarpC Child Bks.

—Titus Bear's Winter. Kozikowski, Renate, illus. LC 85-45688. 14p. (ps). 1987. 3.50 (ISBN 0-694-00071-X). HarpC Child Bks.

Kramer, Remi. The Legend of LoneStar Bear, Bk. One: How LoneStar Got His Name. Kramer, Remi, illus. 64p. 1988. PLB 12.95 (ISBN 0-945887-01-9). Northwind Pr.

—The Legend of LoneStar Bear, Bk. Two: Soaring with Eagles. Kramer, Remi, illus. 72p. 1989. 14.95 (ISBN 0-945887-02-7). Northwind Pr.

—Legend of LoveStar Bear, Bk. 1: How LoveStar Got His Name. rev. ed. (Illus.). 60p. 1989. pap. 12.95 (ISBN 0-945887-08-6). Northwind Pr.

Krause, Ute. Nora & the Great Bear. LC 88-33538. (Illus.). 32p. (ps-3). 1989. 11.95 (ISBN 0-8037-0684-7); PLB 11.89 (ISBN 0-8037-0685-5). Dial Bks Young.

Krensky, Stephen. Big Time Bears. Cocca-Leffler, Maryann, illus. LC 88-30793. (ps-k). 1989. 14.95 (ISBN 0-316-50375-4). Little.

Krueger, Ron, et al. Bearly There at All. French, Marty, illus. 26p. (ps up). 1988. incl. cassette 7.95 (ISBN 1-55578-912-9). Worlds Wonder.

Kurland, Alexandra. Sara's Story: The Bear Nobody Wanted. (Illus.). 64p. (gr. k-4). 1988. 12.95 (ISBN 0-938209-34-5). Bear Hollow Pr.

Kyte, Dennis. Merry Christmas, Bigelow Bear. 1990. 13.95 (ISBN 0-385-26522-0); PLB 14.99 (ISBN 0-385-26523-9). Doubleday.

LaFleur, Tom & Brennan, Gale. Bingo the Bear. Kritchman-Knuteson, Joan, illus. 16p. (Orig.). (gr. k-6). 1981. pap. 1.25 (ISBN 0-685-02454-7). Brennan Bks.

Lansky, Vicki. A New Baby at Koko Bear's House. reissued ed. Prince, Jane, illus. 32p. (Orig.). 1991. pap. 4.95 (ISBN 0-916773-22-1). Book Peddlers.

Lasky, Kathryn. Fourth of July Bear. Cogancherry, Helen, illus. LC 90-37422. 40p. (gr. k up). 1991. 13.95 (ISBN 0-688-08287-4); PLB 13.88 (ISBN 0-688-08288-2, Morrow Jr Bks). Morrow Jr Bks.

Lebrun, Claude. Little Brown Bear Is Ill. Bour, Daniele, illus. 14p. (gr. k-3). 1982. 4.95 (ISBN 0-8120-5499-7). Barron.

—Little Brown Bear Wakes Up. Bour, Daniele, illus. 14p. (gr. k-3). 1982. 4.95 (ISBN 0-8120-5500-4). Barron.

Le Tord, Bijou. Good Wood Bear. Le Tord, Bijou, illus. LC 85-70864. 32p. (ps-2). 1985. 12.95 (ISBN 0-02-756440-1, Bradbury Pr). Macmillan Child Grp.

Little Brown Bear Loses His Clothes. (Illus.). 24p. (ps-3). 1978. 2.50 (ISBN 0-448-46523-X, G&D). Putnam Pub Group.

Lundell, Margo. Teddy Bear's Birthday. DeRosa, Dee, illus. LC 84-82157. 12p. (ps-3). 1985. 3.95 (ISBN 0-448-40876-7, G&D). Putnam Pub Group.

Luttrell, Ida. The Bear Next Door. Stapler, Sarah, illus. LC 90-4153. 64p. (gr. k-3). 1991. 11.95 (ISBN 0-06-024023-7); PLB 11.89 (ISBN 0-06-024024-5). HarpC Child Bks.

McCall, Dan. Jack the Bear. 224p. (gr. 7 up). 1981. pap. 1.95 (ISBN 0-449-70009-7, Juniper). Fawcett.

McCloskey, Robert. Blueberries for Sal. McCloskey, Robert, illus. LC 48-4955. (ps-1). 1976. pap. 3.95 (ISBN 0-14-050169-X, Puffin). Puffin Bks.

—Blueberries for Sal. McCloskey, Robert, illus. LC 48-4955. 56p. (ps-1). 1948. pap. 13.95 (ISBN 0-670-17591-9). Viking Child Bks.

McClung, Robert M. Major: The Story of a Black Bear. McClung, Robert M., illus. LC 87-26126. 64p. (gr. 9-12). 1988. Repr. of 1956 ed. lib. bdg. 14.50 (ISBN 0-208-02201-5, Linnet). Shoe String.

McCue, Lisa, illus. Teddy Dresses. 1983. pap. 2.95 (ISBN 0-671-45490-0, Little Simon). S&S Trade.

McCully, Emily A. Speak up, Blanche! McCully, Emily A., illus. LC 90-36945. 32p. (gr. k-3). 1991. 14.95 (ISBN 0-06-024227-2); PLB 14.89 (ISBN 0-06-024228-0). HarpC Child Bks.

Mack, Stan. Ten Bears in My Bed: A Goodnight Countdown. Mack, Stan, illus. LC 74-151. 32p. (ps-1). 1974. lib. bdg. 10.99 (ISBN 0-394-92902-0). Pantheon.

McKissack, Patricia C. & McKissack, Frederick. Los Tres Osos: (The Three Bears) Bala, Virginia, illus. LC 85-12765. (SPA.). 32p. (ps-2). 1989. PLB 11.93 (ISBN 0-516-32364-4); pap. 3.95 (ISBN 0-516-52364-3). Childrens.

McPhail, David. The Bear's Toothache. (Illus.). 32p. (gr. k-3). 1972. lib. bdg. 12.95 (ISBN 0-316-56312-9, Joy St Bks). Little.
—Henry Bear's Park. McPhail, David, illus. 48p. (gr. 1-3). 1976. lib. bdg. 13.95 (ISBN 0-316-56315-3, Joy St Bks). Little.
—Lost, Vol. 1. (ps-3). 1990. 13.95 (ISBN 0-316-56329-3, Joy St Bks). Little.
Mahan, Benton, illus. Goldilocks & the Three Bears. LC 80-27631. 32p. (gr. k-2). 1981. PLB 9.79 (ISBN 0-89375-470-6); pap. text ed. 1.95 (ISBN 0-89375-471-4). Troll Assocs.
Maison, Della. The Care Bears' Garden. Bracken, Carolyn, illus. LC 82-61566. 32p. (gr. 1-6). 1983. pap. 1.25 saddle-stitched (ISBN 0-394-85827-1). Random.
Margolin, Harriet. Busy Bear's Closet. Nicklaus, Carol, illus. 28p. (ps). 1985. 4.95 (ISBN 0-448-30377-9, G&D). Putnam Pub Group.
—Busy Bear's Cupboard. Nicklaus, Carol, illus. 28p. (ps). 1985. 4.95 (ISBN 0-448-30376-0, G&D). Putnam Pub Group.
—Busy Bear's Room: A Book about Shapes. (Illus.). 28p. 1985. 4.95 (ISBN 0-448-30375-2, G&D). Putnam Pub Group.
Marilue. Bobby Bear & the Friendly Ghost. LC 85-61830. (Illus.). 32p. (ps-1). 1985. 6.95 (ISBN 0-87783-204-8). Oddo.
—Bobby Bear at the Circus. Marilue, illus. LC 89-62708. 32p. (ps-2). 1990. PLB 12.95 (ISBN 0-87783-252-8). Oddo.
—Bobby Bear Meets Cousin Boo. LC 80-82952. (Illus.). 32p. (ps-1). 1981. PLB 9.95 (ISBN 0-87783-155-6). Oddo.
—Bobby Bear's Kite Contest. Marilue, illus. LC 87-62507. 32p. (ps-1). 1988. PLB 11.45 (ISBN 0-87783-219-6). Oddo.
—Bobby Bear's Magic Show. Marilue, illus. LC 89-62707. 32p. (ps-2). 1990. PLB 12.95 (ISBN 0-87783-253-6). Oddo.
—Bobby Bear's New Home. LC 78-190265. (Illus.). 32p. (ps-1). 1973. PLB 9.95 (ISBN 0-87783-054-1); cassette 7.94x (ISBN 0-87783-184-X). Oddo.
—Bobby Bear's Red Raft. LC 71-190266. (Illus.). 32p. (ps-1). 1973. PLB 9.95 (ISBN 0-87783-055-X); cassette 7.94x (ISBN 0-87783-185-8). Oddo.
Martin, Bill, Jr. Brown Bear, Brown Bear, What Do You See? Carle, Eric, illus. LC 83-12779. 24p. (gr. k-2). 1983. 13.95 (ISBN 0-8050-0201-4). H Holt & Co.
—Polar Bear, Polar Bear, What Do You Hear? Carle, Eric, illus. 32p. (ps). 1991. 13.95 (ISBN 0-8050-1759-3). H Holt & Co.
Menten, Ted. Teddy's Bearzaar. LC 88-42753. (Illus.). 96p. (Orig.). 1988. lib. bdg. 19.80 (ISBN 0-89471-638-7); pap. 8.95 (ISBN 0-89471-637-9). Running Pr.
Meyer, Kathleen A. Bear, Your Manners Are Showing. Creative Studios 1, Inc. Staff, illus. 32p. (gr. k-2). 1987. 1.99 (ISBN 0-87403-271-7, 3771). Standard Pub.
—Little Bear's Surprise. Boerke, Carole, illus. (gr. k-2). 1989. 1.99 (ISBN 0-87403-600-3, 3860). Standard Pub.
Miller, Sherry. Lost in the Arctic with Pal Bear. Martinez, Jesse, illus. 32p. (Orig.). (gr. k-5). 1984. pap. 1.95 saddle-stitched (ISBN 0-913379-01-8). Double M Pub.
Miller, Virginia. On Your Potty! LC 90-49221. (Illus.). 32p. (ps up). 1991. 13.95 (ISBN 0-688-10617-X); PLB 13.88 (ISBN 0-688-10618-8). Greenwillow.
Milne, A. A. House at Pooh Corner. Shepard, Ernest H., illus. 192p. (gr. 3-7). 1970. pap. 3.25 (ISBN 0-440-43795-4, YB). Dell.
—The House at Pooh Corner. Shepard, Ernest H., illus. 192p. (ps up). 1988. 9.95 (ISBN 0-525-44444-0, DCB). Dutton Child Bks.
—Pooh & Some Bees. Cremins, Robert, illus. 10p. (ps up). 1987. 7.95 (ISBN 0-525-44339-8, 0674-210, DCB). Dutton Child Bks.
—The Pooh Birthday Book. Shepard, Ernest H., illus. 128p. (ps up). 1985. 5.95 (ISBN 0-525-44212-X, DCB). Dutton Child Bks.
—Pooh Goes Visiting. Cremins, Robert, illus. 10p. (ps up). 1987. 7.95 (ISBN 0-525-44337-1, 0674-210, DCB). Dutton Child Bks.
—Pooh's Library, 4 bks. Shepard, Ernest H., illus. (ps up). 1988. Set. 39.95 (ISBN 0-525-44451-3, DCB). Dutton Child Bks.
—Pooh's Pot O'Honey, 4 vols. Shepard, Ernest H., illus. (ps up). 1985. Boxed Set. 8.95 (ISBN 0-525-37518-X, DCB). Dutton Child Bks.
—A Treasury of Winnie-the-Pooh, 4 bks. Shepard, Ernest H., illus. Incl. Winnie-the-Pooh; The House at Pooh Corner; Now We Are Six; When We Were Very Young. (Illus.). 1987. Boxed set. pap. 13.00 (ISBN 0-440-49580-6). Dell.
—Winnie-the-Pooh. Shepard, Ernest H., illus. 176p. (gr. 3-7). 1981. pap. 3.50 (ISBN 0-440-49571-7, YB). Dell.
—Winnie-the-Pooh. (gr. k-6). 1988. pap. 5.95 (ISBN 0-440-40116-X, Pub. by Yearling Classics). Dell.
—Winnie-the-Pooh: A Pop-Up Book. (Illus.). 12p. (ps up). 1984. 12.95 (ISBN 0-525-44119-0, DCB). Dutton Child Bks.
—Winny de Puh. (SPA.). 7.50 (ISBN 0-685-31015-9). Santillana.
—The World of Christopher Robin. Shepard, Ernest H., illus. (ps up). 1988. 16.95 (ISBN 0-525-44448-3, DCB). Dutton Child Bks.
—The World of Pooh. Shepard, Ernest H., illus. (ps up). 1988. 16.95 (ISBN 0-525-44447-5, DCB). Dutton Child Bks.
—The World of Pooh. (Illus.). (gr. 1-4). 1957. 13.95 (ISBN 0-525-43320-1, 01258-370, Dutton); Incl. "World of Christopher" boxed 29.95 (01258-370). NAL-Dutton.
—The World of Winnie-the-Pooh, 6 bks. Shepard, Ernest H., illus. (ps up). 1988. Set. 33.90 (ISBN 0-525-44452-1, DCB). Dutton Child Bks.
Minarik, Else. Papa Oso Vuelve a Casa. (SPA.). 6.95 (ISBN 0-685-31017-5). Santillana.
Minarik, Else H. Father Bear Comes Home. Sendak, Maurice, illus. LC 59-5794. 64p. (gr. k-3). 1959. 11.95 (ISBN 0-06-024230-2); PLB 11.89 (ISBN 0-06-024231-0). HarpC Child Bks.
—Father Bear Comes Home. Sendak, Maurice, illus. LC 59-5794. (ps-3). 1978. pap. 3.50 (ISBN 0-06-444014-1, Trophy). HarpC Child Bks.
—A Kiss for Little Bear. Sendak, Maurice, illus. LC 68-16820. 32p. (ps-3). 1984. pap. 2.95 (ISBN 0-06-444050-8, Trophy). HarpC Child Bks.
—Little Bear. Sendak, Maurice, illus. 64p. (gr. k-3). 1957. 11.95i (ISBN 0-06-024240-X); PLB 11.89 (ISBN 0-06-024241-8). HarpC Child Bks.
—Little Bear's Friend. Sendak, Maurice, illus. LC 60-6370. 64p. (gr. k-3). 1960. 11.95i (ISBN 0-06-024255-8); PLB 11.89 (ISBN 0-06-024256-6). HarpC Child Bks.
—Little Bear's Friend. Sendak, Maurice, illus. LC 60-6370. 64p. (ps-3). 1985. incl. cassette 5.98 (ISBN 0-694-00031-0, Trophy); pap. 3.50 (ISBN 0-06-444051-6, Trophy). HarpC Child Bks.
—Little Bear's Visit. Sendak, Maurice, illus. LC 61-11451. 64p. (ps-3). 1961. 11.95 (ISBN 0-06-024265-5); PLB 11.89 (ISBN 0-06-024266-3). HarpC Child Bks.
—Little Bear's Visit. Sandal, Maurice, illus. LC 61-11451. 64p. (gr. k-3). 1979. pap. 3.50 (ISBN 0-06-444023-0, Trophy). HarpC Child Bks.
—Little Bear's Visit. Sendak, Maurice, illus. LC 61-11451. 64p. (ps-3). 1985. incl. cassette 5.98 (ISBN 0-694-00032-9, Trophy). HarpC Child Bks.
—Osito. LC 69-14452. (SPA., Illus.). 64p. (ps-3). 1969. PLB 10.89 (ISBN 0-06-024244-2). HarpC Child Bks.
—La Visita de Osito. Sendak, Maurice, illus. (SPA.). (gr. 1-6). pap. 6.95 (ISBN 84-204-3051-X). Santillana.
Mogensen, Jan. Teddy in the Undersea Kingdom. LC 85-26093. (Illus.). 32p. (gr. 3-4). 1985. PLB 11.95 (ISBN 1-55532-000-7). Gareth Stevens Inc.
—When Teddy Woke Early. LC 85-26096. (Illus.). 32p. (gr. 3-4). 1985. PLB 11.95 (ISBN 1-55532-006-6). Gareth Stevens Inc.
Moncure, Jane B. Here We Go 'Round the Year. Hohag, Linda, illus. LC 87-13257. 32p. (ps-2). 1987. PLB 11.97 (ISBN 0-89565-402-4); pap. 6.96 (ISBN 0-89565-435-0). Childs World.
—Where Is Baby Bear? Friedman, Joy, illus. LC 87-12840. 32p. (ps-2). 1987. PLB 11.97 (ISBN 0-89565-405-9); pap. 6.96 (ISBN 0-89565-433-4). Childs World.
Mora, Emma. Gideon the Little Bear Cub. (Illus.). 30p. (ps-1). 1986. 3.95 (ISBN 0-8120-5728-7). Barron.
Morey, Walt. Gentle Ben. 192p. (gr. 4 up). 1976. pap. 2.95 (ISBN 0-380-00743-6, Camelot). Avon.
—Gentle Ben. Schoenherr, John, illus. (gr. 4 up). 1965. 12.95 (ISBN 0-525-30429-0, DCB). Dutton Child Bks.
Morgan, Stephanie. The Witch down the Street. Cooke, Tom, illus. 40p. (ps-3). 1983. cancelled 5.95 (ISBN 0-910313-02-4, 7003). Parker Bros.
Moss, Elaine. Polar. LC 89-2115. (Illus.). 32p. (ps up). 1990. 13.95 (ISBN 0-688-09176-8); lib. bdg. 13.88 (ISBN 0-688-09177-6). Greenwillow.
Mountain, Lee. Bobby Bear & Uncle Sam's Riddle. Marilue, illus. 32p. (ps-1). 1988. PLB 11.45 (ISBN 0-87783-221-8). Oddo.
Muntean, Michaela. Bicycle Bear. Cushman, Doug, illus. LC 83-3980. 48p. (ps-3). 1983. 5.95 (ISBN 0-8193-1103-0); PLB 5.95 (ISBN 0-8193-1104-9). Parents.
Murdocca, Sal. Christmas Bear. (gr. k-3). 1990. pap. 7.95 (ISBN 0-671-64565-X, Little Simon); pap. 3.95 (ISBN 0-671-70849-X). S&S Trade.
Murphy, Jill. Peace at Last. Murphy, Jill, illus. LC 80-66743. 32p. (ps-2). 1980. 12.95 (ISBN 0-8037-6757-9); PLB 12.89 (ISBN 0-8037-6758-7). Dial Bks Young.
—What Next, Baby Bear! Murphy, Jill, illus. LC 83-7316. 32p. (ps-2). 1984. 13.95 (ISBN 0-8037-0027-X). Dial Bks Young.
—What Next, Baby Bear! Murphy, Jill, illus. LC 83-7316. 32p. (ps-2). 1986. pap. 3.95 (ISBN 0-685-37306-1). Dial Bks Young.
The New Adventures of Winnie the Pooh: Masked Offender. (ps up). 1990. PLB 5.98 (ISBN 0-7924-5148-1, Mallard Pr). BDD Promo Bk.
The New Adventures of Winnie the Pooh: Paw & Order. (ps up). 1990. PLB 5.98 (ISBN 0-7924-5150-3, Mallard Pr). BDD Promo Bk.
The New Adventures of Winnie the Pooh: Stripes. (ps up). 1990. PLB 5.98 (ISBN 0-7924-5147-3, Mallard Pr). BDD Promo Bk.
Nims, Bonnie L. Where Is the Bear at School? Tucker, Kathy, ed. Gill, Madelaine, illus. 24p. (ps-1). 1989. 10.95 (ISBN 0-8075-8935-7). A Whitman.
Oana, Katherine. Spacebear Lands on Earth. Baird, Tate, ed. Wallace, Dorathye, illus. LC 86-51210. 16p. (Orig.). (ps up). 1988. pap. 3.72 (ISBN 0-914127-26-8). Univ Class.
Obrist, Jurg. Max & Molly. Obrist, Jurg, illus. 32p. (ps-3). 1989. 13.95 (ISBN 0-399-21630-8, Putnam). Putnam Pub Group.
Oetting, Rae. Bobby Bear's Birthday. Marilue, illus. LC 87-62508. 32p. (ps-1). 1988. PLB 11.45 (ISBN 0-87783-220-X). Oddo.
Oppenheim, Joanne. Could It Be - Bank Street. (ps-3). 1990. PLB 9.99 (ISBN 0-553-05893-2, Little Rooster); pap. 3.50 (ISBN 0-553-34924-4). Bantam.
Osborne, Mary P., compiled by. Bears, Bears, Bears. Schmidt, Karen L., illus. 96p. (ps-2). 1990. 14.95 (ISBN 0-671-69631-9); PLB 18.98 (ISBN 0-671-69630-0). Silver Pr.
Pellowski, Michael J. Karate Bear. Robison, Don, illus. 24p. (gr. k-3). 1987. 1.95 (ISBN 0-87406-250-0, 14-14716-4). Willowisp Pr.
Pene Du Bois, William. Bear Circus. (Illus.). (gr. k-2). 1987. pap. 3.95 (ISBN 0-14-050792-2, Puffin). Puffin Bks.
—Gentleman Bear. LC 84-48320. (Illus.). 80p. (gr. k up). 1985. 14.95 (ISBN 0-374-32533-2). FS&G.
—Gentleman Bear. (Illus.). 80p. (ps up). 1988. pap. 5.95 (ISBN 0-374-42536-1). FS&G.
Phillips, Joan. Walt Disney's Winnie the Pooh & the Toy Airplane. (ps-3). 1990. write for info. (ISBN 0-307-11586-0). Western Pub.
—Walt Disney's Winnie the Pooh & the Very Big Bear. (ps-3). 1990. write for info. (ISBN 0-307-11593-3). Western Pub.
Piequet, Miriam. My Furry Bear. Anyone Can Read Staff, ed. Gregory, Miriam, illus. 43p. (Orig.). (gr. 3-5). 1985. 15.00 (ISBN 0-914275-02-X). Anyone Can Read Bks.
Polter, David. Say Hello to the Care Bear Cousins. Neher, Julie & Redding, Jane, illus. 64p. (ps-3). 1985. pap. 2.95 (ISBN 0-394-87114-6, Random Juv). Random.
Pomerantz, Charlotte. Where's the Bear? Barton, Byron, illus. LC 83-1697. 32p. (ps-1). 1984. 10.25 (ISBN 0-688-01752-5); PLB 10.88 (ISBN 0-688-01753-3). Greenwillow.
Price, Stern & Sloan Staff. Bare Bear's New Clothes. (Illus.). 22p. (gr. 3-6). 1986. 5.95 (ISBN 0-8431-1824-5). Price Stern.
Propper. Bear, Reading Level 3-4. (Illus.). 28p. (gr. 2-5). Date not set. PLB 14.60 (ISBN 0-86592-865-7). Rourke Corp.
Pryor, Bonnie. Grandpa Bear's Christmas. Degen, Bruce, illus. LC 85-29707. 32p. (ps-1). 1986. 12.95 (ISBN 0-688-06063-3, Morrow Junior Books); lib. bdg. 12.88 (ISBN 0-688-06064-1). Morrow.
Pulver, Kathryn. Just Call Me Growler. 1990. 13.95 (ISBN 0-533-08693-0). Vantage.
Punnett, Dick. Does Anyone Have a Spare Bear? Endres, Helen, illus. LC 84-23009. 32p. (gr. k-3). 1985. lib. bdg. 10.95 (ISBN 0-89565-304-4). Childs World.
Reit, Seymour. Rebus Bears-Bank Street. (ps-3). 1989. pap. 3.50 (ISBN 0-553-34689-X). Bantam.
Reit, Seymour V. The Rebus Bears: Level 1. Smith, Kenneth, illus. 1989. 9.99 (ISBN 0-553-05822-3). Bantam.
Reit, Symour. The Rebus Bears, Level 1. Smith, Kenneth, illus. pap. 3.50 (ISBN 0-317-99641-X). Bantam.
Riddell, Chris. The Bear Dance. Riddell, Chris, illus. 32p. (ps-4). 1990. 13.95 (ISBN 0-671-70974-7). S&S Trade.
—Ben & the Bear. LC 85-27123. (Illus.). 32p. (ps-2). 1986. pap. 2.50 (ISBN 0-06-443106-1, Trophy). HarpC Child Bks.
Roberts, Tom. Goldilocks & the Three Bears. Kubinyi, Laszlo, illus. 32p. (gr. k up). 1990. 14.95 (ISBN 0-88708-146-0, Rabbit Ears); incl. cass. 19.95 (ISBN 0-88708-147-9). Picture Bk Studio.
Robinson, Sandra C. The Last Bit-Bear: A Fable. Ditzler, Ellen, illus. (gr. k-6). 1984. pap. 4.95 (ISBN 0-911797-09-2). InterVarsity.
Rockwell, Anne. Bear Child's Book of Hours. Rockwell, Anne, illus. LC 86-24245. 32p. (ps-1). 1991. pap. 4.95 (ISBN 0-06-107410-1). HarpC Child Bks.
—Come to Town. Rockwell, Anne, illus. LC 86-6217. 32p. (ps-1). 1987. 7.95 (ISBN 0-694-00189-9, Crowell Jr Bks); PLB 11.89 (ISBN 0-690-04646-4). HarpC Child Bks.
—The Three Bears & Fifteen Other Stories. LC 74-5381. (Illus.). 128p. (ps-3). 1984. pap. 8.95 flexi-bind (ISBN 0-06-440142-1, Trophy). HarpC Child Bks.
Roose-Evans, James. The Adventures of Odd & Elsewhere. Robb, Brian, illus. 96p. (ps-5). 1988. 10.95 (ISBN 0-233-98310-4). Andre Deutsch.
Root, Clive. Bamboo Bears. (Illus.). 112p. (Orig.). (gr. 8-12). 1990. pap. 17.95 (ISBN 0-920534-61-9, Pub. by Hyperion Pr Ltd CN). Sterling.
Ryan, Will. Grundo Beach Party. Becker, Mary, ed. High, David, et al, illus. 26p. (ps). 1986. 9.95 (ISBN 0-934323-35-6); pre-programmed audio cass. tape incl. Alchemy Comms.
—Lost in Boggley Woods. Becker, Mary, ed. High, David, et al, illus. 26p. (ps). 1986. 9.95 (ISBN 0-934323-38-0); pre-programmed audio cass. tape incl. Alchemy Comms.
—Teddy Ruxpin Christmas. Becker, Mary & Hughes, Margaret A., eds. Hicks, Russell, et al, illus. 34p. (ps). 1986. packaged with preprogrammed audio cass. tape 14.50 (ISBN 0-934323-39-9). Alchemy Comms.
Ryder, Joanne. The Bear on the Moon. Lacey, Carol, illus. LC 89-13133. 32p. (gr. 1 up). Date not set. 13.95 (ISBN 0-688-08109-6); PLB 13.88 (ISBN 0-688-08110-X). Morrow Jr Bks.

BEARS–PICTURES, ILLUSTRATIONS, ETC.

BEARS–POETRY

BEASTS

see Animals

BEATLES, THE

BEAUTY, PERSONAL

see also Cosmetics; Costume; Hair

McCombs, Barbara L. & Brannan, Linda. Good Grooming Habits. (Illus.). 32p. (Orig.). (gr. 7-12). 1990. Set. 10 wkbks. & tchr's. guide 44.95 (ISBN 1-56119-080-2); tchr's. guide 1.95 (ISBN 1-56119-044-6); software 39.95 (ISBN 1-56119-122-1). Educ Pr MD.

Saunders, Rubie. Good Grooming for Girls. Green, Anne C., illus. 96p. (gr. 5-9). 1989. PLB 12.90 (ISBN 0-531-10769-8). Watts.

Zeldis, Yona. Coping with Beauty, Fitness & Fashion. Rosen, Ruth, ed. Daven, Douglas, illus. LC 86-24850. 128p. (gr. 7 up). 1987. PLB 12.95 (ISBN 0-8239-0731-7). Rosen Group.

BEAVERS

Crump, Donald J., ed. Busy Beavers. (Illus.). (gr. k-4). 1988. Set. 10.95 (ISBN 0-685-31765-X); Set. PLB 12.95 (ISBN 0-685-31766-8). Natl Geog.

Dalmais. Beaver, Reading Level 3-4. (Illus.). 28p. (gr. 2-5). Date not set. PLB 14.60 (ISBN 0-86592-859-2). Rourke Corp.

George, William T. Beaver at Long Pond. George, Lindsay B., illus. 24p. (ps-3). 1989. audiocassette pkgd. with bk. as set 17.95 (ISBN 0-924483-22-9). Soundprints.

Hogan, Paula Z. The Beaver. Miyake, Yoshi, illus. LC 79-13305. 32p. (gr. 1-4). 1979. PLB 16.67 (ISBN 0-8172-1502-6). Raintree Pubs.

—The Beaver. LC 79-13305. (Illus.). 32p. (gr. 1-4). 1981. PLB 27.99 incl. cassette (ISBN 0-8172-1848-3); cassette 14.00 (ISBN 0-685-09550-9). Raintree Pubs.

Nentl, Jerolyn. Beaver. LC 83-5323. (Illus.). 48p. (gr. 5). 1983. lib. bdg. 10.95 (ISBN 0-89686-219-4, Crestwood Hse). Macmillan Child Grp.

Rounds, Glen. Wild Orphan. Rounds, Glen, illus. 84p. (gr. 4-6). 1961. 12.95 (ISBN 0-8234-0147-2). Holiday.

Rue, Leonard L., III & Owen, William. Meet the Beaver. (Illus.). 64p. (gr. 3-6). 1986. 11.99g (ISBN 0-399-61236-X, Putnam). Putnam Pub Group.

Ryden, Hope. The Beaver. Ryden, Hope, illus. 64p. (gr. 5 up). 1986. 12.95 (ISBN 0-399-21364-3, Putnam). Putnam Pub Group.

Stone, Lynn. Beavers. (Illus.). 24p. (gr. k-5). 1990. lib. bdg. 11.93 (ISBN 0-86593-041-4); lib. bdg. 8.95s.p. (ISBN 0-685-36338-4). Rourke Corp.

BEAVERS–FICTION

Burgess, Thornton. Paddy the Beaver. 1986. Repr. lib. bdg. 17.95 (ISBN 0-89966-528-4). Buccaneer Bks.

Fisk, George W. Benny, the Lazy Beaver. Barker, Scott J., illus. LC 90-45200. 32p. 1991. 10.99 (ISBN 0-9620507-1-7). Cosmic Concepts Pr.

Gallo, Giovanni. The Lazy Beaver. Samsa, Ermanno, illus. 40p. (ps-3). 1983. pap. 9.95 (ISBN 0-399-20965-4, Philomel). Putnam Pub Group.

George, William T. & George, Lindsay B. Beaver at Long Pond. LC 87-281. (Illus.). 24p. (ps-3). 1988. 13.95 (ISBN 0-688-07106-6); lib. bdg. 13.88 (ISBN 0-688-07107-4). Greenwillow.

Goodman, Robert B. & Spicer, Robert A. The Secret of Beaver Valley. Buffet, Guy, illus. LC 73-77781. (gr. 1-7). 1963. 5.95 (ISBN 0-89610-017-0). Island Heritage.

Grandma Marian, pseud. Beni the Bashful Beaver. Kmiecik, Anne, illus. LC 87-71490. 32p. 1988. 6.95 (ISBN 0-9614989-1-9). Banmar Inc.

Heine, Helme. The Pearl. Heine, Helme, illus. LC 88-3220. 32p. (gr. k-4). 1988. pap. 3.95 (ISBN 0-689-71262-6, Aladdin). Macmillan Child Grp.

Kalas, Sybille & Kalas, Klaus. The Beaver Family Book. Crampton, Patricia, tr. LC 87-13914. (Illus.). (gr. k up). 1987. 15.95 (ISBN 0-88708-050-2). Picture Bk Studio.

MacDonald, Amy. Little Beaver & the Echo. Fox-Davies, Sarah, illus. 32p. 1990. 14.95 (ISBN 0-399-22203-0, Putnam). Putnam Pub Group.

Michaels, Ski. Fun in the Sun. Paterson, Diane, illus. LC 85-14055. 48p. (Orig.). (gr. 1-3). 1986. PLB 9.89 (ISBN 0-8167-0568-2); pap. text ed. 2.95 (ISBN 0-8167-0569-0). Troll Assocs.

Minarik, Elsa H. Percy & the Five Houses. (ps-3). 1990. pap. 3.95 (ISBN 0-14-054209-4, Puffin). Puffin Bks.

Minarik, Else H. Percy & the Five Houses. Stevenson, James, illus. LC 88-4804. 24p. (gr. k up). 1989. 11.95 (ISBN 0-688-08104-5); PLB 11.88 (ISBN 0-688-08105-3). Greenwillow.

Sharmat, Marjorie W. The Story of Bentley Beaver. Hoban, Lillian, illus. LC 82-47715. 64p. (gr. k-3). 1984. PLB 10.89 (ISBN 0-06-025513-7). HarpC Child Bks.

Speare, Elizabeth G. The Sign of the Beaver. 144p. (gr. 5 up). 1983. 12.95 (ISBN 0-395-33890-5). HM.

Thompson-Hoffman, Susan. Delver's Danger. Buzzanco, Eileen M., illus. LC 88-64152. 32p. (gr. k-4). 1989. 11.95 (ISBN 0-924483-02-4); incl. audiocassette 14.95 (ISBN 0-924483-05-9); incl. audiocassette-toy combination 41.95 (ISBN 0-924483-08-3); write for info. incl. audiocassette (ISBN 0-924483-11-3). Soundprints.

Weiss, Clarence B. Grandpa Beaver: His Amazing Tales. Easson, Roger, ed. McKnight, Fred, illus. LC 87-20457. 98p. (Orig.). (gr. 5-12). 1987. pap. 6.95 (ISBN 0-942179-01-3). Shelby Hse.

BECKWOURTH, JAMES PIERSON, 1798-1867

Blassingame, Wyatt. Jim Beckwourth. (Illus.). 80p. (gr. 2-6). 1991. Repr. of 1973 ed. PLB 12.95 (ISBN 0-7910-1404-5). Chelsea Hse.

BEE

see Bees

BEES

see also Honey

Abels, Harriette S. Killer Bees. LC 87-14085. (Illus.). 48p. (gr. 5-6). 1987. PLB 10.95 (ISBN 0-89686-342-5, Crestwood Hse). Macmillan Child Grp.

Bailey, Jill. Life Cycle of a Bee. (ps-3). 1990. PLB 8.99 (ISBN 0-531-18316-5). Watts.

Blau, Melinda E. Killer Bees. LC 77-10010. (Illus.). 48p. (gr. 4 up). 1983. PLB 17.32 (ISBN 0-8172-1055-5); pap. 9.27 (0-8172-2159-X). Raintree Pubs.

Boy Scouts of America. Beekeeping. (Illus.). 56p. (gr. 6-12). 1983. pap. 1.85 (ISBN 0-8395-3362-4, 3362). BSA.

Eastman, David. I Can Read About Bees & Wasps. LC 78-73773. (Illus.). (gr. 2-5). 1979. pap. 1.95 (ISBN 0-89375-203-7). Troll Assocs.

Fischer-Nagel, Andreas & Fischer-Nagel, Heiderose. Life of the Honeybee. Fischer-Nagel, Andreas & Fischer-Nagel, Heiderose, illus. 48p. (gr. 2-5). 1986. lib. bdg. 12.95 (ISBN 0-87614-241-2); pap. 6.95 (ISBN 0-87614-470-9). Carolrhoda Bks.

Fischer-Nagel, Heiderose & Fischer-Nagel, Andreas. Life of the Honeybee. (Illus.). 48p. (gr. 2-5). 1987. pap. 6.95 (ISBN 0-685-18832-9, First Ave Edns). Lerner Pubns.

Harrison, Virginia. The World of Honeybees. Oxford Scientific Films Staff, photos by. LC 89-33936. (Illus.). 32p. (gr. 2-3). 1989. PLB 10.95 (ISBN 0-8368-0142-3). Gareth Stevens Inc.

Hawes, Judy. Bees & Beelines. Aliki, illus. LC 64-10864. 40p. (gr. k-3). 1972. pap. 1.45 (ISBN 0-690-12745-6, Crowell Jr Bks). HarpC Child Bks.

Hogan, Paula Z. The Honeybee. Strigenz, Geri K., illus. LC 78-21165. 32p. (gr. 1-4). 1979. PLB 16.67 (ISBN 0-8172-1256-6). Raintree Pubs.

—The Honeybee. LC 78-21165. (Illus.). 32p. (gr. 1-4). 1984. PLB 27.99 incl. cassette (ISBN 0-8172-2229-4) (ISBN 0-685-09511-8). Raintree Pubs.

Kahkonen, Sharon. Honey Bees. 32p. (gr. 1-4). 1989. PLB 13.32 (ISBN 0-8172-3508-6). Raintree Pubs.

Kerby, Mona. Friendly Bees, Ferocious Bees. Greene, Anne, illus. LC 86-22479. 96p. (gr. 4-8). 1987. lib. bdg. 10.40 (ISBN 0-531-10303-X). Watts.

Life of the Honey Bee. (Illus.). (gr. 4 up). 3.50 (ISBN 0-7214-0722-6). Ladybird Bks.

Mitgutsch, Ali. From Blossom to Honey. Mitgutsch, Ali, illus. 24p. (ps-3). 1981. PLB 6.95 (ISBN 0-87614-146-7). Carolrhoda Bks.

Oda, Hidetomo. Observing Bees & Wasps. Pohl, Kathy, ed. LC 85-28195. (Illus.). 32p. (gr. 3-7). 1986. PLB 16.67 (ISBN 0-8172-2540-4); pap. text ed. 9.27 (ISBN 0-8172-2565-X). Raintree Pubs.

Otani, Takeshi. The Honeybee. Pohl, Kathy, ed. LC 85-28230. (Illus.). 32p. (gr. 3-7). 1986. text ed. 16.67 (ISBN 0-8172-2537-4); pap. text ed. 9.27 (ISBN 0-8172-2562-5). Raintree Pubs.

O'Toole, Christopher. Discovering Bees & Wasps. LC 85-72247. (Illus.). 48p. (gr. k-6). 1986. lib. bdg. 11.90 (ISBN 0-531-18047-6, Pub. by Bookwright Pr). Watts.

Otoole, Christopher. Discovering Bees And Wasps. 1990. pap. 4.95 (ISBN 0-531-18362-9). Watts.

O'Toole, Christopher. The Honeybee in the Meadow. Oxford Scientific Films Staff, photos by. LC 89-33935. (Illus.). 32p. (gr. 4-6). 1989. PLB 10.95 (ISBN 0-8368-0117-2). Gareth Stevens Inc.

Watts, Barrie. Honeybee. (Illus.). 25p. (ps-4). 1990. 6.95 (ISBN 0-382-24013-8); PLB 9.98 (ISBN 0-382-24011-1). Silver Burdett Pr.

BEES–FICTION

Barbie the Bee. (Illus.). (ps-1). 2.98 (ISBN 0-517-46983-9). Outlet Bk Co.

Barrett, Ethel. Buzz Bee. (ps-2). 1978. pap. 5.95 incl. cass. (ISBN 0-8307-0419-1, 5602602). Regal.

Campbell, Peter. Harry's Bee. LC 74-156105. (gr. 1-3). 1971. 5.95 (ISBN 0-672-51587-3, Bobbs). Macmillan.

Carratello, Patty. The Bee & the Seed. Spivak, Darlene, ed. Smythe, Linda, illus. 16p. (gr. k-2). 1988. wkbk. 1.95 (ISBN 1-55734-381-0). Tchr Create Mat.

Cates, Joe W. Buzbee. Cates, Joe W., illus. 96p. (gr. 3-8). 1987. PLB write for info. (ISBN 0-942403-04-5). J Barnaby Dist.

Cormier, Robert. The Bumblebee Flies Anyway. LC 83-2458. 256p. (gr. 8 up). 1983. Knopf.

—The Bumblebee Flies Anyway. 256p. (gr. 5 up). 1984. pap. 3.25 (ISBN 0-440-90871-X, LFL). Dell.

Frederick, Ruth. Where's Tommy? O'Connell, Ruth A., illus. 32p. (gr. 1-2). 1991. pap. 3.99 saddle stitch (ISBN 0-87403-806-5, 24-03896). Standard Pub.

Haker, Loren F. The Li'l Rascals: Timmy & the Bees. (Illus.). 56p. (gr. 1-8). 1984. 7.95 (ISBN 0-9609964-0-0); pap. 4.95 (ISBN 0-9609964-1-9). Haker Books.

Hallin, Emily. Queen Bee. 157p. 1989. pap. 2.25 (ISBN 0-373-88039-1). Harlequin Bks.

Hoban, Brom. Jason & the Bees. Hoban, Brom, illus. LC 78-13902. 64p. (gr. k-3). 1980. 7.64i (ISBN 0-06-022381-2). HarpC Child Bks.

Sand, George. The Mysterious Tale of Gentle Jack & Lord Bumblebee. Spirin, Gennady, illus. LC 87-30490. 80p. (ps up). 1988. 14.95 (ISBN 0-8037-0538-7). Dial Bks Young.

Schwartz, Alvin. Busy Buzzing Bumblebees. Abrams, Kathie, illus. LC 81-48639. 64p. (gr. k-3). 1982. 11.95 (ISBN 0-06-025268-5); PLB 11.89 (ISBN 0-06-025269-3). HarpC Child Bks.

—Busy Buzzing Bumblebees. LC 81-48639. (Illus.). 64p. (gr. k-3). 1982. pap. 3.50 (ISBN 0-06-444036-2, Trophy). HarpC Child Bks.

Stockton, Frank R. The Bee-Man of Orn. Sendak, Maurice, illus. LC 85-45813. 48p. (ps up). 1987. Repr. of 1963 ed. 13.95 (ISBN 0-06-025818-7); PLB 13.89 (ISBN 0-06-025819-5). HarpC Child Bks.

—The Bee-Man of Orn. Sendak, Maurice, illus. LC 85-45813. 48p. (gr. 2 up). 1987. pap. 4.95 (ISBN 0-06-443125-8, Trophy). HarpC Child Bks.

Williams, Effie M. A Hive of Busy Bees. (gr. 5 up). 1976. Repr. of 1939 ed. 3.30 (ISBN 0-686-15479-7). Rod & Staff.

BEETHOVEN, LUDWIG VAN, 1770-1827

Blackwood, Alan. Beethoven. (Illus.). 32p. (gr. 1-6). 1987. PLB 11.90 (ISBN 0-531-18131-6, Pub. by Bookwright Pr). Watts.

Great Composers, Bk. 1: Bach, Mozart, Beethoven. (Illus.). (gr. 5 up). 3.50 (ISBN 0-7214-0230-5). Ladybird Bks.

Greene, Carol. Ludwig Van Beethoven: Musical Pioneer. Dobson, Steven, illus. LC 89-15849. 48p. (gr. k-3). 1989. PLB 15.27 (ISBN 0-516-04208-4); pap. 4.95 (ISBN 0-516-44208-2). Childrens.

Johnson, Ann D. The Value of Giving: The Story of Beethoven. Pileggi, Stephen, illus. LC 78-31545. (gr. k-6). 1979. 9.95 (ISBN 0-916392-34-1, Pub. by Value Communications). Oak Tree Pubns.

Loewen, L. Beethoven. (Illus.). 112p. (gr. 5 up). 1989. lib. bdg. 17.26 (ISBN 0-86592-609-3). Rourke Corp.

McHugh, Elisabet. Beethoven's Cat. (gr. k-6). 1991. pap. 3.25 (ISBN 0-440-40398-7). Dell.

Sage, Alison. Play Beethoven. Gabby, Terry, illus. Bunting, Janet, contrib. by. (Illus.). 32p. (gr. 1-4). 1988. Incl. built-in 22-note electronic keyboard. 12.95 (ISBN 0-8120-5978-6). Barron.

Tames, Richard. Beethoven. LC 90-32377. (Illus.). 32p. 1991. PLB 11.90 (ISBN 0-531-14106-3). Watts.

Thompson, Wendy. Ludwig Van Beethoven. (Illus.). 48p. (gr. 7up). 1991. 16.95 (ISBN 0-670-83678-8). Viking Child Bks.

BEETLES

Beetles. (Illus.). 32p. (gr. 3-7). 1986. PLB 16.67 (ISBN 0-8172-2530-7). Raintree Pubs.

Heymann, Georgianne. Weevils. (Illus.). 32p. (gr. 3-7). 1986. PLB 16.67 (ISBN 0-8172-2713-X); pap. text ed. 9.27 (ISBN 0-8172-2731-8). Raintree Pubs.

Johnson, Sylvia A. Beetles. Kishida, Isao, illus. LC 82-7230. 48p. (gr. 4 up). 1982. lib. bdg. 14.95 (ISBN 0-8225-1476-1). Lerner Pubns.

Oda, Hidetomo. The Diving Beetle. Pohl, Kathy, ed. LC 85-28300. (Illus.). 32p. (gr. 3-7). 1986. PLB 16.67 (ISBN 0-8172-2533-1); pap. text ed. 9.27 (ISBN 0-8172-2558-7). Raintree Pubs.

Still, John. Amazing Beetles. Young, Jerry, illus. LC 91-6516. 32p. (Orig.). (gr. 1-5). 1991. lib. bdg. 9.99 (ISBN 0-679-91519-2); pap. 7.00 (ISBN 0-679-81519-8). Knopf.

BEHAVIOR

see also Christian Life; Courage; Courtesy; Ethics; Etiquette; Friendship; Human Relations; Love; Patriotism; Self-Control; Self-Culture; Social Adjustment; Spiritual Life; Truthfulness and Falsehood

Adderholdt-Elliott, Miriam. Perfectionism: What's Bad about Being Too Good. Espeland, Pamela, ed. LC 86-81130. (Illus.). 136p. (gr. 6 up). 1987. pap. 8.95 (ISBN 0-915793-07-5). Free Spirit Pub.

Albert, Burton. Mine, Yours, Ours. Axeman, Lois, illus. LC 77-9408. (ps). 1977. PLB 9.75 (ISBN 0-8075-5148-1). A Whitman.

Alden, Laura. Houdini. Raskin, Betty, illus. LC 88-34126. 100p. (gr. 3-7). 1989. PLB 12.96 (ISBN 0-89565-456-3); pap. 7.95 (ISBN 0-89565-535-7). Childs World.

Anderson, David A. What You Can See, You Can Be! Jones, Don, illus. 48p. (Orig.). (gr. 3-8). 1988. 11.95 (ISBN 0-87516-603-2). DeVorss.

Anderson, Leone C. Surprise at Muddy Creek. Endres, Helen, illus. 32p. (gr. 1-3). 1990. PLB 10.95 (ISBN 0-89565-698-1). Childs World.

Arnold, Tedd. Mother Goose's Words of Wit & Wisdom: A Book of Months. (Illus.). 64p. 1990. 14.95 (ISBN 0-8037-0825-4); PLB 14.89 (ISBN 0-8037-0826-2). Dial Bks Young.

Ayer, Eleanor. Determination. (gr. 7-12). Date not set. PLB 12.95 (ISBN 0-8239-1226-4). Rosen Group.

Banta, Robert. Grandpa Says: You Can Make It a Wonderful Life. LC 89-52115. 148p. (gr. 2-6). 1990. 7.95 (ISBN 1-55523-312-0). Winston-Derek.

Barton, Charles D. Changes in Youth Morality: What Caused Them, No. 1. rev. ed. Barton, David, illus. 40p. 1988. pap. 3.00 (ISBN 0-317-93057-5). Wallbuilders.

Beatty, Patricia. Behave Yourself, Bethany Brant. LC 86-12517. 160p. (gr. 5-9). 1986. 12.95 (ISBN 0-688-05923-6). Morrow Jr Bks.

Beaudin, Margery. Winning Is Responsibility. LC 80-85339. (gr. 7-10). PLB write for info. (ISBN 0-938762-27-3). Eagle Mktg Corp.

Berger, Melvin. Mind Control. LC 82-46004. 128p. (gr. 5 up). 1985. (Crowell Jr Bks); PLB 10.89 (ISBN 0-690-04349-X, Crowell Jr Bks). HarpC Child Bks.

Berry, Joy. Every Kid's Guide to Being Special. Bartholemew, illus. 48p. (gr. 3-7). 1987. 5.95 (ISBN 0-516-21401-2); PLB 14.60 (ISBN 0-516-01401-3). Childrens.

—Every Kid's Guide to Coping with Childhood Traumas. Bartholomew, illus. 48p. (gr. 3-7). 1988. 5.95 (ISBN 0-516-21426-8); PLB 14.60 (ISBN 0-516-01426-9). Childrens.

—Every Kid's Guide to Decision Making & Problem Solving. Bartholomew, illus. 48p. (gr. 3-7). 1987. 4.95 (ISBN 0-516-21410-1); PLB 14.60 (ISBN 0-516-01410-2). Childrens.

—Every Kid's Guide to Family Rules & Responsibilities. (Illus.). 48p. (gr. 3-7). 1987. 5.95 (ISBN 0-516-21419-5); PLB 14.60 (ISBN 0-516-01419-6). Childrens.

—Every Kid's Guide to Good Manners. (Illus.). 48p. (gr. 3-7). 1987. 4.95 (ISBN 0-516-21420-9); PLB 14.60 (ISBN 0-516-01420-X). Childrens.

—Every Kid's Guide to Handling Disagreements. (Illus.). 48p. (gr. 3-7). 1987. 4.95 (ISBN 0-516-21421-7); PLB 14.60 (ISBN 0-516-01421-8). Childrens.

—Every Kid's Guide to Handling Illness. Bartholomew, illus. 48p. (gr. 3-7). 1988. 4.95 (ISBN 0-516-21427-6); PLB 14.60 (ISBN 0-516-01427-7). Childrens.

—Every Kid's Guide to Intelligent Spending. Bartholomew, illus. 48p. (gr. 3-7). 1988. 4.95 (ISBN 0-516-21428-4); PLB 14.60 (ISBN 0-516-01428-5). Childrens.

—Every Kid's Guide to Using Time Wisely. (Illus.). 48p. (gr. 3-7). 1987. 4.95 (ISBN 0-516-21425-X); PLB 14.60 (ISBN 0-516-01425-0). Childrens.

Berry, Joy W. What to Do When Your Mom or Dad Says: "Be Good!" Kelley, Orly, ed. Bartholomew, illus. LC 83-80509. 48p. (gr. k-6). 4.98 (ISBN 0-941510-15-8). Living Skills.

—What to Do When Your Mom or Dad Says..."Get the Phone!" Batholomew, illus. LC 83-80000507. 48p. (gr. 3 up). 1983. 14.60 (ISBN 0-516-02579-1). Childrens.

—What to Do When Your Mom or Dad Says..."Go to Bed!" Bartholomew, illus. LC 83-80000508. 48p. (gr. 3 up). 1983. 14.60 (ISBN 0-516-02580-5). Childrens.

—What to Do When Your Mom or Dad Says..."Be Good While You're There" Bartholomew, illus. Berry, Joy W., intro. by. LC 82-81202. (Illus.). 48p. (gr. 3-7). 1982. 4.98 (ISBN 0-941510-07-7). Living Skills.

—What to Do When Your Mom or Dad Says..."Don't Hang Around with the Wrong Crowd!" Kelly, Orly, ed. Bartholomew, illus. LC 82-82086. 48p. (gr. k-6). 1982. 4.98 (ISBN 0-941510-10-7). Living Skills.

—What to Do When Your Mom or Dad Says..."Don't Hang Around with the Wrong Crowd!" Bartholomew, illus. LC 82-82000086. (gr. 3 up). 1983. 14.60 (ISBN 0-516-02574-0). Childrens.

—What to Do When Your Mom or Dad Says..."Help!" Kelly, Orly, ed. Bartholomew, illus. LC 82-82088. 48p. (gr. k-6). 1982. 4.98 (ISBN 0-941510-09-3). Living Skills.

—What to Do When Your Mom or Dad Says..."Help!" Bartholomew, illus. LC 82-82000088. 48p. (gr. 3 up). 1983. 14.60 (ISBN 0-516-02577-5). Childrens.

—What to Do When Your Mom or Dad Says..."Don't Overdo with Video Games!" Kelley, Orly, ed. Bartholomew, illus. 48p. (gr. k-6). 4.98 (ISBN 0-941510-25-5). Living Skills.

—What to Do When Your Mom or Dad Says..."Do Something Besides Watching TV" Kelly, Orly, et al, eds. Berry, Joy W., illus. LC 82-82087. 48p. (gr. k-6). 1982. 4.98 (ISBN 0-941510-11-5). Living Skills.

—What to Do When Your Mom or Dad Says..."Do Something Besides Watching TV!" Bartholomew, illus. LC 82-82000087. 48p. (gr. 3 up). 14.60 (ISBN 0-516-02575-9). Childrens.

—What to Do When Your Mom or Dad Says..."Do Your Homework!" Bartholomew, illus. LC 82-82089. 48p. (gr. k-6). 1982. 4.98 (ISBN 0-941510-08-5). Living Skills.

—What to Do When Your Mom or Dad Says..."Do Your Homework!" Bartholomew, illus. LC 82-82000089. 48p. (gr. 3 up). 1983. 14.60 (ISBN 0-516-02576-7). Childrens.

—You Can Be Responsible! Cochran, Nancy & Motycka, Susan, eds. LC 84-52440. (Illus.). 48p. (gr. 1-7). 1985. 4.98 (ISBN 0-941510-48-4). Living Skills.

Birmingham Marketing Staff. Motivational Quotes for Kids & Teens: And Anyone Else Who Wants to Feel Good about Themselves. Watts, Gayle, ed. 76p. (gr. 6-12). 1988. pap. text ed. 8.95 (ISBN 0-945772-01-7). Birmingham Mktg.

Bisignano, Judith & Robinson, Marilyn. Creating Your Future: Activities to Encourage Thinking Ahead, Level 2. Johnson, Dennis, illus. Thoebald, Robert, frwd. by. 64p. (Orig.). (gr. 4-6). 1985. wkbk 6.95 (ISBN 0-934134-38-3). Sheed & Ward MO.

Bisignano, Judy. Relating. Tom, Darcy, illus. 64p. (gr. 3-8). 1985. wkbk. 7.95 (ISBN 0-86653-331-1, GA 678). Good Apple.

Blackburn, Lynn B. I Know I Made It Happen: A Book about Children & Guilt. Johnson, Joy, ed. Borum, Shari, illus. 24p. (Orig.). (ps-6). 1990. pap. 3.50 (ISBN 1-56123-016-2). Centering Corp.

Blake, James L. Common Sense in a Complex World: What Every Young Person Should Know. LC 88-72165. 192p. (Orig.). (gr. 8-11). 1989. pap. 8.95 (ISBN 0-9621230-0-5). CSI Pub.

Bowman, John S. Sportmanship. (Illus.). 64p. (gr. 7-12,RL 4-6). 1990. PLB 12.95 (ISBN 0-8239-1110-1). Rosen Group.

Boyd, Selma & Boyd, Pauline. The How: Making the Best of a Mistake. Luks, Peggy, illus. LC 80-13513. 32p. (ps-3). 1981. 16.95 (ISBN 0-87705-176-3). Human Sci Pr.

Brady, Janeen. Show a Little Love. Grover, Nina, illus. 48p. (gr. k-6). 1981. songbk. 6.95 (ISBN 0-944803-26-1); cassette 7.95 (ISBN 0-944803-28-8). Brite Intl.

—Standin' Tall Forgiveness. Wilson, Grant & Galloway, Neil, illus. 22p. (Orig.). (ps-6). 1981. pap. text ed. 1.50 activity bk. (ISBN 0-944803-39-3); cassette & bk. 8.95 (ISBN 0-944803-40-7). Brite Intl.

—Standin' Tall Honesty. Wilson, Grant & Galloway, Neil, illus. 22p. (Orig.). (ps-6). 1981. pap. text ed. 1.50 activity bk. (ISBN 0-944803-37-7); cassette & bk. 8.95 (ISBN 0-944803-38-5). Brite Intl.

—Standin' Tall Obedience. Wilson, Grant & Galloway, Neil, illus. 22p. (Orig.). (ps-6). 1981. pap. text ed. 1.50 activity bk. (ISBN 0-944803-35-0); cassette & bk. 8.95 (ISBN 0-944803-36-9). Brite Intl.

Brady, Janeen & Woolley, Diane. Standin' Tall Dependability. Galloway, Neil, illus. 22p. (Orig.). (ps-6). 1984. pap. text ed. 1.50 activity bk. (ISBN 0-944803-59-8); cassette & bk. 8.95 (ISBN 0-944803-60-1). Brite Intl.

—Standin' Tall Gratitude. Wilson, Grant, illus. 22p. (Orig.). (ps-6). 1982. pap. text ed. 1.50 activity bk. (ISBN 0-944803-48-2); cassette & bk. 8.95 (ISBN 0-944803-49-0). Brite Intl.

—Standin' Tall Love. Wilson, Grant, illus. 22p. (Orig.). (ps-6). 1982. pap. text ed. 1.50 activity bk. (ISBN 0-944803-50-4); cassette & bk. 8.95 (ISBN 0-944803-51-2). Brite Intl.

—Standin' Tall Self-Esteem. Wilson, Grant, illus. 22p. (Orig.). (ps-6). 1984. pap. text ed. 1.50 activity bk. (ISBN 0-944803-56-3); cassette & bk. 8.95 (ISBN 0-944803-57-1). Brite Intl.

—Standin' Tall Service. Wilson, Grant, illus. 22p. (Orig.). (ps-6). 1984. pap. text ed. 1.50 activity bk. (ISBN 0-944803-52-0); cassette & bk. 8.95 (ISBN 0-944803-53-9). Brite Intl.

Bright, Velma. What Would You Like to Be? Schultz, Patty, illus. 32p. (gr. 1). PLB 10.00 (ISBN 0-9605968-0-1). Bright Bks.

Buerger, Jane. Obedience. rev. ed. Endres, Helen, illus. LC 80-39520. 32p. (gr. k-3). 1981. PLB 11.97 (ISBN 0-89565-206-4). Childs World.

Bundschuh, Rick. A Shadow of a Man. LC 86-22048. 120p. (Orig.). (gr. 6-9). 1986. pap. 4.95 (ISBN 0-8307-1143-0, S185116). Regal.

Burns, Marilyn. I Am Not a Short Adult: Getting Good at Being a Kid. (Illus.). (gr. 5 up). 1977. 14.95 (ISBN 0-316-11745-5); pap. 7.95 (ISBN 0-316-11746-3). Little.

Caldwell, John. Excuses, Excuses: How to Get Out of Practically Anything. Cadwell, John, illus. LC 81-43028. 48p. (gr. 3-6). 1981. PLB 12.89 (ISBN 0-690-04125-X, Crowell Jr Bks). HarpC Child Bks.

Cambridge, Barbara S. And This I Know: Affirmations for Children. rev. ed. Anderson, Lin, illus. 28p. 1987. pap. 6.95 (ISBN 0-317-91380-8). CBridge Pubns.

Carl, Angela R. A Matter of Choice. Speirs, John, illus. 32p. (gr. 1-3). 1990. PLB 10.95 (ISBN 0-89565-699-X). Childs World.

Carswell, Evelyn & Bisignano, Judy. Living. Tom, Darcy, illus. 64p. (gr. 3-8). 1985. wkbk. 7.95 (ISBN 0-86653-332-X, GA 679). Good Apple.

Chapian, Marie. Feeling Small... Walking Tall. 176p. (Orig.). (gr. 8 up). 1989. pap. 6.95 (ISBN 1-55661-029-7). Bethany Hse.

Childre, Doc L. Heart Smarts: Teenage Guide for the Puzzle of Life. Putman, Brian, illus. 126p. (Orig.). (gr. 7-12). 1991. pap. write for info. (ISBN 1-879052-07-5). Planetary Pubns. HEART SMARTS is a powerful, fun, hands-on manual for teenagers, their parents & educators. It gives teenagers the chance to feel & be understood, addressing their kind of day-to-day stress, peer pressures & relationship concerns. The book also provides a "streetsense", nuts & bolts understanding of what to do. It offers fun shortcuts to relieve stress; tools for teens to learn to manage their own energies & improve relationships; & ways to access their own HEART INTELLIGENCE. By getting their head intelligence working together with their heart directives, teens can develop self-security & well-rounded self-esteem - a more mature, self-responsible approach to life. "HEART SMARTS does an excellent job of introducing teenagers to their feelings-& to healthy self-esteem. I applaud Doc Childre for his sensitivity to the needs of young people & for this most excellent tool for teenagers, adults & teachers. I recommend it highly."--Emmett E. Miller, M.D., California Task Force to Promote Self-Esteem. "...Explores the ups 'n' downs of emotion of adolescence with humor & a positive attitude. Compassionately written, the exercises & information provide young people with a way to start building the skills that will enable them to live fully & happily."--Focus on Books.
Publisher Provided Annotation.

Cohen, Susan & Cohen, Daniel. Teenage Competition: A Survival Guide. LC 86-24307. 156p. (gr. 7 up). 1986. 13.95 (ISBN 0-87131-487-8). M Evans.

Cohn-Gilletly, Joanne. Ten Minutes with Me. 3rd ed. (Illus., Orig.). (gr. k-3). 1980. pap. 2.00 (ISBN 0-916634-05-1). Double M Pr.

Coleman, William L. Entering the Teen Zone: Devotions to Guide You. LC 90-43092. 112p. (Orig.). (gr. 7-10). 1991. pap. 4.95 (ISBN 0-8066-2499-X, 9-2499, Augsburg). Augsburg Fortress.

Colonna, Phyllia & Phillips, Ana M. The Power of Caring. LC 81-50388. (gr. k-7). lib. bdg. write for info. (ISBN 0-911712-87-9). Eagle Mktg Corp.

Colonna, Phyllis & Ramussen, Della M. The Power of Courage. LC 80-85338. (gr. k-7). write for info. Eagle Mktg Corp.

Colonna, Phyllis & Rasmussen, Della M. The Power of Cheerfulness. LC 80-85337. (gr. k-7). lib. bdg. write for info. Eagle Mktg Corp.

—The Power of Determination. LC 80-85339. (gr. k-7). lib. bdg. write for info. Eagle Mktg Corp.

—The Power of Enthusiasm. LC 81-50864. (gr. k-7). lib. bdg. write for info. Eagle Mktg Corp.

—The Power of Integrity. LC 81-50390. (gr. k-7). lib. bdg. write for info. (ISBN 0-911712-85-2). Eagle Mktg Corp.

—The Power of Sportsmanship. LC 81-50868. (gr. k-7). lib. bdg. write for info. (ISBN 0-911712-94-1). Eagle Mktg Corp.

—The Power of Trying Again. LC 81-50389. (gr. k-7). lib. bdg. write for info. (ISBN 0-911712-86-0). Eagle Mktg Corp.

Community Intervention, Inc. Staff. Participant Guidebook: My Life... Right Now. (Illus.). 52p. (gr. 7-12). 1988. wkbk. 3.50 (ISBN 0-9613416-9-6). Comm Intervention.

Corey, Dorothy. We All Share. Fay, Ann, ed. LC 80-18988. (Illus.). 32p. (ps-1). 1980. PLB 9.75 (ISBN 0-8075-8696-X). A Whitman.

Coriell, Ron & Coriell, Rebekah. A Child's Book of Character Building, Bk. Two. 128p. (ps-2). 1981. 12.95 (ISBN 0-8007-1265-X). Revell.

Cosby, Bill, et al. Changes: Becoming the Best You Can Be. rev. ed. Barr, Linda & Wojcicki, Marba, eds. Robison, Don, et al, illus. 196p. (gr. 6-8). 1988. pap. text ed. 6.85 (ISBN 0-933419-24-4). Quest Intl.

Cosgrove, Stephen E. Ira Wordworthy. Edelson, Wendy, illus. 32p. (ps-3). 1990. lib. bdg. 12.96 (ISBN 0-89565-658-2). Childs World.

—T. J. Flopp. Edelson, Wendy, illus. 32p. (ps-3). 1990. lib. bdg. 12.96 (ISBN 0-89565-660-4). Childs World.

Cote. Curiosity, Reading Level 2. (Illus.). 32p. (gr. 1-4). Date not set. PLB 13.26 (ISBN 0-86592-442-2). Rourke Corp.

Crouthamel, Thomas G., Sr. It's OK. 2nd ed. Hasty, Patti, illus. LC 86-27694. 36p. (gr. 12 up). 1990. pap. 6.95 (ISBN 0-940701-18-9). Keystone PA. Following the death of his daughter, Thomas Crouthamel began to really listen to what his son & other grieving siblings were saying. He learned that when someone's brother or sister dies, the surviving sibling(s) goes through a traumatic grief process that lasts far longer than people realize. Although the effects of death experienced by a bereaved sibling are common to all grieving siblings, each feels he/she is standing alone in the world, & no one understands. Parents are enveloped in their own grief, peers don't want to hear about it, & teachers don't have the training, or time to cope with a grieving student. IT'S OK is a "Survival Kit" for bereaved siblings. It provides understanding, answers, help, & above all, PERMISSION for surviving siblings to act & feel the way they do. IT'S OK compassionately explains that they are not alone, they are not crazy, that their feelings, frustrations, & emotions are all

"normal" experiences that can happen to anyone following the death of a sister or brother. Although IT'S OK was written for a young age group, favorable reviews have been received from adult bereaved siblings in their 60's & 80's. Sibling grief has no age limits.
Publisher Provided Annotation.

Crowdy, Deborah. Pride. McCallum, Jodie, illus. LC 89-48107. 32p. (gr. k-3). 1990. lib. bdg. 11.97 (ISBN 0-89565-566-7); pap. text ed. 6.96 (ISBN 0-89565-615-9). Childs World.

Crum, Thomas F. Magic of Conflict Workshop for Young People. Heffernan, Cheryl, illus. (gr. 6-12). 1989. multi-media kit 49.95 (ISBN 1-877803-04-9). AIKI Works.

Crutsinger, Carla. Teenage Connection: A Tool for Effective Teenage Communication. LC 87-73063. 225p. (gr. 7-12). 1987. pap. 13.95x (ISBN 0-944662-00-5). Brainworks Inc.

Davies, Leah. Kelly Bear Beginnings, 3 bks. Davies, Joy, illus. 96p. (ps-3). 1991. Set incl. Kelly Bear Feelings; Kelly Bear Behavior; Kelly Bear Health. pap. 13.50 (ISBN 0-9621054-3-0). Kelly Bear Bks.
The "KELLY BEAR" books teach children important life skills such as coping positively with emotions, learning appropriate behavior, making wholesome choices & accepting responsibility for their feelings, actions & bodies. Children identify with the green bear who is a positive role model. The INTERACTION books are to be read by an adult (teacher, librarian, counselor, parent) with a child or children. Throughout the books Kelly Bear asks questions that encourage children to share their thoughts & feelings, as Kelly Bear does. When adults listen with regard, children perceive themselves as valued & their self-esteem thrives. According to Dr. Kevin Swick, Univ. of South Carolina, the KELLY BEAR books have "exemplary situations"... which "have been used successfully with parents & children from every background & cultural orientation." Pam Kent, a teacher, Auburn, Alabama, states, "The books provide invaluable insights...a wonderful teaching tool." The acclaimed series is being used effectively with classrooms of children, in small groups, & with individuals, including high-risk & special education students. The KELLY BEAR books are the mainstay of an eight-week Drug Abuse Prevention Program (D.A.P.P.) $195.00. Kelly Bear Books, Route 3, Box 99, Lafayette, Alabama, (205) 864-8991.
Publisher Provided Annotation.

Davis, Sandra P. That Special Touch. LC 89-92544. (Illus.). 140p. 1990. 39.95 (ISBN 0-9625232-0-8). Special Touch.

Decker, DeLynn. The Power of Patriotism. LC 81-50387. (gr. k-7). lib. bdg. write for info. (ISBN 0-911712-84-4). Eagle Mktg Corp.

Earle, Vana. Honesty. (Illus.). 64p. (gr. 7-12,RL 4-6). 1990. 12.95 (ISBN 0-8239-1109-8). Rosen Group.

Educational Assessment Publishing Co. Staff. Discover: Skills for Life, Level 7: Total Teacher Support System. (Illus.). 396p. Date not set. text ed. 93.25 (ISBN 0-942277-31-7). Educ Assess Pub.

Educational Assessment Publishing Company Staff. Discover: Skills for Life, Level 8: Student Book. (Illus.). 240p. Date not set. text ed. 15.10 (ISBN 0-942277-32-5). Educ Assess Pub.

Educational Assessment Publishing Co. Staff. Discover: Skills for Life, Level 8: Teacher's Edition. (Illus.). 256p. Date not set. text ed. 34.18 (ISBN 0-942277-33-3). Educ Assess Pub.

—Discover: Skills for Life, Level 8: Total Teacher Support System. (Illus.). 396p. Date not set. text ed. 93.25 (ISBN 0-942277-35-X). Educ Assess Pub.

Educational Assessment Publishing Company Staff. Parent - Child Learning Library: Commitment. (Illus.). 32p. (ps). Date not set. text ed. 9.95 (ISBN 0-942277-68-6). Educ Assess Pub.

—Parent - Child Learning Library: Fairness. (Illus.). 32p. (ps). Date not set. text ed. 9.95 (ISBN 0-942277-65-1). Educ Assess Pub.

—Parent - Child Learning Library: Goal Setting. 32p. (ps). Date not set. text ed. 9.95 (ISBN 0-942277-67-8). Educ Assess Pub.

—Parent - Child Learning Library: Honesty English Big Book. (Illus.). 32p. (gr. k-3). Date not set. text ed. 28.50 (ISBN 0-942277-42-2). Educ Assess Pub.

—Parent - Child Learning Library: Honesty Spanish Big Book. (SPA., Illus.). 32p. (gr. k-3). Date not set. text ed. 28.50 (ISBN 0-942277-41-4). Educ Assess Pub.

—Parent - Child Learning Library: Honesty Spanish Edition. (SPA., Illus.). 32p. (ps). Date not set. text ed. 9.95 (ISBN 0-942277-87-2). Educ Assess Pub.

—Parent - Child Learning Library: Honesty. (Illus.). 32p. (ps-k). Date not set. text ed. 9.95 (ISBN 0-942277-59-7). Educ Assess Pub.

—Parent - Child Learning Library: Loyalty. 32p. (gr. k-3). Date not set. text ed. 28.50 (ISBN 0-942277-72-4). Educ Assess Pub.

—Parent - Child Learning Library: Patience. (Illus.). (ps-k). Date not set. text ed. 9.95 (ISBN 0-942277-69-4). Educ Assess Pub.

—Parent - Child Learning Library: Responsibility English Big Book. (Illus.). 32p. Date not set. text ed. 28.50 (ISBN 0-942277-44-9). Educ Assess Pub.

—Parent - Child Learning Library: Responsibility. (Illus.). 32p. (gr. k-3). Date not set. text ed. 9.95 (ISBN 0-942277-58-9). Educ Assess Pub.

—Parent - Child Learning Library: Responsibility Spanish Big Book. (SPA., Illus.). 32p. (gr. k-3). Date not set. text ed. 28.50 (ISBN 0-942277-45-7). Educ Assess Pub.

—Parent - Child Learning Library: Responsibility Spanish Edition. (SPA.). 32p. (ps). Date not set. text ed. 9.95 (ISBN 0-942277-92-9). Educ Assess Pub.

Erickson, P. C. Stand Tall. Pugh, Kayleen, illus. (Orig.). (gr. 4-8). 1978. pap. 2.95 (ISBN 0-89036-111-8). Hawkes Pub Inc.

Everix, Nancy. More Windows to the World. Everix, Nancy, illus. 128p. (gr. 2-8). 1985. wkbk. 10.95 (ISBN 0-86653-316-8, GA 640). Good Apple.

Fiday, Beverly. Patience. Rigo, Christina L., illus. LC 86-12984. 32p. (gr. k-3). 1986. lib. bdg. 11.97 (ISBN 0-89565-358-3). Childs World.

Frykman, John. The Hassle Handbook. rev. ed. LC 84-6851. (Illus.). 108p. 1988. 9.95 (ISBN 0-916147-02-9); pap. 8.95 (ISBN 0-916147-01-0). Regent Pr.

Gajewski, Nancy & Mayo, Patty. SSS: Social Skill Strategies, Bk. A. 336p. (gr. 5-12). 1989. pap. 33.00 (ISBN 0-930599-51-9). Thinking Pubns.

Ganz, Yaffa. The Wonderful World We Live In. Ariel, Liat B., illus. 48p. (gr. k-6). 1989. 10.95 (ISBN 0-89906-964-9); pap. 6.95 (ISBN 0-89906-965-7). Mesorah Pubns.

Gibson, Christine R. & Hargrave, J. Michael. The Tator Tales: A Story & Activity Book on Handling Peer Pressure. Majewski, Chuck, illus. 51p. (gr. 3-5). 1988. pap. 6.95 (ISBN 0-9624285-0-7). Tator Enterprises.

Girard, Linda W. Who Is a Stranger & What Should I Do? Levine, Abby, ed. Cogancherry, Helen, illus. LC 84-17313. 32p. (gr. 2-6). 1985. PLB 10.95 (ISBN 0-8075-9014-2). A Whitman.

Golant, Mitch & Bahr, Amy C. It's OK Books. Burke, Diane O., illus. Incl. It's OK to Be Angry (ISBN 0-528-87143-9); It's OK to Be Shy (ISBN 0-528-87144-7); It's OK to Be Different (ISBN 0-528-87145-5); It's OK to Be Afraid (ISBN 0-528-87146-3). 24p. (ps-2). 1986. pap. write for info. Checkerboard Pr.

Golant, Mitch & Crane, Bob. It's O.K. to Be Different. 128p. (gr. 1-5). 1988. pap. 4.95 (ISBN 0-8125-9462-2). Tor Bks.

—Sometimes It's O.K. to Be Afraid. 128p. (gr. 1-5). 1988. pap. 4.95 (ISBN 0-8125-9464-9). Tor Bks.

Goley. Cooperation, Reading Level 2. (Illus.). 32p. (gr. 1-4). Date not set. PLB 13.26 (ISBN 0-86592-390-6). Rourke Corp.

—Giving, Reading Level 2. (Illus.). 32p. (gr. 1-4). Date not set. PLB 13.26 (ISBN 0-86592-392-2). Rourke Corp.

—Joy, Reading Level 2. (Illus.). 32p. (gr. 1-4). Date not set. PLB 13.26 (ISBN 0-86592-393-0). Rourke Corp.

—Learning, Reading Level 2. (Illus.). 32p. (gr. 1-4). Date not set. PLB 13.26 (ISBN 0-86592-396-5). Rourke Corp.

—Responsibility, Reading Level 2. (Illus.). 32p. (gr. 1-4). Date not set. PLB 13.26 (ISBN 0-86592-394-9). Rourke Corp.

—Self Control, Reading Level 2. (Illus.). 32p. (gr. 1-4). Date not set. PLB 13.26 (ISBN 0-86592-397-3). Rourke Corp.

Goley, Elaine. Caring. (Illus.). 32p. (gr. 1-4). 1987. PLB 13.26 (ISBN 0-86592-381-7). Rourke Corp.

—Helping. (Illus.). 32p. (gr. 1-4). 1987. PLB 13.26 (ISBN 0-86592-384-1). Rourke Corp.

—Honesty. (Illus.). 32p. (gr. 1-4). 1987. PLB 13.26 (ISBN 0-317-60466-X). Rourke Corp.

—Kindness. (Illus.). 32p. (gr. 1-4). 1987. PLB 13.26 (ISBN 0-86592-383-3). Rourke Corp.

—Learn the Value, 10 bks, Set I, Reading Level 2. (Illus.). 320p. (gr. 1-4). Date not set. Set. PLB 132.66 (ISBN 0-86592-375-2). Rourke Corp.

—Patience. (Illus.). 32p. (gr. 1-4). 1987. PLB 10.60 (ISBN 0-86592-379-5). Rourke Corp.

—Trust. (Illus.). 32p. (gr. 1-4). 1987. PLB 13.26 (ISBN 0-86592-378-7). Rourke Corp.

—Understanding Others. (Illus.). 32p. (gr. 1-4). 1987. PLB 13.26 (ISBN 0-86592-382-5). Rourke Corp.

Goley, Elaine, et al. Learn the Value, 18 bks, Set II, Reading Level 2. (Illus.). 576p. (gr. 1-4). Date not set. Set. PLB 238.80 (ISBN 0-86592-391-4). Rourke Corp.

Gonter, Janet. Loving Is... Seward, Lynn, illus. 32p. (gr. 1-4). 1986. casebound 4.95 (ISBN 0-87403-124-9, 3604). Standard Pub.

Gouge, Betty, et al. KidSkills Interpersonal Skill Series, Choices! Choices! Responsibility: Making & Living with Choices. Morse, J. Thomas, ed. Bleck, Linda & Bleck, Cathie, illus. LC 86-45001. 45p. (ps). 1986. PLB 8.95 (ISBN 0-934275-09-2); bk. & cassette 11.95 (ISBN 0-934275-23-8). Fam Skills.

—KidSkills Interpersonal Skill Series, My Feelings & Me: Feelings: Experiencing Feelings. Morse, J. Thomas, et al, eds. Bleck, Linda & Bleck, Cathie, illus. LC 85-81270. 44p. (ps). 1986. 8.95 (ISBN 0-934275-10-6); bk. & cassette 11.95 (ISBN 0-934275-24-6). Fam Skills.

—KidSkills Interpersonal Skill Series, The Rules at My House: Responsibility: Understanding & Accepting Limits. Morse, J. Thomas, et al, eds. Bleck, Linda & Bleck, Cathie, illus. 44p. (ps). 1986. PLB 8.95 (ISBN 0-934275-11-4); bk. & cassette 11.95 (ISBN 0-934275-25-4). Fam Skills.

—KidSkills Interpersonal Skill Series, Wonderful You: Self-Awareness: Accepting & Knowing Myself. Morse, J. Thomas, et al, eds. Bleck, Linda & Bleck, Cathie, illus. LC 85-81270. 42p. (ps). 1986. PLB 8.95 (ISBN 0-934275-12-2); bk. & cassette 11.95 (ISBN 0-934275-26-2). Fam Skills.

Greenspan, Alice. Helping Is Fun. Hoha, Linda, illus. 32p. (gr. k-2). 1990. pasted 2.50 (ISBN 0-87403-027-7, 24-03912). Standard Pub.

Grindley, Sally. I Don't Want To! LC 89-85798. (ps-3). 1990. 13.95 (ISBN 0-316-32893-6, Joy St Bks). Little.

Grunsell, Angela. Bullying. (ps-3). 1990. PLB 10.40 (ISBN 0-531-17213-9). Watts.

Hafford, Jeanette N. Tiny's Self Help Books for Children. (Illus.). 18p. (Orig.). (gr. k-5). 1986. pap. 4.22 (ISBN 0-685-14506-9). Tinys Self Help Bks.

Harmon, Ed & Jarmin, Marge. Taking Charge of My Life: Choices, Changes & Me. Feign, Larry, illus. LC 88-988. 184p. (Orig.). (gr. 5-12). 1988. pap. 9.95 (ISBN 0-918588-10-3). Barksdale Foun.

Hazen, Barbara S. How Can I Help? rev. ed. Sweat, Lynn, illus. 32p. (gr. 2-4). 1990. Repr. of 1988 ed. PLB 9.95 (ISBN 1-878363-13-1). Forest Hse.

Holt, Janice M. Do I Like Myself? Coy, Venture, illus. LC 82-82332. 119p. (gr. 3-9). 1983. pap. 39.95 (ISBN 0-9608812-1-2). Greenlf Pubns.

Hullinger, Annette C. Winning Is Virtue. LC 80-85339. (gr. 7-10). PLB write for info. (ISBN 0-938762-25-7). Eagle Mktg Corp.

Hyde, Margaret O. Is This Kid "Crazy"? Understanding Unusual Behavior. LC 83-16916. 96p. (gr. 5-9). 1983. 9.95 (ISBN 0-664-32707-9, Westminster). Westminster John Knox.

Hyde, Margaret O. & Forsyth, Elizabeth H. The Violent Mind. 144p. (gr. 9-12). 1991. PLB 13.90 (ISBN 0-531-11060-5). Watts.

Johnsen, Karen. The Trouble with Secrets. Forssell, Linda, illus. LC 85-51803. 32p. (Orig.). (ps-3). 1986. lib. bdg. 12.95 (ISBN 0-943990-23-8); pap. 3.95 (ISBN 0-943990-22-X). Parenting Pr.

Johnson, Daniel S. Creative Rebellion: Positive Options for Teens in the 90s. LC 91-61346. (Illus.). 160p. (gr. 6-12). 1991. pap. 11.95 (ISBN 0-922848-11-4). Mystic Garden.

Johnson, Linda C. Responsibility. (Illus.). 64p. (gr. 7-12, RL 4-6). 1990. PLB 12.95 (ISBN 0-8239-1107-1). Rosen Group.

Jordan, Sally. Do I Have To? Philbrook, Diana, illus. 32p. (gr. 4-9). 1986. saddle stitch 0.89 (ISBN 0-87403-033-1, 3531). Standard Pub.

—Good Losers. Philbrook, Diana, illus. 32p. (gr. 5-9). 1986. saddle stitch 0.89 (ISBN 0-87403-034-X, 3532). Standard Pub.

—Is Honesty In? Philbrook, Diana, illus. 32p. (gr. 5-9). 1986. saddle stitch .89 (ISBN 0-87403-035-8, 3533). Standard Pub.

—It's Okay to Be Different. Philbrook, Diana, illus. 32p. (gr. 5-9). 1986. saddle stitch 0.89 (ISBN 0-87403-037-4, 3535). Standard Pub.

—Loneliness. Philbrook, Diana, illus. 32p. (gr. 5-9). 1986. saddle stitch 0.89 (ISBN 0-87403-038-2, 3536). Standard Pub.

—Nobody's Home...Except Me. Philbrook, Diana, illus. LC 87-92234. 32p. (gr. 4-9). 1988. saddle stitch .89 (ISBN 0-87403-439-6, 24-03649). Standard Pub.

—Respect. Philbrook, Diana, illus. 32p. (gr. 5-9). 1986. saddle stitch 0.89 (ISBN 0-87403-039-0, 3537). Standard Pub.

—Saying No. Philbrook, Diana, illus. 32p. (gr. 5-9). 1986. saddle stitch 0.89 (ISBN 0-87403-040-4, 3538). Standard Pub.

—Team Play. Philbrook, Diana, illus. 32p. (gr. 5-9). 1986. saddle stitch 0.89 (ISBN 0-87403-041-2, 3539). Standard Pub.

—Teasing, Taunting, Tormenting...They All Hurt. Philbrook, Diana, illus. LC 87-92233. 32p. (gr. 4-9). 1988. saddle stitched .89 (ISBN 0-87403-438-8, 24-03648). Standard Pub.

—Those Words! Philbrook, Diana, illus. 32p. (gr. 5-9). 1986. saddle stitch 0.89 (ISBN 0-87403-042-0, 3540). Standard Pub.

Kahaner, Ellen. Courage. (Illus.). 64p. (gr. 7-12,RL 4-6). 1990. PLB 12.95 (ISBN 0-8239-1112-8). Rosen Group.

Kalman, Bobbie. Come to My Place. (Illus.). 32p. (gr. k-2). 1985. 6.95 (ISBN 0-86505-062-7); pap. 5.95 (ISBN 0-86505-086-4). Crabtree Pub Co.

—Happy to Be Me. (Illus.). 32p. (gr. k-2). 1985. 6.95 (ISBN 0-86505-060-0); pap. 5.95 (ISBN 0-86505-084-8). Crabtree Pub Co.

Kerr, M. E. Me, Me, Me, Me, Me: Not a Novel. 224p. (gr. 5-9). 1984. 3.50 (ISBN 0-451-13208-4, Sig Vista). NAL-Dutton.

Kino Learning Center Staff & Sanders, Corinne. My Choices & Decisions. Mirocha, Kay, illus. 64p. (gr. 5-9). 1987. pap. 7.95 (ISBN 0-86653-421-0, GA1031). Good Apple.

Kittredge, Elaine. Twelve. Riley, Cyd, illus. 84p. 1989. pap. 9.95 (ISBN 0-9611266-1-2); audiotape, 80 mins. 9.95 (ISBN 0-9611266-2-0). Optext.

Kleckner. Humor, Reading Level 2. (Illus.). 32p. (gr. 1-4). Date not set. PLB 13.26 (ISBN 0-86592-399-X). Rourke Corp.

Kramer, Patricia & Frazer, Linda. The Dynamics of Relationships: A Guide for Developing Self-Esteem & Social Skills for Preteens & Young Children. rev. ed. (Illus.). (gr. 9 up). 1990. pap. text ed. 17.95 tchr's. manual (ISBN 0-929577-03-5). Equal Partners.
The most comprehensive program available dealing with everyday concerns vital to young people takes a preventive approach to such crucial issues as suicide, teen pregnancy, substance abuse, violence, drop-outs & physical & sexual abuse. It was developed to help youth build & maintain a healthy self-esteem, learn to communicate, handle anger & conflict effectively, develop coping & decision-making skills, & develop realistic expectations about adult roles, AIDS, suicide, teen pregnancy, date rape, gangs, etc. It can be: Implemented as a school curriculum. Incorporated into other disciplines (Health, Home Ec/ Family Life, Sex Ed, Social Studies). Used as a resource for treatment centers, substance abuse, mental health & social service programs, youth religious programs, youth clubs & organizations (4-H, Boys/Girls Clubs, Girl/Boy Scouts, etc.) The series is comprised of a teacher's manual & a two-part teen/young adult manual (which includes a separate book on sexuality) & a teacher manual for preteens & youth manual (ages 8-12). Pat Kramer conducts workshops that teach professionals strategies to empower youth & techniques to create positive, supportive environments that can reduce substance abuse, discipline problems, violence & vandalism.
Publisher Provided Annotation.

Lang, Denise V. But Everyone Else Looks So Sure of Themselves: A Guide to Surviving the Teen Years. LC 90-39087. 128p. (Orig.). (gr. 7 up). 1991. pap. 7.95 (ISBN 1-55870-177-X, Shoe Tree Pr) Betterway Pubns.

Lehrman, Fredric. Loving the Earth. (Illus.). 48p. (gr. 6-12). 1990. 17.95 (ISBN 0-89087-603-7). Celestial Arts.

Lenett, Robin, et al. Sometimes It's O. K. to Tell Secrets! 128p. (Orig.). 1986. pap. 3.95 (ISBN 0-8125-9454-1, Dist. by Warner Pub Services & St. Martin's Press). Tor Bks.

Lucas, Betty. For Children's Sake. 1989. 7.95 (ISBN 0-533-08080-0). Vantage.

McDonnell, Janet. Success. Hohag, Linda, illus. LC 88-4348. 32p. (gr. k-3). 1988. PLB 11.97 (ISBN 0-89565-376-1); pap. 6.96 (ISBN 0-89565-488-1). Childs World.

—Thankfulness. Hohag, Linda, illus. LC 88-2657. 32p. (gr. k-3). 1988. PLB 11.97 (ISBN 0-89565-375-3); pap. 5.95 (ISBN 0-89565-487-3). Childs World.

McElmurry, Mary A. Cooperating. Tom, Darcy, illus. 64p. (gr. 3-8). 1985. wkbk. 7.95 (ISBN 0-86653-334-6, GA 680). Good Apple.

McGivney, Walton J. Hot Stuff Planner. McGivney, Walton J., illus. 96p. (gr. 1-8). 1990. pap. 5.99g (ISBN 0-9628095-1-9). Plan Success.

McGuire, J. Victor. No Negatives: A Positive Guide to Successful Leadership. Prado, Jan, ed. Giblin, Tom, pref. by. 130p. (Orig.). (gr. 9-12). 1989. pap. 7.95 wkbk. (ISBN 0-685-26846-2). Spice Pr.

McMillan, Kate. Great Advice from Lila Fenwick. DeGroat, Diane, illus. LC 87-24513. 160p. (gr. 3-7). 1988. 11.95 (ISBN 0-8037-0529-8); PLB 11.89 (ISBN 0-8037-0532-8). Dial Bks Young.

Making Parents Proud. 48p. (gr. 6-8). 1990. pap. 6.95 (ISBN 1-55945-107-6). Group Pub.

Manes, Stephen. Be a Perfect Person in Just Three Days. (ps-7). 1987. pap. 2.50 (ISBN 0-553-15367-6). Bantam.

Margulies, Alice. Compassion. (Illus.). 64p. (gr. 7-12,RL 4-6). 1990. PLB 12.95 (ISBN 0-8239-1108-X). Rosen Group.

Martin, Michael. The Good Behavior Book. Harris, Stephen & Brower, Nancy, eds. Shea, Mikki, illus. (Orig.). (ps up). 1988. pap. 10.95 (ISBN 0-9621191-7-2). Behavior Products.

Mayo, Patty & Gajewski, Nancy. SSS: Social Skill Strategies, Book B: A Curriculum for Adolescents. Krause, Brad, illus. 350p. (Orig.). (gr. 5-12). 1989. pap. text ed. 33.00x (ISBN 0-930599-52-7). Thinking Pubns.

Metten, Patricia. The Power of Attitude. LC 81-50865. (gr. k-7). lib. bdg. write for info. (ISBN 0-911712-91-7). Eagle Mktg Corp.

—The Power of Being Creative. LC 81-50863. (gr. k-7). lib. bdg. write for info. (ISBN 0-911712-89-5). Eagle Mktg Corp.

—The Power of Family. LC 81-50867. (gr. k-7). lib. bdg. write for info. (ISBN 0-911712-93-3). Eagle Mktg Corp.

Min, Kellet I. Modern Informative Nursery Rhymes: Values. Hansen, Heidi, illus. 32p. (Orig.). (ps-3). 1989. pap. 7.95 (ISBN 0-685-26431-9). Rhyme & Reason.

Mitchell, Lorayne. Beautiful Feathers: A Book about Selflessness. Lee, Jeff, illus. 32p. (ps-4). 1987. PLB 12.95 (ISBN 0-943491-01-0). Valued Pubns.

—The Shadow in the Window: A Book about Caring. Lee, Jeff, illus. 32p. (ps-4). 1987. PLB 12.95 (ISBN 0-943491-02-9). Valued Pubns.

Moncure, Jane B. Growing Strong Inside. Hohag, Linda, illus. LC 85-10341. 32p. (gr. k-2). 1985. PLB 11.97 (ISBN 0-89565-333-8). Childs World.

—Happy Healthkins. Axeman, Lois, illus. LC 82-14794. (ps-2). 1982. lib. bdg. 10.95 (ISBN 0-89565-243-9). Childs World.

—Honesty. rev. ed. Karch, Paul, illus. LC 80-39571. 32p. (gr. k-3). 1981. PLB 11.97 (ISBN 0-89565-203-X). Childs World.

—Kindness. rev. ed. Hohag, Linda S., illus. LC 80-39535. 32p. (gr. k-3). 1981. PLB 11.97 (ISBN 0-89565-204-8). Childs World.

Morse, J. Thomas, et al. KidSkills Interpersonal Skill Series, An Island Adventure: Self-Esteem: Being a Friend to Myself. Gouge, Betty, et al, eds. Bleck, Cathie, illus. LC 85-45429. 47p. (gr. 2-3). 1985. PLB 9.95 (ISBN 0-934275-01-7); bk. & cassette 13.95 (ISBN 0-934275-14-9). Fam Skills.

—KidSkills Interpersonal Skill Series, The Feeling Fun House: Feelings: Dealing with Feelings. Gouge, Betty, et al, eds. Bleck, Cathie, illus. LC 85-45423. 45p. (gr. 2-3). 1985. PLB 9.95 (ISBN 0-934275-03-3); bk. & cassette 13.95 (ISBN 0-934275-17-3). Fam Skills.

—KidSkills Interpersonal Skill Series, The Land of Listening: Listening: Getting & Giving Attention. Gouge, Betty, et al, eds. Bleck, Cathie, illus. LC 85-45429. 45p. (gr. 2-3). 1985. PLB 9.95 (ISBN 0-934275-00-9); bk. & cassette 13.95 (ISBN 0-934275-15-7). Fam Skills.

Murphy, Elspeth C. Sometimes I'm Good, Sometimes I'm Bad. Nelson, Jane, illus. 24p. (gr. k-2). 1981. pap. 2.95 (ISBN 0-89191-368-8, 53686). Cook.

Navarra, Tova. Playing It Smart: What to Do When You're on Your Own. Kerr, Tom, illus. 128p. (gr. 2-8). 1989. 12.95 (ISBN 0-8120-6131-4). Barron.

Neilson, Stefan & Thoelke, Shay. Color Me Winning. (Illus.). 50p. (gr. 4-6). 1989. spiral bdg., adult wkbk. 20.00. Aeon-Hierophant.

Noorlun, Lyle J. I Can-Can. 131p. (gr. 9 up). 1989. incl. cassette 16.95 (ISBN 1-877616-00-1). Wholeness Intl.

O'Toole, Donna R. Growing Through Grief: A K-Twelve Curriculum to Help Young People Through All Kinds of Loss. rev. ed. McWhirter, Kore L., illus. 392p. 1989. pap. 59.95 3-ring bdr. (ISBN 1-878321-00-5, Mntn Rainbow). Rainbow NC.
Young People experience an ever growing number of familial, physical, environmental, emotional, & cultural changes - often without the resources, understanding, skills or validation they need to assist growth & development in life constructive ways. The Growing Through Grief Curriculum provides a life cycle, life skills & building block approach so that young people can gain internal & external resources to grow on. Developed in age appropriate groupings, sessions can be taught as a self contained class or can be incorporated into other classes or group or individual settings. "A gift, in an educational format, to parents & teachers. A must for every educator's library."--Jean Shane, Michigan Department of Education. "An exceptional work combining intellectual scholarship with a caring approach. It can be used by both beginners & those who have been working in the field for some time. A major tool for all who care to help children deal more effectively with the world around them."--Robert Stevenson, Ed.D Educator, Author & Grief Counselor. "A practical & compassionate educational tool that provides a hopefulness that is real & without a trace of denial or over optimism. It will be useful for pastoral care in church, school or university ministry settings."--The Rev. Dr. Ted Purcell, Youth & Campus Ministries Division, The Baptist State Convention of N.C.
Publisher Provided Annotation.

Palumbo, Thomas J. Thursday Think Time. Hyndman, Kathryn, illus. 64p. (gr. 3-8). 1985. wkbk. 6.95 (ISBN 0-86653-311-7, GA 650). Good Apple.

Pemberton, Nancy & Riehecky, Janet. Responsibility. Hohag, Linda, illus. LC 87-37557. 32p. (gr. k-3). 1988. PLB 11.97 (ISBN 0-89565-418-0); pap. 6.96 (ISBN 0-89565-521-7). Childs World.

Perez, Demetrio, Jr. Citizens Training Handbook-Manual de Formacion Ciudadana: Discipline-Moral-Covism-Urbanity. (SPA & ENG., Illus.). 315p. 1991. 25.00 (ISBN 0-9628780-0-6). Ed Lncln-Mrt.
Chapter topics are highly practical, including such things as good table manners, the art of conversation, social functions preparations, questions of etiquette, the family & the home, civic morals, character, love, sex education, abortion, prayer in the schools, the danger of drugs, school uniforms, politics, among 57 topics. It is bilingual, Spanish/English. And Perez speaks from years of experience. Since the early 1970s, Perez has directed the "Lincoln-Marti Schools & Day Care Centers" in Miami, Florida. He is also president of the Bilingual Private Schools Association (BIPRISA), director of a weekly tabloid, host of a radio & television talk show & a former elected commissioner & vice-mayor of Miami. Perez believes Citizens Training Handbook, with its emphasis on morality & values, will fill a void in today's school curricula. He writes out of concern for what he sees as a moral crisis in our schools & society in general. In a telling example, he cites a study, which listed the seven major problems in schools during the 1940s as: talking out loud, chewing gum, making noise, running in the halls, cutting into lines, dress code violations, & littering. In contrast,

during the 1980s were: drug abuse, alcohol abuse, teen pregnancy, suicide, rape, theft & assault.
Publisher Provided Annotation.

Peternel, Carolyn R. & Ahern, James. The I Like to Go to School Book. (Illus.). 36p. (Orig.). (gr. k-2). 1983. pap. 2.95 (ISBN 0-9612060-0-4). Primary Progs.

Peterson, Lorraine. If the Devil Made You Do It, You Blew It. 192p. (Orig.). (gr. 8 up). 1989. pap. 6.95 (ISBN 1-55661-052-1). Bethany Hse.

Petrucelli. Consideration, Reading Level 2. (Illus.). 32p. (gr. 1-4). Date not set. PLB 13.26 ea. (ISBN 0-86592-443-0). Rourke Corp.

—Loyalty, Reading Level 2. (Illus.). 32p. (gr. 1-4). Date not set. PLB 13.26 (ISBN 0-86592-441-4). Rourke Corp.

Pincus, Debbie. Feeling Good about Yourself. (Illus.). 96p. (gr. 3-8). 1990. 8.95 (ISBN 0-86653-516-0, GA 1139). Good Apple.

Plastow, John R. Football, Pizza & Success! 130p. (Orig.). (gr. 7-12). 1987. pap. 5.95 (ISBN 0-937382-03-5). Rhinos Pr.

Prather, Hugh E., Jr. Circle of a Thought. 2nd, rev. ed. Helberg, Bob, ed. LC 87-73314. 80p. (gr. 9-12). 1987. pap. 7.95 (ISBN 0-944944-00-0). Amethyst Aura.

Reihecky, Janet. Cooperation. Hutton, Kathryn, illus. LC 89-48284. 32p. (gr. k-3). 1990. lib. bdg. 11.97 (ISBN 0-89565-565-9); pap. text ed. 6.96 (ISBN 0-89565-614-0). Childs World.

Reilly, Jim, et al. Life & Works, 6 bks, Set II. (Illus.). 672p. (gr. 7 up). 1990. Set. PLB 111.60 (ISBN 0-86593-015-5); Set. PLB 83.70s.p. (ISBN 0-685-36350-3). Rourke Corp.

Riehecky, Janet. Good Sportsmanship. Rigo, Cristina, illus. LC 89-29663. 32p. (gr. k-3). 1990. lib. bdg. 11.97 (ISBN 0-89565-563-2); pap. text ed. 6.96 (ISBN 0-89565-612-4). Childs World.

—Sharing. Rigo, Christina, illus. LC 87-26811. 32p. (gr. k-3). 1988. PLB 11.97 (ISBN 0-89565-416-4); pap. 6.96 (ISBN 0-89565-489-X). Childs World.

Riley, Sue. Help! LC 77-16030. (Illus.). (ps-2). 1978. PLB 9.96 (ISBN 0-89565-012-6). Childs World.

—Sharing. LC 77-16293. (Illus.). (ps-2). 1978. PLB 9.96 (ISBN 0-89565-015-0). Childs World.

—Sorry. LC 77-16811. (Illus.). (ps-2). 1978. PLB 9.96 (ISBN 0-89565-013-4). Childs World.

Ross, Tony. The Boy Who Cried Wolf. Ross, Tony, illus. LC 84-23273. 32p. (gr. k up). 1985. 10.95 (ISBN 0-8037-0193-4). Dial Bks Young.

Samuelson, Rita. Sound Strategist. 86p. (gr. k-12). 1989. pap. 33.00 (ISBN 0-930599-50-0). Thinking Pubns.

Sanders, Corinne. Choosing. Tom, Darcy, illus. 64p. (gr. 3-8). 1985. wkbk. 7.95 (ISBN 0-86653-333-8, GA 677). Good Apple.

Schleifer, Jay. Citizenship. (Illus.). 64p. (gr. 7-12,RL 4-6). 1990. PLB 12.95 (ISBN 0-8239-1113-6). Rosen Group.

Schliefer, Jay. The Work Ethic. (gr. 7-12). 1991. PLB 12.95 (ISBN 0-8239-1227-2). Rosen Group.

Schwartz, Linda. What Would You Do? A Kid's Guide to Tricky & Sticky Situations. Armstrong, Beverly, illus. 184p. (gr. 3-6). 1991. pap. 9.95 (ISBN 0-88160-196-9). Learning Wks.

Shaheed, Geraldine M. & Beauchamp, Celestine R. Building My Self-Esteem: (Simple, 9 Vols. rev. ed. (gr. k up). 1988. text ed. write for info.; write for info. tchr's. ed. VF&AL Pub Inc.

Sharma, Vijai P. Insane Jealousy: The Causes, Outcomes, & Solutions When Jealousy Gets Out of Hand: The Triangle of the Mind. Munro, Alistair, intro. by. 224p. (Orig.). (gr. 7-9). 1991. pap. text ed. 16.95 (ISBN 0-9628382-6-8). Mind Pubns.

Shaw, Diana. Make the Most of a Good Thing: You! (gr. 5-9). 1987. 13.95 (ISBN 0-316-78340-4, Joy St Bks); pap. 6.95 (ISBN 0-316-78342-0). Little.

Smith, Wendell. The Roots of Character. (Illus.). 1987. tchr's. ed. 49.95 (ISBN 0-914936-90-5); student wkbk., 168p. 9.95 (ISBN 0-914936-89-1). Bible Temple.

Snider, Dee & Bashe, Philip. Dee Snider's Teenage Survival Guide. LC 86-32963. (gr. 6-12). 1987. (Dolp); pap. 8.95 (ISBN 0-385-23900-9, Dolp). Doubleday.

Somers, Adele. Learn from Everyone! Practical Guidelines to Living. Somers, Stanley E., illus. 192p. (Orig.). (gr. 8 up). 1985. pap. 7.95 (ISBN 0-9615032-0-3). World Relations Pr.

Squire-Buresh, Anne L. To Touch the Sky. LC 89-50050. 44p. (gr. k-3). 1989. 5.95 (ISBN 1-55523-224-8). Winston-Derek.

Stortz, Diane M. Confidence Is... Bishop, Richard, illus. 32p. (gr. 1-4). 1987. casebound 4.95 (ISBN 0-87403-322-5, 3667). Standard Pub.

Students at Risk: Winning Colors Power Pack. (gr. 6-12). 1990. spiral bdg., tchr's. ed., 87p. 30.00; spiral bdg., wkbk., 56p. 20.00 (ISBN 0-685-30818-9). Aeon-Hierophant.

Suttner, Mindy. Winning Is Self-Control. LC 88-90932. (gr. 7-10). PLB write for info. (ISBN 0-938762-26-5). Eagle Mktg Corp.

Swenson, Judy H. & Kunz, Roxane B. Learning My Way: I'm a Winner! LC 86-11577. (Illus.). 48p. (gr. 2-6). 1986. PLB 8.95 (ISBN 0-87518-351-4, Dillon). Macmillan Child Grp.

Swenson, Virginia. The Power of Industry. LC 81-50662. (gr. k-7). lib. bdg. write for info. (ISBN 0-911712-88-7). Eagle Mktg Corp.

Teenage Magazine Editors, compiled by. Boosting Your Self-Confidence. 140p. (Orig.). (gr. 9-12). 1989. pap. 5.95 (ISBN 0-931529-90-5, Teenage Bks). Group Pub.

Thomas, Marlo. Free to Be...You & Me. Steinem, Gloria, intro. by. (gr. 1 up). 1987. pap. 12.95 (ISBN 0-553-34544-3). Bantam.

Thompson, Merita L. & Strange, Johanna. Discover: Skills for Life, Level K: Pupil Edition. (Illus.). 48p. (gr. k-3). Date not set. text ed. 9.65 (ISBN 0-942277-00-7). Educ Assess Pub.

—Discover: Skills for Life, Level K: Spanish Home Worksheets. (SPA., Illus.). 7p. (gr. k-3). Date not set. text ed. 6.87 (ISBN 0-942277-56-2). Educ Assess Pub.

—Discover: Skills for Life, Level K: Student Edition Big Book. (Illus.). 48p. (gr. k-3). Date not set. text ed. 9.65 (ISBN 0-942277-88-0). Educ Assess Pub.

—Discover: Skills for Life, Level K: Teacher's Edition. 80p. (gr. k-3). Date not set. text ed. 31.21 (ISBN 0-942277-01-5). Educ Assess Pub.

—Discover: Skills for Life, Level K: Total Teacher Support System. (Illus.). 168p. (gr. k-3). Date not set. text ed. 87.95 (ISBN 0-942277-03-1). Educ Assess Pub.

—Discover: Skills for Life, Level 1: Pupil Book. (Illus.). 48p. (gr. k-3). Date not set. text ed. 9.65 (ISBN 0-942277-04-X). Educ Assess Pub.

—Discover: Skills for Life, Level 1: Spanish Home Worksheets. (SPA., Illus.). 7p. (gr. 1). Date not set. text ed. 6.87 (ISBN 0-942277-81-3). Educ Assess Pub.

—Discover: Skills for Life, Level 1: Student Edition Big Book. (Illus.). 64p. (gr. k-3). Date not set. text ed. 69.95 (ISBN 0-942277-43-0). Educ Assess Pub.

—Discover: Skills for Life, Level 1: Teacher's Edition. (Illus.). 96p. (gr. k-3). Date not set. text ed. 31.21 (ISBN 0-942277-05-8). Educ Assess Pub.

—Discover: Skills for Life, Level 1: Total Teacher Support System. (Illus.). 168p. Date not set. text ed. 87.95 (ISBN 0-942277-07-4). Educ Assess Pub.

—Discover: Skills for Life, Level 2: Spanish Home Worksheet. (SPA., Illus.). 7p. (gr. 2). Date not set. text ed. 6.87 (ISBN 0-942277-82-1). Educ Assess Pub.

—Discover: Skills for Life, Level 2: Student Book. (Illus.). 64p. (gr. k-3). Date not set. text ed. 9.65 (ISBN 0-942277-08-2). Educ Assess Pub.

—Discover: Skills for Life, Level 2: Teacher's Edition. (Illus.). 112p. (gr. k-3). Date not set. text ed. 31.21 (ISBN 0-942277-09-0). Educ Assess Pub.

—Discover: Skills for Life, Level 2: Total Teacher Support System. (Illus.). (gr. k-3). Date not set. text ed. 87.89 (ISBN 0-942277-11-2). Educ Assess Pub.

—Discover: Skills for Life, Level 3: Student Book. (Illus.). 80p. (gr. k-3). Date not set. text ed. 10.40 (ISBN 0-942277-12-0). Educ Assess Pub.

—Discover: Skills for Life, Level 3: Teacher's Edition. (Illus.). 112p. (gr. k-3). Date not set. text ed. 31.21 (ISBN 0-942277-13-9). Educ Assess Pub.

—Discover: Skills for Life, Level 3: Total Teacher Support System. (Illus.). 186p. (gr. k-3). Date not set. text ed. 87.95 (ISBN 0-942277-15-5). Educ Assess Pub.

—Discover: Skills for Life, Level 4: Spanish Home Worksheets. (SPA., Illus.). 7p. (gr. 4). Date not set. text ed. 6.87 (ISBN 0-942277-84-8). Educ Assess Pub.

—Discover: Skills for Life, Level 4: Student Book. (Illus.). 80p. (gr. k-3). Date not set. text ed. 10.40 (ISBN 0-942277-16-3). Educ Assess Pub.

—Discover: Skills for Life, Level 4: Teacher's Edition. (Illus.). 116p. (gr. k-3). Date not set. text ed. 34.18 (ISBN 0-942277-17-1). Educ Assess Pub.

—Discover: Skills for Life, Level 4: Total Teacher Support. (Illus.). 216p. (gr. k-3). Date not set. text ed. 89.30 (ISBN 0-942277-19-8). Educ Assess Pub.

—Discover: Skills for Life, Level 5: Spanish Home Worksheets. (SPA., Illus.). 7p. (gr. 5). Date not set. text ed. 6.87 (ISBN 0-942277-85-6). Educ Assess Pub.

—Discover: Skills for Life, Level 5: Student Book. (Illus.). 128p. (gr. k-3). Date not set. text ed. 11.50 (ISBN 0-942277-20-1). Educ Assess Pub.

—Discover: Skills for Life, Level 5: Teacher's Edition. (Illus.). 168p. (gr. k-3). Date not set. text ed. 34.18 (ISBN 0-942277-21-X). Educ Assess Pub.

—Discover: Skills for Life, Level 5: Total Teacher Support System. (Illus.). 216p. (gr. k-3). Date not set. text ed. 89.30 (ISBN 0-942277-23-6). Educ Assess Pub.

—Discover: Skills for Life, Level 6: Spanish Home Worksheets. (SPA., Illus.). 7p. (gr. 6). Date not set. text ed. 6.87 (ISBN 0-942277-86-4). Educ Assess Pub.

—Discover: Skills for Life, Level 6: Student Book. (Illus.). 144p. (gr. k-3). Date not set. text ed. 12.40 (ISBN 0-942277-24-4). Educ Assess Pub.

—Discover: Skills for Life, Level 6: Total Teacher Support System. (Illus.). 224p. (gr. k-3). Date not set. text ed. 89.30 (ISBN 0-942277-27-9). Educ Assess Pub.

—Discover: Skills for Life, Level 7: Teacher's Edition. (Illus.). 256p. Date not set. text ed. 34.18 (ISBN 0-942277-29-5). Educ Assess Pub.

—Discover: Skills for Life, Level 9: Student Book. (Illus.). 270p. Date not set. text ed. 41.18 (ISBN 0-942277-36-8). Educ Assess Pub.

Tucker, Jeff & Tucker, Ramona. No Artificial Flavors: 100 Per Cent Friendship: Realistic Devotions for Teens. LC 88-34710. 110p. (gr. 7 up). 1989. pap. text ed. 5.95 (ISBN 0-87788-582-6). Shaw Pubs.

Venti, Pamela R. Why Should I? Asks Jeremy. Spiers, John, illus. 32p. (gr. 1-3). 1990. PLB 10.95 (ISBN 0-89565-700-7). Childs World.

Wassermann, Selma & Wassermann, Jack. The Book of Deciding. Smith, Dennis, illus. LC 89-78073. (gr. k-3). 1990. lib. bdg. 12.85 (ISBN 0-8027-6952-7); pap. 4.95 (ISBN 0-8027-9456-4). Walker & Co.

—The Book of Judging. Smith, Dennis, illus. 32p. (gr. k-3). 1990. lib. bdg. 12.85 (ISBN 0-8027-6950-0); pap. 4.95 (ISBN 0-8027-9455-6). Walker & Co.

Watson, Jane W., et al. Sometimes I Get Angry. Trivas, Irene, illus. 32p. (ps up). 1986. pap. 3.95 (ISBN 0-517-56088-7). Crown.

—Sometimes I'm Afraid. Trivas, Irene, illus. 32p. (ps up). 1986. pap. 3.95 (ISBN 0-517-56087-9). Crown.

Wirths, Claudine G. & Bowman-Kruhm, Mary. Where's My Other Sock? How to Get Organized & Drive Your Parents & Teachers Crazy. Coxe, Molly, illus. LC 88-39338. 128p. (gr. 5 up). 1989. 13.95 (ISBN 0-690-04665-0, Crowell Jr Bks); PLB 13.89 (ISBN 0-690-04667-7, Crowell Jr Bks). HarpC Child Bks.

Wise, C. Dexter, III. Be a Man: Reflections on the Meaning of Manhood in Our Day (An Outline) 30p. (Orig.). (gr. 6 up). 1988. pap. text ed. 5.00 (ISBN 0-685-22586-0). Wise Works Inc.

—I Ain't Into That: (The Book) 48p. (Orig.). (gr. 6-12). 1987. pap. text ed. 5.00 (ISBN 0-685-22587-9); 6.00 (ISBN 0-685-22588-7). Wise Works Inc.

Young, Woody. Clockwise, Vol. One: Quotes on Life. White, Craig, illus. 50p. (Orig.). 1984. pap. text ed. 4.95 (ISBN 0-939513-01-3). Joy Pub SJC.

—Smile Wise. White, Craig, illus. 48p. (Orig.). 1986. pap. text ed. 4.95 (ISBN 0-939513-21-8). Joy Pub SJC.

Ziegler, Sandra. Fairness. (Illus.). 32p. (ps-3). 1989. pap. 3.95 (ISBN 0-516-46316-0). Childrens.

BEHAVIOR–FICTION

Ada, Alma F. The Gold Coin. Waldman, Neil, illus. LC 90-32806. 32p. (gr. k-3). 1991. SBE 12.95 (ISBN 0-689-31633-X, Atheneum Child Bk). Macmillan Child Grp.

Adams, Pam, illus. If I Weren't Me. 24p. (ps-2). 1981. 5.50 (ISBN 0-85953-108-2, Pub. by Child's Play England). Childs Play.

Alexander, Martha. We Never Get to Do Anything. Alexander, Martha, illus. (ps-3). 1985. PLB 7.89 (ISBN 0-8037-9416-9). Dial Bks Young.

Anastasio, Dina. Big Bird Can Share. Leigh, Tom, illus. 32p. (ps-k). 1985. write for info. (ISBN 0-307-12016-3, Pub. by Golden Bks). Western Pub.

Angell, Judie. What's Best for You. LC 90-1599. 192p. (gr. 7 up). 1990. pap. 3.95 (ISBN 0-02-041491-9, Collier Young Ad). Macmillan Child Grp.

Arnold, Tedd. No Jumping on the Bed! Arnold, Tedd, illus. LC 86-13501. 32p. (ps-2). 1987. 13.95 (ISBN 0-8037-0038-5); PLB 13.89 (ISBN 0-8037-0039-3). Dial Bks Young.

Arter, Jim. Gruel & Unusual Punishment. (gr. 3-7). 1991. 13.95 (ISBN 0-385-30298-3). Delacorte.

Bartholomew. Jimmy & the White Lie. (Illus.). 32p. (gr. k-9). 1976. 4.95 (ISBN 0-570-03460-4, 56-1341). Concordia.

Bauer, Marion D. On My Honor. LC 86-2679. 96p. (gr. 4-7). 1986. 12.95 (ISBN 0-89919-439-7, Pub. by Clarion). Ticknor & Fields.

Bennett, Rebecca J. I'm Big Enough. Rigo, Christina, illus. 20p. (ps). casebound 1.59 (ISBN 0-87403-135-4, 2005). Standard Pub.

Blume, Judy. It's Not the End of the World. (gr. k-6). 1986. pap. 3.25 (ISBN 0-440-44158-7, YB). Dell.

—Then Again, Maybe I Won't. 164p. (gr. 5-8). 1986. pap. 3.25 (ISBN 0-440-48659-9, YB). Dell.

Boyd, Lizi. Half Wild & Half Child. (Illus.). 32p. (ps-3). 1991. pap. 3.95 (ISBN 0-14-050825-2, Puffin). Puffin Bks.

Byars, Betsy. Bingo Brown & the Language of Love. (Illus.). 144p. (gr. 3-7). 1991. pap. 3.95 (ISBN 0-14-034141-2, Puffin). Puffin Bks.

Carlson, Nancy. Loudmouth George & the Sixth-Grade Bully. LC 83-7178. (Illus.). 32p. (ps-3). 1983. PLB 9.95 (ISBN 0-87614-217-X). Carolrhoda Bks.

The Cereal Box Adventures. LC 81-68800. (Orig.). (gr. 3-8). 1981. pap. 3.95 (ISBN 0-89191-539-7, 55392). Cook.

Chalmers, Mary. Throw a Kiss, Harry. Chalmers, Mary, illus. LC 89-49064. 32p. (ps-2). 1990. 12.95 (ISBN 0-06-021246-2); PLB 12.89 (ISBN 0-06-021245-4). HarpC Child Bks.

Clark, Barbara R. Reflections. Davis, Ruby & Gerstung, Estella, eds. Clark, Carl R. & Williams, Cecil J. 72p. (Orig.). (gr. 4-12). 1982. pap. 4.95 (ISBN 0-686-37922-5). Williams SC.

Cleary, Beverly. Ramona the Pest. 192p. (gr. 4-7). 1982. pap. 3.25 (ISBN 0-440-47209-1, YB). Dell.

Cohen, Miriam. So What? Hoban, Lillian, illus. LC 81-20101. 32p. (gr. k-3). 1982. PLB 11.88 (ISBN 0-688-01203-5). Greenwillow.

Cole, Joanna. Don't Call Me Names! (Just Right for 4's & 5's) Munsinger, Lynn, illus. LC 89-35412. 32p. (ps). 1990. 4.95 (ISBN 0-679-80258-4); PLB 5.99 (ISBN 0-679-90258-9). McKay.

—Don't Tell the Whole World. Duke, Kate, illus. LC 89-29283. 32p. (gr. k-3). 1990. 13.95 (ISBN 0-690-04809-2, Crowell Jr Bks); PLB 13.89 (ISBN 0-690-04811-4, Crowell Jr Bks). HarpC Child Bks.

Cuyler, Margery. The Trouble with Soap. LC 81-12636. 144p. (gr. 5 up). 1982. 9.95 (ISBN 0-525-45111-0, DCB). Dutton Child Bks.
Dahl, Roald. The Twits. Blake, Quentin, illus. 96p. (gr. 2-6). 1991. pap. 3.95 (ISBN 0-14-034640-6, Puffin). Puffin Bks.
Davidson, Alice J. Beware When Elephants Sneeze. (Illus.). 1986. 4.95 (ISBN 0-8378-5086-X). Gibson.
Davies, Andrew. Conrad's War. 144p. (gr. 5 up). 1986. pap. 1.95 (ISBN 0-440-91452-3, LFL). Dell.
Delton, Judy. I'm Telling You Now. Hoban, Lillian, illus. LC 82-17714. 32p. (ps-k). 1983. 9.95 (ISBN 0-525-44037-2, 0966-290, DCB). Dutton Child Bks.
Dickson, Anna H. Don't Be Shy. Cooke, Tom, illus. LC 86-72402. 32p. (gr. 2-5). 1987. pap. write for info. (ISBN 0-307-12023-6, Pub. by Golden Bks). Western Pub.
Donahue, Laurie. A Promise Is... Seward, Lyn, illus. 32p. (gr. 1-4). 1987. 4.95 (ISBN 0-87403-321-7, 3666). Standard Pub.
Eastman, Patricia. Sometimes Things Change. LC 83-10090. (Illus.). 32p. (ps-2). 1983. PLB 11.93 (ISBN 0-516-02044-7); pap. 2.95 (ISBN 0-516-42044-5). Childrens.
Erickson, Karen. No One Is Perfect. Roffey, Maureen, illus. (ps-k). 1987. pap. 4.95 (ISBN 0-670-81570-5). Viking Child Bks.
Fassler, Joan. Don't Worry Dear. Kranz, Stewart, illus. LC 74-147124. 32p. (ps-3). 1971. 16.95 (ISBN 0-87705-055-4). Human Sci Pr.
Fattah, Michel. Lacey Misbehaves. Voight, Linda, illus. LC 90-52810. 40p. (gr. k-4). Date not set. 12.95 (ISBN 0-915677-53-9). Roundtable Pub.
Friedman, Arthur, illus. The Three Sillies. LC 80-27636. 32p. (gr. k-4). 1981. PLB 9.79 (ISBN 0-89375-486-2); pap. text ed. 1.95 (ISBN 0-89375-487-0). Troll Assocs.
Frost, Marie H. I Can Help. Rigo, Christina, illus. 20p. (ps). 1986. casebound 1.59 (ISBN 0-87403-132-X, 2002). Standard Pub.
Gantos, Jack. Worse Than Rotten, Ralph. Rubel, Nicole, illus. (gr. k-3). 1982. 13.95 (ISBN 0-395-27106-1); pap. 4.95 (ISBN 0-395-32919-1). HM.
Gardner, Richard A. Dr. Gardner's Fables for Our Times. Myers, Robert, illus. LC 80-26098. 125p. (gr. k-6). 1981. 14.95 (ISBN 0-933812-06-X). Creative Therapeutics.
—Dr. Gardner's Stories About the Real World, Vol. I. Lowenheim, Alfred, illus. LC 80-16542. 127p. (gr. k-6). 1980. Repr. of 1972 ed. PLB 14.95 (ISBN 0-933812-04-3). Creative Therapeutics.
—Dr. Gardner's Stories About the Real World, Vol. II. Myers, Robert, illus. LC 80-16592. 95p. (gr. k-6). 1983. 14.95 (ISBN 0-933812-05-1). Creative Therapeutics.
—Dr. Gardner's Stories about the Real World, Vol. III. LC 72-1283. (Illus.). 127p. (gr. k-6). 1985. pap. 3.95 (ISBN 0-933812-07-8). Creative Therapeutics.
Gordon, Shirley. Me & the Bad Guys. Frascino, Edward, illus. 80p. (gr. 3-7). 1984. pap. 2.25 (ISBN 0-440-45520-0, YB). Dell.
Goudge, Eileen. Too Much Too Soon. 160p. (gr. 7-12). 1984. pap. 2.25 (ISBN 0-440-98974-4). Dell.
Grady, Kitten S. Jiggy's Necklace. Grady, Kitten S., illus. LC 87-62211. 40p. (gr. 1-6). 1987. 5.95 (ISBN 0-932433-34-0). Windswept Hse.
Greene, Carol. Wendy & the Whine. (Illus.). 32p. (gr. 1-4). 1987. pap. 4.95 (ISBN 0-570-04157-0, 56-1615). Concordia.
Greene, Constance C. Double-Dare O'Toole. (gr. 4 up). 1990. pap. 3.95 (ISBN 0-14-034541-8, Puffin). Puffin Bks.
Greenwald, Sheila. Give Us a Great Big Smile, Rosy Cole. Greenwald, Sheila, illus. 80p. (gr. 3 up). 1981. 12.95 (ISBN 0-316-32672-0, Joy St Bks). Little.
—Rosy Cole's Great American Guilt Club. Greenwald, Sheila, illus. LC 85-47876. 96p. (gr. 3-7). 1985. 12.95 (ISBN 0-316-32709-3, Joy St Bks). Little.
Grossman, Bill. The Guy Who Was Five Minutes Late. Glasser, Judy, illus. LC 89-36336. 32p. (ps-3). 1990. 13.95 (ISBN 0-06-022268-9); PLB 13.89 (ISBN 0-06-022269-7). HarpC Child Bks.
Groten, Dallas. So What Do I Do Now? LC 89-14. 176p. (Orig.). (gr. 6-12). 1989. pap. 5.95 (ISBN 1-55661-033-5). Bethany Hse.
Gunn, Robin J. Summer Promise: Never Had One Season Held So Much Hope... So Much Heartache. Kobobel, Janet, ed. 171p. (Orig.). 1988. pap. 4.99 (ISBN 0-929608-13-5). Focus Family.
Hargeaves, Roger. Mr. Greedy. 32p. (ps-k). 1980. 1.25 (ISBN 0-8431-0817-7). Price Stern.
Hargreaves, Roger. Little Miss Bossy. Hargreaves, Roger, illus. 32p. (ps-k). 1981. pap. 1.25 (ISBN 0-8431-0893-2). Price Stern.
—Little Miss Helpful. Hargraves, Roger, illus. 32p. (ps-k). 1981. pap. 1.25 (ISBN 0-8431-0897-5). Price Stern.
—Little Miss Late. Hargreaves, Roger, illus. 32p. (ps-k). 1981. pap. 1.25 (ISBN 0-8431-0896-7). Price Stern.
—Little Miss Naughty. Hargreaves, Roger, illus. 32p. (ps-k). 1984. pap. 1.25 (ISBN 0-8431-0889-4). Price Stern.
—Little Miss Neat. Hargreaves, Roger, illus. 32p. (ps-k). 1981. pap. 1.25 (ISBN 0-8431-0894-0). Price Stern.
—Little Miss Scatterbrain. Hargreaves, Roger, illus. 32p. (ps-k). 1981. pap. 1.25 (ISBN 0-8431-0891-6). Price Stern.
—Little Miss Sunshine. Hargreaves, Roger, illus. 32p. 1981. pap. 1.25 (ISBN 0-8431-0899-1). Price Stern.
—Little Miss Trouble. Hargreaves, Roger, illus. 32p. (ps-k). 1981. pap. 1.25 (ISBN 0-8431-0890-8). Price Stern.
—Mr. Bounce. (ps-k). 1976. 1.25 (ISBN 0-8431-0809-6). Price Stern.
—Mr. Bounce. 32p. (ps up). 1976. PLB 8.70s.p. (ISBN 0-87191-814-5); 12.45 (ISBN 0-685-09316-6). Creative Ed.
—Mr. Bump. (ps-k). 1971. 1.25 (ISBN 0-8431-0814-2). Price Stern.
—Mr. Bump. 32p. (ps up). 1971. PLB 8.70s.p. (ISBN 0-87191-815-3); 12.45 (ISBN 0-685-09317-4). Creative Ed.
—Mr. Busy. Hargreaves, Roger, illus. (ps-k). 1980. pap. 1.25 (ISBN 0-8431-0818-5). Price Stern.
—Mr. Busy. 32p. (ps up). 1978. PLB 8.70s.p. (ISBN 0-87191-816-1); 12.45 (ISBN 0-685-09318-2). Creative Ed.
—Mr. Chatterbox. 1p. (ps-k). 1981. 1.25 (ISBN 0-8431-0808-8). Price Stern.
—Mr. Clever. Hargreaves, Roger, illus. 32p. (ps-k). 1982. pap. 1.25 (ISBN 0-8431-1131-3). Price Stern.
—Mr. Clumsy. 32p. (ps up). 1978. PLB 8.70s.p. (ISBN 0-87191-817-X); 12.45 (ISBN 0-685-09320-4). Creative Ed.
—Mr. Daydream. Hargreaves, Roger, illus. 32p. (ps-k). 1982. pap. 1.25 (ISBN 0-8431-1127-5). Price Stern.
—Mr. Dizzy. 32p. (ps up). 1976. PLB 8.70s.p. (ISBN 0-87191-906-0); 12.45 (ISBN 0-685-09321-2). Creative Ed.
—Mr. Forgetful. 32p. (ps-k). 1980. 1.25 (ISBN 0-8431-0805-3). Price Stern.
—Mr. Fussy. 32p. (ps-k). 1980. 1.25 (ISBN 0-8431-0807-X). Price Stern.
—Mr. Fussy. 32p. (ps up). 1976. PLB 8.70s.p. (ISBN 0-87191-818-8); 12.45 (ISBN 0-685-09325-5). Creative Ed.
—Mr. Grumpy. 32p. (ps-k). 1980. 1.25 (ISBN 0-8431-0804-5). Price Stern.
—Mr. Grumpy. 32p. (ps up). 1978. PLB 8.70s.p. (ISBN 0-87191-764-5); 12.45 (ISBN 0-685-09328-X). Creative Ed.
—Mr. Happy. (ps-k). 1980. 1.25 (ISBN 0-8431-0813-4). Price Stern.
—Mr. Happy. 32p. (ps up). 1971. PLB 8.70s.p. (ISBN 0-87191-766-1); 12.45 (ISBN 0-685-09329-8). Creative Ed.
—Mr. Impossible. 32p. (ps up). 1976. PLB 8.70s.p. (ISBN 0-87191-909-5); 12.45 (ISBN 0-685-09330-1). Creative Ed.
—Mr. Mischief. 32p. (ps-k). 1980. 1.25 (ISBN 0-8431-0802-9). Price Stern.
—Mr. Mischief. 32p. (ps up). 1978. PLB 8.70s.p. (ISBN 0-87191-763-7); PLB 12.45 (ISBN 0-685-09333-6). Creative Ed.
—Mr. Muddle. 32p. (ps up). 1976. PLB 8.70s.p. (ISBN 0-87191-910-9); PLB 12.45 (ISBN 0-685-09335-2). Creative Ed.
—Mr. Noisy. 32p. (ps-k). 1980. 1.25 (ISBN 0-8431-0810-X). Price Stern.
—Mr. Nosey. 32p. (ps up). 1971. PLB 8.70s.p. (ISBN 0-87191-821-8); PLB 12.45 (ISBN 0-685-09340-9). Creative Ed.
—Mr. Quiet. 32p. (ps-k). 1980. 1.25 (ISBN 0-8431-0803-7). Price Stern.
—Mr. Quiet. 32p. (ps up). 1978. PLB 8.70s.p. (ISBN 0-87191-822-6); PLB 12.45 (ISBN 0-685-09341-7). Creative Ed.
—Mr. Silly. 32p. (ps-k). 1980. 1.25 (ISBN 0-8431-0811-8). Price Stern.
—Mr. Slow. (Illus.). 32p. (ps-3). 1982. pap. 1.25 (ISBN 0-8431-0881-9). Price Stern.
—Mr. Stingy. 32p. (ps up). 1971. PLB 8.70s.p. (ISBN 0-87191-916-8); PLB 12.45 (ISBN 0-685-09353-0). Creative Ed.
—Mr. Strong. 32p. (ps up). 1976. PLB 8.70s.p. (ISBN 0-87191-917-6); PLB 12.45 (ISBN 0-685-09354-9). Creative Ed.
—Mr. Tall. 32p. (ps up). 1978. PLB 8.70s.p. (ISBN 0-87191-918-4); PLB 12.45 (ISBN 0-685-09356-5). Creative Ed.
—Mr. Tickle. 32p. (ps up). 1971. PLB 8.70s.p. (ISBN 0-87191-759-9); PLB 12.45 (ISBN 0-685-09357-3). Creative Ed.
—Mr. Topsy-Turvy. (Illus.). 32p. 1982. pap. 1.25 (ISBN 0-8431-1129-1). Price Stern.
—Mr. Topsy-Turvy. 32p. (ps up). 1972. PLB 8.70s.p. (ISBN 0-87191-919-2); PLB 12.45 (ISBN 0-685-09358-1). Creative Ed.
—Mr. Uppity. (Illus.). 32p. (ps-3). 1982. pap. 1.25 (ISBN 0-8431-0882-7). Price Stern.
—Mr. Uppity. 32p. (ps up). 1972. PLB 8.70s.p. (ISBN 0-87191-920-6); PLB 12.45. Creative Ed.
—Mr. Worry. 32p. (ps-k). 1980. 1.25 (ISBN 0-8431-0800-2). Price Stern.
—Mr. Worry. 32p. (ps up). 1978. PLB 8.70s.p. (ISBN 0-87191-825-0); PLB 12.45 (ISBN 0-685-09360-3). Creative Ed.
—Mr. Wrong. (Illus.). 32p. (ps-3). 1982. pap. 1.25 (ISBN 0-8431-0879-7). Price Stern.
—Mr. Wrong. 32p. (ps up). 1978. PLB 8.70s.p. (ISBN 0-87191-921-4); PLB 12.45 (ISBN 0-685-09361-1). Creative Ed.
Hayes, Geoffrey. Patrick Goes to Bed. Hayes, Geoffrey, illus. LC 84-6099. 32p. (ps-1). 1989. pap. 2.95 (ISBN 0-679-80161-8, Dragonfly Bks). Knopf.
Heide, Florence P. Tales for the Perfect Child. Chess, Victoria, illus. 80p. (gr. 3-6). 1985. 14.95 (ISBN 0-688-03892-1); PLB 14.88 (ISBN 0-688-03893-X). Lothrop.
Heitler, Susan M. David Decides about Thumbsucking: A Motivating Story for Children & an Informative Guide for Parents. Singer, Paula, illus. LC 85-61019. 52p. (ps-3). 1985. PLB 17.95 (ISBN 0-9614780-1-2); pap. 9.95 (ISBN 0-9614780-0-4). Reading Matters.
Hines, Anna G. Cassie Bowen Takes Witch Lessons. Owens, Gail, illus. LC 85-10302. (gr. 3-7). 1985. 11.95 (ISBN 0-525-44214-6, DCB). Dutton Child Bks.
Hofstrand, Mary. Albion Pig. Hofstrand, Mary, illus. LC 83-17496. 40p. (ps-k). 1984. lib. bdg. 10.99 (ISBN 0-394-96255-9). Knopf.
Holl, Kristi D. Footprints up My Back. LC 84-6176. 168p. (gr. 4-6). 1984. 12.95 (ISBN 0-689-31070-6, Atheneum Child Bk). Macmillan Child Grp.
Hopper, Nancy J. The Seven & One-Half Sins of Stacey Kendall. (gr. 5-9). 1983. pap. 2.75 (ISBN 0-440-47736-0, YB). Dell.
Horwitz, Elinor L. Sometimes It Happens. Jeschke, Susan, illus. LC 79-2687. 40p. (gr. 1-4). 1981. 7.95 (ISBN 0-06-022596-3). HarpC Child Bks.
Hubert, Amelia. Sweet Dreams for Sally. Cooke, Tom, illus. 40p. (ps-3). 1983. 5.95 (ISBN 0-910313-01-6, 7002). Parker Bros.
Hurwitz, Johanna. Class Clown. Hamanaka, Sheila, illus. LC 86-23624. 112p. (gr. 1-4). 1987. 12.95 (ISBN 0-688-06723-9). Morrow Jr Bks.
Keller, Charles, compiled by. Growing up Laughing: Humorists Look at American Youth. (Illus.). (gr. 5 up). 1981. 10.95 (ISBN 0-13-367870-9). P-H.
Keller, Holly. Geraldine's Blanket. Keller, Holly, illus. LC 83-14062. 32p. (ps-1). 1984. 13.95 (ISBN 0-688-02539-0); PLB 13.88 (ISBN 0-688-02540-4). Greenwillow.
—The New Boy. LC 90-41757. (Illus.). 24p. (ps up). 1991. 13.95 (ISBN 0-688-09827-4); PLB 13.88 (ISBN 0-688-09828-2). Greenwillow.
Kirshenbaum, Binnie. Short Subject. LC 89-42538. 208p. (gr. 7 up). 1989. 13.95 (ISBN 0-531-05836-0); PLB 13.99 (ISBN 0-531-08436-1). Orchard Bks Watts.
Kline, Suzy. Don't Touch! Tucker, Kathleen, ed. Leder, Dora, illus. 32p. (ps-1). 1985. 12.95 (ISBN 0-8075-1707-0). A Whitman.
Knorr, Dandi D. Me First. Connelly, Gwen, illus. 32p. (gr. 1-3). 1987. 4.95 (ISBN 0-87403-313-6, 3543). Standard Pub.
Konigsburg, E. L. Up from Jericho Tel. LC 85-20061. 192p. (gr. 5 up). 1986. 13.95 (ISBN 0-689-31194-X, Atheneum Child Bk). Macmillan Child Grp.
Levite, Lily. It Takes a Little More. 32p. 1991. 7.50 (ISBN 0-8062-3447-4). Carlton.
Levy, Elizabeth. Lizzie Lies a Lot. Wallner, John, illus. LC 75-32914. 80p. (gr. 4-6). 1976. 6.95 (ISBN 0-440-04919-9); PLB 6.46 (ISBN 0-440-04920-2). Delacorte.
—Lizzie Lies a Lot. 112p. (gr. 3-5). 1977. pap. 2.75 (ISBN 0-440-44714-3, YB). Dell.
—Take Two, They're Small. (Orig.). (gr. k-6). 1986. pap. 2.95 (ISBN 0-440-48517-7, YB). Dell.
Lindgren, Barbro. Sam's Car. Eriksson, Eva, illus. LC 82-3437. 32p. (gr. k-3). 1982. 6.95 (ISBN 0-688-01263-9). Morrow Jr Bks.
Livingston, Myra C. Higgledy-Piggledy: Verses & Pictures. Peter, Sis, illus. LC 86-8789. 32p. (gr. 3-7). 1986. 11.95 (ISBN 0-689-50407-1, M K McElderry). Macmillan Child Grp.
Lowry, Lois. Taking Care of Terrific. 176p. (gr. 4-7). 1984. pap. 3.25 (ISBN 0-440-48494-4, YB). Dell.
McCrackin, Mark. A Winning Position. 96p. (gr. 7 up). 1982. pap. 1.50 (ISBN 0-440-99483-7, LFL). Dell.
McDaniel, Lurlene. When Dreams Shatter. 128p. (Orig.). (gr. 5-8). 1988. pap. 2.50 (ISBN 0-87406-285-3). Willowisp Pr.
MacDonald, George. Papa's Story & Other Tales. Dorsett, Mary, ed. LC 85-71805. (Illus.). 128p. (gr. 3-8). 1986. 12.95 (ISBN 0-917665-07-4). Bookmakers Guild.
Madison, Winifred. Growing up in a Hurry. (gr. 7-9). 1981. pap. 1.95 (ISBN 0-671-44238-4). PB.
Martinez, Carol. Paco y Ana Aprenden Acerca de la Amabilidad. Stillman, Peter, illus. (SPA.). 32p. (Orig.). (gr. 2-4). 1988. pap. 1.50 (ISBN 0-311-38590-7, Edit Mundo). Casa Bautista.
—Paco y Ana Aprenden Acerca de la Honradez. Stillman, Peter, illus. (SPA.). 32p. (Orig.). (gr. 2-4). 1988. pap. 1.50 (ISBN 0-311-38587-7, Edit Mundo). Casa Bautista.
—Paco y Ana Aprenden Acerca de la Obediencia. Stillman, Peter, illus. (SPA.). 32p. (Orig.). (gr. 2-4). 1988. pap. 1.50 (ISBN 0-311-38588-5, Edit Mundo). Casa Bautista.
Mason, Margo. Ready, Alice? (ps-3). 1990. 9.99 (ISBN 0-553-05816-9). Bantam.
Matranga, Frances C. One Step at a Time. (Illus.). (gr. 4-7). 1987. pap. 3.95 (ISBN 0-570-03642-9, 39-1126). Concordia.
Mayer, Mercer. All By Myself. Mayer & Mercer, illus. 24p. (ps-3). 1985. pap. write for info. (ISBN 0-307-11938-6, Pub. by Golden Bks). Western Pub.
Miles, Betty. Just the Beginning. 148p. (gr. 3 up). 1978. pap. 2.50 (ISBN 0-380-01913-2, Camelot). Avon.
Minarik, Else H. The Little Girl & the Dragon. Gourlault, Martine, illus. LC 90-38495. 24p. (ps up). 1991. 13.95 (ISBN 0-688-09913-0); PLB 13.88 (ISBN 0-688-09914-9). Greenwillow.

Mr. Clumsy. 32p. (ps-k). 1980. 1.25 (ISBN 0-8431-0801-0). Price Stern.

Moncure, Jane B. Caring for My Home. Connelly, Gwen, illus. 32p. (ps-2). 1990. PLB 9.96 (ISBN 0-89565-667-1). Childs World.

—Caring for My Things. Collette, Rondi, illus. 32p. (ps-2). 1990. lib. bdg. 9.96 (ISBN 0-89565-670-1). Childs World.

O'Brien, Anne S. I Don't Want to Go. O'Brien, Anne S., illus. LC 85-82108. 14p. (ps-k). 1986. bds. 3.95 (ISBN 0-8050-0051-8). H Holt & Co.

—It's Hard to Wait. O'Brien, Anne S., illus. LC 85-82106. 14p. (ps-k). 1986. bds. 3.95 (ISBN 0-8050-0050-X). H Holt & Co.

Odor, Ruth S. Please. Indereiden, Nancy, illus. LC 79-25319. (ps-2). 1980. PLB 9.96 (ISBN 0-89565-115-7). Childs World.

Parkison, Ralph F. Big Red & the Fence Post. Withrow, Marion O., ed. Bush, William, illus. 53p. (Orig.). (gr. 2-8). 1988. pap. write for info. Little Wood Bks.

—The Little Flea. Withrow, Marion O., ed. Bush, William, illus. 21p. (Orig.). (gr. 2-8). 1988. pap. write for info. Little Wood Bks.

Peterson, Lorraine. Falling Off Cloud Nine & Other High Places. Dugan, LeRoy, illus. LC 81-38465. 159p. (Orig.). (gr. 8-12). 1981. pap. 5.95 (ISBN 0-87123-167-0). Bethany Hse.

—Radical Advice from the Ultimate Wiseguy. 192p. (Orig.). (gr. 8-12). 1990. pap. 6.95 (ISBN 1-55661-141-2). Bethany Hse.

Pevsner, Stella. Cute Is a Four-Letter Word. 176p. (gr. 7 up). 1989. pap. 2.75 (ISBN 0-671-68845-6, Archway). PB.

Pfeffer, Susan B. Just Between Us. 128p. (gr. k-6). 1981. pap. 2.25 (ISBN 0-440-44194-3, YB). Dell.

Pienkowski, Jan. Small Talk. 12p. (ps-4). 1983. 8.95 (ISBN 0-8431-0982-3). Price Stern.

Platt, Kin. The Ape Inside Me. LC 79-2402. (gr. 7 up). 1979. PLB 11.89 (ISBN 0-685-02078-9, Lipp Jr Bks); PLB 11.89 (ISBN 0-397-31863-4). HarpC Child Bks.

Pryor, Ainslie. The Baby Blue Cat Who Said No. (Illus.). 32p. (ps-1). 1990. pap. 3.95 (ISBN 0-14-050768-X, Puffin). Puffin Bks.

Quackenbush, Robert. I Don't Want to Go, I Don't Know How to Act. Quackenbush, Robert, illus. LC 82-48458. 32p. (gr. k-2). 1983. 11.95i (ISBN 0-397-32033-7, Lipp Jr Bks). HarpC Child Bks.

Quigley, Stacy. Do I Have To? Lexa, Susan, illus. Silverman, Manuel, intro. by. LC 85-24350. (Illus.). 32p. (gr. k-6). 1980. PLB 16.67 (ISBN 0-8172-1352-X). Raintree Pubs.

Radley, Gail. Special Strengths. Boddy, Joe, illus. 64p. (gr. 2-6). 1984. pap. 6.95 (ISBN 0-87743-702-5, Pub. by Bellwood Pr). Baha'i.

Rees, Claudia. The Bird with the Word Talks about Self-Control. Rees, Claudia, illus. (Orig.). (gr. 1-3). 1987. pap. 0.98 (ISBN 0-89274-451-0). Harrison Hse.

Robinson, Nancy K. Wendy & the Bullies. 1989. pap. 2.50 (ISBN 0-590-40780-5). Scholastic Inc.

Rohm, Robert. A Bad Day in Ipsilwhich. (Illus.). (gr. k-3). 1979. pap. text ed. 29.95 6 bks. & 1 cass. (ISBN 0-89290-052-0); pap. text ed. 10.95 1 bk. & 1 cass. (ISBN 0-685-04626-5). Soc for Visual.

—A Box Full of Trouble. LC 78-730967. (Illus.). (gr. k-3). 1979. pap. text ed. 29.95 6 bks. & 1 cass. (ISBN 0-89290-049-0); pap. text ed. 10.95 1 bk. & 1 cass. (ISBN 0-685-04631-1). Soc for Visual.

—The Message in the Sand. LC 78-730967. (Illus.). (gr. k-3). 1979. pap. text ed. 29.95 6 bks. & 1 cass. (ISBN 0-89290-051-2); pap. text ed. 10.95 1 bk. & 1 cass. Soc for Visual.

—The Vanishing Tools. LC 78-730967. (Illus.). (gr. k-3). 1979. pap. text ed. 29.95 6 bks. & 1 cass. (ISBN 0-89290-050-4); pap. text ed. 10.95 1 bk. & 1 cass. Soc for Visual.

Ross, Pat. M & M & the Bad News Babies. Hafner, Marylin, illus. LC 81-18714. 48p. (gr. 6-9). 1983. Knopf.

Roy, Ron. Awful Thursday. Hoban, Lillian, illus. LC 78-14049. (gr. 1-4). 1979. Pantheon.

Rylant, Cynthia. A Fine White Dust. LC 86-1003. 120p. (gr. 6-8). 1986. 12.95 (ISBN 0-02-777240-3, Bradbury Pr). Macmillan Child Grp.

Schultz, Irene. The Woodland Gang & the Hidden Jewels. (Illus.). 128p. (gr. 3 up). 1984. pap. 4.95 (ISBN 0-685-25362-7). Addison-Wesley.

Scott, Elaine. Choices. Thompson, Ellen, illus. LC 88-34537. 192p. (gr. 7 up). 1989. 12.95 (ISBN 0-688-07230-5). Morrow Jr Bks.

Sharmat, Marjorie W. A Big Fat Enormous Lie. McPhail, David, illus. LC 77-15645. (ps-2). 1978. 11.95 (ISBN 0-525-26510-4, DCB). Dutton Child Bks.

Shles, Larry. The Adventure of the Squib Owl: Squib Ser. Shles, Larry, illus. Date not set. pap. 7.95 each (ISBN 0-915190-85-0). Jalmar Pr.
Squib the Owl series, written & whimsically illustrated by Larry Shles, teaches self-esteem & personal & social responsibility as it entertains. The author uses the name Squib to personify the small vunerable part of us all that struggles & at times feels helpless in an enormous world filled with emotions. This Series, five volumes, traces the adventures of this tiny owl as he struggles with his feelings searching at least for understanding. Each of the five titles explores a different vulnerability. MOTHS & MOTHERS, FEATHERS & FATHERS (explores feelings); HOOTS & TOOTS & HAIRY BRUTES (explores disabilities); ALIENS IN MY NEST (explores adolescent behavior); HUGS & SHRUGS (explores inner peace). The latest volume DO I HAVE TO GO TO SCHOOL TODAY? is great for the young reader who needs encouragement from teachers who accept him "just as he is". Brilliantly simple, yet realistically complex, Squib personifies each & every one of us. He is a reflection of what we are, & what we can become. Every reader who has struggled with life's limitations will recognize his own struggles & triumphs in the microcosm of Squib's forest world - in Squib we find a parable for all ages from 8-80.
Publisher Provided Annotation.

Skinner, Richard. Kate the Skate. Parker, Donna, ed. Millar, Pete, illus. LC 79-5201. (Orig.). (gr. 1-5). 1980. pap. text ed. 3.95 (ISBN 0-934360-00-6). Carson Pr.

Slaughter, Hope. The Deeeeelicious Dragon. Heaney, Rhonda K., illus. 32p. (ps-3). 1986. pap. 4.95 (ISBN 0-931093-05-8). Red Hen Pr.

Slepian, Jan. Risk n' Roses. 176p. (gr. 6 up). 1990. 14.95 (ISBN 0-399-22219-7, Philomel Bks). Putnam Pub Group.

Some Things You Just Can't Do by Yourself. (Illus.). (ps-3). 1973. 4.95 (ISBN 0-938678-00-0). New Seed.

Steig, William. Abel's Island. Steig, William, illus. LC 75-35916. 119p. (gr. 1 up). 1985. pap. 3.95 (ISBN 0-374-40016-4, Sunburst). FS&G.

Stouse, Karla F. Three Bears, (Lots of Bees,) & One Pot of Honey. Yanda, Emma, illus. LC 87-70530. 16p. (Orig.). (gr. 2 up). 1987. pap. 7.95 incl. cassette (ISBN 0-87029-206-4). Abbey.

Strasser, Todd. Wildlife. LC 86-19861. 224p. (gr. 7 up). 1987. pap. 14.95 (ISBN 0-385-29560-X). Delacorte.

Stuart, Jesse. A Penny's Worth of Character. Miller, Jim W., et al, eds. Zornes, Rocky, illus. 62p. (gr. 3-6). 1988. 10.00 (ISBN 0-945084-03-X); pap. 3.00 (ISBN 0-945084-04-8). J Stuart Found.

Tangvald, Christine. Oh Yes! Oh No! 1987. bds. 4.95 (ISBN 1-55513-168-9, Chariot Bks). Cook.

Thaler, Mike. Upside down Day. 32p. (gr. k-3). 1986. pap. 2.50 (ISBN 0-380-89999-X, Camelot). Avon.

Tolstoy, Leo. God Sees the Truth, but Waits. LC 85-29920. 32p. (gr. 4 up). 1986. PLB 10.95s.p. (ISBN 0-88682-071-5); 15.65 (ISBN 0-685-12408-8). Creative Ed.

Ulmer, Louise. The Man Who Learned to Give. (gr. k-2). 1977. pap. 1.39 (ISBN 0-570-06109-1, 59-1227). Concordia.

Van Laan, Nancy. A Mouse in My House. Priceman, Marjorie, illus. LC 89-15591. 32p. (ps-3). 1990. 9.95 (ISBN 0-679-80043-3); PLB 10.99 (ISBN 0-679-90043-8). Knopf.

Wade, Barrie. Little Monster. Kew, Katinka, illus. LC 89-37277. 32p. (ps-2). 1990. 13.95 (ISBN 0-688-09596-8); lib. bdg. 13.88 (ISBN 0-688-09597-6). Lothrop.

Waite, Michael P. Handy-Dandy Helpful Hal. LC 87-5275. (gr. k-2). 1987. text ed. 7.95 (ISBN 1-55513-221-9, Chariot Bks). Cook.

Watanabe, Shigeo. I Can Take a Bath. Ohtomo, Yasuo, illus. (ps-k). 1987. 10.95 (ISBN 0-399-21362-7, Philomel). Putnam Pub Group.

Wedell, Robert F. Rolf the Green Ghost. Warners, Sheila B., illus. 69p. (Orig.). (ps-8). 1988. pap. 4.95 (ISBN 0-685-30435-3). Milrob Pr.

Weiss, Ellen. Oh Beans! Starring Jelly Bean. Hall, Susan, illus. LC 88-4904. 32p. (gr. k-3). 1989. PLB 8.79 (ISBN 0-8167-1404-5); pap. text ed. 1.95 (ISBN 0-8167-1405-3). Troll Assocs.

—Oh Beans! Starring Snap Bean. Hall, Susan, illus. LC 88-4900. 32p. (gr. k-3). 1989. PLB 8.79 (ISBN 0-8167-1410-X); pap. text ed. 1.95 (ISBN 0-8167-1411-8). Troll Assocs.

—Oh Beans! Starring Vanilla Bean. Hall, Susan, illus. LC 88-4903. 32p. (gr. k-3). 1989. PLB 8.79 (ISBN 0-8167-1412-6); pap. text ed. 1.95 (ISBN 0-8167-1413-4). Troll Assocs.

Wells, Rosemary. Leave Well Enough Alone. LC 76-42586. (gr. 6 up). 1977. 8.95 (ISBN 0-8037-4754-3). Dial Bks Young.

Williams, Sunnie. The Nomie Book: Growing up from Shy. Crisamore, Naomi, illus. 104p. (Orig.). (gr. 3-6). 1981. pap. 2.75 (ISBN 0-9605444-0-2). Wee Smile.

Winner Takes All, No. 132. 192p. (Orig.). (gr. 7-12). 1987. pap. 2.50 (ISBN 0-553-26790-6). Bantam.

Winterfeld, Henry. Trouble at Timpetill. Lattimore, Deborah N. & Hutchinson, William M., illus. 192p. (gr. 3-7). 1990. pap. 4.95 (ISBN 0-15-290786-6). HarBraceJ.

Wood, Audrey. Tugford Wanted to Be Bad. Wood, Don, illus. LC 83-318. 32p. (ps-3). 1983. pap. 4.95 (ISBN 0-15-291084-0, VoyB). HarBraceJ.

Wood, Ruzena. The Palace of the Moon & Other Tales from Czechoslovakia. Turska, Krystyna, illus. LC 80-2687. 144p. (gr. 2-7). 1981. 9.95 (ISBN 0-233-97206-4). Andre Deutsch.

Woodard, Judy & Tucker, Martha. The Legend of the SunaKorn. LC 89-50138. 40p. 1989. 12.95 (ISBN 0-938021-41-9). Turner Pub Ky.

Wright, Betty R. I Like Being Alone. Toht, Don, illus. Okun, Barbara F., intro. by. LC 80-25513. (Illus.). 32p. (gr. k-6). 1981. PLB 16.67 (ISBN 0-8172-1367-8). Raintree Pubs.

BEHAVIOR PROBLEMS (CHILDREN)
see Problem Children

BELGIUM

Carrick, Noel. Belgium. (Illus.). (gr. 5 up). 1988. 14.95 (ISBN 0-222-00941-1). Chelsea Hse.

Goldstein, Frances. Children's Treasure Hunt Travel to Belgium & France. Goldstein, Frances, illus. LC 80-85012. 230p. (Orig.). (gr. k-12). 1981. pap. 6.95 (ISBN 0-933334-02-8, Dist. by Hippocrene). Paper Tiger Pap.

Lye, Keith. Take a Trip to Belgium. 32p. (gr. k-7). 1984. lib. bdg. 7.99 (ISBN 0-531-04871-3). Watts.

Vandersteen, Willy. The Iron Flowerpotters. Lahey, Nicholas J., tr. from FLE. LC 76-49376. (Illus., Orig.). (gr. 3-8). 1977. pap. 2.50 (ISBN 0-915560-11-9, 11). Hiddigeigei.

BELIEF AND DOUBT

Teller, Hanoch. Courtrooms of the Mind: Stories & Advice on Judging Others Favorably. 2nd ed. 288p. (gr. 12). 1988. Repr. 11.95 (ISBN 0-9614772-4-5). NYC Pub Co.

BELL, ALEXANDER GRAHAM, 1847-1922

Davidson, Margaret. The Story of Alexander Graham Bell: Inventor of the Telephone. Marchesi, Stephen, illus. 92p. (gr. 4-6). 1989. pap. 2.95 (ISBN 0-440-40228-X, YB). Dell.

Dunn, Andrew. Alexander Graham Bell. (Illus.). 48p. (gr. 5-7). 1991. PLB 12.40 (ISBN 0-531-18418-8, Pub. by Bookwright Pr). Watts.

Farr, Naunerle C. Thomas Edison - Alexander Graham Bell. Taloac, Gerry & Trinidad, Angel, illus. (gr. 4-12). 1979. pap. text ed. 2.95 (ISBN 0-88301-357-6); wkbk. 1.25 (ISBN 0-88301-381-9). Pendulum Pr.

Johnson, Ann D. The Value of Discipline: The Story of Alexander Graham Bell. Pileggi, Steve, illus. (gr. k-6). 1985. 9.95 (ISBN 0-7172-1887-2, Pub. by Value Communications). Oak Tree Pubns.

Lewis, Cynthia C. Alexander Graham Bell. (Illus.). 64p. (gr. 3 up). 1991. PLB 10.95 (ISBN 0-87518-461-8, Dillon). Macmillan Child Grp.

Pelta, Kathy. Alexander Graham Bell. (Illus.). 144p. (gr. 5-7). 1989. PLB 13.98 (ISBN 0-382-09529-4). Silver Burdett Pr.

Rider Montgomery, Elizabeth. Alexander Graham Bell: Man of Sound. (Illus.). 80p. (gr. 2-6). 1992. Repr. of 1963 ed. PLB 12.95 (ISBN 0-7910-1423-1). Chelsea Hse.

Shippen, Katherine B. Mr. Bell Invents the Telephone. (Illus.). (gr. 4-6). 1963. lib. bdg. 8.99 (ISBN 0-394-90330-7). Random.

Tames, Richard. Alexander Graham Bell. (Illus.). 32p. (gr. 5-8). 1990. PLB 11.90 (ISBN 0-531-14003-2). Watts.

BEN-GURION, DAVID, 1886-

Silverstein, Herma. David Ben-Gurion. Sloan, Frank, ed. (Illus.). 128p. (gr. 7-12). 1988. 12.90 (ISBN 0-531-10509-1). Watts.

BENCH, JOHNNY, 1947-

Shannon, Mike. Johnny Bench. 1990. 14.95 (ISBN 0-7910-1168-2). Chelsea Hse.

BERLIN

Dudman, J. Division of Berlin. (Illus.). 80p. (gr. 7 up). Date not set. PLB 17.26 (ISBN 0-86592-037-0). Rourke Corp.

Steins, Richar. Berlin. (gr. 7-12). 1991. PLB 14.95 (ISBN 0-8239-1216-7). Rosen Group.

BERMUDA TRIANGLE

Abels, Harriette S. Bermuda Triangle. LC 87-14029. (Illus.). 48p. (gr. 5-6). 1987. PLB 10.95 (ISBN 0-89686-340-9, Crestwood Hse). Macmillan Child Grp.

Collins, Jim. The Bermuda Triangle. LC 77-21808. (Illus.). 48p. (gr. 4 up). 1983. PLB 17.32 (ISBN 0-8172-1050-4); pap. 9.27 (ISBN 0-8172-2153-0). Raintree Pubs.

BERNADETTE SOUBIROUS, SAINT, 1844-1879

Daughters of St. Paul. Light in the Grotto. (gr. 4-9). 1972. pap. 2.00 (ISBN 0-8198-4410-1). Dghtrs St Paul.

BERNARD DE CLAIRVAUX, SAINT, 1091-1153

Daughters of St. Paul. Bells of Conquest. (gr. 3-7). 3.00 (ISBN 0-8198-0228-X); pap. 2.00 (ISBN 0-8198-1109-2). Dghtrs St Paul.

BERNSTEIN, LEONARD, 1918-1990

Deitch, Kenneth M. Leonard Bernstein: America's Maestro. Foley, Sheila, illus.

Stern, Isaac, intro. by. LC 91-70821. (Illus.). 48p. (gr. 5-12). 1991. PLB 17. 95 (ISBN 1-878668-03-X); pap. 7.95 (ISBN 1-878668-07-2). Disc Enter Ltd. LEONARD BERNSTEIN: AMERICA'S MAESTRO by Kenneth M. Deitch & JoAnne B. Weisman begins with an introductory message by Bernstein's close friend & colleague, Isaac Stern. The book highlights Bernstein's family life, education, & accomplishments in the world of music, through interesting anecdotes & original watercolor renderings by Sheila Foley. Although geared for children 10-14, it is truly a book for all ages. Other new titles in Discovery Enterprises, Ltd.'s Picture-book Biography Series include LUCRETIA MOTT: FRIEND OF JUSTICE, with a message from Rosalynn Carter; by Kem Knapp Sawyer, illustrated by Leslie Carow. This biography of Lucretia Mott presents the importance of Mott's Quaker heritage as a guiding force in her quest for world peace & women's rights. Her contributions to the abolitionist movement & her commitment to peace & justice for all are a timely reminder to our nation's young people. Also in the series are W. E.B. DUBOIS: CRUSADER FOR PEACE, with a message from Benjamin L. Hooks; written by Kathryn Cryan Hicks & illustrated by David H. Huckins; CHRISTOPHER COLUMBUS & THE GREAT VOYAGE OF DISCOVERY, with a message by President George Bush; written by JoAnne B. Weisman & Kenneth M. Deitch; & DWIGHT D. EISENHOWER: MAN OF MANY HATS, written by Kenneth M. Deitch. ***Publisher Provided Annotation.***

BERRA, LAWRENCE PETER, 1925-

Appel, Marty. Yogi Berra. (Illus.). 64p. (gr. 3 up). 1992. PLB 14.95 (ISBN 0-7910-1169-0). Chelsea Hse.

BEST BOOKS

see Books and Reading–Best Books

BETHUNE, MARY JANE (MCLEOD) 1875-1955

Greenfield, Eloise. Mary McLeod Bethune. Pinkney, Jerry, illus. LC 76-11522. 40p. (gr. 2-5). 1977. PLB 14.89 (ISBN 0-690-01129-6, Crowell Jr Bks). HarpC Child Bks.

Halasa, Malu. Mary McLeod Bethune. King, Coretta Scott. (Illus.). 112p. (gr. 5 up). 1989. lib. bdg. 17.95x (ISBN 1-55546-574-9). Chelsea Hse.

McKissack, Patricia & McKissack, Frederick. Mary McLeod Bethune: A Great Teacher. Ostendorf, Ned, illus. 32p. (gr. 1-4). 1991. PLB 12.95 (ISBN 0-89490-304-7). Enslow Pubs.

McKissack, Patricia C. Mary McLeod Bethune: A Great American Educator. LC 85-12843. (Illus.). 111p. (gr. 5-8). 1985. PLB 17.27 (ISBN 0-516-03218-6). Childrens.

Mary McLeod Bethune. (gr. 2-6). 1989. pap. 3.50 (ISBN 0-14-042219-6, Puffin). Puffin Bks.

Meltzer, Milton. Mary McCleod Bethune. Marchesi, Stephen, illus. (gr. 2-6). 1988. pap. 3.50 (ISBN 0-317-69647-5, Puffin). Puffin Bks.

BEVERAGES

Charles, Oz. How Does Soda Get Into a Bottle? (Illus.). (gr. 1-5). 1988. pap. 9.95 (ISBN 0-671-63755-X). S&S Trade.

Dineen, Jacqueline. Beverages. 32p. (gr. 4-8). 1988. lib. bdg. 12.95 (ISBN 0-89490-210-5). Enslow Pubs.

Mitgutsch, Ali. From Lemon to Lemonade. Lerner, Mark, tr. from GER. Mitgutsch, Ali, illus. 24p. (ps-3). 1986. lib. bdg. 6.95 (ISBN 0-87614-298-6). Carolrhoda Bks.

Tchudi, Stephen. Soda Poppery: The History of Soft Drinks in America. LC 85-40289. 160p. (gr. 7 up). 1986. 13.95 (ISBN 0-684-18488-5, Scribners Young Read). Macmillan Child Grp.

BIBLE

Alexander, Pat, retold by. Nelson Children's Bible. LC 81-624. 256p. (gr. 2-4). 1991. 9.95 (ISBN 0-8407-6802-8). Nelson.

Aprendamos de la Biblia: Learning about the Bible. (SPA.). 32p. 1987. pap. 1.50 (ISBN 0-311-26612-6). Casa Bautista.

Batchelor, Mary. Children's Bible in Three Hundred Sixty-Five Stories. Haysom, John, illus. 416p. (ps up). 1987. 14.95 (ISBN 0-7459-1333-4). Lion USA.

Beall, Pamela C. & Nipp, Susan H. Wee Sing Bible Songs. Klein, Nancy, illus. 64p. (ps-2). 1986. pap. 2.95 (ISBN 0-8431-1566-1); bk. & cass. 9.95 (ISBN 0-8431-1780-X). Price Stern.

Beegle, Shirley. Bible Quizzes. (gr. 3-6). 1985. pap. 0.69 pocket size (ISBN 0-87239-823-4, 2813). Standard Pub.

Bible. Bible-Kid's Club Bible (Jesus & Me), New King James Version. 210p. 1987. 10.95 (ISBN 0-8407-2765-8). Nelson.

Biffi, Inos. The First Sacraments. Walsh, Kevin, tr. from ITA. Vignazia, Franco, illus. Martini, Carlo, intro. by. LC 88-80658. (Illus.). 94p. (gr. 4-9). 1989. 15.95 (ISBN 0-89870-206-2). Ignatius Pr.

Blankenbaker, Frances. What the Bible Is All about for Young Explorers. LC 86-22488. (Illus.). 364p. (gr. 6-8). 1986. 11.95 (ISBN 0-8307-1179-1, 5111647); pap. 8.95 (ISBN 0-8307-1162-7, 5418877). Regal.

The Children's Bible. (Illus.). (gr. k-12). 1965. write for info. (ISBN 0-307-16520-5, Golden Bks). Western Pub.

Coleman, William. Far Out Facts of the Bible. (gr. 3-7). 1988. pap. 3.69 (ISBN 1-55513-865-9, Chariot Bks). Cook.

Crain, Steve. Bible Fun Book, No. 8. 32p. (Orig.). (gr. k-4). 1981. pap. 1.19 oversized saddle stitched (ISBN 0-87123-772-5). Bethany Hse.

Crisci, Elizabeth. Five-Minute Bible Fun: Lesson Openers. 96p. (gr. 1-5). 1991. 9.95 (ISBN 0-86653-571-3). Good Apple.

Crisci, Elizabeth W. Five-Minute Bible Fun, Closing Activities. 96p. (ps-5). 9.95 (ISBN 0-86653-522-5, SS1819). Good Apple.

Crook, Carol. Puzzles to Learn By. 27p. (Orig.). (gr. 5 up). 1989. pap. text ed. 1.25x (ISBN 0-939399-08-3). Bks of Truth.

Daniel, Sarah. Bible Rebus Quotes. 48p. (gr. 3 up). 1989. 6.95 (ISBN 0-86653-512-8, SS890). Good Apple.

De Fajardo, Vilma, ed. La Biblia Me Ensena. 96p. (ps). 1988. pap. 5.95 (ISBN 0-311-11454-7). Casa Bautista.

Graham, Kathy. Hope for a Troubled Nation. (Illus.). 16p. (Orig.). (gr. 3-6). 1982. pap. 0.60 (ISBN 0-87403-016-1, 2176). Standard Pub.

Gregorowski, Christopher. Bible for Young People. 1990. 6.98 (ISBN 1-55521-588-2). Bk Sales Inc.

Gundersen, Bev. Let the Games Begin: Creative Games for Teaching Scripture. (Illus.). 96p. (gr. 1-6). 1989. wkbk. 7.95 (ISBN 0-87403-586-4, 3081). Standard Pub.

Hagan, Lowell & Westerhof, Jack. Theirs Is the Kingdom. Stoub, Paul, illus. LC 86-11679. 336p. (gr. 3 up). 1986. 14.95 (ISBN 0-8028-5013-8). Eerdmans.

Hand, Phyllis. Breaking into Bible Games. McClure, Nancee, illus. 48p. (gr. 3-6). 1984. wkbk. 6.95 (ISBN 0-317-43001-7, SS 819). Good Apple.

Herr, Amy, ed. Bible Nuture & Reader Series. rev. ed. (gr. 1-4). 1986. write for info. Rod & Staff.

Hruska, Eva J. The Alpha thru Omega Bible Survey. LC 85-90314. (gr. 8-12). 1985. tchr's. ed 7.95 (ISBN 0-9614616-0-8). Eva Hruska.

Illustrated Children's Bible. (Illus.). 256p. (gr. k up). 1986. slipcased 11.95 (ISBN 0-8249-8155-3). Ideals.

Krein, Linda. Bible Crossword Fun. 48p. (gr. 3 up). 1990. 6.95 (ISBN 0-86653-547-0, SS892). Good Apple.

—Bible Crosswords. Hyndman, Kathryn, illus. 48p. (gr. 3 up). 1986. wkbk. 6.95 (ISBN 0-86653-366-4, SS 881). Good Apple.

Larsen, Sandy. Eye-Opening Bible Studies. 32p. (gr. 6-8). 1986. pap. 1.95 (ISBN 0-87788-247-9). Shaw Pubs.

Latta, Richard. Bible Easter Puzzles. 48p. (gr. 3 up). 1988. 6.95 (ISBN 0-86653-427-X, SS885). Good Apple.

Layton, Karen & Layton, Ron. Bible Word Fun. Hyndman, Kathryn, illus. 48p. (gr. 3 up). 1986. wkbk. 6.95 (ISBN 0-86653-367-2, SS 882). Good Apple.

LeCours, Zoe S. Exit Here Please: Puzzles, Games & Mazes about the Book of Exodus. Buckles, Debbie, illus. 64p. (Orig.). (gr. 4-10). 1986. pap. 4.95 (ISBN 0-934661-01-4, 7078). Lions Head Pr.

—To Begin with Puzzles, Games & Mazes about the Book of Genesis. Collins, Diane, illus. 48p. (Orig.). (gr. 2-5). 1985. pap. 4.49 (ISBN 0-934661-00-6, 7077). Lions Head Pr.

Ledyard, Gleason H., tr. Precious Moments Children's Bible: Easy-to-Read, New Life Version. Butcher, Samuel J., illus. 1990. 24.95 (ISBN 0-8010-5664-0). Baker Bk.

Leone, Dee. Vacation Bible School Activities. 96p. (gr. 2-7). 9.95 (ISBN 0-86653-525-X, SS1818). Good Apple.

—The World God Made. 48p. (ps-1). 1991. 6.95 (ISBN 0-86653-636-1, PS-1). Good Apple.

Liljehorn, Linda. Preschool Bible Bulletin Boards. 96p. (ps-1). 1991. 9.95 (ISBN 0-86653-572-1). Good Apple.

Lindvall, Ella K. The Bible Illustrated for Little Children. Turnbaugh, Paul, illus. (gr. 2). 1985. text ed. 12.95 (ISBN 0-8024-0596-7). Moody.

MacKenthun, Carole & Dwyer, Paulinus. Faith. Filkins, Vanessa, illus. 48p. (gr. 2-7). 1986. wkbk. 6.95 (ISBN 0-86653-361-3, SS 874). Good Apple.

—Goodness. Filkins, Vanessa, illus. 48p. (gr. 2-7). 1986. wkbk. 6.95 (ISBN 0-86653-363-X, SS 875). Good Apple.

—Joy. Filkins, Vanessa, illus. 48p. (gr. 2-7). 1986. wkbk. 6.95 (ISBN 0-86653-360-5, SS 873). Good Apple.

—Love. Filkins, Vanessa, illus. 48p. (gr. 2-7). 1986. wkbk. 6.95 (ISBN 0-86653-359-1, SS 872). Good Apple.

—Patience. Filkins, Vanessa, illus. 48p. (gr. 2-7). 1986. wkbk. 6.95 (ISBN 0-86653-364-8, SS 876). Good Apple.

—Peace. Filkins, Vanessa, illus. 48p. (gr. 2-7). 1986. wkbk. 6.95 (ISBN 0-86653-365-6, SS 877). Good Apple.

Mackenzie, Joy. Child's Book of Bible Rhymes. Smith-Fitzpatrick, Kathleen, illus. 32p. (ps-3). 1989. 5.95 (ISBN 0-8249-8393-9). Ideals.

McKissack, Patricia & McKissack, Frederick. My Bible ABC Book. Merrill, Reed, illus. LC 87-70473. (Orig.). (ps-3). 1987. pap. 4.95 (ISBN 0-8066-2271-7, 10-4588, Augsburg). Augsburg Fortress.

McMillan, Mary. Bible Story Bulletin Boards. 96p. (ps-3). 1988. 9.95 (ISBN 0-86653-430-X, SS1828). Good Apple.

Martin, Dianne & Heller, Rachelle. Bible Basic: Advanced. Ostendorf, Ned, illus. 64p. (gr. 5 up). 1986. 5.95 (ISBN 0-87403-052-8, 3192). Standard Pub.

Norton, MaryJane P. Pocketsful of Scripture: Daily Scripture Readings & Activities for Children. LC 88-51473. 60p. (Orig.). 1989. pap. 5.95 (ISBN 0-8358-0595-6). Upper Room.

Persaud, Nancy. Bible Children Puzzles. 48p. (gr. 3 up). 6.95 (ISBN 0-86653-534-9, SS891). Good Apple.

—Bible Number Puzzles. 48p. (gr. 3 up). 1989. 6.95 (ISBN 0-86653-491-1, SS889). Good Apple.

Phillips, Bob. Heavenly Fun. 192p. (Orig.). (gr. 6 up). 1990. pap. 5.99 (ISBN 0-89081-771-5). Harvest Hse.

Piper, John. What's the Difference? Manhood & Womanhood According to the Bible. Elliot, Elisabeth, frwd. by. 64p. (Orig.). 1990. pap. 1.95 (ISBN 0-89107-562-3, Crossway Bks). Good News.

Pliskin, Jacqueline J. The Bible Game & Workbook. 96p. 1990. pap. 5.95 (ISBN 0-944007-84-8). Shapolsky Pubs.

Price, Cheryl. Bible Learning Centers. 96p. (gr. 2-6). 1989. 9.95 (ISBN 0-86653-498-9, SS1817). Good Apple.

Que Linda es la Creacion: Beautiful Creation. (SPA & ENG.). 32p. 1987. pap. 1.50 (ISBN 0-311-26611-8). Casa Bautista.

Rogers, Barbara. God's Chosen King Activity Book. 88p. (Orig.). (ps-1). 1984. pap. 3.00 (ISBN 0-8361-3370-6). Herald Pr.

Rossel, Seymour. Child's Bible: Lessons from the Writings & Prophets, Vol. 2. (gr. 3-5). 1989. pap. text ed. 8.50 (ISBN 0-318-42729-X); tchr's. guide 14.95 (ISBN 0-87441-485-7). Behrman.

Savary, Louis & Frankhausen, Edward. The Bible As Narrated by Jesus, the Storyteller. 1989. 9.95 (ISBN 0-88271-198-9). Regina Pr.

Schlegl, William. Bible Trivia. Leedom, Valerie, illus. 48p. (gr. 3 up). 1986. wkbk. 6.95 (ISBN 0-86653-368-0, SS 883). Good Apple.

Shannon, Foster H. Green Leaf Bible Series, Year Five. 180p. (gr. 3 up). 1989. looseleaf 17.50 (ISBN 0-938462-09-1). Green Leaf CA.

Snyder, Bernadette M. One Hundred Fifty Fun Facts Found in the Bible: For Kids of All Ages. Sharp, Chris, illus. LC 90-70802. 144p. (gr. 1-6). 1990. pap. 5.95 (ISBN 0-89243-330-2). Liguori Pubns.

Steen, Shirley & Edwards, Anne. A Child's Bible. (gr. 1-8). 1986. 9.95 (ISBN 0-8091-2867-5). Paulist Pr.

Stoddard, Sandol. Doubleday Illustrated Children's Bible. Chen, Tony, illus. LC 82-45340. 384p. (gr. 4-6). 1984. 30.00 (ISBN 0-385-18541-3). Doubleday.

Vernon, Louise A. Bible Smuggler. LC 67-15994. (Illus.). 138p. (gr. 4-9). 1967. pap. 5.95 (ISBN 0-8361-1557-0). Herald Pr.

Wangerin, Walter, Jr. The Bible: Its Story for Children. (Illus.). 416p. (ps up). 1981. write for info. Macmillan.

Ward, Elaine M. Growing with the Bible. 64p. (Orig.). (gr. 1-6). 1986. pap. 6.95 (ISBN 0-940754-36-3). Ed Ministries.

Warren, Ramona. Preschool Bible Learning Centers. 96p. (ps-2). 1991. 9.95 (ISBN 0-86653-573-X). Good Apple.

Woggon, Guillermo. Versiculos "Llave" Granberry, Nola, tr. (SPA., Illus.). 16p. (gr. 1-3). 1987. pap. 1.40 (ISBN 0-311-38565-6). Casa Bautista.

BIBLE–ANIMALS

see Bible–Natural History

BIBLE–BIOGRAPHY

see also Apostles; Christian Biography; Prophets; Women in the Bible

Alex, Ben, retold by. Joseph: The Boy Who Learned to Handle His Dreams. Pauzin, Philippe, illus. 32p. (ps-8). 1989. 7.95 (ISBN 0-8028-5032-4). Eerdmans.

Barrett, Ethel. Journey into the Unknown & other Stories about Joshua. Thimsen, Joyce, illus. 154p. 1987. pap. 3.95 (ISBN 0-8307-1235-6, 5811242). Regal.

Barrett, Marsha. Early Christians: Workers for Jesus. Hester, Ron, illus. (gr. 1-6). 1979. 5.95 (ISBN 0-8054-4247-2, 4242-47). Broadman.

Colburn, Rhonda. The Story of Shadrach, Meshach & Abednego. Connelly, Gwen, illus. 24p. (ps-k). 1990. pap. 3.95 (ISBN 0-8249-8421-8). Ideals.

Dugan, LeRoy. Heroes of the Old Testament. 96p. (Orig.). (ps-4). 1981. No. 1. pap. 3.95 oversized, saddle stitched (ISBN 0-87123-704-0); No. 2. pap. 3.95 no. 2 (ISBN 0-87123-705-9). Bethany Hse.

Eisenberg, Ann. Bible Heroes I Can Be. Schanzer, Roz, illus. LC 89-48188. 24p. (ps). 1990. 12.95 (ISBN 0-929371-09-7); pap. 4.95 (ISBN 0-929371-10-0). Kar Ben.

Fulbright, Robert G. Old Testament Friends: Men of Courage. McPheeters, William N., illus. (gr. 1-6). 1979. 5.95 (ISBN 0-8054-4251-0, 4242-51). Broadman.

Healy, Mark. Joshua: Conqueror of Canaan. (Illus.). 52p. (Orig.). (gr. 10 up). 1989. pap. 7.95 (ISBN 1-85314-010-4, Pub. by Firebird Bks UK). Sterling.

—Judas Maccabeus: Rebel of Israel. (Illus.). 52p. (Orig.). (gr. 10 up). 1989. pap. 7.95 (ISBN 1-85314-011-2, Pub. by Firebird Bks UK). Sterling.

—King David: Warlord of Israel. (Illus.). 52p. (Orig.). (gr. 10 up). 1989. pap. 7.95 (ISBN 1-85314-008-2, Pub. by Firebird Bks UK). Sterling.

—Nebuchadnezzar: Scourge of Zion. (Illus.). 52p. (Orig.). (gr. 10 up). 1989. pap. 7.95 (ISBN 1-85314-009-0, Pub. by Firebird Bks UK). Sterling.

Hershey, Katherine. Patriarchs. (Illus.). 51p. (gr. k-6). 1979. pap. text ed. 9.45 (ISBN 1-55976-005-2). CEF Press.

McElrath, William E. Judges & Kings: God's Chosen Leaders. Johnson, Cliff, illus. (gr. 1-6). 1979. 5.95 (ISBN 0-8054-4249-9, 4242-49). Broadman.

McMinn, Tom. Prophets: Preachers for God. Fields, Don, illus. (gr. 1-6). 1979. 5.95 (ISBN 0-8054-4250-2, 4242-50). Broadman.

Marquart, M. Jesus' Second Family. (gr. k-2). 1977. pap. 1.39 (ISBN 0-570-06111-3, 59-1229). Concordia.

People of the Bible. (Illus.). (gr. k-4). 1989. Set of 24 titles, 32 pp. ea. PLB 304.08 (ISBN 0-8172-2045-3). Raintree Pubs.

Seger, Doris. Children of the Bible. Butcher, Sam & Geraldo, Esteban, illus. 64p. (gr. k-6). 1967. pap. text ed. 8.99 (ISBN 1-55976-028-1). CEF Press.

Storr, Catherine. Abraham & Isaac. Rowe, Gavin, illus. LC 84-18076. 32p. (gr. k-4). 1985. PLB 14.65 (ISBN 0-8172-1994-3). Raintree Pubs.

—David & Goliath. Molan, Chris, illus. LC 84-18138. 32p. (gr. k-4). 1985. PLB 14.65 (ISBN 0-8172-1995-1). Raintree Pubs.

—Moses & the Plagues. Russell, Jim, illus. LC 84-18077. 32p. (gr. k-4). 1985. PLB 14.65 (ISBN 0-8172-1999-4). Raintree Pubs.

Storr, Catherine, as told by. Samson & Delilah. (Illus.). 32p. (gr. k-4). 1985. PLB 14.65 (ISBN 0-8172-2044-5). Raintree Pubs.

Thompson, Don. General Joshua. (Illus.). 32p. (gr. 3-5). pap. 1.19 (ISBN 0-87123-697-4). Bethany Hse.

Wiersbe, Warren. Be Challenged! rev. ed. LC 82-12404. (gr. 7). 1982. pap. 3.95 (ISBN 0-8024-1080-4). Moody.

BIBLE–BIRDS

see Bible–Natural History

BIBLE–BOTANY

see Bible–Natural History

BIBLE–COMMENTARIES

Ashworth, L. E. Revelation: Signs of the Times. (Illus.). 240p. (Orig.). (gr. 10). 1990. pap. 5.95 (ISBN 0-9627415-0-7). Advent Times.

Blakeley, Given. What the Bible Says about the Kingdom of God. LC 88-71154. 1988. text ed. 13.95 (ISBN 0-89900-260-9). College Pr Pub.

Chapman, Carl. Who Am I among So Many? An Autobiography Plus Special Articles: The Biggest Exception in the Bible, Paul's Thorn in the Flesh, & Not Discerning the Lord's Body. LC 88-92635. 132p. (Orig.). (gr. 9-12). 1989. pap. 4.99 (ISBN 0-9621529-0-0). C Chapman.

Enriquez, Edmund C. The Golden Gospel: A Pictorial History of the Restoration. Enriquez, Edmund C., illus. 96p. (gr. 6-12). 1981. pap. 6.95 (ISBN 0-88290-198-2). Horizon Utah.

Fischman, Joyce. Bible Work & Play, Vol. 1. rev. ed. Steinberger, Heidi, illus. 80p. (Orig.). (gr. 1-3). 1985. pap. text ed. 5.00 (ISBN 0-8074-0304-0, 103620). UAHC.

Fox, F. Earle. Biblical Sexuality & the Battle for Science. LC 88-80409. 208p. (Orig.). (gr. 9-12). 1988. pap. 5.45 (ISBN 0-945778-00-7). Emmaus Ministries.

George, Alan. My Wonderful Lord. Butcher, Sam & Hilterbrand, Greg, illus. 61p. (gr. k-6). 1987. pap. text ed. 8.99 (ISBN 1-55976-029-X). CEF Press.

MacKenthun, Carole. Biblical Bulletin Boards. Henson, Grace, illus. 48p. (gr. k-4). 1984. wkbk. 6.95 (ISBN 0-86653-197-1, SS 814). Good Apple.

Miles, A. Marie. Bible: Chain of Truth. 168p. (gr. 5 up). pap. 2.00 (ISBN 0-686-29101-8). Faith Pub Hse.

Myers, Bill. Faith Workout. (Illus.). 144p. (gr. 9-12). 1986. 5.95 (ISBN 0-89693-265-6). Victor Bks.

Potter, Jerold C. Books of the Bible. Bowen & Bowen Type Setters Staff, ed. 36p. 1988. pap. text ed. 1.50 (ISBN 0-925306-00-2). WOFPPM.

Schlegl, William. Bible Codes & Messages. (Illus.). 48p. (gr. 3 up). 1989. 6.95 (ISBN 0-86653-479-2, SS887). Good Apple.

Shannon, Foster H. Green Leaf Bible Series: Year Six. 184p. (gr. 3 up). 1991. looseleaf 17.50 (ISBN 0-938462-10-5). Green Leaf Ca.

Shofner, Myra. The Ark Book of Riddles. LC 79-57214. (Illus.). (gr. 3-7). 1980. pap. 3.95 (ISBN 0-89191-250-9). Cook.

Taggart, George. Bible Promises for Tiny Tots, III. Coffen, Richard W., ed. 32p. (Orig.). (ps). 1987. pap. 4.50 (ISBN 0-8280-0375-0). Review & Herald.

Waller, Lynn. How Do We Know the Bible Is True? Reasons a Kid Can Believe It. 64p. (gr. 3-7). 1991. pap. 4.95 (ISBN 0-310-53821-1, Youth Bks). Zondervan.

Weisheit, Eldon. The Gospel for Kids: Series C. (gr. 3-6). 1979. 7.95 (ISBN 0-570-03279-2, 15-2723). Concordia.

Wilhelm, Hans. What Does God Do? 29p. 1987. write for info. (ISBN 0-8499-0712-8). Word Bks.

BIBLE–DICTIONARIES

Layton, Karen & Layton, Ron. Bible Word Play. (Illus.). 48p. (gr. 3 up). 1989. 6.95 (ISBN 0-86653-472-5, SS888). Good Apple.

McElrath, William N. Bible Dictionary for Young Readers. Fields, Don, illus. LC 65-15604. (gr. 4-6). 1965. 11.95 (ISBN 0-8054-4404-1, 4244-04). Broadman.

—Mi Primer Diccionario Biblico. McElrath, Ruth G., tr. from ENG. Fields, Don, illus. (SPA.). 128p. (gr. 4-6). 1986. pap. 4.50 (ISBN 0-311-03656-2). Casa Bautista.

Matthews, Velda & Beard, Ray. Basic Bible Dictionary. Korth, Bob, ed. Wahl, Dick, illus. 128p. (Orig.). (gr. 4-12). 1984. pap. 12.95 (ISBN 0-87239-720-3, 2770). Standard Pub.

Winder, Linda. My First Bible Dictionary: A Sticker-Fun Book. (Illus.). 48p. 1991. pap. 5.95 (ISBN 0-8010-9712-6). Baker Bk.

BIBLE–DRAMA

see Mysteries and Miracle Plays

BIBLE–FESTIVALS

see Fasts and Feasts

BIBLE–FICTION

see Bible–History of Biblical Events–Fiction

BIBLE–FLOWERS

see Bible–Natural History

BIBLE–GARDENS

see Bible–Natural History

BIBLE–HISTORY

Here are entered works on the origin, authorship and composition of the Bible as a book. Works dealing with historical events as described in the Bible are entered under Bible–History of Biblical Events.

Hoffman, Yair & Shamir, Ilana. The World of the Bible for Young Readers. (Illus.). 96p. (gr. 7 up). 1989. pap. 15.95 (ISBN 0-670-81739-2). Viking Child Bks.

Hurlbut, Jesse L. Hurlbut's Story of the Bible. rev. ed. (Illus.). (gr. k-4). 1967. 19.95 (ISBN 0-310-26520-7, 6524). Zondervan.

Unfred, David W. Dinosaurs & the Bible. LC 90-80887. (Illus.). 47p. (gr. 3-8). 1990. 12.95 (ISBN 0-910311-70-6). Huntington Hse.

BIBLE–HISTORY OF BIBLICAL EVENTS

Fishman, Isidore. Remember the Days of Old. (Illus.). (gr. 4-9). 1970. 4.95 (ISBN 0-685-04135-2). Prayer Bk.

Scepters, Swords, & Fire from Heaven. (gr. 4-6). 1990. 1.55 (ISBN 0-89636-113-6, JB 2B). Accent Bks.

Youngman, Bernard R. Patriarchs, Judges, & Kings. (gr. 8-12). pap. 9.95 (ISBN 0-7175-0414-X). Dufour.

BIBLE–HISTORY OF BIBLICAL EVENTS–FICTION

Edington, Andy. Monkeying with the Flood. Eakin, Ed, ed. Messina, Linda, illus. 32p. (gr. 1-2). 1989. 10.95 (ISBN 0-89015-736-7, Pub. by Panda Bks). Eakin Pr.

Head, Constance. The Man Who Carried the Cross for Jesus. (Illus.). (gr. k-4). 1979. 1.39 (ISBN 0-570-06124-5, 59-1242). Concordia.

King-Smith, Dick. Noah's Brother. large type ed. (Illus.). 81p. (gr. 3-8). 1989. Repr. of 1986 ed. PLB 14.95 (ISBN 1-85089-947-9, Pub. by Clio Pr England). ABC-CLIO.

Kramer, Janice. El Buen Samaritano. Rodriguez, Eliseo, tr. from ENG. Mathews, Sally, illus. (SPA.). 32p. (gr. 1-3). 1979. pap. 0.95 (ISBN 0-89922-147-5). Edit Caribe.

Lillington, Kenneth. Jonah's Mirror. (gr. 7 up). 1988. 11.95 (ISBN 0-571-14961-8). Faber & Faber.

Miller, Calvin. The Singer Trilogy: A Mythic Retelling of the Story of the New Testament. LC 90-39944. (Illus.). 494p. 1990. 19.95 (ISBN 0-8308-1300-4, 1300). InterVarsity.

Ryan, John. Mabel & the Tower of Babel. Ryan, John, illus. 32p. (gr. 4-8). 1990. 11.95 (ISBN 0-7459-1742-9). Lion USA.

Van Horn, Brian & Van Horn, Chris. A Boy Full of Joy. Scott, Rita & Van Horn, Brian, illus. (ps-5). Date not set. write for info. (ISBN 1-877765-01-5). Lambgel Family.

—Lain Cain & Label Abel. Scott, Rita & Van Horn, Brian, illus. (gr. k-5). Date not set. write for info. (ISBN 1-877765-02-3). Lambgel Family.

—Leve Eve Believes Werpent the Serpent in the Garden of Eden. Scott, Rita & Van Horn, Brian, illus. (gr. k-5). Date not set. write for info. (ISBN 1-877765-03-1). Lambgel Family.

—Loah Noah & the Ark. Scott, Rita & Van Horn, Brian, illus. (gr. k-5). Date not set. write for info. (ISBN 1-877765-04-X). Lambgel Family.

BIBLE–INTERPRETATION

see Bible–Commentaries

BIBLE–INTRODUCTIONS

see Bible–Study

BIBLE–NATURAL HISTORY

Bright & Beautiful. (Illus.). 8p. (ps). 1984. bds. 2.95 (ISBN 0-7459-1426-8). Lion USA.

Paterson, John & Paterson, Katherine. Consider the Lilies: Flowers of the Bible. Dowden, Anne O., illus. LC 85-43603. 48p. (gr. 7 up). 1986. 13.95 (ISBN 0-690-04461-5, Crowell Jr Bks). HarpC Child Bks.

Peelman, Nancy. The Beasts, Birds & Fish of the Bible. Kocian, Ben F., illus. LC 75-14605. 40p. (Orig.). (gr. 1-8). 1975. pap. 4.50 (ISBN 0-8192-1197-4). Morehouse Pub.

—The Plants of the Bible. Kocian, Ben F., illus. LC 75-14607. 40p. (Orig.). (gr. 1-8). 1975. pap. 4.50 (ISBN 0-8192-1196-6). Morehouse Pub.

Summers, Joan. God's Little Animals: Easy Illustrations & Bible Parallels. (Illus.). 32p. (gr. k-4). 1969. pap. 1.95 (ISBN 0-88243-718-6, 02-0718). Gospel Pub.

Thomas, Mack. Bible Animal Storybook. Hagler, Elizabeth, illus. 224p. (ps-3). 1990. text ed. 15.95 (ISBN 0-945564-35-X). Questar Pubs.

BIBLE–PARABLES

see Jesus Christ–Parables

BIBLE–PICTORIAL WORKS

Beers, V. Gilbert. My Picture Bible to See & to Share. 189p. (ps-4). 1982. text ed. 12.99 (ISBN 0-88207-818-6, Sonflower Bks). SP Pubns.

Clark, Penny, illus. A Coloring Book of Bible Proverbs. 32p. (ps-5). 1988. 2.50 (ISBN 0-9618608-2-0). Lynn's Bookshelf.

Coen, Rena N. Old Testament in Art. LC 77-84410. (Illus.). 72p. (gr. 5 up). 1970. PLB 5.95 (ISBN 0-8225-0168-6). Lerner Pubns.

Ellis, Joyce & Lynn, Claire. Bible Bees. Lautermilch, John, illus. 36p. (gr. k). 1981. 8.00 (ISBN 0-89323-049-9). Bible Memory.

Gaines, M. C., ed. Picture Stories from the Bible: The Old Testament in Full-Color Comic-Strip Form. Cameron, Don, illus. LC 79-66064. 222p. (gr. 3-10). 1979. Repr. of 1943 ed. 12.95 (ISBN 0-934386-01-3). Scarf Pr.

Hook, Frances, illus. New Frances Hook Picture Book. Hayes, Wanda. (Illus.). (gr. k-2). 1989. 10.95 (ISBN 0-87239-243-0, 3548). Standard Pub.

Petts, Ken. The Illustrated Children's Bible. (Illus.). 243p. (gr. k-3). 1985. pap. text ed. 14.95 (ISBN 0-448-14494-8). Putnam Pub Group.

Pittenger, Shari. Listen, Color & Learn: A Coloring Book for Family Devotions, Vol. I, Psalm 1-30. Pittenger, Shari, illus. Harris, Gregg, intro. by. 35p. (Orig.). (ps-6). 1989. pap. text ed. 4.95 (ISBN 0-923463-49-6). Chrstn Life Workshops.

Shissler, Barbara. New Testament in Art. LC 70-84411. (Illus.). 68p. (gr. 5 up). 1970. PLB 5.95 (ISBN 0-8225-0169-4). Lerner Pubns.

Stoddard, Sandol. Doubleday Illustrated Children's Bible. Chen, Tony, illus. LC 82-45340. 384p. (gr. 4-6). 1983. pap. 25.00 (ISBN 0-385-18521-9). Doubleday.

Storr, Catherine. Jesus Begins His Work. Molan, Chris, illus. LC 82-9037. 32p. (gr. k-4). 1982. PLB 14.65 (ISBN 0-8172-1978-1). Raintree Pubs.

Taylor, Kenneth N. Bible in Pictures for Little Eyes. (Illus.). (gr. 2). 1956. 12.95 (ISBN 0-8024-0595-9). Moody.

Tudor, Tasha, illus. The Lord Is My Shepherd: The Twenty-Third Psalm. LC 79-27134. 32p. (gr. 2 up). 1989. 8.95 (ISBN 0-399-20756-2, Philomel). Putnam Pub Group.

BIBLE–PLANTS

see Bible–Natural History

BIBLE–STUDY

Aderman, James. Is He the One? Fischer, William E., ed. Woodfin, James, illus. 64p. (gr. 9-12). 1985. pap. 3.95 leader's guide (ISBN 0-938272-21-7); pap. 3.25 student's guide (ISBN 0-938272-20-9). WELS Board.

The Adventure Bible. 1989. 15.95 (ISBN 0-310-91919-3). Zondervan.

Amstutz, Beverly. Benjamin & the Bible Donkeys. (Illus.). 36p. (gr. k-7). 1981. pap. 2.50x (ISBN 0-937836-03-6). Precious Res.

Bartholomew. The Bible Tells Me. (ps). 1982. pap. 0.85 (ISBN 0-570-04074-4, 56-1377). Concordia.

Beers, Gil. The Early Reader's Bible. Hagler, Elizabeth, illus. 528p. (ps-3). 1991. 15.99 (ISBN 0-945564-43-0). Questar Pubs.

Fun to Learn..Easy to Read! Here's the Bible young children can fully enjoy on their own--& one that's specially designed to strengthen their beginning reader skills! This is a once-in-a-lifetime book for kids, a special companion during a special time in childhood when the discovery of reading unfolds. And this book will help develop not only their love for reading, but also their love for the Bible. "The Early Reader's Bible" is vocabulary-controlled. The text in each story is taken from a 250-word basic vocabulary list developed from public school reading materials. (In each story, an average of three new words are also taught.) The text is written in

short, simple sentences, & set in a clear typeface particularly recommended for children. And on every page of each story is a big, bright, colorful picture to enhance the text! 64 short, easy-to-read Bible stories; Activity pages & fun, life-centered questions following each story; Complete listing of all basic words & all new words used in the text; Bright, colorful pictures on every page; Includes list of moral & spiritual values taught in each story; Complete index to stories & Scriptural references.
Publisher Provided Annotation.

Beers, V. Gilbert. More Little Talks about God & You. LC 87-81042. 224p. (Orig.). (ps-3). 1987. pap. 8.99 (ISBN 0-89081-586-0). Harvest Hse.

Bernstein, David. Parshas Beshalach. Shapiro, Sara, illus. (ENG & HEB.). 192p. (gr. 5-8). 1991. pap. text ed. 6.00 (ISBN 0-914131-96-6, A148). Torah Umesorah.

Berry, Nancee. Jesus Cares for Me. 16p. (ps-1). 1979. pap. 2.15 (ISBN 0-8127-0252-2). Review & Herald.

Biblelearn, 24 vol. set. (gr. 1-6). 1979. 129.95 (ISBN 0-8054-4257-X, 4242-57). Broadman.

Birky, Lela. Truth for Life Bible Studies. (gr. 7-9). pap. write for info (ISBN 0-686-15481-9). Rod & Staff.

Borchardt, Lois M. Learning about God's Love: Word-Picture Activities for Children in Grades 1 & 2. 48p. (gr. 1-2). 1986. pap. 2.95 (ISBN 0-570-04354-9, 61-2017). Concordia.

Brusselmans, Christiane, et al. Sunday: Book of Readings Adapted for Children, Year B. 176p. (ps-8). 1990. text ed. 49.95 (ISBN 0-929496-57-4). Treehaus Comns.

—Sunday: Leaders Weekly Guidebook, Year B. 160p. (ps-8). 1990. text ed. 49.95 (ISBN 0-929496-58-2). Treehaus Comns.

Burrage, Barbara. The Bible Quiz Book. (gr. 5 up). 1979. pap. 2.95 (ISBN 0-8192-1256-3). Morehouse Pub.

Burstein, Chaya M. The Mystery of the Coins. Burstein, Chaya M., illus. 160p. (Orig.). (gr. 4-6). 1988. pap. text ed. 9.95 (ISBN 0-8074-0350-4, 123000). UAHC.

Campbell, Stan. The Saga Begins. 156p. (gr. 8 up). 1988. pap. 5.99 (ISBN 0-89693-656-2). Victor Bks.

—That's the Way the Kingdom Crumbles. 144p. (gr. 8 up). 1988. pap. text ed. 5.99 (ISBN 0-89693-658-9). Victor Bks.

—What's This World Coming To? 144p. (gr. 8 up). 1988. pap. text ed. 5.99 (ISBN 0-89693-865-4). Victor Bks.

Carney, Mary L. Bible Knock-Knocks & Other Fun Stuff. (ps-6). 1988. pap. 3.95 (ISBN 0-687-03180-X). Abingdon.

Case, Riley B., et al. We Believe--Sr. High. rev. ed. 64p. 1988. wkbk. 3.95 (ISBN 0-917851-26-9). Bristol Hse.

Clevenger, Ernest A., Jr. The Church. 104p. (gr. 3 up). 1990. pap. 4.75 (ISBN 0-88428-016-0). Parchment Pr.

Coleman, Sheila S. Be Happy! You Are Special. Plunkett, Mark, ed. Ham, John & Willis, Diane, illus. 32p. (ps). 1988. wkbk. 1.95 (ISBN 0-87403-508-2, 2818). Standard Pub.

Corbin, Linda & Dys, Pat. Jesus Wins the Battle. (Illus., Orig.). (gr. 1-6). 1989. pap. 5.99 wkbk. (ISBN 0-87509-410-4). Chr Pubns.

Coriell, Ron & Coriell, Rebekah. A Child's Book of Character Building, Bk. Two. 128p. (ps-2). 1981. 12.95 (ISBN 0-8007-1265-X). Revell.

Costello, Gwen. A Bible Way of the Cross for Children. Curley, Ed, illus. 32p. (Orig.). (gr. 4-6). 1988. pap. 1.95 (ISBN 0-89622-353-1). Twenty-Third.

Daughters of St. Paul. The Bible for Children. 182p. (gr. 5 up). 1988. 6.00 (ISBN 0-8198-0213-1, CH0070); pap. 5.00 (ISBN 0-8198-0214-X). Dghtrs St Paul.

—The Bible for Young People. 142p. (gr. 4 up). 1988. 6.00 (ISBN 0-8198-0211-5, CH0080); pap. 5.00 (ISBN 0-8198-0212-3). Dghtrs St Paul.

—The Bible for Young Readers. 102p. (ps-3). 1988. 5.00 (ISBN 0-8198-0010-4, CH0090). Dghtrs St Paul.

Dellinger, A. & Fletcher, S. Favorite Bible Verses. (ps-3). pap. 0.59 (ISBN 0-570-08310-9, 56HH1442). Concordia.

Eynon, Dana. Through the Bible in a Year: Pupil Workbook. 64p. (gr. 3-7). 1975. wkbk. 1.95 (ISBN 0-87239-011-X, 3239). Standard Pub.

Fields, Harvey J., ed. A Torah Commentary for Our Times: Genesis, Vol I. Carmi, Giora, illus. (gr. 7 up). 1990. pap. text ed. 12.00 (ISBN 0-8074-0308-3, 164000). UAHC.

Finley, Mitch. Living Scripture: Reproducible Lectionary-Based Reflections on Sunday Scriptures. 112p. (Orig.). 1990. pap. 69.95 (ISBN 1-55612-405-8). Sheed & Ward MO.

Fochman, Joyce. Bible Work & Play, Vol. 3. rev. ed. Lemelman, Martin, illus. 80p. 1986. pap. 5.00 wkbk. (ISBN 0-8074-0305-9, 103640). UAHC.

Fogle, Jeanne S. Teaching the Bible with Puppets. LC 89-50563. (Illus.). 1989. tchr's. ed. 9.95 (ISBN 0-89622-405-8). Twenty-Third.

Following God's Trailblazers: Kings & Prophets 14 Lessons, Vol. 4. (gr. 3-9). 1958. pap. text ed. 3.25 (ISBN 0-86508-033-X); figures text 12.95 (ISBN 0-86508-034-8). BCM Pubn.

Freehof, Lillian S. Bible Legends: An Introduction to Midrash, Vol. 2: Exodus. Schwartz, Howard, ed. Tarlow, Phyllis, illus. 160p. (gr. 4-6). 1988. pap. text ed. 6.95 (ISBN 0-8074-0412-8, 123060). UAHC.

Gaines, M. C., ed. Picture Stories from the Bible: The Old Testament in Full-Color Comic-Strip Form. Cameron, Don, illus. LC 79-66064. 222p. (gr. 3-10). 1979. Repr. of 1943 ed. 12.95 (ISBN 0-934386-01-3). Scarf Pr.

Great Devotional Classics, 29 bklts. 1160p. Date not set. Set. pap. 14.95 (ISBN 0-8358-0332-5). Upper Room.

Grogg, Evelyn. Bible Lessons for Little People: Revised with Learning Centers. rev. ed. Eberle, Sarah, rev. by. LC 80-53878. 144p. (ps). 1981. pap. 7.95 (ISBN 0-87239-430-1, 3368). Standard Pub.

Grunze, Richard. Searching in God's Word-New Testament. Most, Richard, illus. 142p. (gr. 5-6). 1986. 4.95 (ISBN 0-938272-41-1). WELS Board.

—Searching in God's Word-Old Testament. Most, Richard, illus. 140p. (gr. 5-6). 1986. 4.95 (ISBN 0-938272-40-3). WELS Board.

Gundersen, Bev. You Are There Activity Books: Old Testament - New Testament. (Illus.). 96p. (gr. 3-7). 1988. Old Testament. 4.95 (ISBN 0-87403-460-4, 13-02356); New Testament. 4.95 (ISBN 0-87403-461-2, 12-02357). Standard Pub.

Haas, Lois J. Tiny Steps of Faith Series. 1985. pap. text ed. 3.45 (ISBN 0-86508-010-0). BCM Pubn.

Haidle, David & Haidle, Helen. He Is My Shepherd: The Twenty-Third Psalm for Children. Davis, Deena, ed. Haidle, David & Haidle, Helen, illus. LC 89-31428. 32p. (gr. 1-6). 1989. 8.95 (ISBN 0-88070-278-8). Multnomah.

Hammack, Merla F. & Williams, Lisa, eds. The Bible Tells Me So: God's Promises for Kids. Williams, Lisa A., compiled by. (Illus.). 48p. (gr. 3 up). 1989. saddle stitch 1.50 (ISBN 0-87788-081-6). Shaw Pubs.

Hartman, Jack. How to Study the Bible. LC 85-8174. 118p. 1990. pap. 3.50 (ISBN 0-89221-173-3). New Leaf.

Heath, Lou & Taylor, Beth. Reading My Bible in Fall. LC 85-30947. (Orig.). (gr. 1-6). 1986. pap. 4.50 (ISBN 0-8054-4322-3). Broadman.

—Reading My Bible in Spring. (Orig.). (gr. 3-6). 1987. pap. 4.50 (ISBN 0-8054-4320-7). Broadman.

—Reading My Bible in Summer. (Orig.). (gr. 3-6). 1987. pap. 4.50 (ISBN 0-8054-4321-5). Broadman.

—Reading My Bible in Winter. LC 85-30940. (Orig.). (gr. 1-6). 1986. pap. 4.50 (ISBN 0-8054-4323-1). Broadman.

Hillam, Corbin. Preschool Bible Clip & Copy Time-Savers. 96p. (ps-1). 1991. 9.95 (ISBN 0-86653-625-6, SS1887). Good Apple.

Horn, Geoffrey, illus. Bible Stories for Children. Cavanaugh, Arthur. Stewart, Arvis, illus. LC 79-27811. 336p. (gr. 1-5). 1980. 13.95 (ISBN 0-02-554060-2, Mcmillan Child Bk). Macmillan Child Grp.

Horton, Stanley M. What the Bible Says about the Holy Spirit. Zimmerman, Thomas F., frwd. by. LC 75-43154. 316p. (gr. 12). 1976. pap. 7.95 (ISBN 0-88243-647-3, 02-0647). Gospel Pub.

Jordan, Bernice C. Acts: 14 Lessons, Vol. 1. (gr. 3-9). 1954. pap. text ed. 3.25 (ISBN 0-86508-039-9); figure text 11.95 (ISBN 0-86508-040-2). BCM Pubn.

—Acts: 15 Lessons, Vol. 2. (gr. 3-9). 1954. pap. text ed. 3.25 (ISBN 0-86508-041-0); figure text 11.95 (ISBN 0-86508-042-9). BCM Pubn.

—Fighting Giants: Joshua-Solomon 14 Lessons, Vol. 3. (gr. 3-9). 1957. pap. text ed. 3.25 (ISBN 0-86508-031-3); figures text 12.95 (ISBN 0-86508-032-1). BCM Pubn.

—Footsteps to God: Six Basic Bible Truth Lessons. (Illus.). (gr. 3-9). 1970. pap. text ed. 6.50 (ISBN 0-86508-025-9). BCM Pubn.

—Genesis: Fifteen Lessons, Vol. 1. (gr. 3-9). 1960. pap. text ed. 3.25 (ISBN 0-86508-027-5); figures text 12.95 (ISBN 0-86508-028-3). BCM Pubn.

—God's Storehouse: Exodus 16 Lessons, Vol. 2. (Illus.). (gr. 3-9). 1961. pap. text ed. 3.25 (ISBN 0-86508-029-1); 12.95 (ISBN 0-86508-030-5). BCM Pubn.

—Gospels: Fourteen Lessons, Vol. 1. (gr. 3-9). 1955. pap. text ed. 3.25 (ISBN 0-86508-035-6); figures text 12.95 (ISBN 0-86508-036-4). BCM Pubn.

—Gospels: Fourteen Lessons, Vol. 2. (gr. 3-9). 1956. pap. text ed. 3.25 (ISBN 0-86508-037-2); figures text 12.95 (ISBN 0-86508-038-0). BCM Pubn.

Kermond, Carolyn. Little Ways to Heaven. (Illus.). (gr. 3 up). 1988. 6.00 (ISBN 0-8198-4434-9, CH0336). Dghtrs St Paul.

Keyes, Sharrell & Fromer, Margaret. Acts 13-28: Missions Accomplished. DeVelasco, Joe, illus. 93p. (gr. 7-12). 1979. tchrs. ed. 4.95 (ISBN 0-87788-011-5); student ed. 2.95 (ISBN 0-87788-010-7). Shaw Pubs.

Kizer, Kathryn. God Made... Sealy, Kathy, illus. (Orig.). (ps). 1988. pap. 3.50 (ISBN 0-936625-43-0, New Hope AL). Womans Mission Union.

Koenig, John. Narrow Bartholomew. (ps up). 1988. pap. 2.50 (ISBN 0-8198-5104-3, CH0404). Dghtrs St Paul.

Kroecker, Beth. Bible ABC: Primer Pages. 30p. (gr. 1-6). 1987. lib. bdg. 10.95 (ISBN 0-88946-040-X). E Mellen.

Lang, Stephen J. The Illustrated Book of Bible Trivia. (Illus.). 1991. PLB 12.95 (ISBN 0-8423-1613-2). Tyndale.

Larsen, Dale & Larsen, Sandy. It's Up to Me: Choosing God's Way. (Illus.). 32p. (gr. 4-6). 1989. pap. 1.50 camper (ISBN 0-87788-404-8); pap. 3.50 counselor (ISBN 0-87788-405-6). Shaw Pubs.

—Joseph: From Pit to Pyramid. (Illus.). 32p. (gr. 4-6). 1989. pap. 1.50 camper (ISBN 0-87788-435-8); pap. 3.50 counselor (ISBN 0-87788-436-6). Shaw Pubs.

Larsen, Sandy. Choosing: Which Way Do I Go? (Illus.). 32p. (gr. 6-8). 1985. pap. 1.50 camper (ISBN 0-87788-115-4); pap. 3.50 counselor (ISBN 0-87788-116-2). Shaw Pubs.

—Forgiving: Lightening Your Load. (Illus.). 32p. (gr. 6-8). 1985. pap. 1.50 campers (ISBN 0-87788-279-7); pap. 3.50 counselor (ISBN 0-87788-280-0). Shaw Pubs.

Larsen, Sandy & Larsen, Dale. Celebrating Creation: Exploring God's World. 32p. (gr. 10). 1988. pap. 1.50 camper (ISBN 0-87788-109-X); pap. 3.50 counselor (ISBN 0-87788-110-3). Shaw Pubs.

Lashbrook, Marilyn. It's Not My Fault: Man's Big Mistake. Sharp, Chris, illus. LC 90-60459. 32p. (gr. k-3). 1990. 5.95 (ISBN 0-86606-439-7, 870). Roper Pr.

—Too Bad, Ahab! Naboth's Vineyard. Sharp, Chris, illus. LC 90-60457. 32p. (gr. k-3). 1990. 5.95 (ISBN 0-86606-441-9, 872). Roper Pr.

LeFever, Marlene. Survival Kit for Growing Christians. 32p. (gr. 4-6). 1988. pap. 1.50 camper (ISBN 0-685-29582-6); pap. 3.50 counselor (ISBN 0-87788-797-7). Shaw Pubs.

Link, Mark. Path Through Scripture. (Illus.). 288p. (gr. 9-12). 1987. pap. 11.50 (ISBN 0-89505-402-7). Tabor Pub.

—Path Through Scripture: Teacher's Resource Manual. 328p. (gr. 9-12). 1987. 22.95 (ISBN 0-89505-403-5). Tabor Pub.

—The Seventh Trumpet: Teacher's Manual. 207p. (gr. 9-12). 1978. 19.95 (ISBN 0-89505-030-7). Tabor Pub.

Loehrlein, Myrna & Nylin, Dawn. Preschool Bible Lessons. 96p. (ps-1). 1990. 9.95 (ISBN 0-86653-541-1, SS1875). Good Apple.

Lost & Found. (Illus.). 60p. (gr. k-6). 1971. pap. text ed. 8.99 (ISBN 1-55976-025-7). CEF Press.

Lynn, Claire. B-I-B-L-E That's the Book for Me! Lautermilch, John, illus. 18p. (Orig.). (ps-1). 1981. pap. 2.25 (ISBN 0-89323-013-8). Bible Memory.

MacKenzie, Joy. The Big Book of Bible Crafts & Projects. Flint, Russ, illus. 212p. (Orig.). (ps-4). 1981. pap. 12.95 (ISBN 0-310-70151-1, 14019P). Zondervan.

Manley, Deborah. Bible Times. 1990. 4.99 (ISBN 0-517-69616-9). Outlet Bk Co.

Matheny, James F. & Matheny, Marjorie B. Is There a Russian Connection? An Exposition of Ezekiel 37 & 39. 76p. (Orig.). 1987. pap. 3.95 (ISBN 0-939422-01-8). Jay & Assocs.

Mumma, Win. Jesus: The Man with the Miracle Touch. (Illus.). 32p. pap. 5.34 (ISBN 0-8423-1863-1). Tyndale.

My First Bible in Pictures. large type ed. (Illus.). 1989. 9.95 (ISBN 0-8423-4633-3, 01-4633-3); Incl. handle. 13.95 (ISBN 0-8423-4630-9, 01-4630-9). Tyndale.

Nelson, P. C. Bible Doctrines. Zimmerman, Thomas F., intro. by. LC 81-82738. 128p. (gr. 9-12). 1981. pap. 2.95 (ISBN 0-88243-479-9, 02-0479). Gospel Pub.

Newman, Shirley. Introduction to Kings, Later Prophets & Writings, Vol. 3. Rossel, Seymour, ed. Hoban, Brom, illus. 160p. (Orig.). (gr. 4-5). 1981. pap. text ed. 6.95x (ISBN 0-87441-336-2); wkbk. by Morris Sugarman 3.95 (ISBN 0-685-00733-2); tchr's ed. 14. 95x. Behrman.

Nystrom, Carolyn. Angels & Me. (Illus.). (gr. k-2). 1984. pap. 3.95 (ISBN 0-8024-6150-6). Moody.

—Mark: God on the Move. 96p. (gr. 7-12). 1978. pap. 4.95 tchr's ed. (ISBN 0-87788-312-2); student ed. 2.95 (ISBN 0-87788-311-4). Shaw Pubs.

—What Is the Bible? 32p. (gr. 2). 1982. pap. 3.95 (ISBN 0-8024-6157-3). Moody.

Orange, Tom. Scripture Bulletin Boards. 96p. (gr. 2-7). 1987. 9.95 (ISBN 0-86653-397-4, SS1826). Good Apple.

Pape, Donna L., et al. Bible Activities for Kids, No. 1. (Illus.). 64p. (Orig.). (gr. 3-7). 1980. pap. 2.50 (ISBN 0-87123-148-4). Bethany Hse.

Plueddemann, Jim. Keeping Cool in a Crazy World. (Illus.). 32p. (gr. 4-6). 1988. pap. 1.50 camper (ISBN 0-87788-454-4); pap. 3.50 counselor (ISBN 0-87788-455-2). Shaw Pubs.

Raney, Nancy. The Big Bible Broadcast. (Illus.). 144p. (gr. 1-6). 1989. 24.95 (ISBN 1-55513-870-5, 68700). Cook.

Roper, Harlin J. In the Beginning God: Genesis - Exodus 18. 64p. 1989. Repr. wkbk. 4.50 (ISBN 0-86606-350-1, 1). Roper Pr.

Rutan, Debbie. Big Promises for Little People. 30p. 1991. pap. 3.95 (ISBN 0-685-39073-X). Green & White Pub. Big Promises for Little People is a read & color book for children of all ages. It is a thirty page saddle stitch bound glossy covered book. This book captures real life situations that children face every day & then gives a promise to them by citing a scripture

reference from the Bible. Each page has an illustration, some of which are in color & some to be colored by the child. Any parent will be thrilled to have this book added to their child's library. Children will enjoy the themes & activity. This book will be helpful & enjoyable for both Sunday School Departments & Day Care Centers & other teaching facilities. The book was authored by Debbie Rutan of Winona Lake, Indiana & will retail for $3.95 & will be available for ordering after February 15, 1991 through Green & White Publishing, P.O. Box 778, Sturgis, MI 49091. Telephone orders are accepted by calling 616-651-1569. *Publisher Provided Annotation.*

Sanford, Doris. Advanced Theology for Very Tiny Persons, Vol. 1. Davis, Deena, ed. Evans, Graci, illus. (ps). 1988. bds. 12.95 incl. slipcase (ISBN 0-88070-227-3). Multnomah.

Sattgast, L. J. & Elkins, Jan. Teach Me about the Bible. Davis, Deena, ed. Flint, Russ, illus. 32p. (gr. 1-4). 1990. 4.99 (ISBN 0-88070-385-7). Multnomah.

Scheets, Thomas M. The Bible Says: A Look at Current Claims to What the Bible Says. LC 88-62605. 64p. (Orig.). 1989. pap. 4.95 (ISBN 1-55612-239-X). Sheed & Ward MO.

Schramm, Mary. A Look at God's Book. (Illus.). 42p. (gr. k-6). 1973. pap. text ed. 14.99 (ISBN 1-55976-148-2). CEF Press.

Segal, Lore. The Book of Adam to Moses. Baskin, Leonard, illus. LC 87-2581. 144p. (gr. k up). 1987. lib. bdg. 14.99 (ISBN 0-394-96757-7). Knopf.

Shannon, Foster H. The Green Leaf Bible Series, Year One. 174p. (gr. 3 up). 1982. pap. 15.00 (ISBN 0-938462-06-7). Green Leaf CA.

—Green Leaf Bible Series, Year Four. 180p. (gr. 3 up). 1988. looseleaf 17.50 (ISBN 0-938462-08-3). Green Leaf CA.

Sikora, Pat. Small Group Bible Studies: How to Lead Them. 224p. (Orig.). 1991. pap. 9.99 (ISBN 0-87403-858-8, 18-03218). Standard Pub.

Smith, Anne. Thank You, God. 24p. (Orig.). (ps). 1988. pap. text ed. 1.75 (ISBN 0-936625-44-9). Womans Mission Union.

Sorenson, Stephen. Lord, Teach Me Your Ways: Children's Stories with Biblical Parallels. LC 81-2067. 96p. (gr. 3-6). 1982. 0.70 (ISBN 0-687-22660-0). Abingdon.

Stadler, Richard H. Living As a Winner. Fischer, William E., ed. Woodfin, James, illus. 64p. (gr. 9-12). 1985. pap. 2.95 leaders guide (ISBN 0-938272-23-3); pap. 2.95 students guide (ISBN 0-938272-22-5). WELS Board.

Taylor, Kent. Bible in Pictures for Little Eyes. (ps-3). 1991. 18.95 (ISBN 0-8024-0685-8). Moody.

Tonothy, Ruth. Bible Crossword Puzzles. 48p. (gr. 3 up). 1986. pap. 2.95 (ISBN 0-87403-050-1, 2694). Standard Pub.

Tudor, Tasha, illus. And It Was So: Words from the Scripture. 2nd, rev. ed. LC 87-16130. 48p. (ps up). 1988. 8.95 (ISBN 0-664-32724-9, Westminster). Westminster John Knox.

Veerman, David R. Serious Fun. 128p. (gr. 7 up). 1987. pap. 12.99 (ISBN 0-89693-017-3). Victor Bks.

Vos Wezeman, Phyllis & Wiessner, Colleen A. Mary's Memories. 38p. (Orig.). (gr. 1-6). 1989. pap. 5.95 (ISBN 0-940754-72-X). Ed Ministries.

Weinberg, Shnayer. Targilon for Haschalas Chumash: A Chumash Workbook for Beginners. (Illus.). 130p. (Orig.). pap. text ed. 5.50 (ISBN 1-878895-00-1, A135). Torah Umesorah.

Weisheit, Eldon. The Gospel for Little Kids. 1980. pap. 5.95 (ISBN 0-570-03811-1, 12-2920). Concordia.

Wendland, Ernst H. God's Mission in the New Testament. Fischer, William E., ed. 40p. (Orig.). 1986. pap. 2.50 (ISBN 0-938272-55-1). WELS Board.

Youngman, Bernard R. Spreading the Gospel. (gr. 8-12). pap. 9.95 (ISBN 0-7175-0420-4). Dufour.

BIBLE–USE

McElrath, William N. Bible Guidebook. LC 72-79174. 144p. (gr. 3-6). 1972. 11.95 (ISBN 0-8054-4410-6, 4244-10). Broadman.

Maves, Paul B. & Maves, Mary C. Finding Your Way Through the Bible. (Orig.). (gr. 3-4). 1971. pap. 3.95 (ISBN 0-687-13049-2). Abingdon.

BIBLE–ZOOLOGY

see Bible–Natural History

BIBLE. NEW TESTAMENT

Anderson, Julian G. The New Testament in Everyday American English. rev. ed. RKB Studios Staff, illus. x, 886p. (gr. 10 up). 1989. pap. 4.95 (ISBN 0-685-27817-4). Anderson Bks.

Berry, Nancee. Jesus Cares for Me. 16p. (ps-1). 1979. pap. 2.15 (ISBN 0-8127-0252-2). Review & Herald.

Booth, Julianne. Books of the New Testament. (gr. k-4). 1981. pap. 1.39 (ISBN 0-570-06150-4, 59-1305). Concordia.

Bundschuh, Rick. The Church. LC 88-9692. (Illus.). 154p. (Orig.). (gr. 9-12). 1988. pap. 5.95 (ISBN 0-8307-1182-1, S184102). Regal.

Campbell, Stan. Growing Pains: The Church Hits the Road. 144p. (gr. 9-12). 1989. pap. 5.99 (ISBN 0-89693-384-9). Victor Bks.

Dastrup, Linda. I Am a Child of God: My Gospel Principles Book. 14p. (gr. 1-7). 1985. wkbk. 3.95 (ISBN 0-9621898-2-0). Creative Changes.

George, Alan. First Christians. Butcher, Sam, illus. 56p. (gr. k-6). 1991. pap. text ed. 9.45 (ISBN 1-55976-023-0). CEF Press.

The Gospel of John: Jesus' Teachings. 48p. (gr. 9-12). 1990. pap. 6.95 (ISBN 1-55945-208-0). Group Pub.

Hillmann, W. Children's Bible. 95p. (ps-8). 1959. pap. 3.95 (ISBN 0-8146-0120-0). Liturgical Pr.

Jones, Eugene P. Which Was, Which Is, Which Is to Come. (Illus.). 105p. (Orig.). 1989. pap. 24.95 (ISBN 0-925039-00-4). River-Light Pub.

Kreeft, Peter J. Letters to Jesus (Answered) LC 88-83743. 294p. (Orig.). 1989. 17.95 (ISBN 0-89870-243-7); pap. 10.95 (ISBN 0-89870-233-X). Ignatius Pr.

Larsen, Rayola C. Alphabet Talk: Gospel Rhymes for Each Letter of the Alphabet. Perry, Lucille R., illus. LC 89-83429. 32p. (Orig.). (gr. k-3). 1989. pap. 3.95 (ISBN 0-88290-147-8). Horizon Utah.

Mehew, Randall & Mehew, Karen. Gospel Basic Busy Book, Vol. I. Christopherson, Jerry, illus. 100p. 1989. pap. text ed. 6.95 (ISBN 0-910613-13-3). Millenial Pr.

New Testament Psalms Proverbs. 1968. pap. 4.50 (ISBN 0-8361-1279-2). Herald Pr.

Segraves, Daniel. Hair Length in the Bible: A Study of First Corinthians 11: 2-16. Bernard, David, ed. LC 89-37912. 80p. (Orig.). 1989. pap. 4.95 (ISBN 0-932581-57-9). Word Aflame.

Sieg, Robert C. What Mark Says about Jesus: An Interpretation for the Very Young. LC 88-63732. (Illus.). 98p. (Orig.). (gr. k-4). 1988. pap. 7.95 (ISBN 1-55618-041-1). Brunswick Pub.

Smith, Joyce M. Demons, Doubters & Dead Men. 64p. (Orig.). (gr. 4-7). 1986. 2.95 (ISBN 0-8423-0542-4). Tyndale.

Truitt, Gloria A. People of the New Testament: Arch Book Supplement. LC 59-1311. 1983. pap. 1.39 (ISBN 0-570-06173-3). Concordia.

Vos Wezeman, Phyllis & Wiessner, Colleen A. The Mosaic of Mary & Martha. 29p. (Orig.). (gr. 1-6). 1989. pap. 5.95 (ISBN 0-940754-73-8). Ed Ministries.

Wilson, Terry C. The Same: II Timothy 2: 2. 250p. (Orig.). (gr. 12). 1989. pap. 30.00 (ISBN 0-685-28038-1). T C Wilson.

BIBLE. OLD TESTAMENT

Bachrach, Kalman. Olami Sefer Rishon, Bk. 1. rev. ed. Krukman, Tsvi, illus. (HEB.). 59p. (gr. 2). 1943. pap. text ed. 2.00x (ISBN 1-878530-14-3). K Bachrach Co.

—Olami Sefer Sheini, Bk. 2. rev. ed. Krukman, Tsvi, illus. (HEB.). 71p. (gr. 3-4). 1950. pap. text ed. 2.00x (ISBN 1-878530-15-1). K Bachrach Co.

—Olami Sefer Shlishi, Bk. 3. Gutman, Nachum, illus. (HEB.). 92p. (gr. 4-6). 1936. pap. text ed. 2.00x (ISBN 1-878530-16-X). K Bachrach Co.

Daniel, Rebecca. Famous Old Testament Heroes. 48p. (ps-6). 1990. 6.95 (ISBN 0-86653-528-4, SS858). Good Apple.

Davis, Susan. When God Lived in a Tent. (Illus.). (ps-1). 1978. 1.95 (ISBN 0-8127-0181-X). Review & Herald.

Eisenberg, Ann. Bible Heroes I Can Be. Schanzer, Roz, illus. LC 89-48188. 24p. (ps). 1990. 12.95 (ISBN 0-929371-09-7); pap. 4.95 (ISBN 0-929371-10-0). Kar Ben.

Finley, Tom. Ecclesiastes: Survival in the 21st Century. (gr. 9-12). 1989. pap. 5.95 (ISBN 0-8307-1305-0, S185108). Regal.

Graaf, Anne de. Exodus: Moses Leads the People. Montero, Jose P., illus. (gr. 5-7). 1988. 4.95 (ISBN 0-310-52630-2). Zondervan.

Hillmann, W. Children's Bible. 95p. (ps-8). 1959. pap. 3.95 (ISBN 0-8146-0120-0). Liturgical Pr.

MacArthur, John. Elements of True Prayer: Daniel 9.1-19. 1988. pap. 4.25 (ISBN 0-8024-5367-8). Moody.

Newland, Mary R. The Hebrew Scriptures: The Story of God's Promise to Israel & Us. Nagel, Stephan, ed. Abrahamson, Evie, illus. 261p. (Orig.). (gr. 10-11). 1990. pap. text ed. 12.00 (ISBN 0-88489-231-X); tchr's. ed. 18.95 (ISBN 0-88489-232-8). St Mary's.

Orthner, Donald P. Wellsprings of Life: Understanding Proverbs. Thompson, Del, illus. Minnick, Mark, pref. by. (Illus.). xii, 228p. (Orig.). (gr. 9 up). 1989. pap. 7.95 (ISBN 0-317-93833-9). Adon Bks.

Osborne, Richard, compiled by. Proverbs for Kids from the Book. VanRoon, Terry & Kielesinski, Chris, illus. 240p. (gr. k). 1987. 9.95 (ISBN 0-8423-4975-8). Tyndale.

Roper, Harlin J. In the Beginning God: Genesis - Exodus 18. 64p. (gr. 7-12). 1988. Repr. wkbk. 4.50 (ISBN 0-86606-362-5, 1Y). Roper Pr.

—In the Beginning God: Genesis - Exodus 18. (Illus.). 64p. (gr. 4-6). 1989. Repr. of 1956 ed. wkbk. 4.50 (ISBN 0-86606-374-9, 1J). Roper Pr.

Truitt, Gloria A. People of the Old Testament. LC 59-1310. (gr. k-4). 1983. pap. 1.39 (ISBN 0-570-06172-5). Concordia.

BIBLE. OLD TESTAMENT–BIOGRAPHY

Joshua at Jericho. 1989. text ed. 3.95 cased (ISBN 0-7214-5263-9). Ladybird Bks.

Kolbrek, Loyal. The Day God Made It Rain. (gr. k-2). 1977. pap. 1.39 (ISBN 0-570-06108-3, 59-1226). Concordia.

Lashbrook, Marilyn. The Weak Strongman: Samson. Sharp, Chris, illus. LC 90-60456. 32p. (gr. k-3). 1990. 5.95 (ISBN 0-86606-442-7, 873). Roper Pr.

Neff, Lavonne. God's Gift Baby. (gr. k-4). 1977. pap. 1.39 (ISBN 0-570-06113-X, 59-1230). Concordia.

Parry, Linda & Parry, Alan. Jacob & Esau. Parry, Linda & Parry, Alan, illus. 24p. (Orig.). (ps-2). Date not set. pap. 1.49 (ISBN 0-8066-2490-6, 9-2490, Augsburg). Augsburg Fortress.

—Miriam & Moses. Parry, Linda & Parry, Alan, illus. LC 90-80556. 24p. (Orig.). (ps-2). Date not set. pap. 1.49 (ISBN 0-8066-2489-2, 9-2489, Augsburg). Augsburg Fortress.

Porter, Jane. Samson & Super-Strong. Baker, Arthur, illus. 32p. (gr. k-3). 1990. saddle stitched 1.25 (ISBN 0-8028-5062-6). Eerdmans.

Vos Wezeman, Phyllis & Wiessner, Colleen A. A Day with David. 30p. (Orig.). (gr. 1-6). 1988. pap. 5.95 (ISBN 0-940754-57-6). Ed Ministries.

—Gleanings from Ruth. 25p. (Orig.). (gr. 1-6). 1988. pap. 5.95 (ISBN 0-940754-61-4). Ed Ministries.

—Joseph's Jigsaw. 50p. (Orig.). (gr. 1-6). 1988. pap. 5.95 (ISBN 0-940754-59-2). Ed Ministries.

BIBLE. O. T. PSALMS

Clayton, C. Sing a Song of Gladness. (Illus.). 32p. (gr. k-4). 1974. pap. 1.39 (ISBN 0-570-06087-7, 59-1302). Concordia.

Keller, W. Phillip. A Child's Look at the Twenty-Third Psalm. Jarrett, Lauren, illus. LC 84-13718. 96p. (gr. 3 up). 1985. pap. 7.95 (ISBN 0-385-15457-7, Galilee). Doubleday.

Pittenger, Shari. Listen, Color & Learn: A Coloring Book for Family Devotions, Vol. I, Psalm 1-30. Pittenger, Shari, illus. Harris, Gregg, intro. by. 35p. (Orig.). (ps-6). 1989. pap. text ed. 4.95 (ISBN 0-923463-49-6). Chrstn Life Workshops.

BIBLE AS LITERATURE

see also Religious Literature

BIBLE CLASSES

see Bible–Study

BIBLE PLAYS

see Mysteries and Miracle Plays

Langdon, Harry N. Twenty-Six Biblical Playlets for Learning & Liturgy. 64p. (Orig.). 1989. pap. 4.95 (ISBN 0-89243-297-7). Liguori Pubns.

BIBLE STORIES

Abram Talked with God. 24p. (gr. 2-5). 1985. 5.95 (ISBN 0-570-08950-6, 56-1541). Concordia.

Alden, Laura. I Read about God's Care: Grade 2. rev. ed. (Illus.). 128p. (gr. 2). 1983. text ed. 9.95 (ISBN 0-87239-662-2, 2952). Standard Pub.

Bach, Alice & Exum, Cheryl. Moses' Ark: Stories from the Bible. Dillon, Leo & Dillon, Diane, illus. (gr. 4-8). 1989. 14.95 (ISBN 0-685-30899-5). Delacorte.

Baden, Robert. Adam & His Family. (Illus.). 24p. (gr. k-4). 1986. pap. 1.39 (ISBN 0-570-06198-9, 59-1421). Concordia.

Baerg, Harry. Bible Animal Color Book. 14p. 1985. pap. 1.95 (ISBN 0-317-66019-5). Pacific Pr Pub Assn.

Barrett, Ethel. Ethel Barrett Tells Favorite Bible Stories, Vol.3. LC 77-93051. 128p. (gr. 1-7). 1978. pap. 4.95 (ISBN 0-8307-0615-1, 5605806). Regal.

Batchelor, Mary. The Children's Bible in Three Hundred Sixty-Five Stories: Red Gift Edition. (Illus.). 416p. (gr. k up). 1988. 29.95 (ISBN 0-7459-1019-X). Lion USA.

—Children's Bible in Three Hundred Sixty-Five Stories: White Gift Edition. (Illus.). 416p. (gr. k up). 1988. bds. 29.95 (ISBN 0-7459-1375-X). Lion USA.

—The Lion Book of Bible Stories & Prayers. (Illus.). 96p. (gr. 1-5). 1989. 11.95 (ISBN 0-85648-239-0). Lion USA.

Baumann, Kurt, retold by. The Story of Jonah. Reed, Allison, illus. LC 86-62522. 32p. (gr. k-3). 1987. 13.95 (ISBN 1-55858-050-6). North-South Bks NYC.

Baw, Cindy & Brownlow, Paul C. Children of the Bible: Exciting Stories about Children in the Bible. (Illus.). (ps-3). 1984. 8.95 (ISBN 0-915720-19-1). Brownlow Pub Co.

Baxendale, Jean. First Bible Lessons: A Course for Two and Three-Year-Olds. rev. ed. Arthur, Lorraine, illus. LC 81-53021. 144p. (ps). 1982. pap. 7.95 (ISBN 0-87239-486-7, 3369). Standard Pub.

Beers, Gil. The Early Reader's Bible. Hagler, Elizabeth, illus. 528p. (ps-3). 1991. 15.99 (ISBN 0-945564-43-0). Questar Pubs.

Fun to Learn..Easy to Read! Here's the Bible young children can fully enjoy on their own--& one that's specially designed to strengthen their beginning reader skills! This is a once-in-a-lifetime book for kids, a special companion during a special time in childhood when the discovery of reading unfolds. And this book will help develop not only their love for reading, but also their love for the Bible. "The Early Reader's Bible" is vocabulary-controlled. The text in each story is taken from a 250-word basic vocabulary list developed from public

school reading materials. (In each story, an average of three new words are also taught.) The text is written in short, simple sentences, & set in a clear typeface particularly recommended for children. And on every page of each story is a big, bright, colorful picture to enhance the text! 64 short, easy-to-read Bible stories; Activity pages & fun, life-centered questions following each story; Complete listing of all basic words & all new words used in the text; Bright, colorful pictures on every page; Includes list of moral & spiritual values taught in each story; Complete index to stories & Scriptural references.
Publisher Provided Annotation.

Beers, V. Gilbert. Growing up with God's Friends. Endres, Helen, illus. LC 87-81046. 94p. (Orig.). (ps-7). 1987. 12.99 (ISBN 0-89081-528-3). Harvest Hse.
—Growing up with Jesus. Endres, Helen, illus. LC 87-81043. 94p. (Orig.). (ps-7). 1987. 12.99 (ISBN 0-89081-525-9). Harvest Hse.
Berg, Jean H., retold by. The Story of Peter. Palm, Felix, illus. 40p. (Orig.). (gr. k-3). 1990. pap. 9.95 incl. audiocassette (ISBN 0-87510-216-6). Chr Science.
Bergey, Alyce. David & Jonathan. (Illus.). 24p. (gr. k-4). 1987. pap. 1.39 (ISBN 0-570-09006-7, 59-1434). Concordia.
—Young Jesus in the Temple. (Illus.). 24p. (gr. k-4). 1986. pap. 1.39 saddlestitched (ISBN 0-570-06203-9, 59-1426). Concordia.
The Bible: God's Wonderful Book. 10p. (gr. 1-8). 1968. pap. text ed. 3.95 (ISBN 0-86508-150-6). BCM Pubn.
Bible Stories & Activities for Children. 1991. pap. 5.95 (ISBN 0-687-03183-4). Abingdon.
Biffi, Inos. The Story of the Eucharist. Drury, John, tr. from ITA. Vignazia, Franco, illus. LC 85-82173. 125p. (gr. 5 up). 1986. 16.95 (ISBN 0-89870-089-2). Ignatius Pr.
Boone, Pat. Pat Boone's Favorite Bible Stories. Wilheim, Hans, illus. LC 89-80827. 1989. 10.95 (ISBN 0-88419-245-8, Creation Hse). Strang Comms Co.
Bourgeois, Jean-Francois. Los Ninos de la Biblia. Maecha, Alberto, ed. Landgraff, Michael, illus. (SPA.). 40p. (gr. 3-5). 1984. pap. write for info. (ISBN 0-942504-11-9). Overcomer Pr.
Brem, M. M. La Historia de Maria. Mathews, Sally, illus. (SPA.). 32p. (gr. 1-3). 1979. pap. 0.95 (ISBN 0-89922-145-9). Edit Caribe.
Bretschneider, Diana. Bible Puzzle Time, Friends of God. 16p. (gr. 2-7). 1983. pap. 0.60 (ISBN 0-87239-655-X, 2303). Standard Pub.
Brin, Ruth F. The Story of Esther. LC 75-743. (Illus.). 32p. (gr. k-5). 1976. PLB 6.95 (ISBN 0-8225-0364-6). Lerner Pubns.
Brincat, Matthew De. Salt & Light. 56p. (gr. 6up). 1983. pap. 3.00 (ISBN 0-911423-00-1). Bible-Speak.
Brown, Christopher, as told by. Favorite Bible Stories, Vol. 2. (Illus.). 24p. (gr. 3-7). 1985. pap. 2.25 (ISBN 0-89954-416-9). Antioch Pub Co.
Brunelli, Roberto. The Macmillan Book of Three Hundred & Sixty-Six Bible Stories. Clark, Colin, tr. from ITA. Rothero, Chris, illus. LC 88-3507. 192p. (gr. 1-3). 1988. bds. 12.95 (ISBN 0-689-71266-9, Aladdin). Macmillan Child Grp.
Bull, Geoffrey. I Wish I Lived When Noah Did. (gr. 1-6). 1975. 1.95 (ISBN 0-87508-887-2). Chr Lit.
Bull, Norman. Church of Jesus Grows. (gr. 2-7). pap. 10.95 (ISBN 0-7175-0454-9). Dufour.
—Prophets of the Jews. (gr. 2-7). pap. 10.95 (ISBN 0-7175-0979-6). Dufour.
Burke, Patricia A., et al. Adventures from God's Word. rev. ed. Miller, Marge, ed. (Illus.). 128p. (gr. 3). 1983. text ed. 9.95 (ISBN 0-87239-663-0, 2953). Standard Pub.
Burl Ives Bible-Time Stories, 9 bks. (gr. k-3). Set. 6.95 (ISBN 0-89191-299-1, 52993); pap. 14.95 ea., 32p., incl. cassette (52977). Cook.
Burns, Jim. The Greatest Stories Ever Told, Bk. II. (Illus.). 64p. (Orig.). (gr. 9 up). 1988. pap. 4.99 (ISBN 0-89081-640-9). Harvest Hse.
Butterworth, Nick & Inkpen, Mick. The Cat's Story - Jesus at the Wedding. (gr. 3-7). 1988. 4.95 (ISBN 0-310-55800-X, 19089). Zondervan.
—The Fox's Story: Jesus is Born. (gr. 3-7). 1988. 4.95 (ISBN 0-310-55790-9). Zondervan.
—The Mouse's Story: Jesus & the Storm. (gr. 3-7). 1988. 4.95 (ISBN 0-310-55810-7). Zondervan.
—The Nativity Play. Butterworth, Nick & Inkpen, Mick, illus. 32p. (gr. k-3). 1985. 11.95 (ISBN 0-316-11903-2). Little.
Carl, Angela R. & Holmes, Alice C. Growing with Bible Heroes: Grade 4. rev. ed. Miller, Marge, ed. (Illus.). 128p. (gr. 4). 1983. text ed. 9.95 (ISBN 0-87239-664-9, 2954). Standard Pub.
Chaikin, Miriam. Joshua in the Promised land. Frampton, David, illus. (gr. 3-8). 1982. 12.95 (ISBN 0-89919-120-7, Clarion). HM.
Chapman, Geoffrey. Book of Gospels. (Illus.). 672p. 1985. 95.00 (ISBN 0-225-66351-1). Harper SF.
Ching Yee, Janice. God's Busiest Angels. (Illus.). (gr. k-6). 1975. pap. 3.00 (ISBN 0-931420-09-1). Pi Pr.
—God's Naughtiest Angels. (Illus.). (gr. k-6). 1974. pap. 3.00 (ISBN 0-931420-08-3). Pi Pr.
Coe, Joyce. Jesus Rides into Jerusalem. (Illus.). 24p. (gr. k-4). 1987. pap. 1.39 (ISBN 0-570-09007-5, 59-1435). Concordia.
Coleman, Sheila S. The Best Story about Jesus. Ham, John, illus. 32p. (gr. k-2). 1989. pasted 1.99 (ISBN 0-87403-602-X, 3862). Standard Pub.
Coleman, William. Brave & Bashful. (gr. 3-7). 1988. pap. 3.69 (ISBN 0-89191-988-0, Chariot Bks). Cook.
—Kings & Critters. (gr. 3-7). 1989. pap. 3.69 (ISBN 0-89191-989-9, Chariot Bks). Cook.
Couch, Frank. Children's Bible in Story. Codd, Michael, illus. 320p. 1989. 12.95 (ISBN 0-8249-8355-6). Ideals.
Coville, Katherine D., illus. Bible Stories from the Old Testament. Hayward, Linda, retold by. (ps-2). 1987. 11.95 (ISBN 0-448-10351-6, G&D). Putnam Pub Group.
Crain, Steve. Bible Fun Book, No. 7. 32p. (Orig.). (gr. k-4). 1981. oversized saddle stitched 1.19 (ISBN 0-87123-766-0). Bethany Hse.
Crompton, T., illus. The Good Samaritan: Retold by Catherine Storr. 32p. (gr. k-4). 1984. 14.65 (ISBN 0-8172-1988-9, Raintree Childrens Books Belitha Press Ltd. - London). Raintree Pubs.
Daly, Kathleen N. Baby Jesus. Cummins, Jim, illus. 14p. (ps-2). bds. 2.95 (ISBN 0-528-82491-0). Checkerboard Pr.
—Daniel in the Lion's Den. Cummins, Jim, illus. 14p. (ps-2). bds. 2.95 (ISBN 0-528-82492-9). Checkerboard Pr.
—Jonah & the Great Fish. Cummins, Jim, illus. 14p. (ps-2). bds. 2.95 (ISBN 0-528-82495-3). Checkerboard Pr.
—Noah & the Ark. Cummins, Jim, illus. 14p. (gr. 3-7). bds. 2.95 (ISBN 0-528-82490-2). Checkerboard Pr.
Dampier, Joseph H. Workbook on Christian Doctrine. 64p. (Orig.). (gr. 6 up). 1943. pap. 3.95 (ISBN 0-87239-072-1, 3343). Standard Pub.
Daniel, Rebecca. Abraham. Kreitman, Kay M., illus. 32p. (gr. 2-7). 1983. wkbk. 5.95 (ISBN 0-86653-133-5, SS 802). Good Apple.
—Adam & Eve. Kreitman, Kay M., illus. 32p. (gr. 2-7). 1983. wkbk. 5.95 (ISBN 0-86653-131-9, SS 800). Good Apple.
—Daniel. Kreitman, Kay M., illus. 32p. (gr. 2-7). 1983. wkbk. 5.95 (ISBN 0-86653-140-8, SS 809). Good Apple.
—David. Kreitman, Kay M., illus. 32p. (gr. 2-7). 1983. wkbk. 5.95 (ISBN 0-86653-138-6, SS 807). Good Apple.
—Jonah. Kreitman, Kay M., illus. 32p. (gr. 2-7). 1983. wkbk. 5.95 (ISBN 0-86653-141-6, SS 810). Good Apple.
—Joseph. Kreitman, Kay M., illus. 32p. (gr. 2-7). 1983. wkbk. 5.95 (ISBN 0-86653-134-3, SS 803). Good Apple.
—Joshua. Kreitman, Kay M., illus. 32p. (gr. 2-7). 1983. wkbk. 5.95 (ISBN 0-86653-136-X, SS 805). Good Apple.
—Moses. Kreitman, Kay M., illus. 32p. (gr. 2-7). 1983. wkbk. 5.95 (ISBN 0-86653-135-1, SS 804). Good Apple.
—Noah. Kreitman, Kay M., illus. 32p. (gr. 7-12). 1983. wkbk. 5.95 (ISBN 0-86653-132-7, SS 801). Good Apple.
—Samson. Kreitman, Kay M., illus. 32p. (gr. 7-12). 1983. wkbk. 5.95 (ISBN 0-86653-137-8, SS 806). Good Apple.
—Solomon. Kreitman, Kay M., illus. 32p. (gr. 2-7). 1983. wkbk. 5.95 (ISBN 0-86653-139-4, SS 808). Good Apple.
—Women of the Old Testament. Kreitman, Kay M., illus. 32p. (gr. 2-7). 1983. wkbk. 5.95 (ISBN 0-86653-142-4, SS 811). Good Apple.
Daughters of St. Paul. Adventures of Peter & Paul. Gandolfo, C., illus. 120p. (gr. 5-9). 1984. 5.00 (ISBN 0-8198-0726-5). Dghtrs St Paul.
Davidson, Alice J. Alice in Bibleland Storybooks: Prayers & Graces. Marshall, Victoria, illus. 32p. (gr. 3 up). 1986. 4.95 (ISBN 0-8378-5078-9). Gibson.
—Alice in Bibleland Storybooks: Story of David & Goliath. Marshall, Victoria, illus. 32p. (gr. 3 up). 1985. 4.95 (ISBN 0-8378-5070-3). Gibson.
—Alice in Bibleland Storybooks: Story of Daniel & the Lions. Marshall, Victoria, illus. 32p. (gr. 3 up). 1986. 4.95 (ISBN 0-8378-5079-7). Gibson.
—Alice in Bibleland Storybooks: Story of Baby Jesus. Marshall, Victoria, illus. 32p. (gr. 3 up). 1985. 4.95 (ISBN 0-8378-5072-X). Gibson.
—Alice in Bibleland Storybooks: Story of Baby Moses. Marshall, Victoria, illus. 32p. (gr. 3 up). 1985. 4.95 (ISBN 0-8378-5071-1). Gibson.
—Alice in Bibleland Storybooks: Story of Jonah. Marshall, Victoria, illus. 32p. (gr. 3 up). 1984. 4.95 (ISBN 0-8378-5068-1). Gibson.
—Alice in Bibleland Storybooks: Story of Noah. Marshall, Victoria, illus. 32p. (gr. 3 up). 1984. 4.95 (ISBN 0-8378-5067-3). Gibson.
—Alice in Bibleland Storybooks: Story of the Loaves & Fishes. Marshall, Victoria, illus. 32p. (ps-3). 1985. 4.95 (ISBN 0-8378-5073-8). Gibson.
—Alice in Bibleland Storybooks: The Lord's Prayer. (Illus.). (gr. 3 up). 1989. 4.95 (ISBN 0-8378-1868-0). Gibson.
—Alice in Bibleland Storybooks: The Story of Isaac & Rebeckah. (Illus.). (gr. 3 up). 1989. 4.95 (ISBN 0-8378-1852-4). Gibson.
—Alice in Bibleland Storybooks: The Story of Jesus & His Disciples. (Illus.). (gr. 3 up). 1989. 4.95 (ISBN 0-8378-1860-5). Gibson.
—Alice in Bibleland Storybooks: The Story of Ruth & Naomi. (Illus.). (gr. 3 up). 1989. 4.95 (ISBN 0-8378-1855-9). Gibson.
—Alice in Bibleland Storybooks: The Story of Exodus. (Illus.). (gr. 3 up). 1989. 4.95 (ISBN 0-8378-1849-4). Gibson.
—Alice in Bibleland Storybooks: The Story of Joshua. (Illus.). (gr. 3 up). 1989. 4.95 (ISBN 0-8378-1850-8). Gibson.
—Alice in Bibleland Storybooks: The Story of Esther. (Illus.). (gr. 3 up). 1989. 4.95 (ISBN 0-8378-1851-6). Gibson.
—Alice in Bibleland Storybooks: The Story of Paul. (Illus.). (gr. 3 up). 1989. 4.95 (ISBN 0-8378-1853-2). Gibson.
—Alice in Bibleland Storybooks: The Story of the Good Samaritan. (Illus.). (gr. 3 up). 1989. 4.95 (ISBN 0-8378-1854-0). Gibson.
—Alice in Bibleland Storybooks: The Story of the Lost Sheep. (Illus.). (gr. 3 up). 1989. 4.95 (ISBN 0-8378-1865-6). Gibson.
—Alice in Bibleland Storybooks: The Story of the Prodigal Son. (Illus.). (gr. 3 up). 1989. 4.95 (ISBN 0-8378-1848-6). Gibson.
—Alice in Bibleland Storybooks: The Story of the Tower of Babel. (Illus.). (gr. 3 up). 1989. 4.95 (ISBN 0-8378-1866-4). Gibson.
Davoll, Barbara. The Potluck Supper. Hockerman, Dennis, illus. 1988. 4.95 (ISBN 0-685-22774-X); book & cassette 7.95 (ISBN 0-685-22775-8). Zondervan.
—The Shiny Red Sled. Hockerman, Dennis, illus. 24p. 1989. text ed. 5.99 (ISBN 0-89693-498-5); cassette 8.99 (ISBN 0-89693-031-9). Victor Bks.
Dean, Bessie. Paul's Letters of Love. (Illus.). 72p. (Orig.). (gr. k-5). 1981. pap. 5.95 (ISBN 0-88290-170-2). Horizon Utah.
Dede, Vivian H. Elizabeth's Christmas Story. LC 59-1430. (Illus.). 24p. (gr. k-4). 1987. pap. 1.39 (ISBN 0-570-09002-4, 59-1430). Concordia.
De Graaf, Anne. Believing the Truth. (Illus.). 32p. 1989. 4.95 (ISBN 0-310-52770-8). Zondervan.
—Following the Messiah. (Illus.). 32p. 1989. 4.95 (ISBN 0-310-52740-6). Zondervan.
De La Mare, Walter. Stories from the Bible: From the Garden of Eden to the Promised Land. Ardizzone, Edward, illus. 418p. (gr. 3 up). 1985. pap. 5.95 (ISBN 0-571-11086-X). Faber & Faber.
Dellinger, A. & Fletcher, S. N. T. Stories. (ps-3). pap. 0.59 (ISBN 0-570-08312-5, 56HH1444). Concordia.
—O. T. Heroes. (ps-3). pap. 0.59 (ISBN 0-570-08311-7, 56HH1443). Concordia.
Demaree, Doris C. Bible Boys & Girls. (Illus.). (gr. k-4). 1970. pap. 1.50 (ISBN 0-87162-002-2, D1443). Warner Pr.
—Bible Heroes. (gr. k-4). 1970. pap. 1.50 (ISBN 0-87162-004-9, D1444). Warner Pr.
—Exciting Adventures. (gr. k-4). 1974. pap. 1.50 (ISBN 0-87162-235-1, D1445). Warner Pr.
—Followers of God. (gr. k-4). 1974. pap. 1.50 (ISBN 0-87162-236-X, D1446). Warner Pr.
—Helping Others. (gr. k-4). 1970. pap. 1.50 (ISBN 0-87162-237-8, D1447). Warner Pr.
—Living for Jesus. (gr. k-4). 1974. pap. 1.50 (ISBN 0-87162-238-6, D1448). Warner Pr.
DePaola, Tomie. Noah & the Ark. DePaola, Tomie, illus. 40p. (Orig.). (ps-4). 1985. pap. 5.95 (ISBN 0-685-07222-3). Harper SF.
De Paola, Tomie. Queen Esther. rev. ed. Paola, Tomie de, illus. 40p. (Orig.). (gr. k-5). 1987. pap. 8.95 (ISBN 0-06-255540-5). Harper SF.
DePaola, Tomie. Tomie DePaola's Book of Bible Stories. 128p. 1990. 18.95 (ISBN 0-399-21690-1, Putnam). Putnam Pub Group.
DeVries, Betty. One Hundred One Bible Activity Sheets. 144p. (ps up). 1983. pap. 8.95 (ISBN 0-8010-2931-7). Baker Bk.
Doney, Meryl. Bible Stories for Children. 1991. 9.98 (ISBN 0-8317-0829-8). Smithmark.
—How the Bible Came to Us. (Illus.). 48p. (gr. 8 up). 1985. 13.95 (ISBN 0-85648-574-8). Lion USA.
Dowley, Tim. Jesus & the Big Picnic & Other Stories. Deverell, Richard & Deverell, Christine, illus. (gr. 1-7). 1987. pap. 8.95 (ISBN 0-8024-8488-3). Moody.
—Moses & the Great Escape. Deverell, Richard & Deverell, Christine, illus. (gr. 1-7). 1987. 8.95 (ISBN 0-8024-8487-5). Moody.
Draper, Edythe. Wonder. 448p. (gr. 1-4). 1984. 8.95 (ISBN 0-8423-8385-9). Tyndale.
Dugan, LeRoy, illus. Heroes of the New Testament Coloring Book. 96p. (Orig.). (gr. k-4). 1981. saddle-stitched 3.95 (ISBN 0-87123-701-6). Bethany Hse.
—Heroes of the Old Testament, No. 3. 96p. (Orig.). (gr. k-4). 1981. pap. 3.95 saddle-stitched (ISBN 0-87123-703-2). Bethany Hse.
Durepo, Martha. Our Bible. LC 86-17571. (ps). 1987. 5.95 (ISBN 0-8054-4175-1). Broadman.
Easterly, Lane, ed. Great Bible Stories for Children. (Illus.). (gr. 2-4). 9.95 (ISBN 0-8407-5351-9). Nelson.

Egermeier, Elsie E. Egermeier's Bible Story Book. 5th ed. Uptton, Clive, illus. LC 68-23397. (gr. k-6). 1969. 14. 95 (ISBN 0-87162-006-5, D2005); deluxe ed. 15.95 (ISBN 0-87162-007-3, D2006); pap. 8.95 (ISBN 0-87162-229-7, D2008). Warner Pr.
—Egermeier's Favorite Bible Stories. (gr. k-1). 1965. 7.95 (ISBN 0-87162-014-6, D3695). Warner Pr.
Enns, Peter. Stories to Remember: David, God's Champion. Ligon, Terry, illus. 32p. (ps-5). 1987. pap. 2.98 (ISBN 0-943593-04-2); cassette 5.98 (ISBN 0-943593-06-9); coloring bk. 0.98 (ISBN 0-943593-05-0). Kids Intl Inc.
—Stories to Remember: Here Comes Jesus. Ligon, Terry, illus. 32p. (ps-5). 1987. pap. 2.98 (ISBN 0-943593-12-3); coloring bk. 0.98 (ISBN 0-943593-13-1); cassette 5.98 (ISBN 0-943593-14-X). Kids Intl Inc.
Enns, Peter & Forsberg, Glen. Daniel & the Lions & Five Other Stories. Friesen, John H., illus. 24p. (ps-5). 1985. book & cassette 4.95 (ISBN 0-936215-04-6). STL Intl.
—Jesus Is Alive! & Five Other Stories. Friesen, John H., illus. 24p. (ps-5). 1985. book & cassette 4.95 (ISBN 0-936215-06-2). STL Intl.
—Six Stories of Jesus. Friesen, John H., illus. 24p. (ps-5). 1985. 4.95 (ISBN 0-936215-05-4); cassette incl. STL Intl.
Enns, Peter & Ligon, Terry. Stories to Remember: Look What God Made. (Illus.). 32p. (ps-5). 1987. pap. 2.98 (ISBN 0-943593-00-X); coloring bk. 0.98 (ISBN 0-943593-01-8); cassette 5.98 (ISBN 0-943593-02-6). Kids Intl Inc.
Evans, Shirlee. Tree Tall to the Rescue. Ponter, James, illus. LC 87-8615. 144p. (Orig.). (gr. 4-9). 1987. pap. 4.50 (ISBN 0-8361-3444-3). Herald Pr.
Eynon, Dana. Adventures Through the Bible. rev. ed. LC 79-1031. 176p. (gr. 3-6). 1980. pap. 7.95 tchr's book (ISBN 0-87239-378-X, 3234). Standard Pub.
Falk, Cathy. God's Care. 24p. (Orig.). (ps-k). 1983. pap. 1.79 (ISBN 0-87239-676-2, 2451). Standard Pub.
—God's Friends. 24p. (Orig.). (ps-k). 1983. pap. 1.79 (ISBN 0-87239-677-0, 2452). Standard Pub.
—God's Son. 24p. (Orig.). (ps-k). 1983. pap. 1.79 (ISBN 0-87239-678-9, 2453). Standard Pub.
—We Love God. 144p. (Orig.). (ps-k). 1983. pap. 7.95 (ISBN 0-87239-613-4, 3360). Standard Pub.
—We Please God. 24p. (Orig.). (ps-k). 1983. pap. 1.79 (ISBN 0-87239-679-7, 2454). Standard Pub.
Farber, Norma. All Those Mothers at the Manger. Lloyd, Megan, illus. LC 85-42610. 32p. (ps-1). 1985. PLB 12. 89 (ISBN 0-06-021870-3). HarpC Child Bks.
Favorite Bible Stories, Vol. 3. 1989. pap. 2.25 (ISBN 0-89954-597-1). Antioch Pub Co.
Ferntheil, Carol. Bible Adventures Basic Bible Reader. 128p. (gr. 2-4). 1985. pap. 4.95 (2757). Standard Pub.
Finley, Tom. Incredible Stories: Twenty Active Bible Lessons for Your 8 to 12-year-olds. 96p. 1991. pap. 7.95 (ISBN 0-310-53391-0, Pub. by Youth Spec). Zondervan.
Flanders, Michael. Captain Noah & His Floating Zoo. LC 73-7053. (gr. 4-6). 1973. 6.95 (ISBN 0-672-51841-4, Bobbs). Macmillan.
Fletcher, Mary. My Very First Prayer-Time Book. (gr. k-4). 1984. 1.59 (ISBN 0-87162-274-2, D8503). Warner Pr.
Fletcher, Sarah. My Bible Story Book. LC 73-91810. (Illus.). 72p. (ps-3). 1974. 9.95 (ISBN 0-570-03423-X, 56-1171). Concordia.
—My Stories About Jesus. Kueker, Don, illus. 32p. (ps-3). 1974. pap. 2.29 (ISBN 0-570-03427-2, 56-1182). Concordia.
—The Welcoming Party: A Christmas Story. Baker, Arthur, illus. 32p. (gr. k-3). 1990. saddle stitched 1.25 (ISBN 0-8028-5057-X). Eerdmans.
Frank, Penny. Daniel in the Lion's Den. (Illus.). 24p. (gr. 1 up). 1987. 3.95 (ISBN 0-85648-752-X). Lion USA.
—David & Goliath. (Illus.). 24p. (gr. 1 up). 1986. 3.95 (ISBN 0-85648-743-0). Lion USA.
—Elijah & the Prophets of Baal. (Illus.). 24p. (gr. 1-4). 1987. 3.95 (ISBN 0-85648-747-3). Lion USA.
—Gideon Fights for God. (Illus.). 24p. (gr. 1-4). 1987. 3.95 (ISBN 0-85648-738-4). Lion USA.
—Jeremiah & the Great Disaster. (Illus.). 24p. (gr. 1-4). 1987. 3.95 (ISBN 0-85648-750-3). Lion USA.
—Jesus on Trial. (Illus.). 24p. (gr. 1 up). 1987. 3.95 (ISBN 0-85648-772-4). Lion USA.
—Jesus the Teacher. (Illus.). 24p. (gr. 1 up). 1987. 3.95 (ISBN 0-85648-760-0). Lion USA.
—Jonah Runs Away. (Illus.). 24p. (gr. 1-4). 1987. 3.95 (ISBN 0-85648-755-4). Lion USA.
—King David. (Illus.). 24p. (gr. 1 up). 1987. 3.95 (ISBN 0-85648-744-9). Lion USA.
—Mary, Martha & Lazarus. (Illus.). 24p. (gr. 1-4). 1987. 3.95 (ISBN 0-85648-769-4). Lion USA.
—Naaman's Dreadful Secret. (Illus.). 24p. (gr. 1 up). 1987. 3.95 (ISBN 0-85648-748-1). Lion USA.
—Nehemiah's Greatest Day. (Illus.). (gr. 1 up). 1987. pap. 3.95 (ISBN 0-85648-754-6). Lion USA.
—Paul & Friends. (Illus.). 24p. (gr. 1 up). 1987. 3.95 (ISBN 0-85648-776-7). Lion USA.
—Paul the Prisoner. (Illus.). 24p. (gr. 1-4). 1987. 3.95 (ISBN 0-85648-777-5). Lion USA.
—The Story of the Two Brothers. (Illus.). 24p. (gr. 4 up). 1987. 3.95 (ISBN 0-85648-765-1). Lion USA.
Garrison, Eileen & Albanese, Gayle. Eucharistic Manual for Children. Dickinson, Charles, illus. LC 84-60217. 28p. (Orig.). (gr. 1-8). 1984. pap. 4.50 (ISBN 0-8192-1343-8). Morehouse Pub.
Geller, Norman. The First Seven Days. (Illus.). 32p. (gr. 1-4). 1983. pap. 6.95 (ISBN 0-915753-00-6). N Geller Pub.
Gellman, Marc. Does God Have a Big Toe? Stories about Stories in the Bible. De Mejo, Oscar, illus. LC 89-1893. 96p. (gr. 4 up). 1989. 14.95 (ISBN 0-06-022432-0); PLB 14.89 (ISBN 0-06-022433-9). HarpC Child Bks.
Gibson, Katherine. The Tall Book of Bible Stories. Chaiko, Ted, illus. LC 57-10952. 128p. (gr. k-3). 1957. 7.95i (ISBN 0-06-021935-1); PLB 10.89 (ISBN 0-06-021936-X). HarpC Child Bks.
Graaf, Anne de. Canaan: Soldiers of the Lord. Montero, Jose P., illus. (gr. 5-7). 1988. 4.95 (ISBN 0-310-52650-7). Zondervan.
—Egypt: The Years from Joseph to Moses. Montero, Jose P., illus. 32p. (gr. 5-7). 1988. 4.95 (ISBN 0-310-52620-5). Zondervan.
—Genesis: The Beginning. Montero, Jose P., illus. (gr. 5-7). 1988. 4.95 (ISBN 0-310-52600-0). Zondervan.
—Israel: Brother Against Brother. Montero, Jose P., illus. (gr. 5-7). 1988. 4.95 (ISBN 0-310-52610-8). Zondervan.
—Wandering: The Promised Land. Montero, Jose P., illus. (gr. 5-7). 1988. 4.95 (ISBN 0-310-52640-X). Zondervan.
Grant, Amy. Heart to Heart. 96p. 1989. write for info. (ISBN 0-8499-0710-1). Word Bks.
Grant, Myrna. Ivan & the American Journey. LC 88-71169. (gr. 3-7). 1988. 4.95 (ISBN 0-88419-221-0, Creation Hse). Strang Comms Co.
—Ivan & the Hidden Bible. LC 88-71169. (gr. 3-7). 1988. 4.95 (ISBN 0-88419-222-9, Creation Hse). Strang Comms Co.
—Ivan & the Secret in the Suitcase. LC 88-71168. (gr. 3-7). 1988. 4.95 (ISBN 0-88419-223-7, Creation Hse). Strang Comms Co.
Greene, Carol. The Easter Women. (Illus.). 24p. (gr. k-4). 1987. pap. 1.39 (ISBN 0-570-09003-2, 59-1431). Concordia.
Groth, Lynn. With You, Dear Child, in Mind. 16p. (Orig.). (ps). 1985. pap. 1.25 (ISBN 0-938272-77-2). Wels Board.
Gundersen, Bev. Bible Buddies Calendar. Hand, Judy, illus. 32p. (gr. 3-6). 1989. activity 1.95 (ISBN 0-87403-550-3, 2066). Standard Pub.
Haan, Sheri D. Precious Moments Stories from the Bible. Butcher, Samuel, illus. 288p. (gr. 1-6). 1987. 14.95 (ISBN 0-8010-4311-5). Baker Bk.
Haiz, Danah. Jonah's Journey. Hechtkopf, H., illus. LC 72-268. 32p. (gr. k-5). 1973. PLB 6.95 (ISBN 0-8225-0362-X). Lerner Pubns.
Hall, Sarabel. Hannah Hummingbird. Lobley, Robert E., illus. LC 88-30357. 16p. (Orig.). (gr. 1-3). 1989. pap. 6.95 (ISBN 0-86534-131-1). Sunstone Pr.
Hamilton, Dorothy. Jim Musco. LC 71-189563. (Illus.). 104p. (gr. 4-9). 1972. pap. 3.95 (ISBN 0-8361-1668-2). Herald Pr.
Hanna-Barbera Staff. The Greatest Adventure: Stories from the Bible, 3 bks, Vol. 1: Moses; Samson & Delilah; Joshua & the Battle of Jericho. Incl. 2 audiocassettes. pap. 9.95 (ICN 15765X). Abingdon.
Hanna-Barbera, illus. Daniel & the Lion's Den. (Orig.). (gr. k up). 4.95 (ISBN 0-687-15746-3). Abingdon.
—Joshua & the Battle of Jericho. (Orig.). (gr. k up). 4.95 (ISBN 0-687-15743-9). Abingdon.
—Moses Let My People Go. 48p. (Orig.). (gr. k up). 4.95 (ISBN 0-687-15740-4). Abingdon.
—Noah's Ark. (Orig.). (gr. k up). 4.95 (ISBN 0-687-15744-7). Abingdon.
—Samson & Delilah. (Orig.). (gr. k up). 4.95 (ISBN 0-687-15745-5). Abingdon.
Hayes & Hook. Meu Livro de Historias Biblicas. (POR.). (gr. k-6). 1979. 3.00 (ISBN 0-8297-0758-1). Life Pubs Intl.
Hayes, Wanda. A Child's First Book of Bible Stories. LC 83-664. (Illus.). 128p. (ps). 1983. text ed. 9.95 (ISBN 0-87239-659-2, 2949). Standard Pub.
Haywood, Carolyn. Make a Joyful Noise! Bible Verses for Children. LC 84-2401. (Illus.). 96p. (gr. 3-7). 1984. 11.95 (ISBN 0-664-32711-7, Westminster). Westminster John Knox.
Head, Constance. Jeremiah & the Fall of Jerusalem. (Illus.). 24p. (gr. k-4). 1986. pap. 1.39 saddlestitched (ISBN 0-570-06201-2, 59-1424). Concordia.
Heine, Helme. One Day in Paradise. Heine, Helme, illus. LC 85-72492. 32p. (ps-4). 1986. 13.95 (ISBN 0-689-50394-6, M K McElderry). Macmillan Child Grp.

Henley, Karyn. The Beginner's Bible: Timeless Children's Stories. Davis, Dennas, illus. 528p. (ps-5). 1989. 15.95 (ISBN 0-945564-31-7). Questar Pubs. STILL NUMBER ONE on the children's bestseller list in BOOKSTORE JOURNAL (ever since March 1990), this one has sold more than 400,000 copies! Ideal for ages two through eight, THE BEGINNER'S BIBLE includes ninety-five Bible stories told chronologically from Genesis to Revelation. Children will love the more than five hundred pages of Bible stories - with a full-sized, full-color picture on every page! There's also a thorough index to "Favorite Characters, Topics, & Stories," & each story is tagged with a reference line indicating the story's Scripture source. With its clear, young-hearted writing style & charming illustrations, this book is a proven winner!
Publisher Provided Annotation.

Hilliard, Susan E. Death or Deliverance. Ostendorf, Edward, illus. 144p. (gr. 4-7). 1990. pap. 3.95 (ISBN 0-87403-728-X, 24-03988). Standard Pub.
—The Dreamer. Ostendorf, Edward, illus. 144p. (gr. 4-7). 1990. pap. 3.95 (ISBN 0-87403-726-3, 24-03986). Standard Pub.
—Reap the Whirlwind. Ostendorf, Edward, illus. 144p. (gr. 4-7). 1990. pap. 3.95 (ISBN 0-87403-727-1, 24-03987). Standard Pub.
—Trial by Fire. Ostendorf, Edward, illus. 144p. (gr. 4-7). 1990. pap. 3.95 (ISBN 0-87403-725-5). Standard Pub.
Hirsh, Marilyn, illus. The Tower of Babel. LC 80-21196. 32p. (gr. k-3). 1981. reinforced bdg. 6.95 (ISBN 0-8234-0380-7). Holiday.
Hockerman, Dennis. Baby Moses in the Basket. LC 87-70410. 1987. 3.95 (ISBN 1-55513-783-0, Chariot Bks). Cook.
—The Little Children Visit Jesus. LC 87-70411. 1987. 3.95 (ISBN 1-55513-779-2, Chariot Bks). Cook.
—A Young Girl Helps Naaman. LC 87-70409. 1987. 3.95 (ISBN 1-55513-089-5, Chariot Bks). Cook.
Hollingsworth, T. R. Ezra of Galilee. 80p. (Orig.). (gr. 3-6). 1987. pap. text ed. 6.95 (ISBN 0-9617668-0-8). Hollybridge Pubns.
Holt, Pat. Gideon: God's Warrior. Brown, David S., illus. 32p. (gr. 1-6). 1986. 0.50 (ISBN 0-687-14220-2). Abingdon.
Horton, Edna C. & Hadley, Roberta. El Cuidado de Dios. Villasenor, Emma Z., tr. (Illus.). (gr. 1-3). 1983. pap. 1.40 (ISBN 0-311-38555-9). Casa Bautista.
Hunt, P. Bible Stories from the Old Testament. (Illus.). (gr. k-5). 4.98 (ISBN 0-517-43909-3). Outlet Bk Co.
Hunter, Emily. The Bible-Time Nursery Rhyme Book. 96p. 1988. 11.99 (ISBN 0-89081-404-X). Harvest Hse.
Hurlbut, Jesse L. The Bedtime Bible Story Book. Sortor, Toni, ed. Arbuckle, Kathy, illus. 1989. text ed. 17.95 (ISBN 1-55748-096-6); pap. text ed. 9.95 (ISBN 1-55748-095-8); leather bdg. 24.95 (ISBN 1-55748-113-X). Barbour & Co.
Hutton, Warwick. Adam & Eve: The Bible Story. Hutton, Warwick, illus. LC 86-27690. 32p. 1987. 13.95 (ISBN 0-689-50433-0, M K McElderry). Macmillan Child Grp.
—Jonah & the Great Fish. LC 83-15477. (Illus.). 32p. 1984. 13.95 (ISBN 0-689-50283-4, M K McElderry). Macmillan Child Grp.
—Moses in the Bulrushes. Hutton, Warwick, illus. LC 85-72261. 32p. 1986. 13.95 (ISBN 0-689-50393-8, M K McElderry). Macmillan Child Grp.
Ife, Elaine & Sutton, Rosalind. Now You Can Read Stories from the Bible: Moses the Leader. (Illus.). 208p. (gr. 2-4). 1984. 9.95 (ISBN 0-8407-5396-9). Nelson.
Iguchi, Bunshu. The Tiny Sheep. Iguchi, Bunshu, illus. 24p. (ps up). 1986. 9.95 (ISBN 0-8170-1108-0). Judson.
Ingram, Kristen J. Bible Stories for the Church Year. Russell, Joseph P., ed. LC 83-20135. 184p. (Orig.). (gr. 1-6). 1987. pap. 11.95 (ISBN 0-86683-537-7). Harper SF.
International Children's Story Bible. 240p. 1990. write for info. (ISBN 0-8499-0784-5). Word Bks.
Jahsman, Alan H. Holy Bible for Children. (gr. 3-8). 1977. 15.95 (ISBN 0-570-03465-5, 56-1297). Concordia.
Jones, Mary A. Favorite Bible Stories & Verses. 112p. (ps up). 1986. write for info. (ISBN 0-02-689034-8). Macmillan.
Kaiser, Judith B. Quick-Line Stories for Young Children. 1975. spiral bdg. 3.95 (ISBN 0-916406-12-1). Accent Bks.
Kauffman, Suzanne. God Comforts His People: Activity Book. Converse, James, illus. 84p. (Orig.). (gr. k-6). 1986. pap. 3.00 (ISBN 0-8361-3411-7). Herald Pr.
Kendall, Joan. The Story of Samuel. (gr. k-4). 1984. 1.59 (ISBN 0-87162-271-8, D8500). Warner Pr.
Kingsley, Stuart. My Name Is Jesus. (Illus.). 44p. (gr. 3 up). 1988. 6.95 (ISBN 1-55523-127-6). Winston-Derek.
Knecht, F. J. Child's Bible History. Schumacher, Philip, tr. (Illus.). (gr. 5). 1973. pap. 4.00 (ISBN 0-89555-005-9). TAN Bks Pubs.
Knowles, Andrew. The Crossroad Children's Bible. (Illus.). 448p. (gr. 4-8). 1982. pap. 9.95 (ISBN 0-8245-0473-9). Crossroad NY.
Kohls, Tom. Gathering Fruit. 31p. 1987. pap. 3.25 (ISBN 0-8163-0701-6). Pacific Pr Pub Assn.
Kolbrek, Loyal. The Day God Made It Rain. (gr. k-2). 1977. pap. 1.39 (ISBN 0-570-06108-3, 59-1226). Concordia.
—Paul Believes in Jesus. (Illus.). 24p. (gr. k-4). 1987. pap. 1.39 (ISBN 0-570-09008-3, 59-1436). Concordia.

Kostich, Beverly E. Stepping into the Bible. (ps-6). 1988. pap. 2.95 (ISBN 0-687-40060-0). Abingdon.
Kuykendall, Carolyn. Babies of the Bible. Hutton, Kathryn, illus. 24p. (ps-2). 1986. 1.99 (ISBN 0-87403-021-8, 3481). Standard Pub.
Larsen, Sandy. Running the Race: Keeping the Faith. (Illus.). 64p. (Orig.). (gr. 6-12). 1986. pap. 2.95 (ISBN 0-87788-740-3); tchr's. ed. 4.95 (ISBN 0-87788-741-1). Shaw Pubs.
Lashbrook, Marilyn. Don't Rock the Boat: The Story of the Miraculous Catch. Britt, Stephanie M., illus. LC 88-63779. 32p. (ps). 1989. 5.95 (ISBN 0-86606-435-4, 867). Roper Pr.
—God, Please Send Fire: Elijah & the Prophets of Baal. Sharp, Chris, illus. LC 90-60458. 32p. (gr. k-3). 1990. 5.95 (ISBN 0-86606-440-0, 871). Roper Pr.
—Now I See: The Story of the Man Born Blind. Britt, Stephanie M., illus. LC 88-62520. 32p. (ps). 1989. 5.95 (ISBN 0-86606-437-0, 869). Roper Pr.
Le Blanc, Andre, illus. Great Adventures from the Bible. 200p. (Orig.). (gr. 1-8). 1984. pap. 6.95 (ISBN 0-89191-848-5). Cook.
Lehman, Elsie E. God Sends His Son Activity Book. 80p. (Orig.). (gr. 3-9). 1987. pap. 3.00 (ISBN 0-8361-3429-X). Herald Pr.
—God's Wisdom & Power Activity Book. 80p. (ps-1). 1985. pap. 3.00 (ISBN 0-8361-3391-9). Herald Pr.
Lehn, Cornelia. God Keeps His Promise: A Bible Story Book for Young Children. Darwin, Beatrice, illus. LC 76-90377. (gr. k-4). 1970. 12.95 (ISBN 0-87303-291-8). Faith & Life.
Lepon, Shoshana. The Ten Tests of Abraham. Forst, Siegmund, illus. 32p. (Orig.). (gr. k-4). 1986. 7.95 (ISBN 0-317-52412-7); pap. 5.95 (ISBN 0-910818-67-3). Judaica Pr.
Lewis, Shari & Henderson, Florence. One-Minute Bible Stories: New Testament. Ewing, C. S., illus. LC 86-6401. 48p. (ps-3). 1986. PLB 7.95 (ISBN 0-385-23286-1); pap. 7.99 (ISBN 0-385-23287-X). Doubleday.
Linam, Gail. God's People: A Book of Children's Sermons. LC 85-25736. (Orig.). (ps-5). 1986. pap. 4.95 (ISBN 0-8054-4928-0). Broadman.
Lindvall, Ella K. Read-Aloud Bible Stories, Vol. 1. LC 82-2114. 160p. (ps). 1982. 16.95 (ISBN 0-8024-7163-3). Moody.
—Read Aloud Bible Stories, Vol. 3. (ps-3). 1990. 17.95 (ISBN 0-8024-7165-X). Moody.
Linville, Barbara. Christy's Pouting Again. McCallum, Joanne, created by. & illus. 32p. (gr. k-2). 1989. 2.95 (ISBN 0-87403-627-5, 3891). Standard Pub.
—Joey's Too Much TV. McCallum, Joanne, created by. & illus. 32p. (gr. k-2). 1989. 2.95 (ISBN 0-87403-628-3, 3892). Standard Pub.
—Tommy's Afraid to Try. McCallum, Joanne, created by. & illus. 32p. (gr. k-2). 1989. 2.95 (ISBN 0-87403-630-5). Standard Pub.
Little, Emily. David & the Giant. Wilhelm, Hans, illus. LC 86-22079. 48p. (ps-1). 1987. lib. bdg. 6.99 (ISBN 0-394-98867-1, Random Juv); pap. 2.95 (ISBN 0-394-88867-7, Random Juv). Random.
Lockwood, Barbara & McAuley, Marilyn. Bible Surprises. LC 87-71384. 1988. bds. 4.95 (ISBN 1-55513-120-4, Chariot Bks). Cook.
The Lost Son's House. (ps-1). 1988. 3.95 (ISBN 0-8024-0844-3). Moody.
Lovik, Craig J. The Exodus. (Illus.). 24p. (gr. k-4). 1987. pap. 1.39 (ISBN 0-570-09001-6, 59-1429). Concordia.
Lysne, Mary E. Food, Clothes, & Homes of Bible Times. (Illus.). 24p. (gr. k-2). 1989. wkbk. 1.79 (ISBN 0-87403-553-8, 2033). Standard Pub.
McCall, Yvonne H. The Story of Jacob, Rachel & Leah. (Illus.). 24p. (gr. k-4). 1986. pap. 1.39 saddlestitched (ISBN 0-570-06205-5, 59-1428). Concordia.
McElroy. Jesus Forgives Peter. 24p. (Orig.). (gr. k-4). 1985. pap. 1.39 (ISBN 0-570-06192-X, 59-1293). Concordia.
MacHaster, Eve B. God Comforts His People. Converse, James, illus. LC 95-835. 176p. (Orig.). (gr. 3 up). 1985. pap. 5.95 (ISBN 0-8361-3393-5). Herald Pr.
McKellar, Shona. The Beginning of the Rainbow. Kasuya, Masahiro, illus. LC 81-7954. (ps-2). 1982. 8.95g (ISBN 0-687-02770-5). Abingdon.
Macmaster, Eve. God Gives the Land. Converse, James, photos by. LC 83-182. (Illus.). 168p. (Orig.). (ps-1). 1983. pap. 5.95 (ISBN 0-8361-3332-3). Herald Pr.
—God Rescues His People: Stories of God & His People: Exodus, Leviticus, Numbers & Deuteronomy. Converse, James, illus. LC 82-2849. 176p. (Orig.). (ps-1). 1982. pap. 5.95 (ISBN 0-8361-1994-0). Herald Pr.
—God's Chosen King. Converse, James, illus. LC 83-12736. 190p. (Orig.). (gr. 5-6). 1983. pap. 5.95 (ISBN 0-8361-3344-7). Herald Pr.
—God's Justice. Converse, James, illus. LC 84-20514. 168p. (Orig.). (ps-1). 1984. pap. 5.95 (ISBN 0-8361-3381-1). Herald Pr.
McMaster, Eve. God's Wisdom & Power. Converse, James, illus. LC 84-8974. 168p. (Orig.). (gr. 3-8). 1984. pap. 5.95 (ISBN 0-8361-3362-5). Herald Pr.
MacMaster, Eve B. God Builds His Church. Converse, James, illus. LC 87-2875. 184p. (Orig.). (gr. 3 up). 1987. pap. 5.95 (ISBN 0-8361-3446-X). Herald Pr.
—God Sends His Son. Converse, James, illus. LC 86-18342. 160p. (Orig.). (gr. 3-9). 1986. pap. 5.95 (ISBN 0-8361-3420-6). Herald Pr.
—God's Suffering Servant. Converse, James, illus. LC 86-19526. 120p. (Orig.). (gr. 3-9). 1987. pap. 5.95 (ISBN 0-8361-3422-2). Herald Pr.
Mann, Victor. He Remembered to Say "Thank You" (Illus.). 32p. (ps-4). 1976. pap. 1.39 (ISBN 0-570-06103-2, 59-1221). Concordia.
Marquardt, Mervin A. The Temptation of Jesus. (Illus.). 24p. (gr. k-4). 1986. pap. 1.39 saddlestitched (ISBN 0-570-06204-7, 59-1427). Concordia.
Marquart, M. Jesus' Second Family. (gr. k-2). 1977. pap. 1.39 (ISBN 0-570-06111-3, 59-1229). Concordia.
Marshall, Catherine. Catherine Marshall's Story Bible. 200p. (ps-5). 1985. pap. 10.95 (ISBN 0-380-69961-3). Avon.
—Catherine Marshall's Story Bible. (Illus.). 197p. (gr. 1-5). 1984. pap. 10.95 (Chosen Bks). Revell.
Martin, Bill. Fit for the King. Haynes, Glenda, ed. Sweeney, Hazel, illus. 384p. (Orig.). (gr. 7 up). pap. 11.50 (ISBN 0-89114-154-5). Baptist Pub Hse.
Marxhausen, Evelyn. Simeon & the Baby Jesus. (Illus.). 24p. (gr. k-4). 1986. pap. 1.39 saddlestitched (ISBN 0-570-06202-0, 59-1425). Concordia.
Mary & Josephs Home. (gr. 4-6). 1988. 3.95 (ISBN 0-8024-0843-5). Moody.
Maschke, Ruby. Children's Bible Stories Puzzle Book. 48p. 1986. pap. 2.95 (ISBN 0-87403-046-3, 2690). Standard Pub.
Maschke, Ruby A. Bible Puzzles for Children. 64p. (gr. 4-6). 1986. pap. 6.95 (ISBN 0-8170-1095-5). Judson.
Miller, Sarah W. Bible Dramas for Older Boys & Girls. LC 75-95409. (gr. 3-6). 1970. pap. 4.95 (ISBN 0-8054-7506-0). Broadman.
Mills, Brenda. My Bible Story Picture Book. (Illus.). 128p. (gr. k-5). 1982. text ed. 10.99 (ISBN 0-89081-319-1). Harvest Hse.
Mitchell, Robert E. Jesus the Good Shepherd. (Illus.). 24p. (ps-2). 1989. pap. 1.39 (ISBN 0-570-09018-0, 59-1441). Concordia.
Miyoshi, Sekiya. Jonah & the Big Fish. LC 81-3635. (ps-11). 1982. 8.95g (ISBN 0-687-20541-7). Abingdon.
Moeri, Louise. Save Queen of Sheba. 112p. 1990. pap. 2.95 (ISBN 0-380-71154-0, Camelot). Avon.
Molan, Chris, illus. Joseph the Dream Teller: Retold by Catererine Storr. 32p. (gr. k-4). 1984. 14.65 (ISBN 0-8172-1989-7, Raintree Children's Books Belitha Press Ltd. - London). Raintree Pubs.
Moncure, Jane B. I Learn to Read about Jesus: Primer. rev. ed. 128p. (gr. 1). 1983. text ed. 9.95 (ISBN 0-87239-660-6, 2950). Standard Pub.
Mueller, A. C. My Good Shepherd Bible Story Book. LC 70-89876. (gr. 3-5). 1969. bds. 14.95 (ISBN 0-570-03400-0, 56-1126). Concordia.
Mueller, Virginia. Jacob's Ladder. LC 59-1444. (Illus.). 24p. (ps-4). 1990. pap. 1.39 (ISBN 0-570-09021-0). Concordia.
Muir, Virginia J. The One Year Bible Story Book. Hook, Richard & Hook, Frances, illus. 384p. (gr. 5 up). 1988. 12.95 (ISBN 0-8423-2631-6). Tyndale.
Murphy, Elspeth C. Noah's Ark. Tallarico, Tony, illus. 1984. pap. 5.95 (ISBN 1-55513-653-2, 56531). Cook.
Myers, Bill. Jesus: An Eyewitness Account. 144p. (gr. 7 up). 1988. pap. 5.95 (ISBN 0-89693-606-6). Victor Bks.
Neff, Lavonne. God's Gift Baby. (gr. k-4). 1977. pap. 1.39 (ISBN 0-570-06113-X, 59-1230). Concordia.
Odor, Ruth. The Happiest Day. (ps-2). 1985. 5.95 (R4915). Standard Pub.
One Hundred Bible Stories. rev. ed. LC 66-10838. (King James Ed). (gr. 4-6). 1966. 7.95 (ISBN 0-570-03461-2, 56-1063); wkbk. 3.85 (ISBN 0-570-01519-7, 22-1201). Concordia.
O'Neal, Debbie T. My Read-&-Do Bible Storybook. Ebert, Len, illus. LC 89-15184. 128p. (Orig.). (gr. 3-8). 1989. pap. 13.95 kivar (ISBN 0-8066-2431-0, 9-2431). Augsburg Fortress.
Ottow, Harriett. Ruth's Adventures in Israel. LC 87-51493. 44p. (gr. k-2). 1988. 5.95 (ISBN 1-55523-133-0). Winston-Derek.
Overholtzer, Ruth. Joshua. Butcher, Sam & Anderasen, Norma, illus. 62p. (gr. k-6). 1987. pap. text ed. 9.45 (ISBN 1-55976-012-5). CEF Press.
Parker, Gary. Life Before Birth. (Orig.). (gr. 1-8). 1987. 9.95 (ISBN 0-89051-117-9); read-along cassette 5.95 (ISBN 0-317-56094-8). Master Bks.
Parry, Alan & Parry, Linda. The Beginning. (Illus.). 24p. (ps). 1990. pap. 0.99 (ISBN 0-8066-2473-6, 9-2473). Augsburg Fortress.
—The Farmer & the Seed. Parry, Alan, illus. 24p. (ps). 1990. pap. 0.99 (ISBN 0-8066-2474-4, 9-2474). Augsburg Fortress.
Patterson, Kathy C. & Niklaus, Phyllis M. Stories for Communication. Communication & Learning Innovators, Ltd. Staff, et al, eds. Rosado, Yvonne & Niklaus, Rita, illus. 13p. (ps-8). 1985. 6.00 (ISBN 0-932361-01-3); instr. manual, score sheets 80.00. Comm & Learning.
Patterson, Lillie. David, the Story of a King. Cox, Charles, illus. 96p. (gr. 3-6). 1985. PLB 3.95 (ISBN 0-687-10280-4). Abingdon.
Petach, Heidi. Jonah: The Inside Story. Petach, Heidi, illus. 32p. (gr. k-2). 1989. 1.99 (ISBN 0-87403-594-5, 3854). Standard Pub.
Pfrimmer, Mildred. Books to Learn & Live by, 5 bks. Incl. Bk. 1. The ABC's of Creation; Bk. 2. The ABC's of the Flood; Bk. 3. The Aardvark in the Art; Bk. 4. Elephant in Eden; Bk. 5. The Tale of the Whale. (gr. 3-9). 1977. Set. 17.50 (ISBN 0-685-80546-8). Triumph Pub.
Phillips, Cheryl & Harvey, Bonnie C., eds. My Jesus Pocketbook of God's Fruit. Fulton, Ginger A., illus. LC 83-50194. 32p. (ps-3). 1983. pap. 0.69 (ISBN 0-937420-08-5). Stirrup Assoc.
Phillips, Cheryl M. & Harvey, Bonnie C., eds. My Jesus Pocketbook of the Lord's Prayer. Fulton, Ginger A., illus. LC 83-50193. 32p. (ps-3). 1983. pap. 0.69 (ISBN 0-937420-07-7). Stirrup Assoc.
Picture Stories from the Bible. (gr. 4). pap. 5.00 (ISBN 0-87068-598-8). Ktav.
Pilling, Ann. Before I Go to Sleep: A Collection of Bible Stories, Poems & Prayers for Children. Denton, Kady M., illus. LC 89-7816. 96p. 1990. 14.95 (ISBN 0-517-58018-7); PLB 15.99 (ISBN 0-517-58019-5). Crown.
Pingry, Patricia. Daniel & the Lions. Britt, Stephanie, illus. 24p. (Orig.). (ps-3). 1988. pap. 3.95 (ISBN 0-8249-8179-0). Ideals.
—Jonah & the Big Fish. Venturi-Pickett, Stacy, illus. 24p. (Orig.). (ps-3). 1988. pap. 3.95 (ISBN 0-8249-8181-2). Ideals.
Pliskin, Jacqueline J. The Bible Story Activity Book. Pliskin, Jacqueline J., illus. 96p. (gr. 1-4). 1990. pap. 5.95 (ISBN 0-944007-01-5). Shapolsky Pubs.
Polyzoides, G. Stories from the Old Testament. (GRE., Illus.). 71p. (gr. 5 up). 3.20 (ISBN 0-686-80434-1). Divry.
Prescott, D. M. Noah & His Ark. (gr. k-4). 1984. 1.59 (ISBN 0-87162-273-4, D8502). Warner Pr.
Procter, Marjorie. The Little Grey Donkey. (gr. k-4). 1984. 1.59 (ISBN 0-87162-272-6, D8501). Warner Pr.
—The Little Lost Lamb. (gr. k-4). 1984. 1.59 (ISBN 0-87162-276-9, D8505). Warner Pr.
Promises for Kids from the Book. 240p. (gr. 1 up). 1988. 9.95 (ISBN 0-8423-5053-5). Tyndale.
Pucmer, Inka. Rampion. Pucmer, Inka, illus. 25p. (gr. 2-4). 1982. 22.95 (ISBN 0-88010-064-8, Pub. by Walter Keller Pr). Anthroposophic.
Randall, Louise A. Bible Heroes: Stories for Children Ages One to Six. Pardew, Louise, illus. LC 87-82112. 56p. (ps). 1988. pap. 4.95 (ISBN 0-88290-316-0). Horizon Utah.
—Scripture Stories for Tiny Tots: Read-Aloud Stories from the Bible for Children 1 to 6. LC 83-83429. 38p. (Orig.). (gr. k-3). 1983. pap. 3.95 (ISBN 0-88290-209-1). Horizon Utah.
Rathert, Donna R. Job. (Illus.). 24p. (ps-2). 1989. pap. 1.39 (ISBN 0-570-09017-2, 59-1440). Concordia.
Raub, Joyce. Cain & Abel. (Illus.). 24p. (gr. k-4). 1986. pap. 1.39 saddlestitched (ISBN 0-570-06199-7, 59-1422). Concordia.
Regehr, Lydia. Bible Riddles of Birds & Beasts & Creeping Things. (Illus.). 36p. (Orig.). (gr. 7-12). 1982. pap. 2.50 (ISBN 0-89323-030-8). Bible Memory.
Roberts, Jim & Scheck, Joann. Bible Pop-O-Rama Books, 2 vols. Incl. The Brightest Star (ISBN 0-8066-1601-6, 10-0915). (Illus.). (gr. 3 up). 1978. laminated 4.95 ea. (Augsburg). Augsburg Fortress.
Robertson, Jenny. Enciclopedia de Historias Biblicas. LaValle, Maria T., tr. King, Gordon, illus. (SPA.). 272p. (gr. 3-5). 1984. 17.00 (ISBN 0-311-03671-6). Casa Bautista.
Robison, Pamela. Abinadi, Man of God. (Orig.). (gr. 4-7). 1981. pap. 4.50 (ISBN 0-8309-0324-0). Herald Hse.
Rogers, Barbara. God Rescues His People Activity Book. 72p. (Orig.). (ps-1). 1983. pap. 3.00 (ISBN 0-8361-3338-2). Herald Pr.
Samuels, Ruth. Bible Stories for Jewish Children, 2 vols, No. 2. (Illus.). (gr. 3-5). 1973. 7.95x (ISBN 0-87068-965-7). Ktav.
Schoolland, Marian M. Marian's Big Book of Bible Stories. (gr. k-4). 1947. 16.95 (ISBN 0-8028-5003-0). Eerdmans.
Sherlock, Connie. Bible Families. (Illus.). 16p. (Orig.). (gr. 4-8). 1983. pap. 1.95 (ISBN 0-87239-688-6, 2792). Standard Pub.
Silverthorne, Sandy. The Great Bible Adventure. Silverthorne, Sandy, illus. LC 90-36385. 32p. (Orig.). (ps-8). 1990. 10.99 (ISBN 0-89081-842-8). Harvest Hse.
Simon, Mary M. God's Children Pray. 1989. 5.95 (ISBN 0-570-04173-2, 56-1633). Concordia.
Simonelee, Ken. Effy & the Little Glass Soldier. (Orig.). (gr. 5-9). 1991. pap. 4.00 (ISBN 0-915541-83-1). Star Bks Inc.
Singer, Isaac Bashevis. Why Noah Chose the Dove. Shub, Elizabeth, tr. from YID. Carle, Eric, illus. LC 73-87426. 32p. (ps-3). 1974. 13.95 (ISBN 0-374-38420-7); pap. 3.95 (ISBN 0-374-48382-5). FS&G.
—The Wicked City. Fisher, Leonard E., illus. LC 72-175144. 40p. (gr. 3 up). 1972. 8.95 (ISBN 0-374-38426-6). FS&G.
Smith, Katie. God Makes the World. Baker, Arthur, illus. 32p. (gr. k-3). 1990. saddle-stitched 1.25 (ISBN 0-8028-5055-3). Eerdmans.
Spier, Peter. Noah's Ark. Spier, Peter, illus. LC 76-43630. 44p. (gr. k-3). 1977. PLB 15.00 (ISBN 0-385-09473-6); pap. 13.99 (ISBN 0-385-12730-8). Doubleday.
Steiner, Rudolf. And It Came to Pass: An Old Testament, Reader for Children. 1973. lib. bdg. 79.95 (ISBN 0-87968-556-5). Krishna Pr.
Stern, Menahem. The Sun & the Clouds. (gr. 3-6). 1972. 6.95x (ISBN 0-87068-389-6). Ktav.
Stirrup Associates, Inc. Staff. My Jesus Pocketbook of Li'l Critters. Phillips, Cheryl M., ed. Sherman, Erin, illus. LC 82-63139. 32p. (Orig.). (ps-3). 1983. pap. text ed. 17.50 spiral bdg. (ISBN 0-937420-05-0). Stirrup Assoc.

—My Jesus Pocketbook of Manners. Phillips, Cheryl M., ed. Sherman, Erin, illus. LC 82-63141. 32p. (ps-3). 1983. pap. 0.69 (ISBN 0-937420-06-9). Stirrup Assoc.
—My Jesus Pocketbook of the 23rd Psalm. Phillips, Cheryl M., ed. LC 82-63140. (Illus.). 32p. (Orig.). (ps-3). 1983. pap. text ed. 0.69 (ISBN 0-937420-04-2). Stirrup Assoc.
Stoops, Lloyd F. God's Amazing World. rev. ed. Hill, Mildred, illus. 32p. (gr. k-6). 1989. pap. 0.99 (ISBN 0-89216-043-8). Salvation Army.
Storr, Catherine. Noah & His Ark. Russell, Jim, illus. LC 82-7712. 32p. (gr. k-4). 1982. PLB 14.65 (ISBN 0-8172-1975-7). Raintree Pubs.
Storr, Catherine, retold by. Joseph & His Brothers. Molan, Chris, illus. LC 82-9087. 32p. (gr. k-4). 1982. PLB 14.65 (ISBN 0-8172-1976-5). Raintree Pubs.
—Miracles by the Sea. Molan, Christine, illus. LC 82-23022. 32p. (gr. k-4). 1983. PLB 14.65 (ISBN 0-8172-1983-8). Raintree Pubs.
—The Prodigal Son. Rowe, Gavin, illus. LC 82-23011. 32p. (gr. k-4). 1983. PLB 14.65 (ISBN 0-8172-1982-X). Raintree Pubs.
Stowell, Gordon. Jesus Alimenta. Stowell, Gordon, illus. De Martinez, Violeta S., tr. from SPA. (Illus.). 24p. (ps). pap. 0.75 (ISBN 0-311-38614-8). Casa Bautista.
—Jesus Ama. Stowell, Gordon, illus. De Martinez, Violeta S., tr. from SPA. (Illus.). 24p. (ps). 1984. pap. 0.75 (ISBN 0-311-38611-3). Casa Bautista.
—Jesus Cuenta. Stowell, Gordon, illus. De Martinez, Violeta S., tr. from SPA. (Illus.). 24p. (ps). 1984. pap. 0.75 (ISBN 0-311-38613-X). Casa Bautista.
—Jesus Ensena. Stowell, Gordon, illus. De Martinez, Violeta S., tr. from SPA. (Illus.). 24p. (ps). 1984. pap. 0.75 (ISBN 0-311-38609-1). Casa Bautista.
—Jesus Feeds the People. (Illus.). 14p. (gr. 1-5). 1982. pap. 0.59 (ISBN 0-8307-0832-4, 5608167). Regal.
—Jesus Heals. (Illus.). 14p. (gr. 1-5). 1982. pap. 0.59 (ISBN 0-8307-0828-6, 5608122). Regal.
—Jesus Llama. Stowell, Gordon, illus. De Martinez, Violeta S., tr. from SPA. (Illus.). 24p. (ps). 1984. pap. 0.75 (ISBN 0-311-38612-1). Casa Bautista.
—Jesus Loves. 14p. (gr. 1-5). 1982. pap. 0.59 (ISBN 0-8307-0830-8, 5608145). Regal.
—Jesus Nace. De Martinez, Violeta S., tr. from SPA. (Illus.). 24p. (ps). 1984. pap. 0.75 (ISBN 0-311-38608-3). Casa Bautista.
—Jesus Sana. Stowell, Gordon, illus. De Martinez, Violeta S., tr. from ENG. (Illus.). 24p. (ps-1). 1984. pap. 0.75 (ISBN 0-311-38610-5). Casa Bautista.
—Jesus Teaches. (Illus.). 14p. 1982. pap. 0.59 (ISBN 0-8307-0829-4, 5608138). Regal.
—Jesus Tells Some Stories. (Illus.). 14p. (gr. 1-5). 1982. pap. 0.59 (ISBN 0-8307-0833-2, 5608487). Regal.
—Jesus Vive. Stowell, Gordon, illus. De Martinez, Violeta S., tr. from SPA. (Illus.). 24p. (ps-1). 1984. pap. 0.75 (ISBN 0-311-38615-6). Casa Bautista.
Svensson, Borje. Great Stories from the Bible. Mitchell, Vic, illus. 10p. (ps-2). 1985. 8.95 (ISBN 0-89191-939-2, 59394, Chariot Bks). Cook.
Taylor, Kenneth. The Book for Children. 640p. 1985. 12.95 (ISBN 0-8423-2145-4). Tyndale.
Taylor, Kenneth N., ed. My First Bible Stories in Pictures. Hook, Robert & Hook, Frances, illus. Lockwood, Robert P., intro. by. 272p. (gr. k-5). 1990. 14.95 (ISBN 0-87973-245-8, 245); 10.95 (ISBN 0-87973-246-6, 246). Our Sunday Visitor.
Taylor, Paul. The Great Dinosaur Mystery & the Bible. Chong, Jonathan, illus. 64p. (gr. 3-8). 1987. 10.95 (ISBN 0-89051-114-4). Master Bks.
Theaker, Harry G., illus. My First Book of Bible Stories. 64p. (ps-2). 1988. 6.95 (ISBN 0-8249-8265-7). Ideals.
The Thief Who Was Sorry. (gr. k-4). 1982. pap. 1.39 (ISBN 0-570-06154-7, 59-1268). Concordia.
Turner, Philip. The Bible Story. Wildsmith, Brian, illus. 142p. 1987. 19.95 (ISBN 0-19-273104-1). Oxford U Pr.
Ulmer, Louise. Samuel, the Judge. (Illus.). 24p. (gr. k-4). 1986. pap. 1.39 saddlestitched (ISBN 0-570-06200-4, 59-1423). Concordia.
Vos, Catherine F. The Child's Story Bible. (Illus.). 432p. (gr. 3 up). 1983. Repr. of 1934 ed. PLB 16.95 (ISBN 0-8028-5011-1). Eerdmans.
Wallace, Lew. Ben Hur. Larson, Dan, ed. Bohl, Al, illus. 224p. (Orig.). (gr. 6 up). 1990. pap. text ed. 2.50 (ISBN 1-55748-114-8). Barbour & Co.
Walton, Jim & Walton, Kim. Elijah & the Contest. (Illus.). (ps-k). 1987. pap. 3.49 (ISBN 1-55513-042-9, Chariot Bks). Cook.
Walton, John & Walton, Kim. Abraham & His Big Family. LC 86-70678. (Illus.). (ps-k). 1986. pap. 3.49 (ISBN 1-55513-031-3, Chariot Bks). Cook.
—Daniel & the Lions. (Illus.). (ps-k). 1987. pap. 3.49 (ISBN 1-55513-045-3, Chariot Press). Cook.
—David Fights Goliath. 1988. pap. 3.49 (ISBN 1-55513-239-1, Chariot Bks). Cook.
—God & the World He Made. LC 86-70677. (Illus.). (ps-k). 1986. pap. 3.49 (ISBN 1-55513-030-5, Chariot Bks). Cook.
—Jeroboam & the Golden Calves. LC 87-70613. 1988. pap. 3.49 (ISBN 1-55513-240-5, Chariot Bks). Cook.
—Jesus, God's Son, Is Born. LC 87-70612. 1987. pap. 3.49 (ISBN 1-55513-230-8, Chariot Bks). Cook.
—Jonah & the Big Fish. LC 86-70679. (Illus.). (ps-k). 1986. pap. 3.49 (ISBN 1-55513-035-6, Chariot Bks). Cook.
—Paul & the Bright Light. LC 87-70611. 1987. pap. 3.49 (ISBN 1-55513-236-7, Chariot Bks). Cook.
Wangerin, W., Jr. O Happy Day! (gr. k-4). 1981. pap. 1.39 (ISBN 0-570-06093-1, 59-1211). Concordia.
Ward, Elaine M. More Old Testament Stories. 65p. (gr. 1-8). 1984. pap. 6.95 (ISBN 0-940754-23-1). Ed Ministries.
Waybill, Marjorie. God's Justice: Activity Book. 88p. (Orig.). (ps-1). 1985. pap. 3.00 (ISBN 0-8361-3397-8). Herald Pr.
White, J. Edson. Best Stories from the Best Book: And Thou Shalt Teach Them Diligently Unto Thy Children. (Illus.). 160p. (gr. 5 up). 1990. pap. 7.95 (ISBN 0-945460-06-6). Upward Way.
Winthrop, Elizabeth, adapted by. He Is Risen: The Easter Story. Mikolaycak, Charles, illus. LC 84-15869. 32p. (gr. 2-6). 1985. reinforced bdg. 14.95 (ISBN 0-8234-0547-8). Holiday.
Wolf, Bob. Bible Animal Stories, Bk. 1. Lautermilch, John, illus. 86p. (gr. 2-7). 1983. pap. 3.95 (ISBN 0-89323-044-8). Bible Memory.
—Uncle Bob's Bible Stories. Lautermilch, John, illus. 108p. (Orig.). (gr. 4-8). 1982. pap. 3.50 (ISBN 0-89323-028-6). Bible Memory.

BIBLE STORIES–N.T.

Alexander, Pat. My Own Book of Bible Stories. (Illus.). 128p. 1983. 9.95 (ISBN 0-85648-541-1). Lion USA.
Beers, V. Gilbert & Beers, Ronald. Bible Stories to Live by, New Testament. De Jonge, Reint, illus. 96p. (gr. k-3). 1990. 12.99 (ISBN 0-89840-303-0). Heres Life.
Berg, Jean H. The Story of Jesus. Krush, Beth & Krush, Joe, illus. 40p. (Orig.). (gr. k-3). 1977. pap. 9.95 incl. audiocassette (ISBN 0-87510-185-2). Chr Science.
Caffrey, Stephanie & Kenslea, Timothy, eds. The Boy in the Striped Coat. (gr. 3-5). 1978. pap. 1.95 (ISBN 0-8192-1234-2). Morehouse Pub.
Child's Bible: New Testament: Rewritten for Children by Shirley Steen. LC 78-51445. 288p. (gr. 1-8). 1978. pap. 4.95 (ISBN 0-8091-2118-2). Paulist Pr.
Colina, Tessa, ed. Jesus, My Friend. (Illus.). (gr. 1-5). 1978. pap. 1.95 (ISBN 0-87239-270-8, 2442). Standard Pub.
—Jesus, My Lord. (Illus.). (gr. 1-5). 1978. pap. 1.95 (ISBN 0-87239-271-6, 2443). Standard Pub.
—Jesus, My Savior. (Illus.). (gr. 1-5). 1978. pap. 1.95 (ISBN 0-87239-268-6, 2440). Standard Pub.
Daniel, Rebecca. Book I-His Birth. McClure, Nancee, illus. 32p. (gr. 2-7). 1984. wkbk. 5.95 (ISBN 0-86653-213-7, SS 824). Good Apple.
—Book II-His Boyhood. McClure, Nancee, illus. 32p. (gr. 2-7). 1984. wkbk. 5.95 (ISBN 0-86653-223-4, SS 825). Good Apple.
—Book III-Gathering His Disciples. McClure, Nancee, illus. 32p. (gr. 2-7). 1984. wkbk. 4.95 (ISBN 0-86653-224-2, SS 826). Good Apple.
—Book IV-the Teacher. McClure, Nancee, illus. 32p. (gr. 2-7). 1984. wkbk. 5.95 (ISBN 0-86653-225-0, SS 827). Good Apple.
—Book V-The Healer. McClure, Nancee, illus. 32p. (gr. 2-7). wkbk. 5.95 (ISBN 0-86653-226-9, SS 828). Good Apple.
—Book VI-His Miracles. McClure, Nancee, illus. 32p. (gr. 2-7). 1984. wkbk. 5.95 (ISBN 0-86653-227-7, SS 829). Good Apple.
—Book VII-His Parables. McClure, Nancee, illus. 32p. (gr. 2-7). 1984. wkbk. 5.95 (ISBN 0-86653-228-5, SS 830). Good Apple.
—Book VIII-More Parables. McClure, Nancee, illus. 32p. (gr. 2-7). 1984. wkbk. 5.95 (ISBN 0-86653-229-3, SS 831). Good Apple.
—Book XI-His Last Hours. McClure, Nancee, illus. 32p. (gr. 2-7). 1984. wkbk. 5.95 (ISBN 0-86653-232-3, SS 834). Good Apple.
—Book XII-His Resurection. McClure, Nancee, illus. 32p. (gr. 2-7). 1984. wkbk. 5.95 (ISBN 0-86653-233-1, SS 835). Good Apple.
Dean, Bessie. Stories Jesus Told. 72p. 1979. pap. 5.95 (ISBN 0-88290-132-X). Horizon Utah.
Decker, Barbara, ed. A Coloring Book of Bible Verses from the Epistles. Clark, Penny, illus. 32p. (Orig.). 1989. coloring bk 2.50 (ISBN 0-9618608-4-7). Lynn's Bookshelf.
Degering, Etta B. Once upon a Bible Time. Van Dolson, Bobbie J., ed. Nye, Vernon, illus. LC 76-14118. (gr. k-3). 1976. 7.95 (ISBN 0-8280-0052-2). Review & Herald.
Dudley-Smith, Timothy. The Lion Book of Stories of Jesus. (Illus.). 96p. (gr. 1-5). 1989. 11.95 (ISBN 0-85648-906-9). Lion USA.
Hopkins, Margaret. Bible Stories from the New Testament. Coville, Katherine D., illus. 96p. (ps-3). 1989. 12.95 (ISBN 0-448-19184-9, G&D). Putnam Pub Group.
Lashbrook, Marilyn. Nothing to Fear: Jesus Walks on Water. Sharp, Chris, illus. LC 90-61060. 32p. (gr. k-3). 1991. 5.95 (ISBN 0-86606-443-5, 874). Roper Pr.
Lattimore, Deborah N. The Sailor Who Captured the Sea: A Story of the Book of Kells. Lattimore, Deborah N., illus. LC 89-26937. 40p. (gr. 2-5). 1991. 15.95 (ISBN 0-06-023710-4); PLB 15.89 (ISBN 0-06-023711-2). HarpC Child Bks.
O'Connor, Francine M. Special Friends of Jesus: New Testament Stories. Boswell, Kathryn, illus. 64p. (ps-5). 1986. pap. 3.95 (ISBN 0-89243-255-1). Liguori Pubns.
Sattgast, L. J. My Very First Bible. Flint, Russ, illus. (Orig.). (ps-3). 1989. 15.99 (ISBN 0-89081-756-1). Harvest Hse.
Simon, Mary M. Follow That Star. Jones, Dennis, illus. 24p. (ps-1). 1990. pap. 1.99 (ISBN 0-570-04177-5). Concordia.
—Row the Boat. Jones, Dennis, illus. 24p. (ps-1). 1990. pap. 1.99 (ISBN 0-570-04186-4, 56-1645). Concordia.
—Too Tall, Too Small. Jones, Dennis, illus. 24p. (ps-1). 1990. pap. 1.99 (ISBN 0-570-04185-6). Concordia.
Singleton, Kathy. Five Loaves & Two Fish. Baker, Arthur, illus. 32p. (gr. k-3). 1990. saddle stitched 1.25 (ISBN 0-8028-5059-6). Eerdmans.
Stowell, Gordon. Dorcas. Lerin, S. D. de, tr. from ENG. (Illus.). 24p. (gr. 1). 1978. pap. 0.75 (ISBN 0-311-38517-6, Edit Mundo). Casa Bautista.
—Juan el Bautista. Lerin, S. D., tr. from ENG. (Illus.). 24p. (gr. 1). 1981. pap. 0.75 (ISBN 0-311-38515-X, Edit Mundo). Casa Bautista.
—Pablo. Lerin, S. D., tr. from ENG. (Illus.). 24p. (gr. 1). 1981. pap. 0.75 (ISBN 0-311-38518-4, Edit Mundo). Casa Bautista.
—Pedro. Lerin, S. D., tr. from ENG. (Illus.). 24p. (gr. 1). 1981. pap. 0.75 (ISBN 0-311-38516-8, Edit Mundo). Casa Bautista.
Stump, Gladys S. Baby Jesus. (Illus.). (gr. 1). 1978. pap. 2.15 (ISBN 0-8127-0160-7). Review & Herald.
—Paul. (Illus.). (gr. 1). 1978. pap. 1.95 (ISBN 0-8127-0165-8). Review & Herald.
Tiner, John H. Favorite Stories from Acts Word Search. 48p. 1986. pap. 2.95 (ISBN 0-87403-047-1, 2691). Standard Pub.
Truitt, Gloria. The Raising of Jairus' Daughter. (Illus.). 24p. (gr. k-4). 1990. pap. 1.39 (ISBN 0-570-09023-7, 59-1446). Concordia.
Wangerin, Walter, Jr. A Penny Is Everything. (Illus.). 32p. (gr. 1-4). 1974. pap. 1.39 (ISBN 0-570-06084-2, 59-1204). Concordia.
Ward, Elaine M. New Testament Stories. 69p. (Orig.). (gr. 1-8). 1984. pap. 6.95 (ISBN 0-940754-27-4). Ed Ministries.
Winstone, Harold. Gospel for Young Christians. Lescanff, Jacques, illus. 192p. (gr. 3-6). 1985. 3.95 (ISBN 0-225-27392-6). Harper SF.

BIBLE STORIES–O.T.

All the Animals. (ps-1). 1990. pap. 6.95 (ISBN 0-7459-1838-7). Lion USA.
Amoss, Berthe. David & Goliath. (Illus.). 10p. (ps-7). 1989. pap. 2.95 (ISBN 0-922589-12-7). More Than Card.
—Jonah. (Illus.). 10p. (ps-7). 1989. pap. 2.95 (ISBN 0-922589-09-7). More Than Card.
—Noah. (Illus.). 10p. (ps-7). 1989. pap. 2.95 (ISBN 0-922589-10-0). More Than Card.
Animals Two by Two. (ps-1). 1990. pap. 6.95 (ISBN 0-7459-1839-5). Lion USA.
Bach, Alice & Exum, J. Cheryl. Moses & Noah's Ark: Stories from the Bible. Dillon, Leo & Dillon, Diane, illus. LC 89-1069. 181p. 1989. 14.95 (ISBN 0-385-29778-5). Delacorte.
Because God Said So. (gr. 4-6). 1990. 1.55 (ISBN 0-89636-114-4, JB 3B). Accent Bks.
Beers, V. Gilbert & Beers, Ronald. Bible Stories to Live by, Old Testament. rev. ed. De Jonge, Reint, illus. 96p. (gr. k-3). 1991. 12.99 ea. (ISBN 0-89840-302-2). Old Testament. New Testament. Heres Life.
Berg, Jean H. Daniel in the Lions' Den. Darwin, Beatrice, illus. Jareaux, Robin, contrib. by. (Illus.). 32p. (Orig.). (gr. k-3). 1973. pap. 9.95 incl. audiocassette (ISBN 0-87510-178-X). Chr Science.
—Joseph & His Brothers. Krush, Beth & Krush, Joe, illus. 32p. (Orig.). (gr. k-3). 1976. pap. 9.95 incl. audiocassette (ISBN 0-87510-104-6). Chr Science.
—Nehemiah Builds the Wall. Madden, Don, illus. 32p. (Orig.). (gr. k-3). 1978. pap. 9.95 incl. audiocassette (ISBN 0-87510-114-3). Chr Science.
—Noah & the Ark. Madden, Don, illus. 32p. (Orig.). (gr. k-3). 1974. pap. 9.95 incl. audiocassette (ISBN 0-87510-180-1). Chr Science.
Chaikin, Miriam. Exodus. Mikolaycak, Charles, illus. LC 85-27361. 32p. (gr. 2-4). 1987. reinforced bdg. 14.95 (ISBN 0-8234-0607-5). Holiday.
—Joshua in the Promised Land. Frampton, David, illus. (gr. 3-6). 1990. pap. 5.95 (ISBN 0-395-54797-0, Clarion Bks). HM.
Child's Bible: Old Testament: Rewritten for Children by Anne Edwards. LC 78-51444. 384p. (gr. 1-8). 1978. pap. 4.95 (ISBN 0-8091-2117-4). Paulist Pr.
Citrin, Paul J. Joseph's Wardrobe. (Illus.). (gr. 4-6). 1987. pap. 6.95 (ISBN 0-8074-0319-9, 123924). UAHC.
The Creation. (gr. k-3). incl. tape 6.97 (ISBN 0-89191-804-3, 98046). Cook.
Daniel. (gr. k-3). incl. tape 6.97 (ISBN 0-89191-800-0, 98004). Cook.
David. (gr. k-3). incl. tape 6.97 (ISBN 0-89191-803-5, 98038). Cook.
Dimond, Jasper. Noah's Ark. (Illus.). 48p. (gr. k-3). 1983. 8.95 (ISBN 0-13-622951-4). P-H.
Enns, Peter & Forsberg, Glen. Adam & Eve & Five Other Stories. Friesen, John H., illus. 24p. (ps-5). 1985. book & Cassette 4.95 (ISBN 0-936215-01-1). STL Intl.
—David & Goliath & Five Other Stories. Friesen, John H., illus. 24p. (ps-5). 1985. book & Cassette 4.95 (ISBN 0-936215-03-8). STL Intl.
—Joseph the Dreamer & Five Other Stories. Friesen, John H., illus. 24p. (ps-5). 1985. book & cassette 4.95 (ISBN 0-936215-02-X). STL Intl.
Fisher, Leonard E., illus. & adapted by. The Seven Days of Creation. LC 81-2952. 32p. (ps-3). 1981. reinforced bdg. 14.95 (ISBN 0-8234-0398-X); pap. 5.95 (ISBN 0-8234-0757-8). Holiday.

Fletcher, Sarah. My Stories About God's People. Kueker, Don, illus. 32p. (ps-3). 1974. pap. 2.29 (ISBN 0-570-03426-4, 56-1181). Concordia.

Freehof, Lillian S. Bible Legends: An Introduction to Midrash, Vol. 1: Genesis. Schwartz, Howard, ed. (gr. 4-6). 1987. pap. text ed. 6.95 (ISBN 0-8074-0357-1, 123050). UAHC.

Gaines, M. C., ed. Picture Stories from the Bible: The Old Testament in Full-Color Comic-Strip Form. Cameron, Don, illus. LC 79-66064. 222p. (gr. 3-10). 1979. Repr. of 1943 ed. 12.95 (ISBN 0-934386-01-3). Scarf Pr.

Head, Constance. The Story of Deborah. (Illus.). (gr. k-3). 1978. 1.39 (ISBN 0-570-06116-4, 59-1234). Concordia.

Hollender, Betty R. Bible Stories for Little Children, Bk. 1. rev. ed. Bearson, Lee, illus. 80p. (Orig.). (gr. 1-3). 1985. pap. text ed. 6.00 (ISBN 0-8074-0309-1, 103100). UAHC.

—Bible Stories for Little Children, Vol. 2. rev. ed. (Illus.). 80p. (gr. 1-3). 1987. pap. text ed. 6.00 (ISBN 0-8074-0324-5, 103101). UAHC.

—Bible Stories for Little Children, Vol. 3. rev. ed. (Illus.). 80p. (gr. 1-3). 1988. pap. text ed. 6.00 (ISBN 0-8074-0416-0, 103102). UAHC.

—Bible Stories for Little Children, Vol. 4. rev. ed. (Illus.). 80p. (gr. 1-3). 1989. pap. text ed. 6.00 (ISBN 0-8074-0418-7, 103103). UAHC.

Jonah. (gr. k-3). incl. tape 6.97 (ISBN 0-89191-799-3, 97998). Cook.

Joshua. (gr. k-3). incl. tape 6.97 (ISBN 0-89191-610-5, 26104). Cook.

Knox, Joann. Seven Days at Jericho - Rachel Meets the Healer. 64p. (gr. 4-8). 1973. pap. 1.00 (ISBN 0-88243-774-7, 02-0774). Gospel Pub.

Lashbrook, Marilyn. I Don't Want to: The Story of Jonah. Britt, Stephanie M., illus. LC 87-60264. 32p. (ps). 1987. 5.95 (ISBN 0-86606-428-1, 844). Roper Pr.

—The Wall That Did Not Fall: The Story of Rahab's Faith. Britt, Stephanie M., illus. LC 87-63420. 32p. (ps). 1988. 5.95 (ISBN 0-86606-433-8, 864). Roper Pr.

Lenski, Lois. Mr. & Mrs. Noah. LC 48-5989. (Illus.). 48p. (ps-1). 1962. PLB 12.89 (ISBN 0-690-54562-2, Crowell Jr Bks). HarpC Child Bks.

Levinger, Elma E. Beautiful Garden & Other Bible Tales. Robinson, Jessie B., illus. (gr. 3-5). 6.95 (ISBN 0-8197-0253-6). Bloch.

Lewis, Shari. One-Minute Bible Stories: Old Testament. Ewing, C. S., illus. LC 86-2011. 48p. (ps-3). 1986. PLB 7.95 (ISBN 0-385-19565-6); pap. 7.99 (ISBN 0-385-19566-4). Doubleday.

Neusner, Jacob. Meet Our Sages. Hellmuth, Jim, illus. LC 80-12771. 128p. (gr. 5-8). 1980. pap. text ed. 5.95x (ISBN 0-87441-327-3). Behrman.

Noah. (gr. k-3). incl. tape 6.97 (ISBN 0-89191-801-9, 98012). Cook.

Noah's Ark & Other Old Testament Stories. (ps-2). 1989. 9.95 (ISBN 1-55513-812-8). Cook.

O'Connor, Francine M. ABCs of the Old Testament...for Children. Boswell, Kathryn, illus. 32p. (gr. 1-5). 1989. pap. 2.50 (ISBN 0-89243-310-8). Liguori Pubns.

Paamoni, Zev. Aaron, the High Priest. (Illus.). (gr. 5-10). 1970. 3.00 (ISBN 0-914080-27-X). Shulsinger Sales.

—Benjamin, the Littlest Brother. (Illus.). (gr. 5-10). 1970. 3.00 (ISBN 0-914080-28-8). Shulsinger Sales.

—Yitzchak, Son of Abraham. (Illus.). (gr. 5-10). 1970. 4.00 (ISBN 0-914080-25-3). Shulsinger Sales.

Plotka Block, Celia. When Sabbath Came He Rested: A Story-Game for Young Children. 31p. 1989. 6.95 (ISBN 0-533-08513-6). Vantage.

Samuels, Ruth. Bible Stories for Jewish Children, 2 vols, No. 1. (Illus.). (gr. 3-5). 1958. 7.95x (ISBN 0-87068-356-X). Ktav.

Simon, Mary M. Toot! Toot! Jones, Dennis, illus. 24p. (ps-1). 1990. pap. 1.99 (ISBN 0-570-04184-8). Concordia.

Stowell, Gordon. Abraham. Lerin, S. D., tr. from ENG. (Illus.). 24p. (gr. 1). 1981. pap. 0.75 (ISBN 0-311-38511-7, Edit Mundo). Casa Bautista.

—Jonas. Lerin, S. D., tr. from ENG. (Illus.). 24p. (gr. 1). 1978. pap. 0.75 (ISBN 0-311-38514-1, Edit Mundo). Casa Bautista.

—Rut. Lerin, S. D., tr. from ENG. (Illus.). 24p. (gr. 1). 1981. pap. 0.75 (ISBN 0-311-38513-3, Edit Mundo). Casa Bautista.

Stump, Gladys S. Baby Moses. (Illus.). (gr. 1). 1978. pap. 2.15 (ISBN 0-8127-0164-X). Review & Herald.

—Elisha's Room. (Illus.). (gr. 1). 1978. pap. 1.95 (ISBN 0-8127-0162-3). Review & Herald.

—Mordecai's Ride. (Illus.). (gr. 1). 1978. pap. 1.95 (ISBN 0-8127-0161-5). Review & Herald.

The Times of Joshua & the Judges. (gr. 4-6). 1990. 1.55 (ISBN 0-89636-112-8, JB 1B). Accent Bks.

Wengrov, Charles. Tales of the Prophet Samuel. (Illus.). (gr. 5-10). 1969. 4.00 (ISBN 0-914080-22-9). Shulsinger Sales.

BIBLE STUDY

see Bible–Study

BIBLICAL CHARACTERS

see Bible–Biography

BIBLIOGRAPHY–BEST BOOKS

see Books and Reading–Best Books

BIBLIOGRAPHY–REFERENCE BOOKS

see Reference Books

BICYCLE RACING–FICTION

Christopher, Matt. Dirt Bike Runaway. Stewart, Edgar, illus. LC 83-13538. 160p. (gr. 4-6). 1989. 13.95 (ISBN 0-316-13956-4); pap. 3.95 (ISBN 0-316-14002-3). Little.

Crews, Donald. Bicycle Race. LC 84-27912. (Illus.). 24p. (ps-1). 1985. 11.75 (ISBN 0-688-05171-5); lib. bdg. 11.88 (ISBN 0-688-05172-3). Greenwillow.

BICYCLES AND BICYCLING

see also Motorcycles

Abramowski, Dwain. Mountain Bikes. (Illus.). 64p. (gr. 5-8). 1990. PLB 11.90 (ISBN 0-531-10871-6). Watts.

Barnes, F. A. & Kuehne, Tom. Canyon Country: Mountain Biking. LC 87-73014. (Illus.). 144p. (Orig.). (gr. 7 up). 1988. pap. 8.00 (ISBN 0-9614586-5-8). Canyon Country Pubns.

Barrett, Norman. Trailbikes. (Illus.). 32p. (gr. k-3). 1987. PLB 11.40 (ISBN 0-531-10277-7). Watts.

Barrett, Norman S. BMX Bikes. (Illus.). 32p. (gr. k-3). 1987. PLB 11.40 (ISBN 0-531-10272-6). Watts.

BMX Bikes. 48p. (gr. 3-4). 1989. PLB 10.95 (ISBN 0-685-26370-3). Capstone Pr.

Boy Scouts of America. Cycling. (Illus.). 40p. (gr. 6-12). 1984. pap. 1.85 (ISBN 0-8395-3277-6, 3277). BSA.

Brimner, Larry Dane. BXM Freestyle. (Illus.). 72p. (gr. 4-8). 1987. PLB 10.40 (ISBN 0-531-10301-3). Watts.

Chapman. Superbikes. rev. ed. (gr. 4-6). 1984. (Usborne-Hayes); PLB 12.96 (ISBN 0-88110-014-5); pap. 5.95 (ISBN 0-86020-182-1). EDC.

Chlad, Dorothy. Bicycles Are Fun to Ride. Halverson, Lydia, illus. LC 83-23234. 32p. (ps-2). 1984. lib. bdg. 14.60 (ISBN 0-516-01975-9); pap. 3.95 (ISBN 0-516-41975-7). Childrens.

—Es Divertido andar en Bicicleta. Kratky, Lada, tr. Halverson, Lydia, illus. LC 85-23263. (SPA.). 32p. (ps-2). 1986. PLB 14.60 (ISBN 0-516-31975-2); pap. 3.95 (ISBN 0-516-51975-1). Childrens.

Cook, J. Mountain Bikes. (Illus.). 48p. (gr. 6-10). 1991. lib. bdg. 12.96 (ISBN 0-88110-426-4, Usborne); pap. 5.95 (ISBN 0-7460-0520-2, Usborne). EDC.

Coombs, Charles I. BMX: A Guide to Bicycle Motocross. LC 82-20904. (Illus.). 144p. (gr. 4-6). 1983. 13.95 (ISBN 0-688-01867-X). Morrow Jr Bks.

Hart, Cynthia. BMX! A Mini-Poster Book. (Illus.). 32p. (Orig.). (gr. 4 up). 1985. pap. 3.95 (ISBN 0-590-40577-2). Scholastic Inc.

Hoare, Stephen. Bikes. (Illus.). 96p. (gr. 1 up). 1985. PLB 9.90 (ISBN 0-531-19001-3, Gloucester Pr). Watts.

Jennings, Gordon. Minibikes! Coker, Paul, Jr., illus. (gr. 5 up). 1974. P-H.

Kent, J. Racing Bikes. (Illus.). 48p. (gr. 6-10). 1991. lib. bdg. 12.96 (ISBN 0-88110-427-2, Usborne); pap. 5.95 (ISBN 0-7460-0518-0). EDC.

Klingel, Cynthia. Bicycle Safety. (Illus.). 32p. (ps-3). 1986. 10.95s.p. (ISBN 0-88682-085-5); 15.65 (ISBN 0-685-09467-7). Creative Ed.

Lafferty, Peter & Jefferis, David. Pedal Power: The History of Bicycles. (Illus.). 32p. (gr. 5-8). 1990. PLB 11.90 (ISBN 0-531-14084-9). Watts.

Langley, James. The New Bike Book: How to Get the Most Out of Your New Bicycle. LC 89-81204. (Illus.). 128p. (Orig.). 1990. pap. 4.95 (ISBN 0-933201-28-1). Bicycle Books.

Murphy, Jim. Two Hundred Years of Bicycles. LC 81-48608. (Illus.). 64p. (gr. 3-6). 1983. 9.70i (ISBN 0-397-32007-8, Lipp Jr Bks). HarpC Child Bks.

Nielsen, Nancy J. Bicycle Racing. LC 87-30489. (Illus.). 48p. (gr. 5-6). 1988. PLB 10.95 (ISBN 0-89686-361-1, Crestwood Hse). Macmillan Child Grp.

Peck, Robert N. Hub. Lewin, Ted, illus. LC 78-11763. (gr. 3-7). 1979. 5.95 (ISBN 0-394-83968-4). Knopf.

Porter, A. P. Greg LeMond: Premier Cyclist. (Illus.). 56p. (gr. 4-9). 1990. PLB 8.95 (ISBN 0-8225-0476-6). Lerner Pubns.

Pursell, Thomas. Bicycles on Parade. LC 78-27403. (Illus.). 56p. (gr. 4-9). 1980. PLB 9.95 (ISBN 0-8225-0426-X). Lerner Pubns.

Roth, Harold. Bike Factory: A Pantheon Photo Essay. Roth, Harold, photos by. LC 85-3621. (Illus.). 48p. (gr. 3-7). 1985. (Pant Bks Young); (Pant Bks Ypung). Pantheon.

Schlabach, Cara. Touring Cycles. LC 87-20039. (Illus.). 48p. (gr. 5-6). 1987. PLB 10.95 (ISBN 0-89686-355-7, Crestwood Hse). Macmillan Child Grp.

Scioscia, Mary. Bicycle Rider. Young, Ed, illus. LC 82-47702. 48p. (gr. 2-6). 1983. PLB 13.89 (ISBN 0-06-025223-5). HarpC Child Bks.

Stephen, R. J. The Picture World of BMX. (Illus.). 32p. (gr. k-4). 1989. PLB 11.40 (ISBN 0-531-10725-6). Watts.

Sullivan, George. Better Bicycling for Boys & Girls. (Illus.). 64p. (gr. 3-7). 1984. (Putnam); pap. 2.95 (ISBN 0-396-08479-6, Putnam). Putnam Pub Group.

—Better BMX Riding & Racing for Boys & Girls. (Illus.). 64p. (gr. 3-7). 1984. 9.95 (ISBN 0-396-08331-5, Putnam). Putnam Pub Group.

Thompson, Graham. Bikes. LC 86-5701. (Illus.). 24p. (gr. 1-3). 1986. PLB 10.95 (ISBN 1-55532-074-0). Gareth Stevens Inc.

Thomson, H. E. The Tour of the Forest Bike Race: A Guide to Bicycle Racing & the Tour de France. LC 90-80062. (Illus.). 64p. (Orig.). 1990. 9.95 (ISBN 0-933201-35-4). Bicycle Books. The most important events in professional bicycle racing without a doubt are the great international stage races such as the Tour de France. And it is here that Greg LeMond & other American racers have in recent years earned their laurels. Yet many readers - including keen cyclists - don't know just how such a race is run & how the winner is determined. This book explains it all in an easy-to-read & entertaining way. H.E. Thomson's creative paintbrush has captured the atmosphere of the Tour & put it in the perspective of the animals of an imaginary forest who put on their own "Tour of the Forest" each year. Thus the readers find out what a polka dot jersey is all about & what the difference between a team time trial & a regular stage is. "'Tour of the Forest Bike Race' is one of the most informative guides to international stage racing; Thomson manages to cover the subject thoroughly & still be very entertaining." CALIFORNIA BICYCLIST. "Without fully realizing it, the reader is well informed on the art of cycle racing when he's finished reading this short book."--PALATKA DAILY NEWS.
Publisher Provided Annotation.

Todd, Armor. The Marin Mountain Bike Guide. 2nd ed. Todd, Linda, illus. 80p. (gr. 9-12). 1989. pap. 8.95t (ISBN 0-9623537-0-1). A Todd.

Tropea, S. BMX, A Photo-Fact Book. (Illus.). 24p. (Orig.). 1987. pap. 1.95 (ISBN 0-942025-16-4). Kidsbks.

Van der Plas, Rob. Roadside Bicycle Repairs: The Simple Guide to Fixing Your Bike. 2nd ed. Van der Plas, Rob, illus. LC 89-81203. 128p. 1990. pap. 4.95 (ISBN 0-933201-27-3). Bicycle Books.

Wheels! The Kids' Bike Book. (gr. 3-7). 1990. 17.95 (ISBN 0-316-81625-6); pap. 9.95 (ISBN 0-316-81624-8). Little.

Wiley, Jack. Unicycles & Artistic Bicycles Illustrated. LC 86-61015. (Illus.). 168p. (gr. 7 up). 1986. pap. 26.95 (ISBN 0-913999-15-6). Solipaz Pub Co.

Wilhelm, Tim & Wilhelm, Glenda. Bicycling Basics. Seiden, Art, illus. 48p. (gr. 3-7). 1985. pap. 4.95 (ISBN 0-13-077942-3). P-H.

Wood, Tim. Mountain Biking. Fairclough, Chris, photos by. (Illus.). 32p. (gr. k-4). 1989. PLB 10.40 (ISBN 0-531-10829-5). Watts.

BICYCLES AND BICYCLING–FICTION

Andersen, Karen B. What's the Matter, Sylvie, Can't You Ride? Andersen, Karen B., illus. LC 80-12514. 32p. (ps-3). 1981. 9.95 (ISBN 0-8037-9607-2); PLB 9.89 (ISBN 0-8037-9621-8). Dial Bks Young.

Barbot, Daniel. A Bicycle for Rosaura. Fuenmayor, Morella, illus. 24p. (ps-3). 1991. 9.95 (ISBN 0-916291-34-0). Kane-Miller Bk.

Berenstain, Stan & Berenstain, Janice. Bike Lesson. LC 64-11460. (Illus.). 72p. (gr. k-3). 1964. 6.95 (ISBN 0-394-80036-2); lib. bdg. 7.99 (ISBN 0-394-90036-7). Beginner.

Bibee, John. The Magic Bicycle. LC 83-240. (Illus.). 220p. (Orig.). (gr. 4-9). 1983. pap. 6.95 (ISBN 0-87784-348-1). InterVarsity.

Castle, Caroline. Herbert Binns & the Flying Tricycle. Weevers, Peter, illus. LC 86-13441. 32p. (ps-3). 1987. 10.95 (ISBN 0-8037-0041-5). Dial Bks Young.

Christopher, Matt. Tight End. (gr. 4-6). 1986. pap. 3.95 (ISBN 0-316-14054-6). Little.

Fraser, Sheila. I Can Ride a Bike. Kopper, Lisa, illus. 24p. (ps-3). 1991. 5.95 (ISBN 0-8120-6227-2). Barron.

Gillespie, Bonita. Peggy's Problem. Cover, Marilyn, illus. 35p. (gr. 3-8). 1987. 6.95 (ISBN 1-55523-058-X). Winston-Derek.

Gondosch, Linda. The Strawberryland Choo-Choo. Sustendal, Pat, illus. 40p. (ps-3). 1984. cancelled 5.95 (ISBN 0-910313-24-5). Parker Bros.

Harwood, Pearl A. Mr. Bumba Rides a Bicycle. Folger, Joseph, illus. LC 65-27997. 32p. (gr. k-3). 1966. PLB 4.95 (ISBN 0-8225-0109-0). Lerner Pubns.

Holabird, Katharine. Angelina's Birthday Surprise. Craig, Helen, illus. LC 89-3513. 32p. (ps-2). 1989. 11.95 (ISBN 0-517-57325-3, C N Potter Bks). Crown.

Lewis, Rob. The White Bicycle. LC 88-45092. (Illus.). 32p. (ps up). 1988. 9.95 (ISBN 0-374-38384-7). FS&G.

Lloyd, Errol. Sasha & the Bicycle Thieves. (Illus.). 42p. (gr. 2-4). 1989. 3.95 (ISBN 0-8120-6141-1). Barron.

Lynam, Terence. Andy Joins the BMX Bunch. Mostyn, David, illus. LC 87-42802. 32p. (gr. 2-3). 1988. PLB 10.95 (ISBN 1-55532-414-2). Gareth Stevens Inc.

—BMX Bunch, 4 vols. Mostyn, David, illus. 128p. (gr. 2-3). 1987. Set. PLB 43.80 (ISBN 1-55532-413-4). Gareth Stevens Inc.

—The BMX Bunch on Vacation. Mostyn, David, illus. LC 87-42803. 32p. (gr. 2-3). 1988. PLB 10.95 (ISBN 1-55532-416-9). Gareth Stevens Inc.

—The BMX Turns Detective. Mostyn, David, illus. LC 87-42804. 32p. (gr. 2-3). 1988. 10.95 (ISBN 1-55532-417-7). Gareth Stevens Inc.

—Greg's First Race. Mostyn, David, illus. LC 87-42816. 32p. (gr. 2-3). 1988. PLB 10.95 (ISBN 1-55532-415-0). Gareth Stevens Inc.

McLeod, Emilie W. The Bear's Bicycle. McPhail, David, illus. 32p. (gr. k-3). 1986. lib. bdg. 13.95 (ISBN 0-316-56203-3, Joy St Bks); pap. 4.95 (ISBN 0-316-56206-8, Joy St Bks). Little.

McMillan, Bruce. The Remarkable Riderless Runaway Tricycle. rev. ed. (Illus.). 48p. (gr. k-4). 1985. pap. 8.95 (ISBN 0-934313-00-8). Apple Isl Bks.

Miles, Betty. I Would If I Could. LC 81-8458. 128p. (gr. 3-6). 1982. Repr. lib. bdg. 11.99 (ISBN 0-394-93929-8). Knopf.

—I Would If I Could. LC 81-8458. 128p. (gr. 3-6). 1982. Repr. lib. bdg. 11.99 (ISBN 0-394-93929-8). Knopf.

—I Would If I Could. 120p. (gr. 3-6). 1983. pap. 2.95 (ISBN 0-380-63438-4, 60067-5, Camelot). Avon.

Petrie, Catherine. Hot Rod Harry. Sharp, Paul, illus. LC 81-15549. 32p. (ps-2). 1982. PLB 11.93 (ISBN 0-516-03493-6); pap. text ed. 2.95 (ISBN 0-516-43493-4). Childrens.

Quackenbush, Robert. Bicycle to Treachery. Quackenbush, Robert, illus. 48p. (gr. 1-5). 1985. 10.95 (ISBN 0-13-076258-X). P-H.

Radlauer, Ed & Radlauer, Ruth. BMX Winners. LC 84-7818. (Illus.). 48p. (gr. 3 up). 1984. lib. bdg. 13.27 (ISBN 0-516-07813-5). Childrens.

Robinet, Harriette G. Ride the Red Cycle. (Illus.). (gr. 1-5). 1980. 13.95 (ISBN 0-395-29183-6). HM.

Say, Allen. The Bicycle Man. Say, Allen, illus. 48p. (gr. k-3). 1982. 13.95 (ISBN 0-395-32254-5); 11.95 (ISBN 0-685-05704-6). HM.

Thomas, Jane R. Wheels. LC 85-18404. (ps-3). 1986. 12.95 (ISBN 0-317-39001-5). HM.

—Wheels. McCully, Emily A., illus. LC 85-13291. 32p. (ps-3). 1986. 14.95 (ISBN 0-89919-410-9, Pub. by Clarion). Ticknor & Fields.

Warner, Gertrude C. Bicycle Mystery. Cunningham, David, illus. LC 79-126428. 128p. (gr. 3-7). 1970. PLB 9.95 (ISBN 0-8075-0708-3). A Whitman.

Zach, Cheryl. Benny & the Crazy Contest. LC 90-43903. (Illus.). 80p. (gr. 2-6). 1991. SBE 11.95 (ISBN 0-02-793705-4, Bradbury Pr). Macmillan Child Grp.

BIGOTRY

see Toleration

BILINGUAL BOOKS–FRENCH-ENGLISH

De Brunhoff, Laurent. Babar's French Lessons. (Illus.). (ps). 1963. 11.00 (ISBN 0-394-80587-9, Random Juv); lib. bdg. 5.99 (ISBN 0-394-90587-3). Random.

BILINGUAL BOOKS–SPANISH-ENGLISH

Rey, H. A. Jorge el Curioso. (SPA., Illus.). (gr. k-3). 1961. 13.95 (ISBN 0-395-17075-3). HM.

Simon, Norma. What Do I Do: English - Spanish Edition. Lasker, Joe, illus. LC 74-79544. 40p. (ps-2). 1969. PLB 12.95 (ISBN 0-8075-8823-7). A Whitman.

—What Do I Say. Lasker, Joe, illus. LC 67-17420. (ENG & SPA.). (ps-2). 1967. 12.95 (ISBN 0-8075-8828-8); PLB 12.95 (ISBN 0-8075-8826-1). A Whitman.

Tallon, Robert, illus. ABCDEFGHIJKLMNOPQRSTUVWXYZ. LC 76-86987. (ENG & SPA.). 64p. (gr. k-2). 1969. PLB 14.95 (ISBN 0-87460-131-2). Lion Bks.

Williams, Letty. Little Red Hen: La Pequena Gallina Roja. Williams, Herb, illus. LC 78-75684. (ENG & SPA.). (ps-3). 1969. (Pub. by Treehouse); pap. 3.95 (ISBN 0-13-537894-X). P-H.

BILL OF RIGHTS

see U. S. Constitution–Amendments

BILLBOARDS

see Signs and Signboards

BILLS OF CREDIT

see Credit

BIMETALLISM

see Gold; Silver

BINARY SYSTEM (MATHEMATICS)

Watson, Clyde. Binary Numbers. Watson, Wendy, illus. LC 75-29161. 40p. (gr. 1-4). 1977. PLB 12.89 (ISBN 0-690-00993-3, Crowell Jr Bks). HarpC Child Bks.

BINDING OF BOOKS

see Bookbinding

BIOBIBLIOGRAPHY

see Authors

BIOCHEMISTRY

see also Metabolism

BIOGEOGRAPHY

see Geographical Distribution of Animals and Plants

BIOGRAPHY

see also Autobiographies; Christian Biography; Heraldry; Portraits

also names of classes of persons (e.g. Artists; Authors; Musicians; etc.); names of countries, cities, etc. and special subjects with the subdivision Biography (e.g. U. S. –Biography; Blacks–Biography; Religions–Biography; Woman–Biography; etc.) and names of persons for biographies of individuals

Axiom Informaton Resources Staff. Star Guide 1992-1993: Where to Contact over 3200 Movie Stars, TV Stars, Rock Stars, Sports Stars, & Other Famous Celebrities. rev. ed. Robinson, Terry, ed. 200p. 1992. pap. 12.95 (ISBN 0-943213-04-5). Axiom Info Res.

Bliven, Bruce, Jr. American Revolution. (Illus.). (gr. 4-6). 1963. 2.95 (ISBN 0-394-80383-3, Random Juv); lib. bdg. 8.99 (ISBN 0-394-90383-8). Random.

Clarke, Brenda. Caring for Others. LC 89-26296. (Illus.). 48p. (gr. 4-8). 1990. PLB 18.60 (ISBN 0-8114-2751-X). Steck-V.

Cowen, Ida & Gunther, Irene. A Spy for Freedom: The Story of Sarah Aaronsohn. LC 84-10193. (Illus.). 176p. (gr. 5 up). 1984. 14.95 (ISBN 0-525-67150-1, Lodestar Bks). Dutton Child Bks.

Crispin, A. C. Sylvester. 256p. (Orig.). 1985. pap. 2.95 (ISBN 0-8125-8173-3, Dist. by Warner Pub Services & Saint Martin's Press). Tor Bks.

Down, Goldie. You Never Can Tell When You May Meet a Leopard. Davis, Tom, ed. 128p. (gr. 1 up). 1980. pap. 6.95 (ISBN 0-8280-0026-3). Review & Herald.

Famous Men & Women. (Illus.). 96p. (gr. 3-8). 1987. PLB 240.00 set (ISBN 0-317-62823-2); pap. 13.27 (ISBN 0-8172-3056-4). Raintree Pubs.

Goodwin, Bob & Hayes, Dympna. Famous Lives. Kelly, Teri, ed. (Illus.). 48p. (gr. 4). 1987. PLB 14.65 (ISBN 0-88625-171-0); pap. 5.95 (ISBN 0-88625-150-8). Durkin Hayes Pub.

Gudeman, Janice. Creative Encounters with Creative People. Beebe, Mark & Filkins, Vanessa, illus. 144p. (gr. 4 up). 1984. wkbk. 10.95 (ISBN 0-86653-258-7, GA 623). Good Apple.

—Learning from the Lives of Amazing People. 144p. (gr. 4 up). 1988. wkbk. 10.95 (ISBN 0-86653-446-6, GA1055). Good Apple.

Hawthorne, Nathaniel. True Stories from History & Biography. Charvat, William, et al, eds. LC 73-150220. 380p. (gr. 5 up). 1972. 42.00 (ISBN 0-8142-0157-1). Ohio St U Pr.

Johnson, Spencer & Johnson, Donegan. The ValueTale Series, 35 bks. Pileggi, Steve, illus. (ps-5). 1976. 9.95 ea. (ISBN 0-916392-24-4). Oak Tree Pubns.

Through the true stories of real people, ValueTales introduces children between the ages of 3 & 10 to the importance of values like honesty, caring, courage, fairness, love & many others. To date, there are a total of 34 values in 34 volumes. Although the intention of the books is serious, the stories themselves are written to entertain children while telling stories from history, to provide healthy role models, to impart the importance of value systems, & to promote interaction between parents & children. ValueTales provides stories of men & women whose extraordinary accomplishments reflected a strong set of personal principles or values. Each story includes a character designed to be appealing to children, who may be an animal or inanimate object & who provides advice & guidance to the central figure. Among the stories related by the ValueTales are: Louis Pasteur's successful quest to discover the cure for Rabies, despite much ridicule (The Value of Believing in Yourself); Eleanor Roosevelt's compassion for the underprivileged (The Value of Caring); Apache Chief Cochise whose honesty & good faith helped restore faith between the American Indians & white settlers (The Value of Truth & Trust).

Publisher Provided Annotation.

Lee, Betsy. Judy Blume's Story. LC 81-12494. (Illus.). 112p. (gr. 5 up). 1981. PLB 8.95 (ISBN 0-87518-209-7, Dillon). Macmillan Child Grp.

McLeish, Kenneth & McLeish, Valerie. Famous People. LC 90-37910. (Illus.). 96p. (gr. 3-6). 1990. PLB 14.89 (ISBN 0-8167-2238-2); pap. text ed. 6.95 (ISBN 0-8167-2239-0). Troll Assocs.

Magill, Frank N., ed. Great Lives from History, 5 vols. 2527p. (gr. 9-12). 1990. Set. lib. bdg. 350.00x (ISBN 0-89356-565-2). Salem Pr.

Mealy, Virginia. Biography Reports Without Copying. (Illus.). 32p. (gr. 4-9). 1989. pap. 4.95 (ISBN 0-913839-76-0). Bk Lures.

Morgan, et al. What Made Them Great Series, 8 bks. (Illus.). 832p. (gr. 5-8). 1990. Set. PLB 135.84 (ISBN 0-382-09983-4); Set. PLB 101.88s.p.; Set. pap. 71.60 (ISBN 0-382-09984-2); Set. pap. 53.70s.p. Silver Burdett Pr.

People. LC 87-16543. (Illus.). 96p. (gr. 3 up). 1987. lib. bdg. 240.00 set (ISBN 0-317-64434-3); pap. 13.27 (ISBN 0-8172-3052-1). Raintree Pubs.

People Who Have Helped the World, 24 vols. 1360p. 1987. Set. PLB 310.80 (ISBN 1-55532-926-8). Gareth Stevens Inc.

Silvani, Harold. Famous People - Men. 30p. (gr. 4-8). 1975. wkbk. 6.95 (ISBN 1-878669-24-9, 4005). Crea Tea Assocs.

Twenty Names, 10 vols. LC 88-20994. (Illus.). 480p. (gr. 4-10). 1988. Set. 129.95 (ISBN 0-86307-962-8). Marshall Cavendish.

Vasquez, Ely P., et al. The Story of Ana: La Historia de Ana. Guzman, Elia, illus. (SPA & ENG., Illus.). 28p. (Orig.). (gr. 3-6). 1985. PLB 7.95 (ISBN 0-932727-15-8); pap. 2.95 (ISBN 0-932727-01-8). Hope Pub Hse.

Who Were They? 128p. (gr. 3-7). 1990. pap. 7.95 (ISBN 0-671-70943-7). S&S Trade.

BIOLOGY

see also Adaptation (Biology); Anatomy; Cells; Color of Animals; Embryology; Evolution; Fresh-Water Biology; Genetics; Life (Biology); Marine Biology; Natural History; Physiology; Reproduction; Sex; Zoology

Becker, Maurice. Biology Flipper. (Illus.). 49p. (gr. 5 up). 1988. Repr. of 1977 ed. trade edition 5.95 (ISBN 1-878383-05-1). C Lee Pubns.

Bender, Lionel. Simple Creatures. Franklin Watts Ltd., ed. Khan, Aziz, illus. 40p. (gr. 7-9). 1988. PLB 12.40 (ISBN 0-531-17092-6, Gloucester Pr). Watts.

Berman, William. How to Dissect. 4th ed. LC 83-27510. (Illus.). 224p. (Orig.). (gr. 8 up). 1984. pap. 7.95 (ISBN 0-668-05941-9). Prentice Hall Pr.

Biology Encyclopedia. (Illus.). 144p. (gr. 4 up). 1989. text ed. 14.95 (ISBN 0-02-689198-0). Checkerboard Pr.

Chisholm, J. Introduction to Biology. Beeson, D., illus. 48p. (gr. 3-6). 1984. PLB 13.96 (ISBN 0-88110-166-4); pap. 6.95 (ISBN 0-86020-707-2). EDC.

Claridge, Marit & Shackell, John. Living Things: A Simple Introduction. (Illus.). 40p. (gr. 3-6). 1986. 10.95 (ISBN 0-86020-986-5). EDC.

Cleeve, Roger. The Living World. Steltenpohl, Jane, ed. (Illus.). 32p. (gr. 3-5). 1990. PLB 10.98 (ISBN 0-671-68627-5); pap. 4.95 (ISBN 0-671-68630-5). Messner.

Corrick, James A. Recent Revolutions in Biology. LC 86-22464. (Illus.). 128p. (gr. 7 up). 1987. PLB 12.90 (ISBN 0-531-10341-2). Watts.

Day, M. H. Fossil History of Man. 3rd ed. Head, J. J., ed. LC 84-70785. (Illus.). 16p. (gr. 10 up). 1984. pap. 2.15 (ISBN 0-89278-432-6, 45-9632). Carolina Biological.

Evans, Ifor. Biology. (Illus.). 40p. (gr. 4-8). 1984. lib. bdg. 12.40 (ISBN 0-531-04743-1). Watts.

Hanauer, Ethel. Biology Experiments for Children. LC 68-9305. (Illus.). 96p. (gr. 5 up). 1969. pap. 2.95 (ISBN 0-486-22032-X). Dover.

Heller, Richard F. & Heller, Rachael F. AP Exam in Biology. 2nd ed. 288p. (gr. 9-12). 1990. pap. 12.95 (ISBN 0-13-038704-5). Arco.

Jepson, Maud. Illustrated Biology, 2 pts. (Illus.). (gr. 8-12). Animals, Pt. 2. 6.95x (ISBN 0-7195-0734-0). Transatl Arts.

Lanham, Url N. Origins of Modern Biology. LC 68-24478. 273p. (gr. 11-12). 1968. 44.00x (ISBN 0-231-02872-5); pap. 17.00x (ISBN 0-231-08660-1). Columbia U Pr.

LeMaster, Leslie J. Cells & Tissues. LC 85-6695. (Illus.). 45p. (gr. k-3). 1985. PLB 14.60 (ISBN 0-516-01266-5). Childrens.

Mimicry & Camouflage. 64p. (gr. 5 up). 1988. 14.95 (ISBN 0-8160-1657-7). Facts On File.

Nourse, Alan E. Menstruation. rev. ed. Greene, Anne, illus. LC 86-24732. 76p. (gr. 6 up). 1987. PLB 10.40 (ISBN 0-531-10308-0). Watts.

Palmer, J. D. Biological Rhythms & Living Clocks. 2nd ed. Head, J. J., ed. LC 84-70786. (Illus.). 16p. (gr. 10 up). 1984. pap. 2.15 (ISBN 0-89278-192-0, 45-9692). Carolina Biological.

—Human Biological Rhythms. Head, J. J., ed. Khoury, Diana, illus. LC 81-67983. 16p. (gr. 10 up). 1983. pap. 2.15 (ISBN 0-89278-304-4, 45-9704). Carolina Biological.

Schulz, Charles M. Charlie Brown's Super Book of Questions & Answers: About All Kinds of Animals from Snails to People. LC 75-39340. (Illus.). (gr. 3-6). 1976. 10.95 (ISBN 0-394-83249-3, Random Juv). Random.

Seddon, Tony & Bailey, Jill. Living World. LC 86-16800. (Illus.). 160p. (gr. 3 up). 1987. pap. 12.95 (ISBN 0-385-23754-5). Doubleday.

Silver, Donald M. Life on Earth: Biology Today. Wynne, Patricia, illus. 96p. (gr. 5 up). 1983. lib. bdg. 7.99 (ISBN 0-394-95971-X); pap. 1.23 (ISBN 0-394-85971-5). Random.

Stockley, C. Dictionary of Biology: The Facts You Need to Know - At a Glance. (Illus.). 128p. (gr. 6 up). 1987. PLB 15.96 (ISBN 0-88110-229-6); pap. 9.95 (ISBN 0-86020-819-2). EDC.

Taylor, Kim. Too Clever to See. (gr. 2-5). 1991. 9.95 (ISBN 0-385-30216-9); PLB 10.99 (ISBN 0-385-30217-7). Delacorte.

Uhlig, Janie & Ham, Karri. Living Things. Burris, Priscilla, illus. Sussman, Ellen, intro. by. (Illus.). 64p. (gr. 3-6). 1989. pap. 6.95 (ISBN 0-933606-71-0). Monkey Sisters.

Wilbur, Richard. Opposites. LC 72-88175. (Illus., Orig.). (gr. 3-7). 1973. 4.95 (ISBN 0-685-02108-4, HJ). HarBraceJ.

—Opposites. D'Andrade, Diane, ed. (Illus.). 48p. 1991. 11.95 (ISBN 0-15-258720-9). HarBraceJ.

BIOLOGY–ECOLOGY

see Ecology

BIOLOGY, ECONOMIC

see Botany, Economic

BIOLOGY–EXPERIMENTS

Harlow, Rosie & Morgan, Gareth. Energy & Growth. Kuo Kang Chen & Fitzsimmons, Cecilia, illus. 40p. (gr. 5-8). 1991. PLB 12.90 (ISBN 0-531-19124-9, Warwick). Watts.

Tocci, Salvatore. Biology Projects for Young Scientists. 1989. pap. 5.95 (ISBN 0-531-15127-1). Watts.

—Biology Projects for Young Scientists. (Illus.). 128p. (gr. 7-12). 1987. PLB 12.90 (ISBN 0-531-10429-X). Watts.

Vancleave, Janice P. Biology for Every Kid: One Hundred & One Easy Experiments That Really Work. 1990. pap. text ed. 10.95 (ISBN 0-471-50381-9). Wiley.

Ward, Alan. Experimenting with Science about Yourself. Flax, Zena, illus. 48p. (gr. 2-7). 1991. PLB 12.95 (ISBN 0-7910-1512-2). Chelsea Hse.

Wood, Robert W. Thirty-Nine Easy Animal Biology Experiments. (Illus.). 160p. (gr. 3-8). 1991. 16.95 (ISBN 0-8306-6594-3, 3594); pap. 9.95 (ISBN 0-8306-3594-7). TAB Bks.

BIOLOGY, MARINE

see Marine Biology

BIOLOGY–STUDY AND TEACHING

Davis, Mary P. Action Biology - Advanced Placement. (Illus.). 540p. (gr. 11-12). 1988. pap. text ed. 14.85 (ISBN 0-931054-18-4). Clark Pub.

—Action Biology - for the First Year. (Illus.). 494p. (gr. 10). 1988. pap. text ed. 14.85 (ISBN 0-931054-19-2). Clark Pub.

Reep, Marianna L. & Plass, Richard M. New York State Regents Biology Laboratory Manual. (Illus.). 138p. (gr. 8-11). 1989. 5.95 (ISBN 0-685-29317-3). Amer Scholastic.

BIOLUMINESCENCE

Silverstien, Alvin & Silverstein, Virginia. Nature's Living Lights: Fireflies & Other Bioluminescent Creatures. Carroll, Pamela & Carroll, Walter, illus. LC 87-2727. 42p. (gr. 2 up). 1988. 12.95 (ISBN 0-316-79119-9). Little.

BIONICS

Gross, Cynthia S. The New Biotechnology: Putting Microbes to Work. LC 88-18823. (Illus.). 96p. (gr. 5 up). 1988. PLB 15.95 (ISBN 0-8225-1583-0). Lerner Pubns.

Silverstein, Alvin & Silverstein, Virginia B. Futurelife: The Biotechnology Revolution. (Illus.). 96p. (gr. 7 up). 1982. 10.95 (ISBN 0-13-345884-9). P-H.

BIOTECHNOLOGY

see Bionics

BIPLANES

see Airplanes

BIRD HOUSES

Naether, Carl & Vriends, Matthew M. Building an Aviary. (Illus.). 160p. (gr. 8 up). 1989. PLB 12.95 (ISBN 0-685-28494-8, PS-763). TFH Pubns.

BIRD SONG

Milkins, Colin S. Discovering Songbirds. (ps-3). 1990. PLB 11.90 (ISBN 0-531-18312-2). Watts.

BIRD WATCHING

see Birds

BIRDS

see also Birds of Prey; Water Birds

Ames, Felicia. The Bird You Care For. 1970. pap. 1.75 (ISBN 0-451-07527-7, E7527, Sig). NAL-Dutton.

Animals, Birds & Fish. (Illus.). (ps-5). 3.50 (ISBN 0-7214-8003-9); wkbk. B 1.95. Ladybird Bks.

Armstrong, B. Birds. 32p. (gr. 1-6). 1988. 3.95 (ISBN 0-88160-161-6, LW 266). Learning Wks.

Austin, Oliver L., Jr. Families of Birds. Rev. ed. Singer, Arthur, illus. (gr. 9 up). 1985. pap. write for info. (ISBN 0-307-13669-8); pap. write for info. (ISBN 0-307-24015-0, Golden Pr). Western Pub.

Baerg, Harry J. Birds That Can't Fly. Van Dolson, Bobbie J., ed. Baerg, Harry J., illus. LC 82-21535. (Orig.). (gr. 3 up). 1983. pap. 4.50 (ISBN 0-8280-0149-9). Review & Herald.

Bailey, Jill & Seddon, Tony. Birds of Prey. (Illus.). 64p. (gr. 5 up). 1988. 14.95 (ISBN 0-8160-1655-0). Facts On File.

Baines, Chris. The Nest: An Ecology Story Book. Ives, Penny, illus. LC 89-77653. 24p. (ps-3). 1990. 7.95 (ISBN 0-940793-55-5, Crocodile Bks). Interlink Pub.

Barrett, Norman. Flightless Birds. (Illus.). 32p. (gr. k-4). 1991. PLB 11.40 (ISBN 0-531-14112-8). Watts.

Bash, Barbara. Urban Roosts: Where Birds Nest in the City. Bash, Barbara, illus. (gr. 1-5). 1990. 14.95 (ISBN 0-316-08306-2). Little.

Bender, Lionel. Birds & Mammals. Franklin Watts Ltd., ed. Khan, Aziz, illus. 40p. (gr. 7-9). 1988. PLB 12.40 (ISBN 0-531-17091-8, Gloucester Pr). Watts.

Birds. 32p. (Orig.). (ps-1). 1984. pap. 1.25 (ISBN 0-8431-1516-5). Price Stern.

Birds. (gr. 4-6). 1984. 2.95 (ISBN 0-8431-4267-7). Price Stern.

Birds & How They Live. (Illus.). (gr. 4 up). 3.50 (ISBN 0-7214-0124-4). Ladybird Bks.

Birds of Arizona. (Illus.). 32p. (gr. 3 up). 1984. pap. 1.00 (ISBN 0-935810-13-7). Primer Pubs.

Blassingame, Wyatt. Wonders of Egrets, Bitterns, & Herons. 1982. 9.95 (ISBN 0-396-08033-2, Putnam). Putnam Pub Group.

Board, Tessa. Birds. (gr. 4 up). 1983. PLB 11.40 (ISBN 0-531-03472-0). Watts.

Boulton, Carolyn. Birds. Newman, Colin, illus. LC 84-50015. 32p. (gr. 2-4). 1984. PLB 11.90 (ISBN 0-531-04634-6). Watts.

Boy Scouts of America. Bird Study. (Illus.). 64p. (gr. 6-12). 1984. pap. 1.85 (ISBN 0-8395-3282-2, 3282). BSA.

Braithwaite, Althea. Birds. (ps-6). 1988. PLB 7.95 (ISBN 0-88462-178-2); pap. 2.95 (ISBN 0-88462-179-0). Dearborn Finan.

Bremmer. How Birds Live. (gr. 4-6). 1981. (Usborne-Hayes); PLB 13.96 (ISBN 0-88110-082-X); pap. 6.95 (ISBN 0-86020-157-0). EDC.

Brenner, Barbara. Baltimore Orioles. Higgenbottom, J. Winslow, illus. LC 73-14327. 64p. (gr. k-3). 1974. HarpC Child Bks.

—Have You Ever Heard of a Kangaroo Bird? Brady, Irene, illus. 48p. (gr. 3-5). 1980. 7.95 (ISBN 0-698-20446-8, Coward). Putnam Pub Group.

Burnie, David. Bird. Chadwick, Peter, photos by. LC 87-26441. (Illus.). 64p. (gr. 5 up). 1988. 15.00 (ISBN 0-394-89619-X); lib. bdg. 15.99 (ISBN 0-394-99619-4). Knopf.

Burton, Maurice. Birds. (Illus.). 64p. (gr. 4-7). 1985. 15.95 (ISBN 0-8160-1063-3). Facts on File.

Caitlin, Stephen. Amazing World of Birds. Snyder, Joel, illus. LC 89-4968. 32p. (gr. 2-4). 1990. PLB 10.89 (ISBN 0-8167-1747-8); pap. text ed. 2.95 (ISBN 0-8167-1748-6). Troll Assocs.

Cole, Joanna. A Bird's Body. Wexler, Jerome, illus. LC 82-6446. 48p. (gr. k-3). 1982. 12.95 (ISBN 0-688-01470-4); lib. bdg. 12.88 (ISBN 0-688-01471-2, Morrow Jr Bks). Morrow Jr Bks.

Cook, David. Birds. Cook, David, illus. LC 84-11398. 32p. (gr. 3-7). 1985. bds. 5.95 (ISBN 0-517-55431-3). Crown.

Coombs, Charles. Soaring: Where Hawks & Eagles Fly. LC 87-26588. (Illus.). 144p. (gr. k-6). 1988. 13.95 (ISBN 0-8050-0496-3). H Holt & Co.

Cox & Cork. Birds. (gr. 2-5). 1980. (Usborne-Hayes); PLB 11.96 (ISBN 0-88110-072-2); pap. 3.95 (ISBN 0-86020-475-8). EDC.

Forsyth, Adrian & Aziz, Laurel. Exploring the World of Birds: An Equinox Guide to Avian Life. (Illus.). 72p. (gr. 4 up). 1990. 15.95 (ISBN 0-920656-98-6); pap. 9.95 (ISBN 0-920656-94-3). Firefly Bks Ltd.

The fourth in Camden House's series of children's science books, EXPLORING THE WORLD OF BIRDS is an intriguing look at life on the wing. Authors Adrian Forsyth & Laurel Aziz investigate the behaviour of one of our most visible creatures, highlighting the fascinating adaptations birds have made in order to survive in a changing environment. Avoiding the predictable route of simple bird identification, the authors suggest that children can learn much more about their subjects by thoughtful observation: a noisy gang of house sparrows on a telephone wire are not just singing but intimidating a neighbourhood cat; a killdeer with a broken wing is not wounded at all but leading predators away from its nest; the robin standing on your lawn with its head cocked is actually listening for the sound of worms in the earth. Beautifully illustrated with dozens of colour photographs, EXPLORING THE WORLD OF BIRDS is a lively beginner's guide to both the common & cryptic behaviours of the only animal with feathers.

Publisher Provided Annotation.

Fowler, Allan. It Could Still Be a Bird. LC 90-2206. (Illus.). 32p. (ps-2). 1990. PLB 12.60 (ISBN 0-516-04901-1); pap. 30.60 big bk. (ISBN 0-516-49461-9). Childrens.

Friskey, Margaret. Birds We Know. LC 81-7745. (Illus.). 48p. (gr. k-4). 1981. PLB 14.60 (ISBN 0-516-01609-1); pap. 4.95 (ISBN 0-516-41609-X). Childrens.

Ganeri, A. Bird Facts. (Illus.). 48p. (gr. 3-7). 1991. lib. bdg. 12.96 (ISBN 0-88110-530-9, Usborne); pap. 5.95 (ISBN 0-7460-0619-5, Usborne). EDC.

Green, Carl & Sanford, Bill. Dodo. LC 89-7867. (Illus.). 48p. (gr. 4 up). 1989. 10.95 (ISBN 0-89686-455-3, Crestwood Hse). Macmillan Child Grp.

Haley, Neale. Birds for Pets & Pleasure. Carroll, Pamela, illus. LC 80-68740. 224p. (gr. 7 up). 1981. PLB 8.95 (ISBN 0-385-28053-X); pap. 4.95 (ISBN 0-440-00475-6). Delacorte.

Hall, George. Hot Wings of the World. (Illus.). 24p. (Orig.). 1990. pap. 2.50 (ISBN 0-942025-86-5). Kidsbks.

Harner, David L. Attracting & Feeding Wild Birds in the Prescott Area. (Illus.). 96p. (Orig.). (gr. 12). 1989. pap. 3.95 (ISBN 0-685-26081-X). Harner Pubns.

Hiller, Ilo. Introducing Birds to Young Naturalists: From Texas Parks & Wildlife Magazine. LC 89-4398. (Illus.). (gr. 6). 1989. lib. bdg. 21.50x (ISBN 0-89096-412-2); pap. 12.95 (ISBN 0-89096-410-6). Tex A&M Univ Pr.

Hirschi, Ron. What Is a Bird? Walker, Galen B., photos by. (Illus.). (ps-4). 1987. 10.95 (ISBN 0-8027-6720-6); PLB 11.85 (ISBN 0-8027-6721-4). Walker & Co.

—Where Do Birds Live? Walker, Galen B., photos by. (Illus.). (ps-4). 1987. 10.95 (ISBN 0-8027-6722-2); PLB 11.85 (ISBN 0-8027-6723-0). Walker & Co.

Hornblow, Leonora & Hornblow, Arthur. Birds Do the Strangest Things. reissued ed. Singer, Alan D., illus. LC 90-8583. 64p. (gr. 2-4). 1991. PLB 6.99 (ISBN 0-679-91159-6); pap. 3.95 (ISBN 0-679-81159-1). McKay.

Hoyt, George & Hoyt, Doris. A Bird's-Eye View of California. Atkinson, Mary, illus. 48p. (Orig.). (gr. k-4). 1989. pap. 4.95 (ISBN 0-9622364-4-6). Adona Pub.

Hurd, Edith T. Look for a Bird. Hurd, Clement, illus. LC 76-58726. (gr. k-3). 1977. PLB 8.89 (ISBN 0-06-022720-6). HarpC Child Bks.

Illustrated Encyclopedia of Wildlife, Vol. 6: The Birds, Pt. I. 208p. (gr. 7 up). 1990. lib. bdg. write for info. (ISBN 1-55905-042-X). Grey Castle.

Illustrated Encyclopedia of Wildlife, Vol. 7: The Birds, Pt. II. 208p. (gr. 7 up). 1990. lib. bdg. write for info. (ISBN 1-55905-043-8). Grey Castle.

Illustrated Encyclopedia of Wildlife, Vol. 8: The Birds, Pt. III. 208p. (gr. 7 up). 1990. lib. bdg. write for info. (ISBN 1-55905-044-6). Grey Castle.

Jennings, Terry. Birds. LC 89-455. (Illus.). 32p. (gr. 3-6). 1989. PLB 14.60 (ISBN 0-516-08436-4); pap. 4.95 (ISBN 0-516-48436-2). Childrens.

Kaufman, Joe. Joe Kaufman's Big Book about Mammals & Birds. (gr. 1-7). 1989. write for info. (ISBN 0-307-15813-6, Pub. by Golden Bks). Western Pub.

A Kid's First Book of Birdwatching. (Illus.). 64p. (ps up). 1990. incl. cassette 14.95 (ISBN 0-89471-826-6). Running Pr.

Kuchalla, Susan. Birds. Britt, Gary, illus. LC 81-11412. 32p. (gr. k-2). 1982. lib. bdg. 10.89 (ISBN 0-89375-656-3); pap. 2.95 (ISBN 0-89375-657-1). Troll Assocs.

Legg, Gerald. Amazing Tropical Birds. Young, Jerry, photos by. LC 91-6515. (Illus.). 32p. (Orig.). (gr. 1-5). 1991. lib. bdg. 9.99 (ISBN 0-679-91520-6); pap. 7.00 (ISBN 0-679-81520-1). Knopf.

Lohr, J. E. Your First Cockatiel. (Illus.). 36p. (Orig.). 1991. pap. 1.95 (ISBN 0-86622-060-7, YF-104). TFH Pubns.

McGowen, Tom. Album of Birds. (Illus.). 72p. (gr. 3 up). 1982. write for info. (ISBN 0-528-82413-9); PLB write for info. (ISBN 0-528-80076-0). Checkerboard Pr.

McKean, Barb. Birds. Migliore, Ron, illus. 32p. (gr. 3-7). 1985. pap. 3.50 (ISBN 0-88625-116-8). Durkin Hayes Pub.

MacPherson, Mary. Birdwatch: A Young Person's Introduction to Birding. Douglas, Virginia, illus. 144p. (Orig.). (gr. 6 up). 1989. pap. 9.95 (ISBN 0-920197-57-4, Pub. by Summerhill CN). Sterling.

Matthews, Downs. Skimmers. Guravich, Dan, photos by. (Illus.). 40p. (gr. 2-5). 1990. PLB 13.95 (ISBN 0-671-70070-7). S&S Trade.

Milkins, Colin S. Discovering Songbirds. (ps-3). 1990. PLB 11.90 (ISBN 0-531-18312-2). Watts.

Mitchell, Victor. Birds. Mitchell, Victor, illus. 16p. (gr. k up). 1988. pap. 1.95 (ISBN 0-7459-1467-5). Lion USA.

Nero, Robert. Birds, Vol. 1. (Illus.). 40p. (Orig.). (gr. 2-6). 1990. pap. 4.95 (ISBN 0-920534-52-X, Pub. by Hyperion Pr Ltd CN). Sterling.

—Birds, Vol. 2. (Illus.). 40p. (gr. 2-6). 1990. pap. 4.95 (ISBN 0-920534-54-6, Pub. by Hyperion Pr Ltd CN). Sterling.

Noreen, George W. Your First Finch. (Illus.). 36p. (Orig.). 1991. pap. 1.95 (ISBN 0-86622-062-3, YF-106). TFH Pubns.

O'Connor, Karen. The Feather Book. (Illus.). 60p. (gr. 4 up). 1990. lib. bdg. 14.95 (ISBN 0-87518-445-6, Dillon). Macmillan Child Grp.

Parnall, Peter. The Daywatchers. Parnall, Peter, illus. LC 84-5764. 112p. (gr. 7 up). 1984. 18.95 (ISBN 0-02-770190-5, Mcmillan Child Bk). Macmillan Child Grp.

Parramon, J. M. My First Visit to the Aviary. Sales, G., illus. 32p. (ps). 1990. pap. 4.95 (ISBN 0-8120-4303-0). Barron.

Parsons, Alexandra. Amazing Birds. Young, Jerry, photos by. LC 89-38943. (Illus.). (gr. 1-5). 1990. 6.95 (ISBN 0-679-80223-1); PLB 9.99 (ISBN 0-685-31213-5). McKay.

Pasca, Sue-Rhee. Your First Canary. (Illus.). 36p. (Orig.). 1991. pap. 1.95 (ISBN 0-86622-059-3, YF-103). TFH Pubns.

Paysan, Klaus. Birds of the World in Field & Garden. Paysan, Angela & Paysan, Klaus, illus. LC 70-102891. 108p. (gr. 5 up). 1970. PLB 10.95 (ISBN 0-8225-0560-6). Lerner Pubns.

Polette, Nancy. Birds in Literature. (Illus.). 48p. 1990. pap. 5.95 (ISBN 0-913839-86-8). Bk Lures.

Potter, Beatrix. Tale of the Faithful Dove. Angel, Marie, illus. LC 75-109403. (gr. k-3). 1970. 5.95 (ISBN 0-7232-1336-4). Warne.

Reid, Struan. Bird World. (Illus.). 64p. (gr. 4-6). 1991. PLB 13.90 (ISBN 1-56294-009-0). Millbrook Pr.

Roots, Clive. Tropical Birds of the World. Karsten, Peter, illus. 40p. (Orig.). (gr. 2-6). 1990. pap. 4.95 (ISBN 0-920534-82-1, Pub. by Hyperion Pr Ltd CN). Sterling.

Santrey, Laurence. Birds. Johnson, Pamela, illus. LC 84-2731. 32p. (gr. 3-6). 1985. PLB 9.49 (ISBN 0-8167-0192-X); pap. text ed. 2.95 (ISBN 0-8167-0193-8). Troll Assocs.

Schultz, Ellen. I Can Read About Birds. LC 78-73775. (Illus.). (gr. 2-4). 1979. pap. 1.95 (ISBN 0-89375-204-5). Troll Assocs.

Scott, Jack D. Orphans from the Sea. Sweet, Ozzie, illus. 64p. 1982. 10.95 (ISBN 0-399-20858-5, Putnam). Putnam Pub Group.

Selsam, Millicent E. & Hunt, Joyce. A First Look at Birds. Springer, Harriet, illus. LC 73-81404. 32p. (gr. 2-4). 1973. PLB 12.85 (ISBN 0-8027-6164-X). Walker & Co.

Singer, Arthur & Singer, Alan, illus. State Birds. Buckley, Virginia, commentary by. LC 86-2209. 64p. (gr. 4 up). 1990. 16.95 (ISBN 0-525-67177-3, Lodestar Bks); pap. 5.95 (ISBN 0-525-67314-8, Lodestar Bks). Dutton Child Bks.

Singer, Marilyn. Exotic Birds. (gr. 4-7). 1991. pap. 13.99 (ISBN 0-385-26572-7). Doubleday.

Smith, William J. Birds & Beasts. Hnizdovsky, Jacques, illus. (gr. k up). 1990. 18.95 (ISBN 0-87923-865-8). Godine.

Spizzirri Publishing Co. Staff. Birds: Educational Coloring Book. Spizzirri, Linda, ed. Goodman, Marlene, et al, illus. 32p. (gr. 1-8). 1981. pap. 1.95 (ISBN 0-86545-026-9). Spizzirri.

—Prehistoric Birds: An Educational Coloring Book. Spizzirri, Linda, ed. Spizzirri, Peter M., illus. 32p. (gr. 1-8). 1981. pap. 1.95 (ISBN 0-86545-023-4). Spizzirri.

Steele, Philip. Birds. LC 90-42015. (Illus.). 32p. (gr. 5-6). 1991. SBE 9.95 (ISBN 0-89686-583-5, Crestwood Hse). Macmillan Child Grp.

Stone, Lynn. Bird Discovery Library, 6 bks, Reading Level 2. (Illus.). 144p. (gr. k-5). Date not set. Set. PLB 71.60 (ISBN 0-86592-320-5). Rourke Corp.

Stone, Lynn M. Vultures. LC 88-30196. (Illus.). 24p. (gr. 2-4). 1989. PLB 11.93 (ISBN 0-86592-324-8). Rourke Corp.

Storms, Laura. The Bird Book. Lerner, Sharon, illus. LC 82-15189. 32p. (gr. k-3). 1982. lib. bdg. 7.95 (ISBN 0-8225-1116-9). Lerner Pubns.

Wallace, Ian, et al. Bird Life. Quinn, David, et al, illus. 32p. (gr. 4-7). 1985. lib. bdg. 13.96 (ISBN 0-88110-172-9); pap. 5.95 (ISBN 0-86020-841-9). EDC.

Watts, Barrie. Bird's Nest. (Illus.). 24p. (gr. 2-5). 1987. 6.95 (ISBN 0-382-09443-3); PLB 9.98 (ISBN 0-382-09439-5); pap. 3.95 (ISBN 0-382-24015-4). Silver Burdett Pr.

Weston, A. A Step-by-Step Book about Lovebirds. (Illus.). 64p. (gr. 9-12). 1988. pap. 3.95 (ISBN 0-86622-456-4, SK-016). TFH Pubns.

Whyte, Malcolm. North American Birdlife Color & Story Album. (gr. 2 up). pap. 4.50 (ISBN 0-8431-1730-3). Price Stern.

Wiessinger, John. Birds--Right Before Your Eyes. Line, Les, frwd. by. (Illus.). 64p. (gr. 4-10). 1988. lib. bdg. 15.95 (ISBN 0-89490-167-2). Enslow Pubs.

Wildsmith, Brian. Birds by Brian Wildsmith. (Illus.). (gr. k-4). 1967. pap. 5.95 (ISBN 0-19-272117-8). Oxford U Pr.

Zim, Herbert S. & Gabrielson, Ira N. Birds. Irving, James G., illus. (gr. 7 up). 1956. PLB write for info. (ISBN 0-307-24053-3); pap. write for info. (Golden Pr). Western Pub.

BIRDS, AQUATIC

see Water Birds

BIRDS–EGGS AND NESTS

Babson, Jane F. The Nest on the Porch. Babson, Jane F., illus. LC 88-51084. 32p. (Orig.). (ps up). 1989. pap. 4.95 (ISBN 0-940787-01-6). Winstead Pr.

Curran, Eileen. Birds Nests. Johnson, Pamela, illus. LC 84-8658. 32p. (gr. k-2). 1985. PLB 10.89 (ISBN 0-8167-0341-8); pap. text ed. 2.95 (ISBN 0-8167-0342-6). Troll Assocs.

Gans, Roma. It's Nesting Time. Mizumura, Kazue, illus. LC 64-10861. (gr. k-3). 1964. PLB 13.89 (ISBN 0-690-45544-5, Crowell Jr Bks); filmstrip with record 11.95 (ISBN 0-690-45545-3, Crowell Jr Bks); filmstrip with cassette 14.95 (ISBN 0-690-45547-X, Crowell Jr Bks). HarpC Child Bks.

McCauley, Jane R. Baby Birds & How They Grow, 4 vols. Crump, Donald J., ed. LC 83-13150. 32p. (ps-3). 1983. Set. 10.95 (ISBN 0-87044-487-5); lib. bdg. 12.95 (ISBN 0-87044-492-1). Natl Geog.

Reidel, Marlene. From Egg to Bird. Reidel, Marlene, illus. 24p. (ps-3). 1981. PLB 6.95 (ISBN 0-87614-159-9). Carolrhoda Bks.

Selsam, Millicent E., et al. A First Look at Birds' Nest. Springer, Harriett, illus. LC 84-15238. 32p. (gr. 1-4). 1984. lib. bdg. 9.85 (ISBN 0-8027-6565-3). Walker & Co.

BIRDS–FICTION

Aiken, Joan. Mortimer Says Nothing. Blake, Quentin, illus. LC 86-45488. 192p. (gr. 3-6). 1987. PLB 12.89 (ISBN 0-06-020039-1). HarpC Child Bks.

—Nightbirds on Nantucket. 243p. (gr. k-6). 1981. pap. 1.75 (ISBN 0-440-96370-2, YB). Dell.

Amoss, Berthe. The Mockingbird Song. LC 87-45272. 128p. (gr. 4-7). 1988. 12.95i (ISBN 0-06-020061-8); PLB 13.89 (ISBN 0-06-020062-6). HarpC Child Bks.

Anastasio, Dina. Big Bird Can Share. Leigh, Tom, illus. 32p. (ps-k). 1985. write for info. (ISBN 0-307-12016-3, Pub. by Golden Bks). Western Pub.

Andersen, Hans Christian. The Nightingale. Zwerger, Lisbeth, illus. LC 84-9492. (gr. 1 up). 1984. 14.95 (ISBN 0-907234-57-7). Picture Bk Studio.

Baker, Keith. The Dove's Letter. Baker, Keith, illus. LC 87-8530. 32p. (ps-3). 1988. 14.95 (ISBN 0-15-224133-7, HJ). HarBraceJ.

Bang, Molly. The Paper Crane. Bang, Molly, illus. LC 84-13546. 32p. (gr. k-3). 1985. 13.95 (ISBN 0-688-04108-6); lib. bdg. 13.88 (ISBN 0-688-04109-4). Greenwillow.

Berenstain, Stan & Berenstain, Janice. After the Dinosaurs. Berenstain, Stan & Berenstain, Janice, illus. LC 88-42588. 32p. (Orig.). (gr. k-3). 1988. lib. bdg. 5.99 (ISBN 0-394-90518-0, Random Juv); pap. 2.25 (ISBN 0-394-80518-6, Random Juv). Random.

Berliner, Franz. Miserable Marabou. Hedlund, Irene, illus. LC 89-30852. 23p. (gr. k-3). 1989. PLB 12.95 (ISBN 0-8368-0094-X). Gareth Stevens Inc.

Bowman, Margret & Millhouse, Nicholas. Blue-Footed Booby: Bird of the Galapagos. Bowman, Margret, illus. LC 85-27617. 32p. (gr. 1-7). 1986. 11.95 (ISBN 0-8027-6628-5); lib. bdg. 11.85 (ISBN 0-8027-6629-3). Walker & Co.

Bragg, Ruth. Mrs. Muggle's Sparkle. Bragg, Ruth, illus. LC 89-31371. 28p. (ps up). 1990. 14.95 (ISBN 0-88708-106-1). Picture Bk Studio.

Breneman, Steven B. Fly Away Home. LC 84-6252. 74p. (Orig.). (gr. 2-6). 1984. pap. 7.50 (ISBN 0-87743-183-3, Pub. by Bellwood Pr). Baha'i.

Brodzinsky, Anne B. The Mulberry Bird: Story of an Adoption. LC 86-2460. (Illus.). 48p. (gr. k-5). 1986. 9.95 (ISBN 0-9609504-5-1). Perspect Indiana.

This award winning (Catholic Adoptive Parents Association) book uses the story of a mother bird & her much loved baby to explore why a birthparent might make an adoption plan-an area which rarely receives much attention in adoption literature, but the issue which is of the greatest concern to children who were adopted. The author was part of a Rutgers University team which has conducted a longitudinal study of what children understand & when. Well reviewed in adoption periodicals, Small Press Book Review, School Library Journal, etc., this is the best selling children's book from a publisher focusing exclusively on adoption issues. Other adoption related children's books from Perspectives Press include Jane Schnitter's WILLIAM IS MY BROTHER (family built by birth & adoption), Janice Koch's OUR BABY: A BIRTH & ADOPTION STORY (sex education), Ann Angel's REAL FOR SURE SISTER (transracial adoption); Susan Gabel's WHERE THE SUN KISSES THE SEA (international placement), & Susan Gabel's FILLING IN THE BLANKS: A GUIDED LOOK AT GROWING UP ADOPTED (adolescence). Distributed by Ingram, Baker & Taylor or contact the publisher at (317) 872-3055.

Publisher Provided Annotation.

Bulla, Clyde R. White Bird. Cook, Donald, illus. LC 89-70231. 64p. (Orig.). (gr. 2-4). 1990. lib. bdg. 6.99 (ISBN 0-679-90662-2, Random Juv); pap. 2.50 (ISBN 0-679-80662-8, Random Juv). Random.

Burton, Marilee R. Oliver's Birthday. LC 85-45682. (Illus.). 32p. (ps-k). 1986. 11.95 (ISBN 0-06-020879-1). HarpC Child Bks.

Calvert, Patricia. The Snowbird. 192p. (gr. 7 up). 1982. pap. 1.95 (ISBN 0-451-13353-6, AE1354, Sig Vista). NAL-Dutton.

Campbell, Louise A. & Bowers, Grace A. Muffin, The Maine Puffin. Mason, MacAdam L., illus. 40p. (Orig.). (gr. k-3). 1988. pap. 9.95 (ISBN 0-9621949-0-5). Muffin Enter.

There's a lovable, colorful bird that lives off the coast of Maine. He learns to swim, learns to take a bath & learns to eat by himself. He catches a cold & meets a new friend. He's Muffin, an Atlantic Puffin growing up on the islands off the Maine coast. With his mother & father, his friends & the wide open ocean he learns everything a young person would...well, almost everything. Muffin learns to fly, too. MUFFIN, THE MAINE PUFFIN is a children's book written by first-time authors Louise Campbell & Grace Bowers. The colorful illustrations by MacAdam Lee Mason are perfectly matched to these seven stories of the triumphs & obstacles of growing & learning. MUFFIN, THE MAINE PUFFIN is a wonderful idea for children (or grandchildren) 4 to 8 years old.

Publisher Provided Annotation.

Cawthorne, W. A. Who Killed Cockatoo? McRae, Rodney, illus. 32p. 1989. 13.95 (ISBN 0-374-38395-2). FS&G.

Clair, Bevan. Run Roadrunner. LC 80-82912. (ps-6). 1980. pap. 1.50 (ISBN 0-686-30719-4). B A Scott.

Climo, Shirley. King of the Birds. Heller, Ruth, illus. LC 87-47693. 32p. (gr. k-3). 1988. 12.95 (ISBN 0-690-04621-9, Crowell Jr Bks); PLB 14.89 (ISBN 0-690-04623-5). HarpC Child Bks.

Cole, Brock. The Winter Wren. LC 84-1583. (Illus.). 32p. (gr. 2 up). 1984. 13.95 (ISBN 0-374-38454-1, Sunburst); pap. 4.95 (ISBN 0-374-48408-2). FS&G.

Cooke, Tom, illus. Hide-&-Seek with Big Bird: A Sesame Street Book. LC 89-64284. 14p. (ps). 1991. bds. 2.95 (ISBN 0-679-80785-3). Random.

Cosgrove, Stephen. The Nosey Birds. Steelhammer, Ilona, illus. 24p. (gr. k-2). 1990. PLB 10.95 (ISBN 1-878363-22-0). Forest Hse.

Damjan, Mischa. The False Flamingoes. Steadman, Ralph, illus. LC 70-105399. 32p. (ps-3). 7.95 (ISBN 0-87592-016-0). Scroll Pr.

De Paola, Tomie. Bill & Pete. De Paola, Tomie, illus. LC 78-5330. (gr. k-2). 1978. 13.95 (ISBN 0-399-20646-9, Putnam); pap. 5.95 (ISBN 0-399-20650-7, Putnam). Putnam Pub Group.

Eastman, Philip D. Are You My Mother? LC 60-13495. (Illus.). 64p. (gr. 1-2). 1966. 6.95 (ISBN 0-394-80018-4); lib. bdg. 7.99 (ISBN 0-394-90018-9). Beginner.

—Best Nest. Eastman, Philip D., illus. LC 68-28459. 72p. (gr. k-3). 1968. 6.95 (ISBN 0-394-80051-6); lib. bdg. 7.99 (ISBN 0-394-90051-0). Beginner.

—Flap Your Wings. Eastman, Philip D., illus. (ps-2). 1969. (Random Juv). Random.

Estrada, Zilia C. If I Were a Bird. Estrada, Zilia C., illus. (Orig.). (gr. 1 up). 1988. pap. write for info. Blue Flame Pr.

Farmer, Penelope. The Summer Birds. large type ed. 176p. (gr. 3 up). 1990. lib. bdg. 14.95x (ISBN 0-7451-1066-5, Lythway Large Print). G K Hall.

—The Summer Birds. (gr. 5-10). 1991. 14.75 (ISBN 0-8446-6456-1). Peter Smith.

Fender, Kay. Odette: A Springtime in Paris. Dumas, Philippe, illus. 32p. (ps-3). 1991. 10.95 (ISBN 0-916291-33-2). Kane-Miller Bk.

Firmin, Peter. Pinny & the Bird. Firmin, Peter, illus. 32p. (ps-3). 1986. pap. 4.95 (ISBN 0-670-80957-8). Viking Child Bks.

Forman, James. The Life & Death of Yellow Bird. LC 73-82697. 224p. (gr. 7 up). 1973. 13.95 (ISBN 0-374-34408-6). FS&G.

Fox, Mem. Wilfrid Gordon McDonald Partridge. Vivas, Julie, illus. 32p. (gr. k-4). 1989. pap. 7.95 (ISBN 0-916291-26-X). Kane-Miller Bk.

Garland, Sarah. Polly's Puffin. LC 88-24348. (Illus.). 24p. (ps up). 1989. 11.95 (ISBN 0-688-08748-5); PLB 13.88 (ISBN 0-688-08749-3). Greenwillow.

Hague, Kathleen. The Legend of the Veery Bird. Hague, Michael, illus. LC 84-19732. 32p. (ps-3). 1985. 13.95 (ISBN 0-15-243824-6, HJ). HarBraceJ.

Haley, Gail E. Birdsong. Haley, Gail E., illus. (ps up). 1988. pap. 4.95 (ISBN 0-517-57251-6). Crown.

—Birdsong. Haley, Gail E., illus. LC 83-14372. 32p. (gr. k-3). 1984. 10.95 (ISBN 0-517-55051-2). Crown.
Hargreaves, Roger. Shirley Chirp. Jolliffe, Gray, illus. LC 89-60413. 32p. (Orig.). (ps-3). 1989. pap. 1.95 (ISBN 0-679-80119-7). Random.
Hautzig, Deborah. Big Bird Plays the Violin. Mathieu, Joe, illus. LC 90-8967. 40p. (ps-3). 1991. 4.95 (ISBN 0-679-81675-5); PLB 6.99 (ISBN 0-679-91675-X). Random.
Hautzig, Deborah, adapted by. Big Bird Visits the Dodos. Mathieu, Joe, illus. LC 84-43051. 32p. (ps-3). 1985. lib. bdg. 5.99 (ISBN 0-394-97373-9, Random Juv). Random.
—Follow That Bird. LC 84-43052. (Illus.). 48p. (gr. 1-4). 1985. (Random Juv); lib. bdg. 7.99 (ISBN 0-394-97225-2). Random.
Herman, Gail. Big Bird Visits Granny Bird. Nicklaus, Carol, illus. LC 90-60822. 32p. (Orig.). (ps-3). 1991. pap. 1.50 (ISBN 0-679-81050-1). Random.
Hoffman, Beverly. Skipper & Jade: A Love Story. LC 90-71859. 44p. 1991. pap. 6.95 (ISBN 1-55523-411-9). Winston-Derek.
Holling, Holling C. Seabird. Holling, Holling C., illus. (gr. 4-6). 1978. pap. 5.95 (ISBN 0-395-26681-5). HM.
The Ice Bird. 32p. (gr. 1 up). 1981. pap. 4.50 (ISBN 0-941402-01-0). Devon Pub.
Ingoglia, Gina. Sylvester & Tweety: What a Mess. (ps-3). 1990. write for info. (ISBN 0-307-11595-X). Western Pub.
Ishii, Momoko. Tongue-Cut Sparrow. Paterson, Katherine, tr. LC 86-29314. (Illus.). 40p. (ps-3). 1987. 13.95 (ISBN 0-525-67199-4, Lodestar Bks). Dutton Child Bks.
Kamal, Aleph. The Bird Who Was an Elephant. Lessac, Frane, illus. LC 89-14536. 32p. (gr. k-4). 1990. 14.95 (ISBN 0-397-32445-6, Lipp Jr Bks); PLB 14.89 (ISBN 0-397-32446-4, Lipp Jr Bks). HarpC Child Bks.
Kamen, Gloria. The Ringdoves: From the Fables of Bidpai. Kamen, Gloria, illus. LC 87-17404. 32p. (gr. k-3). 1988. 13.95 (ISBN 0-689-31312-8, Atheneum Child Bk). Macmillan Child Grp.
Kent, Jack. Round Robin. Kent, Jack, illus. (ps up). 1989. pap. 12.95 (ISBN 0-671-66698-3); pap. 5.95 (ISBN 0-671-66969-9). S&S Trade.
Klein, Gerda W. Peregrinations: Adventures with the Green Parrot. Chabela, Elizabeth H., illus. LC 86-80966. 48p. (gr. 3-4). 1986. 12.95 (ISBN 0-9616699-0-X); pap. 5.95 (ISBN 0-9616699-1-8). CHB Goodyear Comm.
Klepser, Priscilla. Friends of the Earth. (Illus.). 19p. 1989. 7.95 (ISBN 0-533-08425-3). Vantage.
Kveton, Steven. The Legend of Fredbird. Koehler, Ed, illus. 16p. (Orig.). (ps up). 1986. pap. text ed. 2.95 (ISBN 0-9616799-0-5). Water St Missouri.
Langton, Jane. Fledgling. LC 79-2008. 192p. (gr. 3-7). 1980. PLB 12.89 (ISBN 0-06-023679-5). HarpC Child Bks.
Laurin, Anne. Perfect Crane. Mikolaycak, Charles, illus. LC 80-7912. 32p. (gr. 1-4). 1981. PLB 12.89 (ISBN 0-06-023744-9). HarpC Child Bks.
Lawson, Amy. The Talking Bird & the Story Pouch. Brown, Craig M., illus. LC 86-45493. 96p. (gr. 5up). 1987. 11.95 (ISBN 0-06-023833-X); PLB 11.89 (ISBN 0-06-023834-8). HarpC Child Bks.
Lerner, Sharon. Big Bird's Copycat Day: A Step 1 Book. Jacquet, Jean-Pierre & Mathieu, Joe, illus. LC 84-6869. 32p. (ps-2). 1984. lib. bdg. 6.99 (ISBN 0-394-96912-X, Pub. by BYR); pap. 2.95 (ISBN 0-394-86912-5). Random.
Lewis, Tracey. Where Do All the Birds Go? Lewis, Tracey, illus. LC 88-3743. 32p. (ps-1). 1988. 10.95 (ISBN 0-525-44427-0, DCB). Dutton Child Bks.
Lindgren, Astrid. My Nightingale Is Singing. Otto, Svend, illus. 32p. (gr. k-5). 1986. pap. 10.95 (ISBN 0-670-80997-7). Viking Child Bks.
Lionni, Leo. Inch by Inch. (Illus.). (gr. k-1). 1962. 10.95 (ISBN 0-8392-3010-9). Astor-Honor.
—Pulgada a Pulgada. (SPA., Illus.). (gr. k-1). 1961. 10.95 (ISBN 0-8392-3030-3). Astor-Honor.
Lorenz, Lee. The Feathered Ogre. (Illus.). 48p. (gr. 1-4). 1981. 9.95 (ISBN 0-13-308304-7). P-H.
McCutcheon, Elsie. Storm Bird. LC 87-45013. 176p. (gr. 4 up). 1987. 11.95 (ISBN 0-374-37269-1). FS&G.
Maddox, Tony. Spike, the Sparrow Who Couldn't Sing. Maddox, Tony, illus. 24p. (ps-k). 1989. 5.95 (ISBN 0-8120-6133-0). Barron.
Martchenko, Michael. Bird Feeder Banquet. Martchenko, Michael, illus. 24p. (Orig.). (gr. k-3). 1990. 14.95 (ISBN 1-55037-147-9); pap. 4.95 (ISBN 1-55037-146-0). Firefly Bks Ltd.
Marzilli, Vincent, II. Return of the Nighthawks. Marzilli, Roanne O., illus. 56p. (Orig.). (gr. k-6). 1987. pap. 7.95 (ISBN 0-9617809-1-6). Vincent Marzilli.
Meddaugh, Susan. Tree of Birds. Meddaugh, Susan, illus. 32p. (gr. k-3). 1990. 13.95 (ISBN 0-395-53147-0). HM.
Min, Willemien. The Birdman. Min, Willemien, illus. 32p. (ps-2). 1989. 13.95 (ISBN 0-525-44413-0, DCB). Dutton Child Bks.
Minagawa, Toshio. The Mongoose & the Mynas. 32p. (ps-3). 1991. 6.95 (ISBN 0-8062-3931-X). Carlton.
Mister Tom. Fuzzy Buzzard. Bretlinger, Ted, illus. 32p. (gr. 2-4). 1978. write for info. Oddo.
Moncure, Jane B. Happy Birthday, Word Bird. Hohag, Linda, illus. LC 83-15256. 32p. (gr. k-2). 1983. PLB 11.97 (ISBN 0-89565-256-0). Childs World.
—Hi, Word Bird. Hohag, Linda S., illus. LC 80-15919. 32p. (ps-2). 1981. PLB 11.97 (ISBN 0-89565-159-9). Childs World.
—Word Bird Asks: What? What? What? Gohman, Vera, illus. LC 83-15258. 32p. (gr. k-2). 1983. PLB 11.97 (ISBN 0-89565-258-7). Childs World.
—Word Bird Builds a City. Gohman, Vera, illus. LC 83-15275. 32p. (ps-2). 1983. PLB 11.97 (ISBN 0-89565-257-9). Childs World.
—Word Bird's Circus Surprise. Hohag, Linda, illus. LC 80-29528. 32p. (gr. k-2). 1981. PLB 11.97 (ISBN 0-89565-162-9). Childs World.
—Word Bird's Shapes. Hohag, Linda, illus. LC 83-15255. 32p. (gr. k-2). 1983. PLB 11.97 (ISBN 0-89565-255-2). Childs World.
Moore, Ruth N. Tomas & the Talking Birds. Graber, Esther R., illus. LC 78-23509. 120p. (gr. 3-8). 1979. pap. 3.95 (ISBN 0-8361-1874-X). Herald Pr.
—Tomas y los Pajaros Parlantes. Graber, Esther R., illus. LC 78-70646. (SPA.). 120p. (gr. 3-8). 1979. pap. 3.95 (ISBN 0-8361-1875-8). Herald Pr.
Nystrom, Carolyn. The Lark Who Had No Song. McElrath-Eslick, Lori, illus. 32p. (ps-6). 1991. 11.95 (ISBN 0-7459-1879-4). Lion USA.
Oana, Katherine. Lori Lamb. Baird, Tate, ed. Burtick, Lyn M., illus. 16p. (Orig.). (ps-k). 1989. pap. 4.52 (ISBN 0-914127-09-8). Univ Class.
Oppenheim, Joanne. Have You Seen Birds? Reid, Barbara, illus. 32p. (gr. 3-7). 1987. pap. 8.95 (ISBN 0-590-40585-3, Scholastic Hardcover). Scholastic Inc.
Parkison, Ralph F. The Little Girl, the Lillipop, & the Green Bird, Bk. 1. Withrow, Marion O., ed. Bush, William, illus. 31p. (Orig.). (gr. 2-6). 1988. pap. 4.25 (ISBN 0-929949-00-5). Little Wood Bks.
Peet, Bill. Fly Homer Fly. Peet, Bill, illus. (gr. k-3). 1979. 13.95 (ISBN 0-395-24536-2); pap. 4.95 (ISBN 0-395-28005-2). HM.
Pellowski, Michael J. Maxwell Finds a Friend. Kennedy, Anne, illus. LC 85-14085. 48p. (Orig.). (gr. 1-3). 1986. PLB 9.89 (ISBN 0-8167-0586-0); pap. text ed. 2.95 (ISBN 0-8167-0587-9). Troll Assocs.
Pershall, Mary K. Hello, Barney! Wilson, Mark, illus. 32p. (ps-3). 1989. pap. 11.95 (ISBN 0-670-82406-2). Viking Child Bks.
Rees, Claudia. The Bird with the Word Talks about Self-Control. Rees, Claudia, illus. (Orig.). (gr. 1-3). 1987. pap. 0.98 (ISBN 0-89274-451-0). Harrison Hse.
Roberts, Sarah. Don't Cry, Big Bird. Leigh, Tom, illus. LC 81-4075. 40p. (gr. k-2). 1981. 4.95 (ISBN 0-394-84868-3); lib. bdg. 6.99 (ISBN 0-394-94868-8). Random.
Santos, Elsie S. The Master of Song. Santos, Duarte S., illus. 44p. (Orig.). (ps-1). 1984. pap. 3.95 (ISBN 0-914151-02-9). Shawme Ent.
Scholes, Katherine. The Landing: A Night of Birds. Wong, David, illus. 72p. (gr. 4 up). 1989. 12.95 (ISBN 0-385-26191-8, Zephyr-BFYR). Doubleday.
Searcy, Margaret Z. Race of Flitty Hummingbird & Flappy Crane. (Illus.). (gr. 2-4). 1980. 7.50 (ISBN 0-916620-21-2). Portals Pr.
Segal, Lore. Other Peoples' Houses. 320p. (Orig.). 1986. pap. 3.95 (ISBN 0-449-21149-5, Crest). Fawcett.
Silver, Jody. Rupert, Polly & Daisy. Silver, Jody, illus. LC 83-24979. 48p. (ps-3). 1984. 5.95 (ISBN 0-8193-1124-3). Parents.
Sis, Peter. Rainbow Rhino. Sis, Peter, illus. LC 87-2679. 40p. (ps-1). 1987. 11.95 (ISBN 0-394-89009-4); lib. bdg. 12.99 (ISBN 0-394-99009-9). Knopf.
Snyder, Zilpha K. And Condors Danced. LC 87-5364. 216p. (gr. 4-6). 1987. 14.95 (ISBN 0-385-29575-8). Delacorte.
—And Condors Danced. 224p. (gr. k-6). 1989. pap. 3.25 (ISBN 0-440-40153-4, YB). Dell.
—The Birds of Summer. 192p. (gr. k-12). 1988. pap. 2.95 (ISBN 0-440-20154-3, LE). Dell.
Sobel, Barbara. The Little Bird. Neulinger, Karen, illus. LC 86-81462. 32p. (gr. k-2). 1986. PLB 7.59 (ISBN 0-87386-018-7); pap. 1.95 (ISBN 0-87386-014-4). Jan Prods.
Sommers, Tish. A Bird's Best Friend. Swanson, Maggie, illus. 32p. (ps-k). 1986. write for info. (ISBN 0-307-12018-X, Pub. by Golden Bks). Western Pub.
Southall, Ivan. Blackbird. LC 88-45328. 112p. (gr. 6 up). 1988. 12.95 (ISBN 0-374-30783-0). FS&G.
Spiller, Burton L. Grouse Feathers. 2nd ed. Hunt, Lynn B., illus. 207p. (gr. 10 up). Repr. 35.00 (ISBN 0-685-37781-4). Derrydale Pr.
—More Grouse Feathers. 2nd ed. Hunt, Lynn B., illus. 238p. (gr. 10 up). Repr. of 1938 ed. 35.00 (ISBN 0-685-37780-6). Derrydale Pr.
Stobbs, William. Who Killed Cock Robin? (Illus.). 28p. (ps up). 1990. bds. 12.95 (ISBN 0-19-279862-6). Oxford U Pr.
Stolp, Hans. The Golden Bird. 1990. 11.95 (ISBN 0-8037-0681-2, Dial); PLB 11.89 (ISBN 0-8037-0751-7). Dial Bks Young.
Strodder, Chris. A Sky for Henry. Kennedy, Emilie, illus. 32p. (ps-3). 1985. pap. 4.95 (ISBN 0-931093-03-1). Red Hen Pr.
Talbert, Marc. Dead Birds Singing. (gr. 7 up). 1988. pap. 2.95 (ISBN 0-440-20036-9, LFL). Dell.
Thackray, Patricia. Fanny McFancy: A Passion for Fashion. Forrest, Sandra, illus. 40p. 1988. 12.95 (ISBN 0-88138-113-6). Green Tiger Pr.
Thiele, Colin. Rotten Egg Paterson to the Rescue. Ritz, Karen, illus. LC 90-36189. 144p. (gr. 4-7). 1991. 13.95 (ISBN 0-06-026104-8); PLB 13.89 (ISBN 0-06-026105-6). HarpC Child Bks.
Thompson, Emily. Big Bird's Square Meal: Stories about Shapes & Colors. Brannon, Thomas, illus. LC 87-81933. 32p. (ps-k). 1988. write for info. (ISBN 0-307-13107-6, Pub. by Golden Bks). Western Pub.
The Tidy Bird. (Illus.). (ps-2). 3.50 (ISBN 0-7214-5023-7). Ladybird Bks.
Tolan, Stephanie. A Time to Fly Free. LC 90-31676. 176p. (gr. 3-7). 1990. pap. 3.95 (ISBN 0-689-71420-3, Aladdin). Macmillan Child Grp.
Tusa, Tricia. Maebelle's Suitcase. Tusa, Tricia, illus. LC 86-12434. 32p. (gr. k-3). 1987. 13.95 (ISBN 0-02-789250-6, Mcmillan Child Bk). Macmillan Child Grp.
Weinberger, Jane. Stormy. Kardas, Alek, illus. LC 85-62021. 54p. (gr. 1-6). 1985. 5.95 (ISBN 0-932433-13-8). Windswept Hse.
Whoopi Bird Whistle. 1990. 9.98 (ISBN 0-8317-6170-9). Smithmark.
Wiggin, Kate D. The Birds' Christmas Carol. (Orig.). (gr. k-6). 1988. pap. 3.50 (ISBN 0-440-40121-6, Pub. by Yearling Classics). Dell.
—Birds Christmas Carol. 1989. pap. 2.50 (ISBN 0-590-42118-2). Scholastic Inc.
Wild, Elizabeth. Along Came a Black Bird. LC 87-45882. 192p. (gr. 3-7). 1988. 11.95 (ISBN 0-397-32293-3, Lipp Jr Bks); PLB 11.89 (ISBN 0-397-32294-1, Lipp Jr Bks). HarpC Child Bks.
Wildsmith, Brian. The Apple Bird. (Illus.). 16p. 1987. pap. 2.95 (ISBN 0-19-272136-4). Oxford U Pr.
Williams, Julie S. And the Birds Appeared. Burningham, Robin Y., illus. 32p. (ps-3). 1988. 8.95 (ISBN 0-8248-1194-1, Kolowalu Bk). UH Pr.
Wittman, Sally. Plenty of Pelly & Peak. Wittman, Sally, illus. LC 79-3675. 64p. (gr. k-3). 1980. 7.64i (ISBN 0-06-026563-9). HarpC Child Bks.
Wolff, Ashley. A Year of Birds. (gr. 5-8). 1984. 13.95 (ISBN 0-399-21697-9, Putnam). Putnam Pub Group.
Ziefert, Harriet. Finding Robin Redbreast. 1988. pap. 4.95 (ISBN 0-14-050839-2, Puffin). Puffin Bks.

BIRDS–FLIGHT

see Flight

BIRDS–HABITS AND BEHAVIOR

Arnold, Caroline. Ostriches & Other Flightless Birds. Hewett, Richard R., illus. 48p. (gr. 2-5). 1990. PLB 12.95 (ISBN 0-87614-377-X). Carolrhoda Bks.
Dixon, Franklin W. House on the Cliff. (gr. 5-9). 1927. 4.50 (ISBN 0-448-08902-5, G&D). Putnam Pub Group.
Gans, Roma. When Birds Change Their Feathers. Bond, Felicia, illus. LC 78-20627. 40p. (gr. k-3). 1980. PLB 13.89 (ISBN 0-690-03948-4, Crowell Jr Bks). HarpC Child Bks.
Hoffman, Mary. Bird of Prey. LC 86-17832. (Illus.). 24p. (gr. k-5). 1987. PLB 13.32 (ISBN 0-8172-2701-6). Raintree Pubs.
Hornblow, Leonora & Hornblow, Arthur. Birds Do the Strangest Things. (Illus.). (gr. 2-6). 1965. 6.95 (ISBN 0-394-80061-3, Random Juv); lib. bdg. 8.99 (ISBN 0-394-90061-8). Random.
Horton, et al. Amazing Fact Book of Birds. (Illus.). 32p. 1987. 11.95 (ISBN 0-685-23223-9). Creative Ed.
Johnson, Sylvia A. Albatrosses of Midway Island. Lanting, Frans, illus. 48p. (gr. 2-5). 1990. PLB 12.95 (ISBN 0-87614-391-5). Carolrhoda Bks.

Kalman, Bobbie. Birds at My Feeder. (Illus.). 56p. (gr. 3-4). 1987. 15.95 (ISBN 0-86505-167-4); pap. 7.95 (ISBN 0-86505-187-9). Crabtree Pub Co.
BIRDS AT MY FEEDER, one of the four superbly illustrated books in the North American Wildlife Series is a favorite with all children. BIRDS AT MY FEEDER portrays North American birds that frequent bird feeders. General bird characteristics are featured, from nesting to migration. There are instructions on building your own bird feeders & on how to attract birds to them. The other books in the series are FOREST MAMMALS, OWLS, & ANIMAL BABIES. These big, beautiful, full-color books feature the art of internationally famous wildlife artist Glen Loates.The superb illustrations delight children while the engaging text encourages them to discover a new understanding of the exciting world of wildlife.
Publisher Provided Annotation.

Losito, Linda, et al. Birds: Aerial Hunters. (Illus.). 96p. 1989. 17.95x (ISBN 0-8160-1963-0). Facts on File.
—Birds: The Plant- & Seed-Eaters. (Illus.). 96p. 1989. 17.95x (ISBN 0-8160-1964-9). Facts on File.
Moncure, Jane B. Life Cycles: The Singing Mailbox. Lexa-Senning, Susan, illus. LC 89-24000. 32p. (ps-2). 1990. lib. bdg. 11.97 (ISBN 0-89565-552-7). Childs World.

Morris, Dean. Birds. rev. ed. LC 87-16672. (Illus.). 48p. (gr. 2-6). 1987. PLB 17.32 (ISBN 0-8172-3203-6). Raintree Pubs.

Raintree Publishers Staff. Birds. LC 87-28786. (Illus.). 64p. (Orig.). (gr. 5-9). 1988. PLB 19.99 (ISBN 0-8172-3084-X). Raintree Pubs.

BIRDS–PICTURES, ILLUSTRATIONS, ETC.

Feliciano-Mendoza, Ester & Rodriquez-Baez, Felix. Ala y Trino: Pajaros De Puerto Rico Libro De Ninos Para Colorear. LC 79-24763. (SPA., Orig.). (ps-3). 1980. pap. 4.50 (ISBN 0-8477-3600-8). U of PR Pr.

Gise, Joanne. A Picture Book of Birds. Pistolesi, Roseanna, illus. LC 89-37328. 24p. (gr. 1-4). 1990. lib. bdg. 9.59 (ISBN 0-8167-1898-9); pap. text ed. 2.50 (ISBN 0-8167-1899-7). Troll Assocs.

Stewart, Frances T. & Stewart, Charles P. Birds & Their Environments. Barrett, Rob, illus. 22p. (ps up). 1988. sticker bk. 7.95 (ISBN 0-694-00257-7). HarpC Child Bks.

BIRDS–SONG

see Bird Song

BIRDS' EGGS

see Birds–Eggs and Nests

BIRDS' NESTS

see Birds–Eggs and Nests

BIRDS OF PREY

see also names of birds of prey, e.g. Eagles, etc.

Barrett, Norman. Birds of Prey. (Illus.). 32p. (gr. k-4). 1991. PLB 11.40 (ISBN 0-531-14151-9). Watts.

Gray, Ian. Birds of Prey. LC 90-33768. (Illus.). 32p. (gr. 2-4). 1991. PLB 11.90 (ISBN 0-531-18367-X). Watts.

Hoffman, Mary. Bird of Prey. LC 86-17832. (Illus.). 24p. (gr. k-5). 1987. PLB 13.32 (ISBN 0-8172-2701-6). Raintree Pubs.

Petty, Kate. Birds of Prey. (Illus.). 32p. (gr. 1-6). 1987. PLB 11.90 (ISBN 0-531-17050-0, Gloucester Pr). Watts.

Selsam, Millicent E. & Hunt, Joyce. A First Look at Owls, Eagles, & Other Hunters of the Sky. Springer, Harriet, illus. 32p. (gr. 6-9). 1986. 10.95 (ISBN 0-8027-6625-0); PLB 10.85 (ISBN 0-8027-6642-0). Walker & Co.

Stone, Lynn M. Birds of Prey. LC 82-17909. (Illus.). 48p. (gr. k-4). 1983. PLB 14.60 (ISBN 0-516-01676-8); pap. 4.95 (ISBN 0-516-41676-6). Childrens.

Thomas, Mike & Soothill, Eric. Discovering Birds of Prey. LC 85-73588. (Illus.). 48p. (gr. 4-9). 1986. PLB 11.90 (ISBN 0-531-18052-2, Pub. by Bookwright). Watts.

Wildlife Education, Ltd. Staff. Birds of Prey. Goldman, Kenneth, et al, illus. 20p. (Orig.). (gr. 5 up). 1980. pap. 2.25 (ISBN 0-937934-01-1). Wildlife Educ.

BIRMINGHAM, ALABAMA

White, Marjorie L. Downtown Discovery Tour. rev. ed. (Illus.). 44p. (Orig.). (gr. 3-9). 1984. pap. 5.00 (ISBN 0-317-42237-5). Birmingham Hist Soc.

White, Marjorie L. & Shannon, Katherine. Five Points Heritage Hike Guide. (Illus.). 32p. (Orig.). (gr. 3-9). 1983. pap. 2.00 (ISBN 0-685-11943-2). Birmingham Hist Soc.

BIRTH

see Childbirth

BIRTH CONTROL

Benson, Michael D. Coping with Birth Control. Rosen, Roger, ed. (gr. 7 up). 1988. lib. bdg. 12.95 (ISBN 0-8239-0786-4). Rosen Group.

Emmens, Carol A. The Abortion Controversy. 128p. 1987. lib. bdg. 4.95 (ISBN 0-671-64209-X); PLB 12.98 (ISBN 0-671-62284-6). Messner.

Nourse, Alan E. Birth Control. Kline, M., ed. (Illus.). 160p. (gr. 7 up). 1988. PLB 13.90 (ISBN 0-531-10516-4). Watts.

Terkel, Susan N. Abortion: Facing the Issues. Rosoff, Iris, ed. (Illus.). 160p. (gr. 7 up). 1988. PLB 12.90 (ISBN 0-531-10565-2). Watts.

BIRTHDAYS

Collis, Len. My Little Birthday Book. Reeves, Eira, illus. 24p. (ps-3). 1988. 3.50 (ISBN 0-8120-5919-0). Barron.

De Beer, Hans. Little Polar Bear Birthday Book. De Beer, Hans, illus. 120p. 1990. 7.95 (ISBN 1-55858-081-6). North-South Bks NYC.

Dellosa, Janet & Carson, Patti. Birthday Fun Book. Dellosa, Janet & Carson, Patti, illus. 32p. (ps-2). 1982. pap. 1.59 (ISBN 0-88724-034-8, CD-8005). Carson-Dellos.

Fass, Bernie & Caggiano, Rosemary. Happy Birthday Party Time. 48p. (gr. k-6). 1976. pap. 10.95 (ISBN 0-86704-002-5). Clarus Music.

Gibbons, Gail. Happy Birthday! LC 86-297. (Illus.). 32p. (ps-3). 1986. PLB 14.95 (ISBN 0-8234-0614-8). Holiday.

Glovach, Linda. The Little Witch's Birthday Book. (gr. 1-4). 1981. 7.95 (ISBN 0-13-537977-6). P-H.

Green, Laurel & Beck, Trudy. My Birthday Memories. Nebeker, Kinde, illus. (ps-12). 1985. 5.00 (ISBN 0-9613079-1-9). Greenbeck.

Greenaway, Kate. Birthday Book for Children. (Illus.). (gr. 3-6). 1963. 6.95 (ISBN 0-7232-0216-8). Warne.

Haywood, Carolyn. Happy Birthday from Carolyn Haywood. (gr. 2-4). 1987. pap. 2.95 (ISBN 0-8167-1040-6). Troll Assocs.

Herbert, Janet. Hurray for Birthdays. (gr. k-2). 1986. comb bdg. 3.95 (ISBN 1-55513-040-2, Chariot Bks). Cook.

Jenny, Gerri. Birthday Parties for Children: Activities, Games, Cakes & Fun for Children from 4-10. Macdonald, Roland B. & Gray, Dan, illus. 128p. (gr. k-5). 1991. pap. 9.95 (ISBN 1-878767-15-1). Murdoch Bks. BIRTHDAY PARTIES FOR CHILDREN makes planning the perfect party easy & fun! This is a craft book, a party decorating book, a cake decorating book as well as a games & activities book--a TOTAL party planning book. Each birthday party involves a particular theme--a Balloon Party, for instance, or a Hat Party. All you have to do is follow the directions, copy the patterns, use the illustrations for guidance & you'll have a wonderful time. Each party includes invitations, activities, games, a cake, party favors & costume ideas. So open the book & get started! Spend some time with your child deciding which party to have (& you can mix & match different parts), pick up a few inexpensive materials from the store & have a terrific time with your child! ***Publisher Provided Annotation.***

Moncure, Jane B. Our Birthday Book. Endres, Helen, illus. LC 86-30976. 32p. (ps-3). 1987. PLB 11.97 (ISBN 0-89565-349-4). Childs World.

Motomora, Mitchell. Happy Birthday! (Illus.). 32p. (gr. 1-4). 1989. PLB 13.32 (ISBN 0-8172-3510-8). Raintree Pubs.

Murphy, Elspeth C. It's My Birthday, God: Psalm 90. Nelson, Jane, illus. (ps-2). 1982. misc. format 2.95 (ISBN 0-89191-580-X). Cook.

My Peter Rabbit Birthday Book. (Illus.). (ps up). 1987. 6.95 (ISBN 0-7232-3523-6). Warne.

Neilson, Gena, illus. It's Your Birthday. (ps-1). 1986. spiral bdg. 9.95 (ISBN 0-937763-03-9). Lauri Inc.

Ockenga, Starr & Doolittle, Eileen. Then & Now. Doolittle, Eileen & Ockenga, Starr, illus. 48p. 1990. 16.95 (ISBN 0-395-52153-X). HM.

Perl, Lila. Candles, Cakes, & Donkey Tails: Birthday Symbols & Celebrations. De Larrea, Victoria, illus. LC 84-5803. 80p. (gr. 3-6). 1984. 13.95 (ISBN 0-89919-250-5, Clarion); pap. 4.95 (ISBN 0-89919-315-3). HM.

Potter, Beatrix. Beatrix Potter's Birthday Book. Linder, Enid, ed. Potter, Beatrix, illus. LC 73-89833. 156p. (gr. 1 up). 1974. 6.95 (ISBN 0-7232-1758-0); leather bdg. 11.95 (ISBN 0-7232-1815-3). Warne.

Smith, Dian G. Happy Birthday to Me! A Four-Year Record Book for Birthday Boys & Girls. Franc-Nohain, Marie M., illus. 48p. (gr. 2-5). 1989. pap. 9.95 (ISBN 0-684-19046-X, Scribners Young Read). Macmillan Child Grp.

Vowles, Andrew & Illingworth, Lynn. My Birthday Book. Williams, Harland, illus. 32p. (gr. 1-5). 1985. pap. 2.95 (ISBN 0-88625-061-7). Durkin Hayes Pub.

BIRTHDAYS–FICTION

Anderson, Janet S. The Happy Birthday Hug. Ewers, Joe, illus. LC 85-9476. 32p. (ps-3). 1985. pap. 0.99 (ISBN 0-87372-006-7); 3.50 (ISBN 0-910313-90-3). Parker Bros.

Awdry, W. Happy Birthday, Thomas! A Step 1 Book - Preschool-Gr 1. Bell, Owain, illus. LC 89-49649. 32p. (Orig.). (ps-1). 1990. lib. bdg. 6.99 (ISBN 0-679-90809-9); pap. 2.95 (ISBN 0-679-80809-4). Random.

Bailey, Bobbi M. The Birthday Piano. DeFazzio, Debbie, illus. 30p. (ps-1). 1990. 11.95; pap. 3.95. Wee Pr.

Barker, Marjorie. Magical Hands. Yoshi, illus. LC 89-31373. 32p. (ps up). 1989. 14.95 (ISBN 0-88708-103-7). Picture Bk Studio.

Barrett, Judith. Benjamin's Three Hundred Sixty Five Birthdays. (Illus.). 40p. (ps-1). 1978. pap. 4.95 (ISBN 0-689-70443-7, Aladdin). Macmillan Child Grp.

Bennett, David. The Big Surprise. 24p. (ps-1). 1989. 5.95 (ISBN 0-8120-5912-3). Barron.

Berenstain, Stan & Berenstain, Janice. The Berenstain Bears & Too Much Birthday. Berenstain, Stan & Berenstain, Janice, illus. LC 85-14529. 32p. (ps-1). 1986. lib. bdg. 5.99 (ISBN 0-394-97332-1); pap. 2.25 (ISBN 0-394-87332-7). Random.

Birenbaum, Barbara. The Birthday Wish. LC 88-6026. (Illus.). (gr. 3-5). 1988. pap. 5.95 (ISBN 0-935343-23-7). Peartree.

Birthday Surprise. 1990. 4.98 (ISBN 1-55521-689-7). Bk Sales Inc.

Blair, Anne Denton. Hurrah for Arthur: A Mount Vernon Birthday Party. Watson, Carol, illus. LC 82-10636. 64p. (gr. k-3). 1983. 11.95 (ISBN 0-932020-15-1); pap. 8.95 (ISBN 0-685-05723-2). Seven Locks Pr.

Blocksma, Mary. Grandma Dragon's Birthday. Kalthoff, Sandra C., illus. LC 82-19851. 24p. (ps-2). 1983. PLB 12.33 (ISBN 0-516-01582-6); pap. 3.95 (ISBN 0-516-41582-4). Childrens.

The Bonnie Little Birthday Book. (ps-3). 5.95 (ISBN 0-87741-005-4). Makepeace Colony.

Brown, Marc. Arthur's Birthday. (ps-3). 1991. pap. 4.95 (ISBN 0-316-11074-4). Little.

Brown, Margaret W. The Golden Birthday Book. (Illus.). 48p. (ps up). 1989. write for info. (ISBN 0-307-12096-1, Pub. by Golden Bks). Western Pub.

Cake for Jake. 24p. (ps-2). 1989. pap. 1.29 (ISBN 0-02-898251-7). Checkerboard Pr.

Cameron, Ann. Julian, Dream Doctor. Strugnell, Ann, illus. LC 89-37562. 64p. (Orig.). (gr. 2-4). 1990. PLB 5.99 (ISBN 0-679-90524-3); pap. 1.95 (ISBN 0-679-80524-9). McKay.

Carrick, Carol. Paul's Christmas Birthday. Carrick, Donald, illus. LC 77-28408. 32p. (gr. k-3). 1978. PLB 11.88 (ISBN 0-688-84159-7). Greenwillow.

Caseley, Judith. Three Happy Birthdays. LC 88-18788. (Illus.). 32p. (ps up). 1989. 12.95 (ISBN 0-688-08179-7); PLB 12.88 (ISBN 0-688-08180-0). Greenwillow.

Charlip, Remy & Miller, Mary B. Handtalk Birthday: A Number & Story Book in Sign Language. Ancona, George, illus. LC 86-22755. 48p. 1987. 14.95 (ISBN 0-02-718080-8, Four Winds). Macmillan Child Grp.

Cole, Babette. Babette Cole's Beastly Birthday Book. (ps-4). 1991. 15.95 (ISBN 0-385-41679-2). Doubleday.

Cowley, Joy. The Birthday Cake. Webb, Jenny, illus. 8p. (gr. k-2). 1989. pap. text ed. 15.00 (ISBN 1-55911-275-1). Wright Group.

—The Birthday Cake, 6 bks. Webb, Jenni, illus. 8p. (gr. k-2). 1986. Set. pap. text ed. 12.60 (ISBN 1-55911-339-1). Wright Group.

De Brunhoff, Laurent. Babar's Birthday Surprise. LC 74-123071. (Illus.). 36p. (ps-2). 1970. Repr. of 1970 ed. 10.95 (ISBN 0-394-80591-7, Random Juv); lib. bdg. 11.99 (ISBN 0-394-90591-1). Random.

Delton, Judy. Birthday Bike for Brimhall. (ps-3). 1991. pap. 2.99 (ISBN 0-440-40461-4). Dell.

Devlin, Wende & Devlin, Harry. Cranberry Birthday. Devlin, Wende & Devlin, Harry, illus. LC 88-294. 40p. (gr. k-3). 1988. PLB 13.95 (ISBN 0-02-729210-X, Four Winds). Macmillan Child Grp.

Disney, Walt, Productions Staff. The Mickey Mouse Birthday Book. LC 78-55911. (Illus.). (ps-3). 1978. 3.95 (ISBN 0-394-83963-3, Random Juv); lib. bdg. 4.99 (ISBN 0-394-93963-8). Random.

Dr. Seuss. Happy Birthday to You. Dr. Seuss, illus. (gr. 1-5). 1959. 11.95 (ISBN 0-394-80076-1, Random Juv); PLB 13.99 (ISBN 0-394-90076-6). Random.

Dunbar, Joyce. A Cake for Barney. Boon, Emilie, illus. LC 87-15294. 32p. (ps-2). 1988. 12.95 (ISBN 0-531-05735-6); PLB 12.99 (ISBN 0-531-08335-7). Orchard Bks Watts.

Duvoisin, Roger. Veronica & the Birthday Present. Duvoisin, Roger, illus. (ps-2). 1972. Knopf.

Eisenberg, Lisa. Happy Birthday, Lexie. 144p. (gr. 3-7). 1991. 12.95 (ISBN 0-670-83553-6). Viking Child Bks.

Elliott, Dan. Oscar's Rotten Birthday. Chartier, Normand, illus. LC 81-2398. 40p. (gr. k-2). 1981. 4.95 (ISBN 0-394-84848-9); lib. bdg. 6.99 (ISBN 0-394-94848-3). Random.

Fitzhugh, Louise. I Am Four. Bonners, Susan, illus. LC 82-70309. 48p. (ps-k). 1982. pap. 8.95 (ISBN 0-385-28444-6); pap. 8.89 (ISBN 0-385-28445-4). Delacorte.

—I Am Three. Natti, Sussanns, illus. LC 81-15218. 48p. (ps). 1982. 8.95 (ISBN 0-440-04035-3); PLB 8.89 (ISBN 0-440-04039-6). Delacorte.

Flack, Marjorie. Ask Mr. Bear. Flack, Marjorie, illus. LC 58-8370. 32p. (ps-1). 1971. pap. 3.95 (ISBN 0-02-043090-6, Aladdin). Macmillan Child Grp.

Fleischman, Paul. The Birthday Tree. Sewall, Marcia, illus. LC 78-22155. 32p. (gr. k-3). 1991. pap. 4.50 (ISBN 0-06-443246-7, Trophy). HarpC Child Bks.

Gay, Marie-Louise. Willy Nilly. Levine, Abby, ed. Gay, Marie-Louise, illus. 32p. (gr. 1-3). 1990. 12.95 (ISBN 0-8075-9119-X). A Whitman.

Giff, Patricia R. Happy Birthday, Ronald Morgan! Natti, Susanna, illus. 32p. (Orig.). (ps-3). 1988. pap. 3.95 (ISBN 0-14-050668-3, Puffin). Puffin Bks.

Girard, Linda. You Were Born on Your Very First Birthday. Tucker, Kathy, ed. LC 84-17220. (Illus.). 32p. (ps-3). 1983. PLB 12.95 (ISBN 0-8075-9455-5). A Whitman.

Gordon, Sharon. Surprise Party. Hall, Susan, illus. LC 81-4869. 32p. (gr. k-2). 1981. PLB 10.89 (ISBN 0-89375-521-4); pap. 2.95 (ISBN 0-89375-522-2). Troll Assocs.

Gracia, Debbie. My Birthday on Christmas Day. Aragon, Hilda, illus. 30p. (Orig.). (ps-7). 1980. pap. 3.75 (ISBN 0-915347-05-9). Pueblo Acoma Pr.

Gray, Nigel. Little Pig's Tale. Rees, Mary, illus. LC 90-30642. 32p. (ps-2). 1990. 12.95 (ISBN 0-02-736942-0, Mcmillan Child Bk). Macmillan Child Grp.

Grender, Iris. Did I Ever Tell You about My Birthday Party? (Illus.). 64p. (gr. k-4). 1987. 12.95 (ISBN 0-09-151230-1, Pub. by Hutchinson UK). Trafalgar Sq.

Hallinan, P. K. Today is Your Birthday. (Illus.). 24p. (Orig.). (ps-3). 1991. pap. 3.95 (ISBN 0-8249-8493-5). Ideals.

Happy Birthday, Roger. 24p. 1988. 1.29 (ISBN 0-02-898135-9). Checkerboard Pr.

Hautzig, Deborah. Grover's Bad Dream. Mathieu, Joe, illus. LC 90-32085. 40p. (ps-3). 1990. 4.95 (ISBN 0-679-80898-1); lib. bdg. 6.99 (ISBN 0-679-90898-6). Random.

Heide, Florence P. Treehorn's Wish. Gorey, Edward, illus. LC 83-6240. 64p. (gr. 3-6). 1984. reinforced bdg 8.95 (ISBN 0-8234-0493-5). Holiday.

Heilbroner, Joan. Happy Birthday Present. Chalmers, Mary, illus. LC 61-12094. 64p. (gr. k-3). 1961. PLB 11.89 (ISBN 0-06-022271-9). HarpC Child Bks.

Hertz, Ole. Tobias Has a Birthday. Tobias, Tobi, tr. from DAN. LC 83-27287. (Illus.). 32p. (gr. k-3). 1984. PLB 7.95 (ISBN 0-87614-261-7). Carolrhoda Bks.

Hill, Eric. Spot's Birthday Party. (Illus.). (ps-k). 1982. 10.95 (ISBN 0-399-20903-4, Putnam). Putnam Pub Group.

Hoban, Russell. A Birthday for Frances. Hoban, Lillian, illus. LC 68-24321. (ps-2). 1976. pap. 4.95 (ISBN 0-06-443007-3, Trophy). HarpC Child Bks.

Holabird, Katharine. Angelina's Birthday Surprise. Craig, Helen, illus. LC 89-3513. 32p. (ps-2). 1989. 11.95 (ISBN 0-517-57325-3, C N Potter Bks). Crown.

Hutchins, Pat. Happy Birthday, Sam. LC 78-1295. (Illus.). 32p. (gr. k-3). 1978. PLB 11.88 (ISBN 0-688-84160-0). Greenwillow.

—Happy Birthday, Sam Peter. LC 84-18058. (Illus.). 32p. (ps-1). 1985. pap. 3.50 (ISBN 0-14-050339-0, Puffin). Puffin Bks.

Hynard, Julia. Percival's Party: A Story about Numbers. Thatcher, Francis, illus. LC 82-22114. 32p. (ps-3). 1983. PLB 15.93 (ISBN 0-516-08941-2). Childrens.

Keats, Ezra J. Letter to Amy. Keats, Ezra J., illus. LC 68-24329. (gr. k-3). 1968. 14.95 (ISBN 0-06-023108-4); PLB 14.89 (ISBN 0-06-023109-2). HarpC Child Bks.

Kellogg, Steven. Won't Somebody Play with Me? Kellogg, Steven, illus. 32p. (ps-3). 1985. PLB 9.89 (ISBN 0-8037-9740-0). Dial Bks Young.

Knorr, Dandi D. A Secret Birthday Gift. Connelly, Gwen, illus. 32p. (gr. 1-3). 1987. 4.95 (ISBN 0-87403-314-4, 3544). Standard Pub.

Krauss, Ruth. Birthday Party. Sendak, Maurice, illus. (gr. k-3). 1957. PLB 11.89 (ISBN 0-06-023330-3). HarpC Child Bks.

Levy, Elizabeth. Something Queer at the Birthday Party. 1990. 12.95 (ISBN 0-385-29973-7). Doubleday.

Lorian, Nicole. A Birthday Present for Mama: A Step Two Book. Miller, J. P., illus. LC 83-26849. (ps-2). 1984. (Pub. by BYR); pap. 2.95 (ISBN 0-394-86755-6, Pub. by BYR). Random.

McDonnell, Christine. Lucky Charms & Birthday Wishes. DeGroat, Diane, illus. LC 85-42756. 96p. (gr. 2-5). 1985. pap. 3.95 (ISBN 0-14-031886-0, Puffin). Puffin Bks.

Mackall, Dandi D. Kay's Birthday Surprise. Mathers, Dawn, illus. LC 89-82554. 32p. (ps-2). 1990. pap. 4.95 (ISBN 0-8066-2467-1, 9-2467). Augsburg Fortress.

Magorian, James. Griddlemort Loses His Birthday. LC 88-71604. 32p. (gr. 1-4). 1988. pap. 3.00 (ISBN 0-930674-29-4). Black Oak.

Mariana. Miss Flora McFlimsey's Birthday. rev. ed. Mariana, illus. LC 86-15269. 40p. (ps-2). 1987. 11.95 (ISBN 0-688-04537-5). Lothrop.

Martin, Ann M. Karen's Birthday. (gr. 1-5). 1990. pap. 2.50 (ISBN 0-590-42671-0). Scholastic Inc.

Mealy, Virginia T. Happy Birthday Author. (Illus.). 128p. (gr. 1-6). 1986. pap. 12.95 (ISBN 0-913839-50-7). Bk Lures.

Moncure, Jane B. What's So Special about Today? It's My Birthday. Williams, Jenny, illus. LC 87-21907. 32p. (ps-2). 1987. PLB 11.97 (ISBN 0-89565-414-8). Childs World.

Munsch, Robert. Moira's Birthday. Martchenko, Michael, illus. 32p. (gr. k-3). 1987. 12.95 (ISBN 0-920303-85-4); pap. 4.95 (ISBN 0-920303-83-8). Firefly Bks Ltd.

Noble, Trinka H. Jimmy's Boa & the Big Splash Birthday Bash. Kellog, Steven, illus. LC 88-10933. 32p. (ps-3). 1989. 13.95 (ISBN 0-8037-0539-5); PLB 13.89 (ISBN 0-8037-0540-9). Dial Bks Young.

Oxenbury, Helen. The Birthday Party. Oxenbury, Helen, illus. LC 82-19792. (ps-1). 1983. 3.95 (ISBN 0-8037-0717-7, 0383-120). Dial Bks Young.

Ozman. Jennifer's Birthday Present. LC 73-87798. (Illus.). 32p. (gr. k-3). 1974. PLB 9.95 (ISBN 0-87783-125-4); pap. 3.94 deluxe ed. (ISBN 0-87783-126-2). Oddo.

Parish, Peggy. Be Ready at Eight. Kessler, Leonard, illus. LC 87-1040. 64p. (gr. 1-4). 1987. pap. 3.95 (ISBN 0-689-71163-8, Aladdin). Macmillan Child Grp.

Pearson, Susan. Happy Birthday Grampie. Dillon, Leo & Dillon, Diane, illus. LC 86-31105. 32p. (ps-3). 1987. 10.95 (ISBN 0-8037-3457-3); PLB 10.89 (ISBN 0-8037-3458-1). Dial Bks Young.

—Happy Birthday, Grampie. Fogelman, Phyllis J., ed. Himler, Ronald, illus. LC 85-31105. 32p. (ps-3). 1990. pap. 3.95 (ISBN 0-8037-0779-7). Dial Bks Young.

Peters, Sharon. Feliz Cumpleanos. Harvey, Paul, illus. (SPA.). 32p. (gr. k-2). 1981. PLB 7.06 (ISBN 0-89375-553-2); pap. 1.95 (ISBN 0-685-04948-5). Troll Assocs.

Pittman, Helena C. A Dinosaur for Gerald. Pittman, Helena C., illus. 32p. (gr. k-3). 1990. PLB 12.95 (ISBN 0-87614-431-8). Carolrhoda Bks.

Pomerantz, Charlotte. The Half-Birthday Party. DeSalvo-Ryan, DyAnne, illus. LC 84-4963. 48p. (gr. 1-4). 1984. 13.95 (ISBN 0-89919-273-4, Clarion). HM.

Prager, Annabelle. The Surprise Party. De Paola, Tomie, illus. LC 76-40309. (ps-4). 1977. lib. bdg. 7.99 (ISBN 0-394-93235-8). Pantheon.

—The Surprise Party. De Paola, Tomie, illus. LC 87-20649. 48p. (Orig.). (gr. 1-3). 1988. PLB 6.99 (ISBN 0-318-32684-1, Random Juv); pap. 2.95 (ISBN 0-394-89596-7). Random.

Robins, Dorothy. Katie's Birthday Wish. LC 88-81467. (Illus.). 32p. (Orig.). (ps-2). 1988. pap. 8.95 (ISBN 0-937124-18-4). Kimbo Educ.

Rutherford, Meg. Bluff & Bran & the Birthday. (Illus.). 32p. (ps-3). 1989. 11.95 (ISBN 0-233-98302-3). Andre Deutsch.

Rylant, Cynthia. Birthday Presents. Stevenson, Sucie, illus. LC 87-5485. 32p. (ps-1). 1987. 13.95 (ISBN 0-531-05705-4); PLB 13.99 (ISBN 0-531-08305-5). Orchard Bks Watts.

Sabin, Louis. Birthday Surprise. Magine, John, illus. LC 81-2632. 32p. (gr. k-2). 1981. PLB 10.89 (ISBN 0-89375-527-3); pap. text ed. 2.95 (ISBN 0-89375-528-1). Troll Assocs.

Samuels, Barbara. Happy Birthday, Dolores. LC 88-15469. (Illus.). 32p. (ps-1). 1989. 13.95 (ISBN 0-531-05791-7); PLB 13.99 (ISBN 0-531-08391-8). Orchard Bks Watts.

Sawicki, Norma J. Something for Mom. Weston, Martha, illus. LC 86-34421. 32p. (ps-1). 1987. PLB 12.88 (ISBN 0-688-05590-7). Lothrop.

Schumacher, Claire. Nutty's Birthday. Schumacher, Claire, illus. LC 85-29706. 32p. (ps-2). 1986. 12.95 (ISBN 0-688-06495-7); lib. bdg. 12.88 (ISBN 0-688-06496-5, Morrow Jr Bks). Morrow Jr Bks.

Schweninger, Ann. Birthday Wishes. Schweninger, Ann, illus. LC 85-20178. 32p. (ps-1). 1986. 10.95 (ISBN 0-670-80742-7). Viking Child Bks.

—Birthday Wishes. (Illus.). (ps-1). 1987. pap. 3.95 (ISBN 0-14-050682-9, Puffin). Puffin Bks.

Shaw, Janet. Happy Birthday Kirsten! A Springtime Story. Thieme, Jeanne, ed. Graef, Renne, illus. 72p. (gr. 2-5). 1990. PLB 12.95 (ISBN 0-937295-88-4). Pleasant Co.

Singer, Marilyn. Minnie's Yom Kippur Birthday. Rosner, Ruth, illus. LC 85-14193. 32p. (ps-3). 1989. 12.95 (ISBN 0-06-025846-2); PLB 12.89 (ISBN 0-06-025847-0). HarpC Child Bks.

Springstubb, Tricia. My Minnie Is a Jewel. Lamarche, Jim, illus. LC 80-66712. 48p. (gr. k-4). 1980. PLB 9.95 (ISBN 0-87614-131-9). Carolrhoda Bks.

Spurr, Elizabeth. The Biggest Birthday Cake in the World. Grove, Karen, ed. Litzinger, Rosanne, illus. 32p. (ps-3). 1991. 14.95 (ISBN 0-15-207150-4). HarBraceJ.

Steptoe, John. Birthday. Steptoe, John, illus. LC 72-182782. 32p. (ps-2). 1991. 14.95 (ISBN 0-8050-1849-2). H Holt & Co.

Theriot, David. Leola et la pirogue. Easterling, Mae L., illus. (FRE.). 39p. (gr. 3). 1979. pap. text ed. 1.25 (ISBN 0-911409-03-3). Natl Mat Dev.

Tripp, Valerie. Happy Birthday Molly! A Springtime Story. Thieme, Jeanne, ed. Gaadt, David, illus. 72p. (gr. 2-5). 1990. PLB 12.95 (ISBN 0-937295-90-6). Pleasant Co.

—Happy Birthday Samantha! A Springtime Story. Thieme, Jeanne, ed. Grace, Robert & Niles, Nancy, illus. 72p. (gr. 2-5). 1990. PLB 12.95 (ISBN 0-937295-89-2). Pleasant Co.

Tyler, Linda. The Sick-in-Bed Birthday. Davis, Susan, illus. 32p. (ps-3). 1990. pap. 3.95 (ISBN 0-14-050783-3, Puffin). Puffin Bks.

Wayne, MacKenzie. Teddy's Birthday Party. (Illus.). 24p. (gr. k-3). 1990. 2.95 (ISBN 0-87406-480-5, 26-20331-2). Willowisp Pr.

Whittington, Mary K. The Patchwork Lady. Yolen, Jane, ed. Dyer, Jane, illus. 32p. (ps-3). 1991. 13.95 (ISBN 0-15-259580-5). HarBraceJ.

Wickstrom, Sylvie K. Mothers Can't Get Sick. Wickstrom, Sylvie K., illus. (ps up). 1989. PLB 12.95 (ISBN 0-517-57181-1). Crown.

Willard, Nancy. High Rise Glorious Skittle Skat Roarious Sky Pie Angel Food Cake. Watson, Richard J., illus. 64p. 1990. 15.95 (ISBN 0-15-234332-6). HarbraceJ.

Ziefert, Harriet. Max & Diana & the Birthday Present. Johnson, Lonnie S., illus. LC 86-45338. 32p. (ps-2). 1987. 3.95 (ISBN 0-694-00090-6). HarpC Child Bks.

—The Small Potatoes & the Birthday Party. 64p. (gr. k-6). 1985. pap. 2.75 (ISBN 0-440-48035-3, YB). Dell.

—Where's My Easter Egg? Brown, Richard, illus. LC 84-62004. (gr. 2-6). 1985. pap. 4.95 (ISBN 0-14-050537-7, Puffin). Puffin Bks.

Zion, Gene. No Roses for Harry! Graham, Margaret B., illus. LC 58-7752. 32p. (ps-3). 1976. pap. 3.95 (ISBN 0-06-443011-1, Trophy). HarpC Child Bks.

BIRTHDAYS–POETRY

Damon, Laura. Birthday Buddies. Aiello, Laurel, illus. LC 87-10866. 32p. (gr. k-2). 1988. PLB 10.89 (ISBN 0-8167-1091-0); pap. text ed. 2.95 (ISBN 0-8167-1092-9). Troll Assocs.

Katz, Bobbi, ed. Birthday Bear's Book of Birthday Poems. Walton, Louise & Borgo, Deborah, illus. (gr. 4-8). 1983. lib. bdg. 4.99 (ISBN 0-394-95658-3); pap. 3.95 (ISBN 0-394-85658-9). Random.

Shearer, Marilyn J. Annie's Birthday Party: Learning Colors & Shapes. Truax, Nancy, illus. 16p. (Orig.). (ps-6). 1992. 19.95 (ISBN 0-685-30095-1); pap. 10.95 (ISBN 0-685-30096-X). L Ashley & Joshua.

BISMARCK (BATTLESHIP)

Forester, C. S. The Last Nine Days of the Bismarck. (gr. 7 up). 1959. 14.45 (ISBN 0-685-03074-1). Little.

BISON

Green, Carl R. & Sanford, William R. The Bison. LC 85-6624. (Illus.). 48p. (gr. 4-5). 1985. 10.95 (ISBN 0-89686-275-5, Crestwood Hse). Macmillan Child Grp.

Lepthien, Emilie U. Buffalo. LC 89-457. (Illus.). 48p. (gr. k-4). 1989. PLB 14.60 (ISBN 0-516-01161-8); pap. 4.95 (ISBN 0-516-41161-6). Childrens.

Sanford, William R. & Green, Carl R. The Cape Buffalo. LC 86-32859. (Illus.). 48p. (gr. 4-5). 1987. PLB 10.95 (ISBN 0-89686-321-2, Crestwood Hse). Macmillan Child Grp.

Stone, Lynn. African Buffalo. (Illus.). 24p. (gr. k-5). 1990. lib. bdg. 11.93 (ISBN 0-86593-052-X); lib. bdg. 8.95s.p. (ISBN 0-685-36344-9). Rourke Corp.

Taylor, Dave. The Bison & the Great Plains. (Illus.). 32p. (gr. 3-4). 1990. lib. bdg. 14.95 (ISBN 0-86505-366-9); pap. 7.95 (ISBN 0-86505-396-0). Crabtree Pub Co.

Ziter, Cary B. The Moon of Falling Leaves: The Great Buffalo Hunt. Mayo, Gretchen W., illus. IRosoff, ed. (Illus.). 72p. (gr. 4 up). 1988. PLB 12.90 (ISBN 0-531-10502-4). Watts.

BISON–FICTION

Schnell, Robert W. Bonko. Wilkon, Jozef, illus. LC 77-99446. 28p. (ps-3). 8.95 (ISBN 0-87592-008-X). Scroll Pr.

Slote, Alfred. Finding Buck McHenry. LC 90-39190. 256p. (gr. 3-7). 1991. 13.95 (ISBN 0-06-021652-2); PLB 13.89 (ISBN 0-06-021653-0). HarpC Child Bks.

BLACK ACTORS

Bergman, Carol. Sidney Poitier. King, Coretta Scott, intro. by. (Illus.). 112p. (Orig.). (gr. 5 up). 1988. 17.95 (ISBN 1-55546-605-2); pap. 9.95 (ISBN 0-7910-0209-8). Chelsea Hse.

BLACK AMERICANS

see Blacks

BLACK ARTISTS

Warner, Malcolm-Jamal & Paisner, Daniel. Theo & Me: Growing up Okay. Cosby, Bill & Poussaint, Alvin F. frwd. by. 160p. (gr. 5 up). 1988. 14.95 (ISBN 0-525-24694-0, Dutton). NAL-Dutton.

BLACK ATHLETES

Aaseng, Nathan. Florence Griffith Joyner: Dazzling Olympian. (Illus.). 56p. (gr. 4-9). 1989. PLB 8.95 (ISBN 0-8225-0495-2). Lerner Pubns.

Biracree, Tom. Wilma Rudolph. Horner, Matina, intro. by. (Illus.). 112p. (Orig.). (gr. 7-12). 1989. 17.95 (ISBN 1-55546-675-3); pap. 9.95 (ISBN 0-7910-0217-9). Chelsea Hse.

Jesse Owens. 48p. (gr. 5-6). 1989. PLB 10.95 (ISBN 0-685-26352-5). Capstone Pr.

BLACK AUTHORS

Bishop, Jack. Ralph Ellison. King, Coretta Scott, intro. by. (Illus.). 112p. (Orig.). (gr. 5 up). 1988. 17.95 (ISBN 1-55546-585-4); pap. 9.95 (ISBN 0-7910-0202-0). Chelsea Hse.

Dolan, Sean. Chiang Kai-Shek. Schlesinger, Arthur M., Jr., intro. by. (Illus.). 112p. (gr. 5 up). 1989. lib. bdg. 17.95 (ISBN 0-87754-517-0). Chelsea Hse.

Lyons, Mary E. Sorrow's Kitchen: The Life & Folklore of Zora Neale Hurston. LC 90-8058. (Illus.). 160p. (gr. 7 up). 1990. 13.95 (ISBN 0-684-19198-9, Scribners Young Read). Macmillan Child Grp.

Shuker, Nancy. Maya Angelou. Easton, Emily, ed. (Illus.). 128p. (gr. 7-9). 1990. 14.95 (ISBN 0-382-24036-7); PLB 17.98s.p. (ISBN 0-382-09908-7). Silver Burdett Pr.

Wilson, M. L. Chester Himes. King, Coretta Scott, intro. by. LC 87-30961. (Illus.). 112p. (Orig.). (gr. 5 up). 1988. 17.95 (ISBN 1-55546-591-9); pap. 9.95 (ISBN 0-7910-0212-8). Chelsea Hse.

Yates, Janelle. Zora Neale Hurston: A Storyteller's Life. (Illus.). 104p. (gr. 4-9). 1991. pap. 9.95 (ISBN 0-9623380-7-9). Ward Hill Pr.

BLACK DEATH

see Plague

BLACK FOLKLORE

Bang, Molly. Wiley & the Hairy Man: Adapted from an American Folk Tale. Bang, Molly G., illus. LC 75-38581. 64p. (gr. 1-4). 1976. 9.95 (ISBN 0-02-708370-5, Mcmillan Child Bk). Macmillan Child Grp.

Harris, Joel C. Complete Tales of Uncle Remus. Chase, Richard, ed. (Illus.). 832p. (gr. 7 up). 1955. 35.00 (ISBN 0-395-06799-5). HM.

—Favorite Uncle Remus. Van Santvoord, George & Coolidge, Archibald C., eds. Van Santvoord, George & Coolidge, Archibald C., illus. 320p. (gr. 4-8). 1973. 17.95 (ISBN 0-395-06800-2). HM.

—Uncle Remus. Frost, A. B., illus. LC 65-14828. (gr. 3 up). 1987. Schocken.

BLACK HAWK, SAUK CHIEF, 1767-1838

Hargrove, Jim. The Story of the Black Hawk War. Canaday, Ralph, illus. LC 86-955. 32p. (gr. 3-6). 1986. PLB 13.27 (ISBN 0-516-04696-9). Childrens.

Oppenheim, Joanne. Black Hawk, Frontier Warrior. new ed. LC 78-18049. (Illus.). 48p. (gr. 4-6). 1979. PLB 9.89 (ISBN 0-89375-157-X); pap. 2.95 (ISBN 0-89375-147-2). Troll Assocs.

BLACK MAGIC

see Witchcraft

BLACK MUSICIANS

De Veaux, Alexis. Don't Explain: A Song of Billie Holiday. 151p. (gr. 9 up). 1988. pap. 7.95 (ISBN 0-86316-132-4). Writers & Readers.

Frankl, Ron. Charlie Parker. King, Coretta Scott, intro. by. (Illus.). 112p. (gr. 5 up). 1992. PLB 17.95 (ISBN 0-7910-1134-8). Chelsea Hse.

Gentry, Tony. Dizzy Gillespie. King, Coretta Scott, intro. by. (Illus.). 112p. (gr. 5 up). 1991. PLB 17.95 (ISBN 0-7910-1127-5). Chelsea Hse.

Greenberg, Keith E. Whitney Houston. (Illus.). 32p. (gr. 4-9). 1988. lib. bdg. 9.95 (ISBN 0-8225-1619-5). Lerner Pubns.

Haskins, James. Black Music in America: A History Through Its People. LC 85-47885. (Illus.). 224p. (gr. 7 up). 1987. 12.95 (ISBN 0-690-04460-7, Crowell Jr Bks); PLB 12.89 (ISBN 0-690-04462-3, Crowell Jr Bks). HarpC Child Bks.

Kliment, Bud. Count Basie. King, Coretta Scott, intro. by. (Illus.). 112p. (gr. 5 up). 1992. PLB 17.95 (ISBN 0-7910-1118-6). Chelsea Hse.
—Ella Fitzgerald. King, Coretta Scott, intro. by. (Illus.). 112p. (Orig.). (gr. 5 up). 1989. 17.95 (ISBN 1-55546-586-2); pap. 9.95 (ISBN 0-7910-0220-9). Chelsea Hse.
Mabery, D. L. Janet Jackson. (Illus.). 48p. (gr. 4-9). 1988. pap. 9.95 (ISBN 0-8225-1618-7). Lerner Pubns.
—This Is Michael Jackson. LC 84-10043. (Illus.). 48p. (gr. 4-9). 1984. PLB 9.95 (ISBN 0-8225-1600-4). Lerner Pubns.
Mitchell, Barbara. Raggin' A Story about Scott Joplin. Mitchell, Hetty, illus. 64p. (gr. 3-6). 1987. PLB 9.95 (ISBN 0-87614-310-9). Carolrhoda Bks.
Palmer, Leslie. Lena Horne. King, Coretta Scott. (Illus.). 112p. (gr. 5 up). 1989. lib. bdg. 17.95x (ISBN 1-55546-594-3). Chelsea Hse.
Patterson, Charles. Marian Anderson. Rosoff, Iris, ed. LC 88-10695. (Illus.). 160p. (gr. 7 up). 1988. PLB 13.90 (ISBN 0-531-10568-7). Watts.
Preston, Kitty. Scott Joplin. King, Coretta Scott, intro. by. (Illus.). 112p. (Orig.). (gr. 5 up). 1988. 17.95 (ISBN 1-55546-598-6); pap. 9.95 (ISBN 0-7910-0205-5). Chelsea Hse.
Still, Judith A. Little David Had No Fear. Phillips, Ted, Jr., illus. (Orig.). (gr. 6-8). 1990. write for info. (ISBN 1-877873-03-9); pap. write for info. Master-Player Lib.
Tanenhaus, Sam. Louis Armstrong. King, Coretta Scott, intro. by. (Illus.). 112p. (gr. 5 up). 1989. text ed. 17.95 (ISBN 1-55546-571-4); pap. 9.95 (ISBN 0-7910-0221-7). Chelsea Hse.

BLACK MUSLIMS

Halasa, Malu. Elijah Muhammad. King, Coretta Scott, intro. by. (Illus.). (gr. 5 up). 1990. 17.95 (ISBN 1-55546-602-8). Chelsea Hse.

BLACK POETRY

Adoff, Arnold, ed. My Black Me: A Beginning Book of Black Poetry. LC 73-16445. 96p. (gr. 3 up). 1974. 12.95 (ISBN 0-525-35460-3, DCB). Dutton Child Bks.
—The Poetry of Black America: Anthology of the Twentieth Century. Brooks, Gwendolyn, intro. by. LC 72-76518. 576p. (gr. 7 up). 1973. 24.95 (ISBN 0-06-020089-8); PLB 24.89 (ISBN 0-06-020090-1). HarpC Child Bks.
Hughes, Langston. Dream Keeper. Sewell, Helen, illus. (gr. 7-11). 1962. lib. bdg. 10.99 (ISBN 0-394-91096-6). Knopf.
Madgett, Naomi L., intro. by. Adam of Ife: Black Women in Praise of Black Men. LC 91-61410. (Illus., Orig.). 1991. pap. 15.00 (ISBN 0-916418-80-4). Lotus.
Miller, May. Dust of Uncertain Journey. 1st ed. LC 75-40977. 67p. (gr. 9-12). 1975. pap. 5.00 (ISBN 0-916418-05-7). Lotus.
White, Paulette C. Love Poem to a Black Junkie. 37p. (gr. 7-12). 1975. pap. 4.00x (ISBN 0-916418-04-9). Lotus.

BLACKBOARD DRAWING

see Crayon Drawing

BLACKS

Bellegarde. Black Heroes & Heroines, Bk 5: Benjamin Banneker's Great Achievements. 64p. (gr. 5 up). 1985. 8.95 (ISBN 0-918340-14-4). Bell Ent.
Bibliotheca Press Staff. Black English, Chocolate Slang: or English Too??? 15p. (gr. 9-12). 1989. pap. text ed. 4.00 (ISBN 0-318-42724-9, Pub. by Biblio Pr Ga). Prosperity & Profits.
Daniel, Becky. Portraits in Black. (Illus.). 96p. (gr. 4-7). 1990. 8.95 (ISBN 0-86653-531-4, GA1147). Good Apple.
Farrand, Vernell C. & Farrand, Brent. Afro-Bets Activity & Enrichment Guide: Book of Black Heroes from A to Z. Date not set. pap. 7.95 (ISBN 0-940975-05-X). Just Us Bks.
Haber, Louis. Black Pioneers of Science & Invention. (gr. 4-7). 1991. pap. 4.95 (ISBN 0-15-208566-1, HJ). HarBraceJ.
Hancock, Sibyl. Famous Firsts of Black Americans. Haynes, Jerry, illus. LC 82-612. 128p. (gr. 3-9). 1983. 10.95 (ISBN 0-88289-240-1). Pelican.
Harris, Jacqueline L. Martin Luther King, Jr. (Illus.). 128p. (gr. 7 up). 1983. PLB 13.90 (ISBN 0-531-04588-9). Watts.
Haskins, James. Black Dance in America: A History Through Its People. LC 89-35529. (Illus.). 240p. (gr. 7 up). 1990. 14.95 (ISBN 0-690-04657-X, Crowell Jr Bks); PLB 14.89 (ISBN 0-690-04659-6, Crowell Jr Bks). HarpC Child Bks.
Hudson, Cheryl W. Afro-Bets 1 2 3 Coloring & Activity Book. Date not set. pap. 2.95 (ISBN 0-940975-09-2). Just Us Bks.
Hughes, Langston. Not Without Laughter. LC 79-81544. 320p. (gr. 8 up). 1986. pap. 5.95 (ISBN 0-02-052200-2, Collier). Macmillan.
Johnson, Zenobia M. Afro-American Copy Color Fun. (Illus.). 32p. (Orig.). (ps-1). 1979. wkbk. 3.00 (ISBN 0-9617411-2-0). Z M Johnson.
—Black Footprints. (Illus.). 32p. (Orig.). (gr. 4-7). 1979. wkbk. 3.50 (ISBN 0-9617411-1-2). Z M Johnson.
Miller, Robert. Cowboys. Leonard, Richard, illus. 104p. (gr. 4-7). 1991. PLB 13.98 (ISBN 0-382-24079-0); PLB 8.99s.p.; pap. 7.95 (ISBN 0-382-24084-7); pap. 5.21s.p. Silver Burdett Pr.
Roberts, Paulette & Whaley, Jeanette. Seeds for Progress. LC 89-52122. (Illus.). 140p. 1990. pap. 12.95 (ISBN 0-685-31292-5). Winston-Derek.
Robinson, Dorothy. The Legend of Africania. Temple, Herbert, illus. LC 74-4781. 32p. (gr. k-5). 1974. 10.95 (ISBN 0-87485-037-1). Johnson Chi.
Smead, Howard. The Afro-Americans. Moynihan, Daniel P., intro. by. (Illus.). 120p. (gr. 5 up). 1989. lib. bdg. 17.95 (ISBN 0-87754-854-4); pap. 9.95 (ISBN 0-7910-0256-X). Chelsea Hse.
Spangler, Earl. The Blacks in America. rev. ed. LC 71-150773. (Illus.). 112p. (gr. 5 up). 1980. PLB 11.95 (ISBN 0-8225-0207-0); pap. 3.95 (ISBN 0-8225-1017-0). Lerner Pubns.
Sutton, Charyn, ed. Grio "The Praise Singer" The 1987 Chronicle of Afro-American Heritage, Vol. III. Massey, Cal, et al, illus. 80p. (Orig.). (gr. k-12). 1988. pap. text ed. 9.95 (ISBN 0-936509-00-7); 183.25 (ISBN 0-936509-01-5). Enteracom Inc.
Willis, L. W. Afro-Bets Activity & Enrichment Guide (ABC & 1 2 3 Books) Date not set. pap. 5.95 (ISBN 0-940975-06-8). Just Us Bks.

BLACKS–BIOGRAPHY

Akinsheye, Dexter. African American Inventor Adolphus Samms, Vol. I. Akinsheye, Dayo, ed. Gibbs, C. R., intro. by. (Illus., Orig.). (gr. 1-12). Date not set. pap. 3.00 (ISBN 0-685-26241-3); Set of 39 titles. pap. 78.00 (ISBN 0-685-26242-1). TD Pub.
—African American Inventor Adolphus Samms, Vol. III. Akinsheye, Dayo, ed. Gibbs, C. R., intro. by. (Illus., Orig.). (gr. 1-12). Date not set. pap. 3.00 (ISBN 0-685-26243-X); Set of 39 titles. pap. 78.00 (ISBN 0-685-26244-8). TD Pub.
—African American Inventor Adolphus Samms, Vol. II. Akinsheye, Dayo, ed. Gibbs, C. R., intro. by. (Illus., Orig.). (gr. 1-12). Date not set. pap. 3.00 (ISBN 0-685-26245-6); Set of 39 titles. pap. 78.00 (ISBN 0-685-26246-4). TD Pub.
—African American Inventor Alice H. Parker. Akinsheye, Dayo, ed. Gibbs, C. R., intro. by. (Illus., Orig.). (gr. 1-12). Date not set. pap. 3.00 (ISBN 0-685-26189-1); Set of 39 titles. pap. 78.00 (ISBN 0-685-26190-5). TD Pub.
—African American Inventor Andrew J. Beard. Akinsheye, Dayo, ed. Gibbs, C. R., intro. by. (Illus., Orig.). (gr. 1-12). Date not set. pap. 3.00 (ISBN 0-685-26239-1); Set of 39 titles. pap. 78.00 (ISBN 0-685-26240-5). TD Pub.
—African American Inventor Benjamin F. Jackson. Akinsheye, Dayo, ed. Gibbs, C. R., intro. by. (Illus., Orig.). (gr. 1-12). Date not set. pap. 3.00 (ISBN 0-685-26205-7); Set of 39 titles. pap. 78.00 (ISBN 0-685-26206-5). TD Pub.
—African American Inventor Charles C. Brooks, Vol. II. Akinsheye, Dayo, ed. Gibbs, C. R., intro. by. (Illus., Orig.). (gr. 1-12). Date not set. pap. 3.00 (ISBN 0-685-26207-3); Set of 39 titles. pap. 78.00 (ISBN 0-685-26208-1). TD Pub.
—African American Inventor Charles C. Brooks, Vol. I. Akinsheye, Dayo, ed. Gibbs, C. R., intro. by. (Illus., Orig.). (gr. 1-12). Date not set. pap. 3.00 (ISBN 0-685-26209-X); Set of 39 titles. pap. 78.00 (ISBN 0-685-26210-3). TD Pub.
—African American Inventor Edward R. Lewis. Akinsheye, Dayo, ed. Gibbs, C. R., intro. by. (Illus., Orig.). (gr. 1-12). Date not set. pap. 3.00 (ISBN 0-685-26225-1); Set of 39 titles. pap. 78.00 (ISBN 0-685-26226-X). TD Pub.
—African American Inventor Elijah McCoy. Akinsheye, Dayo, ed. Gibbs, C. R., intro. by. (Illus., Orig.). (gr. 1-12). Date not set. pap. 3.00 (ISBN 0-685-26237-5); Set of 39 titles. pap. 78.00 (ISBN 0-685-26238-3). TD Pub.
—African American Inventor Frederick Jones, Vol. I. Akinsheye, Dayo, ed. Gibbs, C. R., intro. by. (Illus., Orig.). (gr. 1-12). Date not set. pap. 3.00 (ISBN 0-685-26173-5); Set of 39 titles. pap. 78.00 (ISBN 0-685-26174-3). TD Pub.
—African American Inventor Frederick Jones, Vol. II. Akinsheye, Dayo, ed. Gibbs, C. R., intro. by. (Illus., Orig.). (gr. 1-12). Date not set. pap. 3.00 (ISBN 0-685-26177-8); Set of 39 titles. pap. 78.00 (ISBN 0-685-26178-6). TD Pub.
—African American Inventor Garrett T. Morgan, Vol. II. Akinsheye, Dayo, ed. Gibbs, C. R., intro. by. (Illus., Orig.). (gr. 1-12). Date not set. pap. 3.00 (ISBN 0-685-26217-0); Set of 39 titles. pap. 78.00 (ISBN 0-685-26218-9). TD Pub.
—African American Inventor Garrett T. Morgan, Vol. I. Akinsheye, Dayo, ed. Gibbs, C. R., intro. by. (Illus., Orig.). (gr. 1-12). Date not set. pap. 3.00 (ISBN 0-685-26219-7); Set of 39 titles. pap. 78.00 (ISBN 0-685-26220-0). TD Pub.
—African American Inventor George F. Grant. Akinsheye, Dayo, ed. Gibbs, C. R., intro. by. (Illus., Orig.). (gr. 1-12). Date not set. pap. 3.00 (ISBN 0-685-26183-2); Set of 39 titles. pap. 78.00 (ISBN 0-685-26184-0). TD Pub.
—African American Inventor George R. Carruthes. Akinsheye, Dayo, ed. Gibbs, C. R., intro. by. (Illus., Orig.). (gr. 1-12). Date not set. pap. 3.00 (ISBN 0-685-26191-3); Set of 39 titles. pap. 78.00 (ISBN 0-685-26192-1). TD Pub.
—African American Inventor George Toliver. Akinsheye, Dayo, ed. Gibbs, C. R., intro. by. (Illus., Orig.). (gr. 1-12). Date not set. pap. 3.00 (ISBN 0-685-26227-8); Set of 39 titles. pap. 78.00 (ISBN 0-685-26228-6). TD Pub.
—African American Inventor George W. Murray. Akinsheye, Dayo, ed. Gibbs, C. R., intro. by. (Illus., Orig.). (gr. 1-12). Date not set. pap. 3.00 (ISBN 0-685-26199-9); Set of 39 titles. pap. 78.00 (ISBN 0-685-26200-6). TD Pub.
—African American Inventor Gertrude Downing. Akinsheye, Dayo, ed. Gibbs, C. R., intro. by. (Illus., Orig.). (gr. 1-12). Date not set. pap. 3.00 (ISBN 0-685-26213-8); Set of 39 titles. pap. 78.00. TD Pub.
—African American Inventor Granville T. Woods, Vol. II. Akinsheye, Dayo, ed. Gibbs, C. R., intro. by. (Illus., Orig.). (gr. 1-12). Date not set. pap. 3.00 (ISBN 0-685-26231-6); Set of 39 titles. pap. 78.00 (ISBN 0-685-26232-4). TD Pub.
—African American Inventor Granville T. Woods, Vol. I. Akinsheye, Dayo, ed. Gibbs, C. R., intro. by. (Illus., Orig.). (gr. 1-12). Date not set. pap. 3.00 (ISBN 0-685-26233-2); Set of 39 titles. pap. 78.00 (ISBN 0-685-26234-0). TD Pub.
—African American Inventor Harold Linden. Akinsheye, Dayo, ed. Gibbs, C. R., intro. by. (Illus., Orig.). (gr. 1-12). Date not set. pap. 3.00 (ISBN 0-685-26195-6); Set of 39 titles. pap. 78.00 (ISBN 0-685-26196-4). TD Pub.
—African American Inventor Henrietta Bradberry. Akinsheye, Dayo, ed. Gibbs, C. R., intro. by. (Illus., Orig.). (gr. 1-12). Date not set. pap. 3.00 (ISBN 0-685-26175-1); Set of 39 titles. pap. 78.00 (ISBN 0-685-26176-X). TD Pub.
—African American Inventor Henry Blair. Akinsheye, Dayo, ed. Gibbs, C. R., intro. by. (Illus., Orig.). (gr. 1-12). Date not set. pap. 3.00 (ISBN 0-685-26179-4); Set of 39 titles. pap. 78.00 (ISBN 0-685-26180-8). TD Pub.
—African American Inventor Hubert Julian. Akinsheye, Dayo, ed. Gibbs, C. R., intro. by. (Illus., Orig.). (gr. 1-12). Date not set. pap. 3.00 (ISBN 0-685-26181-6); Set of 39 titles. pap. 78.00 (ISBN 0-685-26182-4). TD Pub.
—African American Inventor Jack A. Johnson. Akinsheye, Dayo, ed. Gibbs, C. R., intro. by. (Illus., Orig.). (gr. 1-12). Date not set. pap. 3.00 (ISBN 0-685-26169-7); Set of 39 titles. pap. 78.00 (ISBN 0-685-26170-0). TD Pub.
—African American Inventor James T. Redding. Akinsheye, Dayo, ed. Gibbs, C. R., intro. by. (Illus., Orig.). (gr. 1-12). Date not set. pap. 3.00 (ISBN 0-685-26211-1); Set of 39 titles. pap. 78.00 (ISBN 0-685-26212-X). TD Pub.
—African American Inventor Jan E. Matzeliger. Akinsheye, Dayo, ed. Gibbs, C. R., intro. by. (Illus., Orig.). (gr. 1-12). Date not set. pap. 3.00 (ISBN 0-685-26215-4); Set of 39 titles. pap. 78.00 (ISBN 0-685-26216-2). TD Pub.
—African American Inventor John Pickering. Akinsheye, Dayo, ed. Gibbs, C. R., intro. by. (Illus., Orig.). (gr. 1-12). Date not set. pap. 3.00 (ISBN 0-685-26193-X); Set of 39 titles. pap. 78.00 (ISBN 0-685-26194-8). TD Pub.
—African American Inventor Joseph H. Smith. Akinsheye, Dayo, ed. Gibbs, C. R., intro. by. (Illus., Orig.). (gr. 1-12). Date not set. pap. 3.00 (ISBN 0-685-26235-9); Set of 39 titles. pap. 78.00 (ISBN 0-685-26236-7). TD Pub.
—African American Inventor Lewis H. Latimer, Vol. I. Akinsheye, Dayo, ed. Gibbs, C. R., intro. by. (Illus., Orig.). (gr. 1-12). Date not set. pap. 3.00 (ISBN 0-685-26185-9); Set of 39 titles. pap. 78.00 (ISBN 0-685-26186-7). TD Pub.
—African American Inventor Lewis H. Latimer, Vol. II. Akinsheye, Dayo, ed. Gibbs, C. R., intro. by. (Illus., Orig.). (gr. 1-12). Date not set. pap. 3.00 (ISBN 0-685-26187-5); Set of 39 titles. pap. 78.00 (ISBN 0-685-26188-3). TD Pub.
—African American Inventor Lewis Latimer. Akinsheye, Dayo, ed. Gibbs, C. R., intro. by. (Illus., Orig.). (gr. 1-12). Date not set. pap. 3.00 (ISBN 0-685-26201-4); Set of 39 titles. pap. 78.00 (ISBN 0-685-26202-2). TD Pub.
—African American Inventor Miriam E. Benjamin. Akinsheye, Dayo, ed. Gibbs, C. R., intro. by. (Illus., Orig.). (gr. 1-12). Date not set. pap. 3.00 (ISBN 0-685-26221-9); Set of 39 titles. pap. 78.00 (ISBN 0-685-26222-7). TD Pub.
—African American Inventor Norbert Rillieux. Akinsheye, Dayo, ed. Gibbs, C. R., intro. by. (Illus., Orig.). (gr. 1-12). Date not set. pap. 3.00 (ISBN 0-685-26223-5); Set of 39 titles. pap. 78.00 (ISBN 0-685-26224-3). TD Pub.
—African American Inventor Richard Spikes. Akinsheye, Dayo, ed. Gibbs, C. R., intro. by. (Illus., Orig.). (gr. 1-12). Date not set. pap. 3.00 (ISBN 0-685-26171-9); Set of 39 titles. pap. 78.00 (ISBN 0-685-26172-7). TD Pub.
—African American Inventor Richard Toomey. Akinsheye, Dayo, ed. Gibbs, C. R., intro. by. (Illus., Orig.). (gr. 1-12). Date not set. pap. 3.00 (ISBN 0-685-26229-4); Set of 39 titles. pap. 78.00 (ISBN 0-685-26230-8). TD Pub.
—African American Inventor Sara E. Goode. Akinsheye, Dayo, ed. Gibbs, C. R., intro. by. (Illus., Orig.). (gr. 1-12). Date not set. pap. 3.00 (ISBN 0-685-26203-0); Set of 39 titles. pap. 78.00 (ISBN 0-685-26204-9). TD Pub.
—African American Inventor William B. Purvis. Akinsheye, Dayo, ed. Gibbs, C. R., intro. by. (Illus., Orig.). (gr. 1-12). Date not set. pap. 3.00 (ISBN 0-685-26197-2); Set of 39 titles. pap. 78.00 (ISBN 0-685-26198-0). TD Pub.
Altman, Susan. Extraordinary Black Americans from Colonial to Contemporary Times. LC 88-11977. (Illus.). 240p. (gr. 4 up). 1989. PLB 30.60 (ISBN 0-516-00581-2). Childrens.

Beaton, Margaret. Oprah Winfrey: TV Talk Show Host. LC 90-2150. (Illus). (gr. 4 up). 1990. PLB 17.27 (ISBN 0-516-03270-4). Childrens.

Bellegarde, Ida R. Black Heroes & Heroines, Bk. 4. LC 79-51798. 64p. (gr. 5 up). 1984. 8.95 (ISBN 0-918340-13-6). Bell Ent.

Bernotas, Bob. Amiri Baraka (Le Roi Jones) King, Coretta Scott, intro. by. (Illus). 112p. (gr. 5 up). 1991. PLB 17.95 (ISBN 0-7910-1117-8). Chelsea Hse.

Carwell, Hattie. Blacks in Science: Astrophysicist to Zoologist. Earls, Julian, intro. by. (Illus). 96p. (gr. 8 up). 1988. pap. 7.00 (ISBN 0-682-48911-5); 10.00 (ISBN 0-685-22950-5). H Carwell.

Ceasor, Ebraska, et al. Blacks in Ohio: Seven Portraits. McCluskey, John, ed. (Orig). (gr. 7-12). 1976. pap. 4.25x (ISBN 0-913678-13-9). New Day Pr.

Chaplik, Dorothy. Up with Hope: A Biography of Jesse Jackson. rev. ed. LC 86-11634. (Illus). 128p. (gr. 6 up). 1986. PLB 12.95 (ISBN 0-87518-347-6, Dillon). Macmillan Child Grp.

De Kay, James T. Meet Martin Luther King Jr. LC 78-79789. (gr. 3-6). 1969. 5.95 (ISBN 0-394-80055-9, Random Juv); lib. bdg. 8.99 (ISBN 0-394-90055-3). Random.

Dominy, Jeannine. Katherine Dunham. (Illus). (gr. 5 up). 1992. PLB 17.95 (ISBN 0-7910-1123-2). Chelsea Hse.

Donovan, Richard X. Black Scientists of America. Sorrels, Judith, illus. 134p. (gr. 6 up). 1990. pap. 8.95 (ISBN 0-89420-265-0, 297000). Natl Book.

Ericsson, Mary K. Morrie Turner: Creator of "Wee Pals" LC 85-30846. (Illus). 111p. (gr. 4-7). 1986. PLB 17.27 (ISBN 0-516-03222-4). Childrens.

Ferris, Jeri. Walking the Road to Freedom: A Story about Sojourner Truth. Hanson, Peter E., illus. 64p. (gr. 3-6). 1989. pap. 4.95 (ISBN 0-685-25646-4, First Ave Edns). Lerner Pubns.

Finke, Blythe F. Angela Davis: Traitor or Martyr of the Freedom of Expression? Rahmas, D. Steve, ed. LC 77-190246. 32p. (Orig). (gr. 7-12). 1972. lib. bdg. 4.20 incl. catalog cards (ISBN 0-87157-528-0); pap. 2.95 vinyl laminated covers (ISBN 0-87157-028-9). SamHar Pr.

Fraser, Alison. Walter White. King, Coretta Scott, intro. by. (Illus). 112p. (gr. 5 up). 1991. 17.95 (ISBN 1-55546-617-6). Chelsea Hse.

Freedman, Florence B. Two Tickets to Freedom: The True Story of Ellen & William Craft, Fugitive Slaves. Keats, Ezra J., illus. 96p. (gr. 4 up). 1989. 12.95x (ISBN 0-87226-330-4); pap. 5.95 (ISBN 0-87226-221-9). P Bedrick Bks.

Gaines, Edith M., et al. Black Image Makers. Adrine-Robinson, Kenyette, ed. Belanger, Ray, et al, illus. Gregory, Dick, frwd. by. (Orig). (gr. 5-9). 1988. pap. 8.95 (ISBN 0-913678-17-1). New Day Pr.

Haber, Louis. Black Pioneers of Science & Invention. LC 77-109090. (Illus). (gr. 5 up). 1970. 17.95 (ISBN 0-15-208565-3, HJ). HarBraceJ.

Haskins, James & Benson, Kathleen. Space Challenger: The Story of Guion Bluford. LC 84-4251. (Illus). 64p. (gr. 3-6). 1984. PLB 11.95 (ISBN 0-87614-259-5). Carolrhoda Bks.

Hudson, Wade & Wesley, Valerie W. Afro-Bets Book of Black Heroes from A to Z: An Introduction to Important Black Achievers. LC 87-82951. (Illus). 64p. (gr. 3-6). 1988. pap. 7.95 (ISBN 0-940975-02-5). Just Us Bks.

Humphrey, Perla F. Historic People of Color: The Honorabale H. M. Turner. Spaulding, Ureal, illus. 18p. (Orig). (gr. 3-8). 1990. pap. write for info. (ISBN 1-878910-00-0). Supplemental Learning.

Igus, Toyomi, et al. Book of Black Heroes, Vol. 2: Great Women in the Struggle. 96p. (gr. 4-8). 1991. lib. bdg. 17.95 (ISBN 0-940975-27-0); pap. 10.95 (ISBN 0-940975-26-2). Just Us Bks.

James Rapier: Mini Play. (gr. 5 up). 1977. 6.50 (ISBN 0-89550-360-3). Stevens & Shea.

Johnson, Jacqueline. Stokely Carmichael: The Story of Black Power. Gallin, Richard, ed. Young, Andrew, intro. by. (Illus). 128p. (gr. 5 up). 1990. lib. bdg. 16.98 (ISBN 0-382-09920-6); pap. 7.95 (ISBN 0-382-24056-1). Silver Burdett Pr.

Jones, Margaret. Martin Luther King, Jr. Scott, R., illus. LC 68-9483. 36p. (gr. 1-4). 1968. PLB 13.27 (ISBN 0-516-03524-X); pap. 3.95 (ISBN 0-516-43524-8). Childrens.

Katz, William L. Black People Who Made the Old West. LC 76-7051. (Illus). 160p. (gr. 7 up). 1989. PLB 12.89 (ISBN 0-690-04816-5, Crowell Jr Bks). HarpC Child Bks.

Klots, Steve. Richard Allen. KIng, Coretta Scott, intro. by. (Illus). 112p. (gr. 5 up). 1991. lib. bdg. 17.95 (ISBN 1-55546-570-6). Chelsea Hse.

Koenig, Terry. Tina Turner. LC 86-8950. (Illus). 32p. (gr. 4-5). PLB 9.95 (ISBN 0-89686-305-0, Crestwood Hse). Macmillan Child Grp.

Lawler, Mary. Marcus Garvey. King, Coretta Scott, intro. by. (Illus). 112p. (Orig). (gr. 5 up). 1988. 17.95 (ISBN 1-55546-587-0); pap. 9.95 (ISBN 0-7910-0203-9). Chelsea Hse.

Leder, Jane M. Walter Payton. LC 86-16526. (Illus). 48p. (gr. 5-6). PLB 10.95 (ISBN 0-89686-318-2, Crestwood Hse). Macmillan Child Grp.

Liss, Howard. Great Black Americans in Science - Art - Literature. (Illus). 160p. (gr. 3-9). 1991. lib. bdg. 14.95 (ISBN 0-87460-392-7). Lion Bks.

Machamer, Gene. The Illustrated Black American Profiles. Sager, Linda C., ed. LC 90-82937. (Illus). 192p. (Orig). 1991. pap. 7.95 (ISBN 0-9627369-0-2). Carlisle Pr.

McKissack, Patricia & McKissack, Fredrick. Carter G. Woodson: The Father of Black History. Ostendorf, Ned, illus. 32p. (gr. 1-4). 1991. PLB 12.95 (ISBN 0-89490-309-8). Enslow Pubs.

—George Washington Carver: The Peanut Scientist. Ostendorf, Ned, illus. 32p. (gr. 1-4). 1991. PLB 12.95 (ISBN 0-89490-308-X). Enslow Pubs.

—Great African Americans Series, 10 bks. (Illus). (gr. 1-4). 1991. Set, 32p. ea. PLB 129.50 (ISBN 0-89490-376-4). Enslow Pubs.

Easy-to-read biographies written for young people ages 7-10 about African Americans who have done great things for their country & the world. The Great African Americans series gives young people a better understanding of the contributions African Americans have made to society in many fields such as science, diplomacy, & the arts. Each book contains a glossary with pronunciation hints for hard words, & an index. Illustrated with photos & drawings. Coretta Scott King Award-winning authors, Patricia & Fredrick McKissack introduce their heroes of black history to young people. Titles include: Marian Anderson: A Great Singer; Louis Armstrong: Jazz Musician; Mary McLeod Bethune: A Great Teacher; Ralph J. Bunche: Peacemaker; George Washington Carver: The Peanut Scientist; Frederick Douglass: Leader Against Slavery; Martin Luther King, Jr: Man of Peace; Mary Church Terrell: Leader for Equality; Ida B. Wells-Barnett: A Voice Against Violence; Carter G. Woodson: The Father of Black History. The complete Great African Americans series is available for $129. 50 or individual titles can be purchased for $12.95 each from Enslow Publishers, Inc., Bloy St. & Ramsey Ave., Box 777, Hillside, NJ 07205. To order call (908) 964-7172 or FAX (908) 687-3829. Prices subject to change. *Publisher Provided Annotation.*

—Ida B. Wells-Barnett: A Voice Against Violence. Ostendorf, Ned, illus. LC 90-49848. 32p. (gr. 1-4). 1991. PLB 12.95 (ISBN 0-89490-301-2). Enslow Pubs.

—Mary Church Terrell: Leader for Equality. Ostendorf, Ned, illus. 32p. (gr. 1-4). 1991. PLB 12.95 (ISBN 0-89490-305-5). Enslow Pubs.

Millender, Dharathula H. Crispus Attucks: Black Leader of Colonial Patriots. Morrow, Gray, illus. LC 86-10779. 192p. (gr. 2-6). 1986. pap. 3.95 (ISBN 0-02-041810-8, Aladdin). Macmillan Child Grp.

Miller, Vousette T. Color Me Beautiful Color Me Black. (Illus). 32p. (ps-6). 1988. wkbk. 4.00 (ISBN 0-9619641-0-3). Vous Etes Tres Belle.

Morgan, James A., ed. Profiles in Black History. 19p. (Orig). (gr. 6-8). 1988. pap. text ed. 3.00 (ISBN 0-685-26485-8). Collins Assocs.

Mumford, Donald & Mumford, Esther. From Africa to the Arctic: Five Explorers. Lee, Nancy, illus. 48p. (gr. 1-3). 1992. 9.95 (ISBN 0-9605670-6-2). Ananse Pr.

The exploration of the North American continent by people of African descent began with the travels of Estebanico, a black Morrocan who sought the legendary Seven Cities of Gold in the American Southwest in the 1500s. From 1804 to 1806 York, a slave, accompanied, provisioned, & interpreted for Meriwether Lewis & his

master William Clark, on the historic expedition to explore the recently purchased land west of the Mississippi River. The scout, Jim Beckwourth, discovered the western mountain pass which bears his name today. Stephen Bishop explored, & led parties to, the undiscovered passages of the Mammouth Cave system in Kentucky. From his first journey to the far north in 1891 Matthew Henson prepared himself for the discovery of the North Pole with Robert Peary in 1909. These five men rose from slavery or near-slavery to explore unknown places. The first in a series of the African Diaspora, this book will inform young readers & adult learners of these little-known discoverers. *Publisher Provided Annotation.*

Mumford, Esther H. The Man Who Founded a Town. Kim, Jody, illus. 32p. (Orig). (gr. 2-5). 1990. 8.95 (ISBN 0-9605670-2-X); pap. 4.95 (ISBN 0-9605670-3-8). Ananse Pr.

Naden, Corinne. Ronald McNair. King, Coretta Scott, intro. by. (Illus). 112p. (gr. 5 up). 1991. PLB 17.95 (ISBN 0-7910-1133-X). Chelsea Hse.

Obaba, Al-Imam. Adam Clayton Powell, Jr. (Illus). 43p. (Orig). 1989. pap. 3.95 (ISBN 0-916157-06-7). African Islam Miss Pubns.

—Marcus Mosiah Garvey, Jr. Great Nubian Quiz. (Illus). 43p. (Orig). 1989. pap. 3.95 (ISBN 0-916157-15-6). African Islam Miss Pubns.

Orr, Jack. Black Athlete: His Story in American History. Robinson, Jackie, intro. by. (gr. 6 up). 1969. PLB 14.95 (ISBN 0-87460-104-5). Lion Bks.

Patterson, Lillie & Wright, Cornelia H. Oprah Winfrey: Talk Show Host & Actress. 128p. (gr. 6 up). 1990. 17.95 (ISBN 0-89490-289-X). Enslow Pubs.

Peters, Margaret W. The Ebony Book of Black Achievement. rev. ed. Ferguson, Cecil L., illus. LC 79-128544. 128p. (gr. 4-8). 1974. Repr. 8.95 (ISBN 0-87485-040-1). Johnson Chi.

Richardson, Ben & Fahey, William A. Great Black Americans. 2nd, rev. ed. LC 75-12841. (Illus). 352p. (gr. 5 up). 1976. 16.95 (ISBN 0-690-00994-1, Crowell Jr Bks). HarpC Child Bks.

Richardson, Ben & Foley, William A. Great Black Americans. LC 75-12841. (Illus). 352p. (gr. 7 up). 1990. PLB 16.89 (ISBN 0-690-04791-6, Crowell Jr Bks). HarpC Child Bks.

Rollins, Charlemae H. They Showed the Way: Forty American Negro Leaders. LC 64-20692. 165p. (gr. 4 up). 1964. 14.95 (ISBN 0-690-81612-X, Crowell Jr Bks). HarpC Child Bks.

Ross, H. K. Black American Women, No. 3. (Illus). 160p. (gr. 6-12). 1990. PLB 14.95 (ISBN 0-87460-365-X). Lion Bks.

Santrey, Laurence. Young Frederick Douglass: Fight for Freedom. Dodson, Bert, illus. LC 82-15993. 48p. (gr. 4-6). 1983. PLB 10.79 (ISBN 0-89375-857-4); pap. text ed. 2.95 (ISBN 0-89375-858-2). Troll Assocs.

Sklansky, Jeff. James Farmer. (Illus). (gr. 5 up). 1992. PLB 17.95 (ISBN 0-7910-1126-7). Chelsea Hse.

Sweet, Dovie D. Red Light, Green Light: The Life of Garrett Morgan & His Invention of the Stop Light. 4th ed. (Orig). (gr. 1-6). 1988. pap. 5.00 (ISBN 0-682-49088-1). Kitwardo Pubs.

Tames, Richard. Nelson Mandela. (Illus). 32p. 1991. PLB 11.90 (ISBN 0-531-14124-1). Watts.

Thomas, Anika D. Life in the Ghetto. Thatch, Nancy R., ed. Thomas, Anika D., illus. Melton, David, intro. by. (Illus). 26p. (gr. 5 up). 1991. PLB 12.95 (ISBN 0-933849-34-6). Landmark Edns.

Washington, Booker T. Up from Slavery. Andrews, C. A., intro. by. (gr. 5 up). pap. 2.50 (ISBN 0-8049-0157-0, CL-157). Airmont.

Washington, Jerome. William Hastie. King, Coretta Scott, intro. by. (Illus). 17.95 (ISBN 1-55546-589-7). Chelsea Hse.

Weisbrot, Robert. Father Divine. (Illus). (gr. 5 up). 1992. PLB 17.95 (ISBN 0-7910-1122-4). Chelsea Hse.

Witcover, Paul. Zora Neale Hurston. King, Coretta Scott, intro. by. (Illus). 112p. (gr. 5 up). 1991. PLB 17.95 (ISBN 0-7910-1129-1). Chelsea Hse.

Woods, Geraldine. Oprah Winfrey. (Illus). 80p. (gr. 3 up). 1991. PLB 10.95 (ISBN 0-87518-463-4, Dillon). Macmillan Child Grp.

BLACKS–CIVIL RIGHTS

Douglass, Frederick. Why Is the Negro Lynched. Obaba, Al I., ed. 49p. (Orig). Date not set. pap. text ed. 7.95 (ISBN 0-916157-78-4). African Islam Miss Pubns.

Ella Baker. (Illus). 128p. (gr. 5-8). 1990. lib. bdg. 16.98 (ISBN 0-382-09931-1); pap. 7.95 (ISBN 0-382-24066-9). Silver Burdett Pr.

The History of the Civil Rights Movement, 9 bks. (Illus). (gr. 5-8). 1990. Set, 128p. ea. lib. bdg. 152.82 (ISBN 0-382-09919-2); pap. 71.55 (ISBN 0-382-24055-3). Silver Burdett Pr.

Jones, Margaret. Martin Luther King, Jr. Scott, R., illus. LC 68-9483. 36p. (gr. 1-4). 1968. PLB 13.27 (ISBN 0-516-03524-X); pap. 3.95 (ISBN 0-516-43524-8). Childrens.

Kosof, Anna. The Civil Rights Movement & Its Legacy. (Illus.). 112p. (gr. 7-12). 1989. PLB 12.90 (ISBN 0-531-10791-4). Watts.

McKissack, Patricia & McKissack, Fredrick. The Civil Rights Movement in America from 1865 to the Present. LC 86-9636. (Illus.). 320p. (gr. 4 up). 1987. 39.93 (ISBN 0-516-00580-4). Childrens.

Millender, Dharathula H. Martin Luther King, Jr. Young Man with a Dream. Fiorentino, Al, illus. LC 86-10739. 192p. (gr. 2-6). 1986. pap. 3.95 (ISBN 0-02-042010-2, Aladdin). Macmillan Child Grp.

BLACKS–EDUCATION–FICTION

Clifton, Fred. Darl. (Illus.). 104p. (gr. 2-6). 1973. 5.95 (ISBN 0-89388-098-1). Okpaku Communications.

Hudson, Cheryl W. & Ford, Bernette G. Bright Eyes, Brown Skin. Ford, George, illus. 24p. (ps-2). 1990. 12.95 (ISBN 0-940975-10-6); pap. 6.95 (ISBN 0-940975-23-8). Just Us Bks.

Newell, Hope. Cap for Mary Ellis. LC 53-8547. (gr. 7 up). 1953. PLB 12.89 (ISBN 0-06-024526-3). HarpC Child Bks.

BLACKS–EMPLOYMENT

Marsh, Carole. The Best Book of Black Biographies. (gr. 3-12). 1989. PLB 19.95 (ISBN 1-55609-330-6); pap. 14.95 (ISBN 1-55609-329-2); computer disk 29.95 (ISBN 1-55609-331-4). Gallopade Pub Group.

—Black Business. (gr. 4-12). 1989. PLB 19.95 (ISBN 1-55609-327-6); pap. 14.95 (ISBN 1-55609-326-8); computer disk 29.95 (ISBN 1-55609-328-4). Gallopade Pub Group.

BLACKS–FICTION

Armstrong, William H. Sounder. LC 70-85030. (Illus.). 128p. (gr. 6 up). 1969. 13.95 (ISBN 0-06-020143-6); PLB 13.89 (ISBN 0-06-020144-4). HarpC Child Bks.

—Sounder. Barkley, James, illus. LC 70-85030. 128p. (gr. 6 up). 1972. pap. 2.95 (ISBN 0-06-440020-4, Trophy). HarpC Child Bks.

—Sounder. 116p. (gr. 7 up). pap. 2.50 (ISBN 0-590-40212-9); Teaching Guide. 1.25 (ISBN 0-590-40905-0). Scholastic Inc.

Barrett, Anna P. The Middlebatchers: Throw a Party for the Marriage of Hetty Wish & Lester Leg, Vol. 1. Darst, Shelia S., ed. Russell, Dave, illus. 118p. (Orig.). (gr. 3-7). 1984. pap. 5.95 (ISBN 0-89896-105-X). Larksdale.

Barrett, William E. Lilies of the Field. Silverman, Burt, illus. LC 62-8085. (gr. 7 up). 1967. 3.95 (ISBN 0-685-01491-6, Im); pap. 3.95 (ISBN 0-385-07246-5, Im). Doubleday.

Bonham, Frank. Mystery of the Fat Cat. Smith, Alvin, illus. 160p. (gr. 5-9). 1971. pap. 1.25 (ISBN 0-440-46226-6, YB). Dell.

Boyd, Candy D. Forever Friends. 192p. (gr. 5-9). 1986. pap. 3.95 (ISBN 0-14-032077-6, Puffin). Puffin Bks.

Burgess, Barbara H. Oren Bell. 1991. 15.00 (ISBN 0-385-30325-4). Delacorte.

Byars, Betsy C. The Burning Questions of Bingo Brown. LC 87-21022. 160p. (gr. 3-7). 1988. pap. 12.95 (ISBN 0-670-81932-8). Viking Child Bks.

Campbell, Tammie L. Honey Brown in Search of Her Identity, Vol. 1. Jammer, Cornelius C., Jr., illus. Moon, Felicia, intro. by. (Illus.). 24p. (Orig.). (gr. k-5). 1990. pap. 4.95 (ISBN 0-9623947-0-X). T L Campbell.

Clifton, Lucille. Everett Anderson's Christmas Coming. Gilchrist, Jan S., illus. LC 91-2041. 32p. (ps-4). 1991. 14.95 (ISBN 0-8050-1549-3). H Holt & Co.

Echewa, T. O. How Tables Came to Umu Madu. LC 88-83368. (Illus.). 90p. (gr. 5 up). 19.95 (ISBN 0-86543-127-2); pap. 7.95 (ISBN 0-86543-128-0). Africa World.

Greenfield, Eloise. Daydreamers. Feelings, Tom, illus. (gr. k up). 1981. 11.95 (ISBN 0-8037-2137-4); PLB 11.89 (ISBN 0-8037-2134-X). Dial Bks Young.

Hamilton, Virginia. Bells of Christmas. 1989. 16.95 (ISBN 0-15-206450-8). HarbraceJ.

—A Little Love. 192p. 1984. 12.95 (ISBN 0-399-21046-6, Philomel). Putnam Pub Group.

—M. C. Higgins, the Great. LC 72-92439. 288p. (gr. 7 up). 1974. 14.95 (ISBN 0-02-742480-4, Mcmillan Child Bk). Macmillan Child Grp.

—White Romance. 1989. pap. 3.95 (ISBN 0-15-295888-6). HarbraceJ.

—Zeely. Shimin, Symeon, illus. LC 67-10266. 128p. (gr. 5-7). 1968. 13.95 (ISBN 0-02-742470-7, Mcmillan Child Bk). Macmillan Child Grp.

—Zeely. Shimin, Symeon, illus. LC 86-22197. 128p. (gr. 5-7). 1987. pap. 3.95 (ISBN 0-689-71110-7, Aladdin). Macmillan Child Grp.

Hayes, Sarah. Happy Christmas, Gemma. Ormerod, Jan, illus. LC 85-23674. 32p. (ps-1). 1986. 13.95 (ISBN 0-688-06508-2). Lothrop.

Hill, Elizabeth S. Evan's Corner. (ps-3). 1991. 12.95 (ISBN 0-670-82830-0). Viking Child Bks.

Hooks, William H. The Ballad of Belle Dorcas. Pinkney, Brian, illus. LC 89-2715. 48p. (gr. 2-7). 1990. 13.95 (ISBN 0-394-84645-1); lib. bdg. 14.99 (ISBN 0-394-94645-6). Knopf.

Howard, Ellen. When Daylight Comes. LC 85-7963. 192p. (gr. 5-9). 1985. 14.95 (ISBN 0-689-31133-8, Atheneum Child Bk). Macmillan Child Grp.

Hudson, Cheryl W. & Ford, Bernette G. Bright Eyes, Brown Skin. Ford, George, illus. 24p. (ps-2). 1990. 12.95 (ISBN 0-940975-10-6); pap. 6.95 (ISBN 0-940975-23-8). Just Us Bks.

Hudson, Wade, et al. Jamal's Busy Day. Ford, George, illus. 24p. (gr. 1-3). 1991. lib. bdg. 6.95; pap. write for info. (ISBN 0-940975-24-6). Just Us Bks.

Hulbert, Jay & Kantor, Sid. Armando Asked "Why?" Hoggan, Pat, illus. 24p. (ps-2). 1990. PLB 12.33 (ISBN 0-8172-3576-0). Raintree Pubs.

Humphrey, Margo. The River That Gave Gifts. Rev. ed. LC 78-61980. (Illus.). (gr. 2-9). 1987. 12.95 (ISBN 0-89239-027-1). Children's Book Pr.

Hunt, Irene. William. LC 76-52455. (gr. 5 up). 1977. SBE 11.95 (ISBN 0-684-14902-8, Scribners Young Read). Macmillan Child Grp.

Irwin, Hadley. I Be Somebody. LC 84-490. 180p. (gr. 4-7). 1984. 13.95 (ISBN 0-689-50308-3, M K McElderry). Macmillan Child Grp.

Little Black Sambo. 56p. (ps-3). Repr. of 1920 ed. 11.95 (ISBN 0-916410-58-7, BTime Classics). A D Bragdon.

Mathis, Sharon B. Listen for the Fig Tree. 176p. (gr. 7 up). 1990. pap. 3.95 (ISBN 0-14-034364-4, Puffin). Puffin Bks.

Myers, Walter D. Fast Sam, Cool Clyde, & Stuff. LC 74-32383. 192p. (gr. 7 up). 1975. pap. 12.95 (ISBN 0-670-30874-9). Viking Child Bks.

—The Mouse Rap. LC 89-36419. 192p. (gr. 5-9). 1990. 12.95 (ISBN 0-06-024343-0); PLB 12.89 (ISBN 0-06-024344-9). HarpC Child Bks.

Naidoo, Beverly. Journey to Jo'burg: A South African Story. Velasquez, Eric, illus. LC 85-45508. 96p. (gr. 4-7). 1986. 11.95 (ISBN 0-397-32168-6, Lipp Jr Bks); PLB 13.89 (ISBN 0-397-32169-4, Lipp Jr Bks). HarpC Child Bks.

Nichols, Joan K. All but the Right Folks. LC 85-488. 144p. (gr. 3 up). 1985. PLB 11.95 (ISBN 0-88045-065-7). Stemmer Hse.

Perales, Andre P. Fanfou dans les Bayous: The Adventures of a Bilingual Elephant in Louisiana. Jarlov, Christian, illus. LC 82-15148. 40p. (gr. 1-7). 1982. pap. 5.95 (ISBN 0-88289-378-5); cassette 11.95 (ISBN 0-88289-410-2). Pelican.

Ringgold, Faith. Tar Beach. Ringgold, Faith, illus. LC 90-40410. 32p. (ps-3). 1991. 14.95 (ISBN 0-517-58030-6); lib. bdg. 14.99 (ISBN 0-517-58031-4). Crown.

Rochman, Hazel, ed. Somehow Tenderness Survives: Stories of Southern Africa. LC 88-916. 208p. (gr. 7 up). 1990. pap. 3.25 (ISBN 0-06-447063-6, Trophy). HarpC Child Bks.

Samton, Sheila. Amazing Aunt Agatha. Bandk, Yvette, illus. 24p. (ps-2). 1990. PLB 12.33 (ISBN 0-8172-3575-2). Raintree Pubs.

Smalls, Hector I. Irene & the Big, Fine Nickel, Vol. 1. (ps-3). 1991. 14.95 (ISBN 0-316-79871-1). Little.

Stolz, Mary. Go Fish. Cummings, Pat, illus. LC 90-4860. 80p. (gr. 2-6). 1991. 12.95 (ISBN 0-06-025820-9); PLB 12.89 (ISBN 0-06-025822-5). HarpC Child Bks.

Tate, Eleanora E. Thank You, Dr. Martin Luther King, Jr. 1990. PLB 13.90 (ISBN 0-531-10904-6). Watts.

Taylor, Mildred. Roll of Thunder, Hear My Cry. Pinkney, Jerry, illus. LC 76-2287. (gr. 6 up). 1976. 14.95 (ISBN 0-8037-7473-7). Dial Bks Young.

Taylor, Mildred D. Let the Circle Be Unbroken. LC 81-65854. 432p. (gr. 7 up). 1981. 15.95 (ISBN 0-8037-4748-9). Dial Bks Young.

—Mississippi Bridge. LC 89-27898. (Illus.). 64p. 1990. 12.95 (ISBN 0-8037-0426-7); PLB 12.89 (ISBN 0-8037-0427-5). Dial Bks Young.

—Roll of Thunder, Hear My Cry. large type ed. 304p. 1989. Repr. of 1976 ed. PLB 15.95 (ISBN 1-55736-140-1, Crnrstn Bks). ABC-CLIO.

Thomas, Joyce C. Marked by Fire. 160p. (gr. 7 up). 1982. pap. 2.95 (ISBN 0-380-79327-X, Flare). Avon.

Thurman, Wallace. Blacker the Berry. Larson, Charles R., ed. O'Daniel, Thurman B., illus. (gr. 11 up). 1970. pap. 5.95 (ISBN 0-02-054750-1, Collier). Macmillan.

Voigt, Cynthia. Come a Stranger. 240p. (gr. 6 up). 1987. pap. 3.95 (ISBN 0-449-70246-4, Juniper). Fawcett.

Wagner, Jane. J. T. Parks, Gordon, photos by. (Illus.). 128p. (gr. 3-8). 1972. pap. 3.25 (ISBN 0-440-44275-3, YB). Dell.

Walker, A. & Deeter, C. Finding the Green Stone. 1991. 16.95 (ISBN 0-15-227538-X, HJ). HarBraceJ.

Walker, Mary A. Year of the Cafeteria. Walker, Mary A., illus. LC 79-156109. 144p. (gr. 6-10). 1971. 4.95 (ISBN 0-672-51398-6, Bobbs). Macmillan.

Walter, Mildred P. Mariah Keeps Cool. LC 89-23981. 144p. (gr. 3-7). 1990. 12.95 (ISBN 0-02-792295-2, Bradbury Pr). Macmillan Child Grp.

Washington, Vivian E. I Am Somebody, I Am Me: A Black Child's Credo. Stockett, Thomas & Washington, Luther, illus. 35p. (Orig.). (gr. 2-6). 1986. pap. 8.50 (ISBN 0-935132-07-4). C H Fairfax.

Wilkinson, Brenda. Ludell. LC 75-9390. 176p. (gr. 5 up). 1975. PLB 12.89 (ISBN 0-06-026492-6). HarpC Child Bks.

—Ludell & Willie. LC 76-18402. (gr. 7 up). 1977. PLB 13.89 (ISBN 0-06-026488-8). HarpC Child Bks.

—Ludell's New York Time. LC 79-3173. 192p. (gr. 7 up). 1980. 11.95i (ISBN 0-06-026497-7). HarpC Child Bks.

—Not Separate, Not Equal. LC 85-45847. 192p. (gr. 5 up). 1987. PLB 12.89 (ISBN 0-06-026482-9). HarpC Child Bks.

Williamson, Mel & Ford, George. Walk on. (Illus.). 32p. (gr. 3 up). 1972. 5.95 (ISBN 0-89388-042-6). Okpaku Communications.

Wilson, Beth P. Jenny. Johnson, Delores, illus. LC 89-8135. 32p. (gr. k-3). 1990. 12.95 (ISBN 0-02-793120-X, Mcmillan Child Bk). Macmillan Child Grp.

Wilson, Johnniece. Robin on His Own. (gr. 4-7). 1990. 12.95 (ISBN 0-590-41813-0). Scholastic Inc.

Wisler, G. Clifton. The Raid. LC 85-10152. 128p. (gr. 5-9). 1985. 11.95 (ISBN 0-525-67169-2, Lodestar Bks). Dutton Child Bks.

Yarbrough, Camille. Cornrows. Byard, Carole, illus. LC 78-24010. 48p. (Orig.). (gr. 2-6). 1981. 7.95 (ISBN 0-698-20462-X, Coward); pap. 5.95 (ISBN 0-698-20529-4, Coward). Putnam Pub Group.

BLACKS–HISTORY

Ben-Jochannan, Yosef. Black Man of the Nile & His Family. LC 89-61274. 460p. 1990. pap. 24.95 (ISBN 0-933121-26-1). Black Classic.

Giles, Lucille. Color Me Brown. rev. ed. Holmes, Louis F., illus. 47p. (gr. k-6). 1974. pap. 5.00 (ISBN 0-87485-017-7). Johnson Chi.

Harriott, Jackie. Black Women in Britain. (Illus.). 72p. (gr. 7-11). 1991. 19.95 (ISBN 0-7134-6286-8, Pub. by Batsford UK). Trafalgar Sq.

Just Us Books Editors. Black History Month Activity & Enrichment Handbook. LC 90-60068. 24p. (gr. 3-12). 1990. 8.95 (ISBN 0-940975-25-4); pap. 6.50 (ISBN 0-940975-14-9). Just Us Bks.

Lester, Julius. To Be a Slave. Feelings, Tom, illus. LC 68-28738. (gr. 7-12). 1968. 13.95 (ISBN 0-8037-8955-6). Dial Bks Young.

McCluskey, John, ed. Stories from Black History: Nine Stories, 4 vols. Incl. Mr. Impossible. Gaines, Edith; Can You Count bnd. with Carpetbaggers in Action. Ceasor, Frank G., Sr (ISBN 0-913678-11-2). (204); Little Jess & the Circus bnd with Forty Acres. Shepard, Mary (ISBN 0-913678-10-4). (203); Jubilee Day bnd. with Wildfire. Gaines, Edith & Smith, Martha. (ISBN 0-913678-09-0); Henry Box Brown bnd. with Struggle for Freedom. Pruitt, Pamela & Johnston, Brenda. (ISBN 0-913678-08-2). (201). (Illus., Orig.). (gr. 5 up). 1975. pap. 3.20 per set (ISBN 0-913678-07-4). New Day Pr.

McPherson, James M. Marching Toward Freedom: Blacks in the Civil War, 1861-1865. Scott, John A., ed. (Illus.). 128p. (gr. 7-12). 1990. 16.95 (ISBN 0-8160-2337-9). Facts on File.

Marsh, Carole. Black "Jography" The Paths of Our Black Pioneers. (gr. 3-12). 1989. PLB 19.95 (ISBN 1-55609-321-7); pap. 14.95 (ISBN 1-55609-320-9); computer disk 29.95 (ISBN 1-55609-322-5). Gallopade Pub Group.

—Black Trivia, A-Z. (gr. 3-12). 1989. PLB 19.95 (ISBN 1-55609-318-7); pap. 14.95 (ISBN 1-55609-317-9); computer disk 29.95 (ISBN 1-55609-319-5). Gallopade Pub Group.

—The Color Purple & All That Jazz. (gr. 3-12). 1989. PLB 19.95 (ISBN 1-55609-315-2); pap. 14.95 (ISBN 1-55609-314-4); computer disk 29.95 (ISBN 1-55609-316-0). Gallopade Pub Group.

Martinello, Marian L. & Sance, Melvin M. A Personal History: The Afro-American Texans. (Illus.). 104p. (gr. 5-8). 8.95 (ISBN 0-86701-005-3). U of Tex Inst Tex Culture.

Meltzer, Milton. The Black Americans: A History in Their Own Words. rev. ed. LC 83-46160. (Illus.). 320p. (gr. 7 up). 1984. 14.95i (ISBN 0-690-04419-4, Crowell Jr Bks); PLB 14.89 (ISBN 0-690-04418-6, Crowell Jr Bks). HarpC Child Bks.

—The Black Americans: A History in Their Own Words, 1619-1983. rev. ed. LC 83-46160. (Illus.). 320p. (gr. 7 up). 1987. pap. 9.95 (ISBN 0-06-446055-X, Trophy). HarpC Child Bks.

Miller, Robert. Buffalo Soldiers. Leonard, Richard, illus. 104p. (gr. 4-7). 1991. PLB 13.98 (ISBN 0-382-24080-4); PLB 8.99s.p.; pap. 7.95 (ISBN 0-382-24085-5); pap. 5.21s.p. Silver Burdett Pr.

—Mountain Men. Leonard, Richard, illus. 104p. (gr. 4-7). 1991. PLB 13.98 (ISBN 0-382-24082-0); PLB 8.99s.p.; pap. 7.95 (ISBN 0-382-24087-1); pap. 5.21s.p. Silver Burdett Pr.

—Pioneers. Leonard, Richard, illus. 104p. (gr. 4-7). 1991. PLB 13.98 (ISBN 0-382-24081-2); PLB 8.99s.p.; pap. 7.95 (ISBN 0-382-24086-3); pap. 5.21s.p. Silver Burdett Pr.

—Reflections of a Black Cowboy Series, 4 vols. Leonard, Richard, illus. 416p. (gr. 4-7). 1991. Set. PLB 55.92 (ISBN 0-382-24078-2); Set. PLB 35.94s.p.; Set. pap. 31.80 (ISBN 0-382-24083-9); Set. pap. 20.85s.p. Silver Burdett Pr.

Morgan, James A., ed. Profiles in Black History. 19p. (Orig.). (gr. 6-8). 1988. pap. text ed. 3.00 (ISBN 0-685-26485-8). Collins Assocs.

Myers, Walter D. Now Is Your Time! The African-American Struggle for Freedom. LC 91-314. (Illus.). 320p. (gr. 6 up). 1991. 17.95 (ISBN 0-06-024370-8); PLB 17.89 (ISBN 0-06-024371-6). HarpC Child Bks.

Riley, James A., ed. Black Baseball Journal, Vol. 1, No. 1. (Illus.). 64p. (Orig.). 1990. pap. 6.95 (ISBN 0-9614023-5-0). TK Pubs.

Roberts, Paulette. Activities in African-American History for All Subjects. LC 89-52123. (Illus.). 74p. (gr. 9-12). 1990. pap. 12.95 (ISBN 0-685-31293-3). Winston-Derek.

Sealy, Adrienne V. The Color Your Way into Black History Book. Abantu Industries, illus. 78p. (gr. 2-5). 1980. wkbk. 4.00 (ISBN 0-9602670-6-9). Assn Family Living.

Turner, Morrie. All God's Chillun Got Soul. 64p. (gr. 6). 1980. pap. 7.95 (ISBN 0-8170-0892-6). Judson.

BLACKS–MONTGOMERY, ALABAMA

Stein, R. Conrad. The Story of the Montgomery Bus Boycott. Greene, Nathan, illus. LC 85-31349. 32p. (gr. 3-6). 1986. PLB 13.27 (ISBN 0-516-04697-7); pap. 3.95 (ISBN 0-516-44697-5). Childrens.

BLACKS–POLITICS AND SUFFRAGE

Jakoubek, Robert. Adam Clayton Powell, Jr. King, Coretta Scott, intro. by. (Illus.). 112p. 1988. lib. bdg. 17.95x (ISBN 1-55546-606-0); pap. 9.95 (ISBN 0-7910-0213-6). Chelsea Hse.

BLACKS–SEGREGATION–FICTION

Blume, Judy. Iggie's House. LC 70-104340. 128p. (gr. 4-6). 1982. 12.95 (ISBN 0-02-711040-0, Bradbury Pr). Macmillan Child Grp.

BLACKS–THE WEST

Brenner, Barbara. Wagon Wheels. Bolognese, Don, illus. LC 76-21391. 64p. (gr. k-3). 1978. 10.95i (ISBN 0-06-020668-3); PLB 11.89 (ISBN 0-06-020669-1). HarpC Child Bks.

Katz, William L. Black People Who Made the Old West. LC 76-7051. (Illus.). 160p. (gr. 7 up). 1989. PLB 12.89 (ISBN 0-690-04816-5, Crowell Jr Bks). HarpC Child Bks.

—The Black West. rev. ed. LC 87-28067. (Illus.). 352p. (gr. 8-12). 1987. 29.95 (ISBN 0-940880-17-2); pap. 15.95 (ISBN 0-940880-18-0). Open Hand.

BLACKS IN LITERATURE AND ART

Walter, Mildred P. Trouble's Child. LC 84-16387. 128p. (gr. 4 up). 1985. 11.95 (ISBN 0-688-04214-7). Lothrop.

BLACKWELL, ELIZABETH, 1821-1910

Baker, Rachel. The First Woman Doctor. Copelman, Evelyn, illus. 192p. (gr. 4-6). 1987. pap. 2.50 (ISBN 0-590-40933-6). Scholastic Inc.

Brown, Jordan. Elizabeth Blackwell. Horner, Matina S., intro. by. (Illus.). 112p. (gr. 5 up). 1989. 17.95 (ISBN 1-55546-642-7). Chelsea Hse.

Klingel, Cindy. Women of America: Elizabeth Blackwell. rev. ed. (gr. 2-4). 1987. PLB 11.50s.p. (ISBN 0-88682-169-X); PLB 16.45 (ISBN 0-318-32937-9). Creative Ed.

Latham, Jean L. Elizabeth Blackwell: Pioneer Woman Doctor. Gold, Ethel, illus. 80p. (gr. 2-6). 1991. Repr. of 1975 ed. PLB 12.95 (ISBN 0-7910-1406-1). Chelsea Hse.

Sabin, Francene. Elizabeth Blackwell: The First Woman Doctor. LC 81-23140. (Illus.). 48p. (gr. 4-6). 1982. PLB 10.79 (ISBN 0-89375-756-X); pap. text ed. 2.95 (ISBN 0-89375-757-8). Troll Assocs.

BLAKE, WILLIAM, 1757-1827

Willard, Nancy. A Visit to William Blake's Inn. Provensen, Nancy & Provensen, Martin, illus. LC 80-27403. 48p. (ps-3). 1982. pap. 4.95 (ISBN 0-15-293823-0, VoyB). HarBraceJ.

BLIND

Adler, David A. A Picture Book of Helen Keller. Wallner, John & Wallner, Alexandra, illus. LC 89-77510. 32p. (gr. k-3). 1990. reinforced 14.95 (ISBN 0-8234-0818-3). Holiday.

Alexander, Sally. Mom Can't See Me. Ancona, George, illus. LC 89-13241. 48p. (gr. 1-5). 1990. 14.95 (ISBN 0-02-700401-5, Mcmillan Child Bk). Macmillan Child Grp.

Bergman, Thomas. Seeing in Special Ways: Children Living with Blindness. LC 88-42970. (Illus.). 56p. (gr. 4-5). 1989. PLB 10.95 (ISBN 1-55532-915-2). Gareth Stevens Inc.

Birch, Beverley. Louis Braille: Bringer of Hope to the Blind. Lantier, Patricia, adapted by. LC 90-9969. (Illus.). 64p. (gr. 3-4). 1991. lib. bdg. 12.95 (ISBN 0-8368-0454-6). Gareth Stevens Inc.

Keller, Helen. Story of My Life. LC 54-11951. (Illus.). (gr. 7 up). 1954. 15.95 (ISBN 0-385-04453-4). Doubleday.

BLIND–BIOGRAPHY

Gibson, William. The Miracle Worker. (gr. 6-9). 1984. pap. 3.50 (ISBN 0-553-24778-6). Bantam.

Hall, Candace C. Shelley's Day: The Day of a Legally Blind Child. Hall, Candace C., illus. 24p. (Orig.). (gr. k-6). 1980. pap. 2.95 (ISBN 0-9603840-0-6). Andrew Mtn Pr.

Hunter, Edith F. Child of the Silent Night. Holmes, Bea, illus. 128p. (gr. 2-5). 1991. pap. 3.25 (ISBN 0-440-41223-4, YB). Dell.

Keller, Helen. Story of My Life. Barnett, M. R., intro. by. (gr. 8 up). pap. 2.95 (ISBN 0-8049-0070-1, CL-70). Airmont.

BLIND, DOGS FOR THE

see Guide Dogs

BLIND–EDUCATION

Hunter, Edith F. Child of the Silent Night: The Story of Laura Bridgman. Holmes, Bea, illus. 128p. (gr. 2-5). 1963. 14.95 (ISBN 0-395-06835-5). HM.

Rich, Beverly. Louis Braille: Inventor of a Way to Read & Write That Has Helped Millions of Blind People Communicate with the World. LC 89-4275. (Illus.). 64p. (gr. 5-6). 1989. PLB 12.95 (ISBN 0-8368-0097-4). Gareth Stevens Inc.

BLIND–FICTION

Butler, Beverly. Light a Single Candle. (gr. 7-9). 1989. pap. 2.75 (ISBN 0-671-67712-8, Archway). PB.

Coutant, Helen. The Gift. Mai, Vo-Dinh, illus. LC 82-7810. 48p. (gr. 2-5). 1983. 9.95 (ISBN 0-394-85499-3). Knopf.

Garfield, James B. Follow My Leader. Greiner, Robert, illus. LC 57-1611. 192p. (gr. 4-6). 1957. pap. 13.95 (ISBN 0-670-32332-2). Viking Child Bks.

—Follow My Leader. Sibley, Don, illus. 192p. (gr. 4-6). 1987. pap. 2.50 (ISBN 0-590-40834-8, Pub. by Apple Classics). Scholastic Inc.

Holland, Isabelle. The Unfrightened Dark. LC 89-31570. 128p. (gr. 6-8). 1990. 13.95 (ISBN 0-316-37173-4). Little.

Kent, Deborah. Belonging. (gr. 5 up). 1979. pap. 2.25 (ISBN 0-448-05385-3, Pub. by Tempo). Ace Bks.

Kipling, Rudyard. Light That Failed. (gr. 8 up). 1969. pap. 1.50 (ISBN 0-8049-0199-6, CL-199). Airmont.

Little, Jean. From Anna. Sandin, Joan, illus. LC 72-76505. 208p. (gr. 4-6). 1973. pap. 3.95 (ISBN 0-06-440044-1, Trophy). HarpC Child Bks.

MacLachlan, Patricia. Through Grandpa's Eyes. Ray, Deborah, illus. LC 79-2019. 48p. (gr. 2-4). 1971. PLB 10.89 (ISBN 0-06-022560-2). HarpC Child Bks.

Peck, Richard. Through a Brief Darkness. 144p. (gr. 7 up). 1989. pap. 2.95 (ISBN 0-440-98809-8, LFL). Dell.

Reuter, Margaret. My Mother Is Blind. Lanier, Philip, illus. LC 78-12645. 32p. (ps-3). 1979. PLB 13.27 (ISBN 0-516-02021-8). Childrens.

Taylor, Theodore. Cay. LC 69-15161. 160p. (gr. 6-9). 1987. pap. 13.95 (ISBN 0-385-07906-0). Doubleday.

Whelan, Gloria. Hannah. Bowman, Lealie, illus. LC 90-39554. 64p. (gr. 2-4). 1991. 10.95 (ISBN 0-679-81397-7); PLB 11.99 (ISBN 0-679-91397-1). Knopf.

Yolen, Jane. The Seeing Stick. Charlip, Remy & Maraslis, Demetra, illus. LC 75-6946. 32p. (gr. k up). 1975. PLB 13.89 (ISBN 0-690-00596-2, Crowell Jr Bks). HarpC Child Bks.

Young, Alida E. Is Chelsea Going Blind? 160p. (gr. 5-8). 1988. 2.50 (ISBN 0-87406-367-1). Willowisp Pr.

BLIND–REHABILITATION

see Blind–Education

BLOCK PRINTING

see Wood Engraving

BLOOD

LeMaster, Leslie J. Your Heart & Blood. LC 84-7604. (Illus.). 48p. (gr. k-4). 1984. PLB 14.60 (ISBN 0-516-01933-3); pap. 4.95 (ISBN 0-516-41933-1). Childrens.

Parker, Steve. The Heart & Blood. rev. ed. (Illus.). 48p. (gr. 5 up). 1991. pap. 4.95 (ISBN 0-531-24604-3). Watts.

Ross, Dennis W. Blood. LC 87-70225. (Illus.). 16p. (Orig.). (gr. 10 up). 1988. pap. text ed. 2.15 (ISBN 0-89278-184-X, 45-9784). Carolina Biological.

Showers, Paul. Drop of Blood. Madden, Don, illus. LC 67-23672. (gr. k-3). 1967. PLB 12.89 (ISBN 0-690-24526-2, Crowell Jr Bks). HarpC Child Bks.

—A Drop of Blood. rev. ed. Madden, Don, illus. LC 88-3623. 32p. (gr. k-4). 1989. 13.95 (ISBN 0-690-04715-0, Crowell Jr Bks); PLB 13.89 (ISBN 0-690-04717-7, Crowell Jr Bks). HarpC Child Bks.

Wolfe, Rina E. Charles Richard Drew, M. D. (Illus.). 64p. (gr. 3-6). 1991. PLB 11.90 (ISBN 0-531-20021-3). Watts.

BLOOD–CIRCULATION

Avraham, Regina. The Circulatory System. Koop, C. Everett, intro. by. (Illus.). 112p. (gr. 5-12). 1989. 18.95 (ISBN 0-7910-0013-3). Chelsea Hse.

Bailey, Donna. All about Heart & Blood. LC 90-10052. (Illus.). 48p. (gr. 2-5). 1990. PLB 15.96 (ISBN 0-8114-2779-X). Steck-V.

Dunbar, Robert E. Heart & Circulatory System Projects for Young Scientist. 1989. pap. 5.95 (ISBN 0-531-15132-8). Watts.

Heart & Blood. 48p. (gr. 5-8). 1988. PLB 12.98 (ISBN 0-382-09700-9); 9.74s.p. (ISBN 0-685-24608-6). Silver Burdett Pr.

McGowen, Tom. The Circulatory System: From Harvey to the Artificial Heart. Kline, M., ed. (Illus.). 72p. (gr. 6-9). 1988. PLB 10.40 (ISBN 0-531-10574-1). Watts.

Showers, Paul. Hear Your Heart. Low, Joseph, illus. LC 68-11067. 40p. (gr. k-3). 1968. PLB 12.89 (ISBN 0-690-37379-1, Crowell Jr Bks). HarpC Child Bks.

BLOOD–DISEASES

Payne, Mary. Up & down the Blood Sugar Trail. Berry, Cathy, illus. Smith, Lendon H., intro. by. (Illus., Orig.). (gr. k-4). 1987. pap. 1.98 (ISBN 0-9619326-0-0). MstrWorks Pub.

BLUE JAYS–FICTION

Hurwitz, Johanna. Yellow Blue Jay. Carrick, Donald, illus. LC 85-25868. 128p. (gr. 2-5). 1986. 11.95 (ISBN 0-688-06078-1). Morrow Jr Bks.

BLY, NELLIE

see Cochrane, Elizabeth, 1867-1922

BOAT RACING

Jackson, Al & Tardy, Gene. Drag Boat Racing: The National Championships. (Illus.). 48p. (gr. 3-7). 1973. PLB 6.89x (ISBN 0-914844-05-9); pap. 3.95 (ISBN 0-914844-06-7). J Alden.

BOATBUILDING

see also Shipbuilding

Dolan, Edward F., Jr. Matters of Life & Death. (Illus.). 112p. (gr. 7 up). 1982. PLB 12.90 (ISBN 0-531-04497-1). Watts.

BOATING

see Boats and Boating

BOATS AND BOATING

see also Boatbuilding; Canoes and Canoeing; Houseboats; Motorboats; Rowing; Sailing; Ships; Steamboats; Submarines

Adkins, Jan. Workboats. LC 85-14288. (Illus.). 48p. (gr. 5 up). 1985. 12.95 (ISBN 0-684-18228-9, Scribners Young Read). Macmillan Child Grp.

Barton, Byron. Boats. Barton, Byron, illus. LC 85-47900. 32p. (ps-k). 1986. 4.95 (ISBN 0-694-00059-0, Crowell Jr Bks); PLB 11.89 (ISBN 0-690-04536-0). HarpC Child Bks.

Boating with Cap'n Bob & Matey: An Encyclopedia for Kids of All Ages. LC 88-62045. (Illus.). 32p. (gr. 1-9). 1989. casebound 12.95 (ISBN 0-931595-03-7, Dist. by The Talman Co). Seascape Enters.

Butler, Daphne. First Look at Boats. LC 90-10256. (Illus.). 32p. (gr. 1-2). 1991. lib. bdg. 10.95 (ISBN 0-8368-0502-X). Gareth Stevens Inc.

Gibbons, Gail. Boat Book. Gibbons, Gail, illus. LC 82-15851. 32p. (ps-3). 1983. reinforced bdg. 14.95 (ISBN 0-8234-0478-1); pap. 5.95 (ISBN 0-8234-0709-8). Holiday.

Halsted, Henry F. Boating Basics. Seiden, Art, illus. LC 85-9406. 48p. (gr. 4-9). 1985. 10.95 (ISBN 0-13-078502-4). P-H.

Let's Discover Ships & Boats. LC 80-22959. (Illus.). 80p. (gr. k-6). 1983. pap. text ed. 13.27 (ISBN 0-8172-1774-6). Raintree Pubs.

Lippman, Peter. Busy Boats. LC 79-29636. (Illus.). 32p. (gr. 2-3). 1980. Random.

Matthews, Rupert. Let's Look At Ships & Boats. (ps-3). 1990. PLB 8.90 (ISBN 0-531-18322-X). Watts.

Motorboating. (Illus.). 64p. (gr. 6-12). 1962. pap. 1.85 (ISBN 0-8395-3294-6, 3294). BSA.

Relf, Patricia. The Big Book of Real Boats & Ships. LaPadula, Tom, illus. 48p. (gr. 1-4). 1990. 7.95 (ISBN 0-448-19189-X, G&D). Putnam Pub Group.

Robbins, Ken. Boats. 1989. pap. 12.95 (ISBN 0-590-41157-8). Scholastic Inc.

Rockwell, Anne. Boats. Rockwell, Anne, illus. LC 82-2420. (ps). 1985. 12.95 (ISBN 0-525-44004-6, DCB); pap. 3.95 (ISBN 0-525-44219-7, DCB). Dutton Child Bks.

Rowing. (Illus.). 48p. (gr. 6-12). 1981. pap. 1.85 (ISBN 0-8395-3392-6, 3392). BSA.

Sargent, Ruth. The Nautical Alphabet. Carlson, Kathleen, illus. 32p. (ps-1). 1984. pap. 2.95 saddle-stitched (ISBN 0-89272-190-1). Down East.

Scott, Geoffrey. Egyptian Boats. Carlson, Nancy L., illus. LC 80-27676. 48p. (gr. k-4). 1981. PLB 9.95 (ISBN 0-87614-138-6). Carolrhoda Bks.

Ships & Boats. (Illus.). 80p. (gr. k-6). 1986. pap. 13.27 (ISBN 0-8172-2593-5). Raintree Pubs.

Small-Boat Sailing. (Illus.). 80p. (gr. 6-12). 1989. pap. 1.85 (ISBN 0-8395-3319-5, 3319). BSA.

Steele, Philip. Boats. LC 90-41177. (Illus.). 32p. (gr. 5-6). 1991. SBE 9.95 (ISBN 0-89686-522-3, Crestwood Hse). Macmillan Child Grp.

Thomas, A. Finding Out about Things that Float. (Illus.). 24p. (gr. 2-4). 1987. PLB 11.96 (ISBN 0-88110-295-4); pap. 3.95 (ISBN 0-7460-0102-9). EDC.

BOATS AND BOATING–FICTION

Allen, Pamela. Who Sank the Boat? Allen, Pamela, illus. 32p. (ps-k). 1985. 10.95 (ISBN 0-698-20576-6, Coward); pap. 5.95 (ISBN 0-698-20622-3, Coward). Putnam Pub Group.

Carratello, Patty. My Old Gold Boat. Spivak, Darlene, ed. Smythe, Linda, illus. 16p. (gr. k-2). 1988. wkbk. 1.95 (ISBN 1-55734-383-7). Tchr Create Mat.

Conrad, Pam. Taking the Ferry Home. LC 87-45856. 224p. (gr. 7 up). 1988. 11.95 (ISBN 0-06-021317-5); PLB 11.89 (ISBN 0-06-021318-3). HarpC Child Bks.

Crane, Stephen. The Open Boat. Johnson, V. C., illus. 64p. (gr. 6 up). 1982. PLB 10.95s.p. (ISBN 0-87191-826-9); PLB 15.65 (ISBN 0-685-05630-9). Creative Ed.

Dickinson, Mary. Jilly's Boat Trip. (Illus.). 32p. (gr. k-3). 1987. 10.95 (ISBN 0-233-97890-9). Andre Deutsch.

Fisher, Barbara. Harmony Hurricane Muldoon. Fisher, Barbara, illus. 22p. (Orig.). (gr. 3-5). 1979. pap. 2.00 (ISBN 0-934830-09-6). Ten Penny.

Graham, Margaret B. Benjy's Boat Trip. Graham, Margaret B., illus. LC 77-6393. (ps-3). 1977. PLB 13.89 (ISBN 0-06-022093-7). HarpC Child Bks.

Harwood, Pearl A. Mrs. Moon's Harbor Trip. Overlie, George, illus. LC 67-15692. 32p. (gr. k-3). 1967. PLB 4.95 (ISBN 0-8225-0116-3). Lerner Pubns.

Hest, Amy. A Sort-of Sailor. Rockwell, Lizzie, illus. LC 89-38252. 32p. (gr. k-3). 1990. 13.95 (ISBN 0-02-743641-1, Four Winds). Macmillan Child Grp.

Hobbs, Will. Downriver. 208p. (gr. 6 up). 1991. SBE 13.95 (ISBN 0-689-31690-9, Atheneum Child Bk). Macmillan Child Grp.

Hope, Laura L. Bobbsey Twins on a Houseboat. (gr. 1-4). 1930. 4.50 (ISBN 0-448-08006-0, G&D). Putnam Pub Group.

—Bobbsey Twins' Own Little Ferryboat. (gr. 1-4). 1956. 3.95 (ISBN 0-448-08049-4, G&D). Putnam Pub Group.

Johnson, Pamela. A Mouse's Tale. D'Andrade, Diane, ed. (Illus.). 32p. (gr. k-4). 1991. 11.95 (ISBN 0-15-256032-7). HarBraceJ.

Kelly, Jeff. Tramp Steamer & the Silver Bullet. 192p. (gr. 5-9). 1984. 13.95 (ISBN 0-395-36632-1). HM.

Locker, Thomas. Sailing with the Wind. LC 85-2338. 1990. pap. 4.95 (ISBN 0-8037-0852-1). Dial Bks Young.

Moncure, Jane B. Nanny Goat's Boat. Friedman, Joy, illus. LC 87-12839. 32p. (ps-2). 1987. PLB 11.97 (ISBN 0-89565-404-0); pap. 6.96 (ISBN 0-89565-445-8). Childs World.

Morgan, A. Nicole's Boat. (Illus.). 24p. (ps-8). 1986. 12.95 (ISBN 0-920303-60-9); pap. 4.95 (ISBN 0-920303-61-7). Firefly Bks Ltd.

Page, Michael. The Great Bullocky Race. Ingpen, Robert, illus. 56p. (gr. 4-6). 1988. 11.95 (ISBN 0-396-09200-4, Putnam). Putnam Pub Group.
Pfanner, Louise. Louise Builds a Boat. LC 89-70929. (Illus.). 40p. (ps-1). 1990. 12.95 (ISBN 0-531-05888-3); PLB 12.99 (ISBN 0-531-08488-4). Orchard Bks Watts.
Swolgaard, Carole. Sailboat Coloring Guide: A Great Five Star Super Deluxe Coloring Book. Seablom, Victoria, ed. Seablom, Seth H., illus. 32p. (Orig.). (gr. 1-6). 1979. pap. 2.50 saddle stitched (ISBN 0-918800-07-2). Seablom.
Tubby, I. M., pseud. I'm a Little Tugboat. LC 81-51114. (Illus.). 10p. (ps up). 1982. pap. 2.95 vinyl (ISBN 0-671-44434-4, Little Simon). S&S Trade.
Wise, Francis H. & Wise, Joyce M. Red Sail. (Illus.). (ps-1). 1978. pap. 1.50 (ISBN 0-915766-40-X). Wise Pub.
Wurmfeld, Hope H. Boatbuilder. Wurmfeld, Hope, illus. LC 87-21153. 64p. 1988. 14.95 (ISBN 0-02-793580-9, Mcmillan Child Bk). Macmillan Child Grp.
Young, Ruth. Daisy's Taxi. Sewall, Marcia, illus. LC 90-7735. 32p. (ps-1). 1991. 13.95 (ISBN 0-531-05921-9); PLB 13.99 (ISBN 0-531-08521-X). Orchard Bks Watts.

BOATS AND BOATING–HISTORY

Zeck, Pam & Zeck, Gerry. Mississippi Sternwheelers. LC 81-15553. (Illus.). 32p. (gr. k-4). 1982. PLB 9.95 (ISBN 0-87614-180-7). Carolrhoda Bks.

BODY, HUMAN

see Anatomy; Physiology

BODY AND MIND

see Mind and Body

BODY WEIGHT CONTROL

see Weight Control

BOGS

see Marshes

BOLIVIA

Blair, David N. The Land & People of Bolivia. LC 89-39721. (Illus.). 224p. (gr. 6 up). 1990. 15.95 (ISBN 0-397-32382-4, Lipp Jr Bks); PLB 15.89 (ISBN 0-397-32383-2, Lipp Jr Bks). HarpC Child Bks.
Ikuhara, Yoshiyuki. Children of the World: Bolivia. LC 87-42616. (Illus.). (gr. 5-6). 1988. PLB 12.95 (ISBN 1-55532-321-9). Gareth Stevens Inc.
Lerner Publications, Department of Geography Staff, ed. Bolivia in Pictures. (Illus.). 64p. (gr. 5 up). 1987. PLB 12.95 (ISBN 0-8225-1808-2). Lerner Pubns.
Morrison, Marion. Bolivia. LC 88-10877. (Illus.). 128p. (gr. 5-9). 1988. PLB 25.27 (ISBN 0-516-02705-0). Childrens.
St. John, Jetty. A Family in Bolivia. LC 86-21034. (Illus.). 32p. (gr. 2-5). 1986. PLB 9.95 (ISBN 0-8225-1670-5). Lerner Pubns.

BOLSHEVISM

see Communism

BOMBS, FLYING

see Guided Missiles

BONDS

see also Investments; Stocks

BONES

Balestrino, Philip. Skeleton Inside You. Bolognese, Don, illus. LC 72-132290. (gr. k-3). 1971. (Crowell Jr Bks). HarpC Child Bks.
Bishop, Pamela R. Exploring Your Skeleton: Funny Bones & Not-So-Funny Bones. Callen, Liz, illus. LC 90-31026. 32p. (gr. 1-4). 1991. PLB 12.90 (ISBN 0-531-10970-4). Watts.
Saunderson, Jane. Muscles & Bones. Farmer, Andrew & Green, Robina, illus. LC 90-42882. 32p. (gr. 4-6). 1991. lib. bdg. 11.89 (ISBN 0-8167-2088-6); pap. text ed. 3.95 (ISBN 0-8167-2089-4). Troll Assocs.
Ward, Brian. Bones & Joints: And Their Care. (Illus.). 32p. (gr. 5-8). 1991. PLB 11.40 (ISBN 0-531-14175-6). Watts.

BOOK ILLUSTRATION

see Illustration of Books

BOOK INDUSTRIES AND TRADE

see also Bookbinding; Paper Making and Trade; Printing; Publishers and Publishing

Kehoe, Michael. The Puzzle of Books. Kehoe, Michael, illus. LC 81-17115. 32p. (gr. k-4). 1982. PLB 9.95 (ISBN 0-87614-169-6). Carolrhoda Bks.

BOOK REVIEWS

Barkin, Carol & James, Elizabeth. How to Write Your Best Book Report. Doty, Roy, illus. LC 86-8597. 80p. (gr. 3-7). 1986. 11.88 (ISBN 0-688-05744-6). Lothrop.
Colligan, Louise. The A-Plus Guide to Book Reports. 96p. (gr. 7 up). 1984. pap. 2.25 (ISBN 0-590-33313-5). Scholastic Inc.
Magill, Frank N., ed. Magill's Literary Annual: 1989, 2 vols. 950p. (gr. 9-12). 1989. Set. PLB 65.00x (ISBN 0-89356-289-0, Magill Bks). Salem Pr.

BOOK TRADE

see Book Industries and Trade; Publishers and Publishing

BOOKBINDING

Aliki. How a Book Is Made. Aliki, illus. LC 85-48156. 32p. (gr. k-4). 1988. pap. 5.95 (ISBN 0-06-446085-1, Trophy). HarpC Child Bks.

BOOKS

see also Authors; Illustration of Books; Libraries; Printing; Publishers and Publishing;
also headings beginning with the word Book

Aliki. How a Book Is Made. Aliki, illus. LC 85-48156. 32p. (gr. 2 up). 1986. 12.95 (ISBN 0-690-04496-8, Crowell Jr Bks); PLB 12.89 (ISBN 0-690-04498-4, Crowell Jr Bks). HarpC Child Bks.
Althea. Making a Book. (Illus.). 26p. (gr. 2-5). 1983. pap. 3.95 (ISBN 0-521-27159-2). Cambridge U Pr.
Carroll, Jeri & Dunlavy, Kathy. My Very First Books to Make & Read. 144p. (ps-2). 1990. 10.95 (ISBN 0-86653-557-8, GA1163). Good Apple.
Greene, Carol. How a Book Is Made. (gr. 5-9). 1988. PLB 14.60 (ISBN 0-516-01216-9); pap. 4.95 (ISBN 0-516-41216-7). Childrens.
Greenfeld, Howard. Books: From Writer to Reader. rev. ed. LC 88-11876. (Illus.). 224p. (gr. 4 up). 1988. 19.95 (ISBN 0-517-56840-3); pap. 12.95 (ISBN 0-517-56841-1). Crown.
Merrison, Tim. Books. Stefoff, Rebecca, ed. LC 90-13868. (Illus.). 32p. (gr. 4-8). 1991. PLB 17.26 (ISBN 0-944483-96-8). Garrett Ed Corp.

BOOKS–FICTION

Browne, Anthony. I Like Books. Browne, Anthony, illus. LC 88-8471. 24p. (Orig.). (ps-1). 1989. 10.99 (ISBN 0-394-94186-1); pap. 3.95 (ISBN 0-685-24801-1). Knopf.
Fritz, Jean. The Man Who Loved Books. Hyman, Trina S., illus. 48p. (gr. 7-11). 1981. 9.95 (ISBN 0-399-20715-5, Putnam). Putnam Pub Group.
Furtado, Jo. Sorry, Miss Folio! Joos, Frederic, illus. 32p. (ps-3). 1988. 10.95 (ISBN 0-916291-18-9). Kane-Miller Bk.
Gilson, Jamie. Dial Leroi Rupert, DJ. Wallner, John, illus. 128p. (gr. 3-6). 1990. pap. 2.75 (ISBN 0-671-70252-1, Minstrel Bks). PB.
Hentoff, Nat. The Day They Came to Arrest the Book. 160p. (gr. 7 up). 1983. pap. 3.25 (ISBN 0-440-91814-6, LFL). Dell.
Levinson, Nancy S. Clara & the Bookwagon. Croll, Carolyn, illus. LC 86-45773. 64p. (gr. k-3). 1991. pap. 3.50 (ISBN 0-06-444134-2, Trophy). HarpC Child Bks.
McPhail, David. Fix-It. McPhail, David, illus. LC 83-16459. 24p. (ps-k). 1984. 10.95 (ISBN 0-525-44093-3, DCB). Dutton Child Bks.
Miles, Betty. Maudie & Me & the Dirty Book. LC 79-19783. 160p. (gr. 4-8). 1980. lib. bdg. 10.99 (ISBN 0-394-94343-0). Knopf.
Minsberg, David. The Bookmonster. Matheis, Shelley, illus. 32p. (ps-k). 1981. 7.50 (ISBN 0-940674-00-9); incl. bookmonster doll 27.95 (ISBN 0-685-03087-3). Littlebee.
Smeltzer, Patricia & Smeltzer, Victor. Thank You for a Book to Read. (Illus.). 24p. (gr. k-6). 1983. pap. 2.50 (ISBN 0-86683-719-1, AY8319). Harper SF.

BOOKS–HISTORY

Knowlton, Jack. Books & Libraries. Barton, Harriet, illus. LC 89-70804. 48p. (gr. 2-5). 1991. 14.95 (ISBN 0-06-021609-3); PLB 14.89 (ISBN 0-06-021610-7). HarpC Child Bks.

BOOKS–REVIEWS

see Book Reviews

BOOKS AND READING

see also Book Reviews; Children's Literature; Libraries; Reference Books

Alarie, Julia & Conlon, Betsy. Interactive & Cooperative Book Reports. Sussman, Ellen, intro. by. Burris, Priscilla, illus. 56p. (Orig.). (gr. 3-6). 1990. pap. 6.95 (ISBN 0-933606-85-0, MS-689). Monkey Sisters.
Berksen, Barbara. Island of the Blue Dolphins: A Study Guide. (gr. 4-7). 1984. tchr's. ed. & wkbk. 14.95 (ISBN 0-88122-088-4). LRN Links.
Berry, Marilyn. Help Is on the Way for Book Reports. (Illus.). 48p. (gr. 4-6). 1984. pap. 4.95 (ISBN 0-516-43231-1). Childrens.
Brophy, Susan. The Fighting Ground: A Study Guide. (gr. 4-7). 1988. tchr's. ed. & wkbk. 14.95 (ISBN 0-88122-082-5). LRN Links.
Chapin, Laurie & Flegenheimer-Riggle, Ellen. Leaping into Literature. 144p. (gr. k-3). 1990. 10.95 (ISBN 0-86653-561-6, GA1164). Good Apple.
Collaci, Dorothy. The Contender: A Study Guide. 1989. tchr's. ed. & wkbk. 14.95 (ISBN 0-88122-059-0). LRN Links.
Davis, Bea. Cam Jansen & the Mystery of the Dinosaur Bones: A Study Guide. (gr. 1-3). 1986. tchr's. ed. & wkbk. 14.95 (ISBN 0-88122-068-X). LRN Links.
Davis, Beatrice G. All of a Kind Family: A Study Guide. (gr. 3-6). 1984. tchr's. ed. & wkbk. 14.95 (ISBN 0-88122-072-8). LRN Links.
Davis, Beatrice G., et al. Black Boy: A Study Guide. (gr. 9-12). 1984. tchr's. ed. & wkbk. 14.95 (ISBN 0-88122-105-8). LRN Links.
Direct, R. F. Reading Books for Pay. rev. ed. 192p. (gr. 12). Date not set. pap. text ed. 45.00 (ISBN 0-945661-09-6). PASE Pubns.
Feldman, Enid. Freaky Friday: A Study Guide. (gr. 4-7). 1988. tchr's. ed. & wkbk. 14.95 (ISBN 0-88122-083-3). LRN Links.
Foltzer, Monica. A Sound Track to Reading. 3rd ed. 52p. (gr. 3 up). 1985. pap. text ed. 3.80 (ISBN 0-9607918-4-1, 764921). St Ursula.
Fradken, Ada. The Enormous Egg: A Study Guide. (gr. 4-6). 1986. tchr's. ed. & wkbk. 14.95 (ISBN 0-685-31133-3). LRN Links.
Friedland, Joyce & Kessler, Rikki. The Big Wave: A Study Guide. (gr. 4-6). 1982. tchr's. ed. & wkbk. 14.95 (ISBN 0-88122-000-0). LRN Links.
—Bless the Beasts & the Children: A Study Guide. 1983. tchr's. ed. & wkbk. 14.95 (ISBN 0-88122-023-X). LRN Links.
—Bridge to Teribithia: A Study Guide. (gr. 4-6). 1982. tchr's. ed. & wkbk. 14.95 (ISBN 0-88122-001-9). LRN Links.
—Busybody Nora: A Study Guide. (gr. 2-4). 1982. tchr's. ed. & wkbk. 14.95 (ISBN 0-88122-002-7). Lrn Links.
—Girl Who Owned a City: A Study Guide. (gr. 4-6). 1982. tchr's. ed. & wkbk. 14.95 (ISBN 0-88122-003-5). LRN Links.
Fuhler, Carol. Caddie Woodlawn: A Study Guide. (gr. 4-7). 1988. tchr's. ed. & wkbk. 14.95 (ISBN 0-88122-079-5). Lrn Links.
Gross, Edward, ed. Above & Below: A Guide to Beauty & the Beast. (Illus.). 112p. (Orig.). (gr. 9-12). 1990. pap. 12.95 (ISBN 0-9627508-0-8). Image NY.
Kroll, Carol. The Hobbit: A Study Guide. 1983. tchr's. ed. & wkbk. 14.95 (ISBN 0-88122-036-1). LRN Links.
Leavitt, Joy. Adventures of Huckleberry Finn: A Study Guide. (gr. 10-12). 1983. tchr's. ed. & wkbk. 14.95 (ISBN 0-88122-020-5). LRN Links.
—Adventures of Tom Sawyer: A Study Guide. (gr. 7-12). 1984. tchr's. ed. & wkbk. 14.95 (ISBN 0-88122-103-1). LRN Links.
—All Quiet on the Western Front: A Study Guide. 1983. tchr's. ed. & wkbk. 14.95 (ISBN 0-88122-035-3). LRN Links.
—Death of a Salesman: A Study Guide. (gr. 10-12). 1984. tchr's. ed. & wkbk. 14.95 (ISBN 0-88122-113-9). LRN Links.
Levine, Gloria. Anne of Green Gables: A Study Guide. (gr. 6-8). 1989. tchr's. ed. & wkbk. 14.95 (ISBN 0-88122-056-6). LRN Links.
—Fantastic Mr. Fox: A Study Guide. (gr. 3-5). 1985. tchr's. ed. & wkbk. 14.95 (ISBN 0-88122-076-0). LRN Links.
Littke, Lael. Olympia Odette Presents: Davy Crockett's Bear-ly Believable. Newsom, Tom & Newsom, Carol, illus. 36p. (ps-3). 1990. pap. 15.95 incl. audiocassette (ISBN 1-55999-130-5). LinguiSystems.
—Olympia Odette Presents: Nellie Bly's "In-a-Jam" Telegram. Newsom, Tom & Newsom, Carol, illus. 36p. (ps-3). 1990. pap. 15.95 incl. audiocassette (ISBN 1-55999-131-3). LinguiSystems.
—Olympia Odette Presents: Paul Bunyan's Blue Ox Blues. Newsom, Tom & Newsom, Carol, illus. 36p. (ps-3). 1990. pap. 15.95 incl. audiocassette (ISBN 1-55999-129-1). LinguiSystems.
Marsh, Norma. The Chocolate Touch: A Study Guide. (gr. 2-4). 1989. tchr's. ed. & wkbk. 14.95 (ISBN 0-88122-043-4). Lrn Links.
—A Gift for Mama: A Study Guide. (gr. 2-4). 1989. tchr's. ed. & wkbk. 14.95 (ISBN 0-88122-045-0). LRN Links.
Meyer, Mary. Fahrenheit 451: A Study Guide. 1984. tchr's. ed. & wkbk. 14.95 (ISBN 0-88122-114-7). LRN Links.
Moon, Cliff & Moon, Bernice. Look at... Books, 6 bks, Set 1. Lees, Beverly, et al, illus. (Orig.). (gr. 1-3). 1986. pap. text ed. 23.40 (ISBN 1-55624-068-6, WGO686). Wright Group.
Nebraska Library Commission Staff. Our Books, Our Wings: Books that Nebraskans Read & Treasure. 300p. (Orig.). (gr. 7). 1989. pap. 8.95 (ISBN 0-685-29054-9). NE Library Commission.
Norris, Crystal. Flowers for Algernon: A Study Guide. (gr. 9-11). 1985. tchr's. ed. & wkbk. 14.95 (ISBN 0-88122-115-5). LRN Links.
—Great Expectations: A Study Guide. (gr. 9-12). 1987. tchr's. ed. & wkbk. 14.95 (ISBN 0-88122-116-3). LRN Links.
Nowiszewski, Nancy. Olympia Odette Presents: My Think 'n' Do Adventure Book. DeRosa, Dee, illus. 100p. (ps-3). 1990. spiral bdg., wkbk. 10.95 (ISBN 1-55999-132-1). LinguiSystems.
Polette, Nancy. The Book Report Book for Primary Grades. (Illus.). 32p. 1979. pap. 4.95 (ISBN 0-913839-05-1). Bk Lures.
—Ultimate Book Report Book. (Illus.). 32p. (gr. 4-9). 1989. pap. 4.95 (ISBN 0-913839-75-2). Bk Lures.
Robertson, Debbie. Blast off with Book Reports. Barry, Pat, illus. 64p. (gr. 3-8). 1985. wkbk. 7.95 (ISBN 0-86653-327-3, GA 682). Good Apple.
Sansone, Barbara. Literature in Bloom, 2 bks. Sussman, Ellen, intro. by. Burris, Priscilla, illus. (Orig.). (gr. 3-6). 1989. pap. 6.95 ea. Bk. 1, 56p (ISBN 0-933606-78-8). Bk. 2, 56p (ISBN 0-933606-79-6). Monkey Sisters.
Sheff, Alice. Be a Perfect Person in Just Three Days: A Study Guide. (gr. 1-3). 1989. tchr's. ed. & wkbk. 14.95 (ISBN 0-88122-044-2). LRN Links.
—Freckle Juice: A Study Guide. (gr. 1-4). 1988. tchr's. ed. & wkbk. 14.95 (ISBN 0-88122-066-3). LRN Links.
Sussman, Ellen. Ready to Report. Burris, Priscilla, illus. 76p. (Orig.). (gr. 3-6). 1988. pap. text ed. 7.95 (ISBN 0-933606-66-4). Monkey Sisters.
Tester, Sylvia R. A Visit to the Library. Holmes, Dave, photos by. LC 84-12637. (Illus.). 32p. (gr. k-3). 1985. PLB 14.60 (ISBN 0-516-01492-7). Childrens.
Thorne, Randy. Quick & Short Book Reports. Sussman, Ellen, intro. by. (Illus.). 56p. (gr. 3-5). 1990. pap. 6.95 (ISBN 0-933606-86-9, MS-690). Monkey Sisters.
Tretler, Marcia. Alan & Naomi: A Study Guide. (gr. 4-6). 1989. tchr's. ed. & wkbk. 14.95 (ISBN 0-88122-055-8). LRN Links.
—Anne Frank: The Diary of a Young Girl: A Study Guide. (gr. 6-10). 1987. tchr's. ed. & wkbk. 14.95 (ISBN 0-88122-104-X). LRN Links.
—Call It Courage: A Study Guide. (gr. 4-7). 1987. tchr's ed. & wkbk. 14.95 (ISBN 0-88122-080-9). Lrn Links.
—The Cay: A Study Guide. (gr. 4-7). 1986. tchr's. ed. & wkbk. 14.95 (ISBN 0-88122-081-7). LRN Links.

—From the Mixed-up Files of Mrs. Basil E. Frankweiler: A Study Guide. (gr. 4-7). 1987. tchr's. ed. & wkbk. 14.95 (ISBN 0-88122-084-1). LRN Links.

Tretler, Marcia, et al. Dear Mr. Henshaw: A Study Guide. (gr. 4-6). 1986. tchr's. ed. & wkbk. 14.95 (ISBN 0-88122-074-4). LRN Links.

Tuchman, Anita. The Black Pearl: A Study Guide. (gr. 7-12). 1984. tchr's. ed. & wkbk. 14.95 (ISBN 0-88122-106-6). LRN Links.

Villanella, Rosemary. Charlie & the Chocolate Factory: A Study Guide. (gr. 4-6). 1989. tchr's. ed. & wkbk. 14.95 (ISBN 0-88122-047-7). LRN Links.

Yeager, Natalee. Fun with Children's Classics. (Illus.). 32p. (gr. 4-8). 1987. pap. 4.95 (ISBN 0-913839-66-3). Bk Lures.

BOOKS AND READING FOR CHILDREN
see Children–Books and Reading

BOOKS AND READING–BEST BOOKS

Dibner, Ellen J. & Gustafson, Ronald. Book Finders for Kids: The "Easy to Use" Subject Guide to Finding Non-fiction Books in a Library. Dibner, Ellen J. & Gustafson, Ronald, illus. LC 88-61646. 16p. (Orig.). (gr. 2-8). 1988. pap. 2.95 (ISBN 0-9620888-0-3). Point Publications.

Mealy, Virginia T. Newbery Books. (Illus.). 128p. (gr. 4-8). 1987. pap. 12.95 (ISBN 0-913839-62-0). Bk Lures.

BOOKS FOR CHILDREN
see Children's Literature

BOONE, DANIEL, 1734-1820

Brandt, Keith. Daniel Boone: Frontier Adventures. Lawn, John, illus. LC 82-15915. 48p. (gr. 4-6). 1983. PLB 10.79 (ISBN 0-89375-843-4); pap. text ed. 2.95 (ISBN 0-89375-844-2). Troll Assocs.

Farr, Naunerle C. Davy Crockett-Daniel Boone. Carrillo, Fred & Redondo, Nestor, illus. (gr. 4-12). 1979. pap. text ed. 2.95 (ISBN 0-88301-351-7); wkbk. 1.25 (ISBN 0-88301-375-4). Pendulum Pr.

Hargrove, Jim. Daniel Boone: Pioneer Trailblazer. LC 85-13309. (Illus.). 124p. (gr. 5-7). 1985. PLB 17.27 (ISBN 0-516-03215-1). Childrens.

Lawlor, Laurie. Daniel Boone. Tucker, Kathleen, ed. LC 87-27373. (Illus.). 160p. (gr. 4-8). 1989. PLB 11.50 (ISBN 0-8075-1462-4). A Whitman.

Powell, Thomas. Daniel Boone & the Opening of the Ohio Country. Goetzmann, William H., ed. Collins, Michael, intro. by. (Illus.). 112p. (gr. 5 up). 1991. PLB 18.95 (ISBN 0-7910-1309-X). Chelsea Hse.

Stevenson, Augusta. Daniel Boone: Young Hunter & Tracker. Doremus, Robert, illus. LC 86-10795. 192p. (gr. 2-6). 1986. pap. 3.95 (ISBN 0-02-041830-2, Aladdin). Macmillan Child Grp.

Wilkie, Katharine E. Daniel Boone: Taming the Wilds. Johnson, E. Harper, illus. 72p. (gr. 2-6). 1991. Repr. of 1960 ed. PLB 12.95 (ISBN 0-7910-1407-X). Chelsea Hse.

BOONE, DANIEL, 1734-1820–FICTION

Gleiter, Jan & Thompson, Kathleen. Daniel Boone. LC 84-9816. (Illus.). (gr. 2-5). 1984. PLB 16.67 (ISBN 0-8172-2120-4); PLB 27.99 incl. cassette (ISBN 0-8172-2242-1); pap. 9.27 (ISBN 0-8172-2263-4); pap. 23.95 incl. cassette (ISBN 0-8172-2273-1); cassette 14.00 (ISBN 0-685-09506-1). Raintree Pubs.

BOOTS
see Shoes and Shoe Industry

BORDER LIFE
see Frontier and Pioneer Life

BOSTON

Byers, Helen. Kidding Around Boston: A Young Person's Guide to the City. Blakemore, Sally, illus. 64p. (Orig.). (gr. 3 up). 1990. pap. 9.95 (ISBN 0-945465-36-X). John Muir.

Hughes, Richard. Bound for Boston. Wheeler, Jill, ed. Lowery, Carol, illus. 48p. (gr. 4). 1989. lib. bdg. 10.95 (ISBN 0-939179-44-X). Abdo & Dghtrs.

Monke, Ingrid. Boston. LC 88-20202. (Illus.). 60p. (gr. 3 up). 1988. PLB 12.95 (ISBN 0-87518-382-4, Dillon). Macmillan Child Grp.

BOSTON–FICTION

Forbes, Esther. Johnny Tremain. Ward, Lynd, illus. (gr. 7-9). 1943. 13.95 (ISBN 0-395-06766-9). HM.

Howells, William Dean. Rise of Silas Lapham. Hillerich, R. L., intro. by. (gr. 11 up). pap. 2.95 (ISBN 0-8049-0165-1, CL-165). Airmont.

Lasky, Kathryn. Prank. (gr. 6 up). 1986. pap. 2.75 (ISBN 0-440-97144-6, LFL). Dell.

Lowry, Lois. Taking Care of Terrific. LC 82-23331. 160p. (gr. 5 up). 1983. 13.95 (ISBN 0-395-34070-5). HM.

Marquand, John P. The Late George Apley: A Novel in the Form of a Memoir. (gr. 7 up). 1937. 15.95 (ISBN 0-685-03075-X). Little.

Stratton, Robin L. Raising the Pentagon: Three Ancient Sorcerers Caught in a Time Warp Find Themselves in 20th Century Boston. 240p. (Orig.). 1990. pap. 9.95 (ISBN 0-9626541-1-6). Mockngbrd Square.

BOSTON–HISTORY

Neely, Keith, illus. The Story of the Boston Tea Party. LC 83-27319. (gr. 3-5). 1984. PLB 13.27 (ISBN 0-516-04666-7); pap. 3.95 (ISBN 0-516-44666-5). Childrens.

Phelan, Mary K. The Story of the Boston Massacre. Eitzen, Allan, illus. LC 75-25961. 160p. (gr. 5-9). 1976. 13.95 (ISBN 0-690-00716-7, Crowell Jr Bks). HarpC Child Bks.

—The Story of the Boston Massacre. Eitzen, Allan, illus. LC 75-25961. 160p. (gr. 4-7). 1990. PLB 13.89 (ISBN 0-690-04883-1, Crowell Jr Bks). HarpC Child Bks.

BOSTON TEA PARTY, 1773–FICTION

Knight, James E. Boston Tea Party, Rebellion in the Colonies. Wenzel, David, illus. LC 81-23077. 32p. (gr. 5-9). 1982. PLB 10.79 (ISBN 0-89375-734-9); pap. text ed. 2.95 (ISBN 0-89375-735-7). Troll Assocs.

BOTANY
see also Flowers; Fruit; Leaves; Plants; Seeds; Shrubs; Trees; Vegetables

Back, Christine. Bean & Plant. LC 86-9634. (Illus.). 25p. (gr. 2-5). 1986. 6.95 (ISBN 0-382-09300-3); pap. 9.98 (ISBN 0-382-09286-4); pap. 3.95 (ISBN 0-382-24014-6). Silver Burdett Pr.

Barker, Cicely M., illus. A Flower Fairies Postcard Book. 30p. (ps up). 1991. pap. 7.95 (ISBN 0-7232-3710-7). Warne.

Be a Plant Detective. (gr. 2 up). 1989. 3.99 (ISBN 0-517-68912-X). Outlet Bk Co.

Bonnet, Robert L. & Keen, G. Daniel. Botany: Forty-Nine More Science Fair Projects. (Illus.). 170p. (gr. 4-7). 1990. 16.95 (ISBN 0-8306-7416-0, 3416); pap. 9.95 (ISBN 0-8306-3416-9). TAB Bks.

Botany. (Illus.). (gr. 3-5). 3.50 (ISBN 0-7214-0778-1). Ladybird Bks.

Boy Scouts of America. Botany. (Illus.). 64p. (gr. 6-12). 1983. pap. 1.85 (ISBN 0-8395-3379-9, 3379). BSA.

The Carnival. (Illus.). (ps-5). 3.50 (ISBN 0-7214-0634-3). Ladybird Bks.

Craig, M. Jean & Grimm, William C. Wondrous World of Seedless Plants. LC 73-1757. 1973. 7.95 (ISBN 0-672-51709-4, Bobbs). Macmillan.

Damon, Laura. Wonders of Plants & Flowers. Miyaki, Yoshi, illus. LC 89-5003. 32p. (gr. 2-4). 1989. PLB 10.89 (ISBN 0-8167-1761-3); pap. text ed. 2.95 (ISBN 0-8167-1762-1). Troll Assocs.

Forsthoefel, John & Ransick, Gary. Discovering Botany. Sellers, Marci, illus. 84p. (gr. 3-6). 1982. 8.95 (ISBN 0-88047-005-4, 8206). DOK Pubs.

Nature Encyclopedia. (Illus.). 144p. 1989. Repr. 14.95 (ISBN 0-02-689203-0). Checkerboard Pr.

Pope, Joyce. Practical Plants. 64p. 1990. 15.95x (ISBN 0-8160-2424-3). Facts on File.

Seymour, Peter. How Things Grow. (Illus.). 8p. (gr. k-3). 1988. 6.95 (ISBN 0-525-67243-5, Lodestar Bks). Dutton Child Bks.

Stidworthy, John. Plants & Seeds. 1990. PLB 11.90 (ISBN 0-531-17220-1). Watts.

BOTANY, AGRICULTURAL
see Botany, Economic

BOTANY–ECOLOGY
see also Desert Plants

Sussman, Susan & James, Robert. Big Friend, Little Friend: A Book about Symbiosis. (Illus.). 32p. (gr. 2-5). 1989. 13.95 (ISBN 0-395-49701-9). HM.

BOTANY, ECONOMIC
see also Cotton; Grasses; Plants, Edible; Weeds

Dremann, Craig C. Redwood City Seed Company Catalog of Useful Plants: 1990 Season. Dremann, Craig C. & Dremann, Sue, illus. 28p. (gr. 6-12). 1990. pap. 1.00 (ISBN 0-933421-36-2). Redwood Seed.

BOTANY–GEOGRAPHICAL DISTRIBUTION
see Geographical Distribution of Animals and Plants

BOTANY OF THE BIBLE
see Bible–Natural History

BOUNTY (SHIP)–FICTION

Bligh, William. Mutiny on Board HMS Bounty. Teitel, N. R., intro. by. (gr. 8 up). pap. 1.95 (ISBN 0-8049-0088-4, CL-88). Airmont.

BOURKE-WHITE, MARGARET, 1906-1971

Daffron, Carolyn. Margaret Bourke-White. Horner, Matina, intro. by. (Illus.). 112p. (Orig.). (gr. 5 up). 1988. 17.95 (ISBN 1-55546-644-3); pap. 9.95 (ISBN 0-7910-0411-2). Chelsea Hse.

BOW AND ARROW
see also Archery

BOWDITCH, NATHANIEL, 1773-1838

Latham, Jean L. Carry on, Mr. Bowditch. Cosgrove, John O., illus. LC 55-5219. 256p. (gr. 6 up). 1973. pap. 5.95 (ISBN 0-395-13713-6, Sandpiper). HM.

—Carry on, Mr. Bowditch. Cosgrove, John O., illus. (gr. 6 up). 1955. 13.95 (ISBN 0-395-06881-9). HM.

BOWED INSTRUMENTS
see Stringed Instruments

BOWLING

Lerner, Mark. Bowling Is for Me. Wolfe, Robert L., illus. LC 81-12433. 48p. (gr. 2-5). 1981. PLB 8.95 (ISBN 0-8225-1099-5). Lerner Pubns.

Nardi, Thomas J. Bowling Basics. Gow, Bill, illus. LC 83-22893. 48p. (gr. 3-7). 1984. PLB 10.95 (ISBN 0-13-080516-5). P-H.

BOXERS

Famous Fighters-Coloring Book. 1985. pap. 3.50 (ISBN 0-88388-064-4). Bellerophon Bks.

Lipsyte, Robert. Free to Be Muhammad Ali. LC 77-25640. (gr. 5 up). 1978. PLB 12.89 (ISBN 0-06-023902-6). HarpC Child Bks.

BOXING

Ricciuti, Edward R. How to Box: Boxing for Beginners. Madden, Don, illus. LC 81-43311. 128p. (gr. 3-6). 1982. 12.95 (ISBN 0-690-04180-2, Crowell Jr Bks); (Crowell Jr Bks). HarpC Child Bks.

Rosenthal, Bert. Sugar Ray Leonard: The Baby-faced Boxer. LC 82-4472. (Illus.). (gr. 2-8). 1982. PLB 13.27 (ISBN 0-516-04326-9); pap. 3.95 (ISBN 0-516-44326-7). Childrens.

Sender. Requiem por un Campesino. (gr. 7-12). 1972. pap. 5.95 (ISBN 0-88436-055-5, 70273). EMC.

Thomas, Art & Storms, Laura. Boxing Is for Me. Thomas, Art, photos by. LC 80-20086. (Illus.). 48p. (gr. 2-5). 1982. PLB 8.95 (ISBN 0-8225-1133-9). Lerner Pubns.

BOXING–FICTION

Carrier, Roch. The Boxing Champion. Cohen, Sheldon, illus. 24p. (gr. 3 up). 1991. 14.95 (ISBN 0-88776-249-2). Tundra Bks.

Gifford, Griselda. The Story of Ranald. 104p. (gr. 5-8). 1990. pap. 5.95 (ISBN 0-86241-094-0, Pub. by Cnngt Pub Ltd). Trafalgar Sq.

Peck, Robert N. Dukes. LC 84-4272. 128p. (gr. 5-9). 1984. 9.95 (ISBN 0-910923-06-X). Pineapple Pr.

BOXING–HISTORY

Blady, Ken. The Jewish Boxer's Hall of Fame. LC 88-29367. (Illus.). (gr. 7 up). 1989. 14.95 (ISBN 0-933503-87-3). Shapolsky Pubs.

BOY SCOUTS

Boy Scouts of America. Cub Scout Songbook. (Illus.). 80p. (gr. 3-5). 1969. pap. 2.40x (ISBN 0-8395-3222-9, 3222A). BSA.

Boy Scouts of America Staff. Scoutmaster Handbook. (Illus.). 272p. 1990. pap. 6.50 (ISBN 0-8395-6502-X, 6502). BSA.

Fish & Wildlife Management. 40p. (Orig.). (gr. 6-12). 1990. pap. 1.85 (ISBN 0-685-37947-7, 3307A). BSA.

Murphy, Claire R. Friendship Across Arctic Waters: Alaskan Cub Scouts Visit Their Soviet Neighbors. Mason, Charles, photos by. (Illus.). 48p. (gr. 3-8). 1991. 15.95 (ISBN 0-525-67348-2, Lodestar Bks). Dutton Child Bks.

Orienteering. (Illus.). 32p. (gr. 6-12). 1974. pap. 1.85 (ISBN 0-8395-3385-3, 3385). BSA.

Sheldon, Bill, compiled by. & frwd. by. The Boy Scout Collector's Bibliography. 254p. (Orig.). (gr. 6-12). 1987. pap. 13.50 for info. (ISBN 0-9616668-0-3). B Sheldon.

BOY SCOUTS–FICTION

Delton, Judy. Pee Wee Scout Backpack, 6 vols. (gr. 4-7). 1990. pap. 15.00 (ISBN 0-440-36014-5). Dell.

Tapp, Kathy K. Den Four Meets the Jinx. LC 88-12776. 128p. (gr. 3-6). 1988. 12.95 (ISBN 0-689-50453-5, M K McElderry). Macmillan Child Grp.

BOY SCOUTS–HANDBOOKS, MANUALS, ETC.

Boy Scouts of America. Conservation Skill Book. (Illus.). 32p. (gr. 3-4). 1979. pap. 1.50x (ISBN 0-8395-6584-4); Nineteen Eighty, 12p. tchr's. guide 0.50 (ISBN 0-8395-8224-2); Nineteen Eighty, 24p. Troop leader's can-do-kit 0.50 (ISBN 0-8395-8204-8). BSA.

—Environment Skill Book. (Illus.). 32p. (gr. 3-4). 1979. pap. 1.50x (ISBN 0-8395-6586-0); tchr's. guide 0.50x (ISBN 0-8395-8226-9); troop leader's can-do kit 0.50 (ISBN 0-8395-8206-4). BSA.

—Sea Exploring Manual. 272p. (gr. 6-12). 1987. pap. 8.75 (ISBN 0-8395-3229-6, 3239). BSA.

Boy Scouts of America Staff. Cub Scout Sports: Fishing. 40p. (Orig.). (gr. 2-5). 1988. pap. 1.35 (ISBN 0-8395-2111-1, 2111). BSA.

—My Scout Advancement Trail. (Illus.). 16p. (Orig.). (gr. 5). 1990. pap. 0.95 (ISBN 0-8395-3424-8, 3424). BSA.

—Order of the Arrow Handbook. rev. ed. (Illus.). 96p. (gr. 6 up). 1990. pap. 1.50 (ISBN 0-8395-5000-6, 5000). BSA.

Den Chief Handbook. (Illus.). 128p. (gr. 6-12). 1980. pap. 3.20x (ISBN 0-8395-3211-3, 3211A). BSA.

Wolf Cub Scout Book. rev. ed. (Illus.). 224p. (gr. 2). 1986. pap. 3.00x (ISBN 0-8395-3234-2, 3234). BSA.

BOYLE, ROBERT, 1627-1691

Tiner, John H. Robert Boyle: Trailblazer of Science. (Illus.). (gr. 3-6). 1989. pap. 6.95 (ISBN 0-88062-155-9). Mott Media.

BOYS
see also Boy Scouts; Newsboys; Youth

Buck, Pearl S. The Big Wave. LC 85-45402. (Illus.). 80p. (gr. 3-6). 1986. pap. 2.95 (ISBN 0-06-440171-5, Trophy). HarpC Child Bks.

Filichia, Peter. A Boy's-Eye View of Girls. 128p. (Orig.). (gr. 7 up). 1983. pap. 1.95 (ISBN 0-590-32314-8). Scholastic Inc.

BOYS–EMPLOYMENT
see Child Labor

BOYS–FICTION

Abbott, Jennie. The Boy Who Remembered Everything. Badenhop, Mary, illus. LC 87-14986. 96p. (gr. 3-6). 1988. PLB 9.89 (ISBN 0-8167-1183-6); pap. text ed. 2.95 (ISBN 0-8167-1184-4). Troll Assocs.

Acker, Toni. Tobey: A Tale of Transition. Verrier, Claude, illus. 40p. (gr. 7-12). 1987. pap. 5.95 (ISBN 0-942953-00-2). Wonder Works Studio.

Ahlberg, Allan. Woof! Wegner, Fritz, illus. LC 86-40009. 155p. (gr. 3-7). 1986. pap. 11.95 (ISBN 0-670-80832-6). Viking Child Bks.

Aiello, Barbara & Shulman, Jeffrey. Hometown Hero: Featuring Scott Whittaker. Barr, Loel, illus. 48p. (gr. 3-6). 1989. PLB 12.95 (ISBN 0-941477-04-5). TFC Bks MD.

Alcott, Louisa May. Jo's Boys. 352p. (gr. 4-6). 1984. pap. 2.25 (ISBN 0-14-035015-2, Puffin). Puffin Bks.

—Jo's Boys. Stern, Madelain, afterword by. 304p. (gr. 7-12). 1987. pap. 2.25 (ISBN 0-451-52089-0, Sig Classics). NAL-Dutton.

—Little Men. (Illus.). 384p. (gr. 4 up). 1982. pap. 6.95 (ISBN 0-448-11018-0, G&D). Putnam Pub Group.

—Little Men. 384p. (Orig.). (gr. 4-6). 1987. pap. 2.95 (ISBN 0-590-41279-5, Apple Paperbacks). Scholastic Inc.

Aldridge, James. The True Story of Spit Macphee. LC 87-62396. 208p. (Orig.). (gr. 7 up). 1988. pap. 3.95 (ISBN 0-14-032073-3, Puffin). Puffin Bks.

Alex, Ben. Chebet & the Lost Goat. (Illus.). 32p. (gr. 3-6). 1987. 7.95 (ISBN 0-8028-5020-0). Eerdmans.

Alexander, Martha. Marty McGee's Space Lab, No Girls Allowed. Alexander, Martha, illus. LC 81-2497. 32p. (ps-3). 1981. 7.95 (ISBN 0-8037-5156-7); PLB 7.89 (ISBN 0-8037-5157-5). Dial Bks Young.

Alfie Gets in First. (ps-1). 1987. pap. 3.95 (ISBN 0-688-07036-1, Mulberry Bks). Macmillan.

Amoss, Berthe. Tom in the Middle. Amoss, Berthe, illus. LC 86-42991. 32p. (gr. k-3). 1988. 12.95 (ISBN 0-06-020063-4); PLB 12.89 (ISBN 0-06-020064-2). HarpC Child Bks.

Arkin, Alan. Tony's Hard Work Day. reissued ed. Stevenson, James, illus. LC 76-183161. 32p. (gr. k-3). 1972. 12.95 (ISBN 0-06-020137-1); PLB 12.89 (ISBN 0-06-020138-X). HarpC Child Bks.

Arnold, Tedd. Ollie Forgot. Arnold, Tedd, illus. LC 87-24552. 32p. (ps-3). 1988. 11.95 (ISBN 0-8037-0485-2); PLB 11.89 (ISBN 0-8037-0488-7). Dial Bks Young.

Asimov, Isaac & Sturgeon, Theodore. The Ugly Little Boy - The Widget, the Wadget, & Boff. 1989. 3.50 (ISBN 0-317-93510-0). Tor Bks.

Atlas, Ron. A Room for Benny. Arnold, Ted, illus. (ps). 1987. 5.95 (ISBN 0-671-64078-X, Little Simon). S&S Trade.

Auch, Mary J. Mom Is Dating Weird Wayne. LC 88-45275. 160p. (gr. 4-7). 1988. 13.95 (ISBN 0-8234-0720-9). Holiday.

Avi. The Fighting Ground. Thompson, Ellen, illus. LC 82-47719. 160p. (gr. 5 up). 1984. 12.95 (ISBN 0-397-32073-6, Lipp Jr Bks); PLB 12.89 (ISBN 0-397-32074-4, Lipp Jr Bks). HarpC Child Bks.

—The Fighting Ground. LC 82-47719. 160p. (gr. 4 up). 1987. pap. 3.50 (ISBN 0-06-440185-5, Trophy). HarpC Child Bks.

—Sometimes I Think I Hear My Name. Adams, Jeanette, illus. LC 81-38421. 160p. (gr. 7 up). 1982. 9.95 (ISBN 0-394-85048-3); lib. bdg. 9.99 (ISBN 0-394-95048-8). Pantheon.

Ayal, Ora & Nakao, Naomi. The Adventures of Chester the Chest. LC 81-48642. (Illus.). 32p. (gr. k-3). 1982. 8.61i (ISBN 0-06-020304-8). HarpC Child Bks.

Babbitt, Natalie. Herbert Rowbarge. LC 82-18274. 216p. (gr. 9 up). 1984. (Sunburst); pap. 3.95 (ISBN 0-374-51852-1, Sunburst). FS&G.

Bach, Alice. The Bully of Library Place. (Orig.). 1988. pap. 2.95 (ISBN 0-440-40030-9, YB). Dell.

Baer, Judy. Journey to Nowhere. LC 88-63462. 144p. (Orig.). (gr. 6 up). 1989. pap. 3.95 (ISBN 1-55661-067-X). Bethany Hse.

Baird, Thomas. Finding Fever. LC 81-48646. 224p. (gr. 6 up). 1982. 12.95 (ISBN 0-06-020353-6). HarpC Child Bks.

Baker, Jeannie. Window. LC 90-3922. (Illus.). 32p. (ps up). 1991. 13.95 (ISBN 0-688-08917-8); PLB 13.88 (ISBN 0-688-08918-6). Greenwillow.

Balch, Glenn. Christmas Horse. Crowell, Pers, illus. Woodward, Tim, intro. by. (Illus.). 1990. pap. 9.95 (ISBN 0-931659-10-8). Limberlost Pr.

Balis, Andrea & Reiser, Robert. P. J. (gr. k-6). 1987. pap. 2.95 (ISBN 0-440-46880-9, YB). Dell.

Bang, Molly G. Wiley & the Hairy Man: Adapted from an American Folk Tale. Bang, Molly G., illus. LC 87-2540. 64p. (gr. 1-4). 1987. pap. 3.95 (ISBN 0-689-71162-X, Aladdin). Macmillan Child Grp.

Barrie, J. M. Peter Pan. Shebar, Susan, ed. Lewis, T., illus. LC 87-15480. 48p. (gr. 2-6). 1988. PLB 12.89 (ISBN 0-8167-1199-2); pap. text ed. 3.95 (ISBN 0-8167-1200-X). Troll Assocs.

Barrie, James M. Peter Pan. Ormerod, Jan, illus. (gr. 5 up). 1987. 12.95 (ISBN 0-670-80862-8). Viking Child Bks.

Bates, Betty. Ask Me Tomorrow. LC 87-45329. 144p. (gr. 5 up). 1987. 12.95 (ISBN 0-8234-0659-8). Holiday.

—Tough Beans. Morrill, Leslie, illus. LC 88-45274. 96p. (gr. 3-7). 1988. 11.95 (ISBN 0-8234-0722-5). Holiday.

Batmanglij, M. & Batmanglij, N. The Wonderful Story of Zaal. Franta, illus. LC 86-12665. 48p. (gr. 4 up). 1986. 18.50 (ISBN 0-934211-01-9). Mage Pubs Inc.

Bautista, Bezalie P. The Boy Who Looked Different. Saprid, Pearle R., illus. 24p. (Orig.). (gr. k-2). 1990. pap. 3.50x (ISBN 971-10-0406-2, Pub. by New Day Pub Phillippines). Cellar.

Bawden, Nina. The Finding. LC 84-25069. 160p. (gr. 3 up). 1985. 11.95 (ISBN 0-688-04979-6). Lothrop.

Baylor, Byrd. Amigo. Williams, Garth, illus. 48p. (gr. 1-3). 1989. pap. 4.95 (ISBN 0-689-71299-5, Aladdin). Macmillan Child Grp.

Beatty, Patricia. Charley Skedaddle. 1988. pap. 2.95 (ISBN 0-8167-1317-0). Troll Assocs.

Benchley, Nathaniel. George the Drummer Boy. Bolognese, Don, illus. LC 76-18398. 64p. (gr. k-3). 1987. pap. 3.50 (ISBN 0-06-444106-7, Trophy). HarpC Child Bks.

Bennett, Rodney. Eagle Boy. 164p. (gr. 5-9). 1989. 11.95 (ISBN 0-233-98044-X). Andre Deutsch.

Bergman, Tamar. The Boy from over There. Halkin, Hillel, tr. from HEB. LC 87-36634. 192p. (gr. 3-7). 1988. 12.95 (ISBN 0-395-43077-1). HM.

Bishop, Claire H. The Five Chinese Brothers. Wiese, Kurt, illus. 64p. (ps-3). 1989. pap. 5.95 (ISBN 0-685-36241-8, Pub. by Sandcastle Bks). Putnam Pub Group.

Blackwood, Gary. Wild Timothy. LC 87-937. 160p. (gr. 4-8). 1987. 13.95 (ISBN 0-689-31352-7, Atheneum Child Bk). Macmillan Child Grp.

Blake, Susan. Stealing Josh. 128p. (Orig.). 1990. pap. 3.50 (ISBN 0-449-14606-5). Fawcett.

Blegvad, Lenore. Anna Banana & Me. Blegvad, Erik, illus. LC 86-22220. 32p. (ps-3). 1987. pap. 3.95 (ISBN 0-689-71114-X, Aladdin). Macmillan Child Grp.

Blos, Joan. Brothers of the Heart. LC 85-40293. 176p. (gr. 6 up). 1985. 13.95 (ISBN 0-684-18452-4, Scribners Young Read). Macmillan Child Grp.

—Brothers of the Heart. LC 87-1089. 176p. (gr. 7 up). 1987. pap. 3.95 (ISBN 0-689-71166-2, Aladdin). Macmillan Child Grp.

Blos, Joan W. Old Henry. Gammell, Stephen, illus. LC 86-21745. 32p. (ps-4). 1987. lib. bdg. 13.95 (ISBN 0-688-06399-3); 13.88 (ISBN 0-688-06400-0). Morrow.

Bond, Felicia. The Halloween Performance. LC 82-45920. (Illus.). 32p. (ps-3). 1983. 4.95 (ISBN 0-694-00155-4, Crowell Jr Bks). HarpC Child Bks.

Bonsall, Crosby. And I Mean It, Stanley. LC 73-14324. (Illus.). 32p. (ps-1). 1984. pap. 2.95 (ISBN 0-06-444046-X, Trophy). HarpC Child Bks.

—Who's a Pest? Bonsall, Crosby, illus. LC 62-13310. 64p. (gr. k-3). 1986. pap. 3.50 (ISBN 0-06-444099-0, Trophy). HarpC Child Bks.

Bontemps, Arna. Lonesome Boy. Topolski, Feliks, illus. LC 88-3434. 32p. (gr. k-3). 1988. pap. 4.95 (ISBN 0-8070-8307-0, NL 2). Beacon Pr.

Bosch, Carl. Bully on the Bus. Strecker, Rebekah, illus. LC 88-42650. 64p. (Orig.). (gr. 2-5). 1988. PLB 12.95 (ISBN 0-943990-43-2); pap. 3.95 (ISBN 0-943990-42-4). Parenting Pr.

Bourgeois, Paulette. Hurry up, Franklin. 1991. pap. 3.95 (ISBN 0-590-42621-4). Scholastic Inc.

Boyd, Lizi. Bailey the Big Bully. Boyd, Lizi, illus. 32p. (ps-5). 1989. pap. 11.95 (ISBN 0-670-82719-3). Viking Child Bks.

Bradbury, Ray. Dandelion Wine. (gr. 6 up). 1985. pap. 3.95 (ISBN 0-553-27753-7). Bantam.

Bridgers, Sue E. Notes for Another Life. LC 81-1673. 256p. (gr. 7 up). 1981. Repr. of 1981 ed. lib. bdg. 13.99 (ISBN 0-394-94889-0). Knopf.

Bridwell, Norman. Clifford, We Love You. (ps-3). 1991. pap. 2.25 (ISBN 0-590-43843-3); pap. 5.95 incls. cass. (ISBN 0-590-63604-9). Scholastic Inc.

Briggs, Raymond. Jim & the Beanstalk. Briggs, Raymond, illus. 40p. (ps-2). 1989. pap. 5.95 (ISBN 0-698-20641-X, Sandcastle Bks). Putnam Pub Group.

Brinkley, Charleen L. Jonah & the Glass Mountain. Leatherman, John D., illus. 37p. 1990. 6.95 (ISBN 0-533-08699-X). Vantage.

Brittain, Bill. The Fantastic Freshman. LC 87-35051. 160p. (gr. 5-9). 1988. PLB 12.89 (ISBN 0-06-020719-1). HarpC Child Bks.

Brooks, Walter R. Freddy Goes to Florida. Morrill, Leslie & Wiese, Kurt, illus. LC 86-40424. 208p. (gr. 3-7). 1987. pap. 3.95 (ISBN 0-394-88886-3). Knopf.

Brown, Margaret W. David's Little Indian. Charlip, Remy, illus. 48p. (gr. 2-5). 1989. Repr. of 1954 ed. 10.95 (ISBN 0-929077-02-4, Hopscotch Bks); PLB 10.95 (ISBN 0-317-92547-4, Hopscotch Bks). Watermark Inc.

Browne, Anthony. Willy the Wimp. Browne, Anthony, illus. LC 84-14320. 32p. (ps-3). 1985. 7.95 (ISBN 0-394-87061-1); lib. bdg. 11.99 (ISBN 0-394-97061-6). Knopf.

—Willy the Wimp. Browne, Anthony, illus. LC 84-14320. 32p. (ps-2). 1989. pap. 3.95 (ISBN 0-394-82610-8). Knopf.

Brumpton, Karen B. Freeman Earns a Bike. Feldman, Roper, illus. LC 84-60947. 32p. (ps-4). 1984. 10.95 (ISBN 0-917487-00-1). McVie Pub.

Buchan, Stuart. Guys Like Us. (gr. k-12). 1989. pap. 2.95 (ISBN 0-440-20244-2, LFL). Dell.

Bulla, Clyde R. The Cardboard Crown. Chessare, Michele, illus. LC 83-45049. 96p. (gr. 2-5). 1984. (Crowell Jr Bks); PLB 12.89 (ISBN 0-690-04361-9, Crowell Jr Bks). HarpC Child Bks.

—The Chalk Box Kid. Allen, Thomas B., illus. LC 87-4683. 64p. (gr. 2-4). 1987. lib. bdg. 6.99 (ISBN 0-394-99102-8, Random Juv); pap. 2.50 (ISBN 0-394-89102-3, Random Juv). Random.

Burnett, Frances H. Little Lord Fauntleroy. (Illus.). 252p. 1981. Repr. PLB 21.95x (ISBN 0-89966-288-9). Buccaneer Bks.

—Little Lord Fauntleroy. (gr. k-6). 1986. pap. 4.95 (ISBN 0-440-44764-X, Pub. by Yearling Classics). Dell.

Burningham, John. John Patrick Norman McHennessey: The Boy Who Was Always Late. (Illus.). 32p. (ps-3). 1987. 14.95 (ISBN 0-517-56805-5). Crown.

Burton, Marilee R. Aaron Awoke. LC 81-48638. (Illus.). 40p. (ps-k). 1982. PLB 9.89g (ISBN 0-06-020892-9). HarpC Child Bks.

Burton, Virginia L. Mike Mulligan & His Steam Shovel. (gr. 3 up). 1987. pap. 7.95 incl. cass. (ISBN 0-395-45738-6). HM.

Buscaglia, Leo F. A Memory for Tino. Newsom, Carol, illus. 50p. (ps up). 1988. 12.95 (ISBN 0-688-07482-0). Slack Inc.

Busters Big Chase. 1990. 5.98 (ISBN 1-55521-690-0). Bk Sales Inc.

Butterworth, W. E. Leroy & the Old Man. 168p. (gr. 7 up). 1991. pap. 2.95 (ISBN 0-590-42711-3). Scholastic Inc.

Byars, Besty. The Burning Questions of Bingo Brown. 176p. (gr. 3 up). 1990. pap. 3.95 (ISBN 0-14-032479-8, Puffin). Puffin Bks.

Byars, Betsy. The Eighteenth Emergency. large type ed. 129p. (gr. 4-6). 1988. lib. bdg. 13.95x (ISBN 0-8161-4432-X, Large Print Bks). G K Hall.

Byars, Betsy C. Cracker Jackson. 160p. (gr. 5-9). 1986. pap. 3.95 (ISBN 0-14-031881-X, Puffin). Puffin Bks.

—The Eighteenth Emergency. Grossman, Robert, illus. LC 72-91399. 128p. (gr. 4-6). 1973. pap. 12.95 (ISBN 0-670-29055-6). Viking Child Bks.

Caines, Jeannette. I Need a Lunch Box. Cummings, Pat, illus. LC 85-45829. 32p. (ps-1). 1988. 12.95i (ISBN 0-06-020984-4); PLB 12.89 (ISBN 0-06-020985-2). HarpC Child Bks.

Calhoun, Mary. Jack & the Whoopee Wind. Gackenbach, Dick, illus. LC 86-1630. 32p. (ps-3). 1987. 13.95 (ISBN 0-688-06137-0); lib. bdg. 13.88 (ISBN 0-688-06138-9, Morrow Jr Bks). Morrow Jr Bks.

Calif, Ruth. The Over-the-Hill Ghost. Holub, Joan, illus. 160p. (gr. 3-8). 1988. 10.95 (ISBN 0-88289-667-9). Pelican.

Cameron, Ann. Julian, Secret Agent. Allison, Diane W., illus. LC 88-4428. 64p. (Orig.). (gr. 2-4). 1988. lib. bdg. 6.99 (ISBN 0-394-91949-1, Random Juv); pap. 2.50 (ISBN 0-394-81949-7, Random Juv). Random.

—Julian's Glorious Summer. Leder, Dora, illus. LC 86-33828. 64p. (gr. 2-4). 1987. lib. bdg. 5.99 (ISBN 0-394-99117-6, Random Juv); pap. 2.50 (ISBN 0-394-89117-1, Random Juv). Random.

Cancion De Navidad. (SPA.). 1990. casebound 3.50 (ISBN 0-7214-1397-8). Ladybird Bks.

Cannon, A. E. Will the Real Cal Cameron Please Stand Up? (gr. 7 up). 1988. write for info. Delacorte.

Canty, John. Shadows. Canty, John, illus. LC 87-205. 24p. (gr. k-3). 1987. 12.95 (ISBN 0-06-020988-7). HarpC Child Bks.

Carkeet, David. The Silent Treatment. LC 87-45567. 288p. (gr. 7 up). 1990. pap. 3.25 (ISBN 0-06-447014-8, Trophy). HarpC Child Bks.

Carlson, Nancy. Arnie & the Stolen Markers. (Illus.). 32p. (ps-3). 1989. pap. 3.95 (ISBN 0-14-050707-8, Puffin). Puffin Bks.

—Loudmouth George & The New Neighbors. Carlson, Nancy, illus. (gr. k-3). 1987. incl. cassette 19.95 (ISBN 0-87499-034-3); pap. 12.95 incl. cassette (ISBN 0-87499-032-7); 4 paperbacks, cassette & guide 27.95 (ISBN 0-87499-033-5). Live Oak Media.

Carpenter, Marcos. Carlos, the Street Boy Who Found a Home. Alex, Ben, ed. (Illus.). 32p. (gr. 3-6). 1987. 7.95 (ISBN 0-8028-5019-7). Eerdmans.

Carratello, Patty. This Is Fred. Spivak, Darlene, ed. Brostrom, Eileen, illus. 16p. (gr. k-2). 1988. wkbk. 1.95 (ISBN 1-55734-391-8). Tchr Create Mat.

—Will Bill? Spivak, Darlene, ed. Olsen, Shirley, illus. 16p. (gr. k-2). 1988. wkbk. 1.95 (ISBN 1-55734-388-8). Tchr Create Mat.

Carrick, Carol. Lost in the Storm. Carrick, Donald, illus. LC 74-1051. 32p. (ps-3). 1979. 12.95 (ISBN 0-395-28776-6, Clarion). HM.

—Stay Away from Simon. Carrick, Donald, illus. LC 84-14289. 64p. (gr. 2-5). 1985. 12.95 (ISBN 0-89919-343-9, Clarion). Ticknor & Fields.

—Stay Away from Simon! Carrick, Donald, illus. (gr. 3-6). 1989. pap. 3.95 (ISBN 0-685-37788-1, Pub. by Clarion). Ticknor & Fields.

—What a Wimp! Carrick, Donald, illus. 96p. (gr. 3-6). 1983. 12.95 (ISBN 0-89919-139-8, Clarion). HM.

—What a Wimp! Carrick, Donald, illus. LC 82-9597. (gr. 3-6). 1988. pap. 4.95 (ISBN 0-89919-703-5, Pub. by Clarion). Ticknor & Fields.

Carris, Joan. When the Boys Ran the House. Newsom, Carol, illus. LC 82-47762. 160p. (gr. 4-7). 1982. 12.95 (ISBN 0-397-32019-1, Lipp Jr Bks); (Lipp Jr Bks). HarpC Child Bks.

Caruso, Joseph G. Adam's Diary. (Illus.). 26p. (Orig.). 1989. pap. 3.00 (ISBN 0-88680-313-6); Piano-Vocal Score 15.00 (ISBN 0-88680-314-4). I E Clark.

Caudill, Rebecca. Did You Carry the Flag Today, Charley? Grossman, Nancy, illus. LC 66-11422. 94p. (gr. 2-4). 1966. reinforced bdg. 14.95 (ISBN 0-8050-1201-X); pap. 3.95 (ISBN 0-03-086620-0). H Holt & Co.

Cauley, Lorinda B., retold by. & illus. The Pancake Boy. 32p. (ps-1). 1988. PLB 13.95 (ISBN 0-399-21505-0, Putnam). Putnam Pub Group.

Chapman, Carol. The Tale of Meshka the Kvetch. Lobel, Arnold, illus. LC 80-11225. 32p. (gr. k-3). 1989. pap. 3.95 (ISBN 0-525-44494-7, DCB). Dutton Child Bks.

Chapouton, Anne-Marie. Billy the Brave. Bell, Anthea, tr. from FRE. Claverie, Jean, illus. LC 85-63307. 32p. (gr. k-2). 1986. 8.95 (ISBN 1-55858-070-0). North-South Bks NYC.

Chappell, James A. Little Johnny Raindrop. Shaw, Charles, illus. LC 88-2173. 32p. (ps-3). 1988. 12.95 (ISBN 0-938349-28-7). State House Pr.

Chetwin, Grace. Gom on Windy Mountain. LC 85-18166. (Illus.). 224p. (gr. 6 up). 1986. 12.95 (ISBN 0-688-05767-5). Lothrop.

Christelow, Eileen. Henry & the Dragon. (Illus.). (ps-3). 1990. pap. 4.95 (ISBN 0-395-55697-X, Clarion Bks). HM.

Christian, Mary B. Sebastian & the Bone to Pick Mystery. 64p. 1986. pap. 2.25 (ISBN 0-553-15385-4, Skylark). Bantam.

—Singin' Somebody Else's Song. LC 88-12000. 192p. (gr. 7 up). 1988. 13.95 (ISBN 0-02-718500-1, Mcmillan Child Bk). Macmillan Child Grp.

Christopher, Matt. Johnny Long Legs. Kidder, Harvey, illus. 144p. (gr. 3-6). 1988. pap. 3.95 (ISBN 0-316-14065-1). Little.

Claverie, Jean. Little Lou. Claverie, Jean, illus. LC 90-1531. 48p. 1990. 16.95 (ISBN 1-55670-162-4). Stewart Tabori & Chang.

Cleary, Beverly. Henry & the Paper Route. 196p. (gr. k-6). 1980. pap. 3.25 (ISBN 0-440-43298-7, YB). Dell.

—Henry & the Paper Route. Darling, Louis, illus. LC 57-8562. (gr. 3-7). 1957. 13.95 (ISBN 0-688-21380-4); PLB 13.88 (ISBN 0-688-31380-9). Morrow.
—Henry & the Paper Route. 192p. 1990. pap. 3.50 (ISBN 0-380-70921-X, Camelot). Avon.
—Henry Huggins, 4 vols. (gr. 4-7). 1990. Boxed set. pap. 14.00 (ISBN 0-380-71206-7). Avon.
—Henry Huggins Clubhouse, 6 vols. (gr. 4-7). 1990. pap. 19.50 boxed set (ISBN 0-440-36015-3). Dell.
—Otis Spofford. 192p. (gr. k-6). 1980. pap. 3.25 (ISBN 0-440-46651-2, YB). Dell.
—Runaway Ralph. LC 77-95786. (Illus.). (gr. 3-7). 1970. 14.95 (ISBN 0-688-21701-X); PLB 14.88 (ISBN 0-688-31701-4, Morrow Jr Bks). Morrow Jr Bks.
Clendenin, Mary J. Gonzalo, Coronado's Shepherd Boy. Roberts, Melissa, ed. (Illus.). 128p. (gr. 4-7). 1990. 10.95 (ISBN 0-89015-700-6, Pub. by Panda Bks). Eakin Pr.
Clifford, Eth. I Hate Your Guts, Ben Brooster. 144p. 1990. pap. 2.75 (ISBN 0-590-43534-5). Scholastic Inc.
—The Man Who Sang in the Dark. Owen, Mary B., illus. 96p. (gr. 2-5). 1987. 12.95 (ISBN 0-395-43664-8). HM.
Clifton. Everett Anderson's Nine Month Long. 1988. pap. 4.95 (ISBN 0-8050-0295-2). H Holt & Co.
Clifton, Lucille. The Boy Who Didn't Believe in Spring. Turkle, Brinton, illus. LC 87-27145. 32p. (ps-3). 1988. pap. 3.95 (ISBN 0-525-44365-7, 0383-120, DCB). Dutton Child Bks.
—Everett Anderson's Nine Month Long. Grifalconi, Ann, illus. 32p. (gr. k-2). 1978. 12.95 (ISBN 0-8050-0287-1). H Holt & Co.
—Some of the Days of Everett Anderson. Ness, Evaline, illus. LC 78-98922. (gr. k-2). 10.95 (ISBN 0-8050-0290-1); pap. 5.95 (ISBN 0-8050-0289-8). H Holt & Co.
Clymer, Eleanor. Luke Was There. (Orig.). (gr. k-6). 1989. pap. 2.95 (ISBN 0-440-40139-9, YB). Dell.
Cohen, Miriam. Starring First Grade. Hoban, Lillian, illus. LC 84-5929. 32p. (gr. k-3). 1985. PLB 13.88 (ISBN 0-688-04030-6). Greenwillow.
Cole, Babette. King Change-a-Lot. Cole, Babette, illus. 32p. (ps-3). 1989. 13.95 (ISBN 0-399-21670-7, Putnam). Putnam Pub Group.
—Three Cheers for Errol! Cole, Babette, illus. 32p. (ps-3). 1989. 13.95 (ISBN 0-399-21671-5, Putnam). Putnam Pub Group.
Collier, James L. Outside Looking In. LC 86-21845. 192p. (gr. 5-9). 1987. 13.95 (ISBN 0-02-723100-3, Mcmillan Child Bk). Macmillan Child Grp.
—When the Stars Begin to Fall. LC 86-11619. 224p. (gr. 7 up). 1986. pap. 14.95 (ISBN 0-385-29516-2). Delacorte.
Collodi, Carlo. The Adventures of Pinocchio. Harden, E., tr. from ITA. Innocenti, Roberto, illus. LC 88-8918. 144p. (ps up). 1988. 18.95 (ISBN 0-394-82110-6). Knopf.
Comstock, Esther J. Vallejo & the Four Flags. Comstock, Floyd B., illus. LC 79-21636. xvi, 142p. (gr. 4). 1988. 12.50 (ISBN 0-933994-01-X); pap. 8.75 (ISBN 0-933994-07-9). Comstock Bon.
Conlin, Susan & Friedman, Susan L. Nathan's Day. Smith, M. Kathryn, illus. LC 90-62679. 32p. (Orig.). (ps-k). 1991. lib. bdg. 15.95 (ISBN 0-943990-61-0); pap. 4.95 (ISBN 0-943990-60-2). Parenting Pr.
Cook, Olive R. Trails to Poosey. Sammel, Chelsea, illus. Cook, George R., intro. by. LC 86-8602. (Illus.). 200p. (Orig.). (gr. 3-6). 1986. pap. 5.95 (ISBN 0-930079-01-9). Misty Hill Pr.
Cooney, Barbara. Island Boy. LC 88-175. (ps-3). 1988. pap. 14.95 (ISBN 0-670-81749-X). Viking Child Bks.
Cooper, Susan. The Dark Is Rising. LC 86-3647. 256p. (gr. 6 up). 1986. pap. 2.95 (ISBN 0-689-71087-9, Collier Young Ad). Macmillan Child Grp.
—Greenwitch. LC 86-3324. 148p. (gr. 4-7). 1986. pap. 3.50 (ISBN 0-689-71088-7, Collier Young Ad). Macmillan Child Grp.
—The Grey King. LC 86-3613. 176p. (gr. 6 up). 1986. pap. 3.50 (ISBN 0-689-71089-5, Collier Young Ad). Macmillan Child Grp.
—Silver on the Tree. LC 86-3341. 288p. (gr. 6 up). 1987. pap. 2.95 (ISBN 0-689-71152-2, Collier Young Ad). Macmillan Child Grp.
Corbett, Scott. The Lemonade Trick. Galdone, Paul, illus. (gr. 4-6). 1972. lib. bdg. 14.95 (ISBN 0-316-15694-9, Joy St Bks). Little.
Crawford, Charles. Split Time. LC 87-184. 224p. (gr. 7 up). 1987. 12.95 (ISBN 0-06-021324-8); PLB 12.89 (ISBN 0-06-021380-9). HarpC Child Bks.
Cross, Gillian. Roscoe's Leap. LC 87-45328. 160p. (gr. 7 up). 1987. 13.95 (ISBN 0-8234-0669-5). Holiday.
Crutcher, Chris. The Crazy Horse Electric Game. LC 86-14592. 160p. (gr. 7 up). 1987. 10.25 (ISBN 0-688-06683-6). Greenwillow.
Cummings, Pat. Clean Your Room, Harvey Moon! Cummings, Pat, illus. LC 89-23863. 32p. (ps-2). 1991. RSBE 13.95 (ISBN 0-02-725511-5, Bradbury Pr). Macmillan Child Grp.
Curry, Jane L. Me, Myself & I. LC 87-2681. 160p. (gr. 7 up). 1987. 13.95 (ISBN 0-689-50429-2, M K McElderry). Macmillan Child Grp.
Dahl, Roald. Boy. (Illus.). 160p. (gr. 9-12). Date not set. pap. 4.95 (ISBN 0-685-32894-5, Penguin Bks). Viking Penguin.
—Boy: Tales of Childhood. LC 85-117335. (Illus.). 176p. (gr. 3 up). 1984. 13.95 (ISBN 0-374-37374-4); ltd. ed. 30.00 (ISBN 0-374-37375-2). FS&G.
—Boy: Tales of Childhood. (gr. 4-6). 1986. pap. 4.95 (ISBN 0-14-031890-9, Puffin). Puffin Bks.
—Charlie & Chocolate Factory, Vol. 1. (gr. 4-7). 1977. pap. 2.75 (ISBN 0-553-15248-3). Bantam.
—Charlie & the Chocolate Factory. 176p. (ps up). 1988. pap. 3.95 (ISBN 0-14-032869-6, Puffin). Puffin Bks.
—Charlie & the Chocolate Factory. large type ed. 174p. 1989. Repr. of 1964 ed. 13.95 (ISBN 1-55736-154-1, Crnrstn Bks). ABC CLIO.
—Charlie & the Chocolate Factory: A Play. George, Richard R., adapted by. 320p. (gr. 3-7). 1983. pap. 3.50 (ISBN 0-14-031125-4, Puffin). Puffin Bks.
—Charlie & the Great Glass Elevator. 176p. 1988. pap. 3.95 (ISBN 0-14-032870-X, Puffin). Puffin Bks.
—Charlie & the Great Glass Elevator: The Further Adventures of Charlie Bucket & Willie Wonka, the Chocolate-Maker Extraordinaire. Schindelman, Joseph, illus. (gr. k-7). 1972. 15.00 (ISBN 0-394-82472-5); lib. bdg. 13.99 (ISBN 0-394-92472-X). Knopf.
—Charlie y la Fabrica de Chocolate. (SPA.). 7.95 (ISBN 0-685-31016-7). Santillana.
—Danny & the Champion of the World. 208p. 1988. pap. 3.95 (ISBN 0-14-032873-4, Puffin). Puffin Bks.
—James & the Giant Peach. 112p. 1988. pap. 3.95 (ISBN 0-14-032871-8, Puffin). Puffin Bks.
—James & the Giant Peach. large type ed. (gr. 4-7). 1990. 14.95 (ISBN 1-55736-155-X, Crnrstn Bks). ABC-CLIO.
—James & the Giant Peach. 128p. 1990. Repr. lib. bdg. 19.95x (ISBN 0-89966-702-3). Buccaneer Bks.
—James & the Giant Peach: A Play. 128p. (gr. 3-7). 1983. pap. 3.50 (ISBN 0-14-031464-4, Puffin). Puffin Bks.
—The Wonderful Story of Henry Sugar & Six More. large type, rev. ed. 280p. 1990. PLB 14.95 (ISBN 1-85089-984-3, Crnrstn Bks). ABC-CLIO.
Dana, Barbara. Necessary Parties. LC 85-45267. 352p. (gr. 7 up). 1986. 14.95 (ISBN 0-06-021408-2); PLB 14.89 (ISBN 0-06-021409-0). HarpC Child Bks.
—Zucchini. Christelow, Eileen, illus. LC 80-8448. 128p. (gr. 3-6). 1982. 12.95 (ISBN 0-06-021394-9); PLB 12.89 (ISBN 0-06-021395-7). HarpC Child Bks.
Davoll, Barbara. A Pack of Lies. Hockerman, Dennis, illus. 24p. 1989. pap. 5.99 (ISBN 0-89693-497-7); cassette 8.99 (ISBN 0-89693-030-0). Victor Bks.
Delacre, Lulu. Nathan & Nicholas Alexander. Delacre, Lulu, illus. 32p. (Orig.). (gr. k-3). 1986. pap. 2.50 (ISBN 0-590-41573-5). Scholastic Inc.
Delaney, Michael. Not Your Average Joe. Burke, Chris, illus. 160p. (gr. 4-6). 1990. 12.95 (ISBN 0-525-44538-2, DCB). Dutton Child Bks.
Delton, Judy. I Never Win! Gilchrist, Cathy, illus. LC 80-27618. 32p. (gr. k-4). 1981. PLB 9.95 (ISBN 0-87614-139-4). Carolrhoda Bks.
—Lucky Dog Days. 80p. (gr. k-3). 1988. pap. 2.99 (ISBN 0-440-40063-5, YB). Dell.
—That Mushy Stuff. (Orig.). (gr. k-6). 1989. pap. 2.75 (ISBN 0-440-40176-3, YB). Dell.
Demi. Watch Harry Grow! Demi, illus. LC 84-60109. 26p. (ps-1). 1984. bds. 3.50 (ISBN 0-394-86857-9, Pub. by BYR). Random.
Denzel, Justin. Boy of the Painted Cave. 160p. (gr. 3-7). 1988. 13.95 (ISBN 0-399-21559-X, Philomel Bks). Putnam Pub Group.
DePaola, Tomie. Michael Bird Boy. LC 74-23563. (Illus.). 32p. (gr. k-4). 1987. PLB 12.95 (ISBN 0-671-66468-9); pap. 5.95 (ISBN 0-671-66469-7). S&S Trade.
—Oliver Button Is a Sissy. DePaola, Tomie, illus. (ps-3). 1990. pap. 4.95 (ISBN 0-317-99897-8). HarbraceJ.
Derwent, Lavinia. The Boy from Sula. 158p. (gr. 5-7). 1989. pap. 5.95 (ISBN 0-86241-111-4, Pub. by Cnngt Pub Ltd). Trafalgar Sq.
Dickens, Frank. Albert Herbert Hawkins: The Naughtiest Boy in the World. Dickens, Frank, illus. LC 72-149044. 32p. (ps-3). 7.95 (ISBN 0-87592-000-4). Scroll Pr.
Dickinson, Mary. Alex & Roy. Firmin, Charlotte, illus. 32p. (ps-2). 1982. 9.95 (ISBN 0-233-97347-8). Andre Deutsch.
Diggle, Giles. Inside the Glasshouse. 218p. (gr. 3-6). 1991. 15.95 (ISBN 0-571-14280-X). Faber & Faber.
Diggs, Lucy. Everyday Friends. (gr. 5 up). 1987. pap. 2.95 (ISBN 0-8167-1047-3). Troll Assocs.
—Moon in the Water. LC 87-19310. 240p. (gr. 6 up). 1988. 14.95 (ISBN 0-689-31337-3, Atheneum Child Bk). Macmillan Child Grp.
Dinan, Carolyn. Ben's Brand New Glasses. (Illus.). 32p. (gr. 1-4). 1987. laminated boards 10.95 (ISBN 0-571-14567-1). Faber & Faber.
Dinardo, Jeffrey. Timothy & the Big Bully. Dinardo, Jeffrey, illus. 32p. (ps-3). 1988. pap. 5.95 (ISBN 0-671-66562-6). S&S Trade.
—Timothy & the Night Noises. LC 86-9383. 1990. 11.95 (ISBN 0-671-66807-2); pap. 2.25 (ISBN 0-671-70298-X). S&S Trade.
Dini, Gary. The Heart That Followed Me Home. (Illus.). 32p. (gr. 2-5). 1983. pap. 1.95 (ISBN 0-8091-6548-1). Paulist Pr.
Dixon, Franklin W. The Masked Monkey. (Illus.). 196p. (gr. 5-9). 1972. 4.50 (ISBN 0-448-08951-3, G&D). Putnam Pub Group.
Donovan, John. Wild in the World. LC 74-159044. (gr. 5 up). 1971. PLB 12.89 (ISBN 0-06-021702-2). HarpC Child Bks.
Dorros, Arthur. Splash, Splash. Dorros, Arthur, illus. LC 87-47541. 12p. (ps-1). 1987. 2.95 (ISBN 0-694-00188-0, Crowell Jr Bks). HarpC Child Bks.
Drescher, Joan. Max & Rufus. Drescher, Joan, illus. (gr. k-3). 1982. write for info. HM.
Dubowski, Cathy E. Cave Boy. Dubowski, Mark, illus. LC 87-23427. 32p. (ps-1). 1988. lib. bdg. 6.99 (ISBN 0-394-99571-6, Random Juv); pap. 2.95 (ISBN 0-394-89571-1). Random.
Duckett, Gary. The Return of Talatu'u. LC 86-40285. 150p. (gr. 4-6). 1987. 7.95 (ISBN 1-55523-022-9). Winston-Derek.
Duder, Tessa. In Lane Three, Alex Archer. 180p. (gr. 5-9). 1989. 13.95 (ISBN 0-395-50927-0). HM.
Duffer, Betsy. The Math Wiz. (gr. 4-7). 1990. 11.95 (ISBN 0-670-83422-X). Viking Child Bks.
Duggan, Maurice. Falter Tom & the Water Boy. Rowell, Kenneth, illus. LC 59-12200. (gr. 3-6). 1959. 18.95 (ISBN 0-87599-027-4). S G Phillips.
Edens, Cooper. The Story Cloud. Grant, Kenneth L., illus. 48p. (ps-1). 1991. jacketed, reinforced bdg. 16.00 (ISBN 0-671-74823-8, Green Tiger). S&S Trade.
Eige, Lillian. Cady. Wentworth, Janet, illus. LC 85-45818. 192p. (gr. 3-7). 1987. PLB 11.89 (ISBN 0-06-021793-6). HarpC Child Bks.
Ethridge, Kenneth. Toothpick. 128p. (gr. 7 up). pap. 2.50 (ISBN 0-8167-1316-2). Troll Assocs.
Ets, Marie H. In the Forest. (Illus.). (ps-2). 1976. pap. 3.95 (ISBN 0-14-050180-0, Puffin). Puffin Bks.
—Just Me. (Illus.). (gr. k-2). 1978. pap. 3.95 (ISBN 0-14-050325-0, Puffin). Puffin Bks.
Evans, Shirlee. Tree Tall & the Horse Race. Ponter, James, illus. LC 86-7659. 136p. (Orig.). (gr. 3-8). 1986. pap. 3.95 (ISBN 0-8361-3414-1). Herald Pr.
Farjeon, Eleanor. Jim at the Corner. Ardizzone, Edward, illus. LC 74-163251. 112p. (gr. 2-5). 1990. pap. 2.95 (ISBN 0-394-82583-7). McKay.
Fassler, Joan. The Man of the House. Landa, Peter, illus. LC 73-80122. 32p. (ps-3). 1975. 16.95 (ISBN 0-87705-010-4). Human Sci Pr.
Fenner, Carol. Randall's Wall. LC 90-46490. 96p. (gr. 4-7). 1991. SBE 11.95 (ISBN 0-689-50518-3, M K McElderry). Macmillan Child Grp.
Fenton, Edward. Duffy's Rocks. (gr. k-12). 1989. pap. 3.25 (ISBN 0-440-20242-6, LFL). Dell.
Feuer, Elizabeth. One Friend to Another. LC 87-45363. 192p. (gr. 6 up). 1987. 12.95 (ISBN 0-374-35642-4). FS&G.
Fitzgerald, John D. The Great Brain Does It Again. Mayer, Mercer, illus. LC 74-18600. (gr. 4-7). 1975. 12.95 (ISBN 0-8037-5065-X); PLB 11.89 (ISBN 0-8037-5066-8). Dial Bks Young.
—The Great Brain Reforms. 176p. (gr. k-6). 1975. pap. 3.25 (ISBN 0-440-44841-7, YB). Dell.
—The Great Brain Reforms. LC 72-7601. (Illus.). 176p. (gr. 4-7). 1973. 12.95 (ISBN 0-8037-3067-5); PLB 11.89 (ISBN 0-8037-3068-3). Dial Bks Young.
—Me & My Little Brain. Mayer, Mercer, illus. LC 71-153732. (gr. 4-7). 1985. 12.95 (ISBN 0-8037-5531-7); PLB 11.89 (ISBN 0-8037-5532-5). Dial Bks Young.
—The Return of the Great Brain. 180p. (gr. 3-5). 1975. pap. 2.95 (ISBN 0-440-45941-9, YB). Dell.
Fleischman, Sid. The Whipping Boy. Sis, Peter, illus. (gr. 2-5). 1987. pap. 2.95 (ISBN 0-8167-1038-4). Troll Assocs.
Fosburgh, Liza. Mrs. Abercorn & the Bunce Boys. Downing, Julie, illus. LC 85-29266. 144p. (gr. 7 up). 1986. 12.95 (ISBN 0-02-735460-1, Four Winds). Macmillan Child Grp.
—Mrs. Abercorn & the Bunce Boys. 128p. (gr. k-6). 1989. pap. 2.75 (ISBN 0-440-40154-2, YB). Dell.
Fox, Paula. A Likely Place. Ardizzone, Edward, illus. LC 87-5542. 64p. (gr. 2-6). 1987. Repr. 11.95 (ISBN 0-02-735761-9, Mcmillan Child Bk). Macmillan Child Grp.
—Maurice's Room. Fetz, Ingrid, illus. LC 87-19504. 64p. (gr. 2-6). 1988. pap. 3.95 (ISBN 0-689-71216-2, Aladdin). Macmillan Child Grp.
—Portrait of Ivan. Lambert, Saul, illus. LC 87-1109. 144p. (gr. 6-8). 1987. pap. 3.95 (ISBN 0-689-71167-0, Aladdin). Macmillan Child Grp.
—The Stone-Faced Boy. LC 86-22204. 112p. (gr. 4-6). 1987. pap. 3.95 (ISBN 0-689-71127-1, Aladdin). Macmillan Child Grp.
Freedman, Florence B. Brothers. Parker, Robert A., illus. LC 85-42616. 40p. (gr. k-3). 1985. PLB 11.89 (ISBN 0-06-021872-X). HarpC Child Bks.
French, Michael. Soldier Boy. (gr. 7 up). 1990. pap. 2.95 (ISBN 0-553-28609-X, Starfire). Bantam.
Fujikawa, Gyo. Sam's All-Wrong Day. Fujikawa, Gyo, illus. LC 82-80869. 32p. (Orig.). (gr. k-2). 1982. 3.95 (ISBN 0-448-11755-X, G&D). Putnam Pub Group.
Gackenbach, Dick. Harry & the Terrible Whatzit. Gackenbach, Dick, illus. LC 76-40205. 32p. (ps-3). 1984. pap. 4.95 (ISBN 0-89919-223-8, Pub. byClarion). Ticknor & Fields.
Garden, Nancy. Mystery of the Secret Marks. 192p. (gr. 3 up). 1989. 13.95 (ISBN 0-374-35021-3). FS&G.
Garfield, Leon. Jack Holborn. Maitland, Anthony, illus. (gr. 7 up). 1965. (Random Juv); PLB 5.99 (ISBN 0-685-04259-6). Random.
Geller, Mark. Raymond. LC 87-45282. 128p. (gr. 5-8). 1988. 11.95 (ISBN 0-06-022206-9); PLB 11.89 (ISBN 0-06-022207-7). HarpC Child Bks.
George, Jean C. Water Sky. George, Jean C., illus. LC 86-45496. 224p. (gr. 6 up). 1987. 12.95 (ISBN 0-06-022198-4); PLB 12.89 (ISBN 0-06-022199-2). HarpC Child Bks.

Gerrard, Roy. Mik's Mammoth. (Illus.). 32p. (gr. k-3). 1990. 13.95 (ISBN 0-374-31891-3). FS&G.

Giblin, James C. Chimney Sweeps. Tomes, Margot, illus. LC 81-43878. 64p. (gr. 4-8). 1982. 12.95 (ISBN 0-690-04192-6, Crowell Jr Bks); PLB 12.89 (ISBN 0-690-04193-4, Crowell Jr Bks). HarpC Child Bks.

Giff, Patricia R. Watch Out, Ronald Morgan. Natti, Susanna, illus. 32p. (gr. k-4). 1986. pap. 3.95 (ISBN 0-14-050638-1, Puffin). Puffin Bks.

Gilson, Jamie. Harvey, the Beer Can King. (Illus.). (gr. 4-6). 1988. pap. 2.50 (ISBN 0-671-67423-4, Minstrel Bks). PB.

—Hello, My Name Is Scrambled Eggs. Wallner, John, illus. (gr. 3-6). 1988. pap. 2.95 (ISBN 0-671-74104-7, Minstrel Bks). PB.

—Hobie Hanson, Greatest Hero of the Mall. Riggio, Anita, illus. LC 89-2343. 160p. (gr. 3-6). 1989. 12.95 (ISBN 0-688-08968-2). Lothrop.

—Hobie Hanson, You're Weird. LC 86-15241. 170p. (gr. 4-7). 1987. 12.95 (ISBN 0-688-06700-X). Lothrop.

—Hobie Hanson, You're Weird. Primavera, Elise, illus. 176p. (gr. 3-6). 1988. pap. 2.75 (ISBN 0-671-63971-4, Minstrel Bks). PB.

Glazier, Lyle. Summer for Joey. LC 86-63092. 256p. 1987. pap. 9.95 (ISBN 0-912395-08-7). Millers River Pub Co.

Gleason, Richard. Sprout. LC 86-51074. (Illus.). 84p. (gr. 3-8). 1987. 7.95 (ISBN 1-55523-052-0). Winston-Derek.

Golds, Cassandra. Michael & the Secret War. 208p. (gr. 4-8). 1989. 13.95 (ISBN 0-689-31507-4, Atheneum Child Bk). Macmillan Child Grp.

Gould, Deborah. Terry's Creature. Ivanov, Anatoly, illus. LC 88-13297. 32p. (gr. k-3). 1989. 13.95 (ISBN 0-688-07570-3); PLB 13.88 (ISBN 0-688-07571-1). Lothrop.

Graber, Richard. Doc. LC 85-45034. 160p. (gr. 7 up). 1986. 13.95 (ISBN 0-06-022064-3). HarpC Child Bks.

Graeber, Charlotte T. Fudge. Harness, Cheryl, illus. LC 86-7353. 128p. (gr. 1-4). 1987. 12.95 (ISBN 0-688-06735-2). Lothrop.

—Fudge. 1989. pap. 2.95 (ISBN 0-671-70288-2, Minstrel Bks). PB.

Graham, Amanda. Educating Arthur. Gynell, Donna, illus. LC 87-42756. 32p. (gr. 2-3). 1988. PLB 12.95 (ISBN 1-55532-411-8). Gareth Stevens Inc.

Graham, Bob. Bath Time for John. Graham, Bob, illus. LC 88-80588. (ps-1). 1988. 4.95 (ISBN 0-316-32304-7). Little.

—Here Comes John. Graham, Bob, illus. LC 88-80589. (ps-1). 1988. 4.95 (ISBN 0-316-32305-5). Little.

—Here Comes Theo. Graham, Bob, illus. LC 88-80590. (ps-1). 1988. 4.95 (ISBN 0-316-32307-1). Little.

Gray Boy Renegade Dog on Loose. (gr. 4-7). 1990. pap. 2.95 (ISBN 0-8167-1820-2). Troll Assocs.

Greene, Bette. Get on out of Here, Philip Hall. 144p. (gr. 4-7). 1984. pap. 2.75 (ISBN 0-440-43038-0, YB). Dell.

Greene, Constance C. Just Plain Al. (gr. k-6). 1988. pap. 2.95 (ISBN 0-440-40073-2, YB). Dell.

Greenwald, Sheila. Alvin Webster's Surefire Plan for Success (& How It Failed) Greenwald, Sheila, illus. 96p. (gr. 3-6). 1987. 12.95 (ISBN 0-316-32706-9, Joy St Bks). Little.

—Alvin Webster's Surefire Plan for Success: And How It Failed. (gr. 3-6). 1989. pap. 2.75 (ISBN 0-671-67239-8, Minstrel Bks). PB.

Gretz, Susanna. It's Your Turn, Roger! LC 84-23879. (Illus.). 32p. (ps-3). 1987. pap. 3.95 (ISBN 0-8037-0435-6). Dial Bks Young.

—Roger Loses His Marbles. Gretz, Susanna, illus. LC 88-3753. 32p. (ps-2). 1988. 11.95 (ISBN 0-8037-0565-4). Dial Bks Young.

—Roger Takes Charge! LC 86-24061. (Illus.). 32p. (ps-2). 1987. 12.95 (ISBN 0-8037-0121-7). Dial Bks Young.

—Roger Takes Charge. 1990. pap. 3.95 (ISBN 0-8037-0742-8, Dial Pied Piper). Puffin Bks.

Gripe, Maria. Elvis & His Secret. Gripe, Harald, illus. 208p. (gr. 3-7). 1979. pap. 1.50 (ISBN 0-440-42434-8, YB). Dell.

Grossmann, Cynthia L. Eric's Great Adventure. 32p. (ps-3). 1989. 6.95 (ISBN 0-8062-3581-0). Carlton.

Gutman, Bill. Smitty. (gr. 7-12). 1988. PLB 2.95 (ISBN 0-89872-301-9). Turman Pub.

Guy, Rosa. The Ups & Downs of Carl Davis III. (gr. 5 up). 1989. 13.95 (ISBN 0-385-29724-6). Delacorte.

Haas, Dorothy. The Secret Life of Dilly McBean. 208p. (gr. 3-7). 1988. pap. 2.50 (ISBN 0-590-41169-1, Apple Paperbacks). Scholastic Inc.

Hagstrom, Amy. Strong & Free. Hagstrom, Amy, illus. LC 87-3942. 24p. (gr. 1 up). 1987. PLB 12.95 (ISBN 0-933849-15-X). Landmark Edns.

Hall, Lynn. Danger Dog. LC 86-13914. 112p. (gr. 4-7). 1986. 12.95 (ISBN 0-684-18680-2, Scribners Young Read). Macmillan Child Grp.

—Danza! (gr. 5-7). 1989. pap. 3.95 (ISBN 0-689-71289-8, Aladdin). Macmillan Child Grp.

Hamilton, Dorothy. Busboys at Big Bend. Ponter, James, illus. LC 74-8689. 112p. (gr. 8-12). 1974. o. p. 4.95 (ISBN 0-8361-1744-1); pap. 3.95 (ISBN 0-8361-1745-X). Herald Pr.

Hamilton, Virginia. Junius over Far. LC 84-48344. 288p. (gr. 7 up). 1985. 12.95 (ISBN 0-06-022194-1); PLB 12.89 (ISBN 0-06-022195-X). HarpC Child Bks.

—M. C. Higgins, the Great. LC 87-6330. 288p. (gr. 7 up). 1987. pap. 3.95 (ISBN 0-02-043490-1, Collier Young Ad). Macmillan Child Grp.

Hammer, Charles. Wrong Way Ragsdale. LC 87-21250. 192p. (gr. 5 up). 1987. 12.95 (ISBN 0-374-38657-9). FS&G.

Hamsa, Bobbie. Fast Draw Freddie: Rookie Readers. LC 83-23931. (Illus.). 32p. (ps-2). 1984. lib. bdg. 11.93 (ISBN 0-516-02046-3); pap. 2.95 (ISBN 0-516-42046-1). Childrens.

Handler, Kalindi. The Boy Behind the Counter. 160p. (Orig.). (gr. 7 up). 1989. pap. 2.50 (ISBN 0-380-75646-3, Flare). Avon.

Hannam, Charles. A Boy in Your Situation. 216p. (gr. 7-9). 1989. pap. 9.95 (ISBN 0-233-98279-5, Pub. by A Deutsch England). Trafalgar Sq.

Harrell, John. Here Comes Maurice: A Musical for One Puppet. (Illus.). 15p. (gr. 6 up). 1987. Incls. cassette. pap. 10.95 (ISBN 0-9615389-6-1). York Hse.

Haseley, Dennis. My Father Doesn't Know about the Woods & Me. Hays, Michael, illus. LC 87-30295. 32p. (gr. 1-3). 1988. 13.95 (ISBN 0-689-31365-9, Atheneum Child Bk). Macmillan Child Grp.

Hastings. Rufus & Christopher Series, 3 vols. (Illus.). (gr. 2-4). Set. PLB 29.95 (ISBN 0-87783-168-8); Set. pap. 11.82 deluxe edition (ISBN 0-87783-169-6); cassettes 23.82x (ISBN 0-87783-234-X). Oddo.

Haugaard, Erik C. A Boy's Will. Howell, Troy, illus. LC 83-83. 48p. (gr. 2-5). 1983. 13.95 (ISBN 0-395-33227-3). HM.

—A Boy's Will. (gr. 4-7). 1990. pap. 4.95 (ISBN 0-395-54962-0). HM.

—Cromwell's Boy. (gr. 4-7). 1990. pap. 4.95 (ISBN 0-395-54975-2). HM.

Hautzig, Deborah. Grover's Lucky Jacket. Chartier, Normand, illus. LC 89-30102. 40p. (ps-3). 1989. PLB 6.99 (ISBN 0-679-90077-2); pap. 4.95 (ISBN 0-679-80077-8). Random.

Hawes, Louise. Nelson Malone Meets the Man from Mush-Nut. (gr. 3-7). 1988. pap. 2.50 (ISBN 0-380-70508-7, Camelot). Avon.

Haywood, Carolyn. Eddie's Menagerie. (gr. 2-4). 1987. pap. 2.95 (ISBN 0-8167-1042-2). Troll Assocs.

Heide, Florence P. The Problem with Pulcifer. LC 81-48606. (Illus.). 64p. (gr. 3-6). 1982. PLB 12.89 (ISBN 0-397-32002-7, Lipp Jr Bks). HarpC Child Bks.

Henry, Marguerite. An Innkeeper's Horse. Dennis, Wesley, illus. 24p. (ps-3). 1988. pap. 1.95 (ISBN 0-02-688805-X). Checkerboard Pr.

Herlihy, Dirlie. Ludie's Song. LC 87-30305. 224p. (gr. 5 up). 1988. 14.95 (ISBN 0-8037-0533-6). Dial Bks Young.

Herman, Ben. The Rhapsody in Blue of Mickey Klein. LC 80-28201. 144p. (gr. 7 up). 1981. 8.95 (ISBN 0-916144-68-2). Stemmer Hse.

Hermes, Patricia. Kevin Corbett Eats Flies. Newsom, Carol, illus. LC 85-27086. 160p. (gr. 4-6). 1986. 13.95 (ISBN 0-15-242290-0, HJ). Harbracej.

Hernandez, Betsy, et al. The Boy Who Wanted the Moon. Hilliard, Cindy & French, Marty, illus. 26p. (ps up). 1986. Book & Cassette. 7.95 (ISBN 1-55578-100-4); cass. incl. Worlds Wonder.

Herold, Ann B. The Hard Life of Seymour E. Newton. 96p. (Orig.). (gr. 2-5). 1990. pap. 5.95 (ISBN 0-8361-3532-6). Herald Pr.

Hickey, Tony. Joe in the Middle. 205p. 1988. pap. 5.95 (ISBN 1-85371-021-0, Pub. by Poolbeg Press Ltd Eire). Dufour.

—Spike & the Professor. Ballagh, Robert, illus. LC 89-51005. 160p. (Orig.). (gr. 4-7). 1989. pap. 5.95 (ISBN 1-85371-039-3, Pub. by Poolbeg Press Ltd Eire). Dufour.

Highwater, Jamake. Eyes of Darkness. LC 82-187. 192p. (gr. 6 up). 1985. 13.00 (ISBN 0-688-41993-3). Lothrop.

Hill, Douglas. Blade of the Poisoner. LC 87-3904. 128p. (gr. 7 up). 1987. 13.95 (ISBN 0-689-50418-7, M K McElderry). Macmillan Child Grp.

Hill, Fred D. Christopher & Cumulus Cloud. Young, Elaine & Hill, Charlotte, eds. Rhiney, Sharon, illus. LC 90-80285. 31p. (Orig.). (gr. k-4). 1990. pap. 5.95 (ISBN 0-9620182-1-X). Charill Pubs.

Hiller, B. B. The Karate Kid. 144p. (Orig.). (gr. 7 up). 1984. (Point); 1.25 (ISBN 0-590-40671-X). Scholastic Inc.

—The Karate Kid, Pt. III. Kamen, Robert M., contrib. by. 96p. (gr. 3 up). 1989. pap. 2.95 (ISBN 0-590-43042-4). Scholastic Inc.

Hilts, Len. Timmy O-Dowd & the Big Ditch: A Story of the Glory Days on the Old Erie Canal. 144p. (gr. 3 up). 1988. 13.95 (ISBN 0-15-200606-0, Gulliver Bks). HarBraceJ.

Hines, Anna G. Boys Are Yucko! Lincoln, Pat H., illus. LC 88-18821. 160p. (gr. 5 up). 1989. 12.95 (ISBN 0-525-44344-4, 01160-350, DCB). Dutton Child Bks.

Hoban, Lillian. Arthur's Funny Money. Hoban, Lillian, illus. LC 80-7903. 64p. (gr. k-3). 1984. incl. cassette 5.98 (ISBN 0-694-00173-2, Trophy); pap. 3.50 (ISBN 0-06-444048-6, Trophy). HarpC Child Bks.

—Arthur's Halloween Costume. LC 83-49465. (Illus.). 64p. (gr. k-3). 1986. pap. 3.50 (ISBN 0-06-444101-6, Trophy). HarpC Child Bks.

—Arthur's Loose Tooth. Hoban, Lillian, illus. LC 85-42611. 64p. (ps-3). 1985. 11.95 (ISBN 0-06-022353-7); PLB 11.89 (ISBN 0-06-022354-5). HarpC Child Bks.

Hochman, Doris Z. Kid Koala's Fun Book. Hochman, Doris Z., illus. 44p. (gr. 2-5). 1991. wkbk. 6.95 (ISBN 1-878070-00-2). Three Elves Pr.

Hofmann, Ginnie. Who Wants an Old Teddy Bear? Hofmann, Ginnie, illus. LC 80-10445. 32p. (ps-3). 1980. lib. bdg. 5.99 (ISBN 0-394-93925-5); pap. 2.25 (ISBN 0-394-83925-0). Random.

Holabird, Katharine. Alexander & the Dragon. Craig, Helen, illus. 24p. (ps-2). 1988. 11.95 (ISBN 0-517-56996-5, C N Potter Bks). Crown.

Holland, Isabelle. The Man Without a Face. LC 71-37736. 160p. (gr. 7 up). 1987. pap. 2.95 (ISBN 0-06-447028-8, Trophy). HarpC Child Bks.

Homes, A. M. Jack. LC 89-31061. 208p. (gr. 7 up). 1989. 13.95 (ISBN 0-02-744831-2, Mcmillan Child Bk). Macmillan Child Grp.

Honeycutt, Natalie. The Best-Laid Plans of Jonah Twist. LC 88-7288. 128p. (gr. 3-5). 1988. 12.95 (ISBN 0-02-744850-9, Bradbury Pr). Macmillan Child Grp.

—The Best-Laid Plans of Jonah Twist. 128p. (gr. 2). 1990. pap. 2.95 (ISBN 0-380-70762-4, Camelot). Avon.

Hooks, William H. Mr. Bubble Gum, Level 3. Meisel, Paul, illus. pap. 3.50 (ISBN 0-317-99647-9). Bantam.

—Mr. Bubblegum-Bank Street. (ps-3). 1989. pap. 3.50 (ISBN 0-553-34694-6). Bantam.

—Mr Bubble Gum: Level 3. Meisel, Paul, illus. 1989. 9.99 (ISBN 0-553-05834-7). Bantam.

Horenstein, Henry. Sam Goes Trucking. Horenstein, Henry, illus. (ps-3). 1989. 14.95 (ISBN 0-395-44313-X). HM.

Horenstein, Henry, photos by. Mike Goes Trucking. 1988. write for info. HM.

Hort, Lenny. The Boy Who Held Back the Sea. Locker, Thomas, illus. LC 86-32893. 1987. 15.00 (ISBN 0-8037-0406-2); PLB 14.89 (ISBN 0-8037-0407-0). Dial Bks Young.

Horwitz, Joshua. Only Birds & Angels Fly. LC 85-42632. 192p. (gr. 7 up). 1985. PLB 12.89 (ISBN 0-06-022599-8). HarpC Child Bks.

Howe, E. W. The Moonlight Boy. 1988. Repr. of 1886 ed. lib. bdg. 59.00x (ISBN 0-317-90821-9). Reprint Servs.

Hoye, David. Domino Tommy & His Magna-Cruiser. McEntee, Steve, illus. 20p. (Orig.). (gr. 3). 1989. pap. 2.95 plastic paper (ISBN 0-317-94120-8). Kidzco Pub.

Hudson, Wade, et al. Jamal's Busy Day. Ford, George, illus. 24p. (gr. 1-3). 1991. lib. bdg. 6.95; pap. write for info. (ISBN 0-940975-24-6). Just Us Bks.

Hughes, Dean. Family Pose. LC 88-28501. 192p. (gr. 3-7). 1989. 13.95 (ISBN 0-689-31396-9, Atheneum Child Bk). Macmillan Child Grp.

—Nutty Knows All. LC 88-886. 160p. (gr. 3-7). 1988. 12.95 (ISBN 0-689-31410-8, Atheneum Child Bk). Macmillan Child Grp.

—Theo Zephyr. LC 86-28885. 128p. (gr. 4-8). 1987. 12.95 (ISBN 0-689-31345-4, Atheneum Child Bk). Macmillan Child Grp.

Hughes, Thomas. Tom Brown's School Days. Andrew, C., intro. by. (gr. 7 up). 1968. pap. 1.95 (ISBN 0-8049-0174-0, CL-174). Airmont.

—Tom Brown's Schooldays. 288p. (gr. 4-6). 1984. pap. 2.25 (ISBN 0-14-035022-5, Puffin). Puffin Bks.

Hurd, Edith T. Johnny Lion's Book. Hurd, Clement, illus. LC 65-14490. 64p. (gr. k-3). 1985. pap. 3.50 (ISBN 0-06-444074-5, Trophy). HarpC Child Bks.

Hurwitz, Johanna. Aldo Applesauce. Wallner, John, illus. 128p. (gr. 3-5). 1989. pap. 3.95 (ISBN 0-14-034083-1, Puffin). Puffin Bks.

—Aldo Ice Cream. Wallner, John, illus. 128p. (gr. 3-7). 1989. pap. 3.95 (ISBN 0-14-034084-X, Puffin). Puffin Bks.

—Much Ado about Aldo. Wallner, John, illus. 96p. (gr. 3-7). 1989. pap. 3.95 (ISBN 0-14-034082-3, Puffin). Puffin Bks.

—Rip-Roaring Russell. Hoban, Lillian, illus. LC 83-1019. 96p. (ps-1). 1983. 12.95 (ISBN 0-688-02347-9); lib. bdg. 12.88 (ISBN 0-688-02348-7, Morrow Jr Bks). Morrow Jr Bks.

—Rip-Roarring Russell. Hoban, Lillian, illus. 96p. (gr. 2-5). 1989. pap. 3.95 (ISBN 0-14-032939-0, Puffin). Puffin Bks.

—Russell Rides Again. Hoban, Lillian, illus. 96p. (gr. 2-5). 1989. pap. 3.95 (ISBN 0-14-032941-2, Puffin). Puffin Bks.

—Russell Sprouts. Hoban, Lillian, illus. LC 87-5494. 80p. (ps-2). 1987. 12.95 (ISBN 0-688-07165-1); lib. bdg. 12.88 (ISBN 0-688-07166-X, Morrow Jr Bks). Morrow Jr Bks.

—Russell Sprouts. Hoban, Lillian, illus. 80p. (gr. 2-5). 1989. pap. 3.95 (ISBN 0-14-032942-0, Puffin). Puffin Bks.

Hutchins, Hazel. The Three & Many Wishes of Jason Reid. Tennent, Julie, illus. (gr. 1-4). 1988. 10.95 (ISBN 0-317-69255-0). Viking Penguin.

Hutchins, Pat. You'll Soon Grow into Them, Titch. Hutchins, Pat, illus. LC 82-11755. 32p. (gr. k-3). 1983. 14.95 (ISBN 0-688-01770-3); PLB 14.88 (ISBN 0-688-01771-1). Greenwillow.

Ibbitson, John. The Wimp. 96p. 1986. pap. text ed. 4.50 (ISBN 0-8219-0237-7, 35358); wkbk. 1.20 (ISBN 0-8219-0238-5, 35721). EMC.

Jackson, Alison. My Brother, the Star. 1990. 12.95 (ISBN 0-525-44512-9, DCB). Dutton Child Bks.

Jander, Martha. Philip & the Ethiopian. (Illus.). 24p. (gr. k-4). 1990. pap. 1.39 (ISBN 0-570-09024-5, 59-1447). Concordia.

Jefferies, Richard. Bevis. 384p. (gr. 4-6). 1984. pap. 2.25 (ISBN 0-14-035026-8, Puffin). Puffin Bks.

Johnson, Crockett. A Picture for Harold's Room. Johnson, Crockett, illus. LC 60-6372. 64p. (ps-3). 1985. pap. 3.50 (ISBN 0-06-444085-0, Trophy). HarpC Child Bks.

Johnson, Phyllis. The Boy Toy. Shiffman, Lena, illus. 32p. (gr. k-3). 1988. pap. 5.95 (ISBN 0-914996-26-6). Lollipop Power.

Jones, Diana W. Eight Days of Luke. LC 88-220. 160p. (gr. 7 up). 1988. Repr. of 1975 ed. 11.95 (ISBN 0-688-08006-5). Greenwillow.

—The Lives of Christopher Chant. LC 87-24540. (gr. 7 up). 1988. 11.95 (ISBN 0-688-07806-0). Greenwillow.

—The Lives of Christopher Chant. LC 87-24540. 240p. (gr. 4-7). 1990. pap. 3.50 (ISBN 0-394-82205-6). McKay.

Jones, Rebecca. Germy Blew It. 112p. (gr. 2-9). pap. 2.95 (ISBN 0-8167-1314-6). Troll Assocs.

Jones, Rebecca C. Germy Blew It Again. LC 88-22696. 128p. (gr. 3-6). 1988. 13.95 (ISBN 0-8050-0905-1). H Holt & Co.

Josephs, Anna C. Mountain Boy. LC 85-12238. (Illus.). 32p. (gr. 2-4). 1985. PLB 16.67 (ISBN 0-940742-51-9). Raintree Pubs.

Joy, Flora. Barry & the Three Golden Locks. 48p. (gr. k-4). 1988. wkbk. 5.95 (ISBN 0-86653-456-3, GA1059). Good Apple.

Joyce, William. George Shrinks. Joyce, William, illus. LC 83-47697. 32p. (ps-2). 1987. pap. 3.95 (ISBN 0-06-443129-0, Trophy). HarpC Child Bks.

Kaplan, Lee. Four Eyes. LC 90-71708. 44p. (gr. 1-3). 1991. write for info. Winston-Derek.

Kaplan, Marjorie. Henry & the Boy Who Thought Numbers Were Fleas. Chang, Heidi, illus. LC 90-43852. 64p. (gr. 2-4). 1991. SBE 12.95 (ISBN 0-02-749351-2, Four Winds). Macmillan Child Grp.

Keats, Ezra J. Goggles! Keats, Ezra J., illus. LC 86-28718. 40p. (gr. k-3). 1987. pap. 4.95 (ISBN 0-689-71157-3, Aladdin). Macmillan Child Grp.

—Pet Show! Keats, Ezra J., illus. LC 86-17225. 40p. (gr. k-3). 1987. pap. 4.50 (ISBN 0-689-71159-X, Aladdin). Macmillan Child Grp.

—Peter's Chair. LC 67-4816. (Illus.). 32p. (ps-3). 1983. pap. 4.95 (ISBN 0-06-443040-5, Trophy). HarpC Child Bks.

—The Snowy Day. (Illus.). (ps-k). 1976. pap. 3.95 (ISBN 0-14-050182-7, Puffin). Puffin Bks.

Kemp, Gene. I Can't Stand Losing. 112p. (gr. 7 up). 1987. 9.95 (ISBN 0-571-14773-9). Faber & Faber.

Kennedy, Richard. The Boxcar at the Center of the Universe. Kronen, Jeff, illus. LC 81-47718. 96p. (gr. 6 up). 1982. PLB 11.89 (ISBN 0-06-023187-4). HarpC Child Bks.

Kennedy, William. Charlie Malarkey & the Belly Button Machine. (ps-3). 1990. pap. 4.95 (ISBN 0-14-054239-6, Puffin). Puffin Bks.

Kent, Jack. Joey Runs Away. LC 85-3673. (Illus.). 32p. (gr. k-4). 1989. PLB 12.95 (ISBN 0-671-66461-1); pap. 5.95 (ISBN 0-671-67936-8). S&S Trade.

Kerr, M. E. Dinky Hocker Shoots Smack. LC 72-80366. 208p. (gr. 7 up). 1989. pap. 2.95 (ISBN 0-06-447006-7, Trophy). HarpC Child Bks.

—Fell. LC 86-45776. 160p. (gr. 7 up). 1987. 12.95 (ISBN 0-06-023267-6); PLB 12.89 (ISBN 0-06-023268-4). HarpC Child Bks.

—I Stay Near You. LC 84-48342. 192p. (gr. 7 up). 1985. PLB 12.89 (ISBN 0-06-023105-X). HarpC Child Bks.

Killien, Christi. Rusty Fertlanger, Lady's Man. LC 87-31001. 144p. (gr. 5-9). 1988. 12.95 (ISBN 0-395-46762-4). HM.

King, Christopher. The Boy Who Ate the Moon. Wallner, John, illus. 32p. (ps-2). 1988. PLB 14.95 (ISBN 0-399-21459-3, Philomel Bks). Putnam Pub Group.

King, Larry L. Because of Lozo Brown. Schwartz, Amy, illus. LC 88-3952. (ps-3). 1988. 11.95 (ISBN 0-670-81031-2). Viking Child Bks.

Klein, Norma. No More Saturday Nights. LC 88-678. 288p. (gr. 7 up). 1988. 12.95 (ISBN 0-394-81944-6); lib. bdg. 13.99 (ISBN 0-394-91944-0). Knopf.

—Robbie & the Leap Year Blues. (gr. 3-7). 1990. 3.25 (ISBN 0-394-82305-2, Bullseye Bks). Knopf.

Kline, Susan. Horrible Harry & the Green Slime. Remkiewicz, Frank, illus. 64p. (gr. 2-5). 1989. pap. 10.95 (ISBN 0-670-82468-2). Viking Child Bks.

Kline, Suzy. Herbie Jones. Williams, Richard, illus. LC 84-24915. 96p. (gr. 2-6). 1985. 12.95 (ISBN 0-399-21183-7, Putnam). Putnam Pub Group.

—Horrible Harry & the Ant Invasion. Remkiewicz, Frank, illus. 64p. (gr. 2-5). 1989. pap. 10.95 (ISBN 0-670-82469-0). Viking Child Bks.

—What's the Matter with Herbie Jones? Williams, Richard, illus. (gr. 3-7). pap. 3.95 (ISBN 0-317-62246-3, Puffin). Puffin Bks.

Klingsheim, Arild. Julius. (gr. 4-7). 1991. pap. 4.95 (ISBN 0-440-40431-2). Dell.

Knowles, Tizzie. No, Barnaby. Knowles, Tizzie, illus. 24p. (ps). 1988. 7.95 (ISBN 0-233-98191-8). Andre Deutsch.

Koff, Richard M. Christopher. 160p. 1985. pap. text ed. 2.25 (ISBN 0-553-15363-3). Bantam.

Komaiko, Leah. Earl's Too Cool for Me. Cornell, Laura, illus. LC 87-30803. 40p. (gr. k-3). 1988. 12.95 (ISBN 0-06-023281-1); PLB 12.89 (ISBN 0-06-023282-X). HarpC Child Bks.

Korman, Gordon. I Want to Go Home! 192p. (Orig.). (gr. 3-7). 1991. pap. 2.95 (ISBN 0-590-44210-4). Scholastic Inc.

Kraus, Robert. Herman the Helper. Aruego, Jose & Dewey, Ariane, illus. LC 73-9319. (ps). 1987. pap. 10.95 (ISBN 0-671-66887-0); pap. 5.95 (ISBN 0-671-66270-8). S&S Trade.

—Leo the Late Bloomer. Reissue. ed. Aruego, Jose, illus. LC 70-159154. 32p. (gr. k-3). 1971. 13.95 (ISBN 0-87807-042-7, Crowell Jr Bks); PLB 12.89 (ISBN 0-87807-043-5). HarpC Child Bks.

Krensky, Stephen. Lionel in the Fall. Natti, Susanna, illus. LC 86-32876. 48p. (ps-3). 1987. 9.95 (ISBN 0-8037-0384-8); PLB 9.89 (ISBN 0-8037-0385-6). Dial Bks Young.

Kroll, Steven. One Tough Turkey. Wallner, John, illus. LC 82-2925. 32p. (ps-3). 1982. reinforced bdg. 13.95 (ISBN 0-8234-0457-9). Holiday.

Kropp, Paul. Death Ride. Ruhl, Greg, illus. LC 88-11460. 96p. (Orig.). (gr. 5 up). 1989. pap. 2.95 (ISBN 0-02-041793-4, Collier Young Ad). Macmillan Child Grp.

Krumgold, Joseph. And Now Miguel. Charlot, Jean, illus. LC 53-8415. 245p. (gr. 5 up). 1984. pap. 3.50 (ISBN 0-06-440143-X, Trophy). HarpC Child Bks.

—Onion John. Shimin, Symeon, illus. LC 59-11395. 248p. (gr. 5 up). 1984. pap. 3.50 (ISBN 0-06-440144-8, Trophy). HarpC Child Bks.

Kunhardt, Edith. Where's Peter? LC 86-27061. (Illus.). 24p. (ps-3). 1988. 11.95 (ISBN 0-688-07204-6); lib. bdg. 11.88 (ISBN 0-688-07205-4). Greenwillow.

Kuninori. Jason's Journey into the Rainbow. LC 88-883. (Illus.). 28p. (Orig.). (gr. 1-3). 1988. 11.95 (ISBN 0-943173-02-7); pap. 5.95 (ISBN 0-943173-08-6). Harbinger AZ.

Kurelek, William. A Prairie Boy's Summer. Kurelek, William, illus. 48p. (gr. 5 up). 1975. 14.95 (ISBN 0-88776-058-9); pap. 6.95 (ISBN 0-88776-116-X). Tundra Bks.

—A Prairie Boy's Winter. Kurelek, William, illus. LC 73-8913. 48p. (gr. k-3). 1984. 13.95 (ISBN 0-395-17708-1); pap. 4.95 (ISBN 0-395-36609-7). HM.

—A Prairie Boy's Winter. Kurelek, William, illus. 48p. (gr. 5 up). 1973. 14.95 (ISBN 0-88776-022-8); pap. 6.95 (ISBN 0-88776-102-X). Tundra Bks.

LaFarge, Oliver. Laughing Boy. 245p. 1981. Repr. PLB 18.95 (ISBN 0-89966-367-2). Buccaneer Bks.

La Farge, Oliver. Laughing Boy. 259p. 1981. Repr. PLB 19.95 (ISBN 0-89967-041-5). Harmony Raine.

Langton, Jane. The Hedgehog Boy. Plume, Ilse, illus. LC 83-47698. 40p. (gr. k-3). 1985. 12.95 (ISBN 0-06-023696-5); PLB 12.89 (ISBN 0-06-023697-3). HarpC Child Bks.

Lappin, Peter. Dominic Savio: Teenage Saint. 2nd ed. LC 54-11044. 155p. (gr. 5-10). Date not set. 1.95 (ISBN 0-685-30656-9); pap. write for info. Don Bosco Multimedia.

Lattimore, Deborah N. The Flame of Peace: A Tale of the Aztecs. Lattimore, Deborah N., illus. LC 86-26934. 48p. (gr. k-3). 1987. 13.95 (ISBN 0-06-023708-2); PLB 13.89 (ISBN 0-06-023709-0). HarpC Child Bks.

Lawhead, Steve. Howard Had a Hot Air Ballon. Lawhead, Steve, illus. 32p. (gr. k-3). 7.95 (ISBN 0-7459-1268-0). Lion USA.

Lawson, Robert, illus. Wee Gillis. 72p. (ps-3). 1938. pap. 12.95 (ISBN 0-670-75608-3). Viking Child Bks.

Leaf, Munro. Robert Francis Weatherbee. LC 87-26046. (Illus.). 75p. (ps-3). 1988. Repr. of 1935 ed. PLB 14.50 (ISBN 0-208-02211-2, Linnet). Shoe String.

Lear, Edward. How Pleasant to Know Mr. Lear! LC 82-80822. (Illus.). 136p. (gr. 4-6). 1982. 13.95 (ISBN 0-8234-0462-5). Holiday.

Lelchuk, Alan. On Home Ground. Nacht, Merle, illus. LC 87-8496. 64p. (gr. 5 up). 1987. 9.95 (ISBN 0-15-200560-9, Gulliver Bks). HarBraceJ.

Lewis, Linda. Is There Life after Boys? 165p. (gr. 5-7). 1990. pap. 2.95 (ISBN 0-671-69559-2, Archway). PB.

Lindgren, Astrid. Emil in the Soup Tureen. Seaton, Lilian, tr. Berg, Bjorn, illus. 96p. (gr. 3-7). 1989. pap. 10.95 (ISBN 0-670-82658-8). Viking Child Bks.

—Emil's Pranks. Seaton, Lilian, tr. Berg, Bjorn, illus. 128p. (gr. 3-7). 1989. pap. 10.95 (ISBN 0-670-82659-6). Viking Child Bks.

Lindgren, Barbro. Sam's Potty. Eriksson, Eva, illus. LC 86-864. 32p. (ps-k). 1986. 6.95 (ISBN 0-688-06603-8, Morrow Junior Books). Morrow.

—Sam's Wagon. Eriksson, Eva, illus. LC 86-865. 32p. (ps-k). 1986. 6.95 (ISBN 0-688-05802-7, Morrow Junior Books). Morrow.

Lionni, Leo. Cornelius. Lionni, Leo, illus. LC 82-6442. 40p. (ps-2). 1983. lib. bdg. 13.99 (ISBN 0-394-95419-X). Pantheon.

—Frederick. LC 66-10355. (Illus.). 32p. (ps-3). 1987. pap. 2.95 (ISBN 0-317-53620-6). Knopf.

Lipsyte, Robert. One Fat Summer. LC 76-49746. (gr. 7 up). 1977. PLB 13.89 (ISBN 0-06-023896-8). HarpC Child Bks.

—Summerboy. LC 82-47578. 160p. (gr. 7 up). 1982. 12.95 (ISBN 0-06-023888-7). HarpC Child Bks.

—The Summerboy. 160p. 1984. pap. 2.25 (ISBN 0-553-24130-3). Bantam.

Little, Jean. Different Dragons. (gr. 3-6). 1987. pap. 14.95 (ISBN 0-670-80836-9). Viking Child Bks.

—Different Dragons. Fernandez, Laura, illus. 144p. (gr. 3-7). 1989. pap. 3.95 (ISBN 0-14-031998-0, Puffin). Puffin Bks.

Livingston, Myra C. A Circle of Seasons. Fisher, Leonard E., illus. LC 81-20305. 32p. (ps-3). 1982. Reinforced bdg. 14.95 (ISBN 0-8234-0452-8); pap. 5.95 (ISBN 0-8234-0656-3). Holiday.

Lonergan, Carroll V. Brave Boys of Old Fort Ticonderoga. LC 87-22144. (gr. 6 up). 1987. write for info., 192 p. (ISBN 0-932334-57-1, Empire State Bks); pap. 7.95, 144 p. (ISBN 1-55787-018-7, NY16028, Empire State Bks). Heart of the Lakes.

Lovik, Craig. Andy & the Tire. 32p. (ps-3). 1987. 12.95 (ISBN 0-590-40588-8). Scholastic Inc.

Lowry, Lois. Rabble Starkey. (gr. k-6). 1988. pap. 3.25 (ISBN 0-440-40056-2, YB). Dell.

Lyons, Pam. A Boy Called Simon. (Orig.). (gr. k-12). 1987. pap. 2.50 (ISBN 0-440-91094-3, LFL). Dell.

McArthur, Nancy. The Plant That Ate Dirty Socks. 128p. (Orig.). 1988. pap. 2.95 (ISBN 0-380-75493-2, Camelot). Avon.

McBrier, Michael. Getting Oliver's Goat. Sims, Blanche, illus. LC 87-13870. 96p. (gr. 3-6). 1988. PLB 9.89 (ISBN 0-8167-1145-3); pap. text ed. 2.95 (ISBN 0-8167-1146-1). Troll Assocs.

—Oliver & the Amazing Spy. Sims, Blanche, illus. LC 87-13793. 96p. (gr. 3-6). 1988. PLB 9.89 (ISBN 0-8167-1143-7); pap. text ed. 2.95 (ISBN 0-8167-1144-5). Troll Assocs.

—Oliver Smells Trouble. Sims, Blanche, illus. LC 87-13954. 96p. (gr. 3-6). 1988. PLB 9.89 (ISBN 0-8167-1149-6); pap. text ed. 2.95 (ISBN 0-8167-1150-X). Troll Assocs.

—Oliver's Barnyard Blues. Sims, Blanche, illus. LC 87-13864. 96p. (gr. 3-6). 1988. PLB 9.89 (ISBN 0-8167-1147-X); pap. text ed. 2.95 (ISBN 0-8167-1148-8). Troll Assocs.

McCay, Winsor. The Complete Little Nemo in Slumberland, Vols. I-IV: 1905-1911. Marschall, Richard, intro. by. (Illus.). 96p. (gr. 6 up). Date not set. 139.80 (ISBN 0-924359-00-5). Remco Wrldserv Bks.

McClain, Margaret S. Bellboy: A Muletrain Journey. Stuart, Sara B., illus. LC 89-61681. 154p. (gr. 5 up). 1990. 14.95 (ISBN 0-9622468-1-6). NM Pub Co.

McCloskey, Robert. Homer Price. McCloskey, Robert, illus. (gr. 4-6). 1943. pap. 13.95 (ISBN 0-670-37729-5). Viking Child Bks.

MacDonald, George. At the Back of the North Wind. Mills, Lauren, illus. LC 87-45455. 320p. 1988. 18.95 (ISBN 0-87923-703-1). Godine.

McEvoy, Seth & Wartik, Nancy. Albert's Riddle. (Illus.). 224p. (gr. 6-8). 1989. 9.95 (ISBN 0-318-37482-X). Kipling Pr.

McFall, Gardner. Jonathan's Cloud. Guarnaccia, Steven, illus. LC 85-45259. 32p. (gr. k-3). 1986. PLB 11.89 (ISBN 0-06-024124-1). HarpC Child Bks.

McGrath, Bob. Mr. Sneakers. (Illus.). 48p. (ps-2). 1989. pap. 7.95 incl. audiocassette (ISBN 0-8431-2767-8). Price Stern.

McGuire, Daniel. Portrait of Little Boy in Darkness. LC 86-50144. 205p. (Orig.). (gr. 9 up). 1986. pap. 7.00 (ISBN 0-913793-04-3). Teal Pr.

McIntyre, Vonda N. Barbary. LC 86-9766. 204p. (gr. 6 up). 1986. 12.95 (ISBN 0-395-41029-0). HM.

McKissack, Patricia C. Mirandy & Brother Wind. Pinkney, Jerry, illus. LC 87-349. 32p. (ps-3). 1988. 13.95 (ISBN 0-394-88765-4); lib. bdg. 11.99 (ISBN 0-394-98765-9). Knopf.

MacLachlan, Patricia. Arthur, for the Very First Time. Bloom, Lloyd, illus. LC 79-2007. 128p. (gr. 3-6). 1989. pap. 3.50 (ISBN 0-06-440288-6, Trophy). HarpC Child Bks.

—Arthur for the Very First Time. large type ed. 160p. 1990. Repr. PLB 15.95 (ISBN 1-55736-169-X, Crnrstn Bks). ABC-CLIO.

McPhail, David. Adam's Smile. McPhail, David, illus. LC 87-8888. 32p. (ps-1). 1987. 12.95 (ISBN 0-525-44327-4, DCB). Dutton Child Bks.

Mahy, Margaret. The Boy Who Was Followed Home. Kellogg, Steven, illus. 32p. (ps-3). 1983. pap. 3.95 (ISBN 0-8037-0903-X). Dial Bks Young.

—The Boy with Two Shadows. Williams, Jenny, illus. LC 87-17160. 32p. (ps-3). 1988. 12.95 (ISBN 0-397-32270-4, Lipp Jr Bks); PLB 12.89 (ISBN 0-397-32271-2). HarpC Child Bks.

Mallett, Jerry & Bartch, Marian. Good Old Ernie. 127p. (gr. 4-7). 1978. PLB 7.05 (ISBN 0-8479-1992-7, 120716). Perma Bound.

—Just Old Ernie. 108p. (gr. 4-7). 1988. PLB 7.45 (ISBN 0-8000-5352-4, 167580). Perma Bound.

—Poor Old Ernie. 96p. (gr. 4-7). 1988. Repr. of 1983 ed. PLB 7.85 (ISBN 0-8479-9036-2, 239600). Perma Bound.

Manes, Stephen. Be a Perfect Person in Just Three Days! Huffman, Tom, illus. 64p. (gr. 3-6). 1982. 12.95 (ISBN 0-89919-064-2, Clarion). HM.

Marek, Margot. Matt's Crusade. LC 87-36456. 160p. (gr. 5-9). 1989. pap. 2.95 (ISBN 0-394-82585-3). Knopf.

Marsh, Carole. Columbia Lastname: The Schwarzchild Radius, Bk. 1. (Orig.). (gr. 4 up). 1986. PLB 19.95 (ISBN 1-55609-284-9); pap. text ed. 14.95 (ISBN 0-935326-62-6). Gallopade Pub Group.

Marshall, James. The Cut-Ups. Marshall, James, illus. 32p. (ps-3). 1986. pap. 3.95 (ISBN 0-14-050637-3, Puffin). Puffin Bks.

Martin, Charles E. Sams Saves the Day. Martin, Charles E., illus. LC 86-19594. 32p. (gr. k-3). 1987. 11.75 (ISBN 0-688-06814-6); lib. bdg. 11.88 (ISBN 0-688-06815-4). Greenwillow.

Martin, Rafe. Will's Mammoth. Grammell, Stephen, illus. 32p. (ps-3). 1989. 14.95 (ISBN 0-399-21627-8, Putnam). Putnam Pub Group.

Marzollo, Jean. Cannonball Chris. Sims, Blanche, illus. LC 86-31512. 48p. (gr. 2-3). 1987. lib. bdg. 6.99 (ISBN 0-394-98512-5, Random Juv); pap. 2.95 (ISBN 0-394-88512-0, Random Juv). Random.

Matthews, Phoebe. The Boy on the Cover. (gr. 7 up). 1988. pap. 2.75 (ISBN 0-380-75407-X, Flare). Avon.

Matthias, Catherine. Out the Door. Neill, Eileen M., illus. LC 81-17060. 32p. (ps-2). 1982. PLB 11.93 (ISBN 0-516-03560-6); pap. 2.95 (ISBN 0-516-43560-4). Childrens.

Mauser, Pat R. A Bundle of Sticks. Owens, Gail, illus. LC 87-1074. 176p. (gr. 3-6). 1987. pap. 3.95 (ISBN 0-689-71169-7, Aladdin). Macmillan Child Grp.

Mayer, Mercer. A Boy, a Dog & a Frog. Mayer, Mercer, illus. LC 67-22254. 32p. (ps-2). 1985. pap. 2.95 (ISBN 0-8037-0769-X). Dial Bks Young.

Mayne, William. Gideon Ahoy! (gr. 5-9). 1989. pap. 13.95 (ISBN 0-440-50126-1). Delacorte.

Maynes, William. Corbie. (Illus.). 1986. 9.95 (ISBN 0-13-172602-1). P-H.

Mazer, Norma F. & Mazer, Harry. The Solid Gold Kid. (gr. 7 up). 1989. pap. 2.95 (ISBN 0-553-27851-7, Starfire). Bantam.

Meadow, Herb. The Man Who Stole the Word Beautiful. With, Gerda & Gershen, Helen, illus. LC 87-81223. 44p. (gr. k-4). 1988. 12.95 (ISBN 0-943513-00-6). Voyager BH.

Meyer, Carolyn. Denny's Tapes. LC 87-4038. 224p. (gr. 9 up). 1987. 14.95 (ISBN 0-689-50413-6, M K McElderry). Macmillan Child Grp.

Milne, A. A. World of Christopher Robin. (gr. 1-4). 1958. Boxed with "World of Pooh" 29.95 (ISBN 0-525-43348-1, Dutton); 13.95 (ISBN 0-525-43292-2). NAL-Dutton.

Milne, Teddy. Anthony. LC 86-62446. 197p. (Orig.). (gr. 5 up). 1986. pap. 5.00 (ISBN 0-938875-01-9). Pittenbruach Pr.

Monjo, F. N. The One Bad Thing about Father. Reissue. ed. Negri, Rocco, illus. LC 71-85036. 64p. (gr. k-3). 1970. PLB 11.89 (ISBN 0-06-024334-1). HarpC Child Bks.

Morgan, A. Matthew & the Midnight Money Van. (Illus.). 24p. (ps-8). 1987. 12.95 (ISBN 0-920303-75-7); pap. 4.95 (ISBN 0-920303-72-2). Firefly Bks Ltd.

—Matthew & the Midnight Tow Truck. (Illus.). 24p. (ps-8). 1984. 12.95 (ISBN 0-920303-00-5); pap. 4.95 (ISBN 0-920303-01-3). Firefly Bks Ltd.

—Matthew & the Midnight Turkeys. (Illus.). 24p. (ps-8). 1985. 12.95 (ISBN 0-920303-36-6); pap. 4.95 (ISBN 0-920303-37-4). Firefly Bks Ltd.

Morgan, Allen. Andrew & the Wild Bikes. Beinicke, Steve, illus. 32p. (ps-2). 1990. 12.95 (ISBN 1-55037-083-9); pap. 4.95 (ISBN 1-55037-082-0). Firefly Bks Ltd.

Morgan, L. Peter's Pockets. LC 65-27622. (Illus.). 32p. (gr. k-2). 1968. PLB 9.95 (ISBN 0-87783-029-0). Oddo.

Morgan, Michaela. Edward Hurts His Knee. Porter, Sue, illus. LC 87-71773. 24p. (ps-1). 1988. 8.95 (ISBN 0-525-44371-1, DCB). Dutton Child Bks.

—Edward Loses His Teddy Bear. Porter, Sue, illus. LC 87-71772. 24p. (ps-1). 1988. 8.95 (ISBN 0-525-44373-8, DCB). Dutton Child Bks.

Morton, Jane. No Place for Cal. 112p. (Orig.). 1989. pap. 2.75 (ISBN 0-380-75548-3, Camelot). Avon.

Mountain Boy. (Illus.). 32p. (gr. 2-4). 1985. Incl. audio cassette. PLB 27.99 (ISBN 0-8172-2471-8). Raintree Pubs.

Mueller, Amelia. Sissy Kid Brother. Van Demark, Paul, illus. LC 74-17385. 236p. (gr. 7-10). 1975. pap. 4.95 (ISBN 0-8361-1754-9). Herald Pr.

Mumma, Win. Joseph: The Kid Whose Dreams Came True. (Illus.). 32p. Package of 6. pap. 5.34 (ISBN 0-8423-1958-1). Tyndale.

—Samson: The Kid Who Never Got a Haircut. (Illus.). 32p. pap. 5.34 pkg. of 6 (ISBN 0-8423-5822-6). Tyndale.

Munsch, Robert. Boy in the Drawer. Martchenko, Michael, illus. 32p. (gr. k-3). 1982. 12.95 (ISBN 0-920236-34-0); pap. 4.95 (ISBN 0-920236-36-7). Firefly Bks Ltd.

Myers, Walter D. The Outside Shot. (gr. k-12). 1987. pap. 3.25 (ISBN 0-440-96784-8, LFL). Dell.

Narahashi, Keiko. I Have a Friend. Narahashi, Keiko, illus. LC 86-27628. 32p. (ps-3). 1987. 13.95 (ISBN 0-689-50432-2, M K McElderry). Macmillan Child Grp.

Nasta, Cynthia V. Peter & His Pick-up Truck: An Arizona Children's Tale. Zilka, Pat, illus. LC 89-80352. 24p. (ps-8). 1989. PLB 6.95 (ISBN 0-9622064-1-5); pap. 6.95 (ISBN 0-9622064-2-3). Little Buckaroo.

Naylor, Phyllis R. Beetles, Lightly Toasted. LC 87-911. 144p. (gr. 3-7). 1987. 12.95 (ISBN 0-689-31355-1, Atheneum Child Bk). Macmillan Child Grp.

—Eddie, Incorporated. Sims, Blanche, illus. LC 79-22589. 128p. (gr. 4-6). 1985. pap. 5.95 (ISBN 0-689-71036-4, Aladdin). Macmillan Child Grp.

—The Year of the Gopher. LC 86-17317. 224p. (gr. 7 up). 1987. 14.95 (ISBN 0-689-31333-0, Atheneum Child Bk). Macmillan Child Grp.

Neugeboren, Jay. Poli - a Mexican Boy in Early Texas. Leamon, Tom, illus. LC 88-64094. 120p. (gr. 7 up). 1989. 13.95g (ISBN 0-931722-72-1). Corona Pub.

Newman, Robert. The Case of the Watching Boy. LC 86-28859. 192p. (gr. 3-7). 1987. 13.95 (ISBN 0-689-31317-9, Atheneum Child Bk). Macmillan Child Grp.

El Nino Gigante. (SPA.). (gr. 1-6). 9.95 (ISBN 84-372-1346-0). Santillana.

Nixon, Joan L. Fat Chance, Claude. Pearson, Tracey C., illus. (ps-3). 10.95 (ISBN 0-317-62534-9). Viking Child Bks.

—The Gift. Glass, Andrew, illus. LC 87-22764. 96p. (gr. 3-7). 1988. pap. 3.95 (ISBN 0-689-71217-0, Aladdin). Macmillan Child Grp.

Nolan, Dennis. Wolf Child. Nolan, Dennis, illus. LC 88-35955. 40p. (gr. 1-5). 1989. 13.95 (ISBN 0-02-768141-6, Mcmillan Child Bk). Macmillan Child Grp.

Odom, Melissa W. No Regard Beauregard & the Golden Rule. Rice, James, illus. 132p. (gr. k-6). 1988. 11.95 (ISBN 0-88289-686-5). Pelican.

O'Donnell, Elizabeth L. Maggie Doesn't Want to Move. Schwartz, Amy, illus. LC 86-23684. 32p. (gr. k-3). 1987. PLB 13.95 (ISBN 0-02-768830-5, Pub. by Four Winds Pr). Macmillan Child Grp.

O'Donnell, Thomas. The Journal of Malt Witty. 1989. 10.00 (ISBN 0-533-08038-X). Vantage.

Oke, Janette. Maury Had a Little Lamb. Mann, Brenda, illus. 137p. (Orig.). (gr. 3 up). 1989. pap. 4.95 (ISBN 0-934998-34-5). Bethel Pub.

—Spring's Gentle Promise. LC 89-22. 224p. (Orig.). (gr. 4 up). 1989. pap. 5.95 (ISBN 1-55661-059-9). Bethany Hse.

Oliver Twist. (SPA.). 1990. casebound 3.50 (ISBN 0-7214-1398-6). Ladybird Bks.

Oppenheimer, Joan L. Toughing It Out. (gr. 7 up). 1987. pap. 2.25 (ISBN 0-373-98003-5). S&S Trade.

Oram, Hiawyn. Angry Arthur. Kitamura, Satoshi, illus. 32p. (ps-1). 1989. 12.95 (ISBN 0-525-44471-8, DCB); pap. 3.95 (ISBN 0-525-44472-6). Dutton Child Bks.

—Ned & the Joybaloo. Kitamura, Satoshi, illus. 28p. (ps up). 1989. 11.95 (ISBN 0-374-35501-0). FS&G.

Orczy, Emmuska. Beau Brocade. 275p. (gr. 4 up). 1980. Repr. of 1905 ed. lib. bdg. 13.95x (ISBN 0-89968-194-8). Lightyear.

Ormondroyd, Edward. Broderick. Larrecq, John M., illus. LC 77-83752. 40p. (ps-3). 1984. pap. 4.95 (ISBN 0-395-36170-2, 4-92538). HM.

—Theodore. Larrecq, John M., illus. LC 66-10352. 40p. (ps-3). 1984. pap. 4.95 (ISBN 0-395-36610-0). HM.

Otis, Sharon & Walker, Lois. Jeffrey's Laugh. Hawk, Lee, illus. Goldman, Howard, intro. by. (Illus., Orig.). (ps-6). 1987. wkbk. 6.50 (ISBN 0-9617737-2-3). Total Lrn.

Paige, Harry W. Shadow on the Sun. LC 83-21567. 192p. (gr. 5-9). 1984. 9.95 (ISBN 0-7232-6258-6). Warne.

Palmer, Bernard. Danny Orlis, No. 3: The Race Against Time. 128p. 1989. pap. 3.95 (ISBN 0-8423-0560-2). Tyndale.

—Danny Orlis, No. 4: The Showdown. 128p. 1989. pap. 3.95 (ISBN 0-8423-0557-2). Tyndale.

—Danny Orlis, No. 6: The Sacred Ruins. 128p. 1989. pap. 3.95 (ISBN 0-8423-0561-0). Tyndale.

Parish, Peggy. Good Hunting, Blue Sky. Watts, James, illus. LC 84-43143. 64p. (gr. k-3). 1988. 11.95 (ISBN 0-06-024661-8); PLB 11.89 (ISBN 0-06-024662-6). HarpC Child Bks.

Pascal, Francine. The Hand-Me-Down Kid. 176p. (gr. 3-7). 1990. pap. 2.75 (ISBN 0-590-43391-1). Scholastic Inc.

—Starring Winston. (gr. 4-7). 1990. pap. 2.75 (ISBN 0-553-15836-8). Bantam.

Paterson, Katherine. Jacob Have I Loved. (gr. 7 up). 1981. pap. 2.95 (ISBN 0-380-56499-8, Flare). Avon.

Paulsen, Brendan P. The Luck of the Irish. Connelly, Gwen, illus. (gr. 2-4). 1988. 16.67 (ISBN 0-8172-2752-0). Raintree Pubs.

Paulsen, Gary. Popcorn Days & Buttermilk Nights. 112p. (gr. 5-9). 1989. pap. 3.95 (ISBN 0-14-034204-4, Puffin). Puffin Bks.

Peet, Bill. Huge Harold. Peet, Bill, illus. (gr. k-3). 1982. pap. 4.95 (ISBN 0-395-32923-X). HM.

Pete, Jacelen D. Just Another Busy Day. (Illus.). 32p. 1989. 8.95 (ISBN 0-934601-93-3). Peachtree Pubs.

Petersen, P. J. Good-Bye to Good Ol' Charlie. LC 86-2016. 168p. (gr. 7 up). 1987. pap. 14.95 (ISBN 0-385-29483-2). Delacorte.

Pfeffer, Susan B. About David. 176p. (gr. 7 up). 1982. pap. 3.25 (ISBN 0-440-90022-0, LFL). Dell.

—The Year Without Michael. 176p. (gr. 7-12). 1987. 13.95 (ISBN 0-553-05430-9, Starfire). Bantam.

—The Year Without Michael. (gr. 7-12). 1988. pap. 3.50 (ISBN 0-553-27373-6, Starfire). Bantam.

Pike, Christopher. Christopher Pike, 4 vols. 1990. pap. 11.80 boxed (ISBN 0-671-96377-5). S&S Trade.

Pilling, Ann. Henry's Leg. (gr. 5-9). 1987. pap. 10.95 (ISBN 0-670-80720-6). Viking Child Bks.

Pingry, Patricia. Joseph & a Dream Come True. Spence, James, illus. 24p. (Orig.). (ps-3). 1988. pap. 3.95 (ISBN 0-8249-8182-0). Ideals.

Pinkwater, Daniel. Young Adult Novel. LC 81-43391. 128p. (gr. 7 up). 1982. PLB 11.89 (ISBN 0-690-04189-6, Crowell Jr Bks). HarpC Child Bks.

Pinkwater, Daniel M. The Snarkout Boys & the Baconburg Horror. 1985. pap. 2.50 (ISBN 0-451-13581-4, Sig Vista). NAL-Dutton.

Porte, Barbara A. Harry's Mom. 1990. pap. 2.95 (ISBN 0-440-40362-6, YB). Dell.

—Harry's Visit. (Orig.). (gr. k-6). 1990. pap. 2.95 (ISBN 0-440-40331-6, YB). Dell.

Porter, Bruce. Bill & the Burning Bush. Porter, Bruce, illus. 40p. (Orig.). (gr. 1 up). 1987. pap. 3.95 (ISBN 0-939925-12-5). R C Law & Co.

—Butch & the Bad Baloney. Porter, Bruce, illus. 40p. (Orig.). (gr. 1 up). 1987. pap. 3.95 (ISBN 0-939925-15-X). R C Law & Co.

—Jonah Gets the Jitters. Porter, Bruce, illus. 40p. (Orig.). (gr. 3 up). 1987. pap. 3.95 (ISBN 0-939925-14-1). R C Law & Co.

—Samuel & the Strange Sound. Porter, Bruce, illus. 40p. (Orig.). (gr. 3 up). 1987. pap. 3.95 (ISBN 0-939925-13-3). R C Law & Co.

—Squirt & the Super Soldier. Porter, Bruce, illus. 40p. (Orig.). (gr. 3 up). 1987. pap. 3.95 (ISBN 0-939925-16-8). R C Law & Co.

Porter, Stratton. Freckless. (Orig.). 1988. pap. 4.95 (ISBN 0-440-40050-3, Pub by Yearning Classics). Dell.

Potter, Dan. Crazy Moon Zoo. LC 85-6157. 151p. (gr. 7up). 1985. PLB 12.40 (ISBN 0-531-10076-6). Watts.

Poulin, Stephane. Benjamin & the Pillow Saga. Poulin, Stephane, illus. 1990. 14.95 (ISBN 1-550370-69-3); pap. 5.95 (ISBN 1-550370-68-5). Firefly Bks Ltd.

Powling, Chris. Hiccup Harry. 1990. 10.95 (ISBN 0-525-44558-7, DCB). Dutton Child Bks.

Priestley, Dinah. Hector the Bully. Smith, Wendy, illus. 24p. (ps-3). 1989. PLB 12.95 (ISBN 0-87614-356-7). Carolrhoda Bks.

Prokofiev, Sergei. Peter & the Wolf. Carlson, Maria, tr. Mikolaycak, Charles, illus. (gr. 2-5). 1987. incl. cassette 19.95 (ISBN 0-87499-074-2); pap. 12.95 incl. cassette (ISBN 0-87499-073-4); 4 paperbacks, cassette & guide 27.95 (ISBN 0-87499-075-0). Live Oak Media.

Pryor, Bonnie. Perfect Percy. Smath, Jerry, illus. 1988. pap. 5.95 (ISBN 0-671-65219-2, Little Simon). S&S Trade.

Quintilone, Paul M. Brian Has a Winning Day. (gr. 3-5). Date not set. pap. write for info. (ISBN 0-9616980-2-0). Quintilone Ent.

Rawlings, Marjorie K. The Yearling. 2nd ed. Shenton, Edward, illus. LC 86-20743. 448p. (gr. 5 up). 1988. pap. 4.95 (ISBN 0-02-044931-3, Collier Young Ad). Macmillan Child Grp.

Rayner, Mary. Oh, Paul! Rayner, Mary, illus. 42p. (gr. 2-4). 1989. 13.95 (ISBN 0-8120-6145-4). Barron.

Reece, Colleen L. Escape from Fear. Wheeler, Penny E., ed. 96p. (Orig.). (gr. 6-9). 1988. pap. 4.95 (ISBN 0-8280-0441-2). Review & Herald.

Reuter, Bjarne. Buster's World. LC 89-11919. 112p. (gr. 4 up). 1989. 12.95 (ISBN 0-525-44475-0, DCB). Dutton Child Bks.

Rey, H. A. Curious George Gets a Medal. Rey, H. A., illus. LC 57-7206. 48p. (gr. k-3). 1974. pap. 3.95 (ISBN 0-395-18559-9, Sandpiper). HM.

Ritchie, Alan. Erin McEwan, Your Days Are Numbered. LC 89-2581. 192p. (gr. 3-7). 1991. pap. 3.95 (ISBN 0-394-86578-2, Bullseye Bks). Knopf.

Roberts, Willo D. The View from the Cherry Tree. LC 86-22233. 192p. (gr. 4). 1987. pap. 3.95 (ISBN 0-689-71131-X, Aladdin). Macmillan Child Grp.

Robertson, Keith. Henry Reed, Inc. 224p. (gr. 2-5). 1974. pap. 3.25 (ISBN 0-440-43552-8, YB). Dell.

—Henry Reed, Inc. McCloskey, Robert, illus. 240p. (gr. 4-6). 1989. pap. 3.95 (ISBN 0-14-034144-7, Puffin). Puffin Bks.

—Henry Reed's Baby-Sitting Service. 206p. (gr. 2-5). 1974. pap. 3.25 (ISBN 0-440-43565-X, YB). Dell.

—Henry Reed's Baby-Sitting Service. McCloskey, Robert, illus. 208p. (gr. 4-6). 1989. pap. 3.95 (ISBN 0-14-034146-3, Puffin). Puffin Bks.

—Henry Reed's Big Show. McCloskey, Robert, illus. (gr. 4-6). 1970. pap. 14.95 (ISBN 0-670-36839-3). Viking Child Bks.

—Henry Reed's Big Show. McCloskey, Robert, illus. 208p. (gr. 4-7). 1978. pap. 2.50 (ISBN 0-440-43570-6, YB). Dell.

—Henry Reed's Journey. LC 63-8522. 224p. (gr. 2-5). 1974. pap. 3.25 (ISBN 0-440-43555-2, YB). Dell.

—Henry Reed's Journey. McCloskey, Robert, illus. 224p. (gr. 4-6). 1989. pap. 3.95 (ISBN 0-14-034145-5, Puffin). Puffin Bks.

Robinson, Nancy K. Just Plain Cat. LC 82-18258. 128p. (gr. 3-6). 1984. 12.95 (ISBN 0-02-777350-7, Four Winds). Macmillan Child Grp.

—Just Plain Cat. 28p. (Orig.). (gr. 3-7). 1991. pap. 2.75 (ISBN 0-590-42321-5). Scholastic Inc.

Rochman, Hazel, ed. Somehow Tenderness Survives: Stories of Southern Africa. LC 88-916. 208p. (gr. 7 up). 1990. pap. 3.25 (ISBN 0-06-447063-6, Trophy). HarpC Child Bks.

Rodgers, A. Mary. A Billion for Boris. LC 74-3586. 192p. (gr. 5 up). 1974. PLB 13.89 (ISBN 0-06-025054-2). HarpC Child Bks.

Rodowsky, Colby. H, My Name Is Henley. LC 82-12164. 184p. (gr. 5 up). 1982. 11.95 (ISBN 0-374-32831-5). FS&G.

Roe, Cheryl A. Tym, the Turtle Boy. Hilliard, Peg, illus. 52p. (Orig.). (ps-3). 1989. pap. write for info. (ISBN 0-9623183-0-7). Timeless Sales.

Rogers, Jean. Dinosaurs Are 568. Hafner, Marylin, illus. LC 88-5501. 96p. (gr. 3 up). 1988. 10.95 (ISBN 0-688-07931-8). Greenwillow.

Rollini, Art. When Will Summer Come? Balla, Laszlo, illus. LC 90-70904. 21p. (ps-6). 1991. pap. 5.95 (ISBN 1-55523-354-6). Winston-Derek.

Roos, Stephen. My Favorite Ghost. DeRosa, Dee, illus. LC 87-15186. 128p. (gr. 3-7). 1988. 12.95 (ISBN 0-689-31301-2, Atheneum Child Bk). Macmillan Child Grp.

—Thirteenth Summer. DeRosa, Dee, illus. LC 87-11382. 128p. (gr. 3-6). 1987. 12.95 (ISBN 0-689-31299-7, Atheneum Child Bk). Macmillan Child Grp.
Ross, Tony. Boy Who Cried Wolf. LC 84-23273. 32p. (ps-3). 1991. pap. 3.95 (ISBN 0-8037-0911-0, Dial Pied Piper). Puffin Bks.
Rothberg, Michael. The Cat's-Eye. 16p. (Orig.). 1980. pap. 2.50 (ISBN 0-938370-00-6). Wildflower.
Rudner, Barry. The Littlest Tall Fellow. Carraro, J. M., ed. Fahsbender, Thomas, illus. 28p. (gr. k-6). 1989. pap. 4.95 (ISBN 0-925928-00-3). Tiny Thought.
Ryan, Jeanette M. Misjudged. 192p. (Orig.). (gr. 7 up). 1986. pap. 2.50 (ISBN 0-590-33777-7, Point). Scholastic Inc.
Ryan, Mary C. Frankie's Run. (gr. 3-7). 1987. 12.95 (ISBN 0-316-76370-5). Little.
Sachar, Louis. The Boy Who Lost His Face. LC 88-22622. 208p. (gr. 5-9). 1991. pap. 3.95 (ISBN 0-679-80160-X, Borzoi Sprinters). Knopf.
—Johnny's in the Basement. 128p. (Orig.). (gr. 4-7). 1983. pap. 2.75 (ISBN 0-380-83451-0, 83451-0, Camelot). Avon.
—Johnny's in the Basement. 128p. (gr. 2-6). 1990. Repr. of 1981 ed. PLB 12.99 (ISBN 0-679-90411-5). McKay.
—There's a Boy in the Girl's Bathroom. Foster, Frances, ed. Greenstein, Mina, designed by. LC 86-20100. 224p. (gr. 5 up). 1987. 11.95 (ISBN 0-394-88570-8); lib. bdg. 12.99 (ISBN 0-394-98570-2). Knopf.
Sachs, Betsy. The Boy Who Ate Dog Biscuits. Apple, Margot, illus. LC 89-3905. 64p. (gr. 2-4). 1989. PLB 5.99 (ISBN 0-394-94778-9); pap. 1.95 (ISBN 0-394-84778-4). Random.
Sadler, Marilyn. Alistair Underwater. 1990. pap. 13.95 (ISBN 0-671-69406-5). S&S Trade.
San Souci, Robert. The Boy & the Ghost. Pinkney, J. Brian, illus. (ps-3). 1989. pap. 13.95 (ISBN 0-671-67176-6). S&S Trade.
Sant, Thomas. The Amazing Adventures of Albert & His Flying Machine. DeRosa, Dee, illus. 160p. (gr. 4-7). 1990. 13.95 (ISBN 0-525-67302-4, Lodestar Bks). Dutton Child Bks.
Sargent, Sarah. Jonas McFee, A. T. P. LC 88-19245. 128p. (gr. 3-7). 1989. 11.95 (ISBN 0-02-778041-4, Bradbury Pr). Macmillan Child Grp.
Savage, Cindy. The Great Boyfriend Disaster. 112p. (Orig.). (gr. 6-8). 1988. pap. 2.50 (ISBN 0-87406-240-3). Willowisp Pr.
Savitz, Harriet. The Bullies & Me. 176p. (Orig.). (gr. 3-7). 1991. pap. 2.75 (ISBN 0-590-42975-2). Scholastic Inc.
Schantz, Daniel. Wheeler's Big Catch. Ostendorf, Ned, illus. 96p. (gr. 3-5). 1987. pap. 3.95 (ISBN 0-87403-318-7, 2927). Standard Pub.
—Wheeler's Deal. Ostendorf, Ned, illus. 96p. (gr. 3-5). 1987. pap. 3.95 (ISBN 0-87403-317-9, 2926). Standard Pub.
—Wheeler's Ghost Town. Ostendorf, Ned, illus. 96p. (gr. 3-5). 1987. pap. 3.95 (ISBN 0-87403-319-5, 2928). Standard Pub.
—Wheeler's Good Time. Ostendorf, Ned, illus. 96p. (gr. 3-5). 1987. pap. 3.95 (ISBN 0-87403-320-9, 2929). Standard Pub.
—Wheeler's Swap. Ostendorf, Ned, illus. 96p. (gr. 3-6). 1989. pap. 3.95 (ISBN 0-87403-573-2, 3953). Standard Pub.
Scheidl, Gerda M. Four Candles for Simon. Pfister, Marcus, illus. LC 86-33199. 32p. (gr. k-3). 1987. 13.95 (ISBN 1-55858-065-4). North-South Bks NYC.
Schertle, Alice. Gus Wanders Off. Edwards, Linda S., illus. LC 86-21311. 32p. (ps-2). 1988. 12.95 (ISBN 0-688-04984-2); PLB 12.88 (ISBN 0-688-04985-0). Lothrop.
—In My Treehouse. Dunham, Meredith, illus. LC 82-10016. 32p. (gr. k-3). 1983. 11.95 (ISBN 0-688-01638-3). Lothrop.
—William & Grandpa. Stevenson, D., ed. Dabcovich, Lydia, illus. LC 88-666. 32p. (gr. k-3). 1988. 12.95 (ISBN 0-688-07580-0); PLB 12.88 (ISBN 0-688-07581-9). Lothrop.
Schumacher, Claire. Tim & Jim. (gr. k-3). 1987. 11.95 (ISBN 0-396-09040-0, Putnam). Putnam Pub Group.
Schwartz, Frederick J. The Adventures of Rondy. Olson, Wayne, ed. Kuehn, Christopher, illus. 148p. (gr. k-7). 1985. 7.95 (ISBN 0-9616638-0-4). Rondy Pubns.
Seldon, George. The Cricket in Times Square. large type ed. 192p. 1990. Repr. PLB 15.95 (ISBN 1-55736-170-3, Crnrstn Bks). ABC-CLIO.
Sendak, Maurice. La Cocina de Noche. Sendak, Maurice, illus. (SPA.). (gr. 1-6). 14.95 (ISBN 84-204-4570-3). Santillana.
—Donde Viven Los Monstrous. Sendak, Maurice, illus. (SPA.). (gr. 1-6). 14.95 (ISBN 84-204-3022-6). Santillana.
—Kenny's Window. Sendak, Maurice, illus. LC 56-5148. 64p. (ps up). 1989. pap. 4.95 (ISBN 0-06-443209-2, Trophy). HarpC Child Bks.
Sewall, Marcia. People of the Breaking Day. Sewall, Marcia A., illus. LC 89-18194. 48p. (gr. 1 up). 1990. 14.95 (ISBN 0-689-31407-8, Atheneum Child Bk). Macmillan Child Grp.
Sharmat, Marjorie W. Go to Sleep, Nicholas Joe. Himmelman, John, illus. LC 85-45689. 32p. (ps-3). 1988. PLB 11.89 (ISBN 0-06-025504-8). HarpC Child Bks.
—Nate the Great. Simont, Marc, illus. 48p. (gr. 1-4). 10.95 (ISBN 0-698-20627-4, Coward). Putnam Pub Group.
—What Are We Going to Do about Andrew? Cruz, Ray, illus. LC 88-3357. 32p. (gr. k-4). 1988. pap. 3.95 (ISBN 0-689-71264-2, Aladdin). Macmillan Child Grp.
Sharmat, Mitchell. Gregory the Terrible Eater. Aruego, Jose & Dewey, Ariane, illus. 32p. (gr. k-3). 1984. pap. 2.95 (ISBN 0-590-40250-1). Scholastic Inc.
—Gregory, the Terrible Eater. Aruego, Jose & Dewey, Ariane, illus. 32p. (gr. k-3). 1984. pap. 3.95 (ISBN 0-590-43350-4). Scholastic Inc.
—Sherman Is a Slowpoke. Neuhaus, David, illus. 32p. (gr. k-3). 1988. pap. 12.95 (ISBN 0-590-40938-7, Scholastic Hardcovers). Scholastic Inc.
—Sherman Is a Slowpoke. Newhaus, David, illus. (gr. k-3). 1989. pap. 2.50 (ISBN 0-590-40939-5). Scholastic Inc.
Shute, Linda. Momotaro the Peach Boy. LC 85-9997. (Illus.). 32p. (ps-3). 1986. 13.95 (ISBN 0-688-05863-9); PLB 13.88 (ISBN 0-688-05864-7). Lothrop.
Shyer, Marlene F. Welcome Home, Jellybean. LC 87-19483. 160p. (gr. 3-7). 1988. pap. 3.95 (ISBN 0-689-71213-8, Aladdin). Macmillan Child Grp.
Sierra, Patricia. A Boy I Never Knew. 128p. (gr. 7 up). 1988. pap. 2.50 (ISBN 0-380-75208-5, Flare). Avon.
Simon, Seymour. Einstein Anderson Lights up the Sky. Winkowski, Fred, illus. (gr. 3-7). pap. 3.95 (ISBN 0-317-62300-1, Puffin). Puffin Bks.
—Einstein Anderson, Science Sleuth. Winkowski, Fred, illus. 80p. (gr. 3-7). 1986. pap. 3.95 (ISBN 0-14-032098-9, Puffin). Puffin Bks.
—Einstein Anderson Shocks His Friends. Winkowski, Fred, illus. 80p. (gr. 3-7). 1986. pap. 3.95 (ISBN 0-14-032099-7, Puffin). Puffin Bks.
Singer, Marilyn. The Case of the Cackling Car. Glasser, Judith, illus. LC 84-48333. 64p. (gr. 3-7). 1985. 10.95 (ISBN 0-06-025632-X). HarpC Child Bks.
—A Clue in Code. Glasser, Judith, illus. LC 84-48335. 64p. (gr. 3-7). 1985. PLB 10.89 (ISBN 0-06-025637-0). HarpC Child Bks.
—Leroy Is Missing: A Sam & Dave Mystery. Glasser, Judy, illus. LC 83-48441. 64p. (gr. 3-7). 1987. pap. 2.95 (ISBN 0-06-440208-8, Trophy). HarpC Child Bks.
Sloan, Carolyn. The Sea Child. LC 88-45273. 128p. (gr. 3-7). 1988. 12.95 (ISBN 0-8234-0723-3). Holiday.
Slote, Alfred. Hang Tough, Paul Mather. LC 72-11531. 160p. (gr. 3-7). 1985. pap. 3.50 (ISBN 0-06-440153-7, Trophy). HarpC Child Bks.
—Matt Gargan's Boy. LC 74-26669. 160p. (gr. 3-7). 1985. pap. 3.50 (ISBN 0-06-440154-5, Trophy). HarpC Child Bks.
—My Robot Buddy. LC 85-45393. (Illus.). 96p. (gr. 2-5). 1986. pap. 2.95 (ISBN 0-06-440165-0, Trophy). HarpC Child Bks.
—Omega Station. Kramer, Anthony, illus. LC 85-45395. 160p. (gr. 2-5). 1986. pap. 2.95 (ISBN 0-06-440167-7, Trophy). HarpC Child Bks.
Smath, Jerry. Leon's Prize. LC 87-25800. (Illus.). 40p. (ps-3). 1987. 5.95 (ISBN 0-8193-1169-3). Parents.
Smith, Alison. Billy Boone. LC 88-34839. 128p. (gr. 3-6). 1989. 12.95 (ISBN 0-684-18974-7, Scribners Young Read). Macmillan Child Grp.
Smith, Janice L. It's Not Easy Being George: Stories about Adam Joshua (& His Dog) Gackenbach, Dick, illus. LC 88-33075. 128p. (gr. 1-4). 1991. pap. 3.50 (ISBN 0-06-440338-6, Trophy). HarpC Child Bks.
—The Kid Next Door & Other Headaches: Stories about Adam Joshua. Gackenbach, Dick, illus. LC 83-47689. 160p. (gr. 1-4). 1984. 12.95 (ISBN 0-06-025792-X); PLB 12.89 (ISBN 0-06-025793-8). HarpC Child Bks.
Smith, K. Skeeter. (gr. 6 up). 1989. 13.95 (ISBN 0-395-49603-9). HM.
Smith, Lane. Flying Jake. Smith, Lane, illus. LC 87-25976. 32p. (ps-3). 1988. 14.95 (ISBN 0-02-785830-8, Mcmillan Child Bk). Macmillan Child Grp.
Smith, Mildred S. Where Is Jeffrey's Yo-Yo? (Illus.). 56p. (ps-12). 1988. 8.50 (ISBN 0-9612296-5-9). Williams SC.
Smith, Robert K. Mostly Michael. Coville, Katherine, illus. LC 86-19618. 192p. (gr. 4-6). 1987. pap. 13.95 (ISBN 0-385-29545-6). Delacorte.
—Mostly Michael. 192p. (gr. k-6). 1988. pap. 2.95 (ISBN 0-440-40097-X, YB). Dell.
Snape, Juliet & Snape, Charles. The Boy with Square Eyes: A Case of Televisionitis. (Illus.). 32p. (gr. 3-5). 1988. 12.95 (ISBN 0-13-080524-6, Little Simon). S&S Trade.
Snyder, Diane, retold by. The Boy of the Three-Year Nap. Say, Allen, illus. LC 87-30674. 32p. (ps-3). 1988. 14.95 (ISBN 0-395-44090-4). HM.
Sobel, Barbara. Jake Finds a Penny. Ziffer, Louise, illus. LC 86-81370. 32p. (gr. k-2). 1986. PLB 7.59 (ISBN 0-87386-019-5); pap. 1.95 (ISBN 0-87386-015-2). Jan Prods.
Southall, Ivan. Josh. LC 87-23943. 192p. (gr. 7 up). 1988. 13.95 (ISBN 0-02-786280-1, Mcmillan Child Bk). Macmillan Child Grp.
Speare, Jean. A Candle for Christmas. Blades, Ann, illus. LC 86-61560. 32p. (gr. k-4). 1987. 12.95 (ISBN 0-689-50417-9, M K McElderry). Macmillan Child Grp.
Spinelli, Jerry. Dump Days. (gr. 3-7). 1988. 13.95 (ISBN 0-316-80706-0). Little.
Standish, Burt L. Frank Merriwell Down South. Rudman, Jack, ed. (gr. 9 up). 9.95 (ISBN 0-8373-9305-1); pap. 3.95 (ISBN 0-8373-9005-2). F Merriwell.
—Frank Merriwell in Europe. Rudman, Jack, ed. (gr. 9 up). Date not set. 9.95 (ISBN 0-8373-9308-6); pap. 3.95 (ISBN 0-8373-9008-7). F Merriwell.
—Frank Merriwell's Bravery. Rudman, Jack, ed. (gr. 9 up). Date not set. 9.95 (ISBN 0-8373-9306-X); pap. 3.95 (ISBN 0-8373-9006-0). F Merriwell.
—Frank Merriwell's Hunting Tour. Rudman, Jack, ed. (gr. 9 up). Date not set. 9.95 (ISBN 0-8373-9307-8); pap. 3.95 (ISBN 0-8373-9007-9). F Merriwell.
—Frank Merriwell's Schooldays. Rudman, Jack, ed. (gr. 9 up). 9.95 (ISBN 0-8373-9309-4); pap. 3.95 (ISBN 0-8373-9009-5). F Merriwell.
—Frank Merriwell's Sports Afield. Rudman, Jack, ed. (gr. 9 up). Date not set. 9.95 (ISBN 0-8373-9310-8); pap. 3.95 (ISBN 0-8373-9010-9). F Merriwell.
—Frank Merriwell's Trip West. Rudman, Jack, ed. (gr. 9 up). Date not set. 9.95 (ISBN 0-8373-9304-3); pap. 3.95 (ISBN 0-8373-9004-4). F Merriwell.
Stanley, Monty M. They Call Me a Delinquent. 91p. (Orig.). (gr. 5-12). 1989. 8.95 (ISBN 0-9622667-1-X). Illini Pubns.
Stan-Padilla, Viento. Dream Feather. Stan-Padilla, Viento, illus. LC 87-17823. 72p. (Orig.). (gr. 7 up). 1987. pap. 9.95 (ISBN 0-913990-57-4). Book Pub Co.
Steig, William. Sylvester & the Magic Pebble. Steig, William, illus. 32p. (ps-1). 1988. Bk. & cassette. pap. 6.95 (ISBN 0-671-67144-8). S&S Trade.
Sterman, Betsy & Sterman, Samuel. Too Much Magic. Glasser, Judy, illus. LC 85-45861. 160p. (gr. 3-7). 1987. 12.95 (ISBN 0-397-32186-4, Lipp Jr Bks); PLB 11.89 (ISBN 0-397-32187-2, Lipp Jr Bks). HarpC Child Bks.
Stevenson, James. The Supreme Souvenir Factory. LC 87-33390. (Illus.). 56p. (gr. 1-4). 1988. 13.95 (ISBN 0-688-07782-X). Greenwillow.
Stewart, Winnie. Night on 'Gator Creek. 64p. (Orig.). (RL 3.6). 1984. pap. 3.50 (ISBN 0-88336-215-5). New Readers.
Stion, Rebekah, pseud. SAM's Special Prize. (Illus.). 32p. (gr. k-2). 1989. pasted 1.99 (ISBN 0-87403-596-1, 3856). Standard Pub.
Stolz, Mary. The Bully of Barkham Street. Shortall, Leonard, illus. LC 68-2661. 224p. (gr. 3-7). 1985. pap. 2.50 (ISBN 0-06-440159-6, Trophy). HarpC Child Bks.
—The Explorer of Barkham Street. McCully, Emily A., illus. LC 84-48339. 192p. (gr. 4-6). 1985. 14.95 (ISBN 0-06-025976-0); PLB 12.89 (ISBN 0-06-025977-9). HarpC Child Bks.
—The Explorer of Barkham Street. McCully, Emily A., illus. LC 84-48339. 192p. (gr. 3-7). 1987. pap. 2.50 (ISBN 0-06-440210-X, Trophy). HarpC Child Bks.
Strasser, Todd. Home Alone Movie Tie-In. 1991. pap. 2.75 (ISBN 0-590-44668-1). Scholastic Inc.
Strickland, Alison. Getting Rid of Robert. (Illus.). 64p. (gr. 1-3). 1987. 0.75 (ISBN 0-87406-210-1). Willowisp Pr.
Strohl, Roger R., Jr. Jake & Duke Camp Paw Mountain. 1989. 6.95 (ISBN 0-533-08163-7). Vantage.
Szilagyi, Mary. The Adventures of Charlie & His Wheat-Straw Hat. (gr. k-3). 1986. 14.95 (ISBN 0-399-21704-5, Putnam). Putnam Pub Group.
Talbert, Marc. Toby. LC 87-5333. 176p. (gr. 4 up). 1987. 13.95 (ISBN 0-8037-0441-0). Dial Bks Young.
Talbot, John. Hasn't He Grown! (Illus.). 32p. (ps-2). 1989. 13.95 (ISBN 0-86264-232-9, Pub. by Anderson Pr UK). Trafalgar Sq.
Tamar, Erika. It Happened at Cecilia's. LC 88-28502. 144p. (gr. 6-9). 1989. 12.95 (ISBN 0-689-31478-7, Atheneum Child Bk). Macmillan Child Grp.
Tapp, Kathy K. The Scorpio Ghosts & the Black Hole Gang. LC 86-45492. 192p. (gr. 4-7). 1987. HarpC Child Bks.
Taylor, Judy. My Cat. Cartwright, Reg, illus. LC 87-15267. 24p. (ps-2). 1988. 11.95 (ISBN 0-02-782473-X, Mcmillan Child Bk). Macmillan Child Grp.
Taylor, Mark. Henry the Explorer. Booth, Graham, illus. 48p. (ps-3). 1988. pap. 5.95 (ISBN 0-316-83384-3). Little.
Thaler, Mike. How Far Will a Rubber Band Stretch. 1990. pap. 13.95 (ISBN 0-671-69361-1). S&S Trade.
Thayer, Jane. The Puppy Who Wanted a Boy. McCue, Lisa, illus. LC 85-15465. (ps-3). 1988. pap. 4.95 (ISBN 0-688-08293-9, Mulberry). Morrow.
Thompson, Frederick. Dickon Dicky & Mr. Wheelspoke. 1991. 7.95 (ISBN 0-533-09384-8). Vantage.
Thompson, Julian F. Herb Seasoning. 1990. pap. 12.95 (ISBN 0-590-43023-8). Scholastic Inc.
Tibo, Gilles. Simon & the Wind. Tibo, Gilles, illus. LC 89-50777. 24p. (gr. k-4). 1989. 10.95 (ISBN 0-88776-234-4). Tundra Bks.
—Simon et le Vent d'Automne. Tibo, Gilles, illus. LC 89-50776. (FRE.). 24p. (gr. k-4). 1989. 10.95 (ISBN 0-88776-235-2). Tundra Bks.
Timlock, Jason. Basil, the Loneliest Boy. Colquhoun, Brett, illus. 32p. (ps-2). 1990. 9.95 (ISBN 0-670-83125-5). Viking Child Bks.
Titherington, Jeanne. A Place for Ben. Titherington, Jeanne, illus. LC 86-7656. 24p. (ps-3). 1987. 11.95 (ISBN 0-688-06493-0); PLB 11.88 (ISBN 0-688-06494-9). Greenwillow.
Tolstoy, Leo. Shoemaker Martin. Watts, Bernadette, illus. Hanhart, Brigitte, adapted by. LC 86-60489. (Illus.). 32p. (gr. k-3). 1986. 14.95 (ISBN 1-55858-044-1). North-South Bks NYC.
Towne, Bonnie. Two-Boy Cruise. 128p. (gr. 6-8). 1986. 1.95 (ISBN 0-87406-149-0). Willowisp Pr.
Townsend, John R. Dan Alone. LC 82-49051. 224p. (gr. 5 up). 1983. (Lipp Jr Bks). HarpC Child Bks.

Townsend, Tom. Trader Wooly & the Secret of the Lost Nazi Treasure. Roberts, Melissa, ed. (Illus.). 120p. (gr. 4-7). 1987. 8.95 (ISBN 0-89015-602-6, Pub. by Panda Bks); pap. 3.95 (ISBN 0-89015-634-4). Eakin Pr.

Tulloch, Richard. Danny in the Toybox. Greder, Armin, illus. LC 90-24637. 32p. (ps-3). 1991. 13.95 (ISBN 0-688-10501-7, Tambourine Bks); PLB 13.88 (ISBN 0-688-10502-5, Tambourine Bks). Morrow.

Tusa, Tricia. Chicken. Tusa, Tricia, illus. LC 85-10591. 32p. (gr. k-3). 1986. 12.95 (ISBN 0-02-789320-0, Mcmillan Child Bk). Macmillan Child Grp.

Twain, Mark. Adventures of Huckleberry Finn. facsimile ed. (Illus.). 366p. 1990. Repr. of 1885 ed. miniature 60.00 (ISBN 1-878582-01-1). Childs Min Bk Co.

—Adventures of Huckleberry Finn: A Facsimile of the Manuscript, 2 Vols. Budd, Louis J., intro. by. 758p. 1983. slipcased set 250.00x (ISBN 0-8103-1635-8). Gale.

—The Adventures of Tom Sawyer. facsimile ed. (Illus.). 267p. 1990. Repr. of 1876 ed. miniature 60.00 (ISBN 1-878582-00-3). Childs Min Bk Co.

Tyler, Linda W. My Brother Oscar Thinks He Knows It All. Davis, Susan, illus. 32p. (ps-3). 1989. pap. 11.95 (ISBN 0-670-82533-6). Viking Child Bks.

Ulmer, Louise. The Son Who Said He Wouldn't. (gr. k-4). 1981. pap. 1.39 (ISBN 0-570-06145-8, 59-1262). Concordia.

Unwin, Charlotte. I Want to Be... Kindberg, Sally, illus. LC 87-20037. 24p. (ps-3). 1989. 4.95 (ISBN 0-8037-0508-5). Dial Bks Young.

Van Antwerp, T. Cooper. Hereafter Rising. Graves, Helen, ed. LC 88-50121. 190p. (gr. 3-10). 1988. 8.95 (ISBN 1-55523-139-X). Winston-Derek.

Van De Wetering, Janwillem. Hugh Pine. (Illus.). 96p. (gr. 3 up). 1980. 13.95 (ISBN 0-395-29459-2). HM.

Vann, Donna R. Roberto & the Fountain of Lights. (Illus.). 32p. (gr. 4 up). 8.95 (ISBN 0-7459-1277-X). Lion USA.

Vincent, Gabrielle. Feel Better, Ernest! LC 87-21074. (Illus.). 32p. (ps-3). 1988. Repr. of 1988 ed. 11.95 (ISBN 0-688-07725-0); lib. bdg. 13.88 (ISBN 0-688-07726-9). Greenwillow.

Viorst, Judith. Alexander & the Terrible, Horrible, No Good, Very Bad Day. Cruz, Ray, illus. LC 72-75289. 32p. (gr. k-4). 1972. 12.95 (ISBN 0-689-30072-7, Atheneum Child Bk). Macmillan Child Grp.

—Alexander & the Terrible, Horrible, No Good, Very Bad Day. LC 72-75289. 32p. (gr. k-4). 1976. pap. 2.95 (ISBN 0-689-70428-3, Aladdin). Macmillan Child Grp.

—Alexander & the Terrible, Horrible, No Good, Very Bad Day. Cruz, Ray, illus. LC 87-1087. 32p. (gr. k-4). 1987. pap. 3.95 (ISBN 0-689-71173-5, Aladdin). Macmillan Child Grp.

—Alexander Who Used to be Rich Last Sunday. LC 77-1579. (Illus.). 32p. (ps-4). 1987. pap. 3.95 (ISBN 0-689-71199-9, Aladdin). Macmillan Child Grp.

Voigt, Cynthia. Dicey's Song. large type ed. 334p. 1990. Repr. PLB 15.95 (ISBN 1-55736-166-5, Crnrstn Bks). ABC-CLIO.

Waber, Bernard. Bernard. Waber, Bernard, illus. 48p. (gr. k-3). 1986. 9.95 (ISBN 0-395-31865-3); pap. 3.95 (ISBN 0-395-42648-0). HM.

—Ira Sleeps Over. (gr. 3 up). 1987. pap. 7.95 incl. cass. (ISBN 0-395-45949-4). HM.

—Lyle Finds His Mother. LC 74-5336. (Illus.). 48p. (gr. k-3). 1974. 13.95 (ISBN 0-395-19489-X). HM.

Wallace, Bill. Beauty. LC 88-6422. 192p. (gr. 3-7). 1988. 14.95 (ISBN 0-8234-0715-2). Holiday.

—Snot Stew. McCue, Lisa, illus. 96p. 1990. pap. 2.75 (ISBN 0-671-69335-2, Minstrel Bks). PB.

Walter, Mildred P. Justin & the Best Biscuits in the World. Stock, Catherine, illus. LC 86-7148. 128p. (gr. 3-7). 1986. 12.95 (ISBN 0-688-06645-3). Lothrop.

—My Mama Needs Me. Cummings, Pat, illus. LC 82-12654. 32p. (ps-1). 1983. 14.95 (ISBN 0-688-01670-7); PLB 14.88 (ISBN 0-688-01671-5). Lothrop.

Washington, Anthony. Young Run Away. Adoma, Afua, illus. (Orig.). (gr. 3-6). 1984. pap. 2.98 (ISBN 0-9613078-2-X). Detroit Black.

Weber, Bernard. Ira Says Goodbye. (ps-3). 1991. pap. 4.95 (ISBN 0-395-58413-2). HM.

Weinberger, Jane. That's What Counts. Margit Studio, illus. LC 87-50549. 40p. (gr. k-4). 1988. pap. 5.95 (ISBN 0-932433-33-2). Windswept Hse.

Wells, Rosemary. Don't Spill It Again, James. LC 77-71513. (Illus.). 48p. (ps-3). 1990. 8.95 (ISBN 0-8037-2118-8); pap. 3.95 (ISBN 0-8037-0831-9). Dial Bks Young.

—Shy Charles. Wells, Rosemary, illus. LC 87-27247. 32p. (ps-3). 1988. 11.95 (ISBN 0-8037-0563-8); PLB 11.89 (ISBN 0-8037-0564-6). Dial Bks Young.

Westmoreland, Ronald P. The Wild Horses of Hidden Valley. Roberts, Melissa, ed. (Illus.). 96p. (gr. 4-7). 1990. 8.95 (ISBN 0-89015-717-0). Eakin Pr.

When the Boys Ran the House. Newsom, Carol, illus. 160p. (gr. 3-7). 1983. pap. 3.25 (ISBN 0-440-49450-8, YB). Dell.

Wiggins, Veralee. A Horse for Pat. Wheeler, Gerald, ed. 128p. 1988. pap. 4.95 (ISBN 0-318-32714-7). Review & Herald.

Willey, Margaret. Saving Lenny. (gr. 7 up). 1990. 13.95 (ISBN 0-553-05850-9, Starfire). Bantam.

Williams, Barbara. Albert's Toothache. Chorao, Kay, illus. LC 74-4040. 32p. (ps-1). 1988. pap. 3.95 (ISBN 0-525-44363-0, 0383-120, DCB). Dutton Child Bks.

Wilson, Sarah. The Day That Henry Cleaned His Room. (ps-3). 1990. pap. 13.95 (ISBN 0-671-69202-X). S&S Trade.

Winfield, Arthur. Rover Boys at College. 191p. 1981. Repr. PLB 12.95x (ISBN 0-89966-330-3). Buccaneer Bks.

Winthrop, Elizabeth. Tough Eddie. Hoban, Lillian, illus. LC 84-13664. 32p. (ps-2). 1989. pap. 3.95 (ISBN 0-525-44496-3, DCB). Dutton Child Bks.

Wiseman, David. Adam's Common. LC 84-10936. 192p. (gr. 5 up). 1984. 11.95 (ISBN 0-395-35976-7). HM.

—Jeremy Visick. (gr. 5 up). 1981. 12.95 (ISBN 0-395-30449-0). HM.

—Jeremy Visick. (gr. 4-7). 1990. pap. 3.95 (ISBN 0-395-56153-1). HM.

Wojciechowska, Maia. Shadow of a Bull. LC 86-22199. 160p. (gr. 4). 1987. pap. 3.95 (ISBN 0-689-71132-8, Aladdin). Macmillan Child Grp.

Wolff, Virginia E. Probably Still Nick Swansen. 144p. (gr. 7 up). 1988. 13.95 (ISBN 0-8050-0701-6). H Holt & Co.

Wood, Audrey. Elbert's Bad Word. Wood, Audrey & Wood, Don, illus. LC 86-7557. 32p. (ps-3). 1988. 13. 95 (ISBN 0-15-225320-3, HJ). HarBraceJ.

Wood, Marcia. The Search for Jim McGwynn. LC 88-36583. 160p. (gr. 5-7). 1989. 12.95 (ISBN 0-689-31479-5, Atheneum Child Bk). Macmillan Child Grp.

Wyeth, Sharon D. Boys Wanted. (gr. k-6). 1989. pap. 2.95 (ISBN 0-440-40224-7, YB). Dell.

Yorinks, Arthur. Hey, Al. Egielski, Richard, illus. LC 86-80955. 32p. (gr. k up). 1986. 13.95 (ISBN 0-374-33060-3). FS&G.

—It Happened in Pinsk. Egielski, Richard, illus. LC 83-1727. 32p. (ps up). 1983. 12.95 (ISBN 0-374-33651-2). FS&G.

Young, Helen. What Difference Does It Make, Danny? Blake, Quentin, illus. LC 80-65665. 96p. (gr. 3-6). 1980. 10.95 (ISBN 0-233-97248-X). Andre Deutsch.

Ziefert, Harriet. Goodnight, Everyone. Baruffi, Andrea, illus. LC 88-80666. (ps-3). 1988. 11.95 (ISBN 0-316-98756-5). Little.

—Harry Goes to Fun Land. LC 88-82400. (Illus.). 32p. (ps-3). 1989. pap. 8.95 (ISBN 0-670-82664-2). Viking Child Bks.

—Harry Goes to Fun Land. Smith, Mavis, illus. LC 88-62146. 32p. (ps-3). 1989. pap. 3.50 (ISBN 0-14-050980-1, Puffin). Puffin Bks.

—Harry's Bath. 1990. 9.95 (ISBN 0-553-05863-0, Little Rooster). Bantam.

—I Won't Go to Bed! Baruffi, Andrea, illus. 32p. (ps-3). 1987. 10.95 (ISBN 0-316-98768-9). Little.

—Tim & Jim Take Off. (Illus.). 32p. (ps-2). 1990. pap. 8.95 (ISBN 0-670-83199-9). Viking Child Bks.

—Tim & Jim Take Off. Mandel, Suzy, illus. 32p. (ps-3). 1990. pap. 3.50 (ISBN 0-14-054222-1, Puffin). Puffin Bks.

Zimelman, Nathan. Please Excuse Jasper. Cruz, Ray, illus. 32p. (gr. k-4). 1987. 1.00 (ISBN 0-687-31643-X). Abingdon.

Zindel, Paul. The Amazing & Death-Defying Diary of Eugene Dingman. LC 82-47712. 224p. (gr. 7 up). 1987. 12.95 (ISBN 0-06-026862-X); PLB 12.89 (ISBN 0-06-026863-8). HarpC Child Bks.

Zolotow, Charlotte. But Not Billy. Chorao, Kay, illus. LC 82-47703. 32p. (ps-k). 1983. 12.95 (ISBN 0-06-026963-4); PLB 12.89 (ISBN 0-06-026964-2). HarpC Child Bks.

—My Grandson Lew. Pene du Boid, William, illus. LC 73-1433. 32p. (ps-3). 1985. pap. 3.95 (ISBN 0-06-443066-9, Trophy). HarpC Child Bks.

—Over & Over. Reissue. ed. Williams, Garth, illus. LC 56-8149. 32p. (ps-3). 1957. 7.95 (ISBN 0-694-00195-3); PLB 14.89 (ISBN 0-06-026956-1). HarpC Child Bks.

—Someone New. Blegvad, Erik, illus. LC 77-11838. (ps-3). 1978. 12.95 (ISBN 0-06-027017-9); PLB 12.89 (ISBN 0-06-027018-7). HarpC Child Bks.

—Timothy Too! (ps-3). 1986. 12.95 (ISBN 0-395-39378-7). HM.

BOYS–POETRY

Derwent, Lavinia. Sula. 160p. (gr. 5-7). 1989. pap. 5.95 (ISBN 0-86241-068-1, Pub. by Cnngt Pub Ltd). Trafalgar Sq.

BOYS' CLUBS–FICTION

Brinley, Bertrand R. The Mad Scientists' Club. (gr. 4-6). 1967. pap. 2.25 (ISBN 0-590-32318-0). Scholastic Inc.

Lawrence, James. Binky Brothers & the Fearless Four. Kessler, Leonard, illus. LC 75-77936. 64p. (gr. k-3). 1970. 4.95 (ISBN 0-06-023760-0). HarpC Child Bks.

BRAILLE, LOUIS, 1809-1852

Davidson, Margaret. Louis Braille: The Boy Who Invented Books for the Blind. Compere, illus. (gr. k-3). 1974. pap. 2.50 (ISBN 0-590-41984-6). Scholastic Inc.

Keeler, Stephen. Louis Braille. (Illus.). 32p. (gr. 4-9). 1986. PLB 11.90 (ISBN 0-531-18071-9, Pub. by Bookwright). Watts.

Rich, Beverly. Louis Braille: Inventor of a Way to Read & Write That Has Helped Millions of Blind People Communicate with the World. LC 89-4275. (Illus.). 64p. (gr. 5-6). 1989. PLB 12.95 (ISBN 0-8368-0097-4). Gareth Stevens Inc.

BRAIN

see also Dreams; Mind and Body; Nervous System; Psychology; Sleep

Asimov, Isaac. How Did We Find Out about the Brain. (gr. 5 up). 1987. 10.95 (ISBN 0-8027-6736-2); PLB 11.85 (ISBN 0-8027-6737-0). Walker & Co.

August, Paul. Brain Function. Mendelson, Jack H. & Mello, Nancyintro. by. (Illus.). 104p. (gr. 5 up). 1988. lib. bdg. 18.95x (ISBN 1-55546-204-9). Chelsea Hse.

Bailey, Donna. All about Your Brain. LC 90-41008. (Illus.). 48p. (gr. 2-5). 1990. PLB 15.96 (ISBN 0-8114-2778-1). Steck-V.

The Brain & Nervous System. (Illus.). 48p. (gr. 4up). 1981. PLB 12.40 (ISBN 0-531-04288-X). Watts.

Bruun, Ruth D. & Bruun, Bertel. Brain: What It Is, What It Does. Brunn, Peter, illus. LC 88-21182. 64p. 1989. 12.95 (ISBN 0-688-08453-2); PLB 12.88 (ISBN 0-688-08454-0). Greenwillow.

Facklam, Margery & Facklam, Howard. The Brain: Magnificent Mind Machine. Facklam, Paul, illus. LC 81-47529. (gr. 7 up). 1982. 12.95 (ISBN 0-15-211388-6, HJ). HarBraceJ.

Kettelkamp, Larry. The Human Brain. LC 86-4417. (Illus.). 96p. (gr. 5-12). 1986. PLB 16.95 (ISBN 0-89490-126-5). Enslow Pubs.

LeMaster, Leslie J. Your Brain & Nervous System. LC 84-7635. (Illus.). 48p. (gr. k-4). 1984. PLB 14.60 (ISBN 0-516-01931-7); pap. 4.95 (ISBN 0-516-41931-5). Childrens.

Mathers, Douglas. Brain. Farmer, Andrew & Green, Robina, illus. LC 90-42883. 32p. (gr. 4-6). 1991. PLB 11.89 (ISBN 0-8167-2090-8); pap. 3.95 (ISBN 0-8167-2091-6). Troll Assocs.

Metos, Thomas H. The Human Mind: How We Think & Learn. (Illus.). 128p. (gr. 9-12). 1990. PLB 12.40 (ISBN 0-531-10885-6). Watts.

Moore, Adam. Broken Arrow Boy. Thatch, Nancy R., ed. Melton, David, intro. by. LC 90-5933. (Illus.). 26p. (gr. 3-8). 1990. lib. bdg. 12.95 (ISBN 0-933849-24-9). Landmark Edns.

Parker, Steve. The Brain & Nervous System. rev. ed. (Illus.). 48p. (gr. 5 up). 1991. pap. 4.95 (ISBN 0-531-24600-0). Watts.

—Learning a Lesson: How You See, Think & Remember. (Illus.). 32p. (gr. k-4). 1991. PLB 11.40 (ISBN 0-531-14087-3). Watts.

Platt, Kin. Brogg's Brain. LC 79-9622. 128p. (gr. 6 up). 1981. (Lipp Jr Bks). HarpC Child Bks.

Silverstein, Alvin & Silverstein, Virginia B. The World of the Brain. LC 86-31007. (Illus.). 192p. (gr. 7up). 1986. 12.95 (ISBN 0-688-05777-2). Morrow Jr Bks.

Smith, Kathie B. & Crenson, Victoria. Thinking. Storms, Robert S., illus. LC 87-5886. 24p. (gr. k-3). PLB 9.59 (ISBN 0-8167-1016-3); pap. text ed. 1.95 (ISBN 0-8167-1017-1). Troll Assocs.

Stafford, Patricia. Your Two Brains. Tunney, Linda, illus. LC 85-28575. 96p. (gr. 3-7). 1986. 12.95 (ISBN 0-689-31142-7, Atheneum Child Bk). Macmillan Child Grp.

Tyler. Brain Puzzles. (gr. 2-5). 1980. (Usborne-Hayes); PLB 12.96 (ISBN 0-88110-051-X); pap. 3.95 (ISBN 0-86020-437-5). EDC.

BRASS INSTRUMENTS

see Wind Instruments

BRAVERY

see Courage

BRAZIL

Ashford, Moyra. Brazil. LC 90-19250. (Illus.). 96p. (gr. 6-11). 1991. PLB 18.60 (ISBN 0-8114-2436-7). Steck-V.

Bailey, Donna & Sproule, Anna. Brazil. LC 90-30534. (Illus.). 32p. (gr. 2-5). 1990. PLB 14.64 (ISBN 0-8114-2560-6). Steck-V.

Bender, Evelyn. Brazil. (Illus.). (gr. 5 up). 1990. 14.95 (ISBN 0-7910-1108-9). Chelsea Hse.

Carpenter, Mark. Brazil: An Awakening Giant. LC 87-13417. (Illus.). 128p. (gr. 5 up). 1987. PLB 14.95 (ISBN 0-87518-366-2, Dillon). Macmillan Child Grp.

Cobb, Vicki. This Place Is Wet. Lavallee, Barbara, illus. 32p. (gr. 2-4). 1989. 12.95 (ISBN 0-8027-6880-6); PLB 13.85 (ISBN 0-8027-6881-4). Walker & Co.

Cross, Wilbur. Brazil. LC 84-7602. (Illus.). 128p. (gr. 5-9). 1984. lib. bdg. 25.27 (ISBN 0-516-02753-0). Childrens.

Haverstock, Nathan A. Brazil in Pictures. rev. ed. (Illus.). 64p. (gr. 5 up). 1987. PLB 12.95 (ISBN 0-8225-1802-3). Lerner Pubns.

Jacobsen, Karen. Brazil. LC 89-10042. 48p. (gr. k-4). 1989. PLB 14.60 (ISBN 0-516-01171-5); pap. 4.95 (ISBN 0-516-41171-3). Childrens.

Lye, Keith. Take a Trip to Brazil. (Illus.). 32p. (ps-4). 1984. lib. bdg. 7.99 (ISBN 0-531-04736-9). Watts.

BRAZIL–FICTION

Cohen, Miriam. Born to Dance Samba. Fiammenghi, Gioia, illus. LC 83-47690. 160p. (gr. 4-7). 1984. PLB 12.89 (ISBN 0-06-021359-0). HarpC Child Bks.

Nunes, Lygia B. My Friend the Painter. Pontiero, Giovanni, tr. from POR. 80p. (gr. 4-8). 1991. 13.95 (ISBN 0-15-256340-7). HarBraceJ.

BREAD

see also Baking

Devlin, Wende & Devlin, Harry. Cranberry Thanksgiving. Devlin, Harry, illus. LC 80-17070. 48p. (ps-3). 1984. Repr. of 1971 ed. 13.95 (ISBN 0-02-729930-9, Four Winds). Macmillan Child Grp.

Jones, Judith & Jones, Evan. Knead It, Punch It, Bake It! Jarrett, Lauren, illus. 128p. (gr. 3-6). 1981. (Crowell Jr Bks). HarpC Child Bks.

Mitgutsch, Ali. From Grain to Bread. Mitgutsch, Ali, illus. LC 80-28592. 24p. (ps-3). 1981. PLB 6.95 (ISBN 0-87614-155-6). Carolrhoda Bks.

Moncure, Jane B. What Was It Before It Was Bread? Hygaard, Elizabeth, illus. LC 85-11402. 32p. (ps-2). 1985. PLB 11.97 (ISBN 0-89565-323-0). Childs World.

Morris, Ann. Bread, Bread, Bread. Heyman, Ken, photos by. LC 82-26677. (Illus.). 32p. (ps-2). 1989. 14.95 (ISBN 0-688-06334-9); PLB 14.88 (ISBN 0-688-06335-7). Lothrop.
Oppenneer, Betsy. Betsy's Breads. rev. ed. (Illus.). 40p. (gr. 8 up). 1991. pap. 7.95 (ISBN 0-9627665-2-6). Breadworks.
Patterson, Geoffrey. All about Bread. Patterson, Geoffrey, illus. 32p. (gr. k-3). 1985. 10.95 (ISBN 0-233-97635-3). Andre Deutsch.
Solomon, Hannah. Bake Bread. Stevenson, Edward, illus. LC 76-18807. (gr. 5-12). 1976. (Lipp Jr Bks). HarpC Child Bks.
Story of Bread. (ARA., Illus.). (gr. 3-5). 3.50x (ISBN 0-86685-226-3). Intl Bk Ctr.
Turner, Dorothy. Bread. Yates, John, illus. 32p. (gr. 1-4). 1989. PLB 9.95 (ISBN 0-87614-359-1). Carolrhoda Bks.

BREATHING
see Respiration

BRIDAL CUSTOMS
see Marriage Customs and Rites

BRIDGE (GAME)
Goodwin, Jude & Ellison, Don. Teach Me to Play: A First Book of Bridge. (gr. 3-9). 1988. PLB 10.95 (ISBN 0-944705-03-0); pap. 10.95 (ISBN 0-944705-01-4). Pando Pubns.
Marsh, Carole. Six Puppy Feet: Bridge for Kids. (Illus.). (gr. k-12). 1983. 19.95 (ISBN 1-55609-157-5); pap. 14.95 (ISBN 0-935326-13-8). Gallopade Pub Group.

BRIDGER, JAMES, 1804-1881
Luce, Williard & Luce, Celia. Jim Bridger: Man of the Mountains. Parrish, George I., Jr., illus. 80p. (gr. 2-6). 1991. Repr. of 1966 ed. PLB 12.95 (ISBN 0-7910-1454-1). Chelsea Hse.

BRIDGES
see also names of cities with the subdivision Bridges (e.g. New York City–Bridges) also names of bridges, e.g. Brooklyn Bridge
Ardley, Neil. Bridges. Stefoff, Rebecca, ed. LC 90-40247. (Illus.). 48p. (gr. 4-7). 1990. PLB 17.26 (ISBN 0-944483-74-7). Garrett Ed Corp.
Carlisle, Norman & Carlisle, Madelyn. Bridges. LC 82-17874. (Illus.). 48p. (gr. k-4). 1983. PLB 14.60 (ISBN 0-516-01677-6). Childrens.
Fitzpatrick, Julie. Towers & Bridges. (Illus.). 32p. (gr. 3-5). 1988. PLB 9.96 (ISBN 0-382-09536-7). Silver Burdett Pr.
Kent, Zachary. The Story of the Brooklyn Bridge. LC 88-16220. (Illus.). 32p. (gr. 3-6). 1988. PLB 13.27 (ISBN 0-516-04739-6); pap. 3.95 (ISBN 0-516-44739-4). Childrens.
Mitgutsch, Ali. From Cement to Bridge. Mitgutsch, Ali, illus. LC 81-334. 24p. (ps-3). 1981. PLB 6.95 (ISBN 0-87614-148-3). Carolrhoda Bks.
Pelta, Kathy. Bridging the Golden Gate. (Illus.). 96p. (gr. 4-8). 1987. PLB 11.95 (ISBN 0-8225-1707-8); pap. 4.95 (ISBN 0-8225-9521-4). Lerner Pubns.
Richard, Graham. Bridges. (Illus.). 32p. (gr. 4-6). 1987. lib. bdg. 8.99 (ISBN 0-531-18108-1, Pub. by Bookwright Pr). Watts.

BRIDGES–FICTION
Massi, Jeri. The Bridge. (Illus.). 122p. (Orig.). (gr. 2-4). 1986. pap. 4.95 (ISBN 0-89084-348-1). Bob Jones Univ Pr.
Neville, Emily C. The Bridge. Himler, Ronald, illus. LC 87-24941. 40p. (ps-3). 1988. 13.95 (ISBN 0-06-024385-6); PLB 13.89 (ISBN 0-06-024386-4). HarpC Child Bks.

BRIDGMAN, LAURA DEWEY, 1829-1889
Hunter, Edith F. Child of the Silent Night. Holmes, Bea, illus. 128p. (gr. 2-5). 1991. pap. 3.25 (ISBN 0-440-41223-4, YB). Dell.
—Child of the Silent Night: The Story of Laura Bridgman. Holmes, Bea, illus. 128p. (gr. 2-5). 1963. 14.95 (ISBN 0-395-06835-5). HM.

BRIGANDS
see Robbers and Outlaws

BRITAIN, BATTLE OF, 1940
Black, Wallace B. & Blashfield, Jean F. Battle of Britain. LC 90-46579. (Illus.). 48p. (gr. 5-6). 1991. RSBE 11.95 (ISBN 0-89686-553-3, Crestwood Hse). Macmillan Child Grp.
Skipper, G. C. Battle of Britain. LC 80-15187. (Illus.). 48p. (gr. 3 up). 1980. PLB 14.60 (ISBN 0-516-04781-7). Childrens.

BRITISH COLUMBIA–FICTION
Blades, Ann. A Boy of Tache. LC 76-58698. (Illus.). (gr. 1-5). 1973. 7.95 (ISBN 0-88776-023-6); pap. 5.95 (ISBN 0-88776-034-1). Tundra Bks.

BRITISH IN THE U. S.
Cates, Edwin H. English in America. rev. ed. LC 66-10145. (Illus.). 72p. (gr. 5 up). 1978. PLB 11.95 (ISBN 0-8225-0205-4); pap. 3.95 (ISBN 0-8225-1007-3). Lerner Pubns.
Cornelius, James. The English Americans. LC 89-70801. (Illus.). 112p. (gr. 5 up). 1991. 17.95 (ISBN 0-87754-874-9). Chelsea Hse.

BRITISH IN THE U. S.–FICTION

Weisberg, Valerie H. Three Jolly Stories Include: Three Jollys, Jollys Visit L. A., Jolly Gets Mugged: An ESL Adult-Child Reader. Kolino, Olga, illus. 76p. (Orig.). 1985. pap. text ed. 6.95x (ISBN 0-9610912-4-X). V H Pub.
"Hands across the-sea" tell realistic & humorous situations in three separate stories with questions after each to promote understanding, comprehension & sharing of ideas. The glossary gives definitions for British & American idioms. Earthquakes, mistaken identity & mugging are just a few of the mishaps confronting the British triplets when they visit L.A.--Reviewed by Carol Cunningham, Santa Barbara News Press & Goelta Sun. Its sequel (the genesis of the Jollys) is Little Jollys Find A Home, which is printed on recycled paper & is a timely, delightful story. Found in Farmers Jolly & Dolly's truck, the answer to how they came to be there is a big mystery. However, with good food & loving attention the Jollys grow strong & happy. This sympathetic mystery "will give solace & reassurance to homeless or orphaned children & empathy for others."--Independent Small Press Review, Spring 1991. "The writing & graphics in this story are endearing & in these troubled times, they bring a message of love & hope."
Publisher Provided Annotation.

BROADCASTING
see Radio Broadcasting; Television Broadcasting

BRONTE, CHARLOTTE, 1816-1855
Martin, C. Brontes. (Illus.). 112p. (gr. 7 up). 1989. lib. bdg. 18.60 (ISBN 0-86592-299-3). Rourke Corp.

BRONTE, EMILY JANE, 1818-1848
Martin, C. Brontes. (Illus.). 112p. (gr. 7 up). 1989. lib. bdg. 18.60 (ISBN 0-86592-299-3). Rourke Corp.

BROOKLYN–FICTION
Brown, Kay. Willy's Summer Dream. (gr. 7 up). 1989. 13.95 (ISBN 0-15-200645-1, Gulliver Bks). HarBraceJ.
Chaikin, Miriam. I Should Worry, I Should Care. Egielski, Richard, illus. LC 78-19480. (gr. 3-6). 1979. 12.89 (ISBN 0-06-021174-1). HarpC Child Bks.
Cohen, Miriam. Robert & Dawn Marie 4Ever. LC 85-45269. 160p. (gr. 7 up). 1986. 11.95 (ISBN 0-06-021396-5). HarpC Child Bks.
Rosenblum, Richard. My Block. Rosenblum, Richard, illus. LC 86-28897. 32p. (gr. k-2). 1988. 12.95 (ISBN 0-689-31283-0, Atheneum Child Bk). Macmillan Child Grp.
Shura, Mary F. The Search for Grissi. (gr. 3-7). 1986. 12.95 (ISBN 0-399-21705-3, Putnam). Putnam Pub Group.

BROOKLYN BRIDGE
St. George, Judith. The Brooklyn Bridge: They Said It Couldn't Be Built. (gr. 5 up). Date not set. 13.99 (ISBN 0-399-61282-3, Putnam). Putnam Pub Group.

BROOKLYN DODGERS (BASEBALL TEAM)
Cohen, Barbara. Thank You, Jackie Robinson. Cuffari, Richard, illus. LC 87-29341. (gr. 3-6). 1988. PLB 13.95 (ISBN 0-688-07909-1). Lothrop.

BROTHERS AND SISTERS
Arnold, Eric H. & Loeb, Jeffrey. I'm Telling! Kids Talk about Brothers & Sisters. Karas, G. Brian, illus. (gr. 3-7). 1987. 12.95 (ISBN 0-316-05185-3). Little.
Bode, Janet. Truce: Ending the Sibling War. 144p. (gr. 8-12). 1991. 12.95 (ISBN 0-531-15221-9); PLB 12.90 (ISBN 0-531-10996-8). Watts.
Bunin, Sherry & Bunin, Catherine. Is That Your Sister? LC 76-60. (Illus.). 1976. Pantheon.

Crouthamel, Thomas G., Sr. It's OK. 2nd ed. Hasty, Patti, illus. LC 86-27694. 36p. (gr. 12 up). 1990. pap. 6.95 (ISBN 0-940701-18-9). Keystone PA.
Following the death of his daughter, Thomas Crouthamel began to really listen to what his son & other grieving siblings were saying. He learned that when someone's brother or sister dies, the surviving sibling(s) goes through a traumatic grief process that lasts far longer than people realize. Although the effects of death experienced by a bereaved sibling are common to all grieving siblings, each feels he/she is standing alone in the world, & no one understands. Parents are enveloped in their own grief, peers don't want to hear about it, & teachers don't have the training, or time to cope with a grieving student. IT'S OK is a "Survival Kit" for bereaved siblings. It provides understanding, answers, help, & above all, PERMISSION for surviving siblings to act & feel the way they do. IT'S OK compassionately explains that they are not alone, they are not crazy, that their feelings, frustrations, & emotions are all "normal" experiences that can happen to anyone following the death of a sister or brother. Although IT'S OK was written for a young age group, favorable reviews have been received from adult bereaved siblings in their 60's & 80's. Sibling grief has no age limits.
Publisher Provided Annotation.

Gondosch, Linda. Who Needs a Bratty Brother? Cogancherry, Helen, illus. (gr. 3-7). 1987. pap. 2.50 (ISBN 0-671-62777-5, Minstrel Bks). PB.
Hawkins-Walsh, Elizabeth. Katie's Premature Brother. Johnson, Joy, ed. Borum, Shari, illus. 24p. (Orig.). (ps). 1990. pap. 2.50 (ISBN 1-56123-005-7). Centering Corp.
Lewis, Linda. Want to Trade Two Brothers for a Cat? (Orig.). (gr. 3-6). 1989. pap. 2.75 (ISBN 0-671-66605-3, Minstrel Bks). PB.
Marshak, Samuel. The Month Brothers: A Slavic Tale. Whitney, Thomas P., tr. from RUS. Stanley, Diane, illus. LC 82-7927. 32p. (gr. k up). 1983. PLB 12.88 (ISBN 0-688-01510-7). Morrow Jr Bks.
Mazer, Norma F. Three Sisters. 240p. (gr. 7 up). 1987. pap. 2.50 (ISBN 0-590-33254-6, Point). Scholastic Inc.
Peterson, Jeanne W. I Have a Sister, My Sister Is Deaf. Ray, Deborah, illus. LC 76-24306. (gr. k-3). 1977. 13.95 (ISBN 0-06-024701-0); PLB 13.89 (ISBN 0-06-024702-9). HarpC Child Bks.
Roos, Stephen. My Horrible Secret. Newsom, Carol, illus. 128p. (Orig.). (gr. 4-7). 1991. pap. 3.25 (ISBN 0-440-43956-6, YB). Dell.
Watson, Jane W., et al. Sometimes I'm Jealous. Trivas, Irene, illus. 32p. (ps up). 1986. pap. 2.95 (ISBN 0-517-56062-3). Crown.

BROTHERS AND SISTERS–FICTION
Adams, Edward B., ed. Two Brothers & Their Magic Gourds. Dong-Ho, Choi, illus. 32p. (gr. 3). 1981. 8.95 (ISBN 0-8048-1474-0, Pub. by Seoul Intl Tourist Korea). C E Tuttle.
Adler, C. S. Get Lost, Little Brother. 144p. (gr. 4-7). 1983. 11.95 (ISBN 0-89919-154-1, Clarion). HM.
Adler, Katie & McBride, Rachael. For Sale: One Sister--Cheap! Venezia, Mike, illus. LC 86-11723. 32p. (ps-2). 1986. PLB 13.93 (ISBN 0-516-03476-6); pap. 3.95 (ISBN 0-516-43476-4). Childrens.
Alcock, Vivien. The Cuckoo Sister. large type ed. 256p. (gr. 3-7). 1987. lib. bdg. 15.95x (ISBN 0-7451-0586-6, Pub. by Chivers Pr UK). G K Hall.
—The Cuckoo Sister. (gr. k-6). 1988. pap. 2.95 (ISBN 0-440-40101-1, YB). Dell.
Alcott, Louisa May. Jack & Jill. (Illus.). 352p. (gr. 5 up). 1991. pap. 2.95 (ISBN 0-14-035128-0, Puffin). Puffin Bks.
Alexander, Martha. Nobody Asked Me If I Wanted a Baby Sister. Alexander, Martha, illus. LC 78-153731. (ps-2). 1971. 10.95 (ISBN 0-8037-6401-4); PLB 10.89 (ISBN 0-8037-6402-2). Dial Bks Young.
Aliki. Jack & Jake. Aliki, illus. LC 85-9911. 32p. (ps-1). 1986. 11.75 (ISBN 0-688-06099-4); PLB 11.88 (ISBN 0-688-06100-1). Greenwillow.
Ames, Mildred. The Dancing Madness: A Novel. LC 80-65831. 144p. (gr. 7 up). 1980. 8.95 (ISBN 0-385-28113-7). Delacorte.
Angell, Judie. A Home Is to Share... & Share... & Share. LC 83-21356. 112p. (gr. 4-6). 1984. 12.95 (ISBN 0-02-705830-1, Bradbury Pr). Macmillan Child Grp.
Arthur, Catherine. My Sister's Silent World. Talbot, Nathan, illus. LC 78-13140. 32p. (gr. 3). 1979. PLB 13.27 (ISBN 0-516-02022-6). Childrens.
Ash, Russell. Henry & Caroline at Home. Isles, Joanna, illus. 32p. (gr. 2-4). 1991. 17.95 (ISBN 1-85145-358-X, Pub. by Pavilion UK). Trafalgar Sq.
Auch, Mary J. Pick of the Litter. LC 87-25205. 160p. (gr. 3-7). 1988. 13.95 (ISBN 0-8234-0692-X). Holiday.
Baczewski, Paul. Just for Kicks. LC 90-30528. 192p. (gr. 6 up). 1990. 13.95 (ISBN 0-397-32465-0, Lipp Jr Bks); PLB 13.89 (ISBN 0-397-32466-9, Lipp Jr Bks). HarpC Child Bks.
Baird, Thomas. Walk Out a Brother. LC 82-48859. 288p. (gr. 7 up). 1983. PLB 12.89 (ISBN 0-06-020356-0). HarpC Child Bks.
Banks, Kate. Big, Bigger, Biggest Adventure. Yalowitz, Paul, illus. LC 89-34919. 40p. (ps-3). 1990. 12.95 (ISBN 0-394-89857-5); lib. bdg. 13.99 (ISBN 0-394-99857-X). Knopf.
Bechard, Margaret. My Sister, My Science Report. 96p. (gr. 3-7). 1990. pap. 11.95 (ISBN 0-670-83290-1). Viking Child Bks.

Berenstain, Stan & Berenstain, Janice. The Berenstain Bears: No Girls Allowed. Berenstain, Stan & Berenstain, Janice, illus. LC 85-18246. 32p. (ps-1). 1986. lib. bdg. 5.99 (ISBN 0-394-97331-3); pap. 2.25 (ISBN 0-394-87331-9). Random.

Birdseye, Tom. Tucker. LC 89-46243. 120p. (gr. 3-7). 1990. 13.95 (ISBN 0-8234-0813-2). Holiday.

Bloss, Janet A. How to Snoop in Your Sister's Diary. Robinson, Don, illus. 157p. (gr. 3-6). 1989. pap. 2.50 (ISBN 0-87406-390-6). Willowisp Pr.

—Thirty Ways to Dump a Sister. (Illus.). 144p. (gr. 3-6). 1986. 2.25 (ISBN 0-87406-057-5). Willowisp Pr.

Blume, Judy. Superfudge. 176p. (gr. 2-6). 1981. pap. 3.50 (ISBN 0-440-48433-2, YB). Dell.

—Superfudge. LC 80-10439. 176p. (gr. 3-6). 1980. 11.95 (ISBN 0-525-40522-4, DCB). Dutton Child Bks.

—Superfudge. large type ed. 239p. (gr. 2-6). 1987. Repr. of 1980 ed. lib. bdg. 14.95 (ISBN 1-55736-014-6). ABC-CLIO.

—Tales of a Fourth Grade Nothing. Doty, Roy, illus. LC 70-179050. 128p. (gr. 2-5). 1972. 10.95 (ISBN 0-525-40720-0, DCB). Dutton Child Bks.

Bogart, Jo Ellen. Daniel's Dog. (ps-3). 1990. pap. 11.95 (ISBN 0-590-43402-0). Scholastic Inc.

Bonsall, Crosby N. The Day I Had to Play with My Sister. Bonsall, Crosby N., illus. LC 72-76507. 32p. (ps-2). 1972. PLB 10.89 (ISBN 0-06-020576-8). HarpC Child Bks.

Bottner, Barbara. Big Boss! Little Boss! LC 78-3281. (Illus.). (gr. 1-4). 1978. Pantheon.

Boyd, Lizi. Sam Is My Half Brother. (Illus.). 32p. (ps-2). 1990. pap. 11.95 (ISBN 0-670-83046-1). Viking Child Bks.

Bradman, Tony. The Bluebeards: Peril at the Pirate School. Murphy, Rowan B., illus. 64p. (gr. 2-5). 1990. pap. 2.95 (ISBN 0-8120-4502-5). Barron.

Brandenberg, Franz. I Wish I Was Sick, Too! Aliki, illus. LC 75-46610. 32p. (gr. k-3). 1976. PLB 12.88 (ISBN 0-688-84047-7). Greenwillow.

Brink, Carol R. Magical Melons. Davis, Marguerite, illus. LC 90-144. 208p. (gr. 3-7). 1990. pap. 3.95 (ISBN 0-689-71416-5, Aladdin). Macmillan Child Grp.

Browne, Anthony. The Tunnel. Browne, Anthony, illus. (gr. 1-6). 1990. 11.95 (ISBN 0-394-84582-X); lib. bdg. 12.99 (ISBN 0-685-30419-1). Knopf.

—Tunnel. (gr. 4-8). 1990. 12.99 (ISBN 0-394-94582-4, KNOPF). Random.

Bulla, Clyde R. The Christmas Coat. Wickstrom, Sylvie, illus. LC 89-2380. 48p. (gr. 2-4). 1990. 13.95 (ISBN 0-394-89385-9); PLB 14.99 (ISBN 0-394-99385-3). Knopf.

—Keep Running, Allen! Ichikawa, Satomi, illus. LC 77-23311. (gr. k-2). 1978. PLB 13.89 (ISBN 0-690-01375-2, Crowell Jr Bks). HarpC Child Bks.

Burgess, Barbara H. Oren Bell. 1991. 15.00 (ISBN 0-385-30325-4). Delacorte.

Butler, Beverly. My Sister's Keeper. 224p. (gr. 7-11). 1980. 8.95 (ISBN 0-396-07803-6, Putnam); pap. 3.95 (ISBN 0-396-08744-2, Putnam). Putnam Pub Group.

Byars, Betsy. Bingo Brown, Gypsy Lover. 160p. (gr. 3 up). 1990. 11.95 (ISBN 0-670-83322-3). Viking Child Bks.

—The Not-Just-Anybody Family. Rogers, Jacqueline, illus. LC 85-16184. 160p. (gr. 4-6). 1986. 13.95 (ISBN 0-385-29443-3). Delacorte.

Byars, Betsy C. Go & Hush the Baby. McCully, Emily A., illus. (gr. k-3). 1971. pap. 11.95 (ISBN 0-670-34270-X). Viking Child Bks.

Callen, Larry. Contrary Imaginations. LC 90-33181. (Illus.). 128p. (gr. 6 up). 1991. 12.95 (ISBN 0-688-09961-0). Greenwillow.

Cannon, A. E. Shadow Brothers. 1990. 14.95 (ISBN 0-385-29982-6). Doubleday.

Caple, Kathy. The Coolest Place in Town. Caple, Kathy, illus. 32p. (gr. k-3). 1990. 13.95 (ISBN 0-395-51523-8). HM.

Carlson, Natalie S. A Brother for the Orphelines. (gr. k-6). 1969. pap. 2.75 (ISBN 0-440-40827-X, YB). Dell.

Carlstrom, Nancy W. Heather Hiding. Nolan, Dennis, illus. LC 88-8286. 32p. (ps-1). 1990. 12.95 (ISBN 0-02-717370-4, Mcmillan Child Bk). Macmillan Child Grp.

Chetwin, Grace. Child of the Air. LC 90-47565. 240p. (gr. 5 up). 1991. SBE 14.95 (ISBN 0-02-718317-3, Bradbury Pr). Macmillan Child Grp.

Chorao, Kay. Ups & Downs with Oink & Pearl. Chorao, Kay, illus. LC 85-45264. 64p. (gr. k-3). 1986. PLB 11.89 (ISBN 0-06-021275-6). HarpC Child Bks.

Church, Kristine. My Brother John. Niland, Kilmeny, illus. LC 90-25868. 32p. (ps-3). 1991. 12.95 (ISBN 0-688-10800-8, Tambourine Bks); PLB 12.88 (ISBN 0-688-10801-6, Tambourine Bks). Morrow.

Clark, Sue A. The Rainbow Tree. Clark, Gary B., ed. (Illus.). 18p. (gr. 4-7). 1990. write for info. Point View Pr.

Cleaver, Vera & Cleaver, Bill. Me Too. 160p. (gr. 7-9). 1973. 13.95 (ISBN 0-397-31485-X, Lipp Jr Bks). HarpC Child Bks.

—Trial Valley. Reissue. ed. LC 76-54303. 160p. (gr. 7 up). 1987. PLB 12.89 (ISBN 0-397-32246-1, Lipp Jr Bks). HarpC Child Bks.

Clymer, Eleanor. My Brother Stevie. 96p. (Orig.). (gr. k-6). 1989. pap. 2.95 (ISBN 0-440-40125-9, YB). Dell.

Coleman, Hila. Weekend Sisters. (gr. 6 up). 1988. pap. 2.95 (ISBN 0-449-70206-5, Juniper). Fawcett.

Colman, Hila. Forgotten Girl. LC 89-38482. 160p. (gr. 5-9). 1990. 12.95 (ISBN 0-517-57591-4); PLB 13.99 (ISBN 0-517-57592-2). Crown.

Conford, Ellen. Luck of Pokey Bloom. 1987. pap. 2.50 (ISBN 0-671-63667-7, Minstrel Bks). PB.

Cook, Jean T. Hugs for Our New Baby. (Illus.). (ps-2). 1987. 5.95 (ISBN 0-570-04165-1, 56-1622). Concordia.

Corcoran, Barbara. The Hideaway. LC 86-28849. 128p. (gr. 5-9). 1987. 12.95 (ISBN 0-689-31353-5, Atheneum Child Bk). Macmillan Child Grp.

Coxe, Molly. Whose Footprints? Coxe, Molly, illus. LC 89-70850. 40p. (ps-1). 1990. 14.95 (ISBN 0-690-04835-1, Crowell Jr Bks); PLB 14.89 (ISBN 0-690-04837-8, Crowell Jr Bks). HarpC Child Bks.

Curry, Jane L. Little, Little Sister. Bleguad, Erik, illus. LC 88-13079. 32p. (ps-3). 1989. 11.95 (ISBN 0-689-50459-4, M K McElderry). Macmillan Child Grp.

Deaver, Julie R. First Wedding, Once Removed. LC 90-4184. 224p. (gr. 5-9). 1990. 13.95 (ISBN 0-06-021426-0); PLB 13.89 (ISBN 0-06-021427-9). HarpC Child Bks.

Degen, Bruce. Teddy Bear Towers. Degen, Bruce, illus. LC 90-31937. 32p. (ps-1). 1991. 13.95 (ISBN 0-06-021420-1); PLB 13.89 (ISBN 0-06-021430-9). HarpC Child Bks.

Delton, Judy. Angel in Charge. Morrill, Leslie, illus. LC 84-27862. 152p. (gr. 2-5). 1985. 13.95 (ISBN 0-395-37488-X). HM.

Dixon, Franklin W. Brother Against Brother. 160p. (Orig.). (gr. 7 up). 1989. pap. 2.95 (ISBN 0-671-70712-4, Archway). PB.

Dragonwagon, Crescent. I Hate My Brother Harry. Gackenbach, Dick, illus. LC 82-47706. 32p. (ps-3). 1983. PLB 12.89 (ISBN 0-06-021758-8). HarpC Child Bks.

—I Hate My Brother Harry. Gackenbach, Dick, illus. LC 82-47706. 32p. (gr. k-3). 1989. pap. 3.50 (ISBN 0-06-443193-2, Trophy). HarpC Child Bks.

Dubois, Claude K. He's My Jumbo! (Illus.). 32p. (ps-1). 1990. pap. 9.95 (ISBN 0-670-83029-1). Viking Child Bks.

—Looking for Ginny. (Illus.). 32p. (ps-1). 1990. pap. 9.95 (ISBN 0-670-83030-5). Viking Child Bks.

Edelman, Elaine. I Love My Baby Sister: Most of the Time. Watson, Wendy, illus. LC 85-574. 24p. (ps-3). 1985. pap. 3.95 (ISBN 0-14-050547-4, Puffin). Puffin Bks.

Evans, David. The Famous Hooper Brothers. Labby, Sherman, illus. 101p. (Orig.). 1988. pap. 15.95 (ISBN 0-929422-00-7). Jonah Pr.

Ferguson, Alane. The Practical Joke War. LC 90-45578. 144p. (gr. 3-6). 1991. SBE 12.95 (ISBN 0-02-734526-2, Bradbury Pr). Macmillan Child Grp.

Fox, Paula. Lila & the Lost Boys. large type, unabr. ed. 230p. (gr. 5-7). 1989. lib. bdg. 13.95x (ISBN 0-8161-4725-6). G K Hall.

—Lily & the Lost Boy. LC 87-5778. 160p. (gr. 6-8). 1987. 12.95 (ISBN 0-531-05720-8); PLB 12.99 (ISBN 0-531-08320-9). Orchard Bks Watts.

Franklin, Jonathan. Don't Wake the Baby. (Illus.). 32p. (ps-1). 1991. bds. 13.95 jacketed (ISBN 0-374-31826-3). FS&G.

Galbraith, Kathryn O. Roommates & Rachel. Graham, Mark, illus. LC 90-34768. 48p. (gr. 1-4). 1991. SBE 11.95 (ISBN 0-689-50520-5, M K McElderry). Macmillan Child Grp.

George, Jean C. On the Far Side of the Mountain. 1990. 14.95 (ISBN 0-525-44563-3, DCB). Dutton Child Bks.

Getz, David. Thin Air. 128p. (gr. 6 up). 1990. 14.95 (ISBN 0-8050-1379-2). H Holt & Co.

Gillespie, Bonita. Peggy's Problem. Cover, Marilyn, illus. 35p. (gr. 3-8). 1987. 6.95 (ISBN 1-55523-058-X). Winston-Derek.

Gillham, Bill. My Brother Barry. (Illus.). 96p. (gr. 2-7). 1982. 9.95 (ISBN 0-233-97358-3). Andre Deutsch.

Gondosch, Linda. Who Needs a Bratty Brother? Coganchevy, Helen, illus. LC 85-6943. 112p. (gr. 4-6). 1985. 11.95 (ISBN 0-525-67170-6, Lodestar Bks). Dutton Child Bks.

Goodman, Louise. Ida's Doll. Carter, Debby L., illus. LC 87-25085. 32p. (ps-3). 1989. 12.95 (ISBN 0-06-022275-1); PLB 12.89 (ISBN 0-06-022276-X). HarpC Child Bks.

Graham, Bob. Crusher Is Coming! (Illus.). 32p. (ps-3). 1990. pap. 3.95 (ISBN 0-14-050826-0, Puffin). Puffin Bks.

Grant, Eva. Will I Ever Be Older? Lexa, Susan, illus. Hollingsworth, Charles E., intro. by. LC 80-24782. (Illus.). (gr. k-6). 1981. PLB 16.67 (ISBN 0-8172-1363-5). Raintree Pubs.

Greenfield, Eloise. Sister. Barnett, Moneta, illus. LC 73-22182. 96p. (gr. 5-8). 1987. pap. 3.50 (ISBN 0-06-440199-5, Trophy). HarpC Child Bks.

Gretz, Susanna & Sage, Alison. Teddy Bears Cure a Cold. Gretz, Susanna, illus. 32p. (gr. k-3). 1986. pap. 2.95 (ISBN 0-590-42132-8). Scholastic Inc.

Grimm, Jacob & Grimm, Wilhelm K. Hansel & Gretel. Jeffers, Susan, illus. LC 80-15079. 32p. (gr. k up). 1986. pap. 4.95 (ISBN 0-8037-0318-X). Dial Bks Young.

Haas, Irene. The Maggie B. Haas, Irene, illus. LC 74-18183. 32p. (ps-2). 1975. 14.95 (ISBN 0-689-50021-1, M K McElderry). Macmillan Child Grp.

Hallinan, P. K. We're Very Good Friends, My Brother & I. LC 72-8371. (Illus.). 32p. (gr. k-3). 1973. PLB 13.27 (ISBN 0-516-03659-9). Childrens.

—We're Very Good Friends, My Brother & I. Hallinan, P. K., illus. 24p. (ps-3). 1990. 3.95 (ISBN 0-8249-8469-2). Ideals.

Harper, Anita. It's Not Fair. Hellard, Susan, illus. LC 86-4950. 24p. (ps-k). 1986. 10.95 (ISBN 0-399-21365-1, Philomel). Putnam Pub Group.

Havill, Juanita. It Always Happens to Leona. McCully, Emily, illus. (gr. 2 up). 1989. 12.95 (ISBN 0-517-57227-3). Crown.

Hill, Kirkpatrick. Toughboy & Sister. LC 90-31297. 128p. (gr. 3-7). 1990. 12.95 (ISBN 0-689-50506-X, M K McElderry). Macmillan Child Grp.

Hines, Anna G. They Really Like Me! LC 87-24211. (Illus.). 24p. (ps up). 1989. 11.95 (ISBN 0-688-07733-1); PLB 11.88 (ISBN 0-688-07734-X). Greenwillow.

Hinton, S. E. Tex. LC 78-50448. 224p. (gr. 7 up). 1979. pap. 14.95 (ISBN 0-385-29020-9). Delacorte.

—Tex. 192p. (gr. k up). 1989. pap. 3.50 (ISBN 0-440-97850-5, LFL). Dell.

Hoban, Lillian. Arthur's Prize Reader. Hoban, Lillian, illus. LC 77-25637. 64p. (ps-3). 1978. 11.95 (ISBN 0-06-022379-0); PLB 11.89 (ISBN 0-06-022380-4). HarpC Child Bks.

Holabird, Katharine. Angelina's Baby Sister. (ps). 1991. pap. 13.00 (ISBN 0-517-58600-2). Crown.

Howe, James. Pinky & Rex Got Married. Sweet, Melissa, illus. LC 89-30786. 48p. (gr. k-3). 1990. 11.95 (ISBN 0-689-31454-X, Atheneum Child Bk); 11.95 (ISBN 0-689-31453-1, Atheneum Childrens Bks). Macmillan Child Grp.

Howe, Norma. Game of Life. (gr. 7 up). 1988. 13.95 (ISBN 0-517-57197-8). Crown.

Hughes, Dean. Brothers. LC 85-31208. 105p. (gr. 7-12). 1989. pap. 4.95 (ISBN 0-87579-232-4). Deseret Bk.

Hughes, Shirley. The Big Alfie & Annie Rose Storybook. Hughes, S., illus. LC 88-11149. 64p. (ps-1). 1989. 15.00 (ISBN 0-688-07672-6); PLB 14.88 (ISBN 0-688-07673-4). Lothrop.

Hurwitz, Johanna. Aldo Ice Cream. Wallner, John, illus. LC 80-24371. 128p. (gr. 4-6). 1981. 13.95 (ISBN 0-688-00375-3); PLB 13.88 (ISBN 0-688-00374-5, Morrow Jr Bks). Morrow Jr Bks.

—New Neighbors for Nora. reissued ed. Hoban, Lillian, illus. LC 90-47882. 80p. (ps). 1991. Repr. of 1979 ed. 12.95 (ISBN 0-688-09947-5); PLB 12.88 (ISBN 0-688-09948-3, Morrow Jr Bks). Morrow Jr Bks.

—New Neighbors for Nora. reissued ed. Hoban, Lillian, illus. LC 90-47882. 80p. (ps). 1991. Repr. of 1979 ed. 12.95 (ISBN 0-688-09947-5); PLB 12.88 (ISBN 0-688-09948-3, Morrow Jr Bks). Morrow Jr Bks.

—Nora & Mrs. Mind-Your-Own Business. reissued ed. Hoban, Lillian, illus. LC 90-47882. 80p. (ps up). 1991. Repr. of 1977 ed. 12.95 (ISBN 0-688-09945-9); PLB 12.88 (ISBN 0-688-09946-7, Morrow Jr Bks). Morrow Jr Bks.

—Russell & Elisa. Hoban, Lillian, illus. LC 88-37578. 96p. (gr. k up). 1989. 11.95 (ISBN 0-688-08792-2); lib. bdg. 11.88 (ISBN 0-688-08793-0, Morrow Jr Bks). Morrow Jr Bks.

—Russell & Elisa. (gr. 4 up). 1990. pap. 3.95 (ISBN 0-14-034406-3, Puffin). Puffin Bks.

—School's Out. Hamanaka, Sheila, illus. LC 90-13446. 128p. (gr. 2 up). 1991. 12.95 (ISBN 0-688-09938-6). Morrow Jr Bks.

—Superduper Teddy. Hoban, Lillian, illus. 80p. (gr. 2-5). 1991. pap. 3.95 (ISBN 0-14-034593-0, Puffin). Puffin Bks.

Hutchins, Pat. Tidy Titch. LC 90-38483. (Illus.). 32p. (ps up). 1991. 13.95 (ISBN 0-688-09963-7); PLB 13.88 (ISBN 0-688-09964-5). Greenwillow.

Hyland, Betty. The Girl with the Crazy Brother. LC 86-26762. 137p. (gr. 7-12). 1987. PLB 12.90 (ISBN 0-531-10345-5). Watts.

Inkiow, Dimiter. Me & Clara & Casimir the Cat. Reiner, Walter & Reiner, Traudl, illus. LC 78-31316. (gr. 1-4). 1979. 2.95 (ISBN 0-394-84124-7). Pantheon.

Jarrell, Mary. The Knee-Baby. Shimin, Symeon, illus. LC 73-75295. 32p. (ps up). 1973. 10.95 (ISBN 0-374-34246-6). FS&G.

Johnson, Angela. Do Like Kyla. Ransome, James, illus. LC 89-16229. 32p. (ps-2). 1990. 14.95 (ISBN 0-531-05852-2); PLB 14.99 (ISBN 0-531-08452-3). Orchard Bks Watts.

Just My & My Little Brother. (ps-3). Date not set. write for info. (ISBN 0-307-12628-5, Golden Pr). Western Pub.

Kalman, Maira. Hey Willy, See the Pyramids. (ps-3). 1990. pap. 4.95 (ISBN 0-14-050840-6, Puffin). Puffin Bks.

Keller, Holly. What Alvin Wanted. LC 88-34917. (Illus.). 32p. (ps up). 1990. 12.95 (ISBN 0-688-08933-X); lib. bdg. 12.88 (ISBN 0-688-08934-8). Greenwillow.

Kellogg, Steven. Much Bigger Than Martin. Kellogg, Steven, illus. LC 75-2799. 32p. (ps-3). 1985. 12.95 (ISBN 0-8037-5809-X); PLB 11.89 (ISBN 0-8037-5810-3). Dial Bks Young.

Kerr, M. E. Love Is a Missing Person. LC 75-6299. 176p. (gr. 7 up). 1975. PLB 13.89 (ISBN 0-06-023162-9). HarpC Child Bks.

—Night Kites. LC 85-45386. 192p. (gr. 7 up). 1986. 12.95 (ISBN 0-06-023253-6); PLB 12.89 (ISBN 0-06-023254-4). HarpC Child Bks.

Konigsburg, E. L. From the Mixed-Up Files of Mrs. Basil E. Frankweiler. 1987. pap. 3.95 (ISBN 0-689-71181-6, Aladdin). Macmillan Child Grp.

Kroll, Steven. Loose Tooth. Tusa, Tricia, illus. LC 83-49008. 32p. (ps-3). 1984. 13.95g (ISBN 0-8234-0518-4). Holiday.

Lakin, Patricia. Just Like Me, Vol. 1. 1989. 14.95 (ISBN 0-316-51233-8). Little.

—Oh, Brother! Brewster, Patience, illus. 32p. (gr. 1 up). 1987. 12.95 (ISBN 0-316-51231-1). Little.

Landis, James D. The Sisters Impossible. 160p. 1981. pap. 2.50 (ISBN 0-553-26013-8). Bantam.

—The Sisters Impossible. LC 78-32148. (gr. 4-7). 1979. Knopf.

—The Sisters Impossible. LC 78-32148. 176p. (gr. 4-9). 1990. pap. 3.50 (ISBN 0-679-80219-3, Bullseye Bks). Knopf.

Lasky, Kathryn. Prank. (gr. 6 up). 1986. pap. 2.75 (ISBN 0-440-97144-6, LFL). Dell.

Lawrence, James. Binky Brothers, Detectives. Kessler, Leonard, illus. LC 68-10374. (gr. k-3). 1978. pap. 3.50 (ISBN 0-06-444003-6, Trophy). HarpC Child Bks.

Levine, Arthur. All the Lights in the Night. Ransome, James, illus. LC 90-47496. 32p. (ps-3). 1991. text ed. 14.95 (ISBN 0-688-10107-0). Morrow.

Levinson, Marilyn. And Don't Bring Jeremy. De Groat, Diane, illus. LC 84-22484. 128p. (gr. 4-6). 1985. 10.95 (ISBN 0-8050-0554-4). H Holt & Co.

Lindbergh, Anne. The Shadow on the Dial. LC 86-45783. 160p. (gr. 5-8). 1987. PLB 12.89 (ISBN 0-06-023883-6). HarpC Child Bks.

Lindgren, Astrid. The Children on Troublemaker Street. Wikland, Ilon, illus. 112p. (gr. 1-3). 1991. pap. 3.50 (ISBN 0-689-71515-3, Aladdin). Macmillan Child Grp.

Little, Jean. Listen for the Singing. LC 90-40250. 272p. (gr. 4-7). 1991. pap. 3.95 (ISBN 0-06-440394-7, Trophy). HarpC Child Bks.

—Listen for the Singing. LC 90-40019. 272p. (gr. 4-7). 1991. PLB 14.89 (ISBN 0-06-023910-7). HarpC Child Bks.

Lord, Athena V. The Luck of Z.A.P. & Zoe. Jenkins, Jean, illus. LC 87-5545. 160p. (gr. 4-7). 1987. 13.95 (ISBN 0-02-759560-9, Mcmillan Child Bk). Macmillan Child Grp.

Low, Alice. The Witch Who Was Afraid of Witches. Gundersheimer, Karen, illus. LC 78-3279. (gr. 2-4). 1978. Pantheon.

Lowry, Lois. The One Hundredth Thing about Caroline. 160p. (gr. k-6). 1985. pap. 3.50 (ISBN 0-440-46625-3, YB). Dell.

McCaffrey, Mary. My Brother Ange. Saldutti, Denise, illus. LC 81-43887. 96p. (gr. 3-6). 1982. PLB 11.89 (ISBN 0-690-04195-0, Crowell Jr Bks). HarpC Child Bks.

McCully, Emily. I & Sproggy. (gr. 4 up). 1990. pap. 3.95 (ISBN 0-14-034542-6, Puffin). Puffin Bks.

McDaniel, Becky B. Katie Couldn't. Axeman, Lois, illus. LC 85-11666. 30p. (gr. 1-2). 1985. PLB 11.93 (ISBN 0-516-02069-2); pap. 2.95 (ISBN 0-516-42069-0). Childrens.

—Katie Did It. LC 83-7260. (Illus.). 32p. (ps-2). 1983. PLB 11.93 (ISBN 0-516-02043-9); pap. 2.95 (ISBN 0-516-42043-7). Childrens.

Mcphail, David. Sisters. 1990. pap. 3.95 (ISBN 0-15-275320-6, VoyB). HarbraceJ.

Mahy, Margaret. Seven Chinese Brothers. Tseng, Jean & Mou-sien Tseng, illus. (ps-3). 1990. pap. 12.95 (ISBN 0-590-42055-0). Scholastic Inc.

Manes, Stephen. Chocolate-Covered Ants. 1990. 12.95 (ISBN 0-590-40960-3). Scholastic Inc.

—Monstra vs. Irving. Sours, Michael, illus. 80p. (gr. 2-4). 1989. 12.95 (ISBN 0-8050-0836-5). H Holt & Co.

Manushkin, Fran & Bate, Lucy. Be Brave, Baby Rabbit. De Groat, Diane, illus. LC 89-49460. 32p. (ps-2). 1990. 13.95 (ISBN 0-517-57573-6); PLB 14.99 (ISBN 0-317-99961-3). Crown.

Marcus, Irene W. & Marcus, Paul. Scary Night Visitors: A Story for Children with Bedtime Fears. Jeschke, Susan, illus. 32p. (ps-2). 1990. 16.95 (ISBN 0-945354-26-6); pap. 5.95 (ISBN 0-945354-25-8). Magination Pr.

Margolis, Richard J. Secrets of a Small Brother. Carrick, Donald, illus. LC 84-3478. 40p. (gr. 1-4). 1984. 11.95 (ISBN 0-02-762280-0, Mcmillan Child Bk). Macmillan Child Grp.

Marshall, James. The Cut-Ups. (Illus.). 32p. (gr. 3-8). 1984. pap. 12.95 (ISBN 0-670-25195-X). Viking Child Bks.

Martin, Ann M. Baby-Sitter's Club: Little Sister. 1989. pap. 10.00 (ISBN 0-590-63403-8). Scholastic Inc.

—Inside Out. LC 83-18631. 160p. (gr. 4-9). 1984. 13.95 (ISBN 0-8234-0512-5). Holiday.

—Inside Out. 160p. (gr. 4-6). 1985. pap. 2.50 (ISBN 0-590-40883-6, Apple Paperbacks). Scholastic Inc.

Mason, Margo. Are We There Yet? (ps-3). 1990. 9.99 (ISBN 0-553-05870-3). Bantam.

—Are We There Yet? (ps-3). 1990. pap. 3.50 (ISBN 0-553-34886-8). Bantam.

Matarasso, Janet. Angela's New Sister. Chamberlain, Margaret, illus. 24p. 1988. 11.95 (ISBN 0-521-35640-7). Cambridge U Pr.

Matthews, Ellen. Getting Rid of Roger. LC 77-12311. (Illus.). 96p. (gr. 3-7). 1978. 7.50 (ISBN 0-664-32622-6, Westminster). Westminster John Knox.

Mazer, Norma F. Three Sisters. 240p. (gr. 7 up). 1986. pap. 12.95 (ISBN 0-590-33774-2, Scholastic Hardcover). Scholastic Inc.

Miklowitz, Gloria D. The Love Bombers. LC 80-65836. 160p. (gr. 7 up). 1980. pap. 8.95 (ISBN 0-385-28545-0). Delacorte.

Mills, Claudia. Boardwalk with Hotel. 144p. (gr. 7-12). 1986. pap. 2.50 (ISBN 0-553-15397-8, Skylark). Bantam.

Moncure, Jane B. Caring for My Baby Sister. Martin, Clovis, illus. 32p. (ps-2). 1990. lib. bdg. 9.96 (ISBN 0-89565-669-8). Childs World.

—My Baby Brother Needs a Friend. Hook, Frances, illus. LC 78-21935. (ps-3). 1979. PLB 12.96 (ISBN 0-89565-019-3). Childs World.

—What's So Special about Lauren? She's My Baby Sister. Williams, Jenny, illus. LC 87-21927. 32p. (ps-2). 1987. PLB 9.95 (ISBN 0-89565-413-X). Childs World.

Mulford, Philippa G. The World Is My Eggshell. LC 85-16198. (gr. 7 up). 1986. pap. 14.95 (ISBN 0-385-29432-8). Delacorte.

Myers, Bernice. Cry Baby. Myers, Bernice, illus. LC 89-12342. 32p. (ps-2). 1990. 12.95 (ISBN 0-688-09083-4); lib. bdg. 12.88 (ISBN 0-688-09084-2). Lothrop.

Naylor, Phyllis R. The Solomon System. LC 83-2661. 210p. (gr. 5-9). 1983. 13.95 (ISBN 0-689-30991-0, Atheneum Child Bk). Macmillan Child Grp.

—The Solomon System. LC 86-21758. 216p. (gr. 5-9). 1987. pap. 3.95 (ISBN 0-689-71128-X, Aladdin). Macmillan Child Grp.

Newman, Nanette. Sharing. 1990. 13.95 (ISBN 0-385-41104-9); PLB 14.99 (ISBN 0-385-41105-7). Doubleday.

Noronha, Francis P. The Magic Tree House. LC 85-91383. 42p. (gr. 3-5). 1986. 4.95 (ISBN 0-533-06888-6). Vantage.

O'Donnell, Elizabeth L. Maggie Doesnt Want to Move. LC 89-18207. 32p. (gr. k-3). 1990. pap. 3.95 (ISBN 0-689-71375-4, Aladdin). Macmillan Child Grp.

Oppenheim, Joanne. Left & Right. Litzinger, Rosanne, illus. LC 87-22939. (ps-3). 1989. 13.95 (ISBN 0-15-200505-6, Gulliver Bks). HarBraceJ.

Oppenheimer, Joan. Gardine vs. Hanover. LC 81-43390. 160p. (gr. 5-7). 1982. (Crowell Jr Bks); PLB 9.89 (ISBN 0-690-04191-8). HarpC Child Bks.

Ormerod, Jan. Just Like Me. LC 85-18056. (Illus.). 24p. (ps). 1986. 4.95 (ISBN 0-688-04211-2). Lothrop.

Osborne, Mary P. Last One Home. LC 85-20588. 192p. (gr. 8 up). 1986. 13.95 (ISBN 0-8037-0219-1). Dial Bks Young.

Parish, Peggy. Willy Is My Brother. (Orig.). (gr. k-6). 1989. pap. 2.50 (ISBN 0-440-40163-1, YB). Dell.

Park, Barbara. Operation: Dump the Chump. Sauber, Rob, illus. LC 81-8147. 128p. (gr. 3-6). 1982. 8.95 (ISBN 0-394-85179-X); lib. bdg. 9.99 (ISBN 0-394-95179-4). Knopf.

—Operation: Dump the Chump. 112p. (gr. 3-7). 1983. pap. 2.75 (ISBN 0-380-63974-2, Camelot). Avon.

Pascal, Francine. The Hand-Me-Down Kid. LC 79-5462. (gr. 5-9). 1980. pap. 12.95 (ISBN 0-670-35969-6). Viking Child Bks.

Pearson, Susan. Monnie Hates Lydia. Paterson, Diane, illus. LC 75-9198. 32p. (ps-3). 1985. 7.95 (ISBN 0-8037-5443-4). Dial Bks Young.

Peck, Richard. Those Summer Girls I Never Met. 224p. (gr. 7 up). 1988. 14.95 (ISBN 0-440-50054-0). Delacorte.

Perry, Carol J. Sister vs Sister. 144p. (Orig.). (gr. 4-8). 1990. pap. 2.95 (ISBN 0-87406-523-2). Willowisp Pr.

Petersen, P. J. Corky & the Brothers Cool. LC 84-15579. 192p. (gr. 7 up). 1985. 14.95 (ISBN 0-318-18244-0). Delacorte.

Pevsner, Stella. And You Give Me a Pain, Elaine. LC 78-5857. 192p. (gr. 6 up). 1979. 12.95 (ISBN 0-395-28877-0, Clarion). HM.

Pfeffer, Susan B. Sybil at Sixteen. (gr. 7 up). 1989. 13.95 (ISBN 0-553-05842-8). Bantam.

Pickett, Anola. Old Enough for Magic. Delaney, Ned, illus. LC 88-30320. 64p. (gr. k-3). 1989. 11.95 (ISBN 0-06-024731-2); PLB 11.89 (ISBN 0-06-024732-0). HarpC Child Bks.

Polushkin, Maria. Baby Brother Blues. Weiss, Ellen, illus. LC 85-30880. 32p. (ps-2). 1987. 13.95 (ISBN 0-02-774780-8, Bradbury Pr). Macmillan Child Grp.

Pyrnelle, Louise-Clarke. Diddie, Dumps & Tot. (Illus.). 117p. (gr. 4-8). 1963. 13.95 (ISBN 0-911116-17-6). Pelican.

Ransom, Candice F. My Sister the Meanie. 176p. (gr. 5-8). 1988. pap. 12.95 (ISBN 0-590-41982-X, Scholastic Hardcover). Scholastic Inc.

—My Sister the Meanie. 1989. pap. 2.50 (ISBN 0-590-41527-1). Scholastic Inc.

—My Sister the Meanie. 160p. (gr. 4-7). 1989. pap. 2.75 (ISBN 0-590-44116-7). Scholastic Inc.

Ray, Deborah. Sunday Morning We Went to the Zoo. Ray, Deborah, illus. LC 80-7915. 32p. (ps-2). 1981. 8.95 (ISBN 0-06-024841-6). HarpC Child Bks.

Renner, Beverly H. The Hideaway Summer. Sanderson, Ruth, illus. LC 77-11848. (gr. 4-6). 1978. 8.95i (ISBN 0-06-024862-9). HarpC Child Bks.

Roberts, Willo D. To Grandmother's House We Go. LC 89-34972. 192p. (gr. 3-7). 1990. 13.95 (ISBN 0-689-31594-5, Atheneum Child Bk). Macmillan Child Grp.

Roche, P. K. Webster & Arnold Go Camping. (Illus.). 32p. (ps-3). 1991. pap. 3.95 (ISBN 0-14-050806-6, Puffin). Puffin Bks.

Roe, Eileen. Con Mi Hermano - With My Brother. Casilla, Robert, illus. LC 90-33983. 32p. (ps-3). 1991. RSBE 12.95 (ISBN 0-02-777373-6, Bradbury Pr). Macmillan Child Grp.

Roos, Stephen. My Horrible Secret. Newsom, Carol, illus. LC 82-14954. 128p. (gr. 4-6). 1983. pap. 10.95 (ISBN 0-385-29246-5). Delacorte.

Root, Phyllis. Moon Tiger. Young, Ed, illus. LC 85-7572. 32p. (gr. k-3). 1985. 13.95 (ISBN 0-8050-0896-9). H Holt & Co.

Samuels, Barbara. Faye & Dolores. Samuels, Barbara, illus. LC 87-1419. 40p. (ps-3). 1987. pap. 4.95 (ISBN 0-689-71154-9, Aladdin). Macmillan Child Grp.

Sauer, James. Hank. 1990. 14.95 (ISBN 0-385-30034-4). Doubleday.

Saunders, Susan. Big Sister Stephanie. 128p. 1990. pap. 2.75 (ISBN 0-590-43929-4). Scholastic Inc.

Scarboro, Elizabeth. The Secret Language of the SB. 120p. (gr. 3-7). 1990. pap. 11.95 (ISBN 0-670-83087-9). Viking Child Bks.

Schnitter, Jane. William Is My Brother. LC 90-21364. (Illus.). 32p. (ps-3). 1991. 10.95 (ISBN 0-944934-03-X). Perspect Indiana.
Families expanded by both birth & adoption will enjoy this illustrated story of two brothers--one born to their parents & the other adopted. William & Tony discover that they are alike in many ways & different in many ways, like all brothers, & that what makes each special is his unique qualities, not the way he joined the family. A noted adoption therapist wrote "This book is superb. It addresses all of the information I believe is important. It helps children understand they are born & adopted. It addresses being different & being special, & includes those positive emotions about the process of adopting, stressing the love, excitement & happiness." Warm brown illustrations depict a racially ambiguous family. Other adoption related children's books from Perspectives Press include Janice Koch's OUR BABY: A BIRTH & ADOPTION STORY (sex education), Anne Brodzinsky's THE MULBERRY BIRD (a birthmother's viewpoint), Ann Angel's REAL FOR SURE SISTER (transracial adoption); Susan Gabel's WHERE THE SUN KISSES THE SEA (international placement), & Susan Gabel's FILLING IN THE BLANKS: A GUIDED LOOK AT GROWING UP ADOPTED (adolescence). Distributed by Ingram, Baker & Taylor, or contact the Publisher at (317) 872-3055.
Publisher Provided Annotation.

Simon, Shirley. Benny's Baby Brother. Gregorich, Barbara, ed. (Illus.). 16p. (Orig.). (gr. k-2). 1985. pap. 1.95 (ISBN 0-88743-016-3, 06016). Sch Zone Pub Co.

Singleton, Joy. Almost Twins. (Illus.). 128p. (Orig.). (gr. 3-6). 1991. pap. text ed. 2.50 (ISBN 0-87406-452-X). Willowisp Pr.

Sleator, William. Fingers. 208p. (Orig.). (gr. 7). 1990. pap. 2.95 (ISBN 0-553-25004-3, Starfire). Bantam.

Slier, Debby. Brothers & Sisters. 12p. (ps). 1989. 2.95 (ISBN 1-56288-146-9). Checkerboard Pr.

Slote, Alfred. Moving In. LC 87-45569. 176p. (gr. 3-6). 1989. pap. 3.50 (ISBN 0-06-440294-0, Trophy). HarpC Child Bks.

Smith, Peter. Jenny's Baby Brother. Graham, Bob, illus. (ps-3). 1988. pap. 3.95 (ISBN 0-14-050798-1, Puffin). Puffin Bks.

Snyder, Zilpha K. Blair's Nightmare. LC 83-15677. 204p. (gr. 4-6). 1984. 13.95 (ISBN 0-689-31022-6, Atheneum Child Bk). Macmillan Child Grp.

Sorenson, Jane. The New Pete. Endres, Helen, illus. 144p. (gr. 5-8). 1986. 3.95 (ISBN 0-87403-086-2, 2986). Standard Pub.

Stevenson, James. Worse Than Willy! Stevenson, James, illus. LC 83-14201. 32p. (gr. k-3). 1984. 10.25 (ISBN 0-688-02596-X); PLB 10.88 (ISBN 0-688-02597-8). Greenwillow.

Streatfeild, Noel. Gemma & Sisters. (Orig.). (gr. k-6). 1987. pap. 3.25 (ISBN 0-440-42862-9, YB). Dell.

Tada, Joni E. Ryan & the Circus Wheels. LC 87-26912. 1988. 8.95 (ISBN 1-55513-154-9, Chariot Bks). Cook.

Tapp, Kathy K. Den Four Meets the Jinx. LC 88-12776. 128p. (gr. 3-6). 1988. 12.95 (ISBN 0-689-50453-5, M K McElderry). Macmillan Child Grp.

Temes, Roberta. The Empty Place: A Story for Children. (Illus.). 50p. (gr. 1-6). 1989. 12.95 (ISBN 0-8290-1345-8). Irvington.

Tsutsui, Yoriko. Anna in Charge. Hayashi, Akiko, illus. 32p. (ps-1). 1989. pap. 11.95 (ISBN 0-670-81672-8). Viking Child Bks.

—Anna's Special Present. Hayashi, Akiko, illus. 32p. (ps-3). 1990. pap. 3.95 (ISBN 0-14-054219-1, Puffin). Puffin Bks.

Venezia, Mike. How to Be an Older Brother or Sister. Venezia, Mike, illus. LC 85-27977. 32p. (ps-2). 1986. PLB 13.93 (ISBN 0-516-03494-4); pap. 3.95 (ISBN 0-516-43494-2). Childrens.

Viorst, Judith. I'll Fix Anthony. Lobel, Arnold, illus. LC 78-77942. (ps-3). 1969. 12.95i (ISBN 0-06-026306-7); PLB 11.89 (ISBN 0-06-026307-5). HarpC Child Bks.

Voigt, Cynthia. The Vandemark Mummy. LC 91-7311. 208p. (gr. 5-9). 1991. 13.95 (ISBN 0-689-31476-0, Atheneum Child Bk). Macmillan Child Grp.

Wallace, Bill. Snot Stew. McCue, Lisa, illus. LC 88-31976. 96p. (gr. 3-7). 1989. 13.95 (ISBN 0-8234-0745-4). Holiday.

Walter, Mildred P. Two Too Much. LC 88-14888. 32p. (ps-2). 1990. 12.95 (ISBN 0-02-792290-1, Bradbury Pr). Macmillan Child Grp.

Walton, Sherry. Books Are for Eating. 1990. 11.95 (ISBN 0-525-44554-4, DCB). Dutton Child Bks.

Warrener. Two Bunnykins out to Tea. Corkery, Glenys, illus. LC 83-23531. 24p. (ps-3). 1985. pap. 4.95 (ISBN 0-670-80053-8). Viking Child Bks.

Wartski, Maureen C. My Brother Is Special. 144p. (gr. 7 up). 1981. pap. 3.50 (ISBN 0-451-15856-3, Sig). NAL-Dutton.

Weiss, Nicki. A Family Story. Weiss, Nicki, illus. LC 85-27231. 24p. (ps-3). 1987. 11.75 (ISBN 0-688-06504-X); PLB 11.88 (ISBN 0-688-06505-8). Greenwillow.

—Princess Pearl. Weiss, Nicki, illus. LC 85-17699. 24p. (gr. k-3). 1986. 11.75 (ISBN 0-688-05894-9); PLB 11.88 (ISBN 0-688-05895-7). Greenwillow.

Whitaker, Alexander. Dream Sister. (gr. 5 up). 1986. pap. 12.95 (ISBN 0-395-39377-9). HM.

—Dream Sister. 160p. (gr. k-6). 1989. pap. 2.95 (ISBN 0-440-40156-9, YB). Dell.

Wiesner, David. Hurricane. Wiesner, David, illus. (gr. k-3). 1990. 14.95 (ISBN 0-395-54382-7, Clarion Bks). HM.

Williams, Barbara. Jeremy Isn't Hungry. Alexander, Martha, illus. LC 78-4924. (ps-k). 1989. 10.95 (ISBN 0-525-32760-6, DCB); pap. 3.95 (ISBN 0-525-44536-6, DCB). Dutton Child Bks.

—Mitzi & the Terrible Tyrannosaurus Rex. McCully, Emily A., illus. LC 81-12665. 112p. (gr. 2-4). 1982. 10.95 (ISBN 0-525-45105-6, 0966-290, Dutton). NAL-Dutton.

—Mitzi & the Terrible Tyrannosaurus Rex. McCully, Emily A., illus. 112p. (gr. 3-7). 1983. pap. 1.95 (ISBN 0-440-45673-8, YB). Dell.

Wilson, Johnniece M. Oh, Brother. 128p. (gr. 4-6). 1988. pap. 10.95 (ISBN 0-590-41363-5, Scholastic Haedcovers). Scholastic Inc.

—Oh, Brother. 128p. (gr. 3-7). 1989. pap. 2.50 (ISBN 0-590-41001-6, Apple Paperbacks). Scholastic Inc.

Winthrop, Elizabeth. A Little Demonstration of Affection. LC 74-20390. 160p. (gr. 7 up). 1975. 7.95 (ISBN 0-06-026557-4). HarpC Child Bks.

Wishinsky, Frieda. Oonga Boonga, Vol. 1. (ps-3). 1990. 13.95 (ISBN 0-316-94872-1, Joy St Bks). Little.

Woodruff, Elvira. Tubtime. Stevenson, Sucie, illus. LC 89-36609. 32p. (ps-3). 1990. PLB 14.95 (ISBN 0-8234-0777-2). Holiday.

Wright, Betty R. Ghosts Beneath Our Feet. 144p. (gr. 4-6). 1986. pap. 2.50 (ISBN 0-590-40755-4, Apple Paperbacks). Scholastic Inc.

Young, Alida E. Is My Sister Dying? 144p. (Orig.). (gr. 5-8). 1991. pap. 2.95 (ISBN 0-87406-541-0). Willowisp Pr.

Ziefert, Harriet. My Sister Says Nothing Ever Happens When We Go Sailing. Chwast, Seymour, illus. LC 85-45278. 12p. (ps-2). 1986. 5.95 (ISBN 0-694-00081-7). HarpC Child Bks.

Zolotow, Charlotte. Big Sister & Little Sister. Alexander, Martha, illus. LC 66-8268. 32p. (gr. k-3). 1990. pap. 4.50 (ISBN 0-06-443217-3, Trophy). HarpC Child Bks.

BROWN, JAMES NATHANIEL, 1936-

Loewen, L. James Brown. (Illus.). 112p. (gr. 5 up). 1989. lib. bdg. 17.26 (ISBN 0-86592-607-7). Rourke Corp.

BROWN, JOHN, 1800-1859

Collins, James L. John Brown & the Fight Against Slavery. (Illus.). 32p. (gr. 2-4). 1991. PLB 11.50 (ISBN 1-56294-043-0); pap. 3.95 (ISBN 1-878841-72-6). Millbrook Pr.

Graham, Lorenz. John Brown: A Cry for Freedom. LC 79-7903. (Illus.). 192p. (gr. 7 up). 1980. 11.49i (ISBN 0-690-04023-7, Crowell Jr Bks); PLB 12.89 (ISBN 0-690-04024-5). HarpC Child Bks.

BUCCANEERS

see also Pirates

BUCHANAN, JAMES, PRESIDENT U. S. 1791-1868

Brill, Marlene T. James Buchanan. LC 88-10884. (Illus.). 100p. (gr. 3 up). 1988. PLB 17.27 (ISBN 0-318-41513-5). Childrens.

Collins, David R. James Buchanan: Fifteenth President of the United States. Young, Richard G., ed. LC 89-39948. (Illus.). 128p. (gr. 5-9). 1990. PLB 17.26 (ISBN 0-944483-62-3). Garrett Ed Corp.

BUCK, PEARL (SYDENSTRICKER), 1892-1973

LaFarge, Ann. Pearl Buck. Horner, Matina, intro. by. (Illus.). 112p. (gr. 5 up). 1988. lib. bdg. 17.95 (ISBN 1-55546-645-1). Chelsea Hse.

Mitchell, Barbara. Between Two Worlds: A Story about Pearl Buck. Ritz, Karen, illus. 56p. (gr. 3-6). 1988. PLB 9.95 (ISBN 0-87614-332-X). Carolrhoda Bks.

Schoen, Celin V. Pearl Buck: Famed American Author of Oriental Stories. Rahmas, D. Steve, ed. LC 70-190247. 32p. (Orig.). (gr. 7-12). 1972. lib. bdg. 4.20 incl. catalog cards (ISBN 0-87157-530-2). SamHar Pr.

BUDDHA AND BUDDHISM

Burland, C. A. Way of the Buddha. (gr. 3-7). pap. 7.95 (ISBN 0-7175-0590-1). Dufour.

Gibb, Christopher. The Dalai Lama: The Leader of the Exiled People of Tibet & Tireless Worker for World Peace. LC 89-43119. (Illus.). 68p. (gr. 5-6). 1990. PLB 12.95 (ISBN 0-8368-0224-1). Gareth Stevens Inc.

Hearn, Lafcadio. In Ghostly Japan. LC 79-138068. (Illus.). (gr. 9 up). 1971. pap. 10.95 (ISBN 0-8048-0965-8). C E Tuttle.

Landaw, Jonathan. The Story of Buddha. Basu, R. K., illus. (gr. 3-10). 1979. 7.50 (ISBN 0-89744-140-0). Auromere.

Landaw, Jonathan & Brooke, Janet. Prince Siddhartha. rev. ed. (Illus.). 144p. (gr. 1-8). 1984. 15.95 (ISBN 0-86171-016-9). Wisdom MA.

Morgan, Peggy. Being a Buddhist. (Illus.). 72p. (gr. 7-10). 1989. 19.95 (ISBN 0-7134-6015-6, Pub. by Batsford England). Trafalgar Sq.

—Buddhism. (Illus.). 72p. (gr. 7-12). 1987. 19.95 (ISBN 0-7134-5203-X, Pub. by Batsford England). Trafalgar Sq.

Snelling, John. Buddhist Festivals. (Illus.). 48p. (gr. 3-8). 1987. PLB 14.60 (ISBN 0-86592-980-7). Rourke Corp.

Stewart, Whitney. To the Lion Throne. (Illus.). 60p. (Orig.). (gr. 3 up). 1990. PLB 8.95 (ISBN 0-937938-75-0). Snow Lion.

Swann, Jivan. Tantra: A Handbook for Spiritual Lovers. Westley, Christine, ed. (Illus.). 32p. 1989. pap. 4.00 (ISBN 0-9622052-1-4). Turtle Prints.

BUDDHA AND BUDDHISM–FICTION

Chaitanya, Krishna. Rohanta & Nandriya. Charkravarty, Pranab, illus. (gr. 1-9). 1979. pap. 2.00 (ISBN 0-89744-179-6). Auromere.

Dharma Realm Buddhist University Faculty. Human Roots: Buddhist Stories for Young Readers, Vol. 2. (Illus.). 140p. (Orig.). (gr. 3 up). 1984. pap. 5.00 (ISBN 0-88139-017-8). Buddhist Text.

Hesse, Hermann. Siddhartha. (gr. 10-12). 1982. pap. 3.50 (ISBN 0-553-20884-5). Bantam.

Pharma Realm Buddhist University Faculty Staff, compiled by. Human Roots: Buddhist Stories for Young Readers, Vol. 1. (Illus.). 95p. (Orig.). (gr. 3 up). 1982. pap. 5.00 (ISBN 0-88139-500-5). Buddhist Text.

BUDGERIGARS

Hearne, T. Parakeets. (Illus.). 32p. (gr. 2-5). 1989. lib. bdg. 14.00 (ISBN 0-86625-182-0). Rourke Corp.

Lohr, J. E. Your First Budgerigar. (Illus.). 36p. (Orig.). 1991. pap. 1.95 (ISBN 0-86622-058-5, YF-102). TFH Pubns.

Vrbova, Zuza. Budgerigars. McAulay, Robert, illus. 48p. (gr. 2 up). 1990. PLB 9.95 (ISBN 0-86622-556-0, J-006). TFH Pubns.

BUDGERIGARS–FICTION

Burch, Robert. Traveling Bird. (gr. 1-4). 1959. 9.95 (ISBN 0-8392-3038-9). Astor-Honor.

Paxford, Sandra & Parker, Madeleine. Sandra & Syd. 32p. (gr. 7-10). 1986. pap. 12.00x (ISBN 0-7223-2067-1, Pub. by A H Stockwell England). State Mutual Bk.

BUDGETS, HOUSEHOLD

see also Finance, Personal

BUDGETS, PERSONAL

see Finance, Personal

Wool, John D. Earning, Spending & Saving, Bk. IV. 64p. (gr. 3 up). 1987. pap. text ed. 3.75 (ISBN 0-88323-228-6, 174); tchr's. key 1.50 (ISBN 0-318-33411-9, 224). Pendergrass Pub.

BUFFALO, AMERICAN

see Bison

BUFFALOES–FICTION

Goble, Paul. Buffalo Woman. LC 83-15704. (Illus.). 32p. (gr. k up). 1984. 13.95 (ISBN 0-02-737720-2, Bradbury Pr). Macmillan Child Grp.

BUGLE–FICTION

Baker, Olaf. Where the Buffaloes Begin. Gammell, Stephen, illus. LC 85-5682. 48p. (ps-4). 1989. 14.95 (ISBN 0-670-82760-6); pap. 5.95 (ISBN 0-14-050560-1). Viking Child Bks.

BUGS

see Insects

BUILDING

see also Architecture; Carpentry; Engineering; Masonry

Barton, Byron. Building a House. LC 80-22674. (Illus.). (ps-3). 1990. pap. 4.95 (ISBN 0-688-09356-6, Mulberry). Morrow.

Bates, Robert L. Stone, Clay, Glass: How Building Materials are Found & Used. LC 86-19692. (Illus.). 64p. (gr. 6-12). 1987. PLB 15.95 (ISBN 0-89490-144-3). Enslow Pubs.

Cash, Terry. Bricks. Stefoff, Rebecca, ed. Barber, Ed, photos by. LC 90-40249. (Illus.). 26p. (gr. 3-5). 1990. PLB 15.93 (ISBN 0-944483-68-2). Garrett Ed Corp.

Daniel, Kira. Home Builder. Smolinski, Dick, illus. LC 88-10354. 32p. (gr. k-3). 1989. PLB 10.89 (ISBN 0-8167-1420-7); pap. text ed. 2.50 (ISBN 0-8167-1421-5). Troll Assocs.

Dupasquier, Philippe. The Building Site. Dupasquier, Philippe, illus. 24p. (gr. k-1). 1984. 3.95 (ISBN 0-448-21502-0, G&D). Putnam Pub Group.

Horwitz, Elinor L. How to Wreck a Building. Horwitz, Joshua, illus. LC 81-14185. 56p. (gr. 3-8). 1982. Pantheon.

Isaacson, Phillip M. Round Buildings, Square Buildings & Buildings That Wiggle Like a Fish. Isaacson, Phillip M., illus. LC 87-16967. 128p. (gr. 5 up). 1990. 14.95 (ISBN 0-394-89382-4); lib. bdg. 16.99 (ISBN 0-394-99382-9); pap. 10.95 (ISBN 0-679-80649-0). Knopf.

Lambert, Mark. Building Technology. (Illus.). 48p. (gr. 5-8). 1991. RLB 12.40 (ISBN 0-531-18399-8, Pub. by Boatwright Pr). Watts.

Macaulay, David. Unbuilding. (gr. k-3). 1987. pap. 7.95 (ISBN 0-395-45425-5). HM.

Mills, Jane L. & Johnson, Larry D. Build Like Me. Hebert, Kim T., illus. LC 86-60362. 13p. (Orig.). (ps). 1986. pap. 4.00 (ISBN 0-938155-01-6); pap. 12.00 set of 3 bks. (ISBN 0-685-13524-1). Read A Bol.

Mitgutsch, Ali. From Clay to Bricks. Mitgutsch, Ali, illus. LC 80-29567. 24p. (ps-3). 1981. PLB 6.95 (ISBN 0-87614-149-1). Carolrhoda Bks.

Nash, Paul. Super Structures. Harris, Peter, ed. LC 89-12009. (Illus.). 32p. (gr. 2-4). 1989. PLB 11.93 (ISBN 0-944483-37-2). Garrett Ed Corp.

Pluckrose, Henry. Build It! Fairclough, Chris, photos by. (Illus.). 32p. (gr. k-4). 1990. PLB 10.40 (ISBN 0-531-14062-8). Watts.

Rickard, Graham. Building Homes. (Illus.). 32p. (gr. 2-5). 1989. 9.95 (ISBN 0-8225-2129-6). Lerner Pubns.

Royston, Angela. Buildings, Bridges & Tunnels. Shone, Rob, illus. 40p. (gr. 4-5). 1991. PLB 11.40 (ISBN 0-531-19108-7). Watts.

Royston, Angela & Thompson, Graham. Monster Building Machines. 24p. (ps-2). 1990. 9.95 (ISBN 0-8120-6174-8). Barron.

Walker, Lester. Housebuilding for Children. Hogrogian, Nonny, intro. by. LC 76-47220. (Illus.). 176p. (gr. 2 up). 1977. 16.95 (ISBN 0-87951-059-5). Overlook Pr.

Younker, Richard. On Site: The Construction of a High-Rise. LC 79-7889. (Illus.). (gr. 5-12). 1980. (Crowell Jr Bks). HarpC Child Bks.

BUILDING–FICTION

Enright, Elizabeth. The Four-Story Mistake. (gr. k-6). 1991. 15.00 (ISBN 0-8446-6451-0). Peter Smith.

Hughes, Shirley. The Big Concrete Lorry: A Tale of Trotter Street. Hughes, Shirley, illus. LC 89-8051. 32p. (ps-1). 1990. 13.95 (ISBN 0-688-08534-2); lib. bdg. 13.88 (ISBN 0-688-08535-0). Lothrop.

Kahn, Peggy. The Handy Girls Can Fix It! Jensen, Enola, illus. LC 83-21086. 32p. (ps-5). 1984. pap. 1.95 (ISBN 0-394-86252-X, Random Juv). Random.

Macaulay, David. Unbuilding. (Illus.). (gr. 3 up). 1980. 15.95 (ISBN 0-395-29457-6). HM.

Maynard, Joyce. New House. Bethel, Steve, illus. 32p. (ps-3). 1987. 12.95 (ISBN 0-15-257042-X). HarBraceJ.

Pedersen, Judy. Out in the Country. Pedersen, Judy, illus. LC 90-40032. 40p. (ps-2). 1991. 13.95 (ISBN 0-679-80630-X); PLB 14.99 (ISBN 0-679-90630-4). Knopf.

Tryon, Leslie. Albert's Alphabet. Tryon, Leslie, illus. 40p. (ps-1). 1991. SBE 13.95 (ISBN 0-689-31642-9, Atheneum Child Bk). Macmillan Child Grp.

Wood, Leslie. My House. (Illus.). 16p. (ps up). 1988. pap. 2.95 (ISBN 0-19-272186-0). Oxford U Pr.

BUILDING–REPAIR AND RECONSTRUCTION

Cobb, Vicki. The Secret Life of Hardware: A Science Experiment Book. Morrison, Bill, illus. LC 81-48607. 96p. (gr. 5 up). 1982. 13.95 (ISBN 0-397-31999-1, Lipp Jr Bks); PLB 13.89 (ISBN 0-397-32000-0, Lipp Jr Bks). HarpC Child Bks.

BUILDING REPAIR

see Building–Repair and Reconstruction

BUILDINGS–MAINTENANCE AND REPAIR

see Building–Repair and Reconstruction

BUILDINGS–REMODELING

see Building–Repair and Reconstruction

BULGARIA

Bulgaria. (Illus.). (gr. 7-12). 12.95 (ISBN 0-685-21877-5, 047939). Know Unltd.

Popescu, Julian. Bulgaria. (Illus.). (gr. 5 up). 1988. 14.95 (ISBN 1-55546-177-8). Chelsea Hse.

BULLDOZERS–FICTION

Hoye, David. The Biggest, Most Powerful Bulldozer in the World. McEntee, Steve, illus. 20p. (Orig.). (gr. 2). 1989. pap. 2.95 plastic paper (ISBN 0-317-94119-4). Kidzco Pub.

BULLFIGHTS

Say, Allen. El Chino. Say, Allen, illus. 32p. (gr. 2-8). 1990. 14.95 (ISBN 0-395-52023-1). HM.

BULLFIGHTS–FICTION

Leaf, Munro. El Cuento de Ferdinando: (The Story of Ferdinand) Belpre, Pura, tr. Lawson, Robert, illus. (SPA.). (gr. k-3). 1990. Set; incl. 4 bks., guide, & cass. incl. cass. 19.95 (ISBN 0-87499-189-7); pap. 12.95 incl. cass. (ISBN 0-87499-188-9); pap. 27.95 (ISBN 0-87499-191-9). Live Oak Media.

—The Story of Ferdinand. Lawson, Robert, illus. LC 36-19452. (gr. k-3). 1936. pap. 11.95 (ISBN 0-670-67424-9). Viking Child Bks.

Vandersteen, Willy. The Tender-Hearted Matador: Duck, Lambik, or Your Goose Is Cooked! Lahey, Nicholas J., tr. LC 75-8494. (Illus.). 56p. (Orig.). (gr. 3 up). 1976. pap. 2.50 (ISBN 0-915560-10-0, 10). Hiddigeigei.

BULLION

see Gold; Money; Silver

BUNCHE, RALPH JOHNSON, 1904-1971

Jakoubek, Robert. Ralph Bunche. King, Coretta Scott, intro. by. (Illus.). (gr. 5 up). 17.95 (ISBN 1-55546-576-5). Chelsea Hse.

Johnson, Ann D. The Value of Responsibility: The Story of Ralph Bunche. Pileggi, Steve, illus. LC 78-13960. (gr. k-6). 1978. 9.95 (ISBN 0-916392-29-5, Pub. by Value Communications). Oak Tree Pubns.

McKissack, Patricia & McKissack, Fredrick. Ralph J. Bunche: Peacemaker. Ostendorf, Ned, illus. LC 90-49849. 32p. (gr. 1-4). 1991. PLB 12.95 (ISBN 0-89490-300-4). Enslow Pubs.

BUNYAN, JOHN, 1628-1688

Dengler, Sandy. John Bunyan: Writer of Pilgrim's Progress. (Orig.). (gr. 4-6). 1986. pap. text ed. 3.95 (ISBN 0-8024-4352-4). Moody.

BUNYAN, PAUL

Anderson, J. I. I Can Read About Paul Bunyan. Snyder, Joel, illus. LC 76-54494. (gr. 2-5). 1977. pap. 1.95 (ISBN 0-89375-041-7). Troll Assocs.

Gleeson, Brian. Paul Bunyan. Meyerowitz, Rick, illus. LC 90-8558. 32p. (gr. k up). 1990. 14.95 (ISBN 0-88708-142-8, Rabbit Ears); incl. cass. 19.95 (ISBN 0-88708-143-6). Picture Bk Studio.

Gleiter, Jan & Thompson, Kathleen. Paul Bunyan & Babe the Blue Ox. LC 84-9786. (Illus.). 32p. (gr. k-5). 1984. PLB 16.67 (ISBN 0-8172-2119-0); PLB 27.99 incl. cassette (ISBN 0-8172-2241-3); pap. 9.27 (ISBN 0-685-09503-7); pap. 23.95 incl. cassette (ISBN 0-8172-2272-3); cassette 14.00 (ISBN 0-685-09504-5). Raintree Pubs.

Kellogg, Steven. Paul Bunyan. Kellogg, Steven, illus. LC 83-26684. 1988. pap. 7.95 incl. cassette (ISBN 0-688-08397-8). Morrow.

McCormick, Dell J. Paul Bunyan Swings His Axe. McCormick, Dell J., illus. LC 36-33409. (gr. 4-6). 1936. 8.95 (ISBN 0-87004-093-6). Caxton.

—Tall Timber Tales: More Paul Bunyan Stories. Livesley, Lorna, illus. LC 39-20778. (gr. 4-6). 1939. 7.95 (ISBN 0-87004-094-4). Caxton.

Rounds, Glen. Ol' Paul: The Mighty Logger. LC 75-22163. (Illus.). 96p. (gr. 4-6). 1976. 14.95 (ISBN 0-8234-0269-X); pap. 4.95 (ISBN 0-8234-0713-6). Holiday.

Sabin, Louis. Paul Bunyan. Smolinski, Dick, illus. LC 84-2747. 32p. (gr. 3-6). 1985. PLB 9.49 (ISBN 0-8167-0254-3); pap. text ed. 2.95 (ISBN 0-8167-0255-1). Troll Assocs.

Shephard, Esther. Paul Bunyan. Kent, Rockwell, illus. LC 85-5448. 284p. (gr. 7 up). 1985. 12.95 (ISBN 0-15-259749-2, HJ); pap. 6.95 (ISBN 0-15-259755-7). HarBraceJ.

Turney, Ida V. Paul Bunyan, the Work Giant. (Illus.). (gr. 3 up). 1969. 7.95 (ISBN 0-8323-0163-9). Binford Mort.

BURBANK, LUTHER, 1849-1926

Luther Burbank: Mini-Play. (gr. 5 up). 1978. 6.50 (ISBN 0-89550-330-1). Stevens & Shea.

BURGLARS

see Robbers and Outlaws

BURIAL

see Cemeteries; Funeral Rites and Ceremonies; Mounds and Mound Builders

BURIED CITIES

see Cities and Towns, Ruined, Extinct, etc.

BURIED TREASURE

Colby, C. B. World's Best Lost Treasure Stories. LC 91-14377. (Illus.). 96p. (gr. 3-10). 1991. 12.95 (ISBN 0-8069-8420-1). Sterling.

Gennings, S. Atocha Treasure. (Illus.). 32p. (gr. 4 up). Date not set. PLB 14.00 (ISBN 0-86592-874-6). Rourke Corp.

Gibbons, Gail. Sunken Treasure. Gibbons, Gail, illus. LC 87-30114. 32p. (gr. 1-5). 1988. 12.95 (ISBN 0-690-04734-7, Crowell Jr Bks); PLB 12.89 (ISBN 0-690-04736-3). HarpC Child Bks.

—Sunken Treasure. Gibbons, Gail, illus. LC 87-30114. 32p. (gr. 1-5). 1990. pap. 4.95 (ISBN 0-06-446097-5, Trophy). HarpC Child Bks.

Green, Harriet H. & Martin, Sue G. Treasure Hunts. 144p. (gr. 4-7). 1983. wkbk. 10.95 (ISBN 0-86653-115-7, GA 469). Good Apple.

Kane, Penny. A Hidden Treasure. LC 89-50049. 87p. (gr. 8-11). 1989. pap. 5.95 (ISBN 1-55523-226-4). Winston-Derek.

Lazo, Caroline E. Missing Treasures. (Illus.). 48p. (gr. 5 up). 1990. 10.95 (ISBN 0-89686-510-X, Crestwood Hse). Macmillan Child Grp.

Nesbit, Edith. Story of the Treasure Seekers. (gr. 4-6). 1987. pap. 2.25 (ISBN 0-685-03990-0, Puffin). Puffin Bks.

Sullivan, George. Treasure Hunt: The Sixteen-Year Search for the Lost Treasure Ship Atocha. LC 87-8791. (Illus.). 128p. (gr. 5 up). 1987. 13.95 (ISBN 0-8050-0569-2). H Holt & Co.

Townsend, Lucy. Learning about Hidden Treasure. Halverson, Lydia, illus. LC 87-9396. 48p. (gr. 2-6). 1987. PLB 17.27 (ISBN 0-516-06549-1). Childrens.

Trease, Geoffrey. Hidden Treasure. Molan, Chris, illus. LC 88-21699. 48p. (gr. 4-6). 1989. 14.95 (ISBN 0-525-67270-2, Lodestar Bks). Dutton Child Bks.

Wright, John. Lost Treasures. (Illus.). 48p. (gr. 5-6). 1989. PLB 12.40 (ISBN 0-531-18248-7). Watts.

BURIED TREASURE–FICTION

Armistead, Charles. In Search of the Golden Rainbow. Van Dolson, Bobbie J., ed. (gr. 5-9). 1981. pap. 6.95 (ISBN 0-8280-0086-7). Review & Herald.

Bellairs, John. The Treasure of Alpheus Winterborn. 192p. (gr. 3-8). 1985. pap. 2.75 (ISBN 0-553-15527-X, Skylark). Bantam.

Biggar, Joan R. Treasure at Morning Gulch. (Illus.). 152p. (gr. 5-8). 1991. pap. 3.95 (ISBN 0-570-04193-7). Concordia.

Byars, Betsy. Seven Treasure Hunts. Barrett, Jennifer, illus. LC 90-32043. 80p. (gr. 2-6). 1991. 13.95 (ISBN 0-06-020885-6); PLB 13.89 (ISBN 0-06-020886-4). HarpC Child Bks.

Clements, Bruce. The Treasure of Plunderell Manor. LC 87-25218. 192p. (gr. 7 up). 1987. 12.95 (ISBN 0-374-37746-4); pap. 3.95 (ISBN 0-374-47962-3). FS&G.

Coleman, William. Chesapeake Charlie & Blackbeard's Treasure. LC 80-70573. 128p. (Orig.). (gr. 5-9). 1981. pap. 3.95 (ISBN 0-87123-116-6). Bethany Hse.

Dixon, Franklin W. Hunting for Hidden Gold. (gr. 5-9). 1928. 4.50 (ISBN 0-448-08905-X, G&D). Putnam Pub Group.

Gaskin, Carol. Secret of the Royal Treasure. 144p. (Orig.). 1986. pap. 2.50 (ISBN 0-553-25729-3). Bantam.

Goodman, Julius. Treasure Diver. 128p. (gr. 5-9). 1984. pap. 2.25 (ISBN 0-553-25764-1). Bantam.

Hope, Laura L. Bobbsey Twins' Big Adventure at Home. (gr. 1-4). 1930. 4.50 (ISBN 0-448-08008-7, G&D). Putnam Pub Group.

—The Secret of the Sunken Treasure. (Illus.). (gr. 2-4). 1989. pap. 2.95 (ISBN 0-671-63075-X, Minstrel Bks). PB.

Katz, Welwyn W. Whalesinger. LC 90-34091. 212p. (gr. 7 up). 1991. SBE 13.95 (ISBN 0-689-50511-6, M K McElderry). Macmillan Child Grp.

Kennedy, Richard. Amy's Eyes. Egielski, Richard, illus. LC 82-48841. 448p. (ps up). 1985.. 14.95 (ISBN 0-06-023219-6). HarpC Child Bks.

McArthur, Nancy. The Adventure of the Buried Treasure. Trivas, Irene, illus. 80p. (Orig.). (gr. 1-4). 1990. pap. 2.50 (ISBN 0-590-43466-7). Scholastic Inc.

MacLachlan, Patricia. Unclaimed Treasures. LC 83-47714. 128p. (gr. 5-7). 1987. pap. 3.50 (ISBN 0-06-440189-8, Trophy). HarpC Child Bks.

Micocci, Harriet. Captain Orkle's Treasure. Dora, illus. (gr. 3-7). 1961. 10.95 (ISBN 0-8392-3003-6). Astor-Honor.

Morris, Dave. Buried Treasure. (gr. 4 up). 1990. pap. 2.95 (ISBN 0-440-40391-X). Dell.

Moxley, Susan. Abdul's Treasure. (Illus.). 28p. (ps-3). 1988. 15.95 (ISBN 0-340-38918-4, Pub. by Hodder & Stoughton UK). Trafalgar Sq.

Nesbit, Edith. Story of the Treasure Seekers. (gr. 4-6). 1987. pap. 2.25 (ISBN 0-685-03990-0, Puffin). Puffin Bks.

Orton, Helen F. The Treasure in the Little Trunk. Ball, Robert, illus. 208p. (gr. 4). 1989. pap. text ed. 5.95 (ISBN 0-685-29125-1). Niagara Cnty Hist Soc.

Packard, Edward. Sunken Treasure. 1982. 6.95 (ISBN 0-553-05018-4). Bantam.

Parish, Peggy. Key to the Treasure. 160p. (gr. k-6). 1980. pap. 3.25 (ISBN 0-440-44438-1, YB). Dell.

—Pirate Island Adventure. 176p. (gr. k-6). 1981. pap. 2.95 (ISBN 0-440-47394-2, YB). Dell.

Poskitt, Kjartan. The Mystery of the Pirate's Treasure. Higham, David, illus. 24p. (ps-2). 1990. 7.95 (ISBN 0-8249-8416-1). Ideals.

Saunders, Susan. Lauren's Treasure. 96p. (gr. 3-7). 1988. pap. 2.50 (ISBN 0-590-41695-2). Scholastic Inc.

Shulevitz, Uri. The Treasure. (Illus.). 32p. (gr. k-3). 1986. pap. 3.95 (ISBN 0-374-47955-0). FS&G.

Sobol, Donald J. Encyclopedia Brown & the Case of the Treasure Hunt. Owens, Gail, illus. LC 87-22048. (gr. 3-7). 1988. 12.95 (ISBN 0-688-06955-X). Morrow Jr Bks.

Sohl, Marcia & Dackerman, Gerald. Treasure Island. 16p. (gr. 4-10). 1976. pap. 2.95 (ISBN 0-88301-106-9); pap. 1.25 student activity bk. (ISBN 0-88301-185-9). Pendulum Pr.

Spillane, Mickey. The Day the Sea Rolled Back. Hofheimer, Steven, illus. 1979. 7.95 (ISBN 0-525-61589-X, Dutton). NAL-Dutton.

Stevenson, Robert Louis. Treasure Island. (gr. 7 up). pap. 2.75 (ISBN 0-8049-0002-7, CL-2). Airmont.

—Treasure Island. (Illus.). (gr. 1-9). 1947. deluxe ed. 10.95 (ISBN 0-448-06025-6, G&D). Putnam Pub Group.

—Treasure Island. (Illus.). (gr. 6-9). 1978. 2.95 (ISBN 0-448-14920-6, G&D). Putnam Pub Group.

—Treasure Island. 224p. (gr. 2-5). 1984. pap. 2.25 (ISBN 0-14-035016-0, Puffin). Puffin Bks.

—Treasure Island. Craft, Kinuko Y., illus. Edwards, Jane, adapted by. LC 79-24100. (Illus.). (gr. 4-12). 1983. PLB 17.32 (ISBN 0-8172-1655-3); pap. 9.27 (ISBN 0-8172-2026-7). Raintree Pubs.

—Treasure Island. Peake, Mervyn, illus. LC 78-74010. (gr. 5-12). 1987. pap. 4.95 (ISBN 0-8052-0620-5). Schocken.

—Treasure Island. (gr. 7-12). 1972. pap. 2.25 (ISBN 0-590-40105-X, Schol Pap). Scholastic Inc.

—Treasure Island. Wyeth, N. C., illus. LC 81-8788. 273p. (gr. 3 up). 1981. 22.50 (ISBN 0-684-17160-0, Scribners Young Read). Macmillan Child Grp.

—Treasure Island. write for info. S&S Trade.

—Treasure Island. Letley, Emma, ed. (gr. 7-12). 1985. pap. 2.25 (ISBN 0-19-281681-0). Oxford U Pr.

—Treasure Island. (Illus.). (gr. 7-12). 1982. pap. 4.25 (ISBN 0-19-581379-0). Oxford U Pr.

—Treasure Island. (gr. 7 up). 1965. pap. 1.75 (ISBN 0-451-51917-5, Sig Classics). NAL-Dutton.

—Treasure Island. (gr. k-6). 1986. 7.98 (ISBN 0-685-16845-X, 618168). Outlet Bk Co.

—Treasure Island. Iljinski, Igor, illus. 192p. (gr. 4 up). 1989. 14.95 (ISBN 0-8120-5942-5). Barron.

—Treasure Island. Wyeth, N. C., illus. LC 89-43034. 274p. 1989. Repr. 12.98 (ISBN 0-89471-778-2, Courage Books). Running Pr.

—Treasure Island. abridged ed. Norby, Lisa, adapted by. Fernandez, Fernando, illus. LC 89-70039. 96p. (Orig.). (gr. 2-6). 1990. PLB 5.99 (ISBN 0-679-90402-6); pap. 2.95 (ISBN 0-679-80402-1). Random.

Stover, Marjorie. Midnight in the Dollhouse. Levine, Abby, ed. Loccisano, Karen, illus. (gr. 3-6). 1990. 10.50 (ISBN 0-8075-5124-4). A Whitman.

Treasure Island. (Illus.). 352p. (gr. 3-9). 1981. pap. 7.95 (ISBN 0-448-11025-3, G&D). Putnam Pub Group.

Treasure Island. (Illus.). (gr. 3-5). 3.50 (ISBN 0-7214-0597-5). Ladybird Bks.

Whitney, Phyllis A. Mystery of the Black Diamonds. Gretzer, John, illus. LC 53-8355. 222p. (gr. 4-8). 1954. 7.50 (ISBN 0-664-32099-6, Westminster). Westminster John Knox.

Wibberley, Leonard. Perilous Gold. LC 78-7450. 144p. (gr. 5 up). 1978. 11.95 (ISBN 0-374-35824-9). FS&G.

BURMA

San Suu Kyi Sung. Burma. (Illus.). (gr. 5 up). 1988. 14.95 (ISBN 0-222-00979-9). Chelsea Hse.

BURNETT, FRANCES HODGSON, 1849-1924

Carpenter, Angelica S. & Shirley, Jean. Frances Hodgson Burnett: Beyond the Secret Garden. (Illus.). 128p. (gr. 5 up). 1990. PLB 15.95 (ISBN 0-8225-4905-0). Lerner Pubns.

BURYING GROUNDS

see Cemeteries

BUS DRIVERS

Stamper, Judith. What's It Like to Be a Bus Driver. Garcia, T. R., illus. LC 89-34388. 32p. (gr. k-3). 1989. lib. bdg. 10.89 (ISBN 0-8167-1795-8); pap. text ed. 2.50 (ISBN 0-8167-1796-6). Troll Assocs.

BUSES–FICTION

Awdry, W. Thomas the Tank Engine & the Great Race. Bell, Owain, illus. 7p. (ps-k). 1989. bds. 6.95 with plastic wheels (ISBN 0-679-80000-X, Random Juv). Random.

Cole, Joanna. The Magic School Bus Inside the Earth. Degen, Bruce, illus. 1989. pap. 3.95 (ISBN 0-590-40760-0). Scholastic Inc.

—The Magic School Bus Inside the Human Body. Deger, Bruce, illus. (ps-3). 1990. pap. 3.95 (ISBN 0-590-41427-5). Scholastic Inc.

Cole, Joannna. Magic School Bus at Waterworks. (gr. 1-4). 1986. 13.95 (ISBN 0-590-43739-9). Scholastic Inc.

Cossi, Olga. Gus the Bus. 1990. pap. 2.50 (ISBN 0-590-41614-6). Scholastic Inc.

Crews, Donald. School Bus. Crews, Donald, illus. LC 83-18681. 32p. (gr. k-3). 1984. 14.95 (ISBN 0-688-02807-1); PLB 14.88 (ISBN 0-688-02808-X). Greenwillow.

Fuller, Ted. Barney the Bus. Weinberger, Jane, ed. DeVito, Pamela, illus. LC 88-51276. 48p. (ps-4). 1989. pap. 7.95 (ISBN 0-932433-49-9). Windswept Hse.

Gomi, Taro. Bus Stops. Gomi, Taro, illus. LC 88-10193. 32p. (ps-1). 1988. 10.95 (ISBN 0-87701-551-1). Chronicle Bks.

Grosset & Dunlap Staff. Wheels on the Bus. Smath, Jerry, illus. 18p. (ps). 1991. bds. 2.95 (ISBN 0-448-40124-X, G&D). Putnam Pub Group.

Hutchins, Pat. Follow That Bus! Hutchins, Laurence, illus. LC 76-21822. 112p. (gr. 3-7). 1988. pap. 2.95 (ISBN 0-394-80792-8). Knopf.

Johnson, John E., illus. Here Comes the Bus. 14p. (gr. 2-5). 1985. 2.95 (ISBN 0-394-87544-3, Random Juv). Random.

Kingsland, Robin. Bus Stop Bop. Ayliffe, Alex, illus. 32p. (ps-3). 1991. 14.95 (ISBN 0-670-83919-1). Viking Child Bks.

Muntean, Michaela. The Very Bumpy Bus Ride. Wiseman, Bernard, illus. LC 81-16905. 48p. (ps-3). 1982. 5.95 (ISBN 0-8193-1079-4); 5.95 (ISBN 0-8193-1080-8). Parents.

—The Very Bumpy Bus Ride. Wiseman, B., illus. 48p. (gr. 3-7). 1990. pap. 2.95 (ISBN 0-448-04337-8, G&D). Putnam Pub Group.

Stevens, Florence & Lamont-Clarke, Ginette. Et Si L'Autobus Nous Oublie? Ouellet, Odile, illus. 24p. (ps-2). 1990. 12.95 (ISBN 0-88776-252-2); pap. 6.95 (ISBN 0-88776-260-3). Tundra Bks.

—What If the Bus Doesn't Come? Ouellet, Odile, illus. 24p. (ps-2). 1990. 12.95 (ISBN 0-88776-251-4); pap. 6.95 (ISBN 0-88776-259-X). Tundra Bks.

Zelinsky, Paul O. The Wheels on the Bus: With Pictures that Move. (ps). 1990. 14.95 (ISBN 0-525-44644-3, DCB). Dutton Child Bks.

BUSH, GEORGE, 1924-

Stefoff, Rebecca. George H. W. Bush: Forty-First President of the United States. Young, Richard G., ed. LC 90-2765. (Illus.). 128p. (gr. 5-9). 1990. PLB 17.26 (ISBN 0-944483-67-4). Garrett Ed Corp.

BUSINESS

see also Advertising; Banks and Banking; Credit; Department Stores; Economic Conditions; Manufactures; Marketing; Occupations; Salesmen and Salesmanship; Small Business

Aaseng, Nathan. Close Calls: From the Brink of Ruin to Business Success. (Illus.). 80p. (gr. 5 up). 1990. PLB 13.95 (ISBN 0-8225-0682-3). Lerner Pubns.

American Business. (Illus.). 48p. (gr. 6-12). 1975. pap. 1.85 (ISBN 0-8395-3325-X, 3325). BSA.

Business Kids Staff. The Business Kit. Ashemimry, Nasir M., intro. by. (Illus.). 129p. (gr. 8-12). 1989. tchr's. ed. 14.95 (ISBN 0-9625075-1-2); kit of 5 booklets 49.95 (ISBN 0-9625075-0-4). Lemonade Kids.
Carroll, Jeri & Wells, Candace. Founders. Foster, Tom, illus. 64p. (ps-3). 1986. wkbk. 6.95 (ISBN 0-86653-345-1, GA 695). Good Apple.
Cook, J. Introduction to Business. 48p. (gr. 6 up). 1987. PLB 13.96 (ISBN 0-88110-562-7); pap. 6.95 (ISBN 0-86020-934-2). EDC.
Silver, A. David. Your First Book of Wealth: The Beginner's Guide to Collecting Investing & Starting Your Own Business. 224p. (Orig.). (gr. 9 up). 1989. pap. 10.95 (ISBN 0-934829-47-0). Career Pr Inc.
Winitz, Harris. Business Book Two. Baker, Syd, illus. 50p. (Orig.). (gr. 7 up). 1986. pap. text ed. 8.00 (ISBN 0-939990-46-6); incl. cassette 19.00 (ISBN 0-939990-61-X). Intl Linguistics.

BUSINESS–BIOGRAPHY

Aaseng, Nathan. The Unsung Heroes: Unheralded People Who Invented Famous Products. (Illus.). 80p. (gr. 5 up). 1989. 13.95 (ISBN 0-8225-0676-9). Lerner Pubns.
Haddock, Patricia. Standing up for America: A Biography of Lee Iacocca. LC 86-32965. (Illus.). 128p. (gr. 6 up). 1987. PLB 12.95 (ISBN 0-87518-362-X, Dillon). Macmillan Child Grp.
Mascola. Ray Kroc, Reading Level 2. (Illus.). 24p. (gr. 1-4). Date not set. PLB 12.33 (ISBN 0-86592-433-3). Rourke Corp.

BUSINESS, CHOICE OF

see Vocational Guidance

BUSINESS–FICTION

Aiello, Barbara & Shulman, Jeffrey. Business Is Looking Up: Featuring Renaldo Rodriguez. Barr, Loel, illus. 48p. (gr. 3-6). 1988. PLB 12.95 (ISBN 0-941477-00-2). TFC Bks MD.
Barbour, Karen. Little Nino's Pizzeria. (ps-3). 1990. pap. 4.95 (ISBN 0-15-246321-6, VoyB). HarBraceJ.
Hughes, Dean. Millie Willenheimer & the Chestnut Corporation. LC 82-13758. 144p. (gr. 3-7). 1983. 10. 95 (ISBN 0-689-30958-9, Atheneum Childrens Bks). Macmillan Child Grp.
Kahn, Peggy. The Handy Girls Can Fix It! Jensen, Enola, illus. LC 83-21086. 32p. (ps-5). 1984. pap. 1.95 (ISBN 0-394-86252-X, Random Juv). Random.
Klevin, Jill R. The Turtle Street Trading Co. Edwards, Linda S., illus. LC 82-70312. 144p. (gr. 4-6). 1982. 11. 95 (ISBN 0-385-29043-8); PLB 11.95 (ISBN 0-685-05625-2). Delacorte.
—Turtles Together Forever! Edwards, Linda S., illus. LC 82-70313. 160p. (gr. 4-6). 1982. pap. 9.95 (ISBN 0-385-29045-4); pap. 9.89 (ISBN 0-385-29046-2). Delacorte.
Merrill, Jean. The Toothpaste Millionaire. Palmer, Jan, illus. LC 73-22055. 96p. (gr. 2-5). 1974. 13.95 (ISBN 0-395-18511-4). HM.
Naylor, Phyllis R. Eddie, Incorporated. Sims, Blanche, illus. LC 79-22589. (gr. 3-7). 1980. 12.95 (ISBN 0-689-30754-3, Atheneum Child Bk). Macmillan Child Grp.
Pearson, Tracey C. The Storekeeper. Pearson, Tracey C., illus. LC 87-36602. 32p. (ps-2). 1988. 12.95 (ISBN 0-8037-0370-8); PLB 10.89 (ISBN 0-8037-0371-6). Dial Bks Young.
Pfeffer, Susan B. Kid Power Strikes Back. Grant, Leigh, illus. 128p. (gr. k-8). 1984. lib. bdg. 12.90 (ISBN 0-531-04839-X). Watts.
Robertson, Keith. Henry Reed, Inc. McCloskey, Robert, illus. (gr. 4-6). 1958. pap. 14.95 (ISBN 0-670-36796-6). Viking Child Bks.
Van Leeuwen, Jean. Benjy in Business. Apple, Margot, illus. LC 82-22158. 112p. (gr. 2-6). 1983. 11.95 (ISBN 0-8037-0865-3); PLB 11.89 (ISBN 0-8037-0873-4). Dial Bks Young.

BUSINESS–HISTORY

Aaseng, Nathan. The Rejects: People & Products That Outsmarted the Experts. (Illus.). 80p. (gr. 5 up). 1989. 13.95 (ISBN 0-8225-0677-7). Lerner Pubns.

BUSINESS, SMALL

see Small Business

BUSINESS COLLEGES

see Business Education

BUSINESS DEPRESSIONS

see Depressions; Economic Conditions

BUSINESS EDUCATION

Spencer, Jean. Exploring Careers in the Electronic Office. rev. ed. Rosen, Ruth, ed. (gr. 7-12). 1989. PLB 12.95 (ISBN 0-8239-1009-1). Rosen Group.

BUSINESS ENGLISH

see English Language–Business English

BUSINESS ETHICS

see also Success

BUSINESS LETTERS

see also English Language–Business English

BUSINESS SCHOOLS

see Business Education

BUTTERFLIES

see also Caterpillars; Moths

Allen, Pamela. How to Raise Butterflies. (gr. 4-7). 1990. 11.99 (ISBN 0-399-61286-6). Putnam Pub Group.
Braithwaite, Althea. Butterflies. (ps-6). 1988. PLB 7.95 (ISBN 0-88462-180-4); pap. 2.95 (ISBN 0-88462-181-2). Dearborn Finan.
Brin, Ruth. Butterflies Are Beautiful. Lerner, Sharon, illus. LC 73-21359. 32p. (gr. 3-6). 1974. PLB 5.95 (ISBN 0-8225-0290-9). Lerner Pubns.
Butterflies. (Illus.). (ps-3). 1.95 (ISBN 0-7214-5118-7). Ladybird Bks.
Butterflies & Moths. (Illus.). 32p. (ps-1). 1986. pap. 1.25 (ISBN 0-8431-1523-8). Price Stern.
Cook, David. Small World of Butterflies & Moths. LC 80-85051. (gr. k-3). 1981. PLB 10.40 (ISBN 0-531-03454-2). Watts.
Cox & Cork. Butterflies & Moths. (gr. 2-5). 1980. PLB 11.96 (ISBN 0-88110-073-0); pap. 3.95 (ISBN 0-86020-477-4). EDC.
Cutts, David. Look - a Butterfly. Conner, Eulala, illus. LC 81-11369. 32p. (gr. k-2). 1982. PLB 10.89 (ISBN 0-89375-662-8); pap. text ed. 2.95 (ISBN 0-89375-663-6). Troll Assocs.
Echols, Jean C. Hide a Butterfly. Bergman, Lincoln & Fairwell, Kay, eds. Baker, Lisa H. & Klofkorn, Lisa, illus. Callaway, Jane, et al, photos by. 28p. (Orig.). (gr. 1-3). 1986. pap. 6.50 (ISBN 0-912511-23-0). Lawrence Science.
Fischer-Nagel, Heiderose & Fischer-Nagel, Andreas. Life of the Butterfly. Simon, Noel, tr. from GER. Fischer-Nagel, Heiderose & Fischer-Nagel, Andreas, photos by. (Illus.). 48p. (gr. 2-5). 1987. lib. bdg. 12.95 (ISBN 0-87614-244-7); pap. 6.95 (ISBN 0-87614-484-9). Carolrhoda Bks.
Florian, Douglas. Discovering Butterflies. Florian, Douglas, illus. LC 85-2312. 32p. (ps-2). 1986. 12.95 (ISBN 0-684-18439-7, Scribners Young Read). Macmillan Child Grp.
—Discovering Butterflies. LC 89-37816. 32p. (ps-2). 1990. pap. 3.95 (ISBN 0-689-71376-2, Aladdin). Macmillan Child Grp.
Gattis, L. S., III. Butterflies & Moths for Pathfinders: A Basic Youth Enrichment Skill Honor Packet. (Illus.). 20p. (Orig.). (gr. 5 up). 1987. pap. 5.00 tchr's. ed. (ISBN 0-936241-31-4). Cheetah Pub.
Gibbons, Gail. Monarch Butterfly. Gibbons, Gail, illus. LC 89-1880. 32p. (ps-3). 1989. reinforced bdg. 14.95 (ISBN 0-8234-0773-X). Holiday.
Hogan, Paula Z. The Butterfly. LC 78-26827. (Illus.). 32p. (gr. 1-4). 1979. PLB 16.67 (ISBN 0-8172-1252-3). Raintree Pubs.
—The Butterfly. LC 78-26827. (Illus.). 32p. (gr. k-3). 1984. PLB 27.99 incl. cassette (ISBN 0-8172-2226-X); cassette 14.00 (ISBN 0-685-09516-9). Raintree Pubs.
Josephson, Judith P. The Monarch Butterfly. LC 88-10871. (Illus.). 48p. (gr. 5-6). 1988. PLB 10.95 (ISBN 0-89686-389-1, Crestwood Hse). Macmillan Child Grp.
Jourdan, Eveline. Butterflies & Moths Around the World. LC 80-20086. (Illus.). 108p. (gr. 5 up). 1981. PLB 10. 95 (ISBN 0-8225-0567-3). Lerner Pubns.
Lepthien, Emilie U. Monarch Butterflies. LC 89-456. (Illus.). 48p. (gr. k-4). 1989. PLB 14.60 (ISBN 0-516-01165-0); pap. 4.95 (ISBN 0-516-41165-9). Childrens.
Linton, Margaret & Terry, Trevor. Life Cycle of a Butterfly. Caulkins, Janet, ed. Harland, Jackie, illus. 32p. (gr. 1-6). 1988. PLB 11.90 (ISBN 0-531-18188-X, Pub. by Bookwright). Watts.
Mitchell, Robert & Zim, Herbert S. Butterflies & Moths. Durenceau, Andre, illus. (gr. 5 up). 1964. PLB write for info. (ISBN 0-307-24052-5); pap. write for info. (Golden Pr). Western Pub.
Mitchell, Victor. Butterflies. (Illus.). 16p. (gr. k up). 1988. pap. 1.95 (ISBN 0-7459-1466-7). Lion USA.
Morris, Dean. Butterflies & Moths. rev. ed. LC 87-16666. (Illus.). 48p. (gr. 2-6). 1987. PLB 17.32 (ISBN 0-8172-3204-4). Raintree Pubs.
Norsgaard, Jaediker E. How to Raise Butterflies. Norsgaard, Campbell, photos by. (Illus.). 48p. (gr. 2-5). 1988. 10.95 (ISBN 0-396-09144-X, Putnam). Putnam Pub Group.
Oda, Hidetomo. Butterflies. Pohl, Kathy, ed. LC 85-28196. (Illus.). 32p. (gr. 3-7). 1986. text ed. 16.67 (ISBN 0-8172-2531-5). Raintree Pubs.
—The Swallowtail Butterfly. Pohl, Kathy, ed. LC 85-28229. (Illus.). 32p. (gr. 3-7). 1986. PLB 16.67 (ISBN 0-8172-2542-0); pap. text ed. 9.27 (ISBN 0-8172-2567-6). Raintree Pubs.
Opler, Paul & Strawn, Susan. Butterflies of Eastern North America: A Coloring Album & Activity Book. Strawn, Susan, illus. (gr. 1-6). 1989. pap. 4.95 (ISBN 0-911797-53-X). R Rinehart Inc.
Overbeck, Cynthia. The Butterfly Book. LC 78-7235. (Illus.). 32p. (gr. k-3). 1978. PLB 7.95 (ISBN 0-8225-1111-8). Lerner Pubns.
Penn, Linda. Young Scientists Explore: Butterflies & Moths. Scott, Elaine, illus. 32p. (gr. k-3). 1983. wkbk. 4.95 (ISBN 0-86653-111-4, GA 452). Good Apple.
Porter, Keith. Discovering Butterflies & Moths. LC 85-73664. (Illus.). 48p. (gr. 4-9). 1986. PLB 11.90 (ISBN 0-531-18055-7, Pub. by Bookwright). Watts.
—Discovering Butterflies & Moths. (Illus.). 48p. (gr. 2 up). 1990. pap. 4.95 (ISBN 0-531-18364-5). Watts.
Reidel, Marlene. From Egg to Butterfly. Reidel, Marlene, illus. LC 81-204. 24p. (ps-3). 1981. PLB 6.95 (ISBN 0-87614-153-X). Carolrhoda Bks.
Rowan, James P. Butterflies & Moths. LC 83-7216. (Illus.). 48p. (gr. k-4). 1983. PLB 14.60 (ISBN 0-516-01692-X); pap. 4.95 (ISBN 0-516-41692-8). Childrens.
Sabin, Louis. Amazing World of Butterflies & Moths. Helmer, Jean C., illus. LC 81-7504. 32p. (gr. 2-4). 1982. PLB 10.89 (ISBN 0-89375-560-5); pap. text ed. 2.95 (ISBN 0-89375-561-3); cassette 9.95 (ISBN 0-685-04943-4). Troll Assocs.
Saintsing, David. The World of Butterflies. LC 86-5706. (Illus.). 32p. (gr. 2-3). 1986. 10.95 (ISBN 1-55532-072-4). Gareth Stevens Inc.
Spooner, Sally. How to Raise the Monarch Butterfly. rev. ed. Thomson, Joan, illus. 19p. (Orig.). (gr. 2-6). 1987. pap. text ed. 2.95 incl. tchr's. manual (ISBN 0-318-22509-3). Spooner & Thomson.
Still, John. Amazing Butterflies & Moths. Young, Jerry, photos by. LC 90-19234. (Illus.). 32p. (Orig.). (gr. 1-5). 1991. PLB 9.99 (ISBN 0-679-91515-X); pap. 6.95 (ISBN 0-679-81515-5). Knopf.
Tarrant, Graham. Butterflies. King, Tony, illus. (ps-2). 1983. pap. 6.95 (ISBN 0-399-20927-1, Putnam). Putnam Pub Group.
Watts, Barrie. Butterfly & Caterpillar. LC 86-10050. (Illus.). 28p. (gr. 1-5). 1989. 6.95 (ISBN 0-382-09291-0); PLB 9.98 (ISBN 0-685-19354-3); PLB 9.98 (ISBN 0-382-09282-1); 3.95 (ISBN 0-382-09958-3). Silver Burdett Pr.
Whalley, Mary & Whalley, Paul. Butterfly in the Garden. LC 86-5705. (Illus.). 32p. (gr. 4-6). 1986. 10.95 (ISBN 1-55532-068-6). Gareth Stevens Inc.
Whalley, Paul. Butterfly & Moth. Keates, Colin, et al, photos by. LC 88-1574. (Illus.). 64p. (gr. 5 up). 1988. 13.95 (ISBN 0-394-89618-1); lib. bdg. 14.99 (ISBN 0-394-99618-6). Knopf.
Whyte, Malcolm. Butterflies. (Illus.). 32p. (Orig.). (gr. 1-4). 1989. pap. 3.50 (ISBN 0-8431-1962-4). Price Stern.
Zappler, Liz. A Day in the Life of the Monarch Butterfly. Eakin, Ed, ed. Morris, Aaron, illus. 48p. (gr. 2-6). 1989. 8.85 (ISBN 0-89015-616-6). Eakin Pr.

BUTTERFLIES–FICTION

Andersdatter, Karla M. Follow the Blue Butterfly. Koff, Deborah, illus. (gr. 4-8). 1980. 6.00 (ISBN 0-935430-00-8). In Between.
Dickson, Sandy L. The Story of Smartworms: The Journey Begins. Barrow, Madeline H., ed. Dixon, David, illus. 34p. (gr. k-5). 1989. write for info.; PLB write for info.; pap. write for info. Smartworm Corp.
Fanning, Robbie. One Hundred Butterflies. LC 79-14776. 190p. (gr. 3-6). 1979. 8.95 (ISBN 0-664-32654-4, Westminster). Westminster John Knox.
Fisher, Lucretia. The Butterfly & the Stone. Jardine, Thomas, illus. LC 80-29260. 48p. (Orig.). (ps up). 1981. pap. 3.95 (ISBN 0-916144-69-0). Stemmer Hse.
Fontenot, Mary A. Clovis Crawfish & Petit Papillon. Graves, Keith, illus. LC 83-27325. 52p. (gr. k-5). 1985. Repr. 11.95 (ISBN 0-88289-448-X). Pelican.
Hartmann, Lorice. Who Will Fly with Butterfly? (Illus.). (gr. k-3). 1978. pap. 6.95 (ISBN 0-912760-51-6). Valkyrie Pub Hse.
Lawrence, Louise. Calling B for Butterfly. LC 81-48648. 224p. (gr. 5 up). 1982. 12.02i (ISBN 0-06-023749-X). HarpC Child Bks.
—Calling B for Butterfly. LC 81-48648. 224p. (gr. 7 up). 1988. pap. 3.25 (ISBN 0-06-447036-9, Trophy). HarpC Child Bks.
Oana. Timmy Tiger & the Butterfly Net. LC 80-82954. (Illus.). 32p. (ps-4). 1981. PLB 9.95 (ISBN 0-87783-160-2). Oddo.
Pellowski, Michael J. Professor Possum's Great Adventure. Durrell, Julie, illus. LC 88-1281. 48p. (Orig.). (gr. 1-3). 1988. PLB 9.89 (ISBN 0-8167-1341-3); pap. text ed. 2.95 (ISBN 0-8167-1342-1). Troll Assocs.
Sundgaard, Arnold. The Lamb & the Butterfly. Carle, Eric, illus. LC 88-60092. 32p. (ps-2). 1988. 14.95 (ISBN 0-531-05779-8); PLB 14.99 (ISBN 0-531-08379-9). Orchard Bks Watts.
Trella, Phyllis. Butterflies Have Grandparents, Too. Trella, Phyllis, illus. LC 82-73691. 48p. (gr. 2-6). write for info. (ISBN 0-914201-02-6). Cheeruppet.
Van Pallandt, Nicolas. The Butterfly Night of Old Brown Bear. (ps-3). 1991. bds. 14.95 jacketed (ISBN 0-374-31009-2). FS&G.
West, Tracy. The Butterflies of Freedom. (gr. 6 up). 1988. pap. 2.25 (ISBN 0-317-69512-6). S&S Trade.
Yoshi. The Butterfly Hunt. Yoshi, illus. LC 90-7361. 32p. (gr. k up). 1990. 14.95 (ISBN 0-88708-137-1). Picture Bk Studio.

BUTTONS

Beylon, Cathy, illus. Billy & Belly Button, Getting Dressed. 14p. (ps-3). 1985. 4.95 (ISBN 0-448-41203-9, G&D). Putnam Pub Group.

BUYERS GUIDES

see Consumer Education; Shopping

BY-PRODUCTS

see Waste Products

BYZANTINE EMPIRE

Polyzoides, G. History of Byzantine & Modern Greece. (Illus.). (gr. 4-6). 3.20 (ISBN 0-686-79635-7). Divry.

BYZANTINE EMPIRE–FICTION

Paton Walsh, Jill. The Emperor's Winding Sheet. LC 73-90970. 288p. (gr. 7 up). 1974. 13.95 (ISBN 0-374-32160-4). FS&G.

C

CABEZA DE VACA, ALVAR NUNEZ, 1490?-1557

McCall, Edith. Stalwart Men of Early Texas. Aronson, Lou, illus. LC 78-101296. 128p. (gr. 3-10). 1980. PLB 14.60 (ISBN 0-516-03371-9). Childrens.

CABEZA DE VACA, ALVAR NUNEZ, 1490?-1557–FICTION

Baker, Betty. Walk the World's Rim. LC 65-11458. 192p. (gr. 5 up). 1965. PLB 13.89 (ISBN 0-06-020381-1). HarpC Child Bks.

CABINET WORK

see also Woodwork

CABINS

see Log Cabins

CABLES, SUBMARINE

Nathan, Adele G. First Transatlantic Cable. (Illus.). (gr. 5-9). 1963. lib. bdg. 8.99 (ISBN 0-394-90388-9). Random.

CABOT, JOHN, 1461-1498

Goodnough, David. John Cabot & Son. LC 78-18054. (Illus.). 48p. (gr. 4-7). 1979. PLB 9.89 (ISBN 0-89375-172-3); pap. 2.95 (ISBN 0-89375-164-2). Troll Assocs.

CABRINI, FRANCES XAVIER, SAINT, 1850-1917

Windeatt, Mary F. St. Frances Cabrini. Harmon, Gedge, illus. 32p. (gr. 1-5). 1989. Repr. of 1954 ed. wkbk. 3.00 (ISBN 0-89555-375-9). TAN Bks Pubs.

CACTUS

Bash, Barbara. Desert Giant: The World of the Saguaro Cactus. Bash, Barbara, illus. 32p. (gr. 1-5). 1989. 14.95 (ISBN 0-316-08301-1). Little.

Busch, Phyllis. Cactus in the Desert. Barton, Harriett, illus. LC 78-4771. (gr. k-3). 1979. PLB 12.89 (ISBN 0-690-00292-0, Crowell Jr Bks). HarpC Child Bks.

Cactus of Arizona. (Illus.). 32p. (gr. 3 up). 1984. pap. 1.00 (ISBN 0-935810-15-3). Primer Pubs.

Haselton, Scott E. Cactus & Succulents & How to Grow Them. (gr. 6-12). 1983. 1.25 (ISBN 0-9605656-1-2). Desert Botanical.

Overbeck, Cynthia. Cactus. Hani, Shabo, illus. LC 82-211. 48p. (gr. 4 up). 1982. lib. bdg. 14.95 (ISBN 0-8225-1469-9, First Ave Edns); pap. 5.95 (ISBN 0-8225-9556-7, First Ave Edns). Lerner Pubns.

CAESAR, CAIUS JULIUS, 100-44 B.C.

May, Robin. Julius Caesar & the Romans. (Illus.). 64p. (gr. k-6). 1984. lib. bdg. 12.40 (ISBN 0-531-03823-8). Watts.

Wells, Reuben F. With Caesar's Legions. LC 60-16709. (Illus.). (gr. 7-11). 1951. 18.00 (ISBN 0-8196-0110-1). Biblo.

Whitehead, Albert C. The Standard Bearer: A Story of Army Life in the Time of Caesar. (Illus.). (gr. 7-11). 1943. 18.00 (ISBN 0-8196-0116-0). Biblo.

CAESAR, CAIUS JULIUS, 100-44 B.C.–DRAMA

Shakespeare, William. Julius Caesar. Rudzik, O. H., intro. by. (Illus.). (gr. 9 up). pap. 1.95 (ISBN 0-8049-1004-9, S4). Airmont.

—Julius Caesar. Shaw, Charlie, illus. Stewart, Diana, adapted by. LC 80-16406. (Illus.). 48p. (gr. 4 up). 1983. PLB 17.32 (ISBN 0-8172-1664-2); pap. 9.27 (ISBN 0-8172-2013-5). Raintree Pubs.

CAFETERIAS

see Restaurants, Bars, etc.

CAKE

Drew, Helen. My First Baking Book. LC 91-10239. (Illus.). 48p. (gr. 2-6). 1991. 12.00 (ISBN 0-679-81545-7); lib. bdg. 13.99 (ISBN 0-679-91545-1). Knopf.

CALCULATING MACHINES

see also Computers

Gentry, Roosevelt. Fun with Calculators While Learning. LC 86-72013. 120p. (Orig.). (gr. k-7). 1987. pap. 20.00 (ISBN 0-938991-04-3). Colonial Pr AL.

Lewis, John. Pocket Calculator. (gr. 5-9). 1982. 8.95 (ISBN 0-86020-634-3, Usborne-Hayes); PLB 13.96 (ISBN 0-88110-009-9); pap. 6.95 (ISBN 0-86020-633-5). EDC.

Michunas, Lynn. Kalculator Kids. 64p. (gr. 3-7). 1982. 6.95 (ISBN 0-86653-076-2, GA 410). Good Apple.

CALCULUS

Cohen, Donald. Calculus by & for Young People - Worksheets. Cohen, Donald, illus. 308p. (gr. 1 up). 1991. worksheets 22.95 (ISBN 0-9621674-5-2). D Cohen Mathman.
Problems clearly leading young people to the calculus; with answers & explanations; for young people, parents, & teachers. To accompany CALCULUS BY & FOR YOUNG PEOPLE (ages 7, yes 7, & up). "...The crossings between recreational mathematics, modern calculators, & the track of such pioneers as Newton & Euler make this breezy & personal account, more notebook than book, good fun for the mathematically inclined young person & helpful for any adults who seek freer but solid arithmetic teaching."--SCIENTIFIC AMERICAN, December 1988. $12.00, paper, 177 pages, revised 1989, ISBN 0-9621674-1-X. Videotape #1: "Infinite Series by & for 6 year-olds & up", 24 minutes; $42.95, ISBN 0-9621674-2-8, parallels chapter 1 of Don's book. "... seldom do I see students so excited about their discoveries & sharing their methods..."; "...fun, engaging & eminently practical..."; "an excellent inservice for teachers..." Videotape #2: "Iteration to Infinite Sequences with 6 to 11 year-olds", 38 minutes, $42.95, ISBN 0-9621674-4-4, parallels chapter 8 of Don's book. Children of ages 6 & 7 are shown solving quadratic equations by iteration & iterating functions by hand & with a calculator. *Publisher Provided Annotation.*

—Calculus by & for Young People: (Ages 7, Yes 7 & Up) Cohen, Donald, illus. 177p. (Orig.). (gr. 2 up). 1988. pap. 12.00 spiral bdg. (ISBN 0-9621674-0-1). D Cohen Mathman.

—Calculus by & for Young People: (Ages 7, Yes 7 & Up) rev. ed. (Illus.). 177p. (gr. 1-12). 1989. spiral bdg. 13. 95 (ISBN 0-9621674-1-X). D Cohen Mathman.

Smith, Sanderson M. & Griffin, Frank W. AP Exam in Mathematics: Calculus AB & Calculus BC. 2nd ed. 320p. (gr. 9-12). 1990. pap. 12.95 (ISBN 0-13-019050-0, Pub. by ARCO). Prentice Hall Pr.

CALENDARS

see also Almanacs

Apfel, Necia H. Calendars. LC 85-8814. (Illus.). 88p. (gr. 5-8). 1985. PLB 10.40 (ISBN 0-531-10034-0). Watts.

Bushwick, Nathan. Understanding the Jewish Calander. 114p. (gr. 9-12). 1989. 9.95 (ISBN 0-940118-17-3). Maznaim.

Busy Week. (ps). 1990. text ed. 3.95 cased (ISBN 0-7214-5271-X). Ladybird Bks.

De Beer, Hans. Little Polar Bear Birthday Book. De Beer, Hans, illus. 120p. 1990. 7.95 (ISBN 1-55858-081-6). North-South Bks NYC.

Fisher, Leonard E. Calendar Art: Thirteen Days, Weeks, Months & Years from Around the World. Fisher, Leonard E., illus. LC 86-25835. 64p. 1987. 14.95 (ISBN 0-02-735350-8, Four Winds). Macmillan Child Grp.

Grewe, Georgeann & Glover, Susanne. Calendar Companions for Fall. Grewe, Georgeann, illus. 128p. (gr. 1-6). 1984. wkbk. 9.95 (ISBN 0-317-43005-X, GA 534). Good Apple.

—Calendar Companions for Spring. Grewe, Georgeann, illus. 128p. (gr. 1-6). 1984. wkbk. 9.95 (ISBN 0-86653-171-8, GA 536). Good Apple.

—Calendar Companions for Winter. Grewe, Georgeann, illus. 128p. (gr. 1-6). 1984. wkbk. 9.95 (ISBN 0-86653-168-8, GA 535). Good Apple.

Hughes, Paul. The Days of the Week. Harris, Peter, ed. Burn, Jeffery, illus. LC 89-11758. 62p. (gr. 4-7). 1989. PLB 15.93 (ISBN 0-944483-32-1). Garrett Ed Corp.

Joy, Margaret. Days, Weeks & Months. Renny, Juliet, illus. 112p. (gr. 3 up). 1984. 12.95 (ISBN 0-571-13171-9). Faber & Faber.

Lipkind, William. Days to Remember. Snyder, Jerome, illus. (gr. 3 up). 1961. 10.95 (ISBN 0-8392-3006-0). Astor-Honor.

Milne, A. A. Winnie-the-Pooh's Calendar Book 1988. Shepard, Ernest H., illus. (ps up). 1987. spiral bd. 4.95 (ISBN 0-525-44311-8, Dutton). NAL-Dutton.

Rosenberg, Amye. My Calendar. 66p. (gr. 1-2). 1984. pap. text ed. 4.25 (ISBN 0-87441-385-0). Behrman.

Spizman, Robyn. Bulletin Boards: Ideas for Holidays & Special Days. Pesiri, Evelyn, illus. 64p. (gr. k-6). 1984. wkbk. 6.95 (ISBN 0-86653-211-0, GA 567). Good Apple.

—Bulletin Boards: Monthly Calendars of Learning Fun. Pesiri, Evelyn, illus. 64p. (gr. k-6). 1984. wkbk. 6.95 (ISBN 0-86653-217-X, GA 569). Good Apple.

—Bulletin Boards: Seasonal Ideas & Activities. Pesiri, Evelyn, illus. 64p. (gr. k-6). 1984. wkbk. 6.95 (ISBN 0-86653-218-8, GA 568). Good Apple.

Woods, Jennifer. Month Makers: Reusable Student Calendars for Classroom Activities. Sussman, Ellen, intro. by. Woods, Jennifer, illus. 24p. (Orig.). (gr. 3-6). 1982. pap. text ed. 3.95t (ISBN 0-933606-12-5, MS-613). Monkey Sisters.

Zimmermann, H. Werner. Alphonse Knows...Twelve Months Make a Year. (Illus.). 24p. (ps-2). 1990. bds. 9.95 laminated (ISBN 0-19-540798-9). Oxford U Pr.

CALHOUN, JOHN CALDWELL, 1782-1850

Durwood, Thomas A. John C. Calhoun & the Roots of War. (Illus.). 160p. (gr. 5 up). 1990. lib. bdg. 16.98 (ISBN 0-382-09936-2); pap. 8.95 (ISBN 0-382-24045-6). Silver Burdett Pr.

CALIFORNIA

Brown, Richard, illus. Gulliver's Travels: A Kid's Guide to Southern California. 160p. 1988. 6.95 (ISBN 0-318-33430-5). HarBraceJ.

—A Kid's Guide to Southern California. 160p. (gr. 1 up). 1988. pap. 6.95 (ISBN 0-15-200457-2, Gulliver Bks). HarBraceJ.

Brown, Vinson & Livezey, Robert. The Sierra Nevadan Wildlife Region. 3rd, rev. ed. (Illus.). 192p. (gr 4 up). 1962. 14.95 (ISBN 0-911010-03-3); pap. 7.95 (ISBN 0-911010-02-5). Naturegraph.

Carole Marsh California Books, 31 bks. Set. 638.45 (ISBN 0-7933-1278-7). Gallopade Pub Group.

Carpenter, Allan. California. LC 77-21101. (Illus.). 96p. (gr. 4 up). 1978. PLB 19.93 (ISBN 0-516-04105-3). Childrens.

Endo, Terry, ed. Children's Yellow Pages: Orange County, 1986-87 Edition. Goldstein, Howard, illus. 200p. (Orig.). (gr. k up). 1986. pap. 6.95 (ISBN 0-938789-00-7). Teruko Inc.

Fradin, Dennis. California: In Words & Pictures. Ulm, Robert, illus. LC 76-50600. 48p. (gr. 2-5). 1977. PLB 15.93 (ISBN 0-516-03905-9); pap. 4.95 (ISBN 0-516-43905-7). Childrens.

Gales, Donald M. Handbook of Wildflowers, Weeds, Wildlife & Weather of the South Bay & Palos Verdes (California) 3rd, rev. ed. 240p. (gr. 8 up). 1988. pap. 12.00 (ISBN 0-317-89904-X). D M Gales.

Gray, Anne. The Wonderful World of San Diego. 2nd ed. LC 74-76733. (Illus.). (gr. 4 up). 1975. pap. 3.95 (ISBN 0-88289-081-6). Pelican.

Head, W. S. The California Chaparral: An Elfin Forest. LC 75-24239. 96p. (gr. 4 up). 1972. 13.95 (ISBN 0-87961-003-4); pap. 6.95 (ISBN 0-87961-002-6). Naturegraph.

—The California Chaparral: An Elfin Forest. LC 75-24239. 96p. (gr. 4 up). 1972. 13.95 (ISBN 0-87961-003-4); pap. 6.95 (ISBN 0-87961-002-6). Naturegraph.

Hedgpeth, Joel. Common Seashore Life of Southern California. Hinton, Sam, illus. 64p. (gr. 4 up). 1961. 12.95 (ISBN 0-911010-63-7); pap. 5.95 (ISBN 0-911010-62-9). Naturegraph.

Hoyt, George & Hoyt, Doris. A Bird's-Eye View of California. Atkinson, Mary, illus. 48p. (Orig.). (gr. k-4). 1989. pap. 4.95 (ISBN 0-9622364-4-6). Adona Pub.

Marinacci, Mike. Mysterious California: Strange Places & Eerie Phenomena in the Golden State. (Illus.). 144p. (Orig.). 1988. pap. 7.95 (ISBN 1-882046-02-1). Panpipes Pr.

Marsh, Carole. Avast, Ye Slobs! California Pirate Trivia. (Illus.). (gr. 3-12). 1990. PLB 19.95 (ISBN 0-7933-0184-X); pap. 14.95 (ISBN 0-7933-0183-1); computer disk 29.95 (ISBN 0-7933-0185-8). Gallopade Pub Group.

—The Beast of the California Bed & Breakfast. (Illus.). (gr. 3-12). 1990. PLB 19.95 (ISBN 0-7933-1397-X); pap. 14.95 (ISBN 0-7933-1398-8); computer disk 29. 95 (ISBN 0-7933-1399-6). Gallopade Pub Group.

—California & Other State Greats (Biographies) (Illus.). (gr. 3-12). 1990. PLB 19.95 (ISBN 1-55609-521-X); pap. 14.95 (ISBN 1-55609-520-1); computer disk 29. 95 (ISBN 0-7933-1405-4). Gallopade Pub Group.

—California Bandits, Bushwackers, Outlaws, Crooks, Devils, Ghosts, Desperadoes & Other Assorted & Sundry Characters! (Illus.). (gr. 3-12). 1990. PLB 19. 95 (ISBN 0-7933-0166-1); pap. 14.95 (ISBN 0-7933-0165-3); computer disk 29.95 (ISBN 0-7933-0167-X). Gallopade Pub Group.

—California Classic Christmas Trivia: Stories, Recipes, Activities, Legends, Lore & More! (Illus.). (gr. 3-12). 1990. PLB 19.95 (ISBN 0-7933-0169-6); pap. 14.95 (ISBN 0-7933-0168-8); computer disk 29.95 (ISBN 0-7933-0170-X). Gallopade Pub Group.

—California Coastales. (Illus.). (gr. 3-12). 1990. PLB 19. 95 (ISBN 1-55609-517-1); pap. 14.95 (ISBN 1-55609-516-3); computer disk 29.95 (ISBN 0-7933-1401-1). Gallopade Pub Group.

—The California Hot Air Balloon Mystery. (Illus.). (gr. 2-9). 1990. 19.95 (ISBN 0-7933-2354-1); pap. 14.95 (ISBN 0-7933-2355-X); computer disk 29.95 (ISBN 0-7933-2356-8). Gallopade Pub Group.

—California "Jography" A Fun Run Thru Our State! (Illus.). (gr. 3-12). 1990. PLB 19.95 (ISBN 1-55609-511-2); pap. 14.95 (ISBN 1-55609-510-4); computer disk 29.95. Gallopade Pub Group.

—California Kid's Cookbook: Recipes, How-to, History, Lore & More! (Illus.). (gr. 3-12). 1990. PLB 19.95 (ISBN 0-7933-0178-5); pap. 14.95 (ISBN 0-7933-0177-7); computer disk 29.95 (ISBN 0-7933-0179-3). Gallopade Pub Group.

—California Quiz Bowl Crash Course! (Illus.). (gr. 3-12). 1990. PLB 19.95 (ISBN 1-55609-519-8); pap. 14.95 (ISBN 1-55609-518-X); computer disk 29.95 (ISBN 0-7933-1400-3). Gallopade Pub Group.

—California School Trivia: An Amazing & Fascinating Look at Our State's Teachers, Schools & Students! (Illus.). (gr. 3-12). 1990. PLB 19.95 (ISBN 0-7933-0175-0); pap. 14.95 (ISBN 0-7933-0174-2); computer disk 29.95 (ISBN 0-7933-0176-9). Gallopade Pub Group.

—California Silly Basketball Sportsmysteries, Vol. I. (Illus.). (gr. 3-12). 1990. PLB 19.95 (ISBN 0-7933-0172-6); pap. 14.95 (ISBN 0-7933-0171-8); computer disk 29.95 (ISBN 0-7933-0173-4). Gallopade Pub Group.

—California Silly Basketball Sportsmysteries, Vol. II. (Illus.). (gr. 3-12). 1990. PLB 19.95 (ISBN 0-7933-1574-3); pap. 14.95 (ISBN 0-7933-1575-1); computer disk 29.95 (ISBN 0-7933-1576-X). Gallopade Pub Group.

—California Silly Football Sportsmysteries, Vol. I. (Illus.). (gr. 3-12). 1990. PLB 19.95 (ISBN 1-55609-515-5); pap. 14.95 (ISBN 1-55609-514-7); computer disk 29. 95 (ISBN 0-7933-1396-1). Gallopade Pub Group.

—California Silly Football Sportsmysteries, Vol. II. (Illus.). (gr. 3-12). 1990. PLB 19.95 (ISBN 0-7933-1394-5); pap. 14.95 (ISBN 0-7933-1395-3); computer disk 29.95. Gallopade Pub Group.

—California Silly Trivia! (Illus.). (gr. 3-12). 1990. PLB 19.95 (ISBN 1-55609-509-0); pap. 14.95 (ISBN 1-55609-508-2); computer disk 29.95 (ISBN 0-7933-1390-2). Gallopade Pub Group.

—California's (Most Devastating!) Disasters & (Most Calamitous!) Catastrophies! (Illus.). (gr. 3-12). 1990. PLB 19.95 (ISBN 0-7933-0163-7); pap. 14.95 (ISBN 0-7933-0162-9); computer disk 29.95 (ISBN 0-7933-0164-5). Gallopade Pub Group.

—The Hard-to-Believe-But-True! Book of California History, Mystery, Trivia, Legend, Lore, Humor & More. (Illus.). (gr. 3-12). 1990. PLB 19.95 (ISBN 0-7933-0181-5); pap. 14.95 (ISBN 0-7933-0180-7); computer disk 29.95 (ISBN 0-7933-0182-3). Gallopade Pub Group.

—If My California Mama Ran the World! (Illus.). (gr. 3-12). 1990. PLB 19.95 (ISBN 0-7933-1402-X); pap. 14.95 (ISBN 0-7933-1403-8); computer disk 29.95 (ISBN 0-7933-1404-6). Gallopade Pub Group.

—Let's Quilt California & Stuff It Topographically! (Illus.). (gr. 3-12). 1990. PLB 19.95 (ISBN 1-55609-513-9); pap. 14.95 (ISBN 1-55609-512-0); computer disk 29.95 (ISBN 0-7933-1392-9). Gallopade Pub Group.

O'Connor, Karen. San Diego. (Illus.). 60p. (gr. 3 up). 1990. PLB 12.95 (ISBN 0-87518-439-1, Dillon). Macmillan Child Grp.

Oliver, Rice D. Student Atlas of California. 3rd ed. (Illus.). 72p. (gr. 4 up). 1988. 7.95 (ISBN 0-936778-98-9); tchr's ed. 8.95 (ISBN 0-936778-99-7). Calif Weekly.

—Student Atlas of California. 4th ed. (Illus.). 66p. (gr. 3-8). 1991. PLB 16.95 (ISBN 0-936778-62-8); pap. text ed. 8.95 (ISBN 0-936778-60-1); tchr's. ed. 9.95 (ISBN 0-936778-61-X). Calif Weekly.
Fourth Edition of a unique historical & geographical reference atlas of California directed to upper elementary children & used throughout California. Contains 1990 census figures of state, counties, cities, & Indian reservations. 44 maps: physical & political, natural resources, energy, land, water, historical, cities, communities, counties, & more. Skills: using an atlas, map skills section, historical data, California time line. Topics include: State Seal, Flag & Symbols, A Flight Along the Coast, Finding Distance, Regions of California, Los Angeles Basin, Mountain Ranges, Death Valley, Deserts, Rivers & Drainage, Wilderness Areas, Coastal Islands, Natural Harbors, Earthquake Faults, Indian Groups, Exploration, Missions & Ranchos, Mexican War, Gold Rush & Mother Lode, Transportation, Population Figures, County Seats, Farming & Agriculture, National Parks, Forestry, Water Resources, Weather & Rainfall, Wildlife, Places to Visit, Travel by Bus, Index. "A good addition to any home library."--Pacific Historian.
Publisher Provided Annotation.

Pack, Janet. California. (Illus.). 96p. (gr. 4-9). 1987. PLB 10.40 (ISBN 0-531-10379-X). Watts.

Riegel, Martin P. Ghost Ports of the Pacific, Vol. I: California. LC 89-90772. (Illus.). 52p. (Orig.). 1989. 11.00 (ISBN 0-944871-18-6); pap. 4.95 (ISBN 0-944871-19-4). Riegel Pub.

Salts, Bobbi, ed. California Is for Kids! An Activity Book. Parker, Steve, illus. 32p. (gr. 1-6). 1990. pap. 2.95 (ISBN 0-929526-04-X). Double B Pubns.

Seablom, Seth H. The California Coloring Guide. (Illus.). 32p. (gr. 1-6). 1979. pap. 2.50 (ISBN 0-918800-05-6). Seablom.

Thompson, Kathleen. California. LC 87-16395. 48p. 1987. 17.32 (ISBN 0-86514-462-1); cancelled (ISBN 0-86514-601-2); cancelled Beta video (ISBN 0-86514-087-1); cancelled VHS video (ISBN 0-86514-162-2); cancelled 3/4" video (ISBN 0-86514-237-8). Raintree Pubs.

Todd, Armor. The Marin Mountain Bike Guide. 2nd ed. Todd, Linda, illus. 80p. (gr. 9-12). 1989. pap. 8.95t (ISBN 0-9623537-0-1). A Todd.

Weir, Kim. Northern California Handbook. (Illus.). 759p. (Orig.). (gr. 9-12). 1990. pap. 16.95 (ISBN 0-918373-43-3). Moon Pubns CA.

CALIFORNIA–BIOGRAPHY

Mirko, Vincent W. Grandpa Says. 300p. (Orig.). (gr. 10). 1989. pap. 25.00 (ISBN 0-9623257-0-8). Millsmont Pub.

Yep, Laurence. The Lost Garden. (Illus.). 128p. (gr. 5-7). 1991. 14.98 (ISBN 0-382-24098-7); 9.71s.p.; pap. 12.95 (ISBN 0-382-24090-1); pap. 11.24s.p. Silver Burdett Pr.

CALIFORNIA–FICTION

Cleary, Beverly. The Luckiest Girl. LC 58-6667. 228p. (gr. 7 up). 1958. PLB 12.88 (ISBN 0-688-31741-3). Morrow Jr Bks.

Fleischman, Sid. By the Great Horn Spoon. Von Schmidt, Eric, illus. (gr. 4-6). 1988. 14.95 (ISBN 0-316-28577-3, Joy St Bks); pap. 4.95 (ISBN 0-316-28612-5, Joy St Bks). Little.

Gates, Doris. Blue Willow. Lantz, Paul, illus. LC 40-32435. 176p. (gr. 4-7). 1940. pap. 13.95 (ISBN 0-670-17557-9). Viking Child Bks.

Gorog, Judith. Caught in the Turtle. Sanderson, Ruth, illus. (gr. 5-8). 1983. 10.95 (ISBN 0-399-20981-6, Philomel). Putnam Pub Group.

Gray, Genevieve. How Far, Felipe? Grifalconi, Ann, illus. LC 77-11846. 64p. (gr. k-3). 1978. PLB 11.89 (ISBN 0-06-022108-9). HarpC Child Bks.

Gunn, Robin J. Summer Promise: Never Had One Season Held So Much Hope... So Much Heartache. Kobobel, Janet, ed. 171p. (Orig.). 1988. pap. 4.99 (ISBN 0-929608-13-5). Focus Family.

Harte, Bret. Outcasts of Poker Flat & Other Stories. (gr. 8 up). pap. 1.95 (ISBN 0-8049-0051-5, CL51). Airmont.

Jackson, Helen H. Ramona: Wyeth Edition. Wyeth, N. C., illus. (gr. 6 up). 1939. Repr. of 1884 ed. 17.95 (ISBN 0-316-45467-2). Little.

Katz, Welwyn W. Whalesinger. LC 90-34091. 212p. (gr. 7 up). 1991. SBE 13.95 (ISBN 0-689-50511-6, M K McElderry). Macmillan Child Grp.

Kelso, Mary J. Goodbye, Bodie. Kelso, Mary J., illus. 104p. (Orig.). (gr. 7 up). 1990. pap. 6.95 (ISBN 0-9621406-1-9). MarKel Pr.

Ludwig & Bernal. California Story & Coloring Book. (Illus.). 32p. (Orig.). pap. 2.95 (ISBN 0-930504-01-1). Polaris Pr.

Moeri, Louise. Downwind. 144p. (gr. 4-7). 1984. 13.95 (ISBN 0-525-44096-8, DCB). Dutton Child Bks.

Norris, Frank. Octopus. (gr. 11 up). 1968. pap. 1.95 (ISBN 0-8049-0179-1, CL-179). Airmont.

O'Dell, Scott. Island of the Blue Dolphins. (gr. 7 up). 1960. 13.95 (ISBN 0-395-06962-9). HM.

Pellowski, Michael J. Triple Trouble in Hollywood. Hickman, Estella L., illus. 125p. (gr. 3-6). 1989. pap. 2.75 (ISBN 0-87406-383-3). Willowisp Pr.

Politi, Leo. Song of the Swallows. 1987. 13.95 (ISBN 0-684-18831-7, Scribners Young Read). Macmillan Child Grp.

Snyder, Zilpha K. The Egypt Game. Raible, Alton, illus. LC 67-10467. 224p. (gr. 4-6). 1972. 14.95 (ISBN 0-689-30006-9, Atheneum Child Bk). Macmillan Child Grp.

—Velvet Room. Raible, Alton, illus. LC 65-10474. 224p. (gr. 3-7). 1972. (Atheneum Childrens Bk); pap. 1.95 (ISBN 0-685-00576-3). Macmillan Child Grp.

Steinbeck, John. Of Mice & Men. (gr. 9-12). 1970. pap. 2.75 (ISBN 0-553-26675-6). Bantam.

CALIFORNIA–GOLD DISCOVERIES

Blumberg, Rhoda. The Great American Gold Rush. LC 89-736. (Illus.). 144p. (gr. 5 up). 1989. 16.95 (ISBN 0-02-711681-6, Bradbury Pr). Macmillan Child Grp.

Gold Rush Stories: Mini-Play. (gr. 5 up). 1978. 6.50 (ISBN 0-89550-331-X). Stevens & Shea.

Lake, A. L. Gold Fever. (Illus.). 32p. (gr. 3-8). 1990. PLB 17.26 (ISBN 0-86625-374-2); PLB 12.95s.p. (ISBN 0-685-34710-9). Rourke Corp.

Lyngheim, Linda. Gold Rush Adventure. Garber, Phyllis, illus. LC 87-82679. 96p. (gr. 3-6). 1988. 12.95 (ISBN 0-915369-03-6); pap. 9.95 (ISBN 0-915369-02-8). Langtry Pubns.

McCall, Edith. Gold Rush Adventures. Eckart, Frances, illus. LC 62-9530. 128p. (gr. 3-10). 1980. PLB 14.60 (ISBN 0-516-03328-X). Childrens.

McNeer, May. The California Gold Rush. LC 87-4685. 160p. (gr. 5-9). 1962. Repr. of 1950 ed. lib. bdg. 8.99 (ISBN 0-394-90306-4, Random Juv). Random.

Van Steenwyk, Elizabeth. The California Gold Rush: West with the Forty-Niners. (Illus.). 64p. (gr. 5-8). 1991. PLB 11.90 (ISBN 0-531-20032-9). Watts.

CALIFORNIA–HISTORY

Boule, Mary N. The Missions: California's Heritage, No. 1: Mission San Diego de Alcala. Grim, Ellen & De Batuc, Alfredo, illus. 24p. (Orig.). (gr. 4-6). 1988. pap. 3.50 (ISBN 1-877599-00-X). Merryant Pubs.

—The Missions: California's Heritage, No. 10: Mission Santa Barbara. Grim, Ellen & De Batuc, Alfredo, illus. 24p. (Orig.). (gr. 4-6). 1988. pap. 3.50 (ISBN 1-877599-09-3). Merryant Pubs.

—The Missions: California's Heritage, No. 11: Mission la Purisima Concepcion. Grim, Ellen & De Batuc, Alfredo, illus. 24p. (Orig.). (gr. 4-6). 1988. pap. 3.50 (ISBN 1-877599-10-7). Merryant Pubs.

—The Missions: California's Heritage, No. 12: Mission Santa Cruz. Grim, Ellen & De Batuc, Alfredo, illus. 24p. (Orig.). (gr. 4-6). 1988. pap. 3.50 (ISBN 1-877599-11-5). Merryant Pubs.

—The Missions: California's Heritage, No. 13: Mission Nuestra Senora de la Soledad. Grim, Ellen & De Batuc, Alfredo, illus. 20p. (Orig.). (gr. 4-6). 1988. pap. 3.50 (ISBN 1-877599-12-3). Merryant Pubs.

—The Missions: California's Heritage, No. 14: Mission San Jose. Grim, Ellen & De Batuc, Alfredo, illus. 28p. (Orig.). (gr. 4-6). 1988. pap. 3.50 (ISBN 1-877599-13-1). Merryant Pubs.

—The Missions: California's Heritage, No. 15: Mission San Juan Bautista. Grim, Ellen & De Batuc, Alfredo, illus. 24p. (Orig.). (gr. 4-6). 1988. pap. 3.50 (ISBN 1-877599-14-X). Merryant Pubs.

—The Missions: California's Heritage, No. 16: Mission San Miguel Arcangel. Grim, Ellen & De Batuc, Alfredo, illus. 24p. (Orig.). (gr. 4-6). 1988. pap. 3.50 (ISBN 1-877599-15-8). Merryant Pubs.

—The Missions: California's Heritage, No. 17: Mission San Fernando Rey de Espana. Grim, Ellen & De Batuc, Alfredo, illus. 24p. (Orig.). (gr. 4-6). 1988. pap. 3.50 (ISBN 1-877599-16-6). Merryant Pubs.

—The Missions: California's Heritage, No. 18: Mission San Luis Rey de Francia, 21 Bks. De Batuc, Alfredo & Grim, Ellen, illus. 24p. (Orig.). (gr. 4). 1988. pap. 3.50 (ISBN 1-877599-17-4). Merryant Pubs.

—The Missions: California's Heritage, No. 19: Mission Santa Ines. Grim, Ellen & De Batuc, Alfredo, illus. 24p. (Orig.). (gr. 4-6). 1988. pap. 3.50 (ISBN 1-877599-18-2). Merryant Pubs.

—The Missions: California's Heritage, No. 2: Mission San Carlos Borromeo de Carmelo. Grim, Ellen & De Batuc, Alfredo, illus. 24p. (Orig.). (gr. 4-6). 1988. pap. 3.50 (ISBN 1-877599-01-8). Merryant Pubs.

—The Missions: California's Heritage, No. 20: Mission San Rafael Arcangel. Grim, Ellen & De Batuc, Alfredo, illus. 24p. (Orig.). (gr. 4-6). 1988. pap. 3.50 (ISBN 1-877599-19-0). Merryant Pubs.

—The Missions: California's Heritage, No. 21: Mission San Francisco Solano. Grim, Ellen & De Batuc, Alfredo, illus. 24p. (Orig.). (gr. 4-6). 1988. pap. 3.50 (ISBN 1-877599-20-4). Merryant Pubs.

—The Missions: California's Heritage, No. 3: Mission San Antonio de Padua. Grim, Ellen & De Batuc, Alfredo, illus. 24p. (Orig.). (gr. 4-6). 1988. pap. 3.50 (ISBN 1-877599-02-6). Merryant Pubs.

—The Missions: California's Heritage, No. 4: Mission San Gabriel Arcangel. Grim, Ellen & De Batuc, Alfredo, illus. 24p. (Orig.). (gr. 4-6). 1988. pap. 3.50 (ISBN 1-877599-03-4). Merryant Pubs.

—The Missions: California's Heritage, No. 5: Mission San Luis Obispo de Tolosa. Grim, Ellen & De Batuc, Alfredo, illus. 24p. (Orig.). (gr. 4-6). 1988. pap. 3.50 (ISBN 1-877599-04-2). Merryant Pubs.

—The Missions: California's Heritage, No. 6: Mission San Francisco de Asis. Grim, Ellen & De Batuc, Alfredo, illus. 24p. (Orig.). (gr. 4-6). 1988. pap. 3.50 (ISBN 1-877599-05-0). Merryant Pubs.

—The Missions: California's Heritage, No. 7: Mission San Juan Capistrano. Grim, Ellen & De Batuc, Alfredo, illus. 24p. (Orig.). (gr. 4-6). 1988. pap. 3.50 (ISBN 1-877599-06-9). Merryant Pubs.

—The Missions: California's Heritage, No. 8: Mission Santa Clara de Asis. Grim, Ellen & De Batuc, Alfredo, illus. 24p. (Orig.). (gr. 4-6). 1988. pap. 3.50 (ISBN 1-877599-07-7). Merryant Pubs.

—The Missions: California's Heritage, No. 9: Mission San Buenaventura. Grim, Ellen & De Batuc, Alfredo, illus. 24p. (Orig.). (gr. 4-6). 1988. pap. 3.50 (ISBN 1-877599-08-5). Merryant Pubs.

Brewton, Barney. California Studies. (gr. 4). 1987. text incl. activity program 229.00 (ISBN 0-318-41079-6). Southwinds Pr.

Brock, John M. An Illustrated History of Kern County. Ambriz, Don & Reed, Libby, illus. 83p. (gr. 3-8). 1976. pap. 5.00 (ISBN 0-943500-05-2). Kern Historical.

Junipero Serra. (Illus.). 32p. (gr. 3-6). 1988. PLB 16.67 (ISBN 0-8172-2909-4); pap. 9.27 (ISBN 0-685-28503-0). Raintree Pubs.

Knill, Harry. The Story of Early California & Her Flags. Archambault, Alan, illus. 48p. (Orig.). (gr. 4 up). 1988. pap. 3.95 (ISBN 0-88388-129-2). Bellerophon Bks.

Lyngheim, Linda. Gold Rush Adventure. Garber, Phyllis, illus. LC 87-82679. 96p. (gr. 3-6). 1988. 12.95 (ISBN 0-915369-03-6); pap. 9.95 (ISBN 0-915369-02-8). Langtry Pubns.

McNeer, May. The California Gold Rush. LC 87-4685. 160p. (gr. 5-9). 1962. Repr. of 1950 ed. lib. bdg. 8.99 (ISBN 0-394-90306-4, Random Juv). Random.

Nicholson, Loren. Old Picture Postcards: A Historic Journey along California's Central Coast. (Illus.). 144p. (Orig.). (gr. 9-12). 1989. pap. 12.95 (ISBN 0-9623233-1-4). CA HPA.

Oliver, Rice D. Lone Woman of Ghalas-Hat: The True Story of the Island of the Blue Dolphins. (Illus.). 48p. (gr. 4-8). 1986. PLB 9.95x (ISBN 0-936778-96-2); pap. 3.95x (ISBN 0-936778-95-4). Calif Weekly.

O'Rourke, Everett V. The Highest School in California: A Story of Bodie, California. O'Rourke, Michael E., photos by. (Illus.). 32p. (Orig.). (gr. 1-4). 1978. 4.00 (ISBN 0-685-22567-4). E ORourke.

Reinstedt, Randall A. One-Eyed Charley: The California Whip. Bergez, John, ed. LC 90-81382. (Illus.). 84p. (gr. 3-6). 1990. PLB 9.95 (ISBN 0-933818-23-8). Ghost Town.

Serpico, Phil. Santa Fe Route to the Pacific. Serpico, Phil, illus. LC 87-46360. 150p. (gr. 6 up). 1988. 25.00 (ISBN 0-88418-000-X). Omni Hawthorne.

Stein, R. Conrad. The Story of the Gold at Sutter's Mill. LC 81-6088. (Illus.). 32p. (gr. 3-6). 1981. PLB 13.27 (ISBN 0-516-04617-9). Childrens.

Swindler, William F. & Trover, Ellen L., eds. Chronology & Documentary Handbook of the State of California, No. 5. LC 72-5265. 118p. (gr. 9-12). 1972. PLB 8.50 (ISBN 0-379-16130-3). Oceana.
Van Steenwyk, Elizabeth. The California Gold Rush: West with the Forty-Niners. (Illus.). 64p. (gr. 5-8). 1991. PLB 11.90 (ISBN 0-531-20032-9). Watts.

CALISTHENICS
see Gymnastics; Physical Education and Training

CALLIGRAPHY
see Writing

CAMBISTRY
see Weights and Measures

CAMBODIA
Chandler, David P. The Land & People of Cambodia. LC 90-5907. (Illus.). 224p. (gr. 6 up). 1991. 17.95 (ISBN 0-06-021129-6); PLB 17.89 (ISBN 0-06-021130-X). HarpC Child Bks.
Diep, Bridgette. Trip Through Cambodia. Vaing, Jocelang, illus. LC 73-159478. 32p. (ps-3). 8.95 (ISBN 0-87592-054-3). Scroll Pr.
Roland, Donna. Grandfather's Stories from Cambodia. (gr. 1-3). 1984. pap. 4.50x (ISBN 0-941996-05-0). Open My World.
—More of Grandfather's Stories from Cambodia. (gr. 1-3). 1984. pap. 4.50x (ISBN 0-941996-06-9). Open My World.

CAMELS
Green, Carl R. & Sanford, William R. The Camel. LC 88-5957. (Illus.). 48p. (gr. 5-6). 1988. PLB 10.95 (ISBN 0-89686-385-9, Crestwood Hse). Macmillan Child Grp.
Rothaus, Jim. Camels. 24p. (gr. 3). 1989. 17.10 (ISBN 0-88682-222-X); PLB 11.95s.p. (ISBN 0-318-37903-1). Creative Ed.
Wildlife Education, Ltd. Staff. Camels. Orr, Richard, illus. 20p. (gr. 5 up). 1984. pap. 2.25 (ISBN 0-937934-24-0). Wildlife Educ.

CAMELS–FICTION
Holt-Fortin, Cher. The Ayyam-i Ha Camel. Irvine, Rex J., illus. 48p. (Orig.). (gr. 2-6). 1989. 9.95 (ISBN 0-933770-73-1). Kalimat.
Kipling, Rudyard. How the Camel Got His Hump. Turska, Krystyna, illus. (ps-3). 1988. 4.95 (ISBN 0-7232-3450-7). Warne.
—How the Camel Got His Hump: Just So Stories. Langley, Jonathan, illus. LC 87-29156. 24p. (ps-3). 1988. 5.95 (ISBN 0-399-21553-0, Philomel Bks). Putnam Pub Group.
Klein, Hannah E. Brief Adventures of Agnes, a Camel, & Her Good Friend Shopworth. 1991. 6.95 (ISBN 0-533-09153-5). Vantage.
Peet, Bill. Pamela Camel. (Illus.). (gr. 4-8). 1986. pap. 3.95 (ISBN 0-395-41670-1, Sandpiper). HM.
Ramakrishnan, Prema. King Kamel. Joshi, Jagdish, illus. 24p. (Orig.). (gr. k-3). 1980. pap. 2.50 (ISBN 0-89744-210-5, Pub. by Children's Bk Trust India). Auromere.
Tworkov, Jack. The Camel Who Took a Walk. (Illus.). (gr. k-3). 1974. 13.95 (ISBN 0-525-27393-X, DCB); (DCB). Dutton Child Bks.
—The Camel Who Took a Walk. Duvoisin, Roger, illus. 32p. (ps-3). 1989. pap. 3.95 (ISBN 0-525-44476-9, DCB). Dutton Child Bks.

CAMERAS
Hewett, Joan. Camera. (gr. 4-7). 1990. pap. 5.95 (ISBN 0-395-54788-1, Clarion Bks). HM.
Jervis, Alastair. Camera Technology. (Illus.). 48p. (gr. 5-8). 1991. PLB 12.40 (ISBN 0-531-18385-8). Watts.
Roberts. Fun with Sun Prints & Box Cameras. 1981. 8.95 (ISBN 0-679-20629-9). McKay.

CAMP COOKING
see Outdoor Cookery

CAMPAIGNS, POLITICAL
see Politics, Practical

CAMPAIGNS, PRESIDENTIAL
see Presidents–U. S.–Election

CAMPANELLA, ROY, 1921-
Tackach, James. Roy Campanella. Murray, Jim, intro. by. (Illus.). 64p. (gr. 3 up). 1991. PLB 14.95 (ISBN 0-7910-1170-4). Chelsea Hse.

CAMPING
see also Backpacking; Outdoor Cookery; Outdoor Life; Wilderness Survival
Armstrong, Wayne. Camping Basics. Schoolcraft, Robert, illus. LC 85-9407. 48p. (gr. 3-7). 1985. 10.95 (ISBN 0-13-112657-1). P-H.
Boy Scouts of America. Camping. (Illus.). 96p. (gr. 6-12). 1984. pap. 1.85 (ISBN 0-8395-3256-3, 3256). BSA.
Camping & Walking. (Illus.). 128p. (gr. 3 up). 1987. PLB 15.96 (ISBN 0-88110-287-3); pap. 9.95 (ISBN 0-7460-0129-0). EDC.
Cooke, Tom. Hide & Seek Camping Trip: A Sesame Street Book. 1990. pap. 2.95 (ISBN 0-679-80138-3, Fodor). McKay.
Dolan, Edward. Bicycle Touring & Camping. (Illus.). 192p. (gr. 8 up). 1982. pap. 5.95 (ISBN 0-671-44544-8, Little Simon). S&S Trade.
Felt, Freddi. My Going to Camp Book. Fredman, Foan, illus. 40p. (gr. 1-6). 1988. 5.95 (ISBN 0-9616875-2-5). F & F Pub.
McManus, Patrick F. Kid Camping from Aaaaiii! to Zip. Doty, Roy, illus. LC 79-13152. (gr. 3-8). 1979. 12.95 (ISBN 0-688-41910-0). Lothrop.
Pioneering. (Illus.). 48p. (gr. 6-12). 1974. pap. 1.85 (ISBN 0-8395-3382-9, 3382). BSA.
Zarchy, Harry. Let's Go Camping: A Guide to Outdoor Living. Zarchy, Harry, illus. (gr. 2 up). 1964. lib. bdg. 5.69 (ISBN 0-394-91328-0). Knopf.
Zeleznak, Shirley. Camping. LC 80-425. (Illus.). 32p. (gr. 4 up). 1980. lib. bdg. 9.95 (ISBN 0-89686-071-X, Crestwood Hse). Macmillan Child Grp.

CAMPING–FICTION
Bach, Alice. The Most Delicious Camping Trip Ever. Kellogg, Steven, illus. LC 76-2956. 48p. (gr. k-3). 1976. HarpC Child Bks.
Boynton, Sandra. Hester in the Wild. LC 78-67026. (Illus.). 32p. (ps-3). 1979. HarpC Child Bks.
Carrick, Carol. Sleep Out. Carrick, Donald, illus. LC 72-88539. 32p. (gr. 1-3). 1982. 12.95 (ISBN 0-395-28780-4, Clarion); pap. 4.95 (ISBN 0-89919-083-9, Clarion). HM.
Chodkowski, Dick. Camp Catastrophe. (Illus.). 48p. 1990. pap. 6.95 (ISBN 0-8431-2435-0). Price Stern.
Conford, Ellen. Hail, Hail Camp Timberwood. 144p. (gr. 6 up). 1987. pap. 2.95 (ISBN 0-553-26722-1, Starfire). Bantam.
Dadey, Debbie & Jones, Marcia. Werewolves Don't Go to Summer Camp. 128p. (gr. 2-5). 1991. pap. 2.50 (ISBN 0-590-44061-6). Scholastic Inc.
Gauch, Patricia L. Night Talks. 160p. (gr. 5 up). 1983. pap. 10.95 (ISBN 0-399-20911-5, Putnam). Putnam Pub Group.
Greer, Gary & Ruddick, Bob. This Island Isn't Big Enough for the Four of Us! LC 86-47750. 160p. (gr. 3-7). 1989. pap. 3.95 (ISBN 0-06-440203-7, Trophy). HarpC Child Bks.
Greer, Gery & Ruddick, Bob. This Island Isn't Big Enough for the Four of Us. LC 86-47750. 160p. (gr. 3-7). 1987. 13.95 (ISBN 0-690-04612-X, Crowell Jr Bks); PLB 11.89 (ISBN 0-690-04614-6, Crowell Jr Bks). HarpC Child Bks.
Guild, Anne V. Mickey Mouse in Let's Go...on a Camping Caper. Scholefield, Ron, et al, illus. 26p. (ps up). 1987. pap. 14.95 (ISBN 1-55578-803-3). Worlds Wonder.
Henckel, Mark. It's Tough to Be Small in the Big Outdoors. 1990. pap. 4.95 (ISBN 0-945960-04-2). Outlaw MT.
Henkes, Kevin. Bailey Goes Camping. Henkes, Kevin, illus. LC 84-29027. 24p. (ps-1). 1985. 11.75 (ISBN 0-688-05701-2); lib. bdg. 11.88 (ISBN 0-688-05702-0). Greenwillow.
Hope, Laura L. Bobbsey Twins Camping Out. (gr. 1-4). 1923. 4.50 (ISBN 0-448-08016-8, G&D). Putnam Pub Group.
—Bobbsey Twins on a Bicycle Trip. (gr. 1-4). 1955. 4.50 (ISBN 0-448-08048-6, G&D). Putnam Pub Group.
—Bobbsey Twins on Blueberry Island. (gr. 1-4). 1930. 4.50 (ISBN 0-448-08010-9, G&D). Putnam Pub Group.
Johnson, Annabel & Johnson, Edgar. The Grizzly. Riswold, Gilbert, illus. LC 64-11831. 194p. (gr. 5-9). 1964. PLB 13.89 (ISBN 0-06-022871-7). HarpC Child Bks.
Kaye, Marilyn. Color War! 128p. (Orig.). (gr. 3 up). 1989. pap. 2.95 (ISBN 0-380-75702-8, Camelot). Avon.
—Too Many Counselors. 128p. 1990. pap. 2.95 (ISBN 0-380-75913-6, Camelot). Avon.
Kraft, Jim. Garfield Goes Camping. (Illus.). 24p. 1991. 10.95 (ISBN 0-448-19287-X, G&D). Putnam Pub Group.
L'Engle, Madeleine. The Moon by Night. LC 63-9072. 224p. (gr. 7 up). 1963. 14.95 (ISBN 0-374-35049-3). FS&G.
Levy, Elizabeth. Dracula Is a Pain in the Neck. Gerstein, Mordicai, illus. LC 82-47707. 80p. (gr. 2-6). 1983. 12.95 (ISBN 0-06-023822-4); PLB 12.89 (ISBN 0-06-023823-2). HarpC Child Bks.
Locker, Thomas. Where the River Begins. LC 84-1709. (Illus.). 32p. (gr. k-3). 1984. 15.00 (ISBN 0-8037-0089-X); PLB 14.89 (ISBN 0-8037-0090-3). Dial Bks Young.
Martin, Ann M. Bummer Summer. LC 82-48755. 160p. (gr. 5-9). 1983. 14.95 (ISBN 0-8234-0483-8). Holiday.
—Bummer Summer. 160p. (gr. 4-6). 1984. pap. 2.50 (ISBN 0-590-41308-2, Apple Paperbacks). Scholastic Inc.
Muntean, Michaela. Baby Fozzie Goes Camping. Wilson, Ann, illus. 26p. (ps up). 1987. 12.95 (ISBN 1-55578-604-9). Worlds Wonder.
Norby, Lisa. Crazy Campout. LC 88-14695. 128p. (Orig.). (gr. 3-7). 1989. PLB 5.99 (ISBN 0-394-99607-0); pap. 2.95 (ISBN 0-394-89607-6). Knopf.
Parish, Peggy. Amelia Bedelia Goes Camping. LC 84-7979. (Illus.). 56p. (gr. 1-3). 1985. 12.95 (ISBN 0-688-04058-6); PLB 12.88 (ISBN 0-688-04057-8). Greenwillow.
Pettersen, P. J. I Hate Camping. Remkiewicz, Frank, illus. 80p. (gr. 4-7). 1991. 12.95 (ISBN 0-525-44673-7, DCB). Dutton Child Bks.
Roche, P. K. Webster & Arnold Go Camping. LC 88-1485. 32p. (ps-3). 1989. pap. 12.95 (ISBN 0-670-81993-X). Viking Child Bks.
—Webster & Arnold Go Camping. (Illus.). 32p. (ps-3). 1991. pap. 3.95 (ISBN 0-14-050806-6, Puffin). Puffin Bks.
Schwartz, Joel L. Upchuck Summer. Degen, Bruce, illus. 144p. (gr. 3-7). 1991. pap. 3.50 (ISBN 0-440-49264-5, YB). Dell.
Seton, Ernest T. Two Little Savages. (Illus.). 286p. (gr. 4-8). 1903. pap. 6.95 (ISBN 0-486-20985-7). Dover.
Spindle's Picnic. 1989. 2.99 (ISBN 0-517-69123-X). Outlet Bk Co.
Strohl, Roger R., Jr. Jake & Duke Camp Paw Mountain. 1989. 6.95 (ISBN 0-533-08163-7). Vantage.
Sumiko. My Summer Vacation. Sumiko, illus. LC 89-43164. 32p. (Orig.). (ps-1). 1990. PLB 5.99 (ISBN 0-679-90525-1); pap. 2.25 (ISBN 0-679-80525-7). McKay.
Tafuri, Nancy. Do Not Disturb. LC 86-357. (Illus.). 24p. (ps-3). 1987. 11.75 (ISBN 0-688-06541-4); PLB 11.88 (ISBN 0-688-06542-2). Greenwillow.
Weiss, Ellen. Oh Beans! Starring Half-Baked Bean. Hall, Susan, illus. LC 88-4901. 32p. (gr. k-3). 1989. PLB 8.79 (ISBN 0-8167-1402-9); pap. text ed. 1.95 (ISBN 0-8167-1403-7). Troll Assocs.
Weiss, Nicki. Battle Day at Camp Belmont. (Illus.). 32p. (Orig.). (ps-3). 1988. pap. 3.95 (ISBN 0-14-050761-2, Puffin). Puffin Bks.
Westcott, A. & Symons, C. Whispering River. LC 78-108727. (Illus.). 48p. (gr. 3-5). 1970. PLB 10.95 (ISBN 0-87783-049-5); pap. 3.94 deluxe ed (ISBN 0-87783-116-5). Oddo.
Williams, Vera B. Three Days on a River in a Red Canoe. LC 80-23893. (Illus.). 32p. (gr. k-3). 1981. 14.95 (ISBN 0-688-80307-5); PLB 14.88 (ISBN 0-688-84307-7). Greenwillow.

CAMPS–FICTION
Angell, Judie. In Summertime, It's Tuffy. 192p. (gr. 5 up). 1979. pap. 2.25 (ISBN 0-440-94051-6, LFL). Dell.
Brown, Marc. Arthur Goes to Camp. Brown, Marc, illus. LC 81-15588. 32p. (ps-3). 1984. 14.95 (ISBN 0-316-11218-6, Joy St Bks); pap. 4.95 (ISBN 0-316-11058-2, Joy St Bks). Little.
Carlson, Nancy. Arnie Goes to Camp. 1988. pap. 11.95 (ISBN 0-670-81549-7). Viking Child Bks.
—Arnie Goes to Camp. (Illus.). 32p. (ps-3). 1990. pap. 3.95 (ISBN 0-14-050708-6, Puffin). Puffin Bks.
Conford, Ellen. Hail, Hail Camp Timberwood. Owens, Gail, illus. LC 78-18715. (gr. 3-7). 1978. 14.95 (ISBN 0-316-15291-9). Little.
Cushman, Doug. Camp Big Paw. Cushman, Doug, illus. LC 89-26867. 64p. (gr. k-3). 1990. 11.95 (ISBN 0-06-021367-1); PLB 11.89 (ISBN 0-06-021368-X). HarpC Child Bks.
Danziger, Paula. There's a Bat in Bunk Five. LC 80-64833. 160p. (gr. 7 up). 1980. pap. 10.95 (ISBN 0-385-29013-6); pap. 14.95 (ISBN 0-385-29015-2). Delacorte.
—There's a Bat in Bunk Five. (gr. 4-7). 1982. pap. 3.25 (ISBN 0-440-98631-1). Dell.
Delton, Judy. My Mom Made Me Go to Camp. LC 89-23358. 1990. 12.95 (ISBN 0-385-30040-9). Doubleday.
Gitenstein, Judy. Summer Camp. 64p. (Orig.). (gr. 2-4). 1984. pap. 2.75 (ISBN 0-553-15562-8, Skylark). Bantam.
Hallowell, Tommy. Shot from Midfield. 112p. (gr. 3 up). 1990. pap. 2.95 (ISBN 0-14-032912-9, Puffin). Puffin Bks.
Hannan, Peter. Escape from Camp Wannabarf. Hannan, Peter, illus. LC 90-33203. 32p. (Orig.). (ps-2). 1991. PLB 8.99 (ISBN 0-679-90287-2); pap. 3.95 (ISBN 0-679-80287-8). Knopf.
Kaye, Marilyn. Erin & the Movie Star. 128p. 1991. pap. 2.95 (ISBN 0-380-76181-5, Camelot). Avon.
—Looking for Trouble. 128p. (gr. 4). 1990. pap. 2.95 (ISBN 0-380-75909-8, Camelot). Avon.
—The New & Improved Sarah. 144p. (Orig.). 1990. pap. 2.95 (ISBN 0-380-76180-7, Camelot). Avon.
—A Witch in Cabin Six. 128p. (gr. 3-4). 1990. pap. 2.95 (ISBN 0-380-75912-8, Camelot). Avon.
Lane, Carolyn. Ghost Island. LC 84-28859. 148p. (gr. 3-6). 1985. 11.95 (ISBN 0-395-38207-6). HM.
Levinson, Nancy S. Your Friend Natalie Popper. (gr. 4-7). 1991. 13.95 (ISBN 0-525-67307-5, Lodestar Bks). Dutton Child Bks.
Mckenna, Colleen O. Eenie Meanie Murphy No. 1990. pap. 10.95 (ISBN 0-590-42899-3). Scholastic Inc.
Malcolm, Jahanna N. Camp Clodhopper. (gr. 4-7). 1990. pap. 2.75 (ISBN 0-590-43396-2). Scholastic Inc.
Mallett, Jerry & Bartch, Marian. Goodbye to Camp Crumb. Smith, Mark D., illus. 59p. (gr. 2-5). 1986. PLB 7.05 (ISBN 0-8479-9929-7, 120950). Perma Bound.
Marshall, James. The Cut-ups at Camp Custer. (Illus.). 32p. (ps-3). 1989. pap. 12.95 (ISBN 0-670-82051-2). Viking Child Bks.
Park, Barbara. Buddies. (gr. 7 up). 1986. pap. 2.95 (ISBN 0-380-69992-3, Flare). Avon.
Pravda, Myra & Weiland, Jeanne. Off to Camp! Kiefhaber, Jan, illus. 72p. (Orig.). (gr. 2-7). 1989. pap. 4.95 perfect bdg. (ISBN 0-9622328-0-7). JSP Pub.
Robins, Joan. Addie Runs Away. Truesdell, Sue, illus. LC 88-24350. 32p. (ps-2). 1989. 10.95i (ISBN 0-06-025080-1); PLB 10.89 (ISBN 0-06-025081-X). HarpC Child Bks.
Schneider, Susan. Please Send Junk Food. 160p. (Orig.). (gr. 5 up). 1985. pap. 2.25 (ISBN 0-448-47740-8). Putnam Pub Group.
Schwartz, Joel L. Upchuck Summer's Revenge. 1990. 13.95 (ISBN 0-385-29978-8). Doubleday.
Stine, Bob & Stine, Jane. The Cool Kids' Guide to Summer Camp. Zimmerman, Jerry, illus. 112p. (gr. 7 up). 1983. pap. 2.25 (ISBN 0-590-32389-X, Vagabond). Scholastic Inc.
Stolz, Mary. A Wonderful Terrible Time. Glanzman, Louis S., illus. LC 67-21573. 224p. (ps-7). 1967. PLB 12.89 (ISBN 0-06-026064-5). HarpC Child Bks.
Thompson, Jonathon, Jr. Away at Camp. 20p. (gr. 1-6). 3.00 (ISBN 0-933479-11-5). Thompson.

Ziefert, Harriet. Harry Goes to Day Camp. (Illus.). 32p. (ps-2). 1990. pap. 8.95 (ISBN 0-670-83201-4). Viking Child Bks.
—Harry Goes to Day Camp. Smith, Mavis, illus. 32p. (ps-3). 1990. pap. 3.50 (ISBN 0-14-054223-X, Puffin). Puffin Bks.

CANADA

Ayer, Elizabeth. Canada. (Illus.). 64p. (gr. 7 up). 1990. lib. bdg. 15.93 (ISBN 0-86593-091-0); lib. bdg. 11. 95s.p. (ISBN 0-685-36363-5). Rourke Corp.
Bender, Lionel. Canada. (Illus.). 48p. (gr. 4-8). 1988. PLB 14.98 (ISBN 0-382-09508-1). Silver Burdett Pr.
Brickenden, Jack. Canada. Fairclough, Chris, photos by. Walker, Malcolm, illus. LC 87-32451. 48p. (gr. 5-8). 1989. PLB 12.40 (ISBN 0-531-18185-5, Pub. by Bookwright Pr). Watts.
—We Live in Canada. (Illus.). 64p. (gr. 4-8). 1984. PLB 9.49 (ISBN 0-531-03818-1). Watts.
Bryant, Adam. Canada: Good Neighbor to the World. LC 86-11618. (Illus.). 192p. (gr. 5 up). 1987. PLB 14.95 (ISBN 0-87518-339-5, Dillon). Macmillan Child Grp.
Haaland, Lynn. Acadia Seacoast: A Guidebook for Appreciation. Mills, Louise & Johnson, Mercy, eds. Swensson, Dale I. & Welles, T., illus. 32p. (Orig.). (gr. k up). 1984. pap. 3.00 (ISBN 0-915189-01-1). Oceanus.
Haskins, Jim. Count Your Way Through Canada. Michaels, Steve, illus. 24p. (gr. 1-4). 1989. 11.95 (ISBN 0-87614-350-8); pap. 4.95 (ISBN 0-87614-515-2). Carolrhoda Bks.
Law, Kevin J. Canada. (Illus.). (gr. 5 up). 1988. 14.95 (ISBN 0-222-00912-8). Chelsea Hse.
Lerner Publications, Department of Geography Staff. Canada in Pictures. (Illus.). 64p. (gr. 5 up). 1989. PLB 12.95 (ISBN 0-8225-1870-8). Lerner Pubns.
LeVert, Suzanne. Canada. (Illus.). (gr. 3 up). 1992. PLB 16.95 (ISBN 0-7910-1034-1). Chelsea Hse.
—Canada: Facts & Figures. (Illus.). (gr. 3 up). 1992. PLB 16.95 (ISBN 0-7910-1035-X). Chelsea Hse.
—New Brunswick. (Illus.). (gr. 3 up). 1992. PLB 16.95 (ISBN 0-7910-1029-5). Chelsea Hse.
—Newfoundland. (Illus.). (gr. 3 up). 1992. PLB 16.95 (ISBN 0-7910-1027-9). Chelsea Hse.
—Nova Scotia. (Illus.). (gr. 3 up). 1992. PLB 16.95 (ISBN 0-7910-1028-7). Chelsea Hse.
—Yukon. (Illus.). (gr. 3 up). 1992. PLB 16.95 (ISBN 0-7910-1032-5). Chelsea Hse.
Lye, Keith. Take a Trip to Canada. (Illus.). 32p. (gr. k-3). 1983. PLB 7.99 (ISBN 0-531-03757-6). Watts.
Malcolm, Andrew H. The Land & People of Canada. LC 90-47560. (Illus.). 240p. (gr. 6 up). 1991. 17.95 (ISBN 0-06-022494-0); PLB 17.89 (ISBN 0-06-022495-9). HarpC Child Bks.
Paltrowitz, Stuart & Paltrowitz, Donna. Content Area Reading Skills-Competency Canada: Main Idea. (Illus.). (gr. 4). 1987. pap. text ed. 3.25 (ISBN 0-89525-853-6). Ed Activities.
Redekopp, Elsa. Dream & Wonder: A Child's View of Canadian Village Life. Quiring, Margaret, illus. 119p. (gr. k-7). 1986. pap. 3.95 (ISBN 0-919797-44-X). Kindred Pr.
Sabin, Louis. Canada. Eitzen, Allan, illus. LC 84-40437. 32p. (gr. 3-6). 1985. PLB 9.49 (ISBN 0-8167-0302-7); pap. text ed. 2.95 (ISBN 0-8167-0303-5). Troll Assocs.
Shepherd, J. Canada. LC 87-14626. (Illus.). 128p. (gr. 5-9). 1987. PLB 25.27 (ISBN 0-516-02757-3). Childrens.
Wright, David K. Canada. Wright, David K., photos by. LC 89-43197. (Illus.). 64p. (gr. 5-6). 1991. PLB 12.95 (ISBN 0-8368-0256-X). Gareth Stevens Inc.
Wright, Sarah B. Islands of the Northeastern United States & Eastern Canada. (Illus.). 224p. (Orig.). 1990. pap. text ed. 9.95 (ISBN 0-934601-99-2). Peachtree Pubs.

CANADA–BIOGRAPHY

Canadian Childhoods: A Tundra Anthology. (Illus.). (gr. 4-8). 1989. 24.95 (ISBN 0-88776-208-5). Tundra Bks.
Tykal, Jack B. Etienne Provost: Man of the Mountains. Smith, Monte, ed. Smith, Ralph L., illus. Gowans, Fred, intro. by. (Illus.). 256p. (gr. 9 up). 1989. 15.95 (ISBN 0-943604-24-9); pap. 9.95 (ISBN 0-943604-23-0). Eagles View.
Williams, A. Susan. Canada. (Illus.). 32p. (gr. k-4). 1991. RLB 11.90 (ISBN 0-531-18390-4, Pub. by Boatwright Pr). Watts.

CANADA–DISCOVERY AND EXPLORATION

see America–Discovery and Exploration

CANADA–FICTION

Blades, Ann. Mary of Mile 18. (Illus.). (gr. 1-4). 1971. 11. 95 (ISBN 0-88776-015-5); pap. 6.95 (ISBN 0-88776-059-7). Tundra Bks.
Freedman, Benedict & Freedman, Nancy. Mrs. Mike. (gr. 7 up). 1984. pap. 3.50 (ISBN 0-425-10328-5). Berkley Pub.
Halvorson, Marilyn. Hold on, Geronimo. LC 87-25656. 240p. (gr. 7 up). 1988. pap. 14.95 (ISBN 0-385-29665-7). Delacorte.
Hemon, Louis. Maria Chapdelaine. Brown, Alan, tr. from FRE. Tibo, Gilles, illus. Carrier, Roch, intro. by. LC 89-50775. (Illus.). 96p. (gr. 6 up). 1989. Repr. of 1914 ed. 50.00 (ISBN 0-88776-236-0). Tundra Bks.
—Maria Chapdelaine. Tibo, Gilles, illus. Carrier, Roch, intro. by. LC 89-50774. (FRE., Illus.). 96p. (gr. 6 up). 1989. Repr. of 1914 ed. 50.00 (ISBN 0-88776-239-5). Tundra Bks.
Hope, Laura L. Bobbsey Twins & the Talking Fox Mystery. (Illus.). (gr. 1-4). 1970. 4.50 (ISBN 0-448-08063-X, G&D). Putnam Pub Group.
Lunn, Janet. The Root Cellar. 230p. (gr. 7 up). 1985. pap. 3.95 (ISBN 0-14-031835-6, Puffin). Puffin Bks.
Montgomery, L. M. Anne of Green Gables, 3 vols. (gr. 7-12). 1987. Boxed Set. pap. 8.85 (ISBN 0-553-33307-0); pap. 8.85 (ISBN 0-553-30838-6). Bantam.
Mowat, Farley. Lost in the Barrens. (Illus.). (gr. 7 up). 1956. 15.95 (ISBN 0-316-58638-2, Joy St Bks). Little.
Oke, Janette. When Comes the Spring. LC 85-11261. 224p. (Orig.). (gr. 6). 1985. pap. 5.95 (ISBN 0-87123-795-4). Bethany Hse.
Redekopp, Elsa. Wish & Wonder: A Manitoba Village Child. Goulden, Veleda, illus. 59p. (Orig.). (gr. 3-6). 1982. pap. 3.95 (ISBN 0-919797-21-0). Kindred Pr.

CANADA–HISTORY–TO 1763 (NEW FRANCE)

Anderson, Joan. Pioneer Settlers of New France. 1990. 15.95 (ISBN 0-525-67291-5, Lodestar Bks). Dutton Child Bks.

CANADA–SOCIAL LIFE AND CUSTOMS

Hausherr, Rosmarie. The City Girl Who Went to Sea. Hausherr, Rosmarie, illus. LC 89-27236. 80p. (gr. 3-6). 1990. 14.95 (ISBN 0-02-743421-4, Four Winds). Macmillan Child Grp.

CANADA. ROYAL CANADIAN MOUNTED POLICE–FICTION

Freedman, Benedict & Freedman, Nancy. Mrs. Mike. (gr. 7 up). 1984. pap. 3.50 (ISBN 0-425-10328-5). Berkley Pub.

CANADIAN POETRY–COLLECTIONS

Little, Jean. Hey, World, Here I Am! Truesdell, Sue, illus. LC 88-10987. 96p. (gr. 3-7). 1989. 11.95i (ISBN 0-06-023989-1); PLB 12.89 (ISBN 0-06-024006-7). HarpC Child Bks.

CANALS

Pierce, Anthony. Canal People. (Illus.). 64p. (gr. 7 up). 1978. 14.95 (ISBN 0-7136-1811-6). Dufour.
Scarry, Huck. Life on a Barge: A Sketchbook. Scarry, Huck, illus. 72p. (gr. 3-7). 1982. 10.95 (ISBN 0-13-535831-0). P-H.

CANALS–FICTION

Selberg, Ingrid. Our Changing World. Miller, Andrew, illus. 12p. 1982. 10.95 (ISBN 0-399-20869-0, Philomel). Putnam Pub Group.

CANARIES–FICTION

Frost, Erica. The Story of Matt & Mary. Schumacher, Claire, illus. LC 85-14011. 48p. (Orig.). (gr. 1-3). 1986. PLB 9.89 (ISBN 0-8167-0602-6); pap. text ed. 2.95 (ISBN 0-8167-0603-4). Troll Assocs.
Lofting, Hugh. Doctor Dolittle & the Green Canary. Lofting, Hugh, illus. (gr. 4 up). 1989. 14.95 (ISBN 0-318-41607-7). Delacorte.
—Doctor Doolittle & the Green Canary. Lofting, Hugh, illus. (gr. 4-7). 1989. 14.95 (ISBN 0-385-29748-3). Delacorte.

CANCER

Bergman, Thomas. One Day at a Time: Children Living with Leukemia. LC 88-42972. (Illus.). 48p. (gr. 4-5). 1989. PLB 10.95 (ISBN 1-55532-913-6). Gareth Stevens Inc.
Chamberlain, Shannin. My ABC Book of Cancer. (Illus.). 40p. (Orig.). (ps-8). 1991. pap. 6.95 (ISBN 0-912184-07-8). Synergistic Pr.
Fingert, Howard J. Cancer Therapy. Head, J. J., ed. Steffen, Ann T., illus. LC 86-72194. 16p. (Orig.). (gr. 10 up). 1987. pap. text ed. 2.15 (ISBN 0-89278-370-2, 45-9770). Carolina Biological.
Fradin, Dennis. Cancer. (gr. 5-9). 1988. 14.60 (ISBN 0-516-01210-X); pap. 4.95 (ISBN 0-516-41210-8). Childrens.
Gaes, Jason. My Book for Kids with Cancer. LC 87-60794. (Illus.). 32p. (gr. 3-9). 1988. 12.95 (ISBN 0-937603-04-X). Melius Pub.
Gravelle, Karen & Bertram, John. Teenagers Face-to-Face with Cancer. LC 86-8608. 96p. (gr. 7 up). 1986. lib. bdg. 12.28 (ISBN 0-671-54549-3). Messner.
Greenberg, Jan. No Dragons to Slay. LC 83-17200. 152p. (gr. 7 up). 1983. 11.95 (ISBN 0-374-35528-2); pap. 3.50 (ISBN 0-374-45509-0). FS&G.
Hyde, Margaret O. & Hyde, Lawrence E. Cancer in the Young: A Sense of Hope. LC 84-27126. 96p. (gr. 9 up). 1985. 8.95 (ISBN 0-664-32722-2, Westminster). Westminster John Knox.
Little, Jean. Mama's Going to Buy You a Mockingbird. LC 84-20877. 208p. (gr. 4-6). 1985. pap. 13.95 (ISBN 0-670-80346-4). Viking Child Bks.
Monroe, Judy. Leukemia. LC 90-33663. (Illus.). 48p. (gr. 5-6). 1990. RSBE 10.95 (ISBN 0-89686-532-0, Crestwood Hse). Macmillan Child Grp.
Photopulos, Georgia & Photopulos, Bud. Of Tears & Triumphs: The Family Victory That Has Inspired Thousands of Cancer Patients. 192p. 1988. 16.95 (ISBN 0-86553-197-8). Congdon & Weed.
Rodgers, Joann. Cancer. (Illus.). (gr. 6 up). 1990. 18.95 (ISBN 0-7910-0059-1). Chelsea Hse.
Silverstein, Alvin & Silverstein, Virginia B. Cancer: Can It Be Stopped? new, rev. ed. LC 86-45500. (Illus.). 128p. (gr. 7 up). 1987. 12.95 (ISBN 0-397-32202-X, Lipp Jr Bks); PLB 12.89 (ISBN 0-397-32203-8, Lipp Jr Bks). HarpC Child Bks.
Strauss, Linda. Coping When a Parent Has Cancer. Rosen, Ruth, ed. LC 88-18539. (gr. 7 up). 1988. lib. bdg. 12.95 (ISBN 0-8239-0785-6). Rosen Group.
Swenson, Judy H. & Kunz, Roxane B. Cancer: The Whispered Word. LC 85-6983. (Illus.). 40p. (gr. 2-6). 1986. lib. bdg. 8.95 (ISBN 0-87518-310-7, Dillon). Macmillan Child Grp.

CANDLEMAS

Johnson, Crockett. Will Spring Be Early or Will Spring Be Late? Johnson, Crockett, illus. LC 59-9424. 48p. (gr. k-3). 1961. PLB 12.89 (ISBN 0-690-89423-6, Crowell Jr Bks). HarpC Child Bks.

CANDLES

Benchley, Nathaniel. Bright Candles. LC 73-5477. 264p. (gr. 7 up). 1974. 13.95 (ISBN 0-06-020461-3). HarpC Child Bks.
Faraday, Michael. Faraday's Chemical History of a Candle: Six Illustrated Lectures with Notes & Experiments. (Illus.). (gr. 7-11). 1988. pap. 9.95 (ISBN 1-55652-035-2). Chicago Review.

CANDY

see Confectionery

Stevenson, James W. If I Owned a Candy Factory. Stevenson, James, illus. LC 87-37581. 32p. (ps up). 1989. 11.95 (ISBN 0-688-08106-1); PLB 11.88 (ISBN 0-688-08107-X). Greenwillow.

CANNED GOODS

see Canning and Preserving

CANNING AND PRESERVING

Mitgutsch, Ali. From Fruit to Jam. Mitgutsch, Ali, illus. LC 81-58. 24p. (ps-3). 1981. PLB 6.95 (ISBN 0-87614-154-8). Carolrhoda Bks.

CANOES AND CANOEING

Barrett, Norman. Canoeing. Franklin Watts Ltd., ed. (Illus.). 32p. (ps-9). 1988. PLB 11.40 (ISBN 0-531-10349-8). Watts.
—Canoeing. (Illus.). 32p. (gr. 2 up). 1991. pap. 3.95 (ISBN 0-531-15178-6). Watts.
Boy Scouts of America Staff. Canoeing. (Illus.). 88p. (gr. 6-12). 1989. pap. 1.85 (ISBN 0-8395-3308-X, 3308A). BSA.
Dwier, Lois A. Wilderness Wetlands in Spring: A Canoe Trip in the Pine Barrens of South Jersey. Vivian, V. Eugene, ed. Fink, Frank L., illus. 64p. (gr. 4-12). 1983. 8.95 (ISBN 0-9613007-0-1). Edlo Bks.
Moran, Tom. Canoeing Is for Me. Wolfe, Robert L., illus. LC 83-19957. 48p. (gr. 2-5). 1984. PLB 8.95 (ISBN 0-8225-1142-8). Lerner Pubns.
Penzler, Otto. Danger! White Water. LC 75-21844. (Illus.). 32p. (gr. 5-10). 1976. PLB 10.79 (ISBN 0-89375-004-2); pap. 2.95 (ISBN 0-89375-020-4). Troll Assocs.

CANOES AND CANOEING–FICTION

Roddy, Lee. The Dangerous Canoe Race. Cragg, Shelia, ed. (Orig.). (gr. 3-6). 1990. pap. 4.99 (ISBN 0-929608-62-3). Focus Family.
Slate, Joseph. Mean, Clean, Giant Canoe Machine. Munsinger, Lynn, illus. LC 82-45880. 32p. (gr. k-3). 1983. 11.95 (ISBN 0-690-04293-0, Crowell Jr Bks). HarpC Child Bks.
Williams, Vera B. Three Days on a River in a Red Canoe. LC 80-23893. (Illus.). 32p. (gr. k-3). 1981. 14.95 (ISBN 0-688-80307-5); PLB 14.88 (ISBN 0-688-84307-7). Greenwillow.

CAPE COD–FICTION

Feil, Hila. Blue Moon. LC 89-36915. 208p. (gr. 5-9). 1990. 13.95 (ISBN 0-689-31607-0, Atheneum Child Bk). Macmillan Child Grp.
Weller, Frances W. Boat Song. LC 86-12647. 180p. (gr. 3-7). 1987. 13.95 (ISBN 0-02-792611-7, Mcmillan Child Bk). Macmillan Child Grp.

CAPITAL PUNISHMENT

Flanders, Stephen A. Library in a Book: Capital Punishment. 240p. (gr. 9-12). 1991. 22.95x (ISBN 0-8160-1912-6). Facts on File.
Hays, Scott. Capital Punishment. (Illus.). 64p. (gr. 7 up). 1990. lib. bdg. 15.93 (ISBN 0-86593-074-0); lib. bdg. 11.95s.p. (ISBN 0-685-36322-8). Rourke Corp.
Loeb, Robert H., Jr. Crime & Capital Punishment. rev. ed. 128p. (gr. 7-12). 1986. PLB 12.90 (ISBN 0-531-10209-2). Watts.
O'Sullivan, Carol. Death Penalty: Identifying Propaganda Techniques. (Illus.). 32p. (gr. 3-6). 1990. PLB 8.95 (ISBN 0-89908-636-5). Greenhaven.

CAPITALISTS AND FINANCIERS

Aaseng, Nathan. From Rags to Riches: People Who Started Businesses from Scratch. (Illus.). 80p. (gr. 5 up). 1990. PLB 13.95 (ISBN 0-8225-0679-3). Lerner Pubns.

CAR WHEELS

see Wheels

CARBON

see also Diamonds

CARCINOMA

see Cancer

CARD GAMES

see Cards

CARD TRICKS

see also Fortune Telling

Bailey, Vanessa. Card Tricks: Games & Projects for Children. (Illus.). 32p. (gr. k-4). 1990. PLB 11.40 (ISBN 0-531-17255-4). Watts.

Croxton, William L. Amazing Card Tricks Made Easy to Do. rev. ed. (Illus.). 64p. 1990. pap. 4.95 (ISBN 0-9623230-0-4). WLC Enterprises. YOU CAN BE A MAGICIAN. New Book Makes It Easy. Learn Card Tricks in Minutes. Here are card tricks that can be learned Quickly - No matter whether you are 9 or 90. Let

Bill Croxton teach you how to do AMAZING CARD TRICKS. It's a fascinating book that teaches the reader how to identify unseen cards. Learn how you can mystify friends. Be the life of every party. Get invited back over & over again. AMAZING CARD TRICKS MADE EASY TO DO gives complete step-by-step instructions. There are illustrations so that you know exactly what to do. You'll be the life of every party. And you can learn to do these tricks in only 10 minutes. No trick cards are used. All that you need is a standard deck of playing cards. The simple method that is explained by the author will enable anyone to develop a skill that will last a lifetime. Bill Croxton invites you to try AMAZING BACK CARD TRICKS on a 100% Money Back Guarantee. You'll learn to do the tricks quickly & enjoy performing them. If you are not pleased for any reason, return the book for full refund. It's a great value at only $4.95, available from the publisher. Tel. 205-923-9175.
Publisher Provided Annotation.

Gravatt, Glenn. Fifty Modern Card Tricks You Can Do! 50p. (Orig.). (gr. 7 up). 1977. pap. 3.00 (ISBN 0-915926-07-5). Magic Ltd.

—Fifty More Modern Card Tricks. Walker, Barbara, ed. 60p. (gr. 7 up). 1979. 4.00 (ISBN 0-915926-33-4). Magic Ltd.

CARDIAC DISEASES
see Heart–Diseases

CARDINALS

Roseman, Kenneth. The Cardinal's Snuffbox. Negron, Bill, illus. 128p. (gr. 4-6). 1982. pap. text ed. 6.95 (ISBN 0-8074-0059-9, 140060). UAHC.

CARDS
see also Card Tricks; Fortune Telling

Arnold, Peter. Card Games. (Illus.). 200p. (Orig.). 1989. pap. 14.95 (ISBN 0-87052-730-4). Hippocrene Bks.

Beaton, Clare. Make & Play: Cards. 1990. pap. 2.95 (ISBN 0-531-15159-X). Watts.

Collis, Len. Card Games for Children. Carter, Terry & George, Bob, illus. 96p. (ps up). 1989. pap. 4.95 (ISBN 0-8120-4290-5). Barron.

Old Karankawa Indian Card Game. 1984. 5.95 (ISBN 0-937460-53-2). Hendrick-Long.

Schreiner, Nikki B., et al. The Whole World Kit: American Dream Activity Cards. Weathers, Susan, et al, illus. 60p. (gr. 4-8). 1990. pap. text ed. 215.00 (ISBN 1-879218-29-1). Touch & See Educ.

CARDS, GREETING
see Greeting Cards

CAREER STORIES
see Vocational Stories

CAREERS
see Occupations; Professions; Vocational Guidance; see subject headings with the subdivision Vocational Guidance

CARIBBEAN AREA

Antigua & Barbuda. (Illus.). (gr. 5 up). 1988. 14.95 (ISBN 0-7910-0151-2). Chelsea Hse.

Broberg, Merle. Barbados. (Illus.). 96p. (gr. 5 up). 1989. lib. bdg. 14.95 (ISBN 1-55546-792-X). Chelsea Hse.

Eisenberg, Joyce. Grenada. (Illus.). 96p. (gr. 5 up). 1988. lib. bdg. 14.95 (ISBN 1-55546-777-6). Chelsea Hse.

Haverstock, Nathan A. The Dominican Republic in Pictures. (Illus.). 64p. (gr. 5 up). 1988. PLB 12.95 (ISBN 0-8225-1812-0). Lerner Pubns.

Law, Kevin. St. Lucia. (Illus.). 96p. (gr. 5 up). 1988. lib. bdg. 14.95 (ISBN 1-55546-198-0). Chelsea Hse.

Lessac, Frane. Caribbean Canvas. LC 88-36555. (Illus.). 24p. (ps up). 1989. 14.95 (ISBN 0-397-32367-0, Lipp Jr Bks); PLB 14.89 (ISBN 0-397-32368-9). HarpC Child Bks.

Mason, Antony. The Caribbean. (Illus.). 48p. (gr. 4-8). 1989. PLB 14.98 (ISBN 0-382-09823-4). Silver Burdett Pr.

Springer, Eintou P. The Caribbean. rev ed. (Illus.). 48p. (gr. 5-10). 1988. PLB 16.98 (ISBN 0-382-09469-7); pap. 6.95 (ISBN 0-382-09475-1). Silver Burdett Pr.

CARIBBEAN AREA–FICTION

Haynes, Betsy. Caribbean Adventure. (gr. 4-7). 1990. pap. 2.95 (ISBN 0-553-15831-7, Skylark). Bantam.

Spillane, Mickey. The Day the Sea Rolled Back. Hofheimer, Steven, illus. 1979. 7.95 (ISBN 0-525-61589-X, Dutton). NAL-Dutton.

CARIBOU

Harris, Lorle K. The Caribou. LC 88-18953. (Illus.). 60p. (gr. 3 up). 1988. PLB 12.95 (ISBN 0-87518-391-3, Dillon). Macmillan Child Grp.

Nentl, Jerolyn. The Caribou. LC 83-26254. (Illus.). 48p. (gr. 5-6). 1984. PLB 10.95 (ISBN 0-89686-244-5, Crestwood Hse). Macmillan Child Grp.

Owens, Mary B. A Caribou Alphabet. McCollough, Mark, contrib. by. (Illus.). 40p. (gr. k-6). 1988. 14.95 (ISBN 0-937966-25-8). Tilbury Hse.

CARICATURES
see Cartoons and Caricatures

CARLSBAD CAVERNS

Radlauer, Ruth. Carlsbad Caverns National Park. LC 81-4560. (Illus.). 48p. (gr. 3 up). 1981. PLB 17.27 (ISBN 0-516-07742-2). Childrens.

CARNEGIE, ANDREW, 1835-1919

Bowman, John. Andrew Carnegie. Furstinger, Nancy, ed. (Illus.). 128p. (gr. 7-10). 1989. PLB 13.98 (ISBN 0-382-09582-0). Silver Burdett Pr.

CARNIVALS
see Festivals

CAROLS

Amery, H., compiled by. The Usborne Book of Christmas Carols. (Illus.). 64p. (ps up). 1990. lib. bdg. 13.96 (ISBN 0-88110-447-7, Usborne); pap. 7.95 (ISBN 0-7460-0432-X, Usborne). EDC.

Bowman, Peter. The Christmas Songbook: Favorite Carols with Spinning Pictures. (Illus.). 14p. (ps-1). 1990. 15.95 (ISBN 0-399-21918-8, Putnam). Putnam Pub Group.

Cooper, Don. Merry Christmas Songs & Games. Fritz, Ronald, illus. 32p. (ps-3). 1989. pap. 5.95 incl. cassette (ISBN 0-394-82230-7). Random.

Cosgrove, Shaerie. A Christmas Song. McGlinn, Merry A., illus. Cosgrove, Stephen, contrib. by. (Illus.). 32p. (ps-3). 1989. pap. 4.95 incl. 20 min. cassette (ISBN 0-8249-7343-7). Ideals.

Davie, Helen, illus. Sing with Me Christmas Carols. 24p. (ps up). 1987. pap. 5.95 incl. cassette (ISBN 0-394-89060-4, Random Juv). Random.

De Paola, Tomie. The Friendly Beasts: An Old English Christmas Carol. De Paola, Tomie, illus. 32p. (ps-2). 1981. 13.95 (ISBN 0-399-20739-2, Putnam); pap. 5.95 (ISBN 0-399-20777-5, Putnam). Putnam Pub Group.

—Tomie De Paola's Book of Christmas Carols. De Paola, Tomie, illus. LC 86-755157. 82p. (gr. 1 up). 1987. 17.95 (ISBN 0-399-21432-1, Putnam). Putnam Pub Group.

Glazer, Tom. Tom Glazer's Christmas Songbook. Corrigan, Barbara, illus. 128p. (gr. 3 up). 1989. pap. 14.95 (ISBN 0-385-24641-2, Zephyr-BFYR). Doubleday.

Goode, Diane, illus. Christmas Carols. LC 82-62169. 32p. (ps up). 1988. pap. 1.25 (ISBN 0-394-81940-3, Random Juv). Random.

Hague, Michael. Jingle Bells. Hague, Michael, illus. 32p. (ps up). 1990. 4.95 (ISBN 0-8050-1413-6). H Holt & Co.

Hague, Michael, illus. We Wish You a Merry Christmas. 32p. 1990. 4.95 (ISBN 0-8050-1006-8). H Holt & Co.

Ideals Staff. My First Book of Christmas Carols. Ideals Staff, illus. 24p. (gr. k-6). 1985. pap. 2.95 (ISBN 0-8249-8072-7). Ideals.

Keats, Ezra J. The Little Drummer Boy. LC 68-25714. (gr. k-3). 1972. pap. 4.95 (ISBN 0-02-044090-1, Collier Young Ad). Macmillan Child Grp.

The Keepsake Book of Christmas Carols & Audiocassette. (Illus., Orig.). 1987. 9.95 (ISBN 0-89471-557-7). Running Pr.

McRae, Patrick, illus. O Little Town of Bethlehem. 32p. 1990. 11.95 (ISBN 0-8249-8390-4). Ideals.

Mayr-Pletschen, Heide, illus. A Christmas Carol Book. (gr. 3 up). 2.75 (ISBN 0-685-24603-5). Merry Thoughts.

Morehead, Ruth J., illus. Christmas Is Coming with Ruth J. Morehead's Holly Babes: A Book of Poems & Songs. LC 89-3717. 32p. (Orig.). (ps-1). 1990. pap. 2.25 (ISBN 0-679-80075-1). Random.

Rosenkrans, B., compiled by. My Book of Christmas Carols. Dyer, Jane, illus. 32p. (ps-2). 1986. pap. 1.95 (ISBN 0-448-19079-6, G&D); incl. cassette 5.95 (ISBN 0-448-19085-0). Putnam Pub Group.

Schindler, S. D., illus. The Twelve Days of Christmas. LC 90-22389. 24p. (ps up). 1991. 2.95 (ISBN 0-694-00363-8). HarpC Child Bks.

Tennyson, Noel, illus. Christmas Carols: A Treasury of Holiday Favorites with Words & Pictures. LC 83-60412. 24p. (gr. 1-5). 1983. 2.95 (ISBN 0-394-86125-6). Random.

The Ultimate Christmas Fake Book. 84p. (gr. 4-12). 1985. 10.95 (ISBN 0-88188-381-6, HL00240063). H Leonard Pub Corp.

Wallner, John, illus. Good King Wenceslas. 32p. 1990. 14.95 (ISBN 0-399-21620-0, Philomel Bks). Putnam Pub Group.

Well-Loved Carols. (gr. k-4). 3.50 (ISBN 0-7214-0964-4). Ladybird Bks.

Westcott, Nadine B., illus. Raffi's Christmas Treasury: 14 Illustrated Songs & Musical Arrangements. (ps up). 1988. PLB 17.95 (ISBN 0-517-56806-3). Crown.

CARPENTRY

Here are entered works dealing with the construction of a wooden building or the wooden portion of any building. Works that treat the making and finishing of fine woodwork, such as furniture or interior details, are entered under Cabinet Work.
see also Building; Woodwork

Chadwick, Charley G., et al. Wall Framing. Harrington, Lois G., ed. Smith, George W., Jr. & Edwards, Jason, illus. 72p. (Orig.). (gr. 10-12). 1989. pap. text ed. 8.00 (ISBN 0-89606-266-X, 701); tchr's. key 3.00 (ISBN 0-685-27030-0, 701TK). Am Assn Voc Materials.

Leavitt, Jerome E. Easy Carpentry Projects for Children. 96p. (gr. 2 up). 1986. pap. 3.95 (ISBN 0-486-25057-1). Dover.

Lillegard, Dee. I Can Be a Carpenter. LC 86-9676. (Illus.). 32p. (gr. k-3). 1986. PLB 13.93 (ISBN 0-516-01884-1); pap. 3.95 (ISBN 0-516-41884-X). Childrens.

Martin, John H. A Day in the Life of a Carpenter. Wells, Sarah, illus. LC 84-2420. 32p. (gr. 4-8). 1985. PLB 11.79 (ISBN 0-8167-0093-1); pap. text ed. 2.95 (ISBN 0-8167-0094-X). Troll Assocs.

O'Connor, Patricia. Hitting the Nail on the Head. Trotter, Candace L., ed. 112p. (Orig.). (gr. 8 up). 1991. pap. text ed. 9.95 (ISBN 0-9622684-0-2). Nugget Pub.

Weiss, Harvey. Hammer & Saw. Weiss, Harvey, illus. LC 81-43042. 80p. (gr. 5 up). 1981. PLB 12.89 (ISBN 0-690-04131-4, Crowell Jr Bks). HarpC Child Bks.

CARPENTRY–FICTION

Kinens, Janis J. The Old Woodcutter. Kinens, Janis J., illus. LC 88-81904. 32p. (gr. k-12). 1988. PLB 12.95 (ISBN 0-9620999-0-2); 12.95 (ISBN 0-9620999-1-0). Guzzy Pr.

CARPETS
see also Weaving

CARRIERS, AIRCRAFT
see Aircraft Carriers

CARS (AUTOMOBILES)
see Automobiles

CARS, ARMORED (TANKS)
see Tanks (Military Science)

CARSON, CHRISTOPHER, 1809-1868

Gleiter, Jan & Thompson, Kathleen. Kit Carson. Whipple, Rick, illus. 32p. (gr. 2-5). 1987. PLB 16.67 (ISBN 0-8172-2650-8); pap. 9.27 (ISBN 0-8172-2654-0). Raintree Pubs.

McCall, Edith. Hunters Blaze the Trails. Rogers, Carol, illus. LC 59-3666. 128p. (gr. 3-10). 1980. PLB 14.60 (ISBN 0-516-03332-8). Childrens.

CARSON, RACHEL, 1907-1964

Foster, Leila M. The Story of Rachel Carson & the Environmental Movement. LC 90-2208. (Illus.). 32p. (gr. 3-6). 1990. PLB 13.27 (ISBN 0-516-04753-1); pap. 3.95 (ISBN 0-516-44753-X). Childrens.

Goldberg, Jake. Rachel Carson. (Illus.). 84p. (gr. 3-5). 1991. PLB 12.95 (ISBN 0-7910-1566-1). Chelsea Hse.

Harlan, Judith. Sounding the Alarm: A Biography of Rachel Carson. LC 88-35909. (Illus.). 128p. (gr. 5 up). 1989. lib. bdg. 12.95 (ISBN 0-87518-407-3, Dillon). Macmillan Child Grp.

Jezer, Marty. Rachel Carson. Horner, Matina, intro. by. (Illus.). 112p. (gr. 5 up). 1988. lib. bdg. 17.95 (ISBN 1-55546-646-X). Chelsea Hse.

Kudlinski, Kathleen V. Rachel Carson: Pioneer of Ecology. Lewin, Ted, illus. 64p. (gr. 2-7). 1988. pap. 10.95 (ISBN 0-670-81488-1). Viking Child Bks.

—Rachel Carson: Pioneer of Ecology. Lewin, Ted, illus. 64p. (gr. 2-6). 1989. pap. 3.95 (ISBN 0-14-032242-6, Puffin). Puffin Bks.

Wadsworth, Ginger. Rachel Carson: Voice for the Earth. (Illus.). 128p. (gr. 5 up). 1991. PLB 15.95 (ISBN 0-8225-4907-7). Lerner Pubns.

CARTER, JIMMY, PRESIDENT U. S. 1924-

Richman, Daniel A. James E. Carter: Thirty-Ninth President of the United States. Young, Richard G., ed. LC 88-24562. (Illus.). (gr. 5-9). 1989. PLB 17.26 (ISBN 0-944483-24-0). Garrett Ed Corp.

Smith, Betsy C. Jimmy Carter, President. LC 86-5589. (Illus.). 128p. (gr. 10 up). 1986. 12.95 (ISBN 0-8027-6650-1); PLB 13.85 (ISBN 0-8027-6652-8). Walker & Co.

Wade, Linda R. James Carter. LC 89-33754. 100p. (gr. 3 up). 1989. PLB 17.27 (ISBN 0-516-01372-6). Childrens.

CARTOGRAPHY
see Map Drawing; Maps

CARTOONS AND CARICATURES
see also Comic Books, Strips, etc.

Ames, Lee J. Draw Fifty Famous Cartoons. Ames, Lee J., illus. LC 78-1176. 64p. (gr. 4-6). 1979. pap. 12.95 (ISBN 0-385-13661-7). Doubleday.

Benjamin, Carol L. Cartooning for Kids. Benjamin, Carol L., illus. LC 81-43876. 80p. (gr. 3-7). 1982. PLB 12.89 (ISBN 0-690-04208-6, Crowell Jr Bks). HarpC Child Bks.

Brown, Charlene & Davis, Carolyn. Comic Strip Fun. (Illus.). 64p. (Orig.). 1989. pap. 5.95 (ISBN 0-929261-29-1, BA04). W Foster Pub.

Browne, Dik. Hagar the Horrible, No. 6: Sack Time. 128p. (gr. 2 up). 1986. pap. 2.25 (ISBN 0-441-31471-6, Pub. by Charter Bks). Ace Bks.

—Hi & Lois: Dawg Day Afternoon. 128p. 1986. pap. 1.95 (ISBN 0-8125-6908-3, Dist. by Warner Publisher Services & St. Martin's Press). Tor Bks.

Burness, Tad. Joshua. Burness, Tad, illus. 90p. (Orig.). (gr. 3 up). 1987. pap. 4.95 (ISBN 1-55523-082-2). Winston-Derek.

Byars, Betsy. The Cartoonist. 128p. (gr. k-6). 1981. pap. 1.95 (ISBN 0-440-41046-0, YB). Dell.

Cheatham, Val R. Cartooning for Kids Who Draw & Kids Who Don't Draw. (Illus.). (gr. 4-12). 1976. 4.50 (ISBN 0-914634-34-8, 6531). DOK Pubs.

De Goscinny, Rene. Asterix & Caesar's Gift. 1977. 7.95x (ISBN 0-340-21588-7); pap. 4.95x (ISBN 0-317-00093-4). Intl Learn Syst.

—Asterix & Cleopatra. Uderzo, illus. 1976. 7.95x (ISBN 0-340-04239-7); pap. 4.95x (ISBN 0-686-31734-3). Intl Learn Syst.
—Asterix & the Big Fight. Uderzo, illus. 1976. 7.95x (ISBN 0-340-04238-9); pap. 4.95x (ISBN 0-317-00094-2). Intl Learn Syst.
—Asterix & the Cauldron. Uderzo, illus. 1976. 7.95x (ISBN 0-340-20212-2); pap. 4.95x (ISBN 0-317-00095-0). Intl Learn Syst.
—Asterix & the Chieftain's Shield. 1977. 7.95x (ISBN 0-340-21394-9); pap. 4.95x (ISBN 0-317-00096-9). Intl Learn Syst.
—Asterix & the Goths. Uderzo, illus. 1976. 7.95x (ISBN 0-340-18491-4); pap. 4.95x (ISBN 0-686-31735-1). Intl Learn Syst.
—Asterix & the Great Crossing. Uderzo, illus. 1976. 7.95x (ISBN 0-340-20211-4); pap. 4.95x (ISBN 0-686-31736-X). Intl Learn Syst.
—Asterix & the Laurel Wreath. Uderzo, illus. 1976. 7.95x (ISBN 0-340-19107-4); pap. 4.95x (ISBN 0-686-31737-8). Intl Learn Syst.
—Asterix & the Roman Agent. Uderzo, illus. 1976. 7.95x (ISBN 0-340-16540-5); pap. 4.95x (ISBN 0-317-00097-7). Intl Learn Syst.
—Asterix apud Gothos. Uderzo, illus. (LAT.). 1976. 7.95x (ISBN 0-686-19936-7). Intl Learn Syst.
—Asterix at the Olympic Games. Uderzo, illus. 1976. 7.95x (ISBN 0-340-15591-4); pap. 4.95x (ISBN 0-686-31739-4). Intl Learn Syst.
—Asterix auf Korsika. Uderzo, illus. (GER.). 1976. 7.95x (ISBN 0-686-19937-5). Intl Learn Syst.
—Asterix aux Jeux Olympiques. (FRE.). (gr. 7-9). 19.95 (ISBN 0-685-23424-X, FC884). French & Eur.
—Asterix chez les Bretons. (FRE.). (gr. 7-9). 19.95 (ISBN 0-685-23430-4, FC880). French & Eur.
—Asterix Chez les Helvetes. (FRE., Illus.). (gr. 7-9). 19.95 (ISBN 0-685-28427-1, FC889). French & Eur.
—Asterix e gli Allori di Cesare. (ITA.). 1976. 4.95x (ISBN 0-686-10694-6). Intl Learn Syst.
—Asterix e il Paiolo. Uderzo, illus. (ITA.). 1976. 4.95x (ISBN 0-686-19938-3). Intl Learn Syst.
—Asterix e il Regalo Di Cesare. (ITA.). 1976. 4.95x (ISBN 0-686-10693-8). Intl Learn Syst.
—Asterix en Corcega. Uderzo, illus. (SPA.). 1976. 5.95x (ISBN 84-7419-083-5). Intl Learn Syst.
—Asterix en Hispanie. (FRE., Illus.). (gr. 7-9). 19.95 (ISBN 0-685-28428-X, FC887). French & Eur.
—Asterix en los Juegos Olimpicos. Uderzo, illus. (SPA.). 1976. 5.95x (ISBN 84-7419-045-2). Intl Learn Syst.
—Asterix et Cleopatre. (FRE.). (gr. 7-9). 19.95 (ISBN 0-685-23434-7, FC878). French & Eur.
—Asterix et le Chaudron. (FRE., Illus.). (gr. 7-9). 19.95 (ISBN 0-685-28429-8, FC885). French & Eur.
—Asterix et les Goths. (FRE.). (gr. 7-9). 19.95 (ISBN 0-685-23426-6, FC875). French & Eur.
—Asterix et les Normands. (FRE.). (gr. 7-9). 19.95 (ISBN 0-685-23431-2, FC881). French & Eur.
—Asterix Gallus. Uderzo, illus. (LAT.). 1976. 7.95x (ISBN 0-686-19940-5). Intl Learn Syst.
—Asterix Gladiador. Uderzo, illus. (SPA.). 1976. 5.95x (ISBN 0-686-28601-4). Intl Learn Syst.
—Asterix Gladiateur. (FRE.). (gr. 7-9). 19.95 (ISBN 0-685-23427-4, FC876). French & Eur.
—Asterix Gladiator. Uderzo, illus. (LAT.). 1976. 7.95x (ISBN 0-686-19941-3). Intl Learn Syst.
—Asterix in Britain. Uderzo, illus. 1976. 7.95x (ISBN 0-317-00098-5); pap. 4.95x (ISBN 0-317-00099-3). Intl Learn Syst.
—Asterix in Spain. Uderzo, illus. 1976. 7.95x (ISBN 0-340-14934-5); pap. 4.95x (ISBN 0-686-31741-6). Intl Learn Syst.
—Asterix in Switzerland. Uderzo, illus. 1976. 7.95x (ISBN 0-340-17062-X); pap. 4.95x (ISBN 0-686-34392-1). Intl Learn Syst.
—Asterix la Zizanie. (FRE., Illus.). (gr. 7-9). 19.95 (ISBN 0-685-28426-3, FC888). French & Eur.
—Asterix le Gaulois. (FRE.). (gr. 7-9). 19.95 (ISBN 0-685-23425-8, FC873). French & Eur.
—Asterix Legionnaire. (FRE.). (gr. 7-9). 19.95 (ISBN 0-685-23432-0, FC882). French & Eur.
—Asterix the Gladiator. Uderzo, illus. 1976. 7.95x (ISBN 0-340-10479-1); pap. 4.95x (ISBN 0-317-00100-0). Intl Learn Syst.
—Asterix the Legionary. Uderzo, illus. 1976. 7.95x (ISBN 0-340-10392-2); pap. 4.95x (ISBN 0-686-31743-2). Intl Learn Syst.
—Asterix und Kleopatra. (GER.). 1977. 7.95x (ISBN 0-686-10695-4). Intl Learn Syst.
—The Golden Sickle. Uderzo, illus. 1976. 7.95x (ISBN 2-205-06901-2); pap. 3.95x (ISBN 0-686-31744-0). Intl Learn Syst.
De Goscinny., Rene. La Gran Travesia. Uderzo, illus. (SPA.). 1976. 5.95x (ISBN 84-02-04451-4). Intl Learn Syst.
De Goscinny, Rene. Die Lorbeeren Des Casars. Uderzo, illus. (GER.). 1976. 5.95x (ISBN 0-686-19973-1). Intl Learn Syst.
—The Mansion of the Gods. Uderzo, illus. 1976. 7.95x (ISBN 0-340-17719-5); pap. 4.95x (ISBN 2-2050-6916-0). Intl Learn Syst.
—El Regalo del Cesar. Uderzo, illus. (SPA.). 1976. 5.95x (ISBN 0-686-34393-X). Intl Learn Syst.
—Der Seher. Uderzo, illus. (GER.). 1976. 5.95x (ISBN 0-686-19948-0). Intl Learn Syst.
—The Soothsayer. Uderzo, illus. 1976. 5.95x (ISBN 0-340-19525-8). Intl Learn Syst.
—Die Trabantenstadt. Uderzo, illus. (GER.). 1976. 7.95x (ISBN 0-686-19994-4). Intl Learn Syst.
De Goscinny, Rene & Uderzo, M. La Gran Travesia. (SPA., Illus.). 19.95 (ISBN 0-686-56239-9). French & Eur.
—Der Seher. (GER., Illus.). 19.95 (ISBN 0-686-56267-4). French & Eur.
De Kay, James T. Left-Handed Kids. LC 89-36893. (Illus.). 96p. 1989. pap. 5.95 (ISBN 0-87131-591-2). M Evans.
Edwards, R. Scott & Stobener, Bob. Cel Magic: The Book on Collecting Animation Art. (Illus.). 104p. 1990. pap. 19.95 (ISBN 0-9624792-1-7). Laughs Unltd.
Goscinny, R. & Uderzo, M. El Adivino. (SPA., Illus.). 15.95 (ISBN 0-686-56236-4). French & Eur.
—Der Arvernerschild. (GER., Illus.). 15.95 (ISBN 0-686-56259-3). French & Eur.
—Asterix & the Big Fight. (Illus.). (gr. 7-10). 15.95 (ISBN 0-686-56204-6). French & Eur.
—Asterix & the Roman Agent. (Illus.). (gr. 7-10). 15.95 (ISBN 0-686-56207-0). French & Eur.
—Asterix el Galo. (SPA., Illus.). (gr. 7-10). 15.95 (ISBN 0-686-56223-2). French & Eur.
—Le Cadeau de Cesar. (FRE., Illus.). 15.95 (ISBN 0-686-56245-3). French & Eur.
—The Caldron. (Illus.). 15.95 (ISBN 0-686-56215-1). French & Eur.
—La Cizana. (SPA., Illus.). 15.95 (ISBN 0-686-56232-1). French & Eur.
—El Combate de los Jefes. (SPA., Illus.). 15.95 (ISBN 0-686-56221-6). French & Eur.
—Les Douze Travaux d'Asterix. (FRE., Illus.). 15.95 (ISBN 0-686-56248-8). French & Eur.
—El Escudo Arverno. (SPA., Illus.). 15.95 (ISBN 0-685-01710-9). French & Eur.
—Falx Aurea. (LAT., Illus.). 15.95 (ISBN 0-686-56272-0). French & Eur.
—Das Geschenk Casars. (GER., Illus.). 15.95 (ISBN 0-686-56269-0). French & Eur.
—Die Goldene Sichel. (GER., Illus.). 15.95 (ISBN 0-686-56253-4). French & Eur.
—La Grande Traversee. (FRE., Illus.). 15.95 (ISBN 0-686-56246-1). French & Eur.
—Die Grosse Uberfahrt. (GER., Illus.). 15.95 (ISBN 0-686-56270-4). French & Eur.
—La Hoz de Oro. (SPA., Illus.). 15.95 (ISBN 0-686-56224-0). French & Eur.
—Der Kampf der Hauptlinge. (GER., Illus.). 15.95 (ISBN 0-686-56252-6). French & Eur.
—Der Kupferkessel. (GER., Illus.). 15.95 (ISBN 0-686-56261-5). French & Eur.
—Los Laureles del Cesar. (SPA., Illus.). 15.95 (ISBN 0-686-56235-6). French & Eur.
—Les Lauriers de Cesar. (FRE., Illus.). 15.95 (ISBN 0-686-56243-7). French & Eur.
—Die Lorbeeren des Casar. (GER., Illus.). 15.95 (ISBN 0-686-56266-6). French & Eur.
—The Mansions of the Gods. (Illus.). 15.95 (ISBN 0-686-56210-0). French & Eur.
—Die Normannen. (GER., Illus.). 15.95 (ISBN 0-686-56257-7). French & Eur.
—El Regalo del Cesar. (SPA., Illus.). 15.95 (ISBN 0-686-56238-0). French & Eur.
—La Residencia de los Dioses. (SPA., Illus.). 15.95 (ISBN 0-686-56234-8). French & Eur.
—La Serpe d'Or. (FRE., Illus.). 15.95 (ISBN 0-686-56240-2). French & Eur.
—The Soothsayer. (Illus.). 15.95 (ISBN 0-686-56212-7). French & Eur.
—Streit Um Asterix. (GER., Illus.). 15.95 (ISBN 0-686-56263-1). French & Eur.
—Tour de France. (GER., Illus.). 15.95 (ISBN 0-686-56254-2). French & Eur.
—Le Tour de Gaulle. (FRE., Illus.). 15.95 (ISBN 0-686-56241-0). French & Eur.
—Die Trabantenstadt. (GER., Illus.). 15.95 (ISBN 0-686-56265-8). French & Eur.
—La Vuelta a la Galia. (SPA., Illus.). 15.95 (ISBN 0-686-56226-7). French & Eur.
—La Zizanie. (FRE., Illus.). 15.95 (ISBN 0-686-56242-9). French & Eur.
Goscinny, Rene & Uderzo, M. Asterix bei den Olympischen Spielen. (GER., Illus.). (gr. 7-10). 15.95 (ISBN 0-686-56260-7). French & Eur.
—The Golden Sickle. (Illus.). 15.95 (ISBN 0-686-56213-5). French & Eur.
Goscinny, Rene de. Asterix et la Serpe d'or. (FRE., Illus.). (gr. 3-8). 15.95 (ISBN 0-685-28431-X). French & Eur.
Goscinny, Rene de & Uderzo, M. Asterix als Gladiator. (GER., Illus.). (gr. 7-10). 15.95 (ISBN 0-686-56251-8). French & Eur.
—Asterix als Legionar. (GER., Illus.). (gr. 7-10). 15.95 (ISBN 0-686-56258-5). French & Eur.
—Asterix & Caesar's Gift. (Illus.). (gr. 7-10). 15.95 (ISBN 0-686-56217-8). French & Eur.
—Asterix & Cleopatra. (Illus.). (gr. 7-10). 15.95 (ISBN 0-686-56200-3). French & Eur.
—Asterix & the Chieftain's Shield. (Illus.). (gr. 7-10). 15.95 (ISBN 0-686-56216-X). French & Eur.
—Asterix & the Laurel Wreath. (Illus.). (gr. 7-10). 15.95 (ISBN 0-686-56211-9). French & Eur.
—Asterix & the Normans. (Illus.). (gr. 7-10). 15.95 (ISBN 0-686-56218-6). French & Eur.
—Asterix apud Gothos. (LAT., Illus.). (gr. 7-10). 15.95 (ISBN 0-686-56273-9). French & Eur.
—Asterix at the Olympic Games. (Illus.). (gr. 7-10). 15.95 (ISBN 0-686-56206-2). French & Eur.
—Asterix auf Korsika. (GER., Illus.). (gr. 7-10). 15.95 (ISBN 0-686-56268-2). French & Eur.
—Asterix bei den Briten. (GER., Illus.). (gr. 7-10). 15.95 (ISBN 0-686-56256-9). French & Eur.
—Asterix bei den Schweizern. (GER., Illus.). (gr. 7-10). 15.95 (ISBN 0-686-56264-X). French & Eur.
—Asterix chez les Belges. (FRE., Illus.). (gr. 7-10). 15.95 (ISBN 0-686-56247-X). French & Eur.
—Asterix der Gallier. (GER., Illus.). (gr. 7-10). 15.95 (ISBN 0-686-56249-6). French & Eur.
—Asterix en Bretana. (SPA., Illus.). (gr. 7-10). 15.95 (ISBN 0-686-56222-4). French & Eur.
—Asterix en Corcega. (SPA., Illus.). (gr. 7-10). 15.95 (ISBN 0-686-56237-2). French & Eur.
—Asterix en Corse. (FRE., Illus.). (gr. 7-10). 15.95 (ISBN 0-686-56244-5). French & Eur.
—Asterix en Helvecia. (SPA., Illus.). (gr. 7-10). 15.95 (ISBN 0-686-56233-X). French & Eur.
—Asterix en los Juegos Olimpicos. (SPA., Illus.). (gr. 7-10). 15.95 (ISBN 0-686-56230-5). French & Eur.
—Asterix Gallus. (LAT., Illus.). (gr. 7-10). 15.95 (ISBN 0-686-56271-2). French & Eur.
—Asterix Gladiador. (SPA., Illus.). (gr. 7-10). 15.95 (ISBN 0-686-56227-5). French & Eur.
—Asterix in Spain. (Illus.). 15.95 (ISBN 0-686-56205-4). French & Eur.
—Asterix in Spanien. (GER., Illus.). 15.95 (ISBN 0-686-56262-3). French & Eur.
—Asterix in Switzerland. (Illus.). 15.95 (ISBN 0-686-56208-9). French & Eur.
—Asterix iter Gallicum. (LAT., Illus.). 15.95 (ISBN 0-686-56275-5). French & Eur.
—Asterix Legionario. (SPA., Illus.). 15.95 (ISBN 0-685-01689-7). French & Eur.
—Asterix the Gaul. (Illus.). 15.95 (ISBN 0-686-56199-6). French & Eur.
—Asterix the Gladiator. (Illus.). 15.95 (ISBN 0-686-56201-1). French & Eur.
—Asterix the Legionary. (Illus.). 15.95 (ISBN 0-686-56203-8). French & Eur.
—Asterix und die Goten. (GER., Illus.). 15.95 (ISBN 0-686-56255-0). French & Eur.
—Asterix und Kleopatra. (GER., Illus.). 15.95 (ISBN 0-686-56250-X). French & Eur.
—Asterix y Cleopatra. (SPA., Illus.). 15.95 (ISBN 0-686-56228-3). French & Eur.
—Asterix y el Caldero. (SPA., Illus.). 15.95 (ISBN 0-686-56231-3). French & Eur.
—Asterix y los Godos. (SPA., Illus.). 15.95 (ISBN 0-686-56225-9). French & Eur.
—Asterix y los Normandos. (SPA., Illus.). 15.95 (ISBN 0-686-56229-1). French & Eur.
Herge. The Castafiore Emerald. (gr. k up). 1975. pap. 6.95 (ISBN 0-316-35842-8, Joy St Bks). Little.
Hoff, Syd. How to Draw Cartoons. (Illus.). 32p. (gr. k-3). 1975. pap. 1.95 (ISBN 0-590-10135-8). Scholastic Inc.
—How to Draw Cartoons. (Illus.). 32p. (Orig.). (gr. k-3). 1991. pap. 1.95 (ISBN 0-590-40689-2). Scholastic Inc.
Johnston, Lynn. Is This "One of Those Days," Daddy? Johnston, Lynn, illus. LC 82-72417. 128p. (gr. 5 up). 1982. pap. 7.95 (ISBN 0-8362-1197-9). Andrews & McMeel.
Keane, Bil. Look Who's Here. 1987. pap. 2.25 (ISBN 0-449-13276-5, GM). Fawcett.
Kemsley, James. The Cartoon Book. 64p. (gr. 4 up). 1991. pap. 5.95 (ISBN 0-590-43871-9). Scholastic Inc.
Ketcham, Hank. Dennis the Menace: Everybody's Little Helper. (Illus.). 128p. 1984. pap. 1.95 (ISBN 0-449-12732-X, GM). Fawcett.
—Dennis the Menace: Little Man in a Big Hurry. (Illus.). 128p. 1984. pap. 1.95 (ISBN 0-449-12778-8, Gm). Fawcett.
—Dennis the Menace: Make-Believe Angel. (Illus.). 1981. pap. 1.95 (ISBN 0-449-13902-6, GM). Fawcett.
—Dennis the Menace: Teacher's Threat. (Illus.). 1981. pap. 1.50 (ISBN 0-449-13643-4, GM). Fawcett.
—Dennis the Menace: Voted Most Likely. (Illus.). (gr. 7 up). 1982. pap. 1.75 (ISBN 0-449-13747-3, GM). Fawcett.
—Dennis the Menace: Where the Action Is. (Illus.). 128p. 1981. pap. 1.50 (ISBN 0-449-13669-8, GM). Fawcett.
—Dennis the Menace: Your Friendly Neighborhood Kid. (Illus.). 1979. pap. 1.25 (ISBN 0-449-13778-3, GM). Fawcett.
Mascola. Charles Schulz, Reading Level 2. (Illus.). 24p. (gr. 1-4). Date not set. PLB 12.33 (ISBN 0-86592-429-5). Rourke Corp.
Mickey Mouse et Monte Cristo. (FRE.). (gr. 3-8). 6.25 (ISBN 0-685-28446-8). French & Eur.
Newell, Peter S. Topsys & Turvys. (Illus.). 76p. (gr. 3-7). pap. 3.50 (ISBN 0-486-21231-9). Dover.
Parker, Steve. Draw Partner: How to Draw Wild West Cartoons for Kids. Parker, Steve, illus. 32p. (gr. 1-6). 1990. pap. 2.95 (ISBN 0-929526-08-2). Double B Pubns.
Ross, Dave. More Hugs! LC 83-46167. (Illus.). 32p. (ps up). 1984. 6.95i (ISBN 0-694-00147-3, Crowell Jr Bks). HarpC Child Bks.
Ryan, Tom K. Let'er Rip Tumbleweeds. (Illus.). 128p. 1981. pap. 1.50 (ISBN 0-449-13894-1, GM). Fawcett.
Schultz, Charles. Summers Fly, Winters Walk. (Illus.). 128p. 1991. pap. 5.95 (ISBN 0-8050-1692-9). H Holt & Co.
Schulz, Charles M. Apuros Escolares. (SPA., Illus.). (gr. 3-8). 1.50 (ISBN 0-685-28419-0). French & Eur.
—A Boy Named Charlie Brown. LC 79-80346. 142p. (gr. 5 up). 1969. 7.95 (ISBN 0-03-081861-3). H Holt & Co.

—A Charlie Brown Christmas. LC 76-57940. (Illus.). (gr. k-8). 1977. (Random Juv); PLB 5.99 (ISBN 0-394-83454-2). Random.
—It's a Mystery, Charlie Brown. Schulz, Charles M., illus. 48p. (gr. 1 up). 1975. 4.95 (ISBN 0-394-83101-2, Random Juv); lib. bdg. 4.99 (ISBN 0-394-93101-7). Random.
—Peanuts a Vendre. (FRE.). (gr. 3-8). 1985. pap. 1.95 (ISBN 0-685-23404-5). French & Eur.
—Snoopy & His Sopwith Camel. LC 78-91065. (Illus.). 64p. (gr. 5 up). 1969. 2.95 (ISBN 0-03-083177-6). H Holt & Co.
—Snoopy & the Red Baron. LC 66-22569. (Illus.). 64p. (gr. 5 up). 1966. 2.95 (ISBN 0-03-060560-1). H Holt & Co.
—Strike Three, Charlie Brown. 1987. pap. 2.25 (ISBN 0-449-21290-4, Crest). Fawcett.
—There's No One Like You, Snoopy: Selected Cartoons from "You're You, Charlie Brown, Vol. I. (Illus.). (gr. 1-5). 1985. pap. 2.95 (ISBN 0-449-20776-5, Crest). Fawcett.
—This Is the Best Time of Day, Charlie Brown. 1987. pap. 2.25 (ISBN 0-449-21316-1, Crest). Fawcett.
—Your Choice, Snoopy. 1987. pap. 2.95 (ISBN 0-449-21327-7, Crest). Fawcett.
—You're a Good Sport, Charlie Brown. LC 76-8128. (Illus.). (gr. 1 up). 1976. 4.95 (ISBN 0-394-83297-3, Random Juv). Random.
Sesame Street Staff. Sesame Street Storybook. (Illus.). (ps-4). 1971. 5.95 (ISBN 0-394-82332-X, Random Juv); lib. bdg. 5.99 (ISBN 0-394-92332-4). Random.
Smythe, Reginald. Watch Your Step, Andy Capp. (Illus.). (gr. 4 up). 1979. pap. 1.25 (ISBN 0-449-13562-4, P3562, GM). Fawcett.
Tallarico, Tony. Guide to Drawing Cartoons: A Step by Step Fun Guide. (Illus.). 64p. (gr. 2-7). 1975. pap. 2.95 (ISBN 0-448-11959-5, G&D). Putnam Pub Group.
Tatchell, J. & Evans, C. Young Cartoonist. 72p. (gr. 5 up). 1987. pap. 6.95 (ISBN 0-7460-0083-9). EDC.
Thurber, James. Many Moons. Slobodkin, Louis, illus. LC 43-51250. 48p. (gr. 3-7). 1973. pap. 5.95 (ISBN 0-15-656980-9, VoyB). HarBraceJ.
Tollison, Hal. Cartoon Fun. (Illus.). 64p. (Orig.). 1989. pap. text ed. 5.95 (ISBN 1-56010-033-8, BA07). W Foster Pub.
Turk, Phillip & Degroot, Bob. Leonardo Is a Genius. 48p. 1983. pap. 4.95 (ISBN 2-205-06577-7). Dargaud Pub.
Walt Disney Staff. Alice in Wonderland. 1988. 6.98 (ISBN 0-8317-0287-7, Gallery Bks). Smithmark.

CARVER, GEORGE WASHINGTON, 1864?-1943

Adair, Gene. George Washington Carver. King, Coretta Scott, intro. by. (Illus.). 112p. (Orig.). (gr. 5 up). 1989. 17.95 (ISBN 1-55546-577-3); pap. 9.95 (ISBN 0-7910-0234-9). Chelsea Hse.
Aliki. A Weed Is a Flower: The Life of George Washington Carver. Aliki, illus. 32p. (ps-3). 1988. pap. 12.95 (ISBN 0-671-66118-3, Little Simon); pap. 5.95 (ISBN 0-671-66490-5, Juveniles). S&S Trade.
Benitez, Miena. George Washington Carver, Plant Doctor. 32p. 1989. PLB 13.22 (ISBN 0-8172-3522-1). Raintree Pubs.
Coil, Suzanne M. George Washington Carver. (Illus.). 64p. (gr. 5-8). 1990. PLB 11.90 (ISBN 0-531-10864-3). Watts.
Collins, David. George Washington Carver. Van Seversen, Joe, illus. 131p. (gr. 3-6). 1981. pap. 6.95 (ISBN 0-915134-90-X). Mott Media.
Epstein, Sam & Epstein, Beryl. George Washington Carver. (Orig.). (gr. k-6). 1991. pap. 2.95 (ISBN 0-440-40404-5, Pub. by Yearling Classics). Dell.
Gray, James M. George Washington Carver. Gallin, Richard, ed. (Illus.). 144p. 1990. lib. bdg. 13.98 (ISBN 0-382-09964-8); pap. 7.95 (ISBN 0-382-09969-9). Silver Burdett Pr.
McKissack, Patricia & McKissack, Fredrick. George Washington Carver: The Peanut Scientist. Ostendorf, Ned, illus. 32p. (gr. 1-4). 1991. PLB 12.95 (ISBN 0-89490-308-X). Enslow Pubs.
Means, Florence. Carvers' George. large type ed. (Illus.). 160p. (gr. 4-8). 1991. Repr. of 1952 ed. PLB 17.95 (ISBN 1-55905-075-6). Grey Castle.
Mitchell, Barbara. A Pocketful of Goobers: A Story about George Washington Carver. Hanson, Peter, illus. 64p. (gr. 3-6). 1986. PLB 9.95 (ISBN 0-87614-292-7). Carolrhoda Bks.
Moore, Eva. Story of George Washington Carver. 1990. pap. 2.75 (ISBN 0-590-42660-5). Scholastic Inc.

CARVING, WOOD

see Wood Carving

CASH, JOHNNY

Loewen, L. Johnny Cash. (Illus.). 112p. (gr. 5 up). 1989. lib. bdg. 17.26 (ISBN 0-86592-608-5). Rourke Corp.

CASSATT, MARY, 1845-1926

Cain, Michael. Mary Cassatt. Horner, Matina, intro. by. (Illus.). 112p. (gr. 5 up). 1989. lib. bdg. 17.95 (ISBN 1-55546-647-8). Chelsea Hse.
Meyer, Susan E. Mary Cassatt. (Illus.). 80p. (gr. 7 up). 1990. 18.95 (ISBN 0-8109-3154-0). Abrams.
Venezia, Mike. Mary Cassatt. Venezia, Mike, illus. LC 90-2165. 32p. (ps-4). 1990. PLB 14.60 (ISBN 0-516-02278-4). Childrens.

CASTLES

Cairns, Conrad. Medieval Castles. (Illus.). 52p. (gr. 5 up). 1989. 9.95 (ISBN 0-8225-1235-1). Lerner Pubns.
Campbell, Elizabeth. Castle Hopping in the U. K. with Elizabeth. (Illus.). 60p. (Orig.). (gr. 9-12). 1988. pap. 12.95 (ISBN 0-9618324-0-1). EFC Pub.
Castles of Great Britain. (Illus.). (gr. 5 up). 3.50 (ISBN 0-7214-1090-1). Ladybird Bks.
Clarke, Richard. Castles. LC 85-73661. (Illus.). 32p. (gr. 1-6). 1986. PLB 8.99 (ISBN 0-531-18057-3, Pub. by Bookwright). Watts.
Davison, Brian. Looking at a Castle. Dennis, Peter, illus. LC 87-4834. 32p. (ps-1). 1987. (Random Juv); lib. bdg. 7.99 (ISBN 0-394-99185-0). Random.
Gee, Robyn, ed. Living in Castle Times. McCaig, Rob & Ashman, Iain, illus. 24p. (gr. 3-6). 1982. lib. bdg. 11.96 (ISBN 0-88110-106-0); pap. 4.50 (ISBN 0-86020-621-1). EDC.
Graham, Rickard. Norman Castles. 1990. PLB 10.40 (ISBN 0-531-18323-8). Watts.
James, Alan. Castles & Mansions. (Illus.). 32p. (gr. 2-5). 1989. 9.95 (ISBN 0-8225-2128-8). Lerner Pubns.
Macaulay, David. Castle. Macaulay, David, illus. LC 77-7159. 80p. (gr. 1 up). 1982. 14.95 (ISBN 0-395-25784-0); pap. 7.95 (ISBN 0-395-32920-5). HM.
MacDonald, Fiona. A Medieval Castle: Inside Story. Bergin, Mark, illus. 48p. (gr. 5 up). 1990. 16.95 (ISBN 0-87226-340-1). P Bedrick Bks.
Montes, J. Castles. (Illus.). 48p. (gr. 3-8). Date not set. PLB 18.60 (ISBN 0-86592-456-2). Rourke Corp.
O'Dell, Scott. The Castle in the Sea. 192p. (gr. 7up). 1983. 12.95 (ISBN 0-395-34831-5). HM.
Odor, Ruth S. Learning about Castles & Palaces. Halverson, Lynn, illus. LC 82-9567. 48p. (gr. 2-6). 1982. 17.27 (ISBN 0-516-06537-8). Childrens.
Rom, Christine S. Creepy Castles. LC 89-28986. (Illus.). 48p. (gr. 5 up). 1990. 10.95 (ISBN 0-89686-505-3, Crestwood Hse). Macmillan Child Grp.
Sancha, Sheila. The Castle Story. Sancha, Sheila, illus. 224p. (gr. 7 up). 1982. PLB 15.89 (ISBN 0-690-04146-2, Crowell Jr Bks). HarpC Child Bks.
Smith, Beth. Castles. Green, Ann C., illus. Rakos, Jennie, ed. (Illus.). 96p. (gr. 7-9). 1988. PLB 10.40 (ISBN 0-531-10511-3). Watts.
Spellman, Linda. Castles, Codes, Calligraphy. 112p. (gr. 4-6). 1984. 9.95 (ISBN 0-88160-103-9, LW 904). Learning Wks.
Unstead, R. J., ed. See Inside a Castle. Escott, Dan, et al, illus. (gr. 5-8). 1979. 10.40 (ISBN 0-531-09119-8); PLB 11.90 s&l (ISBN 0-531-09134-1). Watts.
Vaughan, Jenny. Castles. LC 83-50592. (Illus.). 32p. (gr. 2-4). 1984. lib. bdg. 7.99 (ISBN 0-531-04706-7). Watts.

CASTLES–FICTION

Alexander, Lloyd. The Castle of Llyr. 192p. (gr. 5-9). 1980. pap. 3.50 (ISBN 0-440-91125-7, LFL). Dell.
Carlson, Natalie S. The Orphelines in the Enchanted Castle. (gr. k-6). 1988. pap. 2.75 (ISBN 0-440-40015-5, YB). Dell.
Cook, Lyn. The Secret of Willow Castle. Goodwin, Judith, illus. 236p. (Orig.). (gr. 3-10). 1984. pap. 7.95 (ISBN 0-920656-30-7). Camden Hse Pub.
Graves, Robert. An Ancient Castle. Graves, Elizabeth, illus. Thomas, William D., afterword by. LC 81-17204. (Illus.). 72p. (gr. 7 up). 1981. 13.95 (ISBN 0-935576-06-1); pap. 7.95 (ISBN 0-935576-33-9). Kesend Pub Ltd.
Ichikawa, Satomi. Nora's Castle. Ichikawa, Satomi, illus. LC 85-17293. 32p. (gr. 1-3). 1986. 12.95 (ISBN 0-399-21302-3, Putnam). Putnam Pub Group.
McGuire, Leslie. Eureeka's Castle: Magellan Saves the Day. Brannon, Tom, illus. (ps-k). 1991. pap. 1.25 (ISBN 0-307-11512-7, Golden Pr). Western Pub.
Marsh, Carole. Castle Hayne. (Illus.). 60p. (gr. 4-12). 1988. PLB 19.95 (ISBN 1-55609-159-1); pap. 14.95 (ISBN 1-55609-241-5). Gallopade Pub Group.
Montgomery, L. M. The Blue Castle. (gr. 7 up). 1989. pap. 2.95 (ISBN 0-553-28051-1, Starfire). Bantam.
Muchnik, Michoel. The Cuckoo Clock Castle of Shir. LC 79-55560. (Illus.). (ps-3). 1980. 9.95 (ISBN 0-8197-0476-8). Bloch.
Nesbit, Edith. Enchanted Castle. 179p. 1981. Repr. PLB 16.95x (ISBN 0-89967-035-0). Harmony Raine.
Nolan, Dennis. The Castle Builder. Nolan, Dennis, illus. LC 86-23784. 32p. (gr. k-3). 1987. 12.95 (ISBN 0-02-768240-4, Mcmillan Child Bk). Macmillan Child Grp.
O'Dell, Scott. The Castle in the Sea. 160p. (gr. 7 up). 1984. pap. 3.50 (ISBN 0-449-70123-9, Juniper). Fawcett.
Weissman, Anne. The Castle of Chuchurumbel: El Castillo de Churchurumbel. Bailyn, Susan, illus. (ENG & SPA.). 19p. (gr. k-2). 1987. 8.95 (ISBN 968-6217-00-2). Hispanic Bk Dist.
Winthrop, Elizabeth. The Castle in the Attic. Hyman, Trina S., illus. LC 85-5607. 192p. (gr. 4-7). 1985. 13.95 (ISBN 0-8234-0579-6). Holiday.
—The Castle in the Attic. 192p. 1986. pap. 2.95 (ISBN 0-553-15433-8). Bantam.
Zimmerman, Marjorie. The Mystery of the Old Castle. LC 88-6936. (gr. 3-7). 1988. pap. 3.95 (ISBN 1-55513-584-6, Chariot Bks). Cook.

CASTRO, FIDEL, 1927-

Kurland, Gerald. Fidel Castro: Communist Dictator of Cuba. Rahmas, D. Steve, ed. 32p. (Orig.). (gr. 7-12). 1972. lib. bdg. 4.20 incl. catalog cards (ISBN 0-87157-536-1). SamHar Pr.

CAT

see Cats

CATASTROPHES

see Disasters

CATERPILLARS

see also Butterflies; Moths

Selsam, Millicent E. Terry & the Caterpillars. Lobel, Arnold, illus. LC 62-13309. 64p. (gr. k-3). 1962. PLB 11.89 (ISBN 0-06-025406-8). HarpC Child Bks.
Watts, Barrie. Caterpillars. (Illus.). 32p. (gr. k-4). 1989. PLB 10.40 (ISBN 0-531-10719-1). Watts.

CATERPILLARS–FICTION

Bartlett, Jaye. Caterpillar Had a Dream: A Poetic Story about Dreams Coming True. (Illus.). 1991. 8.95 (ISBN 1-878064-02-9). TLC Bks.
"Caterpillar" isn't about pots of gold at the end of the rainbow. "Caterpillar" is about a dream, & the courage to try. Parents & children alike will be thrilled & inspired by Caterpillar's heartening adventure as he finds the courage & determination to make his dream come true.
Publisher Provided Annotation.

—Caterpillar Had a Dream: A Story about Dreams Coming True. Dubina, Alan, illus. 38p. (Orig.). (ps up). 1990. PLB 11.95 incl. cassette (ISBN 1-878064-00-2). New Age CT.
CATERPILLAR HAD A DREAM is a heartening story, written to encourage children to follow their dreams. The poetic book contains 38 pages of magical poetry & endearing color illustrations. CATERPILLAR HAD A DREAM is the first release in a series of twelve planned children's books. The series is being released under the Logo "Tender Loving Caretaker of Planet Earth." A portion of profits from the 'Caretaking Series' is donated to the World Children's Day Foundation, Washington, D.C., to help facilitate & encourage children to become active participant of "Caretaking Projects" in their communities. "CATERPILLAR HAD A DREAM is inspiring & enchanting! It's our two daughters' favorite story book & audio cassette. I feel it's one of the best stories for children I've ever read."--Lee Rector, Publisher, I.S.I. Publications, Tampa, Florida.
Publisher Provided Annotation.

Brown, Ruth. If at First You Do Not See. Brown, Ruth, illus. LC 82-15527. 24p. (gr. k-2). 1983. 11.95 (ISBN 0-8050-1053-X). H Holt & Co.
Carle, Eric. La Oruga Muy Hambrienta. (SPA.). 32p. 1989. 15.95 (ISBN 0-685-32965-8, Philomel Bks). Putnam Pub Group.
—The Very Hungry Caterpillar. Carle, Eric, illus. LC 70-82764. (ps-2). 1981. 15.95 (ISBN 0-399-20853-4, Philomel); plush toy caterpillar 3.00 (ISBN 0-399-21659-6). Putnam Pub Group.
—The Very Hungry Caterpillar. Carle, Eric, illus. 32p. (ps up). 1986. miniature ed. 3.95 (ISBN 0-399-21301-5, Putnam). Putnam Pub Group.
Cosgrove, Stephen. The Dream Tree. James, Robin, illus. (gr. 1-6). 1974. pap. 2.95 (ISBN 0-8431-0553-4). Price Stern.
DeLuise, Dom. Charlie the Caterpillar. Santoro, Christopher, illus. LC 90-31557. 40p. (ps-1). 1990. PLB 13.95 (ISBN 0-671-69358-1). S&S Trade.
Dickson, Sandy L. The Story of Smartworms: The Journey Begins. Barrow, Madeline H., ed. Dixon, David, illus. 34p. (gr. k-5). 1989. write for info.; PLB write for info.; pap. write for info. Smartworm Corp.
The Little Green Caterpillar. (Illus.). 24p. (gr. k-2). 1982. 6.95 (ISBN 0-448-01450-5, G&D). Putnam Pub Group.
Perugini, Donna. The Flight of Orville Wright Caterpillar. (Illus.). 32p. (Orig.). (gr. k-6). 1983. pap. 3.98 (ISBN 0-89274-297-6). Harrison Hse.

CATHEDRALS

Cathedrals of Great Britain. (Illus.). (gr. 5 up). 3.50 (ISBN 0-7214-1092-8). Ladybird Bks.
Gandiol-Coppin, Brigitte. Cathedrals: Stone upon Stone. Bogard, Vicki, tr. from FRE. Thibault, Dominique, illus. LC 89-5361. 38p. (gr. k-5). 1989. 4.95 (ISBN 0-944589-24-3, 024). Young Discovery Lib.
Macaulay, David. Cathedral. (Illus.). (gr. k up). 1981. pap. 7.95 (ISBN 0-395-31668-5). HM.
—Cathedral: The Story of Its Construction. LC 73-6634. (Illus.). 80p. (gr. 1-5). 1973. 15.95 (ISBN 0-395-17513-5). HM.

CATHOLIC CHURCH

Bishops' Committee for Pastoral Research Staff & National Conference of Catholic Bishops Staff. The Sexual Challenge: Growing up Christian. 16p. (Orig.). (gr. 9-12). 1990. pap. 0.95 (ISBN 1-555-86364-7). US Catholic.

Cronin, Gaynell B. & Bellina, Joan. Together at Mass: A Child's Mass Book. Murtagh, Betty, illus. LC 87-70417. 32p. (Orig.). (ps-2). 1987. pap. 2.95 (ISBN 0-87793-357-X). Ave Maria.

Kwatera, Michael. The Ministry of Servers. Stuckenschneider, Placid, illus. 48p. (Orig.). (gr. 6-8). 1982. pap. 1.95 (ISBN 0-8146-1300-4). Liturgical Pr.

Leichner, Jeannine T. Joy Joy, the Mass: Our Family Celebration. (Illus.). (gr. k-3). 1978. pap. 2.95 (ISBN 0-87973-350-0); Spanish Edition. 2.95 (ISBN 0-87973-348-9, 348). Our Sunday Visitor.

McPhee, John, ed. Tu Fe. Diaz, Olimpia, tr. (SPA.). (gr. 9-12). 1980. pap. 2.50 (ISBN 0-89243-124-5, 48290). Liguori Pubns.

O'Connor, Francine M. ABCs of the Mass...for Children. Boswell, Kathryn, illus. 32p. (Orig.). (ps-4). 1988. pap. text ed. 2.95 (ISBN 0-89243-291-8). Liguori Pubns.

O'Connor, Francine M. & Boswell, Kathryn. The ABC'S of the Rosary. (Illus.). 32p. (gr. 1-4). 1984. pap. 2.95 (ISBN 0-89243-221-7). Liguori Pubns.

Senger, Mary C. Let's Learn about the Church & Celebrate Its Message. (Illus.). 64p. (gr. 4-6). 1990. pap. 4.95 (ISBN 0-8146-1888-X). Liturgical Pr.

Stadler, Bernice & Reese, Nancy. Celebrations of the Word for Children: Cycle C. LC 88-90102. 014p. (Orig.). (gr. 3-8). 1988. pap. text ed. 9.95 (ISBN 0-89622-362-0). Twenty-Third.

Windeatt, Mary F. Catholic Story Coloring Books. Harmon, Gedge, illus. 32p. (gr. 1-5). 1989. Repr. of 1954 ed. Set of 24. 48.00 (ISBN 0-89555-381-3). TAN Bks Pubs.

—St. Dominic Savio. Harmon, Gedge, illus. 32p. (gr. 1-5). 1989. Repr. of 1954 ed. wkbk. 3.00 (ISBN 0-89555-370-8). TAN Bks Pubs.

CATHOLIC CHURCH–DICTIONARIES

O'Connor, Francine M. ABCs of the Sacraments...for Children. Nolte, Larry, illus. 32p. (gr. k-3). 1989. pap. 2.95 (ISBN 0-89243-298-5). Liguori Pubns.

CATHOLIC CHURCH–DOCTRINAL AND CONTROVERSIAL WORKS

Canon & Howe, G. E. Stories from The Catechist: Nine Hundred Seven Traditional Catholic Stories Illustrating the Truths of the Catholic Catechism. LC 82-50589. 387p. 1989. pap. 13.50 (ISBN 0-89555-184-5). Tan Bks Pubs.

Center for Learning Network. Fundamentalism: A Catholic Response. 96p. (gr. 9-12). 1986. pap. text ed. 12.95 (ISBN 1-56077-062-7). Ctr Learning.

Crawford, Douglas R. & Mannion, Michael T. Psycho-Spiritual Healing after Abortion. LC 88-63847. 104p. (Orig.). 1989. pap. 5.95 (ISBN 1-55612-246-2). Sheed & Ward MO.

Credo: A Catholic Catechism. 296p. (gr. 7-12). 1984. pap. 8.95 (ISBN 0-225-66343-0). Harper SF.

Hazel, Harry. Power of Persuasion. LC 88-61856. 160p. (Orig.). 1989. pap. 9.95 (ISBN 1-55612-211-X). Sheed & Ward MO.

Mannernach, Janaan & Pfeifer, Carl J. How to Be a Better Catechist: Answers to Questions Catechists Ask Most. LC 89-61927. 112p. (Orig.). 1989. pap. 5.95 (ISBN 1-55612-268-3). Sheed & Ward MO.

Redemptorist Pastoral Publication Staff. How You Live with Jesus: Catechism for Today's Young Catholic. LC 81-80097. 96p. (gr. 4-6). 1981. pap. 4.95 (ISBN 0-89243-137-7). Liguori Pubns.

—Jesus Loves You: A Catholic Catechism for the Primary Grades. LC 82-8000658. 96p. (gr. 1-3). 1982. pap. 5.95 (ISBN 0-89243-157-1). Liguori Pubns.

Sullivan, Francis P. Share the Fire: Cycle A. LC 89-61222. 256p. (Orig.). 1989. pap. 14.95 (ISBN 1-55612-305-1). Sheed & Ward MO.

CATHOLIC CHURCH–FICTION

Benard, Robert. A Catholic Education. (gr. k-12). 1987. pap. 3.50 (ISBN 0-440-91124-9, LFL). Dell.

Meyer, Kathleen A. Father Serra: Traveler on the Golden Chain. LC 89-63335. (Illus.). 72p. (Orig.). 1990. 9.95 (ISBN 0-87973-139-7); pap. 6.50 (ISBN 0-87973-141-9). Our Sunday Visitor.

White, Florence. The Story of Father Junipero Serra. (gr. 3-6). pap. 2.95 (ISBN 0-317-62406-7, YB). Dell.

CATHOLIC CHURCH–HISTORY

White, Florence. Father Junipero Serra & the American. (Orig.). (gr. k-6). 1987. pap. 2.95 (ISBN 0-440-42495-X, YB). Dell.

CATHOLIC CHURCH–MISSIONS

Gray, Charlotte. Mother Teresa: Servant to the World's Suffering People. Ullstein, Susan, adapted by. LC 89-49750. (Illus.). 64p. (gr. 3-4). 1990. PLB 12.95 (ISBN 0-8368-0393-0). Gareth Stevens Inc.

Mother Teresa. (Illus.). (gr. 5-6). 1990. pap. 7.95 (ISBN 0-8192-1523-6). Morehouse Pub.

Pond, Mildred M. Mother Teresa. (Illus.). (gr. 3-5). 1992. PLB 12.95 (ISBN 0-7910-1755-9). Chelsea Hse.

Tames, Richard. Mother Teresa. (Illus.). 32p. (gr. 5 up). 1991. pap. 3.95 (ISBN 0-531-24613-2). Watts.

CATHOLIC LITERATURE

Bitney, James & Nelson, Yvette. Welcome to the Way, Jr. High Student Edition. (Illus.). 80p. (Orig.). (gr. 6-8). 1989. pap. text ed. 6.95 (ISBN 0-89505-585-6). Tabor Pub.

—Welcome to the Way, Sr. High Student Edition. (Illus.). 80p. (gr. 9-12). 1989. pap. text ed. 6.95 (ISBN 0-89505-580-5). Tabor Pub.

McGuire, Michael A. Father McGuire's New, Modern Catechism Know, Love, & Serve: The Holy Father, Our God-Given Supreme Teacher. LC 73-158919. (Illus.). 222p. (gr. 7-8). 1973. pap. 11.00 (ISBN 0-913382-43-4, 103-5). Prow Bks-Franciscan.

—Father McGuire's New, Modern Catechism Know, Love, & Serve, Bk. 1. Sands, Richard J., illus. LC 73-158919. 58p. (ps-1). 1971. pap. 5.25 (ISBN 0-913382-39-6, 103-1). Prow Bks-Franciscan.

—Father McGuire's New, Modern Catechism Know, Love, & Serve: Preparing for First Holy Communion, Bk. 2. LC 73-158919. (Illus.). 90p. (gr. 2). 1971. pap. 6.50 (ISBN 0-913382-40-X, 103-2). Prow Bks-Franciscan.

—Father McGuire's New, Modern Catechism Know, Love, & Serve, Bk. 3. LC 73-158919. (Illus.). 175p. (gr. 3-4). 1972. pap. 9.50 (ISBN 0-913382-41-8, 103-3). Prow Bks-Franciscan.

—Father McGuire's New, Modern Catechism Know, Love, & Serve, Bk. 4. LC 73-158919. (Illus.). 192p. (gr. 5-6). 1973. pap. 10.00 (ISBN 0-913382-42-6, 103-4); write for info. tchr's. manual. Prow Bks-Franciscan.

Mangieri, Rose M. My Companion to Know, Love, & Serve. LC 73-158919. (Illus.). 85p. (Orig.). (ps-1). 1977. pap. 5.50 (ISBN 0-913382-45-0, 103-7). Prow Bks-Franciscan.

Snyder, Bernadette M. Three Hundred Sixty-Five Fun Facts for Catholic Kids. LC 89-84983. 144p. (Orig.). (gr. 4-12). 1989. pap. 5.95 (ISBN 0-89243-309-4). Liguori Pubns.

CATS

Ames, Felicia. The Cat You Care For. 1968. pap. 3.50 (ISBN 0-451-13041-3, Sig). NAL-Dutton.

Animal Answers: Cats. (ps up). 1989. PLB 3.98 (ISBN 0-7924-5066-3, Mallard Pr). BDD Promo Bk.

Aymar, Brant. Personality of the Cat. 1989. 6.99 (ISBN 0-517-00016-4). Outlet BK CO.

Barrett, N. S. Big Cats. FS Staff, ed. (Illus.). 32p. (gr. 1-6). 1988. PLB 11.40 (ISBN 0-531-10527-X). Watts.

Barrett, Norman. Cats. (Illus.). 32p. (gr. k-4). 1990. PLB 11.40 (ISBN 0-531-14041-5). Watts.

—Picture Library: Big Cats. 1990. pap. 3.95 (ISBN 0-531-15203-0). Watts.

—Wild Cats. (Illus.). 32p. (gr. k-4). 1991. PLB 11.40 (ISBN 0-531-14155-1). Watts.

Burton, Jane. Ginger the Kitten. LC 89-11417. (Illus.). 32p. (gr. 2-3). 1989. PLB 10.95 (ISBN 0-8368-0213-6). Gareth Stevens Inc.

Carson, Patti & Dellosa, Janet. Cat Fun Book. Carson, Patti & Dellosa, Janet, illus. 32p. (ps-2). 1984. pap. 1.59 (ISBN 0-88724-021-6, CD-8036). Carson-Dellos.

The Cat Family. Date not set. 5.50 (ISBN 0-317-93753-7). W J Fantasy.

Cats. (Illus.). (ps-2). pap. write for info. (ISBN 0-528-87111-0). Checkerboard Pr.

Cats. (Illus.). 32p. (ps up). 1986. 2.95 (ISBN 0-8431-4283-9). Price Stern.

Clutton-Brock, Juliet. Cat. King, Dave, photos by. LC 91-9399. (Illus.). 64p. (gr. 5 up). 1991. 15.00 (ISBN 0-679-81458-2); lib. bdg. 15.99 (ISBN 0-679-91458-7). Knopf.

De Paola, Tomie. The Kids' Cat Book. LC 79-2090. (Illus.). 32p. (gr. k-3). 1979. reinforced bdg. 14.95 (ISBN 0-8234-0365-3); pap. 5.95 (ISBN 0-8234-0534-6). Holiday.

Dupont, Marie. Your First Kitten. (Illus.). 36p. (Orig.). 1991. pap. 1.95 (ISBN 0-86622-061-5, YF-118). TFH Pubns.

Eisler, Colin. Cats Know Best. Ivory, Lesley A., illus. LC 87-15653. 32p. (ps up). 1988. 13.95 (ISBN 0-8037-0503-4); PLB 13.89 (ISBN 0-8037-0560-3). Dial Bks Young.

Elliott, Joan. Cats. Duenewald, Doris, ed. Allen, Creszentia & Allen, Ted, illus. 1978. 2.95 (ISBN 0-448-16263-6, G&D). Putnam Pub Group.

Fontanel, Beatrice. Cats, Big & Little. Bogard, Vicki, tr. from FRE. Logvinoff, Anne, illus. LC 90-50772. 38p. (gr. k-5). 1991. 4.95 (ISBN 0-944589-27-8, 278). Young Discovery Lib.

Fox, Michael W. & Gates, Wende D. What Is Your Cat Saying? LC 81-4884. (Illus.). 80p. (ps-1). 1982. 9.95 (ISBN 0-698-20443-3, Coward). Putnam Pub Group.

Gag, Wanda. Millions of Cats. Gag, Wanda, illus. 32p. (ps-k). 1928. pap. 4.95 (ISBN 0-698-20637-1, Sandcastle Bks). Putnam Pub Group.

Garrick, Elizabeth. Camelot World: The Mysterious Cat. 128p. (Orig.). 1990. pap. 2.95 (ISBN 0-380-76038-X, Camelot). Avon.

Glovach, Linda. The Little Witch's Cat Book. Glovach, Linda, illus. LC 85-6513. 48p. (gr. 1-3). 1985. 9.95 (ISBN 0-13-537697-1). P-H.

Hamer, Martyn. Cats. (Illus.). 32p. (gr. 2-4). 1983. PLB 7.99 (ISBN 0-531-04510-2). Watts.

Hill, R. Cats & Kittens. 24p. (gr. 1-4). 1983. PLB 11.96 (ISBN 0-88110-085-4); pap. 4.50 (ISBN 0-86020-644-0). EDC.

Hirschi, Ron. What Is a Cat? Younker, Linda Q., illus. 32p. (gr. 1-3). 1991. 12.95 (ISBN 0-8027-8122-5); PLB 13.85 (ISBN 0-8027-8123-3). Walker & Co.

—Where Do Cats Live? Younker, Linda Q., illus. 32p. (gr. 1-3). 1991. 12.95 (ISBN 0-8027-8109-8); PLB 13.85 (ISBN 0-8027-8110-1). Walker & Co.

Jameson, P. Cats. (Illus.). 32p. (gr. 2-5). 1989. lib. bdg. 14.00 (ISBN 0-86625-183-9). Rourke Corp.

Johnson, Esther G. Cats in My Life from Granny to Ginger. Johnson, Dagny, illus. 103p. (Orig.). (gr. 9-12). 1990. pap. 7.95 (ISBN 0-9629143-0-4). E G Johnson.

Kappeler, Markus. Big Cats. (Illus.). 32p. (gr. 4-6). 1991. PLB 11.95 (ISBN 0-8368-0685-9). Gareth Stevens Inc.

McPherson, Mark. Caring for Your Cat. Bernstein, Marianne, illus. LC 84-223. 48p. (gr. 3-7). 1985. PLB 9.89 (ISBN 0-8167-0115-6); pap. text ed. 2.95 (ISBN 0-8167-0116-4). Troll Assocs.

Mattern, Joanne. Picture Book of Cats. Pistolesi, Roseanna, illus. LC 90-42548. 24p. (gr. 1-4). 1991. PLB 9.59 (ISBN 0-8167-2146-7); pap. 2.50 (ISBN 0-8167-2147-5). Troll Assocs.

Moriss, Dean. Cats. rev. ed. LC 87-16699. (Illus.). 48p. (gr. 2-6). 1987. PLB 17.32 (ISBN 0-8172-3205-2). Raintree Pubs.

Naples, Marge. A Step-by-Step Book about Siamese Cats. (Illus.). 64p. (gr. 9-12). 1988. pap. 3.95 (ISBN 0-86622-473-4, SK-021). TFH Pubns.

Nottridge, Rhoda. Let's Look At Big Cats. (ps-3). 1990. PLB 8.90 (ISBN 0-531-18285-1). Watts.

Overbeck, Cynthia. Cats. Yoshino, Shin, illus. LC 83-17530. 48p. (gr. 4 up). 1983. PLB 14.95 (ISBN 0-8225-1480-X). Lerner Pubns.

Parsons, Alexandra. Amazing Cats. Young, Jerry, photos by. LC 90-31885. (Illus.). 32p. (Orig.). (gr. 1-5). 1991. lib. bdg. 9.99 (ISBN 0-679-90690-8); pap. 6.95 (ISBN 0-679-80690-3). Knopf.

Petty, Kate. Gatos. Thompson, George, illus. LC 88-83087. (SPA.). 24p. (gr. k-4). 1991. PLB 10.40 (ISBN 0-531-07916-3). Watts.

Pfloog, Jan. Kittens Are Like That. Pfloog, Jan, illus. LC 75-36469. 32p. (ps-1). 1976. pap. 2.25 (ISBN 0-394-83243-4, Random Juv). Random.

Pope, Joyce. Taking Care of Your Cat. LC 85-51605. (Illus.). 32p. (gr. 4-8). 1987. PLB 10.90 (ISBN 0-531-10159-2). Watts.

Posell, Elsa. Cats. LC 82-23484. (Illus.). 48p. (gr. k-4). 1983. PLB 14.60 (ISBN 0-516-01671-7). Childrens.

Puppies & Kittens. (Illus.). (ps). 3.50 (ISBN 0-7214-0785-4). Ladybird Bks.

Richards, Dorothy S. Fact Finders: The World of Cats. 1989. 6.99 (ISBN 0-517-69085-3). Outlet Bk Co.

Rosenberg, Meir. The Jewish Cat Book: A Different Breed! Feldman, Sara, illus. LC 82-62085. 50p. (gr. 8-12). 1982. pap. 4.50 (ISBN 0-916288-15-3). Micah Pubns.

Rowland, Della. A World of Cats. Gurney, John & Himler, Ronald, illus. 24p. 1989. 8.95 (ISBN 0-8092-4347-4, Calico Bks). Contemp Bks.

Ryden, Hope. Bobcat. LC 82-21621. (Illus.). 64p. (gr. 5 up). 1983. 12.95 (ISBN 0-399-20976-X, Putnam). Putnam Pub Group.

Selsam, Millicent E. & Hunt, Joyce. First Look at Cats. Springer, Harriett, illus. LC 80-7673. 32p. (gr. 1-4). 1981. 7.95 (ISBN 0-8027-6398-7); PLB 9.85 (ISBN 0-8027-6399-5). Walker & Co.

Simon, Seymour. Big Cats. Simon, Seymour, illus. LC 90-36374. 40p. (gr. k-3). 1991. 14.95 (ISBN 0-06-021646-8); PLB 14.89 (ISBN 0-06-021647-6). HarpC Child Bks.

Snell, Nigel. Emma's Kitten. Snell, Nigel, illus. 32p. 1989. 4.95 (ISBN 0-8120-6120-9). Barron.

Sproule, Anna & Sproule, Michael. Cats. Caulkins, Janet, ed. (Illus.). 48p. (gr. 1-6). 1988. PLB 11.90 (ISBN 0-531-18214-2, Pub. by Bookwright Pr). Watts.

Steinberg, Phil. You & Your Pet: Cats. Leo, Judith, illus. LC 78-54353. 64p. (gr. 4 up). 1978. PLB 6.95 (ISBN 0-8225-1252-1). Lerner Pubns.

Steneman, Shep. Garfield: The Complete Cat Book. Davis, Jim, illus. LC 81-50246. 96p. (gr. 5 up). 1981. lib. bdg. 7.99 (ISBN 0-394-94893-9); pap. 5.95 (ISBN 0-394-84893-4). Random.

Stolz, Mary. Cat Walk. Blegvad, Erik, illus. LC 82-47576. 128p. (gr. 3-7). 1983. 12.95 (ISBN 0-06-025974-4); PLB 11.89 (ISBN 0-06-025975-2). HarpC Child Bks.

Stone, Lynn. Big Cat Discover Library, 6 bks, Reading Level 2. (Illus.). (gr. k-5). Date not set. Set. PLB 71.64 (ISBN 0-86592-500-3). Rourke Corp.

Tanaka, Shelley. The Cat Lover's Diary. Fanelli, Jenny, ed. Baron, Elaine, photos by. Reynolds, Nancy L. & Macpherson, Elaine, illus. 176p. (gr. 5 up). 1984. pap. 8.95 (ISBN 0-394-86613-4, Pub. by BYR). Random.

Vrbova, Zuza. Kittens. McAulay, Robert, illus. 48p. (gr. 2 up). 1990. PLB 9.95 (ISBN 0-86622-553-6, J-003). TFH Pubns.

Watson, Carol. If You Were a Kitten. Cony, Sue, illus. 24p. (ps-2). 1990. 1.95 (ISBN 1-878624-31-8, 1553800031). McClanahan Bk.

Waverly, Barney. How Big? How Fast? How Hungry? A Book about Cats. Henry, Steve, illus. 24p. (ps-2). 1990. PLB 12.33 (ISBN 0-8172-3582-5); PLB 9.25 (ISBN 0-685-33579-8). Raintree Pubs.

Wiessinger, John. Cats, Bats, & Bears - Right Before Your Eyes. Wiessinger, John, illus. LC 89-1411. 64p. (gr. 4-10). 1989. PLB 15.95 (ISBN 0-89490-266-0). Enslow Pubs.

Wildlife Education, Ltd. Staff. Big Cats. Meltzer, Dave, et al, illus. 20p. (Orig.). (gr. 5 up). 1981. pap. 2.25 (ISBN 0-937934-04-6). Wildlife Educ.

—Little Cats. Orr, Richard & Stuart, Walter, illus. 200p. (gr. 5 up). 1983. pap. 2.25 (ISBN 0-937934-16-X). Wildlife Educ.

Wilkinson, Sally. Cats Are People Too: By Pattysue, Herself. 47p. (Orig.). (gr. 5 up). 1989. pap. 6.95 (ISBN 0-9623354-5-2). OP Inc.

Winston, Peggy D. Wild Cats. Crump, Donald J., ed. LC 81-47742. 32p. (ps-3). 1981. lib. bdg. 12.95 (ISBN 0-87044-401-8). Natl Geog.

Wolff, George. I Can Read About Cats & Kittens. LC 72-96959. (Illus.). (gr. 2-4). 1973. pap. 1.95 (ISBN 0-89375-056-5). Troll Assocs.

CATS–FICTION

Abercrombie, Barbara. Charlie Anderson. Graham, Mark, illus. LC 89-2449. 32p. (ps-4). 1990. 12.95 (ISBN 0-689-50486-1, M K McElderry). Macmillan Child Grp.

Adler, C. S. The Cat That Was Left Behind. LC 80-28123. 160p. (gr. 3-6). 1981. 13.95 (ISBN 0-395-31020-2, Clarion). HM.

Alexander, Lloyd. The Cat Who Wished to Be a Man. 120p. (gr. 4-7). 1977. 14.95 (ISBN 0-525-27545-2, DCB); (DCB). Dutton Child Bks.

—Time Cat. (gr. k-12). 1985. pap. 3.25 (ISBN 0-440-48677-7, YB). Dell.

—The Town Cats & Other Tales. 144p. (gr. 5 up). 1990. pap. 3.25 (ISBN 0-440-48989-X, YB). Dell.

—The Town Cats & Other Tales. Kubinyi, Laszlo, illus. (gr. 4-7). 1977. 14.95 (ISBN 0-525-41430-4, DCB). Dutton Child Bks.

Allen, Pamela. My Cat Maisie. (Illus.). 32p. (ps-3). 1991. 12.95 (ISBN 0-670-83251-0). Viking Child Bks.

Anderson, Marcie. Ballet Kitty. (Illus.). 24p. (ps-3). 1987. 1.95 (ISBN 0-87406-176-8). Willowisp Pr.

Anderson, Mary. The Catnapping Caper. (gr. k-6). 1989. pap. 2.95 (ISBN 0-440-40236-0, YB). Dell.

Anello, Christine. The Farmyard Cat. Thompson, Sharon, illus. 32p. (ps-1). 1990. pap. 3.95 (ISBN 0-590-42852-7). Scholastic Inc.

Antle, Nancy. The Good Bad Cat. Gregorich, Barbara, ed. (Illus.). 16p. (Orig.). (gr. k-2). 1985. pap. 1.95 (ISBN 0-88743-012-0, 06012). Sch Zone Pub Co.

Apablasa, Bill. Rhymin' Simon & the Mystery of the Fat Cat. Thiesing, Lisa, illus. 64p. (gr. 4-7). 1991. 10.95 (ISBN 0-525-44702-4, DCB). Dutton Child Bks.

Asare, Meshack. Cat in Search of a Friend. LC 86-10583. (Illus.). 32p. (ps-5). 1986. 10.95 (ISBN 0-916291-07-3, Cranky Nell Bk). Kane-Miller Bk.

Asch, Frank & Vagin, Vladimir. Here Comes the Cat! Asch, Frank & Vladimir, Vagin, illus. 1991. pap. 3.95 (ISBN 0-590-41854-8). Scholastic Inc.

Averill, Esther. Fire Cat. Averill, Esther, illus. LC 60-10234. 64p. (gr. k-3). 1960. PLB 11.89 (ISBN 0-06-020196-7). HarpC Child Bks.

—The Fire Cat. LC 60-10234. (Illus.). 64p. (gr. k-3). 1983. pap. 3.50 (ISBN 0-06-444038-9, Trophy). HarpC Child Bks.

—Jenny's Birthday Book. Averill, Esther, illus. LC 54-6589. 32p. (gr. k-3). 1954. PLB 14.89 (ISBN 0-06-020251-3). HarpC Child Bks.

—The School for Cats & Jenny's Moonlight Adventure. Averill, Esther, illus. (gr. k-3). 1990. pap. 2.95 (ISBN 0-553-15362-5). Bantam.

Baba, Noboru. Eleven Cats & a Pig. Baba, Noboru, illus. LC 88-9596. 48p. (gr. k-4). 1988. lib. bdg. 12.95 (ISBN 0-87614-338-9). Carolrhoda Bks.

—Eleven Cats & Albatrosses. Baba, Noboru, illus. LC 88-9598. 48p. (gr. k-4). 1988. lib. bdg. 12.95 (ISBN 0-87614-335-4). Carolrhoda Bks.

—Eleven Cats in a Bag. Baba, Noboru, illus. LC 88-9597. 48p. (gr. k-4). 1988. lib. bdg. 12.95 (ISBN 0-87614-336-2). Carolrhoda Bks.

—Eleven Hungry Cats. LC 88-5419. (Illus.). 48p. (gr. k-4). 1988. PLB 12.95 (ISBN 0-87614-337-0). Carolrhoda Bks.

Babbitt, Natalie. Nellie: A Cat on Her Own. Babbitt, Natalie, illus. (ps up). 1989. 11.95 (ISBN 0-374-35506-1, Di Capua Bks). FS&G.

Bacher, June M. I Never, Ever Heard of Such a Strange Thing! Gardner, K. Lynn, illus. 32p. (ps-1). 1991. 8.99 (ISBN 0-89081-840-1). Harvest Hse.

Baker, Leslie. Third Story Cat. (ps-3). 1990. pap. 4.95 (ISBN 0-316-07836-0). Little.

Ballard, Robin. Cat & Alex & the Magic Flying Carpet. Ballard, Robin, illus. LC 90-33229. 32p. (ps-1). 1991. 14.95 (ISBN 0-06-020389-7); PLB 14.89 (ISBN 0-06-020390-0). HarpC Child Bks.

Bank Street College of Education Staff, et al. No Way, Slippery Slick! LC 90-45163. (Illus.). 32p. (gr. k-3). 1991. pap. 3.50 (ISBN 0-06-107438-1). HarpC Child Bks.

Barber, Antonia. The Mousehole Cat. Bayley, Nicola, illus. LC 90-31533. 40p. (gr. k-3). 1990. 14.95 (ISBN 0-02-708331-4, Mcmillan Child Bk). Macmillan Child Grp.

Barber, Phyllis. Smiley Snake's Adventure. Jordan, Alton, ed. (Illus.). (gr. k-3). 1981. PLB 7.95 (ISBN 0-89868-098-0, Read Res); pap. text ed. 2.95 (ISBN 0-89868-109-X). ARO Pub.

Bare, Colleen S. Critter: The Class Cat. Bare, Colleen S., illus. 32p. (ps-3). 1989. 12.95 (ISBN 0-399-21710-X, Putnam). Putnam Pub Group.

Bayley, Nicola. Crab Cat. Bayley, Nicola, illus. LC 84-773. 24p. (gr. k up). 1984. pap. 3.95 (ISBN 0-394-86499-9). Knopf.

—Spider Cat. Bayley, Nicola, illus. LC 84-772. 24p. (gr. k up). 1984. 3.95 (ISBN 0-394-86500-6). Knopf.

Bell, Clare. Ratha & Thistle-Chaser. 232p. (gr. 7 up). 1990. 14.95 (ISBN 0-689-50462-4, M K McElderry). Macmillan Child Grp.

Bennett, Marian. God Made Kittens. (Illus.). 24p. (ps). 1980. 1.99 (ISBN 0-87239-404-2, 3636). Standard Pub.

Berry, Gail. Kensington Kat. 23p. (ps-7). 1989. 6.95 (ISBN 0-533-08489-X). Vantage.

Bingham, Mindy. Minou. Maeno, Itoko, illus. LC 86-26539. 64p. (gr. k-6). 1987. 12.95 (ISBN 0-911655-36-0). Advocacy Pr.

Bissell, LeClair & Watherwax, Richard. The Cat Who Drank Too Much. (ENG & SPA., Illus.). 48p. (gr. 4 up). 1982. pap. 5.00 (ISBN 0-911153-00-4). Spanish ed., 03/1984 (ISBN 0-911153-01-2). Bibulophile Pr.

Blacker, Terence. You're Under Arrest, Ms. Wiz. Goffe, Toni, illus. 64p. (gr. 2-5). 1990. pap. 2.95 (ISBN 0-8120-4499-1). Barron.

Blume, Judy. The Pain & the Great One. Trivas, Irene, illus. LC 84-11009. 32p. (gr. k-3). 1984. PLB 12.95 (ISBN 0-02-711100-8, Bradbury Pr). Macmillan Child Grp.

Boegehold, Betty. Three to Get Ready. Chalmers, Mary, illus. LC 62-8042. (gr. k-3). 1965. PLB 11.89 (ISBN 0-06-020551-2). HarpC Child Bks.

Boivin, Kelly. Where Is Mittens? Martin, Clovis, illus. LC 90-2220. 32p. (ps-2). 1990. PLB 11.93 (ISBN 0-516-02060-9); pap. 2.95 (ISBN 0-516-42060-7). Childrens.

Boynton, Sandra. Chloe & Maude. Boynton, Sandra, illus. (ps-3). 1985. pap. 6.95 (ISBN 0-316-10491-4). Little.

Bradbury, Thomas E. Scraggly's New Home. Goyette, Ron & Funk, Nancy C., trs. (Illus.). 32p. (Orig.). (gr. k-5). 1987. pap. text ed. write for info. (ISBN 0-9618945-0-4). Tern Pubns.

Braun, Lilian J. The Cat Who Sniffed Glue. 1989. pap. 3.50 (ISBN 0-515-09954-6). Jove Pubns.

Brewster, Patience. Ellsworth & the Cats from Mars. LC 80-16298. (Illus.). 32p. (gr. 1-5). 1981. 13.95 (ISBN 0-395-29612-9, Clarion). HM.

Brown, Margaret W. A Cat Named Sneakers. 1985. PLB 12.89 (ISBN 0-06-020767-1). HarpC Child Bks.

Brown, Ruth. Our Cat Flossie. Monfried, Lucia, ed. Brown, Ruth, illus. 32p. (ps-1). 1990. pap. 3.95 (ISBN 0-525-44608-7, DCB). Dutton Child Bks.

Bryan, Ashley. The Cat's Purr. LC 84-21534. (Illus.). 48p. (ps-3). 1985. SBE 10.95 (ISBN 0-689-31086-2, Atheneum Child Bk). Macmillan Child Grp.

Brychta, Alex. The Arrow. (ps-k). 1987. 2.95 (ISBN 0-19-272166-6). Oxford U Pr.

Buckman, Mary. Magical Muriel. LC 90-60453. (Illus., Orig.). (gr. k-2). 1991. pap. text ed. 12.95 (ISBN 1-879414-07-4). Mary Bee Creat.

Burke, Roma N. Whiskers, a Kitten's Story. LC 87-62417. 120p. (gr. 3-8). 1988. pap. 8.95 (ISBN 0-88100-058-2). Natl Writ Pr.

Burnett, Sharon F. Niko. 32p. 1991. 6.95 (ISBN 0-8062-3802-X). Carlton.

Burns, Theresa. You're Not My Cat. Burns, Theresa, illus. LC 88-8388. 32p. (ps-3). 1989. 12.95 (ISBN 0-397-32340-9, Lipp Jr Bks); PLB 12.89 (ISBN 0-397-32341-7). HarpC Child Bks.

Butler, Beverly. Ghost Cat. 1988. pap. 2.75 (ISBN 0-590-43443-8, SCHOLASTIC). Scholastic Inc.

Calhoun, Mary. Cross-Country Cat. Ingraham, Erick, illus. LC 78-31718. (ps-3). 1986. pap. 4.95 (ISBN 0-688-06519-8, Mulberry). Morrow.

—Cross-Country Cat. Ingraham, Eric, illus. 1988. pap. 7.95 incl. cassette (ISBN 0-688-08398-6). Morrow.

—High-Wire Henry. Ingraham, Erick, illus. LC 89-35642. 40p. (gr. k up). 1991. 13.95 (ISBN 0-688-08983-6); PLB 13.88 (ISBN 0-688-08984-4, Morrow Jr Bks). Morrow Jr Bks.

—Hot-Air Henry. Ingraham, Erick, illus. LC 80-26189. 40p. (gr. k-3). 1984. 12.95 (ISBN 0-688-00501-2); PLB 12.88 (ISBN 0-688-00502-0, Morrow Jr Bks); pap. 4.95 (ISBN 0-688-04068-3, Mulberry Bks). Morrow Jr Bks.

—The Witch of Hissing Hill. McCaffery, Janet, illus. LC 64-15475. (gr. k-3). 1964. PLB 13.88 (ISBN 0-688-31762-6). Morrow.

—The Witch Who Lost Her Shadow. Nobel, Trinka H., illus. (gr. k-3). 1979. 9.57i (ISBN 0-06-020946-1). HarpC Child Bks.

—Wobble the Witch Cat. Duvoisin, Roger, illus. LC 58-5018. 32p. (gr. k-3). 1958. PLB 13.88 (ISBN 0-688-31621-2). Morrow Jr Bks.

Campbell, Rod. Misty's Mischief. LC 84-19617. (Illus.). 20p. (ps-1). 1985. pap. 6.95 (ISBN 0-670-80149-6). Viking Penguin.

Carle, Eric. Have You Seen My Cat? LC 87-15262. (Illus.). (ps up). 1987. 14.95 (ISBN 0-88708-054-5). Picture Bk Studio.

—Have You Seen My Cat? Carle, Eric, illus. 1991. pap. 3.95 (ISBN 0-590-44461-1, Blue Ribbon Bks). Scholastic Inc.

—Let's Paint a Rainbow. 10p. (ps-1). 1982. 4.95 (ISBN 0-399-20881-X, Philomel). Putnam Pub Group.

Carlson, Natalie S. Spooky & the Bad Luck Raven. Glass, Andrew, illus. LC 87-15471. (ps-1). 1988. 12.95 (ISBN 0-688-07650-5); lib. bdg. 12.88 (ISBN 0-688-07651-3). Lothrop.

—Spooky & the Witch's Goat. Stevenson, Dinah, ed. Glass, Andrew, illus. LC 88-21628. 32p. (gr. k-4). 1989. 12.95 (ISBN 0-688-08540-7); PLB 12.88 (ISBN 0-685-22781-2). Lothrop.

Carris, Joan. Witch-Cat. Peck, Beth, illus. LC 83-48448. 160p. (gr. 5 up). 1984. PLB 11.89 (ISBN 0-397-32068-X, Lipp Jr Bks). HarpC Child Bks.

Carris, Joan D. Witch Cat. (gr. 5 up). 1986. pap. 2.95 (ISBN 0-440-49477-X, YB). Dell.

Cassedy, Sylvia. Best Cat Suit of All. LC 87-24659. (ps-3). 1991. 10.95 (ISBN 0-8037-0516-6); PLB 10.89 (ISBN 0-8037-0517-4). Dial Bks Young.

The Cat & the Rat EV, Unit 6. (gr. 2). 1991. 5-pack 21.25 (ISBN 0-88106-750-4). Charlesbridge Pub.

The Cat Who Learned to Sail. LC 89-64308. (Illus.). 32p. (gr. 4-8). 1991. 13.95 (ISBN 0-931595-07-X); pap. 7.95 (ISBN 0-931595-04-5). Seascape Enters.

Cauley, Lorinda B. Puss in Boots. LC 86-7629. (Illus.). 32p. (ps-1). 1988. 13.95 (ISBN 0-15-264227-7, HJ); pap. 3.95 (ISBN 0-15-264228-5). HarBraceJ.

Cecil, Mirabel. Lottie's Cats. Martin, Francesca, illus. LC 89-29038. 32p. (ps-3). 1990. 12.95 (ISBN 0-517-57707-0). Crown.

Chalmers, Mary. Throw a Kiss, Harry. Chalmers, Mary, illus. LC 89-49064. 32p. (ps-2). 1990. 12.95 (ISBN 0-06-021246-2); PLB 12.89 (ISBN 0-06-021245-4). HarpC Child Bks.

Charles, Donald. El Ano de Gato Galano. Kratky, Lada, tr. from GER. Charles, Donald, illus. (SPA.). 32p. (ps-3). 1984. lib. bdg. 14.60 (ISBN 0-516-33461-1); pap. 3.95 (ISBN 0-516-53461-0). Childrens.

—Calico Cat at School. LC 81-6096. (Illus.). 32p. (ps-3). 1981. 14.60 (ISBN 0-516-03445-6); pap. 3.95 (ISBN 0-516-43445-4). Childrens.

—Calico Cat at the Zoo. Charles, Donald, illus. LC 80-25380. 32p. (gr. 3). 1981. PLB 14.60 (ISBN 0-516-03443-X). Childrens.

—Calico Cat Looks at Colors. Charles, Donald, illus. LC 75-12948. 32p. (ps-3). 1975. PLB 14.60 (ISBN 0-516-03437-5). Childrens.

—Calico Cat Looks at Shapes. Charles, Donald, illus. LC 75-12947. 32p. (ps-3). 1975. PLB 14.60 (ISBN 0-516-03436-7). Childrens.

—Count on Calico Cat. Charles, Donald, illus. LC 74-8007. 32p. (ps-3). 1974. PLB 14.60 (ISBN 0-516-03435-9). Childrens.

—Cuenta con Gato Galano. Kratky, Lada, tr. from ENG. Charles, Donald, illus. LC 74-8007. (SPA.). 32p. (ps-3). 1984. lib. bdg. 14.60 (ISBN 0-516-33479-4); pap. 3.95 (ISBN 0-516-53479-3). Childrens.

—Fat, Fat Calico Cat. LC 77-7154. (Illus.). 32p. (gr. 3). 1977. PLB 14.60 (ISBN 0-516-03456-1). Childrens.

—Letters from Calico Cat. Charles, Donald, illus. LC 74-8181. 32p. (ps-3). 1974. PLB 14.60 (ISBN 0-516-03519-3). Childrens.

—El Libro de Ejercicios de Gato Galano. Kratky, Lada, tr. from ENG. Charles, Doanld, illus. LC 82-9640. (SPA.). 32p. (ps-3). 1984. lib. bdg. 14.60 (ISBN 0-516-33457-3); pap. 3.95 (ISBN 0-516-53457-2). Childrens.

—Mira las Formas con Gato Galano. LC 75-12947. (SPA., Illus.). 32p. (ps-3). 1987. PLB 14.60 (ISBN 0-516-33436-0); pap. 3.95 (ISBN 0-516-53436-X). Childrens.

Cherry, Lynne. Archie, Follow Me. (ps-3). 1990. 12.95 (ISBN 0-525-44647-8, DCB). Dutton Child Bks.

Cleary, Beverly. Socks. Darwin, Beatrice, illus. LC 72-10298. 160p. (gr. 3-7). 1973. 11.95 (ISBN 0-688-20067-2); PLB 11.88 (ISBN 0-688-30067-7, Morrow Jr Bks). Morrow Jr Bks.

Coatsworth, Elizabeth. The Cat Who Went to Heaven. Ward, Lynd, illus. LC 58-10917. 72p. (gr. 4-6). 1967. 12.95 (ISBN 0-02-719710-7, Mcmillan Child Bk). Macmillan Child Grp.

—Cat Who Went to Heaven. (gr. 4-6). 1972. pap. 4.95 (ISBN 0-02-042580-5, Aladdin). Macmillan.

—The Cat Who Went to Heaven. Ward, Lynd & Jael, illus. LC 90-175. 80p. (gr. 3-7). 1990. pap. 3.95 (ISBN 0-689-71433-5, Aladdin). Macmillan Child Grp.

Cocca-leffler, Maryann. Wednesday Is Spaghetti Day. (ps-3). 1990. pap. 11.95 (ISBN 0-590-42894-2). Scholastic Inc.

Cook, Veronica L. Mike the Copycat: Adventures & Stories of Cat Tails. Cook, Veronica L., illus. 50p. (Orig.). (ps up). 1989. pap. text ed. write for info. Ronnie Two Pub.

Coon, Alma S. Amy, Ben, & Catalpa the Cat: A Fanciful Story of This & That. Owens, Gail, illus. 40p. (ps-2). 1990. 5.95 (ISBN 0-87935-079-2). Williamsburg.

In this beautifully illustrated, full-color alphabet storybook in verse, Amy, Ben, & Catalpa the Cat take children on a fun-filled day in eighteenth-century Williamsburg. The story, set in early autumn, opens at Amy & Ben's home, where Ben is harvesting pumpkins, Amy is baking apple pies, & playful Catalpa is constantly underfoot. But no sooner does the fifer pass by their window than they are off to the fair! During their adventures in Williamsburg the heroes introduce young readers to George Washington & other eighteenth-century characters as well as to various colonial activities such as a fair, a ride in an oxcart, children's games, & a visit to Tarpley's Store. The inviting illustrations colorfully re-create authentic colonial clothing, architecture, agriculture, & animal husbandry. To order: Colonial

Williamsburg Wholesale Sales, PO Box C, Williamsburg, VA 23187, (804) 220-7178.
Publisher Provided Annotation.

Cosgrove, Stephen. Fanny. James, Robin, illus. 32p. (gr. 5-9). 1986. pap. 2.95 (ISBN 0-8431-1460-6). Price Stern.
Costa, Nicoletta. The Missing Cat. Costa, Nicoletta, illus. 15p. (gr. k-1). 1984. 3.50 (ISBN 0-448-23402-5, G&D). Putnam Pub Group.
Craig, Janet. Muffy & Fluffy: The Kittens Who Didn't Agree. Hall, Susan, illus. LC 87-16227. 32p. (gr. k-2). 1988. PLB 7.06 (ISBN 0-8167-1227-1); pap. text ed. 1.95 (ISBN 0-8167-1228-X). Troll Assocs.
Crooks, Linda H., et al. Kindergang Kindergarten Skills Booklets, Featuring Dandy Dog, Booklet 2. 2nd ed. Crooks, Linda H., illus. (gr. k). 1988. Repr. of 1985 ed. tchr's. ed. 9.19 (ISBN 1-877594-02-4); wkbk. 1.59 (ISBN 0-317-93573-9). I Can.
Crozat, Francois. I Am a Little Cat. 28p. (ps-k). 1990. 7.95 (ISBN 0-8120-6160-8). Barron.
—I Am a Little Cat (Miniature Size) (ps). 1990. 2.95 (ISBN 0-8120-6196-9). Barron.
Cutler, Ebbitt. If I Were a Cat I Would Sit in a Tree. Arnold, Rist, illus. 28p. (gr. k-4). 1985. text ed. 7.95 (ISBN 0-88776-177-1, Dist. by U of Toronto Pr). Tundra Bks.
Dancing Cat. 1991. pap. 14.95 (ISBN 0-671-72637-4). S&S Trade.
Danziger, Paula. The Cat Ate My Gymsuit. 160p. (gr. 5 up). 1980. pap. 3.25 (ISBN 0-440-41612-4, YB). Dell.
Dass, Baba H. Cat & Sparrow. Rich, Andrea, illus. LC 81-51915. 32p. (gr. k-3). 1982. 6.95 (ISBN 0-918100-06-2). Sri Rama.
Davis, Jim. Garfield A to Z Zoo. Fentz, Mike & Kuhn, Dave, illus. LC 83-17697. 24p. (ps-5). 1984. pap. 1.25 (ISBN 0-394-86483-2, Random Juv). Random.
—Garfield Book of the Seasons. Fentz, Mike & Kuhn, Dave, illus. LC 83-17814. 24p. (gr. k-5). 1984. pap. 1.25 (ISBN 0-394-86482-4). Random.
—Garfield Mix & Match Storybook. Davis, Jim, illus. (gr. 1-5). 1982. spiral plastic 3.95 (ISBN 0-394-85444-6). Random.

Davis, Marion M. Sam the Royal Cat, No. 1. Starboard Cove Publishing Staff, ed. Johnston, Anne, illus. 35p. (Orig.). 1989. pap. 5.95x (ISBN 0-9622221-0-0). Starboard Cove. Discover the royal past of the present day Sam. Follow paw marks of this royal cat from his ancestry in China to Maine today. Take your imagination through the years & live the adventure of a cat rich in heritage & fine cat qualities. Published 1989, The Year of the Young Reader.
Publisher Provided Annotation.

DeJong, Meindert. The Easter Cat. Hoban, Lillian, illus. LC 90-24407. 128p. (gr. 3-7). 1991. pap. 3.95 (ISBN 0-689-71468-8, Aladdin). Macmillan Child Grp.
Delton, Judy. Kitty from the Start. LC 86-21481. (gr. 3-5). 1987. 12.95 (ISBN 0-395-42847-5). HM.
Demers, Jan. On Sunday I Lost My Cat. (Illus.). 24p. (gr. k-2). 1986. 2.25 (ISBN 0-87406-129-6). Willowisp Pr.
DePaola, Tomie. Katie, Kit & Cousin Tom. DePaola, Tomie, illus. (ps). 1987. 3.95 (ISBN 0-671-61724-9, Little Simon). S&S Trade.
—Katie's Good Idea. DePaola, Tomie, illus. (ps). 1987. 3.95 (ISBN 0-671-61725-7, Little Simon). S&S Trade.
De Regniers, Beatrice S. So Many Cats. Weiss, Ellen, illus. LC 85-3739. 32p. (ps-3). 1988. 13.95 (ISBN 0-89919-322-6, Clarion); pap. 4.95 (ISBN 0-89919-700-0, Pub. by Clarion). Ticknor & Fields.
Dicks, Terrance. A Cat Called Max: Magnificent Max. Goffe, Toni, illus. 64p. (gr. 3-6). 1990. pap. 2.95 (ISBN 0-8120-4427-4). Barron.
—A Cat Called Max: Max & the Quiz Kids. Goffe, Toni, illus. 64p. (gr. 2-5). 1990. pap. 2.95 (ISBN 0-8120-4501-7). Barron.
Diggs, Lucy. Selene Goes Home. McCully, Emily A., illus. LC 88-7363. 64p. (gr. 2-5). 1989. 11.95 (ISBN 0-689-31464-7, Atheneum Child Bk). Macmillan Child Grp.
Dito, Joan. Calie the Calico Cat & Rory the Spaniel. 32p. (ps-1). 1989. 6.95 (ISBN 0-8062-3542-X). Carlton.
Dr. Seuss. The Cat in the Hat. Dr. Seuss, illus. 64p. (ps-1). 1987. pap. 6.95 book & cassette (ISBN 0-394-89218-6, Random Juv). Random.
—Cat in the Hat Comes Back. Dr. Seuss, illus. LC 58-9017. 72p. (gr. k-3). 1958. 6.95 (ISBN 0-394-80002-8); lib. bdg. 7.99 (ISBN 0-394-90002-2). Beginner.
—The Cat in the Hat Comes Back. (ps-1). 1986. pap. 6.95 incl. cassette (ISBN 0-394-88327-6). Random.
Dubanevich, Arlene. Tom's Tail. (ps-3). 1990. 13.95 (ISBN 0-670-83021-6). Viking Child Bks.
Dueland, Joy. Barn Kitten, House Kitten. (Illus.). (gr. 2-8). 1978. pap. 3.50 (ISBN 0-931942-00-4). Phunn Pubs.
—Dear Tabby. (Illus.). (gr. 4-8). 1978. pap. 2.50 (ISBN 0-931942-02-0). Phunn Pubs.
—Kitten in the Manger. (Illus.). 32p. (gr. 2-8). 1981. pap. 6.95 (ISBN 0-685-08286-5). Phunn Pubs.
Duggan, Alice. Violet's Finest Hour. Stevenson, Harvey, illus. LC 91-52588. 64p. (gr. 1 up). 1991. text ed. 10.95 (ISBN 0-688-09456-2). Lothrop.
Dunn, Judy. The Little Kitten. Dunn, Phoebe, photos by. LC 82-16711. (Illus.). 32p. (ps-4). 1983. lib. bdg. 5.99 (ISBN 0-394-95818-7); pap. 2.25 (ISBN 0-394-85818-2). Random.
Elliott, Lisa E. Old Friends & New Friends, Old Kitties & New Kitties. Caroland, Mary, ed. LC 90-71002. 44p. (gr. k-3). 1991. 5.95 (ISBN 1-55523-364-3). Winston-Derek.
Ernst, Lisa C. Rescue of Aunt Pansy. (ps-2). 1987. pap. 8.95 (ISBN 0-670-81716-3). Viking Child Bks.
Estes, Eleanor. Pinky Pye. Ardizzone, Edward, illus. LC 75-31581. 192p. (gr. 4-6). 1976. pap. 1.75 (ISBN 0-15-671840-5, VoyB). HarBraceJ.
Everitt, Betsy. Frida the Wondercat. 1990. 13.95 (ISBN 0-15-229540-2). HarbraceJ.
Feder, Jane. My Cat Beany. Gundersheimer, Karen, illus. LC 78-10416. 32p. (ps-1). 1989. pap. 3.95 (ISBN 0-394-82594-2, Dragonfly Bks). Knopf.
Fisher, Lois I. Puffy P. Pushycat, Problem Solver. (gr. 3-7). 1983. 8.95 (ISBN 0-396-08119-3, Putnam). Putnam Pub Group.
Five Little Kittens. (Illus.). (ps-k). 3.50 (ISBN 0-7214-0213-5). Ladybird Bks.
Flack, Marjorie. Angus & the Cat. 40p. (ps-k). 1989. PLB 13.99 (ISBN 0-685-01488-6); pap. 12.95 (ISBN 0-685-01489-4). Doubleday.
Foreman, Mark. Sid the Kitten. (Illus.). 32p. (ps-2). 1989. 13.95 (ISBN 0-86264-218-3, Pub. by Anderson Pr UK). Trafalgar Sq.
Foreman, Michael. Cat & Canary. LC 84-9568. (Illus.). 32p. (ps-3). 1987. pap. 4.95 (ISBN 0-8037-0133-0). Dial Bks Young.
Four Little Kittens. (ps-3). 1989. write for info incl. cassette (13686, Pub. by Golden Bks). Western Pub.
Fowler, Richard. Cat's Car. Fowler, Richard, illus. 32p. (ps-1). 1988. 8.95 (ISBN 0-8120-5920-4). Barron.
Fox, Frances M. The Little Cat That Could Not Sleep. Hughes, Shirley, illus. LC 72-89335. 32p. (gr. k-4). 1973. 7.95 (ISBN 0-87592-030-6). Scroll Pr.
Fox, Paula. One-Eyed Cat. Trivas, Irene, illus. LC 84-10964. 192p. (gr. 6-8). 1984. 12.95 (ISBN 0-02-735540-3, Bradbury Pr). Macmillan Child Grp.
—One-Eyed Cat. (gr. k-6). 1985. pap. 3.50 (ISBN 0-440-46641-5, YB). Dell.
Fremantle, Anne. Island of Cats. Sapieha, Christine, illus. (gr. 1-4). 1964. 12.95 (ISBN 0-8392-3011-7). Astor-Honor.
Freschet, Bernice. Furlie Cat. Lewin, Betsy, illus. LC 85-11656. 32p. (ps-3). 1986. 12.95 (ISBN 0-688-05917-1). Lothrop.
Frost, Erica. A Kitten for Rosie. Fiammenghi, Gioia, illus. LC 85-14126. 48p. (Orig.). (gr. 1-3). 1986. PLB 9.89 (ISBN 0-8167-0650-6); pap. text ed. 2.95 (ISBN 0-8167-0651-4). Troll Assocs.
—The Story of Matt & Mary. Schumacher, Claire, illus. LC 85-14011. 48p. (Orig.). (gr. 1-3). 1986. PLB 9.89 (ISBN 0-8167-0602-6); pap. text ed. 2.95 (ISBN 0-8167-0603-4). Troll Assocs.
Frost, Marie H. Five Homes for Five Kittens. Klug, Mikki, illus. 20p. (ps). 1987. 1.59 (ISBN 0-87403-308-X, 2008). Standard Pub.
Fujikawa, Gyo. Fraidy Cat. Fujikawa, Gyo, illus. LC 81-84015. 32p. (gr. k-3). 1982. 3.95 (ISBN 0-448-11753-3, G&D). Putnam Pub Group.
Gag, Wanda. Millions of Cats. Gag, Wanda, illus. 112p. (gr. k-3). 1977. 7.95 (ISBN 0-698-20091-8, Coward); pap. 3.95 (ISBN 0-698-20434-4). Putnam Pub Group.
Galdone, Paul. Puss in Boots. Galdone, Paul, illus. LC 75-25505. 32p. (ps-4). 1979. 13.95 (ISBN 0-395-28808-8, Clarion). HM.
—Puss in Boots. LC 75-25505. 32p. (gr. k-3). 1983. pap. 4.95 (ISBN 0-89919-192-4, Pub. by Clarion). Ticknor & Fields.
—Puss 'N Boots. (ps-3). 1987. incl. cass. 6.95 (ISBN 0-317-64571-4). HM.
Galvani, Maureen. Me & My Cat. Galvani, Maureen, illus. LC 88-33310. 24p. 1989. 10.95 (ISBN 0-87226-410-6, Bedrick Blackie). P Bedrick Bks.
Gantos, Jack. Happy Birthday, Rotten Ralph. Rubel, Nicole, illus. 32p. (ps-3). 1990. 13.95 (ISBN 0-395-53766-5). HM.
—Rotten Ralph. Rubel, Nicole, illus. LC 75-34101. 48p. (gr. k-3). 1976. 13.95 (ISBN 0-395-24276-2); pap. 4.50 (ISBN 0-685-02307-9). HM.
—Rotten Ralph. Rubel, Nicole, illus. (gr. k-3). 1980. pap. 4.95 (ISBN 0-395-29202-6, Sandpiper). HM.
—Rotten Ralph's Rotten Christmas. Rubel, Nicole, illus. LC 84-664. 32p. (ps-3). 1987. 12.95 (ISBN 0-395-35380-7); pap. 17.95 incl. doll (ISBN 0-395-45346-1); pap. 3.95 (ISBN 0-395-45685-1). HM.
—Rotten Ralph's Trick or Treat. Rubel, Nicole, illus. LC 86-7276. 32p. (gr. k-3). 1986. 13.95 (ISBN 0-395-38943-7). HM.
—Worse Than Rotten, Ralph. Rubel, Nicole, illus. (gr. k-3). 1982. 13.95 (ISBN 0-395-27106-1); pap. 4.95 (ISBN 0-395-32919-1). HM.
George, Emma. Quality Time Little Readers: Circus Kitten. 1991. 1.49 (ISBN 0-8317-7270-0). Smithmark.
Gerstein, Mordicai. The New Creatures. LC 90-4128. (Illus.). 32p. (ps-3). 1991. 14.95 (ISBN 0-06-022164-X); PLB 14.89 (ISBN 0-06-022167-4). HarpC Child Bks.
Gillis, Everett A. Goldie. Gillis, Paul, illus. 64p. (Orig.). (gr. 3-7). 1982. pap. 8.00 (ISBN 0-938328-02-6). Pisces Pr TX.
Golden, Nora. Comical Celtic Cat. (gr. 1 up). 1984. 13.95 (ISBN 0-85105-901-5, Pub. by Colin Smythe Ltd Britain). Dufour.
Goldsmith, Melissa. In a Cat State of Mind. Goldsmith, Melissa, illus. LC 90-403394. 120p. (Orig.). (gr. 2-11). 1990. 17.95 (ISBN 0-938921-06-1); pap. text ed. 6.95 (ISBN 0-938921-07-X). Tigertail Ent.
Gormley, Beatrice. Sky Guys to White Cat. McCully, Emily A., illus. 128p. (gr. 3-6). 1991. 12.95 (ISBN 0-525-44743-1, DCB). Dutton Child Bks.
Graboff, Abner. In a Cat's Eye. (Illus.). (gr. 7 up). 1976. pap. 5.00 (ISBN 0-912846-25-9). Bookstore Pr.
Granger, Michele. The Summer House Cat. Strauss, Lindy, illus. 128p. (gr. 2-5). 1989. 11.95 (ISBN 0-525-44488-2, DCB). Dutton Child Bks.
—The Summer House Cat. MacDonald, Patricia, ed. Strauss, Lindy, illus. 128p. (gr. 4-7). 1990. pap. 2.75 (ISBN 0-671-70622-5, Minstrel). PB.
Greaves, Margaret. Cat's Magic. LC 80-8451. 192p. (gr. 5 up). 1981. 10.10i (ISBN 0-06-022122-4). HarpC Child Bks.
Greene, Carol. The Old Ladies Who Liked Cats. Krupinski, Loretta, illus. LC 90-4443. 32p. (gr. k-3). 1991. 14.95 (ISBN 0-06-022104-6); PLB 14.89 (ISBN 0-06-022105-4). HarpC Child Bks.
Haas, Dorothy. Poppy & the Outdoors Cat. Tucker, Kathleen, ed. Apple, Margot, illus. LC 80-19140. 128p. (gr. 2-5). 1982. PLB 9.95 (ISBN 0-8075-6621-7). A Whitman.
—Poppy & the Outdoors Cat. Apple, Margot, illus. 128p. (gr. 2-5). 1985. pap. 2.25 (ISBN 0-590-33567-7, Lucky Star). Scholastic Inc.
Hale, Kathleen. Orlando the Marmalade Cat, a Camping Holiday. (ps-3). 1990. 14.95 (ISBN 0-7232-3648-8). Warne.
Hall, Susan T. Kitty Whiskers. Hall, Susan T., illus. (ps-k). 1991. 5.25 (ISBN 0-307-12902-0, Golden Pr). Western Pub.
Hamer, Sylvia. C. B. & the Pink Pointe Shoes. Hamer, Sylvia, illus. LC 87-70557. 32p. (Orig.). (gr. 3-4). 1987. pap. 9.95 (ISBN 0-942479-00-9). Anderson Pr.
Hamley, Dennis. Tigger & Friends. Briley, D., ed. Rutherford, Meg, illus. LC 88-8385. (gr. k-3). 1989. 12.95 (ISBN 0-688-08606-3); PLB 12.88 (ISBN 0-688-08605-5). Lothrop.
Hammond, Jane. Carlton the Cat. (ps-k). 1983. pap. 1.50 (ISBN 0-87162-290-4, D5604). Warner Pr.
Harwood, Pearl A. Mrs. Moon's Rescue. Overlie, George, illus. LC 67-15694. 32p. (gr. k-3). 1967. PLB 4.95 (ISBN 0-8225-0118-X). Lerner Pubns.
Hausherr, Rosmarie. My First Kitten. Hausherr, Rosmarie, illus. LC 85-42804. 48p. (gr. 1-4). 1985. PLB 12.95 (ISBN 0-02-743420-6, Four Winds). Macmillan Child Grp.
Hautzig, Deborah. Ernie & Bert's New Kitten. Mathieu, Joe, illus. LC 89-10583. 40p. (ps-3). 1990. 4.95 (ISBN 0-679-80420-X); PLB 6.99 (ISBN 0-679-90420-4). McKay.
Hawkins, Colin & Hawkins, Jacqui. Pat the Cat. LC 82-18104. (Illus.). (ps-1). 1986. pap. 9.95 (ISBN 0-399-20957-3, Putnam). Putnam Pub Group.
Hayward, Linda. Rainy Day Kitten. McQueen, Lucinda, illus. 12p. (ps-1). 1986. 5.95 (ISBN 0-448-10451-2, G&D). Putnam Pub Group.
Hayward, Stan. The Millionaire. Godfrey, Bob, illus. (ps-5). 1987. pap. 2.25 (ISBN 0-671-63777-0, Little Simon). S&S Trade.
—The Shutterbug. Godfrey, Bob, illus. (ps-5). 1987. pap. 2.25 (ISBN 0-671-63776-2, Little Simon). S&S Trade.
Heilbroner, Joan. Tom the TV Cat: A Step Two Book. Murdocca, Sal, illus. LC 83-24600. 48p. (ps-2). 1984. lib. bdg. 6.99 (ISBN 0-394-96708-9, Pub. by BYR); pap. 2.95 (ISBN 0-394-86708-4). Random.
Henry, Marguerite. Benjamin West & His Cat Grimalkin. rev. ed. Dennis, Wesley, illus. LC 86-28658. 160p. (gr. 3-7). 1985. 13.95 (ISBN 0-02-743660-8, Mcmillan Child Bk). Macmillan Child Grp.
Herriot, James. Moses the Kitten. Barrett, Peter, illus. LC 84-50930. 32p. (ps up). 1984. 10.95 (ISBN 0-312-54905-9). St Martin.
Hess, Lilo. A Cat's Nine Lives. LC 83-20236. (Illus.). 48p. (gr. 3-6). 1984. 12.95 (ISBN 0-684-18073-1, Scribners Young Read). Macmillan Child Grp.
Hindley, Judy. Mrs. Mary Malarky's Seven Cats. Teasdale, Denise, illus. LC 88-25873. 32p. (ps-2). 1990. 12.95 (ISBN 0-531-05822-0); PLB 12.99 (ISBN 0-531-08422-1). Orchard Bks Watts.
Hoban, Julia. Buzby. Himmelman, John, illus. LC 89-29408. 64p. (gr. k-3). 1990. 11.95 (ISBN 0-06-022399-5); PLB 11.89 (ISBN 0-06-022398-7). HarpC Child Bks.
Hoban, Tana. One Little Kitten. LC 78-31862. (Illus.). 24p. (gr. k-3). 1979. PLB 12.88 (ISBN 0-688-84222-4). Greenwillow.
Hogrogian, Nonny. The Cat Who Loved to Sing. LC 86-27358. (Illus.). 40p. (ps-2). 1988. lib. bdg. 13.99 (ISBN 0-394-99004-8). Knopf.
Hollingsworth, Mary. Charlie & the Shabby Tabby. (Illus.). (ps-3). 1989. 5.95 (ISBN 0-915720-26-4). Brownlow Pub Co.

Howe, James. The Celery Stalks at Midnight. Morrill, Leslie H., illus. 128p. (gr. 3-7). 1984. pap. 3.50 (ISBN 0-380-69054-3, 69054-3, Camelot). Avon.

—Nightly-Nightmare. Morrill, Leslie, illus. LC 86-22334. 128p. (gr. 3-7). 1987. 12.95 (ISBN 0-689-31207-5, Atheneum Child Bk). Macmillan Child Grp.

Hubbell, Andra. Supercat. Dally, Tim, illus. LC 88-63735. 16p. (ps-3). 1989. PLB 16.95 (ISBN 0-9621759-1-9); PLB 11.95 (ISBN 0-317-93727-8). Rochester Pub Lib Dist.

Huck, Charlotte. Princess Furball. Lobel, Anita, illus. LC 88-18780. 40p. (ps up). 1989. 13.95 (ISBN 0-688-07837-0); PLB 13.88 (ISBN 0-688-07838-9). Greenwillow.

Huge, Tom. Garfield & Friends. Fentz, Mike, illus. Incl. Garfield & Arlene Go Picnicking. LC 84-61990; Garfield & Nermal Play Hide-&-Seek. LC 84-61995; Garfield & Odie Go Fishing. LC 84-61988; Garfield & Pooky Feel Lazy. LC 84-61989. 32p. (gr. 5 up). 1985. 6.95 (ISBN 0-394-87350-5, Random Juv). Random.

Hupy, Phyllis. Fancy Cat's Manners School. 1988. 5.95 (ISBN 0-533-07803-2). Vantage.

Hurd, Thacher. Axle the Freeway Cat. Hurd, Thacher, illus. LC 80-8432. 32p. (gr. k-3). 1981. PLB 12.89 (ISBN 0-06-022698-6). HarpC Child Bks.

Ingoglia, Gina. Sylvester & Tweety: What a Mess. (ps-3). 1990. write for info. (ISBN 0-307-11595-X). Western Pub.

Ivory, Lesley A. Meet My Cats. (gr. 2 up). 1989. 13.95 (ISBN 0-8037-0602-2). Dial Bks Young.

Jackson, Neta. The Cat Who Smelled Like Cabbage. Gabbitt, Anne, illus. 25p. (ps-3). 1991. 3.99 (ISBN 0-88070-349-0). Multnomah.

Jacobs, Joseph. King of the Cats. Galdone, Paul, illus. LC 79-16659. 32p. (ps-3). 1980. 13.95 (ISBN 0-395-29030-9, Clarion). HM.

—King of the Cats. Galdone, Paul, illus. LC 79-16659. (gr. k-3). 1985. pap. 4.95 (ISBN 0-89919-400-1, Pub. by Clarion). Ticknor & Fields.

Johansen, Hanna. A Tomcat's Tale. (gr. 4-7). 1991. 13.95 (ISBN 0-525-44583-8, DCB). Dutton Child Bks.

Johnson, Audean, illus. Soft as a Kitten. 14p. (ps). 1982. bds. 8.00 (ISBN 0-394-85517-5). Random.

Johnson, Eleanor. Pirate, the Lighthouse Cat. (gr. 2-5). 1986. pap. 6.95 (ISBN 0-930096-77-0). G Gannett.

Johnston, Johanna & Johnston, Abigail. Great Gravity the Cat. rev. ed. Mathis, Melissa B., illus. LC 88-13351. 64p. (gr. 3-7). 1989. lib. bdg. 15.00 (ISBN 0-208-02223-6, Linnet). Shoe String.

Johnston, Norma. Whisper of the Cat. 192p. (Orig.). 1988. pap. 2.95 (ISBN 0-553-26947-X, Starfire). Bantam.

Jones, Cordelia. Cat Called Camouflage. LC 79-166339. (Illus.). (gr. 7 up). 1971. 18.95 (ISBN 0-87599-189-0). S G Phillips.

Jones, Joyce. A Cat with a Thousand Faces: A Pawto-Biography. Howard, Alvis, ed. Bowen, Richard, illus. 48p. (gr. 1 up). 1991. 15.16 (ISBN 0-9621455-8-0). Honeysuckle.

Joos, Frederic & Joos, Francoise. Puss in Palace. (Illus.). 32p. (gr. k-2). 1990. 13.95 (ISBN 0-86264-235-3, Pub. by Anderson Pr UK). Trafalgar Sq.

Joy, Flora. The Ferocious Feline. 48p. (gr. k-4). 1988. wkbk. 5.95 (ISBN 0-86653-457-1, GA1060). Good Apple.

Kaplan, Marjorie. The Fifteenth Peanut Butter Sandwich. McKeating, Eileen, illus. LC 89-32784. 64p. (gr. 2-4). 1990. 12.95 (ISBN 0-02-749350-4, Four Winds Press). Macmillan Child Grp.

Karen & the Little Lost Kitten. (Illus.). (ps-1). 1982. 5.95 (ISBN 0-8431-0641-7). Price Stern.

Keats, Ezra J. Hi, Cat! 2nd ed. Keats, Ezra J., illus. LC 87-37433. 40p. (gr. k-4). 1988. pap. 4.95 (ISBN 0-689-71258-8, Aladdin). Macmillan Child Grp.

—Hi, Cat! (gr. k-3). 1990. incl. cass. 19.95 (ISBN 0-87499-180-3); pap. 12.95 incl. cass. (ISBN 0-87499-179-X); Set; incl. 4 bks., cass., & guide. pap. 27.95 (ISBN 0-685-38540-X). Live Oak Media.

Kellogg, Steven. The Orchard Cat. Kellogg, Steven, illus. 40p. (ps-3). 1983. pap. 3.75 (ISBN 0-8037-6481-2). Dial Bks Young.

—A Rose for Pinkerton. Kellogg, Steven, illus. LC 81-65848. 32p. (ps-3). 1981. 13.95 (ISBN 0-8037-7502-4); PLB 12.89 (ISBN 0-8037-7503-2). Dial Bks Young.

Kent, Lorna. No, No, Charlie Rascal. LC 88-50448. (Illus.). 32p. (ps-1). 1989. pap. 9.95 (ISBN 0-670-82512-3). Viking Child Bks.

Kern, Phyllis F. Bumble Cat: How She Came to Be. Kern, Phyllis F., illus. 32p. (gr. k-3). 1988. 12.95 (ISBN 0-395-38479-6); pap. 4.95 (ISBN 0-395-47944-4). HM.

Kerr. The Alamo Cat. (Illus.). 64p. (gr. 4-6). 1988. 9.95 (ISBN 0-89015-639-5, Pub. by Panda Bks). Eakin Pr.

Kettner, Christine. An Ordinary Cat. Kettner, Christine, illus. LC 90-19441. 32p. (ps-3). 1991. 13.95 (ISBN 0-06-023172-6); PLB 13.89 (ISBN 0-06-023173-4). HarpC Child Bks.

Kherdian, David. The Cat's Midsummer Jamboree. Hogrogian, Nonny, illus. 32p. (ps-3). 1990. 14.95 (ISBN 0-399-22222-7, Philomel Bks). Putnam Pub Group.

King, Deborah. Cloudy. (Illus.). 32p. (ps-5). 1990. 14.95 (ISBN 0-399-22242-1, Philomel Bks). Putnam Pub Group.

Kingett, Robert P. P. W. Liveaboard Cat. (Illus.). 48p. (Orig.). 1988. pap. write for info. Catalina Creations.

Kipling, Rudyard. Cat That Walked by Himself. 1989. 9.99 (ISBN 0-85953-276-3). Childs Play.

—The Cat That Walked by Himself: A Just So Story. Stobbs, William, illus. LC 83-71483. 32p. (gr. 1-5). 1983. PLB 10.95 (ISBN 0-911745-05-X). P Bedrick Bks.

—The Cat Who Walked by Himself. 1990. pap. 5.95 (ISBN 0-85953-309-3). Childs Play.

Kittens. (gr. k-3). 1962. bds. 3.95 (ISBN 0-448-03082-9, G&D). Putnam Pub Group.

Klimo, Kate, ed. Cats Up. Marshall, Ray & Paul, Korky, illus. 12p. 1982. pop-up 10.50 (ISBN 0-671-45268-1, Little Simon). S&S Trade.

Knotts, Howard. The Summer Cat. Knotts, Howard, illus. LC 79-9610. 48p. (gr. k-4). 1981. 8.61i (ISBN 0-06-023178-5). HarpC Child Bks.

Koci, Marta. Katie's Kitten. LC 82-60893. (Illus.). 28p. (ps-2). 1982. 14.95 (ISBN 0-907234-21-6). Picture Bk Studio.

Kraft, Jim. Garfield At the Gym. Davis, Jim, created by. (Illus.). (gr. k-2). 1991. 4.25 (ISBN 0-307-11696-4, Golden Pr). Western Pub.

—Garfield's Scary Tales. Fentz, Mike, illus. 32p. 1990. 9.95 (ISBN 0-448-40036-7, G&D). Putnam Pub Group.

—Mini-Mysteries Featuring Garfield. Davis, Jim, created by. (Illus.). (ps-3). 1991. pap. 1.75 (ISBN 0-307-12622-6, Golden Pr). Western Pub.

Kroll, Steven. Branigan's Cat & the Halloween Ghost. Ewing, Carolyn, illus. LC 89-77509. 32p. (ps-3). 1990. reinforced 14.95 (ISBN 0-8234-0822-1). Holiday.

Latimer, Heather. Curse of the Painted Cats: A Romantic Suspense Novel. 250p. 1989. 18.95 (ISBN 0-943698-03-0); pap. 4.95 (ISBN 0-943698-04-9); talking bk. with 2 audio cassettes, 3 hrs. 15.95 (ISBN 0-943698-06-5). Papyrus Pubs.

Lawrence, Jim. Shy Little Kitten's Secret Place. (Illus.). 24p. (ps-3). 1989. pap. write for info. (ISBN 0-307-14027-X). Western Pub.

Lear, Edward. The Owl & the Pussycat. (ps-1). 1989. 13.95 (ISBN 0-89919-505-9, Pub. by Clarion); pap. 4.95 (ISBN 0-89919-854-6, Pub. by Clarion). Ticknor & Fields.

Le Guin, Ursula K. Catwings. Schindler, S. D., illus. LC 87-33104. 48p. (gr. 2-5). 1988. 11.95 (ISBN 0-531-05759-3); PLB 11.99 (ISBN 0-531-08359-4). Orchard Bks Watts.

—Catwings Return. Schindler, S. D., illus. LC 88-17902. 56p. (gr. 2-5). 1989. 11.95 (ISBN 0-531-05803-4); PLB 11.99 (ISBN 0-531-08403-5). Orchard Bks Watts.

Leonard, Marcia. Midnight Cat. 1989. bds. 2.95 (ISBN 0-8167-1887-3). Troll Assocs.

Leonard, Marcia, adapted by. Your First Adventure: Little Kitten Sleeps Over, No. 9. Schmidt, Karen, illus. 32p. (Orig.). 1987. pap. 2.50 (ISBN 0-553-15472-9). Bantam.

Lewin, Betsy. Cat Count. (Illus.). 32p. (gr. k-3). 1981. 6.95 (ISBN 0-396-07928-8, Putnam). Putnam Pub Group.

Lillington, Kenneth. The Hallowe'en Cat. Floyd, Gareth, illus. 64p. (gr. 3-5). 1987. laminated boards 9.95 (ISBN 0-571-14690-2). Faber & Faber.

Lindblom, Steven. Let's Give Kitty a Bath. Kelley, True, illus. LC 81-19068. 32p. (ps-2). 1982. PLB 7.70 (ISBN 0-685-00007-9). HarpC Child Bks.

—Let's Give Kitty a Bath. True, Kelly, illus. LC 84-46023. 32p. (ps-2). 1982. 11.95 (ISBN 0-201-10712-0, Crowell Jr Bks). HarpC Child Bks.

Lindgren, Barbro. Sam's Ball. LC 83-722. (ps-k). 1983. 6.95 (ISBN 0-688-02359-2). Morrow Jr Bks.

Lindstrom, Eva. The Cat Hat. Croall, Stephen, tr. from SWE. (Illus.). 40p. (gr. 1-4). 1989. 12.95 (ISBN 0-916291-23-5); pap. 6.95 (ISBN 0-916291-24-3). Kane-Miller Bk.

Lisle, Janet T. The Dancing Cats of Applesap. Shefts, Joelle, illus. LC 83-15696. 176p. (gr. 4-6). 1984. 13.95 (ISBN 0-02-759140-9, Bradbury Pr). Macmillan Child Grp.

—The Dancing Cats of Applesap. Shefts, Joelle, illus. 1985. pap. 2.50 (ISBN 0-553-15348-X, Skylark). Bantam.

Livermore, Elaine. Find the Cat. Livermore, Elaine, illus. LC 75-5401. 48p. (ps-2). 1973. 13.95 (ISBN 0-395-14756-5). HM.

—Three Little Kittens. (Illus.). (ps-3). 1979. 12.95 (ISBN 0-395-28379-5). HM.

Livingston, Myra C., ed. Dog Poems. Morrill, Leslie, illus. LC 89-2061. 32p. (gr. k-3). 1990. reinforced 12.95 (ISBN 0-8234-0776-4). Holiday.

Loveland, Nicole. Boogins Gets a Basket. (Illus.). 32p. (ps-2). 1984. PLB 4.95 (ISBN 0-917107-00-4). Cat-Tales Pr.

McClintock, Barbara. The Heartaches of a French Cat. LC 88-45289. (Illus.). 48p. 1989. 14.95 (ISBN 0-87923-757-0). Godine.

McCue, Lisa, illus. Kitty's Colors. (ps-2). 1983. pap. 2.95 (ISBN 0-671-45489-7, Little Simon). S&S Trade.

McGurn, Patty. Me & Marie. McGurn, Patty, illus. (ps-1). 1989. PLB 12.95 (ISBN 0-517-57218-4). Crown.

McHugh, Elisabet. Beethoven's Cat. Riggio, Anita, illus. LC 87-13704. 160p. (gr. 3-7). 1988. 13.95 (ISBN 0-689-31364-0, Atheneum Child Bk). Macmillan Child Grp.

—Wiggie Wins the West. Riggio, Anita, illus. LC 88-8176. 160p. (gr. 3-7). 1989. 12.95 (ISBN 0-689-31449-3, Atheneum Child Bk). Macmillan Child Grp.

McMillan, Bruce. Kitten Can...a Concept Book. McMillan, Bruce, illus. LC 83-19539. 32p. (ps-1). 1984. 12.95 (ISBN 0-688-02668-0); PLB 12.88 (ISBN 0-688-02669-9). Lothrop.

Magellan, Mauro. Max, the Apartment Cat. Magellan, Mauro, illus. LC 88-32067. 32p. 1989. 12.95 (ISBN 0-89334-117-7). Humanics Ltd.

Mannin, Ethel. The Saga of Sammy-Cat. Kesteven, Peter, illus. (gr. 1-3). 1969. Repr. of 1969 ed. 2.59 (ISBN 0-08-013397-5). Pergamon.

Maril, Nadja. Me, Molly Midnight, the Artist's Cat. Maril, Herman, illus. LC 77-22708. 40p. (gr. k up). 1977. 9.95 (ISBN 0-916144-15-1); pap. 3.95 (ISBN 0-916144-16-X). Stemmer Hse.

—Runaway Molly Midnight, the Artist's Cat. Maril, Herman, illus. LC 80-17097. 40p. (gr. k up). 1980. 9.95 (ISBN 0-916144-62-3). Stemmer Hse.

Marsetta, Midge. Zun Zun. (gr. 1-3). 1989. 8.95 (ISBN 0-533-08059-2). Vantage.

Marzollo, Jean. Three Little Kittens. Thornton, Shelley, illus. 32p. (Orig.). (ps-k). 1986. pap. 2.50 (ISBN 0-590-43713-5). Scholastic Inc.

Matthews, Morgan. Fish for Supper. Miller, Susan, illus. LC 85-14056. 48p. (Orig.). (gr. 1-3). 1986. PLB 9.89 (ISBN 0-8167-0588-7); pap. text ed. 2.95 (ISBN 0-8167-0589-5). Troll Assocs.

Matthias, Catherine. I Love Cats. LC 83-7215. (Illus.). 32p. (ps-2). 1983. PLB 11.93 (ISBN 0-516-02041-2); pap. 2.95 (ISBN 0-516-42041-0). Childrens.

Mayerson, Evelyn W. The Cat Who Escaped from Steerage. LC 90-32890. 80p. (gr. 4-6). 1990. 11.95 (ISBN 0-684-19209-8, Scribners Young Read). Macmillan Child Grp.

Micucci, Charles. A Little Night Music. Micucci, Charles, illus. LC 88-505. 32p. (ps-3). 1989. 10.95 (ISBN 0-688-07900-8); PLB 10.88 (ISBN 0-688-07901-6, Morrow Jr Bks). Morrow Jr Bks.

Miller, Edna. Patches Finds a New Home. Miller, Edna, illus. (ps-4). 1989. pap. 12.95 (ISBN 0-671-66266-X). S&S Trade.

Miller, M. L. The Cat with the Coal-Black Paw. El-Labbad, M., illus. (gr. 6 up). 1986. pap. 2.50 (ISBN 0-88138-056-3, Pub. by Envelope Bks). Green Tiger Pr.

Miller, Minnie T. Grandma's Tiny Kitty. 130p. (gr. k-3). 1975. 5.95 (ISBN 0-87881-014-5). Mojave Bks.

Minarik, Else H. What If? LC 86-7649. (Illus.). 24p. (ps-2). 1987. 11.75 (ISBN 0-688-06473-6); PLB 11.88 (ISBN 0-688-06474-4). Greenwillow.

Mister Tom. Messycat. Spivey, Elvera, illus. LC 77-85397. 36p. (gr. k-4). 1989. pap. 4.95 (ISBN 0-925237-00-0). Ten Pubns.

Moncure, Jane B. Caring for My Kitty. Rigo, Christina, illus. 32p. (ps-2). 1990. PLB 9.96 (ISBN 0-89565-666-3). Childs World.

Mongo, C. Uncle Happy's Cat. (Illus., Orig.). (gr. 2-3). pap. 1.25 (ISBN 0-8198-0167-4). Dghtrs St Paul.

Muntean, Michaela. The Old Man & the Afternoon Cat. Weissman, Bari, illus. LC 81-11047. 48p. (ps-3). 1982. 5.95 (ISBN 0-8193-1071-9); PLB 5.95 (ISBN 0-8193-1072-7). Parents.

Never a Witch's Cat. (Illus.). (gr. 5 up). 1990. pap. 3.50. Ladybird Bks.

Neville, Emily C. It's Like This, Cat. Weiss, Emil, illus. LC 62-21292. 192p. (gr. 5-9). 1964. 12.95 (ISBN 0-06-024390-2); PLB 14.89 (ISBN 0-06-024391-0). HarpC Child Bks.

Newberry, Clare T. April's Kittens. Newberry, Clare T., illus. LC 40-32442. (gr. k-3). 1940. PLB 10.89 (ISBN 0-06-024401-1). HarpC Child Bks.

Nine Lives. (Illus.). (gr. 5 up). 1991. pap. 3.50. Ladybird Bks.

Nodset, Joan L. Come Here, Cat. LC 72-9858. (Illus.). (gr. k-3). 1973. PLB 11.89 (ISBN 0-06-024558-1). HarpC Child Bks.

Oakley, Graham. The Church Mouse. Oakley, Graham, illus. LC 72-75276. 40p. (gr. k-3). 1972. 13.95 (ISBN 0-689-30058-1, Atheneum Child Bk). Macmillan Child Grp.

Oana, Katy D. Shasta & the Shebang Machine. Stephens, Jacquelyn S., illus. LC 77-18350. (gr. k-2). 1978. PLB 5.95 (ISBN 0-89508-066-4). Rainbow Bks.

Oke, Janette. The Prodigal Cat. 160p. (Orig.). (gr. 3). 1984. pap. 4.95 (ISBN 0-934998-19-1). Bethel Pub.

Okimoto, Jean D. Blumpoe Grumpoe Meets Arnold C, Vol. 1. (ps-3). 1990. 13.95 (ISBN 0-316-63811-0, Joy St Bks). Little.

Oldfield, Margaret J. Fat Cat & Ebenezer Geezer: The Teeny Tiny Mouse. 2nd ed. Oldfield, Margaret J., illus. (gr. k-2). 1980. pap. 3.00 (ISBN 0-934876-13-4). Creative Storytime.

Ormerod, Jan. The Saucepan Game. Briley, D., ed. Ormerod, Jan, illus. LC 88-12893. 32p. (ps). 1989. 10.95 (ISBN 0-688-08518-0); PLB 10.88 (ISBN 0-688-08519-9). Lothrop.

Palazzo-Craig, Janet. Case of the Missing Cat. Shire, Ellen, illus. LC 81-7635. 48p. (gr. 2-4). 1982. PLB 10.89 (ISBN 0-89375-594-X); pap. text ed. 2.95 (ISBN 0-89375-595-8). Troll Assocs.

Parish, Peggy. The Cats' Burglar. (gr. k-6). 1988. pap. 2.75 (ISBN 0-440-40054-6, YB). Dell.

Parnall, Peter. Marsh Cat. Parnall, Peter, illus. 112p. (gr. 1-5). 1991. RSBE 12.95 (ISBN 0-02-770120-4, Mcmillan Child Bk). Macmillan Child Grp.

Passen, Lisa. Grammy & Sammy. Passen, Lisa, illus. 32p. (ps-4). 1990. 13.95 (ISBN 0-8050-1415-2). H Holt & Co.

Patterson, Francine. Koko's Kitten. Cohn, Ronald H., photos by. LC 85-2311. (Illus.). 32p. (gr. k up). 1985. 9.95 (ISBN 0-590-33811-0, Scholastic Hardcover). Scholastic Inc.
—Koko's Kitten. Cohn, Ronald H., photos by. (Illus.). 32p. (gr. k up). 1987. pap. 3.95 (ISBN 0-590-33812-9); tchr's. guide 1.25 (ISBN 0-590-41378-3). Scholastic Inc.
—Koko's Kitten. Cohn, Ronald H., photos by. 50p. (gr. k up). 1985. pap. 10.95 (ISBN 0-590-40952-2). Scholastic Inc.
Pepper, Dennis. A Book of Tall Stories. (gr. 5 up). 1987. 12.95 (ISBN 0-19-278101-4). Oxford U Pr.
Peters, Sharon. Five Little Kittens. Rosenberg, Amye, illus. LC 81-2317. 32p. (gr. k-2). 1981. PLB 10.89 (ISBN 0-89375-503-6); pap. 2.95 (ISBN 0-89375-504-4). Troll Assocs.
Petry, Ann. The Drugstore Cat. Suba, Susanna, illus. LC 88-3303. 96p. (gr. k-3). 1988. PLB 15.00 (ISBN 0-318-35207-9, NL3); pap. 6.95 (ISBN 0-8070-8309-7, BP801). Beacon Pr.
Phipson, Joan. The Cats. 176p. (gr. 7 up). 1989. pap. 3.95 (ISBN 0-02-044653-5, Collier Young Ad). Macmillan Child Grp.
Pinkwater, Daniel. The Wuggie Norple Story. DePaola, Tomie, illus. LC 88-878. 40p. (gr. k-4). 1988. pap. 4.50 (ISBN 0-689-71257-X, Aladdin). Macmillan Child Grp.
Pizer, Abigail. Harry's Night Out. LC 86-24065. (Illus.). 32p. (ps-3). 1987. 11.95 (ISBN 0-8037-0055-5). Dial Bks Young.
Poe, Edgar Allan. The Black Cat. Redpath, Ann, ed. Delessert, Etienne, illus. 32p. (gr. 9 up). 1985. PLB 10.95 (ISBN 0-685-10389-7). Creative Ed.
—The Black Cat. rev. ed. (gr. 9-12). 1989. Repr. of 1902 ed. multi-media kit 35.00 (ISBN 0-685-31130-9). Balance Pub.
Polette, Nancy. Little Old Woman & the Hungry Cat. LC 88-18788. (Illus.). 24p. (ps up). 1989. 12.95 (ISBN 0-688-08314-5); PLB 12.88 (ISBN 0-688-08315-3). Greenwillow.
Polushkin, Maria. Kitten in Trouble. Levin, Betsy, illus. LC 85-5753. 32p. (ps-k). 1988. 12.95 (ISBN 0-02-774740-9, Bradbury Pr). Macmillan Child Grp.
Potter, Beatrix. The Complete Adventures of Tom Kitten. (ps-3). 1987. pap. 5.95 (ISBN 0-14-050503-2, Puffin). Puffin Bks.
—El Cuento del Gato Tomas. (SPA., Illus.). 64p. 1988. 4.95 (ISBN 0-7232-3565-1). Warne.
—The Roly-Poly Pudding. 80p. (gr. 1 up). 1986. pap. 2.75 (ISBN 0-486-25099-7). Dover.
—The Tale of Tom Kitten. (Illus.). 58p. (gr. k up). 1983. pap. 1.75 (ISBN 0-486-24502-0). Dover.
—The Tale of Tom Kitten. Atkinson, Allen, illus. 1983. pap. 2.25 (ISBN 0-553-15224-6). Bantam.
—The Tale of Tom Kitten. (Illus.). 64p. (ps-3). 1986. 3.95 (ISBN 0-671-62927-1, Little Simon). S&S Trade.
—The Tale of Tom Kitten. LC 87-40285. (Illus.). (ps up). 1990. incl. audio cassettes 6.95 (ISBN 1-55782-018-X). Warner Bks.
—The Tale of Tom Kitten. (Illus.). (ps-3). 1987. pap. 5.95 (ISBN 0-7232-3467-1). Warne.
—The Tale of Tom Kitten. 1987. pap. 2.25 (ISBN 0-7232-3492-2). Warne.
—The Tale of Tom Kitten. Routledge, Patricia, read by. (ps-3). 1989. pap. 6.95 bk. & tape (ISBN 0-7232-3670-4). Warne.
—Tale of Tom Kitten. 1988. 2.50 (ISBN 0-517-65278-1). Crown.
Potter, Maureen. Theatre Cat. 64p. 1986. 11.95 (ISBN 0-86278-085-3, Pub. by O'Brien Press Ltd Eire). Dufour.
Poulin, Stephane. Can You Catch Josephine? Poulin, Stephane, illus. 24p. (gr. k-4). 1988. 12.95 (ISBN 0-88776-198-4); pap. 6.95 (ISBN 0-88776-214-X). Tundra Bks.
—Peux-tu Attraper Josephine? (FRE., Illus.). 24p. (Orig.). (gr. k-4). 1988. 12.95 (ISBN 0-88776-199-2); pap. 6.95 (ISBN 0-88776-225-5). Tundra Bks.
Price, Susan. The Ghost Drum: A Cat's Tale. LC 86-46032. 176p. (gr. 5 up). 1987. 12.95 (ISBN 0-374-32538-3). FS&G.
Pryor, Ainslie. The Baby Blue Cat & the Dirty Dog Brothers. (Illus.). (ps-3). 1987. 11.95 (ISBN 0-670-81781-3). Viking Child Bks.
—Baby Blue Cat & the Smiley Worm Doll. (ps). 1990. 11.95 (ISBN 0-670-83531-5). Viking Child Bks.
—The Baby Blue Cat & the Whole Batch of Cookies. (Illus.). 32p. (ps-1). 1989. 11.95 (ISBN 0-670-81782-1). Viking Child Bks.
—The Baby Blue Cat & the Whole Batch of Cookies. (Illus.). 32p. (ps-1). 1991. pap. 3.95 (ISBN 0-14-050770-1, Puffin). Puffin Bks.
—The Baby Blue Cat Who Said No. (Illus.). 32p. (ps-1). 1990. pap. 3.95 (ISBN 0-14-050768-X, Puffin). Puffin Bks.
Punnett, Dick. Our Brat Cat. Rauh, Herb, illus. LC 84-23027. 32p. (gr. k-3). 1985. lib. bdg. 10.95 (ISBN 0-89565-303-6). Childs World.
Puss 'n Boots. (FRE.). (gr. k-3). 9.95 (ISBN 0-685-28440-9). French & Eur.
Radke, Martha E. The Cat Who Conducted with His Tail. Tootill, Ginger, illus. LC 81-90803. 28p. (Orig.). (ps-3). 1982. pap. 1.95 (ISBN 0-9607994-0-0). G E Radke.
Reese, Ron. Crazy Cat's Bad Day. Jordan, Alton, ed. (Illus.). (gr. k-3). 1981. PLB 7.95 (ISBN 0-89868-090-5, Read Res); pap. text ed. 2.95 (ISBN 0-89868-101-4). ARO Pub.
Reiser, Lynn. Bedtime Cat. LC 90-30751. (Illus.). 24p. (ps up). 1991. 13.95 (ISBN 0-688-10025-2); PLB 13.88 (ISBN 0-688-10026-0). Greenwillow.
—Dog & Cat. LC 90-3553. (Illus.). 24p. (ps up). 1991. 13.95 (ISBN 0-688-09892-4); PLB 13.88 (ISBN 0-688-09893-2). Greenwillow.
Robertus, Polly. The Dog Who Had Kittens. LC 90-39174. (Illus.). 32p. (ps-3). 1991. PLB 14.95 (ISBN 0-8234-0860-4). Holiday.
Robinson, Nancy K. Just Plain Cat. 127p. (Orig.). (gr. 4-6). 1981. pap. 2.25 (ISBN 0-590-31782-2). Scholastic Inc.
—Just Plain Cat. LC 82-18258. 128p. (gr. 3-6). 1984. 12.95 (ISBN 0-02-777350-7, Four Winds). Macmillan Child Grp.
—Just Plain Cat. 128p. (gr. 3-5). 1985. pap. 2.50 (ISBN 0-590-40778-3, Apple Paperbacks). Scholastic Inc.
Robinson, Tom. Buttons. Bacon, Peggy, illus. (gr. k-2). 1976. pap. 3.95 (ISBN 0-14-050179-7, Puffin). Puffin Bks.
Rockwell, Anne. Honk Honk! LC 79-20267. 32p. (ps-1). 1980. 7.95 (ISBN 0-525-32120-9, DCB). Dutton Child Bks.
Rockwell, Anne, as told by. & illus. Puss in Boots & Other Stories. LC 87-14976. 96p. (gr. k-4). 1988. 15.95 (ISBN 0-02-777781-2, Mcmillan Child Bk). Macmillan Child Grp.
Rodriguez, Agatha A. Catability. Medina, Mary L., illus. 20p. (Orig.). 1990. pap. text ed. 7.95g (ISBN 0-933196-04-0). Bilingue Pubns.

Roe, JoAnn. Marco the Manx Series, 3 bks. Runestrand, Meredith & Mayo, Steve, illus. (gr. k-5). Date not set. Fisherman Cat. PLB 10.95 (ISBN 0-931551-02-1); Alaska Cat. PLB 10.95 (ISBN 0-931551-05-6); Castaway Cat. pap. 5.95 (ISBN 0-931551-03-X); Fisherman Cat. pap. 6.95 (ISBN 0-931551-01-3); Alaska Cat. pap. 6.95 (ISBN 0-931551-04-8). Montevista Pr. "Marco the Manx Series": Each book is a complete story. (1) Castaway Cat, 56 pp, B/W watercolors, color cover, paper only $5.95 (ISBN 0-931551-03-X, 2nd printing). A Manx "city cat," falls off a sailboat, has to survive on an island for the winter. Ocean lore, raccoon fights, eagles. (2) Fisherman Cat, 64 pp, color watercolors, paper $6.95 (ISBN 0-931551-01-3), library binding $10.95 (ISBN 0-931551-02-1). Marco the Manx goes aboard a disabled fishing boat, is trapped below, goes off toward Alaskan fishing grounds. Salmon life cycle, fishing lore. (3) Alaska Cat, 64 pp, color watercolors, paper $6.95 (ISBN 0-931551-04-8); library binding $10.95 (ISBN 0-931551-05-6). Marco's boat is shipwrecked off Sitka, Alaska. Once ashore he encounters bears, is rescued by native children. Totems, etc. Castaway Cat won a national first prize for excellence. Was used in school reading test. Distributors: Pacific Pipeline, 19215 - 66th Avenue South, Kent WA 98032-1171. (206) 872-5523. Alaska News Agency, 325 Potter Street, Anchorage AK 99518. (907) 563-3251. Baker & Taylor, Reno, Momence, etc.
Publisher Provided Annotation.

Roos, Kelley & Roos, Stephen. The Incredible Cat Caper. (gr. 3-6). 1986. pap. 2.75 (ISBN 0-440-44084-X, YB). Dell.
Rosen, Michael. A Cat & Mouse Story. (Illus.). 32p. (gr. k-3). 1983. 9.95 (ISBN 0-233-97484-9). Andre Deutsch.
Ross, Tony. I Want a Cat. (Illus.). 26p. (ps up). 1989. 11.95 (ISBN 0-374-33621-0); pap. 4.95 (ISBN 0-374-43544-8). FS&G.
Rylant, Cynthia. Henry & Mudge & the Happy Cat. Stevenson, Sucie, illus. LC 88-18855. 48p. (gr. 1-3). 1990. 11.95 (ISBN 0-02-778008-2, Bradbury Pr). Macmillan Child Grp.
Sachs, Elizabeth-Ann. A Special Kind of Friend. LC 90-40048. (Illus.). 112p. (gr. 3-7). 1991. pap. 3.95 (ISBN 0-689-71388-6, Aladdin). Macmillan Child Grp.
St. Pierre, Stephanie. Valentine Kittens. 1990. pap. 3.95 (ISBN 0-590-63481-X). Scholastic Inc.
Saki. Tobermory. 32p. (gr. 6). 1990. 10.95s.p. (ISBN 0-88682-305-6); 15.65 (ISBN 0-685-28220-1). Creative Ed.
Salerno, Tony. Kid E. Kat & the Magnificent Riding Machine. LC 90-33473. (Illus.). 32p. (Orig.). (ps-8). 1990. 8.99 (ISBN 0-89081-833-9). Harvest Hse.
Sampson, Fay. Pangur Ban. (Illus.). 128p. (Orig.). (gr. 4-8). 1989. pap. 3.95 (ISBN 0-85648-580-2). Lion USA.
—Serpent of Senargad. (Illus.). 128p. (gr. 4-8). 1989. pap. 3.95 (ISBN 0-7459-1520-5). Lion USA.
—Shape-Shifter. (Illus.). 128p. (gr. 4-8). 1989. pap. 3.95 (ISBN 0-7459-1347-4). Lion USA.
San Souci, Robert D. The White Cat. Spirin, Gennady, illus. LC 88-19698. 32p. (ps-3). 1990. 15.95 (ISBN 0-531-05809-3); PLB 15.99 (ISBN 0-531-08409-4). Orchard Bks Watts.
Santoro, Christopher. Little Kitten. McClain, Mary, illus. 12p. (ps-2). 1982. 3.95 (ISBN 0-671-42547-1, Little Simon). S&S Trade.
Sara. Across Town. LC 90-7982. (Illus.). 32p. (ps-2). 1991. 13.95 (ISBN 0-531-05932-4); PLB 13.99 (ISBN 0-531-08532-5). Orchard Bks Watts.
Sartori, Mario. Tales to Read Aloud to Your Cat: Tiger, Vol. 1. (Illus.). 64p. (gr. 5 up). 1988. 8.95 (ISBN 0-525-24717-3, Dutton). NAL-Dutton.
Saunders, Susan. Mystery Cat, Bk. 1. (Orig.). (ps-3). 1986. pap. 2.25 (ISBN 0-553-15377-3, Skylark). Bantam.
—Mystery Cat & the Chocolate Trap. 96p. (Orig.). 1986. pap. 2.25 (ISBN 0-553-15415-X, Skylark). Bantam.
Savitz, Harriet M. Cats Nobody Wanted. 1989. pap. 2.50 (ISBN 0-590-42196-4). Scholastic Inc.
Scat, Scat! (Illus.). 24p. (ps-3). 1978. 2.50 (ISBN 0-448-46521-3, G&D); PLB 3.59 (ISBN 0-448-13056-4). Putnam Pub Group.
Schertle, Alice. That Olive! Wheeler, Cindy, illus. LC 84-10025. 32p. (ps-1). 1986. PLB 11.88 (ISBN 0-688-04091-8). Lothrop.
Schneidewind, Barbara F. My Name Is: I'm a Cat. (gr. 3-5). 1986. 4.95 (ISBN 0-533-06937-8). Vantage.
Schoch, Tim. Cat Attack. (gr. 3-7). 1988. pap. 2.75 (ISBN 0-380-75520-3, Camelot). Avon.
Schreiber-Wicke, Edith. Cats' Carnival. Laimgruber, Monika, illus. LC 85-45964. 24p. 1986. 13.95 (ISBN 0-87923-627-2). Godine.
Scriven, Gill. White Cat's Holiday. (Illus.). 32p. (gr. 2-4). 1990. 13.95 (Pub. by Collins Pubs UK). Trafalgar Sq.
Segal, Lore. The Story of Mrs. Lovewright & Purrless Her Cat. Zelinsky, Paul, illus. LC 84-25011. 40p. (ps-3). 1985. 12.95 (ISBN 0-394-86817-X); lib. bdg. 12.99 (ISBN 0-394-96817-4). Knopf.
Seidler, Ann & Slepian, Jan. The Cat Who Wore a Pot on Her Head. Martin, Richard E., illus. 32p. (gr. k-3). 1987. pap. 3.95 (ISBN 0-590-43708-9). Scholastic Inc.
Selden, George. Harry Kitten & Tucker Mouse. Williams, Garth, illus. LC 83-16530. 64p. (gr. 2-5). 1986. 11.95 (ISBN 0-374-32860-9). FS&G.
—Harry Kitten & Tucker Mouse. (gr. k-6). 1989. pap. 2.95 (ISBN 0-440-40124-0, YB). Dell.
Selman, LaRue. The Hero, Two. Jordan, Alton, ed. (Illus.). (gr. k-3). 1981. PLB 7.95 (ISBN 0-89868-089-1, Read Res); pap. text ed. 2.95 (ISBN 0-89868-100-6). ARO Pub.
—JD & the Bee. Jordan, Alton, ed. (Illus.). (gr. k-3). 1981. PLB 7.95 (ISBN 0-89868-093-X, Read Res); pap. text ed. 2.95 (ISBN 0-89868-104-9). ARO Pub.
—Rain Frog. Jordan, Alton, ed. (Illus.). (gr. k-3). 1981. PLB 7.95 (ISBN 0-89868-091-3, Read Res); pap. text ed. 2.95 (ISBN 0-89868-102-2). ARO Pub.
—Sammy Skunk Plays the Clown. Jordan, Alton, ed. (Illus.). (gr. k-3). 1981. PLB 7.95 (ISBN 0-89868-097-2, Read Res); pap. text ed. 2.95 (ISBN 0-89868-108-1). ARO Pub.
Sesame Street Staff. Grover's New Kitten. Barrett, John E., photos by. LC 81-50538. (Illus.). 14p. (ps). 1981. bds. 3.95 (ISBN 0-394-84872-1). Random.
Shelley, Purrcy B., ed. Cat-A-Log. (Illus.). 1983. pap. 6.95 (ISBN 0-448-18959-3, G&D). Putnam Pub Group.
Shura, Mary F. The Search for Grissi. (gr. 3-7). 1986. 12.95 (ISBN 0-399-21705-3, Putnam). Putnam Pub Group.
Silverman, Maida. Henry's Cat: Craft Fun. Godfrey, Bob, illus. (gr. 1-5). 1987. pap. 2.25 (ISBN 0-317-66514-6, Little Simon). S&S Trade.
Simon, Norma. Oh, That Cat! Leder, Dora, illus. LC 85-15546. 32p. (ps-4). 1986. 10.95 (ISBN 0-8075-5919-9). A Whitman.
Slate, Joseph. Lonely Lula Cat. Degen, Bruce, illus. LC 84-48345. 32p. (ps-1). 1985. PLB 11.89 (ISBN 0-06-025807-1). HarpC Child Bks.
Slepian, Jan. The Broccoli Tapes. (gr. 3-7). 1989. 13.95 (ISBN 0-399-21712-6, Philomel Bks). Putnam Pub Group.
Slepian, Jan & Seidler, Ann. The Cat Who Wore a Cat on Her Head. Martin, Richard E., illus. 32p. (gr. k-3). 1987. pap. 2.95 (ISBN 0-590-31595-1). Scholastic Inc.
—The Cat Who Wore a Pot on Her Head. Martin, Richard F., illus. 32p. (ps-3). 1981. pap. 2.95 (ISBN 0-590-40977-8). Scholastic Inc.
Smith. Help! There's a Cat Washing Here. (ps-7). 1987. pap. 2.50 (ISBN 0-553-15374-9, Skylark). Bantam.
Smith, Glenna C. The Little Mouse Was a Grouch. Jordan, Alton, ed. (Illus.). (gr. k-3). 1981. PLB 7.95 (ISBN 0-89868-095-6, Read Res); pap. text ed. 2.95 (ISBN 0-89868-106-5). ARO Pub.

Smith, Linda J. Cat's Wedding. (Illus.). 32p. 1989. 12.95 (ISBN 0-8249-8402-1). Ideals.

Snyder, Phillip C. Pa Pong: A Siamese Kitty. Mohrman, Janet S., illus. 28p. (ps-1). 1981. pap. text ed. 3.95 (ISBN 0-940560-03-8). Custom Hse.

Soler, Dona K. Greyball. 80p. (gr. 4-7). 1986. 6.95 (ISBN 0-8059-3006-X). Dorrance.

Sorenson, Jody. The Secret Letters of Mama Cat. LC 87-25333. 122p. (gr. 5-8). 1988. 12.95 (ISBN 0-8027-6779-6); PLB 13.85 (ISBN 0-8027-6791-5). Walker & Co.

Soto, Gary. The Cat's Meow. Soto, Caroline, illus. LC 87-17982. 64p. (Orig.). 1987. pap. 4.95 (ISBN 0-89407-087-8). Strawberry Hill.

Spier, Peter. Peter Spier's Little Cats. LC 82-45494. (Illus.). 14p. (ps-1). 1984. 2.50 (ISBN 0-385-18197-3). Doubleday.

Spirn, Michele. The Cat Who Couldn't Meow. (ps-1). 1988. 8.49 (ISBN 0-87386-054-3); incl. cassette 16.99 (ISBN 0-685-25195-0); pap. 1.95 (ISBN 0-87386-050-0); pap. 9.95 incl. cassette (ISBN 0-685-25196-9). Jan Prods.

Spohn, Kate. Clementine's Winter Wardrobe. LC 89-42531. (Illus.). 32p. (ps-1). 1989. 13.95 (ISBN 0-531-05841-7); PLB 13.99 (ISBN 0-531-08441-8). Orchard Bks Watts.

Stahl, Hilda. Sendi Lee Mason & the Stray Striped Cat. LC 90-80621. 128p. (Orig.). (gr. 2-5). 1990. pap. 4.95 (ISBN 0-89107-580-1, Crossway Bks). Good News.

Stevenson, James. Will You Please Feed Our Cat? Stevenson, James, illus. LC 86-11927. 32p. (gr. k-3). 1987. 11.75 (ISBN 0-688-06847-2); lib. bdg. 11.88 (ISBN 0-688-06848-0). Greenwillow.

Stock, Catherine. Sampson: The Christmas Cat. Stock, Catherine, illus. LC 84-9946. 32p. (ps-3). 1984. 10.95 (ISBN 0-399-21002-4, Putnam). Putnam Pub Group.

Stolz, Mary. Cat Walk. Blegvad, Erik, illus. LC 82-47576. 128p. (gr. 3-7). 1985. pap. 2.95 (ISBN 0-06-440155-3, Trophy). HarpC Child Bks.

Storr, Catherine, as told by. Dick Whittington. LC 85-16904. (Illus.). 32p. (gr. 2-5). 1985. PLB 16.67 (ISBN 0-8172-2507-2); pap. 9.27 (ISBN 0-8172-2515-3). Raintree Pubs.

Stringham, Alene. Kim & Her Kittens. Burris, Priscilla, illus. 60p. (Orig.). (gr. 2-3). 1986. pap. text ed. 5.95 (ISBN 0-933606-46-X, MS-646). Monkey Sisters.

Sullivan, Pat. Felix the Cat. 128p. (Orig.). 1982. pap. 1.75 (ISBN 0-523-49009-7, Dist. by Warner Pub Services & Saint Martin's Press). Tor Bks.

Supraner, Robyn. The Cat Who Wanted to Fly. Goodman, Joan E., illus. LC 85-14119. 48p. (Orig.). (gr. 1-3). 1986. PLB 9.89 (ISBN 0-8167-0612-3); pap. text ed. 2.95 (ISBN 0-8167-0613-1). Troll Assocs.

—Kitty: A Cat's Diary. Paterson, Diane, illus. LC 85-14023. 48p. (Orig.). (gr. 1-3). 1986. PLB 9.89 (ISBN 0-8167-0574-7); pap. text ed. 2.95 (ISBN 0-8167-0575-5). Troll Assocs.

Surprise Cat! (ps-1). 1987. bds. 3.95 (ISBN 0-317-66511-1, Little Simon). S&S Trade.

Suteyev, V. Three Kittens. Ginsburg, Mirra, tr. from RUS. Maestro, Giulio, illus. LC 72-96414. 32p. (ps-1). 1988. PLB 12.95 (ISBN 0-517-50328-X). Crown.

—Three Kittens. Ginsburg, Mirra, tr. Maestro, Giulio, illus. (gr. k-3). 1988. pap. 3.50 (ISBN 0-517-56551-X). Crown.

Taylor, Mildred D. The Gold Cadillac. Hays, Michael, illus. LC 86-11526. 48p. (gr. 2-6). 1987. 12.95 (ISBN 0-8037-0342-2); PLB 11.89 (ISBN 0-8037-0343-0). Dial Bks Young.

Taylor, Theodore. Sniper. LC 89-7415. 227p. (gr. 5-9). 1989. 14.95 (ISBN 0-15-276420-8). HarBraceJ.

Teague, Mark. The Trouble with the Johnsons. (Illus.). (gr. k-3). 1989. pap. 12.95 (ISBN 0-590-42394-0). Scholastic Inc.

Thaler, Mike. Catzilla. (gr. 4-7). 1991. pap. 2.95 (ISBN 0-671-73297-8). S&S Trade.

Thomson, Ross. Moggy Books: Moggy Builds a Beehive; Moggy Bakes Some Bread; Moggy's Seaside Opposites & Moggy Goes on a Picnic, 4 bks. Thomson, Ross, illus. 96p. (gr. k-1). Set. pap. text ed. 24.90 (ISBN 1-55624-252-2). Wright Group.

Three Little Kittens. (Illus.). (ps-1). 1985. 1.98 (ISBN 0-517-47898-6). Outlet Bk Co.

Titus, Eve. Anatole & the Cat. (ps-3). 1990. pap. 4.95 (ISBN 0-553-34871-X). Bantam.

—The Kitten Who Couldn't Purr. Fechner, Amrei, illus. LC 90-13418. 32p. (gr. 3 up). 1991. Repr. 12.95 (ISBN 0-688-09363-9); PLB 12.88 (ISBN 0-688-09364-7, Morrow Jr Bks). Morrow Jr Bks.

Tom Kitten. (Illus.). (ps-2). 1.95 (ISBN 0-7214-5219-1). Ladybird Bks.

Turkle, Brinton. Do Not Open. Turkle, Brinton, illus. LC 80-10289. 32p. (ps-2). 1981. pap. 13.95 (ISBN 0-525-28785-X, 01258-370, DCB). Dutton Child Bks.

Turner, Dona. My Cat Pearl. Turner, Dona, illus. 32p. (ps-1). 1980. PLB 11.89 (ISBN 0-690-03990-5, Crowell Jr Bks). HarpC Child Bks.

Turner, Gladys T. The Autobiography of Tammy: A Gift of Love & Fun. Finney, Frederick M., illus. LC 78-1317. (gr. 3 up). 1978. 6.95 (ISBN 0-89421-007-6); PLB 7.95 (ISBN 0-89421-009-2). Challenge Pr.

Two-Minute Garfield Stories. (ps-k). Date not set. write for info. (ISBN 0-307-12194-1, Golden Pr). Western Pub.

Ungerer, Tomi. No Kiss for Mother. (gr. 4-7). 1991. 13.00 (ISBN 0-385-30384-X); PLB 13.99 (ISBN 0-385-30385-8). Delacorte.

Vagin, Vladimir & Asch, Frank. Here Comes the Cat! Vagin, Vladimir & Asch, Frank, illus. LC 88-3083. (gr. k-3). 1989. pap. 11.95 (ISBN 0-590-41859-9). Scholastic Inc.

Viorst, Judith. The Tenth Good Thing about Barney. Blegvad, Eric, illus. LC 71-154764. 32p. (gr. k-4). 1971. 12.95 (ISBN 0-689-20688-7, Atheneum Child Bk). Macmillan Child Grp.

Voake, Charlotte. Tom's Cat. LC 85-27166. (Illus.). 32p. (ps-2). 1986. pap. 2.50 (ISBN 0-06-443105-3, Trophy). HarpC Child Bks.

—Tom's Cat. Voake, Charlotte, illus. LC 85-23904. 32p. (ps-2). 1986. PLB 11.89 (ISBN 0-397-32195-3, Lipp Jr Bks). HarpC Child Bks.

Wahl, Jan. Dracula's Cat. LC 77-27051. (Illus.). (ps-3). 1981. 6.95 (ISBN 0-685-03842-4); pap. 2.50 (ISBN 0-685-03843-2). P-H.

—Tim Kitten & the Red Cupboard. Degen, Bruce, illus. 32p. (ps-1). 1988. 5.95 (ISBN 0-671-64153-0, Little Simon). S&S Trade.

—Tim Kitten & the Red Cupboard. 1990. pap. 2.25 (ISBN 0-671-70296-3). S&S Trade.

Wallace, Bill. Snot Stew. McCue, Lisa, illus. LC 88-31976. 96p. (gr. 3-7). 1989. 13.95 (ISBN 0-8234-0745-4). Holiday.

Walsh, Abigail M. Momma Cat. Dowling, Marilyn, illus. LC 90-823. 112p. (gr. 2 up). 11.95 (ISBN 0-934745-16-1). Acadia Pub Co.

Weinberger, Jane. Fanny & Sarah. 2nd ed. MacDonald, Karen, illus. LC 84-51987. 40p. (gr. k-4). 1986. pap. 3.95 (ISBN 0-932433-02-2). Windswept Hse.

—Tabitha Jones. 2nd ed. Jones, Renata S., illus. 40p. (Orig.). (ps-4). 1985. pap. 3.95 (ISBN 0-932433-07-3). Windswept Hse.

Weininger, Rachel. Nightshade. Sawyer, Barbara, illus. 64p. (Orig.). (gr. 4-6). 1989. pap. 5.95 (ISBN 0-931093-11-2). Red Hen Pr.

Wellington, Monica. Molly Chelsea & Her Calico Cat. Wellington, Monica, illus. LC 88-3591. 24p. (ps-1). 1988. 11.95 (ISBN 0-525-44403-3, DCB). Dutton Child Bks.

West, Cindy. Henry's Cat Takes a Swim. Godfrey, Bob, illus. (ps). 1987. 3.95 (ISBN 0-671-63772-X, Little Simon). S&S Trade.

Westall, Robert. Blitzcat. (gr. 7 up). 1989. pap. 12.95 (ISBN 0-590-42770-9). Scholastic Inc.

—Blitzcat. 240p. (gr. 7 up). 1990. pap. 2.95 (ISBN 0-590-42771-7). Scholastic Inc.

Whatling, R. C. The Cat Story. 16p. (gr. 7-10). 1986. 15.00X (ISBN 0-7223-2012-4, Pub. by A H Stockwell England). State Mutual Bk.

Wheeler, Cindy. A Good Day, a Good Night. Wheeler, Cindy, illus. LC 79-3017. (ps-2). 1980. 8.61i (ISBN 0-397-31900-2, Lipp Jr Bks). HarpC Child Bks.

—Marmalade's Nap. LC 81-20868. (Illus.). 24p. (ps-1). 1983. lib. bdg. 9.99 (ISBN 0-394-95022-4). Knopf.

Wild, Margaret. The Very Best of Friends. Vivas, Julie, illus. (ps-3). 1990. 13.95 (ISBN 0-15-200625-7, Gulliver Bks). HarbraceJ.

Wildsmith, Brian. Giddy Up. 16p. (ps-k). 1987. pap. 2.95 (ISBN 0-19-272183-6). Oxford U Pr.

—If I Were You. 16p. (ps-k). 1987. pap. 2.95 (ISBN 0-19-272182-8). Oxford U Pr.

Wilkon, Piotr. Rosie the Cool Cat. (ps-3). 1991. 13.95 (ISBN 0-670-83707-5). Viking Child Bks.

Wilson, A. N. Stray. LC 88-36626. 256p. (gr. 7 up). 1989. 15.95 (ISBN 0-531-05840-9); PLB 15.99 (ISBN 0-531-08440-X). Orchard Bks Watts.

—Tabitha. Fox-Davies, Sarah, illus. LC 88-19820. 48p. (gr. 3 up). 1989. 14.95 (ISBN 0-531-05813-1); PLB 14.99 (ISBN 0-531-08413-2). Orchard Bks Watts.

Wilson, Yvonne M. Kitten Without A Name. (Illus.). 23p. (gr. 1-2). 1982. pap. 1.95 (ISBN 0-686-97302-X). Bible Memory.

Winder, Jack. What Are Faces for? Jordan, Alton, ed. (Illus.). (gr. k-3). 1981. PLB 7.95 (ISBN 0-89868-096-4, Read Res); pap. text ed. 2.95 (ISBN 0-89868-107-3). ARO Pub.

Wiseman, Bernard. Cats! Cats! Cats! Wiseman, Bernard, illus. LC 83-27288. 48p. (ps-3). 1984. 5.95 (ISBN 0-8193-1127-8). Parents.

Wolff, Ashley. Only the Cat Saw. (gr. k-3). 1985. 13.95 (ISBN 0-399-21698-7, Putnam). Putnam Pub Group.

Wolski, Slawomir. Tiger Cat. Wilkon, Jozef, illus. Crawford, Elizabeth D., tr. LC 87-43151. (Illus.). 32p. (gr. k-3). 1988. 12.95 (ISBN 1-55858-017-4). North-South Bks NYC.

Wood, Leslie. Sam's Big Day. 16p. (ps-k). 1987. 2.95 (ISBN 0-19-272165-8). Oxford U Pr.

Wood, Phyllis A. Pass Me a Pine Cone. LC 82-1870. 160p. (gr. 7-9). 1982. 11.95 (ISBN 0-664-32692-7, Westminster). Westminster John Knox.

Young, Ed. Up a Tree: A Wordless Picture Book. Young, Ed, illus. LC 82-47733. 32p. (ps-3). 1983. PLB 14.89 (ISBN 0-06-026814-X). HarpC Child Bks.

Young, James. Penelope & the Pirates. Young, James, illus. 32p. (ps-2). 1990. text ed. 12.95 (ISBN 1-55970-074-2). Arcade Pub Inc.

Zaum, Marjorie. Catlore: Tales from Around the World. LC 85-7530. (Illus.). 80p. (gr. 4-6). 1985. SBE 10.95 (ISBN 0-689-31173-7, Atheneum Child Bk). Macmillan Child Grp.

Ziefert, Harriet. Cat Games. Schumacher, Claire, illus. LC 87-25805. 32p. (Orig.). (ps-3). 1988. pap. 2.95 (ISBN 0-14-050809-0, Puffin). Puffin Bks.

—Dr. Cat. Mandel, Suzy, illus. LC 88-62152. 32p. (ps-3). 1989. pap. 3.50 (ISBN 0-14-050985-2, Puffin). Puffin Bks.

—Where's the Cat? Lobel, Arnold, illus. LC 86-45953. 14p. (ps). 1987. 3.50 (ISBN 0-694-00185-6). HarpC Child Bks.

Zirkel, Lynn. Cats Are. Bowman, Peter, illus. 32p. 1990. 8.95 (ISBN 0-8249-8438-2). Ideals.

Zistel, Era. A Cat Called Christopher: The Story of a Cat. Donahue, Judee C., illus. 84p. (Orig.). (gr. 4 up). 1991. pap. 9.95 (ISBN 0-9617426-7-4). J N Townsend.

—Wintertime Cat. rev. ed. Zistel, Era, illus. 64p. 1988. pap. 5.95 (ISBN 0-9617426-4-X). J N Townsend.

CATS–PICTURES, ILLUSTRATIONS, ETC.

Beisner, Monika. Catch That Cat! A Picture Book of Rhymes & Puzzles. (Illus.). 32p. 1990. 13.95 (ISBN 0-374-31226-5). FS&G.

Cole, Joanna. A Cat's Body. Wexler, Jerome, illus. LC 81-22386. 48p. (gr. k-3). 1982. lib. bdg. 12.88 (ISBN 0-688-01054-7, Morrow Jr Bks). Morrow Jr Bks.

Cuddly Kittens & Precious Puppies. (Illus.). 32p. (gr. 1-8). 1989. 3.95 (ISBN 0-87406-549-6, 47-20338-9). Willowisp Pr.

Gorey, Edward, illus. Category. LC 86-10938. (ps up). 1986. Repr. 8.95 (ISBN 0-685-13444-X, Dist. by Watts). Adama Pubs Inc.

Imoto, Yoko, illus. The Picture Book of Cats. Dayton, Linnea & Weller-Watson, Karen, eds. (Illus.). 36p. (ps up). 1985. 7.95 (ISBN 0-915391-14-7, Pub. by Mad Hatter Bks). Slawson Comm.

Isaak, Betty. Classifying Cat. Armstrong, Bev, illus. 24p. (ps). 1982. wkbk. 2.95 (ISBN 0-88160-087-3, LW 123). Learning Wks.

Kittens. (Illus.). (ps-2). pap. write for info. (ISBN 0-528-87110-2). Checkerboard Pr.

Kittens. (Illus.). 1990. 4.98 (ISBN 0-8317-6852-5). Smithmark.

Spizzirri Publishing Co. Staff & Spizzirri, Linda. Cats: An Educational Coloring Book. (Illus.). 32p. (gr. k-5). 1985. pap. 1.95 (ISBN 0-86545-069-2). Spizzirri.

CATS–POETRY

Eliot, T. S. Mr. Mistoffelees with Mungojerrie & Rumpelteazer. Howton, Louise, ed. Le Cain, Errol, illus. 32p. 1991. 13.95 (ISBN 0-15-256230-3). HarBraceJ.

Farjeon, Eleanor. Cats. Lewis, T., illus. 16p. 1989. 3.95 (ISBN 0-8092-4354-7, Calico Bks). Contemp Bks.

—Cats Sleep Anywhere. Jenkins, Mary P., illus. LC 89-77611. 32p. (ps-1). 1990. 9.95 (ISBN 0-397-32463-4, Lipp Jr Bks); PLB 9.89 (ISBN 0-397-32464-2, Lipp Jr Bks). HarpC Child Bks.

Tamar, Erika. It Happened at Cecilia's. 144p. (gr. 7 up). 1991. pap. 3.95 (ISBN 0-02-045395-7, Collier Young Ad). Macmillan Child Grp.

Wheeler, Benson. I, Becky Barrymore. Barrymore, Lionel, illus. (gr. 3 up). 8.95 (ISBN 0-8315-0036-0). Speller.

CATS–TRAINING

Fritzsche, Helga. Cats. (Illus.). 80p. (gr. k-12). 1982. pap. 4.95 (ISBN 0-8120-2421-4). Barron.

CATTLE

see also Cows; Dairying; Livestock; Veterinary Medicine

Chorlian, Ruth W. Long Trail of the Texas Longhorns. 80p. (gr. 4-7). 1986. 7.95 (ISBN 0-89015-540-2, Pub. by Panda Bks). Eakin Pr.

Kaizuki, Kiyonori. A Calf Is Born. Hirano, Cathy, tr. Kaizuki, Kiyonori, illus. LC 89-23091. (JPN.). 40p. (ps-2). 1990. 13.95 (ISBN 0-531-05862-X); PLB 13.99 (ISBN 0-531-08462-0). Orchard Bks Watts.

CATTLE–FICTION

Hancock, Sibyl. Old Blue. Ingraham, Erick, illus. 48p. (gr. 1-4). 1980. PLB 6.99 (ISBN 0-399-61141-X, Putnam). Putnam Pub Group.

CAVE DWELLERS

Al-Islam, Da'i. The Companions of the Cave. 23p. (gr. 1-5). 1985. pap. 3.95 (ISBN 0-940368-55-2). Tahrike Tarsile Quran.

CAVE DWELLERS–FICTION

Carey, Mary V. The Mystery of the Wandering Cave Man. LC 82-3667. (Illus.). 192p. (gr. 4-7). 1982. PLB 7.99 (ISBN 0-394-95278-2). Random.

Little Treasury of the Flintstones, 6 Vol. Boxed Set. 1989. 5.99 (ISBN 0-517-65855-0, Chatham River Pr). Outlet Bk Co.

Turner, Ann. Time of the Bison. Peck, Beth, illus. LC 86-23476. 64p. (gr. 2-6). 1987. 12.95 (ISBN 0-02-789300-6, Mcmillan Child Bk). Macmillan Child Grp.

CAVES

Bender, Lionel. Cave. (Illus.). 32p. (gr. k-6). 1989. PLB 11.90 (ISBN 0-531-10819-8). Watts.

Booth, Eugene. Under the Ground. LC 77-8037. (Illus.). (gr. k-3). 1977. PLB 13.32 (ISBN 0-8393-0110-3). Raintree Pubs.

Brandt, Keith. Caves. Schneider, Rex, illus. LC 84-2573. 32p. (gr. 3-6). 1985. PLB 9.49 (ISBN 0-8167-0142-3); pap. text ed. 2.95 (ISBN 0-8167-0143-1). Troll Assocs.

Gans, Roma. Caves. Maestro, Giulio, illus. LC 76-4881. 40p. (gr. k-3). 1962. PLB 13.89 (ISBN 0-690-01070-2, Crowell Jr Bks). HarpC Child Bks.

Greenberg, Judith E. & Carey, Helen H. Caves. Miyake, Yoshi, illus. 32p. (gr. 2-4). 1990. PLB 16.67 (ISBN 0-8172-3750-X). Raintree Pubs.

Henken, Heidi. Cobb's Cave. Kratoville, Betty L., ed. Lucey, Jack, illus. 64p. (gr. 3-9). 1989. lib. bdg. 4.95 (ISBN 0-87879-655-X, High Noon Books). Acad Therapy.

Langley, Andrew. Under the Ground. LC 85-71730. (Illus.). 32p. (gr. k-6). 1986. PLB 8.99 (ISBN 0-531-18049-2, Pub. by Bookwright Pr). Watts.

Naden, C. J. I Can Read About Caves. new ed. LC 78-66271. (Illus.). (gr. 2-5). 1979. pap. 1.95 (ISBN 0-89375-205-3). Troll Assocs.

Roberts, Allan. Underground Life. LC 82-23582. (Illus.). 48p. (gr. k-4). 1983. PLB 14.60 (ISBN 0-516-01689-X). Childrens.
Wood, Jenny. Caves: An Underground Wonderland. LC 90-55463. (Illus.). 32p. (gr. 3-4). 1990. PLB 11.95 (ISBN 0-8368-0469-4). Gareth Stevens Inc.

CAVES–FICTION

Chew, Ruth. Magic Cave. Chew, Ruth, illus. LC 79-12972. (gr. 2-6). 1978. pap. 8.95 (ISBN 0-8038-4711-4). Hastings.
Misla, Victor M. The Treasure of Camuy's Cave. Misla, Victor M., illus. 30p. (Orig.). (gr. 6-7). 1987. pap. 5.00 (ISBN 0-9626870-1-4). NW Monarch Pr.
Seymour, Peter. What's at the Beach? Carter, David, illus. LC 84-81819. 18p. (ps-k). 1985. 7.95 (ISBN 0-03-002557-5). H Holt & Co.
Steiner, Barbara. Ghost Cave. 1990. 13.95 (ISBN 0-15-230752-4). HarbraceJ.
Zuniega, Thelma M. The Haunted Cave. (Illus.). (ps-3). 1972. 3.00 (ISBN 0-686-09535-9). Cellar.

CELLS

see also D N A; Embryology

Bender, Lionel. Atoms & Cells. (ps-3). 1990. PLB 11.90 (ISBN 0-531-17219-8). Watts.
Fichter, George S. Cells. Green, Anne C., illus. LC 86-5667. 72p. (gr. 4-8). 1986. PLB 10.40 (ISBN 0-531-10210-6). Watts.
LeMaster, Leslie J. Cells & Tissues. LC 85-6695. (Illus.). 45p. (gr. k-3). 1985. PLB 14.60 (ISBN 0-516-01266-5). Childrens.
Miller, Kenneth. Energy & Life. Head, J. J., ed. Steffen, Ann T., illus. LC 86-72192. 16p. (Orig.). (gr. 10 up). 1988. pap. text ed. 2.15 (ISBN 0-89278-168-8, 45-9768). Carolina Biological.
Moner, John G. The Animal Cell. Head, J. J., ed. Steffen, Ann T., illus. LC 83-70597. 32p. (gr. 10 up). 1987. pap. text ed. 2.70 (ISBN 0-89278-347-8, 45-9747). Carolina Biological.
Young, John K. Cells: Amazing Forms & Functions. (Illus.). 128p. (gr. 9-12). 1990. PLB 12.40 (ISBN 0-531-10880-5). Watts.

CEMETERIES

Stein, R. Conrad. The Story of Arlington National Cemetery. Wahl, Richard, illus. LC 79-14350. 32p. (gr. 3-6). 1979. PLB 13.27 (ISBN 0-516-04610-1). Childrens.

CEMETERIES–FICTION

Rodowsky, Colby. The Gathering Room. LC 81-5360. 186p. (gr. 5 up). 1981. 11.95 (ISBN 0-374-32520-0); pap. 3.45 (ISBN 0-374-42520-5). FS&G.

CENTRAL AFRICA

see Africa, Central

CENTRAL AMERICA

Brandt, Keith. Mexico & Central America. Eitzen, Allan, illus. LC 84-2668. 32p. (gr. 3-6). 1985. PLB 9.49 (ISBN 0-8167-0264-0); pap. text ed. 2.95 (ISBN 0-8167-0265-9). Troll Assocs.
Cheney, Glenn Alan. Revolution in Central America. (Illus.). 96p. (gr. 7up). lib. bdg. 12.90 (ISBN 0-531-04761-X). Watts.
Griffiths, J. Crisis in Central America. (Illus.). 80p. (gr. 7 up). Date not set. PLB 17.26 (ISBN 0-86592-034-6). Rourke Corp.
Jacobsen, Peter & Kristensen, Preben. A Family in Central America. LC 85-73585. (Illus.). 32p. (gr. 1-6). 1986. PLB 11.90 (ISBN 0-531-18081-6, Pub. by Bookwright). Watts.
Lye, Keith. Take a Trip to Central America. LC 85-50162. (Illus.). 32p. (gr. 1-6). 1985. PLB 7.99 (ISBN 0-531-10010-3). Watts.
Marklin, Patricia M. Central America & Panama. rev. ed. (Illus.). 96p. (gr. 4 up). 1983. PLB 10.40 (ISBN 0-531-04523-4). Watts.
Morrison, Marion. Central America. (Illus.). 48p. (gr. 4-8). 1989. lib. bdg. 14.98 (ISBN 0-382-09824-2). Silver Burdett Pr.
Wekesser, Carol, et al, eds. Central America: Opposing Viewpoints. rev' ed. LC 90-13922. (Illus.). 240p. (gr. 10 up). 1990. PLB 15.95 (ISBN 0-89908-484-2); pap. text ed. 8.95 (ISBN 0-89908-459-1). Greenhaven.

CENTRAL STATES

see Middle West

CEREBRAL PALSY

Aaseng, Nathan. Cerebral Palsy. (Illus.). 112p. (gr. 9-12). 1991. PLB 12.40 (ISBN 0-531-12529-7). Watts.
Bergman, Thomas. Going Places: Children Living with Cerebral Palsy. Bergman, Thomas, illus. LC 90-48266. 48p. (gr. 4-5). 1991. PLB 10.95 (ISBN 0-8368-0199-7). Gareth Stevens Inc.

CEREMONIES

see Etiquette; Manners and Customs; Rites and Ceremonies

CERTAINTY

see Belief and Doubt

CERVANTES SAAVEDRA, MIGUEL DE, 1547-1616

Busoni, Rafaello. The Man Who Was Don Quixote. (Illus.). 224p. (gr. 5 up). 1982. 9.95 (ISBN 0-13-548107-4, Pub. by Treehouse). P-H.
Milton, Joyce. Don Quixote (Miguel de Cervantes) (gr. 9-12). 1985. pap. 2.50 (ISBN 0-8120-3512-7). Barron.

CEYLON

Caldwell, John C. Sri Lanka. (Illus.). (gr. 5 up). 1988. 14.95 (ISBN 0-222-01017-7). Chelsea Hse.
Lerner Publications, Department of Geography Staff, ed. Sri Lanka in Pictures. (Illus.). 64p. (gr. 5 up). 1988. 12.95 (ISBN 0-8225-1853-8). Lerner Pubns.

CEYLON–FICTION

Williams, Harry. Twins of Ceylon. Paton, Jane, illus. LC 65-12044. (gr. 6-9). 1965. 11.95 (ISBN 0-8023-1108-3). Dufour.

CHAGALL, MARC, 1899-

Greenfeld, Howard. Marc Chagall. (Illus.). 80p. (gr. 7 up). 1990. 18.95 (ISBN 0-8109-3152-4). Abrams.

CHAIRS–FICTION

Browne, Frances. Granny's Wonderful Chair. (gr. 4-6). 1985. pap. 2.25 (ISBN 0-14-035036-5, Puffin). Puffin Bks.
Tennyson, Noel. The Lady's Chair & the Ottoman. Tennyson, Noel, illus. LC 84-11196. 32p. (gr. k-3). 1987. PLB 12.88 (ISBN 0-688-04098-5). Lothrop.
Williams, Vera B. A Chair for My Mother. Williams, Vera B., illus. LC 81-7010. 32p. (gr. k-3). 1982. 13.95 (ISBN 0-688-00914-X); PLB 12.88 (ISBN 0-688-00915-8). Greenwillow.

CHAMELEONS

Schnieper, Claudia. Chameleons. Meier, Max, photos by. (Illus.). 48p. (gr. 2-5). 1989. 12.95 (ISBN 0-87614-341-9); pap. 6.95 (ISBN 0-87614-520-9). Carolrhoda Bks.
Walton, Marilyn J. Chameleon's Rainbow. Salzman, Yuri, illus. LC 84-17760. 32p. (gr. 3-6). 1985. PLB 14.65 (ISBN 0-940742-45-4); incl cassette 27.99 (ISBN 0-8172-2285-5). Raintree Pubs.

CHAMPLAIN, SAMUEL DE, 1567-1635

Zadra, Dan. Explorers of America: Champlain. rev. ed. (gr. 2-4). 1988. PLB 11.50s.p. (ISBN 0-88682-181-9); 16.45 (ISBN 0-318-32948-4). Creative Ed.

CHANGE, SOCIAL

see Social Change

CHAPLIN, CHARLES SPENCER, 1889-

Brown, Pam. Charlie Chaplin: Comic Genius Who Brought Laughter & Hope to Millions. LC 88-27568. (Illus.). 64p. (gr. 5-6). 1991. PLB 12.95 (ISBN 1-55532-838-5). Gareth Stevens Inc.

CHAPMAN, JOHN, 1774-1845

Aliki. Story of Johnny Appleseed. Aliki, illus. (ps-2). 1987. 11.95 (ISBN 0-13-850800-3). P-H.
Johnson, Ann D. The Value of Love: The Story of Johnny Appleseed. Pileggi, Stephen, illus. LC 79-31873. (gr. k-6). 1979. 9.95 (ISBN 0-916392-35-X, Pub. by Value Communications). Oak Tree Pubns.
Le Sueur, Meridel. Little Brother of the Wilderness: The Story of Johnny Appleseed. LC 87-80574. (Illus.). 68p. (gr. 5 up). 1987. Repr. of 1947 ed. 9.95 (ISBN 0-930100-21-2). Holy Cow.
Sabin, Louis. Johnny Appleseed. Smolinski, Dick, illus. LC 84-2732. 32p. (gr. 3-6). 1985. PLB 9.49 (ISBN 0-8167-0220-9); pap. text ed. 2.95 (ISBN 0-8167-0221-7). Troll Assocs.

CHAPMAN, JOHN, 1774-1845–FICTION

Moore, Eva. Johnny Appleseed. (Orig.). (gr. 2-3). pap. 2.50 (ISBN 0-590-40297-8). Scholastic Inc.

CHARACTER EDUCATION

American Institute for Character Education Staff. Character Education Curriculum: The Happy Life Series plus Living with Me & Others Including Our Rights & Responsibilities, Levels A-F. (Illus.). (gr. 1-7). 1984. Set. 820.00 (ISBN 0-685-09646-7); tchr's. ed. 95.00 ea. Level A, 124p (ISBN 0-913413-01-1). Level B, 127p (ISBN 0-913413-02-X). Level C, 148p (ISBN 0-913413-03-8). Level D, 152p (ISBN 0-913413-04-6). Level E, 160p (ISBN 0-913413-05-4). Level F, 6th gr. 95.00 (ISBN 0-685-09647-5); Level G, Middle School#Level K, Kindergarten with film strips. 125.00 (ISBN 0-685-09648-3). Char Ed Inst.

Johnson, Spencer & Johnson, Donegan. The ValueTale Series, 35 bks. Pileggi, Steve, illus. (ps-5). 1976. 9.95 ea. (ISBN 0-916392-24-4). Oak Tree Pubns.
Through the true stories of real people, ValueTales introduces children between the ages of 3 & 10 to the importance of values like honesty, caring, courage, fairness, love & many others. To date, there are a total of 34 values in 34 volumes. Although the intention of the books is serious, the stories themselves are written to entertain children while telling stories from history, to provide healthy role models, to impart the importance of value systems, & to promote interaction between parents & children. ValueTales provides stories of men & women whose extraordinary accomplishments reflected a strong set of personal principles or values. Each story includes a character designed to be appealing to children, who may be an animal or inanimate object & who provides advice & guidance to the central figure. Among the stories related by the ValueTales are: Louis Pasteur's successful quest to discover the cure for Rabies, despite much ridicule (The Value of Believing in Yourself); Eleanor Roosevelt's compassion for the underprivileged (The Value of Caring); Apache Chief Cochise whose honesty & good faith helped restore faith between the American Indians & white settlers (The Value of Truth & Trust).
Publisher Provided Annotation.

Kylie's Song. (gr. 1-4). 1989. video 59.95 (ISBN 0-925159-87-5, 9351). Marshfilm.
Mendoza, George. Hunter I Might Have Been. (Illus.). (gr. 3-5). 1968. 10.95 (ISBN 0-8392-3064-8). Astor-Honor.
Mitchell, Joyce S. Free to Choose: Decision Making for Young Men. LC 76-5589. (gr. 7 up). 1976. 8.95 (ISBN 0-440-02723-3). Delacorte.
Plum, Joan. I Am Special Fun Book. 32p. (Orig.). (ps-2). 1989. pap. 2.95 (ISBN 0-685-26964-7, 55). Our Sunday Visitor.
Rudner, Barry. The Handstand. Fahsbender, Thomas, illus. 32p. 1991. pap. 4.95 (ISBN 0-925928-05-4). Tiny Thought.
—Will I Still Have to Make My Bed In The Morning? (Illus.). 32p. 1991. pap. 4.95 (ISBN 0-925928-10-0). Tiny Thought.
Teller, Hanoch. Above the Bottom Line: Stories & Advice on Integrity. 416p. (gr. 8 up). 1988. write for info. (ISBN 0-9614772-5-3). NYC Pub Co.

CHARACTER EDUCATION–FICTION

Bobo, Carmen P. Sarah's Growing-up Summer. LC 88-62111. 52p. 1989. 5.95 (ISBN 1-55523-187-X). Winston-Derek.
Cosgrove, Stephen. The Grumpling. (Illus.). 32p. (Orig.). (gr. k-4). 1989. pap. 2.95 (ISBN 0-8431-2739-2). Price Stern.
—Poppyseed. (Illus.). 32p. (Orig.). (gr. k-4). 1989. pap. 2.95 (ISBN 0-8431-2738-4). Price Stern.
—Tickle's Tail. (Illus.). 32p. (Orig.). (gr. k-4). 1989. pap. 2.95 (ISBN 0-8431-2736-8). Price Stern.
—Zippity Zoom. (Illus.). 32p. (Orig.). (gr. k-4). 1989. pap. 2.95 (ISBN 0-8431-2737-6). Price Stern.
Gire, Ken. The Booklets' Baking Boo-Boo: A Story about Obeying. Dickenson, John, et al, illus. 32p. 1987. 5.99 (ISBN 0-929608-03-8). Focus Family.
—Limburger's Little White Lie: A Story about Telling the Truth. Dickenson, John, et al, illus. 32p. 1987. 5.99 (ISBN 0-929608-04-6). Focus Family.
—Melody's Kooky Cover-up: A Story about Building Self-Worth. Dickenson, John, et al, illus. 32p. 1987. 5.99 (ISBN 0-929608-02-X). Focus Family.
—Spotlight on Charity: A Story about Overcoming Selfishness. Dickenson, John, et al, illus. 32p. 1988. 5.99 (ISBN 0-929608-10-0). Focus Family.
Groomer, Vera. Good Friends Again: Two - Three. 32p. (ps). 1980. pap. 2.15 (ISBN 0-8127-0272-7). Review & Herald.
Knudson, R. R. You Are the Rain. LC 73-15397. 160p. (gr. 7 up). 1974. pap. 5.95 (ISBN 0-440-08759-7). Delacorte.
Kotrba, Danella G. God's Helper. 32p. (ps). 1980. pap. 2.15 (ISBN 0-8127-0211-5). Review & Herald.
Parkison, Ralph F. The Little Girl & the Inchworm. Withrow, Marion O., ed. Bush, William, illus. 75p. (Orig.). (gr. 2-8). 1988. pap. write for info. Little Wood Bks.
—Santa's Wheat Kernels. Withrow, Marion O., ed. Bush, William, illus. 60p. (Orig.). (gr. 2-8). 1988. pap. write for info. Little Wood Bks.
Rudner, Barry. Nonsense. Fahsbender, Thomas, illus. (gr. k-6). 1990. write for info. (ISBN 0-925928-04-6). Tiny Thought.

CHARACTERS AND CHARACTERISTICS IN LITERATURE

see also Blacks in Literature and Art

CHARLEMAGNE, 742-814–FICTION

Westwood, Jennifer. Stories of Charlemagne. LC 74-12435. (gr. 6 up). 1976. 18.95 (ISBN 0-87599-213-7). S G Phillips.

CHARMS–POETRY

Roy, Cal. What Every Young Wizard Should Know. Roy, Cal, illus. (gr. 2 up). 1963. 8.95 (ISBN 0-8392-3043-5). Astor-Honor.

CHARTOGRAPHY

see Map Drawing; Maps

CHASE, THE

see Hunting

CHATEAUX

see Castles

CHAUCER, GEOFFREY, 1340?-1400

Oetting. The Chieftain of Chaucer. LC 73-87806. (Illus.). 32p. (gr. 2-5). 1974. PLB 9.95 (ISBN 0-87783-137-8); pap. 3.94 deluxe ed. (ISBN 0-87783-138-6). Oddo.

CHAVEZ, CESAR ESTRADA

Cesar Chavez: Mini Play. (gr. 5 up). 1978. 5.00 (ISBN 0-89550-305-0). Stevens & Shea.
Conord, Bruce. Cesar Chavez. (Illus.). (gr. 3-5). 1992. PLB 12.95 (ISBN 0-7910-1757-5). Chelsea Hse.
Franchere, Ruth. Cesar Chavez. Thollander, Earl, illus. LC 85-42999. 48p. (gr. 2-5). 1986. pap. 4.95 (ISBN 0-06-446023-1, Trophy). HarpC Child Bks.

—Cesar Chavez. LC 78-101927. (Illus.). 40p. (gr. 2-5). 1970. PLB 12.89 (ISBN 0-690-18384-4, Crowell Jr Bks). HarpC Child Bks.

Roberts, Maurice. Cesar Chavez & La Causa. LC 85-27980. (Illus.). 31p. (gr. 3-5). 1986. PLB 13.27 (ISBN 0-516-03484-7). Childrens.

CHEERS AND CHEERLEADING

Egbert, Barbara. Cheerleading & Songleading. LC 80-52322. (Illus.). 128p. (gr. 9 up). 1980. pap. 9.95 (ISBN 0-8069-8950-5). Sterling.

Finney, Shan. Cheerleading & Baton Twirling. (Illus.). 72p. (gr. 4-8). 1982. PLB 10.40 (ISBN 0-531-04391-6). Watts.

Haller, Lynda. Cheerleader U. S. A. - Tryouts to Triumph. 68p. (gr. 1-12). 1989. pap. 10.00 spiral bdg. (ISBN 0-317-93086-9). Cheertime USA.

—More Cheers & Chants. rev. ed. Whitman, Rick, photos by. (Illus.). 39p. (Orig.). (gr. 3-12). 1988. pap. text ed. 8.00 (ISBN 0-685-22930-0); cassette 6.00 (ISBN 0-9614174-5-5). Cheertime USA.

Hawkins, Jim W. Cheerleading Is for Me. Moral, Jean D., illus. LC 81-3719. (gr. 2-5). 1981. PLB 8.95 (ISBN 0-8225-1127-4, AACRZ). Lerner Pubns.

Phillips, Betty L. Go! Fight! Win! The NCA Guide for Cheerleaders. Herkimer, Lawrence R., illus. Shepherd, Francis, photos by. LC 79-53607. (Illus.). 160p. (gr. 7 up). 1981. PLB 11.80 (ISBN 0-440-02957-0); pap. 9.95 (ISBN 0-385-29336-4). Delacorte.

CHEETAHS

Arnold, Caroline. Cheetah. Hewett, Richard, photos by. LC 88-39940. (Illus.). 48p. (gr. 2 up). 1989. 12.95 (ISBN 0-688-08143-6); PLB 12.88 (ISBN 0-688-08144-4). Morrow.

Kappeler, Markus. Big Cats. (Illus.). 32p. (gr. 4-6). 1991. PLB 11.95 (ISBN 0-8368-0685-9). Gareth Stevens Inc.

Stone, L. Cheetahs. (Illus.). 24p. (gr. k-5). 1989. lib. bdg. 11.94 (ISBN 0-86592-503-8). Rourke Corp.

CHEMICAL ENGINEERING

see also Metallurgy

CHEMICAL INDUSTRIES

Here are entered works about industries based mainly on chemical processes. Works on the manufacture of chemicals as such are entered under Chemicals.

see also names of industries, e.g. Paper Making and Trade; etc.

CHEMICALS

Jennings, Terry. Everyday Chemicals. LC 88-22888. (Illus.). 32p. (gr. 3-6). 1989. PLB 14.60 (ISBN 0-516-08401-1); pap. 4.95 (ISBN 0-516-48401-X). Childrens.

Landau, Elaine. Chemical & Biological Warfare. 128p. (gr. 5-9). 1991. 14.95 (ISBN 0-525-67364-4, Lodestar Bks). Dutton Child Bks.

CHEMISTRY

see also Color; Explosives; Fire; Pharmacy; Poisons

also headings beginning with the word Chemical

Ardley, Neil. Simple Chemistry. Marffy, Janos, illus. LC 83-51444. 32p. (gr. 4-6). 1985. PLB 11.90 (ISBN 0-531-03778-9). Watts.

Barber, Jacqueline. Chemical Reactions. Bergman, Lincoln & Fairwell, Kay, eds. Baker, Lisa H. & Craig, Rose, illus. Barber, Jacqueline, et al, photos by. 24p. (Orig.). (gr. 7-10). 1986. pap. 6.50 (ISBN 0-912511-13-3). Lawrence Science.

Bronstein, Leona B. & McGrain, Eleanore. Chemistry Flipper. 49p. (gr. 7 up). 1989. Repr. of 1978 ed. trade edition 5.95 (ISBN 1-878383-06-X). C Lee Pubns.

Challand, Helen J. Experiments with Chemistry. LC 88-11862. (Illus.). 48p. (gr. k-4). 1988. PLB 17.27 (ISBN 0-516-01151-0); pap. 4.95 (ISBN 0-516-41151-9). Childrens.

Chemistry. (Illus.). 48p. (gr. 6-12). 1973. pap. 1.85 (ISBN 0-8395-3367-5, 3367). BSA.

Chishom, J. & Lynnington, M. Introduction to Chemistry. Ashman, Iain, illus. 48p. (gr. 6 up). 1983. lib. bdg. 13.96 (ISBN 0-88110-151-6); pap. 6.95 (ISBN 0-86020-709-9). EDC.

Cobb, Vicki. Chemically Active! Experiments You Can Do at Home. Cobb, Theo, illus. LC 83-49490. 160p. (gr. 5-8). 1985. 12.95 (ISBN 0-397-32079-5, Lipp Jr Bks); PLB 12.89 (ISBN 0-397-32080-9, Lipp Jr Bks). HarpC Child Bks.

Conway, Lorraine. Chemistry Concepts. Akins, Linda, illus. 64p. (gr. 5 up). 1983. wkbk. 6.95 (ISBN 0-86653-100-9, GA 460). Good Apple.

Corrick, James A. Recent Revolutions in Chemistry. LC 86-5675. (Illus.). 128p. (gr. 7-12). 1986. PLB 12.90 (ISBN 0-531-10241-6). Watts.

Cunningham, A. Essential Chemistry. (Illus.). 64p. 1992. lib. bdg. 12.96 (ISBN 0-88110-508-2, Usborne); pap. 5.95 (ISBN 0-7460-0727-2). EDC.

Freeman, Mae B. & Freeman, Ira M. The Story of Chemistry. (gr. 3-6). 1962. lib. bdg. 5.99 (ISBN 0-394-90126-6, Random Juv). Random.

Granddad's Wonderful Book of Chemistry. (Illus.). 413p. (gr. 9-12). 1988. lab. manual 17.00 (ISBN 0-318-41069-9). Atlan Formularies.

Hoyt, Marie A. Workbook Game Sheets for Kitchen Chemistry & Front Porch Physics. Green, Victor D. & Loor, Robin, illus. 44p. (Orig.). (gr. 3-8). 1983. pap. text ed. 4.00 (ISBN 0-914911-02-3). Educ Serv Pr.

Kranepool, Harry A. New Investigations in Modern Chemistry. Plass, Richard M., ed. (Illus.). 1989. lab manual & wkbk., 270p. 9.95 (ISBN 0-685-29318-1); 5.95 ea. Lab manual, 116p. Lab reports, 154p. Amer Scholastic.

Mebane, Robert C. & Rybolt, Thomas R. Adventures with Atoms & Molecules: Chemistry Experiments for Young People. Perkins, Ronald I., intro. by. LC 85-10177. (Illus.). 96p. (gr. 4-9). 1985. PLB 16.95 (ISBN 0-89490-120-6). Enslow Pubs.

Rapp, George F. & Erickson, Laura L. Earth's Chemical Clues: The Story of Geochemistry. LC 89-7914. (Illus.). 64p. 1990. lib. bdg. 15.95 (ISBN 0-89490-153-2). Enslow Pubs.

Russo, Tom. MicroChemistry: For High School Chemistry. rev. ed. Stone, Harry, ed. (Illus.). 90p. (gr. 9-12). Date not set. lab manual 15.80 (ISBN 1-877960-05-5, 4-400). Kemtec Educ.

Simple Chemistry. (Illus.). (gr. 3-5). 3.50 (ISBN 0-7214-0660-2). Ladybird Bks.

Walters, Derek. Chemistry. Bishop, Denis, illus. LC 82-50858. 40p. (gr. 4 up). 1983. PLB 11.90 (ISBN 0-531-04581-1). Watts.

Wertheim, J. & Oxlade, C. Dictionary of Chemistry: All the Facts You Need to Know - At a Glance. (Illus.). 128p. (gr. 6 up). 1987. PLB 15.96 (ISBN 0-88110-230-X); pap. 9.95 (ISBN 0-86020-821-4). EDC.

Whyman, Kathryn. Chemical Changes. (Illus.). 32p. (gr. 1-6). 1986. PLB 8.99 (ISBN 0-531-17032-2, Pub. by Gloucester). Watts.

CHEMISTRY–EXPERIMENTS

Challand, Helen J. Activities in the Physical Sciences. LC 83-26224. (Illus.). 96p. (gr. 5 up). 1984. lib. bdg. 17.27 (ISBN 0-516-00504-9). Childrens.

Cobb, Vicki. Chemically Active: Experiments You Can Do at Home. Cobb, Theo, illus. LC 83-49490. 160p. (gr. 6 up). 1990. pap. 4.95 (ISBN 0-06-446101-7, Trophy). HarpC Child Bks.

Gardner, Robert. Famous Experiments You Can Do. (Illus.). 144p. (gr. 9-12). 1990. PLB 12.90 (ISBN 0-531-10883-X). Watts.

—Kitchen Chemistry: Science Experiments to Do at Home. Steltenpohl, Jane, ed. (Illus.). 136p. (gr. 4-8). 1989. PLB 11.98 (ISBN 0-671-67776-4); PLB 8.99s.p.; pap. 4.95 (ISBN 0-671-67576-1); pap. 3.71s.p. Messner.

Granddad's Wonderful Book of Chemistry. (Illus.). 413p. (gr. 9-12). 1988. lab. manual 17.00 (ISBN 0-318-41069-9). Atlan Formularies.

Hoyt, Marie A. Kitchen Chemistry & Front Porch Physics. Finkler, C. Etana, illus. 60p. (Orig.). (gr. 3-8). 1983. pap. 5.00 (ISBN 0-914911-00-7). Educ Serv Pr.

KITCHEN CHEMISTRY & FRONT PORCH PHYSICS for children ages 7-14 has instructions on how to make a SHOEBOX CHEMISTRY SET to be used in performing the 32 science experiments which demystify physics & chemistry. Its use of common materials & everyday household chemicals make the teaching of science fun, safe & in-depth. The simple understandable reading level enables students to discover science concepts by "Hands On" experience. Additionally, the glossary teacher-parent guide along with the Future Scientists of America awards make this book a science treasure to teachers, children, science group leaders & parents of both mainstream & minorities alike. ***Publisher Provided Annotation.***

Johnson, May. Chemistry Experiments. King, Colin, illus. 64p. (gr. 3-6). 1983. lib. bdg. 11.96 (ISBN 0-88110-161-3); pap. 4.95 (ISBN 0-86020-527-4). EDC.

Kramer, Alan. How to Make a Chemical Volcano. 1989. 11.95 (ISBN 0-531-15120-4); PLB 11.90 (ISBN 0-531-10771-X). Watts.

Mullin, Virginia L. Chemistry Experiments for Children. Case, Bernard, illus. LC 68-9306. (gr. 3-10). 1968. pap. 2.95 (ISBN 0-486-22031-1). Dover.

Newton, David E. Consumer Chemistry Projects for Young Scientists. (Illus.). 128p. (gr. 9-12). 1991. PLB 12.90 (ISBN 0-531-11011-7). Watts.

Palder, Edward. Chemistry Magic. Mohrmann, gary, illus. 153p. (gr. 5 up). 1987. pap. 12.95 (ISBN 0-933149-25-5). Woodbine House.

Science in Action, 6 vols. LC 87-36819. 288p. (gr. 5 up). 1988. PLB 89.95 (ISBN 0-86307-020-5). Marshall Cavendish.

Vancleave, Janice P. Chemistry for Every Kid: One Hundred One Easy Experiments that Really Work. 1989. pap. text ed. 10.95 (ISBN 0-471-62085-8). Wiley.

Wood, Robert W. Thirty-Nine Easy Chemistry Experiments. (Illus.). 160p. 1991. 16.95 (ISBN 0-8306-7596-5, 3596); pap. 9.95 (ISBN 0-8306-3596-3). TAB Bks.

Wyler, Rose. Science Fun with a Homemade Chemistry Set. Stewart, Pat, illus. LC 86-21868. 48p. (gr. 2-4). 1987. PLB 11.38 (ISBN 0-671-55575-8); PLB 8.54s.p.; pap. 4.95 (ISBN 0-671-55570-7); pap. 3.71s.p. Messner.

Zubrowski, Bernie. Messing Around with Baking Chemistry: A Children's Museum Activity Book. Hanson, Signe, illus. 64p. (gr. 3-7). 1981. pap. 6.95 (ISBN 0-316-98879-0). Little.

CHEMISTRY, INORGANIC

see also Metals

CHEMISTRY, MEDICAL AND PHARMACEUTICAL

see also Drugs; Pharmacy; Poisons

CHEMISTRY, ORGANIC–SYNTHESIS

see also Plastics

CHEMISTRY, PHYSICAL AND THEORETICAL

see also Atoms; Crystallography; Molecules; Nuclear Physics; Thermodynamics

Rowe, Frederick J. AP Exam in Chemistry. 2nd ed. 208p. (gr. 9-12). 1990. pap. 12.95 (ISBN 0-13-010448-5). Arco.

CHEMISTRY, TECHNICAL

see also Canning and Preserving; Chemicals; Waste Products

also names of specific industries and products, e.g. Clay Industries

CHEMISTS

Grey, Vivian. The Chemist Who Lost His Head: The Story of Antoine Lavoisier. (Illus.). 112p. 1982. 9.95 (ISBN 0-698-20559-6, Coward). Putnam Pub Group.

CHESS

Caldwell, S. Playing Chess. (Illus.). 64p. (gr. 5 up). 1987. PLB 12.96 (ISBN 0-88110-288-1); pap. 6.95 (ISBN 0-7460-0135-5). EDC.

Carroll, David. Make Your Own Chess Set. Carroll, David, photos by. (Illus.). (gr. 5 up). 1975. (Pub. by Treehouse); pap. 2.95 (ISBN 0-13-547786-7). P-H.

James, Richard. Move One! A Chess Course for Beginners. (Illus.). 144p. (Orig.). (gr. 1-4). 1991. pap. 13.95 (ISBN 0-571-14063-7). Faber & Faber.

Keene, Raymond. The Simon & Schuster Pocket Book of Chess. (gr. 4 up). 1989. pap. 12.95 (ISBN 0-671-67923-6); pap. 7.95 (ISBN 0-671-67924-4). S&S Trade.

Lombardy, William & Marshall, Bette. Chess for Children Step by Step: A New, Easy Way to Learn the Game. (Illus.). 1977. 19.95i (ISBN 0-316-53091-3); pap. 18. 95i (ISBN 0-316-53090-5). Little.

Marsh, Carole. Go Queen Go! Chess for Kids. (Illus.). 48p. (gr. k-12). 1983. 19.95 (ISBN 1-55609-160-5); pap. 14.95 (ISBN 0-935326-14-6). Gallopade Pub Group.

Watts, L. & Varley, C. Advanced Chess. (Illus.). 32p. (gr. 5 up). 1991. lib. bdg. 12.96 (ISBN 0-88110-503-1, Usborne); pap. 6.95 (ISBN 0-7460-0617-9, Usborne). EDC.

CHESS–FICTION

Baggiani, J. M. & Tewell, V. M. The Chess Set & Other Stories. Birt, Jane L., illus. 21p. (gr. 2-3). 1966. pap. 3.50 (ISBN 0-934329-07-9). Baggiani-Tewell.

CHIANG, KAI-SHEK, 1896-

Daley, William. The Chinese Americans. Moynihan, Daniel P., intro. by. (Illus.). 112p. (gr. 5 up). 1988. lib. bdg. 17.95 (ISBN 0-87754-867-6). Chelsea Hse.

CHICAGO

Davis, James E. & Hawke, Sharryl D. Chicago. (Illus.). 64p. (gr. 4-9). 1990. PLB 18.00 (ISBN 0-8172-3025-4). Raintree Pubs.

Davis, Lauren. Kidding Around Chicago: A Young Person's Guide to the City. Blakemore, Sally, illus. 64p. (Orig.). (gr. 3 up). 1990. pap. 9.95 (ISBN 0-945465-70-X). John Muir.

Kurland, Gerald. Richard Daley: The Strong Willed Mayor of Chicago. Rahmas, D. Steve, ed. LC 70-190236. 32p. (Orig.). (gr. 7-12). lib. bdg. 4.20 incl. catalog cards (ISBN 0-87157-518-3); pap. 2.95 vinyl laminated covers (ISBN 0-87157-018-1). SamHar Pr.

Pfeiffer, Christine. Chicago. LC 88-20199. (Illus.). 60p. (gr. 3 up). 1988. PLB 12.95 (ISBN 0-87518-385-9, Dillon). Macmillan Child Grp.

Stewart, G. Chicago. (Illus.). 48p. (gr. 5 up). 1989. lib. bdg. 14.60 (ISBN 0-86592-538-0). Rourke Corp.

CHICAGO–FICTION

Herman, Charlotte. Summer on Thirteenth Street. 128p. (gr. 3-7). 1991. 12.95 (ISBN 0-525-44642-7, DCB). Dutton Child Bks.

Sinclair, Upton. The Jungle. (gr. 11 up). pap. 2.95 (ISBN 0-8049-0086-8, CL-86). Airmont.

Turck, Mary. Chicago, Illinois. LC 89-7724. (Illus.). 48p. (gr. 4-5). 1989. 12.95 (ISBN 0-89686-469-3, Crestwood Hse). Macmillan Child Grp.

CHICAGO–HISTORY

Roberts, Maurice. Harold Washington: Mayor with a Vision. LC 87-7247. (Illus.). 30p. (gr. 3-5). 1988. PLB 13.27 (ISBN 0-516-03657-2); pap. 3.95 (ISBN 0-516-43657-0). Childrens.

Simon, Charnan. The Story of the Haymarket Riot. LC 88-22803. (Illus.). 32p. (gr. 3-6). 1988. PLB 13.27 (ISBN 0-516-04740-X); pap. 3.95 (ISBN 0-516-44740-8). Childrens.

Stein, R. Conrad. The Story of the Chicago Fire. Wahl, Richard, illus. LC 81-15543. 32p. (gr. 3-6). 1982. PLB 13.27 (ISBN 0-516-04633-0); pap. 3.95 (ISBN 0-516-44633-9). Childrens.

Warburton, Lois. The Chicago Fire. LC 89-33554. (Illus.). 64p. (gr. 5-8). 1989. PLB 11.95 (ISBN 1-56006-002-6). Lucent Bks.

CHICHESTER, FRANCIS CHARLES, 1901-

Galdone, Paul. Little Red Hen. (ps-3). 1987. incl. cass. 6.95 (ISBN 0-317-64569-2). HM.

CHICKENS–FICTION

Addison-Wesley Staff. La Gallinita Roja Big Book. (SPA., Illus.). 16p. (gr. k-3). 1989. pap. text ed. 31.75 (ISBN 0-201-19936-X). Addison-Wesley.

—La Gallinita Roja, Spanish Little Book. (SPA., Illus.). 16p. (gr. k-3). 1989. pap. text ed. 4.50 (ISBN 0-201-19708-1). Addison-Wesley.

—The Little Red Hen Little Book. (Illus.). 16p. (gr. k-3). 1989. pap. 4.50 (ISBN 0-201-19364-7). Addison-Wesley.

Adshead, Paul. Chicken That Could Swim. (ps-3). 1990. pap. 5.95 (ISBN 0-85953-346-8). Childs Play.

Bond, Felicia. The Chicks' Christmas. LC 82-45918. (Illus.). 32p. (ps-3). 1983. 4.95 (ISBN 0-694-00156-2, Crowell Jr Bks); PLB 11.89 (ISBN 0-690-04333-3). HarpC Child Bks.

Bourgeois, Paulette. Too Many Chicken! (ps-3). 1991. 12.95 (ISBN 0-316-10358-6). Little.

Brambledown: Tiny Chick's Tail. 1990. 3.98 (ISBN 0-8317-0974-X). Smithmark.

Brown, Margaret W. Little Chicken. Weisgard, Leonard, illus. LC 43-16942. 32p. (ps-3). 1943. 12.95 (ISBN 0-06-020739-6); PLB 12.89 (ISBN 0-06-020740-X). HarpC Child Bks.

Burgess, Beverly C. Chicken Little. (Orig.). (gr. 1-3). 1987. 3.98 (ISBN 0-89274-414-6). Harrison Hse.

Byars, Betsy. Good-Bye, Chicken Little. LC 78-19829. 112p. (gr. 5 up). 1990. pap. 2.95 (ISBN 0-06-440291-6, Trophy). HarpC Child Bks.

Casey, Patricia. Cluck, Cluck. LC 87-30435. (Illus.). 32p. (ps-1). 1988. 12.95 (ISBN 0-688-07767-6). Lothrop.

Castoldi, Maggiorina. Chirpy the Chick. 30p. (ps-1). 1987. 3.95 (ISBN 0-8120-5819-4). Barron.

Chicken Licken. (ARA.). (gr. 2-4). 3.50x (ISBN 0-86685-192-5); incl. cassette 12.00x (ISBN 0-685-02568-3). Intl Bk Ctr.

Chicken Sunday. 1991. pap. 13.95 (ISBN 0-671-72750-8). S&S Trade.

Coerr, Eleanor. The Josefina Story Quilt. Degen, Bruce, illus. LC 85-45260. 64p. (gr. k-3). 1986. 11.95 (ISBN 0-06-021348-5); PLB 11.89 (ISBN 0-06-021349-3). HarpC Child Bks.

Cole, Joanna. A Chick Hatches. LC 76-29017. (Illus.). 48p. (gr. k-3). 1976. PLB 13.88 (ISBN 0-688-32087-2). Morrow.

Czernecki, Stefan & Rhodes, Timothy. Nina's Treasures. LC 90-36592. (Illus.). 56p. (gr. 1-6). 1990. pap. 14.95 (ISBN 0-920534-65-1). Sterling.

Dabcovich, Lydia. Mrs. Huggins & Her Hen Hannah. Dabcovich, Lydia, illus. LC 85-4406. 24p. (ps-2). 1988. 12.95 (ISBN 0-525-44203-0, DCB); pap. 3.95 (ISBN 0-525-44368-1, DCB). Dutton Child Bks.

Davis, Jim. U. S. Acres Counts Its Chickens. (Illus.). 128p. (ps up). 1987. pap. 5.95 (ISBN 0-88687-314-2). Pharos Bks NY.

Delaney, Ned. Cosmic Chickens. Delaney, Ned, illus. LC 86-19398. 48p. (ps-3). 1988. 12.95i (ISBN 0-06-021583-6); PLB 12.89 (ISBN 0-06-021584-4). HarpC Child Bks.

Ehrlich, Amy. Buck-Buck the Chicken. Alley, R. W., illus. LC 86-31639. 48p. (gr. 1-3). 1987. lib. bdg. 6.99 (ISBN 0-394-98804-3, Random Juv); pap. 2.95 (ISBN 0-394-88804-9, Random Juv). Random.

Ginsburg, Mirra. The Chick & the Duckling. Suteyev, V., tr. Aruego, Jose & Dewey, Ariane, illus. LC 74-188773. 32p. (ps-1). 1972. 14.95 (ISBN 0-02-735940-9, Mcmillan Child Bk). Macmillan Child Grp.

—Good Morning, Chick. Barton, Byron, illus. LC 80-11352. 32p. (ps). 1980. PLB 12.88 (ISBN 0-688-84284-4). Greenwillow.

Hader, Bertha. Chicken Little. 1990. 3.98 (ISBN 0-8317-4267-4). Smithmark.

Hare, Eric B. Pip Pip the Naughty Chicken. 31p. 1989. pap. 6.95 incl. cassette (ISBN 0-8163-0806-3). Pacific Pr Pub Assn.

Hawkins, Colin & Hawkins, Jacqui. Jen the Hen. LC 84-42955. (Illus.). 22p. (gr. k-1). 1985. 9.95 (ISBN 0-399-21207-8, Putnam). Putnam Pub Group.

Hoban, Julia. Quick Chick. Hoban, Lillian, illus. 32p. (ps-2). 1989. 9.95 (ISBN 0-525-44490-4, DCB). Dutton Child Bks.

Hutchins, Pat. Rosie's Walk. Hutchins, Pat, illus. LC 87-17550. (ps-k). 1971. pap. 3.95 (ISBN 0-02-043750-1, Aladdin). Macmillan Child Grp.

Izawa, Tadasu & Hijkata, Shigemi, illus. The Little Red Hen. 18p. (gr. k-2). 1981. 3.95 (ISBN 0-448-09756-7, G&D). Putnam Pub Group.

Kellog, Steven. Chicken Little. LC 84-25519. (Illus.). (gr. 1 up). 1989. pap. 7.95 bk. & cassette (ISBN 0-688-09041-9, Mulberry). Morrow.

Kwitz, Mary. Little Chick's Big Day. Degen, Bruce, illus. LC 80-7905. 32p. (ps-3). 1981. HarpC Child Bks.

Kwitz, Mary D. La Historica de la Pollita: (Little Chick's Story) Palacios, Argentina, tr. Skekeres, Cindy, illus. (SPA.). 32p. (Orig.). (ps-2). 1987. pap. 2.95 (ISBN 0-590-43457-8). Scholastic Inc.

—Little Chick's Story. Szekeres, Cyndy, illus. LC 77-11841. (ps-3). 1978. 7.64i (ISBN 0-06-023664-7). HarpC Child Bks.

Lane, Megan H. Something to Crow About. (ps-2). 1990. 10.95 (ISBN 0-8037-0697-9); PLB 10.89 (ISBN 0-8037-0698-7). Dial Bks Young.

The Little Red Hen. (ARA., Illus.). (gr. 1-3). 3.50x (ISBN 0-86685-203-4); incl. cassette 12.00x (ISBN 0-685-02575-6). Intl Bk Ctr.

The Little Red Hen. (Illus.). (ps-4). 3.50 (ISBN 0-7214-5010-5). Ladybird Bks.

Macaulay, David. Why the Chicken Crossed the Road. (Illus.). 32p. (gr. 4-6). 1987. 13.95 (ISBN 0-395-44241-9, Clarion). HM.

McKelvey, David. Bobby the Mostly Silky. LC 83-73327. (Illus.). 32p. (gr. 1-3). 1984. lib. bdg. 9.45 (ISBN 0-931722-28-4); pap. 3.95 (ISBN 0-931722-27-6). Corona Pub.

McKissack, Patricia & McKissack, Frederick. The Little Red Hen. Hockerman, Dennis, illus. LC 85-12760. (gr. 1-2). 1985. PLB 11.93 (ISBN 0-516-02363-2); pap. 3.95 (ISBN 0-516-42363-0). Childrens.

McQueen, Lucinda. La Gallinita Roja: (The Little Red Hen) Lopez, Elva R., tr. (SPA.). 32p. (ps-2). 1991. pap. 3.50 (ISBN 0-590-71880-0). Scholastic Inc.

Manes, Stephen. Chicken Trek: A New Oscar J. Noodleman Story. Barrett, Ron, illus. LC 86-23996. (gr. 3-5). 1987. 11.95 (ISBN 0-525-44312-6, DCB). Dutton Child Bks.

Mathers, Petra. Maria Theresa. Mathers, Petra, illus. LC 84-48346. 32p. (ps-3). 1985. 13.95 (ISBN 0-06-024109-8); PLB 13.89 (ISBN 0-06-024112-8). HarpC Child Bks.

Mountain, Lee, et al. The Little Red Hen. (Illus.). 12p. (gr. k-1). 1991. pap. 18.75 (ISBN 0-89061-941-7). Jamestown Pubs.

Myers, Bernice. The Millionth Egg. (gr. k-3). 1991. 13.95 (ISBN 0-688-09886-X). Lothrop.

Oakley, Graham. Hetty & Harriet. Oakley, Graham, illus. LC 81-8024. 32p. (gr. k-3). 1982. 13.95 (ISBN 0-689-30888-4, Atheneum Child Bk). Macmillan.

O'Connor, Jane & O'Connor, Robert. Super Cluck. Lloyd, Megan, illus. LC 90-32832. 64p. (ps-3). 1991. 11.95 (ISBN 0-06-024594-8); PLB 11.89 (ISBN 0-06-024595-6). HarpC Child Bks.

Paul, Jan S. Hortense. Linden, Madekaine G., illus. LC 83-45055. 40p. (ps-2). 1984. 10.10i (ISBN 0-690-04370-8, Crowell Jr Bks). HarpC Child Bks.

Pinkwater, D. Manus. Hoboken Chicken Emergency. LC 76-41910. (Illus.). 94p. (gr. k-3). 1977. pap. 4.95 (ISBN 0-671-66447-6). S&S Trade.

Pinkwater, Daniel M. The Hoboken Chicken Emergency. LC 76-41910. (Illus.). (gr. 3-7). 1984. 10.95 (ISBN 0-13-392514-5); pap. 4.95 (ISBN 0-13-392499-8). P-H.

Pursell, Margaret S. Jessie the Chicken. Hammarberg, Dyan, tr. from FRE. LC 76-29458. (Illus.). 24p. (gr. k-4). 1977. PLB 6.95 (ISBN 0-87614-074-6). Carolrhoda Bks.

Quackenbush, Robert. Sherlock Chick & the Peekaboo Mystery. Quackenbush, Robert, illus. LC 87-3591. 48p. (ps-3). 1987. 5.95 (ISBN 0-8193-1149-9). Parents.

Rausiri, Supa. The Beautiful Chick. Rodriguez, Gloria F., ed. Chang, Phillip, illus. Pinta, Thanom, tr. (Illus.). (gr. k-2). 1979. pap. 3.00x (ISBN 0-686-26620-X, Pub. by New Day Publishers Philippines). Cellar.

Roddie, Shen. Hatch, Egg, Hatch: Touch & Feel Action Flap Book. (ps). 1991. 13.95 (ISBN 0-316-75345-9). Little.

Rubel, Nicole. Goldie. LC 88-32796. (Illus.). 32p. (ps-2). 1989. 11.95 (ISBN 0-06-025096-8); PLB 11.89 (ISBN 0-06-025097-6). HarpC Child Bks.

Schmidt, Karen L., illus. Chicken Little. 18p. (ps). 1986. 3.95 (ISBN 0-448-10223-4, G&D). Putnam Pub Group.

—The Little Red Hen. 16p. (ps). 1984. 3.95 (ISBN 0-448-10218-8, G&D). Putnam Pub Group.

Swan, Walter. Brenda the Cow & the Little White Hen. Swan, Deloris, ed. Asch, Connie, illus. 16p. (Orig.). (gr. 2-3). 1989. pap. 1.50 (ISBN 0-927176-02-5). Swan Enterp.

Tripp, Valerie. Sillyhen's Big Surprise. Martin, Sandra K., illus. LC 89-35758. 24p. (ps-2). 1989. PLB 12.33 (ISBN 0-516-01522-2); pap. 3.95 (ISBN 0-516-41522-0). Childrens.

Wells, Rosemary. Max's Chocolate Chicken. Wells, Rosemary, illus. LC 88-14954. 32p. (ps-2). 1989. 9.95 (ISBN 0-8037-0585-9); PLB 9.89 (ISBN 0-8037-0586-7). Dial Bks Young.

Willis, Val. Silly Little Chick. (Illus.). 32p. (ps-2). 1989. 11.95 (ISBN 0-233-98307-4). Andre Deutsch.

Zemach, Margot. The Little Red Hen: An Old Story. Zemach, Margot, illus. LC 83-14159. 32p. (ps-3). 1983. 11.95 (ISBN 0-374-34621-6). FS&G.

CHIEF JUSTICES

see Judges

CHILD ABUSE

see also Child Molesting

Anderson, Deborah & Finne, Martha. Jason's Story: Going to a Foster Home. Swofford, Jeanette, illus. LC 85-25414. 48p. (gr. 1-4). 1986. lib. bdg. 9.95 (ISBN 0-87518-324-7, Dillon). Macmillan Child Grp.

—Liza's Story: Neglect & the Police. Swofford, Jeanette, illus. LC 85-25379. 48p. (gr. 1-4). 1986. lib. bdg. 9.95 (ISBN 0-87518-319-X, Dillon). Macmillan Child Grp.

—Margaret's Story: Sexual Abuse & Going to Court. Swofford, Jeanette, illus. LC 85-25417. 48p. (gr. 1-4). 1986. lib. bdg. 9.95 (ISBN 0-87518-320-4, Dillon). Macmillan Child Grp.

—Michael's Story: Emotional Abuse & Working with a Counselor. Swofford, Jeanette, illus. LC 85-25400. 48p. (gr. 1-4). 1986. lib. bdg. 9.95 (ISBN 0-87518-322-0, Dillon). Macmillan Child Grp.

—Robin's Story: Physical Abuse & Seeing the Doctor. Swofford, Jeanette, illus. LC 85-25383. 48p. (gr. 1-4). 1986. lib. bdg. 9.95 (ISBN 0-87518-321-2, Dillon). Macmillan Child Grp.

Bliss, Jonathan. Child Abuse. (Illus.). 64p. (gr. 7 up). 1990. lib. bdg. 15.93 (ISBN 0-86593-081-3); lib. bdg. 11.95s.p. Rourke Corp.

Check, William A. Child Abuse. (Illus.). 104p. (gr. 6-12). 1990. PLB 18.95 (ISBN 0-7910-0043-5); pap. 9.95 (ISBN 0-7910-0509-7). Chelsea Hse.

Coalition for Child Advocacy Staff. Touching. Bergsma, Jody, illus. 32p. (Orig.). (ps). 1985. pap. 5.95 (ISBN 0-934671-00-1). Whatcom Cty Opp.

Cooney, Judith. Coping with Sexual Abuse. Rosen, R., ed. 118p. (gr. 7-12). 1987. PLB 12.95 (ISBN 0-8239-0684-1); pap. 7.95 (ISBN 0-8239-0763-5); leader's guide 5.95 (ISBN 0-685-18369-6). Rosen Group.

Elias, Susan C. Strong & Safe: A Children's Guide to Self Protection. Wise, Caroline, illus. 60p. (Orig.). (gr. 1-3). 1989. pap. 8.95 (ISBN 0-317-93904-1). Womansource.

Gil, Eliana M. I Told My Secret: A Book for Kids Who Were Abused. Haskell, Sally, illus. 16p. (Orig.). (gr. 3 up). 1986. pap. 2.00 (ISBN 0-9613205-1-6). Launch Pr.

Grimm, Carol & Montgomery, Becky. T Is for Touching. (gr. k up). 1985. manual & 3-filmstrip series 79.00 (ISBN 0-317-40553-5); manual & videotape one half inch 79.00 (ISBN 0-914633-09-0); manual & videotape three quarter inch 95.00 (ISBN 0-914633-08-2); write for info. manual (ISBN 0-914633-05-8). Rape Abuse Crisis.

Landau, Elaine. Child Abuse: An American Epidemic. rev. ed. 128p. (gr. 7 up). 1990. PLB 12.98 (ISBN 0-671-68874-X); pap. 5.95 (ISBN 0-671-68875-8). Messner.

Morgan, Marcia K. My Feelings. 2nd ed. Hilty, Christi S., illus. (ps). 1984. pap. text ed. 3.95 (ISBN 0-930413-00-8, TX-1-361-947). Equal Just Con.

Mufson, Susan & Kranz, Rachel. Straight Talk about Child Abuse. 128p. 1991. 16.95x (ISBN 0-8160-2376-X). Facts on File.

Park, Angela. Child Abuse. FS-Aladdin Staff, ed. (Illus.). 64p. (gr. 4-12). 1988. PLB 11.90 (ISBN 0-531-17121-3, Gloucester Pr). Watts.

Petty, Kate. Being Careful with Strangers. FS-Aladdin Staff, ed. Kopper, Lisa, illus. 24p. (gr. 1-3). 1988. PLB 5.29 (ISBN 0-531-17107-8, Gloucester Pr). Watts.

Rape & Abuse Crisis Center Staff. Red Flag Green Flag People. Freed, Kecia S., illus. 28p. (gr. k up). 1985. pap. 3.00 (ISBN 0-914633-01-5); revised wkbk. 3.00 (ISBN 0-914633-10-4). Rape Abuse Crisis.

Stark, Evan. Everything You Need to Know about Sexual Abuse. rev. ed. (Illus.). 64p. (gr. 7-12). 1990. 12.95 (ISBN 0-8239-1245-0). Rosen Group.

Stewart, Gail. Child Abuse. LC 89-1386. (Illus.). 48p. (gr. 4 up). 1989. 10.95 (ISBN 0-89686-442-1, Crestwood Hse). Macmillan Child Grp.

Wakcher, Bridget. Child Abuse: Is It Happening to You? Show, Michael, illus. 32p. (Orig.). (gr. 1 up). 1984. pap. 3.50 (ISBN 0-930363-00-0). Teknek.

Ward, Fred & Ward, Betty. About Sexual Abuse: A Program for Teens & Young Adults. Olszewski, Lema J. & Wolff, Kathy, eds. 85p. (Orig.). (gr. 9 up). 1990. pap. text ed. 14.95 (ISBN 1-55896-175-5). Unitarian Univ.

White, Laurie A. & Spencer, Steven L. Take Care with Yourself: A Young Person's Guide to Understanding, Preventing & Healing from the Hurts of Child Abuse. Cohen, Alice E., illus. 36p. (Orig.). (gr. k-7). 1983. English edition. pap. 5.95 (ISBN 0-9612024-0-8); pap. Spanish edition avail. White & Spencer.

CHILD ABUSE–FICTION

Shreve, Susan. Lucy Forever & Miss Rosetree, Shrinks. LC 86-29513. 128p. (gr. 3-7). 1988. pap. 2.95 (ISBN 0-394-80570-4). Knopf.

CHILD AND PARENT

see Parent and Child

CHILD AUTHORS

Here are entered works on children as authors and works written by children.

Allen County Police Officers Assn., compiled by. Kids Talk to Kids. 75p. (gr. 6-12). 1990. pap. write for info. (ISBN 0-9614659-6-4). Cuchullain Pubns.

CHILD ARTISTS

Here are entered works on children as artists and on works of art by children.

Small, Carol B. Art Concepts for Children. Small, Carol B., illus. LC 89-14917. 112p. (Orig.). (gr. 6 up). 1989. pap. 8.95 (ISBN 0-938267-04-3). Bold Prodns.

CHILD BIRTH

see Childbirth

CHILD DEVELOPMENT

see Child Study; Children–Growth

CHILD LABOR

see also Newsboys

Stein, Conrad R. & Neely, Keith. The Story of Child Labor Laws. LC 84-7017. (Illus.). 32p. (gr. 3-6). 1984. lib. bdg. 13.27 (ISBN 0-516-04679-9). Childrens.

CHILD MOLESTING

Anderson, Deborah & Finne, Martha. Margaret's Story: Sexual Abuse & Going to Court. Swofford, Jeanette, illus. LC 85-25417. 48p. (gr. 1-4). 1986. lib. bdg. 9.95 (ISBN 0-87518-320-4, Dillon). Macmillan Child Grp.

Bahr, Amy C. It's OK to Say No. Green, Frederick B., illus. LC 85-80573. 32p. (ps-2). 1986. 4.95 (ISBN 0-448-15328-9, G&D). Putnam Pub Group.

—Your Body Is Your Own. Green, Frederick B., illus. LC 85-80575. 32p. (ps-2). 1986. 4.95 (ISBN 0-448-15326-2, G&D). Putnam Pub Group.

Benedict, Helen. Safe, Strong & Streetwise: The Teenager's Guide to Preventing Sexual Assault. (Illus.). 192p. (gr. 7 up). 1987. 14.95 (ISBN 0-316-08899-4); pap. 5.95 (ISBN 0-87113-100-5). Little.

Cooney, Judith. Coping with Sexual Abuse. Rosen, R., ed. 118p. (gr. 7-12). 1987. PLB 12.95 (ISBN 0-8239-0684-1); pap. 7.95 (ISBN 0-8239-0763-5); leader's guide 5.95 (ISBN 0-685-18369-6). Rosen Group.

Girard, Linda W. My Body Is Private. Tucker, Kathleen, ed. (Illus.). 32p. (gr. k-3). 1984. PLB 10.95 (ISBN 0-8075-5320-4). A Whitman.

Hyde, Margaret & Hyde, Lawrence. Missing Children. LC 85-7323. 104p. (gr. 7up). 1985. PLB 12.90 (ISBN 0-531-10073-1, Gloucester Pr). Watts.

Hyde, Margaret O. Sexual Abuse: Let's Talk about It. rev. & enl. ed. Forsyth, Elizabeth H., intro. by. LC 87-133328. 112p. (gr. 5 up). 1987. 8.95 (ISBN 0-664-32725-7). Westminster John Knox.

Lenett, Robin & Crane, Bob. It's Ok to Say No: A Parent-Child Manual for the Protection of Children. Smith, Frank C., illus. 128p. (Orig.). 1985. pap. 3.95 (ISBN 0-8125-9452-5, Dist. by St. Martin's Press & Warner Pub Services). Tor Bks.

Meyer, Linda D. Safety Zone: A Book Teaching Children Abduction Prevention Skills. Megale, Marina & Walsh, John. (Illus.). 32p. (Orig.). (gr. k-6). 1984. PLB 9.00 (ISBN 0-9603516-8-X). Franklin Pr WA.

Reid, Kathryn G. & Fortune, Marie M. Preventing Child Sexual Abuse: A Curriculum for Children Ages 9-12. LC 89-33084. (Illus.). 96p. (Orig.). 1989. pap. 9.95 (ISBN 0-8298-0810-8). Pilgrim NY.

Russell, Pamela & Stone, Beth. Do You Have a Secret? How to Get Help for Scary Secrets. McKee, Mary, illus. LC 85-27986. 36p. (Orig.). (ps-2). 1986. pap. 6.95 (ISBN 0-89638-098-X, 03467). CompCare.

Satullo, Jane, et al. It Happens to Boys Too... Bookless, Nan, illus. 36p. (Orig.). (ps-6). 1989. pap. 6.50 (ISBN 0-9618618-0-0). RCC-Berkshires Pr.

Sweet, Phyllis. Something Happened to Me. Lindquist, Barbara, illus. LC 81-83422. (gr. 2-5). 1985. pap. 4.95 (ISBN 0-941300-00-5). Mother Courage.

Terkel, Susan N. & Rench, Janice E. Feeling Safe, Feeling Strong: How to Avoid Sexual Abuse & What to Do If It Happens to You. LC 84-9664. (Illus.). 72p. (gr. 4-8). 1984. PLB 11.95 (ISBN 0-8225-0021-3). Lerner Pubns.

Ward, Fred & Ward, Betty. About Sexual Abuse: A Program for Teens & Young Adults. Olszewski, Lema J. & Wolff, Kathy, eds. 85p. (Orig.). (gr. 9 up). 1990. pap. text ed. 14.95 (ISBN 1-55896-175-5). Unitarian Univ.

CHILD MOLESTING–FICTION

Asher, Sandy. Things Are Seldom What They Seem. LC 82-72819. 144p. (gr. 7up). 1983. pap. 11.95 (ISBN 0-385-29250-3). Delacorte.

Caines, Jeannette. Chilly Stomach. Cummings, Pat, illus. LC 85-45250. 32p. (ps-2). 1986. 11.95 (ISBN 0-06-020976-3). HarpC Child Bks.

Cole, Barbara S. Don't Tell a Soul. Rosen, R., ed. 175p. (gr. 7-12). 1987. PLB 12.95 (ISBN 0-8239-0701-5). Rosen Group.

Howard, Ellen. Gillyflower. LC 86-3584. 128p. (gr. 4-8). 1986. 12.95 (ISBN 0-689-31274-1, Atheneum Child Bk). Macmillan Child Grp.

MacLean, John. Mac. 192p. (gr. 7 up). 1987. 12.95 (ISBN 0-395-43080-1). HM.

Nathanson, Laura. The Trouble with Wednesdays. 176p. (gr. 7-12). 1987. pap. 2.95 (ISBN 0-553-26337-4, Starfire). Bantam.

Page, Carole G. Hallie's Secret. 144p. 1987. pap. text ed. 3.95 (ISBN 0-8024-3476-2). Moody.

Patterson, Sherri. No-No the Little Seal: A Story for Very Young Children That Tells about Sexual Abuse. Krupp, Marion N., illus. LC 86-617. 32p. (ps-1). 1986. pap. 4.95 with cassette (ISBN 0-394-88053-6, Random Juv). Random.

Polese, Carolyn. Promise Not to Tell. Barrett, Jennifer, illus. LC 84-19767. 66p. (gr. 3 up). 1985. 16.95 (ISBN 0-89885-239-0). Human Sci Pr.

Sanford, Doris. I Can't Talk about It: A Child's Book about Sexual Abuse. Evans, Graci, illus. LC 86-831. 32p. (ps-5). 1986. 7.95 (ISBN 0-88070-149-8). Multnomah.

Wachter, Oralee. Close to Home. Aaron, Jane, illus. LC 86-6671. 48p. (Orig.). (ps-5). 1986. pap. 12.95 (ISBN 0-590-40330-3). Scholastic Inc.

—No More Secrets for Me. Aaron, Jane, illus. (gr. 1-4). 1984. 14.95 (ISBN 0-316-91490-8); pap. 4.95 (ISBN 0-316-91491-6). Little.

CHILD PSYCHOLOGY

see Child Study

CHILD STUDY

Here are entered works on the psychology, personality, habits, mental development, etc., of the child.

see also Adolescence; Kindergarten; Parent and Child; Play; Problem Children

Anglund, Joan W. Childhood Is a Time of Innocence: Twentieth Anniversary Edition. LC 65-20974. (Illus.). 32p. (gr. k up). 1984. Repr. of 1964 ed. 6.95 (ISBN 0-15-216952-0, HJ). HarBraceJ.

Berry, Joy. About Change & Moving. Bartholomew, illus. 48p. (gr. 3 up). 1990. PLB 14.60 (ISBN 0-516-02951-7); pap. 6.95 (ISBN 0-516-22951-6). Childrens.

Bibeau, Simone. Developing the Early Learner: Level 1. rev. ed. Kruck, Gerry, illus. 64p. (ps-2). 1983. pap. text ed. 4.95 (ISBN 0-940406-01-2). Perception Pubns.

—Developing the Early Learner: Level 2. rev. ed. Kruck, Gerry, illus. 64p. (ps-2). 1983. pap. text ed. 4.95 (ISBN 0-940406-02-0). Perception Pubns.

—Developing the Early Learner: Level 3. rev. ed. Kruck, Gerry, illus. 64p. (ps-2). 1983. pap. text ed. 4.95 (ISBN 0-940406-03-9). Perception Pubns.

—IQ Booster Kit: Developing the Early Learner Levels 1-4. Kruck, Gerry, illus. 256p. (ps-2). 1983. pap. text ed. 85.00 (bks. & cassettes) (ISBN 0-940406-05-5). Perception Pubns.

Coleman, William L. Today I Feel Shy. LC 83-9216. 128p. (Orig.). (gr. 3-4). 1983. pap. 5.95 (ISBN 0-87123-588-9). Bethany Hse.

Fleming, Alice. What to Say When You Don't Know What to Say. LC 82-5782. 128p. (gr. 7 up). 1982. 12.95 (ISBN 0-684-17626-2, Scribners Young Read). Macmillan Child Grp.

Holbrook, Sabra. Fighting Back: The Struggle for Gay Rights. LC 86-19755. 128p. (gr. 7 up). 1987. 13.95 (ISBN 0-525-67187-0, Lodestar Bks). Dutton Child Bks.

Kaufman, Gershen & Raphael, Lev. Stick up for Yourself! Every Kid's Guide to Personal Power & Positive Self-Esteem. 96p. (gr. 3-7). 1990. pap. 8.95 (ISBN 0-915793-17-2). Free Spirit Pub.

Kehoe, Patricia. Something Happened & I'm Scared to Tell: A Book for Young Children Victims of Abuse. Deach, Carol, illus. LC 86-62032. 32p. (Orig.). (ps-1). 1987. PLB 12.95 (ISBN 0-943990-29-7); pap. 3.95 (ISBN 0-943990-28-9). Parenting Pr.

Little People Big Book About Ourselves. 64p. (ps-1). 1989. write for info. (ISBN 0-8094-7458-1); PLB write for info. (ISBN 0-8094-7459-X). Time-Life.

McCoy, Diana L. The Secret: A Child's Story of Sex Abuse, Ages 7-10. Brown, Wynne, illus. Sgroi, Suzanne, intro. by. 32p. (Orig.). (gr. 2-5). 1986. pap. text ed. 6.00 (ISBN 0-9619250-1-9). Magic Lantrn.

Sanchez, Gail J. & Gerbino, Mary. Overeating: Let's Talk about It. Raap, Cynthia, illus. LC 85-25388. 120p. (gr. 4 up). 1986. pap. 9.95 (ISBN 0-87518-319-0, Dillon). Macmillan Child Grp.

Sealy, Adrienne V. No Hill Is Too High. Holder, Stanley, illus. (gr. 2-5). 1978. PLB 4.95 (ISBN 0-9602670-0-X). Assn Family Living.

Semigran, Stu & Wilkinson, Sindy. Making the Best of Me Student Manual: A Handbook for Student Excellence & Self Esteem. 2nd ed. Winborn, Marsha, illus. 171p. (gr. 7-12). Date not set. 19.95 (ISBN 0-940735-05-9). Insight Pub.

Simon, Norma. I Am Not a Crybaby. Cogancherry, Helen, illus. 32p. (ps-3). 1991. pap. 3.95 (ISBN 0-14-054216-7, Puffin). Puffin Bks.

Tiller, David. Wanna Be Number One? Stevens, Bill, illus. 40p. (Orig.). (gr. 4-6). pap. 2.00 (ISBN 0-937170-32-1). Home Mission.

Wittels, Harriet & Greisman, Joan. Things I Hate! LC 73-11053. (Illus.). 32p. (ps-3). 1973. 16.95 (ISBN 0-87705-096-1). Human Sci Pr.

CHILD WELFARE

Here are entered works on the aid, support, and protection of children, by the state or by private welfare organizations.

see also Child Labor; Children–Care and Hygiene; Children–Hospitals; Juvenile Delinquency; Playgrounds

Amstutz, Beverly. Sharing Is Fun. Amstutz, Beverly, illus. 24p. (gr. k-7). 1979. pap. 2.50x (ISBN 0-937836-00-1). Precious Res.

Berry, Joy. Every Kid's Guide to Laws That Relate to Kids in the Community. (Illus.). 48p. (gr. 3-7). 1987. 5.95 (ISBN 0-516-21423-3); PLB 14.60 (ISBN 0-516-01423-4). Childrens.

—Every Kid's Guide to the Juvenile Justice System. (Illus.). 48p. (gr. 3-7). 1987. 5.95 (ISBN 0-516-21422-5); PLB 14.60 (ISBN 0-516-01422-6). Childrens.

Fierstein, Jeff. Kid Contracts. 32p. (gr. 4-8). 1982. 4.95 (ISBN 0-86653-091-6, GA 442). Good Apple.

Fundamental of Child Care Study Aid. 1974. pap. 2.50 (ISBN 0-87738-047-3). Youth Ed.

Maynard, Morlee. Happy Times with People. LC 85-25555. (ps). 1986. 4.95 (ISBN 0-8054-4165-4). Broadman.

O'Connor, Karen. Homeless Children. LC 89-37553. (Illus.). 96p. (gr. 5-8). 1989. PLB 11.95 (ISBN 1-56006-109-X). Lucent Bks.

Rape & Abuse Crisis Center Staff. Annie. rev. ed. Freed, Kecia S., illus. 21p. (ps up). 1985. pap. text ed. 1.50 (ISBN 0-914633-03-1). Rape Abuse Crisis.

Sanford, Doris. Lisa's Parents Fight. Davis, Deena, ed. Evans, Graci, illus. LC 89-31409. 31p. (gr. k-4). 1989. 6.95 (ISBN 0-88070-301-6). Multnomah.

The World's Children, 5 vols. LC 88-21723. (Illus.). 240p. (gr. 4-9). 1988. Set. 69.95 (ISBN 0-86307-987-3). Marshall Cavendish.

CHILD WELFARE–FICTION

Adler, C. S. Fly Free. LC 83-16599. 160p. (gr. 4-8). 1984. 10.95 (ISBN 0-698-20606-1, Coward). Putnam Pub Group.

Moeri, Louise. The Girl Who Lived on the Ferris Wheel. LC 79-11359. (gr. 5-9). 1979. 8.95 (ISBN 0-525-30659-5, DCB). Dutton Child Bks.

Sanford, Doris. Don't Make Me Go Back, Mommy. Davis, Deena, ed. Evans, Graci, illus. (gr. 1-4). 1990. 7.95 (ISBN 0-88070-367-9). Multnomah.

Stanek, Muriel. Don't Hurt Me, Mama. Fay, Ann, ed. LC 83-16771. (Illus.). 32p. (gr. k-3). 1983. PLB 10.95 (ISBN 0-8075-1689-9). A Whitman.

CHILDBIRTH

see also Pregnancy

Allinson, Elaine S. Daniel's Question: A Cesarean Birth Story. DeBiase, Judith, illus. 13p. (ps-5). 1981. staple bdg. 2.95 (ISBN 0-9606960-0-8). Willow Tree NY.

Birth & Growth. 48p. (gr. 5-8). 1988. PLB 12.98 (ISBN 0-382-09708-4); 9.74s.p. (ISBN 0-685-24615-9). Silver Burdett Pr.

Brown, Fern G. Childbirth. Kline, M., ed. (Illus.). 64p. 1988. PLB 12.40 (ISBN 0-531-10573-3). Watts.

—Teen Guide to Childbirth. (Illus.). 64p. (gr. 7 up). 1990. pap. 4.95 (ISBN 0-531-15208-1). Watts.

Cole, Joanna. How You Were Born. LC 83-17314. (Illus.). 48p. (ps-3). 1985. 12.95 (ISBN 0-688-05801-9); PLB 12.88 (ISBN 0-685-10418-4, Morrow Jr Bks); pap. 4.95 (ISBN 0-685-10419-2, Mulberry Bks). Morrow Jr Bks.

Frasier, Debra. On the Day You Were Born. Johnston, Allyn, ed. Frasier, Debra, illus. 32p. 1991. 12.95 (ISBN 0-15-257995-8). HarBraceJ.

Gee, R. Babies: Understanding Conception, Birth & the First Years. 48p. (gr. 5-10). 1986. PLB 13.96 (ISBN 0-88110-336-5); pap. 6.95 (ISBN 0-86020-839-7). EDC.

Holland, Vicki. We Are Having a Baby. (Illus.). (gr. k-1). 1972. 8.95 (ISBN 0-684-12809-8, Scribners Young Read); (Pub. by Scribner). Macmillan Child Grp.

Kitzinger, Sheila. Being Born. Nilsson, Lennart, illus. 64p. (gr. 2-5). 1986. pap. 15.95 (ISBN 0-448-18990-9, G&D). Putnam Pub Group.

Malecki, Maryann. Mom & Dad & I Are Having a Baby! Malecki, Maryann, illus. LC 82-81707. 70p. (Orig.). (ps-3). 1982. pap. 6.95 (ISBN 0-937604-03-8). Pennypress.

Prot, Viviane A. The Story of Birth. Bogard, Vicki, tr. from FRE. Gaudriault, Rozier, illus. LC 90-50777. 38p. (gr. k-5). 1991. 4.95 (ISBN 0-944589-34-0, 340). Young Discovery Lib.

Pursell, Margaret S. A Look at Birth. LC 77-13050. (Illus.). 36p. (gr. 3-6). 1977. PLB 6.95 (ISBN 0-8225-1307-2). Lerner Pubns.

Rhodes, Philip. Childbirth. Head, J. J., ed. LC 78-51690. (Illus.). 16p. (gr. 10 up). 1981. pap. 2.15 (ISBN 0-89278-311-7, 45-9711). Carolina Biological.

Rushnell, Elaine. My Mom's Having a Baby. Duenewald, Doris, ed. LC 77-95422. (Illus.). (gr. k-7). 1978. PLB 6.09 (ISBN 0-448-13486-1, G&D). Putnam Pub Group.

Schoen, Mark. Bellybuttons Are Navels. (Illus.). 40p. (ps-k). 1990. 12.95 (ISBN 0-8290-2409-3). Irvington.

CHILDREN–ADOPTION

see Adoption

CHILDREN–BOOKS AND READING

Here are entered works on the reading interests of children, or lists of books read by or recommended for children. Collections of works published for children are entered under Children's Literature.

Bernhardt, Edythe. ABC's of Thinking with Caldecott Books. Polette, Nancy. (Illus.). 124p. (gr. 1-4). 1988. pap. 12.95 (ISBN 0-913839-70-1). Bk Lures.

Champlin, Connie & Kennedy, Barbara. Books in Bloom: Creativity Through Children's Literature. Wilson, Lois, illus. 106p. (gr. 1-6). 1982. spiral bdg. 13.95 (ISBN 0-938594-01-X). Spec Lit Pr.

Cleary, Florence D. Discovering Books & Libraries: A Handbook for Students in the Middle & Upper Grades. 2nd ed. LC 76-55368. 196p. (gr. 7-12). 1977. pap. 10.00 (ISBN 0-8242-0594-4). Wilson.

Cole, Joanna. Hungry, Hungry Sharks: A Step Two Book. Wynne, Patricia, illus. LC 85-2218. 48p. (gr. 1-3). 1986. lib. bdg. 6.99 (ISBN 0-394-97471-9); pap. 2.95 (ISBN 0-394-87471-4). Random.

Dickson, Sue. Off We Go. rev. ed. Portadino, Norma, illus. 112p. (gr. k-3). 1985. pap. 4.97 (ISBN 1-55574-001-4, WB-130). CBN Publishing.

—Raceway. rev. ed. Portadino, Norma, illus. 96p. (gr. k-3). 1984. pap. 4.97 (ISBN 1-55574-002-2, WB-140). CBN Publishing.

Gillespie, John T. & Lembo, Diana L. Introducing Books: A Guide for the Middle Grades. LC 74-94512. 318p. (gr. 4-6). 1970. 29.95 (ISBN 0-8352-0215-1). Bowker.

Hawthorne, Terri B. & Brown, Diane B. GAIA Celebration for Children: A Workshop & Activities Book. Brown, Diane B., illus. 32p. 1990. pap. 5.99 (ISBN 0-929404-02-5). Tara Educ Servs.

Kowalczyk, Carolyn. Purple Is Part of the Rainbow. Sharp, Gene, illus. LC 85-11693. 32p. (gr. 1-2). 1985. PLB 11.93 (ISBN 0-516-02068-4); pap. 3.95 (ISBN 0-516-42068-2). Childrens.

Lowry, Lois. Anastasia Has the Answers. (gr. 5 up). 1986. 12.95 (ISBN 0-395-41795-3). HM.

Miles, Miska. Annie & the Old One. Parnall, Peter, illus. (gr. 1-3). 1985. pap. 5.95 (ISBN 0-316-57120-2). Little.

Polette, Keith. Try This One! Sharing Books. (Illus.). 32p. (gr. 6-12). 1986. pap. 4.95 (ISBN 0-913839-52-3). Bk Lures.

Polette, Nancy. The ABCs of Books & Thinking Skills. (Illus.). 144p. (gr. 1-8). 1987. pap. 14.95 (ISBN 0-913839-61-2). Bk Lures.

—The Amelia Bedelia Thinking Book. (Illus.). 32p. 1983. pap. 4.95 (ISBN 0-913839-34-5). Bk Lures.

—The Book Bag. (Illus.). 64p. 1986. pap. 7.95 (ISBN 0-913839-46-9). Bk Lures.

—Novel Thinking. (Illus.). 128p. (gr. 6-12). 1987. pap. 12.95 (ISBN 0-913839-47-7). Bk Lures.

—One Hundred Three Book Activities. (Illus.). 32p. (gr. 5-9). 1989. pap. 4.95 (ISBN 0-913839-74-4). Bk Lures.

—Reader's Almanac. (Illus.). 148p. (gr. 4-8). 1985. pap. 14.95 (ISBN 0-913839-44-2). Bk Lures.

—Reading with Music. (Illus.). 32p. (gr. 4-7). 1989. pap. 4.95 (ISBN 0-913839-77-9). Bk Lures.

Polette, Nancy & O'Neal, Kathleen. The Crosby Bonsall Thinking Book. (Illus.). 32p. 1987. pap. 4.95 (ISBN 0-913839-65-5). Bk Lures.

Polette, Nancy & Polette, Keith. Readers Theatre. (Illus.). 48p. (gr. 4-8). 1986. pap. 5.95 (ISBN 0-913839-56-6). Bk Lures.

Rape & Abuse Crisis Center Staff. Annie. rev. ed. Freed, Kecia S., illus. 21p. (ps up). 1985. pap. text ed. 1.50 (ISBN 0-914633-03-1). Rape Abuse Crisis.

Ringstad, M. Adventures on Library Shelves. Pearson, C., illus. LC 68-16398. 48p. (gr. 2 up). 1967. PLB 12.35 prebound (ISBN 0-87783-001-0). Oddo.

Schmeltz, Susan A., ed. This Book Is Just for You. Caudill-Paye, Judythe, illus. LC 81-11928. 100p. (gr. k-6). 1981. 11.95g (ISBN 0-9606586-0-2). Quality MO.

Shelton, Helen, ed. Bibliography of Books for Children. 1988-89 ed. LC 89-345. 112p. (ps-6). 1989. 11.00 (ISBN 0-87173-118-5). ACEI.

Sutherland, Zena, ed. The Best in Children's Books: The University of Chicago Guide to Children's Literature, 1973-1978. LC 79-24331. (gr. 12 up). 1980. lib. bdg. 25.00x (ISBN 0-226-78059-7). U of Chicago Pr.

CHILDREN–CARE AND HYGIENE

Here are entered general works on the physical care of children. Works limited to their physical care in school are entered under School Hygiene.

see also Baby Sitters; Children–Diseases; Children–Hospitals; Health Education; Nurses and Nursing

Arnold, Caroline. Too Fat? Too Thin? Do You Have a Choice? Greenberg, Tony, frwd. by. LC 83-23841. 112p. (gr. 5 up). 1984. PLB 12.88 (ISBN 0-688-02780-6); pap. 5.95 (ISBN 0-688-02779-2, Pub. by Beech Tree Bks). Morrow Jr Bks.

Carroll, Teresa P. Mommy Breastfeeds Our Baby. Gray, Linda, illus. (Orig.). (ps). 1990. pap. 4.95 (ISBN 0-9626614-0-6). NuBaby AL.

Hafford, Jeannette N. Help Mates for Your Playmates. (Illus.). 18p. (ps-7). 1986. pap. 4.22 (ISBN 0-9616549-1-0). Tinys Self Help Bks.

Ispa, Jean. Exploring Careers in Child Care Services. rev. ed. (Illus.). (gr. 7-12). 1990. lib. bdg. 12.95 (ISBN 0-8239-1151-9). Rosen Group.

Lindsay, Jeanne W. Teens Parenting - Your Baby's First Year: A How-to-Parent Book Especially for Teenage Parents. rev. ed. (Illus.). 192p. (gr. 6 up). 1991. text ed. 15.95 (ISBN 0-930934-53-9); pap. text ed. 9.95 (ISBN 0-930934-52-0); write for info. tchrs. ed.; wkbk. 2.50 (ISBN 0-930934-64-4). Morning Glory.

Long, Lynette. On My Own: The Kids' Self Care Book. Hall, Joann, illus. LC 84-463. 160p. (Orig.). (gr. 1-7). 1984. pap. 7.95 (ISBN 0-87491-735-2). Acropolis.

Weiss, Ellen. Bye-Bye, Bottle. (ps). 1991. 3.95 (ISBN 1-56282-026-5). W Disney Pub.

—Bye-Bye, Diapers. (ps). 1991. 3.95 (ISBN 1-56282-023-0). W Disney Pub.

—Bye-Bye, High Chair. (ps). 1991. 3.95 (ISBN 1-56282-024-9). W Disney Pub.

Worth, Bonnie. Bye-Bye, Crib. (ps). 1991. 3.95 (ISBN 1-56282-025-7). W Disney Pub.

Young, Woody. Babysitting Wise. White, Craig, illus. 48p. (Orig.). 1986. pap. text ed. 4.95 (ISBN 0-939513-31-5). Joy Pub SJC.

CHILDREN–CHARITIES, PROTECTION, ETC.

see Child Welfare

CHILDREN, DELINQUENT

see Juvenile Delinquency

CHILDREN–DISCIPLINE

see Children–Management

CHILDREN–DISEASES

see also Children–Hospitals; also names of diseases e.g. Diptheria; etc.

Bock, Glenn N & Hoff, Marshall G., eds. Someone Special. Belding, Pam & Lasley, Susan K., illus. 32p. (gr. k-6). 1981. write for info. (ISBN 0-940210-00-2). Minn Med Found.

Hathaway, Joe & Hathaway, Nancy. How John Was Unique. 12p. (Orig.). (gr. k-3). 1984. pap. text ed. 3.95 (ISBN 0-918335-01-9). Natl Marfan Foun.

Lerner, Marguerite R. Dear Little Mumps Child. Overlie, George, illus. LC 59-15145. (gr. k-5). 1959. PLB 5.95 (ISBN 0-8225-0003-5). Lerner Pubns.

Ogden, John A. The Medibears Guide to the Doctor's Exam: For Children & Parents. Ogden, Ethel F., illus. (gr. k-5). 1991. 9.95 (ISBN 0-8130-1082-9). U Presses Fla.

Ostrow, William & Ostrow, Vivian. All about Asthma. Levine, Abby, ed. Sims, Blanche, illus. 32p. (gr. 3-7). 1989. PLB 10.95 (ISBN 0-8075-0276-6). A Whitman.

"Using his own experiences as illustrations, a young boy gives a clear & thorough picture of living with asthma. The text is well organized; chapters cover what asthma is & isn't, how its causes are determined, how it is treated, & most importantly, how to manage it. The emphasis is upbeat & positive; great care is taken to portray asthmatics as ordinary individuals who can lead normal lives...This is the best treatment of the subject currently available."--SCHOOL LIBRARY JOURNAL. "An excellent introduction for asthma sufferers & for the general public."--KIRKUS REVIEWS. Ages 8-12.

Publisher Provided Annotation.

Richardson, Joy. What Happens When You Catch a Cold? LC 86-3730. (Illus.). 32p. (gr. 2-3). 1986. PLB 10.95 (ISBN 1-55532-104-6). Gareth Stevens Inc.

Royer, Ruth S. Sarah R. Royer - a Young Alzheimer's Patient: My Memory of Her. 1991. 8.95 (ISBN 0-533-09187-X). Vantage.

CHILDREN–DISEASES–FICTION

Aiello, Barbara & Shulman, Jeffrey. A Portrait of Me: Featuring Christine Kontos. (Illus.). 48p. (gr. 3-6). 1989. PLB 12.95 (ISBN 0-941477-05-3). TFC Bks MD.

Barnes, Caroline. It's No Fun to Be Sick! (Illus.). 32p. (ps-k). 1989. write for info. (ISBN 0-307-12031-7, Pub. by Golden Bks). Western Pub.

Blume, Judy. Deenie. 144p. (gr. 7 up). 1991. pap. 3.50 (ISBN 0-440-93259-9, LFL). Dell.

Gehret, Jeanne. Eagle Eyes: A Child's View of Attention Deficit Disorder. Covert, Susan, illus. Gordon, Michael, intro. by. (Illus.). 32p. (Orig.). (gr. 1-5). 1991. pap. 7.95 (ISBN 0-9625136-1-X). Verbal Images Pr.

A warmly-written story for 6 to 10 year-olds about Attention Deficit Disorder (ADD), which affects nearly two million children in the U.S. Clear, comforting explanations & hopeful solutions about a condition few adults understand. Set in the woodlands of upstate New York, Eagle Eyes' rich illustrations hold the interest of young readers (even reluctant ones), & inspires both children & adults to look for the gifts in people who are different. Children with attention problems identify with the book's young hero & benefit from his realization that he is a special person with special talents. Other young readers become sensitized to the needs of their classmates & siblings who have ADD, & parents are inspired to search for their children's hidden abilities & nurture youngsters' self-esteem. Just as Jeanne Gehret's first book, "The Don't-Give-Up Kid," helped children with learning disabilities, this book is already proving itself to be a valuable educational tool in classrooms & homes throughout the country. Recommended by therapists & leading disability groups including the Council for Exceptional Children, Learning Disabilities Association of America, & Children with Attention Deficit Disorders.

Publisher Provided Annotation.

Gilow, Betty & Tickle, Phyllis. It's No Fun to Be Sick by Paula & Her Friends. (Illus.). (gr. 2-6). 1976. 3.95 (ISBN 0-918518-02-4). St Lukes Pr.

Girard, Linda W. Alex, the Kid with AIDS. Levine, Abby, ed. Sims, Blanche, illus. 32p. (gr. 2-5). 1990. PLB 12.95 (ISBN 0-8075-0245-6). A Whitman.

Hannah, Valerie. No More Sugar: Autobiographical Fiction. Herrick, George H., ed. Rudestan, Janice & Bloom, Arnoldintro. by. (Orig.). 1987. 8.95x (ISBN 0-941281-51-5); pap. 6.95x (ISBN 0-941281-50-7). V H Pub.

Hirsch, Linda. The Sick Story. Wallner, John, illus. (gr. k-3). 1976. 7.95 (ISBN 0-8038-6733-6). Hastings.

Jones, Shelley D. When Laughing Isn't Funny. (Illus.). 1990. 6.95 (ISBN 0-533-08541-1). Vantage.

Laird, Elizabeth. Loving Ben. (gr. 5 up). 1989. 14.95 (ISBN 0-385-29810-2). Delacorte.

MacLachlan, Patricia. The Sick Day. Du Bois, William P., illus. LC 78-11686. (gr. k-3). 1979. 6.95 (ISBN 0-394-83876-9). Pantheon.

Roberts, Willo D. Sugar Isn't Everything: A Support Book, in Fiction Form, for the Young Diabetic. LC 86-17275. 208p. (gr. 4 up). 1987. 13.95 (ISBN 0-689-31316-0, Atheneum Child Bk). Macmillan Child Grp.

—Sugar Isn't Everything: A Support Book, in Fiction Form, for the Young Diabetic. LC 88-3358. 192p. (gr. 3-7). 1988. pap. 3.95 (ISBN 0-689-71225-1, Aladdin). Macmillan Child Grp.

Starkman, Neal. Z's Gift. Ellen, G. & Sasaki, Joy, illus. LC 88-71483. 52p. (Orig.). (gr. 4-6). 1988. pap. 5.95 (ISBN 0-935529-08-X). Comprehen Health Educ.

Wolde, Gunilla. Betsy & the Chicken Pox. Wolde, Gunilla, illus. LC 76-9323. 1990. 4.95 (ISBN 0-394-83328-7). Random.

CHILDREN–EDUCATION

see Education, Elementary

CHILDREN, EMOTIONALLY DISTURBED

see Problem Children

CHILDREN–EMPLOYMENT

see Child Labor

CHILDREN–FICTION

Alexander, Lloyd. Beggar Queen. (gr. 6 up). 1984. 14.95 (ISBN 0-525-44103-4, DCB). Dutton Child Bks.

Babbitt, Lucy C. Children of the Maker. LC 88-45482. 208p. (gr. 6 up). 1988. 13.95 (ISBN 0-374-31245-1). FS&G.

Bannerman, Helen. Little Black Quibba. (Illus.). 68p. (ps-4). 1990. Repr. of 1902 ed. 10.95 (ISBN 0-9616844-4-5). Greenhouse Pub.

—The Story of Little Black Mingo. (Illus.). 72p. (ps-4). 1990. Repr. of 1901 ed. 10.95 (ISBN 0-9616844-5-3). Greenhouse Pub.

—The Story of Little Black Quasha. (Illus.). 56p. (ps-4). 1990. Repr. of 1908 ed. 10.95 (ISBN 0-9616844-3-7). Greenhouse Pub.

Barrett, John M. No Time for Me: Learning to Live with Busy Parents. Servello, Joe, illus. LC 78-21257. 32p. (ps-3). 1985. 16.95 (ISBN 0-87705-385-5). Human Sci Pr.

Barrett, Judi. Cloudy with a Chance of Meatballs. Barrett, Ron, illus. (gr. 2-5). 1985. pap. 12.95 incl. cassette (ISBN 0-941078-91-4); PLB incl. cassette 19.95 (ISBN 0-941078-93-0); incl. cassette, 4 paperbacks guide 27.95 (ISBN 0-941078-92-2). Live Oak Media.

Beatty, Patricia. Lupita Manana. LC 81-505. (gr. 7-9). 1981. PLB 12.88 (ISBN 0-688-00359-1). Morrow.

Beckman, Delores. My Own Private Sky. LC 79-23341. 160p. (gr. 4-6). 1980. 9.95 (ISBN 0-525-35510-3, DCB). Dutton Child Bks.

Birenbaum, Barbara. The Hidden Shadow. Birenbaum, Barbara, illus. LC 86-12187. 54p. (gr. 1-4). 1986. pap. 5.95 (ISBN 0-935343-43-1). Peartree.

Bliss, Ronald G. Child of the Field. Berndt, Bethany, illus. LC 82-71046. 104p. (Orig.). (gr. 5-12). 1985. pap. 3.50x (ISBN 0-943864-18-6). Davenport.

Bonsall, Crosby. The Case of the Scaredy Cats. LC 75-159039. (Illus.). 64p. (ps-3). 1984. pap. 3.50 (ISBN 0-06-444047-8, Trophy). HarpC Child Bks.

Bornstein, Ruth. Little Gorilla. Bornstein, Ruth, illus. LC 75-25508. (ps-3). 1986. pap. 4.95 (ISBN 0-89919-421-4, Pub. by Clarion). Ticknor & Fields.

Bornstein, Ruth L. The Seedling Child. LC 86-19581. (Illus.). 40p. (ps-2). 1987. 12.95 (ISBN 0-15-272459-1). HarBraceJ.

Brancato, Robin F. Come Alive at 505. LC 79-19144. 224p. (gr. 7 up). 1980. 8.95 (ISBN 0-394-84294-4); lib. bdg. 8.99 (ISBN 0-394-94294-9). Knopf.

Brinckloe, Julie. Fireflies. LC 85-26767. (Illus.). 32p. (gr. k-2). 1986. pap. 3.95 (ISBN 0-689-71055-0, Aladdin). Macmillan Child Grp.

Burgess, Thornton W. Mother West Wind's Children. Cady, Harrison, illus. 156p. (ps-3). 1985. pap. 6.95 (ISBN 0-316-11657-2). Little.

Busch, Wilhelm. Max & Moritz. Klein, H. Arthur, ed. 216p. (Orig., Bilingual Eng & Ger). (gr. 3-6). 1962. pap. 4.95 (ISBN 0-486-20181-3). Dover.

Carlson, Nancy. Loudmouth George & the Cornet. LC 84-18121. (Illus.). 32p. (ps-3). 1985. pap. 3.95 (ISBN 0-14-050509-1, Puffin). Puffin Bks.

—Loudmouth George & the Cornet. Carlson, Nancy, illus. (gr. k-3). 1986. pap. 12.95 incl. cassette (ISBN 0-87499-011-4); PLB incl. cassette 19.95 (ISBN 0-87499-013-0); incl. cassette 4 paperbacks guide 27.95 (ISBN 0-87499-012-2). Live Oak Media.

—Loudmouth George & the Sixth Grade Bully. LC 84-18120. (Illus.). 32p. (ps-3). 1985. pap. 3.95 (ISBN 0-14-050510-5, Puffin). Puffin Bks.

Caseley, Judith. Ada Potato. LC 87-19738. (Illus.). 24p. (ps up). 1989. 11.95 (ISBN 0-688-07742-0); PLB 11.88 (ISBN 0-688-07743-9). Greenwillow.

Clapp, Patricia C. Witches' Children. (gr. 5-9). 1987. pap. 3.95 (ISBN 0-14-032407-0, Puffin). Puffin Bks.

Cleary, Beverly. Henry & Beezus. Darling, Louis, illus. LC 52-5930. (gr. 3-7). 1952. 13.95 (ISBN 0-688-21383-9); PLB 13.88 (ISBN 0-688-31383-3, Morrow Jr Bks). Morrow Jr Bks.

—Jean & Johnny. 224p. (gr. 6-9). 1981. pap. 2.95 (ISBN 0-440-94358-2, LE). Dell.

—Ramona Quimby, Age Eight. Tiegreen, Alan, illus. LC 80-28425. 192p. (gr. 4-6). 1981. 13.95 (ISBN 0-688-00477-6); PLB 13.88 (ISBN 0-688-00478-4). Morrow.

Conrad, Pam. Staying Nine. LC 87-45862. (Illus.). 80p. (gr. 2-5). 1990. pap. 3.25 (ISBN 0-06-440377-7, Trophy). HarpC Child Bks.

Cooper, Susan. Seaward. LC 86-23234. 180p. (gr. 5 up). 1987. pap. 3.95 (ISBN 0-02-042190-7, Collier Young Ad). Macmillan Child Grp.

Corbett, Scott. The Lemonade Trick. Galdone, Paul, illus. 96p. (gr. 4-6). 1988. pap. 2.95 (ISBN 0-590-32197-8, Apple Paperbacks). Scholastic Inc.

Cosgrove, Stephen. Feather Fin. James, Robin, illus. LC 84-15057. 32p. (Orig.). (gr. k-4). 1983. pap. 2.95 (ISBN 0-8431-0593-3). Price Stern.

Cresswell, Helen. Moondial. LC 87-5626. 208p. (gr. 5-9). 1987. 14.95 (ISBN 0-02-725370-8, Mcmillan Child Bk). Macmillan Child Grp.

Dalgliesh, Alice. The Courage of Sarah Noble. Weisgard, Leonard, illus. LC 54-5922. 60p. (gr. 1-5). 1986. pap. 4.95 (ISBN 0-689-71057-7, Aladdin). Macmillan Child Grp.

Deans, Virginia B. Kate's Scarf. Deans, Virgina B., illus. LC 82-70228. 136p. (Orig.). (gr. 5-12). 1985. pap. 4.50x (ISBN 0-943864-36-4). Davenport.

Deary, Terry. The Custard Kid. Firmin, Charlotte, illus. LC 81-21693. 96p. (gr. 2-6). 1982. PLB 8.95 (ISBN 0-87614-188-2). Carolrhoda Bks.

—The Custard Kid. Firmin, Charlotte, illus. LC 81-21693. 96p. (gr. 3-7). 1991. pap. 3.50 (ISBN 0-06-440360-2, Trophy). HarpC Child Bks.

DeClements, Barthe. No Place for Me. (gr. 5-9). 1987. pap. 12.95 (ISBN 0-670-81908-5). Viking Child Bks.

Delton, Alan T., illus. Huckleberry Hash. 1990. pap. 2.95 (ISBN 0-440-40325-1, YB). Dell.

Delton, Judy. Angel's Mother's Baby. Apple, Margot, illus. 144p. (gr. 2-5). 1989. 13.95 (ISBN 0-395-50926-2). HM.

DePaola, Tomie. Katie & Kit & the Sleepover. 1987. 3.95 (ISBN 0-671-61723-0, Little Simon). S&S Trade.

—Katie & Kit at the Beach. 1987. 3.95 (ISBN 0-671-61722-2, Little Simon). S&S Trade.

Drescher, Joan. I'm in Charge. Drescher, Joan, illus. (gr. 1-3). 1981. 9.95 (ISBN 0-316-19330-5, Pub. by Atlantic Pr). Little.

Duncan, Lois. Wonder Kid Meets the Evil Lunch Snatcher. (gr. 2-4). 1990. pap. 2.95 (ISBN 0-316-19561-8). Little.

Ellis, Terry. The Legend of Willow Wood Springs. LC 85-63828. (Illus.). 180p. (Orig.). (gr. 4 up). 1989. pap. 3.75 (ISBN 0-915677-30-X). Roundtable Pub.

Engh, M. J. The House in the Snow. LC 87-5500. (Illus.). 144p. (gr. 3-5). 1987. 11.95 (ISBN 0-531-05717-8); PLB 11.99 (ISBN 0-531-08317-9). Orchard Bks Watts.

—House in the Snow. 144p. 1990. pap. 2.75 (ISBN 0-590-42658-3). Scholastic Inc.

Enns, Peter & Forsberg, Glen. Stories That Live, 6 vols. Friesen, John H., illus. 144p. (ps-5). 1985. books & cassettes 29.70 (ISBN 0-936215-00-3). STL Intl.

Farjeon, Eleanor. The Glass Slipper. LC 85-45853. 288p. (gr. 3-8). 1986. Repr. of 1956 ed. 11.95 (ISBN 0-397-32180-5, Lipp Jr Bks); (Lipp Jr Bks). HarpC Child Bks.

Ferris, Jean. Looking for Home. 176p. (gr. 8 up). 1989. 12.95 (ISBN 0-374-34649-6). FS&G.

Field, Rachel. Prayer for a Child. Jones, Elizabeth O., illus. LC 84-70991. 32p. (ps-k). 1984. pap. 3.95 (ISBN 0-02-043070-1, Aladdin). Macmillan Child Grp.

Finley, Martha. Elsie's Children. 243p. 1981. Repr. PLB 21.95x (ISBN 0-89966-336-2). Buccaneer Bks.

Fishman, Richard A. The Sandlot Summit. Sutter, Richard, illus. LC 85-63032. 197p. (Orig.). (gr. 4-9). 1985. pap. 3.95 (ISBN 0-9615884-0-3). Sunlakes Pub.

Freedman, Russell. Children of the Wild West. LC 83-5133. (Illus.). 128p. (gr. 3-6). 1983. 14.95 (ISBN 0-89919-143-6, Pub. by Clarion). Ticknor & Fields.

Giff, Patricia R. Spectacular Stone Soup. 80p. (Orig.). (gr. k-6). 1989. pap. 2.75 (ISBN 0-440-40134-8, YB). Dell.

—Today Was a Terrible Day. Natti, Susanna, illus. 1980. 11.95 (ISBN 0-670-71830-0). Viking Child Bks.

Gipson, Fred. Savage Sam. (gr. 1-5). 1976. pap. 4.95 (ISBN 0-06-080377-0, P377, PL). HarperCollins.

Gorman, Carol. Chelsey & the Green-Haired Kid. (gr. 5 up). 1987. 13.95 (ISBN 0-395-41854-2). HM.

Grosset & Dunlap Staff. I'm So Big! (Illus.). 18p. (ps). 1991. bds. 2.95 (ISBN 0-448-40122-3, G&D). Putnam Pub Group.

Ham, Marion, et al. Little Hands. (Illus.). 64p. (ps up). 1986. pap. 2.50 (ISBN 0-916410-19-6). A D Bragdon.

Hastings. Rufus & Christopher & the Box of Laughter. LC 77-190270. (Illus.). 32p. (gr. 2-4). 1972. PLB 9.95 (ISBN 0-87783-060-6); pap. 3.94 deluxe ed. (ISBN 0-87783-106-8); cassette 7.94x (ISBN 0-87783-196-3). Oddo.

Higgins, Betty. Witch Watch. Sun Star Publications Staff, ed. Yazzie, Johnson, illus. August, Clara & Schatt, Paulintro. by. (Illus.). 24p. (Orig.). (gr. 3-8). 1986. pap. 2.95 (ISBN 0-937787-05-1). Sun Star Pubns.

Jarrow, Gail. The Two-ton Secret. 144p. (gr. 5). 1989. pap. 2.95 (ISBN 0-380-75904-7, Camelot). Avon.

Johnson, Sue. At Grandma's House: Story Book for Young Children in Sign Language. Herigstad, Joni, illus. 28p. 1985. pap. 4.50 (ISBN 0-916708-14-4). Modern Signs.

Kaye, Marilyn. Looking for Trouble. 128p. (gr. 4). 1990. pap. 2.95 (ISBN 0-380-75909-8, Camelot). Avon.

Keats, Ezra J. Apartment Three. LC 85-26791. (Illus.). 32p. (gr. 1-5). 1986. pap. 3.95 (ISBN 0-689-71059-3, Aladdin). Macmillan Child Grp.

—Goggles. LC 70-78081. 32p. (ps-3). 1971. pap. 4.95 (ISBN 0-02-044100-2, Collier Young Ad). Macmillan Child Grp.

Keto, C. Tsehloane. Children of Mareng. Keto, Lefa & Keto, Lefanyana, illus. 15p. (Orig.). (gr. 1-3). 1989. pap. write for info. K A Pubns.

Kimmelman, Leslie. Frannie's Fruits. Mathers, Petra, illus. LC 88-17637. 32p. (ps-3). 1989. 12.95 (ISBN 0-06-023143-2); PLB 12.89 (ISBN 0-06-023164-5). HarpC Child Bks.

Klein, Norma. Mom, the Wolfman & Me. (gr. 5 up). 1972. lib. bdg. 9.99 (ISBN 0-394-92470-3). Pantheon.

Klein, Robin. People Might Hear You. (gr. 5-9). 1987. 11.95 (ISBN 0-670-80303-0). Viking Child Bks.

Klevin, Jill R. Turtles Together Forever! Edwards, Linda S., illus. LC 82-70313. 160p. (gr. 4-6). 1982. pap. 9.95 (ISBN 0-385-29045-4); pap. 9.89 (ISBN 0-385-29046-2). Delacorte.

Konigsburg, E. L. Journey to an 800 Number. LC 81-10829. 144p. (gr. 5-9). 1982. 13.95 (ISBN 0-689-30901-5, Atheneum Child Bk). Macmillan Child Grp.

Landsman, Sandra G. I'm Special: An Experiential Workbook for the Child in Us All. Landman, Rodney G., illus. (gr. k up). 1986. pap. 6.95 (ISBN 0-935571-02-7). Treehouse.

Lasky, Kathryn. A Baby for Max. Knight, Christopher G., illus. LC 86-22131. 48p. (ps-2). 1987. pap. 4.95 (ISBN 0-689-71118-2, Aladdin). Macmillan Child Grp.

Lengyel, Emil. Iran. (Illus.). (gr. 4-6). 1981. PLB 10.40 s&l (ISBN 0-531-02242-0). Watts.

Lewis, Luevester. Jackie. Jolly, Cheryl, illus. (gr. k-5). 1970. pap. 1.00. Third World.

Lindgren, Astrid. The Children of Noisy Village. (gr. 3-7). 1988. pap. 3.95 (ISBN 0-14-032609-X, Puffin). Puffin Bks.

—Mischevious Meg. Bothmer, Gerry, tr. Domanska, Janina, illus. LC 85-575. (ps-k). 1985. pap. 4.95 (ISBN 0-14-031954-9, Puffin). Puffin Bks.

Lord, Athena V. Today's Special: Z. A. P. & Zoe. Jenkins, Jean, illus. LC 84-9661. 160p. (gr. 4-7). 1984. 13.95 (ISBN 0-02-761440-9, Mcmillan Child Bk). Macmillan Child Grp.

Lorenz, Lee. Scornful Simkin. Lorenz, Lee, illus. 30p. (Orig.). (gr. k-3). 1982. pap. 3.95 (ISBN 0-13-796730-6, Pub. by Treehouse). P-H.

Lorian, Nicole. Popple Peeking. Beylon, Cathy, illus. 24p. (ps-1). 1986. 5.95 (ISBN 0-394-88040-4). Random.

Low, Joseph. Mice Twice. LC 85-26768. (Illus.). 32p. (ps-3). 1986. pap. 4.95 (ISBN 0-689-71060-7, Aladdin). Macmillan Child Grp.

Lowry, Lois. Rabble Starkey. (gr. 5 up). 1987. 12.95 (ISBN 0-395-43607-9). HM.

McBrier, Page. Spaghetti Breath. 128p. (gr. 4). 1989. pap. 2.50 (ISBN 0-380-75782-6, Camelot). Avon.

—Under Twelve Not Allowed. 128p. (gr. 4). 1989. pap. 2.50 (ISBN 0-380-75780-X, Camelot). Avon.

McCloskey, Robert. Centerburg Tales. (Illus.). (gr. 1-3). 1977. pap. 3.95 (ISBN 0-14-031072-X, Puffin). Puffin Bks.

McDowell, Mildred. The Little People. Whitaker, Arleen, illus. Harman, Sandra L., intro. by. LC 72-133255. (Illus.). 44p. (gr. 1-2). 1971. 2.50 (ISBN 0-87884-002-8). Unicorn Ent.

McRae, Patrick, illus. Peter Cottontail. 24p. (Orig.). (gr. k-6). 1986. pap. 2.95 (ISBN 0-8249-8106-5). Ideals.

Mahy, Margaret. Jam. Craig, Helen, illus. 32p. (ps-3). 1986. 12.95 (ISBN 0-316-54396-9, 543969, Joy St Bks). Little.

Marryat, Captain. The Children of the New Forest. 304p. (gr. 4-6). 1984. pap. 2.25 (ISBN 0-14-035019-5, Puffin). Puffin Bks.

Marshall, James. George & Martha. Marshall, James, illus. LC 74-184250. 48p. (gr. k-3). 1972. 13.95 (ISBN 0-395-16619-5). HM.

Matthews, Morgan. Silly Sidney. Kolding, Richard M., illus. LC 85-14063. 48p. (Orig.). (gr. 1-3). 1986. PLB 9.89 (ISBN 0-8167-0610-7); pap. text ed. 2.95 (ISBN 0-8167-0611-5). Troll Assocs.

—Which Way, Hugo? Miller, Susan, illus. LC 85-14132. 48p. (Orig.). (gr. 1-3). 1986. PLB 9.89 (ISBN 0-8167-0648-4); pap. text ed. 2.95 (ISBN 0-8167-0649-2). Troll Assocs.

Mauser, Patricia R. A Bundle of Sticks. Owens, Gail, illus. LC 81-8098. 176p. (gr. 3-5). 1982. 13.95 (ISBN 0-689-30899-X, Atheneum Child Bk). Macmillan Child Grp.

Moncure, Jane B. Now I Am Five! Endres, Helen, illus. LC 83-25264. 32p. (ps). 1984. PLB 14.60 (ISBN 0-516-01879-5); pap. 3.95 (ISBN 0-516-41879-3). Childrens.

—Now I Am Four! Hutton, Kathryn, illus. LC 83-25270. 32p. (ps). 1984. PLB 14.60 (ISBN 0-516-01878-7); pap. 3.95 (ISBN 0-516-41878-5). Childrens.

—Now I Am Three! Hohag, Linda, illus. LC 83-20892. 32p. (ps). 1984. PLB 14.60 (ISBN 0-516-01877-9); pap. 3.95 (ISBN 0-516-41877-7). Childrens.

—Now I Am Two! Hutton, Kathryn, illus. LC 83-20891. 32p. (ps). 1984. PLB 14.60 (ISBN 0-516-01876-0); pap. 3.95 (ISBN 0-516-41876-9). Childrens.

Nelson, Theresa. Devil Storm. LC 87-5493. 224p. (gr. 5-7). 1987. 12.95 (ISBN 0-531-05711-9); PLB 12.99 (ISBN 0-531-08311-X). Orchard Bks Watts.

Nesbit, Edith. Five Children & It. 182p. 1981. Repr. PLB 19.95 (ISBN 0-89967-036-9). Harmony Raine.

—The Railway Children. (gr. 5-8). 1988. 15.50 (ISBN 0-8446-6345-X). Peter Smith.

Newberry Library Award Staff. The Newberry Library Award. Incl. The Twenty-One Balloons. Pene du Bois, William; The Witch of Blackbird Pond. Speare, Elizabeth; Johnny Tremain. Forbes, Esther; Island of the Blue Dolphins. O'Dell, Scott. 1983. pap. 12.30 boxed set (ISBN 0-440-46256-8). Dell.

O'Brien, Richard. Evil. (Orig.). (gr. 7 up). 1989. pap. 3.50 (ISBN 0-440-20226-4). Dell.

O'Brien, Robert C. Mrs. Frisby & the Rats of NIMH. 248p. (gr. 3-7). 1986. pap. 3.95 (ISBN 0-689-71068-2, Aladdin). Macmillan Child Grp.

Oxenbury, Helen. I Can. Oxenbury, Helen, illus. LC 85-61369. 14p. (ps). 1986. Repr. of 1986 ed. bds. 3.95 (ISBN 0-394-87482-X). Random.

Pascal, Francine. Surprise! Surprise! (ps-3). 1989. pap. 2.75 (ISBN 0-553-15758-2, Skylark). Bantam.

Payne, Sherry N. A Contest. Kyle, Jeff, illus. LC 81-15440. 40p. (gr. 1-4). 1982. PLB 7.95 (ISBN 0-87614-176-9). Carolrhoda Bks.

Peeples, H. I. Meet the Itty-Bitty Kiddies. Montgomery, Michael, illus. 24p. 1989. 7.95 (ISBN 0-8092-4346-6, Calico Bks). Contemp Bks.

Peet, Bill. Jennifer & Josephine. Peet, Bill, illus. (gr. k-3). 1980. 13.95 (ISBN 0-395-18225-5); pap. 3.95 (ISBN 0-395-29608-0). HM.

Pugh, Judith. Wombalong. Pugh, Clifton, illus. 32p. (gr. 2-5). 1986. 9.95 (ISBN 0-915391-20-1, Pub. by Mad Hatter Bks); pap. 6.95 (ISBN 0-915391-19-8, Pub. by Mad Hatter Bks). Slawson Comm.

Quackenbush, Robert. Henry's Important Date. Quackenbush, Robert, illus. LC 81-5026. 48p. (ps-3). 1982. 5.95 (ISBN 0-8193-1067-0); PLB 5.95 (ISBN 0-8193-1068-9). Parents.

The Railway Children. (Illus.). (gr. 3-5). 3.50 (ISBN 0-7214-0824-9). Ladybird Bks.

Ransom, Candice F. Sabrina. 224p. (Orig.). (gr. 7 up). 1986. pap. 2.25 (ISBN 0-590-33845-5, Sunfire). Scholastic Inc.

Ray, Satyajit. Phatik Chand. Ray, Lila, tr. from BEN. 108p. (gr. 6-8). 1984. pap. 8.00 (ISBN 0-86578-230-X). Ind-US Inc.

Reepen, Ronald. Lefty Meets Hefty. Reepen, Ronald, illus. 40p. (gr. 2-7). 1987. 6.95 (ISBN 0-930905-02-4). Platypus Bks.

Rey, H. A. Anybody at Home? (Illus.). 24p. (gr. k-3). 1942. pap. 2.25 (ISBN 0-395-07045-7, Sandpiper). HM.

Roberts, Willo D. Don't Hurt Laurie! Sanderson, Ruth, illus. LC 76-46569. 176p. (gr. 4-6). 1977. 13.95 (ISBN 0-689-30571-0, Atheneum Child Bk). Macmillan Child Grp.

Rodgers, Mary. Freaky Friday. LC 74-183158. 156p. (gr. 5-8). 1972. 12.95 (ISBN 0-06-025048-8); PLB 12.89 (ISBN 0-06-025049-6). HarpC Child Bks.

Roos, Stephen. The Terrible Truth: Secrets of a Sixth-Grader. Newsom, Carol, illus. LC 83-5253. 128p. (gr. 4-6). 1983. 12.95 (ISBN 0-385-29306-2). Delacorte.

Rosenberg, Maxine B. Making a New Home in America. Ancona, George, illus. LC 85-11642. 48p. (gr. 1-4). 1986. 11.95 (ISBN 0-688-05824-8); PLB 11.88 (ISBN 0-688-05825-6). Lothrop.

Rosholt, Malcolm & Rosholt, Margaret. The Child of Two Mothers. Larson, Lynn, illus. LC 83-63177. 108p. (gr. 4 up). 1983. PLB 9.95x (ISBN 0-910417-03-2). Rosholt Hse.

Rylant, Cynthia. Children of Christmas: Stories for the Season. Schindler, S. D., illus. LC 87-1690. 48p. (gr. 3 up). 1987. 11.95 (ISBN 0-531-05706-2); PLB 11.99 (ISBN 0-531-08306-3). Orchard Bks Watts.

Sachs, Marilyn. Class Pictures. LC 80-390. (gr. 4-7). 1980. 13.95 (ISBN 0-525-27985-7, DCB). Dutton Child Bks.

Sargent, Pamela. Alien Child. LC 87-45303. 256p. (gr. 7 up). 1988. 13.95 (ISBN 0-06-025202-2); PLB 13.89 (ISBN 0-06-025203-0). HarpC Child Bks.

Sargent, Sarah. Weird Henry Berg. 160p. (gr. 5 up). 1981. pap. 2.25 (ISBN 0-440-49346-3, YB). Dell.

Schulz, Charles M. Apuros Escolares. (SPA., Illus.). (gr. 3-8). 1.50 (ISBN 0-685-28419-0). French & Eur.

Schwartz, Amy. Bea & Mr. Jones. Schwartz, Amy, illus. 30p. (ps-3). 1983. pap. 3.95 (ISBN 0-14-050439-7, Puffin). Puffin Bks.

Seuling, Barbara. You Can't Sneeze with Your Eyes Open: And Other Freaky Facts about the Human Body. Seuling, Barbara, illus. LC 86-6304. 80p. (gr. 4 up). 1986. 12.95 (ISBN 0-525-67185-4, Lodestar Bks). Dutton Child Bks.

Seymour, Peter. You Can Be Anything. 22p. (ps-1). 1986. 5.95 (ISBN 0-8431-1462-2). Price Stern.

Shearon, Lillian N. Little Mixer. Lohse, W. R., illus. (gr. 2-6). 1945. 3.95 (ISBN 0-672-50357-3, Bobbs). Macmillan.

Shyer, Marlene F. Here I Am, an Only Child. Carrick, Donald, illus. LC 85-40298. 32p. (gr. k-3). 1985. 12.95 (ISBN 0-684-18296-3, Scribners Young Read). Macmillan Child Grp.

—Here I Am, an Only Child. Carrick, Donald, illus. LC 87-1112. 32p. (ps-3). 1987. pap. 3.95 (ISBN 0-689-71156-5, Aladdin). Macmillan Child Grp.

Sidney, Margaret. Five Little Peppers & How They Grew. LC 89-62372. 288p. (gr. 4 up). 1990. pap. 2.95 (ISBN 0-14-035127-2, Puffin). Puffin Bks.

Smith, L. J. The Night of the Solstice. LC 87-11068. 240p. (gr. 5 up). 1987. 14.95 (ISBN 0-02-785840-5, Mcmillan Child Bk). Macmillan Child Grp.

Stanley, Diane. The Good-Luck Pencil. Degen, Bruce, illus. LC 85-13122. 32p. (gr. k-2). 1986. 12.95 (ISBN 0-02-786800-1, Four Winds). Macmillan Child Grp.

Stein, Gertrude. The World Is Round. limited ed. Hurd, Clement, illus. Hurd, Margaret T., intro. by. (Illus.). (gr. 3 up). 1985. 200.00 (ISBN 0-910457-16-6). Arion Pr.

Stolz, Mary. Lands End. LC 73-7139. 176p. (gr. 7 up). 1973. PLB 9.89 (ISBN 0-06-025917-5). HarpC Child Bks.

Strauss, Barbara & Friedland, Helen. See You Later Alligator. D'Elgin, Tershia, illus. 28p. 1986. 6.95 (ISBN 0-8431-1554-8). Price Stern.

Streatfeild, Noel. Thursday's Child. (Orig.). (gr. 5 up). 1986. pap. 3.50 (ISBN 0-440-48687-4, YB). Dell.

Supraner, Robyn. Amazing Mark. Levy, Pam, illus. LC 85-14070. 48p. (Orig.). (gr. 1-3). 1986. PLB 9.89 (ISBN 0-8167-0644-1); pap. text ed. 2.95 (ISBN 0-8167-0645-X). Troll Assocs.

—No Room for a Sneeze! Trivas, Irene, illus. LC 85-14164. 48p. (Orig.). (gr. 1-3). 1986. PLB 9.89 (ISBN 0-8167-0656-5); pap. text ed. 2.95 (ISBN 0-8167-0657-3). Troll Assocs.

Tafuri, Nancy. The Ball Bounced. LC 87-37582. (Illus.). 24p. (ps up). 1989. 11.95 (ISBN 0-688-07871-0). Greenwillow.

Thompson, Julian F. Simon Pure. 336p. (gr. 10-12). 1987. pap. 12.95x (ISBN 0-590-40507-1, Scholastic Hardcover). Scholastic Inc.

Utz. The Simple Pink Bubble That Ended the Trouble with Jonathan Hubble. LC 78-190273. (Illus.). 32p. (gr. 2-3). 1972. PLB 9.95 (ISBN 0-87783-062-2); pap. 3.94 deluxe ed. (ISBN 0-87783-108-4). Oddo.

Vaughan, Marcia K. Wombat Stew. Lofts, Pamela, illus. LC 85-63492. 32p. (ps-3). 1986. 8.95 (ISBN 0-382-09211-2); s.p. 6.71 (ISBN 0-685-12391-X). Silver Burdett Pr.

Von Rosenberg, Marjorie. Max & Martha: Children from Germany in the Texas Hill Country. (Illus.). 48p. (gr. 4-7). 1986. 8.95 (ISBN 0-89015-539-9, Pub. by Panda Bks). Eakin Pr.

Waber, Bernard. Ira Sleeps Over. Waber, Bernard, illus. LC 72-75605. 48p. (gr. k-3). 1973. 13.95 (ISBN 0-395-13893-0). HM.

—You're a Little Kid with a Big Heart. (Illus.). (gr. k-3). 1980. 14.95 (ISBN 0-395-29163-1). HM.

Wahl, Robert. Friend Dog. Ewers, Joe, illus. (ps). 1988. 12.95 (ISBN 0-316-91710-9). Little.

Walker, Mort & Browne, Dik. Hi & Lois: Trixie a la Mode. 128p. 1986. pap. 1.95 (ISBN 0-8125-6904-0, Dist. by Warner Pub Service & St. Martin's Press). Tor Bks.

Walsh, Jill P. A Chance Child. 144p. (gr. 7 up). 1980. pap. 1.95 (ISBN 0-380-48561-3, 48561-3, Flare). Avon.

—A Chance Child. (Illus.). 192p. (gr. 5 up). 1991. pap. 3.95 (ISBN 0-374-41174-3). FS&G.

Warner, Gertrude C. The Boxcar Children Series. 1990. pap. 3.50 ea. A Whitman.

Weiss, Ann E. Good Neighbors? (gr. 5-8). 1985. 12.95 (ISBN 0-317-38803-7). HM.

White, Ellen E. White House Autumn. (Orig.). (gr. 7 up). 1985. pap. 2.95 (ISBN 0-380-89780-6, Flare). Avon.

Will & Nicolas. Finders Keepers. Mordvinoff, Nicolas, illus. LC 51-12326. 32p. (ps-3). 1989. pap. 3.95 (ISBN 0-15-630950-5, VoyB). HarBraceJ.

Yep, Laurence. The Serpent's Children. LC 82-48855. 288p. (gr. 7 up). 1984. PLB 13.89 (ISBN 0-06-026812-3). HarpC Child Bks.

CHILDREN–GROWTH

Ames, Evelyn E. & Trucano, Lucille. Becoming Male & Female. LC 88-63796. (Illus.). 116p. (gr. 9-12). 1988. pap. text ed. 9.95 (ISBN 0-935529-05-5). Comprehen Health Educ.

Harris, Robbie & Levy, Elizabeth. Before You Were Three: How You Began to Walk, Talk, Explore & Have Feelings. Gordillo, Henry E., photos by. LC 76-5587. 160p. (gr. 1 up). 1981. pap. 7.95 (ISBN 0-440-00471-3). Delacorte.

Hutchins, Pat. You'll Soon Grow into Them, Titch. LC 84-22251. (Illus.). 32p. (ps-3). 1985. pap. 3.95 (ISBN 0-14-050434-6, Puffin). Puffin Bks.

Kino Learning Center Staff, et al. My Changing Body. Mirocha, Kay, illus. 64p. (gr. 5-9). 1987. pap. 7.95 (ISBN 0-86653-420-2, GA1030). Good Apple.

—My Journal of Personal Growth. Mirocha, Kay, illus. 64p. (gr. 5-9). 1987. pap. 7.95 (ISBN 0-86653-418-0, GA 1028). Good Apple.

Kirk, Pat & Brown, Alice. Bear Buddies: A Child Learns to Make Friends. (Illus.). (ps-2). 1986. 4.95 (ISBN 0-915720-55-8). Brownlow Pub Co.

—Bear Up: A Child Learns to Handle Ups & Downs. (Illus.). (ps-2). 1986. 4.95 (ISBN 0-915720-51-5). Brownlow Pub Co.

—Bearing Burdens: A Child Learns to Help. (Illus.). (ps-2). 1986. 4.95 (ISBN 0-915720-54-X). Brownlow Pub Co.

—Love Bears All Things: A Child Learns to Love. (Illus.). (ps-2). 1986. 4.95 (ISBN 0-915720-50-7). Brownlow Pub Co.

Moyer, Inez. Responding to Infants. LC 83-71345. 200p. (Orig.). (ps). 1983. pap. 18.95 (ISBN 0-513-01769-0). Denison.

Ortiz, Simon. The Importance of Childhood. Gracia, Fred D., illus. 16p. (Orig.). (ps-7). 1982. pap. 3.75 (ISBN 0-915347-01-6). Pueblo Acoma Pr.

Phifer, Kate G. Tall & Small: A Book about Height. Kendrick, Dennis, illus. LC 86-32401. 96p. (gr. 5 up). 1987. 11.95 (ISBN 0-8027-6684-6); PLB 12.85 (ISBN 0-8027-6685-4). Walker & Co.

Quality Time Workbooks: I Can Look & Learn. 1991. 1.98 (ISBN 0-8317-7299-9). Smithmark.

Quality Time Workbooks: I Can Think & Do. 1991. 1.98 (ISBN 0-8317-7298-0). Smithmark.

Richardson, Joy. What Happens When You Grow? LC 86-3727. (Illus.). 32p. (gr. 2-3). 1986. PLB 10.95 (ISBN 1-55532-106-2). Gareth Stevens Inc.

Sealy, Adrienne V. Mama, Watch Out - I'm Growing Up. (Illus.). (gr. 2-5). 1978. PLB 4.95x (ISBN 0-9602670-1-8). Assn Family Living.

Stanford, Sylvia. I'm Growing. (Illus.). (ps). 1986. 4.95 (ISBN 0-8054-4167-0). Broadman.

Swenson, Allan A. Allan Swenson's Big Fun to Grow Book. (Illus.). (gr. 3-7). 1980. pap. 4.95. McKay.

Thiry, Joan. Discovering the Whole You. Titra, Stephen, illus. 64p. (Orig.). (gr. 5-6). 1991. pap. text ed. 5.25 (ISBN 0-935046-05-4); tchr's. edition 14.00. Chateau Thierry.
DISCOVERING THE WHOLE YOU presents a Family Life Unit in Human Reproduction as related to science units on human reproduction. It is created for use with middle-grade, preteen children. The facts of human reproduction are placed in context of animal reproduction from protozoa to mammals. Human reproduction is taught as part of a total person growth process. An important aspect of this approach is the emphasis on the emotional, mental, moral & social growth of the child entering puberty. The physical growth of the child is kept in the context of the development of all areas of personality growth. Rites of passage for those entering puberty are also presented as part of total personal growth. This total person development is based on the psychology of William Glasser, M.D. It is, therefore, an approach to positive emotional growth. The activities aim to strengthen the child's sense of self-worth, self-respect, self-responsibility. The projects & discussions are multicultural & intergenerational, especially in exploring rites of passage in various cultures. Parent involvement is an important aspect of this approach. There is an accompanying teacher/leader guide.
Publisher Provided Annotation.

Yemm, Marta. Years to Grow. LC 81-68369. (Illus.). 600p. (Orig.). (ps-k). 1981. pap. 31.95 (ISBN 0-513-01724-0). Denison.

CHILDREN–HEALTH

see Children–Care and Hygiene

CHILDREN–HOSPITALS

see also Child Welfare; Children–Diseases

Alsop, Peter, et al. In the Hospital. 64p. (Orig.). (gr. k-6). 1989. pap. 12.98g (ISBN 1-877942-00-6, MS503). Moose Schl Records.

Going to the Hospital. (ps). 1990. 2.99 (ISBN 0-517-69197-3). Outlet Bk Co.

Krall, Charlotte B. & Jim, Judith M. Fat Dog's First Visit: A Child's View of the Hospital. Hull, Nancy, ed. & illus. LC 87-2745. 28p. (Orig.). (ps-3). 1987. pap. text ed. 4.00 (ISBN 0-939838-23-0). Pritchett & Hull.

Livingston, Carole & Ciliotta, Claire. Why Am I Going to the Hospital? Walter, Paul, illus. (gr. 1 up). 1981. 12. 00 (ISBN 0-8184-0316-0). Carol Pub Group.

Rosenstock, Judith D. & Rosenstock, Harvey A. Your Hospital Stay...It'll Be Okay. Sorg, James M., illus. 36p. (Orig.). (gr. 1-5). 1988. pap. 4.95 (ISBN 0-9622172-0-4). D Miller Fndtn.

CHILDREN–MANAGEMENT

Here are entered books on child training and discipline. These books may include psychological matter such as is entered under Child Study, but their content and purpose are more practical. Books on management of children in school are entered under School Discipline.

see also Baby Sitters; Character Education; Problem Children

Allison, Alida. The Toddler's Potty Book. 32p. (ps). 1985. softcover 3.95 (ISBN 0-8431-0673-5). Price Stern.

Connors, Patricia & Perucci, Dorianne. Runaways: Coping at Home & on the Street. Rosen, Ruth, ed. (gr. 7-12). 1989. PLB 12.95 (ISBN 0-8239-1019-9). Rosen Group.

Deakin, Michael. Children on the Hill. LC 73-1731. 128p. 1973. 5.95 (ISBN 0-672-51843-0, Bobbs). Macmillan.

Kleeberg, Irene C. Latchkey Kid. Green, Anne C., illus. LC 85-5077. 102p. (gr. 4-6). 1985. PLB 11.90 (ISBN 0-531-10052-9). Watts.

Monroe, Judy. Latchkey Children. LC 89-1383. (Illus.). 48p. (gr. 4 up). 1989. 10.95 (ISBN 0-89686-438-3, Crestwood Hse). Macmillan Child Grp.

Rogers, Fred. Going to the Potty. Judkis, Jim, illus. 32p. (ps-2). 1986. 12.95 (ISBN 0-399-21296-5, Putnam); pap. 5.95 (ISBN 0-399-21297-3, Putnam). Putnam Pub Group.

Smith, Michael W. & Ridenour, Fritz. Old Enough to Know. 111p. 1989. write for info. (ISBN 0-8499-3162-2). Word Bks.

Spizman, Robyn F. Lollipop Grapes & Clothespin Critters: Quick, On-the-Spot Remedies for Restless of Children 2-10. LC 84-24548. 160p. (ps-5). 1985. pap. 7.64 (ISBN 0-201-06497-9). Addison-Wesley.

CHILDREN–MANAGEMENT–FICTION

Himmel, Roger J. Taking Turns. Manoni, Mary H., ed. Peters, Luther J. & Ross, Connie, illus. (gr. k-3). 1978. pap. text ed. 29.95 6 bks. & 1 cass. (ISBN 0-89290-047-4); pap. text ed. 10.95 1 bk. & 1 cass. Soc for Visual.

Lampert, Emily. A Little Touch of Monster. Kroupa, Melanie, illus. LC 85-26847. 32p. (ps-3). 1986. lib. bdg. 12.95 (ISBN 0-316-51287-7, 512877, Joy St Bks). Little.

Soderstrom, Mary. Maybe Tomorrow I'll Have a Good Time. Wein, Charlotte E., illus. LC 80-25357. 32p. (ps-3). 1981. 16.95 (ISBN 0-89885-012-6). Human Sci Pr.

Wojciechowska, Maia. Don't Play Dead Before You Have To. LC 76-112485. (gr. 7 up). 1970. PLB 11.89 (ISBN 0-06-026568-X). HarpC Child Bks.

CHILDREN–PICTURES, ILLUSTRATIONS, ETC.

Von Zierenberg, Mark. Smalltalk Baby Diary. Young, Geoff, ed. Wyatt, Colin, illus. 60p. (gr. 1). 1988. 24.95 (ISBN 1-877832-00-6). Prism Leisure.

CHILDREN–PSYCHOLOGY

see Child Study

CHILDREN–RELIGIOUS LIFE

Abdu'l-Baha. Tablet of the Heart: God & Me. Fisher, Betty J. & Lundberg, Leslie, eds. Ostovar, Terry, illus. Oldziey, Pepper P., contrib. by. (Illus.). (ps-2). 1987. PLB 14.95 (ISBN 0-87743-207-4). Baha'i.

Anderson, Debby. Thank You, God. Anderson, Debby, illus. (ps up). 1986. plastic comb bdg. 3.95 (ISBN 0-89191-931-7, 59311, Chariot Bks). Cook.

Angers, JoAnn M. My Beginning Mass Book. Read, Maryann, illus. 48p. (Orig.). (gr. 1-4). 1978. pap. 1.95 (ISBN 0-89622-082-6). Twenty-Third.

Bennett, Marian, ed. Twenty-Six Bible Programs for Preschoolers: Featuring Animal Stories with a Purpose. Packard, Olga & Karch, Pat, illus. LC 87-92209. 96p. (ps). 1988. tchr's. ed. 9.95 (ISBN 0-87403-490-6, 13-03424); tchr's. ed. 9.95 (ISBN 0-87403-338-1, 3421). Standard Pub.

Bennett, Rebecca J. God Gives Good Food. Seward, Lyn, illus. 20p. (ps). 1987. 1.59 (ISBN 0-87403-309-8, 2009). Standard Pub.

The Bird That Wouldn't Talk. (Illus.). (ps-3). 1985. pap. 1.19 (ISBN 0-89191-998-8, 59980). Cook.

Blackwell, Muriel F. How Do I Become a Christian? LC 89-34347. (gr. 4-6). 1991. 7.95 (ISBN 0-8054-4341-X). Broadman.

Boykin, Phyllis. I Like to Go to Church. (ps). 1987. 5.95 (ISBN 0-8054-4174-3). Broadman.

Brandt, Catharine. We Light the Candles: Devotions Related to Family Use of the Advent Wreath. 40p. pap. 4.50 (ISBN 0-8066-1544-3, 10-15443, Augsburg). Augsburg Fortress.

Burgess, Beverly Capps. How Can I Please You God? McKee, Vicki, illus. 29p. (Orig.). 1989. pap. text ed. 4.00 (ISBN 0-9618975-1-1). Annette Capps.

Bussard, Paula J. & Jefferson, Patti. Lessons on Praise from Critter County: Helping Children Praise God. 144p. (gr. k-6). 1987. pap. 9.95 (ISBN 0-87403-217-2, 3337). Standard Pub.

Canfield, Anita. The Young Woman & Her Self-Esteem. 93p. (gr. 7-12). 1990. pap. 4.95 (ISBN 0-87579-365-7). Deseret Bk.

Cantoni, Louise B. Leaving Matters to God. Gomez-Milan, Francis, illus. 164p. (gr. 3-8). 1984. 3.00 (ISBN 0-8198-4424-1); pap. 2.00 (ISBN 0-8198-4425-X). Dghtrs St Paul.

Caswell, Helen. God Makes Us Different. (ps-3). 1988. pap. 4.95 (ISBN 0-687-15336-0). Abingdon.

—The Growing in Faith Library, 6 bks. Caswell, Helen, illus. Set. 29.95 (ISBN 0-687-15899-0). I Can Talk with God. I Know Who Jesus Is. God Is Always with Me. My Big Family at Church. God's Love Is for Sharing. God Must Like to Laugh. Abingdon.

Center for Learning Network. Connections: A Bible Program for Children. 84p. (gr. k-3). 1990. pap. text ed. 12.95 (ISBN 1-56077-053-8). Ctr Learning.

—Today Is: Prayer Journal for Teens. 80p. (gr. 6-8). 1988. pap. text ed. 3.95 (ISBN 1-56077-026-0). Ctr Learning.

Chamberlain, Eugene. Carol Beth Learns about Following Jesus. LC 89-38428. (gr. 1-3). 1991. 6.95 (ISBN 0-8054-4340-1). Broadman.

Coe, Rachel. I Have a Family. LC 86-17629. (ps). 1987. 5.95 (ISBN 0-8054-4172-7). Broadman.

Coleman, William. Animals That Show & Tell. LC 85-15122. 144p. (gr. 2-7). 1985. pap. 5.95 (ISBN 0-87123-807-1). Bethany Hse.

—Before You Tuck Me In. LC 85-26703. 128p. (Orig.). (ps-k). 1986. pap. 5.95 (ISBN 0-87123-830-6). Bethany Hse.

—The Warm Hug Book. LC 85-6175. 128p. (Orig.). (ps). 1985. pap. 5.95 (ISBN 0-87123-794-6). Bethany Hse.

Colton, Ann R. Precepts for the Young. 66p. (gr. 1-8). 1959. pap. 2.50 (ISBN 0-917187-15-6). A R C Pub.

Cooper, Charlotte. Fifty Object Stories for Children. (ps-4). 1988. pap. 5.95 (ISBN 0-8010-2523-0). Baker Bk.

Corbin, Linda & Dys, Pat. Jesus Teaches Me. Fieser, Stephen, illus. 35p. (gr. 1-6). 1987. wkbk. 5.99 (ISBN 0-87509-389-2). Chr Pubns.

Crapps, Joyce W. Who Made These Things? LC 86-18773. (ps). 1987. 5.95 (ISBN 0-8054-4178-6). Broadman.

Darcy-Berube, Francoise & Berube, John-Paul. Come, Let Us Celebrate. 64p. (gr. 2-3). 1985. 5.95 (ISBN 0-7773-8007-2, 8514). Harper SF.

Darcy-Berube, Francoise & Berube, John P. Someone's There: Paths to Prayer for Young People. Batet, Carmen, illus. LC 86-82055. 80p. (Orig.). (gr. 3-5). 1987. pap. 4.95 (ISBN 0-87793-350-2). Ave Maria.

Daughters of St. Paul. Gamble for God. Mayer, Maxine, illus. 132p. (gr. 3-8). 1984. 3.00 (ISBN 0-8198-3033-X); pap. 2.00 (ISBN 0-8198-3034-8). Dghtrs St Paul.

Davis, Cos H., Jr. I'm Big Enough. LC 89-24027. (ps-3). 1991. 6.95 (ISBN 0-8054-4342-8). Broadman.

Dean, Bessie. God Hears My Prayers. (Illus.). 24p. (ps-3). 1988. pap. 2.95 (ISBN 0-88290-110-9). Horizon Utah.

—I'm Happy When I'm Good. (Illus.). 24p. (ps-3). 1979. pap. 2.95 (ISBN 0-88290-109-5). Horizon Utah.

De Graaf, Anne. Healing Minds & Bodies. (Illus.). 32p. 1989. 4.95 (ISBN 0-310-52730-9). Zondervan.

—Jesus Touches People. (Illus.). 32p. 1989. 4.95 (ISBN 0-310-52750-3). Zondervan.

Dellinger, A. & Fletcher, S. Proverbs. 16p. (ps-3). pap. 0.59 (ISBN 0-570-08309-5, 56HH1441). Concordia.

—Special Prayers. (ps-3). pap. 0.59 (ISBN 0-570-08315-X, 56HH1447). Concordia.

—Table Prayers. (ps-3). pap. 0.59 (ISBN 0-570-08316-8, 56HH1448). Concordia.

Dellinger, Annetta. Ann Elizabeth Signs With Love. (ps-2). 1991. 8.95 (ISBN 0-570-04192-9, 56-1651). Concordia. Ann Elizabeth can turn cartwheels & count to 100. She plays games, goes fishing, & bakes chocolate chip cookies. Ann Elizabeth is also deaf. But that doesn't stop her from sharing Jesus' love with her family & friends. She uses sign language to tell others of the wonderful God who made each of us special. Ann Elizabeth teaches children how to sign the favorite Bible song, "Jesus Loves Me." Easy-to-follow sign language symbols are illustrated for each word. Ann Elizabeth Signs With Love also assists parents & teachers as they teach children that God loves everyone, even those with disabilities, & helps children feel & share God's love. For children ages 3 to 7. 32 pp. 4-color hardcover. $8.95. Concordia Publishing House. Item no. 56-1651. ISBN 0-570-04192-9 To order -- Call Toll Free 1-800-325-3040. *Publisher Provided Annotation.*

Dellinger, Annetta E. Adopted & Loved Forever. (Illus.). (ps-2). 1987. 5.95 (ISBN 0-570-04167-8, 56-1624). Concordia.

Doerken, Nan. The First Family Car. 59p. (gr. 1-4). 1986. pap. 3.95 (ISBN 0-919797-53-9). Kindred Pr.

Dvir, Azriel & Mashat, Mazal. My Little Siddur. 68p. 8.95 (ISBN 0-915361-87-6). Adama Pubs Inc.

Escape to Egypt. (Illus.). (ps-3). 1985. pap. 1.19 (ISBN 0-89191-946-5, 59469). Cook.

The First Christmas. (Illus.). (ps-3). 1985. pap. 1.19 (ISBN 0-89191-958-9, 59584). Cook.

Fogle, Jeanne S. Seasons of God's Love: The Church Year. Duckert, Mary J. & Lane, Ben, eds. Widener, Bea, illus. LC 88-6414. 32p. 1988. pap. 6.95 (ISBN 0-664-25032-7, Geneva Pr). Westminster John Knox.

Gambill, Henrietta. Are You Listening? Axeman, Lois, illus. LC 85-10349. 32p. (gr. k-2). 1985. PLB 11.97 (ISBN 0-89565-332-X). Childs World.

Gesch, Roy C. Confirmed in Christ. (gr. 7 up). 1983. pap. 2.95 (ISBN 0-570-03911-8, 12-2852). Concordia.

Gibson, Eva. Listening to My Heart. 160p. (Orig.). 1990. special spiral bdg. 10.95 (ISBN 1-55661-132-3). Bethany Hse.

God Made Only One Me. (ps-4). 1987. Set. 10.95 (ISBN 0-570-04155-4, 56-1608); pap. 4.95 (ISBN 0-570-04148-1). Concordia.

Hageman, Marybeth. Thank You, God, for Me. (Illus.). (ps). 1987. pap. 2.95 (ISBN 0-570-09114-4, 56-1589). Concordia.

Hall, Susan T. Perfect Pals God Made for Me. (Illus.). (ps). 1989. 6.95 (ISBN 1-55513-933-7, Chariot Bks). Cook.

Halverson, Delia T. Oak Street Chonicles & the Good News: Everyday Life & Christian Faith. Dotts, M. Franklin, ed. (Illus., Orig.). 1989. pap. 4.25 tchr's. ed., 48p. (ISBN 0-687-75340-6); student ed., 40p. 2.95 (ISBN 0-687-75339-2). Abingdon.

Hansel, Tim. Real Heroes Eat Hamburgers. Harmon, Jeannie & Davis, Cathy, eds. 64p. (gr. 5-7). 1989. pap. 4.50 (ISBN 1-55513-334-7). Cook.

—Real Heroes Wear Jeans. Harmon, Jeannie & Davis, Cathy, eds. 64p. (gr. 5-7). 1989. pap. 4.50 (ISBN 1-55513-333-9). Cook.

Heide, F. God & Me. (Illus.). 32p. (ps). 1987. pap. 3.95 (ISBN 0-570-07792-3, 56-1316). Concordia.

Herbert, Janet. ABC's of Praise. Herbert, Janet, illus. 32p. (ps up). 1986. plastic comb bdg. 3.95 (ISBN 0-89191-926-0, 59261, Chariot Bks). Cook.

Houk, Margaret. That Very Special Person - Me. 136p. (Orig.). 1990. pap. 6.95 (ISBN 0-8361-3514-8). Herald Pr.

Iakovina, Theodore. A Special Gift to God. Buchmiller, Therese, illus. 38p. (gr. k-4). 1986. PLB write for info. Amnos Pubns.

Jackson, James W. A Steward-ship Adventure: Christianomics for Kids. (Illus.). 24p. (Orig.). (gr. 3-6). 1988. wkbk. 2.95 (ISBN 1-55513-840-3, 68403). Cook.

Johnsson, Noelene. Today with My Father. Wheeler, Gerald, ed. Steadham, Richard, illus. 384p. (gr. 1 up). 1984. 9.50 (ISBN 0-8280-0240-1). Review & Herald.

Jones, Rebecca C. I Am Not Afraid. (Illus.). (ps). 1987. pap. 2.29 (ISBN 0-570-09113-6, 56-1588). Concordia.

Kageler, Len. Short Stops with the Lord. 104p. (gr. 9-12). 1984. 8.99 (ISBN 0-87509-348-5). Chr Pubns.

Kraft, Victoreen. Are You Afraid. Chappell, David & Bates, Steve, illus. 20p. (gr. k-6). 1983. pap. text ed. 4.25 (ISBN 1-55976-139-3). CEF Press.

Lawton, Florrie A. God Loves Me. LC 85-24342. (Illus.). (ps). 1986. 4.95 (ISBN 0-8054-4163-8). Broadman.

Lecciones y Actividades Misioneras para Ninos. (SPA.). 96p. (gr. k-1). 1987. pap. text ed. 3.50 (ISBN 0-311-12033-4). Casa Bautista.

Lecciones y Actividades Misioneras para Ninos, No. 2. (SPA.). 96p. (gr. 2-3). 1987. pap. 3.50 (ISBN 0-311-12034-2). Casa Bautista.

Lecciones y Actividades Misioneras para Ninos de 3 y 4 anos, No. 1. (SPA.). 96p. (ps). 1988. pap. 3.50 (ISBN 0-311-12039-3). Casa Bautista.

L'Engle, Madeleine. Trailing Clouds of Glory: Spiritual Values in Children's Books. Brooke, Avery, contrib. by. LC 84-29081. 144p. (gr. 5-9). 1985. 12.95 (ISBN 0-664-32721-4, Westminster). Westminster John Knox.

Linville, Barbara. God Made the One & Only Me. Heaston, Claudia, illus. LC 76-8737. (ps). 1976. pap. text ed. 3.95 (ISBN 0-916406-28-8). Accent Bks.

McDow, Jane. Golden Thoughts for Children. Young, Jack, illus. 48p. (Orig.). (ps-6). 1986. pap. write for info. (ISBN 0-9616464-0-3). Candy Apple Pub.

McKissack, Patricia & McKissack, Fredrick. God Made Something Wonderful. Ching, illus. LC 89-84938. 32p. (Orig.). (gr. 3-5). 1989. pap. 4.95 (ISBN 0-8066-2434-5, 9-2434). Augsburg Fortress.

McMillan, Mary. Christian Parties for Spring & Summer. (Illus.). 96p. (ps-3). 1989. 9.95 (ISBN 0-86653-473-3, SS1814). Good Apple.

Marxhausen, J. If I Should Die-If I Should Live. (Illus.). 48p. (ps). 1987. pap. 4.95 (ISBN 0-570-07793-1, 56HH1317). Concordia.

Mary's Story: Luke 1: 5-2: 18, Mary's Visit to Elizabeth. Bd. with The Little Mouse's Wonderful Journey: Luke 2: 1-18, the Journey to Bethlehem. (ps-3). bk. & cassette 6.95 (ISBN 0-570-08098-3, 59-2149). Concordia.

Meyzlisch, Saul, ed. A Child's Passover Haggadah. (Illus.). 76p. (gr. 1-6). 1987. 9.95 (ISBN 0-915361-70-1, Dist. by Watts). Adama Pubs Inc.

Murphy, Elspeth C. Do You See Me God? Duca, Bill, illus. 32p. (ps-2). 1989. text ed. 6.49 (ISBN 1-55513-457-2, Chariot Bks). Cook.

—God You Fill Us up with Joy. LC 86-4140. (Illus.). (gr. k-2). 1987. pap. 2.95 (ISBN 1-55513-037-2, Chariot Bks). Cook.

The Night the Angels Sang: Luke 2: 8-20, Jesus' Birth. Bd. with Ben's Blanket & the Baby Jesus: Matthew 1: 18-25, the Christmas Story. (ps-3). bk & cassette 6.95 (ISBN 0-570-08085-1, 59-2136). Concordia.

Niquette, Alan & Niquette, Beth. Building Your Christian Defense System. (Orig.). (gr. 9-12). 1988. pap. text ed. 5.95 (ISBN 1-55661-015-7); tchr's. guide 6.95 (ISBN 1-55661-016-5). Bethany Hse.

Owens, Carolyn. Color Me...Cuddly! McLaughlin, Dorthy, illus. 32p. (ps-4). 1982. pap. 1.19 (ISBN 0-87123-695-8). Bethany Hse.

Perkins, Lee & Perkins, Jim. Healthier & Happier Children Through Bedtime Meditations & Prayers, Bks. 1 & 2. 40p. (ps-5). 1982. book & tape set 17.95 (ISBN 0-87604-184-5). ARE Pr.

Peterson, Lorraine. Dying of Embarassment & Living to Tell about It. LC 87-35334. 224p. (Orig.). (gr. 9-12). 1988. pap. 6.95 (ISBN 0-87123-967-1). Bethany Hse.

Plantinga, Cornelius, Jr. A Sure Thing. LC 86-8280. (Illus.). 300p. (gr. 8-10). 1986. text ed. 14.50 (ISBN 0-930265-27-0); tchr's. manual 11.25 (ISBN 0-930265-28-9). CRC Pubns.

Programas y Actividades para Muchachos y Jovencitos, No. 4. (SPA.). 96p. (gr. 4-10). 1987. pap. text ed. 3.50 (ISBN 0-311-12036-9). Casa Bautista.

Programas y Actividades para Ninas y Jovencitas, No. 4. 96p. (gr. 4-10). 1987. pap. text ed. 3.50 (ISBN 0-311-12035-0). Casa Bautista.

Raburn, Terry. Starting Blocks: Running the Race A-G Style. LC 88-80813. 128p. (Orig.). (gr. 7 up). 1988. pap. 2.95 (ISBN 0-88243-860-3, 02-0860); tchr's. guide 4.50 (ISBN 0-88243-200-1, 32-0200). Gospel Pub.

Rezy, Carol. Liturgies for Little Ones: Thirty-Eight Complete Celebrations for Grades One Through Three. Rezy, Carol, illus. LC 78-59926. 160p. (gr. 1-3). 1978. pap. 5.95 (ISBN 0-87793-160-7). Ave Maria.

Richardson, Arleta. Sixteen & Away from Home. (gr. 5 up). 1985. pap. 3.95 (ISBN 0-89191-933-3, 59337). Cook.

Robinson, J. H. & Robinson, R. D. Involving Children in One Hundred Four Sunday School Openings. 72p. pap. 5.95 (ISBN 0-570-03912-6, 12HH2851). Concordia.

Rossel, Seymour. A Child's Bible: The Torah & Its Lessons. (gr. 1 up). 1988. text & activity bk., 160pps. 8.50 (ISBN 0-87441-466-0); tchr's guide, 96pps. 14.95 (ISBN 0-87441-467-9). Behrman.

Rubow, C., illus. God Loves You. 32p. (ps). 4.95 (ISBN 0-570-03434-5, 56HH1189); cassette 5.95 (ISBN 0-570-04100-7, 56HH1468). Concordia.

Schrader, D. Take My Hands. (gr. k-8). 5.95 (ISBN 0-570-04035-3, 41HH1019). Concordia.

Schreivogel, Paul A. More Prayers for Small Children: About Big & Little Things. Goldsborough, June, illus. LC 88-83018. 32p. (Orig.). (gr. 1 up). 1988. pap. 4.95 (ISBN 0-8066-2381-0, 10-4547, Augsburg). Augsburg Fortress.

Simpson, Winifred R. I Can Help Mommy. (Illus.). (ps). 1987. pap. 2.29 (ISBN 0-570-09112-8, 56-1587). Concordia.

A Song for Joseph: Luke 2: 1-20, the Christmas Story. Bd. with The Little Shepherd & the First Christmas: Luke 2: 8-20, the First Christmas. (ps-3). incl. cassette 6.95 (ISBN 0-317-60402-3, 59-2146). Concordia.

Stafford, Tim. Do You Sometimes Feel Like a Nobody? 144p. 1991. pap. 6.95 (ISBN 0-310-71131-2, Campus Life). Zondervan.

Swanson, Steve, et al. Faith Prints: Youth Devotions for Every Day of the Year. LC 85-13466. 224p. (Orig.). (gr. 8 up). 1985. pap. 6.95 (ISBN 0-8066-2178-8, 10-2189, Augsburg). Augsburg Fortress.

Swartzentruber. God Made Me in a Good Way. 1976. 2.45 (ISBN 0-686-18183-2). Rod & Staff.

—We Should Be Thankful. 1976. 2.45 (ISBN 0-686-18188-3). Rod & Staff.

Tangvald, Christine. I Can Talk to God. Goldsborough, June, illus. LC 85-70217. 20p. (ps). 1985. 4.95 (ISBN 0-89191-907-4, 59071). Cook.

—Me, Myself & I. Goldsborough, June, illus. 20p. (ps). 1985. 4.95 (ISBN 0-89191-925-2, 59253). Cook.

—My Own Special Body. Goldsborough, June, illus. 20p. (ps). 1985. pap. 4.95 (ISBN 0-89191-903-1, 59030). Cook.

Tengbom, Mildred. Does It Make Any Difference What I Do? LC 84-14486. 160p. (Orig.). (gr. 3-6). 1984. pap. 5.95 (ISBN 0-87123-448-3). Bethany Hse.

Trammell, Larry. The Highest Calling of All: God's Ultimate Purpose for Each of Us. Kerby, Rob, ed. 176p. (Orig.). (gr. 7 up). 1990. pap. 7.95 (ISBN 0-9624370-0-X). Ablaze Pub.

Truitt, Gloria A. People of the Bible & Their Prayers. (Illus.). 24p. (ps-4). 1987. pap. 1.39 (ISBN 0-570-09005-9, 59-1433). Concordia.

Ureta, Floreal & Malve, Eduardo. Vive Lo Que Crees! - Live What You Believe! (SPA.). 96p. 1990. pap. 3.50 (ISBN 0-311-12349-X). Casa Bautista.

VanderZee, Leonard. Can I Call after Midnight. 76p. (Orig.). (gr. 10-12). 1989. pap. text ed. 16.95 leader's guide (ISBN 0-930265-70-X). CRC Pubns.

Van Seters, Virginia A. Twenty-Six Object Talks for Children's Worship. Briggs, Richard, illus. 48p. 1988. pap. 2.95 (ISBN 0-87403-497-3, 2877). Standard Pub.

Veerman, David R. Any Old Time, Bk. 10. 80p. (gr. 8 up). 1988. pap. text ed. 9.99 (ISBN 0-89693-454-3). Victor Bks.

Wade, Evelyn A. God Is Here, I'm Not Afraid. Rogers, Kathy, illus. LC 88-83019. 32p. (Orig.). 1988. pap. 4.95 (ISBN 0-8066-2382-9, 10-2646, Augsburg). Augsburg Fortress.

Walking with God: Daily Bread, No. 1. (gr. k-4). 1972. pap. text ed. write for info. (ISBN 1-55976-300-0). CEF Press.

The Warm Nest. (Illus.). (ps-3). 1985. pap. 1.19 (ISBN 0-89191-997-X, 59972). Cook.

Weber, Rhiannon. Signposts from Proverbs: An Introduction to Proverbs. Evans, Lawrence L., illus. 128p. (Orig.). 1988. spiral bdg. 9.95 (ISBN 0-85151-517-7). Banner of Truth.

Winn, Alison. Hello God. (gr. k-3). 1985. 3.95 (ISBN 0-87162-405-2, D4310). Warner Pr.

CHILDREN–TRAINING
see Children–Management
CHILDREN, BOOKS AND READING FOR
see Children–Books and Reading
Colligan, Louise. The A-Plus Guide to Book Reports. 1989. pap. 2.50 (ISBN 0-590-42148-4). Scholastic Inc.
CHILDREN IN AFRICA
Children of the World: Nigeria. LC 89-43199. (Illus.). 64p. (gr. 5-6). 1989. PLB 12.45 (ISBN 0-8368-0258-6). Gareth Stevens Inc.
Egypt. LC 87-42578. (Illus.). 64p. (gr. 5-6). 1989. PLB 12.95 (ISBN 1-55532-209-3). Gareth Stevens Inc.
Feelings, Muriel. Moja Means One: A Swahili Counting Book. Feelings, Tom, illus. LC 76-134856. (ps-3). 1987. 13.95 (ISBN 0-8037-5776-X); PLB 13.89 (ISBN 0-8037-5777-8). Dial Bks Young.
Pelnar, Tom & Weber, Valerie, eds. Tanzania. Nakamura, Haruko, photos by. LC 88-42890. (Illus.). 64p. (gr. 5-6). 1989. PLB 12.95 (ISBN 1-55532-210-7). Gareth Stevens Inc.
Rogers, Barbara R. Zambia. Rogers, Stillman, photos by. LC 89-43178. (Illus.). 64p. (gr. 5-6). 1991. PLB 12.95 (ISBN 0-8368-0257-8). Gareth Stevens Inc.
CHILDREN IN AFRICA–FICTION
Black History Series 1, 6 bks. Incl. Vol. 1. George Abraham Jefferson Thinks about Freedom. Smith, Martha. 15p. (gr. 2-3) (ISBN 0-913678-01-5); Vol. 2. Terrible Tuesday. Gaines, Edith. 13p. (gr. 2-3) (ISBN 0-913678-02-3); Vol. 3. Free; The Contraption; The First Freedom Ride. Gaines, Edith & Smith, Martha. 40p. (gr. 3-4) (ISBN 0-913678-03-1); Vol. 4. I Cannot Be a Traitor; the Cannon That Talked Back. Johnston, Brenda & Woodrich, Mary. 31p. (gr. 4-5) (ISBN 0-913678-04-X); Vol. 5. Adventures of Olaudah, the African Boy; Move Feet Move. Hartman, Suzanne & Shepard, Mary. 35p. (gr. 5-6) (ISBN 0-913678-05-8); Vol. 6. The Disguise. Shepard, Mary. 15p. (gr. 5-6) (ISBN 0-913678-06-6). (Illus.). (gr. 2-6). 1988. pap. 10.00x set (ISBN 0-913678-00-7). New Day Pr.
Graham, Lorenz. Song of the Boat. Dillon, Leo & Dillon, Diane, illus. LC 74-5183. 40p. (gr. 2-5). 1975. PLB 12.89 (ISBN 0-690-75232-6, Crowell Jr Bks). HarpC Child Bks.
CHILDREN IN ASIA
Coerr, Eleanor B. Sadako & the Thousand Paper Cranes. Himler, Ronald, illus. LC 76-9872. (gr. 3-5). 1977. 13.95 (ISBN 0-399-20520-9, Putnam). Putnam Pub Group.
Harkonen, Reijo. The Children of Nepal. Pitkanen, Matti A., illus. 48p. (gr. 3-6). 1990. PLB 14.95 (ISBN 0-87614-395-8). Carolrhoda Bks.
Kamatsu, Yoshio. Children of the World: Bhutan. LC 88-21051. (Illus.). 64p. (gr. 5-6). 1988. PLB 12.95 (ISBN 1-55532-867-9). Gareth Stevens Inc.
Kubota, Makota. Children of the World: South Korea. LC 86-42804. (Illus.). 64p. (gr. 5-6). 1987. PLB 12.95 (ISBN 1-55532-168-2). Gareth Stevens Inc.
Miyazima, Yasuhiko. Children of the World: China. LC 87-42576. (Illus.). 64p. (gr. 5-6). 1988. PLB 12.95 (ISBN 1-55532-207-7). Gareth Stevens Inc.
Morieda, Takashi. Children of the World: Burma. LC 86-42799. (Illus.). 64p. (gr. 5-6). 1987. PLB 12.95 (ISBN 1-55532-159-3). Gareth Stevens Inc.
Nurland, Patricia. Vietnam. Vu Viet Dung, photos by. LC 89-43178. (Illus.). 64p. (gr. 5-6). 1991. PLB 12.95 (ISBN 0-8368-0230-6). Gareth Stevens Inc.
Oshihara, Yuzuro. Children of the World: Malaysia. LC 86-42802. (Illus.). 64p. (gr. 5-6). 1987. PLB 12.95 (ISBN 1-55532-160-7). Gareth Stevens Inc.
Ryuichi, Hirokawa. Children of the World: Jordan. LC 87-42618. (Illus.). 64p. (gr. 5-6). 1987. PLB 12.95 (ISBN 1-55532-224-7). Gareth Stevens Inc.
Sumio, Uchiyama. Children of the World: India. LC 87-42577. (Illus.). 64p. (gr. 5-6). 1988. PLB 12.95 (ISBN 1-55532-208-5). Gareth Stevens Inc.
Watanabe, Hitomi. Children of the World: Nepal. LC 86-42806. (Illus.). 64p. (gr. 5-6). 1987. PLB 12.95 (ISBN 1-55532-166-6). Gareth Stevens Inc.
CHILDREN IN AUSTRALIA
Children of the World: Australia. LC 87-42617. (Illus.). 64p. (gr. 5-6). 1987. PLB 12.95 (ISBN 1-55532-222-0). Gareth Stevens Inc.
CHILDREN IN CANADA
Tanobe, Miyuki. Quebec, I Love You: Je t'Aime. Tanobe, Miyuki, illus. 48p. (gr. 5 up). 1971. 3.95 (ISBN 0-88776-072-4); pap. 2.95 (ISBN 0-88776-156-9). Tundra Bks.
Wright, David K. Canada. Wright, David K., photos by. LC 89-43197. (Illus.). 64p. (gr. 5-6). 1991. PLB 12.95 (ISBN 0-8368-0256-X). Gareth Stevens Inc.
CHILDREN IN CHINA–FICTION
Kaye, Geraldine. The Day after Yesterday. Ambrus, Glenys, illus. 96p. (gr. 2-6). 1981. 9.95 (ISBN 0-233-97344-3). Andre Deutsch.
Lewis, Elizabeth F. Young Fu of the Upper Yangtze. new ed. Young, Ed, illus. LC 72-91654. 268p. (gr. 4-6). 1973. 15.95 (ISBN 0-8050-0549-8). H Holt & Co.
CHILDREN IN EUROPE
Allen, Eleanor. Victorian Children. (Illus.). 64p. (gr. 6 up). 1979. 14.95 (ISBN 0-7136-1324-6). Dufour.
Bjener, Tamiko. Children of the World: Finland. LC 87-42580. (Illus.). 64p. (gr. 5-6). 1987. PLB 12.95 (ISBN 1-55532-218-2). Gareth Stevens Inc.
—Children of the World: Sweden. LC 86-42803. (Illus.). 64p. (gr. 5-6). 1987. PLB 12.95 (ISBN 1-55532-164-X). Gareth Stevens Inc.
Brown, Julie & Broen, Robert, eds. Hungary. Nebor, Leos, photos by. LC 88-42888. (Illus.). 64p. (gr. 5-6). 1989. PLB 12.95 (ISBN 1-55532-217-4). Gareth Stevens Inc.
Children of the World: Yugoslavia. LC 88-21053. (Illus.). 64p. (gr. 5-6). 1988. PLB 12.95 (ISBN 1-55532-219-0). Gareth Stevens Inc.
Drighi, Laura. Children of the World: Italy. LC 87-42640. (Illus.). 64p. (gr. 5-6). 1988. PLB 12.95 (ISBN 1-55532-404-5). Gareth Stevens Inc.
Holland, Gini. Poland. LC 89-43181. (Illus.). 64p. (gr. 5-6). 1991. PLB 12.95 (ISBN 0-8368-0233-0). Gareth Stevens Inc.
Nebor, Leos. Children of the World: Czechoslovakia. LC 87-42638. (Illus.). 64p. (gr. 5-6). 1988. PLB 12.95 (ISBN 1-55532-216-6). Gareth Stevens Inc.
Taylor-Boyd, Susan & Brown, Julie, eds. U. S. R. R. Miyajina, Yasuhiko, photos by. LC 88-42891. (Illus.). 64p. (gr. 5-6). 1989. PLB 12.95 (ISBN 1-55532-215-8). Gareth Stevens Inc.
Terushi, Jimbo. Children of the World: West Germany. LC 88-21052. (Illus.). 64p. (gr. 5-6). 1988. PLB 12.95 (ISBN 1-55532-213-1). Gareth Stevens Inc.
Tolan, Sally & Sherwood, Rhoda I., eds. France. Pierre, Philippe, photos by. LC 88-42889. (Illus.). 64p. (gr. 5-6). 1990. PLB 12.95 (ISBN 1-55532-212-3). Gareth Stevens Inc.
Yakoyama, Masami. Children of the World: Spain. LC 86-42808. (Illus.). 64p. (gr. 5-6). 1987. PLB 12.95 (ISBN 1-55532-163-1). Gareth Stevens Inc.
CHILDREN IN FOREIGN COUNTRIES
Ackley, Meredith & Weber, Valerie, eds. Children of the World: Japan. LC 89-11493. (Illus.). 64p. (gr. 5-6). 1989. PLB 12.45 (ISBN 0-8368-0121-0). Gareth Stevens Inc.
Children of the World, 30 vols. 1920p. (gr. 5-6). 1986. Set. PLB 388.50 (ISBN 1-55532-923-3). Gareth Stevens Inc.
O'Brien, John & Taylor-Boyd, Susan, eds. Children of the World: England. Kato, Setsvo, photos by. LC 89-4462. (Illus.). 64p. (gr. 5-6). 1989. PLB 12.95 (ISBN 1-55532-211-5). Gareth Stevens Inc.
Tozuks, Takako. Children of the World: Turkey. Reitci, Rita & Sherwood, Rhoda I., eds. Tozuka, Takako, photos by. LC 88-32745. (Illus.). 64p. (gr. 5-6). 1989. PLB 12.95 (ISBN 1-55532-851-2). Gareth Stevens Inc.
CHILDREN IN ISLANDS OF THE PACIFIC
Bjener, Tamiko. Children of the World: Philippines. LC 86-42805. (Illus.). 64p. (gr. 5-6). 1987. PLB 12.95 (ISBN 1-55532-167-4). Gareth Stevens Inc.
Tozuka, Takako. Children of the World: Indonesia. LC 86-42807. (Illus.). 64p. (gr. 5-6). 1987. PLB 12.95 (ISBN 1-55532-165-8). Gareth Stevens Inc.
Yanagi, Akinobu. Children of the World: New Zealand. LC 86-42801. (Illus.). 64p. (gr. 5-6). 1987. PLB 12.95 (ISBN 1-55532-162-3). Gareth Stevens Inc.
CHILDREN IN ISLANDS OF THE PACIFIC–FICTION
Oetting. Keiki of the Islands. LC 71-108728. (Illus.). 96p. (gr. 3 up). 1970. PLB 10.95 (ISBN 0-87783-018-5); pap. 3.94 deluxe ed. (ISBN 0-87783-096-7). Oddo.
Olsen, E. A. Killer in the Trap. Le Blanc, L., illus. LC 68-16399. 48p. (gr. 3 up). 1970. PLB 10.95 (ISBN 0-87783-019-3); pap. 3.94 deluxe ed. (ISBN 0-87783-097-5); cassette 10.60x (ISBN 0-87783-190-4). Oddo.
CHILDREN IN NORTH AMERICA
Ikuhara, Yoshiyuki. Children of the World: Mexico. LC 86-42800. (Illus.). 64p. (gr. 5-6). 1987. PLB 12.95 (ISBN 1-55532-161-5). Gareth Stevens Inc.
CHILDREN IN SOUTH AMERICA
Ikuhara, Yoshiyuki. Children of the World: Brazil. LC 87-42579. (Illus.). 64p. (gr. 5-6). 1987. PLB 12.95 (ISBN 1-55532-221-2). Gareth Stevens Inc.
CHILDREN IN SOUTH AMERICA–FICTION
Martel, Cruz. Yagua Days. LC 75-27601. (Illus.). 40p. (ps-3). 1987. PLB 11.89 (ISBN 0-8037-9766-4); pap. 4.95 (ISBN 0-8037-0457-7). Dial Bks Young.
CHILDREN IN THE U. S.
Chaback, Elaine & Fortunato, Pat. The Official Kids' Survival Kit: How to Do Things on Your Own. (gr. 4 up). 1981. pap. 10.95 (ISBN 0-316-13531-3). Little.
Children of the World, 30 vols. 1920p. (gr. 5-6). 1986. Set. PLB 388.50 (ISBN 1-55532-923-3). Gareth Stevens Inc.
CHILDREN IN THE U. S.–FICTION
Kerr, M. E. The Son of Someone Famous. LC 73-14338. 234p. (gr. 7 up). 1974. PLB 12.89 (ISBN 0-06-023147-5). HarpC Child Bks.
Oke, Janette. New Kid in Town. Mann, Brenda, illus. 125p. (Orig.). (gr. 3 up). 1983. pap. 4.95 (ISBN 0-934998-16-7). Bethel Pub.
Williams, Cecil & Mirikitani, Janice, eds. I Have Something to Say about This Big Trouble: Children of the Tenderloin Speak Out. (Illus.). 128p. (Orig.). (gr. 3-7). 1989. pap. 9.95 (ISBN 0-9622574-1-9). Glide Word.
CHILDREN'S BOOKS
see Children's Literature
CHILDREN'S DISEASES
see Children–Diseases
CHILDREN'S HOSPITALS
see Children–Hospitals
CHILDREN'S LIBRARIES
see Libraries, Children's; School Libraries
CHILDREN'S LITERATURE
Here are entered collections of works of a cross-genre nature, e.g., Poetry and Prose. Works on the reading interests of children, and or lists of books read by or recommended for children are entered under Children–Books and Reading.
see also Children–Books and Reading; Fairy Tales; Libraries, Children'S; Picture Books; Plays; Poetry; Stories
Ball, Douglas H., et al. Stories Worth Reading. Bruns, Stan & Capron, Michael W., illus. 192p. (Orig.). (gr. 8-11). 1989. pap. text ed. write for info. (ISBN 0-9621844-0-3). Printemps Bks.
Barkan, Joanne, et al. The Muppet Babies in Let's Imagine....A Trip to the Stars. Chauhan, Man har, illus. 26p. (ps up). 1987. pap. 14.95 (ISBN 1-55578-806-8). Worlds Wonder.
—The Muppet Babies in Let's Imagine...The Missing Toy's Adventure. Wilson, Ann, illus. 26p. (ps up). 1987. pap. 14.95 (ISBN 1-55578-805-X). Worlds Wonder.
—The Muppet Babies in Let's Imagine...What Happened in the Nursery. Venning, Sue, illus. (ps up). 1987. pap. 14.95 (ISBN 1-55578-808-4). Worlds Wonder.
Barken, Joanne, et al. The Muppet Babies in Let's Imagine...Music Everywhere. Brannon, Tom, illus. 26p. (ps up). 1987. pap. 14.95 (ISBN 1-55578-807-6). Worlds Wonder.
Beginners Bookshelf, 8 vols. (ps-3). 79.95 (ISBN 0-685-09844-3). Ency Brit Inc.
Bolinske, Janet L., ed. Big Bug Big Book Package, 6 bks. (Illus.). (gr. k-1). 1987. Set of 6 bks., 24 pgs. ea. bk. spiral bdg. 80.00 (ISBN 0-88335-760-7). Milliken Pub Co.
—Children's Classics Big Book Package, 6 bks. (Illus.). (gr. 1-3). 1987. Set of 6 bks., 32 pgs. ea. bk. spiral bdg. 80.00 (ISBN 0-88335-540-X). Milliken Pub Co.
—Children's Classics Hardcover Package, 18 bks. (Illus., Orig.). (gr. 1-3). 1987. Set, 32p. ea. 145.00 (ISBN 0-88335-550-7). Milliken Pub Co.
—Children's Classics Softcover Package, 18 bks. (Illus., Orig.). (gr. 1-3). 1987. Set, 32p. ea. pap. 80.00 (ISBN 0-88335-570-1). Milliken Pub Co.
Bradman, Tony. Baby's Best Book. Kooper, Lisa, illus. LC 87-45275. 48p. (ps). 1988. 11.95 (ISBN 0-06-020716-7); PLB 11.89 (ISBN 0-06-020717-5). HarpC Child Bks.
Brown, J. Aaron, ed. The Rock-a-Bye Collection, Vols. 1 & 2. rev. ed. Vienneau, Jim, illus. 14p. (ps). 1990. incl. cassette 12.95 ea. Vol. 1 (ISBN 0-927945-03-7). Vol. 2 (ISBN 0-927945-04-5). Someday Baby.
Chapin, Laurie & Flegenheimer-Riggle, Ellen. Leaping into Literature. 144p. (gr. k-3). 1990. 10.95 (ISBN 0-86653-561-6, GA1164). Good Apple.
Cole, Joanna & Calmenson, Stephanie. The Laugh Book. Hafner, Marilyn, illus. LC 85-13113. 320p. (gr. 2-6). 1986. 15.95 (ISBN 0-385-18559-6). Doubleday.
Editorial America, S. A. Staff. Los Cuentos Infantiles Mas Famosos Del Mundo. Del Real, Maria E., ed. (SPA., Illus.). 464p. (Orig.). 1990. pap. write for info. (ISBN 0-944499-93-7). Editorial Amer.
Fadiman, Clifton, ed. The World Treasury of Children's Literature, 2 vols. Merrill, Leslie, et al, illus. (ps-3). 1984. in slipcase 45.00 (ISBN 0-316-27302-3). Little.
Frost, Joan. Art, Books & Children: Art Activities Based on Children's Literature. (Illus.). 88p. (gr. 1-6). 1984. spiral bdg. 12.95 (ISBN 0-938594-03-6). Spec Lit Pr.
Geis, Darlene, ed. Walt Disney's Treasury of Cartoon Classics. (Illus.). 224p. (gr. 3 up). 1981. 29.95 (ISBN 0-8109-0813-1). Abrams.

Hammer, Roger A. My Own Book! Reading Is Fundamental (RIF) 20th Anniversary. Schlosser, Cy, illus. LC 86-30410. 128p. (gr. 3-12). 1987. pap. 14.95 (ISBN 0-932991-50-5). Place in the Woods.
Barbara Bush says "...a wonderful momento for one of my favorite projects." 54 delightful essays by multi-cultural children on how their city, state or school got its name. 54 almanacs noting famous minority role models & facts on each state, DC, Puerto Rico, Guam, & the Virgin Islands. 56 case-histories & proven ideas from reading leaders on promoting community literacy. Full text of U.S. Constitution to celebrate bicentennial. Fully-illustrated with nearly 200 four-color photos including all state flags. Perfect-bound, coated enamel cover, index & Table of Multi-Cultural references. To order: 3900 Glenwood Ave, Golden Valley, MN 55422.
Publisher Provided Annotation.

Kidd, Ron. The Nutcracker. Reinert, Rick, illus. 48p. (gr. k-6). 1985. 5.95 (ISBN 0-8249-8095-6). Ideals.

Landau, Elaine. On the Streets: The Lives of Adolescent Prostitutes. LC 86-21825. 112p. (gr. 9 up). 1987. lib. bdg. 12.98 (ISBN 0-671-62135-1). Messner.

Lewis, Shari & O'Kun, Lan. One-Minute Bedtime Stories. Cumings, Art, illus. LC 79-8024. 48p. (ps-3). 1982. pap. 8.95 (ISBN 0-385-15292-2). Doubleday.

Morton, Miriam, ed. A Harvest of Russian Children's Literature. Viguers, Ruth H., frwd. by. LC 67-21384. (Illus.). (ps up). 1967. 47.50x (ISBN 0-520-00886-3). U of Cal Pr.

Newberry Medal Collection, 5 vols, No. 3. (gr. 4 up). 1988. Boxed. pap. 16.25 (ISBN 0-440-36003-X). Dell.

Nophlin, Barbara, ed. Classic Book Collection. (Illus.). (gr. k). Date not set. PLB 129.95 (ISBN 0-88076-127-X, 15665). Kaplan Pr.

Pena, Sylvia C., ed. Kikiriki: Stories & Poems in English & Spanish for Children. 2nd ed. LC 81-68072. (ENG & SPA., Illus.). 116p. (Orig.). (gr. k-6). 1989. pap. 7.50 (ISBN 0-685-34571-8). Arte Publico.

Perez, N. A. One Special Year. LC 84-25258. 200p. (gr. 6-9). 1985. 12.95 (ISBN 0-395-36693-3). HM.

Pogrebin, Letty C. Stories for Free Children. 144p. 1983. text ed. 14.95 (ISBN 0-07-050389-3); pap. text ed. 9.95 (ISBN 0-07-050398-2). McGraw.

Rudin, Ellen, ed. Young Authors of America, Vol. 1. (Illus.). 102p. (gr. 5-8). 1988. pap. 0.60 (ISBN 0-440-84003-1). Dell.

Russell, William F., selected by. Classics to Read Aloud to Your Children. LC 84-7033. 320p. (ps-5). 1984. 18.00 (ISBN 0-517-55404-6). Crown.

Schoch, Tim. Summer Camp Creeps. 160p. (Orig.). (gr. 3-7). 1987. pap. 2.95 (ISBN 0-380-75343-X, Camelot). Avon.

Shaw, Janet, et al. American Girls Collection, 9 bks, No. I. Graef, Renee, et al, illus. (gr. 2-5). 1986. Unboxed Set. 116.55 (ISBN 0-937295-29-9); Unboxed Set. pap. 53.55 (ISBN 0-937295-30-2). Pleasant Co.

Shoemaker, Mrs. J. W., compiled by. Young Folks Recitations: Designed for Young People of Fourteen Years; Containing Selections in Prose & Poetry; Together with Some Short Dialogues & Tableaux. LC 73-2839. (gr. 8-10). 1973. Repr. of 1884 ed. 14.00 (ISBN 0-8369-6413-6). Ayer Co Pubs.

Stroyer, Paul. Treasure Chest of Tales. (Illus.). (gr. 3 up). 1959. 12.95 (ISBN 0-8392-3039-7). Astor-Honor.

Taylor, Kenneth. Stories for the Children's Hour. 2nd ed. (gr. 1-8). 1987. pap. 6.95 (ISBN 0-8024-2227-6). Moody.

Treasury of Disney Little Golden Books. (ps-2). 1972. write for info. (ISBN 0-307-17865-X, Golden Bks). Western Pub.

Veitch, Carol J. & Crawford, Jane. More Literature Puzzles for Elementary & Middle Schools. Mannerberg, Patricia A., illus. LC 86-7161. xiii, 90p. (gr. 1-7). 1986. pap. text ed. 15.50 (ISBN 0-87287-518-0). Libs Unl.

Weber, Chris, ed. Treasures, No. 2: Stories & Art by Students in Oregon. Kimmel, Eric, intro. by. 256p. (Orig.). (gr. k-12). 1988. pap. 11.95 (ISBN 0-9616058-1-2). OR Students Writing.

Witter, Evelyn, et al. More Stories Worth Reading. Penovich, Geraldine & Penovich, Beatrice A., eds. (Illus.). 1989. write for info. Printemps Bks.

Yolen, Jane, et al, eds. Spaceships & Spells. LC 87-175. 224p. (gr. 7-9). 1987. 12.95 (ISBN 0-06-026796-8); PLB 12.89 (ISBN 0-06-026797-6). HarpC Child Bks.

CHILDREN'S LITERATURE–BIBLIOGRAPHY

Comber, Geoffrey & Zeiderman, Howard, eds. Touchstones, Vol. III: Texts for Discussion. Maistrellis, Nicholas, tr. & intro. by. 178p. (Orig.). (gr. 9-12). 1987. pap. text ed. 15.00 (ISBN 1-878461-04-4). CZM Pr.

Mealy, Virginia T. Newbery Books. (Illus.). 128p. (gr. 4-8). 1987. pap. 12.95 (ISBN 0-913839-62-0). Bk Lures.

Miller, Heather S. Children & Gardens: An Annotated Bibliography of Children's Garden Books, 1829-1988. Miasek, Meryl A., ed. 60p. (Orig.). pap. write for info. (ISBN 0-9621791-1-6). CBHL Inc.

Scarry, Richard. Richard Scarry's Storybook Dictionary. LC 99-901821. (Illus.). (gr. k-2). 1966. write for info. (ISBN 0-307-15548-X, Golden Bks). Western Pub.

Shelton, Helen, ed. Bibliography of Books for Children. 1988-89 ed. LC 89-345. 112p. (ps-6). 1989. 11.00 (ISBN 0-87173-118-5). ACEI.

CHILDREN'S LITERATURE–HISTORY AND CRITICSIM

Ash, Russell & Bond, Michael. The Life & Times of Paddington Bear. LC 88-62808. 160p. 1989. pap. 24.95 (ISBN 1-851-45286-9). Viking Penguin.

Gross, Edward, ed. Above & Below: A Guide to Beauty & the Beast. (Illus.). 112p. (Orig.). (gr. 9-12). 1990. pap. 12.95 (ISBN 0-9627508-0-8). Image NY.

Hadlow, Ruth, et al. Children's Books Too Good to Miss. 8th ed. (gr. 1-6). write for info. (ISBN 0-9616276-0-3). Lucas Comns.

San Diego Museum of Art Staff, compiled by. Dr. Seuss from Then to Now. Dr. Seuss, illus. LC 87-4838. 96p. (ps up). 1987. 12.95 (ISBN 0-394-89268-2, Random Juv). Random.

Sullivan, Dianna. Literature Activities for Young Children. Pence, Nedra, illus. 96p. (ps-k). 1989. wkbk. 9.95 (ISBN 1-55734-300-4). Tchr Create Mat.

—Literature Activities for Young Children. Pence, Nedra, illus. 96p. (ps-k). 1989. wkbk. 9.95 (ISBN 1-55734-301-2). Tchr Create Mat.

—Literature Activities for Young Children. Pence, Nedra, illus. 96p. (ps-k). 1989. wkbk. 9.95 (ISBN 1-55734-302-0). Tchr Create Mat.

—Literature Activities for Young Children. Pence, Nedra, illus. 96p. (ps-k). 1989. wkbk. 9.95 (ISBN 1-55734-303-9). Tchr Create Mat.

—Literature Activities for Young Children. Spears, Diane S., illus. 96p. (ps-k). 1990. wkbk. 9.95 (ISBN 1-55734-304-7). Tchr Create Mat.

—Literature Activities for Young Children. Pence, Nedra L., illus. 96p. (ps-k). 1990. wkbk. 9.95 (ISBN 1-55734-305-5). Tchr Create Mat.

—Literature Activities for Young Children. Pence, Nedra L., illus. 96p. (ps-k). 1990. wkbk. 9.95 (ISBN 1-55734-306-3). Tchr Create Mat.

—Literature Activities for Young Children. Pence, Nedra L., illus. 96p. (ps-k). 1990. wkbk. 9.95 (ISBN 1-55734-307-1). Tchr Create Mat.

Yeager, Natalee. Fun with Children's Classics. (Illus.). 32p. (gr. 4-8). 1987. pap. 4.95 (ISBN 0-913839-66-3). Bk Lures.

CHILDREN'S READING

see Children's Literature; Reading

CHILE

Dwyer, Chris. Chile. (Illus.). (gr. 5 up). 1990. 14.95 (ISBN 0-7910-1102-X). Chelsea Hse.

Galvin, Irene F. Chile: Land of Poets & Patriots. (Illus.). 128p. (gr. 5 up). 1990. PLB 14.95 (ISBN 0-87518-421-9, Dillon). Macmillan Child Grp.

Hintz, Martin. Chile. LC 84-23104. (Illus.). 128p. (gr. 5-9). 1985. lib. bdg. 25.27 (ISBN 0-516-02755-7). Childrens.

Lerner Publications, Department of Geography Staff, ed. Chile in Pictures. (Illus.). 64p. (gr. 5 up). 1988. PLB 12.95 (ISBN 0-8225-1809-0). Lerner Pubns.

Mihalik, Paul A. Patagonia Profile. (Illus.). 93p. (Orig.). (gr. 7-12). 1985. pap. text ed. 9.95 (ISBN 0-9615916-0-9). Padre Pio Pubs.

CHIMPANZEES

Alston, Eugenia. Growing up Chimpanzee. Wells, Haru, illus. LC 74-12307. 32p. (gr. 1-4). 1975. (Crowell Jr Bks). HarpC Child Bks.

Birnbaum, Bette. Jane Goodall & the Wild Chimpanzees. (Illus.). 32p. (gr. 1-4). 1989. PLB 13.32 (ISBN 0-8172-3509-4). Raintree Pubs.

Butterworth, Christine & Bailey, Donna. Chimpanzees. LC 90-9928. (Illus.). 32p. (gr. 1-4). 1990. PLB 14.64 (ISBN 0-8114-2642-4). Steck-V.

Chimpanzees. 32p. (gr. 2-7). 1989. pap. 4.95 (ISBN 0-14-034173-0, Puffin). Puffin Bks.

Goodall, Jane. The Chimpanzee Family Book. Neugebauer, Michael, illus. LC 88-33359. 72p. (ps up). 1989. 17.95 (ISBN 0-88708-090-1). Picture Bk Studio.

—Jane Goodall's Animal World: Chimps. (Illus.). 32p. (gr. 3-7). 1989. 11.95 (ISBN 0-689-31467-1, Atheneum Child Bk). Macmillan Child Grp.

—My Life with Chimpanzees. (Illus.). 128p. (gr. 4-6). 1988. pap. 2.75 (ISBN 0-671-66095-0, Minstrel Bks). PB.

Goodall, Jane, ed. Jane Goodall's Animal World: Chimpanzees. (Illus.). 32p. (gr. 3-7). 1989. pap. 3.95 (ISBN 0-689-71320-7, Aladdin). Macmillan Child Grp.

McCormick, Maxine. Chimpanzee. LC 89-28272. (Illus.). 48p. (gr. 5 up). 1990. 10.95 (ISBN 0-89686-514-2, Crestwood Hse). Macmillan Child Grp.

Michel, Anna. Little Wild Chimpanzee. Parnall, Peter & Parnall, Virginia, illus. LC 77-20986. (gr. 1-4). 1978. lib. bdg. 7.99 (ISBN 0-394-93716-3). Pantheon.

Petty, Kate. Chimpanzees. (gr. 4-7). 1990. PLB 10.40 (ISBN 0-531-17193-0). Watts.

Stone, Lynn. Chimpanzees. (Illus.). 24p. (gr. k-5). 1990. lib. bdg. 11.93 (ISBN 0-86593-064-3); lib. bdg. 8.95s.p. (ISBN 0-685-36316-3). Rourke Corp.

CHIMPANZEES–FICTION

Armstrong, Jennifer. That Champion Chimp. (gr. 4-7). 1990. pap. 2.75 (ISBN 0-553-15828-7). Bantam.

Browne, Anthony. I Like Books. Browne, Anthony, illus. LC 88-8471. 24p. (Orig.). (ps-1). 1989. 10.99 (ISBN 0-394-94186-1); pap. 3.95 (ISBN 0-685-24801-1). Knopf.

—Things I Like. Browne, Anthony, illus. LC 88-26632. 24p. (Orig.). (ps-1). 1989. lib. bdg. 10.99 (ISBN 0-394-94192-6); pap. 3.95 (ISBN 0-394-84192-1). Knopf.

Hoban, Lillian. Arthur's Loose Tooth. Hoban, Lillian, illus. LC 85-42611. 64p. (gr. k-3). 1987. pap. 3.50 (ISBN 0-06-444093-1, Trophy). HarpC Child Bks.

Klein, Norma. A Honey of a Chimp. LC 79-20951. (gr. 3-7). 1980. Pantheon.

Landsman, Sandy. Castaways on Chimp Island. LC 85-20071. 216p. (gr. 3-7). 1986. 13.95 (ISBN 0-689-31214-8, Atheneum Child Bk). Macmillan Child Grp.

Pocci, Franz. Chimpanzee, the Darwin Ape. Zahl, Jagna, tr. from ITA. LC 72-84057. 30p. (gr. 1 up). 1973. pap. 3.95 (ISBN 0-8283-1503-5). Branden Pub Co.

Rabe, Berniece. Where's Chimpy? Tucker, Kathleen, ed. Schmidt, Diane, photos by. LC 88-37259. (Illus.). 32p. (ps-2). 1988. PLB 12.95 (ISBN 0-8075-8928-4). A Whitman.

Yolen, Jane. The Boy Who Spoke Chimp. Wiesner, illus. LC 79-27259. 128p. (gr. 3-6). 1981. Knopf.

CHINA

Bliss, Jonathan. China. (Illus.). 64p. (gr. 7 up). 1990. lib. bdg. 15.93 (ISBN 0-86593-090-2); lib. bdg. 11.95s.p. (ISBN 0-685-36364-3). Rourke Corp.

Brightfield, Richard. China: Why Was an Army Made of Clay? 112p. (gr. 4-6). 1989. pap. text ed. 3.95 (ISBN 0-07-047999-2). McGraw.

China (People's Republic of) (Illus.). (gr. 5 up). 1991. 14.95 (ISBN 0-7910-1368-5). Chelsea Hse.

Dudley, William & Swisher, Karin, eds. China. LC 88-24296. (Illus.). 250p. (gr. 10 up). 1988. lib. bdg. 15.95 (ISBN 0-89908-439-7); pap. text ed. 8.95 (ISBN 0-89908-414-1). Greenhaven.

Fisher, Leonard E. The Great Wall of China. Fisher, Leonard E., illus. LC 85-15324. 32p. (gr. 1-5). 1986. 13.95 (ISBN 0-02-735220-X, Mcmillan Child Bk). Macmillan Child Grp.

Fyson, Nance L. & Greenhill, Richard. A Family in China. LC 84-19426. (Illus.). 32p. (gr. 2-5). 1985. PLB 9.95 (ISBN 0-8225-1653-5). Lerner Pubns.

Hacker, Jeffrey H. The New China. LC 85-29414. 96p. (gr. 7-12). 1986. lib. bdg. 12.90 (ISBN 0-531-10156-8). Watts.

Haskins, Jim. Count Your Way Through China. (Illus.). 24p. (gr. 1-4). 1987. lib. bdg. 11.95 (ISBN 0-87614-302-8). Carolrhoda Bks.

Hughes-Stanton, Penelope. See Inside an Ancient Chinese Town. LC 85-52282. (Illus.). 32p. (gr. 4-9). 1986. PLB 11.90 (ISBN 0-531-19009-9, Pub. by Warwick). Watts.

Jacobsen, P. & Kristensen, P. A Family in China. LC 85-71727. (Illus.). 32p. (gr. k-6). 1986. lib. bdg. 11.90 (ISBN 0-531-18035-2, Pub. by Bookwright Pr). Watts.

Johnson, Neil. Step into China. Johnson, Neil, illus. LC 87-20266. 32p. (gr. 3-6). 1988. lib. bdg. 9.98 (ISBN 0-671-64338-X); pap. 5.95 (ISBN 0-671-65852-2). Messner.

Kalman, Bobbie. China - the Culture. (Illus.). 32p. (gr. 4-5). 1989. PLB 14.95 (ISBN 0-86505-209-3); pap. 7.95 (ISBN 0-86505-289-1). Crabtree Pub Co.

—China - the Land. (Illus.). 32p. (gr. 4-5). 1989. lib. bdg. 14.95 (ISBN 0-86505-207-7); pap. 7.95 (ISBN 0-86505-287-5). Crabtree Pub Co.

—China - The People. (Illus.). 32p. (gr. 4-5). 1989. lib. bdg. 14.95 (ISBN 0-86505-208-5); pap. 7.95 (ISBN 0-86505-288-3). Crabtree Pub Co.

China is in the news every day. It has undergone many changes in recent years. In CHINA: THE PEOPLE inviting, candid photographs intimately portray the Chinese people in their homes, going to work, attending school, & enjoying their leisure time. Short paragraphs, a multitude of headings, & easy-to-read text bring the information in CHINA: THE PEOPLE into the realm of a child's experience. CHINA: THE LAND, CHINA: THE PEOPLE, CHINA: THE CULTURE, & TIBET focus on changing China, including recent developments such as the Democracy Movement. The three books on China & one Tibet are part of the LANDS, PEOPLE, & CULTURE SERIES.

Publisher Provided Annotation.

Keeler, Stephen. Passport to China. (Illus.). 48p. (gr. 4-6). 1987. PLB 12.90 (ISBN 0-531-10401-X). Watts.

Kendall, Carol & Yao-wen, Li. Sweet & Sour: Tales from China. LC 78-24349. (Illus.). 112p. (gr. 3-6). 1979. 13.95 (ISBN 0-395-28958-0, Clarion). HM.

Lerner Publications, Department of Geography Staff, ed. China in Pictures. (Illus.). 64p. (gr. 5 up). 1989. 12.95 (ISBN 0-8225-1859-7). Lerner Pubns.

Mason, Sally. Take a Trip to China. (Illus.). 32p. (gr. 1-3). 1981. lib. bdg. 7.99 (ISBN 0-531-04317-7). Watts.

Merton, D. & Yun-Kan, Shio. China: The Land & Its People. rev. ed. LC 85-72107. (gr. 5 up). PLB 15.96 (ISBN 0-382-09253-8). Silver Burdett Pr.

Rau, Margaret. Holding up the Sky: Young People in China. LC 82-20959. (Illus.). 160p. (gr. 5 up). 1983. 12.50 (ISBN 0-525-66718-0, Lodestar Bks). Dutton Child Bks.

Roth, Susan L. Marco Polo. (ps-3). 1991. 14.95 (ISBN 0-385-26495-X); PLB 15.99 (ISBN 0-385-26555-7). Doubleday.

Sabin, Louis. Ancient China. Frenck, Hal, illus. LC 84-2729. 32p. (gr. 3-6). 1985. PLB 9.49 (ISBN 0-8167-0316-7); pap. text ed. 2.95 (ISBN 0-8167-0317-5). Troll Assocs.

Seablom, Seth H. China Coloring Guide. (Illus.). 32p. (gr. 1-6). 1979. pap. 2.50 (ISBN 0-918800-06-4). Seablom.

Stewart, Gail B. China. LC 90-35497. (Illus.). 48p. (gr. 5-6). 1990. RSBE 10.95 (ISBN 0-89686-538-X, Crestwood Hse). Macmillan Child Grp.

Tan, Jennifer. Food in China. LC 88-31644. (Illus.). 32p. (gr. 3-6). 1989. lib. bdg. 13.26 (ISBN 0-86625-338-6). Rourke Corp.

Thompson, Brenda & Overbeck, Cynthia. The Great Wall of China. Austin, Caroline, illus. LC 76-22443. 24p. (gr. k-3). 1977. PLB 5.95 (ISBN 0-8225-1357-9). Lerner Pubns.

Tolhurst, Marilyn. China. (Illus.). 48p. (gr. 4-8). 1988. PLB 14.98 (ISBN 0-382-09510-3). Silver Burdett Pr.

Waterlow, Julia. China. (Illus.). 32p. (gr. k-4). 1991. RLB 11.90 (ISBN 0-531-18393-9, Pub. by Boatwright Pr). Watts.

Wood, Frances. People at Work in China. (gr. 6 up). 1988. 19.95 (ISBN 0-7134-5266-8, Pub. by Batsford England). Trafalgar Sq.

Yungmei, Tang, photos by. China, Here We Come! (Illus.). 64p. (gr. 5-10). 1981. 9.95 (ISBN 0-399-20826-7, Putnam). Putnam Pub Group.

CHINA-BIOGRAPHY

Hoobler, Dorothy & Hoobler, Thomas. Zhou Enlai. Schlesinger, Arthur M., Jr., intro. by. (Illus.). 112p. (gr. 5 up). 1986. 17.95 (ISBN 0-87754-516-2). Chelsea Hse.

Hope, Irene. Ai-Chan's Secret. 1989. pap. 1.95 (ISBN 9971-972-85-9). OMF Bks.

Kurland, Gerald. Mao Tse-Tung: Founder of Communist China. Rahmas, D. Steve, ed. LC 75-190232. 32p. (Orig.). (gr. 7-12). 1972. lib. bdg. 4.20 incl. catalog cards (ISBN 0-87157-514-0); pap. 2.95 vinyl laminated covers (ISBN 0-87157-014-9). SamHar Pr.

CHINA-FICTION

Beyond the Great Wall. (Illus.). (gr. k-9). 1988. pap. 2.50 (ISBN 0-318-36497-2). Scholastic Inc.

Chang, Margaret & Chang, Raymond. In the Eye of War. (gr. 5-9). 1990. 13.95 (ISBN 0-689-50503-5, M K McElderry). Macmillan Child Grp.

Clyde, Ahmad. Cheng Ho's Voyage. Durkee, Noura, illus. LC 81-66951. 32p. (Orig.). (gr. 3-7). 1981. pap. 2.00 (ISBN 0-89259-021-1). Am Trust Pubns.

Cooley, Regina F. The Magic Christmas Pony. Hansen, Han H., illus. 36p. (gr. 1-5). 1991. 19.95 (ISBN 1-880450-04-6). Capstone Pub.
A carousel pony mysteriously disappears in the night, magically reappearing on Christmas Eve in the doorway of Frederick & Valentina's bedroom. With grandparents sleeping unaware in the next room, the Magic Christmas Pony whisks the mystified children to the Forbidden City in China. There they meet the Dragon of Fantasy, a close friend of the Magic Christmas Pony, & enjoy a Dragon banquet. After dining with the many Dragons, their adventure continues. They meet the Emperor & Empress of China & are further entranced by traditional Chinese dances & entertainment. Frederick & Valentina's exposure to the culture & traditions of the Chinese royalty becomes educational as well as entertaining. The Forbidden City comes to life with the rich detail provided by Regina Francoise Cooley, the author, whose thorough research lends a realistic backdrop to this enchanting tale. Hans Henrik Hansen, a well known illustrator from Denmark, has established his reputation in the plate collecting world with collectors plates from both Bing & Grondahl & Royal Copenhagen. His unique use of brilliant saturated color & superb detail has created a book worthy of being called a collectors item. Capstone Publishing Inc. is proud to present this mesmerizing & timeless story.
Publisher Provided Annotation.

DeJong, Meindert. House of Sixty Fathers. Sendak, Maurice, illus. LC 56-8148. 192p. (gr. 5-8). 1956. PLB 13.89 (ISBN 0-06-021481-3). HarpC Child Bks.

Flack, Marjorie. Story about Ping. Wiese, Kurt, illus. LC 33-29356. (ps-2). 1933. pap. 11.95 (ISBN 0-670-67223-8). Viking Child Bks.

Fritz, Jean. China Homecoming. Fritz, Michael, photos by. LC 84-24775. (Illus.). 144p. (gr. 5 up). 1985. 13.95 (ISBN 0-399-21182-9, Putnam). Putnam Pub Group.

Frost, Lesley. Digging Down to China. Hudnut, R., illus. 64p. (gr. 1-4). 1968. 9.95 (ISBN 0-8159-5306-2). Devin.

Handforth, Thomas. Mei Li. Handforth, Thomas, illus. 48p. (gr. k-3). 1955. PLB 14.95 (ISBN 0-385-07401-8); pap. 15.99 (ISBN 0-385-07639-8). Doubleday.

Hwa-I Publishing Co., Staff. Chinese Children's Stories, Vol. 10: The Money Tree, The Coxcomb. Ching, Emily, et al, eds. Wonder Kids Publications Staff, tr. from CHI. Hwa-I Publishing Co., Staff, illus. LC 90-60792. 28p. (gr. 3-6). Repr. of 1988 ed. 7.95x (ISBN 1-56162-010-6). Wonder Kids.

—Chinese Children's Stories, Vol. 100: From Rice into Flowers, The Shy Rainbow. Ching, Emily, et al, eds. Wonder Kids Publications Staff, tr. from CHI. Hwa-I Publishing Co., Staff, illus. LC 90-60811. 28p. (gr. 3-6). Repr. of 1988 ed. 7.95x (ISBN 1-56162-100-5). Wonder Kids.

—Chinese Children's Stories, Vol. 12: The Snail & the Ox, Sparrows Can't Walk. Ching, Emily, et al, eds. Wonder Kids Publications Staff, tr. from CHI. Hwa-I Publishing Co., Staff, illus. LC 90-60793. 28p. (gr. 3-6). Repr. of 1988 ed. 7.95x (ISBN 1-56162-012-2). Wonder Kids.

—Chinese Children's Stories, Vol. 13: Rooster Summons the Sun, The White-Haired Bird. Ching, Emily, et al, eds. Wonder Kids Publications Staff, tr. from CHI. Hwa-I Publishing Co., Staff, illus. LC 90-60793. 28p. (gr. 3-6). Repr. of 1988 ed. 7.95x (ISBN 1-56162-013-0). Wonder Kids.

—Chinese Children's Stories, Vol. 14: Weasel Steals the Chickens, Why is the Crow Black? Ching, Emily, et al, eds. Wonder Kids Publications Staff, tr. from CHI. Hwa-I Publishing Co., Staff, illus. LC 90-60793. 28p. (gr. 3-6). Repr. of 1988 ed. 7.95x (ISBN 1-56162-014-9). Wonder Kids.

—Chinese Children's Stories, Vol. 15: Jiggle in the Wind, The Bat Can't See the Sun. Ching, Emily, et al, eds. Wonder Kids Publications Staff, tr. from CHI. Hwa-I Publishing Co., Staff, illus. LC 90-60793. 28p. (gr. 3-6). Repr. of 1988 ed. 7.95x (ISBN 1-56162-015-7). Wonder Kids.

—Chinese Children's Stories, Vol. 17: The Monkey & the Fire, Lazy Wife & the Bread Ring. Ching, Emily, et al, eds. Wonder Kids Publications Staff, tr. from CHI. Hwa-I Publishing Co., Staff, illus. LC 90-60794. 28p. (gr. 3-6). Repr. of 1988 ed. 7.95x (ISBN 1-56162-017-3). Wonder Kids.

—Chinese Children's Stories, Vol. 18: The Little Bamboo Pole, The Wise Old Man. Ching, Emily, et al, eds. Wonder Kids Publications Staff, tr. from CHI. Hwa-I Publishing Co., Staff, illus. LC 90-60794. 28p. (gr. 3-6). Repr. of 1988 ed. 7.95x (ISBN 1-56162-018-1). Wonder Kids.

—Chinese Children's Stories, Vol. 19: Crow Moves Away, Baby Lion & Baby Rhino. Ching, Emily, et al, eds. Wonder Kids Publications Staff, tr. from CHI. Hwa-I Publishing Co., Staff, illus. LC 90-60794. 28p. (gr. 3-6). Repr. of 1988 ed. 7.95x (ISBN 1-56162-019-X). Wonder Kids.

—Chinese Children's Stories, Vol. 20: Ah-Liu Picks Corn, Cuckoo's Winter. Ching, Emily, et al, eds. Wonder Kids Publications Staff, tr. from CHI. Hwa-I Publishing Co., Staff, illus. LC 90-60794. 28p. (gr. 3-6). Repr. of 1988 ed. 7.95x (ISBN 1-56162-020-3). Wonder Kids.

—Chinese Children's Stories, Vol. 22: The Steal a Bell, The Dropout. Ching, Emily, et al, eds. Wonder Kids Publications Staff, tr. from CHI. Hwa-I Publishing Co., Staff, illus. LC 90-60796. 28p. (gr. 3-6). Repr. of 1988 ed. 7.95x (ISBN 1-56162-022-X). Wonder Kids.

—Chinese Children's Stories, Vol. 23: Dummy Afa, The Fox in a Tiger's Suit. Ching, Emily, et al, eds. Wonder Kids Publications Staff, tr. from CHI. Hwa-I Publishing Co., Staff, illus. LC 90-60796. 28p. (gr. 3-6). Repr. of 1988 ed. 7.95x (ISBN 1-56162-023-8). Wonder Kids.

—Chinese Children's Stories, Vol. 24: Running Fifty vs. One-Hundred Strides, Atu Yanks the Rice Seedlings. Ching, Emily, et al, eds. Wonder Kids Publications Staff, tr. from CHI. Hwa-I Publishing Co., Staff, illus. LC 90-60796. 28p. (gr. 3-6). Repr. of 1988 ed. 7.95x (ISBN 1-56162-024-6). Wonder Kids.

—Chinese Children's Stories, Vol. 25: The Blindmen & the Elephant, Little Frog in the Well. Ching, Emily, et al, eds. Wonder Kids Publications Staff, tr. from CHI. Hwa-I Publishing Co., Staff, illus. LC 90-60796. 28p. (gr. 3-6). Repr. of 1988 ed. 7.95x (ISBN 1-56162-025-4). Wonder Kids.

—Chinese Children's Stories, Vol. 27: Sky-Mending Festival, Decorative Paper for Graves. Ching, Emily, et al, eds. Wonder Kids Publications Staff, tr. from CHI. Hwa-I Publishing Co., Staff, illus. LC 90-60797. 28p. (gr. 3-6). Repr. of 1988 ed. 7.95x (ISBN 1-56162-027-0). Wonder Kids.

—Chinese Children's Stories, Vol. 28: Mih-Ro River, The Herder & the Seamstress. Ching, Emily, et al, eds. Wonder Kids Publications Staff, tr. from CHI. Hwa-I Publishing Co., Staff, illus. LC 90-60797. 28p. (gr. 3-6). Repr. of 1988 ed. 7.95x (ISBN 1-56162-028-9). Wonder Kids.

—Chinese Children's Stories, Vol. 29: Moon Cake, Fei's Adventure. Ching, Emily, et al, eds. Wonder Kids Publications Staff, tr. from CHI. Hwa-I Publishing Co., Staff, illus. LC 90-60797. 28p. (gr. 3-6). Repr. of 1988 ed. 7.95x (ISBN 1-56162-029-7). Wonder Kids.

—Chinese Children's Stories, Vol. 30: La-Ba Porridge, The Stove God. Ching, Emily, et al, eds. Wonder Kids Publications Staff, tr. from CHI. Hwa-I Publishing Co., Staff, illus. LC 90-60797. 28p. (gr. 3-6). Repr. of 1988 ed. 7.95x (ISBN 1-56162-030-0). Wonder Kids.

—Chinese Children's Stories, Vol. 32: Dumplings, Ham. Ching, Emily, et al, eds. Wonder Kids Publications Staff, tr. from CHI. Hwa-I Publishing Co., Staff, illus. LC 90-60798. 28p. (gr. 3-6). Repr. of 1988 ed. 7.95x (ISBN 1-56162-032-7). Wonder Kids.

—Chinese Children's Stories, Vol. 34: The Stuffed Steamed Bao, Miss Freckle's Tofu. Ching, Emily, et al, eds. Wonder Kids Publications Staff, tr. from CHI. Hwa-I Publishing Co., Staff, illus. LC 90-60798. 28p. (gr. 3-6). Repr. of 1988 ed. 7.95x (ISBN 1-56162-034-3). Wonder Kids.

—Chinese Children's Stories, Vol. 35: Monks' Beef Stew, Yue's Tofu Store. Ching, Emily, et al, eds. Wonder Kids Publications Staff, tr. from CHI. Hwa-I Publishing Co., Staff, illus. LC 90-60798. 28p. (gr. 3-6). Repr. of 1988 ed. 7.95x (ISBN 1-56162-035-1). Wonder Kids.

—Chinese Children's Stories, Vol. 37: Confucius' Bookkeeping, The Scissors Shop. Ching, Emily, et al, eds. Wonder Kids Publications Staff, tr. from CHI. Hwa-I Publishing Co., Staff, illus. LC 90-60799. 28p. (gr. 3-6). Repr. of 1988 ed. 7.95x (ISBN 1-56162-037-8). Wonder Kids.

—Chinese Children's Stories, Vol. 38: The Peace Drum, Comb. Ching, Emily, et al, eds. Wonder Kids Publications Staff, tr. from CHI. Hwa-I Publishing Co., Staff, illus. LC 90-60799. 28p. (gr. 3-6). Repr. of 1988 ed. 7.95x (ISBN 1-56162-038-6). Wonder Kids.

—Chinese Children's Stories, Vol. 39: Brush Pen, Duan's Ink-Slab. Ching, Emily, et al, eds. Wonder Kids Publications Staff, tr. from CHI. Hwa-I Publishing Co., Staff, illus. LC 90-6079. 28p. (gr. 3-6). Repr. of 1988 ed. 7.95x (ISBN 1-56162-039-4). Wonder Kids.

—Chinese Children's Stories, Vol. 39: Noodles over the Bridge, Steamed Bread. Ching, Emily, et al, eds. Wonder Kids Publications Staff, tr. from CHI. Hwa-I Publishing Co., Staff, illus. LC 90-60798. 28p. (gr. 3-6). Repr. of 1988 ed. 7.95x (ISBN 1-56162-033-5). Wonder Kids.

—Chinese Children's Stories, Vol. 40: The Ink-Stick, Shiuan Paper. Ching, Emily, et al, eds. Wonder Kids Publications Staff, tr. from CHI. Hwa-I Publishing Co., Staff, illus. LC 90-60799. 28p. (gr. 3-6). Repr. of 1988 ed. 7.95x (ISBN 1-56162-040-8). Wonder Kids.

—Chinese Children's Stories, Vol. 42: Tiger Seeks a Master, Why Are Cats Afraid of Dogs? Ching, Emily, et al, eds. Wonder Kids Publications Staff, tr. from CHI. Hwa-I Publishing Co., Staff, illus. LC 90-60800. 28p. (gr. 3-6). Repr. of 1988 ed. 7.95x (ISBN 1-56162-042-4). Wonder Kids.

—Chinese Children's Stories, Vol. 43: The Bunny's Tail, Fox, Monkey, Rabbit & Horse. Ching, Emily, et al, eds. Wonder Kids Publications Staff, tr. from CHI. Hwa-I Publishing Co., Staff, illus. LC 90-60800. 28p. (gr. 3-6). Repr. of 1988 ed. 7.95x (ISBN 1-56162-043-2). Wonder Kids.

—Chinese Children's Stories, Vol. 44: Snake's Lost Drum, Ox & Buffalo Change Clothes. Ching, Emily, et al, eds. Wonder Kids Publications Staff, tr. from CHI. Hwa-I Publishing Co., Staff, illus. LC 90-60800. 28p. (gr. 3-6). Repr. of 1988 ed. 7.95x (ISBN 1-56162-044-0). Wonder Kids.

—Chinese Children's Stories, Vol. 45: The Goat & the Camel, The Wolf & the Pig. Ching, Emily, et al, eds. Wonder Kids Publications Staff, tr. from CHI. Hwa-I Publishing Co., Staff, illus. LC 90-60800. 28p. (gr. 3-6). Repr. of 1988 ed. 7.95x (ISBN 1-56162-045-9). Wonder Kids.

—Chinese Children's Stories, Vol. 47: The Crane-Riding Immortal, Lyu Dungbin & Guanyin. Ching, Emily, et al, eds. Wonder Kids Publications Staff, tr. from CHI. Hwa-I Publishing Co., Staff, illus. LC 90-60801. 28p. (gr. 3-6). Repr. of 1988 ed. 7.95x (ISBN 1-56162-047-5). Wonder Kids.

—Chinese Children's Stories, Vol. 48: Sir Thunder & Lady Lightning, The Door Guards. Ching, Emily, et al, eds. Wonder Kids Publications Staff, tr. from CHI. Hwa-I Publishing Co., Staff, illus. LC 90-60801. 28p. (gr. 3-6). Repr. of 1988 ed. 7.95x (ISBN 1-56162-048-3). Wonder Kids.

—Chinese Children's Stories, Vol. 49: The Slippery Nose Deity, Under the Moonlight. Ching, Emily, et al, eds. Wonder Kids Publications Staff, tr. from CHI. Hwa-I Publishing Co., Staff, illus. LC 90-60801. 28p. (gr. 3-6). Repr. of 1988 ed. 7.95x (ISBN 1-56162-049-1). Wonder Kids.

—Chinese Children's Stories, Vol. 50: Zung Kuei & the Little Ghost, Earth God & Earth Goddess. Ching, Emily, et al, eds. Wonder Kids Publications Staff, tr. from CHI. Hwa-I Publishing Co., Staff, illus. LC 90-60801. 28p. (gr. 3-6). Repr. of 1988 ed. 7.95x (ISBN 1-56162-050-5). Wonder Kids.

—Chinese Children's Stories, Vol. 52: Joining the Army, Beating up the Tiger. Ching, Emily, et al, eds. Wonder Kids Publications Staff, tr. from CHI. Hwa-I Publishing Co., Staff, illus. LC 90-60802. 28p. (gr. 3-6). Repr. of 1988 ed. 7.95x (ISBN 1-56162-052-1). Wonder Kids.

—Chinese Children's Stories, Vol. 53: Meeting an Angel, The Child in the Deer Skin. Ching, Emily, et al, eds. Wonder Kids Publications Staff, tr. from CHI. Hwa-I Publishing Co., Staff, illus. LC 90-60802. 28p. (gr. 3-6). Repr. of 1988 ed. 7.95x (ISBN 1-56162-053-X). Wonder Kids.

—Chinese Children's Stories, Vol. 54: The Story of Shun, Village of Filial Piety. Ching, Emily, et al, eds. Wonder Kids Publications Staff, tr. from CHI. Hwa-I Publishing Co., Staff, illus. LC 90-60802. 28p. (gr. 3-6). Repr. of 1988 ed. 7.95x (ISBN 1-56162-054-8). Wonder Kids.

—Chinese Children's Stories, Vol. 55: Two Baskets of Mulberries, Trun's Little Daughter. Ching, Emily, et al, eds. Wonder Kids Publications Staff, tr. from CHI. Hwa-I Publishing Co., Staff, illus. LC 90-60802. 28p. (gr. 3-6). Repr. of 1988 ed. 7.95x (ISBN 1-56162-055-6). Wonder Kids.

—Chinese Children's Stories, Vol. 57: The Little-Boy God, A Rooster's Egg. Ching, Emily, et al, eds. Wonder Kids Publications Staff, tr. from CHI. Hwa-I Publishing Co., Staff, illus. LC 90-60803. 28p. (gr. 3-6). Repr. of 1988 ed. 7.95x (ISBN 1-56162-057-2). Wonder Kids.

—Chinese Children's Stories, Vol. 58: Three Princes & the Firewood, Wang's Memory. Ching, Emily, et al, eds. Wonder Kids Publications Staff, tr. from CHI. Hwa-I Publishing Co., Staff, illus. LC 90-60803. 28p. (gr. 3-6). Repr. of 1988 ed. 7.95x (ISBN 1-56162-058-0). Wonder Kids.

—Chinese Children's Stories, Vol. 59: A Tankful of Water, The Little Hero. Ching, Emily, et al, eds. Wonder Kids Publications Staff, tr. from CHI. Hwa-I Publishing Co., Staff, illus. LC 90-60803. 28p. (gr. 3-6). Repr. of 1988 ed. 7.95x (ISBN 1-56162-059-9). Wonder Kids.

—Chinese Children's Stories, Vol. 60: Weighing an Elephant, The Distant Homeland. Ching, Emily, et al, eds. Wonder Kids Publications Staff, tr. from CHI. Hwa-I Publishing Co., Staff, illus. LC 90-60803. 28p. (gr. 3-6). Repr. of 1988 ed. 7.95x (ISBN 1-56162-060-2). Wonder Kids.

—Chinese Children's Stories, Vol. 61: To Catch the Suns, Two Quarrelsome Brothers. Ching, Emily, et al, eds. Wonder Kids Publications Staff, tr. from CHI. Hwa-I Publishing Co., Staff, illus. LC 90-60804. 28p. (gr. 3-6). Repr. of 1988 ed. 7.95x (ISBN 1-56162-062-9). Wonder Kids.

—Chinese Children's Stories, Vol. 63: To Speak or Not, The Dark Village. Ching, Emily, et al, eds. Wonder Kids Publications Staff, tr. from CHI. Hwa-I Publishing Co., Staff, illus. LC 90-60804. 28p. (gr. 3-6). Repr. of 1988 ed. 7.95x (ISBN 1-56162-063-7). Wonder Kids.

—Chinese Children's Stories, Vol. 64: Why Is the Sky So High?, Turning into Stone. Ching, Emily, et al, eds. Wonder Kids Publications Staff, tr. from CHI. Hwa-I Publishing Co., Staff, illus. LC 90-60804. 28p. (gr. 3-6). Repr. of 1988 ed. 7.95x (ISBN 1-56162-064-5). Wonder Kids.

—Chinese Children's Stories, Vol. 65: Lugging Mountains, What's a Life Span? Ching, Emily, et al, eds. Wonder Kids Publications Staff, tr. from CHI. Hwa-I Publishing Co., Staff, illus. LC 90-60804. 28p. (gr. 3-6). Repr. of 1988 ed. 7.95x (ISBN 1-56162-065-3). Wonder Kids.

—Chinese Children's Stories, Vol. 67: The After-Meal Bell, Passing the Three Gorges. Ching, Emily, et al, eds. Wonder Kids Publications Staff, tr. from CHI. Hwa-I Publishing Co., Staff, illus. LC 90-60805. 28p. (gr. 3-6). Repr. of 1988 ed. 7.95x (ISBN 1-56162-067-X). Wonder Kids.

—Chinese Children's Stories, Vol. 68: The Donkey-Riding Poet, The Backyard Song. Ching, Emily, et al, eds. Wonder Kids Publications Staff, tr. from CHI. Hwa-I Publishing Co., Staff, illus. LC 90-60805. 28p. (gr. 3-6). Repr. of 1988 ed. 7.95x (ISBN 1-56162-068-8). Wonder Kids.

—Chinese Children's Stories, Vol. 69: The Young Family, Tsuei's Beautiful Bride. Ching, Emily, et al, eds. Wonder Kids Publications Staff, tr. from CHI. Hwa-I Publishing Co., Staff, illus. LC 90-60805. 28p. (gr. 3-6). Repr. of 1988 ed. 7.95x (ISBN 1-56162-069-6). Wonder Kids.

—Chinese Children's Stories, Vol. 7: Dragon Eye & Cassia Circle, The Conceited Barber. Ching, Emily, et al, eds. Wonder Kids Publications Staff, tr. from CHI. Hwa-I Publishing Co., Staff, illus. LC 90-60792. 28p. (gr. 3-6). Repr. of 1988 ed. 7.95x (ISBN 1-56162-007-6). Wonder Kids.

—Chinese Children's Stories, Vol. 70: Ji's Jokes, The Scrooge. Ching, Emily, et al, eds. Wonder Kids Publications Staff, tr. from CHI. Hwa-I Publishing Co., Staff, illus. LC 90-60805. 28p. (gr. 3-6). Repr. of 1988 ed. 7.95x (ISBN 1-56162-070-X). Wonder Kids.

—Chinese Children's Stories, Vol. 72: The Lotus Child, The Ghost in the Basin. Ching, Emily, et al, eds. Wonder Kids Publications Staff, tr. from CHI. Hwa-I Publishing Co., Staff, illus. LC 90-60806. 28p. (gr. 3-6). Repr. of 1988 ed. 7.95x (ISBN 1-56162-072-6). Wonder Kids.

—Chinese Children's Stories, Vol. 73: Walking through Walls, Who Is the Real Lord Ji? Ching, Emily, et al, eds. Wonder Kids Publications Staff, tr. from CHI. Hwa-I Publishing Co., Staff, illus. LC 90-60806. 28p. (gr. 3-6). Repr. of 1988 ed. 7.95x (ISBN 1-56162-073-4). Wonder Kids.

—Chinese Children's Stories, Vol. 74: Chaos in the Heavenly Palace, Eating the Ginseng Fruit. Ching, Emily, et al, eds. Wonder Kids Publications Staff, tr. from CHI. Hwa-I Publishing Co., Staff, illus. LC 90-60806. 28p. (gr. 3-6). Repr. of 1988 ed. 7.95x (ISBN 1-56162-074-2). Wonder Kids.

—Chinese Children's Stories, Vol. 75: Tang's Strange Journey, Dwarfs & Giants. Ching, Emily, et al, eds. Wonder Kids Publications Staff, tr. from CHI. Hwa-I Publishing Co., Staff, illus. LC 90-60806. 28p. (gr. 3-6). Repr. of 1988 ed. 7.95x (ISBN 1-56162-075-0). Wonder Kids.

—Chinese Children's Stories, Vol. 77: Sir Guan's Big Red Face, Turning Cranes into Words. Ching, Emily, et al, eds. Wonder Kids Publications Staff, tr. from CHI. Hwa-I Publishing Co., Staff, illus. LC 90-60807. 28p. (gr. 3-6). Repr. of 1988 ed. 7.95x (ISBN 1-56162-077-7). Wonder Kids.

—Chinese Children's Stories, Vol. 78: Tang Buohu's Drawings, The General & the Water Tank. Ching, Emily, et al, eds. Wonder Kids Publications Staff, tr. from CHI. Hwa-I Publishing Co., Staff, illus. LC 90-60807. 28p. (gr. 3-6). Repr. of 1988 ed. 7.95x (ISBN 1-56162-078-5). Wonder Kids.

—Chinese Children's Stories, Vol. 79: Black-Faced Sir Bao, Doctor Hwa-Tuo. Ching, Emily, et al, eds. Wonder Kids Publications Staff, tr. from CHI. Hwa-I Publishing Co., Staff, illus. LC 90-60807. 28p. (gr. 3-6). Repr. of 1988 ed. 7.95x (ISBN 1-56162-079-3). Wonder Kids.

—Chinese Children's Stories, Vol. 8: The Millets Won't Go Home, The Immortal Palm. Ching, Emily, et al, eds. Wonder Kids Publications Staff, tr. from CHI. Hwa-I Publishing Co., Staff, illus. LC 90-60792. 28p. (gr. 3-6). Repr. of 1988 ed. 7.95x (ISBN 1-56162-008-4). Wonder Kids.

—Chinese Children's Stories, Vol. 80: The Dwarf Minister, The Fabulous Chimera's Gift. Ching, Emily, et al, eds. Wonder Kids Publications Staff, tr. from CHI. Hwa-I Publishing Co., Staff, illus. LC 90-60807. 28p. (gr. 3-6). Repr. of 1988 ed. 7.95x (ISBN 1-56162-080-7). Wonder Kids.

—Chinese Children's Stories, Vol. 82: The Fish Minister, The Hidden Sword. Ching, Emily, et al, eds. Wonder Kids Publications Staff, tr. from CHI. Hwa-I Publishing Co., Staff, illus. LC 90-60808. 28p. (gr. 3-6). Repr. of 1988 ed. 7.95x (ISBN 1-56162-082-3). Wonder Kids.

—Chinese Children's Stories, Vol. 83: The Revenge of Chao's Orphan, Tien's Wonderful Strategies. Ching, Emily, et al, eds. Wonder Kids Publications Staff, tr. from CHI. Hwa-I Publishing Co., Staff, illus. LC 90-60808. 28p. (gr. 3-6). Repr. of 1988 ed. 7.95x (ISBN 1-56162-083-1). Wonder Kids.

—Chinese Children's Stories, Vol. 84: Who Is the Real Liu Bong?, Kong Borrows the East Wind. Ching, Emily, et al, eds. Wonder Kids Publications Staff, tr. from CHI. Hwa-I Publishing Co., Staff, illus. LC 90-60808. 28p. (gr. 3-6). Repr. of 1988 ed. 7.95x (ISBN 1-56162-084-X). Wonder Kids.

—Chinese Children's Stories, Vol. 85: The Battle of the Fei River, The Princess' Engagement. Ching, Emily, et al, eds. Wonder Kids Publications Staff, tr. from CHI. Hwa-I Publishing Co., Staff, illus. LC 90-60808. 28p. (gr. 3-6). Repr. of 1988 ed. 7.95x (ISBN 1-56162-085-8). Wonder Kids.

—Chinese Children's Stories, Vol. 87: Fan Bridge & Escape Alley, The Stream of Flowers. Ching, Emily, et al, eds. Wonder Kids Publications Staff, tr. from CHI. Hwa-I Publishing Co., Staff, illus. LC 90-60809. 28p. (gr. 3-6). Repr. of 1988 ed. 7.95x (ISBN 1-56162-087-4). Wonder Kids.

—Chinese Children's Stories, Vol. 88: Five Stone Goats, Six-Foot Street. Ching, Emily, et al, eds. Wonder Kids Publications Staff, tr. from CHI. Hwa-I Publishing Co., Staff, illus. LC 90-60809. 28p. (gr. 3-6). Repr. of 1988 ed. 7.95x (ISBN 1-56162-088-2). Wonder Kids.

—Chinese Children's Stories, Vol. 89: Peach Blossom Cave, Mt. Lee. Ching, Emily, et al, eds. Wonder Kids Publications Staff, tr. from CHI. Hwa-I Publishing Co. Staff, illus. LC 90-60809. 28p. (gr. 3-6). Repr. of 1988 ed. 7.95x (ISBN 1-56162-089-0). Wonder Kids.

—Chinese Children's Stories, Vol. 9: The Story of Rice, The Cows & the Trumpet. Ching, Emily, et al, eds. Wonder Kids Publications Staff, tr. from CHI. Hwa-I Publishing Co., Staff, illus. LC 90-60792. 28p. (gr. 3-6). Repr. of 1988 ed. 7.95x (ISBN 1-56162-009-2). Wonder Kids.

—Chinese Children's Stories, Vol. 90: The Dragon Who Puts out Fires, The Golden Hairpin Well. Ching, Emily, et al, eds. Wonder Kids Publications Staff, tr. from CHI. Hwa-I Publishing Co., Staff, illus. LC 90-60809. 28p. (gr. 3-6). Repr. of 1988 ed. 7.95x (ISBN 1-56162-090-4). Wonder Kids.

—Chinese Children's Stories, Vol. 92: White-Rice Magic Cave, Sun-Moon Lake. Ching, Emily, et al, eds. Wonder Kids Publications Staff, tr. from CHI. Hwa-I Publishing Co., Staff, illus. LC 90-60810. 28p. (gr. 3-6). Repr. of 1988 ed. 7.95x (ISBN 1-56162-092-0). Wonder Kids.

—Chinese Children's Stories, Vol. 93: Mt. Anvil & the Sword Well, Two Waters. Ching, Emily, et al, eds. Wonder Kids Publications Staff, tr. from CHI. Hwa-I Publishing Co., Staff, illus. LC 90-60810. 28p. (gr. 3-6). Repr. of 1988 ed. 7.95x (ISBN 1-56162-093-9). Wonder Kids.

—Chinese Children's Stories, Vol. 94: Muddy Water Stream, Sister Lakes & Brother Trees. Ching, Emily, et al, eds. Wonder Kids Publications Staff, tr. from CHI. Hwa-I Publishing Co., Staff, illus. LC 90-60810. 28p. (gr. 3-6). Repr. of 1988 ed. 7.95x (ISBN 1-56162-094-7). Wonder Kids.

—Chinese Children's Stories, Vol. 95: Half-Shield Mountain, The Adopted Daughter Lake. Ching, Emily, et al, eds. Wonder Kids Publications Staff, tr. from CHI. Hwa-I Publishing Co., Staff, illus. LC 90-60810. 28p. (gr. 3-6). Repr. of 1988 ed. 7.95x (ISBN 1-56162-095-5). Wonder Kids.

—Chinese Children's Stories, Vol. 97: Tiger Aunty, Ah-Long & Ah-Hwa. Ching, Emily, et al, eds. Wonder Kids Publications Staff, tr. from CHI. Hwa-I Publishing Co., Staff, illus. LC 90-60811. 28p. (gr. 3-6). Repr. of 1988 ed. 7.95x (ISBN 1-56162-097-1). Wonder Kids.

—Chinese Children's Stories, Vol. 98: Ai-Yu Jello, Granny & the Fox. Ching, Emily, et al, eds. Wonder Kids Publications Staff, tr. from CHI. Hwa-I Publishing Co., Staff, illus. LC 90-60811. 28p. (gr. 3-6). Repr. of 1988 ed. 7.95x (ISBN 1-56162-098-X). Wonder Kids.

—Chinese Children's Stories, Vol. 99: The Underground People, Half-Street Lai. Ching, Emily, et al, eds. Wonder Kids Publications Staff, tr. from CHI. Hwa-I Publishing Co., Staff, illus. LC 90-60811. 28p. (gr. 3-6). Repr. of 1988 ed. 7.95x (ISBN 1-56162-099-8). Wonder Kids.

Kendall, Carol. Sweet & Sour: Tales from China. (gr. 4-7). 1990. pap. 3.95 (ISBN 0-395-54798-9, Clarion Bks). HM.

Lattimore, Deborah N. The Dragon's Robe. Lattimore, Deborah N., illus. LC 89-34512. 32p. (gr. 1-5). 1990. 14.95 (ISBN 0-06-023719-8); PLB 14.89 (ISBN 0-06-023723-6). HarpC Child Bks.

Lattimore, Eleanor. Little Pear. D'Andrade, Diane, ed. (Illus.). 142p. (Orig.). (gr. 4-7). 1991. pap. 4.95 (ISBN 0-15-246685-1, HJ). HarBraceJ.

—Little Pear & His Friends. D'Andrade, Diane, ed. (Illus.). 158p. (Orig.). (gr. 4-7). 1991. pap. 4.95 (ISBN 0-15-246863-3, HJ). HarBraceJ.

Lattimore, Eleanor F. Little Pear. Lattimore, Eleanor F., illus. LC 31-22069. (gr. k-3). 1968. pap. 3.95 (ISBN 0-15-652799-5, VoyB). HarBraceJ.

Lewis, Elizabeth F. Young Fu of the Upper Yangtze. (gr. k-6). 1990. pap. 3.50 (ISBN 0-440-49043-X, YB). Dell.

Lim, Genny. Wings for Lai Ho. Lew, Gordon, tr. Ja, Andrea, illus. 48p. (Orig.). (gr. 5-8). 1982. pap. 5.95 (ISBN 0-934788-01-4). E-W Pub Co.

Mahy, Margaret. Seven Chinese Brothers. Tseng, Jean & Mou-sien Tseng, illus. (ps-3). 1990. pap. 12.95 (ISBN 0-590-42055-0). Scholastic Inc.

Neville, Emily C. The China Year. LC 90-39899. 256p. (gr. 5-9). 1991. 15.95 (ISBN 0-06-024383-X); PLB 15.89 (ISBN 0-06-024384-8). HarpC Child Bks.

Paterson, Katherine. Rebels of the Heavenly Kingdom. LC 83-1529. 224p. (gr. 12 up). 1983. 11.95 (ISBN 0-525-66911-6, Lodestar Bks). Dutton Child Bks.

Pittman, Helena C. A Grain of Rice. LC 84-4670. (Illus.). (gr. k-4). 1986. 12.95 (ISBN 0-8038-2728-8); lib. bdg. 12.95 (ISBN 0-8038-9289-6). Hastings.

Vander Els, Betty. Leaving Point. LC 87-23710. 176p. (gr. 7-12). 1987. 12.95 (ISBN 0-374-34376-4). FS&G.

Wolkstein, Diane. White Wave: A Chinese Tale. Young, Ed, illus. LC 78-4781. (gr. 2 up). 1979. 13.95 (ISBN 0-690-03893-3, Crowell Jr Bks). HarpC Child Bks.

Wonder Kids Publications Group Staff (USA) & Hwa-I Publishing Co., Staff (Taiwan) Animal Tales: Chinese Children's Stories, Vols. 11-15. Ching, Emily, et al, eds. Wonder Kids Publication Staff, tr. from CHI. Hwa-I Publishing Co., Staff, illus. LC 90-60793. 28p. (gr. 3-6). 1991. Repr. of 1988 ed. Five vol. set, 28p. ea. bk. 39.75 (ISBN 1-56162-011-4). Wonder Kids.

—Chinese Sites: Chinese Children's Stories, Vols. 86-90. Ching, Emily, et al, eds. Wonder Kids Publications Staff, tr. from CHI. Hwa-I Publishing Co., Staff, illus. LC 90-60809. (gr. 3-6). 1991. Repr. of 1988 ed. Five vol. set, 28p. ea. bk. 39.75 (ISBN 1-56162-086-6, Lucky Tiger Pr). Wonder Kids.

—Fables: Chinese Children's Stories, Vols. 16-20. Ching, Emily & Ching, Ko-Shee, eds. Wonder Kids Publications Staff, tr. from CHI. Hwa-I Publishing Co., Staff, illus. LC 90-60794. (gr. 3-6). 1991. Repr. of 1988 ed. Five vol. set, 28p. ea. bk. 39.75 (ISBN 1-56162-016-5, Lucky Tiger Pr). Wonder Kids.

—Fairy Tales: Chinese Children's Stories, Vols. 46-50. Ching, Emily, et al, eds. Wonder Kids Publications Staff, tr. from CHI. Hwa-I Publishing Co., Staff, illus. LC 90-60801. (gr. 3-6). 1991. Repr. of 1988 ed. Five vol. set, 28p. ea. bk. 39.75 (ISBN 1-56162-046-7, Lucky Tiger Pr). Wonder Kids.

—Festivals: Chinese Children's Stories, Vols. 26-30. Ching, Emily, et al, eds. Wonder Kids Publications Staff, tr. from CHI. Hwa-I Publishing Co., Staff, illus. LC 90-60797. (gr. 3-6). 1991. Repr. of 1988 ed. Five vol. set, 28p. ea. bk. 39.75 (ISBN 1-56162-026-2, Lucky Tiger Pr). Wonder Kids.

—Filial Piety: Chinese Children's Stories, Vols. 51-55. Ching, Emily, et al, eds. Wonder Kids Publications Staff, tr. from CHI. Hwa-I Publishing Co., Staff, illus. LC 90-60802. (gr. 3-6). 1991. Repr. of 1988 ed. Five vol. set, 28p. ea. bk. 39.75 (ISBN 1-56162-051-3, Lucky Tiger Pr). Wonder Kids.

—Folklore: Chinese Children's Stories,

Vols. 1-5. Ching, Emily, et al, eds. Wonder Kids Publications Staff, tr. from CHI. Hwa-I Publishing Co., Staff, illus. LC 90-60791. 28p. (gr. 3-6). 1991. Repr. of 1988 ed. Five vol. set, 28p. ea. bk. 39.75 (ISBN 1-56162-001-7); Set (100 vols.) 795.00 (ISBN 1-56162-120-X). Wonder Kids. "The most comprehensive collection of children's stories about Chinese culture, customs, philosophy, values, history, literature..."--World Journal. Fashioned together in myths, legends, folktale, fairy tales, fables, & short stories, 200 stories for children are packed with action, magic, love & moral teachings. Recommended for ESL & ages 8-12 reading to promote multi-cultural education & global awareness. Following each short story, a "parental guide" presents supplemental information to further clarify moral messages & cultural meaning. 20 titles of subjects include: Folklore, Tales about Plants, Animal Tales, Fables, Idioms, Festivals, Tales about Food, Inventions, 12 Beasts & the Years, Fairy Tales, Filial Piety, Wonder Kids, Mythology, Literature, Popular Narratives, Heroes, Historical Accounts, Chinese Sites, & Taiwanese Sites. Please refer to the individual subject listing in (Children's) Books in Print for a description of each title of subject in the collection.
Publisher Provided Annotation.

—Heroes: Chinese Children's Stories, Vols. 76- 80. Ching, Emily, et al, eds. Wonder Kids Publication s Staff, tr. from CHI. Hwa-I Publishing Co., Staff, illus. LC 90-60807. (gr. 3-6). 1991. Repr. of 1988 ed. Five vol. set, 28p. ea. bk. 39.75 (ISBN 1-56162-076-9, Lucky Tiger Pr). Wonder Kids.

—Historical Accounts: Chinese Children's Stories, Vols. 81-85. Ching, Emily, et al, eds. Wonder Kids Publications Staff, tr. from CHI. Hwa-I Publishing Co., Staff, illus. LC 90-60808. (gr. 3-6). 1991. Repr. of 1988 ed. Five vol. set, 28p. ea. bk. 39.75 (ISBN 1-56162-081-5, Lucky Tiger Pr). Wonder Kids.

—Idioms: Chinese Children's Stories, Vols. 21- 25. Ching, Emily, et al, eds. Wonder Kids Publications Staff, tr. from CHI. Hwa-I Publishing Co., Staff, illus. LC 90-60796. (gr. 3-6). 1991. Repr. of 1988 ed. Five vol. set, 28p. ea. bk. 39.75 (ISBN 1-56162-021-1, Lucky Tiger Pr). Wonder Kids.

—Inventions: Chinese Children's Stories, Vols. 36-40. Ching, Emily, et al, eds. Wonder Kids Publications Staff, tr. from CHI. Hwa-I Publishing Co., Staff, illus. LC 90-60799. (gr. 3-6). 1991. Repr. of 1988 ed. Five vol. set, 28p. ea. bk. 39.75 (ISBN 1-56162-036-X, Lucky Tiger Pr). Wonder Kids.

—Literature: Chinese Children's Stories, Vols. 66-70. Ching, Emily, et al, eds. Wonder Kids Publications Staff, tr. from CHI. Hwa-I Publishing Co., Staff, illus. LC 90-60805. (gr. 3-6). 1991. Repr. of 1988 ed. Five vol. set, 28p. ea. bk. 39.75 (ISBN 1-56162-066-1, Lucky Tiger Pr). Wonder Kids.

—Mythology: Chinese Children's Stories, Vols. 61-65. Ching, Emily, et al, eds. Wonder Kids Publications Staff, tr. from CHI. Hwa-I Publishing Co., Staff, illus. LC 90-60804. (gr. 3-6). 1991. Repr. of 1988 ed. Five vol. set, 28p. ea. bk. 39.75 (ISBN 1-56162-061-0, Lucky Tiger Pr). Wonder Kids.

—Popular Narratives: Chinese Children's Stories, Vols. 71-75. Ching, Emily, et al, eds. Wonder Kids Publications Staff, tr. from CHI. Hwa-I Publishing Co., Staff, illus. LC 90-60806. (gr. 3-6). 1991. Repr. of 1988 ed. Five vol. set, 28p. ea. bk. 39.75 (ISBN 1-56162-071-8, Lucky Tiger Pr). Wonder Kids.

—Taiwanese Folklore: Chinese Children's Stories, Vols. 96-100. Ching, Emily, et al, eds. Wonder Kids Publication Staff, tr. from CHI. Hwa-I Publishing Co., Staff, illus. LC 90-60811. (gr. 3-6). 1991. Repr. of 1988 ed. Five vol. set, 28p. ea. bk. 39.75 (ISBN 1-56162-096-3, Lucky Tiger Pr). Wonder Kids.

—Taiwanese Sites: Chinese Children's Stories, Vols. 91-95. Ching, Emily, et al, eds. Wonder Kids Publications Staff, tr. from CHI. Hwa-I Publishing Co., Staff, illus. LC 90-60810. (gr. 3-6). 1991. Repr. of 1988 ed. Five vol. set, 28p. ea. bk. 39.75 (ISBN 1-56162-091-2, Lucky Tiger Pr). Wonder Kids.

—Tales about Food: Chinese Children's Stories, Vols. 31-35. Ching, Emily, et al, eds. Wonder Kids Publications Staff, tr. from CHI. Hwa-I Publishing Co., Staff, illus. LC 90-60798. (gr. 3-6). 1991. Repr. of 1988 ed. Five vol. set, 28p. ea. bk. 39.75 (ISBN 1-56162-031-9, Lucky Tiger Pr). Wonder Kids.

—Twelve Beasts & the Years: Chinese Children's Stories, Vols. 41-45. Ching, Emily, et al, eds. Wonder Kids Publications Staff, tr. from CHI. Hwa-I Publishing Co., Staff, illus. LC 90-60800. (gr. 3-6). 1991. Repr. of 1988 ed. Five vol. set, 28p. ea. bk. 39.75 (ISBN 1-56162-041-6, Lucky Tiger Pr). Wonder Kids.

—Wonder Kids: Chinese Children's Stories, Vols. 56-60. Ching, Emily, et al, eds. Wonder Kids Publications Staff, tr. from CHI. Hwa-I Publishing Co., Staff, illus. LC 90-60803. (gr. 3-6). 1991. Repr. of 1988 ed. Five vol. set, 28p. ea. bk. 39.75 (ISBN 1-56162-056-4, Lucky Tiger Pr). Wonder Kids.

CHINA–FOREIGN RELATIONS

Lawson, Don. The Eagle & the Dragon: The History of U. S.-China Relations. LC 85-47531. (Illus.). 192p. (gr. 7 up). 1985. 12.95 (ISBN 0-690-04485-2, Crowell Jr Bks); (Crowell Jr Bks). HarpC Child Bks.

CHINA–HISTORY

Dures, Alan. The Postwar World: China since 1949. (Illus.). 64p. (gr. 7-9). 1988. 19.95 (ISBN 0-7134-5774-0, Pub. by Batsford England). Trafalgar Sq.

Goff, Denise. Early China. rev. ed. (Illus.). 32p. (gr. 4-9). 1986. PLB 11.90 (ISBN 0-531-17025-X, Pub. by Gloucester). Watts.

McLean, Virginia O. Chasing the Moon to China. Cheairs, Nancy & Robinson, Susan, illus. Mitler, Ellen, et al, photos by. LC 87-60411. 40p. (gr. k-6). 1987. PLB 15.95 incl. record (ISBN 0-9606046-1-8). Redbird.

McLenighan, Valjean. China: A History to Nineteen Forty-Nine. LC 83-14260. (Illus.). 128p. (gr. 5-9). 1983. PLB 25.27 (ISBN 0-516-02754-9). Childrens.

Newlon, Clarke. China: The Rise to World Power. (gr. 7-11). 1983. 10.95 (ISBN 0-396-08136-3, Putnam). Putnam Pub Group.

Ross, Frank. Oracles Bones, Stars & the Wheelbarrows: Ancient Chinese Science & Technology. 1990. pap. 4.95 (ISBN 0-395-54967-1). HM.

CHINA (PEOPLE'S REPUBLIC OF CHINA)

Bradley, John. China. (ps-3). 1990. PLB 11.90 (ISBN 0-531-17203-1). Watts.

Jacobsen, Karen. China. LC 90-2200. (Illus.). 48p. (gr. k-4). 1990. PLB 14.60 (ISBN 0-516-01102-2); pap. 4.95 (ISBN 0-516-41102-0). Childrens.

McKillop, Beth. China. Shone, Rob, illus. Franklin Watts Ltd., ed. (Illus.). 32p. (gr. 7-9). 1988. PLB 11.90 (ISBN 0-531-10536-9). Watts.

Major, John S. The Land & People of China. LC 88-23427. (Illus.). 288p. (gr. 6 up). 1989. 14.95 (ISBN 0-397-32336-0, Lipp Jr Bks); PLB 14.89 (ISBN 0-397-32337-9, Lipp Jr Bks). HarpC Child Bks.

Milton, Joyce. A Friend of China. LC 80-19545. (Illus.). 128p. (gr. 7 up). 1980. PLB 9.95 (ISBN 0-8038-2388-6). Hastings.

Thomas, Graham. Timeline: People's Republic of China. (Illus.). 72p. (gr. 7 up). 1990. 19.95 (ISBN 0-85219-791-8, Pub. by Batsford UK). Trafalgar Sq.

CHINA (PEOPLE'S REPUBLIC OF CHINA) –FICTION

McLenighan, Valjean. People's Republic of China. LC 84-7025. (Illus.). 128p. (gr. 5-9). 1984. lib. bdg. 25.27 (ISBN 0-516-02781-6). Childrens.

CHINA (PEOPLE'S REPUBLIC OF CHINA) –HISTORY

Finney, Susan & Kindle, Patricia. China: Then & Now. 64p. (gr. 4-8). 1988. wkbk. 6.95 (ISBN 0-86653-458-X, GA1062). Good Apple.

Lawson, Don. The Long March: Red China under Chairman Mao. LC 82-45580. (Illus.). 160p. (gr. 7 up). 1983. PLB 12.89 (ISBN 0-690-04272-8, Crowell Jr Bks). HarpC Child Bks.

Poole, Frederick K. Mao Zedong. (Illus.). 128p. (gr. 7 up). 1982. PLB 12.90 (ISBN 0-531-04481-5). Watts.

Ross, Stewart. China since Nineteen Forty-Five. (Illus.). 64p. (gr. 7-12). 1989. PLB 12.90 (ISBN 0-531-18220-7). Watts.

CHINA (PEOPLE'S REPUBLIC OF CHINA) –SOCIAL LIFE AND CUSTOMS

McLean, Virginia O. Chasing the Moon to China. Cheairs, Nancy & Robinson, Susan, illus. Mitler, Ellen, et al, photos by. LC 87-60411. 40p. (gr. k-6). 1987. PLB 15.95 incl. record (ISBN 0-9606046-1-8). Redbird.

Rau, Margaret. Young Women in China. LC 88-31045. (Illus.). 160p. (gr. 6 up). 1989. PLB 18.95 (ISBN 0-89490-170-2). Enslow Pubs.

Thomson, Peggy. City Kids in China. Conklin, Paul, illus. LC 90-1993. 128p. (gr. 3-7). 1991. 14.95 (ISBN 0-06-021654-9); PLB 14.89 (ISBN 0-06-021655-7). HarpC Child Bks.

CULTURAL CHANGE

see Social Change

CHINESE IN SAN FRANCISCO–FICTION

Yep, Laurence. Child of the Owl. LC 76-24314. 224p. (gr. 7 up). 1977. PLB 12.89 (ISBN 0-06-026743-7). HarpC Child Bks.

—Dragonwings. LC 74-2625. 256p. (gr. 7 up). 1975. PLB 14.89 (ISBN 0-06-026738-0). HarpC Child Bks.

CHINESE IN THE U. S.

Brownstone, David M. The Chinese-American Heritage. (Illus.). 144p. 1988. 16.95x (ISBN 0-8160-1627-5). Facts on File.

Hamilton, Leni. Clara Barton. Horner, Matina, intro. by. (Illus.). 112p. (gr. 5 up). 1988. lib. bdg. 17.95 (ISBN 1-55546-641-9). Chelsea Hse.

Ludwig, Edward W. & Loo, Jack. Gumshan: The Chinese American Saga. Bernal, Adrienne, illus. 32p. (Orig.). (gr. 4-12). 1982. pap. 2.95 (ISBN 0-930504-02-X). Polaris Pr.

Martinello, Marian & Field, William T., Jr. Who Are the Chinese Texans? Ricks, Thorn, illus. 84p. (Orig.). (gr. 5-8). 8.95 (ISBN 0-933164-36-X); pap. 5.95 (ISBN 0-933164-46-7). U of Tex Inst Tex Culture.

Mayberry, Jodine. Chinese. Daniels, Roger, contrib. by. (Illus.). 64p. (gr. 5-8). 1990. PLB 12.40 (ISBN 0-531-10977-1). Watts.

Meltzer, Milton. The Chinese Americans. LC 79-3419. (Illus.). 192p. (gr. 5 up). 1980. PLB 13.89 (ISBN 0-690-04039-3, Crowell Jr Bks). HarpC Child Bks.

Yep, Laurence. The Lost Garden. (Illus.). 128p. (gr. 5-7). 1991. 14.98 (ISBN 0-382-24098-7); 9.71s.p.; pap. 12.95 (ISBN 0-382-24090-1); pap. 11.24s.p. Silver Burdett Pr.

CHINESE IN THE U. S.–FICTION

Brown, Tricia. Chinese New Year. Ortiz, Fran, photos by. LC 87-8532. (Illus.). 48p. (gr. k-3). 1987. 13.95 (ISBN 0-8050-0497-1). H Holt & Co.

Joe, Jeanne. Ying-Ying: Pieces of a Childhood. Caigoy, Faustino, illus. 112p. (Orig.). (gr. 4 up). 1982. pap. 4.95 (ISBN 0-934788-02-2). E-W Pub Co.

Lim, Sing. West Coast Chinese Boy. Lim, Sing, illus. 64p. (gr. 6-12). 1979. 6.95 (ISBN 0-88776-121-6). Tundra Bks.

Waters, Kate & Slovenz-Low, Madeline. Lion Dancer: Ernie Wan's Chinese New Year. Cooper, Martha, photos by. (Illus.). (gr. k-3). 1990. 12.95 (ISBN 0-685-31010-8). Scholastic Inc.

Yee, Paul. Tales from Gold Mountain: Stories of the Chinese in the New World. Ng, Simon, illus. LC 89-12643. 64p. (gr. k-8). 1990. 14.95 (ISBN 0-02-793621-X, Mcmillan Child Bk). Macmillan Child Grp.

Yep, Laurence. Child of the Owl. LC 76-24314. 224p. (gr. 7 up). 1990. pap. 3.95 (ISBN 0-06-440336-X, Trophy). HarpC Child Bks.

CHINESE LANGUAGE

Chang, Florence C. China Is Farther Than the Sun? A Beginning Chinese-English Reader. LC 80-68256. (Illus.). 51p. (gr. 3-4). 1980. pap. 5.50x incl. wkbk. (ISBN 0-936620-00-5). Ginkgo Hut.

—Maomao & Mimi. Chang, Tao-Yuan, illus. LC 81-80784. 80p. (Orig.). (gr. 5-6). 1981. pap. 4.15x incl. exercises (ISBN 0-936620-05-6). Ginkgo Hut.

—Puppy's Tail. Chang, Tao-Yuan, illus. LC 81-82176. 72p. (Orig.). (gr. 1-2). 1981. pap. 4.15x incl. exercises (ISBN 0-936620-06-4). Ginkgo Hut.

—With Sound & Color: An Intermediate Chinese-English Reader. Chai, Florence, illus. LC 80-68257. 71p. (Orig.). (gr. 7-9). 1980. pap. 6.00x (wkbk. incl.) (ISBN 0-936620-01-3). Ginkgo Hut.

Goldstein, Peggy. Long Is a Dragon: Chinese Writing for Children. LC 90-81148. (Illus.). 32p. (gr. 3-7). 1990. 14.95 (ISBN 0-8351-2375-8). China Bks.

Murray, D. M. & Wong, T. W. Noodle Words: An Introduction to Chinese & Japanese Characters. LC 79-147179. (Illus.). (gr. 9 up). 1971. pap. 6.95 (ISBN 0-8048-0948-8). C E Tuttle.

Sheheen, Dennis, illus. A Child's Picture English-Chinese Dictionary. (gr. k-6). 1987. Repr. 9.95 (ISBN 1-55774-001-1, Dist. by Watts). Adama Pubs Inc.

CHINESE LITERATURE–COLLECTIONS

Ramos, Lindsey. Four Chinese Children's Stories. Troupe, Connie, illus. 14.95 (ISBN 0-9628563-0-4). Lttle Peop Pr. Little Fawn & Baby Swan - A Story of Helping; Pandy the Chinese Panda - A Story of Loving; The Foolish Little Monkey - A Story of Learning; The Village Goats - A Story of Cooperation. These charming stories, new to the USA, are authentic translations of revered Chinese Children's Stories. Four hard-bound volumes come in a sturdy & colorful case. Each is exquisitely illustrated with vivid color & fine detail that will attract young readers. FOUR CHINESE CHILDREN'S STORIES is the first set in an international series by Little People's Press that will present children's stories from many cultures & nations. "Children can experience the paradox of unity & diversity among peoples, & it will encourage a foundation for understanding throughout their lives" says the publisher. "To promote such a foundation is our goal at Little People's Press." Through these animal tales that children love, FOUR CHINESE

CHILDREN'S STORIES lives up to that ideal in a fun & colorful way. *Publisher Provided Annotation.*

CHIPMUNKS
Berenstain, Michael. Peat Moss & Ivy & the Birthday Present. Berenstain, Michael, illus. LC 86-611. 32p. (ps-2). 1986. (Random Juv); pap. 1.95 (ISBN 0-394-87605-9, BYR). Random.
CHIPMUNKS–FICTION
Berenstain, Michael. Peat Moss & Ivy's Backyard Adventure. Berenstain, Michael, illus. LC 85-43097. 32p. (ps-3). 1986. lib. bdg. 5.99 (ISBN 0-394-97604-5); pap. 1.95 (ISBN 0-394-87604-0). Random.
Gruber, Suzanne. Chatty Chipmunk's Nutty Day. Cushman, Doug, illus. LC 84-8665. 32p. (gr. k-2). 1985. PLB 10.89 (ISBN 0-8167-0360-4); pap. text ed. 2.95 (ISBN 0-8167-0440-6). Troll Assocs.
Oana, Katherine. Chirpy Chipmunk. Baird, Tate, ed. Butrick, Lyn M., illus. LC 88-51854. 16p. (Orig.). (ps). 1989. pap. 3.39 (ISBN 0-914127-08-X). Univ Class.
Ryder, Joanne. Chipmunk Song. Cherry, Lynne, illus. LC 86-19786. 32p. (ps-3). 1990. pap. 13.95 (ISBN 0-525-67191-9, Lodestar Bks); pap. 3.95 (ISBN 0-525-67312-1). Dutton Child Bks.
Shook, Jean. Alvin & the Chipmunks: Happy Birthday, Dave! (ps-3). 1990. write for info. (ISBN 0-307-11587-9). Western Pub.
Zalben, Jane B. Oh, Simple! LC 80-22587. (Illus.). 32p. (ps-3). 1981. 8.95 (ISBN 0-374-35604-1). FS&G.
CHISHOLM, SHIRLEY
Hicks, Nancy. The Honorable Shirley Chisholm: Congresswoman from Brooklyn. (gr. 7 up). PLB 11.95 (ISBN 0-87460-259-9). Lion Bks.
CHIVALRY
see also Arthur, King; Civilization, Medieval; Crusades; Feudalism; Heraldry; Knights and Knighthood
Bulfinch, Thomas. Age of Chivalry. (gr. 8 up). pap. 1.95 (ISBN 0-8049-0061-2, CL-61). Airmont.
The End of Chivalry. 64p. (gr. 4-8). 1990. 13.95 (ISBN 0-86307-996-2). Marshall Cavendish.
Westwood, Jennifer. Stories of Charlemagne. LC 74-12435. (gr. 6 up). 1976. 18.95 (ISBN 0-87599-213-7). S G Phillips.
Wright, Sylvia. The Age of Chivalry. JV-Warwick Press Staff, ed. (Illus.). 48p. (gr. 4-9). 1988. PLB 13.90 (ISBN 0-531-19044-7, Warwick). Watts.
CHIVALRY–FICTION
De Cervantes, Miguel. Don Quixote. (gr. 11 up). 1967. pap. 2.75 (ISBN 0-8049-0153-8, CL-153). Airmont.
Green, Roger L. King Arthur & His Knights of the Round Table. (Orig.). (gr. 5-7). 1974. pap. 2.95 (ISBN 0-14-030073-2, Penguin Bks). Viking Penguin.
Lang, Andrew, ed. King Arthur: Tales of the Round Table. Ford, H. J., illus. LC 67-26996. (gr. 5 up). 1987. pap. 7.95 (ISBN 0-8052-0196-3). Schocken.
Lewis, Naomi, tr. Proud Knight, Fair Lady: The Twelve Lais of Marie de France. Barrett, Angela, illus. 128p. (gr. 5 up). 1989. pap. 19.95 (ISBN 0-670-82656-1). Viking Child Bks.
Pyle, Howard. Men of Iron. Bennet, C. L., intro. by. (Illus.). (gr. 6 up). pap. 3.50 (ISBN 0-8049-0093-0, CL-93). Airmont.
CHOCOLATE
Ammon, Richard. The Kids' Book of Chocolate. LC 86-26564. (Illus.). 96p. (gr. 3-7). 1987. 12.95 (ISBN 0-689-31292-X, Atheneum Child Bk). Macmillan Child Grp.
Black, Sonia & Brigandi, Pat. Chocolate, Chocolate, Chocolate: The Complete Book of Chocolate. (gr. 4 up). 1989. pap. 1.95 (ISBN 0-318-41678-6). Scholastic Inc.
Catling, Patrick S. The Chocolate Touch. Apple, Margot, illus. LC 78-31100. 96p. (gr. 4-6). 1979. Repr. of 1952 ed. PLB 11.88 (ISBN 0-688-32187-9). Morrow Jr Bks.
Cormier, Robert. Beyond the Chocolate War. LC 84-22865. 288p. (gr. 9 up). 1985. 11.95 (ISBN 0-394-87343-2); lib. bdg. 11.99 (ISBN 0-394-97343-7). Knopf.
Dahl, Roald. Charlie & the Chocolate Factory. large type ed. 174p. 1989. Repr. of 1964 ed. 13.95 (ISBN 1-55736-154-1, Crnrstn Bks). ABC CLIO.
Mitgutsch, Ali. From Cacao Bean to Chocolate: Translation of Vom Kakao Zur Schokolade. Mitgutsch, Ali, illus. LC 80-29588. 24p. (ps-3). 1981. PLB 6.95 (ISBN 0-87614-147-5). Carolrhoda Bks.
Pinder, Polly. Polly Pinder's Chocolate Cookbook. Pinder, Polly, illus. Search Studios Staff, photos by. (Illus.). 144p. (gr. 7 up). 1988. 24.95 (ISBN 0-85532-603-4, Pub. by Search Pr UK). Pathway Bk Serv.
CHOICE OF BOOKS
see Books and Reading; Books and Reading–Best Books
CHOICE OF PROFESSION
see Vocational Guidance
CHOPIN, FREDERIC FRANCOIS, 1810-1849
Patton, Barbara. Introducing Frederic Chopin. (Illus., Orig.). (gr. 3-9). 1990. pap. 6.95x (ISBN 1-878636-00-6). Soundboard Bks.
CHORAL SPEAKING
Liggett, Clayton E. Concert Theatre. LC 72-104705. (Illus.). (gr. 9 up). 1970. PLB 11.95 (ISBN 0-8239-0194-7). Rosen Group.
CHOREOGRAPHY
see Ballet; Dancing
CHRIST
see Jesus Christ

CHRISTENING
see Baptism
CHRISTIAN ART AND SYMBOLISM
see also Bible–Pictorial Works; Cathedrals; Jesus Christ–Art
Coen, Rena N. Old Testament in Art. LC 77-84410. (Illus.). 72p. (gr. 5 up). 1970. PLB 5.95 (ISBN 0-8225-0168-6). Lerner Pubns.
Currier, Mary. Christian Crafts from Paper Plates. 64p. (ps-5). 1989. 7.95 (ISBN 0-86653-494-6, SS1880). Good Apple.
Hillam, Corbin. Christian Clip & Copy Time-Savers. 96p. (ps up). 1990. 9.95 (ISBN 0-86653-553-5, SS1822). Good Apple.
Ortega, Claudia. Religious Clip Art Book. Ortiz, Gloria, illus. 64p. (Orig.). 1989. pap. 24.95 (ISBN 1-55612-311-6). Sheed & Ward MO.
Schneck, Susan. Christian Clip & Copy Art. 96p. (ps-8). 1989. 9.95 (ISBN 0-86653-503-9, SS1816). Good Apple.
Shissler, Barbara. New Testament in Art. LC 70-84411. (Illus.). 68p. (gr. 5 up). 1970. PLB 5.95 (ISBN 0-8225-0169-4). Lerner Pubns.
Stegenga, Susan J. Christian Crafts - Paper Bag Puppets. 64p. (ps-5). 1990. 7.95 (ISBN 0-86653-552-7, SS1881). Good Apple.
CHRISTIAN BIOGRAPHY
see also Apostles; Cardinals; Clergy; Missionaries; Monasticism and Religious Orders; Pilgrim Fathers; Popes; Saints
African Triumph. (gr. 3-7). 3.00 (ISBN 0-8198-0225-5); pap. 2.00 (ISBN 0-8198-0226-3). Dghtrs St Paul.
Bonniwell, William R. The Life of Blessed Margaret of Castello. LC 83-70524. 113p. (gr. 8). 1983. pap. 5.00 (ISBN 0-89555-213-2). TAN Bks Pubs.
Caldwell, Louise. Timothy: Young Pastor. Karch, Paul, illus. (gr. 1-6). 1978. 5.95 (ISBN 0-8054-4239-1, 4242-39). Broadman.
Daughters of St. Paul. Boy with a Mission. (gr. 4-9). 1967. 3.00 (ISBN 0-8198-0229-8). Dghtrs St Paul.
—God's Secret Agent. (gr. 4-9). 1967. 3.00 (ISBN 0-8198-0236-0); pap. 2.00 (ISBN 0-8198-3036-4). Dghtrs St Paul.
Flores, Kathy. Beauty for Ashes. Cox, Gail, ed. Gobble, Janice, illus. Malvido, Lalo, photos by. 37p. (Orig.). 1990. pap. 3.98 (ISBN 0-9626862-0-4). K Flores Min.
Garrett, Carol. Sam Simpson: Architect of Hope. 192p. (Orig.). 1989. pap. text ed. 6.95 (ISBN 0-936625-63-5, New Hope AL). Womans Mission Union.
Heidebrecht, Paul H. God's Man in the Marketplace: The Story of Herbert J. Taylor. LC 90-37145. 120p. (Orig.). 1990. pap. 7.95 (ISBN 0-8308-1733-6, 1733). InterVarsity.
Hockett, Betty M. Mud on Their Wheels: The Life-Story of Vern & Lois Ellis. Loewen, Janelle, illus. LC 88-81703. 80p. (Orig.). (gr. 3-6). 1988. pap. 3.50 (ISBN 0-943701-14-7). George Fox Pr.
Hollywood, Kathy & Hale, Lorraine. The Heroes & Heroines of the Christian Story. Lloyd, John R., illus. 84p. (gr. 2-7). 1990. write for info. (ISBN 0-9627801-0-3). Allgnc Advntg.
Lappin, Peter. The Falcon & the Dove: The Story of Laura Vicuna. (Illus.). 180p. (gr. 9-12). 1985. pap. 4.95 (ISBN 0-89944-067-3). Don Bosco Multimedia.
—General Mickey. 167p. (Orig.). (gr. 5-10). 1977. pap. 2.95 (ISBN 0-89944-029-0). Don Bosco Multimedia.
McFarlan, Donald. White Queen: Mary Slessor. 1982. pap. 3.95 (ISBN 0-87508-632-2). Chr Lit.
McIndoo, Ethel. Freeda Harris: Woman of Prayer. LC 84-2978. (gr. 4-6). 1984. 5.95 (ISBN 0-8054-4286-3, 4242-86). Broadman.
Martin, Teri. Junipero Serra: God's Pioneer. Novack, Kevin, illus. 64p. (gr. 7-9). 1990. pap. 4.95 (ISBN 0-8091-6589-9). Paulist Pr.
Naish, Jack. Philip: Traveling Preacher. Hester, Ron, illus. (gr. 1-6). 1978. 5.95 (ISBN 0-8054-4241-3, 4242-41). Broadman.
O'Grady, Jim. Dorothy Day: With Love for the Poor. (Illus.). 104p. (gr. 4-9). 1991. pap. 9.95 (ISBN 0-9623380-6-0). Ward Hill Pr.
Olsen, Sue. Kate Magevney & the Christmas Miracle: A Child's Christmas in Memphis (1850) Easson, Roger R., ed. Awsumb, Carl, illus. LC 84-11612. 48p. (gr. 5 up). 1984. 9.95 (ISBN 0-918518-34-2). St Lukes Pr.
Richardson, Arleta. A Heart for God in India. Payne, Peggy & Yoder, Tamra, eds. Ortega, Jennifer, illus. 52p. (Orig.). (gr. 4-6). 1989. pap. 4.00 (ISBN 0-89367-144-4). Light & Life.
Rodino, A. Music Master. (Illus.). (gr. 3-7). 1968. 3.00 (ISBN 0-8198-0105-4). Dghtrs St Paul.
Root, Loretta P. Outflowing Love: Auntie-Bai, Effie Southworth's Life. Benson, Mary C., ed. Benson, John, illus. 124p. (Orig.). 1989. pap. 5.95 (ISBN 0-89367-142-8). Light & Life.
Scott. Slave Ship Captain: John Newton. 1989. pap. 3.95 (ISBN 0-87508-623-3). Chr Lit.
Swift, Catherine. Eric Liddell. 176p. (gr. 8 up). 1990. 3.95 (ISBN 1-55661-150-1). Bethany Hse.
Tallach, John. They Shall Be Mine. 128p. (gr. 9-12). 1981. pap. 6.95 (ISBN 0-85151-320-4). Banner of Truth.
Tozer, A. W. Let My People Go: The Life of Robert A. Jaffray. rev. ed. LC 90-80076. 128p. 1990. pap. 7.99 (ISBN 0-87509-427-9). Chr Pubns.
Turrentine, Jan. Always a Friend: The Story of Mildred McWhorter. 192p. (Orig.). (gr. 7-12). 1988. pap. 4.95 (ISBN 0-936625-35-X, New Hope AL). Womans Mission Union.

Whaley, Richie. Samuel: Prophet & Judge. Shelton, Dean, illus. (gr. 1-6). 1979. 5.95 (ISBN 0-8054-4242-1, 4242-42). Broadman.
White, Kathleen. Jim Elliott. 128p. (gr. 8 up). 1990. Repr. 3.95 (ISBN 1-55661-125-0). Bethany Hse.
Williamson, Denise. River of Danger: A Story of Samuel Kirkland. 112p. (gr. 4-7). 1990. pap. 6.95 (ISBN 1-56121-027-7). Wolgemuth & Hyatt.
Wilson Story, Bettie. Gospel Trailblazer: The Exciting Story of Francis Asbury. 128p. (gr. 4-6). 1984. pap. 1.38 (ISBN 0-687-15652-1). Abingdon.
Windeatt, Mary F. Blessed Kateri Tekakwitha. Harmon, Gedge, illus. 32p. (gr. 1-5). 1989. Repr. of 1954 ed. wkbk. 3.00 (ISBN 0-89555-378-3). TAN Bks Pubs.
CHRISTIAN EDUCATION
see Religious Education
CHRISTIAN ETHICS
Carr, Dan. Cheating. (Illus.). (gr. k-4). 1984. pap. 0.99 (ISBN 0-570-08725-2, 56-1469). Concordia.
—Hurting Others. (Illus.). (gr. k-4). 1984. pap. 0.99 (ISBN 0-570-08727-9, 56-1471). Concordia.
—Lying. (Illus.). (gr. k-4). 1984. pap. 0.99 (ISBN 0-570-08732-5, 56-1476). Concordia.
—My Bad Temper. (Illus.). (gr. 1-3). 1984. pap. 0.99 (ISBN 0-570-08730-9, 56-1474). Concordia.
—Paying Attention. (Illus.). (gr. k-4). 1984. pap. 0.99 (ISBN 0-570-08729-5, 56-1473). Concordia.
—Sharing. (Illus.). (gr. k-4). 1984. pap. 0.99 (ISBN 0-570-08728-7, 56-1472). Concordia.
—Stealing. (Illus.). (gr. k-4). 1984. pap. 0.99 (ISBN 0-570-08731-7, 56-1475). Concordia.
—Vandalism. (Illus.). (gr. k-4). 1984. pap. 0.99 (ISBN 0-570-08726-0, 56-1470). Concordia.
Chappell, Stephen. Dragons & Demons, Angels & Eagles: Morality Tales for Teens. LC 89-63202. 128p. (Orig.). 1990. pap. 4.95 (ISBN 0-89243-314-0). Liguori Pubns.
Christenson, Larry. The Wonderful Way That Babies Are Made. LC 82-12813. 48p. (Orig.). (ps up). 1982. 10.95 (ISBN 0-87123-627-3). Bethany Hse.
Eble, Diane. Personal Best. 160p. 1991. pap. 6.95 (ISBN 0-310-71141-X, Campus Life). Zondervan.
Link, Mark. Decision. 160p. 1987. 6.95 (ISBN 0-89505-655-0). Tabor Pub.
Maston, T. B. & Pinson, William M., Jr. Right or Wrong. rev. 14th ed. LC 75-143282. (gr. 8 up). 1971. pap. 3.95 (ISBN 0-8054-6116-7, 4261-16); 4.50 (ISBN 0-685-00856-8, 4825-37). Broadman.
Reichert, Richard. Making Moral Decisions. rev. ed. LC 83-60316. (Illus.). 191p. (gr. 11-12). 1983. pap. text ed. 8.00x (ISBN 0-88489-150-X); tchrs. guide 9.00x (ISBN 0-88489-151-8); Duplicating Masters. 15.95 (ISBN 0-685-04741-5). St Marys.
Tighe, Mike. I Was Afraid I'd Lose My Soul to a Chocolate Malt... And Other Stories of Everyday Spirituality. LC 89-63837. (Illus.). 96p. (Orig.). 1990. pap. 2.95 (ISBN 0-89243-316-7). Liguori Pubns.
Weakland, Rembert G. Letters to Teens: Hopeful Words from an Archbishop. 48p. (Orig.). (gr. 8-12). 1988. pap. 1.75 (ISBN 0-89243-290-X). Liguori Pubns.
Yorgason, Blaine & Yorgason, Brenton. The Problem with Immorality. 43p. Date not set. pap. text ed. 3.50 (ISBN 0-929985-15-X). Sonos.
Young, Douglas. A Primer of Christianity & Ethics. Hunting, Constance, ed. 200p. (Orig.). (gr. 9-12). 1985. pap. 12.95 (ISBN 0-913006-34-3). Puckerbrush.
CHRISTIAN LIFE
see also Children–Religious Life; Christian Ethics; Faith; Love; Prayer; Religious Education; Spiritual Life
Aaseng, Nathan. I'm Learning, Lord, but I Still Need Help: Story Devotions for Boys. LC 81-65652. 112p. (Orig.). (gr. 3-7). 1981. pap. 4.95 (ISBN 0-8066-1888-4, 10-3202, Augsburg). Augsburg Fortress.
—I'm Searching, Lord, but I Need Your Light. LC 82-72644. 112p. (gr. 3-6). 1983. pap. 4.95 (ISBN 0-8066-1950-3, 10-3203, Augsburg). Augsburg Fortress.
—Which Way Are You Leading Me, Lord? Bible Devotions for Boys. LC 84-21562. 112p. (Orig.). (gr. 3-7). 1984. pap. 4.95 (ISBN 0-8066-2113-3, 10-7099, Augsburg). Augsburg Fortress.
Anderson, Debby. All Year Long. (gr. k-2). 1986. comb bdg. 3.95 (ISBN 1-55513-043-7, Chariot Bks). Cook.
—God Is with Me. (gr. k-2). 1986. comb bdg. 3.95 (ISBN 0-89191-269-X, Chariot Bks). Cook.
Armstrong, Max & Armstrong, Hylma. A Conscience Is... Pride, Barbara, illus. 32p. (gr. 1-4). 1986. casebound 4.95 (ISBN 0-87403-122-2, 3602). Standard Pub.
Ashton, Leila M. My "Feel Good" Secrets. (Illus.). (gr. 1 up). 1978. pap. 1.95 (ISBN 0-8127-0178-X). Review & Herald.
Barker, Shane. Youth Leading Youth. LC 87-22347. 121p. (gr. 7-12). 1987. 9.95 (ISBN 0-87579-111-5). Deseret Bk.
Bartel, Marvin. My Own Picture Book about Getting Older. Bartel, Marvin, illus. LC 89-80248. 43p. (ps-7). 1989. wkbk. 4.95 (ISBN 0-87303-135-0). Faith & Life.
Bartz, Paul A. Letting God Create Your Day, Vol. 1, No. 1: Scripts from the International Broadcast Creation Moments. 84p. (Orig.). 1989. pap. write for info. Colorsong Prodns.
Beckman, Beverly. Senses in God's World. 24p. (ps). 1986. 6.95 (ISBN 0-570-04150-3, 56-1604). Concordia.
Beckmann, Beverly. Emotions in God's World. 24p. (ps-1). 1986. 6.95 (ISBN 0-570-04149-X, 56-1610). Concordia.
—Seasons in God's World. Bowser, Carolyn E., illus. 24p. (gr. 2-5). 1985. 6.95 (ISBN 0-570-04127-9, 56-1538). Concordia.

Beers, V. Gilbert. Friends Are Helpers. Eubank, Mary G., illus. 12p. 1991. 3.95 (ISBN 0-8010-0997-9). Baker Bk.

—Friends Give Good Gifts. Eubank, Mary, illus. 12p. 1991. 3.95 (ISBN 0-8010-0998-7). Baker Bk.

—Friends Play Together. Eubank, Mary G., illus. 12p. 1991. 3.95 (ISBN 0-8010-0999-5). Baker Bk.

—Friends Share. Eubank, Mary G., illus. 12p. 1991. 3.95 (ISBN 0-8010-0996-0). Baker Bk.

Beers, V. Gilbert & Beers, Ronald A. Growing God's Way to See & Share. 192p. (gr. 7 up). 1987. pap. 12.99 (ISBN 0-89693-801-8). Victor Bks.

Bence, Evelyn, ed. New Beginnings. 192p. (gr. 9-12). 1988. 8.95 (ISBN 0-8007-1564-0). Revell.

Bentley, Victor. Possessing Truth in Balance & Anatomy of a Backslider. Bernard, David, ed. LC 89-8945. 128p. (Orig.). 1989. pap. 5.95 (ISBN 0-932581-48-X). Word Aflame.

Bentz, Ron. God, Money & You: How to Be Financially Free. LC 89-60584. 160p. (Orig.). 1989. pap. 8.95 (ISBN 1-55612-180-6). Sheed & Ward MO.

Bernstein, Bob. Thinking Numbers. 96p. (gr. 2-7). 1989. 8.95 (ISBN 0-86653-506-3, GA1094). Good Apple.

Berry, John R. Good Words for New Christians. (Orig.). (gr. 6-12). 1987. pap. 2.95 (ISBN 0-9616900-0-3). J R Berry.

Bibee, John. The Only Game in Town. Turnbaugh, Paul, illus. LC 88-9369. 192p. (ps-6). 1988. pap. 6.95 (ISBN 0-8308-1202-4). InterVarsity.

Bill, J. Brent. Lunch Is My Favorite Subject. LC 86-31312. (Illus.). 180p. (Orig.). (gr. 9-12). 1987. pap. 6.95 (ISBN 0-8007-5239-2). Revell.

Bishops' Committee for Pastoral Research Staff & National Conference of Catholic Bishops Staff. The Sexual Challenge: Growing up Christian. 16p. (Orig.). (gr. 9-12). 1990. pap. 0.95 (ISBN 1-555-86364-7). US Catholic.

Bisignano, Joseph, et al. Creating Your Future: Activities to Encourage Thinking Ahead, Level 3. Theobald, Robert, frwd. by. 64p. (Orig.). (gr. 7-9). 1985. wkbk 6.95 (ISBN 0-934134-39-1). Sheed & Ward MO.

Bitney, James & Nelson, Yvette. Welcome to the Family. 112p. (gr. 4-6). 1988. student ed. 5.95 (ISBN 0-89505-658-5). Tabor Pub.

Bly, Stephen & Bly, Janet. Questions I'd Like to Ask. LC 82-2252. (gr. 5). 1982. 3.95 (ISBN 0-8024-7058-0). Moody.

Bonnici, Roberta L. I'm Scared to Witness! Clore, Chuck, illus. 48p. (Orig.). (gr. 9-12). 1979. pap. 1.50 (ISBN 0-88243-931-6, 02-0931); leader's guide 3.95 (ISBN 0-88243-330-X, 02-0330). Gospel Pub.

—Your Right to Be Different. Clore, Chuck, illus. 48p. (gr. 9-12). 1982. pap. 1.50 (ISBN 0-88243-842-5, 02-0842); leader's guide 3.95 (ISBN 0-88243-333-4, 02-0333). Gospel Pub.

Boone, Debby & Ferrer, Gabriel. Tomorrow Is a Brand New Day. (Illus.). 32p. (Orig.). (ps-3). 1989. 10.99 (ISBN 0-89081-770-7). Harvest Hse.

Britton, Colleen. Celebrate Communion. 79p. (gr. 1-6). 1984. pap. 9.95 (ISBN 0-940754-26-6). Ed Ministries.

Buchanan, Jami L. Letters to My Little Sisters. LC 84-27612. (Orig.). (gr. 7-8). 1985. pap. 4.95 (ISBN 0-8307-0999-1, S185100). Regal.

Burns, Jim. Making Your Life Count. Bundshuh, Rick, illus. 64p. (gr. 8 up). wkbk. 4.99 (ISBN 0-89081-392-2). Harvest Hse.

Cake, J. C. Good Knight Stories. Stickler, Ruth, ed. 190p. (gr. 1 up). 1967. pap. 5.95 (ISBN 0-932785-49-2). Philos Pub.

Carney, Mary L. There's an Angel in My Locker. 112p. (Orig.). (gr. 7-9). 1986. pap. 6.95 (ISBN 0-310-28471-6, 11341P). Zondervan.

Chamberlain, Martha E. Surviving Junior High. LC 88-2937. 296p. (Orig.). (gr. 7-9). 1988. pap. 9.95 (ISBN 0-8361-3462-1). Herald Pr.

Chappell, David, illus. Five Things God Cannot Do. 16p. (gr. k-6). 1989. pap. text ed. 4.25 (ISBN 1-55976-129-6). CEF Press.

Chesney, Sandy. The Zapped Tadpole & More. 93p. 1991. pap. 6.95 (ISBN 0-8163-1029-7). Pacific Pr Pub Assn.

Christie, Les. When You Have to Draw the Line. 132p. (gr. 8 up). 1988. pap. text ed. 6.99 (ISBN 0-89693-439-X). Victor Bks.

Clemmer Steiner, Susan. God Has No Favorites. Shelley, Maynard, ed. LC 89-84827. 97p. (Orig.). (gr. 8-12). 1989. pap. 4.95 (ISBN 0-87303-134-2). Faith & Life.

Coleman, William. Earning Your Wings. LC 84-6299. 140p. (gr. 7 up). 1984. pap. 5.95 (ISBN 0-87123-311-8). Bethany Hse.

—Getting Ready for Our New Baby. LC 84-432. 112p. (ps-2). 1984. pap. 5.95 (ISBN 0-87123-295-2). Bethany Hse.

—The Good Night Book. Coleman, William, illus. LC 79-20002. 128p. (ps). 1980. pap. 5.95 (ISBN 0-87123-187-5). Bethany Hse.

—On Your Mark. LC 79-16458. 112p. (gr. 5-9). 1979. pap. 5.95 (ISBN 0-87123-490-4). Bethany Hse.

Coleman, William L. Entering the Teen Zone: Devotions to Guide You. LC 90-43092. 112p. (Orig.). (gr. 7-10). 1991. pap. 4.95 (ISBN 0-8066-2499-X, 9-2499, Augsburg). Augsburg Fortress.

Corbin, Linda & Dys, Pat. Jesus Is God's Son. (Orig.). (gr. 1-6). 1988. pap. 5.99 (ISBN 0-87509-404-X). Chr Pubns.

Cordova, Laura. God Made Me Special. 64p. (ps-3). 1989. 7.95 (ISBN 0-86653-496-2, SS1857). Good Apple.

Crary, Elizabeth. Mommy Don't Go. Megale, Marina, illus. LC 85-63759. 32p. (Orig.). (ps-2). 1986. lib. bdg. 14.95 (ISBN 0-943990-27-0); pap. 4.95 (ISBN 0-943990-26-2). Parenting Pr.

Cronin, Gaynell B. The Table of the Lord. LC 86-70131. (Illus., Orig.). (gr. 1-3). 1986. Child's Bk, 104 pgs. pap. text ed. 4.50 (ISBN 0-87793-299-9); Director's Manual, 168 pgs. 9.75 (ISBN 0-87793-325-1); Family Bk., 96p. 3.50 (ISBN 0-87793-326-X). Ave Maria.

Crook, Carol. Enter-Praise-Worship. (Illus.). 9p. (Orig.). (gr. 7 up). 1988. pap. 0.75x (ISBN 0-939399-03-2). Bks of Truth.

—God Revealed in Us. 22p. (Orig.). (gr. 7 up). 1989. pap. 1.00x (ISBN 0-939399-04-0). Bks of Truth.

—Spiritual Adoption: Adopted by the Father. (Illus.). 20p. (Orig.). (gr. 7 up). 1989. pap. 1.00x (ISBN 0-939399-13-X). Bks of Truth.

—Thoughts Turn to Actions. 7p. (Orig.). (gr. 5 up). 1989. pap. 0.75x (ISBN 0-939399-10-5). Bks of Truth.

Daniel, Rebecca. Count God's Blessings. 48p. (ps-1). 1991. 8.95 (ISBN 0-86653-626-4, SS1889). Good Apple.

—God's Colorful World. 48p. (ps-1). 1991. 8.95 (ISBN 0-86653-630-2, SS1888). Good Apple.

Daniels, Rebecca. Hallelujah! I'm Special. McClure, Nancee, illus. 48p. (gr. k-3). 1985. wkbk. 6.95 (ISBN 0-86653-174-2, SS 816). Good Apple.

Darden, Bob. The Option Play. 140p. (Orig.). (gr. 9-12). 1990. pap. 6.95 (ISBN 1-55945-050-9, Teenage Bks). Group Pub.

Daughters of St. Paul. A Woman Who Loved. (gr. 3-7). 3.00 (ISBN 0-8198-0240-9); pap. 2.00 (ISBN 0-8198-4708-9). Dghtrs St Paul.

Davidson, Robert G. God Doesn't Make Junk. (gr. 9-12). 1990. 8.00 (ISBN 0-940754-93-2, 8242). Ed Ministries.

—Youth Programming Workbook. 40p. (Orig.). 1989. pap. 8.50 (ISBN 0-940754-67-3). Ed Ministries.

Davis, Ken. How to Live with Your Parents Without Losing Your Mind. (gr. 7 up). 1988. pap. 6.95 (ISBN 0-310-32331-2, 11791P, Pub. by Youth Spec). Zondervan.

DeGrote-Sorensen, Barbara. Everybody Needs a Friend: A Young Christian Book for Girls. LC 86-32152. 112p. (Orig.). (gr. 3-7). 1987. pap. 5.95 (ISBN 0-8066-2247-4, 10-2120, Augsburg). Augsburg Fortress.

De la Cruz Aymes, Maria, et al. Growing with God's Forgiveness & I Celebrate Reconcilation. 72p. (gr. 1-3). 1985. pap. text ed. 5.25 (ISBN 0-8215-2371-6); tchr's. ed. 7.41 (ISBN 0-8215-2373-2); parent pack (10 booklets) 15.39 (ISBN 0-8215-2377-5). Sadlier.

—Growing with the Bread of Life & My Mass Book. 72p. (gr. 1-3). 1985. pap. text ed. 5.25 (ISBN 0-8215-2370-8); tchr's. ed. 7.41 (ISBN 0-8215-2372-4); parent pack (10 booklets) 15.39 (ISBN 0-8215-2376-7). Sadlier.

De Poor, Betty M., tr. Dios, Tu y Tu Familia. 1981. Repr. of 1978 ed. 1.25 (ISBN 0-311-46202-2). Casa Bautista.

Dobson, James. Preparing for Adolescence. rev. ed. Mills, Kathi, ed. LC 89-30455. 175p. 1989. pap. 7.95 (ISBN 0-8307-1258-5, 5419314); 3.95 (ISBN 0-8307-1384-0, 5018928). Regal.

Donze, Mary T. I Can Pray the Rosary! Donze, Mary T., illus. 48p. (Orig.). (gr. 2-4). 1991. pap. 2.95 (ISBN 0-89243-335-3). Liguori Pubns.

Doward, Jan S. Finding the Right Path. 96p. 1990. pap. 6.95 (ISBN 0-8163-0938-8). Pacific Pr Pub Assn.

Eager, George B. Love, Dating & Marriage. Wetmore, Gordon, et al, illus. LC 86-90552. 136p. (Orig.). (gr. 6-12). 1987. pap. 4.95 (ISBN 0-9603752-5-2). Mailbox.

Eder, Enelle G. & Pulham, Grace. Growing in God's Garden - the Greatest Show on Earth: Four Theme-Related Programs to Use with Children, 2 vols. in 1. LC 88-83338. (Illus.). 112p. (gr. 3-6). 1989. tchr's. ed. 9.50 (ISBN 0-88243-555-8, 02-0555). Gospel Pub.

Eubank, Mary G. & Hollingsworth, Mary. King's Workers. 1990. write for info. (ISBN 0-8499-0827-2). Word Bks.

Everett, Betty S. Who Am I, Lord? LC 82-72645. 112p. (Orig.). (gr. 3-6). 1983. pap. 4.95 (ISBN 0-8066-1951-1, 10-7072, Augsburg). Augsburg Fortress.

Feldmeyer, Dean. Just This Once. 144p. (Orig.). (gr. 9-12). 1990. pap. 6.95 (ISBN 1-55945-106-8, Teenage Bks). Group Pub.

Fenske, S. H. My Life in Christ: A Momento of My Confirmation. LC 76-5729. (gr. 8 up). 1976. pap. 2.95 (ISBN 0-8100-0056-3, 16N0514). Northwest Pub.

Fields, Doug. If Life Is a Piece of Cake, Why Am I Still Hungry? (Orig.). (gr. 7 up). 1989. pap. 5.99 (ISBN 0-89081-718-9). Harvest Hse.

Fischer, John. True Believers Don't Ask Why. 192p. (Orig.). (gr. 11-12). 1989. 11.95 (ISBN 1-55661-055-6). Bethany Hse.

Fitzgerald, Annie. Dear God, Bless Our Food. LC 84-71372. 16p. (Orig.). (ps-4). 1984. pap. 1.95 (ISBN 0-8066-2108-7, 10-1859, Augsburg). Augsburg Fortress.

—Dear God, Good Morning. LC 84-71377. 16p. (Orig.). (ps-4). 1984. pap. 1.95 (ISBN 0-8066-2104-4, 10-1860, Augsburg). Augsburg Fortress.

—Dear God, Good Night. LC 84-71374. 16p. (ps-4). 1984. pap. 1.95 (ISBN 0-8066-2105-2, 10-1861, Augsburg). Augsburg Fortress.

—Dear God, I Just Love Birthdays. LC 84-71371. 16p. (Orig.). (ps-4). 1984. pap. 1.95 (ISBN 0-8066-2107-9, 10-1862, Augsburg). Augsburg Fortress.

—Dear God, Thanks for Friends. LC 84-71873. 16p. (Orig.). (ps-4). 1984. pap. 1.95 (ISBN 0-8066-2109-5, 10-1863, Augsburg). Augsburg Fortress.

—Dear God, Thanks for Making Me Me. LC 83-71368. 16p. (Orig.). (ps-4). 1984. pap. 1.95 (ISBN 0-8066-2106-0, 10-1864, Augsburg). Augsburg Fortress.

Foss, Allen J. Living in God's Grace. Rinden, David, ed. 290p. (gr. 6-8). pap. 4.95 (ISBN 0-943167-06-X). Faith & Fellowship Pr.

—Walking in God's Truth: Ten Commandments-Lord's Prayer. rev. ed. Rinden, David, intro. by. Heiman, Lori, illus. 276p. (gr. 6-8). 1989. pap. text ed. 4.95 (ISBN 0-943167-04-3). Faith & Fellowship Pr.

Frades, Ernesto. The Happy Valley of the Elves: A Terry Turtle Adventure. Frades, Ernesto, illus. 48p. (Orig.). (gr. k-3). 1990. pap. write for info. (ISBN 0-9624929-1-4). Little Great Whale.

Frank, Penny. Enemies All Around. (Illus.). 24p. (gr. 1 up). 1986. 3.95 (ISBN 0-85648-749-X). Lion USA.

Franks, Tom. Born to Raze Hell. 112p. (Orig.). 1989. pap. 5.95 (ISBN 1-877717-00-2). Mercedes Ministries.

Freeman, Hobart E. Divine Sovereignty, Human Freedom, & Responsibility in Prophetic Thought. 210p. (Orig.). 1990. pap. 4.50 (ISBN 1-878725-00-9). Faith Min & Pubns.

Fretz, Clarence Y. You & Your Bible-You & Your Life. (gr. 8). pap. 4.10x (ISBN 0-87813-902-8); teachrs guide 13.75x (ISBN 0-87813-903-6). Christian Light.

Friedrich, Elizabeth. The Story of God's Love. 144p. (gr. 6-9). 1985. 9.95 (ISBN 0-570-04122-8, 56-1533). Concordia.

Frost, Marie H. Love Is God. Petach, Heidi, illus. 20p. (ps). 1986. casebound 1.59 (ISBN 0-87403-133-8, 2003). Standard Pub.

Garlow, Willa R. Jesus Is a Special Person. LC 85-24361. (Illus.). (ps). 1986. 4.95 (ISBN 0-8054-4166-2). Broadman.

Gellman, Marc. Where Does God Live. 1991. 11.95 (ISBN 0-8007-3018-6). Revell.

Gonter, Janet. Choosing Is... Pride, Barbara, illus. (gr. 1-4). 1986. casebound 4.95 (ISBN 0-87403-123-0, 3603). Standard Pub.

Gorman, Cinda. Growing up Christian in a Sexy World. 50p. (Orig.). (gr. 5-6). 1989. pap. 8.50 (ISBN 0-940754-78-9). Ed Ministries.

Graham, Rhonda. Yesterday's Tears. 94p. 1991. pap. 6.95 (ISBN 0-8163-1023-8). Pacific Pr Pub Assn.

Gray, Ronald D. Christopher Wren & St. Paul's Cathedral. LC 81-13696. (Illus.). 48p. (gr. 7 up). 1980. pap. 5.95 (ISBN 0-521-21666-4). Cambridge U Pr.

Grimley, Mildred H. Mattie Loves All. Wine, Jeanine M., illus. 22p. (gr. 1-5). 1985. 5.95 (ISBN 0-87178-552-8). Brethren.

Grinstead, Wayne. The Ross Hannas: Living, Laughing, Loving. LC 86-6807. (gr. 4-6). 1986. 5.95 (ISBN 0-8054-4325-8). Broadman.

Grove, Vickie. A Time to Belong. 120p. (Orig.). (gr. 9-12). 1990. pap. 6.95 (ISBN 1-55945-051-7, Teenage Bks). Group Pub.

Grunze, Richard. The Young Christian's Life. (gr. 7-8). 1979. 9.95 (ISBN 0-8100-0104-7, 06N0557). Northwest Pub.

Guest, John. Go for It! Accelerated Christian Growth. LC 88-6638. 120p. (Orig.). (gr. 9-12). 1988. pap. 7.95 (ISBN 0-87788-348-3). Shaw Pubs.

Gundersen, Ben. Memory Verse Bulletin Boards. 96p. (ps-7). 1988. 9.95 (ISBN 0-86653-426-1, SS1827). Good Apple.

Haas, Dorothy. My First Communion. Tucker, Kathleen, ed. McMahon, William F., illus. LC 86-18892. 48p. (gr. k-3). 1987. PLB 10.50 (ISBN 0-8075-5331-X). A Whitman.

Hageman, Marybeth. I Want to Be Like Jesus. LC 89-80615. 32p. (Orig.). 1989. pap. 4.95 (ISBN 0-8066-2419-1, 9-2419). Augsburg Fortress.

Hale, Anita. My Room at Church. LC 85-24344. (Illus.). (ps). 1986. 4.95 (ISBN 0-8054-4168-9). Broadman.

Hamilton, Dorothy. The Castle. Graber, Esther R., illus. LC 75-15599. 112p. (gr. 4-8). 1975. pap. 3.95 (ISBN 0-8361-1776-X). Herald Pr.

Haney, Joy. Behold the Nazarite Woman. Bernard, David, ed. Agnew, Tim, illus. LC 90-30639. 96p. (Orig.). 1990. pap. 4.95 (ISBN 0-932581-63-3). Word Aflame.

Harding, Susan. Tell Me about God: Simple Studies in the Doctrine of God for Children. (Illus.). 64p. (ps-4). 1985. pap. 6.95 (ISBN 0-85151-510-X). Banner of Truth.

Harner, Ruth. Send Someone to Tell Me. Smith, Dale, illus. 16p. (gr. k-6). 1988. pap. text ed. 4.25 (ISBN 1-55976-135-0). CEF Press.

Hartweg, Judy. Loyal Leaders. Henson, Grace, illus. 48p. (gr. 4-6). 1984. wkbk. 6.95 (ISBN 0-86653-238-2, SS 823). Good Apple.

Harty, Annelle & Harty, Robert. Made to Grow. 32p. (gr. 1-3). 1973. 6.95 (ISBN 0-8054-4222-7). Broadman.

Haskin, Dorothy. The One Who Was Different. Butcher, Sam, illus. 16p. (gr. k-6). 1983. pap. text ed. 4.25 (ISBN 1-55976-130-X). CEF Press.

Have You Got a Minute, GOD? Prayers by Teens. (Illus.). 32p. (Orig.). (gr. 7-12). pap. write for info. (ISBN 0-937997-15-3). Hi-Time Pub.

Hayes, Rebecca S. Grant Me a Portion. (gr. 7 up). 1987. pap. 1.25 (ISBN 0-8054-6585-5). Broadman.

Hayhurst, L. W. The Christian Boy, 4 vols. 1964. pap. 2.25 ea. Vol. 1 (CB100). Vol. 2 (CB200). Vol. 3 (CB300). Vol. 4 (CB400). Quality Pubns.

Hayhurst, Mamie W. The Christian Girl, 4 vols. 1964. pap. 2.25 ea. Vol. 1 (CG100). Vol. 2 (CG200). Vol. 3 (CG300). Vol. 4 (CG400). Quality Pubns.
Hershey, Katerine. The Message of a Star. Bates, Stephen & Williamson, Kevin, illus. 9p. (gr. k-6). 1982. pap. 4.25 (ISBN 1-55976-133-4). CEF Press.
Hershey, Katherine. The Christian Soldier. Biel, Bill, et al, illus. 10p. (gr. k-6). 1981. pap. text ed. 4.25 (ISBN 1-55976-138-5). CEF Press.
—A Shepherd for You. (Illus.). 22p. (gr. k-6). 1988. pap. text ed. 4.25 (ISBN 1-55976-149-0). CEF Press.
Higgins, John. Meet God! A Young Christian's Handbook for Knowing God. LC 88-80294. (Illus.). 128p. (gr. 4-6). 1988. 6.50 (ISBN 0-88243-488-8, 02-0488). Gospel Pub.
Hillis, Don W. Stories of Love that Lasts. 80p. (gr. 9-12). 1980. pap. 2.25 (ISBN 0-89323-015-4). Bible Memory.
Hills, Ron, ed. High Fives & High Hopes: Favorite Talks Especially for Youth. LC 90-81267. 150p. (Orig.). (gr. 9-12). 1990. pap. 5.95 (ISBN 0-87579-356-8). Deseret Bk.
Hogan, Jan. Gladdys Makes Peace. Wine, Jeanine M., illus. 22p. (gr. 1-5). 1985. 9.95 (ISBN 0-87178-313-4). Brethren.
Horie, Michiaki & Horie, Hildegard. Steps to Inner Freedom. Huff, Dawn, tr. from GER. Paff, Mike, illus. 120p. (Orig.). (gr. 7 up). 1987. pap. 5.95 (ISBN 0-939925-06-0). R C Law & Co.
How the Dyaks Learned to Give. 20p. (gr. k-6). 1986. pap. text ed. 4.25 (ISBN 1-55976-140-7). CEF Press.
Jafolla, Mary-Alice. Simple Truth. LC 81-69084. 90p. (ps up). 1982. 6.95 (ISBN 0-87159-146-4). Unity School.
Javernick, Ellen. Celebrate the Christian Family. Mohler, Sarah, illus. 144p. (gr. k-6). 1987. pap. 10.95 (ISBN 0-86653-391-5, SS 844). Good Apple.
Jay, Ruth J. Learning from God's Animals. Ratzlaff, Lynette, illus. 36p. (Orig.). (ps-k). 1981. pap. 2.95 (ISBN 0-934998-04-3). Bethel Pub.
—Learning from God's Birds. Ratzlaff, Lynette, illus. 34p. (Orig.). (ps-k). 1981. pap. 2.95 (ISBN 0-934998-05-1). Bethel Pub.
Jefferson, Patti & Wigginton, Shirley. Lessons on Joy from Critter County. Johnson, Diane, illus. 144p. 1989. wkbk. 9.95 (ISBN 0-87403-537-6, 3397). Standard Pub.
Johnson, Betty. Gifts & Rewards. Butcher, Sam, illus. 13p. (gr. k-6). 1981. pap. text ed. 4.25 (ISBN 1-55976-137-7). CEF Press.
—Teach Me Now, Vol. I. (Illus.). 80p. (ps). 1981. pap. text ed. 24.99 kit (ISBN 1-55976-108-3). CEF Press.
—Teach Me Now, Vol. II. (Illus.). 90p. (ps). 1982. pap. text ed. 24.99 kit (ISBN 1-55976-109-1). CEF Press.
—Teach Me Now, Vol. III. (Illus.). 80p. (ps). 1983. pap. text ed. 24.99 kit (ISBN 1-55976-110-5). CEF Press.
—Teach Me Now, Vol. IV. (Illus.). 87p. (ps). 1984. pap. text ed. 24.99 kit (ISBN 1-55976-111-3). CEF Press.
Johnson, Lissa H. Lambs of the Lie. 192p. (gr. 7-12). 1987. pap. 6.95 (ISBN 0-8007-5251-1). Revell.
Johnson, Lois W. You're My Best Friend, Lord. LC 76-3866. 112p. (Orig.). (gr. 4-7). 1976. pap. 4.95 (ISBN 0-8066-1541-9, 10-7490, Augsburg). Augsburg Fortress.
Jones, Chris. What Do I Do Now Lord? LC 76-3860. 112p. (Orig.). (gr. 4-7). 1976. pap. 4.95 (ISBN 0-8066-1539-7, 10-7044, Augsburg). Augsburg Fortress.
Jones, Rebecca C. I Am Not Afraid. (Illus.). (ps). 1987. pap. 2.29 (ISBN 0-570-09113-6, 56-1588). Concordia.
Joy, Flora. Creative Writing Booklets. 64p. (gr. k-6). 1985. 7.95 (ISBN 0-86653-274-9, GA626). Good Apple.
—Creative Writing Booklets, No. 2. 64p. (gr. k-6). 1985. 7.95 (ISBN 0-86653-284-6, GA629). Good Apple.
Juknialis, Joseph J. When God Began in the Middle. Fait, Tom, illus. LC 81-52597. 101p. (Orig.). (gr. 1 up). 1981. pap. text ed. 7.95 (ISBN 0-89390-027-3). Resource Pubns.
Kauffman, Suzanne. God's Suffering Servant Activity Book. 64p. 1988. pap. 3.00 (ISBN 0-8361-3450-8). Herald Pr.
Keck, Saundria. God Made Me. LC 86-17572. (ps). 1987. 5.95 (ISBN 0-8054-4173-5). Broadman.
Kelemen, Julie. Advent Is for Children. 64p. (Orig.). (gr. 3 up). 1988. pap. 1.95 (ISBN 0-89243-292-6). Liguori Pubns.
Kelley, Gail & Hershberger, Carol. Come Mime with Me: A Guide to Preparing Scriptural Dramas for Children. LC 86-62621. 90p. (gr. 1 up). 1987. 10.95 (ISBN 0-89390-089-3). Resource Pubns.
Kenneally, Christy. Miracles & Me: Poems for Children. Ortiz, Gloria C., illus. 64p. (gr. 2-3). 1986. pap. 3.95 (ISBN 0-8091-6558-9). Paulist Pr.
Kesler, Jay & Stafford, Tim. Making Life Make Sense: Answers to Hard Questions about God & You. 176p. 1991. pap. 6.95 (ISBN 0-310-71191-6, Campus Life). Zondervan.
Klaus, Sandra. Life Is Valuable. Hilterbrand, Greg, illus. (gr. k-6). 1987. pap. 4.25 (ISBN 1-55976-152-0). CEF Press.
—Pythons & Book Reports. Bates, Steve, illus. 51p. (gr. k-6). 1987. pap. text ed. 6.99 (ISBN 1-55976-178-4). CEF Press.
Klaus, Tom. If Your Parent Drinks Too Much. 96p. (Orig.). (gr. 9-12). 1990. pap. 7.95 (ISBN 1-55945-006-1, Teenage Bks). Group Pub.
Klein, Patricia, ed. Growing up Born Again. (Illus.). 160p. (gr. 10 up). 1987. pap. 6.95 (ISBN 0-8007-5259-7). Revell.
Knox, Joann. The Midnight Miracle - The Blind Girl Who Sees. 64p. (gr. 4-8). 1973. pap. 1.00 (ISBN 0-88243-775-5, 02-0775). Gospel Pub.
—A New Home for Rhoda. 64p. (gr. 4-8). 1973. pap. 1.00 (ISBN 0-88243-771-2, 02-0771). Gospel Pub.
Korbel, Joseph. Morning Dew. Voisey, Carole, illus. 160p. (gr. 1-8). 1988. 4.50 (ISBN 0-89216-084-5). Salvation Army.
Kownacki, Mary L. & Clark, Carol. Let Peace Begin With Me: Teacher Manual. (gr. 4-6). 1983. pap. 2.95 (ISBN 0-89622-185-7). Twenty-Third.
Kownacki, Mary Lou & Clark, Carol. Let Peace Begin With Me: Peace Book. (gr. 4-6). 1983. pap. 1.00 (ISBN 0-89622-186-5). Twenty-Third.
Laemmlen, Ann & Owen, Jackie. The Articles of Faith Learning Book. 171p. (gr. 3-6). 1990. pap. 7.95 wkbk. (ISBN 0-87579-400-9). Deseret Bk.
Landis, Mary M. Health for the Glory of God. (gr. 4-5). 1976. write for info. (ISBN 0-686-15484-3); tchr's. ed. avail. (ISBN 0-686-15485-1). Rod & Staff.
Larsen, Dale & Larsen, Sandy. Discovering Myself: Who Am I Anyway? (Illus.). 32p. (Orig.). (gr. 7-10). 1987. Camper Ed. pap. 1.50 (ISBN 0-87788-178-2); Counselor Ed. pap. 3.50 (ISBN 0-87788-179-0). Shaw Pubs.
—Got a License, but Where Do I Go? Devotions for Teens on the Move. LC 87-36576. 112p. (Orig.). (gr. 8-12). 1988. pap. 5.95 (ISBN 0-87788-295-9). Shaw Pubs.
—It's a Jungle in Here. LC 87-33131. 150p. (Orig.). (gr. 8-12). 1988. pap. 5.95 (ISBN 0-87788-400-5). Shaw Pubs.
Lashbrook, Marilyn. A Champion Is... Bishop, Richard, illus. 32p. (gr. 1-4). 1986. casebound 4.95 (ISBN 0-87403-121-4, 3601). Standard Pub.
—Digging for Buried Treasure. Bates, Steve, illus. 12p. (gr. k-6). 1984. pap. text ed. 4.25 (ISBN 1-55976-141-5). CEF Press.
—God Speaks to Me. Bates, Stephen, illus. 52p. (gr. k-6). 1985. pap. text ed. 8.99 (ISBN 1-55976-030-3). CEF Press.
Lawson, Michael & Skipp, David. Sexo y Mas: Guia Para la Juventud. (SPA., Illus.). 110p. (Orig.). (gr. 10-12). 1988. pap. 2.95 (ISBN 0-945792-02-6). Editorial Unilit.
LeFever, Marlene. God's Special Creation--Me! (Illus.). 48p. (Orig.). (gr. 4-6). 1987. Camper Ed. pap. 1.50 (ISBN 0-87788-313-0); Counselor Ed. pap. 3.50 (ISBN 0-87788-314-9). Shaw Pubs.
Leichner, Jeannine T. Called to His Supper. (Illus.). 64p. (Orig.). (gr. 1-3). 1990. pap. 3.95 (ISBN 0-87973-138-9, 138). Our Sunday Visitor.
Let the Lord Have His Way. (Illus.). (gr. k-6). 1973. 3.50 (ISBN 3-90117-013-8). CEF Press.
Linam, Gail. God's Fall Gifts. Hester, Ron, illus. (ps). 1991. pap. 3.75 (ISBN 0-8054-4159-X, 4241-59). Broadman.
—God's Summer Gifts. Hester, Ron, illus. (ps). 1991. pap. 3.75 (ISBN 0-8054-4156-5, 4241-56). Broadman.
Link, Mark. Challenge. 160p. (gr. 9-12). 1987. 6.95 (ISBN 0-89505-654-2). Tabor Pub.
—Journey. 144p. 1988. 6.95 (ISBN 0-89505-656-9). Tabor Pub.
Lipson, Greta & Greenberg, Bernice. Extra! Extra! Read All about It! 160p. (gr. 4-8). 1981. 11.95 (ISBN 0-86653-006-1, GA234). Good Apple.
Little Lion & Friends. (Illus.). 24p. (gr. 1 up). 1986. bds. 2.95 (ISBN 0-7459-1029-7). Lion USA.
Living for God: Daily Bread, No. 2. (Illus.). (gr. k-4). 1977. pap. write for info. (ISBN 1-55976-325-6). CEF Press.
Livingston, J. B. If I Were a Teenager: Pupil Book, 4 vols. 1966. pap. 2.25 ea. Quality Pubns.
The Lord Is My Shepherd. (Illus.). (gr. k-6). 1963. 4.99 (ISBN 3-90117-004-9). CEF Press.
Lost & Found Kit. (gr. k-6). 1978. 19.99 (ISBN 1-55976-105-9). CEF Press.
Lowry, James W. In the Whale's Belly & Other Martyr Stories. (Illus.). (gr. 7 up). 1981. 4.70 (ISBN 0-87813-513-8). Christian Light.
Lynn, Claire, compiled by. Build on the Rock. Lautermilch, John & Fearber, Sharon, illus. 52p. (Orig.). (ps-7). 1979. pap. 3.50 (ISBN 0-89323-000-6, 707). Bible Memory.
McAllister, Dawson. Discussion Manual for Student Relationships, Vol. 2. Lamb, Jim, illus. (gr. 5-12). 1976. pap. 8.75 (ISBN 0-923417-07-9). Shepherd Minst.
—Discussion Manual for Student Relationships, Vol. 3. Lamb, Jim, illus. (gr. 5-12). 1978. pap. 8.75 (ISBN 0-923417-08-7). Shepherd Minst.
—Student Relationships, Vol. 1. (gr. 5-12). 1981. pap. 6.95 tchr's. guide (ISBN 0-923417-18-4). Shepherd Minst.
McAllister, Dawson & Kimmel, Tim. Student Relationships, Vol. 2. (gr. 5-12). 1981. pap. 6.95 tchr's. guide (ISBN 0-923417-04-4). Shepherd Minst.
MacAllister, Dawson & Kimmel, Tim. Student Relationships, Vol. 3. (gr. 5-12). 1981. pap. 6.95 tchr's. guide (ISBN 0-923417-19-2). Shepherd Minst.
McAllister, Dawson & Miller, John. Discussion Manual for Student Discipleship, Vol. 2. Lamb, Jim, illus. (gr. 5-12). 1978. pap. 8.50 (ISBN 0-923417-16-8). Shepherd Minst.
McAllister, Dawson & Sharp, Floyd. Handbook for Financial Faithfulness. (Illus.). (gr. 5-12). 1974. pap. 6.95 (ISBN 0-923417-17-6). Shepherd Minst.
McAllister, Dawson & Webster, Dan. Discussion Manual for Student Discipleship, Vol. 1. Lamb, Jim, illus. (gr. 5-12). 1975. pap. 8.50 (ISBN 0-923417-15-X). Shepherd Minst.
—Discussion Manual for Student Relationships, Vol. 1. Lamb, Jim, illus. (gr. 5-12). 1975. pap. 8.75 (ISBN 0-923417-06-0). Shepherd Minst.
McClung, Floyd. Wholehearted: Letting God Shape Your Whole Life. LC 90-37756. 190p. (Orig.). 1990. pap. 8.95 (ISBN 0-8308-1325-X, 1325). InterVarsity.
Machado, Antonio A., et al. Our Lady at Fatima: Prophecies of Tragedy or Hope for America & the World? LC 85-70673. (Illus.). 128p. (Orig.). (gr. 8). 1986. pap. 8.95 (ISBN 1-877-90510-0). TFFACC.
MacKenthum, Carole. Holiday Poems, Prayers & Projects. McClure, Nancee, illus. 48p. (gr. 3-7). 1984. wkbk. 6.95 (ISBN 0-86653-234-X, SS 813). Good Apple.
McKissack, Patricia A. Lights Out, Christopher. Bartholomew, illus. LC 84-71375. 32p. (Orig.). (ps-1). 1984. pap. 5.95 (ISBN 0-8066-2110-9, 10-3870, Augsburg). Augsburg Fortress.
McKissack, Patricia C. It's the Truth, Christopher. Bartholomew, illus. LC 84-71376. 32p. (Orig.). (ps-1). 1984. pap. 5.95 (ISBN 0-8066-2111-7, 10-3457, Augsburg). Augsburg Fortress.
McLellan, Vern. Wise Words from a Wise Guy. (Illus., Orig.). (gr. 7-12). 1989. pap. 3.99 (ISBN 0-89081-775-8). Harvest Hse.
McMillan, Mary. Christian Celebrations for Autumn & Winter. 96p. (gr. 2-7). 1990. 9.95 (ISBN 0-86653-546-2, SS1821). Good Apple.
Maddox, Linda G. Step Toward Freedom. LC 88-8154. (Orig.). (gr. 12). 1991. 7.95 (ISBN 0-8054-5070-X). Broadman.
Mandeville. Lost Sheep. (gr. 2-7). 1979. pap. 3.50 (ISBN 0-7214-0524-X). Chr Lit.
Martin, John D. Living Together on God's Earth. (gr. 3). 1974. 12.95x (ISBN 0-87813-915-X); tchr's. guide 19.65x (ISBN 0-87813-910-9). Christian Light.
Matranga, Frances C. The Perfect Friend. 80p. (Orig.). (gr. 5-7). 1985. pap. 3.95 (ISBN 0-570-04112-0, 56-1523). Concordia.
Maxwell, Arthur S. & Holloway, Cheryl W. Uncle Arthur's Storytime, Vol. 1. Tank, Darrel, et al, illus. 128p. Date not set. PLB 29.90 (ISBN 1-877773-01-8). Family Media.
—Uncle Arthur's Storytime, Vol. 2. Mull, Christ, et al, illus. 128p. Date not set. PLB 29.90 (ISBN 1-877773-02-6). Family Media.
—Uncle Arthur's Storytime, Vol. 3: Children's True Adventures Classic Edition Ser. Mull, Christy, et al, illus. 128p. Date not set. 29.90 (ISBN 1-877773-03-4). Family Media.
Mazak, Lisa. One, Two, Three, Jesus Loves Me. (Illus.). (gr. k-6). 1982. illustrated song 3.99 (ISBN 3-90117-018-9). CEF Press.
Mehew, Randall & Mehew, Karen. Gospel Basic Busy Book, Vol. II. Bales, Marcia, illus. 100p. Date not set. pap. text ed. 6.95 (ISBN 0-910613-08-7). Millenial Pr.
Middleton, Barth & Middleton, Sally. Living God's Way. Bates, Steve, illus. 64p. (gr. k-6). 1985. pap. text ed. 11.99 (ISBN 1-55976-031-1). CEF Press.
—Loving God's Way. Bates, Stephen, illus. 55p. (gr. k-6). 1988. pap. text ed. 7.50 (ISBN 1-55976-033-8). CEF Press.
Milhaven, J. Giles. Good Anger: We Love More Than We Think We Do. LC 89-61217. 224p. 1989. pap. 12.95 (ISBN 1-55612-264-0). Sheed & Ward MO.
Miller, R. Edward. The Flaming Flame. 95p. (Orig.). (gr. 12). 1973. pap. 2.50 (ISBN 0-945818-03-3). Peniel Pubns.
—I Looked & I Saw Mysteries. Schisler, Jack, intro. by. 106p. (gr. 12). 1988. pap. 3.50 (ISBN 0-945818-01-7). Peniel Pubns.
—I Looked & I Saw the Lord. Schisler, Jack, intro. by. 95p. (Orig.). (gr. 12). 1988. pap. 3.50 (ISBN 0-945818-00-9). Peniel Pubns.
—I Looked & I Saw Visions of God. 147p. (Orig.). (gr. 12). 1974. pap. 3.50 (ISBN 0-945818-06-8). Peniel Pubns.
—I Looked & Saw the Heavens Opened... 96p. (Orig.). (gr. 12). 1972. pap. 3.50 (ISBN 0-945818-05-X). Peniel Pubns.
—The Prince & the Three Beggars. 33p. (Orig.). (gr. 12). 1975. pap. 2.00 (ISBN 0-945818-04-1). Peniel Pubns.
—Secrets of the Kingdom. 180p. (Orig.). (gr. 10). 1989. pap. 5.25 (ISBN 0-945818-08-4). Peniel Pubns.
—Thy God Reigneth. Frodsham, Stanley, intro. by. 58p. (gr. 12). 1964. pap. 2.50 (ISBN 0-945818-02-5). Peniel Pubns.
—Victory in Adversity. 168p. (Orig.). (gr. 10). 1988. pap. 4.95 (ISBN 0-945818-07-6). Peniel Pubns.
Morgan, Les. Pulling Weeds. Hartley, Fred, frwd. by. LC 88-93031. 124p. (Orig.). (gr. 9-12). 1989. pap. 5.99 (ISBN 0-87509-414-7). Chr Pubns.
Morris, Hazel. My Family. LC 85-24334. (Illus.). (ps). 1986. 4.95 (ISBN 0-8054-4164-6). Broadman.
Mueller, Charles S. & Bardill, Donald R. Thank God, I'm a Teenager. rev. ed. LC 88-6215. (Illus.). 144p. (gr. 7-12). 1988. pap. 7.95 (ISBN 0-8066-2351-9, 10-6242, Augsburg). Augsburg Fortress.
Myers, Bill. More Hot Topics. 144p. 1989. pap. 5.99 (ISBN 0-89693-670-8). SP Pubns.
Norman, Louise. God's Power Versus Satan's Power: Christian Life Lessons. Snader, Barbara, illus. 64p. (Orig.). (gr. 1-8). 1985. pap. text ed. 11.50 (ISBN 0-86508-062-3). BCM Pubn.

Nye, Julie. Every Perfect Gift. Vogt, Carla, ed. Weikel, Cheryl, illus. 201p. (Orig.). (gr. 9 up). 1990. pap. 4.95 (ISBN 0-89084-499-2). Bob Jones Univ Pr.
Nystrom, Carolyn. What Is a Christian? 32p. (gr. 2). 1981. pap. 3.95 (ISBN 0-8024-6155-7). Moody.
Nystrom, Carolyn & Floding, Matthew. Relationships: Face to Face. (Illus.). 64p. (Orig.). (gr. 7 up). 1986. pap. 2.95 student ed. (ISBN 0-87788-722-5); tchr's ed. 4.95 (ISBN 0-87788-723-3). Shaw Pubs.
O'Connell, Frances H. Giving & Growing: A Student's Guide for Service Projects. Stamschror, Robert P., ed. Mediawerks Staff, illus. 79p. (Orig.). (gr. 7-12). 1990. pap. text ed. 3.50 (ISBN 0-88489-224-7); tchr's. ed. 3.95 (ISBN 0-88489-225-5). St Mary's.
Odor, Harold & Odor, Ruth. Becoming a Christian. Greene, Tom, illus. 16p. (gr. 3-7). 1985. 0.75 (ISBN 0-87239-901-X, 3301). Standard Pub.
Oke, Janette. Love's Long Journey. large type ed. LC 82-9469. 207p. (gr. 4 up). 1985. pap. 7.95 (ISBN 0-685-10671-3). Bethany Hse.
—Love's Unending Legacy. large type ed. LC 84-18412. 224p. (gr. 4 up). 1985. pap. 7.95 (ISBN 0-87123-855-1). Bethany Hse.
O'Neal, Esther. Knowing Christ. (Illus.). 64p. (gr. k-6). 1962. pap. text ed. 8.99 (ISBN 1-55976-026-5). CEF Press.
Orange, Tom & McClure, Nancee. Bulletin Boards That Bless. 48p. (gr. 4-8). 1984. wkbk. 6.95 (ISBN 0-86653-201-3, SS 821). Good Apple.
Our Fathers World. (gr. 2). 4.45 (ISBN 0-686-37694-3). Rod & Staff.
Overholtzer, Ruth P. Life of Peter. Beerhorst, Adrian, illus. 21p. (gr. k-6). 1964. pap. text ed. 9.45 (ISBN 1-55976-013-3). CEF Press.
Peterson, Lorraine. Anybody Can Be Cool, but Awesome Takes Practice. LC 88-19454. (Illus.). 192p. (Orig.). (gr. 9-12). 1988. pap. 6.95 (ISBN 1-55661-040-8). Bethany Hse.
Phillips, Bob. World's Greatest Collection of Daffy Definitions & Riddles. 160p. (Orig.). (gr. 4 up). 1989. pap. 3.99 (ISBN 0-89081-700-6). Harvest Hse.
Pinkston, William S., Jr. With Wings As Eagles. (Illus.). 127p. (gr. 2). 1983. pap. 6.94 (ISBN 0-89084-231-0). Bob Jones Univ Pr.
Plueddemann, Jim. Ready! Get Set! Grow! (Illus.). 48p. 1987. Camper Ed. pap. 1.50 (ISBN 0-87788-715-2); Counselor Ed. pap. 3.50 (ISBN 0-87788-716-0). Shaw Pubs.
Pollinger, Eileen. Building Christian Discipline. 96p. (Orig.). (gr. 8). 1986. pap. 5.95 (ISBN 0-87123-877-2); tchr's. guide 6.95 (ISBN 0-87123-878-0). Bethany Hse.
Potter, Velma M. God Flies Benny's Flag. Russell, Jervis F., ed. (Illus.). 235p. (gr. 4 up). 1989. pap. 12.95 (ISBN 0-939116-20-0). Frontier WA.
Price, Brena. Giving, Christian Stewardship: Teaching Bks. Ressler, William, illus. 14p. (gr. 1-8). 1971. pap. text ed. 3.95 (ISBN 0-86508-154-9). BCM Pubn.
Price, Cheryl. Memory Verse Motivators. 96p. (ps-5). 1990. 9.95 (ISBN 0-86653-550-0, SS1823). Good Apple.
Price, Nelson L. Only the Beginning. LC 79-55662. (gr. 10 up). 1980. 7.95 (ISBN 0-8054-5331-8, 4253-31). Broadman.
Pudaite, Rochunga. Horizons Never End. Lombard, Lynette, illus. 20p. (gr. k-6). 1988. pap. text ed. 4.25 (ISBN 1-55976-144-X). CEF Press.
Quigley, Betty. Our Master's Prayers: A Brief Story of Jesus' Life Based on His Prayers. Quigley, Raymond, ed. Thurman, Nadine, pref. by. (Illus.). 160p. 1991. 8.95 (ISBN 0-9626735-1-X); pap. 6.95 (ISBN 0-9626735-3-6). Rabeth Pub Co.
Repp, Gloria. His Best for God. (Illus.). 24p. (gr. k-6). 1989. pap. text ed. 4.25 (ISBN 1-55976-150-4). CEF Press.
Richmond, Gary. Henry & the Great Flood. 32p. 1990. write for info. (ISBN 0-8499-0745-4). Word Bks.
—Zookeeper Looks at Monkeys. 1991. pap. 3.99 (ISBN 0-8499-0861-2). Word Bks.
—Zookeeper Looks at Mothers & Baby Animals. 1991. pap. 3.99 (ISBN 0-8499-0863-9). Word Bks.
Rives, Elsie. The Shoemakes: God's Helpers. LC 86-4148. (gr. 4-6). 1986. pap. 5.95 (ISBN 0-8054-4328-2). Broadman.
Roberts, Donald. Grace: God's Special Gift. (gr. 1-4). 1982. pap. 3.95 (ISBN 0-570-04060-4, 56-1363). Concordia.
Roehlkepartain, Jolene. Not in My Family. (Orig.). (gr. 9-12). 1990. pap. 6.95 (ISBN 1-55945-022-3, Teenage Bks). Group Pub.
Romona - Evolution of a Christian. LC 84-81703. 93p. 1984. 6.95 (ISBN 0-88290-256-3). Horizon Utah.
Rue, Nancy N. Janis Project. LC 88-70693. 224p. (gr. 9-12). 1988. pap. 7.95 (ISBN 0-89107-486-4, Crossway Bks). Good News.
Runk, Wesley T. Standing Up for Jesus. (gr. k-4). 1985. 4.50 (ISBN 0-89536-725-4, 5809). CSS of Ohio.
S-A-L-V-A-T-I-O-N. (gr. k-6). 1971. illustrated song 2.99 (ISBN 3-90117-012-X). CEF Press.
St. Clair, Barry. Growing On. 144p. (gr. 9-12). 1986. pap. 5.99 (ISBN 0-88207-305-2). Victor Bks.
Salvation, Learning about God's Plan. (Illus.). 19p. (Orig.). (gr. 1-8). 1974. pap. text ed. 3.95 (ISBN 0-86508-151-4). BCM Pubn.
Sapp, Kathy. I Am a Part of Something Big. (Illus.). 32p. (Orig.). (gr. 4-6). 1989. pap. text ed. 3.50 (ISBN 0-936625-66-X, New Hope AL). Womans Mission Union.
Sattgast, L. J. & Elkins, Jan. Teach Me about Salvation. Davis, Deena, ed. Flint, Russ, illus. 32p. (gr. 1-4). 1990. 4.99 (ISBN 0-88070-383-0). Multnomah.
—Teach Me about the Holy Spirit. Davis, Deena, ed. Flint, Russ, illus. 32p. (gr. 1-4). 1990. 4.99 (ISBN 0-88070-384-9). Multnomah.
Schmidt, J. David. More Graffiti: Devotions for Guys. (Illus.). 128p. (gr. 7-12). 1984. pap. 6.95 (ISBN 0-8007-5142-6, Power Bks). Revell.
Sciacca, Fran & Sciacca, Jill. Cliques & Clones. (gr. 7 up). 1987. pap. 3.95 (ISBN 0-89066-100-6). World Wide Pubs.
—Does God Live Here Anymore? 1988. pap. 3.95 (ISBN 0-89066-113-8). World Wide Pubs.
—Good News for a Bad News World. 1989. pap. 3.95 (ISBN 0-685-25653-7). World Wide Pubs.
—Learning to Hope in a Wish-Filled World. 1988. pap. 3.95 (ISBN 0-89066-111-1). World Wide Pubs.
—So What's Wrong with a Big Nose? 1988. pap. 3.95 (ISBN 0-89066-112-X). World Wide Pubs.
—Some Assembly Required. 1989. pap. 3.95 (ISBN 0-685-25748-7). World Wide Pubs.
—Some Things Are Never Discounted. 1988. pap. 3.95 (ISBN 0-89066-114-6). World Wide Pubs.
Shackelford, Robert D. Benefits of Righteousness. 73p. (Orig.). (gr. 9-12). 1988. pap. 3.95 (ISBN 0-9618308-2-4). R Shackelford.
Simpson, Winifred R. I Can Help Mommy. (Illus.). (ps). 1987. pap. 2.29 (ISBN 0-570-09112-8, 56-1587). Concordia.
Six Wonderful Things. 14p. (gr. k-6). 1976. pap. text ed. 4.25 (ISBN 1-55976-126-1). CEF Press.
Smith, Jane D. The Tabernacle. Butcher, Sam, illus. 38p. (gr. k-6). 1972. pap. text ed. 9.45 (ISBN 1-55976-022-2). CEF Press.
Smith, Michael W. & Ridenour, Fritz. Old Enough to Know. large type ed. 111p. 1989. pap. write for info. (ISBN 0-8499-3163-0). Word Bks.
Sorensen, David A. The Friendship Olympics: A Young Christian Book for Boys. LC 86-32259. 112p. (gr. 3-7). 1987. pap. 5.95 (ISBN 0-8066-2248-2, 10-2430, Augsburg). Augsburg Fortress.
—Me, Myself, & God. LC 89-49096. 112p. (Orig.). (gr. 3-7). 1990. pap. 5.95 (ISBN 0-8066-2442-6, 9-2442). Augsburg Fortress.
Stafford, Tim. Love, Sex & the Whole Person: Everything You Want to Know. 280p. 1991. pap. 9.95 (ISBN 0-310-71181-9, Campus Life). Zondervan.
Stanphill, Ira F. Happiness Is the Lord. (Illus.). (gr. k-6). 1987. visualized song 5.99 (ISBN 3-90117-011-1). CEF Press.
Staton, Knofel. Heaven-Bound Living: Light for the Journey. (Orig.). (gr. 7 up). 1989. pap. 2.95 student text (ISBN 0-87403-485-X, 39947); leader's guide 1.95 (ISBN 0-87403-484-1, 39946). Standard Pub.
Stephens, Andrea. Stressed-Out but Hanging Tough. 160p. (gr. 8-12). 1989. pap. 6.95 (ISBN 0-8007-5326-7, Power Bks). Revell.
Stevens, Margaret M. Stepping Stones for Boys & Girls. Stevens, David S., illus. (gr. 5 up). 1977. pap. 4.00 (ISBN 0-87516-248-7). DeVorss.
Stirrup Associates, Inc. Staff. Beautiful Attitudes Matthew 5: 3-12. Phillips, Cheryl M. & Harvey, Bonnie C., eds. Fulton, Ginger A., illus. LC 84-50914. 32p. (ps). 1984. pap. 1.49 (ISBN 0-937420-17-4). Stirrup Assoc.
Stocker, Fern N. Adoniram Judson: Following God's Plan. (Orig.). (gr. 1-6). 1986. pap. 4.50 (ISBN 0-8024-4384-2). Moody.
Swanson, Steve. Is There Life after High School? Making Decisions about Your Future. LC 90-15499. 112p. (Orig.). (gr. 9 up). 1991. pap. 4.95 (ISBN 0-8066-2500-7, 9-2500, Augsburg). Augsburg Fortress.
Tate, Mimi. The Belly Button Brigade. 1974. pap. 1.75 (BBB01). Quality Pubns.
Ten Best Object Lessons. (Illus.). 5p. (gr. k-6). 1956. pap. text ed. 1.25 (ISBN 1-55976-146-6). CEF Press.
Thigpen, Thomas P. Come Sing God's Song. John, Joyce, illus. LC 86-24197. (gr. k-2). 1987. 8.95 (ISBN 1-55513-052-6). Cook.
Tracy, Wesley D. What's a Nice God Like You Doing in a Place Like This? 120p. 1990. pap. 5.95 (ISBN 0-8341-1371-6). Beacon Hill.
Veerman, David R. Any Old Time, Bk. 12. 80p. 1989. pap. 9.99 (ISBN 0-89693-722-4). SP Pubns.
Vivir la Misa. (SPA.). (gr. 6). pap. text ed. 2.75 (ISBN 0-8198-8007-8). Dghtrs St Paul.
Vivo en El Espiritu. (ENG & SPA.). (gr. 5). pap. text ed. 2.75 (ISBN 0-8198-8006-X). Dghtrs St Paul.
Vos Wezeman, Phyllis & Fournier, Jude D. Counting the Days: Twenty-Five Ways. 51p. (Orig.). 1989. pap. 9.95 (ISBN 0-940754-77-0). Ed Ministries.
Vredevelt, Pamela & Rodriguez, Kathryn. Surviving the Secret. 192p. (gr. 9-12). 1987. 9.95 (ISBN 0-8007-1543-8). Revell.
Wallis, Reginald. New Life. (gr. 3-7). pap. 2.95 (ISBN 0-87213-912-3). Loizeaux.
—The New Venture. (gr. 3-7). pap. 0.85 (ISBN 0-87213-914-X). Loizeaux.
Ward, Elaine M. Being with God: Advent Devotions. Lenzen, Diane, illus. 32p. (Orig.). (gr. 1-6). 1988. pap. 4.50 (ISBN 0-940754-66-5). Ed Ministries.
—Gifts of the Spirit. 59p. (Orig.). (gr. 9-12). 1988. pap. 9.95 (ISBN 0-940754-64-9). Ed Ministries.
—In the Summertime: What's There to Do? 1990. pap. 5.95 (ISBN 0-940754-98-3). Ed Ministries.
—Movers of Mountains. 88p. (Orig.). (gr. 7-12). 1984. pap. 12.95 (ISBN 0-940754-24-X, 8196). Ed Ministries.
Warren, Mary P. Lord, I'm Back Again: Story Devotions for Girls. LC 81-65651. 112p. (Orig.). 1981. pap. 4.95 (ISBN 0-8066-1887-6, 10-4098, Augsburg). Augsburg Fortress.
Watson, E. Elaine. Jesus Loves Me All the Time. Arthur, Lorraine, illus. 24p. (ps-2). 1984. 1.99 (ISBN 0-87239-741-6, 3711). Standard Pub.
Waybill, Marjorie. God's Family Activity Book. 64p. (Orig.). (ps-1). 1983. pap. 3.00 (ISBN 0-8361-3336-6). Herald Pr.
Weinandy, Tom. What Must I Do? 32p. (Orig.). (gr. 8 up). 1988. pap. text ed. 9.95 10-pk. (ISBN 0-932085-07-5). Word Among Us.
Weisheit, E. Sixty-One Worship Talks for Children. rev. ed. LC 68-20728. (gr. 3-6). 1975. pap. 6.95 (ISBN 0-570-03714-X, 12-2616). Concordia.
Weisheit, Eldon. God's Love for God's Children: Story Devotion for Family Time. LC 86-3397. (Illus.). 256p. (Orig.). (ps-4). 1986. kivar paper 11.95 (ISBN 0-8066-2213-X, 10-2680, Augsburg). Augsburg Fortress.
Wezeman, Phyllis Vos & Wiessner, Colleen A. Fabric of Faith. Chase, Judith, illus. 47p. (Orig.). (gr. 4-8). 1990. pap. 7.50 (ISBN 1-877871-04-4). Ed Ministries.
Wiersbe, Warren. Be Challenged! rev. ed. LC 82-12404. (gr. 7). 1982. pap. 3.95 (ISBN 0-8024-1080-4). Moody.
Wiggin, Eric & Wiggin, Kate D. Rebecca of Sunnybrook Farm: The Child. Boddy, Joe, illus. 224p. 1990. pap. 9.95 (ISBN 0-943497-95-7). Wolgemuth & Hyatt.
Wilhelm, Carolyn. Early Childhood Bulletin Boards. 96p. (ps-1). 1987. 9.95 (ISBN 0-86653-393-1, SS1825). Good Apple.
Willey, Henry N., Jr. I'm Not Too Little. (Illus.). 8p. (gr. k-6). 1984. visualized song 3.50 (ISBN 3-90117-028-6). CEF Press.
Williams, Bradley B. Out of the Miry Clay. (Orig.). 1989. pap. 5.95 (ISBN 0-9620486-0-7). B B Williams.
Williamson, Kevin, illus. Heaven How to Get There. 6p. (gr. k-6). 1964. pap. text ed. 2.65 (ISBN 1-55976-125-3). CEF Press.
Wilson, Dorothy C. I Will Be a Doctor! LC 83-3862. 160p. (Orig.). (gr. 5 up). 1983. pap. 0.50 (ISBN 0-687-19727-9). Abingdon.
Winder, Linda. My First Question & Answer Book: A Sticker-Fun Book. (Illus.). 48p. 1991. pap. 5.95 (ISBN 0-8010-9713-4). Baker Bk.
Witnessing, Telling Others about Jesus. (Illus.). 15p. (gr. 1-8). 1972. pap. text ed. 3.95 (ISBN 0-86508-155-7). BCM Pubn.
Worrall, Joyce. God Is So Great. Nielsen, Deborah B., illus. 19p. (gr. k-6). 1985. pap. text ed. 4.25 (ISBN 1-55976-132-6). CEF Press.
Your Hand in Mine. 1988. 6.95 (ISBN 0-89954-778-8). Antioch Pub Co.

CHRISTIAN LIFE–FICTION

Andrews, Dorothy W. God's World & Johnny. (gr. 5 up). 1983. pap. 4.35 (ISBN 0-318-01335-5). Rod & Staff.
Ashton, Leila M. Today Is Friday. (Illus.). (ps-1). 1978. pap. 1.95 (ISBN 0-8127-0176-3). Review & Herald.
Bacher, June M. Love Follows the Heart. (Orig.). (gr. 9-12). 1990. pap. 5.99 (ISBN 0-89081-748-0). Harvest Hse.
Baer, Judy. Something Old, Something New. 144p. (Orig.). (gr. 7-9). 1991. pap. 3.95 (ISBN 1-55661-183-8). Bethany Hse.
Bagley, Pat. If You Were a Boy in the Time of the Nephites. Bagley, Pat, illus. 46p. (gr. 3-6). 1989. pap. 4.95. Deseret Bk.
—If You Were a Girl in the Time of the Nephites. Bagley, Pat, illus. 46p. (gr. 3-6). 1989. pap. 4.95 (ISBN 0-87579-249-9). Deseret Bk.
Barger, Eric. From Rock to Rock. LC 87-70776. (Illus.). 190p. 1990. pap. 8.95 (ISBN 0-910311-61-7). Huntington Hse.
Barrett, Ethel. Blister Lamb-Gregory the Grub. (ps-2). 1978. pap. 5.95 incl. cass. (ISBN 0-8307-0420-5, 5602726). Regal.
—Buzz Bee. (ps-2). 1978. pap. 5.95 incl. cass. (ISBN 0-8307-0419-1, 5602602). Regal.
—Gregory the Grub. (ps-1). 1978. pap. 5.95 (ISBN 0-8307-0421-3, 5602807). Regal.
—Quacky & Wacky-Buzz Bee. (ps-1). 1978. pap. 5.95 bk. & cass. pac (ISBN 0-8307-0418-3, 5602593). Regal.
Bauman, Elizabeth H. Coals of Fire. LC 53-12197. (Illus.). (gr. 5-9). 1954. 4.50 (ISBN 0-8361-1957-6). Herald Pr.
Blume, Judy. Are You There, God? It's Me, Margaret. (gr. 4-7). 1991. pap. 3.50 (ISBN 0-440-90419-6, YB). Dell.
Bohl, Al. Zaanan: The Ransom of Renaissance. (Illus.). 224p. (gr. 9-12). 1990. pap. text ed. 2.50 (ISBN 1-55748-136-9). Barbour & Co.
Branch, Mary. Tell Me a Story Book 1. LC 78-53210. (gr. 1-4). 1978. pap. 1.35 (ISBN 0-8163-0210-3, 20079-0). Pacific Pr Pub Assn.
Briscoe, Jill. Harrow Sparrow. Cummings, Ann L., illus. 143p. (gr. 6). 1989. pap. write for info. Jilcoe.
Bull, Geoffrey. I Hid in a House. (gr. k-2). 1975. 1.95 (ISBN 0-87508-884-8). Chr Lit.
—I Wish I Lived When Daniel Did. (gr. 1-3). 1977. 1.95 (ISBN 0-87508-892-9). Chr Lit.
—I Wish I Lived When Esther Did. (gr. 1-3). 1977. 1.95 (ISBN 0-87508-891-0). Chr Lit.
—I Wish I Lived When Gideon Did. (gr. 1-3). 1977. 1.95 (ISBN 0-87508-889-9). Chr Lit.

—I Wish I Lived When Joseph Did. 1977. 1.95 (ISBN 0-87508-888-0). Chr Lit.
Bunyan, John. The Pilgrim's Progress. Larsen, Dan, ed. Bohl, Al, illus. 224p. (gr. 4-8). 1989. pap. text ed. 2.50 (ISBN 1-55748-099-0). Barbour & Co.
Burgess, Beverly C. God Is Never to Busy to Listen. Linder, Elizabeth, illus. (Orig.). (gr. 1-3). 1987. pap. 1.98 (ISBN 0-89274-457-X). Harrison Hse.
Bussard, Paula J. Grandmother Mouse's Secret. Goodridge, Lawrence, illus. 32p. (gr. k-6). 1986. 1.39 (ISBN 0-87403-102-8, 3432). Standard Pub.
—A Loving Touch. Goodridge, Lawrence, illus. 32p. (gr. k-6). 1986. 1.39 (ISBN 0-87403-106-0, 3436). Standard Pub.
—Rascal's Choice. Goodridge, Lawrence, illus. 32p. (gr. k-6). 1986. 1.39 (ISBN 0-87403-103-6, 3433). Standard Pub.
—A Surprise for Lunchbox. Goodridge, Lawrence, illus. 32p. (gr. k-6). 1986. 1.39 (ISBN 0-87403-104-4, 3434). Standard Pub.
—Sydney's Soup-Can Message. Goodridge, Lawrence, illus. 32p. (gr. k-6). 1986. 1.39 (ISBN 0-87403-101-X, 3431). Standard Pub.
—Where Should the Money Go? Goodridge, Lawrence, illus. 32p. (gr. k-6). 1986. 1.39 (ISBN 0-87403-105-2, 3435). Standard Pub.
Canfield, Muriel. Anne. LC 83-73597. 160p. (gr. 8-12). 1984. pap. 3.95 (ISBN 0-87123-423-8). Bethany Hse.
Cannon, Kelly, et al. Becoming Kingdom Kids. (Illus., Orig.). (gr. 2-5). 1989. pap. 5.99 (ISBN 0-89081-727-8). Harvest Hse.
Carney, Mary L. Angel in My Backpack. 128p. (gr. 7-9). 1987. pap. 5.95 (ISBN 0-310-28501-1, 11342P). Zondervan.
Carraway, Mary. Jill. LC 85-71473. 144p. (Orig.). (gr. 6-9). 1985. pap. 3.95 (ISBN 0-87123-847-0). Bethany Hse.
—Wendy. LC 87-72793. 160p. (Orig.). (gr. 9-12). 1988. pap. 3.95 (ISBN 0-87123-942-6). Bethany Hse.
Chisholm, Gloria. Jocelyn. LC 87-72794. 176p. (Orig.). (gr. 9-12). 1988. pap. 3.95 (ISBN 0-87123-846-2). Bethany Hse.
Christian, Mary B. But Everybody Does It: Peer Pressure. Brubaker, Lee W., illus. LC 85-17112. 72p. (Orig.). (gr. 4-7). 1986. pap. 3.95 (ISBN 0-570-03636-4, 39-1098). Concordia.
Clement, Jane T. The Sparrow. Hutteria Society of Brothers Staff, ed. Mow, Kathy, illus. Moody, Ruby, intro. by. LC 68-21133. (Illus.). 212p. (gr. 4 up). 1978. pap. 6.50 (ISBN 0-87486-009-1). Plough.
Conley, Lucy A. Tattletale Sparkie. (gr. 3 up). 1983. 7.50 (ISBN 0-318-01337-1). Rod & Staff.
Cook, Jean T. Hugs for Our New Baby. (Illus.). (ps-2). 1987. 5.95 (ISBN 0-570-04165-1, 56-1622). Concordia.
Cunningham, Dru. It's Fun to Choose. Hackney, Richard, illus. LC 87-91991. 32p. (gr. k-2). 1.99 (ISBN 0-87403-396-9, 24-03806). Standard Pub.
Davoll, Barbara. A Sticky Mystery. Hockerman, Dennis, illus. 24p. 1989. 5.99 (ISBN 0-89693-485-3); cass. 8.99 (ISBN 0-89693-033-5). SP Pubns.
Davoll, Barbara & Hockerman, Dennis. A Short Tail. 24p. 1989. 5.99 (ISBN 0-89693-499-3); cassette 8.99 (ISBN 0-89693-032-7). SP Pubns.
Decker, Marjorie. Christian Mother Goose Humpty Dumpty. (ps). 1989. 3.95 (ISBN 0-529-06683-1). World Bible.
—Christian Mother Goose Little Bo Peep. (ps). 1989. 3.95 (ISBN 0-529-06687-4). World Bible.
—Christian Mother Goose Little Miss Muffet. (ps). 1989. 3.95 (ISBN 0-529-06686-6). World Bible.
—Christian Mother Goose: Little Tommy Tucker. (ps). 1989. 3.95 (ISBN 0-529-06685-8). World Bible.
—Christian Mother Goose Piano Book. (gr. k-4). 1989. 8.95 (ISBN 0-529-06692-0). World Bible.
—Christian Mother Goose Pop-Up Animal Friends. (ps). 1989. 6.95 (ISBN 0-685-31140-6). World Bible.
—Christian Mother Goose Pop-Up Bedtime Rhymes. (ps). 1989. 6.95 (ISBN 0-529-06688-2). World Bible.
—Christian Mother Goose Pop-Up Favorite Rhymes. (ps). 1989. 6.95 (ISBN 0-529-06691-2). World Bible.
—Christian Mother Goose Pop-Up Happy Rhymes. (ps). 1989. 6.95 (ISBN 0-529-06690-4). World Bible.
De Grote-Sorensen, Barbara. Who's That in My Mirror? LC 89-49097. 112p. (Orig.). (gr. 3-7). 1990. pap. 5.95 (ISBN 0-8066-2441-8, 9-2441). Augsburg Fortress.
Dobson, Danae. Woof & the Big Fire. 32p. 1990. write for info. (ISBN 0-8499-8362-2). Word Bks.
—Woof, the Seeing-Eye Dog. 32p. 1990. write for info. (ISBN 0-8499-8363-0). Word Bks.
Doleski, Teddi. The Hurt. (Illus.). 32p. (gr. 2-5). 1983. pap. 2.95 (ISBN 0-8091-6551-1). Paulist Pr.
Doney, Meryl. The Very Worried Sparrow. Geldart, William, illus. 32p. (ps-6). 1991. 11.95 (ISBN 0-7459-1919-7). Lion USA.
Eavey, Louise. A Child's Shining Pathway. Murphy, Emmy L., illus. (ps-1). 1976. pap. 1.95 (ISBN 0-915374-08-0, 08-0). Rapids Christian.
Enns, Peter. God Is Good. Ligon, Terry, illus. 24p. (ps-5). 1985. 4.95 (ISBN 0-936215-21-6); cassette incl. STL Intl.
—Jesus Loves Me. Ligon, Terry, illus. 24p. (ps-5). 1985. 4.95 (ISBN 0-936215-23-2); cassette incl. STL Intl.
—Special Friends. Ligon, Terry, illus. 24p. (ps-5). 4.95 (ISBN 0-936215-22-4); cassette incl. STL Intl.
Eubank, Mary G. & Hollingsworth, Mary. King's Alphabet. (ps-3). 1990. write for info. (ISBN 0-8499-0713-6). Word Bks.
—King's Manners. 1990. write for info. (ISBN 0-8499-0826-4). Word Bks.
Fraser, W. Courage on Mirror Mountain. 128p. (gr. 5-7). 1989. pap. 3.95 (ISBN 1-55513-039-9, Chariot Bks). Cook.
—Mystery on Mirror Mountain. 112p. (gr. 5-7). 1989. pap. 3.95 (ISBN 1-55513-588-9, Chariot Bks). Cook.
Frost, Marie H. Everyone Is Special. Petach, Heidi, illus. 20p. (ps). 1987. 1.59 (ISBN 0-87403-307-1, 2007). Standard Pub.
Fuentes, Vilma M. Pearl Makers: Six Stories about the Children in the Philippines. (Illus., Orig.). (gr. 1-6). 1989. 4.95 (ISBN 0-377-00191-0). Friendship Pr.
Good Little Books for Good Little Children Staff. God Made Me. 12p. (ps). 1986. 3.25 (ISBN 0-8378-5207-2). Gibson.
—The Little Lost Lamb. 12p. (ps). 1986. 3.25 (ISBN 0-8378-5206-4). Gibson.
Groomer, Vera. Dibe Yahzi. (ps). 1980. pap. 1.95 (ISBN 0-8127-0260-3). Review & Herald.
Groton, Dallas. Ordinary Champions: Stories for High School Youth. LC 89-31375. 128p. (Orig.). (gr. 9-12). 1989. pap. 6.95 (ISBN 0-8066-2411-6, 9-2411). Augsburg Fortress.
Gunn, Robin J. Yours Forever. Kobobel, Janet, ed. 160p. (Orig.). (gr. 6-10). 1990. pap. 4.99 (ISBN 0-929608-90-9). Focus Family.
Haffey, Richard. H. R. Cornelius Learns about Love: A Commandments Book for Children. (Illus.). 20p. (Orig.). (gr. 2-5). 1985. pap. 2.95 (ISBN 0-89622-235-7). Twenty-Third.
Hamilton, Dorothy. Winter Girl. Eitzen, Allan, illus. LC 75-40344. 120p. (gr. 3-7). 1976. o. p. 4.95 (ISBN 0-8361-1787-5); pap. 3.95 (ISBN 0-8361-1788-3). Herald Pr.
Hoff, B. J. Song of the Silent Harp. 400p. (Orig.). (gr. 9-12). 1991. 8.95 (ISBN 1-55661-110-2). Bethany Hse.
Hughes, Dean. Under the Same Stars. LC 79-10472. 143p. (gr. 4-8). 1988. pap. 4.95 (ISBN 0-87579-159-X). Deseret Bk.
Johnson, Lois W. Vanishing Footprints. 144p. (Orig.). (ps-8). 1991. pap. 4.95 (ISBN 1-55661-103-X). Bethany Hse.
Johnston, Dorothy. Stop, Look, Listen. (Illus.). 24p. (Orig.). (gr. k-2). 1977. pap. 1.29 (ISBN 0-87239-273-2, 2014). Standard Pub.
Kent, Renee. Kelli's Discovery. (Illus.). 64p. (Orig.). (gr. 4-6). 1989. pap. text ed. 3.50 (ISBN 0-936625-71-6, New Hope AL). Womans Mission Union.
Kerr, Caroline. Young Emotions. Pendleton, Paul, illus. 350p. (Orig.). (gr. 6-9). 1989. pap. 6.95 (ISBN 0-9621392-0-3). Dream Weaver.
Kerr, M. E. What I Really Think of You. LC 81-47735. 224p. (gr. 7 up). 1991. pap. 3.50 (ISBN 0-06-447062-8, Trophy). HarpC Child Bks.
Kiemel, Ann. It's Incredible. (gr. 7 up). 1980. pap. 2.95 (ISBN 0-8423-1818-6). Tyndale.
Kiemel Anderson, Ann. God's Little Dreamer. Lane, Sandy, illus. LC 90-33475. 32p. (ps-8). 1990. 10.99 (ISBN 0-89081-785-5). Harvest Hse.
Klassen, Julie. The Adventures of Heart Longing. LC 86-82881. 128p. (gr. 1-6). 1987. pap. 2.95 (ISBN 0-88243-557-4, 02-0557). Gospel Pub.
Klaus, Sandra. Chris Finds the Answer. Bates, Stephen, illus. 20p. (gr. k-6). 1988. pap. text ed. 4.25 (ISBN 1-55976-127-X). CEF Press.
Klusmeyer, Joann. What about Me? (Illus.). (gr. 4-7). 1987. 3.95 (ISBN 0-570-03641-0, 39-1125). Concordia.
Koenig, Norma E. The Runaway Heart. (Orig.). (gr. 4-6). 1981. pap. 4.95 (ISBN 0-377-00112-0). Friendship Pr.
Landis, Mary. Anthony Gets Ready for Church. 1990. pap. 2.10 (ISBN 0-317-02906-1). Rod & Staff.
Lang, Margaret A. Gramma's Stories & Rhymes for Little Christians. (gr. 2-5). 9.95 (ISBN 0-942242-00-9, A2242). World Bible.
Leeper, John H. The Riddle of the Outlaw Bear & Other Faith-Building Stories. (Illus.). (gr. 1-6). 1984. pap. 4.95 (ISBN 0-8024-7352-0). Moody.
Lehn, Cornelia. I Heard Good News Today. Schlegel, Ralph A., illus. Oyer, Lora S., intro. by. LC 83-80401. (Illus.). 148p. (gr. 1-6). 1983. 12.95 (ISBN 0-87303-073-7). Faith & Life.
Leppard, Lois G. Mandie & the Medicine Man, Bk. 6. LC 85-73426. 150p. (Orig.). (gr. 4-8). 1986. pap. 3.95 (ISBN 0-87123-891-8). Bethany Hse.
—Mandie & the Mysterious Bells, Bk. 10. LC 87-72792. 160p. (Orig.). (gr. 4-8). 1988. pap. 3.95 (ISBN 1-55661-000-9). Bethany Hse.
—Mandie & the Singing Chalet. 160p. (Orig.). (ps-8). 1991. pap. 3.95 (ISBN 1-55661-198-6). Bethany Hse.
Littke, Lael. Where the Creeks Meet. LC 87-15592. 132p. (gr. 6-12). 1989. pap. 4.95 (ISBN 0-87579-229-4). Deseret Bk.
Lloyd, Jeremy. Woodland Gospels: According to Captain Beaky & His Band. Percy, Graham, illus. LC 83-20790. 63p. (gr. k up). 1984. 11.95 (ISBN 0-571-13211-1); pap. 4.95 (ISBN 0-571-14285-0). Faber & Faber.
London, Carolyn. Stolen Ice Cream Bar. Nielson, Deborah, illus. 12p. (gr. k-6). 1981. pap. text ed. 4.25 (ISBN 1-55976-151-2). CEF Press.
MacDonald, George. At the Back of the North Wind. rev. ed. Phillips, Michael, ed. 176p. (ps-2). 1991. 9.95 (ISBN 1-55661-196-X). Bethany Hse.
McFarlan, Donald. Wizard of the Great Lakes. (gr. 5-9). 1975. pap. 3.95 (ISBN 0-87508-631-4). Chr Lit.
McKissack, Patricia. Give It with Love, Christopher: Christopher Learns about Gifts & Giving. Batholomew, illus. 32p. (ps-3). 1988. pap. 5.95 (ISBN 0-8066-2354-3, 10-2554, Augsburg). Augsburg Fortress.
—Speak Up, Christopher: Christopher Learns the Difference Between Right & Wrong. Bartholomew, illus. LC 87-73523. 32p. (ps-6). 1988. pap. 5.95 (ISBN 0-8066-2355-1, 10-5966, Augsburg). Augsburg Fortress.
Marshall, Donald R. The Enchantress of Crumbledown. LC 90-81830. 229p. (gr. 3-6). 1990. 9.95 (ISBN 0-87579-352-5). Deseret Bk.
Matranga, Frances C. One Step at a Time. (Illus.). (gr. 4-7). 1987. pap. 3.95 (ISBN 0-570-03642-9, 39-1126). Concordia.
Mattozzi, Patti. Little Lessons for Little Learners: Angels. 32p. (gr. 2 up). 1989. pap. 3.95 (ISBN 0-8378-1843-5). Gibson.
—Little Lessons for Little Learners: Prayer. 32p. (gr. 1 up). 1989. 3.95 (ISBN 0-8378-1844-3). Gibson.
—Little Lessons for Little Learners: Seasons. 32p. (gr. 2 up). 1989. 3.95 (ISBN 0-8378-1842-7). Gibson.
—Little Lessons for Little Learners: The Lord's House. 32p. (gr. 1 up). 1989. 3.95 (ISBN 0-8378-1845-1). Gibson.
Modica, Terry A. The Dark Secret of the Ouija. Bohl, Al, illus. 224p. (gr. 9-12). 1990. pap. text ed. 2.50 (ISBN 1-55748-138-5). Barbour & Co.
Monaghan, Sue. Willy's Bad Day. Smith, Janet, illus. (Orig.). (gr. 1-3). 1988. pap. 5.95 (ISBN 0-8192-1428-0). Morehouse Pub.
Moore, Ruth N. Wilderness Journey. Eitzen, Allan, illus. LC 79-20489. 182p. (Orig.). (gr. 5-8). 1979. pap. 4.95 (ISBN 0-8361-1907-X). Herald Pr.
Morris, Gilbert. The Dixie Widow. 302p. (Orig.). (gr. 9-12). 1991. text ed. 6.95 (ISBN 1-55661-115-3). Bethany Hse.
Murphy, Elspeth C. Julie Chang. 107p. (gr. 3-7). 1986. 3.95 (ISBN 0-89191-720-9, 57208, Chariot Bks). Cook.
—Pug McConnell. LC 85-26922. 107p. (gr. 3-7). 1986. 3.95 (ISBN 0-89191-728-4, Chariot Bks). Cook.
—Some Words Help, Some Words Hurt. LC 87-31474. 24p. (ps-2). 1988. pap. 3.49 (ISBN 1-55513-164-6, Chariot Bks). Cook.
—That's Not Fair. LC 87-35458. 24p. (gr. 4-7). 1988. pap. 3.49 (ISBN 1-55513-354-1, Chariot Bks). Cook.
Newton, Lucilda A. Big Peanuts in Trouble. (ps-3). 1976. pap. 2.50 (ISBN 0-915374-18-8, 18-8). Rapids Christian.
Oke, Janette. When Breaks the Dawn. LC 86-3405. 250p. (Orig.). (gr. 4 up). 1986. pap. 5.95 (ISBN 0-87123-882-9). Bethany Hse.
Page, Carole G. Heather's Choice. LC 82-3417. 128p. (gr. 7). pap. 3.95 (ISBN 0-8024-3490-8). Moody.
Phillips, Michael & Pella, Judith. Treasure of Stonewycke. LC 88-7531. 352p. (Orig.). (gr. 11 up). 1988. pap. 7.95 (ISBN 0-87123-902-7). Bethany Hse.
Porter, Barbara J. Grandpa & Me & the Wishing Star. Marsh, Dilleen, illus. LC 90-81831. 32p. (ps). 1990. 10.95 (ISBN 0-87579-269-3). Deseret Bk.
Richmond, Gary. Miss Otter Goes to the Movies. 1991. write for info. (ISBN 0-8499-0743-8). Word Bks.
—Prodigal Wolf. 1990. write for info. (ISBN 0-8499-0746-2). Word Bks.
—A Scary Night at the Zoo. 1990. write for info. (ISBN 0-8499-0742-X). Word Bks.
Roddy, Lee. Terror in the Sky. 176p. (Orig.). (ps-8). 1991. pap. 4.95 (ISBN 1-55661-096-3). Bethany Hse.
St. John, Patricia. The Secret at Pheasant Cottage. LC 78-24384. (gr. 6-8). 1979. pap. 3.95 (ISBN 0-8024-7683-X). Moody.
—Secret of the Fourth Candle. LC 81-22400. 128p. 1981. pap. 3.95 (ISBN 0-8024-7681-3). Moody.
—Where the River Begins. LC 80-12304. 128p. (Orig.). (gr. 5-8). pap. 3.95 (ISBN 0-8024-8124-8). Moody.
Schantz, Daniel. Wheeler's Campaign. Ostendorf, Ned, illus. 96p. (Orig.). (gr. 3-6). pap. 3.95 (ISBN 0-87403-454-X, 24-02914). Standard Pub.
Schmid, C. One Hundred Stories. (CHI.). 1980. pap. 2.00 (ISBN 0-8198-5404-2). Dghtrs St Paul.
Schulte, Elaine. Off to a New Start. (gr. 5-7). 1989. pap. 3.95 (ISBN 1-55513-771-7, Chariot Bks). Cook.
Sensenig, Janet. Daryl Borrows a Brother. 166p. 1989. 6.50 (ISBN 0-317-02911-8). Rod & Staff.
Shaffer, Betty. Lisa. LC 82-72149. 141p. (Orig.). (gr. 8-12). 1982. pap. 3.95 (ISBN 0-87123-316-9). Bethany Hse.
Sharp, Christopher. Bad Mouth Christopher. (gr. 1-4). 1980. pap. 4.95 (ISBN 0-570-03482-5, 56-1703). Concordia.
Simpson, Winifred R. Hello, World, You're Mine? (Illus.). (gr. 4-7). 1987. pap. 3.95 (ISBN 0-570-03643-7, 39-1127). Concordia.
Skold, Betty W. Lord, I Have a Question: Story Devotions for Girls. LC 79-50079. (gr. 3-6). 1979. pap. 4.95 (ISBN 0-8066-1718-7, 10-4096, Augsburg). Augsburg Fortress.
Snelling, Lauraine. The Race. 176p. (Orig.). (gr. 7-9). 1991. pap. 4.95 (ISBN 1-55661-161-7). Bethany Hse.
Sollitt, Kenneth. Our Changing Lives. 182p. 1986. pap. 6.95 (ISBN 0-940652-04-8). Sunrise Bks.
Sometimes It's Hard to Be Friends. LC 87-38204. 24p. (ps-2). 1988. pap. 3.49 (ISBN 1-55513-892-6, Chariot Bks). Cook.

Sorenson, Jane. Another Jennifer. Endres, Helen, illus. 144p. (gr. 5-8). 1986. 3.95 (ISBN 0-87403-088-9, 3741). Standard Pub.
—The New Pete. Endres, Helen, illus. 144p. (gr. 5-8). 1986. 3.95 (ISBN 0-87403-086-2, 2986). Standard Pub.
Sorenson, Stephen. Growing up Isn't Easy, Lord: Story Devotions for Boys. LC 79-50080. (gr. 3-6). 1979. pap. 4.95 (ISBN 0-8066-1713-6, 10-2904, Augsburg). Augsburg Fortress.
Stafford, Tim. John Porter in Big Trouble. (Illus.). 32p. (gr. 2-8). 1990. 11.95 (ISBN 0-7459-1807-7). Lion USA.
Stiles, Louise. Little Tree. Torvik, Brian, illus. 32p. (gr. 3 up). 1987. pap. 5.95 (ISBN 0-88144-051-5). Christian Pub.

Stone, Maggie R. The Portrait, Bk. I. Schatz, Bud, intro. by. 161p. (Orig.). (gr. 5-12). 1990. pap. 5.95 (ISBN 0-685-38818-2). M R Stone Minst. Captive in every heart is the desire to love & to serve God. Follow David, Laura & Peter through the entangled web of finding what "true love" really means. David's quiet nature & art abilities, Peter's good looks & social savvy, create a web for Laura that is not of her own spinning. Read how God works in mysterious ways in these lives. The book is being used in the Nashville Public Schools Junior & Senior High Libraries & has also been broadcast over WPLN Talking Library (for blind people in this area). ***Publisher Provided Annotation.***

Stowell, Gordon. God Knows. 14p. (gr. 1-5). 1984. mini-bk 0.59 (ISBN 0-8307-0959-2, 5608425). Regal.
—God Loves. 14p. (gr. 1-5). 1984. mini-bk 0.59 (ISBN 0-8307-0958-4, 5608413). Regal.
—Help Me. 14p. (gr. 1-5). 1984. mini-bk 0.59 (ISBN 0-8307-0961-4, 5608444). Regal.
—I Like. 14p. (ps-2). 1984. mini-bk 0.59 (ISBN 0-8307-0962-2, 5608579). Regal.
—I'm Sorry. 14p. (gr. 1-5). mini-bk 0.59 (ISBN 0-8307-0957-6, 5608524). Regal.
—It's Fun. (gr. 1-5). 1984. mini-bk 0.59 (ISBN 0-8307-0956-8, 5608392). Regal.
—Please God. 14p. (gr. 1-5). 1984. mini-bk 0.59 (ISBN 0-8307-0954-1, 5608381). Regal.
—Thank You God. 14p. (gr. 1-7). 1984. mini-bk 0.59 (ISBN 0-8307-0960-6, 5608436). Regal.
Tada, Joni E. Darcy. LC 87-35712. (gr. 3-7). 1988. pap. 4.49 (ISBN 1-55513-809-8, Chariot Bks). Cook.
Tangvald, Christine. Good for Me! LC 86-72319. 1987. bds. 4.95 (ISBN 1-55513-162-X, Chariot Bks). Cook.
—Guess What? We're Moving. LC 87-34107. 24p. (ps-2). 1988. 7.95 (ISBN 1-55513-481-5, Chariot Bks). Cook.
—Someone I Love Died. 24p. (ps-2). 1988. 7.95 (ISBN 1-55513-490-4, Chariot Bks). Cook.
—We Have a New Baby. LC 87-35457. 24p. (ps-2). 1988. 7.95 (ISBN 1-55513-503-X, Chariot Bks). Cook.
Thoene, Brock & Thoene, Bodie. Gold Rush Prodigal. 224p. (Orig.). (gr. 9-12). 1991. pap. 5.95 (ISBN 1-55661-162-5). Bethany Hse.
Tigunait, Pandit R. Who Is God? Clark, Lawrence, ed. Locano, Graciela, illus. 32p. (Orig.). (gr. k-6). 1989. pap. 4.95t (ISBN 0-89389-118-5). Himalayan Pubs.
Unruh, Sophia. Lenka of Emma Creek. Shelly, Maynard, ed. Unruh, Arch, illus. LC 89-81282. 32p. (Orig.). (ps-7). 1989. pap. 9.95 (ISBN 0-87303-136-9). Faith & Life.
Van Horn, Brian & Van Horn, Chris. No Time in a Jam. Scott, Rita & Van Horn, Brian, illus. (gr. 2-8). Date not set. write for info. (ISBN 1-877765-05-8). Lambgel Family.
Van Leeuwen, Jean. Seems Like This Road Goes on Forever. LC 78-72201. (gr. 8 up). 1979. 8.95 (ISBN 0-8037-7687-X). Dial Bks Young.
Vann, Donna R. Stefan's Secret Fear. Haysom, John, illus. 32p. (gr. 4-8). 1990. 11.95 (ISBN 0-7459-1307-5). Lion USA.
Waite, Michael P. Miggy & Tiggy. 32p. (ps-3). 7.95 (ISBN 1-55513-220-0). Cook.
—Suzy Swoof. LC 87-5269. (ps-3). 1987. 7.95 (ISBN 1-55513-219-7, Chariot Bks). Cook.
Wallace, Barbara B. The Contest Kid Strikes Again. rev. ed. Kamen, Gloria, illus. LC 79-24197. (gr. 4-6). 1988. PLB 0.88 (ISBN 0-687-09590-5); pap. 0.10 (ISBN 0-687-09591-3). Abingdon.
Walters, Julie. Forgiving One Another: Stories About Forgiveness & Reconciliation for Young Children. Swift, Don, illus. 96p. (gr. 2-5). 1979. pap. 2.95 (ISBN 0-87793-179-8). Ave Maria.
Weaver, Anna. Eyes for Benny. (gr. 6 up). 1984. 7.25 (ISBN 0-318-01331-2). Rod & Staff.
Weddle, Linda M. T. J. & the Nobody House. LC 90-8702. 95p. (Orig.). (gr. 3-7). 1990. pap. text ed. 3.95 (ISBN 0-87227-145-5, RBP5174). Reg Baptist.
Weyland, Jack. A New Dawn. LC 83-24049. 181p. (gr. 8 up). 1988. pap. 4.95 (ISBN 0-87579-163-8). Deseret Bk.
Wick, Lori S. A Place Called Home. (gr. 9 up). 1990. pap. 5.99 (ISBN 0-89081-780-4). Harvest Hse.
Wilhelm, Hans. Waldo, Tell Me about Christ. Wilhelm, Hans, illus. 40p. (gr. 3 up). 1988. 4.95 (ISBN 0-8378-1812-5). Gibson.
—Waldo, Tell Me about God. Wilhelm, Hans, illus. 40p. (gr. 3 up). 1988. 4.95 (ISBN 0-8378-1809-5). Gibson.
—Waldo, Tell Me about Guardian Angels. Wilhelm, Hans, illus. 40p. (gr. 3 up). 1988. 4.95 (ISBN 0-8378-1811-7). Gibson.
—Waldo, Tell Me about Me. Wilhelm, Hans, illus. 40p. (gr. 3 up). 1988. 4.95 (ISBN 0-8378-1810-9). Gibson.
Woodson, Meg. Turn It into Glory. Holmes, Marjorie, intro. by. 224p. (gr. 9 up). 1991. 13.95 (ISBN 1-55661-178-1). Bethany Hse.
Wright, Christine. My Sister Katie: How She Sees God's World. Hull, Biz, illus. LC 90-81702. 32p. 1990. text ed. 6.95 (ISBN 0-8066-2497-3, 9-2497). Augsburg Fortress.

CHRISTIAN SCIENCE

Beringer, Joan E. God's Gifts. Leder, Dora, illus. LC 81-82908. 32p. (gr. k-3). 1984. 8.95 (ISBN 0-87510-160-7). Chr Science.
Dueland, Joy. Filled up Full. (Illus.). 30p. (Orig.). (gr. k-3). 1974. pap. 4.95 (ISBN 0-87510-100-3). Chr Science.
—My Best Friend. (Illus.). 27p. (Orig.). (gr. k-3). 1972. pap. 4.95 (ISBN 0-87510-081-3). Chr Science.

CHRISTIAN SYMBOLISM

see Christian Art and Symbolism

CHRISTIAN UNITY

Rosen, Ruth, ed. Jesus for Jews. Owens, Nate, illus. LC 87-20343. 336p. (Orig.). (gr. 12). 1987. 13.95 (ISBN 0-9616148-3-8); pap. 7.95 (ISBN 0-9616148-4-6); pap. 4.95 mass market (ISBN 0-9616148-2-X). Messianic Jewish.

CHRISTIANITY

see also Church; God; Jesus Christ; Missions; Protestantism; Reformation
also names of Christian churches and sects (e.g. Catholic church; Huguenots; etc.) and headings beginning with the words Christian and Church

Billington, Rachel. The First Miracles. Brown, Barbara, illus. 32p. (gr. k-4). 1990. 12.95 (ISBN 0-8028-3687-9). Eerdmans.
Bothwell, H. Roger. My First Book About Communion. (Illus.). (ps). 1978. pap. 1.95 (ISBN 0-8127-0180-1). Review & Herald.
Brown, Alan & Perkins, Judy. Christianity. (Illus.). 68p. (gr. 7-9). 1989. 19.95 (ISBN 0-7134-5319-2, Pub. by Batsford England). Trafalgar Sq.
Landis, Mary. God's Wonderful Trees. 1990. pap. 2.10 (ISBN 0-317-02907-X). Rod & Staff.
—God's Wonderful Water. 1990. pap. 2.10 (ISBN 0-317-02908-8). Rod & Staff.
—My Thank You Book. 1990. pap. 2.10 (ISBN 0-317-02909-6). Rod & Staff.
Lynch, Patricia A. Christianity. (Illus.). 128p. (gr. 7-12). 1991. 17.95x (ISBN 0-8160-2441-3). Facts on File.
Miller, William M. Tales of Persia: A Book for Children. Melton, Lily, illus. 145p. (gr. 1-6). 1988. pap. 5.95 (ISBN 0-87552-292-0). Presby & Reformed.
Montgomery, Herb & Montgomery, Mary. The Christian Pattern Book: Dozens of Creative Activities for Children. St. Marie, Janice, illus. 64p. (gr. 3-12). 1984. wkbk. 10.95 (ISBN 0-86683-831-7). Harper SF.
Orr, Leonard. Physical Immortality for Christians. (gr. 7 up). 1989. pap. 10.00 (ISBN 0-945793-03-0). Inspir Univ.
Orr, Leonard D. Physical Immortality. (gr. 7 up). 1988. pap. 15.00 (ISBN 0-945793-01-4). Inspir Univ.
Orr, Lernard D. Breath Awareness: Breath Awareness for Public Schools, Medical Profession. (gr. 7 up). 1988. pap. 10.00 (ISBN 0-945793-02-2). Inspir Univ.
Oyer, Sharon, et al. Learning to Follow Jesus. (Illus.). 72p. (Orig.). (gr. 2-5). 1988. pap. 5.99 (ISBN 0-89081-663-8). Harvest Hse.
Sciacca, Fran & Sciacca, Jill. No Pain, No Gain. 1989. pap. 3.95 (ISBN 0-685-25654-5). World Wide Pubs.
—Warning: This Christian Is Highly Explosive! 1989. pap. 3.95 (ISBN 0-685-25655-3). World Wide Pubs.
Watkins, Morris. Global Christianity. 64p. (Orig.). (gr. 7 up). 1987. pap. 6.95 (ISBN 0-939925-08-7). R C Law & Co.
Watts, Dorothy E. My Father's Bitter Gift. Woolsey, Raymond H., ed. 96p. (gr. 7-9). 1988. pap. 6.95 (ISBN 0-8280-0494-3). Review & Herald.
Windeatt, Mary F. The Brown Scapular. Harmon, Gedge, illus. 32p. (gr. 1-5). 1989. Repr. of 1954 ed. wkbk. 3.00 (ISBN 0-89555-380-5). TAN Bks Pubs.
—The Rosary. Harmon, Gedge, illus. 32p. (gr. 1-5). 1989. Repr. of 1954 ed. wkbk. 3.00 (ISBN 0-89555-379-1). TAN Bks Pubs.

CHRISTIANITY–HISTORY

see Church History

CHRISTIANITY AND SCIENCE

see Religion and Science

CHRISTMAS

see also Christmas–Fiction; Christmas Entertainments; Christmas Plays; Christmas Poetry; Jesus Christ–Nativity; Santa Claus

ABC Christmas Book. (Illus.). 20p. (ps-5). 1986. pap. 4.00 (ISBN 0-914510-16-9). Evergreen.
Actividades Navidenas: Christmas Activities. 32p. 1987. pap. 1.50 (ISBN 0-311-26613-4). Casa Bautista.
Anderson, Joan. Christmas on the Prairie. Ancona, George, illus. LC 85-4095. 48p. (gr. 2-6). 1985. 13.95 (ISBN 0-89919-307-2, Clarion). Ticknor & Fields.
Anglund, Joan W. Christmas Is a Time of Giving. Anglund, Joan W., illus. LC 61-10106. (gr. k-3). 1961. 9.95 (ISBN 0-15-217863-5, HJ). HarBraceJ.
—Christmas Is Love. (Illus.). 32p. (ps up). 1988. 6.95 (ISBN 0-15-200425-4, Gulliver Bks). HarBraceJ.
Barth, Edna. A Christmas Feast: Poems, Sayings, Greetings, & Wishes. Arndt, Ursula, illus. 176p. (gr. 3-6). 1979. 12.95 (ISBN 0-395-28965-3, Clarion). HM.
—Holly, Reindeer, & Colored Lights: The Story of the Christmas Symbols. Arndt, Ursula, illus. LC 71-157731. 96p. (gr. 3-6). 1985. pap. 4.95 (ISBN 0-89919-037-5, Pub. by Clarion). Ticknor & Fields.
Batchelor, Mary. Lion Christmas Book. (Illus.). 96p. (Orig.). 1988. pap. 7.95 (ISBN 0-7459-1511-6). Lion USA.
Baum, Susan. Merry Tree. Baum, Susan, illus. 16p. (ps-1). 1990. 8.95 (ISBN 0-06-107401-2). HarpC Child Bks.
Baxter, Leon. The Christmas Activity Book. (Illus.). 24p. (gr. k-4). 1990. 5.95 (ISBN 0-8249-8479-X). Ideals.
Beall, Pamela C. & Nipp, Susan H. We Color Wee Sing for Christmas. Klein, Nancy, illus. 48p. (ps-2). 1986. pap. 1.95 (ISBN 0-8431-1781-8); incl. cassette 9.95 (ISBN 0-8431-1782-6). Price Stern.
Beaton, Jane, et al. Family Celebrations: Advent & Christmas. 64p. 1984. pap. 2.50 (ISBN 0-8146-1389-6). Liturgical Pr.
Benjamin, Alan. Christmas Wishes: Chubby Board Book. 1989. 3.95 (ISBN 0-671-68268-7). S&S Trade.
Billy's Christmas Tree. (Illus.). 12p. (ps-3). 1988. bds. 2.95 (ISBN 0-02-688790-8). Checkerboard Pr.
Blackwood, Alan. Christmas. (Illus.). 48p. (gr. 3-8). 1987. PLB 14.60 (ISBN 0-86592-978-5). Rourke Corp.
The Book of Christmas. (Illus.). 144p. (gr. 7 up). 1986. 19.93 (ISBN 0-8094-5261-8); lib. bdg. 25.93 (ISBN 0-8094-5262-6). Time-Life.
Branley, Franklyn M. The Christmas Sky. rev. ed. Fieser, Stephen, illus. LC 89-71210. 48p. (gr. 3-7). 1990. 14.95 (ISBN 0-690-04770-3, Crowell Jr Bks); PLB 14.89 (ISBN 0-690-04772-X, Crowell Jr Bks). HarpC Child Bks.
Brent, Isabelle. The Christmas Story. (Illus.). 1989. 13.95 (ISBN 0-8037-0730-4). Dial Bks Young.
Bridwell, Norman. The Witch's Christmas. Bridwell, Norman, illus. 32p. (gr. k-3). 1986. pap. 1.95 (ISBN 0-590-40434-2). Scholastic Inc.
Brown, Ann. Handmade Christmas Gifts That Are Actually Usable. Small, Carol B., illus. LC 87-31993. 75p. (Orig.). (gr. k-6). 1987. pap. 6.95 (ISBN 0-938267-03-5). Bold Prodns.
Capote, Truman. A Christmas Memory. Peck, Beth, illus. LC 88-36452. 48p. (gr. 2 up). 1989. 14.95 (ISBN 0-679-80040-9); bk. & cassette 19.95 (ISBN 0-394-82500-4). Knopf.
Carlson. A Christmas Lullaby. 24p. (gr. k-4). 1985. pap. 1.39 (ISBN 0-570-06195-4, 59-1296). Concordia.
Carol Time. (ps). 2.95 (ISBN 0-86112-234-8, Pub. by Brimax Bks). Borden.
Carson, Patti & Dellosa, Janet. Christmas Fun Book. Carson, Patti & Dellosa, Janet, illus. 32p. (ps-2). 1981. pap. 1.59 (ISBN 0-88724-053-4, CD-8008). Carson-Dellos.
Carvin, Ruth. Color It Christmas: With Three Christmas Posters. Carvin, Ruth, illus. 8p. (gr. 3 up). 1987. write for info. Carvin Pub.
Cassat, Julie. What I Like Best about Christmas. Rigo, Christina, illus. 14p. (gr. 4-7). Date not set. pap. text ed. 5.95 (ISBN 0-927106-02-7). Prod Concept.
Chapman, Jean. The Sugar-Plum Christmas Book. Niland, Deborah, illus. 190p. (ps-6). 1982. lib. bdg. 23.93 (ISBN 0-516-08952-8). Childrens.
The Children's Christmas Woodbook. (ps). 1986. bds. 9.95 (ISBN 0-8120-5753-8). Barron.
A Child's Christmas. (Illus.). 32p. 1989. pap. text ed. 10.95 (ISBN 0-929648-62-5). Galison.
Chorao, Kay, compiled by. & illus. Baby's Christmas Treasury. LC 90-45872. 48p. (ps). 1991. 10.00 (ISBN 0-679-80198-7, Random Juv); lib. bdg. 10.99 (ISBN 0-679-90198-1). Random.
Christmas Fun & Games. (Illus.). (ps-2). 1.95 (ISBN 0-7214-3182-8). Ladybird Bks.
Christmas Fun Book. (Illus.). (ps-2). 1.95 (ISBN 0-7214-3183-6). Ladybird Bks.
Christmas Is Coming. (ps-k). 1990. bds. 3.95 (ISBN 0-7214-9133-2). Ladybird Bks.
Christmas is Coming! 1990. (Illus.). (ps-7). 1990. 19.95 (ISBN 0-8487-1016-9). Oxmoor Hse.
Christmas: One Hundred Seasonal Favorites. 248p. (gr. 4-12). 1985. 19.95 (ISBN 0-88188-157-0, 00361398). H Leonard Pub Corp.
The Christmas Robin. 3.95 (ISBN 0-7214-5255-8). Ladybird Bks.
Christmas Time. (ps). 2.95 (ISBN 0-86112-197-X, Pub. by Brimax Bks). Borden.
Cooney, Barbara. Christmas. Cooney, Barbara, illus. LC 67-18510. 40p. (gr. k-3). 1967. PLB 12.89 (ISBN 0-690-19201-0, Crowell Jr Bks). HarpC Child Bks.
Corwin, Judith H. Christmas Fun. Corwin, Judith H., illus. 64p. (gr. 3 up). 1982. PLB 10.29 (ISBN 0-671-45944-9); PLB 7.71s.p.; pap. 5.95 (ISBN 0-671-49583-6); pap. 4.46s.p. Messner.
Cracchiolo, Rachelle & Smith, Mary D. Christmas Activities. Crachiolo, Rachelle & Smith, Mary D., illus. 32p. (gr. 1-4). 1985. wkbk. 4.95 (ISBN 1-55734-013-7). Tchr Create Mat.

—Christmas Ornaments from Around the World. Cracchiolo, Rachelle & Smith, Mary D., illus. 32p. (gr. k-3). 1977. wkbk. 4.95 (ISBN 1-55734-003-X). Tchr Create Mat.

Cuyler, Margery. The All-Around Christmas Book. Jones, Corbett, illus. LC 82-3104. 96p. (gr. 2-5). 1982. 11.95 (ISBN 0-03-060387-0); pap. 4.95 (ISBN 0-03-062183-6). H Holt & Co.

Daniel, Becky. The Christmas Story. 16p. (ps-3). 1990. Incl. tchr's. guide. write for info. (ISBN 0-86653-555-1, SS1876). Good Apple.

Delacre, Lulu, selected by. & illus. Las Navidades: Popular Christmas Songs from Latin America. Paz, Elena, contrib. by. (ps up) 1990. 12.95 (ISBN 0-590-43548-5). Scholastic Inc.

Dickens, Charles. A Christmas Carol. LC 85-15815. 96p. (gr. 6 up). 6.95 (ISBN 0-88088-125-9). Peter Pauper.

Dobson, Rebecca J. Christmas Is a Happy Time...To Remember Jesus. Churchville, Barbara, illus. 24p. (ps). 1987. pap. 2.95 (ISBN 0-8170-1126-9). Judson.

Domanska, Janina, illus. The First Noel. LC 85-27084. 24p. (ps up). 1986. 11.75 (ISBN 0-688-04324-0); PLB 11.88 (ISBN 0-688-04325-9). Greenwillow.

Duden, Jane. Christmas. LC 89-28520. (Illus.). 48p. (gr. 4-5). 1990. 10.95 (ISBN 0-89686-497-9, Crestwood Hse.). Macmillan Child Grp.

Ewing, Carolyn, illus. Jingle Bells: A Holiday Book with Lights & Music. 10p. (ps-1). 1990. 10.95 (ISBN 0-689-71431-9, Aladdin). Macmillan Child Grp.

The First Christmas, No. 1. 1989. 3.95 (ISBN 0-7214-5197-7). Chr Lit.

Fletcher, Sarah. The Welcoming Party: A Christmas Story. Baker, Arthur, illus. 32p. (gr. k-3). 1990. saddle stitched 1.25 (ISBN 0-8028-5057-X). Eerdmans.

Fogartie, Arthur F. The Sixteenth Manger. 64p. 1987. pap. 6.95 (ISBN 0-8170-1119-6). Judson.

Fradin, Dennis B. Christmas. 48p. (gr. 2-5). 1990. 12.95 (ISBN 0-89490-258-X). Enslow Pubs.

Getting Ready for Christmas. (Illus.). (ps-2). 1.95 (ISBN 0-7214-3129-1). Ladybird Bks.

Gibbons, Gail. Christmas Time. LC 82-1038. (Illus.). 32p. (ps-3). 1982. reinforced bdg. 14.95 (ISBN 0-8234-0453-6); pap. 5.95 (ISBN 0-8234-0575-3). Holiday.

—Christmas Time. Gibbons, Gail, illus. (gr. k-3). 1985. PLB incl. cassette 19.95 (ISBN 0-941078-84-1); pap. 12.95 incl. Cassette (ISBN 0-941078-82-5); PLB 27.95 incl. cassette, 4 paperbacks, guide (ISBN 0-317-40160-2). Live Oak Media.

Giblin, James C. The Truth about Santa Claus. LC 85-47541. (Illus.). 96p. (gr. 3-7). 1985. 12.95 (ISBN 0-690-04483-6, Crowell Jr Bks); PLB 12.89 (ISBN 0-690-04484-4, Crowell Jr Bks). HarpC Child Bks.

Gibson, Roxie C. Hey, God! What Is Christmas. Gibson, James, illus. LC 82-60192. 64p. (gr. 3-5). 1982. 4.95 (ISBN 0-938232-09-6, 32752). Winston-Derek.

Goode, Diane. Diane Goode's American Christmas. Goode, Diane, illus. 1990. 14.95 (ISBN 0-525-44620-6, DCB). Dutton Child Bks.

Goode, Diane, illus. Diane Goode's Little Library of Christmas Classics. 32p. (gr. 1 up). 1983. boxed set 7.95 (ISBN 0-394-85229-X, Random Juv). Random.

Greene, Carol. Waiting for Christmas: Stories & Activities for Advent. Swisher, Elizabeth, illus. LC 87-70474. 32p. (Orig.). (ps-5). 1987. pap. 4.95 (ISBN 0-8066-2264-4, 10-6915, Augsburg). Augsburg Fortress.

Harrison, Susan. Twelve Days of Christmas. Harrison, Susan, illus. 24p. (ps-3). 1989. pap. 2.95 (ISBN 0-8249-8391-2). Ideals.

Hawthorne, Terri B. & Brown, Diane B. Winter Solstice Celebrations Through the Ages: A Coloring Book for All Ages. Brown, Diane B., illus. 32p. (gr. 3). 1990. pap. 5.99 (ISBN 0-929404-01-7). Tara Educ Servs.

Haywood, Carolyn. Merry Christmas from Eddie. (gr. 2-4). 1987. pap. 2.95 (ISBN 0-8167-1041-4). Troll Assocs.

Herda, D. J. Christmas. (Illus.). 72p. (gr. 4 up). 1983. PLB 10.40 (ISBN 0-531-04524-2). Watts.

Hershey, Katherine. A Very Special Day. Seals, Thelma, et al, illus. 21p. (gr. k-6). 1980. 4.25 (ISBN 1-55976-131-8). CEF Press.

Jaques, Faith. The Christmas Party: A Model Book. Jaques, Faith, illus. 6p. (gr. 2 up). 1986. 8.95 (ISBN 0-399-21393-7, Philomel). Putnam Pub Group.

Jones, Kathy. Celebrate Christmas. Filkins, Vanessa, illus. 144p. (gr. k-6). 1985. wkbk. 10.95 (ISBN 0-86653-279-X, SS 840). Good Apple.

Kalman, Bobbie. Early Christmas. (Illus.). 64p. (gr. 4-5). 1981. 14.95 (ISBN 0-86505-001-5); pap. 7.95 (ISBN 0-86505-003-1). Crabtree Pub Co. EARLY CHRISTMAS is a wonderful historical odyssey taking young readers back to the early days of this country when Christmas traditions were made. Children will read about the special ways the settlers celebrated the most popular holiday of the year. EARLY CHRISTMAS is part of the The Early Settler Life Series, Bobbie Kalman's best-selling books. Illustrated with sepia-colored photographs & etchings, The Early Settler Life Series allows

young readers the opportunity to experience 19th century etchings & photographs that are found only in archival colections. Other books in the series are: EARLY STORES & MARKETS, EARLY LOGGERS & THE SAWMILL, EARLY TRAVEL, EARLY SETTLER CHILDREN, EARLY SETTLER STORYBOOK, EARLY ARTISANS, EARLY PLEASURES & PASTIMES, EARLY VILLAGE LIFE, EARLY FARM LIFE, FOOD FOR THE SETTLER, EARLY CITY LIFE, EARLY HEALTH & MEDICINE, EARLY SCHOOLS, EARLY FAMILY HOME, & EARLY SETTLER ACTIVITY GUIDE.
Publisher Provided Annotation.

—We Celebrate Christmas. (Illus.). 56p. (gr. 3-4). 1985. 15.95 (ISBN 0-86505-040-6); pap. 7.95 (ISBN 0-86505-050-3). Crabtree Pub Co. WE CELEBRATE CHRISTMAS is filled with stories, legends, poems, games, activities & recipes that allow children to experience holiday festivities from around the world. Children can explore the origins & customs of many familiar & colorful festivals & holiday celebrations. They will discover new ways to celebrate holidays & develop an understanding & appreciation of other cultures. WE CELEBRATE CHRISTMAS is part of The Holidays & Festivals Series. Other books in the series are WE CELEBRATE: HANUKKAH, THE HARVEST, HALLOWE'EN, VALENTINE'S DAY, NEW YEAR, FAMILY DAYS, SPRING, WINTER & EASTER. They are all profusely illustrated, fun-filled, multicultural, & easy-to-read.
Publisher Provided Annotation.

Kelley, Emily. Christmas around the World. Kiedrowski, Priscilla, illus 48p. (gr. k-4). 1986. lib. bdg. 9.95 (ISBN 0-87614-249-8). Carolrhoda Bks.

—Christmas Around the World. Kiedrowski, Priscilla, illus. 48p. (ps-4). 1986. pap. 3.95 (ISBN 0-87614-453-9, First Ave Edns). Lerner Pubns.

Kennedy, Pamela. Prayers at Christmastime. Britt, Stephanie M., illus. 24p. (ps-k). 1990. 3.95 (ISBN 0-8249-8480-3). Ideals.

King, Helen. Soul of Christmas. Anderson, Fred, illus. 32p. (gr. k-4). 1972. 4.50 (ISBN 0-87485-057-6). Johnson Chi.

Klug, Ron & Klug, Lyn, eds. The Christian Family Christmas Book. LC 87-1391. (Illus.). 128p. (ps-7). 1987. text ed. 13.95 (ISBN 0-8066-2270-9, 10-1113, Augsburg). Augsburg Fortress.

Kurelek, William. A Northern Nativity. Kurelek, William, illus. (gr. 4 up). 1976. 14.95 (ISBN 0-88776-071-6); pap. 7.95 (ISBN 0-685-04960-4). Tundra Bks.

The Ladybird Christmas Book. (gr. k-3). 1990. 8.95 (ISBN 0-7214-7541-8). Ladybird Bks.

Langstaff, John. What a Morning! The Christmas Story in Black Spirituals. Bryan, Ashley, illus. LC 87-750130. 32p. 1987. 13.95 (ISBN 0-689-50422-5, M K McElderry). Macmillan Child Grp.

Lee, Sharon. Joyous Days: A Collection of Advent & Christmas Activities. 96p. (Orig.). (ps up) 1984. pap. 13.95 (ISBN 0-86683-833-3, 8443). Harper SF.

Leet, Frank R. When Santa Was Late. Winfrey, Buford A., illus. 32p. (ps-4). 1990. 3.95 (ISBN 0-8249-8483-8). Ideals.

Leone, Dee. Christmas A-Z. 96p. (gr. 2-7). 1989. 9.95 (ISBN 0-86653-499-7, SS1892). Good Apple.

A Little Treasury of Christmas Classics, 4 bks. 1990. 8.95 (ISBN 0-8249-8484-6). Ideals.

Low, Alice, compiled by. The Family Read-Aloud Christmas Treasury. Brown, Marc, illus. (ps up). 1989. 17.95 (ISBN 0-316-53371-8, Joy St Bks). Little.

Mackall, Dandi D. Christmas Gifts That Didn't Need Wrapping. Mathers, Dawn, illus. LC 89-82553. 32p. (ps-2). 1990. pap. 4.95 (ISBN 0-8066-2466-3, 9-2466). Augsburg Fortress.

McKissack, Patricia & McKissack, Frederick. The Children's ABC Christmas. Rogers, Kathy, illus. LC 87-73525. (ps-6). 1988. pap. 4.95 (ISBN 0-8066-2356-X, 10-1046, Augsburg). Augsburg Fortress.

Moncure, Jane B. The Gift of Christmas. (ps-2). 1985. 5.95 (R4914). Standard Pub.

—Our Christmas Book. rev. ed. Stasiak, Krystyna & Connelly, Gwen, illus. LC 85-29132. 32p. (ps-3). 1986. lib. bdg. 11.97 (ISBN 0-89565-341-9). Childs World.

Moore, Clement C. The Night Before Christmas. Holt, Shirley, illus. 28p. 16.95 (ISBN 0-9613476-2-7). Shirlee.

—The Night Before Christmas. LC 89-42998. (Illus.). 80p. 1989. 4.95 (ISBN 0-89471-754-5). Running Pr.

—Tectonic History of the Bering Sea & the Evolution of Tertiary Strike-Slip Basins of the Bering Shelf. Wheeler, Jody, illus. 32p. (ps-2). 1991. 42.50 (ISBN 0-8249-8279-7); pap. 10.95 incl. wooden puzzle set (ISBN 0-8249-7269-4). Ideals.

My Big Christmas Book. 1988. 5.98 (ISBN 0-671-07565-9). S&S Trade.

My Christmas Present. (ps-k). 1990. bds. 3.95 (ISBN 0-7214-9128-6). Ladybird Bks.

My First Christmas Book. (ps-k). 1990. bds. 3.95 (ISBN 0-7214-9093-X). Ladybird Bks.

Ogilvy, Carol & Tinkham, Trudy. Classy Christmas Concerts. Renard, Jan, illus. 112p. (gr. k-7). 1986. wkbk. 8.95 (ISBN 0-86653-349-4, GA 795). Good Apple.

O'Leary, Sean C. Christmas Wonder: From Ireland - For Children: Craftwork, Lore, Poems, Songs & Stories. LC 89-50972. (Illus.). 98p. (Orig.). 1989. pap. 12.95 (ISBN 0-86278-177-9, Pub. by O'Brien Press Ltd Eire). Dufour.

Pepper, Dennis. The Oxford Merry Christmas Storybook. (Illus.). 160p. (gr. 1 up). 1990. jacketed 16.95 (ISBN 0-19-278127-8). Oxford U Pr.

Pienkowski, Jan, illus. Christmas. LC 84-5719. 32p. (ps-8). 1989. pap. 9.95 (ISBN 0-394-82609-4). Knopf.

Pistolesi, Roseanna. Let's Celebrate Christmas: A Book of Drawing Fun. Pistolesi, Roseanna, illus. LC 87-61376. 32p. (gr. 2-6). 1988. PLB 10.65 (ISBN 0-8167-1133-X); pap. text ed. 1.95 (ISBN 0-8167-1134-8). Troll Assocs.

Pomaska, Anna. The Little Christmas Activity Book. (ps up). 1988. pap. 1.00 (ISBN 0-486-25679-0). Dover.

Robbins, Ruth. Baboushka & the Three Kings. Sidjakov, Nicholas, illus. LC 60-15036. (ps up). 1960. 13.95 (ISBN 0-395-27673-X, Pub. by Parnassus). HM.

Roberts, Edward. Santa's Puzzle Bag. Hartelius, Margaret A., illus. 32p. (gr. k-3). 1987. pap. 1.50 (ISBN 0-590-40886-0). Scholastic Inc.

Santa Is Coming. (ps). 2.95 (ISBN 0-86112-229-1, Pub. by Brimax Bks). Borden.

Scarry, Patricia M. Sweet Smell of Christmas. Miller, J. P., illus. 32p. (ps-2). 1970. write for info. (ISBN 0-307-13527-6, Golden Bks). Western Pub.

A Sesame Street Christmas. 24p. (ps-3). 1987. pap. write for info. incl. cassette (ISBN 0-307-13997-2, Pub. by Golden Bks). Western Pub.

Simon, Mary M. A Silent Night: Hear Me Read Bible Stories Ser. (Illus.). 24p. (ps-1). 1991. pap. 1.99 (ISBN 0-570-04700-5, 56-1659). Concordia. A Silent Night, the story of Christmas, is one of four new titles in the Hear Me Read Series. There are 14 titles in this series, each one written by noted educator & author Dr. Mary Manz Simon. The Hear Me Read Bible story series is written especially for beginning readers ages 2 to 6, using proven, up-to-date theories about teaching children to read. Each story uses only 25 different words or less, creating a repetitive style that helps children expand their language skills & recognize more words on sight, thus building reader confidence. The simple vocabulary is repeated throughout the story & is listed on the back cover of each book. The books also feature colorful, playful illustrations that capture children's attention. 24pp. 4-color. Paperback. $1.99 each. Concordia Publishing House. Item no. 56-1659. ISBN 0-570-04700-5 To order--Call Toll Free 1-800-325-3040.
Publisher Provided Annotation.

Slawter, Linda. Christmas Activity Book. Slawter, Linda, illus. 32p. (gr. 3-6). 1982. pap. 1.98 (ISBN 0-88724-040-2, CD-8017). Carson-Dellos.

Smith, Elva S., compiled by. Christmas in Legend & Story: A Book for Boys & Girls Illustrated from Famous Paintings. Hazeltine, Alice I., compiled by. LC 72-39390. (gr. 7 up). Repr. of 1915 ed. 18.00 (ISBN 0-8369-6353-9). Ayer Co Pubs.
The Snowman Christmas Book. (Illus.). (ps-2). 1990. 1.95 (ISBN 0-7214-3202-6). Ladybird Bks.
Sparks, Judy, ed. Away in a Manger. Woggon, Bill, illus. 24p. (ps-2). 1985. 1.99 (ISBN 0-87239-871-4, 3671). Standard Pub.
Sullivan, Dianna. Christmas Activities from Around the World. Walhood, Darlene, illus. 48p. (gr. 1-4). 1985. wkbk. 5.95 (ISBN 1-55734-008-0). Tchr Create Mat.
Trent, Robbie. The First Christmas. rev. ed. Simont, Marc, illus. LC 89-29729. 32p. (ps-2). 1990. pap. 3.50 (ISBN 0-06-443249-1, Trophy). HarpC Child Bks.
Tudor, Tasha. Take Joy: The Tasha Tudor Christmas Book. Tudor, Tasha, illus. LC 66-10645. (gr. k up). 1980. 16.95 (ISBN 0-399-20766-X, Philomel); PLB 12.99 (ISBN 0-399-61169-X). Putnam Pub Group.
Vittitow, Mary L. & Liu, Sarah. Fun Things for Kids at Christmastime. Vittitow, Mary L., illus. 64p. (gr. 1-4). 1991. pap. 7.99 wkbk. (ISBN 0-87403-843-X, 28-03063). Standard Pub.
Waddell, Martin. Daisy's Christmas. Langley, Jonathan, illus. 24p. 1990. 11.95 (ISBN 0-8249-8440-4). Ideals.
Watson, Carol. My Little Christmas Box, 4 bks. (Illus.). 32p. (ps-3). 1990. Set. casebound 9.95 (ISBN 0-7459-1837-9). Lion USA.
Wever, Hinke B. Little Lights in the Darkness: Stories & Activities for Advent & Christmas. Vilain, Frederic, tr. from GER. Muller, Anna-Hermine, illus. 99p. (Orig.). 1990. pap. 9.95 (ISBN 0-8198-4444-6). Dghtrs St Paul.
The Whole Christmas Catalog for Kids. (Illus.). 160p. 1988. pap. 12.95 (ISBN 0-89586-742-7). Price Stern.
Willis, Ted. A Problem for Mother Christmas. Bennett, Jill, illus. 160p. (gr. 3-5). 15.95 (ISBN 0-575-03884-5, Pub. by Gollancz England). Trafalgar Sq.
Wilson, Robina B. Merry Christmas! Children at Christmastime Around the World. Ichikawa, Satomi, illus. LC 83-8027. 80p. (gr. k up). 1983. 12.95 (ISBN 0-399-20921-2, Philomel). Putnam Pub Group.
Wolf, Jill. The Story of Christmas. Rudegeair, Jean, illus. 24p. (gr. 3-7). 1986. pap. 2.25 (ISBN 0-89954-459-2). Antioch Pub Co.
Ziefert, Harriet. My Getting-Ready-for-Christmas Book. Smith, Mavis, illus. LC 90-55148. 12p. (ps-1). 1990. 13.95 (ISBN 0-06-107400-4). HarpC Child Bks.

CHRISTMAS–DRAMA

see Christmas Plays

CHRISTMAS–FICTION

Adams, Adrienne. The Christmas Party. Adams, Adrienne, illus. LC 78-16230. 32p. (ps-3). 1978. 13.95 (ISBN 0-684-15930-9, Scribners Young Read). Macmillan Child Grp.
Adams, Edith. Santa's Christmas Surprise. Sustendal, Pat, illus. LC 85-60216. 14p. (gr. 2-6). 1985. bds. 3.95 (ISBN 0-394-87538-9, Random Juv). Random.
Aloia, Gregory F. The Legend of the Golden Straw: A Christmas Story. (ps-4). 1989. 14.95 (ISBN 0-8294-0631-X). Loyola.
Ames, Mildred. Grandpa Jake & the Grand Christmas. LC 90-8527. 112p. (gr. 3-7). 1990. 12.95 (ISBN 0-684-19241-1, Scribners Young Read). Macmillan Child Grp.
Amstutz, Beverly. Too Big for the Bag. (Illus.). (gr. k-7). 1981. pap. 2.50x (ISBN 0-937836-05-2). Precious Res.
Anaya, Rudolfo A. The Farolitos of Christmas: A New Mexican Christmas Story. Sandoval, Richard C., illus. 32p. (Orig.). (gr. k-8). 1987. pap. 6.95 (ISBN 0-937206-06-7). New Mexico Mag.
Anderson, Debbie S. Daniel & the Sand Angel: A Florida Christmas Story. Broderick, Michael, illus. 32p. (Orig.). (ps-4). 1988. pap. 9.95 (ISBN 0-936417-11-0). Axelrod Pub.
Anglund, Joan W. A Christmas Book. (Illus.). 48p. (gr. k-3). 1983. lib. bdg. 7.99 (ISBN 0-394-95551-X). Random.
—Teddy Bear Tales. Anglund, Joan W., illus. LC 85-2238. 48p. (ps up). 1985. (Random Juv); lib. bdg. 7.99 (ISBN 0-394-97171-X, BYR). Random.
Aoki, Hisako. Santa's Favorite Story. 2nd ed. Gantschev, Ivan, illus. LC 82-60895. 28p. (gr. k up). 1990. Repr. of 1982 ed. 4.95 (ISBN 0-88708-153-3). Picture Bk Studio.
Aoki, Hisako & Gantschev, Ivan. Santa's Favorite Story. LC 82-60895. (Illus.). 28p. (ps up). 1982. 14.95 (ISBN 0-907234-16-X). Picture Bk Studio.
Arico, Diane, ed. A Season of Joy: Favorite Stories & Poems for Christmas. San Souci, Daniel, illus. LC 86-29059. 64p. (gr. k-3). 1987. pap. 8.95 (ISBN 0-385-23901-7). Doubleday.
Armstrong, Beverly. Christmas Capers. (Illus.). 24p. (gr. 2-6). 1987. 4.95 (ISBN 0-88160-151-9, LW264). Learning Wks.
Atcheson, Marguerite. Mouse Who Didn't Believe. Atcheson, Marguerite, illus. Davenport, May, intro. by. LC 80-69472. (Illus.). 60p. (Orig.). (gr. k-3). 1980. pap. 1.50x (ISBN 0-9603118-6-6). Davenport.
Awiakta, Marilou. Rising Fawn & the Fire Mystery. Bringle, Beverly, illus. Easson, Roger R., ed. LC 83-13824. (Illus.). 48p. (Orig.). (gr. 5 up). 1984. lib. bdg. 9.95 (ISBN 0-918518-35-0); pap. 6.95 (ISBN 0-918518-29-6). St Lukes Pr.
Bahr, Howard. Home for Christmas: A Child Christmas in the South, Vol. V. (Illus.). 48p. (gr. 5-8). 1987. 9.95 (ISBN 0-918518-51-2). St LUkes Pr.
Bailey, Bobbi M. The Christmas Tree That Cried. Bailey, Mark, ed. Seamon, Omer D., illus. 30p. 11.95; pap. 3.95. Wee Pr.
Baird, Anne. The Christmas Lamb. Baird, Anne, illus. LC 88-5137. 32p. (ps-2). 1989. 12.95 (ISBN 0-688-07774-9); PLB 12.88 (ISBN 0-688-07775-7, Morrow Jr Bks). Morrow Jr Bks.
Barkan, Joanne. The Christmas Toy. Di Fiori, Lawrence, illus. 48p. (gr. k-3). 1987. pap. 3.95 (ISBN 0-685-18381-5). Scholastic Inc.
—Christmas Toy. 1987. pap. 3.95 (ISBN 0-590-40892-5). Scholastic Inc.
Baron-Hall, Daria. Only at the Children's Table. Benton, Mahan, illus. (gr. 2-4). 1988. 16.67 (ISBN 0-318-41753-7). Raintree Pubs.
Baum, L. Frank. The Life & Adventures of Santa Claus. (gr. 2-6). 1985. 4.98 (ISBN 0-517-42062-7). Outlet Bk Co.
—Life & Adventures of Santa Claus. 160p. 1986. pap. 2.25 (ISBN 0-451-52064-5, Sig Classics). NAL-Dutton.
Beachy, J. Wayne. The Extraordinary Ordinary Christmas Matoaca, 1870. Hawkins, Beverly, illus. 20p. (Orig.). (gr. 5). 1984. pap. 2.50 (ISBN 0-9608084-2-6). B Hawkins Studio.
Bedford, Annie N. Frosty the Snowman. Malvern, Corinne, illus. 24p. (ps-1). 1985. Repr. of 1951 ed. write for info. (ISBN 0-307-10201-7, Pub. by Golden Bks). Western Pub.
Bemelmans, Ludwig. Madeline's Christmas. LC 85-40092. (Illus.). 32p. (ps-3). 1985. pap. 13.95 (ISBN 0-670-80666-8). Viking Child Bks.
—Madeline's Christmas. (ps-3). 1988. pap. 3.95 (ISBN 0-14-050666-7, Puffin). Puffin Bks.
Benjamin, Alan. Dear Santa. Woodward, Theresa, illus. & (ps). 1986. pap. 2.95 (ISBN 0-671-62919-0, Little Simon). S&S Trade.
Benteen, John. Los Invasores Apaches. De Villa, Alvaro, tr. from ENG. (SPA.). 160p. 1974. pap. 0.85 (ISBN 0-88473-514-1). Fiesta Pub.
Berenstain, Michael. Peat Moss & Ivy Meet Santa Claus. Berenstain, Michael, illus. LC 86-22029. 32p. (ps-1). 1987. pap. 1.95 (ISBN 0-394-88872-3, Random Juv). Random.
Berenstain, Stan & Berenstain, Janice. The Berenstain Bears' Christmas Tree. LC 80-5087. (Illus.). 72p. (ps-3). 1980. 10.95 (ISBN 0-394-84566-8); lib. bdg. 9.99 (ISBN 0-394-94566-2). Random.
Birenbaum, Barbara. The Lighthouse Christmas. Birenbaum, Barbara & Sapp, Patt, illus. LC 90-7284. 48p. (Orig.). (gr. k-5). 1991. lib. bdg. 8.95 (ISBN 0-935343-25-3); pap. 5.95. Peartree.
Bivens, Christopher, illus. The Perfect Tree & Favorite Christmas Carols. Ingram, John W., ed. Bivins, Christopher, illus. LC 90-34514. 48p. (ps-2). 1990. 4.95 (ISBN 0-88101-104-5). Unicorn Pub.
Black, Auguste R. The Year That Santa Goofed & Other Short Stories. Sherentz, Michael & Horton, Terri, illus. 22p. (Orig.). (gr. 1-5). 1990. pap. 2.95 (ISBN 0-9628010-2-X). A R Black.
Blyton, Enid. Christmas in the Toy Shop. (ps up). 1990. 4.98 (ISBN 0-8317-1291-0). Smithmark.
Bokich, Obren. Christmas Card for Mr. McFizz. (Illus.). 40p. (gr. k-6). 1987. 11.95 (ISBN 0-88138-097-0). Green Tiger Pr.
Bolte, Carl E., Jr. Elvin: The Little Black Elf. Turner, Vernon K., ed. LC 87-28960. 150p. (Orig.). 1988. pap. 8.95 (ISBN 0-89865-554-4). Donning Co.
Bonsall, Crosby. Twelve Bells for Santa. Bonsall, Crosby, illus. LC 76-58714. 64p. (ps-3). 1985. pap. 3.50 (ISBN 0-06-444086-9, Trophy). HarpC Child Bks.
Bonsall, Crosby N. Twelve Bells for Santa. Bonsall, Crosby N., illus. LC 76-58714. 64p. (ps-3). 1977. PLB 11.89 (ISBN 0-06-020582-2). HarpC Child Bks.
Bracken, Carolyn, illus. Santa's Pockets. (ps). 1983. pap. 3.95 (ISBN 0-671-47660-2, Little Simon). S&S Trade.
Brett, Jan. The Wild Christmas Reindeer. Brett, Jan, illus. 32p. (ps-3). 1990. 14.95 (ISBN 0-399-22192-1, Putnam). Putnam Pub Group.
Bridwell, Norman. Clifford's Christmas. Bridwell, Norman, illus. (gr. k-3). 1984. pap. 1.95 (ISBN 0-590-40221-8). Scholastic Inc.
Briggs, Raymond. Father Christmas Goes on Holiday. LC 77-1980. (Illus.). 32p. (gr. k-3). 1977. pap. 3.95 (ISBN 0-14-050187-8, Puffin). Puffin Bks.
Britt, Stephanie, illus. Jingle Bells. 24p. (ps-1). 1988. pap. 2.95 (ISBN 0-8249-8249-5). Ideals.
Broger, Achim, retold by. The Santa Clauses. Krause, Ute, illus. LC 86-2147. 28p. (ps-3). 1986. 11.95 (ISBN 0-8037-0266-3). Dial Bks Young.
—The Santa Clauses. Krause, Ute, illus. LC 86-2147. 28p. (ps-3). 1988. pap. 3.95 (ISBN 0-8037-0557-3). Dial Bks Young.
Brooke, Roger. Santa's Christmas Journey. LC 84-9796. (Illus.). 32p. (gr. k-5). 1984. PLB 16.67 (ISBN 0-8172-2116-6); PLB 27.99 incl. cassette (ISBN 0-8172-2244-8); pap. 9.27 (ISBN 0-8172-2259-6); pap. 23.95 incl. cassette (ISBN 0-8172-2269-3); cassette 14.00 (ISBN 0-685-08347-0). Raintree Pubs.
Brown, Marc. Arthur's Christmas. Brown, Marc, illus. LC 84-4373. (ps-3). 1985. 14.95 (ISBN 0-316-11180-5, Joy St Bks); pap. 4.95 (ISBN 0-316-10993-2). Little.
Brown, Margaret W. Christmas in the Barn. Cooney, Barbara, illus. LC 52-7858. 32p. (gr. k-3). 1961. PLB 13.89 (ISBN 0-690-19272-X, Crowell Jr Bks); PLB 12.89 (ISBN 0-685-04855-1). HarpC Child Bks.
—On Christmas Eve. Montresor, Beni, illus. LC 84-43129. 1985. PLB 12.89 (ISBN 0-06-020764-7). HarpC Child Bks.
Brown, Michael. Santa Mouse. De Witt, Elfrieda, illus. (gr. k-3). 1966. 4.95 (ISBN 0-448-04213-4, G&D); PLB 3.09 (ISBN 0-448-13914-6). Putnam Pub Group.
Bruni, Mary A. Rosita's Christmas Wish. Ricks, Thom, illus. LC 85-52040. 48p. (gr. k-8). 1985. 13.95 (ISBN 0-935857-00-1); ltd. ed. 125.00 (ISBN 0-935857-03-6); write for info. (ISBN 0-935857-09-5); pap. write for info. (ISBN 0-935857-01-X); pap. write for info. (ISBN 0-935857-10-9). Texart.
Bruni, Mary-Ann S. El Sueno de Rosita. De Castro, Rogelio, tr. from ENG. Ricks, Thom, illus. (SPA.). 48p. (gr. k-8). 1987. 13.95 (ISBN 0-935857-02-8); pap. write for info. (ISBN 0-935857-04-4) (ISBN 0-935857-11-7) (ISBN 0-935857-12-5). Texart.
Bryant, Bonnie. Starlight Christmas. (gr. 4-7). 1990. pap. 2.75 (ISBN 0-553-15832-5). Bantam.
Burch, Robert. Christmas with Ida Early. LC 83-5792. 144p. (gr. 3-7). 1983. pap. 12.95 (ISBN 0-670-22131-7). Viking Child Bks.
—Christmas with Ida Early. LC 85-5680. 158p. (gr. 3-7). 1985. pap. 3.95 (ISBN 0-14-031971-9, Puffin). Puffin Bks.
Bures, Ruth A. Here Comes Christmas. 40p. (gr. k-8). 1982. pap. 10.95 (ISBN 0-86704-008-4). Clarus Music.
Buscaglia, Leo F. Seven Stories of Christmas Love. Newsom, Tom, illus. 110p. 1987. 12.95 (ISBN 0-688-07521-5). Slack Inc.
Bush, John. Christmas Fox & Other Winter. 1989. 11.95 (ISBN 0-8037-0723-1). Dial Bks Young.
Capek, Jindra. A Child Is Born. Capek, Jindra, illus. (gr. 5 up). 1987. 12.95 (ISBN 1-55774-007-0, Dist. by Watts). Adama Pubs Inc.
Capote, Truman. A Christmas Memory. Delessert, Etienne, illus. 40p. (gr. 4 up). 1984. PLB 10.95s.p. (ISBN 0-87191-956-7); 15.65 (ISBN 0-685-07722-5). Creative Ed.
—A Christmas Memory. Holm, Celeste, narrated by. Peck, Beth, illus. LC 88-36452. 48p. (gr. 1 up). 1989. incl. cassette 19.95 (ISBN 0-685-32903-8); 12.95 (ISBN 0-685-32904-6). McKay.
Carey, Karla. Julie & Jackie at Christmas-Time: The Narration & Music Book. Nolan, Dennis, illus. 69p. 1990. pap. 18.95 complete pkg. (ISBN 0-685-35761-9); pap. 9.95 (ISBN 1-55768-201-1); cassette 9.95 (ISBN 0-685-35762-7). LC Pub.
Carlson, Anna L. The Mouse Family's Christmas. 1st. ed. (Illus.). 24p. (Orig.). (gr. k-4). 1983. pap. 1.95 (ISBN 0-939938-04-9). Karwyn Ent.
Carrier, Lark. A Christmas Promise. LC 86-12356. (Illus.). 36p. (ps up). 1986. 15.95 (ISBN 0-88708-032-4). Picture Bk Studio.
Cartlidge, Michelle. Teddy's Christmas. Cartlidge, Michelle, illus. 32p. (ps). 1986. pap. 9.95 (ISBN 0-671-62912-3, Little Simon). S&S Trade.
Carty, Margaret F. Christmas in Vermont: Three Stories. Langley, Marilynn, illus. LC 83-62750. 48p. (Orig.). (gr. 5 up). 1983. pap. 2.95 (ISBN 0-933050-21-6). New Eng Pr VT.
Caudill, Rebecca. Certain Small Shepherd. Pene Du Bois, William, illus. LC 65-17604. 48p. (gr. 2-6). 1965. reinforced bdg. 14.95 (ISBN 0-8050-1323-7). H Holt & Co.
Cavendish, Maxwell P. The True Story of Christmas. LeBaudour, RoseMarie, illus. 56p. (Orig.). 1991. pap. 15.00 (ISBN 0-9628016-2-3). Gentian Servs.
Cazet, Denys. Christmas Moon. Cazet, Denys, illus. LC 84-10969. 32p. (ps-2). 1984. 12.95 (ISBN 0-02-717810-2, Bradbury Pr). Macmillan Child Grp.
Chalmers, Mary. A Christmas Story. Chalmers, Mary, illus. LC 56-8143. 24p. (ps-1). 1962. Repr. of 1956 ed. 11.95 (ISBN 0-06-021190-3); PLB 11.89 (ISBN 0-06-021191-1). HarpC Child Bks.
Chartier, Normand, illus. Jingle Bells. bds. 3.95 (ISBN 0-685-29549-4). S&S Trade.
Cheney, Cora. The Christmas Tree Hessian. Price, Edith B., illus. 151p. (gr. 4-6). 1976. pap. 3.95 (ISBN 0-914378-10-4). Countryman.
A Christmas Carol. (gr. 2 up). 1988. pap. 4.87 (ISBN 0-582-01382-8, 70415). Longman.
A Christmas Carol. (Illus.). (gr. 3-5). 3.50 (ISBN 0-7214-0745-5). Ladybird Bks.
A Christmas Story. LC 78-66026. (gr. 4 up). 1978. 4.95 (ISBN 0-934038-00-7). Perish Pr.
Chwast, Seymour. The Little Theater Presents a Christmas Carol. Weaver, Dan, adapted by. Chwast, Seymour, illus. 1986. pap. 15.95 (ISBN 0-670-81033-9). Viking Child Bks.
Ciaravino, John. A Christmas Dream. LC 88-51890. (Illus.). 44p. (gr. k-3). 1989. 5.95 (ISBN 1-55523-215-9). Winston-Derek.
Civardi, Annie. The Secrets of Santa. Scruton, Clive, illus. LC 91-130. 32p. (ps-1). 1991. bds. 13.95 jacketed (ISBN 0-671-74270-1, S&S BYR). S&S Trade.
Clemons, Jack. Gruesome John Frederick: A Tale of Christmas. Hamel, Tom, illus. LC 87-71713. 73p. (Orig.). (gr. 4-5). 1988. pap. 6.00 (ISBN 0-916383-30-X). Aegina Pr.
Clifton, Lucille. Everett Anderson's Christmas Coming. Gilchrist, Jan S., illus. LC 91-2041. 32p. (ps-4). 1991. 14.95 (ISBN 0-8050-1549-3). H Holt & Co.
Climo, Shirley. Cobweb Christmas. Lasker, Joe, illus. LC 81-43879. 32p. (ps-3). 1982. 13.95 (ISBN 0-690-04215-9, Crowell Jr Bks); PLB 13.89 (ISBN 0-690-04216-7). HarpC Child Bks.

Codor, Dick & Teitelbaum, Michael. Follow that Sleigh: The Reindeer Who Saved Christmas. Oren, Rony, contrib. by. (Illus.). (gr. k-5). 1990. 9.95 (ISBN 0-944007-51-1). Shapolsky Pubs.

Cohen, Barbara. The Christmas Revolution. De Groat, Diane, illus. LC 86-21340. 96p. (gr. 3-6). 1987. 12.95 (ISBN 0-688-06806-5). Lothrop.

Collington, Peter. On Christmas Eve. Collington, Peter, illus. LC 90-4202. 32p. 1990. 14.95 (ISBN 0-679-80830-2); PLB 15.99 (ISBN 0-679-90830-7). Knopf.

Coltharp, Barbara. Colonel Neverfail's Christmas. Sandifer, Shannon & Woolfolk, Doug, eds. Turner, James, illus. (Orig.). (gr. 1-3). 1981. 7.95 (ISBN 0-86518-019-9). Moran Pub Corp.

Connolly, Brian A. Bradley's Christmas Adventure. Diamanti, Gina, illus. 38p. (Orig.). (gr. 1-6). 1989. pap. 7.95 (ISBN 0-9624282-0-5). Steele Hollow.

Cooley, Regina F. The Magic Christmas Pony. Hansen, Han H., illus. 36p. (gr. 1-5). 1991. 19.95 (ISBN 1-880450-04-6). Capstone Pub.
A carousel pony mysteriously disappears in the night, magically reappearing on Christmas Eve in the doorway of Frederick & Valentina's bedroom. With grandparents sleeping unaware in the next room, the Magic Christmas Pony whisks the mystified children to the Forbidden City in China. There they meet the Dragon of Fantasy, a close friend of the Magic Christmas Pony, & enjoy a Dragon banquet. After dining with the many Dragons, their adventure continues. They meet the Emperor & Empress of China & are further entranced by traditional Chinese dances & entertainment. Frederick & Valentina's exposure to the culture & traditions of the Chinese royalty becomes educational as well as entertaining. The Forbidden City comes to life with the rich detail provided by Regina Francoise Cooley, the author, whose thorough research lends a realistic backdrop to this enchanting tale. Hans Henrik Hansen, a well known illustrator from Denmark, has established his reputation in the plate collecting world with collectors plates from both Bing & Grondahl & Royal Copenhagen. His unique use of brilliant saturated color & superb detail has created a book worthy of being called a collectors item. Capstone Publishing Inc. is proud to present this mesmerizing & timeless story.
Publisher Provided Annotation.

Cooper, Susan. The Dark Is Rising. Cober, Alan, illus. LC 72-85916. 232p. (gr. 5 up). 1973. 14.95 (ISBN 0-689-30317-3, M K McElderry). Macmillan Child Grp.

Corrin, Sara & Corrin, Stephen, eds. The Faber Book of Christmas Stories. Bennet, Jill, illus. LC 84-13552. 150p. (gr. 3-7). 1984. pap. 9.95 (ISBN 0-571-13348-7). Faber & Faber.

Corrin, Sarah & Corrin, Stephen, eds. Round the Christmas Tree. (gr. 3-7). pap. 3.95 (ISBN 0-317-62263-3, Puffin). Puffin Bks.

Cosgrove, Stephen. Prancer. Heyer, Carol, illus. LC 89-83843. 32p. (gr. k-7). 1990. 14.95 (ISBN 0-685-27179-X); pap. 5.95 (ISBN 1-55868-020-9); pap. 12.95 incl. audio (ISBN 1-55868-041-1). Gr Arts Ctr Pub.
Stephen Cosgrove, master lecturer & storyteller, narrates the audio cassette which accompanies the softcover edition of PRANCER. The original music score enriches this twenty-two minute spellbinding audio tape that brings the magic of PRANCER to life.
Publisher Provided Annotation.

Cothen, Joe. Come to Bethlehem: The Christmas Story. Seago, Robert, illus. LC 75-25503. 64p. (gr. 4 up). 1975. 6.95 (ISBN 0-88289-098-0). Pelican.

Crabtree, Cathy L. & Fowler, Joanne. Poor Me & the Magic of Christmas. rev. ed. Sanor, Peggy, illus. LC 89-84463. 20p. (gr. 2-3). 1989. pap. text ed. 5.95 (ISBN 0-9622719-0-X). Lavender Pr.

Craig, Janet. Little Christmas Star. Miller, Susan, illus. LC 87-10936. 32p. (gr. k-2). 1988. PLB 10.89 (ISBN 0-8167-1097-X); pap. text ed. 2.95 (ISBN 0-8167-1098-8). Troll Assocs.

Crespi, Francesca, illus. Santa Claus Is Coming! 8p. (ps-k). 1987. 3.95 (ISBN 0-8050-0472-6). H Holt & Co.

—Silent Night. 8p. (ps-k). 1987. 3.95 (ISBN 0-8050-0471-8). H Holt & Co.

Crump, Patricia. Jesus' Stocking. Thomas, Ira, illus. 1990. 2.95 (ISBN 0-8091-6591-0). Paulist Pr.

Cruz, Manuel & Cruz, Ruth. A Chicano Christmas Story. Cruz, Manuel, illus. LC 80-69444. (SPA.). 48p. (Orig.). (ps-5). 1981. pap. text ed. 3.95 (ISBN 0-86624-000-4, RM7). Bilingual Ed Serv.

Curtin, Michael. The League Against Christmas. 256p. 1990. 21.95 (ISBN 0-233-98382-1, Pub. by A Deutsch England). Trafalgar Sq.

Daniel, Mark, compiled by. Child's Christmas Treasury. LC 87-36527. (Illus.). 112p. (ps up). 1988. 15.95 (ISBN 0-8037-0484-4). Dial Bks Young.

Davidson, Amanda. Teddy's Christmas Cut-Out. (gr. 4-7). 1990. pap. 2.50 (ISBN 0-8167-2197-1). Troll Assocs.

—Teddy's Countdown to Christmas. (gr. 4-7). 1990. pap. 2.50 (ISBN 0-8167-2198-X). Troll Assocs.

—Teddy's First Christmas. Davidson, Amanda, illus. LC 82-82092. 24p. (ps-2). 1982. 7.95 (ISBN 0-03-062616-1). H Holt & Co.

Davies, Valentine. Miracle on Thirty-Fourth Street. De Paola, Tomie, illus. (gr. k up). 1984. 16.95 (ISBN 0-15-254526-3, HJ). HarBraceJ.

Day, Alexandra. Carl's Christmas. Day, Alexandra, illus. 32p. 1990. bds. 11.95 (ISBN 0-374-31114-5). FS&G.

De Brunhoff, Jean. Babar & Father Christmas. De Brunhoff, Jean, illus. 40p. (gr. k-3). 1987. 16.95 (ISBN 0-394-89265-8, Random Juv). Random.

Delamare, David. The Christmas Secret. (Illus.). 40p. (ps-2). 1991. jacketed, reinforced bdg. 15.00 (ISBN 0-671-74822-X, Green Tiger). S&S Trade.

Delton, Judy. No Time for Christmas. Mitchell, Anastasia, illus. 48p. (gr. k-4). 1988. PLB 9.95 (ISBN 0-87614-327-3); pap. 4.95 (ISBN 0-87614-503-9). Carolrhoda Bks.

—A Pee Wee Christmas. 80p. (Orig.). (gr. k-6). 1988. pap. 2.75 (ISBN 0-440-40067-8, YB). Dell.

Demi. Demi's Christmas Surprise. (Illus.). 10p. 1990. 4.95 (ISBN 0-448-19167-9, G&D). Putnam Pub Group.

Denton, Kady M. Christmas Boot. (ps). 1990. 12.95 (ISBN 0-316-18091-2). Little.

Denver, John. Alfie the Christmas Tree. Robinson, Howard, ed. Pidgeon, Jean, illus. LC 90-36184. 24p. 1990. 11.95 (ISBN 0-945051-25-5, 19427). Natl Wildlife.

DePaola, Tomie. An Early American Christmas. DePaola, Tomie, illus. LC 86-3102. 32p. (gr. k-3). 1987. reinforced bdg. 14.95 (ISBN 0-8234-0617-2). Holiday.

De Paola, Tomie. The First Christmas. (Illus.). 6p. (ps-1). 1984. 13.95 (ISBN 0-399-21070-9, Putnam). Putnam Pub Group.

DePaola, Tomie. Merry Christmas, Strega Nona. DePaola, Tomie, illus. LC 86-4639. 32p. (ps-3). 1986. 14.95 (ISBN 0-15-253183-1, HJ). HarBraceJ.

—Merry Christmas, Strega Nona. DePaola, Tomie, illus. 96p. (gr. k-3). 1986. pap. 12.95 (ISBN 0-318-37359-9, VoyB). HarBraceJ.

Devlin, Wende & Devlin, Harry. Cranberry Christmas. Devlin, Harry, illus. LC 80-16971. 40p. (ps-3). 1984. Repr. of 1976 ed. 13.95 (ISBN 0-02-729900-7, Four Winds). Macmillan Child Grp.

Dewoody, Darrel W. & Dewoody, Betty N. C. T. the Living Christmas Tree. Plunkett, Kathleen, illus. (gr. k-6). 1989. write for info. Old Amer Pr.

Dickens, Charles. Charles Dickens' A Christmas Carol. Richardson, I. M., ed. Kendall, Jane F., illus. LC 87-11270. 32p. (gr. 2-6). 1988. PLB 9.79 (ISBN 0-8167-1053-8); pap. text ed. 1.95 (ISBN 0-8167-1054-6). Troll Assocs.

—Christmas Books. Glancy, Ruth, intro. by. 520p. 1989. pap. 7.95 (ISBN 0-19-281790-6). Oxford U Pr.

—Christmas Carol. LC 85-15815. (gr. 7 up). pap. 2.50 (ISBN 0-8049-0026-4, CL-26). Airmont.

—A Christmas Carol. LC 85-15815. 191p. 1981. Repr. PLB 15.95x (ISBN 0-89966-344-3). Buccaneer Bks.

—A Christmas Carol. LC 85-15815. 150p. 1980. Repr. PLB 13.95x (ISBN 0-89967-017-2). Harmony Raine.

—A Christmas Carol. Foreman, Michael, illus. LC 85-15815. 128p. (gr. 6). 1983. 12.95 (ISBN 0-8037-0032-6). Dial Bks Young.

—A Christmas Carol. Imsand, Marcel, illus. LC 85-15815. 78p. (gr. 4 up). 1984. PLB 10.95s.p. (ISBN 0-87191-955-9); 15.65 (ISBN 0-685-07723-3). Creative Ed.

—A Christmas Carol. LC 85-15815. 240p. (gr. 5 up). 1983. pap. 2.95 (ISBN 0-671-47369-7, WSP). PB.

—A Christmas Carol. Kennedy, Pam, ed. Flint, Russ, illus. 32p. (gr. k-6). 1985. pap. 2.95 (ISBN 0-8249-8099-9). Ideals.

—A Christmas Carol. Cole, Michael, illus. LC 85-15815. 80p. (ps up). 1985. 14.95 (ISBN 0-8120-5705-8). Barron.

—A Christmas Carol. (gr. 4-6). 1986. pap. 1.95 (ISBN 0-590-02102-8). Scholastic Inc.

—A Christmas Carol. Zwerger, Lisbeth, illus. LC 88-15161. 60p. (gr. 5 up). 1988. 19.95 (ISBN 0-88708-069-3). Picture Bk Studio.

—A Christmas Carol. Innocenti, Roberto, illus. LC 90-1335. 152p. 1990. 30.00 (ISBN 1-55670-161-6). Stewart Tabori & Chang.

—A Christmas Carol. abr. ed. Cook, Scott, illus. LC 89-24076. 72p. (gr. 2 up). 1990. 14.95 (ISBN 0-394-82239-0); PLB 15.99 (ISBN 0-394-92239-5). Random.

—A Christmas Carol. Rice, James, illus. & retold by. 48p. 13.95 (ISBN 0-88289-812-4). Pelican.

—A Christmas Carol. 128p. (gr. 4-7). 1987. pap. 2.75 (ISBN 0-590-43527-2). Scholastic Inc.

—Christmas Carol. 1990. pap. 3.75 (ISBN 0-425-12334-0). Berkley Pub.

—Christmas Carol. Sturrock, Walt, illus. 1990. 11.95 (ISBN 0-88101-108-8). Unicorn Pub.

—A Christmas Carol. 1990. pap. 2.50 (ISBN 0-8125-0434-8). Tor Bks.

—A Christmas Carol. Boddy, Joe, illus. LC 91-9054. 48p. (ps-2). 1991. Animal version. 4.95 (ISBN 0-88101-160-6). Unicorn Pub.

—A Christmas Carol: Retold by A. Sweaney. (gr. k-6). 1975. pap. text ed. 4.25x (ISBN 0-19-580724-3). Oxford U Pr.

—Christmas Tales from Dickens. 1990. pap. 5.98 (ISBN 0-8317-1296-1). Smithmark.

—Mickey's Christmas Carol. Disney Studio Staff, ed. LC 84-9491. (Illus.). (gr. k up). 1984. pap. 5.95 (ISBN 0-517-55525-5). Crown.

Dicks, Terrance. Goliath's Christmas. Littlewood, Valerie, illus. 64p. (gr. 2-4). 1987. PLB 7.95 (ISBN 0-8120-5843-7); pap. 2.95 (ISBN 0-8120-3878-9). Barron.

Dinardo, Jeffrey. Timothy & the Christmas Gift. 1989. pap. 12.95 (ISBN 0-671-67959-7). S&S Trade.

Dr. Seuss. How the Grinch Stole Christmas. Dr. Seuss, illus. (gr. k-3). 1957. 8.95 (ISBN 0-394-80079-6, Random Juv); PLB 7.99 (ISBN 0-394-90079-0). Random.

—How the Grinch Stole Christmas! Dr. Seuss, illus. Matthau, Walter, contrib. by. (Illus.). 64p. (ps-1). 1988. pap. 9.95 bk. & cassette pkg. (ISBN 0-394-81339-1, Random Juv). Random.

Duvoisin, Roger. Petunia's Christmas. Duvoisin, Roger, illus. (gr. k-3). 1963. lib. bdg. 12.99 (ISBN 0-394-90868-6). Knopf.

—Petunia's Christmas. Duvoisin, Roger, illus. LC 53-6391. (ps-2). 1990. pap. 4.95 (ISBN 0-679-80696-2, Dragonfly Bks). Knopf.

Edens, Coope. Santa Cows. Lane, Daniel, illus. 40p. (gr. 2 up). 1991. jacketed, reinforced bdg. 14.00 (ISBN 0-671-74863-7, Green Tiger). S&S Trade.

Edler, Timothy J. Crawfish-Man's Night Befo' Christmas. (Illus.). 40p. (gr. k-8). 1984. pap. 10.00 (ISBN 0-931108-12-8). Little Cajun Bks.

—Santa's Cajun Christmas Adventure. (Illus.). 48p. (gr. k-8). 1981. pap. 6.00 (ISBN 0-931108-07-1). Little Cajun Bks.

Eisen, Armand, ed. The Classic Christmas Treasury for Children. LC 89-43004. (Illus.). 56p. (gr. 3 up). 1990. 9.98 (ISBN 0-89471-769-3, Courage Bks). Running Pr.

Enright, Elizabeth. A Christmas Tree for Lydia. Zimdars, Berta, illus. 32p. (gr. 4 up). 1986. PLB 10.45s.p. (ISBN 0-88682-063-4); 14.95 (ISBN 0-685-12423-1). Creative Ed.

Ets, Marie H. & Labastida, Aurora. Nine Days to Christmas. Ets, Marie H., illus. (ps-2). 1959. pap. 13.95 (ISBN 0-670-51350-4). Viking Child Bks.

Fass, Bernie & Wolfson, Mack. Christmas on Main Street. 48p. (gr. 3-12). 1986. pap. 15.95 (ISBN 0-86704-036-X); student bk. 2.95 (ISBN 0-86704-037-8). Clarus Music.

Fisher, Barbara. Philpin's Tree. (Illus.). 12p. (Orig.). (gr. 1-3). 1977. pap. 2.00 (ISBN 0-934830-00-2). Ten Penny.

Fisher, Nell. A Handbell for Hans. 1990. 2.95 (ISBN 0-8378-1885-0). Gibson.

—My Brother's Drum. 1990. 2.95 (ISBN 0-8378-1886-9). Gibson.

Fleming, Denise, illus. The Merry Christmas Book: A First Book of Holiday Stories & Poems. LC 86-3258. 48p. (gr. 3-8). 1986. (Random Juv); (Random Juv). Random.

Folmer, A. P. Barnabys First Christmas. 1989. pap. 5.95 (ISBN 0-590-42892-6). Scholastic Inc.

Franceschelli, Christopher. The First Christmas. 1990. 13.95 (ISBN 0-525-44606-0, DCB). Dutton Child Bks.

Frosty the Snowman. 24p. (ps-3). 1987. pap. write for info incl. cassette (ISBN 0-307-13994-8, Pub. by Golden Bks). Western Pub.

Fujikawa, Gyo. The Night Before Christmas. (Illus.). 24p. (ps-3). 1980. pap. 1.25 (ISBN 0-448-49619-4, G&D). Putnam Pub Group.

Funakoshi, Canna. One Christmas. Izawa, Yohji, illus. LC 90-7445. 40p. (gr. k up). 1990. 12.95 (ISBN 0-88708-140-1). Picture Bk Studio.

Gammell, Stephen. Wake up, Bear...It's Christmas! Gammell, Stephen, illus. LC 81-5019. 32p. (ps-3). 1981. PLB 12.88 (ISBN 0-688-00693-0). Lothrop.

Gantschev, Ivan. The Christmas Train. Gantschev, Ivan, illus. (ps-3). 1984. 13.95 (ISBN 0-316-30346-1). Little.

Gardam, Catharine. The Animals' Christmas. Rowe, Gavin, illus. LC 90-5538. 32p. (gr. k-4). 1990. 13.95 (ISBN 0-689-50502-7, M K McElderry). Macmillan Child Grp.

Gebhardt, Catherine. A Perfect Christmas for Kate Leary. LC 90-70222. 44p. (gr. k-3). 1990. pap. 4.95 (ISBN 1-55523-331-7). Winston-Derek.

Gilcow, Louise. Baby Kermit's Christmas. 1988. write for info. (ISBN 0-02-689160-3). Checkerboard Pr.
Gimbel, Cheryl. Why Does Santa Celebrate Christmas? Lovelady, J., ed. Maners, Wendelin, illus. 36p. (gr. k up). 1990. 12.95 (ISBN 0-915190-67-2, JP9067-2). Jalmar Pr.
Gitkow, Louise. The Christmas Toy. DiSori, Lawrence, illus. (gr. k up). 1987. 12.95 (ISBN 0-685-18060-3, Scholastic Hardcover). Scholastic Inc.
Glovach, Linda. The Little Witch's Christmas Book. Glovach, Linda, illus. 48p. (gr. 1-4). 1982. pap. 4.95 (ISBN 0-13-538090-1, Pub. by Treehouse). P-H.
Godden, Rumer. The Story of Holly & Ivy. Cooney, Barbara, illus. LC 84-25799. 32p. (ps-5). 1985. pap. 13.95 (ISBN 0-670-80622-6). Viking Child Bks.
Gondosch, Linda. Who's Afraid of Haggerty House? LC 86-24265. (gr. 4-6). 1987. 11.95 (ISBN 0-525-67198-6, Lodestar Bks). Dutton Child Bks.
—Who's Afraid of Haggerty House. 1989. pap. 2.75 (ISBN 0-671-67237-1, Minstrel Bks). PB.
Gordon, Shirley. Crystal's Christmas Carol. Frascino, Edward, illus. LC 87-33487. 40p. (gr. k-3). 1989. 12. 95 (ISBN 0-06-022127-5); PLB 12.89 (ISBN 0-06-022239-5). HarpC Child Bks.
Goudge, Eileen. Hawaiian Christmas. (gr. 6 up). 1986. pap. 2.95 (ISBN 0-440-93649-7, LFL). Dell.
Grahame, Kenneth. Mole's Christmas: Or Home Sweet Home. Gooding, Beverly, illus. LC 82-12333. 32p. (gr. k-3). 1983. 10.95 (ISBN 0-13-599738-0). P-H.
Grambling, Lois G. Elephant & Mouse Get Ready for Christmas. Maze, Deborah, illus. 32p. 1990. with dust jacket 12.95 (ISBN 0-8120-6185-3). Barron.
Green, Michelle Y. Willie Pearl. Date not set. write for info (ISBN 0-9627697-0-3). W Ruth Co.
Greenberg, Kenneth R. The Adventures of Tusky & His Friends: A Christmas Mystery. Pearson, Allison K., illus. 64p. (gr. k-4). 1991. PLB 14.95 (ISBN 1-879100-01-0). Tusky Enterprises.
Haas, Dorothy. Bears Upstairs. 1989. pap. 2.75 (ISBN 0-590-42561-7). Scholastic Inc.
Hader, Bertha. Visit from Saint Nick. 1990. 3.98 (ISBN 0-8317-4274-7). Smithmark.
Hall, Lynn. Here Comes Zelda Claus: And Other Holiday Disasters. 1989. 13.95 (ISBN 0-15-233790-3). HarbraceJ.
Hall, Tom T. Christmas & the Old House. Seeley, Laura L., illus. 48p. 1989. 13.95 (ISBN 0-934601-91-7). Peachtree Pubs.
Hamilton, Dorothy. Christmas for Holly. Graber, Esther R., illus. LC 72-141831. 112p. (gr. 4-9). 1971. pap. 3.95 (ISBN 0-8361-1658-5). Herald Pr.
Hamilton, Mary M. Christmas Magic: A Modern Christmas Fable. Miles, Leona & Kelly, Robert T., eds. Babcock, Patricia, illus. 208p. 1989. lib. bdg. 15. 95 (ISBN 0-317-93677-8). Havet Pr.
Hamilton, Virginia. Bells of Christmas. 1989. 16.95 (ISBN 0-15-206450-8). HarbraceJ.
Harder, Geraldine & Harder, Milton. Christmas Goose. Shelly, Maynard, ed. Dyck, Lavonne, illus. LC 90-84535. 80p. (Orig.). (gr. k-6). 1990. pap. 5.95 (ISBN 0-87303-146-6). Faith & Life.
Harris, Leon. Night Before Christmas-in Texas, That Is. Wohlberg, Meg, illus. (gr. k-7). 1977. Repr. of 1952 ed. 8.95 (ISBN 0-88289-175-8). Pelican.
Harvey, Brett. My Prairie Christmas. Ray, Deborah K., illus. LC 90-55104. 32p. (gr. k-3). 1990. reinforced 14. 95 (ISBN 0-8234-0827-2). Holiday.
Haskett, William P. Grandpa Haskett Presents: Original New Christmas Stories for the Young & Young-at-Heart. Haskett, M. R., ed. Haskett, Merelaine, illus. Haskett, M. R., intro. by. (Illus.). 20p. (Orig.). (ps-2). 1982. pap. 3.00g (ISBN 0-9609724-0-4). Haskett Spec.
Hautzig, Deborah, ed. The Christmas Story: Based on the Gospels According to St. Matthew & St. Luke. Beckett, Sheilah, illus. LC 83-60411. 24p. (ps-2). 1983. 2.95 (ISBN 0-394-86124-8). Random.
Hayes, Geoffrey. Christmas in Puttyville. Hayes, Geoffrey, illus. LC 85-2009. 40p. (ps-3). 1985. (Random Juv); lib. bdg. 5.99 (ISBN 0-394-97286-4). Random.
Hayes, Sarah. A Bad Start for Santa. Charteris, Jamie, illus. (ps-3). 12.95 (ISBN 0-87113-093-9). Atlantic Monthly.
—Happy Christmas, Gemma. Ormerod, Jan, illus. LC 85-23674. 32p. (ps-1). 1986. 13.95 (ISBN 0-688-06508-2). Lothrop.
Haywood, Carolyn. Merry Christmas from Betsy. (gr. k-6). 1989. pap. 3.25 (ISBN 0-440-40187-9, YB). Dell.
—Merry Christmas from Eddie. Durrell, Julie, illus. LC 86-2466. 112p. (gr. 1-4). 1986. 12.95 (ISBN 0-688-05828-0, Morrow Junior Books). Morrow.
Hazen, Barbara S. Rudolph the Red-Nosed Reindeer. Scarry, Richard, illus. 24p. (ps-1). 1985. Repr. of 1958 ed. write for info. (ISBN 0-307-10203-3, Pub. by Golden Bks). Western Pub.
Hendry, Diana. Christmas on Exeter Street. Lawrence, John, illus. LC 89-45256. 32p. (gr. k-3). 1989. 12.95 (ISBN 0-679-80134-0); PLB 13.99 (ISBN 0-679-90134-5). Knopf.
Herriot, James. Christmas Day Kitten. Brown, Ruth, illus. LC 86-13890. (ps up). 1986. 10.95 (ISBN 0-312-13407-X). St Martin.
Hildebrandt, Greg. Christmas Treasury. 1990. 11.95 (ISBN 0-88101-107-X). Unicorn Pub.
Hildebrandt, Greg & Hildebrandt, Greg, illus. Twas the Night Before Christmas: And Other Holiday Favorites. LC 90-10976. 48p. (gr. k-2). 1990. 4.95 (ISBN 0-88101-103-7). Unicorn Pub.
Hill, Susan. Can It Be True? A Christmas Story. Barrett, Angela, illus. LC 88-50449. (ps up). 1988. pap. 12.95 (ISBN 0-670-82517-4). Viking Child Bks.
Hisako Aoki. Santa's Favorite Story. Gantschev, Ivan, illus. 24p. 1991. pap. 4.95 (ISBN 0-590-44454-9, Blue Ribbon Bks). Scholastic Inc.
Hoban, Russell. The Mole Family's Christmas. Hoban, Lillian, illus. 48p. (gr. 4-9). 1984. pap. 3.95 (ISBN 0-590-40954-9, Blue Ribbon Bks). Scholastic Inc.
Hoff, Syd. Santa's Moose. Reissue. ed. Hoff, Syd, illus. LC 78-22483. 32p. (ps-3). 1979. 11.95 (ISBN 0-06-022505-X); PLB 10.89 (ISBN 0-06-022506-8). HarpC Child Bks.
Hoffman, E. T. The Nutcracker. Angus, Fay, adapted by. Welply, Michael, illus. (gr. 2 up). 1989. pap. 16.95 (ISBN 0-671-68617-8). S&S Trade.
Hoffmann, E. T. The Nutcracker. Chorao, Kay, illus. Schulman, Janet, adapted by. LC 79-11223. (Illus.). 64p. (gr. 3-7). 1988. pap. 2.95 (ISBN 0-394-82018-5). Knopf.
Holabird, Katharine. Angelina's Christmas. Craig, Helen, illus. LC 85-12389. 32p. (gr. 1 up). 1986. 11.95 (ISBN 0-517-55823-8, C N Potter Bks); pap. 4.95 (ISBN 0-685-22929-7, C N Potter Bks). Crown.
Hollands, Judith. An Elf for Christmas. MacDonald, Patricia, ed. De Rosa, Dee, illus. 80p. (Orig.). (gr. 2-5). 1990. pap. 2.95 (ISBN 0-671-70170-3, Minstrel Bks). PB.
Hollingsworth, Mary. Christmas in Happy Forest. (Illus.). (ps-2). 1990. 6.95 (ISBN 1-877719-05-6). Brownlow Pub Co.
Holmes, Efner T. The Christmas Cat. Tudor, Tasha, illus. LC 76-14802. 32p. (gr. 4 up). 1966. 12.95 (ISBN 0-690-01267-5, Crowell Jr Bks); PLB 12.89 (ISBN 0-690-01268-3). HarpC Child Bks.
Hope, Laura L. Bobbsey Twins' Wonderful Winter Secret. (gr. 1-4). 1931. 4.50 (ISBN 0-448-08024-9, G&D). Putnam Pub Group.
Hornidge, Marilis. Christmas Tales. Weinberger, Jane, ed. DeVito, Pamela, illus. LC 88-51378. 72p. (gr. 1-6). 1988. pap. 7.95 (ISBN 0-932433-50-2). Windswept Hse.
Houston, Gloria M. The Year of the Perfect Christmas Tree: An Appalachian Story. Cooney, Barbara, illus. LC 87-245515. 32p. (ps-3). 1988. 13.95 (ISBN 0-8037-0299-X); PLB 13.89 (ISBN 0-8037-0300-7). Dial Bks Young.
Hover, M. Here Comes Santa Claus. Santoro, Christopher, illus. 14p. (ps). 1982. write for info. (ISBN 0-307-12267-0, Golden Bks.). Western Pub.
Howe, James. The Fright Before Christmas. Morrill, Leslie, illus. LC 87-26280. 48p. (gr. k-3). 1988. 13.95 (ISBN 0-688-07664-5); PLB 13.88 (ISBN 0-688-07665-3, Morrow Jr Bks). Morrow Jr Bks.
—The Fright Before Christmas. Morrill, Leslie H., illus. 48p. 1989. pap. 5.95 (ISBN 0-380-70445-5, Camelot). Avon.
Ideals Staff. Jolly Old Santa Claus. Hinke, George, illus. 24p. (gr. k-6). 1985. pap. 2.95 (ISBN 0-89542-448-7). Ideals.
Impey, Rose. A Letter to Santa Claus. Porter, Sue, illus. 1989. 12.95 (ISBN 0-385-29714-9). Delacorte.
Ingle, Annie. The Smallest Elf. Smath, Jerry, illus. LC 90-30388. 32p. (Orig.). (ps-1). 1990. pap. 2.25 (ISBN 0-679-80846-9). Random.
Jane, Pamela. Noelle of the Nutcracker. Brett, Jan, illus. 64p. (gr. 2-5). 1986. 10.95 (ISBN 0-395-39969-6). HM.
Janice. Little Bear's Christmas. Mariana, illus. LC 64-21191. (gr. k-3). 1964. PLB 12.88 (ISBN 0-688-51076-0). Lothrop.
Jingle Bells. 24p. (ps-3). 1987. pap. write for info incl. cassette (ISBN 0-307-13996-4, Pub. by Golden Bks). Western Pub.
Joey's Special Christmas Gift. (Illus.). 26p. (ps-1). 1988. pap. 2.95 incl. sticker pgs. (ISBN 0-671-66869-2). S&S Trade.
Johnston, Annie F. The Little Colonel's Christmas Vacation. (gr. 5 up). 13.95 (ISBN 0-89201-035-5). Zenger Pub.
Johnston, Tony. Mole & Troll Trim the Tree. (gr. k-6). 1989. pap. 2.95 (ISBN 0-440-40243-3, YB). Dell.
Jones, Cody L. Twinkle Toes. 1991. 7.95 (ISBN 0-533-09261-2). Vantage.
Jones, Jo. Amanda's Tree. Kuse, James A., ed. (gr. 3-6). 1979. pap. 2.95 (ISBN 0-89542-514-9). Jo-Jo Pubns.
—Amanda's Tree. Vansant, Jo, illus. (gr. 3-6). 1977. pap. 3.50 (ISBN 0-9602266-0-5). Jo-Jo Pubns.
Jones, Margaret W. The Christmas Invitation: A Child Chritmas in the South. Easson, Roger R., ed. Robinson, Susan, illus. LC 85-2035. 48p. (gr. 5 up). 1985. 9.95 (ISBN 0-918518-42-3). St Lukes Pr.
Jurie, Jeri. Bizzy Bubbles: Santa's Littlest Elf. Fahs, Anita, illus. LC 77-82535. (gr. k-6). 1977. 10.95x (ISBN 0-686-01311-5); pap. 6.95x (ISBN 0-686-01312-3). Al Fresco.
Karlins, Mark. A Christmas Fable. Hyde, Maureen, illus. LC 89-29321. 32p. (gr. 1-5). 1990. 13.95 (ISBN 0-689-31480-9, Atheneum Child Bk). Macmillan Child Grp.
Kaye, Marilyn. Christmas Reunion. 160p. 1990. pap. 2.95 (ISBN 0-380-76270-6, Camelot). Avon.
Keller, Holly. A Bear for Christmas. Keller, Holly, illus. LC 85-12645. 32p. (ps-3). 1986. 11.75 (ISBN 0-688-05988-0); PLB 11.88 (ISBN 0-688-05989-9). Greenwillow.
Kempadoo, Manghanita. Letters of Thanks. 34p. 1986. pap. 3.95 (ISBN 0-671-62794-5, Fireside). S&S Trade.
Keogh, Brian G. Christmas Magic At the Mall. Keogh, Brian G., illus. 8p. (Orig.). (ps-4). 1991. pap. 1.00 (ISBN 0-9625072-3-7). B G Keogh.

Kimball, Richard S. A Christmas Wrinkle. LC 88-16310. (Illus.). 48p. (Orig.). (gr. 3 up). 1988. pap. 4.95 (ISBN 0-944443-01-X). Green Timber. A different holiday story...for ages eight to adult. Yes, there is a Santa Claus. He lives in each of us who will give him room. That's the message in this Christmas coming-of-age story. Dan, aged 10, is troubled during the holiday season by the contrast between Christmas glitter & the human suffering he discovers not just from the news but in his own back yard, visited daily by a bag lady searching the family garbage cans. Prospects for a pleasant Christmas become dimmer still when Dan's younger sister begins to doubt the magic of Santa Claus. In the cold & dark of earliest Christmas morning, Dan turns from worry to action, rekindles the warmth of Christmas, & sees its meaning by new light. Charcoal drawings throughout the text add warmth & depth of feeling to the story. Full color cover. Paperback, $4.95.
Publisher Provided Annotation.

King, B. A. The Very Best Christmas Tree. McCurdy, Michael, illus. LC 84-47656. 24p. (gr. 2 up). 1984. 9.95 (ISBN 0-87923-539-X). Godine.
King, Tony. The Christmas Junk Box. McCurdy, Michael, illus. LC 87-7386. (gr. k-4). 1987. 9.95 (ISBN 0-87923-694-9). Godine.
Kingman, Lee. The Best Christmas. Cooney, Barbara, illus. (gr. 2-5). 1984. 16.50 (ISBN 0-8446-6160-0). Peter Smith.
Kismaric, Carole, adapted by. A Gift from Saint Nicholas. Mikolaycak, Charles, illus. LC 87-8797. 32p. (gr. k-3). 1988. reinforced bdg. 14.95 (ISBN 0-8234-0674-1). Holiday.
Knapp, Toni. The Gossamer Tree: A Christmas Fable. Brown, Craig M., illus. LC 88-90759. 32p. (Orig.). (gr. 5up). 1988. 13.95 (ISBN 1-882092-00-7); pap. 7.95 (ISBN 1-882092-02-3). Rockrimmon Pr.
Knight, Hilary. Christmas Nutshell Library, 4 bks. Knight, Hilary, illus. Incl. Angels & Berries & Candy Canes (ISBN 0-06-023200-5); Christmas Stocking Story (ISBN 0-06-023205-6); Firefly in a Fir Tree (ISBN 0-06-023190-4); The Night Before Christmas. LC 63-18904. (gr. 1 up). 1963. Set. 10.95 (ISBN 0-06-023165-3). HarpC Child Bks.
Knorr, Dandi D. The Best Christmas Ever. Connelly, Gwen, illus. 32p. (gr. 1-3). 1987. 4.95 (ISBN 0-87403-315-2, 3545). Standard Pub.
Krahn, Fernando. How Santa Had a Long & Difficult Journey Delivering His Presents. (gr. k-6). 1988. pap. 3.95 (ISBN 0-440-40118-6, YB). Dell.
Kraus, Robert. Daddy Long Ears Christmas Surprise. 1989. pap. 4.95 (ISBN 0-671-68150-8). S&S Trade.
Krementz, Jill. A Very Young Circus Flyer. (gr. k-6). 1987. pap. 6.95 (ISBN 0-440-49216-5, YB). Dell.
Kroeber, Theodora. Green Christmas. Larrecq, John M., illus. LC 67-26304. (gr. k-2). 1967. 6.95 (ISBN 0-87466-047-5, Pub. by Parnassus). HM.
Kroll, Steven. Mrs. Claus's Crazy Christmas. Wallner, John, illus. LC 84-25218. 32p. (ps-3). 1985. reinforced bdg. 13.95 (ISBN 0-8234-0563-X). Holiday.
Kunhardt, Edith. Danny's Christmas Star. LC 88-18785. (Illus.). 24p. (ps up). 1989. 12.95 (ISBN 0-688-07905-9); PLB 12.88 (ISBN 0-688-07906-7). Greenwillow.
Kusugak, Michael A. Baseball Bats for Christmas. Krykorka, Vladyana, illus. 24p. (gr. k-3). 1990. 14.95 (ISBN 1-55037-145-2); pap. 5.95 (ISBN 1-55037-144-4). Firefly Bks Ltd.
Kyte, Dennis. Merry Christmas, Bigelow Bear. 1990. 13. 95 (ISBN 0-385-26522-0); PLB 14.99 (ISBN 0-385-26523-9). Doubleday.
Lagerlof, Selma. The Legend of the Christmas Rose. Mikolaycak, Charles, illus. Greene, Ellin, retold by. LC 89-77511. (Illus.). 32p. (ps up). 1990. reinforced 15.95 (ISBN 0-8234-0821-3). Holiday.
La Rochelle, David. A Christmas Guest. Skoro, Martin, illus. 32p. (ps-3). 1988. PLB 12.95 (ISBN 0-87614-325-7); pap. 5.95 (ISBN 0-87614-506-3). Carolrhoda Bks.
Laurence, Margaret. The Christmas Birthday Story. Lucas, Helen, illus. LC 79-27159. 32p. (ps-3). 1980. pap. 6.95 (ISBN 0-394-84361-4). Knopf.
Leeuwen, Jean Van. The Great Christmas Kidnapping Caper. (gr. 3-7). 1976. pap. 2.50 (ISBN 0-440-43220-0, YB). Dell.

Lemoine, Charles A. Santa Clawfish. Lemoine, Charles A., illus. 32p. (Orig.). 1986. pap. 3.20 (ISBN 0-941327-00-0). Charles A Lemoine.

Lemoine, Georges, illus. The Christmas Story According to St. Luke. 32p. 1978. PLB 10.95s.p. (ISBN 0-87191-957-5); 15.65 (ISBN 0-685-07724-1). Creative Ed.

Lemon, Betty. Teton Christmas Tales. Berrey, Phoebe, illus. 45p. (gr. 1 up). 11.50 (ISBN 0-933160-06-2). Teton Bkshop.

L'Engle, Madeleine. The Twenty-Four Days Before Christmas. (gr. k-6). 1987. pap. 2.95 (ISBN 0-440-40105-4, YB). Dell.

Lenski, Lois. Lois Lenski's Christmas Stories. LC 68-24417. (Illus.). 160p. (gr. 4-6). 1968. 12.95 (ISBN 0-397-31031-5, Lipp Jr Bks). HarpC Child Bks.

Leppard, Lois G. Mandie & the Holiday Surprise, Bk. 11. LC 88-71502. 160p. (gr. 3-6). 1988. pap. 3.95 (ISBN 1-55661-036-X). Bethany Hse.

Lewis, Mark. Kaliban's Christmas: A Special Tale of Magic. (gr. 7 up). 1987. pap. 2.95 (ISBN 0-8125-8505-4). Tor Bks.

Lewis, Shari. One Minute Christmas Stories. Palmer, Jan, illus. Matthews, Gerry, contrib. by. LC 86-29146. (Illus.). 48p. (gr. k-3). 1987. pap. 7.95 (ISBN 0-385-23424-4). Doubleday.

Lindgren, Astrid. Christmas in Noisy Village. LC 64-21473. 32p. (ps-3). 1981. pap. 3.95 (ISBN 0-14-050344-7, Puffin). Puffin Bks.

—Christmas in the Stable. LC 62-14449. (Illus.). (gr. 1-3). 1979. PLB 6.99 (ISBN 0-698-30042-4, Coward); pap. text ed. 4.95 (ISBN 0-698-20489-1, Coward). Putnam Pub Group.

—Lotta's Christmas Surprise. Wikland, Ilon, illus. 32p. (ps-3). 1990. 13.95 (ISBN 91-29-59782-X, Pub. by R & S Bks). FS&G.

Lotter, Victoria. Christmas Eve. Buchanan, George C., illus. 28p. (ps-5). 1988. pap. 7.49 (ISBN 0-317-93270-5). Hinterland Pubs.

Luton, Mildred. Christmas Time in the Mountains. Peattie, Gary, illus. 44p. (Orig.). (gr. 1-6). 1981. pap. 5.00 (ISBN 0-87516-434-X). DeVorss.

Lyman, et al. Pee Wee Saves Christmas. Curtis, Peggy H., illus. 80p. 1983. 14.95 (ISBN 0-317-03904-0). Imagination Dust.

M & M & the Santa Secrets. 1985. 9.95 (ISBN 0-670-80624-2). Viking Child Bks.

M & M & the Santa Secrets. (Illus.). 1987. pap. 3.95 (ISBN 0-14-032222-1, Puffin). Puffin Bks.

McAllister, Mimi. Christmas at Gump's. McAllister, Mimi & Becker, Richard, illus. LC 90-60435. 48p. 1990. 16.95 (ISBN 0-9624887-4-7). C Salway Pr.

MacDonald, George. The Christmas Stories of George MacDonald. LC 81-68187. (gr. 1 up). 1981. 12.95 (ISBN 0-89191-491-9, 54916). Cook.

McKenna, Colleen O. Merry Christmas Miss McConnell. (ps-3). 1990. 12.95 (ISBN 0-590-43554-X, Scholastic Hardcover). Scholastic Inc.

McQuilkin, Frank. Forgottenville: The Town That Arrested Santa Claus. Doros Animations, Inc., illus. 48p. (gr. k-7). 1982. 11.95 (ISBN 0-941316-00-9). TSM Books.

McRae, Patrick, illus. The First Noel. 24p. (ps-1). 1988. pap. 2.95 (ISBN 0-8249-8248-7). Ideals.

Mann, Marek. The Animals' Christmas Surprise. Young, Richard G., ed. Mann, Marek, illus. LC 89-11896. 24p. (gr. 1-3). 1989. PLB 13.26 (ISBN 0-944483-51-8). Garrett Ed Corp.

Manushkin, Fran. The Perfect Christmas Picture. Weinhaus, Karen A., illus. LC 79-2678. 64p. (gr. k-3). 1980. 11.95 (ISBN 0-06-024068-7). HarpC Child Bks.

—The Perfect Christmas Picture. Weinhaus, Karen A., illus. LC 79-2678. 64p. (ps-3). 1987. pap. 3.50 (ISBN 0-06-444112-1, Trophy). HarpC Child Bks.

Marie, Nancy. Country Christmas. Ryan, Delores, illus. 36p. (gr. k-5). 1979. 5.95 (ISBN 0-941595-00-5). Heldreth Pub.

Marilue. Bobby Bear's Christmas. LC 77-83628. (Illus.). 32p. (ps-1). 1978. PLB 9.95 (ISBN 0-87783-142-4); cassette o.p. 7.94x (ISBN 0-87783-182-3). Oddo.

Markham, Marion M. The Christmas Present Mystery. McCully, Emily A., illus. 64p. 1990. pap. 2.95 (ISBN 0-380-70966-X, Camelot). Avon.

Marks, Johnny. Rudolph the Red-Nosed Reindeer. Shortall, Leonard, illus. LC 85-60077. 16p. (ps). 1985. bds. 6.95 (ISBN 0-394-87446-3, Random Juv). Random.

Marsh, Carole. The Fortune Cookie Christmas. (Illus., Orig.). (gr. 3 up). 1986. 19.95 (ISBN 1-55609-285-7); pap. 14.95 (ISBN 0-935326-53-7). Gallopade Pub Group.

Marshall, James. Merry Christmas Space Case. 1989. pap. 4.95 (ISBN 0-8037-0653-7, Dial). Doubleday.

Martini, Teri. Feliz Navidad, Pablo. McNichols, William H., illus. 1990. 2.95 (ISBN 0-8091-6597-X). Paulist Pr.

Maxfield, Christine. Christmas in Water Village. Colquhoun, Jean, illus. 32p. (ps-5). 1989. 15.95 (ISBN 0-9621029-0-3). Prima Design.

May, Robert. Rudolph the Red Nosed Reindeer. (ps-3). 1990. 9.95 (ISBN 1-55709-139-0). Applewood.

Mayer, Mercer. Merry Christmas Mom & Dad. Mayer, Mercer, illus. 24p. (ps-3). 1982. pap. write for info. (ISBN 0-307-11886-X, Golden Bks.). Western Pub.

Menotti, Gian-Carlo. Amahl & the Night Visitors. Lemieux, Michele, illus. LC 84-27196. 64p. (ps up). 1986. 15.00 (ISBN 0-688-05426-9); lib. bdg. 14.88 (ISBN 0-688-05427-7, Morrow Jr Bks). Morrow Jr Bks.

Merriam, Eve. The Christmas Box. Small, David, illus. LC 85-5666. 32p. (ps-3). 1985. 12.95 (ISBN 0-688-05255-X); lib. bdg. 12.88 (ISBN 0-688-05256-8, Morrow Jr Bks). Morrow Jr Bks.

Mezek, Karen. Christmas at the Rumpole Mansion. LC 89-31537. (Illus., Orig.). (ps-3). 1989. 9.99 (ISBN 0-89081-710-3). Harvest Hse.

Miller, Edna. Mousekin's Christmas Eve. Miller, Edna, illus. (gr. k-3). 1972. 11.95 (ISBN 0-13-604454-9, Pub. by Treehouse). P-H.

—Mousekin's Christmas Eve. LC 65-25244. (Illus.). 32p. (gr. k-4). 1972. pap. 5.95 (ISBN 0-671-66479-4). S&S Trade.

—Mousekin's Mystery. LC 83-9622. (Illus.). 32p. (gr. k-3). 1983. 11.95 (ISBN 0-13-604330-5). P-H.

Miller, Lynne, ed. Ten Tales of Christmas. 112p. (gr. 4-6). 1988. pap. 2.50 (ISBN 0-590-41447-X). Scholastic Inc.

Moeri, Louise. Star Mother's Youngest Child. Hyman, Trina S., illus. 48p. (ps-2). 1980. 13.95 (ISBN 0-395-21406-8, Sandpiper); pap. 4.95 (ISBN 0-395-29929-2). HM.

Moore, Clement C. The Night Before Christmas. Hague, Michael, illus. LC 80-84842. 12p. (gr. k-2). 1981. 10.95 (ISBN 0-8050-0900-0). H Holt & Co.

—The Night Before Christmas. Evert, Sally, illus. 32p. (ps-2). 1981. pap. 2.95 (ISBN 0-671-44410-7, Little Simon). S&S Trade.

—The Night Before Christmas. Lobel, Anita, illus. LC 84-4342. 32p. (gr. k up). 1984. lib. bdg. 10.99 (ISBN 0-394-96863-8). Knopf.

—The Night Before Christmas. DePaola, Tomie, illus. (gr. k-3). 1984. incl. cassette 19.95 (ISBN 0-317-07112-2); pap. 12.95 incl. cassette (ISBN 0-941078-37-X); incl. 4 bks., cassette, & guide 27.95 (ISBN 0-685-08869-3). Live Oak Media.

—The Night Before Christmas. Tien, illus. 32p. (ps-1). 1986. 5.95 (ISBN 0-671-62209-9, Little Simon). S&S Trade.

—The Night Before Christmas: Or: Account of a Visit from St. Nicholas. Bevis, Phillip & Irwin, Colin, eds. Henley, Clark, illus. 22p. 1984. 150.00 (ISBN 0-923980-03-2). Arundel Pr.

—Two Little Christmas Classics. Goode, Diane, illus. 32p. (ps up). 1989. pap. 4.95 incl. cassette (ISBN 0-394-84629-X). Random.

Moore, Clement C., et al. Mini Bookshelf of Christmas Favorites, 4 bks. (Illus.). 96p. (ps-3). 1989. Set. 7.95 (ISBN 0-8249-8400-5). Ideals.

Moore, J. Thomas. Night after Christmas. (gr. k up). 1990. pap. 5.95 (ISBN 0-925928-07-0). Tiny Thought.

Moore, John T., et al. Christmas Classics for Children. (ps-k). 1981. 14.95 (ISBN 0-570-04058-2, 56-1351). Concordia.

Moore, Ruth N. The Christmas Surprise. Eitzen, Allen, illus. 160p. (Orig.). (gr. 4-8). 1989. pap. 5.95 (ISBN 0-8361-3499-0). Herald Pr.

Morehead, Ruth J. The Christmas Story with Holly Babes. Morehead, Ruth J., illus. LC 85-32305. 32p. (ps-1). 1986. pap. 2.25 (ISBN 0-394-88051-X, Random Juv); cassette pkg. 5.95 (ISBN 0-394-89058-2). Random.

Morris, Dixie G. Who is Santa? Medrano, JoAnn, illus. Robinson, Deborah L., intro. by. (Illus.). 25p. (Orig.). (ps-3). 1988. spiral bdg. 7.50 (ISBN 0-929946-04-9). TACM Inc.

Naylor, Phyllis R. Old Sadie & the Christmas Bear. LC 84-2995. (Illus.). 32p. (ps-2). 1984. 12.95 (ISBN 0-689-31052-8, Atheneum Child Bk). Macmillan Child Grp.

Nelson-Erichsen, Jean. Copito: The Christmas Chihuahua. Atcheson, Marguerite, illus. Davenport, May, intro. by. LC 82-72080. (Illus.). 80p. (gr. k-5). 1982. pap. 3.50x (ISBN 0-943864-07-0). Davenport.

Nerlove, Miriam. Christmas. Tucker, Kathy, ed. Nerlove, Miriam, illus. 24p. (ps-1). 1990. 10.95 (ISBN 0-8075-1148-X). A Whitman.

Nixon, Joan L. The Christmas Eve Mystery. Fay, Ann, ed. Cummins, Jim, illus. LC 81-345. 32p. (gr. 1-3). 1981. PLB 8.95 (ISBN 0-8075-1150-1). A Whitman.

Njoku, Scholastica I. The Miracle of a Christmas Doll. McKay, Suzanne, illus. 29p. (gr. k up). 1986. perfect bdg. 5.95x (ISBN 0-9617833-0-3). S I NJOKU.

Noble, Trinka H. Apple Tree Christmas. Noble, Trinka H., illus. LC 84-1901. 32p. (ps-2). 1988. 12.95 (ISBN 0-8037-0102-0); PLB 12.89 (ISBN 0-8037-0103-9); pap. 3.95 (ISBN 0-8037-0552-2). Dial Bks Young.

Nordqvist, Sven. Merry Christmas, Festus & Mercury. (Illus.). 24p. (ps-3). 1989. PLB 12.95 (ISBN 0-87614-383-4). Carolrhoda Bks.

Oakley, Graham. Church Mice at Christmas. Oakley, Graham, illus. LC 80-14518. 40p. (gr. k-3). 1980. 13.95 (ISBN 0-689-30797-7, Atheneum Child Bk). Macmillan Child Grp.

Odor, Ruth S. What Does Christmas Sound Like? Klug, Mikki, illus. 32p. (gr. k-2). 1987. 1.99 (ISBN 0-87403-282-2, 3782). Standard Pub.

O. Henry. The Gift of the Magi. King, Kevin, illus. 32p. (gr. 5 up). 1988. pap. 12.95 (ISBN 0-671-64706-7). S&S Trade.

—The Gift of the Magi. Sauber, Robert, illus. LC 91-7313. 48p. (gr. 1-6). 1991. 5.95 (ISBN 0-88101-116-9). Unicorn Pub.

—The Gift of the Magi: A Special Christmas Edition. rev. ed. Marshall, Rita, illus. 32p. (gr. 4 up). 1984. PLB 10.95s.p. (ISBN 0-87191-954-0); 15.65 (ISBN 0-685-13439-3). Creative Ed.

O'Keefe, Susan H. A Season for Giving. Keating, Pamela T., illus. 1990. 2.95 (ISBN 0-8091-6592-9). Paulist Pr.

Olson, Arielle N. Hurry Home, Grandma! Dabcovich, Lydia, illus. LC 84-1529. 32p. (ps-1). 1984. 9.95 (ISBN 0-525-44113-1, DCB). Dutton Child Bks.

Oppenheimer, Evelyn. Tilli Comes to Texas. Haverfield, Mary, illus. LC 86-3089. 40p. (gr. k-3). 1986. PLB 9.95 (ISBN 0-937460-21-4). Hendrick-Long.

Ottum, Bob & Wood, JoAnne. Santa's Beard Is Soft & Warm. Ruth, Rod, illus. (ps). 1974. write for info. (ISBN 0-307-12148-8, Golden Bks). Western Pub.

Palumbo, Nancy. Penelope P'Nutt & the Spirit of Christmas: Penelope P'Nutt et L'Ambiance De Noel. Weaver, Judith, illus. 16p. (gr. k-6). 1989. wkbk. 5.95 (ISBN 0-927024-03-9). Crayons Pubns.

—Penelope P'Nutt & the Spirit of Christmas: Penelope P'Nutt y el Espiritu de la Navidad. Weaver, Judith, illus. 16p. (gr. k-6). 1989. wkbk. 5.95 (ISBN 0-927024-02-0). Crayons Pubns.

Parish, Peggy. Merry Christmas, Amelia Bedelia. Sweat, Lynn, illus. LC 85-24919. 64p. (gr. 1-4). 1986. 10.25 (ISBN 0-688-06101-X); PLB 12.88 (ISBN 0-688-06102-8). Greenwillow.

Parker, Ann N. A Christmas Trilogy. Vickery, Diane, illus. (gr. k-4). 1988. pap. 3.95 (ISBN 0-943487-14-5). Sevgo Pr.

Pascal, Francine. Christmas Ghost. (gr. 7-12). 1990. pap. write for info. Bantam.

Paterson, Cynthia & Paterson, Brian. The Foxwood Surprise. (Illus.). 32p. (ps-3). 1988. 6.95 (ISBN 0-8120-5986-7). Barron.

Paterson, Katherine. Angels & Other Strangers: Family Christmas Stories. LC 79-63797. 128p. (gr. 1 up). 1979. 12.95 (ISBN 0-690-03992-1, Crowell Jr Bks). HarpC Child Bks.

—Angels & Other Strangers: Family Christmas Stories. LC 79-63797. 128p. (gr. 7 up). 1988. pap. 3.50 (ISBN 0-06-440283-5, Trophy). HarpC Child Bks.

Patterson, Nancy R. The Christmas Cup. Bowman, Leslie, illus. LC 88-29112. 80p. (gr. 3-5). 1989. 13.95 (ISBN 0-531-05821-2); PLB 13.99 (ISBN 0-531-08421-3). Orchard Bks Watts.

Pearson, Susan. The Day Porkchop Climbed the Christmas Tree. Brown, Rick, illus. (ps up). 1989. 9.95 (ISBN 0-671-66370-4); pap. 2.95 (ISBN 0-671-68884-7). S&S Trade.

—Karin's Christmas Walk. Noble, Trinka H., illus. LC 80-11739. 32p. (ps-3). 1980. 11.95 (ISBN 0-8037-4431-5); PLB 11.89 (ISBN 0-8037-4432-3). Dial Bks Young.

—Karin's Christmas Walk. Noble, Trinka H., illus. LC 80-11739. 32p. (ps-3). 1983. pap. 4.95 (ISBN 0-8037-0020-2). Dial Bks Young.

Pearson, Tracey C., illus. We Wish You a Merry Christmas. LC 82-22224. 32p. (ps up). 1986. 8.95 (ISBN 0-8037-9368-5); PLB 8.89 (ISBN 0-8037-9400-2); pap. 3.95 (ISBN 0-8037-0310-4). Dial Bks Young.

Peet, Bill. Countdown to Christmas. Peet, Bill, illus. LC 72-78394. 48p. (gr. 1-4). 1972. 14.60 (ISBN 0-516-18716-3, Golden Gate); PLB 15.93 (ISBN 0-516-08716-9). Childrens.

Peterkin, Julia. A Plantation Christmas. Hendrickson, David, illus. LC 72-4563. (gr. 7 up). Repr. of 1934 ed. 10.50 (ISBN 0-8369-9119-2). Ayer Co Pubs.

Peters, Lauren. Problems at the North Pole. Thatch, Nancy R., ed. Melton, David, intro. by. LC 90-5929. (Illus.). 26p. (ps-2). 1990. lib. bdg. 12.95 (ISBN 0-933849-25-7). Landmark Edns.

Peters, Sharon. The Tiny Christmas Elf. Durrell, Julie, illus. LC 86-30849. 32p. (gr. k-2). 1987. PLB 7.06 (ISBN 0-8167-0988-2); pap. text ed. 1.95 (ISBN 0-8167-0989-0). Troll Assocs.

Peterson, Carolyn S. & Fenton, Ann D. Christmas Story Programs. Sterchele, Christina L., illus. (ps-6). 1981. 10.00 (ISBN 0-913545-01-5). Moonlight FL.

Pickett, Margaret E. What's Keeping You, Santa? A Christmas Story Book. Brown, Blanche M., illus. LC 83-50122. 64p. (gr. k-5). 1983. PLB 24.95 (ISBN 0-913939-00-5); read a long Cassette 4.95 (ISBN 0-913939-03-X). TP Assocs.

Pierce, Catherine D. Christmas Thief. Gallagher, Jane, illus. (Orig.). (ps-k). 1988. pap. text ed. 4.50 (ISBN 0-9621397-0-X). C D Pierce. From its startling title, CHRISTMAS THIEF, to the enchanting finale (a rendition of OH, LIT-TLE TOWN OF M-OUSE-VILLE)..here is a book for all ages. The size to be held in the hands of the youngest 'reader', it should be purchased by twos; one to be held as the illustrations are studied, one to be read from....Delightful pictures that blossom on every page will be scrutinized & talked about. The setting for the story is a gathering of all the wood creatures to celebrate the holiday. It is presided over by competent & lovable Mrs. Mouse.

Suddenly Tom, her son, discovers that something is missing. The circumstances are sinister & the fear of a thief among them makes for near-panic. Comfortable Mrs. Mouse calms her vindictive son Tom to the point of listening to the words of the tiny thief, a yellow duckling whose handicap has given him a sad history. Author Catherine Doris Pierce does not labor this aspect but the happy conclusion to the story is reached through a lesson in compassion for the hungry little creature who is less fortunate than big, healthy Tom Mouse. The story ends in song & in sighs of bed-time peace. Of course, the lame & lost duckling has a new name & has found a new home. *Publisher Provided Annotation.*

Pilkington, Brian. Grandpa Claus. Pilkington, Brian, illus. 28p. (ps-3). 1990. PLB 12.95 (ISBN 0-87614-436-9). Carolrhoda Bks.
Pippen, Christie. A Very Scraggly Christmas Tree. Beckes, Shirley V., illus. (gr. 2-4). 1988. 16.67 (ISBN 0-8172-2754-7). Raintree Pubs.
Pochocki, Ethel F. The Fox Who Found Christmas. Bell, Thomas P., illus. LC 90-82095. 56p. (Orig.). 1990. pap. 5.95 (ISBN 0-87793-431-2). Ave Maria.
Potter, Beatrix. Peter Rabbit's Christmas Book. (ps-3). 1990. pap. 5.95 (ISBN 0-7232-3778-6). Warne.
Powling, Chris. The Phantom Car Wash. Baylis, Jean, illus. 42p. (gr. 2-4). 1989. 3.95 (ISBN 0-8120-6140-3). Barron.
Prelutsky, Jack. It's Christmas. Hafner, Marylin, illus. 48p. (gr. k-3). 1986. pap. 2.50 (ISBN 0-590-40584-5). Scholastic Inc.
—It's Christmas. Hafner, Marylin, illus. 48p. (Orig.). (gr. k-3). 1986. 2.75 (ISBN 0-590-44048-9); incl. cassette 5.95 (ISBN 0-685-18386-6). Scholastic Inc.
Price, Mathew. The Christmas Stockings. Le Cain, Errol, illus. 20p. (ps-1). 1987. 10.95 (ISBN 0-8120-5870-4). Barron.
The Rand McNally Book of Favorite Christmas Stories. 112p. (ps-3). 1985. write for info. (ISBN 0-528-82678-6). Checkerboard Pr.
Rappaport, Doreen. Mrs. Santa's Christmas Present. LC 88-81465. (Illus.). 32p. (Orig.). (ps-2). 1988. pap. 8.95 (ISBN 0-937124-19-2). Kimbo Educ.
Rice, James. Cajun Night Before Christmas Coloring Book. 32p. (gr. k-4). 1976. pap. 2.50 (ISBN 0-88289-138-3). Pelican.
—Prairie Night Before Christmas. rev. ed. (gr. 1-6). 1986. 11.95 (ISBN 0-88289-630-X). Pelican.
Richardson, I. M. Story of the Christmas Rose. De Kiefte, Kees, illus. LC 87-13817. 32p. (gr. k-4). 1987. PLB 9.79 (ISBN 0-8167-1069-4); pap. text ed. 1.95 (ISBN 0-8167-1070-8). Troll Assocs.
Rigg, Lucy. Baby's Christmas. 1990. 2.95 (ISBN 0-8378-1883-4). Gibson.
—Little Christmas Treasure Books: Christmas Joys. (Illus.). (gr. 2 up). 1989. 2.95 (ISBN 0-8378-1870-2). Gibson.
—Little Christmas Treasure Books: Christmas Cookies. (Illus.). (gr. 2 up). 1989. 2.95 (ISBN 0-8378-1871-0). Gibson.
—Little Christmas Treasure Books: Silent Night. (Illus.). (ps up). 1989. 2.95 (ISBN 0-8378-1872-9). Gibson.
—Little Christmas Treasure Books: The Night Before Christmas. (Illus.). (ps up). 1989. 2.95 (ISBN 0-8378-1869-9). Gibson.
—Thank You, God. 1990. 2.95 (ISBN 0-8378-1884-2). Gibson.
Robinson, Barbara. The Best Christmas Pageant Ever. Brown, Judith G., illus. LC 72-76501. 96p. (gr. 3 up). 1972. 12.95 (ISBN 0-06-025043-7); PLB 13.89 (ISBN 0-06-025044-5). HarpC Child Bks.
—The Best Christmas Pageant Ever. Brown, Judith G., illus. LC 72-76501. 96p. (gr. 3 up). 1988. pap. 28.00 (ISBN 0-06-440278-9, Trophy). HarpC Child Bks.
Rock, Gail. The House Without a Christmas Tree. Gehm, Charles, illus. LC 74-162. 96p. (gr. 2 up). 1974. lib. bdg. 9.99 (ISBN 0-394-92833-4). Knopf.
—The House Without a Christmas Tree. (gr. 4-6). 1985. pap. 2.95 (ISBN 0-440-43394-0, YB). Dell.
Rogers, Jacqueline. The Christmas Pageant. Rogers, Jacqueline, illus. 32p. (ps-2). 1989. 12.95 (ISBN 0-448-40151-7, G&D). Putnam Pub Group.
Rogers, Jean. King Island Christmas. Munoz, Rie, illus. LC 84-25865. 32p. (gr. k-3). 1985. 11.75 (ISBN 0-688-04236-8); lib. bdg. 11.88 (ISBN 0-688-04237-6). Greenwillow.
Royds, Caroline, ed. The Christmas Book: Stories, Poems, & Carols for the Twelve Days of Christmas. Spenceley, Annabel, illus. LC 85-6482. 96p. (ps up). 1985. 12.95 (ISBN 0-399-21284-1, Putnam). Putnam Pub Group.
Rudolph the Red-Nosed Reindeer. (ps-3). Date not set. write for info. incl. cassette (ISBN 0-307-13995-6, 13995, Pub. by Golden Bks). Western Pub.
Rutherford, Meg. Bluff & Bran & the Snowdrift. Rutherford, Meg, illus. 32p. (ps-3). 1988. 10.95 (ISBN 0-233-98076-8). Andre Deutsch.
Rydberg, Viktor. The Christmas Tomten. Wiberg, Harald, illus. 1981. 9.95 (ISBN 0-698-20528-6, Coward). Putnam Pub Group.
Sabin, Fran & Sabin, Lou. The Great Santa Claus Mystery. Trivas, Irene, illus. LC 81-7530. 48p. (gr. 2-4). 1982. PLB 10.89 (ISBN 0-89375-602-4); pap. text ed. 2.95 (ISBN 0-89375-603-2). Troll Assocs.
St. Pierre, Stephanie. Bertie Bears Christmas with Cutter. 1989. pap. 3.95 (ISBN 0-590-43234-6). Scholastic Inc.
Sam, Daniel. Little Wini's Special Christmas Gift. Price, Ellen J., illus. (Illus.). 64p. (ps-6). 1985. 8.95x (ISBN 0-9615453-0-5). Family Herit.
Santa's Special Gift. (Illus.). 12p. (ps-3). 1988. bds. 2.95 (ISBN 0-02-688793-2). Checkerboard Pr.
Santa's Surprise. (Illus.). 12p. (ps-3). 1988. bds. 2.95 (ISBN 0-02-688792-4). Checkerboard Pr.
Santoro, Christopher, illus. Rudolph the Red-Nosed Reindeer. LC 86-62550. 14p. (ps-1). 1987. 5.95 (ISBN 0-394-88923-1, Random Juv). Random.
Scarry, Richard. Richard Scarry's Best Christmas Book Ever. Scarry, Richard, illus. LC 80-5172. 48p. (ps-2). 1981. 8.95 (ISBN 0-394-84936-1); lib. bdg. 5.99 (ISBN 0-394-94936-6). Random.
Scheidl, Gerda. Miriam's Gift. Pfister, Marcus, illus. Lanning, Rosemary, tr. from GER. Pfister, Marcus, illus. LC 89-42611. 32p. (gr. k-3). 1989. 13.95 (ISBN 1-55858-008-5). North-South Bks NYC.
Scheidl, Gerda M. Four Candles for Simon. Bell, Anthea, tr. Pfister, Marcus, illus. (GER.). 32p. (gr. k-3). 1989. pap. 1.95 (ISBN 1-55858-033-6). North-South Bks NYC.
Scholey, Arthur. Dickens Christmas Carol Show. 1979. 5.00 (ISBN 0-87602-119-4). Anchorage.
Schotter, Roni. Efan the Great. Pate, Rodney, illus. LC 84-25070. 32p. (gr. 2-5). 1986. 12.95 (ISBN 0-688-04986-9); PLB 12.88 (ISBN 0-688-04987-7). Lothrop.
Schulz, Charles M. A Charlie Brown Christmas. LC 76-57940. (Illus.). (gr. k-8). 1977. (Random Juv); PLB 5.99 (ISBN 0-394-83454-2). Random.
Schumacher, Claire. Santa's Hat. LC 86-18663. (Illus.). 40p. (ps-3). 1987. PLB 10.95 (ISBN 0-13-791187-4). P-H.
Schur, Maxine R. Samantha's Surprise: A Christmas Story. Lusk, Nancy N., illus. LC 86-60625. 67p. (Orig.). (gr. 2-5). 1986. 12.95 (ISBN 0-937295-21-3); pap. 5.95 (ISBN 0-937295-22-1). Pleasant Co.
—Samantha's Surprise: A Christmas Story. Thieme, Jeanne, ed. Niles, Nancy, illus. 72p. (gr. 2-5). 1990. PLB 12.95 (ISBN 0-937295-86-8). Pleasant Co.
Schweninger, Ann. Christmas Secrets. Schweninger, Ann, illus. LC 83-16983. 32p. (ps). 1984. pap. 10.95 (ISBN 0-670-22109-0). Viking Child Bks.
Scott, Beverly A. Santa's New Suit Funbook. (ps-6). 1973. pap. 3.00 (ISBN 0-686-11715-8). B A Scott.
Sharmat, Marjorie W. I'm Santa Claus & I'm Famous. Hafner, Marylin, illus. LC 90-55106. 32p. (ps-4). 1990. reinforced 14.95 (ISBN 0-8234-0826-4). Holiday.
Sharp, Mary. Bobbi Saves Christmas! Skar, Cynthia S., illus. 28p. (Orig.). (gr. 1-4). 1981. pap. 1.89 (ISBN 0-9603200-1-6). Bobbi Ent.
Shaw, Janet. Kirsten's Surprise: A Christmas Story. Thieme, Jeanne, ed. Graef, Renee, illus. 72p. (gr. 2-5). 1990. PLB 12.95 (ISBN 0-937295-85-X). Pleasant Co.
Siegenthaler, Kathrin. Santa Claus & the Woodcutter. Pfister, Marcus, illus. Crawford, Elizabeth, tr. LC 87-32203. (Illus.). 32p. (gr. k-3). 1988. 14.95 (ISBN 1-55858-027-1). North-South Bks NYC.
Simon, Carly. Boy of the Bells. Datz, Margot, illus. 1990. 14.95 (ISBN 0-385-41587-7); PLB 15.99 (ISBN 0-385-41736-5). Doubleday.
Slate, Joseph. How Little Porcupine Played Christmas. Bond, Felicia, illus. LC 81-43884. 32p. (ps-3). 1982. 12.95 (ISBN 0-690-04237-X, Crowell Jr Bks); PLB 12.89 (ISBN 0-690-04238-8). HarpC Child Bks.
—How Little Porcupine Played Christmas. Bond, Felicia, illus. LC 81-43884. 32p. (gr. k-3). 1988. pap. 3.95 (ISBN 0-06-443164-9, Trophy). HarpC Child Bks.
—Who Is Coming to Our House? Wolff, Ashley, illus. LC 87-7319. 32p. (ps-1). 1988. PLB 13.95 (ISBN 0-399-21537-9, Putnam). Putnam Pub Group.
Smith, Dorothy H. The Tall Book of Christmas. Espenscheid, Gertrude E., illus. LC 54-9002. 96p. (gr. k-3). 1954. 7.95i (ISBN 0-06-025700-8); PLB 10.89 (ISBN 0-06-025701-6). HarpC Child Bks.
Society of Brothers Staff, ed. Behold That Star: A Christmas Anthology: A Collection of Fifteen Christmas Stories. 3rd ed. Maendel, Maria A., illus. LC 67-25968. 368p. (gr. 4 up). 1966. 16.00 (ISBN 0-87486-003-2). Plough.
Solotareff, Gregoire. Noel's Christmas Secret. 1990. 13.95 (ISBN 0-374-35544-4). FS&G.
Speare, Jean. A Candle for Christmas. Blades, Ann, illus. LC 86-61560. 32p. (gr. k-4). 1987. 12.95 (ISBN 0-689-50417-9, M K McElderry). Macmillan Child Grp.
Spier, Peter. Peter Spier's Christmas! Spier, Peter, illus. LC 80-2875. 40p. (ps up). 1983. PLB 13.95 (ISBN 0-385-13184-4); pap. 13.95 (ISBN 0-385-13183-6). Doubleday.
—Peter Spier's Christmas. Spier, Peter, illus. LC 80-2875. 40p. (ps-3). 1988. pap. 6.95 (ISBN 0-385-24580-7). Doubleday.
A Star for Christmas. (Illus.). 26p. (ps-1). 1988. pap. 2.95 incl. sticker pgs. (ISBN 0-671-66870-6). S&S Trade.
Sterchele, Christina L., illus. Twelve Days of Christmas. (ps-6). 1981. 3.50 (ISBN 0-913545-07-4). Moonlight FL.
Stevenson, James. The Night after Christmas. LC 81-1022. (Illus.). 32p. (gr. k-3). 1981. 13.95 (ISBN 0-688-00547-0); PLB 13.88 (ISBN 0-688-00548-9). Greenwillow.
—The Worst Person's Christmas. LC 90-39716. (Illus.). 32p. (ps up). 1991. 13.95 (ISBN 0-688-10210-7); PLB 13.88 (ISBN 0-688-10211-5). Greenwillow.
Still, Kathy. Christmas Cutouts. Still, Kathy, illus. 16p. (ps up). 1988. pap. 10.95 (ISBN 0-06-446086-X, Trophy). HarpC Child Bks.
Stock, Catherine. Christmas Time. Stock, Catherine, illus. LC 89-71249. 32p. (ps-1). 1990. 11.95 (ISBN 0-02-788403-1, Bradbury Pr). Macmillan Child Grp.
—Sampson: The Christmas Cat. Stock, Catherine, illus. LC 84-9946. 32p. (ps-3). 1984. 10.95 (ISBN 0-399-21002-4, Putnam). Putnam Pub Group.
Stone, Jon & Bailey, Joe. Christmas Eve on Sesame Street. Mathieu, Joe, illus. LC 81-50247. 64p. (ps-2). 1991. 7.95 (ISBN 0-394-84733-4, Random Juv); lib. bdg. 6.99 (ISBN 0-394-94733-9, Random Juv). Random.
Story of Christmas. (gr. k-3). incl. tape 6.97 (ISBN 0-89191-602-4, 26021). Cook.
Stout, Robert T. The Noorps Are Coming. Stout, Robert T., illus. 32p. (ps-6). 1982. pap. 3.95 (ISBN 0-911049-05-3). Yuletide Intl.
Sturgis, Matthew. Tosca's Christmas. Mortimer, Anne, illus. 1989. 11.95 (ISBN 0-8037-0722-3). Dial Bks Young.
Summers, Jack L. The Christmas People. LC 88-51480. 180p. 1988. 6.95 (ISBN 1-55523-208-6). Winston-Derek.
Taylor, Mark A. Have You Ever Seen an Angel? Seward, Lyn, illus. 20p. (ps). 1987. 1.59 (ISBN 0-87403-310-1, 2010). Standard Pub.
Tazewell, Charles. Littlest Angel. Leone, S., illus. 32p. (gr. k-6). 1946. PLB 14.60 (ISBN 0-516-03533-9). Childrens.
—The Littlest Angel. 32p. (gr. k-6). 1985. pap. 5.95 (ISBN 0-89542-923-3). Ideals.
Tennyson, Noel, illus. Santa Is Coming. LC 80-54768. 24p. (ps-k). 1981. spiral plastic bdg. 3.95 (ISBN 0-394-84797-0). Random.
Tharlet, Eve. Christmas Won't Wait. Clements, Andrew, tr. from FRE. (Illus.). (gr. k up). 1990. 14.95 (ISBN 0-88708-151-7). Picture Bk Studio.
Thayer, Marjorie. The Christmas Strangers. Freeman, Don, illus. LC 75-38575. 48p. (gr. 2-5). 1976. PLB 17.27 (ISBN 0-516-08719-3, Golden Gate). Childrens.
Theroux, Paul. A Christmas Card. Lawrence, John, illus. 96p. (gr. 4-6). 1978. 13.95 (ISBN 0-395-27204-1). HM.
Thomas, Dylan. A Child's Christmas in Wales. Hyman, Trina S., illus. LC 85-766. 48p. (gr. 4-6). 1985. reinforced bdg. 14.95 (ISBN 0-8234-0565-6). Holiday.
Thomas, Joan G. The Christmas Angel. Thomas, Joan G., illus. 20p. (gr. 1-5). 1988. pap. 3.95 (ISBN 0-8192-1429-9). Morehouse Pub.
Thompson, Kathleen. My Book of Christmas Stories. LC 87-16410. (Illus.). 24p. (gr. 3-5). 1987. PLB 14.65g (ISBN 0-8172-3163-3). Raintree Pubs.
Tift, Tom. Santa & the Captain: A Mystic Christmas Tale. Clover, Barbara, illus. LC 89-81337. 24p. (Orig.). (gr. 2-4). 1989. pap. 6.95 (ISBN 0-9624607-0-2). Hickory Ridge Pr.
Tolstoy, Leo. Papa Panov's Special Day. 2nd ed. Molder, Mig, retold by. Morris, Tony, illus. 32p. 1988. 11.95 (ISBN 0-7459-1358-X). Lion USA.
Tompert, Ann. The Silver Whistle. Peck, Beth, illus. LC 88-1446. 32p. (gr. k-3). 1988. 14.95 (ISBN 0-02-789160-7, Mcmillan Child Bk). Macmillan Child Grp.
Tornqvist, Rita. The Christmas Carp. Kilburn, Greta, tr. Tornqvist, Marit, illus. 32p. (gr. k-3). 1990. 13.95 (ISBN 91-29-59784-6, Pub. by R & S Bks). FS&G.
Trent, Robbie. The First Christmas. rev. ed. Simont, Marc, illus. LC 89-29729. 32p. (ps-2). 1990. 9.95 (ISBN 0-06-026165-X); PLB 9.89 (ISBN 0-06-026166-8). HarpC Child Bks.
Tripp, Valerie. Molly's Surprise: A Christmas Story. Payne, C. F., illus. LC 86-60627. 65p. (Orig.). (gr. 2-5). 1986. 12.95 (ISBN 0-937295-24-8); pap. 5.95 (ISBN 0-937295-25-6). Pleasant Co.
—Molly's Surprise: A Christmas Story. Thieme, Jeanne, ed. Payne, C. F., illus. 72p. (gr. 2-5). 1990. PLB 12.95 (ISBN 0-937295-87-6). Pleasant Co.
Trivas, Irene. Emma's Christmas: An Old Song Re-sung & Pictured. LC 88-1640. (Illus.). 32p. (ps-2). 1988. 13.95 (ISBN 0-531-05780-1); PLB 13.99 (ISBN 0-531-08380-2). Orchard Bks Watts.
Trosclair. A Cajun Night Before Christmas. Jacobs, Howard, ed. Rice, James, illus. LC 74-151725. 48p. (gr. 6-12). 1973. 11.95 (ISBN 0-88289-002-6). Pelican.
Tudor, Tasha. A Book of Christmas. (Illus.). (ps up). 1987. 12.95 (ISBN 0-399-21475-5, Philomel Bks). Putnam Pub Group.
—Dolls' Christmas. Tudor, Tasha, illus. LC 59-12744. (gr. k-3). 1979. 6.95 (ISBN 0-8098-1026-3); pap. 4.95 (ISBN 0-8098-2912-6). McKay.
Turner, Thomas N. Hillbilly Night Afore Christmas. Rice, James, illus. LC 83-4120. 32p. (gr. 1 up). 1983. 11.95 (ISBN 0-88289-367-X). Pelican.
Two-Minute Christmas Stories. (Illus.). 36p. (ps-1). 1989. write for info. (ISBN 0-307-12188-7, Pub. by Golden Bks). Western Pub.

Tyler, Linda W. After Christmas Tree. (ps-3). 1990. 12.95 (ISBN 0-670-83045-3). Viking Child Bks.

Van Allsburg, Chris. Polar Express. Van Allsburg, Chris, illus. LC 85-10907. 32p. (gr. 2 up). 1985. 17.95 (ISBN 0-395-38949-6). HM.

Van Leeuwen, Jean. The Great Christmas Kidnapping Caper. Kellogg, Steven, illus. LC 75-9201. 144p. (gr. 2-6). 1975. 12.95 (ISBN 0-685-01454-1). Dial Bks Young.

—The Great Christmas Kidnapping Caper. Kellogg, Steven, illus. 172p. (gr. 3 up). 1990. pap. 3.95 (ISBN 0-14-034287-7, Puffin). Puffin Bks.

—Oliver & Amanda's Christmas. Schweninger, Ann, illus. 9.95 (ISBN 0-685-29542-7). Dial Bks Young.

—Oliver & Amanda's Christmas. 1989. 9.95 (ISBN 0-8037-0636-7); PLB 9.89 (ISBN 0-8037-0647-2). Dial Bks Young.

VanRynbach, Iris. Cecily's Christmas. LC 87-34083. (Illus.). 32p. (ps-1). 1988. 11.95 (ISBN 0-688-07832-X); lib. bdg. 11.88 (ISBN 0-688-07833-8). Greenwillow.

Vernon, Judy L. All Ears: A Christmas Story. 25p. (Orig.). (gr. 2-8). 1989. pap. 4.95 (ISBN 0-9617776-4-8). J Vernon.

Verschuren, Ineke, compiled by. The Christmas Story Book. 430p. (gr. 4-8). Repr. of 1986 ed. 29.50 (ISBN 0-86315-077-2, Pub. by Floris Bks UK). Gryphon Hse.

Vincent, Gabrielle. Merry Christmas, Ernest & Celestine. Vincent, Gabrielle, illus. LC 83-14155. 32p. (gr. k-3). 1984. PLB 11.88 (ISBN 0-688-02605-2); 12.00 (ISBN 0-688-02606-0). Greenwillow.

Wainwright, Richard M. Poofin: The Cloud That Cried on Christmas. Crompton, Jack, illus. 40p. Repr. 12.95g (ISBN 0-9619566-1-5). Family Life.

Waldrop, Ruth. Santa Grows up in Mother Goose Land. Hendrix, Hurston H., illus. 34p. (ps-3). 1986. pap. 4.95 (ISBN 0-9616894-0-4); cassette incl. RuSk Inc.

Wallace, Bill. The Christmas Spurs. LC 90-55111. 128p. (gr. 3-7). 1990. 13.95 (ISBN 0-8234-0831-0). Holiday.

Walt Disney Company Staff. Reindeer Round-Up: A Merry Christmas at the North Pole. Walt Disney Company Staff, illus. 26p. (ps up). 1988. 19.95 (ISBN 1-55578-313-9). Worlds Wonder.

Walter, Mildred P. Have a Happy... Byard, Carole, illus. LC 88-8962. 144p. (gr. 3-6). 1989. 10.95 (ISBN 0-688-06923-1). Lothrop.

Watson, Clyde. How Brown Mouse Kept Christmas. Watson, Wendy, illus. LC 80-18532. 32p. (ps-3). 1980. 8.95 (ISBN 0-374-33494-3). FS&G.

We Wish You a Merry Christmas. (Illus.). 16.95 (ISBN 0-685-29547-8). Arcade Pub Inc.

Wedell, Robert F. Rolf & the Rainbow Christmas. M. J. Art Concepts Staff, illus. LC 89-91971. 133p. (Orig.). 1989. pap. 5.00 (ISBN 0-9625221-1-2). Milrob Pr.

Wells, Joel. The Manger Mouse. Anderson, Annette B., illus. 1990. 14.95 (ISBN 0-88347-255-4). Thomas More.

Wells, Rosemary. Max Christmas Doll. (ps-3). 1987. 10.95 (ISBN 0-8037-0425-9). Dial Bks Young.

—Max's Christmas. Wells, Rosemary, illus. LC 85-27547. 32p. (ps-2). 1986. 8.95 (ISBN 0-8037-0289-2); PLB 8.89 (ISBN 0-8037-0290-6). Dial Bks Young.

—Morris's Disappearing Bag: A Christmas Story. Wells, Rosemary, illus. LC 75-9202. (ps-3). 1978. pap. 3.95 (ISBN 0-8037-5509-0). Dial Bks Young.

Welser, Matthew W. God Promised Us a Savior. (Illus.). 24p. (ps-4). 1989. pap. 1.39 (ISBN 0-570-09019-9, 59-1442). Concordia.

White, John W. The Christmas Mice. Torres, Dorothy B., illus. 32p. (ps-3). 1984. 10.95 (ISBN 0-913299-15-4, Pub. by Angelfood Bks). Stillpoint.

Wiggin, Kate D. The Birds' Christmas Carol. (Illus.). (gr. 4-6). 13.95 (ISBN 0-395-07205-0). HM.

—Birds Christmas Carol. 1989. pap. 2.50 (ISBN 0-590-42118-2). Scholastic Inc.

—The Birds' Christmas Carol. (Illus.). 69p. 1990. Repr. of 1886 ed. 15.95 (ISBN 0-9616844-6-1). Greenhouse Pub.

Wildsmith, Brian. A Christmas Story. Wildsmith, Brian, illus. LC 89-7959. 32p. (ps-3). 1989. 15.95 (ISBN 0-679-80074-3); PLB 15.99 (ISBN 0-679-90074-8). Knopf.

Wilhelm, Hans. Schnitzels First Christmas. 1989. pap. 13.95 (ISBN 0-671-67977-5). S&S Trade.

—Waldo, Tell Me about Christmas. (Illus.). 40p. (gr. 3 up). 1989. 4.95 (ISBN 0-8378-1846-X). Gibson.

Wilkin, Eloise, illus. Baby's First Christmas. LC 80-80710. 14p. (ps). 1980. 3.95 (ISBN 0-394-84575-7). Random.

Williamson, Duncan. Tell Me a Story for Christmas. (Illus.). 120p. (gr. 5-9). 1989. pap. 11.95 (ISBN 0-86241-243-9, Pub. by Cnngt Pub Ltd). Trafalgar Sq.

Winthrop, Elizabeth. A Child Is Born: The Christmas Story. Mikolaycak, Charles, photos by. LC 82-11728. (Illus.). 32p. (gr. k-3). 1983. reinforced bdg. 14.95 (ISBN 0-8234-0472-2). Holiday.

Wiseman, Bernard. Christmas with Morris & Boris. Wiseman, Bernard, illus. LC 83-11962. 44p. (gr. 1-3). 1983. 12.95 (ISBN 0-316-94855-1). Little.

—Christmas with Morris & Boris. 40p. (gr. k-3). 1986. pap. 1.95 (ISBN 0-590-33257-0). Scholastic Inc.

—Christmas with Morris & Boris. 40p. (gr. k-3). 1991. pap. 2.50 (ISBN 0-590-42434-3). Scholastic Inc.

Wolf, Jill & Moore, Clement C. Teddy Bears Night Before Christmas. Rudegeair, Jean, illus. 24p. (gr. 3-6). 1985. pap. 2.25 (ISBN 0-89954-330-8). Antioch Pub Co.

Wolff, Ashley. Year of Beasts. 1989. pap. 3.95 (ISBN 0-525-44541-2, DCB). Dutton Child Bks.

Wooding, Sharon. Arthur's Christmas Wish. Wooding, Sharon, illus. LC 85-28690. 32p. (gr. k-3). 1986. 12.95 (ISBN 0-689-31211-3, Atheneum Child Bk). Macmillan Child Grp.

Worley, Daryl. Billy & the Christmas Present. Daab, John, illus. 32p. (gr. 2-4). 1989. 9.95 (ISBN 0-924067-01-2). Tyke Corp.

Yeomans, Thomas. For Every Child a Star: A Christmas Story. DePaola, Tomie, illus. LC 84-499. 32p. (gr. k-3). 1986. reinforced bdg. 14.95 (ISBN 0-8234-0526-5). Holiday.

Yorinks, Arthur. Christmas in July. Egielski, Richard, illus. LC 91-55244. 32p. (ps-3). 1991. 14.95 (ISBN 0-06-020256-4); PLB 14.89 (ISBN 0-06-020257-2). HarpC Child Bks.

Zalben, Jane B. Porcupine's Christmas Blues. Zalben, Jane B., illus. 32p. 1982. 9.95 (ISBN 0-399-20893-3, Philomel). Putnam Pub Group.

Zeplin, Zeno. Great Texas Christmas Legends. 2nd ed. Jones, Judy, illus. 156p. (gr. 4 up). 1987. 10.95 (ISBN 0-9615760-2-2); pap. 6.95 (ISBN 0-9615760-3-0). Nel-Mar Pub.

Ziefert, Harriet. Nicky's Christmas Surprise. Brown, Richard, illus. LC 85-5681. 20p. (ps). 1985. pap. 4.95 (ISBN 0-14-050555-5, Puffin). Puffin Bks.

Zimmann, William C., Sr. The Legend of the Christmas Donkey. (gr. k-4). 1984. 1.95 (ISBN 0-89536-989-3, 7540). CSS of Ohio.

Zolotow, Charlotte. The Beautiful Christmas Tree. Robbins, Ruth, illus. 32p. (gr. k-3). 1983. 13.95 (ISBN 0-395-27676-4); pap. 4.95 (ISBN 0-395-34925-7). HM.

CHRISTMAS–POETRY

see Christmas Poetry

CHRISTMAS CARDS

see Greeting Cards

CHRISTMAS CAROLS

see Carols

CHRISTMAS COOKERY

Cuyler, Margery. The All-Around Christmas Book. Jones, Corbett, illus. LC 82-3104. 96p. (gr. 2-5). 1982. 11.95 (ISBN 0-03-060387-0); pap. 4.95 (ISBN 0-03-062183-6). H Holt & Co.

Meyer, Carolyn. Christmas Crafts. Lobel, Anita, illus. LC 74-2608. 160p. (gr. 5 up). 1974. 13.95 (ISBN 0-06-024197-7). HarpC Child Bks.

CHRISTMAS DECORATIONS

Barth, Edna. Holly, Reindeer, & Colored Lights: The Story of the Christmas Symbols. Arndt, Ursula, illus. LC 71-157731. 96p. (gr. 3-6). 1979. 13.95 (ISBN 0-395-28842-8, Clarion). HM.

Crowther, Robert. Punchout Christmas Decorations. 1989. pap. 5.95 (ISBN 0-671-68400-0). S&S Trade.

Davidson, Amanda. Teddy's Christmas Cutout Book. Davidson, Amanda, illus. 10p. (gr. k-2). 1987. 3.95 (ISBN 0-8050-0560-9). H Holt & Co.

De Paola, Tomie. The Family Christmas Tree Book. LC 80-12081. (Illus.). 32p. (gr. k-3). 1980. reinforced bdg. 14.95 (ISBN 0-8234-0416-1); pap. 5.95 (ISBN 0-8234-0535-4). Holiday.

Fowler, Virginia. Christmas Crafts & Customs Around the World. Fowler, Virginia, illus. LC 84-9770. 180p. (gr. 5 up). 1988. 11.95 (ISBN 0-671-66558-8); pap. 5.95 (ISBN 0-671-67057-3). S&S Trade.

Henderson, Kathy. Christmas Trees. LC 89-859. (Illus.). 48p. (gr. k-4). 1989. PLB 14.60 (ISBN 0-516-01162-6); pap. 4.95 (ISBN 0-516-41162-4). Childrens.

Kingshead Corporation Staff. Cut, Color & Create: Make Your Own: Christmas Garland. Kingshead Corporation Staff, illus. 24p. (ps-2). 1987. pap. 2.97 (ISBN 1-55941-020-5). Kingshead Corp.

—Cut, Color & Create: Make Your Own: Christmas Ornaments. Kingshead Corporation Staff, illus. 24p. (gr. 2 up). 1987. pap. 2.97 (ISBN 1-55941-018-3). Kingshead Corp.

—Cut, Color & Create: Make Your Own: Christmas Snowflakes. Kingshead Corporation Staff, illus. 24p. (gr. 3 up). 1987. pap. 2.97 (ISBN 1-55941-019-1). Kingshead Corp.

—Cut, Color & Create: Make Your Own: Easy Christmas Ornaments. Kingshead Corporation Staff, illus. 24p. (ps-2). 1987. pap. 2.97 (ISBN 1-55941-016-7). Kingshead Corp.

—Cut, Color & Create: Make Your Own: Farm. Kingshead Corporation Staff, illus. 24p. (ps-4). 1987. pap. 2.97 (ISBN 1-55941-007-8). Kingshead Corp.

—Cut, Color & Create: Make Your Own: Masks. Kingshead Corporation Staff, illus. 24p. (ps-4). 1988. pap. 2.97 (ISBN 0-685-22520-8). Kingshead Corp.

—Cut, Color & Create: Make Your Own: Number People. Kingshead Corporation Staff, illus. 24p. (ps-3). 1987. pap. 2.97 (ISBN 1-55941-004-3). Kingshead Corp.

—Cut, Color & Create: Make Your Own: Number Blocks. Kingshead Corporation Staff, illus. 24p. (ps-3). 1987. pap. 2.97 (ISBN 1-55941-006-X). Kingshead Corp.

Meyer, Carolyn. Christmas Crafts. Lobel, Anita, illus. LC 74-2608. 160p. (gr. 5 up). 1974. 13.95 (ISBN 0-06-024197-7). HarpC Child Bks.

Purdy, Susan. Christmas Gifts for You to Make. Purdy, Susan, illus. LC 76-10160. (gr. 4-6). 1976. (Lipp Jr Bks); pap. 4.95 o. p. (ISBN 0-397-31696-8, Lipp Jr Bks). HarpC Child Bks.

Spencer, Roberta. Christmas Fun Pack. Merrell, Patrick, illus. 32p. (Orig.). (gr. 1-4). 1984. pap. 3.95 (ISBN 0-590-33422-0). Scholastic Inc.

Supraner, Robyn. Merry Christmas: Things to Make & Do. Barto, Renzo, illus. LC 80-23884. 48p. (gr. 1-5). 1981. PLB 11.89 (ISBN 0-89375-422-6); pap. 2.95 (ISBN 0-89375-423-4). Troll Assocs.

CHRISTMAS ENTERTAINMENTS

see also Christmas Plays

Chancellor, Betty. A Child's Christmas Cookbook. Obering, Kay & Nast, Thomas, illus. 40p. (Orig.). (gr. 1-8). 1969. pap. 4.00 (ISBN 0-914510-00-2). Evergreen.

Christmas Delights. 12p. (gr. 1-6). 1971. pap. 3.25 (ISBN 0-914510-02-9). Evergreen.

Clary, Linda & Harms, Larry. Christmas Music for Little People. Bradley, Richard, ed. (Illus.). 32p. (ps). 1985. bk & cassette 9.95 (ISBN 0-89748-160-7). Bradley Pubns.

Hill, G. L. The Best Birthday: A Christmas Entertainment for Children. (gr. 5-6). 10.95 (ISBN 0-89190-404-2, Pub. by Am Repr). Amereon Ltd.

Menotti, Gian-Carlo. Amahl & the Night Visitors. Lemieux, Michele, illus. LC 84-27196. 64p. (ps up). 1986. 15.00 (ISBN 0-688-05426-9); lib. bdg. 14.88 (ISBN 0-688-05427-7, Morrow Jr Bks). Morrow Jr Bks.

Schlegl, William. Bible Christmas Puzzles. Van Kanegan, Jeff, illus. 48p. (gr. 3 up). 1987. pap. 6.95 (ISBN 0-86653-409-1, SS 884). Good Apple.

Thomas, Dylan. A Child's Christmas in Wales. Ardizzone, Edward, illus. LC 80-66216. 48p. 1980. 13.95 (ISBN 0-87923-339-7); pap. 9.95 (ISBN 0-87923-529-2). Godine.

Webster, George P. & Nast, Thomas. Santa Claus & His Works. (Illus.). 12p. (gr. 1-8). 1972. pap. 3.25 (ISBN 0-914510-03-7). Evergreen.

Zwebner, Janet. The Follow That Sleigh Christmas Activity Book. 48p. (gr. 1-5). 1990. wkbk. 5.95 (ISBN 0-944007-62-7). Shapolsky Pubs.

CHRISTMAS PLAYS

Behrens, June. Christmas-Magic Wagon. Burgeson, Marjorie, illus. LC 75-14007. 32p. (gr. k-4). 1975. PLB 15.93 (ISBN 0-516-08880-7, Golden Gate). Childrens.

Berry, Linda. Christmas Plays for Older Children. (gr. 5-7). 1981. saddle wire 2.95 (ISBN 0-8054-9733-1). Broadman.

Carson, Patti & Dellosa, Janet. Christmas Readiness Activities. (Illus.). 32p. (ps-k). 1983. pap. 1.98 (ISBN 0-88724-049-6, CD-8025). Carson-Dellos.

Dramas Navidenos para Ninos. 32p. (Orig.). (gr. 3-6). 1991. pap. 1.75 (ISBN 0-311-08226-2). Casa Bautista.

Groff, Phylis. The Christmas Nightingale. 1935. 4.50 (ISBN 0-87602-115-1). Anchorage.

Jordan, Myra J. & Grant, Roy E. Santa's Problem. (Illus.). 30p. (Orig.). (ps-1). 1980. pap. 5.00 (ISBN 0-914562-08-8). Merriam-Eddy.

Kamerman, Sylvia E., ed. The Big Book of Christmas Plays. LC 88-15691. (gr. 4-12). 1988. 16.95 (ISBN 0-8238-0288-4). Plays.

—Christmas Play Favorites for Young People. (Orig.). (gr. 4-12). 1982. pap. 12.00 (ISBN 0-8238-0257-4). Plays.

King, Martha B. A Christmas Carol. 1941. 4.50 (ISBN 0-87602-114-3). Anchorage.

Ludwig, Nancy. Christmas Puppets Plays & Art Project Puppets. Fowler, Christopher, illus. 32p. (gr. k-3). 1983. pap. 1.98 (ISBN 0-88724-045-3, CD-8021). Carson-Dellos.

Menotti, Gian-Carlo. Amahl & the Night Visitors. Lemieux, Michele, illus. LC 84-27196. 64p. (ps up). 1986. 15.00 (ISBN 0-688-05426-9); lib. bdg. 14.88 (ISBN 0-688-05427-7, Morrow Jr Bks). Morrow Jr Bks.

Miller, Sarah W. Christmas Drama for Youth. LC 76-20255. 96p. (Orig.). (gr. 7 up). 1976. pap. 4.95 (ISBN 0-8054-7511-7). Broadman.

Pickett, Margaret E. What's Keeping You, Santa? A Christmas Musical Program Package. Brown, Blanche M., illus. 74p. (gr. k-12). 1983. Incl Production Guide with choir arranged songs, cass of songs, thirty slides from bk. 49.95 (ISBN 0-913939-01-3). TP Assocs.

Snyder, J. L. What Christmas Means to Me. Powell, Terry, illus. 43p. (gr. 8-12). 1989. pap. text ed. 2.50 (ISBN 0-87227-134-X). Reg Baptist.

CHRISTMAS POETRY

see also Carols

Arico, Diane, ed. A Season of Joy: Favorite Stories & Poems for Christmas. San Souci, Daniel, illus. LC 86-29059. 64p. (gr. k-3). 1987. pap. 8.95 (ISBN 0-385-23901-7). Doubleday.

Ashley, Jill. Riddles about Christmas. Brook, Bonnie, ed. Gray, Rob, illus. 32p. (ps-3). 1990. 5.95 (ISBN 0-671-70554-7); PLB 10.98 (ISBN 0-671-70552-0). Silver Pr.

Away in a Manger. 1989. 6.95 (ISBN 0-02-689338-X). Checkerboard Pr.

Barry, Robert. Mr. Willoby's Christmas Tree. Galdone, Paul, illus. (gr. k-3). 1963. text ed. 12.95 (ISBN 0-07-003877-5). McGraw.

Brett, Jan. The Twelve Days of Christmas. (Illus.). 32p. 1990. 3.95 (ISBN 0-399-22197-2, Putnam). Putnam Pub Group.

Brett, Jan, illus. The Twelve Days of Christmas. 1990. 14.95 (ISBN 0-399-22037-2, Philomel Bks). Putnam Pub Group.

The Chubby Night Before Christmas. 1984. 3.95 (ISBN 0-671-50952-7, Little Simon). S&S Trade.

Cloonan, Paula, illus. The Twelve Days of Christmas. 24p. (ps-5). 1990. 14.95 (ISBN 0-87226-438-6). P Bedrick Bks.

Counihan, Claire. Twelve Days of Christmas. 1989. pap. 2.50 (ISBN 0-590-42918-3). Scholastic Inc.

Duncan, Beverly K. Christmas in the Stable. (Illus.). 32p. 1990. 14.95 (ISBN 0-15-217758-2). HarbraceJ.

Fleming, Denise, illus. The Merry Christmas Book: A First Book of Holiday Stories & Poems. LC 86-3258. 48p. (gr. 3-8). 1986. (Random Juv); (Random Juv). Random.

Harrison, Michael & Stuart-Clark, Christopher, eds. The Oxford Book of Christmas Poems. (Illus.). 160p. (gr. 3 up). 1988. 16.95 (ISBN 0-19-276051-3); pap. 9.95 (ISBN 0-19-276080-7). Oxford U Pr.

Hillert, Margaret. Sing a Song of Christmas. 2nd ed. Hand, Judy, illus. 32p. (gr. k-2). 1989. 1.99 (ISBN 0-87403-598-8, 3858). Standard Pub.

Hollyn, Lynn. Lynn Hollyn's Christmas Toyland. Anazlone, Lori, illus. LC 84-5212. 40p. (ps-1). 1985. Knopf.

Livingston, Myra C., selected by. Christmas Poems. Hyman, Trina S., illus. LC 83-18559. 32p. (ps-3). 1984. reinforced bdg. 13.95 (ISBN 0-8234-0508-7). Holiday.

Livingston, Myra C., ed. Poems of Christmas. LC 80-13627. 132p. (gr. 5 up). 1980. 13.95 (ISBN 0-689-50180-3, M K McElderry). Macmillan Child Grp.

Lobel, Adrianne. A Small Sheep in a Pear Tree. LC 76-58721. (Illus.). 32p. (gr. k-3). 1977. 12.95 (ISBN 0-06-023952-2); PLB 12.89 (ISBN 0-06-023953-0). HarpC Child Bks.

McGinley, Phyllis. Year Without a Santa Claus. Werth, Kurt, illus. (gr. k-3). 1981. 12.95 (ISBN 0-397-30399-8, Lipp Jr Bks); PLB 14.89 (ISBN 0-397-31969-X). HarpC Child Bks.

Moore, Clement C. The Grandma Moses Night before Christmas. 2nd ed. Moses, Grandma, illus. LC 90-24145. 32p. 1991. 15.00 (ISBN 0-679-81526-0, Random Juv); lib. bdg. 15.99 (ISBN 0-679-91526-5). Random.

—The Night Before Christmas. Trimby, Elisa, illus. LC 77-71994. (gr. 1 up). 1977. pap. 5.95 (ISBN 0-385-13615-3). Doubleday.

—The Night Before Christmas. (Illus.). 16p. (gr. 1-8). 1970. pap. 4.00 (ISBN 0-914510-01-0). Evergreen.

—Night Before Christmas. Fujikawa, Gyo, illus. (ps). 1961. 5.95 (ISBN 0-448-02935-9, G&D). Putnam Pub Group.

—The Night Before Christmas. Weisgard, Leonard, illus. (gr. k-3). 1.95 (ISBN 0-448-04205-3, G&D). Putnam Pub Group.

—The Night Before Christmas. De Paola, Tomie, illus. LC 80-11758. 32p. (ps up). 1980. reinforced bdg. 14.95 (ISBN 0-8234-0414-5); pap. 5.95 (ISBN 0-8234-0417-X). Holiday.

—Night Before Christmas. Moses, Grandma, illus. (gr. k-2). 1962. 10.95 (ISBN 0-394-80741-3, Random Juv). Random.

—The Night Before Christmas. Gorsline, Douglas, illus. 32p. (ps-1). 1985. pap. 5.95 incl. cassette (ISBN 0-394-87658-X). Random.

—The Night Before Christmas. (Illus.). 48p. (gr. k-3). 1988. bds. 12.89 (ISBN 0-8167-1890-3); PLB 11.89 (ISBN 0-8167-1209-3); pap. text ed. 3.95 (ISBN 0-8167-1210-7). Troll Assocs.

—The Night Before Christmas. Goode, Diane, illus. LC 82-62171. 32p. 1988. pap. 1.25 (ISBN 0-394-81938-1, Random Juv). Random.

—The Night Before Christmas. Foreman, Michael, illus. LC 88-50097. (ps up). 1988. pap. 11.95 (ISBN 0-670-82388-0). Viking Child Bks.

—The Night Before Christmas. Amoss, Berthe, illus. 10p. (ps-7). 1989. pap. 3.95 (ISBN 0-922589-06-2). More Than Card.

—The Night Before Christmas. LC 89-42998. (Illus.). 80p. 1989. 4.95 (ISBN 0-89471-754-5). Running Pr.

—The Night Before Christmas. Harness, Cheryl, illus. LC 88-35019. 40p. (ps-8). 1990. 6.95 (ISBN 0-394-82698-1, Random Juv); lib. bdg. 8.99 (ISBN 0-394-92698-6). Random.

—The Night Before Christmas. Clonan, Paula, illus. LC 89-6560. 32p. (ps up). 1990. 12.95 (ISBN 0-87226-416-5, Bedrick Blackie). P Bedrick Bks.

—The Night Before Christmas. Rice, James, illus. 32p. 1990. 13.95 (ISBN 0-88289-755-1). Pelican.

—Night Before Christmas. 1986. 12.95 (ISBN 0-02-689413-0). Macmillan Child Grp.

—Night Before Christmas. 1989. pap. 2.25 (ISBN 0-671-68408-6). S&S Trade.

—The Night Before Christmas. Watson, Wendy, illus. 32p. (ps-1). 1990. 13.95 (ISBN 0-395-53624-3, Clarion Bks). HM.

—The Night Before Christmas. Lobel, Anita, illus. LC 84-4342. 32p. (ps-2). 1988. pap. 3.95 (ISBN 0-394-81968-3). Knopf.

—Night Before Christmas. 1990. 5.98 (ISBN 0-8317-6402-3). Smithmark.

—The Night Before Christmas. Marshall, James, illus. 32p. (ps-3). 1989. 5.95 (ISBN 0-590-33805-6); pap. 5.95 incl. cass. (ISBN 0-590-63330-9); pap. 2.50 (ISBN 0-590-42758-X). Scholastic Inc.

—The Night Before Christmas. Regan, Dana, illus. LC 90-22388. 24p. (ps up). 1991. 2.95 (ISBN 0-694-00365-4). HarpC Child Bks.

—Night Before Christmas Coloring Book. 1986. pap. 2.95 (ISBN 0-671-62959-X). S&S Trade.

—Twas the Night Before Christmas. Hoffer, Linda, illus. LC 85-61305. 24p. (ps up). 1985. 6.95 (ISBN 0-88088-548-3, 885483). Peter Pauper.

—Twas the Night Before Christmas: A Visit from St. Nicholas. Smith, Jessie W., illus. (ps-2). 1912. 13.95 (ISBN 0-395-06952-1). HM.

Nedobeck, Don, illus. Nedobecks Twelve Days of Christmas. (gr. 1-8). 1988. Repr. lib. bdg. 9.95 (ISBN 0-944314-02-3). New Wrinkle.

The Night Before Christmas. 3.95 (ISBN 0-7214-5205-1). Ladybird Bks.

Prelutsky, Jack. It's Christmas. Hafner, Marilyn, illus. LC 81-1100. 48p. (gr. 1-3). 1981. 12.95 (ISBN 0-688-00439-3); PLB 12.88 (ISBN 0-688-00440-7). Greenwillow.

Roche, P. K. At Christmas Be Merry: Poems for Christmas Week. Roche, P. K., illus. LC 84-21917. 32p. (ps-3). 1986. pap. 11.95 (ISBN 0-670-80421-5). Viking Child Bks.

Wilner, Isabel. B Is for Bethlehem: A Christmas Alphabet. Kleven, Elisa, illus. 1990. 13.95 (ISBN 0-525-44622-2, DCB). Dutton Child Bks.

Zabar, Abbie. A Perfectly Irregular Christmas Tree. Zabar, Abbie, illus. 40p. 1991. 14.00 (ISBN 0-517-58608-8, C N Potter Bks). Crown.

CHRISTOLOGY

see Jesus Christ

CHRONOLOGY

see Calendars; Time

CHRONOLOGY, HISTORICAL

Alvarez del Real, Maria E., ed. Fechas Que Han Hecho Historia. (SPA., Illus.). 320p. (Orig.). 1988. pap. 5.00x (ISBN 0-944499-41-4). Editorial Amer.

CHURCH

see also Christian Unity; Christianity

Bennett, Marian. I Go to Church. Dorr, Mary A., illus. 10p. (ps). 1985. 3.95 (ISBN 0-87239-911-7, 2751). Standard Pub.

Campbell, Stan, ed. Any Old Time, Bk. 3. 80p. (gr. 7 up). 1985. pap. 9.99 (ISBN 0-88207-648-5). Victor Bks.

Caswell, Helen. My Big Family at Church. 1990. pap. 4.95 (ISBN 0-687-27533-4). Abingdon.

Cooper, Harold. Believing Truth about the Church. (Illus.). 80p. (gr. 8-9). 1975. pap. 3.50 (ISBN 0-89114-070-0); P. 64. tchr's. ed. 1.50 (ISBN 0-89114-071-9). Baptist Pub Hse.

Hogan, Bernice. The Church Is a Who. Steiger, John, illus. LC 78-24087. (gr. k-3). 1979. 9.95 (ISBN 0-8272-0442-6). CBP.

Richards, H. J. The Mass for Children. 32p. (Orig.). 1991. pap. 3.95 (ISBN 0-8146-2038-8). Liturgical Pr.

Robbins, Duffy. Any Old Time, Bk. 8. 80p. (gr. 7 up). 1987. pap. 9.99 (ISBN 0-89693-514-0). Victor Bks.

Robertson, Everett, ed. Puppet Scripts for Use at Church, No. 2. LC 78-72843. (gr. k up). 1980. saddle-wire 7.95 (ISBN 0-8054-7519-2). Broadman.

Veerman, David R. Any Old Time, Bk. 2. 80p. (gr. 7 up). 1984. pap. 9.99 (ISBN 0-88207-596-9). Victor Bks.

Waybill, Marjorie. God Builds His Church: Activity Book. Converse, James, illus. 72p. (Orig.). (gr. 4-5). 1988. pap. 3.00 (ISBN 0-8361-3457-5). Herald Pr.

Willis, Doris. I Like to Come to My Church. (ps). 1990. 3.95 (ISBN 0-687-03122-2). Abingdon.

CHURCH AND STATE

see also Religious Liberty

Barton, Charles D. The Myth of Separation. 296p. (Orig.). (gr. 7 up). 1989. pap. 7.95 (ISBN 0-925279-04-8). Wallbuilders.

Weiss, Ann E. God & Government: The Separation of Church & State. 160p. (gr. 5-9). 1982. 9.95 (ISBN 0-395-32085-2). HM.

—God & Government: The Separation of Church & State. 1990. pap. 3.95 (ISBN 0-395-54977-9). HM.

CHURCH ARCHITECTURE

see also Cathedrals; Churches

CHURCH BIOGRAPHY

see Christian Biography

CHURCH DENOMINATIONS

see Sects

CHURCH FESTIVALS

see Fasts and Feasts

CHURCH HISTORY

see also Church and State; Jews; Missions; Monasticism and Religious Orders; Popes; Protestantism; Reformation; Sects

also names of countries, states, etc. with the subdivision Church History (e.g. U. S.–Church History; etc.)

Halverson, Sandy. Church History Activity Book: Creative Scripture Learning Experiences about the Restoration for Children 4-12. 36p. (Orig.). (gr. 3-6). 1983. pap. 4.95 (ISBN 0-88290-213-X). Horizon Utah.

Huston, David A. The Light of the Pentecost: A Unique Historical Account of the New Testament Church. Penton, Ben, illus. (gr. 7 up). 1989. pap. 5.95 (ISBN 0-932345-03-4). Antioch Publishes.

Johnson, George, et al. The Story of the Church. LC 80-51329. 521p. (gr. 9). 1980. pap. 16.50 (ISBN 0-89555-156-X). Tan Bks Pubs.

Norwood, Frederick A. & Carr, Jo. Young Reader's Book of Church History. Armstrong, Tom, illus. LC 81-20505. 176p. (gr. 4 up). 1982. 0.90 (ISBN 0-687-46827-2). Abingdon.

Sidwell, Mark, ed. Faith of Our Fathers: Scenes from Church History. 216p. (Orig.). (gr. 9 up). 1989. pap. 6.95 (ISBN 0-89084-492-5). Bob Jones Univ Pr.

Traketellas, Demetrios. Growing in the Knowledge of Christ. 18p. (gr. 12). 1987. pap. 1.25 (ISBN 0-917651-43-X). Holy Cross Orthodox.

Vozdvizhensky, P. Moja pervaja Svjashchennaja Istorija, dlja detjej. (Illus.). 101p. (gr. 3-7). 1968. pap. 4.00 (ISBN 0-317-30407-0). Holy Trinity.

CHURCH HISTORY–FICTION

Lecomte, Eva. Paula, the Waldensian. Strong, W. M., tr. (gr. 3-7). 1942. pap. 5.95 (ISBN 0-87213-511-X). Loizeaux.

Oakley, Graham. The Church Mice & the Moon. Oakley, Graham, illus. LC 74-75569. 40p. (gr. k-3). 1974. 13.95 (ISBN 0-689-30437-4, Atheneum Childrens Bks). Macmillan Child Grp.

CHURCH HISTORY–REFORMATION

see Reformation

CHURCH MUSIC

see also Carols; Hymns

Advance Cal-Tech Inc. Let's Praise & Play: Children's Christian Mini-Piano Book. Kung, Edward, ed. Mc Kig, Susan, illus. Childe, Laura, intro. by. (Illus.). 36p. (ps-6). text ed. write for info. (ISBN 0-943759-00-5). Advance Cal Tech.

Benoit, David & Graff, Charles G. Theft by Deception. (Illus.). 12p. (Orig.). (gr. 7 up). 1987. pap. text ed. 1.50 (ISBN 0-923105-08-5). Glory Ministries.

Howard, Julie. Walk on the Water. 24p. (Orig.). 1990. pap. 5.95 (ISBN 0-8146-2011-6). Liturgical Pr.

Lenski, Lois. Sing for Peace. 16p. (ps-2). 1985. pap. 1.50 (ISBN 0-8361-3396-X). Herald Pr.

Nicol, Mary M. & Roth, Pamela K., eds. Ready, Set... Sing! (Songs for Sunday & Everyday) 96p. (Orig.). 1989. pap. 8.95 (ISBN 0-8170-1155-2). Judson.

Ogilvy, Carol & Tinkham, Trudy. Primary Christmas Concerts. 112p. (gr. k-3). 1989. 9.95 (ISBN 0-86653-485-7, GA1091). Good Apple.

Salvation Song Index. 6p. (gr. k-6). 1957. pap. 0.50 (ISBN 1-55976-204-7). CEF Press.

Songs to Play. (gr. k-3). 1987. 12.95 (ISBN 0-8054-4704-0). Broadman.

CHURCH OF CHRIST OF LATTER DAY SAINTS

see Mormons and Mormonism

CHURCH OF CHRIST, SCIENTIST

see Christian Science

CHURCH UNITY

see Christian Unity

CHURCHES

Here are entered general descriptive and historical works on churches which cannot be entered under Church Architecture. Works relating to the churches of a city are entered under the name of the city with the subdivision Churches.

see also Cathedrals

Johnson, Gordon G. & Putman, Bob. Our Church. LC 83-82990. (Illus.). 147p. (Orig.). (gr. 5-6). 1984. pap. 2.95 (ISBN 0-935797-06-8). Harvest IL.

CHURCHES–FICTION

Barrett, William E. Lilies of the Field. Silverman, Burt, illus. LC 62-8085. (gr. 7 up). 1967. 3.95 (ISBN 0-685-01491-6, Im); pap. 3.95 (ISBN 0-385-07246-5, Im). Doubleday.

Grove, Vicki. He Gave Her Roses. 144p. (Orig.). (gr. 9-12). 1989. pap. 6.95 (ISBN 0-931529-92-1, Teenage Bks). Group Pub.

Murphy, Elspeth C. Danny Petrowski. LC 85-16568. 120p. (Orig.). (gr. 3-5). pap. 3.95 (ISBN 0-89191-730-6). Cook.

—Mary Jo Bennett. 107p. (Orig.). (gr. 3-5). 1985. pap. 3.95 (ISBN 0-89191-711-X, 57117). Cook.

Wilson, Neil. Choice Adventures, No. 1: The Mysterious Old Church. (gr. 4-7). 1991. pap. 3.95 (ISBN 0-8423-5025-X). Tyndale.

CHURCHILL, WINSTON, 1871-1947

Johnson, Ann D. Value of Leadership: The Story of Winston Churchill. (Illus.). (gr. k-6). 1987. 9.95 (ISBN 0-86679-046-2, Pub. by Value Communications). Oak Tree Pubns.

CHURCHILL, SIR WINSTON LEONARD SPENCER, 1874-1965

Bradley, Catherine. Churchill. (ps-3). 1990. PLB 11.90 (ISBN 0-531-17227-9). Watts.

Driemen, J. E. An Unbreakable Spirit: A Biography of Winston Churchill. LC 89-26029. (Illus.). 128p. (gr. 5 up). 1990. 12.95 (ISBN 0-87518-433-2, Dillon); PLB 12.95 (ISBN 0-87518-434-0). Macmillan Child Grp.

Italia, Bob. Winston Churchill. Walner, Rosemary, ed. (Illus.). 32p. (gr. 4). 1990. PLB 11.95 (ISBN 0-939179-78-4). Abdo & Dghtrs.

Keller, Mollie. Winston Churchill. (Illus.). 128p. (gr. 7-12). 1984. lib. bdg. 12.90 (ISBN 0-531-04752-0). Watts.

CHURCHYARDS

see Cemeteries

CID CAMPEADOR

McCaughrean, Geraldine. El Cid. Ambros, Victor G., illus. 128p. (gr. 5 up). 1989. 19.95 (ISBN 0-19-276077-5). Oxford U Pr.

CINEMATOGRAPHY, TRICK

Rimner, I. Movies - FX. (Illus.). 48p. (gr. 3-8). Date not set. PLB 18.60 (ISBN 0-86592-453-8). Rourke Corp.

CIPHERS

see also Cryptography; Writing

Albert, Burton. Code Busters! Levine, Abby, ed. Warshaw, Jerry, illus. 32p. (gr. 3-6). 1985. 10.95 (ISBN 0-8075-1235-4). A Whitman.

The History of Codes & Ciphers in the U. S. During the Period Between the World Wars: Pt. I, 1919-1929. 186p. (gr. 8 up). 1979. lib. bdg. 33.80 (ISBN 0-89412-102-2); pap. text ed. 24.80 (ISBN 0-89412-039-5). Aegean Park Pr.

Mango, Karin N. Codes, Ciphers & Other Secrets. Rosoff, Iris, ed. (Illus.). 96p. (gr. 4-6). 1988. PLB 10. 40 (ISBN 0-531-10575-X). Watts.

CIPHERS–FICTION

Bonsall, Crosby N. The Case of the Double Cross. LC 80-7768. (Illus.). 64p. (gr. k-3). 1980. 11.89 (ISBN 0-06-020602-0); PLB 11.89 (ISBN 0-06-020603-9). HarpC Child Bks.

Janeczko, Paul B. Loads of Codes & Secret Ciphers. LC 84-5791. (Illus.). 144p. (gr. 5-9). 1984. 12.95 (ISBN 0-02-747810-6, Mcmillan Child Bk). Macmillan Child Grp.

CIRCULATION OF THE BLOOD

see Blood–Circulation

CIRCUMNAVIGATION

see Voyages around the World

CIRCUS

see also Animals–Training

Better Homes & Gardens Books Editors. At the Circus. (Illus.). 32p. (ps-8). 1991. 4.95 (ISBN 0-696-01932-9). Meredith Bks.

Caggiano, Rosemary & Martinez, Larry. The Circus. 48p. (gr. k-6). 1978. pap. 10.95 (ISBN 0-86704-000-9). Clarus Music.

Carson, Patti & Dellosa, Janet. Circus Fun Book. Carson, Patti & Dellosa, Janet, illus. 32p. (ps-1). 1982. pap. 1.59 (ISBN 0-88724-056-9, CD-8011). Carson-Dellos.

Cushman, Kathleen. Circus Dreams: The Making of a Circus Artist. (gr. 4-7). 1990. 15.95 (ISBN 0-316-16561-1, Joy St Bks). Little.

Harmer, Mabel. Circus. LC 81-7709. (Illus.). 48p. (gr. k-4). 1981. PLB 14.60 (ISBN 0-516-01610-5). Childrens.

Hoban, Tana. Round & Round & Round. Hoban, Tana, illus. LC 82-11984. 32p. (gr. k-3). 1983. 14.95 (ISBN 0-688-01813-0); PLB 14.88 (ISBN 0-688-01814-9). Greenwillow.

Johnson, John E., illus. Here Comes the Circus. 14p. (gr. 2-5). 1985. 2.95 (ISBN 0-394-87543-5, Random Juv). Random.

Laslo, Cynthia. The Rosen Photo Guide to a Career in the Circus. (Illus.). (gr. 7-12). 1988. lib. bdg. 12.95 (ISBN 0-8239-0819-4). Rosen Group.

Magic of the Circus. (ps-1). pap. 2.49 (ISBN 0-517-48305-X). Outlet Bk Co.

Moss, Miriam. Fairs & Circuses. (Illus.). 32p. (gr. 1-6). 1987. lib. bdg. 8.99 (ISBN 0-531-18144-8, Pub. by Bookwright Pr). Watts.

Schmidt, Diane. I Am a Jesse White Tumbler. Tucker, Kathy, ed. Schmidt, Diane, photos by. (Illus.). 40p. (gr. 2-8). 1990. 13.95 (ISBN 0-8075-3444-7). A Whitman.

CIRCUS–FICTION

Adler, David A. Cam Jansen & the Mystery of the Circus Clown. Natti, Susanna, illus. LC 82-50363. 64p. (gr. 2-4). 1983. pap. 10.95 (ISBN 0-670-20036-0). Viking Child Bks.

Anno, Mitsumasa. Dr. Anno's Magical Midnight Circus. Weatherby, Meredith, tr. from JPN. LC 72-78598. (Illus.). 28p. (gr. k-6). 1972. 6.50 (ISBN 0-8348-2011-0). Weatherhill.

Carey, Karla. Julie & Jackie at the Circus: The Narration & Music Book. Nolan, Dennis, illus. 57p. 1990. pap. 18.95 complete pkg. (ISBN 0-685-35759-7); pap. 9.95 (ISBN 1-55768-202-X); cassette 9.95 (ISBN 0-685-35760-0). LC Pub.

Corcoran, Mark. Night, Circus. Corcoran, Mark, illus. 24p. 1990. 11.95 (ISBN 0-8092-4306-7, Calico Bks). Contemp Bks.

Dr. Seuss. If I Ran the Circus. Dr. Seuss, illus. LC 56-9469. 64p. (gr. k-3). 1980. pap. 3.95 (ISBN 0-394-84546-3, Random Juv). Random.

—If I Ran the Circus. Dr. Seuss, illus. (gr. k-3). 1956. 12. 95 (ISBN 0-394-80080-X, Random Juv); lib. bdg. 10. 99 (ISBN 0-394-90080-4). Random.

Ernst, Lisa C. Ginger Jumps. Ernst, Lisa C., illus. LC 89-38706. 32p. (ps-2). 1990. 14.95 (ISBN 0-02-733565-8, Bradbury Press). Macmillan.

Fitzgerald, Frank. Inside the Circus. Fitzgerald, Frank, illus. 32p. 1989. 12.95 (ISBN 0-8092-4359-8, Calico Bks). Contemp Bks.

Freeman, Don. Bearymore. (Illus.). (ps-3). 1979. pap. 3.95 (ISBN 0-14-050279-3, Puffin). Puffin Bks.

—Bearymore. LC 76-94. (Illus.). 40p. (gr. k-3). 1976. 14. 95 (ISBN 0-670-15174-2). Viking Child Bks.

Harwood, Pearl A. Carnival with Mr. & Mrs. Bumba. Overlie, George, illus. LC 76-156360. 32p. (gr. k-3). 1971. PLB 4.95 (ISBN 0-8225-0128-7). Lerner Pubns.

Haywood, Carolyn. Betsy & the Circus. (gr. k-6). 1989. pap. 3.25 (ISBN 0-440-40197-6). Dell.

—Eddie's Friend Boodles. Stock, Catherine, illus. LC 91-3212. (gr. 6 up). 1991. 12.95 (ISBN 0-688-09028-1). Morrow Jr Bks.

Hope, Laura L. Bobbsey Twins & the Circus Surprise. (gr. 1-4). 1932. 4.50 (ISBN 0-448-08025-7, G&D). Putnam Pub Group.

Hughes, Dean. Jelly's Circus. 168p. (gr. 3-7). 1989. pap. 3.95 (ISBN 0-689-71325-8, Aladdin). Macmillan Child Grp.

Johnson, Crockett. Harold's Circus. LC 59-5318. (ps-3). 1959. PLB 11.89 (ISBN 0-06-022966-7). HarpC Child Bks.

Keremes, Constance A. I Wanted to Go to the Circus. Goffe, Toni, illus. LC 89-1818. 24p. (Orig.). (gr. k-3). 1989. PLB 10.95 (ISBN 0-943173-18-3); pap. 5.95 (ISBN 0-943173-28-0). Harbinger AZ.

Lofting, Hugh. Doctor Dolittle's Circus. Lofting, Hugh, illus. 240p. (gr. 4-7). 1988. 14.95 (ISBN 0-440-50056-7). Delacorte.

—Doctor Dolittle's Circus. (gr. 3-6). 14.75 (ISBN 0-8446-6370-0). Peter Smith.

Lustig, Loretta, illus. The Pop-Up Book of the Circus. LC 78-68789. (ps-3). 1979. 6.95 (ISBN 0-394-84134-4, Random Juv). Random.

Maestro, Betsy. Harriet Goes to the Circus: A Number Concept Book. Maestro, Giulio, illus. LC 76-40204. (ps-1). 1989. Crown.

Manushkin, Fran. Hocus & Pocus at the Circus. Hayes, Geoffrey, illus. LC 82-47704. 64p. (gr. k-3). 1983. 11. 95 (ISBN 0-06-024091-1); PLB 11.89 (ISBN 0-06-024092-X). HarpC Child Bks.

Marilue. Bobby Bear at the Circus. Marilue, illus. LC 89-62708. 32p. (ps-2). 1990. PLB 12.95 (ISBN 0-87783-252-8). Oddo.

Moers, Hermann. Tonio the Great. Wilkon, Jozef, illus. LC 89-43249. 32p. (gr. k-3). 1990. 13.95 (ISBN 1-55858-084-0). North-South Bks NYC.

Moncure, Jane B. Word Bird's Circus Surprise. Hohag, Linda, illus. LC 80-29528. 32p. (gr. k-2). 1981. PLB 11.97 (ISBN 0-89565-162-9). Childs World.

O'Kelley, Mattie L. Circus. O'Kelley, Mattie L., illus. 32p. (ps-3). 1986. 12.95 (ISBN 0-316-63804-8, Joy St Bks). Little.

Otis, James. Toby Tyler. 152p. 1981. Repr. PLB 18.95x (ISBN 0-89966-363-X). Buccaneer Bks.

—Toby Tyler. 188p. 1981. Repr. PLB 19.95 (ISBN 0-89967-037-7). Harmony Raine.

—Toby Tyler or Ten Weeks with a Circus. (gr. 4 up). 1990. pap. 3.50 (ISBN 0-440-40358-8). Dell.

Packard, Edward. The Circus. 64p. 1983. pap. 2.25 (ISBN 0-553-15426-5). Bantam.

Pare, R. Circus Days. (Illus.). 24p. (ps-8). 1988. 12.95 (ISBN 0-685-38505-1); pap. 4.95 (ISBN 1-55037-020-0). Firefly Bks Ltd.

Peet, Bill. Ella. (Illus.). 48p. (gr. k-3). 1964. 13.95 (ISBN 0-395-17577-1). HM.

Pellowski, Michael. Clara Joins the Circus. Kelley, True, illus. LC 80-25602. 48p. (ps-3). 1981. 5.95 (ISBN 0-8193-1057-3); PLB 5.95 (ISBN 0-8193-1058-1). Parents.

Perl, Lila. Tybee Trimble's Hard Times. LC 84-4310. 160p. (gr. 4-7). 1984. 10.95 (ISBN 0-89919-288-2, Clarion). HM.

Piumini, Roberto. The Saint & the Circus. Holmes, Olivia, tr. from ITA. Root, Barrett V., illus. LC 90-23481. 32p. (ps-3). 1991. text ed. 14.95 (ISBN 0-688-10377-4). Morrow.

Potter, Beatrix. The Fairy Caravan. Potter, Beatrix, illus. 192p. (gr. 3-7). 1986. pap. 3.95 (ISBN 0-14-031823-2, Puffin). Puffin Bks.

Poulet, Virginia. Blue Bug's Circus. Maloney, Mary P. & Fleming, Stanley, illus. LC 77-4345. 32p. (ps-3). 1977. PLB 14.60 (ISBN 0-516-03422-7). Childrens.

Rey, H. A. See the Circus. (Illus.). (gr. k-3). 1956. pap. 2.25 (ISBN 0-395-07068-6, Sandpiper). HM.

Saroyan, William. The Circus. Zimdars, Berta, illus. 32p. (gr. 4 up). 1986. PLB 10.95s.p. (ISBN 0-88682-066-9); 15.65 (ISBN 0-685-12422-3). Creative Ed.

Schulz, Charles M. Life Is a Circus, Charlie Brown. Schulz, Charles M., illus. LC 80-28770. 48p. (ps up). 1981. lib. bdg. 5.99 (ISBN 0-394-94826-2). Random.

Vandersteen, Willy. The Circus Baron. Lahey, Nicholas J., tr. from FLE. LC 75-8497. (Illus.). 56p. (Orig.). (gr. 3 up). 1976. pap. 2.50 (ISBN 0-915560-21-6, 21). Hiddigeigei.

Vincent, Gabrielle. Ernest & Celestine at the Circus. LC 88-23220. (Illus.). 32p. (ps up). 1989. 11.95 (ISBN 0-688-08684-5); PLB 11.88 (ISBN 0-688-08685-3). Greenwillow.

Walt Disney Staff. The Circus Book Featuring "Toby Tyler" LC 77-74462. (Illus.). (gr. 2-6). 1978. (Random Juv); lib. bdg. 4.99 (ISBN 0-394-93597-7). Random.

Weil, Lisl. Let's Go to the Circus. Weil, Lisl, illus. LC 87-25201. 32p. (gr. k-3). 1988. reinforced bdg. 13.95 (ISBN 0-8234-0693-8). Holiday.

Wersba, Barbara. Let Me Fall Before I Fly. Hoys, James, illus. LC 86-2686. 48p. (gr. 6 up). 1986. PLB 10.95s.p. (ISBN 0-88682-057-X); 15.65 (ISBN 0-685-12421-5). Creative Ed.

Wiseman, B. Morris & Boris at the Circus. Wiseman, B., illus. LC 87-45682. 64p. (gr. k-3). 1988. 11.95 (ISBN 0-06-026477-2); PLB 11.89 (ISBN 0-06-026478-0). HarpC Child Bks.

—Morris & Boris at the Circus. Wiseman, B., illus. LC 87-45682. 64p. (gr. k-3). 1990. pap. 3.50 (ISBN 0-06-444143-1, Trophy). HarpC Child Bks.

CIRCUS–PICTURES, ILLUSTRATIONS, ETC.

Machotka, Hana. Magic Ring: A Year With The Big Apple Circus. Machotka, Hana, illus. Binder, Paul, intro. by. LC 87-28230. (Illus.). 80p. (gr. 3 up). 1988. 13.95 (ISBN 0-688-07449-9); pap. 8.95 (ISBN 0-688-08222-X, Pub. by Beech Tree Bks). Morrow Jr Bks.

CITIES AND TOWNS

Here are entered works on cities and towns. For works on large cities and their surrounding areas use Metropolitan Areas. General works on the government of cities are entered under Municipal Government. General works on local government other than that of cities are entered under Local Government.

Baylor, Byrd. The Best Town in the World. Himler, Ronald, illus. LC 83-9033. 32p. (gr. 1-3). 1983. 13.95 (ISBN 0-684-18035-9, Scribners Young Read). Macmillan Child Grp.

Bentley, John & Charlton, Bill. Finding Out about Villages. (Illus.). 48p. (gr. 5-8). 1983. 19.95 (ISBN 0-7134-4291-3, Pub. by Batsford England). Trafalgar Sq.

Boney, Lesley, illus. Cities. 48p. (gr. k-5). 1988. pap. 2.95 (ISBN 0-8431-2248-X). Price Stern.

Booth, Eugene. In the City. LC 77-7949. (Illus.). 24p. (gr. k-3). 1985. PLB 13.32 (ISBN 0-8393-0109-X); pap. 9.27 (ISBN 0-8393-0166-9). Raintree Pubs.

Kalman, Bobbie. I Live in a City. (Illus.). 32p. (gr. 2-3). 1986. 6.95 (ISBN 0-86505-070-8); pap. 5.95 (ISBN 0-86505-092-9). Crabtree Pub Co.

Lenski, Lois. Sing a Song of People. Laroche, Giles, photos by. (ps-3). 1987. pap. 14.95 (ISBN 0-316-52074-8). Little.

Little People Big Book about Where We Live. 64p. (ps-1). 1990. write for info. (ISBN 0-8094-7483-2); PLB write for info. (ISBN 0-8094-7484-0). Time-Life.

Macaulay, David. Underground. Macaulay, David, illus. (gr. 1 up). 1983. 15.95 (ISBN 0-395-24739-X); pap. 7.95 (ISBN 0-395-34065-9). HM.

Maestro, Betsy. Delivery Van: Words for Town & Country. Maestro, Giulio, illus. 32p. (ps-2). 1990. 14. 95 (ISBN 0-395-51119-4, Clarion Bks). HM.

—Taxi: A Book of City Words. Maestro, Giulio, illus. LC 88-22867. (ps-2). 1989. 13.95 (ISBN 0-89919-528-8, Pub. by Clarion). Ticknor & Fields.

—Taxi: A Book of City Words. Maestro, Giulio, illus. (ps-3). 1990. pap. 4.95 (ISBN 0-395-54811-X, Clarion Bks). HM.

Maestro, Betsy & DelVecchio, Ellen. Big City Port. Maestro, Giulio, illus. LC 85-4339. 32p. (gr. k-3). 1984. 14.95 (ISBN 0-02-762110-3, Four Winds). Macmillan Child Grp.

Mazer, Norma F. Downtown. LC 84-91105. 192p. (gr. 7 up). 1984. 11.95 (ISBN 0-688-03859-X). Morrow Jr Bks.

More about Carpinteria As It Was, Vol 2. LC 79-83931. (gr. 11 up). 1982. 9.95 (ISBN 0-9608826-1-8). Papillon Pr.

Muller, Jorg. The Changing City. Muller, Jorg, illus. LC 76-46646. (gr. 1 up). 1977. 18.95 (ISBN 0-689-50084-X, M K McElderry). Macmillan Child Grp.

O'Connor, Karen & Crowdy, Deborah. Let's Take a Walk in the City. Axeman, Lois, illus. LC 86-20746. 32p. (ps-2). 1986. lib. bdg. 11.97 (ISBN 0-89565-355-9). Childs World.

Reynolds, Tony. Cities in Crisis. (Illus.). 48p. (gr. 5 up). 1990. lib. bdg. 18.00 (ISBN 0-86592-118-0); lib. bdg. 13.50s.p. (ISBN 0-685-36376-7). Rourke Corp.

Watson. The Town. (gr. k-2). 1980. 6.95 (ISBN 0-86020-391-3, Usborne-Hayes); PLB 11.96 (ISBN 0-88110-070-6); pap. 2.95 (ISBN 0-86020-392-1). EDC.

CITIES AND TOWNS–FICTION

Bell, William. Forbidden City. (gr. 7 up). 1990. 14.95 (ISBN 0-553-07131-9, Starfire); pap. 3.50 (ISBN 0-553-28864-4, Starfire). Bantam.

Berends, Polly B. The Case of the Elevator Duck. Allison, Diane, illus. LC 88-23971. 64p. (gr. 2-4). 1989. PLB 6.99 (ISBN 0-394-92646-3); pap. 1.95 (ISBN 0-394-82646-9). Random.

Carlstrom, Nancy W. Where Does the Night Hide? Allen, Thomas B. & Allen, Laura H., illus. LC 89-32910. 32p. (ps-1). 1990. 13.95 (ISBN 0-02-717390-9, Mcmillan Child Bk). Macmillan Child Grp.

Christopher, John. City of Gold & Lead. LC 67-21245. 224p. (gr. 5-9). 1967. 12.95 (ISBN 0-02-718380-7, Mcmillan Child Bk); (Collier Young Ad). Macmillan Child Grp.

—The City of Gold & Lead. large type ed. 280p. (gr. 3 up). 1990. lib. bdg. 17.95x (ISBN 0-7451-1100-9, Lythway Large Print). G K Hall.

Colman, Hila. Nobody Told Me What I Need to Know. LC 84-8673. 176p. (gr. 7 up). 1984. 11.95 (ISBN 0-688-03869-7). Morrow Jr Bks.

Craft, Ruth. The Day of the Rainbow. Daly, Niki, illus. 32p. (ps-3). 1989. pap. 12.95 (ISBN 0-670-82456-9). Viking Child Bks.

—The Day of the Rainbow. Daly, Niki, illus. 32p. (ps-3). 1991. pap. 4.95 (ISBN 0-14-050935-6, Puffin). Puffin Bks.

Cunningham, Linda. The Copper Angel of Piper's Mill & How She Saved Her Town. Goldberg, Grace, illus. 4p. (gr. 3-5). 1989. 12.95 (ISBN 0-89272-274-6). Down East.

Florian, Douglas. City Street. Florian, Douglas, illus. LC 89-28694. 32p. (ps up). 1990. 12.95 (ISBN 0-688-09543-7); PLB 12.88 (ISBN 0-688-09544-5). Greenwillow.

Forti, Kathleen J. The Door to the Secret City. Brisson, James F., illus. 133p. (Orig.). (gr. 2 up). 1984. cloth 9.95 (ISBN 0-913299-10-3, Pub. by Angelfood Bks). Stillpoint.

Fox, Paula. Maurice's Room. Fetz, Ingrid, illus. LC 85-7200. 64p. (gr. 2-6). 1985. 13.95 (ISBN 0-02-735490-3, Mcmillan Child Bk). Macmillan Child Grp.

—The Village by the Sea. (gr. k-6). 1990. pap. 3.50 (ISBN 0-440-40299-9, Pub. by Yearling Classics). Dell.

Gaeddert, LouAnn. Your Former Friend, Matthew. Schwark, Mary B., illus. 80p. (gr. 3-6). 1984. 11.95 (ISBN 0-525-44086-0, DCB). Dutton Child Bks.

Holman, Felice. Secret City, U. S. A. LC 89-39841. 208p. (gr. 5-9). 1990. 13.95 (ISBN 0-684-19168-7, Scribners Young Read). Macmillan Child Grp.

Hurwitz, Johanna. Hurray for Ali Baba Bernstein. Owens, Gail, illus. LC 88-19107. 112p. (gr. 3-7). 1989. 11.95 (ISBN 0-688-08241-6); PLB 11.88 (ISBN 0-688-08242-4, Morrow Jr Bks). Morrow Jr Bks.

—Nora & Mrs. Mind-Your-Own-Business. Jeschke, Susan, illus. LC 76-54283. 64p. (gr. k-3). 1982. 11.95 (ISBN 0-688-22097-5). Morrow Jr Bks.

Jacobson, Jane. City, Sing, for Me: A Country Child Moves to the City. Rowen, Amy, illus. LC 77-11130. 32p. (gr. 1-5). 1978. 16.95 (ISBN 0-87705-358-8). Human Sci Pr.

Kibbe, Pat. Mrs. Kiddy & the Moonbooms. Rutherford, Jenny, illus. LC 90-24406. 112p. (gr. 1-4). 1991. pap. 2.95 (ISBN 0-689-71469-6, Aladdin). Macmillan Child Grp.

Lewin, Hugh. Jafta: The Town. Kopper, Lisa, illus. LC 84-4950. 24p. (ps-3). 1984. PLB 9.95 (ISBN 0-87614-266-8). Carolrhoda Bks.

Lewis, Thomas P. Frida's Office Day. Cushman, Doug, illus. LC 87-33488. 64p. (gr. k-3). 1989. 11.95 (ISBN 0-06-023843-7); PLB 11.89 (ISBN 0-06-023844-5). HarpC Child Bks.

Lough Roux, Brigette. Fresh Air Kid. (gr. 4-7). 1990. 12.95 (ISBN 0-670-82910-2). Viking Child Bks.

Martin, Melanie. Madison Moves to the Country. Karas, G. Brian, illus. LC 88-1313. 48p. (Orig.). (gr. 1-4). 1989. PLB 9.89 (ISBN 0-8167-1345-6); pap. text ed. 2.95 (ISBN 0-8167-1346-4). Troll Assocs.

Mazer, Harry. Cave under the City. LC 86-45008. 160p. (gr. 3-7). 1989. pap. 3.50 (ISBN 0-06-440303-3, Trophy). HarpC Child Bks.

Myers, Walter D. The Young Landlords. 208p. (gr. 5-9). 1989. pap. 3.95 (ISBN 0-14-034244-3, Puffin). Puffin Bks.

Packard, Edward. Deadwood City. 128p. (gr. 4). 1989. pap. 2.50 (ISBN 0-553-26213-0). Bantam.

Panova, V. On Faraway Street. Gabel, Rya, tr. White, Anne Terry, adapted by. LC 68-12891. (Illus.). 129p. (gr. 3-7). 1968. 3.95 (ISBN 0-8076-0445-3). Braziller.

Peck, Robert N. Justice Lion. 264p. (gr. 7 up). 1981. 13.95 (ISBN 0-316-69658-7). Little.

Phillips, Mildred & Zemach, Margot, illus. The Sign in Mendel's Window. LC 85-5049. 32p. (gr. k-3). 1985. 12.95 (ISBN 0-02-774600-3, Mcmillan Child Bk). Macmillan Child Grp.

Poploff, Michelle. Busy O'Brien & the Great Bubble Gum Blowout. Carter, Abby, illus. 96p. (gr. 2-5). 1990. 12.95 (ISBN 0-8027-6983-7); lib. bdg. 13.85 (ISBN 0-8027-6984-5). Walker & Co.

Priest, Robert. The Town that Got Out of Town. LC 88-46108. (Illus.). 32p. 1989. 14.95 (ISBN 0-87923-786-4). Godine.

Privensen, Alice. Shaker Lane. 1990. pap. 4.95 (ISBN 0-14-050713-2, Puffin). Puffin Bks.

Rockwell, Anne. Come to Town. Rockwell, Anne, illus. LC 86-6217. 32p. (ps-1). 1991. pap. 4.95 (ISBN 0-06-107411-X). HarpC Child Bks.

Rogers, Paul. Tumbledown. Corfield, Robin, illus. LC 87-11558. 32p. (gr. k-3). 1988. 12.95 (ISBN 0-689-31392-6, Atheneum Child Bk). Macmillan Child Grp.

Rylant, Cynthia. But I'll Be Back Again: An Album. LC 88-17860. (Illus.). 80p. (gr. 5-7). 1989. 12.95 (ISBN 0-531-05806-9); PLB 12.99 (ISBN 0-531-08406-X). Orchard Bks Watts.

Scarry, Richard. Richard Scarry's Postman Pig & His Busy Neighbors. LC 77-91646. (Illus.). (ps-2). 1978. lib. bdg. 5.99 (ISBN 0-394-93898-4, Random Juv). Random.

Sharmat, Marjorie W. Mr. Jameson & Mr. Phillips. LC 77-25665. (Illus.). (gr. k-3). 1979. 7.95 (ISBN 0-06-025528-5). HarpC Child Bks.

Simpson, David B. A Nice Day in the City. LC 83-49478. (Illus.). 48p. (gr. 1-4). 1984. HarpC Child Bks.

Skolsky, Mindy W. The Whistling Teakettle & Other Stories about Hannah. LC 76-21395. (Illus.). (gr. 2-5). 1977. 10.89 (ISBN 0-06-025688-5). HarpC Child Bks.

Smucker, Anna E. No Star Nights. Johnson, Steve, illus. LC 88-2782. 48p. (ps-3). 1989. 12.95 (ISBN 0-394-89925-3); lib. bdg. 13.99 (ISBN 0-394-99925-8). Knopf.

Stevens, Carla. Anna, Grandpa & the Big Storm. Tomes, Margot, illus. 48p. (gr. 6-9). 1982. 13.95 (ISBN 0-89919-066-9, Clarion). HM.

Wright, Betty R. Ghosts Beneath Our Feet. 144p. (gr. 4-6). 1986. pap. 2.50 (ISBN 0-590-40755-4, Apple Paperbacks). Scholastic Inc.

CITIES AND TOWNS–HISTORY

Beekman, Daniel. Forest, Village, Town, City. Loewenstein, Bernice, illus. LC 79-7819. 32p. (gr. 3-6). 1982. 10.10i (ISBN 0-690-04084-9, Crowell Jr Bks). HarpC Child Bks.

Codlence, Jean-Michel. The Earliest Cities. Deubelbeiss, Patrick, illus. Ridett, Anthea, tr. from FRE. LC 86-42656. (Illus.). 77p. (gr. 7 up). 1987. 15.96 (ISBN 0-382-09214-7); 10.37s.p. (ISBN 0-685-17550-2). Silver Burdett Pr.

Comes, Pilar & Hernandez, Xavier. Barmi: A Mediterranean City Through the Ages. Ballonga, Jordi, illus. 64p. (gr. 5 up). 1990. 14.95 (ISBN 0-395-54227-8). HM.

Ewing, Juliana H. Our Field. LC 85-31445. 32p. (gr. 4 up). 1986. PLB 10.95s.p. (ISBN 0-88682-074-X); PLB 15.65 (ISBN 0-685-12415-0). Creative Ed.

Kalman, Bobbie. Visiting a Village. (Illus.). 32p. (gr. 3-4). 1990. lib. bdg. 14.95 (ISBN 0-86505-487-8); pap. 7.95 (ISBN 0-86505-507-6). Crabtree Pub Co.

CITIES AND TOWNS–PICTURES, ILLUSTRATIONS, ETC.

Rius, Maria & Parramon, J. M. The City. (ps) 1986. 6.95 (ISBN 0-8120-5748-1); 3.95 (ISBN 0-8120-3700-6). Barron.

CITIES AND TOWNS–POETRY

Brooks, Gwendolyn. Bronzeville Boys & Girls. Solbert, Ronni, illus. LC 56-8152. 48p. (gr. 3-6). 1967. PLB 12.89 (ISBN 0-06-020651-9). HarpC Child Bks.

Larrick, Nancy. On City Streets. LC 68-30505. 160p. (gr. 10 up). 1968. pap. 6.95 (ISBN 0-87131-551-3). M Evans.

CITIES AND TOWNS, RUINED, EXTINCT, ETC.

Corbishley, Mike & Walker, Roger W. Secret Cities. LC 88-31101. (Illus.). 48p. (gr. 4-6). 1989. 14.95 (ISBN 0-525-67275-3, Lodestar Bks). Dutton Child Bks.

Gallant, Roy A. Lost Cities. LC 84-17422. (Illus.). 72p. (gr. 4 up). 1985. lib. bdg. 10.40 (ISBN 0-531-04914-0). Watts.

CITIES AND TOWNS–U. S.

Beekman, Daniel. Forest, Village, Town, City. Loewenstein, Bernice, illus. LC 79-7819. 32p. (gr. 3-6). 1982. 10.10i (ISBN 0-690-04084-9, Crowell Jr Bks). HarpC Child Bks.

Loewen, Nancy & Stewart, Gail. Great Cities of the U. S, 8 bks, Reading Level 6. (Illus.). 384p. (gr. 5 up). Date not set. Set. PLB 116.80 (ISBN 0-86592-537-2). Rourke Corp.

CITIZENSHIP
see also Patriotism

Branson, Margaret & Coombs, Fred. Civics for Today. (Illus.). (gr. 7-9). 1980. text ed. 33.68 (ISBN 0-395-26201-1); tchr's. ed. 40.52 (ISBN 0-395-26202-X); wkbk. 10.52 (ISBN 0-395-26203-8). HM.

Educational Assessment Publishing Company Staff. Parent - Child Learning Library: Citizenship. (Illus.). 32p. Date not set. text ed. 9.95 (ISBN 0-942277-64-3). Educ Assess Pub.

Harik, Elsa M. The Lebanese in America. (Illus.). 96p. (gr. 5 up). 1987. PLB 11.95 (ISBN 0-8225-0234-8); pap. 3.95 (ISBN 0-8225-1032-4). Lerner Pubns.

Kownslar, Allan O. & Smart, Terry L. Civics: Citizens & Society. 2nd ed. (Illus.). 576p. (gr. 7-8). 1983. text ed. 31.88 (ISBN 0-07-035433-2). McGraw.

Meltzer, Milton. The Hispanic Americans. Noren, Catherine & Camhi, Morrie, illus. LC 81-43314. 160p. (gr. 5 up). 1982. 13.95 (ISBN 0-690-04110-1, Crowell Jr Bks); PLB 13.89 (ISBN 0-690-04111-X, Crowell Jr Bks). HarpC Child Bks.

Petersen, Peter L. The Danes in America. (Illus.). 96p. (gr. 5 up). 1987. PLB 11.95 (ISBN 0-8225-0233-X); pap. 3.95 (ISBN 0-8225-1031-6). Lerner Pubns.

Pincus, Debbie & Ward, Richard J. Citizenship. 112p. (gr. 4-9). 1991. 9.95 (ISBN 0-86653-608-6, GA 1327). Good Apple.

Rutledge, Paul. The Vietnamese in America. (Illus.). 64p. (gr. 5 up). 1987. PLB 11.95 (ISBN 0-8225-0235-6); pap. 3.95 (ISBN 0-8225-1033-2). Lerner Pubns.

CITRUS FRUIT
see also names of citrus fruits, e.g. Orange, etc.

Wake, Susan. Citrus Fruits. (Illus.). 32p. (gr. 1-4). 1990. PLB 9.95 (ISBN 0-87614-389-3). Carolrhoda Bks.

CITY LIFE
see Cities and Towns

CITY PLANNING
see also Housing; Urban Renewal

CIVICS
see Citizenship; Political Science; U. S.–Politics and Government

CIVIL DISOBEDIENCE
see Government, Resistance to

CIVIL ENGINEERING
see also Bridges; Canals; Dams; Excavation; Harbors; Irrigation; Masonry; Mining Engineering; Rivers; Roads; Subways; Surveying; Tunnels; Water Supply

CIVIL GOVERNMENT
see Political Science

CIVIL LIBERTY
see Liberty

CIVIL RIGHTS
see also Free Speech; Freedom of the Press; Liberty; Religious Liberty
also names of groups of people with the subdivision Civil rights, e.g. Blacks–Civil Rights

Bach, Julie, ed. Civil Liberties: Opposing Viewpoints. LC 88-1136. (Illus.). 230p. (gr. 10 up). 1988. lib. bdg. 15.95 (ISBN 0-89908-434-6); pap. text ed. 8.95 (ISBN 0-89908-409-5). Greenhaven.

Berry, Joy. Every Kid's Guide to Understanding Human Rights. Bartholemew, illus. 48p. (gr. 3-7). 1987. 4.95 (ISBN 0-516-21407-1); PLB 14.60 (ISBN 0-516-01407-2). Childrens.

Bradley, John. Human Rights. LC 87-80448. (Illus.). 32p. (gr. 4-9). 1987. PLB 8.90 (ISBN 0-531-17055-1, Gloucester Pr). Watts.

Fox, Ken. Everything You Need to Know about Your Legal Rights. (gr. 7-12). 1991. PLB 12.95 (ISBN 0-8239-1322-8). Rosen Group.

Frankel, Marvin & Saideman, Ellen. Out of the Shadows of Night: The Struggle for International Human Rights. (gr. 9 up). 1989. pap. 8.95 (ISBN 0-385-29820-X). Delacorte.

Kronenwetter, Michael. Taking a Stand Against Human Rights Abuses. 1990. PLB 13.40 (ISBN 0-531-10921-6). Watts.

Moore, Yvette. Freedom Songs. LC 88-43073. 176p. (gr. 7 up). 1991. 14.95 (ISBN 0-531-05812-3); PLB 14.99 (ISBN 0-531-08412-4). Orchard Bks Watts.

Sherwin, Jane. Human Rights. (Illus.). 48p. (gr. 5 up). 1990. lib. bdg. 18.00 (ISBN 0-86592-099-0); lib. bdg. 13.50s.p. (ISBN 0-685-36379-1). Rourke Corp.

Totten, Samuel & Kleg, Milton. Human Rights. LC 88-4257. (Illus.). 256p. (gr. 7-12). 1989. lib. bdg. 18.95 (ISBN 0-89490-156-7). Enslow Pubs.

Universal Declaration of Human Rights: An Adaptation for Children. 46p. Date not set. 9.95 (ISBN 92-1-100424-1, 89.1.19); poster 5.95 (ISBN 0-685-39236-8, 90.I.20). UN.

Wilson, Reginald. Our Rights: Civil Liberties in the U. S. rev. ed. 160p. (gr. 7 up). 1991. PLB 15.85 (ISBN 0-8027-8127-6); pap. 8.95 (ISBN 0-8027-7371-0). Walker & Co.

—Think about Our Rights: Civil Liberties & the United States. LC 87-22989. 123p. 1988. 14.85 (ISBN 0-8027-6751-6); pap. 5.95 (ISBN 0-8027-6752-4). Walker & Co.

Zeltmann, Walter F. Human Rights. LC 90-71594. iii, 72p. (Orig.). 1990. 24.90 (ISBN 0-9622705-2-0); pap. 9.90 (ISBN 0-9622705-3-9). Yellow Hook Pr.

CIVIL RIGHTS–BIOGRAPHY

Jacobs, William J. Great Lives: Human Rights. LC 89-37211. (Illus.). 288p. (gr. 4-6). 1990. 22.95 (ISBN 0-684-19036-2, Scribners Young Read). Macmillan Child Grp.

Johnson, Jacqueline. Stokely Carmichael: The Story of Black Power. Gallin, Richard, ed. Young, Andrew, intro. by. (Illus.). 128p. (gr. 5 up). 1990. lib. bdg. 16.98 (ISBN 0-382-09920-6); pap. 7.95 (ISBN 0-382-24056-1). Silver Burdett Pr.

Pround, Benjamin. Nelson Mandela: Strength & Spirit of a Free South Africa. LC 90-24026. (Illus.). 68p. (gr. 5-6). 1991. PLB 13.95 (ISBN 0-8368-0357-4). Gareth Stevens Inc.

Winner, David. Peter Beneson: Taking a Stand Against Injustice-Amnesty International. LC 90-47877. (Illus.). 68p. (gr. 5-6). 1991. PLB 13.95 (ISBN 0-8368-0400-7). Gareth Stevens Inc.

CIVIL RIGHTS–U. S.

Hess, Debra. Thurgood Marshall: The Fight for Equal Justice. Gallin, Richard, ed. Young, Andrew, intro. by. (Illus.). 128p. (gr. 5 up). 1990. lib. bdg. 16.98 (ISBN 0-382-09921-4); pap. 7.95 (ISBN 0-382-24058-8). Silver Burdett Pr.

Knight, H. V. With Liberty & Justice for All: The Meaning of the Bill of Rights Today. LC 66-26725. 318p. (gr. 9 up). 1967. 20.00 (ISBN 0-379-00306-6). Oceana.

Levine, Ellen. If You Lived At the Time of Martin Luther King. 1990. pap. 2.95 (ISBN 0-590-42582-X). Scholastic Inc.

Yette, Samuel F. & Yette, Frederick W. Washington & Two Marches: 1963 & 1983. (Illus.). 1984. 25.00 (ISBN 0-911253-02-5); pap. 16.95 (ISBN 0-911253-03-3); deluxe ed. 50.00 deluxe ltd. ed (ISBN 0-317-11590-1). Cottage Bks.
This is a beautiful, moving pictorial commemorative of two of the greatest demonstrations for human & civil rights in U.S. history. The 1963 March, led by the late Dr. Martin Luther King, Jr., & the 1983 March dedicated to him, are both recorded here with 150 spectacular full color photographs. Also presented is much that took place between the two marches. This is the first visualization of the "Third American Revolution," the extraordinary transformation of the nation's African-American leadership into national leadership & international influence. It is a prized supplement to social studies in scores of public school systems. As a teacher in Delaware put it: "Every school in the country needs a copy of this book. The pictures are so good, the students won't have to read the book. But because the pictures are so good, the kids will want to read it." Jointly recommended by Dr. King's widow, Coretta Scott King, & Dr. Joseph Lowery, president of the Southern Christian Leadership Conference, the book is a testament to the efficacy of democracy, a constitutional primer. Said Dr. Lowery, it documents "the great strides in the struggle for civil rights & the accomplishments that Black people have made...since the signing of the Civil Rights Act in 1964." Wrote the Washington Afro-American: "It is a

work of camera art which should be in every library in the country & in every home...The book not only depicts, in photo-essays, the tremendous & momentous significance of the two marches...but provides an added dimension with its timely, well-researched & brilliant comments about the events covered. It is a classic." ***Publisher Provided Annotation.***

CIVIL RIGHTS DEMONSTRATIONS
see Blacks–Civil Rights
CIVIL SERVICE
Here are entered general works on the history and development of public service. Works on public personnel administration, including the duties of civil service employees, their salaries, pensions, etc., are entered under the name of the country, state or city with the subdivision Officials and Employees.
see also names of countries, cities, etc. with the subdivision Officials and Employees, e.g. U. S.–Officials and Employees
CIVIL WAR–ENGLAND
see Great Britain–History–Civil War and Commonwealth, 1642-1660
CIVIL WAR–U. S.
see U. S.–History–Civil War
CIVILIZATION
see also Anthropology; Archeology; Art; Culture; Education; Ethics; Ethnology; Industry; Inventions; Learning and Scholarship; Manners and Customs; Religions; Social Problems
also names of countries, states, etc. with the subdivision Civilization, e.g. U. S.–Civilization
Carroll, Anne W. Christ the King: Lord of History. 2nd ed. 480p. (gr. 9-12). 1986. pap. 14.95 (ISBN 0-937495-02-6). Trinity Comns.
Merriman, Nick. Early Humans. King, Dave, photos by. LC 88-13431. (Illus.). 64p. (gr. 5 up). 1989. 15.00 (ISBN 0-394-82257-9); lib. bdg. 14.99 (ISBN 0-394-92257-3). Knopf.
Monteith, Jay. A Multicultural Activity Workbook: Africa, Asia & the Americas. (Illus.). 72p. (Orig.). (gr. 1 up). 1991. pap. text ed. 7.95 (ISBN 0-9627366-1-9). Arts & Comns NY.
Reardon, Judy A. & Smock, Raymond W. The Western Civilization Slide Collection Master Guide. rev. ed. 253p. (Orig.). (gr. 7 up). 1988. 25.00 (ISBN 0-923805-01-X). Instruc Resc MD.
—The Western Civilization Slide Collection. (Illus.). 253p. (Orig.). (gr. 7 up). 1988. incl. 2100 slides 895.00 (ISBN 0-923805-02-8); pap. 25.00 (ISBN 0-685-24654-X). Instruc Resc MD.
Tames, Richard. Exploring Other Civilizations. 52p. (gr. 11 up). 1987. pap. 7.95 (ISBN 0-685-19629-1, Pub. by S Thornes). Dufour.
CIVILIZATION, ANCIENT
see also Man, Prehistoric
Chadefaud, Catherine & Coblence, Jean-Michel. The First Empires. Ridett, Anthea, tr. from FRE. Tarride, Michel, illus. 77p. (gr. 7 up). 1988. 15.96 (ISBN 0-382-09481-6); 10.37s.p. (ISBN 0-685-18824-8). Silver Burdett Pr.
Corbishley, Mike & Walker, Roger W. Secret Cities. LC 88-31101. (Illus.). 48p. (gr. 4-6). 1989. 14.95 (ISBN 0-525-67275-3, Lodestar Bks). Dutton Child Bks.
Frazee, Charles & Yopp, Hallie Kay. Early People & the First Civilizations. Frazee, Kathleen & Lumba, Eric, illus. (gr. 6). 1990. write for info. Delos Pubns.
Odijk, Pamela. The Phoenicians. (Illus.). 48p. (gr. 5-8). 1989. PLB 16.98 (ISBN 0-382-09891-9). Silver Burdett Pr.
Szekely, Edmond B. & Bordeaux, Norma N. Messengers from Ancient Civilizations. (Illus.). 44p. (gr. 5 up). 1974. pap. 3.50 (ISBN 0-89564-068-6). IBS Intl.
CIVILIZATION–FICTION
Gardam, Jane. The Hollow Land. Rawlings, Janet, illus. LC 81-6620. 160p. (gr. 5-9). 1982. 10.25 (ISBN 0-688-00873-9). Greenwillow.
CIVILIZATION, GREEK
Cohen, Daniel. Ancient Greece. (gr. 4-7). 1990. 11.95 (ISBN 0-385-26064-4); PLB 12.99 (ISBN 0-385-26065-2). Doubleday.
Powell, Anton. Greece. Shone, Rob, illus. 32p. (gr. 4-6). 1987. PLB 11.90 (ISBN 0-531-10398-6). Watts.
—The Greek World. LC 87-50491. (Illus.). 93p. (gr. 5-9). 1987. PLB 15.90 (ISBN 0-531-19029-3). Watts.
CIVILIZATION–HISTORY
Adams, Jean-Pierre. Mediterranean Civilizations. LC 86-426550. (Illus.). 77p. (gr. 7 up). 1987. 15.96 (ISBN 0-382-09215-5); 10.37s.p. (ISBN 0-685-17551-0). Silver Burdett Pr.
Cairns, Trevor, ed. People Become Civilized. LC 73-20196. (Illus.). 104p. (gr. 5 up). 1974. PLB 10.95 (ISBN 0-8225-0801-X). Lerner Pubns.
Millard. The First Civilization. (gr. 4-9). 1977. (Usborne-Hayes); PLB 13.96 (ISBN 0-88110-107-9); pap. 6.95 (ISBN 0-86020-138-4). EDC.
Scarry, Huck. Our Earth. Schwartz, Betty, ed. (Illus.). 112p. (gr. 3-8). 1984. 12.50 (ISBN 0-671-49846-0, Little Simon). S&S Trade.
CIVILIZATION, MEDIEVAL
see also Chivalry; Feudalism; Middle Ages; Monasticism and Religious Orders
Aliki. A Medieval Feast. LC 82-45923. (Illus.). 32p. (gr. 2-6). 1983. 13.95 (ISBN 0-690-04245-0, Crowell Jr Bks); PLB 13.89 (ISBN 0-690-04246-9, Crowell Jr Bks). HarpC Child Bks.
Cairns, Trevor. Medieval Knights. (Illus.). 64p. 1991. pap. write for info. (ISBN 0-521-38953-4). Cambridge U Pr.
Cairns, Trevor, ed. The Middle Ages. LC 73-22522. (Illus.). 104p. (gr. 5 up). 1975. PLB 10.95 (ISBN 0-8225-0804-4). Lerner Pubns.
Caselli, Giovanni. The Renaissance & the New World. Caselli, Giovanni, illus. LC 85-22900. 48p. (gr. 6-8). 1986. 16.95 (ISBN 0-87226-050-X). P Bedrick Bks.
Corbishley, Mike. Middle Ages. (Illus.). 96p. 1990. 17.95 (ISBN 0-8160-1973-8). Facts on File.
Jones, Madeline. Knights & Castles. (Illus.). 72p. (gr. 7-11). 1991. 19.95 (ISBN 0-7134-6352-X, Pub. by Batsford UK). Trafalgar Sq.
Morgan, Gwyneth. Life in a Medieval Village. LC 81-13735. (Illus.). 52p. (gr. 5 up). 1982. PLB 9.95 (ISBN 0-8225-1207-6). Lerner Pubns.
CIVILIZATION, MODERN
see also History, Modern; Renaissance
Brewton, Sara, et al. Quarks, Quasars & Other Quirks: Quizzical Poems for the Supersonic Age. Blake, Quentin, illus. LC 76-54747. 128p. (gr. 4 up). 1977. 12.95 (ISBN 0-690-01286-1, Crowell Jr Bks). HarpC Child Bks.
Kerrod, Robin. World of Tomorrow. LC 80-50043. (gr. 9 up). 1981. 11.90 (ISBN 0-531-09169-4). Watts.
CLAIRVOYANCE
see also Divination; Extrasensory Perception; Fortune Telling; Hypnotism; Thought Transference
CLARK, WILLIAM, 1770-1838
Stefoff, Rebecca. Lewis & Clark. (Illus.). (gr. 3-5). 1992. PLB 12.95 (ISBN 0-7910-1750-8). Chelsea Hse.
Zadra, Dan. Explorers of America: Lewis & Clark. rev. ed. (gr. 2-4). 1988. PLB 11.50s.p. (ISBN 0-88682-183-5); 16.45 (ISBN 0-318-32947-6). Creative Ed.
CLASS CONFLICT
see Social Conflict
CLASS STRUGGLE
see Social Conflict
CLASSES (MATHEMATICS)
see Set Theory
CLASSICAL ANTIQUITIES
see also Archeology; Art, Greek; Mythology, Classical also names of countries, cities, etc. with the subdivision Antiquities, e.g. Greece–Antiquities
CLASSICAL ART
see Art, Greek
CLASSICAL BIOGRAPHY
see Greece–Biography; Rome–Biography
CLASSICAL LANGUAGES
see Latin Language
CLASSICAL MYTHOLOGY
see Mythology, Classical
CLAY, CASSIUS MARCELLUS, 1942-
see Muhammad Ali, 1942-
CLAY, HENRY, 1777-1852
Kelly, Regina Z. Henry Clay. Walker, C., illus. (gr. 4-6). 1960. (Piper); pap. 2.44 (ISBN 0-395-01717-3). HM.
Peterson, Helen S. Henry Clay: Leader in Congress. Dowd, Vic, illus. 80p. (gr. 2-6). 1991. Repr. of 1964 ed. PLB 12.95 (ISBN 0-7910-1457-6). Chelsea Hse.
CLAY
see also Modeling
Moniot, Janet. Clay Whistles...the Voice of Clay. Rey, Mary L., ed. LC 89-51777. (Illus.). 56p. (Orig.). 1990. pap. 11.95 spiral bdg. (ISBN 0-9624893-0-1); video & book 34.95 (ISBN 0-9624893-1-X). Whistle Pr.
Murphy, Lois. Story Clay. Wilson, Karen, illus. 8p. (gr. 1-8). Date not set. pap. write for info. (ISBN 0-9620672-0-2). Dragon Studio.
CLAY INDUSTRIES
see also Pottery
CLAY MODELING
see Modeling
CLEANING
see also House Cleaning; Soap
Hickman, Martha W. Eeps Creeps, It's My Room. Baer, Mary A., illus. 32p. (gr. 1-3). 1984. 1.00 (ISBN 0-687-11527-2). Abingdon.
It's Fun to Wash. (Illus.). 8p. (ps). 1978. 2.50 (ISBN 0-448-46835-2, G&D). Putnam Pub Group.
CLEANLINESS
see Hygiene
CLEMENS, SAMUEL LANGHORNE, 1835-1910
Hargrove, Jim. Mark Twain: The Story of Samuel Clemens. LC 83-23157. (Illus.). 128p. (gr. 4 up). 1984. lib. bdg. 17.27 (ISBN 0-516-03204-6). Childrens.
Kane, Harnett T. Young Mark Twain & the Mississippi. Bjorklund, L., illus. LC 87-4531. 176p. (gr. 5-9). 1987. lib. bdg. 8.99 (ISBN 0-394-90413-3, Random Juv); pap. 2.95 (ISBN 0-394-89182-1). Random.
Mason, Miriam E. Mark Twain: Young Writer. Gillette, Henry S., illus. LC 90-23768. 192p. (gr. 3-7). 1991. pap. 3.95 (ISBN 0-689-71480-7, Aladdin). Macmillan Child Grp.
Meltzer, Milton. Mark Twain. LC 85-5108. (Illus.). 120p. (gr. 6-9). 1985. PLB 12.90 (ISBN 0-531-10072-3). Watts.
Quackenbush, Robert. Mark Twain? What Kind of Name is That? A Story of Samuel Langhorn Clemens. LC 83-19086. (Illus.). 40p. (gr. 2-6). 1984. PLB 11.95 (ISBN 0-671-66294-5). S&S Trade.
Sabin, Louis. Young Mark Twain. Burns, Ray, illus. LC 89-33982. 48p. (gr. 4-6). 1989. PLB 10.79 (ISBN 0-8167-1783-4); pap. text ed. 2.95 (ISBN 0-8167-1784-2). Troll Assocs.
CLEMENTE, ROBERTO, 1934-1972
Bjarkman, Peter C. Roberto Clemente. Murray, Jim, intro. by. (Illus.). 64p. (gr. 3 up). 1991. PLB 14.95 (ISBN 0-7910-1171-2). Chelsea Hse.
O'Connor, Jim. Story of Roberto Clemente. (gr. 4-7). 1991. pap. 2.95 (ISBN 0-440-40425-8). Dell.
Walker, Paul R. Pride of Puerto Rico: The Life of Roberto Clemente. (gr. 4-7). 1991. pap. 4.95 (ISBN 0-15-263420-7). HarBraceJ.
CLEOPATRA, QUEEN OF EGYPT, 69-30 B.C.
Hoobler, Dorothy & Hoobler, Thomas. Cleopatra. (Illus.). 112p. (gr. 5 up). 1987. lib. bdg. 17.95x (ISBN 0-87754-589-8). Chelsea Hse.
Humphrey, Perla F. Historic People of Color: Cleopatra. Spaulding, Ureal, illus. 22p. (Orig.). (gr. 3-8). 1990. pap. write for info. (ISBN 1-878910-01-9). Supplemental Learning.
Langley, Andrew. Cleopatra & the Egyptians. LC 85-73586. (Illus.). 64p. (gr. 4-9). PLB 12.40 (ISBN 0-531-18079-4, Pub. by Bookwright). Watts.
Shakespeare, William. Antony & Cleopatra. Rudvik, O. H., intro. by. (gr. 10 up). pap. 0.60 (ISBN 0-8049-1011-1, S-11). Airmont.
Shaw, George Bernard. Caesar & Cleopatra. (gr. 11 up). pap. 0.95 (ISBN 0-8049-0119-8, CL-119). Airmont.
CLERGY
see also Monasticism and Religious Orders
DeHart, Jack. So You Want to Serve. Bernard, David, ed. Caito, Mike, illus. 189p. (Orig.). 1990. pap. 6.95 (ISBN 0-932581-77-3). Word Aflame.
Franck, Irene M. & Brownstone, David M. Scholars & Priests. (Illus.). 208p. (gr. 7 up). 1988. 17.95 (ISBN 0-8160-1449-3). Facts on File.
Hutchinson, Duane. Grotto Father: Artist-Priest of the West Bend Grotto. LC 89-39029. 66p. 1989. pap. 4.95 (ISBN 0-934988-20-X). Foun Bks.
Lyngheim, Linda, et al. Father Junipero Serra, the Traveling Missionary. Garber, Phyllis, illus. LC 85-82131. 64p. (gr. 3-5). 1986. 12.95 (ISBN 0-915369-01-X). Langtry Pubns.
Wilson, Jean. Crusader for Christ (Billy Graham) (gr. 6-9). 1973. pap. 3.95 (ISBN 0-87508-602-0). Chr Lit.
CLERGY–FICTION
Barrie, James. Little Minister. (gr. 10 up). 1968. pap. 0.75 (ISBN 0-8049-0187-2, CL-187). Airmont.
Goldsmith, Oliver. Vicar of Wakefield. (gr. 10 up). 1964. pap. 1.25 (ISBN 0-8049-0052-3, CL-52). Airmont.
Vernon, Louise A. A Heart Strangely Warmed. Eitzen, Allan, illus. LC 75-11767. 128p. (gr. 4-9). 1975. pap. 4.95 (ISBN 0-8361-1769-7). Herald Pr.
Wolcott, Leonard T. & Wolcott, Carolyn E. Wilderness Rider. 144p. (Orig.). (gr. 5 up). 1984. pap. 0.40 (ISBN 0-687-45570-7). Abingdon.
CLERGY–VOCATIONAL GUIDANCE
Poling, Nancy W. Most Ministers Wear Sneakers. Ortiz, Gloria C., illus. 32p. (gr. 4-8). 1991. 12.95 (ISBN 0-8298-0907-4, P-0907-4); pap. 6.95 (ISBN 0-8298-0901-5, P-0901-5). Pilgrim NY.
Tierney, Terence. Should You Become a Priest? 64p. (Orig.). (gr. 9 up). 1975. pap. 2.50 (ISBN 0-89243-020-6, 29530). Liguori Pubns.
CLERICAL WORK–TRAINING
see Business Education
CLERKS (SALESMENSHIP)
see Salesmen and Salesmanship
CLEVELAND, GROVER, PRESIDENT U. S. 1837-1908
Collins, David R. Grover Cleveland: 22nd & 24th President of the United States. Young, Richard G., ed. LC 87-35794. (Illus.). (gr. 5-9). 1988. PLB 17.26 (ISBN 0-944483-01-1). Garrett Ed Corp.
Kent, Zachary. Grover Cleveland: Twenty-Second & Twenty-Fourth President of the United States. LC 88-10885. (Illus.). 100p. (gr. 3 up). 1988. PLB 17.27 (ISBN 0-516-01360-2). Childrens.
Vexler, Robert I. Grover Cleveland, 1837-1908: Chronology, Documents, Bibliographical Aids. LC 68-21538. 118p. (gr. 9 up). 1968. PLB 10.00 (ISBN 0-379-12054-2). Oceana.
CLEVELAND–FICTION
Manry, Douglas. The Land the Cleves Built. Sloan, Stephen, ed. Manry, Douglas, illus. 32p. (gr. 2-5). 1989. write for info. (ISBN 0-9622316-0-6). Sloan Manry Pubs.
CLIFF DWELLERS AND CLIFF DWELLINGS
see also Mounds and Mound Builders
Radlauer, Ruth. Mesa Verde National Park. updated ed. Zillmer, Rolf, photos by. LC 76-27350. (Illus.). 48p. (gr. 3 up). 1984. PLB 17.27 (ISBN 0-516-07490-3); pap. 4.95 (ISBN 0-516-47490-1). Childrens.
Trimble, Stephen. The Village of Blue Stone. Dewey, Jennifer O. & Reade, Deborah, illus. LC 88-34194. 64p. (gr. 3-7). 1990. 13.95 (ISBN 0-02-789501-7, Mcmillan Child Bk). Macmillan Child Grp.

CLIMATE
Here are entered works on climate as it relates to man and to plant and animal life, including the effects of changes of climate. Works limited to the climate of a particular region are entered under the name of the place with the subdivision Climate. Works on the state of the atmosphere at a given time and place with respect to heat and cold, wetness or dryness, calm or storm, are entered under Weather. Scientific works on the atmosphere, especially weather factors, are entered under Meteorology.
see also Meteorology; Rain and Rainfall; Seasons; Weather
Duden, Jane. The Ozone Layer. LC 90-36297. (Illus.). 48p. (gr. 5-6). 1990. RSBE 10.95 (ISBN 0-89686-546-0, Crestwood Hse). Macmillan Child Grp.
Facklam, Margery & Facklam, Howard. Changes in the Wind: The Earth's Shifting Climate. Facklam, Paul, illus. LC 85-5475. 128p. (gr. 7-9). 1986. 14.95 (ISBN 0-15-216115-5, HJ). Harbracej.
Flint, David. Weather & Climate: Projects with Geography. (Illus.). 32p. (gr. 5-8). 1991. PLB 11.90 (ISBN 0-531-17321-6, Gloucester Pr). Watts.
Gallant, Roy A. Earth's Changing Climate. Gallant, Roy A., illus. LC 78-22124. 240p. (gr. 7 up). 1984. 14.95 (ISBN 0-02-736840-8, Four Winds). Macmillan Child Grp.
Harris, Jack C. The Greenhouse Effect. LC 90-36294. (Illus.). 48p. (gr. 5-6). 1990. RSBE 10.95 (ISBN 0-89686-543-6, Crestwood Hse). Macmillan Child Grp.
Johnson, Rebecca L. The Greenhouse Effect: Life on a Warmer Planet. (Illus.). 112p. (gr. 5 up). 1990. PLB 17.95 (ISBN 0-8225-1591-1). Lerner Pubns.
Knapp, Brian. Drought. LC 89-19730. (Illus.). 48p. (gr. 5-9). 1990. PLB 17.28 (ISBN 0-8114-2376-X). Steck-V.
Neufeld, Herm & Chaffin, Charles. Climate in Three-D. (Orig.). (gr. 4-9). 1973. pap. 4.50 (ISBN 0-918932-04-1). Activity Resources.
Simon, Seymour. Weather & Climate. (gr. 4-6). 1969. lib. bdg. 4.99 (ISBN 0-394-90804-X). Random.
Stewart, Gail B. Drought. LC 90-36293. (Illus.). 48p. (gr. 5-6). 1990. RSBE 10.95 (ISBN 0-89686-544-4, Crestwood Hse). Macmillan Child Grp.
Torjman, Nathalie. History & Geography of Climates. (gr. 6 up). 1988. 4.95 (ISBN 0-8120-3838-X). Barron.
Updegraff, Imelda & Updegraff, Robert. Continents & Climates. (Illus.). 1981. PLB 9.95 (ISBN 0-89813-040-9); 14.25. Creative Ed.

CLIMATOLOGY
see Climate

CLIPPER SHIPS
Stein, R. Conrad. The Story of the Clipper Ships. LC 81-1299. (Illus.). 32p. (gr. 3-6). 1981. PLB 13.27 (ISBN 0-516-04612-8); pap. 3.95 (ISBN 0-516-44612-6). Childrens.
Whipple, A. B. The Clipper Ships. LC 79-24764. (gr. 7 up). lib. bdg. 21.27 (ISBN 0-8094-2678-1, Pub. by Time-Life). Silver.

CLOCKS AND WATCHES
see also Sundials
Breiter, Herta S. Time & Clocks. rev. ed. LC 87-23229. (Illus.). 48p. (gr. 2-6). 1987. PLB 17.32 (ISBN 0-8172-3262-1); pap. 9.27 (ISBN 0-8172-3287-7). Raintree Pubs.
Gibbons, Gail. Clocks & How They Go. Gibbons, Gail, illus. LC 78-22498. 32p. (gr. k-4). 1979. PLB 13.89 (ISBN 0-690-03974-3, Crowell Jr Bks). HarpC Child Bks.
Zubrowski, Bernie. Clocks: Building & Experimenting with Model Timepieces. Doty, Roy, illus. LC 87-18467. 112p. (gr. 3-7). 1988. lib. bdg. 12.88 (ISBN 0-688-06926-6); pap. 7.95 (ISBN 0-688-06925-8, Pub. by Beech Tree Bks). Morrow Jr Bks.

CLOCKS AND WATCHES–FICTION
Bassett, Lisa. A Clock for Beany. Bassett, Jeni, illus. (gr. 3-8). 1988. pap. 3.95 (ISBN 0-14-050852-X, Puffin). Puffin Bks.
—A Clock for Beany. Bassett, Jeni, illus. 32p. (gr. k-3). 1985. 11.95 (ISBN 0-396-08484-2, Putnam). Putnam Pub Group.
Bellairs, John. The House with a Clock in Its Walls. 192p. (gr. 3 up). 1974. pap. 3.50 (ISBN 0-440-43742-3, YB). Dell.
Brown, Kathryn. Muledred. (Illus.). 32p. (ps-3). 1990. 12.95 (ISBN 0-15-256265-6). HarbraceJ.
Cave, Kathryn. Just in Time. McKenna, Terry, illus. LC 88-33834. 32p. (ps-2). 1989. 8.95 (ISBN 0-517-57311-3, C N Potter Bks). Crown.
Fuchshuber, Annegert. The Cuckoo-Clock Cuckoo. 32p. (gr. k-4). 1988. lib. bdg. 12.95 (ISBN 0-87614-320-6); pap. 5.95 (ISBN 0-87614-499-7). Carolrhoda Bks.
Holland, Margaret & Demers, Jan. Ticktock Around the Clock. Adams, Rhonda, illus. 24p. (gr. k-2). 1987. 1.95 (ISBN 0-87406-233-0, 12-13445-4). Willowisp Pr.
Molesworth, M. L. The Cuckoo Clock. (Orig.). (gr. k-6). 1987. pap. 4.95 (ISBN 0-440-41618-3, Pub. by Yearling Classics). Dell.
Rappoport, Doreen. The Night the Minute Hand Stopped. LC 88-81466. (Illus.). 32p. (Orig.). (ps-2). 1988. pap. 8.95 (ISBN 0-937124-16-8). Kimbo Educ.
Seiden, Art, illus. Tick-Tock. 10p. (ps). 1982. 3.50 (ISBN 0-448-46828-X, G&D). Putnam Pub Group.
Stolz, Mary. Cuckoo Clock. Johnson, Pamela, illus. LC 86-45538. 112p. 1986. 13.95 (ISBN 0-87923-653-1). Godine.
Tompert, Ann. Sue Patch & the Crazy Clocks. 1989. 9.95 (ISBN 0-8037-0656-1). Dial Bks Young.

CLOG DANCING
see Folk Dancing

CLOTHING AND DRESS
Here are entered works dealing with clothing from a practical standpoint including the art of dress. Descriptive and historical works on the costume of particular countries or periods are entered under Costume.
see also Buttons; Costume; Costume Design; Dressmaking; Fashion; Hats; Shoes and Shoe Industry
Accessories. (Illus.). (gr. 5 up). lib. bdg. 14.00 (ISBN 0-86625-281-9). Rourke Corp.
Ball, Jacqueline. Looking Good, 8 bks, Set 11. (Illus.). 64p. (gr. 5 up). 1990. Set. lib. bdg. 112.00 (ISBN 0-86625-287-8). Rourke Corp.
Berry, Joy W. What to Do When Your Mom or Dad Says: "Get Dressed!" Kelley, Orly, ed. Bartholomew, illus. LC 83-80839. 48p. (gr. k-6). 4.98 (ISBN 0-941510-17-4). Living Skills.
—What to Do When Your Mom or Dad Says..."Take Care of Your Clothes!" Bartholomew, illus. Berry, Joy W., intro. by. LC 82-81201. (Illus.). 48p. (gr. 3-7). 1982. 4.98 (ISBN 0-941510-05-0). Living Skills.
Clothing. (Illus.). (gr. 5 up). lib. bdg. 14.00 (ISBN 0-86625-277-0). Rourke Corp.
Cobb, Vicki. Getting Dressed. Hafner, Marylin, illus. LC 87-26097. 32p. (gr. k-3). 1989. 11.95 (ISBN 0-397-32142-2, Lipp Jr Bks); PLB 11.89 (ISBN 0-397-32143-0). HarpC Child Bks.
Costumes & Clothes, 6 vols. LC 88-29281. (Illus.). 192p. (gr. 3-10). 1989. Set. 73.75 (ISBN 0-86307-980-6). Marshall Cavendish.
DePaola, Tomie. Charlie Needs a Cloak. LC 73-16365. (Illus.). 32p. (gr. k-4). 1982. PLB 12.95 (ISBN 0-671-66466-2); pap. 5.95 (ISBN 0-671-66467-0). S&S Trade.
Everett, F. & Garbera, C. Making Clothes. (Illus.). 48p. (gr. 6 up). 1986. PLB 13.96 (ISBN 0-88110-321-7); pap. 5.95 (ISBN 0-86020-981-4). EDC.
Giff, Patricia R. If the Shoe Fits. (Orig.). (gr. k-6). 1988. pap. 2.95 (ISBN 0-440-40086-4, YB). Dell.
Llewellyn, Claire. First Look at Clothes. LC 91-9425. (Illus.). 32p. (gr. 1-2). 1991. PLB 10.95 (ISBN 0-8368-0677-8). Gareth Stevens Inc.
Mitgutsch, Ali. From Cotton to Pants. Mitgutsch, Ali, illus. LC 80-29552. 24p. (ps-3). 1981. PLB 6.95 (ISBN 0-87614-150-5). Carolrhoda Bks.
Oliver, Stephen, photos by. Clothes. LC 90-23999. (Illus.). 24p. (ps-k). 1991. 7.00 (ISBN 0-679-81806-5, Random Juv). Random.
Oxenbury, Helen. Dressing. Oxenbury, Helen, illus. 14p. (ps-k). 1981. 3.95 (ISBN 0-671-42113-1, Little Simon). S&S Trade.
Peeples, H. I. T-Shirt. Moran, Michael, illus. 24p. (gr. 2-5). 1989. 6.95 (ISBN 0-8092-4407-1, Calico Bks). Contemp Bks.
Pluckrose, Henry. Wear It! Fairclough, Chris, photos by. (Illus.). 32p. (gr. k-4). 1990. PLB 10.40 (ISBN 0-531-14065-2). Watts.
Pragoff, Fiona. Clothes. (Illus.). 16p. (ps-k). 1989. 5.95 (ISBN 0-385-26388-0, Zephyr-BFYR). Doubleday.
Ruby, Jennifer. The Nineteen Sixties & Nineteen Seventies. (Illus.). 64p. (gr. 6-9). 1989. 19.95 (ISBN 0-7134-6074-1, Pub. by Batsford England). Trafalgar Sq.
—The Regency. (Illus.). 64p. (gr. 6-9). 1989. 19.95 (ISBN 0-7134-5992-1, Pub. by Batsford England). Trafalgar Sq.
Weil, Lisl. New Clothes: What People Wore - from Cavemen to Astronauts. Weil, Lisl, illus. LC 87-919. 64p. (gr. k-4). 1988. 13.95 (ISBN 0-689-31298-9, Atheneum Child Bk). Macmillan Child Grp.

CLOTHING AND DRESS–FICTION
Austen, Carrie. Rosie's Fashion Show. (gr. 4-7). 1991. pap. 2.95 (ISBN 0-425-12652-8). Berkley Pub.
Beskow, Elsa. Pelle's New Suit. Woodburn, Marion L., tr. from SWE. Beskow, Elsa, illus. 32p. (ps-2). Repr. of 1979 ed. 14.95 (ISBN 0-86315-092-6, Pub. by Floris Bks UK). Gryphon Hse.
Boynton, Sandra. Blue Hat Green Hat. 1984. 3.95 (ISBN 0-671-49320-5). S&S Trade.
Charnas, Suzy M. The Silver Glove. (gr. 7 up). 1989. pap. 2.95 (ISBN 0-318-41646-8, Starfire). Bantam.
Costa, Nicoletta. Dressing Up. Costa, Nicoletta, illus. 16p. (gr. k). 1984. 3.50 (ISBN 0-448-23401-7, G&D). Putnam Pub Group.
Cowley, Joy. Mrs. Grindy's Shoes, 6 bks. Biro, Val, illus. 16p. (Orig.). (gr. k-2). 1987. Set. pap. text ed. 19.80 (ISBN 1-55624-744-3). Wright Group.
—Mrs. Grindy's Shoes. Biro, Val, illus. 16p. (Orig.). (gr. k-2). 1987. pap. text ed. 23.00 (ISBN 1-55624-167-4). Wright Group.
—The Tiny Woman's Coat, 6 bks. Fuller, Elizabeth, illus. 16p. (Orig.). (gr. k-2). 1987. Set. pap. text ed. 19.80 (ISBN 1-55624-741-9). Wright Group.
—The Tiny Woman's Coat. Fuller, Elizabeth, illus. 16p. (Orig.). (gr. k-2). 1987. pap. text ed. 23.00 (ISBN 1-55624-165-8). Wright Group.
De Regniers, Beatrice S. What Can You Do with a Shoe? Sendak, Maurice, illus. LC 55-6429. 32p. (ps-k). 1955. PLB 11.89 (ISBN 0-06-024850-5). HarpC Child Bks.
Estes, Eleanor. The Hundred Dresses. Slobodkin, Louis, illus. LC 73-12940. 80p. (gr. k-3). 1974. pap. 4.95 (ISBN 0-15-642350-2, VoyB). HarBraceJ.
Farjeon, Eleanor. The Glass Slipper. 159p. 1981. Repr. PLB 16.95x (ISBN 0-89966-360-5). Buccaneer Bks.
—The Glass Slipper. 108p. 1981. Repr. PLB 16.95x (ISBN 0-89967-034-2). Harmony Raine.
Gaban, Jesus. Harry Presses Himself. Colorado, Nani, illus. 16p. (ps-1). 1991. PLB 10.95 (ISBN 0-8368-0715-4). Gareth Stevens Inc.
—Harry's Mealtime Mess. Colorado, Nani, illus. 16p. (ps-1). 1991. PLB 10.95 (ISBN 0-8368-0717-0). Gareth Stevens Inc.
—Harry's Sandbox Surprise. Colorado, Nani, illus. 16p. (ps-1). 1991. PLB 10.95 (ISBN 0-8368-0716-2). Gareth Stevens Inc.
Gordon, Sharon. Drip Drop. Page, Don, illus. LC 81-5112. 32p. (gr. k-2). 1981. PLB 10.89 (ISBN 0-89375-507-9); pap. 2.95 (ISBN 0-89375-508-7). Troll Assocs.
Gross, Ruth B. The Emperor's New Clothes. Kent, Jack, illus. 32p. (Orig.). (ps-2). 1991. pap. 2.50 (ISBN 0-590-43267-2). Scholastic Inc.
Harvey, Anne. Flora's Red Socks. McMullan, Bernice, illus. LC 90-41956. 32p. (gr. 4-8). 1991. 12.95 (ISBN 0-87226-447-5). P Bedrick Bks.
Hayes, Geoffrey. Patrick Buys a Coat. Hayes, Geoffrey, illus. LC 84-1659. 32p. (ps-1). 1989. pap. 2.95 (ISBN 0-679-80162-6, Dragonfly Bks). Knopf.
Hilton, Nette. Dirty Dave. Harvey, Roland, illus. LC 89-35402. 32p. (ps-1). 1990. 12.95 (ISBN 0-531-05861-1); PLB 12.99 (ISBN 0-531-08461-2). Orchard Bks Watts.
—A Proper Little Lady. Wilcox, Cathy, illus. LC 89-35399. 32p. (ps-1). 1990. 12.95 (ISBN 0-531-05860-3); PLB 12.99 (ISBN 0-531-08460-4). Orchard Bks Watts.
Klein, David J. Irwin the Sock. (Illus.). 32p. (gr. 2-4). 1987. Incl. audio cassette. 27.99 (ISBN 0-8172-2473-4). Raintree Pubs.
Mack, Bruce. Jesse's Dream Skirt. Buchanan, Marian, illus. LC 79-89892. 35p. (Orig.). (ps-1). 1979. pap. 5.95 (ISBN 0-914996-20-7). Lollipop Power.
Neitzel, Shirley. Jacket I Wear in the Snow. LC 88-18767. (Illus.). 32p. (ps up). 1989. 13.95 (ISBN 0-688-08028-6); PLB 13.88 (ISBN 0-688-08030-8). Greenwillow.
Pascal, Francine. The Hand-Me-Down Kid. 176p. (gr. k-6). 1982. pap. 2.95 (ISBN 0-440-43449-1, YB). Dell.
Rice, Eve. Peter's Pockets. Parker, Nancy W., illus. LC 87-15640. 32p. (ps up). 1989. 12.95 (ISBN 0-688-07241-0); PLB 12.88 (ISBN 0-688-07242-9). Greenwillow.
Rinaldi, Ann. The Last Silk Dress. LC 87-25128. 368p. (gr. 5 up). 1988. 15.95 (ISBN 0-8234-0690-3). Holiday.
Roy, Ron. Whose Shoes Are These? LC 87-24279. (ps-3). 1988. 13.95 (ISBN 0-89919-445-1, Clarion Bks). Ticknor & Fields.
Smithson, Colin & Smithson, Sheila. Joseph's Special Coat. (Illus.). 32p. 1990. 4.95 (ISBN 0-310-56170-1). Zondervan.
Spohn, Kate. Clementine's Winter Wardrobe. LC 89-42531. (Illus.). 32p. (ps-1). 1989. 13.95 (ISBN 0-531-05841-7); PLB 13.99 (ISBN 0-531-08441-8). Orchard Bks Watts.
Streatfeild, Noel. Traveling Shoes. 256p. (gr. 4-7). 1984. pap. 2.95 (ISBN 0-440-48732-3, YB). Dell.
Tamar, Erika. High Cheekbones. 240p. (gr. 7 up). 1990. pap. 12.95 (ISBN 0-670-82843-2). Viking Child Bks.
Thomson, Pat & Ross, Tony. The Treasure Sock. (Orig.). (gr. k-6). 1987. pap. 2.50 (ISBN 0-440-48814-1, YB). Dell.
Watanabe, Shigeo. How Do I Put It on? Ohtomo, Yasuo, illus. LC 79-12714. (gr. 2-4). 1984. PLB 8.95 (ISBN 0-399-20761-9, Philomel); (Philomel); pap. 3.95 (ISBN 0-399-21040-7, Philomel). Putnam Pub Group.
Wells, Rosemary. Max's New Suit. Wells, Rosemary, illus. LC 79-50747. (ps-k). 1979. bds. 3.95 (ISBN 0-8037-6065-5). Dial Bks Young.
Wood, D. No Clothes. (Illus.). 40p. (ps-8). 1990. pap. 5.95 (ISBN 1-55037-089-8). Firefly Bks Ltd.
Ziefert, Harriet. A New Coat for Anna. Lobel, Anita, illus. LC 86-2722. 40p. (ps-3). 1988. pap. 3.95 (ISBN 0-394-89861-3). Knopf.
Zokeisha. Things I Like to Wear. Zokeisha, illus. 16p. (ps-k). 1981. board 2.95 (ISBN 0-671-44452-2, Little Simon). S&S Trade.

CLOTHING TRADE–FICTION
Streatfeild, Noel. Family Shoes. 224p. (gr. 5 up). 1985. pap. 3.50 (ISBN 0-440-42479-8, YB). Dell.
Trella, Phyllis. Jodee's Closet. Trella, Phyllis, illus. LC 82-73689. 48p. (gr. 2-6). write for info. (ISBN 0-914201-04-2). Cheeruppet.

CLOUD SEEDING
see Weather Control

CLOUDS
Cutting, Brian & Cutting, Jillian. Clouds. Bailey, Martin, illus. 16p. (gr. k-2). 1988. pap. text ed. 23.00 (ISBN 1-55911-056-2). Wright Group.
—Clouds, 6 bks. Bailey, Martin, illus. 16p. (Orig.). (gr. k-2). 1988. Set. pap. text ed. 19.80 (ISBN 1-55911-057-0). Wright Group.
DePaola, Tomie. The Cloud Book. De Paola, Tomie, illus. LC 74-34493. 32p. (gr. k-3). 1975. reinforced bdg. 14.95 (ISBN 0-8234-0259-2); pap. 5.95 (ISBN 0-8234-0531-1). Holiday.
Fitzgerald, Bridget. Little Dark Cloud. Alston, Virgil, illus. Harman, Sandra L., intro. by. LC 78-189877. (Illus.). 44p. (gr. 1-2). 1973. 2.50 (ISBN 0-87884-012-5). Unicorn Ent.
Greene, Carol. Hi, Clouds. Sharp, Gene, illus. LC 82-19854. 32p. (ps-2). 1983. PLB 11.93 (ISBN 0-516-02036-6); pap. 2.95 (ISBN 0-516-42036-4). Childrens.
McMillan, Bruce. The Weather Sky. (Illus.). 40p. (gr. 5 up). 1991. 16.95 (ISBN 0-374-38261-1). FS&G.

Peebles, J. Winston. My Funny Cloud. Beach, Bettye, illus. LC 81-50915. 36p. (ps-3). 1981. 4.95 (ISBN 0-938232-00-2). Winston-Derek.
Ray, Deborah K. The Cloud. Ray, Deborah K., illus. LC 83-48438. 48p. (gr. k-3). 1984. HarpC Child Bks.
Scorer, R. S. & Wexler, H. A Colour Guide to Clouds. (Illus.). 72p. (gr. k-7). 1964. text ed. 22.00 (ISBN 0-08-010375-8); pap. text ed. 11.50 (ISBN 0-08-010374-X). Pergamon.
Tomkins, Jasper. Nimby. Tomkins, Jasper, illus. LC 84-144466. 60p. (Orig.). (ps-3). 1983. pap. 7.95 (ISBN 0-914676-83-0). Green Tiger Pr.
Wandelmaier, Roy. Clouds. Jones, John, illus. LC 84-8643. 32p. (gr. k-2). 1985. PLB 10.89 (ISBN 0-8167-0338-8); pap. text ed. 2.95 (ISBN 0-8167-0441-4). Troll Assocs.

CLOWNS

Gaskin, Carol. A Day in the Life of a Circus Clown. Klein, John F., illus. LC 87-10954. 32p. (gr. 4-8). 1988. PLB 11.79 (ISBN 0-8167-1107-0); pap. text ed. 2.95 (ISBN 0-8167-1108-9). Troll Assocs.
Harris, Steven M. This Is My Trunk. Welliver, Norma, illus. LC 85-7462. 32p. (ps-4). 1985. 13.95 (ISBN 0-689-31128-1, Atheneum Child Bk). Macmillan Child Grp.
Sobol, Harriet L. Clowns. Agre, Patricia, photos by. (gr. 6-9). 1982. 9.95 (ISBN 0-698-20558-8, Coward). Putnam Pub Group.
Stolzenberg, Mark. Be a Clown. LC 89-33783. (Illus.). 160p. (gr. 4-12). 1989. pap. 10.95 (ISBN 0-8069-5804-9). Sterling.
Thaler, Mike. The Clown's Smile. Cameron, Tracey, illus. LC 85-45850. 40p. (ps-k). 1986. PLB 10.89 (ISBN 0-06-026052-1). HarpC Child Bks.

CLOWNS–FICTION

Cline, Paul. Fools, Clowns, & Jesters. LC 84-144859. (Illus.). 58p. (gr. 3-10). 1983. pap. 12.95 (ISBN 0-914676-88-1). Green Tiger Pr.
Cole, Joanna. The Clown-Arounds. Smath, Jerry, illus. LC 81-4662. 48p. (ps-3). 1981. 5.95 (ISBN 0-8193-1059-X); PLB 5.95 (ISBN 0-8193-1060-3). Parents.
—The Clown-Arounds Go on Vacation. Smath, Jerry, illus. LC 83-13480. 48p. (ps-3). 1984. 5.95 (ISBN 0-8193-1120-0). Parents.
—Sweet Dreams, Clown-Arounds. Smath, Jerry, illus. LC 85-6348. 48p. (ps-3). 1985. 5.95 (ISBN 0-8193-1138-3). Parents.
Dale, Nora. The Best Trick of All. (Illus.). 32p. (gr. 1-4). 1989. PLB 13.32 (ISBN 0-8172-3505-1). Raintree Pubs.
Gipson, Morrell & Hansson, Peter. Clumsy Clown Willie. Stefoff, Rebecca, ed. LC 90-13793. (Illus.). 24p. (gr. k-3). 1990. PLB 13.26 (ISBN 0-944483-90-9). Garrett Ed Corp.
Johnson, Sharon S. I Want to Be a Clown. Gregorich, Barbara, ed. (Illus.). 16p. (Orig.). (gr. k-2). 1985. pap. 1.95 (ISBN 0-88743-014-7, 06014). Sch Zone Pub Co.
Lacome, Julie. Funny Business. Lacome, Julie, illus. LC 90-36258. 1991. 11.95 (ISBN 0-688-10159-3, Tambourine Bks). Morrow.
Parish, Peggy. Clues in the Woods. 160p. (gr. k-6). 1980. pap. 3.25 (ISBN 0-440-41461-X, YB). Dell.
Pennington, Lillian B. Snafu: The Littlest Clown. Gardner, Earle, illus. LC 73-90113. 32p. (gr. 1-6). 1972. PLB 9.95 (ISBN 0-913532-00-2); cassette 7.94x (ISBN 0-87783-225-0). Oddo.

CLUBS–FICTION

Alcock, Vivien. The Trial of Anna Cotman. (gr. 5-9). 1990. 13.95 (ISBN 0-385-29981-8). Delacorte.
Alexander, Sue. Seymour the Prince. Hoban, Lillian, illus. LC 78-31406. (gr. 2-4). 1979. 6.95 (ISBN 0-685-03943-9). Pantheon.
Berenstain, Michael. The Panda Club's Tree House. (Illus.). 40p. (gr. k-2). 1989. write for info. (ISBN 0-307-11687-5, Pub. by Golden Bks). Western Pub.
Berenstain, Stan & Berenstain, Janice. The Berenstain Bears: No Girls Allowed. Berenstain, Stan & Berenstain, Janice, illus. LC 85-18246. 32p. (ps-1). 1986. lib. bdg. 5.99 (ISBN 0-394-97331-3); pap. 2.25 (ISBN 0-394-87331-9). Random.
Bograd, Larry. The Fourth-Grade Dinosaur Club. Lauter, Richard, illus. LC 88-22876. (gr. 3 up). 1989. 13.95 (ISBN 0-440-50128-8). Delacorte.
Bonsall, Crosby N. The Case of the Double Cross. LC 80-7768. (Illus.). 64p. (gr. k-3). 1980. 11.89 (ISBN 0-06-020602-0); PLB 11.89 (ISBN 0-06-020603-9). HarpC Child Bks.
—Case of the Scaredy Cats. LC 75-159039. (Illus.). 64p. (gr. k-3). 1971. PLB 10.89 (ISBN 0-685-02058-4). HarpC Child Bks.
Cleary, Beverly. Henry & the Clubhouse. Darling, Louis, illus. LC 62-7161. (gr. 3-7). 1962. 12.95 (ISBN 0-688-21381-2); PLB 12.88 (ISBN 0-688-31381-7, Morrow Jr Bks). Morrow Jr Bks.
Cooper, Ilene. Queen of the Sixth Grade. 160p. (gr. 3 up). 1990. pap. 3.95 (ISBN 0-14-034028-9, Puffin). Puffin Bks.
Haynes, Betsy. The Against Taffy Sinclair Club. 112p. (gr. 3-6). 1984. pap. 2.50 (ISBN 0-553-15413-3). Bantam.
Hines, Anna G. Tell Me Your Best Thing. Ritz, Karen, illus. 96p. (gr. 2-4). 1991. 13.95 (ISBN 0-525-44734-2, DCB). Dutton Child Bks.
Jenkins, Jerry B. The Clubhouse Mystery. (gr. 4-7). 1990. pap. 4.50 (ISBN 0-8024-0807-9). Moody.
Klein, Norma. Tomboy. LC 78-4337. 128p. (gr. 3-7). 1989. pap. 2.95 (ISBN 0-394-82044-4). Knopf.
Klevin, Jill R. The Turtle Street Trading Co. Edwards, Linda S., illus. LC 82-70312. 144p. (gr. 4-6). 1982. 11.95 (ISBN 0-385-29043-8); PLB 11.95 (ISBN 0-685-05625-2). Delacorte.
Myrick, Mildred. Secret Three. Lobel, Arnold, illus. LC 63-13323. 64p. (gr. k-3). 1963. PLB 11.89 (ISBN 0-06-024356-2). HarpC Child Bks.
Shusterman, Neal. The Shadow Club. LC 87-35369. 183p. (gr. 7-9). 1988. 12.95 (ISBN 0-316-77540-1). Little.

COACHING (ATHLETICS)

Aaseng, Nathan. College Basketball: You Are the Coach. LC 83-19996. (Illus.). 104p. (gr. 4 up). 1984. lib. bdg. 8.95 (ISBN 0-8225-1555-5). Lerner Pubns.
Beatty, Patricia. The Coach That Never Came. LC 85-15213. 176p. (gr. 5-9). 1985. 11.95 (ISBN 0-688-05477-3). Morrow Jr Bks.

COAL MINES AND MINING

see also Mining Engineering

Davey, John. Mining Coal. (Illus.). 64p. (gr. 6 up). 1976. 14.95 (ISBN 0-7136-1596-6). Dufour.
Davis, Bertha & Whitfield, Susan. The Coal Question. LC 82-4716. (Illus.). 96p. (gr. 7 up). 1982. PLB 12.90 (ISBN 0-531-04484-X). Watts.
Dineen, Jacqueline. Coal. 32p. (gr. 4-8). 1988. lib. bdg. 12.95 (ISBN 0-89490-212-1). Enslow Pubs.
Hansen, Michael C. Coal: How It Is Found & Used. LC 89-34452. 64p. 1990. lib. bdg. 15.95 (ISBN 0-89490-286-5). Enslow Pubs.
Harris, Nathaniel. The Coal Mines. (Illus.). 64p. (gr. 7-12). 1986. 19.95 (ISBN 0-7134-5097-5, Pub. by Batsford England). Trafalgar Sq.
Hendershot, Judith. In Coal Country. Allen, Thomas B., illus. Foster, Frances, ed. Rosenthal, Eileen, designed by. LC 86-15311. (Illus.). 48p. (ps-5). 1987. 14.95 (ISBN 0-394-88190-7); lib. bdg. 14.99 (ISBN 0-394-98190-1). Knopf.
Mitgutsch, Ali. From Swamp to Coal. Mitgutsch, Ali, illus. LC 84-17465. 24p. (ps-3). 1985. PLB 6.95 (ISBN 0-87614-233-1). Carolrhoda Bks.
Stewart, Gail. Coal Miners. LC 88-11860. (Illus.). 48p. (gr. 5-6). 1988. PLB 10.95 (ISBN 0-89686-395-6, Crestwood Hse). Macmillan Child Grp.
Witt, Matt. In Our Blood: Four Coal Mining Families. Dotter, Earl, photos by. LC 78-71518. (Illus., Orig.). (gr. 10-12). 1979. pap. text ed. 6.95 (ISBN 0-9602226-1-8). Highlander.

COAL MINES AND MINING–FICTION

Reilly, Robert T. Rebels in the Shadows. LC 78-66069. 187p. (gr. 3-7). 1979. pap. 8.95 (ISBN 0-8229-5304-8). U of Pittsburgh Pr.

COAL OIL

see Petroleum

COASTAL SIGNALS

see Signals and Signaling

COATS OF ARMS

see Heraldry

COCHISE, APACHE CHIEF, d. 1874

Johnson, Ann D. The Value of Truth & Trust: The Story of Cochise. Pileggi, Steven, illus. LC 77-3294. (gr. k-6). 1977. 9.95 (ISBN 0-916392-10-4, Pub. by Value Communications). Oak Tree Pubns.

COCHRANE, ELIZABETH, 1867-1922

Ehrlich, Elizabeth. Nellie Bly. Horner, Matina S., intro. by. (Illus.). 112p. (gr. 5 up). 1989. 17.95 (ISBN 1-55546-643-5). Chelsea Hse.
Emerson, Kathy L. Making Headlines: A Biography of Nellie Bly. LC 88-35910. (Illus.). 112p. (gr. 5 up). 1989. lib. bdg. 12.95 (ISBN 0-87518-406-5, Dillon). Macmillan Child Grp.

COCKROACHES

Kerby, Mona. Cockroaches. (Illus.). 64p. (gr. 3 up). 1989. PLB 11.90 (ISBN 0-531-10689-6). Watts.

COCOA

see also Chocolate

COCOONS

see Butterflies; Caterpillars; Moths; Silkworms

CODE NAMES

see Ciphers

CODY, WILLIAM FREDERICK, 1846-1917

Buntline, Ned. Buffalo Bill: His Adventures in the West. LC 74-15731. (Illus.). 320p. (gr. 7 up). 1974. Repr. of 1886 ed. 23.00x (ISBN 0-405-06366-0). Ayer Co Pubs.
Harris, Aurand. Buffalo Bill. 1954. 4.50 (ISBN 0-87602-110-0). Anchorage.
McCall, Edith. Hunters Blaze the Trails. Rogers, Carol, illus. LC 59-3666. 128p. (gr. 3-10). 1980. PLB 14.60 (ISBN 0-516-03332-8). Childrens.
Robison, Nancy. Buffalo Bill. (Illus.). 64p. (gr. 3-5). 1991. PLB 11.90 (ISBN 0-531-20007-8). Watts.
Stevenson, Augusta. Buffalo Bill: Frontier Daredevil. Dreany, F. Joseph, illus. LC 90-23767. 192p. (gr. 3-7). 1991. pap. 3.95 (ISBN 0-689-71479-3, Aladdin). Macmillan Child Grp.

COGNITION

see Knowledge, Theory of

COIN COLLECTING

see Coins

COINAGE

see also Gold; Money; Silver

COINS

see also Numismatics

Andersen, Paul. Obsolete Fractional Coinage of the United States. LC 79-55915. (Illus.). 67p. (Orig.). (gr. 9 up). 1980. pap. 4.95 (ISBN 0-9604720-0-2). P Andersen.
Berry, George. Seventeenth Century England: Traders & Tokens. (Illus.). 168p. (gr. 12 up). 1988. PLB 40.00 (ISBN 1-85264-003-0, Pub. by Seaby UK). Numismatic Fine Arts.
Coin Collecting. (Illus.). 32p. (gr. 6-12). 1975. pap. 1.85 (ISBN 0-8395-3390-X, 3390). BSA.
Madous, H. Michael & Newman, Eric P. The First Official U. S. Coins: The Flag Connection. 3rd ed. Alberts, Robert C., et al, eds. 6p. 1989. pap. 2.00 (ISBN 0-934021-33-3). Natl Flag Foun.
Mayhew, Nicholas. Coinage in France from the Dark Ages to Napoleon. (Illus.). 164p. (gr. 10 up). 1988. 38.50 (ISBN 0-900652-87-X, Pub. by Seaby UK). Numismatic Fine Arts.

COINS–FICTION

Gipson, Morrell & Frank, Herta. Tom's Lucky Quarter. Stefoff, Rebecca, ed. LC 90-13796. (Illus.). 24p. (gr. k-3). 1990. PLB 13.26 (ISBN 0-944483-89-5). Garrett Ed Corp.

COLLAGE

Devonshire, Hilary. Collage. FS-Ltd Staff, ed. (Illus.). 32p. (gr. 1-6). 1988. PLB 11.90 (ISBN 0-531-10556-3). Watts.

COLLECTING

see Collectors and Collecting

COLLECTIONS OF LITERATURE

see Short Stories;
also names of literatures and literary forms with the subdivision Collections, e.g. English Literature–Collections; Poetry–Collections

COLLECTIVE SETTLEMENTS

Taylor, Allegra. A Kibbutz in Israel. (Illus.). 32p. (gr. 2-5). 1987. 9.95 (ISBN 0-8225-1678-0). Lerner Pubns.

COLLECTIVISM

see Communism

COLLECTORS AND COLLECTING

see also names of natural specimens with the subdivision Collection and Preservation, e.g. Zoological Specimens–Collection and Preservation

Childress, Casey & McKenzie, Linda. A Beginner's Guide to Baseball Card Collecting: A Step-by-Step Guide for the Young Collector. LC 88-90757. (Illus.). 46p. (Orig.). (gr. 4-8). 1990. Repr. of 1988 ed. vinyl covers 7.95 (ISBN 0-9620167-0-5). C Mack Pub.
Schulz, Charles M. Charlie Brown's Super Book of Things to Do & Collect. Schulz, Charles M., illus. LC 75-7749. 80p. (gr. 3 up). 1975. (Random Juv). Random.

COLLECTORS AND COLLECTING–FICTION

Gilson, Jamie. Harvey, the Beer Can King. Wallner, John, illus. LC 78-1807. 128p. (gr. 4-6). 1983. 13.95 (ISBN 0-688-02382-7). Lothrop.
Manushkin, Fran. Buster Loves Buttons! Zimmer, Dirk, illus. LC 84-48332. 64p. (gr. k-3). 1985. 11.95 (ISBN 0-06-024107-1); PLB 11.89 (ISBN 0-06-024108-X). HarpC Child Bks.
Poskanzer, Susan C. The Superduper Collector. Harvey, Paul, illus. LC 85-14051. 48p. (Orig.). (gr. 1-3). 1986. PLB 9.89 (ISBN 0-8167-0606-9); pap. text ed. 2.95 (ISBN 0-8167-0607-7). Troll Assocs.
Van Pallandt, Nicolas. The Butterfly Night of Old Brown Bear. (ps-3). 1991. bds. 14.95 jacketed (ISBN 0-374-31009-2). FS&G.

COLLECTS

see Prayers

COLLEGE, CHOICE OF

Blaker, Charles W. The College Matchmaker. New, Dwight, illus. LC 80-67604. 56p. (Orig.). (gr. 11-12). 1980. pap. text ed. 3.50 (ISBN 0-9604614-0-X). Rekalb Pr.
Buckalew, Walker. Coping with Choosing a College. Rosen, Roger, ed. 64p. (gr. 7-12). 1990. lib. bdg. 12.95 (ISBN 0-8239-1079-2). Rosen Group.

COLLEGE AND SCHOOL JOURNALISM

Dubrovnin, Vivian. Running a School Newspaper. LC 85-7476. (gr. 4-8). 1985. PLB 10.40 (ISBN 0-531-10046-4). Watts.

COLLEGE ATHLETICS

see Athletics

COLLEGE ENTRANCE REQUIREMENTS

see Colleges and Universities–Entrance Requirements

COLLEGE JOURNALISM

see College and School Journalism

COLLEGE PERIODICALS

see College and School Journalism

COLLEGE TEACHERS

see Educators; Teachers

COLLEGES AND UNIVERSITIES

see also Education, Higher; Scholarships, Fellowships, etc.; Students
also headings beginning with the word College and names of individual institutions

Deegan, Paul. Harvard University. (Illus.). 48p. (gr. 4 up). 1988. lib. bdg. 11.95 (ISBN 0-939179-50-4). Abdo & Dghtrs.
—Rice University. (Illus.). 48p. (gr. 4 up). 1988. lib. bdg. 11.95 (ISBN 0-939179-52-0). Abdo & Dghtrs.
—Stanford University. (Illus.). 48p. (gr. 4 up). 1988. lib. bdg. 11.95 (ISBN 0-939179-53-9). Abdo & Dghtrs.
—University of California of Los Angeles. (Illus.). 48p. (gr. 4 up). 1988. lib. bdg. 11.95 (ISBN 0-939179-48-2). Abdo & Dghtrs.
—University of Chicago. (Illus.). 48p. (gr. 4 up). 1988. lib. bdg. 11.95 (ISBN 0-939179-49-0). Abdo & Dghtrs.
Lundberg, Barbara J. Winning the Selective College Admissions Game: With Strategies & Tactics Explained by Eight Admissions Officers. 100p. (gr. 10-12). 1988. pap. write for info. CPA Old Lyme.

Warren, Christopher. So You're Going to College: Concerns & Strategies for the College-Bound. Gunnell, J., ed. LC 88-82123. (Illus.). 160p. (gr. 11-12). 1989. lib. bdg. 13.95 (ISBN 0-9621001-0-2). Kilroy Pr.

COLLEGES AND UNIVERSITIES–ENTRANCE REQUIREMENTS

Newman, Gerald & Newman, Ebanor W. Writing Your College Admissions Essay. (Illus.). 128p. (gr. 7-12). 1987. PLB 12.90 (ISBN 0-531-10428-1). Watts.

Paul-Matos, Janice. How to Get into College: Step by Step, Vol. 1. 24p. (Orig.). (gr. 9-12). 1985. pap. 5.00 (ISBN 0-9615165-0-X). Coll Acceptance.

Schell, Kent. How to Apply to College Step by Step. 1988. pap. 9.95 (ISBN 0-87738-027-9). Youth Ed.

COLLEGES AND UNIVERSITIES–FICTION

Barba, Harry. Faces of Love. LC 90-93457. 252p. (Orig.). (gr. 9-12). Date not set. 15.95 (ISBN 0-911906-30-4); pap. 5.95 (ISBN 0-911906-31-2). Harian Creative Bks.

Bernard, Robert, ed. All Problems Are Simple & Other Stories: Nineteen Views of the College Years. (gr. 12 up). 1988. 3.50 (ISBN 0-318-37398-X, LF). Dell.

Newton, Suzanne. Where Are You When I Need You? 1991. 13.95 (ISBN 0-670-81702-3). Viking Child Bks.

Singh, Maria E. Carry on, My Friends. LC 88-71123. 64p. (Orig.). 1989. pap. 5.00 (ISBN 0-916383-61-X). Aegina Pr.

COLOMBIA

Haynes, Tricia. Colombia. (Illus.). (gr. 5 up). 1988. 14.95 (ISBN 0-222-00948-9). Chelsea Hse.

Jacobsen, Peter & Kristensen, Preben. A Family in Colombia. LC 85-73677. (Illus.). 32p. (gr. 1-6). 1986. PLB 11.90 (ISBN 0-531-18083-2, Pub. by Bookwright). Watts.

Lerner Publications, Department of Geography Staff, ed. Colombia in Pictures. (Illus.). 64p. (gr. 5 up). 1987. PLB 12.95 (ISBN 0-8225-1810-4). Lerner Pubns.

Morrison, Marion. Colombia. LC 90-36528. (Illus.). 128p. (gr. 5-9). 1990. PLB 25.27 (ISBN 0-516-02722-0). Childrens.

Pearce, Jenny. Colombia. (Illus.). 150p. (gr. 9-12). 1989. 28.00 (ISBN 0-85345-787-5); pap. 18.00 (ISBN 0-85345-788-3). Monthly Rev.

—Colombia: The Drug War. (Illus.). 40p. (gr. 5-8). 1990. PLB 11.90 (ISBN 0-531-17237-6). Watts.

Stewart, Gail B. Colombia. LC 90-47694. (Illus.). 48p. (gr. 5-6). 1991. RSBE 10.95 (ISBN 0-89686-603-3, Crestwood Hse). Macmillan Child Grp.

COLONIAL FURNITURE

see Furniture, American

COLONIAL HISTORY (U. S.)

see U. S.–History–Colonial Period

COLONIAL LIFE AND CUSTOMS (U. S.)

see U. S.–History–Colonial Period; U. S.–Social Life and Customs–Colonial Period

COLOR

Adoff, Arnold. Greens. Lewin, Betsy, illus. LC 85-16631. (gr. 1-5). 1988. 12.95 (ISBN 0-688-04276-7); lib. bdg. 12.88 (ISBN 0-688-04277-5). Lothrop.

Allington, Richard L. Colors. Spangler, Noel, illus. LC 79-19116. 32p. (gr. k-3). 1985. PLB 15.33 (ISBN 0-8172-1280-9); pap. 9.27 (ISBN 0-8172-2477-7). Raintree Pubs.

Anderson, L. W. Light & Color. rev. ed. LC 87-23225. (Illus.). 48p. (gr. 2-6). 1987. PLB 17.32 (ISBN 0-8172-3257-5); pap. 9.27 (ISBN 0-8172-3282-6). Raintree Pubs.

Ardley, Neil. The Science Book of Color. Van Doren, Liz, ed. (Illus.). 28p. (gr. 2-5). 1991. 9.95 (Gulliver Bks). HarBraceJ.

—Science Book of Color. (gr. 4-7). 1991. 9.95 (ISBN 0-15-200576-5). HarBraceJ.

Bradman, Tony. The Bad Babies' Book of Colors. Schulman, Janet, ed. Van der Beek, Debbie, illus. Greenstein, Mina, designed by. LC 86-27860. (Illus.). 32p. (ps-2). 1987. 5.95 (ISBN 0-394-89046-9). Knopf.

Braithwaite, Althea & Gretz, Susanna. Colors of Things. (Illus.). 24p. (ps-2). 1990. 1.95 (ISBN 1-878624-28-8, 1553800028). McClanahan Bk.

Branley, Franklyn M. Color: From Rainbows to Lasers. Roth, Henry, illus. LC 76-46304. 96p. (gr. 6 up). 1978. PLB 13.89 (ISBN 0-690-03847-X, Crowell Jr Bks). HarpC Child Bks.

Brenner, Barbara A. The Color Wizard: Level 1. Dillon, Leo & Dillon, Diane, illus. (ps-3). 1989. 9.99 (ISBN 0-553-05825-8). Bantam.

Brown, Charlene & Davis, Carolyn. Color Fun. Davis, Carolyn, illus. 64p. (Orig.). (gr. k up). 1990. pap. text ed. 5.95 (ISBN 0-929261-27-5, BA02). W Foster Pub.

Brown, Margery W. Afro-Bets: Book of Colors. Blair, Culverson, illus. 24p. (Orig.). (ps-1). 1991. pap. 3.95 (ISBN 0-940975-29-7). Just Us Bks.

Bryant-Mole, K. Colour. (Illus.). 24p. (ps up). 1991. pap. 3.50 (ISBN 0-7460-0594-6, Usborne). EDC.

Carle, Eric. My Very First Book of Colors. reissued ed. Carle, Eric, illus. LC 72-83776. 10p. (ps-1). 1991. bds. 4.95 (ISBN 0-694-00011-6, Crowell Jr Bks). HarpC Child Bks.

Carroll, Jeri. The Complete Color Book. (Illus.). 112p. (ps-3). 1991. 9.95 (ISBN 0-86653-585-3). Good Apple.

Chermayeff, Ivan. Tomato & Other Colors. (ps-3). 1981. 13.55 (ISBN 0-13-924753-X). P-H.

Church, Vivian. Colors Around Me. LC 75-154209. (Illus.). 28p. (gr. k-3). 1971. 4.95 (ISBN 0-910030-15-4). Afro Am.

Color Scheme, Unit 6. (gr. 2). 1991. 5-pack 21.25 (ISBN 0-88106-752-0). Charlesbridge Pub.

Colors. (Illus.). 7p. (ps-1). 1973. 2.50 (ISBN 0-448-09735-4, G&D). Putnam Pub Group.

Colors & Sizes: Recognizing Colors & Comparing Sizes. (ps-3). pap. write for info. incl. cassette (ISBN 0-307-13790-2, Golden Bks). Western Pub.

Courson, Diana. Let's Learn about Colors, Shapes, & Sizes. Skiles, Janet, illus. 64p. (ps-2). 1986. wkbk. 6.95 (ISBN 0-86653-348-6, GA 793). Good Apple.

Davis, Nancy M., et al. Colors. Davis, Nancy M., illus. (Orig.). (ps-2). 1986. pap. 4.95 (ISBN 0-937103-13-6). DaNa Pubns.

DeBruin, Jerry. Light & Color. Swemba, Jeane, illus. 32p. (gr. 4 up). 1986. wkbk. 4.95 (ISBN 0-86653-358-3, GA 690). Good Apple.

De Brunhoff, Laurent. Babar's Book of Color. De Brunhoff, Laurent, illus. LC 84-42737. 36p. (ps-2). 1984. 9.95 (ISBN 0-394-86896-X, Random Juv); lib. bdg. 10.99 (ISBN 0-394-96896-4). Random.

Disney Babies Name the Colors. LC 85-81572. 12p. (ps). 1988. pap. write for info. (ISBN 0-307-06045-4, Pub. by Golden Bks). Western Pub.

Disney, Walt, Productions Staff. Goofy's Book of Colors. LC 82-18630. (Illus.). 32p. (ps-1). 1983. 4.95 (ISBN 0-394-85734-8); lib. bdg. 4.99 (ISBN 0-394-95734-2). Random.

Ehlert, Lois. Color Zoo. Ehlert, Lois, illus. LC 87-17065. 32p. (ps-1). 1989. 11.95 (ISBN 0-397-32259-3, Lipp Jr Bks); PLB 11.89 (ISBN 0-397-32260-7). HarpC Child Bks.

Emberley, Ed E. Green Says Go. LC 68-21165. (Illus.). (ps-3). 1972. lib. bdg. 14.95 (ISBN 0-316-23599-7). Little.

F. J. Strauss Co., Inc. Staff. Color. F. J. Strauss Co., Inc. Staff, illus. 10p. (ps). Date not set. write for info. vinyl (ISBN 0-945987-10-2). F J Strauss.

Frank, Marjorie. I Can Make a Rainbow. LC 76-506. (Illus.). 300p. (gr. k-6). 1976. pap. 16.95 (ISBN 0-913916-19-6, IP 19-6). Incentive Pubns.

Gill, Bob. What Color Is Your World. Gill, Bob, illus. (gr. k-3). 1963. 10.95 (ISBN 0-8392-3042-7). Astor-Honor.

Gregory, Elizabeth. Blinky & the Blends. (Illus.). 1981. 6.95 (ISBN 0-933184-11-5); pap. 4.95 (ISBN 0-933184-12-3). Flame Intl.

Hill, Julie & Hill, Julian. Looking at Light & Color. (Illus.). 48p. (gr. 5-8). 1986. 18.95 (ISBN 0-7134-5153-X, Pub. by Batsford England). Trafalgar Sq.

Hoban, Tana. Of Colors & Things. LC 88-11101. (Illus.). 24p. (ps-12). 1989. 13.95 (ISBN 0-688-07534-7); PLB 13.88 (ISBN 0-688-07535-5). Greenwillow.

—Red, Blue, Yellow Shoe. Hoban, Tana, illus. LC 86-3095. 12p. (ps). 1986. pap. 4.95 (ISBN 0-688-06563-5). Greenwillow.

Howard, Katherine. Do You Know Colors? Miller, J. P., illus. LC 78-1133. (ps-1). 1979. lib. bdg. 5.99 (ISBN 0-394-93957-3, Random Juv); pap. 2.25 (ISBN 0-394-83957-9). Random.

Imershein, Betsy. Finding Red Finding Yellow. Imershein, Betsy, photos by. LC 88-35808. (Illus.). (ps). 1989. 10.95 (ISBN 0-15-200453-X, Gulliver Bks). HarBraceJ.

Jennings, Terry. Light & Color. LC 88-36220. (Illus.). 32p. (gr. 3-6). 1989. PLB 14.60 (ISBN 0-516-08440-2); pap. 4.95 (ISBN 0-516-48440-0). Childrens.

Kahn, Peggy. The Care Bears' Book of Colors. Barto, Bobbi, illus. LC 83-62102. 14p. (ps). 1984. bds. 1.95 (ISBN 0-394-86444-1, Random Juv). Random.

Konigsburg, E. L. Samuel Todd's Book of Great Colors. Konigsburg, E. L., illus. LC 89-6640. 32p. (ps-k). 1990. 13.95 (ISBN 0-689-31593-7, Atheneum Child Bk). Macmillan Child Grp.

Kropa, Susan. Sky Blue, Grass Green. Kropa, Susan, illus. 128p. (gr. 1-3). 1986. wkbk. 9.95 (ISBN 0-86653-355-9, GA 698). Good Apple.

LeGros, Lucy C. Instant Centers - Colors. (Illus.). 40p. (Orig.). (gr. k-2). 1984. pap. 5.95 (ISBN 0-937306-03-7). Creat Res NC.

Lionni, Leo. Little Blue & Little Yellow. (Illus.). (gr. k-1). 1959. 10.95 (ISBN 0-8392-3018-4). Astor-Honor.

McKinnon, Elizabeth S., ed. One-Two-Three Colors: Activities for Introducing Color to Young Children. Warren, Jean, compiled by. Ekberg, Marion H., illus. LC 87-51241. 160p. (Orig.). 1988. pap. 12.95 (ISBN 0-911019-17-0). Warren Pub Hse.

McMillan, Bruce. Growing Colors. McMillan, Bruce, photos by. LC 88-2767. (Illus.). 40p. (ps-2). 1988. 13.95 (ISBN 0-688-07844-3); PLB 13.88 (ISBN 0-688-07845-1). Lothrop.

McMillan, Dana. Color & Concepts. 64p. (gr. k-2). 1985. 6.95 (ISBN 0-912107-35-9). Monday Morning Bks.

Meisenheimer, Sharon. Color Days. (gr. k-3). 1988. pap. 7.95 (ISBN 0-8224-1641-7). Fearon Teach Aids.

Miller, J. P. Learn about Colors with Little Rabbit. Miller, J. P., illus. LC 84-6943. (ps-1). 1984. 3.95 (ISBN 0-394-86671-1, Pub. by BYR); lib. bdg. 4.99 (ISBN 0-394-96671-6). Random.

Moss, David. Colors. 1989. 4.99 (ISBN 0-517-69421-2). Outlet Bk Co.

Oana, Katherine. Learning Words of Color. Baird, Tate, ed. Wallace, Dorathye B., illus. LC 86-50866. 32p. (Orig.). (ps-1). 1986. pap. 2.65 (ISBN 0-914127-79-9). Univ Class.

Oliver, Stephen, photos by. My First Look at Colors. LC 89-63091. (Illus.). 24p. (ps-k). 1990. 6.95 (ISBN 0-679-80535-4). McKay.

Ortiz, Simon. Blue & Red. Aragon, Hilda, illus. 14p. (Orig.). (ps-7). 1981. pap. 3.75 (ISBN 0-915347-08-3). Pueblo Acoma Pr.

Petty, Kate. What's That Color? Kopper, Lisa, illus. 24p. (gr. 1-3). 1986. PLB 7.79 (ISBN 0-531-10257-2). Watts.

Picnic Colors. 1990. text ed. 3.95 cased (ISBN 0-7214-5270-1). Ladybird Bks.

Pienkowski, Jan. Colors. Pienkowski, Jan, illus. (ps). 1989. 2.95 (ISBN 0-671-68134-6). S&S Trade.

Reiss, John J. Colors. Reiss, John J., illus. LC 69-13653. 32p. (ps-2). 1982. 13.95 (ISBN 0-02-776130-4, Bradbury Pr). Macmillan Child Grp.

Ross, Shirley & McCord, Cindy. Color Critters. 64p. (ps-2). 1987. 6.95 (ISBN 0-912107-63-4). Monday Morning Bks.

Scarry, Richard. Richard Scarry's Color Book. Scarry, Richard, illus. LC 75-36465. 14p. (ps-1). 1976. 3.95 (ISBN 0-394-83237-X, Random Juv). Random.

Schwartz, Jeanne. A Handful of Colors. Mansfield, Carol, illus. 32p. 1981. 4.25 (ISBN 0-9604538-2-2). CBH Pub.

Shapes & Colors. (Illus.). (ps-2). 1.95 (ISBN 0-7214-5184-5). Ladybird Bks.

Simon, Hilda. The Magic of Color. Simon, Hilda, illus. LC 81-5044. 56p. (gr. 3 up). 1981. 12.95 (ISBN 0-688-00619-1). Lothrop.

Steig, William. Yellow & Pink. Steig, William, illus. LC 84-80503. 32p. (ps up). 1984. 9.95 (ISBN 0-374-38670-6). FS&G.

Taylor, Barbara. Color & Light. (ps-3). 1990. PLB 11.40 (ISBN 0-531-14015-6). Watts.

—Color & Light. (Illus.). 40p. (gr. k-4). 1991. PLB 11.90 (ISBN 0-531-19127-3, Warwick). Watts.

Thomson, Ruth. All about Colors. Ward, Deborah, illus. LC 87-42588. 32p. (gr. 1-2). 1987. PLB 10.95 (ISBN 1-55532-312-X). Gareth Stevens Inc.

Turner, Gwenda. Colors. (Illus.). 24p. (ps-1). 1990. pap. 9.95 (ISBN 0-670-82552-2). Viking Child Bks.

Washtime Colors. (ps up). 1990. PLB 3.98 (ISBN 0-7924-5362-X, Mallard Pr). BDD Promo Bk.

Watson, Carol, et al. Colors. (Illus.). 24p. (ps-2). 1983. 2.95 (ISBN 0-86020-849-4). EDC.

Wilkes. Colors Book. (gr. k-2). 1979. (Usborne-Hayes); PLB 11.96 (ISBN 0-88110-067-6); pap. 2.95 (ISBN 0-86020-362-X). EDC.

Yenawine, Philip. Colors. (Illus.). (gr. 2-5). 1991. 14.00 (ISBN 0-385-30254-1); PLB 14.99 (ISBN 0-385-30314-9). Delacorte.

COLOR–FICTION

Barrett, John E., photos by. Big Bird Is Yellow: A Sesame Street Book of Colors. LC 89-63996. (Illus.). 14p. (ps). 1990. bds. 3.95 (ISBN 0-679-80752-7). Random.

Boynton, Sandra. Blue Hat Green Hat. 1984. 3.95 (ISBN 0-671-49320-5). S&S Trade.

Charles, Donald. Calico Cat Looks at Colors. Charles, Donald, illus. LC 75-12948. 32p. (ps-3). 1975. PLB 14.60 (ISBN 0-516-03437-5). Childrens.

Childs, Phyllis. Color Me. 35p. (ps-k). 1985. wkbk. 2.95 (ISBN 0-931749-03-4). PJC Lrng Mtrls.

Ehlert, Lois. Color Farm. Ehlert, Lois, illus. LC 89-13561. 40p. (ps-k). 1990. 12.95 (ISBN 0-397-32440-5, Lipp Jr Bks); PLB 12.89 (ISBN 0-397-32441-3, Lipp Jr Bks). HarpC Child Bks.

Freeman, Don. The Chalk Box Story. Freeman, Don, illus. LC 76-10169. 40p. (gr. 1-3). 1976. 13.95 (ISBN 0-397-31699-2). HarpC Child Bks.

Greeley, Valerie. White Is the Moon. Greeley, Valerie, illus. LC 90-40522. 24p. (ps-1). 1991. 12.95 (ISBN 0-02-736915-3, Mcmillan Child Bk). Macmillan Child Grp.

Gundersheimer, Karen. Colors to Know. Gundersheimer, Karen, illus. LC 85-45390. 32p. (ps-1). 1986. 3.95 (ISBN 0-694-00066-3). HarpC Child Bks.

Hoban, Tana. Is It Red? Is It Yellow? Is It Blue? LC 78-2549. (Illus.). 32p. (gr. k-3). 1978. 14.95 (ISBN 0-688-80171-4); PLB 14.88 (ISBN 0-688-84171-6). Greenwillow.

Kim, Joy. Rainbows & Frogs: A Story about Colors. Harvey, Paul, illus. LC 81-4685. 32p. (gr. k-2). 1981. PLB 10.89 (ISBN 0-89375-505-2); pap. text ed. 2.95 (ISBN 0-89375-506-0). Troll Assocs.

Moncure, Jane B. Magic Monsters Look for Colors. Magnuson, Diana, illus. LC 78-23792. (ps-3). 1979. PLB 11.97 (ISBN 0-89565-056-8). Childs World.

Poulet, Virginia. Blue Bug's Book of Colors. Anderson, Peggy P., illus. LC 80-23229. 32p. (ps-3). 1981. PLB 14.60 (ISBN 0-516-03442-1); pap. 3.95 (ISBN 0-516-43442-X). Childrens.

Reiss, John J. Colors. Reiss, John J., illus. LC 69-13653. 32p. (ps-2). 1982. 13.95 (ISBN 0-02-776130-4, Bradbury Pr). Macmillan Child Grp.

Rogers, Alan. Yellow Hippo. Rogers, Alan, illus. LC 90-9834. 16p. (ps-1). 1991. PLB 9.95 (ISBN 0-8368-0405-8). Gareth Stevens Inc.

Sawicki, Norma J. The Little Red House. Goffe, Toni, illus. LC 88-2740. 24p. (ps). 1989. 9.95 (ISBN 0-688-07891-5); PLB 9.88 (ISBN 0-688-07892-3). Lothrop.

Schultz, Betty K. Purple Patches. Sperry, Angela, illus. 32p. (gr. k-3). Date not set. write for info. (ISBN 0-929568-01-X). Raspberry IL.

Sis, Peter. Going Up! A Color Counting Book. LC 87-37203. (Illus.). 24p. (ps up). 1989. 12.95 (ISBN 0-688-08125-8); PLB 12.88 (ISBN 0-685-22783-9). Greenwillow.

Tallarico, Tony. Colors. Tallarico, Tony, illus. 12p. (gr. 3-8). 1982. pap. 2.95 (ISBN 0-89828-304-3). Tuffy Bks.

Testa, Fulvio. If You Take a Paintbrush: A Book of Colors. Testa, Fulvio, illus. LC 82-45512. 32p. (ps-2). 1986. pap. 3.95 (ISBN 0-8037-0282-5). Dial Bks Young.

Williams, Sue. I Went Walking. Vivas, Julie, illus. (ps-3). 1990. 13.95 (ISBN 0-15-200471-8, Gulliver Bks). HarbraceJ.

Young, James. A Million Chameleons. LC 90-52567. (ps-3). 1990. 11.95 (ISBN 0-316-97129-4). Little.

COLOR–POETRY

O'Neill, Mary. Hailstones & Halibut Bones. Weisgard, Leonard, illus. LC 60-7138. 59p. (gr. k-12). 1973. (Zephyr-BFYR); pap. 4.95 (ISBN 0-385-05374-6, Zephyr-BFYR). Doubleday.

—Hailstones & Halibut Bones: Adventures in Color. Wallner, John, illus. 1989. 12.95 (ISBN 0-385-24484-3); PLB 13.99 (ISBN 0-385-24485-1). Doubleday.

COLOR OF ANIMALS

Kipling, Rudyard. How the Leopard Got His Spots. Loestoeter, Lori, illus. LC 89-31374. (ps up). 1989. 14.95 (ISBN 0-88708-111-8, Rabbit Ears); book & cassette package 19.95 (ISBN 0-88708-112-6). Picture Bk Studio.

McDonnell, Janet. Animal Camouflage. LC 88-36642. (Illus.). 48p. (gr. 2-6). 1989. PLB 10.95 (ISBN 0-89565-512-8); pap. 6.96 (ISBN 0-89565-530-6). Childs World.

—Animal Camouflage: Hide & Seek Animals. Magnuson, Diana, illus. LC 89-28083. 32p. (ps-2). 1990. lib. bdg. 11.97 (ISBN 0-89565-562-4). Childs World.

Powzyk, Joyce. Animal Camouflage: A Closer Look. Powzyk, Joyce, illus. LC 89-9848. (gr. 2-9). 1990. 15.95 (ISBN 0-02-774980-0, Bradbury Pr). Macmillan Child Grp.

Selsam, Millicent E. Hidden Animals. LC 72-85020. (Illus.). 64p. (gr. k-3). 1969. PLB 9.89 (ISBN 0-06-025282-0). HarpC Child Bks.

Wright, Rachel. Color & Camouflage. (ps-3). 1990. PLB 10.40 (ISBN 0-531-14000-8). Watts.

COLOR OF MAN

Walton, Darwin. What Color Are You? Franklin, Hal A., photos by. (Illus.). 64p. (gr. 5 up). 1973. 10.95 (ISBN 0-87485-045-2). Johnson Chi.

COLOR SENSE

Colors. (Illus.). (ps-2). 3.50 (ISBN 0-7214-0523-1). Ladybird Bks.

Colors. (Illus.). (ps). 1992. cased 3.50 (ISBN 0-7214-5208-6). Ladybird Bks.

Colors & Shapes. (Illus.). (ps). pap. 1.25 (ISBN 0-7214-9555-9). Ladybird Bks.

Les Couleurs. (FRE., Illus.). 3.50 (ISBN 0-7214-0801-X). Ladybird Bks.

Oxford Scientific Films Editors. Danger Colors. Oxford Scientific Films Staff, illus. 32p. (ps up). 1986. 11.95 (ISBN 0-399-21341-4, Putnam). Putnam Pub Group.

Pauli, Emily. Mokey Fraggles New Colors. 1988. write for info. (ISBN 0-02-689114-X). Checkerboard Pr.

Taulbee, Annette. Colors. (Illus.). 24p. (ps-k). 1986. 3.98 (ISBN 0-86734-060-6, FS-3052). Schaffer Pubns.

—Shapes & Colors. (Illus.). 24p. (ps-k). 1986. 3.98 (ISBN 0-86734-068-1, FS-3061). Schaffer Pubns.

COLOR SENSE–FICTION

Big Bird's Color Game. 14p. (ps). 1980. write for info. (ISBN 0-307-12254-9, Golden Bks). Western Pub.

COLORADO

Aylesworth, Thomas G. & Aylesworth, Virginia L. The Southwest (Texas, New Mexico, Colorado) (Illus.). 64p. (gr. 3 up). 1992. PLB 16.95 (ISBN 0-7910-1048-1). Chelsea Hse.

Barker, Jane V. Trappers & Traders. Downing, Sybil, ed. (Illus.). 36p. (gr. k-6). pap. 3.95 (ISBN 1-878611-03-8). Silver Rim Pr.

Barker, Jane V. & Downing, Sybil. Mountain Treasures. (Illus.). 44p. (gr. k-6). pap. 3.95 (ISBN 1-878611-01-1). Silver Rim Pr.

Carole Marsh Colorado Books, 31 bks. Set. 638.45 (ISBN 0-7933-1280-9). Gallopade Pub Group.

Carpenter, Allan. Colorado. LC 77-13921. (Illus.). 96p. (gr. 4 up). 1978. PLB 19.93 (ISBN 0-516-04106-1). Childrens.

Eccles, Anne. Colorado Activity & Coloring Book. Eccles, Anne, illus. 32p. (ps-8). 1986. pap. 2.95 (ISBN 0-9618555-0-9). Anne M Eccles.

Fischer, Lee, ed. Colorado Is for Kids! An Activity Book for Kids! Parker, Steve, illus. 32p. (gr. 1-6). 1990. pap. 2.95 (ISBN 0-929526-05-8). Double B Pubns.

Fradin, Dennis. Colorado: In Words & Pictures. Wahl, Richard, illus. LC 80-15778. 48p. (gr. k-4). 1980. PLB 15.93 (ISBN 0-516-03906-7); pap. 4.95 (ISBN 0-516-43906-5). Childrens.

Garrity, Leslie & Schecter, Teri. Colorado Geography. (Orig.). (gr. 4-5). 1988. pap. text ed. 8.95 s.p. (ISBN 0-87108-278-0); tchr's. guide s.p. 9.95 (ISBN 0-87108-281-0). Pruett.

Laing, David & Lampiris, Nicholas. Aspen High Country: The Geology, a Pictorial Guide to Roads & Trails. Laing, Jennifer, illus. 144p. (Orig.). (gr. 9-12). 1980. pap. write for info. (ISBN 0-9604274-0-6). Thunder River.

Marsh, Carole. Avast, Ye Slobs! Colorado Pirate Trivia. (Illus.). (gr. 3-12). 1990. PLB 19.95 (ISBN 0-7933-0208-0); pap. 14.95 (ISBN 0-7933-0207-2); computer disk 29.95 (ISBN 0-7933-0209-9). Gallopade Pub Group.

—The Beast of the Colorado Bed & Breakfast. (Illus.). (gr. 3-12). 1990. PLB 19.95 (ISBN 0-7933-1413-5); pap. 14.95 (ISBN 0-7933-1414-3); computer disk 29.95 (ISBN 0-7933-1415-1). Gallopade Pub Group.

—Colorado & Other State Greats (Biographies) (Illus.). (gr. 3-12). 1990. PLB 19.95 (ISBN 1-55609-534-1); pap. 14.95 (ISBN 1-55609-533-3); computer disk 29.95 (ISBN 0-7933-1421-6). Gallopade Pub Group.

—Colorado Bandits, Bushwackers, Outlaws, Crooks, Devils, Ghosts, Desperadoes & Other Assorted & Sundry Characters! (Illus.). (gr. 3-12). 1990. PLB 19.95 (ISBN 0-7933-0190-4); pap. 14.95 (ISBN 0-7933-0189-0); computer disk 29.95 (ISBN 0-7933-0191-2). Gallopade Pub Group.

—Colorado Classic Christmas Trivia: Stories, Recipes, Activities, Legends, Lore & More! (Illus.). (gr. 3-12). 1990. PLB 19.95 (ISBN 0-7933-0193-9); pap. 14.95 (ISBN 0-7933-0192-0); computer disk 29.95 (ISBN 0-7933-0194-7). Gallopade Pub Group.

—Colorado Coastales. (Illus.). (gr. 3-12). 1990. PLB 19.95 (ISBN 1-55609-530-9); pap. 14.95 (ISBN 1-55609-529-5); computer disk 29.95 (ISBN 0-7933-1417-8). Gallopade Pub Group.

—The Colorado Hot Air Balloon Mystery. (Illus.). (gr. 2-9). 1990. 19.95 (ISBN 0-7933-2363-0); pap. 14.95 (ISBN 0-7933-2364-9); computer disk 29.95 (ISBN 0-7933-2365-7). Gallopade Pub Group.

—Colorado "Jography" A Fun Run Thru Our State! (Illus.). (gr. 3-12). 1990. PLB 19.95 (ISBN 1-55609-525-2); pap. 14.95 (ISBN 1-55609-524-4); computer disk 29.95 (ISBN 0-7933-1407-0). Gallopade Pub Group.

—Colorado Kid's Cookbook: Recipes, How-to, History, Lore & More! (Illus.). (gr. 3-12). 1990. PLB 19.95 (ISBN 0-7933-0202-1); pap. 14.95 (ISBN 0-7933-0201-3); computer disk 29.95 (ISBN 0-7933-0203-X). Gallopade Pub Group.

—Colorado Quiz Bowl Crash Course! (Illus.). (gr. 3-12). 1990. PLB 19.95; pap. 14.95 (ISBN 1-55609-531-7); computer disk 29.95 (ISBN 0-7933-1416-X). Gallopade Pub Group.

—Colorado School Trivia: An Amazing & Fascinating Look at Our State's Teachers, Schools & Students! (Illus.). (gr. 3-12). 1990. PLB 19.95 (ISBN 0-7933-0199-8); pap. 14.95 (ISBN 0-7933-0198-X); computer disk 29.95 (ISBN 0-7933-0200-5). Gallopade Pub Group.

—Colorado Silly Basketball Sportsmysteries, Vol. I. (Illus.). (gr. 3-12). 1990. PLB 19.95 (ISBN 0-7933-0196-3); pap. 14.95 (ISBN 0-7933-0195-5); computer disk 29.95 (ISBN 0-7933-0197-1). Gallopade Pub Group.

—Colorado Silly Basketball Sportsmysteries, Vol. II. (Illus.). (gr. 3-12). 1990. PLB 19.95 (ISBN 0-7933-1577-8); pap. 14.95 (ISBN 0-7933-1578-6); computer disk 29.95 (ISBN 0-7933-1579-4). Gallopade Pub Group.

—Colorado Silly Football Sportsmysteries, Vol. I. (Illus.). (gr. 3-12). 1990. PLB 19.95 (ISBN 1-55609-528-7); pap. 14.95 (ISBN 1-55609-527-9); computer disk 29.95 (ISBN 0-7933-1409-7). Gallopade Pub Group.

—Colorado Silly Football Sportsmysteries, Vol. II. (Illus.). (gr. 3-12). 1990. PLB 19.95 (ISBN 0-7933-1410-0); pap. 14.95 (ISBN 0-7933-1411-9); computer disk 29.95 (ISBN 0-7933-1412-7). Gallopade Pub Group.

—Colorado Silly Trivia! (Illus.). (gr. 3-12). 1990. PLB 19.95 (ISBN 1-55609-523-6); pap. 14.95 (ISBN 1-55609-522-8); computer disk 29.95 (ISBN 0-7933-1406-2). Gallopade Pub Group.

—Colorado's (Most Devastating!) Disasters & (Most Calamitous!) Catastrophies! (Illus.). (gr. 3-12). 1990. PLB 19.95 (ISBN 0-7933-0187-4); pap. 14.95 (ISBN 0-7933-0186-6); computer disk 29.95 (ISBN 0-7933-0188-2). Gallopade Pub Group.

—The Hard-to-Believe-But-True! Book of Colorado History, Mystery, Trivia, Legend, Lore, Humor & More. (Illus.). (gr. 3-12). 1990. PLB 19.95 (ISBN 0-7933-0205-6); pap. 14.95 (ISBN 0-7933-0204-8); computer disk 29.95 (ISBN 0-7933-0206-4). Gallopade Pub Group.

—If My Colorado Mama Ran the World! (Illus.). (gr. 3-12). 1990. PLB 19.95 (ISBN 0-7933-1418-6); pap. 14.95 (ISBN 0-7933-1419-4); computer disk 29.95 (ISBN 0-7933-1420-8). Gallopade Pub Group.

—Let's Quilt Colorado & Stuff It Topographically! (Illus.). (gr. 3-12). 1990. PLB 19.95 (ISBN 1-55609-526-0); pap. 14.95 (ISBN 1-55609-126-5); computer disk 29.95 (ISBN 0-7933-1408-9). Gallopade Pub Group.

Moorhead, Carol A. Backyard Wildlife of Colorado. Moorhead, Carol A., illus. 96p. (Orig.). (gr. 6-8). 1991. pap. 8.95 (ISBN 1-879373-08-4). R Rinehart Inc.

Rankin, William. Come Hibernate with Me. Camphouse, Marylyn J., frwd. by. (Illus.). 214p. (Orig.). (gr. 9 up). 1989. 30.00 (ISBN 0-9623948-0-7). M Camphouse.

Thomas, Carolyn S. Kenta Comes to Colorado: A Bilingual Educational Activity Book. Holdorf, Kurt, illus. Romer, Roy, intro. by. (ENG & JPN., Illus.). 64p. (gr. k-4). 1990. pap. 6.95 (ISBN 0-913730-41-6). Robinson Pr.

Thompson, Kathleen. Colorado. LC 87-16374. 48p. (gr. 3 up). 1987. 17.32 (ISBN 0-86514-463-X); cancelled (ISBN 0-86514-603-9); cancelled Beta video (ISBN 0-86514-089-8); cancelled VHS video (ISBN 0-86514-164-9); cancelled 3/4" video (ISBN 0-86514-239-4). Raintree Pubs.

Thumhart, Suzanne. Colorado Wonders. Ayer, Eleanor H., ed. Kline, Jane, illus. 48p. (gr. 4-7). 1986. pap. 6.95x (ISBN 0-939650-16-9). R H Pub.

COLORADO–FICTION

Shirley, Gayle. C Is for Colorado. Bergum, Connie, illus. LC 89-83793. 40p. (Orig.). (gr. k-3). 12.95 (ISBN 0-937959-85-5); pap. 6.95 (ISBN 0-937959-81-2). Falcon Pr MT.

Weber, Lenora M. How Long Is Always? LC 75-1937. 226p. (gr. 7 up). 1970. 14.95 (ISBN 0-690-40680-0, Crowell Jr Bks). HarpC Child Bks.

COLORADO–HISTORY

Ayer, Eleanor H. Hispanic Colorado. Kline, Jane, illus. 48p. (gr. 4-7). 1982. 11.95x (ISBN 0-939650-11-8); pap. 6.95x (ISBN 0-939650-10-X). R H Pub.

—Indians of Colorado. Kline, Jane, illus. 48p. (gr. 4-7). 1981. 11.95x (ISBN 0-939650-08-8); pap. 6.95x (ISBN 0-939650-09-6). R H Pub.

Friggens, Myriam. Tales, Trails & Tommyknockers: Stories from Colorado's Past. Coulter, Gene, illus. LC 79-84876. 144p. (gr. 6 up). 1979. pap. 7.95 (ISBN 0-933472-01-3). Johnson Bks.

Kent, Deborah. Colorado. LC 88-11745. (Illus.). 144p. (gr. 4 up). 1988. PLB 25.27 (ISBN 0-516-00452-2). Childrens.

Skolout, Patricia F. Colorado Springs History A to Z: For Children. Rasmusseu-Frerichs, Cyndy, illus. 37p. (gr. k-6). 1990. Repr. of 1989 ed. activity bk. 3.95 (ISBN 0-9625712-0-2). P F Skolout.

Swindler, William F. & Frech, Mary, eds. Chronology & Documentary Handbook of the State of Colorado, No. 6. LC 73-532. 105p. (gr. 9-12). 1973. PLB 8.50 (ISBN 0-379-16131-1). Oceana.

Thumhart, Suzanne, compiled by. Colorado Businesses. Kline, Jane, illus. 48p. (gr. 4-7). 1984. 11.95x (ISBN 0-939650-21-5). R H Pub.

COLORED PEOPLE (U. S.)

see Blacks

COLORING BOOKS

Baird, Mary & Larrivee-Cohen, Donna, eds. Painting Our Way to a Better Future: An Art-Coloring Book of Contemporary Career Options for Women. Grigsby, Diane, illus. 56p. (Orig.). (gr. 1-9). 1990. pap. 6.95 (ISBN 0-9627833-0-7). Hard Hatted Women.

Caniff, Milton. The Complete Color Terry & the Pirates, Vol. 1. Marschall, Richard, intros. by. Caniff, Milton, illus. Feiffer, Jules. (Illus.). 96p. (gr. 6 up). 1990. 34.95 (ISBN 0-924359-19-6). Remco Wrldserv Bks.

Dinosaurs. (Illus.). (ps-3). 1.95 (ISBN 0-7214-5187-X). Ladybird Bks.

Heller, Ruth. Ruth Heller's Designs for Coloring: Cats. (Illus.). 64p. 1990. pap. 3.95 (ISBN 0-448-03148-5, G&D). Putnam Pub Group.

—Ruth Heller's Designs for Coloring: Snowflakes. (Illus.). 64p. 1990. pap. 3.95 (ISBN 0-448-03145-0, G&D). Putnam Pub Group.

Herriman, George. The Komplete Kolor Krazy Kat, Vol. I: 1935-1936. Marschall, Richard, intros. by. Herriman, George, illus. Waterson, Bill. (Illus.). 96p. (gr. 6 up). 1990. 34.95 (ISBN 0-924359-06-4). Remco WrldServ Bks.

Jemima Puddle-Duck. (Illus.). (ps-2). 1.95 (ISBN 0-7214-5218-3). Ladybird Bks.

Lancaster, Derek. Picture America: States & Capitals. Lancaster, Derek, illus. Anderson, Stevens, ed. (Illus.). 136p. (gr. 5). 1991. pap. 4.95 (ISBN 1-880184-02-8). Compact Classics. PICTURE AMERICA, an illustrated educational product using mnemonic "picture associations", enables any age student to learn more about the United States. In particular, the learner is provided with familiar points of reference ("mnemonic keys") that build natural bridges between states & their capitals. Remembering which capital goes with which state will never be a problem again. Additional details regarding each state (its history, geography, popular name, official flower & bird, demographics, major agricultural & manufacturing interests, etc.) are tied together using exciting descriptions, maps & memory key illustrations. PICTURE AMERICA also contains follow-up worksheets that quiz & prompt the student, further reinforcing what has been taught. This book is both an ideal coloring book & an instructional source for young & old. Families can learn together. PICTURE AMERICA is an entertaining way to learn; a "fun book" rather than a "text book". Most importantly, PICTURE AMERICA

introduces students to a strategy for permanent recall they can make use of again & again. PICTURE AMERICA's vivid state associations won't fade after "the test" is over--they'll remain a lifetime.
Publisher Provided Annotation.

McCay, Winsor. The Complete Little Nemo in Slumberland, Vol. III: 1908-1910. Marschall, Richard, intro. by. (Illus.). 96p. (gr. 6 up). 1990. 34.95 (ISBN 0-924359-03-X). Remco Wrldserv Bks.
—The Complete Little Nemo in Slumberland, Vol. IV: 1910-1911. Marschall, Richard, intro. by. (Illus.). 96p. (gr. 6 up). 1990. 34.95 (ISBN 0-924359-04-8). Remco Wrldserv Bks.
Opposites. (Illus.). (ps-2). 1.95 (ISBN 0-7214-5185-3). Ladybird Bks.
Sterrett, Cliff. The Complete Color Polly & Her Pals, Vol. I: The Surrealist Period, 1926-1927. Marschall, Richard, intros. by. Sterrett, Cliff, illus. Spiegelman, Art. (Illus.). 96p. 1990. 34.95 (ISBN 0-924359-14-5). Remco Wrldserv Bks.
Thomas, M. Angele & Ramey, Mary L. Many Children Coloring Book. (Illus.). 24p. 1988. pap. 1.50 (ISBN 0-9619293-1-6). M A Thomas.
Tom Kitten. (Illus.). (ps-2). 1.95 (ISBN 0-7214-5219-1). Ladybird Bks.
Willhoite, Michael. Families: A Coloring Book. Willhoite, Michael, illus. 32p. (Orig.). (ps-1). 1991. pap. 2.95 saddle-stitched (ISBN 1-55583-192-3). Alyson Pubns.

COLUMBIA RIVER

Baljo, Wallace, Jr. Grand Coulee: A Story of the Columbia River from Molten Lavas & Ice to Grand Coulee Dam. rev. ed. Hemsley, Roberta G., illus. 80p. (gr. 4-6). pap. write for info. (ISBN 0-9606084-0-0). Clipboard.

COLUMBUS, CHRISTOPHER, 1451-1506

Adler, David A. A Picture Book of Christopher Columbus. Wallner, John & Wallner, Alexandra, illus. LC 90-39211. 32p. (gr. k-3). 1991. PLB 14.95 (ISBN 0-8234-0857-4). Holiday.
Asimov, Isaac. Christopher Columbus. LC 90-25836. (Illus.). 64p. (gr. 3-4). 1991. PLB 14.95 (ISBN 0-8368-0556-9). Gareth Stevens Inc.
Bains, Rae. Christopher Columbus. Smolinski, Dick, illus. LC 84-2585. 32p. (gr. 3-6). 1985. lib. bdg. 9.49 (ISBN 0-8167-0150-4); pap. text ed. 2.95 (ISBN 0-8167-0151-2). Troll Assocs.
De Kay, James T. Meet Christopher Columbus. Edens, John, illus. LC 88-19068. 72p. (gr. 2-4). 1989. PLB 6.99 (ISBN 0-394-91963-7); pap. 2.95 (ISBN 0-394-81963-2). Random.
Dodge, Steven. Christopher Columbus & the First Voyages to the New World. Goetzmann, William H., ed. Collins, Michael, intro. by. (Illus.). 112p. (gr. 5 up). 1991. PLB 18.95 (ISBN 0-7910-1299-9); pap. 9.95 (ISBN 0-7910-1522-X). Chelsea Hse.
Fradin, Dennis B. Columbus Day. LC 89-7663. (Illus.). 48p. 1990. PLB 12.95 (ISBN 0-89490-233-4). Enslow Pubs.
—The Nina, the Pinta, & the Santa Maria. (Illus.). 64p. (gr. 5-8). 1991. PLB 11.90 (ISBN 0-531-20034-5). Watts.
Fritz, Jean. Where Do You Think You're Going, Christopher Columbus? Tomes, Margot, illus. 80p. (gr. 3-7). 1981. 13.95 (ISBN 0-399-20723-6, Putnam); pap. 7.95 (ISBN 0-399-20734-1, Putnam). Putnam Pub Group.
Gleiter, Jan & Thompson, Kathleen. Christopher Columbus. Whipple, Rick, illus. 32p. (gr. 2-5). 1986. PLB 16.67 (ISBN 0-8172-2643-5); pap. text ed. 9.27 (ISBN 0-8172-2647-8). Raintree Pubs.
Goodnough, David. Christopher Columbus. new ed. LC 78-18052. (Illus.). 48p. (gr. 4-7). 1979. PLB 9.89 (ISBN 0-89375-170-7); pap. 2.95 (ISBN 0-89375-162-6). Troll Assocs.
Greene, Carol. Christopher Columbus: A Great Explorer. Dobson, Steven, illus. LC 88-37943. 48p. (gr. k-3). 1989. PLB 15.27 (ISBN 0-516-04204-1); pap. 4.95 (ISBN 0-516-44204-X). Childrens.
Haskins, Jim. Christopher Columbus: Admiral of the Ocean Sea. Lasker, Joe, illus. 64p. (gr. 2-5). 1991. pap. 2.95 (ISBN 0-590-42396-7). Scholastic Inc.
Humble, Richard. The Voyages of Columbus. Hook, Richard, illus. 32p. (gr. 5-8). 1991. PLB 11.90 (ISBN 0-531-14189-6). Watts.
Italia, Bob. Christopher Columbus. Walner, Rosemary, ed. (Illus.). 32p. (gr. 4). 1990. PLB 11.95 (ISBN 0-939179-94-6). Abdo & Dghtrs.
Johnson, Spencer. The Value of Curiosity: The Story of Christopher Columbus. Pileggi, Stephen, illus. LC 77-11032. (gr. k-6). 9.95 (ISBN 0-916392-13-9, Pub. by Value Communications). Oak Tree Pubns.
Knight, David. I Can Read About Christopher Columbus. LC 78-73774. (Illus.). (gr. 2-5). 1979. pap. 1.95 (ISBN 0-89375-206-1). Troll Assocs.
Las Casas, Bartholomew. The Log of Christopher Columbus' First Voyage to America: In the Year 1492, As Copied Out in Brief by Bartholomew Las Casas. LC 88-32567. (Illus.). 84p. (gr. 3 up). 1989. Repr. of 1938 ed. lib. bdg. 17.00 (ISBN 0-208-02247-3, Pub. by Linnet). Shoe String.
Levinson, Nancy S. Christopher Columbus: Voyager to the Unknown. (Illus.). (gr. 4-7). 1990. 16.95 (ISBN 0-525-67292-3, Lodestar Bks). Dutton Child Bks.
Lillegard, Dee. My First Columbus Day Book. Raskin, Betty, illus. LC 87-10304. 32p. (ps-2). 1987. PLB 14.60 (ISBN 0-516-02909-6); pap. 3.95 (ISBN 0-516-42909-4). Childrens.
Meltzer, Milton. Columbus & the World Around Him. 1990. 13.95 (ISBN 0-531-15148-4). Watts.
—Columbus & the World Around Him. (gr. 4-7). 1990. PLB 14.90 (ISBN 0-531-10899-6). Watts.
Morgan, Lee & Solarino, Claudio. Christopher Columbus. (Illus.). 104p. (gr. 5-8). 1990. 16.98 (ISBN 0-382-09974-5); pap. 8.95 (ISBN 0-382-24001-4). Silver Burdett Pr.
Morison, Samuel E. Christopher Columbus, Mariner. (Illus.). 192p. (gr. 9-12). 1983. pap. 8.95 (ISBN 0-452-00992-8, Mer). NAL-Dutton.
Osborne, Mary P. Christopher Columbus: Admiral of the Sea. (Orig.). (gr. k-6). 1987. pap. 2.95 (ISBN 0-440-41275-7, YB). Dell.
Parker, Margot. What Is Columbus Day? Bates, Matt, illus. LC 85-12748. 46p. (gr. k-2). 1985. PLB 14.60 (ISBN 0-516-03781-1). Childrens.
Rhodes, Bennie. Christopher Columbus. Smith, A. G. & Smith, A. G., illus. LC 76-5788. (gr. 3-6). 1977. pap. 6.95 (ISBN 0-915134-26-8). Mott Media.
Richards, Dorothy F. Christopher Columbus, Who Sailed on! Nelson, John, illus. LC 78-7664. (gr. k-4). 1978. PLB 10.95 (ISBN 0-89565-032-0). Childs World.
Roop, Peter & Roop, Connie, eds. I, Columbus: My Journal - 1492. Hanson, Peter, illus. 57p. (gr. 4-7). 1990. 13.95 (ISBN 0-8027-6977-2); lib. bdg. 14.85 (ISBN 0-8027-6978-0). Walker & Co.
The Ships of Columbus. 48p. (gr. 4-5). 1989. PLB 10.95 (ISBN 0-685-26412-2). Capstone Pr.
Soule, Gardner. Christopher Columbus: Green Sea of Darkness. large type ed. (Illus.). 112p. (gr. 4-8). 1991. Repr. of 1988 ed. PLB 17.95 (ISBN 1-55905-076-4). Grey Castle.
Stone, Elaine M. Christopher Columbus. (Illus.). (gr. 3-7). 1991. 12.95 (ISBN 0-8423-0468-1). Tyndale.
Stott, Ken, illus. Columbus & the Age of Exploration. LC 84-73568. 64p. (gr. 7-9). 1985. 12.40 (ISBN 0-531-18012-3, Pub. by Bookwright Pr). Watts.
Weisman, JoAnne B. & Deitch, Kenneth M. Christopher Columbus & the Great Voyage of Discovery: With a Message from President George Bush. Eldridge, Marion, illus. Bush, George, contrib. by. LC 90-81362. 40p. (gr. k-6). 1990. PLB 17.95 (ISBN 1-878668-00-5); pap. 7.95g (ISBN 1-878668-01-3). Disc Enter Ltd.
Young, Robert. Christopher Columbus. Brook, Bonnie, ed. Stewart, Arvis, illus. 32p. (gr. k-2). 1990. 5.95 (ISBN 0-671-69110-4); PLB 10.98 (ISBN 0-671-69104-X). Silver Pr.
Zadra, Dan. Explorers of America: Columbus. rev. ed. (gr. 2-4). 1988. PLB 11.50s.p. (ISBN 0-88682-184-3); 16.45 (ISBN 0-318-32946-8). Creative Ed.

COLUMBUS, CHRISTOPHER, 1451-1506–FICTION

Durio, Alice & Rice, James. Cajun Columbus. LC 75-20484. (Illus.). 32p. (gr. 2 up). 1975. 11.95 (ISBN 0-88289-074-3). Pelican.
Litowinsky, Olga. High Voyage: The Final Crossing of Christopher Columbus. (gr. 9-12). 1991. 14.95 (ISBN 0-385-30304-1). Delacorte.
Schlein, Miriam. I Sailed with Columbus. Newsom, Tom, illus. LC 90-24532. 192p. (gr. 3-6). 1991. 13.95 (ISBN 0-06-022513-0); PLB 13.89 (ISBN 0-06-022514-9). HarpC Child Bks.

COLUMBUS DAY

Moncure, Jane B. Our Columbus Day Book. Shackelford, Jean, illus. LC 86-6818. 32p. (ps-3). 1986. lib. bdg. 11.97 (ISBN 0-89565-347-8). Childs World.
Parker, Margot. What Is Columbus Day? Bates, Matt, illus. LC 85-12748. 46p. (gr. k-2). 1985. PLB 14.60 (ISBN 0-516-03781-1). Childrens.
Sandak, Cass. Columbus Day. LC 89-25399. (Illus.). 48p. (gr. 5 up). 1990. 10.95 (ISBN 0-89686-498-7, Crestwood Hse). Macmillan Child Grp.

COLUMNISTS

see Journalists

COMAL (COMPUTER PROGRAM LANGUAGE)

Captain Comal's Staff. Cartridge Graphics & Sound. Hejndorf, Frank, illus. 64p. (Orig.). (gr. 6 up). 1984. pap. 6.95 (ISBN 0-928411-02-8). Comal Users.
Skelton, Mindy. Graphics Primer. Schmidt, Wayne, illus. 84p. (Orig.). (gr. 6 up). 1984. pap. 14.95 (ISBN 0-928411-04-4). Comal Users.

COMEDY

Green, Carl R. & Sanford, William R. Bill Cosby. LC 86-16544. (Illus.). 32p. (gr. 4-5). PLB 9.95 (ISBN 0-89686-297-6, Crestwood Hse). Macmillan Child Grp.
Lucille Ball. 48p. (gr. 5-6). 1989. PLB 10.95 (ISBN 0-685-26348-7). Capstone Pr.

COMETS

Asimov, Isaac. Comets & Meteors. LC 89-4632. 32p. (gr. 3-4). 1989. PLB 11.95 (ISBN 1-55532-400-2). Gareth Stevens Inc.
—How Did We Find Out about Comets? Wool, David, illus. LC 74-78115. 64p. (gr. 5-8). 1975. lib. bdg. 10.85 (ISBN 0-8027-6204-2). Walker & Co.
Bendick, Jeanne. Comets & Meteors: Visitors from Space. (Illus.). 32p. (gr. k-2). 1991. PLB 11.90 (ISBN 1-56294-001-5); pap. 3.95 (ISBN 1-878841-55-6). Millbrook Pr.
Berger, Melvin. Comets, Meteors & Asteroids. (Illus.). 80p. (gr. 7 up). 1981. 9.99 (ISBN 0-399-61148-7, Putnam). Putnam Pub Group.
Branley, Franklyn M. Comets. rev. ed. Maestro, Giulio, illus. LC 83-46161. 32p. (gr. k-3). 1984. (Crowell Jr Bks); PLB 13.89 (ISBN 0-690-04415-1). HarpC Child Bks.
—Comets. Maestro, Giulio, illus. LC 83-46161. 32p. (ps-3). 1987. 7.95 (ISBN 0-694-00199-6, Trophy); (Trophy). HarpC Child Bks.
Couper, Heather. Comets & Meteors. LC 84-52570. (Illus.). 32p. (gr. 5-9). 1985. PLB 11.90 (ISBN 0-531-10000-6). Watts.
Fichter, George S. Comets & Meteors. (Illus.). 72p. (gr. 4 up). 1982. PLB 10.40 (ISBN 0-531-04382-7). Watts.
Fradin, Dennis B. Comets, Asteroids, & Meteors. LC 83-23231. (Illus.). 48p. (gr. k-4). 1984. lib. bdg. 14.60 (ISBN 0-516-01723-3); pap. 4.95 (ISBN 0-516-41723-1). Childrens.
—Halley's Comet. LC 85-17067. (Illus.). 48p. (gr. k-4). 1985. PLB 14.60 (ISBN 0-516-01275-4). Childrens.
Krupp, Edwin C. The Comet & You. Krupp, Robin R., illus. LC 84-20152. 48p. (gr. 1-4). 1985. 13.95 (ISBN 0-02-751250-9, Mcmillan Child Bk). Macmillan Child Grp.
Lyon, Charleen C. The Tale of Halley's Comet: An Educational Coloring Book. (Illus.). 32p. (Orig.). (gr. 3-6). 1985. pap. 2.95 (ISBN 0-9614973-0-0). Niota Pr.
Marsh, Carole. Crazy Comet Classroom Gamebook. (Illus., Orig.). (gr. 3-12). 1986. pap. 19.95 (ISBN 0-935326-87-1). Gallopade Pub Group.
Schatz, Dennis & Osawa, Yasu. The Return of the Comet. Osawa, Yasu, illus. 42p. (gr. 4-9). 1985. pap. 7.95 (ISBN 0-935051-00-7). Pacific Sci Ctr.
Winter, Frank H. Comet Watch: The Return of Halley's Comet. (Illus.). 64p. (gr. 4-10). 1986. PLB 9.95 (ISBN 0-8225-1579-2). Lerner Pubns.

COMIC BOOKS, STRIPS, ETC.

see also Cartoons and Caricatures

Barks, Carl. Walt Disney's Donald & Gladstone Album. (Illus.). 48p. (Orig.). (ps up). 1988. pap. 5.95 (ISBN 0-944599-12-5). Gladstone Pub.
—Walt Disney's Donald Duck Album. Blum, Geoffrey, intro. by. (Illus.). 48p. (Orig.). 1989. pap. 5.95 (ISBN 0-944599-26-5). Gladstone Pub.
—Walt Disney's Donald Duck Album. Blum, Geoffrey, intro. by. (Illus.). 48p. (Orig.). 1989. pap. 5.95 (ISBN 0-944599-23-0). Gladstone Pub.
—Walt Disney's Donald Duck Family Album. Blum, Geoffrey, intro. by. (Illus.). 48p. (Orig.). 1989. pap. 5.95 (ISBN 0-944599-22-2). Gladstone Pub.
—Walt Disney's Uncle Scrooge Album. Blum, Geoffrey, intro. by. (Illus.). 48p. (Orig.). 1989. pap. 5.95 (ISBN 0-944599-24-9). Gladstone Pub.
—Walt Disney's Uncle Scrooge & Donald Duck Giant Album. Blum, Geoffrey, intro. by. (Illus.). 72p. (Orig.). 1989. pap. 8.95 (ISBN 0-944599-27-3). Gladstone Pub.
—Walt Disney's Uncle Scrooge Comic Album. Barks, Carl, illus. Blum, Geoff, intro. by. (Illus.). 48p. (Orig.). 1989. pap. 5.95 (ISBN 0-944599-16-8). Gladstone Pub.
—Walt Disney's Uncle Scrooge Comic Album. Barks, Carl, illus. Blum, Geoff, intro. by. (Illus.). 48p. (Orig.). 1989. pap. 5.95 (ISBN 0-944599-19-2). Gladstone Pub.
Barks, Carl & Hannah, Jack. Walt Disney's Donald Duck Giant Comic Album. Barks, Carl & Hannah, Jack, illus. Blum, Geoff, intro. by. 72p. (gr. k up). 1989. pap. 8.95 (ISBN 0-944599-20-6). Gladstone Pub.
Barks, Carl & Rosa, Don. Walt Disney's Uncle Scrooge Giant Album. Blum, Geoffrey, intro. by. (Illus.). 96p. (Orig.). 1989. pap. 11.95 (ISBN 0-944599-28-1). Gladstone Pub.
Barks, Carl, illus. Walt Disney's Comics in Color, Vol. 4. rev. ed. 192p. 1990. pap. 19.95 (ISBN 0-944599-42-7). Gladstone Pub.
Barks, Carl & Gollub, Mo, illus. Walt Disney's Comics in Color, Vol. 1. rev. ed. 192p. 1990. pap. 19.95 (ISBN 0-944599-39-7). Gladstone Pub.
Barks, Carl & Gottfredson, Floyd, illus. Walt Disney's Comics in Color. rev. ed. 192p. (ps up). Date not set. pap. 19.95 (ISBN 0-944599-35-4). Gladstone Pub.
—Walt Disney's Comics in Color, Vol. 2. rev. ed. 192p. 1990. pap. 19.95 (ISBN 0-944599-40-0). Gladstone Pub.
—Walt Disney's Comics in Color, Vol. 3. rev. ed. 192p. 1990. pap. 19.95 (ISBN 0-944599-41-9). Gladstone Pub.
—Walt Disney's Comics in Color, Vol. 5. rev. ed. 200p. 1990. pap. 19.95 (ISBN 0-944599-38-9). Gladstone Pub.
—Walt Disney's Comics in Color, Vol. 6. rev. ed. 184p. (ps up). 1990. pap. 19.95 (ISBN 0-944599-37-0). Gladstone Pub.
Barks, Carl & Rosa, Don, illus. Walt Disney's Comics in Color, Vol. 7. rev. ed. 206p. (ps up). 1990. pap. 19.95 (ISBN 0-944599-36-2). Gladstone Pub.
Bestall, Alfred & Henderson, James. Rupert Annual: 1988. Harrold, John & Campbell, Doris, illus. 100p. (ps-7). 1988. 12.00 (ISBN 0-85079-179-0, Daily Expres UK). Scholium Intl.
—Rupert Annual: 1989. Harrold, John & Campbell, Doris, illus. 100p. (ps-7). 1989. 12.95 (ISBN 0-85079-187-1, Daily Expres UK). Scholium Intl.
Browne, Dik. Hagar the Horrible: Gangway. 128p. (Orig.). 1985. pap. 1.95 (ISBN 0-685-10966-6, Dist. by Warner Pub Services & St. Martin Press). Tor Bks.

—Hagar the Horrible, No. 5: On the Rack. 128p. (gr. 8-12). 1983. pap. 1.95 (ISBN 0-441-31470-8, Pub. by Charter Bks). Ace Bks.
Caniff, Milton. The Complete Color Terry & the Pirates, Vol. 1. Marschall, Richard, intros. by. Caniff, Milton, illus. Feiffer, Jules. (Illus.). 96p. (gr. 6 up). 1990. 34.95 (ISBN 0-924359-19-6). Remco Wrldserv Bks.
Cummings, Richard. Make Your Own Comics for Fun & Profit. (gr. 7 up). 1985. 8.95 (ISBN 0-679-51208-X). McKay.
Davis, Jim. La Bonne Vie. (FRE.). Date not set. 18.95 (ISBN 0-8288-4581-6). French & Eur.
—La Diete, Jamais! (FRE.). Date not set. 18.95 (ISBN 0-8288-4582-4). French & Eur.
—La Faim Justifie Les Moyens. (FRE.). Date not set. 18.95 (ISBN 0-8288-4583-2, F91530). French & Eur.
—Faut Pas S'En Faire. (FRE.). Date not set. 18.95 (ISBN 0-8288-4584-0, F101551). French & Eur.
—Garfield Prend Du Poids. (FRE.). Date not set. 18.95 (ISBN 0-8288-4586-7, F101550). French & Eur.
—Garfield, Tiens Bon la Rampe. (FRE.). Date not set. 18.95 (ISBN 0-8288-4585-9). French & Eur.
—Moi, On M'Aime. (FRE.). Date not set. 18.95 (ISBN 0-8288-4587-5, M4211). French & Eur.
—Qui Dort Dine. (FRE.). Date not set. 18.95 (ISBN 0-8288-4588-3). French & Eur.
—Tiens Bon la Rampe. (FRE.). Date not set. 18.95 (ISBN 0-8288-4589-1). French & Eur.
—Les Yeux Plus Gros Que le Ventre. (FRE.). Date not set. 18.95 (ISBN 0-8288-4590-5, F91520). French & Eur.
De Goscinny, Rene & Uderzo, Albert. La Gran Travesia. (Illus.). 48p. 7.95 (ISBN 0-685-09538-X). Dargaud Pub.
Disney, Walt. Viking's Eye. 1990. pap. 5.98 (ISBN 0-7924-5404-9). BDD Promo Bk.
The Flintstones. (ps up). 1990. PLB 5.98 (ISBN 0-7924-5152-X, Mallard Pr). BDD Promo Bk.
Gately, George. Heathcliff & the Good Life. 128p. (Orig.). 1985. pap. 3.50 (ISBN 0-8125-1745-8). Tor Bks.
Goscinny, Rene & Uderzo, Albert. Asterix el Galo. (Illus.). 48p. 7.95 (ISBN 0-685-09519-3). Dargaud Pub.
—Asterix en Bretana. (Illus.). 48p. 7.95 (ISBN 0-685-09518-5). Dargaud Pub.
—Certamen Principum. (Illus.). 48p. 7.95 (ISBN 0-685-09551-7). Dargaud Pub.
—La Cizana. (Illus.). 48p. 7.95 (ISBN 0-685-09527-4). Dargaud Pub.
—El Combate de los Jefes. (Illus.). 48p. 7.95 (ISBN 0-685-09517-7). Dargaud Pub.
—El Escudo Arverno. (Illus.). 48p. 7.95 (ISBN 0-686-56220-8). Dargaud Pub.
—La Hoz de Oro. (Illus.). 48p. 7.95 (ISBN 0-685-09520-7). Dargaud Pub.
—Los Laureles del Cesar. (Illus.). 48p. 7.95 (ISBN 0-685-09530-4). Dargaud Pub.
—El Regalo del Cesar. (Illus.). 48p. 7.95 (ISBN 0-685-09536-3). Dargaud Pub.
—La Residencia de los Dioses. (Illus.). 48p. 7.95 (ISBN 0-685-09529-0). Dargaud Pub.
—La Vuelta a la Galia. (Illus.). 48p. 7.95 (ISBN 0-685-09522-3). Dargaud Pub.
Goscinny, Rene, et al. Falx Aurea. (Illus.). 48p. (gr. 10up). 7.95 (ISBN 0-685-09542-8). Dargaud Pub.
Goscinny, Rene de & Uderzo, Albert. Asterix & the Great Crossing. (Illus.). 48p. 1984. pap. 4.95 (ISBN 2-205-06921-7). Dargaud Pub.
—Asterix apud Gothos. (Illus.). 48p. 7.95 (ISBN 0-685-09545-2). Dargaud Pub.
—Asterix en Corcega. (Illus.). 48p. 7.95 (ISBN 0-685-09534-7). Dargaud Pub.
—Asterix en Helvecia. (Illus.). 48p. 7.95 (ISBN 0-685-09528-2). Dargaud Pub.
—Asterix en los Juegos Olimpicos. (Illus.). 48p. 7.95 (ISBN 0-685-09525-8). Dargaud Pub.
—Asterix Gallus. (Illus.). 48p. 7.95 (ISBN 0-685-09540-1). Dargaud Pub.
—Asterix Legionario. (SPA., Illus.). 48p. 7.95 (ISBN 0-686-56219-4). Dargaud Pub.
—Asterix y Cleopatra. (Illus.). 48p. 7.95 (ISBN 0-685-09523-1). Dargaud Pub.
—Asterix y el Caldero. (Illus.). 48p. 7.95 (ISBN 0-685-09526-6). Dargaud Pub.
—Asterix y los Godos. (Illus.). 48p. 7.95 (ISBN 0-685-09521-5). Dargaud Pub.
—Asterix y los Normandos. (Illus.). 48p. 7.95 (ISBN 0-685-09524-X). Dargaud Pub.
Gottfredson, Floyd. Walt Disney's Mickey Mouse Comic Album. Gottfredson, Floyd, illus. Blum, Geoff, intro. by. (Illus.). 48p. (Orig.). 1989. pap. 5.95 (ISBN 0-944599-17-6). Gladstone Pub.
—Walt Disney's Mickey Mouse Comic Album. Gottfredson, Floyd, illus. Blum, Geoff, intro. by. (Illus.). 48p. (Orig.). 1989. pap. 5.95 (ISBN 0-944599-21-4). Gladstone Pub.
—Walt Disney's Mickey Mouse Giant Album. Blum, Geoffrey, intro. by. (Illus.). 72p. (Orig.). 1989. pap. 8.95 (ISBN 0-944599-25-7). Gladstone Pub.
Gray, Harold. Little Orphan Annie in the Great Depression. Gray, Harold, illus. 58p. (Orig.). (gr. 5 up). 1979. pap. 3.95 (ISBN 0-486-23737-0). Dover.
Hall, Katy. Garfield: Jokes, Riddles, & Other Silly Stuff. Fentz, Mike, illus. LC 84-60150. 96p. (gr. 2-5). 1984. pap. 2.95 (ISBN 0-394-86785-8, Pub. by BYR). Random.
Herge. Tintin Games Book, Vol. 1. 1990. pap. 6.95 (ISBN 0-316-35858-4). Little.
Herriman, George. The Komplete Kolor Krazy Kat, Vol. I: 1935-1936. Marschall, Richard, intros. by. Herriman, George, illus. Waterson, Bill. (Illus.). 96p. (gr. 6 up). 1990. 34.95 (ISBN 0-924359-06-4). Remco WrldServ Bks.
Howard, Wayne. The Well. Perle, Ruth L., ed. Howard, Wayne, illus. (gr. k-1). 1977. pap. text ed. 0.60 (ISBN 0-89796-859-X). New Dimens Educ.
The Jetsons. (ps up). 1990. PLB 5.98 (ISBN 0-7924-5153-8, Mallard Pr). BDD Promo Bk.
Jetsons: The Movie. (ps up). 1990. PLB 5.98 (ISBN 0-7924-5155-4, Mallard Pr). BDD Promo Bk.
Lynde, Stan. Rick O'Shay, Hipshot, & Me... a Memoir by Stan Lynde: Includes 10 Complete Stories from the Daily Comic Strip 1959-1977. Gold, Mike, ed. Heston, Charlton, intro. by. LC 90-82941. (Illus.). 250p. (Orig.). (gr. 1 up). 1990. pap. 18.95 (ISBN 0-9626999-0-X). Cttnwd Graphics.

—Stan Lynde's Pardners: The Bonding. (Illus.). (gr. 3 up). 1990. write for info. (ISBN 0-9626999-1-8). Cttnwd Graphics.
An all new graphic novel from internationally syndicated cartoonist Stan Lynde, creator of RICK O'SHAY, & LATIGO. It's a heartwarming, humorous & spirited western adventure. A different kind of western. A different kind of love story. Introducing lone wolf Footloose Fairweather & his spunky young partner, Fancy Free. PARDNERS is historically set in the American West of the 1870's & 80's. A story that all of the family (8-80) will want to read... moral, fresh, wholesome & very entertaining!
Publisher Provided Annotation.

McCay, Winsor. The Complete Little Nemo in Slumberland, Vol. III: 1908-1910. Marschall, Richard, intro. by. (Illus.). 96p. (gr. 6 up). 1990. 34.95 (ISBN 0-924359-03-X). Remco Wrldserv Bks.
—The Complete Little Nemo in Slumberland, Vol. IV: 1910-1911. Marschall, Richard, intro. by. (Illus.). 96p. (gr. 6 up). 1990. 34.95 (ISBN 0-924359-04-8). Remco Wrldserv Bks.
McCoy, James C., et al. Comic Tales Anthology, No. 2. 2nd ed. Davenport, May, intro. by. Walker, Timothy, et al, illus. LC 88-70551. 100p. (Orig.). (gr. 7-12). 1988. pap. 6.95x (ISBN 0-943864-53-4). Davenport.
Merrison, Tim. Comics & Magazines. Stefoff, Rebecca, ed. LC 90-13985. (Illus.). 32p. (gr. 4-8). 1991. PLB 17.26 (ISBN 0-944483-97-6). Garrett Ed Corp.
Peterson, Jim. Broomhilda DewDrop. Peterson, Jim, illus. 32p. (gr. k-5). 1975. 4.95 (ISBN 0-685-63894-4); PLB 5.95 (ISBN 0-685-63895-2). Amhara Corp.
Riebe, Ernest. Mister Block: IWW Comics. Rosemont, Franklin, ed. (Illus.). 36p. lib. bdg. 22.95 (ISBN 0-88286-063-1); pap. 5.95 (ISBN 0-88286-062-3). C H Kerr.
Saavedra, Scott, et al. Collector's Edition, First Issues: Disney Comics. Hoover, Rick, illus. (Illus.). 168p. (gr. 12). 1990. pap. text ed. 29.95 (ISBN 1-56115-110-6). WD Pub.
Salten, Felix. Walt Disney's Bambi Comic Album. Crawford, Mel & Hultgren, Ken, illus. Blum, Geoffrey, intro. by. 48p. (Orig.). (ps up). 1988. pap. 5.95 (ISBN 0-944599-09-5). Gladstone Pub.
Schechter, Harold. Start Collecting Comic Books. LC 90-52740. (Illus.). 128p. (Orig.). (gr. 3 up). 1990. pap. 9.95 (ISBN 0-89471-876-2). Running Pr.
Schulz, Charles. Los Amigos de Snoopy. (SPA.). 64p. 1971. 4.95 (ISBN 0-8288-4507-7). French & Eur.
—Un Amour de Charlie Brown. (FRE.). 1985. 4.95 (ISBN 0-8288-4514-X). French & Eur.
—Apuros Escolares. (SPA.). 64p. 1971. 4.95 (ISBN 0-8288-4504-2). French & Eur.
—Le Beagle Est Revenu Sur Terre. (FRE.). 1985. 9.95 (ISBN 0-8288-4532-8). French & Eur.
—Un Beagle Qui a Du Chien. (FRE.). 1985. 9.95 (ISBN 0-8288-4531-X). French & Eur.
—Belle Mentalite, Snoopy. (FRE.). 1985. 4.95 (ISBN 0-8288-4526-3). French & Eur.
—Bienvenue Snoopy. (FRE.). 45p. 1987. 19.95 (ISBN 0-8288-4538-7). French & Eur.
—Du Calme, Charlie Brown. (FRE.). 1985. 4.95 (ISBN 0-8288-4519-0). French & Eur.
—Carlitos y Snoopy. (SPA.). 64p. 1971. 4.95 (ISBN 0-8288-4512-3). French & Eur.
—Le Chef des Briquets. (FRE.). 1985. 4.95 (ISBN 0-8288-4518-2). French & Eur.
—Al Colegio. (SPA.). 64p. 1971. 4.95 (ISBN 0-8288-4506-9). French & Eur.
—Deportes de Invierno. (SPA.). 64p. 1971. 4.95 (ISBN 0-8288-4508-5). French & Eur.
—Les Dieux du Tennis Etaient Contre Moi. (FRE.). 1985. 9.95 (ISBN 0-8288-4528-X). French & Eur.
—Dis Pas de Betises, Charlie Brown. (FRE.). 1985. 4.95 (ISBN 0-8288-4520-4). French & Eur.
—Elementaire Mon Cher Snoopy. (FRE.). 48p. 1988. 18.95 (ISBN 0-8288-4539-5). French & Eur.
—Fantastique Snoopy. (FRE.). 47p. 1988. 18.95 (ISBN 0-8288-4540-9). French & Eur.
—Feu D'Artifice. (FRE.). 48p. 1989. 19.95 (ISBN 0-8288-4541-7). French & Eur.
—Gente Menuda. (SPA.). 64p. 1971. 4.95 (ISBN 0-8288-4502-6). French & Eur.
—El Gran Jefe. (SPA.). 64p. 1971. 4.95 (ISBN 0-8288-4505-0). French & Eur.
—Le Grand Livre Des Questions, No. 4. (FRE.). 160p. 1982. 29.95 (ISBN 0-8288-4542-5). French & Eur.
—Le Grand Livre Des Questions, No. 5. (FRE.). 158p. 1983. 29.95 (ISBN 0-8288-4543-3). French & Eur.
—Imbattable Snoopy. (FRE.). 48p. 1983. 18.95 (ISBN 0-8288-4544-1). French & Eur.
—Inattaquable Snoopy. (FRE.). 48p. 1986. 18.95 (ISBN 0-8288-4545-X). French & Eur.
—Incroyable Snoopy. (FRE.). 48p. 1982. 18.95 (ISBN 0-8288-4546-8). French & Eur.
—Ineffable Snoopy. (FRE.). 48p. 1985. 18.95 (ISBN 0-8288-4547-6). French & Eur.
—Inegalable Snoopy. (FRE.). 1985. 18.95 (ISBN 0-8288-4536-0). French & Eur.
—Inenarrable Snoopy. (FRE.). 48p. 1987. 18.95 (ISBN 0-8288-4548-4). French & Eur.
—Inepuisable Snoopy. (FRE.). 48p. 1987. 18.95 (ISBN 0-8288-4549-2). French & Eur.
—Intrepide Snoopy. (FRE.). 48p. 1983. 18.95 (ISBN 0-8288-4551-4). French & Eur.
—Invincible Snoopy. (FRE.). 48p. 1985. 18.95 (ISBN 0-8288-4552-2). French & Eur.
—Irresistible Snoopy. (FRE.). 48p. 1985. 18.95 (ISBN 0-8288-4553-0). French & Eur.
—Je Ne T'Ai Jamais Promis un Verger. (FRE.). 1985. 9.95 (ISBN 0-8288-4530-1). French & Eur.
—Joyeuses Paques. (FRE.). 1984. 14.95 (ISBN 0-8288-4537-9). French & Eur.
—L'Infaillible Snoopy. (FRE.). 47p. 1984. 18.95 (ISBN 0-8288-4550-6). French & Eur.
—Meme Mes Critiques Ratent la Cible. (FRE.). 1985. 9.95 (ISBN 0-8288-4533-6). French & Eur.
—Mi Pequeno Mundo. (SPA.). 64p. 1971. 4.95 (ISBN 0-8288-4501-8). French & Eur.
—Misere! Charlie Brown. (FRE.). 1985. 4.95 (ISBN 0-8288-4515-8). French & Eur.
—Ne Me Casse Pas les Oreilles. (FRE.). 1984. 9.95 (ISBN 0-8288-4534-4). French & Eur.
—No Me Comprenden. (SPA.). 64p. 1971. 4.95 (ISBN 0-8288-4511-5). French & Eur.
—El Pajarito Emilio. (SPA.). 64p. 1971. 4.95 (ISBN 0-8288-4510-7). French & Eur.
—Regreso al Colegio. (SPA.). 64p. 1971. 4.95 (ISBN 0-8288-4509-3). French & Eur.
—Reviens, Snoopy. (FRE.). 48p. 1982. 10.95 (ISBN 0-8288-4554-9). French & Eur.
—Reviens, Snoopy: Presses Pocket. (FRE.). 124p. 1989. 10.95 (ISBN 0-8288-4555-7). French & Eur.
—Snoopy Arbitre. (FRE.). 1984. 14.95 (ISBN 0-8288-4559-X). French & Eur.
—Snoopy Connait La Musique. (FRE.). 128p. 1974. 9.95 (ISBN 0-8288-4561-1). French & Eur.
—Snoopy Delire. (FRE.). 50p. 1983. 14.95 (ISBN 0-8288-4562-X). French & Eur.
—Snoopy Detective. (FRE.). 50p. 1983. 14.95 (ISBN 0-8288-4563-8). French & Eur.
—Snoopy: Droles D'Oiseau. (FRE.). 128p. 1975. 9.95 (ISBN 0-8288-4557-3). French & Eur.
—Snoopy Escritor. (SPA.). 64p. 1971. 4.95 (ISBN 0-8288-4503-4). French & Eur.
—Snoopy Et Compagnie. (FRE.). 156p. 1987. write for info. (ISBN 0-8288-4564-6). French & Eur.
—Snoopy Et la Culture. (FRE.). 1975. 9.95 (ISBN 0-8288-4565-4). French & Eur.
—Snoopy Et la St-Valentin. (FRE.). 1984. 14.95 (ISBN 0-8288-4566-2). French & Eur.
—Snoopy Et Ses Freres. (FRE.). 128p. 1974. 9.95 (ISBN 0-8288-4567-0). French & Eur.
—Snoopy Et Son Copain Linus. (FRE.). 128p. 1975. 9.95 (ISBN 0-8288-4568-9). French & Eur.
—Snoopy Grand Coeur. (FRE.). 1975. 9.95 (ISBN 0-8288-4569-7). French & Eur.
—Snoopy: Joyeuses Paques. (FRE.). 1985. 14.95 (ISBN 0-8288-4556-5). French & Eur.
—Snoopy, Le Petit Receuil de Pensees. (FRE.). 1985. write for info. (ISBN 0-8288-4558-1). French & Eur.
—Snoopy Patineur. (FRE.). 1984. 14.95 (ISBN 0-8288-4570-0). French & Eur.
—Snoopy Prestidigitateur. (FRE.). 50p. 1983. 14.95 (ISBN 0-8288-4571-9). French & Eur.
—Snoopy S'En Va-T-En Guerre. (FRE.). 128p. 1974. 9.95 (ISBN 0-8288-4572-7). French & Eur.
—Sois Philosophe, Charlie Brown. (FRE.). 1985. 4.95 (ISBN 0-8288-4517-4). French & Eur.
—T'As Pas de Veine, Charlie Brown. (FRE.). 1985. 4.95 (ISBN 0-8288-4525-5). French & Eur.
—Te Fais Pas de Bile, Charlie Brown. (FRE.). 1985. 4.95 (ISBN 0-8288-4523-9). French & Eur.
—T'Es le Meilleur, Charlie Brown. (FRE.). 1985. 4.95 (ISBN 0-8288-4521-2). French & Eur.
—Tiens Bon, Charlie Brown. (FRE.). 1985. 4.95 (ISBN 0-8288-4527-1). French & Eur.
—Tout Connaitre en S'Amusant: Camions. (FRE.). 32p. 1983. 10.95 (ISBN 0-8288-4578-6). French & Eur.
—Tout Connaitre en S'Amusant: La Ferme. (FRE.). 34p. 1982. 10.95 (ISBN 0-8288-4573-5). French & Eur.

—Tout Connaitre en S'Amusant: La Nature. (FRE.). 34p. 1983. 10.95 (ISBN 0-8288-4574-3). French & Eur.
—Tout Connaitre en S'Amusant: La Plage. (FRE.). 34p. 1982. 10.95 (ISBN 0-8288-4575-1). French & Eur.
—Tout Connaitre en S'Amusant: Les Avions. (FRE.). 34p. 1982. 10.95 (ISBN 0-8288-4576-X). French & Eur.
—Tout Connaitre en S'Amusant: Maisons. (FRE.). 32p. 1983. 10.95 (ISBN 0-8288-4579-4). French & Eur.
—Tout Connaitre En S'Amusant: Saisons. (FRE.). 32p. 1983. 10.95 (ISBN 0-8288-4580-8). French & Eur.
—Tu Cours Apres L'Ete, Et L'Hiver... (FRE.). 1985. 9.95 (ISBN 0-8288-4535-2). French & Eur.
—Tu Te Crois Malin, Charlie Brown. (FRE.). 1985. 4.95 (ISBN 0-8288-4522-0). French & Eur.
—Tu Veux Rire, Charlie Brown. (FRE.). 1985. 4.95 (ISBN 0-8288-4524-7). French & Eur.
—Une Vie de Chien. (FRE.). 1985. 4.95 (ISBN 0-8288-4513-1). French & Eur.
—Vois la Vie en Rose, Snoopy. (FRE.). 1985. 4.95 (ISBN 0-8288-4516-6). French & Eur.
—Y'A Qu'Un Woodstock. (FRE.). 1985. 9.95 (ISBN 0-8288-4529-8). French & Eur.
Schulz, Charles M. It's the Great Pumpkin, Charlie Brown. LC 80-10287. (Illus.). 48p. (gr. 3-5). 1980. Random.
—Love Is Walking Hand in Hand. (Illus.). 64p. (ps up). 1987. pap. 5.95 (ISBN 0-345-34873-7). Pharos Bks NY.
—She Likes You, Charlie Brown. (Illus.). 1985. pap. 2.95 (ISBN 0-449-20788-9, Crest). Fawcett.
—You're on the Wrong Foot Again, Charlie Brown. (Illus.). 128p. (ps up). 1987. pap. 5.95 (ISBN 0-88687-313-4). Pharos Bks NY.
—You're Weird, Sir! LC 82-18658. (Illus.). 192p. (gr. 2-4). 1982. pap. 4.95 (ISBN 0-03-062099-6). H Holt & Co.
Scooby Doo. (ps up). 1990. PLB 5.98 (ISBN 0-7924-5151-1, Mallard Pr). BDD Promo Bk.
Smith, Frank C. I Can Draw Comics & Cartoons. Smith, Frank C., illus. 80p. (Orig.). (gr. 3 up). 1982. pap. 3.95 (ISBN 0-671-44490-5, Little Simon). S&S Trade.
Sterrett, Cliff. The Complete Color Polly & Her Pals, Vol. I: The Surrealist Period, 1926-1927. Marschall, Richard, intros. by. Sterrett, Cliff, illus. Spiegelman, Art. (Illus.). 96p. 1990. 34.95 (ISBN 0-924359-14-5). Remco Wrldserv Bks.
Turk & DeGroot. Leonardo: Non-Stop Genius. (Illus.). 48p. (Orig.). 1984. pap. 4.95 (ISBN 0-317-13162-1). Dargaud Pub.
Walker, Mort. Beetle Bailey: Three's a Crowd. 288p. (Orig.). 1986. pap. 2.95 (ISBN 0-8125-6111-2, Dist. by Warner Pub Service & St. Martin's Press). Tor Bks.
Walt Disney Mickey Mouse Adventures. (ps up). 1990. PLB 5.98 (ISBN 0-7924-5401-4, Mallard Pr). BDD Promo Bk.
Walt Disney Mickey Mouse Adventures: Bing Bong. (ps up). 1990. PLB 5.98 (ISBN 0-7924-5405-7, Mallard Pr). BDD Promo Bk.
Walt Disney Mickey Mouse Adventures: The Barracuda Triangle. (ps up). 1990. PLB 5.98 (ISBN 0-7924-5402-2, Mallard Pr). BDD Promo Bk.
Walt Disney Mickey Mouse Adventures: The Cactus Kid. (ps up). 1990. PLB 5.98 (ISBN 0-7924-5406-5, Mallard Pr). BDD Promo Bk.
Walt Disney Mickey Mouse Adventures: The Phantom Blot. (ps up). 1990. PLB 5.98 (ISBN 0-7924-5403-0, Mallard Pr). BDD Promo Bk.
Walt Disney Staff. Donald & His Friends. 1988. 6.98 (ISBN 0-8317-2392-0). Smithmark.
—Great Mouse Detective. 1988. 6.98 (ISBN 0-8317-3993-2). Smithmark.
—Little Mermaid. 1989. 6.98 (ISBN 0-8317-5605-5). Smithmark.
—Mickey's Christmas Carol. 1988. 6.98 (ISBN 0-8317-5929-1). Smithmark.
—Robin Hood. 1989. 6.98 (ISBN 0-8317-7408-8). Smithmark.
—Sword in the Stone. 1988. 6.98 (ISBN 0-8317-8015-0). Smithmark.
Walt Disney's American Classics: Casey at the Bat. (ps up). 1990. PLB 5.98 (ISBN 0-7924-5051-5, Mallard Pr). BDD Promo Bk.
Walt Disney's American Classics: Davy Crockett. (ps up). 1990. PLB 5.98 (ISBN 0-7924-5054-X, Mallard Pr). BDD Promo Bk.
Walt Disney's American Classics: Johnny Appleseed. (ps up). 1990. PLB 5.98 (ISBN 0-7924-5053-1, Mallard Pr). BDD Promo Bk.
Walt Disney's American Classics: Legend of Sleepy Hollow. (ps up). 1990. PLB 5.98 (ISBN 0-7924-5052-3, Mallard Pr). BDD Promo Bk.
Walt Disney's American Classics: Little Hiawatha. (ps up). 1990. PLB 5.98 (ISBN 0-7924-5455-3, Mallard Pr). BDD Promo Bk.
Walt Disney's American Classics: Old Yeller. (ps up). 1990. PLB 5.98 (ISBN 0-7924-5456-1, Mallard Pr). BDD Promo Bk.
Walt Disney's American Classics: Paul Bunyan. (ps up). 1990. PLB 5.98 (ISBN 0-7924-5056-6, Mallard Pr). BDD Promo Bk.
Walt Disney's American Classics: Pecos Bill. (ps up). 1990. PLB 5.98 (ISBN 0-7924-5457-X, Mallard Pr). BDD Promo Bk.
Watterson, Bill. The Essential Calvin & Hobbes: A Calvin & Hobbes Treasury. Watterson, Bill, illus. Schulz, Charles. 256p. 1988. 19.95 (ISBN 0-8362-1809-4); pap. 12.95 (ISBN 0-8362-1805-1). Andrews & McMeel.
Wenk, Richard. Batman & the Doomsday Prophecy. Delbo, Jose, illus. (gr. 3-6). 1989. pap. 2.75 (ISBN 0-671-68312-8, Archway). PB.
Yogi Bear. (ps up). 1990. PLB 5.98 (ISBN 0-7924-5154-6, Mallard Pr). BDD Promo Bk.

COMIC LITERATURE
see Comedy

COMIC OPERA
see Opera

COMMANDMENTS, TEN
see Ten Commandments

COMMENTARIES, BIBLICAL
see Bible–Commentaries

COMMERCE
see also Banks and Banking; Business; Statistics; Stock Exchange; Stocks; Trade Routes; Transportation
Across Africa & Arabia. (Illus.). 128p. 1990. 17.95x (ISBN 0-8160-1878-2). Facts on File.
Across Asia by Land. (Illus.). 128p. 1990. 17.95x (ISBN 0-8160-1874-X). Facts on File.
The American Way West. (Illus.). 128p. 1990. 17.95x (ISBN 0-8160-1880-4). Facts on File.
Dudley, William, ed. Trade: Opposing Viewpoints. LC 90-24087. (Illus.). 264p. (gr. 10 up). 1991. PLB 15.95 (ISBN 0-89908-176-2); pap. 8.95 (ISBN 0-89908-151-7). Greenhaven.
The Southern World. (Illus.). 128p. 1990. 17.95x (ISBN 0-8160-1881-2). Facts on File.

COMMERCIAL ART
see also Costume Design; Posters

COMMERCIAL AVIATION
see Aeronautics, Commercial

COMMERCIAL EDUCATION
see Business Education

COMMERCIAL PRODUCTS
see also Manufactures; Marine Resources
Free Stuff Editors. Free Stuff for Kids. 12th, rev. ed. (Illus.). 135p. 1988. pap. 4.95 (ISBN 0-88166-116-3). Meadowbrook.
—Free Stuff for Kids 1990. 13th ed. 1989. pap. 5.95 (ISBN 0-88166-170-8, Dist. by Simon & Schuster). Meadowbrook.
Sullivan, George. How Do They Package It? LC 76-18089. (Illus.). 144p. (gr. 7-9). 1976. 7.50 (ISBN 0-664-32601-3, Westminster). Westminster John Knox.

COMMERCIAL SCHOOLS
see Business Education

COMMERCIAL TRAVELERS
see Salesmen and Salesmanship

COMMODORE 64 (COMPUTER)
Buxton, Robin. Commodore 64, Vol. 1. 50p. (gr. 4-12). 1983. pap. text ed. 11.95 (ISBN 0-88193-041-5). Create Learn.
—Commodore 64, Vol. 2. 58p. (gr. 4-12). 1983. pap. text ed. 11.95 (ISBN 0-88193-042-3). Create Learn.
Buxton, Robin & Buxton, Marilyn. Commodore 64, Vol. 3. 59p. (gr. 5-12). 1983. pap. text ed. 11.95 (ISBN 0-88193-043-1). Create Learn.
—Commodore 64, Vol. 4. 59p. (gr. 5-12). 1983. pap. text ed. 11.95 (ISBN 0-88193-044-X). Create Learn.
Captain Comal's Staff. Cartridge Graphics & Sound. Hejndorf, Frank, illus. 64p. (Orig.). (gr. 6 up). 1984. pap. 6.95 (ISBN 0-928411-02-8). Comal Users.
Skelton, Mindy. Graphics Primer. Schmidt, Wayne, illus. 84p. (Orig.). (gr. 6 up). 1984. pap. 14.95 (ISBN 0-928411-04-4). Comal Users.
Stedman, Robert E. & Cosgrove, R. Commodore 64 BASIC for Kids. (Illus.). 352p. (gr. 5-8). 1984. pap. 12.95 (ISBN 0-89303-378-2). Brady Bks.
Watson, Nancy R. Taking off with BASIC on the Commodore 64. (Illus.). 208p. (gr. 5 up). 1984. pap. 12.95 (ISBN 0-89303-868-7). Brady Bks.

COMMONWEALTH, THE
see Political Science

COMMONWEALTH OF ENGLAND
see Great Britain–History–Civil War and Commonwealth, 1642-1660

COMMUNAL LIVING
see Collective Settlements

COMMUNES
see Collective Settlements

COMMUNICABLE DISEASES
see also Bacteriology; Immunity
Arehart, Lynda L. & Torrie, Margaret. Understanding HIV-AIDS: A Workbook Suitable for Mainstreamed Students. (Illus.). 48p. (gr. 9-12). 1990. tchrs. ed. 8.95 (ISBN 0-8138-1619-X); wkbk. 4.95x (ISBN 0-8138-1618-1). Iowa St U Pr.
Diskavich, Laura & Woods, Samuel, Jr. Everything You Need to Know about STD (Sexually Transmitted Diseases) Rosen, Ruth, ed. (gr. 7-12). 1990. PLB 12.95 (ISBN 0-8239-1010-5). Rosen Group.
Donahue, Parnell & Capellaro, Helen. Germs Make Me Sick: A Health Handbook for Kids. Oechsli, Kelly, illus. LC 74-15309. 96p. (gr. 4 up). 1975. Knopf.
Metos, Thomas H. Communicable Diseases. (Illus.). 96p. (gr. 4-9). 1987. PLB 10.40 (ISBN 0-531-10380-3). Watts.
Nourse, Alan E. Lumps, Bumps, & Rashes: A Look at Kids' Diseases. rev. ed. (Illus.). 64p. (gr. 5-8). 1990. PLB 11.90 (ISBN 0-531-10865-1). Watts.
Patent, Dorothy H. Germs! LC 82-48749. (Illus.). 40p. (gr. 3-7). 1983. reinforced bdg. 12.95 (ISBN 0-8234-0481-1). Holiday.

COMMUNICATION
see also Books and Reading; Language and Languages; Newspapers; Postal Service; Writing
Barker, Larry L. Communication Skills: Objectives & Criterion Referenced Exercises for Grades 7-12. (Illus.). 321p. (Orig.). 1988. pap. text ed. 84.95 incl. Listening Skills (ISBN 0-685-27248-6). SPECTRA Inc.
Bernhard, Gwyn K. Gwyn Karon Bernhard's Kids' Talk: Kids' Talk in the Classroom Workbook, No. 1. 125p. (gr. 5-9). 1989. 85.00 (ISBN 1-87-781904-2). Kids Talk CT.
Berry, Joy. Every Kid's Guide to Being a Communicator. (Illus.). 48p. (gr. 3-7). 1987. 5.95 (ISBN 0-516-21418-7); PLB 14.60 (ISBN 0-516-01418-8). Childrens.
Blum, Lila. Tuning in to Spoken Messages: Basic Listening Strategies. 1990. pap. text ed. 8.96 (ISBN 0-8013-0164-5, 75826); cass. 26.21 (ISBN 0-8013-0165-3, 75827). Longman.
Dixon, Malcolm. Communications. (Illus.). 48p. (gr. 5-8). 1991. RLB 12.40 (ISBN 0-531-18411-0, Pub. by Boatwright Pr). Watts.
Educational Assessment Publishing Company Staff. Parent - Child Learning Library: Communication English Big Book. (Illus.). 32p. (gr. k-3). Date not set. text ed. 28.50 (ISBN 0-942277-75-9). Educ Assess Pub.
—Parent - Child Learning Library: Communication Spanish Big Book. (SPA., Illus.). 32p. (gr. k-3). Date not set. text ed. 28.50 (ISBN 0-942277-76-7). Educ Assess Pub.
—Parent - Child Learning Library: Communication Spanish Edition. (SPA.). 32p. (ps). Date not set. text ed. 9.95 (ISBN 0-942277-93-7). Educ Assess Pub.
—Parent - Child Learning Library: Communication. (Illus.). 32p. (ps). Date not set. text ed. 9.95 (ISBN 0-942277-61-9). Educ Assess Pub.
Fant, Louie J., Jr. Intermediate Sign Language. LC 78-61003. (Illus.). 225p. (gr. 7 up). 1980. text ed. 24.95 (ISBN 0-917002-54-7). Joyce Media.
Franck, Irene M. & Brownstone, David M. Communicators. LC 86-8815. (Illus.). 240p. (gr. 7 up). 1986. PLB 17.95 (ISBN 0-8160-1443-4). Facts on File.
Frisch, Carlienne & Balcziak, Bill. Communications, Reading Level 5: Today & Tomorrow, 6 bks. (Illus.). 288p. (gr. 4-8). Date not set. PLB write for info. Rourke Corp.
Geiger, Eve. Two Hundred & Ninety-Two Activities for Literature & Language Arts. (gr. 1-6). 1990. pap. 7.95 (ISBN 0-8224-6746-1). Fearon Teach Aids.
Gilbert, Sara. You Can Speak up in Class. Doty, Roy, illus. 64p. (gr. 3 up). 1991. pap. 6.95 (ISBN 0-688-10304-9, Pub. by Beech Tree Bks). Morrow.
—You Can Speak up in Class. Doty, Roy, illus. 64p. (gr. 3 up). 1991. PLB 12.88 (ISBN 0-688-09867-3). Morrow Jr Bks.
Gregorich, Barbara. Language Skills. Hoffman, Joan, ed. Koontz, Robin M., illus. 32p. (gr. 1). 1988. wkbk. 1.49 (ISBN 0-88743-166-6). Sch Zone Pub Co.
—Language Skills. Hoffman, Joan, ed. Koontz, Robin M., illus. 32p. (gr. 2). 1988. wkbk. 1.49 (ISBN 0-88743-172-0). Sch Zone Pub Co.
—Language Skills: First Grade. Hoffman, Joan, ed. Koontz, Robin M., illus. 32p. (gr. 1). 1990. wkbk. 3.49 (ISBN 0-88743-185-2). Sch Zone Pub Co.
—Language Skills: Second Grade. Hoffman, Joan, ed. Koontz, Robin M., illus. 32p. (gr. 2). 1990. wkbk. 3.49 (ISBN 0-88743-191-7). Sch Zone Pub Co.
—Sequencing & Perceptual Skills: Kindergarten. Hoffman, Joan, ed. Koontz, Robin M., illus. 32p. (gr. k). 1990. wkbk. 3.49 (ISBN 0-88743-178-X). Sch Zone Pub Co.
Gregorich, Barbara & Sliter Johnson, Sharon. Dots & More. Hoffman, Joan, ed. Sandford, John, illus. 32p. (gr. k). 1988. wkbk. 1.49 (ISBN 0-88743-161-5). Sch Zone Pub Co.
—First, Next, Last. Hoffman, Joan, ed. Sandford, John, illus. 32p. (gr. k). 1988. wkbk. 1.49 (ISBN 0-88743-159-3). Sch Zone Pub Co.
—Up-Down In-Out. Hoffman, Joan, ed. Sandford, John, illus. 32p. (gr. k). 1988. wkbk. 1.49 (ISBN 0-88743-158-5). Sch Zone Pub Co.
Hamilton, Harley. Grandfather Moose: Children's Sign Language Book with Rhymes, Games & Chants. 32p. 1989. pap. 9.60 (ISBN 0-916708-21-7). Modern Signs.
Huisingh, Rosemary, et al. ACHIEV-Blue (Activities for Children Involving Everyday Vocabulary) (ps-5). 1989. complete pkg. 186.70 (ISBN 1-55999-002-3). LinguiSystems.
—ACHIEV-Blue Books (Activities for Children Involving Everyday Vocabulary) (ps-5). 1986. spiral manual 49.95 (ISBN 1-55999-004-X). LinguiSystems.
Jordan, Sally. Know What I Mean? Let's Be Clear. Philbrook, Diana, illus. LC 87-92235. 32p. (gr. 4-9). 1988. saddle stitched .89 (ISBN 0-87403-441-8, 24-03651). Standard Pub.
Juntune, Joyce E. Developing Creative Thinking: Fun Book, No. 2. Dougherty, Edie, illus. 26p. (gr. k-4). 1984. pap. 5.00 (ISBN 0-912773-08-1). One Hund Twenty Creat.
Kalman, Bobbie. How We Communicate. (Illus.). 32p. (gr. 2-3). 1986. 14.95 (ISBN 0-86505-074-0). Crabtree Pub Co.

LinguiSystems Staff. ACHIEV-Red Sing-a-Longs Manual (Activities for Children Involving Everyday Vocabulary - Home & Family Vocabulary) (ps-3). 1989. 24.95 (ISBN 1-55999-006-6). LinguiSystems.

Littlefield, Kathy M. & Littlefield, Robert S. Let's Work Together! Stark, Steve, illus. 32p. (Orig.). (gr. 3-6). 1991. pap. text ed. 8.95 (ISBN 1-879340-08-9, K0109). Kidspeak.

—Speak Up! Stark, Steve, illus. 32p. (Orig.). (gr. 3-6). 1989. pap. text ed. 8.95 (ISBN 1-879340-00-3, K0101). Kidspeak.

Littlefield, Robert S. & Ball, Jane A. Who Am I? Who Are They? Stark, Steve, illus. 28p. (Orig.). (gr. 3-6). 1990. pap. text ed. 8.95 (ISBN 1-879340-06-2, K0107). Kidspeak.

McConnell, Nancy L. & Blagden, Carolyn M. RAPP (Resource of Activities for Peer Pragmatics) 1986. spiral reproducible wkbk. 19.95 (ISBN 1-55999-066-X). LinguiSystems.

Mackie, Dan. Communications. Hayes, Cyril & Pelowich, Nadia, eds. Bastien, Charles E., illus. 32p. (gr. 5-9). 1986. lib. bdg. 14.65 (ISBN 0-87617-034-3, Pub. by C Hayes Pr). Penworthy Pub.

The Media, 6 vols. LC 88-29535. (Illus.). 288p. (gr. 7-11). 1989. Set. 73.75 (ISBN 0-86307-973-3). Marshall Cavendish.

Orange County Association Staff. Frases Fundamentales para Comunicarse. (gr. k-12). 1975. 4.77 (ISBN 0-89075-200-1). Crane Pub Co.

Ostuni, Elizabeth E. & Silver, Elaine N. I'm Good at Speech: Music & Activities to Teach Children Good Communication Skills. McTeigue, Susan, illus. 112p. (Orig.). (ps-4). 1990. pap. text ed. 14.95 (ISBN 1-879267-00-4); audiocassette 9.95 (ISBN 1-879267-01-2). Accent Pub NJ.

Palumbo, Thomas. Language Arts Thinking Motivators. 96p. (gr. 2-7). 1988. wkbk. 9.95 (ISBN 0-86653-432-6, GA1050). Good Apple.

Schwartz, Linda. Trivia Trackdown-Communication & Transportation. (Illus.). 32p. (gr. 4-6). 1986. 3.95 (ISBN 0-88160-139-X, LW258). Learning Wks.

Sesame Street Staff. Sesame Street Sign Language Fun. Cooke, Tom, illus. Selkirk, Neil, photos by. LC 79-5570. (Illus.). 72p. (ps-3). 1980. lib. bdg. 10.99 (ISBN 0-394-94212-4); pap. 7.95 (ISBN 0-394-84212-X). Random.

Shadle, Carolyn & Graham, Joan. Building Communication Skills. Franklin, Jean, illus. 48p. (gr. 1-8). 1981. 8.50 (ISBN 0-931724-14-7). Dandy Lion.

Swanson, Norma F. Horizons Plus: A Student's Progress Profile. 1988. write for info. Window World NY.

Travel & Communications. (Illus.). 96p. (gr. 3-8). 1987. PLB 240.00 set (ISBN 0-317-62835-6); pap. 13.27 (ISBN 0-317-62836-4). Raintree Pubs.

Traxler, Mary A. Elementary Language Arts Flipper, No. I. 39p. (gr. 3-6). Date not set. trade edition 5.95 (ISBN 1-878383-15-9). C Lee Pubns.

Weiss, Ann E. Who's to Know? Information, the Media & Public Awareness. 192p. (gr. 5-9). 1990. 14.95 (ISBN 0-395-49702-7). HM.

Zachman, Linda, et al. ACHIEV-Red (Activities for Children Involving Everyday Vocabulary) Package. (ps-5). 1989. complete pkg. 186.70 (ISBN 1-55999-001-5). LinguiSystems.

—ACHIEV-Red Books (Activities for Children Involving Everyday Vocabulary) (ps-5). 1985. spiral manuals 49. 95 (ISBN 1-55999-005-8). LinguiSystems.

Zakim, Shelley P. Communication Workshop: Reproducible Manual & Role-Playing Cards for Social Communication. (gr. 4-12). 1986. spiral reproducible wkbk. 49.95 (ISBN 1-55999-031-7). LinguiSystems.

COMMUNICATION–FICTION

Everett, Louise. Amigo Means Friend. Radinowitz, Sandy, illus. LC 87-11274. 32p. (gr. k-2). 1988. PLB 7.06 (ISBN 0-8167-1000-7); pap. text ed. 1.95 (ISBN 0-8167-1001-5). Troll Assocs.

Lowry, Lois. Anastasia Krupnik. 128p. 1984. pap. 2.95 (ISBN 0-553-15534-2). Bantam.

Nordstrom, Ursula. Secret Language. LC 60-7701. (Illus.). 192p. (gr. 3-5). 1972. pap. 3.50 (ISBN 0-06-440022-0, Trophy). HarpC Child Bks.

Pfeffer, Susan B. What Do You Do When Your Mouth Won't Open? Tomei, Lorna, illus. LC 80-68731. 160p. (gr. 4-6). 1981. 8.95 (ISBN 0-440-09471-2); pap. 9.89 (ISBN 0-385-29140-X). Delacorte.

Schulman, Janet. The Big Hello. Hoban, Lillian, illus. 32p. (gr. 1-4). 1980. pap. 1.95 (ISBN 0-440-40484-3, YB). Dell.

COMMUNICATION–HISTORY

Ardley, Neil. Language & Communications. (Illus.). 40p. (gr. 5-9). 1989. PLB 12.40 (ISBN 0-531-17187-6). Watts.

COMMUNICATION AMONG ANIMALS
see Animal Communication

COMMUNICATIONS RELAY SATELLITES
see Artificial Satellites in Telecommunication

COMMUNISM
see also Individualism; Social Conflict

Trager, Oliver, ed. Communism: The Final Crisis? 224p. 1990. lib. bdg. 29.95x (ISBN 0-8160-2507-X). Facts on File.

COMMUNISM–FICTION

Pride, Mary. The Better Butter Battle. (Illus.). 48p. 1990. 8.95 (ISBN 0-943497-93-0). Wolgemuth & Hyatt.

COMMUNIST CHINA
see China (People's Republic of China)

COMMUNIST COUNTRIES

Trager, Oliver, ed. Communism: The Final Crisis? 224p. 1990. lib. bdg. 29.95x (ISBN 0-8160-2507-X). Facts on File.

COMMUNITY CHESTS
see Fund Raising

COMMUNITY LIFE
see also Cities and Towns

Aten, Jerry. Community Friends. Volpe, Nancee, illus. 64p. (ps-2). 1983. wkbk. 6.95 (ISBN 0-86653-127-0, GA 477). Good Apple.

Clapsadle, Mark & Aemmer, Gail. Community Helpers Fun Book. Clapsadle, Mark, illus. 32p. (ps-2). 1984. pap. 1.59 (ISBN 0-88724-061-5, CD-8050). Carson-Dellos.

Darling, Kathy. Kids & Communities. (Illus.). 64p. (ps-2). 1989. 6.95 (ISBN 0-912107-94-4, MM1911). Monday Morning Bks.

Kalman, Bobbie. Colonial Crafts. 1991. 14.95 (ISBN 0-86505-490-8); pap. 7.95 (ISBN 0-86505-510-6). Crabtree Pub Co.
In COLONIAL CRAFTS your young readers will take a journey into the 18th century & meet the craftspeople who created useful works of art with handmade tools. They will visit the workshops of the wheelwright, cooper, founder, peruker, shoemaker, milliner, gunsmith, & many more. They will find out how the artisans learned their trades through many years of apprenticeship. They will gain an appreciation for the goods made two hundred years ago that are still beautiful today. They will learn why the craftspeople were an essential part of the colonial community.
Publisher Provided Annotation.

—A Colonial Town. 1991. 14.95 (ISBN 0-86505-489-4); pap. 7.95 (ISBN 0-86505-509-2). Crabtree Pub Co.
In A COLONIAL TOWN young readers are introduced to a historic community. They will take a journey into history to a time when people grew their own food & made their own tools. They will travel down the wide cobblestone streets of Williamsburg & enjoy the slow, peaceful pace of the restored city. They will admire the grand estates of long ago & tour the special buildings of Virginia's old capitol. They will find out about the Palace in which the governor lived, the Capitol where laws were made, the Powder Magazine where weapons were kept, & the Gaol where prisoners waited for their punishment. They will meet the apothecary & learn about some of his questionable "cures" & find out how a post mill grinds grain.
Publisher Provided Annotation.

—The Gristmill. (Illus.). 32p. (gr. 3-4). 1990. lib. bdg. 14.95 (ISBN 0-86505-486-X); pap. 7.95 (ISBN 0-86505-506-8). Crabtree Pub Co.
THE GRISTMILL takes a step-by-step look at how a simple water-powered gristmill grinds grain. Detailed diagrams show how the waterwheel, gears, & millstones worked. The book also looks at the role of the miller in the community, the dangers of milling, & the parts of grain that make up wholewheat flour. THE GRISTMILL is part of THE HISTORIC COMMUNITIES SERIES, fun-to-read books that provides a wealth of information for young readers. The series introduces children to the concept of earlier times in history &

looks at community life. THE HISTORIC COMMUNITIES SERIES is beautifully designed, presenting information in two-page spreads through lively text, a multitude of color photographs, & detailed sketches. The books provide a close-up look at each topic, with step-by-step explanations of how tools & processes work. They are excellent for preparing young children for visits to historic sites & provide good follow-up material.
Publisher Provided Annotation.

—Home Crafts. (Illus.). 32p. (gr. 3-4). 1990. lib. bdg. 14.95 (ISBN 0-86505-485-1); pap. 7.95 (ISBN 0-86505-505-X). Crabtree Pub Co.
HOME CRAFTS is a colorful potpourri of the domestic industries carried out by settler men & mostly women. It explains how candles & soap were made, wool & flax were cleaned, spun, & woven, & looks at various needle crafts such as sewing quilts & stitching samplers. HOME CRAFTS also explores the transition of crafts from the home to workshop to factory. HOME CRAFTS is part of The Historic Communities Series, fun-to-read books that provide a wealth of information for young readers. The series introduces children to the concept of earlier times in history & looks at community life. The Historic Communities Series is beautifully designed, presenting information in two-page spreads through lively text, a multitude of color photographs, & detailed sketches. The books provide a close-up look at each topic, with step-by-step explanations of how tools & processes work. They are excellent for preparing young children for visits to historic sites & provide good follow-up material.
Publisher Provided Annotation.

—The Kitchen. (Illus.). 32p. (gr. 3-4). 1990. lib. bdg. 14.95 (ISBN 0-86505-484-3); pap. 7.95 (ISBN 0-86505-504-1). Crabtree Pub Co.
In THE KITCHEN, young readers enter a settler home. They take a close look at the early fireplace, the tools & utensils surrounding it, & the domestic chores that were carried out there such as baking bread & making butter. Comparing an early kitchen with a kitchen of today will allow children to realize the difficulties settlers had just getting food on their tables. Your young readers will gain an understanding of how the settlers made do in a world without refrigerators, toasters, & food processors. THE KITCHEN is part of The Historic Communities Series, fun-to-read books that provide a wealth of information for young readers. The series introduces children to the concept of earlier times in history & looks at community life. The Historic Communities Series is beautifully designed, presenting information in two-page spreads through lively text, a multitude of color photographs, & detailed sketches. The books provide a close-up look at each topic, with step-

by-step explanations of how tools & processes work. They are excellent for preparing young children for visits to historic sites & provide good follow-up material.
Publisher Provided Annotation.

—Tools & Gadgets. 1991. 14.95 (ISBN 0-86505-508-4); pap. 7.95 (ISBN 0-86505-488-6). Crabtree Pub CO.
In the old days people had to rely on tools & their own muscle power to get a job done. In TOOLS & GADGETS your students will have the opportunity to learn about the tools used by farmers, woodworkers, metalworkers, millers, & printers. They will take a close look at the gadgets found in the home, general store, doctor's office, & farm, such as cherry pitters, apple peelers, mustache cups, clock jacks, & fleams. They will be introduced to the gadgets that fascinated children long ago & have the chance to identify some mystery gadgets. This book is an excellent tool to be used before & after visits to historic communities.
Publisher Provided Annotation.

COMMUNITY LIFE–FICTION
Berridge, Celia. On My Street. Berridge, Celia, illus. LC 86-31589. 24p. (ps). 1987. 3.95 (ISBN 0-394-89163-5, Random Juv); PLB 7.99 (ISBN 0-394-88163-X). Random.
Carlson, Nancy. Loudmouth George & the New Neighbors. LC 83-7298. (Illus.). (gr. ps-3). 1983 PLB 9.95 (ISBN 0-87614-216-1). Carolrhoda Bks.
Hamilton, Dorothy. Scamp & the Blizzard Boys. Converse, James, illus. LC 79-23670. 80p. (gr. 5-9). 1980. o. p. 4.95 (ISBN 0-8361-1918-5); pap. 3.95 (ISBN 0-8361-1919-3). Herald Pr.
Hurwitz, Johanna. New Neighbors for Nora. Jeschke, Susan, illus. LC 78-12631. (gr. k-3). 1979. 11.95 (ISBN 0-688-22173-4). Morrow Jr Bks.
Levy, Elizabeth. Something Queer Is Going On. Gerstein, Mordicai, illus. 48p. (gr. 1-4). 1982. pap. 2.75 (ISBN 0-440-47974-6, YB). Dell.
Robertson, Keith. Henry Reed's Think Tank. LC 86-4070. 176p. (gr. 3-7). 1986. pap. 12.95 (ISBN 0-670-80968-3). Viking Child Bks.
Witmer, Edith. Ray's Adventures with New Neighbors. (gr. 3 up). 1981. 6.65 (ISBN 0-686-30774-7). Rod & Staff.

COMMUNITY SCHOOLS
see Schools
COMMUNITY SONGBOOKS
see Songbooks
COMPARATIVE ANATOMY
see Anatomy, Comparative
COMPARATIVE LINGUISTICS
see Language and Languages
COMPARATIVE RELIGION
see Religions
COMPLEXION
see Beauty, Personal; Cosmetics
COMPOSERS
Brownell, David. A Book of Great Composers, Bk. 1. Conkle, Nancy, illus. (gr. 7 up). 1978. pap. 3.95 (ISBN 0-88388-058-X). Bellerophon Bks.
Great Composers, Bks. 1 & 2. (ARA., Illus.). (gr. 5-12). 3.50x ea. Intl Bk Ctr.
Kendall, Catherine W. More Stories of Composers for Young Musicians. (Illus.). 340p. (Orig.). (gr. 1-10). 1985. pap. 12.95 (ISBN 0-9610878-1-1, Dist. by Ability Development Athens, Dist. by Southwestern Stringed instruments & Accessories). Toadwood Pubs.

—Stories of Composers for Young Musicians. LC 83-103936. (Illus.). 192p. (Orig.). (gr. 1-10). 1981. pap. 12.95 (ISBN 0-9610878-0-3). Toadwood Pubs.
Composers, well-known & some not-so-well known, come alive as real & believable people for children ages 6-16. Based on extensive research & study of the composers' lives & their milieu, but without use of excessive dates, pedantic factual material or musicological jargon, each story sets the emotional tone of the life of each musician, beginning with early childhood. The books are set in large

type & wide margins, with portraits of composers, a birthday calendar, & recorded sources of composers' works. "--delightful & charming introduction to the world of music composition & performance" "--gives a feel for some of the exciting common threads that run through the lives of extraordinarily gifted musicians" "--communicates the essence of a composer's life in a warmly, perceptive, quiet way" "--Vividly fleshed out each life" "--careful research has been done"--Susan Grille, music educator, SAA Journal. "Composers are introduced as children, who, like the young readers, take music lessons, have brothers & sisters, & get excited over special events. It eavesdrops on conversations between the composer as a child & his parents & draws the reader into the setting, the lifestyle, & the attitudes of the day".--Phyllis Young, Professor of Cello, American String Teachers Journal. Also available "More Stories of Composers for Young Musicians," 1985, ISBN 0-9610878-1-1.
Publisher Provided Annotation.

Lambert, Lee. Basic Library of the World's Greatest Music. (Illus.). 155p. (gr. 7 up). 1988. pap. text ed. 39.00 (ISBN 0-9621630-1-5). L Lambert.
Nichols, Janet. American Music Makers. (Illus.). 232p. (gr. 7 up). 1990. 19.95 (ISBN 0-8027-6957-8); lib. bdg. 19.85 (ISBN 0-8027-6958-6). Walker & Co.
Tomb, Eric. Early Composers. Conkle, Nancy, illus. 48p. (Orig.). (gr. 7). 1988. pap. 3.50 (ISBN 0-88388-124-1). Bellerophon Bks.
Ventura, Piero. Great Composers. Ventura, Piero, illus. 128p. 1989. 20.95 (ISBN 0-399-21746-0, Putnam). Putnam Pub Group.

COMPOSITION (ART)
see also Painting
COMPOSITION (RHETORIC)
see Rhetoric;
also names of languages with the subdivision Composition and exercises, e.g. English Language–Composition and exercises
COMPULSORY SCHOOL ATTENDANCE
see School Attendance
COMPUTER-ASSISTED INSTRUCTION
Bitter, Gary G. & Camuse, Ruth A. Using a Microcomputer in the Classroom. (gr. k-12). 1983. pap. text ed. 25.00 (ISBN 0-8359-8144-4, Reston). P-H.
Buxton, Marilyn & Buxton, Robin. PET, Vol. 3. 58p. (gr. 5-12). 1983. pap. text ed. 11.95 (ISBN 0-88193-023-7). Create Learn.
—PET, Vol. 4. 54p. (gr. 5-12). 1983. pap. text ed. 11.95 (ISBN 0-88193-024-5). Create Learn.
Buxton, Robin. Commodore 64, Vol. 1. 50p. (gr. 4-12). 1983. pap. text ed. 11.95 (ISBN 0-88193-041-5). Create Learn.
—Commodore 64, Vol. 2. 58p. (gr. 4-12). 1983. pap. text ed. 11.95 (ISBN 0-88193-042-3). Create Learn.
—PET, Vol. 1. 51p. (gr. 4-12). 1983. pap. text ed. 11.95 (ISBN 0-88193-021-0). Create Learn.
—PET, Vol. 2. 51p. (gr. 5-12). 1983. pap. text ed. 11.95 (ISBN 0-88193-022-9). Create Learn.
—PET, Vol. 5. 72p. (gr. 6-12). 1984. pap. text ed. 11.95 (ISBN 0-88193-025-3). Create Learn.
Buxton, Robin & Buxton, Marilyn. Commodore 64, Vol. 3. 59p. (gr. 5-12). 1983. pap. text ed. 11.95 (ISBN 0-88193-043-1). Create Learn.
—Commodore 64, Vol. 4. 59p. (gr. 5-12). 1983. pap. text ed. 11.95 (ISBN 0-88193-044-X). Create Learn.
Levine, Janice R. Microcomputers in Elementary & Secondary Education: A Guide to Resources. 94p. (gr. k-12). 1983. 3.75 (ISBN 0-937597-06-6, IR-65). ERIC Clear.
Pantiel, Mindy & Petersen, Becky. Kids, Teachers, & Computers: A Guide to Computers in the Elementary School. (Illus.). 176p. 1984. pap. text ed. 25.00 (ISBN 0-13-515420-0); pap. text ed. 16.95 (ISBN 0-13-515396-4). P-H.
Preschool Skills. (Illus.). 32p. (ps). 1985. 3.95 (ISBN 0-394-87702-0). Random.
Schwartz, L. Classroom Computer Companion. (gr. 3-6). 1985. 9.95 (ISBN 0-88160-126-8, LW 255). Learning Wks.
Shadow Lawn Press Staff & Birnes, William J. Arco Computer Preparation for the SAT. (gr. 9 up). 1984. Boxed set incl. book, two computer diskettes & instr's. manual. 69.95 (ISBN 0-668-05996-6). Arco.
Taitt, Henry A. Beginning Projects for Adults. 45p. (Prog. Bk.). (gr. 10 up). 1983. pap. text ed. 11.95 (ISBN 0-88193-121-7). Create Learn.

—Beginning Projects for Junior High. 46p. (gr. 7-9). 1983. pap. text ed. 11.95 (ISBN 0-88193-111-X). Create Learn.
Taitt, Jennifer. IBM, Vol. 1. 55p. (gr. 4-12). 1983. pap. text ed. 11.95 (ISBN 0-88193-031-8). Create Learn.
—IBM, Vol. 2. 54p. (gr. 4-12). 1983. pap. text ed. 11.95 (ISBN 0-88193-032-6). Create Learn.
—IBM, Vol. 3. 51p. (gr. 5-12). 1983. pap. text ed. 11.95 (ISBN 0-88193-033-4). Create Learn.
—IBM, Vol. 4. 66p. (gr. 5-12). 1983. pap. text ed. 11.95 (ISBN 0-88193-034-2). Create Learn.
Taitt, Kathy. Apple, Vol. 1. 59p. (gr. 4-12). 1983. pap. text ed. 11.95 (ISBN 0-88193-001-6). Create Learn.
—Apple, Vol. 2. 61p. (gr. 4-12). 1983. pap. text ed. 11.95 (ISBN 0-88193-002-4). Create Learn.
—Apple, Vol. 3. 55p. (gr. 5-12). 1983. pap. text ed. 11.95 (ISBN 0-88193-003-2). Create Learn.
—Apple, Vol. 4. 57p. (gr. 5-12). 1983. pap. text ed. 11.95 (ISBN 0-88193-004-0). Create Learn.
—Apple, Vol. 5. 57p. (gr. 6-12). 1983. pap. text ed. 11.95 (ISBN 0-88193-005-9). Create Learn.
—Apple, Vol. 6. 68p. (gr. 6-12). 1984. pap. text ed. 11.95 (ISBN 0-88193-006-7). Create Learn.
COMPUTER CONTROL
see Automation
COMPUTER CRIMES
Perry, Robert L. Computer Crime. LC 85-26635. 72p. (gr. 4-9). 1986. PLB 10.40 (ISBN 0-531-10113-4). Watts.
COMPUTER ENGINEERING
Davies. Inside the Chip. Round, Grahm, illus. (gr. 6 up). 1984. pap. 3.95 (ISBN 0-86020-729-3). EDC.
COMPUTER GAMES
Best of the Nintendo Comics Systems. 1990. 19.98 (ISBN 0-7924-5529-0). BDD Promo Bk.
Best of the Super Mario Brothers. 1990. 19.98 (ISBN 0-7924-5530-4). BDD Promo Bk.
McCrary, Donald R. Conquering Zelda: The Unauthorized Guide. LC 90-81642. 1990. pap. 7.95 (ISBN 0-87455-239-7). Compute Pubns.
COMPUTER GRAPHICS
Bailey, Harold J., et al. Commodore LOGO: Activities for Exploring Turtle Graphics. (Illus.). 320p. (gr. 5-8). 1984. pap. 14.95 (ISBN 0-89303-376-6). Brady Bks.
Baldwin, Margaret & Pack, Gary. Computer Graphics. 96p. (gr. 6-8). 1984. lib. bdg. 10.40 (ISBN 0-531-04704-0). Watts.
Captain Comal's Staff. Cartridge Graphics & Sound. Hejndorf, Frank, illus. 64p. (Orig.). (gr. 6 up). 1984. pap. 6.95 (ISBN 0-928411-02-8). Comal Users.
Duck, Mike. Using Computer Graphics: Hangman. (gr. 4 up). 1984. 12.40 (ISBN 0-531-03483-6). Watts.
Kettelkamp, Larry. Computer Graphics: How it Works, What it Does. LC 88-38924. (Illus.). 144p. (gr. 7 up). 1989. 12.95 (ISBN 0-688-07504-5). Morrow Jr Bks.
Masterson, Richard. Exploring Careers in Computer Graphics. (gr. 7-12). 1990. 12.95 (ISBN 0-8239-1149-7). Rosen Group.
Petty, Kate. Pictures. West, C. & Barwick, T., illus. LC 85-81979. 32p. (gr. k-6). 1986. lib. bdg. 10.40 (ISBN 0-531-17018-7, Gloucester Pr). Watts.
—Puzzles. West, C. & Barwick, T., illus. LC 85-81980. 32p. (gr. k-6). 1986. lib. bdg. 10.40 (ISBN 0-531-17019-5, Gloucester Pr). Watts.
Reide, Anne M. Coach's Clipboards. (Illus.). 306p. (Orig.). (gr. 5-8). 1986. 10.95 (ISBN 0-931983-02-9, BCLTXT-3). Basic Comp Lit.
Sabato, Olive. An Easy Guide for Creating Computer Graphics in the Elementary Schools, Videocassette - Glenville School Computer Graphics. Tucker, Dorothy, ed. Dunlap, Susan, intro. by. (Illus.). 36p. (gr. 5-6). 1987. pap. 19.95 lesson plan (ISBN 0-942475-06-2); videocassette 39.95, (ISBN 0-942475-05-4). ArtsAmerica.
Skelton, Mindy. Graphics Primer. Schmidt, Wayne, illus. 84p. (Orig.). (gr. 6 up). 1984. pap. 14.95 (ISBN 0-928411-04-4). Comal Users.
Stevens, Lawrence. Computer Graphics Basics. Seiden, Art, illus. LC 84-6826. 48p. (gr. 3-7). 1984. 9.95 (ISBN 0-13-164054-2). P-H.
Tatchell. Computer Graphics. Round, illus. 48p. (gr. 6up). 1984. pap. 3.95 (ISBN 0-86020-739-0). EDC.
COMPUTER INPUT-OUTPUT EQUIPMENT
Herda, D. J. Computer Peripherals. LC 85-7617. (Illus.). 84p. (gr. 5-8). 1985. PLB 10.40 (ISBN 0-531-10036-7). Watts.
COMPUTER LITERACY
Here are entered works on the ability to use and understand computers, including their capabilities, applications, and social implications, in order to function in a computer-based society.
Sodano, Dominick, et al. Computer Literacy & Use. (gr. 4-12). 1983. pap. text ed. 3.25 (ISBN 0-9611246-0-1). Ed Activities.
COMPUTER PROGRAMMING
see Programming (Electronic Computers)
COMPUTER SOFTWARE
see Programming (Electronic Computers)
COMPUTERS
Use for works on modern electronic computers developed after 1945. Works on calculating machines and mechanical computers made before 1945 are entered under Calculating Machines.
see also Calculating Machines; Electronic Data Processing; Information Storage and Retrieval Systems
Aliaga, Barbara. Keyboarding for Kids. (Illus.). 96p. (Orig.). (gr. 1-6). 1985. pap. 7.95 (ISBN 0-88908-606-0, 9538). ISC Pr.

Ardley, Neil. Using the Computer. 32p. (gr. 4-6). 1983. PLB 11.90 (ISBN 0-531-04518-8). Watts.

Asimov, Isaac. How Did We Find Out about Computers? Wool, David, illus. LC 83-40401. 64p. (gr. 5 up). 1984. lib. bdg. 11.85 (ISBN 0-8027-6533-5). Walker & Co.

August, B. Alan. How to Use Lotus 1-2-3. Rinehart, Janice S., ed. Janzen, Dale, illus. 63p. (gr. 9 up). 1983. guide & tapes 119.00 (ISBN 0-917792-23-8). FlipTrack.

Ault, Rosalie S. BASIC Programming for Kids. LC 83-12773. (Illus.). 192p. (gr. 5 up). 1983. 10.95 (ISBN 0-685-06975-3); pap. 9.95 (ISBN 0-395-34920-6). HM.

Bailey, Harold J., et al. Commodore LOGO: Activities for Exploring Turtle Graphics. (Illus.). 320p. (gr. 5-8). 1984. pap. 14.95 (ISBN 0-89303-376-6). Brady Bks.

Baldwin, Margaret & Pack, Gary. Computer Graphics. 96p. (gr. 6-8). 1984. lib. bdg. 10.40 (ISBN 0-531-04704-0). Watts.

Bartoletti, Susan & Lisandrelli, Elaine. Easy Writer: Student Worksheets, Level G. Gompper, Gail, illus. 38p. (Orig.). (gr. 7-9). 1986. pap. text ed. 14.95 (ISBN 0-913935-37-9). ERA-CCR.

—Easy Writer: Student Worksheets, Level H. (Illus.). 38p. (Orig.). (gr. 8-10). 1986. pap. text ed. 14.95 (ISBN 0-913935-38-7). ERA-CCR.

BASIC for Elementary Grades. (gr. 4 up). 1982. write for info. tchr's. guide (ISBN 0-89525-273-2); write for info. 5 filmstrips; Incl. filmstrips & 5 cassettes. tchr's. guide 149.00 (ISBN 0-685-08664-X). Ed Activities.

Berger, Melvin. Computers: A Question & Answer Book. LC 85-47530. 112p. (gr. 5 up). 1985. PLB 12.89 (ISBN 0-690-04480-1, Crowell Jr Bks). HarpC Child Bks.

—Computers in Your Life. LC 80-2452. (Illus.). 128p. (gr. 5 up). 1981. PLB 12.89 (ISBN 0-690-04101-2, Crowell Jr Bks). HarpC Child Bks.

Berke, Tina. Ten (& More) Interesting Uses for Your Home Computer. Collier, Cynthia & Lingham, Gretchen, eds. Verougstraete, Randy & Mozzini, Lisa, illus. 156p. (Orig.). 1990. pap. text ed. 7.95 (ISBN 0-945776-08-X). Comptr Pub Enterprises.

Berliner, Larry & Berliner, Susan. ReWriter, Bk. I. Gompper, Gail, illus. 38p. (Orig.). (gr. 5 up). 1985. pap. text ed. 17.95 ea. Bk. I, gr. 5-8 & high school sp. needs (ISBN 0-913935-28-X). Bk. II, gr. 6-9 & high school sp. needs (ISBN 0-913935-29-8). ERA-CCR.

Bertrand, Armand L., Jr. How to Start Understanding the Computer. LC 83-90306. (Illus.). 208p. (Orig.). (gr. 7 up). 1986. pap. 12.95 (ISBN 0-912447-02-8). Eclectical.

Bitter, Gary G. & Camuse, Ruth A. Using a Microcomputer in the Classroom. (gr. k-12). 1983. pap. text ed. 25.00 (ISBN 0-8359-8144-4, Reston). P-H.

Bly, Janet. Hawaiian Computer Mystery. Turnaugh, Paul, illus. 124p. (Orig.). (gr. 4-8). 1985. pap. 3.95 (ISBN 0-89191-954-6, 59543, Chariot Bks). Cook.

Bonnet, Robert L. Computers: Forty-Nine Science Fair Projects. (Illus.). 160p. (gr. 4-7). 1990. 16.95 (ISBN 0-8306-7524-8, 3524); pap. 9.95 (ISBN 0-8306-3524-6). TAB Bks.

Boren, Sharon. An Apple for Kids. rev. ed. 90p. (gr. 3-8). 1983. pap. 15.95 (ISBN 0-88056-120-3); Apple Wkbk. for kids 9.95 (ISBN 0-88056-119-X, Dist. by Weber Systems). Weber Systems.

Boren, Sharon, et al. An Atari for Kids. 148p. (gr. 3-8). 1984. pap. 15.95 (ISBN 0-88056-123-8, Dist. by Weber Systems). Weber Systems.

Boy Scouts of America. Computers. (Illus.). 80p. (gr. 6-12). 1984. pap. 1.85 (ISBN 0-8395-3338-1, 3338). BSA.

Buxton, Marilyn. Beginning Projects for Children. Harrison, Gaye, illus. 47p. (gr. 4-7). 1983. pap. text ed. 11.95 (ISBN 0-88193-101-2). Create Learn.

—Intermediate Projects for Children. Harrison, Gaye, illus. 60p. (gr. 5-7). 1983. pap. text ed. 11.95 (ISBN 0-88193-103-9). Create Learn.

Buxton, Marilyn & Buxton, Robin. PET, Vol. 3. 58p. (gr. 5-12). 1983. pap. text ed. 11.95 (ISBN 0-88193-023-7). Create Learn.

—PET, Vol. 4. 54p. (gr. 5-12). 1983. pap. text ed. 11.95 (ISBN 0-88193-024-5). Create Learn.

—VIC-20, Vol. 4. 63p. (gr. 5-12). 1983. pap. text ed. 11.95 (ISBN 0-88193-064-4). Create Learn.

Buxton, Marilyn & Buxton, Tammy. TI 99-4A, Vol. 3. 65p. (gr. 5-12). 1983. pap. text ed. 11.95 (ISBN 0-88193-053-9). Create Learn.

—TI 99-4A, Vol. 4. 45p. (gr. 5-12). 1983. pap. text ed. 11.95 (ISBN 0-88193-054-7). Create Learn.

Buxton, Robin. Commodore 64, Vol. 1. 50p. (gr. 4-12). 1983. pap. text ed. 11.95 (ISBN 0-88193-041-5). Create Learn.

—Commodore 64, Vol. 2. 58p. (gr. 4-12). 1983. pap. text ed. 11.95 (ISBN 0-88193-042-3). Create Learn.

—Commodore 64, Vol. 5. 66p. (gr. 6-12). 1984. pap. text ed. 11.95 (ISBN 0-88193-045-8). Create Learn.

—Commodore 64, Vol. 6. 76p. (gr. 6-12). 1984. pap. text ed. 11.95 (ISBN 0-88193-046-6). Create Learn.

—PET, Vol. 1. 51p. (gr. 4-12). 1983. pap. text ed. 11.95 (ISBN 0-88193-021-0). Create Learn.

—PET, Vol. 2. 51p. (gr. 5-12). 1983. pap. text ed. 11.95 (ISBN 0-88193-022-9). Create Learn.

—PET, Vol. 5. 72p. (gr. 6-12). 1984. pap. text ed. 11.95 (ISBN 0-88193-025-3). Create Learn.

—PET, Vol. 6. 56p. (gr. 6-10). 1984. pap. text ed. 11.95 (ISBN 0-88193-026-1). Create Learn.

—VIC-20, Vol. 1. 51p. (gr. 4-12). 1983. pap. text ed. 11.95 (ISBN 0-88193-061-X). Create Learn.

—VIC-20, Vol. 2. 59p. (gr. 4-12). 1983. pap. text ed. 11.95 (ISBN 0-88193-062-8). Create Learn.

—VIC-20, Vol. 3. 59p. (gr. 5-12). 1983. pap. text ed. 11.95 (ISBN 0-88193-063-6). Create Learn.

Buxton, Robin & Buxton, Marilyn. Commodore 64, Vol. 3. 59p. (gr. 5-12). 1983. pap. text ed. 11.95 (ISBN 0-88193-043-1). Create Learn.

—Commodore 64, Vol. 4. 59p. (gr. 5-12). 1983. pap. text ed. 11.95 (ISBN 0-88193-044-X). Create Learn.

Buxton, Tammy. TI 99-4A, Vol. 1. 54p. (gr. 4-12). 1983. pap. text ed. 11.95 (ISBN 0-88193-051-2). Create Learn.

—TI 99-4A, Vol. 2. 53p. (gr. 4-12). 1983. pap. text ed. 11.95 (ISBN 0-88193-052-0). Create Learn.

Captain Comal's Staff. Cartridge Graphics & Sound. Hejndorf, Frank, illus. 64p. (Orig.). (gr. 6 up). 1984. pap. 6.95 (ISBN 0-928411-02-8). Comal Users.

Cassidy, Pat & Close, Jim. Kids, BASIC & the Coleco Adam. (Illus.). 200p. 1984. 17.95 (ISBN 0-13-515446-4). P-H.

Cattoche, Robert J. Computers for the Disabled. LC 86-9184. (Illus.). 96p. (gr. 5-8). 1986. PLB 10.40 (ISBN 0-531-10212-2). Watts.

CES Industries, Inc. Staff. Ed-Lab Experiment Manual: CES 6010 Microwave Training System. (Illus., Orig.). (gr. 9-12). 1984. pap. write for info. (ISBN 0-86711-083-X). CES Industries.

—Ed-Lab Experiment Manual: CES 6016 Telephone Modem. (Illus., Orig.). (gr. 9-12). 1984. pap. write for info. (ISBN 0-86711-085-6). CES Industries.

Computer Design VI. 1989. pap. 1.99 (ISBN 0-394-82369-9). Random.

Computer Design V2. 1989. pap. 1.99 (ISBN 0-394-82370-2). Random.

Computer Design V3. 1989. pap. 1.99 (ISBN 0-394-82371-0). Random.

Crumbaugh, Lee F. How to Use Multiplan. Rinehart, Janice S., ed. Janzen, Dale, illus. 70p. (gr. 7 up). 1983. wkbk. & tapes 89.00 (ISBN 0-917792-20-3). FlipTrack.

Cutler, C. Practice Your BASIC. Reed, Naomi, illus. 48p. (gr. 6 up). 1983. PLB 10.96 (ISBN 0-88110-142-7); pap. 3.95 (ISBN 0-86020-743-9). EDC.

Darling, David. Computers at Home: Today & Tomorrow. Swofford, Jeanette, illus. LC 85-25420. 80p. (gr. 5 up). 1986. lib. bdg. 11.95 (ISBN 0-87518-314-X, Dillon). Macmillan Child Grp.

—Fast, Faster, Fastest: The Story of Supercomputers. Swofford, Jeanette, illus. LC 85-24539. 80p. (gr. 5 up). 1986. lib. bdg. 11.95 (ISBN 0-87518-316-6, Dillon). Macmillan Child Grp.

—Inside Computers: Hardware & Software. LC 85-25411. (Illus.). 80p. (gr. 5 up). 1986. lib. bdg. 11.95 (ISBN 0-87518-312-3, Dillon). Macmillan Child Grp.

—The Microchip Revolution. Swofford, Jeanette, illus. LC 85-24538. 80p. (gr. 5 up). 1986. lib. bdg. 11.95 (ISBN 0-87518-313-1, Dillon). Macmillan Child Grp.

—Robots & the Intelligent Computer. Swofford, Jeanette, illus. LC 85-25369. 80p. (gr. 5 up). 1986. lib. bdg. 11.95 (ISBN 0-87518-315-8, Dillon). Macmillan Child Grp.

Davies. Inside the Chip. Round, Grahm, illus. (gr. 6 up). 1984. pap. 3.95 (ISBN 0-86020-729-3). EDC.

Davies, H. & Whaton, M. Better BASIC. (Illus.). 48p. (gr. 6 up). 1983. lib. bdg. 10.96 (ISBN 0-88110-139-7); pap. 3.95 (ISBN 0-86020-733-1). EDC.

D'Ignazio, Fred. Small Computers. LC 80-85049. (gr. 9 up). 1981. 11.90 (ISBN 0-531-04269-3). Watts.

—The Star Wars Question & Answer Book about Computers. Barr, Ken, illus. LC 82-19030. 64p. (gr. 4-8). 1983. lib. bdg. 7.99 (ISBN 0-394-95686-9). Random.

D'Ignazio, Fred & Wold, Allen L. The Science of Artificial Intelligence. 96p. (gr. 5 up). 1984. lib. bdg. 10.40 (ISBN 0-531-04703-2). Watts.

Duck, Mike. Using Computer Graphics: Hangman. (gr. 4 up). 1984. 12.40 (ISBN 0-531-03483-6). Watts.

Dudley, Art. Word Processing Basics: An Introduction for Young People. Petronella, Michael, illus. LC 84-22315. 48p. (gr. 4-9). 1985. 9.95 (ISBN 0-13-963513-0). P-H.

Duling, Gretchen A. Creative Problem Solving for the Fourth Little Pig. Zilliox, Elaine, illus. 28p. (Orig.). (gr. 4-6). 1984. 6.50 (ISBN 0-88047-043-7, 8412). DOK Pubs.

Egertson, Eric. Developing Computer Skills: Operating Principles for Apple II, IIe & IIGs. 212p. (Orig.). (gr. 7-10). 1989. pap. text ed. 14.95 (ISBN 0-8134-2791-6); 2.95 (ISBN 0-8134-2792-4). Inter Print Pubs.

Elting, Mary. The Answer Book about Computers. Barnes-Murphy, Rowan, illus. (gr. 3-7). 1984. pap. 2.95 (ISBN 0-448-13803-4, G&D). Putnam Pub Group.

Encyclopedia of Computers & Electronics. (Illus.). 144p. (gr. 4 up). 1989. Repr. 14.95 (ISBN 0-02-689200-6). Checkerboard Pr.

Epstein, Lawrence. Exploring Careers in Computer Sales. Rosen, Roger, ed. 64p. (gr. 7-12). 1990. lib. bdg. 12.95 (ISBN 0-8239-0667-1). Rosen Group.

Feeman, Jeff & Feeman, Maryellen. Beginning with BASIC: Beginning Computer Skills. Fowler, Christopher, illus. 64p. (gr. 4-6). 1984. wkbk. 6.95 (ISBN 0-88724-028-3, CD-9040). Carson-Dellos.

—Computer Terms-Hardware. Rittenour, Gary & Fowler, Christopher, illus. 32p. (gr. 3up). 1984. pap. 1.98 (ISBN 0-88724-100-X, CD-9043). Carson-Dellos.

Feeman, Maryellen & Feeman, Jeff. Computer Terms-Software. Fowler, Christopher & Rittenour, Gary, illus. 32p. (gr. 2 up). 1984. pap. 1.98 (ISBN 0-88724-101-8, CD-9044). Carson-Dellos.

—Computer Terms-Word Processing. Rittenour, Gary & Fowler, Christopher, illus. 32p. (gr. 2 up). 1984. pap. 1.98 (ISBN 0-88724-102-6, CD9045). Carson-Dellos.

—People & Computers. Rittenour, Gary & Fowler, Christopher, illus. 32p. (gr. 5 up). 1984. pap. 1.98 (ISBN 0-88724-103-4, CD-9046). Carson-Dellos.

—What Computers Can Do. Rittenour, Gary & Fowler, Christopher, illus. 32p. (gr. 2 up). 1984. pap. 1.98 (ISBN 0-88724-104-2, CD-9047). Carson-Dellos.

First Grade Skills. (Illus.). 32p. (gr. 1). 1985. wkbk. 3.95 (ISBN 0-394-87708-X). Random.

Fry, Edward B. Computer Keyboarding for Children. rev. ed. (gr. 3-6). 1984. pap. text ed. 8.95x (ISBN 0-8077-2754-7). Tchrs Coll.

Gardenier, Turkan K. Songs for Computing & Marching: Adapted from Turkish Melodies. LC 89-90942. (Illus.). (gr. 7-12). 1989. 20.00 (ISBN 0-685-29043-3, 0007). Teka Trends.

Graham, Ian. Computer Games. (gr. 5-9). 1982. pap. 3.95 (ISBN 0-86020-681-5, Usborne-Hayes); PLB 10.96 (ISBN 0-88110-010-2). EDC.

Greene, Laura. Computer Pioneers. LC 84-20864. (Illus.). 96p. (gr. 4 up). 1985. lib. bdg. 10.40 (ISBN 0-531-04906-X). Watts.

Guaraldo, Richard & Zaker, Susan M. Marvel Super Heroes Computer Fun Book I. (Illus.). 96p. (gr. 4-9). 1984. pap. 7.95 (ISBN 0-917657-05-5, Parachute Pr Bks). D I Fine.

—Marvel Super Heroes Computer Fun Book II. (Illus.). 96p. (gr. 4-9). 1984. pap. 7.95 (ISBN 0-917657-06-3, Parachute Pr Bks). D I Fine.

Harbin, Carey E. Fay's New Computer. (Illus.). 30p. (Orig.). (ps-1). 1990. pap. text ed. 2.95 (ISBN 0-918995-03-5). Voc-Offers.

Hargrove, Jim. Microcomputers at Work. LC 84-1715. (Illus.). 48p. (gr. k-4). 1984. lib. bdg. 14.60 (ISBN 0-516-01726-8). Childrens.

Haugo, John E. Introduction to Microcomputers: Apple Set. (Illus.). 40p. (gr. 4-6). 1982. Set. 71.92 (ISBN 0-07-079115-5). McGraw.

—Introduction to Microcomputers: TRS-80 Model III. (Illus.). 40p. (gr. 4-6). 1982. 71.92 (ISBN 0-07-079221-6). McGraw.

Hellman, Hal. Computer Basics. Tvaryanas, Alphonse, illus. LC 82-21483. 48p. (gr. 3-7). 1983. 9.95 (ISBN 0-13-164574-9). P-H.

—Computer Basics. Seiden, Art, illus. 48p. (Orig.). (gr. 3-7). 1986. pap. 5.95 (ISBN 0-13-165697-X). P-H.

Herda, D. J. Computer Maintenance. LC 84-21882. (Illus.). 72p. (gr. 4 up). 1985. lib. bdg. 10.40 (ISBN 0-531-04905-1). Watts.

—Computer Peripherals. LC 85-7617. (Illus.). 84p. (gr. 5-8). 1985. PLB 10.40 (ISBN 0-531-10036-7). Watts.

—Microcomputers. (Illus.). 96p. (gr. 5 up). 1984. lib. bdg. 10.40 (ISBN 0-531-04730-X). Watts.

Hurley, L. ZX-81 TS-1000: Programming for Young Programmers. (Illus.). 96p. (gr. 9up). 1983. pap. text ed. 9.95 (ISBN 0-07-031449-7, BYTE Bks). McGraw.

Hyde, Margaret O. Artificial Intelligence. rev. ed. LC 85-20573. (Illus.). 128p. (gr. 5-12). 1986. PLB 17.95 (ISBN 0-89490-124-9). Enslow Pubs.

Jacobsen, Karen. Computers. LC 81-38451. (Illus.). 48p. (gr. k-4). 1982. PLB 14.60 (ISBN 0-516-01617-2). Childrens.

Jespersen, James & Fitz-Randolph, Jane. Rams, Roms & Robots: The Inside Story of Computers. Hiscock, Bruce, illus. LC 84-3001. 160p. (gr. 7 up). 1984. 13.95 (ISBN 0-689-31063-3, Atheneum Child Bk). Macmillan Child Grp.

Kemnitz, T. M. & Mass, Lynne. Kids Working with Computers: Acorn BASIC. (gr. 2-6). 1984. 4.99 (ISBN 0-89824-086-7). Trillium Pr.

—Kids Working with Computers: Commodore LOGO. (gr. 2-6). 1985. 4.99 (ISBN 0-89824-093-X). Trillium Pr.

—Kids Working with Computers: IBM LOGO. (gr. 2-6). 1985. 4.99 (ISBN 0-89824-094-8). Trillium Pr.

Kemnitz, Thomas M. & Mass, Lynne. Kids Working with Computers: An Apple LOGO Manual. Schlendorf, Lori, illus. 58p. (gr. 4-7). 1983. pap. 4.99 (ISBN 0-89824-073-5). Trillium Pr.

—Kids Working with Computers: The Atari BASIC Manual. Schlendorf, Lori, illus. 48p. (gr. 4-7). 1983. pap. 4.99 (ISBN 0-89824-062-X). Trillium Pr.

—Kids Working with Computers: The Commodore BASIC Manual. Schlendorf, Lori, illus. 48p. (gr. 4-7). 1983. pap. 4.99 (ISBN 0-89824-060-3). Trillium Pr.

—Kids Working with Computers: The IBM BASIC Manual. Schlendorf, Lori, illus. 48p. (gr. 4-7). 1983. pap. 4.99 (ISBN 0-89824-063-8). Trillium Pr.

Kemnitz, Thomas M. & Romanowich, Barabara. Buckfang's Primary LOGO Activity Cards: Commodore & Apple Terrapin. 32p. (gr. k-3). 1985. pap. text ed. 12.99 (ISBN 0-89824-118-9). Trillium Pr.

Kemnitz, Thomas M. & Romanowich, Barbara. Buckfang's Primary LOGO Activity Cards: Apple & IBM LOGO. 32p. (gr. k-3). 1985. pap. text ed. 12.99 (ISBN 0-89824-117-0). Trillium Pr.

Kemntz, T. M. & Mass, Lynne. Kids Working with Computers: TRS-80 Color LOGO. 1984. 4.95 (ISBN 0-89824-078-6). Trillium Pr.

Kerbo, Ronal C. Caves. LC 81-4514. (Illus.). 48p. (gr. 3 up). 1981. PLB 15.93 (ISBN 0-516-07638-8); pap. 4.95 (ISBN 0-516-47638-6). Childrens.

Kidd, Clark & Kidd, Kathy. Compute's IBM PC & PCjr Games for Kids. 384p. (Orig.). 1984. pap. 14.95 (ISBN 0-942386-49-3). Compute Pubns.

Kumbaraci, Turkan & Gardenier, George H. Computer Models: Statistical Methods: Games & Songs. Gardenier, Turhan K., illus. LC 89-90944. 19p. (gr. 1-8). 1989. Incl. manipulatives. 20.00 (ISBN 0-685-29040-9, 0004). Teka Trends.

Lambert, Richard. LOGO & More for the Commodore 64. (Illus.). 128p. (gr. 5 up). 1984. pap. 9.95 (ISBN 0-88056-348-6). Weber Systems.

Lampton, Christopher. CD-ROMS. (Illus.). 96p. (gr. 4-9). 1987. PLB 10.40 (ISBN 0-531-10378-1). Watts.

—How to Create Computer Games. LC 85-26635. 72p. (gr. 4-9). 1986. lib. bdg. 10.40 (ISBN 0-531-10120-7). Watts.

—The Micro Dictionary. (gr. 5 up). 1984. 11.90 (ISBN 0-531-04840-3). Watts.

Lear, Peter. Computer Play. Migliore, Ron, illus. 48p. (gr. 1-5). 1985. pap. 3.95 (ISBN 0-88625-087-0). Durkin Hayes Pub.

—Computers. (Illus.). 32p. (gr. 1-5). 1985. pap. 3.95 (ISBN 0-88625-083-8). Durkin Hayes Pub.

—What Else You Can Do with Your Micro Computer. Horvath, Margaret, illus. 63p. (gr. 4-9). 1984. PLB 14.25 (ISBN 0-88625-078-1). Durkin Hayes Pub.

LeGros, Lucy C. Square One. 41p. (gr. k-2). 1988. tchr's ed. 4.95 (ISBN 0-937306-08-8); 16.95 (ISBN 0-937306-09-6). Creat Res NC.

Mackie, Dean & Mackie, David. BASIC. Migliore, Ron, illus. 48p. (gr. 1-5). 1985. pap. 3.95 (ISBN 0-88625-085-4). Durkin Hayes Pub.

Markle, Sandra. Computer Tutor: An Introduction to Computers. Armstrong, Bev, illus. 64p. (gr. 4-8). 1981. pap. 5.95 (ISBN 0-88160-042-3, LW 227). Learning Wks.

—Computer Tutor Junior. Armstrong, Bev, illus. 48p. (gr. 1-4). 1982. pap. 5.95 (ISBN 0-88160-094-6, LW 120). Learning Wks.

Martin, Dianne & Heller, Rachelle. Bible Basic: Beginner. Ostendorf, Ned, illus. 64p. (gr. 5 up). 1986. 5.95 (ISBN 0-87403-051-X, 3191). Standard Pub.

Mass, Lynne. Kids Working with Computers: The Texas Instruments LOGO Manual. Schlendorf, Lori, illus. 64p. (gr. 4-7). 1983. pap. 4.99 (ISBN 0-89824-074-3). Trillium Pr.

Menges, Patricia A. How to Operate the IBM PC XT-AT. Rinehart, Janice S., ed. Janzen, Dale, illus. 68p. (gr. 5 up). 1985. incl. quick ref. guide & 4 tapes 119.00 (ISBN 0-917792-24-6). FlipTrack.

Mostoller, Dwight E. & Campbell, Margaret F. Ready-to-Use Computer Literacy Activities Kits, Level I. 64p. (gr. 4-6). 1987. student wkbk. 5.95 (ISBN 0-317-66399-2); tchr's. manual 24.95 (ISBN 0-13-762022-5). P-H.

—Ready-to-Use Computer Literacy Activities Kits Level II. 64p. (gr. 7-10). 1987. student wkbk. 5.95 (ISBN 0-317-66401-8); tchr's. manual 24.95 (ISBN 0-13-762048-9). P-H.

Murphy, Linda. Computer Entrepreneurs: People Who Built Successful Businesses Around Computers. Berke, Tina, ed. Verougstraete, Randy, contrib. by. 128p. (Orig.). 1990. pap. text ed. 7.95 (ISBN 0-945776-14-4). Comptr Pub Enterprises.

Nelson, Bonnie E. Science & Computer Activities for Children 3 to 9 Years Old. 2nd, rev. ed. (Illus.). 146p. (gr. k-3). 1988. 28.00x (ISBN 0-931642-21-3). Lintel.

Orsetti, Marion. The Computer Zone. LC 87-42912. 44p. (ps-2). 1988. 8.95 (ISBN 1-55523-111-X). Winston-Derek.

Pantiel, Mindy & Petersen, Becky. Kids, Teachers, & Computers: A Guide to Computers in the Elementary School. (Illus.). 176p. 1984. pap. text ed. 25.00 (ISBN 0-13-515420-0); pap. text ed. 16.95 (ISBN 0-13-515396-4). P-H.

Perry, Robert L. Computer Crime. LC 85-26635. 72p. (gr. 4-9). 1986. PLB 10.40 (ISBN 0-531-10113-4). Watts.

Petty, Kate. Games. West, David, illus. LC 85-70953. 32p. (gr. k-6). 1985. lib. bdg. 10.40 (ISBN 0-531-17008-X, Gloucester Pr). Watts.

Potter. Computer Controlled Robots. Gower, illus. 48p. (gr. 5-8). 1985. PLB 10.96 (ISBN 0-88110-213-X, Pub. by Usborne). EDC.

Preschool Skills. (Illus.). 32p. (ps). 1985. 3.95 (ISBN 0-394-87702-0). Random.

Quiggle, Kevin. COMAL Library of Functions & Procedures. (Illus.). 71p. (Orig.). (gr. 6 up). 1984. pap. 14.95 (ISBN 0-928411-03-6). Comal Users.

Rajaraman, Dharma. Computer: A Child's Play. 120p. 1989. pap. text ed. 11.95 (ISBN 0-9615336-9-2). Silicon Pr.

Rathbone, R. Andrew. The Computer Gamer's Bible. Berke, Tina & Lingham, Gretchen, eds. Verougstraete, Randy, illus. 200p. (Orig.). 1991. pap. text ed. 8.95 (ISBN 0-945776-17-9). Comptr Pub Enterprises.

Reffin & Smith. Computer Programming. (gr. 5-9). 1982. (Usborne-Hayes); PLB 10.96 (ISBN 0-88110-007-2). EDC.

Rego, Paul. Computer Encounters...of the First Kind: "What the Beginner Should Know Before Buying a Computer" (Illus.). 54p. (Orig.). (ps up). 1988. pap. 14.95 (ISBN 0-945876-00-9). Insight Data.

—Computer Encounters...of the Fourth Kind: "What the Beginner Should Know When Exploring the Apple II" Rego, Paul, illus. 139p. (Orig.). (ps up). 1988. pap. 29.95 (ISBN 0-945876-03-3). Insight Data.

—Computer Encounters...of the Second Kind: "What the Beginner Should Know After Buying a Computer" (Illus.). 84p. (Orig.). (ps up). 1988. pap. 32.95 (ISBN 0-945876-01-7). Insight Data.

—Computer Encounters...of the Third Kind: "What the Beginner Should Know When Programming the Apple II" (Illus.). 126p. (Orig.). (ps up). 1988. pap. 29.95 (ISBN 0-945876-02-5). Insight Data.

Reide, Anne M. Coach's Clipboards. (Illus.). 306p. (Orig.). (gr. 5-8). 1986. 10.95 (ISBN 0-931983-02-9, BCLTXT-3). Basic Comp Lit.

Richman, Ellen. Spotlight on Computer Literacy. (gr. 6-8). 1984. pap. 14.00 (ISBN 0-07-480653-X). McGraw.

Sabin, Francene. Computers. Veno, Joseph, illus. LC 84-2708. 32p. (gr. 3-6). 1985. PLB 9.49 (ISBN 0-8167-0314-0); pap. text ed. 2.95 (ISBN 0-8167-0315-9). Troll Assocs.

Schuette, Kim. The Book of Adventure Games, Vol. III. 350p. (Orig.). (gr. k up). 1986. pap. 24.95 (ISBN 0-912003-65-0). Arrays-Continent.

Schwartz, L. Classroom Computer Companion. (gr. 3-6). 1985. 9.95 (ISBN 0-88160-126-8, LW 255). Learning Wks.

Sebranek, Patrick. Computer Folder. (Illus.). (gr. 7-12). 1984. pap. text ed. 0.95x (ISBN 0-9605312-9-7). Write Source.

Shadow Lawn Press Staff & Birnes, William J. Arco Computer Preparation for the SAT. (gr. 9 up). 1984. Boxed set incl. book, two computer diskettes & instr's. manual. 69.95 (ISBN 0-668-05996-6). Arco.

Shigley, Gordon. COMAL Workbook. Hejndorf, Frank, illus. 69p. (Orig.). (gr. 6 up). 1985. pap. text ed. 6.95 (ISBN 0-928411-05-2). Comal Users.

Simon, Seymour. The BASIC Book. Emberley, Barbara & Emberley, Ed E., illus. LC 85-47532. 32p. (gr. k-4). 1985. 13.95 (ISBN 0-690-04472-0, Crowell Jr Bks). HarpC Child Bks.

—The BASIC Book. Emberley, Barbara & Emberley, Ed E., illus. LC 85-42736. 32p. (gr. k-4). 1985. pap. 4.50 (ISBN 0-06-445015-5, Trophy). HarpC Child Bks.

—Bits & Bytes: A Computer Dictionary for Beginners. LC 85-42740. (Illus.). 32p. (gr. k-4). 1985. pap. 4.50 (ISBN 0-06-445014-7, Trophy). HarpC Child Bks.

—Computer Sense, Computer Nonsense. Lindblom, Steven, illus. LC 83-49492. 64p. (gr. 3-7). 1984. (Lipp Jr Bks); (Lipp Jr Bks). HarpC Child Bks.

—How to Talk to Your Computer. Emberley, Ed E. & Emberley, Barbara, illus. LC 84-45337. 32p. (gr. k-4). 1985. 13.95 (ISBN 0-690-04449-6, Crowell Jr Bks); PLB 12.89 (ISBN 0-690-04450-X, Crowell Jr Bks). HarpC Child Bks.

—Meet the Computer. Emberley, Ed E. & Emberley, Barbara, illus. LC 84-45338. 32p. (gr. k-4). 1985. 13.95 (ISBN 0-690-04447-X, Crowell Jr Bks). HarpC Child Bks.

—Meet the Computer. Emberley, Barbara & Emberley, Ed E., illus. LC 84-48533. 32p. (gr. k-4). 1985. pap. 4.50 (ISBN 0-06-445011-2, Trophy). HarpC Child Bks.

—Turtle Talk: A Beginner's Book of Logo. Emberley, Barbara & Emberley, Ed E., illus. LC 85-47890. 32p. (gr. 1-4). 1986. pap. 4.50 (ISBN 0-06-445051-1, Trophy). HarpC Child Bks.

Skelton, Mindy. Graphics Primer. Schmidt, Wayne, illus. 84p. (Orig.). (gr. 6 up). 1984. pap. 14.95 (ISBN 0-928411-04-4). Comal Users.

Smith, Ruffin B. Computers. 32p. (gr. 5-9). 1981. (Usborne-Hayes); PLB 10.96 (ISBN 0-88110-002-1); pap. 3.95 (ISBN 0-86020-542-8). EDC.

Snyder, Gerald S. Let's Talk about Computers. LC 72-91739. (Illus.). (gr. 3-6). 1973. 5.95 (ISBN 0-8246-0152-1). Jonathan David.

Snyder, Thomas F. & O'Neill, Martha. Community Search Apple Set. Cullinan, Dorothy K. & Podgorski, Mary E., illus. (gr. 4-12). 1982. Set. 219.76 (ISBN 0-07-079006-X). McGraw.

—Community Searchbook. Cullinan, Dorothy K. & Podgorski, Mary E., illus. 32p. (gr. 4 up). 1982. pap. text ed. 8.08 reorders (ISBN 0-07-059463-5). McGraw.

Spencer, Donald D. Computer Awareness Book. 3rd ed. 32p. (gr. 4-6). 1990. pap. 3.25 (ISBN 0-89218-099-4, NO. 1094). Camelot Pub.

—Discover Computers. LC 88-6044. 240p. (gr. 6-9). 1988. pap. 14.95 (ISBN 0-89218-121-4, NO. 3083); tchr. resource bk. 19.95 (ISBN 0-89218-123-0, NO. 3084); student wkbk. 6.95 (ISBN 0-89218-122-2, NO. 3085). Camelot Pub.

—Exploring the World of Computers. LC 82-4116. 102p. (gr. 4-6). 1982. 6.95 (ISBN 0-89218-055-2, NO. 1110); pap. 2.95 (ISBN 0-89218-054-4, NO. 1134). Camelot Pub.

—Understanding Computers. 2nd ed. LC 87-27738. 272p. (gr. 7 up). 1988. pap. 16.95 (ISBN 0-89218-092-7, NO. 3025); tchr's. manual 15.95x (ISBN 0-89218-118-4, NO. 3031); student wkbk. 6.95 (ISBN 0-89218-119-2, NO. 3034); test bank 12.95 (ISBN 0-89218-120-6, NO. 3035). Camelot Pub.

—What Computers Can Do. 2nd ed. LC 81-21664. 256p. (gr. 9 up). 1982. 6.95x (ISBN 0-89218-043-9, 1003). Camelot Pub.

Spencer, Jean. Exploring Careers As a Computer Technician. rev. ed. Rosen, Ruth, ed. (gr. 7-12). 1989. PLB 12.95 (ISBN 0-8239-0994-8). Rosen Group.

Stankowich, Mimi. A Child's Guide to Computers, 4 vols. Taylor, Karen & Arkle, Dave, illus. 32p. (ps-3). 1984. 3.95 ea. Bk. 1 (ISBN 0-916881-00-8, ALP701). Bk. 2 (ISBN 0-916881-01-6, ALP702). Bk. 3 (ISBN 0-916881-02-4, ALP703). Bk. 4 (ISBN 0-916881-03-2, ALP704). Advan Learning.

Stedman, Robert E. & Cosgrove, R. Commodore 64 BASIC for Kids. (Illus.). 352p. (gr. 5-8). 1984. pap. 12.95 (ISBN 0-89303-378-2). Brady Bks.

Stevens, Lawrence. Computer Graphics Basics. Seiden, Art, illus. LC 84-6826. 48p. (gr. 3-7). 1984. 9.95 (ISBN 0-13-164054-2). P-H.

Stockley, C. & Watts, L. Computer Jargon. Newton, Martin, illus. 48p. (gr. 6 up). 1983. lib. bdg. 10.96 (ISBN 0-88110-141-9); pap. 3.95 (ISBN 0-86020-737-4). EDC.

Suid, Murray. The Teacher-Friendly Computer Book. 96p. (gr. 2-6). 1984. 8.95 (ISBN 0-912107-19-7). Monday Morning Bks.

Taitt, Henry A. Advanced Projects for Junior High. 51p. (Prog. Bk.). (gr. 7-9). 1984. pap. text ed. 11.95 (ISBN 0-88193-115-2). Create Learn.

—Beginning Projects for Adults. 45p. (Prog. Bk.). (gr. 10 up). 1983. pap. text ed. 11.95 (ISBN 0-88193-121-7). Create Learn.

—Beginning Projects for Junior High. 46p. (gr. 7-9). 1983. pap. text ed. 11.95 (ISBN 0-88193-111-X). Create Learn.

—Intermediate Projects for Junior High. 46p. (gr. 7-9). 1983. pap. text ed. 11.95 (ISBN 0-88193-113-6). Create Learn.

Taitt, Henry A. & Taitt, Jennifer. Atari, Vol. 3. 47p. (gr. 5-12). 1983. pap. text ed. 11.95 (ISBN 0-88193-073-3). Create Learn.

—Atari, Vol. 4. 51p. (gr. 5-12). 1983. pap. text ed. 11.95 (ISBN 0-88193-074-1). Create Learn.

—TRS-80, Vol. 3. 53p. (gr. 5-12). 1983. pap. text ed. 11.95 (ISBN 0-88193-013-X). Create Learn.

—TRS-80, Vol. 4. 56p. (gr. 5-12). 1983. pap. text ed. 11.95 (ISBN 0-88193-014-8). Create Learn.

—TRS-80, Vol. 5. 57p. (gr. 6-12). 1983. pap. text ed. 11.95 (ISBN 0-88193-015-6). Create Learn.

—TRS-80, Vol. 6. 54p. (gr. 6-12). 1984. pap. text ed. 11.95 (ISBN 0-88193-016-4). Create Learn.

Taitt, Henry A. & Taitt, Kathy. TRS-80, Vol. 1. 53p. (gr. 4-12). 1983. pap. text ed. 11.95 (ISBN 0-88193-011-3). Create Learn.

—TRS-80, Vol. 2. 56p. (gr. 4-12). 1983. pap. text ed. 11.95 (ISBN 0-88193-012-1). Create Learn.

Taitt, Jennifer. IBM, Vol. 5. 53p. (gr. 6-12). 1984. pap. text ed. 11.95 (ISBN 0-88193-035-0). Create Learn.

—IBM, Vol. 6. 65p. (gr. 6-12). 1984. pap. text ed. 11.95 (ISBN 0-88193-036-9). Create Learn.

Taitt, Nancy. Atari, Vol. 1. 55p. (gr. 4-12). 1983. pap. text ed. 11.95 (ISBN 0-88193-071-7). Create Learn.

—Atari, Vol. 2. 64p. (Prog. Bk.). (gr. 4-12). 1984. pap. text ed. 11.95 (ISBN 0-88193-072-5). Create Learn.

Tatchell. Computer Graphics. Round, illus. 48p. (gr. 6up). 1984. pap. 3.95 (ISBN 0-86020-739-0). EDC.

Tatchell & Cutter, N. Practical Things to Do with a Microcomputer. Round, Graham, illus. 48p. (gr. 6 up). 1983. pap. 3.95 (ISBN 0-86020-731-5); PLB 10.96 (ISBN 0-88110-140-0). EDC.

Thomas, David A. The Math-Computer Connection. LC 86-10992. (Illus.). 128p. (gr. 7-12). 1986. PLB 11.90 (ISBN 0-531-10231-9). Watts.

Time-Life Books Editors. The Human Body. 128p. (gr. 7 up). 1989. 14.99 (ISBN 0-8094-6062-9); lib. bdg. 23.93 (ISBN 0-8094-6063-7). Time-Life.

Timms, Howard. Measuring & Computing. (Illus.). 40p. (gr. 5-9). 1989. PLB 12.40 (ISBN 0-531-17188-4). Watts.

Trainor, Timothy N. & Krasnewich, Diane. Computer Concepts & Applications. 2nd ed. LC 86-62012. (Illus.). 350p. (gr. 7-8). 1987. pap. text ed. 26.50 (ISBN 0-394-39052-0). Mitchell Pub.

Tyler, J. & Hawarth, L. Write Your Own Adventure Programs. Longworth, Mark, illus. 48p. (gr. 6 up). 1983. lib. bdg. 10.96 (ISBN 0-88110-143-5); pap. 3.95 (ISBN 0-86020-741-2). EDC.

Tyler, Jenny. Creepy Computer Games. Round, Grahm, illus. 16p. (gr. 6 up). 1984. pap. 2.95 (ISBN 0-86020-780-3). EDC.

Vuillequez, Richard J. & Veslocki, Matthew. Technology & the Computer. Gregorio, Frank, ed. Edmonds, Keith, illus. 150p. (gr. 10 up). 1990. pap. text ed. 25.00x (ISBN 0-9627537-0-X). TMC CT.

Waters. Computer Fun. Round, illus. 48p. (gr. 5-8). 1984. PLB 10.96 (ISBN 0-88110-212-1); pap. 3.95 (ISBN 0-86020-803-6). EDC.

Wicks, Keith. Working with Computers. (Illus.). 64p. (gr. 4-7). 15.95 (ISBN 0-8160-1071-4). Facts on File.

Wild, Judith & Zyskowski, Mary. Shaping LOGO on Your Apple. (Illus.). 160p. (gr. 3-8). 1984. pap. 9.95 (ISBN 0-88056-315-X). Weber Systems.

Zomberg, Paul G. Computers. LC 84-9792. (Illus.). 48p. (gr. 4-12). 1984. PLB 15.99 (ISBN 0-8172-1409-7). Raintree Pubs.

COMPUTERS, ELECTRONIC

see Computers

COMPUTERS–FICTION

Anderson, Margaret J. The Ghost Inside the Monitor. LC 89-26848. 128p. (Orig.). (gr. 3-7). 1990. lib. bdg. 11.99 (ISBN 0-679-90359-3, Bullseye Bks). Knopf.

Byars, Betsy C. The Computer Nut. LC 84-7239. 144p. (gr. 3-7). 1984. pap. 12.95 (ISBN 0-670-23548-2). Viking Child Bks.

—The Computer Nut. Byars, Guy, illus. 144p. (gr. 3-7). 1986. pap. 3.95 (ISBN 0-14-032086-5, Puffin). Puffin Bks.

Chetwin, Grace. Out of the Dark World. 160p. (gr. 6 up). 1985. 11.95 (ISBN 0-688-04272-4). Lothrop.

Fettig, Art. The Three Robots Discover Their Pos-Abilities: A Lesson in Goal Setting. Carpenter, Joe, illus. LC 84-81461. (gr. k-7). 1984. pap. 3.95 (ISBN 0-916927-00-8). Growth Unltd.

Francis, Dorothy. Computer Crime. LC 87-4190. 128p. (gr. 7 up). 1987. 12.95 (ISBN 0-525-67192-7, Lodestar Bks). Dutton Child Bks.

Haas, Dorothy. The Secret Life of Dilly McBean. LC 86-8255. 224p. (gr. 5-7). 1986. 13.95 (ISBN 0-02-738200-1, Bradbury Pr). Macmillan Child Grp.

Hoban, Lillian & Hoban, Phoebe. The Laziest Robot in Zone One. Hoban, Lillian, illus. LC 82-48613. 64p. (gr. k-3). 1985. pap. 3.50 (ISBN 0-06-444089-3, Trophy). HarpC Child Bks.

King, Buzz. Silicon Songs. 1990. 14.95 (ISBN 0-385-30087-5). Doubleday.

Leroe, Ellen. Robot Romance. LC 84-48349. 192p. (gr. 6-9). 1985. PLB 12.89 (ISBN 0-06-023746-5). HarpC Child Bks.

Marney, Dean. The Computer That Ate My Brother. 128p. (gr. 5-8). 1987. pap. 2.50 (ISBN 0-590-40267-6, Apple Paperbacks). Scholastic Inc.

—The Computer That Ate My Brother. 128p. (Orig.). (gr. 6-8). 1987. pap. 2.75 (ISBN 0-590-44005-5). Scholastic Inc.

Mister Tom. The Little Computer. Spivey, Elvera, illus. 32p. (gr. 2-4). 1978. write for info. Oddo.

Modell, Frank. Skeeter & the Computer. LC 84-1585. (Illus.). 24p. (ps-3). 1988. 11.95 (ISBN 0-688-03703-8); lib. bdg. 11.88 (ISBN 0-688-03706-2). Greenwillow.

Pantell, Dora. Miss Pickerell & the War of the Computers. (gr. 4 up). 1984. 12.90 (ISBN 0-531-04841-1). Watts.

Rosales, Michael & Sider, Eva. The Adventures of Panchito & Miguel: Panchito's Guide to Computers. Agustini, Michelle, illus. 24p. (Orig.). (gr. 1-4). 1988. pap. text ed. 4.95 (ISBN 0-929297-00-8, 301-158 (005996642)). R & S Books.

Stone, G. H. Fatal Error. LC 90-52580. 144p. (gr. 5 up). 1991. lib. bdg. 7.99 (ISBN 0-679-90587-1). Random.

Strasser, Todd. Complete Computer Popularity Contest. (gr. 4-7). 1991. pap. 3.25 (ISBN 0-440-40436-3). Dell.

COMPUTERS-PROGRAMMING
see Programming (Electronic Computers)

COMPUTING MACHINES (ELECTRONIC)
see Computers

CONCENTRATION CAMPS-FICTION

Aaron, Chester. Gideon. LC 81-48066. 192p. (gr. 7 up). 1982. (Lipp Jr Bks). HarpC Child Bks.

Uchida, Yoshiko. Journey Home. (gr. 4-8). 1982. pap. 3.95 (ISBN 0-689-70755-X, Aladdin). Macmillan Child Grp.

—Journey to Topaz. rev. ed. Carrick, Donald, illus. LC 84-70422. 160p. (gr. 4-12). 1985. pap. 7.95 (ISBN 0-916870-85-5). Creative Arts Bk.

CONCEPTION-PREVENTION
see Birth Control

CONCHOLOGY
see Mollusks; Shells

CONDORS

Schorsch, Nancy. Saving the Condor. (Illus.). 64p. (gr. 3-6). 1991. PLB 11.90 (ISBN 0-531-20010-8). Watts.

Westberg Peters, Lisa. Condor. LC 89-28270. (Illus.). 48p. (gr. 5 up). 1990. 10.95 (ISBN 0-89686-515-0, Crestwood Hse). Macmillan Child Grp.

CONDUCT OF LIFE
see Behavior

Ensor, Sara. Reaching Out. (Illus.). 112p. (Orig.). (gr. 4-5). 1988. pap. text ed. 9.00x (ISBN 1-85239-504-4); tchr's. ed. 5.00 (ISBN 1-85239-505-2). Grosvenor USA.

Waite, Michael P. Eddy & His Amazing Pet. LC 88-16961. (Illus.). 112p. (gr. 3-7). 1988. pap. 4.49 (ISBN 1-55513-641-9). Cook.

CONDUCTING
Here are entered works on orchestral conducting or a combination of orchestral and choral conducting.
see also Bands (Music); Orchestra

CONFECTIONERY

Barkin, Carol & James, Elizabeth. Happy Valentines Day. LC 87-35812. (Illus.). 96p. (gr. 4-7). 1988. 12.95 (ISBN 0-688-06796-4); PLB 12.88 (ISBN 0-688-06797-2). Lothrop.

Blair, Cynthia. The Lollipop Plot. 144p. (Orig.). (gr. 4 up). 1990. pap. 3.95 (ISBN 0-449-70377-0, Juniper). Fawcett.

—The Popcorn Project. (gr. 5 up). 1989. pap. 2.95 (ISBN 0-449-70309-6, Juniper). Fawcett.

Neimark, Jill. Ice Cream. Milone, Karen, illus. LC 84-10915. (gr. 2-6). 1986. 11.95 (ISBN 0-8038-3440-3); pap. 11.95 (ISBN 0-8038-9290-X). Hastings.

Peeples, H. I. Bubble Gum. Payne, Tom, illus. 24p. (gr. 2-5). 1989. 6.95 (ISBN 0-8092-4409-8, Calico Bks). Contemp Bks.

Rice, Karen. Does Candy Grow on Trees? Cohen, Sharon, illus. LC 83-40407. 32p. (gr. 2-5). 1984. 9.95 (ISBN 0-8027-6555-6). Walker & Co.

CONFEDERATION OF AMERICAN COLONIES
see U. S.-History-1783-1809

CONFLICT, SOCIAL
see Social Conflict

CONFUCIUS AND CONFUCIANISM

Johnson, Spencer. The Value of Honesty: The Story of Confucius. Pileggi, Stephen, illus. LC 78-4351. 64p. (gr. k-6). 1979. 9.95 (ISBN 0-916392-36-8, Pub. by Value Communications). Oak Tree Pubns.

CONGO (LEOPOLDVILLE)

Congo. (Illus.). (gr. 5 up). 1990. 14.95 (ISBN 0-7910-1271-9). Chelsea Hse.

CONGRESS-U. S.
see U. S. Congress

CONJURING
see Magic

CONNECTICUT

Carole Marsh Connecticut Books, 31 bks. Set. 638.45 (ISBN 0-7933-1281-7). Gallopade Pub Group.

Carpenter, Allan. Connecticut. LC 79-4173. (Illus.). 96p. (gr. 4 up). 1979. PLB 19.93 (ISBN 0-516-04107-X). Childrens.

Kagan, Myrna. Vision in the Sky: New Haven's Early Years, 1638-1783. LC 89-2762. (Illus.). xiv, 161p. (gr. 4-8). 1989. lib. bdg. 15.00 (ISBN 0-208-02246-5, Linnet). Shoe String.

Macourek, Milos. Max & Sally & the Phenomenal Phone. Herrmann, Dagmar, tr. from CZE. Born, Adolf, illus. LC 88-33871. 82p. (gr. 2-4). 1989. 16.95 (ISBN 0-922984-00-X). Wellington IL.

Marsh, Carole. Avast, Ye Slobs! Connecticut Pirate Trivia. (Illus.). (gr. 3-12). 1990. PLB 19.95 (ISBN 0-7933-0232-3); pap. 14.95 (ISBN 0-7933-0231-5); computer disk 29.95 (ISBN 0-7933-0233-1). Gallopade Pub Group.

—The Beast of the Connecticut Bed & Breakfast. (Illus.). (gr. 3-12). 1990. PLB 19.95 (ISBN 0-7933-1429-1); pap. 14.95 (ISBN 0-7933-1430-5); computer disk 29.95 (ISBN 0-7933-1431-3). Gallopade Pub Group.

—Connecticut & Other State Greats (Biographies) (Illus.). (gr. 3-12). 1990. PLB 19.95 (ISBN 1-55609-547-3); pap. 14.95 (ISBN 1-55609-546-5); computer disk 29.95 (ISBN 0-7933-1437-2). Gallopade Pub Group.

—Connecticut Bandits, Bushwackers, Outlaws, Crooks, Devils, Ghosts, Desperadoes & Other Assorted & Sundry Characters! (Illus.). (gr. 3-12). 1990. PLB 19.95 (ISBN 0-7933-0214-5); pap. 14.95 (ISBN 0-7933-0213-7); computer disk 29.95 (ISBN 0-7933-0215-3). Gallopade Pub Group.

—Connecticut Classic Christmas Trivia: Stories, Recipes, Activities, Legends, Lore & More! (Illus.). (gr. 3-12). 1990. PLB 19.95 (ISBN 0-7933-0217-X); pap. 14.95 (ISBN 0-7933-0216-1); computer disk 29.95 (ISBN 0-7933-0218-8). Gallopade Pub Group.

—Connecticut Coastales. (Illus.). (gr. 3-12). 1990. PLB 19.95 (ISBN 1-55609-543-0); pap. 14.95 (ISBN 1-55609-542-2); computer disk 29.95 (ISBN 0-7933-1433-X). Gallopade Pub Group.

—The Connecticut Hot Air Balloon Mystery. (Illus.). (gr. 2-9). 1990. 19.95 (ISBN 0-7933-2372-X); pap. 14.95 (ISBN 0-7933-2373-8); computer disk 29.95 (ISBN 0-7933-2374-6). Gallopade Pub Group.

—Connecticut "Jography" A Fun Run Thru Our State! (Illus.). (gr. 3-12). 1990. PLB 19.95 (ISBN 1-55609-538-4); pap. 14.95 (ISBN 1-55609-537-6); computer disk 29.95 (ISBN 0-7933-1423-2). Gallopade Pub Group.

—Connecticut Kid's Cookbook: Recipes, How-to, History, Lore & More! (Illus.). (gr. 3-12). 1990. PLB 19.95 (ISBN 0-7933-0226-9); pap. 14.95 (ISBN 0-7933-0225-0); computer disk 29.95 (ISBN 0-7933-0227-7). Gallopade Pub Group.

—Connecticut Quiz Bowl Crash Course! (Illus.). (gr. 3-12). 1990. PLB 19.95 (ISBN 1-55609-545-7); pap. 14.95 (ISBN 1-55609-544-9); computer disk 29.95 (ISBN 0-7933-1432-1). Gallopade Pub Group.

—Connecticut School Trivia: An Amazing & Fascinating Look at Our State's Teachers, Schools & Students! (Illus.). (gr. 3-12). 1990. PLB 19.95 (ISBN 0-7933-0223-4); pap. 14.95 (ISBN 0-7933-0222-6); computer disk 29.95 (ISBN 0-7933-0224-2). Gallopade Pub Group.

—Connecticut Silly Basketball Sportsmysteries, Vol. I. (Illus.). (gr. 3-12). 1990. PLB 19.95 (ISBN 0-7933-0220-X); pap. 14.95 (ISBN 0-7933-0219-6); computer disk 29.95 (ISBN 0-7933-0221-8). Gallopade Pub Group.

—Connecticut Silly Basketball Sportsmysteries, Vol. II. (Illus.). (gr. 3-12). 1990. PLB 19.95 (ISBN 0-7933-1580-8); pap. 14.95 (ISBN 0-7933-1581-6); computer disk 29.95. Gallopade Pub Group.

—Connecticut Silly Football Sportsmysteries, Vol. I. (Illus.). (gr. 3-12). 1990. PLB 19.95 (ISBN 1-55609-541-4); pap. 14.95 (ISBN 1-55609-540-6); computer disk 29.95 (ISBN 0-7933-1425-9). Gallopade Pub Group.

—Connecticut Silly Football Sportsmysteries, Vol. II. (Illus.). (gr. 3-12). 1990. PLB 19.95 (ISBN 0-7933-1426-7); pap. 14.95 (ISBN 0-7933-1427-5); computer disk 29.95 (ISBN 0-7933-1428-3). Gallopade Pub Group.

—Connecticut Silly Trivia! (Illus.). (gr. 3-12). 1990. PLB 19.95 (ISBN 1-55609-536-8); pap. 14.95 (ISBN 1-55609-535-X); computer disk 29.95 (ISBN 0-7933-1422-4). Gallopade Pub Group.

—Connecticut's (Most Devastating!) Disasters & (Most Calamitous!) Catastrophies! (Illus.). (gr. 3-12). 1990. PLB 19.95 (ISBN 0-7933-0211-0); pap. 14.95 (ISBN 0-7933-0210-2); computer disk 29.95 (ISBN 0-7933-0212-9). Gallopade Pub Group.

—The Hard-to-Believe-But-True! Book of Connecticut History, Mystery, Trivia, Legend, Lore, Humor & More. (Illus.). (gr. 3-12). 1990. PLB 19.95 (ISBN 0-7933-0229-3); pap. 14.95 (ISBN 0-7933-0228-5); computer disk 29.95 (ISBN 0-7933-0230-7). Gallopade Pub Group.

—If My Connecticut Mama Ran the World! (Illus.). (gr. 3-12). 1990. PLB 19.95 (ISBN 0-7933-1434-8); pap. 14.95 (ISBN 0-7933-1435-6); computer disk 29.95 (ISBN 0-7933-1436-4). Gallopade Pub Group.

—Let's Quilt Connecticut & Stuff It Topographically! (Illus.). (gr. 3-12). 1990. PLB 19.95 (ISBN 1-55609-539-2); pap. 14.95; computer disk 29.95 (ISBN 0-7933-1424-0). Gallopade Pub Group.

Turner Program Services, Inc. Staff & Clark, James I. Connecticut. 48p. (gr. 3 up). 1985. PLB 17.32 (ISBN 0-86514-426-5); pap. text ed. 9.27 (ISBN 0-86514-501-6). Raintree Pubs.

CONNECTICUT-FICTION

White, Glenn E. Folk Tales of Connecticut, Vol. I. Zangari, Rose M., illus. 61p. (Orig.). (gr. k-12). 1977. pap. 6.50 (ISBN 0-9611926-0-7). GEF White.

—Folk Tales of Connecticut, Vol. II. Zangari, Rose M., illus. 62p. (gr. k-12). 1981. pap. 6.50 (ISBN 0-9611926-1-5). GEF White.

CONNECTICUT-HISTORY

Fradin, Dennis. Connecticut: In Words & Pictures. Wahl, Richard & Meents, Len, illus. LC 79-23292. 48p. (gr. 2-5). 1980. PLB 15.93 (ISBN 0-516-03907-5); pap. 4.95 (ISBN 0-516-43907-3). Childrens.

Kagan, Myrna. Vision in the Sky: New Haven's Early Years, 1638-1783. LC 89-2762. (Illus.). xiv, 161p. (gr. 4-8). 1989. lib. bdg. 15.00 (ISBN 0-208-02246-5, Linnet). Shoe String.

Swindler, William F. & Frech, Mary, eds. Chronology & Documentary Handbook of the State of Connecticut, No. 7. LC 73-533. 139p. (gr. 9-12). 1973. PLB 8.50 (ISBN 0-379-16132-X). Oceana.

CONQUISTADORES
see America-Discovery and Exploration

CONRAD, JOSEPH, 1857-1924

Reilly, Jim. Conrad. (Illus.). 112p. (gr. 7 up). 1990. lib. bdg. 18.60 (ISBN 0-86593-021-X); lib. bdg. 13.95s.p. (ISBN 0-685-36351-1). Rourke Corp.

CONSERVATION OF ENERGY
see Force and Energy

CONSERVATION OF FORESTS
see Forests and Forestry; Natural Resources

CONSERVATION OF NATURAL RESOURCES
see also Natural Resources

Ancona, George. Riverkeeper. (gr. 4-7). 1990. 13.95 (Mcmillan Child Bk). Macmillan Child Grp.

Atwood, Margaret. For the Birds. Bianchi, John, illus. 56p. (gr. 8-12). 1991. pap. 9.95 (ISBN 0-920668-32-1). Firefly Bks Ltd.
Samantha is turned into a bird by her neighbor, who herself becomes a crow, & together they migrate from Canada to a tropical forest in South America. Along the way Samantha learns how urbanization, hunters, rainforest destruction & other problems threaten the birds' ecosystem &, by extension, our own. Sidebar suggestions present a number of practical activities, from the creation of a bird garden in a schoolyard to how to make your own backyard more hospitable to birds. Margaret Atwood, Canada's best-known writer whose most recent works include The Handmaid's Tale & Cat's Eye, is a long-time environmental activist. She is also an avid birdwatcher. Funds from her royalties on this book will be donated to a number of environmental causes. John Bianchi, illustrator of The Dingles, has won acclaim for both his humorous & nature illustrations.
Publisher Provided Annotation.

Boy Scouts of America. Conservation Skill Book. (Illus.). 32p. (gr. 3-4). 1979. pap. 1.50x (ISBN 0-8395-6584-4); Nineteen Eighty, 12p. tchr's. guide 0.50 (ISBN 0-8395-8224-2); Nineteen Eighty, 24p. Troop leader's can-do-kit 0.50 (ISBN 0-8395-8204-8). BSA.

Facklam, Margery. And Then There Was One: The Mysteries of Extinction. Johnson, Pamela, illus. (gr. 3-6). 1990. write for info. Sierra.

Foreman, Michael. One World. (Illus.). 32p. (gr. 2-5). 1991. 14.95 (ISBN 1-55970-108-0). Arcade Pub Inc.

Gates, Richard. Conservation. LC 81-38482. (Illus.). 48p. (gr. k-4). 1982. PLB 14.60 (ISBN 0-516-01618-0). Childrens.

Golland, Derrick. Pressures on the Countryside. (Illus.). 48p. (gr. 7-12). 1986. 19.95 (ISBN 0-85219-625-3, Pub. by Batsford England). Trafalgar Sq.

Goodman, Billy. Camelot World: A Kid's Guide to How to Save the Planet. 128p. (Orig.). 1990. pap. 2.95 (ISBN 0-380-76041-X, Camelot). Avon.

Greene, Carol. Caring for Our People. (Illus.). 32p. (gr. 1-4). 1991. PLB 12.95 (ISBN 0-89490-355-1). Enslow Pubs.

Hare, Tony. Habitat Destruction. (Illus.). 32p. (gr. 5-8). 1991. PLB 11.90 (ISBN 0-531-17307-0, Gloucester Pr). Watts.

—Recycling. (Illus.). 32p. (gr. k-4). 1991. PLB 11.40 (ISBN 0-531-17352-6, Gloucester Pr). Watts.

Hawkes, Nigel. Toxic Waste & Recycling. (Illus.). 32p. (gr. 5-8). 1991. PLB 11.90 (ISBN 0-531-17359-3, Gloucester Pr). Watts.

Hogan, Paula. Dying Oceans. LC 91-10216. (Illus.). 32p. (gr. 3-4). 1991. PLB 12.95 (ISBN 0-8368-0476-7). Gareth Stevens Inc.

—Fragile Mountains. LC 91-2019. (Illus.). 32p. (gr. 3-4). 1991. PLB 12.95 (ISBN 0-8368-0475-9). Gareth Stevens Inc.

Hoyt, Erich. Extinction A-Z. LC 90-23701. 128p. (gr. 6 up). 1991. PLB 17.95 (ISBN 0-89490-325-X). Enslow Pubs.

James, Barbara. Conserving the Polar Regions. LC 90-46064. (Illus.). 48p. (gr. 4-9). 1990. PLB 18.60 (ISBN 0-8114-2393-X). Steck-V.

Javna, John. Fifty Simple Things Kids Can Do to Save the Earth. 156p. 1990. pap. 6.95 (ISBN 0-8362-2301-2). Andrews & McMeel.

Kalman, Bobbie. Buried in Garbage. 32p. (gr. 3-4). 1991. lib. bdg. 14.95 (ISBN 0-86505-424-X); pap. text ed. 7.95 (ISBN 0-86505-454-1). Crabtree Pub Co.
Unfortunately, when garbage is thrown away, it does not disappear. As the population grows by leaps & bounds, we are running out of landfill sites & are literally becoming buried in our own garbage. This thorough book examines the reasons why garbage has become such a worldwide problem & looks at the ways it is being disposed of today. Children will gain an understanding of what a landfill site is, how incineration harms the environment, & the urgency we face in dealing with our garbage problem. Loaded with information & activites, THE CRABTREE ENVIRONMENT SERIES will inform, guide & motivate your students into working towards a cleaner environment.
Publisher Provided Annotation.

—Reducing, Reusing, & Recycling. (Illus.). 32p. (gr. 3-4). 1991. lib. bdg. 14.95 (ISBN 0-86505-426-6); pap. text ed. 7.95 (ISBN 0-86505-456-8). Crabtree Pub Co.
Almost every community around the country has a program for collecting materials that can be broken down to make new & useful products. But recycling is only one solution to the problem of mounting garbage. Children should be made aware that reducing their garbage is the most important goal in helping to save their environment. Helpful information, stories, & activities will empower children to take action concerning their environment.
Publisher Provided Annotation.

Lambert, David. Pollution & Conservation. (Illus.). 32p. (gr. 1-6). 1986. PLB 8.99 (ISBN 0-531-18060-3, Pub. by Bookwright). Watts.

Patent, Dorothy H. The Challenge of Extinction. LC 90-3288. (Illus.). 64p. (gr. 6 up). 1991. PLB 15.95 (ISBN 0-89490-268-7). Enslow Pubs.

Penny, Malcolm. Pollution & Conservation. Furstinger, Nancy, ed. (Illus.). 48p. (gr. 5-8). 1988. PLB 14.98 (ISBN 0-382-09792-0). Silver Burdett Pr.

Pringle, Laurence. Living Treasure: Saving Earth's Threatened Biodiversity. 64p. (gr. 3 up). 1991. 12.95 (ISBN 0-688-07709-9); PLB 12.88 (ISBN 0-688-07710-2, Morrow Jr Bks). Morrow Jr Bks.

Santrey, Laurence. Conservation & Pollution. Maccabe, Richard, illus. LC 84-2703. 32p. (gr. 3-6). 1985. PLB 9.49 (ISBN 0-8167-0260-8); pap. text ed. 2.95 (ISBN 0-8167-0261-6). Troll Assocs.

Schwartz, Linda. Earth Book for Kids: Activities to Help Heal the Environment. Armstrong, Beverly, illus. 184p. (Orig.). (gr. 3-7). 1990. pap. 9.95x (ISBN 0-88160-195-0, LW 289). Learning Wks.

Seidenberg, Steven. Ecology & Conservation. LC 89-11281. (Illus.). 64p. (gr. 4-6). 1990. PLB 12.95 (ISBN 0-8368-0005-2). Gareth Stevens Inc.

CONSERVATION OF THE SOIL
see Soil Conservation
CONSERVATION OF WATER
see Water Conservation
CONSERVATION OF WILD LIFE
see Wild Life–Conservation
CONSTELLATIONS
see Astronomy; Stars
CONSTITUTION
see names of countries and states with subhead constitution, e.g. U. S. Constitution–Amendments
CONSTITUTION (FRIGATE)

Richards, Norman. Story of Old Ironsides. Dunnington, Tom, illus. LC 67-20099. 32p. (gr. 2-5). 1967. PLB 13.27 (ISBN 0-516-04628-4); pap. 3.95 (ISBN 0-516-44628-2). Childrens.

CONSTITUTIONAL AMENDMENTS–U. S.
see U. S. Constitution–Amendments
CONSTITUTIONAL LAW
see also Citizenship; Civil Rights; Democracy; Political Science
also names of countries with the subdivision Constitutional Law, e.g. U. S.–Constitutional Law
CONSTRUCTION
see Architecture; Building; Engineering
CONSTRUCTION OF ROADS
see Roads
CONSUMER EDUCATION
Here are entered works on the selection and most efficient use of consumer goods and services, including methods of educating the consumer. Works on the economic theory of consumption are entered under Consumption (Economics).
see also Shopping

Boy Scouts of America. Consumer Buying. (Illus.). 64p. (gr. 6-12). 1975. pap. 1.85 (ISBN 0-8395-3387-X, 3387). BSA.

Peduzzi, Kelli. Ralph Nader: Crusader for Safe Consumer Products. Tolan, Mary, adapted by. LC 90-9924. (Illus.). 64p. (gr. 3-4). 1990. lib. bdg. 12.95 (ISBN 0-8368-0455-4). Gareth Stevens Inc.

—Ralph Nader: Crusader for Safe Consumer Products & Lawyer for Public Interest. LC 89-4282. (Illus.). 68p. (gr. 5-6). 1990. PLB 12.95 (ISBN 0-8368-0098-2). Gareth Stevens Inc.

Riekes, Linda & Ackerly, Salley M. Young Consumers. 2nd ed. (Illus.). 124p. (gr. 5-9). 1980. pap. text ed. 13.00 (ISBN 0-8299-1021-2); Tchr's. ed. 13.00 (ISBN 0-8299-1022-0). West Pub.

Schmitt, Lois. Smart Spending: A Consumer's Guide. LC 88-29524. 112p. (gr. 5-9). 1989. 11.95 (ISBN 0-684-19035-4, Scribners Young Read). Macmillan Child Grp.

Wool, John D. Buying Power, Bk. III. 64p. (gr. 3 up). 1987. pap. text ed. 3.75 (ISBN 0-88323-241-3, 173); tchr's. key 1.50 (ISBN 0-318-33410-0, 224). Pendergrass Pub.

CONSUMER GOODS
see Manufactures
CONSUMER PROTECTION

Abramowitz, Jack & Uva, Kenneth. Consumers & the Law. (gr. 7-12). 1987. pap. text ed. 3.50 (ISBN 0-89525-871-4). Ed Activities.

Walz, Michael K. & Killen, M. Barbara. The Law & Economics: Your Rights As a Consumer. (Illus.). 88p. (gr. 5 up). 1990. PLB 15.95 (ISBN 0-8225-1779-5). Lerner Pubns.

CONSUMERS' GUIDES
see Consumer Education
CONTACT LENSES
see Eyeglasses
CONTAGION AND CONTAGIOUS DISEASES
see Communicable Diseases
CONTAGIOUS DISEASES
see Communicable Diseases
CONTINENTAL DRIFT

Michel, Francois & Larvor, Yves. The Restless Earth: The Secrets of Earthquakes, Volcanoes, & Continental Drift in Three-Dimensional Moving Pictures. (Illus.). (gr. 5 up). 1990. 15.95 (ISBN 0-670-83361-4). Viking Child Bks.

Miller, Russell. Continents in Collision. (Illus.). 176p. (gr. 7 up). 1983. 18.60 (ISBN 0-8094-4326-0); lib. bdg. 24.60 (ISBN 0-8094-4325-2). Time-Life.

CONTRACEPTION
see Birth Control
CONTRACTIONS
see Ciphers
CONUNDRUMS
see Riddles
CONVICTS
see Crime and Criminals; Prisons
COOK, JAMES, 1728-1779

Blumberg, Rhoda. The Remarkable Voyages of Captain Cook. Lalicki, Barbara, ed. LC 91-11219. (Illus.). 160p. (gr. 5 up). 1991. 18.95 (ISBN 0-02-711682-4, Bradbury Pr). Macmillan Child Grp.

Haney, David. Captain James Cook & the Explorers of the Pacific. Goetzmann, William H., ed. Collins, Michael, intro. by. (Illus.). 112p. (gr. 5 up). 1992. PLB 18.95 (ISBN 0-7910-1310-3). Chelsea Hse.

Harley, Ruth. Captain James Cook. new ed. LC 78-18044. (Illus.). 48p. (gr. 4-7). 1979. PLB 9.89 (ISBN 0-89375-177-4); pap. 2.95 (ISBN 0-89375-169-3). Troll Assocs.

Hoobler, Dorothy & Hoobler, Thomas. The Voyages of Captain Cook. (Illus.). 192p. 1983. pap. 10.95 (ISBN 0-399-20975-1, Philomel). Putnam Pub Group.

Humble, Richard. The Voyages of Captain Cook. Hook, Richard, illus. 32p. (gr. 5-8). 1990. PLB 11.90 (ISBN 0-531-14066-0). Watts.

Johnson, Ann D. The Value of Boldness: The Story of Captain Cook. Pileggi, Steve, illus. 64p. (ps-6). 1986. 9.95 (ISBN 0-86679-025-X, Pub. by Value Communications). Oak Tree Pubns.

Sylvester, David W. Captain Cook & the Pacific. Reeves, Marjorie, ed. (Illus.). 92p. (gr. 7-12). 1971. pap. text ed. 4.75x (ISBN 0-582-20462-3). Longman.

COOK BOOKS
see Cookery
COOKERY
see also Baking; Bread; Confectionery; Desserts; Diet; Food; Outdoor Cookery; Sandwiches; Soups

Aber, Linda. Stuck on Cooking. 96p. (Orig.). (gr. 4 up). 1991. pap. 6.95 (ISBN 0-590-43281-8). Scholastic Inc.

Alarie, Julia & Conlon, Elizabeth. Proofing Is in the Pudding. Sussman, Ellen, ed. (Illus.). 44p. (Orig.). (gr. 3-6). 1983. pap. text ed. 5.95 (ISBN 0-933606-22-2, MS620). Monkey Sisters.

Alvarez del Real, Maria E., ed. Cocina Latino Americana. (SPA., Illus.). 304p. (Orig.). 1988. pap. 4.50x (ISBN 0-944499-44-9). Editorial Amer.

Amari, Suad. Cooking the Lebanese Way. (Illus.). 48p. (gr. 5 up). 1985. PLB 10.95 (ISBN 0-8225-0913-X). Lerner Pubns.

Anderson, Gretchen, ed. The Louisa May Alcott Cookbook. Milone, Karen, illus. 96p. (gr. 3 up). 1985. 12.95 (ISBN 0-316-03951-9). Little.

Bacon, Josephine. Cooking the Israeli Way. Wolfe, Bob, et al, illus. LC 85-18059. 48p. (gr. 5 up). 1986. PLB 10.95 (ISBN 0-8225-0912-1). Lerner Pubns.

Baker, Margaret. Food & Cooking. (Illus.). 64p. (gr. 6 up). 1979. 14.95 (ISBN 0-7136-1465-X). Dufour.

Bartlett, Virginia. Pickles & Pretzels: Pennsylvania's World of Food. LC 79-3996. 1980. pap. 7.95 (ISBN 0-8229-5308-0). U of Pittsburgh Pr.

Bates, Deborah D. Everyone's Cookbook. Bates, James F., ed. & illus. 48p. (gr. 8 up). 1988. pap. text ed. 9.95 (ISBN 0-924563-00-1). Kettle Country Pr.

Baxter, Kathleen M. Come & Get It: A Natural Foods Cookbook for Children. rev. ed. LC 81-70782. (Illus.). 128p. (ps-6). 1989. PLB 13.95 (ISBN 0-9603696-4-3); pap. 8.95 spiral bdg. (ISBN 0-9603696-3-5). Children First.

Beachy, Mary D. & Wolferman, Kristie. When Peanut Butter Is Not Enough. Flick, Deborah M., illus. 100p. (gr. 2-7). 1986. pap. 7.95 (ISBN 0-9616883-0-0). Petit Appetit.

Bell, Peg, intro. by. Batchin' It Specialties: Cooking for "1 or 2" Can Be Fun. rev. ed. LC 88-92429. 198p. (gr. 8). 1988. plastic comb bdg. 12.95 (ISBN 0-9621056-0-0). P A Bell Enterps.

Berry, Joy W. What to Do When Your Mom or Dad Says..."Make Your Breakfast & Lunch!" Kelley, Orly, ed. Bartholomew, illus. LC 83-80840. 48p. (gr. k-6). 4.98 (ISBN 0-941510-18-2). Living Skills.

Better Homes & Gardens Editors. New Junior Cookbook. rev. ed. (Illus.). 96p. (gr. 3-5). 1989. Repr. of 1979 ed. 7.95 (ISBN 0-696-01147-6). Meredith Bks.

Betty Crocker Staff, ed. Betty Crocker's New Boys & Girls Cookbook. (Illus.). 144p. 1990. comb. bdg. 9.95 (ISBN 0-13-083262-6). B Crocker.

Bisignano, Alphonse. Cooking the Italian Way. LC 82-12641. (Illus.). 48p. (gr. 5 up). 1982. PLB 10.95 (ISBN 0-8225-0906-7). Lerner Pubns.

Blanchet, Francoise & Doornekamp, Rinke. What to Do with...a Potato. LC 77-85383. (gr. 3-8). 1979. 4.95 (ISBN 0-8120-5255-2). Barron.

Bourne, Miriam A. A Day in the Life of a Chef. Jann, Gayle, illus. LC 87-13762. 32p. (gr. 4-8). 1988. PLB 11.79 (ISBN 0-8167-1115-1); pap. text ed. 2.95 (ISBN 0-8167-1116-X). Troll Assocs.

Bove, Eugene. Uncle Gene's Breadbook for Kids! Bove, Eugene, illus. 64p. (gr. 5-12). 1986. pap. 11.95 (ISBN 0-937395-00-5). Happibook Pr.

Boy Scouts of America. Cooking Skill Book. (Illus.). 32p. (gr. 6-12). 1975. pap. 1.50x (ISBN 0-8395-6585-2, 6585); tchr's. guide 0.50 (ISBN 0-8395-8225-0); troop leaders can-do kit 1977, 24pp. 0.50 (ISBN 0-8395-8205-6). BSA.

Boys & Girls Cookbook. 64p. 1988. pap. 3.95 (ISBN 0-8249-3079-7). Ideals.

Bragdon, Allen D. Cakes & Pies. Ham, Marion, ed. (Illus.). 64p. (ps up). 1985. pap. 2.50 (ISBN 0-916410-13-7). A D Bragdon.

—Candies & Goodies. Ham, Marion, ed. LC 86-2646. (Illus.). 64p. (ps up). 1985. pap. 2.50 (ISBN 0-916410-14-5). A D Bragdon.

—Gingerbread Tales. Gamon, David, et al, eds. Ringland, Carolyn, illus. 64p. (ps up). 1986. pap. 2.50 (ISBN 0-916410-17-X). A D Bragdon.

Buckman, Mary. The Animal Cookbook. (Illus.). (gr. k-2). 1982. pap. text ed. 9.95 (ISBN 1-879414-01-5). Mary Bee Creat.

—The Count & Cook Book. (Illus.). (gr. k-2). 1982. pap. text ed. 9.95 (ISBN 1-879414-00-7). Mary Bee Creat.

—The Shape & Cook Book. (Illus.). (gr. k-2). 1982. pap. text ed. 9.95 (ISBN 1-879414-02-3). Mary Bee Creat.

Burstein, Chaya M. A First Jewish Holiday Cookbook. Burstein, Chaya M., illus. (gr. 3-8). 1979. (Bonim Bks); pap. 8.95 (ISBN 0-88482-775-5, Bonim Bks). Hebrew Pub.

Chancellor, Betty. A Child's Christmas Cookbook. Obering, Kay & Nast, Thomas, illus. 40p. (Orig.). (gr. 1-8). 1969. pap. 4.00 (ISBN 0-914510-00-2). Evergreen.

Chesnel, Connie. The Rocky Mountain Cookbook. Avakian, Alexandra, photos by. (Illus.). 1989. 24.95 (ISBN 0-517-56090-9, C N Potter Bks). Crown.

Christian, Rebecca. Cooking the Spanish Way. LC 82-4709. (Illus.). 48p. (gr. 5 up). 1982. PLB 10.95 (ISBN 0-8225-0908-3). Lerner Pubns.

Chung, Okwha & Monroe, Judy. Cooking the Korean Way. (Illus.). 48p. (gr. 5 up). 1988. PLB 10.95 (ISBN 0-8225-0921-0). Lerner Pubns.

Cobb, Vicki. More Science Experiments You Can Eat. Maestro, Giulio, illus. LC 78-12732. (gr. 5 up). 1979. 12.95 (ISBN 0-397-31828-6, Lipp Jr Bks); PLB 12.89 (ISBN 0-397-31878-2, Lipp Jr Bks). HarpC Child Bks.

Cobblestone Publishing, Inc Staff. Recipes from Around the World: For Young People 8-14. (Illus.). 36p. (gr. 4-8). 1987. pap. text ed. 4.95 (ISBN 0-942389-03-4). Cobblestone Pub.

Conford, Ellen. What's Cooking, Jenny Archer? Palmisciano, Diane, illus. (gr. 2-4). 1989. 10.95 (ISBN 0-316-15254-4). Little.

Coronado, Rosa. Cooking the Mexican Way. LC 82-254. (Illus.). 48p. (gr. 5 up). 1982. PLB 10.95 (ISBN 0-8225-0907-5). Lerner Pubns.

Corum, Ann K. Easy Cooking: The Island Way. LC 81-19881. (Illus.). 120p. (Orig.). (gr. 8 up). 1982. pap. 5.95 (ISBN 0-916630-24-2). Pr Pacifica.

Corwin, Judith H. Cookie Fun. Corwin, Judith H., illus. 64p. (gr. 3 up). 1985. PLB 10.29 (ISBN 0-671-50797-4); PLB 7.71s.p.; pap. 3.71s.p. Messner.

Coyle, Rena. My First Cookbook. Joyner, Jerry, illus. LC 84-40683. 128p. (Orig.). (gr. 1-5). 1985. pap. 8.95 (ISBN 0-89480-846-X, 846). Workman Pub.

Croft, Karen. Good for Me Cookbook. (Illus.). (gr. k-5). pap. 1.95 (ISBN 0-88247-177-5). R & E Pubs.

Cuyler, Margery. All Around Pumpkin Book. McClintock, Barbara, illus. LC 79-4820. 96p. (gr. 3-7). 1980. pap. 3.95 (ISBN 0-03-056818-8). H Holt & Co.

Disney. Disney Minnie N' Me Cooking Together. 1990. 5.98 (ISBN 0-8317-2348-3). Smithmark.

Dobrin, Arnold. Peter Rabbit's Natural Foods Cookbook. Potter, Beatrix, illus. LC 76-45309. 1977. 10.95 (ISBN 0-7232-6142-3). Warne.

Domke, Lonnie. Kids Cook Too! Creative Cookery for Children & Teens. Domke, Tim, ed. LC 90-84362. (Illus.). 100p. (gr. k up). 1991. 12.95 (ISBN 0-9627795-2-0); pap. 10.95 spiral bdg. (ISBN 0-9627795-1-2). Carolina Cnslts Network.

Kids Cook Too! A neat, innovative book designed for parents & educators. A creative tool that uses cooking as a basis for learning. Loaded with delicious, simple to prepare recipes for the beginner & intermediate young chef. Large, easy to read print with one recipe per page. Includes cooking tips & charts. All recipes used are clearly labeled to indicate level usage. All of these tasty recipes use ingredients that are in the ordinary household pantry. These wonderful little recipes include tasty breakfast foods, main dishes, desserts & fun foods. A unique blend of creative talents has led L. Domke to write this fun filled educational book that we all can savor. A noted educator, L. Domke includes food preparation experiences in her work with youngsters to foster their overall development. A delightfully interesting book brings joy & laughter into all classrooms & home kitchens alike. A learn-by-doing publication that's a breeze to use! A must for every parent & educator. A vital teaching tool & a

memorable gift.
Publisher Provided Annotation.

Dooley, Norah. Everybody Cooks Rice. Thornton, Peter, illus. 32p. (ps-3). 1991. PLB 12.95 (ISBN 0-87614-412-1). Carolrhoda Bks.

Eckstein, Joan & Gleit, Joyce. Fun in the Kitchen. rev. ed. 160p. 1990. pap. 2.95 (ISBN 0-380-75919-5, Camelot). Avon.

Edge, Nellie. Kindergarten Cooks. Leitz, Pierr M., illus. LC 76-48558. 165p. (gr. k-6). 1975. pap. 9.95 (ISBN 0-918146-00-3). Peninsula WA.

Edge, Nellie & Leitz, Pierr M. Kids in the Kitchen. LC 76-48558. (Illus.). 165p. (gr. k-6). 1979. pap. 9.95 (ISBN 0-918146-18-6). Peninsula WA.

Elinsky, Stephen E. Innovations in Cooking. 2nd ed. Summy, Barbara L., illus. 85p. (gr. 7 up). 1988. pap. 17.95 (ISBN 0-9620526-0-4). Elins Laboratories.

Elliott, Allison. Humpty Dumpty Was an Egg: A Coloring Cookbook. (Illus.). 64p. (gr. k-6). 1989. 8.95x (ISBN 0-941099-03-2). Tourmaline Pub.

Emerson, Anne. Peter Rabbit's Cookery Book. Potter, Beatrix, illus. 48p. (gr. k-3). 1986. 6.95 (ISBN 0-7232-3328-4). Warne.

Feig, Barbara K. Now You're Cooking: A Guide to Cooking for Boys & Girls. Haney, Elizabeth M., illus. LC 75-10991. 144p. (gr. 7 up). 1975. pap. 4.95 (ISBN 0-916036-01-0). J B Pal.

Ferguson, David L. Cookbook for Kids: The Kids Can Cook, Too, Cookbook. Ferguson, Jane, ed. Cheney, Glenn L., illus. LC 90-86154. 56p. (Orig.). (gr. 3-6). 1991. cerlox bound 9.95 (ISBN 0-9628148-0-6). Abigail Pubns.

A unique fun, yet practical cookbook for children aged 8 to 12 written by a ten-year old boy who combines his love of sports with the joy of cooking. Recipes are kid-tested & guaranteed to assure success for children who attempt any of the recipes following simple step-by-step directions. Included are snacks, treats, beverages & main meals. Book features only child safe recipes for the blender, toaster or micro-wave oven. No hot greases, range burners or conventional oven use. The inclusion of a story line that runs through the recipes & illustrations helps to make this book both enjoyable & practical. A must for children who enjoy being in the kitchen or for children of working parents who may want to do some of their own cooking. Children enjoy the feeling of success that comes from serving completed recipes to friends, family. Author & publisher have pledged that 20% of net profits will be given to a children's charity. First printing, 2/91, Abigail Publications, 413 Superior Street, Rossford, OH 43460, (419) 666-3333.
Publisher Provided Annotation.

Forte, Imogene. Cookbook: A No Cook & Learn Book. LC 83-80962. (Illus.). 80p. (gr. k-6). 1983. pap. text ed. 3.95 (ISBN 0-86530-089-5, IP-895). Incentive Pubns.

Gattis, L. S., III. Cooking for Pathfinders: A Basic & Advanced Youth Enrichment Skill Honor Packet. (Illus.). 24p. (Orig.). (gr. 5 up). 1989. 5.00 (ISBN 0-936241-49-7). Cheetah Pub.

George, Jean C. The Wild, Wild Cookbook: A Guide for Young Wild-Food Foragers. Kessell, Walter, illus. LC 82-45187. 192p. (gr. 5 up). 1982. PLB 12.89 (ISBN 0-690-04315-5, Crowell Jr Bks). HarpC Child Bks.

Gibson, R. Kitchen Fun. (Illus.). 32p. (ps-3). Date not set. lib. bdg. 13.96 (ISBN 0-88110-456-6, Usborne); pap. 5.95 (ISBN 0-7460-0631-4). EDC.

Glovach, Linda. Little Witch's Black Magic Cookbook. Glovach, Linda, illus. (gr. 1-4). 1975. pap. 3.95 (ISBN 0-13-537936-9, Pub. by Treehouse). P-H.

Goldstein, Helen H. Kids' Cuisine. Bolch, Judy, ed. Pittman, Jackie, illus. LC 83-60306. 64p. (Orig.). (gr. k-7). 1983. pap. 5.95 (ISBN 0-935400-09-5). News & Observer.

Gustafson, Helen. Dinner's Ready, Mom. LC 86-11802. 80p. (Orig.). (gr. k-3). 1986. pap. 8.95 (ISBN 0-89087-470-0). Celestial Arts.

Haim, Nadine. The Artist's Palate. (Illus.). 128p. 1988. 35.00 (ISBN 0-8109-1873-0). Abrams.

Ham, Marion, et al. Breads & Muffins. (Illus.). 64p. (ps up). 1986. pap. 2.50 (ISBN 0-916410-12-9). A D Bragdon.

—Country Cookies. (Illus.). 64p. (ps up). 1986. pap. 2.50 (ISBN 0-916410-15-3). A D Bragdon.

—Herbs & Spices. (Illus.). 64p. (ps up). 1986. pap. 2.50 (ISBN 0-916410-18-8). A D Bragdon.

Hargittai, Magdolna. Cooking the Hungarian Way. (Illus.). 48p. (gr. 5 up). 1986. PLB 10.95 (ISBN 0-8225-0916-4). Lerner Pubns.

Harris, Nancy J. & Marmon, Roma I. Dining In. Harris, William W., illus. 224p. 1979. pap. 6.50 (ISBN 0-918544-34-3). Wimmer Bros.

Harrison, Supenn & Monroe, Judy. Cooking the Thai Way. (Illus.). 48p. (gr. 5 up). 1986. PLB 10.95 (ISBN 0-8225-0917-2). Lerner Pubns.

Hautzig, Esther. Holiday Treats. Yaroslava, illus. LC 83-9347. 96p. (gr. 3 up). 1983. 12.95 (ISBN 0-02-743350-1, Mcmillan Child Bk). Macmillan Child Grp.

Hernandez, Maria. Cocina de Abuela. (SPA.). 176p. (Orig.). 1989. pap. 2.95 (ISBN 0-929281-03-9). Best Pubs Inc.

Hill, Barbara. Cooking the English Way. LC 82-257. (Illus.). 48p. (gr. 5 up). 1982. PLB 10.95 (ISBN 0-8225-0903-2). Lerner Pubns.

Howard, Nina. Classroom Chefs. Rayl, Eleanor, illus. 96p. (gr. 2). 1981. 7.95 (ISBN 0-917206-14-2). Children Learning Ctr.

Huber, Judy. Gardening & Cooking with Children. 60p. (gr. 1-8). 1987. plastic comb. 4.95 (ISBN 0-944793-00-2); pap. 2.95 (ISBN 0-944793-01-0). Prairie Family Pubs.

Hunt, Linda & Frase, Marianne. Loaves & Fishes. LC 80-12165. (Illus.). 176p. (gr. 2-5). 1980. pap. 9.95 spiral bdg. (ISBN 0-8361-1922-3). Herald Pr.

Hunter, Gerald R. & Hoffmann, Peggy. Bake a Snake: How to Survive by Your Own Cooking. Massingill, Susan, illus. LC 81-10293. 68p. (Orig.). (gr. 1-7). 1981. 9.00 (ISBN 0-939710-10-2); pap. 4.75 (ISBN 0-939710-09-9). Meridional Pubns.

Johnson, Barbara. Cup Cooking: Individual Child-Portion Picture Recipes. 12th ed. (Illus.). (ps up). 1990. pap. 2.95 (ISBN 0-317-99815-3). Early Educators.

Johnson, Evelyne & Santoro, Christopher. A First Cookbook for Children: With Illustrations to Color. (Illus.). 48p. (Orig.). (gr. 4 up). 1983. pap. 2.95 (ISBN 0-486-24275-7). Dover.

Kaplan, Lisa. Once upon a Cook Book. Kinne, Kathy, illus. 80p. (Illus.). (gr. k-3). 1984. pap. 4.00 (ISBN 0-937730-01-7). Good Sign.

Kaufman, Cheryl. Cooking the Caribbean Way. (Illus.). 48p. (gr. 5 up). 1988. PLB 10.95 (ISBN 0-8225-0920-2). Lerner Pubns.

Keene, Carolyn. The Nancy Drew Cookbook. 160p. (gr. 4-7). 1973. 3.95 (ISBN 0-448-02856-5, G&D); PLB 4.29 (ISBN 0-448-03795-5). Putnam Pub Group.

Kenda, Margaret. Cooking Wizardry for Kids. (gr. 4-7). 1990. pap. 12.95 (ISBN 0-8120-4409-6); pap. 19.95 incl. chef's apron & hat (ISBN 0-8120-7703-2). Barron.

Kid's Recipes for Success. (Illus.). (gr. 1-6). 1991. write for info. (ISBN 0-9629736-0-2). Riviana Foods.

Kid's Recipes For Success, a cookbook by & for kids, features easy to make items for sensational breakfasts, lunches, snacks, dinners & crafts. The book also features an easy-to-read glossary & kitchen clean-up hints for parents to share with their children. To further assist Mom & Dad, each recipe is coded to indicate the amount of adult supervision & time needed. The cookbook is designed to stimulate creativity & fun in the kitchen, while building self-esteem. For every "Kid's Recipes for Success" cookbook sold a donation will be made to the March of Dimes to benefit its national campaign for healthier babies. All of the simple but delicious recipes have been submitted by children, ages 6 to 12. The recipes were all tested in Riviana's Kitchen & by a kids taste panel.
Publisher Provided Annotation.

Lansky, Vicki. Vicki Lansky's Kid's Cooking. (Illus.). (gr. k-9). 1988. pap. 4.95 (ISBN 0-318-36496-4). Scholastic Inc.

—Vicky Lansky's Kids Cooking. Tunimelly, Nancy McLean, illus. 48p. (gr. 4-6). 1987. pap. 4.95 spiral bnd. (ISBN 0-590-40624-8). Scholastic Inc.

Lemley, Virg & Lemley, Jo. Children's Cookery, Naturally. (Illus.). 57p. (gr. 1-10). 1980. pap. 3.75 (ISBN 0-931798-05-1). Wilderness Hse.

Lesley, Salley M. Cookbook Index Plus. 96p. 1979. pap. 5.95 (ISBN 0-918544-33-5). Wimmer Bros.

Little Red Riding Hood: Story & Recipes. facsimile ed. (Illus.). (ps up). 1987. pap. 2.50 (ISBN 0-916410-45-5). A D Bragdon.

Lurio, David L. More Special Recipes. Mctavish, Michele, illus. LC 84-50054. 128p. 1984. pap. 11.95 (ISBN 0-910423-01-6). Skylight.
McClenahan, Pat & Jaqua, Ida. Cool Cooking for Kids. LC 75-32841. (ps-k). 1976. pap. 7.95 (ISBN 0-8224-1614-X). Fearon Teach Aids.
Macdonald, Kate. The Anne of Green Gables Cookbook. DiLella, Barbara, illus. 48p. 1987. 11.95 (ISBN 0-19-540496-3). Oxford U Pr.
Mac Gregor, Carol. Storybook Cookbook. Cruz, Ray, illus. (gr. 3-7). pap. 1.95 (ISBN 0-13-850842-9, Pub. by Treehouse). P-H.
Madavan, Vijay. Cooking the Indian Way. (Illus.). 52p. (gr. 5 up). 1985. lib. bdg. 10.95 (ISBN 0-8225-0911-3). Lerner Pubns.
Marsh, Carole. The Kitchen House: How Yesterdays Black Women Created Todays American Foods. (gr. 3-12). 1989. PLB 19.95 (ISBN 1-55609-309-8); pap. 14.95 (ISBN 1-55609-308-X); computer disk 29.95 (ISBN 1-55609-310-1). Gallopade Pub Group.
Martel, Jane, ed. Smashed Potatoes: A Kid's Eye View of the Kitchen. LC 74-10947. 96p. (gr. 2 up). 1974. HM.
Meyer, Carolyn. Christmas Crafts. Lobel, Anita, illus. LC 74-2608. 160p. (gr. 5 up). 1974. 13.95 (ISBN 0-06-024197-7). HarpC Child Bks.
Miller, Mary & Richardson, Toni. The Merry Metric Cookbook. Miller, Mary, illus. (Orig.). (gr. k-3). 1974. pap. 4.50 (ISBN 0-918932-32-7). Activity Resources.
Montgomery, Bertha & Nabwire, Constance. Cooking the African Way. (Illus.). 48p. (gr. 5 up). 1988. PLB 10.95 (ISBN 0-8225-0919-9). Lerner Pubns.
Moore, Eva. The Great Banana Cookbook for Boys & Girls. Russo, Susan, illus. 48p. (gr. 1-4). 1983. 13.95 (ISBN 0-89919-150-9, Clarion). HM.
Moore, Marsha. The Teddy Bear Book. (Illus.). 165p. (ps up). 1984. 24.95 (ISBN 0-916410-09-9). A D Bragdon.
Munsen, Sylvia. Cooking the Norwegian Way. LC 82-259. (Illus.). 48p. (gr. 5 up). 1982. PLB 10.95 (ISBN 0-8225-0901-6). Lerner Pubns.
Murphy, Margaret. Bears in the Kitchen. (Illus.). 64p. (ps up). 1986. pap. 2.50 (ISBN 0-916410-11-0). A D Bragdon.
—Fresh Salad Ideas. (Illus.). 64p. (ps up). 1986. pap. 2.50 (ISBN 0-916410-16-1). A D Bragdon.
Nabwire, Constance. Cooking the African Way. 1990. pap. 5.95 (ISBN 0-8225-9564-8). Lerner Pubns.
Neely, Cynthia H. & Lyerly, Elaine M. Mister Cookie Breakfast Cookbook. Lyerly, Elaine M., illus. 32p. (gr. k-4). 1986. pap. 2.50 (ISBN 0-88289-493-5). Pelican.
Nguyen, Chi & Monroe, Judy M. Cooking the Vietnamese Way. (Illus.). 48p. (gr. 5 up). 1985. PLB 10.95 (ISBN 0-8225-0914-8). Lerner Pubns.
Olmsted, Cheryl. Alphabet Cooking Cards. (gr. k-1). 1990. pap. 10.95 (ISBN 0-8224-0454-0). Fearon Teach Aids.
Osborne, Christine. Australian & New Zealand Food & Drink. LC 89-33046. (Illus.). 48p. (gr. 5-9). 1989. PLB 12.40 (ISBN 0-531-18293-2, Pub. by Bookwright Pr). Watts.
—Southeast Asian Food & Drink. (Illus.). 48p. (gr. 7-9). 1990. 12.40 (ISBN 0-531-18234-7). Watts.
Palumbo, Nancy. Rainy Days Are for Baking: Les Recettes Preferee de Penelope P'Nutt. Weaver, Judith, illus. 32p. (gr. k-6). 1989. wkbk. 5.95 (ISBN 0-927024-01-2). Crayons Pubns.
Parents Nursery School Staff. Kids Are Natural Cooks. (Illus.). (ps-6). 1974. pap. 8.95 (ISBN 0-395-18521-1, Sandpiper). HM.
—Kids Are Natural Cooks. McCrady, Lady, illus. LC 73-22054. 144p. (ps-6). 1974. Repr. of 1971 ed. 13.95 (ISBN 0-395-18508-4). HM.
Parnell, Helga. Cooking the South American Way. (Illus.). 48p. (gr. 5 up). 1991. PLB 10.95 (ISBN 0-8225-0925-3). Lerner Pubns.
Paul, Aileen. Kids' Cooking Without a Stove: A Cookbook for Young Children. rev. ed. Inouye, Carol, illus. LC 84-22230. 64p. 1985. pap. 7.95 (ISBN 0-86534-060-9). Sunstone Pr.
Pemberton, Judy. Let's Get Cooking. Anderson, Judith, illus. 103p. (Orig.). (gr. 3-12). 1984. text ed. 7.95 (ISBN 0-317-02695-X). King Fisher Pr.
Penner, Lucille. Colonial Cookbook. (Illus.). 128p. (gr. 4 up). 1976. 14.95 (ISBN 0-8038-1202-7). Hastings.
Perl, Lila. The Hamburger Book: All About Hamburgers & Hamburger Cookery. Goddard, Ragna T., illus. LC 73-7173. 128p. (gr. 5 up). 1979. 8.95 (ISBN 0-395-28921-1, Clarion). HM.
—Hunter's Stew & Hangtown Fry. Cuffari, Richard, illus. LC 77-5366. 176p. (gr. 6 up). 1979. 13.95 (ISBN 0-395-28922-X, Clarion). HM.
Pinder, Polly. Polly Pinder's Chocolate Cookbook. Pinder, Polly, illus. Search Studios Staff, photos by. (Illus.). 144p. (gr. 7 up). 1988. 24.95 (ISBN 0-85532-603-4, Pub. by Search Pr UK). Pathway Bk Serv.
Please Touch Museum Staff. Please Touch Cookbook. Brook, Bonnie, ed. (Illus.). 64p. (ps-2). 1990. pap. 6.95 spiral (ISBN 0-671-70558-X). Silver Pr.
Plotkin, Gregory & Plotkin, Rita. Cooking the Russian Way. (Illus.). 48p. (gr. 5 up). 1986. PLB 10.95 (ISBN 0-8225-0915-6). Lerner Pubns.
Poe, Margie. The No-Cooking Cookbook for Kids. (Illus.). (gr. k-6). 1985. pap. 4.95 (ISBN 0-936985-75-5, 1096A). Kidsmart.
Poskanzer, Susan C. What's It Like to Be a Chef. Pellaton, Karen E., illus. LC 89-34390. 32p. (gr. k-3). 1989. lib. bdg. 10.89 (ISBN 0-8167-1797-4); pap. text ed. 2.50 (ISBN 0-8167-1798-2). Troll Assocs.
Potter, Betty M. The Just for Kids Cookbook. Linehan, Maxene M., illus. 180p. (Orig.). (gr. 1-6). 1985. pap. 9.95 comb. bdg. (ISBN 0-913703-06-0). New Boundary Design.
Potts, Leanna K. & Potts, Evangela. Thyme for Kids. Potts, Leanna K. & Potts, Evangela, illus. 84p. (ps-8). 1990. pap. 7.95 (ISBN 0-935069-24-0). White Oak Pr.
Ransford, Lynn, et al. ABC Crafts & Cooking. (Illus.). 64p. (ps-2). 1987. wkbk. 6.95 (ISBN 1-55734-090-0). Tchr Create Mat.

Redjou, Pat C. No-Gluten Solution: Children's Cookbook. Rader, Marjie, illus. 1991. pap. write for info (ISBN 0-9626052-2-0). Rae Pub.

Robson, Denny. Cooking: Hands-on Projects. (Illus.). 32p. (gr. k-4). 1991. PLB 11.40 (ISBN 0-531-17344-5, Gloucester Pr). Watts.
Rockwell, Anne. The Mother Goose Cookie-Candy Book. LC 82-13268. (Illus.). 32p. (gr. 1-5). 1983. Random.
Rombauer, Irma S. Cookbook for Girls & Boys. (gr. 6-9). 1952. 6.95 (ISBN 0-672-50258-5, Bobbs). Macmillan.
Salaman, Maureen K. Foods That Heal. Scheer, James F., ed. Atkins, Robert, intro. by. 521p. (Orig.). 1989. pap. 19.95 (ISBN 0-913087-02-5). Statford CA.
Sayre School Staff. Yummies for Tummies. (Illus.). 96p. (gr. 4 up). 1977. pap. 4.95 (ISBN 0-918544-37-8). Wimmer Bros.
Scherie, Strom. Stuffin' Muffin: Muffin Pan Cooking for Kids. Konefal, Norma, frwd. by. (Illus.). 100p. (Orig.). (gr. 4-7). 1982. pap. 13.95 (ISBN 0-9606964-9-0). Yng Peoples Pr.
The Sesame Street Cookbook. (Illus.). 48p. (gr. 1-7). 1978. 5.99 (ISBN 0-448-47637-1, G&D). Putnam Pub Group.
Shalant, Phyllis. Look What We've Brought You from Vietnam: Crafts, Games, Recipes, Stories & Other Cultural Activities from New Americans. LC 87-20276. (Illus.). 48p. (gr. 2-6). 1988. lib. bdg. 9.98 (ISBN 0-671-63919-6); pap. 4.95 (ISBN 0-671-65978-2). Messner.
Shirk-Heath, Sandra J. Mom's Metric Cookbook. LC 86-90378. 150p. (gr. 1-6). 1986. PLB write for info. (ISBN 0-9615104-0-4). Shirk-Heath.
Sledge, Sharlande. Guess What I Made!?! Recipes for Children from Around the World. Dillard, Karen, illus. 64p. (Orig.). (gr. 1-6). 1988. pap. 4.50 (ISBN 0-936625-39-2, New Hope AL). Womans Mission Union.
Spence, Lora T., et al. There Once Was a Cook. Baker, Gary G., illus. (gr. k up). 1985. pap. 12.95 (ISBN 0-9614501-0-X). Wesley Inst.
Stabell, B. B. Little Chefs Cook Book. 70p. (gr. 7 up). 1982. pap. 4.75 (ISBN 0-9610872-0-X). B B Stabell.
Stallworth, Lyn. Wond'rous Fare. LC 88-20368. (Illus.). 48p. 1988. 14.95 (ISBN 0-8092-4481-0, Calico Bks). Contemp Bks.
Stewart, J. Kids' Cuisine. (Illus.). 48p. (gr. 2-6). 1988. pap. 4.95 (ISBN 0-88625-153-2). Durkin Hayes Pub.
Stewart, Janet, ed. Kid's Party Cookbook. Rowden, Rick, et al, illus. 32p. (gr. 2-6). 1988. PLB 14.65 (ISBN 0-88625-201-6); pap. 4.95 (ISBN 0-88625-200-8). Durkin Hayes Pub.
Supraner, Robyn. Quick & Easy Cookbook. Barto, Renzo, illus. LC 80-24021. 48p. (gr. 1-5). 1981. PLB 11.89 (ISBN 0-89375-438-2); pap. 2.95 (ISBN 0-89375-439-0). Troll Assocs.
Tabs, Judy & Steinberg, Barbara. Matzah Meals: A Passover Cookbook for Kids. McLean, Chari P., illus. LC 85-40. 72p. (ps up). 1985. pap. 6.95 spiral bd. (ISBN 0-930494-44-X). Kar-Ben.
Takeshita, Jiro. Food in Japan. LC 88-31465. (Illus.). 32p. (gr. 3-6). 1989. lib. bdg. 13.26 (ISBN 0-86625-340-8). Rourke Corp.
Thieme, Jeanne. The American Girls Cookbook: A Peek at Dining in the Past with Meals You Can Cook Today. (Illus.). 64p. (Orig.). (gr. 2-5). 1989. pap. 9.95 (ISBN 0-937295-59-0). Pleasant Co.
Thompson, Kathleen. My Book of Christmas Recipes. LC 87-16416. (Illus.). 24p. (gr. 3-5). 1987. lib. bdg. 14.65 (ISBN 0-8172-3161-7). Raintree Pubs.
Travers, P. L. & Moore-Betty, Maurice. Mary Poppins in the Kitchen: A Cookery Book with a Story. Shepard, Mary, illus. LC 75-10131. 128p. (gr. k up). 1975. 6.95 (ISBN 0-15-252898-9, HJ). HarBraceJ.
Van der Linde, Polly & Van der Linde, Tasha. Around the World in Eighty Dishes. Lemke, Horst, illus. LC 71-160447. 88p. (gr. k-7). 10.95 (ISBN 0-87592-007-1). Scroll Pr.
Villios, Lynne W. Cooking the Greek Way. Wolfe, Robert L., et al, illus. 52p. (gr. 5 up). 1984. PLB 10.95 (ISBN 0-8225-0910-5). Lerner Pubns.
Waldee, Lynne M. Cooking the French Way. LC 82-258. (Illus.). 48p. (gr. 5 up). 1982. PLB 10.95 (ISBN 0-8225-0904-0). Lerner Pubns.
Walker, Barbara. The Little House Cookbook: Frontier Foods from Laura Ingalls Wilder's Classic Stories. Williams, Garth, illus. LC 76-58733. 256p. (gr. 4 up). 1979. 13.95 (ISBN 0-06-026418-7); PLB 13.89 (ISBN 0-06-026419-5). HarpC Child Bks.
Walker, Barbara M. Little House Cookbook. LC 76-58733. (Illus.). 256p. (gr. 4 up). 1989. pap. 6.95 (ISBN 0-06-446090-8, Trophy). HarpC Child Bks.
Watson, N. Cameron. The Little Pigs' First Cookbook. Watson, N. Cameron, illus. 48p. (gr. 1-3). 1987. 12.95 (ISBN 0-316-92467-9). Little.
Weston, Reiko. Cooking the Japanese Way. LC 81-12656. (Illus.). 48p. (gr. 5 up). 1983. PLB 10.95 (ISBN 0-8225-0905-9). Lerner Pubns.
Wilkes, Angela. My First Cookbook. Johnson, David, photos by. LC 88-13798. (Illus.). 48p. (gr. 3-7). 1989. 12.00 (ISBN 0-394-80427-9). Knopf.
Wilms, Barbara. Crunchy Bananas & Other Great Recipes Kids Can Cook. LC 74-31139. (Illus.). 112p. (ps-3). 1984. pap. 5.95 (ISBN 0-87905-507-3, Falcon Books). Gibbs Smith Pub.
Wishik, Cindy. Kids Dish It up...Sugar-Free. LC 82-82188. (Illus.). 160p. (gr. k-3). 1982. pap. 9.95 (ISBN 0-918146-22-4). Peninsula WA.
Wolfe, Bob & Wolfe, Diane, photos by. Holiday Cooking Around the World. Swofford, Jeannette, illus. 52p. (gr. 5 up). 1988. 9.95 (ISBN 0-8225-0922-9). Lerner Pubns.
Wolfe, Robert L. & Wolfe, Diane. Holiday Cooking Around the World. Swofford, Jeannette, illus. 52p. (gr. 5 up). pap. 5.95 (ISBN 0-8225-9573-7). Lerner Pubns.
Wornall, Ruthie. Three Ingredient Cookbook. Classic American Fundraisers Staff, illus. 64p. (gr. 9-12). 1988. pap. 5.95 (ISBN 0-685-29002-6). R Wornall.
Young-Stirs: The Pittsburgh Children's Cookbook. (Illus.). 200p. (Orig.). (ps-12). 1985. pap. 7.95 (ISBN 0-9615457-0-4). Genesis Inc.
Yu, Ling. Cooking the Chinese Way. LC 82-263. (Illus.). 48p. (gr. 5 up). 1982. PLB 10.95 (ISBN 0-8225-0902-4). Lerner Pubns.
Zamojska-Hutchins, Danuta. Cooking the Polish Way. Wolfe, Robert, et al, illus. LC 84-11226. 52p. (gr. 5 up). 1984. PLB 10.95 (ISBN 0-8225-0909-1). Lerner Pubns.
Zweifel, Frances W. Pickle in the Middle & Other Easy Snacks. Zweifel, Frances W., illus. LC 78-19478. 64p. (gr. k-3). 1979. 11.95i (ISBN 0-06-027072-1). HarpC Child Bks.

COOKERY–FICTION

Adams, Pam, illus. The Gingerbread Man. 24p. (ps-2). 1981. 5.50 (ISBN 0-85953-107-4, Pub. by Child's Play England). Childs Play.
Carle, Eric. Pancakes, Pancakes! Carle, Eric, illus. LC 88-32438. 36p. (gr. k up). 1990. Repr. of 1970 ed. 15.95 (ISBN 0-88708-120-7). Picture Bk Studio.
Croll, Carolyn. Too Many Babas. Croll, Carolyn, illus. LC 78-22474. 64p. (gr. k-3). 1979. 7.64i (ISBN 0-06-021383-3). HarpC Child Bks.
Graeber, Charlotte. Mustard. Diamond, Donna, illus. 64p. 1988. pap. 2.75 (ISBN 0-553-15674-8, Skylark). Bantam.
Grey, Judith. Mud Pies. Sims, Deborah, illus. LC 81-4042. 32p. (gr. k-2). 1981. PLB 10.89 (ISBN 0-89375-541-9); pap. 2.95 (ISBN 0-89375-542-7). Troll Assocs.
Hoban, Lillian. Arthur's Christmas Cookies. LC 72-76496. (Illus.). 64p. (gr. k-3). 1972. 11.95 (ISBN 0-06-022367-7); PLB 11.89 (ISBN 0-06-022368-5). HarpC Child Bks.
Hutchins, Pat. The Doorbell Rang. Hutchins, Pat, illus. LC 85-12615. 24p. (ps-3). 1986. 13.95 (ISBN 0-688-05251-7); PLB 13.88 (ISBN 0-688-05252-5). Greenwillow.
Kline, Suzy. Orp & the Chop Suey Burgers. (Illus.). 112p. (gr. 4-8). 1990. 13.95 (ISBN 0-399-22185-9, Putnam). Putnam Pub Group.
Kunhardt, Dorothy. Pudding Is Nice. Kunhardt, Dorothy, illus. LC 75-19948. 64p. (gr. 1 up). 1975. 15.00 (ISBN 0-912846-18-6); pap. 8.00 (ISBN 0-912846-12-7). Bookstore Pr.
Lord, John V. & Burroway, Janet. The Giant Jam Sandwich. Lord, John V., illus. LC 72-13578. 32p. (gr. k-3). 1987. 15.95 (ISBN 0-395-16033-2); pap. 3.95 (ISBN 0-395-44237-0). HM.
Mosely, Francis. The Clever Apple Pie. Mosely, Francis, illus. 32p. (ps-1). 1987. 10.95 (ISBN 0-233-97938-7). Andre Deutsch.
Rockwell, Thomas. How to Eat Fried Worms. McCully, Emily, illus. LC 73-4262. (gr. 4-6). 1973. PLB 12.90 (ISBN 0-531-02631-0). Watts.
Shura, Mary F. Polly Panic. 128p. (gr. 5-8). 1990. 13.95 (ISBN 0-399-22214-6, Putnam). Putnam Pub Group.
Steadman, Ralph. The Jelly Book. Steadman, Ralph, illus. LC 73-99918. 32p. (ps-3). 7.95 (ISBN 0-685-04570-6). Scroll Pr.
Wagner, Karen. Chocolate Chip Cookies. Preiss, Leah P., illus. 32p. (ps-1). 1990. 14.95g (ISBN 0-8050-1268-0). H Holt & Co.
Wayne, Jennifer. Kitchen People. Shortall, Leonard, illus. LC 64-25322. (gr. 3-7). 1965. 3.50 (ISBN 0-672-50351-4, Bobbs). Macmillan.
Weinberger, Jane. The Little Ones. LC 86-50874. (FRE & ENG., Illus.). 54p. (Orig.). (ps-4). 1987. pap. 5.95 (ISBN 0-932433-29-4). Windswept Hse.
Wild, Jocelyn. Florence & Eric Take the Cake. LC 87-639. (Illus.). 32p. (ps-2). 1987. 11.95 (ISBN 0-8037-0305-8). Dial Bks Young.

COOKERY–NATURAL FOODS

Dobrin, Arnold. Peter Rabbit's Natural Foods Cookbook. Potter, Beatrix, illus. LC 76-45309. 1977. 10.95 (ISBN 0-7232-6142-3). Warne.

Isphording, Julie. Food Fun For Kids: A Recipe Coloring Book. Wolterman, Jan, ed. (Illus.). 48p. (gr. 1-6). 1991. pap. 6.95 spiral bdg. (ISBN 0-9629589-0-5). Kids Kitchen.
An entertaining & educational

cookbook for children filled with nourishing adventures. Authored by Julie Isphording, one of America's favorite women marathoners, FOOD FUN FOR KIDS portrays fruit, vegetable, & whole grains as they grow using food caricatures & features delicious recipes high in fiber, low in fat & all sugar-free. Designed for children ages 5 to 10, FOOD FUN FOR KIDS' 48 pages are filled with funny food friend recipes, Foodles, jokes, funny food-facts & puzzles. Blank placemats, with a food alphabet border, are included for children to draw or paint. These placemats can be laminated & used at dinnertime with the family or given as gifts to grandparents & teachers. FOOD FUN FOR KIDS is the answer to that age old question every parent asks, "How can we get our children to eat what's good for them?" FOOD FUN FOR KIDS measures 8 1/2" by 11" with red spiral binding.
Publisher Provided Annotation.

COOKERY-VEGETABLES
Salter, Charles A. The Vegetarian Teen. (Illus.). 112p. (gr. 7 up). 1991. PLB 13.90 (ISBN 1-56294-048-1). Millbrook Pr.
COOKERY-WILD FOODS
Burns, Diane. Sugaring Season: Making Maple Syrup. Nygren, Tord, illus 32p. (gr. k-4). 1990. PLB 12.95 (ISBN 0-87614-420-2). Carolrhoda Bks.
COOKERY, AMERICAN
Avis, Jen & Ward, Kathy. Just for Kids. Johnson, Colleen C., illus. 166p. 1990. spiral bdg. 12.95 (ISBN 0-9628683-1-0). Avis & Ward.
Bartlett, Virginia. Pickles & Pretzels: Pennsylvania's World of Food. LC 79-3996. 1980. pap. 7.95 (ISBN 0-8229-5308-0). U of Pittsburgh Pr.
Cary, Pam. North American Food & Drink. Caulkins, Janet, ed. (Illus.). 48p. (gr. 4-9). 1988. 12.40 (ISBN 0-531-18201-0, Pub. by Bookwright Pr). Watts.
Elliott, Allison. The Cowboy Cookbook. LC 88-51042. (Illus.). 120p. (Orig.). (gr. 1-8). 1989. 8.95x (ISBN 0-941099-02-4). Tourmaline Pub.
Harner, Carol. The Three Sisters Cookbook: Recipes & Remembrances. (Illus.). 164p. (Orig.). (gr. 12). 1989. pap. 9.95 (ISBN 0-685-26082-8). Harner Pubns.
Land, Leslie. The New England Epicure: Reading Between the Recipes. 1988. pap. 9.95 (ISBN 0-440-50078-8, Dell Trade Pbks). Dell.
Penner, Lucille R. Eating the Plates: A Pilgrim Book of Food & Manners. LC 90-5918. (Illus.). 128p. (gr. 1-5). 1991. SBE 14.95 (ISBN 0-02-770901-9, Mcmillan Child Bk). Macmillan Child Grp.
Perl, Lila. Hunter's Stew & Hangtown Fry. Cuffari, Richard, illus. LC 77-5366. 176p. (gr. 6 up) 1979. 13.95 (ISBN 0-395-28922-X, Clarion). HM.
Remole, Mary J. Mary Jane's Cookbook: From the Heart of America. (Illus.). 144p. (gr. 9-12). 1986. text ed. 8.95 (ISBN 0-317-90470-1). Mary Janes Cookbook.
Swendson, Patsy. The Potluck Adventures of Mrs. Marmalade: A Children's Cookbook. Roberts, Melissa, ed. Little, Debbie, illus. 32p. (gr. k-3). 1989. 9.95 (ISBN 0-89015-718-9, Pub. by Panda Bks). Eakin Pr.
COOKERY, AMERICAN-NEW ENGLAND STYLE

Cahill, Robert E. Olde New England's Sugar & Spice & Everything... America's First Cookbook & Food History. Cahill, Keri M., ed. (Illus.). 63p. (Orig.). 1991. pap. 3.95 (ISBN 0-9626162-2-2). Old Saltbox Pub Hse.
The newest addition to the "Olde New England Series," has the subtitle: "The History of Food & America's First Cookbook." Author Bob Cahill has dug up the oldest American recipes he could find, plus weaving a fascinating true adventure about the introduction & development of new foods into the Colonies. He follows the progress of America's "First Fruits," the battles concerning the controversial "love-apple," & merchant intrigue in obtaining spices. He also emphasizes the difficulty of the onion & potato to gain a footing in New England soil, the

beginnings of candy & other sweets in the New World, & humorous stories of preserving meats & fish in the old days. "Sugar & Spice & Everything," provides many first-hand experiences regarding food from our Pilgrim & Puritan ancestors, & is a truly entertaining, information-packed read. It retails for only $4.95. It is 76 pages, soft-cover & has 20 photos. Other titles in the series include: "Curious Customs & Cures," "Strange Superstitions," "Mountain Madness," "Things That Go Bump In The Night," "Mad & Mysterious Men," "Naughty Navy," "Riotous Revolution," "Viking & Indian Wars," "Strange Sea Sagas," "Shipwrecks & Treasures," "The Old Irish of New England," "Ghostly Haunts," "Witches & Wizards," "Pirates & Lost Treasures," & "Horrors of Salem's Witch Dungeon." Order from Old Saltbox, 40 Felt St. Salem, MA 01970.
Publisher Provided Annotation.

COOKERY, CHINESE
Au-Yeung, Cecilia J. First Steps in Chinese Cooking. (CHI & ENG., Illus.). 96p. (gr. 3-9). 1987. 8.95 (ISBN 962-7018-41-4, Pub. by Chpsticks HK). Seven Hills Bk Dists.
COOKERY, FRENCH
LaFargue, Francois. French Food & Drink. (Illus.). 48p. (gr. 4-9). 1987. lib. bdg. 12.40 (ISBN 0-531-18130-8, Pub. by Bookwright Pr). Watts.
COOKERY, GERMAN
Parnell, Helga. Cooking the German Way. (Illus.). 48p. (gr. 5 up). 1988. PLB 10.95 (ISBN 0-8225-0918-0). Lerner Pubns.
COOKERY, GREEK
Villios, Lynne W. Cooking the Greek Way. Wolfe, Robert L., et al, illus. 52p. (gr. 5 up). 1984. PLB 10.95 (ISBN 0-8225-0910-5). Lerner Pubns.
COOKERY, HUNGARIAN
Hargittai, Magdolna. Cooking the Hungarian Way. (Illus.). 48p. (gr. 5 up). 1986. PLB 10.95 (ISBN 0-8225-0916-4). Lerner Pubns.
COOKERY, ITALIAN
Buicchi, Edwina. Italian Food & Drink. (Illus.). 48p. (gr. 4-8). 1987. PLB 12.40 (ISBN 0-531-18120-0, Pub. by Bookwright Pr). Watts.
Gaspari, Claudia. Food in Italy. LC 88-33269. (Illus.). 32p. (gr. 3-6). 1989. lib. bdg. 13.26 (ISBN 0-86625-342-4). Rourke Corp.
Martino, Teresa. Pizza! (Illus.). 32p. (gr. 1-4). 1989. PLB 13.32 (ISBN 0-8172-3533-7). Raintree Pubs.
Pillar, Marjorie. Pizza Man. Pillar, Marjorie, illus. LC 89-35526. 40p. (gr. k-3). 1990. 11.95 (ISBN 0-690-04836-X, Crowell Jr Bks); PLB 11.89 (ISBN 0-690-04838-6, Crowell Jr Bks). HarpC Child Bks.
COOKERY, JEWISH
Burstein, Chaya M. A First Jewish Holiday Cookbook. Burstein, Chaya M., illus. (gr. 3-8). 1979. (Bonim Bks); pap. 8.95 (ISBN 0-88482-775-5, Bonim Bks). Hebrew Pub.
Tabs, Judy & Steinberg, Barbara. Matzah Meals: A Passover Cookbook for Kids. McLean, Chari P., illus. LC 85-40. 72p. (ps up). 1985. pap. 6.95 spiral bd. (ISBN 0-930494-44-X). Kar-Ben.
COOKERY, MEXICAN
Alvarado, Manuel. Mexican Food & Drink. Caulkins, Janet, ed. Wright, John, photos by. (Illus.). 48p. (gr. 4-9). 1988. PLB 12.40 (ISBN 0-531-18199-5, Pub. by Bookwright Pr). Watts.
Fischer, Robert. Tex-Mex Food. FS Staff, ed. Green, Anne C., illus. 72p. (gr. 4-9). 1988. 9.90 (ISBN 0-531-10505-9). Watts.
Gomez, Paolo. Food in Mexico. LC 88-31529. (Illus.). 32p. (gr. 6-9). 1989. lib. bdg. 13.26 (ISBN 0-86625-341-6). Rourke Corp.
COOKERY, NEAR EAST
Osborne, Christine. Middle Eastern Food & Drink. Caulkins, Janet, ed. (Illus.). 48p. (gr. 4-9). 1988. PLB 12.40 (ISBN 0-531-18200-2, Pub. by Bookwright Pr). Watts.
COOKERY, POLISH
Zamojska-Hutchins, Danuta. Cooking the Polish Way. Wolfe, Robert, et al, illus. LC 84-11226. 52p. (gr. 5 up). 1984. PLB 10.95 (ISBN 0-8225-0909-1). Lerner Pubns.
COOKERY, RUSSIAN
Andreev, Tania. Food in Russia. LC 88-32179. (Illus.). 32p. (gr. 3-6). 1989. lib. bdg. 13.26 (ISBN 0-86625-343-2). Rourke Corp.
Plotkin, Gregory & Plotkin, Rita. Cooking the Russian Way. (Illus.). 48p. (gr. 5 up). 1986. PLB 10.95 (ISBN 0-8225-0915-6). Lerner Pubns.

COOKERY, THAI
Harrison, Supenn & Monroe, Judy. Cooking the Thai Way. (Illus.). 48p. (gr. 5 up). 1986. PLB 10.95 (ISBN 0-8225-0917-2). Lerner Pubns.
COOKIES
Carlson, Faith. A Cookie Christmas. Carlson, Faith, illus. 28p. (Orig.). (ps-2). 1986. pap. 5.00 (ISBN 0-932591-05-1). Baggeboda Pr.
Corwin, Judith H. Cookie Fun. Corwin, Judith H., illus. 64p. (gr. 3 up). 1985. PLB 10.29 (ISBN 0-671-50797-4); PLB 7.71s.p.; pap. 3.71s.p. Messner.
Debnam, Betty. Rookie Cookie Cookbook: Everyday Recipes for Kids. (Illus.). 128p. (Orig.). 1989. pap. 7.95 (ISBN 0-8362-4206-8). Andrews & McMeel.
Perry, Josephine. Cookies from Many Lands. 160p. (gr. 6-12). 1972. pap. 4.95 (ISBN 0-486-22832-0). Dover.
St. Pierre. Bunny Bakeshop: Book & Cookie Cutter Set. (ps-1). 1989. pap. 3.95 (ISBN 0-590-63281-7). Scholastic Inc.
St. Pierre, Stephanie & Lovak, Matt. Bunny Bake Shop Cookie-Cutter. (gr. k-3). 1989. pap. 3.95 (ISBN 0-318-41675-1). Scholastic Inc.
COOKING
see Cookery
COOKING, OUTDOOR
see Outdoor Cookery
COOKING UTENSILS
see Household Equipment and Supplies
COOLIDGE, CALVIN, PRESIDENT U. S. 1872-1933
Kent, Zachary. Calvin Coolidge. LC 88-10880. (Illus.). 100p. (gr. 3 up). 1988. PLB 17.27 (ISBN 0-516-01362-9). Childrens.
Stevens, Rita. Calvin Coolidge: Thirtieth President of the United States. Young, Richard G., ed. LC 89-39949. (Illus.). 128p. (gr. 5-9). 1990. PLB 17.26 (ISBN 0-944483-57-7). Garrett Ed Corp.
COPPER
Fodor, R. V. Gold, Copper, Iron: How Metals Are Formed, Found, & Used. LC 87-24464. (Illus.). 96p. (gr. 6-12). 1989. PLB 16.95 (ISBN 0-89490-138-9). Enslow Pubs.
Lambert, M. Copper. (Illus.). 48p. (gr. 5 up). Date not set. PLB 15.93 (ISBN 0-86592-270-5). Rourke Corp.
CORAL REEFS AND ISLANDS
Barrett, Norman. Coral Reef. (Illus.). 32p. (gr. k-4). 1991. PLB 11.40 (ISBN 0-531-14110-1). Watts.
Bender, Lionel. Life on a Coral Reef. (Illus.). 32p. (gr. 3-6). 1989. PLB 11.90 (ISBN 0-531-17163-9, Gloucester Pr). Watts.

Holing, Dwight. Coral Reefs. Leon, Vicki, ed. (Illus.). 40p. (Orig.). 1990. pap. 7.95 (ISBN 0-918303-22-2). Blake Pub.
Although their stony colonies seem impervious to harm, coral reefs are fragile marine communities under seige. 43 dazzling photos compare Indo-Pacific & Caribbean reefs in a photographic bouquet of colors, textures, & patterns. The beauty of the reef extends to the book's design, which continually surprises. More than a pretty face, this book by Dwight Holing talks about the ecology & history of reefs worldwide & introduces reader to the rich, surprising & occasionally droll relationships between coral animals & plants. The lives of characteristic coral inhabitants, such as trigger fish, crinoids, sponges, & star coral, get special treatment. The wide variety of ways in which its citizens eat, hunt, mate & seek refuge are covered in some detail. As with other Blake nature books, readers get a strong environmental message about the reef & how best to protect it & other marine habitats. A detailed list of where to see natural reefs & artifical ones accompanies a world map. A book that divers, artists, students with reports to write, & librarians on limited budgets will like equally.
Publisher Provided Annotation.

Johnson, Rebecca L. A Living Laboratory: Science on the Great Barrier Reef. (Illus.). 64p. (gr. 5 up). 1991. PLB 15.95 (ISBN 0-8225-1596-2). Lerner Pubns.
Orr, Katherine. The Coral Reef Coloring Book. Orr, Katherine, illus. 48p. (gr. 2 up). 1988. pap. 5.95 (ISBN 0-88045-090-8). Stemmer Hse.
Sargent, William. Night Reef: Dusk to Dawn on a Coral Reef. (Illus.). 40p. (gr. 5-8). 1991. 13.95; PLB 13.90 (ISBN 0-531-11073-7). Watts.

Segaloff, Nat & Erickson, Paul. A Reef Comes to Life: Crating an Undersea Exhibit. (Illus.). 48p. (gr. 5-7). 1991. 12.95 (ISBN 0-531-15216-2); PLB 13.90 (ISBN 0-531-10994-1). Watts.

Steere, Susan & Ring, Kathryn M. The Reef & the Wrasse. Steere, Susan, illus. LC 88-24528. 32p. (Orig.). (gr. 4-6). 1988. PLB 12.95 (ISBN 0-943173-05-1); pap. 6.95 (ISBN 0-943173-24-8). Harbinger AZ.

Wood, Jenny. Coral Reefs. (Illus.). 32p. (gr. 3-4). 1992. PLB 12.95 (ISBN 0-8368-0630-1). Gareth Stevens Inc.

CORN

Aliki. Corn Is Maize: The Gift of the Indians. Aliki, illus. LC 75-6928. 40p. (gr. k-3). 1976. PLB 13.89 (ISBN 0-690-00975-5, Crowell Jr Bks). HarpC Child Bks.

—Corn Is Maize: The Gift of the Indians. Aliki, illus. LC 75-6928. 40p. (gr. k-3). 1986. pap. 4.50 (ISBN 0-06-445026-0, Trophy). HarpC Child Bks.

Kellogg, Cynthia. Corn: What It Is, What It Does. LC 88-18784. (Illus.). 48p. 1989. 11.95 (ISBN 0-688-08024-3); PLB 11.88 (ISBN 0-688-08026-X). Greenwillow.

CORONADO, FRANCISCO VASQUEZ DE, 1510?-1554

Zadra, Dan. Explorers of America: Coronado. rev. ed. (gr. 2-4). 1988. PLB 11.50s.p. (ISBN 0-88682-182-7); 16.45 (ISBN 0-318-32944-1). Creative Ed.

CORONARY HEART DISEASES
see Heart–Diseases

CORPULENCE
see Weight Control

CORRECTIONAL INSTITUTIONS
see Prisons

CORRESPONDENCE
see Letter Writing; Letters

CORRUPTION (IN POLITICS)–FICTION

Tunis, John R. City for Lincoln. 1989. pap. 3.95 (ISBN 0-15-218580-1). HarbraceJ.

CORSAIRS
see Pirates

CORTES, HERNANDO, 1485-1547

Castillo, Bernal D. de. Cortez & the Conquest of Mexico by the Spaniards in 1521. Herzog, B. G., abridged by. LC 88-581. xii, 165p. (gr. 5 up). 1988. Repr. of 1942 ed. 17.50 (ISBN 0-318-37415-3, Linnet). Shoe String.

COSBY, WILLIAM HENRY, JR., 1938-

Adams, Barbara Johnston. The Picture Life of Bill Cosby. LC 85-29487. 48p. (gr. k-6). 1986. PLB 7.99 (ISBN 0-531-10168-1). Watts.

Herbert, Solomon & Hill, George. Bill Cosby. (Illus.). (gr. 5 up). 1992. PLB 17.95 (ISBN 0-7910-1121-6). Chelsea Hse.

Martin, Patricia S. Bill Cosby: Superstar. (Illus.). 24p. (gr. 1-4). 1987. PLB 12.33 (ISBN 0-86592-169-5). Rourke Corp.

Rosenberg, Robert. Bill Cosby: The Changing Black Image. (Illus.). 96p. (gr. 7 up). 1991. PLB 19.95 (ISBN 1-878841-17-3). Millbrook Pr.

Woods, Harold & Woods, Geraldine. Bill Cosby: Making America Laugh & Learn. LC 82-23497. (Illus.). 48p. (gr. 3 up). 1983. PLB 10.95 (ISBN 0-87518-240-2, Dillon). Macmillan Child Grp.

COSMETICS

Cobb, Vicki. The Secret Life of Cosmetics: A Science Experiment Book. Cobb, Theo, illus. LC 85-40097. 128p. (gr. 5-9). 1985. 13.95 (ISBN 0-397-32121-X, Lipp Jr Bks); PLB 13.89 (ISBN 0-397-32122-8, Lipp Jr Bks). HarpC Child Bks.

Everett, F. Make-up. (Illus.). 32p. (gr. 6 up). 1987. PLB 13.96 (ISBN 0-88110-242-3); pap. 5.95 (ISBN 0-7460-0075-8). EDC.

Gunter, Annetta, illus. Kitchen Cosmetics: Using Herbs, Fruits & Eatables in Natural Cosmetics. 2nd, rev. ed. 131p. (gr. 8 up). Date not set. pap. 9.95 (ISBN 0-9620838-0-1). Herb Studies.

COSMETICS–FICTION

Stratton-Porter, Gene. Freckles. 254p. 1980. Repr. PLB 21.95 (ISBN 0-89966-224-2). Buccaneer Bks.

COSMOGONY
see Universe

COSMOGONY, BIBLICAL
see Creation

COSMOGRAPHY
see Universe

COSMOLOGY
see Universe

COSMOLOGY, BIBLICAL
see Creation

COSMONAUTS
see Astronauts

COSTA RICA

Cummins, Ronnie & Weber, Valerie. Children of the World: Costa Rica. Welch, Rose, photos by. LC 89-43138. 64p. (gr. 5-6). 1990. PLB 12.95 (ISBN 0-8368-0222-5). Gareth Stevens Inc.

Haynes, Tricia. Costa Rica. (Illus.). (gr. 5 up). 1988. 14.95 (ISBN 0-222-00955-1). Chelsea Hse.

Lerner Publications, Department of Geography Staff. Costa Rica in Pictures. (Illus.). 64p. (gr. 5 up). 1987. PLB 12.95 (ISBN 0-8225-1805-8). Lerner Pubns.

COSTUME

Here are entered descriptive and historical works on the costume of particular countries or periods and for works on fancy costume. Works dealing with clothing from a practical standpoint, including the art of dress, are entered under Clothing and Dress. Works describing the prevailing mode or style in dress are entered under Fashion.

see also Arms and Armor; Clothing and Dress; Cosmetics; Dressmaking; Fashion; Hats; Indians of North America–Costume and Adornment; Jewelry; Make-Up, Theatrical

Baker, Patricia. The Nineteen Forties. (Illus.). 64p. (gr. 6-10). 1992. lib. bdg. 16.95x (ISBN 0-8160-2467-7). Facts on File.

Beaton, Clare. Make & Play: Costumes. 1990. pap. 2.95 (ISBN 0-531-15160-3). Watts.

—Make & Play: T-Shirt Painting. 1990. pap. 2.95 (ISBN 0-531-15164-6). Watts.

Chernoff, Goldie T. Easy Costumes You Don't Have to Sew. LC 76-46428. (Illus.). 48p. (gr. 1-3). 1984. 12.95 (ISBN 0-02-718230-4, Four Winds). Macmillan Child Grp.

Conaway, Judith. Happy Haunting: Halloween Costumes You Can Make. Barto, Renzo, illus. LC 85-28840. 48p. (gr. 1-5). 1986. PLB 11.89 (ISBN 0-8167-0666-2); pap. text ed. 2.95 (ISBN 0-8167-0667-0). Troll Assocs.

—Make Your Own Costumes & Disguises. Barto, Renzo, illus. LC 86-11212. 48p. (gr. 1-5). 1987. PLB 11.89 (ISBN 0-8167-0840-1); pap. text ed. 2.95 (ISBN 0-8167-0841-X). Troll Assocs.

Connikie, Yvonne. The Nineteen Sixties. Cumming, Valerie & Feldman, Elane, eds. (Illus.). Date not set. 16.95x (ISBN 0-8160-2469-3). Facts on File.

Costantino, Maria. The Nineteen Thirties. Cumming, Valerie & Feldman, Elane, eds. (Illus.). 64p. (gr. 6-10). 1992. lib. bdg. 16.95x (ISBN 0-8160-2466-9). Facts on File.

Cunnington, Phillis. Costume. Cunnington, Phillis, intro. by. (Illus.). (gr. 6up). 1970. 14.95 (ISBN 0-7136-0104-3). Dufour.

Harrison, Mary K. How to Dress Dancers: Costuming Techniques for Dance. LC 88-60948. (Illus.). 144p. (gr. 9-12). 1988. pap. 12.95 (ISBN 0-916622-73-8). Princeton Bk Co.

Kingshead Corporation Staff. Cut-Color-&-Create: Make Your Own: Box Magic. Kingshead Corporation Staff, illus. 24p. (ps-1). Date not set. pap. 2.97 (ISBN 1-55941-039-6). Kingshead Corp.

—Cut-Color-&-Create: Make Your Own: Box Magic. Kingshead Corporation Staff, illus. 24p. (ps-1). Date not set. pap. 2.97 (ISBN 1-55941-038-8). Kingshead Corp.

Moss, Miriam. Street Fashion. LC 90-48913. (Illus.). 32p. (gr. 5-6). 1991. RSBE 11.95 (ISBN 0-89686-611-4, Crestwood Hse). Macmillan Child Grp.

Oldfield, Margaret J. Costumes & Customs of Many Lands. (Illus.). (gr. k-3). 1982. pap. 2.95 (ISBN 0-934876-19-3). Creative Storytime.

Polhemus, Ted. Body Styles. (Illus.). 144p. (gr. 8 up). 1989. 27.95 (ISBN 1-85291-008-9, Pub. by Lennard Pub UK). Seven Hills Bk Dists.

Rawson. Disguise & Make-Up. (gr. 2-5). 1979. (Usborne-Hayes); PLB 11.96 (ISBN 0-88110-042-0); pap. 4.50 (ISBN 0-86020-166-X). EDC.

Ruby, Jennifer. Costume in Context: The 1980s. (Illus.). 72p. (gr. 7-11). 1991. 19.95 (ISBN 0-7134-6539-5, Pub. by Batsford UK). Trafalgar Sq.

Wilcox, R. Turner. Folk & Festival Costume of the World. LC 65-23986. (Illus.). 1977. lib. bdg. 50.00x (ISBN 0-684-15379-3, Scribner). Macmillan.

COSTUME–HISTORY

ABC: Costume & Textiles from the Los Angeles County Museum of Art. (Illus.). 32p. (gr. 2 up). 1988. 10.95 (ISBN 0-8109-1877-3). Abrams.

Carnegie, Vicky. The Nineteen Eighties. Cumming, Valerie & Feldman, Elane, eds. (Illus.). 64p. 1990. 16.95x (ISBN 0-8160-2471-5). Facts on File.

Costumes & Clothes, 6 vols. LC 88-29281. (Illus.). 192p. (gr. 3-10). 1989. Set. 73.75 (ISBN 0-86307-980-6). Marshall Cavendish.

First Ladies Gowns. (Illus.). 32p. (ps-6). 1983. pap. 29.50 per set of 10 (ISBN 0-87474-621-3, FLCBP). Smithsonian.

Patteson, Nelda. Clara Driscoll: Savior of the Alamo: Her Life Story Presented Through the Clothes She Wore. (Illus.). 32p. (gr. 4-7). 1991. pap. write for info (ISBN 0-9629001-0-9). Smiley Originals.
This is a children's biography with a difference. On each narrative page B&W photographs & costume sketches in color combine to introduce the elegant, dynamic Mrs. Driscoll. 2 figures with 18 costumes march across color plates representing CLARA DRISCOLL's accomplishments as preservationist, playwright, New York socialite, politician, ambassador's wife, banker, cattlewoman, & philanthropist. At the time of her death in 1945, Time Magazine dubbed her an "empress." Her empires were several: cattle, oil, finance, politics, & philanthropy. Her extraordinary life becomes a costume history from the 1890's to the mid-1940's. Written & illustrated by an artist teacher, CLARA DRISCOLL puts upper elementary & middle school children in touch with greatness. "This book could be used for a book report by students in the fourth through seventh grades," said Nancy Ellis, District-Teacher-of-the-Year, Nixon-Smiley CISD.
Publisher Provided Annotation.

Ruby, Jennifer. Costume in Context: Medieval Times. (Illus.). 64p. (gr. 7-11). 1990. 19.95 (ISBN 0-7134-6075-X, Pub. by Batsford England). Trafalgar Sq.

—Costume in Context: The 1940s & 1950s. (Illus.). 64p. (gr. 7-11). 1990. 19.95 (ISBN 0-7134-6016-4, Pub. by Batsford England). Trafalgar Sq.

—The Edwardians & the First World War. (Illus.). 72p. (gr. 7-9). 1988. 19.95 (ISBN 0-7134-5605-1, Pub. by Batsford England). Trafalgar Sq.

—The Nineteen Twenties & Nineteen Thirties. (Illus.). 64p. (gr. 7-9). 1989. 19.95 (ISBN 0-7134-5773-2, Pub. by Batsford England). Trafalgar Sq.

—The Stuarts. (Illus.). 72p. (gr. 7-9). 1988. 19.95 (ISBN 0-7134-5604-3, Pub. by Batsford England). Trafalgar Sq.

Wilcox, R. Turner. Five Centuries of American Costume. LC 63-9768. (Illus.). 1977. lib. bdg. 35.00 (ISBN 0-684-15161-8, Scribner). Macmillan.

COSTUME DESIGN

Everett, F. Fashion Design: How Clothes are Designed, Made & Sold. (Illus.). (gr. 6 up). 1988. PLB 13.96 (ISBN 0-88110-307-1); pap. 7.95 (ISBN 0-7460-0187-8). EDC.

Glovach, Linda. Little Witch's Black Magic Book of Disguises. (gr. 1-4). 1977. (Pub. by Treehouse); pap. 3.95 (ISBN 0-13-537944-X). P-H.

Molyneux, Lynn & Gordner, Brad. Act It Out: Original Plays Plus Crafts for Costumes & Scenery. Marasco, Pam, illus. 192p. (gr. 2-6). 1986. spiral bdg. 12.95 (ISBN 0-685-29139-1). Trellis Bks Inc.

Moss, Miriam. Fashion Designer. LC 90-48323. (Illus.). 32p. (gr. 5-6). 1991. RSBE 11.95 (ISBN 0-89686-610-6, Crestwood Hse). Macmillan Child Grp.

COSTUME DESIGN–FICTION

Garelick, May. Just My Size. Pene du Bois, William, illus. LC 89-34513. 32p. (ps-3). 1990. 13.95 (ISBN 0-06-022418-5); PLB 13.89 (ISBN 0-06-022419-3). HarpC Child Bks.

Viorst, Judith. Earrings! Malone, Nola L., illus. LC 89-17846. 32p. (gr. 1-4). 1990. 13.95 (ISBN 0-689-31615-1, Atheneum Child Bk). Macmillan Child Grp.

Wegen, Ron. The Halloween Costume Party. LC 83-2069. 32p. (gr. k-3). 1983. 14.95 (ISBN 0-89919-184-3, Clarion). HM.

COTTAGES
see Houses

COTTON

Cotton. (Illus.). (gr. 5 up). lib. bdg. 15.93 (ISBN 0-86592-266-7). Rourke Corp.

Dineen, Jacqueline. Cotton & Silk. 32p. (gr. 4-8). 1988. lib. bdg. 12.95 (ISBN 0-89490-213-X). Enslow Pubs.

Selsam, Millicent E. Cotton. Wexler, Jerome, illus. LC 82-6496. 48p. (gr. k-3). 1982. 12.95 (ISBN 0-688-01499-2); lib. bdg. 14.88 (ISBN 0-688-01500-X, Morrow Jr Bks). Morrow Jr Bks.

Wonsham, Genevieve. Cotton Carta: To Our City Cousins, Big Town, U. S. A. LC 77-83628. (Illus.). (ps-2). 1978. PLB 5.95 (ISBN 0-89508-023-0). Rainbow Bks.

Worsham, Genevieve. Cotton Carta. LC 77-83627. (Illus.). 32p. (gr. 2-4). 1978. PLB 9.95 (ISBN 0-87783-144-0); pap. 3.94 deluxe ed. (ISBN 0-87783-149-1). Oddo.

COTTON MANUFACTURE AND TRADE

Mitgutsch, Ali. From Cotton to Pants. Mitgutsch, Ali, illus. LC 80-29552. 24p. (ps-3). 1981. PLB 6.95 (ISBN 0-87614-150-5). Carolrhoda Bks.

Selsam, Millicent E. Cotton. Wexler, Jerome, illus. LC 82-6496. 48p. (gr. k-3). 1982. 12.95 (ISBN 0-688-01499-2); lib. bdg. 14.88 (ISBN 0-688-01500-X, Morrow Jr Bks). Morrow Jr Bks.

Wonsham, Genevieve. Cotton Carta: To Our City Cousins, Big Town, U. S. A. LC 77-83628. (Illus.). (ps-2). 1978. PLB 5.95 (ISBN 0-89508-023-0). Rainbow Bks.

COUGARS–FICTION

Spanjian, Beth. Baby Cougar. (ps-1). 1990. write for info. (ISBN 0-307-12597-1). Western Pub.

COUNSELING
see also Vocational Guidance

Kramer, Patricia & Frazer, Linda. The Dynamics of Relationships: A Guide for Developing Self-Esteem & Social Skills for Preteens & Young Children. rev. ed. (Illus.). (gr. 9 up). 1990. pap. text ed. 17.95 tchr's. manual (ISBN 0-929577-03-5). Equal Partners.
The most comprehensive program

available dealing with everyday concerns vital to young people takes a preventive approach to such crucial issues as suicide, teen pregnancy, substance abuse, violence, drop-outs & physical & sexual abuse. It was developed to help youth build & maintain a healthy self-esteem, learn to communicate, handle anger & conflict effectively, develop coping & decision-making skills, & develop realistic expectations about adult roles, AIDS, suicide, teen pregnancy, date rape, gangs, etc. It can be: Implemented as a school curriculum. Incorporated into other disciplines (Health, Home Ec/ Family Life, Sex Ed, Social Studies). Used as a resource for treatment centers, substance abuse, mental health & social service programs, youth religious programs, youth clubs & organizations (4-H, Boys/Girls Clubs, Girl/Boy Scouts, etc.) The series is comprised of a teacher's manual & a two-part teen/young adult manual (which includes a separate book on sexuality) & a teacher manual for preteens & youth manual (ages 8-12). Pat Kramer conducts workshops that teach professionals strategies to empower youth & techniques to create positive, supportive environments that can reduce substance abuse, discipline problems, violence & vandalism. ***Publisher Provided Annotation.***

Painter, Carol. Friends Helping Friends: A Manual for Peer Counselors. Sorenson, Don L., ed. 224p. (Orig.). (gr. 9-12). 1989. pap. text ed. 9.95x (ISBN 0-932796-29-X). Ed Media Corp.

COUNTER-REFORMATION

see Reformation

COUNTING BOOKS

Aker, Suzanne. What Comes in Two's, Three's & Four's? 1990. pap. 13.95 (ISBN 0-671-67173-1). S&S Trade.

Alexander, Lloyd. The Book of Three. 192p. (gr. k-6). 1978. pap. 3.50 (ISBN 0-440-40702-8, YB). Dell.

Anno, Mitsumasa. Anno's Counting Book. Anno, Mitsumasa, illus. LC 76-28977. 32p. (ps-3). 1977. 15.95 (ISBN 0-690-01287-X, Crowell Jr Bks); PLB 15.89 (ISBN 0-690-01288-8). HarpC Child Bks.

—Anno's Counting House. (Illus.). 48p. (ps-3). 1982. 15.95 (ISBN 0-399-20896-8, Philomel). Putnam Pub Group.

Ashton, Elizabeth A. An Old-Fashioned One Two Three Book. Smith, Jesse W., illus. 32p. (ps-3). 1991. 14.95 (ISBN 0-670-83499-8). Viking Child Bks.

Astley, Judy. When One Cat Woke Up: A Cat Counting Book. Fogelman, Phyllis J., ed. Astley, Judy, illus. LC 89-23260. 23p. (ps-2). 1990. 10.95 (ISBN 0-8037-0782-7). Dial Bks Young.

Aylesworth, Jim. One Crow: A Counting Rhyme. Young, Ruth, illus. LC 85-45856. 32p. (ps-1). 1990. pap. 4.95 (ISBN 0-06-443242-4, Trophy). HarpC Child Bks.

Baby's First Counting Book. 12p. (ps). 1978. 3.95 (ISBN 0-448-40863-5, G&D). Putnam Pub Group.

Bawden, Juliet. One Year Old: Counting Children 1 to 10. Pask, Helen, illus. LC 89-45802. 24p. (ps). 1990. 9.95g (ISBN 0-8050-1257-5). H Holt & Co.

Big ABC & Counting Book. (Illus.). (ps-k). 8.95 (ISBN 0-7214-7506-X). Ladybird Bks.

Boyle, Sallie, et al. Blends, Digraphs & Counting by Twos, Fives, Tens. (Illus.). 32p. (ps-3). 1984. pap. 1.98 (ISBN 0-88724-162-X, CD-0920). Carson-Dellos.

Brookes, Diane. Passing the Peace: A Counting Book for Kids. (FRE & ENG., Illus.). 24p. 1990. pap. 8.95 (ISBN 0-921254-20-2, Pub. by Penumbra Pr CN). U of Toronto Pr.

Brown, Marc. One Two Three: An Animal Counting Book. 32p. (ps-3). 1976. lib. bdg. 13.95 (ISBN 0-316-11064-7, Joy St Bks). Little.

Carson, Patti & Dellosa, Janet. Beginning Numbers: One Through Ten. (Illus.). 20p. (ps-2). 1984. pap. 5.95 (ISBN 0-88724-136-0, CD-0570). Carson Dellos.

—Numbers, Number Words & Sets: 1-20. Carson, Patti & Dellosa, Janet, illus. 20p. (ps-1). 1984. pap. 5.95 (ISBN 0-88724-153-0, CD-0576). Carson-Dellos.

Charlip, Remy & Joyner, Jerry. Thirteen. LC 75-8875. (Illus.). 40p. (gr. 1-3). 1984. Repr. of 1975 ed. 13.95 (ISBN 0-02-718120-0, Four Winds). Macmillan Child Grp.

Colonial Williamsburg Foundation Staff. The Folk Art Counting Book: From the Abby Aldrich Rockefeller Folk Art Center. (Illus.). 40p. (ps-k). Date not set. 6.95 (ISBN 0-87935-084-9). Williamsburg.

"The Folk Art Counting Book" is designed for young learners but it will be enjoyed by all ages. The images are from the Abby Aldrich Rockefeller Folk Art Center in Williamsburg, Virginia, one of the country's premier collections of American folk art. Folk art is the product of untrained artists who, although unfamiliar with academic artistic rules, somehow solve the technical difficulties encountered & intuitively produce satisfying art. Abby Aldrich Rockefeller's folk art collection of over six hundred pieces is the nucleus of the Abby Aldrich Rockefeller Folk Art Center, a museum of the Colonial Williamsburg Foundation. The present collection numbers over 2,600 objects & continues to grow. Small children can start at one whirligig & soon learn to count up to five weather vanes, ten jungle animals, & twenty eagles. The uncluttered pages with large, clear numbers that are immediately recognizable in a repetitive quilt border make this book easy to use as a learning tool. Outstanding examples of folk art such as the endearing "Baby in Red Chair" & Henry Church's "The Monkey Picture" have been specially selected to enhance young children's appreciation of folk art & to stimulate their visual & cognitive senses. ***Publisher Provided Annotation.***

Conran, Sebastian. My First 1-2-3 Book. Conran, Sebastian, illus. LC 88-6275. 64p. (ps-1). 1988. bds. 7.95 (ISBN 0-689-71267-7, Aladdin). Macmillan Child Grp.

Cory's Counting Game. 22p. (ps). 1979. 5.95 (ISBN 0-8431-0629-8). Price Stern.

Counting. 24p. (Orig.). (ps). 1988. pap. 3.95 (ISBN 0-8431-3137-3); Little Q Answer Wand 7.00 (ISBN 0-318-39953-9). Price Stern.

Counting. (Illus.). (ps-2). 1.95 (ISBN 0-7214-5183-7). Ladybird Bks.

Counting. (Illus.). (ps-2). 3.50 (ISBN 0-7214-0514-2). Ladybird Bks.

Counting Pack, No. 477. (Illus.). (ps-k). incl. chart & activity bk. 6.95 (ISBN 0-7214-5166-7). Ladybird Bks.

Counting Songs. (Illus.). (ps-k). 3.50 (ISBN 0-7214-1123-1). Ladybird Bks.

Crews, Donald. Ten Black Dots. rev. ed. Crews, Donald, illus. LC 85-14871. 32p. (ps-3). 1986. 14.95 (ISBN 0-688-06067-6); PLB 14.88 (ISBN 0-688-06068-4). Greenwillow.

Crowther, Robert. The Most Amazing Hide & Seek Counting Book. Crowther, Robert, illus. 14p. (ps-3). 1981. pap. 13.95 (ISBN 0-670-48997-2). Viking Child Bks.

Dee, Ruby. Two Ways to Count to Ten. Meddaugh, Susan, illus. LC 86-33513. 32p. (ps-1). 1990. pap. 5.95 (ISBN 0-8050-1314-8). H Holt & Co.

Dellosa, Janet & Carson, Patti. Counting (Numerals One to Ten) (Illus.). 32p. (ps-k). 1984. pap. 1.98 (ISBN 0-88724-091-7, CD-7030). Carson-Dellos.

Dellosa, Janet, et al. Colors & Counting Zero Through Nine. (Illus.). 32p. (ps-1). 1984. pap. 1.98 (ISBN 0-88724-158-1, CD-0922). Carson-Dellos.

—Consonants & Counting Zero Through Twenty. (Illus.). 32p. (ps-2). 1984. pap. 1.98 (ISBN 0-88724-161-1, CD-0921). Carson-Dellos.

Disney, Walt, Productions Staff. Mickey's Counting Book. LC 82-18554. (Illus.). 32p. (ps-1). 1983. lib. bdg. 5.99 (ISBN 0-394-95735-0). Random.

Dudley, Dick. Ten Little Lambs. Paris, Pat, illus. 12p. (ps-k). 1988. 8.95 (ISBN 0-8120-5953-0). Barron.

Dunbar, Joyce. Ten Little Mice. 1990. 13.95 (ISBN 0-15-200601-X). HarbraceJ.

Dunn, Phoebe & Lee, Vincent B., photos by. How Many? A Matchem Counting Bk. LC 87-61521. (Illus.). 18p. (ps). 1988. bds. 4.95 (ISBN 0-394-89388-3, Random Juv). Random.

Eichenberg, Fritz. Dancing in the Moon: Counting Rhymes. Eichenberg, Fritz, illus. LC 75-8514. 32p. (gr. k-1). 1975. pap. 3.95 (ISBN 0-15-623811-X, VoyB). HarBraceJ.

F. J. Strauss Co., Inc. Staff. Counting. F. J. Strauss Co., Inc. Staff, illus. 10p. (ps). Date not set. write for info. vinyl (ISBN 0-945987-09-9). F J Strauss.

Feelings, Muriel. Moja Means One: A Swahili Counting Book. LC 76-134856. (Illus.). 32p. (gr. k up). 1976. pap. 4.95 (ISBN 0-8037-5711-5). Dial Bks Young.

Fujikawa, Gyo. Can You Count? (ps-1). 1977. 4.95 (ISBN 0-448-12893-4, G&D). Putnam Pub Group.

—Ten Little Babies. Fujikawa, Gyo, illus. LC 88-60966. 24p. (ps-1). 1989. pap. 4.95 (ISBN 0-394-89033-7). Random.

Gamec, Hazel S. The Magic Pencil Counting Book. Gamec, Hazel S., illus. 12p. 1980. write for info. (ISBN 0-938042-00-9). Printek.

Gould, Ellen. The Blue Number Counting Book. Kelly, Cathy, illus. 13p. (ps-2). pap. 6.00 (ISBN 0-938017-01-2). Learn Tools.

Gregorich, Barbara. Contando del 1 al 10: Counting 1 to 10. Hoffman, Joan, ed. Shepherd-Bartram, tr. from ENG. Pape, Richard, illus. (SPA.). 32p. (Orig.). 1987. wkbk. 1.99 (ISBN 0-938256-79-3). Sch Zone Pub Co.

—Counting Caterpillars. Hoffman, Joan, ed. Alexander, Barbara, et al, illus. 32p. (Orig.). (ps-1). 1986. wkbk. 1.99 (ISBN 0-88743-126-7). Sch Zone Pub Co.

Gretz, Susanna. Teddy Bears 1-10. Gretz, Susanna, illus. LC 86-4795. 24p. (ps-k). 1986. 13.95 (ISBN 0-02-738140-4, Four Winds). Macmillan Child Grp.

Gruenbaum, Hannah. Come, Count with Me. Forst, Sigmund, illus. (ps-1). 1.50 (ISBN 0-685-86207-0). Feldheim.

Haas, Dorothy. The Hugs & Tugs Counting Book. Cooke, Tom, illus. (ps). 5.95 (ISBN 0-317-13462-0). Parker Bros.

Hague, Kathleen. Numbears: A Counting Book. 1986. 10.95 (ISBN 0-03-007194-1). HR&W.

Hawkins, Colin. How Many Are in This Old Car? A Counting Book. Hawkins, Colin, illus. 32p. (ps-k). 1988. 11.95 (ISBN 0-399-21565-4, Putnam). Putnam Pub Group.

Hawksley, Gerald. At Home. Hawksley, Gerald, illus. 10p. (gr. 2-4). 1990. bds. 4.95 (ISBN 1-878624-18-0). McClanahan Bk.

—Farm. Hawksley, Gerald, illus. 10p. (gr. 2-4). 1990. bds. 4.95 (ISBN 1-878624-16-4). McClanahan Bk.

—Trucks. Hawksley, Gerald, illus. 10p. (gr. 2-4). 1990. bds. 4.95 (ISBN 1-878624-17-2). McClanahan Bk.

—Zoo. Hawksley, Gerald, illus. 10p. (gr. 2-4). 1990. bds. 4.95 (ISBN 1-878624-19-9). McClanahan Bk.

Hefter, Richard. Lots of Little Bears. Hefter, Richard, illus. LC 83-2184. 32p. (ps-1). 1983. 5.95 (ISBN 0-911787-04-6). Optimum Res Inc.

Hoban, Tana. One, Two, Three. Hoban, Tana, illus. LC 84-10306. 12p. (ps). 1985. bds. 4.95 (ISBN 0-688-02579-X). Greenwillow.

Holmes, Stephen. Hidden Numbers. LC 89-78486. (Illus.). 20p. (ps-1). 1990. 13.95 (ISBN 0-15-200469-6, Gulliver Bks). HarBraceJ.

Howard, Katherine. I Can Count to One Hundred...Can You? Smollin, Michael J., illus. LC 78-62700. (ps). 1979. lib. bdg. 5.99 (ISBN 0-394-94090-3, Random Juv); pap. 2.25 (ISBN 0-394-84090-9). Random.

Hynard, Julia. Percival's Party: A Story about Numbers. Thatcher, Francis, illus. LC 82-22114. 32p. (ps-3). 1983. PLB 15.93 (ISBN 0-516-08941-2). Childrens.

I Can Count. (ps-k). 3.95 (ISBN 0-7214-5053-9). Ladybird Bks.

Ingle, Annie. Count in the Dark with Glo Worm. Fleming, Denise, illus. LC 84-62883. 14p. (gr. 3-6). 1985. bds. 4.95 (ISBN 0-394-87273-8, Random Juv). Random.

Inkpen, Mick. One Bear at Bedtime. Inkpen, Mick, illus. LC 87-3098. (gr. 2-6). 1988. 12.95 (ISBN 0-316-41889-7). Little.

Jones, Carol. This Old Man. Jones, Carol, illus. 48p. (gr. k-3). 1990. 10.95 (ISBN 0-395-54699-0). HM.

Katz, Bobbi. The Old Woman's Counting Book. Sustendal, Pat, illus. LC 88-61630. 12p. (ps-k). 1989. bds. 3.95 (ISBN 0-394-82224-2). Random.

Katz, Michael J. Ten Potatoes in a Pot & Other Counting Rhymes. Otani, June, illus. LC 89-15583. 32p. (ps-2). 1990. 12.95 (ISBN 0-06-023106-8); PLB 12.89 (ISBN 0-06-023107-6). HarpC Child Bks.

Kingsley, Emily P., et al. Sesame Street One, Two, Three Story Book: Stories About the Numbers from One to Ten. (Illus.). (ps-4). 1973. 6.95 (ISBN 0-394-82694-9, Random Juv); lib. bdg. 6.99 (ISBN 0-394-92694-3). Random.

Kitchen, Bert. Animal Numbers. LC 87-5365. (Illus.). 24p. (ps up). 1987. 12.95 (ISBN 0-8037-0459-3). Dial Bks Young.

—Animal Numbers. LC 87-5365. (Illus.). 24p. (gr. k up). 1991. pap. 4.95 (ISBN 0-8037-0910-2, Dial Pied Piper). Puffin Bks.

Kitman, Carol & Hurwitz, Carol. One Mezuzah: A Jewish Counting Book. (Illus.). 48p. (ps-k). 1984. pap. 6.95 (ISBN 0-940646-54-4). Rossel Bks.

Let's Learn Set. Incl. Positions (7008); Alphabet Sounds & Pictures (7004); Capital & Lower Case Letters (7005); Numbers, Number Words, & Sets (7006); Shapes (7007); Consonants (7009); Color Words (7002); Fun with Numbers (7018); Letters & the Sounds They Make (7017); All about Me (7010); Pre-School & Kindergarten Skills (7015); Printing Practice (7014). 32p. 1984. pap. 285.12 set- 12 each of 12 different "Let's Learn" titles: 144 bks (ISBN 0-88724-099-2). Carson-Dellos.

Lewis, Shari. Baby Lamb Chop Loves Numbers. Beylon, Cathy, illus. 12p. (ps-k). 1991. bds. 3.95 (ISBN 0-679-81724-7). Random.

Livingston, Malcolm, illus. How Many Birds? 16p. (ps). 1986. 2.95 (ISBN 0-86020-962-8). EDC.

—How Many Monkeys? 16p. (ps). 1986. 2.95 (ISBN 0-86020-961-X). EDC.
—How Many Monsters? 16p. (ps). 1986. 2.95 (ISBN 0-86020-960-1). EDC.
MacCarthy, Patricia. Ocean Parade. 1990. 11.95 (ISBN 0-8037-0780-0). Dial Bks Young.
McKissack, Patricia & McKissack, Fredrick. Big Bug Book of Counting. Bartholomew, illus. LC 87-61655. 24p. (Orig.). (gr. k-1). 1987. spiral bdg. 14.95 (ISBN 0-88335-762-3); pap. text ed. 4.95 (ISBN 0-88335-772-0). Milliken Pub Co.
McMillan, Bruce. One Two One Pair. LC 90-37410. (ps-3). 1991. 12.95 (ISBN 0-590-43767-4, Scholastic Hardcover). Scholastic Inc.
Maestro, Betsy. Harriet Goes to the Circus: A Number Concept Book. Maestro, Giulio, illus. LC 76-40204. (ps-1). 1989. Crown.
Manushkin, Fran. Walt Disney's One Hundred One Dalmatians: A Counting Book. Hicks, Russell, illus. LC 90-85426. 32p. (ps-1). 1991. 9.95 (ISBN 1-56282-012-5, Disney Pr); PLB 9.89 (ISBN 1-56282-032-X, Disney Pr). W Disney Pub.
Mathieu, Joe. Sesame Street One Two Three: A Counting Book from 1 to 100. Mathieu, Joe, illus. LC 91-1992. 32p. (ps-1). 1991. 9.00 (ISBN 0-679-81230-X, Random Juv); lib. bdg. 10.99 (ISBN 0-679-91230-4). Random.
Miller, J. P. Learn to Count with Little Rabbit. Miller, J. P., illus. LC 83-21100. 24p. (ps-1). 1984. 3.95 (ISBN 0-394-86149-3, Random Juv). Random.
Miller, Jane. Farm Counting Book. Miller, Jane, illus. 24p. (ps-3). 1986. 8.95 (ISBN 0-13-304790-3); pap. 4.95 (ISBN 0-13-304809-8). P-H.
Moncure, Jane B. Magic Monsters Count to Ten. Fudala, Rosemary, illus. LC 78-23634. (ps-3). 1979. PLB 11.97 (ISBN 0-89565-058-4). Childs World.
Morozumi, Atsuko. One Gorilla: A Counting Book. Morozumi, Atsuko, illus. 26p. (ps-1). 1990. 13.95 (ISBN 0-374-35644-0). FS&G.
Morris, Ann. Night Counting. Roffey, Maureen, illus. LC 85-45332. 16p. (ps). 1986. 3.50 (ISBN 0-694-00074-4). HarpC Child Bks.
My Counting Book. (ps-2). 3.95 (ISBN 0-7214-5146-2). Ladybird Bks.
Nelson, JoAnne. Count by Twos. Beylon, Cathy, illus. 16p. (Orig.). (gr. k-2). 1990. pap. 3.95 (ISBN 1-878624-10-5). McClanahan Bk.
Nikola-Lisa, W. One, Two, Three Thanksgiving! Levine, Abby, ed. Kramer, Robin, illus. 32p. (ps-1). 1991. 12.95 (ISBN 0-8075-6109-6). A Whitman.
Oliver, Stephen, photos by. Counting. LC 90-8577. (Illus.). 24p. (ps-k). 1991. 6.95 (ISBN 0-679-81163-X). Random.
One to Ten. (ps). 1976. 5.50 (ISBN 0-900195-19-3, Brimax Bks). Borden.
One, Two, Three. (Illus.). 32p. (ps-k). 1986. write for info. (ISBN 0-307-05161-7, Pub. by Golden Bks). Western Pub.
Pacovska, Kveta. One, Five, Many. Pacovska, Kveta, illus. 30p. (gr. k-3). 1990. 16.95 (ISBN 0-395-54997-3, Clarion Bks). HM.
Pallotta, Jerry. The Icky Bug Counting Book. (Illus.). 32p. (ps-8). 1991. 14.95 (ISBN 0-88106-497-1); pap. 6.95 (ISBN 0-88106-496-3). Charlesbridge Pub.
Palumbo, Nancy. Lets Color & Count: Colorions et Comptons. Weaver, Judith, illus. 32p. (gr. k-6). 1989. wkbk. 5.95 (ISBN 0-927024-09-8). Crayons Pubns.
Paul, Emily. Count with Baby Kermit. 1988. write for info. (ISBN 0-02-689136-0). Checkerboard Pr.
Peppe, Rodney. The Animal Directory: A First Counting Book. LC 89-18000. (Illus.). 24p. 1990. bds. 9.95 (ISBN 0-87226-421-1, Bedrick Blackie). P Bedrick Bks.
Pienkowski, Jan. Little Monsters: Eggs for Tea. 1990. 5.95 (ISBN 0-385-41343-2). Doubleday.
—Little Monsters: Pet Food. 1990. 5.95 (ISBN 0-385-41344-0). Doubleday.
Pluckrose, Henry. Counting. Fairclough, Chris, photos by. Franklin Watts Ltd., ed. (Illus.). 32p. (ps-6). 1988. PLB 10.40 (ISBN 0-531-10524-5). Watts.
Pomerantz, Charlotte. One Duck, Another Duck. Aruego, Jose & Dewey, Ariane, illus. LC 83-20767. 24p. (ps-1). 1984. 10.25 (ISBN 0-688-03744-5); PLB 10.88 (ISBN 0-688-03745-3). Greenwillow.
Pop-Up Numbers. 12p. (ps-1). 1982. 5.95 (ISBN 0-8431-0968-8). Price Stern.
Pragoff, Fiona. Clothes. (Illus.). 16p. (ps-k). 1989. 5.95 (ISBN 0-385-26388-0, Zephyr-BFYR). Doubleday.
Punnett, Richard D. Count the Possums. Dunnington, Tom, illus. LC 81-21773. 32p. (ps-2). 1982. lib. bdg. 11.97 (ISBN 0-89565-215-3). Childs World.
Quinn, Kaye. Cars, Trucks, Trains, & Planes. (Illus.). 48p. (Orig.). (ps-2). 1989. pap. 2.95 (ISBN 0-8431-2727-9). Price Stern.
—Weird & Wacky Animals. (Illus.). 48p. (Orig.). (ps-2). 1989. pap. 2.95 (ISBN 0-8431-2728-7). Price Stern.
Rae, Mary M. Over in the Meadow: A Counting-Out Rhyme. (Illus.). 32p. (ps-k). 1986. pap. 3.95 (ISBN 0-685-14199-3, Penguin Bks). Viking Penguin.
Reichmeier, Betty, illus. Sing with Me Play-along & Counting Songs. (ps-1). 1987. incl. cassette 5.95 (ISBN 0-394-88810-3, Random Juv). Random.
Reiss, John J. Numbers. Reiss, John J., illus. LC 76-151313. 32p. (ps-2). 1982. 13.95 (ISBN 0-02-776150-9, Bradbury Pr). Macmillan Child Grp.
Rockwell, Anne. Willy Can Count. Rockwell, Anne, illus. 32p. (ps). 1989. 13.95 (ISBN 1-55970-013-0). Arcade Pub Inc.
Rosenburg, Amye, illus. One, Two, Buckle My Shoe. 6p. (ps-k). 1981. cloth 3.50 (ISBN 0-671-42532-3, Little Simon). S&S Trade.
Ross, Harvey. Fraggles Counting Book. 1988. write for info. (ISBN 0-02-689112-3). Checkerboard Pr.
Rylands, Ljiljana. Counting Balloons. (Illus.). 24p. (ps-2). 1990. 1.95 (ISBN 1-878624-21-0, 1553800021). McClanahan Bk.
Scarry, Richard. Fun with Numbers: Grade One. Scarry, Richard, illus. 32p. (ps-2). 1986. pap. 1.95 (ISBN 0-394-87665-2). Random.
—Fun With Numbers: Kindergarten. Scarry, Richard, illus. 32p. (ps-2). 1986. pap. 1.95 (ISBN 0-394-87666-0). Random.
—Richard Scarry's Best Counting Book Ever. Scarry, Richard, illus. LC 74-2544. 48p. (ps-2). 1975. 10.95 (ISBN 0-394-82924-7, Random Juv); PLB 9.99 (ISBN 0-394-92924-1). Random.
Schwartz, David M. How Much Is a Million? Kellogg, Steven, illus. 40p. (gr. k-3). 1986. pap. 2.95 (ISBN 0-590-33966-4). Scholastic Inc.
Scott, Ann H. One Good Horse: A Cowpuncher's Counting Book. LC 89-1984. (Illus.). 32p. (ps up). 1990. 12.95 (ISBN 0-688-09146-6); lib. bdg. 12.88 (ISBN 0-688-09147-4). Greenwillow.
Sendak, Maurice. One Was Johnny: A Counting Book. Sendak, Maurice, illus. 32p. (ps-3). 1962. PLB 12.89 (ISBN 0-06-025540-4). HarpC Child Bks.
—One Was Johnny: A Counting Book. Sendak, Maurice, illus. LC 62-13315. 48p. (ps-3). 1991. pap. 2.95 (ISBN 0-06-443251-3, Trophy). HarpC Child Bks.
Sesame Street Staff. The Count's Counting Book. Cooke, Tom, illus. LC 79-56535. 16p. (ps-3). 1980. pap. 7.95 (ISBN 0-394-84436-X). Random.
Sis, Peter. Going Up! A Color Counting Book. LC 87-37203. (Illus.). 24p. (ps up). 1989. 12.95 (ISBN 0-688-08125-8); PLB 12.88 (ISBN 0-685-22783-9). Greenwillow.
Spencer, Eve. Animal Babies One Two Three. David, Susan, illus. 24p. (ps-2). 1990. PLB 12.33 (ISBN 0-8172-3581-7). Raintree Pubs.
Sugita, Yutaka. Goodnight, One, Two, Three. Sugita, Yutaka, illus. LC 76-149045. 32p. (ps-2). 9.95 (ISBN 0-87592-022-5). Scroll Pr.
Tafuri, Nancy. Who's Counting? Tafuri, Nancy, illus. LC 85-17702. 24p. (ps-1). 1986. 14.95 (ISBN 0-688-06130-3); PLB 14.88 (ISBN 0-688-06131-1). Greenwillow.
Tallarico, Tony, illus. Finger Counting. 28p. (ps-1). 1984. bds. 2.95 (ISBN 0-89828-051-6). Tuffy Bks.
Things to Count. (Illus.). 8p. (ps). 1978. 2.50 (ISBN 0-448-46808-5, G&D). Putnam Pub Group.
Time-Life Books Editors. How Many Hippos? A Mix-&-Match Counting Book. (Illus.). 40p. (ps-2). 1990. write for info. (ISBN 0-8094-9258-X); lib. bdg. write for info. (ISBN 0-8094-9259-8). Time-Life.
Toy Book: Count One to Ten. Date not set. 4.50 (ISBN 0-317-93751-0). W J Fantasy.
Tyler, J. & Round, G. Starting to Count. (Illus.). 24p. (ps up). 1987. pap. 3.50 (ISBN 0-7460-0216-5). EDC.
Walsh, Ellen S. Mouse Count. D'Andrade, Diane, ed. Walsh, Ellen S., illus. 32p. (ps-1). 1991. 11.95 (ISBN 0-15-256023-8). HarBraceJ.
Wells, Rosemary. Max's Toys: A Counting Book. Wells, Rosemary, illus. LC 79-50748. (ps-k). 1979. bds. 3.95 (ISBN 0-8037-6068-X). Dial Bks Young.
Woodard, James & Purdy, Linda. One to Ten Count Again. (Illus.). (ps-k). 1972. PLB 6.89x (ISBN 0-914844-07-5). J Alden.
Worth, Bonnie. Fraggles Adding Fraggles. 1989. write for info. (ISBN 0-02-689262-6). Checkerboard Pr.
Wylie, Joanne & Wylie, David. Cuantos Monstruos?: Un Cuento de Numeros (How Many Monsters? Learning about Counting) LC 85-15136. (SPA., Illus.). 32p. (ps-2). 1988. PLB 14.60 (ISBN 0-516-34494-3); pap. 3.95 (ISBN 0-516-54494-2). Childrens.

Zeldin, Florence. A Mouse in Our Jewish House. Rauchwerger, Lisa, illus. LC 89-40362. 32p. (ps). 1990. 11.95 (ISBN 0-933873-43-3). Torah Aura.
This imaginative counting book, by noted children's author Florence Zeldin, combines the mastery of counting from one to twelve with the introduction of the basic celebrations of the Jewish year. A mouse named Archie Akhbar inhabits this book. Brought to life by the imaginative paper sculptures of Lisa Rauchwerger, Archie eats an escalating number of pieces of food on each subsequent Jewish holiday.
Publisher Provided Annotation.

Ziefert, Harriet. A Dozen Dogs: A Read-&-Count Story. Nicklaus, Carol, illus. LC 84-17797. 32p. (ps-1). 1985. lib. bdg. 6.99 (ISBN 0-394-96935-9, Random Juv); pap. 2.95 (ISBN 0-394-86935-4). Random.
—How Many Eggs? (Illus.). 16p. (ps-1). 1991. pap. 8.95 (ISBN 0-06-107419-5). HarpC Child Bks.

COUNTRY HOUSES
see Architecture, Domestic

COUNTRY LIFE
Here are entered descriptive, popular and literary works on living in the country. Works dealing with social organization and conditions in rural communities are entered under Sociology, Rural.
see also Farm Life; Outdoor Life
Butterworth, Nick & Inkpen, Mick. I Wonder in the Country. 14p. (ps). 1987. pap. 1.95 (ISBN 0-310-55431-4, 19043P). Zondervan.
Crews, Donald. Bigmama's. LC 90-33142. (Illus.). 32p. (ps up). 1991. 13.95 (ISBN 0-688-09950-5); PLB 13.88 (ISBN 0-688-09951-3). Greenwillow.
Jennings, Jay. Moments of Courage. (Illus.). 64p. (gr. 5-7). 1991. PLB 14.98 (ISBN 0-382-24108-8); PLB 11.24s.p.; pap. 8.95 (ISBN 0-382-24114-2); pap. 6.71s.p. Silver Burdett Pr.
North, Sterling. Rascal. (gr. 5 up). 1976. pap. 2.75 (ISBN 0-380-01518-8, Flare). Avon.
Rawcliffe, Micheal. Finding Out about Victorian Country Life. (Illus.). 64p. (gr. 7-12). 1984. 19.95 (ISBN 0-7134-4351-0, Pub. by Batsford England). Trafalgar Sq.
Rius, Maria & Parramon, J. M. The Countryside. (ps). 1986. 6.95 (ISBN 0-8120-5749-X); pap. 3.95 (ISBN 0-8120-3701-4). Barron.
Sancha, Sheila. The Luttrell Village: Country Life in the Middle Ages. Sancha, Sheila, illus. LC 82-45585. 64p. (gr. 6-9). 1983. 13.95 (ISBN 0-690-04323-6, Crowell Jr Bks); PLB 13.89 (ISBN 0-690-04324-4, Crowell Jr Bks). HarpC Child Bks.

COUNTRY LIFE–FICTION
Barklem, Jill. High Hills: Mini Edition. (Illus.). (ps-3). 1991. 9.95 (ISBN 0-399-22271-5, Philomel Bks). Putnam Pub Group.
Burch, Robert. Ida Early Comes Over the Mountain. LC 79-20532. (gr. 5-9). 1980. pap. 13.95 (ISBN 0-670-39169-7). Viking Child Bks.
—Ida Early Comes over the Mountain. (gr. 4 up). 1990. pap. 3.95 (ISBN 0-14-034534-5, Puffin). Puffin Bks.
—Queenie Peavy. 160p. (gr. 3-7). 1987. pap. 3.95 (ISBN 0-14-032305-8, Puffin). Puffin Bks.
Caudill, Rebecca. A Pocketful of Cricket. Ness, Evaline, illus. LC 64-12617. 48p. (gr. k-2). 1964. reinforced bdg. 7.95 (ISBN 0-03-089752-1); pap. 5.95 (ISBN 0-8050-1275-3). H Holt & Co.
Chekhov, Anton. A Day in the Country. Redpath, Ann, ed. Delessert, Etienne, illus. 32p. (gr. 4 up). 1985. PLB 10.95s.p. (ISBN 0-685-10395-1); 15.65 (ISBN 0-685-10396-X). Creative Ed.
Cleaver, Vera & Cleaver, Bill. Lady Ellen Grae. Raskin, Ellen, illus. LC 68-10981. (gr. 4-6). 1968. PLB 12.89 (ISBN 0-397-31012-9, Lipp Jr Bks). HarpC Child Bks.
Dupasquier, Philippe. Our House on the Hill. (Illus.). 32p. (ps-3). 1990. pap. 3.95 (ISBN 0-14-054227-2, Puffin). Puffin Bks.
Enright, Elizabeth. Then There Were Five. Enright, Elizabeth, illus. (gr. k-6). 1987. pap. 2.95 (ISBN 0-440-48806-0, YB). Dell.
Gipson, Fred. Curly & the Wild Boar. Himler, Ronald, illus. LC 77-25644. 96p. (gr. 5 up). 1979. 12.95 (ISBN 0-06-022014-7); PLB 12.89 (ISBN 0-06-022015-5). HarpC Child Bks.
Glines, Edna L. A Turtle on Her Toe. Pierpoint, Marsha W., illus. LC 83-17870. 66p. (ps up). 1984. 9.95 (ISBN 0-9612160-0-X). Tumbleweed Pub Co.
Haseley, Dennis. Shadows. Bowman, Leslie, illus. 80p. (gr. 2-6). 1991. 12.95 (ISBN 0-374-36761-2). FS&G.
Hope, Laura L. Bobbsey Twins' Adventure in the Country. (gr. 1-4). 1930. 4.50 (ISBN 0-448-08002-8, G&D). Putnam Pub Group.
Houston, Gloria. Littlejim. Allen, Thomas, illus. 176p. 1990. 14.95 (ISBN 0-399-22220-0, Philomel Bks). Putnam Pub Group.
Lyon, George-Ella. Come a Tide. Gammell, Stephen, illus. LC 89-35650. 32p. (ps-2). 1990. 14.95 (ISBN 0-531-05854-9); PLB 14.99 (ISBN 0-531-08454-X). Orchard Bks Watts.
Martin, Melanie. Madison Moves to the Country. Karas, G. Brian, illus. LC 88-1313. 48p. (Orig.). (gr. 1-4). 1989. PLB 9.89 (ISBN 0-8167-1345-6); pap. text ed. 2.95 (ISBN 0-8167-1346-4). Troll Assocs.
Montgomery, L. M. Anne of Avonlea. 288p. (gr. 5-8). 1976. pap. 2.95 (ISBN 0-553-24740-9). Bantam.
—Anne of Green Gables. 320p. (gr. 7-12). 1976. pap. 2.95 (ISBN 0-553-24295-4). Bantam.
Muller, Jorg. The Changing Countryside. Muller, Jorg, illus. LC 76-46647. (gr. 1 up). 1977. 18.95 (ISBN 0-689-50085-8, M K McElderry). Macmillan Child Grp.
Nesbit, Edith. The Railway Children. Butts, Dennis, ed. 224p. 1991. pap. 3.95 (ISBN 0-19-282659-X, 11912). Oxford U Pr.
Peck, Robert N. Soup's Goat. Robinson, Charles, illus. LC 83-16245. 112p. (gr. 4-6). 1984. lib. bdg. 12.99 (ISBN 0-394-96322-9); pap. 9.95 (ISBN 0-394-86322-4). Knopf.
Pedersen, Judy. Out in the Country. Pedersen, Judy, illus. LC 90-40032. 40p. (ps-2). 1991. 13.95 (ISBN 0-679-80630-X); PLB 14.99 (ISBN 0-679-90630-4). Knopf.
Pendergraft, Patricia. Brushy Mountain. (gr. 5 up). 1989. 14.95 (ISBN 0-399-21610-3, Philomel Bks). Putnam Pub Group.
Radin, Ruth Y. A Winter Place. O'Kelley, Mattie L., illus. LC 82-15349. 32p. (gr. 3 up). 1982. 15.95 (ISBN 0-316-73218-4, Joy St Bks). Little.
Rylant, Cynthia. Night in the Country. Szilagyi, Mary, illus. LC 85-70963. 32p. (ps-1). 1986. 13.95 (ISBN 0-02-777210-1, Bradbury Pr). Macmillan Child Grp.

—Night in the Country. Szilagyi, Mary, illus. LC 90-1043. 32p. (ps-2). 1991. pap. 4.95 (ISBN 0-689-71473-4, Aladdin). Macmillan Child Grp.
—This Year's Garden. Szilagyi, Mary, illus. LC 86-22224. 32p. (ps-3). 1987. pap. 4.95 (ISBN 0-689-71122-0, Aladdin). Macmillan Child Grp.
Sorensen, Virginia. Miracles on Maple Hill. Davis, Lambert, contrib. by. 192p. (gr. 3-7). 1990. pap. 3.95 (ISBN 0-15-254561-1). HarbraceJ.
Stanley, Diane. A Country Tale. Stanley, Diane, illus. LC 84-14399. 32p. (gr. k-3). 1985. 12.95 (ISBN 0-02-786780-3, Four Winds). Macmillan Child Grp.
Wilder, Laura I. Farmer Boy. rev. ed. Williams, Garth, illus. LC 52-7527. (gr. 2-7). 1961. 14.95 (ISBN 0-06-026425-X); PLB 14.89 (ISBN 0-06-026421-7). HarpC Child Bks.
Zeier, Joan T. The Elderberry Thicket. LC 90-90. 160p. (gr. 4-7). 1990. 12.95 (ISBN 0-689-31612-7, Atheneum Child Bk). Macmillan Child Grp.

COUPS D'ETAT

see Revolutions

COURAGE

see also Fear; Heroes

Brady, Janeen. Standin' Tall Courage. Wilson, Grant, illus. 22p. (Orig.). (ps-6). 1982. pap. text ed. 1.50 activity bk. (ISBN 0-944803-43-1); cassette & bk. 8.95 (ISBN 0-944803-45-8). Brite Intl.
Goley, Elaine. Courage. (Illus.). 32p. (gr. 1-4). 1987. PLB 13.26 (ISBN 0-86592-377-9). Rourke Corp.
Moncure, Jane B. Courage. rev. ed. Endes, Helen, illus. LC 80-39515. 32p. (gr. k-3). 1981. PLB 11.97 (ISBN 0-89565-202-1). Childs World.
Shusterman, Neal. Kid Heroes: True Stories of Rescuers, Survivors & Achievers. 1991. 14.95 (ISBN 0-312-85081-6). Tor Bks.
Sperry, Armstrong. Call It Courage. (gr. 4-7). 1990. pap. 3.95 (ISBN 0-689-71391-6, Aladdin). Macmillan Child Grp.
Stevens, Paul D. & Dillard, Wilson A., eds. The Air Force Cross, for Extraordinary Heroism. LC 88-62544. (Illus.). 96p. (gr. 7 up). 1989. 16.50 (ISBN 0-918495-22-9). Sharp & Dunn.

COURAGE–FICTION

Arvey, Michael. Reincarnation: Opposing Viewpoints. LC 89-37443. (Illus.). 112p. (gr. 3-10). 1989. PLB 13.95 (ISBN 0-89908-067-7). Greenhaven.

Bartlett, Jaye. Caterpillar Had a Dream: A Poetic Story about Dreams Coming True. (Illus.). 1991. 8.95 (ISBN 1-878064-02-9). TLC Bks.
"Caterpillar" isn't about pots of gold at the end of the rainbow. "Caterpillar" is about a dream, & the courage to try. Parents & children alike will be thrilled & inspired by Caterpillar's heartening adventure as he finds the courage & determination to make his dream come true.
Publisher Provided Annotation.

—Caterpillar Had a Dream: A Story about Dreams Coming True. Dubina, Alan, illus. 38p. (Orig.). (ps up). 1990. PLB 11.95 incl. cassette (ISBN 1-878064-00-2). New Age CT.
CATERPILLAR HAD A DREAM is a heartening story, written to encourage children to follow their dreams. The poetic book contains 38 pages of magical poetry & endearing color illustrations. CATERPILLAR HAD A DREAM is the first release in a series of twelve planned children's books. The series is being released under the Logo "Tender Loving Caretaker of Planet Earth." A portion of profits from the 'Caretaking Series' is donated to the World Children's Day Foundation, Washington, D.C., to help facilitate & encourage children to become active participant of "Caretaking Projects" in their communities. "CATERPILLAR HAD A DREAM is inspiring & enchanting! It's our two daughters' favorite story book & audio cassette. I feel it's one of the best stories for children I've ever read."--Lee Rector, Publisher, I.S.I. Publications, Tampa, Florida.
Publisher Provided Annotation.

Church, Kristine. My Brother John. Niland, Kilmeny, illus. LC 90-25868. 32p. (ps-3). 1991. 12.95 (ISBN 0-688-10800-8, Tambourine Bks); PLB 12.88 (ISBN 0-688-10801-6, Tambourine Bks). Morrow.
Crofford, Emily. A Matter of Pride. LaMarche, Jim, illus. LC 81-387. 48p. (gr. 2-6). 1991. Repr. of 1981 ed. PLB 11.95 (ISBN 0-87614-171-8, AACR2). Carolrhoda Bks.
Duncan, Jane. Brave Janet Reachfar. Hedderwick, Mairi, illus. LC 74-8693. 32p. (ps-3). 1975. 7.95 (ISBN 0-8164-3130-2, Clarion). HM.
Erickson, Karen. It's Dark-But I'm Not Scared. Roffey, Maureen, illus. (ps-k). 1987. pap. 4.95 (ISBN 0-670-81571-3). Viking Child Bks.
Henkes, Kevin. Sheila Rae, the Brave. Henkes, Kevin, illus. LC 86-25761. 32p. (gr. k-3). 1987. 13.95 (ISBN 0-688-07155-4); PLB 13.88 (ISBN 0-688-07156-2). Greenwillow.
Holland, Lynda. The Snicker-Snees. LC 90-71710. 44p. 1991. 5.95 (ISBN 1-55523-403-8). Winston-Derek.
Massi, Jeri. Courage by Darkness. 157p. (Orig.). 1987. pap. 4.95 (ISBN 0-89084-412-7). Bob Jones Univ Pr.
Naylor, Phyllis R. One of the Third-Grade Thonkers. Gaffney-Kessell, Walter, illus. LC 88-3130. 144p. (gr. 3-7). 1988. 12.95 (ISBN 0-689-31424-8, Atheneum Child Bk). Macmillan Child Grp.
Reynolds, Susan L. Strandia. (Illus.). 240p. (gr. 9-12). 1991. 14.95 (ISBN 0-374-37274-8). FS&G.
Sperry, Armstrong. Call It Courage. LC 40-4229. (gr. 5-7). 1973. pap. 3.95 (ISBN 0-02-045270-5, Collier Young Ad). Macmillan Child Grp.
Wilson, John. Lucky & the Pot of Gold. (Illus.). (gr. 1-3). Date not set. PLB 4.95 (ISBN 0-9627193-2-3, 428-983). Wilson Investment.
Winthrop, Elizabeth. Being Brave Is Best. Cooke, Tom, illus. 40p. (ps-3). 1984. 5.95 (ISBN 0-910313-19-9). Parker Bros.

COURTESY

see also Behavior; Etiquette

Fiday, Beverly & Crowdy, Deborah. Respect. Hutton, Kathryn, illus. LC 87-36981. 32p. (gr. k-3). 1988. PLB 11.97 (ISBN 0-89565-417-2); pap. 6.96 (ISBN 0-89565-520-9). Childs World.
Fletcher, Sarah. Teen Manners--Why Bother: Showing You Care Helps Others to Like you. (Illus.). 64p. (gr. 7-12). 1987. pap. 3.95 (ISBN 0-570-04449-9, 12-3060). Concordia.
Jordan, Sally. Manners: Don't Leave Home Without Them. Philbrook, Diana, illus. LC 87-92236. 32p. (gr. 4-9). 1988. 0.89 (ISBN 0-87403-440-X, 24-03650). Standard Pub.
Odor, Ruth S. Thanks. Indereiden, Nancy, illus. LC 79-23926. (ps-2). 1980. PLB 9.96 (ISBN 0-89565-113-0). Childs World.

COURTESY–FICTION

Berenstain, Stan & Berenstain, Janice. The Berenstain Bears Forget Their Manners. Berenstain, Stan & Berenstain, Janice, illus. 32p. (ps-1). 1986. pap. 5.95 with cassette (ISBN 0-394-88343-8, Random Juv). Random.
Erickson, Karen. Do I Have to Go Home? Roffey, Maureen, illus. 32p. (ps-k). 1989. pap. 5.95 (ISBN 0-670-82673-1). Viking Child Bks.
Meyer, Kathleen A. Bear, Your Manners Are Showing. Creative Studios 1, Inc. Staff, illus. 32p. (gr. k-2). 1987. 1.99 (ISBN 0-87403-271-7, 3771). Standard Pub.

COURTING

see Dating (Social Customs)

COURTS

see also Judges; Jury; Justice, Administration of

COURTSHIP

see Dating (Social Customs)

COUSTEAU, JACQUES-YVES, 1910-

Davidson, Margaret. Jacques Cousteau: A Biography. 128p. (Orig.). (gr. 3-7). 1991. pap. 2.75 (ISBN 0-685-37725-3). Scholastic Inc.
Greene, Carol. Jacques Cousteau: Man of the Oceans. Dobson, Steven, illus. LC 90-2162. 48p. (gr. k-3). 1990. PLB 15.27 (ISBN 0-516-04215-7); pap. 4.95 (ISBN 0-516-44215-5). Childrens.

COVERLETS

Johnston, Tony. The Quilt Story. De Paola, Tomie, illus. LC 84-18212. 32p. (gr. k-2). 1985. 13.95 (ISBN 0-399-21009-1, Putnam); pap. 5.95 (ISBN 0-399-21008-3). Putnam Pub Group.
Jonas, Ann. The Quilt. Jonas, Ann, illus. LC 83-25385. 32p. (ps-1). 1984. 13.95 (ISBN 0-688-03825-5); PLB 13.88 (ISBN 0-688-03826-3). Greenwillow.
Paul, Ann W. Eight Hands Round: A Patchwork Alphabet. Winter, Jeanette, illus. LC 88-745. 32p. (gr. 3 up). 1991. 14.95 (ISBN 0-06-024689-8); PLB 14.89 (ISBN 0-06-024704-5). HarpC Child Bks.

COW

see Cows

COWBOYS

see also Rodeos

Adams, Andy. Log of a Cowboy. (gr. 7 up). 1969. pap. 1.95 (ISBN 0-8049-0201-1, CL-201). Airmont.
Artman, John. Cowboys: An Activity Book. 64p. (gr. 4 up). 1982. 6.95 (ISBN 0-86653-068-1, GA 417). Good Apple.
Freedman, Russell. Cowboys of the Wild West. LC 85-4200. (Illus.). 128p. (gr. 3-7). 1985. 15.95 (ISBN 0-89919-301-3, Pub. by Clarion). Ticknor & Fields.
—Cowboys of the Wild West. (Illus.). (gr. 3-6). 1990. pap. 5.95 (ISBN 0-395-54800-4, Clarion Bks). HM.
Gorsline, Marie & Gorsline, Douglas. Cowboys. Gorsline, Douglas, illus. LC 78-1131. 32p. (ps-2). 1980. lib. bdg. 5.99 (ISBN 0-394-93935-2, Random Juv); pap. 2.25 (ISBN 0-394-83935-8). Random.
Landau, Elaine. Cowboys. (Illus.). 64p. (gr. 5-8). 1990. PLB 11.90 (ISBN 0-531-10866-X). Watts.
Martini, Teri. Cowboys. LC 81-10049. (Illus.). 48p. (gr. k-4). 1981. PLB 14.60 (ISBN 0-516-01611-3). Childrens.
Matthews, L. Cowboys. (Illus.). 32p. (gr. 3-8). Date not set. PLB 17.26 (ISBN 0-86625-363-7). Rourke Corp.
Seidman, Laurence I. Once in the Saddle: The Cowboy's Frontier, 1866-1896. Scott, John A., ed. (Illus.). 160p. 1990. 16.95x (ISBN 0-8160-2373-5). Facts on File.
Tomb, Ubet. Cowboys. (Illus.). 48p. (gr. 6). 1984. pap. 3.50 (ISBN 0-88388-114-4). Bellerophon Bks.
Williams, Robert L. Cowboy's Caravan. (Illus.). 150p. 1990. 16.95 (ISBN 0-9627534-0-8). Skyspec Pub.

COWBOYS–FICTION

Blackmore, Richard D. Lorna Doone. 378p. 1981. Repr. PLB 23.95 (ISBN 0-89967-024-5). Harmony Raine.
Brooks, Walter R. Freddy the Cowboy. Morrill, Leslie & Wiese, Kurt, illus. LC 86-40423. 240p. (gr. 3-7). 1987. Knopf.
Chandler, Edna W. Cowboy Andy. LC 59-4447. (Illus.). 72p. (gr. 1-2). 1959. 3.95 (ISBN 0-394-80008-7). Beginner.
Downing, Warwick. Kid Curry's Last Ride. LC 88-19822. 176p. (gr. 5-7). 1989. 12.95 (ISBN 0-531-05802-6); PLB 12.99 (ISBN 0-531-08402-7). Orchard Bks Watts.
Erickson, John R. Cowboys Are Partly Human. Holmes, Gerald L., illus. 110p. (Orig.). (gr. 3 up). 1983. 9.95 (ISBN 0-9608612-6-2); pap. 5.95 (ISBN 0-9608612-4-6). Maverick Bks.
Evans, Max. My Pardner. Bjorklund, Lorence, illus. LC 75-187421. 104p. (gr. 5-9). 1972. 3.95 (ISBN 0-395-13725-X). HM.
Findlay, Lois P. The Enchanted Cowboy. Roberts, Anne F., ed. Williams, Exin R., illus. 99p. (Orig.). (gr. 1 up). 1988. pap. 5.00 (ISBN 0-317-89520-6). Libr Commns Servs.
Halvorson, Marilyn. Cowboys Don't Cry. (gr. 6 up). 1986. pap. 3.25 (ISBN 0-440-91303-9, LFL). Dell.
Hancock, Sibyl. Old Blue. Ingraham, Erick, illus. 48p. (gr. 1-4). 1980. PLB 6.99 (ISBN 0-399-61141-X, Putnam). Putnam Pub Group.
Hooker, Ruth. Matthew the Cowboy. Tucker, Kathy, ed. Smith, Cat B., illus. LC 89-21456. 32p. (ps-2). 1990. PLB 12.95 (ISBN 0-8075-4999-1). A Whitman.
Hutchens, Paul. Sugar Creek Gang & the Battle of the Bees. 128p. (gr. 3-7). 1972. pap. 3.50 (ISBN 0-8024-4830-5). Moody.
Kellogg, Steven. Pecos Bill. Kellogg, Steven, illus. LC 86-784. 32p. (ps up). 1986. 15.95 (ISBN 0-688-05871-X); lib. bdg. 15.88 (ISBN 0-688-05872-8, Morrow Jr Bks). Morrow Jr Bks.
Khalsa, Dayal K. Cowboy Dreams. Khalsa, Dayal K., illus. LC 89-22782. 32p. (gr. 1-3). 1990. 13.95 (ISBN 0-517-57490-X); PLB 14.99 (ISBN 0-517-57491-8). McKay.
—Cowboy Dreams. Khalsa, Dayal K., illus. (gr. k-4). 1990. 13.95 (C N Potter Bks). Crown.
Kimmel, Eric A. Four Dollars & Fifty Cents. Rounds, Glen, illus. LC 89-77515. 32p. (gr. k-3). 1990. reinforced 14.95 (ISBN 0-8234-0817-5). Holiday.
Lenski, Lois. Cowboy Small. LC 60-12094. (Illus.). (gr. k-3). 1980. 5.25 (ISBN 0-8098-1021-2). McKay.
Reid, Ace. Cowpokes Comin' Yore Way. 5th ed. Reid, Ace, illus. 64p. (gr. k up). 1985. pap. 5.00 (ISBN 0-917207-05-X). Reid Ent.
—Cowpokes Cookbook & Cartoons. 12th ed. Reid, Ace, illus. 64p. (gr. 5 up). pap. 5.00 (ISBN 0-917207-06-8). Reid Ent.
—Cowpokes Cow Country Cartoons. 14th ed. Reid, Ace, illus. Barker, S. Omar, intro. by. (Illus.). 56p. (gr. 5 up). pap. 5.00 (ISBN 0-917207-00-9). Reid Ent.
—Cowpokes Rarin' to Go. 2nd ed. Reid, Ace, illus. 74p. (gr. 5 up). pap. 5.00 (ISBN 0-917207-09-2). Reid Ent.
—Cowpokes Ride Again. 4th ed. Reid, Ace, illus. 64p. (gr. k up). 1985. pap. 5.00 (ISBN 0-917207-08-4). Reid Ent.
—Cowpokes Tales & Cartoons. 2nd ed. Reid, Ace, illus. Pickens, Slim, intro. by. (Illus.). 64p. (gr. 5 up). pap. 5.00 (ISBN 0-917207-10-6). Reid Ent.
—Cowpokes Wanted. 12th ed. Reid, Ace, illus. Gipson, Fred, intro. by. (Illus.). 62p. (gr. 5 up). pap. 5.00 (ISBN 0-917207-02-5). Reid Ent.
—Draggin' S Ranch Cowpokes. 14th ed. Reid, Ace, illus. 65p. (gr. 5 up). pap. 5.00 (ISBN 0-917207-04-1). Reid Ent.
—More Cowpokes. 14th ed. Reid, Ace, illus. Robertson, FrankC., intro. by. (Illus.). 60p. (gr. 5 up). pap. 5.00 (ISBN 0-917207-01-7). Reid Ent.
Rounds, Glen. Cowboys. Rounds, Glen, illus. LC 90-46501. 32p. (ps-3). 1991. PLB 14.95 (ISBN 0-8234-0867-1). Holiday.
Sewall, Marcia. Riding That Strawberry Roan. LC 84-21904. (Illus.). 32p. (ps-2). 1985. pap. 9.95 (ISBN 0-670-80623-4). Viking Child Bks.
Wister, Owen. Virginian. (gr. 8 up). 1964. pap. 2.95 (ISBN 0-8049-0046-9, CL-46). Airmont.

COWBOYS–SONGS AND MUSIC

Moon, Dolly. My Very First Piano Book of Cowboy Songs: Twenty-Two Favorite Songs Easy in Piano Arrangement. (Illus.). 32p. (gr. 2 up). 1983. pap. 3.50 (ISBN 0-486-24311-7). Dover.

COWS

see also Dairying; Milk

Anders, Rebecca. Clover the Calf. Hammarberg, Dyan, tr. from FRE. LC 76-29448. (Illus.). 24p. (gr. k-4). 1977. PLB 6.95 (ISBN 0-87614-073-8). Carolrhoda Bks.
Braithwaite, Althea. Can You Moo? Rylands, Ljiljana, illus. 24p. (ps-2). 1990. 1.95 (ISBN 1-878624-26-1, 1553800026). McClanahan Bk.
Henderson, Kathy. Dairy Cows. LC 88-11123. 48p. (gr. k-4). 1988. PLB 14.60 (ISBN 0-516-01152-9); pap. 4.95 (ISBN 0-516-41152-7). Childrens.
Hutchings, Tony. Little Spotted Calf. Hutchings, Tony, illus. 12p. (ps-1). 1990. 4.95 (ISBN 1-878624-12-1, 1553800012). McClanahan Bk.
Moncure, Jane B. Ice-Cream Cows & Mitten Sheep. Friedman, Joy, illus. LC 87-14603. 32p. (ps-2). 1987. PLB 11.97 (ISBN 0-89565-403-2); pap. 6.96 (ISBN 0-89565-434-2). Childs World.
Royston, Angela. Cow. (ps-3). 1990. PLB 10.40 (ISBN 0-531-19077-3). Watts.
Stone, Lynn. Cows. (Illus.). 24p. (gr. k-5). 1990. lib. bdg. 11.93 (ISBN 0-86593-039-2); lib. bdg. 8.95s.p. (ISBN 0-685-36309-0). Rourke Corp.

COWS–FICTION

Bernet, Elizabeth C. Wings of Love. Whiting, William T., illus. 40p. (ps). 1988. 11.95 (ISBN 0-88138-109-8). Green Tiger Pr.
Bulla, Clyde R. Dandelion Hill. Degen, Bruce, illus. LC 81-15164. 32p. (ps-1). 1982. 9.75 (ISBN 0-525-45101-3, Dutton). NAL-Dutton.
Cartwright, Stephen. Who Says Moo? (ps up). 1989. PLB 5.98 (ISBN 0-7924-5041-8, Mallard Pr). BDD Promo Bk.
Chase, Edith N. The New Baby Calf. Reid, Barbara, illus. LC 86-3931. (gr. 3-6). 1986. 8.95 (ISBN 0-590-40457-1). Scholastic Inc.
Christison, MaryAnn & Bassano, Sharron. Purple Cows & Potato Chips. (Illus.). 120p. (gr. 5-12). 1987. pap. text ed. 17.95 (ISBN 0-88084-230-X). Alemany Pr.
Cole, Ann & Haas, Carolyn. Purple Cow to the Rescue. LC 82-47913. (Illus.). 160p. (gr. 1-5). 1982. 14.95 (ISBN 0-316-15104-1); pap. 8.95 (ISBN 0-316-15106-8). Little.
Cooper, Susan. The Silver Cow: A Welsh Tale. Hutton, Warwick, illus. LC 82-13928. 32p. (gr. k-4). 1983. 13.95 (ISBN 0-689-50236-2, M K McElderry). Macmillan Child Grp.
The Cow That Went over the Mountain. (ps-3). 1989. Incl. cass. write for info. (13688, Pub. by Golden Bks). Western Pub.
Dennis, Wesley. Flip & the Cows. LC 88-39705. (Illus.). 64p. (ps-2). 1989. Repr. of 1942 ed. lib. bdg. 15.00 (ISBN 0-208-02240-6, Linnet). Shoe String.
Edens, Coope. Santa Cows. Lane, Daniel, illus. 40p. (gr. 2 up). 1991. jacketed, reinforced bdg. 14.00 (ISBN 0-671-74863-7, Green Tiger). S&S Trade.
Forrester, Victoria. The Magnificent Moo. LC 82-13781. (Illus.). 40p. (gr. k-1). 1983. 10.95 (ISBN 0-689-30954-6, Atheneum Childrens Bks). Macmillan Child Grp.
Fussy, Joyce. Cows in the Corn. 168p. 1989. Repr. of 1978 ed. lib. bdg. 18.95 (ISBN 1-85089-309-8, Pub. by Isis Lrg UK). Isis NY.
Greenleaf, E. Who Wants to Nap? LC 68-56820. (Illus.). 32p. (gr. 2-3). PLB 9.95 (ISBN 0-87783-050-9). Oddo.
Hargreaves, Roger. Molly Moo. Jolliffe, Gray, illus. LC 89-60415. 32p. (Orig.). (ps-3). 1989. pap. 1.95 (ISBN 0-679-80122-7). Random.
Herriot, James. Blossom Comes Home. Brown, Ruth, illus. 1988. 10.95 (ISBN 0-312-02169-0). St Martin.
Horvath, Polly. An Occasional Cow. (Illus.). 112p. (gr. 3-7). 1989. 13.95 (ISBN 0-374-35559-2); pap. 3.95 (ISBN 0-374-45573-2). FS&G.
Krasilovsky, Phyllis. Cow Who Fell in the Canal. Spier, Peter, illus. LC 56-8236. 38p. (gr. k-1). 1985. pap. 11.95 (ISBN 0-385-07585-5). Doubleday.
Le Tord, Bijou. A Brown Cow. Le Tord, Bijou, illus. (ps-1). 1989. 12.95 (ISBN 0-316-52166-3). Little.
Lewis, J. Patrick. The Tsar & the Amazing Cow. Henstra, Friso, illus. LC 86-29255. 32p. (ps-3). 1988. 10.95 (ISBN 0-8037-0410-0); PLB 10.89 (ISBN 0-8037-0411-9). Dial Bks Young.
Oppenheim, Joanne. Not Now! Said the Cow, Level 2. Demarest, Chris, illus. pap. 3.50 (ISBN 0-317-99646-0). Bantam.
—The Not Now! Said the Cow-Bank Street. (ps-3). 1989. pap. 3.50 (ISBN 0-553-34691-1). Bantam.
—Not Now! Said the Cow: Level 2. Demarest, Chris, illus. 1989. 9.99 (ISBN 0-553-05826-6). Bantam.
Swan, Walter. Brenda the Cow & the Little White Hen. Swan, Deloris, ed. Asch, Connie, illus. 16p. (Orig.). (gr. 2-3). 1989. pap. 1.50 (ISBN 0-927176-02-5). Swan Enterp.
Wildsmith, Brian. Daisy. Wildsmith, Brian, illus. LC 83-12150. 48p. (ps-1). 1984. (Pant Bks Young); lib. bdg. 11.99 (ISBN 0-394-95975-2). Pantheon.

COYOTES

Ahlstrom, Mark E. The Coyote. LC 85-24290. (Illus.). 48p. (gr. 4-8). 1985. PLB 10.95 (ISBN 0-89686-277-1, Crestwood Hse). Macmillan Child Grp.
Carrick, Carol. Two Coyotes. Carrick, Donald, illus. 32p. (gr. 1-5). 1982. 13.95 (ISBN 0-89919-078-2, Clarion). HM.

COYOTES–FICTION

Bierhorst, John. Doctor Coyote: A Native American Aesop's Fables. Watson, Wendy, illus. LC 86-8669. 48p. (gr. 2-5). 1987. 15.95 (ISBN 0-02-709780-3, Mcmillan Child Bk). Macmillan Child Grp.
Nunes, Susan. Coyote Dreams. Himler, Ronald, illus. LC 87-30288. 32p. (ps-3). 1988. 13.95 (ISBN 0-689-31398-5, Atheneum Child Bk). Macmillan Child Grp.

CRABS

Bailey, Jill. Discovering Crabs & Lobsters. (Illus.). 48p. (gr. 1 up). 1987. lib. bdg. 11.90 (ISBN 0-531-18125-1, Pub. by Bookwright Pr). Watts.
—Life Cycle of a Crab. (ps-3). 1990. PLB 8.99 (ISBN 0-531-18317-3). Watts.
Butterworth, Christine & Bailey, Donna. Crabs. LC 90-36168. (Illus.). 32p. (gr. 1-4). 1990. PLB 14.64 (ISBN 0-8114-2640-8). Steck-V.
Coldrey, Jennifer. The Crab on the Seashore. LC 85-30293. (Illus.). 32p. (gr. 4-6). 1987. 10.95 (ISBN 1-55532-060-0). Gareth Stevens Inc.
—The World of Crabs. LC 85-30294. (Illus.). 32p. (gr. 2-3). 1986. 10.95 (ISBN 1-55532-063-5). Gareth Stevens Inc.
Cutting, Brian & Cutting, Jillian. The Hermit Crab. McCausland, Ian, illus. 16p. (Orig.). (gr. k-2). 1988. pap. text ed. 23.00 (ISBN 1-55911-033-3). Wright Group.
—The Hermit Crab, 6 bks. McCausland, Ian, illus. 16p. (Orig.). (gr. k-2). 1988. Set. pap. text ed. 19.80 (ISBN 1-55911-034-1). Wright Group.
Holling, Holling C. Pagoo. Holling, L. W., illus. (gr. 3-9). 1957. 15.95 (ISBN 0-395-06826-6). HM.
Johnson, Sylvia A. Crabs. Sakurai, Atsushi, illus. LC 82-10056. 48p. (gr. 4 up). 1982. PLB 14.95 (ISBN 0-8225-1471-0). Lerner Pubns.
—Hermit Crabs. Kawashima, Kazunari, illus. 48p. (gr. 4 up). 1989. PLB 14.95 (ISBN 0-8225-1488-5). Lerner Pubns.
McDonald, Megan. Is This a House for Hermit Crab? Schindler, S. D., illus. LC 89-35653. 32p. (ps-1). 1990. 14.95 (ISBN 0-531-05855-7); PLB 14.99 (ISBN 0-531-08455-8). Orchard Bks Watts.
Pohl, Kathleen. Crabs. (Illus.). 32p. (gr. 3-7). 1986. PLB 16.67 (ISBN 0-8172-2716-4); pap. text ed. 9.27 (ISBN 0-8172-2734-2). Raintree Pubs.
—Hermit Crabs. (Illus.). 32p. (gr. 3-7). 1986. PLB 16.67 (ISBN 0-8172-2721-0); pap. 9.27 (ISBN 0-8172-2739-3). Raintree Pubs.

CRABS–FICTION

Cummings, Priscilla. Chadwick & the Garplegrungen. Cohen, A. R., illus. LC 87-71087. 32p. (gr. k-4). 1987. 6.95 (ISBN 0-87033-377-1). Tidewater.
—Chadwick the Crab. Cohen, A. R., illus. LC 85-41005. 32p. (gr. k-4). 1986. 6.95 (ISBN 0-87033-347-X). Tidewater.
—Chadwick's Wedding. Cohen, A. R., illus. LC 88-51677. 30p. (gr. k-4). 1989. 6.95 (ISBN 0-87033-390-9). Tidewater.
Dawson, C. D. Napoleon the Land Crab. (Illus.). 32p. (gr. k-4). 1990. pap. 4.95 (ISBN 0-685-35164-5). Littlepage.
Harriman, Edward. Leroy the Lobster & Crabby Crab. (Illus.). (ps-1). 1967. pap. 6.95 (ISBN 0-89272-000-X). Down East.
Kipling, Rudyard. The Crab That Played With the Sea: A Just So Story. Foreman, Michael, illus. LC 83-71484. 32p. (gr. 1-5). 1983. PLB 10.95 (ISBN 0-911745-06-8). P Bedrick Bks.
Knutson, Barbara. Why the Crab Has No Head: An African Folktale. (Illus.). 24p. (ps-3). 1987. lib. bdg. 9.95 (ISBN 0-87614-322-2); pap. 4.95 (ISBN 0-87614-489-X). Carolrhoda Bks.
Peet, Bill. Kermit the Hermit. (Illus.). (gr. k-3). 1980. 13.95 (ISBN 0-395-15084-1); pap. 4.95 (ISBN 0-395-29607-2). HM.
Tafuri, Nancy. Follow Me! LC 89-23259. (Illus.). 24p. (ps up). 1990. 13.95 (ISBN 0-688-08773-6); lib. bdg. 13.88 (ISBN 0-688-08774-4). Greenwillow.
Tate, Suzanne. Crabby & Nabby: A Tale of Two Blue Crabs. Melvin, James, illus. LC 88-61096. 28p. (Orig.). (gr. k-3). 1988. pap. 3.95 (ISBN 0-9616344-3-X). Nags Head Art.
Watkins, Dawn L. The Cranky Blue Crab: A Tale in Verse. Smith, Anne, ed. Davis, Tim, illus. 32p. (Orig.). (gr. k-1). 1990. pap. write for info. (ISBN 0-89084-506-9). Bob Jones Univ Pr.

CRADLE SONGS

see Lullabies

CRAFTS

see Arts and Crafts; Handicraft

CRANES (BIRDS)

Byars, Betsy C. The House of Wings. Schwartz, Daniel, illus. 136p. (gr. 3-7). 1982. pap. 3.95 (ISBN 0-14-031523-3, Puffin). Puffin Bks.
Horn, Gabriel. The Crane. LC 88-12031. (Illus.). 48p. (gr. 5-6). 1988. PLB 10.95 (ISBN 0-89686-393-X, Crestwood Hse). Macmillan Child Grp.
Patent, Dorothy H. The Whooping Crane: A Comeback Story. Munoz, William, photos by. LC 88-2871. (Illus.). 96p. (gr. 4 up). 1988. 14.95 (ISBN 0-89919-455-9, Pub. by Clarion). Ticknor & Fields.
Roop, Peter & Roop, Connie. Seasons of the Cranes. (Illus.). 32p. (gr. 4-7). 1989. 14.95 (ISBN 0-8027-6859-8); PLB 15.85 (ISBN 0-8027-6860-1). Walker & Co.
Voeller, Edward. The Red-Crowned Crane. LC 89-11718. (Illus.). 60p. (gr. 3 up). 1989. PLB 12.95 (ISBN 0-87518-417-0, Dillon). Macmillan Child Grp.

CRANES, DERRICKS, ETC.

Marston, Hope I. Load Lifters. (Illus.). 64p. (gr. 2-5). 1988. 13.95 (ISBN 0-396-09226-8, Putnam). Putnam Pub Group.
Stephen, R. J. Cranes. LC 85-42089. (Illus.). 32p. (gr. k-6). 1987. lib. bdg. 11.40 (ISBN 0-531-10183-5). Watts.

CRAYON DRAWING

Pluckrose, Henry. Crayons. Fairclough, Chris, photos by. Franklin Watts Ltd., ed. LC 87-50907. (Illus.). 32p. (gr. k-6). 1988. PLB 11.90 (ISBN 0-531-10470-2). Watts.

CRAYON DRAWING–FICTION

Johnson, Crockett. Harold & the Purple Crayon. Johnson, Crockett, illus. LC 55-7683. 64p. (ps-3). 1981. pap. 3.95 (ISBN 0-06-443022-7, Trophy). HarpC Child Bks.
—Harold's ABC. Johnson, Crockett, illus. LC 63-14444. 64p. (ps-3). 1981. pap. 3.95 (ISBN 0-06-443023-5, Trophy). HarpC Child Bks.
—Harold's Circus. Johnson, Crockett, illus. LC 59-5318. 64p. (ps-3). 1981. pap. 2.95 (ISBN 0-06-443024-3, Trophy). HarpC Child Bks.
—Harold's Trip to the Sky. Johnson, Crockett, illus. LC 57-9262. 64p. (ps-3). 1981. pap. 3.95 (ISBN 0-06-443025-1, Trophy). HarpC Child Bks.
—Picture for Harold's Room. Johnson, Crockett, illus. LC 60-6372. (gr. k-3). 1960. PLB 11.89 (ISBN 0-06-023006-1). HarpC Child Bks.

CRAZY HORSE, OGLALA INDIAN, 1842?-1877

Benchley, Nathaniel. Only Earth & Sky Last Forever. LC 72-82891. 204p. (gr. 7 up). 1974. pap. 4.95 (ISBN 0-06-440049-2, Trophy). HarpC Child Bks.
Wheeler, Jill. The Story of Crazy Horse. Deegan, Paul, ed. Dodson, Liz, illus. 32p. (gr. 4). 1989. PLB 11.95 (ISBN 0-939179-66-0). Abdo & Dghtrs.
Zadra, Dan. Indians of America: Crazy Horse. rev. ed. (gr. 2-4). 1987. PLB 11.50s.p. (ISBN 0-88682-163-0); 16.45 (ISBN 0-318-32943-3). Creative Ed.

CREATION

see also Earth; Evolution; Geology; God; Man; Mythology; Universe

All the Animals. (ps-1). 1990. pap. 6.95 (ISBN 0-7459-1838-7). Lion USA.
Animals Two by Two. (ps-1). 1990. pap. 6.95 (ISBN 0-7459-1839-5). Lion USA.
Aronow, Sara. Seven Days of Creation. Seligson, Judith, illus. 32p. (ps-2). 1985. 4.95 (ISBN 0-87203-119-5). Hermon.
Baxendale, Jean. Preschool Bible Activities, 4 vols. Pollard, Nan, illus. 24p. (Orig.). (ps). 1982. No. 1. pap. 1.79 (ISBN 0-87239-487-5, 2459); No. 2. pap. 1.79 (ISBN 0-87239-488-3, 2460); No. 3. pap. 1.79 (ISBN 0-87239-489-1, 2461); No. 4. pap. 1.79 (ISBN 0-87239-490-5, 2462). Standard Pub.
Baynes, Pauline. Let There Be Light. Baynes, Pauline, illus. 32p. (gr. 1 up). 1991. 13.95 (ISBN 0-02-708542-2, Mcmillan Child Bk). Macmillan Child Grp.
Beaude, Pierre-Marie. The Book of Creation. Clements, Andrew, tr. Lemoine, Georges, illus. LC 90-35418. 56p. (gr. 5 up). 1991. 16.95 (ISBN 0-88708-141-X). Picture Bk Studio.
Caffrey, Stephanie & Kenslea, Timothy. How the World Began. 16p. (gr. 3-5). 1978. pap. 1.95 (ISBN 0-8192-1233-4). Morehouse Pub.
Caswell, Helen. God Must Like to Laugh. Caswell, Helen, illus. (ps-3). 1987. pap. 4.95 (ISBN 0-687-15188-0). Abingdon.
Dakenbing, William F. The Creation Book. Hendrickson, et al, illus. Von Braun, Wehrner. LC 75-39840. 70p. (gr. 3 up). 1976. 5.95 (ISBN 0-685-68397-4); pap. 3.95 (ISBN 0-685-68398-2). Triumph Pub.
Daniel, Rebecca & Hierstein, Judy. God's Animal Alphabet. 48p. (ps-1). 1991. 8.95 (ISBN 0-86653-577-2). Good Apple.
Davidson, Alice J. Alice in Bibleland Storybooks: Story of Creation. Marshall, Victoria, illus. 32p. (gr. 3 up). 1984. 4.95 (ISBN 0-8378-5066-5). Gibson.
Eberle, Bob. Warm-Up to Creativity. Weber, June Kern, illus. 64p. (gr. 5 up). 1985. wkbk. 6.95 (ISBN 0-86653-275-7, GA 667). Good Apple.
Erickson, Dean. Seven Days to Care for God's World: Rupert Learns What It Means to Take Care of God's Earth. 1991. pap. 6.95 (ISBN 0-8066-2533-3). Augsburg Fortress.
Gambill, Henrietta D. Seven Special Days. Boddy, Joe, illus. 32p. (gr. k-2). 1987. 1.99 (ISBN 0-87403-281-4, 3781). Standard Pub.
God Made All the Colors. 8p. (ps). 1983. bds. 2.95 (ISBN 0-85648-146-7). Lion USA.
God Made Them All. 8p. (ps). 1983. bds. 2.95 (ISBN 0-85648-147-5). Lion USA.
God's World, Our World. (Illus.). 32p. (ps-2). 1985. 1.95 (ISBN 0-225-66389-9). Harper SF.
Great & Small. 8p. (ps). 1983. bds. 2.95 (ISBN 0-7459-1427-6). Lion USA.
Hamilton, Virginia. In the Beginning: Creation Stories from Around the World. Moser, Barry, illus. 176p. (ps up). 1988. 18.95 (ISBN 0-15-238740-4). HarBraceJ.
Hershey, Katherine. Beginnings. (Illus.). 51p. (gr. k-6). 1979. pap. text ed. 9.45 (ISBN 1-55976-004-4). CEF Press.
Hilliard, Dick & Valenti-Hilliard, Beverly. Surprises! Collopy, George F., illus. 44p. (Orig.). (gr. 1 up). 1981. pap. text ed. 4.95 (ISBN 0-89390-031-1). Resource Pubns.
Jaspersohn, William. How the Universe Began. Accardo, Anthony, illus. LC 85-10545. 48p. (gr. 2-4). 1985. PLB 10.90 (ISBN 0-531-10032-4). Watts.
Kasuya, Masahiro. The Beginning of the World. Kasuya, Masahiro, illus. LC 81-3582. (ps-2). 1982. 8.95g (ISBN 0-687-02765-9). Abingdon.

Lashbrook, Marilyn. Someone to Love: The Story of Creation. Britt, Stephanie M., illus. LC 87-60261. 32p. (ps). 1987. 5.95 (ISBN 0-86606-426-5, 841). Roper Pr.
Lavitt, Edward & McDowell, Robert. In the Beginning Creation Stories. new ed. 156p. (gr. 6-12). 1973. 6.95 (ISBN 0-89388-096-5). Okpaku Communications.
Le Tord, Bijou. The Deep Blue Sea. Le Tord, Bijou, illus. LC 89-16314. 32p. 1990. 13.95 (ISBN 0-531-05853-0); PLB 13.99 (ISBN 0-531-08453-1). Orchard Bks Watts.
McNeil. How Things Began. (gr. 2-5). 1975. (Usborne-Hayes); PLB 13.96 (ISBN 0-88110-114-1); pap. 6.95 (ISBN 0-86020-199-6). EDC.
Mitchell, Stephen. Creation. LC 89-39726. (Illus.). 40p. 1990. 15.95 (ISBN 0-8037-0617-0); PLB 15.89 (ISBN 0-8037-0618-9). Dial Bks Young.
Richards, Larry. It Couldn't Just Happen. 191p. 1989. write for info. (ISBN 0-8499-0715-2). Word Bks.
Swartzentruber. God Made Us in a Wonderful Way. 1976. 2.45 (ISBN 0-686-18184-0). Rod & Staff.
Taylor, Kenneth N. What High School Students Should Know about Creation. (gr. 9-12). 1983. pap. 2.95 (ISBN 0-8423-7872-3). Tyndale.
Ulmer. Adam's Story. LC 59-1292. 24p. (Orig.). (gr. k-4). 1985. pap. 1.39 (ISBN 0-570-06191-1). Concordia.
Waskow, Arthur, et al. Before There Was a Before. LC 84-11177. (Illus.). 88p. (gr. 1-6). 1984. 8.95 (ISBN 0-915361-08-6, Dist. by Watts). Adama Pubs Inc.

CREATION (LITERARY, ARTISTIC, ETC.)

Bashful Bard. Things to Make: The Dew Drop Dell Craft & Activity Book, No. 1. Bashful Bard, illus. 24p. (Orig.). (ps-1). 1989. pap. 2.99 (ISBN 1-877906-07-7). Kenney Pubns.
Bauman, Toni & Zinkgraf, June. Spring Surprises. 240p. (gr. k-6). 1979. 14.95 (ISBN 0-916456-54-4, GA109). Good Apple.
Berry, Joy W. Teach Me about Pretending. Dickey, Kate, ed. LC 85-45091. (Illus.). 36p. (ps). 1986. 4.98 (ISBN 0-685-10731-0). Grolier Inc.
Cline, Starr. Teaching for Talent. Taylor, Christina, illus. Tannenbaum, A. J., intro. by. (Illus.). 56p. (Orig.). (gr. k-6). 1984. 6.95 (ISBN 0-88047-040-2, 8406). DOK Pubs.
Cote. Fairness, Reading Level 2. (Illus.). 32p. (gr. 1-4). Date not set. PLB 13.26 (ISBN 0-86592-445-7). Rourke Corp.
Dellosa, Janet, et al. All about Me. Dellosa, Janet & Carson, Patti, illus. 32p. (ps-1). 1983. pap. 1.98 (ISBN 0-88724-009-7, CD-7010). Carson-Dellos.
Duna, Bill & Duna, Lois. Let's Play & Play & Play... Practice & Assignment Book. (Illus.). 56p. (ps up). 1983. pap. 6.95 (ISBN 0-942928-02-4). Duna Studios.
Espeland, Pamela & Wallner, Rosemary. Making the Most of Today: Daily Readings for Young People on Self-Awareness, Creativity & Self-Esteem. 380p. (Orig.). (gr. 6 up). 1991. pap. 8.95 (ISBN 0-915793-33-4). Free Spirit Pub.
Fearn, Leif. The First First I Think. 91p. (gr. 1-3). 1981. 6.95 (ISBN 0-940444-14-3). Kabyn.
Fearn, Leif & Garner, Irene A. The Alpha Cards. 54p. (gr. 2-9). 1982. card pack 14.00 (ISBN 0-940444-12-7). Kabyn.
—Maneras de Divertirme con Mi Mente. (Illus.). 182p. (gr. 3-9). 1982. 6.50 (ISBN 0-940444-16-X). Kabyn.
Fearn, Leif & Goliaz-Benson, Ursula. Forty-Two Ways to Have Fun with My Mind. Curtner, Rondi L., illus. 58p. (ps-6). 1976. 5.00 (ISBN 0-940444-00-3). Kabyn.
Fearn, Leif & Golisz-Benson, Ursula. Fifty-Two Ways to Have Fun with My Mind. Emmet, Mary, illus. 62p. (gr. 1-3). 1975. 5.00 (ISBN 0-940444-01-1). Kabyn.
—Seventy-Two Ways to Have Fun with My Mind. Curtner, Rondi, illus. 80p. (Orig.). (gr. 4-6). 1976. 5.00 (ISBN 0-940444-03-8). Kabyn.
—Sixty-Two Ways to Have Fun with My Mind. (Illus.). 72p. (Orig.). (gr. 3-6). 1982. 5.00 (ISBN 0-940444-02-X). Kabyn.
Forte, Imogene. Box Crafts: Over 50 Things to Make & Do with Boxes of Every Size. LC 86-82933. (Illus.). 80p. (gr. k-6). 1987. pap. text ed. 3.95 (ISBN 0-86530-123-9, IP 942). Incentive Pubns.
—Crayons & Markers: Artistic Creations, One of a Kind & Made By You. LC 86-82934. (Illus.). 80p. (gr. k-6). 1987. pap. text ed. 3.95 (ISBN 0-86530-162-X, IP 943). Incentive Pubns.
—Dinosaurs: Facts Fun, & Fantastic Crafts. LC 86-82932. (Illus.). 80p. (gr. k-6). 1987. pap. text ed. 3.95 (ISBN 0-86530-149-2, IP 944). Incentive Pubns.
—The Kids' Stuff: Book of Patterns, Projects & Plans to Perk Up Early Learning Programs. LC 82-83051. (Illus.). 200p. (ps-1). 1982. pap. text ed. 12.95 (ISBN 0-86530-054-2, IP 54-2). Incentive Pubns.
Frost, Joan. Exceptional Art--Exceptional Children: Fostering Creativity & Developing Independence. (Illus.). 140p. (gr. 1-8). 1985. spiral bdg. 16.95 (ISBN 0-938594-07-9). Spec Lit Pr.
Fun to Make Witches. 1989. pap. 3.99 (ISBN 0-517-68793-3). Outlet Bk Co.
Gattis, L. S., III. Trailblazer Fun Honors I: Birds, Buttons, Computers, Dress, Kites & Stamps. (Illus.). 20p. (Orig.). (ps-5). 1986. pap. 5.00 tchr's. ed. (ISBN 0-936241-08-X). Cheetah Pub.
Haas, Carolyn B. Look at Me: Creative Learning Activities for Babies & Toddlers. Phillips, Jane B., illus. LC 87-20288. 230p. (Orig.). 1987. pap. 9.95 (ISBN 1-55652-021-2). Chicago Review.
Jackson, Jacqueline. Turn Not Pale, Beloved Snail: A Book about Writing & Other Things. 192p. (gr. 7 up). 1974. 14.95 (ISBN 0-316-45481-8). Little.
Keefe, Betty. Fingerpuppet Tales: Making & Using Puppets with Folk & Fairytales. (Illus.). 148p. (ps-3). 1986. spiral bdg. 17.95 (ISBN 0-938594-08-7). Spec Lit Pr.
Lamping, Ed. The Awareness Book. (Illus.). 40p. (gr. 3-6). 1982. 5.00 (ISBN 0-940444-15-1). Kabyn.
McAllister, Constance. Creative Writing Activities, 2-6. 32p. (gr. 2-6). 1980. pap. 2.95 (ISBN 0-87534-176-4). Highlights.
McGowan, Tom & McGowan, Meredith. Children, Literature & Social Studies: Activities for the Intermediate Grades. (Illus.). 218p. (gr. 4-6). 1986. spiral bdg. 18.95 (ISBN 0-938594-06-0). Spec Lit Pr.
Myers, Garry C. Creative Thinking Activities. Rev. ed. 32p. (gr. 2-6). 1980. pap. 2.95 (ISBN 0-87534-113-6). Highlights.
Nicholas, Robert J. Fifty Creative Exercises, 2 bks. (gr. 7 up). 1991. Set. pap. 28.00 (ISBN 1-879777-02-9); Bk. I. pap. 14.95 (ISBN 1-879777-00-2); Bk. II. pap. 14.95 (ISBN 1-879777-01-0). Leonardos Work.
Osband, Gillian. The Messy Book of Things to Make & Do. Munro, Heather, illus. 32p. (Orig.). (gr. k-3). 1987. pap. 2.50 activity bk. (ISBN 0-590-40888-7). Scholastic Inc.
Outdoor Fun: A-Z Activity Book. 1989. 3.50 (ISBN 0-517-68797-6, Chatham River Pr). Outlet Bk Co.
Petrucelli. Creativity, Reading Level 2. (Illus.). 32p. (gr. 1-4). Date not set. PLB 13.26 (ISBN 0-86592-444-9). Rourke Corp.
Pizzo, Joan E. Little Crumb Fun Book. (Illus.). 32p. (Orig.). (gr. k-6). 1983. pap. 3.95 (ISBN 0-939126-04-4). Back Bay.
Spies & Detectives: Cut & Color Activity Book. 1989. pap. 3.99 (ISBN 0-517-68795-X). Outlet Bk Co.
Spizman, Robyn. All Aboard with Bulletin Boards. Pesiri, Evelyn, illus. 96p. (gr. k-8). 1983. wkbk. 9.95 (ISBN 0-86653-105-X, GA 467). Good Apple.
—Good Apple & Bulletin Board Bonanzas. 144p. (gr. 3-7). 1981. 10.95 (ISBN 0-86653-049-5, GA 281). Good Apple.
Start Anytime Diary Kit. (gr. 4-8). incl. stickers & pens 4.00 (ISBN 0-87406-352-3, 47-14820-1). Willowisp Pr.
Thomas, Sue & Dinges, Susan. Curtain I: A Guide to Creative Drama for Children 5-8 Years Old. (gr. k-3). 1985. 15.00 (ISBN 0-89824-148-0). Trillium Pr.
Watanabe, Shigeo. Get Set! Go! Ohtomo, Yasuo, illus. 32p. (ps-1). 1981. 8.95 (ISBN 0-399-20780-5, Philomel); (Philomel); pap. 13.95 (ISBN 0-399-21038-5, Philomel). Putnam Pub Group.
Whaley, Charles E. & Whaley, Helen F. Future Images: Future Studies for Grades 4-12. (gr. 4-12). 1985. 12.99 (ISBN 0-89824-149-9). Trillium Pr.
Woods, Jennifer. Month Makers: Reusable Student Calendars for Classroom Activities. Sussman, Ellen, intro. by. Woods, Jennifer, illus. 24p. (Orig.). (gr. 3-6). 1982. pap. text ed. 3.95t (ISBN 0-933606-12-5, MS-613). Monkey Sisters.

CREATIVENESS

see Creation (Literary, Artistic, etc.)

Davis, Duane. My Friends & Me Activity Manual. rev. ed. (ps-k). 1988. pap. text ed. 52.00 (ISBN 0-88671-325-0). Am Guidance.

CREDIBILITY

see Truthfulness and Falsehood

CREDIT

see also Banks and Banking

Ortiz, Lucio. Sus Derechos de Credito en Estados Unidos. Garcia, Santos, intro. by. (SPA., Orig.). (gr. 9-12). 1989. pap. 6.00 (ISBN 0-685-28998-2). Publicaciones Nuevos.

CREEDS–COMPARATIVE STUDIES

Richards, H. J. The Creed for Children. 32p. (Orig.). 1991. pap. 3.95 (ISBN 0-8146-2037-X). Liturgical Pr.

CRESTS

see Heraldry

CRETE–FICTION

Cheney, David M. Son of Minos. LC 64-25838. (gr. 7). 18.00 (ISBN 0-8196-0142-X). Biblo.

CREWE, SARA

Burnett, Frances H. A Little Princess. 240p. (gr. 5-9). 1975. pap. 3.50 (ISBN 0-440-44767-4, YB). Dell.

CRICKET–FICTION

Ferguson, Alane. Cricket & the Crackerbox Kid. LC 89-39291. 192p. (gr. 3-7). 1990. 13.95 (ISBN 0-02-734525-4, Bradbury Pr). Macmillan Child Grp.
Selden, George. Chester Cricket's New Home. Williams, Garth, illus. 144p. (gr. 3 up). 1984. pap. 3.25 (ISBN 0-440-41246-3, YB). Dell.

CRICKETS

Cole, Joanna. An Insect's Body. Wexler, Jerome & Mendez, Raymond A., photos by. LC 83-22027. (Illus.). 48p. (ps-3). 1984. 13.95 (ISBN 0-688-02771-7); PLB 13.88 (ISBN 0-688-02772-5, Morrow Jr Bks). Morrow Jr Bks.
Hasegawa, Yo. The Cricket. Pohl, Kathy, ed. LC 85-28201. (Illus.). 32p. (gr. 3-7). 1986. text ed. 16.67 (ISBN 0-8172-2532-3); pap. text ed. 9.27 (ISBN 0-8172-2557-9). Raintree Pubs.
Watts, Barrie. Grasshoppers & Crickets. (Illus.). 32p. (gr. k-4). 1991. PLB 10.40 (ISBN 0-531-14161-6); pap. 3.95 (ISBN 0-531-15618-4). Watts.

CRICKETS–FICTION

Carle, Eric. The Very Quiet Cricket: A Multi-Sensory Book. LC 89-78317. (Illus.). 32p. (ps-1). 1990. 17.95x (ISBN 0-399-21885-8, Philomel Bks). Putnam Pub Group.
Caudill, Rebecca. A Pocketful of Cricket. Ness, Evaline, illus. LC 64-12617. 48p. (gr. k-2). 1964. reinforced bdg. 7.95 (ISBN 0-03-089752-1); pap. 5.95 (ISBN 0-8050-1275-3). H Holt & Co.
—A Pocketful of Cricket. Ness, Evaline, illus. LC 64-12617. 48p. (ps-3). 1989. Repr. of 1964 ed. 15.95 (ISBN 0-8050-1200-1). H Holt & Co.
Keats, Ezra J. Maggie & the Pirate. Keats, Ezra J., illus. LC 85-29347. 32p. (gr. k-3). 1987. Repr. of 1979 ed. 13.95 (ISBN 0-02-749710-0, Four Winds). Macmillan Child Grp.
Kherdian, David. Song in the Walnut Grove. Zelisky, Paul, illus. LC 82-6596. 112p. (gr. 3-7). 1982. lib. bdg. 8.99 (ISBN 0-394-95519-6). Knopf.
Oetting, R. Orderly Cricket. Marilue, illus. LC 68-16395. 32p. (gr. 2-3). 1967. PLB 9.95 (ISBN 0-87783-028-2). Oddo.
Selden, George. Chester Cricket's New Home. Williams, Garth, illus. LC 82-24206. 144p. (gr. 4 up). 1983. 14.95 (ISBN 0-374-31240-0). FS&G.
—Chester Cricket's Pigeon Ride. Williams, Garth, illus. 80p. (gr. 2-6). 1983. pap. 2.75 (ISBN 0-440-41389-3, YB). Dell.
—Cricket in Times Square. Williams, Garth, illus. (gr. 2-7). 1970. pap. 3.50 (ISBN 0-440-41563-2, YB). Dell.
—Tucker's Countryside. Williams, Garth, illus. LC 69-14975. 176p. (gr. 3 up). 1969. 12.95 (ISBN 0-374-37854-1). FS&G.
Stilwell, Alison. Chin Ling, the Chinese Cricket. Stilwell, Alison, illus. LC 81-90045. 48p. (gr. 1-4). 1981. Repr. of 1947 ed. 12.95 (ISBN 0-9605862-0-2). Stilwell Studio.
Wood, Audrey. Quick As a Cricket. Wood, Don, illus. 32p. (ps-2). 1982. 10.00 (ISBN 0-85953-151-1, Pub. by Child's Play England). Childs Play.

CRIME AND CRIMINALS

see also Capital Punishment; Criminal Law; Detectives; Justice, Administration of; Juvenile Delinquency; Pirates; Police; Prisons; Racketeering; Robbers and Outlaws; Smuggling; Trials

Barness, Richard. Graystone College. LC 72-7654. (Illus.). 64p. (gr. 4 up). 1973. PLB 10.95 (ISBN 0-8225-0753-6). Lerner Pubns.
Butterworth, W. E. LeRoy & the Old Man. 168p. (gr. 7 up). 1982. pap. 2.50 (ISBN 0-590-40573-X, Point). Scholastic Inc.
Colby-Newton, Katie. Jack the Ripper: Opposing Viewpoints. LC 90-3835. (Illus.). 112p. (gr. 3-8). 1990. PLB 13.95 (ISBN 0-89908-081-2). Greenhaven.
Crary, Elizabeth. Finders, Keepers. Strecker, Rebekah, illus. LC 87-60369. 64p. (Orig.). (gr. 2-6). 1987. PLB 12.95 (ISBN 0-943990-39-4); pap. 3.95 (ISBN 0-943990-38-6). Parenting Pr.
Davis, Bertha. Instead of Prison. (Illus.). 128p. (gr. 7-12). 1986. PLB 12.90 (ISBN 0-531-10237-8). Watts.
Deming, Richard. Police Lab at Work. LC 66-29903. (Illus.). (gr. 5-7). 4.95 (ISBN 0-672-50433-2, Bobbs). Macmillan.
Dudley, William, ed. Crime & Criminals: Opposing Viewpoints. LC 89-2155. (Illus.). 240p. (gr. 10 up). 1989. lib. bdg. 15.95 (ISBN 0-89908-441-9); pap. text ed. 8.95 (ISBN 0-89908-416-8). Greenhaven.
Earle, Alice M. Curious Punishments of Bygone Days. LC 70-142762. (Illus.). (gr. 9 up). 1972. pap. 8.95 (ISBN 0-8048-0959-3). C E Tuttle.
Francis, Dorothy B. Vandalism: The Crime of Immaturity. LC 82-18333. 128p. (gr. 7 up). 1983. 11.95 (ISBN 0-525-66774-1, Lodestar Bks). Dutton Child Bks.
Freeman, Charles. Terrorists. (Illus.). 72p. (gr. 7-10). 1990. 19.95 (ISBN 0-7134-6076-8, Pub. by Batsford UK). Trafalgar Sq.
Gattis, Lou. Prison Survival & the Inmate Self-Help Sourcebook: A Guide for Those Who "Know-It-All" (Illus.). 254p. (Orig.). (gr. 10 up). 1989. pap. 14.95 (ISBN 0-936241-45-4). Cheetah Pub.
Gustafson, Anita. Guilty or Innocent. LC 85-7608. (Illus.). 160p. (gr. 2-9). 1985. 12.95 (ISBN 0-8050-0555-2). H Holt & Co.
Hamilton, Sue. Public Enemy No. One: Baby Face Nelson. Hamilton, John, ed. (Illus.). 32p. (gr. 4). 1989. PLB 11.95 (ISBN 0-939179-61-X). Abdo & Dghtrs.
—Public Enemy No. One: Bonnie & Clyde. Hamilton, John, ed. (Illus.). 32p. (gr. 4). 1989. PLB 11.95 (ISBN 0-939179-62-8). Abdo & Dghtrs.
—Public Enemy No. One: John H. Dillinger. Hamilton, John, ed. (Illus.). 32p. (gr. 4). 1989. PLB 11.95 (ISBN 0-939179-60-1). Abdo & Dghtrs.
—Public Enemy No. One: Ma Barker. Hamilton, John, ed. (Illus.). 32p. (gr. 4). 1989. PLB 11.95 (ISBN 0-939179-65-2). Abdo & Dghtrs.
—Public Enemy No. One: Machine Gun Kelly. Hamilton, John, ed. (Illus.). 32p. (gr. 4). 1989. PLB 11.95 (ISBN 0-939179-64-4). Abdo & Dghtrs.
—Public Enemy No. One: Pretty Boy Floyd. Hamilton, John, ed. (Illus.). 32p. (gr. 4). 1989. PLB 11.95 (ISBN 0-939179-63-6). Abdo & Dghtrs.
Hill, Bob. Throwaway People: The Story of Seven Convicted Felons & One Convicted Preacher. LC 89-85841. 190p. (Orig.). (gr. 8 up). 1989. 12.95 (ISBN 0-944769-03-9); lib. bdg. 10.95 (ISBN 0-944769-04-7); pap. 4.95 (ISBN 0-944769-00-4). Dearh Pub.
Kyte, Kathy S. Play It Safe: The Kids' Guide to Personal Safety & Crime Prevention. LC 83-6086. (Illus.). 128p. (gr. 5 up). 1983. Knopf.
Langone, John. Violence! Our Fastest Growing Public Health Problem. (gr. 7up). 1984. 14.95 (ISBN 0-316-51431-4). Little.

LeVert, Marianne. Crime in America. Leinwand, Gerald, ed. 128p. (gr. 9-12). 1991. 16.95x (ISBN 0-8160-2102-3). Facts on File.
Loeb, Robert H., Jr. Crime & Capital Punishment. rev. ed. 128p. (gr. 7-12). 1986. PLB 12.90 (ISBN 0-531-10209-2). Watts.
Robins, Dave. Just Punishment. (Illus.). 64p. (gr. 5-8). 1990. PLB 11.90 (ISBN 0-531-17252-X). Watts.
Rohr, Janelle, ed. Violence in America: Opposing Viewpoints. LC 89-25943. (Illus.). 288p. (gr. 10 up). 1990. lib. bdg. 15.95 (ISBN 0-89908-449-4); pap. text ed. 8.95 (ISBN 0-89908-424-9). Greenhaven.
Ryan, Perry T. The Criminal Justice System of Kentucky. (Illus.). 50p. (gr. 9). 1990. pap. 4.95 (ISBN 0-9625504-1-8). P T Ryan.
Stark, Evan. Everything You Need to Know about Street Gangs. (gr. 7-12). 1991. PLB 12.95 (ISBN 0-8239-1319-8). Rosen Group.
Weiss, Karl, ed. The Prison Experience: An Anthology. LC 75-32920. 352p. (gr. 6 up). 1976. pap. 9.95 (ISBN 0-440-06017-6). Delacorte.
Whiting, Roger. Crime & Punishment: A Study Across Time. LC 87-50949. 220p. (Orig.). (gr. 9-12). 1987. pap. text ed. 16.95 (ISBN 0-685-19579-1, Pub. by S. Thornes). Dufour.
Wilkes, A. Fakes & Forgeries. (Illus.). 64p. (gr. 3-7). 1979. lib. bdg. 11.96 (ISBN 0-88110-041-2, Usborne); pap. 4.50 (ISBN 0-86020-231-3). EDC.

CRIME AND CRIMINALS–FICTION

Addy, Sharon. We Didn't Mean to. Blair, Jay, illus. McDermot, Gerald, intro. by. LC 80-24976. (Illus.). 32p. (gr. k-6). 1981. PLB 16.67 (ISBN 0-8172-1370-8). Raintree Pubs Ltd.
Ashley, Bernard. A Kind of Wild Justice. Keeping, Charles, illus. LC 78-10899. (gr. 7 up). 1979. 18.95 (ISBN 0-87599-229-3). S G Phillips.
Bennett, Jay. Deathman, Do Not Follow Me. 144p. (gr. 7 up). 1986. pap. 2.50 (ISBN 0-590-40525-X, Point). Scholastic Inc.
Bradford, Ann & Gezi, Kal. The Mystery at the Tree House. McLean, Mina G., illus. LC 80-15654. 32p. (gr. k-4). 1980. PLB 9.96 (ISBN 0-89565-148-3). Childs World.
Carlson, Nancy. Arnie & the Stolen Markers. (Illus.). 32p. (ps-3). 1987. pap. 11.95 (ISBN 0-670-81548-9). Viking Child Bks.
Christelow, Eileen. The Robbery at the Diamond Dog Diner. LC 86-2682. (Illus.). 32p. (ps-3). 1986. 13.95 (ISBN 0-89919-425-7, Pub. by Clarion); pap. 4.95 (ISBN 0-89919-722-1, Pub. by Clarion). Ticknor & Fields.
Cool, Joyce. The Kidnapping of Courtney Van Allen & What's-Her-Name. LC 80-28455. 192p. (gr. 4-7). 1981. 8.95 (ISBN 0-394-84822-5). Knopf.
Corcoran, Barbara. The Hideaway. 128p. (Orig.). 1989. pap. 2.75 (ISBN 0-380-70635-0, Flare). Avon.
DeClements, Barthe. Five-Finger Discount. (gr. 4-7). 1989. 13.95 (ISBN 0-440-50166-0). Delacorte.
Eige, Lillian E. The Kidnapping of Mr. Huey. LC 82-48610. 160p. (gr. 6 up). 1983. PLB 11.89 (ISBN 0-06-021799-5). HarpC Child Bks.
Ferguson, Alane. Show Me the Evidence. LC 88-39203. 176p. (gr. 7 up). 1989. 12.95 (ISBN 0-02-734521-1, Bradbury Pr). Macmillan Child Grp.
Hamilton, Dorothy. Amanda Fair. Converse, James, illus. LC 80-25073. 136p. (gr. 5-10). 1981. pap. 3.95 (ISBN 0-8361-1943-6). Herald Pr.
—Eric's Discovery. Wind, Betty, illus. LC 79-18537. 120p. (gr. 4-9). 1979. pap. 3.95 (ISBN 0-8361-1903-7). Herald Pr.
Hoban, Lillian. The Case of the Two Masked Robbers. LC 85-45819. (Illus.). 64p. (gr. k-3). 1986. 11.95 (ISBN 0-06-022298-0); PLB 11.89 (ISBN 0-06-022299-9). HarpC Child Bks.
Hyde, Dayton O. The Major, the Poacher, & the Wonderful One-Trout River. LC 84-20442. 168p. (gr. 5 up). 1985. 13.95 (ISBN 0-689-31107-9, Atheneum Child Bk). Macmillan Child Grp.
Lloyd, Errol. Sasha & the Bicycle Thieves. (Illus.). 42p. (gr. 2-4). 1989. 3.95 (ISBN 0-8120-6141-1). Barron.
Morey, Walt. The Lemon Meringue Dog. LC 80-171. 176p. (gr. 4-7). 1980. 13.95 (ISBN 0-525-33455-6, DCB). Dutton Child Bks.
O. Henry. The Ransom of Red Chief. (Illus.). 40p. (gr. 4 up). 1980. PLB 10.95s.p. (ISBN 0-87191-776-9); PLB 15.65 (ISBN 0-685-01266-2). Creative Ed.
Petersen, P. J. Would You Settle for Improbable? A Novel. LC 80-69465. 192p. (gr. 5-9). 1981. 8.95 (ISBN 0-440-09601-4); PLB 8.44 (ISBN 0-440-09672-3). Delacorte.
Poe, Edgar Allan. The Cask of Amontillado. Cutts, David E., adapted by. Toulmin-Rothe, Ann, illus. LC 81-15997. 32p. (gr. 5-10). 1982. PLB 10.79 (ISBN 0-89375-622-9); pap. text ed. 2.95 (ISBN 0-89375-623-7); cassettes avail. Troll Assocs.
Roberts, Willo D. The Pet-Sitting Peril. LC 82-13757. 192p. (gr. 4-6). 1983. 13.95 (ISBN 0-689-30963-5, Atheneum Child Bk). Macmillan Child Grp.
—What Could Go Wrong? LC 88-27484. 176p. (gr. 3-7). 1989. 12.95 (ISBN 0-689-31438-8, Atheneum Child Bk). Macmillan Child Grp.
Schlee, Ann. The Vandal. LC 81-2859. (Illus.). 192p. (gr. 7 up). 1981. 8.95 (ISBN 0-517-54424-5). Crown.
Schwartzman, Lee T. Crippled Detectives or the War of the Red Romer. Mandel, Gerry, ed. (Illus.). (gr. 3-8). 1978. 3.00 (ISBN 0-89409-009-7). Childrens Art.
Sebestyen, Ouida. On Fire. 208p. (gr. 6 up). 1985. 12.45 (ISBN 0-87113-010-6, Joy St Bks). Little.
Slote, Alfred. Tony & Me. LC 74-5182. 160p. (gr. 4-6). 1974. 11.95 (ISBN 0-397-31507-4, Lipp Jr Bks). HarpC Child Bks.
Sobel, Barbara. To Catch a Thief! LC 87-81234. (gr. 3-6). 1987. 7.59 (ISBN 0-87386-047-0); bk. & cassette 16.99 (ISBN 0-317-55326-7); pap. 1.95 (ISBN 0-87386-046-2). Jan Prods.
Stone, G. H. Rough Stuff. LC 88-11904. 144p. (Orig.). (gr. 5 up). 1989. pap. 2.95 (ISBN 0-394-80178-4). Knopf.
Terris, Susan. Baby-Snatcher. 192p. (gr. 5 up). 1985. 11.95 (ISBN 0-374-30473-4). FS&G.
Weiss, Ellen & Friedman, Mel. The Tiny Parents. LC 88-23103. 96p. (Orig.). (gr. 3-7). 1989. lib. bdg. 5.99 (ISBN 0-394-92418-5); pap. 2.95 (ISBN 0-394-82418-0). Knopf.
Wood, Phyllis A. Win Me & You Lose. LC 76-44299. 136p. (gr. 7 up). 1977. 8.95 (ISBN 0-664-32605-6, Westminster). Westminster John Knox.
Zimelman, Nathan. The Crime of Hubie Hemplewhite. Newman, Stephanie, illus. LC 89-39151. 80p. (Orig.). (gr. 1-3). 1990. pap. 7.95 (ISBN 0-943173-56-6). Harbinger AZ.

CRIMES, POLITICAL

see Political Crimes and Offenses

CRIMINAL INVESTIGATION

see also Detectives; Police

Deming, Richard. Police Lab at Work. LC 66-29903. (Illus.). (gr. 5-7). 4.95 (ISBN 0-672-50433-2, Bobbs). Macmillan.
Dixon, Franklin W. & Spina, D. A. Hardy Boys Detective Handbook. rev. ed. (Illus.). 224p. (gr. 4-7). 1972. 4.50 (ISBN 0-448-01990-6, G&D); PLB 3.29 (ISBN 0-448-03227-9, G&D). Putnam Pub Group.
Gustafson, Anita. Guilty or Innocent. LC 85-7608. (Illus.). 160p. (gr. 2-9). 1985. 12.95 (ISBN 0-8050-0555-2). H Holt & Co.

CRIMINAL LAW

see also Capital Punishment; Jury; Trials

Bender, David L. & Leone, Bruno, eds. Criminal Justice Annual, 1989. 144p. (gr. 10 up). 1989. pap. text ed. 5.45 (ISBN 0-89908-551-2). Greenhaven.

CRIMINALS

see Crime and Criminals

CRIMINOLOGY

see Crime and Criminals

CRIPPLES

see Physically Handicapped

CRITICISM

see also Book Reviews

also literature and music subjects with the subdivision History and Criticism, e.g. English Literature–History and Criticism; English Poetry–History and Criticism; Music–History and Criticism

Insel, Eunice & Edson, Ann. Developing Critical Thinking, Bk. 1. (gr. 3-4). 1983. wkbk. 4.25 (ISBN 1-55737-651-4). Ed Activities.

CROCKERY

see Pottery

CROCKETT, DAVID, 1785-1836

Davy Crockett. (Illus.). (gr. 2-5). 1989. 27.99 (ISBN 0-8172-2953-1); pap. 23.95 (ISBN 0-8172-2961-2). Raintree Pubs.
Farr, Naunerle C. Davy Crockett-Daniel Boone. Carrillo, Fred & Redondo, Nestor, illus. (gr. 4-12). 1979. pap. text ed. 2.95 (ISBN 0-88301-351-7); wkbk. 1.25 (ISBN 0-88301-375-4). Pendulum Pr.
McCall, Edith. Hunters Blaze the Trails. Rogers, Carol, illus. LC 59-3666. 128p. (gr. 3-10). 1980. PLB 14.60 (ISBN 0-516-03332-8). Childrens.
Moseley, Elizabeth R. Davy Crockett: Hero of the Wild Frontier. Beecham, Thomas, illus. 80p. (gr. 2-6). 1991. Repr. of 1967 ed. PLB 12.95 (ISBN 0-7910-1409-6). Chelsea Hse.
Parks, Aileen W. Davy Crockett: Young Rifleman. Pearson, Justin, illus. LC 86-10781. 192p. (gr. 2-6). 1986. pap. 3.95 (ISBN 0-02-041840-X, Aladdin). Macmillan Child Grp.
Santrey, Laurence. Davy Crockett: Young Pioneer. Livingston, Francis, illus. LC 82-16040. 48p. (gr. 4-6). 1983. PLB 10.79 (ISBN 0-89375-847-7); pap. text ed. 2.95 (ISBN 0-89375-848-5). Troll Assocs.
Townsend, Tom. Davy Crockett: An American Hero. Eakin, Edwin M., ed. LC 87-16545. (Illus.). 72p. (gr. 4-7). 1987. 9.95 (ISBN 0-89015-643-3, Pub. by Panda Bks); pap. 2.95 (ISBN 0-89015-627-1, Pub. by Panda Bks). Eakin Pr.
Trotman, Felicity & Greenway, Shirley, eds. Davy Crockett. LC 85-16694. (Illus.). 32p. (gr. 2-5). 1985. PLB 16.67 (ISBN 0-8172-2504-8); pap. 9.27 (ISBN 0-8172-2512-9). Raintree Pubs.

CROCKETT, DAVID, 1786-1836–FICTION

Cohen, Caron Lee. Sally Ann Thunder Ann Whirlwind Crockett. Dewey, Ariane, illus. LC 84-7978. 40p. (gr. 1-3). 1985. 11.75 (ISBN 0-688-04006-3); PLB 11.88 (ISBN 0-688-04007-1). Greenwillow.
Dewey, Ariane. The Narrow Escapes of Davy Crockett. Dewey, Ariane, illus. LC 88-34902. (gr. 1 up). 1990. 13.95 (ISBN 0-688-08914-3); PLB 13.88 (ISBN 0-688-08915-1). Greenwillow.

CROCODILES

For the American crocodiles use Alligators.

Barrett, Norman. Cocodrilos y Caimanes. LC 88-51517. (SPA., Illus.). 32p. (gr. k-4). 1991. PLB 11.40 (ISBN 0-531-07919-8). Watts.
—Crocodiles & Alligators. (Illus.). 32p. (gr. k-6). 1990. 11.40 (ISBN 0-531-10705-1). Watts.
Bender, Lionel. Crocodiles & Alligators. FS-Aladdin Staff, ed. LC 88-50513. (Illus.). 32p. (gr. 1-6). 1988. PLB 11.90 (ISBN 0-531-17100-0, Gloucester Pr). Watts.
—First Sight: Crocodiles & Alligators. 1990. pap. 3.95 (ISBN 0-531-17258-9). Watts.
Bright, Michael. Alligators & Crocodiles. (Illus.). 32p. (gr. 5-8). 1990. PLB 11.90 (ISBN 0-531-17245-7). Watts.
Dow, Lesley. Alligators & Crocodiles. 72p. 1990. 17.95x (ISBN 0-8160-2273-9). Facts on File.
Farre, Marie. Crocodiles & Alligators. Matthews, Sarah, tr. from FRE. Wallis, Diz, illus. LC 87-31804. 38p. (gr. k-5). 1988. 4.95 (ISBN 0-944589-01-4, 014). Young Discovery Lib.
Hogan, Paula Z. The Crocodile. Nachreiner, Tom, illus. LC 79-13699. 32p. (gr. 1-4). 1979. PLB 16.67 (ISBN 0-8172-1503-4). Raintree Pubs.
—The Crocodile. LC 79-13699. (Illus.). 32p. (gr. 1-4). 1981. PLB 27.99 incl. cassette (ISBN 0-685-09547-9); cassette 14.00 (ISBN 0-8172-1842-4). Raintree Pubs.
Knight, David. I Can Read About Alligators & Crocodiles. LC 78-73733. (Illus.). (gr. 2-4). 1979. pap. 1.95 (ISBN 0-89375-200-2). Troll Assocs.
Ling, Mary. Amazing Crocodiles & Other Reptiles. Young, Jerry, photos by. LC 90-19239. (Illus.). 32p. (Orig.). (gr. 1-5). 1991. PLB 9.99 (ISBN 0-679-90689-4); pap. 6.95 (ISBN 0-679-80689-X). Knopf.
Petty, Kate. Crocodiles & Alligators. Johnson, Karen, illus. 1990. pap. 2.95 (ISBN 0-531-15153-0). Watts.
Serventy, Vincent. Crocodile & Alligator. LC 84-15890. (Illus.). 24p. (gr. k-5). 1985. PLB 13.32 (ISBN 0-8172-2404-1). Raintree Pubs.
Stone, Lynn. Crocodiles. (Illus.). 24p. (gr. k-5). 1990. lib. bdg. 11.93 (ISBN 0-86593-060-0); lib. bdg. 8.95s.p. (ISBN 0-685-36369-4). Rourke Corp.
Stone, Lynn M. Alligators & Crocodiles. LC 89-9985. 48p. (gr. k-4). 1989. PLB 14.60 (ISBN 0-516-01170-7); pap. 4.95 (ISBN 0-516-41170-5). Childrens.
Wildlife Education, Ltd. Staff. Alligators & Crocodiles. Hoopes, Barbara, illus. 20p. (Orig.). (gr. 5 up). 1984. pap. 2.25 (ISBN 0-937934-25-9). Wildlife Educ.

CROCODILES–FICTION

Aliki. Keep Your Mouth Closed, Dear. Aliki, illus. LC 66-19310. (gr. k-3). 1966. PLB 11.89 (ISBN 0-8037-4418-8). Dial Bks Young.
Aruego, Jose & Dewey, Ariane. Rockabye Crocodile. LC 87-463. (Illus.). 32p. (ps-3). 1988. 13.95 (ISBN 0-688-06738-7); lib. bdg. 13.88 (ISBN 0-688-06739-5). Greenwillow.
Carrick, Carol. The Crocodiles Still Wait. Carrick, Donald, illus. LC 79-23519. 32p. (gr. 1-4). 1980. 14.95 (ISBN 0-395-29102-X, Clarion). HM.
Crocodile Rhythm Block. 1990. 9.98 (ISBN 0-8317-6172-5). Smithmark.
Cutchins, Judy & Johnston, Ginny. The Crocodile & the Crane: Surviving in a Crowded World. LC 86-5339. (Illus.). 64p. (gr. 2-5). 1986. 12.95 (ISBN 0-688-06304-7); lib. bdg. 12.88 (ISBN 0-688-06305-5, Morrow Jr Bks). Morrow Jr Bks.
Dahl, Roald. The Enormous Crocodile. 48p. (Orig.). (gr. 1-3). 1984. pap. 2.95 (ISBN 0-553-15243-2, Skylark). Bantam.
De Paola, Tomie. Bill & Pete. De Paola, Tomie, illus. LC 78-5330. (gr. k-2). 1978. 13.95 (ISBN 0-399-20646-9, Putnam); pap. 5.95 (ISBN 0-399-20650-7, Putnam). Putnam Pub Group.
Fuentes, Vilma M. The Monkey & the Crocodile. Inis, Ninabeth R., illus. 31p. (Orig.). (gr. k-2). 1984. pap. 3.50 (ISBN 971-10-0127-6, Pub. by New Day Philippines). Cellar.
Galdone, Paul. The Monkey & the Crocodile: A Jakata Tale from India. Galdone, Paul, illus. LC 78-79939. 32p. (ps-3). 1987. pap. 4.95 (ISBN 0-89919-524-5, Pub. by Clarion). Ticknor & Fields.
Hoban, Russell. Arthur's New Power. Barton, Byron, illus. LC 77-11550. (gr. 1-5). 1978. PLB 12.89 (ISBN 0-690-01371-X, Crowell Jr Bks). HarpC Child Bks.
—Dinner at Alberta's. Marshall, James, illus. LC 73-94796. 40p. (gr. 1-3). 1975. PLB 11.89 (ISBN 0-690-23993-9, Crowell Jr Bks). HarpC Child Bks.
Moncure, Jane B. Smile, Says Little Crocodile. Hohag, Linda, illus. LC 87-13833. 32p. (ps-2). 1987. PLB 11.97 (ISBN 0-89565-401-6); pap. 6.96 (ISBN 0-89565-449-0). Childs World.
Velthuijs, Max. Elephant & Crocodile. LC 90-55039. 32p. (gr. 4-8). 1990. 12.95 (ISBN 0-374-37675-1). FS&G.
Waber, Bernard. House on East Eighty-Eighth Street. (Illus.). 48p. (gr. k-3). 1973. 13.95 (ISBN 0-395-18157-7). HM.
—The House on East Eighty-Eighth Street. Waber, Bernard, illus. LC 62-8144. 48p. (gr. k-4). 1975. pap. 4.95 (ISBN 0-395-19970-0, Sandpiper). HM.
—Lovable Lyle. LC 69-14728. (Illus.). (gr. k-3). 1977. 13.95 (ISBN 0-395-19858-5); pap. 4.95 (ISBN 0-395-25378-0). HM.
—Lyle & the Birthday Party. (Illus.). (gr. k-3). 1966. 13.95 (ISBN 0-395-15080-9). HM.
—Lyle, Lyle, Crocodile. (Illus.). (gr. k-3). 1965. 13.95 (ISBN 0-395-16995-X). HM.
—Lyle, Lyle Crocodile. LC 65-19305. (ps-3). 1987. pap. 7.95 incl. cass. (ISBN 0-395-45742-4); pap. 4.95 (ISBN 0-395-13720-9). HM.
Waddell, Martin. Harriet & the Crocodiles. Burgess, Mark, illus. (gr. 3-7). 1984. 11.95 (ISBN 0-316-91622-6, Joy St Bks). Little.
Watts, Marjorie-Ann. Crocodile Plaster. Watt, Marjorie-Ann, illus. (gr. k-3). 1984. 9.95 (ISBN 0-233-96962-4). Andre Deutsch.

CROMWELL, OLIVER, 1599-1658
Sarage, Jessica. Cromwell. (Illus.). 64p. (gr. 7-10). 1989. 19.95 (ISBN 0-7134-6033-4, Pub. by Batsford England). Trafalgar Sq.

CROPS
see Farm Produce

CROSS-COUNTRY RUNNING
see Track Athletics

CROSSWORD PUZZLES
Aero Products Research, Inc., Industries Division Staff. Official CB Crossword Puzzles for Big Dummy's. (Illus.). (gr. 8 up). 1977. pap. 1.98 (ISBN 0-912682-18-3). Aero Products.
Chirinian, Helene. Crossword Mysteries: Daring Detectives. 48p. 1990. pap. 2.95 (ISBN 0-8431-2791-0). Price Stern.
—Crossword Mysteries: Super Sleuth Challenge. 48p. 1990. pap. 2.95 (ISBN 0-8431-2789-9). Price Stern.
Cobblestone Publishing Inc. Staff. U. S. History Crosswords: For Young People 8-14. (Illus.). 36p. (gr. 4-8). 1987. pap. text ed. 4.95 (ISBN 0-942389-01-8). Cobblestone Pub.
Cron, Mary. More Phonics Fun: Crossword Puzzles. McMahan, Kelly, illus. 48p. (Orig.). (gr. k-2). 1989. pap. 2.95 incl. chipboard (ISBN 0-8431-2358-3). Price Stern.
Crossword Mysteries: Private Eye. 48p. 1991. pap. 2.95 (ISBN 0-8431-2790-2). Price Stern.
Crossword Puzzle Challenges. (Illus.). 64p. (gr. 2-5). 1990. pap. 1.79 (ISBN 0-671-72335-9). S&S Trade.
Crosswords & Word Games Activity Books. (Illus.). 48p. (gr. 1-4). 1988. pap. 2.95 (ISBN 0-8431-2270-6). Price Stern.
Davis, S. K. Bible Crossword Puzzle Book. (gr. k-3). 1969. pap. 3.95 (ISBN 0-8010-2812-4). Baker Bk.
Glicksburg, Joy B. Crosswords for Language Arts. (gr. 1-5). 1985. pap. 6.95 (ISBN 0-8224-2353-7). Fearon Teach Aids.
Maleska, Eugene T. Children's Word Games & Crossword Puzzles, Vol. 2. (gr. 2-4). 1988. pap. 5.95 (ISBN 0-8129-1692-1, Times Bks). Random.
Moore, Rosalind, ed. The Dell Big Book of Crosswords & Pencil Puzzles, No. 7. (Orig.). 1989. pap. 8.95 (ISBN 0-440-50161-X, Dell Trade Pbks). Dell.
Nowlin, Susan S. Holiday Crossword Puzzles. Spence, Paula, illus. 48p. (gr. 2-5). 1988. wkbk. 5.95 (ISBN 1-55734-366-7). Tchr Create Mat.
Popperwell, Jeral. Science Crossword Puzzles. (Illus.). 48p. (gr. 2-5). 1988. Dinosaurs. pap. 2.95 (ISBN 0-8431-2290-0); Human Body. pap. 2.95 (ISBN 0-8431-2291-9); Wild Animals. pap. 2.95 (ISBN 0-8431-2293-5); Space. pap. 2.95 (ISBN 0-8431-2292-7). Price Stern.
Quinn, Kaye. Science Crosswords: Bizarre Bugs. 48p. 1990. pap. 2.95 (ISBN 0-8431-2811-9). Price Stern.
—Science Crosswords: Freaky Fish. 48p. 1990. pap. 2.95 (ISBN 0-8431-2820-8). Price Stern.
Spivak, Darlene. Crossword Puzzles, Wordsearches & Codes. Spivak, Darlene, illus. 48p. (gr. 2-5). 1986. wkbk. 5.95 (ISBN 1-55734-067-6). Tchr Create Mat.
Spizzirri Publishing Co. Staff. Picture Crosswords: An Educational Activity-Coloring Book. Spizzirr, Linda, ed. (Illus.). 32p. (gr. 1-8). 1986. pap. 1.95 (ISBN 0-86545-081-1). Spizzirri.
Sterling, Mary E. & Nowlin, Susan S. Crossword Puzzles. Spence, Paula & Wright, Terry, illus. 48p. (gr. 2-5). 1988. wkbk. 5.95 (ISBN 1-55734-365-9). Tchr Create Mat.
—Patriotic Wordsearches, Codes & Crossword Puzzles. Spence, Paula, illus. 48p. (gr. 2-5). 1988. wkbk. 5.95 (ISBN 1-55734-367-5). Tchr Create Mat.
Thornton, Christine. Crosswords for Spelling. (gr. 4-6). 1985. pap. 6.95 (ISBN 0-8224-2354-5). Fearon Teach Aids.
Van Ronzelen, George & Oberste, Kenneth, illus. TiL: A Book of Puzzles. LC 88-70805. 264p. (Orig.). (gr. 6 up). 1988. pap. 13.00 (ISBN 0-934426-18-X). NAPSAC Reprods.

CROWS
Blassingame, Wyatt. Wonders of Crows. 1979. 9.95 (ISBN 0-396-07649-1, Putnam). Putnam Pub Group.

CROWS-FICTION
Burgess, Thornton. Blacky the Crow. 93p. 1981. Repr. PLB 17.95 (ISBN 0-89966-351-6). Buccaneer Bks.
—Blacky the Crow. 198p. 1981. Repr. PLB 17.95 (ISBN 0-89967-025-3). Harmony Raine.
Damon, Valerie H. Tea with Adella Dine Crow. Damon, Dave, ed. LC 88-92261. (Illus.). 32p. (ps-5). 1990. 9.95 (ISBN 0-932356-15-X). Star Pubns MO.
George, Jean C. The Cry of the Crow. LC 79-2016. 160p. (gr. 5 up). 1982. pap. 3.50 (ISBN 0-06-440131-6, Trophy). HarpC Child Bks.
Guy, Ginger F. Black Crow, Black Crow. Parker, Nancy W., illus. LC 89-34619. 24p. (ps up). 1991. 13.95 (ISBN 0-688-08956-9); PLB 13.88 (ISBN 0-688-08957-7). Greenwillow.
Harwood, Pearl A. Mrs. Moon Takes a Drive. Overlie, George, illus. LC 67-15695. 32p. (gr. k-3). 1967. PLB 4.95 (ISBN 0-8225-0119-8). Lerner Pubns.
Lionni, Leo. Six Crows. LC 87-3141. (Illus.). 32p. (ps-2). 1988. 12.95 (ISBN 0-394-89572-X); lib. bdg. 12.99 (ISBN 0-394-99572-4). Knopf.

Sampson, Mary Y. & Bertschmann, Harry. Crow. Bertschmann, Mary, ed. Bertschmann, Harry, illus. 48p. 1989. pap. 8.00x (ISBN 0-935505-05-9). Bank St Pr.
With the publication of CROW, The Bank Street Press makes its debut into the world of children's books. This new paperback features the ever-flappable-unflappable Corvus brachyrhynchos making a major breakthrough & having the time of his life. The antics of a crow that loves to walk have been conceived & realized by illustrator Harry Bertschmann & writer Mary York Sampson. In this happy collaboration, they have combined joyful, bold illustrations with a simple, easy-to-read text. Mischievous & fun, CROW will walk right into the hearts of young juveniles everywhere. The review of CROW in THE WASHINGTON POST BOOK WORLD has this to say: "...The concept is sublimely simple: Crow is a strong-minded critter who decides flying is for the birds & sets out to try walking...on stilts, on a cactus, on a birthday cake, on a nose, between the flowers, on ice, in the paint, on the cat, & so on, getting sillier & sillier in a way that will have kids clamoring to join in. The black & white line drawings are equally imitable."
Publisher Provided Annotation.

Shankar, Alaka. Sonali's Friend. Joshi, Jagadish, illus. 16p. (Orig.). (gr. k-3). 1980. pap. 2.50 (ISBN 0-89744-218-0, Pub. by Children's Bk Trust India). Auromere.

CROWS-POETRY
Hellsing, Lennart. Cantankerous Crow. Stroyer, Paul, illus. (gr. k-3). 1962. 9.95 (ISBN 0-8392-3002-8). Astor-Honor.

CRUELTY TO ANIMALS
see Animals–Treatment

CRUSADES
see also Chivalry
Jessops, Joanne. Crusaders. (ps-3). 1990. PLB 10.40 (ISBN 0-531-18324-6). Watts.
Williams, Ann. The Crusaders. 2nd ed. Reeves, Marjorie, ed. (Illus.). 95p. (gr. 7-12). 1975. pap. text ed. 8.60 (ISBN 0-582-31096-2, 78069). Longman.

CRYPTOGRAPHY
see also Ciphers
Barker, Wayne G. Cryptograms. 119p. (gr. 9 up). 1980. lib. bdg. 13.95 (ISBN 0-89412-090-5); pap. text ed. 4.95 (ISBN 0-89412-043-3). Aegean Park Pr.

CRYSTAL GAZING
see Divination

CRYSTALLINE ROCKS
see Rocks

CRYSTALLIZATION
see Crystallography

CRYSTALLOGRAPHY
see also Mineralogy

Singer, Marcia. Crystal Kids: PLAYBook. Rendal, Camille, illus. LC 89-90988. 64p. (Orig.). 1989. pap. 9.95 (ISBN 0-9622543-0-4). PLAY House.
Metaphysics, meditations, creative healing arts & crystal fun for beginners of all ages. Softcover feast of enchanting, colorable illustrations, storyline, songs & "eduP.L.A.Y.tional" activities. Stimulates creativity, self-esteem & imagination skills. Enhances parent-child communications too. Experts recommend it as a year round gift for children & parents to share: "We need more books like this."--Terry Cole-Whittaker. "Wonderful fun tool introducing the world of crystals... topics covered in loving detail."--newsletter Psychic Research Institute (Marcel Vogel). "Every page is a multifaceted lesson/game...creative experience, delightfully endearing artwork."--Lee Perry, Whole Life Times. "My son enjoyed it."--Katrina Raphaell, Crystal Healing. "A light, joyful experience."--Frank Alper, D.D.,

---

Pres. AZ Metaphysical Society. "Fills hole in contemporary literature for children."--Wabun Wind, Lightseeds. "Healthful, helpful, positive, loving tool."--United Sensitive of America. "Inspiring, refreshing for all ages."--Kenny Kingston, Psychic to the Stars. "Delightful drawings, charming & informative text."--Laiura Wilson, (Louise) Hay House "Wondrous journey for the child in us all."--Richard Hatch, "ALL MY CHILDREN" (TV). "Expansive, not violent or condescending...I was tempted to get out my crayons & do a little doodling myself!"--Terry Sweeney, ex "Saturday Night Live" (TV). "Great pictures, songs, pretend games with crystals."--Lezli Censullo, Alternatives Newsletter.
Publisher Provided Annotation.

Stang, Jean. Crystals & Crystal Gardens You Can Grow. (ps-3). 1990. PLB 11.90 (ISBN 0-531-10889-9). Watts.

CRYSTALS
see Crystallography

CUB SCOUTS
see Boy Scouts

CUBA
Crouch, Clifford. Cuba. (Illus.). (gr. 5 up). 1991. 14.95 (ISBN 0-7910-1362-6). Chelsea Hse.
Cummins, Ronald. Cuba. Lopez, Mercedes, illus. LC 89-43170. 64p. (gr. 5-6). 1991. PLB 12.95 (ISBN 0-8368-0219-5). Gareth Stevens Inc.
Garver, Susan & McGuire, Paula. From Mexico, Cuba, & Puerto Rico. (gr. 7-11). pap. 2.50 (ISBN 0-317-13311-X, LFL). Dell.
Grenquist, Barbara. Cubans. (Illus.). 64p. (gr. 5-10). 1991. PLB 12.40 (ISBN 0-531-11107-5). Watts.
Haverstock, Nathan A. Cuba in Pictures. (Illus.). 64p. (gr. 5 up). 1987. PLB 12.95 (ISBN 0-8225-1811-2). Lerner Pubns.
Jose Marti. (Illus.). 32p. (gr. 3-6). 1988. PLB 16.67 (ISBN 0-8172-2906-X); pap. 9.27 (ISBN 0-685-28502-2). Raintree Pubs.
Morris, Emily. Cuba. LC 90-10354. (Illus.). 96p. (gr. 6-11). 1991. PLB 18.60 (ISBN 0-8114-2439-1). Steck-V.
Stubbs, Jean. Cuba. (Illus.). 150p. (gr. 9-12). 1989. 17.50 (ISBN 0-85345-780-8); pap. 8.00 (ISBN 0-85345-781-6). Monthly Rev.
Vazquez, Ana & Casas, Rosa. Cuba. LC 87-10235. (Illus.). 128p. (gr. 5-9). 1987. PLB 25.27 (ISBN 0-516-02758-1). Childrens.

CUBA-HISTORY
Jose Marti. (Illus.). 32p. (gr. 3-6). 1988. PLB 16.67 (ISBN 0-8172-2906-X); pap. 9.27 (ISBN 0-685-28502-2). Raintree Pubs.

CUCKOOS-FICTION
Corbalis, Judy. The Cuckoo Bird. Armitage, David, illus. LC 90-22576. 32p. (gr. 1-4). 1991. 14.95 (ISBN 0-06-021697-2); PLB 14.89 (ISBN 0-06-021698-0). HarpC Child Bks.

CULTS AND SECTS
see Sects

CULTURE
see also Civilization; Education; Learning and Scholarship; Self-Culture
Hirsch, E. D., Jr. The First Dictionary of Cultural Literacy. (Illus.). 352p. (gr. 6-8). 1989. 14.95 (ISBN 0-395-51040-6). HM.

Roland, Donna. Grandfather's Stories. Oden, Ron, illus. (Orig.). (gr. k-3). 1991. pap. 4.50 (ISBN 0-941996-00-X); tchr's. ed. 4.95. Open My World.
"Grandfather's Stories" provides students with a strong sense of personal & social values. At the same time the development of cultural awareness of their own culture & those of their classmates is encouraged. "Grandfather's Stories" is different from most multi-cultural series in that the children are portrayed living in the U.S. but through their grandfather they learn about their cultural background. Grandfather shares information about the country's history, social customs & the values he hopes to pass on to them. Although written on a 2nd grade reading level the series appeals to a wide age range. Its simple concepts yet detailed illustrations attract both

younger & older students. Cultures currently available are: American Indian (Lumbee), Cambodia, Germany, Mexico, the Philippines & Vietnam. Teacher's editions include additional information, activities & skill sheets. A video is also offered. In addition, the sequels, "More of Grandfather's Stories" is also available, which continues the same theme but with grandfather actually telling a folktale from their culture. Published by Open My World Publishing San Diego, California. *Publisher Provided Annotation.*

—**More of Grandfather's Stories.** Oden, Ron, illus. 25p. (Orig.). (gr. k-3). 1991. pap. 4.50 (ISBN 0-941996-02-6); tchr's. ed. 4.95 (ISBN 0-941996-13-1). Open My World.

"More of Grandfather's Stories" develops cultural awareness through cultural folklore. This series is different from most multi-cultural series in that the grandchildren being told the folktale live in the U. S. The selected folktale helps grandfather illustrate the values he hopes to instill. "More of Grandfather's Stories" supports & complements the series "Grandfather's Stories". Although written on a 2nd grade reading level the series appeals to a wide age range. Its simple concepts yet detailed illustrations attract both younger & older students. Cultures currently available are: American Indian (Lumbee), Cambodia, Germany, Mexico, the Philippines & Vietnam. Teacher's editions include additional information, activities & skill sheets. A video is also offered. In addition, "Grandfather's Stories" continues the same theme but grandfather shares information about their homeland's history, customs & the values he hopes to pass on to his grandchildren. Published by Open My World, San Diego, California. *Publisher Provided Annotation.*

Tulling, Virginia. Threatened Cultures. (Illus.). 48p. (gr. 5 up). 1990. lib. bdg. 18.00 (ISBN 0-86592-096-6); lib. bdg. 13.50s.p. (ISBN 0-685-36381-3). Rourke Corp.

CURATES
see Clergy

CURIE, MARIE (SKLODOWSKA) 1867-1934

Birch, Beverley. Marie Curie: Pioneer in the Study of Radiation. LC 89-77762. (Illus.). 64p. (gr. 4-8). 1990. PLB 12.95 (ISBN 0-8368-0388-4). Gareth Stevens Inc.

—Marie Curie: The Polish Scientist Who Discovered Radium & Its Life-Saving Properties. Sherwood, Rhoda, ed. LC 88-2091. (Illus.). 68p. (gr. 5-6). 1988. PLB 12.95 (ISBN 1-55532-818-0). Gareth Stevens Inc.

Birch, Beverly. Marie Curie. (Illus.). (gr. 5-6). 1990. pap. 7.95 (ISBN 0-8192-1522-8). Morehouse Pub.

Brandt, Keith. Marie Curie: Brave Scientist. Milone, Karen, illus. LC 82-16092. 48p. (gr. 4-6). 1983. PLB 10.79 (ISBN 0-89375-855-8); pap. text ed. 2.95 (ISBN 0-89375-856-6). Troll Assocs.

Brown, Pam. Father Damien: Missionary to a Forgotten People. Birch, Beverley, adapted by. LC 89-49751. (Illus.). 64p. (gr. 3-4). 1990. PLB 12.95 (ISBN 0-8368-0389-2). Gareth Stevens Inc.

Dunn, Andrew. Marie Curie. LC 90-37563. (Illus.). 48p. (gr. 5-8). 1991. PLB 12.40 (ISBN 0-531-18375-0, Pub. by Bookwright Pr.). Watts.

Farr, Naunerle. Madame Curie - Albert Einstein. Leonidez, Nestor & Redondo, Nestor, illus. (gr. 4-12). 1979. pap. text ed. 2.95 (ISBN 0-88301-356-8); wkbk. 1.25 (ISBN 0-88301-380-0). Pendulum Pr.

Greene, Carol. Marie Curie: Pioneer Physicist. LC 83-26273. (Illus.). 112p. (gr. 4 up). 1984. lib. bdg. 17.27 (ISBN 0-516-03203-8). Childrens.

Johnson, Ann D. The Value of Learning: The Story of Marie Curie. Pileggi, Stephen, illus. LC 78-6433. (gr. k-6). 1978. 9.95 (ISBN 0-916392-18-X, Pub. by Value Communications). Oak Tree Pubns.

Keller, Mollie. Marie Curie. LC 82-6904. (Illus.). 128p. (gr. 7 up). 1982. PLB 12.90 (ISBN 0-531-04476-9). Watts.

Montgomery, Mary & Baraldi, Severino. Marie Curie. (Illus.). 104p. (gr. 5-8). 1990. lib. bdg. 16.98 (ISBN 0-382-09981-8); pap. 8.95 (ISBN 0-382-24006-5). Silver Burdett Pr.

Sabin, Louis. Marie Curie. Eitzen, Allan, illus. LC 84-2654. 32p. (gr. 3-6). 1985. PLB 9.49 (ISBN 0-8167-0162-8); pap. text ed. 2.95 (ISBN 0-8167-0163-6). Troll Assocs.

Steinke, Ann. Marie Curie. (Illus.). 144p. (gr. 3-6). 1987. pap. 4.95 (ISBN 0-8120-3924-6). Barron.

Tames, Richard. Marie Curie. (Illus.). 32p. (gr. 7-9). 1990. PLB 11.90 (ISBN 0-531-10850-3). Watts.

—Marie Curie. (Illus.). 32p. (gr. 5 up). 1991. pap. 3.95 (ISBN 0-531-24612-4). Watts.

CURIOSITIES AND WONDERS

Allen, Eugenie. The Best Ever Kids' Book of Lists. 128p. (Orig.). 1991. pap. 2.95 (ISBN 0-380-76357-5, Camelot). Avon.

Asher, Sandy. Teddy Teabury's Fabulous Facts. Jones, Bob, illus. 110p. (Orig.). (gr. 4-5). 1985. pap. 2.50 (ISBN 0-440-48576-2, YB). Dell.

Creatures. 48p. (gr. 5-6). 1989. PLB 10.95 (ISBN 0-685-26332-0). Capstone Pr.

Crump, Donald J., ed. The Far-Out Fact Book. LC 79-1793. (Illus.). 104p. (gr. 3-8). 1980. 6.95 (ISBN 0-87044-319-4); PLB 8.50 (ISBN 0-87044-324-0). Natl Geog.

Dann, Max. You'll Never Believe It. Denton, Terry, illus. 128p. (gr. 5 up). 1991. bds. 13.95 laminated (ISBN 0-19-553030-6). Oxford U Pr.

Disappearances. 48p. (gr. 4-5). 1989. PLB 10.95 (ISBN 0-685-26161-1). Capstone Pr.

Doyle, Arthur Conan. The White Company. Wyeth, N. C., illus. Glassman, Peter, afterword by. LC 87-62625. (Illus.). 362p. (ps up). 1988. 17.00 (ISBN 0-688-07817-6). Morrow Jr Bks.

Duncan, David. Strange but True: Twenty-Two Amazing Stories. (gr. 4-6). 1974. pap. 2.25 (ISBN 0-590-03528-2, Cooper Sq Pap). Scholastic Inc.

Edens, Cooper. Caretakers of Wonder. Edens, Cooper, illus. LC 84-144762. 40p. (gr. 3 up). 1981. 11.95 (ISBN 0-914676-78-4, Star & Elephant Bks.); pap. 7.95 (ISBN 0-914676-76-8). Green Tiger Pr.

Edom, H., et al. Finding Out About: Where Things Come from & How Things Are Made. (Illus.). 72p. (gr. 2-4). 1989. 10.95 (ISBN 0-7460-0282-3, Usborne). EDC.

Far & Wide. 48p. (gr. 5-6). 1989. PLB 10.95 (ISBN 0-685-26333-9). Capstone Pr.

Getting There. 48p. (gr. 5-6). 1989. PLB 10.95 (ISBN 0-685-26335-5). Capstone Pr.

Goldman, Phyllis B. Monkeyshines on Strange & Wonderful Facts. Grigni, John, illus. 116p. (Orig.). (ps-8). 1991. pap. 8.95 (ISBN 0-9620900-2-6). NC Learn Inst Fitness. Monkeyshines on Strange & Wonderful Facts, 98 page volume of fascinating facts & miscellany, interesting reference alternative, illus. 8.95 plus 1.00 p/h (ISBN 0-9620900-2-6). Also available, Monkeyshines on the United States Presidents (Games, Puzzles & Trivia) illus., 98p. Interesting, informative & enjoyable view of the lives & work of the first 40 U.S. Presidents 12.95 plus 1.00 p/h (ISBN 0-9620900-1-8). *Publisher Provided Annotation.*

Hagerman, Paul. It's a Weird World. LC 90-37643. (Illus.). 128p. (Orig.). 1990. pap. 5.95 (ISBN 0-8069-7412-5). Sterling.

Hidden Worlds. LC 79-3244. (Illus.). 104p. (gr. 3-8). 1981. 6.95 (ISBN 0-87044-336-4); PLB 8.50 (ISBN 0-87044-341-0). Natl Geog.

Iverson, Carol. I Bet You Didn't Know That Fish Sleep with Their Eyes Open & Other Facts & Curiosities. Lindstrom, Jack, illus. 32p. (gr. 3-6). 1990. PLB 7.95 (ISBN 0-8225-2277-2). Lerner Pubns.

—I Bet You Didn't Know That You Can't Sink in the Dead Sea & Other Facts & Curiosities. Lindstrom, Jack, illus. 32p. (gr. 3-6). 1990. PLB 7.95 (ISBN 0-8225-2278-0). Lerner Pubns.

Land & Water. 48p. (gr. 5-6). 1989. PLB 10.95 (ISBN 0-685-26338-X). Capstone Pr.

Lawless, Joann A. Strange Stories of Life. LC 77-10866. (Illus.). 48p. (gr. 4 up). 1983. PLB 17.32 (ISBN 0-8172-1062-8); pap. 9.27 (ISBN 0-8172-2167-0). Raintree Pubs.

Long, Jack. How Does It Work? rev. ed. McKissack, Vern, illus. 32p. (gr. 2-4). 1990. Repr. of 1988 ed. PLB 9.95 (ISBN 1-878363-17-4). Forest Hse.

—Why Is the Sky Blue? McKissack, Vern, illus. 32p. (gr. 2-4). 1990. Repr. of 1988 ed. PLB 9.95 (ISBN 1-878363-15-8). Forest Hse.

A Look at the Earth Around Us: Plains. (gr. 3-6). 1981. incl. cass. & tchr's. guide 28.95 (ISBN 0-686-74502-7, 04925). Natl Geog.

McLeish, Kenneth. The Seven Wonders of the World. (Illus.). 1989. pap. 6.95 (ISBN 0-521-37911-3). Cambridge U Pr.

Matthews, Rupert. Record Breakers of the Air. LC 89-5212. (Illus.). 32p. (gr. 2-6). 1989. PLB 9.59 (ISBN 0-8167-1921-7); pap. text ed. 2.50 (ISBN 0-8167-1922-5). Troll Assocs.

—Record Breakers of the Land. LC 89-5202. (Illus.). 32p. (gr. 2-6). 1989. PLB 9.59 (ISBN 0-8167-1923-3); pap. text ed. 2.50 (ISBN 0-8167-1924-1). Troll Assocs.

More Far-Out Facts. LC 80-8798. (Illus.). 104p. (gr. 3-8). 1982. 6.95 (ISBN 0-87044-384-4); lib. bdg. 8.50 (ISBN 0-87044-389-5). Natl Geog.

O'Neill, Catherine. Amazing Mysteries of the World. Crump, Donald J., ed. LC 83-13444. 104p. (gr. 3-8). 1983. 6.95 (ISBN 0-87044-497-2); PLB 8.50 (ISBN 0-87044-502-2). Natl Geog.

Pearce, Q. L. Quicksand & Other Earthly Wonders. Steltenpohl, Jane, ed. Fraser, Mary A., illus. 64p. (gr. 4-6). 1989. PLB 12.98 (ISBN 0-671-68530-9); pap. 5.95 (ISBN 0-671-68646-1). Messner.

Places of Mystery. 48p. (gr. 4-5). 1989. PLB 10.95 (ISBN 0-685-26398-3). Capstone Pr.

Rand McNally Fact Books. Rand McNally Fact Books Staff. Incl. Computer World. Hoare, Stephen. write for info. (ISBN 0-528-87857-3); Ships & Other Sea Craft. Williams, Brian. 96p. (gr. 4-7). pap. 3.50 (ISBN 0-528-87858-1). 96p. (gr. 4-7). write for info. Checkerboard Pr.

Schreiber, Brad. Weird Wonders & Bizarre Blunders. 108p. 1989. 4.95 (ISBN 0-88166-174-0, Dist. by S & S). Meadowbrook.

Sobol, Donald J. Encyclopedia Brown's Record Book of Weird & Wonderful Facts. Murdocca, Sal, illus. LC 78-72857. (gr. 3 up). 1979. PLB 9.89 (ISBN 0-440-02330-0). Delacorte.

—Encyclopedia Brown's Second Record Book of Weird & Wonderful Facts. Degen, Bruce, illus. LC 81-790. 160p. (gr. 4-6). 1981. 10.95 (ISBN 0-385-28243-5); PLB 10.95 (ISBN 0-685-01395-2). Delacorte.

Taylor, Paula. The Kids' Whole Future Catalog. LC 82-5279. (Illus.). 256p. (gr. 4-7). 1982. pap. 6.95 (ISBN 0-394-85090-4). Random.

Turner, Dorothy. Man-Made Wonders of the World. LC 86-1340. (Illus.). 32p. (gr. 2 up). 1986. PLB 10.95 (ISBN 0-87518-334-4, Dillon). Macmillan Child Grp.

Warren, William E. The Headless Ghost: True Tales of the Unexplained. Waldman, Neil, illus. LC 85-28214. 144p. (gr. 6 up). 1986. PLB 12.95 (ISBN 0-671-67710-1). S&S Trade.

—The Screaming Skull: True Tales of the Unexplained. Waldman, Neil, illus. LC 87-6909. 144p. (gr. 5 up). 1987. PLB 11.95 (ISBN 0-671-66809-9). S&S Trade.

Wassermann, Selma & Wassermann, Jack. The Book of Hypotheses. Smith, Dennis, illus. LC 89-78082. 32p. (gr. k-3). 1990. PLB 12.85 (ISBN 0-8027-6946-2); pap. 4.95 (ISBN 0-8027-9452-1). Walker & Co.

Winik, J. T. Mysteries. Rowden, Rick, illus. 48p. (gr. 5-9). 1985. pap. 5.95 (ISBN 0-88625-094-3). Durkin Hayes Pub.

Woods, Harold & Woods, Geraldine. The Book of the Unknown. Mathieu, Joe, illus. LC 82-3683. 72p. (gr. 4-7). 1982. lib. bdg. 5.99 (ISBN 0-394-95233-2); pap. 3.95 (ISBN 0-394-85233-8). Random.

World Records & Amazing Facts. (Illus.). 32p. 1985. 3.95 (ISBN 0-394-87697-0). Random.

CURRENCY
see Money

CUSTER, GEORGE ARMSTRONG, 1839-1876

Armstrong, Virgil. The Assassination of General George Armstrong Custer: The True Story Behind the Battle of the Little Big Horn. Whitman, Patricia, ed. 300p. (gr. 9-12). 1990. pap. write for info. (ISBN 0-925390-22-4). Armstrong Assocs.

Bachrach, Deborah. Custer's Last Stand: Opposing Viewpoints. LC 90-36967. (Illus.). 112p. (gr. 3-8). 1990. PLB 13.95 (ISBN 0-89908-077-4). Greenhaven.

Razzi, Jim. Custer & Crazy Horse. (gr. 3-7). 1989. pap. 2.75 (ISBN 0-590-41836-X). Scholastic Inc.

Reynolds, Quentin. Custer's Last Stand. LC 87-4650. (Illus.). 160p. (gr. 5-9). 1987. lib. bdg. 8.99 (ISBN 0-394-90320-X, Random Juv). Random.

CUSTOMS, SOCIAL
see Manners and Customs

CYBERNETICS
see also Bionics; Computers

CYCLES, MOTOR
see Motorcycles

CYCLING
see Bicycles and Bicycling; Motorcycles

CYCLOPEDIAS
see Encyclopedias and Dictionaries

CYTOLOGY
see Cells

CZECHOSLOVAK REPUBLIC

Dominica. (Illus.). (gr. 5 up). 1988. 13.95 (ISBN 0-7910-0152-0). Chelsea Hse.

Lye, Keith. Take a Trip to Czechoslovakia. LC 86-50018. (Illus.). 32p. (gr. 1-6). 1986. PLB 7.99 (ISBN 0-531-10195-9). Watts.

CZECHS IN THE U. S.
Roucek, Joseph S. Czechs & the Slovaks in America. LC 67-15685. (Illus.). 72p. (gr. 5 up). 1967. PLB 11.95 (ISBN 0-8225-0209-7); pap. 3.95 (ISBN 0-8225-1004-9). Lerner Pubns.
Sakson-Ford, Stephanie. Czechoslovakian Americans. Moynihan, Daniel P., intro. by. (Illus.). 112p. (gr. 5 up). 1989. lib. bdg. 17.95 (ISBN 0-87754-870-6). Chelsea Hse.

D

D N A
Asimov, Isaac. How Did We Find Out about DNA? Wool, David, illus. LC 85-15589. 61p. (gr. 9 up). 1985. 9.95 (ISBN 0-8027-6596-3); PLB 10.85 (ISBN 0-8027-6604-8). Walker & Co.
Wilcox, Frank H. DNA: The Thread of Life. (Illus.). 80p. (gr. 5 up). 1988. PLB 12.95 (ISBN 0-8225-1584-9). Lerner Pubns.
DAIRIES
see Dairying
DAIRY CATTLE
see Cows
DAIRY PRODUCTS
see also Dairying;
also names of dairy products, e.g. Milk
DAIRYING
see also Cattle; Cows; Milk
Mitgutsch, Ali. From Grass to Butter. Mitgutsch, Ali, illus. LC 80-28588. 24p. (ps-3). 1981. PLB 6.95 (ISBN 0-87614-156-4). Carolrhoda Bks.
—From Milk to Ice Cream. Mitgutsch, Ali, illus. LC 81-81. 24p. (ps-3). 1981. PLB 6.95 (ISBN 0-87614-158-0). Carolrhoda Bks.
Poskanzer, Susan C. Dairy Farmer. Ulrich, George, illus. LC 88-10040. 32p. (gr. k-2). 1989. PLB 10.89 (ISBN 0-8167-1426-6); pap. text ed. 2.50 (ISBN 0-8167-1427-4). Troll Assocs.
Ross, Catherine. Amazing Milk Book. 1991. pap. 6.68 (ISBN 0-201-57087-4). Addison-Wesley.
Wright, Dare. Look at a Calf. Wright, Dare, illus. LC 73-17369. 48p. 1974. lib. bdg. 4.99 (ISBN 0-394-92776-1, Random Juv). Random.
Ziegler, Sandra. A Visit to the Dairy Farm. LC 87-19692. (Illus.). 32p. (ps-3). 1987. PLB 14.60 (ISBN 0-516-01496-X); pap. 3.95 (ISBN 0-516-41496-8). Childrens.
DAIRYING–FICTION
Gibbons, Gail. The Milk Makers. LC 84-20081. (Illus.). 32p. (gr. k-3). 1985. 13.95 (ISBN 0-02-736640-5, Mcmillan Child Bk). Macmillan Child Grp.
Lindbergh, Anne M. The Hunky-Dory Dairy. Brinckloe, Julie, illus. LC 85-16408. 160p. (gr. 4-6). 1986. 14.95 (ISBN 0-15-237449-3, HJ). HarBraceJ.
DALLAS
Velvin, Elaine. Discover Dallas: A Child's Guide. rev. ed. (Illus.). 68p. (gr. 2-7). 1987. pap. 5.95 (ISBN 0-937460-18-4). Hendrick-Long.
DALLAS COWBOYS (FOOTBALL TEAM)
Alcorta, Joe H., Sr. La Historia de un Famoso Equipo: Los Dallas Cowboys. (SPA., Illus.). 410p. (gr. 9-12). 1989. 14.95 (ISBN 0-685-29025-5). Hermenejildo Pr.
DAMIEN, FATHER, 1840-1889
Brown, Pam. Father Damien: The Man Who Lived & Died for the Victims of Leprosy. Sherwood, Rhoda, ed. LC 88-2106. (Illus.). 68p. (gr. 5-6). 1988. PLB 12.95 (ISBN 1-55532-815-6). Gareth Stevens Inc.
DAMS
Ardley, Neil. Dams. Stefoff, Rebecca, ed. LC 90-40360. (Illus.). 48p. (gr. 4-7). 1990. PLB 17.26 (ISBN 0-944483-75-5). Garrett Ed Corp.
Baljo, Wallace, Jr. Grand Coulee: A Story of the Columbia River from Molten Lavas & Ice to Grand Coulee Dam. rev. ed. Hemsley, Roberta G., illus. 80p. (gr. 4-6). pap. write for info. (ISBN 0-9606084-0-0). Clipboard.
DANCERS
Brighton, Catherine. Nijinsky: Scenes from the Childhood of the Great Dancer. (Illus.). 32p. (ps-3). 1989. 13.95 (ISBN 0-385-24663-3, Zephyr-BFYR); PLB 14.99 (ISBN 0-385-24926-8, Zephyr-BFYR). Doubleday.
Butterworth, Emma M. As the Waltz Was Ending. 262p. (gr. 7 up). 1991. pap. 2.95 (ISBN 0-590-44440-9, Point); tchr's. guide 1.25 (ISBN 0-590-40665-5). Scholastic Inc.
Clarke, Mary & Ashton, Frederick, illus. Antoinette Sibley. Ashton, Frederick, intro. by. 128p. (gr. 8-12). 1981. 29.95 (ISBN 0-903102-64-1, Pub. by Dance Bks UK). Princeton Bk Co.
Gruen, John. People Who Dance. LC 88-60952. (Illus.). 176p. (gr. 9-12). 1988. 24.95 (ISBN 0-916622-74-6). Princeton Bk Co.
Haskins, James. Black Dance in America: A History Through Its People. LC 89-35529. (Illus.). 240p. (gr. 7 up). 1990. 14.95 (ISBN 0-690-04657-X, Crowell Jr Bks); PLB 14.89 (ISBN 0-690-04659-6, Crowell Jr Bks). HarpC Child Bks.
Kozodoy, Ruth. Isadora Duncan. Horner, Matina, intro. by. (Illus.). 112p. (gr. 5 up). 1988. lib. bdg. 17.95x (ISBN 1-55546-650-8). Chelsea Hse.
Linnell, Andrew & Auer, Varvara. The Dance of the Elves. (Illus.). 32p. (Orig.). (ps). 1984. pap. 13.50 (ISBN 0-936132-68-X). Merc Pr NY.
Martin, John H. A Day in the Life of a Ballet Dancer. Jann, Gayle, illus. LC 84-2424. 32p. (gr. 4-8). 1985. PLB 11.79 (ISBN 0-8167-0089-3); pap. text ed. 2.95 (ISBN 0-8167-0090-7). Troll Assocs.
Menning, Viiu. Great Dancers. Conkle, Nancy & Neary, D., illus. (Orig.). (gr. 8). pap. 3.50 (ISBN 0-88388-065-2). Bellerophon Bks.
DANCERS–FICTION
Brenner, Summer. Dancers & the Dance. 144p. (Orig.). 1990. pap. 9.95 (ISBN 0-918273-75-7). Coffee Hse.
Coombs, Karen. Samantha Gill, Belly Dancer. 128p. 1989. pap. 2.75 (ISBN 0-380-75737-0, Camelot). Avon.
Estoril, Jean. Drina Dances Again, No. 5. 1989. pap. 2.95 (ISBN 0-590-42557-9). Scholastic Inc.
—Drina Dances Al, No. 3. 1989. pap. 2.75 (ISBN 0-590-43081-5). Scholastic Inc.
—Drina Dances on Stage, No. 4. 1989. pap. 2.75 (ISBN 0-590-42558-7). Scholastic Inc.
—Drina's Dancing Year, No. 2. 1989. pap. 2.75 (ISBN 0-590-42192-1). Scholastic Inc.
Fox, Paula. The Slave Dancer. (Orig.). (gr. k-6). 1991. pap. 3.50 (ISBN 0-440-40402-9, Pub. by Yearling Classics). Dell.
Gauch, Patricia L. Dance, Tanya. Ichikawa, Satomi, illus. 32p. (ps-3). 1989. 13.95 (ISBN 0-399-21521-2, Philomel Bks). Putnam Pub Group.
Hill, Elizabeth S. The Street Dancers. 192p. (gr. 3-7). 1991. 13.95 (ISBN 0-670-83435-1). Viking Child Bks.
Mathers, Petra. Sophie & Lou. Mathers, Petra, illus. LC 90-37562. 32p. (ps-3). 1991. 14.95 (ISBN 0-06-024071-7); PLB 14.89 (ISBN 0-06-024072-5). HarpC Child Bks.
Smith, Doris B. Karate Dancer. 208p. (gr. 6-9). 1987. 14.95 (ISBN 0-399-21464-X, Putnam). Putnam Pub Group.
Tolles, Martha. Darci & the Dance Contest. 112p. (gr. 4-6). 1987. pap. 2.50 (ISBN 0-590-33824-2, Apple Paperbacks). Scholastic Inc.
DANCING
see also Ballet; Folk Dancing
Ancona, George. Dancing Is. Ancona, George, photos by. (Illus.). 48p. (gr. 1-3). 1981. 13.95 (ISBN 0-525-28490-7, DCB). Dutton Child Bks.
Berger, Melvin. The World of Dance. LC 78-14498. (Illus.). (gr. 7 up). 1978. 21.95 (ISBN 0-87599-221-8). S G Phillips.
Berk, Fred. Chasidic Dance. (gr. 9 up). 1975. pap. 5.00 (ISBN 0-8074-0083-1, 582050). UAHC.
Bessant, P. & Smith, L. Dance. (Illus.). 48p. (gr. 5 up). 1987. PLB 13.96 (ISBN 0-88110-245-8); pap. 6.95 (ISBN 0-7460-0087-1). EDC.
Caney, Steven. Teach Yourself Tap Dancing. LC 89-40726. (Illus.). 64p. (Orig.). (gr. 2-5). 1991. pap. 12.95 (ISBN 0-89480-428-6, 1428). Workman Pub.
Carter, Eneida & Mikalac, Miriam. Break Dance: The Free & Easy Way! Forman, Jan A., illus. 32p. (gr. 7 up). 1984. pap. 9.95 (ISBN 0-916391-00-0). Free & Easy Pubns.
Dunnahoo, Terry. Break Dancing. Sefcik, Robert, illus. LC 84-25801. 72p. (gr. 4-6). 1985. PLB 10.40 (ISBN 0-531-04883-7). Watts.
Heffer, Marjorie & Porter, William. Maggot Pie: Country Dances. 2nd ed. Kennedy, Douglas, intro. by. 55p. (Orig.). (gr. 6 up). 1979. pap. 4.95 (ISBN 0-913714-51-8). Legacy Bks.
Hutchinson-Guest, Ann H. Primer for Dance, Bk. II. 24p. (ps). 1958. pap. text ed. 6.95 (ISBN 0-932582-65-6). Dance Notation.
Johnston, Edith. Regional Dances of the Mexico. (Illus.). 64p. (gr. 3 up). 1983. pap. 6.60 (ISBN 0-8442-7509-3, Passport Bks.). Natl Textbk.
Morrison, Lillian. The Break Dance Kids Poems of Sport, Motion & Locomotion. LC 84-23396. (Illus.). 64p. (gr. 5 up). 1985. PLB 11.88 (ISBN 0-688-04554-5). Lothrop.
Roes, Carol. Children's Christmas Hulas. (gr. k-1). 1965. pap. 35.00 incl. 4 records (ISBN 0-930932-18-8). M Loke.
—Children's Hulas from Hawaii, Bk. 5. Kaiulani, illus. 13p. (gr. 8). 1966. pap. 5.50 (ISBN 0-930932-10-2); record incl. M Loke.
—Introduction to the Hula. (Illus.). 12p. (gr. 1-3). 1961. pap. 2.50 (ISBN 0-930932-07-2). M Loke.
Roes, Carol & Kaiulani. Children's Hulas for Song Stories, Bk. 3. Stone, L., illus. 24p. (gr. 3-4). 1963. pap. 5.50 (ISBN 0-930932-08-0); record incl. M Loke.
—Children's Hulas from Hawaii, Bk. 2. (gr. 4-5). 1962. pap. text ed. 5.50 (ISBN 0-930932-04-8, A572149); record incl. M Loke.
—Hulas for 4 Songs. 18p. (gr. 8 up). 1963. pap. 5.50 (ISBN 0-930932-09-9); record incl. M Loke.
Roes, Carol & Tuulikki. Children's Hulas from Hawaii, Bk. 1. Stone, Lloyd, illus. (gr. k). 1961. pap. text ed. 5.50 (ISBN 0-930932-05-6, A516842); record incl. M Loke.
Sanchez, Sharon S. About Ballet Performance. Bower, Adele, illus. 32p. (ps up). 1990. pap. 5.95 (ISBN 0-9626651-1-8). Dance Data.
Sanchez, Sharon S., ed. About Ballet Class. Bower, Adele, illus. 32p. (Orig.). (ps up). 1990. pap. 5.95 (ISBN 0-9626651-0-X). Dance Data.
Sorine, Daniel S. Imagine That! It's Modern Dance. Sorine, Stephanie R., illus. LC 80-19232. 48p. (ps-3). 1981. lib. bdg. 8.99 (ISBN 0-394-94474-7); PLB 8.95 (ISBN 0-394-84474-2). Knopf.
Thomas, A., et al. Ballet & Dance. (Illus.). 96p. (gr. 5 up). 1987. pap. 10.95 (ISBN 0-7460-0201-7). EDC.
Tolles, Martha. Darci & the Dance Contest. LC 84-28840. 128p. (gr. 4-6). 1985. 11.95 (ISBN 0-525-67166-8, Lodestar Bks). Dutton Child Bks.
Zeck, Gerry. I Love to Dance! LC 82-4232. (Illus.). 64p. (gr. 2-5). 1982. lib. bdg. 9.95 (ISBN 0-87614-198-X). Carolrhoda Bks.
DANCING–FICTION
Appelt, Kathi A. The Boy Who Loved to Dance. Morales, Sioux N., illus. 48p. (ps-3). 1986. PLB 11.95 (ISBN 0-938169-00-9); pap. 6.95 (ISBN 0-938169-01-7). Pecan Tree Pr.
Cone, Molly. Dance Around the Fire. Friedman, Marvin, illus. LC 74-9378. 160p. (gr. 7 up). 1974. 5.95 (ISBN 0-395-19490-3). HM.
Cormier, Larry. The Captain, the Gypsy & the Giant Bird. Bruni, Mary-Ann S., ed. Pressley, Ann, illus. 48p. (gr. k-8). 1986. 12.95 (ISBN 0-935857-07-9); pap. write for info. (ISBN 0-935857-08-7). Texart.
De Paola, Tomie. Oliver Button Is a Sissy. De Paola, Tomie, illus. LC 78-12624. (gr. k-3). 1979. pap. 4.95 (ISBN 0-15-668140-4, VoyB). HarBraceJ.
Edelman, Elaine. Boom-De-Boom. Gundersheimer, Karen, illus. (ps-2). 1980. Pantheon.
Greaves, Margaret. Little Box of Ballet Stories, 3 vols. Crespi, Francesca, illus. Incl. Fire Bird; Petrushka; Coppelia. LC 86-930. 28p. (ps-3). 1986. Boxed Set. 8.95 (ISBN 0-8037-0265-5). Dial Bks Young.
Guard, Jean & Williamson, Ray A. They Dance in the Sky. Stewart, Edgar, illus. (gr. 6 up). 1987. 13.95 (ISBN 0-395-39970-X). HM.
Isadora, Rachel. Max. Isadora, Rachel, illus. LC 76-9088. 32p. (gr. k-3). 1976. 12.95 (ISBN 0-02-747450-X, Mcmillan Child Bk). Macmillan Child Grp.
Kllair, Bevan. Elferina & the Christmas Cha Cha. LC 79-91132. (ps-6). 1979. pap. 3.00 (ISBN 0-935712-00-3). B A Scott.
—The Ziggle Dance at the Zoo. LC 79-91133. (ps-6). 1979. pap. 3.00 (ISBN 0-935712-01-1). B A Scott.
Krementz, Jill. A Very Young Dancer. (gr. 3-6). 1986. pap. 7.95 (ISBN 0-440-49212-2, YB). Dell.
Malcolm, Jahnna N. A Dog Named Toe Shoe. (gr. 4-7). 1991. pap. 2.75 (ISBN 0-590-43398-9). Scholastic Inc.
Marshall, James. The Cut-ups Carry On. (Illus.). 32p. (ps-2). 1990. pap. 12.95 (ISBN 0-670-81645-0). Viking Child Bks.
Martin, Bill, Jr. & Archambault, John. Barn Dance! Rand, Ted, illus. LC 86-14225. 32p. (gr. k-2). 1986. 12.95 (ISBN 0-8050-0089-5). H Holt & Co.
—Barn Dance! Rand, Ted, illus. LC 86-14225. 32p. (gr. k-3). 1988. pap. 4.95 (ISBN 0-8050-0799-7). H Holt & Co.
Rostkowski, Margaret I. After the Dancing Days. LC 85-45810. 224p. (gr. 5-9). 1988. pap. 3.50 (ISBN 0-06-440248-7, Trophy). HarpC Child Bks.
Rylant, Cynthia. Waiting to Waltz: A Childhood. Gammell, Stephen, illus. LC 84-11030. 48p. (gr. 6-8). 1984. 11.95 (ISBN 0-02-778000-7, Bradbury Pr). Macmillan Child Grp.
Shannon, George. Dance Away! Aruego, Jose & Dewey, Ariane, illus. LC 81-6391. 32p. (gr. k-3). 1982. 13.95 (ISBN 0-688-00838-0); PLB 13.88 (ISBN 0-688-00839-9). Greenwillow.
Simon, Carly. Amy the Dancing Bear. Datz, Margot, illus. (ps-3). 1989. 12.95 (ISBN 0-385-26637-5); PLB 13.99 (ISBN 0-385-26721-5). Doubleday.
Skofield, James. Nightdances. Gundersheimer, Karen, illus. LC 80-8943. 32p. (ps-3). 1981. 12.95 (ISBN 0-06-025741-5); PLB 11.89 (ISBN 0-06-025742-3). HarpC Child Bks.
Stapler, Sarah. Cordellia, Dance! LC 89-39352. (Illus.). 32p. (ps-3). 1990. 10.95 (ISBN 0-8037-0792-4); PLB 10.89 (ISBN 0-8037-0793-2). Dial Bks Young.
Streatfeild, Noel. Dancing Shoes. 288p. (gr. k-6). 1980. pap. 3.25 (ISBN 0-440-42289-2, YB). Dell.
Swann, Brian. Tongue Dancing. Dodge, Katherine, illus. 56p. (gr. 7-12). 1984. 12.95g (ISBN 0-937672-12-2). Rowan Tree.
Thesman, Jean. The Last April Dancers. 224p. (gr. 7 up). 1989. pap. 2.75 (ISBN 0-380-70614-8, Flare). Avon.
Tompert, Ann. Savina, the Gypsy Dancer. Nolan, Dennis, illus. LC 90-5902. 32p. (gr. k-3). 1991. RSBE 13.95 (ISBN 0-02-789205-0, Mcmillan Child Bk). Macmillan Child Grp.
Uchida, Yoshiko. The Dancing Kettle. LC 86-70457. 184p. (gr. 5 up). 1986. pap. 7.95 (ISBN 0-88739-014-5). Creative Arts Bk.
Ure, Jean. You Win Some, You Lose Some. LC 85-16134. 182p. (gr. 7 up). 1986. pap. 14.95 (ISBN 0-385-29434-4). Delacorte.
Wallace, Ian. Chin Chiang & the Dragon's Dance. LC 83-13442. (Illus.). 32p. (gr. k-4). 1984. 12.95 (ISBN 0-689-50299-0, M K McElderry). Macmillan Child Grp.
Weyn, Suzanne. Pointing Toward Trouble. Iskowitz, Joel, illus. LC 89-34549. 96p. (gr. 3-5). 1989. PLB 9.89 (ISBN 0-8167-1653-6); pap. text ed. 2.95 (ISBN 0-8167-1654-4). Troll Assocs.
DANDELIONS
Hogan, Paula Z. The Dandelion. LC 78-21155. (Illus.). 32p. (gr. 1-4). 1979. PLB 16.67 (ISBN 0-8172-1250-7). Raintree Pubs.
—The Dandelion. LC 78-21155. (Illus.). 32p. (gr. 1-4). 1984. PLB 27.99 incl. cassette (ISBN 0-8172-2227-8); cassette 14.00 (ISBN 0-685-09513-4). Raintree Pubs.
Pohl, Kathleen. Dandelions. (Illus.). 32p. (gr. 3-7). 1986. pap. text ed. 16.67 (ISBN 0-8172-2708-3); pap. 9.27 (ISBN 0-8172-2726-1). Raintree Pubs.

Watts, Barrie. Dandelion. (Illus.). 24p. (gr. 2-5). 1987. 6.95 (ISBN 0-382-09442-5); PLB 9.98 (ISBN 0-382-09438-7); pap. 3.95 (ISBN 0-382-24016-2). Silver Burdett Pr.

DANIEL, THE PROPHET

Daniel. 1989. 3.95 (ISBN 0-87508-814-7). Chr Lit.

Daniel. (ps-2). 3.95 (ISBN 0-7214-5069-5). Ladybird Bks.

Daniel & the Lions. (ps). 1991. Set of 6. pap. 3.95 (ISBN 0-8007-1168-8). Revell.

De Graaf, Anne. Daniel: Prisoner with a Promise. Montero, Jose P., illus. 32p. (gr. k-4). 1991. 7.95 (ISBN 0-8028-5036-7). Eerdmans.

Heath, Lou. Daniel: Faithful Captive. Myers, William, illus. (gr. 1-6). 1977. bds. 5.95 (ISBN 0-8054-4231-6, 4242-31). Broadman.

Overholtzer, Ruth. Daniel. Butcher, Sam, illus. (gr. k-6). 1988. pap. text ed. 9.45 (ISBN 1-55976-011-7). CEF Press.

Singleton, Kathy. Daniel & the Lions. Baker, Arthur, illus. 32p. (gr. k-3). 1990. saddle stitched 1.25. Eerdmans.

Stirrup Associates, Inc. Staff. My Jesus Pocketbook of Daniel in the Lion's Den. Harvey, Bonnie C. & Phillips, Cheryl M., eds. Fulton, Ginger A., illus. LC 84-50916. 32p. (Orig.). (ps-3). 1984. pap. text ed. 0.69 (ISBN 0-937420-12-3). Stirrup Assoc.

Storr, Catherine, as told by. The Trials of Daniel. (Illus.). 32p. (gr. k-4). 1985. PLB 14.65 (ISBN 0-8172-2040-2). Raintree Pubs.

DANTE ALIGHIERI, 1265-1321–ADAPTATIONS

Tusiani, Joseph. Dante's Inferno. Pfeiffer, Werner, illus. (gr. 5 up). 1965. 9.95 (ISBN 0-8392-3046-X). Astor-Honor.

—Dante's Paradiso. Dore, Gustav, illus. (gr. 7 up). 1969. 9.95 (ISBN 0-685-00563-1). Astor-Honor.

—Dante's Purgatorio. (Illus.). (gr. 5 up). 1968. 9.95 (ISBN 0-8392-3053-2). Astor-Honor.

DARK AGES

see Middle Ages

DARROW, CLARENCE SEWARD, 1857-1938

Clarence Darrow: Mini-Play. (gr. 5 up). 1978. 6.50 (ISBN 0-89550-312-3). Stevens & Shea.

Kurland, Gerald. Clarence Darrow: Attorney for the Damned. Rahmas, D. Steve, ed. LC 75-190240. 32p. (Orig.). (gr. 7-12). 1972. lib. bdg. 4.20 incl. catalog cards (ISBN 0-87157-522-1); pap. 2.95 vinyl laminated covers (ISBN 0-87157-022-X). SamHar Pr.

DARWIN, CHARLES ROBERT, 1809-1882

Hyndley, Kate. The Voyage of the Beagle. Bull, Peter, illus. LC 88-28695. 32p. (gr. 5-9). 1989. PLB 11.40 (ISBN 0-531-18272-X, Pub. by Bookwright Pr). Watts.

Law, Felicia. Darwin & the Voyage of the Beagle. Brook, Judy, illus. LC 84-71817. 96p. (gr. 4 up). 1985. 12.95 (ISBN 0-233-97482-2). Andre Deutsch.

Skelton, Renee. Charles Darwin. LC 87-19564. (Illus.). 144p. (gr. 3-6). 1987. pap. 4.95 (ISBN 0-8120-3923-8). Barron.

Ward, Peter. The Adventures of Charles Darwin: A Story of the Beagle Voyage. LC 81-21751. (Illus.). 96p. (gr. 4-7). 1986. 12.95 (ISBN 0-521-24510-9); pap. 5.95 (ISBN 0-521-31074-1). Cambridge U Pr.

DARWINISM

see Evolution

DATA PROCESSING

see Information Storage and Retrieval Systems

DATA STORAGE AND RETRIEVAL SYSTEMS

see Information Storage and Retrieval Systems

DATE ETIQUETTE

see Dating (Social Customs)

DATING (SOCIAL CUSTOMS)

see also Love; Marriage

Diorio, MaryAnn L. Dating Etiquette for Christian Teens. Crescenzo, Phil, illus. 48p. (Orig.). (gr. 6-12). 1984. pap. 3.95 (ISBN 0-930037-00-6). Daystar Comm.

Dockrey, Karen. Dating: Making Your Own Choices. LC 86-30985. (Orig.). (gr. 7-12). 1987. pap. 4.95 (ISBN 0-8054-5345-8). Broadman.

Dumond, Michael. Coping with the Dating Game. Rosen, R., ed. 115p. (gr. 7-12). 1985. PLB 12.95 (ISBN 0-8239-0637-X). Rosen Group.

Eager, George B. Love, Dating & Sex: What Teens Want to Know. Philbrook, Diana, illus. 208p. (gr. 6 up). 1989. PLB 12.95g (ISBN 0-9603752-9-5). Mailbox.

Hartley, Fred. Dare to Date Differently. (Illus.). 128p. (Orig.). (gr. 8-12). 1988. pap. 6.95 (ISBN 0-8007-5266-X). Revell.

Hunt, Gary & Hunt, Angela. Now That He's Asked You Out: Straight Talk for Girls. LC 89-30704. 132p. (Orig.). (gr. 7-12). 1989. pap. 6.99 (ISBN 0-89840-258-1). Heres Life.

—Now That You've Asked Her Out: Straight Talk for Guys. LC 89-30703. 132p. (Orig.). (gr. 7-12). 1989. pap. 6.99 (ISBN 0-89840-259-X). Heres Life.

Kerley, Joy. Guys vs. Gals: (World War III) (Illus.). pap. text ed. 8.00 (ISBN 0-9614268-1-0). Teen Round Up.

Rue, Nancy N. Coping with Dating Violence. Rosen, Ruth, ed. (gr. 7-12). 1989. PLB 12.95 (ISBN 0-8239-0997-2). Rosen Group.

Schneider, Meg F. Romance! Can You Survive It? A Guide to Sticky Dating Situations. 160p. (Orig.). (gr. 7-12). 1984. pap. 2.25 (ISBN 0-440-97478-X, LFL). Dell.

Scott, Timothy. You Can't Hurry Love: (A Guide to Christian Dating) 10p. (Orig.). (gr. 10-12). 1989. pap. write for info. (ISBN 1-877784-05-2). T Scott Pub.

Sharmat, Marjorie W. How to Meet a Gorgeous Girl. 160p. (Orig.). (gr. k up). 1989. pap. 2.95 (ISBN 0-440-93808-2, LFL). Dell.

Souter, John C. Date. (gr. 7 up). 1981. pap. 4.95 (ISBN 0-8423-0636-6). Tyndale.

Weyn, Suzanne. Boy Trouble. LC 90-11142. 128p. (gr. 4-8). 1990. lib. bdg. 9.89 (ISBN 0-8167-2011-8); pap. text ed. 2.95 (ISBN 0-8167-2012-6). Troll Assocs.

DATING (SOCIAL CUSTOMS)–FICTION

Anderson, Mary. Do You Call That a Dream Date? 176p. (gr. 6 up). 1989. pap. 2.95 (ISBN 0-440-20350-3, LFL). Dell.

Byars, Betsy C. The Cybil War. Owens, Gail, illus. LC 80-26912. 144p. (gr. 8-12). 1981. pap. 12.95 (ISBN 0-670-25248-4). Viking Child Bks.

Conford, Ellen. We Interrupt This Semester for an Important Bulletin. 192p. (Orig.). (gr. 7 up). 1979. pap. 1.95 (ISBN 0-590-32830-1, Vagabond). Scholastic Inc.

Dickenson, Celia. Too Many Boys. 160p. (Orig.). (gr. 5-6). 1984. pap. 2.50 (ISBN 0-553-26615-2). Bantam.

Gelman, Jan. Marci's Secret Book of Dating. LC 90-2255. 96p. (Orig.). (gr. 4-8). 1991. PLB 7.99 (ISBN 0-679-91106-5, Bullseye Bks); pap. 2.95 (ISBN 0-679-81106-0, Bullseye Bks). Knopf.

Greene, Constance C. Al's Blind Date. 128p. (gr. 5-9). 1989. pap. 12.95 (ISBN 0-670-82815-7). Viking Child Bks.

Hall, Lynn. Dagmar Schultz & the Angel Edna. LC 88-36862. 96p. (gr. 5-8). 1989. 11.95 (ISBN 0-684-19097-4, Scribners Young Read). Macmillan Child Grp.

Kenyon, Kate. The Big Date. 160p. (gr. 5-9). 1988. pap. 2.50 (ISBN 0-590-41389-9). Scholastic Inc.

Landis, J. D. Looks Aren't Everything. (gr. 7 up). 1990. 13.95 (ISBN 0-553-05847-9, Starfire). Bantam.

Moore, Sheila. Samson Svenson's Baby. Weinhaus, Karen A., illus. LC 82-48262. 48p. (gr. 1-4). 1983. 11.95 (ISBN 0-06-022612-9). HarpC Child Bks.

Quin-Harkin, Janet. The Great Boy Chase. 192p. (gr. 7-12). 1985. pap. 2.50 (ISBN 0-553-26743-4). Bantam.

Santori, Helen. The Perfect Couple. (gr. 5 up). 1988. pap. 2.95 (ISBN 0-8041-0238-4). Ivy Books.

Steiner, Barbara. Love Match. 128p. (gr. 5-8). 1988. 1.00 (ISBN 0-87406-312-4, 31-16381-3). Willowisp Pr.

Stine, R. L. Broken Date. (gr. 6 up). 1988. write for info. (ISBN 0-373-98021-3). S&S Trade.

Weber, Judith. Dating, No. 47. (gr. 7-12). 1988. pap. 2.50 (ISBN 0-590-41918-8). Scholastic Inc.

Wyeth, Sharon D. Too Cute for Words. (Orig.). (gr. k-6). 1989. pap. 2.95 (ISBN 0-440-40225-5, YB). Dell.

DAVID, KING OF ISRAEL

Alex, Ben, retold by. David: The Brave Shepherd Boy Who Became a Great King. Davot, Francois, illus. 32p. (ps-8). 1989. 7.95 (ISBN 0-8028-5031-6). Eerdmans.

Amoss, Berthe. David & Goliath. (Illus.). 10p. (ps-7). 1989. pap. 2.95 (ISBN 0-922589-12-7). More Than Card.

David. 1989. 3.95 (ISBN 0-87508-813-9). Chr Lit.

David. (ps-2). 3.95 (ISBN 0-7214-5068-7). Ladybird Bks.

Hershey, Katherine. David, Vol. I. Butcher, Sam, illus. 52p. (gr. k-6). 1972. pap. text ed. 9.45 (ISBN 1-55976-020-6). CEF Press.

—David, Vol. II. Butcher, Sam, illus. 55p. (gr. k-6). 1973. pap. text ed. 9.45 (ISBN 1-55976-021-4). CEF Press.

Hollaway, Lee. David: Shepherd, Musician, & King. Karch, Paul, illus. (gr. 1-6). 1977. bds. 5.95 (ISBN 0-8054-4230-8, 4242-30). Broadman.

Lashbrook, Marilyn. I May be Little: The Story of David's Growth. Britt, Stephanie M., illus. LC 87-60262. 32p. (ps). 1987. 5.95 (ISBN 0-86606-429-X, 843). Roper Pr.

McKenna, Una. David Meets Goliath. Baker, Arthur, illus. 32p. (gr. k-3). 1990. saddle-stitched 1.25 (ISBN 0-8028-5053-7). Eerdmans.

McMillan, Mary. King David. Grossman, Dan, illus. 48p. (ps-1). 1987. pap. 6.95 (ISBN 0-86653-392-3, SS 1801). Good Apple.

Segal, Lore. The Story of King Saul & King David. LC 90-52544. (Illus.). 144p. 1991. 19.50 (ISBN 0-8052-4088-8). Pantheon.

Storr, Catherine, as told by. King David. (Illus.). 32p. (gr. k-4). 1985. PLB 14.65 (ISBN 0-8172-2042-9). Raintree Pubs.

DAVID, KING OF ISRAEL–FICTION

Bearman, Jane. David. Bearman, Jane, illus. LC 65-21753. (gr. 3 up). 1975. 3.95 (ISBN 0-8246-0085-1). Jonathan David.

Bull, Geoffrey. I Wish I Lived When David Did. 1975. 1.95 (ISBN 0-87508-890-2). Chr Lit.

DAVIS, ANGELA Y., 1944-

Finke, Blythe F. Angela Davis: Traitor or Martyr of the Freedom of Expression? Rahmas, D. Steve, ed. LC 77-190246. 32p. (Orig.). (gr. 7-12). 1972. lib. bdg. 4.20 incl. catalog cards (ISBN 0-87157-528-0); pap. 2.95 vinyl laminated covers (ISBN 0-87157-028-9). SamHar Pr.

DAVIS, JEFFERSON, 1808-1889

Caldeira, Ernesto. Jefferson Davis Coloring Book. Rice, James, illus. 32p. (Orig.). (gr. 1-6). 1982. pap. 2.50 (ISBN 0-88289-256-8). Pelican.

King, Perry. Jefferson Davis. (Illus.). (gr. 5 up). 1990. 17.95 (ISBN 1-55546-806-3). Chelsea Hse.

DAYAN, MOSHE, 1915-

Amdur, Richard. Moshe Dayan. Schlesinger, Arthur M., intro. by. (Illus.). 112p. (gr. 5 up). 1989. 17.95 (ISBN 1-55546-829-2). Chelsea Hse.

DAYS

see Birthdays; Fasts and Feasts; Holidays

DEAF

Adler, David A. A Picture Book of Helen Keller. Wallner, John & Wallner, Alexandra, illus. LC 89-77510. 32p. (gr. k-3). 1990. reinforced 14.95 (ISBN 0-8234-0818-3). Holiday.

Bergman, Thomas. Finding a Common Language: Children Living with Deafness. LC 88-42969. (Illus.). 48p. (gr. 4-5). 1989. PLB 10.95 (ISBN 1-55532-916-0). Gareth Stevens Inc.

Bourke, Linda & Sullivan, Mary B. A Show of Hands. 96p. (gr. k-3). pap. 2.50 (ISBN 0-590-33961-3). Scholastic Inc.

Charlip, Remy & Miller, Mary B. Handtalk: An ABC of Finger Spelling & Sign Language. Ancona, George, illus. LC 85-3667. 48p. (gr. 1-3). 1984. Repr. of 1974 ed. PLB 15.95 (ISBN 0-02-718130-8, Four Winds). Macmillan Child Grp.

Flodin, Mickey. Signing for Kids: The Fun Way for Anyone to Learn American Sign Language. (Illus.). 144p. (gr. 3-9). 1991. pap. 9.95 (ISBN 0-399-51672-7, Perigee Bks). Putnam Pub Group.

Greene, Laura & Dicker, Eva B. Discovering Sign Language. LC 88-24609. (Illus.). 104p. (gr. 5-12). 1988. pap. 4.95 (ISBN 0-930323-48-3, Kendall Green Pubns). Gallaudet Univ Pr.

—Interpreting Sign Language. (Illus.). 96p. (gr. 5-9). 1990. PLB 12.90 (ISBN 0-531-10773-6). Watts.

—Sign-Me-Fine: Experiencing American Sign Language. Caraway, Caren, illus. LC 90-5148. 110p. (gr. 7-12). 1989. pap. 5.95 (ISBN 0-930323-76-9, Pub. by K Green Pubns). Gallaudet Univ Pr.

Hillebrand, Linda L. & Riekehof, Lottie L. The Joy of Signing Puzzle Book: Have Fun Learning to Sign. (Illus.). 57p. (Orig.). 1989. pap. 2.95 (ISBN 0-88243-676-7, 02-0676). Gospel Pub.

Hunter, Edith F. Child of the Silent Night. Holmes, Bea, illus. 128p. (gr. 2-5). 1991. pap. 3.25 (ISBN 0-440-41223-4, YB). Dell.

Keller, Helen. Story of My Life. LC 54-11951. (Illus.). (gr. 7 up). 1954. 15.95 (ISBN 0-385-04453-4). Doubleday.

LaMore, Gregory S. Now I Understand. Ensing-Keelean, Jan, illus. LC 85-20639. 52p. (gr. 3-6). 1986. 8.95 (ISBN 0-930323-13-0, Kendall Green Pubns). Gallaudet Univ Pr.

Mango, Karin N. Hearing Loss. Perrotta, Mary, ed. (Illus.). 144p. (gr. 7-12). 1991. PLB 12.40 (ISBN 0-531-12519-X). Watts.

Miller, Mary Beth & Ancona, George. Handtalk School. LC 90-24030. (Illus.). 32p. (ps-6). 1991. 14.95 (ISBN 0-02-700912-2, Four Winds). Macmillan Child Grp.

Peterson, Jeanne W. I Have a Sister, My Sister Is Deaf. Ray, Deborah, illus. LC 76-24306. (gr. k-3). 1977. 13.95 (ISBN 0-06-024701-0); PLB 13.89 (ISBN 0-06-024702-9). HarpC Child Bks.

Simko, Carole B. Ear Gear: A Student Workbook on Hearing & Hearing Aids. Skrobisz, Jan, illus. 136p. (gr. 3-6). 1986. 4.50x (ISBN 0-930323-15-7, Clerc Bks). Gallaudet Univ Pr.

Star, Robin R. We Can, 2 vols. (gr. 4 up). 1980. Set. PLB 4.95 (ISBN 0-685-00153-9). Vol. 1 88 pgs (ISBN 0-88200-135-3, C2670). Vol. 2 98 pgs (ISBN 0-88200-136-1, C2786). Alexander Graham.

Starowitz, Anne M. The Day We Met Cindy. LC 88-8979. (Illus.). 16p. (gr. k-3). 1988. pap. 9.50 (ISBN 0-930323-43-2, Kendall Green Pubns). Gallaudet Univ Pr.

Vold, Florence C., et al. Signing with Your Clients: A Practical Manual for Audiologists & Speech - Language Pathologists. LC 90-13968. (Illus.). 329p. spiral bound 29.95x (ISBN 0-930323-53-X, Clerc Bks). Gallaudet Univ Pr.

Walker, Lou Ann. Amy, the Story of a Deaf Child. Abramson, Michael, illus. LC 84-21152. 64p. (gr. 4-6). 1985. 14.95 (ISBN 0-525-67145-5, Lodestar Bks). Dutton Child Bks.

Wolf, Bernard. Anna's Silent World. LC 76-52943. (Illus.). (gr. 1-5). 1977. 12.95 (ISBN 0-397-31739-5, Lipp Jr Bks). HarpC Child Bks.

DEAF–EDUCATION

Bornstein, Harry. All by Myself. 16p. (ps). 1975. pap. 3.50 (ISBN 0-913580-43-0, Pub. by K Green Pubns). Gallaudet Univ Pr.

—Be Careful. 32p. (ps-2). 1976. pap. 5.50 (ISBN 0-913580-55-4, Pub. by K Green Pubns). Gallaudet Univ Pr.

—A Book about Me. 16p. (ps). 1973. pap. 3.50 (ISBN 0-913580-19-8, Pub. by K Green Pubns). Gallaudet Univ Pr.

—Circus Time. 16p. (ps). 1976. pap. 3.50 (ISBN 0-913580-51-1, Pub. by K Green Pubns). Gallaudet Univ Pr.

—The Clock Book. 36p. (ps-2). 1975. pap. 5.95 (ISBN 0-913580-48-1, Pub. by K Green Pubns). Gallaudet Univ Pr.

—Count & Color. 16p. (ps). 1973. pap. 3.50 (ISBN 0-913580-20-1, Pub. by K Green Pubns). Gallaudet Univ Pr.

—The Gingerbread Man. 48p. (ps-2). 1976. pap. 5.95 (ISBN 0-913580-52-X, Pub. by K Green Pubns). Gallaudet Univ Pr.

—I Want to Be a Farmer. 48p. (ps-2). 1972. pap. 5.95 (ISBN 0-913580-14-7). Gallaudet Univ Pr.

—Jack & the Beanstalk. 64p. (ps-2). 1975. pap. 6.50 (ISBN 0-913580-47-3, Pub. by K Green Pubns). Gallaudet Univ Pr.

—Little Lost Sally. 40p. (ps-2). 1975. pap. 5.95 (ISBN 0-913580-40-6). Gallaudet Univ Pr.

—Little Poems for Little People. 56p. (ps-2). 1974. pap. 6.50 (ISBN 0-913580-31-7, Pub. by K Green Pubns). Gallaudet Univ Pr.

—Mouse's Christmas Eve. 44p. (ps-2). 1974. pap. 5.95 (ISBN 0-913580-28-7, Pub by K Green Pubns). Gallaudet Univ Pr.

—My Animal Book. 16p. (ps). 1973. pap. 3.50 (ISBN 0-930323-38-6).

—My Toy Book. 16p. (ps). 1973. pap. 3.50 (ISBN 0-913580-22-8, Pub by K Green Pubns). Gallaudet Univ Pr.

—The Night Before Christmas. 56p. (ps-2). 1973. pap. 6.50 (ISBN 0-913580-15-5, Pub. by K Green Pubns). Gallaudet Univ Pr.

—Night-Day, Work-Play. 48p. (ps-2). 1974. pap. 5.95 (ISBN 0-913580-23-6). Gallaudet Univ Pr.

—Nursery Rhymes from Mother Goose. 56p. (ps-2). 1972. pap. 6.50 (ISBN 0-913580-07-4). Gallaudet Univ Pr.

—Oliver in the City. 56p. (ps-2). 1975. pap. 6.50 (ISBN 0-913580-49-X). Gallaudet Univ Pr.

—The Pet Shop. 16p. (ps). 1976. pap. 3.50 (ISBN 0-913580-54-6, Pub. by K Green Pubns). Gallaudet Univ Pr.

—Police Officer Jones. 16p. (ps). 1976. pap. 3.50 (ISBN 0-913580-53-8, Pub. by K Green Pubns). Gallaudet Univ Pr.

—Questions & More Questions. 52p. (ps-2). 1973. pap. 6.50 (ISBN 0-913580-24-4). Gallaudet Univ Pr.

—Songs in Signed English. 44p. (ps-2). 1973. pap. 9.00 incl. record (ISBN 0-913580-12-0, Pub. by K Green Pubns). Gallaudet Univ Pr.

—Spring Is Green. 52p. (ps-2). 1973. pap. 6.50 (ISBN 0-913580-17-1). Gallaudet Univ Pr.

—Three Little Kittens. 32p. (ps-2). 1973. pap. 5.50 (ISBN 0-913580-16-3). Gallaudet Univ Pr.

—Three Little Pigs. 44p. (ps). 1972. pap. 6.50 (ISBN 0-913580-09-0, Pub. by K Green Pubns). Gallaudet Univ Pr.

—Tommy's Day. 48p. (ps-2). 1973. pap. 5.95 (ISBN 0-913580-10-4). Gallaudet Univ Pr.

—The Ugly Duckling. 48p. (ps-2). 1974. pap. 6.50 (ISBN 0-913580-29-5, Pub. by K Green Pubns). Gallaudet Univ Pr.

—We're Going to the Doctor. 28p. (ps). 1985. pap. 5.95 (ISBN 0-913580-26-0, Pub. by K Green Pubns). Gallaudet Univ Pr.

—With My Legs. 16p. (ps-2). 1975. pap. 3.50 (ISBN 0-913580-42-2, Pub. by K Green Pubns). Gallaudet Univ Pr.

Bornstein, Harry & Saulnier, Karen L. The Signed English Starter. Miller, Ralph R., Sr., illus. LC 84-4042. 232p. (gr-6). 1984. pap. text ed. 13.95 (ISBN 0-913580-82-1, Clerc Bks). Gallaudet Univ Pr.

Dellinger, Annetta. Ann Elizabeth Signs With Love. (ps-2). 1991. 8.95 (ISBN 0-570-04192-9, 56-1651). Concordia.
Ann Elizabeth can turn cartwheels & count to 100. She plays games, goes fishing, & bakes chocolate chip cookies. Ann Elizabeth is also deaf. But that doesn't stop her from sharing Jesus' love with her family & friends. She uses sign language to tell others of the wonderful God who made each of us special. Ann Elizabeth teaches children how to sign the favorite Bible song, "Jesus Loves Me." Easy-to-follow sign language symbols are illustrated for each word. Ann Elizabeth Signs With Love also assists parents & teachers as they teach children that God loves everyone, even those with disabilities, & helps children feel & share God's love. For children ages 3 to 7. 32 pp. 4-color hardcover. $8.95. Concordia Publishing House. Item no. 56-1651. ISBN 0-570-04192-9 To order -- Call Toll Free 1-800-325-3040.
Publisher Provided Annotation.

Johnson, Sue. At Grandma's House: Story Book for Young Children in Sign Language. Herigstad, Joni, illus. 28p. 1985. pap. 4.50 (ISBN 0-916708-14-4). Modern Signs.

Oberkotter, Mildred, et al, eds. The Possible Dream: Mainstream Experiences of Hearing-Impaired Students. 68p. (Orig.). 1990. pap. text ed. 7.95 (ISBN 0-88200-171-X). Alexander Graham.

Rankin, Laura. Handmade Alphabet. 1991. 13.95 (ISBN 0-8037-0974-9). Dial Bks Young.

Sullivan, Mary B., et al. A Show of Hands: Say It in Sign Language. Bourke, Linda, illus. LC 84-48782. 96p. (gr. 2-6). 1985. pap. 4.50 (ISBN 0-06-446007-X, Trophy). HarpC Child Bks.

Andrews, Jean F. Hasta Luego, San Diego. LC 90-27125. 104p. (Orig.). (gr. 3-6). 1991. pap. 4.95 (ISBN 0-930323-83-1, Pub. by K Green Pubns). Gallaudet Univ Pr.

Arthur, Catherine. My Sister's Silent World. Talbot, Nathan, illus. LC 78-13140. 32p. (gr. 3). 1979. PLB 13.27 (ISBN 0-516-02022-6). Childrens.

Bridges, Christina. The Hero. Batten, Linda, illus. 29p. (gr. k-6). 1981. pap. text ed. 8.95 (ISBN 0-917002-39-3). Joyce Media.

Charlip, Remy & Miller, Mary B. Handtalk Birthday: A Number & Story Book in Sign Language. Ancona, George, illus. LC 86-22755. 48p. 1987. 14.95 (ISBN 0-02-718080-8, Four Winds). Macmillan Child Grp.

Cowley. The Silent One. Robinson, Charles, illus. LC 80-21853. (gr. 4-6). 1981. 8.95 (ISBN 0-394-84761-X). Knopf.

Geller, Norman. Talk to God... I'll Get the Message: Black Version. Tomlinson, Albert J., illus. 23p. (gr. 1-4). 1985. pap. 4.95 (ISBN 0-915753-08-1). N Geller Pub.

—Talk to God... I'll Get the Message: Spanish Version. Galway, Bonnie, tr. from ENG. Tomlinson, Albert J., illus. 23p. (gr. 1-4). 1985. pap. 4.95 (ISBN 0-915753-07-3). N Geller Pub.

Hallman, Ruth. Breakaway. LC 80-24977. 94p. (gr. 7 up). 1981. 8.95 (ISBN 0-664-32677-3, Westminster). Westminster John Knox.

Johnston, Catherine D. I Hear the Day. Mark, Joseph, illus. (gr. 2-3). 1977. 9.00 (ISBN 0-914562-04-5); wkbk 3.00 (ISBN 0-914562-05-3). Merriam-Eddy.

Levi, Dorothy. A Very Special Friend. Gold, Ethel, illus. LC 88-33410. 40p. (gr. k-3). 1989. 8.95 (ISBN 0-930323-55-6, Kendall Green Pubns). Gallaudet Univ Pr.

Levine, Edna S. Lisa & Her Soundless World. Kamen, Gloria, illus. (gr. 1-5). 1984. 16.95 (ISBN 0-87705-104-6); pap. 9.95 (ISBN 0-89885-204-8). Human Sci Pr.

Litchfield, Ada B. A Button in Her Ear. Rubin, Caroline, ed. Mill, Eleanor, illus. LC 75-28390. 32p. (gr. 2-4). 1976. PLB 12.95 (ISBN 0-8075-0987-6). A Whitman.

—Words in Our Hands. Tucker, Kathleen, ed. Coganchery, Helen, illus. LC 79-28402. (gr. 2-6). 1980. PLB 12.95 (ISBN 0-8075-9212-9). A Whitman.

Scott, Virginia M. Belonging. Crowe, Patricia, illus. LC 85-31135. 176p. (gr. 7-12). 1987. pap. 2.95 (ISBN 0-930323-33-5, Kendall Green Pubns). Gallaudet Univ Pr.

Shreve, Susan. The Gift of the Girl Who Couldn't Hear. LC 91-2247. 128p. (gr. 3-7). 1991. 12.95 (ISBN 0-688-10318-9, Tambourine Bks). Morrow.

Steel, Danielle. Max & Grandma & Grandpa Winky. (ps-3). 1991. 9.95 (ISBN 0-385-30165-0). Doubleday.

Taylor, Morris. Top of the Hill. 64p. 1988. pap. 4.95 (ISBN 0-87961-183-9). Naturegraph.

Taylor, Theodore. Tuck Triumphant. (gr. 5-7). 1991. 14.95 (ISBN 0-385-41480-3). Doubleday.

Wakeman, Cheryl A. Johnnie Ollie Carri III & His Friend. Womack, Fred, illus. 32p. (ps-3). 1985. 5.95 (ISBN 0-9614819-0-0). R E Moen.
JOHNNIE OLLIE CARRI III & HIS FRIEND is more than just an enjoyable children's book. It teaches a valuable lesson to children of all ages concerning the vital contributions of the elderly & the physically handicapped make to society. Johnnie Ollie walks home through the park each day, just so he can share his school day's activities with his special friend, Mister. The beautiful friendship is obvious to the reader as Johnnie shares happenings from a "typical school day" with which all children can identify. The reader never realizes until the very end that the elderly man has been deaf from birth & that he cannot hear a word Johnnie speaks--but that is not an obstacle in their wonderful relationship. Schools in California, Minnesota & Wisconsin have used this book to supplement units dealing with the elderly, the handicapped & sensitivity to others. Illustrated by noted children's illustrator FRED WOMACK. Full color throughout & printed on durable, high quality color-text paper.
Publisher Provided Annotation.

DEAN, JEROME HERMAN, 1911-
Kavanagh, Jack. Dizzy Dean. Murray, Jim, intro. by. (Illus.). 64p. (gr. 3 up). 1991. PLB 14.95 (ISBN 0-7910-1173-9). Chelsea Hse.

DEATH
Berry, Joy. About Death. Bartholomew, illus. 48p. (gr. 3 up). 1990. PLB 14.60 (ISBN 0-516-02952-5); 6.95 (ISBN 0-516-22952-4). Childrens.

Bisnignano, Judith. Living with Death - Middle School. 64p. (gr. 5-9). 1991. 6.95 (ISBN 0-86653-584-5). Good Apple.

Bratman, Fred. Everything You Need to Know When a Parent Dies. (gr. 7-12). 1991. PLB 12.95 (ISBN 0-8239-1324-4). Rosen Group.

Buntin, Kathleen R., et al. When a Loved One Dies. LC 88-22837. v, 35p. (gr. 3-8). 1988. 7.95 (ISBN 0-87579-142-5). Deseret Bk.

Center for Attitudinal Healing Staff. Another Look at the Rainbow. LC 82-12951. (gr. 1-5). 1983. pap. 7.95 (ISBN 0-89087-341-0). Celestial Arts.

Cera, Mary J. Living with Death - Primary. 64p. (gr. 1-4). 1991. 6.95 (ISBN 0-86653-588-8). Good Apple.

Cohn, Janice. I Had a Friend Named Peter: Talking to Children about the Death of a Friend. Owens, Gail, illus. LC 86-31150. 32p. (ps-2). 1987. 13.00 (ISBN 0-688-06685-2); lib. bdg. 13.88 (ISBN 0-688-06686-0, Morrow Jr Bks). Morrow Jr Bks.

Corley, Elizabeth A. Tell Me about Death, Tell Me about Funerals. Pecoraro, Philip, intro. by. (Illus.). 36p. (Orig.). (gr. 3-6). 1973. pap. text ed. 2.00 (ISBN 0-686-02638-1). Grammatical Sci.

Crouthamel, Thomas G., Sr. It's OK. 2nd ed. Hasty, Patti, illus. LC 86-27694. 36p. (gr. 12 up). 1990. 6.95 (ISBN 0-940701-18-9). Keystone PA.
Following the death of his daughter, Thomas Crouthamel began to really listen to what his son & other grieving siblings were saying. He learned that when someone's brother or sister dies, the surviving sibling(s) goes through a traumatic grief process that lasts far longer than people realize. Although the effects of death experienced by a bereaved sibling are common to all grieving siblings, each feels he/she is standing alone in the world, & no one understands. Parents are enveloped in their own grief, peers don't want to hear about it, & teachers don't have the training, or time to cope with a grieving student. IT'S OK is a "Survival Kit" for bereaved siblings. It provides understanding, answers, help, & above all, PERMISSION for surviving siblings to act & feel the way they do. IT'S OK compassionately explains that they are not alone, they are not crazy, that their feelings, frustrations, & emotions are all "normal" experiences that can happen to anyone following the death of a sister or brother. Although IT'S OK was written for a young age group, favorable reviews have been received from adult bereaved siblings in their 60's & 80's. Sibling grief has no age limits.
Publisher Provided Annotation.

Danesh, Hossain B. The Mysterious Case of the IWS. 32p. (Orig.). 1991. pap. 5.95 (ISBN 1-85168-027-6, Pub. by Oneworld UK). Pub Service.

Daughters of St. Paul. Where's Grandma? (gr. k-2). pap. 1.75 (ISBN 0-8198-8204-6). Dghtrs St Paul.

Fayerweather Street School Staff. The Kids' Book about Death & Dying. Rofes, Eric E., ed. 119p. (gr. 5 up). 1985. 15.95 (ISBN 0-316-75390-4). Little.

Gravelle, Karen & Haskins, Charles. Teenagers Face to Face with Bereavement. Steltenpohl, Jane, ed. 128p. (gr. 7 up). 1989. lib. bdg. 12.98 (ISBN 0-671-65856-5); pap. 5.95 (ISBN 0-671-65975-8). Messner.

Grollman, Earl A. Talking about Death: A Dialogue Between Parent & Child; With Parent's Guide & Recommended Resources. 3rd ed. Heau, Gisela, illus. LC 89-46061. 128p. (gr. k-4). 1990. 16.95 (ISBN 0-8070-2364-7, BP531). Beacon Pr.

Hammond, Janice M. When My Mommy Died: A Child's View of Death. Hammond, Janice M., illus. 27p. (Orig.). 5). 1980. pap. 6.95 (ISBN 0-9604690-0-1). Cranbrook Pub.

Harris, Audrey. Why Did He Die? Dalke, Susan, illus. LC 65-22217. (gr. k-5). 1965. PLB 5.95 (ISBN 0-8225-0256-9). Lerner Pubns.

Heegaard, Marge E. When Someone Very Special Dies: Children Can Learn to Cope with Grief. (Illus.). 32p. (gr. 1-6). 1988. wkbk. 4.95 (ISBN 0-9620502-0-2). Woodland Pr.

Hyde, Margaret O. & Hyde, Lawrence E. Meeting Death. 129p. (gr. 5 up). 1989. 14.95 (ISBN 0-8027-6873-3); PLB 15.85 (ISBN 0-8027-6874-1). Walker & Co.

Johnson, Joy & Johnson, Marvin. Tell Me, Papa: A Family Book for Children's Questions about Death & Funerals. Borum, Shari, illus. 24p. (Orig.). (gr. 2-7). 1978. pap. 2.50 (ISBN 1-56123-011-1). Centering Corp.

Juneau, Barbara F. Sad, but O.K. - My Daddy Died Today: A Child's View of Death. Clemens, Paul M., ed. LC 88-155937. (Illus.). 112p. (Orig.). (gr. 5 up). 1988. pap. 9.95 (ISBN 0-931892-19-8). B Dolphin Pub.

—Sad, but O.K. - My Daddy Died Today: A Child's View of Death. LC 89-7174. 112p. 1989. Repr. of 1988 ed. lib. bdg. 24.95x (ISBN 0-8095-6557-9). Borgo Pr.

Klagsbrun, Francine. Too Young to Die: Youth & Suicide. (gr. 7 up). 1976. 14.95 (ISBN 0-395-24752-7). HM.

Knox, Jean. Death & Dying. Koop, C. Everett, intro. by. (Illus.). 112p. (gr. 6-12). 1989. 18.95 (ISBN 0-7910-0037-0). Chelsea Hse.

LaVelle, Steven. Just Passing Through. (Illus.). 32p. (Orig.). (gr. k-3). 1980. pap. 3.50 (ISBN 0-87516-402-1). DeVorss.

LeShan, Eda J. Learning to Say Good-bye: When a Parent Dies. Giovanopoulous, Paul, illus. LC 76-15155. 96p. (gr. 3 up). 1976. 12.95 (ISBN 0-02-756360-X, Mcmillan Child Bk). Macmillan Child Grp.

Life after Death. 48p. (gr. 4-5). 1989. PLB 10.95 (ISBN 0-685-26163-8). Capstone Pr.

McGuire, Leslie. Death & Illness. (Illus.). 64p. (gr. 7 up). 1990. lib. bdg. 15.93 (ISBN 0-86593-079-1); lib. bdg. 11.95s.p. Rourke Corp.

McHugh. Young People Talk about Death. (gr. 7 up). 1980. PLB 11.90 (ISBN 0-531-02884-4, C10). Watts.

Nystrom, Carolyn. What Happens When We Die? 32p. (gr. 2). 1981. pap. 3.95 (ISBN 0-8024-6154-9). Moody.

Pringle, Laurence. Death Is Natural. LC 90-46402. 64p. (gr. 1 up). 1991. pap. 5.95 (ISBN 0-688-10528-9, Pub. by Beech Tree Bks). Morrow.

—Death Is Natural. LC 90-46402. 64p. (gr. 1 up). 1991. Repr. of 1977 ed. PLB 12.88 (ISBN 0-688-10467-3). Morrow Jr Bks.

Raab, Robert A. Coping with Death. rev. ed. Rosen, Ruth, ed. (gr. 7-12). 1989. PLB 12.95 (ISBN 0-8239-0960-3). Rosen Group.

Richter, Elizabeth. Losing Someone You Love: When a Brother or Sister Dies. LC 85-12395. (Illus.). 80p. (gr. 6 up). 1986. 12.95 (ISBN 0-399-21243-4, Putnam). Putnam Pub Group.

Russell, Katherine B. Guiding Children Through Grief: A Resource Manual of Recommended Books to Help Young Children Cope with Death, Dying & Grief. Russell, Katherine B., illus. 48p. (Orig.). (ps up). 1989. pap. 4.95 (ISBN 0-685-30722-0). Centering Corp.

Stein, Sara B. About Dying. LC 73-15268. (Illus.). 48p. (ps-8). 1984. pap. 7.95 (ISBN 0-8027-7223-4). Walker & Co.

—About Dying. LC 73-15268. (Illus.). 48p. (gr. 1 up). 1974. 10.95 (ISBN 0-8027-6172-0). Walker & Co.

Stewart, Gail. Death. LC 89-31257. (Illus.). 48p. (gr. 4-5). 1989. 10.95 (ISBN 0-89686-446-4, Crestwood Hse). Macmillan Child Grp.

Temes, Roberta. The Empty Place: A Story for Children. (Illus.). 50p. (gr. 1-6). 1989. 12.95 (ISBN 0-8290-1345-8). Irvington.

DEATH–FICTION

Angell, Judie. Ronnie & Rosey. 192p. (gr. 6-9). 1979. pap. 2.25 (ISBN 0-440-97491-7, LFL). Dell.

Bacon, Katharine J. Shadow & Light. LC 86-23789. 208p. (gr. 7 up). 1987. 14.95 (ISBN 0-689-50431-4, M K McElderry). Macmillan Child Grp.

Balter, Lawrence. A Funeral for Whiskers: Understanding Death. Schanzer, Roz, illus. 40p. (ps-3). 1991. 5.95 (ISBN 0-8120-6153-5). Barron.

Bauer, Marion D. Shelter from the Wind. LC 75-28184. 112p. (gr. 6 up). 1979. 13.95 (ISBN 0-395-28890-8, Clarion). HM.

Bierce, Ambrose. An Occurrence at Owl Creek Bridge. Neumeier, Marty, illus. 40p. (gr. 6 up). 1980. PLB 10.95s.p. (ISBN 0-87191-770-X); PLB 15.65 (ISBN 0-685-01263-8). Creative Ed.

Blume, Judy. Tiger Eyes. LC 81-6152. 256p. (gr. 7 up). 1982. 14.95 (ISBN 0-02-711080-X, Bradbury Pr). Macmillan Child Grp.

—Tiger Eyes. 224p. (gr. 7 up). 1982. 3.50 (ISBN 0-440-98469-6, LFL). Dell.

Bosse, Malcolm J. Ganesh. LC 80-2453. 192p. (gr. 7 up). 1981. 11.06i (ISBN 0-690-04102-0, Crowell Jr Bks). HarpC Child Bks.

Boyd, Candy D. Forever Friends. 192p. (gr. 5-9). 1986. pap. 3.95 (ISBN 0-14-032077-6, Puffin). Puffin Bks.

Brown, Margaret W. The Dead Bird. Charlip, Remy, illus. LC 84-43124. 48p. (gr. k-3). 1989. Repr. of 1958 ed. PLB 11.89 (ISBN 0-06-020758-2). HarpC Child Bks.

Bunting, Eve. The Happy Funeral. Vo-Dinh, Mai, illus. LC 81-47719. 48p. (gr. k-4). 1982. HarpC Child Bks.

—A Sudden Silence. 112p. (gr. 12 up). 1988. 14.95 (ISBN 0-15-282058-2). HarBraceJ.

Byars, Betsy. Good-Bye, Chicken Little. LC 78-19829. 112p. (gr. 5 up). 1979. PLB 12.89 (ISBN 0-06-020911-9). HarpC Child Bks.

Cadnum, Michael. Calling Home. 192p. (gr. 7 up). 1991. 14.95 (ISBN 0-670-83566-8). Viking Child Bks.

Cameron, Eleanor. Beyond Silence. LC 80-10350. (gr. 5-9). 1980. 9.95 (ISBN 0-525-26463-9, DCB). Dutton Child Bks.

Carlstrom, Nancy W. Blow Me a Kiss, Miss Lilly. Schwartz, Amy, illus. LC 89-34505. 32p. (ps-3). 1990. 12.95 (ISBN 0-06-021012-5); PLB 12.89 (ISBN 0-06-021013-3). HarpC Child Bks.

Carrick, Carol. The Accident. Carrick, Donald, illus. LC 76-3532. 32p. (ps-3). 1979. 13.95 (ISBN 0-395-28774-X, Clarion); pap. 4.95 (ISBN 0-89919-041-3). HM.

Chambers, Aidan. Dance on My Grave. LC 82-48258. 256p. (gr. 7 up). 1983. PLB 13.89 (ISBN 0-06-021254-3). HarpC Child Bks.

Cohen, Miriam. Jim's Dog Muffins. Hoban, Lillian, illus. LC 83-14090. 32p. (gr. k-3). 1984. 13.95 (ISBN 0-688-02564-1); PLB 13.88 (ISBN 0-688-02565-X). Greenwillow.

Conley, Bruce H. Butterflies, Grandpa & Me. (Illus.). 25p. (gr. 4 up). 1976. pap. 2.00 (ISBN 0-685-65885-6). Thum Print.
Butterflies, Grandpa & Me is a simple story about the unexpected death of a grandfather. Written from a child's point of view, twenty-five pages of text & coloring book pictures follow the main character, Richie, from the first time he learns of grandpa's fatal heart attack, through the funeral & into the first week afterward. Shock & numbness, fear, anger, loss of appetite & loneliness are among the many feelings Richie expresses. In search of answers he runs to the creek where the realities of life & death were gently taught by his loving grandfather. Richie's experience includes going to the funeral home, seeing his grandfather's body & asking questions such as, "where are his feet?", "what are the flowers for...?", & "...is he dead or is he just sleeping?" He spends some time with one of grandpa's older friends, attends the funeral & burial & is surprised to find how hungry he is by the end of the day. In the week that follows, as Richie experiences some of the emptiness of his grandfather's absence he also discovers that doing some of the old things in new ways can bring unexpected pleasure & hope.
Publisher Provided Annotation.

Conrad, Joseph. The Lagoon. 32p. (gr. 6). 1990. 10.95s.p. (ISBN 0-88682-309-9); 15.65 (ISBN 0-685-28224-4). Creative Ed.

Conrad, Pam. My Daniel. LC 88-19850. 144p. (gr. 5 up). 1991. pap. 3.50 (ISBN 0-06-440309-2, Trophy). HarpC Child Bks.

Dabcovich, Lydia. Mrs. Huggins & Her Hen Hannah. Dabcovich, Lydia, illus. LC 85-4406. 24p. (ps-2). 1988. 12.95 (ISBN 0-525-44203-0, DCB); pap. 3.95 (ISBN 0-525-44368-1, DCB). Dutton Child Bks.

Douglas, Eileen. Rachel & the Upside down Heart. (Illus.). 32p. 1990. pap. 6.95 (ISBN 0-8431-2734-1). Price Stern.

Dragonwagon, Crescent. Winter Holding Spring. Himler, Ronald, illus. LC 88-13747. 32p. (gr. 2-5). 1990. 11.95 (ISBN 0-02-733122-9, Mcmillan Child Bk). Macmillan Child Grp.

Fassler, Joan. My Grandpa Died Today. Kranz, Stewart, illus. LC 71-147126. 32p. (ps-3). 1983. 16.95 (ISBN 0-87705-053-8); pap. 9.95 (ISBN 0-89885-174-2). Human Sci Pr.

Field, Shirley. Fire! Fire! 128p. (gr. 7-10). 1990. pap. 3.95 (ISBN 0-7459-1851-4). Lion USA.

Gaeddert, LouAnn. A Summer Like Turnips. 80p. (gr. 3-6). 1989. 13.95 (ISBN 0-8050-0839-X). H Holt & Co.

Gibson, Roxie C. Hey God! What Is Death? LC 90-70219. (Illus.). 50p. (gr. k-5). 1990. 4.95 (ISBN 1-55523-329-5). Winston-Derek.

Giff, Patricia R. The Gift of the Pirate Queen. Rutherford, Jenny, illus. LC 82-70310. 160p. (gr. 4-6). 1982. 11.95 (ISBN 0-385-28338-5); PLB 11.95 (ISBN 0-385-28339-3). Delacorte.

—The Gift of the Pirate Queen. Rutherford, Jenny, illus. LC 82-70310. 160p. (gr. 4-8). 1982. 9.95 (ISBN 0-440-02970-8); PLB 9.89 (ISBN 0-440-02972-4). Delacorte.

Grant, Cynthia D. Phoenix Rising: or How to Survive Your Life. 160p. (gr. 7 up). 1991. pap. 3.50 (ISBN 0-06-447060-1, Trophy). HarpC Child Bks.

Green, Martha G. Grampa's in Heaven. LC 90-71356. (Illus.). 44p. (gr. 3-8). 1991. pap. 5.95 (ISBN 1-55523-399-6). Winston-Derek.

Greenberg, Jan. A Season In-Between. LC 79-17997. 120p. (gr. 5 up). 1979. 11.95 (ISBN 0-374-36564-4). FS&G.

Greene, Constance C. Beat the Turtle Drum. 128p. (gr. 5-8). 1979. pap. 3.25 (ISBN 0-440-40875-X, YB). Dell.

—Beat the Turtle Drum. Diamond, Donna, illus. LC 76-14772. 128p. (gr. 4-6). 1976. 13.95 (ISBN 0-670-15241-2). Viking Child Bks.

Guy, Rosa. Mirror of Her Own. LC 80-69448. 192p. (gr. 7 up). 1981. 8.95 (ISBN 0-385-28636-8). Delacorte.

Hammond, Janice M. When My Dad Died: A Child's View of Death. Hammond, Janice M., illus. 48p. (Orig.). (gr. k-6). 1981. pap. 6.95 (ISBN 0-9604690-3-6). Cranbrook Pub.

Hermes, Patricia. You Shouldn't Have to Say Good-Bye. 128p. (gr. 4-6). 1984. pap. 2.50 (ISBN 0-590-41359-7, Apple Paperbacks). Scholastic Inc.

Hines, Anna G. Remember the Butterflies. Hines, Anna G., illus. LC 90-3536. 32p. (ps-3). 1991. 12.95 (ISBN 0-525-44679-6, DCB). Dutton Child Bks.

Jacobs, Dee. Laura's Gift. Karlsson, Kris, illus. 64p. (Orig.). (gr. 6-12). 1980. PLB 13.95 (ISBN 0-938628-00-3); pap. 8.50 (ISBN 0-938628-01-1). Oriel Pr.

Jewell, Nancy. Time for Uncle Joe. Sandin, Joan, illus. LC 79-2695. 48p. (gr. k-3). 1981. 8.95 (ISBN 0-06-022843-1). HarpC Child Bks.

Joosse, Barbara M. Pieces of the Picture. LC 88-28150. 144p. (gr. 5-7). 1991. pap. 3.50 (ISBN 0-06-440310-6, Trophy). HarpC Child Bks.

King, Buzz. Silicon Songs. 1990. 14.95 (ISBN 0-385-30087-5). Doubleday.

Klause, Annette C. The Silver Kiss. (gr. 9 up). 1990. 14.95 (ISBN 0-385-30160-X). Delacorte.

L'Engle, Madeleine. A Ring of Endless Light. 336p. (gr. 9 up). 1981. pap. 3.50 (ISBN 0-440-97232-9, LE). Dell.

Little, Jean. Mama's Going to Buy You a Mockingbird. 208p. (gr. 5-9). 1986. pap. 3.95 (ISBN 0-14-031737-6, Puffin). Puffin Bks.

Lobel, Arnold. Sapo y Sepo Son Amigos. (SPA.). (gr. 1-6). 8.95 (ISBN 84-204-3043-9). Santillana.

Lowry, Lois. A Summer to Die. Oliver, Jenni, illus. (gr. 3-7). 1977. 13.95 (ISBN 0-395-25338-1). HM.

McDaniel, Lurlene. If I Should Die Before I Wake. 128p. (gr. 5-8). 1985. 0.50 (ISBN 0-87406-077-X). Willowisp Pr.

—Six Months to Live. 144p. (gr. 5-8). 1985. 2.95 (ISBN 0-87406-007-9). Willowisp Pr.

—Why Did She Have to Die? 128p. (gr. 5-8). 1986. 2.50 (ISBN 0-87406-071-0). Willowisp Pr.

Madler, Trudy. Why Did Grandma Die? Lewis, Gloria, intro. by. LC 79-23892. (Illus.). 32p. (gr. k-6). 1980. PLB 16.67 (ISBN 0-8172-1354-6). Raintree Pubs.

Maynard, Frankie. A Tree! for Me! LC 86-51132. (Illus.). 68p. 15.00 (ISBN 0-912783-07-9). Upton Sons.

Mazer, Norma F. After the Rain. LC 86-33270. 304p. (gr. 7 up). 1987. 12.95 (ISBN 0-688-06867-7, Morrow Junior Books). Morrow.

—After the Rain. large type ed. 408p. (gr. 7 up). 1989. lib. bdg. 14.95 (ISBN 0-8161-4807-4, Large Print Bks). G K Hall.

Miles, Betty. The Trouble with Thirteen. LC 78-31678. (gr. 4-7). 1979. 6.95 (ISBN 0-394-83930-7); PLB 12.99 (ISBN 0-394-93930-1). Knopf.

Naughton, Jim. My Brother Stealing Second. LC 88-22035. 288p. (gr. 7 up). 1991. pap. 3.95 (ISBN 0-06-447017-2, Trophy). HarpC Child Bks.

Nesbit, Jeffrey A. All the King's Horses. 192p. (Orig.). (gr. 9-12). 1990. pap. 6.95 (ISBN 0-87788-040-9). Shaw Pubs.

Nystrom, Carolyn. Emma Says Goodbye. (Illus.). 48p. (gr. 4-8). 1990. 7.95 (ISBN 0-7459-1826-3). Lion USA.

O. Henry. The Last Leaf. (Illus.). 32p. (gr. 6 up). 1980. PLB 10.95s.p. (ISBN 0-87191-774-2); 15.65 (ISBN 0-685-01259-X). Creative Ed.

O'Toole, Donna. Aarvy Aardvark Finds Hope: A Read-Aloud Story for People of All Ages. McWhirter, Mary Lou, illus. 80p. (Orig.). (ps up). 1989. pap. 9.95 (ISBN 1-878321-25-0, Mntn Rainbow); tchr's. guide 6.95 (ISBN 1-878321-26-9, Mntn Rainbow); audio tape 9.95 (ISBN 0-685-20985-7, Mntn Rainbow). Rainbow NC.
"Aarvy Aardvark Finds Hope" by Donna O'Toole. This read-aloud story for people of all ages is about loving & losing friendship & hope. Through it readers will learn how healing & growing through even the most devastating losses is possible. "Seldom

does a book come along that has unique appeal & offers something meaningful for all ages. AARVY AARDVARK FINDS HOPE is such a book."--The Grief Support & Education Center, Canton, Ohio. "This is the most wonderful book I have seen - & I have been doing 'death & dying' work for over 15 years."--Helen Fitzgerald, Fairfax, Virginia. "This story has strength, wisdom & beauty. It shows how long it can take to "be yourself" after you've lost so much of importance. Yet it is hopeful - permission giving to open to one's imagination - to once again play in a world so charged by life!"--John Schneider, Ph.D. Dept. of Psychiatry, M.S.U. "A fine book. It belongs in every home, classroom & library."--Ann Isaacs, Publisher The Creative Child & Adult Quarterly. "I love Aarvy Aardvark Finds Hope!"--Elizabeth Kuebler Ross.
Publisher Provided Annotation.

Paterson, Katherine. Bridge to Terabithia. Diamond, Donna, illus. LC 77-2221. (gr. 5 up). 1977. 13.95 (ISBN 0-690-01359-0, Crowell Jr Bks). HarpC Child Bks.

—Bridge to Terabithia. large type ed. Diamond, Donna, illus. 155p. (gr. 2-6). 1987. Repr. of 1977 ed. lib. bdg. 14.95 (ISBN 1-55736-010-3). ABC-CLIO.

—Un Puente Hasta Therabithia. (SPA.). (gr. 1-6). 8.50 (ISBN 84-204-3633-X). Santillana.

Peyton, K. M. A Midsummer's Night Death. 192p. (gr. 7 up). 1982. pap. 1.75 (ISBN 0-440-95615-3, LE). Dell.

Pfeffer, Susan B. About David: A Novel. LC 80-65837. 176p. (gr. 7 up). 1980. 11.95 (ISBN 0-385-28013-0). Delacorte.

Ruckman, Ivy. Who Invited the Undertaker? LC 89-1865. 192p. (gr. 3-7). 1991. pap. 3.50 (ISBN 0-06-440352-1, Trophy). HarpC Child Bks.

Sanford, Doris. It Must Hurt a Lot: A Child's Book About Death. Evans, Graci, illus. LC 86-25009. 32p. (ps-5). 1985. 7.95 (ISBN 0-88070-131-5). Multnomah.

Shott, James. The House Across the Street. LC 87-51498. 30p. (gr. 2-4). 1988. 6.95 (ISBN 1-55523-129-2). Winston-Derek.

Stevens, Margaret. When Grandpa Died. Ualand, Kenneth, illus. LC 78-12360. 32p. (ps-3). 1979. PLB 13.27 (ISBN 0-516-02025-0). Childrens.

Stiles, Norman. I'll Miss You, Mr. Hooper. Mathieu, Joe, illus. LC 83-27013. 24p. (ps-3). 1984. lib. bdg. 4.99 (ISBN 0-394-96600-7, Pub. by BYR). Random.

Talbert, Marc. Dead Birds Singing. LC 85-147. 224p. (gr. 6 up). 1985. 13.95 (ISBN 0-316-83125-5). Little.

Thurman, Chuck. Time for Remembering. 1989. pap. 13.95 (ISBN 0-671-68573-2). S&S Trade.

Tolstoy, Leo. The Death of Ivan Ilych. 112p. (gr. 6). 1990. 10.95s.p. (ISBN 0-88682-298-X); 15.65 (ISBN 0-685-28213-9). Creative Ed.

Velthuijs, Max. Frog & the Birdsong. (ps-3). 1991. bds. 13.95 jacketed (ISBN 0-374-32467-0). FS&G.

Vigna, Judith. Saying Goodbye to Daddy. Levine, Abby, ed. Vigna, Judith, illus. 32p. (gr. k-2). 1990. 12.95 (ISBN 0-8075-7253-5). A Whitman.

Viorst, Judith. The Tenth Good Thing about Barney. Blegvad, Eric, illus. LC 71-154764. 32p. (gr. k-4). 1971. 12.95 (ISBN 0-689-20688-7, Atheneum Child Bk). Macmillan Child Grp.

Warburg, Sandol S. Growing Time. Weisgard, Leonard, illus. LC 69-14729. (gr. k-3). 1975. 13.95 (ISBN 0-395-16966-6). HM.

Westall, Robert. Urn Burial. LC 87-23816. 160p. (gr. 7 up). 1988. 11.95 (ISBN 0-688-07595-9). Greenwillow.

Windsor, Patricia. The Summer Before. 176p. (gr. 7 up). 1974. pap. 1.95 (ISBN 0-440-98382-7, LFL). Dell.

Yolen, Jane. The Stone Silences. 128p. (gr. 7 up). 1984. 10.95 (ISBN 0-399-20971-9, Philomel). Putnam Pub Group.

York, Carol B. Remember Me When I Am Dead. LC 80-13461. (gr. 5-8). 1980. 8.95 (ISBN 0-525-66694-X, Lodestar Bks). Dutton Child Bks.

Young, Alida E. Is My Sister Dying? 144p. (Orig.). (gr. 5-8). 1991. pap. 2.95 (ISBN 0-87406-541-0). Willowisp Pr.

Zemach, Margot. Jake & Honeybunch Go to Heaven. LC 82-71752. (Illus.). 40p. (gr. 3 up). 1982. 14.95 (ISBN 0-374-33652-0). FS&G.

Zindel, Bonnie & Zindel, Paul. A Star for the Latecomer. LC 79-1786. 192p. (gr. 7 up). 1980. 12.95 (ISBN 0-06-026847-6). HarpC Child Bks.

Zindel, Paul & Zindel, Bonnie. A Star for the Latecomer. 160p. (gr. 6 up). 1985. pap. 2.50 (ISBN 0-553-25578-9). Bantam.

DEATH PENALTY
see Capital Punishment

DEATH VALLEY, CALIFORNIA

Salts, Bobbi. Death Valley Discovery! Parker, Steve, illus. 32p. (Orig.). (gr. k-6). 1991. pap. 3.95 (ISBN 1-878900-19-6). DVNH Assn.

DEBATES AND DEBATING
see also Parliamentary Practice

Dunbar, Robert E. How to Debate. (Illus.). 128p. (gr. 7-12). 1987. PLB 12.90 (ISBN 0-531-10335-8). Watts.

Littlefield, Kathy M. & Littlefield, Robert S. Let's Debate! Stark, Steve, illus. 36p. (Orig.). (gr. 3-6). 1989. pap. text ed. 8.95 (ISBN 1-879340-03-8, K0104). Kidspeak.

DECALOGUE
see Ten Commandments

DECISION MAKING

Smith, Sandra L. Coping with Decision Making. Rosen, Ruth, ed. (gr. 7 up). 1989. PLB 12.95 (ISBN 0-8239-1000-8). Rosen Group.

Swanson, Steve. Is There Life after High School? Making Decisions about Your Future. LC 90-15499. 112p. (Orig.). (gr. 9 up). 1991. pap. 4.95 (ISBN 0-8066-2500-7, 9-2500, Augsburg). Augsburg Fortress.

DECLARATION OF INDEPENDENCE
see U. S. Declaration of Independence

DECORATION, INTERIOR
see Interior Decoration

DECORATION AND ORNAMENT
see also Design; Design, Decorative; Enamel and Enameling; Flower Arrangement; Furniture; Gems; Illustration of Books; Interior Decoration; Jewelry; Leather Work; Lettering; Metalwork; Pottery; Sculpture; Tapestry; Wood Carving

Folmer, A. P. Fabulous Holiday Ornaments. (Illus.). 16p. (Orig.). (gr. k up). 1986. pap. 2.95 (ISBN 0-590-33841-2). Scholastic Inc.

DECORATIONS OF HONOR
see also Heraldry

Sherrard, Raymond & Stumpf, George. Badges of the United States Marshals. Esquivel, Jim & Leaf, Richard, illus. LC 89-61859. (Orig.). 1991. 35.45 (ISBN 0-914503-02-2); pap. 22.45 (ISBN 0-914503-03-0). RHS Ent.

DECORATIVE ARTS
see Art Industries and Trade; Arts and Crafts; Decoration and Ornament; Design, Decorative; Interior Decoration

DEDUCTION LOGIC
see Logic

DEEP-SEA DIVING
see Skin Diving

DEEP SEA TECHNOLOGY
see Oceanography

DEER
see also Reindeer

Ahlstrom, Mark. The Whitetail. LC 83-6944. (Illus.). 48p. (gr. 4-5). 1983. lib. bdg. 10.95 (ISBN 0-89686-224-0, Crestwood Hse). Macmillan Child Grp.

Ahlstrom, Mark E. The Mule Deer. LC 87-614. (Illus.). 48p. (gr. 5-6). 1987. PLB 10.95 (ISBN 0-89686-324-7, Crestwood Hse). Macmillan Child Grp.

Bailey, Jill. Discovering Deer. Caulkins, Janet, ed. (Illus.). 48p. (gr. 1-6). 1988. PLB 11.90 (ISBN 0-531-18196-0, Pub. by Bookwright Pr). Watts.

Butterworth, Christine & Bailey, Donna. Deer. LC 90-9960. (Illus.). 32p. (gr. 1-4). 1990. PLB 14.64 (ISBN 0-8114-2638-6). Steck-V.

Chavez, Juana. Mother Deer & Her Spotted Fawns. Aragon, Hilda, illus. 14p. (Orig.). (ps-7). 1981. pap. 3.75 (ISBN 0-915347-10-5). Pueblo Acoma Pr.

Deer. 1990. 2.95 (ISBN 0-8378-2054-5). Gibson.

Fortescue, J. W. The Story of a Red Deer. Armour, G. D., illus. 136p. (gr. 4-7). 1989. 17.95 (ISBN 0-948253-01-0, Pub. by Sportsmans Pr UK). Trafalgar Sq.

Gamlin, Linda. The Deer in the Forest. Oxford Scientific Film Staff, illus. LC 87-9916. 32p. (gr. 4-6). 1987. PLB 10.95 (ISBN 1-55532-273-5). Gareth Stevens Inc.

Long, Evelyn. Grandma Tellmie About...Big Deer, Little Deer...Reindeer. Plott, Dave & Longmeyer, Carole M., eds. 46p. 1985. pap. 3.00 (ISBN 0-931881-01-3). Collaborare Pub.

Royston, Angela. The Deer. Allen, Graham, illus. 24p. (Orig.). (ps-2). 1988. pap. 2.95 (ISBN 0-8249-8242-8). Ideals.

Ryden, Hope. The Little Deer of the Florida Keys. rev. ed. (Illus.). 64p. (Orig.). (gr. 5 up). 1986. 13.95 (ISBN 0-912451-13-0); pap. 8.95 (ISBN 0-912451-14-9). Florida Classics.

Saintsing, David. The World of Deer. Oxford Scientific Films Staff, illus. LC 87-6539. 32p. (gr. 2-3). 1987. PLB 10.95 (ISBN 1-55532-302-2). Gareth Stevens Inc.

Stone, Lynn. Deer. (Illus.). 24p. (gr. k-5). 1990. lib. bdg. 11.93 (ISBN 0-86593-043-0); lib. bdg. 8.95s.p. (ISBN 0-685-36339-2). Rourke Corp.

Tabor, Roger. Survival: Could You Be a Deer? Hayward, Tim, illus. 32p. (gr. 1-6). 1990. 10.95 (ISBN 0-8249-8414-5). Ideals.

Wolpert, Tom. White Tale Magic for Kids. Cox, Daniel S., illus. LC 90-50719. 48p. (gr. 2-3). 1991. lib. bdg. 12.95 (ISBN 0-8368-0661-1). Gareth Stevens Inc.

DEER–FICTION

Aragon, Jane Chelsea. Winter Harvest. Baker, Leslie, illus. LC 87-26489. (ps-3). 1989. 14.95 (ISBN 0-316-04937-9). Little.

Bambi. (FRE.). (gr. 3-8). 13.95 (ISBN 0-685-28447-6, S26622). French & Eur.

Bell, Frederic. Jenny's Corner. Onyshkewych, Zenowij, illus. LC 73-18741. 72p. (gr. 4-6). 1974. 3.95 (ISBN 0-394-82741-4). Random.

Bemelmans, Ludwig. Parsley. Bemelmans, Ludwig, illus. LC 55-7682. 48p. (ps-3). 1955. 14.95 (ISBN 0-06-020455-9). HarpC Child Bks.

Carr, Jan. Bambi. 1988. pap. 2.50 (ISBN 0-590-41664-2). Scholastic Inc.

Carrick, Donald. Harald & the Great Stag. Carrick, Donald, illus. LC 87-17875. 32p. (gr. k-4). 1988. 14.95 (ISBN 0-89919-514-8, Pub. by Clarion). Ticknor & Fields.

—Harald & the Great Stag. Carrick, Donald, illus. 32p. (ps-3). 1990. pap. 4.95 (ISBN 0-395-52596-9). HM.

Forest, Heather, retold by. The Baker's Dozen: A Colonial American Tale. Gaber, Susan, illus. (ps-3). 1988. 13.95 (ISBN 0-15-200412-2, Gulliver Bks). HarBraceJ.

Fortescue, J. W. The Story of a Red Deer. 160p. (gr. 5-8). 1989. pap. 5.95 (ISBN 0-86241-174-2, Pub. by Cnngt Pub Ltd). Trafalgar Sq.

Miller, A. G. Walt Disney's Bambi Gets Lost. (ps-3). 1973. 5.95 (ISBN 0-394-82520-9, Random Juv); lib. bdg. 4.99 (ISBN 0-394-92520-3). Random.

Phillips, Joan. Walt Disney's Bambi's Game. Langley, Bill & Wakeman, Diana, illus. (ps-1). 1991. write for info. (ISBN 0-307-11599-2, Golden Pr). Western Pub.

Prusski, Jeffrey. Bring Back the Deer. Waldman, Neil, illus. 32p. (ps-3). 1988. 13.95 (ISBN 0-15-200418-1, Gulliver Bks). HarBraceJ.

Salten, Felix. Bambi. 134p. 1981. Repr. PLB 16.95x (ISBN 0-89966-358-3). Buccaneer Bks.

—Bambi. 112p. 1981. Repr. PLB 16.95x (ISBN 0-89967-032-6). Harmony Raine.

—Bambi. Cooney, Barbara, illus. (ps up). 1988. pap. 3.50 (ISBN 0-671-66607-X, Minstrel Bks). PB.

—Bambi. Woods, Michael J., illus. LC 90-26533. 160p. (ps up). 1991. jacketed, three-piece bdg. 18.00 (ISBN 0-671-73937-9, S&S BYR). S&S Trade.

Seredy, Kate. The White Stag. (gr. 4-7). 1979. pap. 3.95 (ISBN 0-14-031258-7, Puffin). Puffin Bks.

Sharp, Mary & Niemi, Matt. Bobbi, Father of the Finnish White Tailed Deer. Shappell, Sherry, illus. LC 79-54100. (Orig.). (gr. 4-6). 1979. pap. 5.95 (ISBN 0-9603200-0-8). Bobbi Ent.

Smajda, Michael J. A Deer Love Story. (Illus.). 39p. 1988. text ed. 9.50 (ISBN 0-533-07680-3). Vantage.

Snyder, Zilpha K. A Fabulous Creature. LC 80-18977. 252p. (gr. 5-9). 1981. 10.95 (ISBN 0-689-30829-9, Atheneum Childrens Bks). Macmillan Child Grp.

Vail, Virginia. Oh Deer! 128p. (gr. 3-7). 1990. pap. 2.75 (ISBN 0-590-42802-0). Scholastic Inc.

Walt Disney's Bambi. 24p. (ps-k). 1986. write for info. (ISBN 0-307-10380-3, Pub. by Golden Bks). Western Pub.

Walt Disney's The Bambi Book. 24p. (gr. 2-5). 1987. pap. write for info. (ISBN 0-307-10055-3, Pub. by Golden Bks). Western Pub.

DEERE, JOHN, 1804-1886

Collins, David R. Pioneer Plowmaker: A Story about John Deere. Michaels, Steve, illus. 64p. (gr. 3-6). 1990. PLB 9.95 (ISBN 0-87614-424-5). Carolrhoda Bks.

DEGAS, HILAIRE GERMAIN EDGAR, 1834-1917

Newlands, Anne & National Gallery of Canada Staff. Meet Edgar Degas. Degas, Edgar, illus. LC 88-32035. 32p. (gr. 1 up). 1989. 13.95 (ISBN 0-397-32369-7, Lipp Jr Bks.). HarpC Child Bks.

DEGREES OF LATITUDE AND LONGITUDE
see Geodesy

DELAWARE

Carole Marsh Delaware Books, 31 bks. Set. 638.45 (ISBN 0-7933-1282-5). Gallopade Pub Group.

Carpenter, Allan. Delaware. LC 78-15915. (Illus.). 96p. (gr. 4 up). 1979. PLB 19.93 (ISBN 0-516-04108-8). Childrens.

Fradin, Dennis. Delaware: In Words & Pictures. LC 80-5842. (Illus.). 48p. (gr. 2-5). 1980. PLB 15.93 (ISBN 0-516-03908-3). Childrens.

Marsh, Carole. Avast, Ye Slobs! Delaware Pirate Trivia. (Illus.). (gr. 3-12). 1990. PLB 19.95 (ISBN 0-7933-0256-0); pap. 14.95 (ISBN 0-7933-0255-2); computer disk 29.95 (ISBN 0-7933-0257-9). Gallopade Pub Group.

—The Beast of the Delaware Bed & Breakfast. (Illus.). (gr. 3-12). 1990. PLB 19.95 (ISBN 0-7933-1447-X); pap. 14.95 (ISBN 0-7933-1448-8); computer disk 29.95 (ISBN 0-7933-1449-6). Gallopade Pub Group.

—Delaware & Other State Greats (Biographies) (Illus.). (gr. 3-12). 1990. PLB 19.95 (ISBN 1-55609-558-9); pap. 14.95 (ISBN 1-55609-557-0); computer disk 29.95 (ISBN 0-7933-1455-0). Gallopade Pub Group.

—Delaware Bandits, Bushwackers, Outlaws, Crooks, Devils, Ghosts, Desperadoes & Other Assorted & Sundry Characters! (Illus.). (gr. 3-12). 1990. PLB 19.95 (ISBN 0-7933-0238-2); pap. 14.95 (ISBN 0-7933-0237-4); computer disk 29.95 (ISBN 0-7933-0239-0). Gallopade Pub Group.

—Delaware Classic Christmas Trivia: Stories, Recipes, Activities, Legends, Lore & More! (Illus.). (gr. 3-12). 1990. PLB 19.95 (ISBN 0-7933-0241-2); pap. 14.95 (ISBN 0-7933-0240-4); computer disk 29.95 (ISBN 0-7933-0242-0). Gallopade Pub Group.

—Delaware Coastales. (Illus.). (gr. 3-12). 1990. PLB 19.95 (ISBN 1-55609-554-6); pap. 14.95 (ISBN 1-55609-553-8); computer disk 29.95 (ISBN 0-7933-1451-8). Gallopade Pub Group.

—The Delaware Hot Air Balloon Mystery. (Illus.). (gr. 2-9). 1990. 19.95 (ISBN 0-685-37849-7); pap. 14.95 (ISBN 0-7933-2382-7); computer disk 29.95 (ISBN 0-7933-2383-5). Gallopade Pub Group.

—Delaware "Jography" A Fun Run Thru Our State! (Illus.). (gr. 3-12). 1990. PLB 19.95 (ISBN 1-55609-551-1); pap. 14.95 (ISBN 1-55609-550-3); computer disk 29.95 (ISBN 0-7933-1439-9). Gallopade Pub Group.

—Delaware Kid's Cookbook: Recipes, How-to-, History, Lore & More! (Illus.). (gr. 3-12). 1990. PLB 19.95 (ISBN 0-7933-0250-1); pap. 14.95 (ISBN 0-7933-0249-8); computer disk 29.95 (ISBN 0-7933-0251-X). Gallopade Pub Group.

—Delaware Quiz Bowl Crash Course! (Illus.). (gr. 3-12). 1990. PLB 19.95 (ISBN 1-55609-556-2); pap. 14.95 (ISBN 1-55609-555-4); computer disk 29.95 (ISBN 0-7933-1450-X). Gallopade Pub Group.

—Delaware School Trivia: An Amazing & Fascinating Look at Our State's Teachers, Schools & Students! (Illus.). (gr. 3-12). 1990. PLB 19.95 (ISBN 0-7933-0247-1); pap. 14.95 (ISBN 0-7933-0246-3); computer disk 29.95 (ISBN 0-7933-0248-X). Gallopade Pub Group.

—Delaware Silly Basketball Sportsmysteries, Vol. I. (Illus.). (gr. 3-12). 1990. PLB 19.95 (ISBN 0-7933-0244-7); pap. 14.95 (ISBN 0-7933-0243-9); computer disk 29.95 (ISBN 0-7933-0245-5). Gallopade Pub Group.

—Delaware Silly Basketball Sportsmysteries, Vol. II. (Illus.). (gr. 3-12). 1990. PLB 19.95 (ISBN 0-7933-1456-9); pap. 14.95 (ISBN 0-7933-1457-7); computer disk 29.95 (ISBN 0-7933-1458-5). Gallopade Pub Group.

—Delaware Silly Football Sportsmysteries, Vol. I. (Illus.). (gr. 3-12). 1990. PLB 19.95 (ISBN 0-7933-1441-0); pap. 14.95 (ISBN 0-7933-1442-9); computer disk 29.95 (ISBN 0-7933-1443-7). Gallopade Pub Group.

—Delaware Silly Football Sportsmysteries, Vol. II. (Illus.). (gr. 3-12). 1990. PLB 19.95 (ISBN 0-7933-1444-5); pap. 14.95 (ISBN 0-7933-1445-3); computer disk 29.95 (ISBN 0-7933-1446-1). Gallopade Pub Group.

—Delaware Silly Trivia! (Illus.). (gr. 3-12). 1990. PLB 19.95 (ISBN 1-55609-549-X); pap. 14.95 (ISBN 1-55609-548-1); computer disk 29.95 (ISBN 0-7933-1438-0). Gallopade Pub Group.

—Delaware's (Most Devastating!) Disasters & (Most Calamitous!) Catastrophies! (Illus.). (gr. 3-12). 1990. PLB 19.95 (ISBN 0-7933-0235-8); pap. 14.95 (ISBN 0-7933-0234-X); computer disk 29.95 (ISBN 0-7933-0236-6). Gallopade Pub Group.

—The Hard-to-Believe-But-True! Book of Delaware History, Mystery, Trivia, Legend, Lore, Humor & More. (Illus.). (gr. 3-12). 1990. PLB 19.95 (ISBN 0-7933-0253-6); pap. 14.95 (ISBN 0-7933-0252-8); computer disk 29.95 (ISBN 0-7933-0254-4). Gallopade Pub Group.

—If My Delaware Mama Ran the World! (Illus.). (gr. 3-12). 1990. PLB 19.95 (ISBN 0-7933-1452-6); pap. 14.95 (ISBN 0-7933-1453-4); computer disk 29.95 (ISBN 0-7933-1454-2). Gallopade Pub Group.

—Let's Quilt Delaware & Stuff It Topographically! (Illus.). (gr. 3-12). 1990. PLB 19.95 (ISBN 1-55609-552-X); pap. 14.95 (ISBN 1-55609-063-3); computer disk 29.95 (ISBN 0-7933-1440-2). Gallopade Pub Group.

Thompson, Kathleen. Delaware. 48p. (gr. 3 up). 1986. pap. text ed. 17.32 (ISBN 0-86514-450-8); pap. 9.27 (ISBN 0-86514-525-3); cancelled Beta video (ISBN 0-86514-075-8); cancelled VHS video (ISBN 0-86514-150-9); cancelled 3/4" video (ISBN 0-86514-225-4); cancelled student activity bk. (ISBN 0-86514-375-7); cancelled tchr's. study guide (ISBN 0-86514-300-5); cancelled index. Raintree Pubs.

DELAWARE–HISTORY
Hoffecker, Carol E. Delaware, the First State. (Illus.). 256p. (Orig.). 1987. pap. 9.95 (ISBN 0-912608-47-1). Mid Atlantic.

Swindler, William F. & Frech, Mary, eds. Chronology & Documentary Handbook of the State of Delaware, No. 8. LC 73-524. 90p. (gr. 9-12). 1973. PLB 8.50 (ISBN 0-379-16133-8). Oceana.

DELINQUENCY, JUVENILE
see Juvenile Delinquency

DELIQUENTS
see Crime and Criminals; Juvenile Delinquency

DELUSIONS
see Superstition; Witchcraft

DE MILLE, AGNES, 1908-
Gherman, Beverly. Agnes De Mille: Dancing off the Earth. LC 89-6888. (Illus.). 160p. (gr. 4 up). 1990. 13.95 (ISBN 0-689-31441-8, Atheneum Child Bk). Macmillan Child Grp.

Yuan, Margaret S. Agnes De Mille. Horner, Matina, intro. by. (Illus.). 112p. (gr. 5 up). 1990. lib. bdg. 17.95 (ISBN 1-55546-648-6). Chelsea Hse.

DEMOCRACY
see also Equality; Liberty
Adams, Henry. Democracy, an American Novel. Andrews, C. A., intro. by. (gr. 9 up). pap. 1.50 (ISBN 0-8049-0164-3, CL-164). Airmont.

Aten, Jerry. Democracy for Young Americans. 112p. (gr. 4-8). 1989. 9.95 (ISBN 0-86653-483-0, GA1083). Good Apple.

Eannace, Maryrose. The Pizza Problem: Democracy in Action. 70p. (Orig.). (gr. 6-10). 1990. pap. text ed. 8.75x (ISBN 0-936826-35-5). PS Assocs Croton.

DEMONOLOGY–FICTION
Buck, Pearl S. The Old Demon. Higashi, Sandra, illus. 40p. (gr. 4 up). 1982. PLB 10.95s.p. (ISBN 0-87191-828-5); PLB 15.65 (ISBN 0-685-05631-7). Creative Ed.

DEMONSTRATIONS FOR NEGRO CIVIL RIGHTS
see Blacks–Civil Rights

DENMARK
Andersen, Ulla. We Live in Denmark. LC 83-71633. 64p. (gr. 4-8). 1984. lib. bdg. 9.49 (ISBN 0-531-04782-2, Pub. by Bookwright Pr). Watts.

Levine, Charlotte R. Danish Dependencies. (Illus.). 96p. (gr. 5 up). 1989. lib. bdg. 14.95 (ISBN 1-55546-787-3). Chelsea Hse.

Lye, Keith. Take a Trip to Denmark. (Illus.). 32p. (gr. k-5). 1985. PLB 7.99 (ISBN 0-531-04884-5). Watts.

DENOMINATIONS, RELIGIOUS
see Sects

DENTISTRY
see also Teeth
Berry, Joy W. Teach Me about the Baby Sitter. Dickey, Kate, ed. LC 85-45077. (Illus.). 36p. (ps). 1986. 4.98 (ISBN 0-685-10722-1). Grolier Inc.

—Teach Me about the Dentist. Dickey, Kate, ed. LC 85-45084. (Illus.). 36p. (ps). 1986. 4.98 (ISBN 0-685-10724-8). Grolier Inc.

Boy Scouts of America. Dentistry. (Illus.). 32p. (gr. 6-12). 1975. pap. 1.85 (ISBN 0-8395-3394-2, 3394). BSA.

Bradman, Tony. Dilly Goes to the Dentist. Hellard, Susan, illus. (gr. 2-5). 1987. 10.95 (ISBN 0-670-81683-3). Viking Child Bks.

Braithwaite, Althea. Visiting the Dentist. Newsham, Ian, illus. 24p. (ps-2). 1990. 1.95 (ISBN 1-878624-23-7, 1553800023). McClanahan Bk.

DeSantis, Kenny. A Dentist's Tools. Agre, Patricia A., photos by. LC 87-36505. (Illus.). 48p. (gr. k-3). 1988. 10.95 (ISBN 0-396-09043-5, Putnam); pap. 4.95 (ISBN 0-396-09044-3, Putnam). Putnam Pub Group.

Going to the Dentist. 1990. 2.99 (ISBN 0-517-69198-1). Outlet Bk Co.

Hafford, Jeannette N. Boys & Girls & Doctors & Dentists. 24p. (Orig.). 1986. pap. 7.22 (ISBN 0-9616549-0-2). Tinys Self Help Bks.

Petty, Kate. Going to the Dentist. FS-Aladdin Staff, ed. Kopper, Lisa, illus. 24p. (gr. 1-3). 1988. PLB 5.29 (ISBN 0-531-17104-3, Gloucester Pr). Watts.

Rockwell, Harlow. My Dentist. LC 75-6974. (Illus.). 32p. (ps-3). 1975. 12.95 (ISBN 0-688-80011-4); PLB 12.88 (ISBN 0-688-84004-3). Greenwillow.

Rogers, Fred. Going to the Dentist. Judkis, Jim, photos by. (Illus.). 32p. (Orig.). (ps-2). 1989. 12.95 (ISBN 0-685-25371-6, Putnam); pap. 5.95 (ISBN 0-685-25372-4, Putnam). Putnam Pub Group.

Silverstein, Alvin & Silverstein, Virginia B. So You're Getting Braces: A Guide to Orthodontics. LC 77-16488. (Illus.). 128p. (gr. 5 up). 1978. PLB 12.89 (ISBN 0-397-31786-7, Lipp Jr Bks); pap. 3.95 (ISBN 0-397-31787-5, Lipp Jr Bks). HarpC Child Bks.

Stamper, Judith. What's It Like to Be a Dentist. Gustafson, Dana, illus. LC 89-34392. 32p. (gr. k-3). 1989. lib. bdg. 10.89 (ISBN 0-8167-1799-0); pap. text ed. 2.50 (ISBN 0-8167-1800-8). Troll Assocs.

DENTISTRY–FICTION
Bradman, Tony. Dilly Goes to the Dentist. Hellard, Susan, illus. 64p. (gr. 2-5). 1988. pap. 3.95 (ISBN 0-14-032338-4, Puffin). Puffin Bks.

Civardi, Anne & Cartwright, Stephen. Going to the Dentist. 16p. (ps up). 1987. 2.95 (ISBN 0-7460-0071-5). EDC.

Coles, Allison. Mandy & the Dentist. Charlton, Michael, illus. 28p. (ps up). 1985. 3.95 (ISBN 0-88110-270-9). EDC.

Godfrey, Jan. Me at the Dentist's. (ps-3). 1989. pap. 1.95 (ISBN 0-7459-1732-1). Lion USA.

Kuklin, Susan. When I See My Dentist. LC 87-25695. (Illus.). 32p. (ps-1). 1988. 12.95 (ISBN 0-02-751231-2, Bradbury Pr). Macmillan Child Grp.

Mitra, Annie. Tusk! Tusk! Mitra, Annie, illus. LC 89-77508. 32p. (ps-2). 1990. reinforced 13.95 (ISBN 0-8234-0819-1). Holiday.

DENVER
Corning, Josie. Denver, Colorado. LC 89-32946. (Illus.). 48p. (gr. 4-5). 1989. 12.95 (ISBN 0-89686-464-2, Crestwood Hse). Macmillan Child Grp.

Hawley, Frances, ed. The Children's Pages of Metro Denver - Fall Edition, 1988: A Directory of Products & Services for Children of All Ages & Their Parents. (gr. 7 up). 1988. pap. write for info. (ISBN 0-932439-08-X). Denver Busn Media.

Smith, Barbara A. Historic Denver for Kids. rev. ed. Taylor, Alice, illus. 90p. (Orig.). (gr. k up). 1982. pap. 5.00 (ISBN 0-943804-25-6). U of Denver Teach.

Spies, Karen. Denver. LC 88-20246. (Illus.). 60p. (gr. 3 up). 1988. PLB 12.95 (ISBN 0-87518-386-7, Dillon). Macmillan Child Grp.

DEOXYRIBONUCLEIC ACID
see D N A

DEPARTMENT STORES
see also Salesmen and Salesmanship
Gibbons, Gail. Department Store. LC 83-45053. (Illus.). 32p. (gr. k-4). 1984. (Crowell Jr Bks); PLB 13.89 (ISBN 0-690-04367-8). HarpC Child Bks.

—Department Store. Gibbons, Gail, illus. LC 85-45396. 32p. (gr. k-4). 1986. pap. 4.95 (ISBN 0-06-446028-2, Trophy). HarpC Child Bks.

DEPARTMENT STORES–FICTION
Peck, Richard. Secrets of the Shopping Mall. 192p. (gr. k-6). 1989. pap. 3.25 (ISBN 0-440-40270-0, LFL); pap. 3.50 (ISBN 0-440-98099-2). Dell.

DEPENDENT CHILDREN
see Child Welfare

DEPRESSIONS
Meltzer, Milton. Brother, Can You Spare a Dime: The Great Depression, 1929-1933. Scott, John A., ed. (Illus.). 160p. 1990. 16.95x (ISBN 0-8160-2372-7). Facts on File.

Migneco, Ronald & Biel, Timothy L. The Crash of 1929. LC 89-33556. (Illus.). 64p. (gr. 5-8). 1989. PLB 11.95 (ISBN 1-56006-007-7). Lucent Bks.

Schraff, Anne E. The Great Depression & the New Deal: America's Economic Collapse & Recovery. (Illus.). 128p. (gr. 9-12). 1990. PLB 12.90 (ISBN 0-531-10964-X). Watts.

Stein, R. Conrad. The Story of the Great Depression. Greene, Nathan, illus. LC 85-11039. 31p. (gr. 3-4). 1985. PLB 13.27 (ISBN 0-516-04694-2); pap. 3.95 (ISBN 0-516-44694-0). Childrens.

DEPRESSIONS–FICTION
Ames, Mildred. The Dancing Madness: A Novel. LC 80-65831. 144p. (gr. 7 up). 1980. 8.95 (ISBN 0-385-28113-7). Delacorte.

Cannon, Bettie. A Bellsong for Sarah Raines. LC 87-4299. 192p. (gr. 7 up). 1987. 13.95 (ISBN 0-684-18839-2, Scribners Young Read). Macmillan Child Grp.

Cleaver, Vera & Cleaver, Bill. Mock Revolt. LC 75-151467. 160p. (gr. 6 up). 1971. (Lipp Jr Bks); pap. 1.95 (ISBN 0-397-31237-7). HarpC Child Bks.

Green, Michelle Y. Willie Pearl. Date not set. write for info (ISBN 0-9627697-0-3). W Ruth Co.

Greene, Constance C. Dotty's Suitcase. LC 80-10949. 168p. (gr. 4-6). 1980. pap. 11.95 (ISBN 0-670-28050-X). Viking Child Bks.

Mills, Claudia. What about Annie? LC 84-20862. 128p. (gr. 5 up). 1985. 9.95 (ISBN 0-8027-6573-4). Walker & Co.

Reasonover, Ila. Lottie Daughter of the Depression. Caroland, Mary, ed. LC 90-71004. 154p. (gr. 4-8). 1991. 7.95 (ISBN 1-55523-365-1). Winston-Derek.

Rossiter, Phyllis. Moxie. LC 90-30027. 192p. (gr. 5 up). 1990. 13.95 (ISBN 0-02-777831-2, Four Winds). Macmillan Child Grp.

Schneider, Susan. Please Send Junk Food: A Camp Survival Guide. 100p. 1987. pap. 2.50 (ISBN 0-425-09596-7, Pub. by Berkley-Pacer). Berkley Pub.

Snyder, Zilpha K. Velvet Room. Raible, Alton, illus. LC 65-10474. 224p. (gr. 3-7). 1972. (Atheneum Childrens Bk); pap. 1.95 (ISBN 0-685-00576-3). Macmillan Child Grp.

Stein, Charlotte M. The Stained Glass Window. Sakurai, Jennifer, ed. Stein, Michele P., illus. LC 88-70883. 150p. (Orig.). 1991. incl. wkbk. 16.95 (ISBN 0-916634-13-2); pap. 11.95 incl. wkbk. (ISBN 0-916634-12-4). Double M Pr.

Van Raven, Pieter. A Time of Troubles. LC 90-31409. 192p. 1990. 13.95 (ISBN 0-684-19212-8, Scribners Young Read). Macmillan Child Grp.

DERMATOLOGY
see Skin–Diseases

DESERT ANIMALS
see also Camels
Burton, Robert. Desert. (Illus.). 24p. (gr. k-4). 1991. PLB 13.25 (ISBN 1-878137-17-4). Newington.

Clutterbuck, Mary, illus. Animals & Birds of the Desert. 32p. (gr. 3-5). 1985. 5.95x (ISBN 0-86685-445-2). Intl Bk Ctr.

Pearce, Q. L. & Pearce, W. L. In the Desert. Brook, Bonnie, ed. Bettoli, Delana, illus. 24p. (ps-1). 1990. 4.95 (ISBN 0-671-68829-4); PLB 8.98 (ISBN 0-671-68825-1). Silver Pr.

Plantimal Safari. (ps-6). 1986. 3.00 (ISBN 0-9605656-3-9). Desert Botanical.

DESERT PLANTS
Almeleh, Fiona, illus. Plants & Flowers of the Desert. 32p. (gr. 3-5). 1985. 5.95x (ISBN 0-86685-446-0). Intl Bk Ctr.

Busch, Phyllis. Cactus in the Desert. Barton, Harriett, illus. LC 78-4771. (gr. k-3). 1979. PLB 12.89 (ISBN 0-690-00292-0, Crowell Jr Bks). HarpC Child Bks.

Clutterbuck, Mary, illus. Animals & Birds of the Desert. 32p. (gr. 3-5). 1985. 5.95x (ISBN 0-86685-445-2). Intl Bk Ctr.

Plantimal Safari. (ps-6). 1986. 3.00 (ISBN 0-9605656-3-9). Desert Botanical.

Reading, Susan. Desert Plants. 64p. 1990. 15.95x (ISBN 0-8160-2421-9). Facts on File.

DESERTS
see also Desert Animals; Desert Plants
Adrian, Mary. Wildlife on the Watch. Zallinger, Jean, illus. 64p. (gr. 2-6). 1974. PLB 6.95 (ISBN 0-8038-1553-0). Hastings.

Arnold, Caroline. A Walk in the Desert. Brook, Bonnie, ed. Tanz, Freya, illus. 32p. (ps-1). 1990. 4.95 (ISBN 0-671-68668-2); lib. bdg. 9.98 (ISBN 0-671-68664-X). Silver Pr.

Baker, Lucy. Life in the Deserts. (Illus.). 32p. (gr. 5-8). 1990. PLB 11.40 (ISBN 0-531-10980-1). Watts.

Barrett, Norman. Deserts. (Illus.). 32p. (gr. 2 up). 1991. pap. 3.95 (ISBN 0-531-24619-1). Watts.

—Desiertos. (SPA., Illus.). 32p. (gr. k-4). 1991. PLB 11.40 (ISBN 0-531-07924-4). Watts.

Baylor, Byrd. The Desert Is Theirs. Parnall, Peter, illus. LC 74-24417. 32p. (ps-3). 1975. 13.95 (ISBN 0-684-14266-X, Scribners Young Read). Macmillan Child Grp.

—The Desert Is Theirs. Parnall, Peter, illus. LC 86-17323. 32p. (gr. 1-5). 1987. pap. 4.95 (ISBN 0-689-71105-0, Aladdin). Macmillan Child Grp.

Bender, Lionel. Desert. (Illus.). 32p. (gr. 3-6). 1989. PLB 11.90 (ISBN 0-531-10707-8, Gloucester Pr). Watts.

Brandt, Keith. Deserts. Watling, James, illus. LC 84-8623. 32p. (gr. 3-6). 1985. PLB 9.49 (ISBN 0-8167-0262-4); pap. text ed. 2.95 (ISBN 0-8167-0263-2). Troll Assocs.

Carrie, Christopher. Chase Through the Desert Wilds. (Illus.). 40p. (gr. k up). 1990. 1.59 (ISBN 0-86696-244-1). Binney & Smith.

Catchpole, Clive. Deserts. McIntyre, Brian, illus. LC 83-7757. 32p. (ps-4). 1985. pap. 4.95 (ISBN 0-8037-0037-7, 0481-140). Dial Bks Young.

Chicago Zoological Society Staff, ed. Desert Communities. (Orig.). (gr. 4-6). 1986. pap. text ed. 30.00 (ISBN 0-913934-06-2). Chicago Zoo.

Cowing, Sheila. Searches in the American Desert. LC 88-26883. (Illus.). 224p. (gr. 5 up). 1989. 14.95 (ISBN 0-689-50469-1, M K McElderry). Macmillan Child Grp.

Dewey, Jennifer O. Night & Day in the Desert, Vol. 1. (ps-3). 1991. 15.95 (ISBN 0-316-18210-9). Little.

Hogan, Paula. Expanding Deserts. LC 90-27799. (Illus.). 32p. (gr. 3-4). 1991. PLB 12.95 (ISBN 0-8368-0474-0). Gareth Stevens Inc.

Hughes, Jill. Deserts. rev. ed. Coombs, R. & Wilson, Maurice, illus. 32p. (gr. 4-7). 1987. lib. bdg. 5.99 (ISBN 0-531-17037-3, Gloucester Pr). Watts.

Hunt, Joni P. The Desert. Leon, Vicki, ed. (Illus.). 40p. (Orig.). 1991. pap. 7.95 (ISBN 0-918303-28-1). Blake Pub. Teachers, students, librarians, & nature-lovers alike will relish this sunset-colorful book, the latest in the Blake Habitat series. Easy-to-grasp text sizzles with word pictures about the major plants & animals of the hot & dry lands. 46 magnificent photos, most taken in North American deserts & the balance in Asia, Africa, & South America, show the desert's network of plant & animal interdependency. All are in color. Many are as large as 11 x 17 inches, giving readers a sharp & detailed look at such creatures as bighorn sheep, the oryx, & the roadrunner. Symbiotic relationships--like that of the yucca moth & the Joshua tree are well depicted. Explanations & photos of how plants & animals conserve water are numerous & clear. The issue of desertification & man's impact on the desert also gets coverage. A map of the world's deserts, a list of outstanding desert parks, museums, & displays, & a strong environmental message round out the book.
Publisher Provided Annotation.

A Look at the Earth Around Us: Deserts. (gr. 3-6). 1981. incl. cass. & tchr's. guide 28.95 (ISBN 0-686-73890-X, 04924). Natl Geog.

Lye, Keith. Deserts. (Illus.). 48p. (gr. 5-8). 1987. PLB 14.98 (ISBN 0-382-09501-4). Silver Burdett Pr.

McLeish, Ewan. Spread of Deserts. LC 90-10018. (Illus.). 48p. (gr. 4-9). 1990. PLB 18.60 (ISBN 0-8114-2390-5). Steck-V.

Milner, Cedric. Desert Trek. LC 88-42906. (Illus.). 32p. (gr. 4-5). 1989. PLB 10.95 (ISBN 1-55532-919-5). Gareth Stevens Inc.

Moore, Randy & Vodopich, Darrell S. The Living Desert. LC 90-42243. (Illus.). 64p. (gr. 6 up). 1991. PLB 15.95 (ISBN 0-89490-182-6). Enslow Pubs.

Norden, Carroll R. Deserts. rev. ed. LC 87-23224. (Illus.). 48p. (gr. 2-6). 1987. PLB 17.32 (ISBN 0-8172-3252-4); pap. 9.27 (ISBN 0-8172-3277-X). Raintree Pubs.

Posell, Elsa. Deserts. LC 81-15548. (Illus.). 48p. (gr. k-4). 1982. PLB 14.60 (ISBN 0-516-01613-X); pap. 4.95 (ISBN 0-516-41613-8). Childrens.

Sabin, Louis. Wonders of the Desert. Baldwin-Ford, Pamela, illus. LC 81-7397. 32p. (gr. 2-4). 1982. PLB 10.89 (ISBN 0-89375-574-5); pap. text ed. 2.95 (ISBN 0-89375-575-3); cassette 9.95 (ISBN 0-685-04955-8). Troll Assocs.

Salts, Bobbi. Desert Discovery: An Activity Book for Kids. Parker, Steve, illus. 32p. (gr. 1-6). 1989. pap. text ed. 2.95 (ISBN 0-929526-01-5). Double B Pubns.

Sanders, John. All about Deserts. Boyd, Patti, illus. LC 83-4857. 32p. (gr. 3-6). 1984. lib. bdg. 10.59 (ISBN 0-89375-965-1); pap. text ed. 2.95 (ISBN 0-89375-966-X). Troll Assocs.

Spencer, Guy. A Living Desert. Fuller, Tim, illus. LC 87-3488. 32p. (gr. 3-6). 1988. PLB 10.79 (ISBN 0-8167-1169-0); pap. text ed. 2.95 (ISBN 0-8167-1170-4). Troll Assocs.

Watson, Jane W. Deserts of the World: Future Threat or Promise? (Illus.). 136p. (gr. 10-12). 1981. 13.95 (ISBN 0-399-20785-6, Philomel). Putnam Pub Group.

Watts, Barrie. Twenty-Four Hours in a Desert. (Illus.). 48p. (gr. 5-8). 1991. PLB 11.90 (ISBN 0-531-14187-X). Watts.

Wilkes. Deserts. (gr. 4-6). 1980. (Usborne-Hayes); PLB 11.96 (ISBN 0-88110-080-3); pap. 3.95 (ISBN 0-86020-470-7). EDC.

DESERTS–FICTION

Allard, Harry. The Cactus Flower Bakery. Delaney, Ned, illus. LC 90-36565. 32p. (ps-3). 1991. 14.95 (ISBN 0-06-020046-4); PLB 14.89 (ISBN 0-06-020047-2). HarpC Child Bks.

Baylor, Byrd. Desert Voices. Parnall, Peter, illus. LC 80-17061. 32p. (ps-3). 1981. 13.95 (ISBN 0-684-16712-3, Scribners Young Read). Macmillan Child Grp.

Knox, Joann. Tamar & the Desert Adventure. 64p. (gr. 4-8). 1973. pap. 1.00 (ISBN 0-88243-770-4, 02-0770). Gospel Pub.

L'Engle, Madeleine. Dance in the Desert. Shimin, Symeon, illus. LC 68-29465. 64p. (ps up). 1969. 14.95 (ISBN 0-374-31684-8). FS&G.

Skurzynski, Gloria. Lost in the Devil's Desert. 96p. (gr. 4-8). 1988. 1.00 (ISBN 0-87406-309-4, 33-15904-4). Willowisp Pr.

Williams, Jeffery W. The Four Wheels of Justice Fighting Force: How It Began. Williams, Jeffery W., illus. 26p. (gr. 3 up). 1990. lib. bdg. write for info. (ISBN 1-878392-00-X); pap. 2.95 (ISBN 0-685-30135-4). R Kids Pub.

Woolgar, Jack. Mystery in the Desert. (gr. 6-8). 1967. 6.70 (ISBN 0-8313-0107-4); PLB 6.19 (ISBN 0-685-13778-3). Lantern.

DESIGN

For works on the theory of design.

see also Costume Design

Baxter, Leon. Design. Baxter, Leon, illus. 24p. (gr. 2-7). 1989. pap. 2.95 (ISBN 0-8249-8324-6). Ideals.

Gerson, Trina. Poetic Shapes. Gerson, Janice, illus. 52p. (ps-7). 1981. pap. text ed. 2.95 (ISBN 0-9605878-0-2). Anirt Pr.

McDermott, Catherine. Design. LC 90-10000. (Illus.). 48p. (gr. 6-11). 1990. PLB 18.60 (ISBN 0-8114-2364-6). Steck-V.

Malcolm, Dorothea C. Design: Elements & Principles. LC 71-148087. (Illus.). (gr. 5-12). 1972. 14.95 (ISBN 0-87192-039-5). Davis Mass.

DESIGN, DECORATIVE

see also Decoration and Ornament; Drawing; Lettering; Tapestry

Prints & Patterns. (ARA., Illus.). (gr. 5-12). 3.50x (ISBN 0-86685-219-0). Intl Bk Ctr.

DESSERTS

Cobb, Vicki. The Scoop on Ice Cream. Karas, Brian, illus. 48p. (gr. 4 up). 1985. 11.95 (ISBN 0-316-14895-4). Little.

Klevin, Jill R. Turtles Together Forever! Edwards, Linda S., illus. LC 82-70313. 160p. (gr. 4-6). 1982. pap. 9.95 (ISBN 0-385-29045-4); pap. 9.89 (ISBN 0-385-29046-2). Delacorte.

Mitgutsch, Ali. From Milk to Ice Cream. Mitgutsch, Ali, illus. LC 81-81. 24p. (ps-3). 1981. PLB 6.95 (ISBN 0-87614-158-0). Carolrhoda Bks.

Ondori Publishing Company Staff. Desserts You Can Make: Children's Cookbook, Vol. 2. (Illus.). 64p. (Orig.). (gr. 7 up). 1984. pap. 8.50 (ISBN 0-87040-561-6). Japan Pubns USA.

DETECTIVE STORIES

see Mystery and Detective Stories

DETECTIVES

see also Criminal Investigation; Police; Secret Service

Albert, Burton, Jr. Top Secret! Codes to Crack. Levine, Abby, ed. Warshaw, Jerry, illus. 32p. (gr. 4-7). 1987. PLB 10.95 (ISBN 0-8075-8027-9). A Whitman.

King & Emery. Word Detective Picture Word Book. (gr. k-3). 1982. 11.95 (ISBN 0-86020-662-9, Usborne-Hayes). EDC.

Paige, David. A Day in the Life of a Police Detective. Ruhlin, Roger, photos by. LC 80-54102. (Illus.). 32p. (gr. 4-8). 1981. PLB 11.79 (ISBN 0-89375-442-0); pap. 2.95 (ISBN 0-89375-443-9); cassette avail. Troll Assocs.

Wormser, Richard. Allan Pinkerton: America's First Private Eye. (Illus.). 119p. (gr. 5 up). 1990. 17.95 (ISBN 0-8027-6964-0); lib. bdg. 18.85 (ISBN 0-8027-6965-9). Walker & Co.

DETECTIVES–FICTION

Armstrong, Bev. Dinosaur Detective. Armstrong, Bev, illus. 32p. (gr. k-3). 1979. 3.95 (ISBN 0-88160-075-X, LW 808). Learning Wks.

Avi. The Man Who Was Poe. LC 89-42537. 224p. (gr. 6-8). 1989. 13.95 (ISBN 0-531-05833-6); PLB 13.99 (ISBN 0-531-08433-7). Orchard Bks Watts.

Brooks, Walter R. Freddy the Detective. Morrill, Leslie & Wiese, Kurt, illus. LC 86-40422. 272p. (gr. 3-7). 1987. lib. bdg. 9.99 (ISBN 0-394-98885-X); pap. 4.95 (ISBN 0-394-88885-5). Knopf.

Christian, Mary B. The Phantom of the Operetta. Howell, Kathleen C., illus. LC 86-11497. 80p. (gr. 2-5). 1986. 10.95 (ISBN 0-525-44272-3, DCB). Dutton Child Bks.

Dautrich, Jack & Huff, Vivian. Big City Detective. Huff, Vivian, illus. LC 86-13545. 128p. (gr. 7 up). 1986. 13.95 (ISBN 0-525-67183-8, Lodestar Bks). Dutton Child Bks.

Ehrlich, Amy. Where It Stops, Nobody Knows. LC 88-4095. 192p. (gr. 6 up). 1988. 14.95 (ISBN 0-8037-0575-1). Dial Bks Young.

Eisenberg, Lisa. Mystery at Bluff Point Dunes. LC 87-24454. 176p. (gr. 5 up). 1988. 14.95 (ISBN 0-8037-0527-1). Dial Bks Young.

Johnson, Larry D. & Mills, Jane L. Arnie the Detective. Hebert, Kim T., illus. LC 86-60364. 24p. (ps). 1986. pap. 4.50 (ISBN 0-938155-06-7); pap. 12.00 set of 3 bks. (ISBN 0-685-13514-4). Read A Bol.

Kwitz, Mary D. Gumshoe Goose, Private Eye. Ernst, Lisa C., illus. LC 86-29331. 48p. (ps-3). 1988. 9.95 (ISBN 0-8037-0423-2); PLB 9.89 (ISBN 0-8037-0424-0). Dial Bks Young.

McCay, William. Funny Business. LC 88-31481. 144p. (gr. 5 up). 1989. PLB 6.99 (ISBN 0-394-99981-9). Random.

Platt, Kin. Big Max. Lopshire, Robert, illus. LC 65-14488. (gr. k-3). 1978. pap. 3.50 (ISBN 0-06-444006-0, Trophy). HarpC Child Bks.

Reed, Joyce G. Take a Whistler's Walk. Reed, J., illus. 77p. (gr. 4-9). 1988. 12.95 (ISBN 0-943487-08-0); pap. 4.95 (ISBN 0-943487-07-2). Sevgo Pr.

Rosenberg, Amye & Mason, Patrice G. Sam the Detective & the Alef Bet Mystery. Rossel, Seymour, ed. Rosenberg, Amye, illus. 64p. (Orig.). (gr. 1-3). 1980. pap. text ed. 4.45 (ISBN 0-87441-328-1). Behrman.

Sobol, Donald J. Encyclopedia Brown & the Case of the Mysterious Handprints, No. 16. 128p. 1986. pap. 2.95 (ISBN 0-553-15739-6, Skylark). Bantam.

—Encyclopedia Brown's Book of Wacky Animals. 128p. (Orig.). 1985. pap. 2.25 (ISBN 0-553-15346-3, Skylark). Bantam.

—Encyclopedia Brown's Third Record Book of Weird & Wonderful Facts. 144p. 1985. pap. 2.50 (ISBN 0-553-15372-2, Skylark). Bantam.

Talbert, Marc. The Paper Knife. LC 88-3853. 176p. (gr. 4 up). 1988. 14.95 (ISBN 0-8037-0571-9). Dial Bks Young.

Vestavia Elementary School Fourth Grade Class & Cockrell, Marcille. The Adventures of a Bubble-Bellied Bloopy Droopy Detective. (Illus.). 32p. (gr. k-5). 1989. pap. 3.95 (ISBN 0-943487-22-6). Sevgo Pr.

DEVELOPING COUNTRIES

Rohr, Janelle, ed. The Third World: Opposing Viewpoints. LC 89-36524. (Illus.). 264p. (gr. 10 up). 1989. PLB 15.95 (ISBN 0-89908-447-8); pap. 8.95 (ISBN 0-89908-422-2). Greenhaven.

DEVELOPMENT

see Embryology; Evolution; Growth

DEVELOPMENTAL READING

Dolch, Edward, et al. Gulliver's Stories. Vayssieres, Jean J., illus. (gr. k-3). 1976. pap. 1.95 (ISBN 0-590-09850-0, Schol Pap). Scholastic Inc.

DEVICES (HERALDRY)

see Heraldry; Symbolism

DEVIL

Garden, Nancy. Devils & Demons. LC 75-44461. (gr. 6 up). 1976. (Lipp Jr Bks); pap. 2.95 (ISBN 0-397-31667-4). HarpC Child Bks.

Leslie, Elsie. Is Satan Real? Bates, Stephen, illus. (gr. k-6). 1987. pap. 4.25 (ISBN 1-55976-153-9). CEF Press.

DEVIL–FICTION

Avi. Devil's Race. LC 84-47636. 160p. (gr. 7 up). 1984. 12.95 (ISBN 0-397-32094-9, Lipp Jr Bks); PLB 12.89 (ISBN 0-397-32095-7, Lipp Jr Bks). HarpC Child Bks.

Babbitt, Natalie. The Devil's Storybook. (Illus.). 102p. (gr. 3-7). 1974. 12.95 (ISBN 0-374-31770-4). FS&G.

Beat the Devil. 118p. (Orig.). (gr. 7-12). 1984. pap. 2.50 (ISBN 0-553-26755-8). Bantam.

Benet, Stephen Vincent. The Devil & Daniel Webster. 48p. (gr. 6). 1990. 10.95s.p. (ISBN 0-88682-295-5); 15.65 (ISBN 0-685-28210-4). Creative Ed.

Carey, Valerie S. The Devil & Mother Crump. Lobel, Arnold, illus. LC 87-64. 40p. (gr. k-3). 1987. 11.95 (ISBN 0-06-020982-8); PLB 11.89 (ISBN 0-06-020983-6). HarpC Child Bks.

Hooks, William H. Mean Jake & the Devils. Zimmer, Dirk, illus. LC 81-65846. 64p. (gr. 3-6). 1981. 8.95 (ISBN 0-8037-5563-5). Dial Bks Young.

Marsh, Carole. The Legend of the Devil's Hoofprints. (Illus., Orig.). (gr. 2 up). 1986. PLB 19.95 (ISBN 1-55609-177-X); pap. 14.95 (ISBN 0-935326-57-X). Gallopade Pub Group.

Silsbee, Peter. The Temptation of Kate. LC 90-1351. 160p. (gr. 6-9). 1990. 13.95 (ISBN 0-02-782761-5, Bradbury Pr). Macmillan Child Grp.

Skurzynski, Gloria. Lost in the Devil's Desert. 96p. (gr. 4-8). 1988. 1.00 (ISBN 0-87406-309-4, 33-15904-4). Willowisp Pr.

Tate, Joan. Ling & the Little Devils. Otto, Svend, illus. (ps-3). 9.95 (ISBN 0-317-61896-2). Viking Penguin.

Zemach, Harve. Duffy & the Devil. Zemach, Margot, illus. LC 72-81491. 40p. (ps up). 1986. pap. 3.95 (ISBN 0-374-41897-7, Sunburst). FS&G.

DEVOTION

see Worship

DIABETES

Aiello, Barbara & Shulman, Jeffrey. A Portrait of Me: Featuring Christine Kontos. (Illus.). 48p. (gr. 3-6). 1989. PLB 12.95 (ISBN 0-941477-05-3). TFC Bks MD.

Almonte, Paul & Desmond, Theresa. Diabetes. LC 90-45745. (Illus.). 48p. (gr. 5-6). 1991. RSBE 10.95 (ISBN 0-89686-604-1, Crestwood Hse). Macmillan Child Grp.

Brackenridge, Betty P. Diabetes One Hundred One--Candy Apples, Log Cabins & You: A Pure & Simple Guide for People Who Use Insulin. Hoel, Donna, ed. LC 89-37754. 120p. (Orig.). 1989. pap. 7.95 (ISBN 0-937721-63-8). DCI Publishing.

Connelly, John P. You're Too Sweet. (gr. 4-9). 1968. 9.95 (ISBN 0-8392-1173-2). Astor-Honor.

Dacquino, V. T. Kiss the Candy Days Good-Bye. LC 82-70324. 160p. (gr. 4-6). 1982. pap. 11.95 (ISBN 0-385-28532-9). Delacorte.

Goodheart, Barbara. Diabetes. (Illus.). 128p. (gr. 9-12). 1990. PLB 12.40 (ISBN 0-531-10882-1). Watts.

Hannah, Valerie. No More Sugar: Autobiographical Fiction. Herrick, George H., ed. Rudestan, Janice & Bloom, Arnoldintro. by. (Orig.). 1987. 8.95x (ISBN 0-941281-51-5); pap. 6.95x (ISBN 0-941281-50-7). V H Pub.

Heegaard, Marge. When a Family Gets Diabetes. (Illus.). 50p. (Orig.). (gr. 1-9). 1990. pap. 6.95 (ISBN 0-937721-75-1). DCI Publishing.

Little, Marjorie. Diabetes. (Illus.). (gr. 6-12). 1991. 18.95 (ISBN 0-7910-0061-3). Chelsea Hse.

Pirner, Connie. Even Little Kids Get Diabetes. Tucker, Kathy, ed. Westcott, Nadine B., illus. 24p. (ps-1). 1990. 10.95 (ISBN 0-8075-2158-2). A Whitman.

Silverstein, Virginia B. Sugar Disease: Diabetes. LC 78-11631. (Illus.). 128p. (gr. 5 up). 12.95 (ISBN 0-685-31433-2, Lipp Jr Bks). HarpC Child Bks.

Tiger, Steven. Diabetes. Reingold, Michael, illus. LC 86-23498. 72p. (gr. 4-8). 1987. lib. bdg. 11.98 (ISBN 0-671-63273-6). Messner.

DIALECTICS

see Logic

DIAMONDS

Rickard, G. Diamonds. (Illus.). 48p. (gr. 5 up). Date not set. PLB 15.93 (ISBN 0-86592-271-3). Rourke Corp.

DIARIES

see Autobiographies

DICKENS, CHARLES, 1812-1870

Collins, David R. Tales for Hard Times: A Story about Charles Dickens. Mataya, David, illus. 64p. (gr. 3-6). 1990. PLB 9.95 (ISBN 0-87614-433-4). Carolrhoda Bks.

Hunter, Nigel. Charles Dickens. (Illus.). 32p. (gr. 7-9). 1990. 11.90 (ISBN 0-531-18242-8). Watts.

Johnson, Spencer. The Value of Imagination: The Story of Charles Dickens. Pileggi, Stephen, illus. LC 77-13947. (gr. k-6). 1977. 9.95 (ISBN 0-916392-15-5, Pub. by Value Communications). Oak Tree Pubns.

Martin, Christopher. Dickens. (Illus.). 112p. (gr. 7 up). 1990. lib. bdg. 18.60 (ISBN 0-86593-016-3); lib. bdg. 13.95s.p. (ISBN 0-685-36352-X). Rourke Corp.

DICKINSON, EMILY, 1830-1886

Barth, Edna. I'm Nobody, Who Are You: The Story of Emily Dickinson. Cuffari, Richard, illus. LC 72-129211. 128p. (gr. 3-6). 1979. 14.95 (ISBN 0-395-28843-6, Clarion). HM.

Olsen, Victoria. Emily Dickinson. Horner, Matina S., intro. by. (Illus.). 112p. (gr. 5 up). 1990. 17.95 (ISBN 1-55546-649-4). Chelsea Hse.

Thayer, Bonita E. Emily Dickinson. (Illus.). 144p. (gr. 10-12). 1990. 13.90 (ISBN 0-531-10658-6). Watts.

DICTATORS

Banyard, Peter. The Rise of the Dictators, Nineteen Twenty to Nineteen Thirty-Nine. LC 86-50274. (Illus.). 64p. (gr. 4-12). 1986. PLB 10.29 (ISBN 0-531-10233-5). Watts.

DIET

see also Beverages; Cookery; Digestion; Food; Vegetarianism; Weight Control

Fobel, Jim. Jim Fobels Diet Feasts. 1990. 24.95 (ISBN 0-385-26001-6). Doubleday.

Kamen, Betty. The Chromium Diet, Supplement & Exercise Strategy: An Easy to Follow Routine for Everyone. Rosenbaum, Michael E., intro. by. (Illus.). 216p. (Orig.). 1990. pap. 9.95 (ISBN 0-944501-03-6). Nutrition Encounter.

Ward, Brian R. Diet & Nutrition. (Illus.). 48p. (gr. 4-12). 1987. PLB 12.40 (ISBN 0-531-10259-9). Watts.

Wolhart, Dayna. Anorexia & Bulimia. LC 88-21553. (Illus.). 48p. (gr. 5-6). 1988. PLB 10.95 (ISBN 0-89686-416-2, Crestwood Hse). Macmillan Child Grp.

DIETETICS

see Diet

DIGESTION

see also Diet; Food; Nutrition

All about Our Bodies, Our Digestion. 14p. (gr. k-6). pap. 3.95 (ISBN 0-89346-297-7). Heian Intl.

Avraham, Regina. The Digestive System. (Illus.). (gr. 5-12). 1989. 18.95 (ISBN 0-7910-0015-X). Chelsea Hse.

Bailey, Donna. All about Digestion. LC 90-41010. (Illus.). 48p. (gr. 2-5). 1990. PLB 15.96 (ISBN 0-8114-2781-1). Steck-V.

Erlanger, Ellen. Eating Disorders: A Question & Answer Book about Anorexia Nervosa & Bulimia Nervosa. LC 87-15311. (gr. 6-10). 1988. 11.95 (ISBN 0-8225-0038-8). Lerner Pubns.

Food & Digestion. 48p. (gr. 5-8). 1988. PLB 12.98 (ISBN 0-382-09704-1); 9.74s.p. (ISBN 0-685-24612-4). Silver Burdett Pr.

Parker, Steve. Eating a Meal: How You Eat, Drink & Digest. (Illus.). 32p. (gr. k-4). 1991. PLB 11.40 (ISBN 0-531-14086-5). Watts.

—Food & Digestion. (ps-3). 1990. PLB 12.90 (ISBN 0-531-14027-X). Watts.

—Food & Digestion. rev. ed. (Illus.). 48p. (gr. 5 up). 1991. pap. 4.95 (ISBN 0-531-24603-5). Watts.

Richardson, Joy. What Happens When You Eat? LC 86-3726. (Illus.). 32p. (gr. 2-3). 1986. PLB 10.95 (ISBN 1-55532-105-4). Gareth Stevens Inc.

Showers, Paul. What Happens to a Hamburger. rev. ed. Rockwell, Anne, illus. LC 84-45343. 32p. (ps-3). 1985. 13.95 (ISBN 0-690-04426-7, Crowell Jr Bks); PLB 13.89 (ISBN 0-690-04427-5, Crowell Jr Bks). HarpC Child Bks.

Ward, Brian. Food & Digestion. LC 82-50057. (Illus.). (gr. 4 up). 1982. PLB 12.40 (ISBN 0-531-04458-0). Watts.

Zim, Herbert S. Your Stomach & Digestive Tract. Martin, Rene, illus. LC 72-6734. 64p. (gr. 3-7). 1973. PLB 12.88 (ISBN 0-688-31838-X, Morrow Jr Bks). Morrow Jr Bks.

DINERS

see Restaurants, Bars, Etc.

DINOSAURS

Alden, Laura. Megalosaurus. Magnuson, Diana, illus. 32p. (gr. k-4). 1990. PLB 11.97 (ISBN 0-89565-629-9). Childs World.

—Ornithomimus. Ching, illus. 32p. (gr. k-4). 1990. PLB 11.97 (ISBN 0-89565-630-2). Childs World.

Aliki. Digging up Dinosaurs. Brandenberg, Aliki, illus. LC 80-2250. 40p. (gr. k-3). 1981. (Crowell Jr Bks); PLB 12.89 (ISBN 0-690-04099-7). HarpC Child Bks.

—Digging up Dinosaurs. rev. ed. Aliki, illus. LC 87-29949. 32p. (ps-3). 1988. 13.95i (ISBN 0-690-04714-2, Crowell Jr Bks); PLB 13.89 (ISBN 0-690-04716-9). HarpC Child Bks.

—Digging up Dinosaurs. rev. ed. Aliki, illus. LC 85-42979. 32p. (gr. k-3). 1988. pap. 4.50 (ISBN 0-06-445078-3, Trophy). HarpC Child Bks.

—Dinosaurs Are Different. Aliki, illus. LC 84-45332. 32p. (ps-3). 1985. 13.95 (ISBN 0-690-04456-9, Crowell Jr Bks); PLB 13.89 (ISBN 0-690-04458-5). HarpC Child Bks.

—Dinosaurs Are Different. Aliki, illus. LC 84-45332. 32p. (ps-3). 1988. incl. cassette 7.95 (ISBN 0-694-00236-4, Trophy); pap. 4.50 (ISBN 0-06-445056-2, Trophy). HarpC Child Bks.

—My Visit to the Dinosaurs. rev. ed. Aliki, illus. LC 85-47538. 32p. (ps-3). 1985. 13.95 (ISBN 0-690-04422-4, Crowell Jr Bks); PLB 13.89 (ISBN 0-690-04423-2). HarpC Child Bks.

—My Visit to the Dinosaurs. 2nd ed. Aliki, illus. LC 85-42748. 32p. (ps-3). 1987. incl. cassette 7.95 (ISBN 0-694-00201-1, Trophy); pap. 4.50 (ISBN 0-06-445020-1, Trophy). HarpC Child Bks.

Andrews, Roy C. In the Days of the Dinosaurs. (Illus.). (gr. 3-5). 1959. (Random Juv). Random.

Armstrong, B. Dinosaurs. 32p. (gr. 1-6). 1988. 3.95 (ISBN 0-88160-160-8, LW 265). Learning Wks.

Arnold, Caroline. Dinosaurs Down Under: And Other Fossils from Australia. Hewett, Richard, photos by. (Illus.). 48p. (gr. 3-7). 1990. 14.95 (ISBN 0-89919-814-7). HM.

Asimov, Isaac. Did Comets Kill the Dinosaurs? LC 87-42590. (Illus.). 32p. (gr. 3-4). 1987. PLB 11.95 (ISBN 1-55532-322-7). Gareth Stevens Inc.

—Did Comets Kill the Dinosaurs? 1990. pap. 4.95 (ISBN 0-440-40347-2, YB). Dell.

—How Did We Find Out about Dinosaurs. LC 72-95793. (gr. 5 up). 1981. PLB 11.85 (ISBN 0-8027-6134-8). Walker & Co.

Attalides, Stephanos. Planet of the Dinosaurs: Adventure Box III. Attalides, Stephanos, illus. 12p. (ps up). 1988. 4.95 (ISBN 0-694-00265-8). HarpC Child Bks.

Barlowe, Dorothea & Barlowe, Sy, illus. Dinosaurs. LC 77-70862. (ps-3). 1977. 7.95 (ISBN 0-394-83538-7, Random Juv). Random.

Barton, Byron. Dinosaurs, Dinosaurs. Barton, Byron, illus. LC 88-22938. 40p. (ps-1). 1989. 7.95 (ISBN 0-694-00269-0, Crowell Jr Bks); PLB 13.89 (ISBN 0-690-04768-1). HarpC Child Bks.

—Dinosaurs, Dinosaurs. Barton, Byron, illus. LC 88-22938. 40p. (ps-1). 1991. 19.95 (ISBN 0-06-020410-9). HarpC Child Bks.

Beaufay, Gabriel. Dinosaurs & Other Extinct Animals. (Illus.). 80p. (gr. 7 up). 1987. pap. 4.95 (ISBN 0-8120-3836-3). Barron.

Benton, M. All about Dinosaurs. 1991. 5.98 (ISBN 0-7924-5494-4). BDD Promo Bk.

Benton, Michael. Giant Book of Dinosaurs. 1988. 5.98 (ISBN 0-8317-2290-8). Smithmark.

Benton, Michael J. The Dinosaur Encyclopedia. Barish, Wendy, ed. Channell, Jim, et al, illus. 192p. (gr. 3-7). 1984. 9.29 (ISBN 0-685-09149-X, Little Simon); pap. 6.95 (ISBN 0-671-51046-0). S&S Trade.

Berger, Melvin. Dinosaurs. 128p. 1990. pap. 2.95 (ISBN 0-380-76052-5, Camelot). Avon.

Berkowitz, Henry. The Dinosaurs: An Educational Coloring Book. Berkowitz, Henry, illus. 32p. (Orig.). (gr. 1-9). 1986. pap. 2.50 (ISBN 0-938059-00-9). Henart Bks.

Boney, Lesley, illus. Dinosaurs. 48p. (gr. k-5). 1988. pap. 2.95 (ISBN 0-8431-2245-5). Price Stern.

Branley, Franklyn M. What Happened to the Dinosaurs? Simont, Marc, illus. LC 88-37626. 32p. (gr. k-3). 1989. 13.95 (ISBN 0-690-04747-9, Crowell Jr Bks); PLB 13.89 (ISBN 0-690-04749-5, Crowell Jr Bks). HarpC Child Bks.

—What Happened to the Dinosaurs? Simont, Marc, illus. LC 88-37626. 32p. (gr. k-4). 1991. pap. 4.50 (ISBN 0-06-445105-4, Trophy). HarpC Child Bks.

British Museum Staff. Dinosaurs & Their Living Relatives. 2nd ed. LC 79-14504. (gr. 7 up). 1986. pap. 9.95 (ISBN 0-521-26970-9). Cambridge U Pr.

Burkle, Diane, et al. Big Fearon Book of Dinosaurs. (gr. 1-3). 1989. pap. 11.95 (ISBN 0-8224-0698-5). Fearon Teach Aids.

Butler, Lollie. Erni Cabat's Magical World of Prehistoric Animals. Cabat, Erni, illus. LC 89-84487. 64p. (ps-6). 1989. 16.95 (ISBN 0-925263-02-8). Great Impressions.

Carroll, Susan. How Big Is a Brachiosaurus? Marvin, Frederic, illus. 32p. (ps-2). 1986. pap. 1.95 (ISBN 0-448-19077-X, G&D). Putnam Pub Group.

Chenel, Pascale. Life & Death of Dinosaurs. (Illus.). 80p. (gr. 7 up). 1987. pap. 4.95 (ISBN 0-8120-3840-1). Barron.

Clark, Mary. Dinosaurios: Dinosaurs. Kratky, Lada, tr. from ENG. (SPA., Illus.). 48p. (gr. k-4). 1984. lib. bdg. 13.27 (ISBN 0-516-31612-5); pap. 4.95 (ISBN 0-516-51612-4). Childrens.

Clark, Mary L. Dinosaurs. LC 81-7750. (Illus.). 48p. (gr. k-4). 1981. PLB 14.60 (ISBN 0-516-01612-1); pap. 4.95 (ISBN 0-516-41612-X). Childrens.

Cobb, Vicki. The Monsters Who Died: A Mystery about Dinosaurs. Wenzel, Greg, illus. 64p. (gr. 3-6). 1983. 10.95 (ISBN 0-698-20571-5, Coward). Putnam Pub Group.

Cole, Joanna. Dinosaur Story. Kunstler, Mort, illus. LC 74-5931. 32p. (gr. k-3). 1974. PLB 13.88 (ISBN 0-688-31826-6). Morrow Jr Bks.

Cosner, Shaaron. Dinosaur Dinners. (Illus.). 48p. (gr. 2-4). 1991. PLB 11.90 (ISBN 0-531-20011-6). Watts.

Cowley, Stuart. Quality Time Little Readers: Amazing Dinosaurs. 1991. 1.49 (ISBN 0-8317-7265-4). Smithmark.

Craig, M. Jean. Dinosaurs & More Dinosaurs. Solonevich, George, illus. LC 68-27276. (gr. k-3). 1973. pap. 2.95 (ISBN 0-590-41032-6). Scholastic Inc.

Cremins, Robert. Pop up Baby Brontosaurus. Dudley, Dick, contrib. by. LC 89-31318. (ps-3). 1989. 2.95 (ISBN 0-8037-0726-6). Dial Bks Young.

—Pop up Baby Coelophysis. Dudley, Dick, contrib. by. LC 89-31323. (ps-3). 1989. 2.95 (ISBN 0-8037-0735-5). Dial Bks Young.

—Pop up Baby Pteranodon. Dudley, Dick, contrib. by. LC 89-31320. (ps-3). 1989. 2.95 (ISBN 0-8037-0732-0). Dial Bks Young.

—Pop up Baby Stegosaurus. Dudley, Dick, contrib. by. LC 89-31319. (ps-3). 1989. 2.95 (ISBN 0-8037-0733-9). Dial Bks Young.

—Pop up Baby Triceratops. Dudley, Dick, contrib. by. LC 89-31321. (ps-3). 1989. 2.95 (ISBN 0-8037-0734-7). Dial Bks Young.

—Pop up Baby Tyrannosaurs Rex. Dudley, Dick, contrib. by. LC 89-31322. (ps-3). 1989. 2.95 (ISBN 0-8037-0731-2). Dial Bks Young.

Crenson, Victoria. Discovering Dinosaurs: An Up-to-Date Guide Including the Newest Theories. Walters, Bob & Seward, James, illus. 64p. (gr. 4-8). 1988. 8.95 (ISBN 0-8431-2221-8). Price Stern.

Crump, Donald J., ed. Dinosaur Babies, Bk. 1 of 2. (Illus.). (ps-3). 1991. Set. 19.95 (ISBN 0-317-99619-3). Natl Geog.

—Dinosaurs: Creatures of Long Ago. (Illus.). (ps-5). 1988. Set. 19.95 (ISBN 0-685-31759-5). Natl Geog.

Cutting, Brian & Cutting, Jillian. Dinosaurs. Fowler, Jeff, illus. 16p. (Orig.). (gr. k-2). 1988. pap. text ed. 23.00 (ISBN 1-55911-031-7). Wright Group.

—Dinosaurs, 6 bks. Fowler, Jeff, illus. 16p. (Orig.). (gr. k-2). 1988. Set. pap. text ed. 19.80 (ISBN 1-55911-032-5). Wright Group.

Cutts, David. More about Dinosaurs. Wenzel, Gregory C., illus. LC 81-11432. 32p. (gr. k-2). 1982. PLB 10.89 (ISBN 0-89375-668-7); pap. text ed. 2.95 (ISBN 0-89375-669-5). Troll Assocs.

Davidow-Goodman, Ann. Let's Draw Dinosaurs. Davidow-Goodman, Ann, illus. LC 77-94034. (gr. 1-6). 1978. pap. 2.95 (ISBN 0-448-14990-7, G&D). Putnam Pub Group.

Davidson, Rosalie. Dinosaurs from A to Z. LC 83-7231. (Illus.). 56p. (gr. 3-6). 1983. PLB 16.60 (ISBN 0-516-00516-2). Childrens.

Dimond, Jasper. Dinosaurs. Dimond, Jasper, illus. 48p. (gr. 3-7). 1985. pap. 10.95 (ISBN 0-13-214628-2). P-H.

Dino-Mite. (Illus.). 24p. (Orig.). (gr. 1-5). 1989. pap. 5.95 (ISBN 0-8431-3155-1); Super Q Wand 11.00 (ISBN 0-318-39948-2). Price Stern.

Dinosaur Habitats. (ps-5). 1989. 19.95 (ISBN 0-698-13013-8, Playland Bks). Putnam Pub Group.

The Dinosaur Hunter's Kit. 64p. (Orig.). (gr. 2 up). 1990. pap. 14.95 pkg. with bk. (ISBN 0-89471-804-5). Running Pr.

Dinosaur Poster Book. (Illus.). 48p. (Orig.). 1990. pap. 9.98 (ISBN 0-89471-794-4, Courage Bks). Running Pr.

Dinosaurs. (Illus.). 32p. (ps-6). 1983. pap. 29.50 per set of 10 (ISBN 0-87474-331-1, DICBP). Smithsonian.

Dinosaurs. (Illus.). 32p. (ps up). 1986. 2.95 (ISBN 0-8431-4286-3). Price Stern.

Dinosaurs. (Illus.). 88p. (ps-3). 1989. 15.93 (ISBN 0-8094-4889-0); lib. bdg. 21.27 (ISBN 0-8094-4890-4). Time-Life.

Dinosaurs. 24p. (ps-2). 1989. pap. 1.29 (ISBN 0-02-898254-1). Checkerboard Pr.

Dinosaurs. (Illus.). 20p. (gr. k up). 1990. laminated, wipe clean surface 3.95 (ISBN 0-88679-821-3). Educ Insights.

Dinosaurs. (Illus.). 16p. (gr. k up). 1990. laminated, wipe clean surface 9.95 (ISBN 0-88679-661-X). Educ Insights.

Dinosaurs. (Illus.). (ps-3). 1.95 (ISBN 0-7214-5187-X). Ladybird Bks.

Dinosaurs. (gr. 1-4). 1991. pap. 3.95 (ISBN 0-7214-5319-8). Ladybird Bks.

Dinosaurs. (Illus.). 32p. (gr. 1-6). 1987. 0.50 (ISBN 0-87406-060-5, 46-10821-4). Willowisp Pr.

Dinosaurs-Coloring Book. 1985. pap. 1.50 (ISBN 0-88388-084-9). Bellerophon Bks.

Dinosaurs Pack, No. 484. (Illus.). (ps-k). incl. chart & activity bk. 6.95 (ISBN 0-7214-5136-5). Ladybird Bks.

Dinsmore, Mark. What Really Happened to the Dinosaurs? (Illus.). 24p. (ps-2). 1988. pap. 5.95 (ISBN 0-89051-142-X). Master Bks.

Dixon, Dougal. Be a Dinosaur Detective. Lings, Steve, illus. 36p. (gr. k-4). 1988. 13.95 (ISBN 0-8225-0894-X); pap. 4.95 (ISBN 0-8225-9538-9). Lerner Pubns.

—The First Dinosaurs. Burton, Jane, illus. LC 87-6460. 32p. (gr. 2-3). 1987. PLB 10.95 (ISBN 1-55532-258-1). Gareth Stevens Inc.

—The First Dinosaurs. (Orig.). 1990. pap. 4.95 (ISBN 0-440-40373-1, Pub. by Yearling Classics). Dell.

—Hunting the Dinosaurs. Burton, Jane, illus. LC 87-6461. 32p. (gr. 2-3). 1987. PLB 10.95 (ISBN 1-55532-259-X). Gareth Stevens Inc.

—The Jurassic Dinosaurs. Burton, Jane, illus. LC 87-6462. 32p. (gr. 2-3). 1987. PLB 10.95 (ISBN 1-55532-260-3). Gareth Stevens Inc.

—The Last Dinosaurs. Burton, Jane, illus. LC 87-6463. 32p. (gr. 2-3). 1987. PLB 10.95 (ISBN 1-55532-261-1). Gareth Stevens Inc.

—The Last Dinosaurs. (Orig.). 1990. pap. 4.95 (ISBN 0-440-40377-4, Pub. by Yearling Classics). Dell.

—The Last of the Dinosaurs. Burton, Jane, photos by. LC 89-11335. (Illus.). 32p. (gr. 1-2). 1989. PLB 10.95 (ISBN 0-8368-0153-9). Gareth Stevens Inc.

—Learning about the Dinosaurs. Burton, Jane, photos by. LC 89-4544. (Illus.). 32p. (gr. 1-2). 1989. PLB 10.95 (ISBN 0-8368-0150-4). Gareth Stevens Inc.

—The Very First Dinosaurs. Burton, Jane, photos by. LC 89-11336. (Illus.). 32p. (gr. 1-2). 1989. PLB 10.95 (ISBN 0-8368-0151-2). Gareth Stevens Inc.

—When Dinosaurs Ruled the Earth. Burton, Jane, photos by. LC 89-11337. (Illus.). 32p. (gr. 1-2). 1989. PLB 10.95 (ISBN 0-8368-0152-0). Gareth Stevens Inc.

Dixon, Douglas. Hunting the Dinosaurs. (Orig.). 1990. pap. 4.95 (ISBN 0-440-40372-3, Pub. by Yearling Classics). Dell.

—The Jurassic Dinosaurs. (Orig.). 1990. pap. 4.95 (ISBN 0-440-40375-8, Pub. by Yearling Classics). Dell.

—My First Dinosaur Library, 4 vols. Burton, Jane, illus. (gr. 1-2). 1989. Set. PLB 43.80 (ISBN 0-8368-0149-0). Gareth Stevens Inc.

—The New Dinosaur Library, 4 vols. Burton, Jene, illus. 128p. (gr. 2-3). 1988. Set. PLB 43.80 (ISBN 1-55532-262-X). Gareth Stevens Inc.

Duffee, Dan. A Look Around Dinosaurs. Acosta, Andre, illus. 32p. (Orig.). (gr. 1-4). 1988. pap. 2.50 (ISBN 0-87406-259-4). Willowisp Pr.

Durrell, Gerald. The Fantastic Dinosaur Adventure. Percy, Graham, illus. LC 89-49099. 96p. (gr. 2-5). 1990. PLB 16.95 (ISBN 0-671-70871-6). S&S Trade.

Earthbooks, Inc. Staff. The National Wildlife Federation's Book of Dinosaurs & Other Pre-Historic Animals. Aaestas, Ken, illus. 64p. (Orig.). (gr. 4). 1991. pap. 5.95 (ISBN 1-877731-16-1). Earthbooks Inc.

Eldridge, David. Flying Dragons, Ancient Reptiles That Ruled the Air. Nodel, Norman, illus. LC 79-87965. 32p. (gr. 3-6). 1980. PLB 10.79 (ISBN 0-89375-241-X); pap. 2.95 (ISBN 0-89375-245-2). Troll Assocs.

—The Giant Dinosaurs, Ancient Reptiles That Ruled the Land. Nodel, Norman, illus. LC 79-87967. 32p. (gr. 3-6). 1980. PLB 10.79 (ISBN 0-89375-242-8); pap. 2.95 (ISBN 0-89375-246-0). Troll Assocs.

—Last of the Dinosaurs, the End of an Age. Nodel, Norman, illus. LC 79-64636. 32p. (gr. 3-6). 1980. PLB 10.79 (ISBN 0-89375-243-6); pap. 2.95 (ISBN 0-89375-247-9). Troll Assocs.

Elting, Mary. The Big Golden Book of Dinosaurs. Santoro, Christopher, illus. LC 87-81784. 64p. (gr. 3-6). pap. text ed. write for info. (ISBN 0-307-15567-6, Golden Pr). Western Pub.

—Dinosaurs. Nenzioni, Gabrielle & Cutrona, Mauro, illus. 24p. (ps-3). 1988. pap. write for info. (ISBN 0-307-11912-2, Pub. by Golden Bks). Western Pub.

—Macmillan Book of Dinosaurs & Other Prehistoric Creatures. Hamberger, John, illus. LC 84-4372. 80p. (gr. 2-7). 1984. 15.95 (ISBN 0-02-733430-9, Mcmillan Child Bk). Macmillan Child Grp.

—The Macmillan Book of Dinosaurs & Other Prehistoric Creatures. LC 84-4944. (Illus.). 80p. (gr. 3-7). 1984. pap. 8.95 (ISBN 0-02-043000-0, Aladdin). Macmillan Child Grp.

Elting, Mary & Goodman, Ann. Dinosaur Mysteries. Swan, Susan, illus. LC 79-55035. 64p. (gr. 1-7). 1980. 9.95 (ISBN 0-448-47487-5, G&D); pap. 5.95 (ISBN 0-448-19216-0). Putnam Pub Group.

Emberley, Michael. Dinosaurs! A Drawing Book. Emberley, Michael, illus. 48p. (gr. 3 up). 1985. pap. 4.95 (ISBN 0-316-23631-4). Little.

—Dinosaurs!, Vol. 1: A Drawing Book. 1980. 12.95 (ISBN 0-316-23417-6). Little.

—More Dinosaurs! And Other Prehistoric Beasts. Emberley, Michael, illus. LC 83-9822. 64p. (gr. 3 up). 1983. 13.95 (ISBN 0-316-23424-9). Little.

Farlow, James O. On the Track of Dinosaurs: A Study of Dinosaur Footprints. Tischler, Doris, illus. 64p. (gr. 4-6). 1991. 14.95 (ISBN 0-531-15220-0); PLB 14.90 (ISBN 0-531-10991-7). Watts.

Four Famous Dinosaurs. 32p. (Orig.). (gr. 1-3). 1988. pap. 2.95 (ISBN 0-8431-4324-X). Price Stern.

Freedman, Russell. Dinosaurs & Their Young. Morrill, Leslie, illus. LC 83-6160. 32p. (gr. 1-4). 1983. reinforced bdg. 14.95 (ISBN 0-8234-0496-X). Holiday.

Fuchshuber, Annegert. From Dinosaurs to Fossils. Fuchshuber, Annegert, illus. LC 80-28596. 24p. (ps-3). 1981. PLB 6.95 (ISBN 0-87614-152-1). Carolrhoda Bks.

Gabriele, Joseph. The First Days of the Dinosaurs: Text Edition. Hurst, Marageret, illus. 32p. (Orig.). (gr. 1-3). pap. 1.95 (ISBN 0-911211-55-1, Pub. by Know & Show Bks). Penny Lane Pubns.

—The Great Age of the Dinosaurs. Hurst, Margaret, illus. 32p. (Orig.). (gr. 1-3). 1985. pap. text ed. 1.95 (ISBN 0-911211-56-X, Pub. by Know & Show Bks). Penny Lane Pubns.

—The Last Days of the Dinosaurs: Text Editions. Hurst, Maragaret, illus. 32p. (Orig.). (gr. 1-3). 1985. pap. 1.95 (ISBN 0-911211-57-8, Pub. by Know & Show Bks). Penny Lane Pubns.

Gamiello, Elvira. Dinosaurs Trivia Fun Book. (Illus.). 32p. (Orig.). 1989. pap. 1.50 (ISBN 0-942025-09-1). Kidsbks.

—Giant Word Find Dinosaurs Poster Book. (Illus., Orig.). 1988. pap. 1.95 (ISBN 0-942025-49-0). Kidsbks.

Gay, Tanner O. Dinosaurs & Their Relatives in Action. Cassels, Jean, illus. 16p. (ps-3). 1990. pap. 6.95 (ISBN 0-689-71434-3, Aladdin). Macmillan Child Grp.

Geis, Darlene. Dinosaurs. Shannon, Kenyon, illus. (Orig.). (gr. 4-6). 1960. pap. 2.95 (ISBN 0-8431-4250-2). Wonder.

Gela, Darlene. Dinosaurs & Other Prehistoric Animals. Peterson, Russell F., illus. 108p. (gr. 3-8). 1982. 8.95 (ISBN 0-448-02882-4, G&D). Putnam Pub Group.

Gerver, Jane, ed. Day of the Dinosaur. McCarthy, Kathleen, et al, illus. 32p. (gr. k-3). 1986. wkbk. 3.95 (ISBN 0-394-88169-9). Random.

Gibbons, Gail. Dinosaurs. Gibbons, Gail, illus. LC 87-364. 32p. (ps-3). 1987. 14.95g (ISBN 0-8234-0657-1); pap. 5.95 (ISBN 0-8234-0708-X). Holiday.

Gillette, Lynett. Dinosaur Diary: My Triassic Homeland. Larkin, Catherine, illus. 32p. (gr. 4). 1988. pap. 2.95 (ISBN 0-945695-00-4). Petrified Forest Mus Assn.

Glut, D. F. The Dinosaur Dictionary. Romer, A. S. & Techter, D.intro. by. (Illus.). (gr. 2-6). 1985. pap. 5.98 (ISBN 0-517-45589-7). Outlet Bk Co.

Glut, Donald F. The Dinosaur Dictionary. Romer, Alfred S., intro. by. (gr. 9 up). 1972. 12.50 (ISBN 0-8065-0283-5, Pub. by Citadel Pr). Carol Pub Group.

Granger, Judith. Amazing World of Dinosaurs. Baldwin-Ford, Pamela, illus. LC 81-7476. 32p. (gr. 2-4). 1982. PLB 10.89 (ISBN 0-89375-562-1); pap. text ed. 2.95 (ISBN 0-89375-563-X). Troll Assocs.

Greenberg, Judith E. & Carey, Helen H. Dinosaurs. Birmingham, Lloyd, illus. 32p. (gr. 2-4). 1990. PLB 16.67 (ISBN 0-8172-3751-8). Raintree Pubs.

Halstead, L. B. & Halstead, Jenny. Dinosaurs. LC 87-15142. (Illus.). 170p. (gr. 9 up). 1987. pap. 3.95 (ISBN 0-8069-6626-2). Sterling.

Harvey, Anthony. The World of the Dinosaurs. LC 79-5065. (Illus.). 36p. (gr. 3-6). 1980. PLB 8.95 (ISBN 0-8225-1187-8, First Ave Edns); pap. 4.95 (ISBN 0-8225-9511-7, First Ave Edns). Lerner Pubns.

Haynes, Max. Dinosaur Island. LC 90-48148. (Illus.). 32p. (ps up). 1991. 13.95 (ISBN 0-688-10329-4); PLB 13.88 (ISBN 0-688-10330-8). Lothrop.

Heck, Joseph. Dinosaur Riddles. Barish, Wendy, ed. Hoffman, Sandy, illus. 128p. (gr. 3-7). 1982. pap. 3.80 (ISBN 0-671-45547-8, Little Simon); 9.29 (ISBN 0-685-05613-9). S&S Trade.

Hincks, J. The Rourke Dinosaur Dictionary. (Illus.). 96p. (gr. k-8). Date not set. PLB 26.60 (ISBN 0-86592-049-4). Rourke Corp.

Hopkins, Lee B. Dinosaurs. Tinkleman, Murray, illus. (gr. k up). 1987. 12.95 (ISBN 0-15-223495-0). HarBraceJ.

—Dinosaurs. 1990. pap. 4.95 (ISBN 0-15-223496-9, VoyB). HarbraceJ.

Howard, John. I Can Read About Dinosaurs. (Illus.). (gr. 2-4). 1972. pap. 1.95 (ISBN 0-89375-051-4). Troll Assocs.

Ingoglia, Gina. Let's Look at Dinosaurs. (Illus.). 16p. (ps-1). 1991. bds. 10.95 (ISBN 0-448-40086-3, G&D). Putnam Pub Group.

Jacobs, Francine. Supersaurus. Tyler, D. D., illus. 48p. 1982. 6.99 (ISBN 0-399-61150-9, Putnam). Putnam Pub Group.

Keen, Martin L. Prehistoric Mammals. Hull, John, illus. (gr. 4-6). pap. 2.95 (ISBN 0-8431-4255-3). Wonder.

Knight, David C. The Battle of the Dinosaurs. Ames, Lee J., illus. 96p. (gr. 3-7). 1982. (Pub. by Treehouse); pap. 5.95 (ISBN 0-13-069518-1). P-H.

—Dinosaurs That Swam & Flew. Ames, Lee J., illus. LC 84-24787. 64p. (gr. 3-7). 1986. PLB 11.95 (ISBN 0-671-66292-9). S&S Trade.

Kricher, John C. Peterson First Guide to Dinosaurs. Morrison, Gordon, illus. Peterson, Roger T., frwd. by. (Illus.). 128p. 1990. pap. 4.95 (ISBN 0-395-52440-7). HM.

Kurokawa, Mitsuhiro. The Great Big Book of Dinosaurs. Kurokawa, Mitsuhiro, illus. Obata, Ikuo, contrib. by. LC 88-24779. (Illus.). 32p. (gr. 4-5). 1989. PLB 15.95 (ISBN 0-8368-0000-1). Gareth Stevens Inc.

—The Great Dinosaur Timescape. Strigens, Jerry, illus. (gr. 4-5). 1989. PLB 14.95 (ISBN 0-8368-0001-X). Gareth Stevens Inc.

Lambert, David. Dinosaurs. (ps-3). 1990. PLB 10.90 (ISBN 0-531-19070-6). Watts.

Lambert, David & Halstead, L. B. Dinosaurs. LC 82-9020. (Illus.). 32p. (gr. 2-4). 1982. PLB 10.90 (ISBN 0-531-04371-1). Watts.

Lammers, George E. Dinosaurs. Thorsteinson, Betsy, illus. 40p. (Orig.). (gr. 2-6). 1990. pap. 4.95 (ISBN 0-920534-47-3, Pub. by Hyperion Pr Ltd CN). Sterling.

Lampton, Christopher. Dinosaurs & the Age of Reptiles. (Illus.). 96p. (gr. 4 up). 1983. PLB 10.40 (ISBN 0-531-04526-9). Watts.

—Mass Extinctions: One Theory of Why the Dinosaurs Vanished. (Illus.). 96p. (gr. 7-12). 1986. PLB 12.90 (ISBN 0-531-10238-6). Watts.

—New Theories on the Dinosaurs. (Illus.). 144p. (gr. 7-12). 1989. PLB 13.40 (ISBN 0-531-10781-7). Watts.

Lapp, Rhoda S. God Answers Prayer. (Illus.). 19p. (Orig.). 1989. pap. write for info. R S Lapp.

Latta, Rich. Dinosaur Mazes. 48p. 1990. pap. 2.95 (ISBN 0-8431-2822-4). Price Stern.

Little People Big Book About Dinosaurs. 64p. (ps-1). 1989. write for info. (ISBN 0-8094-7466-2); PLB write for info. (ISBN 0-8094-7467-0). Time-Life.

Long, Robert A. & Welles, Samuel P. All New Dinosaurs. (gr. 7 up). 1975. pap. 3.50 (ISBN 0-88388-031-8). Bellerophon Bks.

McCord. Dinosaurs. (gr. 4-6). 1977. (Usborne-Hayes); PLB 13.96 (ISBN 0-88110-119-2); pap. 6.95 (ISBN 0-86020-126-0). EDC.

McGowen, Tom. Album of Dinosaurs. Ruth, Rod, illus. LC 74-188730. 64p. (gr. 3-12). 1972. write for info. (ISBN 0-528-82024-9). Checkerboard Pr.

—Album of Dinosaurs. Ruth, Rod, illus. 64p. (gr. 3-7). 1987. pap. 4.95 (ISBN 0-02-688500-X). Checkerboard Pr.

McMullan, Kate. Dinosaur Hunters. Jones, John R., illus. LC 88-30742. 48p. (Orig.). (gr. 2-4). 1989. PLB 6.99 (ISBN 0-394-91150-4); pap. 2.95 (ISBN 0-394-81150-X). Random.

Mansell, Dom. Dinosaurs Came to Town. (ps-3). 1991. 12.95 (ISBN 0-316-54584-8). Little.

Minelli, Giuseppe. Dinosaurs & Birds. (Illus.). 64p. 1988. 15.95 (ISBN 0-8160-1559-7). Facts on File.

Moncure, Jane B. Dinosaurs: Back in Time. Hohag, Linda, illus. LC 89-38469. 32p. (ps-2). 1990. lib. bdg. 11.97 (ISBN 0-89565-550-0). Childs World.

Morris, Dean. Dinosaurs & Other First Animal. (ps-3). 1990. pap. 11.99 (ISBN 0-8172-3231-1). Raintree Pubs.

—Dinosaurs & Other First Animals. LC 87-16670. (Illus.). 48p. (gr. 2-6). 1987. PLB 17.32 (ISBN 0-8172-3206-0). Raintree Pubs.

Moseley, Keith. Dinosaurs: A Lost World. Cremins, Robert, illus. 18p. (gr. k-4). 1984. 13.95 (ISBN 0-399-21063-6, Putnam). Putnam Pub Group.

Most, Bernard. Dinosaur Cousins? LC 86-18485. (Illus.). 40p. (gr. k-3). 1987. 13.95 (ISBN 0-15-223497-7, HJ). HarBraceJ.

—A Dinosaur Named after Me. D'Andrade, Diane, ed. Most, Bernard, illus. 32p. (ps-3). 1991. 12.95 (ISBN 0-15-223494-2). HarBraceJ.

—The Littlest Dinosaurs. Most, Bernard, illus. (ps-3). 1989. 12.95 (ISBN 0-15-248125-7). HarBraceJ.

Muller, Carrel & Jacques, Ethel M. Dinosaur Discovery. Muller, Carrel, illus. 32p. (gr. 4-6). 1987. wkbk. 3.75 (ISBN 0-915785-02-1). Bonjour Books.

Neilson, Gena, illus. Dinosaurs. (ps-1). 1986. spiral bdg. 9.95 (ISBN 0-937763-00-4). Lauri Inc.

Nemes, Claire. A Picture Book of Dinosaurs. Kinnealy, Janice, illus. LC 89-37331. 24p. (gr. 1-4). 1990. lib. bdg. 9.59 (ISBN 0-8167-1900-4); pap. text ed. 2.50 (ISBN 0-8167-1901-2). Troll Assocs.

Norell, Mark. All You Need to Know about Dinosaurs. LC 91-21701. (Illus.). 96p. (gr. 2-9). 1991. 12.95 (ISBN 0-8069-8396-5). Sterling.

Norman, David. The Age of Dinosaurs. (Illus.). 32p. (gr. k-6). 1986. lib. bdg. 8.99 (ISBN 0-531-18051-4, Pub. by Bookwright Pr). Watts.

—When Dinosaurs Ruled the Earth. 1985. 6.98 (ISBN 0-671-07522-5). S&S Trade.

Norman, David & Miller, Angela. Dinosaur. Keates, Colin, illus. LC 88-27167. 64p. (gr. 5 up). 1989. 15.00 (ISBN 0-394-82253-6); PLB 14.99 (ISBN 0-394-92253-0). Knopf.

O'Neill, Mary. Dinosaur Mysteries. Bindon, John, illus. LC 89-4789. 32p. (gr. 3-7). 1989. lib. bdg. 12.89 (ISBN 0-8167-1635-8); pap. text ed. 3.95 (ISBN 0-8167-1636-6). Troll Assocs.

—A Family of Dinosaurs. Bindon, John, illus. LC 89-4792. 32p. (gr. 3-7). 1989. lib. bdg. 12.89 (ISBN 0-8167-1633-1); pap. text ed. 3.95 (ISBN 0-8167-1634-X). Troll Assocs.

—Where Are All the Dinosaurs? Bindon, John, illus. LC 89-31165. 32p. (gr. 2-6). 1989. lib. bdg. 12.89 (ISBN 0-8167-1637-4); pap. text ed. 3.95 (ISBN 0-8167-1638-2). Troll Assocs.

Osband, Gillian. The Dinosaur Fun Book. Allen, Jonathan, illus. 32p. (gr. k-3). 1987. pap. 2.50 (ISBN 0-590-40887-9). Scholastic Inc.

Packard, Ann & Stafford, Shirley. Time of the Dinosaurs. 92p. (ps-3). 1981. write for info. (ISBN 0-9607580-1-1). S Stafford.

Packard, Mary. Dinosaurs. Santoro, Chris, illus. 48p. (ps-3). 1981. pap. 8.95 (ISBN 0-671-43040-8, Little Simon). S&S Trade.

Paint, Box Books. Dinosaurs & Their Babies. 1989. pap. 0.71 (ISBN 0-394-82279-X). Random.

Parish, Peggy. Dinosaur Time. Lobel, Arnold, illus. LC 73-14331. 32p. (gr. k-3). 1974. 10.95 (ISBN 0-06-024653-7); PLB 10.89 (ISBN 0-06-024654-5). HarpC Child Bks.

—Dinosaur Time. Lobel, Arnold, illus. LC 73-14331. 32p. (ps-2). 1983. pap. 2.95 (ISBN 0-06-444037-0, Trophy). HarpC Child Bks.

Parker, Steve. Dinosaurs & Their World. (Illus.). 64p. (gr. 2-6). 1988. 7.95 (ISBN 0-448-19217-9, G&D). Putnam Pub Group.

Pearce, Q. L. All about Dinosaurs. Boney, Leslie, illus. (gr. 2 up). 1989. pap. 7.95 (ISBN 0-671-64517-X, Little Simon). S&S Trade.

—Tyrannosaurus Rex & Other Dinosaur Wonders. Fraser, Mary A., illus. 64p. (gr. 4-6). 1990. PLB 12.98 (ISBN 0-671-70687-X); pap. 5.95 (ISBN 0-671-70688-8). Messner.

Penn, Linda. Young Scientist Explore: Dinosaurs. Kasper, Karan, illus. 32p. (gr. k-3). 1985. wkbk. 4.95 (ISBN 0-86653-313-3, GA 652). Good Apple.

Peters, David. A Gallery of Dinosaurs & Other Early Reptiles. Peters, David, illus. LC 88-36400. 64p. (gr. 3 up). 1989. 14.95 (ISBN 0-394-89982-2); lib. bdg. 14.99 (ISBN 0-394-99982-7). Knopf.

Petersen, David. Apatosaurus. LC 88-37654. (Illus.). 48p. (gr. k-4). 1989. PLB 14.60 (ISBN 0-516-01159-6); pap. 4.95 (ISBN 0-516-41159-4). Childrens.

—Tyrannosaurus Rex. LC 88-38054. (Illus.). 48p. (gr. k-4). 1989. PLB 14.60 (ISBN 0-516-01167-7); pap. 4.95 (ISBN 0-516-41167-5). Childrens.

Petty, Kate. Finding Out about Dinosaurs. (Illus.). 32p. (gr. k-3). 1988. 0.50 (ISBN 0-87406-324-8). Willowisp Pr.

Polisar, Barry L. Dinosaurs I Have Known. Stewart, Michael, illus. 48p. (Orig.). (gr. 2-6). 1988. 9.95 (ISBN 0-938663-00-3); pap. 7.95 (ISBN 0-938663-05-4). Rainbow Morn.

Quinn, Kaye. World of the Dinosaurs. Quinn, Kaye, illus. 40p. (gr. 2-4). 1987. pap. 2.50 (ISBN 0-8431-1890-3). Price Stern.

Radlauer, Edward. Dinosaur Mania. Butler, Mary, illus. LC 78-23914. 32p. (gr. k-6). 1979. PLB 14.60 (ISBN 0-516-07470-9, Elk Grove Bks); pap. 3.95 (ISBN 0-516-47470-7). Childrens.

Raham, R. Gary. Sillysaurs: Dinosaurs That Could Have Been. Raham, R. Gary, illus. 16p. (Orig.). (gr. k-4). 1990. write for info. saddle-stitched (ISBN 0-9626301-0-1). Biostration.

Riehecky, Janet. Allosaurus. Hunter, Llyn, illus. LC 88-1693. 32p. (gr. k-4). 1988. PLB 11.97 (ISBN 0-89565-421-0); pap. 5.95 (ISBN 0-89565-490-3). Childs World.

—Anatosaurus. Magnuson, Diana, illus. 32p. (gr. k-4). 1989. lib. bdg. 11.97 (ISBN 0-89565-545-4); pap. 5.95 (ISBN 0-89565-549-7). Childs World.

—Ankylosaurus. Magnuson, Diana, illus. 32p. (gr. k-4). 1990. PLB 11.97 (ISBN 0-89565-621-3). Childs World.

—Ankylosaurus. Magnuson, Diana, illus. 32p. (gr. k-4). 1990. PLB 11.97 (ISBN 0-89565-621-3). Childs World.

—Apatosaurus. Halverson, Lydia, illus. LC 88-1694. 32p. (gr. k-4). 1988. PLB 11.97 (ISBN 0-89565-423-7). Childs World.

—Baryonyx. Conaway, Jim, illus. 32p. (gr. k-4). 1990. PLB 11.97 (ISBN 0-89565-622-1). Childs World.

—Brachiosaurus. Conaway, James, illus. LC 89-22069. 32p. 1989. lib. bdg. 11.97 (ISBN 0-89565-542-X); pap. 6.96 (ISBN 0-89565-546-2). Childs World.

—Coelophysis. Halverson, Lydia, illus. 32p. (gr. k-4). 1990. PLB 11.97 (ISBN 0-89565-623-X). Childs World.

—Compsogathus. Lexa-Senning, Susan, illus. 32p. (gr. k-4). 1990. PLB 11.97 (ISBN 0-89565-624-8). Childs World.

—Compsogathus. Lexa-Senning, Susan, illus. 32p. (gr. k-4). 1990. PLB 11.97 (ISBN 0-89565-624-8). Childs World.

—Deinonychus. Hunter, Llyn, illus. 32p. (gr. k-4). 1990. PLB 10.95 (ISBN 0-89565-625-6). Childs World.

—Dinosaur Relatives. Magnuson, Diana, illus. 32p. (gr. k-4). 1990. lib. bdg. 11.97 (ISBN 0-89565-626-4); pap. text ed. 6.96 (ISBN 0-89565-643-4). Childs World.

—Dinosaur Relatives. Magnuson, Diana, illus. 32p. (gr. k-4). 1990. lib. bdg. 11.97 (ISBN 0-89565-626-4); pap. text ed. 6.96 (ISBN 0-89565-643-4). Childs World.

—Diplodocus. Conaway, Jim, illus. 32p. (gr. k-4). 1990. PLB 11.97 (ISBN 0-89565-627-2). Childs World.

—Discovering Dinosaurs. Endres, Helen, illus. 32p. (gr. k-4). 1990. PLB 11.97 (ISBN 0-89565-620-5). Childs World.

—Discovering Dinosaurs. Endres, Helen, illus. 32p. (gr. k-4). 1990. PLB 11.97 (ISBN 0-89565-620-5). Childs World.

—Hypsilophodon. Ching, illus. 32p. (gr. k-4). 1990. PLB 11.97 (ISBN 0-89565-628-0). Childs World.

—Hypsilophodon. Ching, illus. 32p. (gr. k-4). 1990. PLB 11.97 (ISBN 0-89565-628-0). Childs World.

—Iguanodon. Magnuson, Diana, illus. LC 89-15850. 32p. (gr. k-4). 1989. lib. bdg. 11.97 (ISBN 0-89565-544-6); pap. 6.96 (ISBN 0-89565-548-9). Childs World.

—Maiasaura. Magnuson, Diana, illus. LC 89-22076. 32p. (gr. k-4). 1989. lib. bdg. 11.97 (ISBN 0-89565-543-8); pap. 6.96 (ISBN 0-89565-547-0). Childs World.

—Oviraptor. Magnuson, Diana, illus. 32p. (gr. k-4). 1990. PLB 11.97 (ISBN 0-89565-631-0). Childs World.

—Pachycephalosaurus. Hunter, Llyn, illus. 32p. (gr. k-4). 1990. PLB 11.97 (ISBN 0-89565-632-9). Childs World.

—Parasaurolophus. LeBlanc, Andre, illus. 32p. (gr. k-4). 1990. PLB 11.97 (ISBN 0-89565-633-7). Childs World.

—Parasaurolophus. LeBlanc, Andre, illus. 32p. (gr. k-4). 1990. PLB 11.97 (ISBN 0-89565-633-7). Childs World.

—Protoceratops. Magnuson, Diana, illus. 32p. (gr. k-4). 1990. PLB 11.97 (ISBN 0-89565-634-5). Childs World.

—Protoceratops. Magnuson, Diana, illus. 32p. (gr. k-4). 1990. PLB 11.97 (ISBN 0-89565-634-5). Childs World.

—Saltasaurus. Raskin, Betty, illus. 32p. (gr. k-4). 1990. PLB 11.97 (ISBN 0-89565-635-3). Childs World.

—Stegosaurus. Magnuson, Diana, illus. LC 88-15347. 32p. (gr. k-4). 1988. lib. bdg. 11.97 (ISBN 0-89565-385-0); pap. 6.96 (ISBN 0-89565-494-6). Childs World.

—Triceratops. Magnuson, Diana, illus. LC 88-508. 32p. (gr. k-4). 1988. PLB 11.97 (ISBN 0-89565-422-9); pap. 6.96 (ISBN 0-89565-491-1). Childs World.

—Troodon. Conaway, James, illus. 32p. (gr. k-4). 1990. PLB 11.97 (ISBN 0-89565-636-1). Childs World.

—Tyrannosaurus. Magnuson, Diana L., illus. LC 88-1692. 32p. (gr. k-4). 1988. PLB 11.97 (ISBN 0-89565-424-5); pap. 6.96 (ISBN 0-89565-493-8). Childs World.

Rosenbloom, Joseph. Funniest Dinosaur Book Ever. Wilhelm, Hans, illus. LC 87-7098. 24p. (gr. 1-6). 1987. 12.95 (ISBN 0-8069-6624-6). Sterling.

Rothaus, Jim. Dinosaurs. 24p. (gr. 3). 1988. 17.10 (ISBN 0-88682-223-8); PLB 11.95s.p. (ISBN 0-318-37904-X). Creative Ed.

Rowe, Erna. Los Dinosaurios Gigantes (Giant Dinosaurs) Palacios, Argentina, tr. Smith, Merle, illus. 32p. (ps-2). pap. 3.95 (ISBN 0-590-40647-7). Scholastic Inc.

—Giant Dinosaurs. Smith, Merle, illus. (gr. k-3). 1975. pap. 2.95 (ISBN 0-590-40262-5). Scholastic Inc.

Sandell, Elizabeth. Ankylosaurus: The Armored Dinosaur. Oelerich, Marjorie & Hansen, Harlan S., eds. Vista III Design Staff, illus. LC 88-39806. 32p. (gr. k-5). 1989. PLB 11.95 (ISBN 0-944280-16-1); pap. text ed. 5.95 (ISBN 0-944280-22-6). BSP Pub Inc.

—Apatosaurus: The Deceptive Dinosaur. Oelerich, Marjorie & Hansen, Harlan S., eds. Vista III Design Staff, illus. LC 88-39805. 32p. (gr. k-5). 1989. PLB 11.95 (ISBN 0-944280-12-9); pap. text ed. 5.95 (ISBN 0-944280-18-8). BSP Pub Inc.

—Archaeopteryx: The First Bird. Oelerich, Marjorie & Hansen, Harlan S., eds. Vista III Design Staff, illus. LC 88-39803. 32p. (gr. k-5). 1989. PLB 11.95 (ISBN 0-944280-13-7); pap. text ed. 5.95 (ISBN 0-944280-19-6). BSP Pub Inc.

—Compsognathus: The Smallest Dinosaur. Oelerich, Marjorie & Hansen, Harlan S., eds. Vista III Design Staff, illus. LC 88-39801. 32p. (gr. k-5). 1989. PLB 11.95 (ISBN 0-944280-14-5); pap. text ed. 5.95 (ISBN 0-944280-20-X). BSP Pub Inc.

—Dimetrodon: The Sail-Backed Dinosaur. Oelerich, Marjorie & Hansen, Harlan S., eds. Vista III Design Staff, illus. LC 88-39802. 32p. (gr. k-5). 1989. PLB 11.95 (ISBN 0-944280-15-3); pap. text ed. 5.95 (ISBN 0-944280-21-8). BSP Pub Inc.

—Maiasaura: The Good Mother Dinosaur. Oelerich, Marjorie & Hansen, Harlan S., eds. Vista III Design Staff, illus. LC 88-39799. 32p. (gr. k-5). 1989. PLB 11.95 (ISBN 0-944280-17-X); pap. text ed. 5.95 (ISBN 0-944280-23-4). BSP Pub Inc.

—Plesiosaurus: The Swimming Reptile. Oelerich, Marjorie & Schroeder, Howard, eds. Vista III Design, illus. LC 88-962. 32p. (gr. k-5). 1988. PLB 11.95 (ISBN 0-944280-04-8); pap. 5.95 (ISBN 0-944280-10-2). BSP Pub Inc.

—Pteranodon: The Flying Reptile. Oelerich, Marjorie & Schroeder, Howard, eds. Vista III Design, illus. LC 88-953. 32p. (gr. k-5). 1988. PLB 11.95 (ISBN 0-944280-05-6); pap. 5.95 (ISBN 0-944280-11-0). BSP Pub Inc.

—Seisomasaurus: The Longest Dinosaur. Oelerich, Marjorie & Schroeder, Howard, eds. Vista III Design, illus. LC 88-963. 32p. (gr. k-5). 1988. PLB 11.95 (ISBN 0-944280-03-X); pap. 5.95 (ISBN 0-944280-09-9). BSP Pub Inc.

—Stegosaurus: The Dinosaur with the Smallest Brain. Oelerich, Marjorie & Schroeder, Howard, eds. Vista III Design, illus. LC 88-995. 32p. (gr. k-5). 1988. PLB 11.95 (ISBN 0-944280-02-1); pap. 5.95 (ISBN 0-944280-08-0). BSP Pub Inc.

—Triceratops: The Last Dinosaur. Oelerich, Marjorie & Schroeder, Howard, eds. Vista III Design, illus. LC 88-952. 32p. (gr. k-5). 1988. PLB 11.95 (ISBN 0-944280-01-3); pap. 5.95 (ISBN 0-944280-07-2). BSP Pub Inc.

—Tyrannsasaurus Rex: The Fierce Dinosaur. Oelerich, Marjorie & Schroeder, Howard, eds. Vista III Design, illus. LC 88-958. 32p. (gr. k-5). 1988. PLB 11.95 (ISBN 0-944280-00-5); pap. 5.95 (ISBN 0-944280-06-4). BSP Pub Inc.

Sattler, Helen R. Baby Dinosaurs. Zallinger, Jean D., illus. LC 83-25631. 40p. (ps-3). 1984. 12.95 (ISBN 0-688-03817-4); PLB 12.88 (ISBN 0-688-03818-2). Lothrop.

—Dinosaurs of North America. Rao, Anthony, illus. Ostrom, John H., intro. by. LC 80-27411. (Illus.). 160p. (gr. 2 up). 1981. 17.95 (ISBN 0-688-51952-0). Lothrop.

—The New Illustrated Dinosaur Dictionary. Powzyk, Joyce, illus. 1990. 24.95 (ISBN 0-688-08462-1). Lothrop.

—Tyrannosaurus Rex & Its Kin: The Mesozoic Monsters. Powzyk, Joyce, illus. LC 88-1577. 48p. (gr. 3 up). 1989. 14.95 (ISBN 0-688-07747-1); PLB 13.88 (ISBN 0-688-07748-X). Lothrop.

Schlein, Miriam. Discovering Dinosaur Babies. Colbert, Margaret, illus. LC 89-23496. 40p. (gr. 1-5). 1991. RSBE 14.95 (ISBN 0-02-778091-0, Four Winds). Macmillan Child Grp.

Selsam, Millicent E. Tyrannosaurus Rex. LC 77-25677. (Illus.). (gr. 3-5). 1978. PLB 12.89 (ISBN 0-06-025424-6). HarpC Child Bks.

Selsam, Millicent E. & Hunt, Joyce. A First Look at Dinosaurs. Springer, Harriett, illus. 32p. (gr. 1-4). 1982. PLB 12.85 (ISBN 0-8027-6456-8). Walker & Co.

Shuey, Karen. Dinosaurs. (Illus.). 48p. (gr. k-4). 1987. wkbk. 5.95 (ISBN 1-55734-218-0). Tchr Create Mat.

Silver, Donald & Wynne, Patricia. Dinosaur Life Activity Book. 32p. (gr. 1-3). 1988. pap. 2.50 (ISBN 0-486-25809-2). Dover.

Simon, Seymour. The Largest Dinosaurs. Carroll, Pamela, illus. LC 85-24088. 32p. (gr. k-3). 1986. 12.95 (ISBN 0-02-782910-3, Mcmillan Child Bk). Macmillan Child Grp.

—New Questions & Answers about Dinosaurs. Dewey, Jennifer, illus. LC 88-36226. (gr. k up). 1990. 13.95 (ISBN 0-688-08195-9); PLB 13.88 (ISBN 0-688-08196-7, Morrow Jr Bks). Morrow Jr Bks.

Spizzirri, Linda, ed. Prehistoric Mammals: An Educational Coloring Book. (Illus.). 32p. (gr. 1-8). 1981. pap. 1.95 (ISBN 0-86545-022-6). Spizzirri.

Spizzirri Publishing Co. Staff. Dinosaurs: An Educational Coloring Book. Spizzirri, Linda, ed. Kohn, Arnie, illus. 32p. (gr. 1-8). 1981. pap. 1.95 (ISBN 0-86545-019-6). Spizzirri.

—Dinosaurs of Prey: An Educational Coloring Book. Spizzirri, Linda, ed. (Illus.). 32p. (gr. k-5). 1985. pap. 1.95 (ISBN 0-86545-063-3). Spizzirri.

—Dot-to-Dot Dinosaurs: An Educational Activity-Coloring Book. Spizzirri, Linda, ed. (Illus.). 32p. (gr. 1-8). 1986. pap. 0.99 (ISBN 0-86545-078-1). Spizzirri.

Stewart, Frances T. & Stewart, Charles P. Dinosaurs & Other Creatures of Long Ago. Rogers, Forest & Borland, Cathy, illus. LC 87-45565. (ps up). 1988. sticker bk. 7.95 (ISBN 0-694-00229-1). HarpC Child Bks.

Stewart, J. Dinosaurs: A New Discovery. (Illus.). 32p. (gr. 1-6). 1989. 10.95 (ISBN 0-88625-234-2). Durkin Hayes Pub.

Sullivan, Dianna J. Big & Easy Dinosaurs. Adkins, Lynda, illus. 48p. (ps-2). 1988. wkbk. 5.95 (ISBN 1-55734-103-6). Tchr Create Mat.

Swann, F. Corythosaurus. (Illus.). 24p. (gr. 3 up). Date not set. PLB 14.00 (ISBN 0-86592-521-6). Rourke Corp.

—Psittacosaurus. (Illus.). 24p. (gr. 3 up). Date not set. PLB 14.00 (ISBN 0-86592-518-6). Rourke Corp.

Tallarico, Tony, illus. Dinosaurs. 12p. (ps). 1988. bds. 3.95 (ISBN 0-89828-318-3, 04011). Tuffy Bks.

Unfred, Dave & Schmidt, Doug. Dinosaur Fun Pack. (Illus.). 32p. (ps-2). 1987. pap. 4.95 (ISBN 0-89051-135-7). Master Bks.

Waldrop, Victor H., ed. Ranger Rick's Dinosaur Book. Loomis, Michael E., et al. LC 84-14680. (Illus.). 96p. (gr. 2-7). 1985. Repr. of 1984 ed. PLB 12.95 (ISBN 0-912186-54-2, 19401). Natl Wildlife.

West, Robin. Dinosaur Discoveries: How to Create Your Own Prehistoric World. Wolfe, Bob & Wolfe, Diane, illus. 72p. (gr. 1-5). 1989. PLB 14.95 (ISBN 0-87614-351-6). Carolrhoda Bks.

White, D. Anatosaurus. (Illus.). 24p. (gr. 3 up). Date not set. PLB 14.00 (ISBN 0-86592-520-8). Rourke Corp.

—Rutiodon. (Illus.). 24p. (gr. 3 up). Date not set. PLB 14.00 (ISBN 0-86592-522-4). Rourke Corp.

—Scolosaurus. (Illus.). 24p. (gr. 3 up). Date not set. PLB 14.00 (ISBN 0-86592-519-4). Rourke Corp.

—Spinosaurus. (Illus.). 24p. (gr. 3 up). Date not set. PLB 14.00 (ISBN 0-86592-517-8). Rourke Corp.

Whyte, Malcolm. The Second Dinosaur Action Set. Smith, Dan, illus. 24p. (gr. 7-11). 1988. 5.95 (ISBN 0-8431-1951-9). Price Stern.

—Undersea Dinosaur Action Set. Smith, Dan, illus. 24p. (gr. 1 up). 1988. 5.95 (ISBN 0-8431-1954-3). Price Stern.

Wild, Anne. Dinosaur Mobiles. (Illus.). 28p. (Orig.). (gr. 4 up). 1985. pap. 4.95 (ISBN 0-906212-18-9). Parkwest Pubns.

Wildlife Education, Ltd. Staff. Dinosaurs. Hallett, Mark, illus. 20p. (Orig.). (gr. k-12). 1985. pap. 2.25 (ISBN 0-937934-34-8). Wildlife Educ.

Williams, Geoffrey T. Explorers in Dinosaur World. Cremins, Robert, illus. 32p. (gr. 1-6). 1988. pap. 2.95 (ISBN 0-8431-2264-1); pap. 8.95 incl. cass. (ISBN 0-8431-2265-X). Price Stern.

Wilson, Ron. One Hundred Dinosaurs from A to Z. Fitzsimons, Celia, illus. 64p. (gr. 2-5). 1986. pap. 9.95 (ISBN 0-448-18992-5, G&D). Putnam Pub Group.

World Book, Inc. Staff, ed. Dinosaurs! LC 65-25105. (Illus.). 304p. (gr. 3-7). 1987. PLB write for info. (ISBN 0-7166-0687-9). World BK.

Zallinger, Peter. Dinosaurs. Zallinger, Peter, illus. LC 76-24178. (ps-1). 1977. pap. 2.25 (ISBN 0-394-83485-2, Random Juv). Random.

—Dinosaurs & Other Archosaurs. Risom, Ole & Luke, Melinda, eds. Zallinger, Peter, illus. LC 85-42930. 96p. (gr. 5 up). 1986. lib. bdg. 9.99 (ISBN 0-394-94421-6); pap. 8.95 (ISBN 0-394-84421-1). Random.

Zanini, G. The Dinosaur Book. (Illus.). 72p. (gr. k-6). 1985. 5.98 (ISBN 0-517-42525-4). Outlet Bk Co.

Zim, Herbert S. Dinosaurs. Irving, James G., illus. LC 54-5080. (gr. 3-7). 1954. PLB 11.88 (ISBN 0-688-31239-X). Morrow Jr Bks.

DINOSAURS–FICTION

Ahlberg, Allan. Dinosaur Dreams. LC 90-2943. (Illus.). 24p. (ps up). 1991. 12.95 (ISBN 0-688-09955-6); PLB 12.88 (ISBN 0-688-09956-4). Greenwillow.

Aliki. Digging up Dinosaurs. 32p. (ps-2). Date not set. pap. 6.95 (ISBN 1-55994-302-5, Caedmon). HarperAudio.

—Dinosaur Bones. Aliki, illus. 32p. (gr. k-4). 1990. pap. 4.50 (ISBN 0-06-445077-5, Trophy). HarpC Child Bks.

Ball, Jacqueline A. T. Rex's Missing Tooth. (gr. 4-7). 1991. pap. 2.95 (ISBN 0-06-106055-0, PL). HarperCollins.

Barton, Byron. Bones, Bones, Dinosaur Bones. Barton, Byron, illus. LC 89-71306. 32p. (ps-1). 1990. 9.95 (ISBN 0-690-04825-4, Crowell Jr Bks); PLB 12.89 (ISBN 0-690-04827-0, Crowell Jr Bks). HarpC Child Bks.

Bates, Robin & Simon, Cheryl. The Dinosaurs & the Dark Star. Dewey, Jennifer, illus. LC 84-3922. 48p. (gr. 3-7). 1985. 12.95 (ISBN 0-02-708340-3, Mcmillan Child Bk). Macmillan Child Grp.

Bentley, Ray R. Darby the Dinosaur in Shopping with Darby. Hamby, Michael B., illus. LC 89-51111. 24p. (ps-1). 1989. pap. 2.50 (ISBN 0-9623481-0-4). Darby Dinosaur.

Berenstain, Michael. Flying Dinosaurs - Pterodactyls. Berenstain, Michael, illus. (ps-3). 1991. pap. 1.75 (ISBN 0-307-12620-X, Golden Pr). Western Pub.

Berger, Neal J. The Only Purple Dinosaur. 1991. 6.95 (ISBN 0-533-09141-1). Vantage.

Bliss, Richard B., ed. Dinosaur ABC's Activity Book. rev. ed. Schmitt, Doug, illus. 32p. (gr. k-3). 1986. pap. 3.95 (ISBN 0-89051-113-6). Master Bks.

Booth, Jerry. The Big Beast Book: Dinosaurs & How They Got That Way. Weston, Martha, illus. LC 87-36206. (gr. 3-7). 1988. 14.95 (ISBN 0-316-10263-6); pap. 8.95 (ISBN 0-316-10266-0). Little.

Bradman, Tony. Dilly & the Horror Movie. Hellard, Susan, illus. 64p. (gr. 2-5). 1991. pap. 3.95 (ISBN 0-14-032799-1, Puffin). Puffin Bks.

—Dilly the Dinosaur. Hellard, Susan, illus. LC 86-28985. 52p. (gr. 2-5). 1987. pap. 10.95 (ISBN 0-670-81682-5). Viking Child Bks.

—Dilly the Dinosaur. Hellard, Susan, illus. 64p. (Orig.). (gr. 2-5). 1988. pap. 3.95 (ISBN 0-14-032337-6, Puffin). Puffin Bks.

Brandt, Keith. Case of the Missing Dinosaur. Wallner, John, illus. LC 81-7620. 48p. (gr. 2-4). 1982. PLB 10.89 (ISBN 0-89375-586-9); pap. text ed. 2.95 (ISBN 0-89375-587-7). Troll Assocs.

Brown, Laurie K. Dinosaurs Travel, Vol. 1. (ps-3). 1991. pap. 5.95 (ISBN 0-316-11253-4). Little.

Brown, Marc & Krensky, Stephen. Dinosaurs, Beware! A Safety Guide. Brown, Marc & Krensky, Stephen, illus. LC 82-15207. 32p. (ps-3). 1984. 14.95 (ISBN 0-316-11228-3, Joy St Bks); pap. 5.95 (ISBN 0-316-11219-4, Joy St Bks). Little.

Butler, Lollie. Erni Cabat's Dazzling Dinosaurs. Cabat, Erni, illus. 56p. (ps-6). 1989. 16.95 (ISBN 0-317-94006-6). Great Impressions.

Carmine, Mary. Daniel's Dinosaurs. (gr. 4-7). 1991. 12.95 (ISBN 0-590-44638-X, Scholastic Hardcover). Scholastic Inc.

Carrick, Carol. What Happened to Patrick's Dinosaurs? Carrick, Donald, illus. LC 85-13989. (gr. k-3). 1988. 12.95 (ISBN 0-89919-406-0, Pub. by Clarion); pap. 4.95 (ISBN 0-89919-797-3, Pub. by Clarion). Ticknor & Fields.

Cauley, Lorinda B. The Trouble with Tyrannosaurus Rex. Cauley, Lorinda B., illus. 32p. (gr. 4-8). 1988. 13.95 (ISBN 0-15-290880-3). HarBraceJ.

—The Trouble with Tyrannosaurus Rex. 1990. pap. 4.95 (ISBN 0-15-290881-1, VoyB). HarbraceJ.

Clark, Emma C. The Bouncing Dinosaur. (Illus.). 32p. (ps-3). 1990. 13.95 (ISBN 0-374-30912-4). FS&G.

Cohen, Miriam. Lost in the Museum. Hoban, Lillian, illus. (gr. k-3). 1983. pap. 2.95 (ISBN 0-440-44780-1, YB). Dell.

Coville, Bruce. The Dinosaur That Followed Me Home. Pierard, John, illus. 160p. (Orig.). (gr. 3-6). 1990. pap. 2.75 (ISBN 0-671-64750-4, Minstrel). PB.

Craig, Janet. Little Danny Dinosaur. Harvey, Paul, illus. LC 87-16228. 32p. (gr. k-2). 1988. PLB 7.06 (ISBN 0-8167-1229-8); pap. text ed. 1.95 (ISBN 0-8167-1230-1). Troll Assocs.

Crozat, Francois. I Am a Big Dinosaur. (Illus.). 24p. (ps-k). 1989. 7.95 (ISBN 0-8120-6097-0). Barron.

—I Am a Big Dinosaur-Mini. 24p. (ps). 1990. 2.95 (ISBN 0-8120-6193-4). Barron.

Curran, Eileen. Home for a Dinosaur. Karas, G. Brian, illus. LC 84-8627. 32p. (gr. k-2). 1985. lib. bdg. 10.89 (ISBN 0-8167-0351-5); pap. text ed. 2.95 (ISBN 0-8167-0431-7). Troll Assocs.

Cuyler, Margery. Baby Dot: A Dinosaur Story. Weiss, Ellen, illus. 32p. (ps-1). 1990. 13.95 (ISBN 0-395-51934-9, Clarion Bks). HM.

Demers, Jan. One More Dinosaur. Bird, Lynn, illus. (gr. k-3). 1989. pap. 1.95 (ISBN 0-87406-376-0). Willowisp Pr.

Dial-a-Dinosaur. (Illus.). (gr. k-9). 1989. pap. 3.95 (ISBN 0-318-36481-6). Scholastic Inc.

Dickerson, Karle. Stepmonsters. 128p. (gr. 6-8). 1989. pap. 2.50 (ISBN 0-87406-375-2). Willowisp Pr.

Dolby, K. The Incredible Dinosaur Expedition. (Illus.). 48p. (gr. 3-5). 1987. PLB 10.96 (ISBN 0-88110-300-4); pap. 4.50 (ISBN 0-7460-0149-5). EDC.

Donnelly, Liza. Dinosaur Beach. Donnelly, Liza, illus. 32p. (Orig.). (ps-3). 1991. pap. 2.50 (ISBN 0-590-42176-X). Scholastic Inc.

—Dinosaur Day. 32p. (ps-3). 1987. pap. 2.50 (ISBN 0-590-41800-9). Scholastic Inc.

—Dinosaur Garden. (ps-3). 1990. 12.95 (ISBN 0-590-43173-0, Scholastic Hardcover). Scholastic Inc.

—Dinosaurs' Halloween. (ps-3). 1988. pap. 2.50 (ISBN 0-590-41006-7). Scholastic Inc.

Donnely, Marcus. Squeak the Dinosaur. Young, Debby, illus. 32p. (ps-2). 1987. 9.00 (ISBN 0-938715-02-X). Toy Works Pr.

Emberley, Michael. Dinosaurs! A Drawing Book. Emberley, Michael, illus. 48p. (gr. 3 up). 1985. pap. 4.95 (ISBN 0-316-23631-4). Little.

Giff, Patricia R. In the Dinosaur's Paw. Sims, Blanche, illus. 80p. (gr. k-6). 1985. pap. 2.75 (ISBN 0-440-44150-1, YB). Dell.

Gordon, Sharon. Un Dinosauro en Peligro. Havey, Paul, illus. (SPA.). 32p. (gr. k-2). 1981. PLB 7.06 (ISBN 0-89375-554-0). Troll Assocs.

Greenberg, Robert B. Tyrannosaurus Tex. Zady, Mary, illus. LC 89-4225. 60p. (gr. k-4). 1989. pap. 5.95 (ISBN 0-938349-38-4). State House Pr.

—Tyrannosaurus Tex: First Grade. LC 90-9749. (Illus.). 64p. (gr. k-4). 1991. pap. 6.95 (ISBN 0-938349-56-2). State House Pr.

Hennessy, B. G. The Dinosaur Who Lived in My Backyard. Davis, Susan, illus. 32p. (ps-3). 1990. pap. 3.95 (ISBN 0-14-050736-1, Puffin). Puffin Bks.

Herman, Gail. Time for School, Little Dinosaur. Gorbaty, Norman, illus. LC 89-70331. 24p. (Orig.). (ps-2). 1990. pap. 2.25 (ISBN 0-679-80789-6). Random.

Hilton, Joyce. Dinosaur Days. Roe, Richard, illus. 48p. (gr. k-3). 1988. pap. 5.95 bk. & cassette pkg. (ISBN 0-394-89774-9, Random Juv). Random.

Hobhouse, Sarah & Mackay, David. Wesley & the Dinosaurs, 6 bks. Ross, Tony, illus. 16p. (gr. 1-3). Set. pap. text ed. 19.20 (ISBN 1-55624-146-1, WG1461). Wright Group.

Hoff, Syd. Danny & the Dinosaur. Hoff, Syd, illus. LC 58-7754. 64p. (gr. k-3). 1958. 11.95 (ISBN 0-06-022465-7); PLB 11.89 (ISBN 0-06-022466-5). HarpC Child Bks.

—Danny & the Dinosaur. Hoff, Syd, illus. LC 58-7754. 64p. (ps-3). 1985. incl. cassette 5.98 (ISBN 0-694-00017-5, Trophy); pap. 3.50 (ISBN 0-06-444002-8, Trophy). HarpC Child Bks.

Horner, John & Gorman, James. Maia: A Dinosaur Grows Up. Henderson, Doug, illus. LC 88-43384. 46p. (gr. 2 up). 1989. lib. bdg. 12.90 (ISBN 0-89471-727-8); pap. 5.95 (ISBN 0-89471-691-3). Running Pr.

Horner, John R. & Gorman, James. Maia: A Dinosaur Grows Up. Henderson, Doug, illus. LC 87-13022. 48p. (gr. 3 up). 1987. 8.98 (ISBN 0-89471-552-6, Pub. by Courage Bks.). Running Pr.

Hurd, Edith T. Dinosaur My Darling. Freeman, Don, illus. LC 77-11854. (ps-3). 1978. 6.95 (ISBN 0-06-022743-5). HarpC Child Bks.

Joyce, William. Dinosaur Bob: And His Adventures with the Family Lazardo. Joyce, William, illus. LC 87-30796. 32p. (ps-3). 1988. 14.95 (ISBN 0-06-023047-9); PLB 14.89 (ISBN 0-06-023048-7). HarpC Child Bks.

Kroll, Steven. The Tyrannosaurus Game. DePaola, Tomie, illus. LC 75-37078. 40p. (ps-3). 1976. reinforced bdg. 13.95 (ISBN 0-8234-0275-4); pap. 5.95 (ISBN 0-8234-0620-2). Holiday.

LaFleur, Tom & Brennan, Gale. Isadore the Dinosaur. Berghauer, Meri H., illus. 16p. (Orig.). (gr. k-6). 1981. pap. 1.25 (ISBN 0-685-02456-3). Brennan Bks.

Lasky, Kathryn. Dinosaur Dig. Knight, Christopher G., photos by. LC 89-13212. (Illus.). (gr. 3 up). 1990. 13.95 (ISBN 0-688-08574-1); PLB 13.88 (ISBN 0-688-08575-X, Morrow Jr Bks). Morrow Jr Bks.

Lavie, Arlette. The Dinosaur's Cold. (Illus.). 32p. (gr. k-2). 1988. 15.95 (ISBN 0-340-39946-5, Pub. by Hodder & Stoughton UK). Trafalgar Sq.

Lloyd, David. Dinosaur Days. Cross, Peter, illus. Incl. Early Morning. LC 84-27613. 1985; Silly Games. LC 84-27697. 1985. 3.95 (ISBN 0-394-87380-7); Breakfast. LC 84-27614. 1985. 3.95 (ISBN 0-394-87378-5); Terrible Thing. LC 84-27702. 1985. 3.95 (ISBN 0-394-87381-5). 32p. (ps-1). 1985 (Random Juv). Random.

Logan, Dick, et al. The Egg. 32p. (ps-7). 1987. PLB 10.45 (ISBN 0-87191-781-5); 14.95 (ISBN 0-685-24593-4). Creative Ed.

Longyear, Barry B. The Homecoming. Clark, Alan M., illus. 224p. 1989. 15.95 (ISBN 0-8027-6863-6). Walker & Co.

Malam, John. Pop-Up Dinosaurs. Everitt-Stewart, Andy & Moseley, Dudley, illus. LC 90-60818. 10p. (gr. 1 up). 1991. 7.95 (ISBN 0-679-80871-X). Random.

Mannetti, William. Dinosaurs in Your Backyard. Mannetti, William, illus. LC 81-7998. 160p. (gr. 4-7). 1982. 12.95 (ISBN 0-689-30906-6, Atheneum Child Bk). Macmillan Child Grp.

Manson, Frank A. The Adventures of Prince Albert & the Royal Dinosaurs. Henley, Joan, illus. 144p. (gr. 2-7). 1990. 11.95 (ISBN 0-918339-17-0). Vandamere.

Martin, Rodney. There's a Dinosaur in the Park! Siow, John, illus. LC 86-42811. 31p. (gr. 2-3). 1987. PLB 12.95 (ISBN 1-55532-151-8). Gareth Stevens Inc.

Milton, Joyce. Dinosaur Days. Roe, Richard, illus. LC 84-17861. 48p. (gr. k-3). 1985. lib. bdg. 6.99 (ISBN 0-394-97023-3, Random Juv); pap. 2.95 (ISBN 0-394-87023-9). Random.

Moncure, Jane B. A Wish-for Dinosaur. Gohman, Vera, illus. LC 88-20302. 32p. (ps-2). 1989. PLB 11.97 (ISBN 0-89565-393-1); pap. 6.96 (ISBN 0-89565-515-2). Childs World.

—Word Bird's Dinosaur Day. Hohag, Linda, illus. 32p. (ps-2). 1990. lib. bdg. 11.97 (ISBN 0-89565-617-5); pap. text ed. 6.96 (ISBN 0-89565-619-1). Childs World.

Moser, Cindy & Hummel, Nancy. Dinosaurs Don't Wear Diapers. Parker, Sherry, illus. 16p. (Orig.). (ps). 1990. pap. text ed. 9.95 (ISBN 0-9628204-0-7). Stopher.

Most, Bernard. Dinosaur Cousins? 32p. (ps-3). 1990. pap. 4.95 (ISBN 0-15-223498-5, VoyB). HarBraceJ.

—If the Dinosaurs Came Back. Most, Bernard, illus. LC 77-23911. (ps-2). 1978. 13.95 (ISBN 0-15-238020-5, HJ). HarBraceJ.

—If the Dinosaurs Came Back. Most, Bernard, illus. LC 77-23911. 32p. (ps-3). 1984. pap. 4.95 (ISBN 0-15-238021-3, VoyB). HarBraceJ.

—If the Dinosaurs Came Back. Most, Bernard, illus. 32p. (ps-2). Date not set. pap. write for info. (ISBN 0-15-238022-1). HarBraceJ.

—Whatever Happened to the Dinosaurs? Most, Bernard, illus. LC 84-3779. 40p. (ps-1). 1984. 13.95 (ISBN 0-15-295295-0, HJ). HarBraceJ.

Murphy, Jane. My Pet Tyrannosaurus. LC 88-81468. (Illus.). 32p. (Orig.). (ps-2). 1988. pap. 8.95 (ISBN 0-937124-17-6). Kimbo Educ.

Murphy, Jim. The Last Dinosaur. Weatherby, Mark A., illus. 1991. pap. 3.95 (ISBN 0-590-44875-7, Blue Ribbon Bks). Scholastic Inc.

Nelson, Jeffrey. Dinosaur Jokes & Riddles Book. (Illus.). 24p. (gr. 3 up). 1988. pap. 1.95 (ISBN 0-02-689068-2). Checkerboard Pr.

Night of the Dinosaurs. 1990. text ed. 3.95 cased (ISBN 0-7214-5265-5). Ladybird Bks.

Nixon, Joan L. Watch Out for Dinosaurs. (gr. 4-7). 1991. pap. 2.99 (ISBN 0-440-40459-2). Dell.

Nolan, Dennis. Dinosaur Dream. Nolan, Dennis, illus. LC 89-78208. 32p. (ps-2). 1990. 13.95 (ISBN 0-02-768145-9, Mcmillan Child Bk). Macmillan Child Grp.

Oram, Hiawyn. A Boy Wants a Dinosaur. (ps-3). 1991. bds. 13.95 jacketed (ISBN 0-374-30939-6). FS&G.

Orr, Wendy. Amanda's Dinosaur. Campbell, Gillian, illus. 40p. (ps-3). 1991. pap. 3.95 (ISBN 0-590-42443-2). Scholastic Inc.

Otto, Carolyn. Dinosaur Chase. Hurd, Thacher, illus. LC 90-2021. 32p. (ps-1). 1991. 14.95 (ISBN 0-06-021613-1); PLB 14.89 (ISBN 0-06-021614-X). HarpC Child Bks.

Packard, Edward. A Day with the Dinosaurs, No. 46. 64p. (Orig.). 1988. pap. 2.75 (ISBN 0-553-15612-8, Skylark). Bantam.

Parish, Peggy & Lobel, Arnold. Dinosaur Time. 32p. (ps-2). 1990. pap. 6.95 (ISBN 1-55994-262-2, Caedmon). HarperAudio.

Penn, Audrey. No Bones about Driftiss. Loving, Judy V., illus. LC 89-13326. viii, 146p. (gr. 2-6). 1989. lib. bdg. 14.95 (ISBN 0-939923-11-4); pap. 5.95 (ISBN 0-939923-12-2). M & W Pub Co.

Polhamus, Jean B. Dinosaur Do's & Don'ts. O'Neill, Steven, illus. LC 75-11743. (gr. 1-3). 1975. (Pub. by Treehouse); pap. 2.50 (ISBN 0-13-214668-1). P-H.

Preiss, Byron. Last of the Dinosaurs. (Illus.). 144p. (Orig.). (gr. 7-12). 1988. pap. 2.50 (ISBN 0-553-27007-9). Bantam.

Preiss, Byron & Bischoff, David. Search for Dinosaurs. Henderson, Doug & Nino, Alex, illus. 144p. (Orig.). 1984. pap. 2.25 (ISBN 0-553-25399-9). Bantam.

Ransom, Candice. My Sister, the Traitor. (gr. 4-8). 1989. pap. 12.95 (ISBN 0-590-41981-1). Scholastic Inc.

—My Sister, the Traitor. 1990. pap. 2.75 (ISBN 0-590-41528-X). Scholastic Inc.

Razzi, Jim. Fun with Dinosaurs. Tomasewski, Jim, illus. 48p. (Orig.). (gr. k-3). 1987. pap. 1.95 activity bk. (ISBN 0-590-40786-4). Scholastic Inc.

Reese, Bob. Little Dinosaur. Wasserman, Dan, ed. Reese, Bob, illus. (gr. k-1). 1979. PLB 7.95 (ISBN 0-89868-070-0); pap. 2.95 (ISBN 0-89868-081-6). ARO Pub.
Richler, Mordecai. Jacob Two-Two & the Dinosaur. Foster, Frances, ed. Eyolfson, Norman, illus. Rosenthal, Eileen, designed by. LC 86-20108. (Illus.). 96p. (gr. 1-5). 1987. 11.95 (ISBN 0-394-88704-2); lib. bdg. 11.99 (ISBN 0-394-98704-7). Knopf.
—Jacob Two-Two & the Dinosaur. 96p. (gr. 3-7). 1988. pap. 2.95 (ISBN 0-553-15589-X). Bantam.
Roberts, Sarah. The Adventures of Big Bird in Dinosaur Days. Mathieu, Joe, illus. LC 83-61891. 32p. (ps-3). 1984. pap. 1.25 (ISBN 0-394-85926-X). Random.
Rogers, Jean. Dinosaurs Are Five Hundred Sixty-Eight. (gr. 4-7). 1991. pap. 2.99 (ISBN 0-440-40434-7). Dell.
Ross, Tom, et al. It Zwibble & the Big Birthday Party. 32p. (Orig.). (ps-3). 1990. pap. 2.50 (ISBN 0-590-43861-1). Scholastic Inc.
—It Zwibble, the Star-Touched Dinosaur. Ross, Tom, illus. 32p. (Orig.). (gr. k-3). 1987. pap. 1.95 (ISBN 0-590-40300-1). Scholastic Inc.
—It Zwibble, the Startouched Dinosaur. 32p. (Orig.). (ps-3). 1987. pap. 2.50 (ISBN 0-590-44008-X). Scholastic Inc.
Schatz, Dennis. Dinosaurs - A Journey Through Time: A Children's Activity Book. Quan, Daniel, designed by. 48p. (ps-6). 1987. pap. 9.95 (ISBN 0-935051-01-5). Pacific Sci Ctr.
Senn, Steve. The Double Disappearance of Walter Fozbek. Senn, Steve, illus. 128p. (gr. 3-5). 1983. pap. 2.50 (ISBN 0-380-62737-X, 60064-1, Camelot). Avon.
Silverman, Maida. Dinosaur Babies. Inouye, Carol, illus. LC 88-4690. 1988. pap. 7.95 (ISBN 0-671-65897-2, Little Simon). S&S Trade.
Simon, Seymour. The Smallest Dinosaurs. Rao, Anthony, illus. LC 81-3247. 48p. (gr. k-3). 1988. 12.95 (ISBN 0-517-54425-3). Crown.
—The Smallest Dinosaurs. Rao, Anthony, illus. (gr. k-3). 1988. 4.95 (ISBN 0-517-56550-1). Crown.
Spanjian, Beth. Baby Stegosaurus. (ps-1). 1990. write for info. (ISBN 0-307-12601-3). Western Pub.
—Baby Triceratops. (ps-1). 1990. write for info. (ISBN 0-307-12602-1). Western Pub.
Steiner, Barbara. Oliver Dibbs & the Dinosaur Cause. 160p. 1988. pap. 2.95 (ISBN 0-380-70466-8, Camelot). Avon.
Sundgaard, Arnold. Jethro's Difficult Dinosaur. Mack, Stan, illus. LC 76-29616. (ps-3). 1977. Pantheon.
Thayer, Jane. Quiet on Account of Dinosaur. Fleishman, Seymour, illus. LC 64-10028. 32p. (ps-3). 1964. PLB 12.88 (ISBN 0-688-31632-8); pap. 3.95 (ISBN 0-688-08292-0, Mulberry Bks). Morrow Jr Bks.
Valat, Pierre-Marie. Dinosaur Faces. 1990. 14.95 (ISBN 0-525-44631-1, DCB). Dutton Child Bks.
Van Horn, William. The Big Sneeze. Van Horn, William, illus. 48p. (Orig.). (gr. k-3). 1985. pap. 2.25 (ISBN 0-590-33425-5, Lucky Star). Scholastic Inc.
Wilhelm, Hans. Tyrone the Horrible. Wilhelm, Hans, illus. 32p. (gr. 1-3). 1988. pap. 10.95 (ISBN 0-590-41471-2, Pub. by Scholastic Hardcover). Scholastic Inc.
Williams, Geoffrey T. Dinosaur World. (Illus.). 32p. (Orig.). (gr. 2-5). 1985. pap. 2.95 (ISBN 0-8431-1439-8); pap. 8.95 incl. cass. (ISBN 0-8431-1424-X). Price Stern.
—Lost in Dinosaur World. Svensson, Borje, illus. 32p. (gr. 6-11). 1987. pap. 2.95 (ISBN 0-8431-1878-4); bk. & audiocassete 8.95 (ISBN 0-8431-1885-7). Price Stern.
Wise, William. In the Time of the Dinosaurs. Zacks, Lewis, illus. 64p. (Orig.). (gr. k-3). 1987. pap. 2.50 (ISBN 0-590-41149-7, Hello Reader). Scholastic Inc.

DINOSAURS–POETRY
Dunn, Cynthia T. If You Squint at a Rhinoceros... Lopez, Stella, illus. LC 90-30384. 32p. (gr. 2-5). 1990. 12.95 (ISBN 0-943173-67-1). Harbinger AZ.

DIPLOMACY
Ferrell, Nancy W. Passports to Peace: Embassies & the Art of Diplomacy. LC 85-16006. (Illus.). 96p. (gr. 6 up). 1986. PLB 10.95 (ISBN 0-8225-0644-0). Lerner Pubns.

DIPLOMATIC AND CONSULAR SERVICE–FICTION
Olsen, Viggo. Daktar: Diplomat in Bangladesh. 1990. pap. 9.95 (ISBN 0-8024-1756-6). Moody.

DIPSOMANIA
see Alcoholism

DIPTERA
see Flies; Mosquitoes

DIRECTION, SENSE OF
see Orientation

DIRIGIBLE BALLOONS
see Airships

DISARMAMENT
see also Peace
Dolan, Edward F., Jr. Gun Control. 96p. (gr. 7 up). 1982. PLB 12.90 (ISBN 0-531-02202-1). Watts.
Hawkes, Nigel. The Nuclear Arms Race. 32p. (gr. 4-9). 1986. PLB 8.90 (ISBN 0-531-17029-2, Pub. by Gloucester). Watts.
Smoke, Richard. Think about Nuclear Arms Control: Understanding the Arms Race. (Illus.). 178p. 1988. PLB 14.85 (ISBN 0-8027-6761-3); pap. 5.95 (ISBN 0-8027-6762-1). Walker & Co.
Thro, Ellen. Taking a Stand Against Nuclear War. 1990. PLB 13.40 (ISBN 0-531-10922-4). Watts.
Weiss, Ann E. The Nuclear Arms Race-Can We Survive It? 160p. (gr. 5-9). 1983. 10.95 (ISBN 0-395-34928-1). HM.

DISASTERS
see also Earthquakes; Fires; Floods; Shipwrecks; Storms
Arnold, Caroline. Coping with Natural Disasters. (gr. 5 up). 1988. 13.95 (ISBN 0-8027-6716-8); PLB 14.85 (ISBN 0-8027-6717-6). Walker & Co.
Day, James. The Hindenburg Tragedy. Spender, Nick, illus. LC 88-19879. 32p. (gr. 3-6). 1989. PLB 10.90 (ISBN 0-531-18238-X, Pub. by Bookwright Pr). Watts.
Diamond, Arthur. The Bhopal Chemical Leak. LC 90-6011. (Illus.). 64p. 1990. PLB 11.95 (ISBN 1-56006-009-3). Lucent Bks.
Engholm, Christopher. The Armenian Earthquake. LC 89-33555. (Illus.). 64p. (gr. 5-8). 1989. PLB 11.95 (ISBN 1-56006-004-2). Lucent Bks.
Fradin, Dennis B. Disaster! Blizzards & Winter Weather. LC 83-10074. (Illus.). 64p. (gr. 3 up). 1983. PLB 17.27 (ISBN 0-516-00857-9). Childrens.
—Disaster! Droughts. LC 83-10073. (Illus.). 64p. (gr. 3 up). 1983. PLB 17.27 (ISBN 0-516-00858-7). Childrens.
Keller, David. Great Disasters. 112p. 1990. pap. 2.95 (ISBN 0-380-76043-6, Camelot). Avon.
Marsh, Carole. Maryland's (Most Devastating!) Disasters & (Most Calamitous!) Catastrophies! (Illus.). (gr. 3-8). 1990. PLB 19.95 (ISBN 0-7933-0548-9); pap. 14.95 (ISBN 0-7933-0547-0); disk 29.95 (ISBN 0-7933-0549-7). Gallopade Pub Group.
Nardo, Don. Chernobyl. McGovern, Brian, illus. LC 90-33567. 64p. (gr. 5-8). 1990. PLB 11.95 (ISBN 1-56006-008-5). Lucent Bks.
—Krakatoa. McGovern, Brian, illus. LC 90-6003. 64p. (gr. 5-8). 1990. PLB 11.95 (ISBN 1-56006-011-5). Lucent Bks.
Richard, Graham. The Chernobyl Catastrophe. Bull, Peter, illus. LC 88-5956. 32p. (gr. 3-6). 1989. PLB 10. 90 (ISBN 0-531-18236-3, Pub. by Bookwright Pr). Watts.
Scollins, Richard, illus. The Fire of London. LC 88-5054. 32p. (gr. 3-6). 1989. PLB 10.90 (ISBN 0-531-18237-1, Pub. by Bookwright Pr). Watts.
Standiford, Natalie. The Bravest Dog Ever: The True Story of Balto. Cook, Donald, tr. LC 89-3465. (Illus.). 47p. (Orig.). (gr. 1-3). 1989. PLB 6.99 (ISBN 0-394-99695-X, Random Juv); pap. 2.95 (ISBN 0-394-89695-5). Random.

DISASTERS–FICTION
Voigt, Cynthia. Izzy, Willy-Nilly. LC 85-22933. 276p. (gr. 7 up). 1986. 14.95 (ISBN 0-689-31202-4, Atheneum Child Bk). Macmillan Child Grp.

DISCIPLINE OF CHILDREN
see Children–Management

DISCOVERERS
see Discoveries (In Geography); Explorers

DISCOVERIES (IN GEOGRAPHY)
see also America–Discovery and Exploration; Antarctic Regions; Arctic Regions; Explorers; Northwest Passage; Scientific Expeditions; Voyages and Travels;
also names of countries with the subdivision description and travel, e.g. U. S.–Description and Travel
The Age of Exploration. 64p. (gr. 4-8). 1990. 13.95 (ISBN 0-86307-997-0). Marshall Cavendish.
Crump, Donald J., ed. Beyond the Horizon: Adventures in Faraway Lands. (Illus.). 1992. 8.95 (ISBN 0-317-99620-7); lib. bdg. 9.50 (ISBN 0-317-99621-5). Natl Geog.
Exploring the Past Series, 6 vols. (gr. 4-8). 1990. Set. 83. 70 (ISBN 0-86307-993-8). Marshall Cavendish.
Man, John. Exploration & Discovery. LC 89-11376. (Illus.). 64p. (gr. 4-6). 1990. PLB 12.95 (ISBN 0-8368-0007-9). Gareth Stevens Inc.
—Exploring the World. LC 89-11285. (Illus.). 64p. (gr. 2-3). 1990. PLB 12.95 (ISBN 0-8368-0032-X). Gareth Stevens Inc.
National Geographic Society Staff, ed. Books for Young Explorers, 4 vols, Set 15. (gr. k-4). 1988. Set. 10.95 (ISBN 0-87044-737-8); Set. PLB 12.95 (ISBN 0-87044-742-4). No. 1: Animals in Summer. No. 2: Animals at Play. No. 3: Busy Beavers. No. 4: Let's Explore a River. Natl Geog.
Williams, Brian. Voyages of Discovery. LC 89-26337. (Illus.). 48p. (gr. 4-8). 1990. PLB 18.60 (ISBN 0-8114-2756-0). Steck-V.

DISCOVERIES (IN SCIENCE)
see Inventions; Science

DISCOVERIES, MARITIME
see Discoveries (In Geography)

DISCRIMINATION
For general works on discrimination by race, religion, sex, age, social status, or other factors.
see also Blacks–Civil Rights; Civil Rights; Minorities; Toleration
Smith, Sandra L. Coping with Cross-Cultural & Interracial Relationships. Rosen, Ruth, ed. (gr. 7-12). 1990. lib. bdg. 12.95 (ISBN 0-8239-1157-8, 1157-8). Rosen Group.
Stewart, Gail. Discrimination. LC 89-31259. (Illus.). 48p. (gr. 4-5). 1989. 10.95 (ISBN 0-89686-445-6, Crestwood Hse). Macmillan Child Grp.

DISCRIMINATION–FICTION
Neufeld, John. Edgar Allan. Dunlap, Loren, illus. LC 68-31175. (gr. 5-8). 1968. 18.95 (ISBN 0-87599-149-1). S G Phillips.
Taylor, Mildred. Roll of Thunder, Hear My Cry. Pinkney, Jerry, illus. LC 76-2287. (gr. 6 up). 1976. 14. 95 (ISBN 0-8037-7473-7). Dial Bks Young.
Taylor, Mildred D. Let the Circle Be Unbroken. LC 81-65854. 432p. (gr. 7 up). 1981. 15.95 (ISBN 0-8037-4748-9). Dial Bks Young.
Tunis, John R. Keystone Kids. Brooks, Bruce & Bacom, Paulintro. by. 256p. (gr. 3-7). 1990. pap. 3.95 (ISBN 0-15-242388-5). HarbraceJ.

DISCUSSION
see Debates and Debating

DISEASE (PATHOLOGY)
see Pathology

DISEASE GERMS
see Bacteriology

DISEASES
see also names of diseases and groups of diseases e.g. Communicable Diseases; and subjects with the subdivision Diseases, e.g. Children–diseases; Skin–Diseases
Armstrong, Donald. AIDS. Head, J. J., ed. Johnson, Patricia W., illus. LC 84-45827. 16p. (Orig.). (gr. 10 up). 1986. pap. text ed. 2.15 (ISBN 0-89278-354-0, 45-9754). Carolina Biological.
Asimov, Isaac. How Did We Find Out About Vitamins? Wool, David, illus. LC 73-92453. 64p. (gr. 5-8). 1974. PLB 11.85 (ISBN 0-8027-6184-4). Walker & Co.
Beckelman, Laurie. Alzheimer's Disease. LC 89-25251. (Illus.). 48p. (gr. 4 up). 1989. 10.95 (ISBN 0-89686-489-8, Crestwood Hse). Macmillan Child Grp.
Brown, Fern G. Hereditary Disease. (Illus.). 96p. (gr. 4-9). 1987. PLB 10.40 (ISBN 0-531-10386-2). Watts.
Donahue, Parnell & Capellaro, Helen. Germs Make Me Sick: A Health Handbook for Kids. Oechsli, Kelly, illus. LC 74-15309. 96p. (gr. 4 up). 1975. Knopf.
Eagles, Douglas A. Nutritional Diseases. (Illus.). (gr. 4-8). 1987. PLB 10.40 (ISBN 0-531-10391-9). Watts.
Frank, Julia. Alzheimer's Disease: The Silent Epidemic. (Illus.). 80p. (gr. 5 up). 1985. PLB 9.95 (ISBN 0-8225-1578-4). Lerner Pubns.
French, Barbara. Coping with Bulimia. (Illus.). 160p. (Orig.). (gr. 10 up). 1984. pap. 8.95 (ISBN 0-7225-1380-1). Thorsons SF.
Haensel, Phyllis C. Certain Choices. Hoff, Marshall G. & Bock, Glenn H., eds. Belding, Pam, illus. 32p. (Orig.). (gr. 7-9). 1984. pap. text ed. write for info. (ISBN 0-940210-01-0). Minn Med Found.
Hughes, Barbara. Drug Related Diseases. (Illus.). 96p. (gr. 4-9). 1987. PLB 10.40 (ISBN 0-531-10381-1). Watts.
Kerby, Mona. Asthma. (Illus.). 128p. (gr. 7-12). 1989. PLB 12.40 (ISBN 0-531-10697-7). Watts.
Krementz, Jill. How It Feels to Fight for Your Life. 1989. 15.95 (ISBN 0-316-50364-9). Little.
Landau, Elaine. Alzheimer's Disease. (Illus.). 72p. (gr. 4-9). 1987. PLB 10.40 (ISBN 0-531-10376-5). Watts.
Mactire, Sean P. Lyme Disease. (Illus.). 96p. (gr. 7-12). 1991. PLB 12.40 (ISBN 0-531-12523-8). Watts.
Matthews, John. Library in a Book: Eating Disorders. (Illus.). 240p. (gr. 9-12). 1990. 22.95x (ISBN 0-8160-1911-8). Facts on File.
Nixon, Joan L. The Specter. LC 82-70322. 160p. (gr. 7 up). 1982. pap. 12.95 (ISBN 0-385-28948-0). Delacorte.
Ross, Steven. Winter Rose. (Illus.). 32p. (gr. 7-12). 1988. 5.95 (ISBN 0-8059-3096-5). Dorrance.
Rowe, H. Edward. Microscopic Monster: The Tricky, Devastating AIDS Virus! 32p. (gr. 9 up). 1987. pap. 2.00 ea. (ISBN 0-944373-00-3). Natl AIDS Prevent.
Sanford, Doris. Maria's Grandma Gets Mixed Up. Davis, Deena, ed. Evans, Graci, illus. LC 89-3161. 31p. (gr. k-4). 1989. 6.95 (ISBN 0-88070-298-2). Multnomah.
Taylor, Margaret & Schuett, Virginia E. You & PKU. (Illus.). 43p. 1988. pap. text ed. 5.00 (ISBN 0-299-97065-5). U of Wis Pr.
White, Ryan & Cunningham, Ann M. Ryan White: My Own Story. (Illus.). 144p. (gr. 5 up). 1991. 16.95 (ISBN 0-8037-0977-3). Dial Bks Young.
Zinsser, Hans. Rats, Lice & History. (gr. 9 up). 1984. (Pub. by Atlantic Monthly Pr); pap. 8.95 (ISBN 0-316-98896-0). Little.

DISEASES, COMMUNICABLE
see Communicable Diseases

DISEASES, INFECTIONS
see Communicable Diseases

DISEASES, MENTAL
see Mental Illness; Psychology, Pathological

DISEASES AND PESTS
see Fungi; Insects, Injurious and Beneficial
see names of individual pests (e.g. Locusts)

DISEASES OF ANIMALS
see Veterinary Medicine

DISEASES OF CHILDREN
see Children–Diseases

DISEASES OF THE BLOOD
see Blood–Diseases

DISHES
see Pottery

DISNEY, WALTER ELIAS, 1901-1966
Fisher, Maxine P. The Walt Disney Story. Sporn, Michael, illus. Rakos, Jennie, ed. (Illus.). 72p. (gr. 7 up). 1988. PLB 10.40 (ISBN 0-531-10493-1). Watts.
Ford, Barbara. Walt Disney: A Biography. (Illus.). 160p. (gr. 4-7). 1989. 15.95 (ISBN 0-8027-6864-4); PLB 16. 85 (ISBN 0-8027-6865-2). Walker & Co.
—Walt Disney: A Biography. (Illus.). 160p. (gr. 4-7). 1989. 15.95 (ISBN 0-8027-6864-4); PLB 16.85 (ISBN 0-8027-6865-2). Walker & Co.
Holliss, Richard & Sibley, Brian. Walt Disney's Snow White & the Seven Dwarfs & the Making of the Classic Film. Disney Studio Archives, illus. (ps up). 1987. pap. 14.95 (ISBN 0-671-64439-4). S&S Trade.

The Story of Walt Disney. (gr. k-6). 1989. pap. 2.95 (ISBN 0-440-40240-9, YB). Dell.

DISPLACED PERSONS
see Refugees
DISPOSAL OF REFUSE
see Refuse and Refuse Disposal
DISSENT
Finke, Blythe F. Angela Davis: Traitor or Martyr of the Freedom of Expression? Rahmas, D. Steve, ed. LC 77-190246. 32p. (Orig.). (gr. 7-12). 1972. lib. bdg. 4.20 incl. catalog cards (ISBN 0-87157-528-0); pap. 2.95 vinyl laminated covers (ISBN 0-87157-028-9). SamHar Pr.
DISTRIBUTION (ECONOMICS)
see Commerce; Marketing
DISTRIBUTION OF ANIMALS AND PLANTS
see Geographical Distribution of Animals and Plants
DISTRIBUTION OF WEALTH
see Economics
DISTRICT NURSES
see Nurses and Nursing
DIVIDENDS
see Stocks
DIVINATION
see also Astrology; Dreams; Fortune Telling; Occult Sciences; Superstition
Schwartz, Alvin. Telling Fortunes: Love Magic, Dream Signs, & Other Ways to Learn the Future. Cameron, Tracey, illus. LC 85-45174. 128p. (gr. 4 up). 1987. 12.95 (ISBN 0-397-32132-5, Lipp Jr Bks); PLB 12.89 (ISBN 0-397-32133-3, Lipp Jr Bks). HarpC Child Bks.
DIVINE HEALING
see Christian Science
DIVING
Briggs, Carole S. Diving Is for Me. Sutter, Greg, illus. LC 82-17242. 48p. (gr. 2-5). 1983. PLB 8.95 (ISBN 0-8225-1135-5). Lerner Pubns.
Carson, Charles. Make the Team: Swimming & Diving. (gr. 4-7). 1991. pap. 5.95 (ISBN 0-316-13028-1). Little.
Fischel, E. Swimming & Diving Skills. (Illus.). 48p. (gr. 6-12). 1989. lib. bdg. 12.96 (ISBN 0-88110-395-0, Usborne); pap. 5.95 (ISBN 0-7460-0171-1). EDC.
Goldberg, Bob. Diving Basics. Seiden, Art, illus. 48p. (gr. 3-7). 1986. 10.95 (ISBN 0-13-215963-5). P-H.
Lang, Denise V. Footsteps in the Ocean: Careers in Diving. LC 86-28725. 192p. (gr. 7 up). 1987. 13.95 (ISBN 0-525-67193-5, Lodestar Bks). Dutton Child Bks.
DIVING, SKIN
see Skin Diving
DIVING, SUBMARINE
see Skin Diving
DIVING SUBMARINE
see also Submarines
Conley, Andrea. Window on the Deep: The Adventures of Underwater Explorer Sylvia Earle. (Illus.). 40p. (gr. 5-8). 1991. 13.95 (ISBN 0-531-15232-4); PLB 13.90 (ISBN 0-531-11119-9). Watts.
DIVORCE
see also Marriage
Berry, Joy. About Divorce. Bartholomew, illus. 48p. (gr. 3 up). 1990. PLB 14.60 (ISBN 0-516-02953-3); 6.95 (ISBN 0-516-22953-2). Childrens.
Booher, Dianna D. Coping: When Your Family Falls Apart. LC 79-17342. 192p. (gr. 7 up). 1979. lib. bdg. 11.98 (ISBN 0-671-33083-7). Messner.
Brown, Laurene K. & Brown, Marc. Dinosaurs Divorce: A Guide for Changing Families. Brown, Marc, illus. 32p. (ps-3). 1988. pap. 4.95 (ISBN 0-316-10996-7). Little.
Cain, Barbara & Benedek, Elissa P. What Would You Do? A Child's Book about Divorce. Cummins, James, illus. 50p. 1976. text ed. 9.00 (ISBN 0-88048-300-8). Am Psychiatric.
Carlson, Linda. Everything You Need to Know about Your Parent's Divorce. Rosen, Ruth, ed. (gr. 7-12). 1989. PLB 12.95 (ISBN 0-8239-1012-1). Rosen Group.
Coleman, William L. What Children Need to Know When Parents Get Divorced. LC 83-6006. 91p. (gr. k-5). 1983. pap. 5.95 (ISBN 0-87123-612-5). Bethany Hse.
Craven, Linda. Stepfamilies: New Patterns of Harmony. LC 82-60652. (Illus.). 192p. (gr. 7 up). 1983. lib. bdg. 13.98 (ISBN 0-671-44080-2); pap. 4.95 (ISBN 0-671-49486-4). Messner.
Friedman, Liz. Divorce. FS-Aladdin Staff, ed. (Illus.). 64p. (gr. 4-12). 1988. 11.90 (ISBN 0-531-17122-1, Gloucester Pr). Watts.
Gardner, Richard A. Boys & Girls Book about Divorce. LC 84-2815. (Illus.). 160p. (gr. 7 up). 1983. 25.00 (ISBN 0-87668-664-1). Aronson.
—The Boys & Girls Book about Divorce. (Illus.). (gr. 4 up). 1971. pap. 3.50 (ISBN 0-553-25310-7). Bantam.
Garigan, Elizabeth & Urbanski, Michael. Living with Divorce - Middle School. 64p. (gr. 5-9). 1991. 6.95 (ISBN 0-86653-596-9). Good Apple.
—Living with Divorce - Primary. 64p. (gr. 1-4). 1991. 6.95 (ISBN 0-86653-595-0). Good Apple.
Grollman, Earl A. Talking about Divorce & Separation: A Dialogue Between Parent & Child. Cann., Alison, illus. LC 75-5289. (gr. k-4). pap. 7.95 (ISBN 0-8070-2375-2, BP524). Beacon Pr.
Hazen, Barbara S. Two Homes to Live In: A Child's-Eye View of Divorce. Luks, Peggy, illus. LC 77-21849. 32p. (ps-3). 1978. 16.95 (ISBN 0-87705-313-8); pap. 9.95 (ISBN 0-89885-173-4). Human Sci Pr.
Ives, Sally B., et al. The Divorce Workbook: A Guide for Kids & Families. (Illus.). 160p. (Orig.). (ps-7). 1985. plastic comb bdg. 14.95 (ISBN 0-914525-04-2); pap. 12.95 (ISBN 0-914525-05-0). Waterfront Bks.
Jordan, Sally. Divorce...Love Divided. Philbrook, Diana, illus. LC 87-92231. 32p. (gr. 4-9). 1988. saddle stitched .89 (ISBN 0-87403-436-1, 24-03646). Standard Pub.
Kehle, Mary. In the Middle: What to Do When Your Parents Divorce. LC 86-31319. 96p. (Orig.). (gr. 4-8). 1987. pap. 5.95 (ISBN 0-87788-375-0). Shaw Pubs.
Lazo, Caroline E. Divorce. LC 89-2156. (Illus.). 48p. (gr. 4 up). 1989. 10.95 (ISBN 0-89686-436-7, Crestwood Hse). Macmillan Child Grp.
LeShan, Eda. What's Going to Happen to Me? When Parents Separate or Divorce. rev. ed. Cuffari, Richard, illus. LC 86-10769. 144p. (gr. 3-7). 1986. pap. 3.95 (ISBN 0-689-71093-3, Aladdin). Macmillan Child Grp.
LeShan, Eda J. What's Going to Happen to Me? When Parents Separate or Divorce. Cuffari, Richard, illus. LC 78-4340. 144p. (gr. 3-7). 1984. 13.95 (ISBN 0-02-759230-8, Four Winds). Macmillan Child Grp.
McGuire, Paula. Putting It Together: Teenagers Talk about Family Breakup. LC 86-29238. 224p. (gr. 7 up). 1987. pap. 15.95 (ISBN 0-385-29564-2). Delacorte.
Minnick, Molly A. Divorce Illustrated: Workbook. Minnick, Molly A., illus. 60p. (Orig.). (gr. 4). 1990. pap. 5.00 (ISBN 1-878526-03-0). Pineapple MI.
Nickman, Steven L. When Mom & Dad Divorce. De Groat, Diane, illus. 80p. (gr. 3-6). 1986. lib. bdg. 10.98 (ISBN 0-671-60153-9); pap. 4.95 (ISBN 0-671-62878-X). Messner.
Petty, Kate. Splitting Up. FS-Aladdin Staff, ed. Kopper, Lisa, illus. 24p. (gr. 1-3). 1988. PLB 5.29 (ISBN 0-531-17105-1, Gloucester Pr). Watts.
Prokop, Michael S. Divorce Happens to the Nicest Kids: A Self-Help Book For Kids (3-15) & Adults. Peters, Robert C., ed. Fogarty, Michelle D., illus. LC 85-72180. 224p. (Orig.). (gr. k up). 1986. 18.95 (ISBN 0-933879-25-3); pap. 6.45 Kids' Divorce Wkbk. (ISBN 0-933879-26-1); kids' divorce wkbk. 6.45 (ISBN 0-933879-27-X). Alegra Hse Pubs.
Raab, Robert A. Coping with Divorce. rev. ed. (gr. 7-12). 1984. PLB 12.95 (ISBN 0-8239-0428-8). Rosen Group.
Rofes, Eric, ed. The Kids' Book of Divorce: By, for & about Kids. LC 82-4004. (Illus.). 144p. (gr. 2 up). 1982. pap. 9.00 (ISBN 0-394-71018-5, Vin). Random.
Schuchman, Joan. Two Places to Sleep. LaMarche, Jim, illus. LC 79-88201. 32p. (gr. 1-4). 1979. PLB 7.95 (ISBN 0-87614-108-4). Carolrhoda Bks.
Snyder, James R. What's (Bad) Good about Divorce? 1977. 1st ed. LC 77-84446. (Illus.). 23p. 1977. 6.95 (ISBN 0-9601452-1-4). FIG Ltd.
Stein, Sara B. On Divorce. LC 78-15687. (Illus.). 48p. (ps-8). 1984. pap. 4.95 (ISBN 0-8027-7226-9). Walker & Co.
—On Divorce. Stone, Erika, illus. 48p. 1979. 10.95 (ISBN 0-8027-6344-8). Walker & Co.
Terkel, Susan N. Understanding Child Custody. Rosoff, Iris, ed. 128p. (gr. 7-12). 1991. PLB 12.40 (ISBN 0-531-12521-1). Watts.
Tonner, Leslie. My Mom, Your Dad. 128p. 1989. 14.95 (ISBN 0-89015-720-0, Pub. by Panda Bks). Eakin Pr.
Weyborne, Darlene. When is Daddy Coming Home? A Workbook for Children of Divorce. LC 90-1045. (Illus.). Date not set. 20.00 (ISBN 0-87668-750-8). Aronson.
What Would You Do? A Child's Book about Divorce. (ps). 4.95 (ISBN 0-685-14910-2). Borden.
DIVORCE–FICTION
Abercrombie, Barbara. Cat-Man's Daughter. LC 79-2676. 160p. (gr. 6-9). 1981. HarpC Child Bks.
Aiello, Barbara & Shulman, Jeffrey. On with the Show! Featuring Brenda Dubrowski. Barr, Loel, illus. 56p. (gr. 3-6). 1989. PLB 12.95 (ISBN 0-941477-06-1). TFC Bks MD.
Bechard, Margaret. My Sister, My Science Report. (gr. 3-7). 1990. 13.95 (ISBN 0-670-81646-9, Viking). Viking Child Bks.
Betancourt, Jeanne. The Rainbow Kid. 112p. (Orig.). (gr. 3-7). 1983. pap. 2.50 (ISBN 0-380-84665-9, 84665, Camelot). Avon.
Blume, Judy. It's Not the End of the World. LC 70-181739. 176p. (gr. 5-7). 1982. 12.95 (ISBN 0-02-711050-8, Bradbury Pr). Macmillan Child Grp.
Burns, Peggy. The Splitting Image of Rosie Brown. 128p. (Orig.). (gr. 7-10). 1990. pap. 3.95 (ISBN 0-7459-1831-X). Lion USA.
Carey, Joanna. Where Has Daddy Gone? Osman, Trudy, illus. 32p. (ps-4). 1990. 11.95 (ISBN 0-8249-8457-9). Ideals.
Christiansen, C. B. My Mother's House, My Father's House. (ps-3). 1990. pap. 3.95 (ISBN 0-14-054210-8, Puffin). Puffin Bks.
Cleary, Beverly. Dear Mr. Henshaw. Zelinsky, Paul O., illus. 144p. (gr. k-6). 1984. pap. 3.25 (ISBN 0-440-41794-5, YB). Dell.
—Dear Mr. Henshaw. large type ed. Zelinsky, Paul O., illus. 141p. (gr. 2-6). 1987. Repr. of 1983 ed. lib. bdg. 14.95 (ISBN 1-55736-001-4). ABC-CLIO.
Danziger, Paula. The Divorce Express. LC 82-70318. 144p. (gr. 7 up). 1982. pap. 14.95 (ISBN 0-385-28217-6). Delacorte.
—The Divorce Express. 160p. (gr. 7 up). 1983. pap. 3.25 (ISBN 0-440-92062-0, LFL). Dell.
—The Divorce Express. large type ed. 183p. (gr. 7 up). 1988. lib. bdg. 13.95 (ISBN 0-8161-4413-3, Large Print Bks). G K Hall.
—It's an Aardvark-Eat-Turtle World. large type, unabr. ed. 145p. (gr. 4 up). 1989. lib. bdg. 13.95 (ISBN 0-8161-4704-3). G K Hall.
Fitzhugh, Louise. Sport. 224p. (gr. 7 up). 1980. pap. 1.75 (ISBN 0-440-98350-9, LFL). Dell.
Fleming, Alice. Welcome to Grossville. LC 84-23664. 112p. (gr. 5-7). 1985. 12.95 (ISBN 0-684-18289-0, Scribners Young Read). Macmillan Child Grp.
Goff, Beth. Where Is Daddy? The Story of a Divorce. Perl, Susan, illus. LC 69-14608. 32p. (ps-k). 1969. pap. 4.95 (ISBN 0-8070-2305-1, BP 694). Beacon Pr.
Hillman, Carole D. It's Different Now...a New Beginning. Hillman, Carole D., illus. 10p. (Orig.). 1990. pap. text ed. write for info. (ISBN 0-9624257-1-0). Early Childhood.
Hogan, Paula Z. Will Dad Ever Move Back Home? Leder, Dora, illus. Muir, Martha F., intro. by. LC 79-24058. (Illus.). 32p. (gr. k-6). 1980. PLB 16.67 (ISBN 0-8172-1356-2). Raintree Pubs.
Jones, Cordelia. Cat Called Camouflage. LC 79-166339. (Illus.). (gr. 7 up). 1971. 18.95 (ISBN 0-87599-189-0). S G Phillips.
Kropp, Paul. Moonkid And Liberty. (gr. 3-6). 1990. 13.95 (ISBN 0-316-50485-8, Joy St Bks). Little.
McAfee, A. & Browne, A. Visitors Who Came to Stay. LC 84-40333. 32p. (gr. 4-6). 1985. pap. 11.95 (ISBN 0-670-74714-9). Viking Child Bks.
Mazer, Harry. Guy Lenny. 96p. (gr. 4-8). 1977. pap. 2.95 (ISBN 0-440-93311-0, LFL). Dell.
Mazer, Norma F. Taking Terri Mueller. LC 82-18849. 224p. (gr. 7 up). 1983. 12.95 (ISBN 0-688-01732-0). Morrow Jr Bks.
Nixon, Joan L. Casey & the Great Idea. Rowen, Amy, illus. 144p. (gr. 4-6). 1982. pap. 2.50 (ISBN 0-590-32337-7, Apple Paperbacks). Scholastic Inc.
Park, Barbara. Don't Make Me Smile. LC 81-4880. 128p. (gr. 4-7). 1981. PLB 8.95 (ISBN 0-394-84978-7). Knopf.
—Don't Make Me Smile. 132p. (gr. 4-7). 1983. pap. 2.95 (ISBN 0-380-61994-6, Camelot). Avon.
—Don't Make Me Smile. LC 81-4880. 128p. (gr. 3-7). 1990. pap. 3.25 (ISBN 0-394-84745-8). McKay.
Perry, Patricia & Lynch, Marietta. Mommy & Daddy Are Divorced. LC 77-86268. (Illus.). 27p. (ps-3). 1985. pap. 3.95 (ISBN 0-8037-0233-7). Dial Bks Young.
Pevsner, Stella. A Smart Kid Like You. LC 74-19320. 192p. (gr. 4-8). 1979. 13.95 (ISBN 0-395-28876-2, Clarion). HM.
Pfeffer, Susan B. Dear Dad, Love Laurie. (gr. 4-7). 1989. pap. 10.95 (ISBN 0-590-41681-2). Scholastic Inc.
Sanford, Doris. Please Come Home: A Child's Book about Divorce. Evans, Graci, illus. LC 86-106753. 32p. (ps-5). 1985. 7.95 (ISBN 0-88070-138-2). Multnomah.
Silsbee, Peter. The Temptation of Kate. LC 90-1351. 160p. (gr. 6-9). 1990. 13.95 (ISBN 0-02-782761-5, Bradbury Pr). Macmillan Child Grp.
Smith, Doris B. Kick a Stone Home. LC 74-4209. 192p. (gr. 5 up). 1974. 12.95 (ISBN 0-690-00535-0, Crowell Jr Bks). HarpC Child Bks.
Sommer, Karen. Satch & the Motormouth. (gr. 3-7). 1987. pap. 4.49 (ISBN 1-55513-063-1, Chariot Bks). Cook.
Steiner, Barbara. Tessa. LC 87-31524. 224p. (gr. 7 up). 1988. 12.95 (ISBN 0-688-07232-1, Morrow Junior Books). Morrow.
Stinson, Kathy. Mom & Dad Don't Live Together Anymore. Reynolds, Nancy L., illus. 32p. (gr. k-3). 1984. 12.95 (ISBN 0-920236-92-8); pap. 4.95 (ISBN 0-920236-87-1). Firefly Bks Ltd.
Stolz, Mary. Go & Catch a Flying Fish. LC 78-21785. (gr. 6 up). 1979. PLB 12.89 (ISBN 0-06-025868-3). HarpC Child Bks.
Stowe, Cynthia. Home Sweet Home, Good-bye. (gr. 4-7). 1990. pap. 10.95 (ISBN 0-590-43001-7). Scholastic Inc.
Talbert, Marc. Thin Ice. (gr. 3 up). 1986. 13.95 (ISBN 0-316-83133-6). Little.
Wolitzer, Hilma. Out of Love. LC 76-40983. (Illus.). 160p. (gr. 5 up). 1976. 11.95 (ISBN 0-374-35675-0). FS&G.
Wood, Phyllis A. Song of the Shaggy Canary. LC 73-14785. 156p. (gr. 6 up). 1974. 8.95 (ISBN 0-664-32543-2, Westminster). Westminster John Knox.
—Win Me & You Lose. LC 76-44299. 136p. (gr. 7 up). 1977. 8.95 (ISBN 0-664-32605-6, Westminster). Westminster John Knox.
Zach, Cheryl. Tug of War. 144p. (Orig.). 1988. pap. 2.95 (ISBN 1-55802-073-X). Lynx Bks.
DIX, DOROTHEA LYNDE, 1802-1887
Malone, Mary. Dorothea Dix: Hospital Founder. Sampson, Katharine, illus. 80p. (gr. 2-6). 1991. Repr. of 1968 ed. PLB 12.95 (ISBN 0-7910-1436-3). Chelsea Hse.
DOCKS
see also Harbors
DOCTORS
see Physicians
DODO–FICTION
Baehr, Patricia. Summer of the Dodo. LC 89-39335. 160p. (gr. 3-6). 1990. 12.95 (ISBN 0-02-708135-4, Four Winds). Macmillan Child Grp.
Baender, Margaret W. Tail Waggings of Maggie. Hinkle, Janet W., illus. 64p. (gr. 8-10). 1982. pap. 6.00x (ISBN 0-88100-012-4). Philmar Pub.

DOG
see Dogs
DOG GUIDES
see Guide Dogs
DOGS
see also classes of dog e.g. Guide Dogs; also names of specific breeds

Anderson, J. I. I Can Read About Dogs & Puppies. LC 72-96953. (Illus.). (gr. 2-4). 1973. pap. 1.95 (ISBN 0-89375-053-0). Troll Assocs.
Animal Answers: Dogs. (ps up). 1989. PLB 3.98 (ISBN 0-7924-5063-9, Mallard Pr). BDD Promo Bk.
Ashabranner, Brent. Crazy about German Shepherds. Ashabranner, Jennifer, photos by. LC 90-1303. (Illus.). 96p. (gr. 5 up). 1990. 14.95 (ISBN 0-525-65032-6, Cobblestone Bks). Dutton Child Bks.
Barrett, Norman. Dogs. (Illus.). 32p. (gr. k-4). 1990. PLB 11.40 (ISBN 0-531-14040-7). Watts.
Barton, Byron. Where's Al? Barton, Byron, illus. LC 78-171866. 32p. (ps-3). 1979. 10.95 (ISBN 0-395-28765-0, Clarion). HM.
Boorer, Wendy. Dogs. Coombs, Roy, illus. LC 88-17653. 24p. (Orig.). (gr. 2-5). 1989. lib. bdg. 5.99 (ISBN 0-394-99988-6); pap. 2.95 (ISBN 0-394-89988-1). Random.
Boy Scouts of America. Dog Care. (Illus.). 48p. (gr. 6-12). 1984. pap. 1.85 (ISBN 0-8395-3289-X, 3289). BSA.
Bridwell, Norman. Las Buenas Acciones De Clifford. Palacios, Argentina, tr. Bridwell, Norman, illus. (SPA.). 32p. (gr. k-3). pap. 2.95 (ISBN 0-590-40179-3). Scholastic Inc.
Burton, Jane. Jack the Puppy. LC 89-11422. (Illus.). 32p. (gr. 2-3). 1989. PLB 10.95 (ISBN 0-8368-0209-8). Gareth Stevens Inc.
Casanova, Mary. The Golden Retriever. LC 90-34141. (Illus.). 48p. (gr. 5-6). 1990. RSBE 10.95 (ISBN 0-89686-525-8, Crestwood Hse). Macmillan Child Grp.
Clutton-Brock, Juliet. Dog. Young, Jerry, photos by. LC 91-10135. (Illus.). 64p. (gr. 5 up). 1991. 15.00 (ISBN 0-679-81459-0); lib. bdg. 15.99 (ISBN 0-679-91459-5). Knopf.
Cole, Joanna. A Dog's Body. Wexler, Jerome, illus. LC 85-25885. 48p. (ps-3). 1986. 12.95 (ISBN 0-688-04153-1); lib. bdg. 12.88 (ISBN 0-688-04154-X, Morrow Jr Bks). Morrow Jr Bks.
—My Puppy Is Born. rev. ed. Miller, Margaret, photos by. LC 90-42011. (Illus.). 48p. (ps up). 1991. 13.95 (ISBN 0-688-09770-7); PLB 13.88 (ISBN 0-688-09771-5, Morrow Jr Bks). Morrow Jr Bks.
Cooper, Michael. Racing Sled Dogs: An Original North American Sport. LC 87-25007. (Illus.). 96p. (gr. 4-7). 1988. 13.95 (ISBN 0-89919-499-0, Pub. by Clarion). Ticknor & Fields.
Davidson, Margaret. Five True Dog Stories. 48p. (gr. k-3). 1987. pap. 1.95 (ISBN 0-590-41220-5). Scholastic Inc.
—Five True Dog Stories. 1989. pap. 2.50 (ISBN 0-590-42401-7). Scholastic Inc.
—Seven True Dog Stories. Suba, Susanne, illus. 96p. (gr. 2-5). 1986. Repr. of 1977 ed. 9.95 (ISBN 0-8038-6738-7). Hastings.
Dogs. (Illus.). (ps-2). pap. write for info. (ISBN 0-528-87113-7). Checkerboard Pr.
Ebeling, Jean. Waldo, the Goat Dog. Roberts, Melissa, ed. Arlitt, Nancy, illus. 48p. (gr. 4-7). 1987. 8.95 (ISBN 0-89015-588-7, Pub. by Panda Bks). Eakin Pr.
Elliott, Joan. Dogs. Allen, Creszentia & Allen, Ted, illus. LC 78-58087. 1978. PLB 6.09 (ISBN 0-448-13483-7, G&D). Putnam Pub Group.
Eltinge, et al. The Staffordshire Bull Terrier in America. Eltinge, Steve, ed. Epps, Sarah, illus. Eltinge, Steve, intro. by. 140p. (gr. 4 up). 1986. pap. 24.95 (ISBN 0-9617204-0-9). MIP Pub.
Emert, Phyllis R. Hearing-Ear Dogs. LC 85-12841. (Illus.). 48p. (gr. 5-6). 1985. PLB 10.95 (ISBN 0-89686-283-6, Crestwood Hse). Macmillan Child Grp.
—Military Dogs. LC 85-17488. (Illus.). 48p. (gr. 5-6). 1985. 10.95 (ISBN 0-89686-286-0, Crestwood Hse). Macmillan Child Grp.
—Search & Rescue Dogs. LC 85-18967. (Illus.). 48p. (gr. 5-6). 1985. 10.95 (ISBN 0-89686-285-2, Crestwood Hse). Macmillan Child Grp.
—Sled Dogs. LC 85-14967. (Illus.). 48p. (gr. 5-6). 1985. 10.95 (ISBN 0-89686-288-7, Crestwood Hse). Macmillan Child Grp.
Fischer-Nagel, Heiderose & Fischer-Nagel, Andreas. A Puppy Is Born. Fischer-Nagel, Heiderose & Fischer-Nagel, Andreas, illus. LC 85-3505. 40p. (ps-2). 1985. 10.95 (ISBN 0-399-21234-5, Putnam). Putnam Pub Group.
Gackenbach, Dick. Claude the Dog. 32p. (ps-2). 1979. 13.95 (ISBN 0-395-28792-8, Clarion). HM.
Gill, Margaret B. Everybody Loves Debbie. (Illus.). 22p. (ps-7). 1989. 6.95 (ISBN 0-533-08580-2). Vantage.
Goennel, Heidi. My Dog. LC 88-38706. (Illus.). 32p. (ps-1). 1989. 14.95 (ISBN 0-531-05834-4); PLB 14.99 (ISBN 0-531-08434-5). Orchard Bks Watts.
Hausherr, Rosmarie. My First Puppy. Hausherr, Rosmarie, illus. LC 86-14979. 64p. (gr. 1-4). 1986. 13.95 (ISBN 0-02-743410-9, Four Winds). Macmillan Child Grp.
Herriot, James. Only One Woof. Barrett, Peter, illus. 32p. (ps up). 1985. 10.95 (ISBN 0-312-58583-7). St Martin.
Hill. Dog & Puppies. Goaman, Karen, ed. Kennan, Elaine & Ward, Fredrick, illus. (gr. 2-5). 1983. pap. 4.50 (ISBN 0-86020-646-7); lib. bdg. 11.96 (ISBN 0-88110-086-2). EDC.
Hill, Eric. Spot Goes to School. Hill, Eric, illus. LC 84-42695. 22p. (ps-2). 1984. 10.95 (ISBN 0-399-21073-3, Putnam). Putnam Pub Group.
Jameson, P. Dogs. (Illus.). 32p. (gr. 2-5). 1989. lib. bdg. 14.00 (ISBN 0-86625-184-7). Rourke Corp.
Jons, John A. Studies of the French Dog Sports "Championship of France" (1982-1988) & the Belgian Shepherd Dog Breeds (Malinois, Teruren Groenendael, Laenenois) in Schutzhund Competition in the U. S. A. (1979-1988) 1989. pap. text ed. 12.50 (ISBN 0-685-29411-0). J Jons LA.
Kappeler, Markus. Dogs. (Illus.). 32p. (gr. 4-6). 1991. PLB 11.95 (ISBN 0-8368-0686-7). Gareth Stevens Inc.
Khalsa, Dayal K. I Want a Dog. (Illus.). 24p. (ps up). 1988. 13.95 (ISBN 0-517-56532-3, 557452, C N Potter Bks). Crown.
Leder, Jane M. Stunt Dogs. LC 85-19469. (Illus.). 48p. (gr. 5-6). 1985. 9.95 (ISBN 0-89686-289-5, Crestwood Hse). Macmillan Child Grp.
Lewis, Jean. The Big Book of Dogs. (Illus.). 48p. (gr. 2-6). 1988. PLB 7.95 (ISBN 0-448-09277-8, G&D). Putnam Pub Group.
Ling, Mary. Amazing Wolves, Dogs, & Foxes. Young, Jerry, photos by. LC 91-6514. (Illus.). 32p. (Orig.). (gr. 1-5). 1991. lib. bdg. 9.99 (ISBN 0-679-91521-4); pap. 7.00 (ISBN 0-679-81521-X). Knopf.
Lord, Suzanne. The Labrador Retriever. LC 90-34198. (Illus.). 48p. (gr. 5-6). 1990. RSBE 10.95 (ISBN 0-89686-526-6, Crestwood Hse). Macmillan Child Grp.
McPherson, Mark. Caring for Your Dog. Bernstein, Marianne, illus. LC 84-222. 48p. (gr. 3-7). 1985. PLB 9.89 (ISBN 0-8167-0113-X); pap. 2.95 (ISBN 0-8167-0114-8). Troll Assocs.
Marquardt, Max. Working Dogs. (Illus.). 32p. (gr. 1-4). 1989. PLB 12.33 (ISBN 0-8172-3506-X). Raintree Pubs.
Newman, Matthew. Watch Guard Dogs. LC 85-19542. (Illus.). 48p. (gr. 5-6). 1985. 10.95 (ISBN 0-89686-287-9, Crestwood Hse). Macmillan Child Grp.
Nicholas, Anna K. The Great Dane. (Illus.). 319p. (gr. 7 up). 1988. 19.95 (ISBN 0-86622-122-0, PS-826). TFH Pubns.
Nordmark, Magdalene L. Moss, a Border Collie. Miller, Robert W., illus. Miller, Janus W., prologue by. (Illus.). 37p. (Orig.). 1988. pap. 7.00 (ISBN 0-685-21901-1). Willow Run UT.
O'Neill, Catherine. Dogs on Duty. LC 88-15933. 104p. (gr. 4 up). 1988. 7.95 (ISBN 0-87044-659-2); lib. bdg. 9.50 (ISBN 0-87044-664-9). Natl Geog.
Petty, Kate. Perros. Thompson, George, illus. (SPA.). 24p. (gr. k-4). 1991. PLB 10.40 (ISBN 0-531-07915-5). Watts.
—Puppies. (Illus.). 24p. (gr. k-4). 1990. PLB 10.40 (ISBN 0-531-17232-5). Watts.
Pinkwater, Jill & Pinkwater, Daniel M. Superpuppy: How to Choose, Raise & Train the Best Possible Dog for You. LC 76-8825. (Illus.). 208p. (gr. 6 up). 1982. 13.95 (ISBN 0-395-28878-9, Clarion); pap. 7.95 (ISBN 0-89919-084-7, Clarion). HM.
Pope, Joyce. Taking Care of Your Dog. LC 85-51604. (Illus.). 32p. (gr. 4-8). 1990. PLB 10.90 (ISBN 0-531-10160-6); pap. 3.95 (ISBN 0-531-15166-2). Watts.
Posell, Elsa. Dogs. LC 81-7742. (Illus.). 48p. (gr. k-4). 1981. PLB 14.60 (ISBN 0-516-01614-8). Childrens.
Puppies. (Illus.). (ps-2). pap. write for info. (ISBN 0-528-87112-9). Checkerboard Pr.
Puppies. (Illus.). 1990. 4.98 (ISBN 0-8317-6853-3). Smithmark.
Puppies & Dogs. 32p. (Orig.). (ps-1). 1984. pap. 1.25 (ISBN 0-8431-1508-4). Price Stern.
Puppies & Dogs. (Illus.). (gr. k-9). 1988. pap. 1.25 (ISBN 0-318-36477-8). Scholastic Inc.
Puppies & Kittens. (Illus.). (ps). 3.50 (ISBN 0-7214-0785-4). Ladybird Bks.
Rinard, Judith E. Puppies. Crump, Donald J., ed. LC 82-47857. 32p. (ps-3). 1982. 10.95 (ISBN 0-87044-451-4). Natl Geog.
Rowland, Della. A World of Dogs. Didion, Nancy, illus. 24p. 1990. 8.95 (ISBN 0-8092-4276-1, Calico Bks). Contemp Bks.
Sanford, William & Green, Carl. The Beagle. LC 90-34211. (Illus.). 48p. (gr. 5-6). 1990. RSBE 10.95 (ISBN 0-89686-529-0, Crestwood Hse). Macmillan Child Grp.
—The Cocker Spaniel. LC 90-34059. (Illus.). 48p. (gr. 5-6). 1990. RSBE 10.95 (ISBN 0-89686-531-2, Crestwood Hse). Macmillan Child Grp.
—The Dachshund. LC 90-34058. (Illus.). 48p. (gr. 5-6). 1990. RSBE 10.95 (ISBN 0-89686-530-4, Crestwood Hse). Macmillan Child Grp.
—The German Shepherd. LC 90-34212. (Illus.). 48p. (gr. 5-6). 1990. RSBE 10.95 (ISBN 0-89686-527-4, Crestwood Hse). Macmillan Child Grp.
—The Poodle. LC 90-34199. (Illus.). 48p. (gr. 5-6). 1990. RSBE 10.95 (ISBN 0-89686-528-2, Crestwood Hse). Macmillan Child Grp.
Selsam, Millicent E. Como Crecen los Perritos (How Puppies Grow) Palacios, Argentina, tr. Bubley, Esther, illus. (SPA., Orig.). (ps-3). 1981. pap. 1.95 (ISBN 0-590-31862-4). Scholastic Inc.
—Como Crecen los Perritos: (How Puppies Grow) Palacios, Argentina, tr. Johnson, Neil, photos by. (SPA., Illus.). 32p. (ps-3). 1990. pap. 3.50 (ISBN 0-590-43410-1). Scholastic Inc.
—How Puppies Grow. Johnson, Neil, photos by. (Illus.). 32p. (ps-3). 1990. pap. 2.50 (ISBN 0-590-42736-9). Scholastic Inc.
Selsam, Millicent E. & Hunt, Joyce. A First Look at Dogs. Springer, Harriett, tr. 32p. (gr. 1-4). 1981. 7.95 (ISBN 0-8027-6409-6); lib. bdg. 9.85 (ISBN 0-8027-6421-5). Walker & Co.
Sharmat, Marjorie W. Morris Brookside, a Dog. LC 73-76797. (Illus.). 48p. (gr. k-3). 1973. reinforced bdg. 6.95 (ISBN 0-8234-0225-8). Holiday.
Siegel, Mary-Ellen & Koplin, Hermine M. More Than a Friend: Dogs with a Purpose. (Illus.). 128p. (gr. 4 up). 1984. 10.95 (ISBN 0-8027-6558-0); PLB 11.85 (ISBN 0-8027-6566-1). Walker & Co.
Silverstein, Alvin & Silverstein, Virginia. Dogs: All about Them. LC 84-29723. (Illus.). 256p. (gr. 6 up). 1986. 12.95 (ISBN 0-688-04805-6). Lothrop.
Snell, Nigel. Roy's Puppy. Snell, Nigel, illus. 32p. 1989. 4.95 (ISBN 0-8120-6121-7). Barron.
Sproule, Anna & Sproule, Michael. Dogs. Caulkins, Janet, ed. (Illus.). 48p. (gr. 1-6). 1988. PLB 11.90 (ISBN 0-531-18215-0, Pub. by Bookwright Pr). Watts.
Squire, Ann. Understanding Man's Best Friend: Why Dogs Look & Act the Way They Do. LC 90-30631. (Illus.). 128p. (gr. 3-7). 1991. SBE 14.95 (ISBN 0-02-786590-8, Mcmillan Child Bk). Macmillan Child Grp.
Standiford, Natalie. The Bravest Dog Ever: The True Story of Balto. Cook, Donald, tr. LC 89-3465. (Illus.). 47p. (Orig.). (gr. 1-3). 1989. PLB 6.99 (ISBN 0-394-99695-X, Random Juv); pap. 2.95 (ISBN 0-394-89695-5). Random.
Ullman, H. J. & Ullman, E. Spaniels. (Illus.). (gr. k-12). 1982. pap. 4.95 (ISBN 0-8120-2424-9). Barron.
Unkelbach, Kurt. Both Ends of the Leash: Selecting & Training Your Dog. Petie, Haris, illus. (gr. 3-7). 1968. P-H.
Vrbova, Zuza. Puppies. McAulay, Robert, illus. 48p. (gr. 2 up). 1990. PLB 9.95 (ISBN 0-86622-552-8, J-002). TFH Pubns.
Wild Dog. (Illus.). 24p. (gr. k-5). 1987. PLB 13.32 (ISBN 0-8172-2704-0). Raintree Pubs.
Wildsmith, Brian. Give a Dog a Bone. Wildsmith, Brian, illus. LC 85-3413. 48p. (ps-1). 1985. 10.95 (ISBN 0-394-87709-8, Pant Bks Young). Pantheon.
Zenk, Heather. The Siberian Husky. LC 90-34315. (Illus.). 48p. (gr. 5-6). 1990. RSBE 10.95 (ISBN 0-89686-535-5, Crestwood Hse). Macmillan Child Grp.

DOGS–FICTION

Abbott, Jeanie. The Most Beautiful Dog in the World. Badenhop, Mary, illus. LC 87-14985. 96p. (gr. 3-6). 1988. PLB 9.89 (ISBN 0-8167-1187-9); pap. text ed. 2.95 (ISBN 0-8167-1188-7). Troll Assocs.
Adamson, Charlotte. Tinker's Journey Home. 40p. (ps-8). 1989. 11.95 (ISBN 0-88138-132-2). Green Tiger Pr.
Adler, David A. My Dog & the Birthday Mystery. Gackenbach, Dick, illus. LC 86-14269. 32p. (gr. 1-4). 1987. reinforced bdg. 13.95 (ISBN 0-8234-0632-6); pap. 5.95 (ISBN 0-8234-0710-1). Holiday.
—My Dog & the Green Sock Mystery. Gackenbach, Dick, illus. LC 85-14145. 32p. (gr. 1-4). 1986. reinforced bdg. 13.95 (ISBN 0-8234-0590-7). Holiday.
Adoff, Arnold. Friend Dog. Howell, Troy, illus. LC 80-7773. 48p. (gr. k-5). 1980. PLB 11.89 (ISBN 0-685-02080-0, Lipp Jr Bks); PLB 11.89 (ISBN 0-397-31912-6). HarpC Child Bks.
Allen, Jonathan. My Dog. Allen, Jonathan, illus. LC 89-30857. 32p. (gr. 1-2). 1989. PLB 12.95 (ISBN 0-8368-0095-8). Gareth Stevens Inc.
Ancona, George. Sheep Dog. LC 84-20100. (Illus.). 64p. (gr. 5 up). 1985. 12.95 (ISBN 0-688-04118-3); PLB 12.88 (ISBN 0-688-04119-1). Lothrop.
Anderson, Brad. Marmaduke Hams It up. 256p. (Orig.). 1986. pap. 2.95 (ISBN 0-8125-7346-3, Dist. by Warner Pub Services & St. Martin's Press). Tor Bks.
—Marmaduke...Again? (gr. 5 up). 1977. pap. 1.50 (ISBN 0-590-09085-2). Scholastic Inc.
Anderson, Marilyn D. The Bubble Gum Monster Strikes Again. Hickman, Estella L., illus. 64p. (gr. 1-3). 1989. 2.50 (ISBN 0-87406-405-8, 22-19076-9). Willowisp Pr.
Argueta, Manlio, et al. Magic Dogs of the Volcanoes. Simmons, Elly, illus. (SPA & ENG.). 32p. (gr. k-5). 1990. 12.95 (ISBN 0-89239-064-6). Childrens Book Pr.
Arnosky, Jim. Gray Boy. LC 87-29337. (gr. 4-9). 1988. PLB 13.95 (ISBN 0-688-07345-X). Lothrop.
Avrett, Robert. Timid Pup. (Illus.). (gr. 1-3). PLB 6.70 (ISBN 0-8313-0004-3). Lantern.
Ball, Nancy. Boots: The Story of a Saint. Decker, Tim, illus. LC 88-72340. 44p. (Orig.). (gr. 2-5). 1989. pap. 5.00 (ISBN 0-916383-72-5). Aegina Pr.
Barracca, Sal & Barracca, Debra. The Adventures of Taxi Dog. Fogelman, Phyllis J., ed. Buehner, Mark, illus. LC 89-1056. 32p. (ps-3). 1990. 12.95 (ISBN 0-8037-0671-5); PLB 12.89 (ISBN 0-8037-0672-3). Dial Bks Young.
Barrett, Ethel. Jasper the Jealous Dog. Blankenbaker, Frances, ed. Gaddy, David, illus. LC 89-37545. 24p. (gr. 3-7). 1989. 4.95 (ISBN 0-8307-1378-6, 5111845). Regal.
Benjamin, Carol L. The Wicked Stepdog. Benjamin, Carole L., illus. LC 81-43322. 128p. (gr. 3-7). 1982. PLB 11.89 (ISBN 0-690-04171-3, Crowell Jr Bks). HarpC Child Bks.
—The Wicked Stepdog. 128p. (gr. 5 up). 1986. pap. 2.50 (ISBN 0-380-70089-1, Flare). Avon.
Bennett, Marian. God Made Puppies. (Illus.). 24p. (ps). 1980. 1.99 (ISBN 0-87239-403-4, 3635). Standard Pub.
Best, Ron. Colby: A Dog's Story. 1991. 6.95 (ISBN 0-533-08898-4). Vantage.

Birdwell, Norman. Clifford el Gran Perro Colorado: Clifford the Big Red Dog. Leos, Frances, tr. (Illus.). 32p. (ps-2). 1988. pap. 2.95 (ISBN 0-590-41380-5). Scholastic Inc.

Biros, Florence K. Dog Jack. Libb, Melva, ed. (Illus.). 192p. (Orig.). 1988. pap. 6.95 (ISBN 0-936369-22-1). Son-Rise Pubns.
DOG JACK, real-life mascot of the 102nd Regiment of the Pennsylvania Volunteers, finds his way into the hearts of young readers as they learn of his experiences during the Civil War as told by Florence W. Biros in the novel bearing his name. The actual historic events known about this canine hero are interwoven into this saga of love & adventure about Jed, a runaway slave boy, & his canine companion & friend. The story also shares of the allegiance of the men of the Niagara Volunteers toward their loyal mascot. DOG JACK, 192 page trade paper, is illustrated by a cover portrait by famed artist Ron DiCianni; the final pages are filled with a LIVING HISTORY GALLERY--actual photographs of the reenactment of the 125th Anniversary of the Battle of Gettysburg. DOG JACK, published by Son-Rise Publications, Route 3, Box 202, New Wilmington, PA 16142 retails for $7. 95. Son-Rise phone number: (412) 946-8334.
Publisher Provided Annotation.

Bloss, Janet A. Where Are the Boys? 128p. (gr. 6-8). 1986. 2.50 (ISBN 0-87406-065-6). Willowisp Pr.
Bogart, Jo Ellen. Daniel's Dog. (ps-3). 1990. pap. 11.95 (ISBN 0-590-43402-0). Scholastic Inc.
—Daniel's Dog. Wilson, Janet, illus. LC 89-32558. (ps-1). 1990. 11.95 (ISBN 0-590-73344-3). Scholastic Inc.
Bogart, Jo-Ellen. Daniel's Dog. Wilson, Janet, illus. 1992. pap. 3.95 (ISBN 0-590-43401-2, Blue Ribbon Bks). Scholastic Inc.
Bonsall, Crosby. Amazing the Incredible Super Dog. LC 85-45811. (Illus.). 32p. (gr. k-3). 1986. 11.95 (ISBN 0-06-020590-3); PLB 11.89 (ISBN 0-06-020591-1). HarpC Child Bks.
Bonsall, Crosby N. And I Mean It, Stanley. LC 73-14324. (Illus.). 32p. (gr. k-3). 1974. PLB 9.89. HarpC Child Bks.
Borovsky, Paul. George. Borovsky, Paul, illus. LC 89-2022. (ps up). 1990. 12.95 (ISBN 0-688-09150-4); PLB 12.88 (ISBN 0-688-09151-2). Greenwillow.
Boynton, Sandra. Doggies. 1984. 3.95 (ISBN 0-671-49318-3). S&S Trade.
Braybrooks, Ann, adapted by. Walt Disney's One Hundred One Dalmatians. LC 90-85424. (Illus.). 96p. 1991. 14.95 (ISBN 1-56282-010-9, Disney Pr); PLB 14.89 (ISBN 1-56282-011-7, Disney Pr). W Disney Pub.
—Walt Disney's One Hundred One Dalmatians. LC 90-85425. (Illus.). 72p. (Orig.). (gr. 2-6). 1991. pap. 2.95 (ISBN 1-56282-013-3, Disney Pr). W Disney Pub.
Brenner, Barbara. A Dog I Know. Brenner, Fred, illus. LC 82-47572. 32p. (gr. k-4). 1983. PLB 11.89 (ISBN 0-06-020685-3). HarpC Child Bks.
Brett, Jan. The First Dog. (Illus.). 32p. (ps-3). 1988. 13.95 (ISBN 0-15-227650-5). HarBraceJ.
Bridewell, Norman. Clifford's Puppy Days. (ps-3). 1988. pap. 2.25 (ISBN 0-590-44262-7). Scholastic Inc.
Bridwell, Norman. Clifford & the Grouchy Neighbors. Bridwell, Norman, illus. 32p. (Orig.). (gr. k-3). 1985. pap. 1.95 (ISBN 0-590-33461-1). Scholastic Inc.
—Clifford & the Grouchy Neighbors. Bridwell, Norman, illus. 32p. (gr. k-3). 1989. pap. 2.25 (ISBN 0-590-44261-9); pap. 5.95 incl. cass. (ISBN 0-590-63437-2). Scholastic Inc.
—Clifford at the Circus. Bridwell, Norman, illus. 32p. (gr. k-3). 1985. pap. 1.95 (ISBN 0-590-33588-X). Scholastic Inc.
—Clifford Gets a Job. Bridwell, Norman, illus. 32p. (gr. k-3). 1985. pap. 1.95 (ISBN 0-590-33555-3). Scholastic Inc.
—Clifford Gets a Job. Bridwell, Norman, illus. 32p. (gr. k-3). 1985. pap. 2.25 (ISBN 0-590-44296-1). Scholastic Inc.
—Clifford Goes to Hollywood. Bridwell, Norman, illus. (Orig.). (ps-3). 1986. pap. 1.95 (ISBN 0-590-40115-7). Scholastic Inc.
—Clifford Goes to Hollywood. Bridwell, Norman, illus. 32p. (gr. k-3). 1990. pap. 2.25 (ISBN 0-590-44289-9); pap. 5.95 incl. cass. (ISBN 0-590-63435-6). Scholastic Inc.
—Clifford Takes a Trip. Bridwell, Norman, illus. 32p. (gr. k-3). 1985. pap. 1.95 (ISBN 0-590-33554-5). Scholastic Inc.
—Clifford Takes a Trip. (ps-3). 1985. pap. 2.25 (ISBN 0-590-44260-0). Scholastic Inc.
—Clifford, the Big Red Dog. Bridwell, Norman, illus. 32p. (Orig.). (gr. k-3). 1985. pap. 1.95 (ISBN 0-590-33470-0). Scholastic Inc.
—Clifford the Big Red Dog. Bridwell, Norman, illus. (ps-3). 1988. 2.25 (ISBN 0-590-44297-X); pap. 5.95 incl. cassette (ISBN 0-590-63212-4). Scholastic Inc.
—Clifford the Big Red Dog. Bridwell, Norman, illus. 32p. (ps-3). 1988. pap. 8.95 (ISBN 0-590-40743-0, Pub. by Scholastic Hardcover). Scholastic Inc.
—Clifford the Small Red Puppy. (ps-2). 1988. 2.25 (ISBN 0-590-44294-5); incl. cassette 5.95 (ISBN 0-590-63211-6). Scholastic Inc.
—Clifford the Small Red Puppy. (ps-3). 1990. pap. 8.95 (ISBN 0-590-43496-9). Scholastic Inc.
—Clifford Va de Viaje. rev. ed. Palacios, Argentina, tr. (SPA., Illus.). 32p. (Orig.). (gr. k-3). 1987. pap. 2.95 (ISBN 0-590-40844-5). Scholastic Inc.
—Clifford Wants a Cookie. (Illus.). 16p. (ps-3). 1988. Book & Cookie Cutter Package. pap. 3.95 (ISBN 0-590-63282-5). Scholastic Inc.
—Clifford's ABC. Bridwell, Norman, illus. 32p. (ps-2). 1984. pap. 5.95 (ISBN 0-590-33154-X). Scholastic Inc.
—Clifford's Birthday Party. Bridwell, Norman, illus. 32p. (Orig.). (gr. k-3). 1991. 8.95 (ISBN 0-590-44232-5); pap. 5.95 incl. cassette (ISBN 0-590-63237-X). Scholastic Inc.
—Clifford's Christmas. Bridwell, Norman, illus. (gr. k-3). 1984. pap. 1.95 (ISBN 0-590-40221-8). Scholastic Inc.
—Clifford's Christmas Book-Cassette Prepack. Bridwell, Norman, illus. 32p. (Orig.). (gr. k-3). 1987. 2.25 (ISBN 0-590-44288-0); incl. cassette 5.95 (ISBN 0-590-63210-8). Scholastic Inc.
—Clifford's Family. Bridwell, Norman, illus. 32p. (Orig.). (ps-3). 1984. pap. 1.95 (ISBN 0-590-33849-8). Scholastic Inc.
—Clifford's Family. Bridwell, Norman, illus. 32p. (gr. k-3). 1984. pap. 2.25 (ISBN 0-590-44290-2). Scholastic Inc.
—Clifford's Good Deeds. (Illus.). (ps-3). 1985. pap. 1.95 (ISBN 0-590-33589-8). Scholastic Inc.
—Clifford's Good Deeds. Bridwell, Norman, illus. 32p. (gr. k-3). 1985. pap. 2.25 (ISBN 0-590-44292-9). Scholastic Inc.
—Clifford's Halloween. Bridwell, Norman, illus. 32p. (gr. k-3). 1989. pap. 2.25 (ISBN 0-590-44287-2); pap. 5.95 (ISBN 0-590-63436-4). Scholastic Inc.
—Clifford's Happy Days: A Pop-up Book. Bridwell, Norman, illus. 16p. (Orig.). (gr. k-3). 1990. pap. 12.95 (ISBN 0-590-42926-4). Scholastic Inc.
—Clifford's Kitten. Bridwell, Norman, illus. 32p. (Orig.). (ps-3). 1984. pap. 1.95 (ISBN 0-590-33967-2). Scholastic Inc.
—Clifford's Kitten. Bridwell, Norman, illus. 32p. (gr. k-3). 1984. pap. 2.25 (ISBN 0-590-44280-5). Scholastic Inc.
—Clifford's Manners. Bridwell, Norman, illus. 32p. (gr. k-3). 1987. pap. 2.25 (ISBN 0-590-44285-6). Scholastic Inc.
—Clifford's Pals. Bridwell, Norman, illus. 32p. (gr. k-3). 1985. pap. 1.95 (ISBN 0-590-33582-0). Scholastic Inc.
—Clifford's Pals. Bridwell, Norman, illus. 32p. (gr. k-3). 1985. pap. 2.25 (ISBN 0-590-44295-3). Scholastic Inc.
—Clifford's Puppy Days. 1989. pap. 1.95 (ISBN 0-590-42189-1). Scholastic Inc.
—Clifford's Riddles. Bridwell, Norman, illus. 32p. (Orig.). (ps-3). 1984. pap. 1.95 (ISBN 0-590-33361-5). Scholastic Inc.
—Clifford's Riddles. Bridwell, Norman, illus. 32p. (gr. k-3). 1984. pap. 2.25 (ISBN 0-590-44282-1). Scholastic Inc.
—Clifford's Sticker Book. Bridwell, Norman, illus. 24p. (ps-3). 1984. pap. 3.95 (ISBN 0-590-33657-6). Scholastic Inc.
—Clifford's Tricks. Bridwell, Norman, illus. 32p. (gr. k-3). 1986. pap. 1.95 (ISBN 0-590-33612-6). Scholastic Inc.
—Clifford's Tricks. Bridwell, Norman, illus. 32p. (gr. k-3). 1986. pap. 2.25 (ISBN 0-590-44291-0). Scholastic Inc.
—Clifford's Word Book. Bridwell, Norman, illus. 32p. (Orig.). (ps-1). 1990. pap. 2.25 (ISBN 0-590-43095-5). Scholastic Inc.
—Count on Clifford. (Illus.). 32p. (gr. k-3). 1987. 5.95 (ISBN 0-590-33614-2); pap. 2.25 (ISBN 0-590-44284-8). Scholastic Inc.
—Count on Clifford. (Illus.). 32p. (ps-k). 1987. pap. 1.95 (ISBN 0-590-40566-7). Scholastic Inc.
—Los Trucos de Clifford (Clifford's Tricks) Palacios, Argentina, tr. (SPA.). 32p. (gr. k-3). 1986. pap. 2.95 (ISBN 0-590-40123-8). Scholastic Inc.
Brown, Marc. Arthur's Pet Business. (ps-3). 1990. 14.95 (ISBN 0-316-11262-3, Joy St Bks). Little.
Brown, Margaret W. Indoor Noisy Book. Weisgard, Leonard, illus. LC 42-23589. 42p. (ps-3). 1942. PLB 12.89 (ISBN 0-06-020821-X). HarpC Child Bks.
Brown, Regina. Little Brother. Bornschlegel, Ruth, illus. (gr. 3-7). 1962. 8.95 (ISBN 0-8392-3019-2). Astor-Honor.
Brown, Ruth. Our Puppy's Vacation. (ps-3). 1991. pap. 3.95 (ISBN 0-525-44701-6, Dutton Unicorn). Puffin Bks.
Bruggen, Carol. Letters to Lucy: About Oliver the Dog. Bruggen, Carol, illus. 48p. (ps-4). 1986. 10.95 (ISBN 0-233-97887-9). Andre Deutsch.
Burke, Timothy. Cocoa Puppy. Burke, Ann & Burke, Ann, illus. LC 89-50890. 32p. (Orig.). (ps-3). 1989. 5.00 (ISBN 0-9623227-0-9). Thunder & Ink.
Burningham, John. The Dog. Burningham, John, illus. LC 76-17626. (ps-1). 1985. (Crowell Jr Bks). HarpC Child Bks.
Byars, Betsy. Wanted...Mud Blossom. (gr. 4-7). 1991. 14. 00 (ISBN 0-385-30428-5). Delacorte.
Caitlin, Stephen. You Dirty Dog. LC 87-19182. (Illus.). (gr. k-2). 1987. PLB 10.89 (ISBN 0-8167-1103-8); pap. 2.95 (ISBN 0-8167-1104-6). Troll Assocs.
The Call of the Wild. (Illus.). (gr. 3-12). 1965. deluxe ed. 11.95 (ISBN 0-448-06027-2, G&D); pap. 6.95 (ISBN 0-448-11027-X). Putnam Pub Group.
Campbell, Rod. Henry's Busy Day. Campbell, Rod, illus. LC 83-25905. 18p. (ps-1). 1984. pap. 6.95 (ISBN 0-670-80024-4). Viking Child Bks.
Carlson, Nancy. Harriet & the Roller Coaster. 32p. (gr. k-3). 1984. pap. 3.95 (ISBN 0-14-050467-2, Puffin). Puffin Bks.
—Harriet & Walt. 32p. (gr. k-3). 1984. pap. 3.95 (ISBN 0-14-050463-X, Puffin). Puffin Bks.
—Poor Carl. (Illus.). 32p. (ps-3). 1989. pap. 11.95 (ISBN 0-670-81774-0). Viking Child Bks.
—Poor Carl. (Illus.). 32p. (ps-3). 1991. pap. 3.95 (ISBN 0-14-050773-6, Puffin). Puffin Bks.
Carr, Jan. Lady & the Tramp. 80p. (Orig.). (gr. 4-6). 1987. pap. 2.50 (ISBN 0-590-41450-X). Scholastic Inc.
Carratello, Patty. My Truck & My Pup. Spivak, Darlene, ed. Brostrom, Eileen, illus. 16p. (gr. k-2). 1988. wkbk. 1.95 (ISBN 1-55734-390-X). Tchr Create Mat.
Carrick, Carol. The Foundling. Carrick, Donald, illus. LC 77-1587. 32p. (ps-4). 1979. 13.95 (ISBN 0-395-28775-8, Clarion). HM.
—Lost in the Storm. Carrick, Donald, illus. LC 74-1051. 32p. (ps-3). 1979. 12.95 (ISBN 0-395-28776-6, Clarion). HM.
Carris, Joan. The Greatest Idea Ever. Newsom, Carol, illus. LC 89-34516. 176p. (gr. 3-7). 1990. 11.95 (ISBN 0-397-32378-6, Lipp Jr Bks); PLB 11.89 (ISBN 0-397-32379-4, Lipp Jr Bks). HarpC Child Bks.
Catalanotto, Peter. Dylan's Day Out. LC 88-36440. (Illus.). 32p. (ps-1). 1989. 14.95 (ISBN 0-531-05829-8); PLB 14.99 (ISBN 0-531-08429-9). Orchard Bks Watts.
Cate, Dick. Ghost Dog. (Illus.). 144p. (gr. 5-8). 1989. 19. 95 (ISBN 0-575-03926-4, Pub. by Gollancz England). Trafalgar Sq.
Cavanna, Betty. Going on Sixteen. LC 85-4877. 224p. (gr. 5-9). 1985. Repr. of 1946 ed. 11.95 (ISBN 0-688-05892-2, Morrow Junior Books). Morrow.
—Petey. Krush, Beth & Krush, Jo, illus. LC 73-4351. 144p. (gr. 3-6). 1973. 5.50 (ISBN 0-664-32532-7, Westminster). Westminster John Knox.
Cazet, Denys. Saturday. Cazet, Denys, illus. LC 87-2388. 64p. (gr. 1-4). 1988. pap. 3.95 (ISBN 0-689-71065-8, Aladdin). Macmillan Child Grp.
Charles, Donald. Pickles & Pepper. LC 89-28202. (Illus.). 40p. (gr. k-3). 1990. PLB 13.95 (ISBN 0-671-70345-5). S&S Trade.
—Shaggy Dog's Halloween. Charles, Donald, illus. LC 84-5901. 32p. (ps-3). 1984. lib. bdg. 14.60 (ISBN 0-516-03575-4). Childrens.
—Shaggy Dog's Tall Tale. Charles, Donald, illus. LC 79-26493. 32p. (ps-3). 1980. PLB 14.60 (ISBN 0-516-03616-5). Childrens.
Chorao, Kay. The Cherry Pie Baby. Chorao, Kay, illus. LC 88-2630. 32p. (ps-3). 1989. 12.95 (ISBN 0-525-44435-1, DCB). Dutton Child Bks.
Christian, Mary B. Sebastian (Super Sleuth) & the Purloined Sirloin. McCue, Lisa, illus. LC 85-15238. 64p. (gr. 2-5). 1986. 10.95 (ISBN 0-02-718210-X, Mcmillan Child Bk). Macmillan Child Grp.
—Sebastian (Super Sleuth) & the Stars-In-His-Eyes Mystery. McCue, Lisa, illus. LC 86-21771. 64p. (gr. 2-6). 1987. 10.95 (ISBN 0-02-718540-0, Mcmillan Child Bk). Macmillan Child Grp.
Christopher, Matt. The Dog That Called the Signals. Ogden, Bill, illus. LC 82-15234. 48p. (gr. 3-5). 1982. 12.95 (ISBN 0-316-13980-7). Little.
—The Dog That Pitched a No-Hitter. Vasconcellos, Daniel, illus. (gr. 1-3). 1988. 11.95 (ISBN 0-316-14057-0). Little.
—The Dog That Stole Football Plays. Ogden, Bill, illus. 48p. (gr. 3-5). 1980. 13.95 (ISBN 0-316-13978-5). Little.
Cleary, Beverly. Henry & Ribsy. Darling, Louis, illus. LC 54-6402. 192p. (gr. 3-7). 1954. 12.95 (ISBN 0-688-21382-0); PLB 12.88 (ISBN 0-688-31382-5, Morrow Jr Bks). Morrow Jr Bks.
—Henry Huggins. Darling, Louis, illus. LC 50-8615. (gr. 3-7). 1950. 13.95 (ISBN 0-688-21385-5); PLB 13.88 (ISBN 0-688-31385-X, Morrow Jr Bks). Morrow Jr Bks.
—Ribsy. Darling, Louis, illus. LC 64-13263. (gr. 3-7). 1964. 13.95 (ISBN 0-688-21662-5); PLB 13.88 (ISBN 0-688-31662-X). Morrow.
—Two Dog Biscuits. rev. ed. DeSalvo-Ryan, Dyanne, illus. LC 85-18816. 32p. (ps-1). 1986. 11.95 (ISBN 0-688-05847-7); lib. bdg. 11.88 (ISBN 0-688-05848-5, Morrow Jr Bks). Morrow Jr Bks.
—Two Dog Biscuits. (gr. k-6). 1987. pap. 3.95 (ISBN 0-440-49134-7, YB). Dell.
Clough, Fred. Sal T. Dog. Kirehoff, Dan, illus. 48p. (gr. 1-3). 1990. 12.95 (ISBN 0-89272-281-9). Down East.
Cohen, Miriam. Jim's Dog Muffins. (gr. k-6). 1986. pap. 2.95 (ISBN 0-440-44224-9, YB). Dell.

Coldsborough, June. Little Puppy. McClain, Mary, illus. 12p. (ps-2). 1982. board 4.95 (ISBN 0-671-43159-5, Little Simon). S&S Trade.

Cole, Joanna. My Puppy Is Born. rev. ed. Miller, Margaret, photos by. LC 90-42011. (Illus.). 48p. (ps up). 1991. pap. 4.95 (ISBN 0-688-10198-4, Mulberry). Morrow.

Cone, Molly. Mishmash & The Sauerkraut Mystery. Shortall, Leonard, illus. (gr. 4-6). 1974. pap. 0.95 (ISBN 0-395-18556-4). HM.

—Mishmash & The Substitute Teacher. Shortall, Leonard, illus. (gr. 2-5). 1963. 13.95 (ISBN 0-395-06709-X). HM.

Corbett, Scott. The Disappearing Dog Trick. Galdone, Paul, illus. 112p. (gr. 4-6). 1983. pap. 2.50 (ISBN 0-590-40973-5, Apple Paperbacks). Scholastic Inc.

—The Disappearing Dog Trick. 112p. (gr. 3-7). 1991. pap. 2.75 (ISBN 0-590-42864-0). Scholastic Inc.

Corbin, William. A Dog Worth Stealing. LC 87-5795. 176p. (gr. 5 up). 1987. 12.95 (ISBN 0-531-05712-7); PLB 12.99 (ISBN 0-531-08312-8). Orchard Bks Watts.

Corcoran, Barbara. Annie's Monster. LC 89-28121. 192p. (gr. 3-7). 1990. 13.95 (ISBN 0-689-31632-1, Atheneum Child Bk). Macmillan Child Grp.

Cosgrove, Stephen. Heidi's Rose. Edelson, Wendy, illus. LC 90-71079. 32p. 1991. 14.95 (ISBN 1-55868-033-0). Gr Arts Ctr Pub.
Set high in the mountains at Timberline Lodge, the story begins as a Saint Bernard arrives at the lodge. Wearing a beautiful locket, the huge dog arouses the curiosity of Rose, the innkeeper's daughter. But no one can get close to the animal to see what is in the locket. Accustomed to getting her own way, Rose schemes to get the locket so she can look inside. But adventure overtakes both girl & dog. Stephen Cosgrove is the author of more than 150 children's books. Wendy Edelson's illustrations have won numerous awards.
Publisher Provided Annotation.

Creighton, Susan. Huggins & Kisses. Kong, Emilie, illus. 40p. (ps). 1985. 4.00 (ISBN 0-910313-94-6). Parker Bros.

Crozat, Francois. I Am a Little Dog. 28p. (ps-k). 1990. 7.95 (ISBN 0-8120-6159-4). Barron.

—I Am a Little Dog (Miniature Size) (ps). 1990. 2.95 (ISBN 0-8120-6195-0). Barron.

Davis, Dawn S. A Good Dog to Have Around the House. LC 90-90462. (Illus.). 52p. (Orig.). (gr. 1). 1990. pap. 3.95 (ISBN 1-879318-00-8). Wild Meadows.

—Motorcycle Dog. LC 90-72039. (Illus.). 52p. (Orig.). (gr. 2-4). 1990. pap. 3.95 (ISBN 1-879318-01-6). Wild Meadows.

Day, Alexandra. Good Dog, Carl. Day, Alexandra, illus. LC 85-70419. 36p. (Orig.). (ps up). 1985. 11.95 (ISBN 0-88138-062-8, Star & Elephant Bks.). Green Tiger Pr.

—Paddy's Pay-Day. (Illus.). 32p. (ps up). 1989. pap. 13.95 (ISBN 0-670-82598-0). Viking Child Bks.

DeJong, Meindert. Along Came a Dog. Sendak, Maurice, illus. LC 57-9265. 192p. (gr. 3-6). 1958. PLB 15.89 (ISBN 0-06-021421-X). HarpC Child Bks.

—Along Came a Dog. Sendak, Maurice, illus. LC 57-9265. 192p. (gr. 4-7). 1980. pap. 3.50 (ISBN 0-06-440114-6, Trophy). HarpC Child Bks.

—Hurry Home, Candy. Sendak, Maurice, illus. LC 53-8536. 224p. (gr. 4-7). 1953. PLB 14.89 (ISBN 0-06-021486-4). HarpC Child Bks.

—Hurry Home, Candy. LC 53-8536. (Illus.). 244p. (gr. 4-7). 1972. pap. 3.50 (ISBN 0-06-440025-5, Trophy). HarpC Child Bks.

De Warren, Shaun. The Harris Visits the Garden of Everything. Coupland, Gill, illus. 32p. (ps-3). 1985. cloth 12.95 (ISBN 0-913299-21-9, Dist. by PGW). Stillpoint.

Dicks, Terrance. Goliath at the Seaside. Littlewood, Valerie, illus. 52p. (gr. 2-4). 1989. pap. 2.95 (ISBN 0-8120-4209-3). Barron.

—Goliath Goes to Summer School. Littlewood, Valerie, illus. 52p. (gr. 2-4). 1989. pap. 2.95 (ISBN 0-8120-4210-7). Barron.

Dicks, Terrence. Goliath & the Buried Treasure. Littlewood, Valerie, illus. (gr. k-4). 1987. 7.95 (ISBN 0-8120-5822-4); pap. 2.95 (ISBN 0-8120-3819-3). Barron.

Disney, Walt, Productions Staff. Walt Disney's One Hundred & One Dalmatians. LC 74-10829. (Illus.). 48p. (ps-3). 1975. 6.95 (ISBN 0-394-82571-3, Random Juv); lib. bdg. 4.99 (ISBN 0-394-92571-8). Random.

Dito, Joan. Calie the Calico Cat & Rory the Spaniel. 32p. (ps-1). 1989. 6.95 (ISBN 0-8062-3542-X). Carlton.

Dobson, Danae. Woof & the Big Fire. 32p. 1990. write for info. (ISBN 0-8499-8362-2). Word Bks.

—Woof, the Seeing-Eye Dog. 32p. 1990. write for info. (ISBN 0-8499-8363-0). Word Bks.

A Dog for Keeps (EV, Unit 10. (gr. 3). 1991. 5-pack 21.25 (ISBN 0-88106-781-4). Charlesbridge Pub.

Draper, Cena C. The Worst Hound Around. LC 78-25687. 118p. (gr. 5-8). 1979. 8.95 (ISBN 0-664-32643-9, Westminster). Westminster John Knox.

Duffy, James. Cleaver of the Good Luck Diner. LC 88-29906. (Illus.). 128p. (gr. 3-6). 1989. 12.95 (ISBN 0-684-18969-0, Scribners Young Read). Macmillan Child Grp.

Duncan, Lois. Hotel for Dogs. (gr. 4-7). 1991. pap. 3.25 (ISBN 0-440-40435-5). Dell.

Durrell, Gerald. Keeper. West, Keith, illus. 32p. (gr. 1-4). 1991. 13.95 (ISBN 1-55970-122-6). Arcade Pub Inc.

Eagle, Ellen. Gypsy's Cleaning Day. Eagle, Ellen, illus. LC 89-34315. 32p. (ps up). 1990. 13.95 (ISBN 0-688-07391-3); PLB 13.88 (ISBN 0-688-07392-1, Morrow Jr Bks). Morrow Jr Bks.

Eastman, P. D. Go, Dog, Go! (ps-1). 1986. pap. 6.95 incl. cassette (ISBN 0-394-88328-4). Random.

—Perro Grande...Perro Pequeno: (Big Dog...Little Dog) De Cuenca, Pilar & Alvarez, Ines, trs. Eastman, P. D., illus. LC 81-12070. (SPA.). 32p. (ps-3). 1982. lib. bdg. 5.99 (ISBN 0-394-95142-5); pap. 2.25 (ISBN 0-394-85142-0). Random.

Eastman, Philip D. Big Dog, Little Dog: A Bedtime Story. (Illus.). (ps-1). 1973. pap. 2.25 (ISBN 0-394-82669-8, Random Juv). Random.

—Go, Dog, Go. LC 61-7069. (Illus.). 72p. (gr. 1-3). 1961. 6.95 (ISBN 0-394-80020-6); lib. bdg. 7.99 (ISBN 0-394-90020-0). Beginner.

Engberry, Carrie S. Diary of a Pekingese. 96p. 1990. 9.95 (ISBN 0-8062-3729-5). Carlton.

Erickson, John. The Further Adventures of Hank the Cowdog. 150p. (gr. 3-8). 1988. pap. 3.95 rack-size (ISBN 0-87719-103-4, Lone Star Bks). Gulf Pub.

—Hank the Cowdog. 140p. (gr. 3-8). 1988. pap. 3.95 rack-size (ISBN 0-87719-102-6, Lone Star Bks). Gulf Pub.

Erickson, John R. The Further Adventures of Hank the Cowdog. Holmes, Gerald L., illus. 93p. (Orig.). (gr. 3). 1983. 9.95 (ISBN 0-9608612-7-0); pap. 6.95 (ISBN 0-9608612-5-4); tape 13.95 (ISBN 0-916941-02-7). Maverick Bks.

—Hank the Cowdog: It's a Dog's Life. (Illus.). 100p. (Orig.). (gr. 3). 9.95 (ISBN 0-916941-04-3); pap. 5.95 (ISBN 0-9608612-9-7); talking book 13.95 (ISBN 0-916941-03-5). Maverick Bks.

—Hank the Cowdog: Let Sleeping Dogs Lie. Holmes, Gerald, illus. 19p. (gr. 3 up). 1986. 9.95 (ISBN 0-916941-15-9); pap. 6.95 (ISBN 0-916941-14-0); talking book 13.95 (ISBN 0-916941-16-7). Maverick Bks.

Ernst, Lisa C. Ginger Jumps. Ernst, Lisa C., illus. LC 89-38706. 32p. (ps-2). 1990. 14.95 (ISBN 0-02-733565-8, Bradbury Press). Macmillan.

Estes, Eleanor. Ginger Pye. Estes, Eleanor, illus. LC 51-10446. (gr. 3-7). 1951. 13.95 (ISBN 0-15-230930-6, HJ). HarBraceJ.

—Ginger Pye. Schwartz, Amy, contrib. by. 272p. (gr. 3-7). 1990. pap. 3.95 (ISBN 0-15-230933-0). HarbraceJ.

Evans, Mark. Pepito: The Little Dancing Dog. Cugat, Xavier, illus. LC 78-65354. (gr. k-4). 1979. 6.95 (ISBN 0-87592-063-2). Scroll Pr.

Fairman, Joan. A Penny Saved. (Illus.). (gr. 1-4). 1971. PLB 6.70 (ISBN 0-8313-0036-1). Lantern.

Farley, Walter. The Great Dane Thor. 192p. (gr. 4-7). 1980. pap. 1.50 (ISBN 0-440-93095-2, LFL). Dell.

Fidler, Kathleen. Flash the Sheepdog. (Illus.). 164p. (gr. 5-8). 1989. pap. 5.95 (ISBN 0-86241-071-1, Pub. by Cnngt Pub Ltd). Trafalgar Sq.

—Turk the Border Collie. 160p. (gr. 5-7). 1989. pap. 5.95 (ISBN 0-86241-130-0, Pub. by Cnngt Pub Ltd). Trafalgar Sq.

Flack, Marjorie. Angus & the Cat. 40p. (ps-k). 1989. PLB 13.99 (ISBN 0-685-01488-6); pap. 12.95 (ISBN 0-685-01489-4). Doubleday.

—Angus & the Ducks. (Illus.). 40p. (ps-3). 1989. 12.95 (ISBN 0-385-07213-9, Zephyr-BFYR); PLB 13.99 (ISBN 0-385-07600-2, Zephyr-BFYR). Doubleday.

—Angus Lost. (ps-k). 1989. PLB 12.95 (ISBN 0-385-07214-7); pap. 13.99 (ISBN 0-385-07601-0). Doubleday.

Follow That Puppy. 1991. pap. 13.95 (ISBN 0-671-70780-9). S&S Trade.

Four Puppies. (ps-3). 1989. Incl. cass. write for info. (13686, Pub. by Golden Bks). Western Pub.

Fox, Paula. The Stone-Faced Boy. Mackay, Donald A., illus. LC 68-9053. 112p. (gr. 4-6). 1982. 12.95 (ISBN 0-02-735570-5, Bradbury Pr). Macmillan Child Grp.

Gabriel, Howard W., III. Loving Memories from Dog to Dog. House, David J., illus. 32p. (Orig.). (gr. k-6). 1987. pap. 2.95 (ISBN 0-936997-01-X). M & H Enter.

Gackenbach, Dick. A Bag Full of Pups. LC 80-23230. (Illus.). 32p. (ps-2). 1981. 13.95 (ISBN 0-395-30081-9, Clarion). HM.

—A Bag Full of Pups. LC 80-23230. 32p. (gr. k-3). 1983. pap. 4.95 (ISBN 0-89919-179-7, Pkub. by Clarion). Ticknor & Fields.

—Claude & Pepper. Gackenbach, Dick, illus. LC 75-25507. 32p. (ps-2). 1979. 13.95 (ISBN 0-395-28793-6, Clarion). HM.

—Claude the Dog. Gackenbach, Dick, illus. LC 74-3403. 32p. (ps-2). 1984. pap. 4.95 (ISBN 0-89919-124-X, Pub. by NClarion); pap. 3.60 (ISBN 0-685-02315-X). Ticknor & Fields.

—Dog for a Day. Gackenbach, Dick, illus. LC 86-17514. 32p. (ps-1). 1989. 12.95 (ISBN 0-89919-452-4, Pub. by Clarion); pap. 4.95 (ISBN 0-89919-851-1, Pub. by Clarion). Ticknor & Fields.

—What's Claude Doing? LC 83-14983. (Illus.). 32p. (ps-3). 1986. pap. 4.95 (ISBN 0-89919-464-8, Pub. by Clarion). Ticknor & Fields.

Gag, Wanda. Nothing at All. Gag, Wanda, illus. (gr. 1-3). 1941. PLB 6.99 (ISBN 0-698-30264-8, Coward). Putnam Pub Group.

Gardiner, John R. Stone Fox. Sewall, Marcia, illus. LC 79-7895. 96p. (gr. 2-6). 1980. 12.95 (ISBN 0-690-03983-2, Crowell Jr Bks); PLB 12.89 (ISBN 0-690-03984-0, Crowell Jr Bks). HarpC Child Bks.

Garside, Alice H. The Dog & the Bone. 20p. (Orig.). (gr. k-2). 1990. pap. 2.00 (ISBN 1-882063-11-2). Cottage Pr MA.

—The Dog & the Wolf. 20p. (Orig.). (gr. k-2). 1990. pap. 2.00 (ISBN 1-882063-08-2). Cottage Pr MA.

Geronimi, Clyde. Chips Quips. Geronimi, Clyde, illus. LC 83-72694. 55p. (gr. 4 up). 1983. pap. 3.95 (ISBN 0-939126-09-5). Back Bay.

Gerstein, Mordicai. The New Creatures. LC 90-4128. (Illus.). 32p. (ps-3). 1991. 14.95 (ISBN 0-06-022164-X); PLB 14.89 (ISBN 0-06-022167-4). HarpC Child Bks.

—Roll Over! LC 83-18884. (Illus.). 32p. (ps-1). 1988. 9.95 (ISBN 0-517-55209-4). Crown.

Gilson, Jamie. Double Dare Dog. Primavera, Elise, illus. LC 87-37855. 126p. (gr. 3-5). 1988. 12.95 (ISBN 0-688-07969-5). Lothrop.

—Double Dog Dare. (Illus.). 1989. pap. 2.75 (ISBN 0-671-67898-1, Minstrel Bks). PB.

Gipson, Fred. Old Yeller. LC 56-8780. (Illus.). (gr. 7-9). 1956. 19.95i (ISBN 0-06-011545-9, HarpT). HarperCollins.

—Old Yeller. LC 56-8780. 176p. (gr. 5 up). 1990. pap. 3.50 (ISBN 0-06-440382-3, Trophy). HarpC Child Bks.

Girion, Barbara. Misty & Me. LC 90-31675. 144p. (gr. 3-7). 1990. pap. 3.95 (ISBN 0-689-71442-4, Aladdin). Macmillan Child Grp.

Go Fetch, Bouncer. (ps up). 1990. PLB 5.98 (ISBN 0-7924-5366-2, Mallard Pr). BDD Promo Bk.

Goble, Paul. The Gift of the Sacred Dog. Goble, Paul, illus. LC 80-15843. 32p. (gr. k-2). 1982. Repr. of 1980 ed. 13.95 (ISBN 0-02-736560-3, Bradbury Pr). Macmillan Child Grp.

—Gift of the Sacred Dog. 1984. pap. 4.95 (ISBN 0-02-043280-1, Aladdin). Macmillan Child Grp.

Godden, Rumer. Fu-Dog. Littlewood, Valerie, illus. 64p. (ps-2). 1990. pap. 14.95 (ISBN 0-670-82300-7). Viking Child Bks.

Golder, Stephen & Memling, Lise. Buffy's Orange Leash. LC 88-21293. (Illus.). 32p. (gr. k-3). 1988. 8.95 (ISBN 0-930323-42-4, Kendall Green Pubns). Gallaudet Univ Pr.

Gondosch, Linda. Brutus the Wonder Poodle. Dann, Penny, illus. LC 89-39377. 64p. (Orig.). (gr. 2-4). 1990. PLB 5.99 (ISBN 0-679-90573-1); pap. 1.95 (ISBN 0-679-80573-7). McKay.

Gordon, Sharon. Home for a Puppy. Wheeler, Jody, illus. LC 86-30853. 32p. (gr. k-2). 1988. PLB 7.06 (ISBN 0-8167-0978-5); pap. text ed. 1.95 (ISBN 0-8167-0979-3). Troll Assocs.

Graham, Amanda. Always Arthur. Gynell, Donna, illus. LC 89-4474. 32p. (gr. 2-3). 1990. PLB 12.95 (ISBN 0-8368-0096-6). Gareth Stevens Inc.

Graham, Margaret B. Benjy & His Friend Fifi. Graham, Margaret B., illus. LC 87-29374. 32p. (ps-3). 1988. 11.95 (ISBN 0-06-022252-2); PLB 11.89 (ISBN 0-06-022253-0). HarpC Child Bks.

—Benjy & the Barking Bird. Graham, Margaret B., illus. LC 79-129856. 32p. (ps-3). 1971. 13.95 (ISBN 0-06-022079-1); PLB 13.89 (ISBN 0-06-022080-5). HarpC Child Bks.

—Benjy's Boat Trip. Graham, Margaret B., illus. LC 77-6393. (ps-3). 1977. PLB 13.89 (ISBN 0-06-022093-7). HarpC Child Bks.

—Benjy's Dog House. Graham, Margaret B., illus. LC 72-9854. 32p. (ps-3). 1973. PLB 14.89 (ISBN 0-06-022084-8). HarpC Child Bks.

Griffith, Helen V. Foxy. LC 83-16392. 144p. (gr. 5-9). 1984. reinforced 11.95 (ISBN 0-688-02567-6). Greenwillow.

—Plunk's Dreams. LC 88-34905. (Illus.). 32p. (ps up). 1990. 12.95 (ISBN 0-688-08812-0); lib. bdg. write for info. (ISBN 0-688-08813-9). Greenwillow.

Griffiths, Helen. Grip, a Dog Story. Hall, Douglass, photos by. LC 78-6819. (Illus.). 160p. (gr. 5 up). 1978. 9.95 (ISBN 0-8234-0335-1). Holiday.

Grise, Jeannette. Robert Benjamin & the Great Blue Dog Joke. LC 78-17006. (Illus.). 122p. (gr. 3-6). 1978. 8.95 (ISBN 0-664-32637-4, Westminster). Westminster John Knox.

Gross, Lisa. The Half & Half Dog. Gross, Lisa, illus. LC 88-9347. 26p. (gr. k-6). 1988. lib. bdg. 12.95 (ISBN 0-933849-13-3). Landmark Edns.

Guy, Rosa. Paris, Pee Wee & Big Dog. Binch, Caroline, illus. LC 85-1654. 112p. (gr. 4-6). 1985. 13.95 (ISBN 0-385-29407-7). Delacorte.

Hale, Kathleen. Orlando Keeps a Dog. (ps-3). 1990. 14.95 (ISBN 0-7232-3650-X). Warne.

Hall, Lynn. Letting Go. LC 86-31483. 112p. (gr. 6-9). 1987. 12.95 (ISBN 0-684-18781-7, Scribners Young Read). Macmillan Child Grp.

Hammond, Jane. Daniel the Dog. (ps-k). 1983. pap. 1.50 (ISBN 0-87162-287-4, D5601). Warner Pr.

Hargreaves, Roger. Willie Woof. Jolliffe, Gray, illus. LC 89-60409. 32p. (Orig.). (ps-3). 1989. pap. 1.95 (ISBN 0-679-80116-2). Random.

Harmey, Barbara E. My Very Own Puppy, Playing in the Rain. (ps-k). pap. 4.95 (ISBN 0-317-62509-8). St Martin.

Hart, Sharon M. A Dog for Jesse. Rabinowitz, Sandy, illus. 128p. (gr. 2-5). 1989. pap. 2.50 (ISBN 0-590-41503-4). Scholastic Inc.

Hasenav, Florence A. Pinkey. (Illus.). (gr. 1-6). 1975. 6.00 (ISBN 0-913042-02-1). Holland Hse Pr.

Hathorn, Libby. Thunderwith. 1991. 15.95 (ISBN 0-316-35034-6). Little.

Hawkins, Colin & Hawkins, Jacqui. Tog the Dog. Hawkins, Colin, illus. 22p. (ps-1). 1986. 8.95 (ISBN 0-399-21338-4, Putnam). Putnam Pub Group.

Haywood, Carolyn. Eddie's Friend Boodles. Stock, Catherine, illus. LC 91-3212. (gr. 6 up). 1991. 12.95 (ISBN 0-688-09028-1). Morrow Jr Bks.

Hazen, Barbara S. & Morrill, Leslie H. Stay, Fang. LC 89-32359. (Illus.). 32p. (gr. k-3). 1990. 12.95 (ISBN 0-689-31599-6, Atheneum Child Bk). Macmillan Child Grp.

Heller, Nicholas. Happy Birthday, Moe Dog. LC 87-14851. (Illus.). 24p. (gr. k up). 1988. 11.95 (ISBN 0-688-07670-X); lib. bdg. 11.88 (ISBN 0-688-07671-8). Greenwillow.

Herrold, Tracey. The Puppy Who Needed a Friend. (Illus.). 24p. (Orig.). (gr. k-2). 1989. pap. text ed. 0.99 (ISBN 0-87406-396-5). Willowisp Pr.

Hewett, Joan. Rosalie. Carrick, Donald, illus. LC 86-7333. 32p. (ps-2). 1987. 13.95 (ISBN 0-688-06228-8); PLB 13.88 (ISBN 0-688-06229-6). Lothrop.

Hill, Eric. Cumpleanos de Spot (Spot's Birthday Party) Hill, Eric, illus. (SPA.). 22p. (ps-2). 1983. 11.95 (ISBN 0-399-21020-2, Putnam). Putnam Pub Group.

—Donde Esta Spot? (Where's Spot?) Hill, Eric, illus. (SPA.). 22p. (ps-2). 1983. 11.95 (ISBN 0-399-21018-0, Putnam). Putnam Pub Group.

—El Primer Paseo de Spot. Hill, Eric, illus. (SPA.). (ps-2). 1983. 11.95 (ISBN 0-399-21019-9, Putnam). Putnam Pub Group.

—La Primera Navidad de Spot. Hill, Eric, illus. (SPA.). (ps-2). 1983. 11.95 (ISBN 0-399-21024-5, Putnam). Putnam Pub Group.

—Puppy Love. (Illus.). 32p. (ps-k). 1982. 3.95 (ISBN 0-399-20935-2, Putnam). Putnam Pub Group.

—Spot at Home. (Illus.). 14p. (ps-k). 1991. bds. 3.95 (ISBN 0-399-21774-6, Putnam). Putnam Pub Group.

—Spot at Play. Hill, Eric, illus. LC 84-17848. 14p. (ps-1). 1985. bds. 3.50 (ISBN 0-399-21228-0, Putnam). Putnam Pub Group.

—Spot at the Fair. Hill, Eric, illus. LC 84-17849. 14p. (ps-1). 1985. bds. 3.50 (ISBN 0-399-21229-9, Putnam). Putnam Pub Group.

—Spot Goes Splash! Hill, Eric, illus. 8p. (gr. k-1). 1984. vinyl foam-filled 2.95 (ISBN 0-399-21068-7, Putnam). Putnam Pub Group.

—Spot Goes to the Beach. LC 84-18291. (Illus.). 22p. (gr. k). 1985. 10.95 (ISBN 0-399-21247-7, Putnam). Putnam Pub Group.

—Spot Goes to the Farm. (Illus.). 22p. (ps-1). 1987. 10.95 (ISBN 0-399-21434-8, Putnam). Putnam Pub Group.

—Spot in the Garden. (Illus.). 14p. (ps-k). 1991. bds. 3.95 (ISBN 0-399-21772-X, Putnam). Putnam Pub Group.

—Spot on the Farm. Hill, Eric, illus. LC 84-17850. 14p. (ps-1). 1985. bds. 3.75 (ISBN 0-399-21230-2, Putnam). Putnam Pub Group.

—Spot Sleeps Over. (Illus.). 22p. (ps-k). 1990. 11.95 (ISBN 0-399-21815-7, Putnam). Putnam Pub Group.

—Spot Sleeps Over: (Se Pasa la Noche) (SPA., Illus.). 22p. (ps-k). 1991. 12.95 (ISBN 0-399-21835-1, Putnam). Putnam Pub Group.

—Spot's Birthday Party. (Illus.). 1991. 4.95 (ISBN 0-399-21770-3, Putnam). Putnam Pub Group.

—Spot's First Easter. (Illus.). 22p. (ps-1). 1988. 10.95 (ISBN 0-399-21435-6, Putnam). Putnam Pub Group.

—Spot's First Picnic. Hill, Eric, illus. (ps-2). 1987. 4.95 (ISBN 0-399-21398-8, Putnam). Putnam Pub Group.

—Spot's First Walk. Hill, Eric, illus. 22p. (ps). 1981. 10.95 (ISBN 0-399-20838-0, Putnam). Putnam Pub Group.

—Spot's Friends. Hill, Eric, illus. 8p. (gr. k-1). 1984. vinyl foam-filled 3.50 (ISBN 0-399-21066-0, Putnam). Putnam Pub Group.

—Spot's Toys. Hill, Eric, illus. 8p. (gr. k-1). 1984. 2.95 (ISBN 0-399-21067-9, Putnam). Putnam Pub Group.

—Sweet Dreams, Spot! Hill, Eric, illus. 8p. (gr. k-1). 1984. 2.95 (ISBN 0-399-21069-5, Putnam). Putnam Pub Group.

Hoff, Syd. Barkley. Hoff, Syd, illus. LC 75-6290. 32p. (gr. k-3). 1975. PLB 10.89 (ISBN 0-06-022448-7). HarpC Child Bks.

Holl, Adelaide. Have You Seen My Puppy. Veno, Joe, illus. (ps-1). 1968. (Random Juv). Random.

Holland, Margaret. Look Around Puppies & Dogs. (Illus.). 24p. (Orig.). (ps-3). 1990. pap. 2.50 (ISBN 0-87406-513-5). Willowisp Pr.

Hollands, Judith. Bowser the Beautiful. DeRosa, Dee, illus. (Orig.). (gr. 1-4). 1987. pap. 2.50 (ISBN 0-671-63906-4, Minstrel Bks). PB.

Hooks, William H. Dirty Dozen Dizzy Dogs-Bank Street. (ps-3). 1990. PLB 9.99 (ISBN 0-553-05892-4, Little Rooster); pap. 3.50 (ISBN 0-553-34923-6). Bantam.

Hughes, Shirley. David & Dog. (ps-2). 1981. pap. 3.95 (ISBN 0-13-198044-0, Pub. by Treehouse). P-H.

—Dogger. Hughes, Shirley, illus. LC 87-33787. 32p. (ps-2). 1988. 11.95 (ISBN 0-688-07980-6); PLB 11.88 (ISBN 0-688-07981-4). Lothrop.

Hull, Verne D. Pinky's Dog. (ps-1). 1989. 14.95 (ISBN 0-533-08194-7). Vantage.

Impey, Rose. Desperate for a Dog. Knox, Jolyne, illus. LC 89-1239. 62p. (gr. 1-3). 1989. 10.95 (ISBN 0-525-44513-7, DCB). Dutton Child Bks.

Johnson, Crockett. The Blue Ribbon Puppies. Johnson, Crockett, illus. 32p. (ps-2). 1987. pap. 2.95 (ISBN 0-590-40626-4, Blue Ribbon Bks). Scholastic Inc.

Johnson, Helen. Molly - the Smart Dog. (gr. 1-6). 1991. 6.95 (ISBN 0-8062-3941-7). Carlton.

Jones, Diana W. Dogsbody. LC 76-28715. 256p. (gr. 5-9). 1988. 11.95 (ISBN 0-688-08191-6). Greenwillow.

—Dogsbody. LC 76-28714. 256p. (gr. 4-9). 1990. pap. 3.50 (ISBN 0-394-82031-2). McKay.

Jones, Jo. That Hardhead Cinnamon. Vansant, Jo, illus. LC 89-92753. 36p. (Orig.). (gr. 2-5). 1989. pap. 6.95 (ISBN 0-9602266-1-3). Jo-Jo Pubns.

Joosse, Barbara M. Better with Two. Stock, Catherine, illus. LC 87-30652. 32p. (ps-2). 1988. 11.95 (ISBN 0-06-023076-2); PLB 11.89 (ISBN 0-06-023077-0). HarpC Child Bks.

Kalman, Maira. Max Makes a Million. 1990. 14.95 (ISBN 0-670-83545-5). Viking Child Bks.

Keast, Winifred. What Happened to Duchess's Pups? (Illus.). 92p. (Orig.). (gr. 7 up). 1984. pap. 10.00 (ISBN 0-9613847-0-0); PLB 5.00 (ISBN 0-9613847-1-9). W Keast.

Keats, Ezra J. Whistle for Willie. Keats, Ezra J., illus. LC 64-13595. (ps-1). 1977. pap. 3.95 (ISBN 0-14-050202-5, Puffin). Puffin Bks.

—Whistle for Willie. Keats, Ezra J., illus. (ps-1). 1964. pap. 12.95 (ISBN 0-670-76240-7). Viking Child Bks.

Keller, Holly. Goodbye, Max. Keller, Holly, illus. LC 86-4680. 32p. (ps-3). 1987. 11.75 (ISBN 0-688-06561-9); PLB 11.88 (ISBN 0-688-06562-7). Greenwillow.

Kellogg, Steven. Pinkerton, Behave! Kellogg, Steven, illus. LC 78-31794. (ps-2). 1979. 13.95 (ISBN 0-8037-6573-8); PLB 13.89 (ISBN 0-8037-6575-4). Dial Bks Young.

—Pinkerton, Behave! Kellogg, Steven, illus. 32p. (gr. k-3). 1982. pap. 3.95 (ISBN 0-8037-7250-5). Dial Bks Young.

—A Rose for Pinkerton. Kellogg, Steven, illus. LC 81-65848. 32p. (ps-3). 1981. 13.95 (ISBN 0-8037-7502-4); PLB 12.89 (ISBN 0-8037-7503-2). Dial Bks Young.

—Tallyho, Pinkerton! Kellogg, Steven, illus. LC 82-70198. 32p. (ps-3). 1982. 14.95 (ISBN 0-8037-8731-6); PLB 12.89 (ISBN 0-8037-8743-X). Dial Bks Young.

Key, W. F. Cleo: It's a Dog's Life. (gr. 2-5). 1989. 5.95 (ISBN 0-533-08066-5). Vantage.

Khalsa, Dayal K. I Want a Dog. (Illus.). 24p. (gr. 1 up). 1991. 14.95 (ISBN 0-88776-196-8). Tundra Bks.

—Julian. Khalsa, Dayal K., illus. LC 89-3571. 32p. (gr. 1-3). 1989. 12.95 (ISBN 0-517-57279-6, C N Potter Bks); PLB 13.99 (ISBN 0-517-57410-1). Crown.

—Julian. Khalsa, Dayal K., illus. 24p. (gr. k-8). 1989. 17.95 (ISBN 0-88776-237-9). Tundra Bks.

Kim, Joy. Come on Up. Harvey, Paul, illus. LC 81-2356. 32p. (gr. k-2). 1981. PLB 10.89 (ISBN 0-89375-511-7); pap. text ed. 2.95 (ISBN 0-89375-512-5). Troll Assocs.

Kimmelman, Leslie. Frannie's Fruits. Mathers, Petra, illus. LC 88-17637. 32p. (ps-3). 1989. 12.95 (ISBN 0-06-023143-2); PLB 12.89 (ISBN 0-06-023164-5). HarpC Child Bks.

Kingham-LaChevre, Alice. Roxane, the Blue Dane. LC 88-5062. (Illus.). 156p. (Orig.). (gr. 3-8). 1988. 14.00 (ISBN 0-917665-26-0); pap. 12.00 (ISBN 0-917665-22-8). Bookmakers Guild.

Kjelgaard, Jim. Big Red. 224p. (gr. 4-7). 1982. pap. 3.50 (ISBN 0-553-15434-6, Skylark). Bantam.

—Big Red. Kuhn, Bob, illus. 254p. (gr. 6 up). 1956. 14.95 (ISBN 0-8234-0007-7). Holiday.

—Desert Dog. LC 56-14250. (gr. 5 up). 1975. pap. 2.75 (ISBN 0-553-15491-5). Bantam.

—Irish Red. LC 51-3090. 224p. (gr. 6 up). 1951. 14.95 (ISBN 0-8234-0060-3). Holiday.

—Irish Red: Son of Big Red. large type ed. (gr. 4-8). 1984. pap. 3.50 (ISBN 0-553-15546-6). Bantam.

—Outlaw Red. (gr. 4-8). 1977. pap. 2.75 (ISBN 0-553-15535-0). Bantam.

—Outlaw Red. 230p. (gr. 6 up). 1953. 14.95 (ISBN 0-8234-0084-0). Holiday.

—Snow Dog. 160p. 1980. pap. 2.95 (ISBN 0-553-15365-X). Bantam.

Knight, Eric M. Lassie Come Home. 234p. 1981. Repr. PLB 16.95x (ISBN 0-89966-346-X). Buccaneer Bks.

—Lassie Come Home. (gr. k-6). 1989. pap. 4.95 (ISBN 0-440-40136-4, YB). Dell.

—Lassie Come Home. 224p. 1981. Repr. PLB 12.95x (ISBN 0-89967-020-2). Harmony Raine.

—Lassie Come Home. Kirmse, Marguerite, illus. LC 78-3570. 265p. (gr. 4-6). 1978. 16.95 (ISBN 0-8050-0721-0). H Holt & Co.

Korschunow, Irina. Piebald Pup. Oberlander, Gerhard, illus. (gr. k-3). 1959. 9.95 (ISBN 0-8392-3026-5). Astor-Honor.

Kotzwinkle, William. E. T. The Storybook of the Green Planet. Wiesner, David, illus. 256p. 1985. 15.95 (ISBN 0-399-13063-2, Putnam). Putnam Pub Group.

LaFleur, Tom & Brennan, Gale. Henry the Hound. Flint, Russ, illus. 16p. (Orig.). (gr. k-6). 1982. pap. 1.25 (ISBN 0-685-05556-6). Brennan Bks.

Laird, Elizabeth. The Day Patch Stood Guard. Reeder, Colin, illus. 32p. (gr. k up). 1991. 10.95 (ISBN 0-688-10239-5, Tambourine Bks); PLB 10.88 (ISBN 0-688-10240-9, Tambourine Bks). Morrow.

Langley, Bill & Dias, Ron, illus. Walt Disney's One Hundred One Dalmations. (ps-2). 1991. write for info. (ISBN 0-307-12346-4, Golden Pr). Western Pub.

Lapp, Eleanor J. Orphaned Pup. 144p. (gr. 3-7). 1988. pap. 2.50 (ISBN 0-590-40885-2, Apple Paperbacks). Scholastic Inc.

Lauber, Patricia. Living with Dinosaurs. Henderson, Doug, illus. LC 90-43266. 48p. (gr. 1-5). 1991. SBE 15.95 (ISBN 0-02-754521-0, Bradbury Pr). Macmillan Child Grp.

Lawlor, Laurie. Second-Grade Dog. Levine, Abby, ed. Fiammenghi, Gioia, illus. 40p. (gr. k-3). 1990. 12.95 (ISBN 0-8075-7280-2). A Whitman.

LeeAnet, Loncie & Malloy, Norwood. A Gift for the Whole Family. (gr. 1-3). 1987. 5.95 (ISBN 0-533-06652-2). Vantage.

Leonard, Marcia. Laura Jean the Yard Sale Queen. Brook, Bonnie, ed. Iosa, Ann, illus. LC 89-70304. 24p. (ps-1). 1990. 4.95 (ISBN 0-671-70405-2); PLB 9.98 (ISBN 0-671-70401-X). Silver Pr.

Levine, Jean. Clyde the Terrier. 27p. 1988. 10.95 (ISBN 0-533-07699-4). Vantage.

Lewis, Thomas P. Call for Mr. Sniff. Woldin, Beth W., illus. LC 79-2679. 64p. (gr. k-3). 1981. PLB 11.89 (ISBN 0-06-023815-1). HarpC Child Bks.

Lexau, Joan M. The Dog Food Caper. Hafner, Marilyn, illus. LC 84-1904. 48p. (ps-3). 1987. pap. 4.95 (ISBN 0-8037-0214-0). Dial Bks Young.

—Emily & the Klunky Baby & the Next-Door Dog. Alexander, Martha, illus. LC 77-181789. 40p. (ps-3). 1972. 5.95 (ISBN 0-8037-2309-1); PLB 7.89 (ISBN 0-8037-2310-5). Dial Bks Young.

Lindgren, Barbro. Sam's Cookie. Eriksson, Eva, illus. LC 82-3419. 32p. (gr. k-3). 1982. 6.95 (ISBN 0-688-01267-1). Morrow Jr Bks.

—Sam's Teddy Bear. Eriksson, Eva, illus. LC 82-3418. 32p. (gr. k-3). 1982. 5.95 (ISBN 0-688-01270-1). Morrow Jr Bks.

—The Wild Baby Gets a Puppy: Swedish Edition. Prelutsky, Jack, tr. Eriksson, Eva, illus. LC 87-212. 32p. (ps-3). 1988. Repr. of 1985 ed. 11.95 (ISBN 0-688-06711-5); lib. bdg. 11.88 (ISBN 0-688-06712-3). Greenwillow.

Lippert, Donald F. Shag & the Bouncing Ball. Hedden, Randall, illus. 32p. (ps). Date not set. write for info. Pastel Pubns.

Lippincott, Joseph W. Wilderness Champion: The Story of a Great Hound. Bransom, Paul, illus. LC 44-9586. 192p. (gr. 7-9). 1944. (Lipp Jr Bks); (Lipp Jr Bks). HarpC Child Bks.

Little, Jane. Spook. Larsen, Suzanne K., illus. LC 90-31296. 128p. (gr. 2-5). 1990. pap. 3.95 (ISBN 0-689-71417-3, Aladdin). Macmillan Child Grp.

London, Jack. Call of the Wild. (gr. 6 up). 1964. pap. 2.50 (ISBN 0-8049-0030-2, CL-30). Airmont.

—The Call of the Wild. Kezer, Karel, illus. LC 63-14831. 144p. (gr. 6 up). 1970. 12.95 (ISBN 0-02-759510-2, Macmillan Child Bk). Macmillan Child Grp.

—The Call of the Wild. new ed. Platt, Kin, ed. Carrillo, Fred, illus. LC 73-75461. 64p. (Orig.). (gr. 5-10). 1973. pap. 2.95 (ISBN 0-88301-095-X). Pendulum Pr.

—The Call of the Wild. 128p. (gr. 3-7). 1983. pap. 2.95 (ISBN 0-14-035000-4, Puffin). Puffin Bks.

—The Call of the Wild. 176p. (gr. 6 up). 1987. pap. 2.50 (ISBN 0-590-40594-2, Apple Paperbacks). Scholastic Inc.

—Call of the Wild. Hitchner, Earle, ed. De John, Marie, illus. LC 89-33890. 48p. (gr. 3-6). 1990. PLB 12.89 (ISBN 0-8167-1863-6); pap. text ed. 3.95 (ISBN 0-8167-1864-4). Troll Assocs.

—White Fang. new & abr. ed. Farr, Naunerle, ed. Carrillo, Fred, illus. (gr. 4-12). 1977. pap. text ed. 2.95 (ISBN 0-88301-271-5). Pendulum Pr.

Lorenz, Lee. Hugo & the Spacedog. Lorenz, Lee, illus. LC 82-22960. 30p. (ps-3). 1986. 10.95 (ISBN 0-13-444497-3); pap. 5.95 (ISBN 0-13-444480-9). P-H.

McCue, Lisa, illus. Ten Little Puppy Dogs. LC 86-63577. 28p. (ps). 1987. 2.95 (ISBN 0-394-89149-X, Random Juv). Random.

McElroy, Eugene J. Needle-Nosed Ned. LC 89-50144. (gr. 4-6). 1989. pap. 5.00 (ISBN 0-932433-54-5). Windswept Hse.

McInerney, Judith W. Judge Benjamin: The Superdog Gift. Morrill, Leslie, illus. (gr. 2-4). 1987. pap. 2.95 (ISBN 0-8167-1043-0). Troll Assocs.

—Judge Benjamin: The Superdog Surprise. Morrill, Leslie, illus. 128p. (gr. 4-6). 1990. pap. 2.75 (ISBN 0-671-61283-2, Minstrel Bks). PB.

McKimmie, Elizabeth. Ginger Has Her Pups. 32p. (ps-3). 1990. 6.95 (ISBN 0-8062-3611-6). Carlton.

McMillan, Bruce & McMillan, Brett. Puniddles. McMillan, Bruce, illus. (gr. 2 up). 1982. pap. 4.95 (ISBN 0-395-32076-3). HM.

Maddux, Bob, et al. The Dog That Went Too Fast. French, Marty, et al, illus. 26p. (ps up). 1987. 7.95 (ISBN 1-55578-104-7); cass. incl. Worlds Wonder.

Madokoro, Hisako. The Adventures of Buster the Puppy, 6 vols. Kuroi, Ken, illus. 96p. (gr. k-2). 1991. Set. PLB 65.70 (ISBN 0-8368-0488-0). Gareth Stevens Inc.

—Buster & the Dandelions. Karoi, Ken, illus. LC 90-47926. 24p. (gr. k-2). 1991. PLB 10.95 (ISBN 0-8368-0491-0). Gareth Stevens Inc.
—Buster & the Little Kitten. Kuroi, Ken, illus. LC 90-47947. 24p. (gr. k-2). 1991. PLB 10.95 (ISBN 0-8368-0490-2). Gareth Stevens Inc.
—Buster Catches a Cold. Kuroi, Ken, illus. LC 90-47948. 24p. (gr. k-2). 1991. PLB 10.95 (ISBN 0-8368-0489-9). Gareth Stevens Inc.
—Buster's Blustery Day. Kuroi, Ken, illus. LC 90-47927. 24p. (gr. k-2). 1991. PLB 10.95 (ISBN 0-8368-0494-5). Gareth Stevens Inc.
—Buster's First Snow. Kuroi, Ken, illus. LC 90-47946. 24p. (gr. k-2). 1991. PLB 10.95 (ISBN 0-8368-0492-9). Gareth Stevens Inc.
—Buster's First Thunderstorm. Kuroi, Ken, illus. LC 90-47869. 24p. (gr. k-2). 1991. PLB 10.95 (ISBN 0-8368-0493-7). Gareth Stevens Inc.
Marshak, Samuel. The Pup Grew Up! Pevear, Richard, tr. from RUS. Radunsky, Vladimir, illus. LC 88-28428. 32p. (ps-2). 1989. 13.95 (ISBN 0-8050-0952-3). H Holt & Co.
Marshall, James. Speedboat. Marshall, James, illus. LC 75-40349. 48p. (gr. 1-4). 1976. 13.95 (ISBN 0-395-24384-X). HM.
Martinez, Ruth. Mrs. McDockerty's Knitting. O'Neill, Catharine, illus. 32p. (ps-3). 1990. 13.95 (ISBN 0-395-51591-2). HM.
Matthews, Billie L. & Hurlburt, Virginia E. Davy's Dawg. Welch, Karen E., ed. Boyce, Kenneth, illus. LC 88-32832. 64p. (gr. 3-8). 1989. PLB 9.95 (ISBN 0-937460-58-3). Hendrick-Long.
Mauser, Pat R. Love Is for the Dogs. 1989. pap. 2.50 (ISBN 0-380-75723-0, Flare). Avon.
Mayer, Mercer. A Boy, a Dog & a Frog. LC 67-22254. (Illus.). (ps-3). 1985. 9.95 (ISBN 0-8037-0763-0); PLB 9.89 (ISBN 0-8037-0767-3). Dial Bks Young.
—Frog, Where Are You? Mayer, Mercer, illus. LC 72-85544. (ps-3). 1985. 9.95 (ISBN 0-8037-2737-2); PLB 9.89 (ISBN 0-8037-2732-1). Dial Bks Young.
Meddick, Jim. Robotman II: The Untold Story. (Illus.). 128p. (gr. 6 up). 1986. pap. 5.95 (ISBN 0-88687-279-0). Pharos Bks NY.
Meltabarger, P. J. Livingston: The Pedigreed Pooch of Padre Island. Samuelson, Arnold & Samuelson, Billie, eds. Becher, Ivy, illus. Lynn, E. Russell, intro. by. (Illus.). 150p. (gr. 7-10). 1988. 19.95 (ISBN 0-923133-02-X). JM Pub.
Melton, David. A Boy Called Hopeless. Melton, Todd, illus. LC 86-27557. 232p. (gr. 4 up). 1986. pap. 5.95 (ISBN 0-933849-07-9). Landmark Edns.
—The One & Only Autobiography of Ralph Miller: The Dog Who Knew He Was a Boy. LC 86-27551. (Illus.). 90p. (gr. 2-6). 1987. Repr. of 1979 ed. lib. bdg. 12.95 (ISBN 0-933849-30-3). Landmark Edns.
—The One & Only Second Autobiography of Ralph Miller: The Dog Who Knew He Was a Boy. Melton, David, illus. LC 86-27556. 128p. (gr. 2-6). 1986. pap. 5.95 (ISBN 0-933849-06-0). Landmark Edns.
—The One & Only Second Autobiography of Ralph Miller: The Dog Who Knew He Was a Boy. LC 86-27556. (Illus.). 116p. (gr. 2-6). 1986. Repr. of 1983 ed. lib. bdg. 12.95 (ISBN 0-933849-31-1). Landmark Edns.
Mendelson, Lee. Rock-a-Bye Snoopy. Hill, Frank, illus. 26p. (ps up). 1986. 12.95 (ISBN 1-55578-011-3). Worlds Wonder.
—Snoopy & the Great Pumpkin. Hill, Frank, illus. 26p. (ps up). 1986. 12.95 (ISBN 1-55578-006-7). Worlds Wonder.
—Snoopy at the Dog Show. Hill, Frank, illus. 26p. (ps up). 1986. 12.95 (ISBN 1-55578-008-3). Worlds Wonder.
—Snoopy Goes Camping. Hill, Frank, illus. 26p. (ps up). 1986. 12.95 (ISBN 1-55578-002-4). Worlds Wonder.
—Snoopy Hits the Beach. Hill, Frank, illus. 26p. (ps up). 1986. 12.95 (ISBN 1-55578-004-0). Worlds Wonder.
—Snoopy, Spike & the Cat Next Door. Hill, Frank, illus. 26p. (ps up). 1986. 12.95 (ISBN 1-55578-010-5). Worlds Wonder.
—Snoopy's America. Hill, Frank, illus. 26p. (ps up). 1986. 12.95 (ISBN 1-55578-007-5). Worlds Wonder.
—Snoopy's Band. Hill, Frank, illus. 26p. (ps up). 1986. 12.95 (ISBN 1-55578-009-1). Worlds Wonder.
—Snoopy's Baseball Game. Hill, Frank, illus. 26p. (ps up). 1986. 12.95 (ISBN 1-55578-012-1). Worlds Wonder.
—Snoopy's Birthday Party. Hill, Frank, illus. 26p. (ps up). 1986. 12.95 (ISBN 1-55578-001-6). Worlds Wonder.
—Snoopy's Land of Make Believe. Hill, Frank, illus. 26p. (ps up). 1986. 12.95 (ISBN 1-55578-003-2). Worlds Wonder.
—Snoopy's Show & Tell. Hill, Frank, illus. 26p. (ps up). 1986. 12.95 (ISBN 1-55578-005-9). Worlds Wonder.
—Snoopy's Talent Show. Hill, Frank, illus. 26p. (ps up). 1986. 12.95 (ISBN 1-55578-000-8). Worlds Wonder.
Metoyer, Patrick G. I'm Rattle-Me-Bones III, Esquire. Manchee, Bruce N., illus. LC 87-90349. 24p. (Orig.). (gr. 1-6). 1988. pap. 3.95 (ISBN 0-944523-02-1). Western Slope Pubns.
—No Bones! No Bones! Manchee, Bruce N., illus. LC 87-90350. 24p. (Orig.). (gr. k-2). 1988. pap. 3.95 (ISBN 0-944523-03-X). Western Slope Pubns.
Milnes, Gerald. Granny Will Your Dog Bite? And Other Mountain Rhymes. Root, Kimberly, illus. Bird, Sonja, contrib. by. LC 88-27350. (Illus.). 48p. 1990. Incl. 40 min. cassette. slipcase 18.95 (ISBN 0-394-85363-6). Knopf.
Mitchell, Tucker. The Crystal Whizzard. Graves, Helen, ed. LC 88-50120. 64p. (gr. 2-5). 1988. 12.00 (ISBN 1-55523-146-2). Winston-Derek.
Moncure, Jane B. Polka-Dot Puppy. Endres, Helen, illus. LC 87-15813. 32p. (ps-2). 1987. PLB 11.97 (ISBN 0-89565-407-5); pap. 6.96 (ISBN 0-89565-431-8). Childs World.
—What's So Special about Today? It's My Birthday. Williams, Jenny, illus. LC 87-21907. 32p. (ps-2). 1987. PLB 11.97 (ISBN 0-89565-414-8). Childs World.
Morey, Walt. Kavik, the Wolf Dog. Parnall, Peter, illus. LC 68-24727. (gr. 5-9). 1977. 12.95 (ISBN 0-525-33093-3, DCB); (DCB). Dutton Child Bks.
—Kavik, the Wolf Dog. 1989. pap. 2.75 (ISBN 0-590-40937-9). Scholastic Inc.
Mosley, Marilyn C. Dachshund Tails Down the Yukon. Ross, Sueellen, illus. 112p. (Orig.). (gr. 5). 1988. pap. 5.95 (ISBN 0-9614850-2-7). M C Mosley.
—Dachshund Tails North. Mosley, Rob & Lingle, Bea, illus. LC 82-90167. 50p. (Orig.). (gr. 5). 1982. pap. 4.95 (ISBN 0-9614850-0-0). M C Mosley.
—Dashchund Tails up the Inside Passage. LC 84-90672. (Illus.). 95p. (Orig.). (gr. 5). 1984. pap. 4.95 (ISBN 0-9614850-1-9). M C Mosley.
Murray, Jean G. It's a Ruff Life. LC 82-71950. 70p. (Orig.). (gr. 5-12). 1984. pap. 3.50x (ISBN 0-943864-02-X). Davenport.
Nodset, Joan L. Go Away, Dog. Bonsall, Crosby, illus. LC 63-11162. (gr. k-3). 1963. PLB 11.89 (ISBN 0-06-024556-5). HarpC Child Bks.
Numeroff, Laura J. Digger. LC 82-18242. (Illus.). 32p. (ps-1). 1983. 8.95 (ISBN 0-525-44043-7, Dutton). NAL-Dutton.
Oana, Katy D. The Little Dog Who Wouldn't Be. LC 77-18351. (Illus.). 32p. (gr. 2-4). 1978. PLB 9.95 (ISBN 0-87783-150-5). Oddo.
Odom, Melissa. A Medal for Murphy. Rice, James, illus. 32p. (gr. 1-6). 1987. 11.95 (ISBN 0-88289-635-0). Pelican.
Ollivant, Alfred. Bob, Son of Battle. (Illus.). (gr. 5 up). pap. 2.50 (ISBN 0-8049-0141-4, CL-141). Airmont.
Olsen, E. A. Adrift on a Raft. Le Blanc, L., illus. LC 68-16397. 48p. (gr. 3 up). 1970. PLB 10.95 (ISBN 0-87783-000-2); pap. 3.94 deluxe ed. (ISBN 0-87783-078-9); cassette 10.60x (ISBN 0-87783-176-9). Oddo.
O'Shea, Pat. The Hounds of the Morrigan. LC 85-16435. 469p. (gr. 5 up). 1986. 15.95 (ISBN 0-8234-0595-8). Holiday.
Overbeck, Cynthia. Rusty the Irish Setter. Hammarberg, Dyan, tr. from FRE. LC 76-29463. (Illus.). 24p. (gr. k-4). 1977. PLB 6.95 (ISBN 0-87614-080-0). Carolrhoda Bks.
—Tippy the Fox Terrier. Hammarberg, Dyan, tr. from FRE. LC 76-1230. (Illus.). 24p. (gr. k-4). 1976. PLB 6.95 (ISBN 0-87614-071-1). Carolrhoda Bks.
Paine, Penelope C. & Bingham, Mindy. My Way Sally. Nolt, Christine, ed. Maeno, Itoko, illus. LC 88-2653. 48p. (ps-6). 1988. 13.95 (ISBN 0-911655-27-1). Advocacy Pr.
Parker, Ann N. Home Is Where the Shade Tree Is. Vickery, Diane, illus. 18p. (gr. k-4). 1988. pap. 3.95 (ISBN 0-943487-13-7). Sevgo Pr.
Patrick & the Hungry Puppy. 22p. 1985. 5.95 (ISBN 0-8431-1084-8). Price Stern.
Paulsen, Gary. Dogsong. (gr. 5-9). 1987. pap. 3.95 (ISBN 0-14-032235-3, Puffin). Puffin Bks.
Peet, Bill. Whingdingdilly. Peet, Bill, illus. LC 71-98521. (gr. k-3). 1982. 13.95 (ISBN 0-395-24729-2); pap. 4.95 (ISBN 0-395-31381-3). HM.
Pellowski, Michael J. Copycat Dog. LC 85-14128. (Illus.). 48p. (Orig.). (gr. 1-3). 1986. PLB 9.89 (ISBN 0-8167-0652-2); pap. text ed. 2.95 (ISBN 0-8167-0653-0). Troll Assocs.
—The Puppy Nobody Wanted. Robison, Bill, illus. 24p. (ps-3). 1988. 1.95 (ISBN 0-685-40024-7, 14-17221-2). Willowisp Pr.
—The Puppy Who Wanted a Playmate. (Illus.). 24p. (gr. k-3). 1987. 0.99 (ISBN 0-87406-178-4). Willowisp Pr.
Pels, Richard & Pels, Winslow. The Caribbean Foul Ball Caper. Pels, Winslow, illus. LC 88-19460. 48p. 1988. 13.95 (ISBN 0-8092-4482-9, Calico Bks). Contemp Bks.
Perez, L. King. Belle, the Great American Lap Dog. Norcia, Anne, illus. LC 88-51279. (gr. 4-8). 1988. 4.00 (ISBN 0-932433-45-6). Windswept Hse.
Perkins, Al. Diggingest Dog. Gurney, Eric, illus. LC 67-21920. 72p. (gr. k-3). 1967. 6.95 (ISBN 0-394-80047-8); lib. bdg. 7.99 (ISBN 0-394-90047-2). Beginner.
Peters, Sharon. Maxie the Mutt. Mahan, Ben, illus. LC 87-10914. 32p. (gr. k-2). 1988. PLB 10.89 (ISBN 0-8167-1087-2); pap. text ed. 2.95 (ISBN 0-8167-1088-0). Troll Assocs.
Peterson, Florence. The Big Book of Favorite Dog Stories. Greene, Hamilton, illus. 336p. (gr. 3-9). 7.95 (ISBN 0-448-42640-4, G&D). Putnam Pub Group.
Phillips, Joan. My New Boy. Munsinger, Lynn, illus. LC 85-30129. 32p. (ps-1). 1986. lib. bdg. 6.99 (ISBN 0-394-98277-0, Random Juv); pap. 2.95 (ISBN 0-394-88277-6, Random Juv). Random.
Pinkwater, Daniel. Aunt Lulu. Pinkwater, Daniel, illus. LC 88-1736. 32p. (gr. k-3). 1988. 12.95 (ISBN 0-02-774661-5, Mcmillan Child Bk). Macmillan Child Grp.
—Aunt Lulu. Pinkwater, Daniel, illus. 32p. (gr. k-3). 1991. pap. 3.95 (ISBN 0-689-71413-0, Aladdin). Macmillan Child Grp.
—Jolly Roger: A Dog of Hoboken. LC 84-12629. (Illus.). 64p. (gr. 4-6). 1984. 13.95 (ISBN 0-688-03898-0). Lothrop.
Pinkwater, Daniel M. The Magic Moscow. Pinkwater, Daniel M., illus. LC 80-12785. 64p. (gr. 3-7). 1984. 11.95 (ISBN 0-02-774630-5, Four Winds). Macmillan Child Grp.
Pizer, Abigail. Charlie the Puppy. (Illus.). 32p. (ps-2). 1989. PLB 8.95 (ISBN 0-87614-363-X). Carolrhoda Bks.
Points, Maureen. The Adventures of Pepe the Poodle & Other Stories. Points, Maureen, illus. 1978. pap. 3.50 (ISBN 0-9601594-1-X). Maureen Points.
The Poky Little Puppy. 1990. write for info. (ISBN 0-307-02134-3, Golden Pr). Western Pub.
Porte, Barbara A. Harry's Dog. Abolafia, Yossi, illus. LC 83-14129. 48p. (gr. 1-3). 1983. 13.95 (ISBN 0-688-02555-2); PLB 13.88 (ISBN 0-688-02556-0). Greenwillow.
—The Take-Along Dog. McCully, Emily A., illus. LC 88-18775. 40p. (gr. 1 up). 1989. 11.95 (ISBN 0-688-08053-7); PLB 11.88 (ISBN 0-688-08054-5). Greenwillow.
Pullein-Thompson, Christine. A Home for Jessie. (Illus.). 144p. (gr. 3-6). 1988. 2.50 (ISBN 0-87406-335-3, 33-17187-9). Willowisp Pr.
—Please Save Jessie. (Illus.). 128p. (gr. 3-6). 1989. 2.50 (ISBN 0-87406-430-9, 22-19193-1). Willowisp Pr.
Quayle, Thomas E., ed. Jose' el Diablo: The World's Most Traveled Dog. Quayle, Greg, illus. 95p. (Orig.). 1985. pap. 3.00 (ISBN 0-9623144-0-4). Vilate Pub.
Rand, Gloria. Salty Dog. Rand, Ted, illus. (ps-3). 1989. 13.95 (ISBN 0-8050-0837-3). H Holt & Co.
Rawls, Wilson. Where the Red Fern Grows. 25th anniversary ed. LC 61-9201. 216p. (gr. 5 up). 1961. 14.95 (ISBN 0-385-02059-7); pap. 11.95 (ISBN 0-385-05619-2). Doubleday.
Ray, Deborah K. My Dog, Trip. Ray, Deborah K., illus. LC 87-401. 48p. (gr. 2-4). 1987. reinforced bdg. 12.95 (ISBN 0-8234-0662-8). Holiday.
Rayner, Mary. Marathon & Steve. Rayner, Mary, illus. LC 88-18912. 32p. (ps-2). 1989. 12.95 (ISBN 0-525-44456-4, DCB). Dutton Child Bks.
Razzi, Jim. Sherluck Bones-Mystery Detective Book, No. 1. 48p. (Orig.). 1981. pap. 2.25 (ISBN 0-553-15382-X). Bantam.
Reese, Bob. Sunshine. Wasserman, Dan, ed. Reese, Bob, illus. (gr. k-1). 1979. PLB 7.95 (ISBN 0-89868-073-5); pap. 2.95 (ISBN 0-89868-084-0). ARO Pub.
Reiser, Lynn. Dog & Cat. LC 90-3553. (Illus.). 24p. (ps up). 1991. 13.95 (ISBN 0-688-09892-4); PLB 13.88 (ISBN 0-688-09893-2). Greenwillow.
Rey, Margaret & Rey, H. A. Pretzel. Rey, H. A., illus. LC 44-9584. 32p. (ps-1). 1944. PLB 13.89 (ISBN 0-06-024911-0). HarpC Child Bks.
Rizzo, Alberto, photos by. Snoopy Around the World. Schulz, Charles M., commentaries by. (Illus.). 128p. 1990. 24.95 (ISBN 0-8109-3808-1). Abrams.
Roberts, Thom. Summerdog. (Illus.). 128p. (Orig.). (gr. 1 up). 1978. pap. 2.25 (ISBN 0-380-01950-7, Camelot). Avon.
Roberts, Willo D. Eddie & the Fairy Godpuppy. Morrill, Leslie, illus. LC 83-15678. 136p. (gr. 3-5). 1984. 12.95 (ISBN 0-689-31021-8, Atheneum Child Bk). Macmillan Child Grp.
Robertus, Polly. The Dog Who Had Kittens. LC 90-39174. (Illus.). 32p. (ps-3). 1991. PLB 14.95 (ISBN 0-8234-0860-4). Holiday.
Rockwell, Anne. Hugo at the Park. Rockwell, Anne, illus. LC 89-2417. 32p. (ps-k). 1990. 13.95 (ISBN 0-02-777301-9, Mcmillan Child Bk). Macmillan Child Grp.
Roddy, Lee. D J Dillon & the Mad Dog of Lobo Mountain. 132p. (gr. 8-12). 1986. pap. 4.99 (ISBN 0-89693-482-9). Victor Bks.
Rossbach, Jean. Bernie, the Beagle Who Liked German Cooking. Lalicki, Barbara, ed. Bobak, Cathy, illus. LC 90-21782. 64p. (gr. 1-7). 1991. 13.95 (ISBN 0-02-777787-1, Bradbury Pr). Macmillan Child Grp.
Round, Graham. Hangdog. LC 87-642. (Illus.). 32p. (ps-3). 1987. 7.95 (ISBN 0-8037-0448-8). Dial Bks Young.

Rowan, Barbara C. Does That Goal Count? Manning, Janet, illus. LC 89-61850. 23p. (Orig.). (gr. 4-7). 1989. pap. 4.50 (ISBN 0-9622863-1-1). Bristlecone Pubns.
Does That Goal Count?--an illustrated, short story for eight to twelve year olds, features the love of two young soccer players, Timmy & Mack, & how that love keeps them together, even when the rules of the game, the coach & other players try to break them apart. But don't blame the coach & the players--they've just never heard of a dog playing soccer. Mack, you see, is Timmy's pet sheltie, & the two have been playing with soccer balls since both were young pups. Does That Goal Count?, an off-beat story for children

who love sports & animals, offers exciting descriptions of soccer for the young sports fans, but more importantly, it underscores the virtues of loyalty, love & understanding.
Publisher Provided Annotation.

Ruch, Sandi B. Junkyard Dog. Wunsch, Marjory, illus. LC 89-35652. 96p. (gr. 2-5). 1990. 14.95 (ISBN 0-531-05842-5); PLB 14.99 (ISBN 0-531-08442-6). Orchard Bks Watts.

Rylant, Cynthia. Henry & Mudge & the Bedtime Thumps. Stevenson, Sucie, illus. LC 89-49529. 40p. (gr. 1-3). 1991. RSBE 11.95 (ISBN 0-02-778006-6, Bradbury Pr). Macmillan Child Grp.

—Henry & Mudge & the Happy Cat. Stevenson, Sucie, illus. LC 88-18855. 48p. (gr. 1-3). 1990. 11.95 (ISBN 0-02-778008-2, Bradbury Pr). Macmillan Child Grp.

Sachs, Betsy. The Boy Who Ate Dog Biscuits. Apple, Margot, illus. LC 89-3905. 64p. (gr. 2-4). 1989. PLB 5.99 (ISBN 0-394-94778-9); pap. 1.95 (ISBN 0-394-84778-4). Random.

Sachs, Marilyn. Underdog. LC 84-24676. 128p. (gr. 4-6). 1985. pap. 11.95 (ISBN 0-385-17609-0). Doubleday.

Schneider, Elisa. The Merry-Go-Round Dog. LC 87-4119. (Illus.). 32p. (ps-2). 1988. lib. bdg. 11.99 (ISBN 0-394-99069-2). Knopf.

Schulz, Charles M. Life Is a Circus, Charlie Brown. Schulz, Charles M., illus. LC 80-28770. 48p. (ps up). 1981. lib. bdg. 5.99 (ISBN 0-394-94826-2). Random.

—Snoopy's Getting Married, Charlie Brown. Schulz, Charles M., illus. LC 85-14393. 48p. (gr. 3-7). 1986. Random.

Schweninger, Ann. Wintertime. (ps-3). 1990. 11.95 (ISBN 0-670-83420-3). Viking Child Bks.

Searcy, Margaret Z. Wolf Dog of the Woodland Indians. Brough, Hazel, illus. 112p. (Orig.). (ps-8). 1991. pap. 5.95 (ISBN 0-88289-778-0). Pelican.

Seligson, Susan. Amos Ahoy: A Couch Adventure on Land & Sea. (ps-4). 1990. 14.95 (ISBN 0-316-77403-0, Joy St Bks). Little.

Sendak, Maurice. Higglety Pigglety Pop: Or, There Must Be More to Life. Sendak, Maurice, illus. LC 67-18553. 80p. (gr. k-3). 1967. 14.95 (ISBN 0-06-025487-4). HarpC Child Bks.

Sendak, Maurice & Margolis, Matthew. Some Swell Pup: Or Are You Sure You Want a Dog? Sendak, Maurice, illus. LC 75-42870. 32p. (ps up). 1985. 10.95 (ISBN 0-374-37134-2). FS&G.

Sharmat, Marjorie W. Chasing After Annie. Simont, Marc, illus. LC 80-7906. 64p. (gr. 3-6). 1981. 11.95 (ISBN 0-06-025562-5). HarpC Child Bks.

—I'm the Best. Hillenbrand, Will, illus. LC 90-39176. 32p. (ps-3). 1991. PLB 14.95 (ISBN 0-8234-0859-0). Holiday.

—Morris Brookside, a Dog. LC 73-76797. (Illus.). 48p. (gr. k-3). 1973. reinforced bdg. 6.95 (ISBN 0-8234-0225-8). Holiday.

Shnitzel Gets Lost. 1991. pap. 13.95 (ISBN 0-671-73306-0). S&S Trade.

Singer, Marilyn. Where There's a Will, There's a Wag. Glass, Andrew, illus. LC 85-24837. 96p. (gr. 2-4). 1986. 11.95 (ISBN 0-03-005747-7). H Holt & Co.

Skorpen, Liesel M. His Mother's Dog. Mullin, M. E., illus. LC 76-58707. (ps-3). 1978. HarpC Child Bks.

Smath, Jerry. The Housekeeper's Dog. Smath, Jerry, illus. LC 80-10580. 48p. (ps-3). 1980. 5.95 (ISBN 0-8193-1023-9); PLB 5.95 (ISBN 0-8193-1024-7). Parents.

Smith, Dodie. The Hundred & One Dalmatians. Grahame-Johnstone, Janet & Grahame-Johnstone, Anne, illus. 208p. (gr. 1 up). 1976. pap. 2.50 (ISBN 0-380-00628-6, Camelot). Avon.

—The Hundred & One Dalmatians. (Illus.). 208p. 1989. pap. 14.95 (ISBN 0-670-82660-X). Viking Child Bks.

—The Hundred & One Dalmatians. Dooling, Michael, illus. (gr. 4 up). 1989. pap. 3.95 (ISBN 0-318-41739-1, Puffin). Puffin Bks.

—The One Hundred & One Dalmatians. Dooling, Michael, illus. (gr. 5-9). 1989. pap. 3.95 (ISBN 0-14-034034-3, Puffin). Puffin Bks.

Smith, Elizabeth S. A Service Dog Goes to School: The Story of a Dog Trained to Help the Disabled. Petruccio, Steven, illus. LC 88-17598. 64p. (gr. 1-4). 1988. 12.95 (ISBN 0-688-07648-3); PLB 12.88 (ISBN 0-688-07649-1, Morrow Jr Bks). Morrow Jr Bks.

Smith, Sally Ann. Candle, a Story of Love & Faith. Luther, Luana, ed. Jung, Mary, illus. 42p. 1991. pap. write for info. (ISBN 0-944875-22-X). Doral Pub.

Snow, Pegeen. A Pet for Pat. Dunnington, Tom, illus. LC 83-23159. 32p. (ps-2). 1984. lib. bdg. 11.93 (ISBN 0-516-02049-8); pap. 2.95 (ISBN 0-516-42049-6). Childrens.

Snyder, Phillip C. Poochie. Mohrman, Janet S., illus. 28p. (Orig.). (ps). 1982. pap. 3.95 (ISBN 0-940560-04-6). Custom Hse.

Sohl, Marcia & Dackerman, Gerald. The Call of the Wild Student Activity Book. (Illus.). 16p. (gr. 4-10). 1976. pap. 1.25 (ISBN 0-88301-182-4). Pendulum Pr.

Spot Visits the Hospital. (ps-2). 1987. 4.95 (ISBN 0-399-21397-X, Putnam). Putnam Pub Group.

Stabile, Angie C. The Miracle of My Dog King. 1991. 6.95 (ISBN 0-533-09038-5). Vantage.

Stadler, John. Hector the Accordion-Nosed Dog. 1985. pap. 4.50 (ISBN 0-02-045250-0, Aladdin). Macmillan Child Grp.

Standiford, Natalie. Space Dog & Roy. 80p. 1990. pap. 2.95 (ISBN 0-380-75953-5, Camelot). Avon.

—Space Dog & the Pet Show. 80p. 1990. pap. 2.95 (ISBN 0-380-75954-3, Camelot). Avon.

Steig, William. Caleb & Katie. Steig, William, illus. LC 77-4947. 32p. (ps-3). 1977. 15.95 (ISBN 0-374-31016-5). FS&G.

Steiner, Barbara. Dolby & the Woof-Off. (Illus.). 128p. (gr. 2 up). 1991. 12.95 (ISBN 0-688-08435-4). Morrow Jr Bks.

Stevens, Carla. Trouble for Lucy. Himler, Ronald, illus. LC 79-10445. (gr. 2-6). 1979. 13.95 (ISBN 0-395-28971-8, Clarion). HM.

Stobbs, William. Gregory's Dog. (Illus.). 16p. 1987. pap. 2.95 (ISBN 0-19-272141-0). Oxford U Pr.

Stolz, Mary. Dog on Barkham Street. Shortall, Leonard, illus. LC 60-5787. 176p. (gr. 3-6). 1960. PLB 12.89 (ISBN 0-06-025841-1). HarpC Child Bks.

—A Dog on Barkham Street. Shortall, Leonard, illus. LC 60-5787. 176p. (gr. 3-7). 1985. pap. 3.50 (ISBN 0-06-440160-X, Trophy). HarpC Child Bks.

Stone, Jon. Lovable Furry Old Grover's Resting Places. Smollin, Michael J., illus. LC 83-21087. 32p. (ps-3). 1984. pap. 2.25 (ISBN 0-394-86056-X, Random Juv). Random.

Stone, Lynn. Dingoes. (Illus.). 24p. (gr. k-5). 1990. lib. bdg. 11.93 (ISBN 0-86593-057-0); lib. bdg. 8.95s.p. (ISBN 0-685-36370-8). Rourke Corp.

Strickland, Alison. That Doggone Dog. Robison, Don, illus. 64p. (Orig.). (gr. k-2). 1987. pap. 1.95 (ISBN 0-87406-300-0). Willowisp Pr.

Stuart, Jesse. The Rightful Owner. 2nd ed. Miller, Jim W., et al, eds. Henneberger, Robert, illus. Zornes, Rocky, contrib. by. (Illus.). 96p. (gr. 3-6). 1989. 12.00 (ISBN 0-945084-14-5); pap. 6.00 (ISBN 0-945084-15-3). J Stuart Found.

Szilagyi, Mary. Thunderstorm. Szilagyi, Mary, illus. LC 84-24570. 32p. (ps-2). 1985. 13.95 (ISBN 0-02-788580-1, Bradbury Pr). Macmillan Child Grp.

Taylor, Theodore. Trouble with Tuck. LC 81-43139. 96p. (gr. 4-6). 1989. 13.95 (ISBN 0-385-17774-7); pap. 10.95 (ISBN 0-385-17775-5). Doubleday.

—Tuck Triumphant. (gr. 5-7). 1991. 14.95 (ISBN 0-385-41480-3). Doubleday.

Tell the Time with Benji. (ps). bds. 5.50 (ISBN 0-904494-49-7). Borden.

Terhune, Albert P. Lad: A Dog. 1981. Repr. PLB 24.95 (ISBN 0-89966-348-6). Buccaneer Bks.

—Lad: A Dog. 189p. 1981. Repr. PLB 24.95 (ISBN 0-89967-022-9). Harmony Raine.

—Lad: A Dog. (RL 6). 1978. pap. 2.50 (ISBN 0-451-14626-3, AE1036, Sig). NAL-Dutton.

—Lad: A Dog. 256p. 1978. pap. 3.50 (ISBN 0-451-16417-2, Sig). NAL-Dutton.

Thayer, Jane. The Puppy Who Wanted a Boy. rev. ed. McCue, Lisa, illus. LC 85-15465. 48p. (ps-1). 1986. 12.95 (ISBN 0-688-05944-9); PLB 12.88 (ISBN 0-688-05945-7, Morrow Jr Bks); pap. 4.95 (Mulberry Bks). Morrow Jr Bks.

—The Puppy Who Wanted a Boy. McCue, Lisa, illus. LC 85-15465. (ps-3). 1988. pap. 4.95 (ISBN 0-688-08293-9, Mulberry). Morrow.

Thomas. Comeback Dog. (ps-7). 1983. pap. 2.99 (ISBN 0-553-15521-0, Skylark). Bantam.

Thomas, Allison. Benji. (Orig.). (gr. 5-9). 1980. pap. 1.75 (ISBN 0-515-05749-5). Jove Pubns.

Thomas, Jane R. The Comeback Dog. Howell, Troy, illus. 64p. (gr. 2-6). 1981. 13.95 (ISBN 0-395-29432-0, Clarion). HM.

Tokuda, Wendy & Hall, Richard. Shiro in Love. Sasaki, Karen, illus. 32p. (gr. 1-3). 1989. 11.95 (ISBN 0-89346-306-X). Heian Intl.

Tripp, Valerie. El Perro Cantor (The Singing Dog) Martin, Sandra K., illus. LC 86-14797. (SPA.). 24p. (ps-2). 1990. PLB 12.33 (ISBN 0-516-31578-1). Childrens.

Troy, John. Ben at Large. 1990. pap. 12.50 (ISBN 1-55971-048-9). Northword.

Twinn, Michael. My Friend's Dog. (Illus.). (ps-2). 1977. 2.00 (ISBN 0-85953-071-X, Pub. by Child's Play England). Childs Play.

Vestavia Elementary School Fourth Grade Class & Cockrell, Marcille. The Adventures of a Bubble-Bellied Bloopy Droopy Detective. (Illus.). 32p. (gr. k-5). 1989. pap. 3.95 (ISBN 0-943487-22-6). Sevgo Pr.

Vivelo, Jackie. Beagle in Trouble: Super Sleuth II. LC 85-30155. 112p. (gr. 3-6). 1986. 12.95 (ISBN 0-399-21325-2, Putnam). Putnam Pub Group.

Wahl, Jan. The Adventures of Underwater Dog. Bowers, Tim, illus. 32p. (ps-2). 1989. 8.95 (ISBN 0-448-09313-8, G&D). Putnam Pub Group.

—Dracula's Cat & Frankenstein's Dog. Chorao, Kay, illus. (ps-2). 1990. PLB 13.95 (ISBN 0-671-70820-1). S&S Trade.

Wahl, Robert. Friend Dog. Ewers, Joe, illus. (ps). 1988. 12.95 (ISBN 0-316-91710-9). Little.

Wallace, Bill. A Dog Called Kitty. LC 80-16293. 160p. (gr. 5-9). 1980. 13.95 (ISBN 0-8234-0376-9). Holiday.

—A Dog Named Kitty. (gr. 4-7). 1989. pap. 2.75 (ISBN 0-671-70270-X, Archway). PB.

—Red Dog. LC 86-46202. 192p. (gr. 3-7). 1987. 14.95 (ISBN 0-8234-0650-4). Holiday.

—Red Dog. 176p. (Orig.). (gr. 5-7). 1989. pap. 2.75 (ISBN 0-671-70141-X, Archway). PB.

Walt Disney Staff. Lady & the Tramp. 1987. 6.98 (ISBN 0-8317-5411-7, Gallery Bks). Smithmark.

Warburg, Sandol S. Growing Time. Weisgard, Leonard, illus. LC 69-14729. (gr. k-3). 1975. 13.95 (ISBN 0-395-16966-6). HM.

Wayne. Max, the Dog Who Refused to Die. (ps-7). 1987. pap. 2.25 (ISBN 0-553-25160-0). Bantam.

Weeks, Wilfred H. The White Stone. Schlatter, Becky, illus. LC 85-51932. 37p. (Orig.). (gr. 4-9). 1990. pap. write for info. (ISBN 0-9615677-0-8). Three Riv Ctr.

Weller, Frances W. Riptide. Blake, Robert J., illus. 32p. (ps-3). 1990. 14.95 (ISBN 0-399-21675-8, Philomel Bks). Putnam Pub Group.

Wersba, Barbara. The Farewell Kid. LC 89-36401. 160p. (gr. 7 up). 1990. 12.95 (ISBN 0-06-026378-4); PLB 12.89 (ISBN 0-06-026379-2). HarpC Child Bks.

West, Cindy. Poky Little Puppy's Special Day. (Illus.). 24p. (ps-3). 1989. pap. write for info. (ISBN 0-307-14025-3). Western Pub.

—Poky Little Puppy's Special Day. (Illus.). 24p. (ps-2). 1989. write for info. (ISBN 0-307-12085-6, Pub. by Golden Bks). Western Pub.

West, Colin. Monty, the Dog Who Wears Glasses. (gr. 4-7). 1990. 10.95 (ISBN 0-525-44636-2, DCB). Dutton Child Bks.

—Shape Up, Monty! West, Colin, illus. 64p. (gr. 2-5). 1991. 10.95 (ISBN 0-525-44777-6, DCB). Dutton Child Bks.

Westman, Barbara. Dancing Dogs: Charlotte & Emilio at the Circus. Westman, Barbara, illus. LC 90-23070. 32p. (ps-3). 1991. 14.95 (ISBN 0-06-022459-2); PLB 14.89 (ISBN 0-06-022460-6). HarpC Child Bks.

White Fang. 224p. 1989. pap. 2.50 (ISBN 0-8125-0512-3). Tor Bks.

White, James E. The Triumphs of Trisha & Tripod: Tripod Finds a Home. Senf, Richard L., illus. 22p. 1991. pap. 7.95 (ISBN 0-9629102-0-1). Pyramid TX. About a little handicapped girl named Trisha who dreams of finding a pet to share her love with. The story centers around a three-legged dog named Tripod, who is headed for the humane shelter's version of death row when he is rescued & adopted by Trisha. Trisha always wanted a "big fluffy dog with a fat waggily tail." But, Tripod hardly fitted that description. He's a brown mongrel but to Trisha he was the most wonderful thing that had ever happened in her life. When Trisha sees the doomed Tripod, she understands that just because Tripod lacks a leg, he doesn't lack in an abundance of puppy love. The triumphs of Trisha & Tripod teaches children to love people & animals just for what they are. The world is not perfect & neither are people. As cruel as children may seem at times to other children & other children's pets, they should be taught to be giving. We must learn to love without compromise. That's what the triumphs of Trisha & Tripod is all about.
Publisher Provided Annotation.

Wildsmith, Brian. The Hunter & His Dog. Wildsmith, Brian, illus. 32p. (ps-2). 1979. 12.95 (ISBN 0-19-279725-5); pap. 5.95 (ISBN 0-19-272147-X). Oxford U Pr.

Wilhelm, Hans. I'll Always Love You. Wilhelm, Hans, illus. LC 84-20060. 32p. (ps up). 1988. 11.95 (ISBN 0-517-55648-0); pap. 3.99 (ISBN 0-517-57265-6). Crown.

—A New Home, a New Friend. Wilhelm, Hans, illus. LC 84-18295. 40p. (ps-3). 1985. (Random Juv). Random.

—Schnitzels First Christmas. 1989. pap. 13.95 (ISBN 0-671-67977-5). S&S Trade.

Williams, Vereca R. A Dog Named Sunshine. Shaw, Patricia, illus. 1991. 6.95 (ISBN 0-533-08951-4). Vantage.

Wilson, Towana E. Sam, a Cocker: Sam & His Country Home. Wilson, Towana E., illus. LC 90-87585. (Orig.). (gr. 7 up). 1990. pap. 5.00 (ISBN 0-9623607-1-6). BRAT Pubns.

—Sam, a Cocker: Sam & the Periwinkles. Wilson, Towana E., illus. LC 90-83106. (Orig.). (gr. 7 up). 1990. pap. 5.00 (ISBN 0-9623607-2-4). BRAT Pubns.
SAM & THE PERIWINKLES is the third book in a series about a cocker spaniel who faces real life experiences.

SAM's first encounter was to realize that he was not perfect but that he was important. Self-esteem & adoption were the themes. SAM's second adventure dealt with adjusting to a new home. Now, SAM faces the loss of a companion. SAM living in his country home on the lake, works through the grieving process & leaves the reader with hope. This is one short story for all ages! A child will share pain & hope with SAM. Parents, teachers & clergy can use this book as a springboard into the discussion of grief due to any loss. Remember, there are several losses in a child's life, from the lost toy, pet, perfect "A" grade average to the loss of a family member. This short fiction is based on a true story. This book is long enough to address a very important part of growing up. Yet, it is short enough to allow time for discussion & understanding. This book is for anyone who must help a child through a time when you don't know what to say.
Publisher Provided Annotation.

—Sam a Cocker: Sam Goes Home. Wilson, Towana E., illus. LC 89-92115. 24p. (Orig.). (gr. 5 up). 1989. pap. 5.00 (ISBN 0-9623607-0-8). BRAT Pubns.

Wolff, Ashley. Come with Me. 1990. 12.95 (ISBN 0-525-44555-2, DCB). Dutton Child Bks.

Wolters, Richard A. Home Dog. Hill, Gene, frwd. by. (Illus.). 160p. (gr. 7 up). 1984. 16.95 (ISBN 0-525-24232-5, Dutton). NAL-Dutton.

Wood, Leslie. A Dog Called Mischief. (Illus.). 16p. 1987. pap. 2.95 (ISBN 0-19-272155-0). Oxford U Pr.

Worth, Valerie. Curlicues: The Fortunes of Two Pug Dogs. Babbitt, Natalie, illus. LC 80-15594. 64p. (gr. k up). 1980. 9.95 (ISBN 0-374-31664-3). FS&G.

Wynnejones, Pat. Village Tales, 4 bks. (Illus.). (ps-6). 1991. Set, 24p. ea. 14.95 (ISBN 0-7459-1830-1). Lion USA.

Yeoman, John. Old Mother Hubbard's Dog Dresses Up. Blake, Quentin, illus. LC 89-27026. 24p. (ps-3). 1990. 6.95 (ISBN 0-395-53358-9). HM.

—Old Mother Hubbard's Dog Learns to Play. Blake, Quentin, illus. LC 89-39863. 24p. (ps-3). 1990. 6.95 (ISBN 0-395-53360-0). HM.

—Old Mother Hubbard's Dog Needs a Doctor. Blake, Quentin, illus. LC 89-24448. 24p. (ps-3). 1990. 6.95 (ISBN 0-395-53359-7). HM.

—Old Mother Hubbard's Dog Takes up Sport. Blake, Quentin, illus. LC 89-39942. 24p. (ps-3). 1990. 6.95 (ISBN 0-395-53361-9). HM.

Young, Ed. The Other Bone. LC 83-47706. (Illus.). 32p. (ps-3). 1991. PLB 14.89 (ISBN 0-06-026871-9). HarpC Child Bks.

Young, James. Old Mrs. Mopiter. Young, James, illus. 32p. (gr. 1-3). 1989. 6.95 (ISBN 0-8431-2359-1). Price Stern.

Ziefert, Harriet. Sleepy Dog: A Step One Book. Gorbaty, Norman, illus. LC 84-4775. (ps-2). 1984. PLB 6.99 (ISBN 0-394-96877-8, Pub. by BYR); pap. 2.95 (ISBN 0-394-86877-3). Random.

—Where's the Dog? Lobel, Arnold, illus. LC 86-45952. 14p. (ps). 1987. 3.50 (ISBN 0-694-00184-8). HarpC Child Bks.

Zion, Gene. Harry & the Lady Next Door. Graham, Margaret B., illus. LC 60-9452. 64p. (gr. k-3). 1978. pap. 3.50 (ISBN 0-06-444008-7, Trophy). HarpC Child Bks.

—Harry by the Sea. Graham, Margaret B., illus. LC 65-21302. 32p. (gr. k-3). 1965. 13.95 (ISBN 0-06-026855-7); PLB 13.89 (ISBN 0-06-026856-5). HarpC Child Bks.

—Harry the Dirty Dog. Graham, Margaret B., illus. LC 56-8137. 32p. (gr. k-3). 1956. 13.95 (ISBN 0-06-026865-4); PLB 13.89 (ISBN 0-06-026866-2). HarpC Child Bks.

—Harry the Dirty Dog. Graham, Margaret B., illus. LC 56-8137. 32p. (ps-3). 1976. pap. 3.95 (ISBN 0-06-443009-X, Trophy). HarpC Child Bks.

—No Roses for Harry. Graham, Margaret B., illus. LC 58-7752. (gr. k-3). 1958. 13.95 (ISBN 0-06-026890-5); PLB 13.89 (ISBN 0-06-026891-3). HarpC Child Bks.

Zitzman, Susan M. Dog Food & Other Delights. (gr. 3-7). 1987. pap. 3.95 (ISBN 1-55513-064-X, Chariot Bks). Cook.

Zolotow, Charlotte. The Poodle Who Barked at the Wind. Otani, June, illus. LC 86-42992. 32p. (ps-3). 1987. 12.95i (ISBN 0-06-026965-0); PLB 12.89 (ISBN 0-06-026966-9). HarpC Child Bks.

DOGS–PICTURES, ILLUSTRATIONS, ETC.

Cuddly Kittens & Precious Puppies. (Illus.). 32p. (gr. 1-8). 1989. 3.95 (ISBN 0-87406-549-6, 47-20338-9). Willowisp Pr.

King, Helen B. Sandy. King, Helen B., illus. 18p. (ps-3). 1985. pap. 4.95 (ISBN 0-9615366-4-0). King ME.

Pfloog, Jan. Puppies Are Like That. Pfloog, Jan, illus. LC 74-2542. 32p. (Orig.). (ps-1). 1975. pap. 1.95 (ISBN 0-394-82923-9, Random Juv). Random.

Sanford, Bill & Green, Carl. American Pit Bull Terrier. LC 89-31072. (Illus.). 48p. (gr. 4-5). 1989. 10.95 (ISBN 0-89686-447-2, Crestwood Hse). Macmillan Child Grp.

—Dalmatian. LC 89-31107. (Illus.). 48p. (gr. 4-5). 1989. 10.95 (ISBN 0-89686-449-9, Crestwood Hse). Macmillan Child Grp.

—Doberman Pinscher. LC 89-31071. (Illus.). 48p. (gr. 4-5). 1989. 10.95 (ISBN 0-89686-454-5, Crestwood Hse). Macmillan Child Grp.

—English Springer Spaniel. LC 89-31069. (Illus.). 48p. (gr. 4-5). 1989. 10.95 (ISBN 0-89686-453-7, Crestwood Hse). Macmillan Child Grp.

—Greyhound. LC 89-31113. (Illus.). 48p. (gr. 4-5). 1989. 10.95 (ISBN 0-89686-450-2, Crestwood Hse). Macmillan Child Grp.

—Old English Sheepdog. LC 89-31073. (Illus.). 48p. (gr. 4-5). 1989. 10.95 (ISBN 0-89686-452-9, Crestwood Hse). Macmillan Child Grp.

—Samoyed. LC 89-31070. (Illus.). 48p. (gr. 4-5). 1989. 10.95 (ISBN 0-89686-451-0, Crestwood Hse). Macmillan Child Grp.

—Shih Tzu. LC 89-31108. (Illus.). 48p. (gr. 4-5). 1989. 10.95 (ISBN 0-89686-448-0, Crestwood Hse). Macmillan Child Grp.

Spizzirri Publishing Co. Staff. Dogs: An Educational Coloring Book. Spizzirri, Linda, ed. (Illus.). 32p. (gr. 1-8). 1986. pap. 1.95 (ISBN 0-86545-076-5). Spizzirri.

DOGS–POETRY

Gabriel, Howard W., III. Loving Memories from Dog to Dog. House, David J., illus. 32p. (Orig.). (gr. k-6). 1987. pap. 2.95 (ISBN 0-936997-01-X). M & H Enter.

DOGS–TRAINING

Arnold, Caroline. A Guide Dog Puppy Grows Up. Hewett, Richard, photos by. (Illus.). 48p. (gr. 1 up). 1991. 16.95 (ISBN 0-15-232657-X). HarBraceJ.

Curtis, Patricia. Cindy, a Hearing Ear Dog. Cupp, David, illus. LC 80-24487. (gr. 3-5). 1981. 13.95 (ISBN 0-525-27950-4, DCB). Dutton Child Bks.

Frith, Michael. I'll Teach My Dog One Hundred Words. (Illus.). (ps-1). 1973. 6.95 (ISBN 0-394-82692-2, Random Juv); lib. bdg. 7.99 (ISBN 0-394-92692-7). Random.

Meisterfeld, C. W. Psychological Dog Training: Behavior Conditioning with Respect & Trust. (Illus.). 232p. (Orig.). (gr. 6 up). 1991. pap. 18.00 (ISBN 0-9601292-6-X). M R K.

Unkelbach, Kurt. Both Ends of the Leash: Selecting & Training Your Dog. Petie, Haris, illus. (gr. 3-7). 1968. P-H.

DOGS–TREATMENT

Howard-Moineau, Henrietta. Twiggy: The Abandoned, Diabetic Dog. (Illus.). 73p. (Orig.). (gr. 4 up). 1982. pap. 5.00 (ISBN 0-318-01113-1). Hampshire Pr.

DOGS FOR THE BLIND

see Guide Dogs

DOLL

see Dolls

DOLLHOUSES

Conaway, Judith. Dollhouse Fun! Furniture You Can Make. Barto, Renzo, illus. LC 86-16133. 48p. (gr. 1-5). 1987. PLB 11.89 (ISBN 0-8167-0862-2); pap. text ed. 2.95 (ISBN 0-8167-0863-0). Troll Assocs.

Glubok, Shirley. Dolls' Houses: Life in Miniature. LC 77-25663. (Illus.). 104p. (gr. 5 up). 1984. 16.95i (ISBN 0-06-022016-3). HarpC Child Bks.

Lellie, Herman & Bateson, Margaret. A Victorian Dollhouse. (Illus.). 4p. 1991. bds. 19.95 (ISBN 0-312-06228-1). St Martin.

Pearson, Tracey C. Dollhouse People: A Doll Family You Can Make. LC 83-25992. (Illus.). 80p. (gr. 3-6). 1984. pap. 12.95 (ISBN 0-670-43433-7). Viking Child Bks.

DOLLHOUSES–FICTION

Godden, Rumer. The Doll's House. LC 62-18693. (ps-3). 1976. pap. 3.95 (ISBN 0-14-030942-X, Puffin). Puffin Bks.

Jacobs, Flora G. The Doll House Mystery. (Illus.). 96p. 1958. 5.95 (ISBN 0-686-31594-4). Wash Dolls Hse.

Mariana. Miss Flora McFlimsey & the Baby New Year. rev ed ed. Mariana & Howe, Caroline W., illus. LC 86-15339. 40p. (ps-2). 1988. 11.95 (ISBN 0-688-04533-2); PLB 11.88 (ISBN 0-688-04534-0). Lothrop.

—Miss Flora McFlimsey's Christmas Eve. rev ed ed. Mariana & Howe, Caroline W., illus. LC 86-15259. 40p. (ps-2). 1988. 11.95 (ISBN 0-688-04282-1); PLB 11.88 (ISBN 0-688-04283-X). Lothrop.

Orgel, Doris. Sarah's Room. LC 63-13675. (Illus.). (gr. k-3). 1963. 11.95 (ISBN 0-06-024605-7). HarpC Child Bks.

Wright, Betty R. The Dollhouse Murders. 160p. (gr. 4-6). 1985. pap. 2.50 (ISBN 0-590-33245-7, Apple Paperbacks); tchr's. guide 1.25 (ISBN 0-590-40929-8). Scholastic Inc.

DOLLS

Children's Museum Staff. Original Shirley Temple Dolls in Full Color. (Illus.). 32p. (gr. 2 up). 1988. pap. 3.95 (ISBN 0-486-25461-5). Dover.

Fryer, Jane E. The Mary Francis Sewing Book. Boyer, Jane A., illus. LC 13-22543. 280p. (gr. 4 up). 1981. Repr. of 1913 ed. lib. bdg. 58.00 (ISBN 0-940070-13-8). Doll Works.

Hecht, Joan B. Best Things about Dolls. Hecht, Muriel, illus. 16p. (ps-3). 1987. pap. 4.95 (ISBN 0-931271-08-8). Hi Plains Pr.

Horwitz, Joshua. Doll Hospital. Horwitz, Joshua, photos by. LC 82-14508. (Illus.). 56p. (gr. 3-7). 1983. Pantheon.

The Kachina Doll Book 1. (gr. 1-6). 1972. pap. 3.95 (ISBN 0-918858-00-3). Fun Pub AZ.

The Kachina Doll Book 2. (gr. 1-6). 1973. pap. 3.95 (ISBN 0-918858-01-1). Fun Pub AZ.

McQueen, Lucinda & Guitar, Jeremy, illus. Sybil Sadie. 12p. (gr. 1-5). 1984. 4.00 (ISBN 0-910313-32-6). Parker Bros.

Morgan, Mary H. How to Dress an Old-Fashioned Doll. LC 72-93612. (Illus.). 96p. (gr. 5-8). 1973. pap. 2.95 (ISBN 0-486-22912-2). Dover.

Pfeffer, Susan B. Paperdolls. 160p. (Orig.). (gr. 7-12). 1984. pap. 2.25 (ISBN 0-440-96777-5, LFL). Dell.

Sleator, William. Among the Dolls. Hyman, Trina S., illus. (gr. 2-5). 1975. 11.95 (ISBN 0-525-25563-X, DCB). Dutton Child Bks.

Spizzirri Publishing Co. Staff. Dolls: An Educational Coloring Book. Spizzirri, Linda, ed. Goodman, Marlene & Spizzirri, Peter M., illus. 32p. (gr. 1-8). 1981. pap. 1.95 (ISBN 0-86545-034-X). Spizzirri.

Swanberg, Nancie. American Dolls Coloring & Story Album. 32p. (ps up). 1985. pap. 3.95 (ISBN 0-8431-1753-2). Price Stern.

Tallarico, Tony, illus. Dolls, Dolls, Dolls. 12p. (ps-1). 1990. bds. 3.95 (ISBN 0-89828-405-8). Tuffy Bks.

Taylor, Cora. Yesterday's Doll. 1990. pap. 2.75 (ISBN 0-590-43208-7). Scholastic Inc.

Werner, Vivian. Dolls. 144p. 1991. pap. 2.95 (ISBN 0-380-76044-4, Camelot). Avon.

DOLLS–FICTION

Bailey, Carolyn S. Miss Hickory. Gannett, Ruth, illus. LC 46-7275. (gr. 4-7). 1977. pap. 3.95 (ISBN 0-14-030956-X, Puffin). Puffin Bks.

—Miss Hickory. Gannett, Ruth, illus. (gr. 4-7). 1946. pap. 13.95 (ISBN 0-670-47940-3). Viking Child Bks.

Banner, Mary. Miss Angelina Adorable. Scott, Janet L., illus. LC 28-17283. 102p. (gr. 4 up). 1981. Repr. of 1928 ed. 25.00 (ISBN 0-940070-11-1). Doll Works.

Bawden, Juliet. The Doll's Tea Party. Pask, Helen, photos by. LC 89-6577. (Illus.). 32p. (gr. 2 up). 1989. 12.95 (ISBN 0-87226-413-0, Bedrick Blackie). P Bedrick Bks.

Beard, Patten. The Pantalette Doll. Hubbard, Eleanore M., illus. LC 31-21184. 160p. (gr. 4 up). 1981. Repr. of 1931 ed. lib. bdg. 35.00 (ISBN 0-940070-12-X). Doll Works.

Brink, Carol R. The Bad Times of Irma Baumlein. Hyman, Trina S., illus. LC 76-182018. 144p. (gr. 4-6). 1972. 14.95 (ISBN 0-02-714220-5, Mcmillan Child Bk). Macmillan Child Grp.

—The Bad Times of Irma Baumlein. 2nd ed. Hyman, Trina S., illus. 144p. (gr. 3-7). 1991. pap. 3.95 (ISBN 0-689-71513-7, Aladdin). Macmillan Child Grp.

Brown, Ruth. I Don't Like It! (ps-1). 1990. 13.95 (ISBN 0-525-44559-5, DCB). Dutton Child Bks.

Buffett, Jimmy & Buffett, Savannah J. Trouble Dolls. Ingber, Bonnie V., intro. by. Davis, Lambert, illus. 32p. (ps). 1991. 14.95 (ISBN 0-15-290790-4). HarBraceJ.

Burnett, Frances H. The Racketty-Packetty House. Johnson, Holly, illus. LC 75-8531. 64p. (gr. 2-5). 1975. 12.95 (ISBN 0-397-31642-9, Lipp Jr Bks). HarpC Child Bks.

Collet's Holdings, Ltd. Staff, ed. Raggedy Ann Gets Lost. Gruelle, Johnny, text by. LC 86-61925. (Illus.). 14p. (ps). 1987. 3.95 (ISBN 0-394-88681-X, Random Juv). Random.

Daly, Kathleen N. Raggedy Ann & Andy: Based on the Movie. LC 76-47894. (Illus.). 1977. write for info. (ISBN 0-672-52301-9). Macmillan Child Grp.

Davidson, Michelle. Raggedy Ann's Seashore Adventure. Shackelford, Jean, illus. LC 86-62565. 32p. (ps-1). 1987. pap. 1.25 (ISBN 0-394-88776-X, Random Juv). Random.

Dexter, Catherine. The Oracle Doll. (gr. k-6). 1988. pap. 2.95 (ISBN 0-440-40114-3, YB). Dell.

Dillon, Barbara. The Teddy Bear Tree. MacDonald, Patricia, ed. Rose, David, illus. 80p. (gr. 2-5). 1990. pap. 2.95 (ISBN 0-671-68432-9, Minstrel Bks). PB.

Dolson, Gina, ed. Lisa & the Magic Doll: Russian & Ukrainian Fairy Tales. Mandeville, Jerry & Brodsky, Anna, trs. from RUS & UKR. Mawolski, Stanley M., illus. 56p. (Orig.). (gr. 4-10). 1986. pap. 4.50x (ISBN 0-914265-07-5). New Eng Pub MA.

Duffy, James. The Doll Hospital. 160p. (gr. 3-5). 1989. pap. 11.95 (ISBN 0-590-41860-2). Scholastic Inc.

—Doll Hospital. 1990. pap. 2.75 (ISBN 0-590-41855-6). Scholastic Inc.

Elliott, Dan. My Doll Is Lost! Manthieu, Joe, illus. LC 83-11211. 40p. (ps-3). 1984. 3.95 (ISBN 0-394-86251-1, Random Juv); lib. bdg. 6.99 (ISBN 0-394-96251-6). Random.

Field, Rachel. Hitty: Her First Hundred Years. Lathrop, Dorothy P., illus. LC 29-22704. 220p. (gr. 4-6). 1969. 13.95 (ISBN 0-02-734840-7, Mcmillan Child Bk). Macmillan Child Grp.

Friedman, Tracy. Henriette: The Story of a Doll. Rosenberry, Vera, illus. 64p. (Orig.). (gr. 2-4). 1986. pap. 2.25 (ISBN 0-590-33842-0, Lucky Star). Scholastic Inc.

Gardam, Jane. Through the Dolls' House Door. LC 87-200. (Illus.). 128p. (gr. 5 up). 1987. 10.25 (ISBN 0-688-07447-2). Greenwillow.

—Through the Dolls House Door. (gr. 4-7). 1991. pap. 3.25 (ISBN 0-440-40433-9). Dell.

Garelick, May. Just My Size. Pene du Bois, William, illus. LC 89-34513. 32p. (ps-3). 1990. 13.95 (ISBN 0-06-022418-5); PLB 13.89 (ISBN 0-06-022419-3). HarpC Child Bks.

Gates, Josephine. The Live Doll's House Party. Keep, Virginia, illus. LC 6-28222. 102p. (gr. 4 up). 1981. Repr. of 1906 ed. lib. bdg. 35.00 (ISBN 0-940070-02-2). Doll Works.

—The Live Doll's Party Days. Keep, Virginia, illus. LC 10-26376. 159p. (gr. 4 up). 1981. Repr. of 1910 ed. lib. bdg. 35.00 (ISBN 0-940070-03-0). Doll Works.

—The Live Doll's Play Days. Keep, Virginia, illus. LC 8-25990. 108p. (gr. 4 up). Repr. of 1908 ed. lib. bdg. 35.00 (ISBN 0-940070-04-9). Doll Works.

—The Story of Live Dolls. Keep, Virginia, illus. LC 1-24915. 103p. (gr. 4 up). 1981. Repr. of 1901 ed. lib. bdg. 35.00 (ISBN 0-940070-05-7). Doll Works.

—The Story of the Lost Doll. Keep, Virginia, illus. LC 5-83020. 108p. (gr. 4 up). 1981. Repr. of 1905 ed. lib. bdg. 35.00 (ISBN 0-940070-06-5). Doll Works.

—The Story of the Three Dolls. Keep, Virginia, illus. LC 5-38492. 148p. (gr. 4 up). 1981. Repr. of 1905 ed. lib. bdg. 35.00 (ISBN 0-940070-07-3). Doll Works.

Godden, Rumer. Four Dolls. Baynes, Pauline, illus. LC 83-14157. 144p. (gr. 4-6). 1984. reinforced 13.00 (ISBN 0-688-02801-2). Greenwillow.

—Four Dolls. (gr. 3-7). 1986. pap. 4.95 (ISBN 0-440-42568-9). Dell.

Greenfield, Eloise. My Doll, Keshia. Gilchrist, Jan S., illus. 12p. (ps-1). 1991. bds. 4.95 (ISBN 0-86316-203-7). Writers & Readers.

Gripe, Maria. Agnes Cecilia. Lesser, Rika, tr. from SWE. LC 89-24464. 288p. (gr. 7 up). 1990. 14.95 (ISBN 0-06-022281-6); PLB 14.89 (ISBN 0-06-022282-4). HarpC Child Bks.

Gruelle, Johnny. Original Adventures of Raggedy Ann. LC 88-3684. 1988. 6.99 (ISBN 0-517-66581-6). Outlet Bk Co.

—Raggedy Andy Stories. Gruelle, Johnny, illus. 96p. (ps up). 1987. Repr. PLB 25.95x (ISBN 0-89966-618-3). Buccaneer Bks.

—Raggedy Ann & Andy & the Camel with the Wrinkled Knees. (gr. 1-4). 1977. pap. 1.95 (ISBN 0-440-47390-X). Dell.

Gruelle, Johnny, illus. Little Treasury of Raggedy Ann & Andy. Nash, Corey, retold by. (Illus.). (ps-1). 1984. 5.98 (ISBN 0-517-44730-4). Outlet Bk Co.

Hahn, Mary D. Doll in the Garden. 144p. 1990. pap. 3.50 (ISBN 0-380-70865-5, Camelot). Avon.

Haley, Gail E. Marguerite. Haley, Gail E., illus. (ps-3). 1991. pap. 14.95 (ISBN 0-87460-262-9). Lion Bks.

Higgins, Violet. The Real Story of a Real Doll. (Illus.). 116p. (gr. 4 up). 1981. Repr. of 1929 ed. lib. bdg. 35.00 (ISBN 0-940070-08-1). Doll Works.

Hines, Anna C. Maybe a Band-Aid Will Help. Hines, Anna C., illus. LC 84-1533. 24p. (ps-1). 1984. 8.95 (ISBN 0-525-44115-8, 0869-260, DCB). Dutton Child Bks.

Hines, Anna G. Don't Worry, I'll Find You. Hines, Anna G., illus. LC 85-16129. 24p. (ps-1). 1986. 10.95 (ISBN 0-525-44228-6, DCB). Dutton Child Bks.

Hollands, Judith. The Cry of the Captured Doll. MacDonald, Patricia, ed. De Rosa, Dee, illus. 80p. (Orig.). (gr. 2-5). 1990. pap. 2.75 (ISBN 0-671-66813-7, Minstrel Bks). PB.

Johnson, Phyllis. The Boy Toy. Shiffman, Lena, illus. 32p. (gr. k-3). 1988. pap. 5.95 (ISBN 0-914996-26-6). Lollipop Power.

Kroll, Steven. The Hand-Me-Down Doll. Ness, Evaline, illus. LC 83-4394. 32p. (gr. k-3). 1983. reinforced bdg. 12.95 (ISBN 0-8234-0495-1). Holiday.

Lamm, C. Drew. Anniranni & Mollymishi the Wild-Haired Doll. Ohi, Ruth, illus. 24p. (ps-2). 1990. 14.95 (ISBN 1-55037-105-3); pap. 5.95 (ISBN 1-55037-106-1). Firefly Bks Ltd.

Lippert, Donald F. Mister B. Hedden, Randall, illus. 32p. (ps). Date not set. write for info. Pastel Pubns.

Lunn, Janet. Double Spell. 144p. (gr. 3-7). 1986. pap. 3.95 (ISBN 0-14-031858-5, Puffin). Puffin Bks.

Mcginley, Phyllis. Most Wonderful Doll in World. 1990. 10.95 (ISBN 0-590-43476-4). Scholastic Inc.

McKissack, Patricia C. Nettie Jo's Friends. Cook, Scott, illus. LC 87-14080. 40p. (ps-4). 1989. 13.95 (ISBN 0-394-89158-9); lib. bdg. 13.99 (ISBN 0-394-99158-3). Knopf.

McMillan, Bruce. Ghost Doll. (Illus.). 32p. (gr. k-6). 1989. 15.00 (ISBN 0-317-93062-1). Apple Isl Bks.

Minshull, Evelyn. The Cornhusk Doll. Wallace, Edwin B., illus. LC 86-27125. 72p. (ps). 1987. 14.95 (ISBN 0-8361-3431-1). Herald Pr.

Njoku, Scholastica I. The Miracle of a Christmas Doll. McKay, Suzanne, illus. 29p. (gr. k up). 1986. perfect bdg. 5.95x (ISBN 0-9617833-0-3). S I NJOKU.

O'Connell, Jean S. The Dollhouse Caper. Blegvad, Erik, illus. LC 75-25501. 96p. (gr. 3-7). 1976. 12.95 (ISBN 0-690-01042-7, Crowell Jr Bks). HarpC Child Bks.

Pendergraft, Patricia. The Legend of Daisy Flowerdew. 192p. 1990. 14.95 (ISBN 0-399-22176-X, Philomel Bks). Putnam Pub Group.

Polacco, Patricia. Babushka's Doll. LC 89-6122. (Illus.). 40p. (ps-1). 1990. PLB 14.95 (ISBN 0-671-68343-8). S&S Trade.

Pomerantz, Charlotte. The Chalk Doll. Lessac, Frane, illus. LC 88-872. 32p. (gr. k-3). 1989. 12.95 (ISBN 0-397-32318-2, Lipp Jr Bks); PLB 12.89 (ISBN 0-397-32319-0). HarpC Child Bks.

Raggedy Ann & Andy Second Giant Treasury. Date not set. 5.98 (ISBN 0-517-66719-3). Outlet Bk Co.

Raggedy Ann's Adventure. (ps-1). 1987. write for info. Random.

Rosenberg, Liz. The Scrap Doll. Ballard, Robin, illus. LC 90-35668. 32p. (ps-3). 1991. 13.95 (ISBN 0-06-024864-5); PLB 13.89 (ISBN 0-06-024865-3). HarpC Child Bks.

Sandburg, Carl. The Wedding Procession of the Rag Doll & the Broom Handle & Who Was in It. Pincus, Harriet, illus. LC 67-10211. 32p. (ps-3). 1978. pap. 3.95 (ISBN 0-15-695487-7, VoyB). HarBraceJ.

Schulman, Janet. The Big Hello. Hoban, Lillian, illus. LC 75-33672. (gr. 1-4). 1976. 13.95 (ISBN 0-688-80036-X). Greenwillow.

Shura, Mary F. The Sunday Doll. LC 88-3586. 128p. (gr. 5-7). 1988. 12.95 (ISBN 0-396-09309-4, Putnam). Putnam Pub Group.

Sleator, William. Among the Dolls. Hyman, Trina S., illus. LC 75-5944. 80p. (gr. 3-6). 1991. pap. 2.95 (ISBN 0-679-80347-5, Bullseye Bks). Knopf.

Stover, Marjorie. When the Dolls Woke. Levine, Abby, ed. Loccisano, Karen, illus. 128p. (gr. 3-6). 1985. PLB 9.95 (ISBN 0-8075-8882-2). A Whitman.

Tsutsui, Yoriko. Anna's Special Present. Hayashi, Akiko, illus. 32p. (ps-3). 1990. pap. 3.95 (ISBN 0-14-054219-1, Puffin). Puffin Bks.

Udry, Janice M. Thump & Plunk. Schweninger, Ann, illus. LC 80-8443. 32p. (ps-3). 1981. 12.95 (ISBN 0-06-026149-8); PLB 13.89 (ISBN 0-06-026150-1). HarpC Child Bks.

Unwin, Hilary. Inside the Dollshouse: A Miniature Tale. 32p. 1990. 12.95 (ISBN 0-85683-121-2, Pub. by Shepheard-Walwyn UK). Dufour.

Waddell, Martin. The Hidden House. Barrett, Angela, illus. 32p. (gr. k-6). 1990. 14.95 (ISBN 0-399-22228-6, Philomel Bks). Putnam Pub Group.

Walsum-Quispel, J. van. Tina's Island Home. Leeflang-Oudenarden, C., illus. LC 71-99920. 36p. (gr. k-5). 7.95 (ISBN 0-87592-053-5). Scroll Pr.

Weisman, Jill. Barbie & Her Friends. (gr. 4-7). 1991. pap. 2.95 (ISBN 0-8431-2893-3). Price Stern.

—Barbie Travels Around the World. (gr. 4-7). 1991. pap. 2.95 (ISBN 0-8431-2894-1). Price Stern.

Wilkins, Sarah & Mennella, Roxanna. Dolls. Fisher, Barbara, ed. Wilkins, Sarah & Mennella, Roxanna, illus. 27p. (Orig.). (gr. 4-6). 1984. pap. 2.00 (ISBN 0-934830-34-7). Ten Penny.

Willoughby, Alana. My Dolly. Wasserman, Dan, ed. Reese, Bob, illus. (gr. k-1). 1979. PLB 7.95 (ISBN 0-89868-075-1); pap. 2.95 (ISBN 0-89868-086-7). ARO Pub.

Winthrop, Elizabeth. Katharine's Doll. Hafner, Marylin, illus. LC 83-1408. 32p. (gr. k-3). 1983. 11.95 (ISBN 0-525-44061-5, DCB). Dutton Child BKs.

Wright, Dare. The Lonely Doll. (Illus.). 64p. (ps-3). 1986. pap. 2.95 (ISBN 0-590-40199-8, Blue Ribbon Bks). Scholastic Inc.

—The Lonely Doll. 64p. (gr. k-3). 1986. pap. 3.95 (ISBN 0-590-42320-7). Scholastic Inc.

Zemach, Harve. Mommy, Buy Me a China Doll. 2nd ed. Zemach, Margot, illus. LC 66-16943. 32p. (ps-3). 1975. 10.95 (ISBN 0-374-35005-1, Di Capua Bks). FS&G.

—Mommy, Buy Me a China Doll. Zemach, Margot, illus. 32p. (ps up). 1989. pap. 4.95 (ISBN 0-374-45286-5, Di Capua Bks). FS&G.

Zolotow, Charlotte. William's Doll. Pene Du Bois, William, illus. LC 70-183173. 32p. (ps-3). 1972. 13.95 (ISBN 0-06-027047-0); PLB 13.89 (ISBN 0-06-027048-9). HarpC Child Bks.

DOLPHINS

Anderson, J. I. I Can Read About Whales & Dolphins. LC 72-96955. (Illus.). (gr. 2-4). 1973. pap. 1.95 (ISBN 0-89375-052-2). Troll Assocs.

Barrett, Norman. Delfines. LC 88-51518. (SPA., Illus.). 32p. (gr. k-4). 1991. PLB 11.40 (ISBN 0-531-07920-1). Watts.

Barrett, Norman S. Dolphins. (Illus.). 32p. (gr. k-6). 1989. PLB 11.40 (ISBN 0-531-10706-X). Watts.

Behrens, June. Dolphins! LC 89-33846. 48p. (gr. 1-4). 1989. PLB 14.60 (ISBN 0-516-00517-0); pap. 5.95 (ISBN 0-516-40517-9). Childrens.

Berg, Cami. D Is for Dolphin. Bionoi, Janet, illus. 64p. 1990. 18.95 (ISBN 1-879244-01-2). Windom Bks.

Craig, Janet. Discovering Whales & Dolphins. Johnson, Pamela, illus. LC 89-5004. 32p. (gr. 2-4). 1990. PLB 10.89 (ISBN 0-8167-1759-1); pap. text ed. 2.95 (ISBN 0-8167-1760-5). Troll Assocs.

Crump, Donald J., ed. Dolphins: Our Friends in the Sea. LC 86-18126. (Illus.). 104p. (gr. 4-5). 1986. 6.95 (ISBN 0-87044-609-6); PLB 8.50 (ISBN 0-87044-614-2). Natl Geog.

Davidson, Margaret. Dolphins. (ps-3). 1991. pap. 2.50 (ISBN 0-590-44495-6). Scholastic Inc.

—Nine True Dolphin Stories. 64p. (gr. 2-5). 1990. pap. 2.50 (ISBN 0-590-42399-1). Scholastic Inc.

The Dolphin. (Illus.). (gr. 2-5). 1988. pap. 2.50 (ISBN 0-8167-1576-9). Troll Assocs.

Ginsberg, Daniel. Whales & Dolphins: An Educational Coloring Book. Ginsberg, Daniel, illus. 32p. (Orig.). (gr. 1-4). 1989. pap. 1.99 (ISBN 0-9623284-0-5). Ginsberg Pubns.

Gordon, Sharon. Dolphins & Porpoises. Goldsborough, June, illus. LC 84-8594. 32p. (gr. k-2). 1985. PLB 10.89 (ISBN 0-8167-0340-X); pap. text ed. 2.95 (ISBN 0-8167-0443-0). Troll Assocs.

Green, Carl R. & Sanford, William R. The Bottlenose Dolphin. LC 87-19420. (Illus.). 48p. (gr. 5-6). 1987. PLB 10.95 (ISBN 0-89686-329-8, Crestwood Hse). Macmillan Child Grp.

Hall, Howard. A Charm of Dolphins. Leon, Vicki, ed. (Illus.). 40p. (Orig.). 1991. pap. 7.95 (ISBN 0-918303-27-3). Blake Pub.

Hatherly, Janelle & Nicholls, Delia. Dolphins & Porpoises. 72p. 1990. 17.95x (ISBN 0-8160-2272-0). Facts on File.

Leatherwood, Stephen & Reeves, Randall. The Sea World Book of Dolphins. LC 86-46212. (Illus.). 96p. (Orig.). (gr. 4-8). 1987. 12.95 (ISBN 0-15-271956-3, VoyB); pap. 6.95 (ISBN 0-317-59229-7, VoyB). HarBraceJ.

—The Sea World Book of Dolphins. LC 86-46212. 96p. (gr. 4-7). 1987. pap. 9.95 (ISBN 0-15-271957-1, VoyB). HarBraceJ.

McGowen, Tom. Album of Whales. Ruth, Rod, illus. 64p. (gr. 4-7). 1980. write for info. (ISBN 0-528-82287-X). Checkerboard Pr.

Morris, Robert A. Dolphin. Funai, Mamoru, illus. LC 75-6292. 64p. (gr. k-3). 1975. PLB 11.89 (ISBN 0-06-024342-2). HarpC Child Bks.

—Dolphin. Funai, Mamoru, illus. LC 75-6292. 64p. (gr. k-3). 1983. pap. 3.50 (ISBN 0-06-444043-5, Trophy). HarpC Child Bks.

Palmer, S. Dolphins. (Illus.). (gr. k-5). 1989. lib. bdg. 11.94 (ISBN 0-86592-363-9). Rourke Corp.

Papastavrou, Vassili. Whales & Dolphins. (Illus.). 32p. (gr. k-4). 1991. RLB 11.90 (ISBN 0-531-18394-7, Pub. by Boatwright Pr). Watts.

Patent, Dorothy H. Dolphins & Porpoises. LC 87-45332. (Illus.). 96p. (gr. 4 up). 1987. reinforced bdg. 14.95 (ISBN 0-8234-0663-6). Holiday.

—Looking at Dolphins & Porpoises. LC 88-39985. (Illus.). 48p. (gr. 1-4). 1989. reinforced bdg. 12.95 (ISBN 0-8234-0748-9). Holiday.

Propper. Dolphin, Reading Level 3-4. (Illus.). 28p. (gr. 2-5). Date not set. PLB 14.60 (ISBN 0-86592-861-4). Rourke Corp.

Raintree Publishers Inc. Staff. Dolphins. LC 87-28717. (Illus.). 64p. (Orig.). (gr. 5-9). 1988. PLB 19.99 (ISBN 0-8172-3085-8); pap. 11.93 (ISBN 0-8172-3091-2). Raintree Pubs.

Reed, Don C. The Dolphins & Me. Carroll, Pamela & Carroll, Walter, illus. 144p. (gr. 5 up). 1989. 14.95 (ISBN 0-316-73659-7). Little.

—Dolphins & Me. 1990. pap. 2.75 (ISBN 0-590-43294-X). Scholastic Inc.

Reiss, Diana. Camelot World: The Secrets of the Dolphins. 144p. (Orig.). (gr. 7). 1991. pap. 2.95 (ISBN 0-380-76046-0, Camelot). Avon.

Sabin, Francene. Whales & Dolphins. Johnson, Pamela, illus. LC 84-2709. 32p. (gr. 3-6). 1985. PLB 9.49 (ISBN 0-8167-0286-1); pap. text ed. 2.95 (ISBN 0-8167-0287-X). Troll Assocs.

Saunier, Nadine. The Dolphin. Geneste, Marcelle, illus. 20p. (ps up). 1989. 5.95 (ISBN 0-8120-5981-6). Barron.

Seligson, Marcia. Dolphins at Grassy Key. Ancona, George, illus. LC 88-27143. 48p. (gr. 1 up). 1989. 14.95 (ISBN 0-02-781800-4, Mcmillan Child Bk). Macmillan Child Grp.

Serventy, Vincent. Whale & Dolphin. LC 84-15118. (Illus.). 24p. (gr. k-5). 1985. PLB 13.32 (ISBN 0-8172-2401-7). Raintree Pubs.

—Whale & Dolphin. Serventy, Vincent, illus. 24p. (gr. k-3). 1986. pap. 1.95 (ISBN 0-590-40227-7). Scholastic Inc.

Spizzirri Publishing Co. Staff. Dolphins: An Educational Coloring Book. Spizzirri, Linda, ed. (Illus.). 32p. (gr. 1-8). 1986. pap. 1.95 (ISBN 0-317-56473-0). Spizzirri.

Strachan, Elizabeth. A Closer Look at Whales & Dolphins. rev ed. LC 85-80643. 32p. (gr. 4-7). 1986. lib. bdg. 5.99 (ISBN 0-531-17015-2, Gloucester Pr). Watts.

DOLPHINS–FICTION

Benchley, Nathaniel. Demo & the Dolphin. Gammell, Stephen, illus. LC 80-8434. 96p. (gr. 4-7). 1981. 9.13i (ISBN 0-06-020509-1). HarpC Child Bks.

—Several Tricks of Edgar Dolphin. Funai, Mamoru, illus. LC 79-85038. 64p. (gr. k-3). 1970. PLB 11.89 (ISBN 0-06-020468-0). HarpC Child Bks.

Davidson, Carson. Fast-Talking Dolphin. 1989. pap. 2.75 (ISBN 0-590-42513-7). Scholastic Inc.

Fine, John C. The Boy & the Dolphin. Weinberger, Jane, ed. Kardas, Aleksander, intro. by. (Illus.). 34p. (gr. 4-6). 1990. 15.95 (ISBN 0-932433-68-5); pap. 9.95 (ISBN 0-932433-79-0). Windswept Hse.

Krantz, Hazel. For Love of Jeremy. 1990. 14.95 (ISBN 0-525-67321-0, Lodestar Bks). Dutton Child Bks.

L'Engle, Madeleine. A Ring of Endless Light. 336p. (gr. 9 up). 1981. pap. 3.50 (ISBN 0-440-97232-9, LE). Dell.

O'Dell, Scott. Island of the Blue Dolphins. 192p. (gr. k-6). 1987. pap. 3.50 (ISBN 0-440-43988-4, YB). Dell.

Olsen, E. A. Adrift on a Raft. Le Blanc, L., illus. LC 68-16397. 48p. (gr. 3 up). 1970. PLB 10.95 (ISBN 0-87783-000-2); pap. 3.94 deluxe ed. (ISBN 0-87783-078-9); cassette 10.60x (ISBN 0-87783-176-9). Oddo.

Reynolds, Susan L. Strandia. (Illus.). 240p. (gr. 9-12). 1991. 14.95 (ISBN 0-374-37274-8). FS&G.

Zdanys, Al P. & Beaulieu, Denise. Deliana & Danica. (Illus.). 24p. (Orig.). (ps). 1989. pap. 6.95 (ISBN 0-685-29651-2). Appletree Bks.

DOMESTIC ANIMALS
For general works on farm animals. Books limited to animals as pets are entered under Pets. Books on stock raising as an industry are entered under Livestock; names of all animals are not included in this list but are to be added as needed.
see also Animals–Treatment; Camels; Cats; Cattle; Cows; Dogs; Hogs; Horses; Livestock; Pets; Reindeer; Sheep

Ask about Farm Animals. 64p. (gr. 4-5). 1987. PLB 18.25 (ISBN 0-8172-2881-0); pap. 13.27 (ISBN 0-8172-2893-4). Raintree Pubs.

Baby Animals on the Farm. (Illus.). (ps-k). bds. 3.50 (ISBN 0-7214-9534-6). Ladybird Bks.

Braithwaite, Althea. Farm Animals. McGirr, Barbara, illus. 24p. (ps-2). 1990. 1.95 (ISBN 1-878624-29-6, 1553800029). McClanahan Bk.

Brown, Craig. My Barn. LC 90-41758. (Illus.). 24p. (ps up). 1991. 13.95 (ISBN 0-688-08785-X); PLB 13.88 (ISBN 0-688-08786-8). Greenwillow.

Cook, Brenda. All about Farm Animals. Winterbotham, Ann, illus. 1989. 10.95 (ISBN 0-385-24821-0); PLB 11.99 (ISBN 0-385-24822-9). Doubleday.

Cousins, Lucy. Farm Animals. Cousins, Lucy, illus. LC 90-35893. (ps). 1991. bds. 3.95 (ISBN 0-688-10071-6, Tambourine Bks). Morrow.

Druist, Miriam. Wildlife on the Farm. (gr. 2 up). 1977. 6.35 (ISBN 0-686-23334-4). Rod & Staff.

Dunn, Phoebe. Animal Friends. Dunn, Phoebe, illus. LC 85-2254. 24p. (ps-1). 1985. (Random Juv). Random.

Durrell, Julie, illus. The Pudgy Book of Farm Animals. 16p. (gr. k). 1984. 2.95 (ISBN 0-448-10211-0, G&D). Putnam Pub Group.

Farm Animals. (gr. k). 1982. 3.95 (ISBN 0-448-03079-9, G&D). Putnam Pub Group.

Farm Animals. 32p. (Orig.). (ps-1). 1984. pap. 1.25 (ISBN 0-8431-1513-0). Price Stern.

Farm Animals. LC 90-48332. 24p. (ps-k). 1991. pap. 6.95 (ISBN 0-689-71403-3, Aladdin). Macmillan Child Grp.

Hawksley, Gerald. Farm. Hawksley, Gerald, illus. 10p. (gr. 2-4). 1990. bds. 4.95 (ISBN 1-878624-16-4). McClanahan Bk.

Helweg, Hans. Farm Animals. LC 79-27483. (Illus.). 32p. (ps-3). 1980. lib. bdg. 5.99 (ISBN 0-394-93733-3); pap. 2.25 (ISBN 0-394-83733-9). Random.

Isenbart, Hans-Heinrich. Baby Animals on the Farm. Rau, Ruth, illus. 40p. (gr. k-5). 1984. 11.95 (ISBN 0-399-61225-4, Putnam). Putnam Pub Group.

Jacobsen, Karen. Farm Animals. LC 81-7686. (Illus.). 48p. (gr. k-4). 1981. PLB 14.60 (ISBN 0-516-01619-9); pap. 4.95 (ISBN 0-516-41619-7). Childrens.

Losito, Linda, et al. Pets & Farm Animals. (Illus.). 300p. (gr. 4-9). 1990. 17.95 (ISBN 0-8160-1969-X). Facts on File.

My Book of Baby Farm Animals. (ps-2). 3.95 (ISBN 0-7214-5152-7). Ladybird Bks.

Paladino, Catherine. Our Vanishing Farm Animals: Saving America's Rare Breeds. (ps-3). 1991. 15.95 (ISBN 0-316-68891-6). Little.

Paysan, Klaus. Domestic Pets. Paysan, Klaus & Paysan, Angela, illus. LC 73-171531. 108p. (gr. 5 up). 1972. PLB 10.95 (ISBN 0-8225-0566-5). Lerner Pubns.

Pearce, Q. L. & Pearce, W. J. In the Barnyard. Brook, Bonnie, ed. Bettoli, Delana, illus. 24p. (ps-1). 1990. 4.95 (ISBN 0-671-68828-6); PLB 8.98 (ISBN 0-671-68824-3). Silver Pr.

Scott, Mary. A Picture Book of Farm Animals. Botto, Lisa, illus. LC 90-44888. 24p. (gr. 1-4). 1991. lib. bdg. 9.59 (ISBN 0-8167-2150-5); pap. text ed. 2.50 (ISBN 0-8167-2151-3). Troll Assocs.

Sears, Nancy, illus. Farm Animals. LC 77-70863. (ps-3). 1977. 7.95 (ISBN 0-394-83541-7, Random Juv). Random.

Stone, Lynn. Farm Animals Discovery Library, 6 bks. (Illus.). 144p. (gr. k-5). 1990. Set. lib. bdg. 71.60 (ISBN 0-86593-033-3); Set. lib. bdg. 53.70s.p. (ISBN 0-685-36307-4). Rourke Corp.

Wells, Donna K. What Animals Give Us: So Many Things. Axeman, Lois, illus. LC 89-23991. 32p. (ps-2). 1990. lib. bdg. 11.97 (ISBN 0-89565-557-8). Childs World.

DOMESTIC ANIMALS–DISEASES
see Veterinary Medicine

DOMESTIC ANIMALS–FICTION

Alley, R. W., illus. Old MacDonald Had a Farm. 18p. (ps). 1991. 3.95 (ISBN 0-448-40106-1, G&D). Putnam Pub Group.

Dodds, Siobhan. Elizabeth Hen. Dodds, Siobhan, illus. (ps-3). 1988. 9.95 (ISBN 0-316-18818-2, Joy Street Bks). Little.

Farm Animals. Dunn, Phoebe, photos by. LC 83-61244. (Illus.). 28p. (gr. k-1). 1984. pap. 2.95 (ISBN 0-394-86254-6, Random Juv). Random.

Harrison, David. Wake up, Sun. Wilhelm, Hans, illus. LC 85-30053. 32p. (ps-1). 1986. lib. bdg. 6.99 (ISBN 0-394-98256-8, Random Juv); pap. 2.95 (ISBN 0-394-88256-3, Random Juv). Random.

Hayes, Sarah. Eat up, Gemma. Ormerod, Jan, illus. LC 87-36205. 32p. (ps-1). 1988. 13.00 (ISBN 0-688-08149-5). Lothrop.

Iverson, Diane. Where Are the Babies? Iverson, Diane, illus. 48p. (Orig.). (ps). Date not set. 14.95 (ISBN 0-9623349-1-X); pap. 8.95 (ISBN 0-9623349-2-8). MS Pub.

Klitgaard, Carl E. Roderick Rooster. (Orig.). (gr. k-5). 1982. pap. 6.95 snap binder (ISBN 0-9607516-1-0). Cardot Entpr Inc.

Lorenz, Lee. Hugo & the Spacedog. Lorenz, Lee, illus. LC 82-22960. 30p. (ps-3). 1986. 10.95 (ISBN 0-13-444497-3); pap. 5.95 (ISBN 0-13-444480-9). P-H.

Most, Bernard. The Cow That Went Oink. (Illus.). (ps). 1990. 9.95 (ISBN 0-15-220195-5). HarbraceJ.

Noble, Trinka H. The Day Jimmy's Boa Ate the Wash. Kellogg, Steven, illus. LC 80-15098. 32p. (ps-3). 1984. 13.95 (ISBN 0-8037-1723-7); PLB 13.89 (ISBN 0-8037-1724-5); pap. 3.95 (ISBN 0-8037-0094-6). Dial Bks Young.

Potter, Beatrix. Farmyard Noises. 12p. 1991. bds. 3.50 (ISBN 0-7232-3784-0). Warne.

—The Tale of Jemima Puddle-Duck & Other Farmyard Tales. (Illus.). 80p. (ps-3). 1990. pap. 5.95 (ISBN 0-14-050588-1, Puffin). Puffin Bks.

—The Tale of Jemima Puddle-Duck & Other Farmyard Tales. (ps-3). 1987. 10.95 (ISBN 0-7232-3425-6). Warne.

Provensen, Alice & Provensen, Martin. Our Animal Friends at Maple Hill Farm: Re-issued with New Cover Art. Provensen, Alice, illus. LC 74-828. 64p. (ps-3). 1984. (Pub. by BYR); lib. bdg. 10.99 GLB (ISBN 0-394-92123-2). Random.

Shortall, Leonard, illus. Old MacDonald Had a Farm. LC 84-60028. (ps up). 1984. 5.95 (ISBN 0-394-86797-1, Pub. by BYR). Random.

Tafuri, Nancy. Early Morning in the Barn. Tafuri, Nancy, illus. LC 83-1436. 24p. (ps-1). 1983. 14.95 (ISBN 0-688-02328-2); PLB 14.88 (ISBN 0-688-02329-0). Greenwillow.

DOMESTIC ANIMALS–PICTURES, ILLUSTRATIONS, ETC.

Baby Farm Animals. (Illus.). (ps). pap. 1.25 (ISBN 0-7214-9548-6). Ladybird Bks.

Brown, Margaret W. Big Red Barn. rev. ed. Bond, Felicia, illus. LC 85-45814. 32p. (ps-1). 1989. 11.95 (ISBN 0-06-020748-5); PLB 11.89 (ISBN 0-06-020749-3). HarpC Child Bks.

Cabat, Erni, illus. Erni Cabat's Magical ABC: Animals Around the Farm. Rule, Michael, notes by. LC 90-5242. (Illus.). 64p. (Orig.). (ps-2). 1991. pap. 14.95 (ISBN 0-943173-43-4). Harbinger AZ.

Farm Babies. 1990. 4.98 (ISBN 0-8317-6850-9). Smithmark.

McNaught, Harry. Animal Babies. LC 76-24175. (Illus.). (ps-1). 1977. pap. 2.25 (ISBN 0-394-83570-0, Random Juv). Random.

DOMESTIC APPLIANCES
see Household Equipment and Supplies

DOMESTIC ARCHITECTURE
see Architecture, Domestic

DOMESTIC ARTS
see Home Economics

DOMESTIC RELATIONS
see also Divorce; Marriage; Parent and Child

Berger, Gilda. Violence & the Family. 1990. PLB 12.90 (ISBN 0-531-10906-2). Watts.

Berry, Joy. Every Kid's Guide to Handling Family Arguments. Bartholemew, illus. 48p. (gr. 3-7). 1987. 4.95 (ISBN 0-516-21402-0); PLB 14.60 (ISBN 0-516-01402-1). Childrens.

—Every Kid's Guide to Handling Fights with Brothers & Sisters. Bartholemew, illus. 48p. (gr. 3-7). 1987. 5.95 (ISBN 0-516-21404-7); PLB 14.60 (ISBN 0-516-01404-8). Childrens.

Kurland, Morton L. Coping with Family Violence. rev. ed. Rosen, R., ed. 141p. (gr. 7-12). 1990. PLB 12.95 (ISBN 0-8239-1050-4). Rosen Group.

Stark, Evan. Everything You Need to Know about Family Violence. rev. ed. (Illus.). 64p. (gr. 7-12). 1991. 12.95 (ISBN 0-8239-1314-7). Rosen Group.

DOMESTIC RELATIONS–FICTION

Bernstein, Sharon C. A Family That Fights. Levine, Abby, ed. Ritz, Karen, illus. 32p. (gr. 1-5). 1991. 10.95 (ISBN 0-8075-2248-1). A Whitman.

Gray, Nigel. A Balloon for Grandad. Ray, Jane, illus. LC 87-27867. 32p. (ps-2). 1988. 13.95 (ISBN 0-531-05755-0); PLB 13.99 (ISBN 0-531-08355-1). Orchard Bks Watts.

Greenwald, Sheila. All the Way to Wit's End. (gr. k-6). 1987. pap. 2.75 (ISBN 0-440-40188-7, YB). Dell.

Wells, Rosemary. None of the Above. LC 74-2879. 192p. (gr. 8 up). 1974. 5.95 (ISBN 0-8037-6148-1). Dial Bks Young.

Yep, Laurence. Sea Glass. LC 78-22487. 224p. (gr. 7 up). 1979. HarpC Child Bks.

DOMINIC SAVIO, SAINT, 1842-1857

Daughters of St. Paul. Ahead of the Crowd. (gr. 3-7). 3.00 (ISBN 0-8198-0227-1); pap. 2.00 (ISBN 0-8198-0715-X). Dghtrs St Paul.

DOMINION OF THE SEA
see Sea Power

DONATIONS
see Gifts

DOOLEY, THOMAS ANTHONY, 1927-1961

Brown, Alice H. Tom Dooley, Jungle Doctor. (Illus.). (gr. 1-3). 1979. pap. 1.95 (ISBN 0-03-049441-9). Harper SF.

DOUBLE STARS
see Stars

DOUBT
see Belief and Doubt

DOUGLASS, FREDERICK, 1817?-1895

Davidson, Margaret. Frederick Douglass Fights for Freedom. 80p. (gr. 2-5). 1989. pap. 2.50 (ISBN 0-590-42218-9, Apple Paperbacks). Scholastic Inc.

Gibbs, Carrol R. Friends of Frederick Douglass. Williams, Robert M., illus. 23p. (Orig.). (gr. 5-12). Date not set. pap. 5.00 (ISBN 1-877835-50-1); pap. text ed. 3.75 (ISBN 1-877835-51-X). TD Pub.

McKissack, Patricia & McKissack, Fredrick. Frederick Douglass: Leader Against Slavery. Ostendorf, Ned, illus. 32p. (gr. 1-4). 1991. PLB 12.95 (ISBN 0-89490-306-3). Enslow Pubs.

—Frederick Douglass: The Black Lion. LC 86-32695. (Illus.). 136p. (gr. 4 up). 1987. PLB 17.27 (ISBN 0-516-03221-6); pap. 5.95 (ISBN 0-516-43221-4). Childrens.

Miller, Douglas T. Frederick Douglass & the Fight for Freedom. (Illus.). 144p. (gr. 5 up). 1988. 16.95x (ISBN 0-8160-1617-8). Facts on File.

Russell, Sharman. Frederick Douglass. King, Coretta Scott, intro. by. (Illus.). 112p. (Orig.). (gr. 5 up). 1988. 17.95 (ISBN 1-55546-580-3); pap. 9.95 (ISBN 0-7910-0204-7). Chelsea Hse.

Santrey, Laurence. Young Frederick Douglass: Fight for Freedom. Dodson, Bert, illus. LC 82-15993. 48p. (gr. 4-6). 1983. PLB 10.79 (ISBN 0-89375-857-4); pap. text ed. 2.95 (ISBN 0-89375-858-2). Troll Assocs.

DRAFTING, MECHANICAL
see Mechanical Drawing

DRAG RACING
see Automobile Racing

DRAGONFLIES

Dunkle, Sidney W. Damselflies of Florida, Bermuda, & the Bahamas. (Illus.). 100p. (gr. 9-12). 1990. 19.95 (ISBN 0-945417-86-1); pap. 12.95 (ISBN 0-945417-85-3). Sci Pubs.

Harrison, Virginia. The World of Dragonflies. Oxford Scientific Films Staff, illus. LC 87-42610. 32p. (gr. 2-3). 1988. PLB 10.95 (ISBN 1-55532-310-3). Gareth Stevens Inc.

Losito, Linda. Discover Damselflies & Dragonflies. Caulkins, Janet, ed. (Illus.). 48p. (gr. k-6). 1988. PLB 11.90 (ISBN 0-531-18168-5, Pub. by Bookwright Pr). Watts.

Oda, Hidetomo. Dragonflies. Pohl, Kathy, ed. LC 85-28197. (Illus.). 32p. (gr. 3-7). 1986. text ed. 16.67 (ISBN 0-8172-2534-X); pap. text ed. 9.26 (ISBN 0-8172-2559-5). Raintree Pubs.

O'Toole, Chris. The Dragonfly over the Water. Oxford Scientific Films, photos by. LC 87-42613. (Illus.). 32p. (gr. 4-6). 1988. PLB 10.95 (ISBN 1-55532-306-5). Gareth Stevens Inc.

Overbeck, Cynthia. Dragonflies. Sato, Yuko, illus. LC 82-7221. 48p. (gr. 4 up). 1982. lib. bdg. 14.95 (ISBN 0-8225-1477-X). Lerner Pubns.

Watts, Barrie. Dragonfly. LC 88-18412. (Illus.). 25p. (gr. 1-5). 1989. 6.95 (ISBN 0-382-09800-5); PLB 9.98 (ISBN 0-382-09799-8). Silver Burdett Pr.

DRAKE, SIR FRANCIS, 1540?-1596

Gerrard, Roy. Sir Francis Drake: His Daring Deeds. (Illus.). 32p. (gr. 3 up). 1988. 12.95 (ISBN 0-374-36962-3). FS&G.

Goodnough, David. Francis Drake. LC 78-18056. (Illus.). 48p. (gr. 4-7). 1979. PLB 9.89 (ISBN 0-89375-173-1); pap. 2.95 (ISBN 0-89375-165-0). Troll Assocs.

Hook, Jason. Sir Francis Drake. Caulkins, Janet, ed. (Illus.). 32p. (gr. 1-6). 1988. PLB 11.90 (ISBN 0-531-18202-9, Pub. by Bookwright Pr). Watts.

DRAMA–COLLECTIONS
Use for collections of plays by several authors.
see also Christmas Plays

Foxton, David. Sepia & Song. (Illus.). 96p. (Orig.). 1990. pap. 14.95 (ISBN 0-333-40923-X, McMillan Ed UK). Players Pr.

Garrett, Dan, ed. Friends & Neighbors. (Illus.). 96p. (Orig.). 1990. pap. 14.95 (ISBN 0-333-36054-0, McMillan Ed UK). Players Pr.

—Girls. (Illus.). 96p. (Orig.). 1990. pap. 14.95 (ISBN 0-333-46708-6, McMillan Ed UK). Players Pr.

—Masks & Faces. (Illus.). 96p. (Orig.). 1990. pap. 14.95 (ISBN 0-333-36056-7, McMillan Ed UK). Players Pr.

—Scapegoats. (Illus.). 96p. (Orig.). 1990. pap. 14.95 (ISBN 0-333-36055-9, McMillan Ed UK). Players Pr.

—Taking Issue. (Illus.). 96p. (Orig.). 1990. pap. 14.95 (ISBN 0-333-46709-4, McMillan Ed UK). Players Pr.

Harris, Aurand & Jennings, Coleman. Plays Children Love: A Treasury of Contemporary & Classic Plays for Children. Martin, Mary, intro. by. LC 80-2412. (Illus.). 678p. (gr. k-12). 1981. pap. 19.95 (ISBN 0-385-17096-3). Doubleday.

Ibsen, Henrik. Four Major Plays. Grube, J. Incl. A Doll's House; The Wild Duck; Hedda Gabler; The Master Builder. (gr. 11up). pap. 3.50 (ISBN 0-8049-0120-1, CL-120). Airmont.

Jennings, Coleman A. & Harris, Aurand. Plays Children Love, Vol. II. Channing, Carol, frwd. by. 512p. 1988. 19.95x (ISBN 0-312-01490-2). St Martin.

Jennings, Coleman A. & Berghammer, Gretta, eds. Theatre for Youth: Twelve Plays with Mature Themes. Davis, Jed H., frwd. by. 524p. (gr. 8 up). 1986. 30.00 (ISBN 0-292-78081-8); pap. 15.95 (ISBN 0-292-78085-0). U of Tex Pr.

Kamerman, Sylvia E., ed. The Big Book of Comedies. 1989. 16.95 (ISBN 0-8238-0289-2). Plays.

—The Big Book of Holiday Plays. LC 90-7615. 335p. 1990. 16.95 (ISBN 0-8238-0291-4). Plays.

—Plays of Black Americans. LC 87-12207. (Orig.). (gr. 2-9). 1987. pap. 12.00 (ISBN 0-8238-0279-5). Plays.

Lamb, Wendy, ed. Meeting the Winter Bike Rider & Other Winning Plays. (Orig.). (gr. 5 up). 1986. pap. 3.50 (ISBN 0-440-95548-3, LFL). Dell.

Lambert, Alan & Scott-Hughes, Brian. Junior Drama Workshop. (Illus.). 96p. (Orig.). 1990. pap. 14.95 (ISBN 0-333-43459-5, McMillan Ed UK). Players Pr.

MacDonald, Margaret R. The Skit Book: One Hundred & One Skits from Kids. LC 89-29654. 152p. (gr. 1-9). 1990. 25.00 (ISBN 0-208-02258-9, Pub. by Linnet); pap. 15.00 (ISBN 0-208-02283-X). Shoe String.

Miller, Helen L. Everyday Plays for Boys & Girls. LC 86-8884. (Orig.). (gr. 1-6). 1986. pap. 12.00 (ISBN 0-8238-0274-4). Plays.

Miller, Sarah W. Bible Dramas for Older Boys & Girls. LC 75-95409. (gr. 3-6). 1970. pap. 4.95 (ISBN 0-8054-7506-0). Broadman.

Perry, Shauneille & Jackson, Donald. Mio & Other Plays for Young People. LC 73-92790. (gr. 4 up). 1976. 5.95 (ISBN 0-89388-154-6). Okpaku Communications.

Scott, Louise. Quiet Times. 66p. (ps). 1986. saddle stitched 9.95 (ISBN 0-513-01785-2). Denison.

Tripp, Valerie & Thieme, Jeanne. The American Girls Theater: Plays about Kirsten, Samantha, & Molly for You & Your Friends to Perform, 5 bks. Backes, Nick, et al, illus. 336p. (Orig.). (gr. 2-5). 1989. Set. pap. 14.95 (ISBN 0-937295-58-2). Pleasant Co.

Wallerstein, James S. Adventure: Five Plays for Youth. Goodwin, Chester, illus. Incl. Windigo Island; Bobby & the Time Machine; The Cactus Wild-Cat; Johnny Aladdin; Raymond & the Monster. (gr. 5 up). 1971. 5.95 (ISBN 0-912388-01-3). Aurelon.

—Over the Hills: Four Plays for Youth. Savramis, Nitsa, illus. Incl. The Curse of the Larrabies; Jimmy the Werewolf; Laura & the Magic Trumpet; The Terror of Hoostack Mills. (gr. 5 up). 1971. 5.95 (ISBN 0-912388-02-1). Aurelon.

Willard, Nancy. East of the Sun & West of the Moon: A Play. Moser, Barry, illus. 64p. (gr. 3-5). 1989. 14.95 (ISBN 0-15-224750-5). HarBraceJ.

DRAMA–HISTORY AND CRITICISM

Ibsen, Henrik. The Complete Major Prose Plays of Ibsen: The Complete Major Prose Plays. Fjelde, Rolf, tr. 1152p. (gr. 9-12). 1978. pap. 16.95 (ISBN 0-452-26205-4, Plume). NAL-Dutton.

DRAMA–STUDY AND TEACHING

Olfson, Lewy. Fifty Great Scenes for Student Actors. (gr. 9 up). 1984. pap. 4.95 (ISBN 0-553-25520-7). Bantam.

DRAMATIC ART

see Acting

DRAMA–TECHNIQUE

Korty, Carol. Writing Your Own Plays: Creating, Adapting, Improvising. LC 86-21969. 112p. (gr. 6 up). 1986. 13.95 (ISBN 0-684-18470-2, Scribner). Macmillan.

DRAMATIC MUSIC

see Opera

DRAMATISTS

Glassman, Bruce S. Arthur Miller. (Illus.). 128p. (gr. 7-9). 1990. 17.98 (ISBN 0-382-09904-4); pap. 14.95 (ISBN 0-382-24032-4). Silver Burdett Pr.

DRAWING

see also Anatomy, Artistic; Crayon Drawing; Design, Decorative; Geometrical Drawing; Graphic Methods; Illustration of Books; Landscape Drawing; Mechanical Drawing; Shades and Shadows

Albert, Gretchen D. Scribble Art: Kindergarten & Preschool. Albert, Gretchen D., illus. 85p. (ps-3). 1980. pap. text ed. 5.80 (ISBN 0-686-28105-5). GDA Pubns.

Ames, Lee J. Draw Fifty Airplanes, Aircraft & Spacecraft. Ames, Lee J., illus. LC 76-51554. 64p. (gr. 4-6). 1977. pap. 12.95 (ISBN 0-385-12235-7); pap. 9.95 (ISBN 0-385-12236-5). Doubleday.

—Draw Fifty Animals. Ames, Lee J., illus. LC 73-13083. 64p. (gr. 4-6). 1974. 9.95 (ISBN 0-385-07726-2); pap. 12.95 (ISBN 0-385-07712-2). Doubleday.

—Draw Fifty Animals. Ames, Lee J., illus. LC 73-13083. 64p. (gr. 4-6). 1985. pap. 6.95 (ISBN 0-385-19519-2, Zephyr-BFYR). Doubleday.

—Draw Fifty Boats, Ships, Trucks & Trains. Ames, Lee J., illus. LC 75-19011. 64p. (gr. 4-6). 1976. pap. 12.95 (ISBN 0-385-08903-1). Doubleday.

—Draw Fifty Buildings & Other Structures. Ames, Lee J., illus. LC 79-7483. 64p. (gr. 4-6). 1980. PLB 13.99 (ISBN 0-385-14400-8); pap. 13.99 (ISBN 0-385-14401-6). Doubleday.

—Draw Fifty Cars, Trucks, & Motorcycles. Ames, Lee J., illus. LC 85-13157. 64p. (gr. 4-6). 1986. PLB 12.95 (ISBN 0-385-19059-X); pap. 13.99 (ISBN 0-385-19060-3). Doubleday.

—Draw Fifty Cats. Ames, Lee J., illus. LC 86-8964. 64p. (gr. 4-6). 1986. PLB 12.95 (ISBN 0-385-23484-8); pap. 13.99 (ISBN 0-385-23485-6). Doubleday.

—Draw Fifty Dinosaurs & Other Prehistoric Animals. Ames, Lee J., illus. LC 76-7285. 64p. (gr. 1 up). 1977. pap. 12.95 (ISBN 0-385-11134-7). Doubleday.

—Draw Fifty Dinosaurs & Other Prehistoric Animals. Ames, Lee J., illus. LC 76-7285. 64p. (gr. 4-6). 1985. pap. 6.95 (ISBN 0-385-19520-6, Pub. by Zephyr-BFYR). Doubleday.

—Draw Fifty Dogs. Ames, Lee J., illus. LC 79-6853. 64p. (gr. 4-6). 1981. PLB 10.95 (ISBN 0-385-15686-3); pap. 13.99 (ISBN 0-385-15687-1). Doubleday.

—Draw Fifty Dogs. Ames, Lee J., illus. LC 85-16197. 64p. (gr. 4-6). 1986. pap. 6.95 (ISBN 0-385-23431-7, Pub. by Zephyr-BFYR). Doubleday.

—Draw Fifty Famous Cartoons. Ames, Lee J., illus. LC 78-1176. 64p. (gr. 4-6). 1985. pap. 6.95 (ISBN 0-385-19521-4, Pub. by Zephyr-BFYR). Doubleday.

—Draw Fifty Famous Faces. Ames, Lee J., illus. LC 77-15878. (gr. 4-6). 1978. 9.95 (ISBN 0-385-13217-4); pap. 9.95 (ISBN 0-385-13218-2). Doubleday.

—Draw Fifty Famous Stars: As Selected by Rona Barrett's Hollywood Magazine. Ames, Lee J., illus. LC 81-43238. 64p. (gr. 4-6). 1982. 12.95 (ISBN 0-385-15689-8); pap. 8.95 (ISBN 0-385-15688-X). Doubleday.

—Draw Fifty Horses. Ames, Lee J., illus. LC 81-43646. 64p. (gr. 4-6). 1986. pap. 6.95 (ISBN 0-385-17642-2, Pub. by Zephyr-BFYR). Doubleday.

—Draw Fifty Monsters, Creeps, Superheroes, Demons, Dragons, Nerds, Dirts, Ghoulds, Giants, Vampires, Zombies, & Other Curiosa. Ames, Lee J., illus. LC 80-3006. 64p. (ps up). 1986. pap. 6.95 (ISBN 0-385-17639-2, Pub. by Zephyr-BFYR). Doubleday.

—Draw Fifty Monsters, Creepy Creatures, Superheroes, Demons, Dragons, Nerds, Dirts, Ghouls, Giants, Vampires, Zombies, & Other Curiosa... Ames, Lee J., illus. LC 80-3006. 64p. (gr. 4-6). 1983. 12.95 (ISBN 0-385-17637-6); PLB 9.95 (ISBN 0-385-17638-4). Doubleday.

—Draw Fifty Sharks, Whales, & Other Sea Creatures. (gr. 4-7). 1991. pap. 7.00 (ISBN 0-385-26768-1). Doubleday.

—Draw Fifty Vehicles. Ames, Lee J., illus. LC 77-94862. (gr. 1 up). 1978. pap. 6.95 (ISBN 0-385-14154-8, Zephyr-BFYR). Doubleday.

Ames, Lee J. & Budd, Warren. Draw Fifty Sharks, Whales & Other Sea Creatures. (Illus.). 64p. (gr. 4-6). 1989. 12.95 (ISBN 0-385-24627-7, Zephyr-BFYR); PLB 13.99 (ISBN 0-385-24628-5, Zephyr-BFYR). Doubleday.

Ames, Lee J. & Burns, Ray. Draw Fifty Holiday Decorations. Ames, Lee J. & Burns, Ray, illus. LC 87-15581. 64p. (gr. 4-6). 1987. PLB 13.99 (ISBN 0-385-19058-1); pap. 12.95 (ISBN 0-385-19057-3). Doubleday.

Arnold, Tedd. My First Drawing Book. (Illus.). (ps-2). 1986. bds. 5.95 6 bds. (ISBN 0-89480-350-6, 1350). Workman Pub.

Arnosky, Jim. Sketching Outdoors in Spring. Arnosky, Jim, illus. LC 86-21308. 48p. (gr. 4 up). 1987. 12.95 (ISBN 0-688-06284-9). Lothrop.

Barish, Wendy, ed. I Can Draw Horses. Speirs, Gill, illus. 80p. (gr. 3-7). 1983. pap. 3.95 (ISBN 0-671-46447-7, Little Simon). S&S Trade.

Baxter, Leon. Action. Baxter, Leon, illus. 24p. (gr. 2-7). 1989. pap. 2.95 (ISBN 0-8249-8329-7). Ideals.

—Paper Art. Baxter, Leon, illus. 24p. (gr. 2-7). 1989. pap. 2.95 (ISBN 0-8249-8328-9). Ideals.

—People. Baxter, Leon, tr. (Illus.). (gr. 2-7). 1989. pap. 2.95 (ISBN 0-8249-8327-0). Ideals.

—Plants & Animals. Baxter, Leon, illus. 24p. (gr. 2-7). 1989. pap. 2.95 (ISBN 0-8249-8326-2). Ideals.

Beddow, Bruce R. Draw a Dragon Book: An Artbook for Children Who Draw Their Own Thing. (ps-5). 1991. pap. 6.95 (ISBN 0-533-09240-X). Vantage.

Begin with Lines. 24p. (gr. k up). 1988. pap. 2.95 (ISBN 0-8249-8199-5). Ideals.

Bolognese, Don. Drawing Dinosaurs & Other Prehistoric Animals. (Illus.). 72p. (gr. 4 up). 1982. 4.95 (ISBN 0-531-03588-3). Watts.

—Drawing Horses & Foals. (ps-3). 1990. pap. 3.95 (ISBN 0-531-15200-6). Watts.

—Drawing Spaceships & Other Spacecraft. (Illus.). 64p. (gr. 4-6). 1982. PLB 10.90 (ISBN 0-531-04470-X). Watts.

—Drawing Spaceships & Other Spacecraft. (ps-3). 1990. pap. 3.95 (ISBN 0-531-15201-4). Watts.

Bolognese, Don & Raphael, Elaine. Charcoal & Pastel. (Illus.). 64p. (gr. 4-9). 1986. PLB 11.40 (ISBN 0-531-10226-2). Watts.

—Pen & Ink. LC 86-1552. 64p. (gr. 4-9). 1986. lib. bdg. 10.90 (ISBN 0-531-10133-9). Watts.

—The Way to Draw & Color Dionsaurs. Bolognese, Don & Raphael, Elaine, illus. LC 90-8638. 48p. (Orig.). (gr. 1-7). 1991. lib. bdg. 10.99 (ISBN 0-679-90477-8, Randon Juv); pap. 5.99 (ISBN 0-679-80477-3). Random.

—The Way to Draw & Color Monsters. Bolognese, Don & Raphael, Elaine, illus. LC 90-8637. 48p. (Orig.). (gr. 1-7). 1991. lib. bdg. 10.99 (ISBN 0-679-90478-6, Random Juv); pap. 5.99 (ISBN 0-679-80478-1). Random.

Boy Scouts of America. Art. (Illus.). 48p. (gr. 6-12). 1968. pap. 1.85 (ISBN 0-8395-3320-9, 3320). BSA.

Brook, Bonnie. Let's Celebrate Easter: A Book of Drawing Fun. Klein, Susan, illus. LC 87-50428. 32p. (gr. 2-6). 1988. PLB 10.65 (ISBN 0-8167-1051-1); pap. text ed. 1.95 (ISBN 0-8167-1052-X). Troll Assocs.

Brown, Charlene & Davis, Carolyn. Drawing Fun. Davis, Carolyn, illus. 64p. (Orig.). 1988. pap. text ed. 5.95 (ISBN 0-929261-26-7, BA01). W Foster Pub.

Butterfield, M. How to Draw Machines. 32p. (gr. 2 up). 1988. PLB 12.96 (ISBN 0-88110-316-0); pap. 3.95 (ISBN 0-7460-0175-4). EDC.

Claridge, M. How to Draw Dinosaurs. (Illus.). 32p. (gr. 4 up). 1991. lib. bdg. 12.96 (ISBN 0-88110-502-3, Usborne); pap. 3.95 (ISBN 0-7460-0673-X, Usborne). EDC.

Color. 24p. (gr. k up). 1988. pap. 2.95 (ISBN 0-8249-8204-5). Ideals.

Davidow-Goodman, Ann. Let's Draw Dinosaurs. Davidow-Goodman, Ann, illus. LC 77-94034. (gr. 1-6). 1978. pap. 2.95 (ISBN 0-448-14990-7, G&D). Putnam Pub Group.

Deacon, John. The Drawing Book. (Illus.). 64p. (gr. 4 up). 1989. pap. 5.95 (ISBN 0-590-42142-5). Scholastic Inc.

Dean, Wayne. The Incredible, Spreadable, Magic, Drawing Book. Harryman, Diana L. & Leatherbury, Leven C., eds. Dean, Wayne, illus. 56p. (gr. 3-9). 1983. pap. 9.95 (ISBN 0-9616161-0-5). W Dean Editions.

Dr. Seuss. I Can Draw It Myself: By Me, Myself with a Little Help from My Friend Dr. Seuss. Dr. Seuss, illus. 36p. (gr. k-4). 1987. pap. 6.95 (ISBN 0-685-17592-8, Random Juv). Random.

Emberley, Ed. Ed Emberley's Drawing Book: Make a World. (ps-3). 1991. pap. 5.95 (ISBN 0-316-23644-6). Little.

Emberley, Ed E. Ed Emberley's Big Green Drawing Book. Emberley, Ed E., illus. LC 79-16247. (gr. k up). 1979. 14.95 (ISBN 0-316-23595-4); pap. 8.95 (ISBN 0-316-23596-2). Little.

—Ed Emberley's Big Orange Drawing Book. (Illus.). 96p. (gr. 1-5). 1980. 14.95 (ISBN 0-316-23418-4); pap. 8.95 (ISBN 0-316-23419-2). Little.

—Ed Emberley's Big Purple Drawing Book. Emberley, Ed E., illus. (gr. 1 up). 1981. 14.95 (ISBN 0-316-23422-2); pap. 8.95 (ISBN 0-316-23423-0). Little.

—Ed Emberley's Great Thumbprint Drawing Book. Emberley, Ed E., illus. (gr. 1 up). 1977. lib. bdg. 13.95 (ISBN 0-316-23613-6). Little.

Emberley, Rebecca. Drawing with Numbers & Letters. (gr. 6 up). 1981. 12.95 (ISBN 0-316-23406-0). Little.

Facklam, Margery. And Then There Was One, Vol. 1. (gr. 4-7). 1990. 14.95 (ISBN 0-316-25984-5, Joy St Bks). Little.

Filson, Henry J. Little Hands with First Drawing Practice. (Illus.). 28p. (gr. 10 up). 1978. plasctic bdg. 2.75 (ISBN 0-918554-01-2). Old Violin.

Finding Shapes. (Illus.). 24p. (gr. k up). 1988. pap. 2.95 (ISBN 0-8249-8202-9). Ideals.

Foster, Patience. Guide to Drawing. (gr. 2-5). 1981. (Usborne-Hayes); PLB 13.96 (ISBN 0-88110-025-0); pap. 6.95 (ISBN 0-86020-540-1). EDC.

Frame, Paul. Drawing Cats & Kittens. (ps-3). 1990. pap. 3.95 (ISBN 0-531-15198-0). Watts.

—Drawing Dogs & Puppies. (ps-3). 1990. pap. 3.95 (ISBN 0-531-15199-9). Watts.

—Drawing Reptiles. Frame, Paul, illus. LC 86-10969. 64p. (gr. 4-9). 1986. PLB 10.90 (ISBN 0-531-10225-4). Watts.

Fun to Draw Skateboard Action. 32p. (gr. 1-6). 1988. 0.50 (ISBN 0-87406-368-X). Willowisp Pr.

Hodge, Anthony. Drawing. Hayward, Ron, illus. Kline, M., ed. (Illus.). 32p. (gr. 5-9). 1991. PLB 11.90 (ISBN 0-531-17300-3, Gloucester Pr). Watts.

Hoff, Syd. How to Draw Cartoons. (Illus.). 32p. (gr. k-3). 1975. pap. 1.95 (ISBN 0-590-10135-8). Scholastic Inc.

Holden, Lorraine & Malcarne, Vanessa. Animal Places & Faces: A Drawing Book for Kids Who Care. Arnstrong, Beverly, illus. 30p. 1983. 3.50 (ISBN 0-317-60991-2). NAHEE.

How To Draw Monsters & Other Creatures. 32p. (gr. 2 up). 1987. PLB 12.96 (ISBN 0-88110-274-1); pap. 3.95 (ISBN 0-7460-0081-2). EDC.

Johnson, Pamela. How to Draw the Circus. LC 86-50467. (Illus.). 32p. (gr. 2-6). 1987. PLB 10.65 (ISBN 0-8167-0856-8, Pub. by Watermill Pr); pap. text ed. 1.95 (ISBN 0-8167-0857-6, Pub. by Watermill Pr). Troll Assocs.

Kinnealy, Janice. How to Draw Flowers. LC 86-50468. (Illus.). 32p. (gr. 2-6). 1987. PLB 10.65 (ISBN 0-8167-0846-0, Pub. by Watermill Pr); pap. text ed. 1.95 (ISBN 0-8167-0847-9, Pub. by Watermill Pr). Troll Assocs.

LaPlaca, Michael. How to Draw Boats, Trains, & Planes. Laplaca, Michael, illus. LC 81-52123. 32p. (gr. 2-6). 1982. PLB 10.65 (ISBN 0-89375-682-2); pap. text ed. 1.95 (ISBN 0-89375-497-8). Troll Assocs.

—How to Draw Cars & Trucks. LaPlaca, Michael, illus. LC 81-52122. 32p. (gr. 2-6). 1982. PLB 10.65 (ISBN 0-89375-681-4); pap. text ed. 1.95 (ISBN 0-89375-498-6). Troll Assocs.

—How to Draw Dinosaurs. LaPlaca, Michael, illus. LC 81-52118. 32p. (gr. 2-6). 1982. PLB 10.65 (ISBN 0-89375-683-0); pap. text ed. 1.95 (ISBN 0-89375-496-X). Troll Assocs.

Learning Works Staff. Travel Pack, No. 1: Doodle One. (gr. k-6). 1989. 8.95 (ISBN 0-88160-175-6, LW 290). Learning Wks.

—Travel Pack, No. 2: Doodle Two. (gr. k-6). 1989. 8.95 (ISBN 0-88160-176-4, LW 291). Learning Wks.

—Travel Pack, No. 3: Games. (gr. k-6). 1989. 14.95 (ISBN 0-88160-177-2, LW 292). Learning Wks.

—Travel Pack, No. 4: Dinosaurs. (gr. k-6). 1989. 8.95 (ISBN 0-88160-178-0, LW 293). Learning Wks.

Loh, Carolyn. Let's Celebrate Valentine's Day: A Book of Things to Draw. Loh, Carolyn, illus. LC 87-50429. 32p. (gr. 2-6). 1988. PLB 10.65 (ISBN 0-8167-1035-X); pap. text ed. 1.95 (ISBN 0-8167-1036-8). Troll Assocs.

Lopshire, Robert. I Can Draw! 1988. pap. 2.50 (ISBN 0-590-41278-7). Scholastic Inc.

McKay, Bob. How to Draw Funny People. McKay, Bob, illus. LC 81-69658. 32p. (gr. 2-6). 1982. PLB 10.65 (ISBN 0-89375-688-1); pap. text ed. 1.95 (ISBN 0-89375-408-0). Troll Assocs.

Meiczinger, John. How to Draw Indian Arts & Crafts. Meiczinger, John, illus. LC 88-50807. 32p. (gr. 2-6). 1988. lib. bdg. 10.65 (ISBN 0-8167-1537-8, Pub. by Watermill Pr); pap. text ed. 1.95 (ISBN 0-8167-1515-7, Pub. by Watermill Pr). Troll Assocs.
Niederhauser, Hans R. & Frohlich, Margaret. Form Drawing. Niederhauser, Hans R. & Frohlich, Margaret, illus. 57p. (Orig.). 1974. pap. 10.00 (ISBN 0-318-41110-5). Merc Pr NY.
Oldfield, Margaret J. Lots More Tell & Draw Stories. (Illus.). (ps-3). 1973. PLB 11.95 (ISBN 0-934876-07-X); pap. 6.95 (ISBN 0-934876-03-7). Creative Storytime.
—More Tell & Draw Stories. (Illus.). (ps-3). 1969. PLB 11.95 (ISBN 0-934876-06-1); pap. 6.95 (ISBN 0-934876-02-9). Creative Storytime.
Olson, Margaret J. Tell & Draw Stories. (Illus.). (ps-3). 1963. PLB 11.95 (ISBN 0-934876-05-3); pap. 6.95 (ISBN 0-934876-01-0). Creative Storytime.
Palazzo, Tony. Magic Crayon. Palazzo, Tony, illus. (gr. k-2). 1967. PLB 10.95 (ISBN 0-87460-089-8). Lion Bks.
Picture Squares. (Illus.). 24p. (gr. k up). 1988. pap. 2.95 (ISBN 0-8249-8200-2). Ideals.
Pinkus, Sue. Let's All Draw Cars, Trucks & Other Vehicles. 1991. pap. 16.95 (ISBN 0-8230-2704-X). Watson-Guptill.
—Let's All Draw Cats, Dogs & Other Animals. 1991. pap. 16.95 (ISBN 0-8230-2705-8). Watson-Guptill.
—Let's All Draw Dinosaurs, Pterodactyls & Other Prehistoric Creatures. 1991. pap. 16.95 (ISBN 0-8230-2706-6). Watson-Guptill.
—Let's All Draw Monsters, Ghosts, Gouls & Demons. 1991. pap. 16.95 (ISBN 0-8230-2707-4). Watson-Guptill.
Pistolesi, Roseanna. Let's Celebrate Halloween: A Book of Drawing Fun. Pistolesi, Roseanna, illus. LC 87-50426. 32p. (gr. 2-6). 1988. PLB 10.65 (ISBN 0-8167-1002-3); pap. text ed. 1.95 (ISBN 0-8167-1003-1). Troll Assocs.
Rancan, Janet. How to Draw Cats. Rancan, Janet, illus. LC 81-52121. 32p. (gr. 2-6). 1982. PLB 10.65 (ISBN 0-89375-679-2); pap. text ed. 1.95 (ISBN 0-89375-680-6). Troll Assocs.
Raphael, Elaine. Drawing History: Ancient Rome. (ps-3). 1990. PLB 12.40 (ISBN 0-531-10928-3). Watts.
Raphael, Elaine & Bolognese, Don. Drawing History: Ancient Greece. Raphael, Elaine & Bolognese, Don, illus. 32p. (gr. 5-6). 1989. PLB 12.40 (ISBN 0-531-10738-8). Watts.
Schreiber, Jocelyn. How to Draw Zoo Animals. Schreiber, Jocelyn, illus. LC 87-50427. 32p. (gr. 2-6). 1987. PLB 10.65 (ISBN 0-8167-1004-X, Pub. by Watermill Pr); pap. text ed. 1.95 (ISBN 0-8167-1005-8, Pub. by Watermill Pr). Troll Assocs.
Smith, Frank C. How to Draw Cats & Kittens. Smith, Frank C., illus. 32p. (gr. 1-6). 1986. pap. 1.50 (ISBN 0-590-33831-5). Scholastic Inc.
—How to Draw Cats and Kittens. (ps-3). 1988. pap. 1.95 (ISBN 0-590-44000-4). Scholastic Inc.
—How to Draw Dinosaurs. Smith, Frank C., illus. 32p. (gr. 1-6). 1986. pap. 1.50 (ISBN 0-590-33832-3). Scholastic Inc.
—How to Draw Dinosaurs. (ps-3). 1989. pap. 1.95 (ISBN 0-590-43799-2). Scholastic Inc.
—How to Draw Horses & Ponies. Smith, Frank C., illus. 32p. (gr. 1-6). 1986. pap. 1.50 (ISBN 0-590-33833-1). Scholastic Inc.
—How to Draw Horses & Ponies. (ps-3). 1990. pap. 1.95 (ISBN 0-590-42462-9). Scholastic Inc.
—How to Draw Silly Monsters. Smith, Frank C., illus. 32p. (gr. 1-6). 1986. pap. 1.50 (ISBN 0-590-33834-X). Scholastic Inc.
Snyder, Carrie A. How to Draw Dogs. Snyder, Carrrie A., illus. LC 81-52120. 32p. (gr. 2-6). 1982. PLB 10.65 (ISBN 0-89375-686-5); pap. text ed. 1.95 (ISBN 0-89375-687-3). Troll Assocs.
—How to Draw Horses. Snyder, Carrie A., illus. LC 84-51871. 32p. (gr. 2-6). 1984. PLB 10.65 (ISBN 0-8167-0381-7, Pub. by Watermill Pr); pap. text ed. 1.95 (ISBN 0-8167-0382-5). Troll Assocs.
—You Can Draw Funny Animals. Snyder, Carrie A., illus. LC 81-69659. 32p. (gr. 2-6). 1982. PLB 10.65 (ISBN 0-89375-689-X); pap. text ed. 1.95 (ISBN 0-89375-409-9). Troll Assocs.
Soloff-Levy, Barbara. How to Draw Birds. LC 86-50550. (Illus.). 32p. (gr. 2-6). 1987. PLB 10.65 (ISBN 0-8167-0876-2, Pub. by Watermill Pr); pap. text ed. 1.95 (ISBN 0-8167-0877-0, Pub. by Watermill Pr). Troll Assocs.
—How to Draw Fairy-Tale Characters. LC 90-26789. (Illus.). 32p. (gr. 2-6). 1991. lib. bdg. 10.65 (ISBN 0-8167-2378-8); pap. text ed. 1.95 (ISBN 0-8167-2379-6). Troll Assocs.
—How to Draw Farm Animals. LC 84-51872. (Illus.). 32p. (gr. 2-6). 1984. PLB 10.65 (ISBN 0-89375-797-7, Pub. by Watermill Pr); pap. 1.95 (ISBN 0-89375-798-5). Troll Assocs.
—How to Draw Forest Animals. Soloff-Levy, Barbara, illus. LC 84-51873. 32p. (gr. 2-6). 1984. PLB 10.65 (ISBN 0-8167-0334-5, Pub. by Watermill Pr); pap. text ed. 1.95 (ISBN 0-8167-0335-3). Troll Assocs.
—How to Draw Ghosts, Goblins & Witches: And Other Spooky Characters. Soloff-Levy, Barbara, illus. LC 81-52124. 32p. (gr. 2-6). 1982. PLB 10.65 (ISBN 0-89375-678-4); pap. text ed. 1.95 (ISBN 0-89375-557-5). Troll Assocs.
—How to Draw Sea Creatures. LC 86-50469. (Illus.). 32p. (gr. 2-6). 1987. PLB 10.65 (ISBN 0-8167-0844-4, Pub. by Watermill Pr); pap. text ed. 1.95 (ISBN 0-8167-0845-2, Pub. by Watermill Pr). Troll Assocs.
Sonkin, Susan. How to Draw Baby Animals. Sonkin, Susan, illus. LC 81-52119. 32p. (gr. 2-6). 1982. PLB 10.65 (ISBN 0-89375-684-9); pap. text ed. 1.95 (ISBN 0-89375-685-7). Troll Assocs.
Speirs, Gill. I Can Draw Sharks & Whales. 1986. pap. 3.95 (ISBN 0-671-60477-5). S&S Trade.
Sperling, Anita, et al. Unicorns & Dragons Tracing Fun. Campana, Manny, illus. 16p. (Orig.). (gr. 1-5). 1991. pap. 1.95 (ISBN 0-590-43532-9). Scholastic Inc.
Spiers, Gill. I Can Draw Faces. 1984. pap. 3.95 (ISBN 0-671-49664-6). S&S Trade.
—I Can Draw People. 1985. pap. 3.95 (ISBN 0-671-55343-7, SSJ). S&S Trade.
Start with a Number. (Illus.). 24p. (gr. k up). 1988. pap. 2.95 (ISBN 0-8249-8201-0). Ideals.
Swartz, Susan S. Where & Why. Reeder, Bill, illus. 24p. (Orig.). (ps-6). 1987. pap. 4.50 wkbk. (ISBN 0-943901-00-6). Creare Pubns.
Tallarico, Anthony. I Can Draw Animals. 80p. (Orig.). (gr. 3 up). 1980. pap. 3.95 (ISBN 0-671-41375-9, Little Simon). S&S Trade.
Tallarico, Tony. The Giant I Can Draw Everything. Schneider, Meg, ed. (Illus.). 192p. (Orig.). (gr. 3-7). 1982. pap. 4.95 (ISBN 0-671-44459-X, Little Simon). S&S Trade.
—I Can Draw Cars, Trucks, Trains & Other Wheels. Tallarico, Tony, illus. 80p. (Orig.). (gr. 3 up). 1981. pap. 3.95 (ISBN 0-671-42535-8, Little Simon). S&S Trade.
—I Can Draw Christmas. (Illus.). 80p. (gr. 4 up). 1990. pap. 3.95 perfect bdg. (ISBN 0-671-70446-X). S&S Trade.
—I Can Draw Monsters. 80p. (gr. 3 up). 1980. pap. 3.95 (ISBN 0-671-41374-0, Little Simon). S&S Trade.
—I Can Draw Pets. 1989. pap. 3.95 (ISBN 0-671-67803-5). S&S Trade.
—I Can Draw Sports. (Illus.). 80p. (gr. 4 up). 1990. pap. 3.95 perfect bdg. (ISBN 0-671-70447-8). S&S Trade.
Tatchell, J. How to Draw Animals. 32p. (gr. 2 up). 1988. PLB 12.96 (ISBN 0-88110-315-2); pap. 3.95 (ISBN 0-7460-0177-0). EDC.
—How to Draw Cartoons & Caricatures. 40p. (gr. 2 up). 1987. PLB 12.96 (ISBN 0-88110-273-3); pap. 3.95 (ISBN 0-7460-0067-7). EDC.
What Comes Next? (Illus.). 24p. (gr. k up). 1988. pap. 2.95 (ISBN 0-8249-8203-7). Ideals.
Williams, H. Harland Draws Animals. (Illus.). 32p. (gr. 1-6). 1989. pap. 2.95 (ISBN 0-88625-226-1). Durkin Hayes Pub.
—Harland Draws Cartoons. (Illus.). 32p. (gr. 1-6). 1989. pap. 2.95 (ISBN 0-88625-224-5). Durkin Hayes Pub.
—Harland Draws Wacky & Wierd. (Illus.). 32p. (gr. 1-6). 1989. pap. 2.95 (ISBN 0-88625-232-6). Durkin Hayes Pub.
—Harland Draws 3-D. (Illus.). 32p. (gr. 1-6). 1989. pap. 2.95 (ISBN 0-88625-229-6). Durkin Hayes Pub.
Witty, Ken. A Day in the Life of an Illustrator. Sanacore, Stephen, photos by. LC 80-54100. (Illus.). 32p. (gr. 4-8). 1981. PLB 11.79 (ISBN 0-89375-448-X); pap. 2.95 (ISBN 0-89375-449-8); cassette avail. Troll Assocs.
Zaidenberg, Arthur. How to Draw Heads & Faces. Zaidenberg, Arthur, illus. LC 66-10314. 64p. (gr. 5-10). 1966. PLB 12.89 (ISBN 0-200-03893-1, Crowell Jr Bks). HarpC Child Bks.
—How to Draw the Wild West. LC 71-156848. 64p. (gr. 5-10). 1972. PLB 12.89 (ISBN 0-200-71847-9, B40211, Crowell Jr Books). HarpC Child Bks.

DRAWING–FICTION

Gackenbach, Dick. Mag the Magnificent. Gackenbach, Dick, illus. LC 85-2645. 32p. (ps-3). 1987. 12.95 (ISBN 0-89919-339-0, Clarion); pap. 4.95 (ISBN 0-89919-522-9, Clarion). Ticknor & Fields.
Korschunow, Irina. Adam Draws Himself a Dragon. Skofield, James, tr. from GER. Rahn, Mary, illus. LC 85-45256. 64p. (gr. 1-4). 1988. pap. 3.50 (ISBN 0-06-440229-0, Trophy). HarpC Child Bks.
Nerlove, Miriam. If All the World Were Paper. Tucker, Kathy, ed. Nerlove, Miriam, illus. 32p. (gr. k-3). 1990. 12.95 (ISBN 0-8075-3535-4). A Whitman.
Pittman, Helena C. Gerald-Not-Practical. (Illus.). 32p. (gr. k-3). 1990. PLB 12.95 (ISBN 0-87614-430-X). Carolrhoda Bks.
Testa, Fulvio. If You Take a Pencil. Testa, Fulvio, illus. LC 82-1505. 32p. (ps-2). 1982. 10.95 (ISBN 0-8037-4023-9). Dial Bks Young.
—If You Take a Pencil. LC 82-1505. 32p. (ps-2). 1985. pap. 4.95 (ISBN 0-8037-0165-9). Dial Bks Young.

DRAWING–STUDY AND TEACHING

Aemmer, Gail. Drawing Conclusions. Nemeroff, Patti, illus. 20p. (gr. 2-3). 1985. pap. text ed. 5.95 (ISBN 0-88724-116-6, CD-0544). Carson-Dellos.
—Drawing Conclusions. Black, Rebecca, illus. 20p. (gr. 5-6). 1985. pap. 5.95 (ISBN 0-88724-118-2, CD-0546). Carson-Dellos.
—Drawing Conclusions. Black, Rebecca, illus. 20p. (gr. 3-4). 1985. pap. 5.95 (ISBN 0-88724-117-4, CD-0545). Carson-Dellos.
Ames, Lee J. Draw Fifty Beasties: And Yugglies & Turnover Uglies & Things That Go Bump in the Night. Ames, Lee J., illus. 64p. (gr. 3 up). 1988. PLB 12.95 (ISBN 0-385-24625-0); pap. 13.99 (ISBN 0-385-24626-9). Doubleday.
—Draw Fifty Horses. Ames, Lee J., illus. LC 81-43496. 64p. (gr. 4-6). 1984. PLB 12.95 (ISBN 0-385-17641-4); pap. 12.95 (ISBN 0-385-17640-6). Doubleday.
Armstrong, B. Build a Doodle, No. 1. 32p. (gr. k-4). 1985. 2.95 (ISBN 0-88160-124-1, LW 133). Learning Wks.
—Build a Doodle, No. 2. 32p. (gr. k-4). 1985. 2.95 (ISBN 0-88160-125-X, LW 134). Learning Wks.
Baxter, Leon. The Drawing Book. Baxter, Leon, illus. 64p. (ps-4). 1990. 13.95 (ISBN 0-8249-8475-7). Ideals.
Bonforte, Lisa. I Can Draw Dinosaurs. (Illus.). 64p. (Orig.). (gr. 2-7). 1984. pap. 3.95 (ISBN 0-671-52756-8, Little Simon). S&S Trade.
Dr. Seuss. I Can Draw It Myself. Dr. Seuss, illus. LC 75-117541. (gr. k-4). 1970. pap. 7.95 (ISBN 0-394-80097-4, Random Juv). Random.
DuBosque, D. C. How Do You Draw Dinosaurs? 64p. (Orig.). (gr. 3-9). 1989. pap. 6.95 (ISBN 0-939217-10-4). Peel Prod.
Emberley, Ed E. Ed Emberley's Drawing Book: Make a World. Emberley, Ed E., illus. LC 70-154962. (gr. 2 up). 1972. lib. bdg. 13.95 (ISBN 0-316-23598-9). Little.
Hartophilis, Georgene, illus. How to Draw Dinosaurs. 32p. (Orig.). 1990. pap. 2.95 (ISBN 0-942025-74-1). Kidsbks.
Harwood, Pearl A. Mr. Bumba Draws a Kitten. LC 65-27995. (Illus.). 32p. (gr. k-3). Repr. of 1966 ed. 4.95 (ISBN 0-8225-0107-4). Lerner Pubns.
McKee, Karen A., illus. How to Draw Airplanes. 32p. (Orig.). 1990. pap. 2.95 (ISBN 0-942025-73-3). Kidsbks.
Tallarico, Anthony. Mystery Pictures to Draw. (Illus.). 64p. (Orig.). 1990. pap. 1.95 (ISBN 0-942025-19-9). Kidsbks.
Tallarico, Tony. Guide to Drawing Cartoons: A Step by Step Fun Guide. (Illus.). 64p. (gr. 2-7). 1975. pap. 2.95 (ISBN 0-448-11959-5, G&D). Putnam Pub Group.
Zaidenberg, Arthur. How to Draw & Compose Pictures. LC 78-141862. (gr. 5-10). 1971. PLB 12.89 (ISBN 0-200-71772-3, B36861, Crowell Jr Books). HarpC Child Bks.
—How to Draw Landscapes, Seascapes & Chipscapes. LC 63-10467. (Illus.). 64p. (gr. 4-7). 1963. PLB 12.89 (ISBN 0-200-03949-0, Crowell Jr Bks). HarpC Child Bks.
—How to Draw Landscapes, Seascapes & Cityscapes. Zaidenberg, Arthur, illus. LC 63-10467. (gr. 5-10). 1963. PLB 12.89 (ISBN 0-200-00074-8, B38431, Crowell Jr Books). HarpC Child Bks.
—How to Draw Wild Animals. Zaidenberg, Arthur, illus. LC 57-12534. (gr. 5-10). 1958. PLB 12.89 (ISBN 0-200-71141-5, Crowell Jr Books). HarpC Child Bks.
—How to Draw Wild Animals. LC 57-12534. (Illus.). 64p. (gr. 4-7). 1958. PLB 12.89 (ISBN 0-200-71815-0, Crowell Jr Bks). HarpC Child Bks.
—How to Draw Wild West. LC 71-156848. (Illus.). 64p. (gr. 4-7). 1972. PLB 12.89 (Crowell Jr Bks). HarpC Child Bks.

DRAWING MATERIALS

see Artists' Materials

DREAMS

Berry, Joy. Every Kid's Guide to Understanding Nightmares. Bartholemew, illus. 48p. (gr. 3-7). 1987. 4.95 (ISBN 0-516-21408-X); PLB 14.60 (ISBN 0-516-01408-0). Childrens.
Fujikawa, Gyo. Dreamland. Fujikawa, Gyo, illus. 14p. (ps). 1981. 2.25 (ISBN 0-448-15081-6, G&D). Putnam Pub Group.
Kincher, Jonni. Dreams Can Help: A Journal Guide to Understanding Your Dreams & Making Them Work for You. Morse, Mary & Espeland, Pamela, eds. Staeck, Roy, illus. LC 88-7630. 120p. (Orig.). (gr. 3-9). 1988. pap. 9.95 (ISBN 0-915793-15-6). Free Spirit Pub.
Milios, R. Sleeping & Dreaming. LC 87-14610. (Illus.). 48p. (gr. k-4). 1987. PLB 14.60 (ISBN 0-516-01243-6). Childrens.
Parker, Steve. Dreaming in the Night: How You Rest, Sleep & Dream. (Illus.). 32p. (gr. k-4). 1991. PLB 11.40 (ISBN 0-531-14099-7). Watts.
Uncle Hyggly, pseud. Tad Gonopolis & His Adventures in the Slumberyard, No. 3. Uncle Hyggly, illus. 48p. (gr. 3-6). 1987. pap. 8.95 (ISBN 0-935583-03-3). Wounded Coot.
Wiseman, Ann S. Nightmare Help: A Guide for Adults & Children. Wiseman, Ann S., et al, illus. 137p. (Orig.). (gr. 1-12). 1986. pap. text ed. 9.00 (ISBN 0-937369-00-4). Ansayre Pr.

DREAMS–FICTION

Allgood, Dave & Allgood, Stephanie. Merry Bear Book of Dreams: A Book to Read & Color. 2nd ed. (Illus.). 36p. (ps-3). 1985. pap. 2.95 (ISBN 0-933103-00-X). Merry Bears.
Aylesworth, Jim. The Bad Dream. Fay, Ann, ed. (Illus.). 32p. (ps-2). 1985. 10.95 (ISBN 0-8075-0506-4). A Whitman.
Bartelt, Jeanine, et al. A Fence Too High. French, Marty, et al, illus. 26p. (ps up). 1986. 7.95 (ISBN 1-55578-103-9); cass. incl. Worlds Wonder.
Berger, Barbara H. The Donkey's Dream. Berger, Barbara H., illus. LC 84-18905. 32p. (ps-5). 1986. 13.95 (ISBN 0-399-21233-7, Philomel). Putnam Pub Group.
Brook, Ruth. Toony & the Midnight Monster. Kondo, Vala, illus. LC 86-30739. 32p. (gr. k-3). 1987. lib. bdg. 11.89 (ISBN 0-8167-0910-6); pap. text ed. 2.95 (ISBN 0-8167-0911-4). Troll Assocs.

Brown, Margaret Wise. The Dream Book: First Comes the Dream. Floethe, Richard, illus. 32p. (gr. 1-3). 1990. Repr. of 1950 ed. 9.95. WaterMark Inc.
Cazet, Denys. Daydreams. Cazet, Denys, illus. LC 89-48939. 32p. (ps-2). 1990. 14.95 (ISBN 0-531-05881-6); PLB 14.99 (ISBN 0-531-08481-7). Orchard Bks Watts.
Colonna, Phyllis & Rassmussen, Della M. Power of Dreaming. LC 81-50866. (gr. k-7). PLB write for info. (ISBN 0-911712-92-5). Eagle Mktg Corp.

Cosgrove, Stephen. The Dream Stealer. Heyer, Carol, illus. LC 89-83843. 48p. (gr. 1-4). 1990. 16.95 (ISBN 1-55868-009-8); pap. 5.95 (ISBN 1-55868-021-7); pap. 12.95 incl. audio (ISBN 1-55868-042-X). Gr Arts Ctr Pub.
THE DREAM STEALER is the first of the Dream Maker Classics by Stephen Cosgrove. A twisted, masked gnome, the Dream Stealer, has been taking good dreams from the children of Chimera. The tale is woven around Michael & Gabby's efforts to capture the gnome & release the dreams. Illustrated by Carol Heyer, THE DREAM STEALER is certain to enchant one & all.
Publisher Provided Annotation.

Crossley-Holland, Kevin. Sleeping Nanna. Melnyczuk, Peter, illus. 32p. (ps-1). 1990. 14.95 (ISBN 0-8249-8458-7). Ideals.
Davis, Emmett. Only in Dreams. Wheeler, Cindy, illus. LC 83-8627. 32p. (gr. 3-6). 1983. PLB 14.65 (ISBN 0-940742-15-2). Raintree Pubs.
Denton, Kady M. Dorothy's Dream. Denton, Kady M., illus. LC 88-28589. 32p. (ps-3). 1989. 12.95 (ISBN 0-689-50482-9, M K McElderry). Macmillan Child Grp.
Dickinson, Peter. Merlin Dreams. Lee, Alan, illus. LC 88-3985. 160p. (gr. k-12). 1988. 19.95 (ISBN 0-440-50067-2). Delacorte.
Duncan, Lois. Horses of Dreamland. Diamond, Donna, illus. 32p. (ps-3). 1986. 12.95 (ISBN 0-316-19554-5). Little.
Fabian, Stella. A Pocketful of Dreams. (Illus.). (gr. 3-6). Date not set. write for info. (ISBN 0-922434-37-9). Brighton & Lloyd.
Garrison, Christian. The Dream Eater. Goode, Diane, illus. LC 85-26671. 32p. (ps-2). 1986. pap. 3.95 (ISBN 0-689-71058-5, Aladdin). Macmillan Child Grp.
Gay, Kristin. Herschel's Special Dream. Matsumoto, Allen, illus. 60p. (Orig.). 1986. pap. 5.95 (ISBN 0-945265-08-5). Romar Bks.
Greenfield, Eloise. Daydreamers. Feelings, Tom, illus. (gr. k up). 1981. 11.95 (ISBN 0-8037-2137-4); PLB 11.89 (ISBN 0-8037-2134-X). Dial Bks Young.
Grejniec, Michael. When I Open My Eyes. Grejniec, Michael, illus. 32p. (ps-1). 1990. 15.95 (ISBN 0-8050-1417-9). H Holt & Co.
Hill, Susan. Go Away, Bad Dreams. Julian-Ottie, Vanessa, illus. Lerner, Sharon, ed. LC 84-17759. (Illus.). 32p. (ps-2). 1985. lib. bdg. 5.99 (ISBN 0-394-97222-8, Random Juv); pap. 2.25 (ISBN 0-394-87222-3). Random.
Jarrell, Randall. Fly by Night. Sendak, Maurice, illus. LC 76-27313. 40p. (ps up). 1985. 11.95 (ISBN 0-374-32348-8); pap. 2.95 (ISBN 0-374-42350-4). FS&G.
Lobby, Theodore E. Jessica & the Wolf: A Story for Children Who Have Bad Dreams. Dixon, Tennessee, illus. LC 89-49382. 32p. (gr. k-3). 1990. 15.95 (ISBN 0-945354-22-3); pap. 5.95 (ISBN 0-945354-21-5). Magination Pr.
McPhail, David. The Dream Child. McPhail, David, illus. LC 84-18755. 32p. (ps-3). 1985. 12.95 (ISBN 0-525-44109-3, DCB). Dutton Child Bks.
Maguire, Gregory. Dream Stealer. LC 82-48854. 128p. (gr. 3-7). 1983. HarpC Child Bks.
Mellecker, Judith. Randolph's Dream. Parker, Robert A., illus. LC 90-40612. 48p. 1991. 14.95 (ISBN 0-679-81115-X); lib. bdg. 15.99 (ISBN 0-679-91115-4). Knopf.
Navarra, Jean E. Willowood. 1990. 7.95 (ISBN 0-533-08923-9). Vantage.
Nightingale, S. A Giraffe on the Moon. 1991. 13.95 (ISBN 0-15-230950-0, HJ). HarBraceJ.
Nolan, Dennis. Dinosaur Dream. Nolan, Dennis, illus. LC 89-78208. 32p. (ps-2). 1990. 13.95 (ISBN 0-02-768145-9, Mcmillan Child Bk). Macmillan Child Grp.
Paek, Min. Aekyung's Dream. Paek, Min, illus. (ENG & KOR.). 24p. (gr. 2-7). 1988. 12.95 (ISBN 0-89239-042-5). Childrens Book Pr.
Paulsen, Gary. Night the White Deer Died. 1990. 13.95 (ISBN 0-385-30154-5). Delacorte.
Peck, Richard. Dreamland Lake. 128p. (gr. 7 up). 1990. pap. 3.25 (ISBN 0-440-92079-5, LFL). Dell.
Rhodes, Robert. Bah Koo: Chaser of Bad Dreams. Patterson, Gary, illus. 32p. 1987. (Pub. by Thomas Dunne Bks); book & plush toy 29.95 (ISBN 0-312-01127-X). St Martin.
Riddell, Chris. The Wish Factory. LC 90-34473. (Illus.). 32p. (ps-3). 1990. 14.95 (ISBN 0-8249-8482-X). Ideals.
Ross, Lillian. The Little Old Man & His Dreams. Healy, Deborah, illus. LC 89-34511. 32p. (gr. k-3). 1990. 14.95 (ISBN 0-06-025094-1); PLB 14.89 (ISBN 0-06-025095-X). HarpC Child Bks.
Sharmat, Marjorie W. The Son of the Slime That Ate Cleveland. Pate, Richard, illus. 108p. (Orig.). (gr. k-6). 1985. pap. 2.50 (ISBN 0-440-48086-8, YB). Dell.
Simmonds, Posy. The Chocolate Wedding. Simmonds, Posy, illus. LC 90-4932. 32p. (gr. k-5). 1991. 12.95 (ISBN 0-679-81447-7); PLB 13.99 (ISBN 0-679-91447-1). Knopf.
Snyder, Zilpha K. Blair's Nightmare. (gr. k-6). 1985. pap. 3.25 (ISBN 0-440-40915-2, YB). Dell.
Stevenson, James. Could Be Worse! Stevenson, James, illus. LC 76-28534. 32p. (gr. k-3). 1977. 13.95 (ISBN 0-688-80075-0); PLB 13.88 (ISBN 0-688-84075-2). Greenwillow.
Supraner, Robyn. Molly's Special Wish. Rocklen, Margot, illus. LC 85-14087. 48p. (Orig.). (gr. 1-3). 1986. PLB 9.89 (ISBN 0-8167-0660-3); pap. text ed. 2.95 (ISBN 0-8167-0661-1). Troll Assocs.
Sweetie: A Sugar-Coated Nightmare. 36p. (ps-4). 1985. 8.95 (ISBN 0-88684-175-5); cassette tape avail. Listen USA.
Uchida, Yoshiko. A Jar of Dreams. 131p. (gr. 5-9). 1985. pap. 3.95 (ISBN 0-689-71041-0, Aladdin). Macmillan Child Grp.
Van Allsburg, Chris. Ben's Dream. (Illus.). 32p. (gr. 2 up). 1982. 14.95 (ISBN 0-395-32084-4). HM.
Waller, Wanda W. Unicorns & Dreams. Lopez, Ron, ed. Perrin, Sandra, illus. 39p. (Orig.). (gr. k-6). 1985. pap. 4.95 (ISBN 0-930825-00-4). Lola Library.
Weedn, Flavia. Flavia & the Dream Maker. Weedn, Flavia, illus. 56p. 1988. 14.95 (ISBN 0-929632-00-1). deluxe limited 24.95 (ISBN 0-929632-02-8). Applause Inc.
Wright, Betty R. The Secret Window. LC 82-80816. 160p. (gr. 3-7). 1982. 13.95 (ISBN 0-8234-0464-1). Holiday.
—Why Do I Daydream? Glessner, Marc, illus. Silverman, Manuel S., intro. by. LC 80-25561. (Illus.). 32p. (gr. k-6). 1981. PLB 16.67 (ISBN 0-8172-1371-6). Raintree Pubs Ltd.
Zemach, Harve. Awake & Dreaming. Zemach, Margot, illus. LC 77-125145. 32p. (ps-3). 1970. 10.95 (ISBN 0-374-30462-9). FS&G.
Zemach-Bersin, Kaethe. The Funny Dream. LC 87-18769. (Illus.). 32p. (ps-3). 1988. 11.95 (ISBN 0-688-07500-2); lib. bdg. 11.88 (ISBN 0-688-07501-0). Greenwillow.

DRESS
see Clothing and Dress

DRESSMAKING
see also Sewing

Bradley, Duane. Design It, Sew It, & Wear It: How to Make Yourself a Super Wardrobe Without Commercial Patterns. Corwin, Judith H., illus. LC 76-55732. (gr. 7 up). 1979. write for info. (ISBN 0-690-01297-7, Crowell Jr Bks); PLB 12.89 (ISBN 0-690-03839-9). HarpC Child Bks.
Cobb, Mary. Practical Patterns. (gr. 1-6). 1990. pap. 8.95 (ISBN 0-8224-5151-4). Fearon Teach Aids.

DRINKS
see Beverages

DRIVERS, AUTOMOBILE
see Automobile Drivers

DROMEDARIES
see Camels

DROPOUTS

Sheffield, Anne & Frankel, Bruce, eds. When I Was Young I Loved School: Dropping Out & Hanging In. (gr. 7 up). 1989. 9.95 (ISBN 0-9621641-2-7). CEF Inc.

DROPOUTS–FICTION

Zindel, Paul. I Never Loved Your Mind. 144p. (gr. 9 up). 1984. pap. 2.95 (ISBN 0-553-27323-X). Bantam.
—I Never Loved Your Mind. LC 73-105476. 192p. (gr. 7 up). 1970. PLB 12.89 (ISBN 0-06-026822-0). HarpC Child Bks.

DRUG ADDICTION
see Narcotic Habit

DRUG HABIT
see Narcotic Habit

DRUGS
see also Pharmacy; Poisons
also names of individual drugs, and groups of drugs, e.g. Narcotics

Avraham, Regina. The Downside of Drugs. Mendelson, Jack H. & Mello, Nancyintro. by. (Illus.). 104p. (gr. 5 up). 1988. lib. bdg. 18.95 (ISBN 1-55546-232-4). Chelsea Hse.
—Substance Abuse: Prevention & Treatment. Mendelson, Jack H. & Mello, Nancyintro. by. (Illus.). 104p. (gr. 5 up). 1988. lib. bdg. 18.95 (ISBN 1-55546-219-7). Chelsea Hse.
—Substance Abuse: Prevention & Treatment. 1988. pap. 9.95 (ISBN 0-7910-0807-X). Chelsea Hse.
Baldwin, Dorothy. Health & Drugs. (Illus.). 32p. 1987. PLB 15.93 (ISBN 0-86592-292-6). Rourke Corp.
Berger, Gilda. Drug Abuse: The Impact on Society. Rakos, Jennie, ed. (Illus.). 160p. (gr. 6-12). 1988. PLB 12.90 (ISBN 0-531-10579-2). Watts.
—Making up Your Mind about Drugs. Enik, Ted, illus. LC 88-3609. 80p. (gr. 4-6). 1988. 10.95 (ISBN 0-525-67251-6, Lodestar Bks); pap. 4.95 (ISBN 0-525-67256-7, Lodestar Bks). Dutton Child Bks.
Berger, Gilda & Berger, Melvin. Drug Abuse A-Z. LC 89-1512. (Illus.). 128p. 1990. lib. bdg. 18.95 (ISBN 0-89490-193-1). Enslow Pubs.
Booher, Albert R. Steroids. 11p. (gr. 5-9). 1988. pap. text ed. 5.95 (ISBN 0-685-28967-2). Madonna Edu Syst.
Check, William P. Drugs & Perception. Mendelson, Jack H. & Mello, Nancyintro. by. (Illus.). 104p. (gr. 5 up). 1988. lib. bdg. 18.95 (ISBN 1-55546-214-6). Chelsea Hse.
Chomet, Julian. Speed & Amiphetamines. 1990. PLB 11.90 (ISBN 0-531-10927-5). Watts.
Cleveland, David. That's Life, 9 vols. Pascarella, Sam, illus. (gr. k-8). 1986. tchrs ed. 65.00 (ISBN 0-685-29913-9); wkbk. 3.50 (ISBN 0-685-29914-7). Telesis CA.
Condon, Judith. Pressure to Take Drugs. 1990. PLB 11.90 (ISBN 0-531-10934-8). Watts.
DeStefano, Susan. Focus on Medicines. (Illus.). 64p. (gr. 3-7). 1991. PLB 14.95 (ISBN 0-941477-94-0). TFC Bks MD.
—Focus on Opiates. (Illus.). 68p. (gr. 3-7). 1991. PLB 14.95 (ISBN 0-941477-91-6). TFC Bks MD.
Dolan, Edward F., Jr. Drugs in Sports. LC 85-29521. 128p. (gr. 7-12). 1986. PLB 12.90 (ISBN 0-531-10157-6). Watts.
—International Drug Traffic. LC 84-23440. 112p. (gr. 7-12). 1985. lib. bdg. 11.90 (ISBN 0-531-04937-X). Watts.
Edler, Timothy J. Crawfish-Man's Fifty Ways to Keep Your Kids from Using Drugs. (Illus.). 52p. (gr. k-8). 1982. pap. 6.00 (ISBN 0-931108-08-X). Little Cajun Bks.
Educational Assessment Publishing Company Staff. Parent - Child Learning Library: Drug Information. (Illus.). 32p. (gr. k-3). Date not set. text ed. 9.95 (ISBN 0-942277-54-6). Educ Assess Pub.
—Parent - Child Learning Library: Drug Information English Big Book. (Illus.). 32p. (gr. k-3). Date not set. text ed. 28.50 (ISBN 0-942277-48-1). Educ Assess Pub.
—Parent - Child Learning Library: Drug Information Spanish Big Book. (SPA., Illus.). 32p. (gr. k-3). Date not set. text ed. 28.50 (ISBN 0-942277-49-X). Educ Assess Pub.
—Parent - Child Learning Library: Drug Information Spanish Edition. (SPA., Illus.). 32p. (ps). Date not set. text ed. 9.95 (ISBN 0-942277-90-2). Educ Assess Pub.
Freeman, Sally. Drugs & Civilization. Mendelson, Jack H. & Mello, Nancyintro. by. (Illus.). 104p. (gr. 5 up). 1988. lib. bdg. 18.95 (ISBN 1-55546-222-7). Chelsea Hse.
Friedman, David. Focus on Drugs & the Brain. Neuhaus, David, illus. 64p. (gr. 3-7). 1990. PLB 14.95 (ISBN 0-941477-95-9). TFC Bks MD.
Go Ask Alice. 192p. (gr. 7 up). 1976. pap. 3.50 (ISBN 0-380-00523-9, Flare). Avon.
Grauer, Neil. Drugs & the Law. Mendelson, Jack H. & Mello, Nancyintro. by. (Illus.). 104p. (gr. 5 up). 1988. lib. bdg. 18.95 (ISBN 1-55546-230-8). Chelsea Hse.

Gunn, Jeffrey. Pen Pals Series, No. 1. Wolfe, Debra, illus. (Orig.). (gr. 1). 1991. pap. write for info. (ISBN 1-879146-00-2). Knowldg Pub.
With the growing concern over drugs & drug abuse in today's society, parents tell their child to say no to drugs. But, how many people tell their child why to say no to drugs? This series of 11 children's coloring books will teach them the facts about drugs & drug abuse. These books will also tell your child some of the reasons why kids their age are turning to drugs, & why this is the wrong choice to make. All books are researched & are graphic in nature, to teach the facts the way they really are, no punches pulled. These books are for children 8 & up. Parental help suggested for younger ages. The subtitles for these coloring books are Pen Pals, The Beginning (ISBN 1-879146-01-0), Facts About Pot (ISBN 1-879146-04-5), Facts About Speed (ISBN 1-879146-06-1), Facts About Acid (ISBN 1-879146-08-8), Facts About Heroin (ISBN 1-879146-03-7), Facts About Crack (ISBN 1-879146-09-6), Facts About Downers (ISBN 1-879146-07-x), Facts About Cocaine (ISBN 1-879146-02-9), Facts About Dust (ISBN 1-879146-05-3), Facts About Tobacco (ISBN 1-879146-10-x), Facts About Alcohol (ISBN 1-879146-11-8). 40-46 p. 1991 Knowledge Publishing Company, (218) 828-4341,

915 Welton Road, Baxter, MN 56401.
Publisher Provided Annotation.

—Pen Pals, Vol. 1: The Beginning. Doughty, Virgina, illus. (Orig.). (gr. 3). 1990. pap. write for info. (ISBN 1-879146-01-0). Knowldg Pub.
—Pen Pals, Vol. 2: Facts about Cocaine. Wolfe, Debra, illus. (Orig.). (gr. 3). 1990. pap. write for info. (ISBN 1-879146-02-9). Knowldg Pub.
—Pen Pals, Vol. 3: Facts about Heroin. Wolfe, Debra, illus. (Orig.). (gr. 3). 1990. pap. write for info. (ISBN 1-879146-03-7). Knowldg Pub.
—Pen Pals, Vol. 5: Facts about Dust. Doughty, Virgina, illus. (Orig.). (gr. 3). 1990. pap. write for info. (ISBN 1-879146-05-3). Knowldg Pub.
—Pen Pals, Vol. 6: Facts about Speed. Wolfe, Debra, illus. (Orig.). (gr. 3). 1990. pap. write for info. (ISBN 1-879146-06-1). Knowldg Pub.
—Pen Pals, Vol. 7: Facts about Downers. Wolfe, Debra, illus. (Orig.). (gr. 3). 1990. pap. write for info. (ISBN 1-879146-07-X). Knowldg Pub.
—Pen Pals, Vol. 9: Facts about Crack. Wolfe, Debra, illus. (Orig.). (gr. 3). 1990. pap. write for info. (ISBN 1-879146-09-6). Knowldg Pub.
Hablemos Francamente de las Drogas y el Alcohol. (SPA.). 160p. 1990. 15.95 (ISBN 0-8160-2496-0). Facts on File.
Hawley, Richard. Drugs & Society. 160p. (gr. 7 up). 1991. PLB 15.85 (ISBN 0-8027-8114-4); pap. 8.95 (ISBN 0-8027-7366-4). Walker & Co.
Hemming, Judith. Why Do People Take Drugs? FS-Aladdin Staff, ed. LC 88-50515. (Illus.). 32p. (gr. 1-3). 1988. PLB 10.40 (ISBN 0-531-17113-2, Gloucester Pr). Watts.
Hoobler, Dorothy & Hoobler, Thomas. Drugs & Crime. Mendelson, Jack H. & Mello, Nancyintro. by. (Illus.). 104p. 1988. lib. bdg. 18.95 (ISBN 1-55546-228-6). Chelsea Hse.
Hughes, Barbara. Drug Related Diseases. (Illus.). 96p. (gr. 4-9). 1987. PLB 10.40 (ISBN 0-531-10381-1). Watts.
Hyde, Margaret O. & Hyde, Bruce G. Know about Drugs. 2nd ed. Morrison, Bill, illus. LC 79-13288. 64p. (gr. 4-6). 1979. text ed. 14.95 (ISBN 0-07-031643-0). McGraw.
Hyde, Margaret O., ed. Mind Drugs. 192p. (gr. 7-11). 1986. 10.95 (ISBN 0-396-08813-9, Putnam). Putnam Pub Group.
Inaba, Darryl S. & Cohen, William E. Uppers, Downers & All Arounders. (Illus.). 260p. 1989. 28.95 (ISBN 0-926544-00-4). CNS Prods.
It's O.K. to Say No! (Illus.). (gr. k-9). 1988. pap. 3.95 (ISBN 0-318-36501-4); parent's manual 3.95 (ISBN 0-318-36502-2). Scholastic Inc.
Jussim, Daniel. Drug Tests & Polygraphs: Essential Tools or Violations of Privacy? LC 87-11192. (Illus.). 128p. (gr. 7 up). 1987. lib. bdg. 12.98 (ISBN 0-671-64438-6); pap. 5.95 (ISBN 0-671-65977-4). Messner.
Kamstra, Jerry. Weed: Adventures of a Dope Smuggler. rev. ed. (Illus.). 352p. (gr. 12). pap. text ed. 10.00 (ISBN 0-9617715-0-X). Peer Amid Pr.
Kittredge, Mary. Prescription & OTC Drugs. (Illus.). (gr. 6-12). 1989. 18.95 (ISBN 0-7910-0062-1). Chelsea Hse.
Lincoln, Nigel. Heroin. (Illus.). 64p. (gr. 4-12). 1987. PLB 11.90 (ISBN 0-531-10436-2). Watts.
Lutes, Chris. What Teenagers Are Saying about Drugs & Alcohol. 1990. pap. 7.95 (ISBN 0-310-71051-0, Campus Life). Zondervan.
Martin, Jo. Drugs & the Family. Mendelson, Jack H. & Mello, Nancyintro. by. (Illus.). 104p. (gr. 5 up). 1988. lib. bdg. 18.95 (ISBN 1-55546-220-0); pap. 9.95 (ISBN 0-7910-0797-9). Chelsea Hse.
Monroe, Judy. Drug Testing. LC 89-25425. (Illus.). 48p. (gr. 4 up). 1990. 10.95 (ISBN 0-89686-492-8, Crestwood Hse). Macmillan Child Grp.
—Stimulants & Hallucinogens. LC 88-20350. (Illus.). 48p. (gr. 5-6). 1988. PLB 10.95 (ISBN 0-89686-415-4, Crestwood Hse). Macmillan Child Grp.
Moran, Bill. The Mary Wanna Student Activity Book. Lind, Naomi, illus. Mann, Peggy, intro. by. (Illus.). 23p. (gr. 4-6). 1989. pap. 2.50 (ISBN 0-942493-10-9). Woodmere Press.
Newman, Susan. You Can Say No to a Drink or a Drug: What Every Kid Should Know. (Illus.). 1986. pap. 8.95 (ISBN 0-399-51228-4, Perigee Bks). Putnam Pub Group.
Perry, Robert. Focus on Nicotine & Caffeine. (Illus.). 64p. (gr. 3-7). 1990. PLB 14.95 (ISBN 0-941477-99-1). TFC Bks MD.
Randall, Denise. Drugs & Organized Crime. (ps-3). 1990. PLB 11.90 (ISBN 0-531-10933-X). Watts.
Rodgers, Joann. Drugs & Sexual Behavior. Mendelson, Jack H. & Mello, Nancyintro. by. (Illus.). 104p. (gr. 5 up). 1988. lib. bdg. 18.95 (ISBN 1-55546-215-4). Chelsea Hse.
Schwartz, L. Drug Questions & Answers. (gr. 6-9). 1989. 5.95 (ISBN 0-88160-171-3, LW 282). Learning Wks.
Schwerdtfeger, Don. America Does Not Have a Drug Problem. 131p. (Orig.). 1989. pap. 7.95 (ISBN 0-9624760-0-5). Bding Better People.
Seixas, Judith S. Drugs--What They Are, What They Do. Huffman, Tom, illus. LC 86-33624. 48p. (gr. 1-4). 1987. 12.95 (ISBN 0-688-07399-9); lib. bdg. 12.88 (ISBN 0-688-07400-6). Greenwillow.
Shapiro, Harry. Facts on Drugs in Sports. (Illus.). 32p. (gr. 5-6). 1989. PLB 11.90 (ISBN 0-531-10823-6). Watts.
—Facts on Inhalants. (Illus.). 32p. (gr. 5-6). 1989. PLB 11.90 (ISBN 0-531-10824-4). Watts.
Shulman, Jeffrey. The Drug-Alert Dictionary & Resource Guide. (Illus.). 91p. (gr. 3-7). 1991. PLB 14.95 (ISBN 0-941477-85-1). TFC Bks MD.
—Focus on Cocaine & Crack. Neuhaus, David, illus. 56p. (gr. 3-7). 1990. PLB 14.95 (ISBN 0-941477-98-3). TFC Bks Md.
—Focus on Hallucinogens. (Illus.). 56p. (gr. 3-7). 1991. PLB 14.95 (ISBN 0-941477-92-4). TFC Bks MD.
Stepney, Rob. Inhalants. (Illus.). 64p. (gr. 4-12). 1987. PLB 11.90 (ISBN 0-531-10434-6). Watts.
Stevens, Sarah. Steroids. LC 90-48050. (Illus.). 48p. (gr. 5-6). 1991. RSBE 10.95 (ISBN 0-89686-606-8, Crestwood Hse). Macmillan Child Grp.
Super, Gretchen. Drugs & Our World. 48p. (ps-3). 1990. pap. 3.95 (ISBN 0-8167-2365-6). Troll Assocs.
—What Are Drugs. 48p. (ps-3). 1990. pap. 3.95 (ISBN 0-8167-2364-8). Troll Assocs.
—You Can Say No to Drugs. 48p. (ps-3). 1990. pap. 3.95 (ISBN 0-8167-2366-4). Troll Assocs.
Talmadge, Katherine. Focus on Steroids. (Illus.). 64p. (gr. 3-7). 1991. PLB 14.95 (ISBN 0-941477-93-2). TFC Bks MD.
Theodore, Alan. Origins & Sources of Drugs. Mendelson, Jack & Mello, Nancyintro. by. (Illus.). 104p. (gr. 5 up). 1988. lib. bdg. 18.95 (ISBN 1-55546-234-0). Chelsea Hse.
Turck, Mary C. Crack & Cocaine. LC 89-25409. (Illus.). 48p. (gr. 4 up). 1990. 10.95 (ISBN 0-89686-491-X, Crestwood Hse). Macmillan Child Grp.
Tuttle, Dave. Forever Natural: How to Excel in Sports Drug-Free. (Illus.). 190p. (Orig.). (gr. 9 up). 1990. pap. text ed. 15.95 (ISBN 0-9625740-0-7). Iron Bks.
Twist, Clint. Facts on the Crack & Cocaine Epidemic. (Illus.). 32p. (gr. 5-6). 1989. PLB 11.90 (ISBN 0-531-10822-8). Watts.
Wilker, Debbie A. Deadly Drugs: An Informative Coloring Book. Wilker, Debbie A., illus. (Orig.). (ps-3). 1990. pap. 5.95 (ISBN 1-878282-10-7). St Johann Pr.
Woods, Geraldine. Drug Use & Drug Abuse. rev. ed. LC 85-22531. (Illus.). 72p. (gr. 4-9). 1986. PLB 10.40 (ISBN 0-531-10114-2). Watts.
Woods, Geraldine & Woods, Harold. Cocaine. LC 85-15523. (Illus.). 68p. (gr. 5-8). 1985. PLB 10.40 (ISBN 0-531-10035-9). Watts.
Zeller, Paula K. Focus on Marijuana. (Illus.). 56p. (gr. 3-7). 1990. PLB 14.95 (ISBN 0-941477-97-5). TFC Bks MD.

DRUGS–FICTION

Bank Street College of Education Staff, et al. No Way, Slippery Slick! LC 90-45163. (Illus.). 32p. (gr. k-3). 1991. pap. 3.50 (ISBN 0-06-107438-1). HarpC Child Bks.
Feeney, Mary. Shawn Learns about Drugs. 1990. 7.95 (ISBN 0-533-08640-X). Vantage.
Gibson, Sylvia S. Latawnya, the Naughty Horse, Learns to Say "No" to Drugs. 1990. 6.95 (ISBN 0-533-09102-0). Vantage.
Hinton, S. E. That Was Then, This Is Now. 224p. (gr. k up). 1989. pap. 3.50 (ISBN 0-440-98652-4, LFL). Dell.
Inglehart, Donna W. Breaking the Ring. (gr. 4-7). 1991. 13.95 (ISBN 0-316-41867-6). Little.
Knapp, Paul E. False Positive. LC 89-51296. 167p. 1990. 7.95 (ISBN 1-55523-260-4). Winston-Derek.
Kropp, Paul. Dope Deal. Macpherson, Elaine, illus. LC 81-9766. 96p. (gr. 7-12). 1982. pap. 4.50 (ISBN 0-88436-818-1, 35272); wkbk. 1.20 (ISBN 0-88436-927-7, 35685); read-along cassette 10.00 (ISBN 0-88436-951-X, 35106). EMC.
Mann, Peggy. La Historia de Maria Wanna: O Como te Dana la Marihuana. Ramirez, Gloria & Gatti, Maria N., trs. from ENG. Lind, Naomi, illus. (SPA.). 44p. (Orig.). (gr. 1-6). 1990. pap. text ed. 3.95 (ISBN 0-942493-15-X). Woodmere Press.
Moran, Bill & Mann, Peggy. The Mary Wanna Student Activity Book: Based Upon: The Sad Story of Mary Wanna Or How Marijuana Harms You. rev. ed. Lind, Naomi, illus. 26p. (gr. 4-6). 1990. pap. text ed. 2.95 (ISBN 0-942493-11-7). Woodmere Press.
Strasser, Todd. Angel Dust Blues. LC 78-31735. 1979. 9.95 (ISBN 0-698-20485-9, Coward). Putnam Pub Group.
—Angel Dust Blues. 208p. (gr. 9 up). 1981. pap. 2.95 (ISBN 0-440-90956-2, LE); tchr's guide by Lou Stanek 0.50 (ISBN 0-685-01408-8). Dell.
Strong, Bryan & DeVault, Christine. Christy's Chance. Nelson, Mary, ed. Ransom, Robert D., illus. 72p. (gr. 5-8). 1987. pap. text ed. 3.95 (ISBN 0-941816-33-8). Network Pubns.
Vigna, Judith. My Big Sister Takes Drugs. Mathews, Judith, ed. Vigna, Judith, illus. 32p. (gr. 1-4). 1990. PLB 12.95 (ISBN 0-8075-5317-4). A Whitman.
Wenkart, Henny. Why Would Matthew Do Crack? (gr. 3-7). 1988. write for info. (ISBN 0-911612-00-9). Wenkart.
Wert, Debra L. Mac's Choice: A Story about Choice & Drug Use. Anfenson-Vance, Deborah, et al, eds. Wilson, Miriam J., intro. by. (Illus.). 40p. (gr. 1 up). 1989. pap. 7.95 (ISBN 0-944576-02-8). Rocky River Pubs.
Wingate, Rosalee M. I'll Make It Happen Without Drugs. Sapenter, Marcellus, illus. 44p. (Orig.). (gr. 4-8). 1990. pap. 6.00 (ISBN 0-9625391-0-4). R M Wingate.

DRUGS–LAWS AND REGULATIONS

Lord, Suzanne. Drug Enforcement Agents. LC 89-1343. (Illus.). 48p. (gr. 4 up). 1989. 10.95 (ISBN 0-89686-428-6, Crestwood Hse). Macmillan Child Grp.
Marshall, Eliot. Legalization: A Debate. Mendelson, Jack & Mello, Nancyintro. by. (Illus.). 104p. (gr. 5 up). 1988. lib. bdg. 18.95 (ISBN 1-55546-229-4). Chelsea Hse.

DRUM–FICTION

Gregorich, Barbara. The Gum on the Drum. Hoffman, Joan, ed. Sandford, John, illus. 16p. (Orig.). (gr. k-2). 1984. pap. 1.95 (ISBN 0-88743-004-X, 06004). Sch Zone Pub Co.
Peck, Robert N. Soup's Drum. Robinson, Charles, illus. LC 79-17982. 128p. (gr. 3-6). 1980. 6.95 (ISBN 0-394-84251-0); lib. bdg. 9.99 (ISBN 0-394-94251-5). Knopf.

DRUM MAJORS

Finney, Shan. Cheerleading & Baton Twirling. (Illus.). 72p. (gr. 4-8). 1982. PLB 10.40 (ISBN 0-531-04391-6). Watts.
Hawkins, Jim W. Baton Twirling Is for Me. Bible, William, illus. LC 82-245. 48p. (gr. 2-5). 1982. PLB 8.95 (ISBN 0-8225-1134-7). Lerner Pubns.
Wheelus, Doris. Baton Twirling: A Complete Illustrated Guide. Bolle, Frank, illus. 144p. (gr. 5 up). 1975. 10.95 (ISBN 0-686-67099-X); PLB 7.81 (ISBN 0-87460-310-2); pap. 7.95 (ISBN 0-87460-311-0). Lion Bks.

DRUNKENNESS

see Alcoholism

DRY GOODS

see Textile Industry and Fabrics

DU BOIS, WILLIAM EDWARD BURGHARDT, 1868-1963

Hamilton, Virginia. W. E. B. Dubois: A Biography. LC 70-175106. 192p. (gr. 5-8). 1987. PLB 13.89 (ISBN 0-690-04561-1, Crowell Jr Bks). HarpC Child Bks.
McKissack, Patricia & McKissack, Fredrick. W. E. B. Dubois. (Illus.). 128p. (gr. 9-12). 1990. PLB 13.90 (ISBN 0-531-10939-9). Watts.
Stafford, Mark. W. E. B. Dubois. King, Coretta Scott, intro. by. LC 89-9705. (Illus.). 128p. (Orig.). (gr. 5 up). 1989. PLB 17.95 (ISBN 1-55546-582-X); pap. 8.95 (ISBN 0-7910-0238-1). Chelsea Hse.
W. E. B. Du Bois: Mini Play. (gr. 5 up). 1977. 6.50 (ISBN 0-89550-362-X). Stevens & Shea.

DUCKS

Allred, Gordon. Dori the Mallard. Brown, Margery, illus. (gr. 5 up). 1968. 8.95 (ISBN 0-8392-3052-4). Astor-Honor.
Birchall, Brian. Twelve Little Ducks. LC 90-10054. (Illus.). 16p. (gr. 1-4). 1990. PLB 14.64 (ISBN 0-8114-2692-0). Steck-V.
Blackburn, Lynn B. Timothy Duck: The Story of the Death of a Friend. Johnson, Joy, ed. Borum, Shari, illus. 24p. (Orig.). (gr. 1-6). 1989. pap. 3.50 (ISBN 1-56123-013-8). Centering Corp.
Burton, Jane. Dabble the Duckling. Burton, Jane, photos by. LC 89-11398. (Illus.). 32p. (gr. 2-3). 1989. PLB 10.95 (ISBN 0-8368-0205-5). Gareth Stevens Inc.
Crozat, Francois. I Am a Little Duck. (Illus.). 24p. (ps-k). 1989. 7.95 (ISBN 0-8120-5904-2). Barron.
Dalmais. Duck, Reading Level 3-4. (Illus.). 28p. (gr. 2-5). Date not set. PLB 14.60 (ISBN 0-86592-862-2). Rourke Corp.
Freschet, Berniece. Wood Duck Baby. Arnosky, James, illus. 48p. (gr. 1-3). 1983. pap. 6.99 (ISBN 0-399-61191-6, Putnam). Putnam Pub Group.
Goldin, Augusta. Ducks Don't Get Wet. rev. ed. Kessler, Leonard, illus. LC 88-18073. 32p. (ps-3). 1989. 13.95 (ISBN 0-690-04780-0, Crowell Jr Bks); PLB 13.89 (ISBN 0-690-04782-7, Crowell Jr Bks). HarpC Child Bks.
—Ducks Don't Get Wet. rev. ed. Kessler, Leonard, illus. LC 88-18073. 32p. (ps-3). 1989. pap. 4.50 (ISBN 0-06-445082-1, Trophy). HarpC Child Bks.
Hutchings, Tony. Little Fluffy Duckling. Hutchings, Tony, illus. 12p. (ps-1). 1990. 4.95 (ISBN 1-878624-14-8, 1553800014). McClanahan Bk.
McBrier, Page. Oliver & the Lucky Duck. Sims, Blanche, illus. LC 85-8417. 96p. (gr. 3-6). 1986. PLB 9.89 (ISBN 0-8167-0541-0); pap. text ed. 2.95 (ISBN 0-8167-0542-9). Troll Assocs.
McCue, Lisa, illus. Ducklings Love. LC 90-61308. 24p. (ps-1). 1991. 4.95 (ISBN 0-679-80386-6). Random.
Miller, John P. The Duck Says Quack. Miller, John P., illus. 10p. (ps). 1984. 2.95 (ISBN 0-394-86813-7, Pub. by BYR). Random.
Nentl, Jerolyn. The Mallard. LC 83-2087. (Illus.). 48p. (gr. 4-5). 1983. lib. bdg. 10.95 (ISBN 0-89686-221-6, Crestwood Hse). Macmillan Child Grp.
Rothaus, Jim. Ducks, Geese, & Swans. 24p. (gr. 3). 1988. 17.10 (ISBN 0-88682-224-6); PLB 11.95s.p. (ISBN 0-318-37905-8). Creative Ed.
Royston, Angela. The Duck. Allen, Graham, illus. 24p. (Orig.). (ps-2). 1988. pap. 2.95 (ISBN 0-8249-8243-6). Ideals.
Selsam, Millicent E. & Hunt, Joyce. A First Look at Ducks, Geese & Swans. Springer, Harriet, illus. 32p. (gr. 1-4). 1990. 11.95 (ISBN 0-8027-6975-6); lib. bdg. 12.85 (ISBN 0-8027-6976-4). Walker & Co.
Shaw, Evelyn. A Nest of Wood Ducks. Pape, Cherryl, illus. LC 76-3833. 64p. (gr. k-3). 1976. PLB 11.89 (ISBN 0-06-025592-7). HarpC Child Bks.
Stone, Lynn. Ducks. (Illus.). 24p. (gr. k-5). 1990. lib. bdg. 11.93 (ISBN 0-86593-036-8); lib. bdg. 8.95s.p. (ISBN 0-685-36310-4). Rourke Corp.

Williams, Jane S. Super Duck: A True Story. Pruett, Robert H., ed. Williams, Jane S., illus. 61p. (Orig.). (ps-4). 1990. pap. 9.95 (ISBN 0-9627635-0-0). Brandylane.
For those who love ducks, especially mallard ducks with memorable personalities, & for people who love the Chesapeake Bay region, this true story is sure to delight. Super Duck is an illustrated narrative which tells the story of an uncommon mallard duck raised & nurtured by the author & her husband. Although the book is written primarily for children, Super Duck has broad appeal for children & grown-ups alike. "I believe that this book would be of greatest interest to younger age groups, but also would be appealing to anyone who has an interest in animals & the relationship which people can develop with animals," says Dr. Mitchell Byrd, Dept. of Biology Chairman, William & Mary College, Williamsburg, Virginia. The book includes over 70 original pen & ink drawings by the author, a painter & printmaker of national acclaim. Jane Stouffer Williams has held one person shows at the Galeria Santa Trinita in Florence, Italy, the Gropper Galleries in Boston, & her work is exhibited in collections throughout the US & Europe. She lives in the Northern neck of Virginia near the Chesapeake Bay. ***Publisher Provided Annotation.***

DUCKS–FICTION

Alexander, Martha. No Ducks in Our Bathtub. LC 72-7598. (Illus.). (ps-2). 1977. pap. 2.95 (ISBN 0-8037-6380-8, 0286-090). Dial Bks Young.

Andersen, Hans Christian. The Ugly Duckling. Moore, Lilian, retold by. San Souci, Daniel, illus. 48p. (ps-2). 1988. pap. 3.95 (ISBN 0-590-43794-1); incl. cassette 5.95 (ISBN 0-590-63231-0). Scholastic Inc.

Armstrong the Robot & Earthquack. (Illus.). 1989. write for info. (Mallard Pr). BDD Promo Bk.

Back to the Klondike & Superdoo! (Illus.). 1989. write for info. (Mallard Pr). BDD Promo Bk.

Balan, Bruce. Jeremy Quacks. Meier, David S., illus. LC 89-31372. 32p. (ps up). 1989. 14.95 (ISBN 0-88708-104-5). Picture Bk Studio.

Barks, Carl. Walt Disney's Donald Duck Adventures Album. Barks, Carl, illus. Blum, Geoffrey, intro. by. (Illus.). 48p. (Orig.). (ps up). 1988. pap. 5.95 (ISBN 0-944599-08-7). Gladstone Pub.

—Walt Disney's Donald Duck Adventures Comic Album. Barks, Carl, illus. Blum, Geoffrey, intro. by. (Illus.). 48p. (Orig.). (ps up). 1988. pap. 5.95 (ISBN 0-944599-04-4). Gladstone Pub.

—Walt Disney's Donald Duck Album. Barks, Carl, illus. Blum, Geoffrey, intro. by. (Illus.). 48p. (Orig.). (ps up). 1988. pap. 5.95 (ISBN 0-944599-06-0). Gladstone Pub.

—Walt Disney's Donald Duck Comic Album. Barks, Carl, illus. Blum, Geoffrey, intro. by. (Illus.). 48p. (Orig.). (ps up). 1987. pap. 5.95 (ISBN 0-944599-01-X). Gladstone Pub.

—Walt Disney's Uncle Scrooge Comic Album. Barks, Carl, illus. Blum, Geoffrey, intro. by. (Illus.). 48p. (ps up). 1987. pap. 5.95 (ISBN 0-944599-02-8). Gladstone Pub.

—Walt Disney's Uncle Scrooge Comic Album. Barks, Carl, illus. Blum, Geoffrey, intro. by. (Illus.). 48p. (ps up). 1988. pap. 5.95 (ISBN 0-944599-05-2). Gladstone Pub.

—Walt Disney's Uncle Scrooge Comic Album. Barks, Carl, illus. Blum, Geoffrey, intro. by. (Illus.). 48p. (Orig.). (ps up). 1987. pap. 5.95 (ISBN 0-944599-00-1). Gladstone Pub.

Barrett, Ethel. Quacky & Wacky-Buzz Bee. (ps-1). 1978. pap. 5.95 bk. & cass. pac (ISBN 0-8307-0418-3, 5602593). Regal.

Berends, Polly B. The Case of the Elevator Duck. (Illus.). (gr. 3-6). 1973. lib. bdg. 7.99 (ISBN 0-394-92115-1, Random Juv). Random.

Blocksma, Mary. Donde Esta el Pato? Where's That Duck? Martin, Sandra K., illus. LC 85-15001. (SPA.). 24p. (ps-2). 1990. PLB 12.33 (ISBN 0-516-41587-5); pap. 3.95. Childrens.

Brennan, Mimi. The Golden Egg: A Comic Adventure. Brennan, Mimi, illus. LC 89-20050. 32p. (gr. 2-5). 1990. 12.95 (ISBN 0-8234-0796-9). Holiday.

Bulla, Clyde R. Daniel's Duck. Sandin, Joan, illus. LC 78-22156. 64p. (gr. k-3). 1982. pap. 3.50 (ISBN 0-06-444031-1, Trophy). HarpC Child Bks.

Bunting, Eve. Happy Birthday, Dear Duck. Brett, Jan, illus. LC 87-15694. 32p. (ps-1). 1988. 13.95 (ISBN 0-89919-541-5, Pub. by Clarion). Ticknor & Fields.

—Happy Birthday, Dear Duck. Brett, Jan, illus. 32p. (ps). 1990. pap. 4.95 (ISBN 0-395-52594-2). HM.

Burns, Maurice. Go Ducks Go! Brooks, Ron, illus. 32p. (gr. k-3). 1988. pap. 12.95 (ISBN 0-590-41167-5, Scholastic Hardcovers). Scholastic Inc.

Casey, Patricia. Quack Quack. LC 87-17301. (Illus.). (ps-1). 1988. 12.95 (ISBN 0-688-07765-X). Lothrop.

Conover, Chris. Six Little Ducks. Conover, Chris, illus. LC 75-22155. 32p. (gr. k-2). 1976. PLB 13.89 (ISBN 0-690-01037-0, Crowell Jr Bks). HarpC Child Bks.

Cowley, Joy. Quack, Quack, Quack, 6 bks. Fowler, Jeff, illus. 16p. (Orig.). (gr. k-2). 1987. Set. pap. text ed. 19.80 (ISBN 1-55624-745-1). Wright Group.

—Quack, Quack, Quack! Fowler, Jeff, illus. 16p. (Orig.). (gr. k-2). 1987. pap. text ed. 23.00 (ISBN 1-55624-168-2). Wright Group.

Crozat, Francois. I Am a Little Duck-Mini. 24p. (ps). 1990. 2.95 (ISBN 0-8120-6192-6). Barron.

Dinosaur Ducks & Jungle Duck. (Illus.). 1989. write for info. (Mallard Pr). BDD Promo Bk.

Disney. Duck Tales: Armstrong the Robot & Earthquake. (ps up). 1990. PLB 5.98 (ISBN 0-7924-5234-8, Mallard Pr). BDD Promo Bk.

—Duck Tales: Back to the Klondike & Superdoo. (ps up). 1990. PLB 5.98 (ISBN 0-7924-5237-2, Mallard Pr). BDD Promo Bk.

—Duck Tales: Dinosaur Ducks & Jungle Duck. (ps up). 1990. PLB 5.98 (ISBN 0-7924-5238-0, Mallard Pr). BDD Promo Bk.

—Duck Tales: Sphinx for the Memories & Sir Gyro Gearloose. (ps up). 1990. PLB 5.98 (ISBN 0-7924-5239-9, Mallard Pr). BDD Promo Bk.

—Duck Tales: Sweet Duck of Youth & Double-o-Duck. (ps up). 1990. PLB 5.98 (ISBN 0-7924-5236-4, Mallard Pr). BDD Promo Bk.

Disney Staff. Disney Duck Tales: Master of the Genie & Send in the Clones. (ps up). 1990. PLB 5.98 (ISBN 0-7924-5235-6, Mallard Pr). BDD Promo Bk.

Disney, Walt, Staff. Duck in a Truck. (ps). 1991. 3.95 (ISBN 1-56282-030-3). W Disney Pub.

Dolan, Ellen M. & Bolinske, Janet L., eds. Drakestail. LC 87-61663. (Illus.). 32p. (Orig.). (gr. 1-3). 1987. text ed. 8.95 (ISBN 0-88335-562-0); pap. text ed. 4.95 (ISBN 0-88335-582-5). Milliken Pub Co.

Ducks Can't Count (EV, Unit 1. (gr. 1). 1991. 5-pack 21.25 (ISBN 0-88106-705-9). Charlesbridge Pub.

Ellis, Anne L. Dabble Duck. Truesdell, Sue, illus. LC 83-47692. 32p. (ps-2). 1984. 12.95i (ISBN 0-06-021817-7); PLB 12.89 (ISBN 0-06-021818-5). HarpC Child Bks.

—Dabble Duck. Truesdell, Sue, illus. LC 83-47692. 32p. (ps-3). 1984. pap. 3.95 (ISBN 0-06-443153-3, Trophy). HarpC Child Bks.

Elting, Mary & Folsom, Michael. Q Is for Duck. Kent, Jack, illus. LC 80-13854. 64p. (ps-3). 1980. 13.95 (ISBN 0-395-29437-1, Clarion); pap. 5.95 (ISBN 0-395-30062-2). HM.

Farmer, Patti. What Do You Think I Am... Crazy? Veno, Joe, illus. 32p. (ps-3). 1991. 10.95 (ISBN 0-8120-5979-4). Barron.

Five Little Ducks. 1988. 9.95 (ISBN 0-517-56945-0). Crown.

Flack, Marjorie. Angus & the Ducks. (Illus.). 40p. (ps-3). 1989. 12.95 (ISBN 0-385-07213-9, Zephyr-BFYR); PLB 13.99 (ISBN 0-385-07600-2, Zephyr-BFYR). Doubleday.

—The Story About Ping. Wiese, Kurt, illus. (gr. k-2). 1977. pap. 3.95 (ISBN 0-14-050241-6, Puffin). Puffin Bks.

—Story about Ping. Wiese, Kurt, illus. LC 33-29356. (ps-2). 1933. pap. 11.95 (ISBN 0-670-67223-8). Viking Child Bks.

Friskey, Margaret. Seven Diving Ducks. Morey, Jean, illus. LC 65-20889. 32p. (gr. k-3). 1965. PLB 14.60 (ISBN 0-516-03605-X). Childrens.

Garside, Alice H. The Ant & the Duck. 30p. (Orig.). (gr. k-2). 1990. pap. 2.00 (ISBN 1-882063-07-4). Cottage Pr MA.

Georgiady, Nicholas P. & Romano, Louis G. Gertie the Duck. Wilson, Dagmar, illus. (gr. 1-3). 1982. lib. ed. 2.97 (ISBN 0-695-43363-6); pap. 1.50 (ISBN 0-685-10942-9). Follett Pr.

—Gertie the Duck: Look! I-Can-Read Book. (Illus.). 32p. (gr. k-4). 1988. pap. 3.00 (ISBN 0-695-83363-4). Argee Pubs.

Gerstein, Mordicai. Arnold of the Ducks. Gerstein, Mordicai, illus. LC 82-47735. 64p. (gr. k-3). 1983. 12.95 (ISBN 0-06-022002-3); PLB 12.89 (ISBN 0-06-022003-1). HarpC Child Bks.

—Arnold of the Ducks. Gerstein, Mprdicai, illus. LC 82-47735. 64p. (gr. k-3). 1985. pap. 3.95 (ISBN 0-06-443080-4, Trophy). HarpC Child Bks.

Ginsburg, Mirra. The Chick & the Duckling. Suteyev, V., tr. Aruego, Jose & Dewey, Ariane, illus. LC 74-188773. 32p. (ps-1). 1972. 14.95 (ISBN 0-02-735940-9, Mcmillan Child Bk). Macmillan Child Grp.

Gottfredson, Floyd. Walt Disney's Mickey Mouse Comic Album. Gottfredson, Floyd, illus. Blum, Geoffrey, intro. by. (Illus.). 48p. (Orig.). (ps up). 1987. pap. 5.95 (ISBN 0-944599-03-6). Gladstone Pub.

—Walt Disney's Mickey Mouse Comic Album. Gottfredson, Floyd, illus. Blum, Geoffrey, intro. by. (Illus.). 48p. (Orig.). (ps up). 1988. pap. 5.95 (ISBN 0-944599-07-9). Gladstone Pub.

Green, I. Where Is Duckling Three? Le Blanc, L., illus. LC 68-16402. 32p. (gr. 1-2). 1967. PLB 9.95 (ISBN 0-87783-048-7). Oddo.

Gretz, Susanna. Duck Takes Off. Gretz, Susanna, illus. LC 90-3846. 32p. (ps-1). 1991. SBE 12.95 (ISBN 0-02-737472-6, Four Winds). Macmillan Child Grp.

Hader, Bertha. Ugly Duckling. 1990. 3.98 (ISBN 0-8317-4273-9). Smithmark.

Hayes, Sarah. Nine Ducks Nine. 1990. 12.95 (ISBN 0-688-09534-8); PLB 12.88 (ISBN 0-688-09535-6). Lothrop.

Ingoglia, Gina. The Friendly Duck. (Illus.). 24p. (ps-k). 1989. pap. write for info. (ISBN 0-307-10069-3, Pub. by Golden Bks). Western Pub.

Inkpen, Mick. Gumboot's Chocolatey Day. 1991. 12.99 (ISBN 0-385-41490-0); pap. 11.95 (ISBN 0-385-41489-7). Doubleday.

Johnson, Sylvia A. Downy the Duckling. Hammarberg, Dyan, tr. LC 76-1289. (Illus.). 24p. (gr. k-4). 1976. PLB 6.95 (ISBN 0-87614-063-0). Carolrhoda Bks.

Kelty, Jean M. If You Have a Duck... rev. ed. Ford, Elizabeth, illus. LC 82-51120. 104p. (gr. 1-9). 1982. pap. 9.95 (ISBN 0-910781-00-1). G Whittell Mem.

Kepes, Juliet. The Story of a Bragging Duck. Kepes, Juliet, illus. LC 82-6180. 32p. (gr. k-3). 1983. 8.95 (ISBN 0-395-32863-2). HM.

Kienlen, Helen & Sandercock, Lois. Big Boss Charger. Bower, J. R., illus. 16p. (gr. k-4). 1989. pap. text ed. 4.00 (ISBN 0-9626864-1-7). Holistic Learning.
Just looking at Charger will make you smile. You'll laugh at the funny antics of this tiny yellow duck that was captured in a ring toss by an eight year old boy. This story tells of training Charger to do many tricks. Father's favorite is bring in the morning newspaper. The Patterson family & the beautiful collie dog, Quaker, fall in love with Charger who becomes the neighborhood boss. ***Publisher Provided Annotation.***

Laird, Elizabeth. The Day the Ducks Went Skating. Reeder, Colin, illus. LC 90-25899. 32p. (ps up). 1991. 11.95 (ISBN 0-688-10246-8, Tambourine Bks); PLB 11.88 (ISBN 0-688-10247-6, Tambourine Bks). Morrow.

Lanni, Deborah. What's a Duck Like You Doing in a Place Like This? (Illus.). iv, 23p. (Orig.). (gr. 3-6). 1984. pap. 2.00 (ISBN 0-942788-12-5). Marginal Med.

Leonard, Marcia. Little Duck Finds a Friend. 32p. (ps). 1984. pap. 2.50 (ISBN 0-553-15275-0). Bantam.

—Little Rabbit's Baby Sister. 32p. (Orig.). (ps). 1984. pap. 2.50 (ISBN 0-553-15274-2). Bantam.

LeSieg, Theo. I Wish That I Had Duck Feet. reissued ed. Tobey, B., illus. LC 65-21211. 64p. (ps-2). 1965. 7.99 (ISBN 0-394-90040-5); PLB 7.99 (ISBN 0-685-38459-4). Random.

Leverich, Kathleen. The Hungry Fox & the Foxy Duck. Galdone, Paul, illus. LC 78-11215. 48p. (ps-3). 1979. 5.95 (ISBN 0-8193-0987-7); PLB 5.95 (ISBN 0-8193-0988-5). Parents.

—The Hungry Fox & the Foxy Duck. (Illus.). 48p. (ps-2). 1991. pap. 2.95 (ISBN 0-448-40102-9, G&D). Putnam Pub Group.

Lloyd, David. Duck. Voake, Charlotte, illus. LC 87-26200. 32p. (ps-k). 1990. pap. 3.95 (ISBN 0-06-443169-X, Trophy). HarpC Child Bks.

Lorenz, Lee. A Weekend in the Country. Lorenz, Lee, illus. 32p. (gr. k-3). 1985. 11.95 (ISBN 0-13-947961-9). P-H.

McCloskey, Robert. Make Way for Ducklings. (Illus.). (gr. 1-3). 1976. pap. 3.95 (ISBN 0-14-050171-1, Puffin). Puffin Bks.

—Make Way for Ducklings. McCloskey, Robert, illus. (gr. k-3). 1941. pap. 12.95 (ISBN 0-670-45149-5). Viking Child Bks.

McCue, Lisa, illus. Ducky's Seasons. (ps-2). 1983. pap. 2.95 (ISBN 0-671-45491-9, Little Simon). S&S Trade.

Make Way for Ducklings. (ps-3). 1988. pap. 6.95 incl. cassette (ISBN 0-14-095069-9, Puffin). Puffin Bks.

Mamin-Sibiryak, D. N. Grey Neck. Rudolph, Marguerita, adapted by. Kronz, Leslie S., illus. LC 88-2100. 32p. (gr. k-3). 1988. 13.95 (ISBN 0-88045-068-1). Stemmer Hse.

Masters of the Genie & Send in the Clones. (Illus.). 1989. write for info. (Mallard Pr). BDD Promo Bk.

Matthews, Morgan. Chuck, the Unlucky Duck. Harvey, Paul, illus. LC 88-1284. 48p. (Orig.). (gr. 1-4). 1989. PLB 9.89 (ISBN 0-8167-1333-2); pap. text ed. 2.95 (ISBN 0-8167-1334-0). Troll Assocs.

Mattingley, Christobel. Duck Boy. Mullins, Patricia, illus. LC 85-7521. 96p. (gr. 3-7). 1986. 13.95 (ISBN 0-689-50361-X, M K McElderry). Macmillan Child Grp.

Miller, Edna. Duck Duck. (ps-3). 1981. pap. 3.95 (ISBN 0-685-03845-9). P-H.
Miller, J. P. Little Ducking's Surprise. Miller, J. P., illus. 24p. (ps-1). 1987. 4.95 (ISBN 0-685-17580-4, Random Juv). Random.
—Little Duckling's Surprise. LC 86-62052. (Illus.). 24p. (ps-1). 1987. bk. & doll pkg. 4.95 (ISBN 0-394-88682-8). Random.
Mink, Len. Gospel Duck. Strand, David, illus. 20p. (ps-5). Date not set. pap. text ed. write for info. Mink Ministries.
—Gospel Duck Goes to School. Strand, David, illus. 24p. (ps-6). Date not set. pap. text ed. write for info. Mink Ministries.
Oke, Janette. Ducktails. Mann, Brenda, illus. 131p. (gr. 3 up). 1985. pap. 4.95 (ISBN 0-934998-20-5). Bethel Pub.
Otto, Carolyn. Ducks, Ducks, Ducks. Coxe, Molly, illus. LC 90-42089. 32p. (ps-1). 1991. 14.95 (ISBN 0-06-024637-5); PLB 14.89 (ISBN 0-06-024639-1). HarpC Child Bks.
Paterson, Katherine. The Tale of the Mandarin Ducks. Dillon, Leo & Dillon, Diane, illus. (ps-3). 1990. 14.95 (ISBN 0-525-67283-4, Lodestar Bks). Dutton Child Bks.
El Patito Feo: (The Ugly Little Duck) LC 85-31428. (SPA & ENG.). (ps-2). 1989. PLB 11.93 (ISBN 0-516-33982-6); pap. 3.95 (ISBN 0-516-53982-5). Childrens.
Pellowski, Michael J. The Duck Who Loved Puddles. Paterson, Diane, illus. LC 85-14058. 48p. (Orig.). (gr. 1-3). 1986. PLB 9.89 (ISBN 0-8167-0578-X); pap. text ed. 2.95 (ISBN 0-8167-0579-8). Troll Assocs.
Petrie, Mildred M. Duck, Duck: The Different Duck. Errickson, Shirley V., illus. LC 87-80921. 40p. 1987. 12.95 (ISBN 0-9618241-0-7). Enfield Pubs.
Philip, Neil, ed. Drakestail Visits the King. Underhill, Henry, illus. 32p. (ps-5). 1986. 11.95 (ISBN 0-399-21392-9, Philomel). Putnam Pub Group.
Pinkwater, Daniel M. Ducks. Pinkwater, Daniel M., illus. (gr. 1-3). 1984. 10.95 (ISBN 0-316-70810-0). Little.
Pizer, Abigail. Percy the Duck. (Illus.). 32p. (ps-2). 1989. PLB 8.95 (ISBN 0-87614-365-6). Carolrhoda Bks.
Potter, Beatrix. El Cuento de la Oca Carlota. (SPA., Illus.). 64p. 1988. 5.95 (ISBN 0-7232-3557-0). Warne.
—The Tale of Jemima Puddle-Duck. 64p. (Orig.). (ps). 1984. pap. 2.25 (ISBN 0-553-15251-3). Bantam.
—The Tale of Jemima Puddle-Duck. (Illus.). 64p. (ps-3). 1987. 3.95 (ISBN 0-671-63236-1, Little Simon). S&S Trade.
—The Tale of Jemima Puddle-Duck. LC 87-40284. (Illus.). (ps up). 1990. incl. audio cassettes 6.95 (ISBN 1-55782-017-1). Warner Bks.
—The Tale of Jemima Puddle-Duck. (Illus.). (ps-3). 1987. pap. 5.95 (ISBN 0-7232-3468-X). Warne.
—The Tale of Jemima Puddle-Duck. 1987. pap. 2.25 (ISBN 0-7232-3493-0). Warne.
—The Tale of Jemima Puddle-Duck. Potter, Beatrix, illus. 24p. (ps-2). Date not set. incl. cassette 5.98 (ISBN 1-55886-057-6). Smarty Pants.
—Tale of Jemima Puddle Duck. 1988. 2.50 (ISBN 0-517-65275-7). Crown.
—The Tale of Jemima Puddle-Duck & Other Farmyard Tales. (ps-3). 1987. 10.95 (ISBN 0-7232-3425-6). Warne.
Quackenbush, Robert. Henry Goes West. LC 82-7971. (Illus.). 48p. (ps-3). 1982. 5.95 (ISBN 0-8193-1089-1); PLB 5.95 (ISBN 0-8193-1090-5). Parents.
—Henry's Awful Mistake. Quackenbush, Robert, illus. LC 80-20327. 48p. (ps-3). 1981. 5.95 (ISBN 0-8193-1039-5); PLB 5.95 (ISBN 0-8193-1040-9). Parents.
—Lost in the Amazon: A Miss Mallard Mystery. Quackenbush, Robert, illus. 32p. (gr. 1-4). 1990. PLB 14.95 (ISBN 0-945912-11-0). Pippin Pr.
—Stage Door to Terror. Quackenbush, Robert, illus. LC 84-22295. 48p. (gr. 1-5). 1985. 11.95 (ISBN 0-13-840364-3). P-H.
—Stairway to Doom: A Miss Mallard Mystery. LC 82-21484. (Illus.). 48p. (ps-5). 1983. PLB 9.95 (ISBN 0-13-804595-X). P-H.
—Taxi to Intrigue. Quackenbush, Robert, illus. LC 84-4691. 48p. (gr. 1-5). 1984. 10.95 (ISBN 0-13-886813-1). P-H.
Ruth, Eddie. How Do the Ducks Know? (Illus.). 28p. (Orig.). (gr. 1-4). 1981. pap. 2.50 saddle-stitched (ISBN 0-911826-18-1). Am Atheist.
Sesame Street Staff. One Rubber Duckie. Barrett, John E., photos by. LC 81-86375. (Illus.). (ps). 1982. 3.95 (ISBN 0-394-85309-1). Random.
Sphinx for the Memories & Sir Gyro Gearloose. (Illus.). 1989. write for info. (Mallard Pr). BDD Promo Bk.
Stehr, Frederic. Quack-Quack. Stehr, Frederic, illus. 28p. (ps up). 1988. pap. 3.95 (ISBN 0-374-46141-4). FS&G.
Stott, Dorothy. Too Much. (Illus.). (ps-k). 1990. 10.95 (ISBN 0-525-44569-2, DCB). Dutton Child Bks.
Swan, Walter. Brenda the Cow & the Little White Hen. Swan, Deloris, ed. Asch, Connie, illus. 16p. (Orig.). (gr. 2-3). 1989. pap. 1.50 (ISBN 0-927176-02-5). Swan Enterp.
Sweet Duck of Youth & Double-O-Duck. (Illus.). 1989. write for info. (Mallard Pr). BDD Promo Bk.
Tafuri, Nancy. Have You Seen My Duckling? Tafuri, Nancy, illus. LC 83-17196. 24p. (ps-1). 1984. 15.95 (ISBN 0-688-02797-0); PLB 15.88 (ISBN 0-688-02798-9). Greenwillow.
—Have You Seen My Duckling? Tafuri, Nancy, illus. 32p. (ps-k). 1986. pap. 3.95 (ISBN 0-14-050532-6, Penguin Bks). Viking Penguin.
Teitlebaum, Michael, retold by. The Fuzzy Duckling. Borgo, Deborah, illus. (ps-2). 1991. 5.25 (ISBN 0-307-15700-8, Golden Pr). Western Pub.
Thiele, Colin. Farmer Schulz's Ducks. Milton, Mary, illus. LC 87-21713. 32p. (gr. k-4). 1988. 12.95i (ISBN 0-06-026182-X); PLB 12.89 (ISBN 0-06-026183-8). HarpC Child Bks.
Twohill, Maggie. Who Has the Lucky Duck in Class 4-B. (gr. k-6). 1986. pap. 2.50 (ISBN 0-440-49533-4, YB). Dell.
Tyler, J. & Cartwright, S. Duck & His Friends. Cartwright, Stephen, illus. 16p. (ps). 1988. 2.95 (ISBN 0-7460-0184-3); lib. bdg. 6.96 (ISBN 0-88110-326-8). EDC.
—Duck in Trouble. Cartwright, Stephen, illus. 16p. (ps). 1988. 2.95 (ISBN 0-7460-0185-1); lib. bdg. 6.96 (ISBN 0-88110-327-6). EDC.
—Duck on Holiday. Cartwright, Stephen, illus. 16p. (ps). 1988. 2.95 (ISBN 0-7460-0183-5); lib. bdg. 6.96 (ISBN 0-88110-328-4). EDC.
Weinberger, Jane. Fanny & Sarah. 2nd ed. MacDonald, Karen, illus. LC 84-51987. 40p. (gr. k-4). 1986. pap. 3.95 (ISBN 0-932433-02-2). Windswept Hse.
Wellington, Monica. All My Little Ducklings. Wellington, Monica, illus. LC 88-2284. 32p. (ps-k). 1989. 11.95 (ISBN 0-525-44459-9, DCB). Dutton Child Bks.
West, Cindy. Duck Tales Scrooge Mcduck. 1990. write for info. (ISBN 0-307-11597-6, Golden Pr). Western Pub.
Winthrop, Elizabeth. Bear & Mrs. Duck. Brewster, Patience, illus. LC 87-25129. 32p. (gr. k-3). 1990. 14.95g (ISBN 0-8234-0687-3); pap. 5.95 (ISBN 0-8234-0843-4). Holiday.
Witter, Evelyn. Rocky Duck. Davenport, May, ed. Bd. with Santa's Gift to the Littlest Penguin. Witter, Evelyn; Have You Ever Been in Love. Neal, Eva. LC 81-71557. 64p. (Orig.). (ps-3). 1984. pap. 3.50x (ISBN 0-943864-16-X). Davenport.
Ziegler, J. F. The Duck & the Fox: A Metaphysical Fairy Tale. Butler, Sandra L., ed. Gillard, Dianne & Kirkpatrick, Cindy F., illus. LC 88-32071. 75p. (ps-9). 1988. pap. 9.00 (ISBN 0-9621235-0-1). Hallelujah Pr.

DULLES, JOHN FOSTER, 1888-1959

Finke, Blythe F. John Foster Dulles: Master of Brinksmanship & Diplomacy. Ramas, D. Steve, ed. LC 77-185666. 32p. (Orig.). (gr. 7-12). 1972. lib. bdg. 4.20 incl. catalog cards (ISBN 0-87157-510-8); pap. 2.95 vinyl laminated covers (ISBN 0-87157-010-6). SamHar Pr.
Shivanandan, Mary. Nasser: Modern Leader of Egypt. Rahmas, D. Steve, ed. LC 73-87627. 32p. (Orig.). (gr. 7-12). 1973. lib. bdg. 4.20 incl. catalog cards (ISBN 0-87157-564-7); pap. 2.95 vinyl laminated covers (ISBN 0-87157-064-5). SamHar Pr.

DUMB (DEAF MUTES)

see Deaf

DUNANT, JEAN HENRI, 1828-1910

Gray, Charlotte. Henry Dunant: Founder of the Red Cross, the Relief Organization Dedicated to Helping Suffering People All over the World. Sherwood, Rhoda, ed. LC 88-4917. (Illus.). 68p. (gr. 5-6). 1989. PLB 12.95 (ISBN 1-55532-824-5). Gareth Stevens Inc.

DUNBAR, PAUL LAURENCE, 1872-1906

Gentry, Tony. Paul L. Dunbar. King, Coretta Scott, intro. by. (Illus.). 112p. (Orig.). (gr. 5 up). 1989. 17.95 (ISBN 1-55546-583-8); pap. 9.95 (ISBN 0-7910-0223-3). Chelsea Hse.
McKissack, Patricia. Paul Laurence Dunbar: A Poet to Remember. LC 84-7625. (Illus.). 112p. (gr. 4 up). 1984. lib. bdg. 17.27 (ISBN 0-516-03209-7). Childrens.

DUNES

see Sand Dunes

DUNGEONS

see Prisons

DUNHAM, KATHERINE, 1910-

Haskins, James S. Katherine Dunham. (Illus.). 176p. (gr. 4 up). 1982. 10.95 (ISBN 0-698-20549-9, Coward). Putnam Pub Group.

DURER, ALBRECHT, 1471-1528

Raboff, Ernest. Albrecht Durer. Durer, Albrecht, illus. LC 87-16863. 32p. (gr. 1 up). 1988. Repr. of 1970 ed. 11.95 (ISBN 0-397-32216-X, Lipp Jr Bks). HarpC Child Bks.
—Albrecht Durer. Durer, Albrecht, illus. LC 87-17702. 32p. (gr. 1 up). 1988. pap. 5.95 (ISBN 0-06-446071-1, Trophy). HarpC Child Bks.

DUTCH IN THE U. S.

Olsen, Victoria. The Dutch Americans. Moynihan, Daniel P., intro. by. (Illus.). 112p. (gr. 5 up). 1989. lib. bdg. 17.95 (ISBN 0-87754-873-0). Chelsea Hse.
Tenzythoff, Gerrit J. Dutch in America. LC 68-31505. (Illus.). 80p. (gr. 5 up). 1969. PLB 9.95 (ISBN 0-8225-0220-8); pap. 3.95 (ISBN 0-8225-1005-7). Lerner Pubns.

DWARFS

see also Pygmies

Kuklin, Susan. Thinking Big: The Story of a Young Dwarf. LC 85-10425. (Illus.). 48p. (ps-1). 1986. 12.95 (ISBN 0-688-05826-4); PLB 12.88 (ISBN 0-688-05827-2). Lothrop.

DWARFS–FICTION

Delmun the Dwarf. Date not set. write for info. Songbird & Seabird.
Hugo, Victor. Hunchback of Notre Dame. Canon, R. R., intro. by. (gr. 11 up). pap. 2.25 (ISBN 0-8049-0162-7, CL-162). Airmont.
Kerr, M. E. Little Little. LC 80-8454. 160p. (gr. 7 up). 1981. PLB 12.89 (ISBN 0-06-023185-8). HarpC Child Bks.

DWELLINGS

see Architecture, Domestic; Houses

Lobel, Arnold. Ming Lo Moves the Mountain. Lobel, Arnold, illus. 32p. (ps-3). 1986. pap. 2.95 (ISBN 0-590-33994-X, Blue Ribbon Bks); Bk. & Cassette Set. 6.95 (ISBN 0-590-63097-0). Scholastic Inc.

DYNAMICS

see also Force and Energy; Matter; Motion; Physics; Thermodynamics

E

E S P

see Extrasensory Perception

EAGLES

Andrews, John. How They Live: Eagles. (ps up). 1990. PLB 3.98 (ISBN 0-7924-5145-7, Mallard Pr). BDD Promo Bk.
Bright, Michael. Eagles. Kline, M., ed. (Illus.). 32p. (gr. 4-8). 1991. PLB 11.90 (ISBN 0-531-17262-7). Watts.
Harrison, Virginia & Scott, Jim. The World of Eagles. Shahild, Wendy & Rosinski, Bob, photos by. LC 89-4459. (Illus.). 32p. (gr. 2-3). 1989. PLB 10.95 (ISBN 0-8368-0138-5). Gareth Stevens Inc.
Lang, Aubrey. Eagles. (gr. 4-7). 1990. 14.95 (ISBN 0-316-51387-3). Little.
Lepthien, Emilie U. Bald Eagles. LC 88-38055. (Illus.). 45p. (gr. k-2). 1989. PLB 14.60 (ISBN 0-516-01160-X); pap. 4.95 (ISBN 0-516-41160-8). Childrens.
McConoughey, Jana. Bald Eagle. LC 83-5162. (Illus.). 48p. (gr. 5). 1983. lib. bdg. 10.95 (ISBN 0-89686-218-6, Crestwood Hse). Macmillan Child Grp.
Patent, Dorothy H. Where the Bald Eagles Gather. Munoz, William, illus. LC 83-20852. 64p. (gr. 3-6). 1984. 14.95 (ISBN 0-89919-230-0, Clarion). HM.
Rothaus, Jim. Eagles. 24p. (gr. 3). 1988. 17.10 (ISBN 0-88682-225-4); PLB 11.95s.p. (ISBN 0-318-37906-6). Creative Ed.
Ryden, Hope. America's Bald Eagle. Ryden, Hope, photos by. LC 84-18234. (Illus.). 64p. (gr. 5 up). 1985. 11.95 (ISBN 0-399-21181-0, Putnam). Putnam Pub Group.
Sattler, Helen R. The Book of Eagles. Zallinger, Jean D., illus. LC 88-38806. 64p. (gr. 3 up). 1989. 14.95 (ISBN 0-688-07021-3); PLB 14.88 (ISBN 0-688-07022-1). Lothrop.
Scott, Jim. The Eagle in the Mountains. Shattil, Wendy & Rozinsky, Bob, photos by. LC 89-4461. (Illus.). 32p. (gr. 4-6). 1989. PLB 10.95 (ISBN 0-8368-0113-X). Gareth Stevens Inc.
Selsam, Millicent E. & Hunt, Joyce. A First Look at Owls, Eagles, & Other Hunters of the Sky. Springer, Harriet, illus. 32p. (gr. 6-9). 1986. 10.95 (ISBN 0-8027-6625-0); PLB 10.85 (ISBN 0-8027-6642-0). Walker & Co.
Spizzirri Publishing Co. Staff. Eagles: An Educational Coloring Book. Spizzirri, Linda, ed. (Illus.). 32p. (gr. k-5). 1985. pap. 1.95 (ISBN 0-86545-067-6). Spizzirri.
Stone, Lynn M. Eagles. LC 88-26427. (Illus.). 24p. (gr. 2-4). 1989. PLB 11.93 (ISBN 0-86592-321-3). Rourke Corp.
Van Wormer, Joe. Eagles. Van Wormer, Joe, illus. LC 84-13684. 64p. (gr. 3-6). 1985. 14.95 (ISBN 0-525-67154-4, Lodestar Bks). Dutton Child Bks.
Wildlife Education, Ltd. Staff. Eagles. 1983 ed. Boyer, Trevor, illus. 20p. (gr. 5 up). pap. 2.25 (ISBN 0-937934-14-3). Wildlife Educ.

EAGLES–FICTION

Alvarez, Everett, Jr. & Pitch, Anthony S. Chained Eagle. LC 89-45547. (Illus.). 308p. (gr. 8-12). 1989. 18.95 (ISBN 1-55611-167-3). D I Fine.
Bliss, Ronald G. Eagle Trap. 2nd ed. LC 82-71045. (Illus.). 108p. (gr. 3-5). 1990. pap. 3.50x. Davenport.
Dayrell, Elphinstone. Why the Sun & Moon Live in the Sky. Lent, Blair, illus. 32p. (gr. k-3). 1990. pap. 4.95 (ISBN 0-395-53963-3). HM.
Gothard, Bill. The Eagle Story. LC 81-85536. (Illus.). 64p. (gr. 3-12). 1982. 8.00 (ISBN 0-916888-07-X). Inst Basic Youth.
Jordan, Tina. A Visit to the Eagles' Nest. Jordan, Debra, illus. 20p. (gr. 3-5). 1980. PLB 2.25 (ISBN 0-938574-00-0). Cherubim.
Marshall, James. Yummers Too: The Second Course. Marshall, James, illus. 32p. (gr. k-3). 1990. pap. 3.95 (ISBN 0-395-53967-6). HM.
Mayne, William. Antar & the Eagles. 1990. 13.95 (ISBN 0-385-29977-X). Doubleday.
Patent, Dorothy H. Where the Bald Eagles Gather. Munoz, William, photos by. (Illus.). 56p. (gr. 3-7). 1990. pap. 5.95 (ISBN 0-395-52598-5). HM.

EAR

see also Hearing

Mathers, Douglas. Ears. Farmer, Andrew & Green, Robina, illus. LC 90-42176. 32p. (gr. 4-6). 1991. lib. bdg. 11.89 (ISBN 0-8167-2092-4); pap. text ed. 3.95 (ISBN 0-8167-2093-2). Troll Assocs.
Parker, Steve. The Ear & Hearing. rev. ed. Mayron-Parker, Alan, contrib. by. (Illus.). 48p. (gr. 5-6). 1989. PLB 12.90 (ISBN 0-531-10712-4). Watts.
—The Ear & Hearing. rev. ed. (Illus.). 48p. (gr. 5 up). 1991. pap. 4.95 (ISBN 0-531-24601-9). Watts.

Perkins, Al. Ear Book. O'Brian, Bill, illus. LC 68-28464. (ps-1). 1968. 6.95 (ISBN 0-394-81199-2, Random Juv); lib. bdg. 7.99 (ISBN 0-394-91199-7). Random.

Silverstein, Alvin & Silverstein, Virginia B. The Story of Your Ear. 64p. (gr. 5-9). 1981. lib. bdg. 6.99 (ISBN 0-698-30704-6, Coward). Putnam Pub Group.

Wright, Rachel. Eyes, Ears & Noses. (ps-3). 1990. PLB 10.40 (ISBN 0-531-14001-6). Watts.

EARHART, AMELIA, 1898-1937

Blau, Melinda. Whatever Happened to Amelia Earhart? LC 77-22173. (Illus.). 48p. (gr. 4 up). 1983. PLB 17.32 (ISBN 0-8172-1057-1); pap. 9.27 (ISBN 0-8172-2170-0). Raintree Pubs.

Brown, Fern G. Amelia Earhart Takes Off. Tucker, Kathleen, ed. Halverson, Lydia, illus. 64p. (gr. 3-7). 1985. PLB 10.50 (ISBN 0-8075-0309-6). A Whitman.

Chadwick, Roxane. Amelia Earhart: Aviation Pioneer. (Illus.). 56p. (gr. 4 up). 1987. PLB 9.95 (ISBN 0-8225-0484-7); pap. 4.95 (ISBN 0-8225-9515-X). Lerner Pubns.

Farr, Naunerle C. & Fago, John N. Amelia Earhart - Charles Lindbergh. Vicatan, illus. (gr. 4-12). 1979. pap. text ed. 2.95 (ISBN 0-88301-349-5); wkbk. 1.25 (ISBN 0-88301-373-8). Pendulum Pr.

Kerby, Mona. Amelia Earhart: Courage in the Sky. (gr. 4-7). 1990. pap. 10.95 (ISBN 0-670-83024-0). Viking Child Bks.

Lauber, Patricia. Lost Star: The Story of Amelia Earhart. (Illus.). 96p. (gr. 4-7). 1988. pap. 10.95 (ISBN 0-590-41615-4, Pub. by Scholastic Hardcover). Scholastic Inc.

—Lost Star: The Story of Amelia Earhart. (gr. 4-7). 1990. pap. 2.75 (ISBN 0-590-41159-4). Scholastic Inc.

Leder, Jane. Amelia Earhart: Opposing Viewpoints. LC 89-12028. (Illus.). 112p. (gr. 3-10). 1989. PLB 13.95 (ISBN 0-89908-070-7). Greenhaven.

Parlin, John. Amelia Earhart: Pioneer in the Sky. (Illus.). 80p. (gr. 2-6). 1992. Repr. of 1962 ed. PLB 12.95 (ISBN 0-7910-1437-1). Chelsea Hse.

Quackenbush, Robert. Clear the Cow Pasture I'm Coming. 1990. pap. 11.95 (ISBN 0-671-68548-1, Wallaby). S&S Trade.

Randolph, Blythep. Amelia Earhart. LC 86-26651. (Illus.). 144p. (gr. 7-12). 1987. PLB 13.90x (ISBN 0-531-10331-5). Watts.

Sabin, Francene. Amelia Earhart: Adventure in the Sky. Milone, Karen, illus. LC 82-15987. 48p. (gr. 4-6). 1983. PLB 10.79 (ISBN 0-89375-839-6); pap. text ed. 2.95 (ISBN 0-89375-840-X). Troll Assocs.

Shore, Nancy. Amelia Earhart. Horner, Matina, intro. by. (Illus.). 112p. (Orig.). (gr. 5 up). 1987. 17.95 (ISBN 1-55546-651-6); pap. 9.95 (ISBN 0-7910-0415-5). Chelsea Hse.

Tames, Richard. Amelia Earhart. (Illus.). 32p. (gr. 5 up). 1991. pap. 3.95 (ISBN 0-531-24610-8). Watts.

Zierau, Lillee D. Amelia Earhart: Leading Lady of the Air Age. Rahmas, D. Steve, ed. LC 73-190237. 32p. (gr. 7-12). 1972. lib. bdg. 4.20 incl. catalog cards (ISBN 0-87157-519-1); vinyl laminated covers 2.95 (ISBN 0-87157-019-X). SamHar Pr.

EARTH

see also Antarctic Regions; Arctic Regions; Atmosphere; Creation; Earthquakes; Geodesy; Geography; Geology; Glacial Epoch; Meteorology; Ocean; Oceanography; Physical Geography; Universe

Asimov, Isaac. Earth: Our Home Base. LC 87-42607. (Illus.). 32p. (gr. 3-4). 1988. PLB 11.95 (ISBN 1-55532-362-6). Gareth Stevens Inc.

—How Did We Find Out the Earth Is Round? Selsam, Millicent E., ed. Kalmenoff, Matthew, illus. LC 72-81378. 64p. (gr. 5-8). 1972. PLB 10.85 (ISBN 0-8027-6122-4). Walker & Co.

Baker, D. Earth Observation, Reading Level 3. (Illus.). 32p. (gr. 2-6). Date not set. PLB 13.20 (ISBN 0-86592-974-2). Rourke Corp.

Barnes-Svarney, Patricia L. Clocks in the Rocks: Learning about Earth's Past. LC 89-7698. (Illus.). 64p. (gr. 7-12). 1990. lib. bdg. 15.95 (ISBN 0-89490-275-X). Enslow Pubs.

Behm, Barbara J., ed. Ask about the Earth & the Sky. (Illus.). 64p. (gr. 4-5). 1987. PLB 18.25 (ISBN 0-8172-2876-4); pap. 13.27 (ISBN 0-8172-2888-8). Raintree Pubs.

Bennett, David. Earth. Kightley, Rosalinda, illus. 32p. (ps-12). 1988. pap. 3.95 (ISBN 0-553-05481-3). Bantam.

Berger, Melvin. The New Earth Book: Our Changing Planet. DeGrazio, George, illus. LC 79-7828. 128p. (gr. 5 up). 1980. (Crowell Jr Bks). HarpC Child Bks.

Brandt, Keith. Earth. Jones, John, illus. LC 84-8444. 32p. (gr. 3-6). 1985. PLB 9.49 (ISBN 0-8167-0250-0); pap. text ed. 2.95 (ISBN 0-8167-0251-9). Troll Assocs.

Branley, Franklyn M. The Beginning of the Earth. rev. ed. Maestro, Giulio, illus. LC 87-47765. 32p. (ps-3). 1988. 12.95 (ISBN 0-690-04653-6, Crowell Jr Bks); PLB 13.89 (ISBN 0-690-04654-5, Crowell Jr Bks). HarpC Child Bks.

—The Beginning of the Earth. rev. ed. Maestro, Giulio, illus. LC 87-45677. 32p. (ps-3). 1988. pap. 4.50 (ISBN 0-06-445074-0, Trophy). HarpC Child Bks.

—Mysteries of Planet Earth. Bensusen, Sally J., illus. LC 88-31076. 80p. (gr. 5-9). 1989. 12.95 (ISBN 0-525-67278-8, Lodestar Bks). Dutton Child Bks.

—What Makes Day & Night. rev. ed. Dorros, Arthur, illus. LC 85-40657. 32p. (gr. k-3). 1986. pap. 4.50 (ISBN 0-06-445050-3, Trophy). HarpC Child Bks.

—What Makes Day & Night. rev. ed. Dorros, Arthur, illus. LC 85-47903. 32p. (ps-3). 1986. PLB 13.89 (ISBN 0-690-04524-7, Crowell Jr Bks). HarpC Child Bks.

British Museum, Geological Department Staff. The Age of the Earth. (Illus.). 36p. (gr. 7 up). 1986. pap. 4.50 (ISBN 0-521-32412-2). Cambridge U Pr.

Carratello, John & Carratello, Patty. Hands on Science: Our Changing Earth. Wright, Terry, illus. 32p. (gr. 2-5). 1988. wkbk. 4.95 (ISBN 1-55734-226-1). Tchr Create Mat.

Chisholm. Our Earth: Let's Find Out about. (gr. 2-5). 1982. (Usborne-Hayes); lib. bdg. 11.96 (ISBN 0-88110-016-1); pap. 3.95 (ISBN 0-86020-582-7). EDC.

Cleeve, Roger. The Earth. Steltenpohl, Jane, ed. (Illus.). 32p. (gr. 3-5). 1990. PLB 10.98 (ISBN 0-671-68626-7); pap. 4.95 (ISBN 0-671-68629-1). Messner.

Conway, Lorraine. Earth Science: Tables & Tabulations. Akins, Linda, illus. 64p. (gr. 5 up). 1984. wkbk. 6.95 (ISBN 0-86653-154-8, GA 553). Good Apple.

Cooper, Clare. Earthchange. LC 85-24028. 96p. (gr. 4-8). 1985. 10.95 (ISBN 0-8225-0730-7). Lerner Pubns.

Darling, David. Could You Ever Dig a Hole to China? (Illus.). (gr. 4 up). 1990. RSBE 14.95 (ISBN 0-87518-449-9, Dillon). Macmillan Child Grp.

Dixon, Dougal. The Planet Earth. (Illus.). 40p. (gr. 7-9). 1990. 12.40 (ISBN 0-531-17142-6). Watts.

The Earth. 32p. (Orig.). (gr. 1-3). 1988. pap. 2.95 (ISBN 0-8431-4299-5). Price Stern.

The Earth. (Illus.). 80p. (gr. k-6). 1986. pap. 13.27 (ISBN 0-8172-2585-4). Raintree Pubs.

The Earth. (Illus.). 112p. (gr. 4-9). Date not set. 19.95x (ISBN 1-85435-070-6). Marshall Cavendish.

Earth & Beyond. 96p. (gr. 3-8). 1987. PLB 240.00 (ISBN 0-685-18921-X); pap. 13.25 (ISBN 0-8172-3055-6). Raintree Pubs.

Fisher, David E. The Origin & Evolution of Our Own Particular Universe. LC 88-14108. (Illus.). 192p. (gr. 7 up). 1988. 14.95 (ISBN 0-689-31368-3, Atheneum Child Bk). Macmillan Child Grp.

Fradin, Dennis B. Earth. LC 89-9982. 48p. (gr. k-4). 1989. PLB 13.27 (ISBN 0-516-01172-3); pap. 4.95 (ISBN 0-516-41172-1). Childrens.

Gang, Philip S. Our Planet, Our Home: A Gaia Learning Material. 60p. (gr. 1-9). 1989. Incl. card material. tchr's. ed. 30.00 (ISBN 0-685-27868-9); wkbk. 5.00 (ISBN 0-685-27869-7). Dagaz Pr.

George, Jean C. The Talking Earth. LC 82-48850. 160p. (gr. 6 up). 1983. 12.95i (ISBN 0-06-021975-0); PLB 12.89 (ISBN 0-06-021976-9). HarpC Child Bks.

Guggenheim, Hans. World of Wonderful Difference. (gr. 5-8). 5.00x (ISBN 0-87068-371-3, Pub. by Friendly Hse). Ktav.

Heller, Robert, et al. Earth Science. 2nd ed. (Illus.). 1978. text ed. 32.24 (ISBN 0-07-028037-1). McGraw.

Heslewood, Juliet. Earth, Air, Fire & Water. Lydbury, Jane, et al, illus. 182p. (gr. 4-8). 1989. jacketed 15.95 (ISBN 0-19-278107-3). Oxford U Pr.

Hubley, Faith & Towe, Kenneth M. Enter Life. Hubley, Faith, illus. LC 82-71680. 32p. (gr. 4 up). pap. 9.95 (ISBN 0-440-02357-2, E Friede). Delacorte.

Kalman, Bobbie. Our Earth. (Illus.). 32p. (gr. 2-3). 1987. 14.95 (ISBN 0-86505-078-3); pap. 5.95 (ISBN 0-86505-100-3). Crabtree Pub Co.

Lauber, Patricia. How We Learned the Earth Is Round. Lloyd, Megan, illus. LC 89-49650. 32p. (gr. k-4). 1990. 12.95 (ISBN 0-690-04860-2, Crowell Jr Bks); PLB 12.89 (ISBN 0-690-04862-9, Crowell Jr Bks). HarpC Child Bks.

Lucas, Hazel & Lucas, Ernest. Our World. (Illus.). 48p. (gr. 4 up). 1986. 13.95 (ISBN 0-85648-948-4). Lion USA.

Lye, Keith. The Earth. (Illus.). 64p. (gr. 4-6). 1991. PLB 13.90 (ISBN 1-56294-025-2). Millbrook Pr.

—Our Planet the Earth. LC 79-2346. (Illus.). (gr. 3-6). 1980. PLB 8.95 (ISBN 0-8225-1182-7, First Ave Edns); pap. 4.95 (ISBN 0-8225-9510-9, First Ave Edns). Lerner Pubns.

Mccaughrean, Geraldine. My First Earth Pop-up Book. 1990. 7.95 (ISBN 0-671-67574-5). S&S Trade.

Our World Series, 13 Bks. (Illus.). 480p. (gr. 5-8). 1989. Set. PLB 194.74 (ISBN 0-382-09599-5). Silver Burdett Pr.

Parramon, J. M., et al. Earth. 32p. (ps). 1985. pap. 3.95 (ISBN 0-8120-3596-8). Barron.

—La Tierra. (SPA.). 32p. (ps). 1985. pap. 4.95 (ISBN 0-8120-3618-2). Barron.

Pettigrew, Mark. Planet Earth. (Illus.). 32p. (gr. k-6). 1987. lib. bdg. 8.99 (ISBN 0-531-17043-8, Gloucester Pr). Watts.

Planet Earth. (Illus.). 32p. (Orig.). (gr. 3-6). 1989. pap. 2.95 (ISBN 0-8431-2372-9). Price Stern.

Pomeroy, Johanna P. Content Area Reading Skills Our Earth: Locating Details. (Illus.). (gr. 3). 1989. pap. text ed. 3.25 (ISBN 1-55737-688-3). Ed Activities.

Ruthland, Jonathan. The Violent Earth. Phillipps, Francis & Snook, Charlotte, illus. LC 86-26295. 24p. (gr. 2-5). 1987. lib. bdg. 5.99 (ISBN 0-394-98970-8, Random Juv); pap. 2.95 (ISBN 0-394-88970-3). Random.

Schwartz, Linda. My Earth Book: Puzzles, Projects, Facts & Fun. Armstrong, Beverly, illus. 64p. (gr. 1-4). 1991. pap. 7.95 (ISBN 0-88160-201-9). Learning Wks.

Silver, Donald M. Earth: The Ever-Changing Planet. Wynne, Patricia J., illus. LC 88-11331. 96p. (Orig.). (gr. 5 up). 1989. lib. bdg. 12.99 (ISBN 0-394-99195-8). Random.

Simon, Seymour. Earth: Our Planet in Space. LC 84-28754. (Illus.). 32p. (gr. k-3). 1984. 13.95 (ISBN 0-02-782830-1, Four Winds). Macmillan Child Grp.

Sneider, Cary I. Earth, Moon, & Stars. Bergman, Lincoln & Fairwell, Kay, eds. Baker, Lisa H. & Bevilacqua, Carol, illus. Sneider, Cary I., photos by. 50p. (Orig.). (gr. 5-9). 1986. pap. 9.00 (ISBN 0-912511-18-4). Lawrence Science.

Vancleave, Janice P. Janice Van Cleave's Earth Science for Every Kid: One Hundred & One Experiments That Really Work. 1991. pap. text ed. 10.95 (ISBN 0-471-53010-7). Wiley.

Watson, Nancy, et al. Our Violent Earth. LC 80-8797. (Illus.). 104p. (gr. 3-8). 1982. 6.95 (ISBN 0-87044-383-6); lib. bdg. 8.50 (ISBN 0-87044-388-7). Natl Geog.

Watts & Tyler. The Earth. (gr. 3-6). 1976. pap. 6.95 (ISBN 0-86020-062-0, Usborne-Hayes). EDC.

Williams, Lawrence. The Changing Earth, 6 bks. Burrows, Ray, illus. (Orig.). (gr. 2-4). 1986. pap. text ed. 23.30 incl. tchr's. notes (ISBN 1-55624-009-0). Wright Group.

EARTH–DICTIONARIES

Jugendhandbuch Naturwissen: Erde und Weltall, Vol. 4. (GER.). 128p. 1976. pap. 5.95 (ISBN 3-499-16206-7, M-7489, Pub. by Rowohlt). French & Eur.

Jugendhandbuch Naturwissen: Saeugetiere, Vol. 3. (GER.). 144p. 1976. pap. 5.95 (ISBN 0-686-56619-X, M-7488, Pub. by Rowohlt). French & Eur.

EARTH, EFFECT OF MAN ON

see Man–Influence on Nature

EARTHQUAKES

see also Volcanoes

Archer, Jules. Earthquake! LC 90-45370. (Illus.). 48p. (gr. 5-6). 1991. RSBE 10.95 (ISBN 0-89686-593-2, Crestwood Hse). Macmillan Child Grp.

Asimov, Isaac. How Did We Find Out about Earthquakes? Wool, David, illus. LC 77-78984. (gr. 6 up). 1978. PLB 12.85 (ISBN 0-8027-6306-5). Walker & Co.

Branley, Franklyn M. Earthquakes. Rosenblum, Richard, illus. LC 89-35424. 32p. (gr. k-4). 1990. 13.95 (ISBN 0-690-04661-8, Crowell Jr Bks); PLB 13.89 (ISBN 0-690-04663-4, Crowell Jr Bks). HarpC Child Bks.

British Museum, Geological Department Staff. Earthquakes. (Illus.). 36p. (Orig.). (gr. 7 up). 1986. pap. 4.50 (ISBN 0-521-32411-4). Cambridge U Pr.

Challand, Helen. Earthquakes. LC 82-9699. (Illus.). (gr. k-4). 1982. PLB 14.60 (ISBN 0-516-01636-9); pap. 4.95 (ISBN 0-516-41636-7). Childrens.

Damon, Laura. Discovering Earthquakes & Volcanoes. Jones, John R., illus. LC 89-4974. 32p. (gr. 2-4). 1990. PLB 10.89 (ISBN 0-8167-1757-5); pap. text ed. 2.95 (ISBN 0-8167-1758-3). Troll Assocs.

Deery, Ruth. Earthquakes & Volcanoes. Miller-Ray, Sue E., illus. 48p. (gr. 4-8). 1985. wkbk. 6.95 (ISBN 0-86653-272-2, GA 630). Good Apple.

Elting, Mary. Volcanoes & Earthquakes. Courtney, illus. 48p. (gr. 3-7). 1990. PLB 9.95 (ISBN 0-671-67217-7). S&S Trade.

Engholm, Christopher. The Armenian Earthquake. LC 89-33555. (Illus.). 64p. (gr. 5-8). 1989. PLB 11.95 (ISBN 1-56006-004-2). Lucent Bks.

Fradin, Dennis. Disaster! Earthquakes. LC 81-12263. (Illus.). 64p. (gr. 3 up). 1982. PLB 17.27 (ISBN 0-516-00853-6). Childrens.

Golden, Frederic. The Trembling Earth: Probing & Predicting Quakes. LC 83-3262. (Illus.). 176p. (gr. 7 up). 1983. 13.95 (ISBN 0-684-17884-2, Scribners Young Read). Macmillan Child Grp.

Knapp, Brian. Earthquake. LC 89-21574. (Illus.). 48p. (gr. 5-9). 1990. PLB 17.28 (ISBN 0-8114-2375-1). Steck-V.

Lampton, Christopher. Earthquake. (Illus.). 64p. (gr. 4-6). 1991. PLB 17.25 (ISBN 1-56294-031-7). Millbrook Pr.

Lauber, Patricia. Volcanoes & Earthquakes. 80p. (gr. 4-7). 1991. pap. 2.75 (ISBN 0-590-42592-7). Scholastic Inc.

Merrians, Deborah. I Can Read About Earthquakes & Volcanoes. LC 74-24966. (Illus.). (gr. 2-4). 1975. pap. 1.95 (ISBN 0-89375-067-0). Troll Assocs.

Michel, Francois & Larvor, Yves. The Restless Earth: The Secrets of Earthquakes, Volcanoes, & Continental Drift in Three-Dimensional Moving Pictures. (Illus.). (gr. 5 up). 1990. 15.95 (ISBN 0-670-83361-4). Viking Child Bks.

Poynter, Margaret. Earthquakes: Looking for Answers. 64p. (gr. 6 up). 1990. 15.95 (ISBN 0-89490-274-1). Enslow Pubs.

Radlauer, Ed & Radlauer, Ruth. Earthquakes. LC 87-13772. (Illus.). 48p. (gr. 4 up). 1987. PLB 15.93 (ISBN 0-516-07841-0); pap. 4.95 (ISBN 0-516-47841-9). Childrens.

Santrey, Laurence. Earthquakes & Volcanoes. Jones, John, illus. LC 84-2676. 32p. (gr. 3-6). 1985. PLB 9.49 (ISBN 0-8167-0212-8); pap. text ed. 2.95 (ISBN 0-8167-0213-6). Troll Assocs.

Simon, Seymour. Danger from Below: Earthquakes: Past, Present, & Future. Simon, Seymour, illus. LC 78-22283. 96p. (gr. 3-7). 1984. 12.95 (ISBN 0-02-782800-X, Four Winds). Macmillan Child Grp.

Vogt, Gregory. Predicting Earthquakes. (Illus.). 144p. (gr. 7-12). 1989. PLB 12.90 (ISBN 0-531-10788-4). Watts.

EARTHQUAKES–FICTION

Brandon, Fran. The Day the Woods Went Crazy. LC 89-51294. 44p. (gr. 4-7). 1990. 5.95 (ISBN 1-55523-256-6). Winston-Derek.

Yolen, Jane. The Boy Who Spoke Chimp. Wiesner, illus. LC 79-27259. 128p. (gr. 3-6). 1981. Knopf.

EARTHWORMS

Henwood, Chris. Earthworms. FS-Ltd Staff, ed. Watts, Barrie, photos by. (Illus.). 32p. (gr. 1-3). 1988. PLB 10.40 (ISBN 0-531-10620-9). Watts.

Jennings, Terry. Earthworms. 1990. PLB 10.40 (ISBN 0-531-17097-7); pap. 2.95 (ISBN 0-531-17501-4). Watts.

EAST (FAR EAST)

Fairfield, Sheila. People & Nations of the Far East & the Pacific. Sherwood, Rhoda, ed. LC 88-42918. (Illus.). 64p. (gr. 5-6). 1988. PLB 13.95 (ISBN 1-55532-907-1). Gareth Stevens Inc.

Lum, Peter. Growth of Civilization in East Asia. LC 73-77311. (Illus.). (gr. 8 up). 1969. 25.95 (ISBN 0-87599-144-0). S G Phillips.

EAST AFRICA

see Africa, East

EAST INDIANS IN THE U. S.

Bagai, Leona B. The East Indians & Pakistanis in America. rev. ed. LC 67-15680. (Illus.). 64p. (gr. 5 up). 1972. PLB 9.95 (ISBN 0-8225-0210-0). Lerner Pubns.

Gordon, Susan. Asian Indians. Daniels, Roger, contrib. by. (Illus.). 64p. (gr. 5-8). 1990. PLB 12.40 (ISBN 0-531-10976-3). Watts.

EASTER

Barth, Edna. Lilies, Rabbits, & Painted Eggs: The Story of the Easter Symbols. Arndt, Ursula, illus. LC 74-79033. (gr. 3-6). 1979. 13.95 (ISBN 0-395-28844-4, Clarion); pap. 4.95 (ISBN 0-395-30550-0, Clarion). HM.

Berger, Gilda. Easter & Other Spring Holidays. (Illus.). 72p. (gr. 4 up). 1983. PLB 10.40 (ISBN 0-531-04547-1). Watts.

Bonica, Diane. Biblical Easter & Spring Performances. (Illus.). 96p. (ps-2). 1989. 9.95 (ISBN 0-86653-478-4, SS1869). Good Apple.

Burgess, Beverly C. Is Easter Just for Bunnies? Titolo, Nancy, illus. 30p. (Orig.). (gr. 1-3). 1985. pap. 1.98 (ISBN 0-89274-310-7). Harrison Hse.

Carson, Patti & Dellosa, Janet. Easter Preschool-K Practice. Carson, Patti & Dellosa, Janet, illus. 32p. (ps-k). 1984. pap. 1.98 (ISBN 0-88724-017-8, CD-8032). Carson-Dellos.

—Easter Primary Reading & Art Activities. Carson, Patti & Dellosa, Janet, illus. 32p. (gr. 1-3). 1984. pap. 1.98 (ISBN 0-88724-027-5, CD-8042). Carson-Dellos.

Corwin, Judith H. Easter Fun. (Illus.). (ps up). 1986. pap. 4.95 (ISBN 0-671-60577-1, Little Simon). S&S Trade.

—Easter Fun. Corwin, Judith H., illus. 64p. (gr. 3 up). 1984. PLB 10.29 (ISBN 0-671-50798-2); PLB 7.71s.p.; pap. 5.95 (ISBN 0-671-53108-5); pap. 4.46s.p. Messner.

Daniel, Rebecca & Hierstein, Judy. Easter Week. 16p. (ps-3). 1991. 16.95 (ISBN 0-86653-575-6). Good Apple.

Davis, Nancy M., et al. April & Easter. Davis, Nancy M., illus. 45p. (Orig.). (ps-2). 1986. pap. 5.95 (ISBN 0-937103-10-1). DaNa Pubns.

Dellinger, Annetta E. My First Easter Book. Hohag, Linda, illus. LC 84-21512. 32p. (ps-2). 1985. lib. bdg. 14.60 (ISBN 0-516-02904-5); pap. 3.95 (ISBN 0-516-42904-3). Childrens.

Dellosa, Janet & Carson, Patti. Easter Fun Book. Carson, Patti & Dellosa, Janet, illus. 32p. (ps-1). 1982. pap. 1.59 (ISBN 0-88724-050-X, CD-8004). Carson-Dellos.

Dietz, Sarah S. Easter Activity Book. Rittenour, Gary, illus. 32p. (gr. 3 up). 1984. pap. 1.98 (ISBN 0-88724-067-4, CD-8051). Carson-Dellos.

The Easter Story. 1989. text ed. 3.95 cased (ISBN 0-7214-5287-6). Ladybird Bks.

Fox. Easter, Reading Level 4. (Illus.). 48p. (gr. 3-8). Date not set. PLB 14.60 (ISBN 0-86592-985-8). Rourke Corp.

Gibbons, Gail. Easter. Gibbons, Gail, illus. LC 88-23292. 32p. (ps-3). 1989. reinforced bdg. 14.95 (ISBN 0-8234-0737-3). Holiday.

—Easter. (Illus.). 34p. (gr. k-3). 1989. PLB 14.95; pap. 5.95 (ISBN 0-8234-0866-3). Holiday.

Greene, Carol. Kiri & the First Easter. (Illus.). 32p. (ps-4). 1972. pap. 1.39 (ISBN 0-570-06064-8, 59-1182). Concordia.

Hartwig, Judy. Easter Bulletin Boards. (Illus.). 96p. (ps-8). 1989. 9.95 (ISBN 0-86653-480-6, SS1829). Good Apple.

Hayes, Dan, illus. The Easter Activity Book. 24p. (Orig.). (ps-3). 1991. pap. 4.95 (ISBN 0-8249-8499-4). Ideals.

Heyer, Carol. The Easter Story. Heyer, Carol, illus. 32p. (ps-1). 1990. 10.95 (ISBN 0-8249-8439-0). Ideals.

Huffaker, Alice. Resurrection Day. (ps-3). 1990. pap. 3.95 (ISBN 0-8024-2638-7). Moody.

Kalman, Bobbie. We Celebrate Easter. (Illus.). 56p. (gr. 3-4). 1985. 15.95 (ISBN 0-86505-042-2); pap. 7.95 (ISBN 0-86505-052-X). Crabtree Pub Co.

Kennedy, Pamela. An Easter Celebration: Traditions & Customs from Around the World. Bachleda, F. Lynn, illus. 32p. (gr. 1-5). 1991. 10.95 (ISBN 0-8249-8506-0). Ideals.

Lewis, Lorna. Jesus Is Risen! Baker, Arthur, illus. 32p. (gr. k-3). 1990. saddle-stitched 1.25 (ISBN 0-8028-5054-5). Eerdmans.

McKissack, Patricia & McKissack, Frederick. Oh, Happy, Happy Day! A Child's Easter in Story, Song, & Prayer. Swisher, Elizabeth, illus. LC 88-83017. 32p. 1989. pap. 4.95 (ISBN 0-8066-2394-2, 10-4733, Augsburg). Augsburg Fortress.

Moncure, Jane B. Our Easter Book. Rev. ed. Endres, Helen, illus. LC 86-29876. 32p. (ps-3). 1987. PLB 11.97 (ISBN 0-89565-345-1). Childs World.

My Easter Basket of Little Books, 4 bks. 24p. 1991. Set. 8.95 (ISBN 0-8249-7418-2). Ideals.

Nerlove, Miriam. Easter. Mathews, Judith, ed. Nerlove, Miriam, illus. 24p. (ps-1). 1989. 10.95 (ISBN 0-8075-1871-9). A Whitman.

Rathert, Donna R. Lent Is for Remembering. LC 56-1613. 24p. (Orig.). (ps-1). 1987. pap. 2.95 (ISBN 0-570-04147-3, 56-1613). Concordia.

Riley, Kelly. Celebrate Easter. Filkins, Vanessa, illus. 144p. (gr. k-6). 1987. pap. 10.95 (ISBN 0-86653-385-0, SS 842). Good Apple.

Sandak, Cass. Easter. LC 89-28626. (Illus.). 48p. (gr. 5 up). 1990. 10.95 (ISBN 0-89686-499-5, Crestwood Hse). Macmillan Child Grp.

Stock, Catherine. Easter Surprise. Stock, Catherine, illus. LC 90-1915. 32p. (ps-1). 1991. SBE 11.95 (ISBN 0-02-788371-X, Bradbury Pr). Macmillan Child Grp.

Story of Easter. 1990. 5.98 (ISBN 0-8317-8026-6). Smithmark.

Tangvald, Christine H. Easter Is for Me. LC 88-70663. 24p. (ps). 1989. 2.95 (ISBN 1-55513-741-5). Cook.

Winfrey, Buford A., illus. An Easter Parade of Verse. 24p. (Orig.). (ps-3). 1991. pap. 4.95 (ISBN 0-8249-8504-4). Ideals.

Winthrop, Elizabeth, adapted by. He Is Risen: The Easter Story. Mikolaycak, Charles, illus. LC 84-15869. 32p. (gr. 2-6). 1985. reinforced bdg. 14.95 (ISBN 0-8234-0547-8). Holiday.

Wolf, Jill. Story of Easter. (ps up). 1990. pap. 2.25 (ISBN 0-89954-392-8). Antioch Pub Co.

EASTER–FICTION

Adams, Adrienne. The Easter Egg Artists. Adams, Adrienne, illus. LC 75-39301. 32p. (ps-3). 1976. 13.95 (ISBN 0-684-14652-5, Scribners Young Read). Macmillan Child Grp.

—The Easter Egg Artists. (Illus.). 32p. (gr. k-3). 1981. pap. 2.95 (ISBN 0-689-70479-8, Aladdin). Macmillan.

Black, Sheila. The Story of the Easter Bunny. Officer, Robyn, illus. LC 87-81934. 32p. (ps-1). 1988. write for info. (ISBN 0-307-10415-X, Pub. by Golden Bks). Western Pub.

Chalmers, Mary. Easter Parade. Chalmers, Mary, illus. LC 87-45277. 32p. (ps-1). 1988. 11.95 (ISBN 0-06-021232-2); PLB 11.89 (ISBN 0-06-021233-0). HarpC Child Bks.

Curran, Eileen. Easter Parade. Goodman, Joan E., illus. LC 84-8630. 32p. (gr. k-2). 1985. PLB 10.89 (ISBN 0-8167-0353-1); pap. text ed. 2.95 (ISBN 0-8167-0433-3). Troll Assocs.

Davidson, Alice J. Alice in Bibleland Storybooks: Story of Easter. Marshall, Victoria, illus. 32p. (gr. 3 up). 1988. 4.95 (ISBN 0-8378-1839-7). Gibson.

DeJong, Meindert. The Easter Cat. Hoban, Lillian, illus. LC 90-24407. 128p. (gr. 3-7). 1991. pap. 3.95 (ISBN 0-689-71468-8, Aladdin). Macmillan Child Grp.

DePaola, Tomie. My First Easter. (Illus.). 12p. 1991. 5.95 (ISBN 0-399-21783-5, Putnam). Putnam Pub Group.

Devlin, Wende & Devlin, Harry. Cranberry Easter. Devlin, Harry, illus. LC 88-21370. 40p. (gr. k-3). 1990. PLB 13.95 (ISBN 0-02-729935-X, Four Wind). Macmillan Child Grp.

The Easter Bunny's Helper. 1989. text ed. 3.95 cased (ISBN 0-7214-5233-7). Ladybird Bks.

Easter Is Here. (ps-2). 1988. bds. 3.95 (ISBN 1-55513-980-9, Chariot Bks). Cook.

Gackenbach, Dick. Hattie, Tom, & the Chicken Witch. Gackenbach, Dick, illus. LC 79-2742. 64p. (gr. k-3). 1980. PLB 11.89 (ISBN 0-06-021959-9). HarpC Child Bks.

Gilleo, Alma. The Easter Basket Mystery. Bargielski, Pat, illus. (gr. 1-3). 6 bks. & 1 cass. 29.95 (ISBN 0-89290-011-3); 1 bk. & 1 cass. 10.95 (ISBN 0-685-04639-7). Soc for Visual.

Gipson, Morrell & Mann, Marek. Easter with Friends. Stefoff, Rebecca, ed. LC 90-13794. (Illus.). 24p. (gr. k-3). 1990. PLB 13.26 (ISBN 0-944483-88-7). Garrett Ed Corp.

Grambling, Lois G. Elephant & Mouse Get Ready for Easter. Maze, Debrah, illus. 32p. (ps-3). 1991. 12.95 (ISBN 0-8120-6200-0). Barron.

Hallinan, Patrick. The Small Town Children's Easter. Hallinan, Patrick, illus. 24p. (ps-3). 1989. pap. 2.95 (ISBN 0-8249-8319-X). Ideals.

Heyward, Du Bose. The Country Bunny & the Little Gold Shoes. Flack, Marjorie, illus. 48p. (gr. k-3). 1974. reinforced bdg. 13.95 (ISBN 0-395-15990-3); pap. 4.95 (ISBN 0-395-18557-2, Sandpiper). HM.

Hoban, Lillian. Silly Tilly & the Easter Bunny. Hoban, Lillian, illus. LC 86-7682. 32p. (ps-3). 1987. 10.95 (ISBN 0-06-022392-8); PLB 10.89 (ISBN 0-06-022393-6). HarpC Child Bks.

—Silly Tilly & the Easter Bunny. Hoban, Lillian, illus. LC 86-7682. 32p. (ps-2). 1989. pap. 2.95 (ISBN 0-06-444127-X, Trophy). HarpC Child Bks.

Hoban, Tana. Where Is It? LC 73-8573. (Illus.). 32p. (ps-1). 1974. 12.95 (ISBN 0-02-744070-2, Mcmillan Child Bk). Macmillan Child Grp.

Honey Bunny's Easter Surprise. (Orig.). (ps-1). 1988. pap. 2.95 (ISBN 0-671-64824-1, Little Simon). S&S Trade.

Houselander, Caryll. Petook: An Easter Story. DePaola, Tomie, illus. LC 87-21228. 32p. (gr. k-3). 1988. reinforced bdg. 14.95 (ISBN 0-8234-0681-4). Holiday.

James, Barbara. Easter Basket Book - Easter Egg Hunt. 10p. (ps-3). 1991. pap. 2.95 (ISBN 0-8167-2226-9). Troll Assocs.

—Easter Basket Book - Easter Surprises. 10p. (ps-3). 1991. pap. 2.95 (ISBN 0-8167-2079-7). Troll Assocs.

—Easter Basket Book - Teddy's Easter Basket. 10p. (ps-3). 1991. pap. 2.95 (ISBN 0-8167-2072-X). Troll Assocs.

Jordan, Myra J. & Grant, Roy E. Floppy Rabbit: An Easter Musical. (Illus.). 30p. (Orig.). (ps-1). 1980. pap. 5.00 (ISBN 0-914562-09-6). Merriam-Eddy.

Kraus, Robert. How Spider Saved Easter. (Illus.). 32p. (ps-2). 1988. pap. 2.50 (ISBN 0-590-41092-X). Scholastic Inc.

Kroll, Steven. Big Bunny & the Easter Egg. Stevens, Janet, illus. 32p. (gr. k-3). 1988. pap. 2.95 (ISBN 0-590-41660-X). Scholastic Inc.

—The Big Bunny & the Easter Eggs. LC 81-11613. (Illus.). 32p. (ps-3). 1982. reinforced bdg. 14.95 (ISBN 0-8234-0436-6). Holiday.

Kunhardt, Edith I. Danny & the Easter Egg. LC 88-1164. (Illus.). 24p. (ps up). 1989. 11.95 (ISBN 0-688-08035-9); PLB 11.88 (ISBN 0-688-08036-7). Greenwillow.

The Legend of the Easter Basket. (ps-3). pap. 1.25 (ISBN 0-8198-0199-2). Dghtrs St Paul.

Lewis, Shari. One-Minute Easter Stories. 1990. 8.95 (ISBN 0-385-24960-8). Doubleday.

Lindgren, Astrid. Lotta's Easter Surprise. Wikland, Ilon, illus. Lucas, Barbara, tr. (Illus.). 32p. (ps up). 1991. bds. 13.95 (ISBN 91-29-59862-1, Pub. by R&S Bks). FS&G.

Mayer, Mercer. Happy Easter, Little Critter. Mayer, Mercer, illus. LC 87-81759. 24p. (ps-3). 1988. pap. write for info. (ISBN 0-307-11723-5, Pub. by Golden Bks). Western Pub.

Milhous, Katherine. The Egg Tree. Milhous, Katherine, illus. LC 50-6817. 32p. (gr. 1-4). 1971. 12.95 (ISBN 0-684-12716-4, Scribners Young Read). Macmillan Child Grp.

Miller, Edna. Mousekin's Easter Basket. Miller, Edna, illus. LC 86-22511. (ps-3). 1989. 12.95 (ISBN 0-671-66803-X); pap. 5.95 (ISBN 0-671-67439-0). S&S Trade.

Molan, Chris, illus. The First Easter: Retold by Catherine Storr. 32p. (gr. k-4). 1984. 14.65 (ISBN 0-8172-1987-0, Raintree Childrens Books Belitha Press Ltd. - London). Raintree Pubs.

Myra, Harold. Easter Bunny, Are You for Real? LC 78-21268. (Illus.). (gr. 5-8). 1979. 8.95 (ISBN 0-8407-5148-6). Nelson.

Peeper & the Giant Easter Egg. (Orig.). (ps-1). 1988. pap. 2.95 (ISBN 0-671-64823-3, Little Simon). S&S Trade.

Sabin, Fran & Sabin, Lou. The Great Easter Egg Mystery. Trivas, Irene, illus. LC 81-7610. 48p. (gr. 2-4). 1981. PLB 10.89 (ISBN 0-89375-604-0); pap. text ed. 2.95 (ISBN 0-89375-605-9). Troll Assocs.

San Souci, Daniel, illus. The Easter Treasures. Arico, Diane, compiled by. (ps-4). 1989. 8.95 (ISBN 0-385-24401-0). Doubleday.

Schulz, Charles M. It's the Easter Beagle, Charlie Brown. Schulz, Charles M., illus. LC 75-35553. 48p. (gr. 1 up). 1976. (Random Juv). Random.

Stevenson, James. The Great Big Especially Beautiful Easter Egg. LC 82-11731. (ps-3). 1990. 4.95 (ISBN 0-688-09355-8, Mulberry). Morrow.

Swanson, Harry. Easter Is Not for Bears. Swanson, Harry, illus. 56p. (Orig.). (ps-6). 1989. pap. 5.00 (ISBN 1-878200-04-6). SwanMark Bks.

Tarlow, Nora. An Easter Alphabet. (Illus.). 32p. 1991. 15.95 (ISBN 0-399-22194-8, Putnam). Putnam Pub Group.

Tudor, Tasha. Tale for Easter. Tudor, Tasha, illus. LC 62-8626. (gr. k-3). 1985. 6.95 (ISBN 0-8098-1008-5); pap. 4.95 (ISBN 0-8098-1807-8). McKay.

Wiese, Kurt. Happy Easter. (Illus.). 32p. (ps-1). 1989. pap. 3.95 (ISBN 0-14-050977-1, Puffin). Puffin Bks.

Wilhelm, Hans. More Bunny Trouble. Wilhelm, Hans, illus. 1989. 11.95 (ISBN 0-590-41589-1, Scholastic Hardcover). Scholastic Inc.

Wolf, Winfried. The Easter Bunny. Mathieu, Agnes, illus. LC 85-10115. 32p. (ps-3). 1987. 8.95 (ISBN 0-8037-0239-6). Dial Bks Young.

Wolf, Winifried. The Easter Bunny. Mathieu, Agnes, illus. LC 85-10115. 24p. (ps-3). 1991. pap. 3.95 (ISBN 0-8037-0912-9, Dial Pied Piper). Puffin Bks.

EASTER ISLAND–ANTIQUITIES

Meyer, Miriam W. The Blind Guards of Easter Island. LC 77-14528. (Illus.). 48p. (gr. 4 up). 1983. PLB 17.32 (ISBN 0-8172-1048-2); pap. 9.27 (ISBN 0-8172-2155-7). Raintree Pubs.

EASTERN SEABOARD

see Atlantic States

ECCLESIASTICAL ART

see Christian Art and Symbolism

ECCLESIASTICAL BIOGRAPHY

see Christian Biography

ECCLESIASTICAL FASTS AND FEASTS

see Fasts and Feasts

ECCLESIASTICAL HISTORY

see Church History

ECCLESIASTICAL RITES AND CEREMONIES

see Rites and Ceremonies; Funeral Rites and Ceremonies

ECOLOGY

see also Adaptation (Biology); Botany–Ecology; Geographical Distribution of Animals and Plants; Marine Ecology

Baines, Chris. The Picnic: An Ecology Story Book. Ives, Penny, illus. LC 89-77746. 24p. (ps-3). 1990. 7.95 (ISBN 0-940793-54-7, Crocodile Bks). Interlink Pub.

Bender, David L. & Leone, Bruno, eds. The Environment: Opposing Viewpoints, Vol. I. 464p. (gr. 10 up). 1990. lib. bdg. 19.95 (ISBN 0-89908-553-9). Greenhaven.

Blue & Beautiful: Planet Earth, Our Home. 48p. 1990. 9.95 (ISBN 92-1-100441-1, 90.I.15); poster 5.95 (ISBN 0-685-39198-1, 90.I.19). UN.

Bonnet, Robert L. Environmental Science: Forty-Nine Science Fair Projects. (Illus.). 160p. 1990. 17.95 (ISBN 0-8306-7369-5); pap. 9.95 (ISBN 0-8306-3369-3). TAB Bks.

Boy Scouts of America. Environment Skill Book. (Illus.). 32p. (gr. 3-4). 1979. pap. 1.50x (ISBN 0-8395-6586-0); tchr's. guide 0.50x (ISBN 0-8395-8226-9); troop leader's can-do kit 0.50 (ISBN 0-8395-8206-4). BSA.

—Environmental Science. (Illus.). 72p. (gr. 6-12). 1983. pap. 1.85 (ISBN 0-8395-3363-2, 3363). BSA.

Bright, Michael. The Greenhouse Effect. (Illus.). 32p. (gr. 2-4). 1991. PLB 11.90 (ISBN 0-531-17304-6, Gloucester Pr). Watts.

—Pollution & Wildlife. (Illus.). 32p. (gr. 4-8). 1987. lib. bdg. 8.99 (ISBN 0-531-17046-2, Gloucester Pr). Watts.

Brown, Diane M. The Environment: An Annotated Bibliography. 200p. 1991. PLB 40.00x (ISBN 0-89356-666-7, Magill Bks). Salem Pr.

Brumley, Karen. Saving Our Planet. Altop, Tammy, illus. 40p. (gr. 6). 1991. wkbk. 4.95 (ISBN 1-561894-06-0). Amer Educ Pub.

—Saving Our Planet. Altop, Tammy, illus. 40p. (gr. 5). 1991. wkbk. 4.95 (ISBN 1-561894-05-2). Amer Educ Pub.

—Saving Our Planet. Altop, Tammy, illus. 40p. (gr. 4). Date not set. wkbk. 4.95 (ISBN 1-561894-04-4). Amer Educ Pub.

Burrill, Richard. Guardians of the Planet: Selected California Indian Stories & Environmental Activities for Children. (Illus., Orig.). (ps up). Date not set. pap. write for info. Anthro Co.

Dehr, Roma & Bazar, Ronald. Good Planets Are Hard to Find: An Environmental Information Guide for Kids. Johnson, Nola, illus. 40p. (Orig.). (gr. 4 up). 1990. pap. 4.95 (ISBN 0-919597-09-2). Firefly Bks Ltd.

Diffenderfer, Susan. Ecology: Learning to Love Our Planet. 115p. (gr. k-8). 1984. 16.95 (ISBN 0-913705-01-2, ZP11). Zephyr Pr AZ.

Drutman, Ava & Zuckerman, Susan. Protecting Our Planet. 144p. (gr. 4-8). 1991. 12.95 (ISBN 0-86653-589-6). Good Apple.

Drutman, Ava D. Protecting Our Planet - Primary Grades. 144p. (gr. 1-3). 1991. 12.95 (ISBN 0-86653-619-1, GA1338). Good Apple.

Dudley, William. The Environment: Distinguishing Between Fact & Opinion. (Illus.). 32p. (gr. 3-6). 1990. PLB 8.95 (ISBN 0-89908-603-9). Greenhaven.

Earth Works Project Staff. Fifty Simple Things You Can Do to Save the Earth. (gr. 9 up). 1990. pap. 4.95 (ISBN 0-929634-06-3). Grnleaf Pubs.

Fadely, Jack & Hosler, Virginia. Do the Children Know: Children, Zoos, & Survival. Fadely, Jack & Hosler, Virginia, illus. 164p. (gr. 2-8). 1985. pap. 9.50 (ISBN 0-934293-02-3). Huber-Copeland Pub.

Ferraro, Bonita. Saving Our Planet. Robinson, Don, illus. 40p. (gr. 3). Date not set. wkbk. 4.95 (ISBN 1-561894-03-6). Amer Educ Pub.

—Saving Our Planet. Robinson, Don, illus. 40p. (gr. 2). 1991. wkbk. 4.95 (ISBN 1-561894-02-8). Amer Educ Pub.

—Saving Our Planet. Robinson, Don, illus. 40p. (gr. 1). 1991. wkbk. 4.95 (ISBN 1-561894-01-X). Amer Educ Pub.

Gallant, Roy A. Earth's Vanishing Forests. LC 91-2624. (Illus.). 144p. (gr. 5-9). 1991. 14.95 (ISBN 0-02-735774-0, Mcmillan Child Bk). Macmillan Child Grp.

Greene, Carol. Caring for Our Forest. (Illus.). 32p. (gr. 1-4). 1991. PLB 12.95 (ISBN 0-89490-353-5). Enslow Pubs.

—Caring for Our People. (Illus.). 32p. (gr. 1-4). 1991. PLB 12.95 (ISBN 0-89490-355-1). Enslow Pubs.

Gutnik, Martin A. Ecology Projects for Young Scientists. 1989. pap. 5.95 (ISBN 0-531-15128-X). Watts.

Gutnik, Martin J. Ecology. 96p. (gr. 7 up). 1984. lib. bdg. 12.90 (ISBN 0-531-04765-2). Watts.

Harlow, Rosie & Morgan, Gareth. Energy & Growth. Kuo Kang Chen & Fitzsimmons, Cecilia, illus. 40p. (gr. 5-8). 1991. PLB 12.90 (ISBN 0-531-19124-9, Warwick). Watts.

Herridge, Douglas & Hughes, Susan. The Environmental Detective Kit. LC 90-48247. (Illus.). 80p. (gr. 3 up). 1991. 12.95 (ISBN 0-06-107408-X). HarpC Child Bks.

Hester, Nigel. The Living House. (Illus.). 32p. (gr. 5-8). 1991. PLB 11.40 (ISBN 0-531-14120-9). Watts.

—The Living River. (Illus.). 32p. (gr. 5-8). 1991. PLB 11.40 (ISBN 0-531-14121-7). Watts.

Hoff, Mary & Roders, Mary M. Our Endangered Planet: Tropical Rain Forests. (Illus.). 64p. (gr. 4-6). 1991. PLB 15.95 (ISBN 0-8225-2503-8). Lerner Pubns.

Hogan, Paula. Vanishing Rain Forests. (Illus.). 32p. (gr. 3-4). 1991. PLB 12.95 (ISBN 0-8368-0477-5). Gareth Stevens Inc.

Hogan, Paula & Seidenberg, Steven. Ecology: Our Living Planet. LC 89-11282. (Illus.). 64p. (gr. 2-3). 1990. PLB 12.95 (ISBN 0-8368-0030-3). Gareth Stevens Inc.

Lambert, Mark. Farming & the Environment. LC 90-45614. (Illus.). 48p. (gr. 4-9). 1990. PLB 18.60 (ISBN 0-8114-2392-1). Steck-V.

—The Future for the Environment. (Illus.). 48p. (gr. 4-6). 1986. PLB 12.40 (ISBN 0-531-18075-1, Pub. by Bookwright). Watts.

Leinwand, Gerald. The Environment. 128p. (gr. 7-12). 1990. 16.95x (ISBN 0-8160-2099-X). Facts on File.

Mclaughlin, Molly. Earthworms, Dirt & Rotten Leaves: An Exploration in Ecology. Shetterly, Robert, illus. LC 86-3318. 96p. (gr. 3-7). 1986. 12.95 (ISBN 0-689-31215-6, Atheneum Child Bk). Macmillan Child Grp.

Mcvey, Vicki. Sierra Club Wayfinding Book. (gr. 4-7). 1991. pap. 7.95 (ISBN 0-316-56342-0). Little.

Markle, Sandra. Weather, Electricity, Environmental Investigations. 112p. (gr. 4-6). 1982. 9.95 (ISBN 0-88160-082-2, LW 902). Learning Wks.

Middleton, Nick. Atlas of Environmental Issues. (Illus.). 64p. (gr. 6 up). 1989. 16.95x (ISBN 0-8160-2023-X). Facts on File.

Miles, Betty. Save the Earth! An Ecology Handbook for Kids. Nivola, Claire A., illus. LC 73-15116. 96p. (gr. 2 up). 1974. Knopf.

Miller, Christina G. & Berry, Louise A. Jungle Rescue: Saving the New World Tropical Rain Forests. (Illus.). 128p. (gr. 5-9). 1991. SBE 14.95 (ISBN 0-689-31487-6, Atheneum Child Bk). Macmillan Child Grp.

Norsgaard, E. Jaediker. Nature's Great Balancing Act: In Our Own Backyard. Norsgaard, Campbell, photos by. LC 89-38589. (Illus.). 64p. (gr. 4 up). 1990. 14.95 (ISBN 0-525-65028-8, Cobblehill Bks). Dutton Child Bks.

Pedersen, Anne. The Kid's Environment Book: What's Awry & Why. (Illus.). 192p. (Orig.). (gr. 6 up). 1991. pap. 13.95 (ISBN 0-945465-74-2). John Muir.

Pringle, Laurence. Restoring Our Earth. LC 87-615. (Illus.). 64p. (gr. 7-10). 1987. PLB 15.95 (ISBN 0-89490-143-5). Enslow Pubs.

Radlauer, Ruth & Anderson, Henry M. Reefs. LC 82-17862. (Illus.). 48p. (gr. 4 up). 1983. PLB 15.93 (ISBN 0-516-07836-4). Childrens.

Rosney, Bride, ed. Nature in Action: Young Readers Ecology Handbook. 50p. 1978. Repr. of 1977 ed. 6.95 (ISBN 0-905140-42-7, Pub. by O'Brien Press Ltd Eire). Dufour.

Rothman, Joel. Once There Was a Stream. Roberts, Bruce, photos by. LC 72-90692. (Illus.). 32p. (gr. k-4). 1973. 8.95 (ISBN 0-87592-038-1). Scroll Pr.

Sabin, Francene. Ecosystems & Food Chains. Cumings, Art, illus. LC 84-2707. 32p. (gr. 3-6). 1985. PLB 9.49 (ISBN 0-8167-0282-9); pap. text ed. 2.95 (ISBN 0-8167-0283-7). Troll Assocs.

Schwartz, Linda. Earth Book for Kids: Activities to Help Heal the Environment. Armstrong, Beverly, illus. 184p. (Orig.). (gr. 3-7). 1990. pap. 9.95x (ISBN 0-88160-195-0, LW 289). Learning Wks.

Seidenberg, Steven. Ecology & Conservation. LC 89-11281. (Illus.). 64p. (gr. 4-6). 1990. PLB 12.95 (ISBN 0-8368-0005-2). Gareth Stevens Inc.

Smith, Howard E., Jr. Small Worlds: Communities of Living Things. LC 87-9856. (Illus.). 144p. (gr. 5-7). 1987. 12.95 (ISBN 0-684-18723-X, Scribners Young Read). Macmillan Child Grp.

Spizman, Robyn & Garber, Marianne. What on Earth You Can Do with Kids. 352p. (gr. 1-5). 1991. 23.95 (ISBN 0-86653-623-X, GA1342). Good Apple.

Stevens, Lawrence. Ecology Basics. D'Amato, Janet, illus. 48p. (gr. 3-7). 1986. 10.95 (ISBN 0-13-223215-4). P-H.

Stone, L. Deserts. (Illus.). 48p. (gr. 4-8). 1989. lib. bdg. 14.00 (ISBN 0-86592-438-4). Rourke Corp.

—Prairies. (Illus.). 48p. (gr. 4-8). 1989. lib. bdg. 14.00 (ISBN 0-86592-446-5). Rourke Corp.

—Rain Forests. (Illus.). 48p. (gr. 4-8). 1989. lib. bdg. 14.00 (ISBN 0-86592-437-6). Rourke Corp.

—Temperate Forests. (Illus.). 48p. (gr. 4-8). 1989. lib. bdg. 14.00 (ISBN 0-86592-439-2). Rourke Corp.

—Wetlands. (Illus.). 48p. (gr. 4-8). 1989. lib. bdg. 14.00 (ISBN 0-86592-447-3). Rourke Corp.

Stone, Lynn. Ecozones, 8 bks, Reading Level 6. (Illus.). 384p. (gr. 4-8). Date not set. Set. PLB 112.00 (ISBN 0-86592-434-1). Rourke Corp.

Stone, Lynn M. Marshes & Swamps. LC 82-17861. (Illus.). 48p. (gr. k-4). 1983. PLB 14.60 (ISBN 0-516-01681-4); pap. 4.95 (ISBN 0-516-41681-2). Childrens.

Stwertka, Eve. Rachel Carson. (Illus.). 64p. (gr. 3-6). 1991. PLB 11.90 (ISBN 0-531-20020-5). Watts.

Szekely, Edmond B. Brother Tree. Matinez, Antonielena C., illus. 32p. 1977. pap. 3.50 (ISBN 0-89564-074-0). IBS Intl.

Whitfield, Philip. Can the Whales Be Saved? Questions about the Natural World & the Threats to Its Survival Answered by the Natural History Museum. (Illus.). 96p. (gr. 1 up). 1989. pap. 16.95 (ISBN 0-670-82753-3). Viking Child Bks.

Yanda, Bill. Rads, Ergs, & Cheeseburgers: The Kid's Guide to Energy & the Environment. (Illus.). 108p. (Orig.). (gr. 3 up). 1991. pap. 12.95 (ISBN 0-945465-75-0). John Muir.

ECOLOGY–FICTION

Althea. Rainforest Homes. (Illus.). 24p. (gr. 1 up). 1985. pap. 3.95 (ISBN 0-521-31619-7). Cambridge U Pr.

Bond, Nancy. The Voyage Begun. LC 81-3481. 336p. (gr. 7 up). 1981. 15.95 (ISBN 0-689-50204-4, M K McElderry). Macmillan Child Grp.

Brown, Ruth. The World That Jack Built. Brown, Ruth, illus. 32p. (ps-3). 1991. 13.95 (ISBN 0-525-44635-4, DCB). Dutton Child Bks.

Dexter, Catherine. Gertie's Green Thumb. Eagle, Ellen, illus. LC 82-21664. 128p. (gr. 4-7). 1983. 8.95 (ISBN 0-02-730200-8, Mcmillan Child Bk). Macmillan Child Grp.

Dillon, Barbara. Mrs. Tooey & the Terrible Toxic Tar. LC 87-45985. 96p. (gr. 3-7). 1990. pap. 2.95 (ISBN 0-06-440313-0, Trophy). HarpC Child Bks.

George, Jean C. Who Really Killed Cock Robin? An Ecological Mystery. LC 90-38659. 176p. (gr. 3-7). 1991. 14.95 (ISBN 0-06-021980-7); PLB 14.89 (ISBN 0-06-021981-5). HarpC Child Bks.

Hamilton, Jean. Tropical Rainforests. Leon, Vicki, ed. (Illus.). 40p. (Orig.). 1990. pap. 7.95 (ISBN 0-918303-25-7). Blake Pub.
The worlds' richest terrestrial habitat, the tropical rainforest is an emerald mansion of biological riches. In 5,000 words of text, over 1,000 words of captions, & 40 brilliant color photos, this book presents a roundup look at the world's rainforests, as enchanted & fruitful as they are endangered. To make the diversity of the forest understandable, the book approaches it by levels: the floor, the understory, the canopy, & the pavillion. Like other books in the Blake Habitat series, complex ideas & relationships are presented in a clear & relaxed manner. Unfamiliar terms are used & immediately explained. Captions identify animals & plants & also name their ecological equivalents on other continents. From the photos taken by 18 of the world's best wildlife photographers to the text by a noted writer with a zoology background, no effort has been spared to make this book a quality & good value standout in a forest of competitors.
Publisher Provided Annotation.

Hannah, Valerie. Cyril Squirrel & Sheryl: An Ecological Tale. Herrick, George H., ed. Meek, Barbara, illus. 46p. (Orig.). (gr. k-3). 1991. pap. 8.95 (ISBN 0-941281-78-7). V H Pub.
With "Fun to Answer" questions & printed on recycled paper & Beatrix Potter-like illustrations, this lucid story is about a city squirrel who visits his country cousin Sheryl. When camping in the forest, Cyril only just avoids an ecological disater. "A wonderful reading & learning experience & a child's treasure."--Independent Small Press Review, Spring 1991. "Cyril & Sheryl squirrel share stories of the secrets & exciting places in which they live. This is an enchanting tale full of the quiet wisdom of the ages."--Book Reader, May 1991. "Join the adventures of Cyril, a squirrel who has never seen a tree, who lives an urban environment & skateboards for exercise...This delightful story is populated with many family squirrel members who have plenty to teach Cyril when he goes to the woods to visit his grandparents. Hannah has provided a learning experience for grade school children

(k-3) in this timely ecological adventure."--Bloomsbury Review, May 1991.
Publisher Provided Annotation.

Hoban, Russell. Arthur's New Power. Barton, Byron, illus. LC 77-11550. (gr. 1-5). 1978. PLB 12.89 (ISBN 0-690-01371-X, Crowell Jr Bks). HarpC Child Bks.
Lavie, Arlette. Tower. (ps-3). 1990. 10.95 (ISBN 0-85953-392-1). Childs Play.
O'Brian, Michael. I Helped Save the Earth! (gr. 4-7). 1991. pap. 3.95 (ISBN 0-425-12830-X). Berkley Pub.
Parnall, Peter. The Rock. Parnall, Peter, illus. LC 90-6021. 32p. (gr. k-3). 1991. RSBE 14.95 (ISBN 0-02-770181-6, Mcmillan Child Bk). Macmillan Child Grp.
Scott, Bob. The Backcountry. Arcade, Greg, illus. 24p. (gr. 4-12). 1989. cardstock cover 5.00 (ISBN 0-9621201-0-3). B Scott Bks.
Serendipity. (gr. 1-6). pap. 2.95 (ISBN 0-8431-0562-3). Price Stern.
Thiele, Colin. Fight Against Albatross Two. LC 75-37104. 254p. (gr. 7 up). 1976. PLB 12.89 (ISBN 0-06-026099-8). HarpC Child Bks.
Turner, Ann. Heron Street. Desimini, Lisa, illus. LC 87-24948. 32p. (gr. 1-4). 1989. 12.95i (ISBN 0-06-026184-6); PLB 12.89 (ISBN 0-06-026185-4). HarpC Child Bks.

ECOLOGY, MARINE
see Marine Ecology

ECONOMIC ASSISTANCE
Berger, Gilda. U. S. A. for Africa, Rock Aid in the Eighties. LC 86-24718. (Illus.). 96p. (gr. 7-12). 1987. lib. bdg. 12.90 (ISBN 0-531-10299-8). Watts.

ECONOMIC BOTANY
see Botany, Economic

ECONOMIC CONDITIONS
see also Economic Policy; Statistics; U. S.–Economic Conditions
O'Toole, Thomas. Global Economics. (Illus.). 80p. (gr. 5 up). 1991. PLB 14.95 (ISBN 0-8225-1782-5). Lerner Pubns.

ECONOMIC DEPRESSIONS
see Depressions

ECONOMIC DEVELOPMENT
see Economic Conditions

ECONOMIC ENTOMOLOGY
see Insects, Injurious and Beneficial

ECONOMIC HISTORY
see Economic Conditions

ECONOMIC PLANNING
see Economic Policy

ECONOMIC POLICY
For works on the policy of governments towards economic problems.
see also International Economic Relations
also names of countries and states with the subdivision Economic Policy e.g. U. S.–Economic Policy)
Kronenwetter, Michael. Capitalism vs. Socialism: Economic Policies of the U. S. & the U. S. S. R. LC 85-22579. (Illus.). 103p. (gr. 7-12). 1986. PLB 12.90 (ISBN 0-531-10152-5). Watts.
Rawcliffe, Michael. Timeline: The Welfare State. (Illus.). 72p. (gr. 7 up). 1990. 19.95 (ISBN 0-317-02818-9, Pub. by Batsford UK). Trafalgar Sq.

ECONOMIC RELATIONS, FOREIGN
see International Economic Relations

ECONOMICS
see also Business; Commerce; Credit; Depressions; Economic Conditions; Economic Policy; Finance; Industry; Labor and Laboring Classes; Land; Money; Population
Economics Study Aid. 1987. pap. 3.25 (ISBN 0-87738-045-7). Youth Ed.
Flumiani, C. M. Teenager's Guide to Economics & Finance, 2 vols. in one. LC 72-91789. (Illus.). 70p. (gr. 10-12). 1973. Set. 97.75 (ISBN 0-913314-16-1). Am Classical Coll Pr.
Hess, Karl. Capitalism for Kids. (gr. 5 up). 1987. 12.95 (ISBN 0-685-19725-5); pap. 9.95 (ISBN 0-942103-06-8). Enterprise Del.
Killen, M. Barbara. Introduction to Economic Reasoning. (Illus.). 88p. (gr. 5 up). 1991. PLB 14.95 (ISBN 0-8225-1784-1). Lerner Pubns.
Marsh, Carole. The Teddy Bear Company: Economics for Kids. (Illus.). (gr. 4-8). 1983. 14.95 (ISBN 0-935326-16-2); tchr's. ed. o.p. 6.00 (ISBN 0-935326-90-1). Gallopade Pub Group.
—Teddy Bear's Annual Report. (Illus.). (gr. 4-8). 1983. 14.95 (ISBN 0-935326-26-X). Gallopade Pub Group.
Wyatt, Elaine & Hinden, Stan. The Money Book & Bank. LC 91-13237. (Illus.). 64p. (ps-3). 1991. text ed. 11.95 (ISBN 0-688-10365-0). Morrow.

ECONOMICS–DICTIONARIES
Guenter, H. Jugendlexikon Wirtschaft. (GER.). 192p. 1976. 12.95 (ISBN 3-499-16189-3, M-7492, Pub. by Rowohlt). French & Eur.

ECONOMISTS
Victor, R. F. John Maynard Keynes: Father of Modern Economics. Rahmas, D. Steve, ed. 32p. (Orig.). (gr. 7-12). 1972. lib. bdg. 4.20 incl. catalog cards (ISBN 0-87157-517-5); pap. 2.95 vinyl laminated covers (ISBN 0-87157-017-3). SamHar Pr.

ECUADOR
Cubbit, David & Corkill, David. Ecuador. (Illus.). 130p. (gr. 11-12). 1988. pap. 7.50 (ISBN 0-85345-760-3, Pub. by Lat Am Bur UK). Monthly Rev.
Lepthien, Emilie U. Ecuador. LC 85-26967. (Illus.). 128p. (gr. 5-9). 1986. PLB 25.27 (ISBN 0-516-02760-3). Childrens.
Lerner Publications, Department of Geography Staff. Ecuador in Pictures. (Illus.). 64p. (gr. 5 up). 1987. PLB 12.95 (ISBN 0-8225-1813-9). Lerner Pubns.
Peck, Robert M. Headhunters & Hummingbirds: An Expedition into Ecuador. LC 86-15908. (Illus.). 128p. (gr. 11 up). 1987. 14.95 (ISBN 0-8027-6645-5); PLB 14.85 (ISBN 0-8027-6646-3). Walker & Co.

ECUMENICAL MOVEMENT
see Christian Unity

EDDY, MARY (BAKER) 1821-1910
Sass, Karin. Mary Baker Eddy, a Special Friend. Kieffer, Christa, illus. LC 83-72002. 32p. (gr. k-3). 1983. 8.95 (ISBN 0-87510-165-8). Chr Science.
Smith, Louise. Mary Baker Eddy. Horner, Matina S., intro. by. 112p. (gr. 5 up). 1991. 17.95 (ISBN 1-55546-652-4). Chelsea Hse.

EDIBLE PLANTS
see Plants, Edible

EDISON, THOMAS ALVA, 1847-1931
Adler, David A. Thomas Alva Edison: Great Inventor. Miller, Lyle, illus. LC 89-77507. 48p. (gr. 2-5). 1990. reinforced 13.95 (ISBN 0-8234-0820-5). Holiday.
Buranelli, Vincent. Thomas Alva Edison. (Illus.). 142p. (gr. 5-7). 1989. PLB 13.98 (ISBN 0-382-09522-7). Silver Burdett Pr.
Cousins, Margaret. The Story of Thomas Alva Edison. LC 81-805. (Illus.). 160p. (gr. 5-9). 1981. pap. 3.95 (ISBN 0-394-84883-7). Random.
—Thomas Alva Edison. (Illus.). (gr. 4-8). 1965. lib. bdg. 8.99 (ISBN 0-394-90410-9, Random Juv). Random.
Davidson, Margaret. Story of Thomas Alva Edison: The Wizard of Menlo Park. 1990. pap. 2.50 (ISBN 0-590-42403-3). Scholastic Inc.
Egan, Louise. Thomas A. Edison. (Illus.). 144p. (gr. 3-6). 1987. pap. 4.95 (ISBN 0-8120-3922-X). Barron.
Farr, Naunerle C. Thomas Edison - Alexander Graham Bell. Taloac, Gerry & Trinidad, Angel, illus. (gr. 4-12). 1979. pap. text ed. 2.95 (ISBN 0-88301-357-6); wkbk. 1.25 (ISBN 0-88301-381-9). Pendulum Pr.
Greene, Carol. Thomas Alva Edison: Bringer of Light. LC 84-23247. (Illus.). 128p. (gr. 4 up). 1985. lib. bdg. 17.27 (ISBN 0-516-03213-5). Childrens.
Guthridge, Sue. Thomas A. Edison: Young Inventor. Wook, Wallace, illus. LC 86-10862. 192p. (gr. 2-6). 1986. pap. 3.95 (ISBN 0-02-041850-7, Aladdin). Macmillan Child Grp.
Johnson, Ann D. The Value of Creativity: The Story of Thomas Edison. Pileggi, Steve, illus. LC 80-28152. 64p. (gr. k-6). 1987. 9.95 (ISBN 0-916392-72-4, Pub. by Value Communications). Oak Tree Pubns.
Keller, Jack. Tom Edison's Bright Idea. (Illus.). 32p. (gr. 1-4). 1989. PLB 13.32 (ISBN 0-8172-3532-9). Raintree Pubs.
Lampton, Christopher. Thomas Alva Edison. large type ed. (Illus.). 88p. (gr. 4-8). 1991. Repr. of 1988 ed. PLB 17.95 (ISBN 1-55905-079-9). Grey Castle.
Lampton, Christopher F. Thomas Alva Edison. Solomon, Maury, ed. LC 87-25438. (Illus.). 72p. (gr. 5 up). 1988. PLB 10.40 (ISBN 0-531-10491-5). Watts.
Lowitz, Sadyebeth & Lowitz, Anson. Tom Edison Finds Out. 1979. pap. 0.95 (ISBN 0-440-48384-0, YB). Dell.
Morgan, Nina. Thomas Edison. (Illus.). 48p. (gr. 5-8). 1991. RLB 12.40 (ISBN 0-531-18406-4, Pub. by Boatwright Pr). Watts.
Quackenbush, Robert. What Has Wild Tom Done Now? A Story of Thomas Alva Edison. (gr. 1-4). 1981. 8.95 (ISBN 0-13-952168-2). P-H.
Sabin, Louis. Thomas Alva Edison: Young Inventor. Ulrich, George, illus. LC 82-15889. 48p. (gr. 4-6). 1983. PLB 10.79 (ISBN 0-89375-841-8); pap. text ed. 2.95 (ISBN 0-89375-842-6). Troll Assocs.
Tames, Richard. Thomas Edison. (Illus.). 32p. (gr. 5-8). 1990. PLB 11.90 (ISBN 0-531-14004-0). Watts.

EDITORS AND EDITING
see Journalism; Journalists; Publishers and Publishing

EDUCATION
see also Audio-Visual Education; Books and Reading; Business Education; Character Education; Child Study; Colleges and Universities; Culture; Educators; Learning and Scholarship; Libraries; Military Education; Physical Education and Training; Religious Education; Scholarships, Fellowships, Etc.; Schools; Self-Culture; Study, Method of; Teachers; Teaching
also names of classes of people and social and ethnic groups with the subdivision Education, (e.g. Blacks–Education); subjects with the subdivision Study and Teaching (e.g. Science–Study and Teaching); and headings beginning with the words Education and Educational
Ames, Louise B. Why Am I So Noisy? Why Is She So Shy? 48p. (Orig.). (ps-8). 1991. pap. text ed. 7.95 (ISBN 0-935493-45-X). Programs Educ.
Berry, Joy. Every Kid's Guide to Laws That Relate to School & Work. Bartholomew, illus. 48p. (gr. 3-7). 1987. 4.95 (ISBN 0-516-21412-8); PLB 14.60 (ISBN 0-516-01412-9). Childrens.
Borba, Michele. Esteem Builders: A Self-Esteem Curriculum for Improving Student Achievement, Behavior & School-Home Climate. Taylor-McMillan, Birah, ed. Highpoint Type & Graphics Staff, illus. LC 88-80769. 444p. (Orig.). (gr. k-8). 1989. pap. 39.95 (ISBN 0-915190-53-2, JP9053-2). Jalmar Pr.
Bosch, Carl W. Making the Grade. Strecker, Rebekah, illus. LC 90-62674. 64p. (Orig.). (gr. 3). 1991. lib. bdg. 14.95 (ISBN 0-943990-49-1); pap. 4.95 (ISBN 0-943990-48-3). Parenting Pr.
Caballero, Jane A. & Whordley, Derek. Children Around the World. rev. ed. LC 82-81892. 176p. (Orig.). (ps-4). 1991. pap. 16.95 (ISBN 0-89334-112-6). Humanics Ltd.
Carroll, Jeri. Learning Centers for Little Kids. Foster, Tom, illus. 64p. (ps-2). 1983. wkbk. 6.95 (ISBN 0-86653-103-3, GA 458). Good Apple.
Chapman, Laura. Discover Art - Kindergarten. (gr. k). 1989. kit 179.50 (ISBN 0-87192-219-3, 219-3). Davis Mass.
Class Trips. (gr. 3-5). 3.95 (ISBN 0-317-42452-1). Learning Well.
Colligan, Louise & Colligan, Doug. The A-Plus Guide to Good Grades. 144p. (gr. 7 up). 1984. pap. 2.25 (ISBN 0-590-33314-3). Scholastic Inc.
Cooke, Jean. Projects for Easter. Young, Richard G., ed. Marffy, Janos, illus. LC 89-11792. 32p. (gr. 3-5). 1989. PLB 14.60 (ISBN 0-944483-38-0). Garrett Ed Corp.
De Leeuw, Hendrik, et al. Fireproof Children Education Kit. (Illus.). 308p. (gr. k-6). 1990. 99.95 (ISBN 0-9626076-1-4). Natl Fire Serv Support Systs.
Delisle, James R. Gifted Kids Speak Out: Hundreds of Kids Ages 6-13 Talk about School, Friends, Their Families & the Future. rev. ed. Espeland, Pamela, ed. Urbanovic, Jackie, illus. LC 87-25139. 120p. (Orig.). (gr. 2-7). 1988. pap. 9.95 (ISBN 0-915793-10-5). Free Spirit Pub.
Dixon, Dougal. Dino Dots. 48p. 1988. 4.95 (ISBN 0-88166-122-8, Dist. by Simon & Schuster). Meadowbrook.
Embry, Lynn. Rx for the Classroom Blahs. Filkins, Vanessa, illus. 64p. (gr. 4-8). 1983. wkbk. 6.95 (ISBN 0-86653-104-1, GA 462). Good Apple.
Forte, Imogene. Think about It! Middle Grades. (Illus.). 80p. (gr. 4-6). 1981. pap. text ed. 7.95 (ISBN 0-913916-98-6, IP 98-6). Incentive Pubn.
—Think about It! Primary. (Illus.). 80p. (gr. 1-3). 1981. pap. text ed. 7.95 (ISBN 0-913916-97-8, IP 97-8). Incentive Pubn.
Foster, Elizabeth S. Tutoring: Learning by Helping. rev. ed. Sorenson, Don L., ed. McKee, Mary M., illus. LC 83-80004. 224p. (gr. 9 up). 1983. pap. text ed. 8.95x (ISBN 0-932796-13-3). Ed Media Corp.
Galbraith, Judy. The Gifted Kids Survival Guide: (For Ages Ten & Under) LC 83-83015. (Illus.). 72p. (Orig.). (gr. k-5). 1984. pap. 7.95 (ISBN 0-915793-00-8). Free Spirit Pub.
Kizer, Kathryn. Two Hundred Plus Games & Fun Activities for Teaching Preschoolers. (Illus.). 72p. (Orig.). (ps). 1989. pap. text ed. 4.95 (ISBN 0-936625-70-8, New Hope AL). Womans Mission Union.
Kleman, Mary L. & Kleman, James. Listening Comprehension Training Program: Manuals A-E. 40p. (gr. 4-8). 1982. manual 5.00 (ISBN 0-938464-01-9). JML Enter MD.
Learning Exchange Staff. Seasonal Learning Activities. 112p. (gr. 2-6). 1988. wkbk. 9.95 (ISBN 0-86653-435-0, GA1045). Good Apple.
LeGros, Lucy C. Activities & Games. rev. ed. (Illus.). 75p. (Orig.). (gr. k-2). 1989. pap. 7.95 (ISBN 0-318-41419-8). Creat Res NC.
Liebermann, M. Coloring Books on Events of the Jewish Months: Tishrei, Cheshvan. (ps-2). 1987. 2.50 (ISBN 0-914131-84-2, D710). Torah Umesorah.
Loeper, John J. Going to School in 1776. LC 72-86940. (Illus.). 112p. (gr. 4-7). 1973. 13.95 (ISBN 0-689-30089-1, Atheneum). Macmillan Child Grp.
Lovitt, Chip. Scents-Sational Smelly Sticker Kit. Roper, Robert, illus. 16p. (ps-3). 1986. pap. 3.95 (ISBN 0-590-40538-1). Scholastic Inc.
McDonough, Kathleen L. School Survival Skills: Student Syllabus. (Illus.). 64p. (gr. 8 up). 1985. pap. 7.95 (ISBN 0-89420-246-4, 340025). Natl Book.
McInnes, Celia. Projects for Summer & Holiday Activities. Young, Richard G., ed. Wheele, Stephen, illus. LC 89-11791. 32p. (gr. 3-5). 1989. PLB 14.60 (ISBN 0-944483-39-9). Garrett Ed Corp.
McKinley, Nancy L. & Schwartz, Linda. Make-It-Yourself Barrier Activities. 210p. (gr. k-12). 1987. pap. 33.00 (ISBN 0-930599-16-0). Thinking Pubns.

Maid, Amy & Wallace, Roger. Not Just Schoolwork. LC 76-9524. 201p. (Orig.). 1990. pap. 24.95 (ISBN 0-8290-0354-1). NL Assoc Inc.
"Not Just Schoolwork" is the book that combines superb activities for written expression & creativity. A wonderful tool to motivate both teacher & pupil. Open ended enough to be used from grades 3 through 12. The lessons included can either be used by teachers as resource for additional ideas, or can be reproduced as student activity sheets. The activities are not dependent upon each other even though units do exist & can be built upon.
Publisher Provided Annotation.

Molyneux, Lynn. Active Learning for Young Children. Park, Rosemary, illus. 228p. (ps-3). 1989. 19.95 (ISBN 0-685-29143-X). Trellis Bks Inc.
—Get It Together: Group Projects for Creative Bulletin Boards. Bucur, Mike, illus. 160p. (gr. k-4). 1983. perfect bdg. 9.95 (ISBN 0-685-29141-3). Trellis Bks Inc.
Patacsil, Priscila M. Actividades Educativas Para Preescolares. 172p. (ps). 1988. pap. 6.25 (ISBN 0-311-11049-5). Casa Bautista.
Petreshene, Susan S. More Mind Joggers! One Hundred Two Ready-to-Use Activities That Make Kids Think. 288p. (gr. 1-6). 1988. pap. 22.95x (ISBN 0-87628-584-1). Ctr Appl Res.
Polette, Nancy. Research Book for Gifted Programs K-8. (Illus.). 176p. (gr. 1-8). 1984. pap. 14.95 (ISBN 0-913839-28-0). Bk Lures.
Quality Time Workbooks: I'm Ready for School. 1991. 1.98 (ISBN 0-8317-7297-2). Smithmark.
School Events. (gr. 2-4). wkbk. 3.95 (ISBN 0-317-42450-5). Learning Well.
Steinmetz, Shirley A. Silly Scribbles: A Complete Readiness Program for Young Children. 272p. (ps-k). 1988. pap. 24.95x (ISBN 0-87628-776-3). Ctr Appl Res.
Stuart, Jesse. The Thread That Runs So True. 1977. lib. bdg. 30.00 (ISBN 0-684-15160-X, Scribner); pap. 8.95 (ISBN 0-684-71904-5, Scribner). Macmillan.
Stull, Elizabeth C. Children's Books Activities Kit. 256p. (gr. 1-3). 1988. pap. 24.95x (ISBN 0-87628-014-9). Ctr Appl Res.
Super Activity Books: Dot-to-Dot 3. 48p. 1990. pap. 2.95 (ISBN 0-8431-2786-4). Price Stern.
Super Activity Books: Puzzles & Mazes 2. 48p. 1990. pap. 2.95 (ISBN 0-8431-2787-2). Price Stern.
Thurston, Cheryl M. Extra Book, Level One. Blackstone, Ann, illus. 42p. (Orig.). (gr. 5-12). 1988. pap. text ed. 12.95 (ISBN 1-877673-05-6). Cottonwood Pr.
Welch, Joyce. The Illustrated I Hate School Workbook. Gustafson, Dru, illus. 88p. (Orig.). (gr. 7-9). 1979. pap. 6.95 (ISBN 0-935996-00-1). Wibat Pubns.
Winston, Barbara F. The Hardest Thing about Going to School. Wilson, James P., illus. (Orig.). (gr. k-5). 1987. pap. text ed. 3.95 (ISBN 0-9622810-0-X). B Winston.

EDUCATION–AIMS AND OBJECTIVES

Adams, Pam, illus. Day Dreams. 32p. (Orig.). (ps-2). 1978. 5.50 (ISBN 0-85953-105-8, Pub. by Child's Play England); pap. 4.00 (ISBN 0-85953-082-5). Childs Play.
James, Elizabeth & Barkin, Carol. How to Be School Smart: Secrets of Successful Schoolwork. Doty, Roy, photos by. Greenlaw, M. Jean, intro. by. LC 87-2899. (Illus.). (gr. 4-7). 1988. lib. bdg. 12.88 (ISBN 0-688-06799-9). Lothrop.

EDUCATION–DATA PROCESSING

Eller, Scott. Short Season. 144p. (Orig.). (gr. 4-6). 1985. pap. 2.25 (ISBN 0-590-33573-1, Apple Paperbacks). Scholastic Inc.
Fry, Edward B. Computer Keyboarding for Children. rev. ed. (gr. 3-6). 1984. pap. text ed. 8.95x (ISBN 0-8077-2754-7). Tchrs Coll.
Levine, Janice R. Microcomputers in Elementary & Secondary Education: A Guide to Resources. 64p. (gr. k-12). 1983. 3.75 (ISBN 0-937597-06-6, IR-65). ERIC Clear.

EDUCATION, BUSINESS

see Business Education

EDUCATION, CHARACTER

see Character Education

EDUCATION, CHRISTIAN

see Religious Education

EDUCATION, ELEMENTARY

Armstrong, Bev. Who's Following Directions? Armstrong, Bev, illus. 32p. (gr. 4-7). 1979. wkbk. 3.95 (ISBN 0-88160-072-5, LW 805). Learning Wks.
Armstrong, Beverly. Awards Galore. 48p. (gr. 1-6). 1981. 5.95 (ISBN 0-88160-040-7, LW 225). Learning Wks.
—Outrageous Pages. 32p. (gr. 1-6). 1982. 3.95 (ISBN 0-88160-013-X, LW 116). Learning Wks.
Bauer, Lois M. & Reed, Barbara A. Dance & Play Activities for the Elementary Grades, 2 Vols. (Illus.). (gr. 1-6). 1967. Vol. 1. 4.50 (ISBN 0-910354-02-2); Vol. 2. 4.98 (ISBN 0-910354-07-3). Chartwell.
Fine, Edith & Josephson, Judy. Fantastic Flight. 24p. (ps). 1982. 2.95 (ISBN 0-88160-092-X, LW 130). Learning Wks.
Greanias, Francis. More Pasting Penguins. 24p. (ps). 1980. 3.95 (ISBN 0-88160-060-1, LW 608). Learning Wks.
—Pasting Penguin. 24p. (ps) 1980. 3.95 (ISBN 0-88160-059-8, LW 607). Learning Wks.
Hobby, Janice H. Staying Back. Richardson, Carol, illus. (gr. k-6). 1990. pap. 8.95 (ISBN 0-937404-16-0). Triad Pub FL.
Lerin, Rita. Punctuation Partners. 48p. (gr. 2-4). 1983. 6.95 (ISBN 0-88160-098-9, LW 121). Learning Wks.
Polon, Linda. Paragraph Production. 48p. (gr. 4-6). 1981. 5.95 (ISBN 0-88160-039-3, LW 224). Learning Wks.
Reading, Writing & Arithmetic: Grade 1. 160p. (gr. k-1). 1973. pap. 1.95 (ISBN 0-448-02911-1, G&D). Putnam Pub Group.
Roets, Lois. Student Projects: Ideas & Plans. 272p. (gr. 3 up). 1987. pap. text ed. 30.00 (ISBN 0-911943-11-0). Leadership Pub.
Roets, Lois F. Outline Wizard. 48p. (gr. 4-6). 1980. 5.95 (ISBN 0-88160-034-2, LW 219). Learning Wks.
Schwartz, Linda. The Center Solution. 74p. (gr. 4-6). 1977. 7.95 (ISBN 0-88160-025-3, LW 210). Learning Wks.
Snowball, Marilyn. Preschool Packrat. 112p. (ps). 1982. 9.95 (ISBN 0-88160-011-3, LW 113). Learning Wks.
—Preschool Pelican. 112p. (ps). 1982. 9.95 (ISBN 0-88160-085-7, LW 114). Learning Wks.
Tyler, Sydney B. Young Think Program Two. 90p. (Orig.). (gr. k-1). 1988. pap. text ed. 25.00 report cover (ISBN 0-912781-13-0). Thomas Geale.

EDUCATION, ETHICAL

see Character Education; Religious Education

EDUCATION–FICTION

Bellows, Cathy. Toad School. Bellows, Cathy, illus. LC 89-12562. 32p. (gr. k-3). 1990. 13.95 (ISBN 0-02-708835-9, Mcmillan Child Bk). Macmillan Child Grp.
Bond, Michael. Paddington Takes the Test. (Illus.). (gr. 3-6). 1980. 13.95 (ISBN 0-395-29519-X). HM.
Cosgrove, Stephen. Leo the Lop: Tail Three. James, Robin, illus. 32p. (gr. k-4). 1978. pap. 2.95 (ISBN 0-8431-0577-1). Price Stern.
Hamilton, Dorothy. Jason. LC 73-14813. 120p. (gr. 10-12). 1974. pap. 3.95 (ISBN 0-8361-1728-X). Herald Pr.
Harry Stottlemeier's Discovery. 92p. (gr. 1-5). 6.50 (ISBN 0-686-74918-9); tchr's. manual 30.00 (ISBN 0-686-74919-7). ADL.
Hide & Seek. 22p. (ps-1). 1978. 5.95 (ISBN 0-8431-0633-6). Price Stern.
Kaminski, Gerald. Good Questions. Cooper, Ryan M., illus. 32p. (Orig.). (gr. k-3). 1980. pap. 3.75 (ISBN 0-931896-00-2). Cove View.
Korman, Gordon. Beware the Fish. (Illus., Orig.). (gr. 4-7). 1991. pap. 2.75 (ISBN 0-590-44205-8, Apple Paperbacks). Scholastic Inc.
—Don't Care High. 256p. (gr. 7 up). 1986. pap. 2.50 (ISBN 0-590-40251-X, Point). Scholastic Inc.
—Don't Care High. 1986. pap. 2.95 (ISBN 0-590-43129-3). Scholastic Inc.
Leachman, Clara G. Julie Learns to Write. Winn, Leslie, illus. 22p. (gr. k-1). 1987. pap. 5.50 (ISBN 0-9618517-0-8). C Leachman.
Mr. Cuckoo's Clock Shop. (Illus.). 22p. (ps-1). 1981. 5.95 (ISBN 0-8431-0634-4). Price Stern.
Ritchie, Jo-An. Jonie Goes to Academy. LC 78-21271. (gr. 6-12). 1979. pap. 4.50 (ISBN 0-8127-0193-3). Review & Herald.
—Jonie Graduates. LC 78-27431. (gr. 6-12). 1979. pap. 4.50 (ISBN 0-8127-0201-8). Review & Herald.
Sobol, Donald J. Encyclopedia Brown Tracks Them Down, No. 8. 96p. (gr. 3-6). 1982. pap. 2.50 (ISBN 0-553-15525-3). Bantam.
Squiggly Wiggly. 22p. (ps-1). 1980. 5.95 (ISBN 0-8431-0632-8). Price Stern.

EDUCATION, HIGHER

Blair, Alison. Higher Education. (gr. 10 up). 1988. pap. 2.95 (ISBN 0-8041-0070-5). Ivy Books.

EDUCATION–HISTORY

Lee, Winifred T. A Forest of Pencils. LC 73-1754. (ps-3). 1973. 6.95 (ISBN 0-672-51781-7, Bobbs). Macmillan.

EDUCATION, INTERCULTURAL

see Intercultural Education

EDUCATION, MILITARY

see Military Education

EDUCATION, MORAL

see Character Education

EDUCATION, MUSICAL

see Music–Study and Teaching

EDUCATION, PHYSICAL

see Physical Education and Training

EDUCATION, PRESCHOOL

see Nursery Schools

EDUCATION, PRIMARY

see Education, Elementary

EDUCATION, RELIGIOUS

see Religious Education

EDUCATION, SCIENTIFIC

see Science–Study and Teaching

EDUCATION, SECONDARY

Scott, John I., ed. Getting the Most out of High School. 2nd rev. ed. LC 67-26419. 165p. (gr. 9 up). 1967. 6.50 (ISBN 0-379-00089-X). Oceana.

EDUCATION, THEOLOGICAL

see Religious Education

EDUCATION AND STATE

see also Scholarships, Fellowships, Etc.

EDUCATION OF CHILDREN

see Education, Elementary

EDUCATION OF THE BLIND

see Blind–Education

EDUCATION OF THE DEAF

see Deaf–Education

EDUCATIONAL ADMINISTRATION

see School Administration and Organization

EDUCATIONAL MEASUREMENTS

see Educational Tests and Measurements

EDUCATIONAL PSYCHOLOGY

see also Child Study; Imagination; Perception; Psychology, Applied; Thought and Thinking

EDUCATIONAL TESTS AND MEASUREMENTS

Barton, Charles D. What Happened to SAT Scores, No. 1. rev. ed. Barton, David, illus. 52p. 1988. pap. 3.00 (ISBN 0-317-93056-7). Wallbuilders.
Campbell, John P. Campbell's Middle School Quiz Book, No. 2. 332p. (Orig.). (gr. 5-8). 1986. pap. 13.95x (ISBN 0-9609412-6-6). Patricks Pr.
Donner, Michael. How to Beat the SAT. LC 80-54619. 132p. (gr. 11-12). 1981. pap. 5.95 (ISBN 0-89480-154-6, 460). Workman Pub.
Fredericks & Lipner. Barron's How to Prepare for the Regents Competency Examination: Reading. (gr. 11-12). 1982. pap. 11.95 (ISBN 0-8120-2287-4). Barron.
Gruber, Gary R. Dr. Gary Gruber's Essential Guide to Test Taking for Kids. Guarnaschelli, Maria D., ed. LC 86-8655. 120p. (Orig.). (gr. 3-5). 1986. pap. text ed. 7.95 (ISBN 0-688-06350-0, Quill). Morrow.
—Gruber's Complete Preparation for the SAT - Featuring Critical Thinking Skills. (Orig.). (gr. 10-12). pap. 8.95 (ISBN 0-935475-00-1). Critical Book.
Lawrence, Marcia. How to Take the SAT. 336p. (gr. 9-12). 1979. pap. 9.95 (ISBN 0-452-26296-8, Plume). NAL-Dutton.
Martinson, Thomas. Super Course for the SAT. 784p. (Orig.). (gr. 7-8). 1988. pap. 12.95 (ISBN 0-13-788506-7). S&S Trade.
Sarnoff, Carole & Sennet, Edith. Verbal Command: Power Words SAT Verbal Prep. Monse, Keith, illus. 303p. (gr. 7 up). Date not set. 21.95 (ISBN 1-879871-01-7). Sennet & Sarnoff.
Sommerfield, Elissa B. A Beginner's Guide to the SATs. 85p. (Orig.). (gr. 7-10). 1987. pap. text ed. 10.95 (ISBN 0-9604058-2-8). Ed Skills Dallas.
—Junior SAT Exercises: SAT Exercises for the Ninth & Tenth Grades. 94p. (Orig.). (gr. 9-10). 1987. pap. text ed. 10.95 (ISBN 0-9604058-1-X). Ed Skills Dallas.
World Book, Inc. Staff, ed. The World Book of Test Taking. LC 81-69689. (Illus.). 736p. (gr. 4-12). 1982. write for info. (ISBN 0-7166-3151-2). World Bk.

EDUCATORS

see also Teachers

Kammeraad-Campbell, Susan. Doc: The Story of Dennis Littky & His Fight for a Better School. (Illus.). 18.95 (ISBN 0-8092-4611-2). Contemp Bks.

EDWARD 6TH, KING OF ENGLAND, 1537-1553–FICTION

The Prince & the Pauper. (gr. 4 up). 1988. pap. 4.87 (ISBN 0-582-52284-6, 73812). Longman.
Twain, Mark. Prince & the Pauper. (gr. 5 up). 1964. pap. 2.50 (ISBN 0-8049-0032-9, 32). Airmont.
—The Prince & the Pauper. James, Raymond, ed. Couri, Kathryn A., illus. LC 89-33892. 48p. (gr. 3-6). 1990. lib. bdg. 12.89 (ISBN 0-8167-1873-3); pap. text ed. 3.95 (ISBN 0-8167-1874-1). Troll Assocs.

EGGS

see also Birds–Eggs and Nests

Heller, Ruth. Chicken's Aren't the Only Ones. Heller, Ruth, illus. LC 80-85257. 48p. (ps-1). 1981. 8.95 (ISBN 0-448-01872-1, G&D). Putnam Pub Group.
Johnson, Sylvia A. Inside an Egg. LC 81-17235. (Illus.). 48p. (gr. 4 up). 1982. PLB 14.95 (ISBN 0-8225-1472-9); pap. 5.95 (ISBN 0-8225-9522-2). Lerner Pubns.
Selsam, Millicent E. Egg to Chick. rev. ed. Wolff, Barbara, illus. LC 74-85034. 64p. (ps-3). 1970. PLB 11.89 (ISBN 0-06-025290-1). HarpC Child Bks.
Turner, Dorothy. Eggs. Yates, John, illus. 32p. (gr. 1-4). 1989. PLB 9.95 (ISBN 0-87614-360-5). Carolrhoda Bks.

EGGS–FICTION

Brown, Margaret W. The Golden Egg Book. Wisegard, Leonard, illus. 32p. (ps-1). 1976. write for info. (ISBN 0-307-12045-7, Golden Pr); PLB 9.15 (ISBN 0-685-05367-9). Western Pub.
Butterworth, Oliver. The Enormous Egg. (gr. k-6). 1987. pap. 3.50 (ISBN 0-440-42337-6, YB). Dell.
Casey, Patricia. Quack Quack. LC 87-17301. (Illus.). (ps-1). 1988. 12.95 (ISBN 0-688-07765-X). Lothrop.
Heine, Helme. The Most Wonderful Egg in the World. Heine, Helme, illus. LC 82-49350. 32p. (ps-3). 1983. 13.95 (ISBN 0-689-50280-X, M K McElderry). Macmillan Child Grp.
Lauber, Patricia. What's Hatching Out of That Egg? (Illus.). (gr. 3-6). 1987. pap. 4.95 (ISBN 0-517-56349-5). Crown.
Levitin, Sonia. A Single Speckled Egg. Larrecq, John M., illus. LC 75-4189. 40p. (ps-3). 1976. 6.95 (ISBN 0-87466-074-2, Pub. by Parnassus). HM.
Peet, Bill. Pinkish, Purplish, Bluish Egg. (Illus.). (gr. k-3). 1984. 13.95 (ISBN 0-395-18472-X); pap. 3.95 (ISBN 0-395-36172-9). HM.
Rockwell, Anne. The Gollywhopper Egg. Rockwell, Anne, illus. LC 86-10825. 64p. (gr. 1-4). 1986. pap. 3.95 (ISBN 0-689-71072-0, Aladdin). Macmillan Child Grp.
Roddie, Shen. Hatch, Egg, Hatch: Touch & Feel Action Flap Book. (ps). 1991. 13.95 (ISBN 0-316-75345-9). Little.
Stevenson, James. The Great Big Especially Beautiful Easter Egg. Stevenson, James, illus. LC 82-11731. 32p. (gr. k-3). 1983. 13.95 (ISBN 0-688-01789-4); PLB 13.88 (ISBN 0-688-01791-6). Greenwillow.

EGYPT

Allen. Pharaohs & Pyramids. (gr. 4-9). 1977. (Usborne-Hayes); PLB 13.96 (ISBN 0-88110-103-6); pap. 6.95 (ISBN 0-86020-084-1). EDC.
Bennet, Olivia. A Family in Egypt. LC 84-19468. (Illus.). 32p. (gr. 2-5). 1985. PLB 9.95 (ISBN 0-8225-1652-7). Lerner Pubns.

Browder, Atlantis T. & Browder, Anthony T. My First Trip to Africa. Browder, Anne, ed. Aaron, Malcolm, illus. LC 91-70328. 38p. (Orig.). 1991.

16.95 (ISBN 0-924944-02-1); pap. 8.95 (ISBN 0-924944-01-3). Inst Karmic. Approved for use in New York City's School System two months after publication, MY FIRST TRIP TO AFRICA is the collaborative effort of 8-year-old Atlantis & her father Anthony Browder, author of "From The Browder File, 22 Essays on the African American Experience." MY FIRST TRIP TO AFRICA chronicles the experience of then 7-year-old Atlantis during a 13-day study tour to Egypt in November, 1989. It contains a Parent/Teacher Guide, 27 photographs, 15 illustrations, 3 maps & a 42 word glossary. The Parent/Teacher Guide is an aid providing topics of discussion for children in the classroom, at the dinner table or at bedtime; including activities designed to stimulate a better understanding of all the topics referenced in the narrative. This narrative written specifically for children, will assist them in understanding aspects of personal, world & African history. MY FIRST TRIP TO AFRICA makes good reading for children & adults alike. "Uniquely written from a child's perspective, encompassing historical facts/information every African American of any age should know."--The Capitol Spotlight. "Atlantis's reflections were teamed with photographs taken by Atlantis, her father & her grandmother."--The Washington Post. "...filled with pictures of the historical legacy of Kemet, along with American edifices reminiscent of Ancient Egyptian architecture."--Washington Afro-American.
Publisher Provided Annotation.

Cross, Wilbur. Egypt. LC 82-9465. (Illus.). (gr. 5-9). 1982. PLB 25.27 (ISBN 0-516-02762-X). Childrens.

Department of Geography, Lerner Publications. Egypt in Pictures. (Illus.). 64p. (gr. 5 up). 1988. PLB 12.95 (ISBN 0-8225-1840-6). Lerner Pubns.

Great Civilisations: Egypt. (ARA., Illus.). (gr. 5-12). 3. 50x (ISBN 0-86685-253-0). Intl Bk Ctr.

Harkonen, Reijo. The Children of Egypt. Pitkanen, Matti A., photos by. (Illus.). 40p. (gr. 3-6). 1991. PLB 14.95 (ISBN 0-87614-396-6). Carolrhoda Bks.

Lye, Keith. Take a Trip to Egypt. (Illus.). 32p. (gr. k-3). 1983. PLB 7.99 (ISBN 0-531-03758-4). Watts.

Odijk, Pamela. The Egyptians. (Illus.). 48p. (gr. 5-8). 1989. PLB 16.98 (ISBN 0-382-09886-2). Silver Burdett Pr.

Oliphant, Margaret. The Egyptian World. (Illus.). 96p. (gr. 5-12). 1989. PLB 14.90 (ISBN 0-531-19068-4). Watts.

Unstead, R. J. An Egyptian Town. rev. ed. LC 85-52285. (Illus.). (gr. 4-9). 1986. PLB 11.90 (ISBN 0-531-19012-9, Pub. by Warwick). Watts.

Ventura, Piero. Journey to Egypt. Ventura, Piero, illus. LC 86-40010. 1986. pap. 12.95 (ISBN 0-670-80099-6). Viking Child Bks.

Wilkins, Frances. Egypt. (Illus.). (gr. 5 up). 1988. 14.95 (ISBN 0-222-00925-X). Chelsea Hse.

Worth, Richard. Israel & the Arab States. 96p. (gr. 7 up). 1983. PLB 12.90 (ISBN 0-531-04545-5). Watts.

EGYPT–ANTIQUITIES

Bendick, Jeanne. Egyptians Tombs. (Illus.). 64p. (gr. 3-5). 1989. PLB 11.90 (ISBN 0-531-10462-1). Watts.

Gold, Susan D. Pharaohs Curse. LC 89-25424. (Illus.). 48p. (gr. 5 up). 1990. 10.95 (ISBN 0-89686-511-8, Crestwood Hse). Macmillan Child Grp.

Macaulay, David. Pyramid. Macaulay, David, illus. 80p. (gr. 7 up). 1975. 14.95 (ISBN 0-395-21407-6). HM.

Reiff, Stephanie A. Secrets of Tut's Tomb & the Pyramids. LC 77-22770. (Illus.). (gr. 4 up). 1983. PLB 17.32 (ISBN 0-8172-1051-2); pap. 9.27 (ISBN 0-8172-2166-2). Raintree Pubs.

Santrey, Laurence. Ancient Egypt. Frenck, Hal, illus. LC 84-2728. 32p. (gr. 3-6). 1985. PLB 9.49 (ISBN 0-8167-0248-9); pap. text ed. 2.95 (ISBN 0-8167-0249-7). Troll Assocs.

Smith, Tony, illus. The Great Pyramids & the Sphinx. 48p. (gr. 3-5). 1987. 5.95x (ISBN 0-86685-454-1). Intl Bk Ctr.

Stead, Miriam. Ancient Egypt. McBride, Angus & Thomas, Eric, illus. LC 85-80642. 32p. (gr. 5-7). 1985. PLB 11.90 (ISBN 0-531-17002-0, Gloucester Pr). Watts.

EGYPT–CIVILIZATION

Courtalon, Corinne. On the Banks of the Pharaoh's Nile. Broutin, Christian, illus. LC 87-37195. 38p. (gr. k-5). 1988. 4.95 (ISBN 0-944589-07-3, 073). Young Discovery Lib.

Donnelly, Judy. Tut's Mummy: Lost & Found. Watling, James, illus. LC 87-20790. (Orig.). (gr. 2-3). 1988. lib. bdg. 6.99 (ISBN 0-394-99189-3, Random Juv); pap. 2.95 (ISBN 0-394-89189-9). Random.

Hart, George. Ancient Egypt. Biesty, Stephen, illus. LC 88-30065. 64p. (gr. 5-8). 1989. 14.95 (ISBN 0-15-200449-1). HarBraceJ.

Millard, Anne. Egypt. Shone, Rob, illus. Franklin Watts Ltd., ed. (Illus.). 32p. (gr. 7-9). 1988. PLB 11.90 (ISBN 0-531-10537-7). Watts.

Purdy, Susan & Sandak, Cass R. Ancient Egypt. LC 82-6962. (Illus.). 32p. (gr. 4-6). 1982. PLB 9.90 (ISBN 0-531-04452-1). Watts.

Watson, Lucilla. The Egyptians. Wood, Gerry, illus. LC 86-20277. 24p. (gr. 1-3). 1987. PLB 14.00 (ISBN 0-86592-164-4). Rourke Corp.

EGYPT–FICTION

Bradshaw, Gillian. The Dragon & the Thief. LC 90-48259. (Illus.). (gr. 5 up). 1991. 13.95 (ISBN 0-688-10575-0). Greenwillow.

Carter, Dorothy S. His Majesty, Queen Hatshepsut. Chessare, Michele, illus. LC 85-45855. 256p. (gr. 5 up). 1987. 13.95 (ISBN 0-397-32178-3, Lipp Jr Bks); PLB 13.89 (ISBN 0-397-32179-1, Lipp Jr Bks). HarpC Child Bks.

Ellerby, Leona. King Tut's Game Board. LC 79-91279. 120p. (gr. 4 up). 1980. 9.95 (ISBN 0-8225-0765-X). Lerner Pubns.

Kalman, Maira. Hey Willy, See the Pyramids. (ps-3). 1988. pap. 14.95 (ISBN 0-670-82163-2). Viking Child Bks.

Lepon, Shoshana. The Ten Plagues of Egypt. Goldstein-Alpern, Neva, ed. Forst, Siegmund, illus. 32p. (gr. 4-8). 1988. 8.95 (ISBN 0-910818-77-0); pap. 6.95 (ISBN 0-910818-76-2). Judaica Pr.

Macaulay, David. Pyramid PA. Macaulay, David, illus. (gr. 5 up). 1982. pap. 6.95 (ISBN 0-395-32121-2). HM.

McGraw, Eloise J. Mara, Daughter of the Nile. LC 85-567. 280p. (gr. 5-9). 1985. pap. 3.95 (ISBN 0-14-031929-8, Puffin). Puffin Bks.

Peck, Richard. Blossom Culp & the Sleep of Death. LC 85-16188. 224p. (gr. 4-6). 1986. pap. 14.95 (ISBN 0-385-29433-6). Delacorte.

Snyder, Zilpha K. The Egypt Game. LC 67-2717. (gr. 4-6). 1986. pap. 3.50 (ISBN 0-440-42225-6, YB). Dell.

EGYPT–HISTORY

Ancient Egypt-Coloring Book. 1985. pap. 3.50 (ISBN 0-88388-005-9). Bellerophon Bks.

Burland, Cottie A. Ancient Egypt. (Illus.). (gr. 4-8). 1974. Repr. of 1957 ed. 8.95 (ISBN 0-7175-0014-4). Dufour.

Cohen, Daniel. Ancient Egypt. Lippincott, Gary A., illus. 48p. (gr. 2-6). 1990. 10.95 (ISBN 0-385-24586-6, Zephyr-BFYR); PLB 11.99 (ISBN 0-385-24587-4, Zephyr-BFYR). Doubleday.

Conway, Lorraine. Ancient Egypt. Akins, Linda, illus. 64p. (gr. 4-8). 1987. pap. 6.95 (ISBN 0-86653-399-0, GA 1021). Good Apple.

David, A. Rosalie. The Egyptian Kingdoms. LC 88-820. (Illus.). 160p. 1990. pap. 16.95 (ISBN 0-87226-230-8). P Bedrick Bks.

Giblin, James C. The Riddle of the Rosetta Stone: Key to Ancient Egypt. LC 89-29289. (Illus.). 96p. (gr. 3-7). 1990. 13.95 (ISBN 0-690-04797-5, Crowell Jr Bks); PLB 13.89 (ISBN 0-690-04799-1, Crowell Jr Bks). HarpC Child Bks.

Glubok, Shirley & Tamarin, Alfred. The Mummy of Ramose. LC 76-21392. (Illus.). 1978. PLB 11.89 (ISBN 0-06-022042-2). HarpC Child Bks.

Harper, et al. Flashpoints, 7 bks, Set I, Reading Level 8. (Illus.). 560p. (gr. 7 up). Date not set. Set. PLB 120.82 (ISBN 0-86592-025-7). Rourke Corp.

Harris, Geraldine. Ancient Egypt. (Illus.). 96p. 1990. 17. 95 (ISBN 0-8160-1971-1). Facts on File.

Kerr, James. Egyptian Farmers. (Illus.). 24p. (gr. 2-5). 1991. PLB 10.40 (ISBN 0-531-18374-2, Pub. by Bookwright Pr). Watts.

Langley, Andrew. Cleopatra & the Egyptians. LC 85-73586. (Illus.). 64p. (gr. 4-9). PLB 12.40 (ISBN 0-531-18079-4, Pub. by Bookwright). Watts.

Morley, Jacqueline. An Egyptian Pyramid: Inside Story. Bergin, Mark & James, John, illus. 48p. (gr. 5 up). 1991. 16.95 (ISBN 0-87226-346-0). P Bedrick Bks.

Payne, Elizabeth. The Pharaohs of Ancient Egypt. LC 80-21392. (Illus.). 192p. (gr. 5-9). 1981. pap. 4.95 (ISBN 0-394-84699-0). Random.

Watson, Lucilla. The Egyptians. Wood, Gerry, illus. LC 86-20277. 24p. (gr. 1-3). 1987. PLB 14.00 (ISBN 0-86592-164-4). Rourke Corp.

Woods, Geraldine. Science in Ancient Egypt. Rasof, Henry, ed. (Illus.). 96p. (gr. 5-8). 1988. PLB 10.40 (ISBN 0-531-10486-9). Watts.

EGYPT–KINGS AND RULERS

Payne, Elizabeth. The Pharaohs of Ancient Egypt. LC 80-21392. (Illus.). 192p. (gr. 5-9). 1981. pap. 4.95 (ISBN 0-394-84699-0). Random.

Rosen, Deborah N. Anwar el-Sadat: A Man of Peace. LC 86-9541. (Illus.). 152p. (gr. 4 up). 1986. PLB 17.27 (ISBN 0-516-03214-3). Childrens.

Sullivan, George. Sadat: The Man Who Changed Mid-East History. LC 81-50739. (Illus.). 99p. (gr. 6 up). 1981. reinforced bdg 9.85 (ISBN 0-8027-6435-5). Walker & Co.

EGYPTOLOGY

see Egypt–Antiquities

EIGHTEENTH CENTURY

Ruby, Jennifer. The Eighteenth Century. (gr. 7 up). 1989. 19.95 (ISBN 0-7134-5772-4, Pub. by Batsford England). Trafalgar Sq.

EINSTEIN, ALBERT, 1879-1955

Cwiklik, Robert. Albert Einstein. (Illus.). 144p. (gr. 3-6). 1987. pap. 4.95 (ISBN 0-8120-3921-1). Barron.

Dank, Milton. Albert Einstein. LC 82-23853. (Illus.). 128p. (gr. 7up). 1983. PLB 12.90 (ISBN 0-531-04587-0). Watts.

Einstein, Albert. Albert Einstein. Redpath, Ann, ed. Delessert, Etienne, illus. 32p. (gr. 9 up). 1986. PLB 10.45s.p. (ISBN 0-88682-011-1). Creative Ed.

Farr, Naunerle. Madame Curie - Albert Einstein. Leonidez, Nestor & Redondo, Nestor, illus. (gr. 4-12). 1979. pap. text ed. 2.95 (ISBN 0-88301-356-8); wkbk. 1.25 (ISBN 0-88301-380-0). Pendulum Pr.

Hammontree, Marie. Albert Einstein: Young Thinker. Doremus, Robert, illus. LC 86-10730. 192p. (gr. 2-6). 1986. pap. 3.95 (ISBN 0-02-041860-4, Aladdin). Macmillan Child Grp.

Hunter, Nigel. Einstein. LC 86-50823. (Illus.). 32p. (gr. 4-6). 1987. PLB 11.90 (ISBN 0-531-18092-1, Pub. by Bookwright Pr). Watts.

Ireland, Karin. Albert Einstein. (Illus.). 116p. (gr. 5-7). 1989. PLB 13.98 (ISBN 0-382-09523-5). Silver Burdett Pr.

Reef, Catherine. Albert Einstein. (Illus.). 64p. (gr. 3 up). 1991. PLB 10.95 (ISBN 0-87518-462-6, Dillon). Macmillan Child Grp.

Santrey, Laurence. Young Albert Einstein. Beier, Ellen, illus. LC 89-33940. 48p. (gr. 4-6). 1989. PLB 10.79 (ISBN 0-8167-1777-X); pap. text ed. 2.95 (ISBN 0-8167-1778-8). Troll Assocs.

Smith, Kathie B. Albert Einstein. Steltenpohl, Jane, ed. Seward, James, illus. 24p. (gr. 4-6). 1989. lib. bdg. 7.98 (ISBN 0-671-67514-1); PLB 5.99s.p. (ISBN 0-685-25426-7). Messner.

Smith, Kathie B. & Bradbury, Pamela Z. Albert Einstein. (Illus.). (ps up). 1989. pap. 2.25 (ISBN 0-671-64767-9, Little Simon). S&S Trade.

EISENHOWER, DWIGHT DAVID, PRESIDENT U. S. 1890-1969

Cannon, Marian G. Dwight David Eisenhower: War Hero & President. (gr. 4-7). 1990. PLB 13.90 (ISBN 0-531-10915-1). Watts.

Carpenter. Dwight D. Eisenhower, Reading Level 6. (Illus.). 112p. (gr. 4 up). Date not set. PLB 18.60 (ISBN 0-86625-328-9). Rourke Corp.

Carpenter, Allan. Dwight David Eisenhower...The Warring Peacemaker. (Illus.). 112p. (gr. 4-8). 1987. PLB 74.40 4 bk. set (ISBN 0-317-60502-X); PLB 18. 60 ea. (ISBN 0-317-60503-8). Rourke Corp.

Darby, Jean. Dwight D. Eisenhower. (Illus.). 112p. (gr. 5 up). 1989. 15.95 (ISBN 0-8225-4900-X). Lerner Pubns.

Deitch, Kenneth M. & Weisman, JoAnne B. Dwight D. Eisenhower: Man of Many Hats; With a Message from John S. D. Eisenhower. Connolly, Jay, illus. Eisenhower, John S., intro. by. LC 90-82588. (Illus.). 48p. (gr. 5-12). 1990. PLB 17.95 (ISBN 1-878668-02-1). Disc Enter Ltd.

Dwight David Eisenhower: President. 128p. (gr. 5 up). 1987. 12.95 (ISBN 0-8027-6670-6); PLB 13.85 (ISBN 0-8027-6671-4). Walker & Co.

Ellis, Rafaela. Dwight D. Eisenhower: Thirty-Fourth President of the United States. Young, Richard G., ed. LC 88-24538. (Illus.). (gr. 5-9). 1989. PLB 17.26 (ISBN 0-944483-13-5). Garrett Ed Corp.

Hargrove, Jim. Dwight D. Eisenhower. LC 86-29918. (Illus.). 100p. (gr. 3 up). 1987. PLB 17.27 (ISBN 0-516-01389-0). Childrens.

Sandberg, Peter L. Dwight D. Eisenhower. Schlesinger, Arthur M., Jr., intro. by. (Illus.). 112p. (gr. 5 up). 1986. side sewn 17.95 (ISBN 0-87754-521-9); pap. 9.95 (ISBN 0-7910-0566-6). Chelsea Hse.

Vexler, Robert I. Dwight D. Eisenhower, 1890-1969: Chronology, Documents, Bibliographical Aids. LC 71-95014. 150p. (gr. 9 up). 1970. PLB 10.00 (ISBN 0-379-12070-4). Oceana.

EL SALVADOR

see Salvador

ELECTIONEERING

see Politics, Practical

ELECTIONS

see also Presidents–U. S.–Election

Archer, Jules. Winners & Losers: How Elections Work in America. LC 83-18368. (Illus.). 240p. (gr. 7-12). 1984. 14.95 (ISBN 0-15-297945-X, HJ). HarBraceJ.

Dunnahoo, Terry. How to Win a School Election. Rosenbloom, Richard, illus. 96p. (gr. 10-12). 1990. 12. 40 (ISBN 0-531-10695-0). Watts.

Fradin, Dennis B. Voting & Elections. LC 85-7715. (Illus.). 45p. (gr. k-4). 1985. PLB 14.60 (ISBN 0-516-01274-6); pap. 4.95 (ISBN 0-516-41274-4). Childrens.

Greenberg, Judith & Carey, Helen. Election Special. (gr. 7-12). 1988. Set incl. 10 texts & 1 tchr's. guide (updated annually) pap. text ed. 24.95 (ISBN 0-941342-18-2). Entry Pub.

Modl, Tom, ed. America's Elections: Opposing Viewpoints. LC 87-36788. (Illus.). (gr. 10 up). 1988. lib. bdg. 15.95 (ISBN 0-89908-433-8); pap. text ed. 8.95 (ISBN 0-89908-408-7). Greenhaven.

Priestly, E. J. Finding Out about Elections. (Illus.). 72p. (gr. 7-12). 1983. 19.95 (ISBN 0-7134-3666-2, Pub. by Batsford). Trafalgar Sq.

ELECTIONS–FICTION

Hughes, Dean. Nutty for President. 128p. 1986. pap. 2.50 (ISBN 0-553-15376-5, Skylark). Bantam.

Littke, Lael. Trish for President. LC 84-4587. 160p. (gr. 7 up). 1984. 13.95 (ISBN 0-15-290512-X, HJ). HarBraceJ.

Schulz, Charles M. You're Not Elected, Charlie Brown. (Illus.). (ps up). 1974. Random.

ELECTORAL COLLEGE

see Presidents–U. S.–Election

ELECTRIC APPLIANCES

see Electric Apparatus and Appliances

ELECTRIC APPARATUS AND APPLIANCES

Asimov, Isaac. How Did We Find about Microwaves? Kors, Erika, illus. 64p. (gr. 1-4). 1989. 11.95 (ISBN 0-8027-6837-7); PLB 12.85 (ISBN 0-8027-6838-5). Walker & Co.

ELECTRIC ENGINEERING

see also Electric Apparatus and Appliances; Radio; Telephone

ELECTRIC POWER

Berger, Melvin. Switch On, Switch Off. Croll, Carolyn, illus. LC 88-17638. 32p. (gr. k-3). 1989. (Crowell Jr Bks); PLB 13.89 (ISBN 0-690-04786-X, Crowell Jr. Bks). HarpC Child Bks.

Cobb, Vicki. More Power to You! Ogden, Bill, illus. 64p. (gr. 3-5). 1986. lib. bdg. 11.95 (ISBN 0-316-14899-7). Little.

ELECTRIC WIRING

see also Telephone

ELECTRICAL

see headings beginning with the word Electric

ELECTRICITY

see also Lightning; Magnetism; Radioactivity; Telephone

Amery, H. & Littler, A. The KnowHow Book of Batteries & Magnets: Safe & Simple Experiments, Models & Games. (Illus.). 32p. (gr. 3-6). 1977. pap. 5.95 (ISBN 0-86020-008-6). EDC.

Asimov, Isaac. How Did We Find Out About Electricity? Selsam, Millicent E., ed. Kalmenoff, Matthew, illus. LC 72-81380. 64p. (gr. 5-8). 1973. PLB 10.85 (ISBN 0-8027-6124-0). Walker & Co.

Bailey, Mark W. Electricity. rev. ed. LC 87-20796. (Illus.). 48p. (gr. 2-6). 1988. PLB 17.32 (ISBN 0-8172-3253-2); pap. 9.27 (ISBN 0-8172-3278-8). Raintree Pubs.

Bains, Rae. Discovering Electricity. Snyder, Joel, illus. LC 81-3339. 32p. (gr. 2-4). 1982. PLB 10.89 (ISBN 0-89375-564-8); pap. text ed. 2.95 (ISBN 0-89375-565-6). Troll Assocs.

Berger, Melvin. Switch On, Switch Off. Croll, Carolyn, illus. LC 88-17638. 32p. (gr. k-3). 1989. (Crowell Jr Bks); PLB 13.89 (ISBN 0-690-04786-X, Crowell Jr. Bks). HarpC Child Bks.

—Switch on, Switch Off. Croll, Carolyn, illus. LC 88-17638. 32p. (gr. k-3). 1990. pap. 4.50 (ISBN 0-06-445097-X, Trophy). HarpC Child Bks.

Boltz, C. W. How Electricity Is Made. (Illus.). 32p. (gr. 7 up). 12.95 (ISBN 0-8160-0039-5). Facts on File.

Bortz, Alfred B. Superstuff! Materials That Have Changed Our Lives. (Illus.). 128p. (gr. 9-12). 1990. PLB 12.40 (ISBN 0-531-10887-2). Watts.

Boy Scouts of America Staff. Electricity. rev. ed. LC 89-3236. (Illus.). 48p. (gr. 6-12). 1989. pap. 1.85 (ISBN 0-8395-3206-7, 3206). BSA.

Brandt, Keith. Electricity. Harriton, Chuck, illus. LC 84-2705. 32p. (gr. 3-6). 1985. PLB 9.49 (ISBN 0-8167-0198-9); pap. text ed. 2.95 (ISBN 0-8167-0199-7). Troll Assocs.

Brill, Ethel C. Copper Country Adventure. LC 87-31485. 213p. (gr. 4 up). 1988. 8.50 (ISBN 0-933249-05-5). Mid-Peninsula Lib.

Buban, Peter & Schmitt, Marshall L. Understanding Electricity & Electronics. 3rd ed. 1974. text ed. 28.32 (ISBN 0-07-008675-3, W). McGraw.

Cash, Terry. Electricity & Magnets. Chen, Kuo K. & Bull, Peter, illus. 40p. (gr. 5-6). 1989. PLB 12.90 (ISBN 0-531-19063-3). Watts.

Challand, Helen. Experiments with Electricity. LC 85-30887. (Illus.). 48p. (gr. k-4). 1986. PLB 14.60 (ISBN 0-516-01276-2); pap. 4.95 (ISBN 0-516-41276-0). Childrens.

Chapman, Phil. Electricity. (gr. 5-9). 1976. (Usborne-Hayes); PLB 13.96 (ISBN 0-88110-006-4); pap. 6.95 (ISBN 0-86020-078-7). EDC.

Cosner, Shaaron. The Light Bulb: Inventions That Changed Our Lives. LC 83-40398. 64p. (gr. 5 up). 1984. PLB 10.85 (ISBN 0-8027-6527-0). Walker & Co.

Electricity. 32p. (Orig.). (gr. 1-3). 1988. pap. 2.95 (ISBN 0-8431-4259-6). Price Stern.

Gutnik, Martin J. Electricity: From Faraday to Solar Generators. LC 86-11130. (Illus.). 96p. (gr. 4-9). 1986. PLB 10.40 (ISBN 0-531-10222-X). Watts.

—Simple Electrical Devices. LC 85-26369. (Illus.). 72p. (gr. 4-9). 1986. PLB 10.40 (ISBN 0-531-10127-4). Watts.

Jennings, Terry. Electricity & Magnetism. LC 88-36215. (Illus.). 32p. (gr. 3-6). 1989. PLB 14.60 (ISBN 0-516-08437-2); pap. 4.95 (ISBN 0-516-48437-0). Childrens.

Johnston, Tom. Electricity Turns the World On! Pooley, Sarah, illus. LC 87-42655. 32p. (gr. 4-6). 1987. PLB 10.95 (ISBN 1-55532-410-X). Gareth Stevens Inc.

Jugendhandbuch Naturwissen: Elektrizitaet und Elektronic, Vol. 6. (GER.). 144p. 1976. pap. 5.95 (ISBN 3-499-16208-3, M-7491, Pub. by Rowohlt). French & Eur.

Jugendhandbuch Naturwissen: Energie, Vol. 5. (GER.). 128p. 1976. pap. 5.95 (ISBN 3-499-16207-5, M-7490, Pub. by Rowohlt). French & Eur.

Lillegard, Dee & Stoker, Wayne. I Can Be an Electrician. LC 86-9657. (Illus.). 32p. (gr. k-3). 1986. PLB 13.93 (ISBN 0-516-01896-5). Childrens.

Mackie, Dan. Electricity. Goshorn, Bill, ed. Bastien, Charles, illus. 32p. (gr. 4). 1986. PLB 14.65 (ISBN 0-88625-133-8); pap. 4.95 (ISBN 0-685-30764-6). Durkin Hayes Pub.

Magnets, Bulbs, Batteries. (ARA., Illus.). (gr. 5-12). 3.50x (ISBN 0-86685-206-9). Intl Bk Ctr.

Markle, Sandra. Weather, Electricity, Environmental Investigations. 112p. (gr. 4-6). 1982. 9.95 (ISBN 0-88160-082-2, LW 902). Learning Wks.

Math, Irwin. More Wires & Watts: Understanding & Using Electricity. Keith, Hal, illus. LC 88-15767. 96p. (gr. 7 up). 1988. 14.95 (ISBN 0-684-18914-3, Scribners Young Read). Macmillan Child Grp.

—Wires & Watts: Understanding & Using Electricity. Keith, Hal, illus. LC 88-15767. 96p. (gr. 7 up). 1981. 14.95 (ISBN 0-684-16854-5, Scribners Young Read). Macmillan Child Grp.

—Wires & Watts: Using & Understanding Electricity. Math, Irwin, illus. 96p. (gr. 7 up). 1989. pap. 4.95 (ISBN 0-689-71298-7, Aladdin). Macmillan Child Grp.

Mayes, S. Where Does Electricity Come From? (Illus.). 24p. (gr. 1-4). 1989. lib. bdg. 11.96 (ISBN 0-88110-380-2, Usborne); pap. 3.95 (ISBN 0-7460-0358-7, Usborne). EDC.

Neal, Philip. Energy, Power Sources & Electricity. (Illus.). 48p. (gr. 6-9). 1989. 19.95 (ISBN 0-85219-776-4, Pub. by Batsford England). Trafalgar Sq.

Pomeroy, Johanna P. Content Area Reading Skills Electricity & Magnetism. (Illus.). (gr. 4). 1987. pap. text ed. 3.25 (ISBN 0-89525-859-5). Ed Activities.

Reuben, Gabriel. Electricity Experiments for Children. (Illus.). 88p. (gr. 5-9). pap. 2.95 (ISBN 0-486-22030-3). Dover.

Sanchez, Jesus A. Max Science & the Burned Out Bulb. Sanchez, Brenda L., ed. Sanchez, Jesus A., illus. 24p. (gr. k-5). 1990. pap. 3.95 (ISBN 1-879350-00-9). Max Sci Pub.

Sneider, Cary I., et al. The Magic of Electricity. Bergman, Lincoln & Fairwell, Kay, eds. Sneider, Cary I. & Baker, Lisa H., illus. Sneider, Cary I., photos by. 50p. (Orig.). (gr. 3-6). 1985. pap. 10.00 (ISBN 0-912511-52-4). Lawrence Science.

Swertka, Albert. Superconductors: The Irresistible Future. (Illus.). 96p. (gr. 7-9). 1991. PLB 12.40 (ISBN 0-531-12526-2). Watts.

Taylor, Barbara. Batteries & Magnets. (Illus.). 40p. (gr. k-4). 1991. PLB 11.90 (ISBN 0-531-19130-3, Warwick). Watts.

—Electricity & Magnets. (Illus.). 32p. (gr. 5-8). 1990. PLB 11.40 (ISBN 0-531-14083-0). Watts.

Vogt, Gregory. Electricity & Magnetism. LC 85-10565. (Illus.). 84p. (gr. 5-8). 1985. PLB 10.40 (ISBN 0-531-10038-3). Watts.

—Generating Electricity. LC 85-20202. (Illus.). 72p. (gr. 4-9). 1986. PLB 10.40 (ISBN 0-531-10117-7). Watts.

Ward, Alan. Experimenting with Batteries, Bulbs, & Wires. (Illus.). 48p. (gr. 4-6). 1986. 19.95 (ISBN 0-85219-629-6, Pub. by Batsford England). Trafalgar Sq.

Whyman, Kathryn. Electricity & Magnetism. (Illus.). 32p. (gr. k-6). 1986. PLB 8.99 (ISBN 0-531-17020-9, Gloucester Pr). Watts.

Zubrowski, Bernie. Blinkers & Buzzers: Building & Experimenting with Electricity & Magnetism. Doty, Roy, illus. LC 90-44519. 112p. (gr. 3 up). 1991. pap. 6.95 (ISBN 0-688-09965-3, Pub. by Beech Tree Bks). Morrow.

—Blinkers & Buzzers: Building & Experimenting with Electricity & Magnetism. Doty, Roy, illus. LC 90-44519. 112p. (gr. 3 up). 1991. PLB 12.88 (ISBN 0-688-09966-1). Morrow Jr Bks.

ELECTRICITY–FICTION

Branley, Franklyn M. & Vaughan, Eleanor K. Rusty Rings a Bell. Galdone, Paul, illus. LC 57-7492. (gr. k-3). 1961. (Crowell Jr Bks). HarpC Child Bks.

ELECTROMAGNETISM

Branley, Franklyn M. The Electromagnetic Spectrum: Key to the Universe. Dank, Leonard D., illus. LC 77-26591. (gr. 7 up). 1980. 12.95 (ISBN 0-690-03868-2, Crowell Jr Bks). HarpC Child Bks.

ELECTRONIC COMPUTERS

see Computers

ELECTRONIC DATA PROCESSING

Hellman, Hal. Computer Basics. Tvaryanas, Alphonse, illus. LC 82-21483. 48p. (gr. 3-7). 1983. 9.95 (ISBN 0-13-164574-9). P-H.

ELECTRONIC SPREADSHEETS

Luehrmann, Arthur & Peckham, Herbert. Appleworks Spreadsheets: A Hands-On Guide. (Illus.). 160p. (Orig.). (gr. 7-12). 1987. pap. text ed. 9.25 (ISBN 0-941681-05-X); tchr's. set 18.50 (ISBN 0-941681-12-2). Computer Lit Pr.

—Hands-on Appleworks: A Guide to Word Processing, Data Bases & Spreadsheets. LC 87-836. (Illus.). 478p. (Orig.). (gr. 7-12). 1987. pap. text ed. 19.95 (ISBN 0-941681-07-6); tchr's. set 29.95 (ISBN 0-941681-13-0). Computer Lit Pr.

ELECTRONICS

see also Microelectronics; Transistors

Beasant, Pam & Findly, Ian. Introduction to Electronics. Newton, Martin & Andrews, Jane, illus. 48p. (gr. 5-8). 1985. PLB 13.96 (ISBN 0-88110-218-0, Pub. by Usborne); pap. 6.95 (ISBN 0-86020-809-5). EDC.

The Boy Mechanic, Bk. 1. 470p. 29.95 (ISBN 0-917914-89-9); pap. 17.95 (ISBN 0-917914-88-0). Lindsay Pubns.

Boy Scouts of America. Electronics. (Illus.). 72p. (gr. 6-12). 1977. pap. 1.85 (ISBN 0-8395-3279-2, 3279). BSA.

Buban, Peter & Schmitt, Marshall L. Understanding Electricity & Electronics. 3rd ed. 1974. text ed. 28.32 (ISBN 0-07-008675-3, W). McGraw.

Carter, Alden R. & LeBlanc, Wayne J. Modern Electronics. LC 86-5673. (Illus.). 96p. (gr. 4-9). 1986. PLB 10.40 (ISBN 0-531-10218-1). Watts.

Electronic Office. 1990. 12.95 (ISBN 0-8239-0973-5). Rosen Group.

Encyclopedia of Computers & Electronics. (Illus.). 144p. (gr. 4 up). 1989. Repr. 14.95 (ISBN 0-02-689200-6). Checkerboard Pr.

How Things Work. (Illus.). 88p. (ps-3). 1989. 15.93 (ISBN 0-8094-4873-4); lib. bdg. 21.27 (ISBN 0-8094-4874-2). Time-Life.

Jugendhandbuch Naturwissen: Bausteine des Lebens, 6 vols, Vol. 1. (GER.). 144p. pap. 750.00 (ISBN 3-499-16203-2, M-7486, Pub. by Rowohlt). French & Eur.

Jugendhandbuch Naturwissen: Elektrizitaet und Elektronic, Vol. 6. (GER.). 144p. 1976. pap. 5.95 (ISBN 3-499-16208-3, M-7491, Pub. by Rowohlt). French & Eur.

McPherson, J. G. Fun with Electronics. 64p. (gr. 3-6). 1983. pap. 4.95 (ISBN 0-86020-525-8); lib. bdg. 11.96 (ISBN 0-88110-160-5). EDC.

Tatchell & Cutter, N. Practical Things to Do with a Microcomputer. Round, Graham, illus. 48p. (gr. 6 up). 1983. pap. 3.95 (ISBN 0-86020-731-5); PLB 10.96 (ISBN 0-88110-140-0). EDC.

ELECTRONICS–VOCATIONAL GUIDANCE

Groneman, Chris H. & Feirer, John L. Getting Started in Electricity & Electronics. LC 78-19120. (Illus.). (gr. 7-9). 1979. text ed. 9.52 (ISBN 0-07-024999-7). McGraw.

Larned, Phyllis. Johnny at the Circuits. (Illus.). 40p. (gr. 7-12). 1977. pap. text ed. 2.65 (ISBN 0-915510-20-0). Janus Bks.

ELEMENTARY EDUCATION

see Education, Elementary

ELEPHANTS

Aliki. Wild & Woolly Mammoths. LC 76-18082. (Illus.). 40p. (ps-3). 1983. pap. 4.50 (ISBN 0-06-445005-8, Trophy). HarpC Child Bks.

Barrett, N. S. Elephants. FS Staff, ed. (Illus.). 32p. (gr. 1-6). 1988. PLB 11.40 (ISBN 0-531-10528-8). Watts.

Barrett, Norman. Picture Library: Elephants. 1990. pap. 3.95 (ISBN 0-531-15204-9). Watts.

Bright, Michael. Elephants. (ps-3). 1990. PLB 11.90 (ISBN 0-531-17215-5). Watts.

The Elephant Family. Date not set. write for info. W J Fantasy.

Elephants. (Illus.). 32p. (gr. 2-6). 1989. pap. 4.95 (ISBN 0-14-034175-7, Puffin). Puffin Bks.

Goodall, Jane. Jane Goodall's Animal World: Elephants. 32p. (gr. 3-7). 1990. pap. 3.95 (ISBN 0-689-71395-9, Aladdin). Macmillan Child Grp.

Green, Carl R. & Sanford, William R. Asiatic Elephant. LC 87-20200. (Illus.). 48p. (gr. 5-6). 1987. PLB 10.95 (ISBN 0-89686-333-6, Crestwood Hse). Macmillan Child Grp.

Harrison, Virginia. The World of Elephants. Oxford Scientific Films Staff, photos by. LC 89-11547. (Illus.). 32p. (gr. 2-3). 1989. PLB 10.95 (ISBN 0-8368-0141-5). Gareth Stevens Inc.

Hoffman, Mary. Elephant. LC 84-15119. (Illus.). 24p. (gr. k-5). 1985. PLB 13.32 (ISBN 0-8172-2408-4). Raintree Pubs.

Hogan, Paula Z. The Elephant. Craft, Kinuko Y., illus. LC 79-13307. (gr. 1-4). 1979. PLB 27.99 incl. cassette (ISBN 0-8172-1844-0); PLB 16.67 (ISBN 0-8172-1505-0). Raintree Pubs.

Lavine & Scuro. Wonders of Elephants. 1980. 9.95 (ISBN 0-396-07708-0, Putnam). Putnam Pub Group.

Martin, L. Elephants. (Illus.). 24p. (gr. k-5). Date not set. PLB 11.93 (ISBN 0-86592-998-X). Rourke Corp.

Michel, Anna. Little Wild Elephant. Parnall, Peter & Parnall, Virginia, illus. LC 78-18407. (gr. 1-4). 1979. Pantheon.

Naden, C. J. I Can Read About Elephants. LC 78-65834. (Illus.). (gr. 2-5). 1979. pap. 1.95 (ISBN 0-89375-208-8). Troll Assocs.

Overbeck, Cynthia. Elephants. LC 80-27550. (Illus.). 48p. (gr. 4-10). 1981. PLB 14.95 (ISBN 0-8225-1452-4). Lerner Pubns.

Petty, Kate. Elephants. (ps-3). 1990. PLB 10.40 (ISBN 0-531-17194-9). Watts.

Pfeffer, Pierre. Elephants: Big, Strong & Wise. Matthews, Sarah, tr. from FRE. Mettler, Rene, illus. LC 87-33995. 38p. (gr. k-5). 1988. 4.95 (ISBN 0-944589-04-9, 049). Young Discovery Lib.

Posell, Elsa. Elephants. LC 81-38470. (Illus.). 48p. (gr. k-4). 1982. PLB 14.60 (ISBN 0-516-01621-0). Childrens.

Redmond, Ian. The Elephant in the Bush. Oxford Scientific Films Staff, photos by. LC 89-11297. (Illus.). 32p. (gr. 4-6). 1989. PLB 10.95 (ISBN 0-8368-0116-4). Gareth Stevens Inc.

Rothaus, Jim. Elephants. 24p. (gr. 3). 1988. 17.10 (ISBN 0-88682-226-2); PLB 11.95s.p. (ISBN 0-318-37907-4). Creative Ed.

Schlein, Miriam. Jane Goodall's Animal World: Elephants. Goodall, Jane, intro. by. LC 89-38551. (Illus.). 32p. (gr. 3-7). 1990. 11.95 (ISBN 0-689-31468-X, Atheneum Child Bk). Macmillan Child Grp.

Taylor, Dave. The Elephant & the Scrub Forest. (Illus.). 32p. (gr. 3-4). 1990. lib. bdg. 14.95 (ISBN 0-86505-365-0); pap. 7.95 (ISBN 0-86505-395-2). Crabtree Pub Co.

Mama Tembo, a wise old female elephant, leads her herd from the scrub forest to the rain forest in search of salt licks. The elephants cross the vast, open savannah & meet an incredible variety of animals. Your students will learn about the highly intelligent & affectionate elephants, their fascinating method of communication & the many ways in which they use their trunks! They will also discover the sad plight of these gentle giants as herd populations continue to decline at the hands of unscrupulous poachers. The dynamic, complex relationship between an animal & its habitat is the focus of The Animals & Their Ecosystems Series. Other books in the series include LION & THE SAVANNAH, BISON & THE GREAT PLAINS, & ALLIGATOR & THE EVERGLADES. Dramatic photographs & lively text portray the exciting daily struggle for survival. Each book takes an intimate look at the adventures of a single animal, following it through the important stages of life. The other animals that share the same ecosystem are also highlighted.

Publisher Provided Annotation.

Wax, Wendy & Rowland, Della. Ten Things I Know about Elephants. Payne, Thomas, illus. 24p. 1990. 6.95 (ISBN 0-8092-4302-4, Calico Bks). Contemp Bks.

Wildlife Education, Ltd. Staff. Elephants. Hoopes, Barbara, et al, illus. 20p. (Orig.). (gr. 5 up). 1980. pap. 2.25 (ISBN 0-937934-00-3). Wildlife Educ.

ELEPHANTS–FICTION

Avery, Gillian. The Elephant War. (gr. k-6). 1988. pap. 4.95 (ISBN 0-440-40040-6, Pub by Yearning Classics). Dell.

Awdry, W. Henry & the Elephant: Based on the Railway Series. Bell, Owain, illus. LC 89-62528. 32p. (Orig.). (ps-3). 1990. pap. 1.25 (ISBN 0-679-80408-0). McKay.

—Thomas & the Hide-&-Seek Animals: A Thomas the Tank Engine Flap Book. Bell, Owain, illus. LC 90-62114. 24p. (ps-1). 1991. 7.95 (ISBN 0-679-81316-0). Random.

—Thomas Visits a Farm. Bell, Owain, illus. 10p. (ps). 1991. vinyl 3.95 (ISBN 0-679-81580-5). Random.

Babar au Cirque. (gr. 2-3). pap. 5.95 (ISBN 0-685-33966-1, FC241). French & Eur.

Babar Compeur. 4.95 (ISBN 0-685-33973-4). French & Eur.

Babar et la Vieille Dame. (gr. 2-3). pap. 4.95 (ISBN 0-685-33968-8, FC254). French & Eur.

Barnes, Jill & Teramura, Terua. Elephant Rescue. Rubin, Caroline, ed. Japan Foreign Rights Centre Staff, tr. from JPN. Murakami, Tsutomu, illus. LC 90-37750. 40p. (gr. k-3). 1990. PLB 14.60 (ISBN 0-944483-85-2). Garrett Ed Corp.

Bartlett, Jaye. Freddy the Elephant: The Story of a Sensitive Leader. Dubina, Alan, illus. 45p. (Orig.). (ps up). 1991. pap. 11.95 incl. cassette (ISBN 1-878064-01-0). New Age CT.

Freddy doesn't like himself. He is chubby & can't move very fast. His mentor, Gran-Fada, King of all the Elephants, recognizes Freddy's potential, & encourages Freddy with his majestic understanding. As Freddy grows & learns to accept himself, hope triumphs over low self-esteem. Every child & adult will identify with Freddy's many trials & tribulations, & will cherish the memory of their own "sensitive leader."

Publisher Provided Annotation.

Beittel, Kenneth R. & Beittel, Joan N. Ralph & Deno in Vermont. Beittel, Kenneth R., illus. LC 90-86028. 32p. (Orig.). (gr. 5 up). 1990. pap. 6.00 (ISBN 0-9628511-0-8). HVHA.

Bos, Burny. Ollie the Elephant. De Beer, Hans, illus. LC 89-42608. 32p. (gr. k-3). 1989. 13.95 (ISBN 1-55858-012-3). North-South Bks NYC.

Broker, Loretta. Ellie the Elephant. Meyer, Jacque S., illus. 28p. (Orig.). (ps-k). 1990. pap. 2.95 (ISBN 0-916109-09-7). Summers Pub.

Brunhoff, Jean de. A. B. C. de Babar. new ed. 46p. 1978. 15.95 (ISBN 0-686-54120-0, M11808). French & Eur.

—Babar en Famille. 26p. 1975. 15.95 (ISBN 0-686-54122-7, FC589). French & Eur.

—Babar et le Crocodile. 16p. 1975. 4.95 (ISBN 0-686-54123-5, FC242). French & Eur.

—Babar et le Pere Noel. 29p. 1975. 15.95 (ISBN 0-686-54124-3, FC582). French & Eur.

—Barbar au Cirque. (Illus.). 16p. 1974. 4.95 (ISBN 0-686-54121-9, FC241). French & Eur.

—Le Couronnement de Babar. 16p. 1975. 4.95 (ISBN 0-686-54126-X, FC251). French & Eur.

—L' Enfance de Babar. 16p. 1975. 4.95 (ISBN 0-686-54127-8). French & Eur.

—Histoire de Babar, le Petite Elephant. (Illus.). 16p. 25.00 (ISBN 0-686-54129-4, FC593). French & Eur.

—Vive le Roi Babar. 20p. 1976. 4.95 (ISBN 0-686-54131-6, FC253). French & Eur.

—Le Voyage de Babar. 27p. 1975. 15.95 (ISBN 0-686-54132-4, FC581). French & Eur.

Brunhoff, Laurent de. L' Anniversaire de Babar. 28p. 1975. 15.95 (ISBN 0-686-54133-2, M11806). French & Eur.

—Les Aventures de Babar. 18p. 1977. 15.95 (ISBN 0-686-54134-0). French & Eur.

—Babar a Celesteville. 16p. 1974. 4.95 (ISBN 0-686-54135-9, F12062). French & Eur.

—Babar aux Sports d'Hiver. (Illus.). 20p. 1976. 4.95 (ISBN 0-686-54136-7, FC250). French & Eur.

—Babar Aviateur. 16p. 1974. 4.95 (ISBN 0-686-54137-5, M5989). French & Eur.

—Babar Campeur. 16p. 1974. 4.95 (ISBN 0-686-54138-3). French & Eur.

—Babar dans l'Ile aux Oiseaux. 29p. 15.95 (ISBN 0-686-54139-1, F2002). French & Eur.

—Babar en Amerique. 23p. 1975. 15.95 (ISBN 0-686-54140-5). French & Eur.

—Babar et le Docteur. 16p. 1975. 4.95 (ISBN 0-686-54141-3). French & Eur.

—Babar et le Wouly-Wouly. 26p. 15.95 (ISBN 0-686-54142-1, M11805). French & Eur.

—Babar et Sa Famille. 26p. 1976. 4.95 (ISBN 0-686-54143-X). French & Eur.

—Babar Patissier. 16p. 1975. 4.95 (ISBN 0-686-54144-8). French & Eur.

Carpenter. Elephants Don't Bounce. write for info. HM.

Carrick, Carol. The Elephant. Carrick, Donald, illus. write for info. (Clarion Bks). HM.

—The Elephant in the Dark. Carrick, Donald, photos by. write for info. (Clarion Bks). HM.

—The Elephant in the Dark. Carrick, Donald, illus. LC 88-2591. 144p. (gr. 3-7). 1988. 13.95 (ISBN 0-89919-757-4, Pub. by Clarion). Ticknor & Fields.

—Elephant in the Dark. (gr. 4-7). 1990. pap. 2.75 (ISBN 0-590-42995-7). Scholastic Inc.

Cole, Joanna. Aren't You Forgetting Something, Fiona? Delaney, Ned, illus. LC 83-13457. 48p. (ps-3). 1984. 5.95 (ISBN 0-8193-1121-9). Parents.

Cristaldi, Kathryn. Babar in the Jungle. Fritz, Ronald, illus. LC 88-63342. 32p. (Orig.). (ps-3). 1989. pap. 1.25 (ISBN 0-679-80215-0, Random Juv). Random.

Davidar, E. R. & Joshi, Jagadish. The Runaway Elephant Calf. (Illus.). 24p. (Orig.). (gr. k-3). 1980. pap. 2.75 (ISBN 0-89744-216-4, Pub. by Children's Bk Trust India). Auromere.

Day, Alexandra. Frank & Ernest Play Ball. Day, Alexandra, illus. LC 89-10312. (gr. k-3). 1990. 12.95 (ISBN 0-590-42548-X). Scholastic Inc.

De Brunhoff, Jean. Babar & Father Christmas. De Brunhoff, Jean, illus. Ustinov, Peter, narrated by. LC 40-31350. (Illus.). 48p. (ps up). 1989. pap. 9.95 incl. cassette (ISBN 0-394-84754-7). Random.

—Babar & His Children. Haas, Merle, tr. (Illus.). (ps). 1969. 8.95 (ISBN 0-394-80577-1, Random Juv); lib. bdg. 8.99 (ISBN 0-394-90577-6). Random.

—Babar & His Children. facsimile ed. De Brunhoff, Jean, illus. 48p. 1989. 16.95 (ISBN 0-679-80165-0, Random Juv). Random.

—Babar the King. De Brunhoff, Jean, illus. LC 85-30273. 48p. (ps up). 1989. pap. 4.95 (ISBN 0-394-82938-7, Dragonfly Bks). Knopf.

Debrunhoff, Jean. Babar the King. 1937. 9.95 (ISBN 0-394-80580-1). Random.

De Brunhoff, Jean. Meet Babar & His Family. (Illus.). (ps-1). 1973. pap. 2.25 (ISBN 0-394-82682-5, Random Juv). Random.

—El Rey Babar. (SPA.). 7.50 (ISBN 0-685-31014-0). Santillana.

—The Story of Babar. (Illus.). (ps). 1937. 9.95 (ISBN 0-394-80575-5, Random Juv); PLB 10.99 (ISBN 0-394-90575-X). Random.

—The Story of Babar. De Brunhoff, Jean, illus. 48p. (ps-1). 1984. Oversized Facsimile ed. 18.95 (ISBN 0-394-86823-4, Random Juv). Random.

—The Story of Babar. De Brunhoff, Jean, illus. LC 84-3308. 48p. (ps up). 1989. pap. 4.95 (ISBN 0-394-82940-9, Dragonfly Bks). Knopf.

—Travels of Babar. (Illus.). (ps). 1967. 9.95 (ISBN 0-394-80576-3, Random Juv); lib. bdg. 7.99 (ISBN 0-394-90576-8). Random.

—The Travels of Babar. De Brunhoff, Jean, illus. LC 85-2236. 48p. (ps up). 1985. 18.95 (ISBN 0-394-87453-6, Random Juv). Random.

—The Travels of Babar. De Brunhoff, Jean, illus. LC 85-2236. 48p. (ps up). 1989. pap. 4.95 (ISBN 0-394-82939-5, Dragonfly Bks). Knopf.

—Le Voyage de Babar. (FRE & SPA., Illus.). bds. 15.95 (ISBN 0-685-11626-3). French & Eur.

De Brunhoff, Laurent. Babar a la Mer. (FRE.). (gr. 2-3). 4.95 (ISBN 0-685-11023-0). French & Eur.

—Babar a New York. (Illus.). (gr. 4-6). bds. 15.95 (ISBN 0-685-11024-9). French & Eur.

—Babar & the Ghost: An Easy-to-Read Version: A Step Two Book. De Brunhoff, Laurent, illus. LC 85-11841. 48p. (gr. 1-3). 1986. lib. bdg. 6.99 (ISBN 0-394-97908-7); pap. 2.95 (ISBN 0-394-87908-2). Random.

—Babar Artiste Peintre. (FRE.). (gr. 2-3). 4.95 (ISBN 0-685-28424-7). French & Eur.

—Babar Chez le Docteur. (FRE.). (gr. 2-3). 4.95 (ISBN 0-685-28425-5). French & Eur.

—Babar en Ballon. (FRE.). (gr. 2-3). 4.95 (ISBN 0-685-28422-0). French & Eur.

—Babar en Promenade. (FRE.). (gr. 2-3). 4.95 (ISBN 0-685-11026-5). French & Eur.

—Babar et ce coquin d'Arthur. (FRE., Illus.). (gr. 4-6). bds. 15.95 (ISBN 0-685-11027-3). French & Eur.

—Babar et le Prof. Grifaton. (FRE.). (gr. 2-4). 15.95 (ISBN 0-685-28434-4). French & Eur.

—Babar et ses Enfants. (FRE.). (gr. 2-3). 4.95 (ISBN 0-685-28436-0). French & Eur.

—Babar Fait Du Ski. (FRE.). (gr. 2-3). 4.95 (ISBN 0-685-11029-X). French & Eur.

—Babar Jardinier. (FRE.). (gr. 2-3). 4.95 (ISBN 0-685-11030-3). French & Eur.

—Babar Loses His Crown. De Brunhoff, L., illus. LC 67-21918. 72p. (gr. k-3). 1967. 3.95 (ISBN 0-394-80045-1); lib. bdg. 7.99 (ISBN 0-394-90045-6). Beginner.

—Babar Visits Another Planet. (Illus.). (ps-2). 1972. (Random Juv); PLB 13.99 (ISBN 0-394-92429-0). Random.

—Babar's ABC: Color Book. 1989. pap. 0.94 (ISBN 0-394-83857-2). Random.

—Babar's Birthday Surprise. LC 74-123071. (Illus.). 36p. (ps-2). 1970. Repr. of 1970 ed. 10.95 (ISBN 0-394-80591-7, Random Juv); lib. bdg. 11.99 (ISBN 0-394-90591-1). Random.

—Babar's Bookmobile. De Brunhoff, Laurent, illus. LC 73-22775. 24p. (ps-2). 1974. 9.95 (ISBN 0-394-82660-4, Random Juv). Random.

—Babar's Busy Year: a Book about Seasons: Just Right for 2's & 3's. De Brunhoff, Laurent, illus. LC 88-35726. 24p. (ps). 1989. 4.95 (ISBN 0-394-82882-8, Random Juv). Random.

—Babar's Colors & Shape: Color Book. 1989. pap. 0.94 (ISBN 0-394-83875-0). Random.

—Babar's Family Album: Five Favorite Stories. De Brunhoff, Laurent, illus. LC 90-8748. 112p. (ps-3). 1991. 17.00 (ISBN 0-679-81167-2, Random Juv); lib. bdg. 17.99 (ISBN 0-679-91167-7). Random.

—Babar's French Lessons. (Illus.). (ps). 1963. 11.00 (ISBN 0-394-80587-9, Random Juv); lib. bdg. 5.99 (ISBN 0-394-90587-3). Random.

—Babar's Little Circus Star. De Brunhoff, Laurent, illus. LC 87-14149. 32p. (Orig.). (ps-1). 1988. lib. bdg. 6.99 (ISBN 0-394-98959-7, Random Juv); pap. 2.95 (ISBN 0-394-88959-2). Random.

—Babar's Mystery. De Brunhoff, Laurent, illus. LC 78-55912. 32p. 1990. pap. 4.95 (ISBN 0-679-80836-1, Dragonfly Bks). Knopf.

—Babar's Number Fun: Color Book. 1989. pap. 0.94 (ISBN 0-394-83881-5). Random.

—Babars Paint. 1989. pap. 0.71 (ISBN 0-394-82281-1). Random.

—Babar's Picnic. De Brunhoff, Laurent, illus. LC 90-61349. 24p. (Orig.). (ps-2). 1991. pap. 2.25 (ISBN 0-679-81245-8). Random.

—Babar's Trunk, 4 bks. Incl. Babar at the Seashore; Babar the Gardener; Babar Goes Skiing; Babar on a Picnic. (ps-2). 1969. Set. slipcased 9.95 (ISBN 0-394-80585-2). Random.

—Chateau du Roi Babar. (FRE.). (gr. 3-8). 15.95 (ISBN 0-685-11078-8). French & Eur.

—Le Couronnement de Babar. (FRE.). (gr. 2-3). 4.95 (ISBN 0-685-28420-4). French & Eur.

—Enfance de Babar. (FRE.). (gr. 2-3). 4.95 (ISBN 0-685-28421-2). French & Eur.

—Histoire de Babar. (FRE.). (gr. 2-4). 15.95 (ISBN 0-685-28435-2). French & Eur.

—Isabelle's New Friend: A Babar Book. De Brunhoff, Laurent, illus. LC 89-3727. 32p. (ps-1). 1990. PLB 5.99 (ISBN 0-394-92880-6); pap. 2.25 (ISBN 0-394-82880-1). Random.
—Je Parle Allemand avec Babar. (FRE., Illus.). (gr. 4-6). 15.95 (ISBN 0-685-11271-3). French & Eur.
—Je Parle Anglais avec Babar. (FRE., Illus.). (gr. 4-6). 15.95 (ISBN 0-685-11272-1). French & Eur.
—Je Parle Espagnol avec Babar. (FRE., Illus.). (gr. 4-6). 15.95 (ISBN 0-685-11273-X). French & Eur.
—Je Parle Italien avec Babar. (FRE.). (gr. 4-6). 7.95 (ISBN 0-685-11274-8). French & Eur.
—Meet Babar & His Family. De Brunhoff, Laurent, illus. 32p. (ps-1). 1985. pap. 4.95 incl. cassette (ISBN 0-394-87653-9). Random.
—Roi Babar. (FRE.). (gr. 4-6). 1975. 15.95 (ISBN 0-685-11533-X). French & Eur.
—Vive le Roi Babar. (FRE.). (gr. 2-3). 4.95 (ISBN 0-685-28423-9). French & Eur.
De Brunoff, Laurent. Babar Saves the Day. LC 76-11684. (Illus.). (gr. 3-6). 1976. pap. 2.25 (ISBN 0-394-83341-4, Random Juv). Random.
Delacre, Lulu. Time for School for, Nathan! 1989. pap. 12.95 (ISBN 0-590-41942-0). Scholastic Inc.
Delton, Judy. The Elephant in Duck's Garden. Munsinger, Lynn, illus. LC 85-15531. 32p. (gr. k-3). 1985. 10.95 (ISBN 0-8075-1959-6). A Whitman.
Disney, Walt. Dumbo. 1988. 5.99 (ISBN 0-517-66197-7). Crown.
Dr. Seuss. Horton Hatches the Egg. reissued ed. Crystal, Billy, read by. Dr. Seuss, illus. LC 40-27753. 64p. (ps up). 1991. pap. 10.95 incls. cassette (ISBN 0-394-82956-5). Random.
Elephant's Child. (Illus.). 24p. (ps-k). 1989. 1.29 (ISBN 0-02-898238-X). Checkerboard Pr.
Everett, Louise. Skating on Thin Ice. Kolding, Richard M., illus. LC 86-30857. 32p. (gr. k-2). 1987. PLB 7.06 (ISBN 0-8167-0992-0); pap. text ed. 1.95 (ISBN 0-8167-0993-9). Troll Assocs.
Friessen, Rhinehart. Almost an Elephant. Czerncecki, Stefan, illus. 44p. (Orig.). (gr. 2-6). 1990. pap. 5.95 (ISBN 0-920534-60-0, Pub. by Hyperion Pr Ltd CN). Sterling.
Grambling, Lois G. Elephant & Mouse Get Ready for Christmas. Maze, Deborah, illus. 32p. 1990. with dust jacket 12.95 (ISBN 0-8120-6185-3). Barron.
Greenberg, Kenneth R. The Adventure of Tusky & His Friends, Bk. 2: Tusky Gets Mad at Tusky. Pearson, Allison K., illus. 42p. (gr. k-4). 1991. 15.50 (ISBN 1-879100-02-9). Tusky Enterprises.
—The Adventures of Tusky & His Friends: A Christmas Mystery. Pearson, Allison K., illus. 64p. (gr. k-4). 1991. PLB 14.95 (ISBN 1-879100-01-0). Tusky Enterprises.
—The Adventures of Tusky & His Friends: A Jungle Adventure. Pearson, Allison K., illus. 50p. (gr. k-4). 1991. PLB 13.95 (ISBN 1-879100-00-2). Tusky Enterprises.
—The Adventures of Tusky & His Friends, Vol. 3: Tusky Meets the Green-Eyed Monster. Pearson, Allison K., illus. 66p. (gr. k-4). 1991. 15.95 (ISBN 1-879100-03-7). Tusky Enterprises.
Greenburg, Dan. Jumbo the Boy & Arnold the Elephant. Perl, Susan, illus. LC 87-24931. 48p. (gr. 2-4). 1989. Repr. of 1969 ed. 13.95 (ISBN 0-06-022277-8); PLB 13.89 (ISBN 0-06-022278-6). HarpC Child Bks.
Greene, Carol. The Insignificant Elephant. Gantner, Susan, illus. LC 84-1531. 32p. (ps-3). 1985. 13.95 (ISBN 0-15-238730-7, HJ). HarBraceJ.
Gregorich, Barbara. Elephant & Envelope. Hoffman, Joan, ed. (Illus.). 16p. (Orig.). (gr. k-2). 1985. pap. 1.95 (ISBN 0-88743-017-1, 06017). Sch Zone Pub Co.
Guillot, Rene. The Three Hundred Ninety-Seventh White Elephant. Leatham, Moyra, illus. (gr. 3-7). 1957. 18.95 (ISBN 0-87599-043-6). S G Phillips.
Hemalata. Mahagiri. 7th ed. Biswas, Pulak, illus. 24p. (Orig.). (gr. k-3). pap. 3.00 (ISBN 0-89744-213-X, Pub. by Children's Bk Trust India). Auromere.
Herman, Gail. Babar the Boy King. Prebenna, David, illus. LC 88-63343. 32p. (Orig.). (ps-3). 1989. pap. text ed. 1.25 (ISBN 0-394-84533-1, Random Juv). Random.
Hoff, Syd. Oliver. Hoff, Syd, illus. LC 60-5779. 64p. (gr. k-3). 1960. PLB 11.89 (ISBN 0-06-022516-5). HarpC Child Bks.
—Oliver. Hoff, Syd, illus. LC 60-5779. 64p. (gr. k-3). 1986. pap. 3.50 (ISBN 0-06-444097-4, Trophy). HarpC Child Bks.
Hoppe, Matthias. Mouse & Elephant. (ps-3). 1991. 14.95 (ISBN 0-316-37284-6). Little.
Hunt, Robert. Jamboo the African Elephant. Producciones Ancora, illus. LC 72-736441. (gr. 2-5). 1978. 6 bks. & 1 cass. 29.95 (ISBN 0-89290-026-1); 1 bk. & 1 cass. 10.95 (ISBN 0-685-04651-6). Soc for Visual.
Hurd, Edith T. Stop Stop. Hurd, Clement, illus. LC 61-12095. 64p. (gr. k-3). 1961. PLB 11.89 (ISBN 0-06-022746-X). HarpC Child Bks.
Ingoglia, Gina. Saggy Baggy Elephant No Place for Me. (Illus.). 24p. (ps-2). 1989. write for info. (ISBN 0-307-12086-4, Pub. by Golden Bks). Western Pub.
Jenkin-Pearce, Susie. Boris's Big Ache. Jenkin-Pearce, Susie, illus. LC 88-418. 32p. (ps-2). 1989. 8.95 (ISBN 0-8037-0551-4). Dial Bks Young.
Joyce, Susan. Peel, el Elefante Extraordinario. Sampson, Jennifer, tr. from ENG. DuBosque, D. C., illus. (SPA.). 48p. (ps-7). 1990. lib. bdg. 13.96x (ISBN 0-939217-02-3); pap. 7.95 (ISBN 0-685-30906-1). Peel Prod.
—Peel, the Extraordinary Elephant. DuBosque, D. C., illus. LC 86-61990. 48p. (ps up). 1988. pap. 7.95 sewn bdg. (ISBN 0-939217-01-5). Peel Prod.
Kessler, Ethel & Kessler, Len. Is There an Elephant in Your Kitchen? (Illus.). (ps-k). 1986. 4.95 (ISBN 0-671-62065-7, Little Simon). S&S Trade.
Kipling, Rudyard. The Elephant's Child. Cauley, Lorinda B., illus. LC 85-9098. 48p. (ps-3). 1988. pap. 3.95 (ISBN 0-15-225386-6, HJ). HarBraceJ.
—The Elephant's Child. Frascino, Edward, illus. 32p. (gr. k-3). 1986. 13.95 (ISBN 0-13-273640-3). P-H.
—The Elephant's Child. Cauley, Lorinda B., illus. (gr. 1-4). 1983. 14.95 (ISBN 0-15-225385-8, VoyB). HarBraceJ.
—The Elephant's Child. Mogensen, Jan, illus. LC 89-7787. 48p. 1989. 13.95 (ISBN 0-940793-41-5, Pub. by Crocodile Bks). Interlink Pub.
—The Elephant's Child. Mogensen, Jan, illus. LC 89-7787. 48p. 1991. pap. 6.95 (ISBN 0-940793-77-6, Crocodile Bks). Interlink Pub.
Lobel, Arnold. Uncle Elephant. LC 80-8944. (Illus.). 64p. (gr. k-3). 1986. pap. 3.50 (ISBN 0-06-444104-0, Trophy). HarpC Child Bks.
McNulty, Faith. The Elephant Who Couldn't Forget. Reissue. ed. Simont, Marc, illus. LC 79-2741. 64p. (gr. k-3). 1980. PLB 11.89 (ISBN 0-06-024146-2). HarpC Child Bks.
—The Elephant Who Couldn't Forget. Simont, Mark, illus. LC 79-2741. 64p. (gr. k-3). 1989. pap. 3.50 (ISBN 0-06-444128-8, Trophy). HarpC Child Bks.
Maestro, Betsy. Harriet Goes to the Circus: A Number Concept Book. Maestro, Giulio, illus. LC 76-40204. (ps-1). 1989. Crown.
Mahy, Margaret. Seventeen Kings & Forty-Two Elephants. Fogelman, Phyllis J., ed. MacCarthy, Patricia, illus. LC 87-5311. 32p. (ps-3). 1990. pap. 4.95 (ISBN 0-8037-0781-9). Dial Bks Young.
Manson, Christopher. Two Travelers. Manson, Christopher, illus. LC 89-39064. 32p. (gr. k-3). 1990. 14.95 (ISBN 0-8050-1214-1). H Holt & Co.
Mayer, Mercer. Ah-Choo. (Illus.). (gr. k-2). 1976. 4.95 (ISBN 0-8037-4894-9); PLB 4.58 (ISBN 0-8037-4895-7); pap. 2.95 (ISBN 0-8037-0301-5). Dial Bks Young.
Mills, Joyce C. & Crowley, Richard J. Sammy the Elephant & Mr. Camel: A Story to Help Children Overcome Bedwetting While Discovering Self-Appreciation. Cook, Germaine, illus. LC 88-13581. 48p. (gr. 1 up). 1988. PLB 15.95 (ISBN 0-945354-09-6); pap. 5.95 (ISBN 0-945354-08-8). Magination Pr.
Moser, Erwin. Wilma the Elephant. Agee, Joel, tr. LC 86-1145. (gr. 3-8). 1986. 9.95 (ISBN 0-915361-45-0, Dist. by Watts). Adama Pubs Inc.
Murphy, Jill. All in One Piece. (Illus.). 32p. (ps-1). 1987. 9.95 (ISBN 0-399-21433-X, Putnam). Putnam Pub Group.
—A Piece of Cake. Murphy, Jill, illus. 32p. (ps-3). 1989. 10.95 (ISBN 0-399-21590-5, Putnam). Putnam Pub Group.
New Friends for the Saggy Baggy Elephant. (ps-3). 1989. Incl. cass. write for info. (ISBN 0-307-13681-7, 13681, Pub. by Golden Bks). Western Pub.
Nintendo Staff. Super Mario Bros. Adventures. Nintendo Staff, illus. 32p. (Orig.). (gr. 1-7). 1991. pap. 6.95 incl. cassette (ISBN 0-679-81822-7). Random.
Oetting, Rae. Timmy Tiger & the Elephant. LC 73-108730. (Illus.). 32p. (ps-2). 1970. PLB 9.95 (ISBN 0-87783-041-X); pap. 3.94 deluxe ed (ISBN 0-87783-111-4); cassette 7.94x (ISBN 0-87783-277-3). Oddo.
Packard, Edward. Africa: Where Do Elephants Live Underground. 112p. (gr. 4-6). 1989. pap. text ed. 3.95 (ISBN 0-07-047998-4). McGraw.
Pearce, Philippa. Emily's Own Elephant. Lawrence, John, illus. LC 87-14039. 32p. (gr. k-3). 1988. 11.95 (ISBN 0-688-07678-5); lib. bdg. 11.88 (ISBN 0-688-07679-3). Greenwillow.
Peek, Merle. The Balancing Act. LC 86-17547. 32p. (ps-1). 1987. 12.95 (ISBN 0-89919-458-3, Pub. by Clarion). Ticknor & Fields.
Perl, Lila. Tybee Trimble's Hard Times. LC 84-4310. 160p. (gr. 4-7). 1984. 10.95 (ISBN 0-89919-288-2, Clarion). HM.
Petersham, Maud & Petersham, Miska. Circus Baby. Petersham, Maud & Petersham, Miska, illus. LC 50-9295. 32p. (ps-1). 1968. 13.95 (ISBN 0-02-771670-8, Mcmillan Child Bk). Macmillan Child Grp.
Quilted Elephant. 1991. pap. 13.95 (ISBN 0-671-72496-7). S&S Trade.
Riddell, Chris. The Trouble with Elephants. Riddell, Chris, illus. LC 87-24963. 32p. (ps-2). 1988. 12.95 (ISBN 0-397-32272-0, Lipp Jr Bks); PLB 12.89 (ISBN 0-397-32273-9). HarpC Child Bks.
Roth, Susan L. We'll Ride Elephants Through Brooklyn. (ps up). 1989. 13.95 (ISBN 0-374-38258-1). FS&G.
Royston, Angela. Elephant. Bampton, Bob, illus. 24p. (gr. k-3). 1989. pap. 2.95 (ISBN 0-8249-8368-8). Ideals.
Sadler, Marilyn. Alistair's Elephant. Bollen, Roger, illus. 44p. (Orig.). (gr. k-3). 1986. pap. 5.95 (ISBN 0-13-022773-0). P-H.
Sadler, Marilyn & Bollen, Roger. Alistair's Elephant. LC 82-23091. (Illus.). 48p. (gr. k-4). 1983. PLB 12.95 (ISBN 0-671-66680-0). S&S Trade.
Setterlund, Donna J. Elephant, Please Go Back to the Zoo. Setterlund, Donna J., illus. 30p. 1990. write for info. (ISBN 0-9624342-3-X). Carriage Hse Studio Pubns.
Smath, Jerry. But No Elephants. Smath, Jerry, illus. LC 79-16136. 48p. (ps-3). 1979. 5.95 (ISBN 0-8193-1007-7); PLB 5.95 (ISBN 0-8193-1008-5). Parents.
—Elephant Goes to School. Smath, Jerry, illus. LC 83-23823. 48p. (ps-3). 1984. 5.95 (ISBN 0-8193-1126-X). Parents.
Velthuijs, Max. Elephant & Crocodile. LC 90-55039. 32p. (gr. 4-8). 1990. 12.95 (ISBN 0-374-37675-1). FS&G.
Walters, Jerry. Walt Disney's Dumbo: On Land, on Sea, in the Air. (Illus.). (ps-3). 1973. 6.95 (ISBN 0-394-82518-7, Random Juv); lib. bdg. 4.99 (ISBN 0-394-92518-1). Random.
West, Cathy. Babar to the Rescue. Beylon, Cathy, illus. LC 89-32468. 32p. (Orig.). (ps-1). 1989. pap. 1.95 (ISBN 0-394-84529-3, Random Juv). Random.
Williams, Barbara. Mitzi & the Elephants. McCully, Emily A., illus. LC 84-13743. (gr. 2-4). 1985. 11.95 (ISBN 0-525-44158-1, DCB). Dutton Child Bks.
Yushij, Nima. When the Elephants Came. Evans, Mariam & Batmanglij, M., eds. Evans, Mariam, tr. from PER. Fanta, illus. 32p. (gr. 4 up). 1988. 18.50 (ISBN 0-934211-15-9); English-Persian Version. 18.50 (ISBN 0-934211-09-4). Mage Pubs Inc.

ELEPHANTS–POETRY

Bailey, Jill. Operation Elephant. Green, John, illus. LC 90-46056. 48p. (gr. 3-7). 1991. PLB 17.28 (ISBN 0-8114-2706-4). Steck-V.
Dr. Seuss. Horton Hatches the Egg. Dr. Seuss, illus. (gr. k-3). 1940. 10.95 (ISBN 0-394-80077-X, Random Juv); lib. bdg. 10.99 (ISBN 0-394-90077-4). Random.
Peet, Bill. Ella. (Illus.). 48p. (gr. k-3). 1964. 13.95 (ISBN 0-395-17577-1). HM.

ELEVATORS

Ford, Barbara. The Elevator. LC 82-70440. (Illus.). 64p. (gr. 4-6). 1982. 7.95 (ISBN 0-8027-6450-9); PLB 8.85 (ISBN 0-8027-6451-7). Walker & Co.
Maestro, Betsy & Maestro, Giulio. Through the Year with Harriet. Maestro, Betsy & Maestro, Giulio, illus. LC 84-29339. 32p. (ps-1). 1986. PLB 12.95 (ISBN 0-517-55613-8). Crown.

ELIJAH, THE PROPHET

Colburn, Rhonda. The Story of Elijah. Pickett, Stacy, illus. 24p. (ps-k). 1990. pap. 3.95 (ISBN 0-8249-8419-6). Ideals.
Entz, Angeline J. Elijah: Brave Prophet. Fields, Don, illus. (gr. 1-6). 1978. 5.95 (ISBN 0-8054-4244-8, 4242-44). Broadman.
Kolbrek, Loyal. The Day God Made It Rain. (gr. k-2). 1977. pap. 1.39 (ISBN 0-570-06108-3, 59-1226). Concordia.
Lashbrook, Marilyn. God, Please Send Fire: Elijah & the Prophets of Baal. Sharp, Chris, illus. LC 90-60458. 32p. (gr. k-3). 1990. 5.95 (ISBN 0-86606-440-0, 871). Roper Pr.
Overholtzer, Ruth. Elijah. Butcher, Sam, illus. 36p. (gr. k-6). 1967. pap. text ed. 9.45 (ISBN 1-55976-009-5). CEF Press.
Singer, Isaac Bashevis. Elijah the Slave. Frasconi, Antonio, illus. LC 70-124146. 32p. (ps-3). 1970. 14.95 (ISBN 0-374-32084-5). FS&G.

ELIOT, THOMAS STEARNS, 1888-1965

Reilly, Jim. Eliot. (Illus.). 112p. (gr. 7 up). 1990. lib. bdg. 18.60 (ISBN 0-86593-022-8); lib. bdg. 13.95s.p. (ISBN 0-685-36353-8). Rourke Corp.

ELIZABETH 1ST, QUEEN OF ENGLAND, 1533-1603

Greene, Carol. Elizabeth the First: Queen of England. Dobson, Steven, illus. LC 90-2204. 48p. (gr. k-3). 1990. PLB 15.27 (ISBN 0-516-04214-9); pap. 4.95 (ISBN 0-516-44214-7). Childrens.
Palmer, Michael. Elizabeth I. (Illus.). 64p. (gr. 6-9). 1989. 19.95 (ISBN 0-7134-5660-4, Pub. by Batsford England). Trafalgar Sq.
Stanley, Diane & Vennema, Peter. Good Queen Bess: The Story of Queen Elizabeth I of England. Stanley, Diane, illus. LC 88-37501. 40p. (gr. 1-4). 1990. 14.95 (ISBN 0-02-786810-9, Four Winds). Macmillan Child Grp.

ELIZABETH 2ND, QUEEN OF GREAT BRITAIN, 1926-

Sabin, Francene. Young Queen Elizabeth. Lawn, John, illus. LC 89-33941. 48p. (gr. 4-6). 1989. PLB 10.79 (ISBN 0-8167-1785-0); pap. text ed. 2.95 (ISBN 0-8167-1786-9). Troll Assocs.
Turner, Dorothy. Queen Elizabeth II. LC 84-73574. (Illus.). 32p. (gr. 7-9). 1985. s&l 11.90 (ISBN 0-531-18017-4, Pub. by Bookwright Pr). Watts.

ELK

Ahlstrom, Mark E. The Elk. LC 85-11667. (Illus.). 48p. (gr. 5-6). 1985. 10.95 (ISBN 0-89686-278-X, Crestwood Hse). Macmillan Child Grp.
Arnold, Caroline. Tule Elk. Hewett, Richard R., photos by. (Illus.). 48p. (gr. 2-5). 1989. 12.95 (ISBN 0-87614-343-5). Carolrhoda Bks.

ELK–FICTION

Benander, Carl D. Little Elk. Teasley, Jamie, ed. Beyer, Paul, illus. LC 89-51758. 45p. (gr. k-3). Date not set. 6.95 (ISBN 0-685-31291-7). Winston-Derek.

ELLINGTON, DUKE, 1899-1974

Brown, Gene. Duke Ellington. Easton, Emily, ed. (Illus.). 128p. (gr. 7-9). 1990. lib. bdg. 17.98 (ISBN 0-382-09906-0); pap. 14.95 (ISBN 0-382-24034-0). Silver Burdett Pr.

Frankl, Ron. Duke Ellington. King, Coretta Scott, intro. by. (Illus.). 112p. (Orig.). (gr. 5 up). 1988. 17.95 (ISBN 1-55546-584-6); pap. 9.95 (ISBN 0-7910-0208-X). Chelsea Hse.

King, Coretta Scott, intro. by. Duke Ellington: Bandleader & Composer. (Illus.). 112p. (gr. 7-12). PLB 16.95 (ISBN 0-685-21875-9, 200417). Know Unltd.

ELLIS ISLAND

Fisher, Leonard E. Ellis Island: Gateway to the New World. Fisher, Leonard E., illus. LC 86-2286. 64p. (gr. 3-7). 1986. reinforced 13.95 (ISBN 0-8234-0612-1). Holiday.

Jacobs, William J. Ellis Island: New Hope in a New Land. LC 89-38075. (Illus.). 40p. (gr. 2-5). 1990. 13.95 (ISBN 0-684-19171-7, Scribners Young Read). Macmillan Child Grp.

Stein, R. Conrad. The Story of Ellis Island. Dunnington, Tom, illus. LC 79-12225. 32p. (gr. 3-6). 1979. PLB 13.27 (ISBN 0-516-04613-6); pap. 3.95 (ISBN 0-516-44613-4). Childrens.

ELOCUTION
see Public Speaking

ELVES
see Fairies

EMANCIPATION OF SLAVES
see Slavery in the U. S.

EMBLEMS
see Heraldry; Symbolism

EMBROIDERY

Cherry, Winky. My First Embroidery Book. Cherry, Winky, illus. 40p. (ps-6). 1990. pap. 12.00 (ISBN 0-317-93838-X). ITS Pub.

Hodges, Jean. Smocking Design. 1989. pap. 10.95 (ISBN 0-486-26036-4). Dover.

Thomas, M. Embroidery Book. 320p. (gr. 5-8). 32.50 (ISBN 0-87559-110-8). Shalom.

EMBRYOLOGY
see also Cells; Reproduction

Conway, Lorraine. Heredity & Embryology. (gr. 5 up). 1980. 6.95 (ISBN 0-916456-90-0, GA 179). Good Apple.

EMIGRATION
see Immigration and Emigration

EMOTIONALLY DISTURBED CHILDREN
see Problem Children

EMOTIONS
see also Attitude (Psychology); Belief and Doubt; Fear; Love; Prejudices and Antipathies

Afraid. (ps-3). 1991. 16.67 (ISBN 0-8172-3775-5). Raintree Pubs.

Aliki. Feelings. Aliki, illus. LC 84-4098. 32p. (gr. k-3). 1984. 13.95 (ISBN 0-688-03831-X); PLB 13.88 (ISBN 0-688-03832-8). Greenwillow.

Allington, Richard L. & Krull, Kathleen. Feelings. Cody, Brian, illus. LC 79-27549. 32p. (ps-2). 1985. PLB 15.33 (ISBN 0-8172-1295-7); pap. text ed. 9.27 (ISBN 0-8172-2478-5). Raintree Pubs.

Anderson, Penny S. Feeling Frustrated. Siculan, Dan, illus. LC 82-19910. 32p. (gr. 1-2). 1983. PLB 11.97 (ISBN 0-89565-245-5). Childs World.

Angry. (ps-3). 1991. 16.67 (ISBN 0-8172-3776-3). Raintree Pubs.

Barsuhn, Rochelle N. Feeling Angry. Hutton, Kathryn, illus. LC 82-19911. 32p. (gr. 1-2). 1983. PLB 11.97 (ISBN 0-89565-244-7). Childs World.

Berger, Terry. I Have Feelings. Spivak, I. Howard, photos by. (Illus.). 32p. (ps-3). 1971. 16.95 (ISBN 0-87705-021-X); pap. 9.95 (ISBN 0-89885-342-7). Human Sci Pr.

—I Have Feelings Too. LC 79-15863. 32p. (ps-3). 1979. 16.95 (ISBN 0-87705-441-X). Human Sci Pr.

Berry, Joy. Every Kid's Guide to Handling Feelings. Bartholemew, illus. 48p. (gr. 3-7). 1987. 4.95 (ISBN 0-516-21403-9); PLB 14.60 (ISBN 0-516-01403-X). Childrens.

Davies, Leah. Kelly Bear Beginnings, 3 bks. Davies, Joy, illus. 96p. (ps-3). 1991. Set incl. Kelly Bear Feelings; Kelly Bear Behavior; Kelly Bear Health. pap. 13.50 (ISBN 0-9621054-3-0). Kelly Bear Bks.
The "KELLY BEAR" books teach children important life skills such as coping positively with emotions, learning appropriate behavior, making wholesome choices & accepting responsibility for their feelings, actions & bodies. Children identify with the green bear who is a positive role model. The INTERACTION books are to be read by an adult (teacher, librarian, counselor, parent) with a child or children. Throughout the books Kelly Bear asks questions that encourage children to share their thoughts & feelings, as Kelly Bear does. When adults listen with regard, children perceive themselves as valued & their self-esteem thrives. According to Dr.

Kevin Swick, Univ. of South Carolina, the KELLY BEAR books have "exemplary situations"... which "have been used successfully with parents & children from every background & cultural orientation." Pam Kent, a teacher, Auburn, Alabama, states, "The books provide invaluable insights...a wonderful teaching tool." The acclaimed series is being used effectively with classrooms of children, in small groups, & with individuals, including high-risk & special education students. The KELLY BEAR books are the mainstay of an eight-week Drug Abuse Prevention Program (D.A.P.P.) $195.00. Kelly Bear Books, Route 3, Box 99, Lafayette, Alabama, (205) 864-8991.
Publisher Provided Annotation.

Dombrower, Jan. Getting to Know Your Feelings. Stricklin, Patricia, illus. Johnson, Debbie, ed. 32p. (Orig.). (ps-3). 1990. pap. text ed. 5.95 (ISBN 0-9626348-0-8). Heartwise Pr.
GETTING TO KNOW YOUR FEELINGS is an appealing children's book that helps children to identify & express their feelings. The child will learn how to identify the sensation or "clue" in their body with the help of the little detective character. This will lead children to name & become acquainted with what they are feeling. Appropriate for ages 3 to 8, the book focuses on six emotions including upset, excitement, sadness, fear, anger, & love. The book can be used as a resource for individual feelings that may come up in a day. Simply turn to the page where that specific emotion is & that may lead to an open discussion about it. Presented in a clear & concise style, GETTING TO KNOW YOUR FEELINGS serves as support for the acceptance & expression of emotions & therefore can enhance & validate the child's self esteem. The delightful & charming illustrations capture just the right expressions in the drawings & further illuminate the important ideas being expressed. 32 pages. $3.95; Supplemental lesson plans available. Heartwise Press (415) 537-8630.
Publisher Provided Annotation.

Educational Assessment Publishing Company Staff. Parent - Child Learning Library: Compassion. (Illus.). 32p. (ps). Date not set. text ed. 9.95 (ISBN 0-942277-66-X). Educ Assess Pub.

Freed, Alvyn M. Transactional Analysis: Transactional Analysis for Everybody Ser. (Illus.). (gr. 1-3). Date not set. write for info (ISBN 0-915190-84-2). Jalmar Pr.
Stress, realization of self worth & anxiety are universal problems, bound by neither age nor ethnic background. Tots, teenagers & children of all ages experience these problems. Now there is a way to help them realize their self esteem through Transactional Analysis. The TA books have established "I'M OK YOU'RE OK" as a household concept. TA FOR TOTS (& Other Prinzes) newly revised, deals with a full range of feelings that help tots, from four years old, realize their intrinsic worth as human beings & build & strengthen their self-esteem.

TA FOR KIDS has already proven to be an ideal book to help youngsters, from nine to thirteen years old, develop self-esteem, esteem of others, social & personal responsibility, critical thinking & independent judgement. TA FOR TEENS is aimed at telling teens, from thirteen to eighteen years old, & their (people in charge) that they are OK. Teens is designed to bring teenagers into closer & more satisfying relationships. Dr. Freed offers new choices & options to teenagers dealing with the dilemmas of growing up, in a positive way. Transactional Analysis is a simple-to-use way to understand & respect one's own feelings & those of others. THE ORIGINAL WARM FUZZY TALE originated the concept of Warm Fuzzies & Cold Pricklies, (a fairy tale in every sense, with a moral). A beautifully illustrated book for kids from five to one hundred & five. Great for parents & care-givers.
Publisher Provided Annotation.

Gelinas, Paul J. Coping with Anger. rev. ed. Rosen, Ruth, ed. (gr. 7 up). 1988. lib. bdg. 12.95 (ISBN 0-8239-0780-5). Rosen Group.

—Coping with Your Emotions. rev. ed. Rosen, Ruth, ed. (gr. 7-12). 1989. PLB 12.95 (ISBN 0-8239-0970-0). Rosen Group.

Goldman, Margaret F. My A, B, C, D, E Thinking, Feeling & Doing Book. Era, Diane, illus. Ellis, Albert, intro. by. LC 83-90397. (Illus.). 48p. (ps up). 11.95 (ISBN 0-914237-00-4). L & M Bks.

Hazen, Barbara S. What Are Feelings? rev. ed. Sweat, Lynn, illus. 32p. (gr. 2-4). 1990. Repr. of 1988 ed. PLB 9.95 (ISBN 1-878363-16-6). Forest Hse.

Hurt. (ps-3). 1991. 16.67 (ISBN 0-8172-3777-1). Raintree Pubs.

Jealous. (ps-3). 1991. 16.67 (ISBN 0-8172-3778-X). Raintree Pubs.

Kempler, Susan, et al. A Man Can Be... Dian, Russell, photos by. (Illus.). (ps-3). 1984. 16.95 (ISBN 0-89885-046-0); pap. 9.95 (ISBN 0-89885-208-0). Human Sci Pr.

Kimball, Richard S. A Funny Feeling. Reid, William K., Jr., illus. LC 87-32155. 64p. (Orig.). (gr. 3 up). 1988. pap. 7.95 (ISBN 0-944443-00-1). Green Timber.
This collection of 41 cleverly illustrated poems explores common feelings & sayings about them for entertainment & enlightenment of youngsters aged eight & above. Eight-year olds will identify with Reginald Botts who was "tied up in knots & couldn't get his thoughts undone." Ten-year olds will enjoy the image of Louise being made small by the weight of the grudge she carries. Twelve-year olds will sympathize with Annie who has reached the age "when staying in means being left out" & "going out means being in." Everybody will be delighted by "tongue tied" Sid & by the many other characters & poems. With humor, this book allows readers & listeners to think about their own funny feelings & can open the way for discussion with parents, teachers, counselors, church groups, & friends. Paperback, $7.95.
Publisher Provided Annotation.

Lamb, Jane M. Sharing with Thumpy: My Story of Love & Grief. Dodge, Nancy C., illus. 48p. (gr. k-12). 1985. pap. 8.95 workbook (ISBN 0-918533-10-4). Prairie Lark.

Licata, Renora. Everything You Need to Know about Anger. (gr. 7-12). 1991. PLB 12.95 (ISBN 0-8239-1320-1). Rosen Group.

Lonely. (ps-3). 1991. 16.67 (ISBN 0-8172-3779-8). Raintree Pubs.

McElmurry, Mary A. Appreciating. Herrick, Elizabeth T., illus. 64p. (gr. 2-8). 1983. wkbk. 7.95 (ISBN 0-9607366-1-1, GA 493). Good Apple.

—Belonging. Herrick, Elizabeth T., illus. 64p. (gr. 2-8). 1983. wkbk. 7.95 (ISBN 0-9607366-0-3, GA 492). Good Apple.

—Caring. 64p. (gr. 4-8). 1981. 7.95 (ISBN 0-86653-052-5, GA275). Good Apple.

McElmurry, Mary Anne. Feelings. 80p. (gr. 3-8). 1981. 7.95 (ISBN 0-86653-027-4, GA 276). Good Apple.

Moddy, Marlys. ABC Book of Feelings. (Illus.). 32p. (ps-3). 1991. 7.95 (ISBN 0-570-04190-2, 56-1649). Concordia. The ABC Book of Feelings is a fun, new way to learn the ABC's--& all about feelings at the same time! Journey through the alphabet with a delightful mouse who experiences all kinds of emotions, starting with "A" for "afraid" & ending with "Z" for "zany." Children ages 4 to 8 learn the ABC's & how to express their God-given emotions, realizing that Jesus loves them always & helps them understand their feelings...even when they feel "Y" for "yucky." Award-winning illustrator Joe Buddy's whimsical, colorful illustrations capture children's attention. The charming drawings help children understand what the "feeling" words mean. A wonderful book for parents who want to explain to their children that God has given all people emotions; & assist parents in helping their children express their feelings. 32pp. Hardback. $7.95 Concordia Publishing House. Item no. 56-1649 ISBN 0-570-04190-2 To order--Call toll free 1-800-325-3040.
Publisher Provided Annotation.

Neuman, Stephanie. Feelings: Everybody Has Them. Hankiewicz, Ruth A., illus. LC 84-52602. 104p. (gr. k-6). 1984. pap. 9.95 (ISBN 0-932909-01-9). SNB Pub.

Odor, Ruth S. Moods & Emotions. Bolt, John, illus. LC 81-17008. 112p. (gr. 2-6). 1980. lib. bdg. 11.97 (ISBN 0-89565-210-2). Childs World.

O'Toole, Donna. Healing & Growing Through Grief. (Illus.). 20p. pap. 3.00 (ISBN 0-685-31273-9, HG-02-4). Rainbow NC.

Palmer, Patricia. Liking Myself. Shank, Will, illus. LC 77-88185. 80p. (gr. k-4). 1977. pap. 4.95 (ISBN 0-915166-41-0). Impact Pubs Cal.

—The Mouse, the Monster & Me. Shank, Will, illus. LC 77-88186. 80p. (Orig.). (gr. 3-6). 1977. pap. 4.95 (ISBN 0-915166-43-7). Impact Pubs Cal.

Pincus, Debbie. Sharing. Lasky, Mark, illus. 80p. (gr. 4-8). 1983. wkbk. 7.95 (ISBN 0-86653-117-3, GA 468). Good Apple.

Polland, Barbara K. Feelings: Inside You & Outloud Too. LC 74-25835. (Illus.). 64p. (ps-3). 1984. pap. 6.95 (ISBN 0-89087-006-3). Celestial Arts.

Richards, Joanne & Standley, Marianne V. Dealing with Feelings. 72p. (gr. 2-6). 1982. 7.95 (ISBN 0-88160-015-6, LW 118). Learning Wks.

Riley, Sue. Angry. LC 77-16791. (Illus.). (ps-2). 1978. PLB 9.96 (ISBN 0-89565-014-2). Childs World.

—Sorry. LC 77-16811. (Illus.). (ps-2). 1978. PLB 9.96 (ISBN 0-89565-013-4). Childs World.

Sad. (ps-3). 1991. 16.67 (ISBN 0-8172-3780-1). Raintree Pubs.

Sheehan, Cilla. The Colors That I Am. Elliot, Glen, photos by. LC 80-25351. (Illus.). 32p. (ps-5). 1981. 16.95 (ISBN 0-89885-047-9). Human Sci Pr.

Simon, Norma. How Do I Feel? Lasker, Joe, illus. LC 77-126430. (ps-2). 1970. PLB 12.95 (ISBN 0-8075-3414-5). A Whitman.

Ward, Elaine M. Being Human: Learning Through Feelings. 57p. (Orig.). (gr. 1-6). 1988. pap. 9.95 (ISBN 0-940754-63-0). Ed Ministries.

EMOTIONS–FICTION

Balter, Lawrence. What's the Matter with A. J? Understanding Jealousy. Schanzer, Roz, illus. 40p. (ps-2). 1989. 5.95 (ISBN 0-8120-6119-5). Barron.

Bush, Don. Little Brook Series, 3 bks. (Illus.). (gr. 3). lib. bdg. 16.50 (ISBN 0-943978-03-3). Rolling Hills Pr.

Cain, Barbara S. Double-Dip Feelings: A Book to Help Children Understand Emotions. O'Brien, Ann S., illus. LC 89-49382. 32p. 1990. 15.95 (ISBN 0-945354-23-1); pap. 5.95 (ISBN 0-945354-20-7). Magination Pr.

Conlin, Susan & Friedman, Susan L. Ellie's Day. Smith, M. Kathryn, illus. Illsley-Clarke, Jean, intro. by. LC 89-60334. (Illus.). 32p. (Orig.). (ps-2). 1989. PLB 14.95 (ISBN 0-943990-45-9); pap. 4.95 (ISBN 0-943990-44-0). Parenting Pr.

Cowell, Phyllis F. Your Best Wishes Can Come True. Ewers, Joe, illus. 40p. (ps-3). 1984. 5.95 (ISBN 0-910313-18-0). Parker Bros.

Creighton, Susan. A Hug from the Heart. (ps-3). 1985. 3.50 (ISBN 0-910313-92-X). Parker Bros.

Erickson, Karen. I'm Brave! Roffey, Maureen, illus. 32p. (ps-k). 1989. pap. 5.95 (ISBN 0-670-82676-6). Viking Child Bks.

Giff, Patricia R. Today Was a Terrible Day. Natti, Suzanna, illus. (gr. k-3). 1984. incl. cassette 19.95 (ISBN 0-941078-50-7); pap. 12.95 incl. cassette (ISBN 0-941078-48-5); pap. 27.95 4 bks, cassette, & guide (ISBN 0-941078-49-3); sound fimlstrip 22.95 (ISBN 0-941078-47-7). Live Oak Media.

Haugen, Tormod. The Night Birds. La Farge, Sheila, tr. from NOR. LC 82-70311. 160p. (gr. 4-6). 1982. 11.95 (ISBN 0-385-28735-6, Sey Lawr); pap. 9.89 (ISBN 0-385-28736-4). Delacorte.

Hogan, Paula Z. Sometimes I Get So Mad. Shapiro, Karen, illus. Silverman, Manuel S., intro. by. LC 79-24057. (Illus.). 32p. (gr. k-6). 1980. PLB 16.67 (ISBN 0-8172-1359-7). Raintree Pubs.

Hollands, Judith. The Like Potion. (gr. 3-6). 1989. pap. 2.50 (ISBN 0-671-64151-4, Minstrel Bks). PB.

Klein, Norma. Learning How to Fall. 1989. 14.95 (ISBN 0-553-05809-6, Starfire). Bantam.

Lamb, Jane M. Sharing with Thumpy: My Story of Love & Grief. Dodge, Nancy C., illus. 48p. (gr. k-12). 1985. pap. 8.95 workbook (ISBN 0-918533-10-4). Prairie Lark.

Lester, Julius. This Strange New Feeling. 164p. (gr. 7 up). 1985. pap. 2.50 (ISBN 0-590-41061-X, Point); tchr's. guide 1.25 (ISBN 0-590-40681-7). Scholastic Inc.

Miles, Miska. Gertrude's Pocket. McCully, Emily, illus. (gr. 2-5). 1984. 15.25 (ISBN 0-8446-6164-3). Peter Smith.

Modesitt, Jeanne. The Story of Z. Johnson, Lonnie S., illus. LC 89-3923. 28p. (ps up). 1990. 14.95 (ISBN 0-88708-105-3). Picture Bk Studio.

Nixon, Joan L. The Specter. LC 82-70322. 160p. (gr. 7 up). 1982. pap. 12.95 (ISBN 0-385-28948-0). Delacorte.

Odor, Ruth S. Glad. Indereiden, Nancy, illus. LC 79-26076. (ps-2). 1980. PLB 9.96 (ISBN 0-89565-114-9). Childs World.

Pendergast, Kathleen. Say Another One about How I Feel. Tindal, Pauline, illus. LC 81-90678. 54p. (Orig.). (gr. k-6). 1982. pap. 6.95 (ISBN 0-942178-00-9). Madison Park Pr.

Plum, Carol T. Peter's Angry Toys: I Am Special Childrens Story Books. 32p. (ps-3). 1989. lib. bdg. 9.95 (ISBN 0-87973-015-3, 15); pap. text ed. 5.95 (ISBN 0-87973-012-9, 12). Our Sunday Visitor.

Rozman, Deborah. The Crystal Lady. Royall, Sandy, illus. 72p. (gr. 1 up). 1991. 19.95 (ISBN 1-879052-01-6, Planet Pubns). Planetary Pubns.

Shles, Larry. The Adventure of the Squib Owl: Squib Ser. Shles, Larry, illus. Date not set. pap. 7.95 each (ISBN 0-915190-85-0). Jalmar Pr. Squib the Owl series, written & whimsically illustrated by Larry Shles, teaches self-esteem & personal & social responsibility as it entertains. The author uses the name Squib to personify the small vunerable part of us all that struggles & at times feels helpless in an enormous world filled with emotions. This Series, five volumes, traces the adventures of this tiny owl as he struggles with his feelings searching at least for understanding. Each of the five titles explores a different vulnerability. MOTHS & MOTHERS, FEATHERS & FATHERS (explores feelings); HOOTS & TOOTS & HAIRY BRUTES (explores disabilities); ALIENS IN MY NEST (explores adolescent behavior); HUGS & SHRUGS (explores inner peace). The latest volume DO I HAVE TO GO TO SCHOOL TODAY? is great for the young reader who needs encouragement from teachers who accept him "just as he is". Brilliantly simple, yet realistically complex, Squib personifies each & every one of us. He is a reflection of what we are, & what we can become. Every reader who has struggled with life's limitations will recognize his own struggles & triumphs in the microcosm of Squib's forest world - in Squib we find a parable for all ages from 8-80.
Publisher Provided Annotation.

Smith, Doris B. The First Hard Times. LC 82-60084. 144p. (gr. 3-7). 1983. pap. 12.95 (ISBN 0-670-31571-0). Viking Child Bks.

Tester, Sylvia R. Frustrated. Indereiden, Nancy, illus. LC 79-23804. (ps-2). 1980. PLB 9.96 (ISBN 0-89565-110-6). Childs World.

—Jealous. Indereiden, Nancy, illus. LC 79-24042. (ps-2). 1980. PLB 9.96 (ISBN 0-89565-111-4). Childs World.

—Sad. Indereiden, Nancy, illus. LC 79-26252. (ps-2). 1980. PLB 9.96 (ISBN 0-89565-112-2). Childs World.

Waters, Virginia. Color Us Rational. Lee, Penny, illus. LC 78-71011. (ps-3). 1979. pap. 4.95 (ISBN 0-917476-15-8). Inst Rational-Emotive.

EMPERORS

see Kings and Rulers;

see and names of emperors

EMPLOYEES AND OFFICIALS

see and names of countries, cities, etc. and organizations with the subdivision officials and employees, e.g. U. S. –Officials and Employees

ENAMEL AND ENAMELING

Hawkins, Leslie V. Art Metal & Enameling. 234p. (gr. 9-12). 1974. text ed. 17.60 (ISBN 0-02-662240-8). Bennett IL.

Zechlin, Katharina. Creative Enameling & Jewelry-Making. Kuttner, Paul, tr. LC 65-20877. (gr. 10 up). 1965. 6.95 (ISBN 0-8069-5062-5); PLB 6.69 (ISBN 0-8069-5063-3). Sterling.

ENCYCLOPEDIAS AND DICTIONARIES

Bailey, Kenneth. Enciclopedia Infantil Molino. (SPA.). 234p. 1973. 95.00 (ISBN 84-272-5906-9, S-22860). French & Eur.

Beal, George. The Julian Messner Young Reader's Thesaurus. 1984. pap. 6.95 (ISBN 0-685-09676-9, Little Simon). S&S Trade.

—Simon & Schuster Young Readers' Thesaurus. 1984. pap. 6.95 (ISBN 0-671-50816-4). S&S Trade.

Behm, Barbara, ed. The Index. (Illus.). 96p. (gr. 3-8). 1987. PLB 233.33 set (ISBN 0-317-62824-0); pap. 13.25 (ISBN 0-8172-3062-9). Raintree Pubs.

Calder, S. J. First Facts, 12 bks. Van Wright, Cornelius, illus. (ps-1). 1990. Set, 32p. ea. 59.40 (ISBN 0-671-94108-9); Set, 32p. ea. lib. bdg. 119.76 (ISBN 0-671-94107-0). Messner.

Children's Dictionary. 832p. (gr. 8-12). 1988. 13.95 (ISBN 0-673-12491-6). Scott F.

Child's First Library of Learning, 17 bks. (ps-3). 1990. Set, 88p. ea. 270.81 (ISBN 0-8094-4825-4); Set, 88p. ea. lib. bdg. 361.59 (ISBN 0-8094-4826-2). Time-Life.

Compton's Precyclopaedia, 16 vols. (gr. 1-4). 1988. Set. 269.00 (ISBN 0-85229-479-4). Ency Brit Ed.

Dempsey, Walter. Children's First Encyclopedia. 1985. 6.98 (ISBN 0-671-07744-9). S&S Trade.

Diccionario Enciclopedico, 15 vols. (gr. 7 up). Set. 199.00 (ISBN 0-8347-5189-5). Ency Brit Ed.

Disney, Walt, Staff. My First Muppet Dictionary. (ps-3). 1991. 9.95 (ISBN 1-56282-038-9). W Disney Pub.

Dupre, Jean-Paul. The Barron's Junior Fact-Finder: An Illustrated Encyclopedia for Children. (Illus.). 296p. (gr. 2-6). 1989. 19.95 (ISBN 0-8120-6072-5). Barron.

Eastman, P. D. Cat in the Hat Beginner Book Dictionary. LC 64-1157. (Illus.). 144p. (gr. k-6). 1964. 8.95 (ISBN 0-394-81009-0); lib. bdg. 8.99 (ISBN 0-394-91009-5). Beginner.

Eastman, Philip D. Cat in the Hat Beginner Book Dictionary in Spanish & English. LC 66-10688. (SPA & ENG., Illus.). 144p. (gr. k-3). 1966. 16.00 (ISBN 0-394-81542-4). Beginner.

Elliot, J. Children's Encyclopedia. King, Colin, illus. 128p. (gr. 3-6). 1987. PLB 16.96 (ISBN 0-88110-265-2); pap. 11.95 (ISBN 0-7460-0000-6). EDC.

Enciclopedia Infantil, 10 vols. (SPA.). 2400p. 1974. Set. leather 495.00 (ISBN 84-7254-160-6, S-50480). French & Eur.

Enciclopedia Juvenil Auriga: Inventos Que Conmovieron el Mundo, Descubrimientos e Inventos, Armas Que Conmovieron el Mundo, Historia Ilustrada de los Barcos, Artistas Que Conmovieron el Mundo. (SPA.). 360p. 1977. leatherette 42.00 (ISBN 84-201-0202-4, French & Eur). French & Eur.

Fact Finders, 4 vols. (Illus.). 128p. (gr. 4-5). 1989. Set. PLB 47.80 (ISBN 0-8368-0131-8). Gareth Stevens Inc.

First Picture Dictionary. (Illus.). (ps-1). 1985. 3.98 (ISBN 0-517-48000-X). Outlet Bk Co.

First Picture Dictionary. (Illus.). (ps-2). 3.50 (ISBN 0-7214-0617-3). Ladybird Bks.

Fun Facts & Records. (gr. 2-6). 1990. 7.99 (ISBN 0-517-69601-0). Outlet Bk Co.

Greisman, Joan. First Dictionary. (ps-3). 1990. pap. write for info. (ISBN 0-307-15853-5). Western Pub.

Let's Discover, 16 vols. (Illus.). (gr. k-6). 1981. Set. PLB 330.67 (ISBN 0-8172-1782-7). Raintree Pubs.

The Lincoln Dictionary for Children: The Dictionary for Writing. (gr. 3 up). 1988. 17.95 (ISBN 0-318-33429-1). HarBraceJ.

The Lincoln Writing Dictionary for Children. (Illus.). 896p. (gr. 2-9). 1988. 17.95 (ISBN 0-15-152394-0). HarBraceJ.

The Macmillan Dictionary for Children. rev. ed. 896p. (gr. 3-7). 1989. 14.95 (ISBN 0-02-761561-8, Mcmillan Child Bk). Macmillan Child Grp.
Mi Primer Diccionario Escolar. 4th ed. (SPA.). 480p. 1975. pap. 5.95 (ISBN 84-319-0028-8, S-27087). French & Eur.
Mi Primera Enciclopedia, 2 vols. 7th ed. (SPA.). 420p. 1978. Set. 65.00 (ISBN 84-278-0047-9, S-26910). French & Eur.
Morris, Christopher, et al, eds. The HBJ Student Thesaurus. (Illus.). 320p. 1991. 14.95 (ISBN 0-15-232880-7). HarBraceJ.
My First Dictionary. 1989. 11.95 (ISBN 0-673-28497-2). Scott F.
My First Picture Dictionary. (ps-1). 1985. 5.98 (ISBN 0-517-44379-1). Outlet Bk Co.
Paton, John, ed. Picture Encyclopedia for Children. (gr. 3-6). 1987. 19.95 (ISBN 0-448-18999-2, G&D). Putnam Pub Group.
Reynolds, Jean, ed. New Book of Knowledge. (gr. 3-8). 1989. write for info (ISBN 0-7172-0520-7). Grolier Inc.
Scarry, Richard. Mi Diccionario Infantil. 3rd ed. (SPA.). 96p. 1974. pap. 14.95 (ISBN 0-686-57341-2, S-27628). French & Eur.
—Mi Primer Gran Diccionario Infantil. 4th ed. (SPA.). 90p. 1978. leatherette 13.95 (ISBN 84-02-03836-0, S-26637). French & Eur.
Schulz, Charles M. The Charlie Brown Dictionary. LC 72-12135. (gr. 2-4). 1974. (Random Juv). Random.
Scott, Foresman. My First Dictionary. (ps-3). 1990. 11.95 (ISBN 0-06-017901-5, HarpT). HarperCollins.
—Words for New Readers. (ps-3). 1990. 10.95 (ISBN 0-06-017900-7, HarpT). HarperCollins.
Scott, Foresman Junior Thesaurus. 447p. (gr. 10 up). 1988. 11.95 (ISBN 0-318-37691-1). Scott F.
Second Picture Dictionary. (Illus.). (ps-2). 3.50 (ISBN 0-7214-0618-1). Ladybird Bks.
Simons, Robin. Recyclopedia. (gr. 1 up). 1976. pap. 9.95 (ISBN 0-395-24380-7, Sandpiper). HM.
Snow, Alan. My First Dictionary. 1991. 5.98 (ISBN 0-8317-0225-7). Smithmark.
—My First Encyclopedia. 1991. 5.98 (ISBN 0-8317-0227-3). Smithmark.
Standard Educational Corporation Staff. New Standard Encyclopedia, 20 vols. Downey, Douglas W., et al, eds. LC 91-14723. (gr. 6-12). 1992. write for info. (ISBN 0-87392-197-6). Standard Ed.
Steinberg, Margery A. Dictionary & Word Skills. (Illus.). (gr. 3-5). 1979. pap. 1.25 (ISBN 0-448-16127-3, G&D). Putnam Pub Group.
Student Dictionary. 1328p. (gr. 12 up). 1988. 15.95 (ISBN 0-673-12492-4). Scott F.
Vitale, Miralla. Enciclopedia De la Nina. 3rd ed. (SPA.). 64p. 1979. 29.95 (ISBN 84-7176-201-3, S-50471). French & Eur.
The Webster's II New Riverside Children's Dictionary. 800p. 1985. pap. 8.95 (ISBN 0-395-37884-2). HM.
Webster's Scholastic Dictionary. (gr. 9 up). pap. 2.95 (ISBN 0-8049-2001-X, D1). Airmont.
Wittels, Harriet & Greisman, Joan. The Clear & Simple Thesaurus Dictionary. (Illus.). (gr. 3 up). pap. 7.95 (ISBN 0-448-12198-0, G&D). Putnam Pub Group.
The World Almanac's Infopedia. 408p. 1990. 17.95 (ISBN 0-88687-500-5); pap. 8.95 (ISBN 0-88687-476-9). Pharos Bks NY.
World Book Staff, ed. Childcraft Supplement: Prehistoric Animals, About Dogs, The Magic of Words, The Indian Book, The Puzzle Book, 5 vols. (Illus.). 1520p. (gr. 2-6). 1989. PLB write for info. (ISBN 0-7166-0669-0). World Bk SW.

ENCYCLOPEDIAS AND DICTIONARIES–YEARBOOKS

World Book Staff, ed. The World Book Year Book, 1990. LC 62-4818. (Illus.). 608p. (gr. 6-12). 1990. lib. bdg. write for info. (ISBN 0-7166-0490-6). World Bk.

ENDURANCE, PHYSICAL

see Physical Fitness

ENERGY

see Force and Energy

ENGINEERING

see also specific forms of engineering, e.g. Chemical Engineering

Boring, Mel. Incredible Constructions & the People Who Built Them. LC 84-19522. 96p. (gr. 4 up). 1985. PLB 13.85 (ISBN 0-8027-6560-2). Walker & Co.
Boy Scouts of America. Engineering. (Illus.). 48p. (gr. 6-12). 1978. pap. 1.85 (ISBN 0-8395-3376-4, 3376). BSA.
Dixon, Malcolm. Structures. (Illus.). 48p. (gr. 3-7). 1991. PLB 12.40 (ISBN 0-531-18379-3). Watts.
Gay, Kathlyn. Ergonomics: Making Products & Places Fit People. LC 85-20634. (Illus.). 128p. (gr. 6-12). 1986. PLB 17.95 (ISBN 0-89490-118-4). Enslow Pubs.
Goodwin, Peter. Engineering Projects for Young Scientists. 1989. PLB 12.90 (ISBN 0-531-10339-0); pap. 5.95 (ISBN 0-531-15130-1). Watts.
Nash, Paul. Colossal Constructions. Young, Richard G., ed. LC 89-11714. (Illus.). 32p. (gr. 3-5). 1989. PLB 11.93 (ISBN 0-944483-35-6). Garrett Ed Corp.

ENGINEERING–HISTORY

Crump, Donald J., ed. Builders of the Ancient World: Marvels of Engineering. LC 86-5278. (Illus.). (gr. 8 up). 1986. 7.95 (ISBN 0-87044-585-5); lib. bdg. 9.50 (ISBN 0-87044-590-1). Natl Geog.

ENGINEERING–VOCATIONAL GUIDANCE

Salvadori, Mario. The Art of Construction: Projects & Principles for Beginning Engineers & Architects. 3rd ed. Hooker, Saralinda & Ragus, Christopher, illus. LC 89-49406. 144p. (gr. 5 up). 1990. pap. 9.95 (ISBN 1-55652-080-8). Chicago Review.

ENGINEERING DRAWING

see Mechanical Drawing

ENGINEERING MATERIALS

see Materials

ENGINEERS

Williams, Brian. Karl Benz. (Illus.). 48p. (gr. 5-8). 1991. RLB 12.40 (ISBN 0-531-18404-8, Pub. by Boatwright Pr). Watts.

ENGINEERS–VOCATIONAL GUIDANCE

Harmon, Margaret. Ms. Engineer. LC 79-13620. (Illus.). 186p. (gr. 9 up). 1979. 8.95 (ISBN 0-664-32652-8, Westminster). Westminster John Knox.

ENGINES

see also Automobiles–Engines; Fire Engines; Fuel; Steam Engines

Cole, Joanna. Cars & How They Go. Gibbons, Gail, illus. LC 82-45575. 32p. (gr. 2-6). 1983. 12.95 (ISBN 0-690-04261-2, Crowell Jr Bks); PLB 12.89 (ISBN 0-690-04262-0, Crowell Jr Bks). HarpC Child Bks.

ENGLAND

Goodall, John S. The Story of an English Village. Goodall, John S., illus. LC 78-56242. 60p. 1979. 14.95 (ISBN 0-689-50125-0, M K McElderry). Macmillan Child Grp.
Greene, Carol. England. LC 82-4471. (Illus.). (gr. 5-9). 1982. PLB 25.27 (ISBN 0-516-02763-8). Childrens.

ENGLAND–FICTION

Aiken, Joan. Return to Harken House. (gr. 5-9). 1990. 13.95 (ISBN 0-385-29975-3). Delacorte.
Austen, Jane. Northanger Abbey. 224p. (gr. 9-12). Date not set. pap. 2.50 (ISBN 0-451-51834-9, Sig Classics). NAL-Dutton.
Banks, Lynne R. My Darling Villain. LC 76-58718. 240p. (gr. 7 up). 1977. HarpC Child Bks.
Bond, Michael. Paddington Takes the Test. 128p. (gr. k-6). 1982. pap. 1.95 (ISBN 0-440-47021-8, YB). Dell.
Boston, Lucy M. River at Green Knowe. 1989. pap. 3.95 (ISBN 0-15-267450-0). HarbraceJ.
Chaucer, Geoffrey. The Canterbury Tales. Stewart, Diana, adapted by. Hubrich, Dan, illus. LC 80-22141. 48p. (gr. 4 up). 1983. PLB 17.32 (ISBN 0-8172-1666-9); pap. 9.27 (ISBN 0-8172-2007-0). Raintree Pubs.
Clark, Walter V. The Ox-Bow Incident. 224p. (gr. 9-12). 1943. pap. 4.50 (ISBN 0-451-52386-5, CE1497, Sig Classics). NAL-Dutton.
Cobb, Vicki. Lots of Rot. Schatell, Brian, illus. LC 80-8726. 40p. (gr. 1-3). 1981. PLB 13.89 (ISBN 0-685-02082-7, Lipp Jr Bks); PLB 13.89 (ISBN 0-397-31939-8). HarpC Child Bks.
Cubbage, Jenny. Close Encounters with an English Mind. (Illus.). 64p. (Orig.). (gr. 5-12). 1986. pap. 6.95 (ISBN 0-913853-05-4, 115-065). Freline.
Howker, Janni. Badger on the Barge & Other Stories. LC 84-10293. 208p. (gr. 5-9). 1985. reinforced 11.75 (ISBN 0-688-04215-5). Greenwillow.
—The Nature of the Beast. (gr. 5-9). 1987. pap. 4.95 (ISBN 0-14-032254-X, Puffin). Puffin Bks.
Hoyland, John. The Ivy Garland. Vicary, Richard, illus. 96p. (gr. 10 up). 1987. 9.95 (ISBN 0-8052-8137-1, Pub. by Allison & Busby England). Schocken.
Hughes, Shirley. An Evening at Alfie's. Hughes, Shirley, illus. LC 84-11297. 32p. (ps-1). 1985. 14.95 (ISBN 0-688-04122-1); PLB 14.88 (ISBN 0-688-04123-X). Lothrop.
Jeffries, Roderic. Trapped. LC 79-182580. 160p. (gr. 4-6). 1973. pap. 3.50 (ISBN 0-06-440035-2, Trophy). HarpC Child Bks.
Manley, Seon. A Present for Charles Dickens. LC 82-24862. (Illus.). 124p. (gr. 5 up). 1983. 12.95 (ISBN 0-664-32706-0, Westminster). Westminster John Knox.
Nesbit, Edith. The Railway Children. Butts, Dennis, ed. 224p. 1991. pap. 3.95 (ISBN 0-19-282659-X, 11912). Oxford U Pr.
Phillips, Ann. The Peace Child. (Illus.). 160p. (gr. 5 up). 1988. 13.95 (ISBN 0-19-271560-7). Oxford U Pr.
The Secret Garden. (Illus.). (gr. 3-5). 3.50 (ISBN 0-7214-0632-7). Ladybird Bks.
Swindells, Robert. A Serpent's Tooth. LC 88-24635. 144p. (gr. 4-7). 1989. 13.95 (ISBN 0-8234-0743-8). Holiday.
Thomas, Ruth. The Runaways. LC 88-8229. 304p. (gr. 3-7). 1989. 13.95 (ISBN 0-397-32344-1, Lipp Jr Bks); PLB 13.89 (ISBN 0-397-32345-X, Lipp Jr Bks). HarpC Child Bks.
Twain, Mark. The Prince & the Pauper. James, Raymond, ed. Couri, Kathryn A., illus. LC 89-33892. 48p. (gr. 3-6). 1990. lib. bdg. 12.89 (ISBN 0-8167-1873-3); pap. text ed. 3.95 (ISBN 0-8167-1874-1). Troll Assocs.
Wiseman, David. Thimbles. LC 81-20280. (gr. 4 up). 1982. 7.95 (ISBN 0-395-31867-X). HM.

ENGLAND–HISTORY

see Great Britain–History

ENGLISH AUTHORS

see Authors, English

ENGLISH COMPOSITION

see English Language–Composition and Exercises

ENGLISH DRAMA

see also Mysteries and Miracle Plays

Adams, Richard. Twelfth Night. 1989. pap. text ed. 5.72 (ISBN 0-582-01346-1, 78433). Longman.
Adams, Richard, ed. Midsummer Night's Dream. 1990. pap. text ed. 5.72 (ISBN 0-582-01345-3). Longman.
Ayckbourn, Alan. Confusions. (Illus.). 128p. 1988. pap. 9.95 (ISBN 0-413-53270-4, A0063). Heinemann Ed.
Barrie, James. Peter Pan: The Complete Play. 136p. (gr. 4 up). 1988. pap. 9.95. Tundra Bks.
Birch, Beverly, retold by. Shakespeare's Stories: Tragedies. Kerins, Tony, illus. LC 88-18112. 128p. (gr. 3-7). 1988. 12.95x (ISBN 0-87226-193-X). P Bedrick Bks.
Dekker, Thomas, et al. The Witch of Edmonton. (Illus.). 128p. 1988. pap. 9.95 (ISBN 0-413-53260-7, A0320). Heinemann Ed.
Hamlet. (Illus.). 48p. (gr. 4 up). 1988. PLB 17.32 (ISBN 0-8172-2764-4); pap. 9.27 (ISBN 0-8172-2768-7). Raintree Pubs.
Matchett, William & Schoenbaum, Samuel, eds. King John & Henry VIII. (gr. 9-12). Date not set. pap. 4.95 (ISBN 0-451-52038-6, Sig Classics). NAL-Dutton.
Miles, Bernard. Well-Loved Tales from Shakespeare. Ambrus, Victor G., illus. LC 85-63829. 128p. (gr. 2 up). 1986. 12.95 (ISBN 0-528-82758-8). Checkerboard Pr.
Mulherin, Jennifer. Hamlet. (Illus.). 32p. (gr. 6-12). 1988. 10.96g (ISBN 0-382-09691-6); 8.22s.p. (ISBN 0-382-09697-5). Silver Burdett Pr.
—Macbeth. Scoble, Lesley, illus. LC 87-37225. 32p. (gr. 6-12). 1988. 10.96 (ISBN 0-382-09693-2); 8.22s.p. (ISBN 0-382-09699-1). Silver Burdett Pr.
—The Merchant of Venice. (Illus.). 32p. (gr. 6-12). 1988. 10.96g (ISBN 0-382-09692-4); 8.22s.p. (ISBN 0-685-37318-5); pap. 5.95 (ISBN 0-382-09698-3); pap. 4.46s.p. (ISBN 0-685-37319-3). Silver Burdett Pr.
—A Midsummer Night's Dream. Bancroft-Hunt, Norman, illus. LC 87-37229. 32p. (gr. 6-12). 1988. 10.96g (ISBN 0-382-09690-8). Silver Burdett Pr.
—Romeo & Juliet. Thompson, George, illus. LC 87-37222. 32p. (gr. 6-12). 1988. 10.96 (ISBN 0-382-09688-6); 8.22s.p. (ISBN 0-382-09694-0). Silver Burdett Pr.
—Twelfth Night. Thompson, George, illus. 32p. (gr. 6-12). 1988. 10.96g (ISBN 0-382-09689-4); 8.22s.p. (ISBN 0-685-37320-7); pap. 5.95 (ISBN 0-382-09695-9); pap. 4.46s.p. (ISBN 0-685-37321-5). Silver Burdett Pr.
Shakespeare, William. All's Well That Ends Well. Rowland, Beryl, intro. by. LC 85-4167. (gr. 9 up). 1968. pap. 0.60 (ISBN 0-8049-1022-7, S22). Airmont.
—Antony & Cleopatra. Rudvik, O. H., intro. by. (gr. 10 up). pap. 0.60 (ISBN 0-8049-1011-1, S-11). Airmont.
—As You Like It. Pitt, David G., intro. by. (gr. 10 up). pap. 1.25 (ISBN 0-8049-1006-5, S-6). Airmont.
—Comedy of Errors. Rudzik, O. H., intro. by. (gr. 9 up). 1968. pap. 0.60 (ISBN 0-8049-1023-5, S-23). Airmont.
—Coriolanus. Rowland, Beryl, intro. by. (gr. 10 up). 1968. pap. 0.60 (ISBN 0-8049-1021-9, S-21). Airmont.
—Hamlet. Mattea, Gino, intro. by. (gr. 11 up). pap. 1.95 (ISBN 0-8049-1001-4, S1). Airmont.
—Hamlet. Davidson, Diane, ed. LC 83-12310. (gr. 8-12). 1983. casebound 8.95 (ISBN 0-934048-13-4); pap. 4.95 (ISBN 0-934048-12-6). Swan Books.
—Henry IV, Pts. 1 & 2. Young, Archibald, intro. by. (gr. 10 up). pap. 1.25 ea. Pt. 1 (ISBN 0-8049-1018-9, S18). Pt. 2. pap. 0.60 (ISBN 0-685-00150-4, S19). Airmont.
—Julius Caesar. Rudzik, O. H., intro. by. (Illus.). (gr. 9 up). pap. 1.95 (ISBN 0-8049-1004-9, S4). Airmont.
—Julius Caesar. Davidson, Diane, ed. LC 83-12307. (gr. 8-12). 1983. 8.95 (ISBN 0-934048-05-3); pap. 4.95 (ISBN 0-934048-04-5). Swan Books.
—King John. Rowland, Beryl, intro. by. (gr. 9 up). 1968. pap. 1.95 (ISBN 0-8049-1024-3, S24). Airmont.
—King Lear. Girling, H. K., intro. by. (gr. 11 up). pap. 1.75 (ISBN 0-8049-1012-X, S12). Airmont.
—Macbeth. Duffy, John D., intro. by. (gr. 11 up). pap. 1.95 (ISBN 0-8049-1002-2, S2). Airmont.
—Macbeth. Davidson, Diane, ed. LC 83-12312. (gr. 8-12). 1983. casebound 8.95 (ISBN 0-934048-03-7); pap. 4.95 (ISBN 0-934048-02-9). Swan Books.
—Merchant of Venice. Redekop, Ernest, intro. by. (gr. 9 up). pap. 1.25 (ISBN 0-8049-1003-0, S3). Airmont.
—Merchant of Venice. Davidson, Diane, ed. LC 83-12308. (gr. 8-12). 1983. casebound 8.95 (ISBN 0-934048-09-6); pap. 4.95 (ISBN 0-934048-08-8). Swan Books.
—Midsummer Night's Dream. Pitt, David G., intro. by. (gr. 10 up). pap. 1.95 (ISBN 0-8049-1005-7, S5). Airmont.
—Midsummer Night's Dream. Davidson, Diane, ed. LC 83-12311. (gr. 8-12). 1983. casebound 8.95 (ISBN 0-934048-11-8); pap. 4.95 (ISBN 0-934048-10-X). Swan Books.
—Much Ado about Nothing. Rowland, Beryl, intro. by. (gr. 10 up). pap. 1.95 (ISBN 0-8049-1020-0, S20). Airmont.
—Othello. Rudvik, O. H., intro. by. (gr. 10 up). pap. 1.75 (ISBN 0-8049-1013-8, S13). Airmont.
—Richard Second. Young, Archibald M., intro. by. (gr. 9 up). pap. 0.60 (ISBN 0-8049-1014-6, S14). Airmont.
—Richard Third. Willoughby, John, intro. by. (gr. 9 up). pap. 0.60 (ISBN 0-8049-1015-4, S15). Airmont.
—Romeo & Juliet. Thomas, Clara, intro. by. (gr. 8 up). pap. 1.95 (ISBN 0-8049-1009-X, S9). Airmont.
—Taming of the Shrew. Girling, Z. N., intro. by. (gr. 10 up). pap. 1.75 (ISBN 0-8049-1010-3, S10). Airmont.
—Tempest. Pitt, D. G., intro. by. (gr. 11 up). pap. 1.95 (ISBN 0-8049-1007-3, S7). Airmont.
—Twelfth Night. Pitt, David G., intro. by. (gr. 10 up). pap. 1.75 (ISBN 0-8049-1008-1, S8). Airmont.

Shaw, George Bernard. Caesar & Cleopatra. (gr. 11 up). pap. 0.95 (ISBN 0-8049-0119-8, CL-119). Airmont.
—Man & Superman. Teitel, N. R., intro. by. (gr. 11 up). pap. 2.50 (ISBN 0-8049-0096-5, CL-96). Airmont.
Wilde, Oscar. Five Major Plays. Incl. Lady Windermere's Fan; Importance of Being Earnest; Salome; Woman of No Importance; Ideal Husband. (gr. 10 up). pap. 2.75 (ISBN 0-8049-0208-9, CL-208). Airmont.

ENGLISH ESSAYS

Kaiser, Questa. That Reminds Me... Davenport, May, illus. LC 81-67424. 116p. (Orig.). (gr. 9-12). 1984. pap. 4.50x (ISBN 0-943864-14-3). Davenport.

ENGLISH FOR FOREIGNERS

see English Language–Textbooks for Foreigners

ENGLISH GRAMMAR

see English Language–Grammar

ENGLISH HISTORY

see Great Britain–History

ENGLISH LANGUAGE

Bachman, Barbara. Frisky Phonics Fun I. Bachman, Barbara, illus. 152p. (gr. 1-3). 1984. wkbk. 10.95 (ISBN 0-86653-195-5, GA 548). Good Apple.
—Frisky Phonics Fun II. Bachman, Barbara, illus. 152p. (gr. 1-3). 1984. wkbk. 10.95 (ISBN 0-86653-212-9, GA 549). Good Apple.
Banchek, Linda. Snake In, Snake Out. Arnold, Elaine, illus. LC 78-51935. (ps-1). 1978. (Crowell Jr Bks). HarpC Child Bks.
Burney, Susan L. Prime Time Rhyme Time. (Illus.). 36p. (gr. 2). 1981. spiral binding 4.95 (ISBN 0-89305-039-3). Anna Pub.
Civardi, Anne. Word Finders in English. 48p. (gr. k-3). 1984. 11.95 (ISBN 0-86020-767-6). EDC.
De Brunhoff, Laurent. Je Parle Anglais avec Babar. (FRE., Illus.). (gr. 4-6). 15.95 (ISBN 0-685-11272-1). French & Eur.
Gregory, Elizabeth. The Short & Long. (Illus.). 1981. 6.95 (ISBN 0-933184-09-3); pap. 4.95 (ISBN 0-933184-10-7). Flame Intl.
Hanson, Joan. Homographs: Bow & Bow & Other Words That Look the Same but Sound As Different As Sow & Sow. Hanson, Joan, illus. LC 72-1122. 32p. (ps-3). 1972. PLB 5.95 (ISBN 0-8225-0278-X). Lerner Pubns.
Harlan, Judith. Bilingualism in the United States: Conflict & Controversy. (Illus.). 128p. (gr. 9-12). 1991. PLB 12.90 (ISBN 0-531-13001-0). Watts.
Jenkins, Betty. Vowel Fun. Brown, Virginia, illus. 96p. (gr. 1-3). 1983. wkbk. 8.95 (ISBN 0-86653-107-6, GA 465). Good Apple.
Kindergarten Vocabulary. (Illus.). 24p. (ps-k). 1986. 3.98 (ISBN 0-86734-069-X, FS-3059). Schaffer Pubns.
McMillan, Bruce. Kitten Can...a Concept Book. McMillan, Bruce, illus. LC 83-19539. 32p. (ps-1). 1984. 12.95 (ISBN 0-688-02668-0); PLB 12.88 (ISBN 0-688-02669-9). Lothrop.
—Super, Super, Superwords. Briley, D., ed. McMillan, Bruce, illus. LC 88-9342. 32p. (ps-2). 1989. 12.95 (ISBN 0-688-08098-7); PLB 12.88 (ISBN 0-688-08099-5). Lothrop.
Morley, Diana. Marms in the Marmalade. Rogers, Kathy, illus. LC 83-23982. 24p. (gr. k-4). 1984. PLB 9.95 (ISBN 0-87614-258-7). Carolrhoda Bks.
Terdy, Dennis. Content Area ESL: Social Studies. Mrowicki, Linda, ed. (Illus.). 169p. (gr. 5-12). 1986. pap. 8.95 (ISBN 0-916591-06-9). Linmore Pub.
Thurston, Cheryl M. What's in a Name? Blackstone, Ann, illus. 24p. (Orig.). (gr. 5-12). 1988. pap. text ed. 8.95 (ISBN 1-877673-04-8). Cottonwood Pr.
Winitz, Harris. Text for the Learnables, American English, Bk. 1. 36p. (gr. 3 up). 1990. pap. text ed. 6.50 (ISBN 0-685-38373-3). Intl Linguistics.
—Text for the Learnables, Spanish, Bk. 1. Sagarna, Blanca, tr. (SPA.). 36p. (gr. 3 up). 1990. pap. text ed. 6.50. Intl Linguistics.

ENGLISH LANGUAGE–AMERICANISMS

see Americanisms

ENGLISH LANGUAGE–BUSINESS ENGLISH

Merriss, William E. & Griswold, David H. A Composition Handbook. 3rd ed. 1985. 9.28 (ISBN 0-8013-0074-6, 75738); pap. text ed. 14.80 (ISBN 0-88334-186-7, 76152). Longman.

ENGLISH LANGUAGE–COMPOSITION AND EXERCISES

Alarie, Julia & Conlon, Elizabeth. Tickle My Fancy: Creative Language Arts Activities, Written-Verbal-Artistic. Sussman, Ellen, ed. Smith, Anita, illus. 48p. (Orig.). (gr. 4-6). 1980. pap. text ed. 5.95 (ISBN 0-933606-05-2, MS-606). Monkey Sisters.
Artman, John H. The Write Stuff! Filkins, Vanessa, illus. 64p. (gr. 4-8). 1985. wkbk. 6.95 (ISBN 0-86653-273-0, GA 681). Good Apple.
Basic Skills in English, Bk. 5. (gr. 11). 1980. 19.98 (ISBN 0-88343-790-2); tchr's. manual 10.56 (ISBN 0-88343-791-0); practice bk. 7.17 (ISBN 0-88343-792-9); tchr's. manual with key 10.05 (ISBN 0-88343-793-7). answer key 3.18 (ISBN 0-88343-795-3); answer key to tests 2.48 (ISBN 0-88343-796-1). McDougal-Littell.
Basic Skills in English: Green Level. (gr. 8). 1989. text ed. 21.54 (ISBN 0-8123-5477-X); tchr's. ed. 28.68 (ISBN 0-86609-483-0); practice bk., tchr's. ed. 11.07 (ISBN 0-86609-485-7); tchr's. resource binder 82.50 (ISBN 0-8123-5513-X); practice bk. 7.89 (ISBN 0-86609-484-9); test bklt. 3.09 (ISBN 0-86609-486-5); test bklt. answer key 3.51 (ISBN 0-86609-487-3). McDougal-Littell.
Basic Skills in English: Red Level. (gr. 7). 1989. text ed. 21.54 (ISBN 0-8123-5475-3); tchr's. ed. 26.07 (ISBN 0-86609-477-6); practice bk., tchr's. ed. 11.07 (ISBN 0-86609-479-2); tchr's. resource binder 82.50 (ISBN 0-8123-5507-5); practice bk. 7.80 (ISBN 0-86609-478-4); test bklt. 3.09 (ISBN 0-86609-480-6); test bklt. answer key 3.51 (ISBN 0-86609-481-4). McDougal-Littell.
Bernstein, Bonnie. Writing Crafts Workshop. LC 81-85351. (gr. 3-8). 1982. pap. 8.95 (ISBN 0-8224-9785-9). Fearon Teach Aids.
Black, Ann N. & Smith, Jo R. Ten Tools of Language-Written. 2nd ed. (Illus.). 166p. (gr. 11-12). 1982. pap. text ed. 12.60x (ISBN 0-910513-00-7). Mayfield Printing.
Buchter, Carol & Quigley, Elaine. Developing Basic Writing Skills, Bk. 1. (gr. 3-4). 1983. wkbk. 4.95 (ISBN 0-89525-391-7). Ed Activities.
—Developing Basic Writing Skills, Bk. 2. (gr. 5-6). 1983. wkbk. 4.95 (ISBN 0-89525-392-5). Ed Activities.
Buschemeyer, Robin Q. Word Pal. Launching Pad Studio, Inc. Staff, illus. 40p. (Orig.). (ps-3). 1986. pap. 2.99 (ISBN 0-935609-00-8). Eduplay.
Cahill, Robert B. & Hrebic, Herbert J. Cut the Deck. rev. ed. Barry, Jimi, ed. (gr. 8-9). 1985. text ed. 9.10 (ISBN 0-933282-16-8); pap. text ed. 6.00 (ISBN 0-933282-15-X). Stack the Deck.
Cassedy, Sylvia. In Your Own Words: A Beginner's Guide to Writing. rev. ed. LC 89-78079. 240p. (gr. 5 up). 1990. 13.95 (ISBN 0-690-04821-1, Crowell Jr Bks); PLB 13.89 (ISBN 0-690-04823-8, Crowell Jr Bks). HarpC Child Bks.
—In Your Own Words: A Beginner's Guide to Writing. rev. ed. LC 89-78079. 240p. (gr. 5 up). 1990. pap. 7.95 (ISBN 0-06-446102-5, Trophy). HarpC Child Bks.
Daniel, Becky. Writing Brainstorms. 80p. (gr. 1-4). 1990. 7.95 (ISBN 0-86653-569-1, GA1172). Good Apple.
—Writing Thinker Sheets. 64p. (gr. 4-8). 1989. 7.95 (ISBN 0-86653-490-3, GA1098). Good Apple.
Donovan, Melissa. Teaching Creative Writing. 144p. (gr. 3-8). 1990. 10.95 (ISBN 0-86653-559-4, GA1156). Good Apple.
English Composition Study Aid. 1978. pap. 1.95 (ISBN 0-87738-029-5). Youth Ed.
Fleisher, Paul. Write Now! 80p. (gr. 5-8). 1989. 8.95 (ISBN 0-86653-493-8, GA1088). Good Apple.
Forte, Imogene. Write about It Series, 3 vols. Incl. Beginning Writers. (gr. k-1). 1983. pap. text ed. 7.95 (ISBN 0-86530-044-5, IP 44-5); Primary. (gr. 2-4). 1983. pap. text ed. 7.95 (ISBN 0-86530-045-3, IP 45-3); Middle Grades. (gr. 4-6). 1983. pap. text ed. 7.95 (ISBN 0-86530-046-1, IP 46-1). (Illus., 80 pgs. ea. volume). (gr. k-6). 1983. pap. text ed. 23.50 (ISBN 0-685-06165-5, IP 43-7). Incentive Pubns.
Glover, Susanne & Grewe, Georgeann. Bone up on Book Reports. 64p. (gr. 3-8). 1981. 7.95 (ISBN 0-86653-001-0, GA 228). Good Apple.
Grimm, Gary & Mitchell, Don. Good Apple Creative Writing Book. 112p. (gr. 3-8). 1976. 9.95 (ISBN 0-916456-04-8, GA61). Good Apple.
Hammar, Richard R. Pastor, Church & Law. LC 83-80245. 448p. (gr. 12). 1983. 16.95 (ISBN 0-88243-580-9, 02-0580). Gospel Pub.
Henrich, Stephen & Henrich, Jean. Story Starters on Present Day. rev. ed. Henrich, Jean, illus. 80p. (gr. 4-12). Date not set. write for info. wkbk. (HE 400). Henrich Enter.
—Story Starters on the Future. rev. ed. Henrich, Jean, illus. 80p. (gr. 4-12). Date not set. write for info. wkbk. (HE 500). Henrich Enter.
Hornnes, Esther & Magos, Eunice. Sew & Know: Puppet Projects to Teach Vowel Sounds. Sussman, Ellen, ed. Burris, Priscilla, illus. 40p. (Orig.). (gr. k-2). 1984. pap. text ed. 4.95 (ISBN 0-933606-29-X, MS-628). Monkey Sisters.
Hutson-Nechkash, Peg. Storybuilding: A Guide to Structuring Oral Narratives. 128p. (Orig.). (gr. 3-8). 1990. pap. text ed. 24.00x (ISBN 0-930599-63-2). Thinking Pubns.
James, Elizabeth & Barkin, Carol. How to Write a Great School Report. Greenlaw, M. Jean, intro. by. LC 83-764. (Illus.). 167p. (gr. 3-5). 1983. PLB 11.88 (ISBN 0-688-02283-9). Lothrop.
—How to Write a Term Paper. Jacobs, Leland B., intro. by. LC 80-13734. 96p. (gr. 7 up). 1980. 11.88 (ISBN 0-685-03103-9). Lothrop.
Johnson, Eric. You Are the Editor: Sixty-One Editing Lessons That Improve Writing Skills. (gr. 5 up). 1981. pap. 11.95 (ISBN 0-8224-7696-7); wkbk 3.95 (ISBN 0-8224-7697-5). Fearon Teach Aids.
Kadra, Sheila & Smith, Patricia. Painting with Words. 1987. pap. text ed. 17.20 (ISBN 0-88334-195-6, 76160). Longman.
Lieberman, Leo & Spielberger, Jeffrey. Essential English Composition for College-Bound Students. 224p. (Orig.). (gr. 11-12). 1988. pap. 8.95 wkbk. (ISBN 0-13-286063-5). P-H.
McAllister, Constance. Creative Writing for Beginners. 32p. (Orig.). (gr. 1-3). 1976. pap. 2.95 (ISBN 0-87534-165-9). Highlights.
McBaine, Robert. Student Workbook for Sentence Combining with Exercises & Key. 135p. (Orig.). (gr. 8 up). 1984. pap. 8.90 (ISBN 0-89420-244-8, 261000). Natl Book.
Maid, Amy. Write, from the Beginning. (Illus.). 92p. (Orig.). (gr. 2-4). 1982. pap. 11.95x (ISBN 0-8290-0993-0). Irvington.
Maifair, Linda. Paragraphs Plus, 2 bks. Sussman, Ellen, intro. by. Burris, Priscilla, illus. (Orig.). (gr. 3-6). 1988. pap. 6.95 ea. Level I, 64p (ISBN 0-933606-63-X). Level II o.s.i (ISBN 0-933606-64-8). Monkey Sisters.
Mammen, Lori. TEAMS Vocabulary Plus: Learning & Using TEAMS Vocabulary Words, 3 vols. (Illus.). 120p. 1988. pap. text ed. 7.95 ea. Grade 3 (ISBN 0-944459-00-5). Grade 5 (ISBN 0-944459-01-3). Grade 7 (ISBN 0-944459-02-1). ECS Lrn Systs.
—Writing Prompts Plus: Preparing Students for the TEAMS Composition Test, 4 vols. (Illus.). 160p. 1988. pap. text ed. 7.95 ea. Grade 3 (ISBN 0-944459-03-X). Grade 5 (ISBN 0-944459-04-8). Grade 7 (ISBN 0-944459-05-6). Grade 9 (ISBN 0-944459-06-4). ECS Lrn Systs.
—Writing Warm-Ups: Seven to Twelve. 80p. (gr. 7-12). 1989. pap. text ed. 9.95 (ISBN 0-944459-08-0). ECS Lrn Systs.
Marsh, Carole. A-Plus Very Good! Secrets of Good Writing for Students. (Orig.). (gr. 4-12). 1986. 19.95 (ISBN 1-55609-272-5); pap. text ed. 14.95 (ISBN 0-935326-63-4). Gallopade Pub Group.
Olshtain, Elite, et al. The Junior Files, File 1: English for Today & Tomorrow. rev. ed. Berman, Aaron & Chapman, Charles, eds. (Illus.). 270p. (gr. 6-10). 1991. pap. write for info. (ISBN 1-878598-02-3). Alta Bk Co Pubs.
Richards, Joanne & Standley, Marianne. One for the Books. (Illus.). 128p. (gr. 4-6). 1984. pap. text ed. 8.95 (ISBN 0-86530-023-2, IP 23-2). Incentive Pubns.
Rico, Armando B. School Adventures: Aventuras Escolares. 27p. (Orig.). 1989. pap. text ed. 4.95 (ISBN 1-879219-04-2). Veracruz Pubs.
Ronnholm, Ursula O. & Ronnholm, Paul F. My Book of Words, Songs & Sentences. Enrique, Miguel M., illus. 91p. (gr. k-3). 1986. pap. text ed. 7.00 (ISBN 0-941911-03-9). Two Way Bilingual.
Rothstein, Evelyn & Gess, Diane. EarlyWriter. Gompper, Gail, illus. 80p. (gr. k-1). 1989. pap. text ed. 7.95 (ISBN 0-913935-44-1). ERA-CCR.
Rozakis, Laurie. AP Exam in English Literature & Composition. 2nd ed. 384p. (gr. 9-12). 1990. pap. 10.95 (ISBN 0-13-011629-7). Arco.
Schwartz, L. Pick a Picture - Kit. 40p. (gr. 3-6). 1989. 9.95 (ISBN 0-88160-179-9, LW 285). Learning Wks.
—Select a Story. 40p. (gr. 3-6). 1989. 9.95 (ISBN 0-88160-182-9, LW 286). Learning Wks.
—Sharpen Your Senses. (gr. 1-6). 1978. 3.95 (ISBN 0-88160-056-3, LW 604). Learning Wks.
Segan, Eleanor. How to Write Right, No. 1: From Lists to Letters. (Illus.). 96p. (gr. 7-12). 1986. pap. 5.75 (ISBN 0-941342-15-8, 2115). Entry Pub.
—How to Write Right, No. 2: Forms & More. (Illus.). 64p. (gr. 7-12). 1986. pap. 4.40 (ISBN 0-941342-16-6, 2116). Entry Pub.
Smith, Mary D. & Smith, Brad. Creative Writing Patterns. Tom, Tiana, illus. 48p. (gr. k-4). 1983. wkbk. 5.95 (ISBN 1-55734-130-3). Tchr Create Mat.
Stanish, Bob. Creativity for Kids Through Writing. (Illus.). 64p. (gr. 1 up). 1983. wkbk. 6.95 (ISBN 0-86653-118-1, GA 486). Good Apple.
Suid, Murray. For the Love of Sentences. 64p. (gr. 4-6). 1986. 6.95 (ISBN 0-912107-51-0). Monday Morning Bks.
Tchudi, Susan & Tchudi, Stephen. The Young Writer's Handbook: A Practical Guide for the Beginner Who Is Serious about Writing. LC 87-1463. (Illus.). 176p. (gr. 7 up). 1987. pap. 4.95 (ISBN 0-689-71170-0, Aladdin). Macmillan Child Grp.
Terban, Marvin. Your Foot's on My Feet: And Other Tricky Nouns. Maestro, Giulio, illus. LC 85-19561. (gr. 2-5). 1986. pap. 11.95 (ISBN 0-89919-411-7, Pub. by Clarion); pap. 4.95 (ISBN 0-89919-413-3). Ticknor & Fields.
Thorne, Randy. Week-to-Week Writing. Burris, Priscilla & Wiltshire, Sadelle, illus. 80p. (Orig.). (gr. 2-5). 1989. pap. text ed. 6.95 (ISBN 0-933606-80-X). Monkey Sisters.
Thurston, Cheryl M. Cottonwood Composition Book. 56p. (Orig.). (gr. 5-12). 1986. pap. text ed. 14.95 (ISBN 1-877673-00-5). Cottonwood Pr.
Tilkin, Sheldon. Paragraph & Topic Sentence. Pape, Richard, illus. 24p. (gr. 3-4). 1980. wkbk. 2.95 (ISBN 0-89403-606-8). EDC.
Tyler, J. & Round, G. Ready for Writing. (Illus.). 24p. (ps up). 1989. pap. 3.50 (ISBN 0-7460-0218-1, Usborne). EDC.
Weisberg, Valerie H. Students' Discourse: Comprehensive Examples & Explanations of All Expository Modes & Argument, Precis, Narrative, Examination Writing & MLA Reccomendations for Research Paper Documentation Writing Exposition. 2nd ed. 126p. 1990. pap. 9.95. V H Pub.
Whiteside, Sandra & Whiteside, Rita G. Primary Writing Fun. Whiteside, Saundra & Whiteside, Rita, illus. 80p. (gr. 1-3). 1983. wkbk. 7.95 (ISBN 0-86653-101-7, GA 461). Good Apple.
Winitz, Harris. Basic Structures - American English, Bk. 1: A Textbook for the Learnables. Baker, Syd, illus. 100p. (gr. 7 up). 1990. Incls. cass. tape. pap. text ed. 42.00 incl. 4 cass. tapes. Intl Linguistics.
Writing Help. 32p. (ps-1). 2.95 (ISBN 0-86653-248-X, GA 595). Good Apple.
Writing Help. 32p. (gr. k-2). 2.95 (ISBN 0-86653-249-8, GA 598). Good Apple.
Writing Help. 32p. (gr. 1-3). 2.95 (ISBN 0-86653-250-1, GA 597). Good Apple.

Writing Help. 32p. (gr. 2-4). 2.95 (ISBN 0-86653-251-X, GA 596). Good Apple.

ENGLISH LANGUAGE–CONVERSATION AND PHRASE BOOKS

see English Language–Textbooks for Foreigners; see use subdivision conversation and phrase books for languages other than english

ENGLISH LANGUAGE–DICTIONARIES

Abbs, Brian. Longman Picture Wordbook. (Illus.). (ps-2). 1988. 14.21 (ISBN 0-582-02239-8, 70444). Longman.

Amery & Mila. First Thousand Words in English. (gr. 1-9). 1979. 11.95 (ISBN 0-86020-266-6, Usborne-Hayes). English ed. EDC.

Beal, George. The Simon & Schuster Young Readers' Thesaurus. Barish, Wendy, ed. (Illus.). 192p. (gr. 3-7). 1984. pap. 6.95 (ISBN 0-685-09127-9, Little Simon). S&S Trade.

Beebe, Brooke M. & Rosenblatt, Ruth Y. The Dictionary. Maas, Mieke, illus. LC 77-730283. (gr. 3-5). 1977. pap. text ed. 165.00 4 filmstrips, 4 cass., 24 skill sheets, Guide (ISBN 0-89290-121-7, A151-SATC). Soc for Visual.

Beginning Dictionary. LC 78-27760. (gr. 3-6). 1979. 21.00 (ISBN 0-395-27400-1). HM.

Beginning Dictionary. (Illus.). (gr. 3-6). 1991. pap. text ed. 9.99 (ISBN 0-8123-6931-9); tchr's. notes 2.98 (ISBN 0-8123-6932-7). McDougal-Littell.

Bennett, Archie. New Color-Picture Dictionary for Children. (Illus.). 252p. (gr. k-4). 1981. PLB 22.60 (ISBN 0-516-00820-X). Childrens.

Byrd, Elizabeth L. A Fonalfubet Pronunciation Dictionary of American English Words. (Orig.). (gr. k up). 1986. pap. text ed. 20.00 (ISBN 0-9615393-2-1). U Assocs.

Coogan, John W. A Workbook of Words. 1987. pap. text ed. 21.60 (ISBN 0-8013-0116-5, 75780). Longman.

Cooke, Tom, illus. Open Sesame Picture Dictionary. Malecki, Ed, designed by. (ENG & JPN.). 1987. pap. 5.95 (ISBN 0-19-434170-4). Oxford U Pr.

Dougherty, Margaret M., et al, eds. Instant Spelling Dictionary. (gr. 9 up). 1967. 4.95 (ISBN 0-531-01697-8). Watts.

Eastman, P. D. Cat in the Hat Beginner Book Dictionary. LC 64-1157. (Illus.). 144p. (gr. k-6). 1964. 8.95 (ISBN 0-394-81009-0); lib. bdg. 8.99 (ISBN 0-394-91009-5). Beginner.

Eastman, Philip D. The Cat in the Hat Beginner Book Dictionary. (Illus.). (gr. 2-3). 1984. 8.99 (ISBN 0-685-09231-3). Random.

First Dictionary. 1989. 7.98 (ISBN 0-8317-3359-4). Smithmark.

Foust, Sylvia J. Dictionary Skills. Foust, Sylvia J., illus. 48p. (gr. 2-6). 1986. wkbk. 5.95 (ISBN 1-55734-339-X). Tchr Create Mat.

Goldsmith, Evelyn. First Dictionary for Young Readers. Danns, Penny, illus. 169p. (gr. 1-5). 1989. 11.95 (ISBN 0-531-15121-2). Watts.

Gregorich, Barbara. Dictionary Skills. Pape, Richard, illus. 24p. (gr. 3-4). 1980. wkbk. 2.95 (ISBN 0-89403-605-X). EDC.

Grisewood, John. Simon & Schuster's Illustrated Young Readers' Dictionary. rev. ed. Barish, Wendy, ed. (Illus.). 240p. (gr. 8 up). 1984. pap. 9.79 (ISBN 0-671-50020-1, Little Simon). S&S Trade.

Guralnik, David B., ed. Webster's New World Dictionary: Basic School Edition. 1976. 15.00 (ISBN 0-13-944652-4). P-H.

Hillerich, Robert L. The American Heritage Picture Dictionary. Swanson, Maggie, illus. 144p. (gr. k-1). 1986. 9.95 (ISBN 0-395-42531-X). HM.

Houghton Mifflin Company Staff. The American Heritage School Dictionary. LC 72-75557. (Illus.). 1024p. (gr. 7-10). 1977. 10.95 (ISBN 0-395-24792-6). HM.

Houghton Mifflin Company Staff, ed. The American Heritage Children's Dictionary. Webber, Howard, contrib. by. LC 86-7349. (Illus.). 864p. (gr. 3-6). 1986. 13.95 (ISBN 0-395-42529-8). HM.

Houghton Mifflin Company Staff, ed. & contrib. by. The American Heritage Student's Dictionary. rev. ed. LC 86-7337. (Illus.). 1024p. (gr. 6-9). 1986. 12.95 (ISBN 0-395-40417-7). HM.

Houghton Mifflin Company Staff, ed. Children's Dictionary. Rev. ed. LC 78-27760. (Illus.). 864p. (gr. 3-6). 1979. 12.95 (ISBN 0-395-27512-1). HM.

—First Dictionary. Ulrich, George, illus. LC 78-27760. 864p. (gr. 3-6). 1979. text ed. 11.95 (ISBN 0-685-07955-4). HM.

Houghton Mifflin Primary Dictionary & Workbook-Primary. 1986. 18.40 (ISBN 0-395-38393-5). HM.

Jefferds, Vince. Disney's My Very First Dictionary. LC 88-24135. (Illus.). 95p. (gr. k-3). 1989. 24.95 (ISBN 0-8109-1146-9). Abrams.

Koh, Frances M., ed. English-Korean Picture Dictionary. Vignes, Denise S., illus. LC 87-83309. 49p. (Orig.). (ps up). 1987. pap. 7.95 (ISBN 0-9606090-3-2). EastWest Pr.

Krensky, Stephen, ed. The American Heritage First Dictionary. Ulrich, George, illus. LC 86-7363. (Illus.). (gr. 1-2). 1986. 11.95 (ISBN 0-395-42530-1). HM.

Law, Felicia. Doubleday Children's Picture Dictionary. Holmes, Carol, illus. LC 86-16216. 192p. (gr. k-6). 1987. pap. 13.95 (ISBN 0-385-23711-1). Doubleday.

Levey, Judith, ed. The Macmillan First Dictionary. rev. & expanded ed. LC 90-6062. (Illus.). 416p. (ps-4). 1990. 12.95 (ISBN 0-02-761731-9, Mcmillan Child Bk). Macmillan Child Grp.

Longman Staff. Longman Handy Learner's Dictionary. (gr. 9-12). 1988. pap. text ed. 7.46 (ISBN 0-582-96413-X, 78324). Longman.

Longmeyer, Carole M. What Did You Sayeth? Rhodes, Priscilla, illus. (Orig.). (gr. 4 up). 1983. pap. 14.95 (ISBN 0-935326-45-6). Gallopade Pub Group.

Macmillan Publishing Company Staff. Macmillan Dictionary for Children. rev. ed. LC 81-13651. 784p. (gr. 1-6). 1982. 13.95 (ISBN 0-02-578790-X, Mcmillan Child Bk). Macmillan Child Grp.

—Macmillan Dictionary for Children. rev. ed. (Illus.). (gr. 2 up). 1977. 12.95 (ISBN 0-02-578750-0, Mcmillan Child Bk). Macmillan Child Grp.

—Macmillan Dictionary for Students. LC 84-3880. (Illus.). 1216p. (gr. 6-12). 1984. 16.95 (ISBN 0-02-761560-X, Mcmillan Child Bk). Macmillan Child Grp.

—Macmillan Very First Dictionary: A Magic World of Words. rev. ed. LC 82-22901. (Illus.). 280p. (ps-2). 1983. 10.95 (ISBN 0-02-761730-0). Macmillan.

Merriam-Webster Editorial Staff. Webster's Elementary Dictionary. (Illus.). (gr. 1-6). 1980. 11.95 (ISBN 0-87779-475-8). Merriam-Webster Inc.

Minn, Loretta. Dictionary Digs. Jurgens, Steve, illus. 48p. (gr. 3-8). 1984. wkbk. 5.95 (ISBN 0-86653-169-6, GA 528). Good Apple.

Morehead, Albert H., et al, eds. New American Roget's College Thesaurus in Dictionary Form. (gr. 9 up). 1957. 7.95 (ISBN 0-399-12959-6, Putnam); thumb-indexed ed. o.p. 7.95 (ISBN 0-448-01622-2). Putnam Pub Group.

The New Scholastic Dictionary of American English. 1024p. (gr. 4-7). 1986. pap. 6.95 (ISBN 0-590-40415-6). Scholastic Inc.

Passport Books Staff, ed. Let's Learn English: Picture Dictionary. Goodman, Marlene, illus. 72p. Date not set. 9.95 (ISBN 0-8442-5453-3). Natl Textbk.

Pheby, John A., ed. The Oxford-Duden Pictorial English Dictionary. (Illus.). 824p. (gr. 9 up). 1984. pap. 14.95 (ISBN 0-19-864155-9). Oxford U Pr.

Ridout, Ronald. Activity Picture Dictionary. Wingham, Peter, illus. 48p. (gr. 1 up). 1987. 9.95 (ISBN 0-8120-5844-5). Barron.

Roget's Beginning Thesaurus. (ps-3). 1990. 9.95 (ISBN 0-06-017903-1, HarpT). HarperCollins.

Roget's Beginning Thesaurus. 240p. (gr. 3-7). 1990. 11.95 (ISBN 0-06-017904-X, HarpT). HarperCollins.

Scarry, Huck, illus. My First Picture Dictionary. LC 76-24174. (ps-2). 1978. lib. bdg. 5.99 (ISBN 0-394-93486-5, Random Juv); pap. 2.25 (ISBN 0-394-83486-0). Random.

Schimpff, Jill W. Open Sesame Picture Dictionary: Featuring Jim Henson's Sesame Street Muppets, Children's Television Workshop. Cooke, Tom, illus. (gr. k-6). 1982. 10.95x (ISBN 0-19-503201-2); pap. 5.95x (ISBN 0-19-503035-4); activity book 3.95 (ISBN 0-19-434253-0); Picture Dictionary, English-Chinese. 5.95 (ISBN 0-19-583744-4). Oxford U Pr.

Scott Foresman Co. Staff. Jr. Thesaurus. 1988. 11.95 (ISBN 0-673-12494-0). Scott F.

Sesame Street Staff & Hayward, Linda. The Sesame Street Dictionary. Mathieu, Joe, illus. LC 80-11644. 256p. (ps-3). 1980. bds. 15.95 (ISBN 0-394-84007-0); PLB 17.99 (ISBN 0-394-94007-5). Random.

Sheheen, Dennis, illus. Children's Picture Dictionary: English-Chinese, (gr. k up). 9.95 (ISBN 0-685-18873-6, Dist. by Watts). Adama Pubs Inc.

—A Child's Picture English-Arabic Dictionary. LC 85-15658. (gr. k-2). 1985. 9.95 (ISBN 0-915361-30-2, Dist. by Watts). Adama Pubs Inc.

—A Child's Picture English-Italian Dictionary. LC 86-14052. (gr. k-2). 1986. 9.95 (ISBN 0-915361-57-4, Dist. by Watts). Adama Pubs Inc.

—A Child's Picture English-Yiddish Dictionary. LC 85-15659. (gr. k-2). 1985. 9.95 (ISBN 0-915361-29-9, Dist. by Watts). Adama Pubs Inc.

The Simon & Schuster Young Readers' Illustrated Dictionary. (Illus.). (gr. 3 up). 1985. pap. 6.95 (ISBN 0-671-50821-0, Little Simon). S&S Trade.

Southworth, Mary C. Wordworks. 1986. pap. text ed. 18.00 (ISBN 0-88334-192-1, 76157). Longman.

Spooner, Alan & Weston, John. Oxford Children's Dictionary. (Illus.). (gr. 3 up). 1985. 14.95 (ISBN 0-19-861183-8). Oxford U Pr.

Thompson, Brian. The Viking First Picture Dictionary. (Illus.). 48p. (ps-1). 1988. pap. 8.95 (ISBN 0-670-82154-3). Viking Child Bks.

Thorndike-Barnhart Children's Dictionary. 768p. 1990. 13.95 (ISBN 0-06-017905-8, HarpT). HarperCollins.

Thorndike-Barnhart Student Dictionary. 1310p. (gr. 7 up). 1990. 15.95 (ISBN 0-06-017906-6, HarpT). HarperCollins.

Troll Reference Library Staff. Young People's Dictionary. LC 89-27331. 1991. PLB 14.89 (ISBN 0-8167-2256-0); pap. 9.95. Troll Assocs.

Watson & Folliet. Round the World - English. (gr. 1-9). 1980. 11.95 (ISBN 0-86020-485-5, Usborne-Hayes). French ed (ISBN 0-86020-488-X). Spanish ed (ISBN 0-86020-484-7). EDC.

Webster's Elementary Dictionary. 1990. text ed. 18.75 (ISBN 0-8123-6247-0). McDougal-Littell.

Webster's High School Dictionary. 1990. text ed. 19.80 (ISBN 0-8123-6249-7). McDougal-Littell.

Websters Intermediate Dictionary, No. 79. 1986. 10.95 (ISBN 0-87779-379-4). Merriam-Webster Inc.

Webster's Middle School Dictionary. 1990. text ed. 16.50 (ISBN 0-8123-6248-9). McDougal-Littell.

Webster's New World Dictionaries Staff. Webster's New World Children's Dictionary. Neufeldt, Victoria & De Mello Vianna, Fernando, eds. (Illus.). 912p. 1991. 14.95 (ISBN 0-13-945726-7, Websters New World). Prentice Hall Pr.

Williams, Bill. The New Webster's Comprehensive Dictionary of the English Language. rev. ed. Cayne, Bernard S. & Lechner, Doris E., eds. (Illus.). 1930p. (gr. 3 up). 1989. deluxe ed. 99.99 (ISBN 0-9623476-0-4); lib. bdg. 99.99 (ISBN 0-685-28124-8). Amer Intl Pr.

ENGLISH LANGUAGE–DICTIONARIES–FRENCH

Eastman, Philip D. The Cat in the Hat Beginner Book Dictionary in French & English. LC 65-22650. (Illus.). 144p. (gr. 2-3). 1965. 14.95 (ISBN 0-394-81063-5). Beginner.

Mon Grand Dictionnaire Francais-Anglais. (FRE & ENG.). 23.50 (ISBN 0-685-11402-3). French & Eur.

ENGLISH LANGUAGE–DICTIONARIES–GERMAN

Sheheen, Dennis, illus. A Child's Picture English-German Dictionary. LC 86-13987. (gr. k-2). 1986. 9.95 (ISBN 0-915361-41-8, Dist. by Watts). Adama Pubs Inc.

ENGLISH LANGUAGE–DICTIONARIES–SPANISH

Eastman, Philip D. Cat in the Hat Beginner Book Dictionary in Spanish & English. LC 66-10688. (SPA & ENG., Illus.). 144p. (gr. k-3). 1966. 16.00 (ISBN 0-394-81542-4). Beginner.

Herrera, Ricky. How to Espeak Spenglish. Martinez, Ricardo, illus. 44p. (Orig.). (gr. 7 up). 1987. pap. 1.95 (ISBN 0-9618739-0-6, Lay Back). Humor Us Pubns Inc.

Madrigal, Margarita. Open Door to Spanish, Bk. 2. 222p. (gr. 7-12). 1981. pap. text ed. 5.25 (ISBN 0-88345-427-0, 18470); cassettes 45.00 (ISBN 0-686-77684-4, 58472); ans. key Bk 1, 2 1.50 (ISBN 0-88345-487-4, 18474). Prentice ESL.

ENGLISH LANGUAGE–ETYMOLOGY

Asimov, Isaac. Words from the Myths. Barss, William, illus. 224p. (gr. 5-10). 1961. 14.95 (ISBN 0-395-06568-2). HM.

Graham-Barber, Lynda. Mushy! The Complete Book of Valentine Words. Lewin, Betsy, illus. LC 90-33047. 128p. (gr. 4-10). 1991. 13.95 (ISBN 0-02-736941-2, Bradbury Pr). Macmillan Child Grp.

Steckler, Arthur. One Hundred & One Words & How They Began. LC 78-1012. (Illus.). 96p. 1979. pap. 6.95 (ISBN 0-385-14074-6). Doubleday.

ENGLISH LANGUAGE–GRAMMAR

Adams, Pam, illus. Letters & Words. 16p. (Orig.). (ps-2). 1975. pap. 2.00 (ISBN 0-85953-046-9, Pub. by Child's Play England). Childs Play.

Barrett, Mark, et al. Ready, Set, Grammar! A Beginning Grammar Program for Non-Readers. 1988. spiral reproducible wkbk. 24.95 (ISBN 1-55999-067-8). LinguiSystems.

Basic Skills in English: Green Level. (gr. 8). 1989. text ed. 21.54 (ISBN 0-8123-5477-X); tchr's. ed. 28.68 (ISBN 0-86609-483-0); practice bk., tchr's. ed. 11.07 (ISBN 0-86609-485-7); tchr's. resource binder 82.50 (ISBN 0-8123-5513-X); practice bk. 7.89 (ISBN 0-86609-484-9); test bklt. 3.09 (ISBN 0-86609-486-5); test bklt. answer key 3.51 (ISBN 0-86609-487-3). McDougal-Littell.

Basic Skills in English: Red Level. (gr. 7). 1989. text ed. 21.54 (ISBN 0-8123-5475-3); tchr's. ed. 26.07 (ISBN 0-86609-477-6); practice bk., tchr's. ed. 11.07 (ISBN 0-86609-479-2); tchr's. resource binder 82.50 (ISBN 0-8123-5507-5); practice bk. 7.80 (ISBN 0-86609-478-4); test bklt. 3.09 (ISBN 0-86609-480-6); test bklt. answer key 3.51 (ISBN 0-86609-481-4). McDougal-Littell.

Beller, Janet. A-B-C-ing: An Action Alphabet. Beller, Janet, illus. LC 83-23925. 32p. (ps-1). 1984. pap. text ed. 8.95 (ISBN 0-517-55208-6). Crown.

Berry, Marilyn. Help Is on the Way for Grammar. Bartholomew, illus. 48p. (gr. 4-6). 1987. PLB 13.93 (ISBN 0-516-03280-1). Childrens.

Chapman, John. Welcome to English: Let's Begin. (Illus.). 48p. (gr. 1 up). 1980. pap. 3.25 (ISBN 0-88345-422-X, 18480); tchr's manual 4.50 (ISBN 0-88345-423-8, 18493); tchr's. manual 4-5 7.50 (ISBN 0-88345-368-1, 18499). Prentice ESL.

Collins, Gretchen. English Grammar Flipper: A Guide to Correct English Usage. 49p. (gr. 5 up). 1989. Repr. of 1977 ed. trade edition 5.95 (ISBN 1-878383-01-9). C Lee Pubns.

Coon, Pam. The Vowel Van. 72p. (gr. k-3). 1980. 7.95 (ISBN 0-88160-010-5, LW 112). Learning Wks.

Criscuolo, Nicholas P. & Herman, Barry. Fun With Words. (gr. 2-5). 1988. pap. 6.95 (ISBN 0-8224-3172-6). Fearon Teach Aids.

Crystal, David. Rediscover Grammar. 1987. pap. text ed. 13.96 (ISBN 0-582-00258-3, 78071). Longman.

English Grammar Study Aid. 1978. pap. 1.95 (ISBN 0-87738-028-7). Youth Ed.

Forte, Imogene. I'm Ready to Learn about Beginning Consonants. (Illus.). 64p. (ps-1). 1987. pap. text ed. 1.95 (ISBN 0-86530-155-7, IP 111-4). Incentive Pubns.

—Private "I" LC 84-62933. (Illus.). 80p. (gr. k-6). 1985. wkbk 3.95 (ISBN 0-86530-096-8, IP 91-0). Incentive Pubns.

Gallagher, Nora. How to Stop a Sentence, & Other Methods of Managing Words. LC 84-40761. 1984. (Lipp Jr Bks); text ed. 4.95 (ISBN 0-201-10517-9, Lipp Jr Bks). HarpC Child Bks.

Gregorich, Barbara. Adjectives & Adverbs. Pape, Richard, illus. 24p. (gr. 3-4). 1980. wkbk. 2.95 (ISBN 0-89403-596-7). EDC.
—Beginning Words. Hoffman, Joan, ed. Sandford, John, illus. 32p. (gr. k). 1988. wkbk. 1.49 (ISBN 0-88743-157-7). Sch Zone Pub Co.
—Figures of Speech. Pape, Richard, illus. 24p. (gr. 3-4). 1980. wkbk. 2.95 (ISBN 0-89403-601-7). EDC.
—Letters & Words: Kindergarten. Hoffman, Joan, ed. Koontz, Robin M., illus. 32p. (gr. k). 1990. wkbk. 3.49 (ISBN 0-88743-179-8). Sch Zone Pub Co.
—Opposite Words. Hoffman, Joan, ed. Sandford, John, illus. 32p. (gr. k). 1988. wkbk. 1.49 (ISBN 0-88743-160-7). Sch Zone Pub Co.
—Positional Words & Opposite Words: Kindergarten. Hoffman, Joan, ed. Koontz, Robin M., illus. 32p. (gr. k). 1990. wkbk. 3.49 (ISBN 0-88743-180-1). Sch Zone Pub Co.
—Prefixes, Bases, & Suffixes. Pape, Richard, illus. 24p. (gr. 3-4). 1980. wkbk. 2.95 (ISBN 0-89403-600-9). EDC.
—Prepositions & Conjunctions. Pape, Richard, illus. 24p. (gr. 3-4). 1980. wkbk. 2.95 (ISBN 0-89403-597-5). EDC.
—Word Skills. Hoffman, Joan, ed. Koontz, Robin M., illus. 32p. (gr. 1). 1988. wkbk. 1.49 (ISBN 0-88743-165-8). Sch Zone Pub Co.
—Word Skills. Hoffman, Joan, ed. Koontz, Robin M., illus. 32p. (gr. 2). 1988. wkbk. 1.49 (ISBN 0-88743-171-2). Sch Zone Pub Co.
—Word Skills: First Grade. Hoffman, Joan, ed. Koontz, Robin M., illus. 32p. (gr. 1). 1990. wkbk. 3.49 (ISBN 0-88743-184-4). Sch Zone Pub Co.
—Word Skills: Second Grade. Hoffman, Joan, ed. Koontz, Robin M., illus. 32p. (gr. 2). 1990. wkbk. 3.49 (ISBN 0-88743-190-9). Sch Zone Pub Co.
Heller, Ruth. A Cache of Jewels & Other Collective Nouns. (ps-3). 1989. 10.95 (ISBN 0-448-19211-X, G&D). Putnam Pub Group.
—Kites Sail High: A Book about Verbs. LC 87-82718. (Illus.). 48p. (ps-3). 1988. PLB 10.95 (ISBN 0-448-10480-6, G&D). Putnam Pub Group.
—Merry-Go-Round: A Book about Nouns. (Illus.). 48p. (gr. 1 up). 1990. 13.95 (ISBN 0-448-40085-5, G&D). Putnam Pub Group.
Hoban, Tana. All about Where. LC 90-30849. (Illus.). 32p. (ps up). 1991. 13.95 (ISBN 0-688-09697-2); PLB 13.88 (ISBN 0-688-09698-0). Greenwillow.
Knox, Carolyn W. English for the World of Work. (Illus.). 276p. (gr. 7-12). 1985. text ed. 18.49 (ISBN 0-86601-128-5); tchr's. guide 11.99 (ISBN 0-86601-129-3); wkbk. 4.99 (ISBN 0-86601-130-7). Media Materials.
Koch, Michelle. Just One More. LC 88-17736. (Illus.). 32p. (ps up). 1989. 11.95 (ISBN 0-688-08127-4); PLB 11.88 (ISBN 0-688-08128-2). Greenwillow.
LeGros, Lucy C. Instant Centers - Letters. (Illus.). 46p. (Orig.). (gr. k-2). 1984. pap. 5.95 (ISBN 0-937306-04-5). Creat Res NC.
Lutgendorf, Philip & James, Shirley M. The Parts of Speech. Reichmann, Naczinski & Associates, illus. LC 77-730079. (gr. 7-9). 1976. pap. text ed. 219.00 6 filmstrips, 6 cass., 30 skill sheets, Guide (ISBN 0-89290-118-7, A134-SATC). Soc for Visual.
Phillips, Wanda C. Easy Grammar: Adverbs. (gr. 4-12). 1987. pap. text ed. 11.50 (ISBN 0-936981-04-0). ISHA Enterprises.
—Easy Grammar: Direct Objects & Indirect Objects. 33p. (gr. 4-12). 1986. pap. text ed. 5.50 (ISBN 0-936981-02-4). ISHA Enterprises.
—Easy Grammar: Verbs. 130p. (gr. 4-12). 1986. pap. text ed. 12.50 (ISBN 0-936981-03-2). ISHA Enterprises.
Robinson, Joan. WordBuilding. (gr. 4-8). 1989. pap. 8.95 (ISBN 0-8224-7450-6). Fearon Teach Aids.
—WordStrength. (gr. 4-8). 1989. pap. 8.95 (ISBN 0-8224-7451-4). Fearon Teach Aids.
—WordWise. (gr. 4-8). 1989. pap. 8.95 (ISBN 0-8224-7452-2). Fearon Teach Aids.
Schuster, Slade. The Slade Short Course. 2nd ed. 1982. pap. text ed. 11.00 (ISBN 0-88334-161-1, 76128). Longman.
Schwartz, Linda. Gumball Grammar. 32p. (gr. 4-7). 1979. 3.95 (ISBN 0-88160-068-7, LW 801). Learning Wks.
—Long Vowel Voyage. 20p. (gr. 1-3). 1980. 3.95 (ISBN 0-88160-058-X, LW 606). Learning Wks.
—Short Vowel Voyage. 20p. (gr. 1-3). 1980. 3.95 (ISBN 0-88160-057-1, LW 605). Learning Wks.
Schwartz, Linda & Aleksich, Sue. Grammar Goodies. 48p. (gr. 4-7). 1976. 5.95 (ISBN 0-88160-022-9, LW 206). Learning Wks.
Southworth, Mary C. Wordworks. 1986. pap. text ed. 18.00 (ISBN 0-88334-192-1, 76157). Longman.
Sullivan, Dianna J. Fun with Sight Words. Ecker, Beverly, illus. 48p. (gr. k-3). 1987. wkbk. 5.95 (ISBN 1-55734-080-3). Tchr Create Mat.
Terban, Marvin. I Think I Thought & Other Tricky Verbs. Maestro, Giulio, illus. LC 83-19034. 64p. (Orig.). (ps-4). 1984. 11.95 (ISBN 0-89919-231-9, Pub. by Clarion); pap. 4.95 (ISBN 0-89919-290-4). Ticknor & Fields.
Tilkin, Sheldon. Verbs. Pape, Richard, illus. 24p. (gr. 3-4). 1980. wkbk. 2.95 (ISBN 0-89403-598-3). EDC.
Tilkin, Sheldon L. Nouns & Pronouns. Pape, Richard, illus. 24p. (gr. 3-4). 1980. wkbk. 2.95 (ISBN 0-89403-599-1). EDC.
Tyler, Vicki. The A-Plus Guide to Grammar. 192p. (gr. 7 up). 1984. pap. 2.25 (ISBN 0-590-33316-X). Scholastic Inc.
Walker, Bonnie L. Life Skills English. (Illus.). 291p. (gr. 7-12). 1984. text ed. 18.49 (ISBN 0-86601-073-4); tchr's. guide 11.99 (ISBN 0-86601-074-2); wkbk. 4.99 (ISBN 0-86601-120-X). Media Materials.
Watt, Suzanna M. No Glamour Grammar: Over Four Hundred Reproducible Grammar Worksheets. 1986. spiral reproducible wkbk. 37.95 (ISBN 1-55999-061-9). LinguiSystems.

ENGLISH LANGUAGE–HISTORY

Klausner, Janet. Talk about English: How Words Travel & Change. Doniger, Nancy, illus. LC 89-49116. 208p. (gr. 5 up). 1990. 14.95 (ISBN 0-690-04831-9, Crowell Jr Bks); PLB 14.89 (ISBN 0-690-04833-5, Crowell Jr Bks). HarpC Child Bks.

ENGLISH LANGUAGE–HOMONYMS

Gwynne, Fred. A Chocolate Moose for Dinner. Gwynne, Fred, illus. LC 80-14150. (gr. 1-6). 1988. pap. 11.95 (ISBN 0-671-66685-1); pap. 5.95 (ISBN 0-671-66741-6). S&S Trade.
—The King Who Reigned. Gwynne, Fred, illus. LC 80-12939. (gr. 1-6). 1988. pap. 11.95 (ISBN 0-671-66363-1); pap. 5.95 (ISBN 0-671-66744-0). S&S Trade.
Newhouse, Dora. The Encyclopedia of Homonyms-Sound Alikes: Condensed & Abridged Edition. LC 76-50944. (Illus.). (gr. 6-12). 1978. pap. 6.95 (ISBN 0-918050-00-6). Newhouse Pr.
Newhouse, Dora, illus. Homonyms Plus. (gr. 6-12). 1979. wkbk 6.95 (ISBN 0-918050-42-1); tchr's guide 6.95 (ISBN 0-918050-41-3); activity cards 4.95 (ISBN 0-918050-44-8). Newhouse Pr.

ENGLISH LANGUAGE–IDIOMS

Cox, James A. Put Your Foot in Your Mouth & Other Silly Sayings. Weissman, Sam Q., illus. LC 80-12877. 72p. (gr. 2-5). 1980. bds. 3.95 (ISBN 0-394-84503-X). Random.
Longman Staff. Longman Dictionary of English Idioms. 1979. pap. text ed. 17.96 (ISBN 0-582-05863-5). Longman.
Terban, Marvin. Mad As a Wet Hen & Other Funny Idioms. Maestro, Giulio, illus. LC 86-17575. (gr. 3-6). 1987. 13.95 (ISBN 0-89919-478-8, Pub. by Clarion); pap. 4.95 (ISBN 0-89919-479-6). Ticknor & Fields.

ENGLISH LANGUAGE–ORTHOGRAPHY

see English Language–Spelling

ENGLISH LANGUAGE–PHRASES AND TERMS

see English Language–Terms and Phrases

ENGLISH LANGUAGE–PUNCTUATION

see Punctuation

ENGLISH LANGUAGE–READERS

see Readers;
also subdivision readers for languages other than English, e.g. French Language–Readers

ENGLISH LANGUAGE–RHETORIC

see Rhetoric

ENGLISH LANGUAGE–RIME

Charles, Donald. Time to Rhyme with Calico Cat. LC 77-20994. (Illus.). 32p. (ps-3). 1978. PLB 14.60 (ISBN 0-516-03629-7). Childrens.
Raintree Rhymers, Bk. Two. (Illus.). 32p. (ps-3). 1985. PLB 13.31 (ISBN 0-8172-2452-1); 9.27 (ISBN 0-8172-2457-2). Raintree Pubs.
Raintree Rhymers, Bk. Three. (Illus.). 32p. (ps-4). 1985. PLB 13.31 (ISBN 0-8172-2453-X); pap. 9.27 (ISBN 0-8172-2458-0). Raintree Pubs.
Raintree Rhymers, Bk. One, Bk. Four. (Illus.). 32p. (ps-4). 1985. PLB 13.31 (ISBN 0-8172-2454-8); 9.27 (ISBN 0-8172-2459-9). Raintree Pubs.

ENGLISH LANGUAGE–SPELLING

Alarie, Julia & Conlon, Elizabeth. SOWHAT - Spelling Only Without A Test. Sussman, Ellen, ed. Hauge, Helen, illus. (gr. 3-6). 1980. pap. text ed. 5.95 (ISBN 0-933606-06-0, MS-605). Monkey Sisters.
Baggiani, J. M. & Tewell, V. M. Phonics; a Tool for Better Reading & Spelling, Bk. I. Birt, Jane L., illus. (gr. 1-2). 1982. pap. 9.50 student's copy (ISBN 0-934329-00-1); tchr's. manual 10.75 (ISBN 0-934329-01-X). Baggiani-Tewell.
—Phonics: A Tool for Better Reading & Spelling, Bk. II. Jacobson, Mary M., illus. (gr. 3-6). 1967. pap. 3.50 (ISBN 0-934329-02-8); wkbk. 2.00 (ISBN 0-934329-03-6). Baggiani-Tewell.
—Phonics: A Tool for Better Reading & Spelling, Bk. III. Jacobson, Mary M. & Davis, Mary I., illus. (gr. 5-12). 1984. pap. 5.75 (ISBN 0-934329-04-4); wkbk. 4.00 (ISBN 0-934329-05-2). Baggiani-Tewell.
Brown, Frances. My First Book of Words. LC 78-58344. 144p. (gr. k-6). 1979. Walker Educ.
Carson, Patti & Dellosa, Janet. Consonants: Cut & Paste & More. Carson, Patti & Dellosa, Janet, illus. 32p. (ps-1). 1983. pap. 1.98 (ISBN 0-88724-008-9, CD-7009). Carson-Dellos.
Daniel, Becky. Spelling Thinker Sheets. 64p. (gr. 4-8). 1988. wkbk. 7.95 (ISBN 0-86653-423-7, GA1035). Good Apple.
Daniel, Charlie & Daniel, Becky. Super Spelling Fun. 64p. (gr. 2-6). 1978. 6.95 (ISBN 0-916456-31-5, GA82). Good Apple.
Downey, Tiffany. Spelling Fitness: One Thousand One of the Most Frequently Misspelled Words. Downey, Cynthia, ed. 102p. (Orig.). (gr. 7-12). 1988. 29.95 (ISBN 0-685-22519-4). Infini Educ.
Forte, Imogene & Pangle, Mary Ann. Selling Spelling to Kids. (Illus.). 96p. (gr. 4-6). 1985. guide 8.95 (ISBN 0-86530-060-7, IP 60-7). Incentive Pubns.
Girken, Garland. G. J. B., No. 1: Genuine Junk Book. 32p. 1990. 6.95 (ISBN 0-8062-3606-X). Carlton.
Gordon, Sharon. The Spelling Bee. Garcia, Tom, illus. LC 81-4648. 32p. (gr. k-2). 1981. PLB 10.89 (ISBN 0-89375-535-4); pap. 2.95 (ISBN 0-89375-536-2). Troll Assocs.
Gregorich, Barbara. Spelling. Hoffman, Joan, ed. Koontz, Robin M., illus. 32p. (gr. 1). 1988. wkbk. 1.49 (ISBN 0-88743-167-4). Sch Zone Pub Co.
—Spelling. Hoffman, Joan, ed. Koontz, Robin M., illus. 32p. (gr. 2). 1988. wkbk. 1.49 (ISBN 0-88743-173-9). Sch Zone Pub Co.
Gresko, Bernetta. How Do You Spell...? English Only. Gresko, Bernetta, illus. 44p. (gr. 2-8). 1987. pap. 4.95 (ISBN 0-939755-11-4); wkbk. act sheets 4.95 (ISBN 0-939755-14-9); wkbk. crossword puzzles 4.95 (ISBN 0-939755-06-8). Sunset Prods.
Henry, Marcia K. Words. (gr. 3-9). 1990. write for info. (ISBN 1-878653-00-8). Lex Pr.
Hodgkinson, David. Language Connections Five Student Text: A Spelling Program. (Illus.). 160p. (Orig.). (gr. 5). 1988. pap. text ed. write for info. (ISBN 1-55624-719-2). Wright Group.
—Language Connections Five Studybook: A Spelling Program. (Illus.). 128p. (Orig.). (gr. 5). 1988. pap. text ed. write for info. (ISBN 1-55624-721-4). Wright Group.
Johnson, Eric W. Improve Your Own Spelling. (gr. 6-9). 1977. pap. text ed. 4.95 (ISBN 0-88334-093-3). Longman.
Johnson, Merideth. When I Learn to Spell. 1990. 3.98 (ISBN 0-8317-9370-8). Smithmark.
Kekewich, Jim & Kekewich, Deborah. Language Connections Six Student Text: A Spelling Program. (Illus.). 160p. (Orig.). (gr. 6). 1988. pap. text ed. write for info. (ISBN 1-55624-723-0). Wright Group.
—Language Connections Six Studybook: A Spelling Program. (Illus.). 128p. (Orig.). (gr. 6). 1988. pap. text ed. write for info. (ISBN 1-55624-725-7). Wright Group.
Laurita, Raymond E. The Spelling Doctor Says...,Pt. 1: (Roots 1-10) 87p. (Orig.). 1991. pap. text ed. 11.00 (ISBN 0-914051-20-2). Leonardo Pr.
LeGros, Lucy C. Instant Centers - Holidays. (Illus.). 45p. (Orig.). (gr. k-2). 1985. 5.95 (ISBN 0-937306-06-1). Creat Res NC.

Loomer, Bradley M. & Strege, Maxine G. Useful Spelling: Levels 2-8. 1990. write for info. (ISBN 1-878712-03-9). Useful Lrn.
"What word lists are appropriate for use in spelling programs?" It is clear that a spelling curriculum based upon the 6,000 most frequently used words of the English language will provide youth with over 99 percent of the words they will need during a lifetime. THE NEW IOWA SPELLING SCALE (1954, 1977, 1990) provides a scientific basis for list construction. The lists consider both frequency & difficulty of each word. This study tested 240,000 youth in America. Spelling curricula must be developed utilizing the scientific data of this massive spelling study. Words in USEFUL SPELLING are introduced & reintroduced with the difficulty of each word dictating the frequency of appearance. Persistently difficult words appear more often. The frequency of production influences a student in becoming a good speller. The USEFUL SPELLING text book provides the student internality so necessary for individual achievement. DiStephano & Hagerty (1985) stated: "We recommend THE NEW IOWA SPELLING SCALE for developing word lists. The scale provides reliable information on the average difficulty of each word at each grade. Its 6,236 high frequency words have percentages for the number of students in grade levels 2 through 8 who correctly spelled the words. The USEFUL SPELLING PROGRAM incorporates only research-based learning techniques. Continuous support is provided for students in becoming self-regulated learners. The learning practices (i.e., appropriate practice, proper reinforcement, perceptual discrimination, & knowledge

of results) assist the learner in becoming an efficient speller."-- DiStephano, P. P. & Hagerty, P. J., "Teaching Spelling at Elementary Levels: A Realistic Perspective," THE READING TEACHER, January, 1985.
Publisher Provided Annotation.

Marasco, Toni & Lemire, Cheryl. Language Connections Three Student Text: A Spelling Program. (Illus.). 160p. (Orig.). (gr. 3). 1988. pap. text ed. write for info. (ISBN 1-55624-711-7). Wright Group.

—Language Connections Three Studybook: A Spelling Program. (Illus.). 128p. (Orig.). (gr. 3). 1988. pap. text ed. write for info. (ISBN 1-55624-713-3). Wright Group.

—Language Connections Two Student Text: A Spelling Program. (Illus.). 160p. (Orig.). (gr. 2). 1988. pap. text ed. write for info. (ISBN 1-55624-707-9). Wright Group.

—Language Connections Two Studybook: A Spelling Program. (Illus.). 128p. (Orig.). (gr. 2). 1988. pap. text ed. write for info. (ISBN 1-55624-709-5). Wright Group.

Pen Notes Staff. Learning to Print. (ps up). 1984. 10.95 (ISBN 0-939564-01-7). Pen Notes.

Quildon, Louis. Language Connections Four Student Text: A Spelling Program. (Illus.). 160p. (Orig.). (gr. 4). 1988. pap. text ed. write for info. (ISBN 1-55624-715-X). Wright Group.

—Language Connections Four Studybook: A Spelling Program. (Illus.). 128p. (Orig.). (gr. 4). 1988. pap. text ed. write for info. (ISBN 1-55624-717-6). Wright Group.

Resnick, Jane. Quality Time Little Readers: I Know My Letters. 1991. 1.49 (ISBN 0-8317-7267-0). Smithmark.

Schwartz, Linda. Spelling Speedway. 32p. (gr. 4-7). 1979. 3.95 (ISBN 0-88160-069-5, LW 802). Learning Wks.

Sweeney, Kathy, et al. Spelling. 64p. (gr. 2-4). 1985. 6.95 (ISBN 0-912107-38-3). Monday Morning Bks.

Trisler, Alana & Cardiel, Patrice H. Words I Use When I Write. Trisler, Alana & Cardiel, Patrice H., illus. 36p. (Orig.). (gr. k-3). 1989. pap. text ed. 2.50 (ISBN 0-935493-33-6). Programs Educ.

Wittles, Harriet & Greisman, Joan. How to Spell It: A Dictionary of Commonly Misspelled Words. Wittles, Harriet & Greisman, Joan, illus. 336p. (gr. 1 up). 1982. pap. 7.95 (ISBN 0-448-14756-4, G&D). Putnam Pub Group.

ENGLISH LANGUAGE–STUDY AND TEACHING

Aemmer, Gail. Sequencing. Rittenour, Gary, illus. 20p. (gr. 3-4). 1985. pap. 5.95 (ISBN 0-88724-146-8, CD-0555). Carson-Dellos.

—Sequencing. Rittenour, Gary, illus. 20p. (gr. 5-6). 1985. pap. 5.95 (ISBN 0-88724-147-6, CD-0556). Carson-Dellos.

Claire, Elizabeth. ESL Wonder Workbook, No. 1: This Is Me. Flamm, Jackie, ed. Frazier, J. D., illus. 104p. (Orig.). (gr. 1-6). 1990. pap. 7.65 (ISBN 1-878598-00-7). Alta Bk Co Pubs.

—ESL Wonder Workbook, No. 2: All Around Me. Chapman, Charles, ed. Frazier, J. D., illus. 104p. (Orig.). (gr. 1-6). 1991. pap. write for info. (ISBN 1-878598-01-5). Alta Bk Co Pubs.

Cousins, Michael. English Matters, Vol. 3. (gr. 8-10). pap. 8.95 (ISBN 0-7175-1201-0). Dufour.

Eberle, Bob. A Way with Words. Weber, June K., illus. 96p. (gr. 4-7). 1987. pap. 8.95 (ISBN 0-86653-377-X, GA1009). Good Apple.

Geoffrion, Sondra. Power Study to up Your Grades in English. LC 88-61276. 60p. (Orig.). 1989. pap. text ed. 3.95 (ISBN 0-88247-784-6). R & E Pubs.

Henry, Marcia K. Words. (gr. 3-9). 1990. write for info. (ISBN 1-878653-00-8). Lex Pr.

Joy, Flora. Word Wizardry, Level II. Harroll, Pat, illus. 112p. (gr. 4-12). 1987. pap. 11.95 (ISBN 0-86653-404-0, GA 1017). Good Apple.

—Word Wizardry, Level I. Harroll, Pat, illus. 112p. (gr. 2-8). 1987. pap. 11.95 (ISBN 0-86653-403-2, GA 1016). Good Apple.

Kleman, James A. Short Shots..A Drill a Day: The Easy Way to Language Literacy. 2nd ed. 44p. (gr. 4-8). 1982. manual 5.00 (ISBN 0-938464-09-4). JML Enter MD.

Michener, Dorothy & Muschlitz, Beverly. Bulletin Board Bonanza. (Illus.). 96p. (gr. 2-6). 1981. pap. 7.95 (ISBN 0-86530-028-3, IP-283). Incentive Pubns.

Mylet, Trish & Sheffield, Antoinette. **Children, Today's Joy & Tomorrow's Hope, 8 bks, Set 2. (Illus.). 224p. (gr. 1-3). 1991. Set. pap. text ed. 16.00 (ISBN 0-945590-62-8). Sizzy Bks. CHILDREN, SET 2 contains eight books of short stories & builds on the foundation of CHILDREN, SET 1. Each book consists of six stories. At least one story in each book has an O. Henry-type ending in which the child decides how the story ends. The child**

answers verbally, draws a picture or writes a note on a self expression page. Each story has a state reference page with a large dot-to-dot exercise in the shape of that state's outline. Featured in SET 2 are the District of Columbia & the 45 states not covered in SET 1. While continuing to incorporate geography, phonics (blends, digraphs, long & diverse vowels), number recognition, sentence completion & self-expression as in SET 1, SET 2 also explores the areas of zoology, botany, history & global unity. In the first five books each story is accompanied by a list of its vocabulary. Building on SET 1's themes of fun & fantasy, SET 2 expands & concludes with joy, fact & hope. These warmly written & illustrated books have been well received worldwide by Early Education, Special Education & English as a Second Language teachers, parents & most importantly, children.
Publisher Provided Annotation.

Roberts, John & Roberts, Nedra. Excellence in English. 1987. pap. text ed. 16.00 (ISBN 0-8013-0134-3, 75798). Longman.

Segal, Bertha E. We Learn English Through Action. 106p. (gr. 3-12). 1987. 12.50 (ISBN 0-938395-11-4). B Segal.

Sheffield, Antoinette & Mylet, Trish. **Children, Today's Joy & Tomorrow's Hope, Set 1. (Illus.). 1991. write for info (ISBN 0-945590-74-1). Sizzy Bks. The CHILDREN, TODAY'S JOY & TOMORROW'S HOPE series consists of two sets of books. SET 1 contains 11 beginning reader & activity books. SET 2 contains eight books of short stories. The CHILDREN series consists of positive global readers incorporating geography (the fifty United States & the District of Columbia), phonics (short & long vowels, blends & digraphs), number recognition & self expression. SET 2 expands & explores the areas of zoology, botany, history & global unity. Each book in SET 1 & each story in SET 2 contains a state reference page with a large dot-to-dot exercise in the shape of that state's outline. The first sixteen books include sentence completion exercises & that story's word list. In SET 2 at least one story in each book has an O. Henry-type ending in which the child decides how the story ends. Each series includes a reference guide. Building on SET 1's themes of fun & fantasy, SET 2 expands & concludes with joy, fact & hope. This warmly written & illustrated series has been well received worldwide by Early Education, Special Education & English as a Second Language teachers, parents & most importantly children.**
Publisher Provided Annotation.

ENGLISH LANGUAGE–SYNONYMS AND ANTONYMS

Althea. Opposites of Things. Cony, Frances, illus. 24p. (ps-2). 1990. 1.95 (ISBN 1-878624-30-X, 1553800030). McClanahan Bk.

Bailey, Vanessa. Animal Opposites. (ps). 1991. 5.95 (ISBN 0-8120-6244-2). Barron.

Bellamy, John. Doubleday Children's Thesaurus. Stevenson, Peter, illus. LC 86-16217. 192p. (gr. k-6). 1987. 13.95 (ISBN 0-385-23833-9). Doubleday.

Gillham, Bill & Hulme, Susan. Let's Look for Opposites. Siegieda, Jan, illus. LC 83-24065. 24p. (ps-1). 1984. 4.95 (ISBN 0-698-20614-2, Putnam). Putnam Pub Group.

Hanson, Joan. British-American Synonyms. Hanson, Joan, illus. LC 72-3971. 32p. (gr-3). 1972. PLB 4.95 (ISBN 0-8225-0279-8). Lerner Pubns.

Hellweg, Paul. The Facts on File Student's Thesaurus. 304p. 1991. 24.95x (ISBN 0-8160-1634-8). Facts on File.

Hoban, Tana. Push, Pull, Empty, Full: A Book of Opposites. LC 72-90410. (Illus.). 32p. (ps-2). 1972. 13.95 (ISBN 0-02-744810-X, Mcmillan Child Bk). Macmillan Child Grp.

Koch, Michelle. By the Sea. LC 89-23344. (Illus.). 24p. (ps up). 1991. 13.95 (ISBN 0-688-09549-6); PLB 13.88 (ISBN 0-688-09550-X). Greenwillow.

Laird, Charlton. Webster's New World Thesaurus. 854p. (gr. 9-12). 1987. pap. 10.95 (ISBN 0-13-948126-5). P-H.

Lunn, Carolyn. A Whisper Is Quiet. Martin, Clovis, illus. LC 88-11968. 32p. (ps-2). 1988. PLB 11.93 (ISBN 0-516-02087-0); pap. 2.95 (ISBN 0-516-42087-9). Childrens.

McLenighan, Valjean. Stop-Go, Fast-Slow. Fiddle, Margrit, illus. LC 81-17080. 32p. (ps-2). 1982. PLB 11.93 (ISBN 0-516-03617-3); pap. text ed. 2.95 (ISBN 0-516-43617-1). Childrens.

McMillan, Bruce. Here a Chick, There a Chick. McMillan, Bruce, photos by. LC 82-20348. (Illus.). 32p. (ps-1). 1983. 15.95 (ISBN 0-688-02000-3); PLB 15.88 (ISBN 0-688-02001-1). Lothrop.

My Book of Opposites. (ps-2). 3.95 (ISBN 0-7214-5147-0). Ladybird Bks.

Oliver, Stephen, photos by. Opposites. LC 89-63093. (Illus.). 24p. (ps-k). 1990. Repr. of 1990 ed. 6.95 (ISBN 0-679-80620-2). Random.

Pragoff, Fiona. Opposites. (Illus.). 16p. (ps-k). 1989. 5.95 (ISBN 0-385-26409-7, Zephyr-BFYR). Doubleday.

Roget's Beginning Thesaurus. (ps-3). 1990. 9.95 (ISBN 0-06-017903-1, HarpT). HarperCollins.

Roget's Junior Thesaurus. 448p. (gr. 5-9). Date not set. write for info. HarperCollins.

Tilkin, Sheldon. Synonyms, Antonyms, Homonyms. Pape, Richard, illus. 24p. (gr. 3-4). 1980. wkbk. 2.95 (ISBN 0-89403-603-3). EDC.

Webster's New Thesaurus. (gr. 4 up). 1988. pap. 3.95 (ISBN 0-318-37120-0). Scholastic Inc.

Wittles, Harriet & Greisman, Joan. A First Thesaurus. Block, Alex, illus. 144p. (gr. 2-4). 1985. pap. write for info. (ISBN 0-307-15835-7, Pub. by Golden Bks). Western Pub.

ENGLISH LANGUAGE–TERMS AND PHRASES

Artman, John. Slanguage. 80p. (gr. 4 up). 1980. 7.95 (ISBN 0-916456-60-9, GA 175). Good Apple.

DeWitt, Jim. Means Something Else--"The Doubles" Figures of Speech Writing Book, No. 2. Gleissner, Alex & Nordgren, Steve, illus. 64p. (Orig.). (gr. 6-12). 1987. wkbk. 6.00 (ISBN 0-915199-51-3). Pen-Dec.

Sommer, Elyse. I Read You Loud & Clear: A Kid's Thesaurus of Colorful Phrases. Kirschbaum, John, illus. 128p. 1990. text ed. 10.95 (ISBN 0-88687-575-7, World Almanac). Pharos Bks NY.

Terban, Marvin. In a Pickle & other Funny Idioms. Maestro, Giulio, illus. LC 82-9585. 64p. (gr. 1-4). 1983. 13.95 (ISBN 0-89919-153-3, Pub. by Clarion); pap. 4.95 (ISBN 0-89919-164-9). Ticknor & Fields.

ENGLISH LANGUAGE–TEXTBOOKS FOR FOREIGNERS

Christison, Mary Ann. English Through Poetry. Peterson, Kathleen, illus. 130p. (gr. 3-6). 1982. pap. text ed. 8.95 (ISBN 0-88084-002-1). Alemany Pr.

Davis, Dee G. Real Life Spoken English Basic Version Japanese Version: Hatsuom Henkei Renshu Hearing Course. (JPN.). 99p. 1989. pap. 5.00 (ISBN 0-929350-10-3). Spoken English Pubns.

Graham, Carolyn. The Electric Elephant & Other Stories. (Illus., Orig.). (gr. 7-12). 1982. pap. text ed. 6.50x (ISBN 0-19-503229-2). Oxford U Pr.

Hazzan, Anne-Francoise. Let's Learn English Coloring Book. (Illus.). 64p. 1988. pap. 3.95 (ISBN 0-8442-5451-7, Passport Bks). Natl Textbk.

Keyes, Joan R. Now You're Talking. (gr. 4-9). 1988. wkbk. 4.50 (ISBN 1-55737-067-2). Ed Activities.

McCallum, George P. Visitor from Another Planet & Other Plays. (gr. 4-6). 1982. student's ed. 6.75x (ISBN 0-19-502743-4); tchr's. ed. 7.95x (ISBN 0-19-503167-9). Oxford U Pr.

Scarry, Richard. Getting Ready for Writing. Scarry, Richard, illus. 32p. (ps-k). 1987. pap. 1.95 (ISBN 0-394-89038-8, Random Juv). Random.

Villicana, Solveig. Peanut Butter & Jelly: Reproducible Worksheets for Young Students of ESL. Chapman, Charles, ed. (Illus.). 75p. (Orig.). (gr. 4-8). 1991. pap. write for info. (ISBN 1-878598-08-2). Alta Bk Co Pubs.

ENGLISH LANGUAGE–TEXTBOOKS FOR FOREIGNERS–SPANISH

Kahn, Michele. Mi Libro de Palabras Usadas Cada Dia En Ingles. (gr. k-6). 1982. pap. 11.95 (ISBN 0-8120-5431-8). Barron.

ENGLISH LANGUAGE–VERSIFICATION
see Versification

ENGLISH LITERATURE
see also Authors, English; English Drama; English Essays; English Poetry; English Wit and Humor; Short Stories

Carroll, Lewis. The Alice in Wonderland Pop-up. Thorne, Jenny, illus. LC 80-7615. 12p. (gr. k-4). 1980. pap. 6.95 (ISBN 0-385-28038-6). Delacorte.

Dickens, Charles. A Christmas Carol. abr. ed. Wendt, Michael & Pizar, Kathleen, eds. Sturrock, Walt, illus. 80p. (gr. 2-5). 1988. 5.95 (ISBN 0-88101-087-1). Unicorn Pub.

Wells, H. G. Island of Dr. Moreau. Lowndes, R. A., intro. by. (gr. 7 up). pap. 1.95 (ISBN 0-8049-0110-4, CL-110). Airmont.

Wilde, Oscar. Picture of Dorian Gray. (gr. 9 up). 1964. pap. 2.50 (ISBN 0-8049-0039-6, CL-39). Airmont.

ENGLISH LITERATURE–BIOGRAPHY

see Authors, English

ENGLISH LITERATURE–COLLECTIONS

Rook, Lizzie & Goodfellow, E. J. Tiny Tot's Speaker. facsimile ed. LC 73-160907. (gr. 7 up). Repr. of 1895 ed. 14.00 (ISBN 0-8369-6271-0). Ayer Co Pubs.

ENGLISH POETRY

Blake, Quentin. All Join In. (ps-3). 1991. 14.95 (ISBN 0-316-09934-1). Little.

Coleridge, Samuel Taylor. Portable Coleridge. Richards, Ivor A., ed. (gr. 10 up). 1977. pap. 9.95 (ISBN 0-14-015048-X, P48, Penguin Bks). Viking Penguin.

Crossley-Holland, Kevin. Beowulf. Keeping, Charles, illus. 48p. (gr. 5 up). 1988. 14.95 (ISBN 0-19-279770-0); pap. 6.95 (ISBN 0-19-272184-4). Oxford U Pr.

Dahl, Roald. Roald Dahl's Revolting Rhymes. Blake, Quentin, illus. LC 82-15263. 48p. (gr. 3-6). 1983. 14.00 (ISBN 0-394-85422-5); lib. bdg. 14.99 (ISBN 0-394-95422-X). Knopf.

Hopkins, Lee B. Elves, Fairies & Gnomes. Hoffman, Rosekrans, illus. LC 79-19753. (ps-2). 1980. Knopf.

Jennings, Elizabeth. Secret Brother & Other Poems. Stevens, Meg, illus. LC 69-14765. (gr. 1-5). 1966. 12.95 (ISBN 0-8023-1194-6). Dufour.

Marshall, James. Old Mother Hubbard & Her Wonderful Dog. (ps-3). 1991. 13.95 (ISBN 0-374-35621-1). FS&G.

Milton, John. Paradise Lost. new ed. Tromley, F., intro. by. Bd. with Paradise Regained. (gr. 11up). pap. 2.50 (ISBN 0-8049-0173-2, CL-173). Airmont.

Scott, Walter. Lady of the Lake & Other Poems. Bennet, C. L., intro. by. (gr. 9 up). pap. 1.95 (ISBN 0-8049-0137-6, CL-137). Airmont.

Shakespeare, William. Complete Sonnets & Poems. Fisher, Neil H., intro. by. (gr. 9 up). pap. 0.60 (ISBN 0-8049-1016-2, S-16). Airmont.

Stevenson, Robert Louis. A Child's Garden of Verses. Gregori, Lee, illus. LC 85-12766. (gr. 3 up). 1969. pap. 2.50 (ISBN 0-8049-0195-3, CL-195). Airmont.

ENGLISH POETRY–COLLECTIONS

Elledge, Scott, ed. Wider Than the Sky: Poems to Grow up With. LC 90-4135. 368p. (gr. 5 up). 1990. 19.95 (ISBN 0-06-021786-3); PLB 19.89 (ISBN 0-06-021787-1). HarpC Child Bks.

Heaney, Seamus & Hughes, Ted, eds. The Rattle Bag: An Anthology of Poetry. 498p. (gr. 3 up). 1985. pap. 12.95 (ISBN 0-571-11976-X). Faber & Faber.

Hieatt, Constance B., ed. Beowulf & Other Old English Poems. 2nd, rev. & enl. ed. Hieatt, A. Kent, intro. by. 192p. (gr. 9-12). 1988. pap. 2.95 (ISBN 0-553-21347-4). Bantam.

Palgrave, Francis T. & Press, John, eds. Golden Treasury of the Best Songs & Lyrical Poems in the English Language: From Shakespeare to Larkin. 5th ed. (gr. 5-9). 1987. 35.00 (ISBN 0-19-254156-0); pap. 9.95 (ISBN 0-19-282035-4). Oxford U Pr.

Shakespeare, William. Under the Greenwood Tree. Holdridge, Barbara, ed. DeWitt, Robin & DeWitt, Pat, illus. Rowse, A. L., pref. by. 80p. (gr. 4 up). 1986. 21.95 (ISBN 0-88045-028-2); pap. 14.95 (ISBN 0-88045-029-0); cass. & bk. 23.90 (ISBN 0-88045-103-3); cassette only 8.95 (ISBN 0-88045-100-9). Stemmer Hse.

Stevenson, Robert Louis. A Child's Garden of Verses. Blegvad, Erik, illus. LC 85-12766. (ps-2). 1978. lib. bdg. 5.99 (ISBN 0-394-93739-2, Random Juv). Random.

Williams, Oscar, ed. The Mentor Book of Major British Poets. 576p. (gr. 9-12). 1985. pap. 5.95 (ISBN 0-451-62637-0, Ment). NAL-Dutton.

ENGLISH POETRY–HISTORY AND CRITICISM

Aubrey, Bryan. English Romantic Poetry: An Annotated Bibliography. 200p. 1991. PLB 40.00x (ISBN 0-89356-661-6, Magill Bks). Salem Pr.

ENGLISH SHORT STORIES

see Short Stories

ENGLISH WIT AND HUMOR

Jerome, Jerome K. Diary of a Pilgrimage. (Illus.). 176p. (gr. 6-9). 1990. pap. 8.00 (ISBN 0-86299-010-6). A Sutton Pub.

—Idle Thoughts of an Idle Fellow. (Illus.). 144p. (gr. 6-9). 1990. pap. 8.00 (ISBN 0-86299-009-2). A Sutton Pub.

ENGRAVING

see also Gems; Wood Engraving

ENGRAVING–TECHNIQUE

Bolognese, Don & Raphael, Elaine. Printmaking. (Illus.). 64p. (gr. 4-9). 1987. PLB 10.90 (ISBN 0-531-10316-1). Watts.

ENSEMBLES (MATHEMATICS)

see Set Theory

ENSIGNS

see Flags

ENTERTAINERS

see also Actors and Actresses; Clowns; Dancers

Arts & Entertainment. 96p. (gr. 3-8). 1987. PLB 240.00 set (ISBN 0-685-18919-8); pap. 13.27 (ISBN 0-8172-3060-2). Raintree Pubs.

Hirsch, Linda. You're Going Out There a Kid, but You're Coming Back a Star. Wallner, John, illus. 128p. (Orig.). (gr. 3-7). 1984. pap. 2.25 (ISBN 0-553-15272-6, Skylark). Bantam.

Petrucelli. Jim Henson, Reading Level 2. (Illus.). 24p. (gr. 1-4). Date not set. PLB 12.33 (ISBN 0-86592-426-0). Rourke Corp.

Reisfield, Randi. So You Want to Be a Star: A Teenager's Guide to Breaking into Showbusiness. Clancy, Lisa, ed. (Illus.). 224p. (Orig.). (gr. 6 up). 1990. pap. 2.95 (ISBN 0-671-70192-4, Archway). PB.

Rich, Jason. Celebrity Teen Talk: Exclusive Celebrity Interviews, Video Game Tips & Reviews. (Illus.). 256p. (Orig.). (gr. 4-12). 1991. pap. 6.95 (ISBN 0-9625057-5-7). DMS ID.

Schroeder, Alan. Josephine Baker. King, Coretta Scott, intro. by. (Illus.). 128p. (gr. 5 up). 1991. PLB 17.95 (ISBN 0-7910-1116-X). Chelsea Hse.

ENTERTAINING

see also Amusements; Etiquette; Games

Ball, Jacqueline. Let's Party. (Illus.). 32p. (gr. 5 up). 1990. lib. bdg. 14.00 (ISBN 0-86625-418-8); lib. bdg. 10.50s.p. (ISBN 0-685-36382-1). Rourke Corp.

Fulk, Penny. Children's Parties Made Easy. Durdee, Becky, illus. 142p. (Orig.). pap. 6.00 (ISBN 0-941951-00-6). JJJ Pubs.

Jackson, Sonia. Eeeeaaassy Party Planning. Negrini, Wendy, illus. 80p. (gr. 7 up). 1989. pap. 6.95 (ISBN 0-9619056-0-3). Entrtnmnt Enter.

Jenny, Gerri. Birthday Parties for Children: Activities, Games, Cakes & Fun for Children from 4-10. Macdonald, Roland B. & Gray, Dan, illus. 128p. (gr. k-5). 1991. pap. 9.95 (ISBN 1-878767-15-1). Murdoch Bks. BIRTHDAY PARTIES FOR CHILDREN makes planning the perfect party easy & fun! This is a craft book, a party decorating book, a cake decorating book as well as a games & activities book--a TOTAL party planning book. Each birthday party involves a particular theme--a Balloon Party, for instance, or a Hat Party. All you have to do is follow the directions, copy the patterns, use the illustrations for guidance & you'll have a wonderful time. Each party includes invitations, activities, games, a cake, party favors & costume ideas. So open the book & get started! Spend some time with your child deciding which party to have (& you can mix & match different parts), pick up a few inexpensive materials from the store & have a terrific time with your child!

Publisher Provided Annotation.

Reinhard, Dale W. Simply Celebrating Children. 1991. write for info (ISBN 0-9628888-0-X). Pressed Duck.

Rosen, C. Party Fun. (Illus.). 14p. (gr. 2-6). 1986. pap. 4.50 (ISBN 0-7460-0124-X). EDC.

Wallach, Susan. Great Parties, How to Plan Them. Magnuson, Diana, illus. LC 90-46879. 128p. (gr. 5-9). 1990. PLB 10.89 (ISBN 0-8167-2291-9); pap. text ed. 2.95 (ISBN 0-8167-2292-7). Troll Assocs.

Wilkes, Angela. My First Party Book. LC 90-40331. (Illus.). 48p. (gr. 1-5). 1991. 13.00 (ISBN 0-679-80909-0); PLB 12.99 (ISBN 0-679-90909-5). Knopf.

ENTERTAINING–FICTION

Allard, Harry. The Stupids Have a Ball. Marshall, James, illus. LC 77-27660. (gr. k-3). 1984. 13.95 (ISBN 0-395-26497-9); pap. 3.95 (ISBN 0-395-36169-9). HM.

Bunnikin's Picnic Party. (Illus.). (ps-k). pap. 3.50 (ISBN 0-7214-0206-2, Plume). Ladybird Bks.

Carlson, Nancy. The Talent Show. Carlson, Nancy, illus. LC 85-4122. 32p. (ps-3). 1985. PLB 9.95 (ISBN 0-87614-284-6). Carolrhoda Bks.

Civardi, Anne & Cartwright, Stephen. Going to a Party. 16p. (ps up). 1987. 2.95 (ISBN 0-7460-0072-3). EDC.

Conford, Ellen. To All My Fans, with Love from Sylvie. 192p. (gr. 7 up). 1982. 14.95 (ISBN 0-316-15312-5). Little.

Cooney, Caroline. Saturday Night. 1986. pap. 2.75 (ISBN 0-590-43521-3). Scholastic Inc.

Dubanevich, Arlene. Pig William. 32p. (gr. k-3). 1990. pap. 3.95 (ISBN 0-689-71372-X, Aladdin). Macmillan Child Grp.

Harwood, Pearl A. Mr. Bumba Has a Party. Folger, Joseph, illus. LC 64-19775. 32p. (gr. k-3). 1964. PLB 4.95 (ISBN 0-8225-0106-6). Lerner Pubns.

—Mrs. Moon's Picnic. Overlie, George, illus. LC 67-15690. 32p. (gr. k-3). 1967. PLB 4.95 (ISBN 0-8225-0114-7). Lerner Pubns.

Johnston, Annie F. The Little Colonel's House Party. (gr. 5 up). 13.95 (ISBN 0-89201-039-8). Zenger Pub.

Keats, Ezra J. Hi, Cat! (gr. k-3). 1990. incl. cass. 19.95 (ISBN 0-87499-180-3); pap. 12.95 incl. cass. (ISBN 0-87499-179-X); Set; incl. 4 bks., cass., & guide. pap. 27.95 (ISBN 0-685-38540-X). Live Oak Media.

Kozikowski, Renate. Teddy Bears Picnic. 32p. (ps-2). 1990. 10.95 (ISBN 0-689-71362-2, Aladdin). Macmillan Child Grp.

Randall, Carrie. Dear Diary, No. 1: Party. 1989. pap. 2.75 (ISBN 0-590-42476-9). Scholastic Inc.

—Dear Diary, No. 2: The Party. 1989. pap. 2.75 (ISBN 0-590-42477-7). Scholastic Inc.

—Dear Diary, No. 3: The Dance. 1990. pap. 2.75 (ISBN 0-590-42478-5). Scholastic Inc.

Shreve, Susan. The Masquerade. 160p. (gr. 7 up). 1981. pap. 1.95 (ISBN 0-440-95396-0, LE). Dell.

ENTERTAINMENTS

see Amusements; Skits

ENTOMOLOGY

see Insects

ENTOMOLOGY, ECONOMIC

see Insects, Injurious and Beneficial

ENTRANCE REQUIREMENTS FOR COLLEGE AND UNIVERSITIES

see Colleges and Universities–Entrance Requirements

ENVIRONMENT

see Adaptation (Biology); Ecology; Man–Influence of Environment; Man–Influence on Nature

ENVIRONMENT AND PESTICIDES

see Pesticides and the Environment

ENVIRONMENTAL PROTECTION

see also Conservation of Natural Resources

Arneson, D. J. Toxic Cops. (Illus.). 128p. (gr. 7-12). 1991. PLB 12.40 (ISBN 0-531-12525-4). Watts.

Atwood, Margaret. For the Birds. Bianchi, John, illus. 56p. (gr. 8-12). 1991. pap. 9.95 (ISBN 0-920668-32-1). Firefly Bks Ltd.
Samantha is turned into a bird by her neighbor, who herself becomes a crow, & together they migrate from Canada to a tropical forest in South America. Along the way Samantha learns how urbanization, hunters, rainforest destruction & other problems threaten the bird's ecosystem &, by extension, our own. Sidebar suggestions present a number of practical activities, from the creation of a bird garden in a schoolyard to how to make your own backyard more hospitable to birds. Margaret Atwood, Canada's best-known writer whose most recent works include The Handmaid's Tale & Cat's Eye, is a long-time environmental activist. She is also an avid birdwatcher. Funds from her royalities on this book will be donated to a number of environmental causes. John Bianchi, illustrator of The Dingles, has won acclaim for both his humorous & nature illustrations.

Publisher Provided Annotation.

Bailey, Donna. What We Can Do about Recycling Garbage. (Illus.). 32p. (gr. k-4). 1991. PLB 11.40 (ISBN 0-531-11017-6). Watts.

Bellamy, David. How Green Are You? Dann, Penny, illus. LC 90-19453. 32p. (gr. 1-4). 1991. 14.95 (ISBN 0-517-58429-8, C N Potter Bks); PLB 15.99 (ISBN 0-517-58447-6, C N Potter Bks). Crown.

Berger, Melvin. Hazardous Substances: A Reference. LC 86-8806. (Illus.). 128p. (gr. 6-12). 1986. PLB 17.95 (ISBN 0-89490-116-8). Enslow Pubs.

Bernards, Neal, ed. The Environmental Crisis: Opposing Viewpoints. LC 90-24086. (Illus.). 264p. (gr. 10 up). 1991. PLB 15.95 (ISBN 0-89908-175-4); pap. 8.95 (ISBN 0-89908-150-9). Greenhaven.

Brown, Diane M. The Environment: An Annotated Bibliography. 200p. 1991. PLB 40.00x (ISBN 0-89356-666-7, Magill Bks). Salem Pr.

Dudley, William, et al, eds. Global Resources: Opposing Viewpoints. LC 90-24088. (Illus.). 264p. (gr. 10 up). 1991. PLB 15.95 (ISBN 0-89908-177-0); pap. 8.95 (ISBN 0-89908-152-5). Greenhaven.

Duggleby, John. Pesticides. LC 90-35496. (Illus.). 48p. (gr. 5-6). 1990. RSBE 10.95 (ISBN 0-89686-540-1, Crestwood Hse). Macmillan Child Grp.

Elkington, John, et al. Going Green: A Kid's Handbook to Saving the Planet. Ross, Tony, illus. 96p. (gr. 3 up). 1990. 15.95 (ISBN 0-670-83611-7). Viking Child Bks.

—Going Green: A Kid's Handbook to Saving the Planet. (Illus.). 96p. (gr. 3 up). 1990. pap. 8.95 (ISBN 0-14-034597-3, Puffin). Puffin Bks.

Greene, Carol. Caring for Our Air. (Illus.). 32p. (gr. 1-4). 1991. PLB 12.95 (ISBN 0-89490-351-9). Enslow Pubs.

—Caring for Our Land. (Illus.). 32p. (gr. 1-4). 1991. PLB 12.95 (ISBN 0-89490-354-3). Enslow Pubs.

Hare, Tony. Toxic Waste. (Illus.). 32p. (gr. 5-8). 1991. PLB 11.90 (ISBN 0-531-17308-9, Gloucester Pr). Watts.

—Vanishing Habitats. (Illus.). 32p. (gr. k-4). 1991. PLB 11.40 (ISBN 0-531-17350-X, Gloucester Pr). Watts.

Henricksson, John. Rachel Carson: The Environmental Movement. (Illus.). 96p. (gr. 7 up). 1991. PLB 19.95 (ISBN 1-878841-16-5). Millbrook Pr.

Jakobson, Cathryn. Think About: The Environment. 160p. (gr. 7 up). 1991. PLB 15.85 (ISBN 0-8027-8105-5); pap. 8.95 (ISBN 0-8027-7357-5). Walker & Co.

Kalman, Bobbie. Buried in Garbage. 32p. (gr. 3-4). 1991. lib. bdg. 14.95 (ISBN 0-86505-424-X); pap. text ed. 7.95 (ISBN 0-86505-454-1). Crabtree Pub Co. Unfortunately, when garbage is thrown away, it does not disappear. As the population grows by leaps & bounds, we are running out of landfill sites & are literally becoming buried in our own garbage. This thorough book examines the reasons why garbage has become such a worldwide problem & looks at the ways it is being disposed of today. Children will gain an understanding of what a landfill site is, how incineration harms the environment, & the urgency we face in dealing with our garbage problem. Loaded with information & activites, THE CRABTREE ENVIRONMENT SERIES will inform, guide & motivate your students into working towards a cleaner environment.
Publisher Provided Annotation.

—**Reducing, Reusing, & Recycling. (Illus.). 32p. (gr. 3-4). 1991. lib. bdg. 14.95 (ISBN 0-86505-426-6); pap. text ed. 7.95 (ISBN 0-86505-456-8). Crabtree Pub Co. Almost every community around the country has a program for collecting materials that can be broken down to make new & useful products. But recycling is only one solution to the problem of mounting garbage. Children should be made aware that reducing their garbage is the most important goal in helping to save their environment. Helpful information, stories, & activities will empower children to take action concerning their environment.**
Publisher Provided Annotation.

Koral, April. Our Global Greenhouse. (Illus.). 64p. (gr. 3 up). 1991. pap. 4.95 (ISBN 0-531-15601-X). Watts.

McQueen, Kelly & Fassler, David. Let's Talk Trash: The Kids' Book about Recycling. LC 90-21400. (Illus.). 168p. (ps-6). 1991. pap. 14.95g (ISBN 0-914525-19-0); plastic comb 18.95 (ISBN 0-914525-20-4). Waterfront Bks.

Markham, Adam. The Environment. (Illus.). 48p. (gr. 5 up). Date not set. PLB 18.00 (ISBN 0-86592-286-1). Rourke Corp.

Miles, Betty. Save the Earth: An Action Handbook for Kids. Davis, Nelle, illus. LC 90-46514. 128p. (Orig.). (gr. 5 up). 1991. 13.99 (ISBN 0-679-91731-4); pap. 6.95 (ISBN 0-679-81731-X). Knopf.

Newton, David E. Taking a Stand Against Pollution. 1990. PLB 13.40 (ISBN 0-531-10923-2). Watts.

Pringle, Laurence. Global Warming: Assessing the Greenhouse Threat. (gr. 4-7). 1990. 15.95 (ISBN 1-55970-012-2). Arcade Pub Inc.

Silver, Debbie & Vallely, Bernadette. Earth Action! A Guide to Saving the Planet. Roche, Christine, illus. 144p. (gr. 9-12). 1991. 14.95 (ISBN 0-374-38760-5); pap. 3.95 (ISBN 0-374-41943-4). FS&G.

Steinberg, Michael. Our Wilderness: How the People of New York Found, Changed & Preserved the Adirondacks. LC 91-16550. (Illus.). 112p. (gr. 4-8). 1991. 14.95 (ISBN 0-935272-56-9); 18. 95 (ISBN 0-685-35784-8). ADK Mtn

Club. A history of the 6-million-acre Adirondack Park of New York State, which includes towns & farms, businesses & timberlands as well as 1.2 million acres of wilderness. Written for ages 10 & up (Gr. 4-8). Historic photographs by Stoddard & Apperson. Publication coincides with the 1992 Centennial of the Adirondack Park. Book carries conservationist message.
Publisher Provided Annotation.

Stewart, Gail. Acid Rain. LC 90-5854. (Illus.). 112p. (gr. 5-8). 1990. PLB 11.95 (ISBN 1-56006-111-1). Lucent Bks.

Tesar, Jenny E. Global Warming. Cayne, Bernard S., ed. (Illus.). 128p. (gr. 7-12). 1991. 18.95x (ISBN 0-8160-2490-1). Facts on File.

Wilkes, Angela. My First Green Book. LC 91-4371. (Illus.). 48p. (gr. 2-5). 1991. 12.00 (ISBN 0-679-81780-8); lib. bdg. 13.99 (ISBN 0-679-91780-2). Knopf.

ENZYMES
Berger, Melvin. Enzymes in Action. LC 76-132291. 151p. (gr. 7-9). 1971. 12.95 (ISBN 0-690-26735-5, Crowell Jr Bks). HarpC Child Bks.

Breslow, Ronald. Enzymes: The Machines of Life. Head, J. J., ed. Steffen, Ann T., illus. LC 84-45828. 16p. (Orig.). (gr. 10 up). 1986. pap. text ed. 2.15 (ISBN 0-89278-155-6, 45-9755). Carolina Biological.

EOLITHIC PERIOD
see Stone Age

EPIGRAMS
see also Proverbs; Quotations
Christiansen, Helen E. Trinkets & Treasures: A Collection of Favorite Bits of Wisdom. 130p. (Orig.). (gr. 7 up). 1988. pap. 8.50 (ISBN 0-9621419-0-9). H Christiansen.

Morrison, Lillian, ed. Yours Till Niagara Falls. Bauernschmidt, Marjorie, illus. LC 50-6508. 182p. (gr. 4 up). 1950. 12.95 (ISBN 0-690-91268-4, Crowell Jr Bks). HarpC Child Bks.

EPILEPSY
Kornfield, Elizabeth. Dreams Come True. Kornfield, Lee, ed. (Illus.). 32p. (gr. 3-6). 1986. pap. 5.95 (ISBN 0-940611-00-7). Rocky Mntn Child.

Silverstein, Alvin & Silverstein, Virginia B. Epilepsy. LC 74-31382. (Illus.). 64p. (gr. 4-6). 1990. PLB 12.89 (ISBN 0-397-32413-8, Lipp Jr Bks). HarpC Child Bks.

EPISTEMOLOGY
see Knowledge, Theory of

EQUALITY
see also Democracy
Hilton, Nette. The Long Red Scarf. Power, Margaret, illus. 32p. (ps-3). 1990. PLB 12.95 (ISBN 0-87614-399-0). Carolrhoda Bks.

EQUESTRIANISM
see Horsemanship

ERASMUS, DESIDERIUS, 1466?-1536
Vernon, Louise A. The Man Who Laid the Egg. Eitzen, Allan, illus. LC 77-24939. 120p. (gr. 4-8). 1977. pap. 4.50 (ISBN 0-8361-1828-6). Herald Pr.

ERIE CANAL
Spier, Peter. The Erie Canal. Spier, Peter, illus. LC 70-102055. 36p. (gr. 1-3). 1990. pap. 10.95 (ISBN 0-385-06777-1); pap. 5.95 (ISBN 0-385-05234-0). Doubleday.

Stein, R. Conrad. The Story of the Erie Canal. Neely, Keith, illus. LC 84-28525. 32p. (gr. 3-6). 1985. lib. bdg. 13.27 (ISBN 0-516-04682-9); pap. 3.95 (ISBN 0-516-44682-7). Childrens.

EROSION
see also Soil Conservation
Stille, Darlene. Soil Erosion & Pollution. LC 89-25360. (Illus.). 48p. (gr. k-4). 1990. 14.60 (ISBN 0-516-01188-X); pap. 4.95 (ISBN 0-516-41188-8). Childrens.

ERUPTIONS
see Volcanoes

ERVING, JULIUS
Bell, Marty. The Legend of Dr. J. The Story of Julius Erving. updated & expanded ed. (Illus.). 192p. (gr. 9-12). 1976. pap. 4.95 (ISBN 0-451-15464-9, Sig). NAL-Dutton.

ESCAPES
Stewart, J. & Hamilton, N. Great Escapes. (Illus.). 48p. (gr. 5-9). 1988. PLB 14.65 (ISBN 0-88625-208-3); pap. 5.95 (ISBN 0-88625-207-5). Durkin Hayes Pub.

ESCAPES-FICTION
Holman, Felice. Slake's Limbo. LC 74-11675. 126p. (gr. 4-8). 1974. 12.95 (ISBN 0-684-13926-X, Scribners Young Read). Macmillan Child Grp.

Lewis, C. S. The Silver Chair. Baynes, Pauline, illus. LC 53-12553. 216p. (gr. 4 up). 1988. 12.95 (ISBN 0-02-758780-0, Mcmillan Child Bk); pap. 3.50 (ISBN 0-02-044250-5, Collier). Macmillan Child Grp.

McInerney, Judith W. Judge Benjamin: The Superdog Rescue. Morrill, Leslie, illus. (gr. 4-6). pap. 2.50 (ISBN 0-317-66178-7, Minstrel Bks). PB.

ESKIMOS
Aigner, Jean S. The Eskimo. (Illus.). (gr. 5 up). 1989. 17. 95 (ISBN 1-55546-705-9). Chelsea Hse.

Alexander, Bryan & Alexander, Cherry. An Eskimo Family. (Illus.). 32p. (gr. 2-5). 1985. PLB 9.95 (ISBN 0-8225-1656-X). Lerner Pubns.

Carter, Marilyn. Peluk, an Eskimo Boy. (Illus.). 44p. (gr. 3 up). pap. text ed. 5.95 (ISBN 0-944677-04-5). Aladdin Pub.

Coccola, Raymond de & King, Paul. The Incredible Eskimo. Cameron, J., ed. Houston, James, illus. 435p. (Orig.). (gr. 9). 1986. pap. 16.95 (ISBN 0-88839-189-7). Hancock House.

Davis, Nancy M. Eskimos. Davis, Nancy M., illus. 32p. (Orig.). (ps-5). 1986. pap. 4.95 (ISBN 0-937103-06-3). DaNa Pubns.

Ekoomiak, Normee. Arctic Memories. LC 89-39194. (Illus.). 32p. (gr. 3 up). 1990. 15.95g (ISBN 0-8050-1254-0). H Holt & Co.

Hahn, Elizabeth. Inuit. (Illus.). 32p. (gr. 5-8). 1990. lib. bdg. 13.26 (ISBN 0-86625-386-6); lib. bdg. 9.95s.p. Rourke Corp.

Osinski, Alice. The Eskimo. LC 85-9691. (Illus.). 45p. (gr. 2-3). 1985. PLB 13.27 (ISBN 0-516-01267-3); pap. 4.95 (ISBN 0-516-41267-1). Childrens.

Planche, Bernard. Living with the Eskimos. Matthews, Sarah, tr. from FRE. Grant, Donald, illus. LC 87-31805. 38p. (gr. k-5). 1988. 4.95 (ISBN 0-944589-12-X, 12X). Young Discovery Lib.

Pluckrose, ed. Small World of Eskimos. (gr. k-3). 1980. PLB 10.40 (ISBN 0-531-03418-6, E38). Watts.

Schultz, Ellen. I Can Read About Eskimos. LC 78-73735. (gr. 2-4). 1979. pap. 1.95 (ISBN 0-89375-219-3). Troll Assocs.

Senungetuk, Vivian & Tiulana, Paul. Place for Winter: Paul Tiulana's Story, (A) (Illus.). 120p. (gr. 10-12). 1989. Repr. of 1987 ed. 17.95 (ISBN 0-938227-02-5). CIRI Found.

Smith, J. H. Eskimos-The Inuit of the Arctic. (Illus.). 48p. (gr. 4-8). 1987. PLB 15.33 (ISBN 0-86625-257-6). Rourke Corp.

Vickery, Eugene L. The Ramiluk Stories: Adventures of an Eskimo Family in the Prehistoric Arctic. Tolpo, Lily, illus. 124p. (Orig.). (gr. 5 up). 1989. 16.00 (ISBN 0-937775-11-8); pap. 10.95 (ISBN 0-937775-10-X). Stonehaven Pubs.

ESKIMOS-ART
Morgan, Lael. Art & Eskimo Power: The Life & Times of Alaskan Howard Rock. Sims, Virginia, ed. (Illus.). 260p. (Orig.). (gr. 9-12). 1988. 24.95 (ISBN 0-945397-02-X); pap. 16.95 (ISBN 0-945397-03-8). Epicenter Pr.

ESKIMOS-FICTION
Biggar, Joan R. Danger at Half-Moon Lake. (Illus.). 128p. (gr. 5-8). 1991. 3.95 (ISBN 0-570-04194-5). Concordia.

Chadwick, Roxane. Don't Shoot. Ryan, Edwin H., illus. LC 78-6101. 40p. (gr. 2-9). 1979. PLB 7.95 (ISBN 0-8225-0706-4). Lerner Pubns.

Cohlene, Terri. Ka-Ha-Si & the Loon: An Eskimo Legend. (gr. 4-7). 1990. pap. 3.95 (ISBN 0-8167-2359-1). Troll Assocs.

Craighead-George, Jean. Julie y los Lobos. (SPA.). (gr. 1-6). 8.50 (ISBN 84-204-3206-7). Santillana.

George, Jean C. Julie of the Wolves. Schoenherr, John, illus. LC 72-76509. 180p. (gr. 7 up). 1972. 14.95i (ISBN 0-06-021943-2); PLB 13.89 (ISBN 0-06-021944-0); pap. 3.50 (ISBN 0-06-440058-1). HarpC Child Bks.

—Water Sky. George, Jean C., illus. LC 86-45496. 224p. (gr. 5 up). 1989. pap. 3.95 (ISBN 0-06-440202-9, Trophy). HarpC Child Bks.

Griese, Arnold. The Way of Our People. Wells, Haro, illus. LC 74-23086. 90p. (gr. 4-7). 1975. PLB 12.89 (ISBN 0-690-00707-8, Crowell Jr Bks). HarpC Child Bks.

Houston, James. The Falcon Bow: An Arctic Legend. LC 86-5378. 96p. (gr. 3-7). 1986. 12.95 (ISBN 0-689-50411-X, M K McElderry). Macmillan Child Grp.

Jenness, Aylette & Rivers, Alice. In Two Worlds: A Yup'ik Eskimo Family. Jenness, Aylette, illus. (gr. 6 up). 1989. 13.95 (ISBN 0-395-42797-5). HM.

Kortum, Jeanie. Ghost Vision. Stermer, Dugald, illus. LC 83-4706. 160p. (gr. 5-9). 1983. 10.95 (ISBN 0-394-86190-6, Pant Bks Young). Pantheon.

Kortum, Jeanie & Stermer, Dugald. Ghost Vision. LC 82-19410. (Illus.). 144p. (gr. 5-9). o.s.i 10.95; PLB 10.99. Sierra.

Parish, Peggy. Ootah's Lucky Day. Funai, Mamoru, illus. LC 70-105467. 64p. (gr. k-3). 1970. PLB 11.89 (ISBN 0-06-024645-6). HarpC Child Bks.

Paulsen, Gary. Dogsong. LC 84-20443. 192p. (gr. 7 up). 1985. 13.95 (ISBN 0-02-770180-8, Bradbury Pr). Macmillan Child Grp.

Rogers, Jean. Goodbye, My Island. Munoz, Rie, illus. LC 82-15816. 96p. (gr. 5-7). 1983. 12.95 (ISBN 0-688-01964-1); PLB 12.88 (ISBN 0-688-01965-X). Greenwillow.

ESKIMOS-LEGENDS
Cohlene, Terri. Ka-Ha-Si & the Loon. (Illus.). 48p. (gr. 4-8). 1990. lib. bdg. 19.93 (ISBN 0-86593-002-3); lib. bdg. 14.95s.p. Rourke Corp.

Dearmond, Dale. Boy Who Found the Light. (gr. 4-7). 1990. 16.95 (ISBN 0-316-17787-3). Little.

—The Seal Oil Lamp. DeArmond, Dale, illus. 48p. (gr. k-4). 1988. 14.95 (ISBN 0-316-17786-5). Little.

Houston, James. The White Archer: An Eskimo Legend. LC 79-14458. (Illus.). 96p. (gr. 4-7). 1990. pap. 8.95 (ISBN 0-15-696224-1, VoyB). HarBraceJ.

Sloat, Teri, retold by. & illus. The Eye of the Needle: Based on a Yupik Tale Told by Betty Huffman. (ps-4). 1990. 13.95 (ISBN 0-525-44623-0, DCB). Dutton Child Bks.

ESQUIMAUX

see Eskimos

ESTATE PLANNING

see also Insurance; Investments

ESTHER, QUEEN OF PERSIA–FICTION

Pingry, Patricia. The Story of Esther. Harrison, Susan, illus. 24p. (ps-k). 1990. pap. 3.95 (ISBN 0-8249-8420-X). Ideals.

ETHICAL EDUCATION

see Religious Education

ETHICS

Bernards, Neal, ed. Euthanasia: Opposing Viewpoints. LC 89-2181. (Illus.). 235p. (gr. 10 up). 1989. PLB 15.95 (ISBN 0-89908-442-7); pap. 8.95 (ISBN 0-89908-417-6). Greenhaven.

Cooperation. (gr. 7-12). 1991. PLB 12.95 (ISBN 0-8239-1232-9). Rosen Group.

Garnett, Paul D. Investigating Morals & Values in Today's Society. 160p. (gr. 5-10). 1988. wkbk. 11.95 (ISBN 0-86653-443-1, GA1053). Good Apple.

Hashim, A. S. Islamic Ethics. pap. 5.95 (ISBN 0-686-18404-1); pap. 49.50 entire set (ISBN 0-686-18405-X). Kazi Pubns.

Marsh, Carole. What the Heck Are Ethics? (gr. 4-9). 1988. 19.95 (ISBN 1-55609-342-X); pap. 14.95 (ISBN 0-318-37388-2). Gallopade Pub Group.

Shibles, Warren. Good & Bad Are Funny Things: Ethics in Rhyme for Children. LC 77-93808. (gr. k up). 1978. pap. 6.50 (ISBN 0-912386-14-2). Language Pr.

Sioles, Anna M. An Ethics Primer for Children, Honesty - Kindness - Respect: A Catalyst to Discussion. Sioles, Anna M. & Boethner, Sandra, illus. 83p. (Orig.). (gr. 1-7). 1989. pap. text ed. 7.95x (ISBN 0-9620893-0-3). Agatha Pub Co.

Von Harrison, Grant. Is Kissing Sinful? 16p. 1985. pap. text ed. 2.95 (ISBN 0-929985-27-3). Sonos.

Weiss, Ann E. Bioethics: Dilemmas in Modern Medicine. LC 85-11608. 128p. (gr. 7-12). 1985. lib. bdg. 17.95 (ISBN 0-89490-113-3). Enslow Pubs.

Wilson, Etta. The Value of Excellence. (gr. 7-12). 1991. PLB 15.95 (ISBN 0-8239-1289-2). Rosen Group.

ETHICS, CHRISTIAN

see Christian Ethics

ETHICS, SEXUAL

see Sexual Ethics

ETHIOPIA

Department of Geography, Lerner Publications. Ethiopia in Pictures. (Illus.). 64p. (gr. 5 up). 1988. PLB 12.95 (ISBN 0-8225-1836-8). Lerner Pubns.

Fradin, Dennis B. Ethiopia. LC 88-10882. (Illus.). 128p. (gr. 5-9). 1988. PLB 25.27 (ISBN 0-516-02706-9). Childrens.

Pankhurst, Richard. Ethiopia. (Illus.). (gr. 5 up). 1988. 14.95 (ISBN 0-222-00965-9). Chelsea Hse.

Stewart, Gail B. Ethiopia. LC 90-49795. (Illus.). 48p. (gr. 5-6). 1991. RSBE 10.95 (ISBN 0-89686-601-7, Crestwood Hse). Macmillan Child Grp.

ETHIOPIA–FICTION

Kendall, Jonathan. My Name Is Rachamim. (Illus.). (gr. 2-3). 1987. 7.95 (ISBN 0-8074-0321-0, 123925). UAHC.

ETHNIC GROUPS

see Minorities

ETHNOGRAPHY

see Ethnology

ETHNOLOGY

see also Anthropology; Archeology; Civilization; Color of Man; Costume; Folklore; Language and Languages; Man, Prehistoric; Manners and Customs; Race; Race Problems; Totems and Totemism

Cherryholmes, C. & Manson, G. Studying Cultures. (Illus.). (gr. 4). 1979. text ed. 24.64 (ISBN 0-07-011984-8). McGraw.

Herda, D. J. Ethnic America: The North Central States. (Illus.). 64p. (gr. 5-8). 1991. PLB 13.90 (ISBN 1-56294-016-3). Millbrook Pr.

—Ethnic America: The Northeastern States. (Illus.). 64p. (gr. 5-8). 1991. PLB 13.90 (ISBN 1-56294-014-7). Millbrook Pr.

—Ethnic America: The Northwestern States. (Illus.). 64p. (gr. 5-8). 1991. PLB 13.90 (ISBN 1-56294-018-X). Millbrook Pr.

—Ethnic America: The South Central States. (Illus.). 64p. (gr. 5-8). 1991. PLB 13.90 (ISBN 1-56294-017-1). Millbrook Pr.

—Ethnic America: The Southeastern States. (Illus.). 64p. (gr. 5-8). 1991. PLB 13.90 (ISBN 1-56294-015-5). Millbrook Pr.

—Ethnic America: The Southwestern States. (Illus.). 64p. (gr. 5-8). 1991. PLB 13.90 (ISBN 1-56294-019-8). Millbrook Pr.

Holder, Robyn. Aborigines of Australia. (Illus.). 48p. (gr. 4-8). 1987. 15.33 (ISBN 0-86625-262-2). Rourke Corp.

Langley, Andrew & Butterfield, Maira. People. Young, Norman, illus. LC 89-42986. 48p. (gr. 5-6). 1989. PLB 11.95 (ISBN 0-8368-0132-6). Gareth Stevens Inc.

Langoulant, Allan. Everybody's Different. Langoulant, Allan, illus. LC 90-36811. 32p. (gr. 2-3). 1990. PLB 12.95 (ISBN 0-8368-0435-X). Gareth Stevens Inc.

Lipson, Greta & Romatowski, Jane. Ethnic Pride. Simmons, Sheri, illus. 152p. (gr. 4-9). 1983. wkbk. 11.95 (ISBN 0-86653-121-1, GA 464). Good Apple.

People & Customs. (Illus.). 80p. (gr. k-6). 1986. pap. 13.27 (ISBN 0-8172-2583-8). Raintree Pubs.

Stewart, G. In the Desert. (Illus.). 32p. (gr. 3-8). 1989. lib. bdg. 13.26 (ISBN 0-86592-106-7). Rourke Corp.

Vilsoni, Patricia H. South Pacific Islanders. (Illus.). 48p. (gr. 4-8). 1987. PLB 15.33 (ISBN 0-86625-259-2). Rourke Corp.

Waybill, Marjorie. Chinese Eyes. Cutrell, Pauline, illus. LC 74-5751. 32p. (gr. k-2). 1974. 12.95 (ISBN 0-8361-1738-7). Herald Pr.

Williams, Brenda & Williams, Brian. People & Places. Forsey, Chris, illus. 40p. (gr. 4-5). 1991. PLB 11.40 (ISBN 0-531-19111-7). Watts.

Winter, Frank H. The Filipinos in America. (Illus.). 80p. (gr. 5 up). 1988. 11.95 (ISBN 0-8225-0237-2); pap. 3.95 (ISBN 0-8225-1035-9). Lerner Pubns.

ETIQUETTE

see also Courtesy; Dancing; Dating (Social Customs); Entertaining; Letter Writing; Manners and Customs; also names of countries with the subdivision Social life and customs

Adachi, Kelly. The Kids' Handbook. (Illus.). 112p. (gr. 1 up). 1985. 7.95 (ISBN 0-8184-0365-9); pap. 4.95 (ISBN 0-8184-0368-3). Carol Pub Group.

Adamson, Elizabeth C. Mind Your Manners. 48p. (gr. 1-3). 1981. 5.95 (ISBN 0-86653-014-2, GA 243). Good Apple.

Alden, Laura. Saying I'm Sorry. Siculan, Dan, illus. LC 82-19945. 32p. (gr. 1-2). 1983. PLB 11.97 (ISBN 0-89565-247-1). Childs World.

Berry, Joy W. What to Do When Your Mom or Dad Says: "Go to Bed!" Kelley, Orly, ed. LC 83-80508. (Illus.). 48p. (gr. k-6). 4.98 (ISBN 0-941510-16-6). Living Skills.

—What to Do When Your Mom Or Dad Says..."Be Good!" Bartholomew, illus. LC 83-80000509. 48p. (gr. 3 up). 1983. 14.60 (ISBN 0-516-02578-3). Childrens.

—What to Do When Your Mom or Dad Says..."We Can't Afford It!" Kelley, Orly, ed. Bartholomew, illus. LC 83-80845. 48p. (gr. k-6). 4.98 (ISBN 0-941510-24-7). Living Skills.

—What to Do When Your Mom or Dad Says..."Get the Phone!" Kelley, Orly, ed. Bartholomew, illus. LC 83-80507. 48p. (gr. k-6). 4.98 (ISBN 0-941510-13-1). Living Skills.

—What to Do When Your Mom or Dad Says..."Behave in Public!" Kelley, Orly, ed. Bartholomew, illus. LC 83-80842. 48p. (gr. k-6). 4.98 (ISBN 0-941510-22-0). Living Skills.

—What to Do When Your Mom or Dad Says..."Be Kind to Your Guest" Bartholomew, illus. Berry, Joy W., intro. by. LC 82-81203. (Illus.). 48p. (gr. 3-7). 1982. 4.98 (ISBN 0-941510-06-9). Living Skills.

—What to Do When Your Mom or Dad Says..."Be Kind to Your Guest!" LC 82-81203. (gr. 3 up). 1982. 14.60 (ISBN 0-516-02571-6). Childrens.

—What to Do When Your Mom or Dad Says..."Turn Off the Water & Lights!" Kelley, Orly, ed. Bartholomew, illus. LC 83-80844. 48p. (gr. k-6). 4.98 (ISBN 0-941510-23-9). Living Skills.

—What to Do When Your Mom or Dad Says..."Don't Slurp Your Soup!" Kelley, Orly, ed. Bartholomew, illus. LC 83-80838. 48p. (gr. k-6). 4.98 (ISBN 0-941510-20-4). Living Skills.

—What to Do When Your Mom or Dad Says..."What Should You Say Dear?" Proper Verbal Responses. Bartholomew, illus. LC 83-80000506. 48p. (gr. 3 up). 1983. 14.60 (ISBN 0-516-02581-3). Childrens.

—What to Do When Your Mom or Dad Says..."Write to Grandma!" Kelley, Orly, ed. Bartholomew, illus. LC 83-80841. 48p. (gr. k-6). 4.98 (ISBN 0-941510-21-2). Living Skills.

—What to Do When Your Mom or Dad Says..."Stand Up Straight!" Kelly, Orly, ed. Bartholomew, illus. LC 83-80843. 48p. (gr. k-6). 4.98 (ISBN 0-941510-19-0). Living Skills.

—What to Do When Your Mom or Dad Says: "What Should You Say, Dear?" Kelley, Orly, ed. Bartholomew, illus. LC 83-80506. 48p. (gr. k-6). 4.98 (ISBN 0-941510-14-X). Living Skills.

Brainard, Beth & Behr, Sheila. Soup Should Be Seen, Not Heard! The Kids' Etiquette Book. (Illus.). 107p. (Orig.). (ps-7). 1988. pap. 10.00 (ISBN 0-9621908-0-2). Good Idea Kids.

Brown, Fern G. Etiquette. Green, Anne C., illus. LC 84-20935. 84p. (gr. 4-7). 1985. PLB 10.40 (ISBN 0-531-04908-6). Watts.

Coats, Carolyn & Smith, Pamela. Come Cook with Me! A Cookbook for Kids. Coats, Carolyn, illus. 133p. 1989. pap. 10.00 spiral bound (ISBN 1-878722-06-9). C Coats Bestsellers.

David, Jo. Finishing Touches, Manners with Style. Richey, Donald, illus. LC 90-10888. 128p. (gr. 5-9). 1990. lib. bdg. 10.89 (ISBN 0-8167-2179-3); pap. text ed. 2.95 (ISBN 0-8167-2180-7). Troll Assocs.

Dellinger, Annetta E. Good Manners for God's Children. (ps-k). 1984. pap. 4.95 (ISBN 0-570-04093-0, 56-1461). Concordia.

Donahue, Bob & Donahue, Marilyn. The Right Way to Eat Spaghetti. (Illus.). 128p. (Orig.). (gr. 9-12). 1988. pap. 4.95 (ISBN 0-8423-5597-9). Tyndale.

Educational Assessment Publishing Company Staff. Parent - Child Learning Library: Courtesy English Big Book. (Illus.). 32p. (gr. k-3). Date not set. text ed. 28.50 (ISBN 0-942277-77-5). Educ Assess Pub.

—Parent - Child Learning Library: Courtesy Spanish Big Book. (SPA., Illus.). 32p. (gr. k-3). Date not set. text ed. 28.50 (ISBN 0-942277-78-3). Educ Assess Pub.

—Parent - Child Learning Library: Courtesy Spanish Edition. (SPA.). 32p. Date not set. text ed. 9.95 (ISBN 0-942277-94-5). Educ Assess Pub.

—Parent - Child Learning Library: Courtesy. (Illus.). 32p. (ps). Date not set. text ed. 9.95 (ISBN 0-942277-62-7). Educ Assess Pub.

Everding, Maria P. Pretty As a Picture: A Guide to Manners, Poise & Appearance. 138p. (Orig.). (gr. 4-7). 1986. pap. 14.95 (ISBN 0-9617665-0-6). GME Pub Co.

Frost, Erica. I Can Read about Good Manners. LC 74-24878. (Illus.). (gr. 1-2). 1975. pap. 1.95 (ISBN 0-89375-059-X). Troll Assocs.

Gardner, Richard A. The Girls & Boys Book about Good & Bad Behavior. Lowenheim, Al, illus. LC 90-31241. 221p. (gr. 2-6). 1990. 17.00 (ISBN 0-933812-21-3). Creative Therapeutics.

Goley. Manners, Reading Level 2. (Illus.). 32p. (gr. 1-4). Date not set. PLB 13.26 (ISBN 0-86592-395-7). Rourke Corp.

Hammond, Elizabeth. A Pocket Book of Manners for Young People. Oppenheimer, Jennie, illus. LC 90-90325. 96p. (Orig.). (gr. 4-8). 1990. pap. 5.95 (ISBN 0-9627061-0-8). Trotwood Press.

Hamoy, Carol. What's Wrong? What's Wrong? Hamoy, Carol, illus. (gr. k-3). 1965. 8.95 (ISBN 0-685-00564-X). Astor-Honor.

Hazen, Barbara. Hello Gnu, How Do You Do? (ps-3). 1990. 14.95 (ISBN 0-385-26449-6). Doubleday.

Hill, Shelby & Heffington, Jerri B. The ABC Book of Manners for Children. Barnett, Helmut, illus. LC 88-24082. 60p. (gr. k-3). 1988. 16.95 (ISBN 0-938349-32-5). State House Pr.

Howe, James. The Muppet Guide to Magnificent Manners. Elwell, Peter, illus. LC 83-25063. 64p. (gr. 3-7). 1984. lib. bdg. 5.99 (ISBN 0-394-96351-2, Random Juv); pap. 4.95 (ISBN 0-394-86351-8). Random.

Jefferds, Vince. Disney's Elegant Book of Manners. 1985. pap. 14.95 (ISBN 0-671-60507-0, Little Simon). S&S Trade.

Joslin, Sesyle. What Do You Say, Dear? Sendak, Maurice, illus. LC 84-43140. 48p. 1958. 13.95 (ISBN 0-201-09391-X); PLB 13.89 (ISBN 0-06-023074-6). HarpC Child Bks.

Klare, Judy. Manners. (Illus.). 32p. (gr. 5 up). 1990. PLB 14.00 (ISBN 0-685-36383-X); PLB 10.50 (ISBN 0-685-36384-8). Rourke Corp.

Leaf, Munro. Four-&-Twenty Watchbirds. LC 89-49742. (Illus.). 32p. (ps-3). 1990. lib. bdg. 15.00 (ISBN 0-208-02208-2, Pub. by Linnet). Shoe String.

Learning Forum Staff. Communications & Motivation Personal Growth Set. (gr. 8-12). 1988. 45.00 (ISBN 0-945525-14-1). Supercamp.

Mehew, Randall & Mehew, Karen. The Best Manners Book Ever. Bales, Marcia, illus. 68p. 1990. pap. text ed. 5.95 (ISBN 0-929985-55-9). Sonos.

Moncure, Jane B. Please? Thanks! I'm Sorry. Axeman, Lois, illus. LC 85-11664. 32p. (gr. k-2). 1985. PLB 11.97 (ISBN 0-89565-331-1). Childs World.

—Saying Please. Inderieden, Nancy, illus. LC 82-19927. 32p. (ps-2). 1983. PLB 11.97 (ISBN 0-89565-248-X). Childs World.

Oana, Katherine, et al. Holiday Thank You Notes to Write & Color. (Illus.). 32p. (gr. 2-7). 1983. pap. 1.98 (ISBN 0-88724-041-0, CD-8014). Carson-Dellos.

Parish, Peggy. Mind Your Manners. Hafner, Marylin, illus. LC 77-19096. 56p. (gr. 1-3). 1978. PLB 11.88 (ISBN 0-688-84157-0). Greenwillow.

Polisar, Barry L. Don't Do That: A Child's Guide to Bad Manners, Ridiculous Rules & Inadequate Etiquette. Young, Debby, illus. 64p. (Orig.). (gr. 3-6). 1989. 9.95 (ISBN 0-938663-01-1); pap. 7.95 (ISBN 0-938663-10-0). Rainbow Morn.

Post, Elizabeth L. & Coles, Joan M. Emily Post Talks with Teenagers about Manners & Etiquette. Weber, Jill, illus. LC 86-45135. 143p. (gr. 6 up). 1986. 16.95 (ISBN 0-06-181685-X); pap. 6.95 (ISBN 0-06-096117-1). HarpC Child Bks.

Reece, Colleen L. Saying Thank You. Connelly, Gwen, illus. LC 82-21992. 32p. (gr. 1-2). 1983. PLB 11.97 (ISBN 0-89565-249-8). Childs World.

Riehecky, Janet. May I? Connelly, Gwen, illus. LC 88-16838. 32p. (ps-2). 1989. PLB 9.96 (ISBN 0-89565-388-5); pap. 4.50 (ISBN 0-89565-524-1). Childs World.

—Thank-You. Connelly, Gwen, illus. LC 88-16840. 32p. (ps-2). 1989. PLB 9.96 (ISBN 0-89565-387-7); pap. 6.48 (ISBN 0-89565-523-3). Childs World.

Rittenour, Gary & Aemmer, Gail. Manners Fun Book. Rittenour, Gary, illus. 32p. (ps-3). 1984. pap. 1.59 (ISBN 0-88724-015-1, CD-8030). Carson-Dellos.

Scarry, Richard. Pig Will & Pig Won't: A Book of Manners. Scarry, Richard, illus. LC 83-19177. 24p. (ps-1). 1984. (Random Juv). Random.

—Richard Scarry's Please & Thank You Book. LC 73-2441. (ps-2). 1973. 2.25 (ISBN 0-394-82681-7, Random Juv); lib. bdg. 5.99 (ISBN 0-394-92681-1). Random.

—Richard Scarry's Please & Thank You Book. LC 73-2441. (Illus.). 32p. (ps-1). 1990. pap. 5.95 incl. cassette (ISBN 0-679-80799-3). Random.

Stewart, Marjabelle Y. & Buchwald, Ann. Stand Up, Shake Hands, Say "How Do You Do" What Boys Need to Know about Today's Manners News. rev. ed. LC 77-8159. (gr. 7 up). 1988. 12.95 (ISBN 0-88331-100-3). Luce.

Thiry, Joan. How to Cope with an Artichoke & other Mannerly Mishaps. Walsh, Karen J., illus. 40p. (gr. 7-12). 1982. pap. 4.95 (ISBN 0-935046-04-6). Chateau Thierry.

—How to Entertain a Gnu & Not Disturb Your Family. Walsh, Karen J., illus. 40p. (gr. k-3). 1982. pap. 4.95 (ISBN 0-935046-02-X). Chateau Thierry.

—How to Make a Courtesy Butter Sandwich & Serve it Properly. Walsh, Karen J., illus 40p. (Orig.). (gr. 4-6). 1982. pap. 4.95 (ISBN 0-935046-03-8). Chateau Thierry.

Wathen, Judy & Sussman, Ellen. Teach Me Manners & Courtesy. Burris, Priscilla, illus. 40p. (Orig.). (ps-k). 1989. pap. 4.95 (ISBN 0-933606-74-5); tchr's. guide avail. Monkey Sisters.

World Book, Inc. Staff, ed. Put Your Best Foot Forward with the Alphabet Pals: Right Time for Rosie. LC 89-50457. (Illus.). 20p. (ps). 1989. lib. bdg. write for info. (ISBN 0-7166-1902-4). World Bk.

Young, Marjabelle Y. & Buchwald, Ann. White Gloves & Party Manners. LC 65-25830. (gr. 7 up). 1988. 12.95 (ISBN 0-88331-054-6). Luce.

WHITE GLOVES & PARTY MANNERS, an etiquette guide & Self-Help book for young people, first published in 1965, recently sold its one millionth copy. It was written by Marjabelle Young Stewart & co-author Ann Buchwald (wife of Art Buchwald), who have helped several generations to grow up civilized. The book is even more appropriate for today's world where "the look of good breeding" can be essential for success. The "knowledge of right behavior" described in this book, is still timely. WHITE GLOVES & PARTY MANNERS, is used as a textbook for worldwide courses called "White Gloves & Party Manners" which recently graduated its one millionth young lady. The book for girls, & the companion book for boys, STAND UP, SHAKE HANDS, SAY "HOW DO YOU DO" are delightfully illustrated, simple to understand & refreshing guides for parents & teachers as well. Also available from Robert B. Luce is WHAT TO DO, WHEN, & WHY by Stewart & Buchwald, a companion to the other two books.
Publisher Provided Annotation.

Ziegler, Sandra. Manners. Hutton, Kathryn, illus. LC 88-15013. 32p. (gr. k-3). 1986. PLB 11.97 (ISBN 0-89565-377-X); pap. 6.96 (ISBN 0-89565-527-6). Childs World.

—Manners. (Illus.). 32p. (ps-3) 1989. pap. 3.95 (ISBN 0-516-46315-2). Childrens.

—Understanding. (Illus.). 32p. (ps-3). 1989. pap. 3.95 (ISBN 0-516-46317-9). Childrens.

ETIQUETTE-FICTION

Aliki. Keep Your Mouth Closed, Dear. Aliki, illus. LC 66-19310. 48p. (ps-2). 1985. pap. 3.95 (ISBN 0-8037-4420-X). Dial Bks Young.

American Etiquette Institute Staff. Eddycat & Buddy Entertain a Guest, Bk. 5. (Illus.). 32p. (gr. k-3). 1991. 13.95 (ISBN 1-879322-14-5). Amer Etiquette Inst.

—Eddycat & Gabby Gorilla Babysit, Bk. 9. (Illus.). 32p. (gr. k-3). 1991. 13.95 (ISBN 1-879322-18-8). Amer Etiquette Inst.

—Eddycat Attends Sunshine's Birthday Party, Bk. 3. (Illus.). 32p. (gr. k-3). 1991. 13.95 (ISBN 1-879322-12-9). Amer Etiquette Inst.

—Eddycat Brings Soccer to Mannersville, Bk. 8. (Illus.). 32p. (gr. k-3). 1991. 13.95 (ISBN 1-879322-17-X). Amer Etiquette Inst.

—Eddycat Goes on Vacation with the Ducks, Bk. 11. (Illus.). 32p. (gr. k-3). 1991. 13.95 (ISBN 1-879322-20-X). Amer Etiquette Inst.

—Eddycat Goes Shopping with Becky, Bk. 6. (Illus.). 32p. (gr. k-3). 1991. 13.95 (ISBN 1-879322-15-3). Amer Etiquette Inst.

—Eddycat Helps Sunshine Plan Her Party, Bk. 2. (Illus.). 32p. (gr. k-3). 1991. 13.95 (ISBN 1-879322-11-0). Amer Etiquette Inst.

—Eddycat Introduces Leonardo Lion, Bk. 12. (Illus.). 32p. (gr. k-3). 1991. 13.95 (ISBN 1-879322-21-8). Amer Etiquette Inst.

—Eddycat Introduces Mannersville, USA, Bk. 1. (Illus.). 32p. (gr. k-3). 1991. 13.95 (ISBN 1-879322-10-2). Amer Etiquette Inst.

—Eddycat Serves Grandma's Birthday Brunch, Bk. 10. (Illus.). 32p. (gr. k-3). 1991. 13.95 (ISBN 1-879322-19-6). Amer Etiquette Inst.

—Eddycat Teaches Telephone Skills, Bk. 4. (Illus.). 32p. (gr. k-3). 1991. 13.95 (ISBN 1-879322-13-7). Amer Etiquette Inst.

—Eddycat Visits Wright Street School, Bk. 7. (Illus.). 32p. (gr. k-3). 1991. 13.95 (ISBN 1-879322-16-1). Amer Etiquette Inst.

Davidson, Alice J. Monkeys Never Say Please. (Illus.). 1986. 4.95 (ISBN 0-8378-5085-1). Gibson.

Gabriel, Howard W., III. Growing up with Character: Character Building Stories for Children, Vol. 1. Hasting, Christine Q., illus. 112p. (Orig.). (gr. k-8). 1986. pap. 7.95 (ISBN 0-936997-00-1, 038601). M & H Enter.

Herr, Selma & Piequet, Miriam. Manners Matter. Anyone Can Read Staff, ed. 150p. (Orig.). (gr. 3-7). 1987. pap. 10.50 (ISBN 0-914275-12-7). Anyone Can Read Bks.

Hoban, Russell. Dinner at Alberta's. Marshall, James, illus. LC 73-94796. 40p. (gr. 1-3). 1975. PLB 11.89 (ISBN 0-690-23993-9, Crowell Jr Bks). HarpC Child Bks.

Lewis, Shari. Lamb Chop in the Land of No Manners. (Illus.). 24p. 1989. pap. 3.50 (ISBN 0-685-23303-0) (ISBN 1-55802-290-2). Lynx Bks.

Miller, Virginia. On Your Potty! LC 90-49221. (Illus.). 32p. (ps up). 1991. 13.95 (ISBN 0-688-10617-X); PLB 13.88 (ISBN 0-688-10618-8). Greenwillow.

Piequet, Miriam. The Flying Mule Car. Anyone Can Read Staff, ed. Blanton, Betty, illus. 160p. (Orig.). (gr. 4-6). 1987. pap. 10.95 (ISBN 0-914275-11-9). Anyone Can Read Bks.

Stouse, Karla F. Act Nicely, Please. Yanda, Emma, illus. LC 87-70531. 16p. (gr. 2 up). 1987. pap. 0.95 (ISBN 0-87029-207-2). Abbey.

ETIQUETTE-POETRY

Burgess, Gelett. Goops & How to Be Them: A Manual of Manners for Polite Infants. Burgess, Gelett, illus. LC 68-55603. 96p. (ps-4). 1968. pap. 3.95 (ISBN 0-486-22233-0). Dover.

—More Goops & How Not to Be Them: A Manual of Manners for Impolite Infants. Burgess, Gelett, illus. LC 68-55531. 96p. (ps-4). 1968. pap. 3.95 (ISBN 0-486-22234-9). Dover.

ETYMOLOGY
see names of languages with the subdivision Etymology, e.g. English Language–Etymology, etc.

EUROPE

Bains, Rae. Europe. Eitzen, Allan, illus. LC 84-8598. 32p. (gr. 3-6). 1985. PLB 9.49 (ISBN 0-8167-0304-3); pap. text ed. 2.95 (ISBN 0-8167-0305-1). Troll Assocs.

Fairfield, Sheila. People & Nations of Europe. LC 88-42919. (Illus.). 64p. (gr. 5-6). 1988. PLB 13.95 (ISBN 1-55532-906-3). Gareth Stevens Inc.

Lye, Keith. Europe. Ron Hayward Associates, illus. 40p. (gr. 4-9). 1987. PLB 12.40 (ISBN 0-531-17068-3, Gloucester Pr). Watts.

Roberts, Elizabeth. Europe, 1992. (ps-3). 1990. PLB 11.90 (ISBN 0-531-17204-X). Watts.

EUROPE-DESCRIPTION AND TRAVEL

Georges, D. V. Europe. LC 86-9585. (Illus.). 48p. (gr. k-4). 1986. PLB 14.60 (ISBN 0-516-01292-4); pap. 4.95 (ISBN 0-516-41292-2). Childrens.

Ghazarian, S. H. Armenia. (Illus.). (gr. 5 up). 1990. 14.95 (ISBN 0-7910-0164-4). Chelsea Hse.

Twain, Mark. Innocents Abroad. Gemme, F. R., intro. by. (gr. 9 up). 1967. pap. 3.50 (ISBN 0-8049-0151-1, CL-151). Airmont.

EUROPE, EASTERN

Bradley, John. Eastern Europe: The Road to Democracy. (Illus.). 40p. (gr. 5-8). 1990. PLB 11.90 (ISBN 0-531-17238-4). Watts.

Holm, Anne. North to Freedom. (gr. 5-9). 1984. 16.50 (ISBN 0-8446-6156-2). Peter Smith.

Mayberry, Jodine. Eastern Europeans. Culleton, P., ed. (Illus.). 64p. (gr. 5-8). 1991. PLB 12.40 (ISBN 0-531-11109-1). Watts.

Riordan, James. Eastern Europe. (Illus.). 48p. (gr. 5-10). 1987. PLB 16.98 (ISBN 0-382-09468-9). Silver Burdett Pr.

Ryabko, E. We Live in the European U. S. S. R. (Illus.). 63p. 1984. PLB 9.49 (ISBN 0-531-03794-0). Watts.

EUROPE-FICTION

James, Henry. Portrait of a Lady. Fisher, N. H., intro. by. (gr. 11 up). pap. 2.50 (ISBN 0-8049-0098-1, CL-98). Airmont.

Standish, Burt L. Frank Merriwell in Europe. Rudman, Jack, ed. (gr. 9 up). Date not set. 9.95 (ISBN 0-8373-9308-6); pap. 3.95 (ISBN 0-8373-9008-7). F Merriwell.

EUROPE-HISTORY

Cairns, Trevor. Power for the People. LC 76-30607. (Illus.). 96p. (gr. 7 up). 1978. pap. 9.95 (ISBN 0-521-20902-1). Cambridge U Pr.

Kronenwetter, Michael. The New Eastern Europe. (Illus.). 192p. (gr. 9-12). 1991. PLB 13.90 (ISBN 0-531-11066-4). Watts.

EUROPE-HISTORY-FICTION

Cosman, Madeleine P. The Medieval Baker's Daughter: A Bilingual Adventure in Medieval Life with Costumes, Banners, Music, Food, & a Mystery Play. LC 84-71590. (ENG & SPA., Illus.). 112p. (gr. 3-12). 1984.

pap. 7.95 (ISBN 0-916491-18-8). Bard Hall Pr.

Intelligent young people desiring to know what life was like in medieval England will love this story of Johanna Baxter of Bread Street in the year 1412. This book also recreates medieval clothes, food, talk, song & theater by instructions for creating authentic banners, costumes, recipes, & music, as well as by the script for the amusing newly translated medieval play called Noah's Flood. A useful glossary briefly explains unfamiliar words of Johanna's world. On facing pages, this bilingual book has the Spanish & English texts. The Medieval Baker's Daughter or La Hija de la Panadera Medieval is a successful experiment in cultural unity; students reading & creating together a beautiful medieval feast or festival appreciate one another's talents, interests & languages. Dr. Cosman, an expert in medical law, directs the Medieval & Renaissance Institute at City College, City University of New York. A vivid public lecturer & TV personality, she is the author of many successful books such as Fabulous Feasts: Medieval Cookery & Ceremony (Braziller) & Medieval Holidays & Festivals: A Calendar of Celebrations (Scribner's), she makes glories of the Middle Ages accessible to readers of all ages.
Publisher Provided Annotation.

Treece, Henry. Men of the Hills. Price, Christine, illus. LC 58-5448. (gr. 6-9). 1958. 18.95 (ISBN 0-87599-115-7). S G Phillips.

—Ride into Danger. Price, Christine, illus. LC 59-12203. (gr. 7-10). 1959. 18.95 (ISBN 0-87599-113-0). S G Phillips.

EUROPE-HISTORY-TO 476.

Europe at the Time of Greece & Rome. (Illus.). 80p. (gr. 4 up). 1988. PLB 22.00 (ISBN 0-8172-3305-9). Raintree Pubs.

Frazee, Charles & Yopp, Hallie K. Ancient Europe. Frazee, Kathleen & Lumba, Eric, illus. (gr. 6). 1990. pap. text ed. write for info. Delos Pubns.

—Medieval & Early Modern Europe. Frazee, Kathleen & Lumba, Eric, illus. (gr. 7). 1990. pap. text ed. 5.50 wkbk. Delos Pubns.

The Invaders. LC 79-11934. (Illus.). 64p. (gr. 4 up). 1979. 7.95 (ISBN 0-668-04786-0, 4786-0). Prentice Hall Pr.

Prehistoric & Ancient Europe. (Illus.). 80p. (gr. 4 up). 1988. PLB 22.00 (ISBN 0-8172-3304-0). Raintree Pubs.

EUROPE-HISTORY-476-1492

The Invaders. LC 79-11934. (Illus.). 64p. (gr. 4 up). 1979. 7.95 (ISBN 0-668-04786-0, 4786-0). Prentice Hall Pr.

Sabbagh, Antoine. Europe in the Middle Ages. Ridett, Anthea, tr. from FRE. Morgan, illus. 77p. (gr. 7 up). 1988. 15.96 (ISBN 0-382-09484-0); 10.37s.p. (ISBN 0-685-18823-X). Silver Burdett Pr.

EUROPE-HISTORY-1789-1900

Cairns, Trevor. Europe Around the World. LC 81-13719. (Illus.). 104p. (gr. 5 up). 1975. PLB 10.95 (ISBN 0-8225-0809-5). Lerner Pubns.

—The Old Regime & the Revolution. LC 79-2972. (Illus.). 104p. (gr. 5 up). 1980. PLB 10.95 (ISBN 0-8225-0807-9). Lerner Pubns.

—Power for the People. LC 79-2973. (Illus.). 104p. (gr. 5 up). 1980. PLB 10.95 (ISBN 0-8225-0808-7). Lerner Pubns.

EUROPE-HISTORY-1914-1945
see also World War, 1939-1945

Dolan, Edward F., Jr. Victory in Europe: The Fall of Hitler's Europe. Ribaroff, Margaret, ed. (Illus.). 160p. (gr. 7-12). 1988. PLB 13.90 (ISBN 0-531-10522-9). Watts.

Tames, Richard. Nineteen Thirties. LC 90-32322. (Illus.). 48p. 1991. PLB 12.90 (ISBN 0-531-14059-8). Watts.

EUROPEAN WAR, 1939-1945
see World War, 1939-1945

EVALUATION OF LITERATURE
see Book Reviews; Books and Reading–Best Books; Criticism; Literature–History and Criticism

EVEREST, MOUNT

Rosen, Mike. Conquest of Everest. (ps-3). 1990. PLB 11.40 (ISBN 0-531-18319-X). Watts.

EVERGLADES, FLORIDA–FICTION

Buffett, Jimmy & Buffett, Savannah J. Trouble Dolls. Ingber, Bonnie V., intro. by. Davis, Lambert, illus. 32p. (ps). 1991. 14.95 (ISBN 0-15-290790-4). HarBraceJ.

EVERGLADES NATIONAL PARK

Linn, Christopher. The Everglades: Exploring the Unknown. LC 75-23414. (Illus.). 32p. (gr. 5-10). 1976. PLB 10.79 (ISBN 0-89375-006-9); pap. 2.95 (ISBN 0-89375-022-0). Troll Assocs.

Rom, Christine S. Everglades. LC 88-18644. (Illus.). (gr. 4-8). 1988. PLB 12.95 (ISBN 0-89686-404-9, Crestwood Hse). Macmillan Child Grp.

EVOLUTION

see also Adaptation (Biology); Anatomy, Comparative; Biology; Color of Animals; Color of Man; Creation; Embryology; Man–Influence of Environment; Man–Origin and Antiquity; Religion and Science; Social Change

Althea. How Life Began. (Illus.). 26p. (gr. 2-5). 1983. pap. 3.95 (ISBN 0-521-27167-3). Cambridge U Pr.

Bailey, Marilyn. Evolution: Opposing Viewpoints. LC 90-3837. (Illus.). 112p. (gr. 3-8). 1990. PLB 13.95 (ISBN 0-89908-078-2). Greenhaven.

Baylor, Byrd. If You Are a Hunter of Fossils. Parnall, Peter, illus. LC 79-17926. 32p. (ps-3). 1980. 13.95 (ISBN 0-684-16419-1, Scribners Young Read). Macmillan Child Grp.

Benton, Michael. The Story of Life on Earth. (Illus.). 96p. (gr. 4-12). 1986. PLB 14.90 (ISBN 0-531-19019-6, Pub. by Warwick). Watts.

Childers, Norman H. The Great Monkey Debate. Childers, Norman H., illus. 44p. (gr. k-5). 1988. 14.95g (ISBN 0-940561-12-3). White Rose Pr.

Cole, Joanna. Evolution. Aliki, illus. LC 87-638. 32p. (gr. k-3). 1987. 13.95 (ISBN 0-690-04596-4, Crowell Jr Bks); PLB 13.89 (ISBN 0-690-04598-0, Crowell Jr Bks). HarpC Child Bks.

—Evolution. Aliki, illus. LC 87-638. 32p. (ps-3). 1989. pap. 4.50 (ISBN 0-06-445086-4, Trophy). HarpC Child Bks.

Cork. Evolution: Discoveries & Theories of the Origins of Life. (Illus.). 32p. (gr. 4-8). 1985. PLB 13.96 (ISBN 0-88110-219-9); pap. 6.95 (ISBN 0-86020-867-2). EDC.

Fisher, David E. The Origin & Evolution of Our Own Particular Universe. LC 88-14108. (Illus.). 192p. (gr. 7 up). 1988. 14.95 (ISBN 0-689-31368-3, Atheneum Child Bk). Macmillan Child Grp.

Gallant, Roy A. Before the Sun Dies: The Story of Evolution. LC 88-8284. (Illus.). 208p. (gr. 5 up). 1989. 14.95 (ISBN 0-02-735771-6, Mcmillan Child Bk). Macmillan Child Grp.

McGowen, Tom. The Great Monkey Trial: Science Versus Fundamentalism in America. Gould, Stephen J., frwd. by. (Illus.). 128p. (gr. 9-12). 1990. PLB 12.90 (ISBN 0-531-10965-8). Watts.

Peters, David. From the Beginning: The Story of Human Evolution. LC 90-19187. (Illus.). 128p. (gr. 3 up). 1991. 13.95 (ISBN 0-688-09476-7). Morrow Jr Bks.

Richards, Larry. It Couldn't Just Happen. 191p. 1989. write for info. (ISBN 0-8499-0715-2). Word Bks.

Stein, Sara. The Evolution Book: The Story of 4000 Million Years of Life on Earth. Stein, Sara, illus. LC 84-40682. 400p. (Orig.). (gr. 5-9). 1986. pap. 12.95 (ISBN 0-89480-927-X, 927). Workman Pub.

Taylor, Kenneth N. What High School Students Should Know about Evolution. 70p. (gr. 9-12). 1983. pap. 3.95 (ISBN 0-8423-7873-1). Tyndale.

EXCAVATION

Thompson, Graham. Diggers & Loaders. LC 86-5680. (Illus.). 24p. (gr. 1-2). 1986. PLB 10.95 (ISBN 1-55532-101-1). Gareth Stevens Inc.

EXCAVATIONS (ARCHEOLOGY)

see also Mounds and Mound Builders

EXECUTIONS

see Capital Punishment

EXECUTIVE POWER–U. S.

Stein, R. Conrad. The Story of the Powers of the President. Neely, Keith, illus. LC 84-29257. 32p. (gr. 3-6). 1985. lib. bdg. 13.27 (ISBN 0-516-04684-5). Childrens.

EXERCISE

see also Gymnastics; Physical Education and Training; Physical Fitness;

also names of special kinds of exercises, e.g. Rowing, etc.

Baldwin, Dorothy. Health & Exercise. (Illus.). 32p. (gr. 3-8). 1987. PLB 15.93 (ISBN 0-86592-293-4). Rourke Corp.

Charles, Donald. Calico Cat's Exercise Book. LC 82-9640. (Illus.). (ps-3). 1982. PLB 14.60 (ISBN 0-516-03457-X). Childrens.

Duyff, Roberta L. Big Bug Book of Exercise. McKissack, Patricia & McKissack, Fredrick, eds. Bartholomew, illus. LC 87-61656. 24p. (Orig.). (gr. k-1). 1987. spiral bdg. 14.95 (ISBN 0-88335-761-5); pap. text ed. 4.95 (ISBN 0-88335-771-2). Milliken Pub Co.

Goldstein, Rebecca. The Mind-Body Problem. 304p. (gr. 5 up). 1985. pap. 4.95 (ISBN 0-440-35651-2, LE). Dell.

Isenberg, Barbara & Jaffe, Marjorie. Albert the Running Bear's Exercise Book. De Groat, Diane, illus. LC 84-7064. 64p. (Orig.). (ps-4). 1984. (Clarion); pap. 4.95 (ISBN 0-89919-318-8). HM.

—Albert the Running Bear's Exercise Book. De Groat, Diane, illus. LC 84-7064. 64p. (ps-3). 1987. 13.95 (ISBN 0-317-60201-2, Pub. by Clarion); pap. 4.95 (ISBN 0-685-18671-7). Ticknor & Fields.

Jones, Lucile. Hop, Skip, & Jump. Van Dolson, Bobbie J., ed. 32p. (gr. k up). 1981. pap. 3.95 (ISBN 0-8280-0038-7). Review & Herald.

Kamen, Betty. The Chromium Diet, Supplement & Exercise Strategy: An Easy to Follow Routine for Everyone. Rosenbaum, Michael E., intro. by. (Illus.). 216p. (Orig.). 1990. pap. 9.95 (ISBN 0-944501-03-6). Nutrition Encounter.

Liptak, Karen. Aerobics Basics. D'Amato, Janet, illus. 48p. (gr. 3-7). 1983. 9.95 (ISBN 0-13-018218-4). P-H.

Moncure, Jane B. Healthkins Exercise! Endres, Helen, illus. LC 82-14712. 32p. (ps-2). 1982. lib. bdg. 10.95 (ISBN 0-89565-241-2). Childs World.

Nardo, Don. Exercise. (Illus.). (gr. 5-12). 1992. 18.95 (ISBN 0-7910-0017-6). Chelsea Hse.

Neff, Fred. Keeping Fit Handbook for Physical Conditioning & Better Health. Reid, James, illus. LC 75-38478. 56p. (gr. 5 up). 1977. PLB 8.95 (ISBN 0-8225-1157-6). Lerner Pubns.

Reiss, Elayne & Friedman, Rita. Exercise Expert. (gr. k-1). 10.50 (ISBN 0-89796-866-2). New Dimens Educ.

Richardson, Joy. What Happens When You Run? LC 86-3707. (Illus.). 32p. (gr. 2-3). 1986. PLB 10.95 (ISBN 1-55532-110-0). Gareth Stevens Inc.

EXHIBITIONS

Marsh, Carole. World's Fair Fun Trivia Book. Marsh, Carole, illus. (Orig.). (gr. 4 up). 1982. pap. 4.95 (ISBN 0-935326-06-5). Gallopade Pub Group.

EXILES

see Refugees

EXISTENTIALISM

State of Being Staff. Some States of Being. State of Being Staff, illus. 22p. (Orig.). (gr. 7 up). 1988. pap. 2.00 (ISBN 0-929611-03-9). Plutonium Pr.

EXORCISM

see Witchcraft

EXPEDITIONS, ANTARCTIC AND ARCTIC

see Arctic Regions; Antarctic Regions

EXPEDITIONS, SCIENTIFIC

see Scientific Expeditions

EXPERIMENTS, SCIENTIFIC

see Science–Experiments

EXPLORATION, SUBMARINE

see Underwater Exploration

EXPLORATION, UNDERWATER

see Underwater Exploration

EXPLORATIONS

see America–Discovery and Exploration; Discoveries (In Geography); Explorers

EXPLORERS

see also America–Discovery and Exploration; Discoveries (In Geography); Voyages and Travels

also names of countries with the subdivision Description and Travel and Exploring Expeditions, e.g. U. S. –Description and Travel; U. S.–Exploring Expeditions, etc.; and names of individual explorers

The Age of Exploration. 64p. (gr. 4-8). 1990. 13.95 (ISBN 0-86307-997-0). Marshall Cavendish.

Alper, Ann. Forgotten Voyager: The Story of Amerigo Vespucci. (Illus.). 80p. (gr. 3-6). 1991. PLB 11.95 (ISBN 0-87614-442-3). Carolrhoda Bks.

Artman, John. Explorers. Hyndman, Kathryn, illus. 64p. (gr. 4 up). 1986. 6.95 (ISBN 0-86653-340-0, GA 796). Good Apple.

Asimov, Isaac. Christopher Columbus. LC 90-25836. (Illus.). 64p. (gr. 3-4). 1991. PLB 14.95 (ISBN 0-8368-0556-9). Gareth Stevens Inc.

—Ferdinand Magellan. LC 91-9207. (Illus.). 64p. (gr. 3-4). 1991. PLB 14.95 (ISBN 0-8368-0560-7). Gareth Stevens Inc.

Baker, Susan. Explorers of North America. LC 89-26364. (Illus.). 48p. (gr. 4-8). 1990. PLB 18.60 (ISBN 0-8114-2752-8). Steck-V.

Better Homes & Gardens Books Editors. Let's Go Exploring. (Illus.). 32p. (ps-8). 1991. 4.95 (ISBN 0-696-01933-7). Meredith Bks.

Everett, F. Explorers. (Illus.). 48p. (gr. 4 up). 1991. lib. bdg. 13.96 (ISBN 0-88110-504-X, Usborne); pap. 6.95 (ISBN 0-7460-0514-8). EDC.

Exploring the Past Series, 6 vols. (gr. 4-8). 1990. Set. 83.70 (ISBN 0-86307-993-8). Marshall Cavendish.

Ferris, Jeri. Arctic Explorer: The Story of Matthew Henson. (Illus.). 80p. (gr. 3-6). 1989. PLB 11.95 (ISBN 0-87614-370-2); pap. 5.95 (ISBN 0-87614-507-1). Carolrhoda Bks.

Fisher, Leonard E. Prince Henry the Navigator. Fisher, Leonard E., illus. LC 89-28068. 32p. (gr. 2-6). 1990. 14.95 (ISBN 0-02-735231-5, Mcmillan Child Bk). Macmillan Child Grp.

Fradin, Dennis. Explorers. LC 84-7077. (Illus.). 48p. (gr. k-4). 1984. lib. bdg. 14.60 (ISBN 0-516-01926-0); pap. 4.95 (ISBN 0-516-41926-9). Childrens.

Fritz, Jean. Where Do You Think You're Going, Christopher Columbus? Tomes, Margot, illus. 80p. (gr. 3-7). 1981. 13.95 (ISBN 0-399-20723-6, Putnam); pap. 7.95 (ISBN 0-399-20734-1, Putnam). Putnam Pub Group.

Goetzmann, William H., ed. World Explorers Ser, 33 vols. Collins, Michael, intro. by. (Illus.). 3696p. (gr. 5 up). 1990. PLB 625.35 (ISBN 0-7910-1290-5). Chelsea Hse.

Grosseck, Joyce & Atwood, Elizabeth, eds. Great Explorers. rev. ed. LC 87-81354. (Illus.). 160p. (gr. 4 up). 1988. 1-4 copies 14.95 ea. (ISBN 0-934291-22-5); 5 or more copies 11.95 (ISBN 0-317-91140-6). Gateway Pr MI.

Hargrove, Jim. Ferdinand Magellan: First Around the World. LC 89-15781. (Illus.). 128p. (gr. 3 up). 1990. PLB 25.27 (ISBN 0-516-03051-5). Childrens.

Hernando de Soto. (Illus.). 32p. (gr. 3-5). 1988. PLB 16.67 (ISBN 0-8172-2903-5). Raintree Pubs.

Holden, Raymond P. All about Famous Scientific Expeditions. (Illus.). (gr. 4-6). 1963. 2.95 (ISBN 0-394-80224-1, Random Juv). Random.

Humble, Richard. The Travels of Livingstone. LC 90-32379. (Illus.). 32p. (gr. 5-8). 1991. PLB 11.90 (ISBN 0-531-14101-2). Watts.

—The Voyages of Columbus. Hook, Richard, illus. 32p. (gr. 5-8). 1991. PLB 11.90 (ISBN 0-531-14189-6). Watts.

Italia, Bob. Robert Ballard. Walner, Rosemary, ed. (Illus.). 32p. (gr. 4). 1990. PLB 11.95 (ISBN 0-939179-95-4). Abdo & Dghtrs.

—Will Steger. Walner, Rosemary, ed. (Illus.). 32p. (gr. 4). 1990. PLB 11.95 (ISBN 0-939179-97-0). Abdo & Dghtrs.

Johnson, Spencer. The Value of Curiosity: The Story of Christopher Columbus. Pileggi, Stephen, illus. LC 77-11032. (gr. k-6). 9.95 (ISBN 0-916392-13-9, Pub. by Value Communications). Oak Tree Pubns.

Lillegard, Dee. My First Columbus Day Book. Raskin, Betty, illus. LC 87-10304. 32p. (ps-2). 1987. PLB 14.60 (ISBN 0-516-02909-6); pap. 3.95 (ISBN 0-516-42909-4). Childrens.

Lindsley, Margaret. Andrew Henry: Mine & Mountain Major. (Illus.). 370p. 1990. 19.95 (ISBN 0-936204-79-6); pap. 15.95 (ISBN 0-936204-78-8). Jelm Mtn.

Evokes the era, triumphs & tribulations of the complex & sometimes contradictory man, Andrew Henry. Spanning his lifetime, 1778-1833, as well as awesome mountains, wars & romances, this book defines the man & identifies his rightful place in the history of westward expansion. Wise in the ways of French & Spanish aristocrats & entrepreneurs, boatmen, soldiers, fur trappers, Indians & grizzlies, Henry was comfortable in a wide variety of cultures, from the sophistication of French Ste. Genevieve to the rough & tumble fur-trade forts & Indian camps along the Missouri & Yellowstone Rivers. Miner, militia major, explorer, mountain man, fur trapper, leader of men, he could guide men of diverse backgrounds from St. Louis to the Tetons & back through harsh winters, grizzlies & Blackfeet, yet his first marriage lasted only eighteen days. Associate of Moses Austin, partner of William Ashley, respected contemporary of Manuel Lisa, the Chouteaus, the Valles, Lewis & Clark, he had one Fort Henry in Idaho, two in Montana & one in North Dakota named for him. As were some of the best trout & fly-fishing waters in the world, Henry's Lake & Henry's Fork of the Snake River in Southeastern Idaho.

Publisher Provided Annotation.

Lomask, Milton. Great Lives: Exploration. LC 88-15744. (Illus.). 288p. (gr. 4-6). 1988. 22.95 (ISBN 0-684-18511-3, Scribners Young Read). Macmillan Child Grp.

Matthews, Rupert. Explorer. Stevenson, Jim, illus. LC 91-8428. 64p. (gr. 5 up). 1991. 15.00 (ISBN 0-679-81460-4); lib. bdg. 15.99 (ISBN 0-679-91460-9). Knopf.

Morrison, Dorothy N. Under a Strong Wind: The Adventures of Jessie Benton Fremont. LC 83-6356. (Illus.). 224p. (gr. 5-9). 1983. 14.95 (ISBN 0-689-31004-8, Atheneum Child Bk). Macmillan Child Grp.

Mumford, Donald & Mumford, Esther. From Africa to the Arctic: Five Explorers. Lee, Nancy, illus. 48p. (gr. 1-3). 1992. 9.95 (ISBN 0-9605670-6-2). Ananse Pr.

The exploration of the North American continent by people of African descent began with the travels of Estebanico, a

black Morrocan who sought the legendary Seven Cities of Gold in the American Southwest in the 1500s. From 1804 to 1806 York, a slave, accompanied, provisioned, & interpreted for Meriwether Lewis & his master William Clark, on the historic expedition to explore the recently purchased land west of the Mississippi River. The scout, Jim Beckwourth, discovered the western mountain pass which bears his name today. Stephen Bishop explored, & led parties to, the undiscovered passages of the Mammouth Cave system in Kentucky. From his first journey to the far north in 1891 Matthew Henson prepared himself for the discovery of the North Pole with Robert Peary in 1909. These five men rose from slavery or near-slavery to explore unknown places. The first in a series of the African Diaspora, this book will inform young readers & adult learners of these little-known discoverers.
Publisher Provided Annotation.

Richards, Dorothy F. Christopher Columbus, Who Sailed on! Nelson, John, illus. LC 78-7664. (gr. k-4). 1978. PLB 10.95 (ISBN 0-89565-032-0). Childs World.
Roth, Susan L. Marco Polo. (ps-3). 1991. 14.95 (ISBN 0-385-26495-X); PLB 15.99 (ISBN 0-385-26555-7). Doubleday.
Ryan, Peter. Explorers & Mapmakers. Molan, Chris, illus. LC 89-31824. 48p. (gr. 4-7). 1990. 14.95 (ISBN 0-525-67285-0, Lodestar Bks). Dutton Child Bks.
Sandak, Cass R. Explorers & Discovery. (Illus.). 96p. (gr. 4 up). 1983. PLB 10.40 (ISBN 0-531-04537-4). Watts.
Wilkie, Katherine. Ferdinand Magellan: Noble Captain. Coyle, P., illus. (gr. 4-6). 1963. pap. 2.44 (ISBN 0-395-01751-3, Piper). HM.
Zadra, Dan. Explorers of America: DeSoto. rev. ed. (gr. 2-4). 1988. PLB 11.50s.p. (ISBN 0-88682-185-1); 16.45 (ISBN 0-685-19791-3). Creative Ed.

EXPLORERS–FICTION

Ellis, Terry. Explorers from Willow Wood Springs. LC 85-63827. (Illus.). 180p. (Orig.). (gr. 4 up). 1989. pap. 3.75 (ISBN 0-915677-31-8). Roundtable Pub.
Lee, Rebecca L. Kori & the Island of Enchantment. LC 89-49376. 80p. (Orig.). (gr. 8 up). 1990. pap. 6.95 (ISBN 0-931832-46-2). Fithian Pr.
Moses, Amy. I Am an Explorer. Hackney, Richard, illus. LC 90-38374. 32p. (ps-2). 1990. PLB 11.93 (ISBN 0-516-02059-5); pap. 2.95 (ISBN 0-516-42059-3). Childrens.
Peterson, John. The Littles Go Exploring. (gr. 4-6). 1978. pap. 2.25 (ISBN 0-590-32005-X). Scholastic Inc.

EXPLORING EXPEDITIONS

see names of countries with the subdivision Exploring Expeditions (e.g. U. S.–Exploring Expeditions; etc.) and names of Expeditions, e.g. Lewis and Clark Expedition; etc.

EXPLOSIVES

Fireworks. (Illus.). 12p. (gr. 3-10). 1985. pap. 2.50 (ISBN 0-88138-016-4). Green Tiger Pr.

EXTINCT ANIMALS

see also names of extinct animals, e.g. Mastodon, etc.

Aliki. Wild & Woolly Mammoths. Aliki, illus. LC 76-18082. 40p. (gr. k-3). 1977. PLB 13.89 (ISBN 0-690-01276-4, Crowell Jr Bks). HarpC Child Bks.
Ames, Lee J. Draw Fifty Dinosaurs & Other Prehistoric Animals. Ames, Lee J., illus. LC 76-7285. 64p. (gr. 1 up). 1977. pap. 12.95 (ISBN 0-385-11134-7). Doubleday.
Benton, Michael. Prehistoric Animals: An A-Z Guide. 1989. 7.99 (ISBN 0-517-69190-6). Outlet Bk Co.
Burton, John. Close to Extinction. FS-Aladdin Staff, ed. Hayward, Ron, illus. 32p. (gr. 4-9). 1988. PLB 11.90 (ISBN 0-531-17125-6, Gloucester Pr). Watts.
Crofford, Emily. Great Auk. LC 89-31576. (Illus.). 48p. (gr. 4-5). 1989. 10.95 (ISBN 0-89686-459-6, Crestwood Hse). Macmillan Child Grp.
Dewey, Jennifer & Lyon, Lucy. Prehistoric Swimmers & Flyers of the Southwest. (Illus.). 32p. (gr. 4 up). 1990. pap. text ed. 3.95 (ISBN 0-89013-195-3). Museum NM Pr.
Dixon, Dougal. The Last of the Dinosaurs. Burton, Jane, photos by. LC 89-11335. (Illus.). 32p. (gr. 1-2). 1989. PLB 10.95 (ISBN 0-8368-0153-9). Gareth Stevens Inc.
—The Very First Dinosaurs. Burton, Jane, photos by. LC 89-11336. (Illus.). 32p. (gr. 1-2). 1989. PLB 10.95 (ISBN 0-8368-0151-2). Gareth Stevens Inc.
—When Dinosaurs Ruled the Earth. Burton, Jane, photos by. LC 89-11337. (Illus.). 32p. (gr. 1-2). 1989. PLB 10.95 (ISBN 0-8368-0152-0). Gareth Stevens Inc.
Duggleby, John. Sabertooth Cat. LC 89-31574. (Illus.). 48p. (gr. 4-5). 1989. 10.95 (ISBN 0-89686-462-6, Crestwood Hse). Macmillan Child Grp.
Earthbooks, Inc. Staff. The National Wildlife Federation's Book of Dinosaurs & Other Pre-Historic Animals. Aaestas, Ken, illus. 64p. (Orig.). (gr. 4). 1991. pap. 5.95 (ISBN 1-877731-16-1). Earthbooks Inc.
Eastman, David. I Can Read About Prehistoric Animals. Nodel, Norman, illus. LC 76-54492. (gr. 2-4). 1977. pap. 1.95 (ISBN 0-89375-039-5). Troll Assocs.
Green, Carl & Sanford, Bill. Wooly Mammoth. LC 89-31575. (Illus.). 48p. (gr. 4-5). 1989. 10.95 (ISBN 0-89686-456-1, Crestwood Hse). Macmillan Child Grp.
Horn, Gabriel. Steller's Sea Cow. LC 89-7702. (Illus.). 48p. (gr. k-4). 1990. 10.95 (ISBN 0-89686-460-X, Crestwood Hse). Macmillan Child Grp.
Hornblow, Leonora & Hornblow, Arthur. Prehistoric Monsters Did the Strangest Things. abr. ed. Barlowe, Sy, illus. LC 88-30212. 64p. (gr. 2-4). 1990. lib. bdg. 6.99 (ISBN 0-394-94307-4); pap. 3.95 (ISBN 0-394-84307-X). Random.
Miller, Susanne S. Prehistoric Mammals. Santoro, Christopher, illus. (ps-5). 1984. pap. 7.95 (ISBN 0-671-47976-8, Little Simon). S&S Trade.
Moody, Richard. One Hundred Prehistoric Animals from A to Z. Chasty, Paula, illus. Wilson, Ron, concept by. (Illus.). 64p. (gr. 2-5). 1988. 9.95 (ISBN 0-448-19071-0, G&D). Putnam Pub Group.
Patent, Dorothy H. The Challenge of Extinction. LC 90-3288. (Illus.). 64p. (gr. 6 up). 1991. PLB 15.95 (ISBN 0-89490-268-7). Enslow Pubs.
Pinkus, Sue. Let's All Draw Dinosaurs, Pterodactyls & Other Prehistoric Creatures. 1991. pap. 16.95 (ISBN 0-8230-2706-6). Watson-Guptill.
Prehistoric Animals. 32p. (Orig.). (gr. 1-3). 1988. pap. 2.95 (ISBN 0-8431-4297-9). Price Stern.
Prehistoric Animals & Fossils. (Illus.). (gr. 4 up). 3.50 (ISBN 0-7214-0359-X). Ladybird Bks.
Raintree Publishers Inc. Staff. Prehistoric Animals. (Illus.). 64p. (Orig.). (gr. 5-9). 1988. PLB 19.99 (ISBN 0-8172-3082-3); pap. text ed. 11.93 (ISBN 0-8172-3088-2). Raintree Pubs.
Selsam, Millicent E. Strange Creatures That Lived Long Ago. Dewey, Jennifer, illus. LC 86-29732. 32p. (gr. 4-6). 1987. 13.95 (ISBN 0-590-40707-4, Scholastic Hardcover). Scholastic Inc.
Steele, Philip. Extinct Birds: And Those in Danger of Extinction. (Illus.). 32p. (gr. 5-8). 1991. PLB 11.40 (ISBN 0-531-11027-3). Watts.
—Extinct Reptiles: And Those in Danger of Extinction. (Illus.). 32p. (gr. 5-8). 1991. PLB 11.40 (ISBN 0-531-11030-3). Watts.
Zallinger, Peter. Prehistoric Animals. Zallinger, Peter, illus. 32p. (ps-3). 1981. pap. 2.25 (ISBN 0-394-83737-1). Random.

EXTINCT CITIES

see Cities and Towns, Ruined, Extinct, etc.

EXTACURRICULAR ACTIVITIES

see Student Activities

EXTRASENSORY PERCEPTION

Arvey, Michael. ESP: Opposing Viewpoints. LC 88-24316. (Illus.). 112p. (gr. 3-8). 1988. PLB 13.95 (ISBN 0-89908-057-X). Greenhaven.
Petschek, Joyce. Silver Dreams: A Myth of the Sixth Sense. LC 90-82143. (Illus.). 208p. (gr. 8-12). 1990. 22.95 (ISBN 0-89087-619-3); pap. 19.95 (ISBN 0-89087-620-7). Celestial Arts.
Psychics & ESP. 48p. (gr. 4-5). 1989. PLB 10.95 (ISBN 0-685-26399-1). Capstone Pr.

EXTRASENSORY PERCEPTION–FICTION

Christopher, Matt. The Dog That Stole Football Plays. Ogden, Bill, illus. 48p. (gr. 3-5). 1980. 13.95 (ISBN 0-316-13978-5). Little.
DeClements, Barthe & Greimes, Christopher. Double Trouble. LC 86-28984. (gr. 7 up). 1987. pap. 12.95 (ISBN 0-670-81567-5). Viking Child Bks.
Duncan, Lois. The Third Eye. (gr. 7up). 1984. 14.95 (ISBN 0-316-19553-7). Little.
—The Third Eye. 224p. (gr. 6-12). 1991. pap. 3.50 (ISBN 0-440-98720-2, LFL). Dell.
Hamilton, Virginia. The Gathering. LC 80-12512. 192p. (gr. 7 up). 1980. 11.75 (ISBN 0-688-80269-9); PLB 11.88 (ISBN 0-688-84269-0). Greenwillow.
Kibbe, Pat. The Hocus-Pocus Dilemma. Jones, Dan, illus. LC 78-9906. (gr. 4-7). 1979. Knopf.
McGinnis, Lila. Auras & Other Rainbow Secrets. LC 84-4486. (gr. 3-7). 1984. 10.95 (ISBN 0-8038-0551-9). Hastings.
Peck, Richard. Blossom Culp & the Sleep of Death. LC 85-16188. 224p. (gr. 4-6). 1986. pap. 14.95 (ISBN 0-385-29433-6). Delacorte.
Sleator, William. Into the Dream. Sanderson, Ruth, illus. LC 78-11825. (gr. 4-7). 1979. 13.95 (ISBN 0-525-32583-2, DCB). Dutton Child Bks.
Spicer, Dorothy. Humming Top. LC 68-31176. (gr. 7-11). 1968. 18.95 (ISBN 0-87599-147-5). S G Phillips.
Towne, Mary. Paul's Game. LC 82-72750. 192p. (gr. 7 up). 1983. 13.95 (ISBN 0-385-29248-1). Delacorte.
Vinge, Joan D. Psion. LC 82-70323. 256p. (gr. 7 up). 1982. pap. 12.95 (ISBN 0-385-28780-1). Delacorte.
Wright, Betty R. The Secret Window. LC 82-80816. 160p. (gr. 3-7). 1982. 13.95 (ISBN 0-8234-0464-1). Holiday.

EXTRATERRESTRIAL LIFE

see Life on Other Planets

EYE

see also Optometry; Vision

Amstutz, Beverly. The Fly Has Lots of Eyes. (Illus.). 34p. (gr. k-9). 1981. pap. 2.50x (ISBN 0-937836-04-4). Precious Res.
Bailey, Jill. Eyes. LC 83-13883. (Illus.). 14p. (gr. k-1). 1984. 3.95 (ISBN 0-399-21026-1, Putnam). Putnam Pub Group.
Jedrosz, Aleksander. Eyes. Farmer, Andrew & Green, Robina, illus. LC 90-42177. 32p. (gr. 4-6). 1991. lib. bdg. 11.89 (ISBN 0-8167-2094-0); pap. text ed. 3.95 (ISBN 0-8167-2095-9). Troll Assocs.
Le Sieg, Theodore. Eye Book. McKie, Roy, illus. (ps-1). 1968. 6.95 (ISBN 0-394-81094-5, BE2, Random Juv); lib. bdg. 7.99 (ISBN 0-394-91094-X, BE2). Random.
Osborne, Sonya. The Houses on Socket Street. 21p. (gr. 3-5). 1988. 4.95 (ISBN 0-533-07384-7). Vantage.
Parker, Steve. Eye & Seeing. 1989. PLB 12.90 (ISBN 0-531-10654-3). Watts.
Rahn, Joan E. Eyes & Seeing. Rahn, Joan E., illus. LC 80-23988. 128p. (gr. 5-9). 1981. 10.95 (ISBN 0-689-30828-0, Atheneum Childrens Bks). Macmillan Child Grp.
Smith, Kathie B. & Crenson, Victoria. Seeing. Storms, Robert S., illus. LC 87-5862. 24p. (gr. k-3). 1987. PLB 9.59 (ISBN 0-8167-1008-2); pap. text ed. 1.95 (ISBN 0-8167-1009-0). Troll Assocs.
Thomson, Ruth. Eyes. FS Staff, ed. Galletly, Mike, illus. 32p. (gr. 1-3). 1988. PLB 10.40 (ISBN 0-531-10549-0). Watts.
Ward, Brian. The Eye & Sight. LC 80-54827. (Illus.). 48p. (gr. 4 up). 1981. lib. bdg. 12.40 (ISBN 0-531-04290-1). Watts.
Wright, Rachel. Eyes, Ears & Noses. (ps-3). 1990. PLB 10.40 (ISBN 0-531-14001-6). Watts.

EYEGLASSES

see also Lenses

Stuart, Sandra L. Why Do I Have to Wear Glasses? Robins, Arthur, illus. 48p. Date not set. 12.00 (ISBN 0-8184-0477-9). Carol Pub Group.
Wolff, Angelika. Mom, I Need Glasses. Hill, Dorothy, illus. Saltzman, S. L., intro. by. LC 74-112648. (Illus.). (gr. k-3). 1971. PLB 10.95 (ISBN 0-87460-139-8). Lion Bks.

EYEGLASSES–FICTION

Brown, Marc. Arthur's Eyes. Brown, Marc, illus. LC 79-11734. (ps-3). 1979. lib. bdg. 14.95 (ISBN 0-316-11063-9, Joy St Bks). Little.
Cousins, Lucy. What Can Rabbit See? LC 90-21213. (Illus.). 12p. (ps). 1991. 12.95 (ISBN 0-688-10454-1, Tambourine Bks). Morrow.
Giff, Patricia R. Watch out, Ronald Morgan. Natti, Susanna, illus. LC 84-19623. 24p. (gr. k-3). 1985. pap. 10.95 (ISBN 0-670-80433-9). Viking Child Bks.
Leggett, Linda R. & Andrews, Linda G. The Rose-Colored Glasses: Melanie Adjusts to Poor Vision. Hartman, Laura, illus. LC 79-12501. 32p. (gr. 3 up). 1979. 16.95 (ISBN 0-87705-408-8). Human Sci Pr.
Little, Jean. From Anna. Sandin, Joan, illus. LC 72-76505. 208p. (gr. 4-6). 1972. PLB 14.89 (ISBN 0-06-023912-3). HarpC Child Bks.
Pape, D. L. Liz Dearly's Silly Glasses. LC 68-56824. (Illus.). 48p. (gr. 2-5). 1968. PLB 10.95 (ISBN 0-87783-023-1). Oddo.
Raskin, Ellen. Spectacles. Raskin, Ellen, illus. LC 68-12234. (gr. k-4). 1968. PLB 10.95 (ISBN 0-689-20352-7, Atheneum Childrens Bk). Macmillan Child Grp.
Turin, Adela & Bosnia, Nella. The Real Story of the Bonobos Who Wore Spectacles. (Illus.). 32p. (gr. 3-6). 1980. 6.95 (ISBN 0-904613-18-6). Writers & Readers.
Wolff, Angelika. Mom, I Need Glasses. Hill, Dorothy, illus. Saltzman, S. L., intro. by. LC 74-112648. (Illus.). (gr. k-3). 1971. PLB 10.95 (ISBN 0-87460-139-8). Lion Bks.
Yuki, Mi. Glass for a Hero. Omi, H. & Tsutsumoto, Tracy, illus. 32p. 1991. pap. 3.95 (ISBN 0-89346-333-7). Heian Intl.
—Now I Wear Glasses. Omi, H. & Tsutsumoto, Tracy, illus. 32p. (Orig.). 1991. pap. 3.95 (ISBN 0-89346-334-5). Heian Intl.

F

FABLES

see also Animals–Fiction; Folklore; Parables

Aesop. The Aesop for Children. large type ed. Clauss, J., intro. by. Winter, Nilo, illus. (gr. 1-12). 1976. lib. bdg. 20.95x (ISBN 0-88411-991-2, Pub. by Aeonian Pr). Amereon Ltd.
—Aesop for Children. Winter, Milo, illus. LC 86-73175. 96p. (gr. 2 up). 1984. Repr. of 1919 ed. 12.95 (ISBN 1-56288-039-X). Checkerboard Pr.
—Aesop's Fables. Winder, Blanche, ed. LC 33-31662. (Illus.). (gr. 4 up). pap. 1.95 (ISBN 0-8049-0081-7, CL-81). Airmont.
—Aesop's Fables. Kredel, Fritz, illus. LC 33-31662. (gr. 4-6). 1947-63. Illustrated Junior Library. pap. 7.95 (IJL) (ISBN 0-448-11003-2, G&D); deluxe ed. 11.95 (ISBN 0-448-06003-5); Companion Library. companion lib. o.p. 2.95 (ISBN 0-448-05453-1); pap. ed (IJL) o.p. 4.95 (ISBN 0-686-76870-1). Putnam Pub Group.
—Aesop's Fables. McGovern, Ann, ed. LC 33-31662. (Illus., Orig.). (gr. 4-9). pap. 2.25 (ISBN 0-590-40569-1). Scholastic Inc.
—Aesop's Fables. Riccio, Frank, illus. 196p. 1988. pap. 7.95 (ISBN 0-8092-4485-3, Calico Bks). Contemp Bks.

—Aesop's Fables. Paxton, Tom, retold by. Rayevsky, Robert, illus. LC 88-1652. 40p. (ps-2). 1988. 13.95 (ISBN 0-688-07360-3); PLB 13.88 (ISBN 0-688-07361-1, Morrow Jr Bks). Morrow Jr Bks.
—Aesop's Fables. 1987. 5.98 (ISBN 0-671-08758-4). S&S Trade.
—Aesop's Fables. LC 89-62860. 96p. (ps up). 1990. 4.95 (ISBN 0-89471-795-2). Running Pr.
—Aesop's Fables, 2 bks. (Illus.). (gr. 3-7). 3.50 (ISBN 0-317-03013-2). Bk. 1 (ISBN 0-7214-0358-1). Bk. 2 (ISBN 0-7214-0385-9). Ladybird Bks.
—The Donkey & His Dog. Otto, Svend, illus. (ps-3). 9.95 (ISBN 0-317-61895-4). Viking Penguin.
—The Tortoise & the Hare. Alchemy II, Inc. Staff, illus. 26p. 1988. incl. cassette 9.95 (ISBN 1-55578-902-1). Worlds Wonder.
Aesop & Holder, Heidi. Aesop's Fables. LC 33-31662. (Illus.). 1981. pap. 13.95 (ISBN 0-670-10643-7). Viking Child Bks.
Aesop's Fables. Date not set. 9.98 (ISBN 0-517-67901-9). Outlet Bk Co.
Alley, R. W., retold by. & illus. Seven Fables from Aesop. (gr. k-3). 1986. 12.95 (ISBN 0-396-08820-1, Putnam). Putnam Pub Group.
Andersen, Hans Christian. Emperor's New Clothes. Ford, Pamela B., illus. LC 78-18063. 32p. (gr. k-4). 1979. PLB 9.79 (ISBN 0-89375-132-4); pap. 1.95 (ISBN 0-89375-110-3). Troll Assocs.
Anno, Mitsumasa, retold by. & illus. Anno's Aesop: A Book of Fables by Aesop & Mr. Fox. LC 88-60087. 64p. (ps-2). 1989. 18.95 (ISBN 0-531-05774-7); PLB 18.99 (ISBN 0-531-08374-8). Orchard Bks Watts.
Apy, Deborah. Beauty & the Beast. Hague, Michael, illus. LC 83-4395. 72p. (gr. 4-6). 1983. 12.95 (ISBN 0-8050-1448-9). H Holt & Co.
Bader, Barbara & Geisert, Arthur. Aesop & Company: With Scenes from His Legendary Life. (Illus.). 64p. 1990. 15.95 (ISBN 0-395-50597-6). HM.
Barnett, Carol. Boy Who Cried Wolf. (ps-3). 1990. 7.95 (ISBN 0-8442-9419-5). Natl Textbk.
—Lion & the Mouse. (ps-3). 1990. 7.95 (ISBN 0-8442-9420-9). Natl Textbk.
—Milkmaid & Her Pail. (ps-3). 1990. 7.95 (ISBN 0-8442-9421-7). Natl Textbk.
Bird, E. J. Ten Tall Tales. LC 84-12086. (Illus.). 56p. (gr. 2-6). 1984. PLB 9.95 (ISBN 0-87614-267-6). Carolrhoda Bks.
Biro, Val. Fables from Aesop One to Six, 6 bks. Biro, M. L., notes by. (Illus.). (gr. k-2). 1986. Set. pap. text ed. 18.80 incl. teacher's notes (ISBN 1-55624-002-3). Wright Group.
—Fables from Aesop Seven to Twelve, 6 bks. Biro, M. L., illus. (Orig.). (gr. k-2). 1986. Set. pap. text ed. 18.80 incl. teacher's notes (ISBN 1-55624-003-1). Wright Group.
Biro, Val, retold by. & illus. Fables from Aesop, Nos. 13-18. 72p. (gr. k-2). Set. pap. text ed. 16.80 incl. tchr's. notes (ISBN 1-55624-148-8, WG1488). Wright Group.
Bolliger, Max. Tales of a Late Afternoon. 1989. 13.95 (ISBN 0-525-44546-3, DCB). Dutton Child Bks.
Calder, Alexander. Fables of Aesop According to Sir Roger L'Estrange. (Illus.). 124p. (gr. k-6). pap. 3.95 (ISBN 0-486-21780-9). Dover.
Cauley, Lorinda B. The Town Mouse & the Country Mouse. Cauley, Lorinda B., illus. LC 84-11532. 32p. (ps-3). 1984. 11.95 (ISBN 0-399-21123-3, Putnam); pap. 5.95 (ISBN 0-399-21126-8). Putnam Pub Group.
Clark, Margaret G. Best of Aesop's Fables. (ps-4). 1990. 16.95 (ISBN 0-316-14499-1, Joy St Bks). Little.
Clauss, J., ed. Timeless Children's Tales from Around the World. (Illus.). (gr. 5-6). 1976. lib. bdg. 18.95x (ISBN 0-88411-992-0, Pub. by Aeonian Pr). Amereon Ltd.
Collodi. Pinocchio. (gr. 7-12). pap. 5.95 (ISBN 0-88436-050-4, 55254). EMC.
Constantopoulos, E. Aesop's Fables. (Illus.). 160p. (gr. 2-3). 3.20 (ISBN 0-686-79630-6); wkbk. 2.50 (ISBN 0-686-79631-4). Divry.
Deibert, Alvin N. B. J. & the Language of the Woodland. Joy, Carol, illus. LC 82-24422. 48p. (Orig.). (gr. 2-6). 1983. pap. 7.50 (ISBN 0-87743-701-7, 353-019, Pub. by Bellwood Pr). Baha'i.
Desnos, Robert. Chantefables. Annen, Sharon, tr. from FRE. Annen, Charles, illus. LC 84-61257. 60p. (gr. 1-6). 1988. 17.95 (ISBN 0-9613938-0-7). Penstemon Pr.
Fables de la Fontaine. (FRE.). (gr. 3-8). 8.95 (ISBN 0-685-28444-1). French & Eur.
Fahy, Mary. The Tree That Survived the Winter. Antonucci, Emil, illus. 64p. (gr. 8-12). 1989. pap. 6.95 (ISBN 0-8091-0432-6). Paulist Pr.
Farnagle, A. E. & Smith, W. Hovey. Farnagle's Fables for Children & Adults. Crawford, Kimberly Ann, illus. 64p. (Orig.). (gr. 1-5). 1984. pap. 4.25 (ISBN 0-916565-04-1). Whitehall Pr.
Fisher, Lucretia. Two Monsters: A Fable. Jardine, Thomas, illus. LC 76-21684. 48p. (ps up). 1976. pap. 3.95 (ISBN 0-916144-08-9). Stemmer Hse.
Fujikawa, Gyo, illus. Fairy Tales & Fables. (gr. k-3). 1970. 9.95 (ISBN 0-448-02814-X, G&D). Putnam Pub Group.
Galdone, Paul. Monkey & The Crocodile. Galdone, Paul, illus. LC 78-79939. 32p. (ps-3). 1979. 13.95 (ISBN 0-395-28806-1, Clarion). HM.
—Three Aesop Fox Fables. Galdone, Paul, illus. LC 79-133061. 32p. (ps-2). 1979. 13.95 (ISBN 0-395-28810-X, Clarion). HM.

Garside, Alice H. The Garside Readers. Meeks, Catherine F., illus. Set. pap. 6.25 (ISBN 1-882063-18-X). Cottage Pr MA.
Classic Fables Adapted From Aesop In Phonetically Controlled Natural Language. Appealing, subtle & humorous for all ages. Context written & designed by a well-known diagnostic teacher of dyslexic children & their teachers. Helpful for early readers to make the transition from primary phonic readers to children's literature. Intriguing cover illustrations draw the reader into each story. Each page is approachable--large type & not too many words. The left-hand pages are blank with an attractive border to encourage the student to illustrate what he or she has read. This unique feature encourages creativity & allows a true test of comprehension. A book to read, to hold & to take home with pride. As one student said, "I did my own pictures, & they're nice." Students who have learned the principle of applying the silent "e" will be able to read the Garside Readers. Set One: The Man, The Fox & The Skunk (ISBN 1-882063-07-4); The Fox & The Thrush (ISBN 1-882063-09-0); The Dog & The Wolf (ISBN 1-882063-08-2). Set Two (more difficult): The Ant & The Duck (ISBN 1-882063-07-4); The Dog & The Bone (ISBN 1-882063-11-2; The Fox & The Stork (ISBN 1-882063-10-4). Accompanied by teaching suggestions prepared by Jane Swett, children's literature consultant. Available in sets of three ($6.25) or individual readers ($2.10).
Publisher Provided Annotation.

Grimm, Jacob & Grimm, Wilhelm K. Little Red Cap. Crawford, Elizabeth D., tr. from GER. Zwerger, Lisbeth, illus. LC 82-14211. 24p. (ps-3). 1983. 11.95 (ISBN 0-688-01715-0); PLB 11.88 (ISBN 0-688-01716-9). Morrow.
Gruenbaum, Hannah. A King & His Nose. Forst, Sigmund, illus. (ps-1). 1.50 (ISBN 0-685-86209-7). Feldheim.
—The Mice, the Fox, & the Cheese. Forst, Sigmund, illus. (ps-2). 1.50 (ISBN 0-685-86210-0). Feldheim.
—The Unhappy King. Forst, Sigmund, illus. (ps-3). 1.50 (ISBN 0-685-86208-9). Feldheim.
Guynn, Denise, ed. The Crow & the Pitcher. McKissack, Vernon, illus. 16p. (ps). 1980. pap. 29.95 6 bks. & 1 cass. (ISBN 0-89290-077-6, BC14-5); pap. 10.95 1 bk. & 1 cass. (ISBN 0-685-04637-0, BC14-5). Soc for Visual.
Guynn, Denise W., ed. The Boy Who Cried Wolf. McKissack, Vernon, illus. 16p. (ps). 1980. pap. 29.95 6 bks. & 1 cass. (ISBN 0-89290-076-8, BC14-4); pap. 10.95 1 bk. & 1 cass. (ISBN 0-685-04632-X). Soc for Visual.
—The Country Mouse & the Town Mouse. Flynn, James, illus. 16p. (ps). 1980. pap. 29.95 6 bks. & 1 cass. (ISBN 0-89290-074-1, BC14-2); pap. 10.95 1 bk. & 1 cass. (ISBN 0-685-04636-2, BC14-2). Soc for Visual.
—The Fox & the Crow. Ahern, Frank, illus. LC 74-736152. 16p. (gr. 1-3). 1980. pap. 29.95 6 bks. & 1 cass. (ISBN 0-89290-073-3, BC14-1); pap. 10.95 1 bk. & 1 cass. (ISBN 0-685-04642-7). Soc for Visual.
—The Fox & the Grapes. Corey, Barbara, illus. 16p. (gr. 1-3). 1980. pap. 29.95 6 bks. & 1 cass. (ISBN 0-89290-075-X, BC14-3); pap. 10.95 1 bk. & 1 cass. (ISBN 0-685-04643-5, BC14-3). Soc for Visual.
Hare & the Tortoise. (Illus.). 24p. (ps-k). 1989. 1.29 (ISBN 0-02-898237-1). Checkerboard Pr.
Hegeman, Kathryn T., ed. Aesop's Fables, 4 vols. (gr. 1-3). 1984. Set. 16.00 (ISBN 0-685-10082-0); Vol. I. 5.00 (ISBN 0-89824-051-4); Vol. II. 5.00 (ISBN 0-89824-052-2); Vol. III. 5.00 (ISBN 0-89824-053-0); Vol. IV. 5.00 (ISBN 0-89824-054-9). Trillium Pr.
Jacobs, Joseph, ed. The Fables of Aesop. LC 66-29408. (Illus.). (gr. k up). 1987. pap. 8.95 (ISBN 0-8052-0138-6). Schocken.
Kavanaugh, James. A Village Called Harmony - A Fable. 2nd ed. Biamonte, Daniel, illus. 70p. 1990. pap. 7.95 (ISBN 1-878995-06-5). S J Nash Pub.
Krill, Richard M. Forty Fabulous Fables of Aesop. Grant, Peggy, illus. 90p. (gr. 3-6). 1982. 7.95 (ISBN 0-942624-00-9). Promethean Arts.
La Fontaine. The Hare & the Tortoise. Wildsmith, Brian, illus. 32p. 1987. 12.95 (ISBN 0-19-279625-9); pap. 5.95 (ISBN 0-19-272126-7). Oxford U Pr.
La Fontaine, Jean de. A Hundred Fables of La Fontaine. Billinghurst, P. J., illus. 208p. (gr. 2-6). 2.98 (ISBN 0-517-40206-8). Outlet Bk Co.
Lanhei Kim Park. The Heavenly Pomegranate. 76p. (gr. 5-7). 1973. pap. text ed. 3.00 (ISBN 0-686-05501-2). Simpson Pub.
Leonard, Robert J. Stupid Stories: Nonstop Nonsense for Children of All Ages. Green, Herb, illus. 108p. (Orig.). (gr. 5-10). 1989. pap. 5.95 (ISBN 0-930753-05-4, Pub. by Spectacle Ln Pr). Spect Ln Pr.
Levine, David, selected by. The Fables of Aesop. Gregory, Patrick & Gregory, Justina, trs. Levine, David, illus. LC 84-12894. 108p. (gr. 8). 1984. 13.95 (ISBN 0-87645-074-5, Pub. by Gambit); pap. 8.95 (ISBN 0-87645-116-4). Harvard Common Pr.
Lionni, Leo. Frederick's Fables: A Leo Lionni Treasury of Favorite Stories. Lionni, Leo, illus. Bettelheim, Bruno, intro. by. LC 85-5186. (Illus.). 144p. (ps-3). 1985. 19.95 (ISBN 0-394-87710-1, Pant Bks Young); ltd. ed. 50.00 (ISBN 0-394-87812-4); lib. bdg. 19.99 (ISBN 0-394-97710-6). Pantheon.
Lobel, Arnold. Fables. LC 79-2004. (Illus.). 48p. (gr. 1-4). 1983. pap. 4.95 (ISBN 0-06-443046-4, Trophy). HarpC Child Bks.
—Fabulas. (SPA.). (gr. 1-6). 14.95 (ISBN 84-204-4552-5). Santillana.
MacDonald, George. The Light Princess. rev. ed. Sendak, Maurice, illus. LC 69-14981. 120p. (gr. 1 up). 1969. 10.95 (ISBN 0-374-34455-8); pap. 3.45 (ISBN 0-374-44458-7). FS&G.
Macdonald, Suse. Once Upon Another. LC 89-23478. (Illus.). 32p. (gr. k up). 1990. 12.95 (ISBN 0-8037-0785-1); PLB 12.89 (ISBN 0-8037-0787-8). Dial Bks Young.
McFarland, John. The Exploding Frog: & Other Fables from Aesop. Marshall, James, illus. (gr. 3 up). 1981. pap. 8.70i (ISBN 0-685-03085-7, Pub. by Atlantic Pr) (ISBN 0-316-55577-0). Little.
McGovern, Ann, retold by. Aesop's Fables. 80p. (gr. 4-7). 1990. pap. 2.75 (ISBN 0-590-43880-8). Scholastic Inc.
Magorian, James. The Bonkly Dribblefink Fables. LC 87-70706. 16p. (gr. 1-4). 1987. pap. 3.00 (ISBN 0-930674-24-3). Black Oak.
Marshall, Doris. Work & Play. 1988. 6.95 (ISBN 0-533-07509-2). Vantage.
Martell, Ralph. Aesop's Fables in Song. Martell, Ralph, illus. 21p. (gr. k-5). 1987. bk. & cassette 9.95 (ISBN 0-941977-00-5, RTB-1). Ralmar Enter.
Miller, Edna. Mousekin's Fables. Miller, Edna, illus. 28p. (ps-3). 1982. 11.95 (ISBN 0-13-604165-5). P-H.
Newman, Winifred B. The Spotlessly Leopard. Newman, Winifred B., illus. LC 82-24423. 48p. (Orig.). (gr. 2-6). 1983. pap. 6.95 (ISBN 0-87743-700-9, Pub. by Bellwood Pr). Baha'i.
Nister, Ernest. Golden Tales from Long Ago, 3 vols. Nister, Ernest, illus. LC 80-7614. (24p. ea.). 1980. Set. 6.95 (ISBN 0-440-03015-3). Delacorte.
Oana, Katherine. Kippy Koala. Cooper, William, ed. Butrick, Lyn M., illus. LC 85-51823. 16p. (Orig.). (ps up). 1985. pap. text ed. 3.72x (ISBN 0-914127-21-7). Univ Class.
Parry, Marian, illus. City Mouse - Country Mouse & Two More Mouse Tales from Aesop. (gr. 2-3). 1971. pap. 2.25 (ISBN 0-590-40260-9). Scholastic Inc.
Paxton, Tom. Belling the Cat: And Other Aesop's Fables. Rayevsky, Robert, illus. LC 89-39851. 40p. (ps up). 1990. 13.95 (ISBN 0-688-08158-4); PLB 13.88 (ISBN 0-688-08159-2, Morrow Jr Bks). Morrow Jr Bks.
Plante, Patricia & Bergman, David. The Turtle & the Two Ducks: Animal Fables Retold from La Fontaine. Rockwell, Anne, illus. LC 81-47409. 32p. (ps-2). 1981. (Crowell Jr Bks); PLB 12.89 (ISBN 0-690-04147-0). HarpC Child Bks.
Pride, Mary. Too Many Chickens: Old Wise Tales. 64p. (ps-3). 1990. 8.95 (ISBN 1-56121-010-2). Wolgemuth & Hyatt.
Rackham, Arthur, illus. Aesop's Fables. (gr. 2-9). 5.98 (ISBN 0-517-17198-8). Outlet Bk Co.
Le Rat des Villes et le Rat des Champs. (FRE., Illus.). (gr. 1). 3.50 (ISBN 0-7214-1275-0). Ladybird Bks.
Sanchez, Sonia. Adventures of Small Head, Square Head & Fat Head. new ed. Taiwo, illus. 32p. (gr. 2-6). 1973. 5.95 (ISBN 0-89388-094-9). Okpaku Communications.
Saunders, Susan. The Golden Goose. Saunders, Susan, retold by. (Illus.). (gr. k-3). 1988. pap. 12.95 (ISBN 0-590-41544-1). Scholastic Inc.
Shane, Harold G. Aladdin & the Wonderful Lamp. Clark, William, ed. Winkler, Albert, illus. LC 68-3548. 16p. (gr. 4-8). 1980. pap. 29.95 6 bks. & 1 cass. (ISBN 0-89290-080-6, BC15-3); pap. 10.95 1 bk. & 1 cass. (ISBN 0-685-04624-9, BC15-3). Soc for Visual.
Solomon, L. Ursa. The Rotten Chicken: A Modern Fable. rev., 2nd ed. Cummings, B. Martin, illus. Lewis, Benjamin G., frwd. by. (Illus.). 34p. 1989. Repr. of 1984 ed. wire 7.95 (ISBN 0-9615756-3-8). Henchanted Bks.
Steffens, J. & Carr, J. Myths & Fables. (gr. 7-12). 1984. 9.95 (ISBN 0-88160-113-6, LW 1008). Learning Wks.
Stevens, Janet. The Tortoise & the Hare: An Aesop Fable. Steven, Janet, illus. LC 83-18668. 32p. (ps-3). 1984. reinforced bdg. 14.95 (ISBN 0-8234-0510-9); pap. 5.95 (ISBN 0-8234-0564-8). Holiday.

Tell, Paul. Fun with Aesop: Collector's Edition, Vol. I. Ross, Connie, illus. LC 90-70600. 32p. (gr. 2-6). 1990. pap. 4.95 (ISBN 1-878893-00-9, Telcraft). Tell Pubns OH.
—Fun with Aesop: Collector's Edition, Vol. II. Ross, Connie, illus. LC 90-70600. 32p. (gr. 2-6). 1990. pap. 4.95 (ISBN 1-878893-01-7, Telcraft). Tell Pubns OH.
—Fun with Aesop: Collector's Edition, Vol. III. Ross, Connie, illus. LC 90-70600. 32p. (gr. 2-6). 1990. pap. 4.95 (ISBN 1-878893-02-5, Telcraft). Tell Pubns OH.
—Fun with Aesop: Colletor's Edition, 3 vols. Ross, Connie, illus. LC 90-70600. (gr. 2-6). 1990. Set, 32p. ea. pap. 13.95 (ISBN 1-878893-03-3, Telcraft). Tell Pubns OH.

—Fun with Aesop Reader. Ross, Connie, illus. LC 91-90956. 96p. (gr. 2-6). 1991. 9.95 (ISBN 1-878893-05-X); lib. bdg. 14.95 (ISBN 1-878893-10-6); pap. 5.95 (ISBN 1-878893-04-1). Tell Pubns OH. One year in teacher & parent testing, a collection of Aesop Fables is now available in a unique form, a special contribution to children's literature. "A smash hit with my five year old daughter," writes a major literary agent. "Just excellent!! The children sat absolutely still for the stories. Your expansion into poetry...is a marvelous idea," writes a seasoned 1st grade teacher in a school where grades 1 through 6 are hearing & reading these fables. Written in bright, read-aloud style, each fable ends with a simple question, followed by an answer page. The story is then told in rhythmic verse, this time more particular & personal, like the memories of life. The fresh & deliberately expanded writing remains true to Aesop's classic themes & characters, & with repeated readings the stories won't grow old, only more interesting as they provide wisdom that spans differences in culture, status, & education. Sixty-seven outstanding storybook illustrations create windows for the imagination. The result is hours of enjoyment for children & adults, with ideas that will grow with them. Order from Baker & Taylor; distributed to libraries by Quality Books.
Publisher Provided Annotation.

Testa, Fulvio, illus. Aesop's Fables. 48p. (gr. 2 up). 1989. incl. dust jacket 12.95 (ISBN 0-8120-5958-1). Barron.
Thomas, Vernon. Aesop's Fables. Bhushan, Reboti, illus. 135p. (gr. 1-7). 1981. 7.25 (ISBN 0-89744-231-8, Pub. by Hemkunt India). Auromere.
Warburg, Sandol S. Free. Oliver, Jenni, illus. LC 75-40013. 48p. (gr. 1 up). 1976. PLB 5.95 (ISBN 0-395-24210-X). HM.
Watson. Aesop's Fable. (gr. k-4). 1982. (Usborne-Hayes); PLB 11.96 (ISBN 0-88110-093-5). EDC.
Webber, Irma E. Esta Cosa Se Ve Asi. Urquidi, Maria, tr. Webber, Irma E., illus. LC 76-43571. (SPA.). (gr. k-3). 1978. pap. text ed. 6.88 perfect bound (ISBN 0-918970-23-7). Intl Gen Semantics.
Wildsmith, Brian & LaFontaine, Jean de. The Rich Man & the Shoe-Maker. (Illus.). (ps-3). 1965. pap. 6.95 (ISBN 0-19-272104-6). Oxford U Pr.
Zwerger, Lisbeth, illus. Aesop's Fables. (ps up). 1991. 15.95 (ISBN 0-88708-108-8); pap. 4.95 (ISBN 0-88708-179-7). Picture Bk Studio.

FABRIC PICTURES
see Collage

FABRICS
see Textile Industry and Fabrics

FACETIAE
see Anecdotes; Wit and Humor

FACTORIES
Dupasquier, Philippe. The Factory. Dupasquier, Philippe, illus. 24p. (ps-1). 1984. 3.95 (ISBN 0-448-19052-4, G&D). Putnam Pub Group.
Sundvall, Viveca. Mimi & the Biscuit Factory. Eriksson, Eva, illus. Bibb, Eric, tr. (Illus.). 32p. (ps up). 1989. 12.95 (ISBN 9-12-959142-2, Pub. by R & S Bks). FS&G.
Weisman, Joanne B. Lowell Mill Girls: Life in the Factory. 48p. (gr. 6-9). 1991. pap. 3.50 (ISBN 1-878668-06-4). Disc Enter Ltd.

FACULTY (EDUCATION)
see Educators; Teachers

FAIENCE
see Pottery

FAIRIES
see also Fairy Tales
Alexander, Sue. More Witch, Goblin & Ghost Stories. Winter, Jeanette, illus. LC 78-3280. (gr. 1-4). 1978. 6.95 (ISBN 0-394-83933-1); lib. bdg. 7.99 (ISBN 0-394-93933-6). Pantheon.
Andersdatter, Karla M. Marissa the Tooth Fairy. write for info. In Between.
Banks, Lynne R. The Fairy Rebel. Geldart, William, illus. LC 87-28740. 128p. (gr. 5 up). 1988. 12.95 (ISBN 0-385-24483-5). Doubleday.
Barrie, J. M. Peter Pan. 15.95 (ISBN 0-8488-0427-9). Amereon Ltd.
—Peter Pan in Kensington Gardens. Hollindale, Peter, ed. (Illus.). 288p. 1991. pap. 5.95 (ISBN 0-19-282593-3). Oxford U Pr.
Baum, L. Frank. The Sea Fairies. Neill, John R., illus. 240p. 1987. 17.95 (ISBN 0-929605-03-9); pap. 9.95 (ISBN 0-929605-00-4). Books Wonder.
Briggs, Katharine M. An Encyclopedia of Fairies: Hobgoblins, Brownies, Bogies, & Other Supernatural Creatures. LC 76-12939. (Illus.). (gr. 4 up). 1977. pap. 16.95 (ISBN 0-394-73467-X). Pantheon.
Butterworth, Nick. Amanda's Butterfly. (ps). 1991. 12.95 (ISBN 0-385-30433-1). Delacorte.
Cole, Joanna. Mixed-Up Magic. Donnelly, Judy, ed. Kelley, True, illus. LC 87-14965. 32p. (gr. k-3). 1987. 8.95 (ISBN 0-8038-9298-5). Hastings.
Cosgrove, Stephen. Gnome from Nome. James, Robin, illus. 32p. (gr. 1-6). 1974. pap. 2.95 (ISBN 0-8431-0555-0). Price Stern.
Denan, Corinne. Goblin Tales. LC 79-66326. (Illus.). 48p. (gr. 3-6). 1980. lib. bdg. 9.89 (ISBN 0-89375-320-3); pap. 2.95 (ISBN 0-89375-319-X). Troll Assocs.
Fitzgerald, Jean. The Golden Gate Bridge Troll. Donovan, Karen, illus. 48p. (Orig.). (gr. k-2). 1978. pap. 6.95x (ISBN 0-9618225-0-3). Bridge Troll Pr.
Forest, Heather. The Woman Who Flummoxed the Fairies. Gaber, Susan, illus. (ps-3). 1990. 14.95 (ISBN 0-15-299150-6). HarbraceJ.
Fujikawa, Gyo. Come Follow Me...to the Secret World of Elves & Fairies & Gnomes & Trolls. LC 78-22746. (Illus.). (gr. k-5). 1979. 6.95 (ISBN 0-448-16545-7, G&D). Putnam Pub Group.
Gilligan, Shannon. The Fairy Kidnap. 64p. (Orig.). (gr. 2 up). 1985. pap. 2.25 (ISBN 0-553-15488-5). Bantam.
Good Fairies of Hullen Ridge Staff. The Good Fairies of Hullen Ridge. Woods, Karen J. & Kreisman, Jane, eds. Moore, Lynne M., illus. 24p. (Orig.). (ps-4). 1988. pap. 4.75 (ISBN 0-922597-00-6). GFHR.
—The Legend of the Little Blue Love Puff. Woods, Karen J., ed. Hughs, Lynne M., illus. 24p. (ps-4). 1988. pap. 6.95 (ISBN 0-922597-01-4). GFHR.
Gregory, Sally, illus. Fairies & Phantoms. 28p. (ps-2). 1988. 15.95 (ISBN 0-340-39514-1, Pub. by Hodder & Stoughton UK). Trafalgar Sq.
Hart, Tom. Fairies & Friends. Pearson-Cooper, Michelle, illus. 120p. 1981. 8.95 (ISBN 0-685-01043-0, Pub. by Quartet England). Charles River Bks.
Hunter, Mollie. A Furl of Fairy Wind. Gammell, Stephen, illus. LC 76-58732. 64p. (gr. 2-5). 1977. 12.95 (ISBN 0-06-022675-7). HarpC Child Bks.
Kimmel, Eric A. Hershel & the Hanukkah Goblins. Hyman, Trina S., illus. LC 89-1954. 32p. (gr. k-3). 1989. reinforced 14.95 (ISBN 0-8234-0769-1). Holiday.
Leedy, Loreen. The Potato Party & Other Troll Tales. Leedy, Loreen, illus. LC 89-1746. 32p. (gr. k-3). 1989. reinforced 14.95 (ISBN 0-8234-0761-6). Holiday.
Lemoine, Charles A. Louisiana's Cypress Bayou Elves: Pontain the Trapper. Lemoine, Charles A., illus. 40p. (Orig.). (gr. 1-12). 1986. pap. 5.00 (ISBN 0-941327-01-9). Charles A Lemoine.
Linnell, Andrew & Auer, Varvara. The Dance of the Elves. (Illus.). 32p. (Orig.). (ps). 1984. pap. 13.50 (ISBN 0-936132-68-X). Merc Pr NY.
Littledale, Freya. The Elves & the Shoemaker. Turkle, Brinton, illus. 32p. (ps-4). 1984. pap. 3.95 (ISBN 0-590-33305-4, Blue Ribbon Bks). Scholastic Inc.
McAllister, Frank & McAllister, Fran. The Tooth Fairy Legend. LC 76-9595. (gr. k-4). 1976. 9.95 (ISBN 0-916864-01-4). Block.
Maeterlinck, Maurice. The Blue Bird. Goscinsky, Michael, illus. Poesnecker, Gerald E. & Poesnecker, Gerald E.intro. by. Bd. with The Betrothal. 304p. (gr. 1 up). 1985. 16.95 (ISBN 0-932785-02-6); pap. 10.95 (ISBN 0-932785-01-8). Philos Pub.
Marshall, Edward. Troll Country. Marshall, James, illus. LC 79-19324. 56p. (ps-3). 1980. PLB 9.89 (ISBN 0-8037-6211-9); pap. 4.95 (ISBN 0-8037-6210-0). Dial Bks Young.
Mayne, William. The Green Book of Hob Stories. Benore, Patrick, illus. LC 83-17317. 32p. (gr. k-4). 1984. 7.95 (ISBN 0-399-21039-3, Philomel). Putnam Pub Group.
Mennella, Roxanna, et al. Fairies, Elves & Gnomes. (Illus.). 32p. (Orig.). (gr. 3-8). 1985. pap. 2.00x (ISBN 0-934830-38-X, Dist. by Waterways Project). Ten Penny.
Miner, Carl E. The Original Tooth Fairy Story. Teeter, Melva, illus. LC 85-73462. 24p. (ps-4). 1986. write for info. (ISBN 0-9615985-0-6). Child Ventures.
Morris, Winifred. David & the Ice Elf. Hyde, Maureen, illus. LC 87-27799. 32p. (gr. k-3). 1988. 13.95 (ISBN 0-689-31428-0, Atheneum Child Bk). Macmillan Child Grp.
Myers, Bernice. Sidney Rella & the Glass Sneaker. Myers, Bernice, illus. LC 85-3044. 32p. (gr. k-3). 1985. 13.95 (ISBN 0-02-767790-7, Mcmillan Child Bk). Macmillan Child Grp.
Peters, Sharon. The Tooth Fairy. Sims, Deborah, illus. LC 81-5100. 32p. (gr. k-2). 1981. PLB 10.89 (ISBN 0-89375-519-2); pap. 2.95 (ISBN 0-89375-520-6). Troll Assocs.
Pini, Wendy & Pini, Richard. Elfquest, Book 2. Reynolds, Kay, ed. Pini, Wendy, illus. LC 81-5401. 172p. (Orig.). (gr. 5 up). 1982. pap. 14.95 (ISBN 0-89865-245-6, Starblaze). Donning Co.
—Elfquest, Book 4. Reynolds, Kay, ed. LC 81-5401. (Illus.). 172p. (gr. 5 up). 1984. pap. 14.95 (ISBN 0-89865-377-0, Starblaze); ltd. ed. 40.00 (ISBN 0-89865-378-9, Starblaze). Donning Co.
—Elfquest: Captives of Blue Mountain. rev. ed. (Illus.). 192p. (gr. 4 up). 1988. pap. 17.95 (ISBN 0-936861-08-8, Father Tree Pr). Warp Graphics.
—Elfquest: Fire & Flight. rev. ed. Pini, Wendy, illus. 192p. (gr. 4 up). 1988. pap. 17.95 (ISBN 0-936861-06-1, Father Tree Pr). WARP Graphics.
—Elfquest: Quest's End. rev. ed. (Illus.). 208p. (gr. 4 up). 1988. pap. 17.95 (ISBN 0-936861-09-6, Father Tree Pr). Warp Graphics.
—Elfquest: Siege at Blue Mountain. (Illus.). 144p. (Orig.). (gr. 4 up). 1988. pap. 16.95 (ISBN 0-936861-10-X, Father Tree Pr). Warp Graphics.
—Elfquest: The Forbidden Grove. rev. ed. (Illus.). 208p. (gr. 4 up). 1988. pap. 17.95 (ISBN 0-936861-07-X, Father Tree Pr). Warp Graphics.
—Elfquest: The Secret of Two-Edge. (Illus.). 144p. (Orig.). (gr. 4 up). 1988. pap. 16.95 (ISBN 0-936861-11-8, Father Tree Pr). Warp Graphics.
Pope, Elizabeth M. The Perilous Gard. Cuffari, Richard, illus. LC 73-21648. 272p. (gr. 6 up). 1974. 13.95 (ISBN 0-395-18512-2). HM.
Pratchett, Terry. Truckers. 1990. 14.95 (ISBN 0-385-29984-2). Doubleday.
Stoppel, Florence E. The Adventures of Alfy Elf. (gr. k-2). 1989. 8.95 (ISBN 0-533-07927-6). Vantage.
Wangerin, Walter. Elisabeth & the Water-Troll. Healy, Deborah, illus. LC 90-4359. 64p. (gr. 3-7). 1991. 14.95 (ISBN 0-06-026353-9); PLB 14.89 (ISBN 0-06-026354-7). HarpC Child Bks.

FAIRIES–POETRY
Allingham, William. The Fairies. Hague, Michael, illus. LC 88-28474. 32p. (ps-1). 1988. PLB 13.95 (ISBN 0-8050-1003-3). H Holt & Co.
Hopkins, Lee B. Elves, Fairies & Gnomes. Hoffman, Rosekrans, illus. LC 79-19753. (ps-2). 1980. Knopf.

FAIRS
see also Exhibitions
Moss, Miriam. Fairs & Circuses. (Illus.). 32p. (gr. 1-6). 1987. lib. bdg. 8.99 (ISBN 0-531-18144-8, Pub. by Bookwright Pr). Watts.
Pierce, Jack. The State Fair Book. Pierce, Jack, illus. LC 79-91308. 32p. (gr. k-4). 1980. PLB 9.95 (ISBN 0-87614-124-6). Carolrhoda Bks.
Tudor, Tasha. Corgiville Fair. Tudor, Tash, illus. LC 72-154042. (ps-3). 1971. 14.95i (ISBN 0-690-21791-9, Crowell Jr Bks). HarpC Child Bks.

FAIRS–FICTION
Amery, H. Going to the Fair. (Illus.). 24p. (ps-2). 1987. 3.95 (ISBN 0-7460-0066-9); PLB 7.96 (ISBN 0-88110-262-8). EDC.
Brook, Ruth. Good for You, Lolly. Kondo, Vala, illus. LC 86-30733. 32p. (gr. k-3). 1988. PLB 11.89 (ISBN 0-8167-0914-9); pap. text ed. 2.95 (ISBN 0-8167-0915-7). Troll Assocs.
Casad, Mary B. Bluebonnet at the State Fair. Binder, Pat, illus. 40p. (gr. 2-4). 1985. 9.95 (ISBN 0-89015-530-5). Eakin Pr.
Hall, Lynn. Fair Maiden. LC 90-30629. 128p. (gr. 7 up). 1990. 12.95 (ISBN 0-684-19213-6, Scribners Young Read). Macmillan Child Grp.
Hope, Laura L. Bobbsey Twins & the County Fair Mystery. (gr. 1-4). 1922. 4.50 (ISBN 0-448-08015-X, G&D). Putnam Pub Group.
McCay, William. Funny Business. LC 88-31481. 144p. (gr. 5 up). 1989. PLB 6.99 (ISBN 0-394-99981-9). Random.
Marsh, Carole. Mystery of the World's Fair. Marsh, Carol, illus. (Orig.). (gr. 3-9). 1982. pap. 14.95 (ISBN 0-935326-04-9). Gallopade Pub Group.
Mauser, Pat R. How I Found Myself at the Fair. Howell, Kathleen C., illus. LC 90-30630. 64p. (gr. 1-4). 1990. pap. 2.95 (ISBN 0-689-71414-9, Aladdin). Macmillan Child Grp.
Muntean, Michaela. The Very Bumpy Bus Ride. Wiseman, Bernard, illus. LC 81-16905. 48p. (ps-3). 1982. 5.95 (ISBN 0-8193-1079-4); 5.95 (ISBN 0-8193-1080-8). Parents.
Tudor, Tasha. Corgiville Fair. Tudor, Tasha, illus. LC 72-154042. 56p. (ps-3). 1991. pap. 5.95 (ISBN 0-06-443236-X, Trophy). HarpC Child Bks.

FAIRY PLAYS
Barrie, James M. Peter Pan. abridged ed. Frank, Josette, adapted by. (Illus.). (gr. 1-4). 1965. 3.95 (ISBN 0-394-80749-9, Random Juv); lib. bdg. 4.79 (ISBN 0-394-90749-3). Random.
Le Mair, Henriette W. Granny's Little Rhyme Book. (Illus.). 24p. 1990. 6.95 (ISBN 0-399-22174-3, Philomel Bks). Putnam Pub Group.
Shakespeare, William. Midsummer Night's Dream. Pitt, David G., intro. by. (gr. 10 up). pap. 1.95 (ISBN 0-8049-1005-7, S5). Airmont.

FAIRY TALES

see also Folklore

Absolon, Karel B. The Tale of the Bad Macocha & the Fable of the Underground Punkva River. Absolon, K. B., ed. & illus. 40p. (Orig.). (gr. 4). 1984. pap. text ed. 12.00 (ISBN 0-930329-02-3). KABEL Pubs.

Adventures of Sinbad the Sailor. (gr. 4 up). 1988. pap. 4.87 (ISBN 0-582-54148-4, 74257). Longman.

Aesop. Little Red Riding Hood. Dyer, Jane, illus. LC 85-70289. 18p. (ps). 1985. 3.95 (ISBN 0-448-10227-7, G&D). Putnam Pub Group.

—Town Mouse & the Country Mouse. new ed. LC 78-18062. (Illus.). 32p. (gr. k-3). 1979. PLB 9.79 (ISBN 0-89375-131-6); pap. 1.95 (ISBN 0-89375-109-X). Troll Assocs.

Ahlberg, Allan. Ten in a Bed. Amstutz, Andre, illus. 112p. (gr. 2-6). 1991. pap. 3.95 (ISBN 0-14-032531-X, Puffin). Puffin Bks.

Aiken, Joan. The Stolen Lake: A Novel. LC 81-5015. 256p. (gr. 7 up). 1981. 10.95 (ISBN 0-385-28982-0). Delacorte.

Aladdin. (ARA., Illus.). (gr. 5-12). 3.50x (ISBN 0-86685-182-8). Intl Bk Ctr.

Alchemy II, Inc. Staff, illus. Goldilocks & the Three Bears. 26p. 1988. incl. cassette 9.95 (ISBN 1-55578-906-4). Worlds Wonder.

—Jack & the Beanstalk. 26p. (ps). 1988. incl. cassette 9.95 (ISBN 1-55578-907-2). Worlds Wonder.

Alexander, Lloyd. Black Cauldron. LC 65-13868. (gr. 5-9). 1965. 15.95 (ISBN 0-8050-0992-2). H Holt & Co.

—Book of Three. LC 64-18250. 224p. (gr. 4-6). 1964. 15.95 (ISBN 0-8050-0874-8, HR&W). H Holt & Co.

—Castle of Llyr. LC 66-13461. 204p. (gr. 4-6). 1966. 15.95 (ISBN 0-8050-1115-3). H Holt & Co.

—King's Fountain. Keats, Ezra J., illus. (ps-3). 1989. 13.95 (ISBN 0-525-33240-5, DCB); pap. 4.95 (ISBN 0-525-44537-4, DCB). Dutton Child Bks.

—Taran Wanderer. 272p. (gr. k-6). 1969. pap. 3.50 (ISBN 0-440-48483-9, YB). Dell.

—Taran Wanderer. LC 67-10230. 256p. (gr. 5-9). 1967. 15.95 (ISBN 0-8050-1113-7). H Holt & Co.

—The Town Cats & Other Tales. Kubinyi, Laszlo, illus. (gr. 4-7). 1977. 14.95 (ISBN 0-525-41430-4, DCB). Dutton Child Bks.

Ali Baba: In Arabic. (Illus.). (gr. 4-12). 3.50x (ISBN 0-86685-184-4). Intl Bk Ctr.

Alice in Wonderland. (Illus.). (ps). 1985. bds. 1.98 (ISBN 0-517-48141-3). Outlet Bk Co.

Alice in Wonderland. (gr. 4 up). 1988. pap. 4.87 (ISBN 0-582-52278-1, 73807). Longman.

Alice in Wonderland. write for info. Knopf.

Alice in Wonderland. Date not set. 5.98 (ISBN 0-517-67008-9). Outlet Bk Co.

Alice in Wonderland. (Illus.). (gr. 3-5). 3.50 (ISBN 0-7214-0967-9). Ladybird Bks.

Alice in Wonderland & Through the Looking Glass. 304p. (gr. 4 up). 1981. pap. 7.95 (ISBN 0-448-11004-0, G&D). Putnam Pub Group.

Allan, Nicholas. The Hefty Fairy. (Illus.). 32p. (gr. 1-3). 1990. 13.95 (ISBN 0-09-173751-6, Pub. by Hutchinson UK). Trafalgar Sq.

Amery, H. Cinderella. (gr. 1 up). 1989. 6.96 (ISBN 0-88110-339-X). EDC.

—Little Red Riding Hood. Cartwright, Stephen, illus. 16p. (ps-2). 1987. 2.95 (ISBN 0-7460-0138-X); PLB 6.96 (ISBN 0-88110-290-3). EDC.

Amorso, Lisa, illus. Old Mother Hubbard & Her Dog. LC 86-27321. 32p. (ps-1). 1987. 4.95 (ISBN 0-394-88922-3); lib. bdg. 7.99 (ISBN 0-394-98922-8). Knopf.

Amoss, Berthe. Cinderella. Amoss, Berthe, illus. 10p. (ps-7). 1989. pap. 2.95 (ISBN 0-922589-04-6). More Than Card.

—Little Red Riding Hood. (Illus.). 10p. (ps-7). 1989. pap. 2.95 (ISBN 0-922589-11-9). More Than Card.

Andersen, Hans Christian. Andersen's Fairy Tales. LC 58-6191. (Illus.). 352p. (gr. 3-9). pap. 10.95 (ISBN 0-448-11005-9, G&D); deluxe ed. 11.95 (ISBN 0-448-06005-1). Putnam Pub Group.

—Dulac's the Snow Queen: And Other Stories. Haugaard, Erik C., tr. Dulac, Edmund, illus. LC 76-7308. 144p. (ps up). 9.95 (ISBN 0-385-11678-0). Doubleday.

—Emperor & the Nightingale. Watling, James, illus. LC 78-18065. 32p. (gr. k-4). 1979. PLB 9.79 (ISBN 0-89375-134-0); pap. 1.95 (ISBN 0-89375-112-X). Troll Assocs.

—The Emperor's New Clothes. Rockwell, Anne, retold by. & illus. LC 83-19610. 32p. (ps-3). 1982. PLB 12.89 (ISBN 0-690-04149-7, Crowell Jr Bks). HarpC Child Bks.

—The Emperor's New Clothes. Burton, Virginia L., illus. LC 83-19610. 48p. (gr. k-3). 1979. pap. 5.95 (ISBN 0-395-28594-1). HM.

—Emperor's New Clothes. Delano, Jack & Delano, Irene, eds. LC 83-19610. (Illus.). (gr. 2-6). 1971. (Random Juv). Random.

—The Emperor's New Clothes. Westcott, Nadine B., illus. (ps-3). 1984. 14.95 (ISBN 0-316-93123-3); pap. 5.95 (ISBN 0-316-93124-1). Little.

—The Emperor's New Clothes. Duntze, Dorothee, illus. LC 86-2509. 32p. (gr. k-3). 1986. 14.95 (ISBN 1-55858-036-0). North-South Bks NYC.

—The Emperor's New Clothes. Alchemy II, Inc. Staff, illus. 26p. (ps). 1988. incl. cassette 9.95 (ISBN 1-55578-901-3). Worlds Wonder.

—Favorite Tales of Hans Andersen. James, M. R., tr. from DAN. Jacques, Robin, illus. 168p. (gr. 2-5). 1986. pap. 6.95 (ISBN 0-571-13927-2). Faber & Faber.

—The Fir Tree. Imsand, Marcel & Marshall, Rita, illus. 40p. (gr. 6 up). 1983. PLB 10.95s.p. (ISBN 0-87191-949-4); 15.65 (ISBN 0-685-07717-9). Creative Ed.

—Hans Andersen: His Classic Fairy Tales. Haugaard, Erik C., tr. Foreman, Michael, illus. LC 77-74792. 196p. (gr. 1 up). 1978. 15.95 (ISBN 0-385-13364-2). Doubleday.

—Hans Andersen's Fairy Tales. Kingsland, L. W., tr. Birkett, Rachel, illus. 268p. (ps-6). 1987. 18.95 (ISBN 0-19-274532-8). Oxford U Pr.

—Hans Andersen's Fairy Tales: A Selection. Frolich, Lorenz & Pedersen, Vilhelm, illus. Kingsland, L. W., tr. from DAN. Lewis, Naomi, intro. by. LC 84-7120. 1985. pap. 3.95 (ISBN 0-19-281699-3). Oxford U Pr.

—Hans Christian Andersen's Fairy Tales. Gotlieb, Jules, illus. LC 58-6191. (gr. 3 up). pap. 2.50 (ISBN 0-8049-0169-4, CL-169). Airmont.

—Little Match Girl. Lent, Blair, illus. LC 68-28050. (gr. k-3). 1975. 12.95 (ISBN 0-395-21625-7); pap. 1.95 (ISBN 0-685-02294-3). HM.

—Little Mermaid. 1987. write for info. (ISBN 0-8499-8530-7). Word Bks.

—The Little Mermaid: A Step Three Book. Hautzig, Deborah, adapted by. May, Darcy, illus. LC 91-6632. 48p. (Orig.). (gr. 2-3). 1991. lib. bdg. 6.99 (ISBN 0-679-92241-5, Random Juv); pap. 2.95 (ISBN 0-679-82241-0). Random.

—The Marsh King's Daughter. Gentry, Linnea, retold by. Klages, Ricki, illus. LC 88-22417. 56p. (gr. k up). 1990. PLB 16.95 (ISBN 0-943173-04-3); pap. 9.95 (ISBN 0-943173-13-2). Harbinger AZ.

—Michael Hague's Favourite Hans Christian Andersen Fairy Tales. Hague, Michael, illus. LC 81-47455. 168p. (gr. 4-6). 1981. 18.95 (ISBN 0-8050-0659-1). H Holt & Co.

—Nightingale. Le Gallienne, Eva, tr. Burkert, Nancy E., illus. LC 64-18574. 48p. (gr. 3 up). 1965. PLB 14.89 (ISBN 0-06-023781-3). HarpC Child Bks.

—The Nightingale. (Illus.). 44p. (gr. 1-4). 1986. 7.95 (ISBN 0-8120-5710-4); Creative Character Building ed. 7.95 (ISBN 0-8120-5718-X). Barron.

—The Nightingale. Demi, illus. (gr. 3 up). 1988. pap. 3.95 (ISBN 0-15-257428-X, VoyB). HarBraceJ.

—The Nightingale. Darke, Alison C., illus. 32p. (ps-3). 1989. 13.95 (ISBN 0-385-26081-4, Zephyr-BFYR); PLB 14.99 (ISBN 0-385-26082-2, Zephyr-BFYR). Doubleday.

—The Nightingale. Zwerger, Lisbeth, illus. 1991. pap. 3.95 (ISBN 0-590-44458-1, Blue Ribbon Bks). Scholastic Inc.

—The Princess & the Pea. Galdone, Paul, illus. LC 77-12707. (ps-2). 1979. 14.95 (ISBN 0-395-28807-X, Clarion). HM.

—The Princess & the Pea. Stevens, Janet, adapted by. LC 81-13395. (Illus.). 32p. (gr. k-2). 1982. reinforced bdg. 14.95 (ISBN 0-8234-0442-0); pap. 5.95 (ISBN 0-8234-0753-5). Holiday.

—The Princess & the Pea. Duntze, Dorothee, illus. LC 85-7199. 32p. (gr. k-2). 1985. 14.95 (ISBN 1-55858-034-4). North-South Bks NYC.

—The Princess & the Pea. Alchemy II, Inc. Staff, illus. 26p. (ps). 1988. incl. cassette 9.95 (ISBN 1-55578-909-9). Worlds Wonder.

—The Red Shoes. (gr. 7-12). 1983. pap. 2.25x (ISBN 0-19-421741-8). Oxford U Pr.

—Seven Tales by Hans Christian Andersen. reissued ed. Le Gallienne, Eva, tr. from DAN. Sendak, Maurice, illus. LC 59-16151. 144p. (gr. 3 up). 1959. 13.95 (ISBN 0-06-023790-2); PLB 13.89 (ISBN 0-06-023791-0). HarpC Child Bks.

—The Snow Queen. Lewis, Naomi, adapted by. Bogdanovic, Toma, illus. LC 68-17218. 32p. (ps-5). 9.95 (ISBN 0-87592-048-9). Scroll Pr.

—The Snow Queen. Jeffers, Susan, illus. LC 82-70199. 40p. (gr. k up). 1989. 15.95 (ISBN 0-8037-8011-7); PLB 12.89 (ISBN 0-8037-8029-X); pap. 4.95 (ISBN 0-8037-0692-8). Dial Bks Young.

—The Snow Queen. Hess, Dick & Eidrigewcius, Stasys, illus. LC 83-71172. 48p. (gr. 6 up). 1984. PLB 10.95s.p. (ISBN 0-87191-950-8); PLB 15.65 (ISBN 0-685-07718-7). Creative Ed.

—The Snow Queen. (Illus.). 44p. (gr. 1-4). 1986. 7.95 (ISBN 0-8120-5709-0); Creative Character Building ed. 7.95 (ISBN 0-8120-5717-1). Barron.

—Snow Queen. 1987. 15.95 (ISBN 0-8050-0485-8). H Holt & Co.

—The Steadfast Tin Soldier. Galdone, Paul, illus. LC 79-4325. (ps-4). 1979. 14.95 (ISBN 0-395-28964-5, Clarion). HM.

—The Steadfast Tin Soldier. Lemoine, Georges, illus. 32p. 1983. PLB 10.95s.p. (ISBN 0-87191-948-6); PLB 15.65 (ISBN 0-685-07716-0). Creative Ed.

—Thumbelina. Jeffers, Susan, illus. LC 79-50146. (ps-3). 1979. 14.95 (ISBN 0-8037-8815-0); PLB 14.89 (ISBN 0-8037-8814-2). Dial Bks Young.

—Thumbelina. Nigoghossian, Christine W., illus. LC 78-18080. 32p. (gr. k-4). 1979. PLB 9.79 (ISBN 0-89375-141-3); pap. 1.95 (ISBN 0-89375-119-7). Troll Assocs.

—Thumbelina. abr. ed. Hautzig, Deborah, adapted by. Kaila, Kaarina, illus. Collins, Judy, contrib. by. (Illus.). 32p. (ps-5). 1990. Incl. 30 min. cassette. slipcased 15.95 (ISBN 0-679-80810-8). Knopf.

—Thumbelina. abr. ed. Hautzig, Deborah, adapted by. Kaila, Kaarina, illus. LC 89-29700. 32p. (ps-3). 1990. 9.95 (ISBN 0-679-80667-9); PLB 10.99 (ISBN 0-679-90667-3). Knopf.

—Thumbelina & Other Stories. LC 88-43554. 160p. 1989. 4.95 (ISBN 0-89471-722-7). Running Pr.

—Thumbeline. Zwerger, Lisbeth, illus. LC 85-12062. 28p. (gr. 1 up). 1985. 14.95 (ISBN 0-88708-006-5). Picture Bk Studio.

—The Tin Soldier. (gr. k-6). 1983. pap. 2.25x (ISBN 0-19-421742-6). Oxford U Pr.

—The Ugly Duckling. Bogdanovic, Toma, illus. LC 75-145207. 32p. (ps-3). 9.95 (ISBN 0-87592-055-1). Scroll Pr.

—Ugly Duckling. Williams, Jennie, illus. LC 78-18059. 32p. (gr. k-2). 1979. PLB 9.79 (ISBN 0-89375-128-6); pap. 1.95 (ISBN 0-89375-106-5). Troll Assocs.

—The Ugly Duckling. (gr. k-6). 1983. pap. 2.25x (ISBN 0-19-421704-3). Oxford U Pr.

—The Ugly Duckling. (Illus.). 44p. (gr. 1-4). 1986. 7.95 (ISBN 0-8120-5708-2); Creative Character Building ed. 7.95 (ISBN 0-8120-5716-3). Barron.

—The Ugly Duckling. Moore, Lillian, retold by. San Souci, Daniel, illus. 48p. (gr. 3-7). 1987. 12.95 (ISBN 0-590-40957-3, Scholastic Hardcover). Scholastic Inc.

—The Ugly Duckling. Mayer, Marianna, retold by. Locker, Thomas, illus. LC 85-23869. 40p. 1987. 16.95 (ISBN 0-02-765130-4, Mcmillan Child Bk). Macmillan Child Grp.

—The Ugly Duckling. Howell, Troy, retold by. & illus. 40p. 1990. 15.95 (ISBN 0-399-22158-1, Putnam). Putnam Pub Group.

—The Ugly Duckling. (Illus.). 24p. (ps up). 1990. write for info. (ISBN 0-307-12106-2, Pub. by Golden Bks). Western Pub.

—The Ugly Duckling: A Classic Tale. Jose, Eduard, adapted by. McDonnell, Janet, tr. from SPA. Asensio, Augusti, illus. LC 88-36795. 32p. (gr. 1-4). 1988. PLB 10.95 (ISBN 0-89565-474-1). Childs World.

—The Wild Swans. Milone, Karen, illus. LC 80-27685. 32p. (gr. k-4). 1981. PLB 9.79 (ISBN 0-89375-480-3); pap. text ed. 1.95 (ISBN 0-89375-481-1). Troll Assocs.

Angelina & the Princess. Holabird, Katharine. Craig, Helen, illus. LC 84-6818. 24p. (ps-2). 1988. 11.95 (ISBN 0-517-55273-6, C N Potter Bks). Crown.

L' Apprenti Sorcier. (FRE., Illus.). (gr. 3). 3.50 (ISBN 0-7214-1290-4). Ladybird Bks.

Ariana. Sleeping Beauty Retold: For Those Who Can't Wait 100 Years for a Happy Ending. Carleton, Marci, illus. 22p. (Orig.). (gr. 1-6). 1983. pap. 3.50 (ISBN 0-916549-00-3). Ariana Prods.

Atkinson, Allen. Old King Cole & Other Favorites. (Illus.). 64p. (Orig.). 1986. pap. 2.50 (ISBN 0-553-15355-2). Bantam.

Babbitt, Natalie. Kneeknock Rise. Babbitt, Natalie, illus. LC 79-105622. 96p. (gr. 3 up). 1984. (Sunburst); pap. 3.50 (ISBN 0-374-44260-6). FS&G.

—The Search for Delicious. Babbitt, Natalie, illus. LC 69-20374. 176p. (gr. 3 up). 1969. 14.95 (ISBN 0-374-36534-2, Sunburst); pap. 3.50 (ISBN 0-374-46536-3, Sunburst). FS&G.

Baby's First Mother Goose. 12p. (ps). 1978. 3.95 (ISBN 0-448-40862-7, G&D). Putnam Pub Group.

Balducci, Rita, retold by. Little Red Riding Hood. Eubank, Mary G., illus. (ps-k). 1991. pap. 1.25 (ISBN 0-307-11511-9, Golden Pr). Western Pub.

Balian, Lorna. Leprechauns Never Lie. LC 79-25950. (Illus.). 32p. (gr. k-3). 1980. 8.95 (ISBN 0-687-21371-1); PLB 8.95 (ISBN 0-685-00020-6). Abingdon.

Banks, Lynne R. The Fairy Rebel. 128p. (gr. 4). 1989. pap. 2.95 (ISBN 0-380-70650-4, Camelot). Avon.

Barnett, Carol. Goldilocks & the Three Bears. (ps-3). 1990. 7.95 (ISBN 0-8442-9416-0). Natl Textbk.

—Little Red Hen. (ps-3). 1990. 7.95 (ISBN 0-8442-9418-7). Natl Textbk.

Barrie, J. M. Peter Pan. (Illus.). (ps). 1985. bds. 1.00 (ISBN 0-517-48144-8). Outlet Bk Co.

—Peter Pan. Hague, Michael, illus. LC 87-403. 168p. (gr. 3-6). 1987. 16.95 (ISBN 0-8050-0276-6). H Holt & Co.

—Peter Pan in Kensington Gardens. 175p. 1981. Repr. PLB 16.95x (ISBN 0-89966-328-1). Buccaneer Bks.

—Peter Pan: Return to Never-Never Land. Forten, Ron, adapted by. (Illus.). 56p. 1991. pap. write for info. (ISBN 1-56398-016-9). Malibu Graphics.

Barrie, James M. Peter Pan. abridged ed. Frank, Josette, adapted by. (Illus.). (gr. 1-4). 1965. 3.95 (ISBN 0-394-80749-9, Random Juv); lib. bdg. 4.79 (ISBN 0-394-90749-3). Random.

—Peter Pan. Hyman, Trina S., ed. LC 80-14510. (Illus.). 192p. (gr. k up). 1980. 18.95 (ISBN 0-684-16611-9, Scribners Young Read). Macmillan Child Grp.

—Peter Pan. 1986. pap. 2.25 (ISBN 0-14-035066-7, Puffin). Puffin Bks.

—Peter Pan. Lurie, Alison, afterword by. 208p. 1987. pap. 2.50 (ISBN 0-451-52088-2, Sig Classics). NAL-Dutton.

—Peter Pan. Frank, Josette, adapted by. Goode, Diane, illus. Redgrave, Lynn, contrib. by. (Illus.). 72p. (ps-5). 1987. incl. cassette 13.95 (ISBN 0-394-89226-7, Random Juv). Random.

—Peter Pan: The Complete Book. Hudson, Susan, illus. 180p. (Orig.). (gr. 4 up). 1988. pap. 9.95 (ISBN 0-88776-206-9). Tundra Bks.

Bartos-Hoppner, Barbara. The Pied Piper of Hamelin. Fuchshuber, Annegert, illus. LC 87-45150. 32p. (gr. k-3). 1987. 9.95 (ISBN 0-397-32239-9, Lipp Jr Bks). HarpC Child Bks.

Battaglia, Aurelius, illus. Mother Goose. LC 73-2447. (ps-2). 1978. lib. bdg. 5.99 (ISBN 0-394-92661-7, Random Juv). Random.

Baum, Arline & Baum, Joseph. Opt: An Illusionary Tale. LC 86-28130. (ps-3). 1987. pap. 11.95 (ISBN 0-670-80870-9). Viking Child Bks.

Baum, L. Frank. Animal Fairy Tales. Bull, Charles L., illus. 48p. (ps-3). 1989. 12.95 (ISBN 0-929605-05-5); pap. 6.95 (ISBN 0-929605-04-7). Books Wonder.

—Dorothy & the Wicked Witch. Naden, C. J., adapted by. LC 79-84149. (Illus.). 32p. (gr. 2-5). 1980. PLB 10.79 (ISBN 0-89375-195-2); pap. 2.95 (ISBN 0-89375-191-X). Troll Assocs.

—Dorothy & the Wizard. Naden, C. J., adapted by. LC 79-84150. (Illus.). 32p. (gr. 2-5). 1980. PLB 10.79 (ISBN 0-89375-196-0); pap. 2.95 (ISBN 0-89375-192-8). Troll Assocs.

—Dorothy & the Wizard in Oz. (gr. 4 up). 16.50 (ISBN 0-8446-6141-4). Peter Smith.

—Land of Oz. (Illus.). (gr. 4 up). 1968. pap. 1.25 (ISBN 0-8049-0181-3, CL-181). Airmont.

—Marvelous Land of Oz. Neill, John R., illus. Gardner, M., intro. by. (Illus.). xvii, 287p. (gr. 4-6). 1969. pap. 5.95 (ISBN 0-486-20692-0). Dover.

—Marvelous Land of Oz. (gr. k-3). 1970. pap. 1.95 (ISBN 0-590-08565-4). Scholastic Inc.

—Off to See the Wizard. Naden, C. J., adapted by. LC 79-84171. 32p. (gr. 2-5). 1980. PLB 10.79 (ISBN 0-89375-194-4); pap. 2.95 (ISBN 0-89375-190-1). Troll Assocs.

—Ozma of Oz. (gr. 5 up). 17.75 (ISBN 0-8446-6180-5). Peter Smith.

—Queen Zixi of Ix: Or, the Story of the Magic Cloak. Richardson, Frederick, illus. Gardner, M., intro. by. (Illus.). 231p. (gr. 1-3). 1971. pap. 4.95 (ISBN 0-486-22691-3). Dover.

—The Road to Oz. LC 79-88480. 1986. pap. 4.95 (ISBN 0-345-33467-1). Ballantine.

—Surprising Adventures of the Magical Monarch of Mo & His People. Ver Beck, Frank, illus. (ps-4). 1968. pap. 6.95 (ISBN 0-486-21892-9). Dover.

—Wizard of Oz. Copelman, Evelyn, et al, illus. (gr. 4-6). 1956. il. jr. lib. o.p. 5.95 (ISBN 0-448-05826-X, G&D); deluxe ed. 11.95 (ISBN 0-448-06026-4); Companion Lib. Ed. 2.95 (ISBN 0-448-05470-1). Putnam Pub Group.

—The Wizard of Oz. Granger, L. Frank, illus. (gr. 2-4). 1984. pap. 2.25 (ISBN 0-590-40442-3). Scholastic Inc.

—The Wizard of Oz. Hague, Michael, illus. LC 82-1109. 232p. (gr. 2-4). 1982. 19.95 (ISBN 0-8050-0221-9). H Holt & Co.

—The Wizard of Oz. (gr. 3-7). 1983. pap. 2.95 (ISBN 0-14-035001-2, Puffin). Puffin Bks.

—The Wizard of Oz. Smith, Jos A., illus. Hautzig, Deborah, adapted by. LC 83-13792. (Illus.). 64p. (ps-3). 1984. (Random Juv); lib. bdg. 8.99 (ISBN 0-394-95331-2). Random.

—The Wonderful Wizard of Oz. Krenkel, Roy, illus. (gr. 4 up). pap. 2.25 (ISBN 0-8049-0069-8, CL-69). Airmont.

—The Wonderful Wizard of Oz. 139p. 1981. Repr. PLB 15.95x (ISBN 0-89966-347-8). Buccaneer Bks.

—Wonderful Wizard of Oz. Denslow, W. W., illus. Gardner, Martin, intro. by. (Illus.). vii, 268p. (gr. k-6). 1960. pap. 7.95 (ISBN 0-486-20691-2). Dover.

—The Wonderful Wizard of Oz. Leach, William R., ed. 188p. 1991. pap. text ed. write for info. (ISBN 0-534-14736-4). Wadsworth Pub.

Beauty & the Beast. (Illus.). (ps-4). 3.50 (ISBN 0-7214-0642-4). Ladybird Bks.

La Belle au Bois Dormant. (FRE., Illus.). (gr. 2). 3.50 (ISBN 0-7214-1284-X). Ladybird Bks.

Bennett, Anna E. Little Witch. Stone, Helen, illus. LC 52-1374. (gr. 3-5). 1953. PLB 12.89 (ISBN 0-397-30261-4, Lipp Jr Bks). HarpC Child Bks.

Berger, Terry, ed. Black Fairy Tales. White, David O., illus. LC 70-75517. (gr. 3-7). 1974. (Atheneum Childrens Bk); pap. 3.95 (ISBN 0-689-70402-X). Macmillan Child Grp.

Biro, Val. Jack & the Beanstalk. (Illus.). 32p. (ps up). 1990. bds. 9.95 (ISBN 0-19-278218-5). Oxford U Pr.

—Tales from Hans Christian Andersen One to Four, 4 bks. (Illus., Orig.). (gr. 2-3). 1986. Set. pap. text ed. 19.80 (ISBN 1-55624-007-4). Wright Group.

Bishop, Claire H. The Five Chinese Brothers. (Illus.). (gr. k-3). 1938. 7.95 (ISBN 0-698-20044-6, Coward). Putnam Pub Group.

Black, Sheila, ed. Andersen's Fairy Tales. LC 90-55649. (Illus.). 56p. (gr. 1-4). 1991. 9.98 (ISBN 0-89471-981-5, Courage Bks). Running Pr.

Blanche Neige et les Sept Nains. (FRE., Illus.). (gr. 3). 3.50 (ISBN 0-7214-1294-7). Ladybird Bks.

Le Bonhomme de Pain d'Epice. (FRE., Illus.). (gr. 1). 3.50 (ISBN 0-7214-1279-3). Ladybird Bks.

Book of Classic Fairy Tales. (ps). 1978. 6.95 (ISBN 0-904494-88-8). Borden.

Boston, Lucy M. Sea Egg. Boston, Peter, illus. LC 67-10200. (gr. 2-5). 1967. 8.95 (ISBN 0-15-271050-7, HJ). HarBraceJ.

Boucle d'Or et les Trois Ours. (FRE., Illus.). (gr. 1). 3.50 (ISBN 0-7214-1271-8). Ladybird Bks.

The Brave Little Tailor. (Illus.). (ps-4). 3.50 (ISBN 0-7214-0791-9). Ladybird Bks.

Brett, Jan. Beauty & the Beast. (ps-3). 1990. pap. 5.95 (ISBN 0-395-55702-X, Clarion Bks). HM.

Brett, Jan, retold by. & illus. Goldilocks & the Three Bears. (gr. k-3). 1987. 13.95 (ISBN 0-396-08925-9, Putnam). Putnam Pub Group.

Briggs, Raymond. The Fairy Tale Treasury. Haviland, Virginia, ed. (gr. k up). 1986. pap. 8.95 (ISBN 0-440-42556-5, YB). Dell.

—The Mother Goose Treasury. Briggs, Raymond, illus. 1986. pap. 8.95 (ISBN 0-440-46408-0, YB). Dell.

Briggs, Raymond, ed. & illus. Mother Goose Treasury. (ps-3). 1966. PLB 16.95 (ISBN 0-698-20094-2, Coward). Putnam Pub Group.

Bros. Grimm. King of the Golden Mountain. Cutts, David, ed. Watling, James, illus. LC 87-11262. 32p. (gr. 2-4). 1988. PLB 9.79 (ISBN 0-8167-1055-4); pap. text ed. 1.95 (ISBN 0-8167-1056-2). Troll Assocs.

Brown, Beth, compiled by. Fairy Tales of Birds & Beasts, Vol. 1. (Illus.). 128p. (gr. 3-7). 1991. PLB 13.95 (ISBN 0-87460-375-7). Lion Bks.

Brown, Marcia & Perrault, Charles. Cinderella. Brown, Marcia, illus. 32p. (gr. 1-5). 1981. pap. 4.95 (ISBN 0-689-70484-4, Aladdin). Macmillan Child Grp.

—Cinderella. (Illus.). (ps-5). 1971. 13.95 (ISBN 0-684-12676-1, Scribners Young Read). Macmillan Child Grp.

Buj, Moira, illus. Mother Goose. 12p. (ps-2). 1977. pap. 2.00 (ISBN 0-85953-080-9, Pub. by Child's Play England). Childs Play.

Burgess, Beverly C. Jack & the Beanstalk. (gr. k-6). 1985. pap. 3.98 (ISBN 0-89274-384-0). Harrison Hse.

Byars, Betsy C. After the Goat Man. Himler, Ronald, illus. LC 74-8200. 128p. (gr. 5-9). 1974. pap. 13.95 (ISBN 0-670-10908-8). Viking Child Bks.

Calhoun, Mary. Hungry Leprechaun. Duvoisin, Roger, illus. LC 62-7214. 32p. (gr. k-3). 1962. PLB 12.88 (ISBN 0-688-31713-8). Morrow Jr Bks.

Carey, Mary V. Walt Disney's Peter Pan & Captain Hook. (Illus.). (ps-3). 1973. 6.95 (ISBN 0-394-82517-9, Random Juv); lib. bdg. 4.99 (ISBN 0-394-92517-3). Random.

Carlyon, Richard. The Dark Lord of Pengersick. Ellison, Pauline, illus. LC 80-13360. 176p. (gr. 4 up). 1980. 12. 95 (ISBN 0-374-31700-3). FS&G.

Carroll, Lewis. Alice au Pays de Merveilles. (FRE.). (gr. 3-8). 19.95 (ISBN 0-685-28445-X, M5497). French & Eur.

—Alice in Wonderland. 215p. 1981. Repr. PLB 15.95x (ISBN 0-89966-345-1). Buccaneer Bks.

—Alice in Wonderland. Tenniel, John, illus. 160p. (ps up). 1985. pap. 2.25 (ISBN 0-590-33960-5). Scholastic Inc.

—Alice in Wonderland. Tenniel, John, illus. 160p. (gr. 3-6). 1988. pap. 2.50 (ISBN 0-590-42035-6, Apple Classics). Scholastic Inc.

—Alice in Wonderland: A Classic Tale. Jose, Eduard, adapted by. Riehecky, Janet, tr. from SPA. Rovira, Francesc, illus. LC 88-35309. 32p. (gr. 1-4). 1988. PLB 10.95 (ISBN 0-89565-467-9). Childs World.

—Alice in Wonderland & Through the Looking Glass. Tenniel, John, illus. (gr. 4-6). 1946-63. 11.95 (ISBN 0-448-06004-3, G&D). Putnam Pub Group.

—Alice in Wonderland & Through the Looking Glass. Lewis, T., illus. 296p. 1988. pap. 7.95 (ISBN 0-8092-4488-8, Calico Bks). Contemp Bks.

—Alice's Adventures in Wonderland. Tenniel, John, illus. Bd. with Through the Looking Glass. LC 82-242973. (gr. 5 up). pap. 1.95 (ISBN 0-8049-0079-5, CL-79). Airmont.

—Alice's Adventures in Wonderland. Bd. with Through the Looking Glass. LC 82-242973. 315p. (gr. 4-6). 1962. pap. 2.95 (ISBN 0-02-042350-0, Collier Young Ad). Macmillan Child Grp.

—Alice's Adventures in Wonderland. Hall, David, illus. Sibley, Brian, afterword by. (Illus.). (ps up). 1986. pap. 14.95 (ISBN 0-671-63565-4, Little Simon). S&S Trade.

—Alice's Adventures in Wonderland. Hague, Michael, illus. LC 85-856. (ps up). 1985. 14.95 (ISBN 0-8050-0212-X). H Holt & Co.

—Alice's Adventures in Wonderland. Browne, Anthony, illus. LC 88-522. 128p. (ps up). 1988. 19.95 (ISBN 0-394-80592-5); lib. bdg. 19.99 (ISBN 0-394-90592-X). Knopf.

—Alice's Adventures in Wonderland & Through the Looking Glass. (RL 4). 1960. pap. 2.50 (ISBN 0-451-52320-2, Sig Classics). NAL-Dutton.

—Alice's Adventures in Wonderland & Through the Looking Glass. Tenniel, John, illus. Cohen, Morton N., intro. by. (Illus.). 256p. 1984. pap. 2.50 (ISBN 0-553-21345-8, Bantam Classics Spectra). Bantam.

—Alice's Adventures in Wonderland: The Ultimate Illustrated Edition. Edens, Cooper, compiled by. (ps up). 1989. 19.95 (ISBN 0-553-05385-X). Bantam.

—Alice's Adventures Underground. Carroll, Lewis, illus. Gardner, Martin. (Illus.). 128p. (gr. 4-9). 1965. pap. 2.95 (ISBN 0-486-21482-6). Dover.

—Aventures D'Alice au Pays des Merveilles. Bue, Henri, tr. from ENG. Tenniel, John, illus. Cohen, Morton N., intro. by. (FRE., Illus.). 196p. (gr. 4-8). 1972. pap. 4.95 (ISBN 0-486-22836-3). Dover.

—The Little Alice Editions: Alice's Adventures in Wonderland; Through the Looking-Glass. Tenniel, John, illus. 416p. (ps up). 1988. slipcased set 12.95 (ISBN 0-8037-0589-1). Dial Bks Young.

—Reader's Digest Best Loved Books for Young Readers: Alice's Adventures in Wonderland & Through the Looking Glass. Ogburn, Jackie, ed. Tenniel, John, illus. 192p. (gr. 4-12). 1989. 3.99 (ISBN 0-945260-21-0). Choice Pub NY.

—Through the Looking-Glass. Baker, Kyle, adapted by. 1990. pap. 3.75 (ISBN 0-425-12022-8, Pub. by Berkley-Pacer). Berkley Pub.

—Through the Looking Glass. Tenniel, John, illus. 224p. 1991. Repr. 14.95 (ISBN 0-312-80374-5). St Martin.

—Through the Looking-Glass & What Alice Found There (California-Pennyroyal Edition) Goodacres, Selwyn H. & Kincaid, James R.intro. by. Incl. Deluxe Edition. 198p. 225.00 (ISBN 0-520-05026-6). LC 83-47520. 198p. (gr. 8 up). 1983. 35.00 (ISBN 0-520-05039-8). U of Cal Pr.

Carroll, Lewis & Tenniel, Sir John. Alice's Adventures in Wonderland. LC 82-242973. (Illus.). (gr. 5 up). 1977. 9.95 (ISBN 0-312-01821-5). St Martin.

Carruth, Jane. My Giant Treasury of Fairy Tales. 1988. 9.98 (ISBN 0-671-09118-2). S&S Trade.

Carter, Angela, tr. Sleeping Beauty & Other Favourite Fairy Tales. Foreman, Michael, illus. LC 84-1451. 128p. (gr. 1-8). 1984. 12.95 (ISBN 0-8052-3921-9). Schocken.

Cauley, Lorinda B. The Ugly Duckling. Canley, Lorinda B., illus. LC 79-12340. 48p. (gr. k-3). 1979. pap. 4.95 (ISBN 0-15-692528-1, VoyB). HarBraceJ.

Cauley, Lorinda B., retold by. & illus. Jack & the Beanstalk. 32p. (gr. k-4). 1983. 12.95 (ISBN 0-399-20901-8, Putnam); pap. 5.95 (ISBN 0-399-20902-6, Putnam). Putnam Pub Group.

Cavanaugh, Kate. I Can't Sleep with Those Elves Watching Me. Kiner, K. C., illus. 24p. (ps-8). Date not set. pap. text ed. 4.95 (ISBN 0-9622353-1-8). KAC.

Chapman, Kim W. The Magic Hat. 2nd ed. LC 76-20842. (Illus.). 46p. (gr. k up). 1976. 5.95 (ISBN 0-914996-10-X). Lollipop Power.

Chardiet, Bernice. Rapunzel. 1990. pap. 2.50 (ISBN 0-590-42281-2). Scholastic Inc.

Chase, Richard. Jack Tales. (Illus.). 202p. (gr. 4-6). 1943. 13.95 (ISBN 0-395-06694-8). HM.

Le Chat Botte. (FRE., Illus.). (gr. 2). 3.50 (ISBN 0-7214-1280-7). Ladybird Bks.

Le Chat, le Chien, l'Ane et les Voleurs. (FRE., Illus.). (gr. 2). 3.50 (ISBN 0-7214-1286-6). Ladybird Bks.

Chicken Licken. (Illus.). 28p. (ps up). 1987. 3.95 (ISBN 0-7214-5029-6). Ladybird Bks.

Chicken Licken. (Illus.). (ps-4). 3.50 (ISBN 0-7214-0693-9). Ladybird Bks.

Children's Treasury: Traditional Fairy Tales. 1990. 7.98 (ISBN 0-8317-1363-1). Smithmark.

Chorao, Kay. Child's Fairy Tale Book. (ps-3). 1990. 14.95 (ISBN 0-525-44630-3, DCB). Dutton Child Bks.

Chwast, Seymour, illus. Bushy Bride: Norwegian Fairy Tale. LC 83-71174. 32p. (gr. 6 up). 1983. PLB 10. 95s.p. (ISBN 0-87191-952-4); 15.65 (ISBN 0-685-07720-9). Creative Ed.

Cincerelli, Carol J. The Tales of Hans Christian Andersen. 144p. (gr. 1-6). 1990. 10.95 (ISBN 0-86653-544-6, GA1159). Good Apple.

—The Tales of the Brothers Grimm. 144p. (gr. 1-6). 1990. 10.95 (ISBN 0-86653-562-4, GA1160). Good Apple.

Cinderella. (ps-3). 1979. pap. 3.95 (ISBN 0-448-09747-8, G&D). Putnam Pub Group.

Cinderella. (ARA., Illus.). (gr. 2-5). 3.50x (ISBN 0-86685-193-3). Intl Bk Ctr.

Cinderella. (Illus.). (ps-3). 1985. 1.98 (ISBN 0-517-28807-9). Outlet Bk Co.

Cinderella. (Illus.). (ps-1). 1.98 (ISBN 0-517-39461-8). Outlet Bk Co.

Cinderella. Date not set. 5.98 (ISBN 0-517-67010-0). Outlet Bk Co.

Cinderella. (Illus.). 20p. (ps-2). 1990. 5.95 (ISBN 0-8120-6168-3). Barron.

Cinderella. (ps-1). 1989. 2.99 (ISBN 0-517-69215-5). Outlet Bk Co.

Cinderella. (Illus.). (ps-2). 3.95 (ISBN 0-7214-5058-X). Ladybird Bks.

Cinderella. (Illus.). (gr. k-1). 3.50 (ISBN 0-7214-5125-X). Ladybird Bks.

Cinderella. (Illus.). (ps-4). 3.50 (ISBN 0-7214-0647-5). Ladybird Bks.

Clark, Joan. Thomasina & the Trout Tree. Hiscox, Ingeborg, illus. LC 72-179431. 40p. (gr. 2 up). 1971. 4.95 (ISBN 0-88776-018-X). Tundra Bks.

Cloke, Rene. Beauty & the Beast & Other Fairy Tales. 1991. 3.98 (ISBN 0-8317-4912-1). Smithmark.

—Cinderella And Other Fairy Tales. 1991. 3.98 (ISBN 0-8317-4915-6). Smithmark.

—Jack And the Beanstalk And Other Fairy Tales. 1991. 3.98 (ISBN 0-8317-4914-8). Smithmark.

—Red Riding Hood And Other Fairy Tales. 1991. 3.98 (ISBN 0-8317-4911-3). Smithmark.

—Sleeping Beauty And Other Fairy Tales. 1991. 3.98 (ISBN 0-8317-4913-X). Smithmark.

—Snow White And Other Fairy Tales. 1991. 3.98 (ISBN 0-8317-4910-5). Smithmark.

Coatsworth, Elizabeth. The Cat Who Went to Heaven. Ward, Lynd, illus. LC 58-10917. 72p. (gr. 4-6). 1967. 12.95 (ISBN 0-02-719710-7, Mcmillan Child Bk). Macmillan Child Grp.

Cohen, Lynn. Fairy Tale World. 64p. (ps-k). 1986. 6.95 (ISBN 0-912107-48-0). Monday Morning Bks.

Cole, Joanna. Mixed-Up Magic. Kelly, True, illus. 32p. (Orig.). (gr. k-3). 1987. pap. 2.50 (ISBN 0-590-40789-9). Scholastic Inc.

Collins, Meghan. The Willow Maiden. Gal, Laszlo, illus. LC 85-1533. 40p. (gr. k up). 1985. 11.95 (ISBN 0-8037-0217-5); PLB 11.89 (ISBN 0-8037-0218-3). Dial Bks Young.

Collodi, Carlo. The Adventures of Pinocchio. Spinner, Stephanie, adapted by. Goode, Diane, illus. 64p. (gr. k-3). 1983. 6.95 (ISBN 0-394-85910-3); lib. bdg. 8.99 (ISBN 0-394-95910-8). Random.

—The Adventures of Pinocchio. Wainwright, Francis, tr. & illus. LC 86-45047. 96p. (gr. 2-4). 1986. 16.95 (ISBN 0-8050-0027-5). H Holt & Co.

—Pinocchio. (FRE., Illus.). (gr. 3-8). 5.95 (ISBN 0-685-11495-3, S16273). French & Eur.

—Pinocchio: A Classic Tale. Jose, Eduard, adapted by. Moncure, Jane B., tr. from SPA. Asensio, Augusti, illus. LC 88-35308. 32p. 1988. PLB 10.95 (ISBN 0-89565-458-X). Childs World.

—Walt Disney's Pinocchio. Walt Disney Studios Staff, illus. 80p. 1989. 19.95 (ISBN 0-8109-1467-0). Abrams.

The Complete Brothers Grimm Fairy Tales. (gr. 2-6). 6.98 (ISBN 0-517-33631-6). Outlet Bk Co.

The Complete Hans Christian Andersen Fairy Tales. (gr. 2-6). 6.98 (ISBN 0-517-33632-4). Outlet Bk Co.

Cooney, Barbara. Snow White & Rose Red. (ps-3). 1991. PLB 14.99 (ISBN 0-385-30176-6); pap. 13.95. Delacorte.

Cooper, Susan, retold by. Tam Lin. Hutton, Warwick, illus. LC 90-5571. 32p. (gr. k-4). 1991. SBE 13.95 (ISBN 0-689-50505-1, M K McElderry). Macmillan Child Grp.

Le Cordonnier et les Lutins. (FRE., Illus.). (gr. 1). 3.50 (ISBN 0-7214-1273-4). Ladybird Bks.

Corrin, Sara & Corrin, Stephen, eds. The Faber Book of Favourite Fairy Tales. Wijngaard, Juan, illus. 160p. (gr. k-6). 1988. 18.95 (ISBN 0-571-14854-9). Faber & Faber.

—The Faber Book of Modern Fairy Tales. Strugnell, Ann, illus. 320p. (gr. 3 up). 1981. 15.95 (ISBN 0-571-11768-6). Faber & Faber.

—More Stories for Under-Fives. Julian-Ottie, Vanessa, illus. 116p. (ps). 1990. 11.95 (ISBN 0-571-15058-6); pap. 9.95 (ISBN 0-571-12921-8). Faber & Faber.

Courson, Diana. Let's Learn about Fairy Tales & Nursery Rhymes. 64p. (ps-2). 1988. wkbk. 6.95 (ISBN 0-86653-437-7, GA1040). Good Apple.

Craig, M. Jean. The Three Wishes. Salzman, Yuri, illus. 48p. (Orig.). (gr. k-3). 1986. pap. 2.50 (ISBN 0-590-41744-4). Scholastic Inc.

Croll, Carolyn, adapted by. & illus. The Little Snowgirl. 32p. (ps-k). 1989. 13.95 (ISBN 0-399-21691-X, Putnam). Putnam Pub Group.

Crump, Fred. Afrotina & the Three Bears: (A Retold Story) Crump, Fred, illus. LC 88-51222. 44p. (gr. k-2). Date not set. pap. 4.95 (ISBN 1-55523-195-0). Winston-Derek.

—Little Red Riding Hood: (A Retold Story) Crump, Fred, illus. LC 88-51219. 44p. (gr. k-2). 1989. pap. 4.95 (ISBN 1-55523-193-4). Winston-Derek.

—Mama Goose: A Retold Story. Crump, Fred, illus. LC 88-51224. 44p. (gr. k-2). 1989. pap. 4.95 (ISBN 1-55523-194-2). Winston-Derek.

—Thumblina: A Retold Story. Crump, Fred, illus. LC 88-51223. 44p. (gr. k-2). 1989. pap. 4.95 (ISBN 1-55523-191-8). Winston-Derek.

Crump, Fred, Jr. Beauty & the Beast. Crump, Fred, Jr., illus. 44p. (gr. k-2). 1991. pap. 4.95 (ISBN 1-55523-379-1). Winston-Derek.

—McGambo & the Tiger. Crump, Fred, Jr., illus. 44p. (gr. k-2). 1991. pap. 4.95 (ISBN 1-55523-410-0). Winston-Derek.

—Rapunzel. Crump, Fred, Jr., illus. 272p. (gr. k-2). 1991. pap. 4.95 (ISBN 1-55523-408-9). Winston-Derek.

Cummings, e. e. Fairy Tales. Eaton, John, illus. LC 65-18727. 48p. (ps-3). 1975. pap. 3.95 (ISBN 0-15-629895-3, VoyB). HarBraceJ.

Cutburth, Ronald W. Love from the Sea. Naumann, Cynthia E., ed. Percels, Beth, illus. 27p. (Orig.). (gr. 4-7). 1990. pap. 3.50 (ISBN 1-878291-01-7). Love From Sea.

Cutts, David, retold by. Gingerbread Boy. Goodman, Joan E., illus. LC 78-18069. 32p. (gr. k-2). 1979. PLB 9.79 (ISBN 0-89375-122-7); pap. 1.95 (ISBN 0-89375-100-6). Troll Assocs.

Dahl, Roald. James & the Giant Peach. Burkert, Nancy E., illus. (gr. 3 up). 1962. 17.95 (ISBN 0-394-81282-4); lib. bdg. 17.99 (ISBN 0-394-91282-9). Knopf.

—Magic Finger. Pene DuBois, William, illus. LC 66-18657. 46p. (gr. 3-6). 1966. 13.95 (ISBN 0-06-021381-7); PLB 13.89 (ISBN 0-06-021382-5). HarpC Child Bks.

Daniels, Patricia. Aladdin & the Magic Lamp. LC 79-27304. (Illus.). 24p. (gr. k-5). 1980. PLB 13.31 (ISBN 0-8393-0257-6). Raintree Pubs.

—Aladdin & the Magic Lamp. LC 79-27304. (Illus.). 24p. (gr. k-5). 1981. PLB 27.99 incl. cassette (ISBN 0-8172-1832-7); cassette 14.00 (ISBN 0-685-09552-5). Raintree Pubs.

—Ali Baba & the Forty Thieves. LC 79-27042. (Illus.). (gr. k-5). 1981. PLB 27.99 with cassette (ISBN 0-8172-1837-8); PLB 13.31 (ISBN 0-685-09553-3); cassette 14.00. Raintree Pubs.

—Beauty & the Beast. Large, Annabel, illus. LC 79-28433. 24p. (gr. k-5). 1980. PLB 13.31 (ISBN 0-8393-0258-4). Raintree Pubs.

—Beauty & the Beast. LC 79-28433. (Illus.). 24p. (gr. k-5). 1981. PLB 27.99 incl. cassette (ISBN 0-8172-1833-5); cassette 14.00 (ISBN 0-685-09554-1). Raintree Pubs.

—Cinderella. Read, Maggie, illus. LC 79-28526. 24p. (gr. k-5). 1980. PLB 27.99 incl. cassette (ISBN 0-8172-1834-3); PLB 13.31 (ISBN 0-8393-0253-3); cassette 14.00 (ISBN 0-685-04209-X). Raintree Pubs.

—Rumpelstiltskin. Nightingale, Sandy, illus. LC 79-27140. 24p. (gr. k-5). 1980. PLB 13.31 (ISBN 0-8393-0252-5). Raintree Pubs.

—Rumpelstiltskin. LC 79-27140. (Illus.). 24p. (gr. k-5). 1981. PLB 27.99 incl. cassette (ISBN 0-8172-1831-9); cassette 14.00 (ISBN 0-685-09555-X). Raintree Pubs.

—Sinbad the Sailor. Webb, Roger, illus. LC 79-28588. 24p. (gr. k-5). 1980. PLB 13.31 (ISBN 0-8393-0256-8). Raintree Pubs.

—Sinbad the Sailor. LC 79-28588. (Illus.). 24p. (gr. k-5). 1980. PLB 27.99 incl. cassette (ISBN 0-8172-1835-1). Raintree Pubs.

—Sleeping Beauty. Tarrant, Carol, illus. LC 79-26974. 24p. (gr. k-5). 1980. PLB 13.31 (ISBN 0-8393-0254-1). Raintree Pubs.

—Sleeping Beauty. LC 79-26974. (Illus.). 24p. (gr. k-5). 1980. PLB 27.99 incl. cassette (ISBN 0-8172-1838-6); cassette 14.00 (ISBN 0-685-09556-8). Raintree Pubs.

—Snow White & the Dwarfs. Spalding, Tony, illus. LC 79-28431. 24p. (gr. k-5). 1980. PLB 13.31 (ISBN 0-8393-0251-7). Raintree Pubs.

—Snow White & the Dwarfs. LC 79-28431. (Illus.). 24p. (gr. k-5). 1980. PLB 27.99 (ISBN 0-8172-1836-X); cassette 14.00 (ISBN 0-685-09557-6). Raintree Pubs.

Dasent, George W. East o' the Sun & West o' the Moon. LC 70-97214. (Illus.). xv, 418p. (gr. 1 up). 1970. pap. 8.95 (ISBN 0-486-22521-6). Dover.

David, Alfred & Meek, Mary E. The Twelve Dancing Princesses & Other Fairy Tales. LC 73-16517. (Illus.). 320p. (gr. 1-6). 1974. pap. 10.95x (ISBN 0-253-20173-X). Ind U Pr.

Dawood, N. J. Aladdin: And Other Tales from the Arabian Nights. 176p. (gr. 4 up). 1990. pap. 2.25 (ISBN 0-14-035105-1, Puffin). Puffin Bks.

De Paola, Tomie. Helga's Dowry. De Paola, Tomie, illus. LC 76-54953. 32p. (ps-3). 1977. pap. 3.95 (ISBN 0-15-640010-3, VoyB). HarBraceJ.

—The Story of the Three Wise Kings. LC 83-4609. (Illus.). (ps-5). 1983. 13.95 (ISBN 0-399-20998-0, Putnam); pap. 5.95 (ISBN 0-399-20999-9). Putnam Pub Group.

De Paola, Tomie, illus. Tomie dePaola's Mother Goose. LC 84-26314. 127p. (ps-2). 1985. 17.95 (ISBN 0-399-21258-2, Putnam). Putnam Pub Group.

De Regniers, Beatrice S. Jack & the Beanstalk. Wilsdorf, Anne, illus. LC 89-18663. 48p. (ps-2). 1990. pap. 4.95 (ISBN 0-689-71421-1, Aladdin). Macmillan Child Grp.

—Red Riding Hood. LC 89-38024. 48p. (gr. k-3). 1990. pap. 4.95 (ISBN 0-689-71373-8, Aladdin). Macmillan Child Grp.

Diamantes, Kitty, illus. Favorite Tales from Grimm. 96p. (gr. 3 up). 1988. 9.95 (ISBN 0-02-689060-7). Checkerboard Pr.

Dick Whittington. (ARA., Illus.). (gr. 4-12). 3.50x (ISBN 0-86685-196-8). Intl Bk Ctr.

Disney, Walt. Snow White & the Seven Dwarfs. (gr. 2 up). 1979. pap. 0.95 (ISBN 0-448-15923-6, G&D). Putnam Pub Group.

Disney, Walt, Productions Staff. The Book of Tall Tales: Featuring "The Shaggy Dog" LC 77-74466. (Illus.). (gr. 2-6). 1978. (Random Juv); lib. bdg. 4.99 (ISBN 0-394-93596-9). Random.

—Walt Disney's Cinderella. LC 74-22325. (Illus.). 48p. (ps-3). 1974. 6.95 (ISBN 0-394-82552-7, Random Juv); lib. bdg. 4.99 (ISBN 0-394-92552-1). Random.

—Walt Disney's Peter & the Wolf. LC 74-6423. (Illus.). 48p. (ps-3). 1974. (Random Juv); lib. bdg. 5.99 (ISBN 0-394-92563-7). Random.

—Walt Disney's Snow White & the Seven Dwarfs. (Illus.). (ps-3). 1973. 6.95 (ISBN 0-394-82625-6, Random Juv); lib. bdg. 5.99 (ISBN 0-394-92625-0). Random.

Dixon, Peter W., intro. by. Great Tales of Old. LC 87-83338. (Illus.). 312p. (gr. k-3). 1988. text ed. 15.95 (ISBN 0-945161-01-8); pap. 9.95 (ISBN 0-945161-00-X). Lantern Bks.

Dodge, Mary M. Hans Brinker. (gr. k-6). 1985. pap. 4.95 (ISBN 0-440-43446-7, Pub. by Yearling Classics). Dell.

Dodson, Bert, illus. Lazy Jack. LC 78-18070. 32p. (gr. k-4). 1979. PLB 9.79 (ISBN 0-89375-123-5); pap. 1.95 (ISBN 0-89375-101-4). Troll Assocs.

Dolan, Ellen M. & Bolinske, Janet L., eds. Aladdin & the Magic Lamp. Lie, Eula, illus. LC 87-61661. 32p. (Orig.). (gr. 1-3). 1987. text ed. 8.95 (ISBN 0-88335-564-7); pap. text ed. 4.95 (ISBN 0-88335-584-1). Milliken Pub Co.

Les Douze Princesses. (FRE., Illus.). (gr. 1). 3.50 (ISBN 0-7214-1278-5). Ladybird Bks.

Dreizler, Loch A. Princess Pickle Head. Mallord, Lauri, illus. LC 88-80123. 42p. (Orig.). (ps-4). 1988. pap. 2.95 (ISBN 0-9620053-0-4). LAD Redondo Beach.

Dunster, Mark. Marsh King. 10p. (Orig.). 1990. pap. 4.00 (ISBN 0-89642-184-8). Linden Pubs.

—Zond. 45p. (Orig.). 1989. pap. 5.00 (ISBN 0-89642-168-6). Linden Pubs.

Eastman, David. Peter & the Wolf. Atkinson, Allen, illus. LC 87-11275. 32p. (gr. k-3). 1988. PLB 9.79 (ISBN 0-8167-1057-0); pap. text ed. 1.95 (ISBN 0-8167-1058-9). Troll Assocs.

Edelman, Heinz, illus. Prince Ring: Icelandic Fairy Tale. 32p. (gr. 6 up). 1983. PLB 10.95s.p. (ISBN 0-87191-951-6); PLB 15.65 (ISBN 0-685-07719-5). Creative Ed.

Edens, Cooper, ed. & intro. by. Beauty & the Beast. abr. ed. LC 88-81988. (Illus.). 1989. 14.95 (ISBN 0-88138-115-2). Green Tiger Pr.

Ehrlich, Amy. Pome & Peel. Gal, Laszlo, illus. (ps-3). 1990. 11.95 (ISBN 0-8037-0287-6); PLB 11.89 (ISBN 0-8037-0288-4). Dial Bks Young.

—Rapunzel. Waldherr, Kris, illus. LC 88-25918. 32p. (ps-3). 1989. 12.95 (ISBN 0-8037-0654-5); PLB 12.89 (ISBN 0-8037-0655-3). Dial Bks Young.

Ehrlich, Amy, adapted by. The Random House Book of Fairy Tales. Goode, Diane, illus. LC 83-13833. 224p. (gr. k-4). 1985. bds. 17.00 (ISBN 0-394-85693-7, Random Juv); lib. bdg. 17.99 (ISBN 0-394-95693-1, Random Juv). Random.

Eisen, Armand. Little Red Riding Hood. Ferris, Lynn B., illus. LC 87-46241. 24p. 1988. 9.95 (ISBN 0-394-55883-9). Knopf.

Elves & the Shoemaker. (ARA., Illus.). (gr. 3-5). 3.50x (ISBN 0-86685-199-2); incl. cassette 12.00x (ISBN 0-685-02571-3). Intl Bk Ctr.

Elves & the Shoemaker. (Illus.). (ps-k). 3.50 (ISBN 0-7214-5132-2). Ladybird Bks.

The Elves & the Shoemaker. (Illus.). (ps-4). 3.50 (ISBN 0-7214-1199-1). Ladybird Bks.

Elwell, Peter. Cinderella. Elwell, Peter, illus. 32p. 1988. 12.95 (ISBN 0-8092-4484-5, Calico Bks). Contemp Bks.

L' Empereur et le Rossignol. (FRE., Illus.). (gr. 2). 3.50 (ISBN 0-7214-1283-1). Ladybird Bks.

The Emperor & the Nightingale. (Illus.). (ps-4). 3.50 (ISBN 0-7214-1054-5). Ladybird Bks.

The Emperor's New Clothes. (Illus.). (ps-4). 3.50 (ISBN 0-7214-5006-7). Ladybird Bks.

The Enormous Turnip. (ARA., Illus.). (gr. 3-5). 3.50x (ISBN 0-86685-200-X). Intl Bk Ctr.

The Enormous Turnip. (Illus.). (ps-k). 3.50 (ISBN 0-7214-5129-2). Ladybird Bks.

The Enormous Turnip. (Illus.). (ps-4). 3.50 (ISBN 0-7214-0731-5). Ladybird Bks.

Enright, Elizabeth. Tatsinda. Johnston, Allyn, ed. Treherne, Katie T., illus. 72p. (gr. k-5). 1991. 16.95 (ISBN 0-15-284280-2). HarBraceJ.

Erben, Karel J. Listen, Kids... Czech Fairy Tales. Ciuffreda, Lillian, ed. Kalnoky, Julius, tr. Jelinek, Otakar, illus. LC 87-83652. 65p. (gr. 3-8). 1988. 13.95 (ISBN 0-9619982-0-2). Kalnoky Pr.

Erickson, Jon. The Steadfast Tin Soldier. Mogensen, Jan, illus. LC 87-42582. 32p. (gr. 2-4). 1987. PLB 10.95 (ISBN 1-55532-320-0). Gareth Stevens Inc.

—The Top & the Ball. Mogensen, Jan, illus. LC 87-42584. 32p. (gr. 2-4). 1987. PLB 10.95 (ISBN 1-55532-318-9). Gareth Stevens Inc.

—The Woman with the Eggs. Mogensen, Jan, illus. LC 87-42583. 32p. (gr. 2-4). 1987. PLB 10.95 (ISBN 1-55532-319-7). Gareth Stevens Inc.

Evans, Eugene. Bremen Town Musicians. Boddy, Joe & Boddy, Joe, illus. LC 90-10974. 48p. (gr. 1-5). 1990. 5.95 (ISBN 0-88101-102-9). Unicorn Pub.

Fairy Tales Clippers. (Illus.). (gr. k-5). 1989. Complete Package: 8 clippers. PLB 223.92 (ISBN 0-8172-1830-0). Raintree Pubs.

Fairy Tales from Many Lands. Date not set. 9.98 (ISBN 0-517-67951-5). Outlet Bk Co.

Faulkner, Matt. Jack & the Beanstalk. (Illus.). 48p. (Orig.). (gr. k-3). 1986. pap. 2.50 (ISBN 0-590-40164-5). Scholastic Inc.

Faulkner, William. Wishing Tree. (Illus.). (gr. 4 up). 1967. 8.95 (ISBN 0-394-45222-4). Random.

Favorite Tales of Hans Christian Andersen. 96p. (gr. 2 up). 1988. 9.95 (ISBN 0-02-688550-6). Checkerboard Pr.

Ferris, Lynn B., retold by. & illus. Goldilocks & the Three Bears. LC 86-46154. 24p. (gr. k up). 1987. 9.95 (ISBN 0-394-55882-0). Knopf.

Field, Eugene. Wynken, Blyken & Nod. 1989. pap. 2.95 (ISBN 0-590-42422-X). Scholastic Inc.

—Wynken, Blynken, & Nod. Beckett, Sheilah, illus. 18p. (ps). 1986. 3.95 (ISBN 0-448-10225-0, G&D). Putnam Pub Group.

—Wynken, Blynken & Nod. Berg, Ron, illus. 24p. (gr. k-3). Big Book. 19.50 (ISBN 0-317-69655-6); pap. 2.50 (ISBN 0-590-71589-5). Scholastic Inc.

Finger, Charles J. Tales from Silver Lands. Honore, Paul, illus. 225p. (gr. 7 up). 1965. 16.95 (ISBN 0-685-01496-7). Doubleday.

The Firebird. (Illus.). (ps-4). 3.50 (ISBN 0-7214-0848-6). Ladybird Bks.

Five Famous Fairy Tales. (gr. 4 up). 1988. pap. 4.87 (ISBN 0-582-54147-6, 74256). Longman.

Foreman, Michael. Fairy Tales. large type ed. Foreman, Michael, illus. 200p. (gr. 3-8). 1989. Repr. of 1981 ed. PLB 14.95 (ISBN 1-85089-975-4, Pub. by Clio Pr England). ABC-CLIO.

Fowler, Richard. Ted & Dolly Fairytale Flight. (Illus.). 24p. (ps-3). 1984. 9.95 (ISBN 0-88110-190-7). EDC.

—Ted & Dolly's Magic Carpet Ride. 24p. (ps-1). 1984. 9.95 (ISBN 0-88110-155-9). EDC.

The Fox & the Hound. Date not set. 5.98 (ISBN 0-517-67007-0). Outlet Bk Co.

Fuentes, Vilma M. The Fairy of Masara. Inis, Ninabeth R., illus. 24p. (Orig.). (gr. k-3). 1984. pap. 3.50 (ISBN 971-10-0211-6, Pub by New Day Philippines). Cellar.

Fujikawa, Gyo. Fairy Tales. (Illus.). 24p. (ps-3). 1980. pap. 1.25 (ISBN 0-448-49615-1, G&D). Putnam Pub Group.

Fujikawa, Gyo, illus. Fairy Tales & Fables. (gr. k-3). 1970. 9.95 (ISBN 0-448-02814-X, G&D). Putnam Pub Group.

Fujita, Miho. Princess And the Pea-Board Book. 1991. 3.98 (ISBN 0-8317-3122-2). Smithmark.

Gackenbach, Dick, retold by. & illus. The Princess & the Pea. 32p. (ps-3). 1986. pap. 3.95 (ISBN 0-14-050571-7, Puffin). Puffin Bks.

Gag, Wanda. Snow White & the Seven Dwarfs. Gag, Wanda, illus. (gr. 2-4). 1938. PLB 6.99 (ISBN 0-698-30320-2, Coward). Putnam Pub Group.

Gag, Wanda & Tomes, Margot. The Sorcerer's Apprentice. LC 78-23990. (Illus.). (gr. k-3). 1979. 6.95 (ISBN 0-698-20481-6, Coward). Putnam Pub Group.

Galdone, Paul. Henny Penny. Galdone, Paul, illus. LC 68-24735. 32p. (ps-2). 1979. 13.95 (ISBN 0-395-28800-2, Clarion). HM.

—Rumpelstiltskin. Galdone, Paul, illus. LC 84-12741. 32p. (ps-3). 1985. 13.95 (ISBN 0-89919-266-1, Clarion). HM.

Galdone, Paul, illus. Little Red Riding Hood. LC 74-6426. 32p. (gr. k-3). 1974. text ed. 14.95 (ISBN 0-07-022732-2). McGraw.

Gardner, Richard A. Dr. Gardner's Fairy Tales for Today's Children. Lowenheim, Alfred, illus. LC 80-16187. 96p. (gr. 1-6). 1978. Repr. of 1974 ed. PLB 14.95 (ISBN 0-933812-02-7). Creative Therapeutics.

—Dr. Gardner's Modern Fairy Tales. Lowenheim, Al, illus. LC 83-40149. 106p. (gr. 2-6). Repr. 14.95 (ISBN 0-933812-09-4). Creative Therapeutics.

Geis, Darlene, ed. Walt Disney's Treasury of Children's Classics. (Illus.). (gr. 5 up). 1978. 29.95 (ISBN 0-8109-0812-3). Abrams.

Gerstein, Mordicai, retold by. & illus. Beauty & the Beast. 48p. (ps-2). 1989. 12.95 (ISBN 0-525-44510-2, DCB); bk. & cassette 17.95 (ISBN 0-525-44511-0). Dutton Child Bks.

Gikow, Louise, retold by. Muppet Babies Classic Children's Tales. (Illus.). 32p. 1990. 14.95 (ISBN 0-88363-690-5). H L Levin.

Gilleo, Alma, ed. The Elves & the Shoemaker. Laite, Gordon, illus. LC 65-2642. (gr. 1-3). 1977. pap. 29.95 6 bks. & 1 cass. (ISBN 0-89290-013-X); pap. 10.95 1 bk. & 1 cass. (ISBN 0-685-04640-0). Soc for Visual.

—The Four Servants. Don Robison, Don, illus. LC 74-734828. 16p. 1976. pap. 29.95 6 bks. & 1 cass. (ISBN 0-89290-009-1); pap. 10.95 1 bk. & 1 cass. (ISBN 0-685-04641-9). Soc for Visual.

—The Golden Buttons, 6 bks. Sharp, Gene, illus. LC 74-734827. 16p. (ps). 1976. pap. 29.95 6 bks. & 1 cass. (ISBN 0-89290-008-3); pap. 10.95 1 bk. & 1 cass. (ISBN 0-685-70098-4). Soc for Visual.

—The Goose-Girl. Biegel, Cecilia, illus. LC 74-734823. 16p. (gr. 1-3). 1976. Set. 6 bks. & 1 cass. 29.95 (ISBN 0-89290-005-9); 1 bk. & 1 cass. 10.95 (ISBN 0-685-04647-8). Soc for Visual.

—Hans Clodhopper. Hamblin, George, illus. LC 76-730154. (gr. 1-3). 1976. Set. 6 bks. & 1 cass. 29.95 (ISBN 0-89290-002-4); 1 bk. & 1 cass. 10.95 (ISBN 0-685-04649-4). Soc for Visual.

—King Grisly-Beard. Stasiak, Krystyna, illus. LC 74-734822. 16p. (gr. 1-3). 1976. 6 bks. & 1 cass. 29.95 (ISBN 0-89290-004-0); 1 bk. & 1 cass. 10.95 (ISBN 0-685-04655-9). Soc for Visual.

—The Little Mermaid, 6 bks. Shelton, Harley, illus. LC 76-730155. (gr. 1-3). 1976. 6 bks. & 1 cass. 29.95 (ISBN 0-89290-003-2); 1 bk. & 1 cass. 10.95 (ISBN 0-685-70093-3). Soc for Visual.

—The Water of Life. Robertson, Robert, illus. LC 74-734825. 1976. Set. 6 bks. & 1 cass. 29.95 (ISBN 0-89290-006-7); 1 bk. & 1 cass. 10.95. Soc for Visual.

—The Wild Swans, 6 bks. Stasiak, Krystyna, illus. LC 76-730152. (gr. k-3). 1976. 6 bks. & 1 cass. 29.95 (ISBN 0-89290-000-8); 1 bk. & 1 cass. 10.95. Soc for Visual.

The Gingerbread Boy. (Illus.). (ps-4). 3.50 (ISBN 0-7214-5012-1). Ladybird Bks.

The Gingerbread Man. (Illus.). 28p. (ps up). 1987. 3.95 (ISBN 0-7214-5030-X). Ladybird Bks.

Gingerbread Man. (Illus.). (gr. k-1). 3.50 (ISBN 0-7214-5168-3). Ladybird Bks.

Gipson, Morrell. Rip Van Winkle. San Souci, Daniel, illus. LC 83-20624. 32p. (gr. k-3). 1987. pap. 4.95 (ISBN 0-385-23965-3, Pub. by Zephyr-BFYR). Doubleday.

Goldberg, Moses. Rumpelstiltskin: A Participation Play. (gr. k-3). 1987. pap. 4.50 playscript (ISBN 0-87602-269-7). Anchorage.

Golden Foot. (Illus.). (gr. 1-6). 1984. pap. 5.95 (ISBN 0-913546-67-4). Dharma Pub.

The Golden Goose. (Illus.). (ps-4). 3.50 (ISBN 0-7214-0626-2). Ladybird Bks.

Goldilocks. (Illus.). (ps-3). 1985. 2.98 (ISBN 0-517-28808-7). Outlet Bk Co.

Goldilocks. (Illus.). (ps-1). 2.49 (ISBN 0-517-39462-6). Outlet Bk Co.

Goldilocks & the Three Bears. 2nd ed. 44p. (ps-2). 1980. pap. 5.50 (ISBN 0-913580-06-6, Pub. by K Green Pubns). Gallaudet Univ Pr.

Goldilocks & the Three Bears. (Illus.). 18p. (ps-1). 1979. 3.95 (ISBN 0-448-09748-6, G&D). Putnam Pub Group.

Goldilocks & the Three Bears. (ARA., Illus.). (gr. 1-5). 3.50x (ISBN 0-685-82827-1). Intl Bk Ctr.

Goldilocks & the Three Bears. (Illus.). 20p. (ps-2). 1990. 5.95 (ISBN 0-8120-6165-9). Barron.

Goldilocks & the Three Bears. (Illus.). (ps-1). 1989. 2.98 (ISBN 0-517-69217-1). Outlet Bk Co.

Goldilocks & the Three Bears. (Illus.). (ps-2). 3.95 (ISBN 0-7214-5060-1). Ladybird Bks.

Goldilocks & the Three Bears. (Illus.). (ps-k). 3.50 (ISBN 0-7214-5086-5). Ladybird Bks.

Goldilocks & the Three Bears. (Illus.). (ps-4). 3.50 (ISBN 0-7214-1173-8). Ladybird Bks.

Gooc, Van. Goldilocks & Three Bears. 1989. 4.99 (ISBN 0-517-69318-6). Outlet Bk Co.

Goodall, John S. Puss in Boots. Goodall, John S., illus. LC 90-38606. 56p. (ps-3). 1990. 14.95 (ISBN 0-689-50521-3, M K McElderry). Macmillan Child Grp.

Goodnight Stories. (Illus.). 58p. (ps up). 1987. 8.95 (ISBN 0-7214-5034-2). Ladybird Bks.

Gool, Van. Emperor's New Clothes. 1989. 4.99 (ISBN 0-517-69316-X). Outlet Bk Co.

—Puss in Boots. 1989. 4.99 (ISBN 0-517-69319-4). Outlet Bk Co.

The Goose Girl. (Illus.). (ps-4). 3.50 (ISBN 0-7214-0764-1). Ladybird Bks.

Grahame, Kenneth. Reluctant Dragon. Shepard, Ernest H., illus. 58p. (gr. 3-6). 1953. 8.95 (ISBN 0-8234-0093-X); pap. 4.95 (ISBN 0-8234-0755-1). Holiday.

—Wind in the Willows. (gr. 4 up). pap. 2.75 (ISBN 0-8049-0105-8, CL-105). Airmont.

—Wind in the Willows. 234p. 1981. Repr. lib. bdg. 14.95x (ISBN 0-89966-305-2). Buccaneer Bks.

—The Wind in the Willows. Green, Peter, ed. (gr. 5 up). 1983. pap. 2.95 (ISBN 0-19-281640-3). Oxford U Pr.

—Wind in the Willows, Vol. 1. 1972. 12.95 (ISBN 0-684-12819-5, Scribners Young Read). Macmillan Child Grp.

Greaves, Margaret. Tattercoats. Chamberlain, Margaret, illus. LC 90-6919. 32p. (ps-2). 1990. 13.95 (ISBN 0-517-58026-8); PLB 14.99 (ISBN 0-517-58027-6). Crown.

Greer, Blanche. The Black Swan & the Green See Saw. Sarnoff, Arthur, illus. LC 75-261399. (gr. 5 up). 1977. 3.95 (ISBN 0-930422-07-4). Dennis-Landman.

Grimm, Jacob. The Shoemaker & the Elves. Adams, Adrienne, illus. Grimm, Wilhelm K. LC 60-12607. (Illus.). 32p. (ps-3). 1972. 12.95 (ISBN 0-684-12982-5, Scribners Young Read). Macmillan Child Grp.

—Snow White & Red Rose. 1988. 13.95 (ISBN 0-8050-0738-5). H Holt & Co.

Grimm, Jacob & Grimm, Wilhelm K. About Wise Men & Simpletons: Twelve Tales from Grimm. Shub, Elizabeth, tr. Hogrogian, Nonny, illus. LC 85-15330. 128p. (gr. 3-7). 1986. 13.95 (ISBN 0-02-737450-5, Mcmillan Child Bk). Macmillan Child Grp.

—The Bear & the Kingbird. Segal, Lore, tr. from GER. Conover, Chris, illus. LC 79-118605. 32p. (ps up). 1979. 12.95 (ISBN 0-374-30618-4). FS&G.

—Brave Little Tailor. Corcoran, Mark, illus. LC 78-18075. 32p. (gr. 1-4). 1979. PLB 9.79 (ISBN 0-89375-137-5); pap. 1.95 (ISBN 0-89375-115-4). Troll Assocs.

—Bremen Town Musicians. Ford, Pamela B., illus. LC 78-18064. 32p. (gr. k-4). 1979. PLB 9.79 (ISBN 0-89375-133-2); pap. 1.95 (ISBN 0-89375-111-1). Troll Assocs.

—Children's Classics: Grimm's Fairy Tales. 1989. 5.98 (ISBN 0-671-08756-8). S&S Trade.

—The Classic Grimm's Fairy Tales. Eisen, Armand, ed. LC 89-43005. (Illus.). 56p. (gr. 1-8). 1989. 9.98 (ISBN 0-89471-768-5, Courage Bks). Running Pr.

—The Complete Grimm's Fairy Tales. Scharl, Josef, illus. Stern, James, ed. LC 44-40373. (Illus.). 1976. pap. 14.95 (ISBN 0-394-70930-6). Pantheon.

—The Devil with the Three Golden Hairs. Hogrogian, Nonny, illus. LC 82-12735. 40p. (gr. k-3). 1983. 10.95 (ISBN 0-394-85560-4); lib. bdg. 10.99 (ISBN 0-394-95560-9). Knopf.

—The Elves & the Shoemaker. LC 80-27634. (Illus.). 32p. (gr. k-3). 1981. PLB 9.79 (ISBN 0-89375-472-2); pap. text ed. 1.95 (ISBN 0-89375-473-0). Troll Assocs.

—The Falling Stars. Sopko, Eugene, illus. LC 85-7193. 32p. (gr. k-3). 1985. 10.95 (ISBN 0-8050-0173-5). H Holt & Co.

—The Fisherman & His Wife. Jarrell, Randall, tr. from GER. Zemach, Margot, illus. LC 79-3248. 32p. (ps-3). 1980. 13.95 (ISBN 0-374-32340-2). FS&G.

—The Fisherman & His Wife. Howe, John, illus. 32p. (gr. 6 up). 1983. PLB 10.95s.p. (ISBN 0-87191-937-0); 15.65 (ISBN 0-685-07705-5). Creative Ed.

—The Fisherman & His Wife. Jarrell, Randall, tr. from GER. Zemach, Margot, illus. 32p. (ps up). 1987. pap. 4.95 (ISBN 0-374-42326-1). FS&G.

—The Fisherman & His Wife. Richardson, I. M., ed. Lippincott, Gary, illus. LC 87-10902. 32p. (gr. k-4). 1988. PLB 9.79 (ISBN 0-8167-1075-9); pap. text ed. 1.95 (ISBN 0-8167-1076-7). Troll Assocs.

—Fitcher's Bird. Arisman, Marshall, illus. 32p. (gr. 9 up). 1983. PLB 10.95s.p. (ISBN 0-87191-942-7); 15.65 (ISBN 0-685-07710-1). Creative Ed.

—Frog Prince. Baxter, Robert, illus. LC 78-18073. 32p. (gr. k-4). 1979. PLB 9.79 (ISBN 0-89375-126-X); pap. 1.95 (ISBN 0-89375-104-9). Troll Assocs.

—The Frog Prince. Alchemy II, Inc. Staff, illus. 26p. (ps). 1988. incl. cassette 9.95 (ISBN 1-55578-900-5). Worlds Wonder.

—The Frog Prince. Lewis, Naomi, tr. from GER. Schroeder, Binette, illus. LC 89-42613. (GER.). 32p. (gr. k-3). 1989. 14.95 (ISBN 1-55858-015-8). North-South Bks NYC.

—The Golden Goose. Paterson, Diane, illus. LC 80-29207. 32p. (gr. k-3). 1981. PLB 9.79 (ISBN 0-89375-476-5); pap. 1.95 (ISBN 0-89375-477-3). Troll Assocs.

—The Goose Girl. Perret, Paul, illus. 32p. (gr. 4 up). 1984. PLB 10.95s.p. (ISBN 0-87191-934-6); 15.65 (ISBN 0-685-07702-0). Creative Ed.

—Grimms' Fairy Tales. Gotlieb, Jules, illus. (gr. 3 up). pap. 2.50 (ISBN 0-8049-0168-6, CL-168). Airmont.

—Grimms' Fairy Tales. (Illus.). 1981. 7.95 (ISBN 0-448-11009-1, G&D); deluxe ed. 13.95 (ISBN 0-448-06009-4, G&D). Putnam Pub Group.

—Grimm's Fairy Tales. Barish, Wendy, ed. Atkinson, Allen, illus. 304p. 1982. 15.95 (ISBN 0-671-43792-5, Little Simon). S&S Trade.

—Grimm's Fairy Tales. Carter, Peter, ed. & tr. Richardson, Peter, illus. 238p. (ps-6). 1987. 18.95 (ISBN 0-19-274529-8). Oxford U Pr.

—Grimm's Tales for Young & Old: The Complete Stories. Manheim, Ralph, tr. LC 76-56318. 648p. (gr. k-12). 1983. 14.95 (ISBN 0-385-11005-7); pap. 15.95 (ISBN 0-385-18950-8). Doubleday.

—Hansel & Gretel. Jeffers, Susan, illus. LC 80-15079. 32p. (gr. k up). 1980. 14.95 (ISBN 0-8037-3492-1); PLB 14.89 (ISBN 0-8037-3491-3). Dial Bks Young.

—Hansel & Gretel. Felix, Monique, illus. 32p. (gr. 6 up). 1983. PLB 10.95s.p. (ISBN 0-87191-935-4); 15.65 (ISBN 0-685-07703-9). Creative Ed.

—Hansel & Gretel. LC 85-6286. (Illus.). 32p. (gr. k-3). 1985. 11.95 (ISBN 0-13-383654-1). P-H.

—Hansel & Gretel. Browne, Anthony, illus. LC 87-25993. 32p. (ps-3). 1988. pap. 3.95 (ISBN 0-394-89859-1). Knopf.

—Hansel & Gretel. Zwerger, Lisbeth, illus. 32p. (ps-2). 1991. pap. 3.95 (ISBN 0-590-44459-X, Blue Ribbon Bks). Scholastic Inc.

—Household Stories of the Brothers Grimm. Crane, Lucy, tr. Crane, Walter, illus. x, 269p. (gr. 3-9). 1886. pap. 4.95 (ISBN 0-486-21080-4). Dover.

—Household Tales. Peake, Mervyn, illus. Hoban, Russell, intro. by. LC 79-64122. (Illus.). (gr. 3-9). 1987. Schocken.

—Jorinda & Joringel. Cutts, David, ed. Rickman, David, illus. LC 87-10937. 32p. (gr. k-4). 1988. PLB 9.79 (ISBN 0-8167-1065-1); pap. text ed. 1.95 (ISBN 0-8167-1066-X). Troll Assocs.

—The Juniper Tree: And Other Tales from Grimm, 2 vols. Segal, Lore & Jarrell, Randall, trs. from GER. Sendak, Maurice, illus. LC 73-82698. 332p. (ps up). 1973. Boxed Set. 25.00 (ISBN 0-374-18057-1); (Sunburst). FS&G.

—King Grisly-Beard. Sendak, Maurice, illus. Taylor, Edgar, tr. from GER. LC 73-77911. (Illus.). (ps-3). 1973. 11.95 (ISBN 0-374-34133-8); bds. 6.95 (ISBN 0-374-34134-6). FS&G.

—Little Red Riding Hood. Pincus, Harriet, ed. LC 68-11505. (Illus.). 32p. (ps-3). 1989. pap. 10.95 (ISBN 0-15-652850-9, AVB75, VoyB). HarBraceJ.

—Little Red Riding Hood. Mahan, Benton, illus. LC 80-27684. 32p. (gr. k-3). 1981. PLB 9.79 (ISBN 0-89375-488-9); pap. 1.95 (ISBN 0-89375-489-7). Troll Assocs.

—Little Red Riding Hood. Hyman, Trina S., retold by. & illus. LC 82-7700. 32p. (ps-3). 1982. reinforced binding 14.95 (ISBN 0-8234-0470-6); pap. 5.95 (ISBN 0-8234-0653-9). Holiday.

—Little Red Riding Hood. Alchemy II, Inc. Staff, illus. 26p. (ps). 1988. incl. cassette 9.95 (ISBN 1-55578-903-X). Worlds Wonder.

—The Queen Bee. Dumas, Phillipe, illus. 32p. (gr. 4 up). 1984. PLB 10.95s.p. (ISBN 0-87191-939-7); PLB 15.65 (ISBN 0-685-07707-1). Creative Ed.

—Ragamuffins. Watts, Bernadette, illus. LC 89-42609. 32p. (gr. k-3). 1989. 13.95 (ISBN 1-55858-014-X). North-South Bks NYC.

—Rapunzel. Dodson, Bert, illus. LC 78-18066. 32p. (gr. k-3). 1979. PLB 9.79 (ISBN 0-89375-135-9); pap. 1.95 (ISBN 0-89375-113-8). Troll Assocs.

—Rapunzel. Rogasky, Barbara, retold by. Hyman, Trina S., illus. LC 81-6419. 32p. (ps-3). 1982. Reinforced bdg. 14.95 (ISBN 0-8234-0454-4); pap. 5.95 (ISBN 0-8234-0652-0). Holiday.

—Rapunzel. Hague, Michael, illus. 32p. (gr. 6 up). 1986. PLB 10.95s.p. (ISBN 0-87191-936-2); PLB 15.65 (ISBN 0-685-07704-7). Creative Ed.

—Rumpelstiltskin. Hockerman, Dennis, illus. LC 78-18079. 32p. (gr. k-3). 1979. PLB 9.79 (ISBN 0-89375-140-5); pap. 1.95 (ISBN 0-89375-118-9). Troll Assocs.

—Rumpelstiltskin. Zelinsky, Paul O., retold by. & illus. LC 86-4482. (gr. k up). 1986. 13.95 (ISBN 0-525-44265-0, DCB). Dutton Child Bks.

—Rumpelstiltskin. Alchemy II, Inc. Staff, illus. 26p. 1988. incl. cassette 9.95 (ISBN 1-55578-910-2). Worlds Wonder.

—The Shoemaker & the Elves. Hughes, Margaret A., adapted by. (Illus.). 26p. (ps). 1987. Packaged with pre-programmed audio cass. tape. 9.95 (ISBN 0-934323-65-8). Alchemy Comms.

—The Sleeping Beauty. Alchemy II, Inc. Staff, illus. 26p. (ps). 1988. incl. cassette 9.95 (ISBN 1-55578-908-0). Worlds Wonder.

—Snow White & Rose Red. Weren, James, illus. LC 78-18074. 32p. (gr. k-3). 1979. PLB 9.79 (ISBN 0-89375-136-7); pap. 1.95 (ISBN 0-89375-114-6). Troll Assocs.

—Snow White & Rose Red. Topor, Roland, illus. 32p. (gr. 6 up). 1984. PLB 10.95s.p. (ISBN 0-87191-938-9); PLB 15.65 (ISBN 0-685-07706-3). Creative Ed.

—Snow White & Rose Red. Wallner, John, illus. LC 84-4910. 32p. (gr. k-3). 1984. 10.95 (ISBN 0-13-815234-9). P-H.

—Snow White & Rose Red. Watts, Bernadette, illus. LC 87-72036. 32p. (gr. k-3). 1988. 13.95 (ISBN 1-55858-054-9). North-South Bks NYC.

—Snow White & the Seven Dwarfs. (FRE., Illus.). (gr. 3-8). 8.95 (ISBN 0-685-11566-6). French & Eur.

—Snow-White & the Seven Dwarfs. Jarrell, Randall, tr. from GER. Burkert, Nancy E., illus. LC 28-1489. 32p. (ps up). 1972. 14.95 (ISBN 0-374-37099-0). FS&G.

—Snow White & the Seven Dwarfs. Iwasaki, Chihiro, illus. LC 85-12158. 40p. (gr. 1 up). 1985. 15.95 (ISBN 0-88708-012-X). Picture Bk Studio.

—Snow-White & the Seven Dwarfs. Jarrell, Randall, tr. from GER. Burkert, Nancy E., illus. 32p. (ps up). 1987. pap. 5.95 (ISBN 0-374-46868-0). FS&G.

—The Table, the Donkey & the Stick. Galdone, Paul, illus. (ps-3). 1976. PLB 7.95 (ISBN 0-07-022701-2). McGraw.

—Tales from the Brothers Grimm. 1987. 1.98 (ISBN 0-671-08490-9). S&S Trade.

—Three Feathers. Schmid, Eleanor, illus. 32p. (gr. 4 up). 1984. PLB 10.95s.p. (ISBN 0-87191-941-9); PLB 15.65 (ISBN 0-685-07709-8). Creative Ed.

—Three Languages. Chermayeff, Ivan, illus. 32p. (gr. 4 up). 1984. PLB 10.95s.p. (ISBN 0-87191-940-0); PLB 15.65 (ISBN 0-685-07708-X). Creative Ed.

—Twelve Dancing Princesses. Hockerman, Dennis, illus. LC 78-18077. 32p. (gr. k-4). 1979. PLB 9.79 (ISBN 0-89375-139-1); pap. 1.95 (ISBN 0-89375-117-0). Troll Assocs.

—The Twelve Dancing Princesses. Carter, Anne, retold by. Dalton, Anne, illus. LC 88-13794. 32p. (ps-4). 1989. 13.95 (ISBN 0-397-32372-7, Lipp Jr Bks); PLB 13.89 (ISBN 0-397-32373-5, Lipp Jr Bks). HarpC Child Bks.

—Wolf & the Seven Kids. new ed. Craft, Kinuko Y., illus. LC 78-18076. 32p. (gr. 1-4). 1979. PLB 9.79 (ISBN 0-89375-138-3); pap. 1.95 (ISBN 0-89375-116-2). Troll Assocs.

Grimm, Wilhelm K. Hansel & Gretel. Zelinsky, Paul O. & Lesser, Rika, eds. (Illus.). 48p. (gr. k-3). 1985. 14.95 (ISBN 0-399-21733-9, Putnam). Putnam Pub Group.

Gross, Ruth B. Emperor's New Clothes. Kent, Jack, illus. LC 83-19610. 32p. (gr. k-3). 1971. pap. 1.95 (ISBN 0-590-40148-3); pap. 3.95 (ISBN 0-590-04354-4); record incl. Scholastic Inc.

—Hansel & Gretel. Pels, Winslow, illus. 48p. (ps-2). 1990. pap. 5.95 incl. cass. (ISBN 0-590-63297-3); pap. 2.50 (ISBN 0-590-41797-5). Scholastic Inc.

Gross, Ruth B., retold by. Hansel & Gretel. Pels, Winslow P., illus. 48p. (ps-2). 1988. pap. 12.95 (ISBN 0-590-41793-2). Scholastic Inc.

Gruelle, Johnny. Raggedy Ann & Andy Giant Treasury: Four Adventures Plus 12 Short Stories. Golden, N., retold by. Nash, C., frwd. by. (ps-1). 1985. 5.98 (ISBN 0-517-45594-3). Outlet Bk Co.

Grundtvig, Sven. Danish Fairy Tales. Cramer, J. Grant, tr. from DAN. Van Heusen, Drew, illus. vii, 115p. (gr. k-5). 1972. pap. 4.95 (ISBN 0-486-22891-6). Dover.

Gulliver's Travels. (gr. 4 up). 1988. pap. 4.87 (ISBN 0-582-52285-4, 73813). Longman.

Hader, Bertha. Hansel & Gretel. 1990. 3.98 (ISBN 0-8317-4268-2). Smithmark.

—Humpty Dumpty. 1990. 3.98 (ISBN 0-8317-4269-0). Smithmark.

Hague, Michael, illus. Mother Goose: A Collection of Classic Nursery Rhymes. LC 83-22559. (ps-4). 1984. 15.95 (ISBN 0-8050-0214-6). H Holt & Co.

Haley, Gail. Sea Tale. Haley, Gale E., illus. LC 89-34453. (gr. 1-4). 1990. 13.95 (ISBN 0-525-44567-6, DCB). Dutton Child Bks.

Haley, Gail E., illus. Jack & the Bean Tree. 48p. (gr. k-3). 1986. 13.95 (ISBN 0-517-55717-7). Crown.

Hall, Avery & Korty, John. Twice upon a Time. (Illus.). 48p. 1983. 6.95 (ISBN 0-671-45633-4, Little Simon). S&S Trade.

Hamilton, Virginia. The Dark Way: Stories from the Spirit World. Davis, Lambert, illus. 176p. (gr. 3 up). 1990. 19.95 (ISBN 0-15-222340-1); Numbered, signed & Ltd. ed. 100.00 (ISBN 0-15-222341-X). HarBraceJ.

Hansel & Gretel. (Illus.). (ps). 1985. bds. 1.00 (ISBN 0-517-48142-1). Outlet Bk Co.

Hansel & Gretel. (Illus.). (ps-3). 1985. 2.98 (ISBN 0-517-28803-6). Outlet Bk Co.

Hansel & Gretel. (Illus.). (ps-1). 2.98 (ISBN 0-517-45985-X). Outlet Bk Co.

Hansel & Gretel. (Illus.). (ps-k). 2.98 (ISBN 0-517-41274-8). Outlet Bk Co.

Hansel & Gretel. (Illus.). 20p. (ps-2). 1990. 5.95 (ISBN 0-8120-6167-5). Barron.

Hansel & Gretel. (Illus.). (ps-2). 3.95 (ISBN 0-7214-5101-2). Ladybird Bks.

Hansel & Gretel. (Illus.). (ps-k). 3.50 (ISBN 0-7214-5130-6). Ladybird Bks.

Hansel & Gretel. (Illus.). (ps-4). 3.50 (ISBN 0-7214-0730-7). Ladybird Bks.

Hansel et Grete. (FRE., Illus.). (gr. 2). 3.50 (ISBN 0-7214-1282-3). Ladybird Bks.

The Happy Prince. (Illus.). (gr. 3-5). 3.50 (ISBN 0-7214-0790-0). Ladybird Bks.

Hare & the Tortoise. 1990. 5.98 (ISBN 0-8317-3882-0). Smithmark.

Harper, Wilhelmina, ed. Gunniwolf. Wiesner, William, illus. LC 67-22387. (ps-3). 1970. 11.95 (ISBN 0-525-31139-4, DCB). Dutton Child Bks.

Haviland, Virginia, selected by. Favorite Fairy Tales Told Around the World. Schindler, S. D., illus. (ps-6). 1985. 19.95 (ISBN 0-316-35044-3). Little.

Hearn, Michael P. The Victorian Fairy Tale Book. LC 87-36039. (Illus.). 1988. 19.95 (ISBN 0-394-56594-0). Pantheon.

Heide, Florence P. The Shrinking of Treehorn. Gorey, Edward, illus. LC 78-151753. 64p. (gr. 3-6). 1971. 11.95 (ISBN 0-8234-0189-8). Holiday.

Heidi. (Illus.). 336p. (gr. 3-7). 1981. deluxe ed. 11.95 (ISBN 0-448-06012-4, G&D); pap. 7.95 (ISBN 0-448-11012-1, G&D). Putnam Pub Group.

Helldorfer, M. C. The Mapmaker's Daughter. Hunt, Jonathan, illus. LC 89-39330. 40p. (ps-3). 1991. RSBE 14.95 (ISBN 0-02-743515-6, Bradbury Pr). Macmillan Child Grp.

Hepburn, Katharine, retold by. World of Stories. Lee, Brian & Humphreys, Ginny, illus. LC 88-45076. 128p. (gr. 2-6). 1988. Incl. cassette. 21.95 (ISBN 0-06-022296-4). HarpC Child Bks.

Hill, Eric. Fairy Tales. 24p. (Orig.). (ps-k). 1985. 4.95 (ISBN 0-8431-0919-X). Price Stern.

Hjelm, J. Thaddeus Jones & the Dragon. LC 68-56830. (Illus.). 64p. (gr. 2-5). 1968. PLB 10.95 (ISBN 0-87783-039-8); pap. 3.94 deluxe ed. (ISBN 0-87783-110-6). Oddo.

Hoffmann, E. T. The Nutcracker. Sendak, Maurice, illus. Manheim, Ralph, tr. LC 83-25266. (Illus.). 120p. (gr. 3 up). 1984. 40.00 (ISBN 0-517-55285-X). Crown.

—The Nutcracker. Bell, Anthea, adapted by. Zwerger, Lisbeth, illus. LC 87-15249. (gr. 1 up). 1987. 14.95 (ISBN 0-88708-051-0). Picture Bk Studio.

—Nutcracker. Madden, Andrea C., tr. Goodrich, Carter, illus. LC 86-45271. 104p. 1987. 14.95 (ISBN 0-394-55384-5). Knopf.

—The Nutcracker. 2nd, abr. ed. Bell, Anthea, tr. Zwerger, Lisbeth, illus. LC 87-15249. 28p. (gr. k up). 1990. Repr. of 1987 ed. 4.95 (ISBN 0-88708-156-8). Picture Bk Studio.

—The Nutcracker. Delamare, David, illus. LC 91-2167. 48p. (gr. 1-5). 1991. 5.95 (ISBN 0-88101-115-0). Unicorn Pub.

Hoffmann, E. T. & Schulman, Janet. The Nutcracker. Chorao, Kay, illus. LC 79-11223. (gr. 1-5). 1979. 11.95 (ISBN 0-525-36245-2, DCB). Dutton Child Bks.

Hooks, William A. Gruff Brothers. 1990. 9.99 (ISBN 0-553-05855-X). Bantam.

Hooks, William H. Moss Gown. Carrick, Donald, illus. (gr. k-4). 1987. 13.95 (ISBN 0-89919-460-5, Pub. by Clarion). Ticknor & Fields.

Horio, Seishi. The Monkey & the Crab. Ooka, D. T., tr. from JPN. Murakami, Tsutomu, illus. 32p. 1985. 11.95 (ISBN 0-89346-246-2). Heian Intl.

Housman, Laurence. Rocking - Horse Land. Rodanas, Kristina, illus. LC 89-45902. 32p. (gr. k-3). 1990. 13.95 (ISBN 0-688-09014-1); lib. bdg. 13.88 (ISBN 0-688-09015-X). Lothrop.

Howe, John. Jack & the Beanstalk, Vol. 1. 1989. 14.95 (ISBN 0-316-37579-9). Little.

Hughes, Margaret A. Jack & the Beanstalk. Forsse, Ken & Becker, Mary, eds. Hicks, Russell, et al, illus. 26p. (ps). 1986. 9.95 (ISBN 0-934323-25-9); pre-programmed audio cass. tape incl. Alchemy Comms.

—The Sleeping Beauty. Forsse, Ken & Becker, Mary, eds. Hicks, Russell, et al, illus. 26p. (ps). 1986. 9.95 (ISBN 0-934323-27-5). Alchemy Comms.

Hughes, Margaret A. & Forsse, Ken. Goldilocks & the Three Bears. Becker, Mary, ed. Hicks, Russell, et al, illus. 26p. (ps). 1986. 9.95 (ISBN 0-934323-26-7); pre-programmed audio cass. tape avail. Alchemy Comms.

Hughes, Margaret A. & Forsse, Ken, eds. Peter & the Wolf. Hicks, Russell, et al, illus. 26p. (ps). 1986. packaged with preprogrammed audio cass. tape 9.95 (ISBN 0-934323-33-X). Alchemy Comms.

Hughes, Margaret A., et al, eds. The Princess & the Pea. (Illus.). 26p. (ps). 1986. with pre-programmed audio cass. tape 9.95 (ISBN 0-934323-29-1). Alchemy Comms.

—The Emperor's New Clothes. Hicks, Russell & Mazurek, Theresa, illus. 26p. (ps). 1986. incl. pre-programmed audio cass. tape 9.95 (ISBN 0-934323-30-5). Alchemy Comms.

—The Frog Prince. Hicks, Russell, et al, illus. 26p. (ps). 1986. packaged with pre-programmed audio cass. tape 9.95 (ISBN 0-934323-28-3). Alchemy Comms.

—Little Red Riding Hood. Hicks, Russell & McCarthy, Douglas, illus. 26p. (ps). 1986. 9.95 (ISBN 0-934323-31-3); incl. pre-programmed audio cass. tape. Alchemy Comms.

—Rumpelstiltskin. Hicks, Russell, et al, illus. 26p. (ps). 1986. packaged with preprogrammed audio cass. tape 9.95 (ISBN 0-934323-32-1). Alchemy Comms.

Hunter, Mollie. A Furl of Fairy Wind. Gammell, Stephen, illus. LC 76-58732. 64p. (gr. 2-5). 1977. 12.95 (ISBN 0-06-022675-7). HarpC Child Bks.

—A Stranger Came Ashore. LC 75-10814. (gr. 4-8). 1977. pap. 3.50 (ISBN 0-06-440082-4, Trophy). HarpC Child Bks.

Hutchins, Pat. Changes, Changes. Hutchins, Pat, illus. LC 70-123133. 32p. (ps-k). 1973. text ed. 13.95 (ISBN 0-02-745570-9, Aladdin); pap. 0.95 (ISBN 0-02-043770-6). Macmillan Child Grp.

Hutton, Warwick. Beauty & the Beast. Hutton, Warwick, illus. LC 84-48441. 32p. 1985. 13.95 (ISBN 0-689-50316-4, M K McElderry). Macmillan Child Grp.

Hyman, Trina S. The Sleeping Beauty. LC 75-43769. (Illus.). (gr. 1 up). 1983. 14.95 (ISBN 0-316-38702-9); pap. 6.95 (ISBN 0-316-38708-8). Little.

Irving, Washington. Rip Van Winkle. Wyeth, N. C., illus. Glassman, Peter, afterword by. LC 87-60720. (Illus.). 110p. (ps up). 1987. 15.00 (ISBN 0-688-07459-6). Morrow Jr Bks.

Isadora, Rachel. The Princess & the Frog. LC 88-61. (Illus.). 32p. (ps up). 1989. 12.95 (ISBN 0-688-06373-X); PLB 12.88 (ISBN 0-688-06374-8). Greenwillow.

Isele, Elizabeth. The Frog Princess: A Russian Tale Retold. Hague, michael, illus. LC 81-43883. 32p. (ps up). 1984. (Crowell Jr Bks); PLB 12.89 (ISBN 0-690-04218-3). HarpC Child Bks.

Izawa, Tadasu & Hijikata, Shigemi, illus. A Puppet Treasure Book of Fairy Tales. 98p. (ps-1). 1981. 7.95 (ISBN 0-448-12290-1, G&D). Putnam Pub Group.

Izawa, Tadasu & Hijkata, Shigemi, illus. Hansel & Gretel. 18p. (gr. k-2). 1981. 3.95 (ISBN 0-448-09754-0, G&D). Putnam Pub Group.

Jack & the Beanstalk. (ARA., Illus.). (gr. 2-5). 3.50x (ISBN 0-86685-258-1); incl. cassette 12.00x (ISBN 0-685-02572-1). Intl Bk Ctr.

Jack & the Beanstalk. (Illus.). 20p. (ps-2). 1990. 5.95 (ISBN 0-8120-6164-0). Barron.

Jack & the Beanstalk. (Illus.). (gr. k-1). 3.50 (ISBN 0-7214-5122-5). Ladybird Bks.

Jack & the Beanstalk. (Illus.). (ps-4). 3.50 (ISBN 0-7214-0688-2). Ladybird Bks.

Jack & the Beanstalk Favorite. 1989. 5.99 (ISBN 0-517-69320-8). Crown.

Jacobs, Joseph. English Fairy Tales. 160p. (gr. 4 up). 1990. pap. 2.25 (ISBN 0-14-035108-6, Puffin). Puffin Bks.

Jacobs, Joseph, ed. Celtic Fairy Tales. Batten, John D., illus. LC 67-24223. xvi, 267p. (ps-6). 1968. pap. 5.95 (ISBN 0-486-21826-0). Dover.

—English Fairy Tales. Batten, John D., illus. LC 67-19703. xv, 261p. (gr. 3-6). 1898. pap. 5.95 (ISBN 0-486-21818-X). Dover.

—Indian Fairy Tales. Batten, John D., illus. LC 76-9897. (gr. 4-6). 1976. 17.00x (ISBN 0-8486-0205-6). Roth Pub Inc.

—Indian Fairy Tales. Batten, John D., illus. xvi, 255p. (ps-4). 1969. pap. 6.95 (ISBN 0-486-21828-7). Dover.

—More Celtic Fairy Tales. Batten, John D., illus. LC 67-24224. x, 234p. (ps-6). 1968. pap. 5.95 (ISBN 0-486-21827-9). Dover.

Janssen, James S. The Elves of Bellaire Drive. Dietrich, Helen R., ed. Hunn, Diane, illus. Roniger, Mary S., frwd. by. (Illus.). 66p. (Orig.). 1989. pap. 5.95 (ISBN 0-944784-02-X). Habersham. This handy sized book is a collection of stories about three good-natured but shy little fellows that live in a hollow oak tree in the backyard of the author's house. While he has never met his three timid neighbors, he has kept in touch with Ajax, Brice & Calvin by eavesdropping, warning them of potential hazards, swapping gifts & other such neighborly actions. He has kept track of their activities & adventures & told stories of them to his three children & ten grandchildren. The elves' enthusiastic pursuits have gotten them into & out of trouble & joyous encounters with other little people, big people (like us), all kinds of animals- cats, dogs, skunks, rabbits & birds. They lead a pleasing life & have fun, & you & your children will too as you read this delightful book. The author was inspired to write these stories when he saw how much his grandchildren enjoyed his telling these charming anecdotes to his own little people. And the many illustrations by Diane Hunn, a local artist, are equally charming & add much to the children's enjoyment of the stories.
Publisher Provided Annotation.

—Further Adventures of the Elves of Bellaire Drive. Hunn, Diane, illus. Roiniger, Mary Sue, intro. by. (Illus.). (ps-5). 1991. pap. 5.95 (ISBN 0-9619160-1-X). W S Nelson & Co. When the book "The Elves of Bellaire Drive" appeared in 1989, it became

immediately popular among the children, especially those that live in the same neighborhood as Ajax, Brice & Calvin. There has been a steady stream of these young fans of the miniature heroes, who come to visit. While they know that they cannot actually see the Elves, who only come out at night, they love to see their yard furniture & to knock on the tiny red door in the old hollow oak tree & to shout out their loving greetings. In turn the Elves have indicated a love for the children of the neighborhood in what few ways they can. They have set a good example of good behavior, they have assisted various animals, as well as fairies & even Santa Claus. They have proved to be an asset to the neighborhood & a joy to the children. Again we were fortunate to have our artist, Diane Hunn, prepare many illustrations to embellish the various stories.
Publisher Provided Annotation.

Jarrell, Randall. Animal Family. Sendak, Maurice, illus. LC 65-20659. (gr. 3 up). 1985. 16.95 (ISBN 0-394-81043-0). Pantheon.
Jeffers, Susan. Wild Robin. Jeffers, Susan, illus. (ps-3). 1976. 12.95 (ISBN 0-525-42787-2, DCB). Dutton Child Bks.
Jensen, Karen. Goldilocks & the Three Bears. Rigg, Lucy, illus. 32p. (ps up). 1987. 9.95 (ISBN 0-910079-05-6). Lucy & Co.
Jones, Terry. Terry Jones' Fairy Tales. Foreman, Michael, illus. 128p. (ps up). 1986. pap. 8.95 (ISBN 0-14-031642-6, Puffin). Puffin Bks.
Jose, Eduard, adapted by. Aladdin's Lamp: A Classic Tale. Suire, Diane D., tr. from SPA. Lavarello, Jose M., illus. LC 88-35312. 32p. (gr. 1-4). 1988. PLB 10.95 (ISBN 0-89565-481-4). Childs World.
—Fearless John: A Classic Tale. Moncure, Jane B., tr. from SPA. Lavarello, Jose M., illus. LC 88-35215. 32p. (gr. 1-4). 1988. PLB 10.95 (ISBN 0-89565-470-9). Childs World.
—The Old Sandman: A Classic Tale. Riehecky, Janet, tr. from SPA. Asensio, Augusti, illus. LC 88-36793. 32p. (gr. 1-4). 1988. PLB 10.95 (ISBN 0-89565-461-X). Childs World.
The Jungle Book. Date not set. 5.98 (ISBN 0-517-67006-2). Outlet Bk Co.
Kanzawa, Toshiko & Inoue, Yosuke. Selfish Old Woman. (ps-2). 5.95 (ISBN 0-672-51581-4, Bobbs). Macmillan.
Kase-Baker, Judith. Snow White & the Seven Dwarfs. (ps-6). 1984. pap. 4.50 (ISBN 0-87602-256-5). Anchorage.
Kendall, Carol. Whisper of Glocken. Gobbato, Imero & Garcia, Manuel, illus. LC 85-17634. 256p. (Orig.). (gr. 3 up). 1986. pap. 4.95 (ISBN 0-15-295699-9, VoyB). HarBraceJ.
Kennedy, Richard. Inside My Feet: The Story of a Giant. Himler, Ronald, illus. LC 78-19479. 80p. (gr. 2-6). 1979. 8.61i (ISBN 0-06-023118-1); PLB 11.89 (ISBN 0-06-023119-X). HarpC Child Bks.
Kent, Jack. Jack Kent's Happy-Ever-After Book. LC 75-43289. (Illus.). (ps-3). 1976. (Random Juv). Random.
Kimmel, Eric A., retold by. Baba Yaga: A Russian Folktale. Lloyd, Megan, illus. LC 90-39215. 32p. (ps-3). 1991. PLB 14.95 (ISBN 0-8234-0854-X). Holiday.
Kindle, Patricia & Finney, Susan. Fantasy & Fairy Tales. McKay, Ardis, illus. 64p. (gr. 4-8). 1985. wkbk 6.95 (ISBN 0-86653-317-6, GA 669). Good Apple.
Kipling, Rudyard. The Elephant's Child. (ps-2). 1988. 4.95 (ISBN 0-7232-3449-3). Warne.
—Just So Stories. 1987. 13.95 (ISBN 0-670-80242-5). Viking Child Bks.
Knight, Hilary. Cinderella. Knight, Hilary, illus. LC 80-18660. 32p. (ps-2). 1982. lib. bdg. 5.99 (ISBN 0-394-93759-7); pap. 1.95 (ISBN 0-394-83759-2). Random.
Koshland, Ellen. Magic Lollipop. Koshland, Ellen, illus. LC 73-149481. (gr. k-3). 1971. lib. bdg. 5.99 (ISBN 0-394-92163-1). Knopf.
Kroll, Steven. Princess Abigail & the Wonderful Hat. Brewster, Patience, illus. LC 90-39213. 32p. (ps-3). 1991. PLB 14.95 (ISBN 0-8234-0853-1). Holiday.
Krulik, Nancy E. Nutcracker: A Story to Color. 1987. pap. 1.95 (ISBN 0-590-41231-0). Scholastic Inc.

Kuehn-Radtke, Erica. Katja & Nicol. Fee, Karin & Rohl, Ludwig, illus. 28p. (Orig.). (gr. 3 up). 1991. pap. 8.95 (ISBN 0-916639-00-2). Kuehn Radtke. A heart warming story about two little children & their village. Once upon a time there lived in a little village in Austria, near a rocky mountain, two little children, Katja & Nicol. The little hamlet was so beautiful, we called it Camelot. It was the domain of the God of the Mountains, our beloved Ruebezahl. Katja & Nicol is a part of a true experiment with the Beings of the Elements & the God of the Mountains. --This is book one. Three more will follow; also, this book will be on tape, & so will the others that follow. It is written for the ones who believe that around us & in our world are greater powers than human power. Powers of Light & Protection. Anyone who can accept this will enjoy the book. It is a book without crime & violence. It is the balance back to life. Don't buy the book if you believe in war, crime or violence, & that dope & hate are necessary to survive...Crime, hate & war are HUMAN CREATIONS & HAVE NO PLACE IN A GOOD, CLEAN GOD-WAY OF LIFE.
Publisher Provided Annotation.

Landes, William-Alan. Aladdin n' His Magic Lamp: Music & Lyrics. rev. ed. (gr. 3-12). 1985. pap. text ed. 15.00 (ISBN 0-88734-002-4). Players Pr.
—Rumpelstiltskin. rev. ed. LC 89-43683. 52p. (gr. 3-12). 1985. pap. text ed. 6.00 (ISBN 0-88734-104-7); tchr's. ed. 30.00 (ISBN 0-88734-005-9). Players Pr.
Landes, William-Alan & Lasky, Mark A. Grandpa's Bedtime Story. rev. ed. LC 89-63868. (gr. 3-12). 1985. pap. text ed. 6.00 (ISBN 0-88734-505-0). Players Pr.
Landes, William-Alan & Rizzo, Jeff. Rumpelstiltskin: Music & Lyrics. rev. ed. (gr. 3-12). 1985. pap. text ed. 15.00 (ISBN 0-88734-004-0). Players Pr.
Lang, Andrew. The Crimson Fairy Book. Ford, H. J., illus. LC 67-17988. (gr. 4-8). 17.50 (ISBN 0-8446-0753-3). Peter Smith.
—Green Fairy Book. LC 34-28314. (Illus.). (gr. 4 up). 1969. pap. 2.95 (ISBN 0-8049-0197-X, CL-197). Airmont.
—The Olive Fairy Book. Ford, H. J., illus. (gr. 2 up). 17.00 (ISBN 0-8446-0754-1). Peter Smith.
—Pink Fairy Book. Ford, Henry J., illus. 360p. (gr. 4-6). 1966. pap. 6.95 (ISBN 0-486-21792-2). Dover.
—The Pink Fairy Book. Ford, H. J., illus. (gr. 2 up). 17.50 (ISBN 0-8446-0755-X). Peter Smith.
—The Red Fairy Book. Ford, H. J. & Speed, illus. (gr. 2 up). 17.50 (ISBN 0-8446-0756-8). Peter Smith.
—The Violet Fairy Book. Ford, H. J., illus. (gr. 2 up). 17.50 (ISBN 0-8446-0757-6). Peter Smith.
—The Yellow Fairy Book. Ford, H. J., illus. (gr. 2 up). 17.50 (ISBN 0-8446-0758-4). Peter Smith.
Lang, Andrew, ed. Arabian Nights Entertainments. Ford, H. J., illus. LC 69-17098. xv, 424p. (gr. k-6). 1969. pap. 6.95 (ISBN 0-486-22289-6). Dover.
—Blue Fairy Book. LC 34-28315. (Illus.). (gr. 4 up). 1969. pap. 2.95 (ISBN 0-8049-0196-1, CL-196). Airmont.
—Blue Fairy Book. Ford, Henry J. & Hood, G. P., illus. LC 34-28315. 390p. (gr. 1-6). 1965. pap. 6.95 (ISBN 0-486-21437-0). Dover.
—Brown Fairy Book. Ford, Henry J., illus. (gr. 1-6). pap. 6.95 (ISBN 0-486-21438-9). Dover.
—Crimson Fairy Book. Ford, Henry J., illus. LC 67-17988. 371p. (gr. 4-6). 1966. pap. 6.95 (ISBN 0-486-21799-X). Dover.
—Green Fairy Book. Ford, Henry J., illus. LC 34-28314. 366p. (gr. 4-6). 1965. pap. 6.95 (ISBN 0-486-21439-7). Dover.
—Grey Fairy Book. Ford, Henry J., illus. LC 67-17983. 387p. (gr. 4-6). 1900. pap. 6.95 (ISBN 0-486-21791-4). Dover.
—Lilac Fairy Book. Ford, H. J., illus. 367p. (ps-4). 1968. pap. 6.95 (ISBN 0-486-21907-0). Dover.
—Olive Fairy Book. Ford, H. J., illus. 330p. (gr. 4-6). 1966. pap. 5.95 (ISBN 0-486-21908-9). Dover.
—Orange Fairy Book. Ford, H. J., illus. 358p. (gr. 1-6). 1968. pap. 6.95 (ISBN 0-486-21909-7). Dover.
—Red Fairy Book. Ford, Henry J. & Speed, Lancelot, illus. 367p. (gr. 4-6). pap. 6.95 (ISBN 0-486-21673-X). Dover.
—Violet Fairy Book. Ford, Henry J & Lang, H. J., illus. (gr. 4-6). pap. 6.95 (ISBN 0-486-21675-6). Dover.
—Yellow Fairy Book. Ford, Henry J., illus. 321p. (gr. 4-6). pap. 6.95 (ISBN 0-486-21674-8). Dover.
Laughlin, Florence. Little Leftover Witch. Greenwald, Sheila, illus. LC 60-11815. (gr. 2-5). 1973. pap. 3.95 (ISBN 0-02-044180-0, Collier Young Ad). Macmillan Child Grp.
Leamy, Edmund. Fairy Minstrel of Glenmalure & Other Stories for Children. Casseau, Vera, illus. LC 76-9901. (gr. 4-6). 1976. Repr. of 1913 ed. 15.00x (ISBN 0-8486-0210-2). Roth Pub Inc.
—Golden Spears & Other Fairy Tales. Turner, Corinne, illus. LC 76-9902. (gr. 4-6). 1976. Repr. of 1928 ed. 15.00x (ISBN 0-8486-0211-0). Roth Pub Inc.
Lear, Edward. The Owl & the Pussycat. Cauley, Lorinda B., illus. LC 84-24897. 32p. (ps-1). 1986. 12.95 (ISBN 0-399-21254-X, Putnam); pap. 4.95 (ISBN 0-399-21253-1, Putnam). Putnam Pub Group.
Leeds, Barbara. Fairy Tale Rap: "Jack & the Beanstalk" & Other Stories. Hamilton, Craig, illus. 32p. (Orig.). (gr. k-8). 1990. pap. 5.95 (ISBN 0-9624932-0-1); pap. 12.95 incl. cass. (ISBN 0-9624932-2-8); cassette 8.95 (ISBN 0-9624932-1-X). Miramonte Pr.
Le Guin, Ursula K. The Tombs of Atuan. Garraty, Gail, illus. LC 70-154753. 176p. (gr. 6-9). 1971. 15.95 (ISBN 0-689-20680-1, Atheneum Child Bk). Macmillan Child Grp.
Leprince de Beaumont's, Marie. Beauty & the Beast. Howard, Richard, tr. Knight, Hilary, illus. Cocteau, Jean. (Illus.). 48p. (gr. 1-5). 1990. PLB 14.95 (ISBN 0-671-70720-5). S&S Trade.
Lesser, Rika, retold by. Hansel & Gretel. Zelinsky, Paul O., illus. 48p. (ps-3). 1989. pap. 5.95 (ISBN 0-399-21725-8, Sandcastle Bks). Putnam Pub Group.
Lewis, Naomi. Hans Andersen's Fairy Tales. 1988. pap. 2.25 (ISBN 0-14-035085-3, Puffin). Puffin Bks.
Lindgren, Astrid. The Tomten. Wiberg, Harald, illus. LC 61-10658. (gr. 1-3). 1979. 8.95 (ISBN 0-698-20147-7, Coward); (Coward); pap. 6.95 (ISBN 0-698-20487-5, Coward). Putnam Pub Group.
Lipton, Alfred. Cinderella, Vol. 512. rev. ed. Caban, Janice, ed. & illus. 10p. (gr. k). 1989. pap. 2.00 (ISBN 1-878501-01-1). Ntrl Science Indus.
—Goldilox & the Three Bears, Vol. 514. rev. ed. Caban, Janice, ed. & illus. 10p. (gr. k). 1989. pap. 2.00 (ISBN 1-878501-02-X). Ntrl Science Indus.
—Jack & the Beanstalk, Vol. 510. rev. ed. Caban, Janice, ed. & illus. 10p. (gr. k). 1989. pap. 2.00 (ISBN 1-878501-00-3). Ntrl Science Indus.
—Little Red Riding Hood, Vol. 520. rev. ed. Caban, Janice, ed. & illus. 10p. (gr. k). 1989. pap. 2.00 (ISBN 1-878501-05-4). Ntrl Science Indus.
—Pinocchio, Vol. 516. rev. ed. Caban, Janice, ed. & illus. 10p. (gr. k). 1989. pap. 2.00 (ISBN 1-878501-03-8). Ntrl Science Indus.
—Sleeping Beauty, Vol. 518. rev. ed. Caban, Janice, ed. & illus. 10p. (gr. k). 1989. pap. 2.00 (ISBN 1-878501-04-6). Ntrl Science Indus.
Little People Big Book about Magical Worlds. 64p. (ps-1). 1990. write for info. (ISBN 0-8094-7495-6); PLB write for info. (ISBN 0-8094-7496-4). Time-Life.
The Little Red Hen. (Illus.). 28p. (ps up). 1987. 3.95 (ISBN 0-7214-5028-8). Ladybird Bks.
The Little Red Hen. (Illus.). (ps-4). 3.50 (ISBN 0-7214-5010-5). Ladybird Bks.
Little Red Riding Hood. (ARA., Illus.). (gr. 3-5). 3.50x (ISBN 0-86685-204-2). Intl Bk Ctr.
Little Red Riding Hood. (Illus.). (ps-4). 3.50 (ISBN 0-7214-1113-4). Ladybird Bks.
Littledale, Freya. The Magic Fish: Easy to Read Folktales Ser. Pels, Winslow P., illus. 32p. (Orig.). (gr. k-3). 1986. pap. 2.50 (ISBN 0-590-33843-9). Scholastic Inc.
—Snow White. (gr. k-3). 1980. pap. 2.95 (ISBN 0-590-31280-4). Scholastic Inc.
Littledale, Freya, retold by. The Twelve Dancing Princesses. Seltzer, Isadore, illus. 32p. (gr. 1-4). 1988. pap. 2.50 (ISBN 0-590-41185-3). Scholastic Inc.
Lobel, Anita. The Dwarf Giant. Lobel, Anita, illus. LC 90-39214. 32p. (ps-3). 1991. PLB 14.95 (ISBN 0-8234-0852-3). Holiday.
Lobel, Arnold. Giant John. Lobel, Arnold, illus. LC 64-16639. 32p. (gr. k-3). 1964. PLB 13.89 (ISBN 0-06-022946-2). HarpC Child Bks.
—Prince Bertram the Bad. Lobel, Arnold, illus. LC 63-8741. 32p. (gr. k-3). 1963. PLB 12.89 (ISBN 0-06-023976-X). HarpC Child Bks.
Lopez, N. C. King Pancho & the First Clock. Gutierrez, M., illus. LC 63-16396. 32p. (gr. 2-7). 1967. PLB 9.95 (ISBN 0-87783-020-7); pap. 3.94 deluxe ed. (ISBN 0-87783-098-3); cassette 7.94x (ISBN 0-685-03701-0). Oddo.
Lopez, Norbert. Cuento Del Rey Pancho y el Primer Reloj. LC 70-108730. (Illus.). 32p. (gr. 2-7). 1970. PLB 9.95 (ISBN 0-87783-010-X); pap. 3.94 deluxe ed. (ISBN 0-87783-104-1); cassette 7.94x (ISBN 0-685-03700-2). Oddo.
Lubin, Leonard, adapted by. Aladdin & His Wonderful Lamp. Burton, Richard F., tr. from ARA. Lubin, Leonard, illus. LC 82-70308. 48p. (gr. 1-4). 1982. 10.95 (ISBN 0-440-00302-4); PLB 10.89 (ISBN 0-440-00304-0). Delacorte.
Lundbergh, Holger, tr. from SWE. Great Swedish Fairy Tales. Bauer, John, illus. LC 73-132364. 224p. (gr. 4-6). 1973. (Sey Lawr); pap. 10.95 (ISBN 0-440-03041-2). Delacorte.
McAllister, Angela. Enchanted Flute. 1991. 14.95 (ISBN 0-385-30326-2). Delacorte.
McAllister, Stephen F. The Tooth Fairy Legend. (Illus.). 40p. (gr. k-8). 1991. write for info. (ISBN 0-915677-54-7). Roundtable Pub.
McCaughrean, Geraldine. One Thousand & One Arabian Nights. Lavis, Stephen, illus. 260p. 1987. 18.95 (ISBN 0-19-274530-1). Oxford U Pr.
Macdonald, George. At the Back of the North Wind. Thomas, A. M., intro. by. LC 64-21758. (Illus.). (gr. 5 up). pap. 1.50 (ISBN 0-8049-0100-7, CL-100). Airmont.

—At the Back of the North Wind. Mozley, George, illus. LC 77-17650. (gr. 5 up). 1987. pap. 8.95 (ISBN 0-8052-0595-0). Schocken.
—The Complete Fairy Tales of George MacDonald. Hughes, Arthur, illus. Green, Roger L., intro. by. LC 77-80272. (Illus.). (gr. 3-9). 1987. Schocken.
—Princess & the Goblin. Hogan, A. H., intro. by. (gr. 3 up). 1967. pap. 1.50 (ISBN 0-8049-0156-2, CL-156). Airmont.
—Princess & the Goblin. (gr. 1-4). 1984. pap. 2.25 (ISBN 0-14-035029-2, Puffin). Puffin Bks.
—The Princess & the Goblin. Smith, J. A., illus. LC 85-70808. 256p. (gr. 3 up). 1985. deluxe ed. 11.95 (ISBN 0-448-18973-9, G&D). Putnam Pub Group.
—Sir Gibbie. Yates, Elizabeth, ed. LC 79-64123. (gr. 7-12). 1987. pap. 8.95 (ISBN 0-8052-0637-X). Schocken.
McEwan, Chris. Pinocchio. 1990. 13.95 (ISBN 0-385-41327-0); PLB 14.99 (ISBN 0-385-41328-9). Doubleday.
McGovern, Ann. Stone Soup. Pels, Winslow P., illus. 32p. (Orig.). (gr. k-2). 1986. pap. 2.50 (ISBN 0-590-41602-2). Scholastic Inc.
McKinley, Robin. Beauty: A Retelling of the Story of Beauty & the Beast. LC 77-25636. 256p. (gr. 7-9). 1978. 13.95 (ISBN 0-06-024149-7); PLB 13.89 (ISBN 0-06-024150-0). HarpC Child Bks.
—The Door in the Hedge. LC 80-21903. 224p. (gr. 7 up). 1981. reinforced bdg. 11.75 (ISBN 0-688-00312-5). Greenwillow.
McKissack, Patricia & McKissack, Frederick. Cinderella. Dunnington, Tom, illus. LC 85-12764. (gr. 1-2). 1985. PLB 11.93 (ISBN 0-516-02361-6); pap. 3.95 (ISBN 0-516-42361-4). Childrens.
MacManus, Seumas, ed. Donegal Fairy Stories. Verbeck, Frank, illus. xii, 256p. (gr. 4-6). 1968. pap. 5.95 (ISBN 0-486-21971-2). Dover.
Madame d'Aulnoy's Collection Staff. Jack & the Beanstalk. Francois, Andre, illus. 32p. (gr. 4 up). 1983. PLB 10.95s.p. (ISBN 0-87191-947-8); 15.65 (ISBN 0-685-07715-2). Creative Ed.
Madame de Villeneuve. Beauty & the Beast. Delessert, Etienne, illus. 48p. (gr. 4 up). 1984. 10.95s.p. (ISBN 0-87191-946-X); 15.65 (ISBN 0-685-07714-4). Creative Ed.
The Magic Porridge Pot. (ARA., Illus.). (gr. 3-5). 3.50x (ISBN 0-86685-205-0). Intl Bk Ctr.
Manniche, Lise, tr. The Prince Who Knew His Fate. (Illus.). 40p. 1982. 10.95 (ISBN 0-399-20850-X, Philomel). Putnam Pub Group.
Marshall, James. Hansel & Gretel. LC 89-26011. (Illus.). 32p. (ps-3). 1990. 12.95 (ISBN 0-8037-0827-0); PLB 12.89 (ISBN 0-8037-0828-9). Dial Bks Young.
Matthews, Morgan. Squeaky Shoes. Karas, Brian, illus. LC 85-14014. 48p. (Orig.). (gr. 1-3). 1986. PLB 9.89 (ISBN 0-8167-0642-5); pap. text ed. 2.95 (ISBN 0-8167-0643-3). Troll Assocs.
—Tricky Alex. Mahan, Ben, illus. LC 85-14018. 48p. (Orig.). (gr. 1-3). 1986. PLB 9.89 (ISBN 0-8167-0598-4); pap. text ed. 2.95 (ISBN 0-8167-0599-2). Troll Assocs.
Mayer, Marianna. Aladdin & the Enchanted Lamp. McDermott, Gerald, illus. LC 84-4894. 96p. (gr. 4-6). 1985. 15.95 (ISBN 0-02-765360-9, Mcmillan Child Bk). Macmillan Child Grp.
—Beauty & the Beast. Mayer, Marianna, illus. LC 78-54679. 48p. (gr. k up). 1984. 15.95 (ISBN 0-02-765270-X, Four Winds). Macmillan Child Grp.
—Beauty & the Beast. Mayer, Mercer, illus. LC 87-1095. 48p. (ps up). 1987. pap. 5.95 (ISBN 0-689-71151-4, Aladdin). Macmillan Child Grp.
—The Prince & the Princess: A Bohemian Fairy Tale. Rogers, Jacqueline, illus. 64p. (gr. 3 up). 1989. 13.95 (ISBN 0-553-05843-6). Bantam.
—The Sorcerer's Apprentice: A Greek Fable. Weisner, David, illus. (gr. 3 up). 1989. 13.95 (ISBN 0-553-05844-4). Bantam.
—The Spirit of the Blue Light. Gal, Laszlo, illus. LC 86-12524. 40p. (gr. k-3). 1990. 15.95 (ISBN 0-02-765350-1, Mcmillan Child Bk). Macmillan Child Grp.
Mayer, Mercer. East of the Sun & West of the Moon. Mayer, Mercer, illus. LC 80-11496. 48p. (gr. k up). 1984. 13.95 (ISBN 0-02-765190-8, Four Winds). Macmillan Child Grp.
—Terrible Troll. Mayer, Mercer, illus. LC 68-28730. (gr. k-3). 1968. PLB 11.89 (ISBN 0-8037-8621-2). Dial Bks Young.
Mayer, Mercer, retold by. The Sleeping Beauty. LC 84-7195. (Illus.). 48p. (gr. k up). 1984. 14.95 (ISBN 0-02-765340-4, Mcmillan Child Bk). Macmillan Child Grp.
Micocci, Harriet. Captain Orkle's Treasure. Dora, illus. (gr. 3-7). 1961. 10.95 (ISBN 0-8392-3003-6). Astor-Honor.
Milne, A. A. House at Pooh Corner. Shepard, Ernest H., illus. (gr. k up). 1985. 9.95 (ISBN 0-525-32302-3, Dutton). NAL-Dutton.
—Now We Are Six. Shepard, Ernest H., illus. 112p. (gr. 1-3). 1970. pap. 3.25 (ISBN 0-440-46485-4, YB). Dell.
—The Pooh Story Book. Shepard, Ernest H., illus. (gr. k-4). 1965. 11.95 (ISBN 0-525-37546-5, DCB). Dutton Child Bks.
—Winnie-the-Pooh. Shepard, Ernest H., illus. (gr. 1-5). 1961. 9.95 (ISBN 0-525-43035-0, Dutton). NAL-Dutton.
—Winnie-the-Pooh. Shepard, Ernest H., illus. 176p. (ps up). 1988. 9.95 (ISBN 0-525-44443-2, DCB). Dutton Child Bks.
Milone, Karen, illus. Beauty & the Beast. LC 81-612. 32p. (gr. k-4). 1981. PLB 9.79 (ISBN 0-89375-464-1); pap. text ed. 1.95 (ISBN 0-89375-465-X). Troll Assocs.
Minard, Rosemary, ed. Womenfolk & Fairy Tales. LC 74-26555. (Illus.). 176p. (gr. 2-5). 1975. 13.95 (ISBN 0-395-20276-0). HM.
Miner, Carl E. Why the Tooth Fairy Didn't Arrive Last Night. (Illus.). 24p. 1986. write for info. Child Ventures.
Moon, Cliff. Once upon a Time Five to Eight, 4 bks. Sharpe, Caroline, illus. (Orig.). (gr. 1-2). 1986. Set. pap. text ed. 19.80 (ISBN 1-55624-006-6). Wright Group.
—Once upon a Time One to Four, 4 bks. Sharpe, Caroline, illus. 24p. (Orig.). (gr. 1-2). 1986. pap. text ed. 19.80 (ISBN 1-55624-005-8). Wright Group.
Mora, Emma. Snow White & the Seven Dwarfs. (Illus.). 30p. (ps-1). 1986. 3.95 (ISBN 0-8120-5726-0). Barron.
Morgan, Gwenda, illus. Grimm's Other Tales. 160p. (gr. 4-8). 1989. 22.95 (ISBN 0-86241-066-5, Pub. by Cnngt Pub Ltd). Trafalgar Sq.
Morgan, Hal & Tucker, Kerry. Jack & the Beanstalk; with an Inflatable Beanstalk. Marsh, Susan, illus. 10p. (ps-3). 1987. pap. 4.95 (ISBN 0-942820-21-5). Steam Pr MA.
Mother Goose. (Illus.). 58p. (ps up). 1987. 8.95 (ISBN 0-7214-5033-4). Ladybird Bks.
Mother Goose. 1990. 2.98 (ISBN 0-8317-7254-9). Smithmark.
The Mother Goose Book. (ps-1). 1990. write for info. (ISBN 0-307-10092-8, 10092). Western Pub.
Mother Goose Staff. Little Red Riding Hood. Facsimile ed. LC 86-11772. (Illus.). 56p. (gr. k-5). 1986. Repr. of 1924 ed. 11.95 (ISBN 0-916410-35-8). A D Bragdon.
Motomora, Mitchell. Lazy Jack & the Silent Princess. (Illus.). 32p. (gr. 1-4). 1989. PLB 13.32 (ISBN 0-8172-3529-9). Raintree Pubs.
Mountain, Lee, et al. The Gingerbread Man. (Illus.). 20p. (gr. k-1). 1991. pap. 18.75 (ISBN 0-89061-943-3). Jamestown Pubs.
—Goldilocks & the Three Bears. (Illus.). 16p. (gr. k-1). 1991. pap. 18.75 (ISBN 0-89061-942-5). Jamestown Pubs.
Mulherin, Jennifer, ed. Favorite Fairy Tales. (Illus.). (gr. k-4). 1983. 7.95 (ISBN 0-448-01339-8, G&D). Putnam Pub Group.
My Big Book of Fairy Tales: A Treasury of Favorite Stories for Children. 1987. 8.98 (ISBN 0-671-08503-4). S&S Trade.
My Book of Favorite Fairy Tales. 1985. 5.98 (ISBN 0-671-06930-6). S&S Trade.
Myers, Walter D. The Dragon Takes a Wife. LC 71-172340. (gr. 2-4). 7.95 (ISBN 0-672-51586-5, Bobbs). Macmillan.
Nesbit, E. Melisande. 1989. 13.95 (ISBN 0-15-253164-5). HarbraceJ.
Nesbit, Edith. Beauty & the Beast. Christie, Julia, illus. (ps-3). 1988. 4.95 (ISBN 0-7232-3540-6). Warne.
Neubacher, G. Little Red Riding Hood. (Illus.). 32p. (gr. 1-4). 1989. PLB 8.95 (ISBN 0-88625-214-8). Durkin Hayes Pub.
Newell, Peter S. Topsys & Turvys. (Illus.). 76p. (gr. 3-7). pap. 3.50 (ISBN 0-486-21231-9). Dover.
Newman, Matt H., ed. Goldilocks & the Three Bears. Laite, Gordon, illus. LC 66-3459. 18p. (gr. 1-3). 1980. pap. 29.95 6 bks. & 1 cass. (ISBN 0-89290-085-7, BC13-2); pap. 10.95 1 bk. & 1 cass. (ISBN 0-685-04646-X). Soc for Visual.
—Little Red Riding Hood. Kane, Sharon, illus. LC 66-3456. 18p. (gr. 1-3). 1980. pap. 29.95 6 bks. & 1 cass. (ISBN 0-89290-084-9, BC13-1); pap. 10.95 1 bk. & 1 cass. (ISBN 0-685-04658-3, BC13-1). Soc for Visual.
Nightingale, Sandy A., illus. Hansel & Gretel. LC 85-2222. 24p. (ps-1). 1985. (Random Juv); lib. bdg. 4.99 (ISBN 0-394-97022-5). Random.
Nister, Ernest, illus. Peeps into Fairyland. 1987. 14.95 (ISBN 0-399-21394-5, Philomel). Putnam Pub Group.
Nones, Eric J. Canary Prince. (ps up). 1991. 14.95 (ISBN 0-374-31029-7). FS&G.
North, Carol. Hansel & Gretel. 1990. pap. write for info. (ISBN 0-307-10033-2, Golden Pr). Western Pub.
Norton, Mary. Are All the Giants Dead? Froud, Brian, illus. LC 78-6622. (gr. 4-6). 1978. pap. 9.95 (ISBN 0-15-607888-0, VoyB). HarBraceJ.
—Borrowers. Krush, Beth & Krush, Joe, illus. LC 53-7870. (gr. 3 up). 1953. 13.95 (ISBN 0-15-209987-5, HJ). HarBraceJ.
—Borrowers Afield. Krush, Beth & Krush, Joe, illus. LC 55-11011. (gr. 3 up). 1955. 12.95 (ISBN 0-15-210166-7, HJ). HarBraceJ.
—Borrowers Afloat. Krush, Beth & Krush, Joe, illus. LC 59-5630. (gr. 3 up). 1959. 12.95 (ISBN 0-15-210345-7, HJ). HarBraceJ.
—Borrowers Aloft. Krush, Beth & Krush, Joe, illus. LC 61-11751. (gr. 3 up). 1961. 12.95 (ISBN 0-15-210524-7, HJ). HarBraceJ.
—Poor Stainless. Krush, Beth & Krush, Joe, illus. LC 70-140781. 32p. (gr. 3-7). 1985. 7.95 (ISBN 0-15-263221-2, HJ). HarBraceJ.
Nuebacher, G. The Frog Prince. (Illus.). 32p. (gr. 1-4). 1989. 8.95 (ISBN 0-88625-216-4). Durkin Hayes Pub.
—Pinocchio. (Illus.). 32p. (gr. 1-4). 1989. 8.95 (ISBN 0-88625-218-0). Durkin Hayes Pub.
—Sleeping Beauty. (Illus.). 32p. (gr. 1-4). 1989. 8.95 (ISBN 0-88625-220-2). Durkin Hayes Pub.
Offerman, Lynn, ed. Gregg Hildebrandt's Favorite Fairy Tales. Hildebrandt, Gregory, illus. 224p. (gr. 3 up). 1984. pap. 12.95 (ISBN 0-671-50327-8, Little Simon). S&S Trade.
Okawa, Essei. The Adventures of the One Inch Boy. Ooka, D. T., tr. from JPN. Endo, Teruyo, illus. 32p. (gr. k-6). 1985. 11.95 (ISBN 0-89346-258-6). Heian Intl.
—The Fisherman & the Grateful Turtle. Ooka, D. T., tr. from JPN. Murakami, Koichi, illus. 32p. (gr. k-6). 1985. PLB 11.95 (ISBN 0-89346-257-8). Heian Intl.
Olu Easmon, Carol. Bisi & the Golden Disc. LC 89-77347. (Illus.). 32p. 1990. 13.95 (ISBN 0-940793-56-3, Pub. by Crocodile Bks). Interlink Pub.
Olujic, Grozdana. Rose of Mother-of-Pearl. Kessler, Jascha, tr. Jacobi, Kathy, illus. (SER & CRO.). 19p. (Orig.). (gr. 4 up). 1983. pap. 6.00 (ISBN 0-915124-90-4, Pub. by Toothpaste). Coffee Hse.
Omnibus of Fairy Tales. (ps). pap. 9.95 (ISBN 0-86112-024-8, Brimax Bks). Borden.
Osborne, Mary P., retold by. Beauty & the Beast. Pels, Winslow P., illus. 40p. (gr. 1-4). 1991. pap. 3.95 (ISBN 0-590-40166-1). Scholastic Inc.
Ozaki, Yei T., compiled by. The Japanese Fairy Book. LC 70-109415. (Illus.). 320p. (gr. 3-8). 1970. pap. 9.95 (ISBN 0-8048-0885-6). C E Tuttle.
Paget, Francis E. & Churne, William. The Hope of the Katzekopfs: A Fairy Tale. LC 68-18214. (ps-3). 1968. Repr. of 1844 ed. 21.00 (ISBN 0-384-44510-1). Johnson Repr.
Pape, D. L. King Robert, the Resting Ruler. LC 68-56823. (Illus.). 48p. (gr. 2-5). 1968. PLB 10.95 (ISBN 0-87783-021-5). Oddo.
—Three Thinkers of Thay-Lee. LC 68-56828. (Illus.). 48p. (gr. 2-5). 1968. PLB 10.95 (ISBN 0-87783-040-1). Oddo.
Parker, Ed, illus. Three Billy Goats Gruff. LC 78-18068. 32p. (gr. k-3). 1979. PLB 9.79 (ISBN 0-89375-121-9); pap. 1.95 (ISBN 0-89375-099-9); cassette 9.95 (ISBN 0-685-04953-1). Troll Assocs.
Patterson, Eleanora. Twice-upon-a-Time: Born & Adopted. Prey, Barbara E., illus. LC 87-92071. 48p. (gr. k-4). 1988. pap. 5.95 (ISBN 0-9607432-1-9). E P Press.
Pearson, Susan, retold by. Jack & the Beanstalk. Warhola, James, illus. (ps-3). 1989. pap. 13.95 (ISBN 0-671-67196-0). S&S Trade.
Perrault, Charles. Cinderella. (Fr.). (gr. 3-8). 9.95 (ISBN 0-685-23349-9). French & Eur.
—Cinderella. new ed. Smith, Phil, illus. LC 78-18067. 32p. (gr. k-3). 1979. PLB 9.79 (ISBN 0-89375-120-0); pap. 1.95 (ISBN 0-89375-098-0). Troll Assocs.
—Cinderella. Innocenti, Roberto, illus. 32p. (gr. 4 up). 1983. 10.95s.p. (ISBN 0-87191-945-1); 15.65 (ISBN 0-685-07713-6). Creative Ed.
—Cinderella. Jeffers, Susan, illus. Ehrlich, Amy, retold by. LC 85-1685. (Illus.). 32p. (ps-3). 1985. 12.95 (ISBN 0-8037-0205-1); PLB 12.89 (ISBN 0-8037-0206-X). Dial Bks Young.
—Cinderella. Lange, Jessica, ed. Goode, Diane, tr. from FRE. & illus. LC 87-16886. 48p. (ps up). 1988. 11.95 (ISBN 0-394-89603-3); incl. cassette 14.95 (ISBN 0-685-19731-X); lib. bdg. 12.99 (ISBN 0-685-19732-8). Knopf.
—Cinderella. Alchemy II, Inc. Staff, illus. 26p. (ps). 1988. incl. cassette 9.95 (ISBN 1-55578-911-0). Worlds Wonder.
—Cinderella. 2nd ed. Brown, Marcia, tr. from FRE. & illus. LC 87-34920. 32p. (ps-3). 1988. pap. 4.50 (ISBN 0-689-71261-8, Aladdin). Macmillan Child Grp.
—Cinderella. (ps-3). 1990. pap. 4.95 (ISBN 0-8037-0830-0, Dial Pied Piper). Puffin Bks.
—Cinderella: And Other Tales from Perrault. Hague, Michael, illus. 96p. (gr. 1-5). 1989. 18.95 (ISBN 0-8050-1004-1). H Holt & Co.
—Cinderella; or, The Little Glass Slipper. Le Cain, Errol, illus. (gr. 1 up). 1977. pap. 3.95 (ISBN 0-14-050137-1, Puffin). Puffin Bks.
—Little Red Riding Hood. Moon, Sarah, photos by. (Illus.). 32p. (gr. 9 up). 1983. PLB 10.95s.p. (ISBN 0-87191-943-5); 15.65 (ISBN 0-685-07711-X). Creative Ed.
—Perrault's Fairy Tales. Dore, Gustave, illus. LC 72-79522. viii, 117p. (gr. 4-6). 1969. pap. 5.95 (ISBN 0-486-22311-6). Dover.
—Ricky the Tuft: A Classic Tale. Jose, Eduard, adapted by. Moncure, Jane B., tr. from SPA. Lavarello, Jose M., illus. LC 88-36792. 32p. (gr. 1-4). 1988. PLB 10.95 (ISBN 0-89565-473-3). Childs World.
—Sleeping Beauty & Other Stories. LC 88-43558. 160p. 1989. 4.95 (ISBN 0-89471-721-9). Running Pr.
—The Sleeping Beauty in the Woods. Collier, John, illus. 32p. (gr. 6 up). 1984. PLB 10.95s.p. (ISBN 0-87191-944-3); PLB 15.65 (ISBN 0-685-07712-8). Creative Ed.
—Three Wishes. Lightbown, Meredith, illus. LC 78-18060. 32p. (gr. k-3). 1979. PLB 9.79 (ISBN 0-89375-129-4); pap. 1.95 (ISBN 0-89375-107-3). Troll Assocs.
Peter & the Wolf. (Illus.). (gr. k). 3.50 (ISBN 0-7214-5128-4). Ladybird Bks.
Peter & the Wolf. (Illus.). (ps-4). 3.50 (ISBN 0-7214-1116-9). Ladybird Bks.
Peter Pan. Date not set. 5.98 (ISBN 0-517-68647-3). Outlet Bk Co.
Peter Rabbit. (gr. k-3). 1987. 4.95 (ISBN 0-932715-05-2). Evans FL.

Peterson, John. The Littles. Clark, Roberta C., illus. 80p. (gr. 2-5). 1986. pap. 2.50 (ISBN 0-590-41601-4). Scholastic Inc.
—The Littles & the Trash Tinies. Clark, Roberta C., illus. (gr. 4-6). 1977. pap. 2.25 (ISBN 0-590-32011-4). Scholastic Inc.
Le Petit Chaperon Rouge. (FRE., Illus.). (gr. 2). 3.50 (ISBN 0-7214-1285-8). Ladybird Bks.
La Petite Poule Rousse. (FRE., Illus.). (gr. 1). 3.50 (ISBN 0-7214-1276-9). Ladybird Bks.
La Petite Sirene. (FRE., Illus.). (gr. 3). 3.50 (ISBN 0-7214-1289-0). Ladybird Bks.
Pierre et le Loup. (FRE., Illus.). (gr. 3). 3.50 (ISBN 0-7214-1293-9). Ladybird Bks.
Pinocchio. (FRE.). 6.25 (ISBN 0-685-33974-2). French & Eur.
Play Mask Books: Cinderella. (ps up). 1990. PLB 5.98 (ISBN 0-7924-5445-6, Mallard Pr). BDD Promo Bk.
Play Mask Books: Goldilocks & the Three Bears. (ps up). 1990. PLB 5.98 (ISBN 0-7924-5447-2, Mallard Pr). BDD Promo Bk.
Play Mask Books: Little Red Riding Hood. (ps up). 1990. PLB 5.98 (ISBN 0-7924-5448-0, Mallard Pr). BDD Promo Bk.
Play Mask Books: Sleeping Beauty. (ps up). 1990. PLB 5.98 (ISBN 0-7924-5446-4, Mallard Pr). BDD Promo Bk.
Polette, Nancy. Activities with Folktales & Fairytales. (Illus.). 32p. (gr. 4-7). 1979. pap. 4.95 (ISBN 0-913839-00-0). Bk Lures.
—Thinking Skills with Fairy Tales. (Illus.). 32p. (gr. 3-6). 1983. pap. 4.95 (ISBN 0-913839-12-4). Bk Lures.
Porazinska, Janina. The Enchanted Book: A Tale from Krakow. Smith, Bozena, tr. Brett, Jan, photos by. LC 86-22918. 32p. (gr. k-4). 1987. 13.95 (ISBN 0-15-225950-3). HarBraceJ.
Postma, Lidia. The Stolen Mirror. Postma, Lidia, illus. LC 75-43888. 32p. (ps-3). 1976. McGraw.
Potter, Beatrix. The Complete Tales of Beatrix Potter. Potter, Beatrix, illus. 384p. (ps-6). 1989. 35.00 (ISBN 0-7232-3618-6). Warne.
—The Fairy Caravan. (Illus.). 226p. (ps-4). 1985. 10.95 (ISBN 0-7232-3307-1). Warne.
—The Tale of Benjamin Bunny. Stewart, Pat, illus. LC 74-78812. 59p. (gr. 2 up). 1974. pap. 1.75 (ISBN 0-486-21102-9). Dover.
—The Tale of Timmy Tiptoes. (Illus.). 64p. (gr. 3 up). 1987. pap. 1.75 (ISBN 0-486-25541-7). Dover.
—A Treasury of Peter Rabbit & Other Stories. (Illus.). (gr. k up). 1985. 5.98 (ISBN 0-517-23948-5). Outlet Bk Co.
Poucette. (FRE., Illus.). (gr. 1). 3.50 (ISBN 0-7214-1274-2). Ladybird Bks.
The Princess & the Frog. (ARA., Illus.). (gr. 4-6). 3.50x (ISBN 0-86685-217-4); incl. cassette 12.00x. Intl Bk Ctr.
The Princess & the Frog. (Illus.). (ps-4). 3.50 (ISBN 0-7214-0766-8). Ladybird Bks.
Princess & the Pea. (ARA., Illus.). (gr. 4-6). 3.50 (ISBN 0-86685-218-2); incl. cassette 12.00x (ISBN 0-685-02577-2). Intl Bk Ctr.
The Princess & the Pea. (Illus.). (ps-4). 3.50 (ISBN 0-7214-5007-5). Ladybird Bks.
La Princesse et la Grenouille. (FRE., Illus.). (gr. 3). 3.50 (ISBN 0-7214-1287-4). Ladybird Bks.
La Princesse et le Petit Pois. (FRE., Illus.). (gr. 1). 3.50 (ISBN 0-7214-1272-6). Ladybird Bks.
Prokofieff, Sergei. Peter & the Wolf. Alchemy II, Inc. Staff, illus. 26p. (ps). 1988. incl. cassette 9.95 (ISBN 0-317-89541-9). Worlds Wonder.
Pushkin, Aleksandr. The Snow Storm. Redpath, Ann, ed. 40p. (gr. 6 up). 1983. PLB 10.95s.p. (ISBN 0-87191-923-0); PLB 15.65 (ISBN 0-685-07658-X). Creative Ed.
Puss in Boots. (ARA., Illus.). (gr. 2-6). 3.50x (ISBN 0-86685-220-4). Intl Bk Ctr.
Puss in Boots. (ps-1). 1.79 (ISBN 0-517-46234-6). Outlet Bk Co.
Puss in Boots. (Illus.). (ps-1). 1.98 (ISBN 0-517-39464-2). Outlet Bk Co.
Puss in Boots. (Illus.). (gr. k). 3.50 (ISBN 0-7214-5170-5). Ladybird Bks.
Puss in Boots. (Illus.). (ps-4). 3.50 (ISBN 0-7214-0086-8). Ladybird Bks.
Pyle, Howard. The Wonder Clock or, Four & Twenty Marvelous Tales, Being One for Each Hour of the Day. (Illus.). xiv, 319p. (gr. 3-6). pap. 7.95 (ISBN 0-486-21446-X). Dover.
Rackham, Arthur. Sleeping Beauty. Rackham, Arthur, illus. 110p. (gr. k-4). 1920. pap. 3.95 (ISBN 0-486-22756-1). Dover.
Ransome, Arthur. The Fool of the World & the Flying Ship. Shulevitz, Uri, illus. LC 68-54105. 48p. (ps-3). 1968. 15.95 (ISBN 0-374-32442-5). FS&G.
Rapunzel. (Illus.). (gr. k). 3.50 (ISBN 0-7214-5167-5). Ladybird Bks.
Rapunzel in Arabic. (Illus.). (gr. 4-6). 3.50x (ISBN 0-86685-264-6). Intl Bk Ctr.
Red Riding Hood. (Illus.). (ps-1). 1.29 (ISBN 0-517-47346-1). Outlet Bk Co.
Red Riding Hood. (Illus.). (ps-2). 3.95 (ISBN 0-7214-5103-9). Ladybird Bks.
La Reine des Neiges. (FRE., Illus.). (gr. 3). 3.50 (ISBN 0-7214-1291-2). Ladybird Bks.
Richardson, Frederick, illus. Mother Goose: The Original Volland Edition. (gr. k up). 1985. 7.95 (ISBN 0-517-43619-1). Outlet Bk Co.
Richardson, Lee & Holt, Shirley, eds. Little Red Riding Hood. (Illus.). 28p. (gr. 3-8). 1985. 16.95 (ISBN 0-9613476-1-9). Shirlee.
Ringi, Kjell. Stranger. Ringi, Kjell, illus. LC 68-23661. (ps-2). 1968. 3.95 (ISBN 0-394-81571-8). Random.
Riordan, James, retold by. Peter & the Wolf. Ambrus, Victor G., illus. 24p. (ps-6). 1987. 13.95 (ISBN 0-19-279824-3). Oxford U Pr.
Rip Van Winkle. (Illus.). (ps-3). 1985. 1.98 (ISBN 0-517-28806-0). Outlet Bk Co.
Robbie, Dorothy & Hand, Desmond. Alice in Wonderland. (gr. k up). 1970. pap. 1.50x (ISBN 0-912262-19-2). Proscenium.
Robbins, John. The Tooth Fairy Is Broke. Gemmill, Courtenay, ed. Owings, Rae, illus. 48p. (gr. k-5). 1988. 13.95 (ISBN 0-945938-01-2). Clark Davis.
Roberts, Jo-Anna. Alligator & the Toothfairy. Kinnell, Shannon, illus. 56p. (ps-2). 1991. 11.50g (ISBN 1-879212-00-5). Desert Star Intl.
Roberts, Tom. Goldilocks & the Three Bears. Kubinyi, Laszlo, illus. 32p. (gr. k up). 1990. 14.95 (ISBN 0-88708-146-0, Rabbit Ears); incl. cass. 19.95 (ISBN 0-88708-147-9). Picture Bk Studio.
Rogasky, Barbara, retold by. The Water of Life. Hyman, Trina S., illus. LC 84-19226. 40p. (gr. k-3). 1986. reinforced bdg. 14.95 (ISBN 0-8234-0552-4). Holiday.
Rojankovsky, Feodor. Tall Book of Nursery Tales. Rojankovsky, Feodor, illus. LC 44-3881. (ps-1). 1944. 7.95 (ISBN 0-06-025065-8). HarpC Child Bks.
Rose-Blanche et Rose-Rouge. (FRE., Illus.). (gr. 2). 3.50 (ISBN 0-7214-1288-2). Ladybird Bks.
Ross, Tony. Mrs. Goat & Her Seven Little Kids. Ross, Tony, illus. LC 89-17933. 24p. (gr. 1-3). 1990. 13.95 (ISBN 0-689-31624-0, Atheneum Child Bk). Macmillan Child Grp.
Rowland, Jada, illus. Rapunzel. 32p. (gr. 2-5). 1989. 12.95 (ISBN 0-8092-4400-4, Calico Bks). Contemp Bks.
Royds, Caroline, selected by. The Dragon, Giant & Monster Treasury. Spenceley, Annabel, illus. 96p. 1988. 13.95 (ISBN 0-399-21587-5, Putnam). Putnam Pub Group.
Rumpelstiltskin. (ARA., Illus.). (gr. 4-6). 3.50x (ISBN 0-86685-265-4). Intl Bk Ctr.
Le Ruse Renard et la Petite Poule Rousse. (FRE., Illus.). (gr. 1). 3.50 (ISBN 0-7214-1277-7). Ladybird Bks.
Rymer, Alta M. Up from Uzam. Rymer, Alta M., illus. 28p. (Orig.). (gr. 2-4). 1987. pap. 11.50 (ISBN 0-9600792-8-9). Rymer Bks.
Sage, Jacqueline I., illus. Many Furs: A Grimm's Fairy Tale. LC 81-947. 32p. (gr. 1-4). 1990. 9.95 (ISBN 0-89742-041-1). Celestial Arts.
Saint-Exupery, Antoine de. Little Prince. Woods, Katherine, tr. Saint-Exupery, Antoine de, illus. LC 67-1144. (gr. 3-7). 1943. 12.95 (ISBN 0-15-246503-0, HJ). HarBraceJ.
Sakade, Florence. Japanese Children's Favorite Stories. Kurosaki, Yoshio, illus. LC 58-11620. (gr. 1-4). 1958. bds. 16.95 (ISBN 0-8048-0284-X). C E Tuttle.
Salter-Mathieson, Nigel. Little Chief Mischief. Gruen, Chuck, illus. (gr. 2-7). 1962. 10.95 (ISBN 0-8392-3020-6). Astor-Honor.
San Souci, Daniel, illus. The Bedtime Book: A Collection of Fairy Tales. LC 85-12898. 48p. (gr. k-3). 1985. pap. 7.95 (ISBN 0-671-60505-4, Little Simon). S&S Trade.
Sans Souci, Daniel. Bedtime Book: A Collection of Fairy Tales. 1985. 11.79 (ISBN 0-671-60506-2). S&S Trade.
Saponaro, Sabina. The Ugly Duckling. (Illus.). 30p. (ps-1). 1986. 3.95 (ISBN 0-8120-5725-2). Barron.
Scally, Kevin. Story of Red Riding Hood. Scally, Kevin, illus. 32p. (ps-3). 1984. 3.95 (ISBN 0-448-11126-8, G&D). Putnam Pub Group.
—The Three Bears. Scally, Kevin, illus. 32p. (ps-3). 1984. 3.95 (ISBN 0-448-11129-2, G&D). Putnam Pub Group.
Schiller, Justin G. Alice's Adventures in Wonderland: An 1865 Printing Re-described. (Illus.). 112p. 1990. 75.00x (ISBN 0-9627110-0-4). Battledore Ltd.
Scott, Michael. Irish Fairytales. Gervin, Joseph, illus. LC 89-50977. 142p. (gr. 2-5). 1989. pap. 11.95 (ISBN 0-85342-866-2, Pub. by Mercier Press Ltd Eire). Dufour.
Seltzer, Richard W., Jr. The Lizard of Oz. Couture, Christin, illus. LC 74-20172. 128p. (Orig.). (gr. 7 up). 1974. pap. 4.50 (ISBN 0-915232-01-4). B & R Samizdat.
—Now & Then & Other Tales from Ome. Seltzer, Richard W., Jr., illus. LC 76-12138. (gr. 5). 1976. 4.50 (ISBN 0-915232-03-0); pap. 1.95 (ISBN 0-915232-02-2). B & R Samizdat.
Severance, Charles L. Tales of the Thumb. 2nd ed. LC 72-86863. (Illus.). (gr. 3-6). pap. 4.75 (ISBN 0-932411-00-2). Pub Div JCS.
Shane, Harold G. King Arthur & the Magic Sword. Clark, William, ed. Maltman, Chauncey, illus. LC 68-3547. 16p. (gr. 4-8). 1980. pap. 29.95 6 bks. & 1 cass. (ISBN 0-89290-079-2, BC15-2); pap. 10.95 1 bk. & 1 cass. (ISBN 0-685-04654-0, BC15-2). Soc for Visual.
Shearer, Marilyn J. Sleeping Beauty. Walker, Larry, illus. 16p. (ps-6). Date not set. 19.95 (ISBN 0-685-30099-4); pap. 10.95 (ISBN 0-685-30100-1). L Ashley & Joshua.
Shibano, Tamizo. The Old Man Who Made the Trees Bloom. Ooka, D. T., tr. from JPN. Iguchi, Bunshu, illus. 32p. 1985. 11.95 (ISBN 0-89346-247-0). Heian Intl.
Shulevitz, Uri. One Monday Morning. Shulevitz, Uri, illus. LC 66-24483. (gr. k-3). 1974. 14.95 (ISBN 0-684-13195-1, Scribners Young Read). Macmillan Child Grp.
Siberell, Anne. A Journey to Paradise. Siberell, Anne, illus. LC 89-39793. 32p. (ps-3). 1990. 14.95 (ISBN 0-8050-1212-5). H Holt & Co.
Singer, Isaac Bashevis. Alone in the Wild Forest. Shub, Eliz, tr. from YID. Zemach, Margot, illus. LC 78-161372. 80p. (gr. 1 up). 1971. 8.95 (ISBN 0-374-30238-3). FS&G.
—Mazel & Shlimazel or the Milk of a Lioness. Zemach, Margot, illus. LC 67-19887. 48p. (ps-3). 1979. 14.95 (ISBN 0-374-34884-7). FS&G.
—When Shlemiel Went to Warsaw & Other Stories. Zemach, Margot, illus. Shub, Elizabeth, tr. from YID. LC 68-30932. (Illus.). 128p. (gr. 4 up). 1969. 13.95 (ISBN 0-374-38316-2). FS&G.
Singer, S. B. Naftali the Storyteller & His Horse, Sus. (gr. 4 up). 1979. pap. 1.50 (ISBN 0-440-46642-3). Dell.
Sleeping Beauty. (SPA & FRE.). (gr. k-3). Span. ed. 6.25 (ISBN 0-685-28438-7); Fr. ed. 9.95 (ISBN 0-685-28439-5). French & Eur.
Sleeping Beauty. (Illus.). (ps-3). 1985. 1.98 (ISBN 0-517-28811-7). Outlet Bk Co.
Sleeping Beauty. (Illus.). (ps-1). 1.29 (ISBN 0-517-47347-X). Outlet Bk Co.
Sleeping Beauty. Date not set. 5.98 (ISBN 0-517-67009-7). Outlet Bk Co.
Sleeping Beauty. (Illus.). (ps-2). 3.95 (ISBN 0-7214-5100-4). Ladybird Bks.
Sleeping Beauty. (Illus.). (ps-k). 3.50 (ISBN 0-7214-5133-0). Ladybird Bks.
Sleeping Beauty. (Illus.). (ps-4). 3.50 (ISBN 0-7214-0953-9). Ladybird Bks.
Sly Fox & Red Hen. (Illus.). (ps-k). 3.50 (ISBN 0-7214-5131-4). Ladybird Bks.
The Sly Fox & the Little Red Hen. (Illus.). (ps-4). 3.50 (ISBN 0-7214-0950-4). Ladybird Bks.
The Snow Queen. (Illus.). (ps-4). 3.50 (ISBN 0-7214-0763-3). Ladybird Bks.
Snow White. (Illus.). (ps-1). 1.98 (ISBN 0-517-39465-0). Outlet Bk Co.
Snow White. (Illus.). (ps-1). 1.29 (ISBN 0-318-12084-4). Outlet Bk Co.
Snow White. 1990. 2.98 (ISBN 0-8317-7257-3). Smithmark.
Snow White & Rose Red. (ARA., Illus.). (gr. 4-6). 3.50x (ISBN 0-86685-225-5). Intl Bk Ctr.
Snow White & Rose Red. (Illus.). (ps-4). 3.50 (ISBN 0-7214-0593-2). Ladybird Bks.
Snow White & the Seven Dwarfs. (ARA., Illus.). (gr. 1-12). pap. 3.50x (ISBN 0-86685-268-9); incl. cassette 12.00x. Intl Bk Ctr.
Snow White & the Seven Dwarfs. (Illus.). (ps-2). 3.95 (ISBN 0-7214-5062-8). Ladybird Bks.
Snow White & the Seven Dwarfs. (Illus.). (gr. k-1). 3.50 (ISBN 0-7214-5172-1). Ladybird Bks.
Snow White & the Seven Dwarfs. (Illus.). (ps-4). 3.50 (ISBN 0-7214-0648-3). Ladybird Bks.
Snow White & the Seven Little Men: For Those Who Find Great Things in Small Packages. (Illus.). 26p. (Orig.). (gr. 1-6). 1984. pap. 3.50 (ISBN 0-916549-01-1). Ariana Prods.
The Sorcerer's Apprentice. (Illus.). (ps-4). 3.50 (ISBN 0-7214-0765-X). Ladybird Bks.
So-Un, Kim. Story Bag: A Collection of Korean Folk Tales. Higashi, Setsu, tr. Eui-Hwan, Kim, illus. LC 55-13738. (gr. 2-5). 1955. pap. 10.95 (ISBN 0-8048-0548-2). C E Tuttle.
Spier, Peter. London Bridge Is Falling Down. Spier, Peter, illus. LC 67-17695. (ps). 1985. pap. 10.95 (ISBN 0-385-08717-9). Doubleday.
Stanley, Diane. Fortune. Stanley, Diane, illus. LC 88-13204. (ps-4). 1990. 12.95 (ISBN 0-688-07210-0); PLB 12.88 (ISBN 0-688-07211-9, Morrow Jr Bks). Morrow Jr Bks.
Steig, William. Caleb & Katie. Steig, William, illus. LC 77-4947. 32p. (ps-3). 1977. 15.95 (ISBN 0-374-31016-5). FS&G.
Stevens, Janet. The Princess & the Pea. 32p. (gr. k-3). 1984. pap. 1.95 (ISBN 0-590-33111-6). Scholastic Inc.
Stevens, Janet, retold by. Goldilocks & the Three Bears. LC 85-27312. (Illus.). 32p. (ps-2). 1986. reinforced bdg. 14.95 (ISBN 0-8234-0608-3). Holiday.
Stevens, Janet, illus. The Emperor's New Clothes: Adapted from Hans Christian Andersen. LC 85-728. 32p. (ps-2). 1985. reinforced 14.95 (ISBN 0-8234-0566-4). Holiday.
Stockton, Frank. The Bee-Man of Orn. Delessert, Etienne, illus. LC 85-23272. 40p. (gr. 4 up). 1986. PLB 10.95s.p. (ISBN 0-88682-055-3); 15.65 (ISBN 0-685-12402-9). Creative Ed.
Storer, Ronald, ed. Sleeping Beauty & Bluebeard. (gr. k-6). 1972. pap. 2.25x (ISBN 0-19-421746-9). Oxford U Pr.
Story, Rita, retold by. Goldilocks & the Three Bears. Rosato, Amelia, illus. LC 90-52572. 32p. 1990. pap. 7.95 (ISBN 0-915391-37-6, MH37). Slawson Comm.
—The Ugly Duckling. Rosato, Amelia, illus. 32p. 1990. pap. 7.95 (ISBN 0-915391-38-4, MH38, Pub. by Mad Hatter Bks). Slawson Comm.
Swift, Jonathan. Gulliver's Travels. LC 47-31082. (gr. 8 up). 1964. pap. 2.95 (ISBN 0-8049-0015-9, CL-15). Airmont.
—Gulliver's Travels. Watson, Aldren, illus. LC 47-31082. 352p. (gr. 4-6). 1947. 12.95 (ISBN 0-448-05461-2, G&D); (G&D); (G&D). Putnam Pub Group.

FAIRY TALES-INDEXES

FAITH

FAITH CURE–FICTION

Robinson, Barbara. My Brother Louis Measures Worms: and Other Louis Stories. LC 87-45302. 160p. (gr. 5 up). 1990. pap. 3.50 (ISBN 0-06-440362-9, Trophy). HarpC Child Bks.

FALCONS

Arnold, Caroline. Saving the Peregrine Falcon. Hewett, Richard R., photos by. LC 84-15576. (Illus.). 48p. (gr. 2-5). 1985. PLB 12.95 (ISBN 0-87614-225-0); pap. 6.95 (ISBN 0-685-08654-2). Carolrhoda Bks.

Birkhead, Mike. The Falcon over the Town. Oxford Scientific Films, photos by. LC 87-42615. (Illus.). 32p. (gr. 4-6). 1988. PLB 10.95 (ISBN 1-55532-304-9). Gareth Stevens Inc.

Green, Carl R. & Sanford, William R. The Peregrine Falcon. LC 86-2670. (Illus.). 48p. (gr. 4-5). 1986. PLB 10.95 (ISBN 0-89686-271-2, Crestwood Hse). Macmillan Child Grp.

Harrison, Virginia. The World of a Falcon. Oxford Scientific Films Staff, photos by. LC 87-42611. (Illus.). 32p. (gr. 2-3). 1988. PLB 10.95 (ISBN 1-55532-308-1). Gareth Stevens Inc.

FALCONS–FICTION

Deliz, Wenceslao S. Adios Falcon. Marichal, Poli, illus. LC 85-1116. (SPA.). (ps-3). 1985. pap. 2.00 (ISBN 0-8477-3530-3). U of PR Pr.

George, Jean C. On the Far Side of the Mountain. 1990. 14.95 (ISBN 0-525-44563-3, DCB). Dutton Child Bks.

—The Summer of the Falcon. George, Jean C., illus. LC 62-16543. 153p. (gr. 5 up). 1979. pap. 3.50 (ISBN 0-06-440095-6, Trophy). HarpC Child Bks.

Girzone, Joseph F. Kara: The Lonely Falcon. Molloy, Eideen, illus. LC 78-63393. 52p. (gr. 2 up). 1985. Repr. of 1979 ed. 8.95 (ISBN 0-911519-05-X). Richelieu Court.

FALL

see Autumn

FALLACIES

see Logic

FALLING STARS

see Meteors

FALSEHOOD

see Truthfulness and Falsehood

FAMILY

see also Divorce; Domestic Relations; Marriage; Parent and Child

also names of members of the family, e.g., Fathers; Mothers; etc.

Amstutz, Beverly. I Love My Foster Grandparents. (Illus.). 24p. (gr. k-7). 1981. pap. 2.50x (ISBN 0-937836-06-0). Precious Res.

Barmat, Jeanne. Foster Families. LC 90-46834. (Illus.). 48p. (gr. 5-6). 1991. RSBE 10.95 (ISBN 0-89686-605-X, Crestwood Hse). Macmillan Child Grp.

Berry, Joy. Step Families. Bartholomew, illus. 48p. (gr. 3 up). 1990. 14.60 (ISBN 0-516-02955-X); pap. 6.95 (ISBN 0-516-22955-9). Childrens.

Bledsoe, Jane L. & Jones, S. D. An American Family. (gr. 5 up). 1989. Vol. I. PLB 3.90 (ISBN 0-8224-4751-7, Fearon Educ); Vol. II. PLB 3.90 (ISBN 0-8224-4752-5); Vol. III. PLB 3.90 (ISBN 0-8224-4753-3); Vol. IV. PLB 3.90 (ISBN 0-8224-4754-1); Vol. V. PLB 3.90 (ISBN 0-8224-4755-X); Vol. VI. PLB 3.90 (ISBN 0-8224-4756-8); Vol. VII. PLB 3.50 (ISBN 0-8224-4757-6); Vol. VIII. PLB 3.90 (ISBN 0-318-41438-4). Fearon Teach Aids.

Chernow, Fred B. & Chernow, Carol. That's Life. (Illus.). 36p. (gr. 1-7). pap. 2.49 (ISBN 0-9610742-2-1). Purcell Prods.

Cline, Ruth K. J. Focus on Families: A Reference Handbook. 230p. (gr. 9-12). 1989. lib. bdg. 35.00 (ISBN 0-87436-508-2). ABC Clio.

Cooney, Caroline B. Family Reunion. (gr. 7 up). 1989. 14.95 (ISBN 0-553-05836-3, Starfire). Bantam.

Families & Friends. (Illus.). 32p. (ps-2). 1985. 1.95 (ISBN 0-225-66390-2). Harper SF.

Fisher, Leonard E. The Tanners. Fisher, Loenard E., illus. LC 66-10136. 48p. (gr. 3 up). 1986. pap. 5.95 (ISBN 0-87923-609-4). Godine.

Glassman, Bruce. Everything You Need to Know about Stepfamilies. rev. ed. (Illus.). 64p. (gr. 7-12). 1991. 12.95 (ISBN 0-8239-1313-9). Rosen Group.

Hazen, Barbara S. If It Weren't for Benjamin: (I'd Always Get to Lick the Icing Spoon) Hartman, Laura, illus. LC 78-26403. 32p. (ps-3). 1979. 16.95 (ISBN 0-87705-384-7); pap. 9.95 (ISBN 0-89885-172-6). Human Sci Pr.

Hill, Margaret. Coping with Family Expectations. Rosen, Ruth, ed. (gr. 7-12). 1990. lib. bdg. 12.95 (ISBN 0-8239-1159-4). Rosen Group.

Hodges, Margaret. Making a Difference: The Story of an American Family. LC 88-31131. (Illus.). 208p. (gr. 7 up). 1989. 13.95 (ISBN 0-684-18979-8, Scribners Young Read). Macmillan Child Grp.

Jenness, Aylette. Families: A Celebration of Diversity, Commitment & Love. (Illus.). 48p. (gr. 3-5). 1990. 13.95 (ISBN 0-395-47038-2). HM.

Kalman, Bobbie. People in My Family. (Illus.). 32p. (gr. k-2). 1985. 14.95 (ISBN 0-86505-061-9); pap. 6.95 (ISBN 0-86505-085-6). Crabtree Pub Co.

Koftan, Jenelle & Koftan, Kenneth. Long-Distance Grandparenting. (Illus.). 96p. (Orig.). (ps-k). 1988. pap. 12.95 (ISBN 0-945184-00-X). Spring Creek Pubns.

—Long-Distance Grandparenting. (Illus.). 96p. (Orig.). (gr. k-2). 1988. pap. 12.95 (ISBN 0-945184-01-8). Spring Creek Pubns.

—Long-Distance Grandparenting. (Illus.). 112p. (Orig.). (gr. 3-5). 1988. pap. 12.95 (ISBN 0-945184-02-6). Spring Creek Pubns.

McFarland, Rhoda. Drugs & Your Brothers & Sisters. (gr. 7-12). 1991. PLB 14.95 (ISBN 0-8239-1266-3). Rosen Group.

Parramon, J. M., et al. Children. 32p. (gr. 3-5). pap. 3.95 ea.; Eng. ed. pap. 4.95 (ISBN 0-8120-3850-9). Span. ed.: Los Ninos (ISBN 0-8120-3854-1). Barron.

—Grandparents. 32p. (gr. 3-5). Eng. ed. pap. 3.95 (ISBN 0-8120-3853-3); Span. ed.: Los Abuelos. pap. 4.95 (ISBN 0-8120-3857-6). Barron.

Pendergast, Kathleen. Say Another One about My Family. Tindal, Pauline, illus. LC 82-61139. 54p. (gr. k-6). 1982. pap. 6.95 (ISBN 0-942178-01-7). Madison Park Pr.

Regan, Mary. A Family in France. LC 84-19392. (Illus.). 32p. (gr. 2-5). 1985. PLB 9.95 (ISBN 0-8225-1651-9). Lerner Pubns.

Rosofsky, Iris. My Aunt Ruth. LC 90-4940. 224p. (gr. 7 up). 1991. 13.95 (ISBN 0-06-025087-9); PLB 13.89 (ISBN 0-06-025088-7). HarpC Child Bks.

Rudstrom, Lennart. A Family. Larsson, Carl, illus. 32p. (gr. 1-12). 1980. 10.95 (ISBN 0-399-20700-7, Putnam). Putnam Pub Group.

Schaffer, Patricia. How Babies & Family Are Made-There Is More Than One Way! Corbett, Susanne, illus. LC 86-23087. 64p. (gr. k-4). 1988. pap. 6.95 (ISBN 0-935079-17-3). Tabor Sarah Bks.

Simon, Norma. All Kinds of Families. Rubin, Caroline, ed. Lasker, Joe, illus. LC 75-42283. 40p. (gr. k-2). 1975. PLB 12.95 (ISBN 0-8075-0282-0). A Whitman.

Stein, Sara B. That New Baby. LC 73-15271. (Illus.). 48p. (gr. 1 up). 1974. 12.95 (ISBN 0-8027-6175-5). Walker & Co.

Tigwell, Tony. A Family in India. LC 84-19446. (Illus.). 32p. (gr. 2-5). 1985. PLB 9.95 (ISBN 0-8225-1654-3). Lerner Pubns.

FAMILY–FICTION

Ackerman, Karen. The Leaves in October. LC 90-550. 128p. (gr. 3-7). 1991. SBE 12.95 (ISBN 0-689-31583-X, Atheneum Child Bk). Macmillan Child Grp.

Ancona, George. Helping Out. (ps-3). 1991. pap. 127.60 (ISBN 0-395-55774-7, Clarion Bks). HM.

Anshaw, Carol. Latchkey Kids. (ps-3). 1991. pap. 2.75 (ISBN 0-590-43188-9). Scholastic Inc.

Arter, Jim. Gruel & Unusual Punishment. (gr. 3-7). 1991. 13.95 (ISBN 0-385-30298-3). Delacorte.

Bloss, Janet A. One Hundred & One Ways to a Perfect Family. (Illus.). 128p. (Orig.). (gr. 3-6). 1990. pap. text ed. 2.50 (ISBN 0-87406-462-7). Willowisp Pr.

Boyd, Lizi. Not-So-Wicked Stepmother. LC 86-26737. (ps-4). 1987. pap. 11.95 (ISBN 0-670-81589-6). Viking Child Bks.

Brandenberg, Franz. Aunt Nina & Her Nephews & Nieces. Aliki, illus. LC 82-12004. 32p. (gr. k-3). 1983. PLB 11.88 (ISBN 0-688-01870-X); 11.75 (ISBN 0-688-01869-6). Greenwillow.

—Aunt Nina, Good Night. Aliki, illus. LC 88-18777. 32p. (ps up). 1989. 12.95 (ISBN 0-688-07463-4); PLB 12.88 (ISBN 0-688-07464-2). Greenwillow.

Bunn, Scott. Just Hold On. LC 82-70316. 160p. (gr. 7 up). 1982. pap. 9.95 (ISBN 0-385-28490-X). Delacorte.

Busselle, Rebecca. A Frog's-Eye View. LC 90-30645. 208p. (gr. 7 up). 1990. 14.95 (ISBN 0-531-05907-3); PLB 14.99 (ISBN 0-531-08507-4). Orchard Bks Watts.

Carney, Mary L. Too Tough to Hurt. 128p. 1991. pap. 5.95 (ISBN 0-310-28621-2, Youth Bks). Zondervan.

Carris, Joan. Aunt Morbelia & the Screaming Skulls. Cushman, Doug, illus. (gr. 3-7). 1990. 14.95 (ISBN 0-316-12945-3). Little.

Christian, Mary B. Linc. 128p. (gr. 7 up). 1991. 12.95 (ISBN 0-02-718580-X, Mcmillan Child Bk). Macmillan Child Grp.

Christopher, Matt. The Fox Steals Home. Johnson, Lary, illus. LC 78-17526. (gr. 4-6). 1985. 13.95 (ISBN 0-316-13976-9); pap. 3.95 (ISBN 0-316-13986-6). Little.

Colman, Hila. Diary of a Frantic Kid Sister. (gr. 4-6). 1985. pap. 2.50 (ISBN 0-671-61926-8, Archway). PB.

Cormier, Robert. Eight Plus One. 1991. pap. 3.95 (ISBN 0-440-20838-6, LFL). Dell.

Cunningham, Carolyn. All Kinds of Separation. Mortenson, Bob, illus. 24p. (gr. k-6). 1988. wkbk. 3.95 (ISBN 0-685-20040-X, 0494). Kidsrights.

Curry, Jane L. The Big Smith Snatch. LC 89-8036. 192p. (gr. 4-7). 1989. 13.95 (ISBN 0-689-50478-0, M K McElderry). Macmillan Child Grp.

Delavan, Elizabeth. Peter & George & Uncle Henry. (Illus.). 48p. (gr. 3-4). 1988. pap. 2.95 (ISBN 1-55787-020-9, NY75041). Heart of the Lakes.

DiSalvo-Ryan, Dyanne. Uncle Willie & the Soup Kitchen. DiSalvo-Ryan, Dyanne, illus. LC 90-6375. 32p. (gr. 1 up). 1991. 13.95 (ISBN 0-688-09165-2); PLB 13.88 (ISBN 0-688-09166-0, Morrow Jr Bks). Morrow Jr Bks.

Ellis, Sarah. A Family Project. LC 87-22818. 144p. (gr. 4-7). 1988. Repr. of 1986 ed. 12.95 (ISBN 0-689-50444-6, M K McElderry). Macmillan Child Grp.

—A Family Project. (Orig.). (gr. k-6). 1991. pap. 3.25 (ISBN 0-440-40397-9, Pub. by Yearling Classics). Dell.

Enright, Elizabeth. Then There Were Five. Enright, Elizabeth, illus. (gr. k-6). 1987. pap. 2.95 (ISBN 0-440-48806-0, YB). Dell.

Epperley, Mike. The BucketHead Families: Givers & Takers. Erb, Sherry, illus. 32p. (Orig.). (gr. k-5). 1990. pap. 4.95 (ISBN 0-9621214-3-6). Student Sccss.

Estes, Eleanor. The Moffat Museum. Estes, Eleanor, illus. LC 83-8427. 262p. (gr. 3-7). 1983. 10.95 (ISBN 0-15-255086-0, HJ). HarBraceJ.

Fassler, Joan. All Alone with Daddy: A Young Girl Plays the Role of Mother. Gregory, Dorothy L., illus. LC 76-80120. 32p. (ps-3). 1975. 16.95 (ISBN 0-87705-009-0). Human Sci Pr.

—One Little Girl. Smyth, M. Jane, illus. LC 76-80120. 32p. (ps-3). 1969. 16.95 (ISBN 0-87705-008-2). Human Sci Pr.

Fitzhugh, Louise. Nobody's Family Is Going to Change. (Illus.). 221p. (gr. 5-9). 1986. pap. 3.50 (ISBN 0-374-45523-6). FS&G.

Garland, Michael. My Cousin Katie. Garland, Michael, illus. (ps-1). 1990. 13.89. HarpC Child Bks.

Gates, Josephine S. The Live Dolls Busy Days. Keep, Virginia, illus. (gr. 4 up). Repr. of 1907 ed. 35.00 (ISBN 0-940070-15-4). Doll Works.

Giff, Patricia R. The Winter Worm Business. Morrill, Leslie, illus. (gr. 4-6). 1981. pap. 8.95 (ISBN 0-385-29152-3); pap. 8.89 (ISBN 0-385-29154-X). Delacorte.

Gipson, Morrell & Mangold, Paul. Walkers Go Hiking. LC 90-13797. (Illus.). 24p. (gr. k-3). 1990. PLB 13.26 (ISBN 0-944483-91-7). Garrett Ed Corp.

Goldman, Susan. Cousins Are Special. Rubin, Caroline, ed. Goldman, Susan, illus. LC 75-11924. (ps-2). 1978. PLB 9.75 (ISBN 0-8075-1317-2). A Whitman.

Gordon, Shirley. The Boy Who Wanted a Family. 96p. (gr. 1-4). 1982. pap. 2.95 (ISBN 0-440-40786-9, YB). Dell.

Greenfield, Eloise. Sister. Barnett, Moneta, illus. LC 73-22182. 96p. (gr. 5-12). 1974. 13.95 (ISBN 0-690-00497-4, Crowell Jr Bks). HarpC Child Bks.

Haas, Jessie. Keeping Barney. LC 81-7029. 160p. (gr. 5-9). 1982. reinforced bdg. 11.75 (ISBN 0-688-00859-3). Greenwillow.

Hamilton, Dorothy. The Gift of a Home. LC 73-13989. 120p. (gr. 9-11). 1974. pap. 3.95 (ISBN 0-8361-1727-1). Herald Pr.

—Ken's Bright Room. Converse, James L., photos by. LC 82-23351. (Illus.). 88p. (Orig.). (gr. 7-10). 1982. pap. 3.95 (ISBN 0-8361-3328-5). Herald Pr.

Hartling, Peter. Old John. Crawford, Elizabeth D., tr. from GER. LC 89-12976. 128p. (gr. 4-9). 1990. 11.95 (ISBN 0-688-08734-5). Lothrop.

Hayashi, Nancy. Cosmic Cousin. Hayashi, Nancy, illus. LC 87-34192. 80p. (gr. 2-5). 1988. 10.95 (ISBN 0-525-44387-8, DCB). Dutton Child Bks.

Henkes, Kevin. Chester's Way. Henkes, Kevin, illus. 32p. (ps-3). 1989. pap. 3.95 (ISBN 0-14-054053-9, Puffin). Puffin Bks.

—Two under Par. Henkes, Kevin, illus. LC 86-7556. 128p. (gr. 2-6). 1987. 10.25 (ISBN 0-688-06708-5). Greenwillow.

Hensley, Sam, Jr. Family Portrait. FS Staff, ed. 256p. (gr. 9-12). 1988. 12.90 (ISBN 0-531-10611-X). Watts.

Hest, Amy. Where in the World Is the Perfect Family? LC 88-20391. 112p. (gr. 4-7). 1989. 12.95 (ISBN 0-89919-659-4, Clarion Bks). HM.

Hill, Elizabeth S. When Christmas Comes. 208p. (gr. 5-7). 1989. pap. 11.95 (ISBN 0-670-82201-9). Viking Child Bks.

Hines, Anna G. Mean Old Uncle Jack. Hines, Anna G., illus. 32p. 1990. 13.95 (ISBN 0-395-52137-8). HM.

Hoguet, Susan R. I Unpacked My Grandmother's Trunk. Houget, Susan R., illus. LC 83-1701. 58p. (ps-3). 1983. 13.95 (ISBN 0-525-44069-0, DCB). Dutton Child Bks.

Hughes, Dean. Family Picture. 1990. pap. 2.75 (ISBN 0-590-43356-3). Scholastic Inc.

Hughes, Shirley. An Evening at Alfie's. Hughes, Shirley, illus. LC 84-11297. 32p. (ps-1). 1985. 14.95 (ISBN 0-688-04122-1); PLB 14.88 (ISBN 0-688-04123-X). Lothrop.

Impey, Rose. My Mom & Our Dad. (ps-3). 1991. 12.95 (ISBN 0-670-83663-X). Viking Child Bks.

Jewell, Nancy. The Family under the Moon. Kessler, Leonard, illus. LC 76-2344. (ps-3). 1976. PLB 14.89i (ISBN 0-06-022827-X). HarpC Child Bks.

Johnson, Annabel & Johnson, Edgar. The Grizzly. Riswold, Gilbert, illus. LC 64-11831. 194p. (gr. 5-9). 1964. PLB 13.89 (ISBN 0-06-022871-7). HarpC Child Bks.

Jones, Diana W. Aunt Maria. LC 90-24742. (Illus.). (gr. 7 up). 1991. 13.95 (ISBN 0-688-10611-0). Greenwillow.

Joosse, Barbara M. The Pitiful Life of Simon Schultz. LC 90-22352. 192p. (gr. 5-9). 1991. 13.95 (ISBN 0-06-022486-X); PLB 13.89 (ISBN 0-06-022487-8). HarpC Child Bks.

Keller, Holly. Cromwell's Glasses. Keller, Holly, illus. LC 81-6644. 32p. (gr. k-3). 1982. 14.95 (ISBN 0-688-00834-8). Greenwillow.

Kerr, M. E. I'll Love You When You're More Like Me. LC 76-58709. 160p. (gr. 7 up). 1977. PLB 14.89 (ISBN 0-06-023137-8). HarpC Child Bks.

Kherdian, David. A Song for Uncle Harry. Hogrogian, Nonny, illus. 80p. (gr. 3-7). 1989. 13.95 (ISBN 0-399-21895-5, Philomel Bks). Putnam Pub Group.

Kirkland, Dianna K. I Have a Stepfamily but... Orlowski, Dennis, illus. 40p. (Orig.). (ps-5). 1981. pap. 6.50 (ISBN 0-685-00148-2); counseling activity guide-stepfamilies 6.50 (ISBN 0-686-96649-X). Aid-U Pub.

Korman, Gordon. Who Is Bugs Potter. 1991. pap. 2.95 (ISBN 0-590-44207-4). Scholastic Inc.

Kuchler, Lena. My Hundred Children. (Orig.). (gr. k-12). 1987. pap. 3.50 (ISBN 0-440-95263-8, LFL). Dell.

LeVert, John. The Flight of the Cassowary. 228p. (gr. 7 up). 1986. 14.95 (ISBN 0-316-52196-5, Pub. by Joy Street Bks). Little.

McCloskey, Robert. One Morning in Maine. McCloskey, Robert, illus. (gr. k-3). 1952. pap. 13.95 (ISBN 0-670-52627-4). Viking Child Bks.

MacLachlan, Patricia. Arthur, for the Very First Time. Bloom, Lloyd, illus. LC 79-2007. 128p. (gr. 4-7). 1980. PLB 13.89 (ISBN 0-06-024047-4). HarpC Child Bks.

Mahy, Margaret. Aliens in the Family. LC 86-3908. 192p. (gr. 7 up). 1986. pap. 12.95 (ISBN 0-590-40320-6, Scholastic Hardcover). Scholastic Inc.

—Aliens in the Family. large type ed. 210p. (gr. 3-8). 1989. Repr. of 1986 ed. PLB 14.95 (ISBN 1-85089-974-6, Pub. by Clio Pr England). ABC-CllO.

—My Wonderful Aunt, Story 1. rev. ed. Gardiner, Deirdre, illus. 24p. (gr. 1-3). pap. text ed. 4.40 Americanized version (ISBN 1-55624-081-3, WP081-3). Wright Group.

—My Wonderful Aunt, Story 2. rev. ed. Gardiner, Deirdre, illus. 24p. (gr. 1-3). pap. text ed. 4.40 Americanized version (ISBN 1-55624-082-1, WP0821). Wright Group.

—My Wonderful Aunt, Story 3. Gardiner, Deirdre, illus. 24p. (gr. 1-2). pap. text ed. 4.40 (ISBN 1-55624-083-X, WP083X). Wright Group.

—My Wonderful Aunt, Story 4. Gardiner, Deirdre, illus. 24p. (gr. 1-2). pap. text ed. 4.40 (ISBN 1-55624-084-8, WP0848). Wright Group.

—My Wonderful Aunt, Story 3: Big Book. Gardiner, Deirdre, illus. 24p. (gr. 1-2). pap. text ed. 26.00 (ISBN 1-55624-154-2, WP1542). Wright Group.

—My Wonderful Aunt, Story 4: Big Book. Gardiner, Deirdre, illus. 24p. (gr. 1-2). pap. text ed. 26.00 (ISBN 1-55624-155-0, WP1550). Wright Group.

Martin, Ann M. Ten Kids, No Pets. (gr. 3-7). 1989. pap. 2.75 (ISBN 0-590-42244-8, Apple Paperbacks). Scholastic Inc.

Morris-Vann, Artie M. My Dad Is Unemployed... But. Orlowski, Dennis, illus. 40p. (Orig.). (ps-5). 1981. pap. 6.50 (ISBN 0-940370-01-8); counseling activity guide-unemployed families 6.50 (ISBN 0-685-00149-0). Aid-U Pub.

Norris, Carolyn. In Our House: Story for Young Children in Sign Language. Norris, Carolyn, illus. 32p. (Orig.). (ps-3). 3.25 (ISBN 0-916708-11-X). Modern Signs.

Nostlinger, Christine. The Cucumber King. Bell, Anthea, tr. 126p. (gr. 3-7). 1984. 9.95 (ISBN 0-930267-01-X). Bergh Pub.

Orgel, Doris. Midnight Soup & a Witch's Hat. Newsom, Carol, illus. 96p. (gr. 2-5). 1989. pap. 3.95 (ISBN 0-14-032212-4, Puffin). Puffin Bks.

Parish, Peggy. Amelia Bedelia's Family Album. Sweat, Lynn, illus. LC 87-15641. 48p. (gr. 3-9). 1988. 11.95 (ISBN 0-688-07676-9); lib. bdg. 11.88 (ISBN 0-688-07677-7). Greenwillow.

Parker, Nancy W. Love from Aunt Betty. (Illus.). 32p. (gr. k-3). 1983. 10.95 (ISBN 0-396-08135-5, Putnam). Putnam Pub Group.

Pearson, Gayle. Fish Friday. 192p. (gr. 3-7). 1989. pap. 3.95 (ISBN 0-689-71324-X, Aladdin). Macmillan Child Grp.

Peck, Robert N. Soup's Uncle. Robinson, Charles, illus. LC 87-37538. 112p. (gr. 4-7). 1988. 13.95 (ISBN 0-440-50062-1). Delacorte.

Peterson, John. Littles & the Lost Children. (gr. 4-7). 1991. pap. 2.50 (ISBN 0-590-43026-2). Scholastic Inc.

—The Littles to the Rescue. Peterson, John, illus. 48p. (ps-3). 1981. 6.95 (ISBN 0-448-47491-3, G&D). Putnam Pub Group.

Pevsner, Stella. Sister of the Quints. LC 86-17565. 192p. (gr. 5-9). 1987. 12.95 (ISBN 0-89919-498-2, Pub. by Clarion). Ticknor & Fields.

Pfeffer, Susan B. Claire at Sixteen. 1989. 13.95 (ISBN 0-553-05819-3, Starfire). Bantam.

Pople, Maureen. The Other Side of the Family. LC 87-32929. 176p. (gr. 5-9). 1988. 13.95 (ISBN 0-8050-0758-X). H Holt & Co.

—The Other Side of the Family. LC 87-32929. 176p. (gr. 7 up). 1990. pap. 3.25 (ISBN 0-394-83854-8). McKay.

Ratera, Rosario K. A Gift. (Illus.). (gr. 1-3). 1972. 3.00 (ISBN 0-686-09524-3, Pub. by New Day Pub Philippines). Cellar.

Rush, Alison. The Last of Danu's Children. LC 82-2981. (gr. 7 up). 1982. 9.95 (ISBN 0-395-32270-7); write for info. HM.

St. Peter, Joyce. Always Abigail. LC 81-47103. (Illus.). 128p. (gr. 3-5). 1981. 9.13i (ISBN 0-397-31934-7, Lipp Jr Bks). HarpC Child Bks.

Schwartz, Alvin. There Is a Carrot in My Ear & Other Noodle Tales. Weinhaus, Karen A., illus. LC 80-8442. 64p. (gr. k-3). 1982. PLB 11.89 (ISBN 0-06-025234-0). HarpC Child Bks.

Sebestyen, Ouida. Far from Home. 192p. (gr. 7 up). 1980. 15.95 (ISBN 0-316-77932-6, Joy St Bks). Little.

Sidney, Margaret. The Five Little Peppers & How They Grew. 302p. 1981. Repr. PLB 21.95x (ISBN 0-89966-340-0). Buccaneer Bks.

—Five Little Peppers & How They Grew. 1989. pap. 2.95 (ISBN 0-590-42520-X). Scholastic Inc.

—Five Little Peppers Grown up. 334p. 1981. Repr. lib. bdg. 21.95x (ISBN 0-89966-341-9). Buccaneer Bks.

Skurzynski, Gloria. Trapped in Slickrock Canyon. Soucie, Daniel S., illus. LC 83-14988. 128p. (gr. 4-6). 1984. 13.95 (ISBN 0-688-02688-5). Lothrop.

Smith, Doris B. The First Hard Times. 144p. (gr. 5-9). 1984. pap. 2.50 (ISBN 0-440-42532-8, YB). Dell.

Smith, Miriam. Kimi & the Watermelon. Armitage, David, illus. 32p. (ps-3). 1989. pap. 3.95 (ISBN 0-14-050950-X, Puffin). Puffin Bks.

Sobol, Harriet L. We Dont't Look Like Our Mom & Dad. Agre, Patricia, illus. 32p. (gr. 4-7). 1984. 11.95 (ISBN 0-698-20608-8, Coward). Putnam Pub Group.

Stretton, Barbara. The Truth of the Matter. 256p. 1984. pap. write for info. (ISBN 0-399-21147-0, Perigee Bks). Putnam Pub Group.

Tafuri, Nancy. All Year Long. Tafuri, Nancy, illus. LC 82-9275. 32p. (gr. k-2). 1983. PLB 10.88 (ISBN 0-688-01416-X). Greenwillow.

Taylor, Sydney. Ella of All-of-a-Kind Family. 144p. (gr. k-6). 1980. pap. 3.25 (ISBN 0-440-42252-3, YB). Dell.

Van Steenwyk, Elizabeth. Three Dog Winter. (gr. 4-9). 1987. 13.95 (ISBN 0-8027-6718-4). Walker & Co.

Walter, Mildred P. Mariah Keeps Cool. LC 89-23981. 144p. (gr. 3-7). 1990. 12.95 (ISBN 0-02-792295-2, Bradbury Pr). Macmillan Child Grp.

Watts, C. Ellen. Moving Again! I'm Not Going. 112p. 1989. pap. 4.95 (ISBN 0-87403-589-9, 3992). Standard Pub.

Willard, Nancy. Uncle Terrible: More Adventures of Anatole. McPhail, David, illus. LC 82-47940. 120p. (gr. 5 up). 1985. pap. 5.95 (ISBN 0-15-292794-8, HJ). HarBraceJ.

Wooldridge, Rhoda. Johnny Tread Water. 1983. pap. 8.00 (ISBN 0-8309-0354-2). Ind Pr MO.

Zolotow, Charlotte. The Quarreling Book. Lobel, Arnold, illus. LC 63-14445. 32p. (gr. k-3). 1963. 12.95 (ISBN 0-06-026975-8); PLB 11.89 (ISBN 0-06-026976-6). HarpC Child Bks.

—The Sky Was Blue. Williams, Garth, illus. LC 62-13328. (gr. k-3). 1963. PLB 13.89 (ISBN 0-06-027001-2). HarpC Child Bks.

FAMILY LIFE

Amstutz, Beverly. Sprouts: A Diary for the Foster Child. Amstutz, Beverly, illus. 38p. (Orig.). (gr. k-7). 1982. pap. 2.50x (ISBN 0-937836-07-9). Precious Res.

Ancona, George. Helping Out. Ancona, George, illus. LC 84-14995. 48p. (ps-4). 1985. 12.95 (ISBN 0-89919-278-5, Clarion). Ticknor & Fields.

Anglund, Joan W. All about My Family. Anglund, Joan W., illus. 48p. (ps up). 1987. pap. 6.95 (ISBN 0-590-40828-3). Scholastic Inc.

Arnstein, Helene S. Billy & Our New Baby. Smyth, M. Jane, illus. LC 73-7951. 32p. (ps-3). 1973. 16.95x (ISBN 0-87705-093-7). Human Sci Pr.

Bailey, Marilyn. Stepfamilies. LC 89-25325. (Illus.). 48p. (gr. 4 up). 1990. 10.95 (ISBN 0-89686-495-2, Crestwood Hse). Macmillan Child Grp.

Bennett, Gay. A Family in Sri Lanka. LC 85-6891. (Illus.). 32p. (gr. 2-5). 1985. PLB 9.95 (ISBN 0-8225-1661-6). Lerner Pubns.

Bennett, Olivia. A Family in Brazil. (Illus.). 32p. (gr. 2-5). 1986. lib. bdg. 9.95 (ISBN 0-8225-1665-9). Lerner Pubns.

Berry, Joy W. Teach Me about Brothers & Sisters. Dickey, Kate, ed. LC 85-45079. (Illus.). 36p. (ps). 1986. 4.98 (ISBN 0-685-10718-3). Grolier Inc.

—Teach Me about Relatives. Dickey, Kate, ed. LC 85-45080. (Illus.). 36p. (ps). 1986. 4.98 (ISBN 0-685-10719-1). Grolier Inc.

—What to Do When Your Mom or Dad Says..."Be Prepared!" LC 81-83790. (Illus.). 48p. (gr. 3 up). 1982. lib. bdg. 14.60 (ISBN 0-516-02566-X). Childrens.

—What to Do When Your Mom or Dad Says..."Earn Your Allowance!" LC 81-83791. (Illus.). 48p. (gr. 3 up). 1982. lib. bdg. 14.60 (ISBN 0-516-02568-6). Childrens.

Booher, Dianna D. Coping: When Your Family Falls Apart. LC 79-17342. 192p. (gr. 7 up). 1979. lib. bdg. 11.98 (ISBN 0-671-33083-7). Messner.

Clifton, Lucille, et al. Everett Anderson's Goodbye. Grifalconi, Ann, illus. LC 82-23426. 32p. (ps-1). 1983. 10.95 (ISBN 0-8050-0235-9). H Holt & Co.

Cosby, Clair G. Lord, Help Me Love My Sister. LC 86-4831. 80p. (Orig.). (gr. 3-10). 1986. pap. 4.95 (ISBN 0-8361-3413-3). Herald Pr.

Crary, Elizabeth. Mommy Don't Go. Megale, Marina, illus. LC 85-63759. 32p. (Orig.). (ps-2). 1986. lib. bdg. 14.95 (ISBN 0-943990-27-0); pap. 4.95 (ISBN 0-943990-26-2). Parenting Pr.

Crews, Donald. Bigmama's. LC 90-33142. (Illus.). 32p. (ps up). 1991. 13.95 (ISBN 0-688-09950-5); PLB 13.88 (ISBN 0-688-09951-3). Greenwillow.

Davis, Diane. Something Is Wrong at My House. Megale, Marina, illus. LC 84-62129. 40p. (Orig.). (ps-6). 1985. PLB 12.95 (ISBN 0-943990-11-4); pap. 3.95 (ISBN 0-943990-10-6). Parenting Pr.

Dellinger, A. & Fletcher, S. Family Devotions. (ps-3). pap. 0.59 (ISBN 0-570-08313-3, 56HH1445). Concordia.

Fast, Suellen M. Celebrations of Daughterhood. 2nd, rev. ed. Serman, Gina L., ed. 70p. (gr. k up). 1988. pap. 8.00 (ISBN 0-317-57532-5). Daughter Cult.

Forever Amy, Amy's Grandma. 1990. 7.95 (ISBN 0-533-08996-4). Vantage.

Friedrich, Liz. Married Life. (Illus.). 64p. (gr. 7-12). 1989. PLB 12.40 (ISBN 0-531-10836-8). Watts.

Gay, Kathlyn. The Changing Families: Meeting Today's Challenges. LC 86-19708. (Illus.). 128p. (gr. 6-12). 1988. lib. bdg. 17.95 (ISBN 0-89490-139-7). Enslow Pubs.

Getzoff, Ann & McClenahan, Carolyn. Stepkids: A Survival Guide for Teenagers in Stepfamilies...& for Stepparents Doubtful of Their Own Survival. 171p. (gr. 5 up). 1985. pap. 8.95 (ISBN 0-8027-7236-6). Walker & Co.

Gilbreth, Frank B., Jr. & Carey, Ernestine G. Cheaper by the Dozen. (gr. 6 up). pap. 3.50 (ISBN 0-553-25018-3). Bantam.

Gooden, Kimberly W. Coping with Family Stress. Rosen, Ruth, ed. (gr. 7-12). 1989. PLB 12.95 (ISBN 0-8239-0980-8). Rosen Group.

Goom, Bridget. A Family in Singapore. (Illus.). 32p. (gr. 2-5). 1986. lib. bdg. 9.95 (ISBN 0-8225-1663-2). Lerner Pubns.

Gunner, Emily & McConky, Shirley. A Family in Australia. (Illus.). 32p. (gr. k-6). 1984. lib. bdg. 11.90 (ISBN 0-531-03824-6). Watts.

Hautzig, Esther. Endless Steppe: Growing up in Siberia. LC 68-13582. 243p. (gr. 7 up). 1968. 13.95 (ISBN 0-690-26371-6, Crowell Jr Bks). HarpC Child Bks.

Hermes, Patricia. Who Will Take Care of Me? LC 82-48757. 128p. (gr. 3-7). 1983. 11.95 (ISBN 0-15-296265-4, HJ). HarBraceJ.

Holland, Vicki. We Are Having a Baby. (Illus.). (gr. k-1). 1972. 8.95 (ISBN 0-684-12809-8, Scribners Young Read); (Pub. by Scribner). Macmillan Child Grp.

Jacobsen & Kristensen. A Family in Hong Kong. LC 84-73580. (Illus.). 32p. (gr. 3-5). 1985. 11.90 (ISBN 0-531-18001-8, Pub. by Bookwright Pr). Watts.

Jacobsen, P. & Kristensen, P. A Family in China. LC 85-71727. (Illus.). 32p. (gr. k-6). 1986. lib. bdg. 11.90 (ISBN 0-531-18035-2, Pub. by Bookwright Pr). Watts.

Jacobsen, P & Kristensen, P. A Family in Iceland. LC 85-62086. (Illus.). 32p. (gr. k-6). 1986. lib. bdg. 11.90 (ISBN 0-531-18036-0, Pub. by Bookwright Pr). Watts.

Jacobsen, P. & Kristensen, P. A Family in Japan. (Illus.). 32p. (gr. k-6). 1984. lib. bdg. 11.90 (ISBN 0-531-03825-4). Watts.

—A Family in Thailand. (Illus.). 32p. (gr. k-6). 1986. lib. bdg. 11.90 (ISBN 0-531-18038-7, Pub. by Bookwright Pr). Watts.

—A Family in the U. S. S. R. LC 85-62086. (Illus.). 32p. (gr. k-6). 1986. lib. bdg. 11.90 (ISBN 0-531-18037-9, Pub. by Bookwright Pr). Watts.

Jacobsen, Peter & Kristensen, Preben. A Family in Central America. LC 85-73585. (Illus.). 32p. (gr. 1-6). 1986. PLB 11.90 (ISBN 0-531-18081-6, Pub. by Bookwright). Watts.

—A Family in Colombia. LC 85-73677. (Illus.). 32p. (gr. 1-6). 1986. PLB 11.90 (ISBN 0-531-18083-2, Pub. by Bookwright). Watts.

—A Family in Greenland. (Illus.). 32p. (gr. 1-6). 1986. PLB 11.90 (ISBN 0-531-18082-4, Pub. by Bookwright). Watts.

—A Family in Hawaii. LC 85-73677. (Illus.). 32p. (gr. 1-6). 1986. PLB 11.90 (ISBN 0-531-18084-0, Pub. by Bookwright). Watts.

—A Family in Switzerland. LC 84-73578. 32p. (gr. 7-9). 1985. s&l 11.90 (ISBN 0-531-18002-6, Pub. by Bookwright Pr). Watts.

—A Family in the Persian Gulf. LC 84-73579. (Illus.). 32p. (gr. 2-5). 1985. PLB 11.90 s&l (ISBN 0-531-18003-4, Pub. by Bookwright Pr). Watts.

—A Family in West Africa. LC 84-73577. (Illus.). 32p. (gr. 1-6). 1985. PLB 11.90 (ISBN 0-531-18000-X, Pub. by Bookwright Pr). Watts.

Leiner, Katherine. Something's Wrong in My House. Kline, M., ed. (Illus.). 64p. (gr. k-6). 1988. PLB 10.90 (ISBN 0-531-10506-7). Watts.

Lewis, Claudia. Up in the Mountains: And Other Poems of Long Ago. Fontaine, Joel, illus. LC 90-4439. 64p. (gr. 3-7). 1991. 13.95 (ISBN 0-06-023810-0); PLB 13.89 (ISBN 0-06-023812-7). HarpC Child Bks.

Little, Jean. Kate. LC 70-148419. 174p. (gr. 5-8). 1971. PLB 12.89 (ISBN 0-06-023914-X). HarpC Child Bks.

Little People Big Book about Families. 64p. (ps-1). 1990. write for info. (ISBN 0-8094-7491-3); PLB write for info. (ISBN 0-8094-7492-1). Time-Life.

Lowry, Lois. Anastasia Again! De Groat, Diane, illus. 160p. (gr. 3-6). 1981. 13.95 (ISBN 0-395-31147-0). HM.

Moran, Tom. A Family in Ireland. (Illus.). 32p. (gr. 2-5). 1986. lib. bdg. 9.95 (ISBN 0-8225-1668-3). Lerner Pubns.

Nicoll, Helen & Pienkowski, Jan. Meg's Veg. (Illus.). 32p. (ps-1). 1983. 13.95 (ISBN 0-434-95639-2, Pub. by W Heinemann Ltd). Trafalgar Sq.

—Mog's Mumps. (Illus.). 32p. (ps-1). 1983. 15.95 (ISBN 0-434-95640-6, Pub. by W Heinemann Ltd). Trafalgar Sq.

Paris, Susan. Mommy & Daddy Are Fighting. Labinski, Gail, illus. LC 85-22193. 24p. (Orig.). (ps-4). 1986. pap. 8.95 (ISBN 0-931188-33-4). Seal Pr Feminist.

Perovskaya, Olga. Wolf in Olga's Kitchen. Glagoleva, Fainna, tr. Culfogienis, Angie, illus. LC 69-12440. (gr. 4-8). 1969. 5.50 (ISBN 0-672-50590-8, Bobbs). Macmillan.

Robson, John, ed. Me & You. (Illus.). 48p. (Orig.). (gr. 6-9). 1982. pap. 2.50 (ISBN 0-936098-33-3). Intl Marriage.

—You & Your Family. (Illus.). 30p. (Orig.). (gr. 2-4). 1981. pap. 2.50 (ISBN 0-936098-30-9). Intl Marriage.

Rosenberg, Maxine B. Finding a Way: Living with Exceptional Brothers & Sisters. Ancona, George, photos by. LC 88-6776. 48p. (gr. 1-4). 1988. 12.95 (ISBN 0-688-06873-1); PLB 12.88 (ISBN 0-688-06874-X). Lothrop.

St. John, Jetty. A Family in Chile. (Illus.). 32p. (gr. 2-5). 1986. lib. bdg. 9.95 (ISBN 0-8225-1667-5). Lerner Pubns.

Siegel, Eli. Children's Guide to Parents & Other Matters: Little Essays for Children & Others. LC 78-171393. (Illus.). (gr. 1-6). 1971. text ed. 6.50 (ISBN 0-910492-16-6). Definition.
Stewart, Judy. A Family in Morocco. (Illus.). 32p. (gr. 2-5). 1986. lib. bdg. 9.95 (ISBN 0-8225-1664-0). Lerner Pubns.
—A Family in Sudan. (Illus.). 32p. (gr. 2-5). 1988. lib. bdg. 9.95 (ISBN 0-8225-1682-9). Lerner Pubns.
Velez, Jose S. Cuando en Casa No Nos Comprenden - When We Are Not Understood at Home. (SPA.). 112p. (Orig.). (gr. 9 up). 1991. pap. 3.95 (ISBN 0-311-46263-4). Casa Bautista.
Weddle, Linda M. Handling the Hassles at Home. large type ed. Date not set. 2.95 (ISBN 0-8474-0505-2). Back to Bible.
Wilkins, Frances. Family Life from Nineteen Thirty to the Nineteen Eighties. (Illus.). 72p. (gr. 7-12). 1986. 19.95 (ISBN 0-7134-4818-0, Pub. by Batsford England). Trafalgar Sq.
Yu, Ling. A Family in Taiwan. (Illus.). 32p. (gr. 2-5). 1990. PLB 9.95 (ISBN 0-8225-1685-3). Lerner Pubns.

FAMILY LIFE–FICTION

Adler, C. S. In Our House Scott Is My Brother. LC 79-20693. 144p. (gr. 5-9). 1980. 12.95 (ISBN 0-02-700140-7, Mcmillan Child Bk). Macmillan Child Grp.
—One Sister Too Many. 176p. (gr. 3-7). 1991. pap. 3.95 (ISBN 0-689-71521-8, Aladdin). Macmillan Child Grp.
—One Sister Too Many: A Sequel to Split Sisters. LC 88-13144. 176p. (gr. 4-8). 1989. 12.95 (ISBN 0-02-700271-3, Mcmillan Child Bk). Macmillan Child Grp.
—Split Sisters. Wimmer, Mike, illus. LC 85-15411. 156p. (gr. 4-8). 1986. 12.95 (ISBN 0-02-700380-9, Mcmillan Child Bk). Macmillan Child Grp.
—Split Sisters. (gr. 4-7). 1990. pap. 3.95 (ISBN 0-689-71369-X, Aladdin). Macmillan Child Grp.
Agee, James. Death in the Family. 320p. (gr. 10 up). 1971. pap. 3.95 (ISBN 0-553-23392-0). Bantam.
Alcott, Louisa May. Eight Cousins. (gr. k-6). 1986. pap. 3.50 (ISBN 0-440-42231-0, Pub. by Yearling Classics). Dell.
—Eight Cousins or the Aunt Hill. 272p. (gr. 5 up). 1989. pap. 2.95 (ISBN 0-14-035112-4, Puffin). Puffin Bks.
—Jo's Boys. Date not set. 18.95 (ISBN 0-8488-0411-2). Amereon Ltd.
—Jo's Boys. 1989. Repr. of 1886 ed. lib. bdg. 79.00 (ISBN 0-685-27398-9). Reprint Servs.
—Little Men. (gr. 4-6). 1971. 5.95 (ISBN 0-448-02363-6, G&D). Putnam Pub Group.
—Little Men. (Illus.). (gr. 4-6). (G&D); 12.95 (ISBN 0-448-06018-3, G&D). Putnam Pub Group.
—Little Men. 1989. Repr. of 1861 ed. lib. bdg. 79.00 (ISBN 0-685-27393-8). Reprint Servs.
—Little Women. (Illus.). (gr. 6 up). pap. 2.95 (ISBN 0-8049-0106-6, CL-106). Airmont.
—Little Women. Magagna, Anna M. & Jambor, Louis, illus. (gr. 4-6). 1981. Illustrated Junior Library. pap. 9.95 (ISBN 0-448-11019-9, G&D); deluxe ed. 14.95 (ISBN 0-448-06019-1); Companion Library 3.95 (ISBN 0-448-05466-3). Putnam Pub Group.
—Little Women. 59.95 (ISBN 0-8490-0547-7). Gordon Pr.
—Little Women. Smith, Jessie W., illus. (gr. 7 up). 1968. 17.95 (ISBN 0-316-03095-3). Little.
—Little Women. 320p. (gr. 3-7). 1983. pap. 2.25 (ISBN 0-14-035008-X, Puffin). Puffin Bks.
—Little Women. 1963. 37.50 (ISBN 0-685-20188-0, 144-7). Saphrograph.
—Little Women. Barish, Wendy, ed. Cheng, Judith, illus. 576p. 1982. 15.95 (ISBN 0-671-44447-6, Little Simon). S&S Trade.
—Little Women. 1983. Repr. lib. bdg. 18.95x (ISBN 0-89966-408-3). Buccaneer Bks.
—Little Women. Bedall, Madelon, intro. by. 1981. pap. 6.00 (ISBN 0-685-06605-3, Modern Lib). Random.
—Little Women. Douglas, Ann, intro. by. 480p. (gr. 3 up). 1983. pap. 3.95 (ISBN 0-451-52341-5, Sig Classic). NAL-Dutton.
—Little Women. Edwards, Gunvor, illus. Gliberry, Lysbeth, retold by. (Illus.). 48p. (gr. 7-12). 1975. pap. text ed. 2.25x (ISBN 0-19-421804-X). Oxford U Pr.
—Little Women. LC 62-20197. (gr. 4 up). 1986. pap. 3.95 (ISBN 0-02-041240-1, Collier). Macmillan.
—Little Women. (gr. 2 up). 8.98 (ISBN 0-517-63489-9). Outlet Bk Co.
—Little Women. (Orig.). (gr. k-6). 1987. pap. 6.95 (ISBN 0-440-44768-2, Pub. by Yearling Classics). Dell.
—Little Women. 256p. (gr. 3-7). 1986. pap. 2.50 (ISBN 0-590-40498-9, Pub. by Apple Classics). Scholastic Inc.
—Little Women. James, Derek, illus. LC 87-45450. 512p. 1988. 18.95 (ISBN 0-394-56279-8). Knopf.
—Little Women. Showalter, Elaine, intro. by. 608p. 1989. pap. 5.95 (ISBN 0-14-039069-3, Penguin Classics). Viking Penguin.
—Little Women. 1989. Repr. of 1867 ed. lib. bdg. 79.00 (ISBN 0-685-27395-4). Reprint Servs.
—Little Women. Auerbach, Nina, afterword by. 480p. 1983. pap. 3.95 (ISBN 0-553-21275-3, Bantam Classics Spectra). Bantam.
—Little Women, 4 vols. large type ed. (gr. 7 up). Repr. of 1946 ed. Set. write for info. NAVH.
—Little Women. large type ed. 336p. 1987. 15.95 (ISBN 0-7089-8384-7, Charnwood). Ulverscroft.
—Little Women. 1986. pap. 2.95 (ISBN 0-590-43797-6). Scholastic Inc.
—Little Women. 1988. 2.98 (ISBN 0-671-09222-7). S&S Trade.
—Little Women. Smith, Jessie W., illus. 388p. (gr. 4 up). 1986. 12.95 (ISBN 0-681-40055-2). Longmeadow Pr.
—Little Women, Vol. 2: The Sisters Grow Up. Lindskoog, Kathryn, ed. (Illus.). (gr. 3-7). 1991. pap. 6.99 (ISBN 0-88070-463-2). Multnomah.
—A Modern Mephistopheles. Date not set. 14.95 (ISBN 0-8488-0412-0). Amereon Ltd.
—Reader's Digest Best Loved Books for Young Readers: Little Women. Ogburn, Jackie, ed. English, Mark, illus. 176p. (gr. 4-12). 1989. 3.99 (ISBN 0-945260-25-3). Choice Pub NY.
—Works of Louisa May Alcott. (gr. 5-6). 35.95 (ISBN 0-88411-173-3, Pub. by Aeonian Pr). Amereon Ltd.
Alexander, Martha. Nobody Asked Me If I Wanted a Baby Sister. Alexander, Martha, illus. LC 78-153731. (ps-2). 1971. 10.95 (ISBN 0-8037-6401-4); PLB 10.89 (ISBN 0-8037-6402-2). Dial Bks Young.
Alexander, Sue. World Famous Muriel. Demarest, Chris L., illus. LC 82-17186. (ps-3). 1984. 14.95 (ISBN 0-316-03131-3). Little.
Allard, Harry. The Stupids Have a Ball. Marshall, James, illus. LC 77-27660. (gr. k-3). 1984. 13.95 (ISBN 0-395-26497-9); pap. 3.95 (ISBN 0-395-36169-9). HM.
—The Stupids Step Out. Marshall, James, illus. LC 73-21698. 32p. (gr. k-3). 1977. 13.95 (ISBN 0-395-18513-0); pap. 3.95 (ISBN 0-395-25377-2). HM.
Allison, Diane W. In Window Eight, the Moon Is Late. Allison, Diane W., illus. (ps-3). 1988. 12.95 (ISBN 0-316-03435-5). Little.
Ashley, Bernard. All My Men. LC 78-12683. (gr. 6 up). 1978. 18.95 (ISBN 0-87599-228-5). S G Phillips.
Auch, Mary J. Cry Uncle! LC 87-45330. 224p. (gr. 4-7). 1987. 13.95 (ISBN 0-8234-0660-1). Holiday.
Auster, Benjamin. I Like It When... Winborn, Marsha, illus. 24p. (ps-2). 1990. PLB 12.33 (ISBN 0-8172-3578-7); PLB 9.25 (ISBN 0-685-33575-5). Raintree Pubs.
Bach, Alice. A Father Every Few Years. LC 76-24303. 144p. (gr. 7 up). 1977. HarpC Child Bks.
Baker, Barbara. Oh, Emma. Stock, Catharine, illus. 96p. (gr. 2-5). 1991. 12.95 (ISBN 0-525-44771-7, DCB). Dutton Child Bks.
Bang, Molly G. Dawn. LC 83-886. 32p. (gr. 4-7). 1983. PLB 13.88 (ISBN 0-688-02404-1). Morrow Jr Bks.
Barrett, Joyce D. Willie's Not the Hugging Kind. Cummings, Pat, illus. LC 89-1868. 32p. (gr. k-3). 1991. pap. 4.95 (ISBN 0-06-443264-5, Trophy). HarpC Child Bks.
Barrington, Margaret. My Cousin Justin. 288p. (Orig.). (gr. 10-12). 1991. pap. text ed. 11.95 (ISBN 0-85640-456-X, Pub. by Blackstaff Pr Belfast). Dufour.
Bawden, Nina. The Peppermint Pig. LC 74-26922. 192p. (gr. 3-6). 1975. PLB 13.89 (ISBN 0-397-31618-6, Lipp Jr Bks). HarpC Child Bks.
Belden, Wilanne S. Frankie! LC 86-33507. (Illus.). 176p. (gr. 2-7). 1987. 14.95 (ISBN 0-15-229380-9). HarBraceJ.
Beni, Ruth. The Family Next Door. (Illus.). 48p. (gr. 2-4). 1990. pap. 6.95 (ISBN 0-233-98383-X, Pub. by A Deutsch UK). Trafalgar Sq.
Birdwell, Norman. La Familia de Clifford. (SPA.). (ps-2). 1989. pap. 2.95 (ISBN 0-590-41992-7). Scholastic Inc.
Blaine, Marge. The Terrible Thing That Happened at Our House. Wallner, John, illus. LC 86-4827. 40p. (ps-3). 1984. Repr. of 1975 ed. 13.95 (ISBN 0-02-710720-5, Four Winds). Macmillan Child Grp.
Blakeslee, Ann. After the Fortune Cookies. 128p. (gr. 3-7). 1989. 14.95 (ISBN 0-399-21562-X, Putnam). Putnam Pub Group.
Blume, Judy. Fudge-A-Mania. (gr. 3-7). 1990. 12.95 (ISBN 0-525-44672-9, DCB). Dutton Child Bks.
—Just as Long as We're Together. LC 87-7980. 304p. (gr. 5-8). 1987. 12.95 (ISBN 0-531-05729-1); PLB 12.99 (ISBN 0-531-08329-2). Orchard Bks Watts.
—Starring Sally J. Freedman As Herself. LC 76-57805. 296p. (gr. 4-7). 1982. 14.95 (ISBN 0-02-711070-2, Bradbury Pr). Macmillan Child Grp.
—Superfudge. 176p. (gr. 2-6). 1981. pap. 3.50 (ISBN 0-440-48433-2, YB). Dell.
—Superfudge. LC 80-10439. 176p. (gr. 3-6). 1980. 11.95 (ISBN 0-525-40522-4, DCB). Dutton Child Bks.
—Superfudge. large type ed. 239p. (gr. 2-6). 1987. Repr. of 1980 ed. lib. bdg. 14.95 (ISBN 1-55736-014-6). ABC-CLIO.
—Then Again, Maybe I Won't. LC 77-156548. 176p. (gr. 5-7). 1982. 13.95 (ISBN 0-02-711090-7, Bradbury Pr). Macmillan Child Grp.
Bond, Michael. More about Paddington. Fortnum, Peggy, illus. 128p. (gr. 3-7). 1979. pap. 2.95 (ISBN 0-440-45825-0, YB). Dell.
—Paddington at Large. Fortnum, Peggy, illus. 128p. (gr. 3-7). 1970. pap. 2.95 (ISBN 0-440-46801-9, YB). Dell.
—Paddington at Work. 128p. (gr. k-8). 1971. pap. 2.95 (ISBN 0-440-40797-4, YB). Dell.
Bonsall, Crosby. And I Mean It, Stanley. 32p. (ps-2). 1990. pap. 6.95 (ISBN 1-55994-265-7, Caedmon). HarperAudio.
Bonsall, Crosby N. The Day I Had to Play with My Sister. Bonsall, Crosby N., illus. LC 72-76507. 32p. (ps-2). 1972. PLB 10.89 (ISBN 0-06-020576-8). HarpC Child Bks.
Bradburne, Elizabeth & Voller, Katheen. Happy Families. (gr. 4-7). 1989. 4.25 (ISBN 0-901269-20-4). Grosvenor USA.
Brochmann, Elizabeth. What's the Matter, Girl? LC 79-2022. 128p. (gr. 7 up). 1980. 8.95 (ISBN 0-06-020677-2). HarpC Child Bks.
Brooks, Jerome. Naked in Winter. LC 89-35651. 224p. (gr. 7 up). 1990. 14.95 (ISBN 0-531-05866-2); PLB 14.99 (ISBN 0-531-08466-3). Orchard Bks Watts.
Brown, Faye. Chinch Bugs, Chinky Pins, & Chinie-Berry Beads. Brown, Trillie, illus. 191p. (Orig.). 1990. pap. 7.95 (ISBN 0-943487-24-2). Sevgo Pr.
Byars, Betsy. Good-Bye, Chicken Little. LC 78-19829. 112p. (gr. 5 up). 1979. PLB 12.89 (ISBN 0-06-020911-9). HarpC Child Bks.
—The Night Swimmers. Howell, Troy, illus. LC 79-53597. 160p. (gr. 4-6). 1980. 9.95 (ISBN 0-685-01397-9); pap. 11.95 (ISBN 0-385-28709-7). Delacorte.
—The Not-Just-Anybody Family. (gr. k-6). 1987. pap. 2.95 (ISBN 0-440-45951-6, YB). Dell.
—Wanted...Mud Blossom. (gr. 4-7). 1991. 14.00 (ISBN 0-385-30428-5). Delacorte.
Byars, Betsy C. The Cartoonist. Cuffari, Richard, illus. LC 77-12782. 128p. (gr. 3-7). 1978. pap. 13.95 (ISBN 0-670-20556-7). Viking Child Bks.
—The Glory Girl. (ps-3). 1985. pap. 3.95 (ISBN 0-14-031785-6, Puffin). Puffin Bks.
—Summer of the Swans. CoConis, Ted, illus. (gr. 7 up). 1970. pap. 12.95 (ISBN 0-670-68190-3). Viking Child Bks.
Byers, Rinda M. Mycca's Baby. Tamura, David, illus. LC 88-27320. 32p. (ps-2). 1990. 13.95 (ISBN 0-531-05828-X); PLB 13.99 (ISBN 0-531-08428-0). Orchard Bks Watts.
Caines, Jeannette. Window Wishing. LC 79-2698. (Illus.). 32p. (gr. k-3). 1980. PLB 12.89 (ISBN 0-06-020934-8). HarpC Child Bks.
Cameron, Ann. Julian, Dream Doctor. Strugnell, Ann, illus. LC 89-37562. 64p. (Orig.). (gr. 2-4). 1990. PLB 5.99 (ISBN 0-679-90524-3); pap. 1.95 (ISBN 0-679-80524-9). McKay.
—More Stories Julian Tells. Strugnell, Ann, illus. LC 84-10095. 96p. (gr. k-4). 1986. 13.95 (ISBN 0-394-86969-9); lib. bdg. 13.99 (ISBN 0-394-96969-3). Knopf.
Cameron, Eleanor. Julia & the Hand of God. Owens, Gail, illus. LC 77-4507. (gr. 4-7). 1977. 12.95 (ISBN 0-525-32910-2, DCB). Dutton Child Bks.
—Julia's Magic. Owens, Gail, illus. LC 84-8118. 144p. (gr. 2-5). 1984. 10.95 (ISBN 0-525-44114-X, DCB). Dutton Child Bks.
—The Private World of Julia Redfern. 224p. (gr. 5 up). 1990. pap. 4.95 (ISBN 0-14-034043-2, Puffin). Puffin Bks.
—A Room Made of Windows. (gr. 7 up). 1971. 15.95 (ISBN 0-316-12523-7, Joy St Bks). Little.
—That Julia Redfern. Owens, Gail, illus. LC 82-2405. 144p. (gr. 2-5). 1982. 12.95 (ISBN 0-525-44015-1, DCB). Dutton Child Bks.
Carlson, Nancy. The Perfect Family. Carlson, Nancy, illus. LC 85-4123. 32p. (ps-3). 1985. PLB 9.95 (ISBN 0-87614-280-3). Carolrhoda Bks.
—Take Time to Relax. (ps-3). 1991. 13.95 (ISBN 0-670-83287-1). Viking Child Bks.
Carrick, Carol. Left Behind. Carrick, Donald, illus. (ps-3). 1991. pap. 4.95 (ISBN 0-395-54380-0, Clarion Bks). HM.
Caseley, Judith. Hurricane Harry. LC 90-13809. (Illus.). 128p. (gr. 1 up). 1991. 13.95 (ISBN 0-688-10027-9). Greenwillow.
Caudill. Happy Little Family. (gr. k-6). 1989. pap. 2.75 (ISBN 0-440-40164-X, YB). Dell.
Caudill, Rebecca. Saturday Cousins. (gr. k-6). 1989. pap. 2.75 (ISBN 0-440-40208-5, YB). Dell.
Cave, Hugh B. The Voyage. LC 87-24004. 192p. (gr. 3-7). 1988. 13.95 (ISBN 0-02-717780-7, Mcmillan Child Bk). Macmillan Child Grp.
Chaikin, Miriam. Finders Weepers. Egielski, Richard, illus. LC 79-9608. 128p. (gr. 3-6). 1980. PLB 12.89. HarpC Child Bks.
—I Should Worry, I Should Care. Egielski, Richard, illus. LC 78-19480. (gr. 3-6). 1979. 12.89 (ISBN 0-06-021174-1). HarpC Child Bks.
Chang, Margaret & Chang, Raymond. In the Eye of War. (gr. 5-9). 1990. 13.95 (ISBN 0-689-50503-5, M K McElderry). Macmillan Child Grp.
Christiansen, C. B. A Small Pleasure. LC 87-19313. 144p. (gr. 7 up). 1988. 12.95 (ISBN 0-689-31369-1, Atheneum Child Bk). Macmillan Child Grp.
Christopher, Matt. Tight End. 128p. (gr. 3 up). 1981. 12.95 (ISBN 0-316-14017-1). Little.
Cleary, Beverly. Dear Mr. Henshaw. Zelinsky, Paul O., illus. LC 83-5372. 144p. (gr. 3-7). 1983. 12.95 (ISBN 0-688-02405-X); PLB 12.88 (ISBN 0-688-02406-8, Morrow Jr Bks). Morrow Jr Bks.
—The Growing-Up Feet. DiSalvo-Ryan, DyAnne, illus. LC 86-12585. 32p. (ps-1). 1987. 11.95 (ISBN 0-688-06619-4); lib. bdg. 11.88 (ISBN 0-688-06620-8). Morrow.
—Mitch & Amy. Porter, George, illus. LC 67-10041. 224p. (gr. 3-7). 1967. 15.95 (ISBN 0-688-21688-9); PLB 15.88 (ISBN 0-688-31688-3, Morrow Jr Bks). Morrow Jr Bks.
—Ramona & Her Father. Tiegreen, Alan, illus. LC 77-1614. 192p. (gr. 3-7). 1977. 13.95 (ISBN 0-688-22114-9); PLB 13.88 (ISBN 0-688-32114-3). Morrow.
—Ramona & Her Mother. 208p. (gr. k-6). 1980. pap. 3.25 (ISBN 0-440-47243-1, YB). Dell.
—Ramona, Forever. 192p. (gr. k-6). 1985. pap. 3.25 (ISBN 0-440-47210-5, YB). Dell.

—Ramona Quimby, Age 8. large type ed. Tiegreen, Alan, illus. 142p. (gr. 2-6). 1987. Repr. of 1981 ed. lib. bdg. 14.95 (ISBN 1-55736-000-6). ABC-CLIO.
—Sister of the Bride. Krush, Beth & Krush, Joe, illus. LC 63-8802. 256p. (gr. 7 up). 1963. PLB 13.88 (ISBN 0-688-31742-1). Morrow Jr Bks.
Cleaver, Vera. Belle Pruitt. LC 87-45879. 176p. (gr. 4-7). 1988. 12.95 (ISBN 0-397-32304-2, Lipp Jr Bks); PLB 12.89 (ISBN 0-397-32305-0, Lipp Jr Bks). HarpC Child Bks.
—Sugar Blue. Nomes, Eric J., illus. LC 83-19910. 160p. (gr. 5 up). 1984. 13.00 (ISBN 0-688-02720-2). Lothrop.
—Sweetly Sings the Donkey. LC 85-40098. 160p. (gr. 5-9). 1985. 12.95 (ISBN 0-397-32156-2, Lipp Jr Bks); PLB 12.89 (ISBN 0-397-32157-0, Lipp Jr Bks). HarpC Child Bks.
Cleaver, Vera & Cleaver, Bill. Delpha Green & Company. LC 79-172141. 144p. (gr. 6 up). 1972. (Junior Bks); pap. 2.95 (ISBN 0-397-31344-6, LSC-8). HarperCollins.
—Dust of the Earth. LC 75-18939. 160p. (gr. 7 up). 1975. 13.95 (ISBN 0-397-31650-X, Lipp Jr Bks). HarpC Child Bks.
—Mock Revolt. LC 75-151467. 160p. (gr. 6 up). 1971. (Lipp Jr Bks); pap. 1.95 (ISBN 0-397-31237-7). HarpC Child Bks.
Climo, Shirley. Month of Seven Days. 192p. (gr. 2-9). pap. 2.95 (ISBN 0-8167-1476-2). Troll Assocs.
Clymer, Eleanor. A Search for Two Bad Mice. Gill, Margery, illus. 80p. (gr. 1-3). 1991. pap. 3.50 (ISBN 0-689-71537-4, Aladdin). Macmillan Child Grp.
Collier, James L. The Winchesters. LC 88-5364. 176p. (gr. 5 up). 1988. 13.95 (ISBN 0-02-722831-2, Mcmillan Child Bk). Macmillan Child Grp.
Colman, Hila. Suddenly. LC 86-28460. 160p. (gr. 7 up). 1987. 12.95 (ISBN 0-688-05865-5). Morrow Jr Bks.
Conrad, Pam. Prairie Visions: The Life & Times of Solomon Butcher. Zudeck, Darryl, illus. LC 90-38658. 96p. (gr. 5 up). 1991. 16.95 (ISBN 0-06-021373-6); PLB 16.89 (ISBN 0-06-021375-2). HarpC Child Bks.
Cooney, Caroline B. Family Reunion. 1990. pap. 2.95 (ISBN 0-553-28573-4). Bantam.
Corlett, William. The Bloxworth Blue. LC 85-42916. 192p. (gr. 7 up). 1985. PLB 12.89 (ISBN 0-06-021344-2). HarpC Child Bks.
Cowell, Phyllis. A Hugga Bunch Hello. Kong, Emilie, illus. 40p. (ps). 1985. 4.00 (ISBN 0-910313-87-3). Parker Bros.
Cresswell, Helen. Bagthorpes Abroad. (gr. 3-7). 1987. pap. 3.95 (ISBN 0-14-031972-7, Puffin). Puffin Bks.
—Bagthorpes vs. the World: Being the Fourth Part of the Bagthorpe Saga. LC 79-13260. 204p. (gr. 5 up). 1979. 13.95 (ISBN 0-02-725420-8, Mcmillan Child Bk). Macmillan Child Grp.
—Ordinary Jack: Being the First Part of the Bagthorpe Saga. LC 77-5146. 192p. (gr. 5 up). 1977. 13.95 (ISBN 0-02-725540-9, Mcmillan Child Bk). Macmillan Child Grp.
Crew, Linda. Someday I'll Laugh about This. 1990. 14.95 (ISBN 0-385-30083-2). Doubleday.
Crofford, Emily. Stories from the Blue Road. Nobens, C. A., illus. LC 81-21229. 168p. (gr. 4-8). 1981. PLB 8.95 (ISBN 0-87614-189-0). Carolrhoda Bks.
Cuyler, Margery. Daisy's Crazy Thanksgiving. Kramer, Robin, illus. 32p. (gr. k-3). 1990. 14.95 (ISBN 0-8050-0559-5). H Holt & Co.
Dana, Barbara. Necessary Parties. 320p. 1987. pap. 3.50 (ISBN 0-553-26984-4, Starfire). Bantam.
Danziger, Paula. Can You Sue Your Parents for Malpractice? LC 78-72856. 266p. (gr. 7 up). 1979. 14.95 (ISBN 0-385-28112-9). Delacorte.
—Everyone Else's Parents Said Yes. (gr. 3-7). 1989. 13.95 (ISBN 0-385-29805-6). Delacorte.
Davis, Jenny. Good-bye & Keep Cold. LC 87-5794. 224p. (gr. 7 up). 1987. 12.95 (ISBN 0-531-05715-1); PLB 12.99 (ISBN 0-531-08315-2). Orchard Bks Watts.
De Lint, Charles. The Dreaming Place. Froud, Brian, illus. LC 90-488. 144p. (gr. 7 up). 1990. 14.95 (ISBN 0-689-31571-6, Atheneum Child Bk). Macmillan Child Grp.
Delton, Julie. My Uncle Nikos. Simont, Marc, illus. LC 81-43317. 32p. (gr. 1-4). 1983. 10.53i (ISBN 0-690-04164-0, Crowell Jr Bks). HarpC Child Bks.
Draper, C. G. A Holiday Year. (gr. 5-9). 1988. 12.95 (ISBN 0-316-19203-1). Little.
Duder, Tessa. Jellybean. 112p. (gr. 3-7). 1986. pap. 10.95 (ISBN 0-670-81235-8). Viking Child Bks.
Duffy, James. Cleaver & Company. (Illus.). 128p. (gr. 4-6). 1991. 12.95 (ISBN 0-684-19371-X, Scribners Young Read). Macmillan Child Grp.
Eastern, Anne G. The Picolinis. 160p. (Orig.). (gr. 2-5). 1988. pap. 2.75 (ISBN 0-553-15566-0, Skylark). Bantam.
Ehrlich, Amy. Zeek Silver Moon. Parker, Robert A., illus. LC 70-181787. 32p. (ps-3). 1972. Dial Bks Young.
Ellis, Jana. The Best of Everything. LC 88-12380. 160p. (gr. 7 up). 1988. pap. text ed. 2.50 (ISBN 0-8167-1356-1). Troll Assocs.
—Two for One. LC 88-12384. 160p. (gr. 7 up). 1988. pap. text ed. 2.50 (ISBN 0-8167-1354-5). Troll Assocs.
Engel, Diana. Gino Badino. Engel, Diana, illus. LC 90-36456. 32p. (ps up). 1991. 13.95 (ISBN 0-688-09502-X); PLB 13.88 (ISBN 0-688-09503-8, Morrow Jr Bks). Morrow Jr Bks.
Estes, Eleanor. The Middle Moffats. (gr. k-6). 1989. pap. 3.25 (ISBN 0-440-40180-1, YB). Dell.
—Moffats. Slobodkin, Louis, illus. LC 41-51893. (gr. 4-6). 1941. 14.95 (ISBN 0-15-255095-X, HJ). HarBraceJ.
—The Moffats. (gr. k-6). 1989. pap. 3.25 (ISBN 0-440-40177-1, YB). Dell.
—Rufus M. Slobodkin, Louis, illus. LC 43-51239. (gr. 3-7). 1943. 15.95 (ISBN 0-15-269415-3, HJ). HarBraceJ.
Fitzhugh, Louise. Nobody's Family Is Going to Change. 224p. (gr. 3-7). 1975. pap. 1.75 (ISBN 0-440-46454-4, YB). Dell.
Fleischman, Sid. Humbug Mountain. Von Schmidt, Eric, illus. LC 78-9419. (gr. 4-6). 1978. 14.95i (ISBN 0-316-28569-2, Pub. by Atlantic Monthly Pr). Little.
—Mr. Mysterious & Company. Von Schmidt, Eric, illus. (gr. 4-6). 1962. 14.95 (ISBN 0-316-28578-1, Joy St Bks). Little.
Fosburgh, Liza. Wrong Way Home. 1990. 14.95 (ISBN 0-553-05883-5). Bantam.
Fox, Paula. Maurice's Room. Fetz, Ingrid, illus. LC 85-7200. 64p. (gr. 2-6). 1985. 13.95 (ISBN 0-02-735490-3, Mcmillan Child Bk). Macmillan Child Grp.
Gardner, Richard A. The Boys & Girls Book about Stepfamilies. Lowenheim, Alfred, illus. 180p. (gr. 3-10). 1985. pap. 3.95 (ISBN 0-933812-13-2). Creative Therapeutics.
Gates, Doris. Blue Willow. Lantz, Paul, illus. LC 40-32435. (gr. 4-6). 1976. pap. 3.95 (ISBN 0-14-030924-1, VS30, Puffin). Puffin Bks.
Gelfand. The Jeffersons. (Illus.). 32p. (gr. 4 up). 1985. PLB 8.95. Creative Ed.
George, Jean C. The Cry of the Crow. LC 79-2016. 160p. (gr. 5 up). 1980. PLB 12.89 (ISBN 0-06-021957-2). HarpC Child Bks.
Gerson, Corinne. Tread Softly. LC 78-72199. (gr. 4-7). 1979. 7.95 (ISBN 0-8037-9058-9). Dial Bks Young.
Giff, Patricia R. Fourth Grade Celebrity. Morrill, Leslie, illus. LC 79-50678. (gr. 4-6). 1979. 8.95 (ISBN 0-440-02725-X); PLB 8.89 (ISBN 0-440-02726-8). Delacorte.
Gilbreth, Frank B., Jr. & Carey, Ernestine G. Cheaper by the Dozen. (gr. 6 up). 1984. pap. 3.50 (ISBN 0-553-27250-0, Starfire). Bantam.
Godden, Rumer. Thursday's Children. (gr. k-12). 1987. pap. 3.25 (ISBN 0-440-98790-3, LFL). Dell.
Goffstein, Brooke. Our Prairie Home: A Picture Album. Goffstein, Brooke, illus. LC 87-30795. 32p. (ps up). 1988. 12.95 (ISBN 0-06-022290-5); PLB 12.89 (ISBN 0-06-022291-3). HarpC Child Bks.
Gracious Plenty. 1991. pap. 13.95 (ISBN 0-671-73566-7). S&S Trade.
Greene, Constance C. Beat the Turtle Drum. Diamond, Donna, illus. LC 76-14772. 128p. (gr. 4-6). 1976. 13.95 (ISBN 0-670-15241-2). Viking Child Bks.
Greenfield, Eloise. Talk about a Family. 64p. (gr. 3-7). 1989. pap. 2.50 (ISBN 0-590-42247-2, Apple Paperbacks). Scholastic Inc.
Griffin, Peni R. A Dig in Time. LC 90-47388. 192p. (gr. 4-7). 1991. SBE 13.95 (ISBN 0-689-50525-6, M K McElderry). Macmillan Child Grp.
Growing Pains. (gr. k-9). 1988. pap. 2.95 (ISBN 0-318-37109-X). Scholastic Inc.
Guiberson, Brenda Z. Turtle People. LC 90-388. 112p. (gr. 3-6). 1990. 12.95 (ISBN 0-689-31647-X, Atheneum Child Bk). Macmillan Child Grp.
Hall, Barbara. Dixie Storms. 1990. 15.95 (ISBN 0-15-223825-5). HarbraceJ.
Hall, Lynn. Flyaway. LC 87-12824. 128p. (gr. 7 up). 1987. 12.95 (ISBN 0-684-18888-0, Scribners Young Read). Macmillan Child Grp.
Hamilton, Dorothy. Rosalie. Unada, illus. LC 76-39961. 128p. (gr. 3-10). 1977. pap. text ed. 3.95 (ISBN 0-8361-1807-3). Herald Pr.
Hamilton, Virginia. Cousins. 128p. (gr. 5 up). 1990. 14.95 (ISBN 0-399-22164-6, Philomel Bks). Putnam Pub Group.
—Sweet Whispers, Brother Rush. 224p. (gr. 7 up). 1982. 12.95 (ISBN 0-399-20894-1, Philomel). Putnam Pub Group.
Harris, Mark J. Come the Morning. LC 88-24213. 176p. (gr. 5-9). 1989. 13.95 (ISBN 0-02-742750-1, Bradbury Pr). Macmillan Child Grp.
Harwood, Pearl A. Mr. Bumba Keeps House. Folger, Joseph, illus. LC 64-19772. 32p. (gr. k-3). 1964. PLB 4.95 (ISBN 0-8225-0103-1). Lerner Pubns.
Haven, Susan. Maybe I'll Move to the Lost & Found. 160p. (gr. 5 up). 1988. 14.95 (ISBN 0-399-21509-3, Putnam). Putnam Pub Group.
Hazen, Nancy. Grownups Cry Too: Los Adultos Tambien Lloran-English-Spanish Text. 2nd ed. Cotera, Martha P., tr. LC 78-71542. (Illus.). 25p. (ps-1). 1978. pap. 5.00 (ISBN 0-914996-19-3). Lollipop Power.
Head, Ann. Mr & Mrs. Bo Jo Jones. (Illus.). 192p. (gr. 9-12). 1968. pap. 3.95 (ISBN 0-451-16319-2, Sig). NAL-Dutton.
Heide, Florence P. Time Flies! Hafner, Marylin, illus. LC 84-47833. 112p. (gr. 3-7). 1984. 12.95 (ISBN 0-8234-0542-7). Holiday.
—Time Flies! 112p. 1985. pap. 2.50 (ISBN 0-553-15370-6, Skylark). Bantam.
Heitz, True. Mommy Moon & the Rainbow Children. Mattos, D., illus. 13p. (Orig.). (ps-2). 1982. pap. 3.00 (ISBN 0-686-37664-1). True Heitz.
Henkes, Kevin. Grandpa & Bo. Henkes, Kevin, illus. LC 85-14869. 32p. (ps-3). 1986. 11.75 (ISBN 0-688-04956-7); PLB 11.88 (ISBN 0-688-04957-5). Greenwillow.
Hennessy, B. G. When You Were Just a Little Girl. (ps-3). 1991. 12.95 (ISBN 0-670-82998-6). Viking Child Bks.
Hessell, Jenny. Staying at Sam's. Williams, Jenny, illus. LC 89-14561. 32p. (ps-3). 1990. 10.95 (ISBN 0-397-32432-4, Lipp Jr Bks); PLB 10.89 (ISBN 0-397-32433-2, Lipp Jr Bks). HarpC Child Bks.
Hill, Elizabeth S. Evan's Corner. (ps-3). 1991. 12.95 (ISBN 0-670-82830-0). Viking Child Bks.
Himmelman, John. The Day-Off Machine. Brook, Bonnie, ed. Himmelman, John, illus. 48p. (ps-3). 1990. lib. bdg. 8.98 (ISBN 0-671-69635-1); pap. 3.50 (ISBN 0-671-69639-4). Silver Pr.
—The Great Leaf Blast-Off. Brook, Bonnie, ed. Himmelman, John, illus. 48p. (ps-3). 1990. lib. bdg. 8.98 (ISBN 0-671-69634-3); pap. 3.50 (ISBN 0-671-69638-6). Silver Pr.
Hindley, J., et al. Time Traveller's Omnibus. (Illus.). 32p. 1977. text ed. 17.95 (ISBN 0-86020-222-4). EDC.
Hinton, S. E. Outsiders. large type, unabr. ed. 298p. (gr. 7 up). 1989. lib. bdg. 14.95 (ISBN 0-8161-4630-6). G K Hall.
Hirsh, Marilyn. Could Anything Be Worse? Hirsh, Marilyn, illus. LC 73-17364. 32p. (gr. k-3). 1987. pap. 5.95 (ISBN 0-8234-0655-5). Holiday.
Hobbs, Will. Changes in Latitudes. LC 87-17462. 176p. (gr. 7 up). 1988. 13.95 (ISBN 0-689-31385-3, Atheneum Child Bk). Macmillan Child Grp.
Hoberman, Mary Ann. Mr. & Mrs. Muddle. Hoberman, Mary Ann, illus. LC 87-27320. 32p. (gr. k-4). 1988. 13.95 (ISBN 0-316-36735-4, Joy St Bks). Little.
Holl, Kristi D. Footprints up My Back. LC 84-6176. 168p. (gr. 4-6). 1984. 12.95 (ISBN 0-689-31070-6, Atheneum Child Bk). Macmillan Child Grp.
—No Strings Attached. LC 87-22688. 128p. (gr. 3-7). 1988. 12.95 (ISBN 0-689-31399-3, Atheneum Child Bk). Macmillan Child Grp.
Honeycutt, Natalie. Ask Me Something Easy. LC 90-7765. 160p. (gr. 6-9). 1991. 13.95 (ISBN 0-531-05894-8); PLB 13.99 (ISBN 0-531-08494-9). Orchard Bks Watts.
Hooks, William H. A Flight of Dazzle Angels. LC 88-11913. 176p. 1988. 13.95 (ISBN 0-02-744430-9, Mcmillan Child Bk). Macmillan Child Grp.
Howard, Ellen. Sister. LC 90-196. 160p. (gr. 3-7). 1990. 12.95 (ISBN 0-689-31653-4, Atheneum Child Bk). Macmillan Child Grp.
Hurst, James. The Scarlet Ibis: A Classic Story of Brotherhood. (Illus.). (gr. 4 up). 1987. PLB 10.95s.p. (ISBN 0-88682-000-6); PLB 15.65 (ISBN 0-685-11037-0). Creative Ed.
Hurwitz, Johanna. The Rabbi's Girls. Johnson, Pamela, illus. LC 82-2102. 192p. (gr. 4-6). 1982. 11.95 (ISBN 0-688-01089-X). Morrow Jr Bks.
—Tough-Luck Karen. Groat, Diane de, illus. LC 82-6443. 160p. (gr. 4-6). 1982. 12.95 (ISBN 0-688-01485-2). Morrow Jr Bks.
Hutchins, Pat. Titch. Hutchins, Pat, illus. LC 77-146622. 32p. (ps-1). 1971. 12.95 (ISBN 0-02-745880-6, Mcmillan Child Bk). Macmillan Child Grp.
Irwin, Hadley. Abby, My Love. LC 84-24571. 168p. (gr. 7 up). 1985. 13.95 (ISBN 0-689-50323-7, M K McElderry). Macmillan Child Grp.
James, Simon. The Day Jake Vacuumed. (ps-3). 1989. pap. 7.95 (ISBN 0-553-05840-1). Bantam.
Johnston, Norma. Glory in the Flower. 200p. (gr. 4 up). 1990. pap. 3.95 (ISBN 0-14-034292-3, Puffin). Puffin Bks.
—The Keeping Days. 240p. (gr. 4 up). 1990. pap. 3.95 (ISBN 0-14-034291-5, Puffin). Puffin Bks.
Jones, Diana W. The Ogre Downstairs. LC 89-11741. 192p. (gr. 5 up). 1990. 12.95 (ISBN 0-688-09195-4). Greenwillow.
Jukes, Mavis. No One Is Going to Nashville. Bloom, Lloyd, illus. LC 82-18901. 48p. (gr. 2-5). 1983. 8.95 (ISBN 0-394-85609-0); lib. bdg. 10.99 (ISBN 0-394-95609-5). Knopf.
Keating, August. Uncle Wooley. LC 87-82084. 55p. (Orig.). (gr. 9 up). 1988. pap. 5.00 (ISBN 0-916383-47-4). Aegina Pr.
Keats, Ezra J. Louie's Search. Keats, Ezra J., illus. LC 80-10176. 32p. (gr. k-3). 1984. 13.95 (ISBN 0-02-749700-3, Four Winds). Macmillan Child Grp.
—Peter's Chair. Keats, Ezra J., illus. LC 67-4816. (gr. k-3). 1967. 13.95i (ISBN 0-06-023111-4); PLB 13.89 (ISBN 0-06-023112-2). HarpC Child Bks.
Kellogg, Steven, retold by. & illus. There Was an Old Woman. 48p. (ps-3). 1984. 13.95 (ISBN 0-02-749780-1, Four Winds). Macmillan.
Kerr, M. E. If I Love You, Am I Trapped Forever? LC 72-9860. 176p. (gr. 7 up). 1973. PLB 12.89 (ISBN 0-06-023149-1). HarpC Child Bks.
—Night Kites. LC 85-45386. 192p. (gr. 7 up). 1986. 12.95 (ISBN 0-06-023253-6); PLB 12.89 (ISBN 0-06-023254-4). HarpC Child Bks.
—What I Really Think of You. LC 81-47735. 224p. (gr. 7 up). 1982. 12.95 (ISBN 0-06-023188-2). HarpC Child Bks.
Killilea, Marie. Wren. Riger, Robert, illus. (gr. 3-7). 1981. pap. 0.95 (ISBN 0-440-49704-3, YB). Dell.
Kirby, Susan E. Shadow Boy. LC 90-7687. 160p. (gr. 7 up). 1991. 13.95 (ISBN 0-531-05869-7); PLB 13.99 (ISBN 0-531-08469-8). Orchard Bks Watts.
Klein, Norma. Breaking Up. LC 80-10953. 224p. 1980. Pantheon.
—Confessions of an Only Child. Cwffari, Richard, illus. LC 73-14750. 112p. (gr. 3-7). 1974. Pantheon.

Konigsburg, E. L. Father's Arcane Daughter. LC 76-5495. 128p. (gr. 4-8). 1976. SBE 12.95 (ISBN 0-689-30524-9, Atheneum Child Bk). Macmillan Child Grp.
Kuskin, Karla. Something Sleeping in the Hall. Kuskin, Karla, illus. LC 82-47721. 64p. (gr. k-3). 1985. 11.95 (ISBN 0-06-023633-7); PLB 11.89 (ISBN 0-06-023634-5). HarpC Child Bks.
Lansing, Karen E. Time to Fly. 104p. (Orig.). (gr. 4-8). 1991. pap. 5.95 (ISBN 0-8361-3560-1). Herald Pr.
Lawrence, Louise. Children of the Dust. LC 85-42618. 192p. (gr. 7 up). 1985. HarpC Child Bks.
—Sing & Scatter Daisies. LC 76-21393. (gr. 7 up). 1977. 8.95 (ISBN 0-06-023772-4). HarpC Child Bks.
L'Engle, Madeleine. Meet the Austins. 192p. (gr. 5-9). 1981. pap. 3.50 (ISBN 0-440-95777-X, LE). Dell.
Lester, Alison. Bumping & Bouncing. (Illus.). 16p. (ps-k). 1989. pap. 3.50 (ISBN 0-670-81991-3). Viking Child Bks.
Levin, Betty. The Trouble With Gramary. LC 87-22702. 192p. (gr. 5up). 1988. 13.95 (ISBN 0-688-07372-7). Greenwillow.
Levitin, Sonia. Silver Days. 192p. (gr. 5 up). 1989. 13.95 (ISBN 0-689-31563-5, Atheneum Child Bk). Macmillan Child Grp.
Lisle, Janet T. Afternoon of the Elves. LC 88-35099. 128p. (gr. 4-6). 1989. 12.95 (ISBN 0-531-05837-9); PLB 12.99 (ISBN 0-531-08437-X). Orchard Bks Watts.
Litchfield, Ada B. Making Room for Uncle Joe. Tucker, Kathleen, ed. LC 83-17036. (Illus.). 32p. (gr. 2-5). 1984. PLB 10.95 (ISBN 0-8075-4952-5). A Whitman.
Little, Jean. Home from Far. Lazare, Jerry, illus. (gr. 5 up). 1989. 14.95 (ISBN 0-316-52792-0); pap. 4.95 (ISBN 0-316-52802-1). Little.
—Look Through My Window. Sandin, Joan, illus. LC 71-105470. 270p. (gr. 4-7). 1970. PLB 13.89 (ISBN 0-06-023924-7). HarpC Child Bks.
Little Women. (gr. 4 up). 1988. pap. 4.87 (ISBN 0-582-54162-X, 74269). Longman.
Little Women. (Illus.). (gr. 3-5). 3.50 (ISBN 0-7214-5005-9). Ladybird Bks.
Lothrop, Harriet M. The Five Little Peppers & How They Grew. (Orig.). (gr. k-6). 1985. pap. 4.95 (ISBN 0-440-42505-0, Pub. by Yearling Classics). Dell.
Lowry, Lois. Anastasia on Her Own. LC 84-22432. 131p. (gr. 5-7). 1985. 13.95 (ISBN 0-395-38133-9). HM.
—A Summer to Die. Oliver, Jenni, illus. (gr. 3-7). 1977. 13.95 (ISBN 0-395-25338-1). HM.
—Us & Uncle Fraud. (gr. k-6). 1985. pap. 3.25 (ISBN 0-440-49185-1, YB). Dell.
McCusker, Paul. Strange Journey Back: An Adventure in Odyssey. Craig, Sheila, ed. Loccisano, Karen, illus. 85p. (Orig.). (gr. 3-6). 1991. pap. 3.99 (ISBN 1-56179-021-4). Focus Family.
McDonald, Joyce. Mail-Order Kid. 128p. (gr. 3-7). 1988. 12.95 (ISBN 0-399-21513-1, Putnam). Putnam Pub Group.
Macdonald, Maryann. Rosie Runs Away. Sweet, Melissa, illus. LC 89-27575. 32p. (ps-2). 1990. 12.95 (ISBN 0-689-31625-9, Atheneum Child Bk). Macmillan Child Grp.
McKenna, Colleen O. Too Many Murphys. 144p. (gr. 3-7). 1988. pap. 10.95 (ISBN 0-590-41731-2, Pub. by Scholastic Hardcover). Scholastic Inc.
MacLachlan, Patricia. Sarah, Plain & Tall. LC 83-49481. 64p. (gr. 3-5). 1985. 10.95 (ISBN 0-06-024101-2); PLB 10.89 (ISBN 0-06-024102-0). HarpC Child Bks.
—Seven Kisses in a Row. Marella, Maria P., illus. LC 82-47718. 64p. (gr. 2-5). 1983. 12.95 (ISBN 0-06-024083-0); PLB 12.89 (ISBN 0-06-024084-9). HarpC Child Bks.
McPhail, David. Sisters. LC 84-3775. (Illus.). 32p. (ps-3). 1984. 11.95 (ISBN 0-15-275319-2, HJ). HarBraceJ.
Major, Kevin. Hold Fast. 176p. (gr. 7 up). 1981. pap. 3.25 (ISBN 0-440-93756-6, LE). Dell.
Markus, Julia. Uncle. 1987. pap. 3.95 (ISBN 0-440-39187-3, LE). Dell.
Marron, Carol A. When Great Aunt Zelda Comes. Collins, Fry, illus. LC 84-17733. 32p. (gr. 3-6). 1985. PLB 14.65 (ISBN 0-940742-42-X). Raintree Pubs.
Marron, Carol A. & Root, Phyllis. Just One of the Family. Karn, George, illus. LC 84-17680. 32p. (gr. 3-6). 1985. PLB 27.99 incl. cassette (ISBN 0-8172-2287-1); PLB 14.65 (ISBN 0-940742-47-0); cassette 14.00 (ISBN 0-685-09933-4). Raintree Pubs.
Marshall, James. George & Martha. LC 74-184250. (Illus.). 48p. (gr. k-3). 1974. pap. 4.95 (ISBN 0-395-19972-7, Sandpiper). HM.
—George & Martha Back in Town. Marshall, James, illus. LC 83-22842. 32p. (gr. k-3). 1984. 13.95 (ISBN 0-395-35386-6, 5-90939); pap. 3.95 (ISBN 0-685-07886-8). HM.
Martin, Ann M. Me & Katie (the Pest) Sims, Blanche, illus. LC 85-5558. 160p. (gr. 4-7). 1985. 12.95 (ISBN 0-8234-0580-X). Holiday.
—Me & Katie the Pest. 1990. pap. 2.75 (ISBN 0-590-43618-X). Scholastic Inc.
—Ten Kids, No Pets. LC 87-25206. 184p. (gr. 3-7). 1988. 13.95 (ISBN 0-8234-0691-1). Holiday.
Marzollo, Jean. Uproar on Holler Cat Hill. Kellogg, Steven, illus. LC 79-22201. (ps-2). 1980. 8.95 (ISBN 0-8037-9027-9). Dial Bks Young.
Masters, Susan R. The Secret Life of Hubie Hartzel. Mayo, Gretchen W., illus. LC 89-36402. 144p. (gr. 3-7). 1990. 11.95 (ISBN 0-397-32399-9, Lipp Jr Bks); PLB 11.89 (ISBN 0-397-32400-6, Lipp Jr Bks). HarpC Child Bks.
Mathis, Sharon B. The Hundred-Penny Box. Dillon, Leo & Dillon, Diane, illus. 48p. (gr. k-3). 1975. pap. 13.95 (ISBN 0-670-38787-8). Viking Child Bks.
Matthews, Ellen. Getting Rid of Roger. LC 77-12311. (Illus.). 96p. (gr. 3-7). 1978. 7.50 (ISBN 0-664-32622-6, Westminster). Westminster John Knox.
Maury, Inez. My Mother & I Are Growing Strong. (SPA & ENG., Illus.). (ps-4). 1978. 6.95 (ISBN 0-938678-06-X). New Seed.
Mearian, Judy F. Two Ways About It. LC 79-10029. (gr. 5 up). 1985. 7.95 (ISBN 0-8037-8797-9). Dial Bks Young.
Meyer, Carolyn. Killing the Kudu. LC 90-6089. 208p. (gr. 9 up). 1990. 14.95 (ISBN 0-689-50508-6, M K McElderry). Macmillan Child Grp.
Miklowitz, Gloria D. Suddenly Super Rich. (gr. 7 up). 1989. 13.95 (ISBN 0-553-05845-2, Starfire). Bantam.
Miles, Betty. Just the Beginning. Bacon, Paul, illus. LC 75-28545. 152p. (gr. 4-8). 1988. PLB 10.99 (ISBN 0-394-93226-9). Knopf.
Miller, Mary Jane. Me & My Name. (gr. 4-7). 1990. 11.95 (ISBN 0-670-83196-4). Viking Child Bks.
Mohr, Nicholasa. Felita. Cruz, Ray, illus. LC 79-50149. (gr. 3-6). 1979. PLB 12.89 (ISBN 0-8037-3144-2). Dial Bks Young.
—Going Home. (gr. 4-7). 1989. pap. 2.95 (ISBN 0-553-15699-3, Skylark). Bantam.
Moncure, Jane B. I Never Say I'm Thankful, But I Am. Hook, Frances, illus. LC 78-21577. (ps-3). 1979. PLB 12.96 (ISBN 0-89565-023-1). Childs World.
Munsil, Ritchie. Dinner at Auntie Rose's. (Illus.). 24p. (ps-8). 1984. 12.95 (ISBN 0-920236-96-0); pap. 4.95 (ISBN 0-920236-63-4). Firefly Bks Ltd.
Naylor, Phyllis R. Send No Blessings. LC 89-28024. 240p. (gr. 7 up). 1990. 13.95 (ISBN 0-689-31582-1, Atheneum Child Bk). Macmillan Child Grp.
Nesbit, Edith. The Five Children & It. (gr. 4-6). 1986. pap. 3.50 (ISBN 0-440-42586-7, Pub. by Yearling Classics). Dell.
Nielsen, Shelly. Take a Bow, Victoria. 130p. (gr. 5-6). 1986. pap. 3.95 (ISBN 0-89191-470-6). Cook.
Norton, Andre & Miller, Phyllis. House of Shadows. LC 83-16197. 216p. (gr. 5-9). 1984. 14.95 (ISBN 0-689-50298-2, M K McElderry). Macmillan Child Grp.
Nystrom, Carolyn. Mike's Lonely Summer. Baum, Ann, illus. 48p. (gr. 1-6). 1986. 7.95 (ISBN 0-7459-1016-5). Lion USA.
O'Brien, Anne S. It Hurts! O'Brien, Anne S., illus. LC 85-82107. 14p. (ps-k). 1986. bds. 3.95 (ISBN 0-8050-0048-8). H Holt & Co.
Parish, Peggy. Amelia Bedelia's Family Album. 48p. 1989. pap. 5.95 (ISBN 0-380-70760-8, Camelot). Avon.
Park, Barbara. My Mother Got Married: (And Other Disasters) LC 88-27257. 128p. (gr. 3-7). 1989. 13.00 (ISBN 0-394-82149-1); lib. bdg. 11.99 (ISBN 0-394-92149-6). Knopf.
—My Mother Got Married: (And Other Disasters) LC 88-27257. 144p. (gr. 3-7). 1990. pap. 3.50 (ISBN 0-394-85059-9, Bullseye Bks). Knopf.
Pascal, Francine. Hangin' out with Cici. (gr. 5-9). 1977. pap. 12.95 (ISBN 0-670-36045-7). Viking Child Bks.
—The Parent Plot. 1990. pap. 2.95 (ISBN 0-553-28611-0). Bantam.
Paton Walsh, Jill. Goldengrove. LC 72-81484. 130p. (gr. 6 up). 1985. pap. 3.45 (ISBN 0-374-42587-6, Sunburst). FS&G.
Pevsner, Stella. Keep Stompin' till the Music Stops. LC 76-27845. 144p. (gr. 4-7). 1979. 13.95 (ISBN 0-395-28875-4, Clarion). HM.
Peyton, K. M. Darkling. 1990. 14.95 (ISBN 0-385-30086-7). Doubleday.
Pfeffer, Susan B. Kid Power Strikes Back. Grant, Leigh, illus. 128p. (gr. k-8). 1984. lib. bdg. 12.90 (ISBN 0-531-04839-X). Watts.
Platt, Kin. Crocker. LC 82-48456. 128p. (gr. 7 up). 1983. 11.95i (ISBN 0-397-32025-6, Lipp JR Bks). HarpC Child Bks.
Porte, Barbara A. I Only Made up the Roses. LC 86-18307. 128p. (gr. 7 up). 1987. reinforced 10.25 (ISBN 0-688-05216-9). Greenwillow.
Pryor, Bonnie. The Plum Tree War. Leder, Dora, illus. LC 88-32426. 128p. (gr. 3-6). 1989. 11.95 (ISBN 0-688-08142-8). Morrow Jr Bks.
—Vinegar Pancakes & Vanishing Cream. Owens, Gail, illus. LC 86-31085. 128p. (gr. 2-5). 1987. 12.95 (ISBN 0-688-06728-X, Morrow Junior Books). Morrow.
Raskin, Ellen. Figgs & Phantoms. Raskin, Ellen, illus. LC 73-17309. 160p. (gr. 4-7). 1977. pap. 15.95 (ISBN 0-525-29680-8, 01063-320, DCB); (DCB). Dutton Child Bks.
Reiss, Johanna. The Journey Back. LC 76-12615. 128p. (gr. 5 up). 1976. 12.95 (ISBN 0-690-01252-7, Crowell Jr Bks). HarpC Child Bks.
Repp, Gloria. The Stolen Years. 152p. (Orig.). (gr. 9-12). 1989. pap. 4.95 (ISBN 0-89084-481-X). Bob Jones Univ Pr.
Reynolds, Phyllis. The Keeper. 192p. (gr. 6 up). 1987. pap. 2.95 (ISBN 0-553-26882-1, Starfire). Bantam.
Rigby, Shirley L. Smaller Than Most. Carter, Debby L., illus. LC 85-42636. 32p. (gr. k-3). 1985. HarpC Child Bks.
Riley, Jocelyn. Only My Mouth Is Smiling. LC 81-18688. 224p. (gr. 7-9). 1982. 12.95 (ISBN 0-688-01087-3). Morrow Jr Bks.
Roberts, Willo D. Megan's Island. LC 87-17505. 192p. (gr. 3-7). 1988. 13.95 (ISBN 0-689-31397-7, Atheneum Child Bk). Macmillan Child Grp.
—Megan's Island. (gr. 4-7). 1990. pap. 3.95 (ISBN 0-689-71387-8, Aladdin). Macmillan Child Grp.
Robinson, Barbara. My Brother Louis Measures Worms: And Other Louis Stories. LC 87-45302. 160p. (gr. 3-7). 1988. 11.95 (ISBN 0-06-025082-8); PLB 12.89 (ISBN 0-06-025083-6). HarpC Child Bks.
Robinson, Nancy K. Angela, Private Citizen. LC 89-5918. 146p. (gr. 3-6). 1989. pap. 10.95 (ISBN 0-590-41726-6). Scholastic Inc.
—Just Plain Cat. LC 82-18258. 128p. (gr. 3-6). 1984. 12.95 (ISBN 0-02-777350-7, Four Winds). Macmillan Child Grp.
—Oh Honestly, Angela! LC 85-2102. 128p. (gr. 3-6). 1985. 9.95 (ISBN 0-590-32983-9, Scholastic Hardcover). Scholastic Inc.
—Veronica Knows Best. 160p. (gr. 3-7). 1989. pap. 2.75 (ISBN 0-590-40510-1, Apple Paperbacks). Scholastic Inc.
Root, Phyllis. Hidden Places. San Souci, Daniel, illus. LC 83-8615. 32p. (gr. 3-6). 1983. PLB 14.65 (ISBN 0-940742-30-6). Raintree Pubs.
—My Cousin Charlie. Marella, Pia, illus. LC 84-16079. 32p. (gr. 3-6). 1985. PLB 14.65 (ISBN 0-940742-40-3). Raintree Pubs.
Rylant, Cynthia. A Blue-Eyed Daisy. LC 84-21554. 112p. (gr. 5-7). 1985. 11.95 (ISBN 0-02-777960-2, Bradbury Pr). Macmillan Child Grp.
—The Relatives Came. Gammell, Stephen, illus. LC 85-10929. 32p. (ps-2). 1985. 13.95 (ISBN 0-02-777220-9, Bradbury Pr). Macmillan Child Grp.
Sachs, Marilyn. Baby Sister. 160p. 1987. pap. 2.95 (ISBN 0-380-70358-0, Flare). Avon.
St. George, Judith. What's Happening to My Junior Year? 160p. (gr. 5 up). 1986. 13.95 (ISBN 0-399-21316-3, Putnam). Putnam Pub Group.
St. John, Patricia. Where the River Begins. LC 80-12304. 128p. (Orig.). (gr. 5-8). pap. 3.95 (ISBN 0-8024-8124-8). Moody.
Sandin, Joan. The Long Way to a New Land. Sandin, Joan, illus. LC 80-8942. 64p. (gr. k-3). 1986. pap. 3.50 (ISBN 0-06-444100-8, Trophy). HarpC Child Bks.
Saunders, Susan. Sleepover Friends: Stephanie's Family Secret, No. 11. 1989. pap. 2.50 (ISBN 0-590-41845-9). Scholastic Inc.
Schneider, Rex. That's Not All! Gregorich, Barbara, ed. (Illus.). 16p. (Orig.). (gr. k-2). 1985. pap. 1.95 (ISBN 0-88743-019-8, 06019). Sch Zone Pub Co.
Schultz, Betty K. Morn of Mystery. (Illus., Orig.). (gr. 4-6). Date not set. pap. write for info. (ISBN 0-929568-02-8). Raspberry IL.
Schwartz, Amy. Her Majesty, Aunt Essie. LC 84-11003. (Illus.). 32p. (gr. k-2). 1984. 13.95 (ISBN 0-02-781450-5, Bradbury Pr). Macmillan Child Grp.
Scott, Ann H. Sam. Shimin, Symeon, illus. (ps-3). 1967. text ed. 14.95 (ISBN 0-07-055803-5). McGraw.
Segal, Lore. Tell Me a Mitzi. Pincus, Harriet, illus. LC 69-14980. 40p. (ps-3). 1982. 13.95 (ISBN 0-374-37392-2); pap. 5.95 (ISBN 0-374-47502-4). FS&G.
—Tell Me a Trudy. Wells, Rosemary, illus. LC 77-24123. 40p. (ps-3). 1977. 14.95 (ISBN 0-374-37395-7). FS&G.
Seredy, Kate. The Good Master. (Illus.). 196p. (gr. 5-9). 1986. pap. 4.95 (ISBN 0-14-030133-X, Puffin). Puffin Bks.
Sharmat, Marjorie W. Get Rich Mitch! 96p. (gr. 3-7). 1986. pap. 2.50 (ISBN 0-380-70170-7, Camelot). Avon.
—Mitchell Is Moving. Aruego, Jose & Dewey, Ariane, illus. LC 78-6816. 48p. (gr. 1-4). 1978. RSBE 11.95 (ISBN 0-02-782410-1, Mcmillan Child Bk). Macmillan Child Grp.
Shevrin, Aliza, selected by. & tr. from YID. Around the Table: Family Stories of Sholom Aleichem. Gowing, Toby, illus. 128p. (gr. 5-8). 1991. 12.95 (ISBN 0-684-19237-3, Scribners Young Read). Macmillan Child Grp.
Simon, Shirley. Get Lost, Becka! Gregorich, Barbara, ed. (Illus.). 16p. (Orig.). (gr. k-2). 1985. pap. 1.95 (ISBN 0-88743-013-9, 06013). Sch Zone Pub Co.
Singer, A. L. Little Monsters. 1989. pap. 2.95 (ISBN 0-590-42742-3). Scholastic Inc.
Skolsky, Mindy W. Carnival & Kopeck & More about Hannah. Weinhaus, Karen A., illus. LC 77-25643. 80p. (gr. 2-5). 1979. PLB 12.89 (ISBN 0-06-025692-3). HarpC Child Bks.
Smith, Doris B. The First Hard Times. (gr. 4 up). 1990. pap. 3.95 (ISBN 0-14-034538-8, Puffin). Puffin Bks.
—Tough Chauncey. 224p. (gr. 3-7). 1986. pap. 3.95 (ISBN 0-14-031928-X, Puffin). Puffin Bks.
Smith, Robert K. The War with Grandpa. Lauter, Richard, illus. LC 83-14366. 128p. (gr. 4-8). 1984. pap. 12.95 (ISBN 0-385-29314-3). Delacorte.
Smith, Rukshana. Sumitra's Story. LC 82-19794. 168p. (gr. 6). 1983. 9.95 (ISBN 0-698-20579-0, Coward). Putnam Pub Group.
Snyder, Carol. The Leftover Kid. 160p. 1987. pap. 2.50 (ISBN 0-425-09709-9). Berkley Pub.
Spinelli, Jerry. Who Put That Hair in My Toothbrush? LC 83-20716. (gr. 5-9). 1984. 14.95 (ISBN 0-316-80712-5). Little.
—Who Put That Hair in My Toothbrush? (gr. 5-9). 1986. pap. 3.25 (ISBN 0-440-99485-3, LFL). Dell.
Springer, Nancy. Not on a White Horse. LC 87-3477. 192p. (gr. 5 up). 1988. 13.95 (ISBN 0-689-31366-7, Atheneum Child Bk). Macmillan Child Grp.
Stanek, Muriel. I Won't Go Without a Father. Mill, Eleanor, illus. LC 78-188435. 32p. (gr. 1-4). 1972. PLB 10.95 (ISBN 0-8075-3524-9). A Whitman.

Stevenson, James. When I Was Nine. Stevenson, James, illus. LC 85-9777. 32p. (gr. k-3). 1986. 12.95 (ISBN 0-688-05942-2); PLB 12.88 (ISBN 0-688-05943-0). Greenwillow.

Stevenson, Ralph L., Jr. Sam's Stamp Store. Wolgamott, Elizabeth, illus. O'Neil, Greg, intro. by. (Illus.). 28p. (Orig.). (ps-2). 1983. pap. 3.50 (ISBN 0-9610762-0-8). Sirius Leag.

Stevenson, Robert Louis. Reader's Digest Best Loved Books for Young Readers: Kidnapped - The Adventures of David Balfour. Ogburn, Jackie, ed. Wyeth, N. C., illus. 136p. (gr. 4-12). 1989. 3.99 (ISBN 0-945260-32-6). Choice Pub NY.

Stiles, Martha B. Kate of Still Waters. LC 90-5546. 240p. (gr. 4-7). 1990. 14.95 (ISBN 0-02-788395-7, Mcmillan Child Bk). Macmillan Child Grp.

Stolz, Mary. By the Highway Home. LC 71-159046. (gr. 7 up). 1971. PLB 13.70 (ISBN 0-06-025831-4). HarpC Child Bks.

—Ferris Wheel. LC 76-41511. 144p. (gr. 4-7). 1977. PLB 12.89 (ISBN 0-06-025860-8). HarpC Child Bks.

—What Time of Night Is It? LC 80-7917. 224p. (gr. 6 up). 1981. PLB 12.89 (ISBN 0-06-026062-9). HarpC Child Bks.

Strasser, Todd. Turn It Up! (gr. 6-12). 1985. pap. 2.50 (ISBN 0-440-99059-9, LFL). Dell.

Sumiko. My Summer Vacation. Sumiko, illus. LC 89-43164. 32p. (Orig.). (ps-1). 1990. PLB 5.99 (ISBN 0-679-90525-1); pap. 2.25 (ISBN 0-679-80525-7). McKay.

Surprise, Surprise! 160p. (Orig.). (gr. 5-9). 1989. pap. 2.95 (ISBN 1-55802-075-6). Lynx Bks.

Sweeney, Joyce. The Dream Collector. (gr. 7 up). 1989. 14.95 (ISBN 0-385-29813-7). Delacorte.

Tangvald, Christine. My Family Is Special. LC 86-71797. 1987. bds. 4.95 (ISBN 1-55513-169-7, Chariot Bks). Cook.

Tapp, Kathy K. Smoke from the Chimney. LC 85-18713. 132p. (gr. 4-7). 1986. 12.95 (ISBN 0-689-50389-X, M K McElderry). Macmillan Child Grp.

Taylor, Sydney. All-of-a-Kind Family. John, Helen, illus. 192p. (gr. k-6). 1980. pap. 3.25 (ISBN 0-440-40059-7, YB). Dell.

—All-of-a-Kind Family. John, Helen, illus. 189p. (gr. 3-6). 1988. Repr. of 1951 ed. 11.95 (ISBN 0-929093-00-3). Taylor Prodns.
ALL-OF-A-KIND FAMILY by Sydney Taylor, was first published in 1951, after winning the Follett Children's Book Contest, & has been in print continuously since then. It was highly acclaimed & adored by readers from its first appearance & has become a classic, as have the other titles in this series, described below. It was followed over the years by four other books about this immigrant family growing up on New York's Lower East Side in the years immediately before & during the First World War, & each in turn, received the same enthusiastic reception. They are: ALL-OF-A-KIND FAMILY DOWNTOWN (ISBN 0-929093-01-1); MORE ALL-OF-A-KIND FAMILY (ISBN 0-929093-02-X); ALL-OF-A-KIND FAMILY UPTOWN (ISBN 0-929093-03-8); ELLA OF ALL-OF-A-KIND FAMILY (ISBN 0-929093-04-6). Over the years, each new book was greeted with glowing reviews from the children's major media. More importantly, perhaps, is the fact that readers welcomed each...& that these readers continue to remember the books fondly & order them for their own children & grandchildren. This family of five girls, later joined by a baby brother, has been taken to the heart of America & has created a firmly entrenched place in its children's literature. Distributed by the Talman Company, 150 Fifth Avenue, New York, NY 10011. Each book is hardcovered & is $11.95.
Publisher Provided Annotation.

—All-of-a-Kind Family Downtown. 188p. (gr. k-6). 1973. pap. 2.95 (ISBN 0-440-42032-6, YB). Dell.

—All-of-a-Kind Family Downtown. Krush, Beth & Krush, Joe, illus. 187p. 1988. Repr. of 1972 ed. 11.95 (ISBN 0-929093-01-1). Taylor Prodns.

—All-of-a-Kind Family Uptown. Stevens, Mary, illus. 160p. (gr. 4-7). 1981. pap. 3.25 (ISBN 0-440-40091-0, YB). Dell.

—All-of-a-Kind Family Uptown. Stevens, Mary, illus. 160p. 1988. Repr. of 1958 ed. 11.95 (ISBN 0-929093-03-8). Taylor Prodns.

—Ella of All of a Kind Family. (Illus.). (gr. 4-7). 1978. 9.95 (ISBN 0-525-29238-1, DCB). Dutton Child Bks.

—Ella of All-of-a-Kind Family. Rosner, Meryl, illus. 133p. (gr. 4-8). 1988. Repr. of 1978 ed. 11.95 (ISBN 0-929093-04-6). Taylor Prodns.

—More All-of-a-Kind Family. Stevens, Mary, illus. (gr. 3-7). 1923. pap. 3.25 (ISBN 0-440-45813-7, YB). Dell.

—More All-of-a-Kind Family. Stevens, Mary, illus. 160p. (gr. 3-6). 1988. Repr. of 1954 ed. 11.95 (ISBN 0-929093-02-X). Taylor Prodns.

Terris, Susan. The Latchkey Kids. 167p. (gr. 5 up). 1986. 12.95 (ISBN 0-374-34363-2). FS&G.

—No Scarlet Ribbons. LC 80-28501. 154p. (gr. 5 up). 1981. 11.95 (ISBN 0-374-35532-0). FS&G.

Tester, Sylvia R. A Day of Surprises. Hook, Frances, illus. LC 78-23263. (ps-3). 1979. PLB 12.96 (ISBN 0-89565-022-3). Childs World.

Thomas, Marlo, et al. Free to Be...A Family. LC 87-47581. (Illus.). 160p. 1990. 19.95 (ISBN 0-553-05235-7); pap. 12.95 (ISBN 0-553-34559-1). Bantam.

Thompson, Jean. Don't Forget Michael. Apple, Margot, illus. LC 79-16637. 64p. (gr. k-3). 1979. 11.95 (ISBN 0-688-22196-3); (Morrow Jr Bks). Morrow Jr Bks.

Tolan, Stephanie S. The Great Skinner Getaway. LC 86-22874. 204p. (gr. 7 up). 1987. 13.95 (ISBN 0-02-789361-8, Four Winds). Macmillan Child Grp.

Tulloch, Richard. Stories from Our House. Vivas, Julie, illus. 32p. (ps-3). 1987. 11.95 (ISBN 0-521-33485-3). Cambridge U Pr.

Uchida, Yoshiko. The Best Bad Thing. LC 85-26790. 136p. (gr. 4-7). 1986. pap. 3.95 (ISBN 0-689-71069-0, Aladdin). Macmillan Child Grp.

Ure, Jean. If It Weren't For Sebastian. LC 84-15568. 192p. (gr. 7 up). 1985. 14.95 (ISBN 0-385-29380-1). Delacorte.

—If It Weren't for Sebastian. (gr. k-12). 1987. pap. 2.95 (ISBN 0-440-93996-8, LFL). Dell.

Van Laan, Nancy. Possum Come A-Knocking. Booth, George, illus. LC 88-12751. 32p. (ps-3). 1990. 14.00 (ISBN 0-394-82206-4); lib. bdg. 12.99 (ISBN 0-394-92206-9). Knopf.

Van Leeuwen, Jean. Seems Like This Road Goes on Forever. LC 78-72201. (gr. 8 up). 1979. 8.95 (ISBN 0-8037-7687-X). Dial Bks Young.

Vogel, Ilse-Margret. My Summer Brother. Vogel, Ilse-Margret, illus. LC 80-7911. 96p. (gr. 2-5). 1981. 8.95i (ISBN 0-06-026324-5). HarpC Child Bks.

Voigt, Cynthia. Homecoming. LC 80-36723. 320p. (gr. 5 up). 1981. 14.95 (ISBN 0-689-30833-7, Atheneum Child Bk). Macmillan Child Grp.

Waber, Bernard. Funny, Funny Lyle. Waber, Bernard, illus. LC 86-27772. 40p. (gr. k-3). 1987. 13.95 (ISBN 0-395-43619-2). HM.

Waddell, Martin. Once There Were Giants. Dale, Penny, illus. LC 88-33586. (gr. k-3). 1989. 13.95 (ISBN 0-385-29806-4). Delacorte.

Waggoner, Karen. Dad Gummit & Ma Foot. Riggio, Anita, illus. LC 89-70983. 32p. (ps-2). 1990. 14.95 (ISBN 0-531-05891-3); PLB 14.99 (ISBN 0-531-08491-4). Orchard Bks Watts.

Walker, Barbara, ed. The Little House Diary. LC 84-48754. (Illus.). 160p. (ps up). 1985. pap. 9.95 (ISBN 0-06-446006-1). HarpC Child Bks.

Walker, Mary A. Brad's Box. LC 87-33658. 128p. (gr. 6-9). 1988. SBE 12.95 (ISBN 0-689-31426-4, Atheneum Child Bk). Macmillan Child Grp.

—Year of the Cafeteria. Walker, Mary A., illus. LC 79-156109. 144p. (gr. 6-10). 1971. 4.95 (ISBN 0-672-51398-6, Bobbs). Macmillan.

Walton, Marilyn J. Those Terrible Terwilliger Twins. DiSalvo-Ryan, Dyanne, illus. LC 84-17732. 32p. (gr. 3-6). 1985. PLB 14.65 (ISBN 0-940742-39-X). Raintree Pubs.

Wangerin, Walter, Jr. Thistle. Sewell, Marcia, illus. LC 82-47717. 48p. (gr. 2-4). 1983. PLB 11.89 (ISBN 0-06-026352-0). HarpC Child Bks.

Wells, Rosemary. None of the Above. LC 74-2879. 192p. (gr. 8 up). 1974. 5.95 (ISBN 0-8037-6148-1). Dial Bks Young.

—Unfortunately Harriet. Wells, Rosemary, illus. LC 76-181786. 32p. (ps-3). 1972. PLB 4.58 (ISBN 0-8037-9169-0). Dial Bks Young.

Wickstrom, Lois. Oliver. (Illus.). 32p. 1991. 14.95 (ISBN 0-9611872-5-5). Our Child Pr.

Wiggin, Eric & Wiggin, Kate D. Rebecca of Sunnybrook Farm: The Girl. 256p. (gr. 4-7). 1990. 9.95 (ISBN 1-56121-004-8). Wolgemuth & Hyatt.

Willard, Barbara. The Eldest Son. (gr. k-12). 1989. pap. 3.25 (ISBN 0-440-20412-7, LFL). Dell.

Williams, Vera B. A Chair for My Mother. Williams, Vera B., illus. LC 81-7010. 32p. (gr. k-3). 1982. 13.95 (ISBN 0-688-00914-X); PLB 12.88 (ISBN 0-688-00915-8). Greenwillow.

—Music, Music for Everyone. Williams, Vera B., illus. LC 83-14196. 32p. (gr. k-3). 1984. 13.95 (ISBN 0-688-02603-6); PLB 13.88 (ISBN 0-688-02604-4). Greenwillow.

—Something Special for Me. Williams, Vera B., illus. LC 82-11884. 32p. (gr. k-3). 1983. 13.95 (ISBN 0-688-01806-8); PLB 13.88 (ISBN 0-688-01807-6). Greenwillow.

Wojciechowska, Maia. Hey, What's Wrong with This One? Sandin, Joan, illus. LC 67-14071. 90p. (gr. 3-6). 1969. PLB 12.89 (ISBN 0-06-026579-5). HarpC Child Bks.

Wolitzer, Hilma. Toby Lived Here. (gr. 5-11). 1986. pap. 3.45 (ISBN 0-374-47924-0). FS&G.

Wyss, J. D. The Swiss Family Robinson. (gr. 4-6). 1986. pap. 2.25 (ISBN 0-14-035044-6, Puffin). Puffin Bks.

Wyss, Johann. Swiss Family Robinson. (gr. 5 up). 1964. pap. 2.95 (ISBN 0-8049-0013-2, CL-13). Airmont.

—The Swiss Family Robinson. James, Raymond, ed. Beier, Ellen, illus. LC 89-33888. 48p. (gr. 3-6). 1990. lib. bdg. 12.89 (ISBN 0-8167-1875-X); pap. text ed. 3.95 (ISBN 0-8167-1876-8). Troll Assocs.

Wyss, Johann D. The Swiss Family Robinson. 1990. pap. 2.95 (ISBN 0-451-52481-0, Sig Classics). NAL-Dutton.

Zable, Rona S. Landing on Marvin Gardens. (gr. 7 up). 1989. 13.95 (ISBN 0-553-05839-8, Starfire). Bantam.

Zach, Cheryl. More Than Friends. 160p. (Orig.). (gr. 5-9). 1989. pap. 2.95 (ISBN 1-55802-074-8). Lynx Bks.

Zindel, Paul. Effect of Gamma Rays on Man-in-the-Moon Marigolds. Kingman, D., illus. (gr. 9 up). 1984. pap. 3.95 (ISBN 0-553-28028-7). Bantam.

Zolotow, Charlotte. A Father Like That. Shecter, Ben, illus. LC 70-135778. (ps-3). 1971. PLB 12.89 (ISBN 0-06-026950-2). HarpC Child Bks.

—May I Visit? Reissue. ed. Blegvad, Erik, illus. LC 75-25405. 32p. (gr. k-3). 1976. 12.95 (ISBN 0-06-026932-4); PLB 12.89 (ISBN 0-06-026933-2). HarpC Child Bks.

FAMILY LIFE EDUCATION

Matiella, Ana C. Cultural Pride Student Workbook. Salinas, Ron, illus. 96p. (Orig.). (gr. 5-8). 1988. pap. 7.95 (ISBN 0-941816-68-0). Network Pubns.

—La Familia Student Workbook. Salinas, Ron, illus. 96p. (Orig.). (gr. 5-8). 1988. pap. 7.95 (ISBN 0-941816-70-2). Network Pubns.

FAMILY PLANNING

see Birth Control

FAMILY RELATIONS

see Domestic Relations

FAMINE

Fine, John C. The Hunger Road. Fine, John C., illus. LC 87-27794. 160p. (gr. 5 up). 1988. 13.95 (ISBN 0-689-31361-6, Atheneum Child Bk). Macmillan Child Grp.

Fradin, Dennis. Disaster! Famines. LC 85-31847. (Illus.). 64p. (gr. 3 up). 1986. PLB 17.27 (ISBN 0-516-00859-5). Childrens.

Timberlake, Lloyd. Famine in Africa. LC 85-81982. (Illus.). 32p. (gr. 4-8). 1986. PLB 8.90 (ISBN 0-531-17017-9, Gloucester Pr). Watts.

FANTASTIC FICTION

see also Ghost Stories; Science Fiction

Adler, C. S. Eddie's Blue-Winged Dragon. 144p. (gr. 5-8). 1988. 14.95 (ISBN 0-399-21535-2, Putnam). Putnam Pub Group.

—Eddie's Blue-Winged Dragon. 144p. 1990. pap. 2.95 (ISBN 0-380-70768-3, Camelot). Avon.

Ahlberg, Janet & Ahlberg, Allan. Jeremiah in the Dark Woods. (Illus.). 48p. (ps-3). 1990. pap. 3.95 (ISBN 0-14-032811-4, Puffin). Puffin Bks.

Aiken, Joan. The Erl King's Daughter. Warren, Paul, illus. 42p. (gr. 2-4). 1989. 3.95 (ISBN 0-8120-6137-3). Barron.

—Up the Chimney Down. LC 85-42642. 256p. (gr. 5 up). 1985. 12.95 (ISBN 0-06-020036-7). HarpC Child Bks.

Alexander, Sue. World Famous Muriel & the Scary Dragon. Demarest, Chris L., illus. 48p. (gr. 1-3). 1985. 14.95 (ISBN 0-316-03134-8). Little.

Alpert, Lou. Dancing with the Shadows in My Room. Alpert, Lou, illus. 32p. (ps-5). 1991. 12.95 (ISBN 1-879085-06-2). Whsprng Coyote Pr.

Amthor, Terry K. Teeth of Mordor. Fenlon, Peter C., ed. Martin, David & Martin, Elissa, illus. 32p. (gr. 10-12). 1988. pap. 6.00 (ISBN 0-915795-96-5, 8202). Iron Crown Ent Inc.

Andersen, Hans Christian. Thumbelina. Jeffers, Susan, illus. LC 79-50146. 32p. (ps-3). 1985. pap. 4.95 (ISBN 0-8037-0232-9). Dial Bks Young.

Arthur, Lanai. Journey to the Land of the Crystal Sun. 1988. pap. 5.95 (ISBN 0-533-07712-5). Vantage.

Asch, Frank. Journey to Terezor. LC 88-45866. 176p. (gr. 4-8). 1991. pap. 3.95 (ISBN 0-679-80425-0, Bullseye Bks). Knopf.

Asher, Sandy. Missing Pieces. (gr. 6 up). 1986. pap. 2.50 (ISBN 0-440-95716-8, LFL). Dell.

Asimov, Isaac & Greenberg, Martin H., eds. Visions of Fantasy. Elmore, Larry, illus. 192p. (gr. 5 up). 1989. 14.95 (ISBN 0-385-26359-7, Zephyr-BFYR). Doubleday.

Asimov, Isaac, et al, eds. Mutants. LC 83-48444. 256p. (gr. 7 up). 1988. pap. 2.95 (ISBN 0-06-447019-9, Trophy). HarpC Child Bks.

Asimov, Janet & Asimov, Isaac. Norby & the Invaders. LC 85-13635. 138p. (gr. 3-5). 1985. 10.95 (ISBN 0-8027-6599-8); PLB 10.85 (ISBN 0-8027-6607-2). Walker & Co.

—Norby & the Oldest Dragon. (gr. 4-9). 1990. 14.95 (ISBN 0-8027-6909-8); PLB 15.85 (ISBN 0-8027-6910-1). Walker & Co.

Avi. Bright Shadow. LC 85-5719. 144p. (gr. 5-7). 1985. 12.95 (ISBN 0-02-707750-0, Bradbury Pr). Macmillan Child Grp.

—Who Stole the Wizard of Oz? James, Derek, illus. LC 81-884. 128p. (gr. 3-6). 1990. pap. 2.95 (ISBN 0-394-84992-2). McKay.

Babbitt, Natalie. Tuck Everlasting. LC 75-33306. 160p. (gr. 3 up). 1975. 14.95 (ISBN 0-374-37848-7, Sunburst); pap. 3.95 (ISBN 0-374-48009-5, Sunburst). FS&G.

Bank Street Book of Creepy Tales. 1989. pap. 3.95 (ISBN 0-671-63147-0). S&S Trade.

Banks, Lynne R. The Fairy Rebel. large type ed. (Illus.). 227p. 1989. PLB 15.95 (ISBN 1-55736-124-X, Crnrstn Bks). ABC-CLIO.

—Farthest-Away Mountain. (gr. 4-7). 1991. 14.95 (ISBN 0-385-41534-6). Doubleday.

Barber, Antonia. The Ghosts. (gr. 6-9). 1989. pap. 2.95 (ISBN 0-671-70714-0, Archway). PB.

Barklem, Jill. The Four Seasons of Brambly Hedge. (Illus.). 144p. (gr. 3 up). 1990. 24.95 (ISBN 0-399-21869-6, Philomel Bks). Putnam Pub Group.

Barrie, J. M. Peter Pan. Dubowski, Cathy, adapted by. Zallinger, Jean, illus. LC 90-23077. 96p. (Orig.). (gr. 2-7). 1991. lib. bdg. 5.99 (ISBN 0-679-91044-1, Random Juv); pap. 2.95 (ISBN 0-679-81044-7). Random.

—Peter Pan in Kensington Gardens. 150p. 1980. Repr. PLB 16.95x (ISBN 0-89967-006-7). Harmony Raine.

—Peter Pan: Return to Never-Never Land. Forten, Ron, adapted by. (Illus.). 56p. 1991. pap. write for info. (ISBN 1-56398-016-9). Malibu Graphics.

Barrie, James. Peter Pan. (gr. k-5). 8.98 (ISBN 0-517-63222-5). Outlet Bk Co.

Baum, L. Frank. Adventures in Oz: Ozma of Oz & Marvelous Land of Oz, The Original Editions Complete & Unabridged. 575p. (gr. 2 up). 1985. pap. 11.90 (ISBN 0-486-24880-1). Dover.

—Glinda of Oz. 224p. 1985. pap. 3.95 (ISBN 0-345-33394-2, Del Rey). Ballantine.

—Little Wizard Stories of Oz. (Illus.). 96p. 1988. pap. 2.95 (ISBN 0-553-15617-9, Skylark). Bantam.

—El Mago de Oz. (SPA.). 9.95 (ISBN 0-685-31013-2). Santillana.

—Marvelous Land of Oz. McKee, David, illus. 192p. (gr. 4-6). 1985. pap. 2.25 (ISBN 0-14-035041-1, Puffin). Puffin Bks.

—The Marvelous Land of Oz. Neill, John R., illus. LC 85-4856. 288p. (gr. 4-6). 1985. 15.00 (ISBN 0-688-05439-0). Morrow Jr Bks.

—Over the Rainbow. Naden, C. J., ed. Morrison, Bill, illus. LC 79-84151. 32p. (gr. 2-5). 1980. PLB 10.79 (ISBN 0-89375-197-9); pap. text ed. 2.95 (ISBN 0-89375-193-6). Troll Assocs.

—Ozma of Oz. 272p. (gr. 2 up). 1985. pap. 5.95 (ISBN 0-486-24779-1). Dover.

—Ozma of Oz. Neill, John R., illus. LC 88-63291. 288p. 1989. 19.95 (ISBN 0-688-06632-1). Morrow Jr Bks.

—Patchwork Girl of Oz. 1990. pap. 6.95 (ISBN 0-486-26514-5). Dover.

—The Road to Oz. Neill, John R., illus. Glassman, Peter, afterword by. LC 90-48349. (Illus.). 272p. 1991. Repr. of 1909 ed. 16.95 (ISBN 0-688-09997-1). Morrow Jr Bks.

—Tik Tok of Oz. (Illus.). 192p. (gr. 5 up). 1991. pap. 2.25 (ISBN 0-14-035124-8, Puffin). Puffin Bks.

—The Wizard of Oz. (gr. 3-5). 1989. pap. 2.50 (ISBN 0-590-41746-0, Pub. by Apple Classics). Scholastic Inc.

—The Wonderful Wizard of Oz. 193p. 1981. Repr. PLB 11.95x (ISBN 0-89967-021-0). Harmony Raine.

—The Wonderful Wizard of Oz. (gr. 5-6). 17.95 (ISBN 0-88411-772-3, Pub. by Aeonian Pr). Amereon Ltd.

—The Wonderful Wizard of Oz. Moser, Barry, illus. 1986. 29.95 (ISBN 0-520-05822-4). U of Cal Pr.

—The Wonderful Wizard of Oz. large type ed. Denslow, W. W., illus. 188p. (gr. 2-6). 1987. lib. bdg. 13.95 (ISBN 1-55736-013-8). ABC-CLIO.

Baum, Roger S. Dorothy of Oz. Miles, Elizabeth, illus. LC 89-6918. 176p. 1989. 14.95 (ISBN 0-688-07848-6). Morrow Jr Bks.

Bawden, Nina. Squib. LC 82-75. (Illus.). 160p. (gr. 4-6). 1982. 12.95 (ISBN 0-688-01299-X). Lothrop.

Beatty, Patricia. Charley Skedaddle. LC 87-12270. 192p. (gr. 5-9). 1987. 12.95 (ISBN 0-688-06687-9). Morrow Jr Bks.

Bell, Clare. Clan Ground. (gr. k-12). 1987. pap. 2.95 (ISBN 0-440-91287-3, LFL). Dell.

Benedek, Elek & Illyes, Gyula. The Prince & His Magic Horse. 72p. (gr. 3 up). 1987. 13.95 (ISBN 963-13-2534-2, Pub. by Corvina Kiado HU). Intl Spec Bk.

Bennett, Jill. Teeny Tiny. De Paola, Tomie, illus. LC 85-12347. 32p. (ps-1). 1986. 8.95 (ISBN 0-399-21293-0, Putnam). Putnam Pub Group.

Benson, Robert B. The Wizard of Bergen. 100p. (Orig.). (gr. 7-12). 1987. pap. 7.50 (ISBN 0-9616327-1-2). Brandt Bks.

Berends, Polly. Ozma & the Wayward Wand. Rose, David, illus. LC 84-17972. 80p. (gr. 2-6). 1985. (Random Juv); pap. 1.95 (ISBN 0-394-87068-9). Random.

Berger, Barbara H. Gwinna. (Illus.). 128p. 1990. 18.95 (ISBN 0-399-21738-X, Philomel Bks). Putnam Pub Group.

Bhaktipada, Swami. Lila in the Land of Illusion: A Re-Telling of Lewis Carroll's Alice in Wonderland. New Vrindaban Community Artists, illus. LC 87-18626. 127p. (gr. 3-8). 1987. 12.95 (ISBN 0-932215-22-X); pap. text ed. 7.95 (ISBN 0-932215-19-X). Palace Pub.

Bibee, John. Bicycle Hills: How One Halloween Almost Got out of Hand. LC 89-15316. (Illus.). 201p. (Orig.). (gr. 7-8). 1989. pap. 6.95 (ISBN 0-8308-1203-2, 1203). InterVarsity.

—The Last Christmas. LC 90-4870. (Illus.). 204p. (Orig.). (gr. 3-8). 1990. pap. 6.95 (ISBN 0-8308-1204-0, 1204). InterVarsity.

Bicknell, Treld, compiled by. Seven Is Heaven. LC 86-45415. (Illus.). (gr. 2). 1986. 8.95 (ISBN 0-15-200580-3, Gulliver Bks). HarBraceJ.

Biro, Val. Gumdrop & the Secret Switches. LC 82-14786. (Illus.). 32p. (ps up). PLB 9.95. Creative Ed.

—Gumdrop Finds a Friend. LC 82-17688. (Illus.). 32p. (ps up). PLB 9.95. Creative Ed.

—Gumdrop Gets His Wings. LC 82-17716. (Illus.). 32p. (ps up). PLB 9.95. Creative Ed.

Blathwayt, Benedict. Tangle & the Firesticks. Blathwayt, Benedict, illus. LC 87-2591. (gr. k-3). 1987. 9.95 (ISBN 0-394-88827-8); lib. bdg. 11.99 (ISBN 0-394-98827-2). Knopf.

—Tangle & the Silver Bird. Blathwayt, Benedict, illus. LC 88-22024. 32p. (gr. k-3). 1989. 12.95 (ISBN 0-394-82780-5); lib. bdg. 13.99 (ISBN 0-394-92780-X). Knopf.

Blume, Judy. Otherwise Known As Sheila the Great. (gr. 3-6). 1972. 11.95 (ISBN 0-525-36455-2, DCB). Dutton Child Bks.

—Superfudge. LC 80-10439. 176p. (gr. 3-6). 1980. 11.95 (ISBN 0-525-40522-4, DCB). Dutton Child Bks.

Bond, Nancy. A String in the Harp. LC 75-28181. 384p. (gr. 4-8). 1976. 14.95 (ISBN 0-689-50036-X, M K McElderry). Macmillan Child Grp.

Bradbury, Ray. The Halloween Tree. 192p. (gr. 7 up). 1984. pap. 3.95 (ISBN 0-553-25823-0). Bantam.

Brett, Jan. Beauty & the Beast. Brett, Jan, illus. LC 88-16965. 48p. (gr. 1-7). 1989. 14.95 (ISBN 0-89919-497-4, Clarion Bks). HM.

Brightfield, Richard. Escape from the Kingdom of Frome, No. 4: The Battle of Astar. 128p. (Orig.). 1987. pap. 2.50 (ISBN 0-553-26290-4, Starfire). Bantam.

—The Forest of the King. 128p. (Orig.). (gr. 7-12). 1986. pap. 2.50 (ISBN 0-553-26155-X). Bantam.

—Star System Tenopia, No. 4. 144p. (Orig.). 1986. pap. 2.50 (ISBN 0-553-25637-8). Bantam.

—Terror on Kabran. 144p. (Orig.). 1986. pap. 2.50 (ISBN 0-553-25636-X). Bantam.

—Trapped in the Sea Kingdom. 128p. 1986. pap. 2.50 (ISBN 0-553-25473-1). Bantam.

Brown, Jeff. A Lamp for the Lambchops. Wheeling, Lynn, illus. LC 82-48628. 96p. (gr. 2-6). 1983. PLB 11.89 (ISBN 0-06-020694-2). HarpC Child Bks.

Brown, John R. Living Legends. LC 89-50186. 124p. (Orig.). 1990. pap. 5.95 (ISBN 0-916383-89-X). Aegina Pr.

Brunn, Robert. The Initiation. (gr. 5 up). 1982. pap. 1.95 (ISBN 0-440-94047-8, LFL). Dell.

Buckley, John. The Magical Round Wall. 1991. 6.95 (ISBN 0-533-08849-6). Vantage.

Burgess, Gelett. Goop Tales. LC 72-93766. (Illus.). 128p. (gr. 1-6). 1973. pap. 3.95 (ISBN 0-486-22914-9). Dover.

Burgess, Thornton W. Mother West Wind's Children. Cady, Harrison, illus. 156p. (ps-3). 1985. pap. 6.95 (ISBN 0-316-11657-2). Little.

Bush, Max. The Troll & the Elephant Prince. (gr. 4 up). 1985. pap. 4.50 (ISBN 0-87602-254-9). Anchorage.

Butler, Dorothy. A Happy Tale. Hurford, John, illus. LC 90-34500. 32p. (ps-5). 1990. 11.95 (ISBN 0-940793-61-X, Crocodile Bks). Interlink Pub.

Byars, Betsy. The Blossoms & the Green Phantom. Rogers, Jacqueline, illus. 160p. (gr. 4-6). 1987. pap. 14.95 (ISBN 0-385-29533-2). Delacorte.

—The Two-Thousand Pound Goldfish. large type ed. 160p. 1989. Repr. of 1982 ed. PLB 15.95 (ISBN 1-55736-131-2, Crnrstn Bks). ABC-CLIO.

Byrne, John & Giordano, Dick. Superman: The Man of Steel. (ps up). 1988. pap. 12.95 (ISBN 0-317-69500-2). Fawcett.

Cahn, Joseph M. The Teenie Weenies Book: The Life & Art of William Donahey. Kishbaugh, Allan, intro. by. LC 84-80569. (Illus.). 128p. (Orig.). (gr. 7-12). 1986. 16.95 (ISBN 0-88138-035-0). Green Tiger Pr.

Carabis, Anne. The Magic Rocking Chair. Carabis, Anne, illus. 28p. (Orig.). (ps-3). 1980. pap. 3.50 (ISBN 0-9605802-0-4). Carabis.

Card, Orson S. Enders Game & Speaker for the Dead. (gr. 7 up). 1987. pap. 3.95 (ISBN 0-317-57062-5). Tor Bks.

Carrick, Carol. Aladdin & the Wonderful Lamp. Carrick, Donald, illus. (ps-3). 1989. 12.95 (ISBN 0-590-41679-0, Scholastic Hardcover). Scholastic Inc.

Carroll, Lewis. Alice in Wonderland. 299p. 1981. Repr. PLB 12.95x (ISBN 0-89967-019-9). Harmony Raine.

—Alice in Wonderland. Maraja, illus. LC 85-81652. 120p. (gr. 5 up). 1986. pap. 10.95 (ISBN 0-448-18983-6, G&D). Putnam Pub Group.

—Alice in Wonderland. 1990. 7.98 (ISBN 0-8317-1351-8). Smithmark.

—Alice's Adventures in Wonderland. (Illus.). (gr. 7-12). 1973. pap. 4.25x (ISBN 0-19-580713-8). Oxford U Pr.

—Alice's Adventures in Wonderland. Weevers, Peter, illus. 224p. (gr. 3 up). 1989. 19.95 (ISBN 0-399-22241-3, Philomel Bks). Putnam Pub Group.

—Alice's Adventures in Wonderland. Tenniel, John, illus. 224p. 1991. Repr. 13.95 (ISBN 0-312-01820-7). St Martin.

—Through the Looking Glass. 176p. (gr. 7 up). 1985. pap. 2.25 (ISBN 0-14-035039-X, Puffin). Puffin Bks.

—Through the Looking Glass, & What Alice Found There. Tenniel, John, illus. LC 84-60960. 184p. (gr. 2 up). 1984. Repr. of 1941 ed. 6.95 (ISBN 0-88088-991-8, 889918). Peter Pauper.

—Through the Looking-Glass: And What Alice Found There. Todd, Justin, illus. LC 68-21827. 176p. (ps up). 1988. 16.95 (ISBN 0-8052-4036-5). Schocken.

Castle, Caroline. Herbert Binns & the Flying Tricycle. 1990. pap. 3.95 (ISBN 0-8037-0739-8, Dial Pied Piper). Puffin Bks.

Chaikin, Miriam. Yossi Asks the Angels for Help. Mathers, Petra, illus. LC 84-48351. 64p. (gr. 3-5). 1985. 11.95 (ISBN 0-06-021195-4). HarpC Child Bks.

Cheetham, Ann. The Pit. (gr. 5-8). 1990. 14.95 (ISBN 0-8050-1142-0). H Holt & Co.

Cheever, John. The Enormous Radio. 32p. (gr. 6 up). 1983. PLB 10.95s.p. (ISBN 0-87191-959-1); 15.65 (ISBN 0-685-07727-6). Creative Ed.

Chetwin, Grace. The Riddle & the Rune. LC 87-10284. 256p. (gr. 5 up). 1987. 14.95 (ISBN 0-02-718312-2, Bradbury Pr). Macmillan Child Grp.

—The Starstone. LC 88-30249. 256p. (gr. 5 up). 1989. 14.95 (ISBN 0-02-718315-7, Bradbury Pr). Macmillan Child Grp.

Chew. Trouble with Magic. (ps-3). pap. 2.25 (ISBN 0-590-10343-1, Schol Pap). Scholastic Inc.

Chew, Ruth. Summer Magic. Chew, Ruth, illus. (gr. k-3). 1977. pap. 2.25 (ISBN 0-590-10421-7). Scholastic Inc.

—Trapped in Time. Chew, Ruth, illus. 128p. (Orig.). (gr. 2-3). 1986. pap. 2.50 (ISBN 0-590-33813-7, Lucky Star). Scholastic Inc.

Christian, Mary B. The Toady & Dr. Miracle. Ohlsson, Ib, illus. LC 84-21278. 56p. (gr. 1-4). 1985. PLB 9.95 (ISBN 0-02-718470-6). Macmillan.

Christopher, Matt. The Kid Who Only Hit Homers. Kidder, Harvey, illus. (gr. 4-6). 1972. lib. bdg. 13.95 (ISBN 0-316-13918-1). Little.

Cissom, Joan. The Enchanted Unicorn. Transue, David, illus. 20p. (Orig.). 1989. pap. 3.95 (ISBN 0-929560-01-9). Southern Rose Prodns.

Clarke, J. The Torment of Mr. Gully. 144p. (gr. 7 up). 1991. 14.95 (ISBN 0-8050-1421-7). H Holt & Co.

Cole, Babette. The Trouble with Gran. 32p. (ps-3). 1987. 13.95 (ISBN 0-399-21428-3, Putnam). Putnam Pub Group.

Cole, Joanna. The Magic School Bus Inside the Earth. Degen, Bruce, illus. LC 87-4563. 48p. (gr. k-3). 1987. pap. 13.95 (ISBN 0-590-40759-7). Scholastic Inc.

—The New Baby at Your House. Hammid, Hella, photos by. LC 85-10653. (Illus.). 48p. (ps-3). 1985. 11.95 (ISBN 0-688-05806-X); lib. bdg. 11.88 (ISBN 0-688-05807-8, Morrow Jr Bks); pap. 5.95 (ISBN 0-688-07418-9, Mulberry Bks). Morrow Jr Bks.

Cone, Molly. The Amazing Memory of Harvey Bean. (Illus.). 112p. (gr. 3-6). 1980. 13.95 (ISBN 0-395-29181-X). HM.

Coombs, Patricia. Dorrie & the Dreamyard Monsters. Coombs, Patricia, illus. 48p. (gr. k-6). 1982. pap. 2.25 (ISBN 0-440-40896-2, YB). Dell.

Cooper, Louise. The Master. 288p. (Orig.). (gr. 7 up). 1987. pap. 3.50 (ISBN 0-8125-3396-8, Dist. by St. Martin's Pr & Warner Pub Servs). Tor Bks.

Cooper, Susan. The Dark Is Rising. Cober, Alan, illus. LC 72-85916. 232p. (gr. 5 up). 1973. 14.95 (ISBN 0-689-30317-3, M K McElderry). Macmillan Child Grp.

—The Grey King. Heslop, Michael, illus. LC 75-8526. 224p. (gr. 4-8). 1975. 14.95 (ISBN 0-689-50029-7, M K McElderry). Macmillan Child Grp.

Corbin, Linda & Dys, Pat. Jesus Helps Me Grow. Fieser, Stephen, illus. 28p. (Orig.). (gr. 1-6). 1986. pap. 5.99 (ISBN 0-87509-374-4). Chr Pubns.

Corddry, Thomas. Kibby & the Red Elephant. Kock, Carl, illus. LC 72-13771. (gr. 3-6). 1973. 6.95 (ISBN 0-87955-106-2). O'Hara.

Corrin, Sara & Corrin, Stephen, eds. Imagine That! Fifteen Fantastic Tales. Bennett, Jill, illus. LC 86-2164. 192p. (gr. 3-6). 1986. 12.95 (ISBN 0-571-13843-8). Faber & Faber.

Cosgrove, Stephen. Balderdash. Gedrose, Ed, illus. 32p. (ps up). 1991. 14.95 (ISBN 1-55868-045-4). Gr Arts Ctr Pub.

There was a place called Bugaboo where elfin creatures called Woodsprites lived. But also there, in the darkened shadows of Bugaboo, lived Balderdash, the king of twisty snakes & skittering things. He was the leader of any puffery shaded black & grey that whisked about the night scaring wit & wisdom from those not wise. So frightened were the Woodsprites of Balderdash & all that they commanded that they wouldn't work in the garden for fear of the daytime shadows. No one would gather

nuts or berries for fear of being away from the protective wrap of the nighttime fires. With no one to work the garden & no one to gather berries, there was no food, & without food, the Woodsprites were very hungry indeed. Thus begins Stephen Cosgrove's classic tale of BALDERDASH as illustrated by Ed Gedrose, one of the Northwest's premier fantasy artists.
BALDERDASH is added with great pride as the fourth book in the DreamMaker Classic series. Children of all ages learn not to fear the dark, the shadows, & those things that imagination can make.
Publisher Provided Annotation.

—Dragolin. James, Robin, illus. LC 85-14400. (Orig.). (gr. k-5). 1978. pap. 2.95 (ISBN 0-8431-1165-8). Price Stern.

—The Dream Stealer. Heyer, Carol, illus. LC 89-83843. 48p. (gr. 1-4). 1990. 16.95 (ISBN 1-55868-009-8); pap. 5.95 (ISBN 1-55868-021-7); pap. 12.95 incl. audio (ISBN 1-55868-042-X). Gr Arts Ctr Pub.
THE DREAM STEALER is the first of the Dream Maker Classics by Stephen Cosgrove. A twisted, masked gnome, the Dream Stealer, has been taking good dreams from the children of Chimera. The tale is woven around Michael & Gabby's efforts to capture the gnome & release the dreams. Illustrated by Carol Heyer, THE DREAM STEALER is certain to enchant one & all.
Publisher Provided Annotation.

—Flutterby Fly. James, Robin, illus. LC 85-14353. (Orig.). (gr. k-4). 1984. pap. 2.95 (ISBN 0-8431-1162-3). Price Stern.

Cosgrove, Stephen E. Gigglesnitcher. James, Robin, illus. 48p. (gr. k-9). 1991. 16.95 (ISBN 1-55868-034-9). Gr Arts Ctr Pub.
The GIGGLESNITCHER has stolen all of Levity Tree's giggle blossoms & laughing leaves, & now nothing is as it should be on the island of Serendipity. The birds have stopped singing, the animals are grumpy, & the Muffin Muncher is so upset his tears are creating a flood in the village! Leo the Lop & magical Flutterby, the winged horse, come to the rescue & try to persuade the thief to change his ways. This is a Serendipity adventure by Stephen Cosgrove to warm the hearts of readers young & old. The illustrations by Robin James are the perfect accompaniment to this enchanting tale.
Publisher Provided Annotation.

—Terrybrook Dragon. McNatt, Richard, illus. 32p. (gr. k-7). 1990. 14.95 (ISBN 1-55868-036-5). Gr Arts Ctr Pub.
TERRYBROOK DRAGON is a tale about the banished prince who must protect his mother, the queen, & his princess sister from the terrible Terrybrook Dragon. The prince's father left the three alone to go out into the world & secure a new castle for his family - much like fathers now, who are forced to leave home to find better jobs to support their families. This is a timeless story of families separated by

circumstances beyond their control. It is a metaphor relating to family problems, values, & personal worth. The combination of Cosgrove & McNatt is not new. Together they created the 6-book series, "The Snuffin Chronicles." McNatt also did extensive work for Disney Studios where he illustrated many of the "Winnie the Pooh" books.
Publisher Provided Annotation.

Costello, Melina P. Tutti-Frutti Town: Blinky Blueberry Finds a Friend. Costello, Melina P., illus. 32p. (Orig.). (gr. k-3). 1991. pap. 6.50 (ISBN 1-878130-01-3). Bang A Drum.
Cover, Arthur B. Blade of the Guillotine. 144p. (Orig.). (gr. 7-12). 1986. pap. 2.50 (ISBN 0-553-26038-3). Bantam.
Coville, Bruce. Sarah & the Dragon. Peck, Beth, illus. LC 83-48447. 48p. (gr. k-3). 1984. PLB 11.89 (ISBN 0-685-07683-0, Lipp Jr Bks); PLB 11.89 (ISBN 0-397-32070-1). HarpC Child Bks.
Crenshaw, George. Belvedere: Flapjacks, No. 4. 256p. (Orig.). 1983. pap. 2.50 (ISBN 0-523-49082-8, Dist. by Warner Pub. Services & Saint Martin's Press). Tor Bks.
Cresswell, Helen. Bagthorpes Haunted: Being the Sixth Part of the Bagthorpe Saga. 192p. (gr. 5-9). 1985. 13.95 (ISBN 0-02-725380-5, Mcmillan Child Bk). Macmillan Child Grp.
—The Secret World of Polly Flint. Felts, Shirley, illus. 176p. (gr. 3-7). 1991. pap. 3.95 (ISBN 0-689-71532-3, Aladdin). Macmillan Child Grp.
Cross, Gillian. The Demon Headmaster. large type ed. 208p. (gr. 3 up). 1990. lib. bdg. 16.95x (ISBN 0-7451-1150-5, Lythway Large Print). G K Hall.
Cross, Peter. Trouble for Trumpets. Cross, Peter, illus. LC 83-43115. (gr. 3 up). 1984. 9.95 (ISBN 0-394-86513-8, Random Juv). Random.
Crutchfield, Charlie. Assassins of Dol Amroth. Fenlon, Peter C., ed. McBride, Angus, illus. (Orig.). (gr. 10-12). 1987. pap. 6.00 (ISBN 0-915795-98-1, 8106). Iron Crown Ent Inc.
Cunningham, Julia. Dorp Dead. Spanfeller, James, illus. LC 65-11441. 96p. (gr. 3-7). 1987. PLB 9.99 (ISBN 0-317-58791-9); pap. 2.95 (ISBN 0-394-89267-4). Knopf.
Cutting, Edith. Ithamar - Achsah. Grossman, Dan, illus. 48p. (gr. 2-7). 1985. wkbk. 2.48 (ISBN 0-86653-303-6). Good Apple.
—Jorim-Abigail. Grossman, Dan, illus. 48p. (gr. 2-7). 1985. wkbk. 2.48 (ISBN 0-86653-305-2). Good Apple.
—Timna - Azor. Grossman, Dan, illus. 48p. (gr. 2-7). 1985. wkbk. 2.48 (ISBN 0-86653-308-7). Good Apple.
Dalton, Annie. Out of the Ordinary. LC 89-39787. 256p. (gr. 7 up). 1990. 14.95 (ISBN 0-06-021424-4); PLB 14.89 (ISBN 0-06-021425-2). HarpC Child Bks.
D'Aulaire, Ingri & D'Aulaire, Edgar P. D'Aulaire's Norse Gods & Giants. LC 86-11677. (Illus.). 168p. (gr. up). 1986. pap. 13.95 (ISBN 0-385-23692-1, Pub. by Zephyr-BFYR). Doubleday.
Davids, Paul. The Fountain of Youth. Davids, Paul, photos by. (Illus.). 56p. (Orig.). (gr. 5-9). pap. text ed. 9.95 (ISBN 0-939031-01-9). Pictorial Legends.
Degen, Bruce. Jamberry. Degen, Bruce, illus. LC 82-47708. 32p. (ps-1). 1990. 12.95 (ISBN 0-06-021416-3). HarpC Child Bks.
DeLeeuw, Adele. The Boy with Wings. LC 74-15860. (gr. 1-6). 1971. 8.95 (ISBN 0-87874-001-5, Nautilus). Galloway.
De Paola, Tomie. Songs of the Fog Maiden. LC 78-12822. (Illus.). 32p. (ps-3). 1979. reinforced bdg. 8.95 (ISBN 0-8234-0341-6). Holiday.
Dexter, Catherine. Mazemaker. Ingraham, Erick, illus. LC 88-32349. 224p. (gr. 5-9). 1989. 11.95 (ISBN 0-688-07383-2). Morrow Jr Bks.
Dickens, Charles. A Child's Story. Ingpen, Robert, illus. 32p. 9.95 (ISBN 0-9587845-4-X, AA04, Pub. by Mad Hatter Bks). Slawson Comm.
Dickey, James. Bronwen, the Traw, & the Shape-Shifter. Watson, Richard J., illus. LC 85-27082. 32p. (ps-3). 1986. 13.95 (ISBN 0-15-212580-9, HJ). HarBraceJ.
Dickinson, Peter. A Box of Nothing. LC 87-25660. 128p. (gr. 3-6). 1988. pap. 14.95 (ISBN 0-385-29664-9). Delacorte.
—The Weathermonger. (gr. k-12). 1988. pap. 2.95 (ISBN 0-440-20003-2). Dell.
Disney Classics: Oliver & Company. 1990. 6.98 (ISBN 0-8317-6574-7). Smithmark.
Disney, Walt, Productions Staff. Return to Oz. LC 84-43005. (Illus.). 48p. (ps-3). 1985. (Random Juv); lib. bdg. 5.99 (ISBN 0-394-97183-3). Random.
Disney, Walt, Staff. Blue Kangaroo. (ps) 1991. 3.95 (ISBN 1-56282-029-X). W Disney Pub.
Doyle, Arthur Conan. The Lost World. (Illus.). 272p. (gr. 5 up). 1991. pap. 2.95 (ISBN 0-14-035013-6, Puffin). Puffin Bks.
Doyle, Debra & Macdonald, James. The City by the Sea. Mitchell, Judy, illus. LC 89-5213. 144p. (gr. 5-9). 1990. PLB 9.89 (ISBN 0-8167-1830-X); pap. text ed. 2.95 (ISBN 0-8167-1831-8). Troll Assocs.

—School of Wizardry. Mitchell, Judy, illus. LC 89-33882. 144p. (gr. 5-9). 1989. PLB 9.89 (ISBN 0-8167-1826-1); pap. text ed. 2.95 (ISBN 0-8167-1827-X). Troll Assocs.
—Tournament & Tower. Mitchell, Judy, illus. LC 89-33881. 144p. (gr. 5-9). 1989. PLB 9.89 (ISBN 0-8167-1828-8); pap. text ed. 2.95 (ISBN 0-8167-1829-6). Troll Assocs.
Dravich, Jay E. Dreams of Cloud Dancing. Gullikson, Karen, illus. 150p. (Orig.). (gr. 4-12). 1982. 15.00 (ISBN 0-9604258-2-9); pap. 6.00 (ISBN 0-9604258-3-7). Tari Bk Pubs.
Dr. Seuss. Great Day for Up! Blake, Quentin, illus. LC 74-5517. 36p. (ps-1). 1974. 6.95 (ISBN 0-394-82913-1, Random Juv); lib. bdg. 7.99 (ISBN 0-394-92913-6). Random.
—Hunches in Bunches. Dr. Seuss, illus. 48p. (gr. 1-5). 1982. lib. bdg. 10.99 (ISBN 0-394-95502-1, Random Juv); pap. 10.95 (ISBN 0-394-85502-7). Random.
Duane, Diane. High Wizardry. 1990. 14.95 (ISBN 0-385-29983-4). Doubleday.
Dubowski, Cathy E., adapted by. Willow: The Storybook Based on the Movie. (Illus.). 64p. (gr. k-5). 1988. lib. bdg. 8.99 (ISBN 0-394-99574-0, Random Juv); (Random Juv). Random.
Duncan, Lois. Locked in Time. (gr. 6 up). 1986. pap. 3.50 (ISBN 0-440-94942-4, LFL). Dell.
—Stranger with My Face. 176p. (gr. 7 up). 1990. pap. 3.50 (ISBN 0-440-98356-8, LFL). Dell.
Dunham, Katharine. Kasamance: A Fantasy. LC 73-92612. (gr. 7 up). 1974. 6.95 (ISBN 0-89388-128-7). Okpaku Communications.
Eager, Edward. Half Magic. Bodecker, N. M., illus. LC 54-5153. (gr. 4-6). 1954. 12.95 (ISBN 0-15-233078-X, HJ). HarBraceJ.
—Half Magic. Treherne, Katie T. & Bodecker, N. M., illus. 208p. (gr. 3-7). 1989. pap. 3.95 (ISBN 0-15-233081-X). HarBraceJ.
—Knight's Castle. Bodecker, N. M., illus. (gr. 4-6). 16.75 (ISBN 0-8446-6232-1). Peter Smith.
—Knight's Castle. Treherne, Katie T. & Bodecker, N. M., illus. 208p. (gr. 3-7). 1989. pap. 3.95 (ISBN 0-15-243105-5). HarBraceJ.
—Magic by the Lake. Treherne, Katie T. & Bodecker, N. M., illus. 208p. (gr. 3-7). 1989. pap. 3.95 (ISBN 0-15-250444-3). HarBraceJ.
—Magic or Not? Bodecker, N. M., illus. (gr. 4-6). 1984. 16.75 (ISBN 0-8446-6154-6). Peter Smith.
—Magic or Not? Treherne, Katie T. & Bodecker, N. M., illus. 208p. (gr. 3-7). 1989. pap. 3.95 (ISBN 0-15-251160-1). HarBraceJ.
—Seven-Day Magic. (gr. 4-6). 15.75 (ISBN 0-8446-6381-6). Peter Smith.
—Seven-Day Magic. Treherne, Katie T. & Bodecker, N. M., illus. 208p. (gr. 3-7). 1989. pap. 3.95 (ISBN 0-15-272916-X). HarBraceJ.
—The Time Garden. Bodecker, N. M., illus. (gr. 4-6). 17.50 (ISBN 0-8446-6233-X). Peter Smith.
—The Time Garden. Treherne, Katie T. & Bodecker, N. M., illus. 192p. (gr. 3-7). 1990. pap. 4.95 (ISBN 0-15-288193-X). HarBraceJ.
—The Well-Wishers. (gr. 3-7). 17.50 (ISBN 0-8446-6382-4). Peter Smith.
—The Well Wishers. Treherne, Katie T. & Bodecker, N. M., illus. 192p. (gr. 3-7). 1990. pap. 4.95 (ISBN 0-15-294994-1). HarBraceJ.
Edwards, Julie. The Last of the Really Great Whangdoodles. Kubinyi, Laszlo, illus. LC 73-5482. (gr. 3-7). 1974. 13.95 (ISBN 0-06-021805-3). HarpC Child Bks.
Ellis, Anne L. The Dragon of Middlethorpe. (Illus.). 192p. (gr. 4-7). 1991. 14.95 (ISBN 0-8050-1713-5). H Holt & Co.
Emert, Phyllis R. Monsters, Strange Dreams & UFO's. 1990. pap. 2.50 (ISBN 0-8125-9425-8). Tor Bks.
Engdahl, Sylvia. Enchantress from the Stars. (gr. 6-10). 1991. 15.75 (ISBN 0-8446-6448-0). Peter Smith.
Esbensen, Barbara J. The Star Maiden: An Ojibway Tale. Davie, Helen K., illus. (ps-3). 1988. 14.95 (ISBN 0-316-24951-3). Little.
Evslin, Bernard. Jason & the Argonauts. Dodson, Bert, illus. LC 86-32114. 176p. (gr. 5 up). 1986. 13.00 (ISBN 0-688-06245-8). Morrow Jr Bks.
Farris, Stella. The Magic Blanket. Farris, Stella, illus. LC 79-2393. 30p. (ps-2). 1987. 4.95 (ISBN 0-694-00171-6). HarpC Child Bks.
—The Magic Bubble Pipe. Farris, Stella, illus. LC 78-54674. 30p. (ps-2). 1987. 4.95 (ISBN 0-694-00170-8). HarpC Child Bks.
—The Magic Castle. Farris, Stella, illus. LC 78-54676. 30p. (ps-2). 1987. 4.95 (ISBN 0-694-00169-4). HarpC Child Bks.
Faucher, Elizabeth. Honey, I Shrunk the Kids. 1989. pap. 2.95 (ISBN 0-590-42115-8). Scholastic Inc.
Feiertag, Sarah C. Mineland. 1990. 7.95 (ISBN 0-533-08924-7). Vantage.
Fleischman, Sid. McBroom Tells a Lie. Lorraine, Walter H., illus. 64p. (gr. 4-6). 1976. 13.95 (ISBN 0-316-28572-2, Joy St Bks). Little.
Florescu, Radu R. Dracula, Prince of Many Faces, Vol. 1. 1989. 19.95 (ISBN 0-316-28655-9). Little.
Foley, Pat. Edge. (Illus.). 19p. (Orig.). (gr. k-1). 1989. pap. 5.00 (ISBN 0-9624315-0-8). Pajari Pr.
Forrester, John. The Secret of the Round Beast. LC 87-45281. 160p. (gr. 7 up). 1988. pap. 2.75 (ISBN 0-06-447025-3, Trophy). HarpC Child Bks.
Freeman, Don. The Paper Party. (Illus.). (gr. 1 up). 1977. pap. 3.95 (ISBN 0-14-050212-2, Puffin). Puffin Bks.

Froman, Robert. Seeing Things: A Book of Poems. Barber, Ray, illus. LC 73-18494. 64p. (gr. 4-8). 1987. (Crowell Jr Bks); PLB 13.89 (ISBN 0-690-04625-1, Crowell Jr Bks). HarpC Child Bks.
Gag, Wanda. The Earth Gnome. Tomes, Margot, illus. LC 84-23804. 48p. (gr. 1-4). 1985. 8.95 (ISBN 0-698-20618-5, Coward). Putnam Pub Group.
Galdone, Paul, illus. History of Mother Twaddle & the Marvelous Achievements of Her Son Jack. LC 73-9726. (ps-2). 1979. 12.95 (ISBN 0-395-28801-0, Clarion). HM.
Gannett, Ruth S. The Dragons of Blueland. Gannett, Ruth C., illus. LC 86-27480. 96p. (gr. 2-5). 1963. lib. bdg. 9.99 (ISBN 0-394-91092-3); pap. 3.95 (ISBN 0-394-89050-7). Knopf.
—Elmer & the Dragon. Gannett, Ruth C., illus. LC 86-27479. 96p. (gr. 2-5). 1987. PLB 3.95 (ISBN 0-394-89049-3); pap. 3.95 (ISBN 0-317-58797-8). Knopf.
—My Father's Dragon. Gannett, Ruth C., illus. LC 86-27635. 96p. (gr. 2-5). 1987. pap. 3.95 (ISBN 0-394-89048-5). Knopf.
—Three Tales of My Father's Dragon. Gannett, Ruth C., illus. 96p. (gr. 2-5). 1987. Set. pap. 12.00 (ISBN 0-394-89136-8). Knopf.
Ganz, Yaffa. Sauta Simcha & the Cinnamon Tree. Gewirtz, Bina & Poppins, Jewish M., illus. (gr. 6-10). 10.95 (ISBN 0-87306-354-6). Feldheim.
Garden, Graeme. The Skylighters. Canning, Neil, illus. 32p. (gr. 1 up). 1988. 13.95 (ISBN 0-19-520642-8). Oxford U Pr.
Gaskin, Carol. The Forbidden Towers. Price, T. Alexander, illus. LC 84-16219. 128p. (gr. 3-7). 1985. lib. bdg. 9.49 (ISBN 0-8167-0324-8); pap. text ed. 2.95 (ISBN 0-8167-0325-6). Troll Assocs.
—Legend of Hiawatha, No. 2. 80p. (Orig.). 1986. pap. 2.50 (ISBN 0-553-15450-8). Bantam.
—The Magician's Ring. Price, T. Alexander, illus. LC 84-8499. 128p. (gr. 3-7). 1985. PLB 9.49 (ISBN 0-8167-0320-5); pap. text ed. 2.95 (ISBN 0-8167-0321-3). Troll Assocs.
—Master of Mazes. Price, T. Alexander, illus. LC 84-24015. 128p. (gr. 3-7). 1985. PLB 9.49 (ISBN 0-8167-0322-1); pap. text ed. 2.95 (ISBN 0-8167-0323-X). Troll Assocs.
Gelfand. E. T. (Illus.). 32p. (gr. 4 up). 1985. PLB 8.95 (ISBN 0-89813-113-8); 12.80. Creative Ed.
Geringer, Laura. Molly's New Washing Machine. Mathers, Petra, illus. LC 85-45839. 32p. (gr. k-3). 1986. 11.95 (ISBN 0-06-022150-X); PLB 11.89 (ISBN 0-06-022151-8). HarpC Child Bks.
Gibson, Andrew. Ellis & the Hummick. Riddell, Chris, illus. 132p. (gr. 3-7). 1990. 10.95 (ISBN 0-571-15233-3). Faber & Faber.
—Ellis & the Hummick. Riddell, Chris, illus. 132p. (gr. 3-6). 1990. pap. 3.95 (ISBN 0-571-14412-8). Faber & Faber.
Gilden, Mel. Monster Mashers. 96p. (Orig.). (gr. 5 up). 1989. pap. 2.75 (ISBN 0-380-75785-0, Camelot). Avon.
Gilson, Jamie. Thirteen Ways to Sink a Sub. Edwards, Linda S., illus. (gr. 3-7). 1982. 12.95 (ISBN 0-688-01304-X). Lothrop.
Ginsburg, Mirra. Across the Stream. Tafuri, Nancy, illus. (ps). 1985. pap. 3.50 (ISBN 0-14-050436-2, Penguin Bks). Viking Penguin.
Gipe, George. Gremlins. (Illus.). 77p. (gr. 3-7). 1984. pap. 2.95 (ISBN 0-380-89003-8, Camelot). Avon.
Glatzer. Quest for the Cities of Gold, No. 16. 144p. (Orig.). (ps-6). 1987. pap. 2.50 (ISBN 0-553-26295-5). Bantam.
The Goblin. Date not set. write for info. Songbird & Seabird.
Gorog, Judith. Three Dreams & a Nightmare: And Other Tales of the Dark. 160p. (gr. 4 up). 1988. 13.95 (ISBN 0-399-21578-6, Philomel Bks). Putnam Pub Group.
Grahame, Kenneth. The Reluctant Dragon. Hague, Michael, illus. LC 83-209. 32p. (gr. 3-6). 1988. pap. 5.95 (ISBN 0-8050-0802-0). H Holt & Co.
Gramatky, Hardie & Gramatky, Dorothea C. Little Toot & the Loch Ness Monster. Gramatky, Hardie, illus. 48p. (ps-3). 1989. 13.95 (ISBN 0-399-21684-7, Putnam). Putnam Pub Group.
Graves, Robert. Big Green Book. 64p. (gr. 1-4). 1990. pap. 4.95 (ISBN 0-689-71402-5, Aladdin). Macmillan Child Grp.
Green, Phyllis. Eating Ice Cream with a Werewolf. (gr. 4-6). 1985. pap. 2.95 (ISBN 0-440-42182-9, YB). Dell.
Greer, Gery & Ruddick, Bob. Max & Me & the Time Machine. LC 82-48762. 140p. (gr. 4-6). 1983. 13.95 (ISBN 0-15-253134-3, HJ). HarBraceJ.
Griffith, Helen V. Emily & the Enchanted Frog. Lamb, Susan C., illus. LC 88-16511. 32p. (gr. 1 up). 1989. 12.95 (ISBN 0-688-08483-4); PLB 12.88 (ISBN 0-688-08484-2). Greenwillow.
Guderjahn, Ernie L. A Children's Trilogy: Ali's Flying Rug, the Shadow Workers, & the Magic Cricket. (Orig.). (gr. 3 up). 1984. pap. text ed. 6.00 (ISBN 0-88734-504-2). Players Pr.
Gulliver's Travels. (Illus.). 48p. (gr. 4 up). 1988. PLB 17.32 (ISBN 0-8172-2763-6); pap. 9.27 (ISBN 0-8172-2767-9). Raintree Pubs.
Gutierrez, Douglas. The Night of the Stars. Dearden, Carmen D., tr. from SPA. Oliver, Maria F., illus. 24p. (ps-1). 1988. 9.95 (ISBN 0-916291-17-0). Kane-Miller Bk.
Haas, Dorothy. Dorothy & Old King Crow. Ewing, C. S., illus. LC 86-3824. 48p. (gr. 2-3). 1986. (Random Juv); pap. 2.95 (ISBN 0-394-88227-X). Random.
Hall, Lynn. Flyaway. LC 87-12824. 128p. (gr. 7 up). 1987. 12.95 (ISBN 0-684-18888-0, Scribners Young Read). Macmillan Child Grp.
Hamilton, Virginia. Dustland. 1989. pap. 3.95 (ISBN 0-15-224315-1). HarbraceJ.
—The Gathering. 1989. pap. 3.95 (ISBN 0-15-230592-0). HarbraceJ.
—Justice & Her Brother. 1989. pap. 3.95 (ISBN 0-15-241640-4). HarbraceJ.
—The Mystery of Drear House: The Conclusion of the Dies Drear Chronicle. LC 88-2887. 224p. (gr. 7 up). 1988. pap. 3.95 (ISBN 0-02-043480-4, Collier Young Ad). Macmillan Child Grp.
Hamley, Dennis. Pageants of Despair. LC 74-10841. 180p. (gr. 7-10). 1974. 18.95 (ISBN 0-87599-205-6). S G Phillips.
Harris, Geraldine. The Dead Kingdom. (gr. k-12). 1987. pap. 2.50 (ISBN 0-440-91810-3, LFL). Dell.
Haugaard, Erik C. The Samurai's Tale. 256p. (gr. 7 up). 1984. 14.95 (ISBN 0-395-34559-6, 5-87439). HM.
Hawthorne, Julian. Rumpty-Dudget's Tower. Goode, Diane, illus. 48p. (gr. 1-4). 1987. Repr. of 1879 ed. Knopf.
Haynes, Betsy. The Power. (Orig.). (gr. 5 up). 1982. pap. 1.95 (ISBN 0-440-97164-0, LFL). Dell.
Haynes, James. Voices in the Dark. (Orig.). (gr. 5 up). 1982. pap. 1.95 (ISBN 0-440-99317-2, LFL). Dell.
Heller, Nicholas. A Troll Story. LC 88-34906. (Illus.). 24p. (ps up). 1990. 12.95 (ISBN 0-688-08970-4); PLB 14.88 (ISBN 0-688-08971-2). Greenwillow.
Herzig, Alison C. & Mali, Jane L. Sam & the Moon Queen. 176p. (gr. 4-8). 1990. 13.95 (ISBN 0-395-53342-2, Clarion Bks). HM.
Hill, Douglas. Goblin Party. Demeyer, Paul, illus. 44p. (gr. 3-5). 1990. 13.95 (ISBN 0-575-04338-5, Pub. by Gollancz England). Trafalgar Sq.
—Master of Fiends. LC 88-12847. 192p. (gr. 7 up). 1988. 13.95 (ISBN 0-689-50419-5, M K McElderry). Macmillan Child Grp.
Hiller, B. Honey, I Shrunk the Kids. (gr. 4-7). 1989. pap. 2.95 (ISBN 0-590-42119-0). Scholastic Inc.
Hissey, Jane. Jolly Tall. (Illus.). 32p. (ps-3). 1990. 14.95 (ISBN 0-399-21827-0, Philomel Bks). Putnam Pub Group.
Hodgell, P. C. Dark of the Moon. 368p. 1987. pap. 3.50 (ISBN 0-425-09561-4). Berkley Pub.
Hodges, Margaret, adapted by. St. George & the Dragon. Hyman, Trina S., illus. LC 83-19980. (gr. 6-8). 1984. 14.95 (ISBN 0-316-36789-3). Little.
Hoffman, Mary. Dracula's Daughter. Riddell, Chris, illus. 42p. (gr. 2-4). 1989. 3.95 (ISBN 0-8120-6135-7). Barron.
Holabird, Katharine. Alexander & the Magic Boat. Craig, Helen, illus. 24p. (ps-2). 1990. 11.95 (ISBN 0-517-58142-6); PLB 12.99 (ISBN 0-517-58149-3). Crown.
Holl, Kristi D. Footprints up My Back. (gr. 3-6). 1986. pap. 2.95 (ISBN 0-440-42649-9, YB). Dell.
Holling, Holling C. Pagoo. Holling, Lucille W., illus. 96p. (gr. 4-6). 1990. pap. text ed. 7.95 (ISBN 0-395-53964-1). HM.
Horwitz, Elinor L. When the Sky Is Like Lace. Cooney, Barbara, illus. LC 75-9664. 32p. (gr. 1-3). 1987. PLB 13.89 (ISBN 0-685-02092-4, Lipp Jr Bks); PLB 13.89 (ISBN 0-397-32137-6). HarpC Child Bks.
Houston, James. Ice Swords: An Undersea Adventure. Houston, James, illus. LC 85-7328. 168p. (gr. 5-9). 1985. 13.95 (ISBN 0-689-50333-4, M K McElderry). Macmillan Child Grp.
Hunt, Roderick. Ghosts, Witches & Things Like That... (Illus.). 144p. (ps-6). 1987. 14.95 (ISBN 0-19-278108-1). Oxford U Pr.
Hutchins, Hazel. The Three & Many Wishes of Jason Reid. Tennent, Julie, illus. 96p. (gr. 1-4). 1990. pap. 3.95 (ISBN 0-14-032178-0, Puffin). Puffin Bks.
Jackson, Steve & Livingstone, Ian. Appointment with F.E.A.R. (Orig.). (gr. 5 up). 1986. pap. 2.50 (ISBN 0-440-90258-4, LFL). Dell.
—Demons of the Deep. (Orig.). (gr. k-12). 1987. pap. 2.50 (ISBN 0-440-91843-X, LFL). Dell.
Jacobs, Joseph. Adventures of Tom Thumb. Cutts, David, adapted by. Fuka, illus. LC 87-10980. 32p. (gr. k-3). 1988. PLB 9.79 (ISBN 0-8167-1071-6); pap. text ed. 1.95 (ISBN 0-8167-1072-4). Troll Assocs.
Jalbert, Louise. The Diverting Tale of the Radish & the Shoe. LC 83-82781. (Illus.). 40p. (Orig.). (gr. k up). 1984. pap. 8.95 (ISBN 0-88138-023-7). Green Tiger Pr.
James, Betsy. Long Night Dance. LC 88-38837. 176p. (gr. 7 up). 1989. 13.95 (ISBN 0-525-44485-8, DCB). Dutton Child Bks.
Jansson, Tove. Comet in Moominland. Portch, Elizabeth, tr. (Illus.). 192p. (gr. 2-5). 1990. 13.95 (ISBN 0-374-31526-4); pap. 3.95 (ISBN 0-374-41331-2). FS&G.
—Finn Family Moomintroll. Portch, Elizabeth, tr. (Illus.). 174p. (gr. 2-5). 1990. pap. 3.50 (ISBN 0-374-42307-5, Sunburst). FS&G.
—Moominsummer Madness. (gr. 4-7). 1991. 13.95 (ISBN 0-374-35039-6). FS&G.
Jarrell, Randall. Fly by Night. Sendak, Maurice, illus. LC 76-27313. 40p. (ps up). 1985. 11.95 (ISBN 0-374-32348-8); pap. 2.95 (ISBN 0-374-42350-4). FS&G.
Jenkins, Gerald & Bear, Magdalen. The Compound of the Five Cubes. (Illus.). 24p. (Orig.). (gr. 5-9). 1986. pap. 4.95 (ISBN 0-906212-47-2, Tarquin). Parkwest Pubns.
—The Final Stellation of the Icosahedron. (Illus.). 24p. (Orig.). (gr. 5-9). 1986. pap. 4.95 (ISBN 0-906212-48-0, Tarquin). Parkwest Pubns.
Jennings, Michael. Mattie Fritts & the Cuckoo Caper. LC 75-30872. (Illus.). 128p. (gr. 4 up). 1976. 6.95 (ISBN 0-672-52202-0, Bobbs). Macmillan.
Johnson, Philip R. Chase of the Sorceress. LC 89-50958. 152p. (gr. 7-12). 1989. pap. 8.25x (ISBN 0-943864-58-5). Davenport.
Jones, Diana W. Castle in the Air. LC 90-30266. (Illus.). 208p. (gr. 6 up). 1991. 13.95 (ISBN 0-688-09686-7). Greenwillow.
—A Charmed Life. LC 77-18414. 224p. (gr. 3-7). 1989. pap. 2.95 (ISBN 0-394-82032-0, Bullseye Bks). Knopf.
—Fire & Hemlock. LC 84-4084. 352p. (gr. 7 up). 1984. reinforced bdg. 13.00 (ISBN 0-688-03942-1). Greenwillow.
—Hidden Turnings. LC 89-11742. (gr. 7 up). 1990. 12.95 (ISBN 0-688-09163-6). Greenwillow.
—Howl's Moving Castle. LC 85-21981. 224p. (gr. 7 up). 1986. reinforced bdg. 10.25 (ISBN 0-688-06233-4). Greenwillow.
—The Magicians of Caprona. pap. 2.25 (ISBN 0-441-51556-8, Pub. by Ace Science Fiction). Ace Bks.
—A Tale of Time City. LC 86-33304. (Illus.). 288p. (gr. 7 up). 1987. 11.75 (ISBN 0-688-07315-8). Greenwillow.
—A Tale of Time City. LC 86-33304. 288p. (gr. 5-9). 1989. pap. 3.95 (ISBN 0-394-82030-4). Knopf.
Jones, Terry. Nicobobinus. Foreman, Michael, illus. LC 85-28630. 176p. (gr. k-6). 1986. 16.95 (ISBN 0-87226-065-8). P Bedrick Bks.
Josse, Barbara M. The Thinking Place. Chorao, Kay, illus. LC 81-515. 36p. (ps-2). 1982. lib. bdg. 8.99 (ISBN 0-394-94908-0). Knopf.
Juster, Norton. The Phantom Tollbooth. Feiffer, Jules, illus. LC 61-13202. 256p. (gr. 3-7). 1988. pap. 3.95 (ISBN 0-394-82037-1). Knopf.
—The Phantom Tollbooth. large type ed. 320p. (gr. 3-7). 1989. lib. bdg. 14.95 (ISBN 0-8161-4801-5, Large Print Bks). G K Hall.
Karl, Jean. Search For the Ten-Winged Dragon. (ps-3). 1990. PLB 14.95 (ISBN 0-385-26493-3); pap. 15.99 (ISBN 0-385-26494-1). Doubleday.
Karl, Jean E. Strange Tomorrow. LC 84-28609. 144p. (gr. 4-7). 1985. 12.95 (ISBN 0-525-44162-X, DCB). Dutton Child Bks.
—The Turning Place: Stories of a Future Past. 224p. (gr. 5-6). 1976. 9.95 (ISBN 0-525-41573-4, DCB). Dutton Child Bks.
Katz, Wilton W. The Third Magic. 208p. (gr. 6-10). 1989. 14.95 (ISBN 0-689-50480-2, M K McElderry). Macmillan Child Grp.
Keller, Beverly. A Small, Elderly Dragon. Malone, Nola L., illus. LC 83-13632. 144p. (gr. 5 up). 1984. 12.95 (ISBN 0-688-02553-6). Lothrop.
Kendall, Carol. The Gammage Cup. Garcia, Manuel, contrib. by. 224p. (gr. 3-7). 1990. pap. 3.95 (ISBN 0-15-230575-0). HarbraceJ.
Kent, Lorna. Shazam. (Illus.). 32p. (ps-2). 1990. pap. 9.95 (ISBN 0-670-83073-9). Viking Child Bks.
Key, Alexander. The Forgotten Door. 144p. (gr. 3-7). 1986. pap. 2.50 (ISBN 0-590-40398-2, Apple Paperbacks). Scholastic Inc.
—The Forgotten Door. 144p. (gr. 3-7). 1986. pap. 2.75 (ISBN 0-590-43130-7). Scholastic Inc.
Khanna & Ridley. RoleMaster Companion II. Velez, Walter, illus. 112p. (Orig.). (gr. 10-12). 1987. pap. 12.00 (ISBN 0-915795-97-3, 1600). Iron Crown Ent Inc.
Kilian, Crawford. Wonders, Inc. Larrecq, John M., illus. (gr. 1 up). 1968. 6.95 (ISBN 0-87466-058-0, Pub. by Parnassus). HM.
Kindle, Patricia & Finney, Susan. Fantasy & Fairy Tales. McKay, Ardis, illus. 64p. (gr. 4-8). 1985. wkbk 6.95 (ISBN 0-86653-317-6, GA 669). Good Apple.
King, Stephen. The Eyes of the Dragon. Palladini, David, illus. 336p. 1987. pap. 21.95 (ISBN 0-670-81458-X). Viking Child Bks.
Kirwan-Vogel, Anna. The Jewel of Life. Yolen, Jane, ed. 128p. 1991. 15.95 (ISBN 0-15-200750-4, J Yolen Bks). HarBraceJ.
Kiu. Date not set. write for info. Songbird & Seabird.
Kjelgaard, Jim. Wild Trek. 272p. 1981. pap. 2.75 (ISBN 0-553-15466-4). Bantam.
Klein, Robin. Came Back to Show You I Could Fly. 196p. (gr. 4 up). 1990. pap. 11.95 (ISBN 0-670-82901-3). Viking Child Bks.
Kline, Suzy. Orp. 96p. 1990. pap. 2.95 (ISBN 0-380-71038-2, Camelot). Avon.
Klipper, Ilse. Magic Journey. Osborne, Gretchen, illus. 83p. (Orig.). (gr. k-5). 1983. pap. 5.95 (ISBN 0-9605022-1-1). Pathwys Pr CA.
Koertge, Ron. Boy in the Moon, Vol. 1. (gr. 4-7). 1990. 14.95 (ISBN 0-316-50102-6, Joy St Bks). Little.
Koller, Jackie F. Dragonling. LC 89-27145. (ps-4). 1990. 10.95 (ISBN 0-316-50148-4). Little.
Konwicki, Tadeusz. Anthropos-Specter-Beast. Korwin-Rodziszewski, George & Korwin-Rodziszewski, Audrey, trs. from POL. LC 77-13500. 320p. (gr. 9 up). 1977. 18.95 (ISBN 0-87599-218-8). S G Phillips.
Kornblatt, Marc. Flame of the Inquisition, No. 15. 144p. 1986. pap. 2.50 (ISBN 0-553-26160-6). Bantam.
Kraus, Robert. Jack Galaxy, Space Cop. (ps-3). 1990. pap. 2.75 (ISBN 0-553-15777-9, Skylark). Bantam.
Krulik, Nancy. Honey I Shrunk the Kids - Storybook. (ps-3). 1989. pap. 2.50 (ISBN 0-590-42120-4). Scholastic Inc.
Krulik, Nancy E. Superman IV: The Quest for Peace - Picture Book. (Illus.). (ps-3). 1987. pap. 2.50 (ISBN 0-590-41227-2). Scholastic Inc.

—The Littles Have a Wedding. 96p. (gr. 2-5). 1986. pap. 2.25 (ISBN 0-590-40135-1). Scholastic Inc.
—The Littles Take a Trip. 96p. (gr. 2-5). 1986. pap. 2.50 (ISBN 0-590-42713-X). Scholastic Inc.
Phillips, Terry. The Soulforger. LC 85-90158. (Illus.). 192p. (gr. 5-7). 1985. pap. 2.50 (ISBN 0-685-11035-4). Random.
Pierce, Meredith A. A Gathering of Gargoyles. 272p. 1985. pap. 2.95 (ISBN 0-8125-4902-3, Dist. by Warner Pub Services & Saint Martin's Press). Tor Bks.
Pierce, Tamora. Lioness Rampant: Song of the Lioness, Bk. Four. LC 88-6213. 336p. (gr. 6 up). 1988. 15.95 (ISBN 0-689-31116-8, Atheneum Child Bk). Macmillan Child Grp.
Pilkey, Dav. Dragon Gets By. LC 90-46027. (Illus.). 48p. (gr. 1-3). 1991. 12.95 (ISBN 0-531-05935-9); PLB 12.99 (ISBN 0-531-08535-X). Orchard Bks Watts.
Ploss, Douglas A. The Tweens at Deep Lake: An Original American Fantasy. Ploss, Douglas A., illus. LC 79-90996. 88p. (gr. 3 up). 1979. PLB 13.50 (ISBN 0-9603632-0-3); pap. 8.50 (ISBN 0-9603632-1-1). OPC.
Poe, Edgar Allan. Reader's Digest Best Loved Books for Young Readers: Tales of Poe. Ogburn, Jackie, ed. Liebman, Oscar, illus. 152p. (gr. 4-12). 1989. 3.99 (ISBN 0-945260-24-5). Choice Pub NY.
Polcovar, Jane. The Charming. 160p. (Orig.). (gr. 7-12). 1984. pap. 2.50 (ISBN 0-553-26691-8). Bantam.
Polikarpus, Viido & King, Tappan. Down Town. 304p. (gr. 7 up). 1987. pap. 2.95 (ISBN 0-8125-4937-6). Tor Bks.
Porter-Lane, Esther. St. George & the Dragon. (Orig.). (gr. 4 up). 1985. pap. 4.50 (ISBN 0-87602-249-2). Anchorage.
Potter, Beatrix. The Tale of Mrs. Tiggy-winkle. (Illus.). 57p. (gr. k-6). 1973. pap. 1.75 (ISBN 0-486-20546-0). Dover.
—Tale of Mrs. Tiggy Winkle. (Illus.). (ps). 1991. pap. 1.99 (ISBN 0-7232-3770-0). Warne.
Pratchett, Terry. Diggers: The Second Book of the Bromeliad. (gr. 4-7). 1991. pap. 14.95 (ISBN 0-385-30152-9). Doubleday.
Prater, John. The Gift. Prater, John, illus. 32p. (ps-3). 1986. pap. 9.95 (ISBN 0-670-80952-7). Viking Child Bks.
Purtill, Richard. Enchantment at Delphi. LC 85-30556. (gr. 7 up). 1986. 14.95 (ISBN 0-15-200447-5, Gulliver Bks). HarBraceJ.
Randall, E. T. Cosmic Kidnappers. Rogers, Jacqueline, illus. LC 84-8579. 128p. (gr. 3-7). 1985. PLB 9.49 (ISBN 0-8167-0328-0); pap. text ed. 2.95 (ISBN 0-8167-0329-9). Troll Assocs.
—Target: Earth. Rogers, Jacqueline, illus. LC 84-2740. 128p. (gr. 3-7). 1985. PLB 9.49 (ISBN 0-8167-0326-4); pap. text ed. 2.95 (ISBN 0-8167-0327-2). Troll Assocs.
—Thieves from Space. Rogers, Jacqueline, illus. LC 84-8538. 128p. (gr. 3-7). 1985. PLB 9.49 (ISBN 0-8167-0330-2); pap. text ed. 2.95 (ISBN 0-8167-0331-0). Troll Assocs.
—Town in Terror. Rogers, Jacqueline, illus. LC 84-5617. 128p. (gr. 3-7). 1985. PLB 9.49 (ISBN 0-8167-0332-9); pap. 2.95 (ISBN 0-8167-0333-7). Troll Assocs.
Raskin, Ellen. Figgs & Phantoms. Raskin, Ellen, illus. LC 73-17309. 160p. (gr. 4-7). 1977. pap. 15.95 (ISBN 0-525-29680-8, 01063-320, DCB); (DCB). Dutton Child Bks.
Reed, Louis. The Wicks & the Wacks. LC 85-70443. (ps-2). 1985. pap. 5.00 (ISBN 0-916383-00-8, Univ Edtns). Aegina Pr.
Reiling, Robert J. The Dragon's Smile. Reiling, Robert J., illus. 48p. (gr. 3-9). 1988. pap. 7.95 (ISBN 0-533-07430-4). Vantage.
Reit, Seymour V. & Navaroo, Jose G. Voyage with Columbus. 96p. (Orig.). 1986. pap. 2.50 (ISBN 0-553-15431-1). Bantam.
Relf, Patricia. Sweet Sea: The Princess of Coral Kingdom. Dubin, Jill, illus. 48p. (ps-3). 1985. 6.95 (ISBN 0-448-18974-7, G&D). Putnam Pub Group.
Reynolds, Alfred. Kiteman. 208p. (gr. 6 up). 1986. pap. 2.75 (ISBN 0-553-26036-7, Spectra). Bantam.
—Kiteman of Karanga. LC 84-14351. (Illus.). 224p. (gr. 7 up). 1985. Knopf.
Rhys, Morgana. Dragonfire: Castle Beneath the Sea. (Illus.). 128p. 1990. pap. 2.95 (ISBN 0-8431-2716-3). Price Stern.
—Dragonfire: The Curse of Peredur. (Illus.). 128p. 1990. pap. 2.95 (ISBN 0-8431-2717-1). Price Stern.
—Dragonfire: Thieves of NIR. (Illus.). 128p. 1990. pap. 2.95 (ISBN 0-8431-2715-5). Price Stern.
Rice, James. Lyn & the Fuzzy. Rice, James, illus. LC 75-19096. 40p. (gr. 2-6). 1975. 11.95 (ISBN 0-88289-087-5). Pelican.
Riddell, Ruth. Haunted Journey. LC 88-938. 224p. (gr. 6-9). 1988. 14.95 (ISBN 0-689-31429-9, Atheneum Child Bk). Macmillan Child Grp.
Rinaldi, Ann. Time Enough for Drums. LC 85-24869. 256p. (gr. 7 up). 1986. 14.95 (ISBN 0-8234-0603-2). Holiday.
Robbins, Trina. Catswalk: The Growing of Girl. (Illus.). 96p. (Orig.). (gr. 3-6). 1990. pap. 16.95 (ISBN 0-89087-608-8). Celestial Arts.
Rockwell, Thomas. How to Eat Fried Worms. McCully, Emily, illus. LC 73-4262. (gr. 4-6). 1973. PLB 12.90 (ISBN 0-531-02631-0). Watts.
Rodda, Emily. The Best Kept Secret. Young, Noela, illus. 128p. (gr. 2-4). 1990. 14.95 (ISBN 0-8050-0936-1). H Holt & Co.
Rowe, W. W. Gully's Travels in Space-Time. LC 90-71370. 61p. (gr. k-3). 1991. pap. 5.95 (ISBN 1-55523-385-6). Winston-Derek.
Ryder, Joanne. Where Butterflies Grow. Cherry, Lynne, illus. LC 88-37989. 32p. (ps-3). 1989. 13.95 (ISBN 0-525-67284-2, Lodestar Bks). Dutton Child Bks.
Sadler, Marilyn. Alistair's Time Machine. Bollen, Roger, illus. 40p. (ps up). 1989. pap. 5.95 (ISBN 0-671-68493-0). S&S Trade.
Sampson, Fay. Chris & the Dragon. Bennett, Jill, illus. 96p. (gr. 4-6). 1987. 14.95 (ISBN 0-575-03661-3, Pub. by Gollancz England). Trafalgar Sq.
Sandburg, Carl. Rootabaga Stories, Pt. 1. Hague, Michael, contrib. by. 256p. (gr. 3-7). 1990. pap. 3.95 (ISBN 0-15-269065-4). HarbraceJ.
San Souci, Robert D. The Enchanted Tapestry. Gal, Laszlo, illus. LC 85-29283. 32p. (ps-3). 1987. 11.95 (ISBN 0-8037-0304-X); PLB 11.89 (ISBN 0-8037-0306-6). Dial Bks Young.
—The Enchanted Tapestry. Fogelman, Phyllis J., ed. Gal, Laszio, illus. LC 85-29283. 32p. (ps-3). 1990. pap. 3.95 (ISBN 0-8037-0862-9). Dial Bks Young.
Schubert, Ingrid & Schubert, Dieter. The Magic Bubble Trip. LC 84-25071. (Illus.). 32p. (ps-3). 1985. 9.95 (ISBN 0-916291-02-2); pap. 6.95 (ISBN 0-916291-03-0). Kane Miller Bk.
Scott, Hugh. The Plant That Ate the World: A Novel of the Near Future. 106p. (gr. 3-6). 1991. 14.95 (ISBN 0-571-15440-9). Faber & Faber.
Seidler, Tor. The Tar Pit. LC 87-74338. 160p. 1987. 11.95 (ISBN 0-374-37383-3); pap. 3.50 (ISBN 0-374-47452-4). FS&G.
Sendak, Maurice. Outside Over There. Sendak, Maurice, illus. LC 79-2682. 40p. (gr. k up). 1981. 19.95 (ISBN 0-06-025523-4); PLB 19.89 (ISBN 0-06-025524-2). HarpC Child Bks.
Service, Pamela F. Stinker from Space. LC 87-25266. 96p. (gr. 3-5). 1988. 12.95 (ISBN 0-684-18910-0, Scribners Young Read). Macmillan Child Grp.
Sidney, Margaret. Five Little Peppers Midway. (Orig.). (gr. k-6). 1987. pap. 4.95 (ISBN 0-440-42589-1, Pub. by Yearling Classics). Dell.
Singer, Marilyn. Horsemaster. LC 88-10945. 192p. (gr. 7 up). 1988. pap. 3.50 (ISBN 0-02-044991-7, Collier Young Ad). Macmillan Child Grp.
Slater, Teddy, adapted by. Walt Disney's Alice in Wonderland. Maten, Franc, illus. (ps-2). 1991. write for info. (ISBN 0-307-12341-3, Golden Pr). Western Pub.
Sleator, William. Singularity. LC 84-26075. 192p. (gr. 7 up). 1985. 12.95 (ISBN 0-525-44161-1, DCB). Dutton Child Bks.
Slote, Alfred. My Trip to Alpha I. Berson, Harold, illus. LC 85-45394. 96p. (gr. 2-5). 1986. pap. 3.95 (ISBN 0-06-440166-9, Trophy). HarpC Child Bks.
Smith, Agnes. An Edge of the Forest. Sharkey, J. Thomas, illus. 207p. (gr. 7 up). 1974. 9.00 (ISBN 0-87012-171-5). Westwind Pr.
Smith, Sherwood. Wren to the Rescue. 228p. (gr. 7 up). 1990. 15.95 (ISBN 0-15-200975-2, J Yolen Bks). HarbraceJ.
Smith, Susan. Changing Places. 176p. (Orig.). (gr. 7 up). 1986. pap. 2.50 (ISBN 0-590-33580-4, Point). Scholastic Inc.
Sochard, Ruth. Weathertop, the Tower of the Wind. Fenlon, Pete, ed. Martin, David & Martin, Elissa, illus. 32p. (Orig.). (gr. 10-12). 1987. pap. 6.00 (ISBN 0-915795-89-2, 8201). Iron Crown Ent Inc.
Spirin, Gennady, illus. Enchanter's Spell: Five Famous Tales. LC 86-24063. 96p. (ps up). 1988. 14.95 (ISBN 0-8037-0320-1). Dial Bks Young.
Springer, Nancy. Red Wizard. LC 88-29376. 144p. (gr. 4 up). 1990. 12.95 (ISBN 0-689-31485-X, Atheneum Child Bk). Macmillan Child Grp.
Spurr, Elizabeth. Mrs. Minetta's Car Pool. Sims, Blanche, illus. LC 90-35. 32p. (gr. k-3). 1990. pap. 3.95 (ISBN 0-689-71430-0, Aladdin). Macmillan Child Grp.
Stafford, Greg. Runequest: Deluxe. Peterson, Sandy, ed. (Illus.). 96p. (gr. 8 up). 1989. 29.95 (ISBN 0-911605-51-7). Avalon Hill.
Stanley, Diane. Captain Whiz-Bang. Stanley, Diane, illus. LC 86-16432. 32p. (ps-2). 1987. 12.95 (ISBN 0-688-06226-1); lib. bdg. 12.88 (ISBN 0-688-06227-X, Morrow Jr Bks). Morrow Jr Bks.
Staplehurst, Graham. Minas Tirith. Fenlon, Peter C., ed. McBride, Angus, illus. 192p. (gr. 10-12). 1988. 18.00 (ISBN 1-55806-001-4, 8301). Iron Crown Ent Inc.
—The Phantom of the Northern Marches. Fenlon, Peter, ed. Horne, Daniel, illus. 32p. (Orig.). (gr. 10-12). 1986. pap. 6.00 (ISBN 0-915795-47-7, 8102). Iron Crown Ent Inc.
Steele, Mary Q. Journey Outside. (gr. 5-9). 1984. 15.50 (ISBN 0-8446-6169-4). Peter Smith.
Steig, William. The Amazing Bone. Steig, William, illus. LC 76-26479. 32p. (ps-3). 1983. 16.95 (ISBN 0-374-30248-0). FS&G.
Steiner, Claude. A Warm Fuzzy Tale. Dick, Joann, illus. Freed, Alvyn M., intro. by. LC 77-77981. (Illus., Orig.). (gr. k up). 1977. 7.95 (ISBN 0-915190-08-7, JP9008-7). Jalmar Pr.
Stevenson, Robert Louis. Dr. Jekyll & Mr. Hyde. (gr. 9-12). 1991. pap. text ed. 4.87 (ISBN 0-582-01818-8, 78330). Longman.
Stewart, Celeste. The Blue Dragon. Watts, James K., illus. 54p. (gr. 4-8). 1985. PLB 3.95 (ISBN 0-932433-06-5). Windswept Hse.
Stouffer, Nancy. Silver Linings. Stouffer, Nancy, illus. 48p. (gr. 2-5). 1989. pap. 2.95 (ISBN 0-927008-65-3). BCI-Bk Cook Inc.
Stuart, W. J. Forbidden Planet. 212p. (gr. 5 up). 1990. pap. 3.95 (ISBN 0-374-42445-4, Sunburst). FS&G.
Sutton, Scott E. The Family of Ree. Sutton, Scott E., illus. 45p. (gr. 2-4). 1986. 12.95 (ISBN 0-9617199-1-5). Sutton Pubns.
—More Altitude, Quick! (Illus.). 51p. (gr. 2-4). 1988. 12.95 (ISBN 0-9617199-4-X). Sutton Pubns.
Swados, Elizabeth. Inside Out: A Musical Adventure. LC 89-31327. (Illus.). 124p. (gr. 4-6). 1990. 14.95 (ISBN 0-316-82466-6). Little.
Swindells, Robert. Follow a Shadow. LC 90-55109. 160p. (gr. 3-7). 1990. 13.95 (ISBN 0-8234-0839-6). Holiday.
Tallarico, Beatrice & Stone, S. Callis. The Weeuns Journey of Two Cousins. Stone, S. Callis, illus. 39p. (gr. 2-8). 1984. 12.95 (ISBN 0-936191-13-9). Tallstone Pub.
Tallis, Robyn. Mountain of Stolen Dreams. (gr. 6 up). 1988. pap. 2.95 (ISBN 0-8041-0201-5). Ivy Books.
—Night of Two New Moons. (gr. 6 up). 1989. pap. 2.95 (ISBN 0-8041-0209-0). Ivy Books.
—Visions from the Sea. (gr. 6 up). 1989. pap. 2.95 (ISBN 0-8041-0206-6). Ivy Books.
—Zero-Sum Games. (gr. 6 up). 1989. pap. 2.95 (ISBN 0-8041-0207-4). Ivy Books.
Thomas, Roy. The Dragonlance Saga, Bk. 3. Yeates, Tom & Oliff, Steve, illus. LC 88-50405. 80p. (Orig.). (gr. 5 up). 1988. pap. 9.95 (ISBN 0-88038-611-8). TSR Inc.
Tidy, Bill. Incredible Bed. (Illus.). 32p. (ps-1). 1991. 13.95 (ISBN 0-86264-268-X, Pub. by Andersen Pr UK). Trafalgar Sq.
Titchenell, Elsa-Brita. Once Round the Sun. Gruelle, Justin C. & Russell, Elizabeth A., illus. LC 81-52615. iv, 57p. (gr. 1 up). 1981. Repr. of 1950 ed. 8.50 (ISBN 0-911500-61-8). Theos U Pr.
Tolkien, J. R. R. The Hobbit. Hague, Michael, illus. 300p. (ps up). 1989. pap. 12.95 (ISBN 0-395-52021-5, Sandpiper). HM.
Tom Swift: Terror on the Moons of Jupiter. 192p. (gr. 3-7). 1981. 8.95 (ISBN 0-671-41182-9, Little Simon); pap. 2.75 (ISBN 0-671-41183-7). S&S Trade.
Tomalin, Ruth. The Green Wishbone. Rowe, Gavin, illus. 154p. (gr. k-2). 1991. pap. 3.95 (ISBN 0-571-15438-7). Faber & Faber.
Travers, P. L. Mary Poppins in Cherry Tree Lane. Shepard, Mary, illus. LC 82-71383. 96p. (gr. 4-6). 1982. 12.95 (ISBN 0-385-28601-5); PLB 10.95 (ISBN 0-685-05624-4). Delacorte.
Tripp, Wallace. A Great Big Ugly Man Came Up & Tied His Horse to Me: A Book of Nonsense Verse. (Illus.). 48p. (gr. k-12). 1974. lib. bdg. 14.95 (ISBN 0-316-85280-5); pap. 6.95 (ISBN 0-316-85281-3). Little.
Troll. Wizard of Oz Activity Book. 64p. (ps-3). 1991. pap. 1.95 (ISBN 0-8167-2283-8). Troll Assocs.
Turner, Ann. Rosemary's Witch. LC 90-39779. 176p. (gr. 6 up). 1991. 13.95 (ISBN 0-06-026127-7); PLB 13.89 (ISBN 0-06-026128-5). HarpC Child Bks.
Updike, David. Seven Times Eight. Lorenz, Lee, illus. 40p. (gr. 2-5). 1990. PLB 14.95 (ISBN 0-945912-10-2). Pippin Pr.
Uttley, Alison. Lavender Shoes: Eight Tales of Enchantment. Ede, Janina, illus. 84p. (gr. k-2). 1991. pap. 3.95 (ISBN 0-571-15344-5). Faber & Faber.
Van Allsburg, Chris. The Garden of Abdul Gasazi. (Illus.). 32p. (gr. 1-12). 1979. 16.95 (ISBN 0-395-27804-X). HM.
Vandersteen, Willy. An Island Called Hoboken. Lahey, Nicholas, tr. from FLE. LC 75-8496. (Illus.). 56p. (Orig.). (gr. 3 up). 1976. pap. 2.50 (ISBN 0-915560-01-1, 1). Hiddigeigei.
—The Merry Musketeers. Lahey, Nicholas J., tr. from FLE. LC 75-8495. (Illus.). 56p. (Orig.). (gr. 3 up). 1976. pap. 2.50 (ISBN 0-915560-18-6, 18). Hiddigeigei.
Van Leeuwen, Jean. Benjy & the Power of Zingies. Apple, Margot, illus. LC 82-1513. 112p. (gr. 2-6). 1985. 10.95 (ISBN 0-8037-0379-1); PLB 10.89 (ISBN 0-8037-0380-5). Dial Bks Young.
VanRynbach, Iris. The Soup Stone. LC 86-31830. (Illus.). 32p. (ps-3). 1988. 11.95 (ISBN 0-688-07254-2); lib. bdg. 11.88 (ISBN 0-688-07255-0). Greenwillow.
Verne, Jules. Twenty Thousand Leagues under the Sea. James, Raymond, ed. Geehan, Wayne, illus. LC 89-34248. 48p. (gr. 3-6). 1990. PLB 12.89 (ISBN 0-8167-1879-2); pap. text ed. 3.95 (ISBN 0-8167-1880-6). Troll Assocs.
—Twenty Thousand Leagues under the Sea. rev. ed. Grund, Diane F., ed. (Illus.). 128p. 1990. pap. 1.95 (ISBN 0-942025-85-7). Kidsbks.
Los Viajes De Gulliver. (SPA.). 1990. casebound 3.50 (ISBN 0-7214-1403-6). Ladybird Bks.
Viorst, Judith. My Mama Says There Aren't Any Zombies, Ghosts, Vampires, Creatures, Demons, Monsters, Fiends, Goblins, or Things. Chorao, Kay, illus. LC 73-76331. 48p. (gr. k-4). 1973. 12.95 (ISBN 0-689-30102-2, Atheneum Child Bk). Macmillan Child Grp.
Vogt, Esther. The Shiny Dragon. Converse, James, illus. LC 83-12981. 104p. (Orig.). (gr. 5-8). 1983. pap. 3.95 (ISBN 0-8361-3348-X). Herald Pr.

Volkov, Alexander. The Wizard of Emerald City & Urfin Jus & His Wooden Soldiers. Blystone, Peter L., tr. from RUS. LC 90-62416. (gr. 4 up).

1991. 11.95 (ISBN 1-878941-16-X). Red Branch Pr.
L. Frank Baum's The Wizard of Oz has been an American classic for over 90 years. But did you know that, during half that period, it's also been a Russian classic? Alexander Volkov published his Russian translation/ adaptation of it in 1939 & 1959, retelling the tale in his own way & giving it a uniquely Russian flavor. Soviet children loved it so much that Volkov eventually wrote five wonderful "Magic Land" sequels for them. What are these six novels like? How does our American classic look through Russian eyes? This volume with translations of the first two novels, provides an answer. Volkov's WIZARD is quite different from Baum's: most characters have new names, & the young heroine, along with her other problems, must contend with an Ogre & survive a deluge! The second novel tells of her return to Magic Land to defeat a wicked sorcerer who has constructed an army of wooden soldiers & seized power there. Two additional volumes, now in preparation, will complete the cycle, thus making all six novels available in English. Anyone liking the American Wizard will enjoy Volkov & want to read all six delightful tales. Don't miss out! Order your copy today!
Publisher Provided Annotation.

Vorhees, Duance & Mueller, Mark. The Ogres' Magic Clubs. Kim, Yon-Kyong, illus. 46p. (gr. 2-5). 1991. PLB 9.95 (ISBN 0-930878-88-4). Hollym Intl.
—The Seven Brothers & the Big Dipper. Pak, Mi-Son, illus. 46p. (gr. 2-5). 1991. PLB 9.95 (ISBN 0-930878-74-4). Hollym Intl.
Vorhees, Duance & Mueller, Mark, eds. Mr. Moon & Miss Sun. Kim, Yon-Kyong, illus. 45p. (gr. 2-5). 1990. PLB 9.95 (ISBN 0-930878-72-8). Hollym Intl.
Vrooman, Christine W. Willowby's World of Fluffits. Sidaras, Nanci, illus. 56p. (Orig.). (gr. 2-6). 1984. pap. 8.95 with stickers incl. (ISBN 0-910349-02-9). Cloud Ten.
Wahl, Jahn. Mooga Mega Mekki. Krahn, Fernando, illus. LC 73-16818. 48p. (gr. 2-4). 1974. 7.95 (ISBN 0-87955-111-9). O'Hara.
Wahl, Jan, adapted by. The Wizard of Oz Movie Storybook. (Illus.). 48p. (ps-3). 1989. write for info. (ISBN 0-307-12093-7, Pub. by Golden Bks). Western Pub.
Walker Books Staff. The Jungle of Peril. Graham, Alistair, illus. 48p. (gr. 1-5). 1986. 4.95 (ISBN 0-671-60718-9, Little Simon). S&S Trade.
—The Planet of Terror. Graham, Alastair, illus. 48p. (gr. 1-5). 1986. 4.95 (ISBN 0-671-60717-0, Little Simon). S&S Trade.
Walt Disney Staff. Peter Pan. 1987. 6.98 (ISBN 0-8317-6799-5, Gallery Bks). Smithmark.
Walton, Robert M. Joel in Tananar. (Illus.). (gr. 4-9). 1982. 8.95 (ISBN 0-914598-05-8). Pr MacDonald & Reinecke.
Waltz, Marjorie. The Dragon, the Winds & the Witches. Waltz, Catherine, illus. LC 86-72867. 64p. (Orig.). (gr. k-2). 1987. pap. 5.00 (ISBN 0-916383-14-8). Aegina Pr.
Wangerin, Walter, Jr. Book of the Dun Cow. LC 77-25641. 256p. (gr. 7-9). 1978. 12.95 (ISBN 0-06-026346-6); PLB 12.89 (ISBN 0-06-026347-4). HarpC Child Bks.
Waterton, Kulyn. Orff, Twenty-Seven Dragons & a Snarkel. (Illus.). 24p. (ps-8). 1984. pap. 4.95 (ISBN 0-920303-03-X). Firefly Bks Ltd.
Weinberg, Larry, adapted by. Star Wars. LC 84-18151. (Illus.). 72p. (ps-5). 1985. (Random Juv). Random.
Wells, H. G. Invisible Man. (gr. 4-7). 1990. pap. 2.95 (ISBN 0-590-44016-0). Scholastic Inc.
—The Time Machine. Powell, Ivan, illus. Wright, Betty R., adapted by. LC 81-4097. (Illus.). 48p. (gr. 4 up). 1983. PLB 17.32 (ISBN 0-8172-1675-8); pap. 9.27 (ISBN 0-8172-2024-0). Raintree Pubs.
West, Mark I., ed. Before Oz: Juvenile Fantasy Stories from Nineteenth-Century America. LC 89-35643. (Illus.). 229p. 1989. lib. bdg. 27.50 (ISBN 0-208-02234-1, Archon Bks). Shoe String.
White, Celeste. The Legend of the Flying Hotdog. (Illus.). 32p. 1989. 11.95 (ISBN 0-88138-131-4). Green Tiger Pr.
White, John. Gaal the Conqueror. Stockman, Jack, illus. LC 89-19821. 312p. (Orig.). (gr. 7-9). 1989. pap. 10.95 (ISBN 0-87784-591-3, 591). InterVarsity.
—The Iron Sceptre. (Illus.). 404p. (Orig.). (gr. 4-7). 1981. pap. 10.95 (ISBN 0-87784-589-1). InterVarsity.
White, Viola G. Sam & the Doodlebugs. 25p. 1989. 5.95 (ISBN 0-533-07856-3). Vantage.
Wignell, Edel. Escape by Deluge. LC 89-36008. 152p. (gr. 5-9). 1990. 13.95 (ISBN 0-8234-0802-7). Holiday.
Williams, Leslie. A Bear in the Air. Vendrell, Carme S., illus. LC 80-10290. 28p. (gr. k up). 1980. 7.95 (ISBN 0-916144-54-2). Stemmer Hse.
Williams-Ellis, Anabel. Tales from the Enchanted World. Kemp, Moira, illus. (gr. 3-7). 1988. 17.95 (ISBN 0-316-94133-6). Little.
Williamson, Louis. The Year Christmas Was Almost Spoiled. Galinat, William, illus. 1990. pap. 5.95 (ISBN 0-533-08481-4). Vantage.
Winterfeld, Henry. Castaways in Lilliput. Lattimore, Deborah N. & Hutchinson, William M., illus. 192p. (gr. 3-7). 1990. pap. 4.95 (ISBN 0-15-214822-1). HarBraceJ.
Winthrop, Elizabeth. The Castle in the Attic. (gr. k-9). 1988. pap. 2.75 (ISBN 0-318-37103-0). Scholastic Inc.
Wizard of Oz. (Illus.). (gr. k-1). 3.50 (ISBN 0-7214-5127-6). Ladybird Bks.
Wood, Audrey. Moonflute. Wood, Don, illus. LC 86-4666. (ps-3). 1986. 13.95 (ISBN 0-15-255337-1). HarBraceJ.
Wood, Marcia. The Secret Life of Hilary Thorne. LC 87-30263. 128p. (gr. 5-9). 1988. 12.95 (ISBN 0-689-31405-1, Atheneum Child Bk). Macmillan Child Grp.
Woodcock, John. Trouble in Space. 64p. (Orig.). (gr. 6 up). 1984. pap. 2.25 (ISBN 0-553-15501-6). Bantam.
Woodruff, Elvira. Awfully Short for the Fourth Grade. Hillenbrand, Will, illus. LC 89-2082. 112p. (gr. 3-6). 1989. 13.95 (ISBN 0-8234-0785-3). Holiday.
Wrightson, Patricia. Night Outside. Peck, Beth, illus. LC 85-7529. 64p. (gr. 4-7). 1985. 12.95 (ISBN 0-689-50363-6, M K McElderry). Macmillan Child Grp.
Yep, Laurence. Dragon Cauldron. LC 90-39584. (Illus.). 320p. (gr. 7 up). 1991. 16.95 (ISBN 0-06-026753-4); PLB 16.89 (ISBN 0-06-026754-2). HarpC Child Bks.
—Dragon of the Lost Sea. LC 81-48644. 224p. (gr. 6 up). 1988. pap. 3.95 (ISBN 0-06-440227-4, Trophy). HarpC Child Bks.
—Dragon Steel. LC 84-48338. 288p. (gr. 7 up). 1985. 12.95 (ISBN 0-06-026748-8); PLB 12.89 (ISBN 0-06-026751-8). HarpC Child Bks.
—Dragonwings. large type ed. 282p. 1990. Repr. of 1975 ed. lib. bdg. 15.95 (ISBN 1-55736-168-1, Crnrstn Bks). ABC-CLIO.
Yolen, Jane. The Acorn Quest. Natti, Susanna, illus. LC 80-2755. 64p. (gr. 3-6). 1981. PLB 12.89 (ISBN 0-690-04107-1, Crowell Jr Bks). HarpC Child Bks.
—Heart's Blood. LC 83-14978. 224p. (gr. 7 up). 1984. 14.95 (ISBN 0-385-29316-X). Delacorte.
—The Rainbow Rider. Foreman, Michael, illus. LC 73-19700. 32p. (ps-3). 1974. PLB 12.89 (ISBN 0-690-00311-0, Crowell Jr Bks). HarpC Child Bks.
—The Transfigured Hart. Diamond, Donnal, illus. LC 75-2377. 96p. (gr. 4 up). 1975. 12.95 (ISBN 0-690-00736-1, Crowell Jr Bks). HarpC Child Bks.
Zettner, Pat. The Shadow Warrior. LC 89-440. 224p. (gr. 7 up). 1990. 13.95 (ISBN 0-689-31486-8, Atheneum Child Bk). Macmillan Child Grp.
Ziefert, Harriet. Under the Water. (Illus.). 32p. (ps-2). 1990. pap. 8.95 (ISBN 0-670-83198-0). Viking Child Bks.
Zion, Gene. All Falling Down. Graham, Margaret B., illus. LC 51-12571. 32p. (ps-1). 1951. PLB 13.89 (ISBN 0-06-026831-X). HarpC Child Bks.
Zolna, Ed. Fran an' Maabl: Rel. (Illus.). 64p. (Orig.). (gr. 9-12). 1988. pap. 2.50 (ISBN 0-945975-00-7). E Zolna Inc.

FAR EAST
see East (Far East)

FARADAY, MICHAEL, 1791-1867
Brophy, Michael. Michael Faraday. LC 90-33893. (Illus.). 48p. (gr. 4-8). 1991. PLB 12.40 (ISBN 0-531-18376-9). Watts.

FARM ANIMALS
see Domestic Animals; Livestock

FARM CROPS
see Farm Produce

FARM IMPLEMENTS
see Agricultural Machinery

FARM LIFE
see also Country Life; Ranch Life
Anderson, George. American Family Farm. 1989. 18.95 (ISBN 0-15-203025-5). HarbraceJ.
Arnow, Jan. Hay from Seed to Feed. Arnow, Jan, illus. LC 86-2843. 48p. (gr. 3-7). 1986. lib. bdg. 11.99 (ISBN 0-394-96508-6). Knopf.
Cook, Brenda. All about Farm Animals. Winterbotham, Ann, illus. 1989. 10.95 (ISBN 0-385-24821-0); PLB 11.99 (ISBN 0-385-24822-9). Doubleday.
DeWitt, Jamie. Jamie's Turn. LC 84-13973. (Illus.). 32p. (gr. 3-6). 1984. PLB 16.67 (ISBN 0-940742-37-3). Raintree Pubs.
Fass, Bernie, et al. Old MacDonald Had a Farm. 32p. (gr. k-4). 1981. pap. 10.95 (ISBN 0-86704-007-6). Clarus Music.
Fun at the Farm. (Illus.). (ps-5). 3.50 (ISBN 0-7214-0478-2); No. 4. wkbk. 1.95; Series S05, Set 1. flash cards 4.75; Series S05, Set 2. flash cards 4.75. Ladybird Bks.
Gildemeister, Jerry. Around the Cat's Back. Gildemeister, Jerry, illus. 128p. (gr. 4-12). 1989. 32.50 (ISBN 0-936376-06-6). Bear Wallow Pub.
Glotzbach, Gerri, et al. The Family, 6 bks. (Illus.). 384p. (gr. 7 up). 1990. Set. lib. bdg. 95.60 (ISBN 0-86593-075-9). Rourke Corp.
Goodall, John S. The Story of a Farm. Goodall, John S., illus. (gr. 1 up). 1989. 14.95 (ISBN 0-689-50479-9, M K McElderry). Macmillan Child Grp.
Graham-Cameron, M. The Farmer. (Illus.). 26p. (gr. 2-5). 1983. pap. 3.95 (ISBN 0-521-27162-2). Cambridge U Pr.
Hellen, Nancy. On the Farm: Match It Up. 1989. 3.99 (ISBN 0-517-68250-8). Outlet Bk Co.
Henderson, Kathy. I Can Be a Farmer. LC 88-37716. (Illus.). 32p. (gr. k-3). 1989. PLB 13.93 (ISBN 0-516-01923-6); pap. 4.95 (ISBN 0-516-41923-4). Childrens.
Larsson, Carl & Rudstrom, Lennart. A Farm. LC 76-2130. (Illus.). 32p. (gr. 3 up). 1976. 13.95 (ISBN 0-399-20541-1, Putnam). Putnam Pub Group.
Lee, Valerie. Dysfunctional Families. (Illus.). 64p. (gr. 7 up). 1990. lib. bdg. 15.93 (ISBN 0-86593-077-5); lib. bdg. 11.95s.p. (ISBN 0-685-36296-5). Rourke Corp.
Lenski, Lois. Little Farm. Lenski, Lois, illus. LC 58-12902. (gr. k-3). 1980. 5.25 (ISBN 0-8098-1009-3). McKay.
Matthews, Morgan. What's It Like to Be a Farmer. Kennedy, Anne, illus. LC 89-34386. 32p. (gr. k-3). 1989. lib. bdg. 10.89 (ISBN 0-8167-1803-2); pap. text ed. 2.50 (ISBN 0-8167-1804-0). Troll Assocs.
Miller, Jane. Farm Alphabet Book. LC 83-19277. (Illus.). 24p. (gr. k-4). 1984. PLB 8.95 (ISBN 0-671-66550-2). S&S Trade.
—Farm Noises. Miller, Jane, photos by. (Illus.). (ps-3). 1989. pap. 8.95 (ISBN 0-671-67450-1). S&S Trade.
—Seasons on the Farm. Miller, Jane, illus. 32p. (gr. k-3). 1986. 10.95 (ISBN 0-13-797275-X). P-H.
Provensen, Alice & Provensen, Martin. The Year at Maple Hill Farm. LC 77-18518. (Illus.). (ps-2). 1981. 15.95 (ISBN 0-689-30642-3, Atheneum Child Bk). Macmillan Child Grp.
—The Year at Maple Hill Farm. Provensen, Alice & Provensen, Martin, illus. LC 88-10367. 32p. (ps-2). 1988. pap. 3.95 (ISBN 0-689-71270-7, Aladdin). Macmillan Child Grp.
Taylor, Barbara. Ready Set Go: On the Farm. 1991. 4.98 (ISBN 0-8317-7357-X). Smithmark.

FARM LIFE–FICTION
Adams, Pam, illus. Old MacDonald. 16p. (ps-2). 1978. 8.00 (ISBN 0-85953-054-X, Pub. by Child's Play England). Childs Play.
—Old MacDonald Had a Farm. (Orig.). (ps-2). 1975. pap. 5.00 (ISBN 0-85953-053-1, Pub. by Child's Play England). Childs Play.
Addison-Wesley Staff. The Farmer & the Beet Little Book. (Illus.). 16p. (gr. k-3). 1989. pap. text ed. 4.50 (ISBN 0-201-19053-2). Addison-Wesley.
Allen, Thomas B. On Grandaddy's Farm. Allen, Thomas B., illus. LC 88-23374. 48p. (ps-3). 1989. 13.95 (ISBN 0-394-89613-0); lib. bdg. 14.99 (ISBN 0-394-99613-5). Knopf.
Amery, H. Barn on Fire. (Illus.). 16p. (ps). 1989. 2.95 (ISBN 0-7460-0260-2, Usborne); lib. bdg. 7.96 (ISBN 0-88110-375-6, Usborne). EDC.
—The Usborne Book of Farmyard Tales. (Illus.). 64p. (ps). 1989. 8.95 (ISBN 0-7460-0263-7, Usborne). EDC.
Andrews, Jan. The Auction. Reczuch, Karen, illus. LC 90-41378. 32p. (ps-3). 1991. RSBE 12.95 (ISBN 0-02-705535-3, Macmillan Child Bk). Macmillan Child Grp.
Bacon, Katharine J. Shadow & Light. LC 86-23789. 208p. (gr. 7 up). 1987. 14.95 (ISBN 0-689-50431-4, M K McElderry). Macmillan Child Grp.
Baehr, Patricia. Louisa Eclipsed. LC 88-17709. 160p. (gr. 7 up). 1988. 12.95 (ISBN 0-688-07682-3). Morrow Jr Bks.
Bates, Kathy F. & Fahlman, Dorothy. Old MacDonald's Farm. 24p. (ps-3). 1989. pap. write for info. (ISBN 0-307-14032-6). Western Pub.
Bax, Martin. Edmond Went Far Away. Foreman, Michael, illus. (ps up). 1989. 12.95 (ISBN 0-15-225105-7, HJ). HarBraceJ.
Berst, Barbara. We Are Farmers. Berst, Barbara, illus. 24p. (Orig.). (ps-2). Date not set. acid-free cotton paper 25.00, (ISBN 0-9614126-3-1); pap. 9.95 (ISBN 0-9614126-2-3). Natl Lilac Pub.
Bright, Velma. The Story of the Little Round Barn. Schultz, Patty, illus. LC 81-65540. 48p. (Orig.). (gr. 2-3). 1981. 10.00x (ISBN 0-9605968-2-8); pap. 5.00 (ISBN 0-9605968-3-6). Bright Bks.
Brown, Craig. My Barn. LC 90-41758. (Illus.). 24p. (ps up). 1991. 13.95 (ISBN 0-688-08785-X); PLB 13.88 (ISBN 0-688-08786-8). Greenwillow.
—Patchwork Farmer. LC 88-29229. 24p. (ps up). 1989. 12.95 (ISBN 0-688-07735-8); PLB 12.88 (ISBN 0-688-07736-6). Greenwillow.
Brown, Margaret W. Big Red Barn. Bond, Felicia, illus. LC 85-45814. 32p. (ps-1). 1991. 19.95 (ISBN 0-06-020750-7). HarpC Child Bks.
Brown, Ruth. The Big Sneeze. LC 84-23385. (Illus.). 32p. (ps-1). 1985. 13.95 (ISBN 0-688-04665-7); lib. bdg. 12.88 (ISBN 0-688-04666-5). Lothrop.
Bunting, Eve. The Big Red Barn. Knotts, Howard, illus. LC 78-12186. (gr. k-3). 1979. pap. 6.95 (ISBN 0-15-611938-2, VoyB). HarBraceJ.
Burch, Robert. Tyler, Wilkin & Skee. LC 89-28245. 160p. (gr. 4-6). 1990. Repr. 14.95 (ISBN 0-8203-1194-4). U of Ga Pr.

Byars, Betsy C. The Midnight Fox. Grifalconi, Ann, illus. (gr. 3-7). 1981. pap. 3.95 (ISBN 0-14-031450-4, Puffin). Puffin Bks.
—The Midnight Fox. Grifalconi, Ann, illus. LC 68-27566. (gr. 3-7). 1968. pap. 13.95 (ISBN 0-670-47473-8). Viking Child Bks.
Campbell, Rod. Oh Dear! Campbell, Rod, illus. LC 84-3993. 20p. (ps-1). 1986. 8.95 (ISBN 0-02-716430-6, Four Winds). Macmillan Child Grp.
Cannon, Bettie. Begin the World Again. LC 90-46596. 192p. (gr. 7 up). 1991. SBE 13.95 (ISBN 0-684-19292-6, Scribners Young Read). Macmillan Child Grp.
Carrick, Carol. In the Moonlight, Waiting. Carrick, Donald, illus. 32p. (ps-1). 1990. 13.95 (ISBN 0-89919-867-8). Clarion Pr.
Carrie, Christopher. Mixed up Farm. (Illus.). 32p. (Orig.). (ps-k). 1990. 1.99 (ISBN 0-86696-236-0). Binney & Smith.
Carter, Alden R. Growing Season. 300p. (gr. 6 up). 1984. 13.95 (ISBN 0-698-20599-5, Coward); pap. 2.25 (ISBN 0-448-47749-1). Putnam Pub Group.
Casey, Patricia. Quack Quack. LC 87-17301. (Illus.). (ps-1). 1988. 12.95 (ISBN 0-688-07765-X). Lothrop.
Cather, Willa. Neighbor Rosicky. LC 85-46058. 88p. (gr. 6 up). 1986. PLB 10.95s.p. (ISBN 0-88682-065-0); PLB 15.65 (ISBN 0-685-12414-2). Creative Ed.
Cauley, Lorinda B. The Cock, the Mouse & the Little Red Hen. (Illus.). 32p. (ps-1). 1982. 9.95 (ISBN 0-399-20740-6, Putnam); pap. 4.95 (ISBN 0-399-20930-1). Putnam Pub Group.
Cleary, Beverly. Emily's Runaway Imagination. Krush, Joe & Krush, Beth, illus. LC 61-10939. 224p. (gr. 3-7). 1961. 12.95 (ISBN 0-688-21267-0); PLB 12.88 (ISBN 0-688-31267-5, Morrow Jr Bks). Morrow Jr Bks.
Cleaver, Vera & Cleaver, Bill. Dust of the Earth. LC 75-18939. 160p. (gr. 7 up). 1975. 13.95 (ISBN 0-397-31650-X, Lipp Jr Bks). HarpC Child Bks.
Climo, Lindee. Chester's Barn. Climo, Lindee, illus. (gr. 1-5). 1982. pap. 6.95 (ISBN 0-88776-155-0). Tundra Bks.
Clymer, Susan. Four Month Friend. Rabinowitz, Sandy, illus. LC 89-10618. 144p. (ps-3). 1990. pap. 10.95 (ISBN 0-590-42544-7). Scholastic Inc.
Cosgrove, Stephen. The Fine Family Farm. Steelhammer, Ilona, illus. 24p. (gr. k-2). 1990. PLB 10.95 (ISBN 1-878363-19-0). Forest Hse.
Crofford, Emily. Stories from the Blue Road. Nobens, C. A., illus. LC 81-21229. 168p. (gr. 4-8). 1981. PLB 8.95 (ISBN 0-87614-189-0). Carolrhoda Bks.
Crowther, Robert. How Many Babies on the Farm? (Illus.). 10p. (ps-k). 1991. bds. 5.95 (ISBN 0-671-73157-2, Little Simon). S&S Trade.
—Who Lives on the Farm? (Illus.). 10p. (ps-k). 1991. bds. 5.95 (ISBN 0-671-73156-4, Little Simon). S&S Trade.
Crozat, Francois. I Am a Little Pig. (Illus.). (ps-3). 1991. large 7.95 (ISBN 0-8120-6201-9); miniature 2.95 (ISBN 0-8120-6222-1). Barron.
Dahl, Roald. The Wonderful Story of Henry Sugar & Six More. LC 77-5354. 32p. (gr. 5 up). 1991. 15.00 (ISBN 0-394-83604-9). Knopf.
Dalgliesh, Alice. The Little Wooden Farmer. reissued ed. Lobel, Anita, illus. LC 68-12061. 32p. (ps-1). 1988. 12.95 (ISBN 0-02-725590-5, Mcmillan Child Bk). Macmillan Child Grp.
De Angeli, Marguerite. Yonie Wondernose. (Illus.). 48p. (gr. 1-5). 1955. 15.95 (ISBN 0-385-07573-1, Zephyr-BFYR). Doubleday.
De Armond, Dale. Berry Woman's Children. De Armond, Dale, illus. LC 84-29760. 40p. (gr. 1 up). 1985. 10.25 (ISBN 0-688-05814-0); lib. bdg. 10.88 (ISBN 0-688-05815-9). Greenwillow.
DeJong, Meindert. Along Came a Dog. Sendak, Maurice, illus. LC 57-9265. 192p. (gr. 3-6). 1958. PLB 15.89 (ISBN 0-06-021421-X). HarpC Child Bks.
Demuth, Patricia. Joel: Growing up a Farm Man. (Illus.). 96p. (gr. 3-7). 1982. 12.95 (ISBN 0-396-07997-0, Putnam). Putnam Pub Group.
Devons, Sonia. Shut the Gate! Rayner, Shoo, illus. LC 89-18544. 32p. (ps). 1990. 10.95 (ISBN 0-87226-426-2). P Bedrick Bks.
D'Ham, Claude, illus. On the Farm. (Orig.). (ps-2). 1975. pap. 2.00 (ISBN 0-85953-036-1, Pub. by Child's Play England). Childs Play.
Doherty, Berlie. White Peak Farm. LC 89-23060. 128p. (gr. 5 up). 1990. 12.95 (ISBN 0-531-05867-0); PLB 12.99 (ISBN 0-531-08467-1). Orchard Bks Watts.
Domanska, Janina. Busy Monday Morning. Domanska, Janina, illus. LC 83-25362. 32p. (ps-1). 1985. 13.00 (ISBN 0-688-03833-6); PLB 12.88 (ISBN 0-688-03834-4). Greenwillow.
Dunrea, Olivier. Eppie M. Says... Dunrea, Olivier, illus. LC 89-3134. 32p. (ps-2). 1990. 12.95 (ISBN 0-02-733205-5, Mcmillan Child Bk). Macmillan Child Grp.
Dutton, Sandra. The Cinnamon Hen's Autumn Day. Dutton, Sandra, illus. LC 87-30290. 32p. (ps-2). 1988. 12.95 (ISBN 0-689-31414-0, Atheneum Child Bk). Macmillan Child Grp.
Enright, Elizabeth. Thimble Summer. (gr. k-6). 1987. pap. 3.25 (ISBN 0-440-48681-5, YB). Dell.
—Thimble Summer. Enright, Elizabeth, illus. LC 38-27586. 134p. (gr. 4-6). 1938. 15.95 (ISBN 0-8050-0306-1). H Holt & Co.
Fiday, Beverly & Fiday, David. Time to Go. Allen, Thomas B., illus. (ps-3). 1990. 14.95 (ISBN 0-15-200608-7). HarbraceJ.
Fleischman, Paul. The Animal Hedge. Dabcovich, Lydia, illus. LC 82-2404. (gr. 2-5). 1983. 9.95 (ISBN 0-525-44002-X, DCB). Dutton Child Bks.
Florian, Douglas. A Year in the Country. LC 88-16026. (Illus.). 32p. (ps up). 1989. 12.95 (ISBN 0-688-08186-X); lib. bdg. 12.88 (ISBN 0-688-08187-8). Greenwillow.
Frances, Marian. Mr. Mac-A-Doodle. (Illus.). (gr. 1). 1972. pap. 1.95 (ISBN 0-89375-045-X). Troll Assocs.
Frascino, Edward. Nanny Noony & the Dust Queen. Frascino, Edward, illus. 32p. (gr. k-3). 1990. PLB 14.95 (ISBN 0-945912-09-9). Pippin Pr.
Gammell, Stephen. Once upon Macdonald's Farm. LC 89-17792. 32p. (gr. k-3). 1990. pap. 3.95 (ISBN 0-689-71379-7, Aladdin). Macmillan Child Grp.
Garland, Michael. My Cousin Katie. Garland, Michael, illus. LC 88-356. 32p. (ps-1). 1989. 13.95 (ISBN 0-690-04738-X, Crowell Jr Bks); PLB 14.89 (ISBN 0-690-04740-1). HarpC Child Bks.
Gibson, Betty. Story of Little Quack. (ps-3). 1991. 12.95 (ISBN 0-316-30966-4, Joy St Bks). Little.
Graeber, Charlotte. The Fluff Puff Farm. French, Marty & Lamb, Jim, illus. 26p. (ps up). 1988. incl. cassette 7.95 (ISBN 1-55578-917-X). Worlds Wonder.
Graeker, Charlotte. The Fluff Puff Farm. French, Marty, et al, illus. 26p. (ps up). 1986. Book & Cassette. 7.95 (ISBN 1-55578-110-1). Worlds Wonder.
Hall, Barbara. Dixie Storms. 1990. 15.95 (ISBN 0-15-223825-5). HarbraceJ.
Hall, Lynn. The Leaving. LC 80-18636. 128p. (gr. 7 up). 1980. 12.95 (ISBN 0-684-16716-6, Scribners Young Read). Macmillan Child Grp.
Hamilton, Virginia. Zeely. Shimin, Symeon, illus. LC 67-10266. 128p. (gr. 5-7). 1968. 13.95 (ISBN 0-02-742470-7, Mcmillan Child Bk). Macmillan Child Grp.
Hampton's Happy Farms. 1990. 5.98 (ISBN 1-55521-691-9). Bk Sales Inc.
Hawkins, Colin. Old MacDonald Had a Farm. (ps-3). 1991. 9.95 (ISBN 0-8431-2884-4). Price Stern.
Hellen, Nancy. Old MacDonald Had a Farm. LC 89-25587. (Illus.). 18p. (ps-1). 1990. 13.95 (ISBN 0-531-05872-7). Orchard Bks Watts.
Hoff, Syd. My Aunt Rosie. Hoff, Syd, illus. LC 72-76513. 32p. (ps-3). 1972. PLB 11.89 (ISBN 0-06-022504-1). HarpC Child Bks.
Hol, Coby. A Visit to the Farm. Hol, Coby, illus. LC 88-25366. 32p. (gr. k-3). 1989. 13.95 (ISBN 1-55858-000-X). North-South Bks NYC.
Holmes, Efner T. Amy's Goose. Tudor, Tasha, illus. LC 77-3027. 32p. (gr. 1-3). 1977. 12.95 (ISBN 0-690-03800-3, Crowell Jr Bks); PLB 12.89 (ISBN 0-690-03801-1). HarpC Child Bks.
Hoppe, Joanne. Pretty Penny Farm. 224p. (gr. 7 up). pap. 2.50 (ISBN 0-8167-1326-X). Troll Assocs.
Howard, Ellen. Sister. LC 90-196. 160p. (gr. 3-7). 1990. 12.95 (ISBN 0-689-31653-4, Atheneum Child Bk). Macmillan Child Grp.
Iverson, Diane. Where Are the Babies? Iverson, Diane, illus. 48p. (Orig.). (ps). Date not set. 14.95 (ISBN 0-9623349-1-X); pap. 8.95 (ISBN 0-9623349-2-8). MS Pub.
Jake & Jenny on the Farm. 18p. 1990. 7.95 (ISBN 0-8431-2853-4). Price Stern.
Jakubowsky, Frank. Frank on a Farm. 60p. (Orig.). 1988. pap. 4.95 (ISBN 0-932588-11-5). Jesus Bks.
Johnson, John E., illus. Here Comes the Farmer. 14p. (ps-3). 1985. 2.95 (ISBN 0-394-87552-4, Random Juv). Random.
Kindergarden, Henry O. The Farmer's Huge Carrot. (Illus.). 24p. (Orig.). (gr. k-3). 1990. pap. text ed. 2.95 (ISBN 0-87406-437-6). Willowisp Pr.
King, P. E. Down on the Funny Farm. Graham, Alastair, illus. 48p. (gr. 2-3). 1986. pap. 5.95 (ISBN 0-394-88333-0, Random Juv). Random.
King-Smith, David. Cuckoobush Farm. Kazuko, illus. LC 87-14871. 32p. (ps-1). 1988. Repr. of 1987 ed. 11.95 (ISBN 0-688-07680-7); lib. bdg. 11.88 (ISBN 0-688-07681-5). Greenwillow.
King-Smith, Dick. Pigs Might Fly. (gr. 4 up). 1990. pap. 3.95 (ISBN 0-14-034537-X, Puffin). Puffin Bks.
Kinsey-Warnock, Natalie. The Canada Geese Quilt. Bowman, Leslie W., illus. LC 88-32661. 64p. (gr. 4 up). 1989. 12.95 (ISBN 0-525-65004-0, Cobblehill Bks). Dutton Child Bks.
Kunhardt, Edith. Which Pig Would You Choose? LC 88-35588. (Illus.). (ps up). 1990. 12.95 (ISBN 0-688-08981-X); lib. bdg. 12.88 (ISBN 0-688-08982-8). Greenwillow.
Laird, Elizabeth. The Day Patch Stood Guard. Reeder, Colin, illus. 32p. (gr. k up). 1991. 10.95 (ISBN 0-688-10239-5, Tambourine Bks); PLB 10.88 (ISBN 0-688-10240-9, Tambourine Bks). Morrow.
—The Day Sidney Ran Off. Reeder, Colin, illus. LC 90-11154. 32p. (gr. k up). 1991. 10.95 (ISBN 0-688-10241-7, Tambourine Bks); PLB 10.88 (ISBN 0-688-10242-5, Tambourine Bks). Morrow.
—The Day Veronica Was Nosy. Reeder, Colin, illus. LC 90-24063. 32p. (ps up). Date not set. 11.95 (ISBN 0-688-10248-4, Tambourine Bks); PLB 11.88 (ISBN 0-688-10249-2, Tambourine Bks). Morrow.
Landis, Mary M. The Coon Tree Summer: Merry Brook Farm Story. (gr. 5 up). 1978. 8.80 (ISBN 0-686-22987-8). Rod & Staff.
Lenski, Lois. Strawberry Girl. Lenski, Lois, illus. 208p. (gr. k-6). 1987. pap. 3.50 (ISBN 0-440-48347-6, YB). Dell.
Lillie, Patricia. When the Rooster Crowed. Parker, Nancy W., illus. LC 90-30783. 32p. (ps up). 1991. 13.95 (ISBN 0-688-09378-7); PLB 13.88 (ISBN 0-688-09379-5). Greenwillow.
Lindbergh, Reeve. Benjamin's Barn. Jeffers, Susan, illus. 32p. (ps-3). 1990. 13.95 (ISBN 0-8037-0613-8); PLB 13.89 (ISBN 0-8037-0614-6). Dial Bks Young.
—The Midnight Farm. Jeffers, Susan, illus. LC 86-1722. 32p. (ps-2). 1987. 14.95 (ISBN 0-8037-0331-7); PLB 14.89 (ISBN 0-8037-0333-3). Dial Bks Young.
The Little Red Hen. 24p. 1988. pap. 1.29 (ISBN 0-02-898132-4). Checkerboard Pr.
Littledale, Freya. The Farmer in the Soup. Delaney, Molly, illus. 32p. (Orig.). (gr. 1-3). 1987. pap. 2.25 (ISBN 0-590-40194-7). Scholastic Inc.
—The Farmer in the Soup. Delaney, Molly, illus. 32p. (Orig.). (gr. k-3). 1987. pap. 2.50 (ISBN 0-590-42535-8). Scholastic Inc.
Lussert, Anneliese. The Farmer & the Moon. Wilkon, Jozef, illus. LC 86-42944. 32p. (gr. k-3). 1987. 13.95 (ISBN 1-55858-049-2). North-South Bks NYC.
MacDonald, Betty. Hello, Mrs. Piggle-Wiggle. Knight, Hilary, illus. LC 57-5613. (gr. k-3). 1957. 12.95 (ISBN 0-397-31715-8, Lipp Jr Bks). HarpC Child Bks.
—Mrs. Piggle-Wiggle. rev. ed. Knight, Hilary, illus. LC 47-1876. (gr. k-3). 1957. 13.95 (ISBN 0-397-31712-3, Lipp Jr Bks). HarpC Child Bks.
—Mrs. Piggle-Wiggle's Farm. Sendak, Maurice, illus. LC 54-7299. (gr. k-3). 1954. 13.95 (ISBN 0-397-31713-1, Lipp Jr Bks). HarpC Child Bks.
—Mrs. Piggle-Wiggle's Magic. new ed. Knight, Hilary, illus. LC 49-11124. (gr. k-3). 1957. 12.95 (ISBN 0-685-02083-5, Lipp Jr Bks). HarpC Child Bks.
McGuire, Leslie. This Farm Is a Mess. McGuire, Leslie, illus. LC 80-25811. 48p. (ps-3). 1981. 5.95 (ISBN 0-8193-1045-X); PLB 5.95 (ISBN 0-8193-1046-8). Parents.
McPhail, David. Farm Morning. D'Andrade, Diane, ed. (Illus.). 32p. (Orig.). (gr. k-3). 1991. pap. 3.95 (ISBN 0-15-227300-X, HJ). HarBraceJ.
Maiboroda, Tanya. Farm. (Illus.). 48p. (gr. 4-7). 1987. pap. 2.95 (ISBN 0-8431-1880-6). Price Stern.
Miller, Jane. Farm Alphabet Book. 32p. (ps-2). 1984. 8.95 (ISBN 0-13-304767-9). P-H.
Montgomery, Lucy M. Anne of Green Gables. 1987. Boxed set. pap. 8.95 (ISBN 0-553-33306-2). Bantam.
Nilsson, Ulf. If You Didn't Have Me. Eriksson, Eva, illus. Blecher, Lone T. & Blecher, George, trs. LC 86-21327. (Illus.). 128p. (gr. 2-5). 1987. 11.95 (ISBN 0-689-50406-3, M K McElderry). Macmillan Child Grp.
Noble, Trinka H. Apple Tree Christmas. Noble, Trinka H., illus. LC 84-1901. 32p. (ps-2). 1988. 12.95 (ISBN 0-8037-0102-0); PLB 12.89 (ISBN 0-8037-0103-9); pap. 3.95 (ISBN 0-8037-0552-2). Dial Bks Young.
O'Kelley, Mattie L. Circus. O'Kelley, Mattie L., illus. 32p. (ps-3). 1986. 12.95 (ISBN 0-316-63804-8, Joy St Bks). Little.
Otto, Carolyn. That Sky, That Rain. Lloyd, Megan, illus. LC 89-36582. 32p. (ps-3). 1990. 12.95 (ISBN 0-690-04763-0, Crowell Jr Bks); PLB 12.89 (ISBN 0-690-04765-7, Crowell Jr Bks). HarpC Child Bks.
Paris, Pat. Old MacDonald Had a Farm. (Illus.). 12p. (ps-1). 1989. text ed. 9.95 (ISBN 0-8120-6107-1). Barron.
Passwaters, Tiffany & Dyer, Rod. Who Likes Rain? (Illus.). 28p. (ps-1). 1990. 10.95 (ISBN 0-87701-697-6). Chronicle Bks.
Pearson, Susan. Well, I Never! Warhola, James, illus. LC 89-48016. 40p. (ps-1). 1990. PLB 13.95 (ISBN 0-671-69199-6). S&S Trade.
Peck, Robert N. Trig. 64p. (gr. 4-6). 1979. pap. 1.25 (ISBN 0-440-49098-7, YB). Dell.
Pellowski, Anne. First Farm in the Valley: Anna's Story. Watson, Wendy, illus. 192p. (gr. 3-6). 1982. 9.95 (ISBN 0-399-20887-9, Philomel). Putnam Pub Group.
—Willow Wind Farm: Betsy's Story. Watson, Wendy, illus. 176p. (gr. 9-12). 1981. 8.95 (ISBN 0-399-20781-3, Philomel). Putnam Pub Group.
Platenius, Agnes H. Polliwog Pool. 1988. 6.95 (ISBN 0-533-07789-3). Vantage.
—With Peter on the Farm. 35p. 1988. 5.95 (ISBN 0-533-07790-7). Vantage.
Richards, Nancy W. Farmer Joe's Hot Day. Zimmerman, Werner, illus. 24p. (gr. k-3). Big Book. 19.50 (ISBN 0-590-71714-6); pap. 2.25 (ISBN 0-590-71713-8). Scholastic Inc.
Richardson, Arleta. Eighteen & on Her Own. LC 85-29050. 173p. (gr. 4 up). 1986. pap. 3.95 (ISBN 0-89191-512-5). Cook.
Rossiter, Phyllis. Moxie. LC 90-30027. 192p. (gr. 5 up). 1990. 13.95 (ISBN 0-02-777831-2, Four Winds). Macmillan Child Grp.
Roundabout Red Gate Farm. (ps-1). 1987. 5.95 (ISBN 0-448-11326-0, G&D). Putnam Pub Group.
Ryno, Marie. Birthday Girl. (Illus.). (gr. 1-3). 1989. 7.95 (ISBN 0-533-08073-8). Vantage.

Saban, Vera. Right Now Forever. Mills, Janie, illus. LC 90-39763. 130p. (Orig.). (gr. 4-6). 1990. pap. write for info. (ISBN 0-914565-34-6). Capstan Pubns.
Ten seemed a magic number to Jennie Barnes, & she had become ten years old January of that year of 1915.

Surely, she thought, this must be the best age of all, & she wished she could stay ten forever. So the story begins of a little girl on a tenant farm in old Nebraska. The book was critiqued by fourth & fifth graders: Jeff commented, "I think the story was similar to the story WHERE THE RED FERN GROWS. I wouldn't mind reading it over & over again." And Greg said he "Liked this book, because I like people who are poor & still get the things they want." The teacher's comment: "This book captivated the students & kept their interest. Even when I had reached the end of a chapter with just a few minutes of class left, they wanted me to keep reading!"--Douglas Walton of Nelson, Nebraska. Illustrations by Janie Mills add interest & value. To order this book & for additional information on other TimberTrails Books, call (307) 568-2604.
Publisher Provided Annotation.

St. George, Judith. Do You See What I See. LC 82-12367. 158p. 1982. 9.95 (ISBN 0-399-20912-3, Putnam). Putnam Pub Group.

Schatell, Brian. Farmer Goff & His Turkey Sam. Schatell, Brian, illus. LC 81-47756. 32p. (gr. 1-3). 1982. PLB 13.89 (ISBN 0-397-31983-5, Lipp Jr Bks). HarpC Child Bks.

Seredy, Kate. Good Master. Seredy, Kate, illus. LC 85-43043. (gr. 4-6). 1935. pap. 13.95 (ISBN 0-670-34592-X). Viking Child Bks.

—Singing Tree. (gr. 4 up). 1990. pap. 4.95 (ISBN 0-14-034543-4, Puffin). Puffin Bks.

Sesame Street Staff. Big Bird's Farm. Barrett, John E., photos by. LC 81-50537. (Illus.). 14p. (ps). 1981. bds. 3.95 (ISBN 0-394-84812-8). Random.

Shriver, Jean A. Mayflower Man. 1991. 14.95 (ISBN 0-385-30295-9). Delacorte.

Smith, E. Boyd. The Farm Book. Smith, E. Boyd, illus. 64p. (gr. 3-5). 1982. 12.95 (ISBN 0-395-32951-5). HM.

—The Farm Book. Smith, E. Boyd, illus. 64p. (ps up). 1990. pap. 4.95 (ISBN 0-395-54951-5). HM.

Sommer-Bodenburg, Angela. The Vampire on the Farm. Greenberg, Ann, ed. Glienke, Amelie, illus. 144p. (gr. 3-6). 1990. pap. 2.95 (ISBN 0-671-70236-X, Minstrel Bks). PB.

Stauffer, Patricia I. Farming Is OK. Mattingly, Jennie, ed. Taylor, Neil, illus. LC 87-50262. 44p. (gr. 1-3). 1987. 6.95 (ISBN 1-55523-077-6). Winston-Derek.

Steig, William. Farmer Palmer's Wagon Ride. Steig, William, illus. LC 74-9949. 32p. (ps up). 1974. 11.95 (ISBN 0-374-32288-0). FS&G.

Stevens, Kathleen. Molly, McCullough, & Tom the Rogue. Zemach, Margot, illus. LC 82-45584. 32p. (gr. 2-6). 1983. (Crowell Jr Bks); PLB 11.89 (ISBN 0-690-04296-5). HarpC Child Bks.

Stiles, Martha B. Kate of Still Waters. LC 90-5546. 240p. (gr. 4-7). 1990. 14.95 (ISBN 0-02-788395-7, Mcmillan Child Bk). Macmillan Child Grp.

Stratton-Porter, Gene. The Harvester. 560p. 1977. PLB 24.95 (ISBN 0-89966-225-0). Buccaneer Bks.

Swan, Walter. The Little Green Tractor. Swan, Deloris, ed. Asch, Connie, illus. 16p. (Orig.). (gr. 2-4). 1989. pap. 1.50 (ISBN 0-927176-04-1). Swan Enterp.

Tolliver, Ruby C. Blind Bess, Buddy, & Me. Welch, Karen, ed. Miller, Lyle L., illus. 104p. (gr. 4 up). 1990. lib. bdg. 12.95 (ISBN 0-937460-63-X). Hendrick-Long.

Van Kirk, Eileen. Promise to Keep. 1990. 14.95 (ISBN 0-525-67319-9, Lodestar Bks). Dutton Child Bks.

Waechter, Friederich K. The Farmers in the Well. Dobak, Annelies, tr. LC 85-1240. (Illus.). (gr. k-3). 1985. 9.95 (ISBN 0-915361-16-7, Dist. by Watts). Adama Pubs Inc.

Wiggen, Kate D. Rebecca of Sunnybrook Farm. Bixler, Phyllis, afterword by. 1991. pap. 2.95 (ISBN 0-451-52483-7, Sig Classics). NAL-Dutton.

Wiggin, Kate D. Rebecca of Sunnybrook Farm. 259p. 1981. Repr. PLB 21.95 (ISBN 0-89967-028-8). Harmony Raine.

—Rebecca of Sunnybrook Farm. 288p. (gr. 4-6). 1988. pap. 2.95 (ISBN 0-590-41343-0). Scholastic Inc.

—Rebecca of Sunnybrook Farm. 279p. (gr. 5 up). 1986. pap. 2.25 (ISBN 0-14-035046-2, Puffin). Puffin Bks.

Wild, Margaret. The Very Best of Friends. Vivas, Julie, illus. (ps-3). 1990. 13.95 (ISBN 0-15-200625-7, Gulliver Bks). HarbraceJ.

Wilder, Laura I. Farmer Boy. rev. ed. Williams, Garth, illus. LC 52-7527. (gr. 2-7). 1961. 14.95 (ISBN 0-06-026425-X); PLB 14.89 (ISBN 0-06-026421-7). HarpC Child Bks.

York, Carol B. Febold Feboldson, the Fix It Farmer. LC 79-66321. (Illus.). 48p. (gr. 3-6). 1980. lib. bdg. 9.89 (ISBN 0-89375-312-2); pap. 2.95 (ISBN 0-89375-311-4). Troll Assocs.

Ziefert, Harriet. Noisy Barn! Taback, Simms, illus. 16p. (ps-1). 1990. 4.95 (ISBN 0-06-107405-5). HarpC Child Bks.

Zokeisha. Farm House. Klimo, Kate, ed. (Illus.). 16p. 1983. 2.85 (ISBN 0-671-46130-3, Little Simon). S&S Trade.

FARM MACHINERY
see Agricultural Machinery

FARM MECHANICS
see Agricultural Machinery

FARM PRODUCE

Cochrane, Jennifer. Food Plants. LC 90-37226. (Illus.). 48p. (gr. 5-9). 1990. PLB 18.60 (ISBN 0-8114-2733-1). Steck-V.

FARM PRODUCE–MARKETING

Bertoldi, Joyce. Aguacates (Avacados) Cultivando, Cosechando y Vendiendo. LC 89-71328. (SPA., Illus.). 42p. (gr. 3-6). 1989. pap. 4.95 (ISBN 0-942884-04-3). Observational.

FARMING
see Agriculture

FARMS

Battaglia, Aurelius, illus. A Farm. LC 77-83860. (gr. 1-3). 1978. pap. 0.95 (ISBN 0-448-49605-4, G&D). Putnam Pub Group.

Bushey, Jerry. Farming the Land: Modern Farmers & Their Machines. Bushey, Jerry, photos by. (Illus.). 40p. (gr. k-4). 1987. PLB 12.95 (ISBN 0-87614-314-1); pap. 4.95 (ISBN 0-87614-493-8). Carolrhoda Bks.

Butterworth, Nick & Inkpen, Mick. I Wonder on the Farm. 14p. (ps). 1987. pap. 1.95 (ISBN 0-310-55421-7, 19042P). Zondervan.

Damon, Laura. Hide-&-Seek on the Farm. Kramer, Robin, illus. LC 87-13737. 32p. (gr. k-2). 1988. PLB 7.06 (ISBN 0-8167-1231-X); pap. text ed. 1.95 (ISBN 0-8167-1232-8). Troll Assocs.

Dellosa, Janet & Carson, Patti. Farm Fun Book. Dellosa, Janet & Carson, Patti, illus. 32p. (ps-2). 1984. pap. 1.59 (ISBN 0-88724-020-8, CD-8035). Carson-Dellos.

Epstein, Sam & Epstein, Beryl. You Call That a Farm? Raising Leeches, Alligators, Weeds, & Other Unusual Things. (Illus.). 64p. (gr. 2-5). 1991. 13.95 (ISBN 0-374-38705-2). FS&G.

Fradin, Dennis. Farming. LC 83-15110. (Illus.). 48p. (gr. k-4). 1983. PLB 14.60 (ISBN 0-516-01693-8). Childrens.

Gorman, Carol. America's Farm Crisis. (Illus.). 128p. (gr. 7-12). 1987. lib. bdg. 12.90 (ISBN 0-531-10408-7). Watts.

Parramon, J. M. Mi Primera Vista a La Granja. 1990. pap. 4.95 (ISBN 0-8120-4400-2). Barron.

—My First Visit to a Farm. 1990. pap. 5.95 (ISBN 0-8120-4305-7). Barron.

Tudor, Tasha. Seasons of Delight: A Year on an Old-Fashioned Farm. Tudor, Tasha, illus. 12p. (gr. 1 up). 1986. 13.95 (ISBN 0-399-21308-2, Philomel). Putnam Pub Group.

FARRAGUT, DAVID GLASGOW, 1801-1870

Latham, Jean L. David Farragut: Our First Admiral. Frame, Paul, illus. 80p. (gr. 2-6). 1991. Repr. of 1967 ed. PLB 12.95 (ISBN 0-7910-1438-X). Chelsea Hse.

FARRELL, JEFF

Henning, Jean M. Six Days to Swim-Jeff Farrell: A Story of Olympic Courage. Daland, P., intro. by. LC 71-103031. (Illus.). (gr. 6-12). 1970. 3.50 (ISBN 0-911822-02-X). Swimming.

FASCISM–GERMANY
see National Socialism

FASHION
For works describing the prevailing mode or style in dress. Historical works on styles of particular countries or periods are entered under Costume.
see also Clothing and Dress; Costume; Dressmaking

Baker, Patricia. The Nineteen Forties. (Illus.). 64p. (gr. 6-10). 1992. lib. bdg. 16.95x (ISBN 0-8160-2467-7). Facts on File.

Costantino, Maria. The Nineteen Thirties. Cumming, Valerie & Feldman, Elane, eds. (Illus.). 64p. (gr. 6-10). 1992. lib. bdg. 16.95x (ISBN 0-8160-2466-9). Facts on File.

Hodgman, Ann. A Day in the Life of a Fashion Designer. Jann, Gayle, illus. LC 87-13394. 32p. (gr. 4-8). 1988. PLB 11.79 (ISBN 0-8167-1119-4); pap. text ed. 2.95 (ISBN 0-8167-1120-8). Troll Assocs.

FASTS AND FEASTS
see also Christmas; Easter; Holidays

Ahsan, M. M. Muslim Festivals. (Illus.). 48p. (gr. 3-8). 1987. PLB 14.60 (ISBN 0-86592-979-3). Rourke Corp.

Barz, Brigitte. Festivals with Children. 1988. pap. 10.50 (ISBN 0-86315-055-1, 20241). Gryphon Hse.

Everix, Nancy. Ethnic Celebrations Around the World. 160p. (gr. 3-8). 1991. 11.95 (ISBN 0-86653-607-8, GA1326). Good Apple.

Kapoor. Sikh Festivals, Reading Level 4. (Illus.). 48p. (gr. 3-8). Date not set. PLB 14.60 (ISBN 0-86592-984-X). Rourke Corp.

Lovato, Rebecca. Carlos at the Fiesta (Carlos en la Fiesta) Cardona, Consuelo M., tr. LC 76-42856. (gr. 6-12). 1976. pap. 5.95 (ISBN 0-89430-000-8). Palos Verdes.

McLeish, Kenneth, et al. Celebrations, 6 bks. Lynch, Maurice, notes by. (Illus.). 32p. (Orig.). (gr. 4-6). 1986. Set. pap. text ed. 29.70 incl. teacher's notes (ISBN 1-55624-011-2). Wright Group.

Saypol, Judyth R. & Wikler, Madeline. My Very Own Sukkot Book. Wikler, Madeline, illus. LC 83-26738. 40p. (gr. k-5). 1980. pap. 2.95 (ISBN 0-930494-09-1). Kar Ben.

FASTS AND FEASTS–FICTION

Cohen, Barbara. Yussel's Prayer. Deraney, Michael J., illus. LC 80-25377. 32p. (gr. k-4). 1981. PLB 12.88 (ISBN 0-688-00461-X). Lothrop.

Dennison, George. And Then a Harvest Feast. (Illus.). (gr. 2-6). 1973. Random.

Feder, Harriet K. Not Yet, Elijah! Halpern, Joan, illus. LC 89-1744. 32p. (gr. k-3). 1989. pap. 4.95 (ISBN 0-930494-95-4). Kar Ben.

FASTS AND FEASTS–JUDAISM
see also names of individual fasts and feasts, e.g. Yom Kippur, etc.

Adler, David. Jewish Holiday Fun. 64p. (Orig.). (gr. 2-6). 1987. pap. 3.95 (ISBN 0-930494-72-5). Kar Ben.

Adler, David A. A Picture Book of Jewish Holidays. Heller, Linda, illus. LC 81-2765. 32p. (gr. k-3). 1981. reinforced bdg. 13.95 (ISBN 0-8234-0396-3); pap. 5.95 (ISBN 0-8234-0756-X). Holiday.

Burstein, Chaya M. A First Jewish Holiday Cookbook. Burstein, Chaya M., illus. (gr. 3-8). 1979. (Bonim Bks); pap. 8.95 (ISBN 0-88482-775-5, Bonim Bks). Hebrew Pub.

Cashman, Greer F. & Frankel, Alona. Jewish Days & Holidays. LC 86-70789. (Illus.). 64p. (ps up). 1986. 9.95 (ISBN 0-915361-58-2, Dist. by Watts). Adama Pubs Inc.

Chaikin, Miriam. Shake a Palm Branch: The Story & Meaning of Sukkot. Friedman, Marvin, illus. LC 84-5022. 80p. (gr. 3-6). 1986. 12.95 (ISBN 0-89919-254-8, Pub. by Clarion); pap. 4.95 (ISBN 0-89919-428-1, Pub. by Clarion). Ticknor & Fields.

Cohen, Barbara. First Fast. (Illus.). 32p. (gr. 4-6). 1987. 7.95 (ISBN 0-8074-0354-7, 101066). UAHC.

Corwin, Judith H. Jewish Holiday Fun. Corwin, Judith H., illus. LC 86-16201. 64p. (gr. 3 up). 1987. PLB 10.29 (ISBN 0-671-60230-6); PLB 7.71s.p.; pap. 4.46s.p. Messner.

Englander, Lois, et al. The Jewish Holiday Do-Book. new ed. (gr. 3 up). 1977. 9.95x (ISBN 0-685-76976-3). Bloch.

Epstein, Morris. My Holiday Story Book. rev. ed. (gr. 4-5). 1958. pap. 4.50x (ISBN 0-87068-368-3). Ktav.

Gamoran, Mamie G. Fun Ways to Holidays. (gr. 4-6). 1951. pap. 2.00 (ISBN 0-8074-0136-6, 321400). UAHC.

Garvey, Robert. First Book of Jewish Holidays. (Illus.). (gr. 1-2). 1954. pap. 4.50x (ISBN 0-87068-362-4). Ktav.

Geller, Norman. Color Me Happy: It's Rosh Hashannah & Yom Kippur. Cruchow, Jane C., illus. 36p. (gr. k-4). 1986. pap. 2.95 (ISBN 0-915753-10-3). N Geller Pub.

Gellman, Ellie. It's Rosh-Hashanah. Kahn, Katherine J., illus. LC 85-80783. 12p. (ps). 1985. bds. 4.95 (ISBN 0-930494-50-4). Kar Ben.

Greenberg, Judith E. & Carey, Helen H. Jewish Holidays. LC 84-20983. (Illus.). 32p. (gr. 4-6). 1985. lib. bdg. 10.40 (ISBN 0-531-04913-2). Watts.

Grishaver, Joel L. Building Jewish Life: High Holy Days. LC 87-13949. (Illus.). 48p. (gr. k-3). 1988. pap. text ed. 4.95 (ISBN 0-933873-17-4). Torah Aura.

—Building Jewish Life Passover Haggadah. (HEB & ENG., Illus.). 48p. (Orig.). (gr. 4-8). 1989. pap. 2.95 (ISBN 0-933873-41-7). Torah Aura.

—Our Exodus: A Family Haggadah. (HEB & ENG., Illus.). 48p. (Orig.). (gr. 4-8). 1989. pap. 3.85 (ISBN 0-933873-42-5). Torah Aura.

—Sukkot & Simhat Torah. (Illus.). 48p. 1988. pap. text ed. 4.95 (ISBN 0-933873-13-1). Torah Aura.

Jaffe, Leonard. The Pitzel Holiday Book. (Illus.). (gr. 5-8). 1962. 7.95x (ISBN 0-87068-359-4). Ktav.

Kleinbard, Gitel. Oh, Zalmy! Or, Tales of Two Esthers, Bk. 3. Vorhand, Rachel, illus. (gr. 1-4). 1979. pap. 3.95 (ISBN 0-917274-05-9). Mah Tov Pubns.

Kozodoy, Ruth. The Book of Jewish Holidays. Rossel, Seymour, ed. Suba, Suzanne, illus. 192p. (Orig.). (gr. 4-5). 1981. pap. text ed. 7.95x (ISBN 0-87441-334-6); tchr's. guide with duplicating masters by Moshe Ben-Aharon 12.50x (ISBN 0-87441-367-2); By Morris J. Sugarman. student's activity bk. 4.25 (ISBN 0-87441-338-9). Behrman.

Lemelman, Martin, illus. Jewish Holiday Book. 10p. 1989. bds. 4.95 (ISBN 0-8074-0431-4, 102004). UAHC.

Mack, Grace C. My Special Book of Jewish Celebrations. (Illus.). 36p. (Orig.). (ps-2). 1984. pap. 8.95 (ISBN 0-9602338-4-9). Rockdale Ridge.

Marcus, Audrey F. & Zwerin, Raymond A. Shabbat Can Be. Saltzman, Yuri, illus. Syme, Daniel B., ed. (Illus.). (gr. k-3). 1979. 10.95 (ISBN 0-8074-0023-8). UAHC.

Pliskin, Jacqueline. The Jewish Holiday Game & Workbook. (Illus.). (gr. 8-12). 1989. pap. 5.95 (ISBN 0-933503-85-7). Shapolsky Pubs.

—My Very Own Animated Jewish Holiday Activity Book. (Illus.). 96p. (gr. 4-8). 1987. pap. 5.95 (ISBN 0-933503-16-4). Shapolsky Pubs.

Schaffer, Patricia. Chag Sameach! A Jewish Holiday Book for Children. (Illus.). 28p. (Orig.). (ps-4). 1985. pap. 5.95 (ISBN 0-935079-16-5). Tabor Sarah Bks.

Schlein, Miriam. Our Holidays. Kahn, Katherine, illus. 128p. (gr. k-3). 1983. pap. text ed. 7.95x (ISBN 0-87441-382-6). Behrman.

Schram, Peninnah. The Big Sukkah. Kahane, Jacqueline, illus. LC 86-7520. 32p. (ps-3). 1986. 10.95 (ISBN 0-930494-56-3); pap. 4.95 (ISBN 0-930494-57-1). Kar Ben.

Sidon, Ephraim. The Animated Megillah. 54p. (gr. 1-5). 1987. 14.95 (ISBN 0-8246-0324-9). Jonathan David.

Simon, Norma. Tu Bishvat. Weiss, Harvey, illus. (ps-k). 1961. plastic cover 4.50 (ISBN 0-8381-0709-5). United Syn Bk.

Sokoloff, David. The New Jewish Holiday Activity & Coloring Book. 96p. (ps-8). 1990. pap. 5.95 (ISBN 0-944007-92-9). Shapolsky Pubs.

Turck, Mary. Jewish Holidays. (Illus.). 48p. (gr. 3 up). 1990. 10.95 (ISBN 0-89686-502-9, Crestwood Hse). Macmillan Child Grp.

Turner. Jewish Festivals, Reading Level 4. (Illus.). 48p. (gr. 3-8). Date not set. Set. PLB 14.60 (ISBN 0-86592-977-7). Rourke Corp.

Wark, Mary A. We Tell It to Our Children: The Story of Passover: A Haggadah for Seders with Young Children. 2nd ed. Oskow, Craig, illus. Lerner, Leigh D., frwd. by. LC 88-92282. (Illus.). 126p. (Orig.). (ps-6). 1988. pap. 5.95 wire bdg. (ISBN 0-9619880-8-8). Mensch Makers Pr.

Wark, MaryAnn B. We Tell It to Our Children: The Story of Passover (Leader Edition with Puppets) A Haggadah for Seders with Young Children. Oskow, Cragi, illus. Lerner, Leigh D., frwd. by. LC 87-63604. (Illus.). 150p. (Orig.). (ps-6). 1988. pap. 11.95 wire-o (ISBN 0-9619880-9-6). Mensch Makers Pr.
Children's active participatory Haggadah makes Passover story into an engaging drama of the Exodus story. A complete guide, including multi-national recipes, for putting on the traditional Seder meal for passover. Text is a musical puppet show with Judaically-meaningful lyrics set to simple American folk tunes. Everyone participates in singing throughout the service. This Leader edition has 9 cut out puppets who are the "guests" from the past, who in a "you-are-there" style tell the story of the Exodus. Parts for non-readers & early readers. Guest edition - no puppets with full text also available. Endorsed by rabbis, religious educators (Jewish & Christian), children's book store owners, preschool teachers, parents & grandparents nationwide. For home or model seders. Authentically Jewish; easy for non-Jews. Developmentally appropriate for children. Downright fun for adults. Other unique features include the Passover food sysmbols, like matzah, explained at the appropriate time in the story; special sections to personalize & teach about world Jewry. Difficult concepts like slavery are taught through action, songs, & pictures. Lyrics respond to children's thinking while tackling complicated issues surrounding freedom. Plentiful, detailed drawings emphasize immediacy of ideas & illustrate every idea & ceremonial symbol.
Publisher Provided Annotation.

Youdovin, Susan S. Why Does It Always Rain on Sukkot? Levine, Abby, ed. Nerlove, Miriam, illus. 32p. (ps-3). 1990. PLB 12.95 (ISBN 0-8075-9079-7). A Whitman.

Zeldin, Florence. A Mouse in Our Jewish House. Rauchwerger, Lisa, illus. LC 89-40362. 32p. (ps). 1990. 11.95 (ISBN 0-933873-43-3). Torah Aura.
This imaginative counting book, by noted children's author Florence Zeldin, combines the mastery of counting from one to twelve with the introduction of the basic celebrations of the Jewish year. A mouse named Archie Akhbar inhabits this book. Brought to life by the imaginative paper sculptures of Lisa Rauchwerger, Archie eats an escalating number of pieces of food on each subsequent Jewish holiday.
Publisher Provided Annotation.

FATHERS

Byers, Ken. The Father & Son Survival Kit: A Journey into the Wilderness of Relationships. (gr. 9 up). 1988. 19.95 (ISBN 0-9619040-1-1); pap. 12.95 (ISBN 0-9619040-0-3); wkbk. 12.95 (ISBN 0-9619040-2-X). Journeys Together.

Hallinan, P. K. We're Very Good Friends, My Father & I. Hallinan, P. K., illus. LC 88-35167. 32p. (ps-3). 1989. PLB 13.27 (ISBN 0-516-03651-3). Childrens.

Merriam, Eve. Daddies at Work. Fernandes, Eugenie, illus. 32p. (ps-2). 1991. pap. 2.25 (ISBN 0-671-73276-5, Little Simon). S&S Trade.

Nelson, Theresa. The Twenty-Five Cent Miracle. 224p. (gr. 4-7). 1989. pap. 3.95 (ISBN 0-689-71326-6, Aladdin). Macmillan Child Grp.

Simon, Norma. I Wish I Had My Father. Tucker, Kathleen, ed. LC 83-1287. (Illus.). 32p. (gr. 1-4). 1983. PLB 10.95 (ISBN 0-8075-3522-2). A Whitman.

FATHERS–FICTION

Aiken, Joan. Dido & Pa. LC 86-2061. 256p. (gr. 7 up). 1986. 14.95 (ISBN 0-385-29480-8). Delacorte.

Allen, Suzanne. Almost Starring Dad. (gr. 4-7). 1990. pap. 2.75 (ISBN 0-425-12218-2). Berkley Pub.

Asch, Frank. Just Like Daddy. (Illus.). 32p. (gr. k-4). 1984. PLB 12.95 (ISBN 0-671-66456-5); pap. 4.95 (ISBN 0-671-66457-3). S&S Trade.

Bawden, Nina. The Robbers. LC 79-4152. (Illus.). 160p. (gr. 4-7). 1989. Repr. of 1979 ed. 12.95 (ISBN 0-688-41902-X). Lothrop.

Baynton, Martin. Why Do You Love Me? LC 89-1861. (Illus.). 32p. (ps up). 1990. 12.95 (ISBN 0-688-09156-3); PLB 12.88 (ISBN 0-688-09157-1). Greenwillow.

Bograd, Larry. Travelers. LC 85-45172. 192p. (gr. 7 up). 1986. 11.95 (ISBN 0-397-32128-7, Lipp Jr Bks); PLB 11.89 (ISBN 0-397-32129-5). HarpC Child Bks.

Brighton, Catherine. Five Secrets in a Box. Brighton, Catherine, illus. 32p. (ps-3). 1987. 11.95 (ISBN 0-525-44318-5, 01160-350, DCB). Dutton Child Bks.

Burgess, Gelett. The Little Father. Egielski, Richard, illus. 32p. (ps up). pap. 3.95 (ISBN 0-374-44486-2). FS&G.

Burstein, Fred. Anna's Rain. Stevenson, Harvey, illus. LC 89-42533. 32p. (ps-1). 1990. 14.95 (ISBN 0-531-05827-1); PLB 14.99 (ISBN 0-531-08427-2). Orchard Bks Watts.

Calvert, Patricia. The Hour of the Wolf. LC 83-14184. 160p. (gr. 7 up). 1983. 12.95 (ISBN 0-684-17961-X, Scribners Young Read). Macmillan Child Grp.

Cannon, Bettie. A Bellsong for Sarah Raines. LC 87-4299. 192p. (gr. 7 up). 1987. 13.95 (ISBN 0-684-18839-2, Scribners Young Read). Macmillan Child Grp.

Carter, Alden R. Robodad. 144p. 1990. 14.95 (ISBN 0-399-22191-3, Putnam). Putnam Pub Group.

Cleaver, Vera. Sugar Blue. (gr. 3-6). 1986. pap. 2.95 (ISBN 0-440-48422-7, YB). Dell.

Close, Jessie. The Warping of Al. LC 90-4058. 288p. (gr. 7 up). 1990. 15.95 (ISBN 0-06-021280-2); PLB 15.89 (ISBN 0-06-021281-0). HarpC Child Bks.

Collins, Judith G. Josh's Scary Dad. Paterson, Diane, illus. 32p. (Orig.). (gr. 3-5). 1983. pap. 0.20 (ISBN 0-687-20546-8). Abingdon.

Dahl, Roald. Danny: The Champion of the World. Bennett, Jill, illus. 208p. (gr. 3 up). 1975. lib. bdg. 13.99 (ISBN 0-394-93103-3). Knopf.

Declements, Barthe. Monkey See, Monkey Do. (gr. 7 up). 1990. 13.95 (ISBN 0-385-30158-8). Delacorte.

DeJong, Meindert. The House of Sixty Fathers. Sendak, Maurice, illus. LC 56-8148. 192p. (gr. 5-8). 1987. pap. 3.50 (ISBN 0-06-440200-2, Trophy). HarpC Child Bks.

De Pressense, Domitille. Natalie: The Spanking. (Illus.). 28p. (ps-1). 1990. pap. 3.95 (ISBN 0-8120-4506-8). Barron.

Dickens, Charles. Dombey & Son. (ps-8). 1990. Repr. lib. bdg. 29.95x (ISBN 0-89966-678-7). Buccaneer Bks.

Fassler, Joan. All Alone with Daddy: A Young Girl Plays the Role of Mother. Gregory, Dorothy L., illus. LC 76-80120. 32p. (ps-3). 1975. 16.95 (ISBN 0-87705-009-0). Human Sci Pr.

Fleischman, Paul. Rear-View Mirrors. LC 85-45387. 128p. (gr. 7 up). 1986. 12.95 (ISBN 0-06-021866-5); PLB 12.89 (ISBN 0-06-021867-3). HarpC Child Bks.

Fox, Paula. Blowfish Live in the Sea. 128p. (gr. 6-8). 1986. pap. 3.95 (ISBN 0-689-71092-5, Aladdin). Macmillan Child Grp.

—Portrait of Ivan. reissue ed. Lambert, Saul, illus. LC 74-93085. 144p. (gr. 5-7). 1985. 12.95 (ISBN 0-02-735510-1, Bradbury Pr). Macmillan Child Grp.

Friend, David. Baseball, Football, Daddy & Me. Brown, Rick, illus. 32p. (ps-3). 1990. 12.95 (ISBN 0-670-82420-8). Viking Child Bks.

Gifaldi, David. One Thing for Sure. LC 86-2677. 160p. (gr. 4-7). 1986. 13.95 (ISBN 0-89919-462-1, Pub. by Clarion). Ticknor & Fields.

Grant, Cynthia D. Keep Laughing. LC 90-6816. 192p. (gr. 7 up). 1991. 14.95 (ISBN 0-689-31514-7, Atheneum Child Bk). Macmillan Child Grp.

Greenfield, Eloise. My Daddy & I. Gilchrist, Jan S., illus. 12p. 1991. bds. 4.95 (ISBN 0-86316-206-1). Writers & Readers.

Hallinan, P. K. We're Very Good Friends, My Father & I. Hallinan, P. K., illus. (ps-k). 1990. pap. 3.95 (ISBN 0-8249-8427-7). Ideals.

—We're Very Good Friends, My Mother & I. Hallinan, P. K., illus. 24p. (ps-k). 1990. pap. 3.95 (ISBN 0-8249-8519-2). Ideals.

Hamm, Diane J. Bunkhouse Journal. LC 90-8062. 96p. (gr. 7 up). 1990. 11.95 (ISBN 0-684-19206-3, Scribners Young Read). Macmillan Child Grp.

Haseley, Dennis. My Father Doesn't Know about the Woods & Me. Hays, Michael, illus. LC 87-30295. 32p. (gr. 1-3). 1988. 13.95 (ISBN 0-689-31365-9, Atheneum Child Bk). Macmillan Child Grp.

Hawks, Robert. This Stranger, My Father. LC 87-26245. 228p. (gr. 5-9). 1988. 13.95 (ISBN 0-395-44089-0). HM.

—This Stranger, My Father. 240p. (gr. 4). 1990. pap. 2.95 (ISBN 0-380-70739-X, Flare). Avon.

Helm, Lynn Z. Living with Dad. (gr. 5-7). 1990. pap. 2.75 (ISBN 0-590-43011-4). Scholastic Inc.

Hess, Donna L. A Father's Promise. (Illus.). 268p. (Orig.). (gr. 6). 1987. pap. 6.94 (ISBN 0-89084-379-1). Bob Jones Univ Pr.

Hickman, Martha W. When Andy's Father Went to Prison. rev. ed. Levine, Abby, ed. Raymond, Larry, illus. LC 89-77318. 40p. (gr. 2-5). 1990. PLB 10.95 (ISBN 0-8075-8874-1). A Whitman.

—When Can Daddy Come Home? Livingston, Francis, illus. 48p. (gr. 1-3). 1983. 1.00 (ISBN 0-687-44969-3). Abingdon.

Hines, Anna G. Daddy Makes the Best Spaghetti. Hines, Anna G., illus. LC 85-13993. (ps-1). 1986. 11.95 (ISBN 0-89919-388-9, Pub. by Clarion). Ticknor & Fields.

—Sky All Around. Hines, Anna G., illus. 32p. (gr. 4-7). 1989. 13.95 (ISBN 0-89919-801-5, Pub. by Clarion). HM.

Hoopes, Lyn L. Daddy's Coming Home. Degen, Bruce, illus. LC 83-47693. 32p. (ps-2). 1984. HarpC Child Bks.

Horlacher, Bill & Horlacher, Kathy. I'm Glad I'm Your Dad. Hutton, Kathryn, illus. 24p. (ps-2). 1985. 1.99 (ISBN 0-87239-875-7, 3675). Standard Pub.

Howker, Janni. The Nature of the Beast. (gr. 5-9). 1987. pap. 4.95 (ISBN 0-14-032254-X, Puffin). Puffin Bks.

Hunt, Irene. The Everlasting Hills. LC 85-2449. 192p. (gr. 6-8). 1985. 13.95 (ISBN 0-684-18340-4, Scribners Young Read). Macmillan Child Grp.

Isadora, Rachel. At the Crossroads. LC 90-30751. (Illus.). 32p. (ps up). 1991. 13.95 (ISBN 0-688-05270-3); PLB 13.88 (ISBN 0-688-05271-1). Greenwillow.

Joyce, James. Eveline. 32p. (gr. 6). 1990. 10.95s.p. (ISBN 0-88682-308-0); 15.65 (ISBN 0-685-28223-6). Creative Ed.

Kidd, Nina. June Mountain Secret. Kidd, Nina, illus. LC 90-31574. 32p. (gr. k-3). 1991. 14.95 (ISBN 0-06-023167-X); PLB 14.89 (ISBN 0-06-023168-8). HarpC Child Bks.

Konigsburg, E. L. Father's Arcane Daughter. (gr. 5-8). 1986. pap. 3.25 (ISBN 0-440-42496-8, YB). Dell.

Kroll, Steven. Gone Fishing. Stevenson, Harvey, illus. LC 89-22241. 48p. (ps-2). 1990. 12.95 (ISBN 0-517-57589-2); PLB 13.99 (ISBN 0-517-57590-6). Crown.

—Happy Father's Day. Hafner, Marylin, illus. LC 87-7559. 32p. (ps-3). 1988. 14.95g (ISBN 0-8234-0671-7). Holiday.

Lewin, Hugh. Jafta's Father. Kopper, Lisa, illus. LC 82-12837. 24p. (ps-3). 1983. PLB 9.95 (ISBN 0-87614-209-9); pap. 3.95 (ISBN 0-87614-496-2). Carolrhoda Bks.

—Jafta's Father. Kopper, Lisa, illus. 24p. (ps-3). 1989. pap. 3.95 (ISBN 0-685-24886-0, First Ave Edns). Lerner Pubns.

Lindenbaum, Pija. Else-Marie & Her Seven Little Daddies. LC 91-9077. (Illus.). 32p. (ps-2). 1991. 14.95 (ISBN 0-8050-1752-6). H Holt & Co.

Lyle, Letcher L. Dark but Full of Diamonds. (gr. 12 up). 1981. 9.95 (ISBN 0-698-20517-0, Coward). Putnam Pub Group.

Mandelbaum, Pili. You Be Me, I'll Be You. (Illus.). 40p. (ps-3). 1990. 12.95 (ISBN 0-916291-27-8). Kane-Miller Bk.

Mayer, Mercer. Just Me & My Dad. (Illus.). 24p. (ps-3). 1977. pap. write for info. (ISBN 0-307-11839-8, Golden Bks). Western Pub.

Meyer, Carolyn. Wild Rover. 208p. (gr. 7-10). 1989. 13.95 (ISBN 0-689-50475-6, M K McElderry). Macmillan Child Grp.

Monjo, F. N. The One Bad Thing about Father. Reissue. ed. Negri, Rocco, illus. LC 71-85036. 64p. (gr. k-3). 1970. PLB 11.89 (ISBN 0-06-024334-1). HarpC Child Bks.

Morgan, A. Daddy-Care. (Illus.). 24p. (ps-8). 1986. 12.95 (ISBN 0-920303-58-7); pap. 4.95 (ISBN 0-685-38506-X). Firefly Bks Ltd.

Munsch, Robert. David's Father. Martchenko, Michael, illus. 32p. (gr. k-3). 1983. 12.95 (ISBN 0-920236-62-6); pap. 4.95 (ISBN 0-920236-64-2). Firefly Bks Ltd.

Murphy, Jill. Worlds Apart. LC 88-5814. 144p. (gr. 3-7). 1989. 13.95 (ISBN 0-399-21566-2, Putnam). Putnam Pub Group.

Naylor, Phyllis R. The Keeper. LC 85-20029. 228p. (gr. 5 up). 1986. 13.95 (ISBN 0-689-31204-0, Atheneum Child Bk). Macmillan Child Grp.

Okimoto, Jean D. Norman Schnurman, Average Person. 128p. 1982. 9.95 (ISBN 0-399-20913-1, Putnam). Putnam Pub Group.

Ormerod, Jan. Dad's Back. LC 84-12614. (Illus.). 24p. (ps). 1985. 4.95 (ISBN 0-688-04126-4). Lothrop.

—Reading. LC 84-12628. (Illus.). 24p. (ps). 1985. 4.95 (ISBN 0-688-04127-2). Lothrop.

Otey, Mimi. Daddy Has a Pair of Striped Shorts. LC 90-55289. (Illus.). 32p. (ps-3). 1990. 13.95 (ISBN 0-374-31675-9). FS&G.

Oxenbury, Helen. Tom & Pippo Read a Story. Oxenbury, Helen, illus. LC 87-37438. 14p. (ps-k). 1988. bds. 5.95 (ISBN 0-689-71252-9, Aladdin). Macmillan Child Grp.

Parker, Kristy. My Dad the Magnificent. Monfried, Lucia, ed. Hoban, Lillian, illus. (ps-2). 1987. 10.95 (ISBN 0-525-44314-2, DCB). Dutton Child Bks.

—My Dad the Magnificent. Monfried, Lucia, ed. Hoban, Lillian, illus. 32p. (ps-2). 1990. pap. 3.95 (ISBN 0-525-44607-9, DCB). Dutton Child Bks.

Peck, Richard. Father Figure. (gr. k-12). 1988. pap. 2.95 (ISBN 0-440-20069-5, LFL). Dell.

Pfeffer, Susan B. Dear Dad, Love Laurie. 1990. pap. 2.75 (ISBN 0-590-41682-0). Scholastic Inc.

Pollock, Penny. Summer Captive. LC 86-63075. 176p. (gr. 7 up). 1987. 14.95 (ISBN 0-936915-06-4, Shoe Tree Pr). Betterway Pubns.

Porter, Bruce. The Parable of Pa Diggle's Son. Porter, Bruce, illus. 40p. (Orig.). (gr. 3 up). 1987. pap. 3.95 (ISBN 0-939925-11-7). R C Law & Co.

Porter-Gaylord, Laurel. I Love My Daddy Because... Wolff, Ashley, illus. LC 90-2865. 24p. (ps). 1991. 5.95 (ISBN 0-525-44624-9, DCB). Dutton Child Bks.

Ray, Deborah K. My Daddy Was a Soldier: A World War Two Story. Ray, Deborah K., illus. LC 89-20056. 40p. (gr. 1-4). 1990. PLB 12.95 (ISBN 0-8234-0795-0). Holiday.

Ready, Ann C. Her Father's Daughter. 192p. (Orig.). (gr. 6-12). 1981. pap. 1.95 (ISBN 0-448-14688-6). Ace Bks.

Roberts, Bethany. Waiting-for-Papa Stories. Stapler, Sarah, illus. LC 89-36589. 32p. (ps-3). 1990. 12.95 (ISBN 0-06-025050-X); PLB 12.89 (ISBN 0-06-025051-8). HarpC Child Bks.

Rosen, David. Henry's Tower. Feldman, Lynne, illus. LC 84-61581. 36p. (gr. k-5). 1984. 10.95 (ISBN 0-930905-01-6); pap. 4.95 (ISBN 0-930905-00-8). Platypus Bks.

Seeger, Pete. Abiyoyo: South African Lullaby & Folk Story. Hays, Michael, illus. LC 85-15341. 48p. (ps-4). 1986. 15.95 (ISBN 0-02-781490-4, Mcmillan Child Bk). Macmillan Child Grp.

Shaw, Richard C. My Dad Sells Insurance. Snyder, Dan, illus. 40p. (ps-5). 1988. PLB write for info. (ISBN 0-944900-00-3). Shaw & Co.

Shusterman, Neal. What Daddy Did. 1991. pap. 15.95 (ISBN 0-316-78906-2). Little.

Smith, Beatrice S. The Road to Galveston. LC 72-7657. (Illus.). 132p. (gr. 4 up). 1973. PLB 7.95 (ISBN 0-8225-0755-2). Lerner Pubns.

Steadman, Ralph. That's My Dad. Steadman, Ralph, illus. 32p. (gr. k-2). 1987. 11.95 (ISBN 0-86264-133-0, Pub. by Anderson Pr UK). Trafalgar Sq.

Steel, Danielle. Martha's New Daddy. Rogers, Jacqueline, illus. (ps-2). 1989. 8.95 (ISBN 0-385-29799-8). Delacorte.

Steptoe, John. Daddy Is a Monster...Sometimes. Steptoe, John, illus. LC 77-4464. 32p. (gr. k-3). 1980. PLB 12.89 (ISBN 0-397-31893-6, Lipp Jr Bks). HarpC Child Bks.

—Daddy Is a Monster...Sometimes. LC 77-4464. (Illus.). 32p. (gr. k-3). 1983. pap. 6.95 (ISBN 0-06-443042-1, Trophy). HarpC Child Bks.

Strohl, Roger R., Jr. Jake & Duke Camp Paw Mountain. 1989. 6.95 (ISBN 0-533-08163-7). Vantage.

Taylor, Sydney. A Papa Like Everyone Else. (gr. k-6). 1989. pap. 2.95 (ISBN 0-440-40129-1, YB). Dell.

Todd, Leonard. Squaring Off. (gr. 7 up). 1990. 13.95 (ISBN 0-670-83377-0). Viking Child Bks.

Tyler, Linda W. When Daddy Comes Home. Davis, Susan, illus. (ps-1). 1988. pap. 3.95 (ISBN 0-14-050615-2, Puffin). Puffin Bks.

Voigt, Cynthia. Sons from Afar. LC 87-1857. 224p. (gr. 7 up). 1987. 14.95 (ISBN 0-689-31349-7, Atheneum Child Bk). Macmillan Child Grp.

Watanabe, Shigeo. Daddy, Play With Me. Ohtomo, Yasuo, illus. LC 84-14818. 32p. (ps). 1985. 9.95 (ISBN 0-399-21211-6, Philomel Bks). Putnam Pub Group.

—Daddy, Play with Me! Ohtomo, Yasuo, illus. (ps). 1986. 3.95 (ISBN 0-399-21334-1, Philomel). Putnam Pub Group.

—Where Is My Daddy? Ohtomo, Yasuo, illus. 32p. 1985. pap. 3.95 (ISBN 0-399-21049-0, Philomel). Putnam Pub Group.

—Where's My Daddy? Ohtomo, Yasuo, illus. LC 79-19347. 32p. (ps-1). 1982. PLB 8.95 (ISBN 0-399-20899-2, Philomel). Putnam Pub Group.

Weller, Frances W. Boat Song. LC 86-12647. 180p. (gr. 3-7). 1987. 13.95 (ISBN 0-02-792611-7, Mcmillan Child Bk). Macmillan Child Grp.

Wood, Phyllis A. Win Me & You Lose. LC 76-44299. 136p. (gr. 7 up). 1977. 8.95 (ISBN 0-664-32605-6, Westminster). Westminster John Knox.

Yolen, Jane. All Those Secrets of the World. (ps-3). 1991. 14.95 (ISBN 0-316-96891-9). Little.

Ziefert, Harriet. Keeping Daddy Awake on the Way Home from the Beach. Chwast, Seymour, illus. LC 85-45277. 12p. (ps-2). 1986. 5.95 (ISBN 0-694-00080-9). HarpC Child Bks.

—When Daddy Had the Chicken Pox. Kalish, Lionel, illus. LC 90-43559. 32p. (ps-3). 1991. 13.95 (ISBN 0-06-026906-5); PLB 13.89 (ISBN 0-06-026907-3). HarpC Child Bks.

Zolotow, Charlotte. A Father Like That. Shecter, Ben, illus. LC 70-135778. (ps-3). 1971. PLB 12.89 (ISBN 0-06-026950-2). HarpC Child Bks.

FAUNA

see Animals; Zoology

FEAR

see also Courage

Barsuhn, Rochelle N. Feeling Afraid. Connelly, Gwen, illus. LC 82-19946. (gr. 1-2). 1983. PLB 11.97 (ISBN 0-89565-246-3). Childs World.

Being Alone. 48p. (gr. 3-4). 1989. PLB 10.95 (ISBN 0-685-26362-2). Capstone Pr.

The Dark. 48p. (gr. 3-4). 1989. PLB 10.95 (ISBN 0-685-26363-0). Capstone Pr.

Doctors & Dentists. 48p. (gr. 3-4). 1989. PLB 10.95. Capstone Pr.

Dragonwagon, Crescent. Will It Be Okay? Shecter, Ben, illus. LC 76-48859. (ps-3). 1977. PLB 12.89 (ISBN 0-06-021738-3). HarpC Child Bks.

Frandsen, Karen G. I'd Rather Get a Spanking Than Go to the Doctor. Frandsen, Karen G., illus. LC 86-11735. 32p. (ps-3). 1987. PLB 13.93 (ISBN 0-516-03498-7); pap. 3.95 (ISBN 0-516-43498-5). Childrens.

Gackenbach, Dick. Harry & the Terrible Whatzit. Gackenbach, Dick, illus. LC 76-40205. 32p. (ps-2). 1979. 12.95 (ISBN 0-395-28795-2, Clarion). HM.

Gross, Alan. Sometimes I Worry. Venezia, Mike, illus. LC 78-8019. 32p. (gr. k-3). 1978. PLB 13.93 (ISBN 0-516-03670-X). Childrens.

Hipp, Earl. Fighting Invisible Tigers: A Stress Management Guide for Teens. Galbraith, Judy, intro. by. LC 85-80632. (Illus.). 120p. (Orig.). (gr. 6-12). 1985. pap. 9.95 (ISBN 0-915793-04-0). Free Spirit Pub.

Jones, Rebecca C. I Am Not Afraid. (Illus.). (ps). 1987. pap. 2.29 (ISBN 0-570-09113-6, 56-1588). Concordia.

Marcus, Irene W. & Marcus, Paul. Scary Night Visitors: A Story for Children with Bedtime Fears. Jeschke, Susan, illus. 32p. (ps-2). 1990. 16.95 (ISBN 0-945354-26-6); pap. 5.95 (ISBN 0-945354-25-8). Magination Pr.

Moving Away. 48p. (gr. 3-4). 1989. PLB 10.95 (ISBN 0-685-26365-7). Capstone Pr.

Nardo, Don. Anxiety & Phobias. (Illus.). (gr. 6-12). 1992. 18.95 (ISBN 0-7910-0041-9). Chelsea Hse.

St. George, Judith. Who's Scared? Not Me! 160p. (gr. 5 up). 1987. 13.95 (ISBN 0-399-21481-X, Putnam). Putnam Pub Group.

Scary Places. 48p. (gr. 3-4). 1989. PLB 10.95 (ISBN 0-685-26366-5). Capstone Pr.

Snakes. 48p. (gr. 3-4). 1989. PLB 10.95 (ISBN 0-685-26367-3). Capstone Pr.

Stein, Sara B. About Phobias. LC 78-65615. (Illus.). 48p. (ps-8). 1984. pap. text ed. 7.95 (ISBN 0-8027-7219-6). Walker & Co.

—About Phobias. Stone, Erika, illus. (ps-8). 1979. 10.95 (ISBN 0-8027-6348-0). Walker & Co.

Storms. 48p. (gr. 3-4). 1989. PLB 10.95 (ISBN 0-685-26368-1). Capstone Pr.

Strangers. 48p. (gr. 3-4). 1989. PLB 10.95 (ISBN 0-685-26369-X). Capstone Pr.

FEAR–FICTION

Alexander, Liza. Scared of the Dark. Cooke, Tom, illus. 32p. (ps-k). 1986. write for info. (ISBN 0-307-12020-1, Pub by Golden Bks). Western Pub.

Alexander, Sally. Sarah's Surprise. Kastner, Jill, illus. LC 89-36780. 32p. (gr. k-3). 1990. 13.95 (ISBN 0-02-700391-4, Mcmillan Child Bk). Macmillan Child Grp.

Balter, Lawrence. Linda Saves the Day: Understanding Fear. Schanzer, Roz, illus. 40p. (ps-2). 1989. 5.95 (ISBN 0-8120-6117-9). Barron.

Bell, Mary & Yates, Steve. I'm Not Afraid. Burger, Nola, illus. 24p. (ps-2). 1989. PLB write for info. Kids Ink Pr.

Berenstain, Stan & Berenstain, Janice. The Berenstain Bears Get Stage Fright. Berenstain, Stan & Berenstain, Janice, illus. LC 85-25716. 32p. (gr. 3-6). 1986. lib. bdg. 5.99 (ISBN 0-394-97337-2, Random Juv); pap. 1.95 (ISBN 0-394-87337-8, Random Juv). Random.

Bond, Felicia. Poinsettia & the Firefighters. LC 83-46169. (Illus.). 32p. (ps-3). 1984. PLB 14.89 (ISBN 0-690-04401-1, Crowell Jr Bks). HarpC Child Bks.

Bonsall, Crosby N. Who's Afraid of the Dark? LC 79-2700. (Illus.). 32p. (ps-3). 1980. 11.95 (ISBN 0-06-020598-9); PLB 11.89 (ISBN 0-06-020599-7). HarpC Child Bks.

Browne, Anthony. Changes. Browne, Anthony, illus. LC 90-4283. 32p. (ps-3). 1991. Repr. of 1990 ed. 14.95 (ISBN 0-679-81029-3); PLB 15.99 (ISBN 0-679-91029-8). Knopf.

—The Tunnel. Browne, Anthony, illus. (gr. 1-6). 1990. 11.95 (ISBN 0-394-84582-X); lib. bdg. 12.99 (ISBN 0-685-30419-1). Knopf.

Bussard, Paula. Guess Who's Afraid. Goodridge, Larry, illus. 28p. (gr. k-3). 1985. 1.39 (ISBN 0-87239-966-4, 3386). Standard Pub.

Carrick, Carol. The Climb. Carrick, Donald, illus. 32p. (gr. k-4). 1980. 14.95 (ISBN 0-395-29431-2, Clarion). HM.

Christelow, Eileen. Henry & the Dragon. Christelow, Eileen, illus. LC 83-14405. 32p. (ps-2). 1984. 13.95 (ISBN 0-89919-220-3, Clarion). HM.

Church, Kristine. My Brother John. Niland, Kilmeny, illus. LC 90-25868. 32p. (ps-3). 1991. 12.95 (ISBN 0-688-10800-8, Tambourine Bks); PLB 12.88 (ISBN 0-688-10801-6, Tambourine Bks). Morrow.

Coles, Allison. Michael in the Dark. Charlton, Michael, illus. 28p. (ps up). 1985. 3.95 (ISBN 0-88110-267-9). EDC.

Colman, Penny. Dark Closets & Noises in the Night. 1991. pap. 3.95 (ISBN 0-8091-6600-3). Paulist Pr.

Dalgliesh, Alice. The Courage of Sarah Noble. Weisgard, Leonard, illus. LC 54-5922. 64p. (gr. 1-5). 1987. Repr. of 1954 ed. 12.95 (ISBN 0-684-18830-9, Scribners Young Read). Macmillan Child Grp.

Dinardo, Jeffrey. Timothy & the Night Noises. Dinardo, Jeffrey, illus. LC 86-9383. 32p. (ps-2). 1986. 11.95 (ISBN 0-13-922048-8). P-H.

Feldman, Eva B. Seymour, the Formerly Fearful. LC 89-35668. 160p. (gr. 3-6). 1990. 12.95 (ISBN 0-02-734371-5, Four Winds Press). Macmillan Child Grp.

Freschet, Bernice. Furlie Cat. Lewin, Betsy, illus. LC 85-11656. 32p. (ps-3). 1986. 12.95 (ISBN 0-688-05917-1). Lothrop.

Goss, Janet L. & Harste, Jerome C. It Didn't Frighten Me! Book & Cassette. Rommey, Steve, illus. 24p. (gr. k-3). 1985. 4.95 (ISBN 0-87406-062-1). Willowisp Pr.

Gruber, Suzanne. Monster under My Bed. Britt, Stephanie, illus. LC 84-45687. 32p. (gr. k-2). 1985. PLB 10.89 (ISBN 0-8167-0456-2); pap. text ed. 2.95 (ISBN 0-8167-0457-0). Troll Assocs.

Hest, Amy. A Sort-of Sailor. Rockwell, Lizzie, illus. LC 89-38252. 32p. (gr. k-3). 1990. 13.95 (ISBN 0-02-743641-1, Four Winds). Macmillan Child Grp.

Jannson, Tove. The Fillyjonk Who Believed in Disasters. 32p. (gr. 6). 1990. 10.95s.p. (ISBN 0-88682-299-8); 15.65 (ISBN 0-685-28214-7). Creative Ed.

Klein, Norma. Visiting Pamela. Chorao, Kay, illus. LC 78-72203. (ps-3). 1979. PLB 6.46 (ISBN 0-8037-9308-1). Dial Bks Young.

Lankton, Stephen R. The Blammo-Surprise! Book: A Story to Help Children Overcome Fears. LC 88-13566. (Illus.). 48p. (gr. 1 up). 1988. PLB 15.95 (ISBN 0-945354-11-8); pap. 5.95 (ISBN 0-945354-10-X). Magination Pr.

LeRoy, Gen. Cold Feet. 192p. (gr. 7 up). 1986. pap. 1.75 (ISBN 0-440-91336-5, LE). Dell.

McMillan, Sally H. I Used to Be Afraid. Robison, Don, illus. LC 85-51100. 24p. (gr. k-4). 1986. 7.95 (ISBN 0-87406-023-0); pap. 4.95 incl. cassette (ISBN 0-685-10919-4). Willowisp Pr.

Martin, Ann M. Stage Fright. Sims, Blanche, illus. 144p. (gr. 4-6). 1986. pap. 2.50 (ISBN 0-590-40874-7, Apple Paperbacks). Scholastic Inc.

Martin, Jacqueline B. Bizzy Bones & Uncle Ezra. Ormai, Stella, illus. LC 83-25618. 32p. (ps-2). 1984. PLB 12.88 (ISBN 0-688-03782-8). Lothrop.

Melton, David. A Boy Called Hopeless. Melton, Todd, illus. LC 86-27557. 231p. (gr. 4-8). 1986. Repr. of 1976 ed. lib. bdg. 12.95 (ISBN 0-933849-32-X). Landmark Edns.

Mogensen, Jan. Teddy & the Chinese Dragon. LC 85-26091. (Illus.). 32p. (gr. 3-4). 1985. PLB 11.95 (ISBN 1-55532-002-3). Gareth Stevens Inc.

Morris, Winifred. What If the Shark Wears Tennis Shoes? Lewin, Betsy, illus. LC 89-38150. 32p. (ps-2). 1990. 12.95 (ISBN 0-689-31587-2, Atheneum Child Bk). Macmillan Child Grp.

Pittman, Helena C. Once When I Was Scared. Rand, Ted, illus. LC 88-3598. 32p. (gr. k-3). 1988. 13.95 (ISBN 0-525-44407-6, DCB). Dutton Child Bks.

Polisar, Barry L. The Snake Who Was Afraid of People. Clark, David, illus. 48p. (gr. 2-6). 1989. 9.95 (ISBN 0-938663-08-9); pap. 7.95 (ISBN 0-938663-09-7). Rainbow Morn.

—Snakes! & the Boy Who Was Afraid of Them. Clark, David, illus. 48p. (gr. 2-6). 1988. 9.95 (ISBN 0-938663-06-2); pap. 7.95 (ISBN 0-938663-07-0). Rainbow Morn.

Rae, Judy. Bye, Bye Boogieman. Rev. ed. Lalo, illus. Timm, Stephen A., intro. by. LC 83-70412. (Illus.). 42p. (Orig.). (ps-3). 1984. pap. 3.95 (ISBN 0-939728-09-5). Steppingstone Ent.

Riley, Sue. Afraid. LC 77-15627. (Illus.). (gr. k-2). 1978. PLB 9.95 (ISBN 0-89565-011-8). Childs World.

Rockwell, Anne E. & Rockwell, Harlow. The Night We Slept Outside. Rockwell, Anne & Rockwell, Harlow, illus. LC 86-3473. 48p. (gr. 1-4). 1986. pap. 3.95 (ISBN 0-689-71070-4, Aladdin). Macmillan Child Grp.

Rodgers, Frank. Who's Afraid of the Ghost Train? Rodgers, Frank, illus. 32p. (ps-1). 1989. 12.95 (ISBN 0-15-200642-7, Gulliver Bks). HarBraceJ.

Sabraw, John. I Wouldn't Be Scared. LC 88-23352. (Illus.). 32p. (ps-1). 1989. 13.95 (ISBN 0-531-05818-2); PLB 13.99 (ISBN 0-531-08418-3). Orchard Bks Watts.

Sharmat, Marjorie W. Who's Afraid of Ernestine? Chambliss, Maxie, illus. LC 85-14911. 48p. (gr. 1-4). 1985. lib. bdg. 7.99 (ISBN 0-698-30746-1, Coward). Putnam Pub Group.

Shaw, Diana. Lessons in Fear. 176p. (gr. 7 up). pap. 2.50 (ISBN 0-8167-1315-4). Troll Assocs.

Simms, Laura. The Squeaky Door. Wickstrom, Sylvie, illus. LC 89-23895. 32p. (ps-2). 1991. 12.95 (ISBN 0-517-57583-3); PLB 13.99 (ISBN 0-517-57584-1). Crown.

Tester, Sylvia R. Sometimes I'm Afraid. Hook, Frances, illus. LC 78-23262. (ps-3) 1979. PLB 12.96 (ISBN 0-89565-021-5). Childs World.

Tompert, Ann. The Tzar's Bird. Rayevsky, Robert, illus. LC 89-31376. 32p. (gr. k-3). 1990. 14.95 (ISBN 0-02-789401-0, Mcmillan Child Bk). Macmillan Child Grp.

Wardlaw, Lee. The Eye & I. Stouffer, Deborah, illus. 75p. (Orig.). 1988. pap. 2.95 (ISBN 0-931093-10-4). Red Hen Pr.

Woods, Audrey. Scaredy Cats. Woods, Audrey, illus. 32p. (ps-2). 1981. 5.50 (ISBN 0-85953-110-4, Pub. by Child's Play England). Childs Play.

Ziefert, Harriet. Good Night' Lewis! Nicklaus, Carol, illus. LC 85-14306. 32p. (ps-2). 1986. pap. 1.95 (ISBN 0-394-87617-2). Random.

FEASTS
see Fasts and Feasts

FEEBLE MINDED
see Mentally Handicapped

FEELING
see Perception; Touch

FEELINGS
see Emotions

FEET
see Foot

FELLOWSHIPS
see Scholarships, Fellowships, Etc.

FELONY
see Crime and Criminals

FEMINISM
see also Women'S Rights

Carabillo, Toni & Meuli, Judith. The Feminization of Power. Smeal, Eleanor, intro. by. (Illus). 166p. (Orig.). (gr. 8-12). 1988. pap. 8.95 (ISBN 0-929037-02-2). Fund Feminist Majority.

Hanmer, Trudy J. Taking a Stand Against Sexism & Sex Discrimination. (Illus). 144p. (gr. 9-12). 1990. PLB 13.40 (ISBN 0-531-10962-3). Watts.

Henry, Sondra & Taitz, Emily. Betty Friedan: Fighter for Women's Rights. 128p. (gr. 6 up) 1990. 17.95 (ISBN 0-89490-292-X). Enslow Pubs.

Hinding, Andrea, ed. Feminism: Opposing Viewpoints. LC 86-3096. (Illus). 250p. (Orig.). (gr. 9 up). 1986. PLB 15.95 (ISBN 0-89908-388-9); pap. 8.95 (ISBN 0-89908-363-3). Greenhaven.

Schneir, Miriam, ed. Feminism. (gr. 9-12). 1971. pap. 7.95 (ISBN 0-394-71738-4, Vin). Random.

Smith, Karina. Women in Protest. (Illus). 75p. (gr. 7-11). 1991. 19.95 (ISBN 0-7134-6223-X, Pub. by Batsford UK). Trafalgar Sq.

Taylor-Boyd, Susan. Betty Friedan. LC 90-9691. (Illus). 64p. (gr. 5-6). 1990. PLB 12.95 (ISBN 0-8368-0104-0). Gareth Stevens Inc.

FENCING
Thomas, Art. Fencing Is for Me. Sheehan-Burke, Julia, illus. LC 81-20716. 48p. (gr. 2-5). 1982. PLB 8.95 (ISBN 0-8225-1129-0). Lerner Pubns.

FERMENTATION
see also Bacteriology

FERRIES
Conrad, Pam. Taking the Ferry Home. LC 87-45856. 224p. (gr. 7 up). 1990. 3.25 (ISBN 0-06-447011-3, Trophy). HarpC Child Bks.

FERRIES–FICTION
Maestro, Betsy. Ferryboat. Maestro, Giulio, illus. LC 85-47887. 32p. (ps-3). 1986. 12.95 (ISBN 0-690-04519-0, Crowell Jr Bks); PLB 12.89 (ISBN 0-690-04520-4). HarpC Child Bks.

FESTIVALS
see also Fasts and Feasts; Holidays; Pageants

Crews, Donald. Carousel. Crews, Donald, illus. LC 82-3062. 32p. (ps-1). 1982. PLB 13.88 (ISBN 0-688-00909-3). Greenwillow.

Weilerstein, Sadie R. What the Moon Brought. (Illus). 159p. (gr. 1-3). 1942. pap. 7.95 (ISBN 0-8276-0265-0). JPS Phila.

Wersba, Barbara. The Carnival in My Mind. LC 81-48640. 224p. (gr. 7 up). 1982. PLB 12.89 (ISBN 0-06-026410-1). HarpC Child Bks.

FESTIVALS–FICTION
Abler, David A. & Natti, Susanna. Cam Jansen & Mystery Carnival Prize. LC 84-3617. (Illus). 64p. (gr. 2-5). 1984. pap. 10.95 (ISBN 0-670-20034-4). Viking Child Bks.

Dorros, Arthur. Tonight Is Carnaval. Club De Madres Virgen Del Carmen Staff, illus. LC 90-32391. 32p. (ps-3). 1991. 13.95 (ISBN 0-525-44641-9, DCB). Dutton Child Bks.

Hall, Lynn. A Killing Freeze. LC 88-5143. 128p. (gr. 7 up). 1988. 12.95 (ISBN 0-688-07867-2). Morrow Jr Bks.

Potter, Beatrix. The Tale of Jemima Puddle-duck. (Illus). 64p. 1984. pap. 1.75 (ISBN 0-486-24634-5). Dover.

Wheels Go Round. (Illus). 24p. (gr. k-2). 1982. 6.95 (ISBN 0-448-01452-1, G&D). Putnam Pub Group.

FESTIVALS–JEWS
see Fasts and Feasts–Judaism

FEUDALISM
see also Chivalry; Middle Ages

Jones, Madeline. Knights & Castles. (Illus). 72p. (gr. 7-11). 1991. 19.95 (ISBN 0-7134-6352-X, Pub. by Batsford UK). Trafalgar Sq.

FEVER
see also names of fevers, e.g. malaria, etc.

FIBERS
see also Cotton; Paper; Silk

FICTION–HISTORY AND CRITICISM
Fabian, William M. Fiction Finder Manual. (gr. 4-12). 1984. 6.95 (ISBN 0-916625-08-7). Computer Assis.

Greenwald, Sheila. It All Began with Jane Eyre: Or, the Secret Life of Franny Dillman. 128p. (gr. 5 up) 1981. pap. 1.75 (ISBN 0-440-94136-9, LE). Dell.

FICTION–TECHNIQUE
Asher, Sandy. Where Do You Get Your Ideas? Hellard, Susan, illus. 96p. (gr. 5 up). 1987. 12.95 (ISBN 0-8027-6690-0); PLB 13.85 (ISBN 0-8027-6691-9). Walker & Co.

Polette, Nancy. U. S. Historical Fiction: A Whole Language Approach. (Illus). 48p. (gr. 5-8). 1990. pap. 5.95 (ISBN 0-913839-85-X). Bk Lures.

FICTITIOUS ANIMALS
see Animals, Mythical

FIEFS
see Feudalism

FIELD ATHLETICS
see Track Athletics

FIELD SPORTS
see Hunting; Sports

FIESTAS
see Fasts and Feasts

FIGHTER PLANES
Cave, Ron & Cave, Joyce. What about...Fighters. West, David, illus. 32p. (gr. k-3). 1983. PLB 10.90 (ISBN 0-531-03468-2). Watts.

Emert, Phyllis. Fighter Planes. (Illus). 64p. (gr. 5-9). 1990. PLB 12.98 (ISBN 0-671-68959-2); pap. 5.95 (ISBN 0-671-68964-9). Messner.

Lowe, Malcolm V. Fighters. Sarson, Peter, et al, illus. LC 84-7941. 48p. (gr. 5 up). 1985. PLB 9.95 (ISBN 0-8225-1376-5, First Ave Edns); pap. 4.95 (ISBN 0-8225-9506-0, First Ave Edns). Lerner Pubns.

Messenger, Charles. Combat Aircraft. (Illus). 48p. (gr. 6 up). 1984. PLB 11.90 (ISBN 0-531-04867-5). Watts.

Stein, R. Conrad. Fighter Planes. LC 85-30890. (Illus). 48p. (gr. 4-8). 1986. PLB 14.60 (ISBN 0-516-04766-3). Childrens.

Sullivan, George. Modern Fighter Planes. 128p. (gr. 6-10). Date not set. lib. bdg. 17.95x (ISBN 0-8160-2352-2). Facts on File.

FIGHTING
see Battles; Boxing; Bullfights; Fencing; Self-Defense; War

FIGURE SKATING
see Skating

FIJI ISLANDS
Ball, John & Fairclough, Chris. Fiji. (Illus). (gr. 5 up). 1988. 14.95 (ISBN 0-222-00984-5). Chelsea Hse.

FILLING STATIONS
see Automobiles–Service Stations

FINANCE
see also Banks and Banking; Commerce; Credit; Finance, Personal; Insurance; Investments; Money; Stock Exchange

Buhay, Debra. Black & White of Finance. 30p. (gr. 12). Date not set. pap. 2.00 (ISBN 1-878056-02-6). D Hockenberry.

Lubov, Andrea. Taxes & Government Spending. (Illus). 88p. (gr. 5 up). 1990. 15.95 (ISBN 0-8225-1777-9). Lerner Pubns.

FINANCE, PERSONAL
see also Insurance; Investments

Berry, Joy. Every Kid's Guide to Making & Managing Money. Bartholemew, illus. 48p. (gr. 3-7). 1987. 4.95 (ISBN 0-516-21405-5); PLB 14.60 (ISBN 0-516-01405-6). Childrens.

Berry, Joy W. What to Do When Your Mom or Dad Says..."Earn Your Allowance" Bartholemew, illus. Berry, Joy W., intro. by. LC 81-83791. (Illus). 48p. (gr. 3-7). 1982. 4.98 (ISBN 0-941510-03-4). Living Skills.

Burkett, Larry. Get a Grip on Your Money - Student: A Teen Study in Financial Management. Haystead, Wes, ed. Slonim, David, illus. 128p. (gr. 9-12). 1990. pap. text ed. 4.95 (ISBN 0-929608-92-5). Focus Family.

—Get a Grip on Your Money - Student Text: A Teen Study in Christian Financial Management. Haystead, Wes, ed. Slonim, David, illus. 136p. (Orig.). (gr. 9-12). 1990. pap. text ed. 4.95 (ISBN 0-929608-75-5). Focus Family.

—Get a Grip on Your Money - Teacher's Guide: A Teen Study in Christian Financial Management. Haystead, Wes, ed. Slonim, David, illus. 116p. (Orig.). (gr. 9-12). 1990. pap. text ed. 10.95 (ISBN 0-929608-74-7). Focus Family.

—Get a Grip on Your Money: A Teen Study in Financial Management. Haystead, Wes, ed. Slonim, David, illus. 112p. 1990. pap. text ed. 12.95 (ISBN 0-929608-91-7). Focus Family.

—Surviving the Money Jungle - Student Workbook: A Junior High Study in Handling Money. Haystead, Wes, ed. Day, Bruce, illus. 72p. (Orig.). (gr. 7-9). 1990. pap. text ed. 4.95 (ISBN 0-929608-77-1). Focus Family.

Canario, Jack. Be Ad-Wise. (Illus). 64p. (gr. 7-12). 1983. pap. 3.95 (ISBN 0-915510-54-5). Janus Bks.

Chan, Janis F. Pay by Check. (Illus). 64p. (gr. 7-12). 1981. pap. 3.95 (ISBN 0-915510-52-9). Janus Bks.

Drew, Bonnie J. & Drew, O. Noel. Fast Cash for Kids. (Illus). 168p. (Orig.). (gr. 4-9). 1987. pap. 9.95 (ISBN 0-939445-01-8). Homeland Pubns.

Kelsey & Gundlach. More for Your Money. (Illus). 64p. (gr. 7-12). 1981. pap. 3.95 (ISBN 0-915510-53-7). Janus Bks.

Long, J., ed. Budgeting Know-How. 48p. (gr. 4-5). 1988. pap. text ed. write for info. (ISBN 0-8428-7172-1). Cambridge Bk.

Marsh, Carole. A Kid's Book of Smarts: How to Think, Make Decisions, Figure Things Out, Budget Your Time, Money, Plan Your Day, Week, Life & Other Things Adults Wish They'd Learned When They Were Kids! (Illus). 68p. (gr. 4-12). 1983. PLB 19.95 (ISBN 1-55609-173-7); pap. 14.95 (ISBN 0-935326-18-9). Gallopade Pub Group.

Schwartz, David M. If You Made a Million. Kellogg, Steven, illus. LC 88-12819. 40p. (gr. 1-5). 1989. 14.95 (ISBN 0-688-07017-5); PLB 14.88 (ISBN 0-685-22780-4). Lothrop.

Stine, Jane & Stine, Jovial B. Everything You Need to Survive: Money Problems. Murdocca, Sal, illus. LC 82-23117. 96p. (gr. 5-9). 1983. pap. 1.95 (ISBN 0-394-85247-8). Random.

Sullivan, Mick. Spare Time Cash: Every Student's Guide to Making Money on the Side. Moe, Mary, ed. 114p. (Orig.). (gr. 10 up). 1989. pap. 12.95 (ISBN 1-878330-00-4). Sullivan MT.

Temple, Todd. How to Become a Teenage Millionaire. 204p. (Orig.). (gr. 9-12). 1991. pap. 8.95 (ISBN 0-8407-9579-3). Oliver-Nelson.

Wilkinson, Elizabeth. Making Cents: Every Kid's Guide to Money, Vol. 1. 1989. 14.95 (ISBN 0-316-94101-8); pap. 8.95 (ISBN 0-316-94102-6). Little.

Wilson, Rachel. Master Your Money. (Illus). 64p. (gr. 7-12). 1981. pap. 3.95 (ISBN 0-915510-51-0). Janus Bks.

FINANCIERS
see Capitalists and Financiers

FINGER PLAY
Un Arana Encantadora - Spider Magic. LC 90-62626. (Illus). 12p. 1991. bds. 5.95 incl. finger puppet (ISBN 1-877779-21-0). Schneider Educational.

Brown, Marc. Finger Rhymes. LC 80-10173. (Illus). 32p. (ps-2). 1980. 11.95 (ISBN 0-525-29732-4, DCB). Dutton Child Bks.

Cahill, Chris. Un Conejito Encantador - Bunny Magic. LC 90-62627. (Illus). 12p. 1991. bds. 5.95 incl. finger puppet (ISBN 1-877779-20-2). Schneider Educational.

—Un Osito Encantador - Bear Magic. LC 90-62628. (Illus). 12p. 1991. bds. 5.95 incl. finger puppet (ISBN 1-877779-19-9). Schneider Educational.

Grayson, Marion. Let's Do Fingerplays. Weyl, Nancy, illus. LC 62-10217. (ps-3). 1962. 12.95 (ISBN 0-88331-003-1). Luce.

Lindsay, Vachel. Una Tortuga Encantadora - Turtle Magic. LC 90-62625. (Illus). 12p. 1991. bds. 5.95 incl. finger puppet (ISBN 1-877779-22-9). Schneider Educational.

Self, Margaret, compiled by. Two Hundred Two Things to Do. LC 68-16267. (Illus., Orig.). (gr. k-2). 1968. pap. 3.95 (ISBN 0-8307-0026-9, 5001102). Regal.

Weimer, Tonja E. Fingerplays & Action Chants: Animals, Vol. 1. Kozlina, Yvonne, illus. 42p. (Orig.). (gr. k-1). 1986. pap. text ed. 8.95 (ISBN 0-936823-00-3); cassette 8.95 (ISBN 0-936823-01-1). Pearce Evetts.
Tonja Evetts Weimer is that rare combination - a truly remarkable teacher who has the talent to transfer her magic with young children, into materials for others to use. The two volumes of Fingerplays & Chants (Vol. 1, Animals; Vol. 2, Family & Friends) are jewels. Each book is extensively illustrated, with all the words & actions to do each fingerplay. The audio cassettes that complement the books are full of humor, sound effects & Tonja's special voice. Identical sequence in tape & book allows children to follow the book as they hear the tape - & so encourages learning of pre-reading skills. Tonja Weimer's other materials include two Creative Dance & Music Videos: FROLICKING FROGS (ISBN 0-936823-10-0) $19.95 & RHYMES & RAINBOWS (ISBN 0-936823-09-7) $19.95. These delightful 30 minute videos each contain an illustrated story, folksongs & fingerplays. The videos foster the natural creativity of young children as they teach, & encourage each child to do their best. Children from two to six simply LOVE them. For more information on her materials please call 1-800-842-9571.
Publisher Provided Annotation.

—Fingerplays & Action Chants: Family & Friends, Vol. 2. Kozlina, Yvonne, illus. 44p. (Orig.). (ps-1). 1986. pap. text ed. 8.95 (ISBN 0-936823-02-X); cassette 8.95 (ISBN 0-936823-03-8). Pearce Evetts.

FINGERPRINTS

Ahouse, Jeremy J. Fingerprinting. Bergman, Lincoln & Fairwell, Kay, eds. Klofkorn, Lisa, illus. Hoyt, Richard, photos by. (Illus.). 38p. (Orig.). (gr. 4-8). 1987. pap. 6.50 (ISBN 0-912511-21-4). Lawrence Science.

Fingerprinting. 36p. (gr. 6-12). 1983. pap. 1.85 (ISBN 0-8395-3287-3, 3287). BSA.

FINLAND

Hintz, Martin. Finland. LC 82-17856. (Illus.). 128p. (gr. 5-9). 1983. PLB 25.27 (ISBN 0-516-02764-6). Childrens.

Lander, Patricia S. & Charbonneau, Claudette. The Land & People of Finland. LC 88-27144. (Illus.). 224p. (gr. 6 up). 1990. 14.95 (ISBN 0-397-32357-3, Lipp Jr Bks); PLB 14.89 (ISBN 0-397-32358-1, Lipp Jr Bks). HarpC Child Bks.

Sanes, Alan. Finland. (Illus.). (gr. 5 up). 1988. 14.95 (ISBN 0-222-01037-1). Chelsea Hse.

FINLAND–FICTION

Sharp, Mary & Niemi, Matt. Bobbi, Father of the Finnish White Tailed Deer. Shappell, Sherry, illus. LC 79-54100. (Orig.). (gr. 4-6). 1979. pap. 5.95 (ISBN 0-9603200-0-8). Bobbi Ent.

FIR

Andersen, Hans Christian. The Fir Tree. Burkert, Nancy E., illus. LC 73-121800. 48p. (gr. 3-6). 1970. 13.95 (ISBN 0-06-020077-4); PLB 13.89 (ISBN 0-06-020078-2). HarpC Child Bks.

Fischer-Nagel, Heiderose & Fischer-Nagel, Andreas. Fir Trees. Fischer-Nagel, Heidrose & Fischer-Nagel, Andreas, photos by. (Illus.). 48p. (gr. 2-5). 1989. 12.95 (ISBN 0-87614-340-0). Carolrhoda Bks.

FIRE

see also Fires; Fuel; Heat

Fire. (Illus.). 48p. (gr. 2-6). 1987. PLB 17.32 (ISBN 0-8172-3254-0); pap. 9.27 (ISBN 0-8172-3279-6). Raintree Pubs.

Knapp, Brian. Fire. LC 89-11423. (Illus.). 48p. (gr. 5-9). 1990. PLB 17.28 (ISBN 0-8114-2377-8). Steck-V.

Parramon, J. M. & Vendrell, C. S. El Fuego. (SPA.). 32p. (ps). 1985. pap. 3.95 (ISBN 0-8120-3619-0). Barron.

Petty, Kate. Fire. (Illus.). 32p. (gr. k-4). 1990. PLB 11.90 (ISBN 0-531-14060-1). Watts.

Van Laan, Nancy. Rainbow Crow. Vidal, Beatriz, illus. LC 88-12967. 40p. (ps-3). 1989. 12.95 (ISBN 0-394-89577-0); lib. bdg. 13.99 (ISBN 0-394-99577-5). Knopf.

FIRE–FICTION

Bauer, Marion D. Rain of Fire. LC 83-2065. 160p. (gr. 4-8). 1983. 13.95 (ISBN 0-89919-190-8, Clarion). HM.

Brown, Lynn. Fire & Firecrackers. 3rd ed. Walker, Granville, Jr., ed. Jackson, Gregory A., illus. 14p. (Orig.). (ps-6). 1982. pap. 2.97x (ISBN 0-9608466-1-1). Fun Reading.

Eichelberger, Rosa K. Big Fire in Baltimore. LC 78-31311. (Illus.). (gr. 3 up). 1979. pap. 7.95 (ISBN 0-916144-37-2). Stemmer Hse.

Hooks, William H. Circle of Fjre. LC 82-3982. 144p. (gr. 5-9). 1982. 12.95 (ISBN 0-689-50241-9, M K McElderry). Macmillan Child Grp.

FIRE BALLS

see Meteors

FIRE DEPARTMENTS

Bundt, Nancy. The Fire Station Book. Bundt, Nancy, illus. LC 80-16617. 32p. (gr. k-4). 1981. PLB 9.95 (ISBN 0-87614-126-2). Carolrhoda Bks.

Williams, Brenda. Fighting a Fire. MacDonald, Andrew, illus. LC 87-4643. 32p. (ps-1). 1987. 3.95 (ISBN 0-394-89187-2, Random Juv); lib. bdg. 7.99 (ISBN 0-394-99187-7, Random Juv). Random.

Wolf, Bernard. Firehouse. LC 83-1174. 96p. (gr. 5 up). 1983. 11.95 (ISBN 0-688-01734-7); PLB 11.88 (ISBN 0-688-01735-5, Morrow Jr Bks). Morrow Jr Bks.

FIRE ENGINES

Barrett, Norman. Picture World of Fire Engines. LC 90-31035. (Illus.). 32p. (gr. k-4). 1991. PLB 11.40 (ISBN 0-531-14091-1). Watts.

Bracken, Carolyn, illus. Fast Rolling Fire Trucks. (ps). 1984. 5.95 (ISBN 0-448-09876-8, G&D). Putnam Pub Group.

Bushey, Jerry. Building a Fire Truck. Bushey, Jerry, illus. LC 81-6182. 32p. (gr. k-4). 1981. PLB 9.95 (ISBN 0-87614-170-X). Carolrhoda Bks.

Marston, Hope I. Fire Trucks. (Illus.). 64p. (gr. k-3). 1984. 11.95 (ISBN 0-396-08451-6, Putnam). Putnam Pub Group.

Rockwell, Anne. Fire Engines. Rockwell, Anne, illus. (ps-1). 1986. 12.95 (ISBN 0-525-44259-6, DCB). Dutton Child Bks.

Slater, Teddy. All Aboard Fire Trucks. (Illus.). 32p. (ps-2). 1991. pap. 1.95 (ISBN 0-448-34360-6, G&D). Putnam Pub Group.

FIRE ENGINES–FICTION

Fowler, Richard. Mr. Little's Noisy Fire Engine. (Illus.). 20p. 1990. 11.95 (ISBN 0-448-40042-1, G&D). Putnam Pub Group.

Greydanus, Rose. Un Carro De Bomberos Grande y Rojo. Harvey, Paul, illus. (SPA.). 32p. (gr. k-2). 1981. PLB 7.06 (ISBN 0-89375-555-9); pap. 1.95 (ISBN 0-685-04944-2). Troll Assocs.

Haywood, Carolyn. Eddie & the Fire Engine. Haywood, Carolyn, illus. LC 49-9873. 192p. (gr. 1-5). 1949. PLB 12.88 (ISBN 0-688-31252-7). Morrow.

Kraus, Robert. Freddy the Fire Engine. Kraus, Robert, illus. 18p. (ps). 1985. 3.50 (ISBN 0-448-10219-6, G&D). Putnam Pub Group.

Smith, Dennis. Little Fire Engine That Saved the City. 1990. 9.95 (ISBN 0-385-26257-4). Doubleday.

FIRE ENGINES–HISTORY

Hatmon, Paul W. Yesterday's Fire Engines. LC 80-11158. (Illus.). 48p. (gr. 4-9). 1980. PLB 9.95 (ISBN 0-8225-0430-8). Lerner Pubns.

FIRE EXTINCTION

see also Fire Engines

Broekel, Ray. Fire Fighters. LC 81-7655. (Illus.). 48p. (gr. k-4). 1981. PLB 14.60 (ISBN 0-516-01620-2); pap. 4.95 (ISBN 0-516-41620-0). Childrens.

Chlad, Dorothy. Cuando hay un incendio sal para afuera. Kratky, Lada, tr. from ENG. Halverson, Lydia, illus. LC 85-9636. (SPA.). 32p. (ps-2). 1984. lib. bdg. 14.60 (ISBN 0-516-31986-8); pap. 3.95 (ISBN 0-516-51986-7). Childrens.

Gibbons, Gail. Fire! Fire! LC 83-46162. (Illus.). 40p. (gr. k-4). 1984. 13.95 (ISBN 0-690-04417-8, Crowell Jr Bks); PLB 12.89 (ISBN 0-690-04416-X). HarpC Child Bks.

Hannum, Dotti. A Visit to the Fire Station. Holmes, Dave & Markson, Sue, illus. LC 84-12155. 32p. (gr. k-3). 1985. PLB 14.60 (ISBN 0-516-01491-9); pap. 3.95 (ISBN 0-516-41491-7). Childrens.

FIRE ISLAND–FICTION

Estes, Eleanor. Pinky Pye. Ardizzone, Edward, illus. LC 58-5708. (gr. 4-6). 1958. 10.95 (ISBN 0-15-262076-1, HJ). HarBraceJ.

FIRE PREVENTION

see also Fire Extinction;
also names of cities with the subdivision Fires and Fire Prevention, e.g. Chicago–Fires and Fire Prevention, etc.

Bester, Roger. Fireman Jim. Bester, Roger, photos by. LC 81-9694. (Illus.). 32p. (gr. k-3). 1987. 9.95 (ISBN 0-517-54290-0). Crown.

Chlad, Dorothy. Cuando hay un incendio sal para afuera. Kratky, Lada, tr. from ENG. Halverson, Lydia, illus. LC 85-9636. (SPA.). 32p. (ps-2). 1984. lib. bdg. 14.60 (ISBN 0-516-31986-8); pap. 3.95 (ISBN 0-516-51986-7). Childrens.

De Leeuw, Hendrik, et al. Fireproof Children Education Kit. (Illus.). 308p. (gr. k-6). 1990. 99.95 (ISBN 0-9626076-1-4). Natl Fire Serv Support Systs.

Firemanship. (Illus.). 72p. (gr. 6-12). 1987. pap. 1.85 (ISBN 0-8395-3317-9, 3317). BSA.

Franklin, Herb. Fireman Fred's, Fire Safety Coloring Book. Miller, Jackie, illus. 8p. (gr. 1-5). 1990. pap. 0.50 (ISBN 0-945145-02-0). Miller Family Pubns.

Maas, Robert. Fire Fighters. Maas, Robert, photos by. (Illus.). 32p. (gr. k-3). 1989. pap. 12.95 (ISBN 0-590-41459-3). Scholastic Inc.

Morrison, Ellen E. Guardian of the Forest: A History of the Smokey Bear Program. 2nd, rev. ed. LC 89-60719. (Illus.). 144p. (gr. 6). 1989. 12.95 (ISBN 0-9622537-3-1). Morielle Pr.

FIRE PREVENTION–FICTION

Cox, Mike, et al. Fire Drill. Wasserman, Dan, ed. Reese, Bob, illus. (gr. k-1). 1979. PLB 7.95 (ISBN 0-89868-071-9); pap. 2.95 (ISBN 0-89868-082-4). ARO Pub.

Leonard, Marcia. Jeffrey Lee, Future Fireman. Brook, Bonnie, ed. Chambliss, Maxie & Iosa, Ann, illus. LC 90-31299. 24p. (ps-1). 1990. 4.95 (ISBN 0-671-70407-9); lib. bdg. 9.98 (ISBN 0-671-70403-6). Silver Pr.

FIREARMS

Colby, C. B. Civil War Weapons: Small Arms, & Artillery of the Blue & Gray. (Illus.). (gr. 4-7). 1962. PLB 6.99 (ISBN 0-698-30046-7, Coward). Putnam Pub Group.

Harris, Jack C. Gun Control. (Illus.). 48p. (gr. 4 up). 1990. 10.95 (ISBN 0-89686-493-6, Crestwood Hse). Macmillan Child Grp.

Hawkes, Nigel. Gun Control. FS-Aladdin Staff, ed. Hayward, Ron, illus. LC 88-50524. 32p. (gr. 4-9). 1988. PLB 11.90 (ISBN 0-531-17111-6, Gloucester Pr). Watts.

Horton, et al. Amazing Fact Book of Weapons. (Illus.). 32p. 1987. 11.95 (ISBN 0-88682-170-3). Creative Ed.

Landau, Elaine. Armed America. (Illus.). 128p. (gr. 6 up). 1991. lib. bdg. 12.98 (ISBN 0-671-72386-3); pap. 5.95 (ISBN 0-671-72387-1). Messner.

O'Sullivan, Carol. Gun Control: Distinguishing Between Fact & Opinion. (Illus.). 32p. (gr. 3-6). 1990. PLB 8.95 (ISBN 0-89908-638-1). Greenhaven.

Rowland-Entwhistle, Theodore. Guns. Caulkins, Janet, ed. (Illus.). 32p. (gr. 1-6). 1988. PLB 8.99 (ISBN 0-531-18209-6, Pub. by Bookwright Pr). Watts.

Strahinich, Helen. Guns in America. 160p. (gr. 7 up). 1991. PLB 15.85 (ISBN 0-8027-8104-7); pap. 8.95 (ISBN 0-8027-7356-7). Walker & Co.

FIREARMS–HISTORY

Colby, C. B. Two Centuries of Weapons: 1776-1976. LC 75-10459. (Illus.). 48p. (gr. 4-7). 1976. PLB 6.99 (ISBN 0-698-30596-5, Coward). Putnam Pub Group.

FIREFLIES

Brinckloe, Julie. Fireflies! Brinckloe, Julie, illus. LC 84-20158. 32p. (gr. k-2). 1985. 12.95 (ISBN 0-02-713310-9, Mcmillan Child Bk). Macmillan Child Grp.

Edwards, Roger. Max Science & the Glowing Firefly. Sanchez, Brenda L., ed. Beard, Derrick, illus. 26p. (gr. k-5). 1991. pap. 3.95 (ISBN 1-879350-01-7). Max Sci Pub.

Hawes, Judy. Fireflies in the Night. LC 63-15088. (Illus.). (gr. k-3). 1963. pap. 4.95 (ISBN 0-690-01259-4, Crowell Jr Bks). HarpC Child Bks.

Johnson, Sylvia A. Fireflies. Kuribayashi, Satoshi, illus. 48p. (gr. 4 up). 1986. PLB 14.95 (ISBN 0-8225-1485-0). Lerner Pubns.

Ryder, Joanne. Fireflies. Bolognese, Don, illus. LC 76-58695. 64p. (gr. k-3). 1977. PLB 9.89 (ISBN 0-06-025154-9). HarpC Child Bks.

Yajima, Minoru. The Firefly. Pohl, Kathy, ed. LC 85-28193. (Illus.). 32p. (gr. 3-7). 1986. pap. text ed. 16.67 (ISBN 0-8172-2535-8); pap. text ed. 9.27 (ISBN 0-8172-2560-9). Raintree Pubs.

FIREFLIES–FICTION

Swartzentruber. God Made the Firefly. 1976. 2.45 (ISBN 0-686-18186-7). Rod & Staff.

FIREMEN

Bornstein, Harry. Fire Fighter Brown. Tom, Linda C., illus. 16p. (ps). 1976. pap. 3.50 (ISBN 0-913580-50-3, Pub. by K Green Pubns). Gallaudet Univ Pr.

Elliott, Dan. A Visit to the Sesame Street Firehouse. Mathieu, Joe, illus. LC 83-4606. 32p. (ps-3). 1983. lib. bdg. 5.99 (ISBN 0-394-96029-7); pap. 2.25 (ISBN 0-394-86029-2). Random.

Hankin, Rebecca. I Can Be a Fire Fighter. LC 84-29282. (Illus.). 32p. (gr. k-3). 1985. lib. bdg. 13.93 (ISBN 0-516-01847-7); pap. 3.95 (ISBN 0-516-41847-5). Childrens.

Hepworth, R. Firefighters. (Illus.). 32p. (gr. 4 up). Date not set. PLB 14.00 (ISBN 0-86592-412-0). Rourke Corp.

Here Comes the Firemen, 2 vols. in 1. (ps-1). 1990. 3.99 (ISBN 0-517-69585-5). Outlet Bk Co.

Johnson, Jean. Firefighters: A to Z. Johnson, Jean, photos by. LC 85-5348. (Illus.). 39p. (gr. 1-3). 1985. 11.95 (ISBN 0-8027-6589-0); PLB 11.85 (ISBN 0-8027-6590-4). Walker & Co.

Marion, Kenneth P. Volunteer Firefighter. Beyer, Beverly, illus. 32p. (ps-2). 1990. pap. 4.00 (ISBN 0-945878-00-1). JK Pub.

Pellowski, Michael J. Fire Fighter. Lawn, John, illus. LC 88-10353. 32p. (gr. k-2). 1989. PLB 10.89 (ISBN 0-8167-1428-2); pap. text ed. 2.50 (ISBN 0-8167-1429-0). Troll Assocs.

Puedo Ser Bombero: (I Can Be a Firefighter) LC 84-29282. (SPA & ENG.). (gr. k-3). 1989. PLB 13.93 (ISBN 0-516-31847-0); pap. 3.95 (ISBN 0-516-51847-X). Childrens.

Smith, Betsy. A Day in the Life of a Firefighter. Noren, Catherine, photos by. LC 80-54099. (Illus.). 32p. (gr. 4-8). 1980. PLB 11.79 (ISBN 0-89375-444-7); pap. 2.95 (ISBN 0-89375-445-5); cassettes avail. Troll Assocs.

FIREMEN–FICTION

Brown, Margaret W. The Little Fireman. Slobodkina, Esphyr, illus. LC 84-43127. 40p. 1952. 11.95 (ISBN 0-201-09261-1). HarpC Child Bks.

Godfrey, Martyn. Fire! Fire! 96p. (gr. 7-12). 1986. pap. text ed. 4.50 (ISBN 0-8219-0233-4, 35360); 1.20 (ISBN 0-8219-0234-2, 35719). EMC.

Seymour, Peter. Fire Fighters. (ps-3). 1990. 12.95 (ISBN 0-525-67295-8, Lodestar Bks). Dutton Child Bks.

Zokeisha. Firehouse. Klimo, Kate, ed. Zokeisha, illus. 16p. (ps-k). 1983. 2.95 (ISBN 0-671-46128-1, Little Simon). S&S Trade.

FIRES

see also Fire Extinction; Fire Prevention; Forest Fires

Chlad, Dorothy. When There Is a Fire Go Outside. LC 81-18018. (Illus.). (gr. k-3). 1982. PLB 14.60 (ISBN 0-516-01986-4); pap. 3.95 (ISBN 0-516-41986-2). Childrens.

Fradin, Dennis. Disaster! Fires. LC 82-9404. (Illus.). (gr. 3 up). 1982. PLB 17.27 (ISBN 0-516-00855-2). Childrens.

Gibbons, Gail. Fire! Fire! Gibbons, Gail, illus. LC 83-46162. 40p. (gr. k-4). 1987. pap. 4.95 (ISBN 0-06-446058-4, Trophy). HarpC Child Bks.

Kent, Zachary. The Story of the Triangle Factory Fire. LC 88-36223. (Illus.). 32p. (gr. 3-6). 1989. PLB 13.27 (ISBN 0-516-04742-6); pap. 3.95 (ISBN 0-516-44742-4). Childrens.

Scollins, Richard, illus. The Fire of London. LC 88-5054. 32p. (gr. 3-6). 1989. PLB 10.90 (ISBN 0-531-18237-1, Pub. by Bookwright Pr). Watts.

FIRES–FICTION

Laster, Jim. The Birthday Gift That Beeped. Knight, George, ed. Erwin, Julie, illus. LC 83-176266. 56p. (gr. k-4). 1983. 10.95 (ISBN 0-9612780-0-5). J Laster Pub Co.

Robinet, Harriette G. Children of the Fire. LC 91-9484. 144p. (gr. 4-7). 1991. 13.95 (ISBN 0-689-31655-0, Atheneum Child Bk). Macmillan Child Grp.

FIREWORKS–FICTION

Brown, Lynn. Fire & Firecrackers. 3rd ed. Walker, Granville, Jr., ed. Jackson, Gregory A., illus. 14p. (Orig.). (ps-6). 1982. pap. 2.97x (ISBN 0-9608466-1-1). Fun Reading.

FIRST AID

Boy Scouts of America. First Aid. (Illus.). 96p. (gr. 6-12). 1988. pap. 1.85 (ISBN 0-8395-3276-8, 3276A). BSA.

Carter, Sharon, et al. Coping with Medical Emergencies. rev. ed. 121p. (gr. 7-12). 1988. lib. bdg. 12.95 (ISBN 0-8239-0782-1). Rosen Group.

Chaback, Elaine & Fortunato, Pat. The Official Kids' Survival Kit: How to Do Things on Your Own. (gr. 4 up). 1981. pap. 10.95 (ISBN 0-316-13531-3). Little.

Cole, Joanna. Cuts, Breaks, Bruises, & Burns: How Your Body Heals. Kelley, True, illus. LC 84-45335. 48p. (gr. 2-6). 1985. 12.95 (ISBN 0-690-04437-2, Crowell Jr Bks); PLB 12.89 (ISBN 0-690-04438-0). HarpC Child Bks.

Gilbert, Sara. Get Help: Solving the Problems in Your Life. Friedman, Ellen, illus. LC 88-32352. 144p. (gr. 5 up). 1989. 12.95 (ISBN 0-688-08010-3); pap. 6.95 (ISBN 0-688-08928-3, Pub. by Beech Tree Bks). Morrow Jr Bks.

Greeley, Sheila. S.T.A.R. Junior First Aid. Strong, Susan, illus. 32p. (gr. k-5). 1989. write for info. spiral bdg. FAFCTPC.

Kittredge, Mary. Emergency Medicine & First Aid. 112p. (gr. 6 up). 1991. PLB 18.95 (ISBN 0-7910-0063-X). Chelsea Hse.

Richardson, Joy. What Happens When You Hurt Yourself? LC 86-3678. (Illus.). 32p. (gr. 2-3). 1986. PLB 10.95 (ISBN 1-55532-107-0). Gareth Stevens Inc.

Snyder, Carol. Dear Mom & Dad, Don't Worry. (gr. 7 up). 1989. 13.95 (ISBN 0-553-05801-0, Starfire). Bantam.

Ward, Brian R. First Aid. (Illus.). 48p. (gr. 4-12). 1987. PLB 12.40 (ISBN 0-531-10260-2). Watts.

FISH

see Fishes

FISH CULTURE

Selsam, Millicent E. & Hunt, Joyce. A First Look at Fish. Springer, Harriet, illus. LC 72-81377. 32p. (gr. 2-4). 1972. PLB 9.85 (ISBN 0-8027-6120-8). Walker & Co.

Waters, John F. Sea Farmers. LC 71-98059. (Illus.). 128p. (gr. 6-9). 1970. PLB 8.95 (ISBN 0-8038-6690-9). Hastings.

Wax, Wendy. Inside the Aquarium. Murray, Joe, illus. 32p. 1989. 12.95 (ISBN 0-8092-4357-1, Calico Bks). Contemp Bks.

FISH HATCHERIES

see also Fish Culture

FISHERIES

Here are entered works on the fishing industry.

see also Fishes

Fish. (Illus.). 20p. (gr. k up). 1990. laminated, wipe clean surface 3.95 (ISBN 0-88679-820-5). Educ Insights.

Illustrated Encyclopedia of Wildlife, Vol. 10: The Fishes. 304p. (gr. 7 up). 1990. lib. bdg. write for info. (ISBN 1-55905-046-2). Grey Castle.

Klein, John F. & Gaskin, Carol. A Day in the Life of a Commercial Fisherman. Klein, John F., illus. LC 87-10949. 32p. (gr. 4-8). 1988. PLB 11.79 (ISBN 0-8167-1109-7); pap. text ed. 2.95 (ISBN 0-8167-1110-0). Troll Assocs.

Lionni, Leo. Fish Is Fish. LC 78-117452. (Illus.). 32p. (ps-6). 1974. pap. 2.95 (ISBN 0-394-82799-6). Knopf.

New England Aquarium Staff & Kaufman, Les. Do Fishes Get Thirsty? Questions Answered by the New England Aquarium. (Illus.). 40p. (gr. 5 up). 1991. 12.95 (ISBN 0-531-15214-6). Watts.

Rogers, Daniel. Food from the Sea. (Illus.). 32p. (gr. 5-8). 1991. RLB 11.90 (ISBN 0-531-18388-2, Pub. by Boatwright Pr). Watts.

FISHERIES–FICTION

Fox, Paula. Blowfish Live in the Sea. (gr. 6-8). 1991. 16.50 (ISBN 0-8446-6449-9). Peter Smith.

Himmelman, John. Ellen & the Goldfish. Himmelman, John, illus. LC 89-34475. 32p. (ps-3). 1990. 12.95 (ISBN 0-06-022416-9); PLB 12.89 (ISBN 0-06-022417-7). HarpC Child Bks.

Sharmat, Marjorie W. Nate the Great & the Fishy Prize. (gr. k-6). 1988. pap. 2.99 (ISBN 0-440-40039-2, YB). Dell.

Whittle, Emily. The Fisherman's Tale. Burdick, Jeri, illus. 32p. 1988. 10.95 (ISBN 0-88138-101-2). Green Tiger Pr.

FISHES

see also Aquariums; Fish Culture; Fisheries; Fishing; Tropical Fish;

also names of fishes, e.g. Salmon, etc.

Animals, Birds & Fish. (Illus.). (ps-5). 3.50 (ISBN 0-7214-8003-9); wkbk. B 1.95. Ladybird Bks.

Armstrong, B. Fishes. 32p. (gr. 1-6). 1988. 3.95 (ISBN 0-88160-163-2, LW 268). Learning Wks.

Arnosky, Jim. Freshwater Fish & Fishing. 1989. pap. 2.75 (ISBN 0-590-41730-4). Scholastic Inc.

Bender, Lionel. Fish to Reptiles. Franklin Watts Ltd., ed. Khan, Aziz, illus. 40p. (gr. 7-9). 1988. PLB 12.40 (ISBN 0-531-17093-4, Gloucester Pr). Watts.

Braithwaite, Althea. Fish. (ps-6). 1988. PLB 7.95 (ISBN 0-88462-182-0); pap. 2.95 (ISBN 0-88462-183-9). Dearborn Finan.

Broekel, Ray. Dangerous Fish. LC 82-4464. (gr. k-4). 1982. 14.60 (ISBN 0-516-01635-0); pap. 4.95 (ISBN 0-516-41635-9). Childrens.

Carson, Patti & Dellosa, Janet. Fish Fun Book. Carson, Patti & Dellosa, Janet, illus. 32p. (ps-2). 1984. pap. 1.59 (ISBN 0-88724-013-5, CD-8012). Carson-Dellos.

Cole, Joanna. A Fish Hatches. LC 78-13445. (Illus.). (gr. k-3). 1978. PLB 12.88 (ISBN 0-688-32153-4, Morrow Jr Bks). Morrow Jr Bks.

Cross, Frank B. & Collins, Joseph T. Illustrated Guide to Fishes in Kansas. Robertson, Jeanne L., illus. 14p. (gr. 4-6). 1976. pap. 1.00 (ISBN 0-89338-000-8). U of KS Mus Nat Hist.

Doan, Kenneth. Fish. Osen, Richard, illus. 40p. (Orig.). (gr. 2-6). 1990. pap. 4.95 (ISBN 0-920534-41-4, Pub. by Hyperion Pr Ltd CN). Sterling.

Eastman, David. What Is a Fish? Sweat, Lynn, illus. LC 81-11373. 32p. (gr. k-2). 1982. lib. bdg. 10.89 (ISBN 0-89375-660-1); pap. text ed. 2.95 (ISBN 0-89375-661-X). Troll Assocs.

Evanoff, Vlad. A Complete Guide to Fishing. rev. ed. LC 80-2251. (Illus.). (gr. 7 up). 1981. PLB 12.89 (ISBN 0-690-04091-1, Crowell Jr Bks). HarpC Child Bks.

Fish. (Illus.). 20p. (gr. k up). 1990. laminated, wipe clean surface 3.95 (ISBN 0-88679-820-5). Educ Insights.

Fitzsimons, Cecilia. My First Fishes & Other Waterlife: Pop-Up Field Guide. Fitzsimons, Cecilia, illus. LC 86-45489. 12p. (gr. k-4). 1987. 8.95 (ISBN 0-06-021873-8). HarpC Child Bks.

Freedman, Russell. Killer Fish. LC 81-85089. (Illus.). 40p. (gr. 1-4). 1982. reinforced bdg. 12.95 (ISBN 0-8234-0449-8). Holiday.

Halton, Cheryl M. Those Amazing Eels. (Illus.). 112p. (gr. 4 up). 1990. PLB 12.95 (ISBN 0-87518-431-6, Dillon). Macmillan Child Grp.

Harris, Jack C. A Step-by-Step Book about Guppies. (Illus.). 64p. (gr. 9-12). 1988. pap. 3.95 (ISBN 0-86622-464-5, SK-035). TFH Pubns.

Hornblow, Leonora & Hornblow, Arthur. Fish Do the Strangest Things. Frith, Michael K., illus. (ps-3). 1966. 5.95 (ISBN 0-394-80062-1, Random Juv); lib. bdg. 8.99 (ISBN 0-394-90062-6). Random.

—Fish Do the Strangest Things. Eggert, John F., illus. LC 88-30202. 64p. (gr. 2-4). 1990. lib. bdg. 6.99 (ISBN 0-394-94309-0); pap. 3.95 (ISBN 0-394-84309-6). Random.

Horton, et al. Amazing Fact Book of Fish. (Illus.). 32p. 1987. 11.95 (ISBN 0-685-23225-5). Creative Ed.

Joseph, James, et al. Tuna & Billfish: Fish Without a Country. 2nd ed. Mattson, George, illus. Revelle, Roger, intro. by. LC 80-81889. (Illus.). 53p. (Orig.). (gr. 7-12). 1980. pap. 7.95 (ISBN 0-9603078-1-8). Inter-Am Tropical.

Keller, Gunter. A Step-by-Step Book about Discus. (Illus.). 64p. (gr. 9-12). 1988. pap. 3.95 (ISBN 0-86622-465-3, SK-008). TFH Pubns.

Ling, Mary. Amazing Fish. Young, Jerry, photos by. LC 90-49651. (Illus.). 32p. (Orig.). (gr. 1-5). 1991. PLB 9.99 (ISBN 0-679-91516-8); pap. 6.95 (ISBN 0-679-81516-3). Knopf.

Losito, Linda, et al. Fish. (Illus.). 96p. 1989. 17.95x (ISBN 0-8160-1966-5). Facts on File.

McPherson, Mark. Caring for Your Fish. Bernstein, Marianne, illus. LC 84-8563. 48p. (gr. 3-7). 1985. PLB 9.89 (ISBN 0-8167-0109-1); pap. text ed. 2.95 (ISBN 0-8167-0110-5). Troll Assocs.

Mitchell, Victor. Fish. Mitchell, Victor, illus. 16p. (gr. k up). 1988. pap. 1.95 (ISBN 0-7459-1468-3). Lion USA.

Noel, Spike. Fish & the Sea. (Illus.). 64p. (gr. 7 up). 1972. 14.95 (ISBN 0-7136-1239-8). Dufour.

Overbeck, Cynthia. The Fish Book. Lerner, Sharon, illus. LC 78-7205. 32p. (gr. k-3). 1978. PLB 7.95 (ISBN 0-8225-1110-X). Lerner Pubns.

Parker, Steve. Fish. King, Dave & Keates, Colin, photos by. LC 89-36445. (Illus.). 64p. (gr. 5 up). 1990. 15.00 (ISBN 0-679-80439-0); PLB 14.99 (ISBN 0-679-90439-5). McKay.

Pierce, Q. L. Find the Mistakes Science: Fantastic Fish. (gr. 4-7). 1991. pap. 2.95 (ISBN 0-8431-2816-X). Price Stern.

Pohl, Kathleen. Killifish. (Illus.). 32p. (gr. 3-7). 1986. PLB 16.67 (ISBN 0-8172-2720-2); pap. 9.27 (ISBN 0-8172-2738-5). Raintree Pubs.

—Stickleback Fish. (Illus.). 32p. (gr. 3-7). 1986. PLB 16.67 (ISBN 0-8172-2722-9); pap. text ed. 9.27 (ISBN 0-8172-2740-7). Raintree Pubs.

Pope, Joyce. Taking Care of Your Fish. Franklin Watts Ltd., ed. (Illus.). 32p. (gr. 7-9). 1990. PLB 10.90 (ISBN 0-531-10192-4); pap. 3.95 (ISBN 0-531-15167-0). Watts.

Quinn, Kaye. Look at Fish. Quinn, Kaye, illus. 40p. (gr. 2-6). 1986. pap. 2.50 (ISBN 0-8431-1891-1). Price Stern.

Ricciuti, Edward R. Donald & the Fish That Walked. Hoff, Syd, illus. LC 74-2609. 64p. (gr. k-3). 1974. 6.95 (ISBN 0-06-024997-8). HarpC Child Bks.

Sabin, Louis. Fish. Helmer, Jean C., illus. LC 84-2624. 32p. (gr. 3-6). 1985. PLB 9.49 (ISBN 0-8167-0178-4); pap. text ed. 2.95 (ISBN 0-8167-0179-2). Troll Assocs.

Seafood. (Illus.). (gr. 5 up). lib. bdg. 15.93 (ISBN 0-86592-265-9). Rourke Corp.

Segaloff, Nat & Erickson, Paul. Fish Tales. LC 89-26279. (Illus.). 32p. 1990. 12.95 (ISBN 0-8069-7322-6); PLB 15.69 (ISBN 0-8069-7323-4). Sterling.

Spizzirri, Linda, ed. Prehistoric Fish: Educational Coloring Book. (Illus.). 32p. (gr. 1-8). 1981. pap. 1.95 (ISBN 0-86545-021-8). Spizzirri.

Spizzirri Publishing Co. Staff & Spizzirri, Linda. Deep-Sea Fish: An Educational Coloring Book. (Illus.). 32p. (gr. k-5). 1985. pap. 1.95 (ISBN 0-86545-064-1). Spizzirri.

Stewart, Frances T. & Stewart, Charles P., III. Fishes & Other Sea Creatures in Their Environments. Koss, Martin R., Jr., illus. LC 87-45853. 22p. (ps up). 1988. sticker book 7.95 (ISBN 0-694-00256-9). HarpC Child Bks.

Stratton, Barbara R. What Is a Fish? (Illus.). 32p. (gr. k-4). 1991. 12.95 (ISBN 0-531-15223-5); PLB 12.90 (ISBN 0-531-11020-6). Watts.

Sutton, Felix. Fish. Koehler, Cynthia & Koehler, Alvin, illus. (gr. 4-6). pap. 2.95 (ISBN 0-8431-4270-7). Price Stern.

Takeuchi, Hiroshi. The World of Fishes. Pohl, Kathy, ed. LC 85-28212. (Illus.). 32p. (gr. 3-7). 1986. PLB 16.67 (ISBN 0-8172-2548-X); pap. text ed. 9.27 (ISBN 0-8172-2573-0). Raintree Pubs.

Tate, Suzanne. Billy Bluefish: A Tale of Big Blues. Melvin, James, illus. LC 88-92517. 28p. (Orig.). (gr. k-3). 1988. pap. 3.95 (ISBN 0-9616344-4-8). Nags Head Art.

Wheeler, Alwyne. Discovering Saltwater Fish. Caulkins, Janet, ed. (Illus.). 48p. (gr. k-6). 1988. PLB 11.90 (ISBN 0-531-18171-5, Pub. by Bookwright Pr). Watts.

Wiessinger, John. Fish, Frogs & Snakes - Right Before Your Eyes. LC 89-1511. (Illus.). 64p. (gr. 4-10). 1989. PLB 15.95 (ISBN 0-89490-265-2). Enslow Pubs.

Wildsmith, Brian. Fishes. (Illus.). 32p. 1987. 11.95 (ISBN 0-19-279639-9); pap. 5.95 (ISBN 0-19-272151-8). Oxford U Pr.

FISHES–FICTION

Brown, Margaret W. The Fish with the Deep Sea Smile: Stories & Poems for Reading to Young Children. LC 87-26227. (Illus.). 128p. (ps-3). 1988. Repr. of 1938 ed. PLB 18.00 (ISBN 0-208-02193-0, Linnet). Shoe String.

Bush, John. The Fish Who Could Wish. Paul, Korky, illus. 32p. (ps-3). 1991. 12.95 (ISBN 0-916291-35-9). Kane-Miller Bk.

Byars, Betsy. Two-Thousand-Pound Goldfish. (gr. 4-6). 1983. pap. 2.50 (ISBN 0-590-40224-2, Apple Paperbacks). Scholastic Inc.

—The Two-Thousand-Pound Goldfish. 160p. (gr. 4-6). 1988. pap. 2.50 (ISBN 0-590-40562-4). Scholastic Inc.

—The Two-Thousand-Pound Goldfish. 160p. (gr. 3-7). 1991. pap. 2.75 (ISBN 0-590-42368-1). Scholastic Inc.

Cazet, Denys. A Fish in His Pocket. Cazet, Denys, illus. LC 87-5462. 32p. (ps-2). 1987. 13.95 (ISBN 0-531-05713-5); PLB 13.99 (ISBN 0-531-08313-6). Orchard Bks Watts.

Clements, Andrew. Big Al. 2nd ed. Yoshi, illus. LC 88-15129. 32p. (gr. k up). 1990. Repr. of 1988 ed. 4.95 (ISBN 0-88708-154-1). Picture Bk Studio.

Cohen, Barbara. The Carp in the Bathtub. Halpern, Joan, illus. 48p. (gr. 1-5). 1972. PLB 13.88 (ISBN 0-688-51627-0). Lothrop.

Dr. Seuss. One Fish Two Fish Red Fish Blue Fish. Dr. Seuss, illus. 64p. (ps-1). 1987. pap. 6.95 incl. cassette (ISBN 0-394-89224-0, Random Juv). Random.

Ehlert, Lois. Fish Eyes: A Book You Can Count On. Ehlert, Lois, illus. 1990. 14.95 (ISBN 0-15-228050-2). HarbraceJ.

Farrington, S. Kip. Tony the Tuna. (gr. 4-5). 1976. 6.95 (ISBN 0-911660-25-9). Yankee Peddler.

Fayville, Barry. Stanley's Aquarium. 152p. (gr. 7 up). 1990. jacketed 14.95 (ISBN 0-19-558197-0). Oxford U Pr.

Fish Stew. (Illus.). (gr. 5 up). 1990. pap. 3.50. Ladybird Bks.

Fontenot, Mary A. Clovis Crawfish & Etienne Escargot. Vincent, Eric, illus. LC 84-18895. 32p. (gr. k-6). 1982. 11.95 (ISBN 0-88289-368-8). Pelican.

—Clovis Crawfish & His Friends. rev. ed. Graves, Keith, illus. LC 85-16994. 32p. (gr. k-6). 1985. 11.95 (ISBN 0-88289-479-X). Pelican.

George, William T. & George, Lindsay B. Fishing at Long Pond. LC 89-77514. (Illus.). 24p. (ps up). 1991. 13.95 (ISBN 0-688-09401-5); PLB 13.88 (ISBN 0-688-09402-3). Greenwillow.

Gomi, Taro. Where's the Fish? Gomi, Taro, illus. LC 85-15282. 32p. (ps-k). 1986. 11.95 (ISBN 0-688-06241-5); lib. bdg. 11.88 (ISBN 0-688-06242-3, Morrow Jr Bks). Morrow Jr Bks.

Graeber, Charlotte. In, Out & about Catfish Pond. Stockman, Jack, illus. (gr. 1-4). 1984. 4.95 (ISBN 0-89191-841-8); pap. 3.95 (ISBN 0-89191-798-5). Cook.

Huan Ching & the Golden Fish. (Illus.). 32p. (gr. 2-4). 1988. Incl. audio cassette. PLB 27.99 (ISBN 0-8172-2466-1). Raintree Pubs.

Kalan, Robert. Blue Sea. Crews, Donald, illus. LC 78-18396. 24p. (gr. k-3). 1979. 14.95 (ISBN 0-688-80184-6); PLB 14.88 (ISBN 0-688-84184-8). Greenwillow.

Lionni, Leo. Fish Is Fish. Lionni, Leo, illus. LC 78-117452. (gr. k-3). 1970. lib. bdg. 13.99 (ISBN 0-394-90440-0). Pantheon.

Littledale, Freya. The Magic Fish. Pels, Winslow P., illus. 32p. (Orig.). (gr. k-3). 1986. pap. 2.50 (ISBN 0-590-41100-4). Scholastic Inc.

Luenn, Nancy. Nessa's Fish. Waldman, Neil, illus. LC 89-10548. 32p. (gr. k-3). 1990. SBE 13.95 (ISBN 0-689-31477-9, Atheneum Child Bk). Macmillan Child Grp.

Maddern, Eric. Curious Clownfish. (ps-3). 1990. 14.95 (ISBN 0-316-48894-1, Joy St Bks). Little.

Moskowitz, Stewart. Patchwork Fish Tale. Klimo, Kate, ed. Moskowitz, Stewart, illus. 32p. 1982. 4.95 (ISBN 0-671-45327-0, Little Simon). S&S Trade.

Niedergeses, Catherine. Peter the Ship Eater. LC 88-51703. (Illus.). 44p. (gr. k-3). 1988. pap. 5.95 (ISBN 1-55523-210-8). Winston-Derek.

Palmer, Helen. A Fish Out of Water. LC 61-9579. (Illus.). 72p. (ps-3). 1961. 6.95 (ISBN 0-394-80023-0); lib. bdg. 7.99 (ISBN 0-394-90023-5). Beginner.

Reese, Bob. Ocean Fish School. LC 82-23572. (Illus.). 24p. (ps-2). 1983. PLB 11.27 (ISBN 0-516-02314-4); pap. 2.95 (ISBN 0-516-42314-2). Childrens.

—Oola Oyster. LC 82-23609. (Illus.). 24p. (ps-2). 1983. PLB 11.27 (ISBN 0-516-02311-X); pap. 2.95 (ISBN 0-516-42311-8). Childrens.
—Spongee Sponge. LC 82-23608. (Illus.). 24p. (ps-2). 1983. PLB 11.27 (ISBN 0-516-02315-2); pap. 2.95 (ISBN 0-516-42315-0). Childrens.
Reeser, Michael. Huan Ching & the Golden Fish. Sakahara, Dick, illus. 32p. (gr. 2-4). 1988. PLB 16.67 (ISBN 0-8172-2751-2). Raintree Pubs.
Schatell, Brian. Midge & Fred. Schatell, Brian, illus. LC 82-48540. 32p. (ps-2). 1983. 8.61i (ISBN 0-397-32046-9, Lipp Jr Bks). HarpC Child Bks.
Stowell, Gordon. Ana. Lerin, S. D., tr. from ENG. (Illus.). 24p. (gr. 1). 1981. pap. 0.75 (ISBN 0-311-38512-5, Edit Mundo). Casa Bautista.
Super, Terri, illus. A Fish & a Frog. 10p. (ps). 1984. vinyl bk. 2.95 (ISBN 0-448-41226-8, G&D). Putnam Pub Group.
Tate, Suzanne. Flossie Flounder: A Tale of Flat Fish. Melvin, James, illus. LC 88-92679. 28p. (Orig.). (gr. k-3). 1989. pap. 3.95 (ISBN 0-9616344-5-6). Nags Head Art.
—Flossie Flounder: Un Cuento Del Pez Chato. LC 90-61962. (Illus.). 28p. (Orig.). (gr. k-3). 1990. pap. 4.95 (ISBN 1-878405-01-2). Nags Head Art.
—Lucky Lookdown: A Tale of a Funny Fish. Melvin, James, illus. LC 89-92221. 28p. (Orig.). (gr. k-3). 1989. pap. 3.95 (ISBN 0-9616344-8-0). Nags Head Art.
—Sammy Shrimp: A Tale of a Little Shrimp. Melvin, James, illus. LC 90-61002. 28p. (Orig.). (gr. k-3). 1990. pap. 3.95 (ISBN 1-878405-00-4). Nags Head Art.
—Spunky Spot: A Tale of One Smart Fish. Melvin, James, illus. LC 88-63784. 28p. (Orig.). (gr. k-3). 1989. pap. 3.95 (ISBN 0-9616344-6-4). Nags Head Art.
—Spunky Spot: Un Cuento De Un Pez Inteligente. LC 90-61966. (Illus.). 28p. (Orig.). (gr. k-3). 1990. pap. 4.95 (ISBN 1-878405-02-0). Nags Head Art.
Tubby, I. M., pseud. I'm a Little Fish. LC 81-51113. (Illus.). 10p. (ps up). 1982. pap. 2.95 vinyl (ISBN 0-671-44435-2, Little Simon). S&S Trade.
Wylie, Joanne. Un Cuento Curioso de Colores. Kratky, Lada, tr. from ENG. Wylie, David, illus. LC 83-7448. (SPA.). 32p. (ps-2). 1984. lib. bdg. 14.60 (ISBN 0-516-32983-9); pap. 3.95 (ISBN 0-516-52983-8). Childrens.
—Un Cuento de un Pez Grande. Kratky, Lada, tr. from ENG. Wylie, David, illus. LC 83-7449. (SPA.). 32p. (ps-2). 1984. lib. bdg. 14.60 (ISBN 0-516-32982-0); pap. 3.95 (ISBN 0-516-52982-X). Childrens.
Wylie, Joanne & Wylie, David. A Big Fish Story. LC 83-7449. (Illus.). 32p. (ps-2). 1983. PLB 14.60 (ISBN 0-516-02982-7); pap. 3.95 (ISBN 0-516-42982-5). Childrens.
—A Fishy Alphabet Story. LC 83-7510. (Illus.). 32p. (ps-2). 1983. PLB 14.60 (ISBN 0-516-02981-9); pap. 3.95 (ISBN 0-516-42981-7). Childrens.
—A Fishy Color Story. LC 83-7448. (Illus.). 32p. (ps-2). 1983. PLB 14.60 (ISBN 0-516-02983-5); pap. 3.95 (ISBN 0-516-42983-3). Childrens.
—A Fishy Shape Story. Wylie, David, illus. LC 83-25222. 32p. (ps-2). 1984. lib. bdg. 14.60 (ISBN 0-516-02985-1); pap. 3.95 (ISBN 0-516-42985-X). Childrens.
—A Funny Fish Story. Wylie, David, illus. LC 83-24058. 32p. (ps-2). 1984. lib. bdg. 14.60 (ISBN 0-516-02986-X); pap. 3.95 (ISBN 0-516-42986-8). Childrens.
Yorinks, Arthur. Louis the Fish. Egielski, Richard, illus. LC 80-16855. 32p. (ps up). 1980. 13.95 (ISBN 0-374-34658-5). FS&G.
—Louis the Fish. Egielshi, Richard, illus. 32p. (ps up). 1986. pap. 3.95 (ISBN 0-374-44598-2). FS&G.

FISHING

Arnosky, Jim. Fish in a Flash! A Personal Guide to Spin-Fishing. LC 90-45832. (gr. 4-9). 1991. 14.95 (ISBN 0-02-705854-9, Bradbury Pr). Macmillan Child Grp.
—Freshwater Fish & Fishing. LC 81-12520. (Illus.). 64p. (gr. 3-7). 1984. 12.95 (ISBN 0-02-705850-6, Four Winds). Macmillan Child Grp.
—Freshwater Fish & Fishing. 1989. pap. 2.75 (ISBN 0-590-41730-4). Scholastic Inc.
Bailey, Donna. Fishing. LC 90-9958. (Illus.). 32p. (gr. 1-4). 1990. PLB 14.64 (ISBN 0-8114-2851-6). Steck-V.
Broughton, Bruno. Fishing. (Illus.). 32p. (gr. k-4). 1991. RLB 11.40 (ISBN 0-531-18432-3, Pub. by Boatwright Pr). Watts.
Civardi, A. & Rashbrook, F. The KnowHow Book of Fishing: A Simple Guide to Making Tackle & Catching Fish. (Illus.). 32p. (gr. 3-6). 1977. pap. 5.95 (ISBN 0-86020-032-9). EDC.
Connett, Eugene V. Fishing a Trout Stream. 2nd ed. Smith, Lawrence, photos by. (Illus.). 138p. (gr. 10 up). Repr. of 1934 ed. 35.00 (ISBN 0-685-37778-4). Derrydale Pr.
Craig, Janet. Fisherman. Eitzen, Allan, illus. LC 88-10045. 32p. (gr. k-2). 1989. PLB 10.89 (ISBN 0-8167-1438-X); pap. text ed. 2.50 (ISBN 0-8167-1439-8). Troll Assocs.
Evanoff, Vlad. A Complete Guide to Fishing. rev. ed. LC 80-2251. (Illus.). (gr. 7 up). 1981. PLB 12.89 (ISBN 0-690-04091-1, Crowell Jr Bks). HarpC Child Bks.
Ferrell, Nancy W. The Fishing Industry. (Illus.). 72p. (gr. 4-8). 1984. lib. bdg. 10.40 (ISBN 0-531-04823-3). Watts.
Fishing. (Illus.). 80p. (gr. 6-12). 1988. pap. 1.85 (ISBN 0-8395-3295-4, 3295). BSA.
Gibbons, Gail. Surrounded by Sea: Life on a New England Fishing Island. (ps-3). 1991. 14.95 (ISBN 0-316-30961-3). Little.
Haker, Loren F. The Li'l Rascals: Tale of a Fish. Haker, Loren F., illus. 66p. (gr. 1-8). 1984. 7.95 (ISBN 0-9609964-2-7); pap. 4.95 (ISBN 0-9609964-3-5). Haker Books.
Hausherr, Rosmarie. The City Girl Who Went to Sea. Hausherr, Rosmarie, illus. LC 89-27236. 80p. (gr. 3-6). 1990. 14.95 (ISBN 0-02-743421-4, Four Winds). Macmillan Child Grp.
Randolph, John. Fishing Basics. Seiden, Art, illus. 48p. (gr. 3-7). 1985. pap. 4.95 (ISBN 0-13-319732-8). P-H.
Scarry, Huck. Life on a Fishing Boat: A Sketchbook. LC 83-9631. (Illus.). 72p. (gr. 3-5). 1983. 10.95 (ISBN 0-13-535856-6). P-H.
Sobol, Donald J. Encyclopedia Brown's Book of the Wacky Outdoors. (Orig.). (gr. 5 up). 1988. pap. 2.50 (ISBN 0-553-15599-9). Bantam.
Thomas, Art. Fishing Is for Me. LC 80-13442. (Illus.). 48p. (gr. 2-5). 1980. PLB 8.95 (ISBN 0-8225-1096-0). Lerner Pubns.

FISHING–FICTION

Abolafia, Yossi. A Fish for Mrs. Gardenia. LC 87-17907. (Illus.). 32p. (gr. k-3). 1988. 11.95 (ISBN 0-688-07467-7); lib. bdg. 11.88 (ISBN 0-688-07468-5). Greenwillow.

Bozanich, Tony L. Captain Flounder, His Sole Brothers & Friends. Isaksen, Lisa A., ed. Isaksen, Patricia, illus. 16p. (ps-4). 1984. pap. 4.95 (ISBN 0-930655-00-1). Antarctic Pr.
Who is Captain Flounder? Skipper Tony L. Bozanich has created this famous flatfish fisherman who finds his life's reward on the bottom of the sea. This enchanting fish story, a series of rhymes which capture the true spirit of the sea, is a delightful children's book entitled "Captain Flounder, His Sole Brothers & Friends". With salty characters colorfully illustrated by Lisa A. Isaksen, Captain Flounder comes alive in an underwater wonderland for kids to explore! Bozanich, owner & skipper of the purse seiner "Antarctic", has been on the water for over 50 years. He has fished the Pacific Coastal waters from Alaska to California but calls the Puget Sound his home. He has a wealth of information, stories, & anecdotes about the high times & the disastrous times of fishing. His experience of the sea enables him to create this salty story now being read & enjoyed by all ages.
Publisher Provided Annotation.

Carlson, Nancy. Loudmouth George & the Fishing Trip. LC 82-22159. (Illus.). 32p. (ps-3). 1983. PLB 9.95 (ISBN 0-87614-213-7). Carolrhoda Bks.
—Loudmouth George & the Fishing Trip. LC 84-18119. (Illus.). 32p. (ps-3). 1985. pap. 3.95 (ISBN 0-14-050508-3, Puffin). Puffin Bks.
—Loudmouth George & the Fishing Trip. Carlson, Nancy, illus. (gr. k-3). 1986. pap. 12.95 incl. cassette (ISBN 0-87499-017-3); PLB incl. cassette 19.95 (ISBN 0-87499-019-X); write for info. incl. cassette, 4 paperbacks guide (ISBN 0-87499-018-1). Live Oak Media.
Delacre, Lulu. Nathan's Fishing Trip. (Illus.). 1988. pap. 12.95 (ISBN 0-590-41281-7). Scholastic Inc.
—Nathan's Fishing Trip. (ps-2). 1989. pap. 2.50 (ISBN 0-590-41282-5). Scholastic Inc.
Ferguson, Susan Y. Uncle Lester's Lemonade Lure. Ferguson, Susan Y., illus. 15p. (Orig.). 1988. lib. bdg. write for info. (ISBN 0-9621556-0-8). SYF Enter.
Gilmartin, Thelma. What Happens to Me When I Fish the Sea & a Fish Catches Me. Barton, Kent, illus. LC 76-12929. 36p. (Orig.). (gr. 1-3). 1976. pap. 2.95 (ISBN 0-89317-009-7). Windward Pub.
Goffstein, M. B. Fish for Supper. LC 75-27598. (Illus.). 32p. (gr. k-2). 1976. PLB 8.89 (ISBN 0-8037-2572-8). Dial Bks Young.
Gray, Catherine & Gray, James. Tammy & the Gigantic Fish. Joyce, William, illus. LC 82-47732. 32p. (ps-1). 1991. pap. 4.95 (ISBN 0-06-443263-7, Trophy). HarpC Child Bks.
Gray, Catherine D. & Gray, James. Tammy & the Gigantic Fish. Williams, illus. LC 82-47732. 32p. (ps-2). 1983. PLB 12.89 (ISBN 0-685-06177-9). HarpC Child Bks.
Heller, Nicholas. Fish Stories. Heller, Nicholas, illus. LC 86-14906. 24p. (gr. k-3). 1987. 11.75 (ISBN 0-688-06931-2); PLB 11.88 (ISBN 0-688-06932-0). Greenwillow.
Henckel, Mark. Sis' Revenge: Oh Brother, This Is Fishing. Walton, Jeri D., ed. Potter, John, illus. 32p. (ps-2). 1989. pap. 4.95 (ISBN 0-945960-03-4). Outlaw MT.
Hertz, Ole. Tobias Catches Trout. Tobias, Tobi, tr. from DAN. Hertz, Ole, illus. LC 83-27224. 32p. (gr. k-3). 1984. PLB 7.95 (ISBN 0-87614-263-3). Carolrhoda Bks.
—Tobias Goes Ice Fishing. Tobias, Tobi, tr. from DAN. Hertz, Ole, illus. LC 83-26356. 32p. (gr. k-3). 1984. PLB 7.95 (ISBN 0-87614-260-9). Carolrhoda Bks.
Kidd, Nina. June Mountain Secret. Kidd, Nina, illus. LC 90-31574. 32p. (gr. k-3). 1991. 14.95 (ISBN 0-06-023167-X); PLB 14.89 (ISBN 0-06-023168-8). HarpC Child Bks.
Kipling, Rudyard. Captains Courageous. (gr. 6 up). 1964. pap. 1.75 (ISBN 0-8049-0027-2, CL-27). Airmont.
Lisle, Janet T. The Lampfish of Twill. Halperin, Wendy A., illus. LC 91-8279. 176p. (gr. 5 up). 1991. 15.95 (ISBN 0-531-05963-4); RLB 15.99 (ISBN 0-531-08563-5). Orchard Bks Watts.
Long, Earlene R. Gone Fishing. Brown, Richard, illus. LC 83-22558. 32p. (ps-3). 1987. 13.95 (ISBN 0-395-35570-2, 5-90090); pap. 3.95 (ISBN 0-395-44236-2). HM.
McCloskey, Robert. Burt Dow: Deep-Water Man. McCloskey, Robert, illus. LC 68-364. 64p. (gr. 4-6). 1963. pap. 15.95 (ISBN 0-670-19748-3). Viking Child Bks.
—Burt Dow, Deep-Water Man. (Illus.). 64p. (ps-3). 1989. pap. 4.95 (ISBN 0-14-050978-X, Puffin). Puffin Bks.
Maris, Ron. Bernard's Boring Day. 1990. 12.95 (ISBN 0-385-29948-6). Doubleday.
Real, Rory. The Fishing Derby. (Illus.). 32p. (ps-3). 1990. pap. 3.95 (ISBN 0-8120-4394-4). Barron.

Roe, JoAnn. Marco the Manx Series, 3 bks. Runestrand, Meredith & Mayo, Steve, illus. (gr. k-5). Date not set. Fisherman Cat. PLB 10.95 (ISBN 0-931551-02-1); Alaska Cat. PLB 10.95 (ISBN 0-931551-05-6); Castaway Cat. pap. 5.95 (ISBN 0-931551-03-X); Fisherman Cat. pap. 6.95 (ISBN 0-931551-01-3); Alaska Cat. pap. 6.95 (ISBN 0-931551-04-8). Montevista Pr. "Marco the Manx Series": Each book is a complete story. (1) Castaway Cat, 56 pp, B/W watercolors, color cover, paper only $5.95 (ISBN 0-931551-03-X, 2nd printing). A Manx "city cat," falls off a sailboat, has to survive on an island for the winter. Ocean lore, raccoon fights, eagles. (2) Fisherman Cat, 64 pp, color watercolors, paper $6.95 (ISBN 0-931551-01-3), library binding $10.95 (ISBN 0-931551-02-1). Marco the Manx goes aboard a disabled fishing boat, is trapped below, goes off toward Alaskan fishing grounds. Salmon life cycle, fishing lore. (3) Alaska Cat, 64 pp, color watercolors, paper $6.95 (ISBN 0-931551-04-8); library binding $10.95 (ISBN 0-931551-05-6). Marco's boat is shipwrecked off Sitka, Alaska. Once ashore he encounters bears, is rescued by native children. Totems, etc. Castaway Cat won a national first prize for excellence. Was used in school reading test. Distributors: Pacific Pipeline, 19215 - 66th Avenue South, Kent WA 98032-1171. (206) 872-5523. Alaska News Agency, 325 Potter Street, Anchorage AK 99518. (907) 563-3251. Baker & Taylor, Reno, Momence, etc.
Publisher Provided Annotation.

Stewig, John W., retold by. The Fisherman & His Wife. Tomes, Margot, illus. LC 88-1698. 32p. (gr. k-3). 1988. reinforced bdg. 13.95 (ISBN 0-8234-0714-4). Holiday.
Stock, Catherine. Armien's Fishing Trip. Stock, Catherine & Stock, Catherine, illus. LC 89-3266. 40p. (gr. 1 up). 1990. 13.95 (ISBN 0-688-08395-1); PLB 13.88 (ISBN 0-688-08396-X, Morrow Jr Bks). Morrow Jr Bks.
Stolz, Mary. Go Fish. Cummings, Pat, illus. LC 90-4860. 80p. (gr. 2-6). 1991. 12.95 (ISBN 0-06-025820-9); PLB 12.89 (ISBN 0-06-025822-5). HarpC Child Bks.

Swayne, Dick & Savage, Peter. I Am a Fisherman. LC 77-10977. (Illus.). 32p. (gr. 1-3). 1978. (Lipp Jr Bks); PLB 2.95 (ISBN 0-397-31796-4, JBL-J). HarpC Child Bks.

Ward, Sally G. Punky Goes Fishing. LC 90-35538. (Illus.). 32p. (ps-3). 1991. 11.95 (ISBN 0-525-44681-8, DCB). Dutton Child Bks.

Wichman, Juliet R. Moki Learns to Fish. 1981. pap. 4.75 (ISBN 0-686-86236-8). Kauai Museum.

Wylie, Joanne & Wylie, David. A More or Less Fish Story. Wylie, David, illus. LC 83-25223. 32p. (ps-2). 1984. lib. bdg. 14.60 (ISBN 0-516-02984-3); pap. 3.95 (ISBN 0-516-42984-1). Childrens.

Ziefert, Harriet. A Wish for a Fish. Childers, Argus, illus. LC 89-3976. 24p. (Orig.). (ps-1). 1989. pap. 1.95 (ISBN 0-394-81998-5, Random Juv). Random.

FISHING INDUSTRY

see Fisheries

FLAGS

see also Signals and Signaling

Armbruster, Ann. The American Flag. (Illus.). 64p. (gr. 5-8). 1991. PLB 11.90 (ISBN 0-531-20045-0). Watts.

Boros, Ladislav J. Flagorama: Exploring Our World with Flags. Boros, Ladislav J., illus. LC 73-84143. (gr. 3-10). 1973. pap. 4.50 (ISBN 0-915236-02-8). Focus Quality.

Caudill, Rebecca. Did You Carry the Flag Today, Charley? Grossman, Nancy, illus. LC 66-11422. 94p. (gr. 2-4). 1966. reinforced bdg. 14.95 (ISBN 0-8050-1201-X); pap. 3.95 (ISBN 0-03-086620-0). H Holt & Co.

Crampton, William. Flag. Plomer, Martin & Shone, Karl, illus. LC 88-27174. 64p. (gr. 5 up). 1989. 13.95 (ISBN 0-394-82255-2); PLB 14.99 (ISBN 0-394-92255-7). Knopf.

Fradin, Dennis B. The Flag of the United States. LC 88-15436. (Illus.). 48p. (gr. k-4). 1988. PLB 14.60 (ISBN 0-516-01158-8); pap. 4.95 (ISBN 0-516-41158-6). Childrens.

Gilbert, Charles E., Jr. Flags of Texas. Rice, James, illus. 96p. (gr. 6 up). 1989. 13.95 (ISBN 0-88289-721-7). Pelican.

Mayer, Albert I. Story of Old Glory. LC 79-110036. (Illus.). 32p. (gr. 4-8). 1970. PLB 14.60 (ISBN 0-516-04629-2). Childrens.

Miller, Natalie. Story of the Star-Spangled Banner. Wilde, G., illus. LC 65-1221. (gr. 2-5). 1965. PLB 13.27 (ISBN 0-516-04636-5); pap. 3.95 (ISBN 0-516-44636-3). Childrens.

Parrish, Thomas. The American Flag. LC 72-92156. (Illus.). (gr. 5 up). 1973. 7.95 (ISBN 0-671-65204-4, Little Simon). S&S Trade.

Swanson, June. I Pledge Allegiance. Hanson, Rick, illus. 40p. (gr. k-4). 1990. PLB 9.95 (ISBN 0-87614-393-1). Carolrhoda Bks.

White, D. Flags. (Illus.). 48p. (gr. 3-8). Date not set. PLB 18.60 (ISBN 0-86592-454-6). Rourke Corp.

Williams, Earl P., Jr. What You Should Know about the American Flag. rev. ed. Prosser, Les, illus. Sheads, Scott S., frwd. by. (Illus.). 68p. (gr. 4-6). 1989. pap. text ed. 4.95 (ISBN 0-939631-10-5). Thomas Publications.

FLEAS–FICTION

Lionni, Leo. A Flea Story: I Want to Stay Here! I Want to Go There! Lionni, Leo, illus. LC 77-4322. (ps-2). 1977. Pantheon.

Pellowski, Michael J. No Fleas, Please! Jones, John, illus. LC 85-14066. 48p. (Orig.). (gr. 1-3). 1986. PLB 9.89 (ISBN 0-8167-0608-5); pap. text ed. 2.95 (ISBN 0-8167-0609-3). Troll Assocs.

Wood, Audrey. The Napping House. Wood, Don, illus. LC 83-13035. 32p. (ps-3). 1984. 13.95 (ISBN 0-15-256708-9, HJ). HarBraceJ.

FLEMING, ALEXANDER, SIR, 1881-1955

Tames, Richard. Alexander Fleming. (Illus.). 32p. (gr. 5-8). 1990. PLB 11.90 (ISBN 0-531-14005-9). Watts.

FLIES

McClintock, Mike. Fly Went By. LC 58-9018. (Illus.). (gr. 1-3). 1958. 6.95 (ISBN 0-394-80003-6); lib. bdg. 7.99 (ISBN 0-394-90003-0). Beginner.

FLIGHT

see also Aeronautics

Ardley, Neil. Science Book of Air. (gr. 4-7). 1991. 9.95 (ISBN 0-15-200578-1). HarBraceJ.

Aust, Siegfried. Flight! Free As a Bird. Poppel, Hans, illus. 32p. (gr. 2-5). 1991. PLB 12.95 (ISBN 0-8225-2150-4). Lerner Pubns.

Balibar, Francoise & Maury, Jean-Pierre. How Things Fly. 80p. (gr. 8 up). 1989. pap. 4.95 (ISBN 0-8120-4215-8). Barron.

Berliner, Don. Aerobatics. LC 80-10914. (Illus.). 48p. (gr. 4-9). 1980. PLB 9.95 (ISBN 0-8225-0436-7). Lerner Pubns.

Booth, Eugene. In the Air. LC 77-7984. (Illus.). 24p. (gr. k-3). 1977. PLB 13.32 (ISBN 0-8393-0105-7). Raintree Pubs.

Boyne, Walter J. The Smithsonian Book of Flight for Young People. LC 88-985. 128p. (gr. 3-7). 1988. pap. 10.95 (ISBN 0-689-71212-X, Aladdin). Macmillan Child Grp.

Crews, Donald. Flying. Crews, Donald, illus. LC 85-27022. 32p. (ps-3). 1986. 11.75 (ISBN 0-688-04318-6); PLB 11.88 (ISBN 0-688-04319-4). Greenwillow.

—Flying. LC 85-27022. 32p. (ps-3). 1989. pap. 4.95 (ISBN 0-688-09235-7, Mulberry). Morrow.

Dixon, Malcolm. Flight. LC 90-38122. (Illus.). 48p. (gr. 3-7). 1991. PLB 12.40 (ISBN 0-531-18380-7). Watts.

Fitzpatrick, Julie. In the Air. LC 84-40839. (Illus.). 32p. (gr. 2-5). PLB 9.96 (ISBN 0-382-09060-8). Silver Burdett Pr.

Flight. (Illus.). (gr. 5 up). 3.50 (ISBN 0-7214-0833-8). Ladybird Bks.

Flying. 80p. (gr. k-3). 1983. pap. 13.27 (ISBN 0-8172-2093-3). Raintree Pubs.

Let's Discover Flying. (Illus.). 80p. (gr. k-6). 1986. pap. 13.27 (ISBN 0-8172-2594-3). Raintree Pubs.

Livingston, Myra C. Up in the Air. Fisher, Leonard E., illus. LC 88-23293. 32p. (gr. k-3). 1989. reinforced bdg. 14.95 (ISBN 0-8234-0736-5). Holiday.

Llewellyn, Claire. First Look in the Air. (Illus.). 32p. (gr. 1-2). 1991. PLB 10.95 (ISBN 0-8368-0701-4). Gareth Stevens Inc.

Martin, Ann M. Karen's Plane Trip. 144p. (gr. 2-4). 1991. pap. 2.95 (ISBN 0-590-44834-X). Scholastic Inc.

Miller, Edna. Mousekin's ABC. LC 72-176159. (Illus.). 32p. (gr. k-4). 1972. PLB 11.95 (ISBN 0-13-604125-6). P-H.

Stewart, Frances T. & Stewart, Charles P., III. Flight. Gaadt, George S., illus. LC 86-45757. 10p. (ps up). 1987. 7.95 (ISBN 0-694-00178-3). HarpC Child Bks.

Taylor, Barbara. Air & Flight. (Illus.). 40p. (gr. k-4). 1991. PLB 11.90 (ISBN 0-531-19129-X, Warwick). Watts.

—Air & Flying. (Illus.). 32p. (gr. 5-8). 1991. PLB 11.40 (ISBN 0-531-14183-7). Watts.

Tessendorf, K. C. Wings Around the World: The American World Flight of 1924. (Illus.). 96p. (gr. 4 up). 1991. SBE 14.95 (ISBN 0-689-31550-3, Atheneum Child Bk). Macmillan Child Grp.

Ward, Alan. Flight & Floating. King, Colin, illus. 64p. (gr. 3-6). 1983. pap. 4.95 (ISBN 0-86020-529-0); lib. bdg. 11.96 (ISBN 0-88110-162-1). EDc.

Weston, Graham. In the Air. Wood, Gerald, illus. LC 83-71636. 32p. (gr. 3-6). 1983. PLB 10.90 (ISBN 0-531-04699-0). Watts.

FLIGHT–FICTION

Bantock, Nick. Wings: A Pop-up Book of Things That Fly. Bantock, Nick, illus. LC 90-60979. 12p. (ps-5). 1991. 14.95 (ISBN 0-679-81041-2). Random.

Barrie, James M. Peter Pan. Frank, Josette, adapted by. Goode, Diane, illus. LC 82-13288. 72p. (ps-4). 1983. lib. bdg. 8.99 (ISBN 0-394-95717-2); pap. 8.95 (ISBN 0-394-85717-8). Random.

Brock, Betty. No Flying in the House. Tripp, Wallace, illus. LC 79-104755. 144p. (gr. 2-5). 1982. pap. 3.50 (ISBN 0-06-440130-8, Trophy). HarpC Child Bks.

Durrell, Gerald. The Fantastic Flying Journey. Percy, Graham, illus. (gr. 2 up). 1989. pap. 17.95 (ISBN 0-671-64982-5). S&S Trade.

Eastman, Elizabeth. Fly Beyond the Mountain. Large, Hazel, illus. ii, 18p. (Orig.). (gr. k-4). 1985. pap. 1.49 (ISBN 0-9615959-0-6). JAARS Inc.

Florian, Douglas. Airplane Ride. LC 83-45048. (Illus.). 32p. (ps-2). 1984. 10.53i (ISBN 0-690-04364-3, Crowell Jr Bks). HarpC Child Bks.

Gildemeister, Jerry. The Fancy of Flight. Gildemeister, Jerry & Larson, Tim, illus. LC 90-85379. (gr. 9-12). 1991. 38.50 (ISBN 0-936376-07-4). Bear Wallow Pub.

Gormley, Beatrice. Mail-Order Wings. McCully, Emily A., illus. 176p. (gr. 3-6). 1981. 12.95 (ISBN 0-525-34450-0, DCB). Dutton Child Bks.

Hughes, Shirley. Up & Up. LC 85-24166. (Illus.). 32p. (gr. k-2). 1986. Repr. of 1979 ed. 11.95 (ISBN 0-688-06261-X). Lothrop.

Kveton, Steven P. If I Could Fly. 14p. (Orig.). (ps-6). 1987. pap. text ed. 0.75 (ISBN 0-9616799-1-3). Water St Missouri.

McPhail, David. First Flight. McPhail, David, illus. LC 86-28804. (ps-3). 1987. 13.95i (ISBN 0-316-56323-4, Joy St Bks). Little.

Murphy, Shirley R. Tattie's River Journey. De Paola, Tomie, illus. LC 82-45508. 32p. (ps-3). 1983. 11.95 (ISBN 0-8037-8767-7); PLB 11.89 (ISBN 0-8037-8770-7). Dial Bks Young.

Pevsner, Stella. Lindsay, Lindsay, Fly Away Home. LC 83-2115. 192p. (gr. 6up). 1983. 10.95 (ISBN 0-89919-186-X, Clarion). HM.

Provensen, Alice & Provensen, Martin. The Glorious Flight. (gr. 4-6). 1987. pap. 4.95 (ISBN 0-14-050729-9, Puffin). Puffin Bks.

—The Glorious Flight. (gr. 3-5). 1987. incl. bk. & cassette 19.95 (ISBN 0-87499-062-9); pap. 27.95 incl. 4 bks. & cassette (ISBN 0-87499-063-7); pap. 12.95 incl. bk. & cassette (ISBN 0-87499-061-0). Live Oak Media.

Savage, Deborah. The Flight of the Albatross. (gr. 7 up). 1989. 14.95 (ISBN 0-395-45711-4). HM.

Strodder, Chris. A Sky for Henry. Kennedy, Emilie, illus. 32p. (ps-3). 1985. pap. 4.95 (ISBN 0-931093-03-1). Red Hen Pr.

Woodruff, Elvira. The Wing Shop. Gammell, Stephen, illus. LC 90-55094. 32p. (ps-3). 1991. PLB 14.95 (ISBN 0-8234-0825-6). Holiday.

FLIGHT TO THE MOON

see Space Flight to the Moon

FLIGHT TRAINING

see Airplanes–Piloting

FLIGHTS AROUND THE WORLD

see Aeronautics–Flights

FLOODS–FICTION

Dahlstedt, Marden A. The Terrible Wave: Memorial Edition. Robinson, Charles, illus. LC 72-76687. 125p. (gr. 7 up). 1988. pap. 5.00 (ISBN 0-9621827-0-2). R R Dahlstedt.

Friermood, Elisabeth H. Promises in the Attic. LC 60-12790. (gr. 5-9). 1975. pap. 4.95 (ISBN 0-913428-14-0). Landfall Pr.

Gilson, Jamie. Hobie Hanson, Greatest Hero of the Mall. Riggio, Anita, illus. 160p. (gr. 3-6). 1990. pap. 2.95 (ISBN 0-671-70646-2, Minstrel Bks). PB.

Milton, Hilary. Tornado! 160p. (gr. 4 up). 1983. PLB 12.90 (ISBN 0-531-04542-0). Watts.

Palmer, Bernard & Palmer, Marjorie. The Flood. Webb, Gary A., illus. 32p. (Orig.). (ps-k). 1982. pap. 3.95 (ISBN 0-934998-10-8). Bethel Pub.

Ruckman, Ivy. No Way Out. LC 87-47817. 224p. (gr. 6 up). 1988. 12.95 (ISBN 0-690-04669-3, Crowell Jr Bks); PLB 12.89 (ISBN 0-690-04671-5, Crowell Jr Bks). HarpC Child Bks.

FLOODS

see also Rivers

Fradin, Dennis. Disaster! Floods. LC 82-9402. (Illus.). (gr. 3 up). 1982. PLB 17.27 (ISBN 0-516-00856-0). Childrens.

Knapp, Brian. Flood. LC 89-11437. (Illus.). 48p. (gr. 5-9). 1990. PLB 17.28 (ISBN 0-8114-2374-3). Steck-V.

Micallef, Mary. Floods & Droughts. Micallef, Mary, illus. 48p. (gr. 4-8). 1985. wkbk. 6.95 (ISBN 0-86653-323-0, GA 632). Good Apple.

Waters, John. Flood! LC 90-45371. (Illus.). 48p. (gr. 5-6). 1991. RSBE 10.95 (ISBN 0-89686-596-7, Crestwood Hse). Macmillan Child Grp.

FLORA

see Botany; Plants

FLORAL DECORATION

see Flower Arrangement

FLORAL DESIGN

see Design, Decorative

FLORIDA

Bertsch, Aida C. & Bertsch, Werner J. Florida: Educational & Historical Coloring Book. (Illus.). 24p. (Orig.). (gr. 1-6). 1989. pap. 2.99 (ISBN 1-877833-01-0). Pro Pub Inc.

Carole Marsh Florida Books, 31 bks. Set. 638.45 (ISBN 0-7933-1284-1). Gallopade Pub Group.

Carpenter, Allan. Florida. LC 78-8108. (Illus.). 96p. (gr. 4 up). 1979. PLB 19.93 (ISBN 0-516-04109-6). Childrens.

Coil, Suzanne M. Florida. (Illus.). 96p. (gr. 4-9). 1987. PLB 10.40 (ISBN 0-531-10384-6). Watts.

Davis, T. Frederick. History of Jacksonville, Florida & Vicinity 1513 to 1924. 3rd ed. (Illus.). 513p. (gr. 8 up). Repr. of 1925 ed. 22.50 (ISBN 0-935259-06-6). San Marco Bk.

Fichter, George S. Floridians All. Cardin, George, illus. 96p. (ps-8). 1991. 10.95 (ISBN 0-88289-804-3). Pelican.

Fischer, Marsha. Miami. (Illus.). 60p. (gr. 3 up). 1990. 12.95 (ISBN 0-87518-428-6, Dillon); PLB 12.95 (ISBN 0-685-33007-9). Macmillan Child Grp.

Fradin, Dennis. Florida: In Words & Pictures. Wahl, Richard, illus. LC 80-16681. 48p. (gr. 2-5). 1980. PLB 15.93 (ISBN 0-516-03909-1); pap. 4.95 (ISBN 0-516-43909-X). Childrens.

A Kid's Guide to Florida. 160p. (gr. 1 up). 1989. pap. 6.95 (ISBN 0-15-200461-0, Gulliver Bks). HarBraceJ.

Marsh, Carole. Avast, Ye Slobs! Florida Pirate Trivia. (Illus.). (gr. 3-12). 1990. PLB 19.95 (ISBN 0-7933-0304-4); pap. 14.95 (ISBN 0-7933-0303-6); computer disk 29.95 (ISBN 0-7933-0305-2). Gallopade Pub Group.

—The Beast of the Florida Bed & Breakfast. (Illus.). (gr. 3-12). 1990. PLB 19.95 (ISBN 0-7933-1493-3); pap. 14.95 (ISBN 0-7933-1494-1); computer disk 29.95 (ISBN 0-7933-1495-X). Gallopade Pub Group.

—Florida & Other State Greats (Biographies) Florida Bks. (Illus.). (gr. 3-12). 1990. PLB 19.95 (ISBN 1-55609-426-4); pap. 14.95 (ISBN 1-55609-425-6); computer disk 29.95 (ISBN 0-7933-1501-8). Gallopade Pub Group.

—Florida Bandits, Bushwackers, Outlaws, Crooks, Devils, Ghosts, Desperadoes & Other Assorted & Sundry Characters! (Illus.). (gr. 3-12). 1990. PLB 19.95 (ISBN 0-7933-0286-2); pap. 14.95 (ISBN 0-7933-0285-4); computer disk 29.95 (ISBN 0-7933-0287-0). Gallopade Pub Group.

—Florida Classic Christmas Trivia: Stories, Recipes, Activities, Legends, Lore & More! (Illus.). (gr. 3-12). 1990. PLB 19.95 (ISBN 0-7933-0289-7); pap. 14.95 (ISBN 0-7933-0288-9); computer disk 29.95 (ISBN 0-7933-0290-0). Gallopade Pub Group.

—Florida Coastales. (Illus.). (gr. 3-12). 1990. PLB 19.95 (ISBN 1-55609-422-1); pap. 14.95 (ISBN 1-55609-118-4); computer disk 29.95 (ISBN 0-7933-1497-6). Gallopade Pub Group.

—The Florida Hot Air Balloon Mystery. (Illus.). (gr. 2-9). 1990. 19.95 (ISBN 0-7933-2399-1); pap. 14.95 (ISBN 0-7933-2400-9); computer disk 29.95 (ISBN 0-7933-2401-7). Gallopade Pub Group.

—Florida "Jography" A Fun Run Thru Our State! (Illus.). (gr. 3-12). 1990. PLB 19.95 (ISBN 1-55609-418-3); pap. 14.95 (ISBN 1-55609-048-X); computer disk 29.95 (ISBN 0-7933-1487-9). Gallopade Pub Group.

—Florida Kid's Cookbook: Recipes, How-To, History, Lore & More! (Illus.). (gr. 3-12). 1990. PLB 19.95 (ISBN 0-7933-0298-6); pap. 14.95 (ISBN 0-7933-0297-8); computer disk 29.95 (ISBN 0-7933-0299-4). Gallopade Pub Group.

—Florida Quiz Bowl Crash Course! (Illus.). (gr. 3-12). 1990. PLB 19.95 (ISBN 1-55609-424-8); pap. 14.95 (ISBN 1-55609-423-X); computer disk 29.95 (ISBN 0-7933-1496-8). Gallopade Pub Group.

—Florida School Trivia: An Amazing & Fascinating Look at Our State's Teachers, Schools & Students! (Illus.). (gr. 3-12). 1990. PLB 19.95 (ISBN 0-7933-0295-1); pap. 14.95 (ISBN 0-7933-0294-3); computer disk 29. 95 (ISBN 0-7933-0296-X). Gallopade Pub Group.
—Florida Silly Basketball Sportsmysteries, Vol. I. (Illus.). (gr. 3-12). 1990. PLB 19.95 (ISBN 0-7933-0292-7); pap. 14.95 (ISBN 0-7933-0291-9); computer disk 29. 95 (ISBN 0-7933-0293-5). Gallopade Pub Group.
—Florida Silly Basketball Sportsmysteries, Vol. II. (Illus.). (gr. 3-12). 1990. PLB 19.95 (ISBN 0-7933-1502-6); pap. 14.95 (ISBN 0-7933-1503-4); computer disk 29. 95 (ISBN 0-7933-1504-2). Gallopade Pub Group.
—Florida Silly Football Sportsmysteries, Vol. I. (Illus.). (gr. 3-12). 1990. PLB 19.95 (ISBN 1-55609-421-3); pap. 14.95 (ISBN 1-55609-420-5); computer disk 29. 95 (ISBN 0-7933-1489-5). Gallopade Pub Group.
—Florida Silly Football Sportsmysteries, Vol. II. (Illus.). (gr. 3-12). 1990. PLB 19.95 (ISBN 0-7933-1490-9); pap. 14.95 (ISBN 0-7933-1491-7); computer disk 29. 95 (ISBN 0-7933-1492-5). Gallopade Pub Group.
—Florida Silly Trivia! (Illus.). (gr. 3-12). 1990. PLB 19.95 (ISBN 1-55609-417-5); pap. 14.95 (ISBN 1-55609-037-4); computer disk 29.95 (ISBN 0-7933-1486-0). Gallopade Pub Group.
—Florida's (Most Devastating!) Disasters & (Most Calamitous!) Catastrophies! (Illus.). (gr. 3-12). 1990. PLB 19.95 (ISBN 0-7933-0283-8); pap. 14.95 (ISBN 0-7933-0282-X); computer disk 29.95 (ISBN 0-7933-0284-6). Gallopade Pub Group.
—The Hard-to-Believe-But-True! Book of Florida History, Mystery, Trivia, Legend, Lore, Humor & More. (Illus.). (gr. 3-12). 1990. PLB 19.95 (ISBN 0-7933-0301-X); pap. 14.95 (ISBN 0-7933-0300-1); computer disk 29.95 (ISBN 0-7933-0302-8). Gallopade Pub Group.
—If My Florida Mama Ran the World! (Illus.). (gr. 3-12). 1990. PLB 19.95 (ISBN 0-7933-1498-4); pap. 14.95 (ISBN 0-7933-1499-2); computer disk 29.95 (ISBN 0-7933-1500-X). Gallopade Pub Group.
—Let's Quilt Florida & Stuff It Topographically! (Illus.). (gr. 3-12). 1990. PLB 19.95 (ISBN 1-55609-419-1); pap. 14.95 (ISBN 1-55609-055-2); computer disk 29. 95 (ISBN 0-7933-1488-7). Gallopade Pub Group.
Mathews, Sally. Travel & Learn Florida: A Children's Activity Book. (Illus.). 48p. (ps-8). 1991. pap. 7.95 (ISBN 0-941263-24-X). Sentinel Bks.
Morgan, Cheryl K. The Everglades. Morgan, Cheryl K., illus. LC 89-5175. 32p. (gr. 3-6). 1989. PLB 10.79 (ISBN 0-8167-1733-8); pap. text ed. 2.95 (ISBN 0-8167-1734-6). Troll Assocs.
Shore, Carol. The Official Florida Natives: A Friendly Introduction. LC 84-91492. (Illus.). 56p. (ps-7). 1985. pap. 2.98 (ISBN 0-9612136-2-0). C Shore Pr.
Stephenson, Sallie. Orlando, Florida. LC 89-32947. (Illus.). 48p. (gr. 4-5). 1989. 12.95 (ISBN 0-89686-463-4, Crestwood Hse). Macmillan Child Grp.
Stone, Lynn M. Florida. LC 87-9391. (Illus.). 144p. (gr. 4 up). 1987. PLB 25.27 (ISBN 0-516-00455-7). Childrens.
Swindler, William F. & Frech, Mary, eds. Chronology & Documentary Handbook of the State of Florida, No. 9. LC 73-567. 106p. (gr. 9-12). 1973. PLB 8.50 (ISBN 0-379-16134-6). Oceana.
Turner Program Services, Inc. Staff & Clark, James I. Florida. 48p. (gr. 3 up). 1985. pap. text ed. 17.32 (ISBN 0-86514-427-3); pap. text ed. 9.27 (ISBN 0-86514-502-4); cancelled Beta video (ISBN 0-86514-052-9); cancelled VHS video (ISBN 0-86514-127-4); cancelled 3/4" video (ISBN 0-86514-202-5); cancelled tchr's. guide (ISBN 0-86514-277-7); cancelled student activity bk. (ISBN 0-86514-352-8); cancelled index. Raintree Pubs.

FLORIDA–FICTION

Brooks, Walter R. Freddy Goes to Florida. Morrill, Leslie & Wiese, Kurt, illus. LC 86-40424. 208p. (gr. 3-7). 1987. pap. 3.95 (ISBN 0-394-88886-3). Knopf.
Griffith, Helen V. Foxy. LC 83-16392. 144p. (gr. 5-9). 1984. reinforced 11.95 (ISBN 0-688-02567-6). Greenwillow.
Peck, Robert N. Arly. 160p. (gr. 5 up). 1989. 16.95 (ISBN 0-8027-6856-3). Walker & Co.
Sansevere, Carol Q. New Girl in Town. 128p. (Orig.). (gr. 7 up). 1989. pap. 2.95 (ISBN 1-55802-200-7). Lynx Bks.
—Stolen Kisses. 144p. (Orig.). (gr. 5-9). 1989. pap. 2.95 (ISBN 1-55802-201-5). Lynx Bks.
Whittaker, Dorothy. Angels of the Swamp. 160p. (gr. 6-9). 1991. 15.95 (ISBN 0-8027-8129-2). Walker & Co.

FLORISTS DESIGNS

see Flower Arrangement

FLOWER ARRANGEMENT

Bauzen, Peter & Bauzen, Susanne. Flower Pressing. Kuttner, Paul, tr. from GER. LC 77-167661. (gr. 7 up). 1982. pap. 4.95 (ISBN 0-8069-7674-8). Sterling.

FLOWER GARDENING

Here are entered works on the cultivation of flowering plants for either commercial or private purposes.
see also Flowers; House Plants; Plant Propagation

FLOWER PAINTING AND ILLUSTRATION

Crowell, Robert L. The Lore & Legends of Flowers. Dowden, Anne O., illus. LC 79-7829. 88p. (gr. 7 up). 1982. 14.95 (ISBN 0-690-03991-3, Crowell Jr Bks); PLB 14.89 (ISBN 0-690-04035-0, Crowell Jr Bks). HarpC Child Bks.

FLOWERS

see also Flower Arrangement; Flower Painting and Illustration; Plants; State Flowers; Wild Flowers

Barker, Cicely M. Flower Fairies of the Spring. Barker, Cicely M., illus. (ps up). 1991. 5.95 (ISBN 0-7232-3753-0). Warne.
—Flower Fairies of the Summer. Barker, Cicely M., illus. (ps up). 1991. 5.95 (ISBN 0-7232-3754-9). Warne.
—Flower Fairies of the Trees. Barker, Cicely M., illus. (ps up). 1991. 5.95 (ISBN 0-7232-3760-3). Viking Child Bks.
Bragdon, Allen D. A Gift of Flowers. Gamon, David, et al, eds. Ringland, Carolyn, illus. 64p. (ps up). 1986. pap. 2.50 (ISBN 0-916410-21-8). A D Bragdon.
Braithwaite, Althea. Flowers. (ps-6). 1988. PLB 7.95 (ISBN 0-88462-184-7); pap. 2.95 (ISBN 0-88462-185-5). Dearborn Finan.
Broughton, Jacqueline P. Garden Flowers to Color. (Illus.). 32p. (ps-2). 1972. pap. 1.25 (ISBN 0-913456-51-9). Interbk Inc.
Cutting, Brian & Cutting, Jillian. The Dandelion. Beard, Angela, illus. 16p. (Orig.). (gr. k-2). 1988. pap. text ed. 23.00 (ISBN 1-55911-035-X). Wright Group.
—The Dandelion, 6 bks. Beard, Angela, illus. 16p. (Orig.). (gr. k-2). 1988. Set. pap. text ed. 19.80 (ISBN 1-55911-036-8). Wright Group.
Dowden, Anne O. The Clover & the Bee: A Book of Pollination. Dowden, Anne O., illus. LC 87-30116. 96p. (gr. 5 up). 1990. 17.95 (ISBN 0-690-04677-4, Crowell Jr Bks); PLB 17.89 (ISBN 0-690-04679-0, Crowell Jr Bks). HarpC Child Bks.
—State Flowers. Reissue. ed. Dowden, Anne O., illus. LC 78-41927. 96p. (gr. 5 up). 1978. PLB 13.89 (ISBN 0-690-03884-4, Crowell Jr Bks). HarpC Child Bks.
Flowers. (Illus.). (ps-3). 1.95 (ISBN 0-7214-5117-9). Ladybird Bks.
Flowers & Trees. (Illus.). 88p. (ps-3). 1989. 15.93 (ISBN 0-8094-4857-2); lib. bdg. 21.27 (ISBN 0-8094-4858-0). Time-Life.
Hildebrand, June. A Book of Flowers. (Illus.). 72p. (Orig.). 1982. write for info. Claremount Pr.
Ichikawa, Satomi & Laird, Elizabeth. Rosy's Garden: A Child's Keepsake of Flowers. (Illus.). 48p. 1990. 16.95 (ISBN 0-399-21881-5, Philomel Bks). Putnam Pub Group.
Jennings, Terry. Flowers. LC 88-37553. (Illus.). 32p. (gr. 3-6). 1989. PLB 14.60 (ISBN 0-516-08439-9); pap. 4.95 (ISBN 0-516-48439-7). Childrens.
Johnson, Sylvia A. Morning Glories. Sato, Yuko, illus. 48p. (gr. 4-10). 1985. PLB 14.95 (ISBN 0-8225-1462-1). Lerner Pubns.
—Roses Red, Violets Blue: Why Flowers Have Colors. (Illus.). 64p. (gr. 5 up). 1991. PLB 14.95 (ISBN 0-8225-1594-6). Lerner Pubns.
Kirkpatrick, Rena K. Look at Flowers. rev. ed. Milne, Annabel & Stebbing, Peter, illus. LC 84-26227. 32p. (gr. 2-4). 1985. PLB 15.99 (ISBN 0-8172-2352-5); pap. text ed. 9.27 (ISBN 0-8172-2377-0). Raintree Pubs.
Mayes, S. What Makes a Flower Grow? (Illus.). 24p. (gr. 1-4). 1989. lib. bdg. 11.96 (ISBN 0-88110-381-0, Usborne); pap. 3.95 (ISBN 0-7460-0275-0, Usborne). EDC.
Mitchell, Victor. Flowers. Mitchell, Victor, illus. 16p. (gr. k up). 1988. pap. 1.95 (ISBN 0-7459-1470-5). Lion USA.
Orange, Anne. The Flower Book. Lerner, Sharon, illus. LC 74-12743. 32p. (gr. k-3). 1975. PLB 7.95 (ISBN 0-8225-0294-1). Lerner Pubns.
Overbeck, Cynthia. Sunflowers. LC 80-27797. (Illus.). 48p. (gr. 4 up). 1981. PLB 14.95 (ISBN 0-8225-1457-5). Lerner Pubns.
Patent, Dorothy H. Flowers for Everyone. Munoz, William, photos by. LC 89-23937. (Illus.). 64p. (gr. 5 up). 1990. 14.95 (ISBN 0-525-65025-3, Cobblehill Bks). Dutton Child Bks.
Pohl, Kathleen. Morning Glories. (Illus.). 32p. (gr. 3-7). 1986. PLB 16.67 (ISBN 0-8172-2711-3); pap. 9.27 (ISBN 0-8172-2729-6). Raintree Pubs.
—Sunflowers. (Illus.). 32p. (gr. 3-7). 1986. PLB 16.67 (ISBN 0-8172-2710-5); pap. text ed. 9.27 (ISBN 0-8172-2728-8). Raintree Pubs.
—Tulips. (Illus.). 32p. (gr. 3-7). 1986. PLB 16.67 (ISBN 0-8172-2709-1); pap. 9.27 (ISBN 0-8172-2727-X). Raintree Pubs.
Sabin, Louis. Plants, Seeds & Flowers. Moylan, Holly, illus. LC 84-2720. 32p. (gr. 3-6). 1985. PLB 9.49 (ISBN 0-8167-0226-8); pap. text ed. 2.95 (ISBN 0-8167-0227-6). Troll Assocs.
Tsuchida, Yoshiharu. The Flowers in My Garden. (Illus.). 22p. (ps-1). 1981. 3.50 (ISBN 0-89346-195-4). Heian Intl.
Wexler, Jerome. Flowers Fruits Seeds. LC 86-30616. (Illus.). 32p. (ps-3). 1987. PLB 12.95 (ISBN 0-671-66372-0). S&S Trade.

FLOWERS–ARRANGEMENT

see Flower Arrangement

FLOWERS–FICTION

Andersen, Hans Christian. Little Ida's Flowers. Allen, Linda, illus. 32p. (gr. k-4). 1990. 13.95 (ISBN 0-399-21571-9, Philomel Bks). Putnam Pub Group.
Cernobous, Wayne J. Millie Milkweed Seed Meets the Genny Geranium Gang. Wyman, Helen B., illus. 46p. (Orig.). (gr. k-5). 1984. pap. 5.95 (ISBN 0-9615065-0-4). Kinnickinnic Pr.
Cox, Mike & Cox, Kris. Flowers. Wasserman, Dan, ed. Reese, Bob, illus. (gr. k-1). 1979. PLB 7.95 (ISBN 0-89868-076-X); pap. 2.95 (ISBN 0-89868-087-5). ARO Pub.
Cox, Willis F. & Cox, Rosemary C. Phillip's Daffodil. (Orig.). (gr. k-8). 1987. pap. 2.95 (ISBN 0-9610758-4-8). W F Cox.
DePaola, Tomie. The Legend of the Indian Paintbrush. (Illus.). 32p. (ps-3). 1991. pap. 5.95 (ISBN 0-399-21777-0, Putnam). Putnam Pub Group.
Foslien, Dagmar. The Fantastic Fashion Show. Paris, Pat & Shackelford, Jeane, illus. 40p. (ps-3). 1984. 5.95 (ISBN 0-910313-50-4). Parker Bros.
Freeman, Don. Dandelion. Freeman, Don, illus. (gr. k-3). 1982. incl. cassette 19.95 (ISBN 0-941078-11-6); pap. 12.95 incl. cassette (ISBN 0-941078-09-4); user's guide incl. 4 pbs. & cassette 27.95 (ISBN 0-941078-10-8). Live Oak Media.
Garfield, Leon. The December Rose. 208p. (gr. 5-9). 1988. pap. 3.95 (ISBN 0-14-032070-9, Puffin). Puffin Bks.
Hayes, Joe. Mariposa, Mariposa. Jelinek, Lucy, illus. (SPA & ENG.). 32p. (Orig.). (gr. k-5). 1988. pap. 3.95 (ISBN 0-939729-08-3); Bk. & cass. pkg. 7.95 (ISBN 0-939729-09-1). Trails West Pub.
Hendry, Diana. The Rainbow Watchers. Wickstrom, Thor, illus. LC 91-52853. 48p. (gr. 1 up). 1991. text ed. 10.95 (ISBN 0-688-10305-7). Lothrop.
Hutchins, Pat. Titch. Hutchins, Pat, illus. LC 77-146622. 32p. (ps-1). 1971. 12.95 (ISBN 0-02-745880-6, Mcmillan Child Bk). Macmillan Child Grp.
Laroche, Michel. The Snow Rose. Laroche, Sandra, illus. LC 85-16391. 32p. (gr. k-3). 1986. 12.95 (ISBN 0-8234-0594-X). Holiday.
Lobel, Arnold. The Rose in My Garden. Lobel, Anita, illus. LC 83-14097. 40p. (gr. k-3). 1984. 13.95 (ISBN 0-688-02586-2); PLB 13.88 (ISBN 0-688-02587-0). Greenwillow.
Nathan, Beverly & Bizer, Linda. King Size Coloring & Activity Book. Paris, Pat & Kong, Emilie, illus. 128p. (ps-8). 1984. pap. 2.50 (ISBN 0-910313-57-1). Parker Bros.
Nicolai, D. Miles. The Summer the Flowers Had No Scent. 3rd ed. Poyser, Victoria, illus. 28p. (gr. 3-5). 1977. pap. 2.75 (ISBN 0-933992-19-X). Coffee Break.
Paris, Pat & All, Wendy, illus. Rose-Petal. 12p. (ps-3). 1984. cancelled 4.00 (ISBN 0-910313-53-9). Parker Bros.
—Sunny Sunflower. 14p. (ps-3). 1984. cancelled 4.00 (ISBN 0-910313-55-5). Parker Bros.
Paris, Pat & Lipking, Ron, illus. A Garden of Love to Share: A Panorama. (ps-3). 1984. 4.00 (ISBN 0-910313-56-3). Parker Bros.
Pirotta, Saviour. The Flower from Outer Space. Stewart, Sarah-Jane, illus. LC 87-33374. 32p. (gr. 4-8). 1988. 12.95 (ISBN 0-87226-183-2, Bedrick Blackie). P Bedrick Bks.
Poulet, Virginia. Blue Bug's Surprise. Maloney, Mary & Fleming, Stan, illus. LC 76-50670. 32p. (gr. k-3). 1977. PLB 14.60 (ISBN 0-516-03427-8). Childrens.
Prieto. Pablo's Petunias. LC 72-190269. (Illus.). 32p. (gr. 3-5). 1972. PLB 9.95 (ISBN 0-87783-058-4); pap. 3.94 deluxe ed. (ISBN 0-87783-102-5). Oddo.
Sisson, Joan. Marigold. Sisson, Joan, illus. 24p. (Orig.). (ps-5). 1988. pap. 4.00 (ISBN 0-317-93622-0). J Sisson.
Slote, Elizabeth. Lilly's Garden. Slote, Elizabeth, illus. 32p. (ps-1). 1991. 13.95 (ISBN 0-688-10013-9, Tambourine Bks); PLB 13.88 (ISBN 0-688-10014-7, Tambourine Bks). Morrow.
Van Leeuwen, Jean. Timothy's Flower. (Illus.). (ps-3). 1967. 3.50 (ISBN 0-394-81896-2). Random.

FLOWERS, STATE

see State Flowers

FLOWERS, WILD

see Wild Flowers

FLOWERS IN ART

see Design, Decorative; Flower Painting and Illustration

FLOWERS IN LITERATURE

Jangl, Alda M. & Jangl, James F. Ancient Legends of the Twelve Birthflowers. Jangl, Alda M., illus. 40p. (gr. 9-12). 1987. pap. 3.95 (ISBN 0-942647-01-7). Prisma Pr.

FLY

see Flies

FLY-CASTING

Wylie, Joanne & Wylie, David. Un Cuento de Peces, Mas o Menos. LC 83-25223. (SPA., Illus.). 32p. (ps-2). 1987. PLB 14.60 (ISBN 0-516-32984-7); pap. 3.95 (ISBN 0-516-52984-6). Childrens.

FLYING

see Flight

FLYING BOMBS

see Guided Missiles

FLYING SAUCERS

Around the World. 48p. (gr. 5-6). 1989. PLB 10.95 (ISBN 0-685-26346-0). Capstone Pr.
Arvey, Michael. UFO's: Opposing Viewpoints. LC 89-11645. (Illus.). 111p. (gr. 6 up). 1989. PLB 13.95 (ISBN 0-89908-060-X). Greenhaven.
Asimov, Isaac. Unidentified Flying Objects. LC 87-42604. (Illus.). (gr. 3-4). 1988. PLB 11.95 (ISBN 1-55532-355-3). Gareth Stevens Inc.
—Unidentified Flying Objects. 1990. pap. 4.95 (ISBN 0-440-40349-9, YB). Dell.
Berger, Melvin. UFOs, ETs & Visitors from Space. (Illus.). 80p. (gr. 5 up). 1988. 11.95 (ISBN 0-399-61218-1, Putnam). Putnam Pub Group.

Butts, Donna R. & Corder, S. Scott. UFO Contact, the Four. Stevens, Wendelle C., ed. Butts, Donna R., illus. Caulfield, William, intro. by. (Illus.). 240p. (gr. 9-12). 1989. PLB 17.95 (ISBN 0-934269-18-1). UFO Photo.

Christian, Mary B. UFO's. LC 87-9008. (Illus.). 48p. (gr. 5-6). 1987. PLB 10.95 (ISBN 0-89686-347-6, Crestwood Hse). Macmillan Child Grp.

Cohen, Daniel. A Close Look at Close Encounters. (Illus.). 192p. (gr. 7-11). 1981. 9.95 (ISBN 0-396-07927-X, Putnam). Putnam Pub Group.

—Creatures from UFOs. (Illus.). 112p. (gr. 7-12). 1978. 8.95 (ISBN 0-396-07582-7, Putnam). Putnam Pub Group.

Collins, Jim. Unidentified Flying Objects. LC 77-13040. (Illus.). 48p. (gr. 4 up). 1983. PLB 17.32 (ISBN 0-8172-1065-2); pap. 9.27 (ISBN 0-8172-2169-7). Raintree Pubs.

The Flying Saucer. (Illus.). (ps-2). 3.50 (ISBN 0-7214-0912-1); parent-teacher guide avail. Ladybird Bks.

Gelman, Rita & Seligson, Marcia. UFO Encounters. (gr. 4-6). 1978. pap. 1.50 (ISBN 0-590-05403-1). Scholastic Inc.

The History. 48p. (gr. 5-6). 1989. PLB 10.95 (ISBN 0-685-26345-2). Capstone Pr.

Keene, Carolyn. Nancy Drew: Flying Saucer Mystery. (Illus.). (gr. 3-7). 1980. 8.95 (ISBN 0-671-95514-4, Little Simon); pap. 3.50 (ISBN 0-671-95601-9). S&S Trade.

Kitamura, Satoshi. UFO Diary. (ps up). 1989. 12.95 (ISBN 0-374-38026-0); pap. 4.95 (ISBN 0-374-48041-9). FS&G.

Participants? 48p. (gr. 5-6). 1989. PLB 10.95 (ISBN 0-685-26347-9). Capstone Pr.

Photos & Art. 48p. (gr. 5-6). 1989. PLB 10.95 (ISBN 0-685-26344-4). Capstone Pr.

Physical Evidence. 48p. (gr. 5-6). 1989. PLB 10.95 (ISBN 0-685-26343-6). Capstone Pr.

Rasmussen, Richard M. The UFO Challenge. LC 90-32962. (Illus.). 96p. (gr. 5-8). 1990. PLB 11.95 (ISBN 1-56006-122-7). Lucent Bks.

Riehecky, Janet. UFOs. Siculan, Dan, illus. LC 88-25730. 100p. (gr. 3-7). 1989. PLB 12.96 (ISBN 0-89565-453-9); pap. 6.95 (ISBN 0-89565-536-5). Childs World.

Rutland, Jonathan. UFOs. Full, Roger, illus. LC 87-4793. 24p. (gr. 2-5). 1987. lib. bdg. 5.99 (ISBN 0-394-99211-3, Random Juv); (BYR). Random.

Sightings. 48p. (gr. 5-6). 1989. PLB 10.95 (ISBN 0-685-26342-8). Capstone Pr.

Spellman, Linda. Monsters, Mysteries, UFOs. 112p. (gr. 4-6). 1984. 9.95 (ISBN 0-88160-095-4, LW 903). Learning Wks.

Stevens, Wendelle C. UFO...Contact from Reticulum, Update. Stevens, Wendelle C., et al, illus. 444p. (gr. 9-12). 1989. PLB 18.95 (ISBN 0-934269-15-7). UFO Photo.

—UFO...Contact from the Pleiades: A Supplementary Investigation Report. Stevens, Wendelle C., illus. 552p. (gr. 9-12). 1989. PLB 29.95 (ISBN 0-9608558-4-X). UFO Photo.

What If They're Real? 48p. (gr. 5-6). 1989. PLB 10.95 (ISBN 0-685-26341-X). Capstone Pr.

When Worlds Meet. 48p. (gr. 5-6). 1989. PLB 10.95 (ISBN 0-685-26340-1). Capstone Pr.

Wilding-White. UFO's. 32p. (gr. k-6). 1977. pap. 5.95 (ISBN 0-86020-150-3). EDC.

FOG–FICTION

Alexander, Frances. Mother Goose on the Rio Grande. (Illus.). 96p. (gr. 4 up). 1983. pap. 5.95 (ISBN 0-8442-7641-3, Passport Bks). Natl Textbk.

Bacheller, Irving. Lost in the Fog. Krupinski, Loretta, adapted by. & illus. LC 88-25923. (gr. k-3). 1990. 14.95 (ISBN 0-316-07462-4). Little.

Ryder, Joanne. Fog in the Meadow. Owens, Gail, illus. LC 77-25650. (ps-3). 1979. 9.57i (ISBN 0-06-025148-4). HarpC Child Bks.

Tresselt, Alvin R. Hide & Seek Fog. Duvoisin, Roger, illus. LC 65-14087. 32p. (gr. k-2). PLB 14.88 (ISBN 0-688-51169-4). Lothrop.

FOG SIGNALS

see Signals and Signaling

FOLIAGE

see Leaves

FOLK ART

Here are entered general and historical works on peasant and popular art in the fields of decorative arts, music, dancing, theater, etc.

see also Art Industries and Trade; Arts and Crafts

Abernethy, Jane F. & Tune, Suelyn C. Made in Hawaii. Williams, Julie S., illus. LC 83-4895. 140p. (gr. 3-12). 1983. pap. 5.95 (ISBN 0-8248-0870-3). UH Pr.

Colonial Williamsburg Foundation Staff. The Folk Art Counting Book: From the Abby Aldrich Rockefeller Folk Art Center. (Illus.). 40p. (ps-k). Date not set. 6.95 (ISBN 0-87935-084-9). Williamsburg. "The Folk Art Counting Book" is designed for young learners but it will be enjoyed by all ages. The images are from the Abby Aldrich Rockefeller Folk Art Center in Williamsburg, Virginia, one of the country's premier collections of American folk art. Folk art is the product of untrained artists who, although unfamiliar with academic artistic rules, somehow solve the technical difficulties encountered & intuitively produce satisfying art. Abby Aldrich Rockefeller's folk art collection of over six hundred pieces is the nucleus of the Abby Aldrich Rockefeller Folk Art Center, a museum of the Colonial Williamsburg Foundation. The present collection numbers over 2,600 objects & continues to grow. Small children can start at one whirligig & soon learn to count up to five weather vanes, ten jungle animals, & twenty eagles. The uncluttered pages with large, clear numbers that are immediately recognizable in a repetitive quilt border make this book easy to use as a learning tool. Outstanding examples of folk art such as the endearing "Baby in Red Chair" & Henry Church's "The Monkey Picture" have been specially selected to enhance young children's appreciation of folk art & to stimulate their visual & cognitive senses. ***Publisher Provided Annotation.***

Esterman, M. M. A Fish That's a Box: Folk Art from the National Museum of American Art, Smithsonian Institution. LC 90-3802. (Illus.). 32p. (gr. k-5). 1990. 12.95 (ISBN 0-915556-21-9). Great Ocean.

Fowler, Virginie. Folk Arts Around the World. Fowler, Virginie, illus. 168p. (gr. 5 up). 1984. pap. 6.95 (ISBN 0-13-322975-0). P-H.

Horwitz, Elinor L. Contemporary American Folk Artists. Horwitz, Joshua, photos by. LC 75-14353. (Illus.). (gr. 6 up). 1975. 8.50i (ISBN 0-397-31626-7, Lipp Jr Bks). HarpC Child Bks.

Rochester Folk Art Guild Staff. Little Shooter of Birds & the Great Sun. (ps-7). 1981. 9.50 (ISBN 0-686-33125-7). Rochester Folk Art.

Stanislaw, Mary Anne. Kalagas: The Wall Hangings of Southeast Asia. Stedman, Robert, photos by. 64p. (Orig.). (gr. 7 up). 1987. pap. 12.50 (ISBN 0-9618445-0-7). Ainslie's.

FOLK DANCING

Cone, Molly. Dance Around the Fire. Friedman, Marvin, illus. LC 74-9378. 160p. (gr. 7 up). 1974. 5.95 (ISBN 0-395-19490-3). HM.

Duke, Jerry. Clog Dance in the Appalachians. (Illus.). 96p. (Orig.). 1984. pap. 7.95 (ISBN 0-9613727-0-2). Duke Pub Co.

Hansen, Carol, et al. Shilpa: Folk Dances, Music, Crafts & Puppetry of India. rev. ed. LC 90-12985. (Illus.). 205p. 1990. tchr. looseleaf 44.95 (ISBN 0-930141-38-5). World Eagle.

Roes, Carol. Hulas from Hawaii. 15p. (gr. k-8). 1978. pap. 5.50 (ISBN 0-930932-03-X); record incl. M Loke.

FOLK LORE

see Folklore

FOLK MUSIC

see Folk Songs

FOLK SONGS

see also Ballads; Carols; Folklore; National Songs

Beall, Pamela C. & Nipp, Susan H. Wee Sing Fun 'n Folk Songs. (Illus.). 64p. (Orig.). (ps-2). pap. 2.95 (ISBN 0-8431-2760-0); bk. & cassette 9.95 (ISBN 0-8431-2759-7). Price Stern.

Berger, Melvin. The Story of Folk Music. LC 76-18159. (Illus.). (gr. 6 up). 1976. PLB 21.95 (ISBN 0-87599-215-3). S G Phillips.

Chusid, Nancy. Favorite Folk Songs. Chusid, Nancy, illus. 32p. (Orig.). (gr. 2-6). 1990. pap. 6.95 incl. cassette (ISBN 1-878624-07-5). McClanahan Bk.

Durell, Ann, compiled by. The Diane Goode Book of American Folk Tales & Songs. Goode, Diane, illus. LC 89-1097. (ps-5). 1989. 14.95 (ISBN 0-525-44458-0, DCB). Dutton Child Bks.

Ochs, Bill. The Clarke Learn to Play Tin Whistle Set. (Illus.). 80p. (Orig.). (gr. 3 up). 1988. Incl cass. pap. 15.95 (ISBN 0-9623456-0-1). Incl. tin whistle & cassette in blister package. pap. 24.95 (ISBN 0-9623456-2-8). Pnnywhstlrs Pr.

Rochester Folk Art Guild Staff. Sunlight in the Morning: Songs from the Farm. (Illus.). 40p. (gr. k-6). 1983. 13.00 (ISBN 0-686-40298-7); cassette tape 6.00 (ISBN 0-317-00393-3). Rochester Folk Art.

Teutsch, Betsy. One Little Goat: Had Gadya. LC 89-18298. (Illus.). 32p. 1990. 16.95 (ISBN 0-87668-824-5). Aronson.

Watson, Wendy. Wendy Watson's Frog Went A-Courting. Watson, Wendy, illus. LC 89-63022. 32p. (ps-2). 1990. 13.95 (ISBN 0-688-06539-2); lib. bdg. 13.88 (ISBN 0-688-06540-6). Lothrop.

Westcott, Nadine B. There's a Hole in the Bucket. Westcott, Nadine B., illus. LC 89-34538. 32p. (ps-2). 1990. 12.95 (ISBN 0-06-026422-5); PLB 12.89 (ISBN 0-06-026423-3). HarpC Child Bks.

FOLK SONGS, AFRICAN

Goss, Linda & Goss, Clay. The Baby Leopard: An African Folktale. Bailey-Jones, Suzanne & Jones, Michael R., illus. 32p. (ps-3). 1989. pap. 3.95 (ISBN 0-553-34648-2); audiocassette 7.95 (ISBN 0-318-41503-8). Bantam.

FOLK SONGS, AMERICAN

see Folk Songs–U. S.

FOLK SONGS, ENGLISH

Cauley, Lorinda B., illus. Old MacDonald Had a Farm. 32p. (ps-3). 1989. 13.95 (ISBN 0-399-21628-6, Putnam). Putnam Pub Group.

De Paola, Tomie. The Friendly Beasts: An Old English Christmas Carol. De Paola, Tomie, illus. 32p. (ps-2). 1981. 13.95 (ISBN 0-399-20739-2, Putnam); pap. 5.95 (ISBN 0-399-20777-5, Putnam). Putnam Pub Group.

Rounds, Glen, illus. I Know an Old Lady Who Swallowed a Fly. LC 89-46244. 32p. 1990. PLB 14.95 (ISBN 0-8234-0814-0). Holiday.

FOLK SONGS, FRENCH

Shulevitz, Uri. One Monday Morning. LC 85-28583. (Illus.). 32p. (ps-3). 1986. pap. 4.95 (ISBN 0-689-71062-3, Aladdin). Macmillan Child Grp.

FOLK SONGS, SPANISH

West, Patricia M. Hispanic Folk Songs of the Southwest: For Bilingual Programs (Part II) 33p. (gr. k-12). 1982. 5.00. U of Denver Teach.

West, Patricia M. & Otero, George G. Hispanic Folk Songs of the Southwest: An Introduction (Part I) updated ed. 33p. (Orig.). (gr. k-12). 1982. pap. 5.00 (ISBN 0-943804-11-6). U of Denver Teach.

FOLK SONGS–U. S.

Blocher, Arlo. Folk. LC 75-39815. (Illus.). 32p. (gr. 5-10). 1976. PLB 10.79 (ISBN 0-89375-013-1); pap. 2.95 (ISBN 0-89375-029-8). Troll Assocs.

McCarthy, Bobette. Buffalo Girls. McCarthy, Bobette, illus. (ps-6). 1987. PLB 10.95 (ISBN 0-517-56568-4). Crown.

Pearson, Tracey C., illus. Old MacDonald Had a Farm. LC 83-18815. 32p. (ps-2). 1984. 11.95 (ISBN 0-8037-0068-7); PLB 9.89 (ISBN 0-8037-0070-9). Dial Bks Young.

Quackenbush, Robert. Go Tell Aunt Rhody. LC 72-8711. 32p. (gr. 1-4). 1973. 11.95 (ISBN 0-397-31718-2, Lipp Jr bks). HarpC Child Bks.

—She'll Be Comin' 'Round the Mountain. Reissue. ed. Quackenbush, Robert, illus. LC 73-2943. 40p. (ps up). 1988. Repr. of 1973 ed. PLB 12.89 (ISBN 0-397-32266-6, Lipp Jr Bks). HarpC Child Bks.

—There'll Be a Hot Time in the Old Town Tonight: The Great Chicago Fire of 1871 Told with Song & Pictures. Reissue. ed. Quackenbush, Robert, illus. LC 74-4283. 32p. (ps up). 1988. Repr. of 1974 ed. PLB 13.89 (ISBN 0-397-32267-4, Lipp Jr Bks). HarpC Child Bks.

Rounds, Glen. Old MacDonald Had a Farm. Rounds, Glen, illus. LC 88-24640. 32p. (ps-3). 1989. reinforced bdg. 14.95 (ISBN 0-8234-0739-X); pap. 5.95 (ISBN 0-8234-0846-9). Holiday.

Seeger, Ruth C. American Folk Songs for Children. Cooney, Barbara, illus. 192p. (gr. k-12). 1980. pap. 10.00 (ISBN 0-385-15788-6, Zephyr-BFYR). Doubleday.

Tolman, Newton F. Quick Tunes & Good Times. (gr. 7 up). 1972. 7.50 (ISBN 0-87233-018-4). Bauhan.

FOLK TALES

see Folklore

FOLKLORE

see also Devil; Folk Songs; Ghosts; Grail; Halloween; Proverbs; Superstition; Witchcraft

Aesop. The Miller, His Son & Their Donkey. Sopko, Eugen, illus. LC 85-7198. 32p. (gr. k-3). 1988. 14.95 (ISBN 1-55858-067-0); pap. 4.95 (ISBN 1-55858-063-8). North-South Bks NYC.

Aladdin. (Illus.). (gr. 3-7). 3.50 (ISBN 0-7214-0387-5). Ladybird Bks.

Ali Baba. (Illus.). (gr. 3-7). 3.50 (ISBN 0-7214-0386-7). Ladybird Bks.

Amoss, Berthe. Cinderella. Amoss, Berthe, illus. 10p. (ps-7). 1989. pap. 2.95 (ISBN 0-922589-04-6). More Than Card.

—Little Red Riding Hood. (Illus.). 10p. (ps-7). 1989. pap. 2.95 (ISBN 0-922589-11-9). More Than Card.

Ananse & the Sky God. (Illus.). (gr. 1). 3.50 (ISBN 0-7214-5175-6). Ladybird Bks.

Baden, Robert. And Sunday Makes Seven. Mathews, Judith, ed. Edwards, Michelle, illus. 32p. (ps-3). 1990. 12.95 (ISBN 0-8075-0356-8). A Whitman.

Barnett, Carol. Boy & the Donkey. (ps-3). 1990. 7.95 (ISBN 0-8442-9417-9). Natl Textbk.

Bendick, Jeanne. Scare a Ghost, Tame a Monster. Bendick, Jeanne, illus. LC 82-23696. 120p. (gr. 3-6). 1983. 11.95 (ISBN 0-664-32701-X, Westminster). Westminster John Knox.

Biro, Val. Jack & the Beanstalk. (Illus.). 32p. (ps up). 1990. bds. 9.95 (ISBN 0-19-278218-5). Oxford U Pr.

Bishop, Dorothy S. The City Mouse & the Country Mouse. (FRE & ENG., Illus.). 72p. 1989. pap. 4.95 (ISBN 0-8442-1086-2, Passport Bks). Natl Textbk.

—The Lion & the Mouse. (FRE & ENG., Illus.). 72p. 1989. pap. 4.95 (ISBN 0-8442-1084-6, Passport Bks). Natl Textbk.

Brett, Jan. The Mitten: A Ukranian Folktale. Brett, Jan, illus. 32p. (ps-3). 1990. 14.95 (ISBN 0-399-21920-X, Putnam). Putnam Pub Group.

Brown, Jerome C. Folk Tale PaperCrafts. (gr. k-5). 1989. pap. 7.95 (ISBN 0-8224-3156-4). Fearon Teach Aids.
Bryan, Ashley. Beat the Story-Drum, Pum-Pum. Bryan, Ashley, illus. LC 86-20598. 80p. (gr. 4-6). 1987. pap. 6.95 (ISBN 0-689-71107-7, Aladdin). Macmillan Child Grp.
Butler, Stephen. Henny Penny. Butler, Stephen, illus. LC 90-35115. 32p. (ps-1). 1991. 12.95 (ISBN 0-688-09921-1, Tambourine Bks); PLB 12.88 (ISBN 0-688-09922-X, Tambourine Bks). Morrow.
Butterworth, Ben. Tales from Long Ago, 8 bks, Nos. 1-8. Ives, Penny, et al, illus. (Orig.). (gr. 2-3). 1986. Set. pap. text ed. 27.90 (ISBN 1-55624-004-X). Wright Group.
Byer, Carol, illus. Henny Penny. LC 80-28146. 32p. (gr. k-3). 1981. PLB 9.79 (ISBN 0-89375-490-0); pap. text ed. 1.95 (ISBN 0-89375-491-9). Troll Assocs.
Carrick, Malcolm. Happy Jack. LC 78-19476. (Illus.). 64p. (gr. k-3). 1979. 7.64i (ISBN 0-06-021121-0). HarpC Child Bks.
Climo, Shirley. The Egyptian Cinderella. Heller, Ruth, illus. LC 88-37547. 32p. (gr. k-3). 1989. 14.95 (ISBN 0-690-04822-X, Crowell Jr Bks); PLB 14.89 (ISBN 0-690-04824-6, Crowell Jr Bks). HarpC Child Bks.
Cohen, Daniel. Southern Fried Rat & Other Gruesome Tales. Brier, Peggy, illus. LC 82-25120. 128p. (gr. 7 up). 1982. 9.95 (ISBN 0-87131-400-2). M Evans.
Cothran, Jean, ed. Whang Doodle: Folk Tales from the Carolinas. LC 72-86904. (Illus.). (gr. 3-7). 1972. Repr. of 1989 ed. 5.95 (ISBN 0-87844-052-6). Sandlapper Pub Co.
Cowsill, Virginia. Favorite Childhood Tales Set. Kempster, Teddy, ed. Holtman, Noelle M., illus. (Orig.). (gr. 2-4). 1989. pap. text ed. 8.50 (ISBN 0-88336-981-8). New Readers.
Davison, Kathy. Porcupine & the Sky Mirrors: And Other Stories about the Moon & Its Magic. Morrison, Cathy, illus. 48p. 1991. text ed. 14.95 (ISBN 0-917665-49-X). Bookmakers Guild.
Denan, Corinne. Once upon a Time Tales. LC 79-66337. (Illus.). 48p. (gr. 2-6). 1980. lib. bdg. 9.89 (ISBN 0-89375-340-8); pap. 2.95 (ISBN 0-89375-339-4). Troll Assocs.
—Troll Tales. new ed. LC 79-66327. (Illus.). 48p. (gr. 3-6). 1980. lib. bdg. 9.89 (ISBN 0-89375-322-X); pap. 2.95 (ISBN 0-89375-321-1); cassette avail. Troll Assocs.
De Paola, Tomie. Helga's Dowry. De Paola, Tomie, illus. LC 76-54953. 32p. (ps-3). 1977. 13.95 (ISBN 0-15-233701-6, HJ). HarBraceJ.
Elkin, Benjamin. Six Foolish Fishermen. Evans, K., illus. (gr. k-4). 1957. PLB 14.60 (ISBN 0-516-03601-7); pap. 3.95 (ISBN 0-516-43601-5). Childrens.
Fairy Tales from Many Lands. Date not set. 9.98 (ISBN 0-517-67951-5). Outlet Bk Co.
Foley, Tom, illus. Sakshi Gopal: A Witness for the Wedding. Greene, Joshua, retold by. (Illus.). 16p. (gr. 1-4). 1981. pap. 2.00 (ISBN 0-89647-036-9). Bala Bks.
Gag, Wanda. The Funny Thing. (Illus.). 32p. (ps-3). 1991. pap. 5.95 (ISBN 0-698-20676-2, Putnam). Putnam Pub Group.
Galdone, Paul. Little Tuppen. Galdone, Paul, illus. LC 67-10364. 32p. (ps-3). 1979. 9.95 (ISBN 0-395-28804-5, Clarion). HM.
—The Magic Porridge Pot. Galdone, Paul, illus. LC 76-3531. 32p. (ps-3). 1979. 13.95 (ISBN 0-395-28805-3, Clarion). HM.
—Three Little Pigs. Galdone, Paul, illus. LC 75-123456. (ps-3). 1979. 13.95 (ISBN 0-395-28813-4, Clarion). HM.
Geis, Darlene, ed. Walt Disney's Treasury of Children's Classics. (Illus.). (gr. 5 up). 1978. 29.95 (ISBN 0-8109-0812-3). Abrams.
The Gingerbread Boy. 24p. (ps). 1988. pap. 1.29 (ISBN 0-02-898136-7). Checkerboard Pr.
Greene, Joshua, retold by. Krishna, Master of All Mystics. Amendola, Dominique, illus. 16p. (gr. 1-4). 1981. pap. 4.00 (ISBN 0-89647-035-0). Bala Bks.
Grimm, Jacob & Grimm, Wilhelm K. The Falling Stars. Sopko, illus. LC 85-7193. 1988. 13.95 (ISBN 1-55858-041-7). North-South Bks NYC.
—The Frog King & Other Tales of the Brothers Grimm. 315p. (ps-8). 1989. pap. 2.95 (ISBN 0-451-52379-2, Sig Classics). NAL-Dutton.
Hausman, Gerald. Beth: The Little Girl of Pine Knoll. Totten, Bob, illus. LC 74-82228. 32p. (gr. 6 up). 1974. 15.00 (ISBN 0-912846-08-9). Bookstore Pr.
Hawthorne, Nathaniel. Twice Told Tales. Gemme, F. R., intro. by. (gr. 9 up). pap. 2.50 (ISBN 0-8049-0066-3, CL-66). Airmont.
Hodges, Margaret. Buried Moon, Vol. 1. (ps-3). 1990. 14.95 (ISBN 0-316-36793-1). Little.
Jacobs, Joseph. Tattercoats. Tomes, Margot, illus. 32p. (gr. k-4). 1989. 14.95 (ISBN 0-399-21584-0, Putnam). Putnam Pub Group.
Jose, Eduard, adapted by. The Three Little Pigs: A Classic Tale. McDonnell, Janet, tr. from SPA. Asensio, Augusti, illus. LC 88-35314. 32p. (gr. 1-4). 1988. PLB 10.95 (ISBN 0-89565-459-8). Childs World.
Joyce, Susan. Naro, the Ancient Spider: The Creation of the Sun & Moon. DuBosque, D. C., illus. (gr. 4). 1990. 12.00 (ISBN 0-939217-04-X). Peel Prod.
Kamerman, Sylvia E., ed. The Big Book of Folktale Plays. 336p. (gr. 3-7). 1991. 16.95 (ISBN 0-8238-0294-9). Plays.
Kerven, Rosalind. King Leopard's Gift: And Other Legends of the Animal World. Waldman, Bryna, illus. 32p. 1990. 12.95 (ISBN 0-521-36180-X). Cambridge U Pr.
—Legends of the Animal World. (Illus.). 32p. (gr. 3-7). 1986. 11.95 (ISBN 0-521-30576-4). Cambridge U Pr.
Lang, Andrew. Pink Fairy Book. Ford, Henry J., illus. 360p. (gr. 4-6). 1966. pap. 6.95 (ISBN 0-486-21792-2). Dover.
Lang, Andrew, ed. Blue Fairy Book. Ford, Henry J. & Hood, G. P., illus. LC 34-28315. 390p. (gr. 1-6). 1965. pap. 6.95 (ISBN 0-486-21437-0). Dover.
—Brown Fairy Book. Ford, Henry J., illus. (gr. 1-6). pap. 6.95 (ISBN 0-486-21438-9). Dover.
—Crimson Fairy Book. Ford, Henry J., illus. LC 67-17988. 371p. (gr. 4-6). 1966. pap. 6.95 (ISBN 0-486-21799-X). Dover.
—Green Fairy Book. Ford, Henry J., illus. LC 34-28314. 366p. (gr. 4-6). 1965. pap. 6.95 (ISBN 0-486-21439-7). Dover.
—Grey Fairy Book. Ford, Henry J., illus. LC 67-17983. 387p. (gr. 4-6). 1900. pap. 6.95 (ISBN 0-486-21791-4). Dover.
—Lilac Fairy Book. Ford, H. J., illus. 367p. (ps-4). 1968. pap. 6.95 (ISBN 0-486-21907-0). Dover.
—Olive Fairy Book. Ford, H. J., illus. 330p. (gr. 4-6). 1966. pap. 5.95 (ISBN 0-486-21908-9). Dover.
—Orange Fairy Book. Ford, H. J., illus. 358p. (gr. 1-6). 1968. pap. 6.95 (ISBN 0-486-21909-7). Dover.
—Red Fairy Book. Ford, Henry J. & Speed, Lancelot, illus. 367p. (gr. 4-6). pap. 6.95 (ISBN 0-486-21673-X). Dover.
—Violet Fairy Book. Ford, Henry J. & Lang, H. J., illus. (gr. 4-6). pap. 6.95 (ISBN 0-486-21675-6). Dover.
—Yellow Fairy Book. Ford, Henry J., illus. 321p. (gr. 4-6). pap. 6.95 (ISBN 0-486-21674-8). Dover.
Lester, Julius. The Knee-High Man & Other Tales. Pinto, Ralph, illus. LC 72-181785. 32p. (ps-3). 1985. 12.95 (ISBN 0-8037-4593-1). Dial Bks Young.
Lipson, Greta. Fact, Fantasy, Folklore. 160p. (gr. 3-12). 1977. 11.95 (ISBN 0-916456-11-0, GA71). Good Apple.
—Famous Fables for Little Troupers. Kropa, Susan, illus. 168p. (gr. k-6). 1984. 11.95 (ISBN 0-86653-202-1, GA 554). Good Apple.
Little People Big Book about Magical Worlds. 64p. (ps-1). 1990. write for info. (ISBN 0-8094-7495-6); PLB write for info. (ISBN 0-8094-7496-4). Time-Life.
Little Red Riding Hood. (ps-1). 3.95 (ISBN 0-448-09749-4, G&D). Putnam Pub Group.
Lurie, Alison. Clever Gretchen & Other Forgotten Folktales. Tomes, Margot, illus. LC 78-22512. 128p. (gr. 4-6). 1980. PLB 12.89 (ISBN 0-690-03944-1, Crowell Jr Bks). HarpC Child Bks.
McCloskey, Robert. Centerburg Tales. McCloskey, Robert, illus. LC 51-10675. 192p. (gr. 4-6). 1951. pap. 14.95 (ISBN 0-670-20977-5). Viking Child Bks.
Mace, Jean. Home Fairy Tales. Booth, Mary L., tr. from FRE. LC 78-74517. (Illus.). (gr. 4-5). 1979. Repr. of 1867 ed. 24.75x (ISBN 0-8486-0220-X). Roth Pub Inc.
McGovern, Ann. Stone Soup. Pels, Winslow P., illus. LC 86-10098. 32p. (gr. k-3). 1986. pap. 11.95 (ISBN 0-590-40526-8, Scholastic Hardcover). Scholastic Inc.
McQueen, Lucinda, illus. The Little Red Hen. 32p. (Orig.). (gr. k-2). 1985. Big book. 19.50 (ISBN 0-590-71718-9); pap. 2.50 (ISBN 0-590-41145-4); incl. cassette 5.95 (ISBN 0-590-63067-9). Scholastic Inc.
Maggi, Tolstoy M. Fables & Folk Tales. (Illus.). 30p. (ps-1). 1986. 3.95 (ISBN 0-8120-5727-9). Barron.
Mahan, Benton, illus. Goldilocks & the Three Bears. LC 80-27631. 32p. (gr. k-2). 1981. PLB 9.79 (ISBN 0-89375-470-6); pap. text ed. 1.95 (ISBN 0-89375-471-4). Troll Assocs.
Moroney, Lynn, adapted by. Elinda Who Danced in the Sky: An Eastern European Folktale from Estonia. Reisberg, Veg, illus. 32p. (gr. 1-7). 1990. 12.95 (ISBN 0-89239-066-2). Childrens Book Pr.
Ormerod, Jan. The Story of Chicken Licken. Ormerod, Jan, illus. LC 85-7911. 32p. (ps-1). 1986. 13.00 (ISBN 0-688-06058-7). Lothrop.
Oxenbury, Helen, retold by. & illus. The Helen Oxenbury Nursery Story Book. LC 84-28887. 80p. (ps-1). 1985. lib. bdg. 12.99 (ISBN 0-394-97519-7); PLB 12.95 (ISBN 0-394-87519-2). Knopf.
Paton, Alan. Tales from a Troubled Land. 1977. 20.00 (ISBN 0-684-15135-9, Scribner); (Scribner). Macmillan.
Le Petit Chaperon Rouge. (FRE., Illus.). (gr. 2). 3.50 (ISBN 0-7214-1285-8). Ladybird Bks.
La Petite Poule Rousse. (FRE., Illus.). (gr. 1). 3.50 (ISBN 0-7214-1276-9). Ladybird Bks.
Pevear, Richard. Our King Has Horns! Payevsky, Robert, illus. LC 86-23525. 32p. (gr. k-3). 1987. 14.95 (ISBN 0-02-773920-1, Mcmillan Child Bk). Macmillan Child Grp.
Phelps, Ethel J. The Maid of the North: Feminist Folk Tales from Around the World. Bloom, Lloyd, illus. LC 80-21500. 192p. (gr. 2-9). 1982. pap. 8.95 (ISBN 0-8050-0679-6). H Holt & Co.
Pizzo, Joan E. Amy Avocet. Geronimi, Clyde, illus. LC 83-70739. (gr. k-6). 1983. 8.95 (ISBN 0-939126-06-0). Back Bay.
Polette, Nancy. Activities with Folktales & Fairytales. (Illus.). 32p. (gr. 4-7). 1979. pap. 4.95 (ISBN 0-913839-00-0). Bk Lures.
—Thinking Skills with Tall Tales. (Illus.). 32p. (gr. 3-6). 1983. pap. 4.95 (ISBN 0-913839-13-2). Bk Lures.
Pomerantz, Charlotte. Whiff, Sniff, Nibble, & Chew: The Gingerbread Boy Retold. Incisa, Monica, illus. LC 83-14179. 24p. (gr. k-3). 1984. PLB 8.59 (ISBN 0-688-02552-8). Greenwillow.
Rapunzel. (Illus.). (gr. k). 3.50 (ISBN 0-7214-5167-5). Ladybird Bks.
Rojankovsky, Feodor. Tall Book of Nursery Tales. Rojankovsky, Feodor, illus. LC 44-3881. (ps-1). 1944. 7.95 (ISBN 0-06-025065-8). HarpC Child Bks.

Roland, Donna. Grandfather's Stories. Oden, Ron, illus. (Orig.). (gr. k-3). 1991. pap. 4.50 (ISBN 0-941996-00-X); tchr's. ed. 4.95. Open My World.
"Grandfather's Stories" provides students with a strong sense of personal & social values. At the same time the development of cultural awareness of their own culture & those of their classmates is encouraged. "Grandfather's Stories" is different from most multi-cultural series in that the children are portrayed living in the U.S. but through their grandfather they learn about their cultural background. Grandfather shares information about the country's history, social customs & the values he hopes to pass on to them. Although written on a 2nd grade reading level the series appeals to a wide age range. Its simple concepts yet detailed illustrations attract both younger & older students. Cultures currently available are: American Indian (Lumbee), Cambodia, Germany, Mexico, the Philippines & Vietnam. Teacher's editions include additional information, activities & skill sheets. A video is also offered. In addition, the sequels, "More of Grandfather's Stories" is also available, which continues the same theme but with grandfather actually telling a folktale from their culture. Published by Open My World Publishing San Diego, California.
Publisher Provided Annotation.

—More of Grandfather's Stories. Oden, Ron, illus. 25p. (Orig.). (gr. k-3). 1991. pap. 4.50 (ISBN 0-941996-02-6); tchr's. ed. 4.95 (ISBN 0-941996-13-1). Open My World.
"More of Grandfather's Stories" develops cultural awareness through cultural folklore. This series is different from most multi-cultural series in that the grandchildren being told the folktale live in the U. S. The selected folktale helps grandfather illustrate the values he hopes to instill. "More of Grandfather's Stories" supports & complements the series "Grandfather's Stories". Although written on a 2nd grade reading level the series appeals to a wide age range. Its simple concepts yet detailed illustrations attract both younger & older students. Cultures currently available are: American Indian (Lumbee), Cambodia, Germany, Mexico, the Philippines & Vietnam. Teacher's editions include additional information, activities & skill sheets. A video is also offered. In addition, "Grandfather's Stories" continues the same theme but grandfather shares information about their homeland's history, customs & the values he hopes to pass on to his grandchildren. Published by Open My World, San Diego, California.
Publisher Provided Annotation.

Ross, Tony. The Three Pigs. Ross, Tony, illus. LC 83-2356. 32p. (gr. 2-4). 1983. 10.95 (ISBN 0-394-86143-4, Pant Bks Young). Pantheon.

Le Ruse Renard et la Petite Poule Rousse. (FRE., Illus.). (gr. 1). 3.50 (ISBN 0-7214-1277-7). Ladybird Bks.

Sanfield, Steve. The Feather Merchants: & Other Tales of the Fools of Chelm. Magaril, Mikhail, illus. LC 90-29273. 112p. (gr. 3 up). 1991. 15.95 (ISBN 0-531-05958-8); RLB 15.99 (ISBN 0-531-08558-9). Orchard Bks Watts.

Schwartz, Alvin. All of Our Noses Are Here & Other Noodle Tales. Weinhaus, Karen A., illus. LC 84-48330. 64p. (gr. k-3). 1985. PLB 10.89 (ISBN 0-685-09667-X). HarpC Child Bks.

—Tales of Trickery from the Land of Spoof. Christiana, David, illus. 88p. (gr. 3 up). 1988. pap. 3.50 (ISBN 0-374-47426-5). FS&G.

Shannon, George. More Stories to Solve: Fifteen Folktales from Around the World. Sis, Peter, illus. LC 89-7413. 64p. (gr. k up). 1991. 12.95 (ISBN 0-688-09161-X). Greenwillow.

Shearer, Marilyn J. The Crown of Fools: Based on: The Tortoise & the Hare. 16p. (ps-6). 1992. 19.95 (ISBN 0-685-30101-X); pap. 10.95 (ISBN 0-685-30102-8). L Ashley & Joshua.

Shulevitz, Uri. One Monday Morning. LC 85-28583. (Illus.). 32p. (ps-3). 1986. pap. 4.95 (ISBN 0-689-71062-3, Aladdin). Macmillan Child Grp.

Stroyer, Paul. Second Treasure Chest of Tales. (Illus.). (gr. 3 up). 1960. 12.95 (ISBN 0-8392-3032-X). Astor-Honor.

Tales of the Heart. LC 89-11509. 80p. (gr. 3-9). 1990. PLB 13.96 (ISBN 0-8114-4158-X). Steck-V.

Thompson, Stith, ed. One Hundred Favorite Folktales. LC 68-27355. (Illus.). 456p. 1968. 29.95 (ISBN 0-253-15940-7); pap. 12.95x (ISBN 0-253-20172-1). Ind U Pr.

Three Little Pigs. (Illus.). (ps-1). 1985. 1.98 (ISBN 0-517-47899-4). Outlet Bk Co.

The Three Little Pigs. 32p. (ps-1). 1985. 2.49 (ISBN 0-517-46242-7). Outlet Bk Co.

Tompert, Ann. It May Come in Handy Someday. Cayard, Bruce, illus. LC 74-19487. 48p. (gr. 4-6). 1975. text ed. 5.95 (ISBN 0-07-064932-4); text ed. 5.72 (ISBN 0-07-064933-2). McGraw.

Troughton, Joanna. Joanna Troughton's Folk Tales: What Made Tiddalik Laugh; Mouse-Deer's Market; How Night Came; Who Will Be the Sun?; The Magic Mill & Tortoise's Dream, 6 bks. Troughton, Joanna, illus. 32p. (gr. 1-3). Set. pap. text ed. 28.90 (ISBN 1-55624-498-3). Wright Group.

Vorhees, Duance & Mueller, Mark. The Lazy Man. Kang, Mi-Suk, illus. 46p. (gr. 2-5). 1991. PLB 9.95x (ISBN 0-930878-73-6). Hollym Intl.

Vorhees, Duance & Mueller, Mark, eds. The Woodcutter & the Heavenly Maiden. Kim, Yon-Kyong, illus. 45p. (gr. 2-5). 1990. PLB 9.95x (ISBN 0-930878-71-X). Hollym Intl.

Wallner, John. City Mouse - Country Mouse & Two More Tales from Aesop. Wallner, John, illus. 32p. (Orig.). (gr. k-3). 1987. pap. 2.50 (ISBN 0-590-41155-1). Scholastic Inc.

Wilson, Barbara K. The Turtle & the Island: A Folktale from Papua New Guinea. Lessac, Frane, illus. LC 89-134444. 32p. (gr. k-4). 1990. Repr. of 1990 ed. 13.95 (ISBN 0-397-32438-3, Lipp Jr Bks); PLB 13.89 (ISBN 0-397-32439-1, Lipp Jr Bks). HarpC Child Bks.

Yolen, Jane. The Girl Who Cried Flowers & Other Tales. Palladini, David, illus. LC 73-8903. 64p. (gr. 3-6). 1974. 12.95 (ISBN 0-690-00216-5, Crowell Jr Bks); (Crowell Jr Bks). HarpC Child Bks.

—Neptune Rising: Songs & Tales of the Undersea Folk. Wiesner, David, illus. LC 82-5281. 149p. 1982. 11.95 (ISBN 0-399-20918-2, Philomel). Putnam Pub Group.

Zimmerman, H. Werner. Henny Penny. 1989. pap. 9.95 (ISBN 0-590-42390-8). Scholastic Inc.

FOLKLORE–AFRICA

Aardema, Verna. Bimwili & the Zimwi. Meddaugh, Susan, illus. LC 85-4449. 32p. (ps-3). 1985. 12.95 (ISBN 0-8037-0212-4); PLB 12.89 (ISBN 0-8037-0213-2). Dial Bks Young.

Aardema, Verna, retold by. Traveling to Tondo: A Tale of the Nkundo of Zaire. Hillenbrand, Will, illus. LC 90-39419. 40p. (gr. k-4). 1991. 13.00 (ISBN 0-679-80081-6); PLB 13.99 (ISBN 0-679-90081-0). Knopf.

Akinde, Akindele. Atu's Prophecy: An African Epic Story for the Entire Family. Oyeleye, Bola, illus. LC 90-83347. 40p. (Orig.). (gr. 8). 1990. pap. write for info. (ISBN 0-9627363-0-9). Apala Prodns.

Appiah, Peggy. Tales of an Ashanti Father. Dickson, Mona, illus. LC 88-19059. 160p. (gr. 2-6). 1989. lib. bdg. 12.95 (ISBN 0-8070-8312-7); pap. 5.95 (ISBN 0-8070-8313-5, NL4). Beacon Pr.

Arnott, Kathleen. African Myths & Legends. Kiddell-Monroe, Joan, illus. 224p. (gr. 4 up). 1990. pap. 8.95 (ISBN 0-19-274143-8). Oxford U Pr.

Berger, Terry, ed. Black Fairy Tales. White, David O., illus. LC 70-75517. (gr. 3-7). 1974. (Atheneum Childrens Bk); pap. 3.95 (ISBN 0-689-70402-X). Macmillan Child Grp.

Blakely, Nora B. Shani on the Hill. Gilchrist, Jan S., illus. (gr. 1). 1988. pap. 3.95 (ISBN 0-88378-123-9). Third World.

Bryan, Ashley. Lion & the Ostrich Chicks & Other African Folk Tales. Ashley, Bryan, illus. LC 86-3349. 96p. (gr. 2-6). 1986. 13.95 (ISBN 0-689-31311-X, Atheneum Child Bk). Macmillan Child Grp.

Greaves, Nick. When Hippo Was Hairy & Other Tales from Africa. Clement, Rod, illus. 144p. (gr. 3-12). 1988. 12.95 (ISBN 0-8120-4131-3). Barron.

—When Hippo Was Hairy & Other Tales from Africa. Clement, Rod, illus. 144p. (gr. k up). 1991. pap. 7.95 (ISBN 0-8120-4548-3). Barron.

Haley, Gail E. A Story, A Story. Haley, Gail E., illus. LC 69-18961. 36p. (ps-3). 1970. 14.95 (ISBN 0-689-20511-2, Atheneum Child Bk). Macmillan Child Grp.

Knutson, Barbara. Why the Crab Has No Head: An African Folktale. (Illus.). 24p. (ps-3). 1987. lib. bdg. 9.95 (ISBN 0-87614-322-2); pap. 4.95 (ISBN 0-87614-489-X). Carolrhoda Bks.

Lottridge, Celia B., retold by. The Name of the Tree: A Bantu Folktale. Wallace, Ian, illus. LC 89-2430. 36p. (gr. 1-5). 1990. PLB 14.95 (ISBN 0-689-50490-X, M K McElderry). Macmillan Child Grp.

Madhubuti, Safisha. Story of Kwanzaa. (gr. 1). 1989. pap. 5.95 (ISBN 0-88378-001-1). Third World.

Pitcher, Diana. The Mischief Maker. Dove, Sally, illus. 64p. 1990. pap. 5.95 (ISBN 0-86486-106-0, Pub. by D Philip South Africa). Interlink Pub.

—Tokoloshi: African Folk Tales Retold. Rutherford, Meg, illus. LC 80-28470. 64p. (gr. 3 up). 1990. 9.95 (ISBN 0-89742-049-7). Celestial Arts.

Poland, Marguerite. The Wood-Ash Stars. Altshuler, Shanne, illus. 64p. 1990. pap. 5.95 (ISBN 0-86486-089-7, Pub. by D Philip South Africa). Interlink Pub.

Robertson, Graeme. The Battle of Bongerhoohoo. Szmid, Gordon, illus. LC 79-11855. (gr. 3-7). 1979. PLB 8.95 (ISBN 0-672-52592-5, Bobbs). Macmillan.

Tadjo, Veronique. Lord of the Dance: An African Retelling. Tadjo, Veronique, illus. LC 89-2785. 32p. (gr. 1-4). 1989. 12.95 (ISBN 0-397-32351-4, Lipp Jr Bks); PLB 12.89 (ISBN 0-397-32352-2, Lipp Jr Bks). HarpC Child Bks.

Troughton, Joanna, retold by. Tortoise's Dream: An African Folk Tale. Troughton, Joannna, illus. LC 85-15065. 28p. (ps-2). 1986. 14.95 (ISBN 0-87226-039-9, Bedrick Blackie). P Bedrick Bks.

FOLKLORE–AFRICA, CENTRAL

Grifalconi, Ann. Village of Round & Square Houses. Grifalconi, Ann, illus. 32p. (gr. k-3). 1986. lib. bdg. 14.95 (ISBN 0-316-32862-6). Little.

Savory, Phyllis. Congo Fireside Tales. Tolford, Joshua, illus. (gr. 4-6). 1962. 6.95g (ISBN 0-8038-1112-8). Hastings.

FOLKLORE–AFRICA, SOUTH

Berger, Terry, ed. Black Fairy Tales. White, David O., illus. LC 70-75517. (gr. 3-7). 1974. (Atheneum Childrens Bk); pap. 3.95 (ISBN 0-689-70402-X). Macmillan Child Grp.

FOLKLORE–AFRICA, WEST

Aardema, Verna. Why Mosquitoes Buzz in People's Ears: A West African Tale. Dillon, Leo & Dillon, Diane, illus. LC 77-71514. (ps-3). 1978. pap. 4.95 (ISBN 0-8037-6088-4). Dial Bks Young.

—Why Mosquitoes Buzz in People's Ears: A West African Tale. Dillon, Leo & Dillon, Diane, illus. LC 74-2886. 32p. (ps-3). 1975. 14.95 (ISBN 0-8037-6089-2); PLB 14.89 (ISBN 0-8037-6087-6). Dial Bks Young.

Anderson, David A. & Sankofa. The Origin of Life on Earth: A Yoruba Creation Myth. Wilson, Kathleen A., illus. 64p. Date not set. PLB 15.95 (ISBN 0-9629978-5-4). Sights Prods. POWERFUL AFRICAN FOLKLORE. This beautiful book lavishly illustrated by Kathleen Atkins Wilson, features Dr. David Anderson's retelling of an ancient Yoruban myth. Dr. Anderson is a storyteller who is as expressive as the tales he tells. The story tells of the time when there were only two domains: the sky above & the water below & of the adventures of Obatala, a deity who journeys down from the sky to create the world. Obatala lowers himself on a golden chain clutching a snail shell full of sand, a bird's egg & a bag of nuts & seeds. With these items & help from the other deities he creates the Earth & its inhabitants. The mythology comes from the ancient Yoruba, a West African culture that lived in city-states located in lands known today as Nigeria & Benin. The Yoruba religion underscores the creation myth upon which this folklore is based.
Publisher Provided Annotation.

Courlander, Harold & Herzog, George. The Cow-Tail Switch & Other West African Stories. Chastain, Madye L., illus. LC 47-30108. 160p. (gr. 2-4). 1988. pap. 12.95 (ISBN 0-8050-0288-X). H Holt & Co.

Omoleye, Amoke. Yoruba Children's Tales. Omoleye, Amoke, illus. 33p. (Orig.). (gr. k-8). 1990. pap. 5.95 (ISBN 0-9625699-1-7). Amoke Omoleye Pub.

FOLKLORE–ALASKA

Welsh-Smith, Susan. Andy: An Alaskan Tale. Munoz, Rie, illus. 24p. 1988. 11.95 (ISBN 0-521-35535-4). Cambridge U Pr.

FOLKLORE–ARABIA

Aladdin. (ARA., Illus.). (gr. 5-12). 3.50x (ISBN 0-86685-182-8). Intl Bk Ctr.

Aladdin. (Illus.). (gr. 3-7). 3.50 (ISBN 0-7214-0387-5). Ladybird Bks.

Ali Baba. (Illus.). (gr. 3-7). 3.50 (ISBN 0-7214-0386-7). Ladybird Bks.

Ali Baba: In Arabic. (Illus.). (gr. 4-12). 3.50x (ISBN 0-86685-184-4). Intl Bk Ctr.

Bull, Rene. The Arabian Knights. (gr. 2-6). 1986. 8.98 (ISBN 0-685-16864-6, 619342). Outlet Bk Co.

Eastman, David, adapted by. Aladdin & the Wonderful Lamp. Waldman, Bryna, illus. LC 87-13756. 32p. (gr. 1-4). 1988. PLB 9.79 (ISBN 0-8167-1073-2); pap. text ed. 1.95 (ISBN 0-8167-1074-0). Troll Assocs.

Jose, Eduard, adapted by. Aladdin's Lamp: A Classic Tale. Suire, Diane D., tr. from SPA. Lavarello, Jose M., illus. LC 88-35312. 32p. (gr. 1-4). 1988. PLB 10.95 (ISBN 0-89565-481-4). Childs World.

—Ali Baba & the Forty Thieves: A Classic Tale. Riehecky, Janet, tr. from SPA. Rovira, Francesc, illus. LC 88-36871. 32p. (gr. 1-4). 1988. PLB 10.95 (ISBN 0-89565-485-7). Childs World.

—Sinbad the Sailor: A Classic Tale. Riehecky, Janet, tr. from SPA. Rovira, Francesc, illus. LC 88-36872. 32p. (gr. 1-4). 1988. PLB 10.95 (ISBN 0-89565-472-5). Childs World.

Lang, Andrew, ed. Arabian Nights Entertainments. Ford, H. J., illus. LC 69-17098. xv, 424p. (gr. k-6). 1969. pap. 6.95 (ISBN 0-486-22289-6). Dover.

Riordan, James. Tales from the Arabian Nights. Ambrus, Victor G., illus. LC 84-62456. 128p. (gr. 4 up). 1985. 11.95 (ISBN 0-528-82672-7). Checkerboard Pr.

Swan, ed. Tales from the Arabian Nights. (Illus.). 1989. pap. 4.87 (ISBN 0-582-54151-4, 78036). Longman.

Thomas, Vernon. Stories from the Arabian Nights. Basu, R. K., illus. (gr. 8-12). 1979. 7.25 (ISBN 0-89744-142-7). Auromere.

Twain, Mark. Arabian Nights. Goodenow, Earle, illus. (gr. 4-9). pap. 7.95 illus. jr. lib (ISBN 0-448-11006-7, G&D); deluxe ed. 11.95 (ISBN 0-448-06006-X). Putnam Pub Group.

FOLKLORE–ARMENIA

Bider, Djemma. A Drop of Honey. Kojoyian, Armen, illus. (ps-4). 1989. pap. 14.95 (ISBN 0-671-66265-1). S&S Trade.

Hogrogian, Nonny. The Contest. LC 75-40389. (Illus.). 32p. (gr. k-3). 1976. PLB 12.88 (ISBN 0-688-84042-6). Greenwillow.

FOLKLORE–ASIA

Asian Cultural Center for UNESCO. Folk Tales from Asia for Children Everywhere, Bk. 2. LC 74-82605. (Illus.). 56p. (gr. 3-6). 1975. 6.50 (ISBN 0-8348-1033-6). Weatherhill.

—Folk Tales from Asia for Children Everywhere, Bk. 5. LC 74-82605. (Illus.). 64p. (gr. 3-6). 1977. 6.50 (ISBN 0-8348-1036-0). Weatherhill.

—Folk Tales from Asia for Children Everywhere, Bk. 6. LC 74-82605. (Illus.). 64p. (gr. 3-6). 1978. 6.50 (ISBN 0-8348-1037-9). Weatherhill.

—Folktales from Asia for Children Everywhere, Bk. 1. LC 74-82605. (Illus.). 56p. (gr. 1-4). 1975. 6.50 (ISBN 0-8348-1032-8). Weatherhill.

Asian Cultural Center for UNESCO, ed. Folk Tales from Asia for Children Everywhere, Bk. 3. LC 74-82605. (Illus.). 64p. (gr. 3-6). 1976. 6.50 (ISBN 0-8348-1034-4). Weatherhill.

Candappa, Beulah. Tales of South Asia, 4 bks. Collard, Derek, et al, illus. 64p. (Orig.). (gr. 4-7). 1986. Set. pap. text ed. 23.80 incl. teacher's notes (ISBN 1-55624-012-0). Wright Group.

Harris, Edward N., compiled by. The Rice Fairy: Karen Stories from Southeast Asia. LC 89-21946. (Illus.). 105p. (gr. 4-6). 1989. Repr. of 1987 ed. lib. bdg. 20.00 (ISBN 0-929225-33-3). Simplicity Pr.

Ra, Ruth, illus. Many Lands, Many Stories: Asian Folk Tales for Children. Conger, David, contrib. by. LC 87-50167. (Illus.). 94p. 1987. 11.95 (ISBN 0-8048-1527-5). C E Tuttle.

Revich, S. J. The Camel Boy. Hinlicky, Gregg, illus. 158p. (gr. 5-8). 1987. 9.95 (ISBN 0-935063-44-7); pap. 7.95 (ISBN 0-935063-45-5). CIS Comm.

—The Poet & the Thief. Hinlicky, Gregg, illus. 158p. (gr. 5-7). 1989. 10.95 (ISBN 0-935063-71-4); pap. 7.95 (ISBN 0-935063-72-2). CIS Comm.

Troughton, Joanna, retold by. & illus. The Quail's Egg: A Folk Tale from Sri Lanka. LC 87-33376. (ps-3). 1988. 14.95 (ISBN 0-87226-185-9, Bedrick Blackie). P Bedrick Bks.

FOLKLORE–ASIA, SOUTHEASTERN

Xiong, Blia, ed. Nine-in-One Grr! Grr! Spagnoli, Cathy, as told by. (Illus.). 32p. (ps-5). 1989. 12.95 (ISBN 0-89239-048-4). Childrens Book Pr.

FOLKLORE–AUSTRALIA

Lofts, Pamela, retold by. & illus. The Echidna & the Shade Tree. 32p. (gr. 1-6). 1985. pap. 3.95 (ISBN 0-915391-05-8, Pub. by Mad Hatter Bks). Slawson Comm.

Trezise, Percy. The Rainbow Serpent. Keller, Kathy, intro. by. Trezise, Percy, illus. LC 88-20122. 32p. (gr. 2-3). 1988. PLB 12.95 (ISBN 1-55532-949-7). Gareth Stevens Inc.

Troughton, Joanna, retold by. & illus. What Made Tiddalik Laugh: An Australian Aborigine Folk Tale. LC 86-1234. 32p. (ps-2). 1986. 14.95 (ISBN 0-87226-081-X, Bedrick Blackie). P Bedrick Bks.

FOLKLORE, BLACK
see Black Folklore

FOLKLORE–CANADA

Ardizzone, Edward. Tim in Danger. (Illus.). 48p. (ps-3). 1987. pap. 6.95 (ISBN 0-19-272106-2). Oxford U Pr.

FOLKLORE–CARIBBEAN AREA

Jones, Evan. Tales of the Caribbean, 4 bks. Norhtway, Jenny, et al, illus. 48p. (Orig.). (gr. 4-7). 1986. Set. pap. text ed. 23.80 incl. teacher's notes (ISBN 1-55624-014-7). Wright Group.

Lewis, Theresa. Caribbean Folk Legends. LC 89-81981. 90p. (gr. 6-12). 1990. 19.95 (ISBN 0-86543-158-2); pap. 7.95 (ISBN 0-86543-159-0). Africa World.

Makhanlall, David. Brer Anansi & the Boat Race: A Folk Tale from the Caribbean. Rosato, Amelio, illus. LC 88-925. (ps-3). 1988. 14.95 (ISBN 0-87226-184-0, Bedrick Blackie). P Bedrick Bks.

FOLKLORE, CELTIC

Jacobs, Joseph, ed. Celtic Fairy Tales. Batten, John D., illus. LC 67-24223. xvi, 267p. (ps-6). 1968. pap. 5.95 (ISBN 0-486-21826-0). Dover.

—More Celtic Fairy Tales. Batten, John D., illus. LC 67-24224. x, 234p. (ps-6). 1968. pap. 5.95 (ISBN 0-486-21827-9). Dover.

FOLKLORE–CHINA

Ai-Ling, Louie, retold by. Yeh-Shen: A Cinderella Story from China. (Illus.). (ps-3). 1988. 13.95 (ISBN 0-317-99866-8, Ideals). Putnam Pub Group.

Birdseye, Tom. A Song of Stars. Ju-Hong Chen, illus. LC 89-20066. 32p. (gr. 4-8). 1990. 14.95 (ISBN 0-8234-0790-X). Holiday.

Carpenter, Frances. Tales of a Chinese Grandmother. Hasselriie, Malthe, illus. LC 72-77514. 302p. (gr. 3-8). 1972. pap. 8.95 (ISBN 0-8048-1042-7). C E Tuttle.

Carpenter, Francis. Tales of a Chinese Grandmother. 293p. (gr. 5-6). Repr. of 1937 ed. lib. bdg. 19.95x (ISBN 0-89190-481-6, Pub. by River City Pr). Amereon Ltd.

Chin, Yin-lien C., et al, eds. Traditional Chinese Folktales. (Illus.). 192p. (gr. 8-12). 1989. 19.95 (ISBN 0-87332-507-9). M E Sharpe.

Day, David. The Sleeper. Entwisle, Mark, illus. 32p. (gr. k-4). 1990. 13.95 (ISBN 0-8249-8456-0). Ideals.

Demi. Chen Ping & His Magic Axe. (Illus.). 32p. (gr. 5-8). 1987. 12.95 (ISBN 0-396-08907-0, G&D). Putnam Pub Group.

—The Empty Pot. Demi, illus. LC 89-39062. 32p. (ps-2). 1990. 15.95 (ISBN 0-8050-1217-6). H Holt & Co.

—The Magic Boat. Demi, illus. 32p. (ps-2). 1990. 15.95 (ISBN 0-8050-1141-2). H Holt & Co.

Denman, Cherry. The Little Peacock's Gift: A Folk Tale from China. Denman, Cherry, illus. LC 87-17504. 28p. (gr. k-5). 1988. 14.95 (ISBN 0-87226-175-1, Bedrick Blackie). P Bedrick Bks.

Heyer, Marilee. The Weaving of a Dream. Heyer, Marilee, illus. 32p. (ps-3). 1989. pap. 4.95 (ISBN 0-14-050528-8, Puffin). Puffin Bks.

—The Weaving of a Dream: A Chinese Folktale. Heyer, Marilee, illus. LC 85-20187. 32p. (gr. k-6). 1986. pap. 14.95 (ISBN 0-670-80555-6). Viking Child Bks.

Hong, Lily T. How the Ox Star Fell from Heaven. Fay, Ann, ed. Hong, Lily T., illus. 32p. (gr. k-3). 1990. 13.95 (ISBN 0-8075-3428-5). A Whitman.

Hume, Lotta C. Favorite Children's Stories from China & Tibet. Lo-Koon-Chiu, illus. LC 61-6219. (gr. 1-4). 1962. pap. 14.95 (ISBN 0-8048-1605-0). C E Tuttle.

Kendall, Carol. The Wedding of the Rat Family. Watts, James, illus. LC 88-2197. 32p. (gr. 2-5). 1988. 13.95 (ISBN 0-689-50450-0, M K McElderry). Macmillan Child Grp.

Lee, Jeanne M., retold by. & illus. The Legend of the Milky Way. LC 81-6906. 32p. (gr. k-3). 1982. 11.50 (ISBN 0-8050-0217-0). H Holt & Co.

Li, Xiao M., tr. from CHI. The Mending of the Sky & Other Chinese Myths. Wu, Shan M., illus. Buckley, Cicely, intro. by. (Illus.). 54p. (Orig.). (gr. 5 up). 1989. pap. 9.00 (ISBN 0-9617481-3-3). Oyster River Pr. Beautifully illustrated with calligraphy & halftones from watercolors by Shan Ming Wu. Brief bibliography & a note on Chinese names. "Young & old will marvel at how the ingenuity of gods & humans helped people survive natural disasters, political strife, & how pottery, silk, cooking, herbal medicine & the written language came to be invented for the benefit of humankind.

Provides a window on ancient & present-day China."--A. Shipman, UNH Dept. Classics. "Straightforward renderings with colorful, dramatic phrases, enhanced by Shan Ming Wu's fine illustrations with the charm of traditional Chinese paintings."--Small Press Book Review. On the invention of the writing system: Cang Xie had a broad dragon-like face with four shining eyes. As a child...he spent hours observing celestial bodies & earthly creatures...When his characters were first brought to light,...the whole world was shocked, & ghosts cried at night. It was feared people might give up farming & become interested in playing with the other characters...
Publisher Provided Annotation.

Ludwig, Lyndell. The Little White Dragon. Ludwig, Lyndell, illus. 23p. (gr. 5 up). 1989. pap. 4.95 (ISBN 0-9621782-0-9). Star Dust Bks. "THE LITTLE WHITE DRAGON" This timeless, well loved tale from ancient China takes you into the world of a wonderful little dragon intent on exploring everything both inside & outside of his realm. At one point he even changes himself into a little fish so he can dive into the waters of the deep sea. However, after numerous adventures, including a miraculous escape, he decides that, after all, it is much better just to be the dragon he really is, with untold worlds yet to discover. The third in a series of authentic Chinese tales in picture book form, delightfully told & illustrated by the author who is well qualified both as an illustrator & in her knowledge of the Chinese language. ("Like the tales of Rudyard Kipling 'these stories' transport children to another time & a different, fascinating world."--Creative Arts). Children are important! As the world changes cultures are blending. And stories from distant lands such as China are enormously valuable in broadening the scope for growth & understanding. They are also fun to read. TS'AO CHUNG WEIGHS AN ELEPHANT ("...splendid, vibrantly colored paintings..."--Publishers Weekly) & THE SHOEMAKER'S GIFT are also available from Star Dust Books at $4.95 each. Publisher Provided Annotation.

Miller, Moira. The Moon Dragon. Deuchar, Ian, illus. LC 88-3902. 32p. (ps-3). 1989. 12.95 (ISBN 0-8037-0566-2). Dial Bks Young.

Morris, Jill. Monkey & the White Bone Demon. Sheng, Lin, et al, illus. LC 83-17670. 32p. 1984. pap. 10.95 (ISBN 0-670-48574-8). Viking Child Bks.

Mosel, Arlene. Tikki Tikki Tembo. Lent, Blair, illus. LC 68-11839. 48p. (gr. k-2). 1968. 14.95 (ISBN 0-8050-0662-1). H Holt & Co.

Wang, Rosalind C., retold by. The Fourth Question: A Chinese Folktale. Ju-Hong Chen, illus. LC 90-43536. 32p. (ps-3). 1991. PLB 14.95 (ISBN 0-8234-0855-8). Holiday.

Williams, Jay. Everyone Knows What a Dragon Looks Like. Mayer, Mercer, illus. LC 84-29589. 32p. (gr. k-3). 1984. 14.95 (ISBN 0-02-793090-4, Four Winds). Macmillan Child Grp.

Wonder Kids Publications Group Staff (USA) & Hwa-I Publishing Co., Staff (Taiwan) Folklore: Chinese Children's Stories, Vols. 1-5. Ching, Emily, et al, eds. Wonder Kids Publications Staff, tr. from CHI. Hwa-I Publishing Co., Staff, illus. LC

90-60791. 28p. (gr. 3-6). 1991. Repr. of 1988 ed. Five vol. set, 28p. ea. bk. 39.75 (ISBN 1-56162-001-7); Set (100 vols.) 795.00 (ISBN 1-56162-120-X). Wonder Kids.
"The most comprehensive collection of children's stories about Chinese culture, customs, philosophy, values, history, literature..."--World Journal. Fashioned together in myths, legends, folktale, fairy tales, fables, & short stories, 200 stories for children are packed with action, magic, love & moral teachings. Recommended for ESL & ages 8-12 reading to promote multi-cultural education & global awareness. Following each short story, a "parental guide" presents supplemental information to further clarify moral messages & cultural meaning. 20 titles of subjects include: Folklore, Tales about Plants, Animal Tales, Fables, Idioms, Festivals, Tales about Food, Inventions, 12 Beasts & the Years, Fairy Tales, Filial Piety, Wonder Kids, Mythology, Literature, Popular Narratives, Heroes, Historical Accounts, Chinese Sites, & Taiwanese Sites. Please refer to the individual subject listing in (Children's) Books in Print for a description of each title of subject in the collection. Publisher Provided Annotation.

Wriggins, Sally. White Monkey King: A Chinese Fable. Solbert, Ronni, illus. LC 76-44281. (gr. 1-5). 1977. Pantheon.

Yang, Jwing-Ming. YMAA Children's Book Series: Volume One, Stories One & Two. 32p. (Orig.). (gr. 4 up). 1989. pap. 6.00 (ISBN 0-940871-09-2). Yangs Martial Arts.

Yep, Laurence. The Rainbow People. Wiesner, David, illus. LC 88-21203. 208p. (gr. 3-7). 1989. 15.95 (ISBN 0-06-026760-7); PLB 13.89 (ISBN 0-06-026761-5). HarpC Child Bks.

—Tongues of Jade. Wiesner, David, illus. LC 91-2119. 192p. (gr. 3-7). 1991. 14.95 (ISBN 0-06-022470-3); PLB 14.89 (ISBN 0-06-022471-1). HarpC Child Bks.

Young, Ed, tr. from CHI. & illus. Lon Po Po: A Red Riding Hood Story from China. 32p. (gr. k-4). 1989. 14.95 (ISBN 0-399-21619-7, Philomel Bks). Putnam Pub Group.

Yuan Hsi Kuo & Louise Hsi Kuo. Chinese Folk Tales. LC 75-9082. (gr. 7 up). 1976. pap. 6.95 (ISBN 0-89087-074-8). Celestial Arts.

FOLKLORE–CZECHOSLOVAKIA

Gag, Wanda. Gone Is Gone. Gag, Wanda, illus. (gr. k-3). 1960. PLB 5.99 (ISBN 0-698-30179-X, Coward). Putnam Pub Group.

Hill, Mary B., retold by. Natasha's Gift: A Folktale from Czechoslovakia. Koczar, Gwenda, illus. Hill, Mary B, intro. by. (Illus.). 32p. (gr. 2 up). 1990. 14.95g (ISBN 0-917665-46-5). Bookmakers Guild.

Horejs, Vit. Twelve Iron Sandals: And other Czechoslovak Tales. Spanfeller, Jim, illus. LC 84-22272. 128p. (gr. 4-6). 1985. 11.95 (ISBN 0-13-934159-5). P-H.

Nemcova, B. Fairy Tales from Czechoslovakia, Vol. I. Velinsky, L., tr. Kabel Pub Staff, illus. Absolon, K., intro. by. (CZE., Illus.). 305p. (Orig.). (gr. 4 up). 1987. pap. 39.50 (ISBN 0-685-19314-4). Kabel Pubs.

FOLKLORE–DENMARK

Andersen, Hans Christian. The Emperor's Nightingale: A Classic Tale. Jose, Eduard, adapted by. Moncure, Jane B., tr. from SPA. Lavarello, Jose M., illus. LC 88-35209. 32p. (gr. 1-4). 1988. PLB 11.95 (ISBN 0-89565-484-9). Childs World.

—The Little Match Girl: A Classic Tale. Jose, Eduard, adapted by. Suire, Diane D., tr. from SPA. Rovira, Francesc, illus. LC 88-36868. 32p. (gr. 1-4). 1988. PLB 10.95 (ISBN 0-89565-476-8). Childs World.

—The Little Mermaid: A Classic Tale. Jose, Eduard, adapted by. Moncure, Jane B., tr. from SPA. Lavarello, Jose M., illus. LC 88-36869. 32p. (gr. 1-4). 1988. PLB 10.95 (ISBN 0-89565-477-6). Childs World.

—The Princess & the Pea: A Classic Tale. Jose, Eduard, adapted by. Riehecky, Janet, tr. from SPA. Rovira, Francesc, illus. LC 88-35206. 32p. (gr. 1-4). 1988. PLB 10.95 (ISBN 0-89565-486-5). Childs World.

—The Steadfast Tin Soldier: A Classic Tale. Jose, Eduard, adapted by. Moncure, Jane B., tr. from SPA. Asensio, Augusti, illus. LC 88-35207. 32p. (gr. 1-4). 1988. PLB 10.95 (ISBN 0-89565-468-7). Childs World.

—Thumbelina: A Classic Tale. Jose, Eduard, adapted by. Riehecky, Janet, tr. from SPA. Rovira, Francesc, illus. LC 88-35307. 32p. (gr. 1-4). 1988. PLB 10.95 (ISBN 0-89565-466-0). Childs World.

Conover, Chris. The Wizard's Daughter: A Viking Legend. Conover, Chris, illus. LC 84-12613. 32p. (gr. 3-5). 1984. 14.95 (ISBN 0-316-15314-1). Little.

Haviland, Virginia. The Talking Pot, Vol. 1: A Danish Folktale. (ps-4). 1990. 14.95 (ISBN 0-316-35060-5, Joy St Bks). Little.

The Little Mermaid. (Illus.). (ps-4). 3.50 (ISBN 0-7214-0627-0). Ladybird Bks.

Tales from Hans Andersen. 1989. pap. 4.87 (ISBN 0-582-54149-2, 78035). Longman.

FOLKLORE–EGYPT

Green, Roger L. Tales of Ancient Egypt. (gr. k-3). 1990. pap. 2.95 (ISBN 0-14-035101-9, Puffin). Puffin Bks.

FOLKLORE–ENGLAND

Amoss, Berthe. Jack & the Beanstalk. Amoss, Berthe, illus. 10p. (ps-7). 1989. pap. 2.95 (ISBN 0-922589-00-3). More Than Card.

Dick Whittington. (Illus.). (gr. k). 3.50 (ISBN 0-7214-5171-3). Ladybird Bks.

Dick Whittington. (Illus.). (ps-4). 3.50 (ISBN 0-7214-0952-0). Ladybird Bks.

Galdone, Paul. The Teeny-Tiny Woman. Galdone, Paul, illus. LC 84-4311. 32p. (ps-3). 1984. 13.95 (ISBN 0-89919-270-X, Clarion). HM.

—The Three Sillies. LC 80-22197. (Illus.). 40p. (ps-3). 1981. 9.95 (ISBN 0-395-30172-6, Clarion). HM.

Greenburg, Joanne. Jack in the Beanstalk. Walsh, Michael S., illus. 48p. (gr. 3 up). 1980. 12.25 (ISBN 0-8299-1033-6). West Pub.

Howe, John. Jack & the Beanstalk, Vol. 1. 1989. 14.95 (ISBN 0-316-37579-9). Little.

Izawa, Tadasu & Hijkata, Shigemi, illus. Jack & the Beanstalk. 18p. (gr. k-2). 1981. 3.95 (ISBN 0-448-09758-3, G&D). Putnam Pub Group.

Jack & the Beanstalk. (Illus.). (ps-3). 1985. 2.98 (ISBN 0-517-28804-4). Outlet Bk Co.

Jack & the Beanstalk. (Illus.). 24p. (ps-k). 1989. 1.29 (ISBN 0-02-898241-X). Checkerboard Pr.

Jacobs, Joseph, ed. English Fairy Tales. Batten, John D., illus. LC 67-19703. xv, 261p. (gr. 3-6). 1898. pap. 5.95 (ISBN 0-486-21818-X). Dover.

Marks, Alan, retold by. & illus. Childe Roland: An English Folk Tale. LC 88-19429. 32p. 1989. 14.95 (ISBN 0-87226-400-9, Bedrick Blackie). P Bedrick Bks.

Mockler, Anthony. King Arthur & His Knights. Harris, Nick, illus. 308p. 1987. jacketed 18.95 (ISBN 0-19-274531-X). Oxford U Pr.

O'Connor, Jane, retold by. The Teeny Tiny Woman. Alley, R. W., illus. LC 86-485. 32p. (ps-1). 1986. lib. bdg. 6.99 (ISBN 0-394-98320-3, Random Juv); pap. 2.95 (ISBN 0-394-88320-9, Random Juv). Random.

Parker, Ed, illus. Jack & the Beanstalk. LC 78-18072. 32p. (gr. k-4). 1979. PLB 9.79 (ISBN 0-89375-125-1); pap. 1.95 (ISBN 0-89375-103-0). Troll Assocs.

Robin Hood. (Illus.). (gr. 3-7). 3.50 (ISBN 0-7214-0885-0). Ladybird Bks.

Schmidt, Karen, illus. The Gingerbread Man. 32p. (gr. k-2). 1985. pap. 2.50 (ISBN 0-590-41056-3). Scholastic Inc.

Service, Pamela F. Wizard of Wind & Rock. Marshall, Laura, illus. LC 89-32865. 32p. (gr. k-5). 1990. 13.95 (ISBN 0-689-31600-3, Atheneum Child Bk). Macmillan Child Grp.

FOLKLORE, ESKIMO

Ridley, Ruth. Eagle Han Huch'inn Hodok: Stories in Eagle Han Huch'inn. Jamieson, Sandy, illus. Krauss, Michael, intro. by. (Illus.). 37p. (Orig.). (gr. 1-8). 1983. pap. 4.00 (ISBN 0-933769-14-8). Alaska Native.

FOLKLORE–EUROPE

Bornstein, Harry & Saulnier, Karen. Little Red Riding Hood. Pomeroy, Bradley O., illus. 48p. (gr. 1-6). 1990. PLB 14.95 (ISBN 1-878363-26-3). Forest Hse.

Brodmann, Aliana. Such a Noise! Fillingham, David, tr. from GER. Poppel, Hans, illus. 32p. (gr. k-3). 1989. 11.95 (ISBN 0-916291-25-1). Kane-Miller Bk.

Cincerelli, Carol J. A Russian Folktale - My Mother Is the Most Beautiful Woman in the World. 96p. (gr. 1-6). 1990. 8.95 (ISBN 0-86653-539-X, GA1162). Good Apple.

Einhorn, David. Seventh Candle & Other Folk Tales of Eastern Europe. Pashin, Gertrude, tr. Einhorn, David, illus. LC 68-10968. (gr. 6-8). 1968. 7.95x (ISBN 0-87068-369-1). Ktav.

Lorenz, Lee. Big Gus & Little Gus. Lorenz, Lee, illus. 32p. (gr. k-3). 1984. pap. 5.95 (ISBN 0-13-078122-3). P-H.

FOLKLORE–FINLAND

Troughton, Joanna, retold by. & illus. The Magic Mill: A Finnish Folk Tale from the Kalevala. LC 88-24170. 32p. 1989. 14.95 (ISBN 0-87226-405-X, Bedrick Blackie). P Bedrick Bks.

FOLKLORE–FRANCE

Beauty & the Beast. (Illus.). (ps-4). 3.50 (ISBN 0-7214-0642-4). Ladybird Bks.

Brown, Marcia. Stone Soup. Brown, Marcia, illus. LC 47-11630. 48p. (ps-4). 1979. 12.95 (ISBN 0-684-92296-7, Scribners Young Read); pap. 5.95 (ISBN 0-684-16217-2, Scribner). Macmillan Child Grp.

Deuchar, Ian. Prince & the Mermaid. 1990. 12.95 (ISBN 0-8037-0638-3). Dial Bks Young.

Heyer, Carol, retold by. & illus. Beauty & the Beast. 32p. (ps-3). 1989. 13.95 (ISBN 0-8249-8359-9). Ideals.

Mayer, Marianna. Beauty & the Beast. Mayer, Mercer, illus. LC 87-1095. 48p. (ps up). 1987. pap. 5.95 (ISBN 0-689-71151-4, Aladdin). Macmillan Child Grp.

Milone, Karen, illus. Beauty & the Beast. LC 81-612. 32p. (gr. k-4). 1981. PLB 9.79 (ISBN 0-89375-464-1); pap. text ed. 1.95 (ISBN 0-89375-465-X). Troll Assocs.

Pagnol. Le Chateau de ma Mere. (gr. 7-12). pap. 5.95 (ISBN 0-88436-045-8, 40278). EMC.

Paterson, Diane, illus. Stone Soup. LC 80-27947. 32p. (gr. 1-4). 1981. PLB 9.79 (ISBN 0-89375-478-1); pap. text ed. 1.95 (ISBN 0-89375-479-X). Troll Assocs.

Perrault, Charles. Perrault's Fairy Tales. Dore, Gustave, illus. LC 72-79522. viii, 117p. (gr. 4-6). 1969. pap. 5.95 (ISBN 0-486-22311-6). Dover.

—Puss in Boots. new ed. Da Riff, Andrea, illus. LC 78-18061. 32p. (gr. k-3). 1979. PLB 9.79 (ISBN 0-89375-130-8); pap. 1.95 (ISBN 0-89375-108-1). Troll Assocs.

—Puss in Boots: A Classic Tale. Jose, Eduard, adapted by. Suire, Diane D., tr. from SPA. Asensio, Augusti, illus. LC 88-35316. 32p. (gr. 1-4). 1988. PLB 10.95 (ISBN 0-89565-482-2). Childs World.

Puss in Boots. (Illus.). (gr. k). 3.50 (ISBN 0-7214-5170-5). Ladybird Bks.

Puss in Boots. (Illus.). (ps-4). 3.50 (ISBN 0-7214-0086-8). Ladybird Bks.

Radiguet, Raymond. Le Diable au Corps. (gr. 7-12). pap. 5.95 (ISBN 0-88436-059-8, 40273). EMC.

Saunders, Susan. Puss in Boots. 1989. pap. 2.50 (ISBN 0-590-41888-2). Scholastic Inc.

Stewig, John W., retold by. Stone Soup. Tomes, Margot, illus. LC 90-46502. 32p. (ps-3). 1991. PLB 14.95 (ISBN 0-8234-0863-9). Holiday.

Stone Soup. (Illus.). 24p. (ps-k). 1989. write for info. (ISBN 0-02-898167-7). Checkerboard Pr.

FOLKLORE–GERMANY

Amery, H. Cinderella. 1989. 2.95 (ISBN 0-7460-0250-5, Usborne). EDC.

Amoss, Berthe. Hansel & Gretel. Amoss, Berthe, illus. 10p. (ps-7). 1989. pap. 2.95 (ISBN 0-922589-05-4). More Than Card.

—Rumpelstiltskin. Amoss, Berthe, illus. 10p. (ps-7). 1989. pap. 2.95 (ISBN 0-922589-03-8). More Than Card.

—Snow White & the Seven Dwarfs. Amoss, Berthe, illus. 10p. (ps-7). 1989. pap. 2.95 (ISBN 0-922589-01-1). More Than Card.

Andersen, Hans Christian. Thumbeline. Zwerger, Lisbeth, illus. LC 85-12062. 28p. (gr. 1 up). 1985. 14.95 (ISBN 0-88708-006-5). Picture Bk Studio.

Anglund, Joan W. Nibble Nibble Mousekin: A Tale of Hansel & Gretel. Anglund, Joan W., illus. LC 62-14422. (ps-3). 1962. 10.95 (ISBN 0-15-257400-X, HJ). HarBraceJ.

Bailey, Emma. Quality Time Little Readers: Three Bears. 1991. 1.49 (ISBN 0-8317-7275-1). Smithmark.

La Belle au Bois Dormant. (FRE., Illus.). (gr. 2). 3.50 (ISBN 0-7214-1284-X). Ladybird Bks.

Birch Lane Press Staff. Cinderella. (ps-3). 1990. 12.95 (ISBN 1-55972-054-9, Birch Ln Pr). Carol Pub Group.

—Jack & the Beanstalk. (ps). 1990. 12.95 (ISBN 1-55972-048-4, Birch Ln Pr). Carol Pub Group.

Blanche Neige et les Sept Nains. (FRE., Illus.). (gr. 3). 3.50 (ISBN 0-7214-1294-7). Ladybird Bks.

Boll. Die Erzahlungen. (gr. 7-12). pap. 5.95 (ISBN 0-88436-108-X, 45275). EMC.

Bornstein, Harry & Saulnier, Karen L. Little Red Riding Hood: Told in Signed English. Pomeroy, Bradley O., illus. LC 90-3477. 40p. (ps-2). 1990. 13.95 (ISBN 0-930323-63-7, Pub. by K Green Pubns). Gallaudet Univ Pr.

The Brementown Musicians. (Illus.). 24p. (ps-k). 1989. 1.29 (ISBN 0-02-898239-8). Checkerboard Pr.

Browning, Robert. The Pied Piper of Hamelin. rev. ed. Small, Terry, illus. 64p. (gr. 1 up). 1988. 10.95 (ISBN 0-15-200566-8, Gulliver Bks). HarBraceJ.

Chmielarz, Sharon, adapted by. The Pied Piper of Hamelin. DeWitt, Pat & DeWitt, Robin, illus. 40p. (gr. k-6). 1990. 14.95 (ISBN 0-88045-115-7). Stemmer Hse.

Cooney, Barbara. Snow White & Rose Red. (ps-3). 1991. PLB 14.99 (ISBN 0-385-30176-6); pap. 13.95. Delacorte.

Corrin, Stephen & Corrin, Sara, eds. The Pied Piper of Hamelin. Le Cain, Errol, illus. 32p. (ps up). 1989. 14.95 (ISBN 0-15-261596-2, HJ). HarBraceJ.

Crump, Fred, Jr. Sleeping Beauty: A Retold Story. Crump, Fred, Jr., illus. LC 89-51788. 44p. (gr. k-2). Date not set. pap. 4.95 (ISBN 1-55523-300-7). Winston-Derek.

Dolan, Ellen M. & Bolinske, Janet L., eds. Hansel & Gretel. Nichol, Bee, illus. LC 87-61670. 32p. (Orig.). (gr. 1-3). 1987. text ed. 8.95 (ISBN 0-88335-555-8); 4.95 (ISBN 0-88335-545-0); pap. text ed. 3.95 (ISBN 0-88335-575-2). Milliken Pub Co.

Eden, Cooper, intro. by. Goldilocks. abr. ed. (Illus.). 48p. (gr. 9-12). 1989. 14.95 (ISBN 0-88138-135-7). Green Tiger Pr.

Edens, Cooper. Jack & the Beanstalk. 1990. 14.95 (ISBN 0-88138-139-X). Green Tiger Pr.

Edens, Cooper, intro. by. Little Red Riding Hood. (Illus.). 60p. 1989. 14.95 (ISBN 0-88138-128-4). Green Tiger Pr.

Fujita, Miho. Cinderella-board Book. 1991. 3.98 (ISBN 0-8317-3120-6). Smithmark.

—Goldilocks - Board Book. 1991. 3.98 (ISBN 0-8317-3121-4). Smithmark.

—Red Riding Hood-board Book. 1991. 3.98 (ISBN 0-8317-3119-2). Smithmark.

—Sleeping Beauty-board Book. 1991. 3.98 (ISBN 0-8317-3124-9). Smithmark.

—Snow White-Board Book. 1991. 3.98 (ISBN 0-8317-3123-0). Smithmark.

Gag, Wanda. Snow White & the Seven Dwarfs. Gag, Wanda, illus. (gr. 2-4). 1938. PLB 6.99 (ISBN 0-698-30320-2, Coward). Putnam Pub Group.

Gag, Wanda & Tomes, Margot. The Sorcerer's Apprentice. LC 78-23990. (Illus.). (gr. k-3). 1979. 6.95 (ISBN 0-698-20481-6, Coward). Putnam Pub Group.

Galdone, Paul. The Elves & the Shoemaker. Galdone, Paul, illus. LC 83-14979. 32p. (ps-3). 1986. 13.95 (ISBN 0-89919-226-2, Pub. by Clarion); pap. 4.95 (ISBN 0-89919-422-2, Pub. by Clarion). Ticknor & Fields.

Goes. Das Brandopfer. (gr. 7-12). pap. 5.95 (ISBN 0-88436-057-1, 45274). EMC.

Goodall, John S. Little Red Riding Hood. LC 87-34245. (Illus.). 60p. (ps-3). 1988. 14.95 (ISBN 0-689-50457-8, M K McElderry). Macmillan Child Grp.

Grimm, Jacob. The Shoemaker & the Elves. Adams, Adrienne, illus. Grimm, Wilhelm K. LC 60-12607. (Illus.). 32p. (ps-3). 1972. 12.95 (ISBN 0-684-12982-5, Scribners Young Read). Macmillan Child Grp.

Grimm, Jacob & Grimm, Wilhelm K. Cinderella: A Classic Tale. Jose, Eduard, adapted by. Moncure, Jane B., tr. from SPA. Asensio, Augusti, illus. LC 88-35317. 32p. (gr. 1-4). 1988. PLB 10.95 (ISBN 0-89565-483-0). Childs World.

—The Fisherman & His Wife. Jarrell, Randall, tr. from GER. Zemach, Margot, illus. 32p. (ps up). 1987. pap. 4.95 (ISBN 0-374-42326-1). FS&G.

—German Folk Tales. Krappe, Alexander H. & Magoun, Francis P., Jr., trs. LC 59-5095. 682p. (gr. 5 up). 1969. pap. 15.95x (ISBN 0-8093-0356-6). S Ill U Pr.

—Grimm's Fairy Tales. Crikshank, G., tr. (Illus.). (gr. 7 up). 1985. pap. 2.25 (ISBN 0-14-035070-5, Puffin). Puffin Bks.

—Grimm's Fairy Tales. Barish, Wendy, ed. Atkinson, Allen, illus. 304p. 1982. 15.95 (ISBN 0-671-43792-5, Little Simon). S&S Trade.

—Hansel & Gretel. Jeffers, Susan, illus. LC 80-15079. 32p. (gr. k up). 1980. 14.95 (ISBN 0-8037-3492-1); PLB 14.89 (ISBN 0-8037-3491-3). Dial Bks Young.

—Hansel & Gretel: A Classic Tale. Jose, Eduard, adapted by. Riehecky, Janet, tr. from SPA. Asensio, Augusti, illus. LC 88-35212. 32p. (gr. 1-4). 1988. PLB 10.95 (ISBN 0-89565-480-6). Childs World.

—Household Stories of the Brothers Grimm. Crane, Lucy, tr. Crane, Walter, illus. x, 269p. (gr. 3-9). 1886. pap. 4.95 (ISBN 0-486-21080-4). Dover.

—Rumpelstiltskin: A Classic Tale. Moncure, Jane B., tr. from SPA. Asensio, Augusti, illus. LC 88-35315. 32p. (gr. 1-4). 1988. PLB 10.95 (ISBN 0-89565-463-6). Childs World.

—Snow White & the Seven Dwarfs. Iwasaki, Chihiro, illus. LC 85-12158. 40p. (gr. 1 up). 1985. 15.95 (ISBN 0-88708-012-X). Picture Bk Studio.

Hastings, Selina. Peter & the Wolf. Cartwright, Reg, illus. (ps-2). 1990. 5.95 (ISBN 0-8050-1362-8). H Holt & Co.

Hautzig, Deborah, retold by. The Pied Piper of Hamelin: A Step 2 Book. Schindler, S. D., illus. LC 89-3968. 48p. (Orig.). (gr. 1-3). 1989. lib. bdg. 6.99 (ISBN 0-394-96579-5, Random Juv); pap. 2.95 (ISBN 0-394-86579-0, Random Juv). Random.

Hyman, Trina S. The Sleeping Beauty. LC 75-43769. (Illus.). (gr. 1 up). 1983. 14.95 (ISBN 0-316-38702-9); pap. 6.95 (ISBN 0-316-38708-8). Little.

Janisch, Heinz. Till Eulenspiegel's Merry Pranks. Bell, Anthea, tr. from GER. Zwerger, Lisbeth, illus. LC 90-7168. 32p. (gr. 3 up). 1990. 15.95 (ISBN 0-88708-150-9). Picture Bk Studio.

Jose, Eduard, adapted by. Goldilocks & the Three Bears: A Classic Tale. McDonnell, Janet, tr. from SPA. Lavarello, Jose M., illus. LC 88-36870. 32p. (gr. 1-4). 1988. PLB 10.95 (ISBN 0-89565-465-2). Childs World.

—Snow White & the Seven Dwarves: A Classic Tale. McDonnell, Janet, tr. from SPA. Asensio, Augusti, illus. LC 88-35210. 32p. (gr. 1-4). 1988. PLB 10.95 (ISBN 0-89565-479-2). Childs World.

—Till Eulenspiegel's Merry Pranks: A Classic Tale. Riehecky, Janet, tr. from SPA. Rovira, Francesc, illus. LC 88-36794. 32p. (gr. 1-4). 1988. PLB 10.95 (ISBN 0-89565-475-X). Childs World.

Kastner. Drei Manner Im Schnee. (gr. 7-12). pap. 5.95 (ISBN 0-88436-038-5, 45271). EMC.

Kimmel, Eric A. Nanny Goat & the Seven Little Kids. Stevens, Janet, illus. LC 89-20058. 32p. (ps-3). 1990. PLB 14.95 (ISBN 0-8234-0789-6). Holiday.

Little Red Riding Hood. (Illus.). 32p. (ps-1). 1985. 2.49 (ISBN 0-517-46240-0); bds. 1.00 (ISBN 0-517-48143-X). Outlet Bk Co.

Little Red Riding Hood. (ps-3). Date not set. write for info. incl. cassette (ISBN 0-307-13970-0, 13970, Pub. by Golden Bks). Western Pub.

Mayer, Marianna. The Spirit of the Blue Light. Gal, Laszlo, illus. LC 86-12524. 40p. (gr. k-3). 1990. 15.95 (ISBN 0-02-765350-1, Mcmillan Child Bk). Macmillan Child Grp.

Musicians of Bremen. (Illus.). (ps-4). 3.50 (ISBN 0-7214-1209-2). Ladybird Bks.

Ormerod, Jan & LLoyd, David. The Frog Prince. Omerod, Jan, illus. LC 89-12977. 32p. (ps-3). 1990. 12.95 (ISBN 0-688-09568-2); lib. bdg. 12.88 (ISBN 0-688-09569-0). Lothrop.

Perrault, Charles. Little Red Riding Hood: A Classic Tale. Jose, Eduard, ed. Moncure, Jane B., tr. from SPA. Lavarello, Jose M., illus. LC 88-37088. 32p. (gr. 1-4). 1988. PLB 10.95 (ISBN 0-89565-457-1). Childs World.

—Sleeping Beauty: A Classic Tale. Jose, Eduard, adapted by. Moncure, Jane B., tr. from SPA. Asensio, Agusti, illus. LC 88-35212. 32p. (gr. 1-4). 1988. PLB 10.95 (ISBN 0-89565-478-4). Childs World.

—Tom Thumb: A Classic Tale. Jose, Eduard, adapted by. Riehecky, Janet, tr. from SPA. Rovira, Francesc, illus. LC 88-35211. 32p. (gr. 1-4). 1988. PLB 10.95 (ISBN 0-89565-462-8). Childs World.

The Pied Piper. (Illus.). (gr. k-1). 3.50 (ISBN 0-7214-5173-X). Ladybird Bks.

The Pied Piper. (Illus.). (ps-4). 3.50 (ISBN 0-7214-0847-8). Ladybird Bks.

Red Riding Hood. (Illus.). (ps-3). 1985. 2.98 (ISBN 0-517-28810-9). Outlet Bk Co.

Rogasky, Barbara, retold by. The Water of Life. Hyman, Trina S., illus. LC 84-19226. 40p. (gr. k-3). 1986. reinforced bdg. 14.95 (ISBN 0-8234-0552-4). Holiday.

Ross, Tony. Hansel & Gretel. (Illus.). 32p. (gr. k-3). 1990. 13.95 (ISBN 0-86264-210-8, Pub. by Anderson Pr UK). Trafalgar Sq.

—Mrs. Goat & Her Seven Little Kids. Ross, Tony, illus. LC 89-17933. 24p. (gr. 1-3). 1990. 13.95 (ISBN 0-689-31624-0, Atheneum Child Bk). Macmillan Child Grp.

Rowland, Jada. The Elves & the Shoemakers. (Illus.). 32p. 1989. 12.95 (ISBN 0-8092-4355-5, Calico Bks). Contemp Bks.

Sanderson, Ruth, retold by. The Twelve Dancing Princesses. (gr. 2-4). 1990. 14.95 (ISBN 0-316-77017-5). Little.

San Souci, Robert D., ed. Grimm's the Six Swans. San Souci, Daniel, illus. (ps-3). 1989. pap. 14.95 (ISBN 0-671-65848-4). S&S Trade.

Snow White & the Seven Dwarfs. (Illus.). (ps-3). 1985. 2.98 (ISBN 0-517-28812-5). Outlet Bk Co.

Stevenson, Peter. Play Mask Book - Cinderella. 12p. (ps-3). 1991. pap. 5.95 (ISBN 0-8167-2371-0). Troll Assocs.

Walt Disney Staff. Pinocchio. 1987. 6.98 (ISBN 0-8317-6889-4, Gallery Bks). Smithmark.

Whitten, Patricia. Quality Time Little Readers: Red Riding Hood. 1991. 1.49 (ISBN 0-8317-7271-9). Smithmark.

FOLKLORE–GREAT BRITAIN

Galdone, Paul. Henny Penny. Galdone, Paul, illus. LC 68-24735. 32p. (ps-2). 1979. 13.95 (ISBN 0-395-28800-2, Clarion). HM.

—The Teeny-Tiny Woman. LC 84-4311. (Illus.). 32p. (ps-3). 1986. pap. 4.95 (ISBN 0-89919-463-X, Pub. by Clarion). Ticknor & Fields.

McLeish, Kenneth. Tales of the British Isles, 4 bks. Collard, Derek, et al, illus. 64p. (Orig.). (gr. 4-7). 1986. Set. pap. text ed. 23.80 incl. teacher's notes (ISBN 1-55624-015-5). Wright Group.

FOLKLORE–GREECE

Lines, Kathleen, ed. The Faber Book of Greek Legends. Jacques, Faith, illus. 272p. (gr. 4 up). 1986. pap. 11.95 (ISBN 0-571-13920-5). Faber & Faber.

FOLKLORE, GYPSY

Miller, Joseph. Wandering Gypsies. LC 72-87908. (Illus.). (gr. 6-12). 1969. text ed. 10.00 (ISBN 0-912472-08-1). Miller Bks.

FOLKLORE–HAITI

Johnson, Gyneth. How the Donkeys Came to Haiti & Other Folk Tales. Di Benedetto, Angelo, illus. 124p. (gr. 4-9). 12.95 (ISBN 0-8159-5706-8). Devin.

Wolkstein, Diane, ed. The Magic Orange Tree: And Other Haitian Folktales. Henriquez, Elsa, illus. LC 79-22787. (gr. 10 up). 1987. pap. 14.95 (ISBN 0-8052-0650-7). Schocken.

FOLKLORE–HAWAII

Aguiar, Elithe. Legends of Hawaii As Told By Lani Goose. Aguiar, Elithe & Sakamoto, Dean, illus. 20p. (gr. k up). 1986. pap. 8.95 incl. audio cassette (ISBN 0-944264-00-X). Lani Goose Pubns.

Brown, Marcia. Backbone of the King. (Illus.). 180p. (gr. 4-8). 1984. Repr. of 1966 ed. 12.95 (ISBN 0-8248-0963-7). UH Pr.

Kahn, Elithe M. Legends of Maui As Told by Lani Goose. Shiu, Tom, illus. 20p. (gr. k-6). 1989. pap. 8.95 incl. audiocassette (ISBN 0-944264-04-2). Lani Goose Pubns.

Kalakaua. The Legends & Myths of Hawaii: The Fables & Folk-Lore of a Strange People. Daggett, R. M., ed. & illus. LC 72-77519. (gr. 9 up). 1972. pap. 12.95 (ISBN 0-8048-1032-X). C E Tuttle.

Thompson, Vivian L. Hawaiian Myths of Earth, Sea, & Sky. Kahalewai, Marilyn, illus. LC 88-1325. 88p. (gr. 3-8). 1988. pap. 8.50 (ISBN 0-8248-1171-2, Kolowalu Bk). UH Pr.

—Kawelo, Roving Chief. Wozniak, Patricia A., illus. 96p. (gr. 4-6). 1991. 14.95 (ISBN 0-8248-1339-1, Kolowalu Bk). UH Pr.

Tune, Suelyn C. How Maui Slowed the Sun. Burningham, Robin Y., illus. LC 88-4548. 32p. (gr. k up). 1988. 8.95 (ISBN 0-8248-1083-X). UH Pr.

—Maui & the Secret of Fire. Burningham, Robin Y., illus. LC 90-27175. 32p. (ps-4). 1991. 9.95 (ISBN 0-8248-1391-X, Kolowalu Bk). UH Pr.

Williams, Julie S. Maui Goes Fishing. Burningham, Robin Y., illus. LC 90-27176. 32p. (ps-4). 1991. 9.95 (ISBN 0-8248-1390-1, Kolowalu Bk). UH Pr.

FOLKLORE–HUNGARY

Benedek, Elek. Palko, the Piper: Hungarian Folktales. (Illus.). 28p. (ps-8). 1988. 13.95 (ISBN 963-13-2531-8, Pub. by Corvina Budapest). Intl Spec Bk.

Biro, Val. Tobias & the Dragon: A Hungarian Folk Tale. Biro, Val, illus. LC 89-18492. 32p. (ps). 1990. 12.95 (ISBN 0-87226-427-0). P Bedrick Bks.

Ginsburg, Mirra. Two Greedy Bears: Adapted from a Hungarian Folk Tale. Aruego, Jose & Dewey, Ariane, illus. LC 76-8819. 32p. (ps-2). 1976. 13.95 (ISBN 0-02-736450-X, Mcmillan Child Bk). Macmillan Child Grp.

The Three Wishes: Hungarian Folktales. (Illus.). 32p. 1989. 12.95 (ISBN 963-13-2563-6, Pub. by Corvina Kiado HU). Intl Spec Bk.

FOLKLORE–ICELAND

Helgadottir, Gudrun. Flumbra: An Icelandic Folktale. Sanders, Christopher, tr. from ICE. Pilkington, Brian, illus. LC 86-6173. 32p. (gr. 1-6). 1986. lib. bdg. 12.95 (ISBN 0-87614-243-9). Carolrhoda Bks.

FOLKLORE–INDIA

Beven, Annette. The Spade Sage. Hall, Diane, illus. 24p. (gr. 1-5). 1984. pap. 5.95 (ISBN 0-913546-71-2). Dharma Pub.

Black, Deborah, illus. The King & the Goat. Tulku, Tarthang, intro. by. LC 86-19829. (Illus.). 32p. (Orig.). (gr. 1-4). 1986. PLB 12.95 (ISBN 0-89800-159-5); pap. 5.95 (ISBN 0-89800-145-5). Dharma Pub.

Brown, Marcia. Once a Mouse. Brown, Marcia, illus. LC 61-14769. 32p. (ps-3). 1972. 13.95 (ISBN 0-684-12662-1, Scribners Young Read). Macmillan Child Grp.

Carlson, Jeanne, et al, illus. A King, a Hunter & a Golden Goose. Tulku, Tarthang, intro. by. LC 86-24154. 32p. (gr. 1-4). 1987. PLB 12.95 (ISBN 0-89800-155-2); pap. 5.95 (ISBN 0-89800-141-2). Dharma Pub.

Choudhary, Bani. Story of Mahabharata. (ps up). 1988. 7.50 (ISBN 0-318-37379-3). Auromere.

Choudhary, Bani R. Stories from Panchatantra. Bhushan, Reboti, illus. (gr. 3-10). 1979. 7.50 (ISBN 0-89744-136-2). Auromere.

Clemmons, Bradley & Witwer, Julia, illus. The Fish King's Power of Truth. Tulku, Tarthang, intro. by. LC 86-24159. 32p. (gr. k-4). 1987. PLB 12.95 (ISBN 0-89800-158-7); pap. 5.95 (ISBN 0-89800-144-7). Dharma Pub.

Cook, Elizabeth, adapted by. Rabbit Who Overcame Fear: A Jataka Tale. Meller, Eric, illus. Tulku, Tarthang, intro. by. (Illus.). 32p. (Orig.). (gr. k-4). 1991. 12. 95 (ISBN 0-89800-212-5); pap. 5.95 (ISBN 0-89800-211-7). Dharma Pub. The latest in a series of children's stories drawn from the rich storytelling tradition of ancient India, China & Tibet, presented for the first time in large picture-book format. Stories in the Jataka Tales promote the values of compassion, peace, friendship, & kindness, opening the door for parent & child to discuss the importance of these issues. In this story, a young rabbit, startled from sleep by a loud noise & shaking, springs into flight in fear of an earthquake. His panic spreads, endangering other animals who follow his blind rush toward a cliff. They are saved by a compassionate lion who teaches them how to investigate the source of fear before jumping to unwise conclusions. An instructive tale told with warmth & humor. Vibrant color. Ages 3-8. Available in English, Portuguese, German, Dutch. Valuable for multicultural education, English as second language classes. Call Dharma Publishing, (800) 873-4276 for a free brochure of other books in this series. *Publisher Provided Annotation.*

Demi, adapted by. & illus. The Hallowed Horse: A Folktale from India. (gr. k-3). 1987. 14.95 (ISBN 0-396-08908-9, Putnam). Putnam Pub Group.

Giles, Anne E. Merwan: Stories of Meher Baba for Children. Lesnik, D., illus. LC 80-53858. 96p. (Orig.). (gr. 3-7). 1980. pap. 4.95 (ISBN 0-913078-41-7). Sheriar Pr.

Jacobs, Joseph, ed. Indian Fairy Tales. Batten, John D., illus. xvi, 255p. (ps-4). 1969. pap. 6.95 (ISBN 0-486-21828-7). Dover.

McSweeney, Terry, illus. Great Gift & the Wish-Fulfilling Gem. Tulku, Tarthang, intro. by. LC 86-19767. (Illus.). 32p. (gr. k-5). 1987. PLB 12.95 (ISBN 0-89800-157-9); pap. 5.95 (ISBN 0-89800-143-9). Dharma Pub.

Newton, Pam, retold by. & illus. The Stonecutter: An Indian Folktale. 32p. (ps-3). 1990. 14.95 (ISBN 0-399-22187-5, Putnam-Whitebird). Putnam Pub Group.

Panday, Daulat. The Tales of India, Vol. 2. 126p. (gr. 3-8). 1985. pap. 5.95 (ISBN 0-89071-331-6, Pub. by Sri Aurobindo Ashram India). Aurobindo Assn.

The Parrot & the Fig Tree. Harmon, Michael, illus. Tulku, Tarthang, intro. by. LC 86-24159. (Illus.). 32p. (Orig.). (gr. k-4). 1987. PLB 12.95 (ISBN 0-89800-156-0); pap. 5.95 (ISBN 0-89800-142-0). Dharma Pub.

Ram, Govinder. Rama & Sita: A Folk Tale from India. Ram, Govinder, illus. LC 87-14333. 28p. (gr. k-5). 1988. 14.95 (ISBN 0-87226-171-9, Bedrick Blackie). P Bedrick Bks.

Savitri. Tales from Indian Classics, Bk. I. Biswas, Pulak, illus. (gr. 3-9). 1979. 4.50 (ISBN 0-89744-167-2). Auromere.

—Tales from Indian Classics, Bk. II. Biswas, Pulak, illus. (gr. 3-9). 1979. 4.50 (ISBN 0-89744-168-0). Auromere.

—Tales from Indian Classics, Bk. III. Chatterjee, Sukumar, illus. (gr. 3-9). 1979. 4.50 (ISBN 0-89744-169-9); pap. write for info. Auromere.

Shankar. Treasury of Indian Tales: Book I. Mukerji, Debrabrata, illus. (gr. 8-12). 1979. 4.95 (ISBN 0-89744-170-2). Auromere.

—Treasury of Indian Tales: Book II. Vyas, Anil, illus. (gr. 8-12). 1979. 4.95 (ISBN 0-89744-171-0). Auromere.

Shanta. Nala Damayanti. Sonkaria, Gyan, illus. (gr. 1-9). 1979. pap. 3.00 (ISBN 0-89744-158-3). Auromere.

Stamler, Suzanne. Three Wise Birds. Nolan, Gary, illus. (gr. 1-6). pap. 5.95 (ISBN 0-913546-68-2). Dharma Pub.

Tagore, Abindranath. The Cheese Doll. Mukherjee, Meenakshi, tr. from BEN. (Illus.). (gr. 3-11). 1979. 6.25 (ISBN 0-89744-143-5). Auromere.

Thomas, Vernon, ed. Folk Tales from India. Ghosh, R. B., illus. (gr. 3-10). 1979. 7.50 (ISBN 0-89744-141-9). Auromere.

Troughton, Joanna. The Wizard Punchkin: A Folk Tale from India. Troughton, Joanna, illus. LC 87-11517. 28p. (gr. k-5). 1988. 14.95 (ISBN 0-87226-162-X, Bedrick Blackie). P Bedrick Bks.

The Value of Friends. LC 86-24164. 32p. (Orig.). (gr. k-4). 1986. PLB 12.95 (ISBN 0-89800-154-4); pap. 5.95 (ISBN 0-89800-140-4). Dharma Pub.

Wheeler, M. J. Fox Tales. Gustafson, Dana, illus. LC 83-21001. 56p. (gr. k-4). 1984. PLB 9.95 (ISBN 0-87614-255-2). Carolrhoda Bks.

FOLKLORE, INDIAN

see also Indians of North America–Legends

Bierhorst, John, ed. The Girl Who Married a Ghost & Other Tales from the North American Indian. LC 77-21515. (Illus.). (gr. 7 up). 1984. 12.95 (ISBN 0-02-709740-4, Four Winds). Macmillan Child Grp.

Bruchac, Joseph. Return of the Sun: Native American Tales from the Northeast Woodlands. Carpenter, Gary, illus. 200p. (Orig.). 1990. pap. 8.95 (ISBN 0-89594-343-3). Crossing Pr.

Connolly, James E., ed. Why the Possum's Tail Is Bare: And Other North American Indian Nature Tales. Adams, Andrea, illus. LC 84-26871. 56p. (gr. 3 up). 1985. PLB 13.95 (ISBN 0-88045-069-X). Stemmer Hse.

Crofts, Trudy. The Hunter & the Quail. Childers, Peggy, illus. 24p. (gr. 1-6). 1977. pap. 5.95 (ISBN 0-913546-30-5). Dharma Pub.

Davis, Grania. The King & the Mangoes. Hoffman, Sheila, illus. 24p. (gr. 1-4). 1983. pap. 5.95 (ISBN 0-913546-69-0). Dharma Pub.

—The Proud Peacock & the Mallard. Christman, Anne, illus. 24p. (gr. k-4). 1983. pap. 5.95 (ISBN 0-913546-70-4). Dharma Pub.

De Angulo, Jaime. Indian Tales. De Angulo, Jaime, illus. 256p. (gr. 5 up). 1984. 8.95 (ISBN 0-374-52163-8, Am Century). FS&G.

Goble, Paul, retold by. & illus. Iktomi & the Ducks: A Plains Indian Tale. LC 89-71025. 32p. (ps-1). 1990. 14.95 (ISBN 0-531-05883-2); PLB 14.99 (ISBN 0-531-08483-3). Orchard Bks Watts.

Greison, Betty, et al. Black Hawk & Jim Thorp: Super Heroes; Sauk Indian Stories for Children. (gr. 5-12). 1983. pap. 4.95 (ISBN 0-89992-085-3). Coun India Ed.

Gupta, Rupa. Tales from Indian Classics. Basu, R. K., illus. 136p. (gr. 1-9). 1981. 7.50 (ISBN 0-89744-233-4, Pub. by Hemkunt India). Auromere.

Lacapa, Michael. The Flute Player: An Apache Folktale. Lacapa, Michael, illus. LC 89-63749. 64p. (gr. 1-3). 1990. 14.95 (ISBN 0-87358-500-3). Northland AZ.

Law, Katheryn. Salish Folk Tales. (gr. 2-8). 1972. 2.95 (ISBN 0-89992-028-4). Coun India Ed.

Leech, Jay & Spencer, Zane. Moon of the Big-Dog. Funai, Mamoru, illus. LC 79-7893. 64p. (gr. 2-6). 1980. (Crowell Jr Bks); PLB 8.89 (ISBN 0-690-04002-4). HarpC Child Bks.

McDermott, Gerald. Arrow to the Sun: A Pueblo Indian Tale. McDermott, Gerald, illus. (gr. 1 up). 1977. pap. 4.95 (ISBN 0-14-050211-4, Puffin). Puffin Bks.

Mayo, Gretchen W. Earthmaker's Tales: North American Indian Stories about Earth Happenings. Mayo, Gretchen W., illus. LC 88-20515. 96p. (gr. 5 up). 1989. 11.95 (ISBN 0-8027-6839-3); PLB 12.85 (ISBN 0-8027-6840-7). Walker & Co.

—North American Indian Stories: Earthmaker's Tales. Mayo, Gretchen W., illus. 48p. (gr. 5 up). 1991. pap. 5.95 (ISBN 0-8027-7343-5). Walker & Co.

—North American Indian Stories: More Earthmaker's Tales. Mayo, Gretchen W., illus. 48p. (gr. 5 up). 1991. pap. 5.95 (ISBN 0-8027-7344-3). Walker & Co.

—North American Indian Stories: More Star Tales. Mayo, Gretchen W., illus. 48p. (gr. 5 up). 1991. pap. 5.95 (ISBN 0-8027-7347-8). Walker & Co.

—North American Indian Stories: Star Tales. Mayo, Gretchen W., illus. 48p. (gr. 5 up). 1991. pap. 5.95 (ISBN 0-8027-7345-1). Walker & Co.

—Star Tales: North American Indian Stories about the Stars. 96p. (gr. 5 up). 1987. 11.95 (ISBN 0-8027-6672-2); PLB 12.85 (ISBN 0-8027-6673-0). Walker & Co.

Norman, Howard. How Glooskap Outwits the Ice Giants: And Other Tales of the Maritime Indians, Vol. 1. 1989. 14.95 (ISBN 0-316-61181-6, Joy St Bks). Little.

Reed, Evelyn D. Coyote Tales from the Indian Pueblos. Strock, Glen, illus. LC 86-14544. 96p. (gr. 4 up). 1988. pap. 8.95 (ISBN 0-86534-094-3). Sunstone Pr.

Troughton, Joanna, retold by. & illus. Who Will Be the Sun? A North American Indian Folk Tale. LC 85-15074. 28p. (gr. k-4). 1986. 14.95 (ISBN 0-87226-038-0, Bedrick Blackie). P Bedrick Bks.

FOLKLORE–IRELAND

Danaher, Kevin. Children's Book of Irish Folktales. Berson, Harold, illus. 108p. 1984. pap. 9.95 (ISBN 0-85342-718-6, Pub. by Mercier Press Ltd Eire). Dufour.

Dillon, Eilis. Lost Island. 204p. 1987. pap. 7.95 (ISBN 0-86278-118-3, Pub. by O'Brien Press Ltd Eire). Dufour.

Fritz, Jean. Brendan the Navigator. Arno, Enrico, illus. LC 78-13247. (gr. 2-5). 1979. 7.95 (ISBN 0-698-20473-5, Coward). Putnam Pub Group.

Gregory, Isabella. Irish Legends for Children. (Illus.). 90p. (ps-8). 1983. pap. 5.95 (ISBN 0-85342-691-0, Pub. by Mercier Press Ltd Eire). Dufour.

Lenihan, Edmund. Strange Irish Tales for Children. (Illus.). 116p. (ps-8). 1987. pap. 9.95 (ISBN 0-85342-833-6, Pub. by Mercier Press Ltd Eire). Dufour.

Lynch, Patricia. Tales of Irish Enchantment. (Illus.). 108p. 1980. pap. 8.95 (ISBN 0-85342-790-9, Pub. by Mercier Press Ltd Eire). Dufour.

McDermott, Gerald. Daniel O'Rourke: An Irish Tale. 1988. pap. 3.95 (ISBN 0-14-050673-X, Puffin). Puffin Bks.

McGowan, Hugh. Leprechauns, Legends & Irish Tales. Haigh, Peter, illus. 128p. (gr. 7 up). 1990. 24.95 (ISBN 0-575-04261-3, Pub. by Gollancz England). Trafalgar Sq.

MacLiammoir, Michael. Faery Nights: Stories on Ancient Irish Festivals. 104p. (ps-8). 1987. 13.95 (ISBN 0-86278-074-8, Pub. by O'Brien Press Ltd Eire); (Pub. by O'Brien Press Ltd Eire). Dufour.

O'Leary, Peter. Seadna. O'Ceirn, Cyril & O'Ceirn, Kit, trs. from IRI. (Illus.). 166p. (Orig.). (gr. k up). 1989. pap. 11.95 (ISBN 0-907606-60-1, Pub. by Glendale Pr). Irish Bks Media.

Ryan, Joan & Snell, Gordon, eds. The Haunted Hills: Ghost Tales of Ireland for Children. (Illus.). 158p. (gr. 4-8). 1984. 10.95 (ISBN 0-907606-20-2, Pub. by Glendale Pr). Irish Bks Media.

FOLKLORE–ISLANDS OF THE PACIFIC

Hashimoto, Yasuko & Edades, Jean. Tales of a Japanese Grandmother, 5 Vols. Kubota, Kenji, illus. (Orig.). (gr. k-3). 1982. Set. pap. 12.50 (ISBN 0-686-37564-5, Pub. by New Day Philippines). Cellar.

Intia, Peria S. Three Tales from Bicol. Dia, Benjamin A. & Lopez, Ben, illus. 45p. (Orig.). (gr. 4-6). 1982. pap. 4.00 (ISBN 971-10-0029-6, Pub. by New Day Philippines). Cellar.

FOLKLORE–ITALY

Cossi, Olga. Orlanda & the Contest of Thieves. Sarmo, Tom, illus. LC 89-15107. 32p. (gr. 1-6). 1989. 14.95 (ISBN 0-917665-32-5). Pelican.

DePaola, Tomie. The Clown of God. De Paola, Tomie, illus. LC 78-3845. (gr. k up). 1978. 13.95 (ISBN 0-15-219175-5, HJ). HarBraceJ.

De Paola, Tomie. The Legend of Old Befana. De Paola, Tomie, illus. LC 80-12293. 32p. (gr. k-3). 1980. 14.95 (ISBN 0-15-243816-5, HJ). HarBraceJ.

—The Legend of Old Befana. De Paola, Tomie, illus. LC 80-12293. 32p. (gr. k-3). 1980. pap. 3.95 (ISBN 0-15-243817-3, VoyB). HarBraceJ.

DePaola, Tomie. Strega Nona. LC 75-11565. (Illus.). 32p. (ps-4). 1979. PLB 13.95 (ISBN 0-671-66283-X); pap. 6.95 (ISBN 0-671-66606-1). S&S Trade.

—Tony's Bread. DePaola, Tomie, illus. 32p. (ps-3). 1989. 13.95 (ISBN 0-399-21693-6, Putnam). Putnam Pub Group.

Giannini, Enzo. Little Parsley. (ps-3). 1990. pap. 13.95 (ISBN 0-671-67197-9). S&S Trade.

Manson, Christopher. The Crab Prince. Manson, Christopher, illus. LC 90-26626. 32p. (gr. k-3). 1991. 14.95 (ISBN 0-8050-1215-X). H Holt & Co.

Nones, Eric J. Canary Prince. (ps up). 1991. 14.95 (ISBN 0-374-31029-7). FS&G.

Rayevsky, Inna, retold by. The Talking Tree. Ravesky, Robert, illus. 32p. (gr. k-4). 1990. 14.95 (ISBN 0-399-21631-6, Putnam). Putnam Pub Group.

FOLKLORE–JAMAICA

Sherlock, Philip K. Anansi, the Spider Man. Brown, Marcia, illus. LC 54-5619. 112p. (gr. 3-7). 1954. 14.95 (ISBN 0-690-08905-8, Crowell Jr Bks). HarpC Child Bks.

FOLKLORE–JAPAN

Goodman, Robert B. & Spicer, Robert A. Urashima Taro. Tabrah, Ruth, ed. Suyeoka, George, illus. LC 73-79570. (gr. 1-7). 1973. 5.95 (ISBN 0-89610-013-8). Island Heritage.

Haugaard, Erik & Haugaard, Masako. The Story of Yuriwaka. (Illus.). 64p. (gr. 3-6). 1991. 12.95 (ISBN 1-879373-02-5, Arpel Gra CO). R Rinehart Inc.

Hearn, Lafcadio. In Ghostly Japan. LC 79-138068. (Illus.). (gr. 9 up). 1971. pap. 10.95 (ISBN 0-8048-0965-8). C E Tuttle.

Hodges, Margaret. Wave. Lent, Blair, illus. (gr. k-3). 1964. 3.50 (ISBN 0-395-06817-7). HM.

Johnston, Tony. The Badger & the Magic Fan: A Japanese Folktale. DePaola, Tomie, illus. 32p. (ps-3). 1990. 13.95 (ISBN 0-399-21945-5, Putnam). Putnam Pub Group.

Kendall, Carol, retold by. Haunting Tales from Japan. LC 85-50684. (Illus.). 40p. (Orig.). (gr. 6-9). 1985. pap. 6.00 (ISBN 0-913689-22-X). Spencer Muse Art.

Mcalpine, Helen & Mcalpine, William, eds. Japanese Tales & Legends. (Illus.). 218p. 1989. pap. 8.95 (ISBN 0-19-274140-3). Oxford U Pr.

Motomora, Mitchell. Peach Boy. (Illus.). 32p. (gr. 1-3). 1989. PLB 12.33 (ISBN 0-8172-3513-2). Raintree Pubs.

Ozaki, Yei T., compiled by. The Japanese Fairy Book. LC 70-109415. (Illus.). 320p. (gr. 3-8). 1970. pap. 9.95 (ISBN 0-8048-0885-6). C E Tuttle.

Rampo, Edogawa. Japanese Tales of Mystery & Imagination. Harris, James B., tr. LC 56-6804. (Illus.). (gr. 9 up). 1956. pap. 9.95 (ISBN 0-8048-0319-6). C E Tuttle.

Sakade, Florence. Japanese Children's Favorite Stories. Kurosaki, Yoshio, illus. LC 58-11620. (gr. 1-4). 1958. bds. 16.95 (ISBN 0-8048-0284-X). C E Tuttle.

—Little One-Inch & Other Japanese Children's Favorite Stories. (Illus.). (gr. 1-5). 1958. pap. 8.95 (ISBN 0-8048-0384-6). C E Tuttle.

—Peach Boy & Other Japanese Children's Favorite Stories. Kurosaki, Yoshisuke, illus. (gr. 1-5). 1958. pap. 8.95 (ISBN 0-8048-0469-9). C E Tuttle.

Sakade, Florence, ed. Urashima Taro & Other Japanese Children's Stories. (Illus.). (gr. 1-6). 1958. pap. 8.95 (ISBN 0-8048-0609-8). C E Tuttle.

Stamm, Claus. Three Strong Women. Tseng, Jean & Tseng, Mou-sien, illus. 32p. (gr. 2-5). 1990. pap. 12.95 (ISBN 0-670-83323-1). Viking Child Bks.

Terrible Eek. 1991. pap. 13.95 (ISBN 0-671-73737-6). S&S Trade.

Uchida, Yoshiko. The Two Foolish Cats. Zemach, Margot, illus. LC 86-12660. 32p. (ps-3). 1987. 13.95 (ISBN 0-689-50397-0, M K McElderry). Macmillan Child Grp.

Yagawa, Sumiko. The Crane Wife. Paterson, Katherine, tr. from JPN. Akaba, Suekichi, illus. LC 80-29278. 32p. (ps-3). 1981. pap. 4.95 (ISBN 0-685-03413-5, Mulberry Bks). Morrow Jr Bks.

Yamaguchi, Marianne. The Sea of Gold & Other Tales from Japan. LC 87-72797. (Illus.). 144p. (gr. 7-12). 1988. pap. 7.95 (ISBN 0-88739-056-0). Creative Arts Bk.

FOLKLORE, JEWISH

Alder, David A. The Children of Chelm. Friedman, Arthur, illus. (gr. 1-5). 1979. (Bonim Bks); pap. 4.50 (ISBN 0-88482-773-9, Bonim Bks). Hebrew Pub.

Chaikin, Miriam. Hinkl & Other Shlemiel Stories. Posner, Marcia, illus. LC 86-29755. 96p. (Orig.). (gr. 7 up). 1987. pap. 6.95 (ISBN 0-933503-37-7). Shapolsky Pubs.

Freehof, Lillian S. Bible Legends: An Introduction to Midrash, Vol. 1: Genesis. Schwartz, Howard, ed. (gr. 4-6). 1987. pap. text ed. 6.95 (ISBN 0-8074-0357-1, 123050). UAHC.

Freeman, Florence B. It Happened in Chelm: A Story of the Legendary Town of Fools. Krevitsky, Nik, illus. 64p. (gr. 3-8). 1990. pap. text ed. 9.95 (ISBN 0-933503-22-9). Shapolsky Pubs.

Ganz, Yaffa. Tali's Slippers, Tova's Shoes. Ariel, Liat B., illus. 32p. (gr. k-6). 1989. 5.95 (ISBN 0-89906-502-3). Mesorah Pubns.

Gauz, Yaffa. Savta Simcha & the Seven Splendid Gifts. Gewirtz, Bina, illus. (gr. 4-7). 1987. 11.95 (ISBN 0-87306-437-2). Feldheim.

Geras, Adele. My Grandmother's Stories: A Collection of Jewish Folk Tales. Jordan, Jael, illus. LC 90-4309. 96p. (gr. 3-7). 1990. 17.95 (ISBN 0-679-80910-4); PLB 18.99 (ISBN 0-679-90910-9). Knopf.

Gershator, Phillis. Honi & His Magic Circle. Rieger, Shay, illus. LC 79-84931. (gr. k-4). 1979. 6.95 (ISBN 0-8276-0167-0). JPS Phila.

Jaffe, Nina. The Three Riddles: A Jewish Folktale. Waldman, Bryna, illus. (ps-3). 1989. incl. cassette 7.95 (ISBN 0-553-45910-4). Bantam.

—The Three Riddles: A Jewish Folktale. Waldman, Bryna, illus. (ps-3). 1989. pap. 3.95 (ISBN 0-553-34649-0). Bantam.

Kleinbard, Gitel. Oh, Zalmy! Or, the Tale of the Porcelain Pony, Bk. 1. (Illus.). (gr. k-3). 1976. 5.95 (ISBN 0-917274-04-0); pap. 3.95 (ISBN 0-917274-01-6). Mah Tov Pubns.

Margolin, Miriam. Little Stories for Little Children. Ryback, Issachar, illus. 32p. (gr. k-3). 1986. Repr. of 1922 ed. 11.75x (ISBN 0-918825-55-5); 11.95 (ISBN 0-918825-53-9). Moyer Bell Limited.
These are simple stories of shtetl life that attain an astonishing immediacy throughout the Picassoesque black-&-white drawings of Issachar Ryback, a Russian artist often compared with Marc Chagall. First published in 1922 by the Jewish Section of Comissariat for Folk Education, USSR.
Publisher Provided Annotation.

Omer, Devorah. Once There Was a Hassid. Shvo, Aaron, illus. 28p. (gr. 4 up). 1987. 9.95 (ISBN 0-915361-73-6, Dist. by Watts). Adama Pubs Inc.

Shulevitz, Uri. The Treasure. Shulvitz, Uri, illus. LC 78-12952. 32p. (ps-3). 1979. 13.95 (ISBN 0-374-37740-5). FS&G.

Simon, Solomon. Adventures of Simple Shmerel. Fischel, Lillian, illus. (gr. 3-7). 1942. 4.95 (ISBN 0-87441-127-0). Behrman.

—Wise Men of Helm. (gr. 3-7). 1942. pap. 6.50 (ISBN 0-87441-125-4). Behrman.

Singer, Isaac Bashevis. Elijah the Slave. Frasconi, Antonio, illus. 32p. (ps up). 1988. pap. 4.95 (ISBN 0-374-42047-5). FS&G.

—When Shlemiel Went to Warsaw & Other Stories. Zemach, Margot, illus. 161p. (gr. 3-7). 1986. pap. 3.50 (ISBN 0-374-48365-5). FS&G.

Sofer, G. A Story a Day, Vol. I: Tishrei-Cheshvan. Weinbach, Shaindel, tr. from HEB. Bardugo, Miriam, illus. 206p. (gr. 7-12). 1989. 12.95 (ISBN 0-89906-950-9); pap. 9.95 (ISBN 0-89906-951-7). Mesorah Pubns.

—A Story a Day, Vol. II: Kislev-Teves. Weinbach, Shaindel, tr. from HEB. Bardugo, Miriam, illus. 232p. (gr. 7-12). 1988. 12.95 (ISBN 0-89906-952-5); pap. 9.95 (ISBN 0-89906-953-3). Mesorah Pubns.

—A Story a Day, Vol. III: Shevat-Adar. Weinbach, Shaindel, tr. from HEB. Bardugo, Miriam, illus. 224p. (gr. 7-12). 1989. 12.95 (ISBN 0-89906-954-1); pap. 9.95 (ISBN 0-89906-955-X). Mesorah Pubns.

—A Story a Day, Vol. IV: Nissan-Iyar. Weinbach, Shaindel, tr. from HEB. Bardugo, Miriam, illus. 210p. (gr. 7-12). 1989. 12.95 (ISBN 0-89906-956-8); pap. 9.95 (ISBN 0-89906-957-6). Mesorah Pubns.

—A Story a Day, Vol. V: Sivan-Tammuz. Weinbach, Shaindel, tr. from HEB. Bardugo, Miriam, illus. 210p. (gr. 7-12). 1989. 12.95 (ISBN 0-89906-958-4); pap. 9.95 (ISBN 0-89906-959-2). Mesorah Pubns.

—A Story a Day, Vol. VI: Ev-Elul. Weinbach, Shaindel, tr. from HEB. Bardugo, Miriam, illus. 210p. (gr. 7-12). 1989. 12.95 (ISBN 0-89906-960-6); pap. 9.95 (ISBN 0-89906-961-4). Mesorah Pubns.

Weinstock, Y. Tales from the Gemara, Vol. II: Shabbos. Weinstock, Shaindel, tr. from HEB. (Illus.). 160p. (gr. 5-12). 1989. 11.95 (ISBN 0-89906-814-6); pap. 8.95 (ISBN 0-89906-815-4). Mesorah Pubns.

FOLKLORE–KOREA

Adams, Edward B., ed. Blindman's Daughter. Choi, Dong Ho, illus. 32p. (gr. 3). 1981. 8.95 (ISBN 0-8048-1472-4, Pub. by Seoul Intl Publishing House). C E Tuttle.

—Korean Cinderella. Choi, Dong Ho, illus. 32p. (gr. 3). 1982. 8.95 (ISBN 0-8048-1473-2, Pub. by Seoul Intl Publishing House). C E Tuttle.

Carpenter, Frances. Tales of a Korean Grandmother. LC 72-77515. (Illus.). (gr. 3-8). 1972. pap. 8.95 (ISBN 0-8048-1043-5). C E Tuttle.

Ginsburg, Mirra, ed. The Chinese Mirror. Zemach, Margot, illus. LC 86-22940. 32p. (gr. 4-8). 1988. 15.95 (ISBN 0-15-200420-3, Gulliver Bks). HarBraceJ.

Hyun, Peter, ed. Korea's Favorite Tales & Lyrics. Park, Dong-Il, illus. 124p. 1986. 12.95 (ISBN 0-318-32535-7, Pub. by Seoul Intl Pub Hse Korea). C E Tuttle.

Kim, Yong-Kol. Brave Hong Kil-Dong: The Man Who Bought the Shade of a Tree. Kang, Mi-Sun & Kim, Yong-Kyong, illus. 46p. (gr. 2-5). 1990. PLB 9.95x (ISBN 0-930878-91-4). Hollym Intl.

So-Un, Kim. Story Bag: A Collection of Korean Folk Tales. Higashi, Setsu, tr. Eui-Hwan, Kim, illus. LC 55-13738. (gr. 2-5). 1955. pap. 10.95 (ISBN 0-8048-0548-2). C E Tuttle.

Vorhees, Duance & Mueller, Mark. The Faithful Daughter Shim Ch'ong: The Little Frog Who Never Listened. Kang, Mi-Sun & Kim, Yon-Kyong, illus. 46p. (gr. 2-5). 1990. PLB 9.95x (ISBN 0-930878-92-2). Hollym Intl.

—The Greedy Princess: The Rabbit & the Tiger. Pak, Mi-Son & Kim, Yon-Kyong, illus. 46p. (gr. 2-5). 1990. PLB 9.95x (ISBN 0-930878-90-6). Hollym Intl.

—The Snail Lady: The Magic Vase. Kang, Mi-Sun, illus. 46p. (gr. 2-5). 1990. PLB 9.95x (ISBN 0-930878-89-2). Hollym Intl.

—The Son of the Cinnamon Tree: The Donkey's Egg. Kim, Yon-Kyong & Kang, Mi-Sun, illus. 46p. (gr. 2-5). 1990. PLB 9.95x (ISBN 0-930878-93-0). Hollym Intl.

Yoo, Grace S. Two Korean Brothers: The Story of Hungbu & Nolbu. LC 73-18023. (gr. k-3). 1970. 6.95 (ISBN 0-912580-01-1). Far Eastern Res.

FOLKLORE–LATIN AMERICA

Baden, Robert. Y Domingo, Siete. Mathews, Judith, ed. Ada, Alma F., tr. Edwards, Michelle, illus. (SPA.). 32p. (ps-3). 1990. 12.95 (ISBN 0-8075-9355-9). A Whitman.

Green, Belva. How the Robin Got Its Red Breast. Beitler, Stanley, ed. White, Monica, illus. LC 90-80399. 32p. (ps-3). 1990. 12.95 (ISBN 0-945740-01-8). Indp Pubs.

Petersen, Arona. Food & Folklore of the Virgin Islands. 300p. (Orig.). (gr. 9-12). 1990. 20.00 (ISBN 0-9626577-0-0). A Petersen.

FOLKLORE–MEXICO

Blackmore, Vivian, retold by. Why Corn Is Golden: Stories about Plants. Martinez-Ostos, Susana, illus. LC 82-17280. (gr. k-3). 1984. 12.95 (ISBN 0-316-54820-0). Little.

De Paola, Tomie. The Lady of Guadalupe. De Paola, Tomie, illus. LC 79-19610. 48p. (gr. k-4). 1980. reinforced bdg. 14.95 (ISBN 0-8234-0373-4); pap. 5.95 (ISBN 0-8234-0403-X). Holiday.

Hayes, Joe. Monday, Tuesday, Wednesday, Oh! Lunes, Martes, Miercoles, O! Jelinek, Lucy, illus. 32p. (Orig.). (gr. 2-5). 1987. pap. 3.95 (ISBN 0-939729-04-0); bk. & cassette 7.95, (ISBN 0-939729-05-9). Trails West Pub.

—The Terrible Tragadabas: El Terrible Tragadabas. Jelinek, Lucy, illus. 32p. (Orig.). (ps-4). 1987. pap. 3.95 (ISBN 0-939729-02-4); bk. & cassette 7.95, (ISBN 0-939729-03-2). Trails West Pub.

Hinojosa, Francisco. The Old Lady Who Ate People: Frightening Stories. Maciel, Leonel, illus. LC 82-17247. (gr. k-3). 1984. 12.95 (ISBN 0-316-54220-2). Little.

Montejo, Victor. The Bird Who Cleans the World: Mayan Fables. Kaufman, Wallace, tr. from SPA. (Illus.). 1991. 22.95 (ISBN 0-915306-93-X). Curbstone.

Parapan, S. M. A Mexican Legend: Quetzalcoat! The Bird-Serpent. Castillo, L., illus. 24p. (Orig.). (gr. k-3). 1989. pap. text ed. write for info.; write for info. tchr's. activity guide. Parapan.

Rohmer, Harriet & Anchondo, Mary. How We Came to the Fifth World. Lopez, Graciela C., illus. LC 76-7240. (ENG & SPA.). 24p. (gr. 2-6). 1988. 12.95 (ISBN 0-89239-024-7). Childrens Book Pr.

Roland, Donna. More of Grandfather's Stories from Mexico. (gr. 1-3). 1986. pap. 4.50 (ISBN 0-941996-10-7). Open My World.

Ryder, Virginia P. Three Monkey Saves the Day. Kilgore, Julia, illus. 21p. (Orig.). (gr. k-12). 1991. pap. 8.95 (ISBN 0-935098-04-6). Amigo Pr. An imaginative story drawn from animal myths of the ancient Mexican codices. Ideal for ethnic studies as Latinos find magic & pride in their Pre-Columbian heritage. All the children will love the antics of Mexico's typical animals; the Mexican hairless dog, the ocelot & the howler monkey. The story illustrates contemporary ways of thinking about & protecting wild animals. The title of the story is based on the Aztec calendar. The calendar-stone, as well as the gold, carnelian & jade gifts can be viewed today at one of the world's greatest archaeological museums which is in Mexico City. The peoples of meso-America believed that the world came to an end every 52 years. Tzintzin, the priest in the story, helps to save the world by capturing a new day. He performs his secret priestly duties with his helpers, Oco, a howling monkey, Chichi, a blue Mexican hairless dog & the eagle. The priest recalls how he found & captured his animal friends in the jungle. Children will love coloring the large line drawings of each of the animals. A favorite picture is of the priest when he finds the old ocelot asleep in the tall grasses. He cares for the ocelot until it dies a natural death from old age. The ocelot wills the priest his fur coat to use as a rug when he no longer needs it. The story is a little sad but quite beautiful. Each of the incidents of the story can promote lively discussions on ethnicity, environmental literacy, archaeology, geography, & many other topics.
Publisher Provided Annotation.

FOLKLORE–MIDDLE EAST

Manson, Christopher, retold by. & illus. A Gift for the King: A Persian Tale. LC 88-28430. 32p. (ps-2). 1989. PLB 14.95 (ISBN 0-8050-0951-5). H Holt & Co.

FOLKLORE–MOROCCO

Chimenti, Elisa. Tales & Legends of Morocco. Benamy, Arnon, tr. (Illus.). (gr. 5 up). 1965. 10.95 (ISBN 0-8392-3049-4). Astor-Honor.

FOLKLORE–NEAR EAST

Aardema, Verna. What's So Funny, Ketu? Brown, Marc, illus. LC 82-70195. 32p. (ps-2). 1982. 9.95 (ISBN 0-8037-9364-2); PLB 9.89 (ISBN 0-8037-9370-7). Dial Bks Young.

Gold, Sharlya & Caspi, Mishael M. The Answered Prayer: And Other Yemenite Folktales. Wunsch, Marjory, illus. 80p. (gr. 3-5). 1990. 13.95 (ISBN 0-8276-0354-1). JPS Phila.

Hashim, A. S. Al-Khulafe al-Rashidoon. pap. 5.95 (ISBN 0-686-18406-8); pap. 49.50 entire ser. (ISBN 0-686-18407-6). Kazi Pubns.

Yushij, Nima. When the Elephants Came. Evans, Mariam & Batmanglij, M., eds. Evans, Mariam, tr. from PER. Fanta, illus. 32p. (gr. 4 up). 1988. 18.50 (ISBN 0-934211-15-9); English-Persian Version. 18.50 (ISBN 0-934211-09-4). Mage Pubs Inc.

FOLKLORE, NEGRO

see Black Folklore

FOLKLORE–NIGERIA

Bryan, Ashley. Beat the Story-Drum, Pum-Pum. LC 80-12045. (Illus.). 80p. (gr. 4-6). 1980. 10.95 (ISBN 0-689-30769-1, Atheneum Childrens Bk). Macmillan Child Grp.

FOLKLORE–NORWAY

Appleby, Ellen. The Three Billy-Goats Gruff. (Illus.). 32p. (gr. k-2). 1985. pap. 2.50 (ISBN 0-590-41121-7). Scholastic Inc.

Dasent, George W. East o' the Sun & West o' the Moon. LC 70-97214. (Illus.). xv, 418p. (gr. 1 up). 1970. pap. 8.95 (ISBN 0-486-22521-6). Dover.

Feldman, Eve. The Squire Takes a Wife. Weissman, Barry, illus. 24p. (ps-2). 1990. PLB 12.33 (ISBN 0-8172-3580-9); PLB 9.25 (ISBN 0-685-33577-1). Raintree Pubs.

FOLKLORE, ORIENTAL

Piequet, Miriam. Ting-Li's Tales Told on the Devil's Mountain. Anyone Can Read Staff, ed. Yin-Chwang, Wang Tsen-Zan. (Illus.). 60p. (Orig.). (gr. 3-7). 1987. pap. write for info. (ISBN 0-914275-13-5). Anyone Can Read Bks.

FOLKLORE–PHILIPPINE ISLANDS

De La Paz, Myrna J. Abadeha: The Philippine Cinderella. De Leon, Romeo, illus. 28p. (gr. k-7). 1991. 11.95 (ISBN 0-9629255-0-0). Pazific Queen. This version of Cinderella is an enchanting story of the struggles & the eventual triumph of a young girl against her oppressors through an enduring faith in the benevolent forces of nature. Set in one of the many lovely & exotic islands of the Philippines. This tale captures the mystical charm of the native culture of the Filipinos. Educational & entertaining. All 28 pages of the book are rendered with large full-color illustrations depicting many fascinating cultural elements of pre-colonial Philippine life. Colorful images of Philippine scenery, traditional outfits, architecture, arts, crafts & folkways vividly enhance the lively narrative. Along with the enchantment, this heartwarming tale conveys the deep respect & reverence for nature & the earth inherent in the indigenous culture of the Philippines.
Publisher Provided Annotation.

Fuentes, Vilma M. Manggob & His Golden Top. Inis, Ninabeth R., illus. 48p. (Orig.). (gr. k-3). 1985. pap. 4.00 (ISBN 971-10-0218-3, Pub. by New Day Philippines). Cellar.

Montero, Jaime A. Gatan & Talaw. (Illus., Orig.). (gr. 1-3). 1984. pap. 3.50 (ISBN 971-10-0164-0, Pub. by New Day Philippines). Cellar.

FOLKLORE–PUERTO RICO

Rohmer, Harriet & Rea, Jesus G. Atariba & Niguayona. Castillo, Consuelo M., illus. LC 76-17495. (ENG & SPA.). 24p. (gr. 2-6). 1988. 12.95 (ISBN 0-89239-026-3). Childrens Book Pr.

FOLKLORE–SCANDINAVIA

Hague, Kathleen & Hague, Michael. East of the Sun & West of the Moon. LC 80-13499. (Illus.). 48p. (gr. k-3). 1989. pap. 3.95 (ISBN 0-15-224703-3, VoyB). HarBraceJ.

Synge, Ursula. Weland: Smith of the Gods. Keeping, Charles, illus. LC 73-5945. 94p. (gr. 7 up). 1973. 18.95 (ISBN 0-87599-200-5). S G Phillips.

FOLKLORE–SCOTLAND

Cooper, Susan. The Selkie Girl. Hutton, Warwick, illus. LC 90-39982. 32p. (gr. k-8). 1991. pap. 4.95 (ISBN 0-689-71467-X, Aladdin). Macmillan Child Grp.

Jacobs, Joseph. The Stars in the Sky. Amtmann, Airdrie, illus. LC 78-11718. 32p. (ps up). 1979. 8.95 (ISBN 0-374-37229-2). FS&G.

Robertson, Joanne. Sea Witches. (ps-3). 1991. 14.95 (ISBN 0-8037-1070-4). Dial Bks Young.

Wilson, Barbara K. Scottish Folk-Tales & Legends. Kiddell-Moore, Joan, illus. 224p. (ps-7). 1990. pap. 8.95 (ISBN 0-19-274141-1). Oxford U Pr.

FOLKLORE–SERBIA

Gaidar. Cyk i Gek. (gr. 7-12). pap. 5.95 (ISBN 0-88436-051-2, 65250). EMC.

FOLKLORE, SLAVIC

De Regniers, Beatrice S. Little Sister & the Month Brothers. Tomes, Margot, illus. LC 75-4594. 48p. (ps-3). 1976. 8.95 (ISBN 0-8164-3147-7, Clarion). HM.

Galdone, Joanna. The Little Girl & the Big Bear. Galdone, Paul, illus. 40p. (ps-3). 1980. 14.95 (ISBN 0-395-29029-5, Clarion). HM.

FOLKLORE–SOUTH AMERICA

Alexander, Ellen. Llama & the Great Flood: A Folktale from Peru. Alexander, Ellen, illus. LC 88-1194. 40p. (gr. k-4). 1989. 13.95 (ISBN 0-690-04727-4, Crowell Jr Bks); PLB 13.89 (ISBN 0-690-04729-0). HarpC Child Bks.

Bierhorst, John. The Mythology of South America. LC 87-26237. (Illus.). 256p. (gr. 7 up). 1988. 15.95 (ISBN 0-688-06722-0). Morrow Jr Bks.

Finger, Charles J. Tales from Silver Lands. Honore, Paul, illus. 225p. (gr. 7 up). 1965. 16.95 (ISBN 0-685-01496-7). Doubleday.

Troughton, Joanna, retold by. & illus. How Night Came: A Folk Tale from the Amazon. LC 86-10917. 32p. (ps-2). 1986. 14.95 (ISBN 0-87226-093-3, Bedrick Blackie). P Bedrick Bks.

—How the Birds Changed Their Feathers: A South American Folk Tale. LC 86-1251. 32p. (ps-2). 1986. 14.95 (ISBN 0-87226-080-1, Bedrick Blackie). P Bedrick Bks.

FOLKLORE–SOVIET UNION

Afanasyev, Alexander. Fool & the Fish: A Tale from Russia. Hort, Lenny, retold by. Spirin, Gennady, illus. 32p. (ps-3). 1990. 12.95 (ISBN 0-8037-0861-0). Dial Bks Young.

Croll, Carolyn, adapted by. & illus. The Little Snowgirl. 32p. (ps-k). 1989. 13.95 (ISBN 0-399-21691-X, Putnam). Putnam Pub Group.

Disney, Walt, Productions Staff. Walt Disney's Peter & the Wolf. LC 74-6423. (Illus.). 48p. (ps-3). 1974. (Random Juv); lib. bdg. 5.99 (ISBN 0-394-92563-7). Random.

Downing, Charles. Russian Tales & Legends. Kiddell-Monroe, Joan, illus. 224p. (gr. 4 up). 1990. pap. 8.95 (ISBN 0-19-274144-6). Oxford U Pr.

Druts, Yefim & Gessler, Alexei, eds. Russian Gypsy Tales. Horse, Harry, illus. 142p. (gr. 5-8). 1989. 17.95 (ISBN 0-86241-082-7, Pub. by Cnngt Pub Ltd). Trafalgar Sq.

Mikolaycak, Charles. Babushka: An Old Russian Folktale. Mikolaycak, Charles, illus. LC 84-500. 32p. (ps-3). 1984. reinforced bdg. 14.95 (ISBN 0-8234-0520-6); pap. 5.95 (ISBN 0-8234-0712-8). Holiday.

Milhous, Katherine & Dalgiesh, Alice. The Turnip: An Old Russian Folktale. Morgan, Pierr, illus. 32p. (ps-3). 1990. 13.95 (ISBN 0-399-22229-4, Philomel Bks). Putnam Pub Group.

Prokofiev, Sergei & Chappell, Warren. Peter & the Wolf. (Illus.). (gr. 4 up). 1973. pap. 1.95 (ISBN 0-394-82613-2). Knopf.

Ransome, Arthur. The Fool of the World & the Flying Ship. Shulevitz, Uri, illus. LC 68-54105. 48p. (ps-3). 1968. 15.95 (ISBN 0-374-32442-5). FS&G.

—Old Peter's Russian Tales. Jaques, Faith, illus. 256p. (gr. 5-9). 1975. pap. 3.50 (ISBN 0-14-030696-X, Penguin Bks). Viking Penguin.

Ransome, Arthur, ed. The Fool of the World & the Flying Ship: A Russian Tale. Shulevitz, Uri, illus. (ps up). 1987. pap. 4.95 (ISBN 0-374-42438-1). FS&G.

Reyher, Becky. My Mother Is the Most Beautiful Woman in the World. Gannett, Ruth, illus. 40p. (gr. k-3). 1945. PLB 14.88 (ISBN 0-688-51251-8). Lothrop.

Robbins, Ruth. Baboushka & the Three Kings. Sidjakov, Nicholas, illus. LC 60-15036. (ps up). 1960. 13.95 (ISBN 0-395-27673-X, Pub. by Parnassus). HM.

Small, Ernest & Lent, Blair. Baba Yaga. (Illus.). 48p. (gr. k-3). 1966. 13.95 (ISBN 0-395-16975-5). HM.

Tate, Carole. Pancakes & Pies: A Russian Folk Tale. LC 88-38111. 32p. (gr. 2 up). 1989. 14.95 (ISBN 0-87226-407-6, Bedrick Blackie). P Bedrick Bks.

Tolstoy, Leo. Chozjain I Rabotnik. (gr. 7-12). pap. 5.95 (ISBN 0-88436-054-7, 65252). EMC.

Winter, Jeanette. The Girl & the Moon Man: A Siberian Folktale. Winter, Jeanette, illus. LC 83-19462. 32p. (gr. 1-3). 1984. (Pant Bks Young). Pantheon.

Winthrop, Elizabeth, adapted by. Vasilissa the Beautiful: A Russian Folktale. Koshkin, Alexander, illus. LC 89-26903. 40p. (gr. 1-5). 1991. 15.95 (ISBN 0-06-021662-X); PLB 15.89 (ISBN 0-06-021663-8). HarpC Child Bks.

Zemach, Harve & Zemach, Margot. Salt. Zemach, Margot, illus. LC 65-12312. 32p. (ps-3). 1977. 13.95 (ISBN 0-374-36385-4). FS&G.

FOLKLORE–SPAIN

Caperucita Roja. (SPA.). (gr. 2). 1990. casebound 3.50 (ISBN 0-7214-1409-5). Ladybird Bks.

La Cenicienta. (SPA.). (gr. 3). 1990. casebound 3.50 (ISBN 0-7214-1405-2). Ladybird Bks.

Los Duendes y el Zapatero. (SPA.). (gr. 1). 1990. casebound 3.50 (ISBN 0-7214-1411-7). Ladybird Bks.

Guareschi. Don Camillo. (gr. 7-12). 1972. pap. 5.95 (ISBN 0-88436-121-7, 55255). EMC.

Irving, Washington. Spanish Papers. Irving, Pierre, ed. LC 78-74516. (gr. 7 up). 1979. Repr. of 1868 ed. 42.50x (ISBN 0-8486-0219-6). Roth Pub Inc.

Vernon, Adele, retold by. The Riddle: Based on an Old Catalan Story. Rayevsky, Robert & Radunsky, Vladimir, illus. (gr. k-3). 1987. 12.95 (ISBN 0-396-08920-8, Putnam). Putnam Pub Group.

FOLKLORE–SWEDEN

Rydberg, Viktor. The Christmas Tomten. Wiberg, Harald, illus. 1981. 9.95 (ISBN 0-698-20528-6, Coward). Putnam Pub Group.

FOLKLORE–TIBET

Cook, Elizabeth, adapted by. Rabbit Who Overcame Fear: A Jataka Tale. Meller, Eric, illus. Tulku, Tarthang, intro. by. (Illus.). 32p. (Orig.). (gr. k-4). 1991. 12.95 (ISBN 0-89800-212-5); pap. 5.95 (ISBN 0-89800-211-7). Dharma Pub. The latest in a series of children's stories drawn from the rich storytelling tradition of ancient India, China & Tibet, presented for the first time in large picture-book format. Stories in the Jataka Tales promote the values of compassion, peace, friendship, & kindness, opening the door for parent & child to discuss the importance of these issues. In this story, a young rabbit, startled from sleep by a loud noise & shaking, springs into flight in fear of an earthquake. His panic spreads, endangering other animals who follow his blind rush toward a cliff. They are saved by a compassionate lion who teaches them how to investigate the source of fear before jumping to unwise conclusions. An instructive tale told with warmth & humor. Vibrant color. Ages 3-8. Available in English, Portuguese, German, Dutch. Valuable for multicultural education, English as second language classes. Call Dharma Publishing, (800) 873-4276 for a free brochure of other books in this series. ***Publisher Provided Annotation.***

Gretchen, Sylvia, ed. & tr. from TIB. Hero of the Land of Snow. Witwer, Julia, illus. LC 89-25603. vi, 32p. (gr. 5-8). 1990. 14.95 (ISBN 0-89800-201-X, 795); pap. 6.95 (ISBN 0-89800-202-8). Dharma Pub.

Hume, Lotta C. Favorite Children's Stories from China & Tibet. Lo-Koon-Chiu, illus. LC 61-6219. (gr. 1-4). 1962. pap. 14.95 (ISBN 0-8048-1605-0). C E Tuttle.

FOLKLORE–TURKEY

Walker, Barbara K. A Treasury of Turkish Folktales for Children. LC 88-6859. xii, 155p. (gr. 3 up). 1988. lib. bdg. 17.50 (ISBN 0-208-02206-6, Linnet). Shoe String.

—Watermelons, Walnuts & the Wisdom of Allah: And Other Tales of the Hoca. Berson, Harold, illus. 72p. 1991. Repr. of 1967 ed. 17.50 (ISBN 0-89672-254-6). Tex Tech Univ Pr.

FOLKLORE–UKRAINE

Kismaric, Carole, adapted by. The Rumor of Pavel & Paali: A Ukranian Folktale. Mikolaycak, Charles, illus. LC 87-19958. 32p. (gr. 1-3). 1988. 13.95i (ISBN 0-06-023277-3); PLB 13.89 (ISBN 0-06-023278-1). HarpC Child Bks.

Tresselt, Alvin R. Mitten. Mills, Yaroslava, illus. LC 64-14436. 30p. (gr. k-3). 1964. PLB 12.88 (ISBN 0-688-51053-1). Lothrop.

FOLKLORE–U. S.

Allen, Linda & Snider, Chrystle L., eds. Washington Songs & Lore. Green, Donald A., illus. 200p. (gr. 1-12). 1988. pap. 15.95 (ISBN 0-9616441-3-3); Abridged ed., 72 pg. comb bdg. 8.95 (ISBN 0-9616441-4-1). Melior Dist.

Anderson, J. I. I Can Read About Johnny Appleseed. Krasnoborski, William, illus. LC 76-54445. (gr. 2-5). 1977. pap. 1.95 (ISBN 0-89375-037-9). Troll Assocs.

Arnold, Caroline. The Terrible Hodag. Davis, Lambert, illus. 32p. (gr. 5-8). 1989. 14.95 (ISBN 0-15-284750-2). HarBraceJ.

Ata, Te, as told by. Baby Rattlesnake. Moroney, Lynn, adapted by. Reisberg, Veg, illus. 32p. (ps-5). 1989. 12.95 (ISBN 0-89239-049-2). Childrens Book Pr.

Bang, Molly G. Wiley & the Hairy Man: Adapted from an American Folk Tale. Bang, Molly G., illus. LC 87-2540. 64p. (gr. 1-4). 1987. pap. 3.95 (ISBN 0-689-71162-X, Aladdin). Macmillan Child Grp.

Bierhorst, John, ed. The Naked Bear: Folktales of the Iroquois. Zimmer, Dirk, illus. LC 86-21836. 144p. (gr. 3 up). 1987. 14.95 (ISBN 0-688-06422-1). Morrow Jr Bks.

Chase, Richard. Grandfather Tales. (Illus.). 240p. (gr. 4-6). 1973. 13.95 (ISBN 0-395-06692-1). HM.

—Jack Tales. (Illus.). 202p. (gr. 4-6). 1943. 13.95 (ISBN 0-395-06694-8). HM.

Durell, Ann, compiled by. The Diane Goode Book of American Folk Tales & Songs. Goode, Diane, illus. LC 89-1097. (ps-5). 1989. 14.95 (ISBN 0-525-44458-0, DCB). Dutton Child Bks.

Edler, Timothy J. T-Boy in Mossland. (Illus.). 48p. (gr. k-8). 1978. pap. 6.00 (ISBN 0-931108-03-9). Little Cajun Bks.

—T-Boy the Little Cajun. Judice, Van, illus. 36p. (gr. k-8). 1978. pap. 6.00 (ISBN 0-931108-01-2). Little Cajun Bks.

Ferguson, Joe. The Deathless White Stallion & Other Tales. Sky Rivers & Eakin, Edwin M., eds. Morris, Aaron, illus. 64p. (gr. 4-6). 1989. 10.95 (ISBN 0-89015-702-2, Pub. by Panda Bks); pap. 3.95 (ISBN 0-89015-712-X). Eakin Pr.

Galbreath, Bob. Tennessee Red Berry Tales. Garrett, Deborah G., ed. 97p. (Orig.). (gr. 3 up). 1986. pap. 7.95 (ISBN 0-9616918-0-8). Whites Creek Pr.

Gianni, Gary, retold by. & illus. John Henry. 32p. (gr. 6 up). 1989. 9.95 (ISBN 0-943718-18-X). Kipling Pr.

Gleiter, Jan & Thompson, Kathleen. Casey Jones. Balistreri, Francis, illus. 32p. (gr. 2-5). 1987. PLB 16.67 (ISBN 0-8172-2653-2); pap. 9.27 (ISBN 0-8172-2657-5). Raintree Pubs.

Hamilton, Virginia. The People Could Fly. Dillon, Leo & Dillon, Diane, illus. LC 84-25020. 192p. (ps-12). 1985. 16.95 (ISBN 0-394-86925-7); lib. bdg. 16.99 (ISBN 0-394-96925-1). Knopf.

—The People Could Fly: American Black Tales. Jones, James Earl, contrib. by. (ps up). 1988. 9.95 (ISBN 0-394-89301-8); cassette avail. Knopf.

Harper, Wilhelmina, ed. Gunniwolf. Wiesner, William, illus. LC 67-22387. (ps-3). 1970. 11.95 (ISBN 0-525-31139-4, DCB). Dutton Child Bks.

Harris, Joel C. Uncle Remus & Br'er Rabbit. 1986. Repr. lib. bdg. 17.95x (ISBN 0-89966-540-3). Buccaneer Bks.

Harris, Joel C. & Metaxas, Eric, eds. Brer Rabbit & the Wonderful Tar Baby. Drescher, Henrik, illus. LC 90-7166. 32p. (gr. k up). 1990. 14.95 (ISBN 0-88708-144-4, Rabbit Ears); incl. cass. 19.95 (ISBN 0-88708-145-2). Picture Bk Studio.

Hayes, Joe. La Llorona. Treog-Hill, Vicki, illus. 32p. (Orig.). (gr. 1-9). 1986. pap. 4.95 (ISBN 0-938317-02-4). Cinco Puntos.

Krauss, Ruth. A Very Special House. Sendak, Maurice, illus. LC 53-7115. 32p. (ps-1). 1990. pap. 4.95 (ISBN 0-06-443228-9, Trophy). HarpC Child Bks.

Lester, Julius & Fogelman, Phyllis J., eds. Further Tales of Uncle Remus: The Misadventures of Brer Rabbit, Brer Fox, Brer Wolf, the Doodang, & All the Other Creatures. Pinkney, Jerry, illus. LC 88-20223. 160p. (ps up). 1990. 15.00 (ISBN 0-8037-0610-3); PLB 14.89 (ISBN 0-8037-0611-1). Dial Bks Young.

Lisker, Tom. Tall Tales: American Myths. LC 77-11104. (Illus.). (gr. 4-5). 1977. PLB 14.65 (ISBN 0-8172-1039-3). Raintree Pubs.

Lobel, Arnold. Fables. Lobel, Arnold, illus. LC 79-2004. 48p. (gr. 1-4). 1980. 14.95 (ISBN 0-06-023973-5); PLB 14.89 (ISBN 0-06-023974-3). HarpC Child Bks.

Ludwig, Warren. Good Morning, Granny Rose: An Arkansas Folktale. (Illus.). 32p. (ps-3). 1990. 13.95 (ISBN 0-399-21950-1, Putnam). Putnam Pub Group.

Lyman, Nanci A. Paul Bunyan. new ed. LC 79-66320. (Illus.). 48p. (gr. 3-6). 1980. lib. bdg. 9.89 (ISBN 0-89375-310-6); pap. 2.95 (ISBN 0-89375-309-2). Troll Assocs.

—Pecos Bill. LC 79-66319. (Illus.). 48p. (gr. 3-6). 1980. lib. bdg. 9.89 (ISBN 0-89375-308-4); pap. 2.95 (ISBN 0-89375-307-6). Troll Assocs.

Moore, Mary S. Fireside Tales. Clay, Cliff, illus. 21p. (Orig.). (gr. 5-12). 1990. pap. 7.95 (ISBN 0-913678-18-X); paper & audiocassette 10.00 (ISBN 0-913678-19-8). New Day Pr.

Naden, C. J. John Henry, the Steeldriving Man. new ed. LC 79-66317. (Illus.). 48p. (gr. 3-6). 1980. lib. bdg. 9.89 (ISBN 0-89375-304-1); pap. 2.95 (ISBN 0-89375-303-3). Troll Assocs.

Petersham, Maud & Petersham, Miska. The Rooster Crows. Petersham, Maud & Petersham, Miska, illus. LC 46-446. 64p. (ps-2). 1969. 13.95 (ISBN 0-02-773100-6, Mcmillan Child Bk). Macmillan Child Grp.

Sanfield, Steve. The Adventures of High John the Conqueror. Ward, John, illus. LC 88-17946. 128p. (gr. 3 up). 1989. 12.95 (ISBN 0-531-05807-7); PLB 12.99 (ISBN 0-531-08407-8). Orchard Bks Watts.

—A Natural Man: The True Story of John Henry. Thornton, Peter, illus. LC 85-45965. 32p. (gr. 2-6). 1990. pap. 9.95 (ISBN 0-87923-844-5). Godine.

San Souci, Robert. Legend of Sleepy Hollow. San Souci, Daniel, illus. LC 86-2064. 32p. (ps-3). 1986. 11.95 (ISBN 0-385-23396-5, Zephyr-BFYR); PLB 11.95 (ISBN 0-385-23397-3, Zephyr-BFYR). Doubleday.

—Talking Eggs. 1989. PLB 13.89 (ISBN 0-8037-0620-0). Dial Bks Young.

Schwartz, Alvin. Flapdoodle: Pure Nonsense from American Folklore. O'Brien, John, illus. LC 79-9618. 128p. (gr. 5 up). 1990. PLB 12.89 (ISBN 0-397-31920-7, Lipp Jr Bks). HarpC Child Bks.

—Tomfoolery: Trickery & Foolery with Words. Rounds, Glen, illus. LC 72-12900. 128p. (gr. 4 up). 1973. 12.95 (ISBN 0-685-02088-6, Lipp Jr Bks). HarpC Child Bks.

—A Twister of Twists, a Tangler of Tongues. Rounds, Glen, illus. LC 72-1434. 126p. (gr. 4 up). 1972. 13.95 (ISBN 0-397-31387-X, Lipp Jr Bks). HarpC Child Bks.

Schwartz, Alvin, ed. Whoppers: Tall Tales & Other Lies Collected from American Folklore. Rounds, Glen, illus. LC 74-32024. 128p. (gr. 4 up). 1990. pap. 3.95 (ISBN 0-06-446091-6, Trophy). HarpC Child Bks.

Varney, Sharon. Cranberry Ridge Tales. 72p. (Orig.). (gr. 7 up). 1986. pap. 7.95 (ISBN 0-685-17323-2). S Varney.

Whedbee, Charles H. Legends of the Outer Banks & Tar Heel Tidewater. LC 66-23049. (Illus.). 165p. (gr. 5 up). 1979. 9.95 (ISBN 0-910244-41-3). Blair.

Wolkstein, Diane, retold by. The Legend of Sleepy Hollow. Alley, R. W., illus. LC 86-23596. 32p. (gr. 1-4). 1987. 13.00 (ISBN 0-688-06532-5); (Morrow Junior Books). Morrow Jr Bks.

Word, Christine. Ghosts Along the Bayou: Tales of Haunted Places in Southwestern Louisiana. Fuchs, Jeff, illus. 160p. (gr. 6-12). 1988. 12.95 (ISBN 0-937614-09-2). Acadiana Pr.

York, Carol B. Casey Jones. new ed. LC 79-66313. (Illus.). 48p. (gr. 3-6). 1980. PLB 9.89 (ISBN 0-89375-298-3); pap. 2.95 (ISBN 0-89375-297-5). Troll Assocs.

—Johnny Appleseed. LC 79-66312. (Illus.). 48p. (gr. 3-6). 1980. lib. bdg. 9.89 (ISBN 0-89375-296-7); pap. 2.95 (ISBN 0-89375-295-9). Troll Assocs.

—Mike Fink. LC 79-66315. (Illus.). 48p. (gr. 3-6). 1980. lib. bdg. 9.89 (ISBN 0-89375-302-5); pap. 2.95 (ISBN 0-89375-301-7). Troll Assocs.

—Old Stormalong: The Seafaring Sailor. LC 79-66322. (Illus.). 48p. (gr. 3-6). 1980. lib. bdg. 9.89 (ISBN 0-89375-314-9); pap. 2.95 (ISBN 0-89375-313-0). Troll Assocs.

—Sam Patch, the Big Time Jumper. new ed. LC 79-66318. (Illus.). 48p. (gr. 3-6). 1980. lib. bdg. 9.89 (ISBN 0-89375-306-8); pap. 2.95 (ISBN 0-89375-305-X); cassette avail. Troll Assocs.

FOLKLORE–VIETNAM

Graham, Gail B. The Beggar in the Blanket. Bryan, Brigitte, illus. LC 77-85548. 96p. (gr. 1-5). 1988. 12.95 (ISBN 0-8037-0664-2); PLB 12.89 (ISBN 0-8037-0663-4). Dial Bks Young.

Lucas, Alice. Voices of Liberty. Tang, You-shan, illus. (gr. 4-12). 1990. pap. text ed. 7.00 16p. ea. (ISBN 0-936434-27-9, Pub. by Zellerbach Fam Fund); 12p. ea. tchr's. guide 6.00 (ISBN 0-936434-28-7, Pub. by Zellerbach Fam Fund). SF Study Ctr.

Vuong, Lynette D. The Brocaded Slipper & Other Vietnamese Tales. Vo, Dinh M., illus. LC 84-40746. 1982. 13.95 (ISBN 0-201-08088-5, Lipp Jr Bks). HarpC Child Bks.

FOLKLORE–WEST INDIES

Berry, James. Spiderman Anancy. Olubo, Joseph, illus. 144p. (gr. 5-9). 1989. 13.95 (ISBN 0-8050-1207-9). H Holt & Co.

De Sauza, James, as told by. Brother Anansi & the Cattle Ranch: (El Hermano Anansi y el Rancho) Zubizarreta, Rosalma, tr. Rohmer, Harriet, adapted by. Von Mason, Stephen, illus. (SPA & ENG.). 32p. (ps-7). 1989. 12.95 (ISBN 0-89239-044-1). Childrens Book Pr.

Sherlock, Philip M. West Indian Folk Tales. Kiddell-Monroe, Joan, illus. 151p. (gr. 3 up). 1988. pap. 8.95 (ISBN 0-19-274127-6). Oxford U Pr.

FOLKWAYS

see Manners and Customs

FOOD

see also Beverages; Cookery; Diet; Farm Produce; Fruit; Nutrition; Poultry; Vegetables; Vegetarianism; Vitamins also names of foods, e.g. Bread, etc.

Ask about the World of Food. 64p. (gr. 4-5). 1987. PLB 18.25 (ISBN 0-8172-2885-3); pap. 13.27 (ISBN 0-8172-2897-7). Raintree Pubs.

Baldwin, Dorothy. Health & Food. (Illus.). 32p. (gr. 3-8). 1987. PLB 15.93 (ISBN 0-86592-294-2). Rourke Corp.

Bennett, Rebecca J. God Gives Good Food. Seward, Lyn, illus. 20p. (ps). 1987. 1.59 (ISBN 0-87403-309-8, 2009). Standard Pub.

Brooks, F. Food & Eating. (Illus.). 24p. (gr. 2-4). 1989. lib. bdg. 11.96 (ISBN 0-88110-399-3, Usborne); pap. 3.95 (ISBN 0-7460-0452-4, Usborne). EDC.

Burns, Marilyn. Good for Me! All about Food in 32 Bites. Clifford, Sandy, illus. LC 78-6727. (gr. 5 up). 1978. 14.95 (ISBN 0-316-11749-8); pap. 8.95 (ISBN 0-316-11747-1). Little.

Cahill, Robert E. Olde New England's Sugar & Spice & Everything... America's First Cookbook & Food

History. Cahill, Keri M., ed. (Illus.). 63p. (Orig.). 1991. pap. 3.95 (ISBN 0-9626162-2-2). Old Saltbox Pub Hse. The newest addition to the "Olde New England Series," has the subtitle: "The History of Food & America's First Cookbook." Author Bob Cahill has dug up the oldest American recipes he could find, plus weaving a fascinating true adventure about the introduction & development of new foods into the Colonies. He follows the progress of America's "First Fruits," the battles concerning the controversial "love-apple," & merchant intrigue in obtaining spices. He also emphasizes the difficulty of the onion & potato to gain a footing in New England soil, the beginnings of candy & other sweets in the New World, & humorous stories of preserving meats & fish in the old days. "Sugar & Spice & Everything," provides many first-hand experiences regarding food from our Pilgrim & Puritan ancestors, & is a truly entertaining, information-packed read. It retails for only $4.95. It is 76 pages, soft-cover & has 20 photos. Other titles in the series include: "Curious Customs & Cures," "Strange Superstitions," "Mountain Madness," "Things That Go Bump In The Night," "Mad & Mysterious Men," "Naughty Navy," "Riotous Revolution," "Viking & Indian Wars," "Strange Sea Sagas," "Shipwrecks & Treasures," "The Old Irish of New England," "Ghostly Haunts," "Witches & Wizards," "Pirates & Lost Treasures," & "Horrors of Salem's Witch Dungeon." Order from Old Saltbox, 40 Felt St. Salem, MA 01970.
Publisher Provided Annotation.

Carratello, Patricia. Food & Nutrition. Carratello, Patricia, illus. 38p. (gr. 1-4). 1980. wkbk. 5.95 (ISBN 1-55734-212-1). Tchr Create Mat.

Cavanagh, Mary. Favorite Menus. Kubo, Chad & Filarca, Josie, illus. 13p. (gr. 3-5). 1980. pap. 3.95 (ISBN 0-8431-2573-X). Enrich.

Clark, Elizabeth. Fish. (Illus.). 32p. (gr. 1-4). 1990. PLB 9.95 (ISBN 0-87614-376-1). Carolrhoda Bks.

—Meat. (Illus.). 32p. (gr. 1-4). 1990. PLB 9.95 (ISBN 0-87614-375-3). Carolrhoda Bks.

Cobb, Vicki. The Scoop on Ice Cream. Karas, Brian, illus. 48p. (gr. 4 up). 1985. 11.95 (ISBN 0-316-14895-4). Little.

Corey, Melinda. Let's Visit a Spaghetti Factory. Emmerich, Donald, illus. LC 89-5110. 32p. (gr. 2-4). 1990. PLB 10.79 (ISBN 0-8167-1741-9); pap. text ed. 2.95 (ISBN 0-8167-1742-7). Troll Assocs.

De Paola, Tomie. The Popcorn Book. LC 77-21456. (Illus.). 32p. (gr. k-3). 1978. reinforced bdg. 14.95 (ISBN 0-8234-0314-9); pap. 5.95 (ISBN 0-8234-0533-8). Holiday.

Dineen, Jacqueline. Food from Dairy & Farmyard. 32p. (gr. 4-8). 1988. lib. bdg. 12.95 (ISBN 0-89490-215-6). Enslow Pubs.

—Food from the Sea. 32p. (gr. 4-8). 1988. lib. bdg. 12.95 (ISBN 0-89490-216-4). Enslow Pubs.

Disney, Walt, Staff. Banana in a Bandanna: A Book about Things to Eat. (ps). 1991. 3.95 (ISBN 1-56282-028-1). W Disney Pub.

Downer, Lesley. Japanese Food & Drink. Caulkins, Janet, ed. (Illus.). 48p. (gr. k-6). 1988. PLB 12.40 (ISBN 0-531-18174-X, Pub. by Bookwright Pr). Watts.

Fischer, Robert. Pizza. FS Staff, ed. Green, Anne C., illus. 72p. (gr. 4-9). 1988. 10.90 (ISBN 0-531-10503-2). Watts.

Geraghty, Paul. Over the Steamy Swamp. Geraghty, Paul, illus. 32p. (ps up). 1989. 13.95 (ISBN 0-15-200561-7, Gulliver Bks). HarBraceJ.

Gill, Nancy. Using Cereal Boxes. McGinnity, Molly, illus. 13p. (gr. 4-6). 1980. pap. 3.95 (ISBN 0-8431-2574-8). Enrich.

Gokay, Nancy H. Sugarbush: Making Maple Syrup. LC 80-17582. (Illus.). 32p. (Orig.). (gr. 3-4). 1980. pap. 2.00 (ISBN 0-910726-95-7). Hillsdale Educ.

Goodwin, Mary T. & Pollen, Gerry. Creative Food Experiences for Children. 2nd rev. ed. Versel, Lauren, illus. 256p. (gr. k-6). 1980. pap. 7.95 (ISBN 0-89329-027-0). Ctr Sci Public.

Gross, Ruth B. What's on My Plate? Seltzer, Isadore, illus. LC 87-22057. 32p. (gr. k-3). 1990. 12.95 (ISBN 0-02-737000-3, Mcmillan Child Bk). Macmillan Child Grp.

Hamilton, Mary. Wild Edibles. (Illus.). 50p. (gr. 2-6). 1990. pap. 4.95 (ISBN 0-920534-51-1, Pub. by Hyperion Pr Ltd CN). Sterling.

Horwitz, Joshua. Night Markets: Bringing Food to a City. Horwitz, Joshua, illus. LC 85-45401. 96p. (gr. 2-6). 1986. pap. 3.95 (ISBN 0-06-446046-0, Trophy). HarpC Child Bks.

—Night Markets: Bringing Food to the City. LC 83-45242. (Illus.). 96p. (gr. 3-7). 1984. 12.95 (ISBN 0-690-04378-3, Crowell Jr Bks); PLB 12.89 (ISBN 0-690-04379-1, Crowell Jr Bks). HarpC Child Bks.

Jennings, Terry. Food. LC 88-22866. (Illus.). 32p. (gr. 3-6). 1989. PLB 14.60 (ISBN 0-516-08402-X); pap. 4.95 (ISBN 0-516-48402-8). Childrens.

Johnson, Sylvia A. Potatoes. Suzuki, Masaharu, illus. 48p. (gr. 4 up). 1984. lib. bdg. 14.95 (ISBN 0-8225-1459-1). Lerner Pubns.

Kalman, Bobbie. The Food We Eat. (Illus.). 32p. (gr. 2-3). 1986. 14.95 (ISBN 0-86505-073-2); pap. 6.95 (ISBN 0-86505-095-3). Crabtree Pub Co.

Kelley, True. Let's Eat. Kelley, True, illus. LC 88-25699. 32p. (ps-1). 1989. 11.95 (ISBN 0-525-44482-3, DCB). Dutton Child Bks.

Kolodny, Nancy J. When Food's a Foe: How to Confront & Conquer Eating Disorders. (Illus.). 224p. (gr. 7 up). 1987. 14.95 (ISBN 0-316-50167-0). Little.

Kowtaluk. Discovering Food. (gr. 7-9). 1982. 14.00 (ISBN 0-02-663350-7). Bennett IL.

Lapenkova, Valentina & Lambton, Edward. Russian Food & Drink. Caulkins, Janet, ed. (Illus.). 48p. (gr. k-6). 1988. 12.40 (ISBN 0-531-18175-8, Pub. by Bookwright Pr). Watts.

Llewellyn, Claire. First Look at Growing Food. LC 91-9424. (Illus.). 32p. (gr. 1-2). 1991. PLB 10.95 (ISBN 0-8368-0678-6). Gareth Stevens Inc.

McCoy, J. J. How Safe Is Our Food Supply? (Illus.). 144p. (gr. 9-12). 1990. PLB 12.90 (ISBN 0-531-10935-6). Watts.

Mumaw, Catherine & Voran, Marilyn. The Whole Thing. 24p. (gr. 6-11). 1981. pap. 1.50 (ISBN 0-8361-1962-2). Herald Pr.

Ontario Science Center Staff. Foodworks: Over One Hundred Science Activities & Fascinating Facts That Explore the Magic of Food. LC 87-1796. 96p. (gr. 7-12). 1987. pap. 8.61 (ISBN 0-201-11470-4). Addison-Wesley.

Parker, Steve. Food & Digestion. rev. ed. (Illus.). 48p. (gr. 5 up). 1991. pap. 4.95 (ISBN 0-531-24603-5). Watts.

Patent, Dorothy H. Where Food Comes From. Munoz, William, illus. LC 90-49833. 40p. (gr. 3-7). 1991. PLB 14.95 reinforced (ISBN 0-8234-0877-9). Holiday.

Peeples, H. I. Bubble Gum. Payne, Tom, illus. 24p. (gr. 2-5). 1989. 6.95 (ISBN 0-8092-4409-8, Calico Bks). Contemp Bks.

Penny, Malcolm. The Food Chain. Caulkins, Janet, ed. (Illus.). 32p. (gr. k-6). 1988. PLB 8.99 (ISBN 0-531-18167-7, Pub. by Bookwright Pr). Watts.

Perl, Lila. Junk Food, Fast Food, Health Food: What America Eats & Why. 192p. (gr. 5 up). 1980. 13.95 (ISBN 0-395-29108-9, Clarion). HM.

—Slumps, Grunts, & Snickerdoodles: What Colonial America Ate & Why. Cuffari, Richard, illus. LC 75-4894. 128p. (gr. 6 up). 1979. 13.95 (ISBN 0-395-28923-8, Clarion). HM.

Reece, Colleen L. What Was It Before It Was Ice Cream? Axeman, Lois, illus. LC 85-13262. 32p. (ps-2). 1985. PLB 11.97 (ISBN 0-89565-325-7). Childs World.

Sanders, Pete. Food & Hygiene. (Illus.). 32p. (gr. 2-5). 1990. PLB 10.40 (ISBN 0-531-17243-0). Watts.

Seixas, Judith S. Junk Food--What It Is, What It Does. Huffman, Tom, illus. LC 83-14135. 48p. (gr. 1-3). 1984. 12.95 (ISBN 0-688-02559-5); PLB 12.88 (ISBN 0-688-02560-9). Greenwillow.

Smalley, Guy, illus. My Very Own Book of What's for Lunch. 24p. (ps-2). 1989. 9.95 (ISBN 0-929793-05-6). Camex Bks Inc.

Sproule, Anna. Food for the World. LC 87-80099. (Illus.). 48p. (gr. 1-4). 1987. 12.95x (ISBN 0-8160-1783-2). Facts on File.

Tan, Jennifer, et al. International Foods, 6 bks, Reading Level 4. (Illus.). 192p. (gr. 3-6). Date not set. Set. PLB 79.60 (ISBN 0-86625-337-8). Rourke Corp.

Tavalarios, Irene. Greek Food & Drink. Caulkins, Janet, ed. (Illus.). 48p. (gr. k-6). 1988. 12.40 (ISBN 0-531-18172-3, Pub. by Bookwright Pr). Watts.

Tesar, Jenny. Food & Water: Threats, Shortages & Solutions. Cayne, Bernard S., ed. (Illus.). 128p. (gr. 7-12). 1992. lib. bdg. 18.95x (ISBN 0-8160-2495-2). Facts on File.

Watanabe, Shigeo. What a Good Lunch! Ohtomo, Yasuo, illus. 32p. (gr. k). 1981. 8.95 (ISBN 0-399-20811-9, Philomel); pap. 3.95 (ISBN 0-399-21048-2, Philomel). Putnam Pub Group.

FOOD, CANNED

see Canning and Preserving

FOOD–FICTION

Addeo, Pat. Mrs. Blake's Cakes. 1991. 6.95 (ISBN 0-533-08807-0). Vantage.

The Adventures of Rowena & the Wonderful Jam & Jelly Factory. 40p. 1987. 16.95 (ISBN 0-944345-11-5). S C Toof.

Anderheggen, George C. Willie the Weenie Whiner. (Illus.). 20p. (Orig.). (gr. 5 up). 1983. 3.95 (ISBN 0-910717-01-X). Bookling Pubs.

Asch, Frank. Milk & Cookies. (Illus.). 48p. (ps-2). 1991. pap. 2.95 (ISBN 0-448-40103-7, G&D). Putnam Pub Group.

Baker, Bonnie J. A Pear by Itself. LC 82-4430. 32p. (ps-2). 1982. 11.93 (ISBN 0-516-02032-3); pap. 2.95 (ISBN 0-516-42032-1). Childrens.

Barrett, Judith. Cloudy with a Chance of Meatballs. Barrett, Ron, illus. LC 78-2945. 32p. (ps-3). 1978. 13.95 (ISBN 0-689-30647-4, Atheneum Child Bk). Macmillan Child Grp.

Bjork, Christina. Elliot's Extraordinary Cookbook. Sandin, Joan, tr. Anderson, Lena, illus. 60p. 1991. 11.95 (ISBN 91-29-59658-0, Pub. by R & S Bks). FS&G.

Borden, Margie. Mincemeat Pie. Graves, Helen, ed. 54p. (gr. 4-8). 1987. 5.95 (ISBN 1-55523-048-2). Winston-Derek.

Brenner, Barbara. Beef Stew. Siracusa, Catherine, illus. LC 89-36769. 32p. (Orig.). (ps-1). 1990. lib. bdg. 6.99 (ISBN 0-394-95046-1); pap. 2.95 (ISBN 0-394-85046-7). Random.

Brown, Marc. Pickle Things. (Illus.). 48p. (ps-2). 1991. pap. 2.95 (ISBN 0-448-40105-3, G&D). Putnam Pub Group.

Buchanan, J. Nothing Else but Yams for Supper. (Illus.). 24p. (ps-8). 1988. pap. 4.95 (ISBN 0-88753-182-2). Firefly Bks Ltd.

Buckman, Mary. Wiggle Worm. LC 89-63502. (Illus., Orig.). (gr. k-2). 1989. pap. text ed. 12.95 (ISBN 1-879414-06-6). Mary Bee Creat.

Carlson, Anna L. The Candy Cruncher. 2nd. ed. LC 80-83738. (Illus.). 24p. (gr. k-4). 1983. pap. 1.95 (ISBN 0-939938-03-0). Karwyn Ent.

—The Cookie Looker. 2nd. ed. LC 80-82182. (Illus.). (gr. k-4). 1983. pap. 1.95 (ISBN 0-939938-01-4). Karwyn Ent.

Cartwright, Stephen. Who Likes Honey? (ps up). 1989. PLB 5.98 (ISBN 0-7924-5042-6, Mallard Pr). BDD Promo Bk.

Cohen, Peter. Olson's Meat Pies. Landstrom, Olof, illus. Fisher, Richard E., tr. (Illus.). (gr. k-4). 1989. 12.95 (ISBN 9-129-59180-5, Pub. by R & S Bks). FS&G.

Cormier, Robert. Beyond the Chocolate War. (gr. 6 up). 1986. pap. 3.25 (ISBN 0-440-90580-X, LFL). Dell.

Cowley, Joy. Huggles' Breakfast. Fuller, Elizabeth, illus. 8p. (gr. k-2). 1989. pap. text ed. 15.00 (ISBN 1-55911-276-X). Wright Group.

—Huggles' Breakfast, 6 bks. Fuller, Elizabeth, illus. 8p. (gr. k-2). 1986. Set. pap. text ed. 12.60 (ISBN 1-55911-337-5). Wright Group.

—Ice Cream. Allpress, Jill, illus. 8p. (gr. k-2). 1989. pap. text ed. 15.00 (ISBN 1-55911-284-0). Wright Group.

—Ice Cream, 6 bks. Allpress, Jill, illus. 8p. (gr. k-2). 1986. Set. pap. text ed. 12.60 (ISBN 1-55911-355-3). Wright Group.

Cushman, Doug. Possum Stew. (ps-1). 1990. 12.95 (ISBN 0-525-44566-8, DCB). Dutton Child Bks.

Dalmais, Anne-Marie. The Busy Day of Mamma Pizza. Percy, Graham, illus. 32p. (ps-3). 1990. 5.95 (ISBN 0-374-31007-6). FS&G.

Danziger, Paula. The Pistachio Prescription. (gr. k-12). 1988. pap. 2.95 (ISBN 0-317-67249-5). Dell.

Davoll, Barbara. The Potluck Supper. Hockerman, Dennis, illus. 24p. 1988. 5.99 (ISBN 0-89693-406-3); cassette 8.99 (ISBN 0-89693-617-1). Victor Bks.

Delton, Judy. Cookies & Crutches. 80p. (Orig.). (gr. k-6). 1988. pap. 2.50 (ISBN 0-440-40010-4, YB). Dell.

Demarest, Chris L. No Peas for Nellie. Demarest, Chris L., illus. 32p. (gr. k-3). 1991. pap. 3.95 (ISBN 0-689-71474-2, Aladdin). Macmillan Child Grp.

De Paola, Tomie. Pancakes for Breakfast. De Paola, Tomie, illus. LC 77-15523. 32p. (ps-3). 1978. pap. 3.95 (ISBN 0-15-670768-3, VoyB). HarBraceJ.

Doyle, Charlotte. Freddie's Spaghetti. Reilly, Nicholas, illus. LC 90-61003. 24p. (Orig.). (ps-2). 1991. pap. 2.25 (ISBN 0-679-81160-5). Random.

Dragonwagon, Crescent. Coconut. Tafuri, Nancy, illus. LC 83-47691. 32p. (ps-3). 1984. PLB 14.89 (ISBN 0-06-021760-X). HarpC Child Bks.

Dr. Seuss. Green Eggs & Ham. Dr. Seuss, illus. 64p. (ps-1). 1987. pap. 6.95 incl. cassette (ISBN 0-394-89220-8, Random Juv). Random.

Du Quette, Keith. Rippening Day for a Picnic. (ps-3). 1990. 12.95 (ISBN 0-670-83311-8). Viking Child Bks.

Duyff, Roberta L. The Bread That Grew. McKissack, Patricia & McKissack, Fredrick, eds. Dorenkamp, Michelle, illus. LC 87-61646. 32p. (Orig.). (gr. 1-3). 1987. text ed. 8.95 (ISBN 0-88335-725-9); pap. text ed. 4.95 (ISBN 0-88335-745-3). Milliken Pub Co.

Elish, Dan. Worldwide Dessert Contest. (gr. 4 up). 1990. pap. 3.50 (ISBN 0-553-15820-1). Bantam.

Gaban, Jesus. Harry's Mealtime Mess. Colorado, Nani, illus. 16p. (ps-1). 1991. PLB 10.95 (ISBN 0-8368-0717-0). Gareth Stevens Inc.

Goffstein, M. B. Fish for Supper. Goffstein, M. B., illus. LC 75-27598. 32p. (ps-2). 1986. pap. 3.50 (ISBN 0-8037-0284-1). Dial Bks Young.

Grey, Judith. Yummy, Yummy. Goodman, Joan E., illus. LC 81-2360. 32p. (gr. k-2). 1981. PLB 10.89 (ISBN 0-89375-543-5); pap. 2.95 (ISBN 0-89375-544-3). Troll Assocs.

Gustafson, Scott. Alphabet Soup: A Feast of Letters. (Illus.). 48p. 1990. 14.95 (ISBN 0-8092-4299-0). Contemp Bks.

Haddon, Mark. Toni & the Tomato Soup. Haddon, Mark, illus. 32p. (ps-1). 1989. 12.95 (ISBN 0-15-200610-9, Gulliver Bks). HarBraceJ.

Harrison, D. James. Saturn Storm's Broccoli Adventure. LC 89-51459. (Illus.). 44p. (gr. k-3). 1989. 5.95 (ISBN 1-55523-278-7). Winston-Derek.
Hayes, Daniel. The Trouble with Lemons. LC 89-46192. 128p. (gr. 6 up). 1991. 14.95 (ISBN 0-87923-825-9). Godine.

Hayes, Frederick & Hayes, Jean. The Chile Pot. 1988. 6.95 (ISBN 0-925605-00-X). Pinto Pub. THE CHILE POT portrays the humorous efforts of one courageous pinto bean who avoids becoming just another bean in the "big pot of chile." With the often reluctant help of his sidekick, Chapulin, he manages to escape the long spoon of the frustrated old lady, & so, happily, rides off on the grasshopper, Chapulin, into the sunset, singing his song, THE FRIJOLE ROAD. THE CHILE POT is our first effort in this new series THE ADVENTURES OF PINTO BEAN & CHAPULIN. Our second book entitled THE CAT THAT COULDN'T MEOW will be published in middle September. It is a hilarious story of how Greta, the cat, finds her meow & also her great love. Our Christmas book, SANTA'S MYSTERIOUS PRESENT will be ready for the holidays. This heart-warming story features Pinto Bean & Chapulin & the mountain with two mouths. Each book has an accompanying cassette that tells the story & songs that children will love. Each of the above books may be purchased from the PINTO PUBLISHING COMPANY at 3610 Calle del Monte, NE, Albuquerque, NM 87110. THE CHILE POT price is $6.95. Postage will be paid by the PINTO PUBLISHING COMPANY with sales coming from this listing.
Publisher Provided Annotation.

Hayes, Geoffrey. Patrick Eats His Dinner. Hayes, Geoffrey, illus. LC 84-5924. 32p. (ps-1). 1989. pap. 2.95 (ISBN 0-679-80163-4, Dragonfly Bks). Knopf.
Heide, Florence P. Banana Blitz. 128p. (gr. 3-7). 1984. pap. 2.50 (ISBN 0-553-15258-0, Skylark). Bantam.
Hennessy, B. G. Jak Baked the Cake. Morgan, Mary, illus. 32p. (ps-3). 1990. pap. 12.95 (ISBN 0-670-82237-X). Viking Child Bks.
Higham, Jon A. Aardvark's Picnic. Higham, Jon A., illus. (ps-3). 1987. pap. 10.95 (ISBN 0-316-36085-6). Little.
Hoban, Russell. Dinner at Alberta's. Marshall, James, illus. 48p. (gr. k-6). 1980. pap. 2.95 (ISBN 0-440-41864-X, YB). Dell.
Hodgman, Ann. The Cookie Caper. (gr. 4-7). 1990. pap. 2.75 (ISBN 0-425-12132-1). Berkley Pub.
—French Fried Aliens. 1990. pap. 2.75 (ISBN 0-425-12170-4). Berkley Pub.
—Frog Punch. (gr. 4 up). 1990. pap. 2.75 (ISBN 0-425-12092-9). Berkley Pub.
Hughes, Shirley. Another Helping of Chips. Hughes, Shirley, illus. LC 86-20958. 64p. (gr. 2-4). 1987. 11.95 (ISBN 0-688-06871-5); PLB 11.88 (ISBN 0-688-06872-3). Lothrop.
Hurlbut, Phillip R., Jr. Jeraboam & the Amazing Spaghetti Mountain. Renfroe, Dan, illus. LC 79-90933. 123p. (Orig.). (gr. 3 up). 1979. pap. 2.95 (ISBN 0-936086-00-9). Entertainment Factory.
Hurwitz, Johanna. Much Ado about Aldo. Wallner, John, illus. (gr. 4-6). 1978. PLB 13.88 (ISBN 0-688-32160-7). Morrow Jr Bks.
Joosse, Barbara M. Jam Day. McCully, Emily A., illus. LC 86-46117. 32p. (gr. k-3). 1987. 12.95 (ISBN 0-06-023096-7); PLB 12.89 (ISBN 0-06-023097-5). HarpC Child Bks.
Jukes, Mavis. Blackberries in the Dark. Allen, Thomas B., illus. LC 85-4259. 48p. (gr. 7-11). 1985. lib. bdg. 11.99 (ISBN 0-394-97599-5). Knopf.
Kandoian, Ellen. Is Anybody Up? Kandoian, Ellen, illus. 32p. (ps-3). 1989. 14.95 (ISBN 0-399-21749-5, Putnam). Putnam Pub Group.
Kent, Jack. Socks for Supper. Kent, Jack, illus. LC 78-6224. 40p. (ps-3). 1978. 5.95 (ISBN 0-8193-0964-8); PLB 5.95 (ISBN 0-8193-0965-6). Parents.
Khalsa, Dayal K. How Pizza Came to Our Town. Khalsa, Dayal K., illus. 32p. (gr. k-8). 1989. 14.95 (ISBN 0-88776-231-X). Tundra Bks.
—How Pizza Came to Queens. Khalsa, Dayal K., illus. (gr. 1 up). 1989. PLB 13.95 (ISBN 0-517-57126-9, C N Potter Bks). Crown.
Kingston, Arlene. The Bagels Are Coming. Kingston, Arlene, illus. 40p. (ps up). 1988. pap. 5.95 (ISBN 0-929934-00-8). Child Time Pubs.
Latterman, Terry. The Watermelon Treat. Hawkins, Mary E., ed. Lattermen, Terry, illus. LC 85-63266. 48p. (gr. 1-4). 1987. 8.95 (ISBN 0-934739-03-X); pap. 5.95 (ISBN 0-934739-04-8). Pussywillow Pub.
Lord, John V. & Burroway, Jane. The Giant Jam Sandwich. (Illus.). 1990. 7.95 (ISBN 0-395-53966-8). HM.
McDaniel, Lurlene. The Pony That Nobody Wanted. (Illus.). 96p. (gr. 2-5). 1982. 0.50 (ISBN 0-87406-074-5). Willowisp Pr.
MacDonald, Elizabeth. Mr. MacGregor's Breakfast Egg. Ayliffe, Alex, illus. 32p. (ps-1). 1990. pap. 12.95 (ISBN 0-670-83256-1). Viking Child Bks.
McLean, Bill. The Best Peanut Butter Sandwich in the Whole World. Helmer, Katherine, illus. 28p. (ps-2). 1990. pap. 4.95 (ISBN 0-88753-207-1). Firefly Bks Ltd.
McLenighan, Valjean. One Whole Doughnut...One Doughnut Hole. LC 82-12838. (Illus.). (ps-2). 1982. PLB 11.93 (ISBN 0-516-02031-5); pap. 2.95 (ISBN 0-516-42031-3). Childrens.
Modell, Frank. Ice Cream Soup. LC 87-21097. (Illus.). 24p. (ps-3). 1988. 11.95 (ISBN 0-688-07770-6); lib. bdg. 11.88 (ISBN 0-688-07771-4). Greenwillow.
Nordqvist, Sven. Pancake Pie. Wilhelm, Hans, illus. LC 84-16640. 32p. (ps-3). 1985. 11.95 (ISBN 0-688-04141-8); PLB 11.88 (ISBN 0-688-04142-6, Morrow Jr Bks). Morrow Jr Bks.
Paulsen, Gary. Popcorn Days & Buttermilk Nights. LC 83-9015. 160p. (gr. 7 up). 1983. 10.95 (ISBN 0-525-66770-9, Lodestar Bks). Dutton Child Bks.
Pearson, Tracey C. A Apple Pie. Pearson, Tracey C., illus. LC 85-13125. 32p. (ps-2). 1986. 5.95 (ISBN 0-8037-0252-3). Dial Bks Young.
Peck, Robert N. Soup on Fire. Robinson, Charles, illus. LC 87-5261. 112p. (gr. 4-7). 1987. pap. 13.95 (ISBN 0-385-29580-4). Delacorte.
—Soup on Ice. Robinson, Charles, illus. LC 85-218. 128p. (gr. 3-7). 1985. lib. bdg. 9.99 (ISBN 0-394-97613-4). Knopf.
—Soup on Wheels. (gr. 3-7). 1986. pap. 2.95 (ISBN 0-440-48190-2, YB). Dell.
—Soup's Drum. (gr. k-6). 1988. pap. 2.95 (ISBN 0-440-40003-1). Dell.
Peifer, Jane. The Biggest Popcorn Party Ever in Center County. Nolt, Marilyn P., illus. LC 86-27063. 32p. (Orig.). (ps-1). 1987. pap. 4.95 (ISBN 0-8361-3435-4). Herald Pr.
Potter, Beatrix. The Roly-Poly Pudding. 64p. (Orig.). 1984. pap. 2.25 (ISBN 0-553-15249-1). Bantam.
Pryor, Bonnie. Vinegar Pancakes & Vanishing Cream. 128p. (gr. k-6). 1989. pap. 2.95 (ISBN 0-440-40173-9, YB). Dell.
Rifas, Leonard. Food First Comic. Goldenman, Gretta, ed. 24p. (Orig.). (gr. 7-12). 1982. pap. 1.00 (ISBN 0-935028-11-0). Inst Food & Develop.
Roald Dahl's Charlie & the Chocolate Factory, 4 vols. 1988. Boxed Set. pap. 8.70. Bantam.
Robart, Rose. The Cake That Mack Ate. Kovalski, Maryann, illus. LC 86-47709. (ps-3). 1987. 12.95 (ISBN 0-316-74890-0). Little.
Roffey, Maureen. Mealtime. Roffey, Maureen, illus. LC 89-48006. 32p. (ps). 1990. pap. 4.95 (ISBN 0-689-70809-2, Aladdin). Macmillan Child Grp.
Rohmer, Harriet, et al, eds. Mister Sugar Came to Town (La Visita del Senor Azucar) Zubizarreta, Rosalina & Zubizarreta, Rosalna, trs. Chagoya, Enrique, illus. (SPA & ENG.). 32p. (ps-5). 1989. 12.95 (ISBN 0-89239-045-X). Childrens Book Pr.
Ross, Tony. Stone Soup. LC 86-16580. (Illus.). 32p. (ps-3). 1987. 10.95 (ISBN 0-8037-0400-3); PLB 10.89 (ISBN 0-8037-0401-1). Dial Bks Young.
Schwartz, Alvin. There Is a Carrot in My Ear & Other Noodle Tales. Weinhaus, Karen A., illus. LC 80-8442. 64p. (gr. k-3). 1986. pap. 3.50 (ISBN 0-06-444103-2, Trophy). HarpC Child Bks.
Schwartz, Joel L. The Great Spaghetti Showdown. 160p. (gr. k-6). 1988. pap. 2.75 (ISBN 0-440-40099-6, YB). Dell.
Sendak, Maurice. La Cocina de Noche. Sendak, Maurice, illus. (SPA.). (gr. 1-6). 14.95 (ISBN 84-204-4570-3). Santillana.
Sewall, Marcia. Riding That Strawberry Roan. LC 84-21904. (Illus.). 32p. (ps-2). 1985. pap. 9.95 (ISBN 0-670-80623-4). Viking Child Bks.
Sherman, Eileen B. The Odd Potato. Kahn, Katherine J., illus. LC 84-17186. 32p. (gr. k-5). 1984. pap. 4.95 (ISBN 0-930494-37-7). Kar-Ben.
Simons-Ailes, Sandra, illus. Mrs. Ortiz Makes Fry Bread. 30p. (Orig.). (ps-7). 1979. pap. 3.00 (ISBN 0-915347-06-7). Pueblo Acoma Pr.
Slepian, Jan & Seidler, Ann. The Hungry Thing Returns. Martin, Richard E., illus. LC 89-6350. (ps-3). 1990. pap. 11.95 (ISBN 0-590-42890-X). Scholastic Inc.
Smith, Doris B. A Taste of Blackberries. Wimmer, Mike, illus. LC 88-45077. 64p. (gr. 3-6). 1988. pap. 3.50 (ISBN 0-06-440238-X, Trophy). HarpC Child Bks.
Smith, Robert K. Chocolate Fever. Fiammenghi, Gioia, illus. 96p. (gr. 2-5). 1989. 10.99 (ISBN 0-399-61224-6, Putnam). Putnam Pub Group.
Stamaty, Mark A. Minnie Maloney & Macaroni. LC 76-2281. (Illus.). 40p. (ps-3). 1976. PLB 4.58 (ISBN 0-8037-5589-9). Dial Bks Young.
Stevenson, James. Yuck! LC 83-25421. (Illus.). (ps-3). 1986. 3.95 (ISBN 0-688-06524-4, Mulberry). Morrow.
Swan, Walter. Teeny Weeny. Swan, Deloris, ed. Asch, Connie, illus. 16p. (Orig.). (ps). 1989. pap. 1.50 (ISBN 0-927176-01-7). Swan Enterp.
Theriot, David. Les Trois Petits Amis et la Decouverte du Gumbo. Easterling, Mae L., illus. (FRE.). 41p. (gr. 3). 1979. pap. 1.25 (ISBN 0-911409-04-1). Natl Mat Dev.
Thill, Larry. The Adventures of Alice in Nutritionland: A Nutritional Storybook for Children. Thill, Michael, illus. 31p. (Orig.). (gr. k-6). 1989. pap. 8.00 (ISBN 0-317-93500-3). Impressive Pubns.
Turnbull, Ann. Make It, Break It. McTaggart, David, illus. 32p. (ps-2). 1990. pap. 12.95 (ISBN 0-670-83359-2). Viking Child Bks.
Walter, Mildred P. Justin & the Best Biscuits in the World. Stock, Catherine, illus. LC 86-7148. 128p. (gr. 3-6). 1990. pap. 3.25 (ISBN 0-679-80346-7, Bullseye Bks). Knopf.
Wells, Rosemary. Max's Breakfast. Wells, Rosemary, illus. LC 84-14968. 12p. (ps-k). 1985. bds. 3.95 (ISBN 0-8037-0161-6). Dial Bks Young.
Wilson, Sarah. Muskrat, Muskrat, Eat Your Peas! Wilson, Sarah, illus. (ps). 1989. pap. 13.95 (ISBN 0-671-67515-X). S&S Trade.
Wilson-Kelly, Becky. Mother Grumpy's Dog Biscuits. Wilson-Kelly, Becky, illus. LC 89-24553. 32p. (ps-3). 1990. 12.95 (ISBN 0-8050-1287-7). H Holt & Co.
Wojciechowski, Susan. Patty Dillman of Hot Dog Fame. LC 88-22565. 176p. (gr. 4-8). 1990. pap. 3.50 (ISBN 0-679-80170-7, Bullseye Bks). Knopf.
Yummy Books: Biggest of All. 1991. 1.98 (ISBN 0-8317-9975-7). Smithmark.
Ziefert, Harriet. Chocolate Mud Cake. Gundersheimer, Karen, illus. LC 87-12139. 36p. (ps-1). 1988. 02716030 11.95 (ISBN 0-06-026883-2); PLB 11.89 (ISBN 0-06-026892-1). HarpC Child Bks.
—Dinner's Ready, Jessie! Smith, Mavis, illus. LC 90-55149. 32p. (ps-1). 1990. 4.95 (ISBN 0-06-107402-0). HarpC Child Bks.
—The Small Potatoes Busy Beach Day. (gr. k-3). 1986. pap. 2.75 (ISBN 0-440-48045-0, YB). Dell.
Zokeisha. Things I Like to Eat. Zokeisha, illus. 16p. (ps-k). 1981. 2.95 (ISBN 0-671-44449-2, Little Simon). S&S Trade.

FOOD–PRESERVATION
see also Canning and Preserving
MacManiman, Gen. Dry It-You'll Like It. 3rd ed. Calderon, Paula B., illus. 80p. (gr. 5 up). pap. 4.95 (ISBN 0-9611998-0-6). Macmaniman.

FOOD CONTROL
see Food Supply

FOOD PLANTS
see Plants, Edible

FOOD POISONING
Lobstein, Tim. Poisoned Food? 1990. PLB 8.90 (ISBN 0-531-17208-2). Watts.

FOOD PRESERVATION
see Food–Preservation

FOOD SUPPLY
see also Food–Preservation
Aaseng, Nathan. Ending World Hunger. (Illus.). 144p. (gr. 9-12). 1991. PLB 12.90 (ISBN 0-531-11007-9). Watts.
Dando, William A. & Dando, Caroline Z. A Reference Guide to World Hunger. 128p. (gr. 6 up). 1991. PLB 17.95 (ISBN 0-89490-326-8). Enslow Pubs.
Gibb, Christopher. Food or Famine. (Illus.). 48p. (gr. 5 up). 1987. Set. PLB 72.00 (ISBN 0-317-60377-9); PLB 18.00 (ISBN 0-86592-279-9). Rourke Corp.
Versfield, Ruth. Why Are People Hungry? Franklin Watts Ltd., ed. (Illus.). 32p. (gr. k-3). 1988. 10.40 (ISBN 0-531-17082-9, Gloucester Pr). Watts.

FOOD TRADE
see Farm Produce–Marketing

FOOT
Aliki. My Feet. Aliki, illus. LC 89-49357. 32p. (ps-1). 1990. 12.95 (ISBN 0-690-04813-0, Crowell Jr Bks); PLB 12.89 (ISBN 0-690-04815-7, Crowell Jr Bks). HarpC Child Bks.
Cobb, Vicki. Sneakers Meet Your Feet. Cobb, Theo, illus. 48p. (gr. 4-6). 1985. 11.95 (ISBN 0-316-14896-2). Little.
Damon, Laura. Funny Fingers, Funny Toes. Kennedy, Anne, illus. LC 87-10915. 32p. (gr. k-2). 1988. PLB 10.89 (ISBN 0-8167-1089-9); pap. text ed. 2.95 (ISBN 0-8167-1090-2). Troll Assocs.
Dr. Seuss. Foot Book. Dr. Seuss, illus. LC 68-28462. (ps-1). 1968. 6.95 (ISBN 0-394-80937-8, Random Juv); lib. bdg. 7.99 (ISBN 0-394-90937-2). Random.
Hughes, Shirley. Alfie's Feet. Hughes, Shirley, illus. LC 82-13012. 32p. (ps-1). 1983. 14.95 (ISBN 0-688-01658-8); PLB 14.88 (ISBN 0-688-01660-X). Lothrop.
Machotka, Hana. What Neat Feet! Machotka, Hana, photos by. LC 90-40886. (Illus.). 32p. (gr. k up). 1991. 13.95 (ISBN 0-688-09474-0); PLB 13.88 (ISBN 0-688-09475-9, Morrow Jr Bks). Morrow Jr Bks.
Parnall, Peter. Feet! Parnall, Peter, illus. LC 88-5272. 32p. (ps-1). 1988. 13.95 (ISBN 0-02-770110-7, Mcmillan Child Bk). Macmillan Child Grp.
Pluckrose, Henry. Feet. FS Staff, ed. Galletly, Mike, photos by. (Illus.). 32p. (gr. 1-3). 1988. PLB 10.40 (ISBN 0-531-10615-2). Watts.
Reiss, Elayne & Friedman, Rita. Fantastic Funny Feet. (gr. k-1). 10.50 (ISBN 0-89796-867-0). New Dimens Educ.

FOOTBALL
see also Soccer

Aaseng, Nathan. College Football: You Are the Coach. LC 83-22193. (Illus.). 104p. (gr. 4 up). 1984. lib. bdg. 8.95 (ISBN 0-8225-1556-3). Lerner Pubns.

—College Football's Hottest Rivalries. (Illus.). 80p. (gr. 4 up). 1987. PLB 9.95 (ISBN 0-8225-1531-8). Lerner Pubns.

—Football: It's Your Team. (Illus.). 104p. (gr. 4 up). 1985. PLB 8.95 (ISBN 0-8225-1557-1). Lerner Pubns.

—Football: You Are the Coach. LC 82-269. (Illus.). 104p. (gr. 4up). 1983. PLB 8.95 (ISBN 0-8225-1551-2). Lerner Pubns.

—Football's Cunning Coaches. LC 80-29252. (Illus.). 80p. (gr. 4 up). 1981. PLB 7.95 (ISBN 0-8225-1065-0). Lerner Pubns.

—Football's Fierce Defenses. Aaseng, Nathan, photos by. LC 79-16315. (Illus.). 72p. (gr. 4 up). 1980. PLB 7.95 (ISBN 0-8225-1057-X). Lerner Pubns.

—Football's Incredible Bulks. (Illus.). 80p. (gr. 4 up). 1987. PLB 9.95 (ISBN 0-8225-1532-6). Lerner Pubns.

—Football's Most Controversial Calls. (Illus.). 72p. (gr. 4 up). 1985. PLB 9.95 (ISBN 0-8225-1528-8). Lerner Pubns.

—Football's Most Shocking Upsets. (Illus.). 80p. (gr. 4 up). 1985. PLB 9.95 (ISBN 0-8225-1529-6). Lerner Pubns.

—Football's Steadiest Kickers. LC 80-28863. (Illus.). 80p. (gr. 4 up). 1981. PLB 7.95 (ISBN 0-8225-1069-3). Lerner Pubns.

—You Are the Coach: College Football. (gr. 6-12). 1985. pap. 2.25 (ISBN 0-440-99840-9, LFL). Dell.

—You Are the Coach: Football. 112p. (gr. 5 up). 1983. pap. 2.50 (ISBN 0-440-99136-6, LFL). Dell.

Anderson, Dave. The Story of Football. LC 85-7195. (Illus.). 192p. (gr. 5 up). 1985. 13.95 (ISBN 0-688-05634-2); pap. 8.95 (ISBN 0-688-05635-0, Pub. by Beech Tree Bks). Morrow Jr Bks.

Beall, Alan. Braves on the Warpath: The Fifty Greatest Games in the History of the Washington Redskins. Baugh, Sammy, frwd. by. LC 88-81470. (Illus.). 400p. (gr. 6-12). 1988. 24.95 (ISBN 0-929639-00-6). Kinloch Bks.

Blinn, William. Brian's Song. (Illus.). 128p. (Orig.). (gr. 6 up). 1983. pap. 3.50 (ISBN 0-553-26618-7). Bantam.

Bloom, Marc. Know Your Game: Football. (gr. 4-7). 1990. pap. 2.95 (ISBN 0-590-43312-1). Scholastic Inc.

Brenner, Richard J. The Complete Super Bowl Story: Games I-XXIII. (Illus.). 112p. (gr. 5 up). 1989. PLB 10.95 (ISBN 0-8225-1503-2). Lerner Pubns.

Broekel, Ray. Football. LC 81-15484. (Illus.). 48p. (gr. k-4). 1982. PLB 14.60 (ISBN 0-516-01629-6); pap. 4.95 (ISBN 0-516-41629-4). Childrens.

Bryce, James & Polick, Bill. The Power Basics of Football. LC 84-22838. 112p. 1986. 5.95 (ISBN 0-13-688318-4, Busn). P-H.

Carroll, Bob. The Official Pro Football Hall of Fame Fun & Fact Sticker Book. (Illus.). 96p. (gr. 3 up). 1990. pap. 7.95 incl. 80 stickers (ISBN 0-671-68696-8). S&S Trade.

Cohen, Daniel. The Restless Dead: Ghostly Tales from Around the World. (gr. 4 up). 1987. pap. 2.50 (ISBN 0-671-64373-8, Archway). PB.

De Luca, Sam. Junior Football Playbook. LC 73-80413. (Illus.). 128p. (gr. 4-8). 1973. 5.95 (ISBN 0-8246-0150-5). Jonathan David.

Dickmeyer, Lowell A. Football Is for Me. Oddie, Alan, photos by. LC 79-15445. (Illus.). 48p. (gr. 2-5). 1979. PLB 8.95 (ISBN 0-8225-1087-1). Lerner Pubns.

Ferrell, John M. Playing Flag Football. 32p. (gr. 1-6). 1983. pap. write for info. (ISBN 0-88035-052-0, 3029, Pub. by YMCA USA). Human Kinetics.

Football Basics Study Aid. 1975. pap. 2.50 (ISBN 0-87738-048-1). Youth Ed.

Football Card Collecting Kit, 1990. (Illus.). 1990. pap. write for info. (ISBN 0-942025-80-6). Kidsbks.

Fox, Larry. Football Basics. Gow, Bill, illus. (gr. 3-7). 1981. 9.95 (ISBN 0-13-323998-5). P-H.

Gelman, Mitch. Super Bowl Sunday, No. 4. (Orig.). (gr. 9 up). 1984. pap. 2.25 (ISBN 0-671-47578-9, Archway). PB.

Greene, Carol. I Can Be a Football Player. LC 84-9609. (Illus.). 32p. (gr. k-3). 1984. lib. bdg. 13.93 (ISBN 0-516-01839-6); pap. 3.95 (ISBN 0-516-41839-4). Childrens.

Gutman, Bill. Gamebreakers of the NFL. (Illus.). (gr. 5 up). 1973. (Random Juv); lib. bdg. 3.69 (ISBN 0-394-92501-7). Random.

—Go for It: Football. Brown, Ben, illus. 64p. (gr. 3-7). 1989. PLB 16.50 (ISBN 0-942545-85-0). Grey Castle.

Harris, Richard. I Can Read About Football. Milligan, John, illus. LC 76-54398. (gr. 2-5). 1977. pap. 1.95 (ISBN 0-89375-033-6). Troll Assocs.

Hawkes, Bob. Playbook: Football, No. 2. (gr. 4-7). 1991. pap. 4.95 (ISBN 0-316-34349-8). Little.

Horrigan, Joe. The Official Pro Football Hall of Fame Answer Book. (Illus.). 96p. (gr. 3 up). 1990. pap. 6.95 (ISBN 0-671-68695-X); pap. 11.95 reinforced trade (ISBN 0-671-71001-X). S&S Trade.

Kessler, Leonard. Kick, Pass, & Run. Kessler, Leonard, illus. LC 66-18656. 64p. (ps-3). 1966. PLB 11.89 (ISBN 0-06-023160-2). HarpC Child Bks.

Korch, Rick. The Official Pro Football Hall of Fame Playbook. (Illus.). 64p. (gr. 3 up). 1990. pap. 4.95 (ISBN 0-671-68698-4); PLB 11.95 (ISBN 0-671-71002-8). S&S Trade.

Liss, Howard. Making of a Rookie. (Illus.). (gr. 5-9). 1968. lib. bdg. 3.69 (ISBN 0-394-90199-1, Random Juv). Random.

—Playoff: Professional Football's Great Championship Games. LC 66-10675. (Illus.). (gr. 7 up). 1966. pap. 4.50 (ISBN 0-440-06939-4). Delacorte.

Madden, John. The First Book of Football. (gr. 3 up). 1988. bds. 10.95 (ISBN 0-517-56981-7). Crown.

Nash, Bruce & Zullo, Allan. The Football Hall of Shame: Young Fans' Edition. (Illus.). 128p. (gr. 4 up). 1989. pap. 2.75 (ISBN 0-671-72922-5, Archway). PB.

—Little Football Big Leaguers: Amazing Boyhood Stories of Today's Football Stars. (Illus.). 96p. (gr. 1 up). 1990. pap. 7.95 incl. 45 trading cards (ISBN 0-671-70850-3). S&S Trade.

Nuwer, Hank. Strategies of the Great Football Coaches. Solomon, Maury, ed. (Illus.). 144p. (gr. 7 up). 1988. PLB 12.90 (ISBN 0-531-10518-0). Watts.

Rothaus, James R. Atlanta Falcons. 48p. (gr. 4 up). 1991. PLB 10.45 (ISBN 0-88682-359-5). Creative Ed.

—Denver Broncos. (gr. 4 up). 1986. PLB 12.95 (ISBN 0-88682-365-X); 18.50 (ISBN 0-685-14308-2). Creative Ed.

—Detroit Lions. 48p. (gr. 4 up). 1986. PLB 12.95 (ISBN 0-88682-366-8); 18.50 (ISBN 0-685-14310-4). Creative Ed.

Sakurai, Jennifer. Rules of the Game: Football. 48p. 1990. pap. 3.95 (ISBN 0-8431-2433-4). Price Stern.

Scheffel, Vernon L. Flag Football: How to Play It. LC 87-51055. (Illus.). 90p. (gr. 7-12). 1987. pap. 6.95 (ISBN 0-944450-00-8). LLU Pr.

Smith, Alias & Pelkowski, Robert. Football: Frankie Fumble in Football Friends. 32p. (ps-3). 1989. pap. 3.95 (ISBN 0-8120-4242-5). Barron.

Smith, Don R. The Official Pro Football Hall of Fame Book of Superstars. (Illus.). 40p. (gr. 3 up). 1990. pap. 4.95 (ISBN 0-671-68697-6). S&S Trade.

Stanley, Jerry W. The Football Player's Training Diary. 120p. (gr. 7-12). 1988. plastic bdg. 7.95 (ISBN 0-685-24024-X). Sports Diary Pub.

Sullivan, George. All about Football. (Illus.). 128p. (gr. 3-7). 1990. 10.95 (ISBN 0-396-09095-8, Putnam); pap. 6.95 (ISBN 0-399-21907-2, Putnam). Putnam Pub Group.

—Better Football for Boys. (Illus.). 64p. (gr. 3-7). 1980. 9.95 (ISBN 0-396-07843-5, Putnam); pap. 2.95 (ISBN 0-396-08241-6, Putnam). Putnam Pub Group.

—Football Kids. (gr. 4-7). 1990. 13.95 (ISBN 0-525-65040-7, Cobblehill Bks). Dutton Child Bks.

—Quarterback. Madden, Don, illus. LC 81-43889. 64p. (gr. 4 up). 1982. 11.95 (ISBN 0-690-04241-8, Crowell Jr Bks). HarpC Child Bks.

Taylor, Valerie. Til Death Did Us Part. 67p. (gr. 12). 1985. pap. 6.95 (ISBN 0-917117-01-8). Creat Concern.

Teitelbaum, Michael. Playbook! Football: You're the Quarterback, You Call the Shots. (gr. 9-12). 1990. pap. 4.95 (ISBN 0-316-83623-0). Little.

Ward. Super Bowl II: Green Bay Packers vs. Oakland Raiders. (Illus.). 32p. (gr. 3-8). PLB 8.95. Creative Ed.

Webb, Equilla B. An Amateur's Guide to Football & Recruiting. 192p. (Orig.). (gr. 9-12). 1990. pap. text ed. 45.00 (ISBN 0-9624771-1-7). Equilla Enterprises.

Weber, Bruce. Weber's Inside Pro Football, 1990. 1990. pap. 2.25 (ISBN 0-590-43464-0). Scholastic Inc.

FOOTBALL–BIOGRAPHY

Aaseng, Nathan. Football's Breakaway Backs. LC 80-16691. (Illus.). 72p. (gr. 4 up). 1980. PLB 7.95 (ISBN 0-8225-1063-4). Lerner Pubns.

—Football's Sure-Handed Receivers. LC 80-17762. (Illus.). 72p. (gr. 4 up). 1980. PLB 7.95 (ISBN 0-8225-1064-2). Lerner Pubns.

—Football's Winning Quarterbacks. LC 80-12074. (Illus.). 80p. (gr. 4 up). 1980. PLB 7.95 (ISBN 0-8225-1062-6). Lerner Pubns.

Alfano, Pete. Super Bowl Superstars: The Most Valuable Players in the NFL's Championship Game. LC 82-368. (Illus.). 144p. (gr. 5-9). 1982. pap. 1.81 (ISBN 0-394-85017-3). Random.

Balzar, Howard. Football Super Stars. Allison, B., intro. by. (Illus.). 23p. (Orig.). (gr. 1-8). 1990. pap. 2.50 (ISBN 0-943409-13-6). Marketcom.

—Quarterbacks of the NFL. Allison, B., intro. by. (Illus.). 23p. (Orig.). (gr. 1-8). 1990. pap. 2.50 (ISBN 0-943409-12-8). Marketcom.

Balzer, Howard. Football All Pro Defense. Allison, B., intro. by. Focus on Sports-New York Staff, illus. 28p. (Orig.). 1989. pap. 2.50 (ISBN 0-943409-10-1). Marketcom.

—Football All Pro Offense. Allison, B., intro. by. Focus On Sports-New York Staff, illus. (Orig.). 1989. pap. 2.50 (ISBN 0-943409-09-8). Marketcom.

—Football All Pro Super Stars. Allison, B., ed. Focus On Sports-New York Staff, illus. 28p. (Orig.). 1989. pap. 2.50 (ISBN 0-943409-11-X). Marketcom.

Benagh, Jim. Sports Great Herschel Walker. 64p. (gr. 4-10). 1990. 15.95 (ISBN 0-89490-207-5). Enslow Pubs.

Buck, Ray. Jim Plunkett: The Comeback Kid. LC 84-7711. 48p. (gr. 2-8). 1984. lib. bdg. 13.27 (ISBN 0-516-04340-4). Childrens.

Devaney, John. Winners of the Heisman Trophy. 2nd ed. (Illus.). (gr. 5 up). 1990. 14.95 (ISBN 0-8027-6906-3); lib. bdg. 15.85 (ISBN 0-8027-6907-1). Walker & Co.

Goodman, Michael E. Lawrence Taylor. LC 87-29023. (Illus.). 48p. (gr. 5-6). 1988. PLB 10.95 (ISBN 0-89686-365-4, Crestwood Hse). Macmillan Child Grp.

Great Offensive Players of the NFL: Touchdown! (Illus.). (gr. k-9). 1988. pap. 2.50 (ISBN 0-318-36485-9). Scholastic Inc.

Hewitt, Brian. Jim McMahon: The Zany Qaurterback. LC 86-9583. (Illus.). 48p. (gr. 2-8). 1986. PLB 13.27 (ISBN 0-516-04359-5); pap. 3.95 (ISBN 0-516-44359-3). Childrens.

Kaplan, Richard. Great Linebackers of the NFL. (Illus.). (gr. 5-9). 1970. (Random Juv). Random.

Leder, Jane M. Marcus Allen. (Illus.). 48p. (gr. 5-6). 1985. PLB 10.95 (ISBN 0-89686-251-8, Crestwood Hse). Macmillan Child Grp.

—Walter Payton. LC 86-16526. (Illus.). 48p. (gr. 5-6). PLB 10.95 (ISBN 0-89686-318-2, Crestwood Hse). Macmillan Child Grp.

Liss, Howard. Making of a Rookie. (Illus.). (gr. 5-9). 1968. lib. bdg. 3.69 (ISBN 0-394-90199-1, Random Juv). Random.

Monroe, Judy. John Elway. LC 87-27430. (Illus.). 48p. (gr. 5-6). 1988. PLB 10.95 (ISBN 0-89686-367-0, Crestwood Hse). Macmillan Child Grp.

Nielsen, Nancy J. Eric Dickerson. LC 87-27560. (Illus.). 48p. (gr. 5-6). 1988. PLB 10.95 (ISBN 0-89686-366-2, Crestwood Hse). Macmillan Child Grp.

Raber, Thomas R. Joe Montana: Comeback Quarterback. 1990. pap. 3.95 (ISBN 0-8225-9572-9). Lerner Pubns.

Raber, Tom. Joe Montana: Comeback Quarterback. (Illus.). 64p. (gr. 4-9). 1989. PLB 8.95 (ISBN 0-8225-0486-3). Lerner Pubns.

Rainbolt, Richard. Football's Rugged Running Backs. LC 74-27469. (Illus.). 72p. (gr. 4 up). 1975. PLB 7.95 (ISBN 0-8225-1052-9). Lerner Pubns.

Roberts, Andre. William Perry: The Refrigerator. LC 86-4184. (Illus.). 48p. (gr. 2-8). 1986. PLB 13.27 (ISBN 0-516-04358-7). Childrens.

Rolfe, John. Bo Jackson. (gr. 4-7). 1991. pap. 4.95 (ISBN 0-316-75457-9). Little.

Rubin, Bob. All-Stars of the NFL. LC 76-8133. (Illus.). (gr. 5 up). 1976. (Random Juv). Random.

—Dan Marino: Wonder Boy Quarterback. LC 85-9724. (Illus.). 48p. (gr. 2-5). 1985. PLB 13.27 (ISBN 0-516-04347-1); pap. 3.95 (ISBN 0-516-44347-X). Childrens.

Stein, Conrad R. Walter Payton: Record-Breaking Runner. LC 87-13241. (Illus.). 48p. (gr. 2 up). 1987. PLB 13.27 (ISBN 0-516-04363-3); pap. 3.95 (ISBN 0-516-44363-1). Childrens.

Sufrin, Mark. Payton. LC 88-15751. (Illus.). 160p. (gr. 7 up). 1988. 13.95 (ISBN 0-684-18940-2, Scribners Young Read). Macmillan Child Grp.

FOOTBALL–DICTIONARIES

Lorimer, Lawrence T. & Devaney, John. The Football Book. LC 77-74461. (Illus.). (gr. 5 up). 1977. lib. bdg. 7.99 (ISBN 0-394-93574-8, Random Juv); pap. 2.44 (ISBN 0-394-83574-3). Random.

Olgin, Joseph. Illustrated Football Dictionary for Young People. Sutton, Larry, illus. (gr. 4 up). 1978. pap. 2.50 (ISBN 0-13-450874-2, Pub. by Treehouse). P-H.

FOOTBALL–FICTION

Aaseng, Nathan. At Left Linebacker, Chip Demory. LC 87-30905. 1988. pap. 4.49 (ISBN 1-55513-921-3, Chariot Bks). Cook.

—Football: It's Your Team. (gr. k-12). 1987. pap. 2.50 (ISBN 0-440-92648-3, LFL). Dell.

Bernstein, Joanne E. & Cohen, Paul. Touchdown Riddles. Levine, Abby, ed. Signorino, Slug, illus. 32p. (gr. 2-6). 1989. 8.95g (ISBN 0-8075-8036-8). A Whitman.

Blessing, Richard. A Passing Season. LC 82-47912. 228p. (gr. 6 up). 1982. 14.95 (ISBN 0-316-09957-0). Little.

—A Passing Season. LC 82-47912. 228p. (gr. 6 up). 1982. 14.95 (ISBN 0-316-09957-0). Little.

Boss, David. From First Down to Touchdown. 1990. 5.98 (ISBN 0-8317-9400-3). Smithmark.

Carpenter, Jerry & Dimeglio, Steve. Phil Simms. Deegan, Paul, ed. (Illus.). 32p. (gr. 4). 1990. PLB 9.95 (ISBN 0-939179-25-3). Abdo & Dghtrs.

Christopher, Matt. Catch That Pass, Vol. 1. Kidder, Harvey, illus. LC 77-77442. (gr. 4-6). 1989. lib. bdg. 12.95 (ISBN 0-316-13932-7); pap. 3.95 (ISBN 0-316-13924-6). Little.

—The Counterfeit Tackle. (gr. 4-7). 1990. pap. 3.95 (ISBN 0-316-14243-3). Little.

—Football Fugitive. Johnson, Larry, illus. 128p. (gr. 4-6). 1988. 11.95 (ISBN 0-316-13971-8); pap. 3.95 (ISBN 0-316-14064-3). Little.

—The Great Quarterback Switch. Jones, Eric, illus. LC 83-25628. (gr. 4-6). 1984. 13.95 (ISBN 0-316-13903-3). Little.

—Tackle Without a Team. Sanfilippo, Margaret, illus. LC 88-22644. 128p. (gr. 3-7). 1989. 13.95 (ISBN 0-316-14067-8). Little.

—Touchdown for Tommy. Caddell, Foster, illus. 145p. (gr. 4-6). 1985. lib. bdg. 12.95 (ISBN 0-316-13938-6); pap. 3.95 (ISBN 0-316-13982-3). Little.

—Tough to Tackle. Kidder, Harvey, illus. 152p. (gr. 4-6). 1987. pap. 3.95 (ISBN 0-316-14058-9). Little.

Dygard, Thomas J. Forward Pass. LC 89-33427. (Illus.). 192p. (gr. 7 up). 1989. 11.95 (ISBN 0-688-07961-X). Morrow Jr Bks.

—Forward Pass. (gr. 4 up). 1990. pap. 3.95 (ISBN 0-14-034562-0, Puffin). Puffin Bks.

—Halfback Tough. LC 85-25987. 224p. (gr. 7 up). 1986. 12.95 (ISBN 0-688-05925-2). Morrow Jr Bks.

—Halfback Tough. 224p. (gr. 5 up). 1989. pap. 3.95 (ISBN 0-14-034113-7, Puffin). Puffin Bks.

—Quarterback Walk-On. LC 81-18715. 224p. (gr. 7-9). 1982. 13.65 (ISBN 0-688-01065-2). Morrow Jr Bks.

—Quaterback Walk-On. 224p. (gr. 5 up). 1989. pap. 3.95 (ISBN 0-14-034115-3, Puffin). Puffin Bks.

—Winning Kicker. 192p. (gr. 4 up). 1990. pap. 3.95 (ISBN 0-14-034117-X, Puffin). Puffin Bks.

Foley, Louise M. Tackle Twenty-Two. Heinly, John, illus. 48p. (ps-3). 1981. pap. 1.75 (ISBN 0-440-48484-7, YB). Dell.

Gault, William C. Super Bowl Bound. LC 80-1015. 160p. (gr. 7-11). 1980. 7.95 (ISBN 0-396-07889-3, Putnam). Putnam Pub Group.

Halecroft, David. Breaking Loose. (gr. 4 up). 1990. pap. 2.95 (ISBN 0-14-034546-9, Puffin). Puffin Bks.

Hallowell, Tommy. Last Chance Quarterback. 112p. (gr. 3 up). 1990. pap. 2.95 (ISBN 0-14-032909-9, Puffin). Puffin Bks.

—Last Chance Quarterback. (gr. 4-7). 1991. 12.95 (ISBN 0-670-83731-8). Viking Child Bks.

Hermes, Patricia. What If They Knew. 128p. (gr. k-6). 1981. pap. 2.95 (ISBN 0-440-49515-6, YB). Dell.

Hill, Laurence D. A Season of Dreams. LC 90-37674. 320p. 1990. 19.95 (ISBN 0-8397-7591-1). Eriksson.

Horenstein, Henry. Go, Team, Go! Horenstein, Henry, illus. LC 88-10019. 56p. (gr. 3-7). 1988. 13.95 (ISBN 0-02-744420-1, Mcmillan Child Bk). Macmillan Child Grp.

Jenkins, Jerry. The Mysterious Football Team. (Orig.). (gr. 9-12). 1986. pap. text ed. 3.95 (ISBN 0-8024-8234-1). Moody.

Kessler, Leonard. Kick, Pass & Run. Kessler, Leonard, illus. LC 66-18656. (gr. k-3). 1978. pap. 3.50 (ISBN 0-06-444012-5, Trophy). HarpC Child Bks.

—Super Bowl. LC 80-10171. (Illus.). 56p. (gr. 1-4). 1980. PLB 12.88 (ISBN 0-688-84270-4). Greenwillow.

—Super Bowl. (gr. k-6). 1991. pap. 2.95 (ISBN 0-440-40403-7, Pub. by Yearling Classics). Dell.

Knudson, R. R. Zanballer. 176p. (gr. 5-9). 1986. pap. 3.95 (ISBN 0-14-032168-3, Puffin). Puffin Bks.

Korman, Gordon. The Zucchini Warriors. 208p. (gr. 4-7). 1988. pap. 10.95 (ISBN 0-590-41335-X, Pub. by Scholastic Hardcover). Scholastic Inc.

—Zucchini Warriors. 1990. pap. 2.75 (ISBN 0-590-41334-1). Scholastic Inc.

Kuskin, Karla. The Dallas Titans Get Ready for Bed. Simont, Marc, illus. LC 83-49470. 48p. (gr. k-3). 1986. 11.95 (ISBN 0-06-023562-4); PLB 11.89 (ISBN 0-06-023563-2). HarpC Child Bks.

Lee, S. C. Young Bear: The Legend of Bear Bryant's Boyhood. LC 77-14848. (gr. 7-12). 1983. pap. 6.95 (ISBN 0-87397-250-3). Strode.

Malmgren, Dallin. The Whole Nine Yards. (gr. 7 up). 1987. pap. 2.95 (ISBN 0-440-99575-2, LFL). Dell.

Myers, Bernice. Sidney Rella & the Glass Sneaker. Myers, Bernice, illus. LC 85-3044. 32p. (gr. k-3). 1985. 13.95 (ISBN 0-02-767790-7, Mcmillan Child Bk). Macmillan Child Grp.

Nichols, Paul. Blitz: Rookie Quarterback, No. 1. (gr. 3 up). 1988. pap. 2.95 (ISBN 0-345-35108-8). Ballantine.

—Touchdown. (gr. 4 up). 1989. pap. 2.95 (ISBN 0-345-35114-2). BAllantine.

—Tough Tackle. 1988. pap. 2.95 (ISBN 0-345-35109-6). Ballantine.

Sherman, Harold M. Interference, & Other Football Stories. facsimile ed. LC 70-178460. (gr. 7 up). Repr. of 1932 ed. 18.00 (ISBN 0-8369-4061-X). Ayer Co Pubs.

Tunis, John R. All-American. 1989. pap. 3.95 (ISBN 0-15-202292-9). HarbraceJ.

Twohill, Maggie. Superbowl Upset. LC 90-47412. 160p. (gr. 3-6). 1991. SBE 12.95 (ISBN 0-02-789691-9, Bradbury Pr). Macmillan Child Grp.

Van Leeuwen, Jean. Benjy the Football Hero. Owens, Gail, illus. LC 84-21459. 192p. (gr. 2-6). 1985. 11.95 (ISBN 0-8037-0189-6); PLB 11.89 (ISBN 0-8037-0190-X). Dial Bks Young.

FOOTBALL–HISTORY

Aaseng, Nathan. Football's Super Bowl Champions: I-VIII. LC 81-13659. (Illus.). 80p. (gr. 4 up). 1982. PLB 7.95 (ISBN 0-8225-1072-3). Lerner Pubns.

—Football's Super Bowl Champions: IX-XVI. LC 82-10099. (Illus.). 72p. (gr. 4 up). 1982. PLB 7.95 (ISBN 0-8225-1333-1). Lerner Pubns.

Gutman, Bill. Sport's Illustrated: Pro Football Record Breakers. (Illus.). 1990. pap. 2.75 (ISBN 0-671-68623-2, Archway). PB.

Jarrett, William. Timetables of Sports History: Football. (Illus.). 96p. (gr. 6 up). 1989. 17.95 (ISBN 0-8160-1919-3). Facts on File.

King, Gary. An Autumn Remembered: Reflections of College Football's Greatest Team. King, Charlyce, ed. LC 87-73386. 300p. (Orig.). (gr. 9 up). 1988. pap. 12.95 (ISBN 0-9619712-0-7). Red Earth OK.

Marks, Henry S. Who Was Who in Alabama. LC 74-188627. (gr. 9-12). 1972. 14.95 (ISBN 0-87397-017-9). Strode.

Resciniti, Angelo. Hot Superbowl Battles. 208p. (gr. 3-8). 1988. pap. 1.95 (ISBN 0-87406-608-5). Willowisp Pr.

Snypp, Wilbur & Hunter, Bob. Buckeyes: Ohio State Football. (Illus.). 352p. (gr. 6-12). 1988. 16.95 (ISBN 0-87397-307-0). Strode.

The Super Book of Football. (gr. 3-7). 1990. 19.95 (ISBN 0-316-57370-1). Little.

The Super Bowl. 32p. (gr. 4). 1990. 12.95s.p. (ISBN 0-88682-315-3); 18.50 (ISBN 0-685-28230-9). Creative Ed.

FOOTBALL–YEARBOOKS

Aaseng, Nathan. A Decade of Champions: Super Bowls XVI-XXIV. (Illus.). 64p. (gr. 5 up). 1991. PLB 10.95 (ISBN 0-8225-1504-0). Lerner Pubns.

NFL Team Book, 1987. (Illus.). (gr. k-9). 1988. pap. 3.95 (ISBN 0-318-36495-6). Scholastic Inc.

FOOTBALL CLUBS

Rothaus, James R. The Indianapolis Colts. (gr. 4 up). 1986. PLB 12.95 (ISBN 0-88682-369-2); 18.50 (ISBN 0-685-17913-3). Creative Ed.

FORAGE PLANTS

see also Grasses

FORCE AND ENERGY

see also Mechanics; Motion

Adler, David. Wonders of Energy. Johnson, Lewis, illus. LC 82-20042. 32p. (gr. 3-6). 1983. PLB 10.59 (ISBN 0-89375-884-1); pap. text ed. 2.95 (ISBN 0-89375-885-X). Troll Assocs.

Althea. What Makes Things Move? Green, Robina, illus. LC 90-10924. 32p. (gr. k-3). 1990. PLB 10.89 (ISBN 0-8167-2124-6); pap. text ed. 2.95 (ISBN 0-8167-2125-4). Troll Assocs.

Breitter, Herta S. Fuel & Energy. rev. ed. LC 87-20804. (Illus.). 48p. (gr. 2-6). 1987. PLB 17.32 (ISBN 0-8172-3255-9); pap. 9.27 (ISBN 0-8172-3280-X). Raintree Pubs.

Catherall, Ed. Exploring Uses of Energy. LC 90-46703. (Illus.). 48p. (gr. 3-7). 1990. PLB 18.60 (ISBN 0-8114-2598-3). Steck-V.

Cobb, Vicki. Why Doesn't the Earth Fall Up? And Other Not Such Dumb Questions about Motion. Enik, Ted, illus. LC 88-11108. 40p. (gr. 2-5). 1989. 12.95 (ISBN 0-525-67253-2, Lodestar Bks). Dutton Child Bks.

—Why Doesn't the Sun Burn Out? (gr. 4-7). 1990. 13.95 (ISBN 0-525-67301-6, Lodestar Bks). Dutton Child Bks.

Cohen, Lynn. Energy & Machines. 64p. (ps-2). 1988. 6.95 (ISBN 0-912107-78-2, MM982). Monday Morning Bks.

Conway, Lorraine. Energy. Akins, Linda, illus. 64p. (gr. 5 up). 1985. wkbk. 6.95 (ISBN 0-86653-267-6, GA 639). Good Apple.

Goldin, Augusta. Small Energy Sources: Choices That Work. LC 87-167. (Illus.). 176p. (gr. 7 up). 1988. 17.95 (ISBN 0-15-276215-9, HJ). HarBraceJ.

Grolier Editors & Douglas, John H. The Future World of Energy. LC 84-10886. (Illus.). 112p. (gr. 7-9). 1984. PLB 12.90 (ISBN 0-531-04881-0). Watts.

Johnston, Tom. Energy: Making It Work. Pooley, Sarah, illus. LC 87-42751. 32p. (gr. 4-6). 1987. PLB 10.95 (ISBN 1-55532-405-3). Gareth Stevens Inc.

—The Forces with You! Pooley, Sarah, illus. LC 87-42753. 32p. (gr. 4-6). 1987. PLB 10.95 (ISBN 1-55532-408-8). Gareth Stevens Inc.

Johnstone, Hugh. Facts on Future Energy Possibilities. 1990. 11.90 (ISBN 0-531-14067-9). Watts.

Jugendhandbuch Naturwissen: Energie, Vol. 5. (GER.). 128p. 1976. pap. 5.95 (ISBN 3-499-16207-5, M-7490, Pub. by Rowohlt). French & Eur.

Lafferty, Peter. Energy & Light. (Illus.). 40p. (gr. 7-9). 1990. 12.40 (ISBN 0-531-17144-2). Watts.

Langley, Andrew. Energy. (Illus.). 32p. (gr. 1-6). 1986. PLB 8.99 (ISBN 0-531-18085-9, Pub. by Bookwright). Watts.

Neal, Philip. Energy, Power Sources & Electricity. (Illus.). 48p. (gr. 6-9). 1989. 19.95 (ISBN 0-85219-776-4, Pub. by Batsford England). Trafalgar Sq.

Raintree Publishers Inc. Staff. Energy. LC 87-28699. (Illus.). 64p. (Orig.). (gr. 5-9). 1988. PLB 19.99 (ISBN 0-8172-3076-9); pap. 11.93 (ISBN 0-8172-3093-9). Raintree pubs.

Rickard, Graham. Bioenergy. (Illus.). 32p. (gr. 4-6). 1991. PLB 11.95 (ISBN 0-8368-0707-3). Gareth Stevens Inc.

Taylor, Barbara. Force & Movement. (Illus.). 32p. (gr. 5-8). 1990. PLB 11.40 (ISBN 0-531-14081-4). Watts.

Ward, Alan. Experimenting with Energy. Flax, Zena, illus. 48p. (gr. 2-7). 1991. PLB 12.95 (ISBN 0-7910-1510-6). Chelsea Hse.

Whyman, Kathryn. Heat & Energy. (Illus.). 32p. (gr. 1-6). 1986. PLB 11.90 (ISBN 0-531-17022-5, Pub. by Gloucester). Watts.

FORD, GERALD, PRES. U. S., 1913-

Collins, David R. Gerald R. Ford: Thirty-Eighth President of the United States. Young, Richard G., ed. LC 89-39945. (Illus.). 128p. (gr. 5-9). 1990. PLB 17.26 (ISBN 0-944483-65-8). Garrett Ed Corp.

Randolph, Sallie. Gerald R. Ford: President. LC 86-16333. 128p. (gr. 5 up). 1987. 12.95 (ISBN 0-8027-6666-8); PLB 13.85 (ISBN 0-8027-6667-6). Walker & Co.

FORD, HENRY, 1863-1947

Aird, Hazel B. & Ruddiman, Catherine. Henry Ford: Young Man with Ideas. Wood, Wallace, illus. LC 86-10756. 192p. (gr. 2-6). 1986. pap. 3.95 (ISBN 0-02-041910-4, Aladdin). Macmillan Child Grp.

Harris, Jacqueline L. Henry Ford. 128p. (gr. 7 up). 1984. lib. bdg. 12.90 (ISBN 0-531-04754-7). Watts.

Kent, Zachary. The Story of Henry Ford & the Automobile. LC 90-2163. (Illus.). 32p. (gr. 3-6). 1990. PLB 13.27 (ISBN 0-516-04751-5); pap. 3.95 (ISBN 0-516-44751-3). Childrens.

Killingray, David. Henry Ford. Yapp, Malcolm, et al, eds. (Illus.). 32p. (gr. 6-11). 1980. pap. text ed. 2.95 (ISBN 0-89908-024-3). Greenhaven.

Mitchell, Barbara. We'll Race You, Henry: A Story about Henry Ford. Haubrich, Kathy, illus. 64p. (gr. 3-6). 1986. PLB 9.95 (ISBN 0-87614-291-9); pap. 4.95 (ISBN 0-87614-471-7). Carolrhoda Bks.

Sipiera, Paul. Gerald Ford. LC 89-33745. 100p. (gr. 3 up). 1989. PLB 17.27 (ISBN 0-516-01371-8). Childrens.

FORECASTING WEATHER

see Weather Forecasting

FOREIGN AID PROGRAM

see Economic Assistance

FOREIGN ECONOMIC RELATIONS

see International Economic Relations

FOREIGN MISSIONS

see Missions

FOREIGN POLICY

see names of countries with the subdivision. foreign relations, e. g. U. S.–Foreign Relations; etc.

FOREIGN POPULATION

see Immigration and Emigration

FOREIGN RELATIONS

see International Relations;

see names of countries with subdivision Foreign Relations

FOREIGNERS

see Citizenship

FOREST CONSERVATION

see Forests and Forestry

FOREST FIRES

Guth, A. Richard & Cohen, Stan B. Red Skies of Eighty-Eight: The 1988 Forest Fire Season in the Northern Rockies, the Northern Great Plains & the Greater Yellowstone Area. LC 89-50399. (Illus.). 136p. (Orig.). 1989. pap. text ed. 12.95. Pictorial Hist.

Lampton, Christopher. Forest Fire. (Illus.). 64p. (gr. 4-6). 1991. PLB 17.25 (ISBN 1-56294-033-3). Millbrook Pr.

Morrison, Ellen E. Guardian of the Forest: A History of the Smokey Bear Program. 2nd, rev. ed. LC 89-60719. (Illus.). 144p. (gr. 6). 1989. 12.95 (ISBN 0-9622537-3-1). Morielle Pr.

Vogel, Carole G. Great Yellowstone Fire, Vol. 1. 1990. 14.95 (ISBN 0-316-90522-4). Little.

Vogt, Gregory. Forests on Fire: The Fight to Save Our Trees. (Illus.). 144p. (gr. 9-12). 1990. PLB 12.90 (ISBN 0-531-10940-2). Watts.

FOREST PRODUCTS

see also Lumber and Lumbering; Rubber; Wood

FORESTRY

see Forests and Forestry

FORESTS AND FORESTRY

see also Lumber and Lumbering; Trees; Wood

Anderson, David & Holland, I. I., eds. Forests & Forestry. 4th ed. (gr. 10-12). 1990. 35.95 (ISBN 0-8134-2855-6); text ed. 26.95 (ISBN 0-685-33565-8). Inter Print Pubs.

Arnold, Caroline. A Walk by the Seashore. Brook, Bonnie, ed. Tanz, Freya, illus. 32p. (ps-1). 1990. 4.95 (ISBN 0-671-68666-6); lib. bdg. 9.98 (ISBN 0-671-68662-3). Silver Pr.

—A Walk in the Woods. Brook, Bonnie, ed. Tanz, Freya, illus. 32p. (ps-1). 1990. 4.95 (ISBN 0-671-68665-8); lib. bdg. 9.98 (ISBN 0-671-68661-5). Silver Pr.

Arnosky, Jim. In the Forest. Arnosky, Jim, illus. LC 89-2341. 32p. (gr. 4 up). 1989. 13.95 (ISBN 0-688-08162-2); PLB 13.88 (ISBN 0-688-09138-5). Lothrop.

Bains, Rae. Forests & Jungles. Snyder, Joel, illus. LC 84-8641. 32p. (gr. 3-6). 1985. PLB 9.49 (ISBN 0-8167-0312-4); pap. text ed. 2.95 (ISBN 0-8167-0313-2). Troll Assocs.

Baker, Lucy. Life in the Rainforests. (Illus.). 32p. (gr. 5-8). 1990. PLB 11.40 (ISBN 0-531-10983-6). Watts.

Bellamy, David. Our Changing World: The Forest. Dow, Jill, illus. 24p. (gr. 1-4). 1988. bds. 9.95 (ISBN 0-517-56800-4, C N Potter Bks). Crown.

Booth, Basil. Temperate Forests. Furstinger, Nancy, ed. (Illus.). 48p. (gr. 5-8). 1988. PLB 14.98. Silver Burdett Pr.

Bright, Michael. Tropical Rainforest. (Illus.). 32p. (gr. 2-4). 1991. PLB 11.90 (ISBN 0-531-17301-1, Gloucester Pr). Watts.

Butler, Daphne. First Look in the Forest. LC 90-10240. (Illus.). 32p. (gr. 1-2). 1991. lib. bdg. 10.95 (ISBN 0-8368-0506-2). Gareth Stevens Inc.

Coucher, Helen. Rain Forest. (Illus.). 32p. (ps up). 1988. 13.95 (ISBN 0-374-36167-3). FS&G.

Cowcher, Helen. Rain Forest. (Illus.). 32p. (ps-3). 1989. incl. audiocassette 17.95 (ISBN 0-924483-20-2). Soundprints.

Craig, Janet. Wonders of the Rain Forest. Schindler, S. D., illus. LC 89-5001. 32p. (gr. 2-4). 1989. PLB 10.89 (ISBN 0-8167-1763-X); pap. text ed. 2.95 (ISBN 0-8167-1764-8). Troll Assocs.

Crump, Donald J., ed. The Emerald Realm: Earth's Precious Rain Forests. (Illus.). 1990. 8.95 (ISBN 0-87044-795-5). Natl Geog.

—Explore a Tropical Forest, No. 1. (Illus.). (ps-3). 1989. 19.95 (ISBN 0-87044-757-2). Natl Geog.

Curran, Eileen. Life in the Forest. Harvey, Paul, illus. LC 84-16455. 32p. (gr. k-2). 1985. PLB 10.89 (ISBN 0-8167-0446-5); pap. text ed. 2.95 (ISBN 0-8167-0447-3). Troll Assocs.

Dorros, Arthur. Rainforest Secrets. 1990. 13.95 (ISBN 0-590-43369-5, Scholastic Hardcover). Scholastic Inc.

Ekey, Robert. Fire! in Yellowstone. Mayer, Larry, illus. LC 89-43156. 32p. (gr. 2-4). 1989. lib. bdg. 10.95 (ISBN 0-8368-0226-8). Gareth Stevens Inc.

Forestry. (Illus.). 80p. (gr. 6-12). 1984. pap. 1.85 (ISBN 0-8395-3302-0, 3302). BSA.

Forsyth, Andrian. Journey Through a Tropical Jungle. (gr. 3-7). 1989. pap. 14.95 (ISBN 0-671-66262-7). S&S Trade.

Gallant, Roy A. Earth's Vanishing Forests. LC 91-2624. (Illus.). 144p. (gr. 5-9). 1991. 14.95 (ISBN 0-02-735774-0, Mcmillan Child Bk). Macmillan Child Grp.

George, Jean C. One Day in the Tropical Rain Forest. Allen, Gary, illus. LC 89-36583. 64p. (gr. 4-7). 1990. 11.95 (ISBN 0-690-04767-3, Crowell Jr Bks); PLB 11.89 (ISBN 0-690-04769-X, Crowell Jr Bks). HarpC Child Bks.

Gordon, Sharon. Trees. Trivas, Irene, illus. LC 82-20291. 32p. (gr. k-2). 1982. lib. bdg. 10.89 (ISBN 0-89375-901-5); pap. text ed. 2.95 (ISBN 0-8167-0879-7). Troll Assocs.

Gould, G. Forests of Africa, Reading Level 5. (Illus.). 32p. (gr. 3-6). Date not set. PLB 13.26. Rourke Corp.

Greenaway, Theresa. Fir Trees. LC 90-9640. (Illus.). 48p. (gr. 5-9). 1990. PLB 18.60 (ISBN 0-8114-2727-7). Steck-V.

Greenberg, Judith E. & Carey, Helen H. The Rain Forest. Masheris, Bob, illus. 32p. (gr. 2-4). 1990. PLB 16.67 (ISBN 0-8172-3753-4). Raintree Pubs.

Greene, Carol. Caring for Our Forest. (Illus.). 32p. (gr. 1-4). 1991. PLB 12.95 (ISBN 0-89490-353-5). Enslow Pubs.

Hamilton, Jean. Tropical Rainforests. Leon, Vicki, ed. (Illus.). 40p. (Orig.). 1990. pap. 7.95 (ISBN 0-918303-25-7). Blake Pub.
The worlds' richest terrestrial habitat, the tropical rainforest is an emerald mansion of biological riches. In 5,000 words of text, over 1,000 words of captions, & 40 brilliant color photos, this book presents a roundup look at the world's rainforests, as enchanted & fruitful as they are endangered. To make the diversity of the forest understandable, the book approaches it by levels: the floor, the understory, the canopy, & the pavillion. Like other books in the Blake Habitat series, complex ideas & relationships are presented in a clear & relaxed manner. Unfamiliar terms are used & immediately explained. Captions identify animals & plants & also name their ecological equivalents on other continents. From the photos taken by 18 of the world's best wildlife photographers to the text by a noted writer with a zoology background, no effort has been spared to make this book a quality & good value standout in a forest of competitors.
Publisher Provided Annotation.

Hare, Tony. Rainforest Destruction. (Illus.). 32p. (gr. 5-8). 1990. PLB 11.90 (ISBN 0-531-17248-1). Watts.

Hogan, Paula. Vanishing Rain Forests. (Illus.). 32p. (gr. 3-4). 1991. PLB 12.95 (ISBN 0-8368-0477-5). Gareth Stevens Inc.

Kuhn, Dwight, photos by. The Hidden Life of the Forest. Schwartz, David M., text by. (Illus.). 40p. (gr. 1 up). 1988. PLB 12.95 (ISBN 0-517-57058-0). Crown.

Landau, Elaine. Tropical Rain Forests Around the World. (Illus.). 64p. (gr. 3 up). 1991. pap. 4.95 (ISBN 0-531-15600-1). Watts.

Miller, Christina G. & Berry, Louise A. Jungle Rescue: Saving the New World Tropical Rain Forests. (Illus.). 128p. (gr. 5-9). 1991. SBE 14.95 (ISBN 0-689-31487-6, Atheneum Child Bk). Macmillan Child Grp.

Mitchell, Victor. Woodlands. Mitchell, Victor, illus. 16p. (gr. k up). 1988. pap. 1.95 (ISBN 0-7459-1472-1). Lion USA.

Nations, James D. Tropical Rainforests: Endangered Environments. Rasof, Henry, ed. LC 88-5695. (Illus.). 144p. (gr. 7-12). 1988. PLB 12.90 (ISBN 0-531-10604-7). Watts.

Newton, James R. Rain Shadow. Bonners, Susan, illus. LC 82-45927. 32p. (gr. 2-6). 1983. 12.95 (ISBN 0-690-04344-9, Crowell Jr Bks); PLB 12.89 (ISBN 0-690-04345-7, Crowell Jr Bks). HarpC Child Bks.

Page, Jake. Forest. (Illus.). 176p. (gr. 7 up). 1983. 18.60 (ISBN 0-8094-4344-9); lib. bdg. 24.60 (ISBN 0-8094-4345-7). Time-Life.

Paige, David. A Day in the Life of a Forest Ranger. Mauney, Michael, photos by. LC 78-68809. (Illus.). 32p. (gr. 4-8). 1980. PLB 11.79 (ISBN 0-89375-227-4); pap. 2.95 (ISBN 0-89375-231-2). Troll Assocs.

Pearce, Q. L. Piranhas & Other Wonders of the Jungle. Fraser, Mary A., illus. 64p. (gr. 4-6). 1990. PLB 12.98 (ISBN 0-671-70689-6); pap. 5.95 (ISBN 0-671-70690-X). Messner.

Pearce, Q. L. & Pearce, W. L. In the Forest. Brook, Bonnie, ed. Bettoli, Delana, illus. 24p. (ps-1). 1990. 4.95 (ISBN 0-671-68830-8); PLB 8.98 (ISBN 0-671-68826-X). Silver Pr.

Pellowski, Michael J. Forest Ranger. Ulrich, George, illus. LC 88-10355. 32p. (gr. k-2). 1989. PLB 10.89 (ISBN 0-8167-1422-3); pap. text ed. 2.50 (ISBN 0-8167-1423-1). Troll Assocs.

Pope, Joyce. A Closer Look at Jungles. rev. ed. Orr, Richard, illus. 32p. (gr. 4 up). 1984. lib. bdg. 5.99 (ISBN 0-531-03478-X, Gloucester Pr). Watts.

—Plants of the Tropics. 64p. 1990. 15.95x (ISBN 0-8160-2423-5). Facts on File.

Prosser, Robert. Disappearing Rainforest. (gr. 6 up). 1988. 19.95 (ISBN 0-7134-7195-6, Pub. by Batsford England). Trafalgar Sq.

Sabin, Francene. Wonders of the Forest. Willard, Michael, illus. LC 81-7401. 32p. (gr. 2-4). 1982. PLB 10.89 (ISBN 0-89375-572-9); pap. text ed. 2.95 (ISBN 0-89375-573-7). Troll Assocs.

Schoonmaker, Peter K. The Living Forest. LC 89-33603. (Illus.). 64p. 1990. lib. bdg. 15.95 (ISBN 0-89490-270-9). Enslow Pubs.

Seymour, Peter. What's in the Prehistoric Forest? Carter, David A., illus. LC 90-80885. 18p. (ps-2). 1990. 10.95 (ISBN 0-8050-1450-0). H Holt & Co.

Spencer, Guy. An Ancient Forest. Staub, Frank J., illus. LC 87-3487. 32p. (gr. 3-6). 1987. PLB 10.79 (ISBN 0-8167-1167-4); pap. text ed. 2.95 (ISBN 0-8167-1168-2). Troll Assocs.

Thomas, Heather S. A Week in the Woods. Woolsey, Raymond H., ed. 64p. (gr. 2-4). 1988. pap. 4.95 (ISBN 0-8280-0435-8). Review & Herald.

Watts, Barrie. Twenty-Four Hours in a Forest. (Illus.). 48p. (gr. 5-8). 1990. PLB 11.90 (ISBN 0-531-14036-9). Watts.

Whipple, Jane B. Forest Resources. LC 84-20939. (Illus.). 64p. (gr. 5-8). 1985. lib. bdg. 10.40 (ISBN 0-531-04909-4). Watts.

Wilderness Society Staff. Color the Ancient Forest. (Illus.). 48p. (Orig.). (ps-3). 1991. saddle-stitched 4.95 (ISBN 1-879326-07-8). Living Planet Pr.

Willow, Diane. At Home in the Rainforest. (Illus.). 32p. (ps-8). 1991. 14.95 (ISBN 0-88106-485-8). Charlesbridge Pub.

Zuckerman, Seth. Saving Our Ancient Forests. (Illus.). 128p. (Orig.). 1991. pap. 5.95 (ISBN 0-9626072-9-0). Living Planet Pr.

FORESTS AND FORESTRY–FICTION

Abrams, Jodell. The Enchanted Forest Color & Story Album. (Illus.). 32p. (Orig.). 1981. pap. 3.95 (ISBN 0-8431-1712-5). Troubador Pr.

Alexander, Martha. I'll Protect You from the Jungle Beasts. Alexander, Martha, illus. LC 73-6015. 32p. (ps-2). 1980. pap. 1.95 (ISBN 0-8037-3900-1). Dial Bks Young.

Arvetis, Chris & Palmer, Carole. What Is a Jungle? Buckley, James, illus. 32p. (ps-3). 1984. Repr. 3.95 (ISBN 0-528-82825-8). Checkerboard Pr.

Babbitt, Natalie. Phoebe's Revolt. LC 68-13679. (Illus.). 40p. (ps up). 1978. 11.95 (ISBN 0-374-35907-5). FS&G.

Baker, Jeannie. Where the Forest Meets The Sea. LC 87-7551. (Illus.). 32p. (ps-3). 1988. 13.95 (ISBN 0-688-06363-2); lib. bdg. 13.88 (ISBN 0-688-06364-0). Greenwillow.

Catterwell, Thelma. Aldita & the Forest. Stone, Derrick, illus. (ps-3). 1989. 14.95 (ISBN 0-395-50925-4). HM.

Cherry, Lynne. Great Kapok Tree: A Tale of the Amazon Rain Forest. 1990. 14.95 (ISBN 0-15-200520-X). HarbraceJ.

Cowcher, Helen. Rain Forest. (Illus.). 32p. (ps-3). 1990. pap. 4.95 (ISBN 0-374-46190-2, Sunburst). FS&G.

Cristini, Ermanno & Puricelli, Luigi. In the Woods. Cristini, Ermanno & Puricelli, Luigi, illus. LC 83-8153. 28p. (ps up). 1985. 12.95 (ISBN 0-907234-31-3). Picture Bk Studio.

Evans, Olive. Secrets of the Forest. (gr. 3-12). 1985. pap. text ed. 6.00 (ISBN 0-88734-502-6). Players Pr.

Gile, John. The First Forest. Heflin, Tom, illus. LC 89-91458. 40p. (gr. k up). 1989. 13.95 (ISBN 0-910941-01-7). J Gile Comm.

Goldsborough, June. What's in the Woods? LC 76-10271. (Illus.). 32p. 1981. pap. 2.95 (ISBN 0-13-955047-X). P-H.

Grange, Wallace B. Those of the Forest. Petrie, Chuck, ed. Murie, Olaus J., illus. Johnson, Dan, intro. by. (Illus.). 336p. (gr. 6 up). 1989. Repr. of 1953 ed. 19.50 (ISBN 0-932558-49-6). Willow Creek Pr.

Hackman, Martha. The Lost Forest. Cesari, Aura, illus. 12p. (gr. 7-9). 1982. pap. 2.50 (ISBN 0-914676-97-0). Green Tiger Pr.

Hanson, Fred E. Simon. Hanson, Ann R., illus. 64p. (gr. 4-6). pap. 9.95 (ISBN 0-9624292-1-X). Black Willow Pr.

Hasenau, James. Fuzzy Bear. LC 82-81828. (Illus.). (gr. k-4). 1985. 6.00 (ISBN 0-913042-15-3). Holland Hse Pr.

Hollingsworth, Mary. Polka Dots, Stripes, Humps 'n Hatracks: How God Created Happy Forest. (Illus.). (ps-2). 1990. 6.95 (ISBN 1-877719-00-5). Brownlow Pub Co.

—Twizzler, the Unlikely Hero. (Illus.). (ps-2). 1990. 6.95 (ISBN 1-877719-01-3). Brownlow Pub Co.

Lasky, Kathryn. Sugaring Time. Knight, Christopher G., illus. & photos by LC 82-23928. 64p. (gr. 3-7). 1983. 11.95 (ISBN 0-02-751680-6, Mcmillan Child Bk). Macmillan Child Grp.

Morey, Walt. Canyon Winter. (gr. 4 up). 1972. 15.95 (ISBN 0-525-27410-3, DCB). Dutton Child Bks.

Morreale, Vin, Jr. The Day the Woods Were One. (Orig.). (gr. 3 up). 1985. pap. text ed. 6.00 (ISBN 0-88734-507-7). Players Pr.

Newton, James. A Forest Is Reborn. Bonners, Susan, illus. LC 81-43882. 32p. (gr. 2-5). 1982. (Crowell Jr Bks); (Crowell Jr Bks). HarpC Child Bks.

Rhea, Celeste. The Acorn Sprout & His Forest Friends. (Illus.). 23p. (Orig.). (gr. 1-4). 1978. pap. 1.95 (ISBN 0-89323-010-3, 025). Bible Memory.

Ryder, Joanne. When the Woods Hum. LC 90-37879. (Illus.). 32p. (gr. 1 up). 1991. 13.95 (ISBN 0-688-07057-4); PLB 13.88 (ISBN 0-688-07058-2, Morrow Jr Bks). Morrow Jr Bks.

Siegenthaler, Kathrin. Santa Claus & the Woodcutter. Crawford, Elizabeth, tr. from GER. Pfister, Marcus, illus. 32p. (gr. k-3). 1989. pap. 1.95 (ISBN 1-55858-032-8). North-South Bks NYC.

Spohn, David. Winter Wood. LC 90-49944. (Illus.). 32p. (gr. k up). 1991. 13.95 (ISBN 0-688-10093-7); PLB 13.88 (ISBN 0-688-10094-5). Lothrop.

Spring in the Enchanted Forest. (Illus.). (ps-1). 1985. 2.98 (ISBN 0-517-46980-4). Outlet Bk Co.

Springer, Jean. The Great Forest. Peterson, Pete, ed. French, Ed, illus. 169p. (gr. 3-6). 1986. pap. 3.95 (ISBN 0-934998-25-6). Bethel Pub.

Taylor, Mildred. Song of the Trees. Pinkney, Jeny, illus. LC 74-18598. 56p. (gr. 2-5). 1985. 12.95 (ISBN 0-8037-5452-3); PLB 11.89 (ISBN 0-8037-5453-1). Dial Bks Young.

Tejima. Woodpecker Forest. Tejima, illus. 48p. (ps-3). 1989. 14.95 (ISBN 0-399-21618-9, Philomel Bks). Putnam Pub Group.

Thoreau, Henry David. Walden. Lowe, Steve, ed. Sabuda, Robert, illus. 32p. 1990. 14.95 (ISBN 0-399-22153-0, Philomel Bks). Putnam Pub Group.

FORESTS AND FORESTRY–VOCATIONAL GUIDANCE

Greene, Carol. I Can Be a Forest Ranger. LC 88-37717. (Illus.). 32p. (gr. k-3). 1989. PLB 13.93 (ISBN 0-516-01924-4); pap. 3.95 (ISBN 0-516-41924-2). Childrens.

Paige, David. A Day in the Life of a Forest Ranger. Mauney, Michael, photos by. LC 78-68809. (Illus.). 32p. (gr. 4-8). 1980. PLB 11.79 (ISBN 0-89375-227-4); pap. 2.95 (ISBN 0-89375-231-2). Troll Assocs.

FORGERY OF WORKS OF ART

Waldron, Ann. True or False? Amazing Art Forgeries. (Illus.). 160p. (gr. 3-7). 1983. PLB 12.95 (ISBN 0-8038-7220-8). Hastings.

Wilkes, A. Fakes & Forgeries. (Illus.). 64p. (gr. 3-7). 1979. lib. bdg. 11.96 (ISBN 0-88110-041-2, Usborne); pap. 4.50 (ISBN 0-86020-231-3). EDC.

FORM, MUSICAL

see Musical Form

FORMOSA

Edmonds, I. G. Taiwan: The Other China. LC 70-156112. (gr. 6-10). 7.95 (ISBN 0-672-51598-9, Bobbs). Macmillan.

Lerner Publications, Department of Geography Staff, ed. Taiwan in Pictures. (Illus.). 64p. (gr. 5 up). 1989. PLB 12.95 (ISBN 0-8225-1865-1). Lerner Pubns.

Wee, Jerrie. Taiwan. (Illus.). (gr. 5 up). 1988. 14.95 (ISBN 1-55546-180-8). Chelsea Hse.

FORTIFICATION

Mulvihill, Margaret. Roman Forts. 1990. PLB 11.90 (ISBN 0-531-17201-5). Watts.

FORTS

see Fortification

FORTUNE

see Success

FORTUNE, AMOS, 1709?-1801

Yates, Eliizabeth. Amos Fortune, Free Man. Unwin, Nora S., illus. 192p. (gr. 3-7). 1989. pap. 3.95 (ISBN 0-14-034158-7, Puffin). Puffin Bks.

Yates, Elizabeth. Amos Fortune, Free Man. Unwin, Nora S., illus. (gr. 7 up). 1967. 13.95 (ISBN 0-525-25570-2, DCB). Dutton Child Bks.

FORTUNE TELLING

see also Astrology; Cards; Dreams

Gibson, Litzkah R. How to Read Palms. Adelman, Sherri, ed. (Illus.). 184p. (gr. 10-12). 1989. pap. 8.95 (ISBN 0-8119-0033-9). Lifetime.

Schwartz, Alvin. Telling Fortunes: Love Magic, Dream Signs, & Other Ways to Learn the Future. Cameron, Tracey, illus. LC 85-45174. 128p. (gr. 4 up). 1987. 12.95 (ISBN 0-397-32132-5, Lipp Jr Bks); PLB 12.89 (ISBN 0-397-32133-3, Lipp Jr Bks). HarpC Child Bks.

—Telling Fortunes: Love Magic, Dream Signs, & Other Ways to Learn the Future. Cameron, Tracey, illus. LC 85-45174. 128p. (gr. 4 up). 1990. pap. 4.95 (ISBN 0-06-446094-0, Trophy). HarpC Child Bks.

Shimano, Jimmei. Oriental Fortune Telling. LC 65-18960. (Illus.). (gr. 9 up). 1965. pap. 9.95 (ISBN 0-8048-0448-6). C E Tuttle.

FOSSIL MAMMALS

see Mammals, Fossil

FOSSILS

see also Extinct Animals; Mammals, Fossil; Reptiles, Fossil

Aliki. Fossils Tell of Long Ago. Aliki, illus. LC 78-170999. 40p. (gr. k-3). 1972. PLB 12.89 (ISBN 0-690-31379-9, Crowell Jr Bks). HarpC Child Bks.

—Fossils Tell of Long Ago. rev. ed. Aliki, illus. LC 89-17247. 32p. (gr. k-4). 1990. 13.95 (ISBN 0-690-04844-0, Crowell Jr Bks); PLB 13.89 (ISBN 0-690-04829-7, Crowell Jr Bks). HarpC Child Bks.

—Fossils Tell of Long Ago. rev. ed. Aliki, illus. LC 89-17247. 32p. (gr. k-4). 1990. 13.95 (ISBN 0-690-04844-0, Crowell Jr Bks); PLB 13.89 (ISBN 0-690-04829-7, Crowell Jr Bks). HarpC Child Bks.

—Fossils Tell of Long Ago. rev. ed. Aliki, illus. LC 89-15468. 32p. (gr. k-4). 1990. pap. 4.50 (ISBN 0-06-445093-7, JS093, Trophy). HarpC Child Bks.

Andrews, Roy C. In the Days of the Dinosaurs. (Illus.). (gr. 3-5). 1959. (Random Juv). Random.

Arnold, Caroline. Trapped in Tar: Fossils from the Ice Age. LC 86-17614. (Illus.). 64p. (gr. 3-6). 1987. 12.95 (ISBN 0-89919-415-X, Pub. by Clarion). Ticknor & Fields.

—Trapped in Tar: Fossils from the Ice Age. (gr. 4-7). 1990. pap. 5.95 (ISBN 0-395-54783-0, Clarion Bks). HM.

Bains, Rae. Prehistoric Animals. Acosta, Andres, illus. LC 84-2735. 32p. (gr. 3-6). 1985. PLB 9.49 (ISBN 0-8167-0296-9); pap. text ed. 2.95 (ISBN 0-8167-0297-7). Troll Assocs.

Baylor, Byrd. If You Are a Hunter of Fossils. Parnall, Peter, illus. LC 79-17926. 32p. (gr. 3-6). 1984. pap. 4.95 (ISBN 0-689-70773-8, Aladdin). Macmillan Child Grp.

Benton, Michael. Prehistoric Animals: An A-Z Guide. 1989. 7.99 (ISBN 0-517-69190-6). Outlet Bk Co.

Berger, Melvin. Monsters. 128p. 1991. pap. 2.95 (ISBN 0-380-76053-3, Camelot). Avon.

Burton, Virginia L. Life Story. (Illus.). (gr. k-3). 1989. 15.95 (ISBN 0-395-16030-8); pap. 6.95 (ISBN 0-395-52017-7). HM.

Cohen, Daniel. Prehistoric Animals. Johnson, Pamela F., illus. LC 86-19666. 48p. (gr. k-3). 1988. 9.95 (ISBN 0-385-23416-3); PLB 10.99 (ISBN 0-385-23417-1). Doubleday.

Cork, B. & Bramwell, M. Rocks & Fossils. Jackson, I. & Suttie, A., illus. 32p. (gr. 5-8). 1983. PLB 13.96 (ISBN 0-88110-159-1); pap. 6.95 (ISBN 0-86020-765-X). EDC.

Craig, Janet. Discovering Prehistoric Animals. Watling, James, illus. LC 89-4973. 32p. (gr. 2-4). 1990. PLB 10.89 (ISBN 0-8167-1755-9); pap. text ed. 2.95 (ISBN 0-8167-1756-7). Troll Assocs.

Curtis, Neil. Fossils. Atkinson, Mike, illus. LC 83-51439. 32p. (gr. 3-5). 1984. PLB 7.99 (ISBN 0-531-03773-8). Watts.

Dixon, Dougal. Hunting the Dinosaurs. Burton, Jane, illus. LC 87-6461. 32p. (gr. 2-3). 1987. PLB 10.95 (ISBN 1-55532-259-X). Gareth Stevens Inc.

Dixon, Douglas. Be a Fossil Detective. (gr. 2 up). 1989. 3.99 (ISBN 0-517-68022-X). Outlet Bk Co.

Gallant, Roy A. Fossils. LC 84-19477. (Illus.). 72p. (gr. 4 up). 1985. lib. bdg. 10.40 (ISBN 0-531-04910-8). Watts.

Gela, Darlene. Dinosaurs & Other Prehistoric Animals. Peterson, Russell F., illus. 108p. (gr. 3-8). 1982. 8.95 (ISBN 0-448-02882-4, G&D). Putnam Pub Group.

Goldish, Meish. What is a Fossil? (Illus.). 32p. (gr. 1-4). 1989. PLB 13.32 (ISBN 0-8172-3535-3). Raintree Pubs.

Harrison, Virginia & Rowland-Entwistle, Theodore. The Prehistoric World. LC 89-11276. (Illus.). 64p. (gr. 2-3). 1990. PLB 12.95 (ISBN 0-8368-0031-1). Gareth Stevens Inc.

Hornblow, Leonora & Hornblow, Arthur. Prehistoric Monsters Did the Strangest Things. abr. ed. Barlowe, Sy, illus. LC 88-30212. 64p. (gr. 2-4). 1990. lib. bdg. 6.99 (ISBN 0-394-94307-4); pap. 3.95 (ISBN 0-394-84307-X). Random.

Howard, John. I Can Read About Fossils. Nodel, Norman, illus. LC 76-54446. (gr. 2-5). 1977. pap. 1.95 (ISBN 0-89375-038-7). Troll Assocs.

Kaufmann, John. Flying Giants of Long Ago. LC 81-43881. (Illus.). 40p. (gr. k-3). 1984. (Crowell Jr Bks); (Crowell Jr Bks). HarpC Child Bks.

Lammers, George E. Time & Life: Fossils Tell the Earth's Story. Thorsteinson, Betsy, illus. 40p. (Orig.). (gr. 3-9). 1990. pap. 4.95 (ISBN 0-920534-39-2, Pub. by Hyperion Pr Ltd CN). Sterling.

Lauber, Patricia. Dinosaurs Walked Here & Other Stories Fossils Tell. LC 86-8239. (Illus.). 64p. (gr. 2-4). 1987. 15.95 (ISBN 0-02-754510-5, Bradbury Pr). Macmillan Child Grp.

Prehistoric Animals & Fossils. (Illus.). (gr. 4 up). 3.50 (ISBN 0-7214-0359-X). Ladybird Bks.

Prehistoric Encyclopedia. (Illus.). 144p. (gr. 4 up). 1989. Repr. 14.95 (ISBN 0-02-688539-5). Checkerboard Pr.

Rhodes, Frank H., et al. Fossils. Perlman, Raymond, illus. (gr. 6 up). 1962. PLB write for info. (ISBN 0-307-63515-5); pap. write for info. (ISBN 0-307-24411-3, Golden Pr). Western Pub.

Roberts, Allan. Fossils. LC 82-23521. (Illus.). 48p. (gr. k-4). 1983. PLB 14.60 (ISBN 0-516-01678-4); pap. 4.95 (ISBN 0-516-41678-2). Childrens.

Rowland-Entwistle, Theodore. Prehistoric Life. LC 89-11373. (Illus.). 64p. (gr. 4-6). 1990. PLB 12.95 (ISBN 0-8368-0006-0). Gareth Stevens Inc.

Rydell, Wendy. Discovering Fossils. Burns, Ray, illus. LC 83-4832. 32p. (gr. 3-6). 1984. lib. bdg. 10.59 (ISBN 0-89375-973-2); pap. text ed. 2.95 (ISBN 0-89375-974-0). Troll Assocs.

Sabin, Louis. Fossils. Maccabe, Richard, illus. LC 84-2716. 32p. (gr. 3-6). 1985. PLB 9.49 (ISBN 0-8167-0228-4); pap. text ed. 2.95 (ISBN 0-8167-0229-2). Troll Assocs.

Sandberg, Phillip. Stereogram Book of Fossils. (gr. 7 up). plastic comb bdg. 6.95 (ISBN 0-8331-1702-5). Hubbard Sci.

Taylor, Paul. Fossil. Keates, Colin, photos by. LC 89-36444. (Illus.). 64p. (gr. 5 up). 1990. 15.00 (ISBN 0-679-80440-4); PLB 14.99 (ISBN 0-679-90440-9). McKay.

Zim, Herbert S. Dinosaurs. Irving, James G., illus. LC 54-5080. (gr. 3-7). 1954. PLB 11.88 (ISBN 0-688-31239-X). Morrow Jr Bks.

FOSTER HOME CARE–FICTION

Amstutz, Beverly. That Boy, That Girl. LC 80-80372. (Illus.). 24p. (gr. k-7). 1979. pap. 2.50x (ISBN 0-937836-01-X). Precious Res.

Byars, Betsy. The Pinballs. LC 76-41518. 144p. (gr. 5 up). 1977. 14.95 (ISBN 0-06-020917-8); PLB 14.89 (ISBN 0-06-020918-6). HarpC Child Bks.

Hermes, Patricia. Heads, I Win. Newsome, Carol, illus. LC 87-19249. 128p. (gr. 3-7). 1988. 12.95 (ISBN 0-15-233659-1, HJ). HarBraceJ.

Holl, Kristi D. Just Like a Real Family. LC 82-16239. 132p. (gr. 4-6). 1983. 12.95 (ISBN 0-689-30970-8, Atheneum Child Bk). Macmillan Child Grp.

Kidd, Diana. Onion Tears. Montgomery, Lucy, illus. LC 90-43011. 72p. (gr. 2-5). 1991. 12.95 (ISBN 0-531-05870-0); PLB 12.99 (ISBN 0-531-08470-1). Orchard Bks Watts.

MacLachlan, Patricia. Mama One, Mama Two. Bornstein, Ruth, illus. LC 81-47795. 32p. (gr. 1-3). 1982. 12.95 (ISBN 0-06-024081-4); PLB 12.89 (ISBN 0-06-024082-2). HarpC Child Bks.

Myers, Walter D. Won't Know Till I Get There. LC 81-71128. 192p. (gr. 7 up). 1982. pap. 11.95 (ISBN 0-670-77862-1). Viking Child Bks.

Paterson, Katherine. La Gran Gilly Hopkins. (SPA.). (gr. 1-6). 6.95 (ISBN 84-204-3222-9). Santillana.

—The Great Gilly Hopkins. LC 77-27075. (gr. 5 up). 1978. 13.95i (ISBN 0-690-03837-2, Crowell Jr Bks); PLB 13.89 (ISBN 0-690-03838-0, Crowell Jr Bks). HarpC Child Bks.

—The Great Gilly Hopkins. large type ed. 170p. (gr. 2-6). 1987. Repr. of 1978 ed. lib. bdg. 14.95 (ISBN 1-55736-011-1). ABC-CLIO.

St. John, Patricia. Where the River Begins. LC 80-12304. 128p. (Orig.). (gr. 5-8). pap. 3.95 (ISBN 0-8024-8124-8). Moody.

Wieler, Diana. Last Chance Summer. 1991. 15.00 (ISBN 0-385-30317-3). Delacorte.

Wolitzer, Hilma. Toby Lived Here. LC 78-4550. 147p. (gr. 5 up). 1978. 11.95 (ISBN 0-374-37625-5). FS&G.

Wood, Phyllis A. The Revolving Door Stops Here. Garrick, Jacqueline, illus. LC 89-23891. 192p. (gr. 6 up). 1990. 14.95 (ISBN 0-525-65022-9, Cobblehill Bks). Dutton Child Bks.

FOURTH OF JULY

Anderson, Joan. The Glorious Fourth at Prairietown. Ancona, George, photos by. LC 85-28417. (Illus.). 48p. (gr. 2-6). 1986. 11.95 (ISBN 0-688-06246-6); lib. bdg. 11.88 (ISBN 0-688-06247-4, Morrow Jr Bks). Morrow Jr Bks.

Dalgliesh, Alice. Fourth of July Story. Nonnast, Marie, illus. LC 56-6138. 32p. (ps-3). 1972. 13.95 (ISBN 0-684-13164-1, Scribners Young Read); (Scribner). Macmillan Child Grp.

Giblin, James C. Fireworks, Picnics, & Flags: The Story of the Fourth of July Symbols. Arndt, Ursula, illus. LC 82-9612. 96p. (gr. 3-6). 1983. 13.95 (ISBN 0-89919-146-0, Pub. by Clarion); pap. 4.95 (ISBN 0-89919-174-6, PUb. by Clarion). Ticknor & Fields.

Phelan, Mary K. Fourth of July. Shimin, Symeon, illus. LC 65-25909. 40p. (gr. k-3). 1966. PLB 12.89 (ISBN 0-690-31415-9, Crowell Jr Bks). HarpC Child Bks.

Schultz, Ellen. I Can Read About July Fourth, Seventeen Seventy-Six. LC 78-68470. (Illus.). (gr. 3-5). 1979. pap. 1.95 (ISBN 0-89375-211-8). Troll Assocs.

Shachtman, Tom. America's Birthday: The Fourth of July. Saaf, Chuck, photos by. LC 85-24207. (Illus.). 48p. (gr. 3-7). 1986. 13.95 (ISBN 0-02-782870-0, Mcmillan Child Bk). Macmillan Child Grp.

FOURTH OF JULY–FICTION

Lasky, Kathryn. Fourth of July Bear. Cogancherry, Helen, illus. LC 90-37422. 40p. (gr. k up). 1991. 13.95 (ISBN 0-688-08287-4); PLB 13.88 (ISBN 0-688-08288-2, Morrow Jr Bks). Morrow Jr Bks.

FOXES

Ahlstrom, Mark. The Foxes. LC 83-5324. (Illus.). 48p. (gr. 5-6). 1983. lib. bdg. 10.95 (ISBN 0-89686-220-8, Crestwood Hse). Macmillan Child Grp.

Braithwaite, Althea. Foxes. (ps-6). 1988. PLB 7.95 (ISBN 0-88462-186-3); pap. 2.95 (ISBN 0-88462-187-1). Dearborn Finan.

Burton, Jane. Fancy the Fox. Burton, Jane, photos by. LC 88-2729. (Illus.). 24p. (Orig.). 1988. lib. bdg. 5.99 (ISBN 0-394-99963-0, Random Juv); pap. 1.95 (ISBN 0-394-89963-6, Random Juv). Random.

—Trill the Fox Cub. LC 89-11370. (Illus.). 32p. (gr. 2-3). 1989. PLB 10.95 (ISBN 0-8368-0212-8). Gareth Stevens Inc.

Bush, John. Christmas Fox & Other Winter. 1989. 11.95 (ISBN 0-8037-0723-1). Dial Bks Young.

Butterworth, Christine & Bailey, Donna. Foxes. LC 90-36169. (Illus.). 32p. (gr. 1-4). 1990. PLB 14.64 (ISBN 0-8114-2641-6). Steck-V.

Fox. 1990. 2.95 (ISBN 0-8378-2050-2). Gibson.

LaBonte, Gail. The Arctic Fox. LC 88-18967. (Illus.). 60p. (gr. 3 up). 1989. PLB 12.95 (ISBN 0-87518-390-5, Dillon). Macmillan Child Grp.

Lavine, Sigmund A. Wonders of Foxes. 1986. 10.95 (ISBN 0-396-08857-0, Putnam). Putnam Pub Group.

Ling, Mary. Amazing Wolves, Dogs, & Foxes. Young, Jerry, photos by. LC 91-6514. (Illus.). 32p. (Orig.). (gr. 1-5). 1991. lib. bdg. 9.99 (ISBN 0-679-91521-4); pap. 7.00 (ISBN 0-679-81521-X). Knopf.

MacQuitty, Miranda. Discovering Foxes. Caulkins, Janet, ed. (Illus.). 48p. (gr. 1-6). 1988. PLB 11.90 (ISBN 0-531-18197-9, Pub. by Bookwright Pr). Watts.

Royston, Angela. The Fox. Allen, Graham, illus. 24p. (Orig.). (ps-2). 1988. pap. 2.95 (ISBN 0-8249-8244-4). Ideals.

Schnieper, Claudia. On the Trail of the Fox. Scherer, Elise, tr. (GER., Illus.). 48p. (gr. 2-5). 1986. lib. bdg. 12.95 (ISBN 0-87614-287-0); pap. 6.95 (ISBN 0-87614-480-6). Carolrhoda Bks.

—On the Trail of the Fox. (Illus.). 48p. (gr. 1-5). 1987. pap. 6.95 (ISBN 0-685-18833-7, First Ave Edns). Lerner Pubns.

FOXES–FICTION

Abolafia, Yossi. Fox Tale. LC 89-77501. (Illus.). 32p. (ps up). 1991. 13.95 (ISBN 0-688-09541-0); PLB 13.88 (ISBN 0-688-09542-9). Greenwillow.

Anders, Rebecca. Ali the Desert Fox. Hammarberg, Dyan, tr. from FRE. LC 76-29469. (Illus.). (gr. k-4). 1977. PLB 6.95 (ISBN 0-87614-076-2). Carolrhoda Bks.

Anderson, Rachel & Bradby, David. Renard the Fox. (Illus.). 80p. (gr. 5-8). 1987. 17.95 (ISBN 0-19-274129-2). Oxford U Pr.

Arnosky, Jim. Watching Foxes. LC 84-20157. (Illus.). 24p. (ps-3). 1984. 12.95 (ISBN 0-688-04259-7); PLB 12.88 (ISBN 0-688-04260-0). Lothrop.

Berrill, Margaret. Chanticleer. Bottomley, Jane, illus. LC 86-6746. 32p. (gr. 2-5). PLB 16.67 (ISBN 0-8172-2626-5). Raintree Pubs.

Brown, Margaret W. Fox Eyes. Williams, Garth, illus. LC 76-43086. (ps-3). 1977. Pantheon.

Byars, Betsy C. The Midnight Fox. Grifalconi, Ann, illus. LC 68-27566. (gr. 3-7). 1968. pap. 13.95 (ISBN 0-670-47473-8). Viking Child Bks.

Carrick, Malcolm. Mr. Tod's Trap. Carrick, Malcolm, illus. LC 79-2012. 64p. (gr. k-3). 1980. 7.64i (ISBN 0-06-021113-X). HarpC Child Bks.

Chaucer, Geoffrey. Chanticleer & the Fox. Cooney, Barbara, illus. LC 58-10449. 40p. (ps-3). 1961. 12.95 (ISBN 0-690-18561-8, Crowell Jr Bks); PLB 13.89 (ISBN 0-690-18562-6); pap. 3.95 (ISBN 0-690-04318-X). HarpC Child Bks.

—Chanticleer & the Fox. Cooney, Barbara, illus. LC 58-10449. 32p. (gr. k-3). 1982. pap. 4.95 (ISBN 0-06-443087-1, Trophy). HarpC Child Bks.

Christopher, Matt. The Fox Steals Home. Johnson, Lary, illus. LC 78-17526. (gr. 4-6). 1985. 13.95 (ISBN 0-316-13976-9); pap. 3.95 (ISBN 0-316-13986-6). Little.

Clifford, Eth. Flatfoot Fox & the Case of the Missing Eye. Lies, Brian, illus. 48p. (gr. 2-5). 1990. 12.95 (ISBN 0-395-51945-4). HM.

Dahl, Roald. Fantastic Mr. Fox. (gr. 4-8). 1978. pap. 2.50 (ISBN 0-553-15390-0, Skylark). Bantam.

—Fantastic Mr. Fox. Chaffin, Donald, illus. LC 74-118704. 72p. (gr. 3-6). 1986. 14.95 (ISBN 0-394-80497-X); lib. bdg. 14.99 (ISBN 0-394-90497-4). Knopf.

Dr. Seuss. Fox in Socks. (ps-1). 1986. pap. 6.95 incl. cassette (ISBN 0-394-88322-5). Random.

Firmin, Peter. Hungry Mr. Fox. (gr. k-6). 1990. pap. 2.95 (ISBN 0-440-40340-5, YB). Dell.

Galdone, Paul. What's in Fox's Sack. Galdone, Paul, illus. 32p. (ps-1). 1982. 13.95 (ISBN 0-89919-062-6, Clarion). HM.

—What's in Fox's Sack? LC 81-10251. (Illus.). (gr. 1-3). 1987. pap. 4.95 (ISBN 0-89919-491-5, Pub. by Clarion). Ticknor & Fields.

Gardiner, John R. Stone Fox. Sewall, Marcia, illus. LC 79-7895. 96p. (gr. 2-6). 1983. pap. 3.50 (ISBN 0-06-440132-4, Trophy). HarpC Child Bks.

Garside, Alice H. The Fox & the Stork. 40p. (Orig.). (gr. k-2). 1990. pap. 2.00 (ISBN 1-882063-10-4). Cottage Pr MA.

—The Fox & the Thrush. 20p. (Orig.). (gr. k-2). 1990. pap. 2.00 (ISBN 1-882063-09-0). Cottage Pr MA.

Gosselin, Shirley A. The Tale of Fabian & Gilead Brown. (Illus., Orig.). (gr. k-6). 1986. pap. 14.95 (ISBN 0-914339-13-3). P E Randall Pub.

Gregorich, Barbara. The Fox on the Box. Hoffman, Joan, ed. Masheris, Robert, illus. 16p. (Orig.). (gr. k-2). 1984. pap. 1.95 (ISBN 0-88743-005-8, 06005). Sch Zone Pub Co.

Hastings, Selina, retold by. Reynard the Fox. Percy, Graham, illus. LC 90-11105. 80p. (gr. 2-4). 1991. 16.95 (ISBN 0-688-09949-1, Tambourine Bks); PLB 16.88 (ISBN 0-688-10156-9, Tambourine Bks). Morrow.

Kellogg, Steven, retold by. & illus. Chicken Little. LC 84-25519. 32p. (ps-3). 1985. 13.95 (ISBN 0-688-05690-3); PLB 12.88 (ISBN 0-688-05691-1, Morrow Jr Bks); pap. 3.95 (ISBN 0-688-07045-0, Mulberry Bks). Morrow Jr Bks.

Kent, Jack. Silly Goose. Kent, Jack, illus. LC 82-21441. 32p. (ps-3). 1986. 10.95 (ISBN 0-13-809947-2); pap. 5.95 (ISBN 0-13-810177-9). P-H.

King-Smith, Dick. The Fox Busters. Miller, Jon, illus. LC 87-37409. 128p. (gr. 4-7). 1988. 13.95 (ISBN 0-440-50064-8). Delacorte.

Kjelgaard, Jim. Haunt Fox. 160p. 1981. pap. 2.50 (ISBN 0-553-15547-4). Bantam.

Koralek, Jenny. The Friendly Fox. Gooding, Beverley, illus. (ps-3). 1989. 12.95 (ISBN 0-316-50179-4). Little.

Korschunow, Irina. The Foundling Fox. Skofield, James, tr. from GER. Michl, Reinhard, illus. LC 84-47631. 48p. (gr. k-3). 1984. 13.95 (ISBN 0-06-023243-9). HarpC Child Bks.

Lane, Margaret. The Fox. Lilly, Kennethk, illus. LC 82-71355. 32p. (ps-4). 1982. 9.95 (ISBN 0-8037-2491-8). Dial Bks Young.

Leverich, Kathleen. The Hungry Fox & the Foxy Duck. (Illus.). 48p. (ps-2). 1991. pap. 2.95 (ISBN 0-448-40102-9, G&D). Putnam Pub Group.

Lindgren, Astrid. The Tomten & the Fox. Wiberg, Harald, illus. 32p. (ps-3). 1989. pap. 5.95 (ISBN 0-698-20644-4, Sandcastle Bks). Putnam Pub Group.

McKissack, Patricia C. Flossie & the Fox. Isadora, Rachel, illus. LC 86-2024. 32p. (ps-3). 1986. 12.95 (ISBN 0-8037-0250-7); PLB 11.89 (ISBN 0-8037-0251-5). Dial Bks Young.

Marshall, Edward. Fox All Week. Marshall, James, illus. LC 84-1708. (ps-3). 1984. 8.95 (ISBN 0-8037-0062-8); PLB 8.89 (ISBN 0-8037-0066-0). Dial Bks Young.

—Fox All Week. Marshall, James, illus. LC 84-1708. 48p. (ps-3). 1987. pap. 4.95 (ISBN 0-8037-0008-3). Dial Bks Young.

—Fox & His Friends. Marshall, James, illus. LC 81-68769. 56p. (ps-3). 1982. PLB 10.89 (ISBN 0-8037-2669-4); pap. 4.95 (ISBN 0-8037-2668-6). Dial Bks Young.

—Fox at School. Marshall, James, illus. LC 82-45506. 48p. (ps-3). 1983. PLB 9.89 (ISBN 0-8037-2675-9); pap. 4.95 (ISBN 0-8037-2674-0). Dial Bks Young.

—Fox in Love. Marshall, James, illus. LC 82-70190. 56p. (ps-3). 1982. PLB 9.89 (ISBN 0-8037-2433-0); pap. 4.95 (ISBN 0-8037-2426-8). Dial Bks Young.

—Fox on Wheels. Marshall, James, illus. LC 83-5254. 48p. (ps-3). 1983. PLB 9.89 (ISBN 0-8037-0002-4); pap. 4.95 (ISBN 0-8037-0001-6). Dial Bks Young.

Marshall, James. Fox Be Nimble. Fogelman, Phyllis J., ed. Marshall, James, illus. LC 89-7933. 48p. (ps-3). 1990. 9.95 (ISBN 0-8037-0760-6); PLB 9.89 (ISBN 0-8037-0761-4). Dial Bks Young.

—Fox on the Job. 1990. pap. 4.95 (ISBN 0-8037-0746-0, Dial Easy to Read). Puffin Bks.

Michaels, Ski. Felix, the Funny Fox. Mahan, Ben, illus. LC 85-14097. 48p. (Orig.). (gr. 1-3). 1986. PLB 9.89 (ISBN 0-8167-0590-9); pap. text ed. 2.95 (ISBN 0-8167-0591-7). Troll Assocs.

Nordqvist, Sven. The Fox Hunt. Nordqvist, Sven, illus. LC 87-28197. 32p. (ps-2). 1988. 12.95 (ISBN 0-688-06881-2); PLB 12.88 (ISBN 0-688-06882-0, Morrow Jr Bks). Morrow Jr Bks.

Ross, Tony. Foxy Fables. Ross, Tony, illus. LC 85-27436. 32p. (ps-3). 1986. 11.95 (ISBN 0-8037-0291-4). Dial Bks Young.

Shepherd, C. A., et al. The Sly Fox. (Orig.). (gr. 3-12). 1985. pap. text ed. 6.00 (ISBN 0-88734-503-4). Players Pr.

Singer, Bill. The Fox with Cold Feet. Kendrick, Dennis, illus. LC 80-10288. 48p. (ps-3). 1980. 5.95 (ISBN 0-8193-1021-2); PLB 5.95 (ISBN 0-8193-1022-0). Parents.

Spier, Peter. Fox Went Out on a Chilly Night. LC 60-7139. (Illus.). (gr. 1-3). 1989. pap. 5.95 (ISBN 0-385-01065-6, Zephyr). Doubleday.

Tejima, Keizaburo. Fox's Dream. Tejima, Keizaburo, illus. (ps-1). 1987. 13.95 (ISBN 0-399-21455-0, Philomel Bks). Putnam Pub Group.

—Fox's Dream. (Illus.). 48p. (gr. 5 up). 1990. pap. 5.95 (ISBN 0-399-22017-8, Philomel Bks). Putnam Pub Group.

Thomas, Jane R. Fox in a Trap. Howell, Troy, illus. 96p. (gr. 2-5). 1990. pap. 3.95 (ISBN 0-395-54426-2, Clarion Bks). HM.

Tompert, Ann. Grandfather Tang's Story. Parker, Robert A., illus. LC 89-22205. 32p. (ps-2). 1990. 12.95 (ISBN 0-517-57487-X); PLB 14.99 (ISBN 0-517-57272-9). Crown.

—Little Fox Goes to the End of the World. Wallner, John, illus. (gr. k-3). 1979. pap. 2.95 (ISBN 0-590-12101-4, Schol Pap). Scholastic Inc.

—Little Fox Goes to the End of the World. Wallner, John, illus. 40p. (ps-4). 1984. pap. 2.95 (ISBN 0-590-40439-3, Blue Ribbon Bks). Scholastic Inc.

Voss-Bark, Doris L. Philip the Fox & Other Stories. Brown, Denise, illus. LC 66-10511. (gr. 3-6). 1967. 10. 95 (ISBN 0-8023-1105-9). Dufour.

Walt Disney Staff. Fox & the Hound. 1988. 6.98 (ISBN 0-8317-3472-8). Smithmark.

Watson, Clyde. Tom Fox & the Apple Pie. Watson, Wendy, illus. LC 74-171010. (ps-3). 1972. 11.95 (ISBN 0-690-82783-0, Crowell Jr Bks). HarpC Child Bks.

Wheeler, M. J. Fox Tales. Gustafson, Dana, illus. LC 83-21001. 56p. (gr. k-4). 1984. PLB 9.95 (ISBN 0-87614-255-2). Carolrhoda Bks.

Wyllie, Stephen. Dinner with Fox. LC 89-25899. (Illus.). 24p. (ps-3). 1990. 12.95 (ISBN 0-8037-0796-7). Dial Bks Young.

FOXES–SONGS AND MUSIC

Spier, Peter. Fox Went Out on a Chilly Night. Spier, Peter, illus. LC 60-7139. 42p. (gr. k-3). 1961. pap. 11. 95 (ISBN 0-385-07990-7). Doubleday.

FRACTIONS

Burke, Jeanne M. Focus on Fractions. (Illus.). 113p. (gr. 6-12). 1988. pap. 12.00 (ISBN 1-878371-00-2). Educ Ideas.

—Focus on Fractions: Teacher's Guide - Grades 6-12. Delzeith, Keith, illus. (Illus.). 127p. (Orig.). (gr. 6-12). 1988. pap. 15.00 (ISBN 1-878371-01-0). Educ Ideas.

Daniel, Becky. Hooray for Fraction Facts! 80p. (gr. 2-5). 1990. 9.95 (ISBN 0-86653-568-3, GA1165). Good Apple.

Daniel, Charlie & Daniel, Becky. Freaky Fractions. 48p. (gr. 1-5). 1978. 5.95 (ISBN 0-916456-19-6, GA77). Good Apple.

Dennis, J. Richard. Fractions Are Parts of Things. LC 73-127603. (Illus.). 40p. (gr. 2-4). 1972. PLB 12.89 (ISBN 0-690-31521-X, Crowell Jr Bks). HarpC Child Bks.

Ockenga, Earl & Rucker, Walt. Place Value to One Hundred. Dawson, Dave, illus. 16p. (gr. 1). 1990. pap. text ed. 1.25 (ISBN 1-56281-115-0, M115). Extra Eds.

Smart, Margaret & Tuel, Patricia. Focus on Fractions, 3 vols. Laycock, Mary, intro. by. (Illus.). (gr. 6-9). 1977. pap. text ed. 6.50 ea.; Set. 16.50 (ISBN 0-918932-69-6). Vol. 1 (ISBN 0-918932-14-9). Vol. 2 (ISBN 0-918932-15-7). Vol. 3 (ISBN 0-918932-16-5). Activity Resources.

FRACTURES–FICTION

Wolff, Angelika. Mom, I Broke My Arm. Glueckselig, Leo, illus. LC 69-18646. (gr. k-3). 1969. PLB 10.95 (ISBN 0-87460-121-5). Lion Bks.

FRANCE

Bailey, Donna & Sproule, Anna. France. LC 90-9647. (Illus.). 32p. (gr. 2-5). 1990. PLB 14.64 (ISBN 0-8114-2561-4). Steck-V.

Balerdi, Susan. France: The Crossroads of Europe. LC 83-23198. (Illus.). 142p. (gr. 5 up). 1984. PLB 14.95 (ISBN 0-87518-248-8, Dillon). Macmillan Child Grp.

Bender, Lionel. France. (Illus.). 48p. (gr. 4-8). 1988. PLB 14.98 (ISBN 0-382-09505-7). Silver Burdett Pr.

Getting to Know France. 48p. 7.95 (ISBN 0-8442-1410-8, Passport Bks). Natl Textbk.

Goldstein, Frances. Children's Treasure Hunt Travel to Belgium & France. Goldstein, Frances, illus. LC 80-85012. 230p. (Orig.). (gr. k-12). 1981. pap. 6.95 (ISBN 0-933334-02-8, Dist. by Hippocrene). Paper Tiger Pap.

James, Ian. France. Fairclough, Chris, photos by. (Illus.). 32p. (gr. 3-6). 1989. PLB 11.90 (ISBN 0-531-10640-3). Watts.

Moss, Peter & Palmer, Thelma. France. LC 86-9628. (Illus.). 128p. (gr. 5-9). 1986. PLB 25.27 (ISBN 0-516-02761-1). Childrens.

Norbrook, Dominique. Passport to France. (Illus.). 48p. (gr. 4-8). 1986. PLB 12.90 (ISBN 0-531-10014-6). Watts.

Somerville, L. First Book of France. (Illus.). 32p. 1989. PLB 13.96 (ISBN 0-88110-391-8); pap. 6.95 (ISBN 0-7460-0322-6). EDC.

Stevens, Rita. French Overseas Departments & Territories. (Illus.). (gr. 5 up). 1988. 14.95 (ISBN 1-55546-188-3). Chelsea Hse.

Tomlins, James. We Live in France. (gr. 6-8). 1984. PLB 9.49 (ISBN 0-531-04688-5). Watts.

FRANCE–FICTION

Albert, Gilbert. Les Champs et Les Forets. Ganim, Barbara, illus. (FRE.). 28p. (gr. 6-8). 1986. pap. text ed. 3.95 (ISBN 0-911409-46-7). Natl Mat Dev.

Balzac. Le Pere Goriot. (gr. 7-12). pap. 5.95 (ISBN 0-88436-043-1, 40280). EMC.

Banks, Lynne R. Melusine: A Mystery. LC 88-32798. 256p. (gr. 7 up). 1989. 12.95 (ISBN 0-06-020394-3); PLB 12.89 (ISBN 0-06-020395-1). HarpC Child Bks.

Birchman, David F. Victorious Paints the Great Ballooon. LC 90-1746. 64p. (gr. 2-6). 1991. 13.95 (ISBN 0-02-710111-8, Bradbury Pr). Macmillan Child Grp.

Carlson, Natalie S. Happy Orpheline. Williams, Garth, illus. LC 57-9260. 112p. (gr. 3-6). 1957. PLB 13.89 (ISBN 0-06-021007-9). HarpC Child Bks.

De Brunhoff, L. La Fete de Celesteville. (gr. 4-6). 15.95 (ISBN 0-685-33969-6). French & Eur.

Flaubert, Gustave. Madame Bovary. (gr. 11 up). pap. 2.50 (ISBN 0-8049-0089-2, CL-89). Airmont.

Fournier. Le Grand Meaulnes. (gr. 7-12). pap. 5.95 (ISBN 0-88436-110-1, 40272). EMC.

Guillot, Rene. Wind of Chance. Dale, Norman, tr. Collot, Pierre, illus. (gr. 6-9). 1958. 18.95 (ISBN 0-87599-048-7). S G Phillips.

Lear, Edward & Depaola, Tomie. Bonjour, Mister Satie. (Illus.). (ps-3). 1991. 15.95 (ISBN 0-399-21782-7, Putnam). Putnam Pub Group.

Maupassant. Mon Oncle Jules. (gr. 7-12). pap. 5.95 (ISBN 0-88436-044-X, 40281). EMC.

Renard. Poil de Carotte. (gr. 7-12). pap. 4.95 (ISBN 0-88436-046-6, 40264). EMC.

Simenon. Les Enigmes. (gr. 7-12). pap. 5.95 (ISBN 0-88436-058-X, 40269). EMC.

Simenon, Georges. Maigret et le Clochard. pap. 5.95 (ISBN 0-88436-047-4, 40270). EMC.

Supervielle, Jules. Le Voleur D'enfants. pap. 4.95 (ISBN 0-88436-111-X, 40265). EMC.

FRANCE–HISTORY

Blackwood, Alan & Chosson, Brigitte. France. Caulkins, Janet, ed. (Illus.). 48p. (gr. 1-6). 1988. PLB 12.40 (ISBN 0-531-18186-3, Pub. by Bookwright Pr). Watts.

Harris, Nathan. The Fall of the Bastille. 64p. (gr. 6-8). 1987. 19.95 (ISBN 0-85219-670-9, Pub. by Batsford England). Trafalgar Sq.

Sookram, Brian. France. (Illus.). (gr. 5 up). 1990. 14.95 (ISBN 0-7910-1111-9). Chelsea Hse.

FRANCE–HISTORY–FICTION

Dumas, Alexandre. Three Musketeers. Price, Norman & Van Swearingen, E. C., illus. (gr. 4-6). 1953-59. pap. 6.95 (ISBN 0-448-11024-5, G&D); deluxe ed. 11.95 (ISBN 0-448-06024-8). Putnam Pub Group.

Storr, Catherine, as told by. The Three Musketeers. (Illus.). 32p. (gr. k-5). 1985. PLB 16.67 (ISBN 0-8172-2500-5); pap. 9.27 (ISBN 0-8172-2508-0). Raintree Pubs.

FRANCE–HISTORY–TO 1328–FICTION

Konigsburg, E. L. A Proud Taste for Scarlet & Miniver. Konigsburg, E. L., illus. LC 73-76320. 208p. (gr. 5-9). 1973. 13.95 (ISBN 0-689-30111-1, Atheneum Child Bk). Macmillan Child Grp.

FRANCE–HISTORY–HOUSE OF VALOIS, 1328-1589

Hugo, Victor. The Hunchback of Notre Dame. Shaw, Charles, illus. Stewart, Diana, adapted by. LC 81-5151. (Illus.). 48p. (gr. 4 up). 1983. PLB 17.32 (ISBN 0-8172-1671-5); pap. 9.27 (ISBN 0-8172-2010-0). Raintree Pubs.

FRANCE–HISTORY–HOUSE OF VALOIS, 1328-1589–FICTION

Dana, Barbara. Young Joan. LC 90-39494. 384p. (gr. 7 up). 1991. 17.95 (ISBN 0-06-021422-8); PLB 17.89 (ISBN 0-06-021423-6). HarpC Child Bks.

Hugo, Victor. The Hunchback of Notre Dame. Shaw, Charles, illus. Stewart, Diana, adapted by. LC 81-5151. (Illus.). 48p. (gr. 4 up). 1983. PLB 17.32 (ISBN 0-8172-1671-5); pap. 9.27 (ISBN 0-8172-2010-0). Raintree Pubs.

The Hunchback of Notre Dame. (gr. 4 up). 1988. Incl. 26 cards. 22.00 (ISBN 0-8172-2180-8). Raintree Pubs.

Scott, Walter. Quentin Durward. Bennet, C. L., intro. by. (gr. 9 up). pap. 2.50 (ISBN 0-8049-0132-5, CL-132). Airmont.

Sohl, Marcia & Dackerman, Gerald. Hunchback of Notre Dame: Student Activity Book. (Illus.). (gr. 4-10). 1976. wkbk 1.25 (ISBN 0-88301-189-1). Pendulum Pr.

FRANCE–HISTORY–BOURBONS, 1589-1789–FICTION

Dumas, Alexandre. Man in the Iron Mask. Hillerich, R., intro. by. (gr. 9 up). 1967. pap. 2.75 (ISBN 0-8049-0150-3, CL-150). Airmont.

—Three Musketeers. (gr. 8 up). pap. 3.95 (ISBN 0-8049-0127-9, CL-127). Airmont.

The Three Musketeers. (gr. 4 up). 1988. pap. 4.87 (ISBN 0-582-01384-4, 70417). Longman.

The Three Musketeers. (Illus.). (gr. 3-5). 3.50 (ISBN 0-7214-0633-5). Ladybird Bks.

FRANCE–HISTORY–REVOLUTION, 1789-1799

Banfield, Susan. The Rights of Man, the Reign of Terror: The Story of the French Revolution. LC 89-2742. 224p. (gr. 7 up). 1990. 14.95 (ISBN 0-397-32353-0, Lipp Jr Bks); PLB 14.89 (ISBN 0-397-32354-9, Lipp Jr Bks). HarpC Child Bks.

Cairns, Trevor. Power for the People. LC 76-30607. (Illus.). 96p. (gr. 7 up). 1978. pap. 9.95 (ISBN 0-521-20902-1). Cambridge U Pr.

Mitchell, Crohan. The Napoleonic Wars. (Illus.). 72p. (gr. 7-10). 1989. 19.95 (ISBN 0-7134-5729-5, Pub. by Batsford England). Trafalgar Sq.

Mulvihill, Margaret. The French Revolution. Wood, Gerald, illus. LC 88-31564. 32p. (gr. 3-6). 1989. PLB 11.90 (ISBN 0-531-17167-1). Watts.

FRANCE–HISTORY–REVOLUTION, 1789-1799–FICTION

Dickens, Charles. Tale of Two Cities. (gr. 9 up). 1964. pap. 2.75 (ISBN 0-8049-0021-3, CL-21). Airmont.

—Tale of Two Cities. Busoni, Rafaello, illus. (gr. 4-6). 1948. pap. 5.95 (ISBN 0-448-11023-7, G&D); deluxe ed. 11.95 (ISBN 0-448-06023-X). Putnam Pub Group.

—A Tale of Two Cities. Shaw, Charles, illus. Krapesh, Patti, adapted by. LC 79-24746. (Illus.). (gr. 4 up). 1983. PLB 17.32 (ISBN 0-8172-1658-8); pap. 9.27 (ISBN 0-8172-2022-4). Raintree Pubs.

Orczy, Emmuska. Scarlet Pimpernel. (gr. 7 up). 1964. pap. 2.95 (ISBN 0-8049-0028-0, CL-28). Airmont.

A Tale of Two Cities. (Illus.). (gr. 3-5). 3.50 (ISBN 0-7214-0710-2). Ladybird Bks.

FRANCE–HISTORY–CONSULATE AND EMPIRE, 1799-1815–FICTION

Wheeler, Thomas G. Fanfare for the Stalwart. LC 67-22813. (gr. 8 up). 1967. 18.95 (ISBN 0-87599-139-4). S G Phillips.

FRANCE–SOCIAL LIFE AND CUSTOMS

Harris, Jonathan. The Land & People of France. LC 88-19211. (Illus.). 256p. (gr. 6 up). 1989. 14.95 (ISBN 0-397-32320-4, Lipp Jr Bks); PLB 14.89 (ISBN 0-397-32321-2, Lipp Jr Bks). HarpC Child Bks.

Kollay, Jocelyne. French Holiday Activity Workbook. (FRE & ENG., Illus.). 100p. (Orig.). (gr. 9-12). 1988. wkbk. 16.95 (ISBN 0-9617764-1-2). PS Enterprises.

Powell, Jillian. France. (Illus.). 32p. (gr. k-3). 1991. PLB 11.90 (ISBN 0-531-18372-6, Pub. by Bookwright Pr). Watts.

FRANCIS OF ASSISI, SAINT, 1182-1226

DePaola, Tomie. Francis: The Poor Man of Assisi. DePaola, Tomie, illus. LC 81-6984. 48p. (gr. k-3). 1990. PLB 15.95 (ISBN 0-8234-0435-8); pap. 6.95 (ISBN 0-8234-0812-4). Holiday.

Windeatt, Mary F. St. Francis of Assisi. Harmon, Gedge, illus. 32p. (gr. 1-5). 1989. Repr. of 1954 ed. wkbk. 3.00 (ISBN 0-89555-368-6). TAN Bks Pubs.

FRANCIS OF ASSISI, SAINT, 1182-1126–FICTION

O'Dell, Scott. The Road to Damietta. 256p. (gr. 6 up). 1985. 14.95 (ISBN 0-395-38923-2). HM.

—The Road to Damietta. 240p. 1987. pap. 3.50 (ISBN 0-449-70233-2, Juniper). Fawcett.

FRANCIS XAVIER, SAINT, 1506-1552

Daughters of St. Paul. Flame in the Night. (gr. 4-9). 1967. 3.00 (ISBN 0-8198-0234-4); pap. 2.00 (ISBN 0-8198-2610-3). Dghtrs St Paul.

FRANKLIN, BENJAMIN, 1706-1790

Adler, David A. A Picture Book of Benjamin Franklin. Wallner, John & Wallner, Alexandra, illus. LC 89-20059. 32p. (gr. k-3). 1990. 14.95g (ISBN 0-8234-0792-6). Holiday.

—A Picture Book of Benjamin Franklin. Wallner, Alexandra & Wallner, John, illus. 1991. pap. 5.95 (ISBN 0-8234-0882-5). Holiday.

Alico, Stella H. Benjamin Franklin-Martin Luther King Jr. Cruz, E. R., illus. (gr. 4-12). 1979. pap. text ed. 2.95 (ISBN 0-88301-353-3); wkbk 1.25 (ISBN 0-88301-377-0). Pendulum Pr.

Aliki. The Many Lives of Benjamin Franklin. Aliki, illus. 32p. (ps-3). 1988. pap. 12.95 (ISBN 0-671-66119-1, Little Simon); pap. 5.95 (ISBN 0-671-66491-3, Juveniles). S&S Trade.

Cousins, Margaret. Ben Franklin of Old Philadelphia. LC 81-806. 160p. (gr. 5-9). 1981. pap. 4.95 (ISBN 0-394-84928-0). Random.

Feldman, Eve B. Benjamin Franklin: Scientist & Inventor. (Illus.). 64p. (gr. 5-8). 1990. PLB 11.90 (ISBN 0-531-10867-8). Watts.

Franklin, Benjamin. Autobiography of Benjamin Franklin. Bigoness, J. W., intro. by. LC 80-26312. (gr. 8 up). pap. 2.75 (ISBN 0-8049-0071-X, CL-71). Airmont.

Fritz, Jean. What's the Big Idea, Ben Franklin? (Illus.). 48p. (gr. 2-6). 1982. 9.95 (ISBN 0-698-20365-8, Coward); pap. 5.95 (ISBN 0-698-20543-X, Coward). Putnam Pub Group.

Graves, Charles P. Benjamin Franklin: Man of Ideas. (Illus.). 80p. (gr. 2-6). 1992. Repr. of 1960 ed. PLB 12.95 (ISBN 0-7910-1422-3). Chelsea Hse.

Greene, Carol. Benjamin Franklin: A Man with Many Jobs. Dobson, Steven, illus. LC 88-15011. 48p. (gr. k-3). 1988. PLB 15.27 (ISBN 0-516-04202-5); pap. 4.95 (ISBN 0-516-44202-3). Childrens.

Johnson, Spencer. The Value of Saving: The Story of Benjamin Franklin. Pileggi, Stephen, illus. LC 78-8652. 64p. (gr. k-6). 1978. 9.95 (ISBN 0-916392-17-1, Pub. by Value Communications); pap. 8.95 incl. cassette (ISBN 0-86679-067-5). Oak Tree Pubns.

Kurland, Gerald. Benjamin Franklin: America's Universal Man. Rahmas, D. Steve, ed. LC 72-190250. 32p. (Orig.). (gr. 7-12). 1972. lib. bdg. 4.20 incl. catalog cards (ISBN 0-87157-533-7); pap. 2.95 vinyl laminated covers (ISBN 0-87157-033-5). SamHar Pr.

Lawson, Robert. Ben & Me. (gr. 3-6). 1973. pap. 2.75 (ISBN 0-440-42038-5, YB). Dell.

Looby, Christopher. Benjamin Franklin. Schlesinger, Arthur M., Jr. (Illus.). 112p. (gr. 5 up). 1990. 17.95x (ISBN 1-55546-808-X). Chelsea Hse.

Meltzer, Milton. Benjamin Franklin: The New American. Vestal, Jeanne, ed. LC 88-17015. (Illus.). 176p. (gr. 6-9). 1988. PLB 14.90 (ISBN 0-531-10582-2). Watts.

Osborne, Mary P. The Many Lives of Benjamin Franklin. (Illus.). (gr. 5 up). 1990. 13.95 (ISBN 0-685-31008-6). Dial Bks Young.

—The Many Lives of Benjamin Franklin. LC 88-38369. (Illus.). 144p. (gr. 4-7). 1990. 13.95 (ISBN 0-8037-0679-0); PLB 13.89 (ISBN 0-8037-0680-4). Dial Bks Young.

Quackenbush, Robert. Benjamin Franklin & His Friends. Quackenbush, Robert, illus. 32p. (gr. 2-6). 1991. 13.95 (ISBN 0-945912-14-5). Pippin Pr.

Santrey, Laurence. Young Ben Franklin. LC 81-23067. (Illus.). 48p. (gr. 4-6). 1982. PLB 10.79 (ISBN 0-89375-768-3); pap. text ed. 2.95 (ISBN 0-89375-769-1). Troll Assocs.

Scarf, Maggi. Meet Benjamin Franklin. Beckhoff, Harry, illus. (gr. 2-6). 1968. 2.95 (ISBN 0-394-80070-2, Random Juv). Random.

—Meet Benjamin Franklin. Fogarty, Pat, illus. LC 88-17657. 64p. (gr. 2-4). 1989. PLB 6.99 (ISBN 0-394-91961-0); pap. text ed. 2.95 (ISBN 0-394-81961-6). Random.

Stevenson, Augusta. Benjamin Franklin: Young Printer. Quigley, Ray, illus. LC 86-10786. 192p. (gr. 2-6). 1986. pap. 3.95 (ISBN 0-02-041920-1, Aladdin). Macmillan Child Grp.

FRANKLIN, BENJAMIN, 1706-1790–FICTION

Lawson, Robert. Ben & Me. Lawson, Robert, illus. 1939p. (gr. 7-10). 1988. 14.95 (ISBN 0-316-51732-1); pap. 4.95 (ISBN 0-316-51730-5). Little.

FRAUD

see also Impostors and Imposture

FRAUD–FICTION

Colman, Hila. The Double Life of Angela Jones. LC 87-33246. 160p. (gr. 7 up). 1988. 12.95 (ISBN 0-688-06781-6). Morrow Jr Bks.

Duncan, Lois. Stranger with My Face. (gr. 8 up). 1981. 14.95 (ISBN 0-316-19551-0). Little.

Fleischman, Sid. McBroom Tells the Truth. Lorraine, Walter H., illus. LC 81-1035. 48p. (gr. 3-7). 1981. 12.45i (ISBN 0-316-28550-1, Pub. by Atlantic Pr). Little.

Melville, Herman. Confidence Man. Grube, J., intro. by. (gr. 11 up). pap. 1.95 (ISBN 0-8049-0121-X, CL-121). Airmont.

FREAKS

see Monsters

FREDERICK 2ND, DER GROSSE, KING OF PRUSSIA, 1712-1786

Kittredge, Mary. Frederick the Great. Schlesinger, Arthur M., Jr., intro. by. (Illus.). 112p. (gr. 5 up). 1988. lib. bdg. 17.95 (ISBN 0-87754-525-1). Chelsea Hse.

FREE SPEECH

Deegan, Paul. Freedom of Speech. Abbott, Phyllis, et al, eds. Wadsworth, Elaine, illus. 32p. (gr. 4). 1987. lib. bdg. 10.95 (ISBN 0-939179-22-9). Abdo & Dghtrs.

Evans, J. Edward. Freedom of Speech. (Illus.). 88p. (gr. 4 up). 1990. PLB 10.95 (ISBN 0-8225-1753-1). Lerner Pubns.

Hentoff, Nat. The First Freedom: The Tumultuous History of Free Speech in America. LC 87-32182. 336p. (gr. 7 up). 1988. pap. 16.95 (ISBN 0-385-29643-6). Delacorte.

—The First Freedom: The Tumultuous History of Free Speech in America. LC 78-72860. (gr. 7 up). 1980. 11.95 (ISBN 0-440-03850-2). Delacorte.

Trager, Oliver, ed. The Arts & Media in America: Freedom or Censorship? 224p. 1991. 29.95x (ISBN 0-8160-2578-9). Facts on File.

FREEBOOTERS

see Pirates

FREEDOM

see Liberty

FREEDOM MARCHES

see Blacks–Civil Rights

FREEDOM OF RELIGION

see Religious Liberty

FREEDOM OF SPEECH

see Free Speech

FREEDOM OF THE PRESS

Evans, J. Edward. Freedom of the Press. (Illus.). 72p. (gr. 5 up). 1990. PLB 10.95 (ISBN 0-8225-1752-3). Lerner Pubns.

Pfeffer, Susan B. A Matter of Principle. LC 81-15288. 192p. (gr. 7 up). 1982. 11.95 (ISBN 0-385-28649-X). Delacorte.

Zerman, Melvyn B. Taking on the Press: Constitutional Rights in Conflict. Rather, Dan, frwd. by. LC 85-47896. (Illus.). 192p. (gr. 7 up). 1986. 11.95 (ISBN 0-690-04301-5, Crowell Jr Bks); PLB 11.89 (ISBN 0-690-04302-3, Crowell Jr Bks). HarpC Child Bks.

FREEDOM OF WORSHIP

see Religious Liberty

FREEZING

see Ice

FREIGHT AND FREIGHTAGE

see also Aeronautics, Commercial

FREMONT, JOHN CHARLES, 1813-1890

Harris, Edward. John Charles Fremont & the Great Western Reconnaisance. Goetzmann, William H., ed. Collins, Michael, intro. by. (Illus.). 112p. (gr. 5 up). 1990. lib. bdg. 18.95 (ISBN 0-7910-1312-X). Chelsea Hse.

FRENCH AND INDIAN WAR

see U. S.–History–French and Indian War, 1755-1763

FRENCH IN AMERICA

Kunz, Virginia B. The French in America. LC 66-10146. (Illus.). 96p. (gr. 5 up). PLB 8.95 (ISBN 0-8225-0204-6); pap. 3.95 (ISBN 0-8225-1008-1). Lerner Pubns.

Morrice, Polly. The French Americans. Moynihan, Daniel P. (Illus.). 112p. (gr. 5 up). 1988. lib. bdg. 17.95 (ISBN 0-87754-878-1). Chelsea Hse.

FRENCH LANGUAGE

Atkin, K. Le Francais Sans Souci. 304p. (gr. 4-6). 1987. pap. text ed. 27.81 (ISBN 0-201-17624-6). Addison-Wesley.

Colvin, L. & Irving, N. Essential French. (Illus.). 64p. 1990. lib. bdg. 12.96 (ISBN 0-88110-420-5); pap. 5.95 (ISBN 0-7460-0316-1). EDC.

Gattegno, Caleb. The Silent Way for French. (Orig.). (gr. k-12). 1965. 3.50; Mille Phrases. 3.50 (ISBN 0-87825-082-4); Trente-Six Instantanes. 2.95 (ISBN 0-87825-099-9); Huit Contes. 2.50 (ISBN 0-87825-095-6); Worksheets. 2.00 (ISBN 0-87825-083-2); Wall Pictures. 10.00 (ISBN 0-87825-052-2); Word Charts. 55.00 (ISBN 0-87825-075-1); One chart, expanded Fidel. 30.00 (ISBN 0-87825-078-6); Expanded Fidel. 5.00 (ISBN 0-87825-098-0). Ed Solutions.

—The Silent Way for Spanish. (Orig.). (gr. k-12). 1965. Mil Frases. 3.50 (ISBN 0-87825-047-6); Narraciones Breves. 3.50 (ISBN 0-87825-048-4); Ocho Cuentos. 3.50 (ISBN 0-87825-049-2); Worksheets. 2.50 (ISBN 0-87825-084-0); Wall Pictures. 10.00 (ISBN 0-87825-045-X); Word Charts. 25.00 (ISBN 0-87825-076-X); Spanish Fidel (European) 5.00 (ISBN 0-87825-079-4); Spanish Fidel (S. American) 2.25 (ISBN 0-87825-080-8). Ed Solutions.

Hazzan, Anne-Francoise. Let's Learn French Coloring Book. (Illus.). 64p. (gr. 4 up). 1988. pap. 3.95 (ISBN 0-8442-1389-6, Passport Bks). Natl Textbk.

Lionni, Leo. Pouce par Pouce. (FRE., Illus.). (gr. k-1). 1961. 10.95 (ISBN 0-8392-3028-1). Astor-Honor.

Martinez, Eliseo R. & Martinez, Irma C. French Readiness Skills, Vol. 1. Mahak, Francine T., tr. (Illus.). 87p. 1987. wkbk. 9.50 (ISBN 1-878300-02-4). Childrens Work.

Les Nombres. (FRE., Illus.). 3.50 (ISBN 0-7214-0798-6). Ladybird Bks.

O'Halloran, Tim. Words Around Us in French. O'Halloran, Tim, illus. (FRE.). 48p. (ps-k). 1985. 10.95 (ISBN 0-88625-125-7). Durkin Hayes Pub.

Rice, James. A Cajun Alphabet. LC 76-28490. (Illus.). 96p. (gr. 1-4). 1976. 13.95 (ISBN 0-88289-136-7). Pelican.

Rich, Beatrice. ABCDEFGHIJKLMNOPQRSTUVWXYZ in English & French. LC 81-20838. (Illus.). 64p. (gr. k-2). 1983. PLB 12.95 (ISBN 0-87460-353-6). Lion Bks.

Slack, Anne, et al. French for Communication, One. LC 77-87429. (Illus.). (gr. 9). 1979. write for info. complete program. HM.

Taylor, Maurie. Easy French Vocabulary Games. (FRE., Illus.). 64p. (gr. 4 up). 1988. pap. 4.95 (ISBN 0-8442-1323-3, Passport Bks). Natl Textbk.

Wilkes, Angela. French for Beginners. (Illus.). 48p. (gr. 4 up). 1988. 7.95 (ISBN 0-8442-1413-2, Passport Bks). Natl Textbk.

Wordfinder in French. (Illus.). 48p. (gr. 2-6). 1984. 11.95 (ISBN 0-86020-770-6). EDC.

FRENCH LANGUAGE–CONVERSATION AND PHRASE BOOKS

Berlitz. Berlitz Jr. French. (FRE., Illus.). 64p. (Orig.). (ps-2). 1989. bds. 19.95 incl. cassette (ISBN 0-689-71314-2, Aladdin). Macmillan Child Grp.

Jacob, Suzanne, ed. Children's Living French. (Illus.). 1987. manual 5.00 (ISBN 0-517-56331-2); dictionary 5.00 (ISBN 0-517-56332-0); cassettes 20.00 (ISBN 0-517-56329-0). Crown.

Kahn, Michele. My Everyday French Word Book. LC 79-89631. 44p. (gr. 1-6). 1981. 10.95 (ISBN 0-8120-5344-3). Barron.

Page, Brian. Franc-Parler. (FRE.). 208p. 1988. pap. 10.95 (ISBN 0-8219-0340-3, 40306); tchr's. guide 5.95 (ISBN 0-8219-0341-1, TG-40825). EMC.

Poulin, Stephane. As-Tu Vu Josephine? Poulin, Stephane, illus. LC 86-51044. (FRE.). 24p. (gr. k-4). 1988. 12.95 (ISBN 0-88776-188-7); pap. 6.95 (ISBN 0-88776-224-7). Tundra Bks.

—Have You Seen Josephine? Poulin, Stephane, illus. LC 86-51043. 24p. (gr. k-4). 1988. 12.95 (ISBN 0-88776-180-1); pap. 6.95 (ISBN 0-88776-215-8). Tundra Bks.

Segal, Bertha E. Apprenons le Francais au Moyen de l'Action. Raileanu, Lia, tr. from ENG. (FRE.). 106p. (Orig.). (gr. 3-12). 1987. pap. text ed. 12.50 (ISBN 0-938395-13-0). B Segal.

Waggoner, Carmen. Descriptions de Dessins: Picture Descriptions in French. Parr, Frederique & Winitz, Harris, eds. Baker, Syd, illus. (FRE.). 65p. (Orig.). (gr. 7 up). 1989. pap. text ed. 32.00 incl. 2 cassettes (ISBN 0-939990-77-6). Intl Linguistics.

White, Judith. Summer Talk: Phrase-a-Day French for Families. Macbain, Carol, illus. 27p. (ps-6). 1986. wkbk. 6.25 (ISBN 0-937531-01-4). Fgn Lang Young Child.

FRENCH LANGUAGE–DICTIONARIES

A Child's Picture English-French Dictionary. LC 84-71800. 48p. (gr. k-6). 1984. 9.95 (ISBN 0-915361-12-4, Dist. by Watts). Adama Pubs Inc.

Let's Learn Picture Dictionaries: French. (Illus.). 72p. 1989. 9.95 (ISBN 0-8442-1392-6, Passport Bks). Natl Textbk.

FRENCH LANGUAGE–DICTIONARIES–ENGLISH

Eastman, Philip D. The Cat in the Hat Beginner Book Dictionary in French & English. LC 65-22650. (Illus.). 144p. (gr. 2-3). 1965. 14.95 (ISBN 0-394-81063-5). Beginner.

French-English - English-French Dictionary. (gr. 4 up). 1988. pap. 2.25 (ISBN 0-318-37108-1). Scholastic Inc.

FRENCH LANGUAGE–GRAMMAR

Gauduchon, Michaele. French Grammar Flipper. 49p. (gr. 5 up). Date not set. trade edition 5.95 (ISBN 1-878383-12-4). C Lee Pubns.

Roussy de Sales, R. de. Jeux de Grammaire. (FRE., Illus.). 64p. (gr. 5 up). 1983. pap. 4.95 (ISBN 0-8442-1380-2, Passport Bks.). Natl Textbk.

FRENCH LANGUAGE–READERS

Amery, Heather. First Thousand Words in French. Cartwright, Stephen, illus. 50p. (ps-7). 1980. 11.95 (ISBN 0-86020-267-4). EDC.

—Word Detective in French. Cartwright, Stephen, illus. 50p. (gr. 3-7). 1983. 11.95 (ISBN 0-86020-663-7). EDC.

Carlson, Natalie S. Talking Cat & Other Stories of French Canada. Duvoisin, Roger, illus. LC 52-5429. 92p. (gr. 3-6). 1952. PLB 12.89 (ISBN 0-06-021081-8). HarpC Child Bks.

Conroy, Joseph F. Danger sur la Cote d'azur: Reader 4. Bakke, Eric, illus. LC 81-7820. (FRE.). 40p. (Orig.). (gr. 7-12). 1982. pap. 2.50 (ISBN 0-88436-857-2, 40262). EMC.

—Destination: France! Reader 1. Bakke, Eric, illus. LC 81-7816. (FRE.). 40p. (Orig.). (gr. 7-12). 1982. pap. 2.50 (ISBN 0-88436-854-8, 40259). EMC.

—Sur la Route de la Contrebande. Bakke, Eric, illus. LC 81-7817. (FRE.). 40p. (Orig.). (gr. 7-12). pap. 2.50 (ISBN 0-88436-856-4, 40261). EMC.

Henry, Charles L., et al. French Study-Aid. 1974. pap. 2.75 (ISBN 0-87738-032-5). Youth Ed.

Potter, Beatrix. Pierre Lapin: Peter Rabbit. (FRE., Illus.). (gr. 3-7). 1973. 5.00 (ISBN 0-7232-0650-3). Warne.

Roussy de Sales, R. de. Easy French Crossword Puzzles. (FRE., Illus.). 64p. (gr. 5 up). 1983. pap. 4.95 (ISBN 0-8442-1330-6, Passport Bks). Natl Textbk.

FRENCH LANGUAGE–STUDY AND TEACHING

Mahoney, Judy & Cronan, Mary. Teach Me More French. (FRE., Illus.). 20p. (ps-5). 1989. incl. cassette 13.95 (ISBN 0-934633-11-8). Teach Me.

FRENCH REVOLUTION

see France–History–Revolution, 1789-1799

FRESH-WATER ANIMALS

see also Aquariums; Marine Animals;

also names of individual fresh-water animal, e.g. Beavers, etc.

Grimmer, Glenna. Things That Swim in Texas Waters Alphabetically Speaking: And in Other Coastal States of the Gulf of Mexico. Eakin, Edwin M., ed. Hoese, H. Dickson, illus. 48p. (gr. 4-6). 1989. 11.95 (ISBN 0-89015-694-8, Pub. by Panda Bks). Eakin Pr.

Kaufman, Les & NEA Staff. Alligators to Zooplankton: A Dictionary of Water Babies. (Illus.). 64p. (gr. 5-7). 1991. 13.95 (ISBN 0-531-15215-4); PLB 14.90 (ISBN 0-531-10995-X). Watts.

Taylor, Kim. Hidden Under Water. (gr. 4-7). 1990. 9.95 (ISBN 0-385-30184-7). Delacorte.

FRESH-WATER BIOLOGY

see also Aquariums; Fresh-Water Animals; Marine Biology

Amos, William H. Life in Ponds & Streams. Crump, Donald J., ed. LC 81-47745. 32p. (ps-3). 1981. lib. bdg. 10.95 (ISBN 0-87044-404-2); PLB 12.95 (ISBN 0-87044-409-3). Natl Geog.

Curran, Eileen. Life in the Pond. Ellis, Elizabeth, illus. LC 84-16285. 32p. (gr. k-2). 1985. lib. bdg. 10.89 (ISBN 0-8167-0452-X); pap. text ed. 2.95 (ISBN 0-8167-0453-8). Troll Assocs.

Dewey, Jennifer O. At the Edge of the Pond. Dewey, Jennifer O., illus. 48p. (gr. 1-5). 1987. 14.95 (ISBN 0-316-18208-7). Little.

Friedman, Judi C. The ABC of a Summer Pond. new ed. Dommers, John, photos by. LC 73-92631. (Illus.). (gr. k-4). 1975. 5.95 (ISBN 0-910812-14-4); pap. 3.25 (ISBN 0-910812-15-2). Johnny Reads.

Headstrom, Richard. Adventures with Freshwater Animals. (Illus.). 217p. (gr. 5 up). 1983. pap. 5.95 (ISBN 0-486-24453-9). Dover.

Jennings, Terry. Pond Life. LC 88-22880. (Illus.). 32p. (gr. 3-6). 1989. PLB 14.60 (ISBN 0-516-08406-2); pap. 4.95 (ISBN 0-516-48406-0). Childrens.

Kirkpatrick, Rena K. Look at Pond Life. rev. ed. Milne, Annabel & Stebbing, Peter, illus. LC 84-26249. 32p. (gr. 2-4). 1985. PLB 15.99 (ISBN 0-8172-2355-X); pap. text ed. 9.27 (ISBN 0-8172-2380-0). Raintree Pubs.

Kuhn, Dwight, photos by. The Hidden Life of the Pond. Schwartz, David M., text by. (Illus.). 40p. (gr. 1 up). 1988. PLB 12.95 (ISBN 0-517-57060-2). Crown.

Lavies, Bianca. Lily Pad Pond. Lavies, Bianca, photos by. (Illus.). 32p. (ps-2). 1989. 13.95 (ISBN 0-525-44483-1, DCB). Dutton Child Bks.

Reid, George K. Pond Life. Zim, Herbert S., ed. Kaicher, Sally & Dolan, Tom, illus. (gr. 7 up). 1967. pap. write for info. (ISBN 0-307-24017-7, Golden Pr). Western Pub.

Rockwell, Jane. All about Ponds. Veno, Joseph, illus. LC 83-4835. 32p. (gr. 3-6). 1984. lib. bdg. 10.59 (ISBN 0-89375-971-6); pap. text ed. 2.95 (ISBN 0-89375-972-4). Troll Assocs.

Sabin, Francene. Wonders of the Pond. Grant, Leigh, illus. LC 81-7407. 32p. (gr. 2-4). 1982. PLB 10.89 (ISBN 0-89375-576-1); pap. text ed. 2.95 (ISBN 0-89375-577-X); cassette 9.95 (ISBN 0-685-04956-6). Troll Assocs.

Snow, John. Secrets of Ponds & Lakes. Jack, Susan, ed. Dowling, Jak, intro. by. (Illus.). 96p. (Orig.). (gr. 4-10). 1982. pap. 3.95 (ISBN 0-930096-30-4). G Gannett.

Stone, Lynn M. Pond Life. LC 83-7311. (Illus.). 48p. (gr. k-4). 1983. PLB 14.60 (ISBN 0-516-01705-5); pap. 4.95 (ISBN 0-516-41705-3). Childrens.

Tordjman, Nathalie. The Living Pond. Bogard, Vicki, tr. from FRE. Bour, Laura, illus. LC 90-50780. 38p. (gr. k-5). 1991. 4.95 (ISBN 0-944589-38-3, 383). Young Discovery Lib.

Wells, Donna K. Pond Life: The Fishing Trip. Ching, illus. LC 90-1644. 32p. (ps-2). 1990. lib. bdg. 11.97 (ISBN 0-89565-581-0). Childs World.

Wyler, Rose. Puddles & Ponds. Petruccio, Steven, illus. 32p. (gr. k-2). 1990. PLB 11.98 (ISBN 0-671-66348-8); pap. 4.95 (ISBN 0-671-66352-6). Messner.

FRESH-WATER PLANTS

see also Aquariums; Marine Plants

FRIENDS, SOCIETY OF

Hinshaw, Mary E. Quaker Adventures: Three Hundred Years in Carolina. (Illus.). 74p. (Orig.). (gr. 5-7). 1971. pap. 1.50x (ISBN 0-942727-01-0). NC Yrly Pubns Bd.

Hinshaw, Seth B. Carolina Quakers. (Illus.). 74p. (Orig.). (gr. 5-7). 1971. pap. 1.50x (ISBN 0-942727-15-0). NC Yrly Pubns Bd.

Zach, Cheryl. More Than Friends. 160p. (Orig.). (gr. 5-9). 1989. pap. 2.95 (ISBN 1-55802-074-8). Lynx Bks.

FRIENDS, SOCIETY OF–FICTION

De Angeli, Marguerite. Thee, Hannah! (Illus.). 96p. (gr. 2-5). 1970. 15.95 (ISBN 0-385-07525-1, Zephyr-BFYR). Doubleday.

Luttrell, Ida. The Bear Next Door. Stapler, Sarah, illus. LC 90-4153. 64p. (gr. k-3). 1991. 11.95 (ISBN 0-06-024023-7); PLB 11.89 (ISBN 0-06-024024-5). HarpC Child Bks.

Smith, Susan. Angela & the King-Size Crusade. (gr. 3-7). 1988. pap. 2.50 (ISBN 0-317-69592-4). PB.

—Sonya Begonia & the Eleventh Birthday Blues. (gr. 3-7). 1988. pap. 2.50 (ISBN 0-317-69590-8). PB.

Turkle, Brinton. Obadiah the Bold. Turkle, Brinton, illus. LC 65-13350. (gr. k-3). 1977. pap. 3.95 (ISBN 0-14-050233-5, Puffin). Puffin Bks.

—Obadiah the Bold. Turkle, Brinton, illus. (gr. k-3). 1965. pap. 13.95 (ISBN 0-670-52001-2). Viking Child Bks.

FRIENDSHIP

see also Love

Anderson, Debby. Friends. Anderson, Debby, illus. 32p. (ps up). 1986. plastic comb bdg. 3.95 (ISBN 0-89191-932-5, 59329, Chariot Bks). Cook.

Barratt, Dorothy, et al. Becoming Friends, What Friends Believe. Eichorn, Chris & Nelson, Lois, illus. 78p. (gr. 5-6). 1990. tchr's. ed. 7.50 (ISBN 0-943701-16-3). George Fox Pr.

Berry, Joy. Every Kid's Guide to Making Friends. Bartholemew, illus. 48p. (gr. 3-7). 1987. 5.95 (ISBN 0-516-21406-3); PLB 14.60 (ISBN 0-516-01406-4). Childrens.

Berry, Joy W. Teach Me about Friends. Dickey, Kate, ed. LC 85-45083. (Illus.). 36p. (ps). 1986. 4.98 (ISBN 0-685-10721-3). Grolier Inc.

Carter, Sharon. Coping Through Friendship. Rosen, Roger, ed. (gr. 7 up). 1988. lib. bdg. 12.95 (ISBN 0-8239-0789-9). Rosen Group.

Coleman, William L. The Friendship Factory. LC 86-17137. 128p. (ps-2). 1986. pap. 5.95 (ISBN 0-87123-670-2). Bethany Hse.

Cunningham, Julia. Wolf Roland. LC 82-19068. 96p. (gr. 5 up). 1983. Pantheon.

Daniel, Becky. Count on Your Friends. 32p. (ps-k). 1991. 7.95 (ISBN 0-86653-582-9). Good Apple.

Dellinger, Annetta E. Hugging. Williams, Jenny, illus. LC 84-21505. 32p. (gr. k-3). 1985. lib. bdg. 11.97 (ISBN 0-89565-301-X). Childs World.

Families & Friends. (Illus.). 32p. (ps-2). 1985. 1.95 (ISBN 0-225-66390-2). Harper SF.

First Graders of Samuel S. Nixon School. Friendship for Three. (Illus.). 24p. (gr. k-2). 1988. 2.95 (ISBN 0-317-93828-2). Willowisp Pr.

Fulton, Ginger A. Let's Be Friends. (Illus.). (ps). 1988. pap. 3.25 (ISBN 0-8024-3014-7). Moody.

Goley, Elaine. Friendship. (Illus.). 32p. (gr. 1-4). 1987. PLB 13.26 (ISBN 0-86592-376-0). Rourke Corp.

Gouge, Betty, et al. KidSkills Interpersonal Skill Series, Let's Share: Friendship: Sharing. Morse, J. Thomas, et al, eds. Bleck, Linda & Bleck, Cathie, illus. LC 86-81270. 48p. (ps). 1986. PLB 8.95 (ISBN 0-934275-13-0); bk. & cassette 11.95 (ISBN 0-934275-27-0). Fam Skills.

Hallinan, P. K. That's What a Friend Is. Hallinan, P. K., illus. 32p. (gr. k-6). 1985. pap. 2.95 (ISBN 0-8249-8006-9). Ideals.

Heine, Helme. Friends: A Celebration of Friendship That Bridges Separations. Heine, HElme, illus. 32p. pap. 3.95 (ISBN 0-685-31272-0, OF-02-2). Rainbow NC.

Jackson, Tim. Friends & Choices. Jackson, Tim, illus. & intro. by. 24p. (Orig.). (gr. 6-12). 1987. pap. 1.95 (ISBN 0-942675-05-3). Creative License.

—Just Like a Happy Family. Jackson, Tim, illus. 17p. (gr. 4 up). 1985. pap. 1.95 (ISBN 0-942675-00-2). Creative License.

—That's All They're Good For. Jackson, Tim, illus. & intro. by. 20p. (gr. 5-9). 1986. pap. 1.95 (ISBN 0-942675-02-9). Creative License.

Johnson, Lois W. Thanks for Being My Friend. Peck, Virginia, illus. LC 88-60473. 180p. (Orig.). 1988. pap. 4.95 (ISBN 0-89109-234-X). NavPress.

Jones, Bill. Friendships: Making the Best of Them. LC 89-83736. 64p. (Orig.). (gr. 7-12). 1989. pap. 4.50 (ISBN 0-89840-257-3). Heres Life.

Kalman, Bobbie. Fun with My Friends. (Illus.). 32p. (gr. k-2). 1985. 14.95 (ISBN 0-86505-063-5); pap. 6.95 (ISBN 0-86505-087-2). Crabtree Pub Co.

Karlsberg, Elizabeth. How to Make & Keep Friends. Magnuson, Diana, illus. LC 90-48252. 128p. (gr. 5-9). 1990. lib. bdg. 10.89 (ISBN 0-8167-2295-1); pap. text ed. 2.95 (ISBN 0-8167-2296-X). Troll Assocs.

Kelly, Kathleen M. River Friends. Kelly, Kathleen M., illus. LC 87-35140. 32p. (gr. k-3). 1988. 13.95 (ISBN 0-689-31412-4, Atheneum Child Bk). Macmillan Child Grp.

Kino Learning Center Staff, et al. My Relationships with Others. Mirocha, Kay, illus. 64p. (gr. 5-9). 1987. pap. 7.95 (ISBN 0-86653-419-9, GA 1029). Good Apple.

Knowles, Anne. Under the Shadow. LC 82-48857. 128p. (gr. 5 up). 1983. PLB 11.89 (ISBN 0-06-023222-6). HarpC Child Bks.

Leshan, Eda. When Kids Drive Kids Crazy: How to Get Along with Your Friends & Enemies. (gr. 5 up). 1990. 12.95 (ISBN 0-8037-0866-1). Dial Bks Young.

Lionni, Leo. Frederick & His Friends. Lionni, Leo, illus. (ps-2). 1989. bk. & cassette 14.95 (ISBN 0-394-82784-8). Knopf.

Macaulay, David. Mill. Macaulay, David, illus. 128p. (gr. 6 up). 1983. 15.95 (ISBN 0-395-34830-7). HM.

MacMillan, Dianne & Freeman, Dorothy. My Best Friend Martha Rodriquez: Meeting a Mexican-American Family. Fricke, Warren, illus. LC 86-5342. 48p. (gr. 3-6). 1986. lib. bdg. 9.98 (ISBN 0-671-61973-X). Messner.

Mahy, Margaret. Making Friends. (ps-3). 1990. 13.95 (ISBN 0-689-50498-5, M K McElderry). Macmillan Child Grp.

Making Friends--Keeping Friends. 128p. (Orig.). (gr. 9-12). 1989. pap. 5.95 (ISBN 0-931529-89-1). Group Pub.

Marzollo, Jean & Marzollo, Claudio. Ruthie's Rude Friends. Meddaugh, Susan, illus. LC 84-1707. 48p. (ps-3). 1987. pap. 4.95 (ISBN 0-8037-0378-3). Dial Bks Young.

Miller, E. Lorraine. Friendship. Browne, Rob, illus. LC 77-79105. (ps up). 1977. 5.00 (ISBN 0-89566-000-8). Miller Ent.

Miller, Judi. How to be Friends with a Boy - How to be Friends with a Girl. 96p. (gr. 5-9). 1990. pap. 2.75 (ISBN 0-590-42806-3). Scholastic Inc.

Morris, Brenda. Friends Help Me. LC 86-18769. (ps). 1987. 5.95 (ISBN 0-8054-4179-4). Broadman.

Morse, J. Thomas, et al. KidSkills Interpersonal Skill Series, A Lasting Friend: Friendship: Making Friends. Gouge, Betty, et al, eds. Bleck, Cathie, illus. LC 85-45422. 45p. (gr. 2-3). 1985. PLB 9.95 (ISBN 0-934275-06-8); bk. & cassette 13.95 (ISBN 0-934275-20-3). Fam Skills.

—KidSkills Interpersonal Skill Series, Lair of the Jade Tiger: Friendship: Keeping Friends. Gouge, Betty, et al, eds. Bleck, Cathie, illus. LC 85-81270. 48p. (gr. 2-3). 1986. PLB 9.95 (ISBN 0-934275-07-6); bk. & cassette 13.95 (ISBN 0-934275-21-1). Fam Skills.

My Best Friend, 4 bks. (Illus.). (gr. 3-5). 1990. Set, 48p. ea. lib. bdg. 39.92 (ISBN 0-671-94193-3). Messner.

Oxenbury, Helen. Friends. Oxenbury, Helen, illus. 14p. (ps-k). 1981. 3.95 (ISBN 0-671-42111-5, Little Simon). S&S Trade.

Painter, Carol. Leading a Friends Helping Friends Program. Sorenson, Don L., ed. 160p. (Orig.). (gr. 9-12). 1989. pap. text ed. 8.95x (ISBN 0-932796-28-1). Ed Media Corp.

Pike, Christopher. The Party. (gr. 9 up). 1989. pap. 2.95 (ISBN 0-671-68808-1, Archway). PB.

Rabinowich, Ellen. Underneath I'm Different. LC 82-14919. 192p. (gr. 7 up). 1983. 12.95 (ISBN 0-685-06447-6). Delacorte.

Ranieri, Ralph F. Friends: Making & Keeping Them. LC 89-84592. 64p. (Orig.). 1989. pap. 1.95 (ISBN 0-89243-304-3). Liguori Pubns.

Roberts, Sharon L. Friendship. Hohag, Linda, illus. LC 86-9641. 32p. (gr. k-3). 1986. lib. bdg. 11.97 (ISBN 0-89565-350-8). Childs World.

Robison, Deborah. Bye-Bye, Old Buddy. LC 83-5149. (Illus.). 32p. (gr. k-3). 1983. 10.95 (ISBN 0-89919-185-1, Clarion). HM.

Rockwell, Thomas. How to Fight a Girl. 1987. 12.95 (ISBN 0-531-15082-8). Watts.

Sachs, Marilyn. Just Like a Friend. LC 89-1168. 168p. (gr. 5-9). 1989. 14.95 (ISBN 0-525-44524-2, DCB). Dutton Child Bks.

Schwartz, L. Feelings about Friends. (gr. 3-6). 1988. 4.95 (ISBN 0-88160-168-3, LW 281). Learning Wks.

Sciacca, Fran & Sciacca, Jill. Burger, Fries & a Friend to Go. (gr. 7 up). 1987. pap. 3.95 (ISBN 0-89066-097-2). World Wide Pubs.

Somethings It's O.K. to Tell Secrets. (gr. k-9). 1988. pap. 3.95 (ISBN 0-318-36510-3). Scholastic Inc.

Stone, J. David & Keefauver, Larry. Friend to Friend: Helping Your Friends Through Problems. rev. ed. LC 90-81968. 74p. (gr. 8-12). 1990. pap. 6.95x (ISBN 0-932796-31-1). Ed Media Corp.

Varenhorst, Barbara B. Real Friends: Becoming the Friend You'd Like to Have. LC 82-48412. (Illus.). 160p. (Orig.). 1983. pap. 8.95 (ISBN 0-06-250890-3, CN4048). Harper SF.

Warburg, Sandol S. I Like You. Chwast, Jacqueline, illus. LC 65-11020. 48p. (gr. 1-3). 1965. 4.95 (ISBN 0-395-07176-3). HM.

Yingling, Phyllis S. My Best Friend Elena Pappas: Meeting a Greek-American Family. Zimic, Tricia, illus. LC 86-5310. 48p. (gr. 3-6). 1986. lib. bdg. 9.98 (ISBN 0-671-62090-8). Messner.

Youngs, Bettie B. Friendship Is Forever, Isn't It? 141p. (Orig.). (gr. 4 up). 1990. pap. 8.95x (ISBN 0-940221-05-5). Lrng Tools-Bilicki Pubns.

Ziegler, Sandra. Friends: A Handbook about Getting Along Together. Fleishman, Seymour, illus. LC 81-17025. 112p. (gr. 2-6). 1980. PLB 11.97 (ISBN 0-89565-207-2). Childs World.

FRIENDSHIP–FICTION

Abbott, Jennie. Costume Party. Badenhop, Mary, illus. LC 87-14987. 96p. (gr. 3-6). 1988. PLB 9.89 (ISBN 0-8167-1189-5); pap. text ed. 2.95 (ISBN 0-8167-1190-9). Troll Assocs.

Ackerman, Karen. The Tin Heart. Hays, Michael, illus. LC 89-6528. 32p. (gr. 1-3). 1990. 13.95 (ISBN 0-689-31461-2, Atheneum Child Bk). Macmillan Child Grp.

Adler, C. S. Always & Forever Friends. LC 87-18230. 192p. (gr. 4-7). 1988. 12.95 (ISBN 0-89919-681-0, Pub. by Clarion). Ticknor & Fields.

—Always & Forever Friends. 176p. 1990. pap. 3.50 (ISBN 0-380-70687-3, Camelot). Avon.

—Binding Ties. (gr. k-12). 1989. pap. 2.95 (ISBN 0-440-20413-5, LFL). Dell.

—Some Other Summer. (gr. 3-7). 1988. pap. 2.50 (ISBN 0-380-70515-X, Camelot). Avon.

Adler, Carole S. Kiss the Clown. LC 85-17138. (gr. 7 up). 1986. 12.95 (ISBN 0-89919-419-2, Pub. by Clarion). Ticknor & Fields.

Adoff, Arnold. Flamboyan. Barbour, Karen, illus. 32p. (ps-3). 1988. 14.95 (ISBN 0-15-228404-4, HJ). HarBraceJ.

Adorjan, Carol. That's What Friends Are For. 1990. pap. 2.75 (ISBN 0-590-42454-8). Scholastic Inc.

Agee, Jon. Ludlow Laughs. Agee, John, illus. LC 85-45466. 32p. (ps up). 1985. 12.95 (ISBN 0-374-34666-6); (Sunburst). FS&G.

Ahlberg, Allan. Ten in a Bed. Amstutz, Andre, illus. 112p. 1989. pap. 11.95 (ISBN 0-670-82042-3). Viking Child Bks.

Aiello, Barbara & Shulman, Jeffrey. Friends for Life: Featuring Amy Wilson. Barr, Loel, illus. LC 88-29251. 48p. (gr. 3-6). 1988. PLB 12.95 (ISBN 0-941477-03-7). TFC Bks MD.

—Secrets Aren't (Always) for Keeps: Featuring Jennifer Hauser. Barr, Loel, illus. 48p. (gr. 3-6). 1988. PLB 12. 95 (ISBN 0-941477-01-0). TFC Bks MD.

Aiken, Joan. The Cuckoo Tree. (gr. 4-6). 15.25 (ISBN 0-8446-6380-8). Peter Smith.

Albright, Molly. Best Friends. DeRosa, Dee, illus. LC 87-13874. 96p. (gr. 3-6). 1988. PLB 9.49 (ISBN 0-8167-1151-8); pap. text ed. 2.95 (ISBN 0-8167-1152-6). Troll Assocs.
—The Big Showoffs. DeRosa, Dee, illus. LC 87-13872. 96p. (gr. 3-6). 1988. PLB 9.89 (ISBN 0-8167-1155-0); pap. text ed. 2.95 (ISBN 0-8167-1156-9). Troll Assocs.
—The Dream Team. DeRosa, Dee, illus. LC 87-13821. 96p. (gr. 3-6). 1988. PLB 9.89 (ISBN 0-8167-1153-4); pap. text ed. 2.95 (ISBN 0-8167-1154-2). Troll Assocs.
Alcock, Vivien. The Trial of Anna Cotman. (gr. 5-9). 1990. 13.95 (ISBN 0-385-29981-8). Delacorte.
Alexander, Martha. My Outrageous Friend Charlie. (ps-2). 1989. 10.95 (ISBN 0-8037-0587-5); PLB 11.89 (ISBN 0-8037-0588-3). Dial Bks Young.
Aliki. Feelings. LC 84-4098. (Illus.). (ps-3). 1986. 3.95 (ISBN 0-688-06518-X, Mulberry). Morrow.
—Overnight at Mary Bloom's. Aliki, illus. LC 86-7719. 32p. (ps-3). 1987. 11.75 (ISBN 0-688-06764-6); lib. bdg. 11.88 (ISBN 0-688-06765-4). Greenwillow.
—We Are Best Friends. Aliki, illus. LC 81-6549. 32p. (gr. k-3). 1982. 14.95 (ISBN 0-688-00822-4); PLB 14.88 (ISBN 0-688-00823-2). Greenwillow.
All That Jazz: Pink Parrots, No. 2. (gr. 3-7). 1990. pap. 3.50 (ISBN 0-316-12445-1). Little.
Allen, Suzanne. Scrambled Eggs, No. 3. (gr. 3 up). 1990. pap. 2.75 (ISBN 0-425-12476-2). Berkley Pub.
Alter, Judy. Katie & the Recluse. LC 90-23695. 192p. (gr. 4-9). 1991. pap. 5.95 (ISBN 0-936650-13-3). E C Temple.
Amdur, Nikki. One of Us. Sanderson, Ruth, illus. LC 81-65847. (gr. 3-6). 1981. 8.95 (ISBN 0-8037-6742-0); PLB 8.89 (ISBN 0-8037-6743-9). Dial Bks Young.
Amstutz, Beverly. You Are Number One! (Illus.). 30p. (gr. k-9). 1982. pap. 2.50x (ISBN 0-937836-08-7). Precious Res.
Anderson, Janet. A Hug for a New Friend. Kong, Emilie, illus. 40p. (ps). 4.00 (ISBN 0-910313-88-1). Parker Bros.
Anderson, Mary. Who Says Nobody's Perfect? LC 87-5336. 160p. (gr. 7 up). 1987. pap. 14.95 (ISBN 0-385-29582-0). Delacorte.
Anglund, Joan W. A Friend Is Someone Who Likes You: Silver Anniversary Edition. Anglund, Joan W., illus. LC 58-8624. 32p. (ps-3). 1983. 8.95 (ISBN 0-15-229678-6, HJ). HarBraceJ.
Ardizzone, Edward. Tim & Ginger. Ardizzone, Edward, illus. 48p. (ps-3). 1987. pap. 6.95 (ISBN 0-19-272113-5). Oxford U Pr.
—Tim's Friend Towser. Ardizzone, Edward, illus. 48p. (ps-3). 1987. pap. 6.95 (ISBN 0-19-272112-7). Oxford U Pr.
Argent, Kerry. Wombat & Bandicoot: Best Friends. Argent, Kerry, illus. LC 89-13041. (ps-2). 1990. 13.95 (ISBN 0-316-05096-2, Joy St Bks). Little.
Arneson, D. J. Friend Indeed. LC 80-23062. (gr. 4 up). 1981. PLB 11.90 (ISBN 0-531-04257-X). Watts.
Ashwill, Beverley. Marlina & McGee. Ashwill, Betty J., illus. LC 86-73031. 32p. (ps-3). 1987. pap. 5.95 (ISBN 0-941381-00-5). BJO Enterprises.
—The Runaways. Ashwill, Betty, illus. LC 87-72441. 48p. (gr. 4-8). 1988. 12.95 (ISBN 0-941381-02-1); pap. 5.95 (ISBN 0-941381-01-3). BJO Enterprises.
Atkinson, John. Bamboo & Friends. Engel, Michael, illus. LC 88-50844. 104p. (gr. 1-12). 1988. 13.95 (ISBN 0-929155-05-X). Windward Bks.
Atlas, Yehuda. It's Me! Kerman, Danny, illus. Lacks, Roslyn, tr. LC 85-1239. (Illus.). 48p. (gr. 4 up). 1985. 9.95 (ISBN 0-915361-20-5, Dist. by Watts). Adama Pubs Inc.
Avery, Lorraine. The Runaway Winner. Thomas, Linda, illus. LC 89-34369. 96p. (gr. 4-6). 1989. PLB 9.89 (ISBN 0-8167-1708-7); pap. text ed. 2.95 (ISBN 0-8167-1709-5). Troll Assocs.
Avi. S. O. R. Losers. 96p. (gr. 3-7). 1986. pap. 2.95 (ISBN 0-380-69993-1, Camelot). Avon.
Baehr, Patricia. Summer of the Dodo. LC 89-39335. 160p. (gr. 3-6). 1990. 12.95 (ISBN 0-02-708135-4, Four Winds). Macmillan Child Grp.
Baer, Judy. New Girl in Town. LC 88-71504. 176p. (Orig.). (gr. 10-12). 1988. pap. 3.95 (ISBN 1-55661-022-X). Bethany Hse.
—Tomorrow's Promise. 144p. (Orig.). (gr. 6-9). 1990. pap. 3.95 (ISBN 1-55661-143-9). Bethany Hse.
—Trouble with a Capital T. LC 88-71503. 176p. (Orig.). (gr. 10-12). 1988. pap. 3.95 mass market (ISBN 1-55661-021-1). Bethany Hse.
—Yesterday's Dream. 144p. (Orig.). (gr. 8-10). 1990. pap. 3.95 (ISBN 1-55661-142-0). Bethany Hse.
Baker, Barbara. Digby & Kate Again. Winborn, Marsha, illus. LC 88-25677. 48p. (ps-2). 1989. 9.95 (ISBN 0-525-44477-7, DCB). Dutton Child Bks.
—NO Spells No. (gr. 4-7). 1991. 10.95 (ISBN 0-525-44639-7, DCB). Dutton Child Bks.
Balian, Lorna. Wilbur's Space Machine. Balian, Lorna, illus. LC 90-55095. 32p. (ps-3). 1990. reinforced 14.95 (ISBN 0-8234-0836-1). Holiday.
Bargar, Gary W. Life Is Not Fair. LC 83-15299. 180p. (gr. 4-7). 1984. 13.95 (ISBN 0-89919-218-1, Clarion). HM.
Barr, Linda. Best Friends Don't Tell Lies. 128p. (Orig.). (gr. 5-8). 1989. pap. text ed. 2.95 (ISBN 0-87406-423-6). Willowisp Pr.
—I Won't Let Them Hurt You. 112p. (Orig.). (gr. 6-9). 1988. pap. 2.95 (ISBN 0-87406-314-0). Willowisp Pr.
Barrett, Joyce D. Willie's Not the Hugging Kind. Cummings, Pat, illus. LC 89-1868. 32p. (gr. k-3). 1989. 12.95 (ISBN 0-06-020416-8); PLB 12.89 (ISBN 0-06-020417-6). HarpC Child Bks.
Bashful Bard. What Does It Mean to Be a Friend. (Illus.). 28p. (Orig.). (ps-1). 1989. pap. 2.99 (ISBN 1-877906-10-7). Kenney Pubns.
Bassett, Lisa. Beany & Scamp. Bassett, Jeni, illus. (gr. k-3). 1987. 12.95 (ISBN 0-399-21703-7, Putnam). Putnam Pub Group.
Bastin, Marjolein. My Name Is Vera. (Illus.). 28p. (ps-2). 1985. 2.95 (ISBN 0-8120-5690-6). Barron.
—Vera & Her Friends. (Illus.). 28p. (ps-2). 1985. 2.95 (ISBN 0-8120-5689-2). Barron.
—Vera's Dresses Up. 28p. (ps-2). 1985. 2.95 (ISBN 0-8120-5691-4). Barron.
Bates, Betty. Thatcher Payne-in-the-Neck. (gr. k-6). 1987. pap. 2.95 (ISBN 0-440-48598-3, YB). Dell.
Bauer, Marion D. On My Honor. (gr. k-6). 1987. pap. 2.95 (ISBN 0-440-46633-4, YB). Dell.
Baum, Louis. One More Time. Bouma, Paddy, illus. LC 85-31050. 32p. (ps-k). 1986. lib. bdg. 11.88 (ISBN 0-688-06587-2, Morrow Jr Bks). Morrow Jr Bks.
Bawden, Nina. Rebel on a Rock. LC 77-10686. 160p. (gr. 7 up). 1988. PLB 13.89 (ISBN 0-397-32140-6, Lipp Jr Bks). HarpC Child Bks.
—The Robbers. LC 79-4152. (Illus.). 160p. (gr. 4-7). 1989. Repr. of 1979 ed. 12.95 (ISBN 0-688-41902-X). Lothrop.
Bayles, Miriam. Si Bantay, Si Puti, at Si Ngaw. Bayles, Arthur, illus. (TAG., Orig.). (gr. k-2). 1988. pap. 3.75x (ISBN 971-10-0359-7, Pub. by New Day Pub Philippines). Cellar.
Baylor, Byrd. And It Is Still That Way. Jelinek, Lucy, illus. 96p. (gr. k-8). 1987. pap. 6.95 (ISBN 0-939729-06-7). Trails West Pub.
Baynton, Martin. Fifty Saves His Friend. Baynton, Martin, illus. LC 85-17064. 32p. (ps-1). 1986. bds. 5.95 (ISBN 0-517-56022-4). Crown.
Beerbohm, Max. The Happy Hypocrite. DeHoff, George, illus. LC 85-70301. 40p. 1985. 16.95 (ISBN 0-88138-038-5, Star & Elephant Bks.). Green Tiger Pr.
Behrens, Michael. At the Edge. 208p. (gr. 7 up). 1988. pap. 2.95 (ISBN 0-380-75610-2, Flare). Avon.
—Freestyle. (gr. 7 up). 1988. pap. 2.50 (ISBN 0-318-37142-1, Flare). Avon.
Bell, Mary & Yates, Steve. Friends. MacDonald, Robert G. & Ross, Brenda, illus. 24p. (ps-2). 1989. PLB write for info. Kids Ink Pr.
Benard, Robert. Do You Like It Here? (gr. 10-12). 1989. pap. 3.50 (ISBN 0-440-20435-6, LFL). Dell.
Benard, Robert, ed. All Problems Are Simple. (Orig.). (gr. k-12). 1988. pap. 3.95 (ISBN 0-440-20164-0, LFL). Dell.
Berenstain, Michael. The Dwarks at the Mall. 48p. (Orig.). (gr. 2 up). 1985. pap. 2.25 (ISBN 0-553-15341-2). Bantam.
Bergman, Thomas. Don't Turn Away, 5 vols. Bergman, Thomas, illus. 56p. (gr. 4-5). 1989. Set. PLB 54.75 (ISBN 1-55532-941-1). Gareth Stevens Inc.
Bergstrom, Corinne. Losing Your Best Friend. Rosamilia, Patricia, illus. LC 79-20622. 32p. (ps-3). 1980. 16.95 (ISBN 0-87705-471-1). Human Sci Pr.
Bernard, Elizabeth. Starting Over. (gr. 6 up). 1989. pap. 3.50 (ISBN 0-449-14547-6). Fawcett.
Bess, Clayton. Big Man & the Burn-Out. LC 85-11822. 208p. (gr. 5 up). 1985. 12.95 (ISBN 0-395-36173-7). HM.
Best of Friends: Sixth Grade Can Really Kill You; Sixth Grade Sleepover; Sixth Grade Secrets; & A Really Popular Girl. (gr. 2-6). 1989. pap. 11.00 boxed set (ISBN 0-590-63454-2). Scholastic Inc.
Better Homes & Gardens Books Editors. A Tree Full of Friends. 32p. 1989. 4.95 (ISBN 0-696-01910-8). Meredith Bks.
Birdseye, Tom. I'm Going to Be Famous. LC 86-45401. 144p. (gr. 3-7). 1986. 13.95 (ISBN 0-8234-0630-X). Holiday.
—I'm Going to Be Famous. (gr. k-6). 1989. pap. 2.95 (ISBN 0-440-40212-3, YB). Dell.
Birnhack, Sara. Promise Me Tomorrow. LC 90-82061. (gr. 6 up). 1990. 12.95 (ISBN 1-56062-025-0); pap. 9.95 (ISBN 1-56062-026-9). CIS Comm.
Bishop, Claire H. The Man Who Lost His Head. McCloskey, Robert, illus. 64p. (ps-3). 1989. pap. 3.95 (ISBN 0-14-050976-3, Puffin). Puffin Bks.
Blair, Cynthia. The Double-Dip Disguise. (gr. 4 up). 1988. pap. 2.95 (ISBN 0-449-70256-1, Juniper). Fawcett.
Blair, Shannon. Kiss & Tell. 176p. (Orig.). (gr. 5 up). 1985. pap. 2.50 (ISBN 0-553-26843-0). Bantam.
Blaustein, Muriel. Make Friends, Zachary! Blaustein, Muriel, illus. LC 88-6308. 32p. (ps-2). 1990. 12.95 (ISBN 0-06-020545-8); PLB 12.89 (ISBN 0-06-020546-6). HarpC Child Bks.
Blos, Joan W. A Gathering of Days: A New England Girl's Journal, 1830-1832. LC 90-32. 160p. (gr. 3-7). 1990. pap. 3.95 (ISBN 0-689-71419-X, Aladdin). Macmillan Child Grp.
Bloss, Janet A. The Creep's at It Again. Robison, Don, illus. 128p. (Orig.). (gr. 3-6). 1988. pap. 1.00 (ISBN 0-87406-345-0). Willowisp Pr.
Blume, Judy. Just as Long as We're Together. LC 87-7980. 304p. (gr. 5-8). 1987. 12.95 (ISBN 0-531-05729-1); PLB 12.99 (ISBN 0-531-08329-2). Orchard Bks Watts.
Bograd, Larry. Bad Apple. 152p. (gr. 9 up). 1986. pap. 3.45 (ISBN 0-374-40476-3). FS&G.
Bonnette, Jeanne. Three Friends. (ps-2). 1982. pap. 2.95 (ISBN 0-89992-066-7). Coun India Ed.
Botner, Barbara. The World's Greatest Expert on Everything...Is Crying. (gr. 3-7). 1986. pap. 2.95 (ISBN 0-440-49739-6, YB). Dell.
Bottner, Barbara. Dumb Old Casey Is a Fat Tree. LC 78-19474. (Illus.). 64p. (gr. 1-4). 1991. pap. 3.50 (ISBN 0-06-440346-7, Trophy). HarpC Child Bks.
—Nothing in Common. (gr. 5 up). 1988. pap. 2.95 (ISBN 0-553-27060-5, Starfire). Bantam.
Bradford, Jan. Caroline Zucker Gets Even. Ramsey, Marcy D., illus. LC 89-20630. 96p. (gr. 2-5). 1991. lib. bdg. 9.89 (ISBN 0-8167-2015-0); pap. text ed. 2.95 (ISBN 0-8167-2016-9). Troll Assocs.
Brancato, Robin F. Winning. LC 77-5632. 224p. 1987. lib. bdg. 12.99 (ISBN 0-394-93581-0). Knopf.
Brandenberg, F. Leo & Emily. (gr. k-6). 1990. pap. 2.95 (ISBN 0-440-40294-8, YB). Dell.
Brandenberg, Franz. Leo & Emily. Aliki, illus. LC 80-19657. 56p. (gr. 1-3). 1981. 13.95 (ISBN 0-688-80292-3). Greenwillow.
—Nice New Neighbors. Aliki, illus. LC 77-1651. 56p. (gr. 1-4). 1977. PLB 13.88 (ISBN 0-688-84105-8). Greenwillow.
—Nice New Neighbors. (ps-3). 1980. pap. 2.25 (ISBN 0-685-04526-9). Scholastic Inc.
Brandt, Betty. Special Delivery. Haubrich, Kathy, illus. 48p. (gr. k-4). 1988. lib. bdg. 9.95 (ISBN 0-87614-312-5). Carolrhoda Bks.
Branscum, Robbie. The Girl. LC 85-45826. 128p. (gr. 5 up). 1986. PLB 10.89 (ISBN 0-06-020703-5). HarpC Child Bks.
Bridgers, Sue E. All Together Now. LC 78-12244. 256p. (gr. 7 up). 1979. Repr. of 1979 ed. lib. bdg. 13.99 (ISBN 0-394-94098-9). Knopf.
—Notes for Another Life. 208p. (gr. 7 up). 1989. pap. 2.95 (ISBN 0-553-27185-7). Bantam.
Brimner, Larry D. Cory Coleman, Grade Two. Ritz, Karen, illus. 64p. (gr. 2-4). 1990. 12.95 (ISBN 0-8050-1312-1). H Holt & Co.
Brisson, Pat. Your Best Friend, Kate. Brown, Rick, illus. LC 88-6037. 40p. (gr. k-3). 1989. 12.95 (ISBN 0-02-714350-3, Bradbury Pr). Macmillan Child Grp.
Broger, Achim. The Day Chubby Became Charles. Cafiero, Renee V., tr. from GER. McCully, Emily A., illus. LC 89-13112. 96p. (gr. 2-5). 1990. 12.95 (ISBN 0-397-32144-9, Lipp Jr Bks); PLB 12.89 (ISBN 0-397-32145-7, Lipp Jr Bks). HarpC Child Bks.
Bronin, Andrew. Gus & Buster Work Things Out. Szekeres, Cyndy, illus. 64p. (gr. k-4). 1990. pap. 2.95 (ISBN 0-440-43318-5, YB). Dell.
Brook, Ruth. Jingle's Big Race. Kondo, Vala, illus. LC 86-30729. 32p. (gr. k-3). 1988. PLB 11.89 (ISBN 0-8167-0902-5); pap. text ed. 2.95 (ISBN 0-8167-0903-3). Troll Assocs.
—Jump for Joy, Betty. Kondo, Vala, illus. LC 86-30731. 32p. (gr. k-3). 1988. PLB 11.89 (ISBN 0-8167-0908-4); pap. text ed. 2.95 (ISBN 0-8167-0909-2). Troll Assocs.
—Sweet Hearts for Dolly. Kondo, Vala, illus. LC 86-30732. 32p. (gr. k-3). 1987. PLB 11.89 (ISBN 0-8167-0906-8); pap. text ed. 2.95 (ISBN 0-8167-0907-6). Troll Assocs.
Brooks, Bruce. Everywhere. LC 90-4073. 80p. (gr. 4 up). 1990. 12.95 (ISBN 0-06-020728-0); PLB 12.89 (ISBN 0-06-020729-9). HarpC Child Bks.
—Midnight Hour Encores. LC 86-45035. 288p. (gr. 7 up). 1986. 13.95 (ISBN 0-06-020709-4); PLB 13.89 (ISBN 0-06-020710-8). HarpC Child Bks.
—The Moves Make the Man. LC 83-49476. 288p. (gr. 7 up). 1987. pap. 2.95 (ISBN 0-06-447022-9, Trophy). HarpC Child Bks.
Brown, Marc. The True Francine. Brown, Marc, illus. 32p. (ps-3). 1981. 14.95 (ISBN 0-316-11212-7, Joy St Bks). Little.
Brown, Palmer. Hickory. Brown, Palmer, illus. LC 77-11849. 48p. (ps-3). 1978. PLB 9.57i (ISBN 0-06-020887-2). HarpC Child Bks.
Browne, Anthony. Willy the Champ. Browne, Anthony, illus. LC 85-10053. 32p. (ps-3). 1986. lib. bdg. 9.99 (ISBN 0-394-97907-9). Knopf.
Bryant, Bonnie. Horse Wise. (gr. 4 up). 1990. pap. 2.95 (ISBN 0-553-15805-8). Bantam.
Buchan, Stuart. When We Lived with Pete. (Orig.). (gr. 4-7). 1986. pap. 2.95 (ISBN 0-440-49483-4, YB). Dell.
Bulla, Clyde R. Last Look. McCully, Emily A, illus. LC 78-22507. 96p. (gr. 3-5). 1979. PLB 12.89 (ISBN 0-690-03966-2, Crowell Jr Bks). HarpC Child Bks.
Bunting, Eve. If I Asked You, Would You Stay? LC 82-49052. 160p. (gr. 7 up). 1984. PLB 12.89x (ISBN 0-397-32066-3, Trophy); pap. 2.75 (ISBN 0-06-447023-7, Trophy). HarpC Child Bks.
—Sixth-Grade Sleepover. LC 86-4679. 96p. (gr. 4-6). 1986. 13.95 (ISBN 0-15-275350-8, HJ). HarBraceJ.
—Sixth Grade Sleepover. (Illus.). (gr. k-9). 1988. pap. 2.50 (ISBN 0-318-36508-1). Scholastic Inc.
—Such Nice Kids. 160p. (gr. 4-9). 1990. 13.95 (ISBN 0-395-54998-1, Clarion Bks). HM.
Burke, Timothy. Cocoa Puppy. Burke, Ann & Burke, Ann, illus. LC 89-50890. 32p. (Orig.). (ps-3). 1989. 5.00 (ISBN 0-9623227-0-9). Thunder & Ink.
Bush, Max. Thirteen Bells of Boglewood. (Orig.). (gr. k-3). 1987. pap. 4.50 (ISBN 0-87602-272-7). Anchorage.
Buttenwieser, Paul. Their Pride & Joy. (gr. 6 up). 1988. pap. 8.95 (ISBN 0-440-50073-7, LE). Dell.

Butterworth, Nick & Inkpen, Mick. Nice or Nasty. Butterworth, Nick & Inkpen, Mick, illus. (ps-3). 1987. pap. 12.95 (ISBN 0-316-11915-6). Little.
Byars, Betsy. Beans on the Roof. Rosales, Melodye, illus. 80p. (gr. k-3). 1988. pap. 13.95 (ISBN 0-440-50055-9). Delacorte.
—Beans on the Roof. 1990. pap. 2.95 (ISBN 0-440-40314-6, YB). Dell.
—A Blossom Promise. Rogers, Jacqueline, illus. 160p. (gr. k-6). 1989. pap. 2.95 (ISBN 0-440-40137-2, YB). Dell.
—The Pinballs. LC 76-41518. 144p. (gr. 5 up). 1987. pap. 3.50 (ISBN 0-06-440198-7, Trophy). HarpC Child Bks.
Byars, Betsy C. The Cybil War. Owens, Gail, illus. 144p. (gr. 3 up). 1990. pap. 3.95 (ISBN 0-14-034356-3, Puffin). Puffin Bks.
Capote, Truman. Miriam: A Classic Story of Loneliness. (Illus.). (gr. 4 up). 1982. PLB 10.95s.p. (ISBN 0-87191-829-3); 15.65. Creative Ed.
Carkeet, David. The Silent Treatment. LC 87-45567. 288p. (gr. 7 up). 1988. PLB 13.89 (ISBN 0-06-020979-8). HarpC Child Bks.
Carlson, Nancy. Harriet & Walt. LC 81-18137. (Illus.). 32p. (ps-3). 1982. lib. bdg. 9.95 (ISBN 0-87614-185-8). Carolrhoda Bks.
—Harriet & Walt. Carlson, Nancy, illus. (gr. k-3). 1984. bk. & cassette 19.95 (ISBN 0-941078-59-0); pap. 12. 95 bk. & cassette (ISBN 0-317-14688-2); cassette, 4 paperbacks & guide 27.95 (ISBN 0-317-14689-0). Live Oak Media.
Carr, Jan, adapted by. Oliver & Company. 64p. (gr. 2-7). 1988. pap. 2.50 (ISBN 0-590-42049-6). Scholastic Inc.
Carrick, Carol. Some Friend! Carrick, Donald, illus. LC 79-11490. 112p. (gr. 6 up). 1979. 13.95 (ISBN 0-395-28966-1, Clarion). HM.
—Some Friend. Carrick, Donald, illus. LC 79-11490. 112p. (gr. 3-6). 1987. pap. 3.95 (ISBN 0-89919-525-3, Pub. by Clarion). Ticknor & Fields.
Caseley, Judith. Harry & Willy & Carrothead. LC 90-30291. (Illus.). 24p. (ps up). 1991. 13.95 (ISBN 0-688-09492-9); PLB 13.88 (ISBN 0-688-09493-7). Greenwillow.
Cassedy, Sylvia. M. E. & Morton. LC 85-48251. 288p. (gr. 4-7). 1987. 13.95 (ISBN 0-690-04560-3, Crowell Jr Bks); PLB 12.89 (ISBN 0-690-04562-X, Crowell Jr Bks). HarpC Child Bks.
Casterline, Charlotte L. My Friend Has Asthma. Zabroski, Patricia, illus. 24p. (Orig.). (ps-6). 1985. pap. 4.95 (ISBN 0-9617218-0-4). Info All Bk.
—Sam the Allergen. (Illus.). 26p. (Orig.). (ps-6). 1985. pap. 4.95 (ISBN 0-9617218-1-2). Info All Bk.
Cave, Hugh B. Conquering Kilmarnie. LC 88-29978. 192p. (gr. 3-7). 1989. 13.95 (ISBN 0-02-717781-5, Mcmillan Child Bk). Macmillan Child Grp.
Chaikin, Miriam. Getting Even. Egielski, Richard, illus. LC 81-48647. 128p. (gr. 3-7). 1982. PLB 12.89 (ISBN 0-06-021165-2). HarpC Child Bks.
—Lower! Higher! You're a Liar! Egielski, Richard, illus. LC 83-48445. 160p. (gr. 3-7). 1984. 12.95 (ISBN 0-06-021186-5); PLB 12.89 (ISBN 0-06-021187-3). HarpC Child Bks.
Chambers, Aidan. NIK: Now I Know. LC 87-30836. 288p. (gr. 7 up). 1988. 13.95 (ISBN 0-06-021208-X); PLB 13.89 (ISBN 0-06-021209-8). HarpC Child Bks.
Chambless, Jane. Tucker & the Bear. (ps-2). 1989. pap. 13.95 (ISBN 0-671-67357-2). S&S Trade.
Chang, Heidi. Elaine & the Flying Frog. Chang, Heidi, illus. LC 90-33721. 64p. (Orig.). (gr. 2-4). 1991. PLB 6.99 (ISBN 0-679-90870-6); pap. 2.50 (ISBN 0-679-80870-1). Random.
Chapouton, Anne-Marie. Ben Finds a Friend. Wensell, Ulises, illus. 32p. (ps-2). 1986. lib. bdg. 7.95 (ISBN 0-399-21268-X, Putnam). Putnam Pub Group.
Chardiet, Bernice & Maccarone, Grace. School Friends. Karas, G. Brian, illus. 32p. (ps-2). 1991. 2.50 (ISBN 0-590-43306-7). Scholastic Inc.
Chetwin, Grace. The Crystal Stair: From Tales of Gom in the Legends of Ulm. LC 87-27395. 240p. (gr. 5 up). 1988. 14.95 (ISBN 0-02-718311-4, Bradbury Pr). Macmillan Child Grp.
Child Study Children's Book Committee. Friends Are Like That! Stories to Read to Yourself. Grant, Leigh, illus. LC 78-22513. (gr. 3-6). 1979. 12.95i (ISBN 0-690-03979-4, Crowell Jr Bks). HarpC Child Bks.
Childress, Alice. A Hero Ain't Nothin' but a Sandwich. large type ed. 144p. 1989. PLB 15.95 (ISBN 1-55736-112-6, Crnrstn Bks). ABC-CLIO.
Chorao, Kay. George Told Kate. (ps). 1990. pap. 3.95 (ISBN 0-525-44649-4, DCB). Dutton Child Bks.
Christian, Mary B. Penrod Again. Dyer, Jane, illus. LC 90-29. 56p. (gr. 1-4). 1990. pap. 3.95 (ISBN 0-689-71432-7, Aladdin). Macmillan Child Grp.
—Penrod's Party. Schindler, S. D., illus. LC 89-37203. 48p. (gr. 1-4). 1990. 11.95 (ISBN 0-02-718525-7, Mcmillan Child Bk). Macmillan Child Grp.
—Singin' Somebody Else's Song. 192p. (gr. 5 up). 1990. pap. 3.95 (ISBN 0-14-034169-2, Puffin). Puffin Bks.
Clardy, Andrea F. Dusty Was My Friend. Alexander, Eleanor, illus. 32p. (gr. 5 up). 1984. 16.95 (ISBN 0-89885-141-6). Human Sci Pr.
Clarke, Pauline. Return of the Twelve. (Orig.). (gr. 3-7). 1986. pap. 4.95 (ISBN 0-440-47536-8). Dell.
Cleary, Beverly. The Beezus & Ramona Diary. Tiegreen, Alan, illus. 224p. (gr. 5-7). 1986. pap. 9.95 (ISBN 0-688-06353-5, Pub. by Beech Tree Bks). Morrow.
—Mitch & Amy. 224p. (gr. k-6). 1980. pap. 3.25 (ISBN 0-440-45411-5, YB). Dell.
—Mitch & Amy. 224p. 1991. pap. 3.50 (ISBN 0-380-70925-2, Camelot). Avon.
—Ramona & Her Friends. pap. 9.00 (ISBN 0-440-47222-9). Dell.
Cleaver. Moonlake Angel. (gr. k-6). 1989. pap. 2.95 (ISBN 0-440-40165-8, YB). Dell.
Cleaver, Vera & Cleaver, Bill. Mock Revolt. LC 75-151467. 160p. (gr. 6 up). 1971. (Lipp Jr Bks); pap. 1.95 (ISBN 0-397-31237-7). HarpC Child Bks.
Clements, Bruce. Coming About. LC 83-47841. 180p. (gr. 5 up). 1984. 11.95 (ISBN 0-374-31457-8). FS&G.
—Two Against the Tide. 224p. (gr. 4 up). 1987. pap. 3.50 (ISBN 0-374-48016-8). FS&G.
Clifford, Eth. I Hate Your Guts, Ben Brooster. 112p. (gr. 3-7). 1989. 13.95 (ISBN 0-395-51079-1). HM.
—I Never Wanted to be Famous. (gr. 3-5). 1986. 12.95 (ISBN 0-395-40420-7). HM.
—Just Tell Me When We're Dead! (gr. 5-7). 1985. pap. 2.75 (ISBN 0-590-44010-1). Scholastic Inc.
Clifton, Lucille. Everett Anderson's Goodbye. Grifalconi, Ann, illus. LC 82-23426. 32p. (Orig.). (gr. k-3). 1988. pap. 5.95 (ISBN 0-8050-0800-4). H Holt & Co.
—Lucky Stone. Payson, Dale, illus. (gr. 2-5). 1986. pap. 2.75 (ISBN 0-440-45110-8, YB). Dell.
Cline, Don. Antrim & Billy. Metz, Leon, intro. by. LC 90-1598. (Illus.). 170p. 1990. 21.95 (ISBN 0-932702-48-1). Creative Texas.
Clymer, E. The Spider, the Cave, & the Pottery Bowl. 80p. (gr. k-6). 1989. pap. 2.75 (ISBN 0-440-40166-6, YB). Dell.
Clymer, Susan. Four Month Friend. (ps-3). 1991. pap. 2.75 (ISBN 0-590-42545-5). Scholastic Inc.
Coburn, John B. Anne & the Sand Dobbies. LC 86-12650. 121p. (gr. 7-12). 1986. pap. 8.95 (ISBN 0-8192-1354-3). Morehouse Pub.
Cohen, Barbara. Headless Roommate. (gr. 7-12). 1987. pap. 2.25 (ISBN 0-553-26679-9). Bantam.
—Tell Us Your Secret. 1989. 13.95 (ISBN 0-553-05810-X, Starfire). Bantam.
—Thank You, Jackie Robinson. Cuffari, Richard, illus. LC 87-29341. (gr. 3-6). 1988. PLB 13.95 (ISBN 0-688-07909-1). Lothrop.
Cohen, Charles. See You Tomorrow, Charles. 32p. (gr. k-6). 1989. pap. 2.95 (ISBN 0-440-40162-3, YB). Dell.
Cohen, Miriam. It's George. (gr. k-6). 1989. pap. 2.95 (ISBN 0-440-40198-4). Dell.
—Liar, Liar, Pants on Fire! (gr. k-6). 1987. pap. 2.95 (ISBN 0-440-44755-0, YB). Dell.
—So What? (gr. k-6). 1988. pap. 2.95 (ISBN 0-440-40048-1, YB). Dell.
Cole, Babette. Silly Book. (ps-3). 1990. 13.99 (ISBN 0-385-41238-X). Doubleday.
Cole, Joanna. Bully Trouble: A Step Two Book. Hafner, Marilyn, illus. LC 89-3757. 48p. (Orig.). (gr. 1-3). 1989. lib. bdg. 6.99 (ISBN 0-394-94949-8, Random Juv); pap. 2.95 (ISBN 0-394-84949-3). Random.
—Don't Call Me Names! (Just Right for 4's & 5's) Munsinger, Lynn, illus. LC 89-35412. 32p. (ps). 1990. 4.95 (ISBN 0-679-80258-4); PLB 5.99 (ISBN 0-679-90258-9). McKay.
—The Missing Tooth. Hafner, Marilyn, illus. LC 88-1903. 48p. (Orig.). (gr. 1-3). 1988. lib. bdg. 6.99 (ISBN 0-394-99279-2, Random Juv); pap. 2.95 (ISBN 0-394-89279-8, Random Juv). Random.
Conford, Ellen. Anything for a Friend. LC 78-27843. (gr. 3-7). 1979. 14.95 (ISBN 0-316-15308-7). Little.
—Why Me? 156p. (gr. 5 up). 1985. 14.95 (ISBN 0-316-15326-5). Little.
—Why Me? (gr. 7 up). 1987. pap. 2.75 (ISBN 0-671-62841-0, Archway). PB.
—You Can Never Tell. 160p. (gr. 7 up). 1988. pap. 2.75 (ISBN 0-671-66182-5, Archway). PB.
Conrad, Pam. Holding Me Here. LC 85-45254. 192p. (gr. 7 up). 1986. 11.95 (ISBN 0-06-021338-8); PLB 11.89 (ISBN 0-06-021339-6). HarpC Child Bks.
Cooney, Caroline B. Among Friends. 176p. (gr. 6 up). 1987. 13.95 (ISBN 0-553-05446-5, Starfire). Bantam.
Cooper, Ilene. Frances Dances. LC 90-49469. (Illus.). 112p. (Orig.). (gr. 3-6). 1991. PLB 8.99 (ISBN 0-679-91111-1, Bullseye Bks); pap. 2.95 (ISBN 0-679-81111-7, Bullseye Bks). Knopf.
—Frances Takes a Chance. LC 90-2622. (Illus.). 112p. (Orig.). (gr. 3-6). 1991. PLB 8.99 (ISBN 0-679-91110-3, Bullseye Bks); pap. 2.95 (ISBN 0-679-81110-9, Bullseye Bks). Knopf.
Corcoran, Barbara. You Put up with Me, I'll Put up with You. LC 86-17217. 176p. (gr. 5-9). 1987. SBE 12.95 (ISBN 0-689-31305-5, Atheneum Child Bk). Macmillan Child Grp.
—You Put up with Me, I'll Put up with You. 176p. (gr. 3-7). 1989. pap. 2.50 (ISBN 0-380-70558-3, Camelot). Avon.
Coret, Harriette. Better off Without Me. Billups, Annie, ed. Forstadt, Fran, illus. 80p. (Orig.). 1989. pap. text ed. 3.50 (ISBN 0-88336-762-9). New Readers.
Corey, Deirdre. Friends 4-Ever: P.S. We'll Miss You, No. 1. 1990. pap. 2.75 (ISBN 0-590-42627-3). Scholastic Inc.
Cory, Deirdre. Friends 'til the Ocean Waves. 128p. (gr. 3-7). 1990. pap. 2.75 (ISBN 0-590-44028-4). Scholastic Inc.
Cosgrove, Stephen. Misty Morgan. (Illus.). 32p. (gr. k-4). 1987. PLB 12.66 (ISBN 0-86592-368-X). Rourke Corp.
—Morgan Morning. James, Robin, illus. 32p. (gr. 1-6). 1982. pap. 2.95 (ISBN 0-8431-0591-7). Price Stern.
—Raz-Ma-Taz. James, Robin, illus. 32p. (gr. 1-6). 1982. pap. 2.95 (ISBN 0-8431-0588-7). Price Stern.
Cosgrove, Stephen E. Hannah & Hickory. Edelson, Wendy, illus. 32p. (ps-3). 1990. lib. bdg. 12.96 (ISBN 0-89565-664-7). Childs World.
—Persimmony. Edelson, Wendy, illus. 32p. (ps-3). 1990. lib. bdg. 12.96 (ISBN 0-89565-661-2). Childs World.
Cossi, Olga. Adventure on the Graveyard of the Wrecks. 144p. (Orig.). (gr. 9-12). 1991. pap. 5.95 (ISBN 0-88289-808-6). Pelican.
Costa, Nicoletta. A Friend Comes to Play. Costa, Nicoletta, illus. 16p. (gr. k-1). 1984. 3.50 (ISBN 0-448-23403-3, G&D). Putnam Pub Group.
Coutant, Helen. The Gift. Mai, Vo-Dinh, illus. LC 82-7810. 48p. (gr. 2-5). 1983. 9.95 (ISBN 0-394-85499-3). Knopf.
Craig, Helen. A Welcome for Annie. Craig, Helen, illus. LC 85-12683. 32p. (ps-2). 1986. Knopf.
Cresswell, Helen. Bagthorpes Unlimited: Being the Third Part of the Bagthorpe Saga. LC 77-3561. 192p. (gr. 5 up). 1978. 13.95 (ISBN 0-02-725430-5, Mcmillan Child Bk). Macmillan Child Grp.
Cross, Gillian. Chartbreaker. (gr. k-12). 1989. pap. 2.95 (ISBN 0-440-20312-0, LFL). Dell.
—On the Edge. (gr. k-12). 1987. pap. 2.75 (ISBN 0-440-96666-3, LFL). Dell.
Cummings, Priscilla. Oswald & the Timberdoodles. Cohen, A. R., illus. LC 90-70723. 30p. (gr. k-5). 1990. 8.95 (ISBN 0-87033-411-5). Tidewater.
Cunningham, Julia. Oaf. Sis, Peter, illus. LC 85-14654. 128p. (gr. 2-6). 1986. Knopf.
Cuyler, Margery. The Trouble with Soap. LC 81-12636. 144p. (gr. 5 up). 1982. 9.95 (ISBN 0-525-45111-0, DCB). Dutton Child Bks.
Dahan, Andre. My Friend the Moon. (ps-3). 1987. pap. 12.95 (ISBN 0-670-81569-1). Viking Child Bks.
Dahl, Roald. The BFG. large type ed. (Illus.). 320p. (gr. 3-8). 1989. Repr. of 1982 ed. PLB 14.95 (ISBN 1-85089-957-6, Pub. by Clio Pr England). ABC-CLIO.
—George's Marvelous Medicine. (gr. 2-4). 1987. pap. 2.75 (ISBN 0-553-15394-3, Skylark). Bantam.
Damon, Valerie H. Willo Mancifoot (and the Mugga Killa Whomps) Damon, Dave, ed. LC 83-50739. (Illus.). (gr. 2-6). 1985. 14.95 (ISBN 0-932356-07-9); ltd. art ed. 100.00 (ISBN 0-932356-08-7). Star Pubns Mo.
Dana, Barbara. Zucchini. Christelow, Eileen, illus. 160p. (gr. 3-6). pap. 2.75 (ISBN 0-553-15437-0, Skylark). Bantam.
Dana, Maggie. If Wishes Were Horses. Ruff, Donna, illus. LC 87-16201. 128p. (gr. 4-8). 1988. PLB 9.89 (ISBN 0-8167-1197-6); pap. text ed. 2.95 (ISBN 0-8167-1198-4). Troll Assocs.
—Jumping into Trouble. Ruff, Donna, illus. LC 87-16248. 128p. (gr. 4-8). 1988. PLB 9.89 (ISBN 0-8167-1193-3); pap. text ed. 2.95 (ISBN 0-8167-1194-1). Troll Assocs.
—No Time for Secrets. Ruff, Donna, illus. LC 87-19027. 128p. (gr. 4-8). 1988. PLB 9.89 (ISBN 0-8167-1191-7); pap. text ed. 2.95 (ISBN 0-8167-1192-5). Troll Assocs.
—Racing for the Stars. Ruff, Donna, illus. LC 87-16246. 128p. (gr. 4-8). 1987. PLB 9.89 (ISBN 0-8167-1195-X); pap. text ed. 2.95 (ISBN 0-8167-1196-8). Troll Assocs.
Davidson, Linda. Fast Forward. (gr. 10 up). 1989. pap. 2.95 (ISBN 0-8041-0246-5). Ivy Books.
Davis, Gibbs. Swann Song. 176p. (gr. 7 up). 1989. pap. 2.50 (ISBN 0-380-75609-9, Flare). Avon.
Davis, Jenny. Good-Bye & Keep Cold. 1989. pap. 2.95 (ISBN 0-440-20481-X, LFL). Dell.
Davis, Maggie S. The Rinky-Dink Cafe. Sandford, John, illus. LC 87-35435. 32p. (ps-3). 1988. pap. 12.95 (ISBN 0-671-66408-5). S&S Trade.
Day, Alexandra. Frank & Ernest. Day, Alexandra, illus. 1991. pap. 3.95 (ISBN 0-590-41556-5, Blue Ribbon Bks). Scholastic Inc.
Dean, Karen S. Cammy Takes a Bow. (gr. 3-7). 1988. pap. 2.50 (ISBN 0-380-75400-2, Camelot). Avon.
Deaver, Julie R. First Wedding, Once Removed. LC 90-4184. 224p. (gr. 5-9). 1990. 13.95 (ISBN 0-06-021426-0); PLB 13.89 (ISBN 0-06-021427-9). HarpC Child Bks.
DeClements, Barthe. Nothing's Fair in Fifth Grade. LC 80-54195. 144p. (gr. 3-7). 1981. pap. 12.95 (ISBN 0-670-51741-0). Viking Child Bks.
De la Mare, Walter. Visitors. LC 86-6244. 40p. (gr. 4 up). 1986. PLB 10.95s.p. (ISBN 0-88682-070-7); PLB 15. 65 (ISBN 0-685-12420-7). Creative Ed.
Delton, Judy. Angel in Charge. (gr. k-6). 1990. pap. 2.95 (ISBN 0-440-40264-6, YB). Dell.
—Angel's Mother's Boyfriend. Apple, Margot, illus. LC 82-27054. 176p. (gr. 2-5). 1986. 12.95 (ISBN 0-395-39968-8). HM.
—Blue Skies, French Fries. 80p. (Orig.). (gr. k-6). 1988. pap. 2.75 (ISBN 0-440-40064-3, YB). Dell.
—The Pee Wee Jubilee. (gr. k-6). 1989. pap. 2.50 (ISBN 0-440-40226-3, YB). Dell.
—Rosy Noses, Freezing Toes. Tiegreen, Alan, illus. (Orig.). 1990. pap. 2.75 (ISBN 0-440-40384-7, YB). Dell.
—Scary, Scary Huckleberry. Tiegreen, Alan, illus. (Orig.). (gr. k-6). 1990. pap. 2.95 (ISBN 0-440-40336-7, YB). Dell.
De Maupassant, Guy. Two Friends. Redpath, Ann, ed. Delessert, Etienne, illus. 32p. (gr. 4 up). 1985. PLB 10.95s.p. (ISBN 0-88682-003-0); PLB 15.65 (ISBN 0-685-10403-6). Creative Ed.
De Paola, Tomie. Bill & Pete Go Down the Nile. De Paola, Tomie, illus. 32p. (ps-1). 1987. 12.95 (ISBN 0-399-21395-3, Putnam). Putnam Pub Group.

De Regniers, Beatrice. How Joe the Bear & Sam the Mouse Got Together. Myers, Bernice, illus. LC 89-12110. 32p. (ps-2). 1990. 12.95 (ISBN 0-688-09079-6); lib. bdg. 12.88 (ISBN 0-688-09080-X). Lothrop.
De Regniers, Beatrice S. A Week in the Life of Best Friends: And Other Poems of Friendship. Doyle, Nancy, illus. LC 85-28680. 48p. (gr. 3-7). 1986. 11.95 (ISBN 0-689-31179-6, Atheneum Child Bk). Macmillan Child Grp.
Devlin, Wende & Devlin, Harry. Cranberry Valentine. Devlin, Wende & Devlin, Harry, illus. LC 85-24047. 32p. (gr. k-3). 1986. 13.95 (ISBN 0-02-729200-2, Four Winds). Macmillan Child Grp.
Dickerson, Karle. Best Friend Blues. 144p. (Orig.). (gr. 6-9). 1988. pap. 2.75 (ISBN 0-87406-319-1). Willowisp Pr.
Dickinson, Peter. Heartease. (gr. 7 up). 1988. pap. 2.95 (ISBN 0-317-69490-1, LFL). Dell.
Dines, Carol. Best Friends Tell the Best Lies. LC 88-29433. (gr. 7 up). 1989. 14.95 (ISBN 0-385-29704-1). Delacorte.
Dodd, Lynley. Hairy Maclary's Bone. Dodd, Lynley, illus. LC 85-9772. 32p. (gr. 1-2). 1985. PLB 10.95 (ISBN 0-918831-06-7). Gareth Stevens Inc.
Dodson, Susan. Shadows Across the Sand. (gr. 7 up). pap. 2.25 (ISBN 0-449-70114-X, Juniper). Fawcett.
Donovan, John. Remove Protective Coating a Little at a Time. LC 73-4977. 108p. (gr. 7 up). 1973. PLB 12.89 (ISBN 0-06-021720-0). HarpC Child Bks.
Dubanevich, Arlene. Pig William. Dubanevich, Arlene, illus. LC 85-5776. 32p. (ps-2). 1985. 13.95 (ISBN 0-02-733200-4, Bradbury Pr). Macmillan Child Grp.
Dunrea, Olivier. Mogwogs on the March. Dunrea, Olivier, illus. LC 85-5493. 32p. (ps-1). 1985. pap. 5.95 (ISBN 0-8234-0845-0). Holiday.
Dunster, Mark. Doricio. 11p. (Orig.). 1989. pap. 4.00 (ISBN 0-89642-170-8). Linden Pubs.
Edens, Cooper. Hugh's Hues. Edens, Cooper, illus. LC 88-81935. 32p. 1988. 11.95 (ISBN 0-88138-114-4). Green Tiger Pr.
—With Secret Friends. LC 84-149490. (Illus.). 48p. (gr. 7-12). 1981. pap. 8.95 (ISBN 0-914676-57-1). Green Tiger Pr.
Edwards, Dorothy. My Naughty Little Sister & Bad Harry's Rabbit. Hughes, Shirley, illus. (ps-2). 1981. 8.95x (ISBN 0-13-608935-6). P-H.
Edwards, Pat. Little John & Plutie. 180p. (gr. 3-7). 1988. 13.95 (ISBN 0-395-48223-2). HM.
Effinger, Marta. Bunker & Me: Summer Adventures of Best Friends, Vol. I. Lawrence & Penny, ed. Effinger, Michael, illus. Washington, Pat, intro. by. (Illus.). 30p. (gr. 3-5). 1990. 12.95xg (ISBN 0-929917-02-2). Magnolia PA.
Eggleston, Edward. Mister Blake's Walking Stick. 1988. Repr. of 1870 ed. lib. bdg. 59.00x (ISBN 0-317-90257-1). Reprint Servs.
Ehrlich, Amy. Leo, Zack & Emmie. Kellogg, Steven, illus. LC 81-2604. 64p. (ps-3). 1981. PLB 9.89 (ISBN 0-8037-4761-6). Dial Bks Young.
—Leo, Zack & Emmie Together Again. LC 86-16810. (Illus.). 56p. (ps-3). 1987. 9.95 (ISBN 0-8037-0381-3); PLB 9.89 (ISBN 0-8037-0382-1). Dial Bks Young.
—Leo, Zack, & Emmie Together Again. LC 86-16810. (Illus.). 56p. (ps-3). 1990. pap. 3.95 (ISBN 0-8037-0837-8). Dial Bks Young.
Elliott, Paula. Fluffy & Sparky: A Story about True Buddies. Royall, Sandy, illus. 32p. (ps up). 1991. 12.95 (ISBN 1-879052-00-8). Planetary Pubns.
Ellis, Carol. Cry in the Night. 1990. pap. 2.75 (ISBN 0-590-42845-4). Scholastic Inc.
Ellis, Jana. Never Stop Smiling. LC 88-12390. 160p. (gr. 7 up). 1988. pap. text ed. 2.50 (ISBN 0-8167-1360-X). Troll Assocs.
Ellis, Sarah. Next-Door Neighbors. LC 89-37923. 160p. (gr. 4-7). 1990. 11.95 (ISBN 0-689-50495-0, M K McElderry). Macmillan Child Grp.
Enright, Elizabeth. The Saturdays. Enright, Elizabeth, illus. 184p. (gr. 2-6). 1988. 12.95 (ISBN 0-8050-0291-X). H Holt & Co.
Eriksson, Eva. Hocus Pocus. Eriksson, Eva, illus. LC 84-26340. 32p. (ps-3). 1985. PLB 8.95 (ISBN 0-87614-235-8). Carolrhoda Bks.
—One Short Week. Eriksson, Eva, illus. LC 84-17644. 32p. (ps-3). 1985. PLB 8.95 (ISBN 0-87614-234-X). Carolrhoda Bks.
Escudie, Rene. Paul & Sebastian. Townley, Roderick, tr. from FRE. Wensell, Ulises, illus. LC 88-12768. 32p. (ps-3). 1988. 10.95 (ISBN 0-916291-19-7). Kane-Miller Bk.
Ethridge, Kenneth E. Toothpick. LC 85-42883. 128p. (gr. 7 up). 1985. 12.95 (ISBN 0-8234-0585-0). Holiday.
Eyerly, Jeannette. Seth & Me & Rebel Make Three. LC 82-48463. 128p. (gr. 7 up). 1983. 12.95i (ISBN 0-397-32042-6, Lipp Jr Bks). HarpC Child Bks.
Fabian, Margaret W. My Friend Luke, the Stenciller. Fabian, Margaret W., illus. LC 83-50689. 35p. (gr. 3-4). 1987. pap. 8.95 over boards (ISBN 0-931474-25-6). TBW Bks.
Fabian, Stella. The Opal Mystery. LC 90-83465. (Illus.). 192p. (Orig.). (gr. 3-7). 1991. pap. 3.25 (ISBN 0-922434-39-5). Brighton & Lloyd.
Farnette, Cherrie, et al. People Need Each Other. rev. ed. 80p. (gr. 4-7). 1989. pap. text ed. 7.95 (ISBN 0-86530-070-4, IP 63-3). Incentive Pubns.
Farrar, Susan C. Samantha on Stage. Sanderson, Ruth, illus. 164p. (gr. 3 up). 1990. pap. 3.95 (ISBN 0-14-034328-8, Puffin). Puffin Bks.
Fassler, Joan. The Boy with a Problem: Johnny Learns to Share His Troubles. LC 78-147125. (Illus.). 32p. (ps-3). 1971. 16.95 (ISBN 0-87705-054-6). Human Sci Pr.
Feinberg, Anna. Wiggy & Boa. James, Ann, illus. 112p. (gr. 3-7). 1990. 13.95 (ISBN 0-395-53704-5). HM.
Feldman, Eve. We Are Friends. (Illus.). 32p. (gr. 1-4). 1989. PLB 13.32 (ISBN 0-8172-3517-5). Raintree Pubs.
Fender, Kay. Odette: A Springtime in Paris. Dumas, Philippe, illus. 32p. (ps-3). 1991. 10.95 (ISBN 0-916291-33-2). Kane-Miller Bk.
Fernstrom, Russell & Fernstrom, Beverly. Weepy the Swoose & Other Stories. 48p. (ps-7). 1990. 6.95 (ISBN 0-8062-3647-7). Carlton.
Ferris, Jean. The Stainless Steel Rule. LC 85-45731. 192p. (gr. 7 up). 1986. 13.95 (ISBN 0-374-37212-8). FS&G.
Ferry, Charles. Raspberry One. LC 82-25476. 224p. (gr. 7 up). 1983. 11.95 (ISBN 0-395-34069-1). HM.
Fobes, Jacqueline. A Papago Boy & His Friends. (gr. 1-4). 1980. pap. 1.50 (ISBN 0-686-32641-5). Impresora Sahuaro.
Foley, Patricia. John & the Fiddler. Sewall, Marcia, illus. LC 89-34514. 64p. (gr. 1-5). 1990. 12.95 (ISBN 0-06-021841-X); PLB 12.89 (ISBN 0-06-021842-8). HarpC Child Bks.
Fontenot, Mary A. Clovis Crawfish & the Curious Crapaud. Kidder, Christine, illus. LC 86-4997. 32p. (gr. k-5). 1986. 11.95 (ISBN 0-88289-610-5). Pelican.
Fosburgh, Liza. Bella Arabella. 112p. 1987. pap. 2.50 (ISBN 0-553-15484-2, Skylark). Bantam.
Fox, Paula. Lily & the Lost Boy. (gr. k-6). 1989. pap. 3.25 (ISBN 0-440-40235-2, YB). Dell.
Freeman, Don. Corduroy. Freeman, Don, illus. (gr. k-3). 1982. incl. cass. 19.95 (ISBN 0-941078-08-6); pap. 12.95 incl. cass. (ISBN 0-941078-06-X); user's guide incl. 4 pbs. & cass. 27.95 (ISBN 0-941078-07-8). Live Oak Media.
—Corduroy: (Edicion Espanola) Freeman, Don, illus. (SPA.). (ps-3). 1990. incl. cass. 19.95 (ISBN 0-87499-192-7); pap. 12.95 incl. cass. (ISBN 0-87499-213-3); Set; incl. 4 bks., guide, & cass. pap. 27.95 (ISBN 0-87499-193-5). Live Oak Media.
—Mop Top. Freeman, Don, illus. (gr. k-3). 1982. incl. cass. 19.95 (ISBN 0-941078-14-0); pap. 12.95 incl. cass. (ISBN 0-941078-12-4); user's guide incl. 6 pbs. & cass. 27.95 (ISBN 0-941078-13-2). Live Oak Media.
—A Pocket for Corduroy. Freeman, Don, illus. (gr. k-3). 1982. incl. cass. 19.95 (ISBN 0-941078-17-5); pap. 12.95 incl. cass. (ISBN 0-941078-15-9); user's guide incl. 4 pbs. & cass. 27.95 (ISBN 0-941078-16-7). Live Oak Media.
—A Rainbow of My Own. Freeman, Don, illus. (gr. k-3). 1982. incl. cass. 19.95 (ISBN 0-941078-20-5); pap. 12.95 incl. cass. (ISBN 0-941078-18-3); user's guide incl. 4 pbs. & cass. 27.95 (ISBN 0-941078-19-1). Live Oak Media.
Freeman, Lydia. Corduroy's Day. McCue, Lisa, illus. LC 84-40477. 14p. (ps). 1985. pap. 3.95 (ISBN 0-670-80521-1). Viking Child Bks.
French, Michael. Us Against Them. (gr. 7-12). 1989. pap. 2.95 (ISBN 0-553-27647-6, Starfire). Bantam.
Friends Forever. 1986. pap. 9.50 (ISBN 0-590-63122-5). Scholastic Inc.
Friends in Fern Hollow. (Illus.). (ps). 1985. bds. 1.49 (ISBN 0-318-45846-2). Outlet Bk Co.
Fritz, Jean. Early Thunder. Ward, Lynd, illus. (gr. 5-9). 1987. pap. 3.95 (ISBN 0-14-032259-0, Puffin). Puffin Bks.
Frost, Robert. You Come Too. Nason, Thomas W., illus. Hyde, Cox, frwd. by. LC 59-12940. (Illus.). 96p. (gr. 4 up). 1959. 14.95 (ISBN 0-8050-0299-5); pap. 5.95 (ISBN 0-8050-0316-9). H Holt & Co.
Gabhart, Ann. Only in Sunshine. (gr. 7 up). 1988. pap. 2.95 (ISBN 0-380-75395-2). Avon.
Gackenbach, Dick. What's Claude Doing? Gackenbach, Dick, illus. LC 83-14983. 32p. (ps-2). 1984. 13.95 (ISBN 0-89919-224-6, Clarion). HM.
—What's Claude Doing? LC 83-14983. (Illus.). 32p. (ps-3). 1986. pap. 4.95 (ISBN 0-89919-464-8, Pub. by Clarion). Ticknor & Fields.
Gaeddart, Louann. Your Former Friend, Matthew. 80p. 1985. pap. 2.25 (ISBN 0-553-15345-5, Skylark). Bantam.
Gaeddert, LouAnn. Your Former Friend, Matthew. Schwark, Mary B., illus. 80p. (gr. 3-6). 1984. 11.95 (ISBN 0-525-44086-0, DCB). Dutton Child Bks.
Ganz, Yaffa. Sharing a Sunshine Umbrella: A Mimmy & Simmy Story. Klineman, Harvey, illus. 1989. 8.95 (ISBN 0-87306-496-8). Feldheim.
Garcia, Maria. Read-A-Long with "The Adventures of Connie & Diego" 1988. incl. audiocassette 22.95 (ISBN 0-89239-033-6). Childrens Book Pr.
Garfield, Leon. The December Rose. large type ed. 344p. (gr. 3-7). 1987. lib. bdg. 15.95x (ISBN 0-7451-0588-2, Pub. by Chivers Pr UK). G K Hall.
—Footsteps. (gr. k-6). 1988. pap. 3.25 (ISBN 0-440-40102-X, YB). Dell.
Garrigue, Sheila. The Eternal Spring of Mr. Ito. LC 85-5687. 176p. (gr. 5-7). 1985. 13.95 (ISBN 0-02-737300-2, Bradbury Pr). Macmillan Child Grp.
Garrigue, Shelia. Between Friends (R) 1986. pap. 2.50 (ISBN 0-590-40773-2). Scholastic Inc.
Gauch, Patricia L. Night Talks. 160p. (gr. 5 up). 1983. pap. 10.95 (ISBN 0-399-20911-5, Putnam). Putnam Pub Group.
Geller, Mark. The Strange Case of the Reluctant Partners. LC 89-29409. 96p. (gr. 5-9). 1990. 13.95 (ISBN 0-06-021972-6); PLB 13.89 (ISBN 0-06-021973-4). HarpC Child Bks.
George, Gail. The Popples' Pajama Party. Sustendal, Pat, illus. LC 85-19403. 32p. (ps-3). 1986. pap. 2.25 (ISBN 0-394-88041-2). Random.
George, Lindsay B. William & Boomer. George, Lindsay B., illus. 24p. (ps-3). 1990. incl. audiocassette 17.95 (ISBN 0-924483-23-7). Soundprints.
Gerson, Corrine. Passing Through. 208p. (gr. 8 up). 1980. pap. 1.50 (ISBN 0-440-96958-1, LFL). Dell.
Gerstein, Mordicai. The Room. LC 83-47709. (Illus.). 32p. (ps-3). 1984. 11.95 (ISBN 0-06-021998-X). HarpC Child Bks.
Gibson, Eva. Laina. LC 85-73423. 150p. (Orig.). (gr. 9-12). 1986. pap. 3.95 (ISBN 0-87123-896-9). Bethany Hse.
Giff, Patricia R. All about Stacy. Sims, Blanche, illus. 80p. (Orig.). (gr. k-6). 1988. pap. 2.95 (ISBN 0-440-40088-0, YB). Dell.
—B-E-S-T Friends. 80p. (Orig.). (gr. k-6). 1988. pap. 2.95 (ISBN 0-440-40090-2, YB). Dell.
—The Candy Corn Contest. 80p. (Orig.). (ps-6). 1984. pap. 2.75 (ISBN 0-440-41072-X, YB). Dell.
—December Secrets. Sims, Blanche, illus. 80p. (gr. k-6). 1984. pap. 2.75 (ISBN 0-440-41795-3, YB). Dell.
—Fish Face. Sims, Blanche, illus. 80p. (Orig.). (gr. 1-4). 1984. pap. 2.75 (ISBN 0-440-42557-3, YB). Dell.
—Love, from the Fifth-Grade Celebrity. (gr. k-6). 1987. pap. 2.75 (ISBN 0-440-44948-0, YB). Dell.
—Tootsie Tanner, Why Dont You Talk. (gr. k-6). 1990. pap. 2.95 (ISBN 0-440-40239-5, YB). Dell.
Gilden, Mel. Born to Howl. Pierard, John, illus. 96p. 1987. pap. 2.50 (ISBN 0-380-75425-8, Camelot). Avon.
Gillham, Bill. The Rich Kid. Mosley, Francis, illus. LC 85-71252. 112p. (gr. 3-7). 1985. 10.95 (ISBN 0-233-97684-1). Andre Deutsch.
Gipson, Morrell & Mayer, Lene. Let's Be Friends. Stefoff, Rebecca, ed. LC 90-13795. (Illus.). 24p. (gr. k-3). 1990. PLB 13.26 (ISBN 0-944483-92-5). Garrett Ed Corp.
Gire, Ken. Rhythm & Blues: A Story about Doing Right When You Feel Wronged. Dickenson, John, et al, illus. 30p. 1988. 5.99 (ISBN 0-929608-11-9). Focus Family.
Girion, Barbara. Portfolio to Fame. (Orig.). (gr. k-12). 1987. pap. 2.50 (ISBN 0-440-97148-9, LFL). Dell.
—Prescription for Success. (gr. 7 up). 1987. pap. 2.50 (ISBN 0-440-97165-9). Dell.
Gold, Porter. Who's There? (Illus.). 32p. (gr. 1-4). 1989. PLB 13.22 (ISBN 0-8172-3514-0). Raintree Pubs.
Golding, Leila P. Rachel. LC 88-71304. 176p. (Orig.). (gr. 10-12). 1988. pap. 3.95 (ISBN 0-87123-963-9). Bethany Hse.
—Shelly. LC 85-73424. 150p. (Orig.). (gr. 9-12). 1986. pap. 3.95 (ISBN 0-87123-867-5). Bethany Hse.
Gondosch, Linda. Who's Afraid of Haggerty House? LC 86-24265. (gr. 4-6). 1987. 11.95 (ISBN 0-525-67198-6, Lodestar Bks). Dutton Child Bks.
—Who's Afraid of Haggerty House. 1989. pap. 2.75 (ISBN 0-671-67237-1, Minstrel Bks). PB.
Goodman, Roger B. A Bed for the Wind. Root, Kimberly B., illus. 32p. (gr. 1-4). 1988. pap. 12.95 (ISBN 0-671-66117-5, Little Simon). S&S Trade.
Gordon, Christine W. Mee Glows with Health & Happiness. Gordon, Christine W., illus. LC 87-90587. 32p. (Orig.). (ps-2). 1987. pap. 5.00 (ISBN 0-9618854-1-6). Mee Enterp.
—Mee, Who Is Hardly Any Size at All. Gordon, Christine W., illus. LC 87-90588. (Orig.). (ps-k). 1987. pap. 4.00 (ISBN 0-9618854-0-8). Mee Enterp.
Gordon, Sharon. Playground Fun. Karas, G. Brian, illus. LC 86-30854. 32p. (gr. k-2). 1987. lib. bdg. 7.06 (ISBN 0-8167-0990-4); pap. text ed. 1.95 (ISBN 0-8167-0991-2). Troll Assocs.
Gordon, Sheila. Waiting for the Rain. LC 87-7638. 224p. (gr. 7 up). 1987. 12.95 (ISBN 0-531-05726-7); PLB 12.99 (ISBN 0-531-08326-8). Orchard Bks Watts.
Gormley, Beatrice. Best Friend Insurance. McCully, Emily A., illus. (gr. 3-6). 1983. 10.95 (ISBN 0-525-44066-6, DCB). Dutton Child Bks.
—Best Friend Insurance. McCully, Emily A., illus. 160p. (gr. 3-7). 1985. pap. 2.50 (ISBN 0-380-69854-4, Camelot). Avon.
Goudge, Eileen. Don't Say Goodbye. 153p. (Orig.). (gr. 6-12). 1985. pap. 2.25 (ISBN 0-440-92108-2, LFL). Dell.
—Looking for Love. (Orig.). 1986. pap. 2.25 (ISBN 0-440-94730-8, LFL). Dell.
—Night after Night. (gr. 6-12). 1986. pap. 2.25 (ISBN 0-440-96369-9, LFL). Dell.
—Smart Enough to Know. (Orig.). (gr. 7-12). 1984. pap. 2.25 (ISBN 0-440-98168-9, LFL). Dell.
Gould, Deborah. Brendan's Best-Timed Birthday. Rogers, Jacqueline, illus. LC 87-19886. 32p. (ps-1). 1988. 13.95 (ISBN 0-02-737390-8, Bradbury Pr). Macmillan Child Grp.
Gould, Marilyn. The Twelfth of June. LC 85-45173. 192p. (gr. 4-7). 1986. PLB 11.89 (ISBN 0-685-12399-5, Lipp Jr Bks); PLB 11.89 (ISBN 0-397-32131-7). HarpC Child Bks.
Graham, Bob. The Adventures of Charlotte & Henry. (ps-3). 1987. 10.95 (ISBN 0-670-81660-4). Viking Child Bks.
—Crusher Is Coming! (Illus.). 32p. (ps-3). 1990. pap. 3.95 (ISBN 0-14-050826-0, Puffin). Puffin Bks.

—Pete & Roland. (ps-3). 1988. pap. 3.95 (ISBN 0-318-32773-2, Puffin). Puffin Bks.

Grahame, Kenneth. Open Road. 1987. pap. 2.25 (ISBN 0-671-63626-X, Little Simon). S&S Trade.

—River Bank. 1987. pap. 2.25 (ISBN 0-671-63627-8, Little Simon). S&S Trade.

Grant, Cynthia D. Kumquat May, I'll Always Love You. (gr. 7-12). 1987. pap. 2.95 (ISBN 0-553-26416-8, Starfire). Bantam.

Greenberg, Jan. The Iceberg & Its Shadow. LC 80-20060. 132p. (gr. 7 up). 1980. 10.95 (ISBN 0-374-33624-5). FS&G.

Greenberg, Kenneth R. The Adventures of Tusky & His Friends: A Jungle Adventure. Pearson, Allison K., illus. 50p. (gr. k-4). 1991. PLB 13.95 (ISBN 1-879100-00-2). Tusky Enterprises.

Greene, Bette. Get on out of Here, Philip Hall. LC 79-50151. 160p. (gr. 3-6). 1981. 14.95 (ISBN 0-8037-2871-9); PLB 14.89 (ISBN 0-8037-2872-7). Dial Bks Young.

Greene, Constance C. A Girl Called Al. Barton, Byron, illus. (gr. 6-8). 1969. pap. 12.95 (ISBN 0-670-34153-3). Viking Child Bks.

—Isabelle & Little Orphan Frannie. 128p. (gr. 8-12). 1988. pap. 11.95 (ISBN 0-670-82266-3). Viking Child Bks.

—Your Old Pal, Al. 160p. (gr. k-6). 1981. pap. 2.95 (ISBN 0-440-49862-7, YB). Dell.

Greenfield, Eloise. Big Friend, Little Friend. Gilchrist, Jan S., illus. 12p. (ps-1). 1991. bds. 4.95 (ISBN 0-86316-204-5). Writers & Readers.

Greenwald, Sheila. The Atrocious Two. (Orig.). (gr. k-6). 1989. pap. 2.95 (ISBN 0-440-40141-0, YB). Dell.

Gregorich, Barbara. My Friend Goes Left. Hoffman, Joan, ed. John, Joyce, illus. 16p. (Orig.). (gr. k-2). 1984. pap. 1.95 (ISBN 0-88743-008-2, 06008). Sch Zone Pub Co.

Grimes, Francis H. Kiss & Tell. 160p. (Orig.). 1989. pap. 2.95 mass mrkt. (ISBN 1-55802-077-2). Lynx Bks.

Grove, Vicki. The Fastest Friend in the West. 176p. (gr. 4-8). 1990. 14.95 (ISBN 0-399-22184-0, Putnam). Putnam Pub Group.

Guy, Rosa. The Friends. LC 72-11068. 208p. (gr. 4 up). 1973. 10.95 (ISBN 0-03-007876-8). H Holt & Co.

—The Friends. (gr. 7-12). 1983. pap. 2.95 (ISBN 0-553-26519-9). Bantam.

Haas, Dorothy. New Friends. (gr. 1-4). 1988. pap. 2.75 (ISBN 0-590-41506-9, Apple Paperbacks). Scholastic Inc.

Hahn, Mary D. Tallahassee Higgins. 1988. pap. 2.95 (ISBN 0-380-70500-1, Camelot). Avon.

Hall, Lynn. The Giver. LC 86-23259. 128p. (gr. 7). 1987. pap. 3.95 (ISBN 0-02-043290-9, Collier Young Ad). Macmillan Child Grp.

Hallinan, P. K. That's What a Friend Is. Hallinan, P. K., illus. LC 76-27744. 32p. (gr. k-3). 1977. PLB 13.27 (ISBN 0-516-03628-9); pap. 3.95 (ISBN 0-516-43628-7). Childrens.

—We're Very Good Friends, My Brother & I. LC 72-8371. (Illus.). 32p. (gr. k-3). 1973. PLB 13.27 (ISBN 0-516-03659-9). Childrens.

—We're Very Good Friends, My Uncle & I. Hallinan, P. K., illus. LC 89-17264. 32p. (ps-3). 1989. PLB 13.27 (ISBN 0-516-03650-5). Childrens.

Halvorson, Marilyn. Let It Go. (gr. 5 up). 1988. pap. 2.95 (ISBN 0-440-20053-9, LFL). Dell.

Ham, Karri, et al. All Booked Up! Burris, Priscilla, illus. 64p. (Orig.). (gr. 4-8). 1986. pap. 6.95 (ISBN 0-933606-43-5, MS-642). Monkey Sisters.

Hamilton, Dorothy. Bittersweet Days. Graber, Esther R., illus. LC 77-18867. 128p. (gr. 4-8). 1978. pap. 3.95 (ISBN 0-8361-1846-4). Herald Pr.

—The Castle. Graber, Esther R., illus. LC 75-15599. 112p. (gr. 4-8). 1975. pap. 3.95 (ISBN 0-8361-1776-X). Herald Pr.

—Holly's New Year. Graber, Esther R., illus. LC 81-4098. 112p. (gr. 3-9). 1981. pap. 3.95 (ISBN 0-8361-1961-4). Herald Pr.

Hamilton, Virginia. The Planet of Junior Brown. Pinkney, Jerry, photos by. LC 85-16651. (Illus.). 224p. (gr. 5-9). 1986. pap. 3.95 (ISBN 0-02-043540-1, Collier Young Ad). Macmillan Child Grp.

—White Romance. 1989. pap. 3.95 (ISBN 0-15-295888-6). HarbraceJ.

Hammond, Elizabeth. My Rainbow Friends. Taylor, Neil, illus. LC 87-51495. 44p. (ps). 1989. 5.95 (ISBN 1-55523-023-7). Winston-Derek.

Hansen, Joyce. The Gift-Giver. LC 79-13812. 128p. (gr. 4-8). 1980. 13.95 (ISBN 0-395-29433-9, Clarion). HM.

—Yellow Bird & Me. LC 85-484. (gr. 3-7). 1986. 12.95 (ISBN 0-89919-335-8, Pub. by Clarion). Ticknor & Fields.

Harmey, Barbara E. I Used to Be Older. (ps-k). pap. 4.95 (ISBN 0-317-62508-X). St Martin.

—Once upon a Time. (ps-k). 4.95 (ISBN 0-317-62506-3). St Martin.

Harper, Anita. Just a Minute! Hellard, Susan, illus. (ps-1). 1987. 9.95 (ISBN 0-399-21461-5). Putnam Pub Group.

Harris, Emily. Hilary & Lars. LC 88-50753. 82p. (gr. 5-8). 1988. 6.95 (ISBN 1-55523-148-9). Winston-Derek.

Harwood, Pearl A. Mrs. Moon & Her Friends. Overlie, George, illus. LC 67-15688. 32p. (gr. k-3). 1967. PLB 4.95 (ISBN 0-8225-0112-0). Lerner Pubns.

Haskins, Francine. I Remember One Hundred Twenty-One. (Illus.). 32p. (gr. k-5). 1991. 13.95 (ISBN 0-89239-100-6). Childrens Book Pr.

Hassler, Jon. Jemmy. (gr. 5 up). 1988. pap. 3.50 (ISBN 0-449-70302-9, Juniper). Fawcett.

Hautzig, Deborah. It's Not Fair. Leigh, Tom, illus. LC 85-30154. 40p. (ps-3). 1986. 4.95 (ISBN 0-394-88151-6, Random Juv). Random.

—Why Are You So Mean to Me? Cooke, Tom, illus. LC 85-18434. 40p. (ps-3). 1986. 4.95 (ISBN 0-394-88060-9); lib. bdg. 6.99 (ISBN 0-394-98060-3). Random.

Havill, Juanita. Jamaica's Find. O'Brien, Anne S., illus. LC 85-14542. 32p. (gr. 4-8). 1987. pap. 4.95 (ISBN 0-395-45357-7). HM.

—Leona & Ike. McCully, Emily, illus. LC 90-40411. 128p. (gr. 2-6). 1991. 13.95 (ISBN 0-517-57687-2); PLB 14.99 (ISBN 0-517-57688-0). Crown.

Hawkins, Colin & Hawkins, Jacqui. When I Was One. (Illus.). 32p. (ps). 1990. pap. 11.95 (ISBN 0-670-81154-8). Viking Child Bks.

Hay, John. Rover & Coo Coo. Solliday, Tim, illus. 32p. (gr. 3-6). 1986. 12.95 (ISBN 0-88138-078-4). Green Tiger Pr.

Hayes, Sheila. You've Been Away All Summer. LC 85-30756. 160p. (gr. 4-7). 1986. 12.95 (ISBN 0-525-67182-X, Lodestar Bks). Dutton Child Bks.

Haynes, Betsy. The Boys Only Club. (gr. 4 up). 1990. pap. 2.95 (ISBN 0-553-15809-0). Bantam.

—The Bragging War. 120p. (gr. 5-7). 1989. pap. 2.75 (ISBN 0-553-15651-9). Bantam.

—Celebrity Auction. (gr. 4 up). 1990. pap. 2.75 (ISBN 0-553-15784-1). Bantam.

—Grade Me. (gr. 7). 1989. pap. 2.75 (ISBN 0-685-33584-4). Bantam.

—The Popularity Trap: The Fabulous Five, No. 3. (gr. 4-7). 1988. pap. 2.75 (ISBN 0-553-15634-9, Skylark). Bantam.

—Seventh-Grade Menace. (gr. 4 up). 1989. pap. 2.75 (ISBN 0-553-15763-9). Bantam.

—Taffy Sinclair & the Melanie Makeover. (gr. 2-6). 1988. pap. 2.75 (ISBN 0-553-15604-7, Skylark). Bantam.

—Taffy Sinclair & the Secret Admirer Epidemic. (gr. 2-6). 1988. pap. 2.50 (ISBN 0-553-15582-2, Skylark). Bantam.

—Taffy Sinclair, Baby Ashley, & Me. 128p. (gr. 4-7). 1988. pap. 2.50 (ISBN 0-553-15557-1, Skylark). Bantam.

Haywood, Carolyn. Eddie & His Big Deals. 190p. (gr. 3-7). 1990. Repr. of 1955 ed. 3.95 (ISBN 0-688-10075-9, Pub. by Beech Tree Bks). Morrow.

—Little Eddie. 160p. (gr. 3-7). 1990. Repr. of 1947 ed. 3.95 (ISBN 0-688-10074-0, Pub. by Beech Tree Bks). Morrow.

Henkes, Kevin. Chester's Way. LC 87-14882. (Illus.). 32p. (ps-3). 1988. 13.95 (ISBN 0-688-07607-6); lib. bdg. 13.88 (ISBN 0-688-07608-4). Greenwillow.

—Jessica. LC 87-38087. (Illus.). 24p. (gr. k up). 1989. 11.95 (ISBN 0-688-07829-X); PLB 11.88 (ISBN 0-688-07830-3). Greenwillow.

—A Weekend with Wendell. Henkes, Kevin, illus. LC 85-24822. 32p. (ps-3). 1986. 13.95 (ISBN 0-688-06325-X); PLB 13.88 (ISBN 0-688-06326-8). Greenwillow.

Herlihy, Dirlie. Ludie's Song. 224p. (gr. 4 up). 1990. pap. 3.95 (ISBN 0-14-034245-1, Puffin). Puffin Bks.

Hermes, Patricia. Friends Are Like That. 128p. (gr. 5-8). 1985. pap. 2.50 (ISBN 0-590-33558-8, Apple Paperbacks). Scholastic Inc.

—Friends Are Like That. 160p. (gr. 7-9). 1988. pap. 2.50 (ISBN 0-590-40757-0). Scholastic Inc.

—I Hate Being Gifted. 144p. 1990. 14.95 (ISBN 0-399-21687-1, Putnam). Putnam Pub Group.

Herz, Roger J. Claude Humphrey Dwickens: The Old Man with the Mustache. Aldworth, Susan, illus. 32p. (Orig.). (ps-6). 1988. pap. text ed. 3.95 (ISBN 0-9619560-0-3). TGNW Pr.

Hest, Amy. Pete & Lily. (gr. k-6). 1989. pap. 2.75 (ISBN 0-440-40145-3, YB). Dell.

Heuck, Sigrid. Pony & Bear Are Friends. Heuck, Sigrid, illus. LC 89-77711. 32p. (ps-1). 1990. 9.95 (ISBN 0-394-82311-7); PLB 10.99 (ISBN 0-394-92311-1). Knopf.

Hines, Anna G. Cassie Bowen Takes Witch Lessons. Owens, Gail, illus. LC 85-10302. (gr. 3-7). 1985. 11.95 (ISBN 0-525-44214-6, DCB). Dutton Child Bks.

Hinton, S. E. Rumble Fish. large type ed. 128p. (gr. 9-12). 1990. Repr. PLB 14.90 (ISBN 1-85089-996-7, Windbrush). ABC-CLIO.

Hinton, Susie E. That Was Then, This Is Now. (gr. 7 up). 15.50 (ISBN 0-8446-6371-9). Peter Smith.

Hirsch, Karen. Becky. Egenberger, Carl, illus. LC 80-27619. 40p. (gr. 1-4). 1981. PLB 7.95 (ISBN 0-87614-144-0). Carolrhoda Bks.

Hissey, Jane. Best Friends: More Old Bear Tales. Hissey, Jane, illus. 80p. (ps-3). 1989. 16.95 (ISBN 0-399-21674-X, Philomel Bks). Putnam Pub Group.

Hoban, Lillian. Arthur's Pen Pal. Hoban, Lillian, illus. LC 75-6289. 64p. (gr. k-3). 1976. PLB 11.89 (ISBN 0-06-022372-3). HarpC Child Bks.

—Arthur's Pen Pal. Hoban, Lillian, illus. 32p. (ps-2). Date not set. pap. 6.95 (ISBN 0-00-004236-6, Caedmon). HarperAudio.

Hoban, Russell. Best Friends for Frances. Hoban, Lillian, illus. LC 71-77935. (ps-2). 1976. pap. 4.95 (ISBN 0-06-443008-1, Trophy). HarpC Child Bks.

—The Rain Door. Blake, Quentin, illus. LC 86-47719. 32p. (ps-3). 1987. 11.95 (ISBN 0-690-04575-1, Crowell Jr Bks); PLB 11.89 (ISBN 0-690-04577-8). HarpC Child Bks.

Hockett, Betty M. Down a Winding Road. (Illus.). 80p. (gr. 3-8). 1985. pap. 3.50 (ISBN 0-943701-11-2). George Fox Pr.

—From Here to There & Back Again. Cammack, Phyllis, illus. LC 84-81034. 80p. (Orig.). (gr. 3-8). 1984. pap. 3.50 (ISBN 0-943701-09-0). George Fox Pr.

—Happiness under the Indian Trees. LC 86-81349. (Illus.). 80p. (gr. 3-8). 1986. pap. 3.50 (ISBN 0-943701-12-0). George Fox Pr.

—What Will Tomorrow Bring? LC 85-70504. (Illus.). 80p. (gr. 3-8). 1985. pap. 3.50 (ISBN 0-943701-10-4). George Fox Pr.

Hodgman, Ann. There's a Bat Wing in My Lunchbox. Pierard, John, illus. 96p. 1988. pap. 2.95 (ISBN 0-380-75426-6, Camelot). Avon.

Hoff, Syd. Who Will Be My Friends? Hoff, Syd, illus. 32p. (gr. k-2). 1960. PLB 10.89 (ISBN 0-06-022556-4). HarpC Child Bks.

Hoffman, Phyllis. Meatball. McCully, Emily A., illus. LC 89-49425. 32p. (ps-2). 1991. 14.95 (ISBN 0-06-022563-7); PLB 14.89 (ISBN 0-06-022564-5). HarpC Child Bks.

Hogan, Paula Z. I Hate Boys-I Hate Girls. Hockerman, Dennis, illus. McDonald, Paula & McDonald, Dickintro. by. LC 79-24056. (Illus.). 32p. (gr. k-6). 1980. PLB 16.67 (ISBN 0-8172-1358-9). Raintree Pubs.

Hoh, Diane. Funhouse. 1990. pap. 2.95 (ISBN 0-590-43050-5). Scholastic Inc.

Holabird, Katharine. Angelina & Alice. Craig, Helen, illus. (ps-2). 1988. 11.95 (ISBN 0-517-56074-7, C N Potter Bks). Crown.

Holcomb, Nan. Patrick & Emma Lou. Yoder, Dot, illus. 32p. (ps-2). 1989. pap. 5.95 (ISBN 0-944727-03-4). Jason & Nordic Pubs.

Hole, Dorothy. Real Friends. 144p. (Orig.). (gr. 5-8). 1988. pap. 1.95 (ISBN 0-87406-341-8). Willowisp Pr.

Holl, Kristi. Two of a Kind. Skivington, Janice, illus. 128p. (Orig.). (gr. 3-6). 1990. pap. 4.99 (ISBN 0-87403-748-4, 24-03968). Standard Pub.

Holl, Kristi D. First Things First. (gr. k-6). 1989. pap. 2.95 (ISBN 0-440-40147-X, YB). Dell.

Holland, Isabelle. Henry & Grudge. Guida, Liisa C., illus. 64p. (gr. 3-6). 1986. 10.95 (ISBN 0-8027-6611-0); lib. bdg. 10.85 (ISBN 0-8027-6612-9). Walker & Co.

—Now Is Not Too Late. 160p. (gr. 4 up). 1985. pap. 2.75 (ISBN 0-553-15548-2). Bantam.

Holmes, Barbara W. Charlotte the Starlet. Himmelman, John, illus. LC 87-11938. 128p. (gr. 3-6). 1989. pap. 2.95 (ISBN 0-06-440292-4, Trophy). HarpC Child Bks.

Honeycutt, Natalie. The All New Jonah Twist. LC 85-28048. 128p. (gr. 3-5). 1986. 10.95 (ISBN 0-02-744840-1, Bradbury Pr). Macmillan Child Grp.

—Invisible Lissa. 128p. (gr. 3-7). 1986. pap. 2.75 (ISBN 0-380-70120-0, Camelot). Avon.

Hopkins, Lee B., ed. Best Friends. Watts, James, illus. LC 85-45257. 48p. (gr. k-4). 1986. PLB 11.89 (ISBN 0-06-022562-9). HarpC Child Bks.

Howard, Milly. On Yonder Mountain. (Illus.). 127p. (Orig.). (gr. 1-6). 1989. pap. 5.50 (ISBN 0-89084-462-3). Bob Jones Univ Pr.

Howe, James. I Wish I Were a Butterfly. Young, Ed, illus. LC 86-33635. 40p. (ps-3). 1987. 14.95 (ISBN 0-15-200470-X, Gulliver Bks). HarBraceJ.

—A Night Without Stars. 192p. (gr. 7 up). 1985. pap. 2.95 (ISBN 0-380-69877-3, Flare). Avon.

—Pinky & Rex & the Spelling Bee. Sweet, Melissa, illus. LC 89-78305. 48p. (gr. k-3). 1991. SBE 11.95 (ISBN 0-689-31618-6, Atheneum Child Bk). Macmillan Child Grp.

—Pinky & Rex Got Married. Sweet, Melissa, illus. LC 89-30786. 48p. (gr. k-3). 1990. 11.95 (ISBN 0-689-31454-X, Atheneum Child Bk); 11.95 (ISBN 0-689-31453-1, Atheneum Childrens Bks). Macmillan Child Grp.

Howe, Norma. In With the Out Crowd. 208p. (gr. 7 up). 1986. 12.95 (ISBN 0-395-40490-8). HM.

Hughes, Dean. Lucky Breaks Loose. LC 90-30850. 136p. (Orig.). (gr. 3-6). 1990. pap. 4.95 (ISBN 0-87579-194-8). Deseret Bk.

—Lucky's Crash Landing. LC 90-30991. 160p. (Orig.). (gr. 3-6). 1990. pap. 4.95 (ISBN 0-87579-193-X). Deseret Bk.

—Nutty Can't Miss. LC 86-20556. 144p. (gr. 3-7). 1987. 12.95 (ISBN 0-689-31319-5, Atheneum Child Bk). Macmillan Child Grp.

—Nutty Can't Miss. 144p. (gr. 2-5). 1988. pap. 2.75 (ISBN 0-553-15584-9, Skylark). Bantam.

Hughes, Shirley. Alfie Gives a Hand. LC 83-14883. (Illus.). (ps-3). 1986. 4.95 (ISBN 0-688-06521-X, Mulberry). Morrow.

—Lucy & Tom's Day. Hughes, Shirley, illus. 32p. (ps-1). 1986. pap. 3.50 (ISBN 0-14-050068-5, Puffin). Puffin Bks.

—Moving Molly. Hughes, Shirley, illus. LC 87-34250. 32p. (ps-2). 1988. 11.95 (ISBN 0-688-07982-2); PLB 11.88 (ISBN 0-688-07984-9). Lothrop.

Hunt, Angela E. Cassie Perkins, No. 2: A Friend Forever. (gr. 4-7). 1991. pap. 3.95 (ISBN 0-8423-0462-2). Tyndale.

Hunt, Irene. No Promises in the Wind. 100p. 1987. pap. 2.75 (ISBN 0-425-09969-5, Pub. by Berkley-Pacer). Berkley Pub.

Hunt, Joyce. Four of Us & Victoria Chubb. (gr. 4-7). 1990. pap. 2.75 (ISBN 0-590-42976-0). Scholastic Inc.

Hurwitz, Johanna. Aldo Applesauce. Wallner, John, illus. LC 79-16200. 128p. (gr. 4-6). 1979. 12.95 (ISBN 0-688-22199-8); PLB 12.88 (ISBN 0-688-32199-2, Morrow Jr Bks). Morrow Jr Bks.

—Bunk Mates. (Illus.). (gr. k-9). 1988. pap. 2.50 (ISBN 0-318-36498-0). Scholastic Inc.

—Russell Rides Again. Hoban, Lillian, illus. LC 85-7287. 96p. (ps-2). 1985. 12.95 (ISBN 0-688-04628-2); lib. bdg. 12.88 (ISBN 0-688-04629-0, Morrow Jr Bks). Morrow Jr Bks.

—Teacher's Pet. Hamamaka, Sheila, illus. LC 87-24003. 128p. (gr. 2-5). 1988. 12.95 (ISBN 0-688-07506-1). Morrow Jr Bks.

In the Meadow, Unit 4. (gr. 1). 1991. 7.45 (ISBN 0-88106-728-8). Charlesbridge Pub.

In the Meadow Activity Book, Unit 4. (gr. 1). 1991. 3.90 (ISBN 0-88106-730-X). Charlesbridge Pub.

In the Meadow Activity Book (EV, Unit 4. (gr. 1). 1991. 3.90 (ISBN 0-88106-729-6). Charlesbridge Pub.

Irwin, Hadley. Kim-Kimi. LC 86-21416. 208p. (gr. 7 up). 1987. 13.95 (ISBN 0-689-50428-4, M K McElderry). Macmillan Child Grp.

—Moon & Me. LC 80-24052. 168p. (gr. 5-9). 1981. 13.95 (ISBN 0-689-50194-3, M K McElderry). Macmillan Child Grp.

Isadora, Rachel. Friends. LC 88-11753. (Illus.). (ps up). 1990. 13.95 (ISBN 0-688-08264-5); PLB 13.88 (ISBN 0-688-08265-3). Greenwillow.

Isele, Elizabeth. Pooks. Demarest, Chris L., illus. LC 82-48462. 32p. (ps-3). 1983. (Lipp Jr Bks); PLB 8.89g (ISBN 0-397-32045-0). HarpC Child Bks.

Jenkins-Pearce, Susie. Percy Short & Cuthbert. (ps-3). 1991. 12.95 (ISBN 0-670-82803-3). Viking Child Bks.

Johnson, Pete. Catch You on the Flip Side. 135p. (gr. 7-9). 1989. pap. 9.95 (ISBN 0-233-98074-1, Pub. by A Deutsch England). Trafalgar Sq.

Johnson, Ward. Ben's New Buddy. Cooke, Tom, illus. 40p. (ps-3). 1984. 5.95 (ISBN 0-910313-16-4). Parker Bros.

—A Koosa for the Kids. Yealdhall, Gary, illus. (ps-3). 1985. pap. 0.99 (ISBN 0-87372-007-5). Parker Bros.

Jones, Janice. Secrets of a Summer Spy. LC 89-38156. 192p. (gr. 5-9). 1990. 13.95 (ISBN 0-02-747861-0, Bradbury Pr). Macmillan Child Grp.

Jones, Linda K. Fear Strikes at Midnight. 128p. 1990. pap. 5.95 (ISBN 0-8361-3507-5). Herald Pr.

Jones, Rebecca C. Matthew & Tilly. Peck, Beth, illus. LC 90-3730. 32p. (ps-3). 1991. 13.95 (ISBN 0-525-44684-2, DCB). Dutton Child Bks.

Jones, Rhodri. Different Friends. 122p. (gr. 6-9). 1990. pap. 9.95 (ISBN 0-233-98096-2, Pub. by A Deutsch England). Trafalgar Sq.

Jones, Toeckey. Skindeep. LC 85-45843. 256p. (gr. 7 up). 1986. 12.95 (ISBN 0-06-023051-7); PLB 12.89 (ISBN 0-06-023052-5). HarpC Child Bks.

Jordan, P. D. Cooper Street. 147p. (Orig.). (gr. 5-12). 1989. pap. 4.25 (ISBN 0-929885-21-X). Haypenny Pr.

Jorgensen, Dan. Dawn's Diamond Defense. LC 87-11735. 1988. pap. 4.49 (ISBN 1-55513-062-3, Chariot Bks). Cook.

Jukes, Mavis. Getting Even. LC 87-25053. 160p. (gr. 4-7). 1988. 11.95 (ISBN 0-394-89594-0); lib. bdg. 12.99 (ISBN 0-394-99594-5). Knopf.

—Like Jake & Me. Bloom, Lloyd, illus. LC 83-8380. 32p. (gr. k up). 1984. 12.95 (ISBN 0-394-85608-2); PLB 13.99 (ISBN 0-394-95608-7). Knopf.

Kahaner, Ellen. Fourth Grade Loser. Henderson, David F., illus. LC 90-26791. 96p. (gr. 3-5). 1991. lib. bdg. 9.89 (ISBN 0-8167-2384-2); pap. text ed. 2.95 (ISBN 0-8167-2385-0). Troll Assocs.

Kaldhol, Marit. Goodbye Rune. Crosby-Jones, Michael, tr. from NOR. Yen, Wenche, illus. (NOR.). 32p. (ps-5). 1987. 12.95 (ISBN 0-916291-11-1). Kane-Miller Bk.

Kassem, Lou. Secret Wishes. 144p. (gr. 3-7). 1989. pap. 2.95 (ISBN 0-380-75544-0, Camelot). Avon.

Kastner, Erich. Lisa & Lottie. Books, Cyrus, tr. De Larrea, Victoria, illus. 136p. (gr. 3-7). 1982. pap. 2.95 (ISBN 0-380-57117-X, 60070-6, Camelot). Avon.

Katchen, Carole. Your Friend Annie. 1989. pap. 2.75 (ISBN 0-590-42732-6). Scholastic Inc.

Kaye, Marilyn. Cabin Six Plays Cupid. 128p. (Orig.). (ps-8). 1989. pap. 2.95 (ISBN 0-380-75701-X, Camelot). Avon.

—No Boys Allowed. 128p. (Orig.). (ps-8). 1989. pap. 2.95 (ISBN 0-380-75700-1, Camelot). Avon.

—Three of a Kind, No. 1: With Friends Like These, Who Needs Enemies. (gr. 4-7). 1990. pap. 3.50 (ISBN 0-06-106001-1, Harp PBks). HarperCollins.

—Three of a Kind, No. 4: Two's Company, Four's a Crowd. (gr. 4-7). 1991. pap. 3.50 (ISBN 0-06-106058-5, Harp PBks). HarperCollins.

—Three of a Kind, No. 5: Cat Morgan, Working Girl. (gr. 4-7). 1991. pap. 3.50 (ISBN 0-06-106059-3, Harp PBks). HarperCollins.

—Too Many Counselors. 128p. 1990. pap. 2.95 (ISBN 0-380-75913-6, Camelot). Avon.

—Will You Cross Me? Delaney, Ned, illus. LC 84-47633. 32p. (gr. k-3). 1985. PLB 10.89 (ISBN 0-06-023103-3). HarpC Child Bks.

Keats, Ezra J. Louie. Keats, Ezra J., illus. LC 75-6766. 32p. (gr. k-3). 1983. PLB 14.88 (ISBN 0-688-02383-5). Greenwillow.

—Maggie & the Pirate. Keats, Ezra J., illus. LC 85-29347. 32p. (gr. k-3). 1987. Repr. of 1979 ed. 13.95 (ISBN 0-02-749710-0, Four Winds). Macmillan Child Grp.

Keene, Carolyn. Between the Lines. 160p. (Orig.). (gr. 6 up). 1990. pap. 2.95 (ISBN 0-671-67763-2, Archway). PB.

Keller, Charles. Norma Lee I Don't Knock on Doors: Knock Knock Jokes. Galdone, Paul, illus. LC 82-21549. 44p. (gr. 3-7). 1983. 9.95 (ISBN 0-13-623587-5). P-H.

Kellogg, Steven. Best Friends. Kellogg, Steven, illus. LC 85-15971. 32p. (ps-3). 1986. 13.95 (ISBN 0-8037-0099-7); PLB 13.89 (ISBN 0-8037-0101-2). Dial Bks Young.

Kennedy, Elba Harness. Danny & Tommy Show & Tell. (Illus.). 89p. 1988. 6.95 (ISBN 0-533-07489-4). Vantage.

Kerr, M. E. Night Kites. LC 85-45386. 224p. (gr. 7 up). 1987. pap. 3.50 (ISBN 0-06-447035-0, Trophy). HarpC Child Bks.

Kherdian, David. Song in the Walnut Grove. Zelisky, Paul, illus. LC 82-6596. 112p. (gr. 3-7). 1982. lib. bdg. 8.99 (ISBN 0-394-95519-6). Knopf.

Kidd, Ronald. Dunker. 176p. (gr. 5 up). pap. 2.50 (ISBN 0-553-26431-1). Bantam.

Kiesel, Stanley. Skinny Malinky Leads the War for Kidness. 176p. (gr. 7 up). 1985. pap. 2.50 (ISBN 0-380-69875-7, Flare). Avon.

Killien, Christi. Putting on an Act. (gr. 5 up). 1986. 12.95 (ISBN 0-395-41027-4). HM.

King, Larry L. Because of Lozo Brown. (ps-3). 1990. pap. 3.95 (ISBN 0-14-050593-8, Puffin). Puffin Bks.

King-Smith, Dick. Harry's Mad. (gr. k-6). 1988. pap. 3.25 (ISBN 0-440-40112-7, YB). Dell.

Klass, Sheila S. The Bennington Stitch. 144p. (gr. 7-12). 1986. pap. 2.50 (ISBN 0-553-26049-9). Bantam.

—Page Four. 176p. 1988. pap. 2.95 (ISBN 0-553-26901-1, Starfire). Bantam.

Klaveness, Jan O. The Griffin Legacy. (gr. 4-6). 1985. pap. 3.25 (ISBN 0-440-43165-4, YB). Dell.

Klein, Norma. Just Friends. LC 89-11148. 192p. (gr. 7 up). 1990. 12.95 (ISBN 0-679-80213-4); PLB 13.99 (ISBN 0-679-90213-9). McKay.

—Just Friends. (gr. 7 up). 1990. 12.95. Knopf.

—Just Friends. 160p. 1991. pap. 3.95 (ISBN 0-449-70352-5, Juniper). Fawcett.

—Naomi in the Middle. Grant, Leigh, illus. LC 74-2878. 64p. (gr. 1-4). 1989. pap. 2.95 (ISBN 0-394-82307-9). Knopf.

—Now That I Know. LC 87-32080. 160p. (gr. 7 up). 1988. 13.95 (ISBN 0-553-05472-4). Bantam.

Klein, Robin. Enemies. Young, Noela, illus. LC 88-27318. 64p. (gr. 2-5). 1989. 11.95 (ISBN 0-525-44479-3, DCB). Dutton Child Bks.

Klevin, Jill R. The Best of Friends. 176p. (Orig.). (gr. 7 up). 1981. pap. 2.25 (ISBN 0-590-33782-3, Wildfire). Scholastic Inc.

Kline, Suzy. Horrible Harry in Room 2B. Remkiewicz, Frank, illus. 64p. (gr. 2-5). 1990. pap. 2.95 (ISBN 0-14-032825-4, Puffin). Puffin Bks.

—What's the Matter with Herbie Jones? Williams, Richard, illus. (gr. 2-6). 1986. 11.95 (ISBN 0-399-21315-5, Putnam). Putnam Pub Group.

Klingsheim, Trygve B. Julius. Jakobsen, Arild, illus. LC 87-6846. 64p. (ps-3). 1987. 11.95 (ISBN 0-385-29611-8). Delacorte.

Knaff, Jean C. Manhattan. Knaff, Jean C., illus. LC 89-2748. 32p. (ps-2). 1989. pap. 4.95 (ISBN 0-394-84780-6, Dragonfly Bks). Knopf.

Knorr, Dandi D. A Super Friend. Connelly, Gwen, illus. 32p. (gr. 1-3). 1987. 4.95 (ISBN 0-87403-316-0, 3546). Standard Pub.

Knowles, John. A Separate Peace. LC 60-5312. 186p. (gr. 7 up). 1987. 35.00 (ISBN 0-02-564850-0, Scribner). Macmillan.

Koenig, Glennis. Solution for Randy's Problem. 32p. 1990. 6.95 (ISBN 0-8062-3612-4). Carlton.

Kong, Emilie, illus. A Hug Is for Happiness. 12p. (ps). 1985. 2.65 (ISBN 0-317-18485-7). Parker Bros.

—One-Two-Three Hug. 12p. (ps). 1985. 2.65 (ISBN 0-910313-93-8). Parker Bros.

Konigsburg, E. L. George. 160p. (gr. k-6). 1985. pap. 3.25 (ISBN 0-440-42847-5, YB). Dell.

—Jennifer, Hecate, Macbeth, William McKinley & Me, Elizabeth. Konigsburg, E. L., illus. LC 67-10458. 128p. (gr. 3-5). 1971. 12.95 (ISBN 0-689-30007-7, Atheneum Child Bk). Macmillan Child Grp.

—Jennifer, Hecate, Macbeth, William McKinley & Me, Elizabeth. 128p. (gr. 3-6). 1985. pap. 3.25 (ISBN 0-440-44162-5, YB). Dell.

—A Proud Taste for Scarlet & Miniver. 208p. (gr. 5-8). 1985. pap. 3.25 (ISBN 0-440-47201-6, YB). Dell.

Korman, Gordon. Our Man Weston. 240p. (gr. 4-6). 1986. pap. 2.50 (ISBN 0-590-41848-3, Apple Paperbacks). Scholastic Inc.

—The War with Mr. Wizzle. 192p. (gr. 3-7). 1990. pap. 2.75 (ISBN 0-590-44206-6). Scholastic Inc.

Korth-Sander, Irmtraut. Will You Be My Friend? Korth-Sander, Irmtraut, illus. Lanning, Rosemary, tr. from GER. LC 86-60485. (Illus.). 32p. (gr. k-2). 1986. 13.95 (ISBN 1-55858-071-9). North-South Bks NYC.

Kraus, Robert. Three Friends. Arvego, Jose & Dewey, Ariane, illus. (gr. k-3). 1975. (Dutton); pap. 2.95 (ISBN 0-525-62346-9). NAL-Dutton.

Krensky, Stephan. Scoop after Scoop: A History of Ice Cream. Rosenblum, Richard, illus. LC 86-3597. 56p. (gr. 4-7). 1986. 12.95 (ISBN 0-689-31276-8, Atheneum Child Bk). Macmillan Child Grp.

Kropp, Paul. Getting Even. 192p. 1986. pap. 3.50 (ISBN 0-7704-2112-1). Bantam.

Krull, Kathleen. Alex Fitzgerald, TV Star. (ps-3). 1991. 10.95 (ISBN 0-316-50479-3). Little.

Krumgold, Joseph. Onion John. Shimin, Symeon, illus. LC 59-11395. 248p. (gr. 5 up). 1987. 13.95 (ISBN 0-690-59957-9, Crowell Jr Bks); PLB 13.89 (ISBN 0-690-04698-7, Crowell Jr Bks). HarpC Child Bks.

Kuskin, Karla. Just Like Everyone Else. LC 59-5320. (Illus.). 32p. (ps-3). 1982. pap. 2.95 (ISBN 0-06-443032-4, Trophy). HarpC Child Bks.

Lager, Claude. Jeanette & Josie. Dubois, Claude K., illus. 32p. (ps-3). 1989. pap. 12.95 (ISBN 0-670-82657-X). Viking Child Bks.

Laird, Elizabeth. The Miracle Child. Gabriel, Abba A. W., illus. LC 85-45374. 32p. (gr. 2-4). 1985. 12.95. H Holt & Co.

Landis, James D. Joey & the Girls. 192p. (Orig.). (gr. 7-12). 1987. pap. 2.95 (ISBN 0-553-26415-X, Starfire). Bantam.

Lantz, Fran. Making It on Our Own. (gr. 6-12). 1986. pap. 2.75 (ISBN 0-440-95202-6, LFL). Dell.

Lasky, Kathryn. Home Free. (gr. 7 up). 1988. pap. 2.95 (ISBN 0-440-20038-5, LFL). Dell.

Lawlor, Laurie. Addie's Dakota Winter. Tucker, Kathy, ed. Gowing, Toby, tr. (Illus.). 160p. (gr. 2-6). 1989. PLB 10.50 (ISBN 0-8075-0171-9). A Whitman.

—How To Survive Third Grade. Levine, Abby, ed. (Illus.). 72p. (gr. 2-5). 1988. PLB 8.95 (ISBN 0-8075-3433-1). A Whitman.

L'Engle, Madeleine. And Both Were Young. (Orig.). (gr. 7 up). 1983. pap. 3.50 (ISBN 0-440-90229-0, LFL). Dell.

—And Both Were Young. LC 82-72751. 240p. (gr. 7 up). 1983. 14.95 (ISBN 0-385-29237-6). Delacorte.

Leppard, Lois G. Mandie & the Charleston Phantom, Bk. 7. LC 86-7098. 128p. (Orig.). (gr. 4-7). 1986. pap. 3.95 (ISBN 0-87123-650-8). Bethany Hse.

Lester, Helen. The Wizard, the Fairy, & the Magic Chicken. Munsinger, Lynn, illus. LC 82-21302. 32p. (gr. k-3). 1988. pap. 4.95 (ISBN 0-395-47945-2). HM.

Levene, Nancy. Cherry Cola Champions. LC 88-12294. (Illus.). 120p. (gr. 3-7). 1988. pap. 4.49 (ISBN 1-55513-519-6, Chariot Bks). Cook.

Levene, Nancy S. Mint Cookie Miracles. LC 88-11902. 120p. (gr. 3-7). 1988. pap. 4.49 (ISBN 1-55513-514-5, Chariot Bks). Cook.

Leverich, Kathleen. Best Enemies. Lamb, Susan C., illus. LC 88-19150. (gr. 1 up). 1989. 10.95 (ISBN 0-688-08316-1). Greenwillow.

—Best Enemies Again. Lorraine, Walter, illus. LC 90-30303. 96p. (gr. 2 up). 1991. 13.95 (ISBN 0-688-09440-6). Greenwillow.

Levinson, Marilyn. The Fourth-Grade Four. Bowman, Leslie, illus. LC 89-31109. 80p. (gr. 2-4). 1989. 12.95 (ISBN 0-8050-1082-3). H Holt & Co.

Levitin, Sonia. A Season for Unicorns. LC 85-20051. 204p. (gr. 5-9). 1986. 13.95 (ISBN 0-689-31113-3, Atheneum Child Bk). Macmillan Child Grp.

Levoy, Myron. Alan & Naomi. LC 76-41522. 176p. (gr. 6 up). 1977. PLB 12.89. (ISBN 0-06-023800-3). HarpC Child Bks.

—Alan & Naomi. LC 76-41522. 176p. (gr. 6 up). 1987. pap. 3.50 (ISBN 0-06-440209-6, Trophy). HarpC Child Bks.

—Three Friends. LC 83-47713. 192p. (gr. 7 up). 1984. 12.95 (ISBN 0-06-023826-7). HarpC Child Bks.

Levy, Elizabeth. Something Queer at the Birthday Party. 1990. 12.95 (ISBN 0-385-29973-7). Doubleday.

Levy, Marilyn. No Way Home. 160p. 1990. pap. 3.95 (ISBN 0-449-70326-6, Juniper). Fawcett.

—Remember to Remember Me. (gr. 5 up). 1988. pap. 2.95 (ISBN 0-449-70278-2, Juniper). Fawcett.

Lewis, Harriet. Pampoody & Max. 72p. 1977. pap. 4.50 (ISBN 0-933294-01-8). Backroads.

Lexau, Joan. Striped Ice Cream. LC 68-10774. (Illus.). 96p. (gr. k-3). 1968. PLB 12.89 (ISBN 0-397-31047-1, Lipp Jr Bks). HarpC Child Bks.

Lichtman, Wendy. Telling Secrets. LC 85-45271. 256p. (gr. 7 up). 1986. PLB 13.89 (ISBN 0-06-023885-2). HarpC Child Bks.

Lieberman, Lillian. Comprehension. 64p. (gr. 2-5). 1987. 6.95 (ISBN 0-912107-66-9). Monday Morning Bks.

Lillie, Patricia. Jake & Rosie. LC 87-14939. (Illus.). 24p. (ps up). 1989. 11.95 (ISBN 0-688-07624-6); PLB 11.88 (ISBN 0-688-07625-4). Greenwillow.

Lindberg, Anne. The Worry Week. (gr. 3-7). 1988. pap. 2.95 (ISBN 0-380-70394-7, Camelot). Avon.

Lindbergh, Anne M. The Worry Week. Hewitt, Kathryn, illus. LC 84-19299. 131p. (gr. 3-6). 1985. 12.95 (ISBN 0-15-299675-3, HJ). HarBraceJ.

Lindbergh, Anne M. & Hoguet, Susan. Next Time, Take Care. (Illus.). 32p. (ps-3). 1988. 13.95 (ISBN 0-15-257200-7, HJ). HarBraceJ.

Lindquist, Marie. Untamed Heart. 160p. (Orig.). (gr. 7-12). 1987. pap. 2.50 (ISBN 0-553-26474-5, Starfire). Bantam.

Lindroos, Marianne. Engine People. (Illus.). 32p. (gr. 3-5). 1989. 4.25 (ISBN 0-901269-54-9). Grosvenor USA.

Lionni, Leo. It's Mine. Lionni, Leo, illus. LC 85-190. 32p. (ps-1). 1986. 15.00 (ISBN 0-394-87000-X); lib. bdg. 15.99 (ISBN 0-394-97000-4). Knopf.

—Swimmy. LC 63-8504. (Illus.). 32p. (ps-6). 1987. pap. 2.95 (ISBN 0-317-53621-4). Knopf.

Little, Jean. Kate. LC 70-148419. 174p. (gr. 5-8). 1971. PLB 12.89 (ISBN 0-06-023914-X). HarpC Child Bks.

—Kate. LC 20-148419. 174p. (gr. 5-8). 1973. pap. 3.95 (ISBN 0-06-440037-9, Trophy). HarpC Child Bks.

—Look Through My Window. Sandin, Joan, illus. LC 71-105470. 270p. (gr. 4-7). 1970. PLB 13.89 (ISBN 0-06-023924-7). HarpC Child Bks.

Lobe, Mira. Ben & the Child of the Forest. Sklenitzka, Franz S., illus. 96p. (gr. 3-4). 1988. pap. 2.95 (ISBN 0-8120-3936-X). Barron.

Lobel, Arnold. Days with Frog & Toad. LC 78-21786. (Illus.). 64p. (gr. k-3). 1979. 11.95i (ISBN 0-06-023963-8); PLB 11.89 (ISBN 0-06-023964-6). HarpC Child Bks.

—Dias con Sapo y Sepo. (SPA.). (gr. 1-6). 8.95 (ISBN 84-204-3743-3). Santillana.

Lomasney, Eileen. What Do You Do with the Rest of the Day, Mary Ann? 1991. pap. 3.95 (ISBN 0-8091-6601-1). Paulist Pr.

Long, Kathy. A Surprise for Mrs. Dodds: A Little Boy's Friendship Changes a Lonely Woman's Life. Rogers, Kathy, illus. LC 89-84939. 32p. (gr. 3-5). 1989. pap. 4.95 (ISBN 0-8066-2437-X, 9-2437). Augsburg Fortress.

Lovelace, Maud H. Betsy & Tacy Go Downtown. LC 43-51264. (Illus.). (gr. 3-6). 1979. pap. 2.95 (ISBN 0-06-440098-0, Trophy). HarpC Child Bks.

—Betsy & Tacy Go over the Big Hill. Lenski, Lois, illus. LC 42-23557. (gr. 3-6). 1979. pap. 2.95 (ISBN 0-06-440099-9, Trophy). HarpC Child Bks.

—Betsy-Tacy. LC 40-30965. (Illus.). (gr. 2-5). 1979. pap. 2.95 (ISBN 0-06-440096-4, Trophy). HarpC Child Bks.

—Betsy-Tacy & Tib. Lenski, Lois, illus. LC 41-18714. (gr. 2-5). 1979. pap. 3.50 (ISBN 0-06-440097-2, Trophy). HarpC Child Bks.

—Betsy-Tacy Books, 6 vols. (gr. 4-6). 1981. Boxed Set. pap. 12.95 (ISBN 0-06-440127-8, Trophy). HarpC Child Bks.

Lowry, Lois. Find a Stranger, Say Good-Bye. LC 78-1024. 192p. (gr. 5 up). 1978. 14.95 (ISBN 0-395-26459-6). HM.

—Switcharound. (gr. k-6). 1991. pap. 3.50 (ISBN 0-440-48415-4, YB). Dell.

Lund, Doris. Eric. 268p. (gr. 7 up). 1979. pap. 2.95 (ISBN 0-440-94586-0, LFL). Dell.

Lustig, Blanche. Morris, Boris, & ?? 1988. 5.95 (ISBN 0-533-07958-6). Vantage.

Lustig, Loretta, illus. Skip to My Lou. 1989. bk. & cassette 5.95 (ISBN 0-553-45908-2). Bantam.

Luttrell, Ida. Lonesome Lester. Lloyd, Megan, illus. LC 83-47701. 48p. (gr. k-3). 1984. PLB 12.89 (ISBN 0-06-024030-X). HarpC Child Bks.

—Tillie & Mert. Cushman, Doug, illus. LC 85-42641. 64p. (gr. k-3). 1985. PLB 11.89 (ISBN 0-06-024028-8). HarpC Child Bks.

Luttrell, Jean. Winning Isn't Everything. Luttrell, Chuck, illus. 76p. (Orig.). (gr. 3-5). 1990. pap. 6.95 (ISBN 0-9617609-2-3). Shade Tree NV.

Lyon, George E. A Regular Rolling Noah. Grammell, Stephen, illus. LC 86-8312. 32p. (ps-2). 1986. 13.95 (ISBN 0-02-761330-5, Bradbury Pr). Macmillan Child Grp.

McBrier, Page. First Course: Trouble. 128p. 1990. pap. 2.50 (ISBN 0-380-75783-4, Camelot). Avon.

—Rats. 128p. 1990. pap. 2.95 (ISBN 0-380-75901-2, Camelot). Avon.

McConnell, Christine. Don't Be Mad, Ivy. De Groat, Diane, photos by. (gr. 2-5). 1988. pap. 3.95 (ISBN 0-14-032329-5, Puffin). Puffin Bks.

McCusker, Paul. The Secret Cave of Robinwood: An Adventure in Odyssey. Craig, Sheila, ed. Loccisano, Karen, illus. 85p. (Orig.). (gr. 3-6). 1991. pap. 3.99 (ISBN 1-56179-023-0). Focus Family.

McDaniel, Lurlene. Goodbye Doesn't Mean Forever. (gr. 7 up). 1989. pap. 2.95 (ISBN 0-553-28007-4, Starfire). Bantam.

—I Want to Live. 128p. (gr. 5-8). 1987. 1.50 (ISBN 0-87406-237-3). Willowisp Pr.

—Three's a Crowd. 128p. (Orig.). (gr. 6-8). 1987. pap. 2.50 (ISBN 0-87406-274-8). Willowisp Pr.

MacDonald, Betty. Mrs. Piggle-Wiggle, 4 vols. 1986. Boxed Set. pap. 11.80 (ISBN 0-06-440152-9, Trophy). HarpC Child Bks.

MacDonald, George. Alec Forbes & His Friend Annie. Phillips, Michael R., ed. 256p. (gr. 2-7). 1990. 9.95 (ISBN 1-55661-140-4). Bethany Hse.

—The Peasant Girl's Dream. rev. ed. Phillips, Michael R., ed. LC 88-33336. 224p. (gr. 11 up). 1989. pap. 6.95 (ISBN 1-55661-023-8). Bethany Hse.

Macdonald, Mary A. Hedgehog Bakes a Cake - Bank Street. (ps-3). 1990. 9.99 (ISBN 0-553-05872-X). Bantam.

—Hedgehog Bakes a Cake - Bank Street. (ps-3). 1990. pap. 3.50 (ISBN 0-553-34890-6). Bantam.

McDonnell, Christine. Don't Be Mad, Ivy. DeGroat, Diane, illus. LC 81-65850. 80p. (gr. 1-5). 1981. PLB 8.89 (ISBN 0-8037-2128-5). Dial Bks Young.

—Just for the Summer. De Groat, Diane, illus. 128p. (gr. 2-6). 1989. pap. 3.95 (ISBN 0-14-032147-0, Puffin). Puffin Bks.

McDonnell, Margot B. My Own Worst Enemy. LC 84-7722. 192p. (gr. 7 up). 1984. 11.95 (ISBN 0-399-21102-0, Putnam). Putnam Pub Group.

McHargue, Georgess. See You Later, Crocodile. 192p. (gr. 5-9). 1988. 14.95 (ISBN 0-440-50052-4). Delacorte.

MacKeen, Leslie A. Who Can Fix It? Thatch, Nancy R., ed. MacKeen, Leslie A., illus. Melton, David, intro. by. LC 89-31819. (Illus.). 26p. (gr. k-3). 1989. lib. bdg. 12.95 (ISBN 0-933849-19-2). Landmark Edns.

Maclean, Moira. There Was an Old Woman. 1990. 9.95 (ISBN 0-385-41224-X). Doubleday.

Mclerran, Alice. Secrets. 128p. 1990. 12.95 (ISBN 0-688-09545-3). Lothrop.

McMullan, Kate. Great Advice from Lila Fenwick. De Groat, Diane, illus. 176p. (gr. 5-9). 1989. pap. 3.95 (ISBN 0-14-034086-6, Puffin). Puffin Bks.

—The Great Ideas of Lila Fenwick. DeGroat, Diane, illus. LC 85-29348. 128p. (gr. 3-7). 1986. 11.95 (ISBN 0-8037-0316-3); PLB 11.89 (ISBN 0-8037-0317-1). Dial Bks Young.

McNamara, John. Revenge of the Nerd. 128p. (gr. 5 up). 1985. pap. 2.50 (ISBN 0-440-97353-8, LFL). Dell.

Magorian, Michelle. Back Home. LC 84-47629. 352p. (gr. 7 up). 1984. 14.95 (ISBN 0-685-08449-3); PLB 14.89 (ISBN 0-06-024104-7). HarpC Child Bks.

—Good Night, Mr. Tom. LC 80-8444. 336p. (gr. 5-9). 1986. pap. 3.95 (ISBN 0-06-440174-X, Trophy). HarpC Child Bks.

Mahy, Margaret. Memory. (gr. k-12). 1989. pap. 3.25 (ISBN 0-440-20433-X, LFL). Dell.

—The Tricksters. LC 86-33761. 272p. (gr. 9 up). 1987. 14.95 (ISBN 0-689-50400-4, M K McElderry). Macmillan Child Grp.

Major, Kevin. Hold Fast. LC 79-17544. (gr. 9-12). 1980. 9.95 (ISBN 0-440-03506-6). Delacorte.

Maloney, Ray. The Impact Zone. (gr. k-12). 1987. pap. 2.95 (ISBN 0-440-94013-3, LFL). Dell.

Mango, Karin M. Just for the Summer. LC 89-36568. 208p. (gr. 7 up). 1990. 13.95 (ISBN 0-06-024038-5); PLB 13.89 (ISBN 0-06-024039-3). HarpC Child Bks.

Mark, Jan. Handles. LC 84-20467. 160p. (gr. 5-9). 1985. 13.95 (ISBN 0-689-31140-0, Atheneum Child Bk). Macmillan Child Grp.

Markus, Julia. Friends along the Way. (gr. k-12). 1987. pap. 4.95 (ISBN 0-440-32761-X, LE). Dell.

Marney, Dean. You, Me, & Gracie Makes Three. (gr. 6-8). 1989. pap. 2.50 (ISBN 0-590-41637-5, Apple Paperbacks). Scholastic Inc.

—You, Me, & Gracie Makes Three. 144p. (Orig.). (gr. 6-8). 1989. pap. 2.75 (ISBN 0-590-43996-0). Scholastic Inc.

Marshall, Anthony D. Basti. Weinberger, Jane, ed. LC 87-51167. (Illus.). 78p. (gr. 5 up). 1987. pap. 5.95 (ISBN 0-932433-37-5). Windswept Hse.

Marshall, Edward. Fox All Week. Marshall, James, illus. LC 84-1708. (ps-3). 1984. 8.95 (ISBN 0-8037-0062-8); PLB 8.89 (ISBN 0-8037-0066-0). Dial Bks Young.

Marshall, James. The Cut-ups Cut Loose. (Illus.). 32p. (ps-3). 1989. pap. 3.95 (ISBN 0-14-050672-1, Puffin). Puffin Bks.

—George & Martha Tons of Fun. (Illus.). 48p. (gr. k-3). 1986. 13.95 (ISBN 0-395-29524-6); pap. 3.95 (ISBN 0-395-42646-4). HM.

Martinez, Carol. Paco y Ana Aprenden Acerca de la Amistad. Stillman, Peter, illus. (SPA., Orig.). (gr. 2-4). 1988. pap. 1.50 (ISBN 0-311-38589-3, Edit Mundo). Casa Bautista.

Marzollo, Jean. Best Friends Club. 1990. pap. 2.50 (ISBN 0-590-42726-1). Scholastic Inc.

Mason, Margo. Two Good Friends. (ps-3). 1990. 9.99 (ISBN 0-553-05869-X). Bantam.

—Two Good Friends. (ps-3). 1990. pap. 3.50 (ISBN 0-553-34885-X). Bantam.

Massi, Jeri. Abandoned. 136p. (Orig.). (gr. 5-8). 1989. pap. 4.95 (ISBN 0-89084-467-4). Bob Jones Univ Pr.

Masterson, Audrey. The Day the Gypsies Came to Town. Oudekerk, Douglas, illus. LC 83-7319. 32p. (gr. 3-6). 1983. PLB 14.65 (ISBN 0-940742-22-5). Raintree Pubs.

Mathis, Sharon B. Sidewalk Story. 64p. (gr. 2-6). 1986. pap. 3.95 (ISBN 0-14-032165-9, Puffin). Puffin Bks.

Matranga, Frances C. One Step at a Time. (Illus.). (gr. 4-7). 1987. pap. 3.95 (ISBN 0-570-03642-9, 39-1126). Concordia.

Matthews, Phoebe. Switchstance. 176p. (Orig.). (gr. 7 up). 1989. pap. 2.95 (ISBN 0-380-75729-X, Flare). Avon.

Mayer, Mercer. This Is My Friend. (Illus.). 40p. (gr. k-2). 1989. write for info. (ISBN 0-307-11685-9, Pub. by Golden Bks). Western Pub.

Mayne, William. The Blue Book of Hob Stories. Benson, Patrick, illus. 32p. (ps-k). 1984. 7.95 (ISBN 0-399-21037-7, Philomel). Putnam Pub Group.

—A House in Town. Fox-Davies, Sarah, illus. 32p. (ps-3). 1988. 9.95 (ISBN 0-13-395880-9, Little Simon). S&S Trade.

Mazer, Harry. When the Phone Rang. 192p. (gr. 7 up). 1991. pap. 2.95 (ISBN 0-590-44773-4). Scholastic Inc.

Mazer, Norma. C, My Name Is Cal. (gr. 4-7). 1990. 13. 95 (ISBN 0-590-41833-5). Scholastic Inc.

Mazer, Norma F. A, My Name Is Ami. 160p. (Orig.). (gr. 3-7). 1991. pap. 2.95 (ISBN 0-590-43896-4, Apple Paperbacks). Scholastic Inc.

—Silver. LC 88-18652. 272p. (gr. 7 up). 1988. 12.95 (ISBN 0-688-06865-0). Morrow Jr Bks.

Mazer, Norma F. & Mazer, Harry. Heartbeat. 1989. 14. 95 (ISBN 0-553-05808-8, Starfire). Bantam.

Mebs, Gudren. Sunday's Child. (gr. k-6). 1989. pap. 2.95 (ISBN 0-440-40167-4, YB). Dell.

Merriam, Eve. Blackberry Ink. Wilhelm, Hans, illus. LC 84-16633. 40p. (ps-2). 1985. 12.95 (ISBN 0-688-04150-7); PLB 12.88 (ISBN 0-688-04151-5, Morrow Jr Bks). Morrow Jr Bks.

—Jamboree. 96p. (Orig.). (ps-6). 1984. pap. 2.50 (ISBN 0-440-44199-4, YB). Dell.

Michaels, Scott, ed. Freddy & Betty, Vol. 1. Morton, Tom, illus. (gr. 1-6). Date not set. tchr's. ed. 2.50 (ISBN 0-317-93682-4). S Michaels Pub.

Miles, Betty. I Would If I Could. 120p. (gr. 3-6). 1983. pap. 2.95 (ISBN 0-380-63438-4, 60067-5, Camelot). Avon.

—Maudie & Me & the Dirty Book. 140p. (gr. 4-7). 1981. pap. 2.95 (ISBN 0-380-55541-7, Camelot). Avon.

—Maudie & Me & the Dirty Book. LC 79-19783. 144p. (gr. 4-7). 1989. pap. 2.95 (ISBN 0-394-82595-0, Bullseye Bks). Knopf.

—The Trouble with Thirteen. LC 78-31678. (gr. 4-7). 1979. 6.95 (ISBN 0-394-83930-7); PLB 12.99 (ISBN 0-394-93930-1). Knopf.

Miller, Julano. Life Line Series, 5 in 1 set. (Illus.). 48p. 1985. Set. pap. 15.00 (ISBN 0-87879-484-0, High Noon Books). Acad Therapy.

Mills, Claudia. Hannah on Her Way. 160p. (gr. 3-7). 1991. SBE 12.95 (ISBN 0-02-767011-2, Mcmillan Child Bk). Macmillan Child Grp.

Millward, David W. Jenny & Bob. (ps). 1991. 15.00 (ISBN 0-385-30431-5). Delacorte.

Modrell, Dolores. Tales of Tiddly. Eagle, Ellen, illus. 48p. (ps-1). 1990. PLB 13.95 (ISBN 0-671-69204-6). S&S Trade.

Mogensen, Jan. Teddy's Christmas Gift. LC 82-26095. (Illus.). 32p. (gr. 3-4). 1985. PLB 11.95 (ISBN 1-55532-004-X). Gareth Stevens Inc.

Moncure, Jane B. My Baby Brother Needs a Friend. Hook, Frances, illus. LC 78-21935. (ps-3). 1979. PLB 12.96 (ISBN 0-89565-019-3). Childs World.

Montgomery, L. M. Rainbow Valley. 240p. (gr. 6 up). 1985. pap. 2.95 (ISBN 0-553-25213-5). Bantam.

Moore, Emily. Just My Luck. 112p. (gr. 4-7). 1983. 10.95 (ISBN 0-525-44009-7, Dutton). NAL-Dutton.

Moore, Lilian. I'll Meet You at the Cucumbers. Wooding, Sharon, illus. (gr. 1-4). 1989. pap. 2.75 (ISBN 0-553-15705-1, Skylark). Bantam.

Morgan & Yew. Cosgrove, Stephen. 32p. (gr. 1-6). 1982. pap. 2.95 (ISBN 0-8431-0589-5). Price Stern.

Morgenstern, Susie S. It's Not Fair. Abrams, Kathie, photos by & illus. LC 83-81535. 100p. (gr. 4 up). 1983. 10.95 (ISBN 0-374-33649-0). FS&G.

Morris, Carroll H. Saddle Shoe Blues. LC 87-595. 168p. 1987. 9.95 (ISBN 0-87579-077-1). Deseret Bk.

Morrison, Dorothy N. Whisper Goodbye. 192p. (gr. 2-9). pap. 2.95 (ISBN 0-8167-1045-7). Troll Assocs.

Mulford, Philippa G. If It's Not Funny, Why Am I Laughing? LC 82-70321. 144p. (gr. 7 up). 1982. 9.95 (ISBN 0-440-03961-4). Delacorte.

—The World Is My Eggshell. (gr. k-12). 1989. pap. 2.95 (ISBN 0-440-20243-4, LFL). Dell.

Munro, Roxie. Blimps. Munro, Roxie, illus. 32p. (gr. 2-5). 1988. 12.95 (ISBN 0-525-44441-6, DCB). Dutton Child Bks.

Murphy, Elspeth C. Curtis Anderson. Kenyon, Tony, illus. LC 86-8819. 120p. (gr. 3-5). 1986. pap. 3.95 (ISBN 1-55513-027-5). Cook.

—Danny Petrowski. LC 85-15568. 120p. (Orig.). (gr. 3-5). pap. 3.95 (ISBN 0-89191-730-6). Cook.

—The Littlest One. LC 87-7106. (ps-k). 1987. 3.95 (ISBN 1-55513-268-5, Chariot Bks). Cook.

—Mary Jo Bennett. 107p. (Orig.). (gr. 3-5). 1985. pap. 3.95 (ISBN 0-89191-711-X, 57117). Cook.

—Too Many Bunnies. LC 87-70609. 1988. pap. 3.95 (ISBN 1-55513-247-2, Chariot Bks). Cook.

Murray, Marguerite. Like Seabirds Flying Home. LC 88-4396. 192p. 1988. 13.95 (ISBN 0-689-31459-0, Atheneum Child Bk). Macmillan Child Grp.

Myers, Bill & Johnson, Ken. McGee & Me! No. 2: Star in the Breaking. 1989. pap. 3.95 (ISBN 0-8423-4168-4); video 19.95 (ISBN 0-8423-4153-6). Tyndale.

—McGee & Me! No. 4: Skate Expectations. 1989. pap. 3.95 (ISBN 0-8423-4165-X); video 19.95 (ISBN 0-8423-4155-2). Tyndale.

—McGee & Me: The Big Lie. 1989. pap. 3.95 (ISBN 0-8423-4169-2). Tyndale.

Myers, Walter D. Fast Sam, Cool Clyde, & Stuff. LC 74-32383. 192p. (gr. 7 up). 1975. pap. 12.95 (ISBN 0-670-30874-9). Viking Child Bks.

—Motown & Didi. (gr. k-12). 1987. pap. 3.50 (ISBN 0-440-95762-1, LFL). Dell.

Naylor, Phyllis R. The Agony of Alice. LC 85-7957. 144p. (gr. 4-9). 1985. 12.95 (ISBN 0-689-31143-5, Atheneum Child Bk). Macmillan Child Grp.

—A String of Chances. LC 82-1790. 252p. (gr. 6 up). 1982. 11.95 (ISBN 0-689-30935-X, Atheneum Childrens Bks). Macmillan Child Grp.

Neighborhood Friends. (Illus.). 64p. (gr. k-1). 1984. pap. 1.25 (ISBN 0-448-16137-0, G&D); pap. 30.00 set of 24 (ISBN 0-448-81730-6, G&D). Putnam Pub Group.

Nelson, Theresa. And One for All. (gr. 4-7). 1991. pap. 3.50 (ISBN 0-440-40456-8). Dell.

Neville, Emily C. It's Like This, Cat. Weiss, Emil, illus. LC 62-21292. 192p. (gr. 5-9). 1964. 12.95 (ISBN 0-06-024390-2); PLB 14.89 (ISBN 0-06-024391-0). HarpC Child Bks.

Nimeth, Albert J. I Like You, Just Because. LC 79-139971. (Illus.). (gr. 5 up). 1971. 5.00 (ISBN 0-8199-0422-8). Franciscan Herald.

Nister, Ernest. Special Days. Nister, Ernest, illus. (gr. k up). 1989. 4.95 (ISBN 0-399-21694-4, Philomel Bks). Putnam Pub Group.

Nixon, Joan L. A Family Apart. 176p. (gr. 7-12). 1987. 14.95 (ISBN 0-553-05432-5, Starfire). Bantam.

—Maggie, Too. LC 84-19766. 96p. (gr. 3-6). 1985. 11.95 (ISBN 0-15-250350-1, HJ). HarBraceJ.

—A Place to Belong. 1990. pap. 3.50 (ISBN 0-553-28485-1). Bantam.

Noelle of the Nutcracker. 1988. pap. 2.75 (ISBN 0-553-15673-X, Skylark). Bantam.

Norby, Lisa. The Holly Hudnut Admiration Society. LC 87-36566. 128p. (Orig.). (gr. 3-7). 1989. lib. bdg. 5.99 (ISBN 0-394-99604-6); pap. 2.95 (ISBN 0-394-89604-1). Knopf.
North, Emily. Old Friends, New Friends. Sims, Lynda, illus. LC 79-22046. 32p. (gr. k-3). 1980. PLB 13.27 (ISBN 0-516-01479-X). Childrens.
Nunes, Lygia B. My Friend the Painter. Pontiero, Giovanni, tr. from POR. 80p. (gr. 4-8). 1991. 13.95 (ISBN 0-15-256340-7). HarBraceJ.
O'Brien, Anne S. Don't Say No! O'Brien, Anne S., illus. LC 85-82109. 14p. (ps-k). 1986. bds. 3.95 (ISBN 0-8050-0049-6). H Holt & Co.
O'Connor, Jane. Just Good Friends. LC 82-44851. 192p. (gr. 6-9). 1983. PLB 12.89 (ISBN 0-06-024591-3). HarpC Child Bks.
—Molly the Brave & Me. Hamanaka, Sheila, illus. LC 89-10864. 48p. (Orig.). (gr. 1-3). 1990. lib. bdg. 6.99 (ISBN 0-394-94175-6); pap. 2.95 (ISBN 0-394-84175-1). Random.
Okimoto, Jean D. Take a Chance, Gramps, Vol. 1. (gr. 4-7). 1990. 13.95 (ISBN 0-316-63812-9, Joy St Bks). Little.
Oneal, Zibby. Turtle & Snail. Tomes, Margot, illus. LC 78-14826. (gr. k-2). 1979. 11.95i (ISBN 0-397-31829-4, Lipp Jr Bks). HarpC Child Bks.
Orgel, Doris. The Devil in Vienna. LC 78-51319. (gr. 7 up). 1978. 8.95 (ISBN 0-8037-1920-5). Dial Bks Young.
Orlev, Uri. The Island on Bird Street. Halkin, Hillel, tr. from HEB. 176p. (gr. 5 up). 1984. 13.95 (ISBN 0-395-33887-5, 5-92515). HM.
Ormondroyd, Edward. Time at the Top. 1990. pap. 2.95 (ISBN 0-553-15420-6). Bantam.
Osborne, Mary P. Mo & His Friends. DiSalvo-Ryan, DyAnne, illus. LC 87-15655. 48p. (ps-3). 1989. 9.95 (ISBN 0-8037-0504-2); 9.89 (ISBN 0-8037-0505-0). Dial Bks Young.
—Mo & His Friends. (ps-3). 1991. pap. 3.95 (ISBN 0-8037-0924-2, Dial Easy to Read). Puffin Bks.
—Mo to the Rescue. Disalvo-Ryan, Dyanne, illus. LC 84-28796. 56p. (ps-3). 1985. 8.95 (ISBN 0-8037-0180-2); PLB 8.89 (ISBN 0-8037-0182-9). Dial Bks Young.
Paige, Rob. Some of My Best Friends Are Monsters. Yalowitz, Paul, illus. LC 87-29973. 32p. (ps-2). 1988. 12.95 (ISBN 0-02-769640-5, Bradbury Pr). Macmillan Child Grp.
Pare, R. A Friend Like You. (Illus.). 24p. (ps-8). 1984. pap. 4.95 (ISBN 0-920303-05-6). Firefly Bks Ltd.
Park, Barbara. Almost Starring Skinnybones. LC 87-28752. (gr. 3-7). 1988. 10.95 (ISBN 0-394-89831-1); lib. bdg. 11.99 (ISBN 0-394-99831-6). Knopf.
—Beanpole. 160p. (gr. 5 up). 1984. pap. 2.95 (ISBN 0-380-69840-4, Flare). Avon.
—Buddies. LC 84-12521. 144p. (gr. 5-9). 1985. 9.95 (ISBN 0-394-86934-6); lib. bdg. 9.99 (ISBN 0-394-96934-0). Knopf.
—Buddies. (gr. 7 up). 1986. pap. 2.95 (ISBN 0-380-69992-3, Flare). Avon.
Parker, Cam. Camp Off-the-Wall. LC 86-25921. 128p. (gr. 3-7). 1987. pap. 2.50 (ISBN 0-380-75196-8, Camelot). Avon.
Pascal, Francine. Best Friends. 112p. (Orig.). (gr. 7-12). 1986. pap. 2.99 (ISBN 0-553-15655-1, Skylark). Bantam.
—Friend Against Friend. (gr. 9-12). 1990. pap. 2.95 (ISBN 0-553-28636-6). Bantam.
—Hangin' out with Cici. 160p. (gr. 5 up). 1985. pap. 2.95 (ISBN 0-440-93364-1, LFL). Dell.
—One of the Gang, No. 10. 1987. pap. 2.50 (ISBN 0-553-15531-8, Skylark). Bantam.
—Runaway. 176p. (Orig.). (gr. 5 up). 1985. pap. 2.75 (ISBN 0-553-26682-9). Bantam.
Passen, Lisa. Fat, Fat Rose Marie. Passen, Lisa, illus. LC 90-21112. 32p. (ps-3). 1991. 14.95 (ISBN 0-8050-1653-8). H Holt & Co.
Paterson, Katherine. Bridge to Terabithia. Diamond, Donna, illus. LC 77-2221. (gr. 5 up). 1977. 13.95 (ISBN 0-690-01359-0, Crowell Jr Bks). HarpC Child Bks.
—Bridge to Terabithia. Diamond, Donna, illus. LC 77-2221. 144p. (gr. 5-9). 1987. pap. 3.50 (ISBN 0-06-440184-7, Trophy). HarpC Child Bks.
—Bridge to Terabithia. Diamond, Donna, illus. LC 77-2221. 144p. (gr. 5 up). 1987. Repr. of 1977 ed. PLB 13.89 (ISBN 0-690-04635-9, Crowell Jr Bks). HarpC Child Bks.
—Come Sing, Jimmy Jo. 192p. (gr. 5 up). 1986. pap. 3.50 (ISBN 0-380-70052-2, Flare). Avon.
—Un Puente Hasta Therabithia. (SPA.). (gr. 1-6). 8.50 (ISBN 84-204-3633-X). Santillana.
Paulsen, Gary. The Foxman. 128p. (gr. 4 up). 1990. pap. 3.95 (ISBN 0-14-034311-3, Puffin). Puffin Bks.
Pearce, Phillippa. Fresh. Zimdars, Berta, illus. 64p. 1987. PLB 15.65 (ISBN 0-88682-125-8); PLB 10.95 s.p. (ISBN 0-685-23214-X). Creative Ed.
Pearson, Kit. The Daring Game. (Illus.). 240p. (gr. 3-7). 1991. pap. 3.95 (ISBN 0-14-031932-8, Puffin). Puffin Bks.
Peck, Richard. Remembering the Good Times. LC 84-19962. 192p. (gr. 7 up). 1985. pap. 14.95 (ISBN 0-385-29396-8). Delacorte.
—Remembering the Good Times. (gr. 5-12). 1986. pap. 3.25 (ISBN 0-440-97339-2, LFL). Dell.
—Those Summer Girls I Never Met. (gr. k up). 1989. pap. 3.50 (ISBN 0-440-20457-7, LFL). Dell.
Peck, Robert N. Soup. (gr. 3 up). 1979. pap. 2.95 (ISBN 0-440-48186-4, YB). Dell.
—Soup. Gehm, Charles, illus. LC 73-15117. 104p. (gr. 3 up). 1974. 4.95 (ISBN 0-394-82700-7); lib. bdg. 9.99 (ISBN 0-394-92700-1). Knopf.
—Soup & Me. Lilly, Charles, illus. LC 75-9514. 112p. (gr. 3-6). 1975. 4.95 (ISBN 0-394-83157-8); lib. bdg. 9.99 (ISBN 0-394-93157-2). Knopf.
—Soup for President. Lewin, Ted, illus. LC 77-3548. (gr. 6 up). 1978. 5.95 (ISBN 0-394-83675-8); lib. bdg. 9.99 (ISBN 0-394-93675-2). Knopf.
—Soup in the Saddle. Robinson, Charles, illus. LC 82-14010. 96p. (gr. 3-6). 1983. 9.95 (ISBN 0-394-85294-X); lib. bdg. 9.99 (ISBN 0-394-95294-4). Knopf.
Peppy. 1990. 2.98 (ISBN 0-8317-7255-7). Smithmark.
Perkins, Myrna. Bored Betty's Wish. Perkins, William C. & Perkins, Lani, illus. 32p. (Orig.). (gr. 2-5). 1986. pap. 5.95 (ISBN 0-937729-02-7). Markins Enter.
Perl, Lila. Me & Fat Glenda. 160p. (gr. 4-6). 1985. pap. 2.50 (ISBN 0-671-60503-8, Archway). PB.
Perlman, Ruthy. Working It Out. LC 90-82185. (gr. 7 up). 1990. 12.95 (ISBN 1-56062-033-1); pap. 9.95 (ISBN 1-56062-035-8). CIS Comm.
Perry, Carol. Thirteen & Loving It. 156p. (gr. 5-8). 1989. pap. 2.95 (ISBN 0-87406-371-X). Willowisp Pr.
Petersen, P. J. Corky & the Brothers Cool. (gr. 6 up). 1986. pap. 2.75 (ISBN 0-440-91624-0, LFL). Dell.
—Nobody Else Can Walk It for You. 224p. (gr. 6 up). 1984. pap. 2.95 (ISBN 0-440-96733-3, LFL). Dell.
Peterson, George C. Stuck in the Mud, Vol. 1. Peterson, George, illus. 208p. (Orig.). (gr. 9-12). Date not set. pap. write for info. (ISBN 0-9621320-0-4). G Peterson.
Petroske, Mimi. Boy My Very Special Friend. Caroland, Mary, ed. (Illus.). 44p. (gr. k-3). 1991. 5.95 (ISBN 1-55523-381-3). Winston-Derek.
Pfeffer, Susan B. Darcy Downstairs. 144p. (gr. 4-7). 1990. 13.95 (ISBN 0-8050-1307-5). H Holt & Co.
—The Friendship Pact. 112p. (Orig.). (gr. 4-6). 1986. pap. 2.50 (ISBN 0-590-32143-9, Apple Paperbacks). Scholastic Inc.
—Just Between Us. 128p. (gr. k-6). 1981. pap. 2.25 (ISBN 0-440-44194-3, YB). Dell.
—Starring Peter & Leigh. LC 78-72855. 1978. 7.95 (ISBN 0-440-08226-9). Delacorte.
Pfister, Marcus. Where Is My Friend? Pfister, Marchus, illus. LC 85-63301. 12p. (ps-k). 1986. 3.95 (ISBN 1-55858-043-3). North-South Bks NYC.
Phelan, Terry W. Best Friends, Hands Down. Hafner, Marylin, illus. LC 85-63838. 48p. (Orig.). (gr. 2-5). 1986. 9.95 (ISBN 0-936915-00-5, Shoe Tree Pr); pap. 3.95 (ISBN 0-936915-01-3). Betterway Pubns.
Phipson, Joan. Hit & Run. LC 85-7522. 132p. (gr. 7 up). 1985. 12.95 (ISBN 0-689-50362-8, M K McElderry). Macmillan Child Grp.
Pike, Christopher. The Dance. (gr. 9 up). 1989. pap. 2.95 (ISBN 0-671-70011-1, Archway). PB.
—Fall into Darkness. 224p. 1990. pap. 3.50 (ISBN 0-671-73684-1, Archway). PB.
—Weekend. 230p. (Orig.). (gr. 7 up). 1986. pap. 2.50 (ISBN 0-590-40753-8, Point). Scholastic Inc.
—Weekend. 1986. pap. 2.75 (ISBN 0-590-42968-X). Scholastic Inc.
Pilkey, Dav. A Friend for Dragon. LC 90-45219. (Illus.). 48p. (gr. 1-3). 1991. 12.95 (ISBN 0-531-05934-0); PLB 12.99 (ISBN 0-531-08534-1). Orchard Bks Watts.
Pinkwater, Daniel. Doodle Flute. Pinkwater, Daniel, illus. LC 90-6622. 32p. (gr. k-3). 1991. RSBE 12.95 (ISBN 0-02-774635-6, Mcmillan Child Bk). Macmillan Child Grp.
Pinsker, Judith. A Lot Like You. (gr. 5 up). 1989. pap. 2.95 (ISBN 0-553-27852-5, Starfire). Bantam.
Pitts, Paul. For a Good Time, Don't Call Claudia. LC 86-90772. 128p. (gr. 7 up). 1986. pap. 2.50 (ISBN 0-380-75117-8, Flare). Avon.
Polushkin, Maria. Mother, Mother, I Want Another. Dawson, Diane, illus. 32p. (ps-1). 1988. pap. 3.95 (ISBN 0-517-55947-1). Crown.
Porter, Gene S. Freckles. George, Jean C., afterword by. (gr. 5 up). 1988. pap. 4.95 (ISBN 0-317-68987-8, Pub. by Yearling Classics). Dell.
Poskanzer, Susan C. A Surprise for Baby Blueberry Muffin. Sustendal, Pat, illus. 40p. (ps-3). 1984. cancelled 5.95 (ISBN 0-910313-23-7). Parker Bros.
Potter, Beatrix. Mrs. Tiggy Winkle & Friends. 1987. pap. 3.95 (ISBN 0-14-032047-4, Puffin). Puffin Bks.
Pryor, Bonnie. Amanda & April. DeGroat, Diane, illus. LC 85-15308. 32p. (ps-1). 1986. 14.95 (ISBN 0-688-05869-8, Morrow Junior Books); lib. bdg. 14.88 (ISBN 0-688-05870-1). Morrow.
Quin-Harkin, Janet. The Graduates. 176p. (Orig.). (gr. 7-12). 1986. pap. 2.50 (ISBN 0-553-25723-4). Bantam.
—Old Friends, New Friends. 224p. (Orig.). (gr. 6 up). 1986. pap. 2.50 (ISBN 0-553-26186-X). Bantam.
—On Our Own. 176p. (Orig.). (gr. 6 up). 1986. pap. 2.50 (ISBN 0-685-13234-X). Bantam.
—Roadtrip. (gr. 6 up). 1989. pap. 2.95 (ISBN 0-8041-0336-4). Ivy Books.
Rabinowitz, Ann. Bethie. LC 88-22840. 208p. (gr. 7 up). 1989. 14.95 (ISBN 0-02-775661-0, Mcmillan Child Bk). Macmillan Child Grp.
Radin, Ruth Y. Tac's Island. Owens, Gail, illus. LC 85-23119. 80p. (gr. 3-6). 1986. 10.95 (ISBN 0-02-775780-3, Mcmillan Child Bk). Macmillan Child Grp.
Rand, Suzanne. The Good Luck Girl. 192p. (Orig.). (gr. 7-12). 1986. pap. 2.50 (ISBN 0-553-25644-0). Bantam.
Ransom, Candice F. Thirteen. 192p. (Orig.). (gr. 6 up). 1986. pap. 2.50 (ISBN 0-590-40192-0, Apple Paperbacks). Scholastic Inc.
Raskin, Ellen. Figgs & Phantoms. (Illus.). 160p. (gr. 5-9). 1989. pap. 4.95 (ISBN 0-14-032944-7, Puffin). Puffin Bks.
Ravilious, Robin. Two in a Pocket. (ps-3). 1991. 14.95 (ISBN 0-316-73449-7). Little.
Reaver, Chap. Mote. 1990. 14.95 (ISBN 0-385-30163-4). Delacorte.
Reeves, Faye C. Howie Merton & the Magic Dust. Buller, Jon, illus. LC 90-38341. 64p. (Orig.). (gr. 2-4). 1991. lib. bdg. 6.99 (ISBN 0-679-91527-3, Random Juv); pap. 2.50 (ISBN 0-679-81527-9). Random.
Regan, Dian C. Game of Survival. 144p. (Orig.). 1989. pap. 2.75 (ISBN 0-380-75585-8, Flare). Avon.
Reit, Ann. I Thought You Were My Best Friend. 144p. (gr. 6-8). 1988. pap. 2.50 (ISBN 0-590-40445-8). Scholastic Inc.
Resciniti, Angelo. The Ketchup Kid. Robison, Don, illus. 96p. (Orig.). (gr. 3-5). 1987. pap. 2.25 (ISBN 0-87406-228-4). Willowisp Pr.
Reynolds, Susan L. Strandia. (Illus.). 240p. (gr. 9-12). 1991. 14.95 (ISBN 0-374-37274-8). FS&G.
Richardson, Arleta. New Faces, New Friends. (gr. 3-7). 1988. pap. 3.95 (ISBN 1-55513-985-X, Chariot Bks). Cook.
Richemont, Enid. The Time Tree. (gr. 3-7). 1990. 12.95 (ISBN 0-316-74452-2). Little.
Richler, Mordecai. Jacob Two-Two Hooded Fang. (ps-7). 1987. pap. 2.50 (ISBN 0-317-64199-9, Skylark). Bantam.
Robins, Joan. Addie Meets Max. Truesdell, Sue, illus. LC 84-48329. 32p. (ps-3). 1985. 9.95 (ISBN 0-06-025063-1); PLB 10.89 (ISBN 0-06-025064-X). HarpC Child Bks.
Rocklin, Joanne. Sonia Begonia. Downing, Julie, illus. LC 85-23120. 96p. (gr. 3-7). 1986. 12.95 (ISBN 0-02-777310-8, Mcmillan Child Bk). Macmillan Child Grp.
Rockwell, Thomas. How to Fight a Girl. Fiammenghi, Gioia, illus. 128p. (gr. 4-6). 1987. PLB 12.90 (ISBN 0-531-10140-1). Watts.
Rodgers, Dorothy. Polka Dots & Friendship. 1988. 5.95 (ISBN 0-533-07728-1). Vantage.
Rodgers, Raboo. Magnum Fault. 192p. (gr. 5 up). 1984. 11.95 (ISBN 0-685-07882-5, 5-95260). HM.
Rodowsky, Colby. P. S. Write Soon. 158p. (gr. 5 up). 1987. pap. 3.50 (ISBN 0-374-46032-9). FS&G.
Roffey, Maureen. Bathtime. Roffey, Maureen, illus. LC 89-18413. 32p. (ps). 1990. pap. 4.95 (ISBN 0-689-70808-4, Aladdin). Macmillan Child Grp.
Rogers, Fred. Making Friends. Judkis, Jim, photos by. (Illus.). (ps-1). 1987. 12.95 (ISBN 0-399-21382-1, Putnam); pap. 5.95 (ISBN 0-399-21385-6, Putnam). Putnam Pub Group.
Rogers, Paul & Rogers, Emma. What's Wrong, Tom? Robinson, Colin, illus. 32p. (ps-1). 1989. pap. 11.95 (ISBN 0-670-82394-5). Viking Child Bks.
Romain, Trevor C. The Bad Mood. Thornblad, Vernon, illus. 32p. 1989. 13.95 (ISBN 0-87719-164-6, Lone Star Bks). Gulf Pub.
Roos, Stephen. The Fair-Weather Friends. DeRosa, Dee, illus. LC 86-17246. 124p. (gr. 3-6). 1987. 12.95 (ISBN 0-689-31297-0, Atheneum Child Bk). Macmillan Child Grp.
—Fair-Weather Friends. 128p. (gr. 2-9). pap. 2.95 (ISBN 0-8167-1306-5). Troll Assocs.
—You'll Miss Me When I'm Gone. (gr. k-12). 1989. pap. 2.95 (ISBN 0-440-20485-2, LE). Dell.
Rosen, Michael. Mind Your Own Business. Blake, Quentin, illus. LC 74-9969. 96p. (gr. 3 up). 1974. 18.95 (ISBN 0-87599-209-9). S G Phillips.
Rosenblatt, Arthur. Keep on Caring. Cook, Tom, illus. 40p. (ps-3). 1985. 5.95 (ISBN 0-910313-84-9). Parker Bros.
Roser, Wiltrud. Lena & Leopold. (Illus.). 32p. (ps-3). 1988. pap. 3.95 (ISBN 0-14-050818-X, Puffin). Puffin Bks.
Ross, Anna. Be My Friend. Gorbaty, Norman, illus. LC 89-24389. 24p. (ps). 1991. 3.95 (ISBN 0-394-85496-9). Random.
Ross, Pat. M & M & the Super Child Afternoon. Hafner, Marylin, illus. 48p. (gr. 1-4). 1989. pap. 3.95 (ISBN 0-14-032145-4, Puffin). Puffin Bks.
—M & M & the Superchild Afternoon. Hafner, Marylin, illus. LC 86-28128. (gr. 1-4). 1987. pap. 9.95 (ISBN 0-670-81208-0). Viking Child Bks.
Rostkowski, Margaret I. The Best of Friends. LC 88-33077. 192p. (gr. 7 up). 1989. 12.95 (ISBN 0-06-025104-2); PLB 12.89 (ISBN 0-06-025105-0). HarpC Child Bks.
Rothstein, Chaya L. Mentchkins Make Friends. (gr. 4-8). 1988. pap. 4.95 (ISBN 0-87306-453-4). Feldheim.
Roy, Ron. Frankie Is Staying Back. Kessell, Walter, illus. 64p. (gr. 2-5). 1981. 8.95 (ISBN 0-395-31025-3, Clarion). HM.
Ruckman, Ivy. This Is Your Captain Speaking. (gr. 5 up). 1987. 14.95 (ISBN 0-8027-6734-6). Walker & Co.
Ruffell, Ann. Blood Brother. LC 80-80538. 160p. (gr. 7 up). 1980. PLB 8.90 (ISBN 0-531-04177-8). Watts.
Rutherford, Meg. Bluff & Bran & the Treehouse. (Illus.). 32p. (ps-3). 1987. 10.95 (ISBN 0-233-97889-5). Andre Deutsch.
Rylant, Cynthia. Henry & Mudge: The First Book of Their Adventures. Stevenson, Suzie, illus. LC 86-13615. 40p. (gr. 1-3). 1987. 11.95 (ISBN 0-02-778001-5, Bradbury Pr). Macmillan Child Grp.
Sachar, Louis. The Boy Who Lost His Face. LC 88-22622. 192p. (gr. 5-9). 1989. 11.95 (ISBN 0-394-82863-1); PLB 12.99 (ISBN 0-394-92863-6). Knopf.

—The Worst Person in the World. LC 77-22141. (Illus.). 32p. (gr. k-3). 1978. PLB 13.88 (ISBN 0-688-84127-9). Greenwillow.

Stolz, Mary. Bully of Barkham Street. Shortall, Leonard, illus. LC 68-2661. 224p. (gr. 3-6). 1963. PLB 14.89 (ISBN 0-06-025821-7). HarpC Child Bks.

—Noonday Friends. Glanzman, Louis S., illus. LC 65-20257. 192p. (gr. 3-7). 1965. PLB 14.89 (ISBN 0-06-025946-9). HarpC Child Bks.

—Noonday Friends. LC 65-20257. (Illus.). 192p. (gr. 4-7). 1971. pap. 3.95 (ISBN 0-06-440009-3, Trophy). HarpC Child Bks.

—Quentin Corn. Johnson, Pamela, illus. LC 84-48321. 128p. (gr. 1-7). 1985. 14.95 (ISBN 0-87923-553-5). Godine.

Stouffer, Nancy. The Land of the Nother-One. Stouffer, Nancy, illus. 48p. (gr. 1-4). 1989. pap. 2.95 (ISBN 0-927008-13-0). BCI-Bk Cook Inc.

Stouse, Karla F. Diff'rent Is Kind of Nice. Yanda, Emma, illus. LC 87-70532. 16p. (gr. 2 up). 1987. pap. 0.95 (ISBN 0-87029-208-0). Abbey.

—Nellie & the Nasty Nast. Yanda, Emma, illus. LC 87-70533. 16p. (Orig.). (gr. 2 up). 1987. pap. 0.95 (ISBN 0-87029-205-6). Abbey.

Strasser, Todd. Friends till the End. 224p. (gr. 7 up). 1982. pap. 3.25 (ISBN 0-440-92625-4, LFL). Dell.

—A Very Touchy Subject. (gr. 6 up). 1986. pap. 2.95 (ISBN 0-440-98851-9, LFL). Dell.

Streatfeild, Noel. Good-Bye Gemma. (Orig.). (gr. k-6). 1987. pap. 3.25 (ISBN 0-440-42871-8, YB). Dell.

Stringham, Alene. Kate & Nate. Burris, Priscilla, illus. 60p. (Orig.). (gr. 1-2). 1986. pap. text ed. 5.95 (ISBN 0-933606-45-1, 645). Monkey Sisters.

Strommen, Judith B. Grady the Great. 144p. (gr. 4-6). 1990. 13.95 (ISBN 0-8050-1405-5). H Holt & Co.

Sundgaard, Arnold. Meet Jack Appleknocker. Samton, Sheila, illus. LC 87-2568. 32p. (ps-2). 1988. PLB 13.95 (ISBN 0-399-21472-0, Philomel Bks). Putnam Pub Group.

Sutton. Me & the Weirdos. (ps-7). 1987. pap. 2.25 (ISBN 0-553-15395-1, Skylark). Bantam.

Sutton, Laverne. Peacock Feathers. 23p. 1988. 4.95 (ISBN 0-533-07722-2). Vantage.

Suzanne, Jamie. Best Friends. large type ed. Pascal, Francine, created by. 104p. (gr. 7-12). 1990. Repr. of 1986 ed. 9.95 (ISBN 1-55905-064-0). Grey Castle.

Swallow, Pamela C. No Promises. 176p. (gr. 5 up). 1989. 13.95 (ISBN 0-399-21561-1, Putnam). Putnam Pub Group.

Sweeney, Joyce. Face the Dragon. 1990. 14.95 (ISBN 0-385-30164-2). Delacorte.

Tada, Joni E. Meet My Friends. LC 87-22344. (gr. 4-8). 1987. pap. 4.49 (ISBN 1-55513-808-X, Chariot Bks). Cook.

Tafuri, Nancy. My Friends. Tafuri, Nancy, illus. LC 86-29388. 12p. (ps). 1987. Board book. 3.95 (ISBN 0-688-07187-2). Greenwillow.

Talbert, Marc. Rabbit in the Rock. (gr. 7 up). 1989. 14.95 (ISBN 0-8037-0693-6). Dial Bks Young.

Talbott, Hudson. Going Hollywood! A Dinosaur's Dream. Talbott, Hudson, illus. LC 89-1190. 32p. (ps-3). 1989. 12.95 (ISBN 0-517-57354-7). Crown.

Tangvald, Christine. My Friends Are Special. LC 86-71795. 1987. bds. 4.95 (ISBN 1-55513-170-0, Chariot Bks). Cook.

Taylor, Judy. Sophie & Jack. Gantner, Susan, illus. 32p. (ps-2). 1983. PLB 9.95 (ISBN 0-399-20947-6, Philomel). Putnam Pub Group.

Taylor, Mark A. A Friend Is... McInturfp, Steve, illus. 32p. (gr. 1-4). 1987. casebound 4.95 (ISBN 0-87403-324-1, 3669). Standard Pub.

Taylor, Mildred D. The Friendship. Ginsburg, Max, illus. LC 86-29309. 56p. (gr. 2-6). 1987. 12.95 (ISBN 0-8037-0417-8); PLB 13.89 (ISBN 0-8037-0418-6). Dial Bks Young.

—The Friendship & the Gold Cadillac. (gr. 2-6). 1989. pap. 2.95 (ISBN 0-553-15765-5, Skylark). Bantam.

Tempski, Armine von. Born in Paradise. LC 84-27345. 342p. 1985. 27.50 (ISBN 0-918024-65-X); pap. 14.95 (ISBN 0-918024-34-X). Ox Bow.

Thaler, Mike. The Moon & the Balloon. LC 82-14965. (Illus.). 32p. (ps-3). 1982. 8.95 (ISBN 0-8038-4744-0). Hastings.

Thomas, Janet. Newcomer. 33p. (Orig.). (gr. k-3). 1987. pap. 4.50 playscript (ISBN 0-87602-268-9). Anchorage.

Thompson, Pat. My Friend Mr. Morris. (gr. k-6). 1988. pap. 2.50 (ISBN 0-440-40061-9). Dell.

Thornton, Terry & Thornton, Sandy. Recess. (Illus.). 32p. (gr. 2-5). 1987. pap. 0.30 (ISBN 0-687-35660-1). Abingdon.

Thorpe, Jean J. Kirtpatrick's Kritters. Thorpe, Jean J., illus. 50p. (gr. k-6). 1988. pap. 7.95 (ISBN 0-317-93347-7). Art & Earth.

Timm, Stephen A. The Floor That Said "No More" Neidigh, Sherry, illus. LC 86-60276. 48p. 1986. pap. 5.95 (ISBN 0-939728-12-5). Steppingstone Ent.

Tingle, Dolli. Going to Be a Bride. (Illus.). 32p. 1987. 5.95 (ISBN 0-8378-5080-0). Gibson.

Tolan, Stephanie S. A Good Courage. (gr. 7 up). 1989. pap. 2.95 (ISBN 0-449-70329-0, Juniper). Fawcett.

Tomkins, Jasper. My Secret Sunrise. (Illus.). 60p. (Orig.). 1989. 11.95 (ISBN 0-88138-136-5); pap. 7.95 (ISBN 0-88138-130-6). Green Tiger Pr.

Tomlinson, Theresa. Summer Witches. LC 90-38162. 96p. (gr. 2-7). 1991. SBE 11.95 (ISBN 0-02-789206-9, Mcmillan Child Bk). Macmillan Child Grp.

Tsutsui, Yoriko. Anna's Special Present. Hayashi, Akiko, illus. 32p. (ps-3). 1988. pap. 11.95 (ISBN 0-670-81671-X). Viking Child Bks.

Turkle, Brinton. Thy Friend, Obadiah. (Illus.). 40p. (gr. k-3). 1982. pap. 4.95 (ISBN 0-14-050393-5, Puffin). Puffin Bks.

Tusa, Tricia. Miranda. LC 84-21764. (Illus.). 32p. (gr. 7 up). 1985. 12.95 (ISBN 0-02-789520-3, Mcmillan Child Bk). Macmillan Child Grp.

Twain, Mark. A Story Without an End. LC 85-30885. 32p. (gr. 4 up). 1986. PLB 10.95s.p. (ISBN 0-88682-064-2); PLB 15.65 (ISBN 0-685-12417-7). Creative Ed.

Twohill, Maggie. Big Mouth. (gr. k-6). 1989. pap. 2.95 (ISBN 0-440-40223-9, YB). Dell.

—Valentine Frankenstein. Lalicki, Barbara, ed. LC 90-24459. 144p. (gr. 3-6). 1992. 12.95 (ISBN 0-02-789692-7, Bradbury Pr). Macmillan Child Grp.

Uchida, Yoshiko. The Happiest Ending. LC 85-6245. 120p. (gr. 3-7). 1985. 12.95 (ISBN 0-689-50326-1, M K McElderry). Macmillan Child Grp.

Ure, Jean. After Thursday. LC 86-19635. 176p. (gr. 7 up). 1987. pap. 14.95 (ISBN 0-385-29548-0). Delacorte.

—The Other Side of the Fence. LC 87-27184. 176p. (gr. 7 up). 1988. 14.95 (ISBN 0-385-29627-4). Delacorte.

Van Curen, Barbara. When the Zebras Came for Lunch. Manierre, Betsy, illus. 64p. (ps-2). 1989. pap. text ed. 5.95 (ISBN 0-922510-01-6). Lucky Bks.

Van Steenwyk, Elizabeth. Can You Keep a Secret? 128p. (Orig.). (gr. 4-6). 1990. pap. text ed. 2.50 (ISBN 0-87406-465-1). Willowisp Pr.

Veith, Jan T. Boundless Imagination. 112p. (gr. 3-6). 1987. 9.95 (ISBN 0-912107-55-3). Monday Morning Bks.

Vickery, Eugene L. New Friends in a New World: Thanksgiving Story of Children with New Friends. Tolpo, Lily, illus. 20p. (Orig.). (gr. k-8). 1986. pap. 1.95 (ISBN 0-937775-03-7). Stonehaven Pubs.

Vincent, Gabrielle. Ernest & Celestine. LC 81-6392. (Illus.). (ps-3). 1986. 3.95 (ISBN 0-688-06525-2, Mulberry). Morrow.

Vinge, Joan D. Psion. 352p. (gr. k-12). 1985. pap. 2.95 (ISBN 0-440-97192-6, LFL). Dell.

Viorst, Judith. If I Were in Charge of the World & Other Worries. LC 81-2342. (Illus.). 64p. (gr. 2 up). 1984. pap. 3.95 (ISBN 0-689-70770-3, Aladdin). Macmillan Child Grp.

—Rosie & Michael. Tomei, Lorna, illus. LC 74-75571. 40p. (gr. 1-4). 1974. 13.95 (ISBN 0-689-30439-0, Atheneum Child Bk). Macmillan Child Grp.

—Rosie & Michael. 2nd ed. Tomei, Lorna, illus. LC 86-13969. 40p. (gr. 1-4). 1988. pap. 3.95 (ISBN 0-689-71272-3, Aladdin). Macmillan Child Grp.

Voigt, Cynthia. A Solitary Blue. LC 83-6007. 204p. (gr. 7 up). 1983. 14.95 (ISBN 0-689-31008-0, Atheneum Child Bk). Macmillan Child Grp.

—Tell Me if the Lovers Are Losers. LC 81-8079. 252p. (gr. 7 up). 1982. 14.95 (ISBN 0-689-30911-2, Atheneum Child Bk). Macmillan Child Grp.

Vreeken, Elizabeth. Kenny & Jane Make Friends. Rosenthal, Constance, illus. LC 63-8586. 63p. (gr. 4). 1963. 3.95 (ISBN 0-379-00158-6). Oceana.

Vuong, Lynette D. A Friend for Carlita. Boddy, Joe, illus. 32p. (gr. k-2). 1989. pasted 1.99 (ISBN 0-87403-593-7, 3853). Standard Pub.

Waddell, Martin. Joe's Gang: Making a Monster; The Space Rocket; The Shop; The Big Show; Building a House & The Band, 6 bks. King, Pauline, illus. 96p. (gr. k-1). Set. pap. text ed. 28.90 (ISBN 1-55624-497-5). Wright Group.

—We Love Them. Firth, Barbara, illus. LC 89-8226. 32p. (ps-2). 1990. 12.95 (ISBN 0-688-09331-0); lib. bdg. 12.88 (ISBN 0-688-09332-9). Lothrop.

Wagner, Donald R. No Tears for My Mary. Horwitz, Janet, ed. LC 87-90522. 40p. (gr. 7 up). 1989. 8.95 (ISBN 0-910583-02-1); pap. 4.95 (ISBN 0-318-32717-1). Shamrock Pr.

Wahl, Robert. Friend Dog. Ewers, Joe, illus. (ps). 1988. 12.95 (ISBN 0-316-91710-9). Little.

Waite, Michael P. Buzzle Billy. LC 87-5282. 1987. 7.95 (ISBN 1-55513-218-9, Chariot Bks). Cook.

Wakeman, Cheryl A. Johnnie Ollie Carri III & His Friend. Womack, Fred, illus. 32p. (ps-3). 1985. 5.95 (ISBN 0-9614819-0-0). R E Moen.

JOHNNIE OLLIE CARRI III & HIS FRIEND is more than just an enjoyable children's book. It teaches a valuable lesson to children of all ages concerning the vital contributions of the elderly & the physically handicapped make to society. Johnnie Ollie walks home through the park each day, just so he can share his school day's activities with his special friend, Mister. The beautiful friendship is obvious to the reader as Johnnie shares happenings from a "typical school day" with which all children can identify. The reader never realizes until the very end that the elderly man has been deaf from birth & that he cannot hear a word Johnnie speaks--but that is not an obstacle in their wonderful relationship. Schools in California, Minnesota & Wisconsin have used this book to supplement units dealing with the elderly, the handicapped & sensitivity to others. Illustrated by noted children's illustrator FRED WOMACK. Full color throughout & printed on durable, high quality color-text paper.

Publisher Provided Annotation.

Walley, Susan. Best of Friends. Lyall, Elizabeth, ed. Halverson, Tom, illus. 156p. (Orig.). (gr. 4-8). 1989. pap. 4.95 (ISBN 0-89084-486-0). Bob Jones Univ Pr.

Ware, Martin E. Carly's & Amy's, Friends & Fables. (Illus.). 40p. (gr. 3-8). 1991. 7.50 (ISBN 0-8059-3194-5). Dorrance.

Webb, Angela. Reflections. Fairclough, Chris, photos by. Franklin Watts Ltd., ed. (Illus.). 32p. (ps-6). 1988. 10.90 (ISBN 0-531-10457-5). Watts.

Weber, Ane & Krueger, Ron. A Tailor-Made Friendship. French, Marty & Iwai, Noel, illus. 26p. (ps up). 1988. incl. cassette 7.95 (ISBN 1-55578-913-7). Worlds Wonder.

Weber, Ane, et al. A Tailor-Made Friendship. French, Marty & Iwia, Noel, illus. 26p. (ps up). 1986. Book & Cassette. 7.95 (ISBN 1-55578-107-1). Worlds Wonder.

Webster, Jean. Dear Enemy. (gr. 4-7). 1991. pap. 3.50 (ISBN 0-440-40440-1). Dell.

Weiss, Anne E. Lies, Deception, & Truth. 160p. (gr. 5-9). 1988. 13.95 (ISBN 0-395-40486-X). HM.

Weiss, Nicki. Maude & Sally. Weiss, Nicki, illus. LC 82-12003. 32p. (gr. k-3). 1983. 10.25 (ISBN 0-688-01859-9); PLB 10.88 (ISBN 0-688-01861-0). Greenwillow.

—Maude & Sally. (ps-3). 1988. pap. 3.95 (ISBN 0-14-050760-4, Puffin). Puffin Bks.

Wells, Rosemary. Stanley & Rhoda. Wells, Rosemary, illus. LC 78-51874. 40p. (ps-2). 1981. pap. 3.95 (ISBN 0-8037-7995-X, 0383-120). Dial Bks Young.

Wersba, Barbara. Crazy Vanilla. LC 85-45956. 192p. (gr. 7 up). 1986. PLB 11.89 (ISBN 0-06-026369-5). HarpC Child Bks.

Westlake, Diane. Will & the Grace. Galas, Julie, illus. 80p. (Orig.). (gr. 6-12). 1985. pap. 9.00 (ISBN 0-9614438-0-4). Fen Winnie.

Weyn, Suzanne. All Alone in the Eighth Grade. LC 91-10162. 128p. (gr. 7-9). 1991. lib. bdg. 9.89 (ISBN 0-8167-2394-X); pap. text ed. 2.95 (ISBN 0-8167-2395-8). Troll Assocs.

—Star Magic. LC 90-11151. 128p. (gr. 4-8). 1990. lib. bdg. 9.89 (ISBN 0-8167-2013-4); pap. text ed. 2.95 (ISBN 0-8167-2014-2). Troll Assocs.

Whisper's Rainbow Treasure. (gr. 4-7). 1990. pap. 2.25 (ISBN 0-89954-965-9). Antioch Pub Co.

White, Ellen E. Life Without Friends. LC 86-28056. (Illus.). 256p. (gr. 7 up). 1987. pap. 12.95 (ISBN 0-590-33781-5, Scholastic Hardcover). Scholastic Inc.

—Life Without Friends. 256p. (gr. 7 up). 1988. pap. 2.75 (ISBN 0-590-33829-3). Scholastic Inc.

Wiethorn, Randall J. Rock Finds a Friend. Wiethorn, Randall J., illus. 32p. 1988. 9.95 (ISBN 0-88138-110-1). Green Tiger Pr.

Wild, Margaret. Mr. Nick's Knitting. Huxley, Dee H., illus. (ps-3). 1989. 12.95 (ISBN 0-15-200518-8, Gulliver Bks). HarBraceJ.

Wilde, Oscar. The Devoted Friend. LC 86-2609. 32p. (gr. 4 up). 1986. PLB 10.95s.p. (ISBN 0-88682-067-7); 15.65 (ISBN 0-685-12404-5). Creative Ed.

—The Devoted Friend. Batmanglij, N. Khalili, tr. from ENG. Fanta, illus. 28p. (gr. 4 up). 1988. 15.00 (ISBN 0-934211-16-7); Bilingual Eng.-Persian. 15.00 (ISBN 0-934211-10-8). Mage Pubs Inc.

Willey, Margaret. Finding David Dolores. LC 85-45252. 192p. (gr. 7 up). 1986. PLB 10.89 (ISBN 0-06-026484-5). HarpC Child Bks.

Winthrop, Elizabeth. The Best Friends Club. Weston, Martha, illus. LC 88-13406. 32p. (ps-3). 1989. 12.95 (ISBN 0-688-07582-7); PLB 12.88 (ISBN 0-688-07583-5). Lothrop.

—Lizzie & Harold. Weston, Martha, illus. LC 83-14858. 32p. (gr. k-3). 1985. 12.95 (ISBN 0-688-02711-3); PLB 12.88 (ISBN 0-688-02712-1). Lothrop.

—Miranda in the Middle. (gr. 4 up). 1990. pap. 3.95 (ISBN 0-14-034392-X, Puffin). Puffin Bks.

Wojciechowska, Maia. Don't Play Dead Before You Have To. LC 76-112485. (gr. 7 up). 1970. PLB 11.89 (ISBN 0-06-026568-X). HarpC Child Bks.

Wolde, Gunilla. Betsy & Peter Are Different. Wolde, Gunilla, illus. LC 78-66265. (ps). Date not set. 1.95 (ISBN 0-685-04256-1, Random Juv); lib. bdg. write for info. (ISBN 0-394-95423-8). Random.

Wolkoff, Judie. In a Pig's Eye. Rutherford, Jenny, illus. LC 85-29974. 144p. (gr. 3-5). 1986. 12.95 (ISBN 0-02-793370-9, Bradbury Pr). Macmillan Child Grp.

—In a Pig's Eye. (gr. k-6). 1989. pap. 2.95 (ISBN 0-440-40140-2, YB). Dell.

Wood, Audrey. Orlando's Littlewhile Friends. Wood, Audrey, illus. (ps-2). 1981. 6.00 (ISBN 0-85953-111-2, Pub. by Child's Play England); pap. 5.50 (ISBN 0-85953-106-6). Childs Play.
—Orlando's Littlewhile Friends. 1989. 10.99 (ISBN 0-85953-283-6). Childs Play.
Wood, Vivian B. You're a Very Special Person. Wood, David & Wood, Vivian, illus. 38p. (Orig.). (gr. 1). 1988. pap. 5.95 (ISBN 0-9621567-0-1). V B Wood.
Woodson, Jacqueline. Last Summer with Maizon. 1990. 13.95 (ISBN 0-385-30045-X). Doubleday.
Wright, Alexandra & Wright, Elena. Will We Miss Them? (Illus.). 32p. (ps-8). 1991. 14.95 (ISBN 0-88106-489-0). Charlesbridge Pub.
Wyeth, Sharon D. Handle with Care. (gr. k-6). 1990. 2.95 (ISBN 0-440-40267-0, YB). Dell.
—No Creeps Need Apply. (gr. k-6). 1989. pap. 2.95 (ISBN 0-440-40241-7, YB). Dell.
—P. S. Forget It. (gr. k-6). 1989. pap. 2.95 (ISBN 0-440-40230-1, YB). Dell.
—Pen Pals: Stolen Pen Pals, No. 9. (gr. 4-7). 1990. pap. 2.95 (ISBN 0-440-40342-1). Dell.
—Sam the Sham. (gr. k-6). 1989. pap. 2.95 (ISBN 0-440-40250-6, YB). Dell.
Wynne, Carrie E. That Looks Like a Nice House. LC 87-82078. (Illus.). 42p. (Orig.). (gr. 8). 1987. pap. 4.95 (ISBN 0-9613205-3-2). Launch Pr.
Yarbro, Chelsea Q. Floating Illusions. LC 85-45825. 224p. (gr. 7 up). 1986. PLB 12.89 (ISBN 0-06-026643-0). HarpC Child Bks.
Yeatman, Linda. Buttons. Casson, Hugh, illus. 64p. (gr. 2-5). 1988. pap. 2.95 (ISBN 0-8120-3956-4). Barron.
—Perkins. Gon, Adriano, illus. 64p. (gr. 2-5). 1988. pap. 3.50 (ISBN 0-8120-3993-9). Barron.
Yep, Laurence. Kind Hearts & Gentle Monsters. LC 81-47738. 192p. (gr. 7 up). 1982. PLB 12.89 (ISBN 0-06-026733-X). HarpC Child Bks.
Yolen, Jane. Owl Moon. Schoenherr, John, illus. (ps-1). 1987. 14.95 (ISBN 0-399-21457-7, Philomel Bks). Putnam Pub Group.
—The Rainbow Rider. Foreman, Michael, illus. LC 73-19700. 32p. (ps-3). 1974. PLB 12.89 (ISBN 0-690-00311-0, Crowell Jr Bks). HarpC Child Bks.
Yorgason, Blaine M. & Yorgason, Brenton. Pardners: Three Stories on Friendship. Durfee, John C. & Durfee, Gaylie, illus. 64p. (Orig.). (gr. 9 up). 1988. pap. 3.95 (ISBN 0-929985-05-2). Sonos.
York, Carol B. Miss Know It All... 96p. (Orig.). (gr. 4 up). 1985. pap. 2.50 (ISBN 0-553-15408-7, Skylark). Bantam.
—Miss Know-It-All & the Three Ring Circus. (Illus.). 96p. (Orig.). 1988. pap. 2.75 (ISBN 0-553-15590-3, Skylark). Bantam.
You Are Special! 36p. (ps-4). 1985. 8.95 (ISBN 0-88684-176-3); cassette tape avail. Listen USA.
Young, Alida E. I Never Got to Say Good-Bye. 128p. (Orig.). (gr. 6-9). 1988. pap. 2.95 (ISBN 0-87406-359-0). Willowisp Pr.
Zadra, Dan. Dare to Be Different. (Illus.). 32p. (gr. 6 up). 1986. PLB 10.95s.p. (ISBN 0-88682-016-2); 15.65. Creative Ed.
—Mistakes Are Great! (Illus.). 32p. (gr. 6 up). 1986. PLB 10.95s.p. (ISBN 0-88682-019-7); 15.65. Creative Ed.
—More Good Time for You. (Illus.). 32p. (gr. 6 up). 1986. PLB 10.95s.p. (ISBN 0-88682-022-7); PLB 15.65. Creative Ed.
Zalben, Jane B. Here's Looking at You, Kid. (gr. k-12). 1987. pap. 2.50 (ISBN 0-440-93573-3, LFL). Dell.
—Porcupine's Christmas Blues. Zalben, Jane B., illus. 32p. 1982. 9.95 (ISBN 0-399-20893-3, Philomel). Putnam Pub Group.
Zelonky, Joy. My Best Friend Moved Away. Adams, Angela, illus. Silverman, Manuel, intro. by. LC 79-24111. (Illus.). (gr. k-6). 1980. PLB 16.67 (ISBN 0-8172-1353-8). Raintree Pubs.
Ziefert, Harriet. Mike & Tony: Best Friends. Siracusa, Catherine, illus. (ps-3). 1987. pap. 8.95 (ISBN 0-670-81719-8). Viking Child Bks.
—Nicky Upstairs & Down. Brown, Richard, illus. (ps-3). 1987. pap. 8.95 (ISBN 0-670-81717-1, Puffin); pap. 3.50 (ISBN 0-14-050742-6, Puffin). Puffin Bks.
—Say Goodnight! Siracusa, Catherine, illus. (ps-3). 7.95 (ISBN 0-317-62548-9); pap. 2.95 (ISBN 0-317-62549-7). Viking Child Bks.
—The Small Potatoes & the Sleep-Over. Brown, Richard, illus. (Orig.). (gr. k-6). 1985. pap. 2.75 (ISBN 0-440-48036-1, YB). Dell.
Zindel, Bonnie. Hollywood Dream Machine. 192p. (gr. 7-12). 1985. pap. 2.50 (ISBN 0-553-25240-2, Starfire). Bantam.
Zindel, Paul. A Begonia for Miss Applebaum. LC 88-11010. 192p. (gr. 7 up). 1989. 13.95i (ISBN 0-06-026877-8); PLB 13.89 (ISBN 0-06-026878-6). HarpC Child Bks.
—Harry & Hortense at Hormone High. 160p. (gr. 7-12). 1985. pap. 2.95 (ISBN 0-553-25175-9, Starfire). Bantam.
Zolotow, Charlotte. The Hating Book. Shecter, Ben, illus. LC 69-14444. 32p. (ps-3). 1969. 11.95 (ISBN 0-06-026923-5); PLB 11.89 (ISBN 0-06-026924-3). HarpC Child Bks.
—The Hating Book. Schecter, Ben, illus. LC 69-14444. 32p. (gr. k-3). 1989. pap. 3.95 (ISBN 0-06-443197-5, Trophy). HarpC Child Bks.
—Hold My Hand. Reissue. ed. Di Grazia, Thomas, illus. LC 72-76506. 32p. (gr. k-3). 1972. 12.95 (ISBN 0-06-026951-0); PLB 12.89 (ISBN 0-06-026952-9). HarpC Child Bks.
—Janey. Himler, Ronald, illus. LC 72-9861. 24p. (ps-3). 1973. PLB 12.89 (ISBN 0-06-026928-6). HarpC Child Bks.
—The New Friend. McCully, Emily A., illus. LC 80-67856. 32p. (ps-3). 1981. PLB 11.89 (ISBN 0-685-02101-7, Crowell Jr Bks). HarpC Child Bks.
—The Unfriendly Book. Pene Du Bois, William, illus. LC 74-19581. 32p. (ps-3). 1975. PLB 12.89 (ISBN 0-06-026931-6). HarpC Child Bks.

FRIENDSHIP–POETRY

Hallinan, P. K. That's What a Friend Is. Hallinan, P. K., illus. LC 76-27744. 32p. (gr. k-3). 1977. PLB 13.27 (ISBN 0-516-03628-9); pap. 3.95 (ISBN 0-516-43628-7). Childrens.
Kellogg, Steven. Best Friends. Fogelman, Phyllis J., ed. Kellogg, Steven, illus. LC 85-15971. 32p. (ps-3). 1990. pap. 3.95 (ISBN 0-8037-0829-7). Dial Bks Young.
Maris, Ron. Is Anyone Home? Maris, Ron, illus. LC 85-5436. 32p. (ps-2). 1986. 11.95 (ISBN 0-688-05899-X). Greenwillow.
Peck, Robert N. Justice Lion. 264p. (gr. 7 up). 1981. 13.95 (ISBN 0-316-69658-7). Little.
Roy, Cal. Friend Can Be. (Illus.). (gr. 2 up). 1969. 9.95 (ISBN 0-8392-3075-3). Astor-Honor.

FROGMEN

see Skin Diving

FROGS

Back, Christine & Watts, Barrie. Tadpole & Frog. LC 86-10049. (Illus.). 24p. 1986. 6.95 (ISBN 0-382-09293-7); PLB 9.98 (ISBN 0-382-09285-6); pap. 3.95 (ISBN 0-382-24021-9). Silver Burdett Pr.
Braithwaite, Althea. Frogs. (ps-6). 1989. PLB 8.95 (ISBN 0-88462-188-X). Dearborn Finan.
Burton, Jane. Hoppy the Toad. Burton, Jane, photos by. LC 89-42690. (Illus.). 24p. (Orig.). (ps-3). 1989. Random.
—Taddy the Toad. LC 89-11409. (Illus.). 32p. (gr. 2-3). 1989. PLB 10.95 (ISBN 0-8368-0211-X). Gareth Stevens Inc.
Chang, Heidi. Elaine, Mary Lewis, & the Frogs. (Illus.). 64p. (gr. 2-5). 1988. PLB 8.95 (ISBN 0-517-56752-0). Crown.
Clarke, Barry. Amazing Frogs & Toads. Young, Jerry, photos by. LC 90-31882. (Illus.). 32p. (Orig.). (gr. 1-5). 1991. lib. bdg. 9.99 (ISBN 0-679-90688-6); pap. 6.95 (ISBN 0-679-80688-1). Knopf.
Coldrey, Jennifer. Frog in the Pond. LC 85-30300. (Illus.). 32p. (gr. 4-6). 1987. 10.95 (ISBN 1-55532-059-7). Gareth Stevens Inc.
—The World of Frogs. LC 85-30297. (Illus.). 32p. (gr. 2-3). 1987. 10.95 (ISBN 1-55532-024-4). Gareth Stevens Inc.
Cole, Joanna. A Frog's Body. Wexler, Jerome, illus. LC 80-10705. 48p. (gr. k-3). 1980. PLB 12.88 (ISBN 0-688-32228-X, Morrow Jr Bks). Morrow Jr Bks.
Dallinger, Jane & Johnson, Sylvia A. Frogs & Toads. LC 80-27667. (Illus.). 48p. (gr. 4 up). 1982. PLB 14.95 (ISBN 0-8225-1454-0, First Ave Edns); pap. 5.95 (ISBN 0-8225-9502-8, First Ave Edns). Lerner Pubns.
Florian, Douglas. Discovering Frogs. Florian, Douglas, illus. LC 86-6731. 32p. (ps-3). 1986. 12.95 (ISBN 0-684-18688-8, Scribners Young Read). Macmillan Child Grp.
Hogan, Paula Z. The Frog. Strigenz, Geri K., illus. LC 78-21240. 32p. (gr. 1-4). 1979. PLB 16.67 (ISBN 0-8172-1253-1). Raintree Pubs.
—The Frog. LC 78-21240. (Illus.). 32p. (gr. 1-4). 1984. PLB 27.99 incl. cassette (ISBN 0-8172-2228-6); cassette 14.00 (ISBN 0-685-09512-6). Raintree Pubs.
Johnson, Sylvia A. Tree Frogs. Masuda, Modoki, illus. LC 86-2721. 48p. (gr. 4 up). 1986. PLB 14.95 (ISBN 0-8225-1467-2). Lerner Pubns.
Lacey, Elizabeth A. The Complete Frog: A Guide for the Very Young Naturalist. Santoro, Christopher, illus. LC 88-9343. 72p. (gr. k-4). 1989. 12.95 (ISBN 0-688-08017-0); PLB 12.88 (ISBN 0-688-08018-9). Lothrop.
Linley, Mike. Discovering Frogs & Toads. LC 85-73666. (Illus.). 48p. (gr. 4-9). PLB 11.90 (ISBN 0-531-18053-0, Pub. by Bookwright). Watts.
Lovett, Sarah, text by. Extremely Weird Frogs. (Illus.). 48p. (gr. 3 up). 1991. 9.95 (ISBN 1-56261-006-6). John Muir.
Morris, Dean. Frogs & Toads. rev. ed. LC 87-16698. (Illus.). 48p. (gr. 2-6). 1987. PLB 17.32 (ISBN 0-8172-3208-7). Raintree Pubs.
—Frogs & Toads. (ps-3). 1990. pap. 11.99 (ISBN 0-8172-3233-8). Raintree Pubs.
Oda, Hidetomo. The Tadpole. Pohl, Kathy, ed. LC 85-28202. (Illus.). 32p. (gr. 3-7). 1986. PLB 16.67 (ISBN 0-8172-2545-5); pap. text ed. 9.27 (ISBN 0-8172-2570-6). Raintree Pubs.
—The Tree Frog. annual Pohl, Kathy, ed. LC 85-28194. (Illus.). 32p. (gr. 3-7). 1986. PLB 16.67 (ISBN 0-8172-2546-3); pap. text ed. 9.27 (ISBN 0-8172-2571-4). Raintree Pubs.
Petty, Kate. Frogs & Toads. Baker, Alan, illus. 32p. (gr. k-3). 1990. pap. 2.95 (ISBN 0-531-15154-9). Watts.
Schultz, Ellen. I Can Read About Frogs & Toads. LC 78-73714. (Illus.). (gr. 2-5). 1979. pap. 1.95 (ISBN 0-89375-210-X). Troll Assocs.
Selsam, Millicent E. & Hunt, Joyce. A First Look at Frogs, Toads & Salamanders. Spunger, Harriett, illus. 32p. (gr. 2-4). 1976. PLB 12.85 (ISBN 0-8027-6244-1). Walker & Co.
Webster, David. Frog & Toad Watching. LC 86-7237. (Illus.). 80p. (gr. 3-6). 1986. lib. bdg. 9.79 (ISBN 0-671-60024-9). Messner.
Williams, John. The Life Cycle of a Frog. Caulkins, Janet, ed. LC 87-71472. (Illus.). 32p. (gr. k-6). 1988. PLB 11.90 (ISBN 0-531-18161-8, Pub. by Bookwright Pr). Watts.

FROGS–FICTION

Aardema, Verna. The Vingananee & the Tree Toad. Weiss, Ellen, illus. (gr. 3-8). 1988. pap. 4.95 (ISBN 0-14-050890-2, Puffin). Puffin Bks.
Aardema, Verna, retold by. The Vingananee & the Tree Toad. Weiss, Ellen, illus. LC 82-13473. 48p. (gr. 1-4). 1983. 12.95 (ISBN 0-7232-6217-9). Warne.
Anderson, Ethel. The Lonely Frog. 39p. 1988. 5.95 (ISBN 0-533-07593-9). Vantage.
Barbaresi, Nina. Frog Went A-Courting. Barbaresi, Nina, illus. 32p. (Orig.). (gr. k-3). 1985. pap. 2.50 (ISBN 0-590-33301-1, Seesaw Bks). Scholastic Inc.
Barkan, Joanne. Kermit's Mixed-up Message. Attinello, Lauren, illus. 32p. (Orig.). (gr. 1-4). 1987. pap. 2.75 (ISBN 0-590-44011-X). Scholastic Inc.
Bellows, Cathy. Toad School. Bellows, Cathy, illus. LC 89-12562. 32p. (gr. k-3). 1990. 13.95 (ISBN 0-02-708835-9, Mcmillan Child Bk). Macmillan Child Grp.
Blake, Quentin. The Story of the Dancing Frog. Blake, Quentin, illus. LC 84-12222. 32p. (ps-3). 1985. lib. bdg. 9.99 (ISBN 0-394-97033-0). Knopf.
—The Story of the Dancing Frog. Blake, Quentin, illus. LC 84-12222. 32p. (ps-2). 1990. pap. 4.95 (ISBN 0-394-84506-4). McKay.
Boericke, Arthur, et al. The Complete Adventures of Olga da Polga. Helweg, Hans, illus. LC 82-72753. 512p. (gr. 4-6). 1983. 16.95 (ISBN 0-440-00981-2). Delacorte.
Brown, Marc, illus. Can You Jump Like a Frog? 8p. (ps-k). 1989. 5.95 (ISBN 0-525-44463-7, DCB). Dutton Child Bks.
Carlson, Anna L. Toady Tales. 2nd. ed. LC 80-83018. 24p. (gr. k-4). 1983. pap. 1.95 (ISBN 0-939938-02-2). Karwyn Ent.
Cleveland, David. The Frog on Robert's Head. Ernst, Lisa C., illus. (gr. 1-4). 1981. 8.95 (ISBN 0-698-20512-X, Coward). Putnam Pub Group.
Conover, Chris. Froggie Went A-Courting. LC 86-45289. (Illus.). 32p. (ps up). 1986. 12.95 (ISBN 0-374-32466-2). FS&G.
Corey, Deirdre. Friends Four-Ever Minus One. 144p. (gr. 3-7). 1991. pap. 2.75 (ISBN 0-590-44029-2, Apple Paperbacks). Scholastic Inc.
Dauer, Rosamond. Bullfrog & Gertrude Go Camping. 64p. (gr. k-6). 1988. pap. 2.95 (ISBN 0-440-40074-0). Dell.
—Bullfrog Grows Up. (gr. k-6). 1988. pap. 2.95 (ISBN 0-440-40007-4). Dell.
Duke, Kate. Seven Froggies Went to School. Duke, Kate, illus. LC 84-1371. 32p. (ps-1). 1985. 11.95 (ISBN 0-525-44160-3, DCB). Dutton Child Bks.
Edwards, Davina. The Hoppy Frog. Geiger, Irene R., illus. 36p. (gr. 1-12). 1990. pap. write for info. (ISBN 0-8198-3329-0). Dghtrs St Paul.
Elliott, Donald. Frogs & Ballet. Arrowood, Clinton, illus. LC 78-19566. (gr. 1 up). 1979. smythe sewn 12.95 (ISBN 0-87645-099-0, Pub. by Gambit); pap. 8.95 (ISBN 0-87645-119-9). Harvard Common Pr.
Emery, C. F. Horny. Le Blanc, L., illus. LC 68-17304. 48p. (gr. 2 up). 1967. PLB 9.26 (ISBN 0-87783-017-7). Oddo.
Erickson, Russell E. Warton & the Contest. Di Fiori, Lawrence, illus. LC 86-102. 96p. (ps-4). 1986. 11.95 (ISBN 0-688-05818-3); PLB 11.88 (ISBN 0-688-05819-1). Lothrop.
Freddy Frog. (Illus.). (ps). 1.79 (ISBN 0-517-46417-9). Outlet Bk Co.
Gackenbach, Dick. Crackle Gluck & the Sleeping Toad. LC 78-12635. (Illus.). 32p. (gr. 1-3). 1979. 7.95 (ISBN 0-395-28953-X, Clarion). HM.
Gage, Wilson. Mike's Toads. Rounds, Glen, illus. LC 88-34907. 96p. (gr. 3 up). 1990. 12.95 (ISBN 0-688-08834-1). Greenwillow.
Garcia, Joseph G. Jump for the Apple! The Story of Lily Pond, a Soccer-Playing Frog with Long, Long Legs. Day, Rhonda, ed. Garcia, Joseph G., illus. 28p. (gr. 4up). 1983. pap. 5.95 (ISBN 0-9612350-0-4). Goal Ent.
Gilbert, Jane. Grouchy Old Fuddley. 1991. 6.95 (ISBN 0-533-09110-1). Vantage.
Gordon, Margaret. The Frogs' Holiday. (ps-2). 1987. pap. 9.95 (ISBN 0-670-80854-7). Viking Child Bks.
Graham, Amanda. Picasso the Green Tree Frog. Siow, John, illus. LC 86-42809. 1987p. (gr. 2-3). 1987. PLB 12.95 (ISBN 1-55532-152-6). Gareth Stevens Inc.
Grahame, Kenneth. The Adventures of Toad. Shepard, Ernest, illus. LC 90-45374. 48p. (ps-3). 1991. pap. 4.95 POB (ISBN 0-689-71498-X, Aladdin). Macmillan Child Grp.
Gregorich, Barbara. Jog, Frog, Jog. Hoffman, Joan, ed. Schneider, Rex, illus. 16p. (Orig.). (gr. k-2). 1984. pap. 1.95 (ISBN 0-88743-006-6, 06006). Sch Zone Pub Co.
Gretz, Susanna. Frog in the Middle. Gretz, Susanna, illus. LC 90-3842. 32p. (ps-1). 1991. SBE 12.95 (ISBN 0-02-737471-8, Four Winds). Macmillan Child Grp.
Greydanus, Rose. Federiquito el Sapo. Garcia, Tom, illus. (SPA.). 32p. (gr. k-2). 1981. PLB 7.06 (ISBN 0-89375-549-4); pap. 1.95 (ISBN 0-685-04947-7). Troll Assocs.
Griffith, Helen V. Emily & the Enchanted Frog. Lamb, Susan C., illus. LC 88-16511. 32p. (gr. 1 up). 1989. 12.95 (ISBN 0-688-08483-4); PLB 12.88 (ISBN 0-688-08484-2). Greenwillow.

Grimm, Jacob & Grimm, Wilhelm K. The Frog Prince & The Pear Tree. (Illus.). 48p. (gr. 1-4). 1985. 5.95 (ISBN 0-88110-251-2). EDC.

Gwynee, Fred. Pondlarker. LC 90-9524. (Illus.). 40p. (gr. k-4). 1990. PLB 13.95 (ISBN 0-671-70846-5). S&S Trade.

Harwood, Pearl A. Mrs. Moon's Polliwogs. Overlie, George, illus. LC 67-15689. 32p. (gr. k-3). 1967. PLB 4.95 (ISBN 0-8225-0113-9). Lerner Pubns.

Kellogg, Steven. The Mysterious Tadpole. Kellogg, Steven, illus. LC 77-71517. 32p. (ps-3). 1979. pap. 3.95 (ISBN 0-8037-6244-5). Dial Bks Young.

Kepes, Juliet. Frogs Merry. Kepes, Juliet, illus. (ps-2). 1963. lib. bdg. 6.99 (ISBN 0-394-91176-8). Pantheon.

Krauss, Robert. Mert the Blurt. Aruego, Jose & Dewey, Ariane, illus. LC 80-14508. (ps). 1987. pap. 10.95 (ISBN 0-671-66537-5); pap. 5.95 (ISBN 0-671-66539-1). S&S Trade.

Langstaff, John & Rojankovsky, Feodor. Frog Went A-Courtin' Rojankovsky, Feodor, illus. LC 55-5237. (gr. 1-4). 1972. pap. 3.95 (ISBN 0-15-633900-5, VoyB). HarBraceJ.

Larke, Joe. The Bullfrog & the Grasshopper & Other "Tails" Larke, Karol, illus. 72p. (gr. k-6). 1987. 10.00 (ISBN 0-9620112-0-7). Grin A Bit.

Le Blanc, L. Little Frog Learns to Sing. Le Blanc, L., illus. LC 68-16394. 32p. (ps-2). 1967. PLB 9.95 (ISBN 0-87783-022-3). cassette 7.94x (ISBN 0-87783-191-2). Oddo.

Lee, Jeanne M., retold by. & illus. Toad Is the Uncle of Heaven. LC 85-5639. 32p. (gr. k-2). 1985. 13.95 (ISBN 0-8050-1146-3). H Holt & Co.

Lobel, Arnold. Days with Frog & Toad. LC 78-21786. (Illus.). 64p. (gr. k-3). 1979. 11.95i (ISBN 0-06-023963-8); PLB 11.89 (ISBN 0-06-023964-6). HarpC Child Bks.

—Frog & Toad All Year. LC 76-2343. (Illus.). 64p. (gr. k-3). 1976. 11.95 (ISBN 0-06-023950-6); PLB 11.89 (ISBN 0-06-023951-4). HarpC Child Bks.

—Frog & Toad Are Friends. Lobel, Arnold, illus. LC 73-105492. 64p. (gr. k-3). 1970. 11.95 (ISBN 0-06-023957-3); PLB 11.89 (ISBN 0-06-023958-1). HarpC Child Bks.

—The Frog & Toad Pop-Up Book. Lobel, Arnold, illus. LC 85-45373. 12p. (ps-3). 1986. 9.95i (ISBN 0-06-023986-7). HarpC Child Bks.

—Frog & Toad Together. Lobel, Arnold, illus. LC 73-183163. 64p. (gr. k-3). 1972. 11.95 (ISBN 0-06-023959-X); PLB 11.89 (ISBN 0-06-023960-3). HarpC Child Bks.

—Sapo y Sepo Inseparables. (SPA.). 7.95 (ISBN 0-685-31020-5). Santillana.

Luderer, Lynn. The Toad Intruder. DeGroat, Diane, illus. (gr. 1-4). 1982. 7.95 (ISBN 0-395-32081-X). HM.

McCue, Lisa, illus. Froggie's Treasure. (ps-2). 1983. pap. 2.85 (ISBN 0-671-45488-9, Little Simon). S&S Trade.

McDonnell, Christine. Toad Food & Measle Soup. DeGroat, Diane, illus. LC 82-70204. 128p. (gr. 1-5). 1982. 9.95 (ISBN 0-8037-8476-7, 01063-320); PLB 10.89 (ISBN 0-8037-8488-0). Dial Bks Young.

—Toad Food & Measle Soup. De Groat, Diane, illus. 112p. 1984. pap. 3.95 (ISBN 0-14-031724-4, Puffin). Puffin Bks.

Mayer, Mercer. A Boy, a Dog & a Frog. LC 67-22254. (Illus.). (ps-3). 1985. 9.95 (ISBN 0-8037-0763-0); PLB 9.89 (ISBN 0-8037-0767-3). Dial Bks Young.

—Four Frogs in a Box, 4 vols. LC 75-9197. (Illus.). (gr. k-5). 1976. boxed set 7.95 (ISBN 0-8037-2776-3). Dial Bks Young.

—Frog Goes to Dinner. Mayer, Mercer, illus. LC 74-2881. 32p. (ps-2). 1985. 8.95 (ISBN 0-8037-3386-0); PLB 8.89 (ISBN 0-8037-3381-X). Dial Bks Young.

—Frog Goes to Dinner. Mayer, Mercer, illus. (gr. k-2). 1977. pap. 2.95 (ISBN 0-8037-2733-X). Dial Bks Young.

—Frog on His Own. Mayer, Mercer, illus. LC 73-6018. 32p. (ps-2). 1985. 8.95 (ISBN 0-8037-2701-1); PLB 8.89 (ISBN 0-8037-2695-3). Dial Bks Young.

—Frog on His Own. Mayer, Mercer, illus. LC 73-6018. 32p. (ps-2). 1980. pap. 2.95 (ISBN 0-8037-2716-X). Dial Bks Young.

—Frog, Where Are You? Mayer, Mercer, illus. LC 72-85544. (ps-3). 1985. 9.95 (ISBN 0-8037-2737-2); PLB 9.89 (ISBN 0-8037-2732-1). Dial Bks Young.

—Frog, Where Are You? Mayer, Mercer, illus. LC 72-85544. 32p. (ps-2). 1980. pap. 2.95 (ISBN 0-8037-2729-1). Dial Bks Young.

Mayer, Mercer & Mayer, Marianna. One Frog Too Many. Mayer, Mercer, illus. LC 75-6325. 32p. (ps-2). 1985. 9.95 (ISBN 0-8037-4838-8); PLB 9.89 (ISBN 0-8037-4858-2). Dial Bks Young.

—One Frog Too Many. LC 75-6325. (Illus.). (ps-2). 1977. pap. 2.95 (ISBN 0-8037-6734-X). Dial Bks Young.

Nichols, Freeda B. Little Bug Eyes: The Little Frog Who Did. LC 89-91965. (Illus.). 24p. (Orig.). (gr. k-6). pap. 4.95 (ISBN 0-9623980-0-4). Baker Seaforth.

One Green Frog. (Illus.). 24p. (gr. k-2). 1982. 6.95 (ISBN 0-448-01453-X, G&D). Putnam Pub Group.

Paris, Pat. Pop up Frog. 1989. 4.95 (ISBN 0-671-67554-0). S&S Trade.

Potter, Beatrix. Meet Jeremy Fisher. (Illus.). 12p. (ps). 1987. bds. 2.95 (ISBN 0-7232-3453-1). Warne.

—The Tale of Jeremy Fisher. Bloom, Claire, narrated by. 1984. pap. 5.95 with cassette (ISBN 0-89845-502-2, TBC5022, Caedmon). HarperAudio.

—The Tale of Mr. Jeremy Fisher. Atkinson, Allen, illus. 1983. pap. 2.25 (ISBN 0-553-15221-1). Bantam.

Pursell, Margaret S. Sprig the Tree Frog. Hammarberg, Dyan, tr. from FRE. LC 76-1224. (Illus.). 24p. (gr. k-4). 1976. PLB 6.95 (ISBN 0-87614-064-9). Carolrhoda Bks.

Randall, Carrie. The Roommate. 144p. (gr. 3-7). 1991. pap. 2.75 (ISBN 0-590-44023-3, Apple Paperbacks). Scholastic Inc.

Redhead, Janet S. The Turkeygobbling Frog Show. Clark, Tracey, illus. LC 90-10074. 24p. (gr. 1-4). 1990. PLB 15.96 (ISBN 0-8114-2696-3). Steck-V.

Royston, Angela. Frog. Pledger, Maurice, illus. 24p. (gr. k-3). 1989. pap. 2.95 (ISBN 0-8249-8370-X). Ideals.

Sadler, Marilyn. Alistair Underwater. 1990. pap. 13.95 (ISBN 0-671-69406-5). S&S Trade.

Saunders, Susan. Kate the Winner! 128p. (gr. 3-7). 1991. pap. 2.75 (ISBN 0-590-43925-1, Apple Paperbacks). Scholastic Inc.

Schneider, Rex. The Wide-Mouthed Frog. LC 80-13449. (Illus.). 32p. (gr. k up). 1980. 13.95 (ISBN 0-916144-58-5). Stemmer Hse.

Solotareff, Gregoire. The Ogre & the Frog King. LC 87-8531. (FRE., Illus.). 32p. (ps-1). 1988. 11.95 (ISBN 0-688-07078-7); lib. bdg. 11.88 (ISBN 0-688-07079-5). Greenwillow.

Steig, William. Gorky Rises. Steig, William, illus. LC 80-68068. 32p. (ps up). 1980. 13.95 (ISBN 0-374-32752-1). FS&G.

—Gorky Rises. (Illus.). 32p. (ps up). 1986. pap. 4.95 (ISBN 0-374-42784-4). FS&G.

Stouffer, Nancy. The Fat Frog. Stouffer, Nancy, illus. 48p. (ps-1). 1989. pap. 2.95 (ISBN 0-927008-00-9). BCI-Bk Cook Inc.

Super, Terri, illus. A Fish & a Frog. 10p. (ps). 1984. vinyl bk. 2.95 (ISBN 0-448-41226-8, G&D). Putnam Pub Group.

Temko, Florence. Paper Pandas & Jumping Frogs. Jackson, Paul, illus. Petersen, Richard, et al, photos by. LC 86-70960. (Illus.). 135p. (gr. 3-6). 1986. pap. 11.95 (ISBN 0-8351-1770-7). China Bks.

Thomson, Pat. Thank You for the Tadpole. (gr. k-6). 1988. pap. 2.50 (ISBN 0-440-40027-9, YB). Dell.

Twain, Mark. The Jumping Frog. (Illus.). 78p. (gr. 7 up). 1986. 25.00 (ISBN 0-932458-31-9); pap. 5.95 (ISBN 0-932458-30-0). Star Rover.

Velthuijs, Max. Frog & the Birdsong. (ps-3). 1991. bds. 13.95 jacketed (ISBN 0-374-32467-0). FS&G.

Velthuis, Max. Frog in Love. Bell, Anthea, tr. (ps up). 1989. 11.95 (ISBN 0-374-32465-4); pap. 4.95 (ISBN 0-374-42470-5). FS&G.

Wang, Mary L. El Principe Rana: (The Frog Prince) Connelly, Gwen, illus. LC 86-11796. (SPA.). 32p. (ps-2). 1989. PLB 11.93 (ISBN 0-516-33983-4); pap. 3.95 (ISBN 0-516-53983-3). Childrens.

Williams, George, III. Mark Twain: Jackass Hill & the Jumping Frog. Dalton, Bill, ed. (Illus.). 112p. (gr. 5 up). 1989. text ed. 12.95 (ISBN 0-935174-20-6); pap. 6.95 (ISBN 0-935174-19-2). Tree by River.

Wood, Leslie. The Frog & the Fly. (Illus.). 16p. 1987. pap. 2.95 (ISBN 0-19-272154-2). Oxford U Pr.

Yolen, Jane. Commander Toad & the Intergalactic Spy. Degen, Bruce, illus. 64p. (ps-4). 1986. lib. bdg. 9.99 (ISBN 0-698-30747-X, Coward); pap. 5.95 (ISBN 0-698-20623-1, Coward). Putnam Pub Group.

—Commander Toad & the Planet of the Grapes. Degen, Bruce, illus. 64p. (gr. 1-4). 1982. lib. bdg. 9.99 (ISBN 0-698-30736-4, Coward); pap. 5.95 (ISBN 0-698-20540-5). Putnam Pub Group.

—Commander Toad in Space. Degen, Bruce, illus. 64p. (gr. 3-5). 1980. PLB 8.99 (ISBN 0-698-30724-0, Coward); pap. 5.95 (ISBN 0-698-20522-7). Putnam Pub Group.

Zemach, Harve & Zemach, Kaethe. The Princess & Froggie. Zemach, Margot, illus. LC 75-697. 48p. (ps-3). 1975. 9.95 (ISBN 0-374-36116-9). FS&G.

FRONTIER AND PIONEER LIFE

see also Cowboys; Indians of North America–Captivities; Overland Journeys to the Pacific; Ranch Life

American Pioneer Family. (Illus.). (gr. 3-8). lib. bdg. 14.00 (ISBN 0-86592-138-5). Rourke Corp.

Anderson, Joan. Christmas on the Prairie. Ancona, George, illus. LC 85-4095. 48p. (gr. 2-6). 1985. 13.95 (ISBN 0-89919-307-2, Clarion). Ticknor & Fields.

—Pioneer Children of Appalachia. Ancona, George, illus. LC 86-2624. 48p. (gr. 2-5). 1986. 13.95 (ISBN 0-89919-440-0, Pub. by Clarion). Ticknor & Fields.

—Pioneer Settlers of New France. 1990. 15.95 (ISBN 0-525-67291-5, Lodestar Bks). Dutton Child Bks.

—Spanish Pioneers of the Southwest. Ancona, George, photos by. LC 88-16121. (Illus.). 64p. (gr. 3-6). 1989. 14.95 (ISBN 0-525-67264-8, Lodestar Bks). Dutton Child Bks.

Anderson, Joan W. Pioneer Children of Appalachia. (gr. 4-7). 1990. pap. 5.95 (ISBN 0-395-54792-X, Clarion Bks). HM.

Anderson, William & Kelly, Leslie A. Little House Country: A Photo Guide to the Homesites of Laura Ingalls Wilder. (Illus.). 48p. 1989. 9.95 (ISBN 0-9610088-8-1). Anderson MI.

Bragg, Bea. The Very First Thanksgiving: Pioneers on the Rio Grande. LC 89-15562. (Illus.). 64p. (Orig.). (gr. 3-5). 1989. pap. 7.95 (ISBN 0-943173-22-1). Harbinger AZ.

Chambers, Catherine E. Frontier Dream: Life on the Great Plains. Smolinski, Dick, illus. LC 83-18282. 32p. (gr. 5-9). 1984. PLB 10.79 (ISBN 0-8167-0039-7); pap. text ed. 2.95 (ISBN 0-8167-0040-0). Troll Assocs.

Cooper, James Fenimore. The Leatherstocking Saga. (gr. 5-6). 32.95 (ISBN 0-8488-0059-1, Pub. by Amereon Hse). Amereon Ltd.

Fradin, Dennis. Pioneers. LC 84-9418. (Illus.). 48p. (gr. k-4). 1984. lib. bdg. 14.60 (ISBN 0-516-01927-9). Childrens.

Gorsline, Marie & Gorsline, Douglas. The Pioneers. reissued ed. Gorsline, Marie & Gorsline, Douglas, illus. LC 78-54960. 32p. (gr. k-4). 1982. pap. 2.25 (ISBN 0-394-83905-6). Random.

Gunby, Lise. Early Farm Life. (Illus.). 80p. (gr. 3-4). 1983. 15.95 (ISBN 0-86505-027-9); pap. 7.95 (ISBN 0-86505-026-0). Crabtree Pub Co.

Gurasich, Marj. Letters to Oma, a Young German Girl's Account of Her First Year in Texas, 1847. Whitehead, Barbara, illus. LC 88-38747. 162p. (gr. 4-8). 1989. pap. 9.95 (ISBN 0-87565-037-6). Tex Christian.

Hamilton, Dorothy. Daniel Forbes: A Pioneer Boy. King, Barbara L., illus. (Orig.). (gr. 3-5). 1980. pap. 3.95 (ISBN 0-686-32860-4). Barnwood Pr.

Hartley, Al. Yankee Doodle on the Frontier. Hartley, Al, illus. LC 89-8350. 45p. (gr. 3-6). 1989. 6.95 (ISBN 0-88070-294-X). Multnomah.

Jones, Helen H. Over the Mormon Trail. Rogers, Carol, illus. LC 63-9706. 128p. (gr. 3-10). 1980. PLB 14.60 (ISBN 0-516-03354-9). Childrens.

Kalman, Bobbie. Early Artisans. (Illus.). 64p. (gr. 4-5). 1983. 14.95 (ISBN 0-86505-023-6); pap. 7.95 (ISBN 0-86505-022-8). Crabtree Pub Co.

—Early Christmas. (Illus.). 64p. (gr. 4-5). 1981. 14.95 (ISBN 0-86505-001-5); pap. 7.95 (ISBN 0-86505-003-1). Crabtree Pub Co.
EARLY CHRISTMAS is a wonderful historical odyssey taking young readers back to the early days of this country when Christmas traditions were made. Children will read about the special ways the settlers celebrated the most popular holiday of the year. EARLY CHRISTMAS is part of the The Early Settler Life Series, Bobbie Kalman's best-selling books. Illustrated with sepia-colored photographs & etchings, The Early Settler Life Series allows young readers the opportunity to experience 19th century etchings & photographs that are found only in archival colections. Other books in the series are: EARLY STORES & MARKETS, EARLY LOGGERS & THE SAWMILL, EARLY TRAVEL, EARLY SETTLER CHILDREN, EARLY SETTLER STORYBOOK, EARLY ARTISANS, EARLY PLEASURES & PASTIMES, EARLY VILLAGE LIFE, EARLY FARM LIFE, FOOD FOR THE SETTLER, EARLY CITY LIFE, EARLY HEALTH & MEDICINE, EARLY SCHOOLS, EARLY FAMILY HOME, & EARLY SETTLER ACTIVITY GUIDE.
Publisher Provided Annotation.

—Early City Life. (Illus.). 64p. (gr. 4-5). 1983. 14.95 (ISBN 0-86505-029-5); pap. 7.95 (ISBN 0-86505-028-7). Crabtree Pub Co.

—The Early Family Home. (Illus.). 64p. (gr. 4-5). 1982. 14.95 (ISBN 0-86505-017-1); pap. 7.95 (ISBN 0-86505-016-3). Crabtree Pub Co.

—Early Pleasures & Pastimes. (Illus.). 96p. (gr. 4-5). 1983. 15.95 (ISBN 0-86505-025-2); pap. 7.95 (ISBN 0-86505-024-4). Crabtree Pub Co.

—Early Settler Children. (Illus.). 64p. (gr. 4-5). 1982. 14.95 (ISBN 0-86505-019-8); pap. 7.95 (ISBN 0-86505-018-X). Crabtree Pub Co.

—Early Stores & Markets. (Illus.). 64p. (gr. 4-5). 1981. 14.95 (ISBN 0-86505-002-3); pap. 7.95 (ISBN 0-86505-004-X). Crabtree Pub Co.

—Early Travel. (Illus.). 64p. (gr. 4-5). 1981. 14.95 (ISBN 0-86505-007-4); pap. 7.95 (ISBN 0-86505-008-2). Crabtree Pub Co.

—Early Village Life. (Illus.). 64p. (gr. 4-5). 1981. 14.95 (ISBN 0-86505-009-0); pap. 7.95 (ISBN 0-86505-010-4). Crabtree Pub Co.

—Food for the Settler. (Illus.). 96p. (gr. 4-5). 1982. 15.95 (ISBN 0-86505-013-9); pap. 7.95 (ISBN 0-86505-012-0). Crabtree Pub Co.

—Visiting a Village. (Illus.). 32p. (gr. 3-4). 1990. lib. bdg. 14.95 (ISBN 0-86505-487-8); pap. 7.95 (ISBN 0-86505-507-6). Crabtree Pub Co.

Levine, Ellen. If You Traveled West in a Covered Wagon. Shaw, Charles, illus. 80p. (Orig.). (gr. 2-5). 1986. pap. 2.95 (ISBN 0-590-42229-4). Scholastic Inc.

Lindbergh, Reeve. Johnny Appleseed. Jakoben, Kathy, illus. (ps-4). 1990. 14.95 (ISBN 0-316-52618-5, Joy St Bks). Little.

Lindsley, Margaret. Andrew Henry: Mine & Mountain Major. (Illus.). 370p. 1990. 19.95 (ISBN 0-936204-79-6); pap. 15.95 (ISBN 0-936204-78-8). Jelm Mtn.
Evokes the era, triumphs & tribulations of the complex & sometimes contradictory man, Andrew Henry. Spanning his lifetime, 1778-1833, as well as awesome mountains, wars & romances, this book defines the man & identifies his rightful place in the history of westward expansion. Wise in the ways of French & Spanish aristocrats & entrepreneurs, boatmen, soldiers, fur trappers, Indians & grizzlies, Henry was comfortable in a wide variety of cultures, from the sophistication of French Ste. Genevieve to the rough & tumble fur-trade forts & Indian camps along the Missouri & Yellowstone Rivers. Miner, militia major, explorer, mountain man, fur trapper, leader of men, he could guide men of diverse backgrounds from St. Louis to the Tetons & back through harsh winters, grizzlies & Blackfeet, yet his first marriage lasted only eighteen days. Associate of Moses Austin, partner of William Ashley, respected contemporary of Manuel Lisa, the Chouteaus, the Valles, Lewis & Clark, he had one Fort Henry in Idaho, two in Montana & one in North Dakota named for him. As were some of the best trout & fly-fishing waters in the world, Henry's Lake & Henry's Fork of the Snake River in Southeastern Idaho.
Publisher Provided Annotation.

McCall, Edith. Cowboys & Cattle Drives. Rogers, Carol, illus. LC 64-19886. 128p. (gr. 3-10). 1980. PLB 14.60 (ISBN 0-516-03312-3). Childrens.
—Cumberland Gap & Trails West. Rogers, Carol, illus. LC 61-10102. 128p. (gr. 3-10). 1980. PLB 14.60 (ISBN 0-516-03311-5). Childrens.
—Explorers in a New World. Borja, Robert, illus. LC 60-6675. 128p. (gr. 3-10). 1980. PLB 14.60 (ISBN 0-516-03318-2). Childrens.
—Forts in the Wilderness. Wiskur, Darrell, illus. LC 68-24378. 128p. (gr. 3-10). 1980. PLB 14.60 (ISBN 0-516-03324-7). Childrens.
—Gold Rush Adventures. Eckart, Frances, illus. LC 62-9530. 128p. (gr. 3-10). 1980. PLB 14.60 (ISBN 0-516-03328-X). Childrens.
—Heroes of Western Outposts. Tanis, William, illus. LC 60-11155. 128p. (gr. 3-10). 1980. PLB 14.60 (ISBN 0-516-03331-X). Childrens.
—Hunters Blaze the Trails. Rogers, Carol, illus. LC 59-3666. 128p. (gr. 3-10). 1980. PLB 14.60 (ISBN 0-516-03332-8). Childrens.
—Mail Riders. Eckart, Frances, illus. LC 61-10103. 128p. (gr. 3-10). 1980. PLB 14.60 (ISBN 0-516-03347-6). Childrens.
—Pioneering on the Plains. Rogers, Carol, illus. LC 62-15638. 128p. (gr. 3-10). 1980. PLB 14.60 (ISBN 0-516-03358-1). Childrens.
—Pioneers on Early Waterways. Rogers, Carl, illus. LC 61-10104. 128p. (gr. 3-10). 1980. PLB 14.60 (ISBN 0-516-03357-3). Childrens.
—Settlers on a Strange Shore. Rogers, Carol, illus. LC 60-11154. 128p. (gr. 3-10). 1980. PLB 14.60 (ISBN 0-516-03367-0). Childrens.
—Wagons Over the Mountains. Rogers, Carol, illus. LC 61-10101. 128p. (gr. 3-10). 1980. PLB 14.60 (ISBN 0-516-03376-X). Childrens.
Mayers, Florence C. ABC: The Wild West Buffalo Bill Historical Center, Cody, Wyoming. LC 90-440. (Illus.). 32p. 1990. 12.95 (ISBN 0-8109-1903-6). Abrams.
Naden, C. J. I Can Read About Pioneers. LC 78-65835. (Illus.). (gr. 3-6). 1979. pap. 1.95 (ISBN 0-89375-214-2). Troll Assocs.
Parish, Peggy. Let's Be Early Settlers with Daniel Boone. LC 67-14068. (Illus.). 96p. (gr. 3-5). 1967. PLB 14.89 (ISBN 0-06-024648-0). HarpC Child Bks.

Perez, Robert H. Southwest Borderlands: Veins of Silver & Gold. (Illus.). 160p. (gr. 10-12). 1982. pap. text ed. 7.50 (ISBN 0-940870-13-4); tchr's man. 2.50 (ISBN 0-940870-14-2). U of AZ Ed Mat.
Perl, Lila. Hunter's Stew & Hangtown Fry. Cuffari, Richard, illus. LC 77-5366. 176p. (gr. 6 up). 1979. 13.95 (ISBN 0-395-28922-X, Clarion). HM.
Pioneers in Change, 10 bks., 6 vols. (Illus.). (gr. 5-7). 1990. Set, 144p. ea. lib. bdg. 139.80 (ISBN 0-382-09930-3); pap. 47.70 (ISBN 0-382-24161-4). Silver Burdett Pr.
Sabin, Francene. Pioneers. Frenck, Hal, illus. LC 84-2580. 32p. (gr. 3-6). 1985. PLB 9.49 (ISBN 0-8167-0120-2); pap. text ed. 2.95 (ISBN 0-8167-0121-0). Troll Assocs.
Smith, Carter, ed. Daily Life: A Sourcebook on Colonial America. (Illus.). 96p. (gr. 5 up). 1991. PLB 14.90 (ISBN 1-56294-038-4); pap. write for info. (ISBN 1-878841-68-8). Millbrook Pr.
—Explorers & Settlers: A Sourcebook on Colonial America. (Illus.). 96p. (gr. 5 up). 1991. PLB 19.95 (ISBN 1-56294-035-X); pap. write for info. (ISBN 1-878841-64-5). Millbrook Pr.
Stenson, Elizabeth. Early Settler Activity Guide. (Illus.). 128p. (gr. 4-5). 1983. pap. 15.95 (ISBN 0-86505-036-8). Crabtree Pub Co.
Stewart, Gail. Frontiersmen. (Illus.). 32p. (gr. 3-8). 1990. PLB 17.26 (ISBN 0-86625-406-4); PLB 12.95s.p. (ISBN 0-685-34709-5). Rourke Corp.
—Lumberman. (Illus.). 32p. (gr. 3-8). 1990. lib. bdg. 17.26 (ISBN 0-86625-407-2). Rourke Corp.
—Rivermen. (Illus.). 32p. (gr. 3-8). 1990. PLB 17.26 (ISBN 0-86625-409-9). Rourke Corp.
—Scouts. (Illus.). 32p. (gr. 3-8). 1990. PLB 17.26 (ISBN 0-86625-404-8). Rourke Corp.
—Trappers & Traders. (Illus.). 32p. (gr. 3-8). 1990. PLB 17.26 (ISBN 0-86625-401-3). Rourke Corp.
Strait, Treva A. The Price of Free Land. LC 78-24287. (Illus.). (gr. 4-6). 1979. (Lipp Jr Bks). HarpC Child Bks.
Tunis, Edwin. Frontier Living. Tunis, Edwin, illus. LC 75-29639. 168p. (gr. 7 up). 1976. 25.95 (ISBN 0-690-01064-8, Crowell Jr Bks). HarpC Child Bks.
Vickery, Eugene L. Frontier Adventures: Stories in Verse of Young People in Kentucky & the South West. Vickery, Millie M., ed. Tolpo, Lily, illus. 40p. (Orig.). (gr. 1-8). 1987. pap. 4.95 perfect bdg. (ISBN 0-937775-06-1). Stonehaven Pubs.

FRONTIER AND PIONEER LIFE–BIOGRAPHY
Artman, John. Pioneers. Hyndman, Kathryn, illus. 64p. (gr. 4 up). 1987. pap. 6.95 (ISBN 0-86653-401-6, GA 1027). Good Apple.
Byrne, Pamela R. & Kinnell, Susan K. Pioneers & Explorers in North America: Summaries of Biographical Articles in History Journals. 132p. (gr. 9-12). 1988. pap. text ed. 18.00 (ISBN 0-87436-540-6). ABC Clio.
Crawford, Ann F. Jane Long - Frontier Woman. Baxter, Rosario, illus. 64p. (gr. 4-7). 1990. lib. bdg. 12.95 (ISBN 0-87443-090-9). Benson.
—Lizzie - Queen of the Cattle Trails. Fain, Cheryl G., illus. 64p. (gr. 4-7). 1990. lib. bdg. 12.95 (ISBN 0-87443-091-7). Benson.
Hargrove, Jim. Daniel Boone: Pioneer Trailblazer. LC 85-13309. (Illus.). 124p. (gr. 5-7). 1985. PLB 17.27 (ISBN 0-516-03215-1). Childrens.
Laura Ingalls Wilder. (gr. 2-6). 1988. pap. 3.95 (ISBN 0-14-032074-1, Puffin). Puffin Bks.

Lindsley, Margaret. Andrew Henry: Mine & Mountain Major. (Illus.). 370p. 1990. 19.95 (ISBN 0-936204-79-6); pap. 15.95 (ISBN 0-936204-78-8). Jelm Mtn.
Evokes the era, triumphs & tribulations of the complex & sometimes contradictory man, Andrew Henry. Spanning his lifetime, 1778-1833, as well as awesome mountains, wars & romances, this book defines the man & identifies his rightful place in the history of westward expansion. Wise in the ways of French & Spanish aristocrats & entrepreneurs, boatmen, soldiers, fur trappers, Indians & grizzlies, Henry was comfortable in a wide variety of cultures, from the sophistication of French Ste. Genevieve to the rough & tumble fur-trade forts & Indian camps along the Missouri & Yellowstone Rivers. Miner, militia major, explorer, mountain man, fur trapper, leader of men, he could guide men of diverse backgrounds from St. Louis to the Tetons & back through harsh winters, grizzlies & Blackfeet, yet his first marriage lasted only eighteen days. Associate of Moses

Austin, partner of William Ashley, respected contemporary of Manuel Lisa, the Chouteaus, the Valles, Lewis & Clark, he had one Fort Henry in Idaho, two in Montana & one in North Dakota named for him. As were some of the best trout & fly-fishing waters in the world, Henry's Lake & Henry's Fork of the Snake River in Southeastern Idaho.
Publisher Provided Annotation.

FRONTIER AND PIONEER LIFE–FICTION
Ackerman, Karen. Araminta's Paint Box. Lewin, Betsy, illus. LC 88-35033. 32p. (gr. 1-3). 1990. 12.95 (ISBN 0-689-31462-0, Atheneum Child Bk). Macmillan Child Grp.
Alter, Judith M. Luke & the Van Zandt County War. Conoly, Walli, illus. LC 84-101. 132p. (gr. 4 up). 1984. 10.95 (ISBN 0-912646-88-8). Tex Christian.
Brink, Carol R. Caddie Woodlawn. Hyman, Trina S., illus. LC 73-588. 288p. (gr. 4-6). 1973. 14.95 (ISBN 0-02-713670-1, Mcmillan Child Bk). Macmillan Child Grp.
Byars, Betsy. The Golly Sisters Go West. Truesdell, Sue, illus. LC 84-48474. 64p. (gr. k-3). 1986. 11.95 (ISBN 0-06-020883-X); PLB 11.89 (ISBN 0-06-020884-8). HarpC Child Bks.
—Hooray for the Golly Sisters! Truesdell, Sue, illus. LC 89-48147. 64p. (gr. k-3). 1990. 11.95 (ISBN 0-06-020898-8); PLB 11.89 (ISBN 0-06-020899-6). HarpC Child Bks.
Byars, Betsy C. Trouble River. Negri, Rocco, illus. (gr. 3-7). 1969. pap. 13.95 (ISBN 0-670-73257-5). Viking Child Bks.
—Trouble River. Negri, Rocco, illus. 160p. (gr. 3-7). 1989. pap. 3.95 (ISBN 0-14-034243-5, Puffin). Puffin Bks.
Canfield, Dorothy. The Bent Twig. 334p. 1981. Repr. PLB 17.95x (ISBN 0-89966-343-5). Buccaneer Bks.
Chambers, Catherine E. California Gold Rush: Search for Treasure. Eitzen, Alan, illus. LC 83-18280. 32p. (gr. 5-9). 1984. PLB 10.79 (ISBN 0-8167-0051-6); pap. text ed. 2.95 (ISBN 0-8167-0052-4). Troll Assocs.
—Daniel Boone & the Wilderness Road. Guzzi, George, illus. LC 83-18291. 32p. (gr. 5-9). 1984. PLB 10.79 (ISBN 0-8167-0037-0); pap. text ed. 2.95 (ISBN 0-8167-0038-9). Troll Assocs.
—Flatboats on the Ohio: Westward Bound. Lawn, John, illus. LC 83-18278. 32p. (gr. 5-9). 1984. PLB 10.79 (ISBN 0-8167-0049-4); pap. text ed. 2.95 (ISBN 0-8167-0050-8). Troll Assocs.
—Frontier Farmer: Kansas Adventures. Epstein, Len, illus. LC 83-18279. 32p. (gr. 5-9). 1984. PLB 10.79 (ISBN 0-8167-0053-2); pap. text ed. 2.95 (ISBN 0-8167-0054-0). Troll Assocs.
—Frontier Village: A Town Is Born. Smolinski, Dick, illus. LC 83-18271. 32p. (gr. 5-9). 1984. PLB 10.79 (ISBN 0-8167-0045-1); pap. text ed. 2.95 (ISBN 0-8167-0046-X). Troll Assocs.
—Indiana Days: Life in a Frontier Town. Lawn, John, illus. LC 83-18283. 32p. (gr. 5-9). 1984. PLB 10.79 (ISBN 0-8167-0055-9); pap. text ed. 2.95 (ISBN 0-8167-0056-7). Troll Assocs.
—Log Cabin Home: Pioneers in the Wilderness. Eitzen, Alan, illus. LC 83-18277. 32p. (gr. 5-9). 1984. PLB 10.79 (ISBN 0-8167-0041-9); pap. text ed. 2.50 (ISBN 0-8167-0042-7). Troll Assocs.
—Texas Roundup: Life on the Range. Lawn, John, illus. LC 83-18281. 32p. (gr. 5-9). 1984. PLB 10.79 (ISBN 0-8167-0047-8); pap. text ed. 2.95 (ISBN 0-8167-0048-6). Troll Assocs.
—Wagons West: Off to Oregon. Smolinski, Dick, illus. LC 83-18276. 32p. (gr. 5-9). 1984. PLB 10.79 (ISBN 0-8167-0043-5); pap. text ed. 2.95 (ISBN 0-8167-0044-3). Troll Assocs.
Coerr, Eleanor. The Josefina Story Quilt. Degen, Bruce, illus. LC 85-45260. 64p. (gr. k-3). 1989. pap. 3.50 (ISBN 0-06-444129-6, Trophy). HarpC Child Bks.
Cooper, James Fenimore. The Deerslayer. 528p. (gr. 9-12). 1991. pap. 3.50 (ISBN 0-553-21085-8, Bantam Classics). Bantam.
—The Deerslayer: or The First War-Path. Wyeth, N. C., illus. LC 90-34326. 480p. 1990. 22.95 (ISBN 0-684-19224-1, Scribners Young Read); deluxe ed. 75.00 (ISBN 0-684-19234-9, Scribner). Macmillan Child Grp.
—Pathfinder. (gr. 6 up). 1964. pap. 2.95 (ISBN 0-8049-0035-3, CL-35). Airmont.
—Pioneers. (gr. 8 up). 1964. pap. 1.95 (ISBN 0-8049-0049-3, CL-49). Airmont.
—Prairie. (gr. 8 up). 1964. pap. 1.95 (ISBN 0-8049-0041-8, CL-41). Airmont.
Dalgliesh, Alice. The Courage of Sarah Noble. Weisgard, Leonard, illus. LC 54-5922. 64p. (gr. 1-5). 1987. Repr. of 1954 ed. 12.95 (ISBN 0-684-18830-9, Scribners Young Read). Macmillan Child Grp.
—The Courage of Sarah Noble. 2nd ed. Weisgard, Leonard, illus. 64p. (gr. 1-5). 1991. pap. 4.95 (ISBN 0-689-71540-4, Aladdin). Macmillan Child Grp.
Donahue, Marilyn C. The Valley in Between. (gr. 5 up). 1987. 14.95 (ISBN 0-8027-6731-1); PLB 15.85 (ISBN 0-8027-6733-8). Walker & Co.

Forbes, Esther. Johnny Tremain. 1987. pap. 3.50 (ISBN 0-440-44250-8). Dell.

Fritz, Jean. The Cabin Faced West. Rojankovsky, Feodor, illus. (gr. 4-7). 1958. 8.95 (ISBN 0-698-20016-0, Coward). Putnam Pub Group.

—The Cabin Faced West. Rojanovsky, Feodor, illus. (gr. 1-7). 1987. pap. 3.95 (ISBN 0-14-032256-6, Puffin). Puffin Bks.

Harrison, Nick. While Yet We Live. 224p. Date not set. pap. write for info. (ISBN 0-940652-08-0). Sunrise Bks.

Henry, Marguerite. San Domingo: The Medicine Hat Stallion. Longheed, Robert, illus. LC 72-7416. 224p. (gr. 2-9). 1986. 8.95 (ISBN 0-528-82443-0). Macmillan Child Grp.

Howard, Ellen. The Chickenhouse House. LC 90-38007. (Illus.). 64p. (gr. 2-5). 1991. SBE 11.95 (ISBN 0-689-31695-X, Atheneum Child Bk). Macmillan Child Grp.

Kerr, Rita. The Ghost of Panna Maria. Eakin, Ed, ed. Kerr, Rita, illus. 96p. (gr. 2-4). 1990. 9.95 (ISBN 0-89015-791-X); pap. 3.95 (ISBN 0-89015-803-7). Eakin Pr.

—Texas Marvel. Roberts, Melissa, ed. 120p. (gr. 4-7). 1987. 7.95 (ISBN 0-89015-597-6, Pub. by Panda Bks). Eakin Pr.

Lasky, Kathryn. The Bone Wars. 384p. (gr. 5-9). 1989. pap. 4.95 (ISBN 0-14-034168-4, Puffin). Puffin Bks.

Laurgaard, Rachel K. Patty Reed's Doll: The Story of the Donner Party. Michaels, Elizabeth, illus. 144p. (gr. 3-6). 1989. pap. 7.95 (ISBN 0-9617357-2-4). Tomato Enter.

Mason, Miriam E. Young Mister Meeker & His Exciting Journey to Oregon. (gr. 3-6). 1952. 4.95 (ISBN 0-672-50599-1, Bobbs). Macmillan.

Monjo, F. N. Indian Summer. Lobel, Anita, illus. LC 78-20264. 192p. (gr. k-3). 1968. PLB 11.89 (ISBN 0-06-024328-7). HarpC Child Bks.

Moore, Robin. The Bread Sister of Sinking Creek. LC 89-36400. (Illus.). 160p. (gr. 4-7). 1990. 14.95 (ISBN 0-397-32418-9, Lipp Jr Bks); PLB 12.89 (ISBN 0-397-32419-7, Lipp Jr Bks). HarpC Child Bks.

—Maggie among the Seneca. rev. ed. LC 89-77110. 112p. (gr. 4-7). 1990. 13.95 (ISBN 0-397-32455-3, Lipp Jr Bks); PLB 13.89 (ISBN 0-397-32456-1, Lipp Jr Bks). HarpC Child Bks.

Murrow, Liza K. West Against the Wind. LC 87-45337. 240p. (gr. 7 up). 1987. 14.95 (ISBN 0-8234-0668-7). Holiday.

Nielsen, Shelly. More Victoria. 130p. (gr. 5-6). 1986. pap. 3.95 (ISBN 0-89191-453-6). Cook.

O'Dell, Scott. Carlota. O'Dell, Scott, illus. LC 77-9468. 176p. (gr. 5-9). 1977. 13.95 (ISBN 0-395-25487-6). HM.

Reuther, Ruth E. Meet at the Falls: The Story of the Pioneers. McCall, Jody, ed. (Illus.). 1989. pap. text ed. write for info. (ISBN 0-9622632-1-4). Wee-Chee-Taw.

Richter, Conrad. Light in the Forest. Chappell, Warren, illus. (gr. 6 up). 1966. 17.95 (ISBN 0-394-43314-9). Knopf.

Shay, Myrtle. Adventures of Ricky & Chub. Kennedy, Paul, illus. (gr. 4-8). PLB 6.70 (ISBN 0-685-02937-9). Lantern.

Speare, Elizabeth G. The Sign of the Beaver. 144p. (gr. 5-9). 1984. pap. 3.50 (ISBN 0-440-47900-2, YB). Dell.

Steele, William O. Buffalo Knife. 1990. pap. 3.95 (ISBN 0-15-213212-0). HarbraceJ.

—Flaming Arrows. 1990. pap. 3.95 (ISBN 0-15-228427-3). HarbraceJ.

—Winter Danger. Galdone, Paul, illus. LC 54-5157. (gr. 4-6). 1954. 6.75 (ISBN 0-685-02109-2, HJ). HarBraceJ.

Stevens, Carla. Trouble for Lucy. Himler, Ronald, illus. LC 79-10445. (gr. 2-6). 1979. 13.95 (ISBN 0-395-28971-8, Clarion). HM.

Stewart, George R. The Pioneers Go West. LC 87-4568. 160p. (gr. 5-9). 1987. lib. bdg. 8.99 (ISBN 0-394-90342-0, Random Juv); pap. 2.95 (ISBN 0-394-89180-5, Random Juv). Random.

Stoutenburg, Adrien. American Tall Tales. Powers, Richard M., illus. (gr. 3-7). 1976. pap. 3.95 (ISBN 0-14-030928-4, Puffin). Puffin Bks.

Turner, Ann. Dakota Dugout. Himler, Ronald, illus. 32p. (ps-3). 1989. pap. 3.95 (ISBN 0-689-71296-0, Aladdin). Macmillan Child Grp.

Wells, Marian. Out of the Crucible. LC 88-21121. 256p. (Orig.). 1988. pap. 6.95 (ISBN 1-55661-037-8). Bethany Hse.

Wilder, Laura I. By the Shores of Silver Lake. rev. ed. Williams, Garth, illus. LC 52-7529. 292p. (gr. 4-7). 1961. 14.95 (ISBN 0-06-026416-0); PLB 14.89 (ISBN 0-06-026417-9). HarpC Child Bks.

—Little House in the Big Woods. rev. ed. Williams, Garth, illus. LC 52-7525. (gr. 1-6). 1953. 14.95i (ISBN 0-06-026430-6); PLB 14.89 (ISBN 0-06-026431-4). HarpC Child Bks.

—Little House on the Prairie. rev. ed. Williams, Garth, illus. LC 52-7526. 238p. (gr. 3-7). 1953. 14.95i (ISBN 0-06-026445-4); PLB 14.89 (ISBN 0-06-026446-2). HarpC Child Bks.

—Little House on the Prairie. (gr. 4-6). 1975. pap. 4.95 (ISBN 0-06-080357-6, P357, PL). HarperCollins.

—Little Town on the Prairie. rev. ed. Williams, Garth, illus. LC 52-7531. 308p. (gr. 4-8). 1953. 14.95 (ISBN 0-06-026450-0); PLB 14.89 (ISBN 0-06-026451-9). HarpC Child Bks.

—The Long Winter. rev. ed. Williams, Garth, illus. LC 52-7530. 334p. (gr. 4-8). 1953. 14.95 (ISBN 0-06-026460-8); PLB 14.89 (ISBN 0-06-026461-6). HarpC Child Bks.

—On the Banks of Plum Creek. rev. ed. Williams, Garth, illus. LC 52-7528. 340p. (gr. 3-7). 1953. 14.95 (ISBN 0-06-026470-5); PLB 14.89 (ISBN 0-06-026471-3). HarpC Child Bks.

—On the Way Home. Lane, Rose W., ed. LC 62-17966. (Illus.). 112p. (gr. 7 up). 1962. 12.95 (ISBN 0-06-026489-6); PLB 12.89 (ISBN 0-06-026490-X). HarpC Child Bks.

—On the Way Home. Lane, Rose W., ed. LC 62-17966. (Illus.). 112p. (gr. 7 up). 1976. pap. 2.95 (ISBN 0-06-440080-8, Trophy). HarpC Child Bks.

—These Happy Golden Years. rev. ed. Williams, Garth, illus. LC 52-7532. 289p. (gr. 5-9). 1961. 14.95 (ISBN 0-06-026480-2); PLB 14.89 (ISBN 0-06-026481-0). HarpC Child Bks.

FRONTIER AND PIONEER LIFE–THE WEST

Alter, Judith. Growing up in the Old West. (Illus.). 64p. (gr. 3-5). 1989. PLB 11.90 (ISBN 0-531-10746-9). Watts.

—Women of the Old West. (Illus.). 64p. (gr. 3-5). 1989. PLB 11.90 (ISBN 0-531-10756-6). Watts.

Collins, James L. Lawmen of the Old West. (ps-3). 1990. PLB 11.90 (ISBN 0-531-10893-7). Watts.

Killingray, Margaret. Settlers in the American West. (Illus.). 64p. (gr. 7-10). 1989. 19.95 (ISBN 0-7134-5839-9, Pub. by Batsford England). Trafalgar Sq.

Landau, Elaine. Cowboys. (Illus.). 64p. (gr. 5-8). 1990. PLB 11.90 (ISBN 0-531-10866-X). Watts.

Matthews, L. Gunfighters. (Illus.). 32p. (gr. 3-8). Date not set. PLB 17.26 (ISBN 0-86625-361-0). Rourke Corp.

—Pioneers. (Illus.). 32p. (gr. 3-8). Date not set. PLB 17.26 (ISBN 0-86625-362-9). Rourke Corp.

Putman, Alice. Westering. 1990. 12.95 (ISBN 0-525-67299-0, Lodestar Bks). Dutton Child Bks.

Stein, R. Conrad. The Story of the Homestead Act. Koenig, Cathy, illus. LC 78-4839. 32p. (gr. 3-6). 1978. PLB 13.27 (ISBN 0-516-04616-0). Childrens.

Tykal, Jack B. Etienne Provost: Man of the Mountains. Smith, Monte, ed. Smith, Ralph L., illus. Gowans, Fred, intro. by. (Illus.). 256p. (gr. 9 up). 1989. 15.95 (ISBN 0-943604-24-9); pap. 9.95 (ISBN 0-943604-23-0). Eagles View.

FROST, ROBERT, 1874-1963

Bober, Natalie S. A Restless Spirit: The Story of Robert Frost. (Illus.). 192p. (gr. 5 up). 1991. 19.95 (ISBN 0-8050-1672-4). H Holt & Co.

Longo, Lucas. Robert Frost: Twentieth Century Modern American Poet Laureate. Rahmas, D. Steve, ed. LC 70-190239. 32p. (gr. 7-12). 1972. lib. bdg. 4.20 incl. catalog cards (ISBN 0-87157-521-3). SamHar Pr.

FRUIT

see also Citrus Fruit; Fruit Culture;
also names of fruits, e.g. Apple, etc.

Dineen, Jacqueline. Fruit. 32p. (gr. 4-8). 1988. lib. bdg. 12.95 (ISBN 0-89490-217-2). Enslow Pubs.

Dowden, Anne O. From Flower to Fruit. LC 83-46163. (Illus.). 64p. (gr. 7 up). 1984. 14.95 (ISBN 0-690-04402-X, Crowell Jr Bks). HarpC Child Bks.

Ehlert, Lois. Eating the Alphabet: Fruits & Vegetables from A to Z. 32p. (gr. 3-6). 1989. 13.95 (ISBN 0-15-224435-2). HarBraceJ.

Mitgutsch, Ali. From Seed to Pear. Mitgutsch, Ali, illus. LC 81-83. 24p. (ps-3). 1981. PLB 6.95 (ISBN 0-87614-163-7). Carolrhoda Bks.

Pohl, Kathleen. Gourds. (Illus.). 32p. (gr. 3-7). 1986. PLB 16.67 (ISBN 0-8172-2712-1); pap. 9.27 (ISBN 0-8172-2730-X). Raintree Pubs.

Wexler, Jerome. Flowers Fruits Seeds. LC 86-30616. (Illus.). 32p. (ps-3). 1987. PLB 12.95 (ISBN 0-671-66372-0). S&S Trade.

FRUIT–CANNING

see Canning and Preserving

FRUIT–MARKETING

see Farm Produce–Marketing

FRUIT CULTURE

see also Plant Propagation

Bertoldi, Joyce. Aguacates (Avacados) Cultivando, Cosechando y Vendiendo. LC 89-71328. (SPA., Illus.). 42p. (gr. 3-6). 1989. pap. 4.95 (ISBN 0-942884-04-3). Observational.

—Avocados: Growing, Harvesting & Marketing. Bertoldi, Art, illus. LC 89-3432. 42p. (gr. 3-6). 1989. pap. 4.95 (ISBN 0-942884-03-5). Observational.

FRUIT CULTURE–FICTION

Ancona, George. Bananas: From Manolo to Margie. Ancona, George, illus. 48p. (gr. 3-6). 1982. 14.95 (ISBN 0-89919-100-2, Clarion). HM.

Balan, Bruce. The Cherry Migration. Lane, Dan, illus. 32p. 1988. 12.95 (ISBN 0-88138-098-9). Green Tiger Pr.

The Pineapple Story. LC 78-60645. (Illus.). 39p. (gr. 3 up). 1978. 5.00 (ISBN 0-916888-03-7). Inst Basic Youth.

Riskind, Mary. Apple Is My Sign. 160p. (gr. 5-8). 1981. 12.95 (ISBN 0-395-30852-6). HM.

Williams, Vera B. Cherries & Cherry Pits. Williams, Vera B., illus. LC 85-17156. 40p. (ps up). 1986. 13.95 (ISBN 0-688-05145-6); PLB 13.88 (ISBN 0-688-05146-4). Greenwillow.

FRUSTRATION

see Attitude (Psychology); Emotions

FRY, ELIZABETH (GURNEY) 1780-1845

Johnson, Spencer. The Value of Kindness: The Story of Elizabeth Fry. 2nd ed. Pileggi, Steve, illus. LC 76-55339. (gr. k-6). 1976. 9.95 (ISBN 0-916392-09-0, Pub. by Value Communications). Oak Tree Pubns.

FUEL

see also Wood

Baker, Susan. First Look at Using Energy. LC 91-2372. (Illus.). 32p. (gr. 1-2). 1991. PLB 10.95 (ISBN 0-8368-0680-8). Gareth Stevens Inc.

Brown, A. S. Fuel Resources. (Illus.). 72p. (gr. 4 up). 1985. lib. bdg. 10.40 (ISBN 0-531-04911-6). Watts.

Brown, Julie & Brown, Robert. Earth's Energy & Fuel. LC 91-2803. (Illus.). 64p. (gr. 2-3). 1991. PLB 12.95 (ISBN 0-8368-0077-X). Gareth Stevens Inc.

Rice, Dale. Energy from Fossil Fuels. Daniels, Pat, ed. LC 82-9805. (Illus.). 48p. (gr. 4 up). 1985. PLB 15.99 (ISBN 0-8172-1417-8); pap. 9.27 (ISBN 0-8172-1430-5). Raintree Pubs.

Santrey, Laurence. Energy & Fuels. Burns, Raymond, illus. LC 84-2704. 32p. (gr. 3-6). 1985. PLB 9.49 (ISBN 0-8167-0290-X); pap. text ed. 2.95 (ISBN 0-8167-0291-8). Troll Assocs.

Seidenberg, Steven. Fuel & Energy. LC 90-23743. (Illus.). 64p. (gr. 4-6). 1991. PLB 12.95 (ISBN 0-8368-0052-4). Gareth Stevens Inc.

Twist, Clint. Facts on Fossil Fuels. 1990. 11.90 (ISBN 0-531-14068-7). Watts.

FULLER, RICHARD BUCKMINSTER, 1895-

Potter, Robert R. Buckminster Fuller. Gallin, Richard, ed. (Illus.). 144p. 1990. lib. bdg. 13.98 (ISBN 0-382-09967-2); pap. 7.95 (ISBN 0-382-09972-9). Silver Burdett Pr.

FULTON, ROBERT, 1765-1815

Henry, Joanne L. Robert Fulton: Steamboat Builder. Mawicke, Tran, illus. 80p. (gr. 2-6). 1991. Repr. of 1975 ed. PLB 12.95 (ISBN 0-7910-1411-8). Chelsea Hse.

Landau, Elaine. Robert Fulton. (Illus.). 64p. (gr. 3-5). 1991. PLB 11.90 (ISBN 0-531-20016-7). Watts.

Quackenbush, Robert. Watt Got You Started, Mr. Fulton? Quackenbush, Robert, illus. 39p. (gr. 1-4). 1982. 7.95 (ISBN 0-13-944397-5). P-H.

FUND RAISING

Kleeberg, Irene C. Fund Raising. Rakos, Jennie, ed. LC 88-5655. (Illus.). 72p. (gr. 4-9). 1988. 10.40 (ISBN 0-531-10583-0). Watts.

FUNDS

see Finance

FUNERAL RITES AND CEREMONIES

Berrill, Margaret. Mummies, Masks, & Mourners. 1990. 14.95 (ISBN 0-525-67282-6, Lodestar Bks). Dutton Child Bks.

Syme, Daniel B. Jewish Mourning. 1989. pap. 3.00 (ISBN 0-8074-0332-6, 388494). UAHC.

FUNGI

see also Bacteriology; Mushrooms

Coldrey, Jennifer. Discovering Fungi. Caulkins, Janet, ed. (Illus.). 48p. (gr. k-6). 1988. PLB 11.90 (ISBN 0-531-18170-7, Pub. by Bookwright Pr). Watts.

Gattis, L. S., III. Fungi for Pathfinders: A Basic Youth Enrichment Skill Honor Packet. (Illus.). 20p. (Orig.). (gr. 5 up). 1987. pap. 5.00 tchr's. ed. (ISBN 0-936241-20-9). Cheetah Pub.

Madgwick, Wendy. Fungi & Lichens. LC 90-9571. (Illus.). 48p. (gr. 5-9). 1990. PLB 18.60 (ISBN 0-8114-2728-5). Steck-V.

FUNNIES

see Comic Books, Strips, Etc.

FUR-BEARING ANIMALS

see also names of fur-bearing animals, e.g. Beavers, etc.

FUR SEALS

see Seals (Animals)

FUR TRADE

Siegel, Beatrice. Fur Trappers & Traders: The Indians, the Pilgrims, & the Beaver. Bock, William S., illus. LC 80-7671. 64p. (gr. 3-7). 1987. PLB 11.85 (ISBN 0-8027-6397-9). Walker & Co.

FURNITURE

see also Wood Carving
also names of articles of furniture, e.g. Chairs; Mirrors; etc.

Mitgutsch, Ali. From Tree to Table. Mitgutsch, Ali, illus. LC 81-672. 24p. (ps-3). 1981. PLB 6.95 (ISBN 0-87614-165-3). Carolrhoda Bks.

Watson, Aldren A. Country Furniture. LC 73-18013. (Illus.). 256p. (gr. 7-12). 1974. 19.95 (ISBN 0-690-00190-8, Crowell Jr Bks). HarpC Child Bks.

FURNITURE, AMERICAN

Watson, Aldren A. Country Furniture. LC 73-18013. (Illus.). 256p. (gr. 7-12). 1974. 19.95 (ISBN 0-690-00190-8, Crowell Jr Bks). HarpC Child Bks.

FURNITURE, COLONIAL

see Furniture, American

G

G.I.S.

see Soldiers–U. S.

GALAPAGOS ISLANDS

Root, Phyllis & McCormick, Maxine. Galapagos Islands. LC 89-7918. (Illus.). 48p. (gr. 4-5). 1989. 12.95 (ISBN 0-89686-434-0, Crestwood Hse). Macmillan Child Grp.

GALES
see Winds
GALILEI, GALILEO, 1564-1642
McTavish, Douglas. Galileo. (Illus.). 48p. (gr. 5-8). 1991. RLB 12.40 (ISBN 0-531-18405-6, Pub. by Boatwright Pr). Watts.
Rosen, Sidney. Galileo & the Magic Numbers. Stein, Harve, illus. (gr. 7 up). 1958. 13.95 (ISBN 0-316-75704-7). Little.
GALLERIES (ART)
see Art–Galleries and Museums
GAMA, VASCO DA, 1469?-1524
Knight, David. Vasco Da Gama. LC 78-18057. (Illus.). 48p. (gr. 4-7). 1979. PLB 9.89 (ISBN 0-89375-175-8); pap. 2.95 (ISBN 0-89375-167-7). Troll Assocs.
GAME AND GAME BIRDS
see also Hunting; Trapping
also names of animals and birds, e.g. Deer; Pheasants; etc.
GAME PRESERVES
Barton, Miles. Zoos & Game Reserves. Franklin Watts Ltd., ed. (Illus.). 32p. (gr. 7-9). 1988. PLB 8.99 (ISBN 0-531-17090-X, Pub. by Gloucester Pr). Watts.
GAMES
see also Amusements; Cards; Kindergarten; Olympic Games; Play; Singing Games; Sports;
also names of games, e.g. Chess; Tennis; etc.
Adams, Pam, illus. What Is It? (Orig.). (ps-2). 1975. pap. 2.00 (ISBN 0-85953-044-2, Pub. by Child's Play England). Childs Play.
Adler, David A. Passover Fun Book: Puzzles, Riddles, Magic & More. (Illus.). (gr. k-5). 1978. saddlewire bdg. 3.95 (ISBN 0-88482-759-3, Bonim Bks). Hebrew Pub.
Alderson, Frederick. Outdoor Games. (Illus.). 64p. (gr. 6 up). 1980. 14.95 (ISBN 0-7136-2031-5). Dufour.
Andrews, Ed. Caravans of Mars. Hasenauer, Richard, illus. 64p. (Orig.). 1989. pap. 8.00 (ISBN 1-55878-023-8). Game Designers.
Aulson, Pam. Placemat Pets 'n Playmates. (Illus.). 24p. (gr. 6 up). 1980. pap. 3.00 (ISBN 0-9601896-2-9). Patch As Patch.
Ball Games. 48p. (gr. 3-8). 1990. 16.95 (ISBN 1-85435-077-3). Marshall Cavendish.
Barr, Bill. The Famous Name Guessing Game. (Illus.). 48p. (gr. 6 up). 1988. pap. 2.95 (ISBN 0-8431-2306-0). Price Stern.
Baylor, Byrd. Guess Who My Favorite Person Is? Parker, Robert A., illus. LC 77-7151. 32p. (Orig.). (gr. 1-5). 1985. pap. 4.95 (ISBN 0-689-71052-6, Aladdin). Macmillan Child Grp.
Beall, Pamela C. & Nipp, Susan. Wee Sing & Play. (Illus.). 64p. (Orig.). (ps-6). 1983. pap. 2.95 (ISBN 0-8431-0391-4); pap. 9.95 incl. cassette (ISBN 0-8431-0743-X). Price Stern.

Beaver, Edmund. Travel Games. (gr. 4 up). 1974. pap. 1.00 (ISBN 0-910208-01-8). Beavers.
TRAVEL GAMES is an illustrated 32 page FAMILY FUN BOOK. This is a proven "FUN ON RUN" book for restless travelers of all ages. ALL members in the car can enjoy the games together. Young eyes are trained to become more observing. This pocket size book is filled with treasure hunt activities & exciting contests. Here is an excellent gift for restless travelers. TRAVEL GAMES has received favorable recognition from nation wide books & magazines. The popular children's book FREE STUFF FOR KIDS has promoted TRAVEL GAMES IN EVERY EDITION. Retail $1.00. Wholesale Discount 50%; 24 copies including shipping $13.80; 50 copies including shipping $27.20; 100 copies including shipping $54.00. Order from THE BEAVERS, (218) 224-2182, HCR 70, Box 537, La Porte, MN 56461.
Publisher Provided Annotation.

Benarde, Anita. Games from Many Lands. Benarde, Anita, illus. Winskill, Mary, frwd. by. LC 71-86975. (Illus.). 64p. (gr. 3-7). 1971. PLB 12.95 (ISBN 0-87460-147-9). Lion Bks.
Bentley, William G. Indoor & Outdoor Games. (gr. k-6). 1966. pap. 6.95 (ISBN 0-8224-3910-7). Fearon Teach Aids.
Bernstein, Bob. Friday Afternoon Fun. Schmidt, Ross, illus. 64p. (gr. 2-6). 1984. wkbk. 6.95 (ISBN 0-86653-206-4, GA 558). Good Apple.
Bernstein, Bonnie. Patterns & Props. 112p. (gr. k-3). 1984. 9.95 (ISBN 0-912107-21-9). Monday Morning Bks.
Black, Sonia. Across the U. S. A. Game. 1989. pap. 2.95 (ISBN 0-590-42156-5). Scholastic Inc.
Bond, Larry. Data Annex Upgrade. Venters, Steve, illus. 136p. (Orig.). 1990. pap. 10.00 (ISBN 1-55878-053-X). Game Designers.
Brady, Maxine. The Monopoly Book. (Illus.). (gr. 7 up). 1976. pap. 4.95 (ISBN 0-679-14401-3). McKay.
Brown, Marzella. Cooperative Learning: Great Games for Cooperative Learning. Rivera, Doreen, et al, illus. 48p. (gr. 2-5). 1990. wkbk. 5.95 (ISBN 1-55734-108-7). Tchr Create Mat.
Buskin, David. Outdoor Games. Kline, Dick, illus. Thompson, Morton, intro. by. (Illus.). (gr. k-4). 1966. PLB 11.95 (ISBN 0-87460-090-1). Lion Bks.
Butterfield, M. Air Travel Games: Puzzles, Games & Things to Do on a Journey Or at Home. (Illus.). 32p. (gr. 2 up). 1986. pap. 4.95 (ISBN 0-86020-997-0). EDC.
Butterfield, S. Gold Medal Games. (gr. 1-4). 3.95 (ISBN 0-88160-106-3, LW 125). Learning Wks.
Campbell, Andrea. Great Games for Great Parties: How to Throw a Perfect Party. LC 91-22983. (Illus.). 160p. (gr. 1-9). 1991. pap. 14.95 (ISBN 0-8069-8318-3). Sterling.
Campbell, Rod. Book of Board Games. (Illus.). 12p. 1984. 5.95 (ISBN 0-13-079872-X). P-H.
Caney, Steven. Steven Caney's Playbook. LC 75-9816. (Illus.). 240p. (ps-5). 1975. pap. 8.95 (ISBN 0-911104-38-0, 050). Workman Pub.
Chadwick, Frank. Cloud Captains of Mars. Aulisio, Janet, illus. 64p. (Orig.). 1989. pap. 8.00 (ISBN 1-55878-043-2). Game Designers.
—Ironclads & Ether Flyers. Deitrick, David, illus. 112p. (Orig.). 1990. pap. 12.00 (ISBN 0-943580-96-X). Game Designers.
Chadwick, Frank A. Conklin's Atlas. Ryan, Shea, illus. 80p. (Orig.). 1989. pap. 10.00 (ISBN 1-55878-024-6). Game Designers.
—Soldier's Companion. Hasenauer, Richard, illus. 192p. (Orig.). 1989. pap. 15.00 (ISBN 1-55878-026-2). Game Designers.
—Twilight: Two Thousand. Harris, Dell, illus. 280p. (Orig.). 1990. pap. 20.00 (ISBN 1-55878-070-X). Game Designers.
Chadwick, Frank S. Cadillacs & Dinosaurs. Schultz, Mark, illus. 144p. (Orig.). (gr. 9-12). 1990. pap. 18.00 (ISBN 1-55878-073-4). Game Designers.
Charlton, S. Coleman. Creatures & Treasures. (Illus.). 96p. (gr. 10-12). 1985. 12.00 (ISBN 0-915795-30-2, 1400). Iron Crown Ent Inc.
Charlton, S. Coleman & Ruemmler, John D. Middle-Earth Role Playing (MERP) (Illus.). 128p. (gr. 10-12). 1986. pap. 10.00 (ISBN 0-915795-31-0, 8000). Iron Crown Ent Inc.
Chase, Richard. Singing Games & Playparty Games. Tolford, Joshua, illus. 63p. (gr. 1-4). 1949. pap. 2.50 (ISBN 0-486-21785-X). Dover.
Chasing Games. 48p. (gr. 3-8). 1990. PLB 16.95 (ISBN 1-85435-078-1). Marshall Cavendish.
Church, Ellen C. Learning Things: Games That Make Learning Fun for Children 3-8 Years Old. LC 81-82033. (ps-3). 1982. pap. 10.95 (ISBN 0-8224-4268-X). Fearon Teach Aids.
Cobb, Vicki. How to Really Fool Yourself: Illusions for All Your Senses. LC 79-9620. (Illus.). 160p. (gr. 5 up). 1981. 12.95 (ISBN 0-397-31906-1, Lipp Jr Bks); PLB 12.89 (ISBN 0-397-31907-X, Lipp Jr Bks). HarpC Child Bks.
Colborn, Mark. Rolemaster Companion. Charlton, S. C., ed. McBride, Angus, illus. 96p. (gr. 10-12). 1986. pap. 12.00 (ISBN 0-915795-12-4, 1500). Iron Crown Ent Inc.
Collins, David R. The Game of Think. LC 82-71553. 23p. (ps-3). 1984. 3.50x (ISBN 0-943864-39-9). Davenport.
Cooper, Don. Happy Birthday Songs & Games. Freeze, Marla, illus. Elkins, Stephen, contrib. by. (Illus.). 32p. (Orig.). (ps-3). 1988. pap. 5.95 bk. & cassette pkg. (ISBN 0-394-80826-6, Random Juv). Random.
Corbett, Pie. Playtime Treasury. 1990. 16.95 (ISBN 0-385-26448-8). Doubleday.
Deitrick, David R., illus. Tales from the Ether. 64p. (Orig.). (gr. 9-12). 1989. pap. 8.00 (ISBN 1-55878-011-4). Game Designers.
Demi. Find Demi's Dinosaurs: An Animal Game Book. Demi, illus. 50p. (ps-3). 1989. 40.00x (ISBN 0-448-19020-6, G&D). Putnam Pub Group.
Dobbs, Katy. My First Gamebook. Joyner, Jerry, illus. LC 85-40524. (ps-2). 1986. 6 bds. 5.95 (ISBN 0-89480-945-8, 945). Workman Pub.
Donaldson, Judith E. Travel Games: Vol. 2, Five to Ten Years. Brown, George H., ed. Donaldson, Judith E., illus. 36p. (gr. k-5). pap. text ed. 1.50 (ISBN 0-939942-06-2). Larkspur.
Durlacher, Ed, ed. The Play Party Book: Singing Games for Children. Bare, Arnold E., illus. 38p. (ps-5). 1945. 9.50 (ISBN 0-8159-6505-2). Devin.
Eberle, Bob. Scamper On. Weber, June K., illus. 64p. (Orig.). (gr. k-12). 1984. 6.95 (ISBN 0-88047-047-X, 8413). DOK Pubs.
Einon, Dorothy. Play with a Purpose: Learning Games for Children Six Weeks to Ten Years. Farndon, Jon, illus. LC 85-6301. 256p. (ps-5). 1986. pap. 9.95 (ISBN 0-394-74214-1). Pantheon.
Emberley, Ed E. Ed Emberley's Crazy Mixed-up Face Game. Emberley, Ed E., illus. 32p. (gr. 1 up). 1981. pap. 15.95 (ISBN 0-316-23420-6). Little.
Evans, Delphine. What Shall We Do Today? (Illus.). 128p. (ps). 1987. 13.95 (ISBN 0-09-160400-1, Pub. by Hutchinson UK). Trafalgar Sq.
Fenlon, Peter C. Moria. (Illus.). 72p. (gr. 10-12). 1984. 12.00 (ISBN 0-915795-27-2, 2900). Iron Crown Ent Inc.
Fenlon, Peter C. & Colborn, Mark. Lords of Middle-Earth, Vol 1. McBride, Angus, illus. 96p. (Orig.). 1986. pap. 12.00 (ISBN 0-915795-26-4, 8002). Iron Crown Ent Inc.
Folson, Marcia & Folson, Michael. Easy As Pie: A Guessing Game of Saying. Kent, Jack, illus. LC 84-14978. 64p. (Orig.). (ps-3). 1985. 13.95 (ISBN 0-89919-303-X, Pub. by Clarion); pap. 5.95 (ISBN 0-89919-351-X). Ticknor & Fields.
Forte, Imogene. Games: Some Old, Some New, All Fun to Do. LC 83-82331. (Illus.). 80p. (gr. k-6). 1983. pap. text ed. 3.95 (ISBN 0-86530-093-3, IP 93-3). Incentive Pubns.
Foster, Sally. Simon Says...Let's Play. Foster, Sally, photos by. LC 89-9776. (Illus.). 48p. (gr. 1-6). 1990. 13.95 (ISBN 0-525-65019-9, Cobblestone Bks). Dutton Child Bks.
Frem, Margie, illus. Conversation Games: Vol. III, Solutions. Rev. ed. Freeman, Harold, Jr., intro. by. (Illus.). 134p. (ps-6). 1981. pap. 17.00 (ISBN 0-939632-23-3). ILM.
Friedland, Dave. Fieldtrip. Pondsmith, Mike & Bryant, Linda, eds. Ruggles, Scott, illus. 36p. (gr. 5-12). 1987. game bk. 8.00 (ISBN 0-937279-03-X, TS 2101). R Talsorian.
Gamble, Donna T. Games to Go, 5 bklets. (ps-5). 1989. 27.95 (ISBN 1-55999-041-4). LinguiSystems.
Gamec, Hazel S. The Disappearing ABC Game Book. Gamec, Hazel S., illus. 12p. write for info. (ISBN 0-938042-02-5). Printek.
—Looking Out of the Window. Gamec, Hazel S., illus. 12p. 1980. write for info. (ISBN 0-938042-01-7). Printek.
—The Magic Pencil Counting Book. Gamec, Hazel S., illus. 12p. 1980. write for info. (ISBN 0-938042-00-9). Printek.
Games Around the World. 48p. (gr. 5-6). 1989. PLB 10.95 (ISBN 0-685-26334-7). Capstone Pr.
Games Children Play Series, 8 vols. LC 88-28773. (Illus.). 384p. (gr. 3-8). 1990. Set. 135.60 (ISBN 1-85435-076-5). Marshall Cavendish.
Games of Skill & Strength. 48p. (gr. 3-8). 1990. PLB 16.95 (ISBN 1-85435-084-6). Marshall Cavendish.
Games with Rope & String. 48p. (gr. 3-8). 1990. PLB 16.95 (ISBN 1-85435-081-1). Marshall Cavendish.
Gee, John. Hidden Pictures: Favorites by John Gee. (Illus.). 32p. (Orig.). (gr. 1-6). 1981. pap. 2.95 (ISBN 0-87534-230-2). Highlights.
Gehman, Christian. Riders of Rohan. (Illus.). 48p. (gr. 10-12). 1985. pap. 12.00 (ISBN 0-915795-29-9, 3100). Iron Crown Ent Inc.
Gemme, Leila B. T-Ball Is Our Game. Marshall, Richard, photos by. LC 77-17173. (Illus.). 32p. (gr. k-3). 1978. PLB 15.93 (ISBN 0-516-03630-0). Childrens.
Glovach, Linda. Little Witch's Black Magic Book of Games. (gr. 1-4). 1973. 7.95 (ISBN 0-13-537928-8). P-H.
Greenaway, Kate. Kate Greenaway's Book of Games. (Illus.). 64p. (gr. 2 up). 1987. 9.95x (ISBN 0-312-01175-X). St Martin.
Greenwood, Donald J. Advanced Squad Leader: WWII Tactical Warfare. Keebler, Charlie, illus. 200p. (gr. 9 up). 1989. 45.00 (ISBN 0-911605-50-9). Avalon Hill.
Grossman, Roz & Gewirtz, Gladys. Let's Play Dreidel. Springer, Sally, illus. LC 89-34892. 16p. (ps-3). 1989. incl. tape & dreidel 8.95 (ISBN 0-929371-00-3). Kar Ben.
Grummer, Arnold E. The Great Balloon Game Book & More Balloon Activities. Wenger-Marsh, Beth, illus. 112p. (gr. 2 up). 1987. 12.95 (ISBN 0-938251-00-7). G Markim.
Gryski, Camilla. Cat's Cradle, Owl's Eyes: A Book of String Games. Sankey, Tom, illus. LC 84-9075. 80p. (gr. 3 up). 1984. PLB 12.88 (ISBN 0-688-03940-5); pap. 6.95 (ISBN 0-688-03941-3, Pub. by Beech Tree Bks). Morrow Jr Bks.
—Many Stars & More String Games. Sankey, Tom, illus. LC 85-4875. 80p. (gr. 3 up). 1985. lib. bdg. 11.88 (ISBN 0-688-05793-4); pap. 7.95 (ISBN 0-688-05792-6, Pub. by Beech Tree Bks). Morrow Jr Bks.
—Super String Games. Sankey, Tom, illus. LC 88-18365. 80p. (gr. 3 up). 1988. lib. bdg. 11.88 (ISBN 0-688-07685-8); pap. 6.95 (ISBN 0-688-07684-X, Pub. by Beech Tree Bks). Morrow Jr Bks.
Gundersheimer, Karen. One Two Three Play with Me. LC 84-47628. (Illus.). 32p. (ps-1). 1985. PLB 10.89 (ISBN 0-06-022177-1). HarpC Child Bks.
Hand, Phyllis. Breaking into Bible Games. McClure, Nancee, illus. 48p. (gr. 3-6). 1984. wkbk. 6.95 (ISBN 0-317-43001-7, SS 819). Good Apple.
Harris, Frank. Great Games to Play with Groups. (gr. 1 up). 1989. 7.95 (ISBN 0-8224-3379-6). Fearon Teach Aids.
Hart, Bruce & Hart, Carole. Waiting Games. 320p. (gr. 7 up). 1981. pap. 3.50 (ISBN 0-380-79012-2, Flare). Avon.
Highlights Editors. Hidden Pictures & Other Challengers. (Illus.). 32p. (Orig.). (gr. 1-6). 1981. pap. 2.95 (ISBN 0-87534-227-2). Highlights.
—Hidden Pictures & Other Fun. (Illus.). 32p. (Orig.). (gr. 1-6). 1981. pap. 2.95 (ISBN 0-87534-178-0). Highlights.
—Hidden Pictures & Other Puzzlers. (Illus.). 32p. (Orig.). (gr. 1-6). 1981. pap. 2.95 (ISBN 0-87534-180-2). Highlights.

—Hidden Pictures Plus Brain Benders. (Illus.). 32p. (Orig.). (gr. 1-6). 1986. pap. 2.95 (ISBN 0-87534-104-7). Highlights.
—Hidden Pictures Plus Brain Stretchers. (Illus.). 32p. (Orig.). (gr. 1-6). 1986. pap. 2.95 (ISBN 0-87534-103-9). Highlights.
—Hidden Pictures Plus Brain Teasers. (Illus.). 32p. (Orig.). (gr. 1-6). 1986. pap. 2.95 (ISBN 0-87534-102-0). Highlights.
—Hidden Pictures Plus Fun for Masterminds. (Illus.). 32p. (Orig.). (gr. 1-6). 1986. pap. 2.95 (ISBN 0-87534-101-2). Highlights.
—Hidden Pictures with Picture Clues & Other Games. (Illus.). 32p. (Orig.). (gr. 1-6). 1981. pap. 2.95 (ISBN 0-87534-226-4). Highlights.
Highlights Staff, ed. Hidden Pictures Plus Thinking Fun. (Illus.). 32p. (Orig.). (gr. 1-6). 1986. pap. 2.95 (ISBN 0-87534-105-5). Highlights.
Hillery, Mable & Hall, Patricia. A Guide to the Use of Street-Folk-Musical Games in the Classroom: Chanting Games. rev. ed. Kendrick, John & May, Warren, illus. Freeman, Harold, Jr., intro. by. 77p. (ps-6). 1982. pap. 12.00 (ISBN 0-939632-05-5). ILM.
Hodgson, Harriet. Gameworks. 64p. (gr. k-3). 1986. 6.95 (ISBN 0-912107-41-3). Monday Morning Bks.
Isynwill, L. N. & Hike, Herbert. At Your Door: A Modern-Day Campaign. Willis, Lynn & Herber, Keith, eds. Gibbons, Lee, illus. 162p. (Orig.). (gr. 12 up). 1990. pap. 17.95 (ISBN 0-933635-64-8, 2326). Chaosium.
Jackson, Steve & Livingstone, Ian. The Rings of Kether. (Orig.). (gr. 6-12). 1986. pap. 2.50 (ISBN 0-440-97407-0, LFL). Dell.
Kalbfleisch, Susan. Jump! The New Jump Rope Book. McGugan, Laurie, illus. LC 86-23578. 128p. (gr. 3 up). 1987. 12.95 (ISBN 0-688-06929-0); pap. 6.95 (ISBN 0-688-06930-4, Pub. by Beech Tree Bks). Morrow Jr Bks.
Kalter, Joanmarie. The World's Best String Games. LC 89-32404. (Illus.). 128p. (gr. 3-12). 1990. pap. 4.95 (ISBN 0-8069-6921-0). Sterling.
Keeler, Ronald F. Games for Children: For Indoors & Outdoors. 64p. (ps-2). 1982. pap. 3.95 (ISBN 0-8010-5478-8). Baker Bk.
Keith, William H., Jr. Allegheny Uprising. Venters, Steve, illus. 49p. (Orig.). (gr. 9-12). 1987. pap. 7.00 (ISBN 0-943580-29-3). Game Designers.
—The Fire City of Krakow. Ventus, Steve & Danforth, Liz, illus. 49p. (Orig.). 1985. pap. 7.00 (ISBN 0-943580-51-X). Game Designers.
Kelemen, Julie. Advent Is for Children. 64p. (Orig.). (gr. 3 up). 1988. pap. 1.95 (ISBN 0-89243-292-6). Liguori Pubns.
Klutz Press Staff. The Klutz Book of Jacks. (Illus.). 30p. (Orig.). 1989. pap. 6.95 incl. jacks, ball & pouch (ISBN 0-932592-21-X). Klutz Pr.
—The Klutz Book of Marbles. (Illus.). 30p. (Orig.). 1989. pap. 6.95 incl. marbles, shooter & pouch (ISBN 0-932592-22-8). Klutz Pr.
Korner, David. Come out & Play. Korner, David, illus. LC 86-82811. 56p. (gr. 1-5). pap. 9.95 (ISBN 0-317-59042-1). Korn Kompany.
Kraychy, Juliet. Do You Have Your Own Cloud? 32p. 1989. 6.95 (ISBN 0-8062-3571-3). Carlton.
Kroll, Steven. The Tyrannosaurus Game. DePaola, Tomie, illus. 1988. bk. & cassette 19.95 (ISBN 0-87499-096-3); bk. & cassette 12.95 (ISBN 0-87499-095-5); 4 cassettes & guide 27.95 (ISBN 0-87499-097-1). Live Oak Media.
Kubasch, Heike. Bree & the Barrow-Downs. (Illus.). 40p. (gr. 10-12). 1984. pap. 7.00 (ISBN 0-915795-16-7, 8010). Iron Crown Ent Inc.
Langley, Andrew. Travel Games for Kids. rev. ed. LC 90-84702. (Illus.). 96p. (gr. k-8). 1991. pap. 10.95 (ISBN 0-936399-09-0). Berkshire Hse.
Langstaff, Nancy & Langstaff, John. Sally Go Round the Moon & Other Revels Songs & Singing Games for Young Children. Pienkowski, Jan, illus. LC 86-90535. 127p. (ps-1). 1986. pap. 12.95 (ISBN 0-9618334-0-8). Revels Pubns.
Leokum, Arkady. Quizzes, Tricks, Stunts, Puzzles & Brain Teasers from Tell Me Why. Huehnergarth, John, illus. 80p. (gr. 1-7). 1973. 4.95 (ISBN 0-448-11536-0, G&D). Putnam Pub Group.
Let's Play a Game Everyone Wins. 36p. (ps-4). 1985. 8.95 (ISBN 0-88684-178-X); cassette tape avail. Listen USA.
Lipscomb, Susan D. & Zuanich, Margaret A. BASIC Fun: Computer Games, Puzzles & Problems Children Can Write. 176p. (gr. k-7). 1982. pap. 2.95 (ISBN 0-380-80606-1, Camelot). Avon.
Little People Big Book about Playtime. 64p. (ps-1). 1990. write for info. (ISBN 0-8094-7516-2); lib. bdg. write for info. (ISBN 0-8094-7517-0). Time-Life.
Liu, Sarah & Vittitow, Mary L. Learning Games Without Losers. (Illus.). 96p. (gr. 2-6). 1985. guide 8.95 (ISBN 0-86530-039-9, IP 39-9). Incentive Pubns.
Lopshire, Robert. ABC Games. Lopshire, Robert, illus. LC 85-47883. 64p. (ps-1). 1986. 10.95 (ISBN 0-690-04443-7, Crowell Jr Bks); PLB 10.89 (ISBN 0-690-04444-5). HarpC Child Bks.
Love, Marla. Twenty Decoding Games. (gr. 2-6). 1982. pap. 10.95 (ISBN 0-8224-5801-2). Fearon Teach Aids.
—Twenty Word Structure Games. (gr. 2-6). 1983. pap. 10.95 (ISBN 0-8224-5802-0). Fearon Teach Aids.
Lucas, Katherine & Lucas, Louise. Who Owns the Unicorn. (Illus., Orig.). (gr. 4-12). 1980. pap. text ed. 7.50 (ISBN 0-914634-69-0, 7918). DOK Pubs.
McAlister, George A. & McLeod, Lloyd. Dominoes Texas Style. (Illus.). 164p. (Orig.). (gr. 9). 1977. pap. 5.95 (ISBN 0-924307-02-1). Docutex Inc.
McInnes, Terry. COACC. Farley, A. C., illus. 96p. (Orig.). 1989. pap. text ed. 10.00 (ISBN 0-943580-72-2). Game Designers.
McKeage, Jeff. Hillmen of the Trollshaws. (Illus.). 36p. (gr. 10-12). 1984. pap. 7.00 (ISBN 0-915795-24-8, 8040). Iron Crown Ent Inc.
Magos, Eunice & Hornnes, Esther. Simon Says, "Let's Play Learning Games" Sussman, Ellen, ed. Burris, Priscilla, illus. 48p. (Orig.). (ps-1). 1985. tchr's ed. 5.95 (ISBN 0-933606-40-0, MS-640). Monkey Sisters.
Marsh, Carole. The Biltmore House Classroom Gamebook. (Illus., Orig.). (gr. 1-12). 1986. PLB 19.95 (ISBN 0-935326-83-9). Gallopade Pub Group.
—The Lost Colony Classroom Gamebook. (Illus., Orig.). (gr. 3-12). 1986. pap. 19.95 (ISBN 0-935326-86-3). Gallopade Pub Group.
—The Missing Head Mystery Classroom Gamebook. (Illus., Orig.). (gr. 3-6). 1986. pap. 19.95 (ISBN 0-935326-84-7). Gallopade Pub Group.
Martin, Julia. Rotten to the Core. Aulisio, Janet, illus. 64p. (Orig.). 1990. pap. 8.00 (ISBN 1-55878-059-9). Game Designers.
Martin, Kathy. Party Shakers. Biancalana, Tim, illus. Martin, Kathy. LC 82-21729. (Illus.). 47p. (gr. k-8). 1982. pap. 3.95 (ISBN 0-942752-00-7). C A M Co.
Melton, Dana D. & Ledbetter, Frances M. Hooked on Games. Melton, Dana D., illus. 150p. (Orig.). (gr. k-6). 1989. pap. 9.95 (ISBN 0-685-29409-9). Hooked Games.
Meretzky, S. Eric. Zork: The Cavern of Doom, No. 3. Harris, Dell, illus. (gr. 4-6). 1984. pap. 1.95 (ISBN 0-8125-7985-2, Pinnacle Bks). Tor Bks.
—Zork: The Forces of Krill, No. 1. Van Munching, Paul, illus. 126p. (gr. 4-6). 1984. pap. 1.95 (ISBN 0-8125-7975-5, Pinnacle Bks). Tor Bks.
—Zork: The Malifestro Quest, No. 2. (Illus.). 127p. (gr. 4-6). 1984. pap. 1.95 (ISBN 0-8125-7980-1, Pinnacle Bks). Tor Bks.
Miller, Marc W. ASW Forms. Venters, Steve, illus. 49p. (Orig.). 1990. pap. 8.00 (ISBN 1-55878-057-2). Game Designers.
—Fighting Ships. Ellis, Kevin, illus. 96p. (Orig.). 1990. pap. 10.00 (ISBN 1-55878-050-5). Game Designers.
—Sub Forms. Venters, Steve, illus. 49p. (Orig.). 1989. pap. 8.00 (ISBN 1-55878-019-X). Game Designers.
Mills, Jane L. & Johnson, Larry D. Peek-a-Boo. Hebert, Kim T., illus. LC 86-60380. 13p. (Orig.). (ps). 1986. pap. 3.50 (ISBN 0-938155-04-0); pap. 12.00 set of 3 bks. (ISBN 0-685-13530-6). Read A Bol.
Monroe, John B., ed. Blood Brothers: B-Movie Monsters & Adventures. (Illus.). 128p. (Orig.). (gr. 12 up). 1990. pap. 18.95 (ISBN 0-933635-69-9, 2329). Chaosium.
Nilsen, David. Ranger. Bostick, Angela, illus. 64p. (Orig.). 1989. pap. 8.00 (ISBN 1-55878-016-5). Game Designers.
Novak, Greg. Over the Top. Doubet, Amy, illus. 120p. (Orig.). (gr. 9-12). 1990. pap. 12.00 (ISBN 1-55878-012-2). Game Designers.
Oakley, Ruth. Board & Card Games. LC 88-28710. (Illus.). 48p. (gr. 4-8). 1990. PLB 16.95 (ISBN 1-85435-082-X). Marshall Cavendish.
—Chanting Games. LC 88-28774. (Illus.). 48p. (gr. 4-8). 1990. PLB 16.95 (ISBN 1-85435-080-3). Marshall Cavendish.
—Games with Papers & Pencils. LC 88-28711. (Illus.). 48p. (gr. 4-8). 1989. PLB 16.95 (ISBN 1-85435-083-8). Marshall Cavendish.
—Games with Sticks, Stones & Shells. LC 88-28773. (Illus.). 48p. (gr. 4-8). 1989. PLB 16.95 (ISBN 1-85435-079-X). Marshall Cavendish.
Pagnucci, Susan. Games to Cut. (Illus.). 20p. (Orig.). (gr. k-3). 1978. Incl. 5 reading & math games to make & use. 4.25 (ISBN 0-929326-03-2). Bur Oak Pr Inc.
Pat-a-Cake. (Illus.). 8p. (ps). 1978. 2.50 (ISBN 0-448-46833-6, G&D). Putnam Pub Group.
Pearson, Craig. Make Your Own Games Workshop. (gr. 3-8). 1982. pap. 8.95 (ISBN 0-8224-9782-4). Fearon Teach Aids.
Peterson, Steve & McDonald, George, eds. Enemies. Williams, Mark, illus. 24p. (gr. 10-12). 1986. pap. 6.00 (ISBN 0-915795-51-5, 02). Iron Crown Ent Inc.
Phillips, Louis. The World by Sevens: A Kid's Book of Lists. (Illus.). 96p. (gr. 4 up). 1981. lib. bdg. 12.90 (ISBN 0-531-02883-6). Watts.
Phillips, Martin A. The Official National Table Hockey League Handbook, Vol. 1. Phillips, Zoe A., ed. Rullestad, Chris, illus. LC 89-91696. 66p. (Orig.). (gr. 12). Date not set. write for info. (ISBN 0-9623588-0-0); pap. write for info. (ISBN 0-9623588-1-9). Gnu Wine Pr.
Phillips, Peter. Survivors Guide to the U. K. Bradstreet, Tim, illus. 49p. (Orig.). 1990. pap. 7.00 (ISBN 1-55878-009-2). Game Designers.
Pondsmith, Michael. Cyberpunk. Liu, Sam, et al, illus. Fisk, Colin, contrib. by. 98p. (gr. 10-12). 1988. game bk. 20.00 (ISBN 0-937279-05-6, CP 3001). R Talsorian.
—Mekton II. 2nd ed. Bryant, Linda, et al, eds. Dunn, Benn, et al, illus. 93p. (gr. 7-12). 1987. game bk. 12.00 (ISBN 0-937279-04-8, MK 1002). R Talsorian.
Potter, Beatrix. The Peter Rabbit Make-a-Mobile Book. 20p. 1990. pap. 5.95. Warne.
Potter, T. Car Travel Games: Puzzles, Games & Things to Do on a Journey-or at Home. (Illus.). 32p. (gr. 2 up). 1986. pap. 4.95 (ISBN 0-86020-926-1). EDC.
Potter, T. & Butterfield, M. Travel Games. (Illus.). 64p. (gr. 2 up). 1986. pap. 7.95 (ISBN 0-86020-999-7, Usborne). EDC.
Razzi, Jim. Spooky Action Cut-Outs. Myers, Bernice, illus. 32p. (gr. 1-3). pap. 1.95 (ISBN 0-590-31242-1). Scholastic Inc.
Reid, Mary. Anytime Parties for Children. Arthur, Lorraine, illus. 80p. (gr. 1-5). 1987. wkbk. 5.95 (ISBN 0-87403-290-3, 2802). Standard Pub.
Robinson, Andrew M. The Gadgets! 48p. (gr. 10-12). 1986. pap. 8.00 (ISBN 0-915795-64-7, 23). Iron Crown Ent Inc.
Rockwell, Anne. Games (& How to Play Them) Rockwell, Anne, illus. LC 72-10936. 48p. (gr. 1 up). 1973. 13.95 (ISBN 0-690-32159-7, Crowell Jr Bks). HarpC Child Bks.
Rowen, Larry. Beyond Winning: Group Centered Games & Sports. (gr. 2-6). 1990. pap. 7.95 (ISBN 0-8224-3380-X). Fearon Teach Aids.
Rowland, Marcus L. Canal Priests of Mars. Harris, Dell, illus. 64p. (Orig.). 1990. pap. 8.00 (ISBN 1-55878-039-4). Game Designers.
Royer, Katherine. Nursery Happy Times Book. (Illus.). 48p. (ps). 1957. pap. 2.95x (ISBN 0-8361-1277-6). Herald Pr.
Ruemmler, John D. Rangers of the North. (Illus.). 56p. (gr. 10-12). 1985. pap. 12.00 (ISBN 0-915795-22-1, 3000). Iron Crown Ent Inc.
Runyan, Cathy C. Knuckles Down! A Fun Guide to Marble Play. 2nd ed. (Illus.). 36p. (gr. 1-6). 1990. pap. 4.95 (ISBN 0-935295-01-1). Right Brain.
Ryan, Tim & White, Scott G. Bear's Den. Holloway, Jim, illus. 49p. (Orig.). 1989. pap. 7.00 (ISBN 1-55878-030-0). Game Designers.
Scarry, Richard. Richard Scarry's Best Coloring Activity Book Ever. LC 74-6872. (Illus.). 176p. (ps-4). 1974. 6.95 (ISBN 0-394-83018-0, Random Juv). Random.
Schick, Lawrence. Heroic Worlds: A History & Guide to Role-Playing Games. (Illus.). 380p. (Orig.). (gr. 6 up). 1991. 34.95x (ISBN 0-87975-652-7); pap. 16.95 (ISBN 0-87975-653-5). Prometheus Bks.
Schmitz, Dorothy C. The Fabulous Frisbee. LC 78-7416. (Illus.). 32p. (gr. 3 up). 1978. PLB 9.95 (ISBN 0-913940-88-7, Crestwood Hse). Macmillan Child Grp.
Smith, Lester W. Beastman of Mars. Aulisio, Janet, illus. 64p. (Orig.). 1989. pap. 8.00 (ISBN 1-55878-022-X). Game Designers.
—Deathwatch Program. Aulisio, Janet, illus. 64p. (Orig.). 1990. pap. 8.00 (ISBN 1-55878-051-3). Game Designers.
—Earth - Cybertech Sourcebook. Aulisio, Janet, illus. 96p. (Orig.). (gr. 9-12). 1989. pap. 10.00 (ISBN 1-55878-014-9). Game Designers.
Sochard, Ruth. Dagorlad & the Dead Marshes. (Illus.). 36p. (gr. 10-12). 1984. pap. 7.00 (ISBN 0-915795-20-5, 8020). Iron Crown Ent Inc.
—Pirates of Pelargir. Fenlon, Peter, ed. McBride, Angus, illus. 32p. (Orig.). (gr. 10-12). 1987. pap. 6.00 (ISBN 0-915795-44-2, 8104). Iron Crown Ent Inc.
Sperling, Anita, et al. Funny Faces Tracing Fun. Wildman, George, illus. 24p. (gr. k-3). 1987. pap. 1.95 (ISBN 0-590-40889-5). Scholastic Inc.
Spivak, Darlene. Sequence Fun. Wright, Theresa, illus. 32p. (gr. k-2). 1988. wkbk. 4.95 (ISBN 1-55734-121-4). Tchr Create Mat.
Stafford, Greg. Prince Valiant: The Storytelling Game. Dunn, Bill & Willis, Lynn, eds. Foster, Hal, illus. 128p. (Orig.). (gr. 6 up). 1989. pap. 19.95 (ISBN 0-933635-50-8, 2801). Chaosium.
Staplehurst, Graham. Robin Hood. Fenlon, Peter & Charlton, S. Coleman, eds. McBride, Angus, illus. 160p. (Orig.). (gr. 10-12). 1987. pap. 15.00 (ISBN 0-915795-28-0, 1010). Iron Crown Ent Inc.
Steig, William. C D C? (Illus.). 64p. (gr. 3 up). 1986. pap. 3.50 (ISBN 0-374-41024-0). FS&G.
Sterling, Mary E. Clothespin Games. Vasconcelles, Keith, illus. 28p. (ps-k). 1989. wkbk 7.95 (ISBN 1-55734-172-9). Tchr Create Mat.
—File Folder Games. Vasconcelles, Keith, illus. 28p. (ps-k). 1989. wkbk 7.95 (ISBN 1-55734-171-0). Tchr Create Mat.
—Synonym-Antonym-Homonym Word Games. Spence, Paula, illus. 48p. (gr. 2-5). 1988. wkbk. 5.95 (ISBN 1-55734-368-3). Tchr Create Mat.
—Wheel Games. Vasconcelles, Keith, illus. 28p. (ps-k). 1989. wkbk 7.95 (ISBN 1-55734-170-2). Tchr Create Mat.
Stuart, Sally E. & Young, Woody. One-Hundred Plus Party Games. Dongarra, Kathryn, ed. White, Craig, illus. 96p. (Orig.). 1988. pap. text ed. 7.95 (ISBN 0-939513-61-7). Joy Pub SJC.
Suid, Murray. For the Love of Words. 112p. (gr. 2-6). 1983. 9.95 (ISBN 0-912107-02-2). Monday Morning Bks.
Swedish Intelligence Editors & Morrison, Jim. Sparkerpolice Guidebook: How to Play Sparkerpolice. Rundqvist, Per, tr. (Illus.). (gr. 11-12). Date not set. 35.00 (ISBN 0-915628-17-1). Zeppelin.
Swerdlick, Harriet & Reiter, Edith. President Games: Puzzles, Quizzes, & Mind Teasers for Every George, Abe, & Lyndon! 48p. (Orig.). (gr. 3 up). 1988. pap. 2.95 incl. chipboard (ISBN 0-8431-2240-4). Price Stern.
Tabor, Roger. Survival: Could You Be a Fox? Morgan, Dee, illus. 32p. (gr. 2-7). 1989. 9.95 (ISBN 0-8249-8360-2). Ideals.

—Survival: Could You Be an Otter? Morgan, Dee, illus. 32p. (gr. 2-7). 1989. 9.95 (ISBN 0-8249-8361-0). Ideals.

Tallarico, Tony. Mr. Merlin's Puzzle & Game Book. Klimo, Kate, ed. Tallarico, Tony, illus. 64p. (Orig.). (gr. 3-6). 1981. pap. 2.95 (ISBN 0-671-44492-1, Little Simon). S&S Trade.

Tallarico, Tony, illus. Disney's Five Board Games to Go. 12p. (ps-5). 1990. bds. 16.95 (ISBN 0-89828-386-8). Tuffy Bks.

—Five Wacky Games to Go. 12p. (ps-3). 1991. 14.95 (ISBN 0-89828-387-6). Tuffy Bks.

Theisen, John A. Steppelords of Mars. Harris, Dell, illus. 64p. (Orig.). 1989. pap. 8.00 (ISBN 1-55878-025-4). Game Designers.

Thieme, Jeanne & Hansen, Robyn. The American Girls Games: Three Antique American Games That Kirsten, Samantha, & Molly Played. (Illus.). 32p. (Orig.). (gr. 2-5). 1989. pap. 17.95 (ISBN 0-937295-61-2). Pleasant Co.

Thompson, Kathleen. My Book of Christmas Games. LC 87-16392. (Illus.). 24p. (gr. 3-5). 1987. lib. bdg. 14.65 (ISBN 0-8172-3162-5). Raintree Pubs.

Toys & Games. (ARA., Illus.). (gr. 4-6). 3.50x (ISBN 0-86685-241-7). Intl Bk Ctr.

Van der Meer, Ron. The World's First Ever Pop-Up Games Book. Van der Meer, Ron, illus. 8p. (gr. k-3). 1982. 9.95 (ISBN 0-440-06943-2). Delacorte.

Vecchione, Glen. The World's Best Street & Yard Games. LC 88-38273. (Illus.). 128p. (gr. 2-8). 1989. 12.95 (ISBN 0-8069-6900-8). Sterling.

Warren, Jean. Learning Games. 80p. (gr. k-2). 1983. 7.95 (ISBN 0-912107-06-5). Monday Morning Bks.

Webb, Phila H. & Corby, Jane. Little Book of Hand Shadows. LC 90-52549. (Illus.). 80p. (gr. 1 up). 1990. 4.95 (ISBN 0-89471-852-5). Running Pr.

Webster, Harriet. Going Places: The Young Traveler's Guide & Activity Book. Owens, Gail, illus. LC 89-24201. 112p. (gr. 4-7). 1991. SBE 12.95 (ISBN 0-684-19078-8, Scribners Young Read). Macmillan Child Grp.

Weigle, Marta. Follow My Fancy: The Book of Jacks & Jack Games. (Illus.). 94p. pap. 2.95 (ISBN 0-486-22081-8). Dover.

Wergin, Joseph P. Cribbage for Kids. Gansen, Ed, illus. Corvi, Becky S., intro. by. LC 90-82436. (Illus.). 116p. (Orig.). (gr. 4-6). 1990. pap. 10.00x (ISBN 0-9627003-0-4); tchr's. ed. 20. 00x (ISBN 0-9627003-1-2). Intl Gamester.

CRIBBAGE FOR KIDS is a family oriented manuscript designed for the dual purpose of learning & entertainment. The work features dialogue with a puppy love story, generous illustrations, a beautiful designed book cover, & text graphics that depict the great strategy moves in Cribbage; however Grandparents will enjoy the large print & the opportunity to read this book. It truly is a book for all ages! In the book CRIBBAGE FOR KIDS, you will come to know Jessica & how she learned to play winning Cribbage; Uncle Joe the wise old professor of this 400 year old card game; Mark the brother who truly believes that girls can't play cards; David whose affection grows out of respect for her Cribbage game skills; & a cast of neighborhood characters who provide the background for an exciting Cribbage tournament. This 400 year old board game of numbers & strategy is regarded by many educators as not only an excellent method but a painless one in teaching math skills to students. If you play Cribbage, by all means teach your children to play. It is not only a game of numbers but it also trains the younger learner to reason out situations & to make logical decisions. The young learner, age 8-12, is taught to lose gracefully, to be a good sport, & a modest winner. The BEAUTY of this game is that grade school children can play well enough to win over grandparents. This splendid work CRIBBAGE FOR KIDS by Joseph Petrus Wergin is available by mail order from The International Gamester, Ltd., Postal Box 2116, Ann Arbor, MI 48106 USA for only $10.00 postpaid. This children's work can also be purchased in a Deluxe Gift Set including a Drueke Walnut Cribbage Board & the International Gamester's custom deck of playing cards, for only $20.00 postpaid. Remember the Gamester always pays the shipping.
Publisher Provided Annotation.

Wieck, Stewart, et al. White Wolf: Temples, Demons, & Ships of War. Petersen, Sandy & Dunn, Bill, eds. Purcell, Steve & Overbey, Taylor, illus. 56p. (Orig.). (gr. 8 up). 1987. pap. 8.95 (ISBN 0-933635-42-7, 2108). Chaosium.

Willner, Carl. Goblin-Gate & Eagle's Eyrie. (Illus.). 32p. (gr. 10-12). 1985. pap. 7.00 (ISBN 0-915795-40-X, 8070). Iron Crown Ent Inc.

—Havens of Gondor, Land of Belfalas. Fenlon, Peter, ed. McBride, Angus, illus. 64p. (Orig.). (gr. 10-12). 1987. pap. 12.00 (ISBN 0-915795-25-6, 3300). Iron Crown Ent Inc.

—Tower of Cirith Ungol & Shelob's Lair. (Illus.). 32p. (gr. 10-12). 1984. pap. 7.00 (ISBN 0-915795-21-3, 8030). Iron Crown Ent Inc.

Wiseman, Loren K. American Combat Vehicle Handbook. Farley, A. C., illus. 104p. (Orig.). (gr. 9-12). 1990. pap. 12.00 (ISBN 1-55878-061-0). Game Designers.

—Infantry Weapons of the World. Venters, Steve, illus. 104p. (Orig.). (gr. 9-12). 1991. pap. 12.00 (ISBN 1-55878-068-8). Game Designers.

—Merc: Two Thousand. Larkin, Bob, illus. 120p. (Orig.). (gr. 9-12). 1990. pap. 16.00 (ISBN 1-55878-072-6). Game Designers.

—More Tales from the Ether. Aulisio, Janet, illus. 64p. (Orig.). 1989. pap. 8.00 (ISBN 1-55878-028-9). Game Designers.

—Return to Warsaw. Holloway, Jim, illus. 49p. (Orig.). 1989. pap. 7.00 (ISBN 1-55878-018-1). Game Designers.

—Soviet Combat Vehicle Handbook. Venters, Steve, illus. 104p. (Orig.). (gr. 9-12). 1990. pap. 12.00 (ISBN 1-55878-067-X). Game Designers.

—White Eagle. Holloway, Jim, illus. 49p. (Orig.). 1990. pap. 7.00 (ISBN 1-55878-033-5). Game Designers.

Wiswell, Phil. Kids' Games: Traditional Indoor & Outdoor Activities for Children of All Ages. LC 86-23955. (Illus.). 176p. (ps up). 1987. pap. 12.95 (ISBN 0-385-23405-8). Doubleday.

Yektai, Niki. What's Silly? Ryan, Suzannah, illus. LC 88-22883. 32p. (gr. 2-4). 1989. 13.95 (ISBN 0-89919-746-9, Pub. by Clarion). Ticknor & Fields.

Zavisca, Ernest & Beltowski, Gary. How to Conquer Dragon's Lair. LC 84-60273. (Illus.). 60p. (Orig.). (gr. 5 up). 1984. pap. 2.95 (ISBN 0-941126-06-4). Meadowlark.

GAMES–FICTION

Bridwell, Norman. Fun with Clifford Activity Book. 1989. pap. 1.95 (ISBN 0-590-42032-1). Scholastic Inc.

Bunting, Eve. The Waiting Game. LC 80-8793. 64p. (gr. 7 up). 1981. (Lipp Jr Bks); PLB 9.89 (ISBN 0-397-31942-8). HarpC Child Bks.

Capote, Truman. Jug of Silver. Hoys, James, illus. LC 86-4230. 48p. (gr. 4 up). 1986. PLB 10.95s.p. (ISBN 0-88682-076-6); 15.65 (ISBN 0-685-12419-3). Creative Ed.

Crutcher, Chris. The Crazy Horse Electric Game. (gr. k-12). 1988. pap. 3.50 (ISBN 0-440-20094-6). Dell.

Gretz, Susanna. Hide-&-Seek. Gretz, Susanna, illus. LC 85-13008. 10p. (ps-k). 1986. PLB 2.95 (ISBN 0-02-737400-9, Four Winds). Macmillan Child Grp.

Hess, Joan. Red Rover, Red Rover. (gr. 6 up). 1988. pap. 2.25 (ISBN 0-373-98016-7). S&S Trade.

Hutchins, Pat. What Game Shall We Play? LC 89-34621. (Illus.). 24p. (ps up). 1990. 12.95 (ISBN 0-688-09196-2); PLB 12.88 (ISBN 0-688-09197-0). Greenwillow.

Justus. Jumping Jack. LC 73-87803. (Illus.). 32p. (gr. k-3). 1974. PLB 9.95 (ISBN 0-87783-123-8); pap. 3.94 deluxe ed. (ISBN 0-87783-124-6); cassette o.s.i. 7.94x (ISBN 0-87783-189-0). Oddo.

Kay, Gene. Speedy O'Hare's Sun Valley Race. Kay, Gene, illus. 36p. (ps-7). 1987. pap. 8.95 (ISBN 0-945222-24-6). Gazelle Prodns.

Klein, Robin. Games. (gr. 5-9). 11.95 (ISBN 0-317-62539-X). Viking Child Bks.

McToots, Rudi. Best-Ever Book of Indoor Games. LC 84-72575. (Illus.). 128p. (gr. 2 up). 1985. pap. 4.95 (ISBN 0-668-06295-9). Prentice Hall Pr.

Nister, Ernest. Playtime Surprises. Nister, Ernest, illus. LC 84-16579. 12p. (gr. k up). 1985. 10.95 (ISBN 0-399-21214-0, Philomel). Putnam Pub Group.

Rodda, Emily. Finders Keepers. LC 90-47850. (Illus.). (gr. 5 up). 1991. 13.95 (ISBN 0-688-10516-5). Greenwillow.

Stine, Jovial Bob. Pork & Beans: Play Date. Aruego, Jose & Dewey, Ariane, illus. (ps-2). 1989. pap. 12.95 (ISBN 0-590-41579-4). Scholastic Inc.

Todd, H. E. Bobby Brewster's Jigsaw Puzzle. Biro, Val, illus. 96p. (gr. 5-7). 1989. 13.95 (ISBN 0-340-42087-1, Pub. by Hodder & Stoughton UK). Trafalgar Sq.

Ure, Jean. You Win Some, You Lose Some. (gr. k-12). 1988. pap. 2.95 (ISBN 0-440-99845-X, LFL). Dell.

Wain, John. The Free Zone Starts Here. LC 83-14373. 196p. (gr. 7 up). 1984. 13.95 (ISBN 0-385-29315-1). Delacorte.

Whittington, Mary K. Troll Games. Day, Betsy, illus. LC 90-83. 32p. (gr. k-3). 1991. SBE 13.95 (ISBN 0-689-31630-5, Atheneum Child Bk). Macmillan Child Grp.

Wood, Don. Piggies. (ps). 1991. 13.95 (ISBN 0-15-256341-5). HarBraceJ.

GAMES, OLYMPIC

see Olympic Games

GANDHI, INDIRA, 1917-

Currimbhoy, Nayana. Indira Gandhi. LC 85-10506. (Illus.). 116p. (gr. 7up). 1985. PLB 12.90 (ISBN 0-531-10064-2). Watts.

Greene, Carol. Indira Nehru Gandhi: Ruler of India. LC 85-359. (Illus.). 32p. (gr. 2-5). 1985. lib. bdg. 13.27 (ISBN 0-516-03478-2). Childrens.

GANDHI, MOHANDAS KARAMCHAND, 1869-1948

Bains, Rae. Gandhi, Peaceful Warrior. Snow, Scott, illus. LC 89-5101. 48p. (gr. 4-6). 1990. lib. bdg. 10.79 (ISBN 0-8167-1767-2); pap. text ed. 2.95 (ISBN 0-8167-1768-0). Troll Assocs.

Cheney, Glenn A. Mohandas Gandhi. (Illus.). 128p. (gr. 7 up). 1983. PLB 12.90 (ISBN 0-531-04600-1). Watts.

Faber, Doris & Faber, Harold. Mahatma Gandhi. LC 86-8734. (Illus.). 128p. (gr. 5 up). 1986. lib. bdg. 10.98 (ISBN 0-671-60176-8). Messner.

Fischer, Louis. Gandhi: His Life & Message for the World. 192p. (gr. 9-12). 1982. pap. 4.50 (ISBN 0-451-62742-3, Ment). NAL-Dutton.

Freitas, F. Bapu. Freitas, F., illus. (gr. 1-9). 1979. Pt. I. pap. 2.50 (ISBN 0-89744-173-7); Pt. II. pap. 1.50 (ISBN 0-89744-174-5). Auromere.

Gandhi, Mahatma. Mahatma Gandhi. Redpath, Ann, ed. Delessert, Etienne, illus. 32p. (gr. 4 up). 1985. PLB 10.45s.p. (ISBN 0-88682-010-3); 14.95 (ISBN 0-685-10400-1). Creative Ed.

Hunter, Nigel. Gandhi. (Illus.). 32p. (gr. 4-8). 1987. PLB 11.90 (ISBN 0-531-18093-X, Pub. by Bookwright Pr). Watts.

Joshi, Uma. Stories from Bapu's Life. Patel, Mickey, illus. (gr. 1-9). 1979. pap. 2.50 (ISBN 0-89744-180-X). Auromere.

Nicholoson, Michael. Mahatma Gandhi: Champion of Human Rights. Birch, Beverley, adapted by. LC 89-77589. (Illus.). 64p. (gr. 3-4). 1990. PLB 12.95 (ISBN 0-8368-0390-6). Gareth Stevens Inc.

Nicholson, Michael. Mahatma Gandhi: The Man Who Freed India & Led the World in Nonviolent Change. Sherwood, Rhoda, ed. LC 88-2098. (Illus.). 68p. (gr. 5-6). 1988. PLB 12.95 (ISBN 1-55532-813-X). Gareth Stevens Inc.

Rawding, F. W. Gandhi. LC 79-11008. (Illus.). 48p. (gr. 7 up). 1980. pap. 5.95 (ISBN 0-521-20715-0). Cambridge U Pr.

Shankar, R. Story of Gandhi. (Illus.). (gr. 3-10). 1979. 5.00 (ISBN 0-89744-166-4). Auromere.

GANGS

see Crime and Criminals; Juvenile Delinquency

GANGS–FICTION

Bunting, Eve. Someone Is Hiding on Alcatraz Island. LC 84-5019. 144p. (gr. 5-8). 1984. 12.95 (ISBN 0-89919-219-X, Clarion). HM.

Cooper, Susan. Dawn of Fear. Gill, Margery, illus. LC 71-115755. (gr. 3-7). 1988. 14.95 (ISBN 0-15-266201-4, HJ). HarBraceJ.

Fleischman, Sid. The Case of Princess Tomorrow. Morrison, Bill, illus. LC 80-19518. 64p. (gr. 2-5). 1981. Random.

—The Case of the Cackling Ghost. Woodrun, Jim, illus. LC 80-20059. 64p. (gr. 2-4). 1981. Random.

Hinton, S. E. Rumble Fish. LC 75-8004. 112p. (gr. 7 up). 1975. pap. 13.95 (ISBN 0-385-28675-9). Delacorte.

Hutchens, Paul. On the Mexican Border. (gr. 3-7). 1968. pap. 3.50 (ISBN 0-8024-4818-6). Moody.

—Sugar Creek Gang & the Cemetery Vandals. 128p. (gr. 3-7). 1972. pap. 3.50 (ISBN 0-8024-4829-1). Moody.

Murphy, Barbara B. & Wolkoff, Judie. Ace Hits the Big Time. 192p. (gr. 7 up). 1982. pap. 3.50 (ISBN 0-440-90328-9, LFL). Dell.

Neville, Emily C. Seventeenth-Street Gang. LC 66-7116. (Illus.). 160p. (gr. 4-7). 1972. pap. 2.95 (ISBN 0-06-440019-0, Trophy). HarpC Child Bks.

Peck, Richard. Secrets of the Shopping Mall. 192p. (gr. k-6). 1989. pap. 3.25 (ISBN 0-440-40270-0, LFL); pap. 3.50 (ISBN 0-440-98099-2). Dell.

Spinelli, Jerry. Bathwater Gang. (gr. 4-7). 1990. 10.95 (ISBN 0-316-80720-6). Little.

Sudbury, Rodie. The Silk & the Skin. 144p. (gr. 3-7). 1982. 8.95 (ISBN 0-233-96816-4). Andre Deutsch.

GARBAGE

see Refuse and Refuse Disposal

GARDEN PESTS

see Insects, Injurious and Beneficial

GARDENING

Use for practical works on the cultivation of flowers, fruits, lawns, vegetables, etc.

see also Fruit Culture; Insects, Injurious and Beneficial; Plant Propagation; Plants; Plants, Cultivated; Vegetable Gardening; Weeds

Brown, Marc. Your First Garden Book. Brown, Marc, illus. (gr. 1 up). 1981. 12.45i (ISBN 0-316-11217-8, Pub. by Atlantic Pr); pap. 5.95 (ISBN 0-316-11215-1). Little.

Butterworth, Nick & Inkpen, Mick. I Wonder in the Garden. 14p. (ps). 1987. pap. 1.95 (ISBN 0-310-55401-2, 19040P). Zondervan.

Davis, A. This Is My Garden. (Illus.). 12p. (ps-1). 1987. 2.50 (ISBN 0-88625-138-9). Durkin Hayes Pub.

Fell, Derek. A Kid's First Book of Gardening with Greenhouse & Seeds. (Illus.). 96p. (Orig.). (gr. 2 up). 1990. pap. 12.98 (ISBN 0-89471-751-0, Pub. by Courage Bks). Running Pr.

Fujikawa, Gyo. Let's Grow a Garden. Fujikawa, Gyo, illus. (gr. k-3). 1978. 3.50 (ISBN 0-448-14613-4, G&D). Putnam Pub Group.

Grow Lab: A Complete Guide to Gardening in the Classroom. LC 87-90726. 127p. (ps-8). 1988. pap. 19.95 (ISBN 0-915873-31-1). Natl Gardening Assn.

Huber, Judy. Gardening & Cooking with Children. 60p. (gr. 1-8). 1987. plastic comb. 4.95 (ISBN 0-944793-00-2); pap. 2.95 (ISBN 0-944793-01-0). Prairie Family Pubs.

Huff, Barbara A. Greening the City Streets: The Story of Community Gardens. Ziebel, Peter, photos by. (Illus.). 80p. (gr. 3-7). 1990. 15.95 (ISBN 0-89919-741-8, Clarion Bks). HM.

Hunt, Linda, et al. Celebrate the Seasons. LC 83-12657. 176p. (Orig.). (ps-2). 1983. pap. 7.95 (ISBN 0-8361-3337-4). Herald Pr.

McCann, Sean. Growing Things. LC 89-51018. 138p. (Orig.). 1989. pap. 5.95 (ISBN 1-85371-029-6, Pub. by Poolbeg Press Ltd Eire). Dufour.

Maris, Ron. In My Garden. LC 87-8773. (Illus.). 32p. (ps-1). 1988. Repr. of 1987 ed. 13.00 (ISBN 0-688-07631-9). Greenwillow.

Markmann, Erika. Grow It! An Indoor - Outdoor Gardening Guide for Kids. Konemund, Gisela, illus. LC 90-45043. 48p. (gr. 2-7). 1991. PLB 11.99 (ISBN 0-679-91528-1); pap. 6.95 (ISBN 0-679-81528-7). Random.

Oechsli, Helen & Oechsli, Kelly. In My Garden: A Child's Gardening Book. Oechsli, Kelly, illus. LC 84-21285. 32p. (ps-2). 1985. 12.95 (ISBN 0-02-768510-1, Mcmillan Child Bk). Macmillan Child Grp.

Parkinson, Cornelia M. Alex Livingston, the Tomato Man. (Illus.). 20p. (gr. 4 up). 1985. pap. 1.50 (ISBN 0-938404-05-9, AWL). Hist Tales.

Raferty, Kim G. & Raftery, Kevin. Kids Gardening: A Kid's Guide to Messing Around in the Dirt. M'Guinness, Jim, illus. 84p. (Orig.). 1989. pap. 12.95 incl. 15 varieties of seeds (ISBN 0-932592-25-2). Klutz Pr.

Robson, Denny. Grow It for Fun: Hands-on Projects. (Illus.). 32p. (gr. k-4). 1991. PLB 11.40 (ISBN 0-531-17343-7, Gloucester Pr). Watts.

Schnatz, Grace. A Child's Introduction to a Garden. Schnatz, Grace, illus. 33p. (gr. 4-8). 1984. PLB 4.75 (ISBN 0-9614145-0-2). G Schnatz Pubns.

Woggon, Guillermo. Cultivemos una Huerta. Granberry, Nola, tr. (SPA., Illus.). 16p. (gr. 1-3). 1987. pap. 1.40 (ISBN 0-311-38564-8). Casa Bautista.

GARDENING–FICTION

Bjork, Christina. Linnea in Monet's Garden. Sandin, Joan, tr. from SWE. Anderson, Lena, illus. 56p. (gr. 3-6). 1987. 11.95 (ISBN 9-12-958314-4, R & S Bks). FS&G.

Brautigan, Richard. In Watermelon Sugar. 176p. (gr. 9 up). 1973. pap. 1.75 (ISBN 0-440-34026-8). Dell.

Carlson, Nancy. Harriet & the Garden. LC 81-18136. (Illus.). 32p. (ps-3). 1982. lib. bdg. 9.95 (ISBN 0-87614-184-X). Carolrhoda Bks.

—Harriet & the Garden. Carlson, Nancy, illus. (gr. k-3). 1985. bk. & cassette 19.95 (ISBN 0-941078-66-3); pap. 12.95 bk. & cassette (ISBN 0-317-14686-6); cassette, 4 paperbacks & guide 27.95 (ISBN 0-317-14687-4). Live Oak Media.

Cristini, Ermanno & Puricelli, Luigi. In My Garden. Cristini, Ermanno & Puricelli, Luigi, illus. LC 85-9402. 28p. (ps up). 1985. 12.95 (ISBN 0-907234-05-4). Picture Bk Studio.

De Brunhoff, Laurent. Babar Jardinier. (FRE.). (gr. 2-3). 4.95 (ISBN 0-685-11030-3). French & Eur.

Ehlert, Lois. Growing Vegetable Soup. (ps-3). 1990. pap. 4.95 (ISBN 0-15-232580-8, VoyB). HarBraceJ.

—Growing Vegetable Soup. Ehlert, Lois, illus. 32p. (ps-3). Date not set. pap. write for info. (ISBN 0-15-232581-6). HarBraceJ.

—Growing Vegetable Soup. (ps-3). 1987. 13.95 (ISBN 0-15-232575-1, HJ). HarBraceJ.

Florian, D. Vegetable Garden. 1991. 13.95 (ISBN 0-15-293383-2, HJ). HarBraceJ.

Kemp, Anthea & Metcalfe, Penny. Mr. Percy's Magic Greenhouse. (Illus.). 32p. (ps-2). 1988. 15.95 (ISBN 0-575-03870-5, Pub. by Gollancz England). Trafalgar Sq.

Lewis, Richard, ed. In a Spring Garden. Keats, Ezra J., illus. 32p. (ps up). 1989. pap. 4.95 (ISBN 0-8037-4033-6, Dial Pied Piper). Puffin Bks.

Lobel, Arnold. The Rose in My Garden. Lobel, Anita, illus. 40p. (ps-2). 1985. pap. 3.95 (ISBN 0-590-41530-1). Scholastic Inc.

Lobel, Arnold & Lobel, Anita. The Rose in My Garden. Lobel, Anita, illus. 40p. (ps-2). 1985. pap. 2.95 (ISBN 0-590-40356-7, Blue Ribbon Bks). Scholastic Inc.

Lord, John V. Mr. Mead & His Garden. LC 74-20766. (Illus.). (gr. k-3). 1975. PLB 6.95 (ISBN 0-395-20278-7). HM.

Moncure, Jane B. Word Bird's Rainy-Day Dance. Hohag, Linda, illus. LC 90-31693. 32p. (ps-2). 1990. lib. bdg. 11.97 (ISBN 0-89565-579-9); pap. text ed. 6.96 (ISBN 0-89565-610-8). Childs World.

Muller, Gerda. The Garden in the City. Muller, Gerda, illus. 40p. (gr. k-3). 1991. 13.95 (ISBN 0-525-44697-4). Dutton Child Bks.

Muntean, Michaela. A Garden for Miss Mouse. Santoro, Christopher, illus. LC 82-2135. 48p. (ps-3). 1982. 5.95 (ISBN 0-8193-1083-2); lib. bdg. 5.95 (ISBN 0-8193-1084-0). Parents.

Newman, Winifred B. The Secret in the Garden. (Illus.). 32p. (Orig.). (gr. k-5). 1980. pap. 4.50 (ISBN 0-87743-159-0, 353-014). Baha'i.

Rockwell, Anne & Rockwell, Harlow. How My Garden Grew. LC 81-17145. (Illus.). 24p. (ps-k). 1982. 8.95 (ISBN 0-02-777660-3, Mcmillan Child Bk). Macmillan Child Grp.

Stobbs, William. Gregory's Garden. (Illus.). 16p. 1987. pap. 2.95 (ISBN 0-19-272140-2). Oxford U Pr.

Williams, Sarah, ed. Round & Round the Garden. Beck, Ian, illus. 48p. (ps). 14.95 (ISBN 0-19-279766-2); pap. 5.95 (ISBN 0-19-272132-1); cassette 7.95 (ISBN 0-19-279852-9). Oxford U Pr.

Wolf, Janet. The Rosy Fat Magenta Radish. (ps-1). 1990. 14.95 (ISBN 0-316-95045-9, Joy St Bks). Little.

Zavos, Judy. Murgatroyd's Garden. Zak, Drahos, illus. 32p. (gr. k-3). 1988. 9.95 (ISBN 0-312-01629-8). St Martin.

GARDENING–POETRY

Disch, Thomas M. The Tale of Dan De Lion. McClun, Rhonda, illus. 25p. (ps up). 1986. 9.95 (ISBN 0-918273-30-7). Coffee Hse.

Steele, Mary Q. Anna's Garden Songs. Anderson, Lena, illus. LC 88-5660. 32p. (gr. k up). 1989. 11.95 (ISBN 0-688-08217-3); PLB 11.88 (ISBN 0-688-08218-1). Greenwillow.

GARDENS–FICTION

Avery, Helen P. The Secret Garden. (Orig.). (gr. k-3). 1987. pap. 5.00 playscript (ISBN 0-87602-271-9). Anchorage.

Burnett, Frances. The Secret Garden. 1989. pap. 2.50 (ISBN 0-451-52080-7). NAL-Dutton.

Burnett, Frances H. The Secret Garden. 302p. 1981. Repr. PLB 19.95x (ISBN 0-89966-326-5). Buccaneer Bks.

—Secret Garden. (gr. k-6). 1989. pap. 3.50 (ISBN 0-440-47709-3, Pub. by Yearling Classics); pap. 2.75 (ISBN 0-440-97709-6, Dell Trade Pbks). Dell.

—The Secret Garden. (gr. 4-6). 1987. pap. 2.25 (ISBN 0-14-035004-7, Puffin). Puffin Bks.

—The Secret Garden. Mitchell, Kathy, illus. 320p. (gr. 4 up). 1987. 12.95 (ISBN 0-448-06029-9, G&D). Putnam Pub Group.

—The Secret Garden. Tudor, Tasha, illus. LC 62-17457. 256p. (gr. 4-8). 1987. pap. 3.50 (ISBN 0-06-440188-X, Trophy). HarpC Child Bks.

—The Secret Garden. McNulty, Faith, afterword by. 1987. pap. 2.95 (ISBN 0-451-52417-9, Sig Classics). NAL-Dutton.

—The Secret Garden. Allen, Thomas B., illus. Howe, James, adapted by. LC 86-17788. (Illus.). 72p. (gr. k-5). 1987. 13.95 (ISBN 0-394-86467-0, Random Juv); lib. bdg. 12.99 (ISBN 0-394-96467-5). Random.

—The Secret Garden. (gr. k-6). 8.98 (ISBN 0-517-63225-X). Outlet Bk Co.

—The Secret Garden. Hague, Michael, illus. LC 86-22780. 240p. (gr. 4-6). 1987. 18.95 (ISBN 0-8050-0277-4). H Holt & Co.

—The Secret Garden. 304p. (Orig.). (gr. 4-6). 1987. pap. 2.95 (ISBN 0-590-40720-1, Pub. by Apple Classics). Scholastic Inc.

—The Secret Garden. Lowry, Lois, intro. by. 256p. 1987. pap. 2.95 (ISBN 0-553-21201-X, Bantam Classics). Bantam.

—The Secret Garden. Betts, Louise, adapted by. LC 87-15490. (Illus.). (gr. 3-6). 1987. PLB 12.89 (ISBN 0-8167-1203-4); pap. 3.95 (ISBN 0-8167-1204-2). Troll Assocs.

—The Secret Garden. 360p. 1987. pap. 4.95 (ISBN 0-19-281772-8). Oxford U Pr.

—The Secret Garden. Sanderson, Ruth, illus. LC 86-46002. 240p. 1988. 18.95 (ISBN 0-394-55431-0). Knopf.

—The Secret Garden. Hughes, Shirley, illus. 240p. (gr. 5 up). 1989. pap. 18.95 (ISBN 0-670-82571-9). Viking Child Bks.

—The Secret Garden. 304p. (gr. 4-7). 1987. pap. 2.95 (ISBN 0-590-43346-6). Scholastic Inc.

—Secret Garden. 1987. pap. 3.50 (ISBN 0-440-40055-4). Dell.

—Secret Garden. 288p. 1990. pap. 2.50 (ISBN 0-8125-0501-8). Tor Bks.

—Secret Garden. Howell, Troy, illus. 272p. (gr. 4 up). 1987. 10.95 (ISBN 0-681-40056-0). Longmeadow Pr.

—Secret Garden. 1991. pap. 3.99 (ISBN 0-8125-1910-8). Tor Bks.

Burnett, Francis H. The Secret Garden: A Young Reader's Edition of the Classic Story. Abr. ed. Crawford, Dale, illus. LC 90-80198. 56p. (gr. 1 up). 1990. 9.98 (ISBN 0-89471-860-6, Courage Bks). Running Pr.

Carlson, Nancy. Harriet & the Garden. Carlson, Nancy, illus. 32p. (ps-3). 1985. pap. 3.95 (ISBN 0-14-050466-4, Puffin). Puffin Bks.

Collette, Paul & Wright, Robert. Huddles. (Orig.). (gr. 3-12). 1985. pap. text ed. 6.00 (ISBN 0-88734-512-3). Players Pr.

Hahn, Mary D. Doll in the Garden. 144p. 1990. pap. 3.50 (ISBN 0-380-70865-5, Camelot). Avon.

Harwood, Pearl A. Mr. Bumba Plants a Garden. Folger, Joseph, illus. LC 64-19771. 32p. (gr. k-3). 1964. PLB 4.95 (ISBN 0-8225-0102-3). Lerner Pubns.

El Jardin Secreto. (SPA.). 1990. casebound 3.50 (ISBN 0-7214-1404-4). Ladybird Bks.

Klipper, Ilse. My Magic Garden. Green, Maureen, et al, illus. 91p. (Orig.). (gr. 2-6). 1980. pap. 5.95 (ISBN 0-9605022-0-3). Pathwys Pr CA.

Leonard, Marcia. Gregory & Mr. Grump. Brook, Bonnie, ed. Chambliss, Maxie & Iosa, Ann, illus. 24p. (ps-1). 1990. 4.95 (ISBN 0-671-70406-0); lib. bdg. 9.98 (ISBN 0-671-70402-8). Silver Pr.

Rylant, Cynthia. This Year's Garden. Szilagyi, Mary, illus. LC 86-22224. 32p. (ps-3). 1987. pap. 4.95 (ISBN 0-689-71122-0, Aladdin). Macmillan Child Grp.

St. John, Patricia M. Rainbow Garden. (gr. 2-5). pap. 4.50 (ISBN 0-8024-0028-0). Moody.

The Secret Garden. (gr. 4 up). 1988. pap. 4.87 (ISBN 0-582-54152-2, 74259). Longman.

Stevenson, James. Grandpas Too-Good Garden. LC 88-18786. (Illus.). 32p. (gr. k up). 1989. 12.95 (ISBN 0-688-08485-0); PLB 12.88 (ISBN 0-688-08486-9). Greenwillow.

GARFIELD, JAMES ABRAM, PRESIDENT U. S., 1831-1881

Brown, Fern G. James A. Garfield: Twentieth President of the United States. Young, Richard G., ed. LC 89-39953. (Illus.). 128p. (gr. 5-9). 1990. PLB 17.26 (ISBN 0-944483-63-1). Garrett Ed Corp.

Lillegard, Dee. James A. Garfield. LC 87-18200. (Illus.). 100p. (gr. 3 up). 1987. PLB 17.27 (ISBN 0-516-01394-7). Childrens.

GARIBALDI, GIUSEPPE, 1807-1882

Viola, Herman & Viola, Susan. Giuseppe Garibaldi. (Illus.). (gr. 5 up). 1988. 17.95 (ISBN 0-87754-526-X). Chelsea Hse.

GARMENT MAKING

see Dressmaking

GAS AND OIL ENGINES

see also Automobiles–Engines

Dineen, Jacqueline. Oil & Gas. 32p. (gr. 4-8). 1988. lib. bdg. 12.95 (ISBN 0-89490-219-9). Enslow Pubs.

GAS ENGINES

see Gas and Oil Engines

GAS STATIONS

see Automobiles–Service Stations

GASES

Bailey, Donna. Energy from Oil & Gas. LC 90-39300. (Illus.). 48p. (gr. 2-5). 1990. PLB 15.96 (ISBN 0-8114-2518-5). Steck-V.

Barber, Jacqueline. Solids, Liquids, & Gases. Bergman, Lincoln & Fairwell, Kay, eds. Baker, Lisa H. & Peterson, Adria, illus. Barber, Jacqueline, et al, photos by. 56p. (Orig.). (gr. 3-6). 1986. pap. 10.00 (ISBN 0-912511-69-9). Lawrence Science.

Berger, Melvin. Solids, Liquids & Gases: From Superconductors to the Ozone Layer. (Illus.). 80p. (gr. 5 up). 1989. 11.99 (ISBN 0-399-21731-2, Putnam). Putnam Pub Group.

Gas. LC 80-54728. (gr. 4 up). 1981. PLB 11.90 (ISBN 0-531-04198-0). Watts.

Gas. (Illus.). (gr. 5 up). lib. bdg. 15.93 (ISBN 0-86592-264-0). Rourke Corp.

GASOLINE ENGINES

see Gas and Oil Engines

GASTRONOMY

see Cookery; Food

GAUCHOS

see Cowboys

GAZETTEERS

see also Names, Geographical

GEESE

Ahlstrom, Mark. The Snow Goose. LC 85-29933. (Illus.). 48p. (gr. 5-6). 1986. PLB 10.95 (ISBN 0-89686-293-3, Crestwood Hse). Macmillan Child Grp.

Kalas, Sybille. The Goose Family Book. Crampton, Patricia, tr. LC 85-30986. (Illus.). 53p. (gr. 1 up). 1986. 15.95 (ISBN 0-88708-019-7). Picture Bk Studio.

Rothaus, Jim. Ducks, Geese, & Swans. 24p. (gr. 3). 1988. 17.10 (ISBN 0-88682-224-6); PLB 11.95s.p. (ISBN 0-318-37905-8). Creative Ed.

Selsam, Millicent E. & Hunt, Joyce. A First Look at Ducks, Geese & Swans. Springer, Harriet, illus. 32p. (gr. 1-4). 1990. 11.95 (ISBN 0-8027-6975-6); lib. bdg. 12.85 (ISBN 0-8027-6976-4). Walker & Co.

GEESE–FICTION

Ahlstrom, Mark. The Canada Goose. LC 83-24015. (Illus.). 48p. (gr. 5-6). 1984. PLB 10.95 (ISBN 0-89686-243-7, Crestwood Hse). Macmillan Child Grp.

Asch, Frank. Macgooses' Grocery. Marshall, James, illus. LC 77-86270. 32p. (ps-2). 1980. pap. 1.95 (ISBN 0-8037-5328-4). Dial Bks Young.

Duvoisin, Roger. Petunia. Duvoisin, Roger, illus. (gr. k-3). 1962. lib. bdg. 8.99 (ISBN 0-394-90865-1). Knopf.

—Petunia. Duvoisin, Roger, illus. LC 72-9552. 32p. (ps-2). 1989. pap. 3.95 (ISBN 0-394-82589-6). Knopf.

—Petunia, I Love You. Duvoisin, Roger, illus. (gr. k-3). 1965. lib. bdg. 12.99 (ISBN 0-394-90870-8). Knopf.

—Petunia's Christmas. Duvoisin, Roger, illus. (gr. k-3). 1963. lib. bdg. 12.99 (ISBN 0-394-90868-6). Knopf.

Gallico, Paul. Snow Goose. (gr. 9 up). 1941. 10.95 (ISBN 0-394-44593-7). Knopf.

George, Lindsay B. William & Boomer. George, Lindsay B., illus. 24p. (ps-3). 1990. incl. audiocassette 17.95 (ISBN 0-924483-23-7). Soundprints.

Grimm, Jacob & Grimm, Wilhelm K. The Golden Goose. Duntze, Dorothee, illus. Bell, Anthea, tr. LC 87-32108. (Illus.). 32p. (gr. k-3). 1988. 12.95 (ISBN 1-55858-047-6). North-South Bks NYC.

Hunt, Robert. Windy: The Snow Goose. Burridge, Marge O., illus. LC 74-735894. (gr. 2-5). 1978. 6 bks. & 1 cass. 29.95 (ISBN 0-89290-035-0); 1 bk. & 1 cass. 10.95 (ISBN 0-685-04676-1). Soc for Visual.

Kent, Jack. Silly Goose. Kent, Jack, illus. LC 82-21441. 32p. (ps-3). 1986. 10.95 (ISBN 0-13-809947-2); pap. 5.95 (ISBN 0-13-810177-9). P-H.

—Silly Goose. LC 82-21441. (Illus.). 32p. (gr. k-4). 1983. PLB 10.95 (ISBN 0-671-66676-2); pap. 5.95 (ISBN 0-671-66677-0). S&S Trade.

Langton, Jane. The Fledgling. LC 79-2008. 192p. (gr. 3-7). 1981. pap. 3.50 (ISBN 0-06-440121-9, Trophy). HarpC Child Bks.

Lindbergh, Reeve. Day the Goose Got Loose. Kellogg, Steven, illus. LC 87-28959. 32p. (ps-3). 1990. 12.95 (ISBN 0-8037-0408-9); PLB 12.89 (ISBN 0-8037-0409-7). Dial Bks Young.

McKelvey, David. Commander the Gander. Asklin, William O., illus. LC 84-72455. 48p. (gr. 4-6). 1984. lib. bdg. 9.45 (ISBN 0-931722-31-4); pap. 3.95 (ISBN 0-931722-30-6). Corona Pub.

Marshall-Noke, Dorothy. Feathers. Weinberger, Jane, ed. Christian, Marilynn V., illus. LC 88-51278. 64p. (gr. 1-4). 1990. pap. 7.95 (ISBN 0-932433-52-9). Windswept Hse.

Mister Tom. Gilly the Goose. Bonnett, Niki, illus. 32p. (Orig.). (gr. k-4). 1989. pap. 5.95 (ISBN 0-925237-02-7). Ten Pubns.

Pierce, Meredith A. Where the Wild Geese Go. Henterly, Jamichael, illus. LC 87-24514. 60p. (ps up). 1988. 15.00 (ISBN 0-525-44379-7, 01456-440, DCB). Dutton Child Bks.

Saunders, Susan. The Golden Goose. Seltzer, Isadore, illus. 32p. (Orig.). (gr. k-3). 1987. pap. 2.50 (ISBN 0-590-41049-0); Book-Cassette pkg. 5.95 (ISBN 0-317-59404-4). Scholastic Inc.

—The Golden Goose. Selzer, Isadore, illus. 32p. (gr. k-3). 1988. pap. 2.50 (ISBN 0-590-41715-0). Scholastic Inc.

Sharmat, Marjorie W. Griselda's New Year. Chartier, Normand, illus. 32p. (gr. 1-4). 1989. pap. 3.95 (ISBN 0-689-71341-X, Aladdin). Macmillan Child Grp.

Simon, Shirley. Foolish Goose. Gregorich, Barbara, ed. (Illus.). 16p. (Orig.). (gr. k-2). 1985. pap. 1.95 (ISBN 0-88743-015-5, 06015). Sch Zone Pub Co.

White, Sylvia. Home Is Best. Weinberger, Jane & Black, Albert, eds. DeVito, Pamela, illus. LC 88-50315. 44p. (gr. 1-4). 1988. pap. 3.95 (ISBN 0-932433-48-0). Windswept Hse.

GEHRIG, HENRY LOUIS, 1903-1941

Brandt, Keith. Lou Gehrig, Pride of the Yankees. Lawn, John, illus. LC 85-1075. 48p. (gr. 4-6). 1986. lib. bdg. 10.79 (ISBN 0-8167-0549-6); pap. text ed. 2.95 (ISBN 0-8167-0550-X). Troll Assocs.

Curato, Guy, pseud. Batting One Thousand - Baseball's Leading Hitters: A Tribute to Lou Gehrig. LC 88-82916. 124p. (Orig.). (gr. 9). 1989. pap. write for info. (ISBN 0-9621591-0-7). T Assicurato.

Van Riper, Guernsey, Jr. Lou Gehrig: One of Baseball's Greatest. Robinson, Jerry, illus. LC 86-10951. 192p. (gr. 2-6). 1986. pap. 3.95 (ISBN 0-02-041930-9, Aladdin). Macmillan Child Grp.

GEMS

For works on cut and polished precious stones treated from the point of view of art or antiquity. Works on uncut stones treated from the mineralogical point of view are entered under Precious Stones. Works on gems in which the interest is in the setting are entered under Jewelry.

see also Precious Stones

Jangl, James F. Birthstone Coloring Book: Birthstone Legends & Other Gem Folklore. Jangl, Alda M. & Jangl, James F., illus. 32p. (gr. k up). 1987. pap. 3.50 (ISBN 0-942647-03-3). Prisma Pr.

Lutz, Tim. Gem Hunter's Kit. (Illus.). 64p. (Orig.). (gr. 3 up). 1990. package 16.95 (ISBN 0-89471-828-2). Running Pr.

Mercer, Ian. Gemstones. (Illus.). 32p. (gr. 1-6). 1987. lib. bdg. 11.90 (ISBN 0-531-17057-8, Gloucester Pr). Watts.

Swinburne, Laurence & Swinburne, Irene. The Deadly Diamonds. LC 77-10764. (Illus.). 48p. (gr. 4 up). 1983. PLB 17.32 (ISBN 0-8172-1064-4); pap. 9.27 (ISBN 0-8172-2158-1). Raintree Pubs.

GENEALOGY

see also Biography; Heraldry

Beller, Susan P. Roots for Kids: Genealogy Anyone Can Understand. LC 88-35134. 128p. (Orig.). (gr. 6 up). 1989. pap. 7.95 (ISBN 1-55870-112-5). Betterway Pubns.

Bonsey, Lynn & Healey, Lorna. It's All Relative: How to Create Your Own Personal Family History Trivia Game. Richards, Christine A., illus. 108p. (Orig.). (gr. 12). 1988. pap. 9.95 (ISBN 1-55613-148-8). Heritage Books.

Brown, Abram E. Beneath Old Rooftrees. (Illus.). xiv, 350p. (gr. 9-12). 1988. pap. 25.00 (ISBN 1-55613-107-0). Heritage Bk.

Chorzempa, Rosemary A. My Family Tree Workbook: Genealogy for Beginners. 64p. (gr. 5 up). 1982. pap. 2.50 (ISBN 0-486-24229-3). Dover.

Cooper, Kay. Where Did You Get Those Eyes: A Guide to Discovering Your Family History. Accardo, Anthony, illus. (gr. 5 up). 1988. 13.95 (ISBN 0-8027-6802-4); PLB 14.85 (ISBN 0-8027-6803-2). Walker & Co.

Crosby, Nina E. & Marten, Elizabeth H. Don't Teach Let Me Learn about Presidents, of the U. S. People, Genealogy, Immigrants. (Illus.). 80p. (Orig.). (gr. 3-9). 1979. pap. 8.95 tchr's. enrichment manual (ISBN 0-914634-67-4, 7912). DOK Pubs.

Genealogy. (Illus.). 64p. (gr. 6-12). 1988. pap. 1.85 (ISBN 0-8395-3383-7, 3383). BSA.

Perl, Lila. The Great Ancestor Hunt. LC 88-36211. (Illus.). 112p. (gr. 4 up). 1989. 15.95 (ISBN 0-89919-745-0, Clarion Bks). HM.

—Great Ancestor Hunt: The Fun of Finding Out Who You Are. (gr. 4-7). 1990. pap. 5.95 (ISBN 0-395-54790-3, Clarion Bks). HM.

Styx, Sherrie A. Genealogy Just for Kids! (Illus.). 28p. (gr. k-4). 1989. wkbk. 2.50 (ISBN 1-882121-25-2). Styx Enter.

—Our Colorful Family Tree. (Illus.). 10p. (ps-2). 1989. write for info. (ISBN 1-882121-00-7). Styx Enter.

Thieme, Jeanne. The American Girls Album: A Picture Frame & Memory Book to Record Your Family History. (Illus.). 48p. (Orig.). (gr. 2-5). 1989. pap. 12.95 (ISBN 0-937295-57-4). Pleasant Co.

Wolfman, Ira. Do People Grow on Family Trees? Genealogy for Kids & Other Beginners. LC 88-51586. (Illus.). 192p. (Orig.). (gr. 3-7). 1991. pap. 9.95 (ISBN 0-89480-348-4, 1348). Workman Pub.

Wubben, Pamela G. Living Genealogy for Children. 65p. (ps-7). 1981. pap. 9.95 (ISBN 0-935442-03-0). One Percent.

GENERALS

Brown, Warren. Colin Powell. (Illus.). (gr. 5 up). 1992. PLB 17.95 (ISBN 0-7910-1647-1); pap. 9.95 (ISBN 0-7910-1648-X). Chelsea Hse.

Caldwell, Willie W. Stonewall Jim: A Biography of General James A. Walker, C. S. A. Savage, Lon, ed. Butler, M. Caldwell, intro. by. (Illus.). 280p. (gr. 10-12). 1990. 24.95 (ISBN 0-9617256-4-8); pap. 12.95 (ISBN 0-9617256-5-6). Northcross Hse.

Fritz, Jean. Stonewall. (Illus.). (gr. 3-7). 1979. 14.95 (ISBN 0-399-20698-1, Putnam). Putnam Pub Group.

Landau, Elaine. Colin Powell: Four Star General. (Illus.). 64p. (gr. 5-8). 1991. PLB 11.90 (ISBN 0-531-20143-0). Watts.

Shelley, Mary V. Dr. Ed: The Story of General Edward Hand. Weatherlow, Regina, illus. LC 78-10331. 36p. (gr. 4-7). 1978. 5.75 (ISBN 0-915010-24-0). Sutter House.

GENERATION

see Reproduction

GENETICS

see also Adaptation (Biology); Evolution; Life (Biology); Reproduction

Arnold, Caroline. Genetics: From Mendel to Gene Splicing. LC 86-5668. (Illus.). 72p. (gr. 4-9). 1986. PLB 10.40 (ISBN 0-531-10223-8). Watts.

Asimov, Isaac. How Did We Find Out about Our Genes? Wool, David, illus. LC 83-1211. 64p. (gr. 5-8). 1983. PLB 10.85 (ISBN 0-8027-6500-9). Walker & Co.

Bornstein, Sandy. What Makes You What You Are: A First Look at Genetics. Steltenpohl, Jane, ed. (Illus.). 128p. (gr. 7 up). 1989. PLB 11.98 (ISBN 0-671-63711-8); pap. 6.95 (ISBN 0-671-68650-X). Messner.

Dudley, William, ed. Genetic Engineering: Opposing Viewpoints. LC 89-25765. (Illus.). 264p. (gr. 10 up). 1990. lib. bdg. 15.95 (ISBN 0-89908-477-X); pap. text ed. 8.95 (ISBN 0-89908-452-4). Greenhaven.

Edelson, Edward. Genetics & Heredity. (Illus.). (gr. 5 up). 1991. 18.95 (ISBN 0-7910-0018-4). Chelsea Hse.

Edwards, R. G. Test-Tube Babies. Head, J. J., ed. Khoury, Diana, illus. LC 79-50741. 16p. (gr. 10 up). 1981. pap. 2.15 (ISBN 0-89278-289-7, 45-9689). Carolina Biological.

Gerbi, Susan A. From Genes to Proteins. Head, J. J., ed. Steffen, Ann T., illus. LC 84-45830. 16p. (Orig.). (gr. 10 up). 1987. pap. text ed. 2.15 (ISBN 0-89278-358-3, 45-9758). Carolina Biological.

Goldstein, Philip. Genetics Is Easy. rev. ed. (Illus.). (gr. 9 up). 8.05 (ISBN 0-8313-1539-3). Lantern.

Gutnik, Martin. Genetics. 128p. (gr. 7-12). 1985. PLB 12.90 (ISBN 0-531-04936-1). Watts.

—Genetics Projects for Young Scientists. 1989. pap. 5.95 (ISBN 0-531-15131-X). Watts.

Higgins, Jane H. Discovering Genetics. West, James A., illus. 48p. (Orig.). (gr. 4-12). 1983. pap. text ed. 8.95 tchr's. enrichment bk. (ISBN 0-88047-033-X, 8315). DOK Pubs.

Lampton, Christopher. Gene Technology: Confronting the Issues. (Illus.). 144p. (gr. 9-12). 1990. PLB 12.90 (ISBN 0-531-10951-8). Watts.

Olesky, Walter. Miracles of Genetics. LC 85-30852. (Illus.). 127p. (gr. 6-9). 1986. PLB 21.27 (ISBN 0-516-00531-6). Childrens.

Silverstein, Alvin & Silverstein, Virginia B. Genes, Medicine, & You. LC 88-37353. (Illus.). 160p. (gr. 6 up). 1989. PLB 18.95 (ISBN 0-89490-154-0). Enslow Pubs.

Sully, Nina. Looking at Genetics. (Illus.). 48p. (gr. 5-8). 1985. 18.95 (ISBN 0-7134-4775-3, Pub. by Batsford England). Trafalgar Sq.

GEODESY

see also Surveying

Lauber, Patricia. Seeing Earth from Space. LC 89-77523. (Illus.). 80p. (gr. 5 up). 1990. 19.95 (ISBN 0-531-05902-2); PLB 19.99 (ISBN 0-531-08502-3). Orchard Bks Watts.

GEOGRAPHICAL ATLASES

see Atlases

GEOGRAPHICAL DISTRIBUTION OF ANIMALS AND PLANTS

see also Animals–Migration; Desert Animals; Desert Plants; Fresh-Water Animals; Marine Animals; Marine Plants

Animal Friends of the Northwest. (gr. 4-7). pap. 2.00 (ISBN 0-915266-08-3). Awani Pr.

Animal Friends of the Rockies. (gr. 4-7). pap. 2.00 (ISBN 0-915266-09-1). Awani Pr.

Animal Friends of the Sierra. (gr. 4-7). pap. 2.00 (ISBN 0-915266-06-7). Awani Pr.

Animal Friends of the Southwest. (gr. 4-7). pap. 2.00 (ISBN 0-915266-07-5). Awani Pr.

Animal Friends of the Yellowstone. (gr. 4-7). pap. 2.00 (ISBN 0-915266-10-5). Awani Pr.

Wolff, Robert. Animals of Europe. Dallet, Robert, illus. LC 77-78379. 160p. (gr. 3-9). 1969. PLB 29.95 (ISBN 0-87460-092-8). Lion Bks.

—Animals of the Americas. Dallet, Robert, illus. LC 73-78378. (gr. 3-9). 1969. PLB 29.95 (ISBN 0-87460-093-6). Lion Bks.

GEOGRAPHICAL DISTRIBUTION OF MAN

see Ethnology

GEOGRAPHICAL NAMES

see Names, Geographical

GEOGRAPHY

For general works, frequently textbooks, which describe the surface of the earth with its various peoples, animals, natural products and industries. For travel books limited to one country or region, use the name of the place with the subdivision Description and Travel. Works that treat only of the physical features of the earth's surface and its atmosphere are entered under Physical Geography.

see also Atlases; Discoveries (In Geography); Ethnology; Maps; Physical Geography; Surveying; Voyages and Travels

also names of countries, states, etc. with the subdivision Description and Travel, and Geography, e.g. U. S. –Description and Travel

Aten, Jerry. Understanding Our World Through Geography. 208p. (gr. 4-8). 1991. 13.95 (ISBN 0-86653-592-6). Good Apple.

Balsley, Irol W. Where on Earth? 144p. (gr. 4-8). 1986. wkbk. 10.95 (ISBN 0-86653-336-2, GA 691). Good Apple.

Bresler, L. Earth Facts: Records-Lists-Facts-Comparisons. (Illus.). 48p. (gr. 3-7). 1987. PLB 12.96 (ISBN 0-88110-239-3); pap. 5.95 (ISBN 0-7460-0022-7). EDC.

Brewton, Barney. California Studies. (gr. 4). 1987. text incl. activity program 229.00 (ISBN 0-318-41079-6). Southwinds Pr.

Carratello, John & Carratello, Patty. World Geography. Chellton, Anna, illus. 48p. (gr. 3-6). 1989. wkbk. 5.95 (ISBN 1-55734-161-3). Tchr Create Mat.

Churchill, E. Richard. Geography Flipper. 49p. (gr. 5 up). 1989. Repr. of 1987 ed. trade edition 5.95 (ISBN 1-878383-07-8). C Lee Pubns.

Cohen, Lynn. Me & My World. Pinkerton, Susan, illus. 64p. 1986. 6.95x (ISBN 0-912107-46-4, Dist. by Good Apple). Monday Morning Bks.

Cooper, Kay. Where in the World Are You? Novak, Justin, illus. 80p. (gr. 3-7). 1990. 13.95 (ISBN 0-8027-6912-8); lib. bdg. 14.85 (ISBN 0-8027-6913-6). Walker & Co.

Countries of the World Facts: Records-Lists-Facts-Comparisons. (Illus.). 48p. (gr. 3-7). 1986. PLB 12.96 (ISBN 0-88110-227-X); pap. 5.95 (ISBN 0-86020-977-6). EDC.

Crawford, Sue. Lands of Legend. (Illus.). 48p. (gr. 5-6). 1989. PLB 12.40 (ISBN 0-531-18247-9). Watts.

Crump, Donald J., ed. Along a Rocky Shore. (Illus.). (gr. k-4). 1990. Set. 13.95 (ISBN 0-87044-822-6); lib. bdg. write for info. (ISBN 0-87044-823-4). Natl Geog.

—Books for Young Explorers: Along a Rocky Shore; Animal Families; Lions & Tigers & Leopards: The Big Cats; Our Amazing Animal Friends, 4 bks, Set 17. (gr. k-4). 1990. Set. PLB 13.95 (ISBN 0-87044-821-8). Natl Geog.

—Geo-Whiz! 104p. (gr. 3-8). 1988. 6.95 (ISBN 0-87044-657-6); PLB 8.50 (ISBN 0-87044-662-2). Natl Geog.

Dempsey, Michael W. Children's First Geography Encyclopedia. 1985. 6.98 (ISBN 0-671-07746-5). S&S Trade.

Dixon, Dougal. Geography. 40p. (gr. 4 up). 1984. lib. bdg. 11.40 (ISBN 0-531-04744-X). Watts.

Fradin, Dennis. Continents. LC 86-9580. (Illus.). 48p. (gr. k-4). 1986. PLB 14.60 (ISBN 0-516-01291-6); pap. 4.95 (ISBN 0-516-41291-4). Childrens.

Frinks, Donna. All about Me. (gr. k). 1989. text incl. activity program 160.00 (ISBN 0-318-41077-X). Southwinds Pr.

Gakken Co. Ltd. Editors. Famous Places. Time-Life Books Inc. Editors, tr. 90p. (gr. k-3). 1989. write for info. (ISBN 0-8094-4893-9); PLB write for info. (ISBN 0-8094-4894-7). Time-Life.

Geography Encyclopedia. (Illus.). 144p. (gr. 4 up). 1989. Repr. 14.95 (ISBN 0-02-689199-9). Checkerboard Pr.

Hargreaves, Margaret & Davis, Pat. At Home & School. (Illus.). (gr. 1). 1988. text incl. activity program 259.00 (ISBN 0-318-41078-8). Southwinds Pr.

—Extending My World. (gr. 3). 1988. text incl. activity program 259.00 (ISBN 0-318-41080-X). Southwinds Pr.
—My Neighborhood & Me. (gr. 2). 1988. text incl. activity program 259.00 (ISBN 0-318-41081-8). Southwinds Pr.
Jennings, Terry. Exploring Our World, 6 vols. (Illus.). 288p. (gr. 4-8). 1987. Set. lib. bdg. 83.70x (ISBN 0-86307-818-4). Marshall Cavendish.
Jones, Earl, Sr. Map Rap: A Fun Way to Learn Geography Through Rap. Smallwood, James, illus. Coleman, Booker T., intro. by. LC 90-84037. (Illus.). 60p. (Orig.). (gr. 2-12). 1990. pap. 12.75 (ISBN 0-935132-18-X). C H Fairfax.
Kalman, Bobbie. People & Places. (Illus.). 32p. (gr. 2-3). 1987. 14.95 (ISBN 0-86505-079-1); pap. 6.95 (ISBN 0-86505-101-1). Crabtree Pub Co.
Kruger, Herbert O., et al. World Geography Study Aid. 1986. pap. 1.95 (ISBN 0-87738-044-9). Youth Ed.
Liptak, Karen. Pangaea: The Mother Continent. Steere, Susan, illus. LC 89-15495. 36p. (Orig.). (gr. 4-6). 1989. 15.95 (ISBN 0-943173-36-1); pap. 8.95 (ISBN 0-943173-42-6). Harbinger AZ.
Little People Big Book about Faraway Places. 64p. (ps-1). 1990. write for info. (ISBN 0-8094-7504-9); PLB write for info. (ISBN 0-8094-7505-7). Time-Life.
Magos, Eunice & Mornnes, Esther. Learning Journeys, 2 Bks. Burris, Priscilla, illus. (Orig.). (gr. 3-5). 1985. Bk. I. pap. text ed. 5.95 (ISBN 0-933606-34-6); Bk. II. pap. text ed. 5.95 (ISBN 0-933606-35-4). Monkey Sisters.
Maifair, Linda. People & Places. Burris, Priscilla, illus. Sussman, Ellen, intro. by. (Illus.). 64p. (gr. 3-6). 1989. pap. 6.95 (ISBN 0-933606-72-9). Monkey Sisters.
Manley, Deborah. People & Places. 1990. 4.99 (ISBN 0-517-69614-2). Outlet Bk Co.
Moon, Bernice & Moon, Cliff. My Country. LC 85-22397. (Illus.). 1280p. (gr. 2-5). 1986. lib. bdg. 199.00x (ISBN 0-86307-476-6). Marshall Cavendish.
Naylor, Sue. Natural Wonders of the World. LC 86-2026. (Illus.). 32p. (gr. 2 up). 1986. PLB 10.95 (ISBN 0-87518-331-X, Dillon). Macmillan Child Grp.
Nero, Ann B. Essential Skills in Geography. Radner, Barbara, ed. (Illus.). 94p. (Orig.). (gr. 4-9). 1987. pap. text ed. 3.96 (ISBN 0-528-17918-7); tchrs. ed 7.92 (ISBN 0-528-17919-5). Rand McNally.
People & Places Series, 24 bks. (Illus.). 1152p. (gr. 4-8). 1989. Set. PLB 359.52 (ISBN 0-382-09600-2). Silver Burdett Pr.
Schroeder, Mary. Extending U. S. History & Geography. West, James A., illus. 32p. (Orig.). (gr. 3-6). 1984. 5.95 (ISBN 0-88047-041-0, 8404). DOK Pubs.
Silver Burdett Countries. (gr. 5 up). 1990. Set, 6 bks., 48p. ea. lib. bdg. 319.20 (ISBN 0-382-09648-7); Set, 6 bks., 48p. ea. pap. 41.70 (ISBN 0-382-09650-9). Silver Burdett Pr.
Simon & Schuster Staff. Where Is It: Questions & Answers. 1989. pap. 7.95 (ISBN 0-671-68468-X). S&S Trade.
Singer, Marilyn. Nine O'Clock Lullaby. Lessac, Frane, illus. LC 90-32116. 32p. (ps-3). 1991. 14.95 (ISBN 0-06-025647-8); PLB 14.89 (ISBN 0-06-025648-6). HarpC Child Bks.
Steck-Vaughn Company Staff. Voices from Around the World. LC 90-10133. (Illus.). 128p. (gr. 5-8). 1990. PLB 18.60 (ISBN 0-8114-2772-2). Steck-V.
Stoltman, Joseph P. Goode's Atlas Place Location Study Guide. Radner, Barbara, ed. (Illus.). 96p. (Orig.). (gr. 8-12). 1987. Student ed. pap. 3.96 (ISBN 0-528-17753-2); tchrs. ed 7.92 (ISBN 0-528-17754-0). Rand McNally.
Tyler. World Geography. (Illus.). 160p. (gr. 3-6). 1986. 17.95 (ISBN 0-86020-193-7). EDC.
Where It's At: Geography for the Quick. (gr. 4-8). 1.95. Trillium Pr.

GEOGRAPHY, COMMERCIAL
see also Economic Conditions; Trade Routes

GEOGRAPHY-DICTIONARIES
Enciclopedia Geografica Juvenil, 13 vols. (SPA.). 1280p. 1974. Set. pap. 250.00 (ISBN 84-201-0410-8). French & Eur.
Knowlton, Jack. Geography from A to Z: A Picture Glossary. Barton, Harriett, illus. LC 86-4594. 48p. (gr. 2-5). 1988. 12.95 (ISBN 0-690-04616-2, Crowell Jr Bks); PLB 13.89 (ISBN 0-690-04618-9). HarpC Child Bks.

GEOGRAPHY, HISTORICAL-MAPS
see Atlases, Historical

GEOGRAPHY, PHYSICAL
see Physical Geography

GEOGRAPHY-PICTORIAL WORKS
see Views

GEOGRAPHY-VOCATIONAL GUIDANCE
Sipiera, Paul. I Can Be a Geographer. LC 90-2198. (Illus.). 32p. (gr. k-3). 1990. PLB 13.93 (ISBN 0-516-01961-9). Childrens.

GEOLOGY
see also Coral Reefs and Islands; Creation; Earth; Earthquakes; Glaciers; Mineralogy; Mountains; Oceanography; Physical Geography; Rocks; Submarine Geology; Volcanoes
Aylesworth, Thomas G. Moving Continents: Our Changing Earth. 64p. (gr. 6 up). 1990. 15.95 (ISBN 0-89490-273-3). Enslow Pubs.
Baylor, Byrd. If You Are a Hunter of Fossils. Parnall, Peter, illus. LC 79-17926. 32p. (ps-3). 1980. 13.95 (ISBN 0-684-16419-1, Scribners Young Read). Macmillan Child Grp.
Boy Scouts of America. Geology. (Illus.). 96p. (gr. 6-12). 1985. pap. 1.85 (ISBN 0-8395-3284-9, 3284). BSA.
Boyer, Robert E. & Snyder, P. B. Geology Fact Book. 2nd ed. LC 75-138627. (Illus.). 48p. (gr. 4-7). 1986. pap. text ed. 5.95 (ISBN 0-8331-0572-8). Hubbard Sci.
Bryan, T. Scott. Geysers: What They Are & How They Work. (Illus.). 48p. (Orig.). 1990. pap. 5.95 (ISBN 0-911797-74-2). R Rinehart Inc.
Butler, Daphne. First Look under the Ground. LC 90-10250. (Illus.). 32p. (gr. 1-2). 1991. lib. bdg. 10.95 (ISBN 0-8368-0507-0). Gareth Stevens Inc.
Catherall, Ed. Exploring Soil & Rocks. LC 90-10024. (Illus.). 48p. (gr. 3-7). 1990. PLB 18.60 (ISBN 0-8114-2595-9). Steck-V.
Diagram Group & Lambert, David. The Field Guide to Geology. (Illus.). 256p. (gr. 9). 1988. 24.95 (ISBN 0-8160-1697-6). Facts on File.
Dixon, Dougal. Geology. Bishop, Denis, illus. 40p. (gr. 4 up). 1983. PLB 12.40 (ISBN 0-531-04582-X). Watts.
Ingoglia, Gina. Look Inside the Earth. (Illus.). 16p. (ps-1). 1991. bds. 10.95 (ISBN 0-448-40087-1, G&D). Putnam Pub Group.
Lye, Keith. The Earth. (Illus.). 64p. (gr. 4-6). 1991. PLB 13.90 (ISBN 1-56294-025-2). Millbrook Pr.
McNulty, Faith. How to Dig a Hole to the Other Side of the World. Simont, Marc, illus. LC 78-22479. 32p. (ps-3). 1979. PLB 12.89 (ISBN 0-685-02061-4). HarpC Child Bks.
Mayes, S. What's under the Ground? (Illus.). 24p. (gr. 1-4). 1989. lib. bdg. 11.96 (ISBN 0-88110-378-0, Usborne); pap. 3.95 (ISBN 0-7460-0357-9, Usborne). EDC.
Osband, Gillian. Our Living Earth. Clifton-Dey, Richard, illus. 12p. (gr. 5-8). 1987. 14.95 (ISBN 0-399-21447-X, Putnam). Putnam Pub Group.
Pomeroy, Johanna P. Content Area Reading Skills Geology: Detecting Sequence. (Illus.). (gr. 4). 1987. pap. text ed. 3.25 (ISBN 1-55737-085-0). Ed Activities.
Rossbocher, Lisa A. Recent Revolutions in Geology. LC 86-9236. (Illus.). 128p. (gr. 7-12). 1986. PLB 12.90 (ISBN 0-531-10242-4). Watts.
Sipiera, Paul. I Can Be a Geologist. LC 86-9598. (Illus.). 32p. (gr. k-3). 1986. PLB 13.93 (ISBN 0-516-01897-3); pap. 3.95 (ISBN 0-516-41897-1). Childrens.

GEOLOGY, ECONOMIC
see also Mines and Mineral Resources; Soils

GEOLOGY, HISTORICAL
see Geology, Stratigraphic
Stanley, Steven M. Earth & Life Through Time. 2nd ed. LC 88-16454. (Illus.). 704p. 1988. text ed. 42.95 (ISBN 0-7167-1975-4). W H Freeman.

GEOLOGY-MAPS
Raymo, Chet. Geologic & Topographic Profile of the United States along Interstate 80. Raymo, Chet, illus. 21p. (Orig.). (gr. 6-12). 1982. pap. text ed. 6.95 (ISBN 0-8331-1714-9, 473). Hubbard Sci.

GEOLOGY-NORTH AMERICA
Frye, Keith. Roadside Geology of Virginia. Alt, David & Hyndman, Donald, eds. Venkatakrishnan, Rames, illus. Milici, Robert C., frwd. by. LC 86-8755. (Illus.). 256p. (Orig.). (gr. 5 up). 1986. pap. 9.95 (ISBN 0-87842-199-8). Mountain Pr.
Smith, W. Hovey. Guide to the Geology of Bartow County, Georgia. (Illus.). 46p. (Orig.). (gr. 8-12). 1985. pap. text ed. 5.00 (ISBN 0-916565-07-6). Whitehall Pr.

GEOLOGY, STRATIGRAPHIC
see also Fossils
Spizzirri Publishing Co. Staff. Paleozoic Life: An Educational Coloring Book. Spizzirri, Linda, ed. Spizzirri, Peter M., illus. 32p. (gr. 1-8). 1981. pap. 1.95 (ISBN 0-86545-024-2). Spizzirri.

GEOLOGY, SUBMARINE
see Submarine Geology

GEOMETRICAL DRAWING
see also Graphic Methods; Mechanical Drawing
Macmahon, Horace. Stereogram Book of Contours. LC 74-188860. 32p. (gr. 1 up). 1972. pap. 3.95 plastic comb bdg. (ISBN 0-8331-1705-X). Hubbard Sci.

GEOMETRY
see also Geometrical Drawing
Amir-Moez, Ali R. & Menzel, Donald H. Fun with Numbers, Lines & Angles. 32p. (gr. 3-6). 1981. pap. 2.95 (ISBN 0-87534-179-9). Highlights.
Brownlee, Juanita. Tangram Geometry in Metric. Merrick, Paul, illus. (Orig.). (gr. 5-10). 1976. pap. 6.95 (ISBN 0-918932-43-2, 0140701407). Activity Resources.
Churchill, Eric R. Geometry Flipper. 49p. (gr. 5 up). 1989. Repr. of 1988 ed. trade edition 5.95 (ISBN 1-878383-04-3). C Lee Pubns.
Fisher, Leonard E. Look Around! A Book about Shapes. (ps-k). 1987. pap. 11.95 (ISBN 0-670-80869-5). Viking Child Bks.
Froman, Robert. Angles Are Easy As Pie. Barton, Byron, illus. LC 75-6608. 40p. (gr. k-3). 1976. PLB 12.89 (ISBN 0-690-00916-X, Crowell Jr Bks). HarpC Child Bks.
Gillham, Bill & Hulme, Susan. Let's Look for Shapes. Siegieda, Jan, illus. LC 83-25177. 24p. (ps-1). 1984. 4.95 (ISBN 0-698-20615-0, Putnam). Putnam Pub Group.
Hewavisenti, Latshmi. Shapes & Solids. (Illus.). 32p. (gr. k-4). 1991. PLB 11.40 (ISBN 0-531-17320-8, Gloucester Pr). Watts.
Hoban, Tana. Circles, Triangles & Squares. Hoban, Tana, illus. LC 72-93305. 32p. (ps-2). 1974. 13.95 (ISBN 0-02-744830-4, Mcmillan Child Bk). Macmillan Child Grp.
—Shapes, Shapes, Shapes. Hoban, Tana, photos by. LC 85-17569. (Illus.). 32p. (ps-3). 1986. 14.95 (ISBN 0-688-05832-9); PLB 14.88 (ISBN 0-688-05833-7). Greenwillow.
Jenkins, Lee, et al. Geoblocks & Geojackets. (gr. 3-10). 1976. 7.95 (ISBN 0-918932-22-X). Activity Resources.
Kahn, Peggy. The Care Bears' Circus of Shapes. Bracken, Carolyn, illus. LC 83-51590. 14p. (ps-1). 1984. bds. 3.95 (ISBN 0-394-86726-2, Pub. by BYR). Random.
Kirk, Jim. Environmental Geometry. (Illus.). (gr. 3-8). 1975. incl. activity cards 4.95 (ISBN 0-918932-61-0). Activity Resources.
Laycock, Mary & Dominques, Manuel. Discover It! 32p. (Orig.). (gr. 5-10). 1986. pap. 6.50 (ISBN 0-918932-87-4). Activity Resources.
Navarro, C. F. Early Geometry. (Illus.). 64p. (Orig.). (gr. 2-3). 1990. pap. text ed. 6.50 (ISBN 1-878396-04-8). Start Smart Bks.
Nichols, Frank, illus. Circles. (Orig.). (ps-2). 1976. pap. 2.00 (ISBN 0-85953-047-7). Childs Play.
Nickel, Shirley. Experiments in Geometry. Gerbrandt, Stan, illus. 50p. (gr. 4-9). 1974. wkbk. 6.95 (ISBN 1-878669-26-5, 4168). Crea Tea Assocs.
Rogers, Paul. The Shapes Game. Tucker, Sian, illus. LC 89-19957. 32p. (ps-1). 1990. 12.95g (ISBN 0-8050-1280-X). H Holt & Co.
Serra, Michael. Discovering Geometry: An Inductive Approach. 756p. (gr. 9-12). 1989. 24.95 (ISBN 0-913684-08-2). Key Curr Pr.
Shapes & Sizes. (Illus.). 32p. (ps). 1985. 3.95 (ISBN 0-394-87704-7). Random.
Vellozi, Joseph A. Plane & Coordinate Geometry Study Aid. 1974. pap. 2.50 (ISBN 0-87738-040-6). Youth Ed.
Wiley, Larry. Introductory Geometrics. 278p. (Orig.). (gr. 10-12). 1986. pap. text ed. 15.00 (ISBN 0-89824-065-4); tchr's. ed. 7.50 (ISBN 0-89824-066-2). Trillium Pr.
Zimmerman, H. Werner. Alphonse Knows...A Circle Is Not a Valentine. (Illus.). 24p. (ps-2). 1991. bds. 9.95 laminated (ISBN 0-19-540744-X). Oxford U Pr.

GEOMETRY, PLANE
see Geometry

GEOMETRY, SOLID
see Geometry

GEOPHYSICS
see also Meteorology; Oceanography

GEORGE WASHINGTON BRIDGE-FICTION
Swift, Hildegarde H. & Ward, Lynd. Little Red Lighthouse & the Great Gray Bridge. Ward, Lynd, illus. LC 42-36286. (gr. k-3). 1942. 15.95 (ISBN 0-15-247040-9, HJ). HarBraceJ.

GEORGIA
Carole Marsh Georgia Books, 31 bks. Set. 638.45 (ISBN 0-7933-1285-X). Gallopade Pub Group.
Carpenter, Allan. Georgia. LC 79-12095. (Illus.). 96p. (gr. 4 up). 1979. PLB 19.93 (ISBN 0-516-04110-X). Childrens.
Fradin, Dennis. Georgia: In Words & Pictures. Wahl, Richard, illus. LC 80-26768. 48p. (gr. 2-5). 1981. PLB 15.93 (ISBN 0-516-03910-5). Childrens.
Fradin, Dennis B. The Georgia Colony. LC 89-34954. 160p. (gr. 4 up). 1989. PLB 22.60 (ISBN 0-516-00392-5). Childrens.
Kytle, Elizabeth. Willie Mae: Elizabeth Kytle. rev. ed. Kytle, Calvin, ed. Ladner, Joyce A., frwd. by. 272p. (gr. 8-12). 1991. pap. 12.95 (ISBN 0-939009-45-5). EPM Pubns.
Loewen, N. Atlanta. (Illus.). 48p. (gr. 5 up). 1989. lib. bdg. 14.60 (ISBN 0-86592-543-7). Rourke Corp.
Marsh, Carole. Avast, Ye Slobs! Georgia Pirate Trivia. (Illus.). (gr. 3-12). 1990. PLB 19.95 (ISBN 0-7933-0328-1); pap. 14.95 (ISBN 0-7933-0327-3); computer disk 29.95 (ISBN 0-7933-0329-X). Gallopade Pub Group.
—The Beast of the Georgia Bed & Breakfast. (Illus.). (gr. 3-12). 1990. PLB 19.95 (ISBN 0-7933-1512-3); pap. 14.95 (ISBN 0-7933-1513-1); computer disk 29.95 (ISBN 0-7933-1514-X). Gallopade Pub Group.
—Georgia & Other State Greats (Biographies) (Illus.). (gr. 3-12). 1990. PLB 19.95 (ISBN 1-55609-392-6); pap. 14.95 (ISBN 1-55609-391-8); computer disk 29.95 (ISBN 0-7933-1520-4). Gallopade Pub Group.
—Georgia Bandits, Bushwackers, Outlaws, Crooks, Devils, Ghosts, Desperadoes & Other Assorted & Sundry Characters! (Illus.). (gr. 3-12). 1990. PLB 19.95 (ISBN 0-7933-0310-9); pap. 14.95 (ISBN 0-7933-0309-5); computer disk 29.95 (ISBN 0-7933-0311-7). Gallopade Pub Group.
—Georgia Classic Christmas Trivia: Stories, Recipes, Activities, Legends, Lore & More! (Illus.). (gr. 3-12). 1990. PLB 19.95 (ISBN 0-7933-0313-3); pap. 14.95 (ISBN 0-7933-0312-5); computer disk 29.95 (ISBN 0-7933-0314-1). Gallopade Pub Group.
—Georgia Coastales. (Illus.). (gr. 3-12). 1990. PLB 19.95 (ISBN 1-55609-233-4); pap. 14.95 (ISBN 1-55609-117-6); computer disk 29.95 (ISBN 0-7933-1516-6). Gallopade Pub Group.
—The Georgia Hot Air Balloon Mystery. (Illus.). (gr. 2-9). 1990. 19.95 (ISBN 0-7933-2408-4); pap. 14.95 (ISBN 0-7933-2409-2); computer disk 29.95 (ISBN 0-7933-2410-6). Gallopade Pub Group.

—Georgia Jography: A Fun Run Through the Peach State. (Illus.). 50p. (Orig.). (gr. 4-8). 1986. pap. 14.95 (ISBN 0-935326-93-6). Gallopade Pub Group.

—Georgia Kid's Cookbook: Recipes, How-To, History, Lore & More! (Illus.). (gr. 3-12). 1990. PLB 19.95 (ISBN 0-7933-0322-2); pap. 14.95 (ISBN 0-7933-0321-4); computer disk 29.95 (ISBN 0-7933-0323-0). Gallopade Pub Group.

—Georgia Quiz Bowl Crash Course! (Illus.). (gr. 3-12). 1990. PLB 19.95 (ISBN 1-55609-384-5); pap. 14.95 (ISBN 1-55609-383-7); computer disk 29.95 (ISBN 0-7933-1515-8). Gallopade Pub Group.

—Georgia School Trivia: An Amazing & Fascinating Look at Our State's Teachers, Schools & Students! (Illus.). (gr. 3-12). 1990. PLB 19.95 (ISBN 0-7933-0319-2); pap. 14.95 (ISBN 0-7933-0318-4); computer disk 29.95 (ISBN 0-7933-0320-6). Gallopade Pub Group.

—Georgia Silly Basketball Sportsmysteries, Vol. I. (Illus.). (gr. 3-12). 1990. PLB 19.95 (ISBN 0-7933-0316-8); pap. 14.95 (ISBN 0-7933-0315-X); computer disk 29.95 (ISBN 0-7933-0317-6). Gallopade Pub Group.

—Georgia Silly Basketball Sportsmysteries, Vol. II. (Illus.). (gr. 3-12). 1990. PLB 19.95 (ISBN 0-7933-1521-2); pap. 14.95 (ISBN 0-7933-1522-0); computer disk 29.95 (ISBN 0-7933-1523-9). Gallopade Pub Group.

—Georgia Silly Football Sportsmysteries, Vol. I. (Illus.). (gr. 3-12). 1990. PLB 19.95 (ISBN 1-55609-394-2); pap. 14.95 (ISBN 1-55609-393-4); computer disk 29.95 (ISBN 0-7933-1508-5). Gallopade Pub Group.

—Georgia Silly Football Sportsmysteries, Vol. II. (Illus.). (gr. 3-12). 1990. PLB 19.95 (ISBN 0-7933-1509-3); pap. 14.95 (ISBN 0-7933-1510-7); computer disk 29.95 (ISBN 0-7933-1511-5). Gallopade Pub Group.

—Georgia Silly Trivia Book. (Illus.). 48p. (Orig.). (gr. 2-12). 1985. pap. 14.95 (ISBN 0-935326-61-8). Gallopade Pub Group.

—Georgia's (Most Devastating!) Disasters & (Most Calamitous!) Catastrophies! (Illus.). (gr. 3-12). 1990. PLB 19.95 (ISBN 0-7933-0307-9); pap. 14.95 (ISBN 0-7933-0306-0); computer disk 29.95 (ISBN 0-7933-0308-7). Gallopade Pub Group.

—The Hard-to-Believe-But-True! Book of Georgia History, Mystery, Trivia, Legend, Lore, Humor & More. (Illus.). (gr. 3-12). 1990. PLB 19.95 (ISBN 0-7933-0325-7); pap. 14.95 (ISBN 0-7933-0324-9); computer disk 29.95 (ISBN 0-7933-0326-5). Gallopade Pub Group.

—If My Georgia Mama Ran the World! (Illus.). (gr. 3-12). 1990. PLB 19.95 (ISBN 0-7933-1517-4); pap. 14.95 (ISBN 0-7933-1518-2); computer disk 29.95 (ISBN 0-7933-1519-0). Gallopade Pub Group.

—Let's Quilt Georgia & Stuff It Topographically! (Illus.). (gr. 3-12). 1990. PLB 19.95 (ISBN 1-55609-382-9); pap. 14.95 (ISBN 1-55609-054-4); computer disk 29.95 (ISBN 0-7933-1507-7). Gallopade Pub Group.

Pedersen, Anne. Kidding Around Atlanta: A Young Person's Guide to the City. (Illus.). 64p. (gr. 3 up). 1989. pap. 9.95 (ISBN 0-945465-35-1). John Muir.

Snow, Pegeen. Atlanta. LC 88-20243. (Illus.). 60p. (gr. 3 up). 1988. PLB 12.95 (ISBN 0-87518-389-1, Dillon). Macmillan Child Grp.

Turner Programs Services, Inc. Staff & Clark, James I. Georgia. 48p. (gr. 3 up). 1985. pap. text ed. 15.99 (ISBN 0-86514-428-1); pap. text ed. 9.27 (ISBN 0-86514-503-2); cancelled Beta video (ISBN 0-86514-053-7); cancelled VHS video (ISBN 0-86514-128-2); cancelled 3/4" video (ISBN 0-86514-203-3); cancelled tchr's. guide (ISBN 0-86514-278-5); cancelled student activity bk. (ISBN 0-86514-353-6); cancelled index. Raintree Pubs.

GEORGIA–FICTION

Beatty, Patricia. Turn Homeward, Hannalee. LC 84-8960. 208p. (gr. 5-9). 1984. 12.95 (ISBN 0-688-03871-9). Morrow Jr Bks.

Blackburn, Joyce. The Bloody Summer of Seventeen Forty-Two: A Colonial Boy's Journal. Graham, Critt, illus. 64p. (gr. 5-8). 1985. pap. 4.25 (ISBN 0-930803-00-0). Fort Frederica.
This book vividly details an account of a child's life in colonial Georgia. The journal recounts the life of a young Scottish boy named Johnny "Little Jack" McLeod in the weeks surrounding the decisive battle for English/Spanish control over Georgia. Johnny lived in Frederica Town, the fortified settlement & southern military headquarters for British North America. The British victory at Bloody Marsh on St. Simons Island ended Spain's claims to Georgian lands. Frederica Town is brought to life through vibrant accounts of the boy's observations of the soldiers, craftsmen & families living in this bustling 18th century military town. This journal

sparks a child's imagination & appreciation of Georgia's rich heritage. The 63 page bound paperback book is written to a mid-elementary grade reader level. It is handsomely illustrated by Critt Graham. Author Joyce Blackburn is a noted biographer of James Oglethorpe, Georgia's founder, & other prize winning historical novels for young readers. The book retails for $4.25, plus shipping & handling & is available from the Fort Frederica Association, Rt. #9, Box 286-C, St. Simons Island, GA 31522. (912) 638-3639. A 40% discount is available to booksellers. Library or educator discounts are also available. *Publisher Provided Annotation.*

L'Engle, Madeleine. The Other Side of the Sun. 344p. 1971. 6.95 (ISBN 0-374-22805-1). FS&G.

Wilkinson, Brenda. Ludell. LC 75-9390. 176p. (gr. 5 up). 1975. PLB 12.89 (ISBN 0-06-026492-6). HarpC Child Bks.

—Ludell & Willie. LC 76-18402. (gr. 7 up). 1977. PLB 13.89 (ISBN 0-06-026488-8). HarpC Child Bks.

GEORGIA–HISTORY

Swindler, William F. & Frech, Mary, eds. Chronology & Documentary Handbook of the State of Georgia, No. 10. LC 73-499. 119p. (gr. 9-12). 1973. PLB 8.50 (ISBN 0-379-16135-4). Oceana.

GEOSCIENCE
see Geology

GERBILS

Barrett, Norman. Gerbils. (Illus.). 32p. (gr. k-4). 1990. PLB 11.40 (ISBN 0-531-14030-X). Watts.

Hearne, T. Gerbils. (Illus.). 32p. (gr. 2-5). 1989. lib. bdg. 14.00 (ISBN 0-86625-186-3). Rourke Corp.

Henrie. Gerbils. (gr. 2-5). 1980. PLB 10.90 (ISBN 0-531-04121-2, E40). Watts.

Petty, Kate. Gerbils. Thompson, George, illus. LC 89-50454. 32p. (gr. k-2). 1989. PLB 10.40 (ISBN 0-531-17158-2, Gloucester Pr). Watts.

Pope, Joyce. Taking Care of Your Gerbil. (Illus.). 32p. (gr. 4-8). 1987. PLB 10.90 (ISBN 0-531-10190-8). Watts.

Snell, Nigel. Nita's Gerbil. Snell, Nigel, illus. 32p. 1989. 4.95 (ISBN 0-8120-6122-5). Barron.

Sproule, Anna & Sproule, Michael. Gerbils. (Illus.). 48p. (gr. 7-9). 1990. 11.90 (ISBN 0-531-18251-7). Watts.

Wexler, Jerome. Pet Gerbils. Tucker, Kathy, ed. (Illus.). 48p. (gr. 2-8). 1989. PLB 13.95 (ISBN 0-8075-6523-7). A Whitman.

GERBILS–FICTION

Manes, Stephen. The Great Gerbil Roundup. McKinley, John, illus. 144p. (gr. 3 up). 1988. 13.95 (ISBN 0-15-232490-9, HJ). HarBraceJ.

Swallow, Pamela C. Melvil & Dewey in the Chips. Brown, Judith, illus. LC 86-61092. 48p. (Orig.). (gr. 1-3). 1986. o. p. 9.95 (ISBN 0-936915-02-1, Shoe Tree Pr); pap. 4.95 (ISBN 0-936915-03-X). Betterway Pubns.

GERMAN LANGUAGE–CONVERSATIONS AND PHRASE BOOK

Beeck, Johannes, et al. Telefon. Baker, Syd, illus. Winitz, Harris, intro. by. (GER., Illus.). 50p. (gr. 7 up). 1990. Incls. cass. tape. pap. text ed. 20.00. Intl Linguistics.

Brinckmann, Caren, et al. Beforderung. Baker, Syd, illus. Winitz, Harris, intro. by. (GER., Illus.). 40p. (gr. 7 up). 1990. Incls. cass. tape. pap. text ed. 21.00 (ISBN 0-939990-71-7). Intl Linguistics.

Colvin, L. & Irving, N. Essential German. (Illus.). 64p. 1990. lib. bdg. 12.96 (ISBN 0-88110-419-1); pap. 5.95 (ISBN 0-7460-0318-8). EDC.

Hazzan, Anne-Francoise. Let's Learn German Coloring Book. (Illus.). 64p. (gr. 4 up). 1988. pap. 3.95 (ISBN 0-8442-2164-3, Passport Bks). Natl Textbk.

Hildebrand, Sigrid S. & Hildebrand, Eckart. Gehen. Rohrer, Josef, ed. Baker, Syd, illus. Winitz, Harris, intro. by. (GER., Illus.). 85p. (gr. 7 up). 1990. Incls. cass. tape. pap. 20.00. Intl Linguistics.

—Stellen, Legen und Setzen. Rohrer, Josef, ed. Baker, Syd, illus. Winitz, Harris, intro. by. (GER., Illus.). 80p. (Orig.). (gr. 7 up). 1990. Incls. cass. tape. pap. text ed. 21.00 (ISBN 0-939990-65-2). Intl Linguistics.

Let's Learn Picture Dictionaries: German. (Illus.). 72p. 1989. 9.95 (ISBN 0-8442-2167-8, Passport Bks). Natl Textbk.

Liedloff, Helmut. Ohne Muhe! LC 79-84596. (Illus.). (gr. 9-10). 1980. pap. 7.32 (ISBN 0-395-27931-3). HM.

Mahoney, Judy. Teach Me More German. Kamstra, Angela, illus. (GER.). 20p. (ps-5). 1990. pap. 13.95 incl. 45 min. cass. (ISBN 0-934633-23-1). Teach Me.

Nash, Rod. In Germany. (GER.). 80p. (gr. 7-12). 1984. pap. text ed. 8.95 (ISBN 0-8219-0056-0, 45285); tchr's. wkbk. 4.50 (ISBN 0-8219-0274-1, 45820); 3.95 (ISBN 0-8219-0273-3, 45660). EMC.

Stehr, Tamara. The Pappenheimers: An Animation & Vocabulary Guide. Garbers, Fred, illus. (gr. k-6). 1983. text ed. 10.95 (ISBN 3-468-96795-0). Langenscheidt.

Trim, John. Ganz Spontan! (GER.). 352p. 1988. pap. text ed. 11.50 (ISBN 0-8219-0346-2, 45295); tchr's. guide 5.95 (ISBN 0-8219-0347-0, TG-45823). EMC.

Wilkes, Angela. German for Beginners. (Illus.). 48p. (gr. 4 up). 1988. 7.95 (ISBN 0-8442-2165-1, Passport Bks). Natl Textbk.

Winitz, Harris. Hauser und Gebaude: Houses & Buildings in German. Rohrer, Josef, ed. Baker, Syd, illus. (GER.). 50p. (Orig.). (gr. 7 up). 1989. pap. text ed. 20.00 incl. cassette (ISBN 0-939990-76-8). Intl Linguistics.

GERMAN LANGUAGE–GRAMMAR

Stehr, Tamara. The Pappenheimers: An Animation & Vocabulary Guide. Garbers, Fred, illus. (gr. k-6). 1983. text ed. 10.95 (ISBN 3-468-96795-0). Langenscheidt.

GERMAN LANGUAGE–READERS

Amery, Heather. First Thousand Words in German. Cartwright, Stephen, illus. 50p. (ps-7). 1979. 11.95 (ISBN 0-86020-268-2). EDC.

—Word Detective in German: Word Detective Ser. Cartwright, Stephen, illus. 50p. (gr. 3-7). 1983. 11.95 (ISBN 0-86020-664-5). EDC.

Civardi, Anne. Word Finder in German. Cartwright, Stephen, illus. 48p. (gr. k-3). 1984. 11.95 (ISBN 0-86020-771-4). EDC.

Cooper, Lee. Fun with German. Githens, Elizabeth, illus. (gr. 3 up). 1972. lib. bdg. 15.95 (ISBN 0-316-15588-8). Little.

Curtis, David, et al. German Study-Aid. 1977. pap. 2.75 (ISBN 0-87738-034-1). Youth Ed.

De Brunhoff, Laurent. Je Parle Allemand avec Babar. (FRE., Illus.). (gr. 4-6). 15.95 (ISBN 0-685-11271-3). French & Eur.

Meyer, Ursula & Wolfson, Alice. Abenteur in Deutschland. (Illus.). (gr. 9-12). 1976. pap. text ed. 4.75 (ISBN 0-88345-276-6, 18485). Prentice ESL.

GERMAN POETRY–COLLECTIONS

Busch, Wilhelm. Max & Moritz. Arndt, Walter, tr. LC 85-1241. (Illus.). (gr. 4 up). 1985. 9.95 (ISBN 0-915361-19-1, Dist. by Watts). Adama Pubs Inc.

GERMANS IN PENNSYLVANIA
see Pennsylvania Dutch

GERMANS IN THE U. S

Franck, Irene M. The German-American Heritage. (Illus.). 160p. 1988. 16.95x (ISBN 0-8160-1629-1). Facts on File.

Galicich, Anne. The German Americans. Moynihan, Daniel P. (Illus.). 112p. (gr. 5 up). 1989. lib. bdg. 17.95 (ISBN 1-55546-141-7); pap. 9.95 (ISBN 0-7910-0265-9). Chelsea Hse.

Kunz, Virginia B. The Germans in America. LC 66-10147. (Illus.). 88p. (gr. 5 up). 1966. PLB 11.95 (ISBN 0-8225-0208-9); pap. 3.95 (ISBN 0-8225-1009-X). Lerner Pubns.

GERMANY

Adler, Ann. A Family in West Germany. LC 85-6981. (Illus.). 32p. (gr. 2-5). 1985. PLB 9.95 (ISBN 0-8225-1658-6). Lerner Pubns.

Ayer, Eleanor. Germany. (Illus.). 64p. (gr. 7 up). 1990. lib. bdg. 15.93 (ISBN 0-86593-093-7); lib. bdg. 11.95s.p. (ISBN 0-685-36365-1). Rourke Corp.

Fairclough, Chris. Take a Trip to West Germany. (Illus.). 32p. (gr. 1-3). 1981. lib. bdg. 7.99 (ISBN 0-531-04320-7). Watts.

Getting to Know Germany. 48p. 1989. 7.95 (ISBN 0-8442-2168-6, Passport Bks). Natl Textbk.

Pfeiffer, Christine. Germany: Two Nations, One Heritage. LC 86-32954. (Illus.). 176p. (gr. 5 up). 1987. PLB 14.95 (ISBN 0-87518-361-1, Dillon). Macmillan Child Grp.

Phillpotts, Beatrice. Germany. (Illus.). 48p. (gr. 4-8). 1989. lib. bdg. 14.98 (ISBN 0-382-09794-7). Silver Burdett Pr.

Schloredt, Valerie. West Germany. (Illus.). 48p. (gr. 5-10). 1988. PLB 15.96 (ISBN 0-382-09471-9). Silver Burdett Pr.

Stadtler, Christa. West Germany. (Illus.). 32p. (gr. k-3). 1991. PLB 11.90 (ISBN 0-531-18371-8, Pub. by Bookwright Pr). Watts.

GERMANY (FEDERAL REPUBLIC)

Adler, Anne. Passport to West Germany. LC 85-50173. (Illus.). 48p. (gr. 4-9). 1986. PLB 12.90 (ISBN 0-531-10017-0). Watts.

Dolan, Sean. West Germany: On the Road to Reunification. (Illus.). (gr. 5 up). 1991. 14.95 (ISBN 0-7910-1367-7). Chelsea Hse.

Einhorn, Barbara. West Germany. Caulkins, Janet, ed. (Illus.). 48p. (gr. 1-6). 1988. PLB 12.40 (ISBN 0-531-18187-1, Pub. by Bookwright Pr). Watts.

Hintz, Martin. West Germany. LC 82-17882. (Illus.). 128p. (gr. 5-9). 1983. PLB 25.27 (ISBN 0-516-02793-X). Childrens.

Stadtler, Christa. West Germany. (Illus.). 32p. (gr. k-3). 1991. PLB 11.90 (ISBN 0-531-18371-8, Pub. by Bookwright Pr). Watts.

GERMANY–FICTION

Carter, Peter. Bury the Dead. LC 85-45995. 354p. (gr. 6 up). 1987. 14.95 (ISBN 0-374-31011-4). FS&G.

Degens, T. On the Third Ward. LC 89-77451. 256p. (gr. 6 up). 1990. 14.95 (ISBN 0-06-021428-7); PLB 14.89 (ISBN 0-06-021429-5). HarpC Child Bks.

Jerome, Jerome K. Three Men on the Bummel. (Illus.). 240p. (gr. 6-9). 1991. pap. 8.00 (ISBN 0-86299-029-7). A Sutton Pub.

Kastner. Mein Onkel Franz. (gr. 7-12). pap. 4.95 (ISBN 0-88436-037-7, 45259). EMC.

Lenz. Lotte Soll Nicht Sterben. (gr. 7-12). pap. 4.95 (ISBN 0-88436-039-3, 45260). EMC.
Roesler. Gansebraten. (gr. 7-12). pap. 4.95 (ISBN 0-88436-109-8, 45262). EMC.
Roland, Donna. Grandfather's Stories from Germany. (gr. 1-3). 1984. pap. 4.50x (ISBN 0-941996-03-4). Open My World.
—More of Grandfather's Stories from Germany. (gr. 1-3). 1984. pap. 4.50x (ISBN 0-941996-04-2). Open My World.
Schnurre. Die Tat. pap. 5.95 (ISBN 0-88436-040-7, 45272). EMC.
Winnig. Romerzimmer. (gr. 7-12). pap. 4.95 (ISBN 0-88436-041-5, 45261). EMC.
Zweig. Novellen. (gr. 7-12). pap. 5.95 (ISBN 0-88436-042-3, 45273). EMC.

GERMANY-HISTORY

Stewart, Gail B. Germany. LC 90-2244. (Illus.). 48p. (gr. 5-6). 1990. RSBE 10.95 (ISBN 0-89686-548-7, Crestwood Hse). Macmillan Child Grp.

GERMANY-HISTORY-FICTION

Richter, Hans P. I Was There. (gr. 5-9). 1987. pap. 4.95 (ISBN 0-14-032206-X, Puffin). Puffin Bks.

GERMANY-HISTORY-20TH CENTURY

Finke, Blythe F. Konrad Adenauer: Architect of the New Germany. Rahmas, D. Steve, ed. LC 79-190241. 32p. (Orig.). (gr. 7-12). 1972. lib. bdg. 4.20 incl. catalog cards (ISBN 0-87157-523-X); pap. 2.95 vinyl laminated covers (ISBN 0-87157-023-8). SamHar Pr.

GERMANY-HISTORY-1933-1945

Chrisp, Peter. Blitzkrieg. (Illus.). 64p. (gr. 7-10). 1991. PLB 12.90 (ISBN 0-531-18373-4). Watts.
Tames, Richard. Nazi Germany. (Illus.). 72p. (gr. 7-12). 1985. 19.95 (ISBN 0-7134-3538-0, Pub. by Batsford England). Trafalgar Sq.
Wolff, Marion F. The Shrinking Circle: Memories of Nazi Berlin, 1933-39. 128p. (gr. 7-9). 1989. pap. 7.95 (ISBN 0-8074-0419-5, 147501). UAHC.

GERMS

see Bacteriology; Microorganisms

GERONIMO, APACHE CHIEF, 1829-1909

Jeffrey, David. Geronimo. Viola, Herman, intro. by. (Illus.). 32p. (gr. 3-6). 1990. PLB 16.67 (ISBN 0-8172-3404-7). Raintree Pubs.
Kent, Zachary. The Story of Geronimo. LC 88-37005. (Illus.). 32p. (gr. 3-6). 1989. PLB 13.27 (ISBN 0-516-04743-4); pap. 3.95 (ISBN 0-516-44743-2). Childrens.
Wheeler, Jill. The Story of Geronimo. Deegan, Paul, ed. Dodson, Liz, illus. 32p. (gr. 4). 1989. PLB 11.95 (ISBN 0-939179-68-7). Abdo & Dghtrs.
Zadra, Dan. Indians of America: Geronimo. rev. ed. (gr. 2-4). 1987. PLB 11.50s.p. (ISBN 0-88682-159-2); 16. 45 (ISBN 0-318-32939-5). Creative Ed.

GERONTOLOGY

see Old Age

GERSHWIN, GEORGE, 1898-1937

Kresh, Paul. American Rhapsody: The Story of George Gershwin. LC 87-24469. (Illus.). 160p. (gr. 5-9). 1988. 14.95 (ISBN 0-525-67233-8, Lodestar Bks). Dutton Child Bks.
Mitchell, Barbara. America, I Hear You: A Story about George Gershwin. Smith, Jan H., illus. 64p. (gr. 3-6). 1987. PLB 9.95 (ISBN 0-87614-309-5). Carolrhoda Bks.

GETTYSBURG, BATTLE OF, 1863

Coffey, Vincent J. Battle of Gettysburg. rev. ed. (Illus.). 64p. (gr. 5 up). 1989. pap. 7.95 (ISBN 0-382-09911-7). Silver Burdett Pr.
Johnson, Neil. The Battle of Gettysburg. Johnson, Neil, illus. LC 88-30414. 64p. (gr. 5 up). 1989. 14.95 (ISBN 0-02-747831-9, Four Winds). Macmillan Child Grp.
Kantor, MacKinlay. Gettysburg. LC 87-4576. (Illus.). (gr. 5-9). 1987. lib. bdg. 8.99 (ISBN 0-394-90323-4, Random Juv); pap. 3.95 (ISBN 0-394-89181-3). Random.

GETTYSBURG, BATTLE OF, 1863-FICTION

Cregar, Elyse. Gettysburg: By the Third Sun Setting. Guy, Ed, illus. (Orig.). (gr. 6-12). 1988. pap. 5.95 (ISBN 0-9621292-0-8). Tamerac Pub.

GHANA

Barnett, Jeanie M. Ghana. (Illus.). 96p. (gr. 5 up). 1989. lib. bdg. 14.95 (ISBN 1-55546-789-X). Chelsea Hse.
Hintz, Martin. Ghana. LC 86-29935. (Illus.). 128p. (gr. 5-9). 1987. PLB 25.27 (ISBN 0-516-02773-5). Childrens.
Lerner Publications, Department of Geography Staff. Ghana in Pictures. (Illus.). 64p. (gr. 5 up). 1988. 12.95 (ISBN 0-8225-1829-5). Lerner Pubns.

GHOST STORIES

Abbott, Jennie. The Ghost of Hanover Hill. Badenhop, Mary, illus. LC 87-14983. 96p. (gr. 3-6). 1988. PLB 9.89 (ISBN 0-8167-1185-2); pap. text ed. 2.95 (ISBN 0-8167-1186-0). Troll Assocs.
Adler, C. S. Ghost Brother. 160p. (gr. 4-8). 1990. 13.95 (ISBN 0-395-52592-6). HM.
Adler, David A. Jeffrey's Ghost & the Fifth Grade Dragon. Jenkins, Jean, illus. LC 85-886. 64p. (gr. 2-4). 1985. 9.95 (ISBN 0-8050-0480-7). H Holt & Co.
—Jeffrey's Ghost & the Ziffel Fair Mystery. Jenkins, Jean, illus. LC 86-14594. 64p. (gr. 2-4). 1987. 10.95 (ISBN 0-8050-0278-2). H Holt & Co.
Aiken, Joan. Return to Harken House. (gr. 5-9). 1990. 13. 95 (ISBN 0-385-29975-3). Delacorte.
—The Shadow Guests. (gr. 5 up). 1986. pap. 2.95 (ISBN 0-440-48226-7, YB). Dell.
—The Shadow Guests: A Novel. LC 80-65830. 144p. (gr. 7 up). 1980. pap. 11.95 (ISBN 0-385-28889-1). Delacorte.
Alcock, Vivien. The Haunting of Cassie Palmer. LC 81-15230. 160p. (gr. 4-6). 1982. pap. 11.95 (ISBN 0-385-28402-0). Delacorte.
Alexander, Sue. Witch, Goblin & Ghost in the Haunted Woods. Winter, Jeanette, illus. LC 80-20863. 72p. (gr. 1-4). 1981. 6.95 (ISBN 0-394-84443-2); lib. bdg. 7.99 (ISBN 0-394-94443-7). Pantheon.
—Witch, Goblin, & Sometimes Ghost: Six Read-Alone Stories. Winter, Jeanette, illus. LC 76-8657. (ps-3). 1976. 6.95 (ISBN 0-394-83216-7); lib. bdg. 11.99 (ISBN 0-394-93216-1). Pantheon.
Alley, Robert. The Ghost in Dobbs Diner. Alley, Robert, illus. LC 81-4864. 48p. (ps-3). 1981. 5.95 (ISBN 0-8193-1055-7); lib. bdg. 5.95 (ISBN 0-8193-1056-5). Parents.
Anderson, Mary. Terror under the Tent. (gr. k-6). 1987. pap. 2.50 (ISBN 0-440-48633-5, YB). Dell.
—The Three Spirits of Vandermeer Manor. (Orig.). (gr. k-6). 1987. pap. 2.75 (ISBN 0-440-48810-9, YB). Dell.
Astrop, John. John Astrop's Ghastly Games. Astrop, John, illus. 24p. (ps-3). 1983. pop-up bk. 9.95 (ISBN 0-385-29307-0). Delacorte.
Avi. Something Upstairs: A Tale of Ghosts. LC 88-60094. 128p. (gr. 5-7). 1988. 11.95 (ISBN 0-531-05782-8); PLB 11.99 (ISBN 0-531-08382-9). Orchard Bks Watts.
Bang, Molly, ed. & illus. The Goblins Giggle & Other Stories. (gr. 3-5). 1988. 17.25 (ISBN 0-8446-6360-3). Peter Smith.
Bellairs, John. The Revenge of the Wizard's Ghost. Gorey, Edward, illus. LC 85-4550. 160p. (gr. 5 up). 1985. 13.95 (ISBN 0-8037-0170-5); PLB 11.89 (ISBN 0-8037-0177-2). Dial Bks Young.
—The Revenge of the Wizard's Ghost. 160p. 1986. pap. 3.50 (ISBN 0-553-15451-6). Bantam.
Benchley, Nathaniel. Ghost Named Fred. Shecter, Ben, illus. LC 68-24322. 64p. (gr. k-3). 1968. PLB 11.89 (ISBN 0-06-020474-5). HarpC Child Bks.
—A Ghost Named Fred. Shecter, Ben, illus. LC 68-24322. 64p. (gr. k-3). 1979. pap. 3.50 (ISBN 0-06-444022-2, Trophy). HarpC Child Bks.
Blair, L. E. The Ghost of Eagle Mountain. 128p. (gr. 2 up). 1990. pap. write for info. (ISBN 0-307-22006-0, Pub. by Golden Bks). Western Pub.
Bodie, Idella. Ghost in the Capitol. Kovach, Gay H., illus. 116p. (gr. 5-9). 1986. pap. 6.95 (ISBN 0-87844-072-0). Sandlapper Pub Co.
Bright, Robert. Georgie. Bright, Robert, illus. 44p. (gr. k-1). 1944. pap. 7.95 (ISBN 0-385-07307-0). Doubleday.
—Georgie. 48p. (gr. k-3). pap. 1.50 (ISBN 0-590-01617-2). Scholastic Inc.
—Georgie & the Robbers. Bright, Robert, illus. LC 63-11384. 28p. (ps-1). 1963. pap. 5.95 (ISBN 0-385-04483-6); pap. 2.50 (ISBN 0-385-13341-3). Doubleday.
Brittain, Bill. Who Knew There'd Be Ghosts? Chessare, Michele, illus. LC 84-48496. 128p. (gr. 4-7). 1985. 12. 95 (ISBN 0-06-020699-3); PLB 12.89 (ISBN 0-06-020700-0). HarpC Child Bks.
Buffie, Margaret. The Haunting of Frances Rain. 1989. pap. 12.95 (ISBN 0-590-42834-9). Scholastic Inc.
—Haunting of Francis Rain. 1990. pap. 2.95 (ISBN 0-590-42835-7). Scholastic Inc.
Bulla, Clyde R. Ghost of Windy Hill. Bolognese, Don, illus. LC 68-11059. (gr. 3-7). 1968. PLB 12.89 (ISBN 0-690-32764-1, Crowell Jr Bks). HarpC Child Bks.
—The Ghost of Windy Hill. 96p. (Orig.). (gr. 2-5). 1990. pap. 2.50 (ISBN 0-590-43286-9). Scholastic Inc.
Bunting, Eve. Ghost Behind Me. (gr. 7-9). 1986. pap. 2.50 (ISBN 0-671-62211-0, Archway). PB.
—Ghost's Hour, Spook's Hour. Carrick, Donald, illus. LC 86-31674. 32p. (ps-1). 1987. 12.95 (ISBN 0-89919-484-2, Pub. by Clarion). Ticknor & Fields.
—Ghost's Hour, Spook's Hour. Carrick, Donald, illus. 1990. pap. 7.95 incl.cassette (ISBN 0-395-56244-9, Clarion Bks). HM.
—The Ghosts of Departure Point. 114p. (gr. 7 up). 1984. pap. 2.25 (ISBN 0-590-33116-7, Point). Scholastic Inc.
—In the Haunted House. Meddaugh, Susan, illus. LC 89-77663. 32p. (ps-3). 1990. 13.95 (ISBN 0-395-51589-0, Clarion Bks). HM.
Butler, Beverly. Ghost Cat. 192p. (gr. 3-7). 1988. pap. 2.50 (ISBN 0-590-41837-8, Pub. by Apple Paperbacks). Scholastic Inc.
Calif, Ruth. The Over-the-Hill Ghost. Holub, Joan, illus. 160p. (gr. 3-8). 1988. 10.95 (ISBN 0-88289-667-9). Pelican.
Carrie, Christopher. Mystery of the Forest Phantom. (Illus.). 40p. (gr. k up). 1990. pap. 1.59 (ISBN 0-86696-243-3). Binney & Smith.
Carson, Patti & Dellosa, Janet. Spooky Fun Book. Carson, Patti & Dellosa, Janet, illus. 32p. (ps-1). 1981. pap. 1.59 (ISBN 0-88724-051-8, 8006). Carson-Dellos.
Cates, Emily. The Ghost in the Attic. Cates, Emily, illus. (gr. 3-7). 1990. pap. 2.95 (ISBN 0-553-15826-0, Skylark). Bantam.
Celli, Rose, tr. A Ghost, a Witch & a Goblin. (gr. k-3). 1970. pap. 1.50 (ISBN 0-590-04447-8). Scholastic Inc.
Chambers, Aidan, ed. A Haunt of Ghosts. LC 86-45486. 192p. (gr. 7 up). 1987. 12.95 (ISBN 0-06-021206-3); PLB 12.89 (ISBN 0-06-021207-1). HarpC Child Bks.
Charbonneau, Eileen. The Ghosts of Stony Clove. LC 87-20321. 160p. (gr. 5 up). 1988. 13.95 (ISBN 0-531-05739-9); PLB 13.99 (ISBN 0-531-08339-X). Orchard Bks Watts.
Climo, Shirley. T.J.'s Ghost. Berenzy, Alix, illus. LC 87-42931. 160p. (gr. 5 up). 1989. 11.95 (ISBN 0-690-04689-8, Crowell Jr Bks); PLB 11.89 (ISBN 0-690-04691-X, Crowell Jr Bks). HarpC Child Bks.
Cohen, Daniel. The Headless Roommate & Other Tales of Terror. LC 80-18821. (Illus.). 128p. (gr. 8 up). 1980. 11.95 (ISBN 0-87131-327-8). M Evans.
—Phone Call from a Ghost: Strange Tales from Modern America. 128p. (gr. 4 up). 1988. 10.95 (ISBN 0-396-09266-7, Putnam). Putnam Pub Group.
—Real Ghosts. (Illus.). 128p. (gr. 4 up). 1986. pap. 2.50 (ISBN 0-671-62670-1, Archway). PB.
—The Restless Dead: Ghostly Tales from Around the World. (gr. 4 up). 1987. pap. 2.50 (ISBN 0-671-64373-8, Archway). PB.
—The World's Most Famous Ghost. (Illus.). 112p. (gr. 3-6). 1989. pap. 2.75 (ISBN 0-671-69145-7, Minstrel Bks). PB.
Cohen, Miriam. Starring First Grade. (gr. k-6). 1987. pap. 2.95 (ISBN 0-440-48250-X, YB). Dell.
Colby, C. B. World's Best "True" Ghost Store Stories. LC 88-11703. (Illus.). 128p. (Orig.). (gr. 6-12). 1989. pap. 3.95 (ISBN 0-8069-6898-2). Sterling.
—World's Best "True" Ghost Stories. LC 88-11703. (Illus.). 128p. (gr. 6-12). 1988. 12.95 (ISBN 0-8069-6876-1). Sterling.
Conrad, Pam. Stonewords: A Ghost Story. LC 89-36382. 144p. (gr. 5 up). 1990. 12.95 (ISBN 0-06-021315-9); PLB 12.89 (ISBN 0-06-021316-7). HarpC Child Bks.
Cook, Emilie C. Winnie the Witch & the Frightened Ghost. Gilleo, Alma, ed. McKissick, Vernon, illus. LC 74-734865. (gr. 1-3). 1977. 6 bks. & 1 cass. 29.95 (ISBN 0-89290-012-1); 1 bk. & 1 cass. 10.95 (ISBN 0-685-04677-X). Soc for Visual.
Coombs, Patricia. Dorrie & the Haunted House. 48p. (gr. k-6). 1980. pap. 1.50 (ISBN 0-440-42212-4, YB). Dell.
—Dorrie & the Screebit Ghost. Coombs, Patricia, illus. LC 79-4443. (gr. 1-4). 1979. 9.95 (ISBN 0-688-41883-X). Lothrop.
Corbett, Scott. The Red Room Riddle. (Illus.). 128p. (gr. 4-6). 1975. lib. bdg. 14.95 (ISBN 0-316-15719-8, Joy St Bks). Little.
Courtney, Dayle. Secret of Pirates' Cave. rev. ed. 160p. (gr. 6-9). 1991. pap. 4.99 (ISBN 0-87403-834-0, 24-03884). Standard Pub.
Coville, Bruce. The Ghost Wore Grey. 128p. (Orig.). 1988. pap. 2.75 (ISBN 0-553-15610-1, Skylark). Bantam.
Cresswell, Helen. Bagthorpes Haunted. (gr. 3-7). 1988. pap. 3.95 (ISBN 0-14-032172-1, Puffin). Puffin Bks.
Cross, Gilbert B. A Witch Across Time. LC 89-38474. 224p. (gr. 6-9). 1990. 14.95 (ISBN 0-689-31602-X, Atheneum Child Bk). Macmillan Child Grp.
Crossley-Holland, Kevin. Storm. (Illus.). 42p. (gr. 2-4). 1989. 3.95 (ISBN 0-8120-6143-8). Barron.
Cuyler, Margery. Sir William & the Pumpkin Monster. Winborn, Marsha, illus. LC 84-610. 32p. (gr. k-2). 1984. 9.95 (ISBN 0-8050-0247-2). H Holt & Co.
Dearest Grand-Ma. 1991. pap. 13.95 (ISBN 0-385-41843-4). Doubleday.
De Brunhoff, Laurent. Babar & the Ghost. De Brunhoff, Laurent, illus. LC 80-5753. 32p. (gr. k-3). 1981. PLB 11.99 (ISBN 0-394-94660-X); pap. 4.95 boards (ISBN 0-394-84660-5). Random.
Deem, James M. How to Find a Ghost. Kelley, True, illus. 144p. (gr. 5-9). 1988. 13.95 (ISBN 0-395-46846-9). HM.
—How to Find a Ghost. 144p. 1990. pap. 3.25 (ISBN 0-380-70829-9, Camelot). Avon.
Delton, Judy. Camp Ghost-Away. 80p. (Orig.). (gr. k-6). 1988. pap. 2.50 (ISBN 0-440-40062-7, YB). Dell.
Denan, Corinne. Hair-Raising Tales. LC 79-66334. (Illus.). 48p. (gr. 5-7). 1980. PLB 9.89 (ISBN 0-89375-334-3); pap. 2.95 (ISBN 0-89375-333-5). Troll Assocs.
—Haunted House Tales. Toulmin-Rothe, Ann, illus. LC 79-66335. 48p. (gr. 5-7). 1980. PLB 9.89 (ISBN 0-89375-336-X); pap. text ed. 2.95 (ISBN 0-89375-335-1); cassette avail. Troll Assocs.
—Strange & Eerie Tales. new ed. LC 79-66336. (Illus.). 48p. (gr. 4-6). 1980. lib. bdg. 9.89 (ISBN 0-89375-338-6); pap. 2.95 (ISBN 0-89375-337-8). Troll Assocs.
Denholtz, Roni S. The Ghost in the New House. Fontalvo, Nelsy, illus. LC 86-81369. 32p. (gr. k-2). 1986. PLB 7.59 (ISBN 0-87386-017-9); pap. 1.95 (ISBN 0-87386-013-6). Jan Prods.
Detorie, Rick. Ghost in the Closet. 24p. (gr. k-3). pap. 1.95 (ISBN 0-8167-1457-6). Troll Assocs.
—Haunted Elevator. 24p. (gr. k-3). pap. 1.95 (ISBN 0-8167-1459-2). Troll Assocs.
—Haunted Tool Shed. 24p. (gr. k-3). pap. 1.95 (ISBN 0-8167-1456-8). Troll Assocs.
—Red-Headed Gooseberry Ghost. 24p. (gr. k-3). pap. 1.95 (ISBN 0-8167-1458-4). Troll Assocs.
Dickens, Charles. The Signalman. Richardson, I. M., adapted by. Ashmead, Hal, illus. LC 81-19819. 32p. (gr. 5-10). 1982. PLB 10.79 (ISBN 0-89375-630-X); pap. text ed. 2.95 (ISBN 0-89375-631-8). Troll Assocs.
Disney, Walt, Productions Staff. Walt Disney Productions Presents "The Haunted House" LC 75-16430. (Illus.). 48p. (ps-3). 1976. 5.95 (ISBN 0-394-82570-5, Random Juv); lib. bdg. 4.99 (ISBN 0-394-92570-X). Random.
Dixon, Franklin W. The Hardy Boys Ghost Stories. 144p. 1989. pap. 3.50 (ISBN 0-671-69133-3, Minstrel Bks). PB.
Drinkwater, Carol. The Haunted School. (gr. 5-9). 1988. pap. 3.95 (ISBN 0-317-69631-9, Puffin). Puffin Bks.
Dunlop, Eileen. House on the Hill. 160p. (gr. 2-9). pap. 2.95 (ISBN 0-8167-1323-5). Troll Assocs.

Eldin, Peter. Spookster's Handbook. LC 89-32659. (Illus.). 96p. (Orig.). (gr. 3-9). 1990. 12.95 (ISBN 0-8069-5742-5); pap. 3.95 (ISBN 0-8069-5743-3). Sterling.

Estern, Anne G. The Picolinis & the Haunted House. Frenck, Hal, illus. 115p. (gr. 3-5). 1989. pap. 2.95 (ISBN 0-553-15771-X, Skylark). Bantam.

Fleischman, Sid. The Case of the Cackling Ghost. Woodrun, Jim, illus. LC 80-20059. 64p. (gr. 2-4). 1981. Random.

—The Ghost in the Noonday Sun. Sis, Peter, illus. LC 88-11066. (gr. 5 up). 1989. 11.95 (ISBN 0-688-08410-9). Greenwillow.

—The Ghost in the Noonday Sun. 144p. (gr. 3-7). 1991. pap. 2.75 (ISBN 0-590-43662-7, Apple Paperbacks). Scholastic Inc.

—The Ghost on Saturday Night. Von Schmidt, Eric, illus. 64p. (gr. 4-6). 1974. 13.95 (ISBN 0-316-28583-8, Joy St Bks). Little.

Flora, James. Grandpa's Ghost Stories. LC 78-51999. (Illus.). 32p. (gr. k-4). 1978. 12.95 (ISBN 0-689-50112-9, M K McElderry). Macmillan Child Grp.

Frost, Erica. I Can Read about Ghosts. LC 74-24964. (Illus.). (gr. 2-4). 1975. pap. 1.95 (ISBN 0-89375-065-4). Troll Assocs.

Furman, A. L., ed. Ghost Stories. (gr. 5-8). 1986. pap. 2.50 (ISBN 0-671-62488-1, Archway). PB.

Furman, Abraham L., ed. More Teen-Age Ghost Stories. (gr. 6-10). 1963. PLB 6.70 (ISBN 0-8313-0052-3). Lantern.

—More Teen-Age Haunted Stories. (gr. 5-10). 1967. PLB 6.70 (ISBN 0-8313-0057-4). Lantern.

Gage, Wilson. The Ghost of Five Owl Farm. (gr. 4-8). 1986. pap. 2.50 (ISBN 0-671-56085-9, Archway). PB.

—Mrs. Gaddy & the Ghost. Hafner, Marylin, illus. LC 78-16366. 56p. (gr. 1-3). 1979. 10.95 (ISBN 0-688-80179-X). Greenwillow.

Gantz, David. Ms. Agatha in the Goblins Are Coming. Gantz, David, illus. 26p. (ps-3). 1988. pap. 2.95 incl. full-color stickers (ISBN 0-671-64205-7). S&S Trade.

—The Spookiest Day. Gantz, David, illus. 32p. (Orig.). (gr. k-3). 1986. pap. 2.50 (ISBN 0-590-40325-7). Scholastic Inc.

Garfield, Leon. Footsteps: A Novel. LC 80-65834. 192p. (gr. 7 up). 1980. 12.95 (ISBN 0-385-28294-X). Delacorte.

—Mister Corbett's Ghost. Maitland, Antony, illus. (gr. 3-7). 10.95 (ISBN 0-317-62538-1). Viking Child Bks.

—The Wedding Ghost. Keeping, Charles, illus. 66p. (gr. 6 up). 1987. bds. 14.95 laminated (ISBN 0-19-279779-4). Oxford U Pr.

Garfield, Vivien & Alcock, Vivien. Ghostly Companions. (gr. k-6). 1990. pap. 2.95 (ISBN 0-440-40276-X, YB). Dell.

Ghost in the Attic. 1990. text ed. 3.95 cased (ISBN 0-7214-5268-X). Ladybird Bks.

Ghostbusters Storybook. 1987. write for info (Little Simon). S&S Trade.

Gilligan, Shannon. The Haunted Swamp. (gr. 4-7). 1991. pap. 2.95 (ISBN 0-553-15856-2). Bantam.

Great Ghost Stories. (Illus.). 140p. (gr. 4-8). 1991. lib. bdg. 14.95 (ISBN 0-87460-370-6). Lion Bks.

Haas, Dorothy. The Haunted House, No. 3. 96p. (gr. 2-4). 1988. pap. 2.50 (ISBN 0-590-41508-5). Scholastic Inc.

Hahn, Mary D. The Doll in the Garden: A Ghost Story. 160p. (gr. 4-6). 1989. 13.95 (ISBN 0-89919-848-1, Pub. by Clarion). HM.

—Wait Till Helen Comes: A Ghost Story. LC 86-2648. 144p. (gr. 4-7). 1986. 12.95 (ISBN 0-89919-453-2, Pub. by Clarion). Ticknor & Fields.

Hancock, Sibyl. Esteban & the Ghost. Zimmer, Dirk, illus. LC 82-22125. 32p. (ps-3). 1983. 10.95 (ISBN 0-8037-2443-8); PLB 10.89 (ISBN 0-8037-2411-X). Dial Bks Young.

Harter, Walter. The Phantom Hand. Totten, Robert, illus. 128p. (gr. 4 up). 1976. pap. 5.96 (ISBN 0-13-661843-X, Pub. by Treehouse). P-H.

Haunted House. 1989. pap. 0.66 (ISBN 0-394-82301-X). Random.

Haunted House on Hoover Hill. (ps-3). 1990. pap. 2.95 (ISBN 0-8167-2192-0). Troll Assocs.

Haunted House Stories. (Illus.). (gr. k-9). 1988. pap. 1.95 (ISBN 0-318-36489-1). Scholastic Inc.

Hearne, Betsy G. Eli's Ghost. Himler, Ronald, illus. LC 86-21096. 112p. (gr. 3-7). 1987. 12.95 (ISBN 0-689-50420-9, M K McElderry). Macmillan Child Grp.

Helldorfer, M. C. Spook House. LC 88-30026. 160p. (gr. 4 up). 1989. 12.95 (ISBN 0-02-743514-8, Bradbury Pr). Macmillan Child Grp.

Hezlep, William. Ghost Town. (Orig.). (gr. 3-12). 1985. pap. text ed. 5.00 (ISBN 0-88734-402-X). Players Pr.

Hildick, E. W. The Ghost Squad & the Ghoul of Grunberg. LC 85-29350. 160p. (gr. 5-9). 1986. 11.95 (ISBN 0-525-44229-4, 01063-320, DCB). Dutton Child Bks.

—The Ghost Squad & the Halloween Conspiracy. LC 85-6835. 176p. (gr. 5-9). 1985. 13.95 (ISBN 0-525-44111-5, DCB). Dutton Child Bks.

—The Ghost Squad & the Menace of the Malevs. 160p. (gr. 5-9). 1988. 12.95 (ISBN 0-525-44439-4, DCB). Dutton Child Bks.

—The Ghost Squad & the Prowling Hermits. LC 87-8889. (gr. 5-9). 1987. 12.95 (ISBN 0-525-44330-4, DCB). Dutton Child Bks.

—The Ghost Squad Breaks Through. LC 84-3985. 112p. (gr. 5-9). 1984. 12.95 (ISBN 0-525-44097-6, 01063-320, DCB). Dutton Child Bks.

Hitchcock, Alfred, ed. Alfred Hitchcock's Ghostly Gallery. (Illus.). (gr. 5-8). 1962. 6.95 (ISBN 0-394-81226-3, Random Juv). Random.

—Alfred Hitchcock's Ghostly Gallery. LC 62-14298. (Illus.). 272p. (gr. 5 up). 1984. pap. 3.95 (ISBN 0-394-86762-9, Pub. by BYR). Random.

—Alfred Hitchcock's Haunted Houseful. LC 84-15949. (Illus.). 272p. (gr. 4-9). 1985. lib. bdg. 6.99 (ISBN 0-394-91224-1, Random Juv); pap. 3.95 (ISBN 0-394-87041-7, Random Juv). Random.

Hoke, Helen, ed. Tales of Fear & Frightening Phenomena. LC 82-7299. 144p. (gr. 7 up). 1982. pap. 10.50 (ISBN 0-525-66789-X, Lodestar Bks). Dutton Child Bks.

Holl, Kristi D. The Haunting of Cabin Thirteen. (gr. k-6). 1989. pap. 2.95 (ISBN 0-440-40182-8, YB). Dell.

—The Haunting of Cabin 13. LC 86-17274. 128p. (gr. 3-7). 1987. 12.95 (ISBN 0-689-31321-7, Atheneum Child Bk). Macmillan Child Grp.

Homer, Larona. The Shore Ghosts & Other Stories of New Jersey. Bock, William S., illus. 154p. (gr. 4-8). 1986. 8.95 (ISBN 0-912608-14-5). Mid Atlantic.

Howe, James. Nighty-Nightmare. 128p. (gr. 3-7). 1988. pap. 3.50 (ISBN 0-380-70490-0, Camelot). Avon.

Hubner, Carol K. The Haunted Shul. Kramer, Devorah, illus. (gr. 3-8). 1979. 6.95 (ISBN 0-910818-14-2). Judaica Pr.

Hutchinson, Duane. Storyteller's Ghost Stories. 2nd ed. LC 89-23689. 112p. (gr. 4 up). 1989. pap. 6.95 (ISBN 0-934988-32-3). Foun Bks.

—A Storyteller's Ghost Stories, Bk. 2. LC 90-3122. 96p. (gr. 3 up). 1990. pap. 5.95 (ISBN 0-934988-18-8). Foun Bks.

Ibbotson, Eva. Great Ghost Rescue. large type ed. 172p. (gr. 3-8). 1989. Repr. of 1975 ed. PLB 14.95 (ISBN 1-85089-951-7, Pub. by Clio Pr England). ABC-Clio.

Irving, Washington. Legend of Sleepy Hollow & Other Stories. (gr. 6 up). 1964. pap. 2.75 (ISBN 0-8049-0050-7, CL-50). Airmont.

James, Henry. Turn of the Screw. Andrews, C. A., intro. by. (gr. 9 up). 1967. pap. 1.75 (ISBN 0-8049-0155-4, CL-155). Airmont.

—The Turn of the Screw. Shaw, Charles, illus. Stewart, Diana, adapted by. LC 81-5217. (Illus.). 48p. (gr. 4 up). 1983. PLB 17.32 (ISBN 0-8172-1672-3); pap. 9.27 (ISBN 0-8172-2027-5). Raintree Pubs.

Jerome, Jerome K. After Supper Ghost Stories: And Other Tales. 176p. (gr. 6-9). 1990. pap. 8.00 (ISBN 0-86299-762-3). A Sutton Pub.

Kahn, Joan. Ready or Not: Here Come Fourteen Frightening Stories! LC 86-31875. (Illus.). 176p. (gr. 7 up). 1987. 11.75 (ISBN 0-688-07167-8). Greenwillow.

Kaplan, Carol B. The Haunted Picnic. Bolinske, Janet L., ed. Quenell, Midge, illus. LC 87-62999. 24p. (Orig.). (ps-k). 1988. 17.95 (ISBN 0-88335-754-2); pap. write for info. (ISBN 0-88335-077-7). Milliken Pub Co.

Kassem, Lou. A Haunting in Williamsburg: A Ghost Story. 112p. (gr. 5-6). 1990. pap. 2.95 (ISBN 0-380-75892-X, Camelot). Avon.

Keene, Carolyn. Nancy Drew Ghost Stories. 160p. 1989. pap. 3.50 (ISBN 0-671-69132-5, Minstrel Bks). PB.

Kenyon, Kate. Who's Haunting the Eighth Grade, No. 13. 176p. (gr. 5-9). 1988. pap. 2.50 (ISBN 0-590-41787-8). Scholastic Inc.

Klaveness, Jan O. Ghost Island. (gr. k-12). 1987. pap. 2.95 (ISBN 0-440-93097-9, LFL). Dell.

Kroll, Steven. Amanda & the Giggling Ghost. Gackenbach, Dick, illus. LC 79-28379. 40p. (ps-3). 1980. reinforced bdg. 12.95 (ISBN 0-8234-0408-0). Holiday.

Landon, Lucinda. Meg Mackintosh & the Mystery At C. (gr. 4-7). 1990. 12.95 (ISBN 0-316-51367-9, Joy St Bks). Little.

Lawrence, Louise. Sing & Scatter Daisies. LC 76-21393. (gr. 7 up). 1977. 8.95 (ISBN 0-06-023772-4). HarpC Child Bks.

Leach, Maria. Thing at the Foot of the Bed. Werth, Kurt, illus. LC 59-6658. 128p. (gr. 3-5). 1987. PLB 12.95 (ISBN 0-399-21496-8, Philomel). Putnam Pub Group.

Leppard, Lois G. Mandie & the Ghost Bandits, Bk. 3. LC 84-71151. 128p. (Orig.). (gr. 5-7). 1984. pap. 3.95 (ISBN 0-87123-442-4). Bethany Hse.

Leroe, Ellen. The Peanut Butter Poltergeist. LC 87-8882. 128p. (gr. 4 up). 1987. 12.95 (ISBN 0-525-67241-9, Lodestar Bks). Dutton Child Bks.

Levin, Betty. The Keeping Room. LC 80-23931. (Illus.). 248p. 1989. Repr. of 1981 ed. 11.95 (ISBN 0-688-80300-8). Greenwillow.

Lindgren, Astrid. The Ghost Skinny Jack. Wikland, Ilon, illus. LC 87-50371. 32p. (ps-3). 1988. pap. 10.95 (ISBN 0-670-81913-1). Viking Child Bks.

Lively, Penelope. The Ghost of Thomas Kempe. Maitland, Anthony, illus. 192p. (gr. 3-6). 1973. 14.95 (ISBN 0-525-30495-9, DCB). Dutton Child Bks.

—Uninvited Ghosts. Lawrence, John, illus. LC 84-26035. 128p. (gr. 4-7). 1985. 11.95 (ISBN 0-525-44165-4, DCB). Dutton Child Bks.

Lynn, Ruth. Ester: The Story of a Small Ghost. Wagner, R. M., ed. Lynn, Ruth, illus. LC 81-69693. 28p. (gr. 5 up). 1981. 12.95 (ISBN 0-941674-00-2). Woodcock Pr.

McBratney, Sam. The Ghosts of Hungryhouse Lane. Thiesing, Lisa, illus. 128p. (gr. 4-7). 1989. 13.95 (ISBN 0-8050-0985-X). H Holt & Co.

—The Ghosts of Hungryhouse Lane. 128p. (gr. 3-7). 1990. pap. 2.75 (ISBN 0-590-43462-4). Scholastic Inc.

McBrier, Page. Adventure in the Haunted House. Sims, Blanche, illus. LC 85-8436. 96p. (gr. 3-6). 1986. PLB 9.89 (ISBN 0-8167-0539-9); pap. text ed. 2.95 (ISBN 0-8167-0540-2). Troll Assocs.

Maccarone, Grace. Ghost on the Hill. 1990. pap. 2.50 (ISBN 0-590-42978-7). Scholastic Inc.

—The Haunting of Grade Three. Oechsli, Ke-ly, illus. 96p. (Orig.). (gr. 4-6). 1987. pap. 2.50 (ISBN 0-590-40921-2, Lucky Star). Scholastic Inc.

—The Haunting of Grade Three. 96p. (Orig.). (gr. 2-5). 1987. pap. 2.50 (ISBN 0-590-43868-9). Scholastic Inc.

—Return of the Third-Grade Ghosthunters. 1989. pap. 2.50 (ISBN 0-590-41944-7). Scholastic Inc.

McGinnis, Lila. The Ghost Upstairs. LC 81-20337. (Illus.). 128p. (gr. 4-7). 1982. 12.95 (ISBN 0-8038-2716-4); lib. bdg. 12.89 (ISBN 0-8038-9286-1). Hastings.

Mahy, Margaret. The Haunting. LC 82-3983. 144p. (gr. 5-9). 1982. 12.95 (ISBN 0-689-50243-5, M K McElderry). Macmillan Child Grp.

—Haunting. (gr. 4-7). 1991. pap. 3.25 (ISBN 0-440-40408-8). Dell.

Manes, Stephen. The Hooples' Haunted House. Weston, Martha, illus. LC 81-2216. 128p. (gr. 4-6). 1981. pap. 11.95 (ISBN 0-385-28416-0). Delacorte.

Marar, Eve. More Haunted House Stories. (Illus.). 96p. (Orig.). 1988. pap. 1.95 (ISBN 0-942025-64-4). Kidsbks.

Marlin, J. Getting out the Ghost. LC 84-7669. 176p. (gr. 7 up). 1984. 11.95 (ISBN 0-399-21130-6, Putnam). Putnam Pub Group.

Marshall, Edward. Four on the Shore. Marshall, James, illus. LC 84-1708. 48p. (ps-3). 1985. 9.95 (ISBN 0-8037-0155-1); PLB 9.89 (ISBN 0-8037-0142-X). Dial Bks Young.

Martin, Bill & Archambault, John. The Ghost-Eye Tree. LC 85-8422. (Illus.). 32p. (gr. k-2). 1985. 13.95 (ISBN 0-8050-0208-1). H Holt & Co.

Martin, Bill, Jr. & Archambault, John. The Ghost-Eye Tree. Rand, Ted, illus. LC 85-8422. 32p. (Orig.). (gr. k-3). 1988. pap. 4.95 (ISBN 0-8050-0947-7). H Holt & Co.

Miller, Judi. Ghost a La Mode. (gr. 3-7). 1989. pap. 2.75 (ISBN 0-553-15755-8, Skylark). Bantam.

—Ghost in My Soup. (gr. 3-7). 1985. pap. 2.75 (ISBN 0-553-15622-5, Skylark). Bantam.

Montgomery, Raymond A. The Haunted House. 64p. 1981. pap. 2.25 (ISBN 0-553-15428-1). Bantam.

Moore, Ruth N. Ghost Town Mystery. Gerig, Sibyl G., illus. LC 87-2874. 144p. (gr. 4 up). 1987. pap. 4.95 (ISBN 0-8361-3445-1). Herald Pr.

Mooser, Stephen. Shadows on the Graveyard Trail. (Orig.). (gr. 5-7). 1986. pap. 2.75 (ISBN 0-440-40805-9, YB). Dell.

Mullin, Penn. The Ghosts of Black Point. Kratoville, Betty L., ed. Lucey, Jack, illus. 64p. (gr. 3-9). 1989. PLB 4.95 (ISBN 0-87879-653-3, High Noon Books). Acad Therapy.

Naylor, Phyllis R. Bernie & the Bessledorf Ghost. LC 88-29389. 144p. (gr. 3-7). 1990. 12.95 (ISBN 0-689-31499-X, Atheneum Child Bk). Macmillan Child Grp.

Nixon, Joan L. The Ghosts of Now. (gr. 7 up). 1986. pap. 3.25 (ISBN 0-440-93115-0, LFL). Dell.

—Haunted Island. 128p. (Orig.). (gr. 3-7). 1987. pap. 2.50 (ISBN 0-590-40203-X, Apple Paperbacks). Scholastic Inc.

—Haunted Island. 128p. (Orig.). (gr. 3-7). 1987. pap. 2.75 (ISBN 0-590-43134-X). Scholastic Inc.

Norton, Andre & Miller, Phyllis. House of Shadows. LC 83-16197. 216p. (gr. 5-9). 1984. 14.95 (ISBN 0-689-50298-2, M K McElderry). Macmillan Child Grp.

O'Connor, Jane & O'Connor, Jim. The Ghost in Tent Nineteen. Williams, Richard, illus. LC 87-82372. 64p. (Orig.). (gr. 2-4). 1988. lib. bdg. 6.99 (ISBN 0-394-99800-6, Random Juv); pap. 1.95 (ISBN 0-394-89800-1). Random.

O'Connor, Jane, retold by. The Teeny Tiny Woman. Alley, R. W., illus. LC 86-485. 32p. (ps-1). 1986. lib. bdg. 6.99 (ISBN 0-394-98320-3, Random Juv); pap. 2.95 (ISBN 0-394-88320-9, Random Juv). Random.

Odorizzi, De D. Georgie the Ghost. 1990. 6.95 (ISBN 0-533-08991-3). Vantage.

Oetting. The Gray Ghosts of Gotham. LC 73-87804. (Illus.). 32p. (gr. 2-5). 1974. PLB 9.95 (ISBN 0-87783-135-1); pap. 3.94 deluxe ed. (ISBN 0-87783-136-X). Oddo.

O'Huigin, Sean. The Ghost Horse of the Mounties. Moser, Barry, illus. LC 87-46287. (gr. 4-6). 1991. 14.95 (ISBN 0-87923-721-X). Godine.

Oliver, Stephen R. The Gitter, the Googer, & the Ghost. Wyman, Cherie R., illus. LC 83-5281. 112p. (gr. 2-6). 1983. PLB 8.95 (ISBN 0-87614-250-1). Carolrhoda Bks.

Osborne, Will. Thirteen Ghosts: Strange but True Ghost Stories. 1988. pap. 2.75 (ISBN 0-590-44511-1). Scholastic Inc.

Palin, Michael. The Mirrorstone: A Ghost Story with Holograms. Lee, Alan, illus. Seymour, Richard, designed by. LC 86-7375. (Illus.). 32p. (gr. 5 up). 1986. 14.95 (ISBN 0-394-88353-5). Knopf.

Parish, Peggy. The Ghosts of Cougar Island. (Orig.). (gr. 2-4). 1986. pap. 3.25 (ISBN 0-440-42872-6, YB). Dell.

—Haunted House. 160p. (gr. k-6). 1981. pap. 3.25 (ISBN 0-440-43459-9, YB). Dell.

—Haunted House. (gr. 4-6). 1991. 15.00 (ISBN 0-8446-6391-3). Peter Smith.

Pascal, Francine. The Ghost of Tricia Martin. 1990. pap. 2.95 (ISBN 0-553-28487-8). Bantam.

—Ghosts in the Graveyard. (gr. 4-7). 1990. pap. 3.50 (ISBN 0-553-15801-5). Bantam.
Peck, Richard. The Ghost Belonged to Me. LC 74-34218. 184p. (gr. 7 up). 1975. pap. 14.95 (ISBN 0-670-33767-6). Viking Child Bks.
—The Ghost Belonged to Me. 192p. (gr. 5 up). 1983. pap. 3.25 (ISBN 0-440-93075-8, LFL). Dell.
—The Ghost Belonged to Me. (gr. k-6). 1987. pap. 3.25 (ISBN 0-440-42861-0, YB). Dell.
—The Ghost Belonged to Me. large type ed. 230p. 1989. Repr. of 1975 ed. PLB 15.95 (ISBN 1-55736-116-9, Crnrstn Bks). ABC-CLIO.
—Ghosts I Have Been. 256p. (gr. 5 up). 1979. pap. 3.25 (ISBN 0-440-92839-7, LFL). Dell.
—Ghosts I Have Been. (gr. k-6). 1987. pap. 2.95 (ISBN 0-440-42864-5, YB). Dell.
Pellowski, Michael J. Ghost in the Library. Durham, Robert, illus. LC 88-1236. 48p. (Orig.). (gr. 1-4). 1989. PLB 9.89 (ISBN 0-8167-1337-5); pap. text ed. 2.95 (ISBN 0-8167-1338-3). Troll Assocs.
Peters, Sharon. The Goofy Ghost. Garcia, Tom, illus. LC 81-2573. 32p. (gr. k-2). 1981. PLB 10.89 (ISBN 0-89375-533-8); pap. 2.95 (ISBN 0-89375-534-6). Troll Assocs.
Pienkowski, Jan. The Haunted House. (Illus.). (ps-3). 1979. 12.95 (ISBN 0-525-31520-9, DCB). Dutton Child Bks.
Platt, Kin. The Ghost of Hellsfire Street. LC 80-10446. 256p. (gr. 4-6). 1980. 12.95 (ISBN 0-385-28317-2). Delacorte.
Radford, Ken. The Cellar. LC 88-24708. 184p. (gr. 4-7). 1989. 13.95 (ISBN 0-8234-0744-6). Holiday.
Raskin, Ellen. Ghost in a Four-Room Apartment. Raskin, Ellen, illus. LC 69-13521. 48p. (gr. k-3). 1978. (Aladdin); pap. 1.95 (ISBN 0-689-70446-1, Aladdin). Macmillan Child Grp.
Razzi, Jim. The Ghost in the Mirror: And Other Ghost Stories. Kretschmann, Karin, illus. 64p. 1990. 8.99 (ISBN 0-448-40059-6, G&D); pap. 2.95 (ISBN 0-448-40058-8, G&D). Putnam Pub Group.
Redmond, Marilyn. Henry Hamilton, Graduate Ghost. Redmond, Marilyn, illus. LC 81-22693. 159p. (gr. 6 up). 1982. 9.95 (ISBN 0-88289-303-3). Pelican.
Riddell, Ruth. Shadow Witch. 208p. (gr. 6-9). 1989. 13.95 (ISBN 0-689-31484-1, Atheneum Child Bk). Macmillan Child Grp.
Robinson, Marileta. The Big Bicycle Race. Morrill, Leslie, illus. 1984. incl. cassette 7.95; 5.95 (ISBN 0-910313-29-6). Parker Bros.
Roddy, Lee. D J Dillon Ghost of the Moaning Mansion. 132p. (gr. 3-7). 1987. pap. 4.99 (ISBN 0-89693-349-0). Victor Bks.
Ross, Pat. M & M & the Haunted House Game. Hafner, Marilyn, illus. 48p. (gr. 1-3). 1981. pap. 1.25 (ISBN 0-440-45544-8, YB). Dell.
—M & M & the Haunted House Game. Hafner, Marilyn, illus. (gr. 1-4). 1980. Pantheon.
Rossetti, Christina. Goblin Market. (Illus.). 48p. (gr. 4-7). 1989. pap. 9.95 (ISBN 0-575-04389-X, Pub. by Gollancz England). Trafalgar Sq.
Russell, Jean, ed. Supernatural Stories: Thirteen Tales of the Unexpected. LC 87-7881. 160p. (gr. 4-7). 1987. 11.95 (ISBN 0-531-05723-2); PLB 11.99 (ISBN 0-531-08323-3). Orchard Bks Watts.
Ryan, Joan & Snell, Gordon, eds. The Haunted Hills: Ghost Tales of Ireland for Children. (Illus.). 158p. (gr. 4-8). 1984. 10.95 (ISBN 0-907606-20-2, Pub. by Glendale Pr). Irish Bks Media.
Sabin, Fran & Sabin, Lou. Secret of the Haunted House. Trivas, Irene, illus. LC 81-8751. 48p. (gr. 2-4). 1982. PLB 10.89 (ISBN 0-89375-598-2); pap. text ed. 2.95 (ISBN 0-89375-599-0). Troll Assocs.
St. George, Judith. Haunted. 160p. (gr. 6 up). 1986. pap. 2.50 (ISBN 0-553-26047-2). Bantam.
Salway, Lance. A Nasty Piece of Work & Other Ghost Stories. Ford, Jeremy, illus. LC 84-17641. 128p. (gr. 4-8). 1985. 10.95 (ISBN 0-89919-360-9, Clarion). HM.
Schertle, Alice. Hob Goblin & the Skeleton. (ps-3). 1982. 10.25 (ISBN 0-685-05955-3); PLB 10.88. Lothrop.
Schneider, Meg. The Ghost in the Picture. 144p. (gr. 3-7). 1988. pap. 2.50 (ISBN 0-590-41670-7). Scholastic Inc.
Schrade, Arlene O. Gabriel, the Happy Ghost. Incl. Gabriel en Mexico (Gabriel Learns About the Day of the Dead (ISBN 0-8442-7211-6, 7211-6); Gabriel en Espana (Gabriel in Pampiona (ISBN 0-8442-7222-1, 7222-1); Gabriel en Puerto Rico (Gabriel in the Caribbean (ISBN 0-8442-7224-8, 7224-8). (ENG & SPA., Illus.). 32p. (gr. 4 up). 1983. pap. 4.95 ea. (Passport Bks.). Natl Textbk.
Schumacher, Claire W. Ghostly Tales of Lake Superior. Kopari, Catherine, illus. LC 87-91292. 94p. (Orig.). (gr. 9). 1987. PLB 6.95 (ISBN 0-917378-06-7). Zenith City.
Schwartz, Betty, ed. Great Ghost Stories. Geiger, Paul, illus. 192p. (gr. 4-8). 1985. pap. 6.95 (ISBN 0-671-60179-2, Little Simon). S&S Trade.
Seuling, Barbara. The Teeny Tiny Woman: An Old English Ghost Tale. Seuling, Barbara, illus. (gr. k-3). 1978. pap. 3.95 (ISBN 0-14-050266-1, Puffin). Puffin Bks.
Sharmat, Marjorie W. Two Ghosts on a Bench. Langner, Nola, illus. LC 81-47734. 64p. (gr. k-3). 1982. HarpC Child Bks.
Sheldon, Ann. Linda Craig: The Haunted Valley. Barish, Wendy, ed. 192p. (gr. 3-7). 1982. 8.50 (ISBN 0-671-45551-6, Little Simon); pap. 2.95 (ISBN 0-671-45550-8). S&S Trade.
Sherrow, Victoria. There Goes the Ghost. Lloyd, Megan, illus. LC 83-49485. 32p. (gr. k-3). 1985. 11.95 (ISBN 0-06-025509-9). HarpC Child Bks.
Simon, Seymour. Ghosts. Gammell, Stephen, illus. LC 75-37520. 80p. (gr. 4-6). 1988. PLB 13.89 (ISBN 0-397-32346-8, Lipp Jr Bks). HarpC Child Bks.
Sine, Megan & Sine, Willam H. Max Is Back. (Illus.). 80p. (gr. 4 up). 1989. pap. 3.95 (ISBN 0-449-90415-6, Columbine). Fawcett.
Singer, Marilyn. Ghost Host. LC 86-45778. 192p. (gr. 5 up). 1987. 11.95 (ISBN 0-06-025623-0); PLB 11.89 (ISBN 0-06-025624-9). HarpC Child Bks.
—Ghost Host. 208p. (gr. 7 up). 1988. pap. 2.50 (ISBN 0-590-41547-6, Point). Scholastic Inc.
Snape, Juliet & Snape, Charles. I'm Not Frightened of Ghosts. (Illus.). 32p. (gr. 2-5). 1987. 11.95 (ISBN 0-13-451246-4). P-H.
Sonntag, Linda, ed. The Ghost Story Treasury. Spenceley, Annabel, illus. 96p. (gr. 7 up). 1987. 12.95 (ISBN 0-399-21477-1, Putnam). Putnam Pub Group.
Spearing, Judith. Ghosts Who Went to School. Glass, Marvin, illus. 160p. (gr. 4-6). 1986. pap. 2.50 (ISBN 0-590-40452-0, Apple Paperbacks). Scholastic Inc.
—Ghosts Who Went to School. 1986. pap. 2.75 (ISBN 0-590-42859-4). Scholastic Inc.
Stark, John. Haunted House Stories. (Illus.). 96p. (Orig.). 1988. pap. 1.95 (ISBN 0-942025-17-2). Kidsbks.
Starkey, Dinah. Ghosts & Bogles. Pienkowski, Jan, illus. 124p. (gr. 3-5). 1987. 17.95 (ISBN 0-434-96440-9, Pub. by W Heinemann Ltd). Trafalgar Sq.
Stine, Jovial B. Ghostbusters II Storybook. 1989. pap. 4.95 (ISBN 0-590-42907-8). Scholastic Inc.
Stine, Megan & Stine, H. William. Christmas Visitors. (Illus.). 80p. 1988. pap. 2.95 (ISBN 0-449-90328-1, Columbine). Fawcett.
—Haunted Halloween. (Illus.). 80p. 1988. pap. 2.95 (ISBN 0-449-90327-3, Columbine). Fawcett.
—Mysterious Max. (Illus.). 80p. 1988. pap. 2.95 (ISBN 0-449-90326-5, Columbine). Fawcett.
Stine, Megan & Stine, William H. Baseball Card Fever. (Illus.). 80p. (gr. 4 up). 1989. pap. 3.95 (ISBN 0-449-90416-4, Columbine). Fawcett.
—Max's Secret Formula. (Illus.). 80p. (gr. 4 up). 1989. pap. 3.95 (ISBN 0-449-90417-2, Columbine). Fawcett.
Storr, Catherine. Cold Marble & Other Ghost Stories. LC 85-10319. 129p. (gr. 6-9). 1985. 13.95 (ISBN 0-571-13582-X). Faber & Faber.
Storr, Catherine, as told by. The Flying Dutchman. LC 85-16711. (Illus.). 32p. (gr. k-5). 1985. PLB 16.67 (ISBN 0-8172-2501-3); pap. 9.27 (ISBN 0-8172-2509-9). Raintree Pubs.
Supraner, Robyn. The Ghost in the Attic. LC 78-18039. (Illus.). 48p. (gr. 2-4). 1979. PLB 10.89 (ISBN 0-89375-095-6); pap. 2.95 (ISBN 0-89375-083-2). Troll Assocs.
Suzanne, Jamie. The Haunted House. large type ed. Pascal, Francine, created by. 106p. (gr. 7-12). 1990. Repr. of 1986 ed. 9.95 (ISBN 1-55905-066-7). Grey Castle.
Swarthout, Glendon & Swarthout, Kathryn. The Ghost & the Magic Saber. (Illus.). (gr. 4-7). 1963. lib. bdg. 4.99 (ISBN 0-394-91194-6). Random.
Tapp, Kathy K. The Ghostmobile. 160p. (gr. 3-7). 1991. pap. 2.75 (ISBN 0-590-43441-1). Scholastic Inc.
Thacker, Nola. All on a Winter's Day. 144p. (gr. 7 up). 1990. pap. 2.95 (ISBN 0-590-43416-0). Scholastic Inc.
Thayer, Jane. Gus Loved His Happy Home. Fleishman, Seymour, illus. LC 88-36962. 32p. (ps-2). 1989. PLB 13.95 (ISBN 0-208-02249-X, Pub. by Linnet). Shoe String.
Thompson, Jonathon. Haunted House Hoax. 10p. (gr. 3-6). 2.50 (ISBN 0-933479-12-3). Thompson.
Todd, H. E. The Silly Silly Ghost. Biro, Val, illus. 32p. (gr. k-3). 1989. 13.95 (ISBN 0-340-41155-4, Pub. by Hodder & Stoughton UK). Trafalgar Sq.
Tropea, Maria. Look & Look Again, Lost in the Haunted Mansion. Tallarico, Anthony, illus. 24p. (Orig.). (gr. 4-7). 1990. pap. 1.95 (ISBN 1-878890-03-4). Palisades Prodns.
VanOosting, James. Maxie's Ghost. LC 87-19800. 112p. (gr. 4-6). 1987. 10.95 (ISBN 0-374-34873-1). FS&G.
Waddell, Martin. Harriet & the Haunted School. Burgess, Mark, illus. (gr. 2-6). 1986. pap. 2.50 (ISBN 0-671-62215-3, Minstrel Bks). PB.
Wainwright, Richard M. The Gift from Obadiah's Ghost. Crompton, Jack, illus. 40p. 1990. 12.95 (ISBN 0-9619566-2-3). Family Life.
—A Tiny Miracle. Crompton, Jack, illus. 40p. Repr. 12. 95g (ISBN 0-9619566-0-7). Family Life.
Westall, Robert. Ghost Abbey. LC 88-23945. (gr. 7 up). 1989. pap. 12.95 (ISBN 0-590-41692-8). Scholastic Inc.
—Ghost Abbey. 1990. pap. 2.95 (ISBN 0-590-41693-6). Scholastic Inc.
—Ghosts & Journeys. large type ed. 192p. (gr. 3-8). 1989. Repr. of 1988 ed. PLB 14.95 (ISBN 1-85089-950-9, Pub. by Clio Pr England). ABC-CLIO.
Wibberley, Leonard. The Crime of Martin Coverly. LC 79-28538. 184p. (gr. 5 up). 1980. 11.95 (ISBN 0-374-31656-2). FS&G.
Wilde, Nicholas. Into the Dark. 1990. 12.95 (ISBN 0-590-43424-1). Scholastic Inc.
Windsor, Patricia. How a Weirdo & a Ghost Can Change Your Entire Life. (gr. k-6). 1988. pap. 2.75 (ISBN 0-440-40094-5). Dell.
Wippersberg, W. J. Bad Times for Ghosts. Bhend-Zaugg, Kathi, illus. LC 86-45058. 160p. (gr. 3-7). 1986. 13.95 (ISBN 0-15-200413-0, Gulliver Bks); pap. 6.95 (ISBN 0-15-200414-9). HarBraceJ.
Wright, Betty R. Christina's Ghost. LC 85-42880. 128p. (gr. 3-7). 1985. 13.95 (ISBN 0-8234-0581-8). Holiday.
—Christina's Ghost. 112p. (Orig.). (gr. 4-6). 1987. pap. 2.50 (ISBN 0-590-40284-6, Apple Paperbacks). Scholastic Inc.
—A Ghost in the Window. LC 87-45331. 160p. (gr. 3-7). 1987. 13.95 (ISBN 0-8234-0661-X). Holiday.
—A Ghost in the Window. (gr. 3-7). 1988. pap. 2.50 (ISBN 0-590-41839-4). Scholastic Inc.
—The Ghost of Ernie P. LC 90-55108. 128p. (gr. 3-7). 1990. 13.95 (ISBN 0-8234-0835-3). Holiday.
—Ghosts Beneath Our Feet. LC 84-47835. 144p. (gr. 3-7). 1984. 13.95 (ISBN 0-8234-0538-9). Holiday.
—Ghosts Beneath Our Feet. 144p. (gr. 4-6). 1986. pap. 2.50 (ISBN 0-590-40755-4, Apple Paperbacks). Scholastic Inc.
—Ghosts Beneath Our Feet. 144p. (gr. 3-7). 1986. pap. 2.75 (ISBN 0-590-43444-6). Scholastic Inc.
Wyeth, Sharon D. The Ghost Show. 1990. pap. 2.75 (ISBN 0-553-15829-5). Bantam.
York, Carol B. Nights in Ghostland. (gr. 5-7). 1987. pap. 2.50 (ISBN 0-671-63793-2, Archway). PB.
Zeplin, Zeno. The Cross-Eyed Ghost. Jones, Judy, illus. 154p. (gr. 3-6). 1991. PLB 11.95 casebound (ISBN 1-877740-05-5); pap. text ed. 6.95 (ISBN 1-877740-06-3). Nel-Mar Pub.
—The Haunted Classroom. Jones, Judy, illus. 136p. (gr. 4-7). 1989. text ed. 10.95 (ISBN 0-9615760-8-1); pap. text ed. 6.95 (ISBN 0-9615760-9-X). Nel-Mar Pub.

GHOST TOWNS

see Cities and Towns, Ruined, Extinct, Etc.

GHOSTS

see also Apparitions; Psychical Research; Superstition

Adams, Pam & Jones, Ceri, illus. A Book of Ghosts. 32p. (Orig.). (ps-2). 1974. 5.50 (ISBN 0-85953-073-6, Pub. by Child's Play England); pap. 4.00 (ISBN 0-85953-028-0). Childs Play.
Beckett, John. World's Weirdest "True" Ghost Stories. Hayhurst, Steve, illus. LC 91-15408. 96p. (gr. 3-10). 1991. 12.95 (ISBN 0-8069-8410-4). Sterling.
Brittain, Bill. Who Knew There'd Be Ghosts? Chessare, Michele, illus. LC 84-48496. 128p. (gr. 4-7). 1988. pap. 2.95 (ISBN 0-06-440224-X, Trophy). HarpC Child Bks.
Cartwright & Rawson. Gnomes, Goblins & Fairies. (gr. k-4). 1980. 6.95 (ISBN 0-86020-385-9, Usborne-Hayes); pap. 3.95 (ISBN 0-86020-384-0). EDC.
—Princes, Wizards & Gnomes. (gr. k-4). 1980. 10.95 (ISBN 0-86020-508-8, Usborne-Hayes). EDC.
Cohen, Daniel. America's Very Own Ghosts. (Illus.). 48p. (gr. 3-7). 1985. 10.95 (ISBN 0-396-08505-9, Putnam). Putnam Pub Group.
—The Ghosts of War. 96p. (gr. 5-8). 1990. 14.95 (ISBN 0-399-22200-6, Putnam). Putnam Pub Group.
—Great Ghosts. (gr. 4-7). 1990. 12.95 (ISBN 0-525-65039-3, Cobblehill Bks). Dutton Child Bks.
—Phantom Animals. 96p. 1991. 14.95 (ISBN 0-399-22230-8, Putnam). Putnam Pub Group.
—Phone Call from a Ghost: Strange Tales from Modern America. MacDonald, Patricia, ed. Lynn, David, illus. 112p. (gr. 5-7). 1990. pap. 2.75 (ISBN 0-671-68242-3, Minstrel). PB.
—Real Ghosts. (gr. 9-12). Date not set. 8.95 (ISBN 0-396-07454-5, Putnam). Putnam Pub Group.
—The World's Most Famous Ghosts. (Illus.). 1978. 8.95 (ISBN 0-396-07543-6, Putnam). Putnam Pub Group.
Coombs, Patricia. Dorrie & the Haunted House. 48p. (gr. k-6). 1980. pap. 1.50 (ISBN 0-440-42212-4, YB). Dell.
Cuyler, Margery. Sir William & the Pumpkin Monster. Winborn, Marsha, illus. LC 84-610. 32p. (ps-2). 1989. pap. 4.95 (ISBN 0-8050-1017-3). H Holt & Co.
Farrant, Don W. Real Ghosts Don't Wear Sheets. Kusmierz, James P., illus. 80p. (Orig.). pap. 7.00 (ISBN 0-935604-02-2). Ivystone.
Friedhoffer & Brown, Harriet. How to Haunt a House for Halloween. Kaufman, Richard, illus. White, Timothy, photos by. (Illus.). 96p. (gr. 3 up). 1989. pap. 6.95 (ISBN 0-531-15122-0). Watts.
Ghosts & Poltergeists. 48p. (gr. 4-5). 1989. PLB 10.95 (ISBN 0-685-26162-X). Capstone Pr.
Hancock, Sibyl, adapted by. Esteban & the Ghost. (Illus.). 32p. (ps-3). 1985. pap. 3.95 (ISBN 0-8037-0230-2). Dial Bks Young.
Hoffman, Elizabeth P. This House Is Haunted! LC 77-10981. (Illus.). (gr. 4-5). 1977. PLB 14.65 (ISBN 0-8172-1033-4). Raintree Pubs.
Keene, Carolyn. Ghosts in the Gallery. LC 74-10467. (Illus.). 196p. (gr. 4-7). 1975. 2.95 (ISBN 0-448-09093-7, G&D). Putnam Pub Group.
Knight, David C. Best True Ghost Stories of the Twentieth Century. Waldman, Neil, illus. LC 83-23075. 64p. (gr. 3-7). 1984. PLB 11.95 (ISBN 0-671-66556-1). S&S Trade.
McSherry, Frank D., Jr., et al, eds. Western Ghosts. LC 90-8072. 224p. (Orig.). (gr. 8 up). 1990. pap. 9.95 (ISBN 1-558-53069-X). Rutledge Hill Pr.
Matthews, Rupert. Ghosts. Bragg, Michael, illus. LC 89-715. 48p. (gr. 4-6). 1989. PLB 12.40 (ISBN 0-531-18290-8). Watts.
Mayard. Ghosts. 32p. (gr. k-6). 1977. pap. 5.95 (ISBN 0-86020-148-1). EDC.

Nixon, Joan L. The Specter. LC 82-70322. 160p. (gr. 7 up). 1982. pap. 12.95 (ISBN 0-385-28948-0). Delacorte.

Reinstedt, Randall A. The Strange Case of the Ghosts of the Robert Louis Stevenson House. Bergez, John, ed. LC 88-81933. (Illus.). 70p. (gr. 3-6). 1988. lib. bdg. 9.95 (ISBN 0-933818-22-X). Ghost Town.

Riehecky, Janet. Haunted Houses. Halverson, Lydia & Siculan, Dan, illus. LC 88-38780. 100p. (gr. 3-7). 1989. PLB 12.96 (ISBN 0-89565-454-7); pap. 7.95 (ISBN 0-89565-534-9). Childs World.

Roberts, Nancy. America's Most Haunted Places. (Illus.). 95p. (gr. 5 up). 1987. pap. 5.95 (ISBN 0-87844-074-7). Sandlapper Pub Co.

—Ghosts & Specters of the Old South. Roberts, Bruce, photos by. LC 73-20909. (Illus.). 93p. (gr. 4-12). 1984. pap. 5.95 (ISBN 0-87844-058-5). Sandlapper Pub Co.

—Southern Ghosts. (Illus.). 72p. (gr. 5 up). 1987. pap. 5.95 (ISBN 0-87844-075-5). Sandlapper Pub Co.

Simon, Seymour. Ghosts. LC 75-37520. (gr. 1-3). 1976. (Pub. by Lipp Jr Bks); pap. 2.95 (ISBN 0-397-31665-8). HarpC Child Bks.

Smith, Curtis W. Spirits of London: A Psychobiography for Travelers. LC 87-91611. 108p. (Orig.). (gr. 11 up). 1988. pap. 4.95 (ISBN 0-944208-00-2). Seventh Wing Pubns.

Sotnak, Lewann. Haunted Houses. LC 89-70792. (Illus.). 48p. (gr. 5 up). 1990. 10.95 (ISBN 0-89686-508-8, Crestwood Hse). Macmillan Child Grp.

Stevenson, Drew. One Ghost Too Many: A Sarah Capshaw Mystery. Kelly, Kathleen M., illus. 128p. (gr. 4-6). 1991. 13.95 (ISBN 0-525-65052-0, Cobblehill Bks). Dutton Child Bks.

Stine, R. L. Haunted. MacDonald, Patricia, ed. 176p. (Orig.). (gr. 6-9). 1990. pap. 2.95 (ISBN 0-671-70242-4, Archway). PB.

Weinberg, Alyce T. Spirits of Frederick. LC 79-54039. (Illus.). 73p. (Orig.). 1979. pap. 3.95x (ISBN 0-9604552-0-5). A T Weinberg.

Windham, Kathryn T. Jeffrey Introduces Thirteen More Southern Ghosts. Foster, Sharon, illus. LC 70-170663. 128p. (gr. 6 up). 1987. pap. 9.50 (ISBN 0-8173-0381-2). U of Ala Pr.

—Jeffrey's Latest Thirteen: More Alabama Ghosts. Gilbert, John, illus. LC 82-50029. 147p. 1987. pap. 9.50 (ISBN 0-8173-0380-4). U of ala Pr.

—Thirteen Georgia Ghosts & Jeffrey. Lanier, Frances, illus. LC 73-87004. 154p. (gr. 6 up). 1987. pap. 9.50 (ISBN 0-8173-0377-4). U of Ala Pr.

—Thirteen Mississippi Ghosts & Jeffrey. Russell, H. R., illus. LC 74-15509. 148p. (gr. 6 up). 1987. pap. 9.50 (ISBN 0-8173-0379-0). U of Ala Pr.

—Thirteen Tennessee Ghosts & Jeffrey. Brogdon, Lecia, illus. LC 73-87004. 160p. (gr. 6 up). 1987. pap. 9.50 (ISBN 0-8173-0378-2). U of Ala Pr.

Windham, Kathryn T. & Figh, Margaret G. Thirteen Alabama Ghosts & Jeffrey. Atkins, Delores E., illus. LC 71-94443. 120p. (gr. 6 up). 1987. pap. 9.50 (ISBN 0-8173-0376-6). U of Ala Pr.

Word, Christine. Ghosts Along the Bayou: Tales of Haunted Places in Southwestern Louisiana. Fuchs, Jeff, illus. 160p. (gr. 6-12). 1988. 12.95 (ISBN 0-937614-09-2). Acadiana Pr.

Wright, Betty R. Christina's Ghost. 112p. (gr. 3-7). 1987. pap. 2.75 (ISBN 0-590-42709-1). Scholastic Inc.

GIANTS

Naden, C. J. I Can Read About All Kinds of Giants. LC 78-65833. (Illus.). (gr. 2-4). 1979. pap. 1.95 (ISBN 0-89375-201-0). Troll Assocs.

Rawson. Giants. (gr. k-4). 1980. 6.95 (ISBN 0-86020-339-5, Usborne-Hayes); pap. 3.95 (ISBN 0-86020-338-7). EDC.

GIANTS–FICTION

Allen, Linda, retold by. & illus. The Giant Who Had No Heart. 40p. (ps-3). 1988. 13.95 (ISBN 0-399-21446-1, Philomel Bks). Putnam Pub Group.

Carrick, Donald. Harald & the Giant Knight. 32p. (gr. 1-3). 1982. 14.95 (ISBN 0-89919-060-X, Clarion). HM.

Carroll, John. Donkey Nina & the Giant. Chamberlain, Sarah, illus. LC 88-33552. (gr. k-3). 1989. 12.95 (ISBN 0-525-44478-5, DCB). Dutton Child Bks.

Cincerelli, Carol J. The Selfish Giant by Oscar Wilde. 96p. (gr. 1-6). 1990. 8.95 (ISBN 0-86653-537-3, GA1158). Good Apple.

Cole, Brock. The Giant's Toe. LC 85-20569. 32p. (ps up). 1986. 13.95 (ISBN 0-374-32559-6). FS&G.

Coville, Bruce & Coville, Katherine. The Foolish Giant. LC 77-18522. (Illus.). (gr. k-2). 1978. PLB 12.89 (ISBN 0-397-31800-6, Lipp Jr Bks). HarpC Child Bks.

Dahl, Roald. The BFG. Blake, Quentin, illus. LC 85-566. 221p. (gr. 1 up). 1982. 14.95 (ISBN 0-374-30469-6). FS&G.

—The BFG. Blake, Quentin, illus. 1989. pap. 3.95 (ISBN 0-14-034019-X, Puffin). Puffin Bks.

Denan, Corinne. Giant Tales. LC 79-66330. (Illus.). 48p. (gr. 3-6). 1980. lib. bdg. 9.89 (ISBN 0-89375-328-9); pap. 2.95 (ISBN 0-89375-327-0). Troll Assocs.

—Tales of the Ugly Ogres. Craft, Kinuko Y., illus. LC 79-66333. 48p. (gr. 3-6). 1980. PLB 9.89 (ISBN 0-89375-332-7); pap. text ed. 2.95 (ISBN 0-89375-331-9). Troll Assocs.

De Paola, Tomie. The Mysterious Giant of Barletta. De Paola, Tomie, illus. LC 83-18445. 32p. (ps-3). 1988. pap. 3.95 (ISBN 0-15-256349-0, HJ). HarBraceJ.

De Regniers, Beatrice S. Jack the Giant Killer. Wilsdorf, Anne, illus. LC 86-3606. 32p. (gr. k-3). 1987. 12.95 (ISBN 0-689-31218-0, Atheneum Child Bk). Macmillan Child Grp.

Du Bois, William P. The Giant. (Orig.). (gr. k-6). 1987. pap. 4.95 (ISBN 0-440-42994-3, Pub. by Yearling Classics). Dell.

Feldman, Eve. A Giant Surprise. (Illus.). 32p. (gr. 1-4). 1989. PLB 13.32 (ISBN 0-8172-3527-2). Raintree Pubs.

Gaeddert, LouAnn. Gustav the Gourmet Giant. Kellog, Steven, illus. LC 76-2282. (ps-3). 1979. Repr. of 1976 ed. PLB 6.46 (ISBN 0-8037-3338-0). Dial Bks Young.

Galdone, Paul. Jack & the Beanstalk. Galdone, Paul, illus. LC 73-9726. 32p. (ps-3). 1982. pap. 4.95 (ISBN 0-89919-085-5, Pub. by Clarion). Ticknor & Fields.

The Giant's Child (EV, Unit 5. (gr. 2). 1991. 5-pack 21.25 (ISBN 0-88106-743-1). Charlesbridge Pub.

Goffe, Toni. Joe Giant's Missing Boot. 32p. 1990. 12.95 (ISBN 0-688-09532-1); PLB 12.88 (ISBN 0-688-09533-X). Lothrop.

Grater, Michael. On Sunday the Giant...; On Monday the Giant...; On Tuesday the Giant...; On Wednesday the Giant...; On Thursday the Giant...& On Friday the Giant.., 6 bks. Grater, Michael, illus. 84p. (gr. k-2). Set. pap. text ed. 28.90 (ISBN 1-55624-496-7, WG4975). Wright Group.

Green, John F. Alice & the Beauty Giant. 1990. pap. 12.95 (ISBN 0-590-43428-4). Scholastic Inc.

Haley, Patrick. The Little Person. Kool, Jonna, illus. LC 81-65114. 64p. (gr. 2-3). 1981. PLB 9.00 (ISBN 0-9605738-0-1). East Eagle.

Hayes, Sarah. Mary Mary. Craig, Helen, illus. LC 90-5964. 32p. (gr. k-3). 1990. 13.95 (ISBN 0-689-50514-0, M K McElderry). Macmillan Child Grp.

The Helpful Giant, Unit 5. (gr. 2). 1991. 5-pack 21.25 (ISBN 0-88106-745-8). Charlesbridge Pub.

Hughes, Ted. The Iron Giant: A Story in Five Nights. Zimmer, Dirk, illus. LC 87-45089. 64p. (gr. 3-7). 1988. 11.95 (ISBN 0-06-022638-2); PLB 11.89 (ISBN 0-06-022639-0). HarpC Child Bks.

—The Iron Giant: A Story in Five Nights. Zimmer, Dirk, illus. LC 87-45089. 64p. (gr. 3-7). 1988. pap. 3.95 (ISBN 0-06-440214-2, Trophy). HarpC Child Bks.

Kennedy, Richard. Inside My Feet: The Story of a Giant. Himler, Ronald, illus. LC 78-19479. 80p. (gr. 2-6). 1979. 8.61i (ISBN 0-06-023118-1); PLB 11.89 (ISBN 0-06-023119-X). HarpC Child Bks.

Kroll, Steven. Big Jeremy. Carrick, Donald, illus. LC 88-35812. 32p. (gr. k-3). 1989. reinforced bdg. 14.95 (ISBN 0-8234-0759-4). Holiday.

Martin, Melanie. Itsy-Bitsy Giant. Cushman, Doug, illus. LC 88-1234. 48p. (Orig.). (gr. 1-3). 1989. PLB 9.89 (ISBN 0-8167-1335-9); pap. text ed. 2.95 (ISBN 0-8167-1336-7). Troll Assocs.

Munsch, Robert. Giant. Tibo, Gilles, illus. 32p. (gr. k-3). 1989. 14.95 (ISBN 1-550370-71-5); pap. 5.95 (ISBN 1-550370-70-7). Firefly Bks Ltd.

Pene Du Bois, William. The Giant. (gr. 3-6). 15.50 (ISBN 0-8446-6379-4). Peter Smith.

Porter, Sue. Little Wolf & the Giant. (ps-1). 1990. pap. 13.95 (ISBN 0-671-70363-3). S&S Trade.

Ringi, Kjell. Stranger. Ringi, Kjell, illus. LC 68-23661. (ps-2). 1968. 3.95 (ISBN 0-394-81571-8). Random.

Root, Phyllis. Soup for Supper. Truesdell, Sue, illus. LC 85-45273. 32p. (ps-2). 1986. 12.95 (ISBN 0-06-025070-4); PLB 12.89 (ISBN 0-06-025071-2). HarpC Child Bks.

Wilde, Oscar. The Selfish Giant. Zwerger, Lisbeth, illus. LC 83-24930. 28p. (gr. 1 up). 1984. 15.95 (ISBN 0-907234-30-5). Picture Bk Studio.

—The Selfish Giant. LC 86-2593. 32p. (gr. 4 up). 1986. PLB 10.95s.p. (ISBN 0-88682-068-5); PLB 15.65 (ISBN 0-685-12416-9). Creative Ed.

—The Selfish Giant. Mansell, Dom, illus. LC 86-9356. 32p. (gr. 1-4). 1986. 10.95 (ISBN 0-13-803586-5). P-H.

—The Selfish Giant. Mansell, Dom, illus. 1986. PLB 10.95 (ISBN 0-671-66847-1). S&S Trade.

—The Selfish Giant. Zwerger, Lisbeth, illus. 1991. pap. 3.95 (ISBN 0-590-44460-3). Scholastic Inc.

Wilkes. Gulliver's Travels. (gr. 3-6). 1982. PLB 11.96 (ISBN 0-88110-064-1); pap. 3.95 (ISBN 0-86020-612-2). EDC.

Yorinks, Arthur. Sid & Sol. Egielski, Richard, illus. LC 77-24126. 32p. (ps up). 1977. 10.95 (ISBN 0-374-36904-6). FS&G.

GIBSON, ALTHEA, 1917-

Biracree, Tom. Althea Gibson. Horner, Matina, intro. by. (Illus.). 112p. (gr. 5 up). 1990. lib. bdg. 17.95 (ISBN 1-55546-654-0). Chelsea Hse.

Fago, John N. & Farr, Naunerle C. Jim Thorpe - Althea Gibson. Redondo, Frank & Carrillo, Fred, illus. (gr. 4-12). 1979. pap. text ed. 2.95 (ISBN 0-88301-360-6); wkbk. 1.25 (ISBN 0-88301-384-3). Pendulum Pr.

GIFTED CHILDREN–FICTION

Levy, Nathan & Levy, Janet. There Are Those. Edwards, Joan, illus. LC 82-81111. 32p. (ps up). 1990. 21.95 (ISBN 0-9608240-0-6). NL Assoc Inc.
If you have gifted children in your life, this book "There Are Those," will put their special qualities into poetic words for you. The joy, excitement, challenge & frustration that the very bright children bring to themselves & to those around them are brought alive in this highly acclaimed poem. This hardcover book is illustrated with brilliant designs in vivid color. Destined to become a classic, this book will be loved by children from 8-88!
Publisher Provided Annotation.

Rimm, Sylvia B. & Priest, Christine. Gifted Kids Have Feelings Too: And Other Not-So-Fictitious Stories for & about Teenagers. Maas, Katherine, illus. LC 90-81442. 162p. (Orig.). (gr. 6-12). 1990. pap. text ed. 15.00 (ISBN 0-937891-06-1); pap. text ed. 15.00 discussion book (ISBN 0-937891-07-X). Apple Pub Wisc.

Warren, Sandra, ed. Being Gifted: Because You're Special from the Rest. 68p. (Orig.). (ps-6). 1987. pap. 9.99 (ISBN 0-89824-173-1). Trillium Pr.

GIFTS

Amoss, Berthe. Car Seat Games. (Illus.). 10p. (ps-7). 1989. pap. 2.95 (ISBN 0-922589-14-3). More Than Card.

Cheng, Andrea. Let's Make a Present! Easy to Make Gifts for Friends & Relatives of Any Age. Macdonald, Roland B. & Gray, Dan, illus. 128p. (gr. k-5). 1991. pap. 9.95 (ISBN 1-878767-16-X). Murdoch Bks.
"Did you make this? For me!" In an age of mass-produced toys nothing stands out like a present the giver has made especially for a friend. Andrea Cheng presents wonderful projects for you & your child to make, so your child can proudly proclaim, "& I made it for you, all by myself!" Each section of the book describes the right sort of present to make for children of different ages. In learning about what sorts of presents are appropriate for different children, your child will also learn a great deal about herself--why shapes & colors are important for newborns, why intricate patterns will frustrate a preschooler & so on. The presents described in the book are easy to make & generally don't require expensive materials. The book includes full-sized patterns, step-by-step instructions & color illustrations, so making the perfect present is easy--even if you've never been a "craft mom."
Publisher Provided Annotation.

Silbert, Linda P. & Silbert, Alvin J. The Wonderful World of Gift Giving. (gr. 3-7). 1983. wkbk. 4.98 (ISBN 0-89544-024-5). Silbert Bress.

Sullivan, Dianna J. Gifts for Holidays & Everyday. Adkins, Lynda, illus. 96p. (gr. k-4). 1987. wkbk. 9.95 (ISBN 1-55734-091-9). Tchr Create Mat.

Wilkes, A. & Rosen, C. Making Presents. (Illus.). 14p. (gr. 2-6). 1986. pap. 4.50 (ISBN 0-7460-0123-1). EDC.

GIFTS–FICTION

Better Homes & Gardens Editors. The Best-Ever Gift. 32p. Date not set. 4.95 (ISBN 0-696-01901-9). Meredith Bks.

Bunting, Eve. The Mother's Day Mice. Brett, Jan, illus. LC 85-13991. (ps-3). 1986. 12.95 (ISBN 0-89919-387-0, Pub. by Clarion). Ticknor & Fields.

Delton, Judy. No Time for Christmas. Mitchell, Anastasia, illus. 48p. (gr. k-4). 1988. PLB 9.95 (ISBN 0-87614-327-3); pap. 4.95 (ISBN 0-87614-503-9). Carolrhoda Bks.

—No Time for Christmas. Mitchell, Anastasia, illus. 48p. (gr. k-4). 1989. pap. 4.95 (ISBN 0-685-25640-5, First Ave Edns). Lerner Pubns.

Emberley, Michael. Present, Vol. 1. (ps-3). 1991. 14.95 (ISBN 0-316-23411-7). Little.

Hansen, Joyce. The Gift-Giver. (gr. 3-6). 1989. pap. 3.95 (ISBN 0-89919-852-X, Pub. by Clarion). Ticknor & Fields.

Holroyd, Angela. Lost Present. 1990. 4.98 (ISBN 0-8317-5649-7). Smithmark.

Kiser, SuAnn & Kiser, Kevin. The Birthday Thing. Abolafia, Yossi, illus. LC 87-38085. 24p. (gr. k up). 1989. 11.95 (ISBN 0-688-07772-2); PLB 11.88 (ISBN 0-688-07773-0). Greenwillow.

Kushner, Donn. The Violin-Maker's Gift. Panton, Doug, illus. LC 81-19406. 74p. (gr. 2 up). 1982. 8.95 (ISBN 0-374-38155-0). FS&G.

Little, Lessie J. & Greenfield, Eloise. I Can Do It by Myself. Byard, Carole, illus. LC 77-11554. (gr. k-2). 1978. 14.95 (ISBN 0-690-01369-8, Crowell Jr Bks); PLB 14.89 (ISBN 0-690-03851-8). HarpC Child Bks.

Marzollo, Jean. Best Present Ever. 1989. pap. 2.50 (ISBN 0-590-42724-5). Scholastic Inc.

O. Henry. Gift of the Magi. Wheeler, Jody, illus. 24p. (ps-3). 1989. pap. 2.95 (ISBN 0-8249-8388-2). Ideals.

Palumbo, Nancy. A Birthday Present for Ree-Ree: Un Cadeau d'Anniversaire Pour Ree-Ree. Weaver, Judith, illus. 32p. (Orig.). (ps-6). 1989. wkbk. 5.95 (ISBN 0-927024-15-2). Crayons Pubns.

—A Birthday Present for Ree-Ree: Un Regalo Cumpleanos Para Ree-Ree. Weaver, Judith, illus. 32p. (Orig.). (gr. k-6). 1989. wkbk. 5.95 (ISBN 0-927024-14-4). Crayons Pubns.

Patterson, Nancy R. The Christmas Cup. Bowman, Leslie, illus. LC 88-29112. 80p. (gr. 3-5). 1989. 13.95 (ISBN 0-531-05821-2); PLB 13.99 (ISBN 0-531-08421-3). Orchard Bks Watts.

Rinehart, Kimberly R. The Greatest Gift of All. Rettmer, Georgia M., illus. 70p. 1987. 12.95 (ISBN 0-942865-02-2). It Takes Two.

Rodanas, Kristina. The Story of Wali Dad. Rodanas, Kristina, illus. LC 86-34423. 32p. (gr. k-3). 1988. 13.95 (ISBN 0-688-07262-3); PLB 13.88 (ISBN 0-688-07263-1). Lothrop.

Williams, Vera B. Something Special for Me. LC 82-11884. (Illus.). (ps-3). 1986. 4.95 (ISBN 0-688-06526-0, Mulberry). Morrow.

Wolf, Janet. The Best Present Is Me. LC 82-48853. (Illus.). 32p. (gr. k-3). 1984. HarpC Child Bks.

GILBRETH FAMILY

Gilbreth, Frank B. & Carey, Ernestine G. Cheaper by the Dozen. rev. ed. Vasiliy, illus. LC 63-20411. (gr. 7 up). 1963. 15.45i (ISBN 0-690-18632-0, Crowell Jr Bks). HarperCollins.

GIPSIES

see Gypsies

GIRAFFES

Arnold, Caroline. Giraffe. Hewett, Richard, illus. LC 87-1502. 48p. (gr. 2-5). 1987. 12.95 (ISBN 0-688-07069-8); lib. bdg. 12.88 (ISBN 0-688-07070-1, Morrow Jr Bks). Morrow Jr Bks.

Green, Carl R. & Sanford, William R. The Giraffes. LC 87-1363. (Illus.). 48p. (gr. 5-6). 1987. PLB 10.95 (ISBN 0-89686-332-8, Crestwood Hse). Macmillan Child Grp.

Hoffman, Mary. Giraffe. LC 86-6770. (Illus.). 24p. (gr. k-5). 1986. PLB 13.32 (ISBN 0-8172-2397-5). Raintree Pubs.

Propper. Giraffe, Reading Level 3-4. (Illus.). 28p. (gr. 2-5). Date not set. PLB 14.60 (ISBN 0-86592-860-6). Rourke Corp.

Sattler, Helen R. Giraffes: The Sentinels of the Savannas. Santoro, Christopher, illus. LC 89-2287. 80p. (gr. 3 up). 1990. 14.95 (ISBN 0-688-08284-X); PLB 14.88 (ISBN 0-688-08285-8). Lothrop.

Stone, Lynn. Giraffes. (Illus.). 24p. (gr. k-5). 1990. lib. bdg. 14.60 (ISBN 0-86593-050-3); lib. bdg. 8.95s.p. (ISBN 0-685-36346-5). Rourke Corp.

Wildlife Education, Ltd. Staff. Giraffes. Francis, John, et al, illus. 20p. (Orig.). (gr. 5 up). 1982. pap. 2.25 (ISBN 0-937934-09-7). Wildlife Educ.

GIRAFFES–FICTION

Dahl, Roald. The Giraffe & the Pelly & Me. Blake, Quentin, illus. LC 85-47593. 32p. (gr. 2 up). 1985. 11.95 (ISBN 0-374-32602-9). FS&G.

Dartez, Cecilia C. Jenny Giraffe Discovers the French Quarter. Wilson, Shelby, illus. 32p. (ps-8). 1991. 11.95 (ISBN 0-88289-819-1). Pelican.

Grandma, Marian, pseud. Georgie the Jovial Giraffe. Sott, Donna, illus. LC 85-71331. 32p. (gr. 3 up). 1985. text ed. write for info. (ISBN 0-9614989-0-0). Banmar Inc.

Hammond, Jane. Ginger the Giraffe. (ps-k). 1983. pap. 1.50 (ISBN 0-87162-289-0, D5603). Warner Pr.

Hunt, Robert. Necki the African Giraffe. Producciones Ancora, illus. LC 72-736445. (gr. 2-5). 1978. 6 bks. & 1 cass. 29.95 (ISBN 0-89290-030-X); 1 bk. & 1 cass. 10.95. Soc for Visual.

Rey, H. A. Cecily G. & the Nine Monkeys. Rey, H. A., illus. 32p. (gr. 1-3). 1974. 12.95 (ISBN 0-395-18430-4). HM.

GIRL SCOUTS

Cadette & Senior Girl Scout Interest Projects. (Illus.). 160p. (gr. 6-12). 1987. pap. 5.50 (ISBN 0-88441-343-8, 20-792). Girl Scouts USA.

Games for Girl Scouts. (Illus.). 128p. (ps up). 1990. pap. 6.00 (ISBN 0-88441-347-0, 20-902). Girl Scouts USA.

Girl Scout Badges & Signs. (Illus.). 250p. (gr. 3-7). 1990. pap. 5.75 (ISBN 0-88441-346-2, 20-900). Girl Scouts USA.

Girl Scouts of the U. S. A. Staff. More Brownie Girl Scout Try-Its. (Illus.). 88p. (gr. 1-3). 1989. pap. 4.00 (ISBN 0-88441-345-4, 20-784). Girl Scouts USA.

—Sing Together: A Girl Scout Songbook. (Illus.). 192p. (gr. 1-12). 1973. spiral bdg. 7.50 (ISBN 0-88441-309-8, 20-206). Girl Scouts USA.

Kudlinski, Kathleen V. Juliette Gordon Low: America's First Girl Scout. Hamanaka, Sheila, illus. (gr. 2-6). 1988. pap. 10.95 (ISBN 0-670-82208-6). Viking Child Bks.

Outdoor Education in Girl Scouting. (Illus.). 172p. (gr. 6-12). 1984. pap. 7.00 (26-217). Girl Scouts USA.

Steelsmith, Shari. Juliette Gordon Low: Founder of the Girl Scouts. Pope, Connie J., illus. LC 89-62673. 32p. (Orig.). (ps-4). 1990. lib. bdg. 15.95 (ISBN 0-943990-37-8); pap. 5.95 (ISBN 0-943990-36-X). Parenting Pr.

World Association of Girl Guides & Girl Scouts Staff. Trefoil Round the World. rev. ed. (Illus.). 392p. (gr. 4-12). 1986. 7.00 (ISBN 0-900827-41-6, 23-962). Girl Scouts USA.

GIRL SCOUTS–FICTION

Greenwald, Sheila. It All Began with Jane Eyre: Or, the Secret Life of Franny Dillman. (Illus.). (gr. 3-7). 1980. 14.95 (ISBN 0-316-32671-2, Joy St Bks). Little.

GIRL SCOUTS–HANDBOOKS, MANUALS, ETC

Brownie Girl Scout Handbook. (Illus.). 192p. (gr. 1-3). 1986. pap. 5.00 (ISBN 0-88441-337-3, 20-787). Girl Scouts USA.

Cadette & Senior Girl Scout Handbook. (Illus.). 176p. (gr. 6-12). 1987. pap. 7.00 (ISBN 0-88441-342-X, 20-791). Girl Scouts USA.

Girl Scouts of the U. S. A. Staff. Wide World of Girl Guiding & Girl Scouting. (Illus.). 88p. (gr. 1-6). 1980. pap. text ed. 7.00 (ISBN 0-88441-143-5, 19-713). Girl Scouts USA.

GIRLS

Blair, L. E. Peer Pressure Girl Talk, No. 9. 1991. pap. 2.95 (ISBN 0-307-22009-5). Western Pub.

Cleary, Beverly. A Girl from Yamhill. (gr. k-6). 1989. pap. 3.95 (ISBN 0-440-40185-2, YB). Dell.

—A Girl from Yamhill: A Memoir. LC 87-31554. (Illus.). 320p. (gr. 7 up). 1988. 15.95 (ISBN 0-688-07800-1). Morrow Jr Bks.

Coerr, Eleanor. Sadako & the Thousand Paper Cranes. Himler, Ronald, illus. 64p. (gr. 2-5). 1979. pap. 2.95 (ISBN 0-440-47465-5, YB). Dell.

Filichia, Peter. A Boy's-Eye View of Girls. 128p. (Orig.). (gr. 7 up). 1983. pap. 1.95 (ISBN 0-590-32314-8). Scholastic Inc.

Forrester, Victoria. Poor Gabriella: A Christmas Story. Boulet, Susan B., illus. LC 86-3607. 32p. 1986. 13.95 (ISBN 0-689-31265-2, Atheneum Child Bk). Macmillan Child Grp.

Galicich, Anne. Samantha Smith: A Journey for Peace. LC 87-13614. (Illus.). 64p. (gr. 3 up). 1987. PLB 10.95 (ISBN 0-87518-367-0, Dillon). Macmillan Child Grp.

Lukes, Bonnie L. How to Be a Reasonably Thin Teenage Girl (Without Starving, Losing Your Friends, or Running Away from Home) Niclaus, Carol, illus. LC 86-3347. 96p. (gr. 6 up). 1986. 12.95 (ISBN 0-689-31269-5, Atheneum). Macmillan Child Grp.

Madaras, Lynda & Madaras, Area. Lynda Madaras' Growing-Up Guide for Girls. Aher, Jackie, illus. LC 86-23719. 224p. (gr. 4-10). 1986. 16.95 (ISBN 0-937858-87-0); pap. 9.95 (ISBN 0-937858-74-9). Newmarket.

Marzollo, Jean. Getting Your Period: A Book about Menstruation. Williams, Kent, illus. Storch, Marcia, intro. by. LC 88-3986. (Illus.). 112p. (gr. 4 up). 1989. 13.95 (ISBN 0-8037-0355-4); 6.95 (ISBN 0-8037-0356-2). Dial Bks Young.

Rau, Margaret. Young Women in China. LC 88-31045. (Illus.). 160p. (gr. 6 up). 1989. PLB 18.95 (ISBN 0-89490-170-2). Enslow Pubs.

Rodowsky, Colby. Julie's Daughter. LC 85-47589. 231p. (gr. 7 up). 1985. 13.95 (ISBN 0-374-33963-5). FS&G.

Setterlund, Donna J. A Dream & a Promise: From a Child to a Woman with a Mother's Help along the Way. (Illus.). 240p. (gr. 8 up). 1990. write for info. (ISBN 0-9624342-2-1); pap. write for info. Carriage Hse Studio Pubns.

Weston, Carol. Girltalk: All the Stuff Your Sister Never Told You. 1985. pap. 8.95 (ISBN 0-06-463711-5, B&N Bks). HarperCollins.

Yothers, Tina & Plutzik, Roberta. Being Your Best: Tina Yothers' Guide for Girls. (gr. 4-7). 1987. pap. 2.50 (ISBN 0-671-63128-4, Archway). PB.

GIRLS–EMPLOYMENT

see Child Labor

GIRLS–FICTION

Adams, Laurie. Alice Whipple Shapes Up. (gr. 4-7). 1990. pap. 2.75 (ISBN 0-553-15803-1). Bantam.

Adler, C. S. Carly's Buck. LC 86-17183. 160p. (gr. 4-8). 1987. 12.95 (ISBN 0-89919-480-X). Ticknor & Fields.

—If You Need Me. LC 87-36467. 160p. (gr. 4-8). 1988. 12.95 (ISBN 0-02-700420-1, Mcmillan Child Bk). Macmillan Child Grp.

Adler, Susan S. Meet Samantha: An American Girl. Lusk, Nancy M., illus. LC 86-60467. 61p. (Orig.). (gr. 2-5). 1986. 12.95 (ISBN 0-937295-03-5); pap. 5.95 (ISBN 0-937295-04-3). Pleasant Co.

—Meet Samantha: An American Girl. Thieme, Jeanne, ed. Niles, Nancy, illus. 72p. (gr. 2-5). 1990. PLB 12.95 (ISBN 0-937295-80-9). Pleasant Co.

—Samantha Learns a Lesson: A School Story. Lusk, Nancy N., illus. LC 86-60624. 61p. (Orig.). (gr. 2-5). 1986. 12.95 (ISBN 0-937295-12-4); pap. 5.95 (ISBN 0-937295-13-2). Pleasant Co.

—Samantha Learns a Lesson: A School Story. Thieme, Jeanne, ed. Niles, Nancy, illus. 72p. (gr. 2-5). 1990. PLB 12.95 (ISBN 0-937295-83-3). Pleasant Co.

Adler, Susan S., et al. Samantha's Boxed Set, 6 bks. (Illus.). 432p. (gr. 2-5). 1990. Boxed set. pap. 34.95 (ISBN 0-937295-77-9). Pleasant Co.

Agee, Una S. Gertrude's Salad & Other Stories. 32p. (ps-8). 1991. 6.95 (ISBN 0-8062-3999-9). Carlton.

Agnew, Robin. Rebecca of Grand Hotel. Agnew, Robin, illus. 72p. 1990. text ed. 15.95 (ISBN 0-9627301-0-6). Grand Hotel.

Ai-Ling, Louie, retold by. Yeh-Shen: A Cinderella Story from China. Young, Ed, illus. (ps-3). 1988. pap. 4.95 (ISBN 0-399-21594-8, Sandcastle Bks). Putnam Pub Group.

Akiko Sueyoshi. Jessica's Friend. Young, Richard G., ed. Kaisei-sha, tr. Akiko Hayashi, illus. LC 89-12050. 32p. (gr. 1-3). 1989. PLB 13.26 (ISBN 0-944483-47-X). Garrett Ed Corp.

Albright, Molly. Video Stars. Connor, Eulala, illus. LC 88-15880. 96p. (gr. 3-6). 1988. PLB 9.89 (ISBN 0-8167-1480-0); pap. text ed. 2.95 (ISBN 0-8167-1481-9). Troll Assocs.

Alcott, Louisa May. An Old-Fashioned Girl. (Orig.). (gr. k-6). 1987. pap. 4.95 (ISBN 0-440-46609-1, Pub. by Yearling Classics). Dell.

—Rose in Bloom. (gr. k-6). 1986. pap. 4.95 (ISBN 0-440-47588-0, YB). Dell.

—Rose in Bloom. 336p. (gr. 5 up). 1989. pap. 2.95 (ISBN 0-14-035125-6, Puffin). Puffin Bks.

Alexander, Martha. Sabrina. Alexander, Martha, illus. LC 72-134855. 32p. (ps-2). 1991. pap. 2.95 (ISBN 0-8037-0842-4, Dial Pied Piper). Puffin Bks.

Allard, Harry & Marshall, James. Miss Nelson Is Back. (Illus.). (gr. k-3). 1982. 13.95 (ISBN 0-395-32956-6); pap. 3.95 (ISBN 0-395-41668-X). HM.

Allee, Marjorie H. Jane's Island. De Gogorza, Maitland, illus. 236p. (gr. 6 up). 1988. Repr. of 1931 ed. 13.95 (ISBN 0-9611374-2-8). Woods Hole Hist.

Allen, Jeffrey. Mary Alice Returns. Marshall, James, illus. (ps-3). 1986. lib. bdg. 13.95i (ISBN 0-316-03429-0). Little.

Alter, Judy. Maggie & Devildust Ridin' High. Shaw, Charles, illus. LC 89-2683. 176p. (Orig.). (gr. 4-9). 1990. pap. 5.95 (ISBN 0-936650-10-9). E C Temple.

Alvarez, Julia. How the Garcia Girls Lost Their Accents. 308p. (gr. 10 up). 1991. 16.95 (ISBN 0-945575-57-2). Algonquin Bks.

Amadio, Nadine. The New Adventures of Alice in Rainforest Land. Blackman, Charles, illus. 80p. 7.95 (ISBN 0-9587845-3-1, AA07, Pub. by Mad Hatter Bks). Slawson Comm.

Ammon, Richard. Growing up Amish. LC 88-27493. (Illus.). 80p. (gr. 3 up). 1989. 12.95 (ISBN 0-689-31387-X, Atheneum Child Bk). Macmillan Child Grp.

Anders, Jeanne. Leslie. LC 86-72892. 160p. (gr. 9 up). 1987. pap. 3.95 (ISBN 0-87123-927-2). Bethany Hse.

Andersen, Hans Christian. The Little Match Girl. Erickson, Jon, retold by. Morgansen, Jan, illus. LC 87-42585. 32p. (gr. 2-4). 1987. PLB 10.95 (ISBN 1-55532-317-0). Gareth Stevens Inc.

—The Little Match Girl. Isadora, Rachel, illus. 32p. (ps-3). 1990. pap. 5.95 (ISBN 0-399-22007-0, Putnam). Putnam Pub Group.

—Thumbelina. Demi, adapted by. & illus. 32p. (ps-3). 1989. 13.95 (ISBN 0-396-09241-1, G&D). Putnam Pub Group.

Anderson, Margaret J. Searching for Shona. LC 77-17056. 160p. (gr. 4-7). 1989. pap. 2.95 (ISBN 0-394-82587-X, Bullseye Bks). Knopf.

Angell, Judie. Dear Lola: How to Build Your Own Family. 144p. (gr. 5-9). 1986. pap. 1.95 (ISBN 0-440-91787-5, LFL). Dell.

—Tina Gogo. 160p. (gr. 5 up). 1980. pap. 1.75 (ISBN 0-440-98738-5, LFL). Dell.

Aragon, Jane Chelsea. Winter Harvest. Baker, Leslie, illus. LC 87-26489. (ps-3). 1989. 14.95 (ISBN 0-316-04937-9). Little.

Argiroff, Louise. Pollen Pie. Argiroff, Louise, illus. LC 87-3462. 32p. (gr. k-4). 1988. 13.95 (ISBN 0-689-31359-4, Atheneum Child Bk). Macmillan Child Grp.

Armstrong, Jennifer. Hilary to the Rescue. (gr. 3-6). 1990. pap. 2.75 (ISBN 0-553-15812-0). Bantam.

Arrick, Fran. Nice Girl from Good Home. 208p. (gr. 7 up). 1986. pap. 2.75 (ISBN 0-440-96358-3, LFL). Dell.

—Steffie Can't Come Out to Play. 160p. (gr. 7 up). 1979. pap. 2.50 (ISBN 0-440-97635-9, LFL). Dell.

Asher, Sandy. Mary in the Middle. Tang, Susan & Weatherbee, illus. 64p. (gr. 2-4). 1990. pap. 2.50 (ISBN 0-590-43836-0). Scholastic Inc.

Auch, Mary Jane. Glass Slippers Give You Blisters. 1990. pap. 2.75 (ISBN 0-590-43501-9). Scholastic Inc.

Austen, Carrie. Becky's Super Secret. (gr. 4-7). 1990. pap. 2.75 (ISBN 0-425-12131-3). Berkley Pub.

—Julie's Outrageous Idea. (gr. 4-7). 1991. pap. 3.75 (ISBN 0-425-12552-1). Berkley Pub.

—Party Line, No. 8: Rosie's Mystery on Ice. 1990. pap. 2.75 (ISBN 0-425-12440-1). Berkley Pub.

—Party Line, No. 9. 1991. pap. 2.75 (ISBN 0-425-12486-X). Berkley Pub.

—Rosie's Popularity Plan. 1990. pap. 2.75 (ISBN 0-425-12169-0). Berkley Pub.

Avi. Bright Shadow. LC 88-3339. 176p. (gr. 6-9). 1988. pap. 3.95 (ISBN 0-689-71256-1, Aladdin). Macmillan Child Grp.

Babbitt, Natalie. Phoebe's Revolt. (Illus.). 40p. (ps up). 1988. pap. 3.95 (ISBN 0-374-45792-1). FS&G.

Baer, Judy. Adrienne. LC 87-71605. 176p. (Orig.). (gr. 7-12). 1987. pap. 3.95 (ISBN 0-87123-949-3). Bethany Hse.

—The Intruder. 160p. (Orig.). (gr. 7 up). 1989. pap. 3.95 (ISBN 1-55661-088-2). Bethany Hse.

—Jennifer's Secret. LC 88-63463. 128p. (Orig.). (gr. 6 up). 1989. pap. 3.95 (ISBN 1-55661-058-0). Bethany Hse.

Balian, Lorna. Amelia's Nine Lives. LC 85-30835. (gr. 5-8). 1986. 13.95 (ISBN 0-687-01250-3); PLB 5.95 (ISBN 0-687-37096-5). Abingdon.

Ball, Nancy. Shy Ann. Christie, Robert D., illus. LC 88-51305. 55p. (Orig.). (gr. k-4). 1989. pap. 3.95 (ISBN 0-931563-03-8). Wishing Rm.
Balzola, Asun. Munia & the Red Shoes. (Illus.). 1989. 11.95 (ISBN 0-521-37142-2). Cambridge U Pr.
Bang, Molly. Delphine. Bang, Molly, illus. LC 87-34958. 32p. (gr. 2 up). 1988. 12.95 (ISBN 0-688-05636-9); PLB 12.88 (ISBN 0-688-05637-7, Morrow Jr Bks). Morrow Jr Bks.
Barbour, Karen. Nancy. (Illus.). (ps-3). 1989. 13.95 (ISBN 0-15-256675-9). HarBraceJ.
Barkan, Joanne. Anna Marie's Blanket. Maze, Deborah, illus. 32p. 1990. 12.95 (ISBN 0-8120-6124-1). Barron.
Barker, Julia. Jenny & Sukey. 1990. 6.95 (ISBN 0-533-08906-9). Vantage.
Bauer, Caroline F. Too Many Books! Paterson, Diane, illus. 32p. (ps-3). 1986. pap. 3.95 (ISBN 0-14-050632-2, Puffin). Puffin Bks.
Baum, L. Frank. Patchwork Girl of Oz. 1990. pap. 6.95 (ISBN 0-486-26514-5). Dover.
Bawden, Nina. The Outside Child. LC 88-27349. (Illus.). 160p. (gr. 4-9). 1989. 12.95 (ISBN 0-688-08965-8). Lothrop.
Bayer, Jane. A, My Name Is Alice. Kellogg, Steven, illus. LC 84-7059. 32p. (ps-2). 1987. pap. 4.95 (ISBN 0-8037-0130-6). Dial Bks Young.
Beatty, Patricia. Be Ever Hopeful Hannalee. 216p. (gr. 5-9). 1990. pap. 2.95 (ISBN 0-8167-2259-5). Troll Assocs.
—Sarah & Me & Lady from the Sea. LC 89-33624. 224p. (gr. 5 up). 1989. 11.95 (ISBN 0-688-08045-6). Morrow Jr Bks.
—Turn Homeward, Hannalee. 193p. (gr. 5-9). 1990. pap. 2.95 (ISBN 0-8167-2260-9). Troll Assocs.
Becker, Lois & Stratton, Mark. Mistress Mary. Alchemy II, Inc. Staff, illus. 26p. (ps). Date not set. incl. cassette 9.95 (ISBN 1-55578-920-X). Worlds Wonder.
Bee, Cindy. A Big House, a Little Girl & a Few Things That Made Them Laugh. Jesionowski, Mary & Schnickel, Jacob, illus. 20p. (Orig.). (ps-5). 1990. pap. 2.75 (ISBN 0-9616308-1-7). Hearthstn Inn.
Beiler, Edna. Mattie Mae. Graber, E. R., illus. LC 67-24800. 128p. (gr. 3-7). 1967. pap. 3.95 (ISBN 0-8361-1789-1). Herald Pr.
Bemelmans, Ludwig. Madeline's House: Includes: Madeline; Madeline's Rescue; Madeline & the Bad Hat. Bemelmans, Ludwig, illus. (ps-3). 1989. pap. 11.95 (ISBN 0-14-095028-1, Puffin). Puffin Bks.
Benson, B. J. Tandy. LC 88-50930. 179p. 1989. pap. 6.95 (ISBN 1-55523-169-1). Winston-Derek.
Benziger, John. The Corpuscles: Adventurers in Inner Space. Benziger, John & Benziger, Mary, illus. LC 88-92390. 64p. (gr. k-6). 1989. 11.95 (ISBN 0-9620961-0-5). Corpuscles Intergalactica.
Bernard, Elizabeth. Satin Slippers: Temptations. (gr. 6 up). 1988. pap. 2.95 (ISBN 0-449-14543-3). Fawcett.
Blackmore, R. D. Lorna Doone. (gr. 9-12). 1991. pap. text ed. 4.87 (ISBN 0-582-01814-5, 78332). Longman.
Blackmore, Richard. Lorna Doone. 345p. 1981. Repr. PLB 23.95 (ISBN 0-89966-350-8). Buccaneer Bks.
Blaine, Marge. The Terrible Thing That Happened at Our House. Wallner, John C., illus. 32p. (gr. 1-4). 1991. pap. 3.95 (ISBN 0-590-42371-1). Scholastic Inc.
Blair, Cynthia. Starstruck. (gr. 6 up). 1986. pap. 2.95 (ISBN 0-449-70218-9, Juniper). Fawcett.
Blakeslee, Ann R. After the Fortune Cookies. 128p. (gr. 3-7). 1990. pap. 2.75 (ISBN 0-590-43947-2). Scholastic Inc.
Blaustein, Muriel. Lola Koala & the Ten Times Worse Than Anything. Blaustein, Muriel, illus. LC 86-22811. 32p. (ps-2). 1987. 7.95 (ISBN 0-694-00220-8); PLB 11.89 (ISBN 0-06-020539-3). HarpC Child Bks.
Blegvad, Lenore. Anna Banana & Me. Blegvad, Erik, illus. LC 84-547. 32p. (gr. k-3). 1985. 12.95 (ISBN 0-689-50274-5, M K McElderry). Macmillan Child Grp.
Blos, Joan W. A Gathering of Days: A New England Girl's Journal, 1830-1832. LC 90-32. 160p. (gr. 3-7). 1990. pap. 3.95 (ISBN 0-689-71419-X, Aladdin). Macmillan Child Grp.
Bloss, Janet A. The Girl with Green Hair. (Illus.). 125p. (Orig.). (gr. 3-6). 1989. pap. text ed. 2.50 (ISBN 0-87406-416-3). Willowisp Pr.
Blume, Judy. Are You There, God? It's Me, Margaret. 156p. (gr. 5-8). 1972. pap. 3.50 (ISBN 0-440-40419-3, YB). Dell.
—Blubber. LC 73-94116. 160p. (gr. 4-6). 1982. 12.95 (ISBN 0-02-711010-9, Bradbury Pr). Macmillan Child Grp.
—Deenie. LC 73-80197. 192p. (gr. 6-8). 1982. 13.95 (ISBN 0-02-711020-6, Bradbury Pr). Macmillan Child Grp.
—Judy Blume: Judy Blume & You, Friends for Life, 4 vols. (gr. 4-7). 1990. pap. 12.65 boxed set (ISBN 0-440-36013-7). Dell.
—Otherwise Known As Sheila the Great. 128p. (gr. 3-6). 1976. pap. 3.50 (ISBN 0-440-46701-2, YB). Dell.
—Starring Sally J. Freedman As Herself. LC 76-57805. 296p. (gr. 4-7). 1982. 14.95 (ISBN 0-02-711070-2, Bradbury Pr). Macmillan Child Grp.
Bobo, Carmen P. Sarah's Growing-up Summer. LC 88-62111. 52p. 1989. 5.95 (ISBN 1-55523-187-X). Winston-Derek.
Bodecker, N. M. Hurry, Hurry, Mary Dear! LC 76-14841. (Illus.). 128p. 1976. text ed. 10.95 (Pub. by M K McElderry). Macmillan Child Grp.
Bograd, Larry. Poor Gertie. Zimmer, Dirk, illus. LC 86-3091. 96p. (gr. 3-6). 1986. pap. 12.95 (ISBN 0-385-29487-5). Delacorte.
Boissard, Janine. Cecile. (gr. 9 up). 1989. pap. 2.95 (ISBN 0-449-70338-X, Juniper). Fawcett.
Borntrager, Mary C. Rebecca. 176p. (Orig.). (gr. 8-12). 1989. pap. 5.95 (ISBN 0-8361-3500-8). Herald Pr.
Bottner, Barbara. Nothing in Common. LC 85-45834. 176p. (gr. 7 up). 1986. 12.95 (ISBN 0-06-020604-7). HarpC Child Bks.
Bourgeois, Paulette. Big Sarah's Little Boots. Clark, Brenda, illus. 1992. pap. 3.95 (ISBN 0-590-42623-0). Scholastic Inc.
Boutis, Victoria. Looking Out. LC 87-36455. 144p. (gr. 5-9). 1988. 12.95 (ISBN 0-02-711830-4, Four Winds). Macmillan Child Grp.
Boyd, Candy D. Charlie Pippin. LC 86-23780. 192p. (gr. 3-7). 1987. 13.95 (ISBN 0-02-726350-9, Mcmillan Child Bk). Macmillan Child Grp.
Bracken, Carolyn, illus. The Little Frosty Library: Frosty Stocking Stuffer Books. (ps-k). 1987. Four slipcased books - Frosty & the Christmas Kitten; Frosty & the Ice Skates; Frosty & the Christmas Dinner; Frosty & the New Hat. 6.95 (ISBN 0-671-92412-5, Little Simon). S&S Trade.
Bradford, Jan. Caroline Zucker Makes a Big Mistake. Ramsey, Marcy, illus. LC 90-11160. 96p. (gr. 2-5). 1990. PLB 9.89 (ISBN 0-8167-2023-1); pap. text ed. 2.95 (ISBN 0-8167-2024-X). Troll Assocs.
Bradman, Tony. Dilly Tells the Truth. Hellard, Susan, illus. 64p. (gr. 2-5). 1988. pap. 10.95 (ISBN 0-670-82350-3). Viking Child Bks.
—Wait & See. Browne, Eileen, illus. 32p. (ps up). 1988. 10.95 (ISBN 0-19-520644-4). Oxford U Pr.
Brancato, Robin F. Sweet Bells Jangled Out of Tune. 182p. (gr. 7 up). 1991. pap. 2.75 (ISBN 0-590-42865-9). Scholastic Inc.
Brandt, Betty. The Adventures of Nicolet. Brandt, Laura, ed. Craig, Jennifer, illus. 160p. (Orig.). (gr. 8-12). 1991. 12.95 (ISBN 0-9622014-2-1). Beaver Valley.
Brenner, Barbara A. Annie's Pet: Level 2. Ziegler, Jack, illus. (ps-3). 1989. 9.99 (ISBN 0-553-05833-9); pap. 3.50 (ISBN 0-553-34693-8). Bantam.
Brewster, Patience. Nobody. Brewster, Patience, illus. 32p. (ps-3). 1982. 13.95 (ISBN 0-89919-110-X, Clarion). HM.
Bridgers, Sue E. All Together Now. 192p. (gr. 7 up). 1980. pap. 2.75 (ISBN 0-553-26845-7). Bantam.
—Sara Will. 1986. 14.95i (ISBN 0-06-020691-8). HarpC Child Bks.
Bright, Robert. Jorgito: (Georgie) Palacios, Argentina, tr. (SPA.). 48p. (ps-3). 1991. pap. 3.95 (ISBN 0-590-42127-1). Scholastic Inc.
Brighton, Catherine. Five Secrets in a Box. Brighton, Catherine, illus. 32p. (ps-3). 1987. 11.95 (ISBN 0-525-44318-5, 01160-350, DCB). Dutton Child Bks.
Brillhart, Julie. Anna's Goodbye Apron. Mathews, Judith, ed. Brillhart, Julie, illus. 32p. (ps-1). 1990. PLB 12.95 (ISBN 0-8075-0375-4). A Whitman.
Brinckloe, Julie. Playing Marbles. Brinckloe, Julie, illus. LC 88-1608. 32p. (gr. k-3). 1988. 12.95 (ISBN 0-688-07143-0); PLB 12.88 (ISBN 0-688-07144-9, Morrow Jr Bks). Morrow Jr Bks.
Brink, Carol R. The Bad Times of Irma Baumlein. LC 76-182018. 144p. (gr. 4-6). 1974. pap. 3.95 (ISBN 0-02-041900-7, Aladdin). Macmillan Child Grp.
—Caddie Woodlawn. (Illus.). 288p. (gr. 4-6). 1990. 3.95 (ISBN 0-689-71370-3, Aladdin). Macmillan Child Grp.
Brodeur, Ruth W. Stories from the Big Chair. De Groat, Diane, illus. LC 88-35230. 48p. (gr. 1-4). 1989. 11.95 (ISBN 0-689-50481-0, M K McElderry). Macmillan Child Grp.
Bronte, Charlotte. Jane Eyre. (gr. 9 up). 1964. pap. 3.75 (ISBN 0-8049-0017-5, CL-17). Airmont.
Brooks, Ilsley D. Jennifer Ilsley Deering Brooks. Stearns, Helen M., ed. Urbahn, Clara, illus. 48p. (ps up). 1987. 8.95 (ISBN 0-9614281-3-9). Cricketfield Pr.
Brooks, Sandra. I Can Pray to God. Connelly, Gwen, tr. 32p. (gr. k-2). 1989. pasted 1.99 (ISBN 0-87403-601-1, 3861). Standard Pub.
Brown, Marc. The True Francine. Brown, Marc, illus. (ps-3). 1987. pap. 5.95 (ISBN 0-316-11243-7, Joy St Bks). Little.
Buchan, Stuart. Love & Lucy Bloom. (gr. 7 up). 1988. pap. 2.25 (ISBN 0-373-98022-1). S&S Trade.
Bulla, Clyde R. The Cardboard Crown. Chessare, Michele, illus. LC 83-45049. 96p. (gr. 2-5). 1984. (Crowell Jr Bks); PLB 12.89 (ISBN 0-690-04361-9, Crowell Jr Bks). HarpC Child Bks.
—Shoeshine Girl. Grant, Leigh, illus. LC 75-8516. 64p. (gr. 2-5). 1989. pap. 3.50 (ISBN 0-06-440228-2, Trophy). HarpC Child Bks.
—Shoeshine Girl. LC 75-8516. (Illus.). 80p. (gr. 3-5). 1989. PLB 13.89 (ISBN 0-690-04830-0, Crowell Jr Bks). HarpC Child Bks.
Bunting, Eve. Jane Martin, Dog Detective. Schwartz, Amy, illus. 48p. 1988. pap. 3.95 (ISBN 0-15-239587-3, VoyB). HarBraceJ.
—Karen Kepplewhite Is the World's Best Kisser. LC 83-2066. 96p. (gr. 3-6). 1983. 12.95 (ISBN 0-89919-182-7, Clarion). HM.
—Sixth Grade Sleepover. 112p. (gr. 3-7). 1987. pap. 2.75 (ISBN 0-590-42882-9). Scholastic Inc.
—Surrogate Sister. LC 83-49483. 192p. (gr. 7 up). 1984. PLB 13.89 (ISBN 0-397-32099-X, Lipp Jr Bks). HarpC Child Bks.
Burnett, Frances H. A Little Princess. Tudor, Tasha, illus. LC 63-15435. 240p. (gr. 4-8). 1987. pap. 3.50 (ISBN 0-06-440187-1, Trophy). HarpC Child Bks.
—Sara Crewe. 96p. (gr. 3-7). 1986. pap. 2.75 (ISBN 0-590-42323-1). Scholastic Inc.
Burnett, Francis H. Sara Crewe. Wildsmith, Brian, illus. 96p. (gr. 4-6). 1986. pap. 2.50 (ISBN 0-590-40733-3, Apple Paperbacks). Scholastic Inc.
Burstein, Fred. Rebecca's Nap. Cogancherry, Helen, illus. LC 88-1041. 32p. (ps-1). 1988. 13.95 (ISBN 0-02-715620-6, Bradbury Pr). Macmillan Child Grp.
Busselle, Rebecca. Bathing Ugly. LC 88-17929. 192p. (gr. 7 up). 1989. 12.95 (ISBN 0-531-05801-8); PLB 12.99 (ISBN 0-531-08401-9). Orchard Bks Watts.
Byars, Betsy C. The Glory Girl. LC 83-5927. 144p. (gr. 5-9). 1983. pap. 12.95 (ISBN 0-670-34261-0). Viking Child Bks.
Bylinsky, Tatyana. Before the Wildflowers Bloom. Bylinsky, Tatyana, illus. 80p. (gr. 3 up). 1988. 12.95 (ISBN 0-517-57052-1). Crown.
Caines, Jeannette. Just Us Women. Cummings, Pat, illus. LC 81-48655. (gr. k-3). 1982. 14.95i (ISBN 0-06-020941-0); PLB 12.89 (ISBN 0-06-020942-9). HarpC Child Bks.
Calhoun, Mary. Depend on Katie John. Frame, Paul, illus. LC 61-7328. 208p. (gr. 3-6). 1961. PLB 12.89 (ISBN 0-06-020926-7). HarpC Child Bks.
—Depend on Katie John. Frame, Paul, illus. LC 61-7328. 208p. (gr. 3-7). 1972. pap. 3.50 (ISBN 0-06-440029-8, Trophy). HarpC Child Bks.
—Honestly, Katie John. Frame, Paul, illus. LC 63-8473. 224p. (gr. 4-7). 1963. PLB 12.89 (ISBN 0-06-020936-4). HarpC Child Bks.
—Julie's Tree. LC 87-45857. 160p. (gr. 2-5). 1988. 11.95 (ISBN 0-06-020995-X); PLB 11.89 (ISBN 0-06-020996-8). HarpC Child Bks.
—Julie's Tree. LC 87-45857. 144p. (gr. 3-6). 1990. pap. 3.50 (ISBN 0-06-440247-9, Trophy). HarpC Child Bks.
—Katie John. Frame, Paul, illus. LC 60-5775. (gr. 3-6). 1960. PLB 12.89 (ISBN 0-06-020951-8). HarpC Child Bks.
—Katie John. LC 60-5775. (Illus.). 128p. (gr. 3-6). 1972. pap. 3.50 (ISBN 0-06-440028-X, Trophy). HarpC Child Bks.
—Katie John & Heathcliff. LC 80-7770. 160p. (gr. 3-7). 1989. pap. 3.50 (ISBN 0-685-22791-X, Trophy). HarpC Child Bks.
Call, Val. Trust Me, Jennifer. Davenport, May, illus. LC 82-72081. 176p. (Orig.). (gr. 5-12). 1985. pap. 4.50x (ISBN 0-943864-01-1). Davenport.
Calvert, Patricia. Hadder MacColl. 144p. (gr. 5-9). 1986. pap. 3.95 (ISBN 0-14-032158-6, Puffin). Puffin Bks.
—When Morning Comes. LC 89-5854. 160p. (gr. 7 up). 1989. 12.95 (ISBN 0-684-19105-9, Scribners Young Read). Macmillan Child Grp.
Cameron, Eleanor. Julia & the Hand of God. Owens, Gail, illus. 176p. (gr. 3-7). 1989. pap. 3.95 (ISBN 0-14-034042-4, Puffin). Puffin Bks.
—Julia's Magic. Owens, Gail, illus. 160p. (gr. 3-7). 1989. pap. 3.95 (ISBN 0-14-034040-8, Puffin). Puffin Bks.
—That Julia Redfern. Owens, Gail, illus. 144p. (gr. 3-7). 1989. pap. 3.95 (ISBN 0-14-034041-6, Puffin). Puffin Bks.
Canfield, Dorothy. Understood Betsy. 219p. 1981. Repr. PLB 16.95 (ISBN 0-89966-342-7). Buccaneer Bks.
—Understood Betsy. 213p. 1980. Repr. PLB 16.95 (ISBN 0-89967-016-4). Harmony Raine.
Caple, Kathy. The Purse. Caple, Kathy, illus. LC 86-2889. 32p. (gr. k-3). 1986. 12.95 (ISBN 0-395-41852-6). HM.
Carratello, Patty. Dot's Pot. Spivak, Darlene, ed. Brostrom, Eileen, illus. 16p. (gr. k-2). 1988. wkbk. 1.95 (ISBN 1-55734-389-6). Tchr Create Mat.
—Gail's Paint Pail. Spivak, Darlene, ed. Olsen, Shirley, illus. 16p. (gr. k-2). 1988. wkbk. 1.95 (ISBN 1-55734-385-3). Tchr Create Mat.
—Skate, Kate, Skate. Spivak, Darlene, ed. Smythe, Linda, illus. 16p. (gr. k-2). 1988. wkbk. 1.95 (ISBN 1-55734-380-2). Tchr Create Mat.
Carroll, Lewis. Alice in Wonderland. 1990. 7.98 (ISBN 0-8317-1351-8). Smithmark.
Caseley, Judith. Cousins. LC 88-34903. (Illus.). 24p. (ps up). 1990. 12.95 (ISBN 0-688-08433-8); lib. bdg. 12.88 (ISBN 0-688-08434-6). Greenwillow.
Casey, Barbara W. Leilani Zan. LC 90-71707. 113p. (gr. 9-12). Date not set. 7.95 (ISBN 1-55523-405-4). Winston-Derek.
Catley, Alison. Ellie's Doorstep. (Illus.). 1989. 10.95 (ISBN 0-8120-5966-2). Barron.
Cavanna, Betty. Paintbox Summer. 212p. 1981. Repr. PLB 19.95 (ISBN 0-89966-357-5). Buccaneer Bks.
—Wanted: A Girl for the Horses. LC 83-19289. 224p. (gr. 7 up). 1984. 12.95 (ISBN 0-688-02757-1). Morrow.
Chase, Emily. Happy Birthday, Jane. 192p. (Orig.). (gr. 5-9). 1988. pap. 2.50 (ISBN 0-590-41516-6). Scholastic Inc.
—Here Comes the Bridesmaid, No. 31. (gr. 6-10). 1988. pap. 2.50 (ISBN 0-590-41673-1). Scholastic Inc.
—Keeping Secrets. 176p. (Orig.). (gr. 7 up). 1984. pap. 2.50 (ISBN 0-590-41417-8). Scholastic Inc.
—Make Me a Star. 176p. (Orig.). (gr. 6 up). 1985. pap. 2.25 (ISBN 0-590-40440-7). Scholastic Inc.
—One Boy Too Many. 176p. (Orig.). (gr. 5-9). 1986. pap. 2.50 (ISBN 0-590-41277-9). Scholastic Inc.
—Our Roommate Is Missing, No. 2. (gr. 6-10). 1984. pap. 2.50 (ISBN 0-590-42048-8). Scholastic Inc.
—The Roommate & the Cowboy. 160p. (gr. 6-10). 1988. pap. 2.50 (ISBN 0-590-41390-2). Scholastic Inc.

—A Roommate Returns. 176p. (gr. 5-9). 1988. pap. 2.50 (ISBN 0-590-41671-5). Scholastic Inc.
—With Friends Like That. 192p. (Orig.). (gr. 7 up). 1985. pap. 2.25 (ISBN 0-590-40869-0). Scholastic Inc.
—You're No Friend of Mine. 192p. (Orig.). (gr. 7 up). 1984. pap. 2.25 (ISBN 0-590-40080-0). Scholastic Inc.
Child, Lydia M. Girls Own Book. (ps-3). 1991. pap. 12.95 (ISBN 1-55709-134-X). Applewood.
Chriestenson, Shawna, et al. The Biggest Little Girl. French, Marty & Warter, Fred, illus. 26p. (ps up). 1988. incl. cassette 7.95 (ISBN 1-55578-916-1). Worlds Wonder.
Christiansen, C. B. A Small Pleasure. 128p. (gr. 7 up). 1989. pap. 2.95 (ISBN 0-380-70699-7, Flare). Avon.
Clapp, Patricia C. Constance. 256p. (gr. 5 up). 1986. pap. 4.95 (ISBN 0-14-032030-X, Puffin). Puffin Bks.
Cleary, Beverly. Beezus & Ramona. 160p. (gr. 5-6). 1990. pap. 3.50 (ISBN 0-380-70918-X, Camelot). Avon.
—Cutting up with Ramona! Scribner, JoAn L., illus. 24p. (gr. 1-5). 1983. pap. 3.95 (ISBN 0-440-41627-2, YB). Dell.
—Ellen Tebbits. 160p. 1990. pap. 3.50 (ISBN 0-380-70913-9, Camelot). Avon.
—Ramona & Her Father. 192p. (gr. 5-6). 1990. pap. 3.50 (ISBN 0-380-70916-3, Camelot). Avon.
—Ramona & Her Mother. 208p. 1990. pap. 3.50 (ISBN 0-380-70952-X, Camelot). Avon.
—Ramona, Forever. Tiegreen, Alan, illus. LC 84-704. 192p. (gr. 3-7). 1984. 13.95 (ISBN 0-688-03785-2); PLB 13.88 (ISBN 0-688-03786-0, Morrow Jr Bks). Morrow Jr Bks.
—Ramona Forever. large type ed. 192p. 1989. Repr. of 1984 ed. PLB 15.95 (ISBN 1-55736-139-8, Crnrstn Bks). ABC-CLIO.
—Ramona Quimby, 5 vols. (gr. 4-7). 1990. pap. 16.25 boxed set (ISBN 0-440-36027-7). Dell.
—Ramona Quimby, Age Eight. Tiegreen, Alan, illus. 192p. (gr. 3-7). 1982. pap. 3.25 (ISBN 0-440-47350-0, YB). Dell.
—The Ramona Quimby Diary. Tiegreen, Alan, illus. 160p. (gr. 3-7). 1984. pap. 8.95 spiral bdg. (ISBN 0-688-03883-2, Pub. by Beech Tree Bks). Morrow.
—Ramona the Brave. large type ed. (Illus.). 143p. (gr. k-6). 1990. Repr. PLB 15.95 (ISBN 1-55736-159-2, Crnrstn Bks). ABC-CLIO.
—Ramona the Pest. Palacios, Argentina, tr. Darling, Louis, illus. LC 83-23805. (SPA.). 208p. (gr. 3-7). 1984. 12.95 (ISBN 0-688-02783-0). Morrow.
—Ramona the Pest. large type ed. (Illus.). 175p. (gr. k-6). 1990. Repr. PLB 15.95 (ISBN 1-55736-158-4, Crnrstn Bks). ABC-CLIO.
—Sister of the Bride. 128p. (gr. 6-9). 1981. pap. 2.75 (ISBN 0-440-97596-4, LE). Dell.
—Socks. 160p. (gr. k-6). 1980. pap. 3.25 (ISBN 0-440-48256-9, YB). Dell.
Cleaver, Vera. Ellen Grae. Raskin, Ellen, illus. LC 67-10623. 96p. 1967. PLB 12.89 (Lipp Jr Bks). HarpC Child Bks.
—Hazel Rye. LC 85-42741. 192p. (gr. 5-8). 1985. pap. 3.95 (ISBN 0-06-440156-1, Trophy). HarpC Child Bks.
—Moon Lake Angel. LC 86-15242. 160p. (gr. 7 up). 1987. 12.95 (ISBN 0-688-04952-4). Lothrop.
Clements, Andrew. Big Al. Yoshi, illus. 1991. pap. 3.95 (ISBN 0-590-44455-7, Blue Ribbon Bks). Scholastic Inc.
Cliburn, Alan. Tracey the Great. 124p. (gr. 3-6). 1989. pap. 0.50 (ISBN 0-87406-323-X). Willowisp Pr.
Clifford, Eth. Leah's Song. (gr. 3-7). 1989. pap. 2.50 (ISBN 0-590-42193-X, Apple Paperbacks). Scholastic Inc.
Cohen, Barbara. The Christmas Revolution. De Groat, Diane, illus. LC 86-21340. 96p. (gr. 3-6). 1987. 12.95 (ISBN 0-688-06806-5). Lothrop.
—Molly's Pilgrim. Deraney, Michael J., illus. (gr. k-3). 1990. pap. 2.75 (ISBN 0-553-15833-3). Bantam.
Cole, Babette. Princess Smartypants. Cole, Babette, illus. LC 86-12381. (ps-3). 1987. 12.95 (ISBN 0-399-21409-7, Putnam). Putnam Pub Group.
—Princess Smartypants. (Illus.). 32p. (ps-3). 1991. pap. 5.95 (ISBN 0-399-21779-7, Putnam). Putnam Pub Group.
Colen, Kimberly. My Birthday Book. Hudson, Carol, illus. 24p. (Orig.). (gr. 2-5). 1988. pap. 2.95 (ISBN 0-590-41351-1). Scholastic Inc.
Collier, James L. & Collier, Christopher. Who Is Carrie? (gr. k-6). 1987. pap. 3.25 (ISBN 0-440-49536-9, YB). Dell.
—The Winter Hero. 132p. (gr. 9 up). 1985. pap. 2.75 (ISBN 0-590-42604-4). Scholastic Inc.
Colton, Debie. Messy Marcy MacIntyre. LC 89-42629. 32p. (gr. 1-2). 1990. PLB 12.95 (ISBN 0-8368-0108-3). Gareth Stevens Inc.
Conford, Ellen. A Case For Jenny Archer. (ps-3). 1990. pap. 2.95 (ISBN 0-316-15352-4). Little.
—Dreams of Victory. Rockwell, Gail, illus. 144p. (gr. 4-6). 1973. 14.95 (ISBN 0-316-15294-3). Little.
—Felicia the Critic. Stewart, Arvis, illus. (gr. 4-6). 1985. pap. 2.25 (ISBN 0-671-60039-7, Archway). PB.
—Felicia, the Critic. Stewart, Arvis, illus. (gr. 4-6). 1973. 14.95 (ISBN 0-316-15295-1). Little.
—Jenny Archer. (ps-3). 1991. pap. 2.95 (ISBN 0-316-15353-2). Little.
—Jenny Archer to the Rescue: What Happens When You Want to Be a Hero But Can't Find a Willing... (ps-3). 1990. 10.95 (ISBN 0-316-15351-6). Little.
—The Luck of Pokey Bloom. Lowenstein, Bernice, illus. 144p. (gr. 4-6). 1975. 14.95 (ISBN 0-316-15305-2). Little.
Conrad, Pam. Seven Silly Circles. Wimmer, Mike, illus. LC 85-45835. 64p. (gr. 2-5). 1987. 11.95 (ISBN 0-06-021333-7); PLB 11.89 (ISBN 0-06-021334-5). HarpC Child Bks.
—Staying Nine. Wimmer, Mike, illus. LC 87-45862. 80p. (gr. 2-5). 1988. 12.95 (ISBN 0-06-021319-1); PLB 11.89 (ISBN 0-06-021320-5). HarpC Child Bks.
—What I Did for Roman. LC 86-45497. 192p. (gr. 7 up). 1987. PLB 12.89 (ISBN 0-06-021332-9). HarpC Child Bks.
Cookson, C. Our Kate. large type ed. Date not set. 13.95 (ISBN 0-685-34778-8). Ulverscroft.
Coolidge, Susan. What Katy Did. 176p. (gr. 3-7). 1983. pap. 2.25 (ISBN 0-14-035011-X, Puffin). Puffin Bks.
—What Katy Did. 190p. 1988. Repr. lib. bdg. 19.95x (ISBN 0-89966-585-3). Buccaneer Bks.
—What Katy Did Next. (gr. k-6). 1989. pap. 3.50 (ISBN 0-440-40244-1, Pub. by Yearling Classics). Dell.
Cooney, Barbara. Miss Rumphius. LC 85-40447. (Illus.). 32p. (ps-3). 1985. pap. 4.95 (ISBN 0-14-050539-3, Puffin). Puffin Bks.
Cooney, Caroline B. The Face on the Milk Carton. (gr. 7 up). 1990. 14.95 (ISBN 0-553-05853-3). Bantam.
—Last Dance. 224p. (Orig.). (gr. 9 up). 1991. pap. 2.95 (ISBN 0-590-44629-0). Scholastic Inc.
—New Year's Eve. 224p. (Orig.). (gr. 7 up). 1988. pap. 2.50 (ISBN 0-590-40941-7). Scholastic Inc.
Corbalis, Judy. The Wrestling Princess & Other Stories. Craig, Helen, illus. 160p. (gr. 3-6). 1986. 11.95 (ISBN 0-233-97852-6). Andre Deutsch.
Corcoran, Barbara. The Potato Kid. 192p. (gr. 3-7). 1989. 13.95 (ISBN 0-689-31589-9, Atheneum Child Bk). Macmillan Child Grp.
Corey, Deirdre. Sealed with a Hug. (gr. 4-7). 1990. pap. 2.75 (ISBN 0-590-44027-6). Scholastic Inc.

Cosgrove, Stephen. Heidi's Rose. Edelson, Wendy, illus. LC 90-71079. 32p. 1991. 14.95 (ISBN 1-55868-033-0). Gr Arts Ctr Pub.
Set high in the mountains at Timberline Lodge, the story begins as a Saint Bernard arrives at the lodge. Wearing a beautiful locket, the huge dog arouses the curiosity of Rose, the innkeeper's daughter. But no one can get close to the animal to see what is in the locket. Accustomed to getting her own way, Rose schemes to get the locket so she can look inside. But adventure overtakes both girl & dog. Stephen Cosgrove is the author of more than 150 children's books. Wendy Edelson's illustrations have won numerous awards.
Publisher Provided Annotation.

Craft, Ruth. Fancy Nancy in Disguise. Smee, Nicola, illus. 96p. (gr. 1-3). 1990. 11.95 (Pub. by Collins Pubs UK). Trafalgar Sq.
Cross, Gillian. Chartbreaker. LC 86-46199. 184p. (gr. 7 up). 1987. 13.95 (ISBN 0-8234-0647-4). Holiday.
Cunningham, Julia. Viollet. Cober, Alan E., illus. (gr. 4-7). 1966. PLB 6.99 (ISBN 0-394-91821-5). Pantheon.
Cusick, Richie T. The Lifeguard. 192p. (Orig.). (gr. 9 up). 1988. pap. 2.75 (ISBN 0-590-43203-6). Scholastic Inc.
Cuyler, Margery. Freckles & Jane. Morrill, Leslie H., illus. LC 88-32068. (ps-2). 1990. pap. 4.95 (ISBN 0-8050-1479-9). H Holt & Co.
Dadey, Debbie & Jones, Marcia. Vampires Don't Wear Polka Dots. 96p. (Orig.). (gr. 2-5). 1990. pap. 2.50 (ISBN 0-590-43411-X). Scholastic Inc.
Dahl, Roald. Matilda. large type ed. 1989. Repr. of 1988 ed. PLB 15.95 (ISBN 1-55736-123-1, Crnrstn Bks). ABC-CLIO.
—Matilda. 240p. (gr. 3-7). 1990. pap. 3.95 (ISBN 0-14-034294-X, Puffin). Puffin Bks.
Daly, Maureen. Seventeenth Summer. 293p. 1981. Repr. PLB 19.95x (ISBN 0-89966-355-9). Buccaneer Bks.
Daneman, Meredith. Francie & the Boys. (Illus.). 192p. (gr. 6-9). 1989. 14.95 (ISBN 0-440-50137-7). Delacorte.
Davidson, Alan. The Bewitching of Alison Allbright. 164p. (gr. 5-9). 1989. 12.95 (ISBN 0-670-82015-6). Viking Child Bks.
Davis, Gibbs. Lucky Socks. (gr. 4-7). 1991. pap. 2.75 (ISBN 0-553-15865-1). Bantam.
—Major-League Melissa. (gr. 4-7). 1991. pap. 2.75 (ISBN 0-553-15866-X). Bantam.
—Maud Flies Solo. (gr. 4-7). 1990. pap. 3.50 (ISBN 0-553-15786-8). Bantam.
—The Other Emily. Shute, Linda, illus. LC 83-18913. 32p. (gr. k-3). 1984. 14.95 (ISBN 0-395-35482-X, 5-84351). HM.
—The Other Emily. Shute, Linda, illus. 32p. (gr. k-3). 1990. pap. 4.95 (ISBN 0-395-54947-7). HM.
Davis, Leslie. Pretending. 160p. (gr. 6-9). 1988. pap. 2.50 (ISBN 0-590-41638-3). Scholastic Inc.
Day, S. Monica's Mother Said No. (Illus.). 24p. (ps-8). 1987. pap. 4.95 (ISBN 0-88753-158-X). Firefly Bks Ltd.
Deary, Terry. Calamity Kate. Firmin, Charlotte, illus. LC 82-1326. 112p. (gr. 2-6). 1982. lib. bdg. 8.95 (ISBN 0-87614-195-5). Carolrhoda Bks.
—Calamity Kate. Firmin, Charlotte, illus. LC 82-1326. 112p. (gr. 3-7). 1991. pap. 3.50 (ISBN 0-06-440361-0, Trophy). HarpC Child Bks.
De Brunhoff, Laurent. Babar's Little Girl. De Brunhoff, Laurent, illus. LC 68-42962. 36p. (ps-3). 1987. lib. bdg. 9.99 (ISBN 0-394-98689-X, Random Juv); pap. 6.95 (ISBN 0-394-88689-5). Random.
Deedy, Carmen A. Agatha's Feather Bed: Not Just Another Wild Goose Story. Seeley, Laura L., illus. 32p. (ps-5). 1991. 14.95 (ISBN 1-56145-008-1). Peachtree Pubs.
De la Mare, Walter. Molly Whuppie. Le Cain, Errol, illus. LC 82-83099. 32p. (gr. 1 up). 1983. 11.95 (ISBN 0-374-35000-0). FS&G.
Delaney, A. The Gunnywolf. Delaney, A., illus. LC 87-29351. 32p. (ps-3). 1988. 11.95 (ISBN 0-06-021594-1); PLB 11.89 (ISBN 0-06-021595-X). HarpC Child Bks.
Delton, Judy. I Never Win. (ps-3). 1991. pap. 2.95 (ISBN 0-440-40414-2). Dell.
—Kitty in High School. LC 84-523. 128p. (gr. 2-5). 1984. 10.95 (ISBN 0-395-35334-3, 5-84405). HM.
Demarest, Chris L. No Peas for Nellie. LC 87-14167. (Illus.). 32p. (ps-2). 1988. 13.95 (ISBN 0-02-728460-3, Mcmillan Child Bk). Macmillan Child Grp.
DePaola, Tomie. Marianna May & Nursey. DePaola, Tomie, illus. LC 82-9364. 32p. (ps-3). 1983. reinforced bdg. 14.95 (ISBN 0-8234-0473-0); pap. 5.95 (ISBN 0-8234-0623-7). Holiday.
De Pressense, Domitille. Natalie: I'm Going to Tell My Mom. (Illus.). 28p. (ps-1). 1990. pap. 3.95 (ISBN 0-8120-4510-6). Barron.
Derby, Pat. Goodbye Emily, Hello. (gr. 7 up). 1989. 13.95 (ISBN 0-374-32744-0). FS&G.
De Regniers, Beatrice S. The Way I Feel... Sometimes. Meddaugh, Susan, illus. LC 87-18245. 48p. (gr. 1-4). 1988. 13.95 (ISBN 0-89919-647-0, Pub. by Clarion). Ticknor & Fields.
De Weese, Gene. The Calvin Nullifier. (gr. k-6). 1989. pap. 2.95 (ISBN 0-440-40214-X, YB). Dell.
Dickens, Charles. Little Dorrit. (ps-8). 1990. Repr. lib. bdg. 39.95x (ISBN 0-89966-680-9). Buccaneer Bks.
Dickens, Lucy. Rosy's Pool. 1991. 13.95 (ISBN 0-670-83577-3). Viking Child Bks.
Dickinson, Peter. Emma Tupper's Diary. 224p. (gr. 3 up). 1988. pap. 3.25 (ISBN 0-440-40080-5, YB). Dell.
—Eva. (gr. 7 up). 1989. 14.95 (ISBN 0-440-50129-6). Delacorte.
Dixon, Jeanne. The Tempered Wind. LC 87-1379. 224p. (gr. 7 up). 1987. 14.95 (ISBN 0-689-31339-X, Atheneum Child Bk). Macmillan Child Grp.
Dobrin, Arnold. Josephine's 'Magination. 48p. (gr. 2-5). 1991. pap. 3.95 (ISBN 0-590-43494-2). Scholastic Inc.
Doherty, Berlie. Granny Was a Buffer Girl. LC 87-25080. 160p. (gr. 5 up). 1988. 12.95 (ISBN 0-531-05754-2); PLB 12.99 (ISBN 0-531-08354-3). Orchard Bks Watts.
Donahue, Marilyn. Reach with All Your Heart. LC 88-14807. (gr. 3-7). 1988. pap. 4.49 (ISBN 1-55513-755-5, Chariot Bks). Cook.
Doren, Marion W. Borrowed Summer. LC 85-45816. 160p. (gr. 3-7). 1986. PLB 11.89 (ISBN 0-06-021724-3). HarpC Child Bks.
Dott, A. Eric. Hide a Book: They Meet. Talbot, Jim, illus. 22p. (ps-1). 1987. PLB 5.95 (ISBN 0-939871-00-9). Monarch Toy.
Douglas, Anna J. The Goofy Gamble. LC 89-2634. 112p. (Orig.). (gr. 3-7). 1989. pap. 2.95 (ISBN 0-679-80062-X, Bullseye Bks). Knopf.
Douglas-Wiggins, Kate. Rebecca of Sunnybrook Farm. Hinkle, Don, ed. Elwell, Peter, illus. LC 87-15475. 48p. (gr. 3-6). 1987. PLB 12.89 (ISBN 0-8167-1217-4); pap. text ed. 3.95 (ISBN 0-8167-1218-2). Troll Assocs.
Downer, Ann. The Glass Salamander. LC 88-35034. 224p. 1989. 13.95 (ISBN 0-689-31413-2, Atheneum Child Bk). Macmillan Child Grp.
—The Spellkey. LC 86-28709. 232p. (gr. 7 up). 1987. 14.95 (ISBN 0-689-31329-2, Atheneum Child Bk). Macmillan Child Grp.
Dragonwagon, Crescent. Always, Always. Zeldich, Arieh, illus. LC 83-22199. 32p. (gr. 1-4). 1984. 11.95 (ISBN 0-02-733080-X, Mcmillan Child Bk). Macmillan Child Grp.
—Katie in the Morning. Day, Betsy, illus. LC 82-47709. 32p. (ps-3). 1983. PLB 12.89 (ISBN 0-06-021730-8). HarpC Child Bks.
—Margaret Ziegler Is Horse-Crazy. Elwell, Peter, illus. LC 87-23975. 32p. (gr. 1-4). 1988. 12.95 (ISBN 0-02-733230-6, Mcmillan Child Bk). Macmillan Child Grp.
Dubov, Christine. Aleksandra, Where Are Your Toes? Schnieder, Josef, photos by. (Illus.). 14p. (ps). 1986. 3.95 (ISBN 0-312-01717-0). St Martin.
Duffy, James. Missing. LC 87-25295. 144p. (gr. 4-7). 1988. 12.95 (ISBN 0-684-18912-7, Scribners Young Read). Macmillan Child Grp.
Du Jardin, Rosamond. Practically Seventeen. 224p. (gr. 4-9). 1949. PLB 14.89 (ISBN 0-397-30153-7, Lipp Jr Bks). HarpC Child Bks.

Dunbar, Joyce. The Raggy Taggy Toys. Lynch, P. J., illus. 32p. (gr. k-3). 1988. 10.95 (ISBN 0-8120-4130-5). Barron.
Dunlop, Beverly. The Poetry Girl. 216p. (gr. 6-8). 1989. 13.95 (ISBN 0-395-49679-9). HM.
Dunlop, Eileen. Clementina. LC 86-22913. 160p. (gr. 7 up). 1987. 12.95 (ISBN 0-8234-0642-3). Holiday.
—The Valley of Deer. LC 89-1931. 152p. (gr. 4-7). 1989. 13.95 (ISBN 0-8234-0766-7). Holiday.
Dutton, Sandra. Tales of Belva Jean Copenhagen. Dutton, Sandra, illus. LC 88-27492. 80p. (gr. 3-6). 1989. 11.95 (ISBN 0-689-31463-9, Atheneum Child Bk). Macmillan Child Grp.
Eakin, Edwin M., ed. Last Summer I Got in Trouble. (gr. 4-7). 1987. 8.95 (ISBN 0-89015-612-3, Pub. by Panda Bks). Eakin Pr.
Easton, Patricia H. Stable Girl: Working for the Family. Ferguson, Herb, illus. 48p. (gr. 1-7). 1991. write for info. (ISBN 0-15-278340-7). HarBraceJ.
Edwards, Julie. Mandy. reissued ed. Brown, Judith G., illus. LC 76-157901. 192p. (gr. 4-7). 1971. PLB 13.89 (ISBN 0-06-021803-7). HarpC Child Bks.
Ehrlich, Amy. Where It Stops, Nobody Knows. 224p. (gr. 6 up). 1990. pap. 3.95 (ISBN 0-14-034266-4, Puffin). Puffin Bks.
Eisenberg, Lisa. Leave It to Lexie. 144p. (gr. 2-7). 1989. pap. 11.95 (ISBN 0-670-82844-0). Viking Child Bks.
Emerson, Kathy L. Julia's Mending. LC 87-5793. 144p. (gr. 5 up). 1987. 11.95 (ISBN 0-531-05719-4); PLB 11.99 (ISBN 0-531-08319-5). Orchard Bks Watts.
Epp, Margaret & Wiens, Ruth. Sarah & the Persian Shepherd. 123p. (Orig.). (gr. 3-6). 1982. pap. 4.95 (ISBN 0-919797-06-7). Kindred Pr.
Ernst, Lisa C. Nattie Parsons' Good-Luck Lamb. LC 87-13700. (Illus.). 32p. (ps-3). 1988. pap. 11.95 (ISBN 0-670-81778-3). Viking Child Bks.
Ewing, Katherine. A Really Popular Girl. (gr. 3-7). 1989. pap. 2.50 (ISBN 0-590-41856-4, Apple Paperbacks). Scholastic Inc.
Fadely, Jack & Hosler, Virginia. The Forest of Can: A Fable of Mind. Fadely, Jack & Hosler, Virginia, illus. 88p. (gr. 2-8). pap. 7.50 (ISBN 0-934293-05-8); pap. 17.50 with tapes (ISBN 0-317-38466-X). Huber-Copeland Pub.
Farmer, Penelope. Charlotte Sometimes. (Orig.). (gr. k-6). 1987. pap. 4.95 (ISBN 0-440-41261-7, Pub. by Yearling Classics). Dell.
—Emma in Winter. (gr. k-6). 1987. pap. 2.95 (ISBN 0-440-42308-2, YB). Dell.
Ferris, Jean. Invincible Summer. 176p. (gr. 7 up). 1989. pap. 2.95 (ISBN 0-380-70619-9, Flare). Avon.
Fiday, David J. Sweet Surprises. Rigo, Christina, illus. 32p. (gr. k-2). 1989. pasted 1.99 (ISBN 0-87403-597-X, 3857). Standard Pub.
Field, Rachel. Calico Bush. reissued ed. Lewis, Allen, illus. LC 66-19095. 224p. (gr. 5-9). 1987. 13.95 (ISBN 0-02-734610-2, Mcmillan Child Bk). Macmillan Child Grp.
—General Store. Laroche, Giles, illus. LC 87-37218. (ps-3). 1988. 15.95 (ISBN 0-316-28163-8). Little.
—Hitty, Her First Hundred Years. (gr. k-6). 1990. pap. 3.95 (ISBN 0-440-40337-5, YB). Dell.
Filichia, Peter. Girls Can't Do It. 224p. (Orig.). 1990. pap. 2.95 (ISBN 0-380-75784-2, Flare). Avon.
Finley, Martha. Elsie Dinsmore. LC 74-15737. (Illus.). 342p. (gr. 7 up). 1975. Repr. of 1896 ed. 24.00x (ISBN 0-405-06372-5). Ayer Co Pubs.
—Elsie Dinsmore. 332p. Repr. PLB 21.95x (ISBN 0-89966-332-X). Buccaneer Bks.
—Elsie's Girlhood. 273p. 1981. Repr. PLB 21.95x (ISBN 0-89966-334-6). Buccaneer Bks.
Fisher, Dorothy C. Understood Betsy. (gr. k-6). 1987. pap. 4.95 (ISBN 0-440-49179-7, Pub. by Yearling Classics). Dell.
Fitzhugh, Louise. Harriet the Spy. 304p. (gr. 5 up). 1979. pap. 3.50 (ISBN 0-440-43447-5, YB). Dell.
Fox, Robert J. Charity, Morality, Sex & Young People. 180p. (gr. 7-12). 1987. pap. 8.95 (ISBN 0-937495-14-X). Trinity Comns.
Fradin, Dennis. How I Saved the World. LC 86-11585. 160p. (gr. 4-6). 1986. PLB 10.95 (ISBN 0-87518-355-7, Dillon). Macmillan Child Grp.
French, Fiona. Snow White in New York. 32p. 1990. pap. 6.95 (ISBN 0-19-272210-7). Oxford U Pr.
Friedland, Joyce & Kessler, Rikki. Maggie Marmelstein: A Study Guide. (gr. 4-6). 1982. tchr's. ed. & wkbk. 14. 95 (ISBN 0-88122-006-X). LRN Links.
Friedman, Frieda. Dot for Short. 173p. 1981. Repr. PLB 14.95x (ISBN 0-686-73781-4). Buccaneer Bks.
Friedman, Melanie. Jennifer. 1991. pap. 2.95 (ISBN 0-425-12614-5). Berkley Pub.
—No Way, Jennifer, No. 2. 1991. pap. 2.75 (ISBN 0-425-12604-8). Berkley Pub.
—What's Next Jennifer, No. 1. 1991. pap. 2.75 (ISBN 0-425-12603-X). Berkley Pub.
Fritz, Jean. Brady. Ward, Lynd, illus. (gr. 5-9). 1987. pap. 3.95 (ISBN 0-14-032258-2, Puffin). Puffin Bks.
Fujikawa, Gyo. Me Too! Fujikawa, Gyo, illus. LC 81-84014. 32p. (gr. k-3). 1982. 3.95 (ISBN 0-448-11752-5, G&D). Putnam Pub Group.
Funakoshi, Canna. One Evening. Izawa, Yohji, illus. LC 87-29243. (ps up). 1988. 11.95 (ISBN 0-88708-063-4). Picture Bk Studio.
Galbraith, Kathryn O. Waiting for Jennifer. Trivas, Irene, illus. LC 86-27628. 32p. (ps-3). 1987. 12.95 (ISBN 0-689-50430-6, M K McElderry). Macmillan Child Grp.
Gallaz, Chrsitophe. Rose Blanche: Based on the Original Idea of Roberto Innocenti. Delessert, Etienne & Redpath, Ann, eds. Coventry, Martha, tr. from FRE. LC 85-70219. (Illus.). 32p. (gr. 6 up). 1986. PLB 16. 95s.p. (ISBN 0-87191-994-X); PLB 24.25 (ISBN 0-685-10118-5). Creative Ed.
Garcia, Lola. A Girlfriend at Acoma, Siyu, & an Invitation to Supper. Aragon, Sherry, illus. 14p. (Orig.). (ps-7). 1981. pap. 3.75 (ISBN 0-915347-09-1). Pueblo Acoma Pr.
Gardam, Jane. A Few Fair Days. LC 88-5477. 128p. (gr. 5 up). 1988. 11.95 (ISBN 0-688-07602-5). Greenwillow.
—A Long Way from Verona. LC 88-5254. 192p. (gr. 7 up). 1988. 13.95 (ISBN 0-02-735781-3, Mcmillan Child Bk). Macmillan Child Grp.
Garfield, Vivien & Alcock, Vivien. The Sylvia Game. (gr. k-6). 1990. pap. 2.95 (ISBN 0-440-40266-2, YB). Dell.
Gates, Doris. Blue Willow. Lantz, Paul, illus. LC 40-32435. (gr. 4-6). 1976. pap. 3.95 (ISBN 0-14-030924-1, VS30, Puffin). Puffin Bks.
Gates, Susan. The Burnhope Wheel. LC 89-1934. 96p. (gr. 4-7). 1989. 12.95 (ISBN 0-8234-0767-5). Holiday.
George, Jean C. One Day in the Woods. Allen, Gary, illus. LC 87-21712. 48p. (gr. 4-7). 1988. 11.95 (ISBN 0-690-04722-3, Crowell Jr Bks); PLB 11.89 (ISBN 0-690-04724-X, Crowell Jr Bks). HarpC Child Bks.
Gerber, Merrill J. Also Known As Sadzia! The Belly Dancer! LC 86-45484. 192p. (gr. 7 up). 1987. 12.95i (ISBN 0-06-022162-3); PLB 12.89 (ISBN 0-06-022163-1). HarpC Child Bks.
Giff, Patricia R. Emily Arrow Promises to Do Better This Year. (Orig.). 1990. pap. 2.75 (ISBN 0-440-40369-3, Pub. by Yearling Classics). Dell.
—The Girl Who Knew It All. Morrill, Leslie, illus. (gr. 4-6). 1984. 6.95 (ISBN 0-385-28362-8); PLB 6.95 (ISBN 0-385-28363-6). Delacorte.
—The Girl Who Knew It All. Morrill, Leslie, illus. LC 79-50677. (gr. 4-6). 1979. 6.95 (ISBN 0-440-03137-0); PLB 6.89 (ISBN 0-440-03138-9). Delacorte.
—Have You Seen Hyacinth Macaw? Kramer, Anthony, illus. (gr. 4-6). 1981. 11.95 (ISBN 0-385-28389-X); pap. 12.95 (ISBN 0-385-28390-3). Delacorte.
—I Love Saturday. Remkiewicz, Frank, illus. 32p. (ps-3). 1989. 12.95 (ISBN 0-685-26817-9). Viking Child Bks.
Gilman, Dorothy. Girl in Buckskin. 144p. (gr. 7 up). 1990. pap. 3.50 (ISBN 0-449-70380-0, Juniper). Fawcett.
Gilman, Phoebe. Jillian Jiggs. Gilman, Phoebe, illus. 40p. (Orig.). (gr. k-3). 1988. pap. 2.50 (ISBN 0-590-41340-6). Scholastic Inc.
Gleeson, Libby. Eleanor, Elizabeth. LC 89-36009. 136p. (gr. 5-9). 1990. 13.95 (ISBN 0-8234-0804-3). Holiday.
Goble, Paul. The Girl Who Loved Wild Horses. Goble, Paul, illus. LC 86-3321. 32p. (gr. k-3). 1986. pap. 3.95 (ISBN 0-689-71082-8, Aladdin). Macmillan Child Grp.
Godden, Rumer. The Peacock Spring. 286p. (gr. 7 up). 1986. pap. 3.95 (ISBN 0-14-032005-9, Penguin Bks). Viking Penguin.
Goldman, Dara. The Hiccup Cure. Goodman, Dara, illus. 32p. (ps-1). 1989. 9.95 (ISBN 0-399-21663-4, Putnam). Putnam Pub Group.
Goldshlag-Cooks, Roberta. Gittel & the Bell. Martz, Susan, illus. LC 87-2828. (gr. k-4). 1987. 10.95 (ISBN 0-930494-68-7); pap. 4.95 (ISBN 0-930494-69-5). Kar Ben.
Goode, Diane, illus. The Nutcracker: The Story Based on the Ballet. LC 82-62170. 32p. 1988. pap. 1.25 (ISBN 0-394-81939-X, Random Juv). Random.
Gormley, Beatrice. More Fifth Grade Magic. McCully, Emily A., illus. LC 88-25683. 112p. (gr. 3-6). 1989. 11.95 (ISBN 0-525-44486-6, DCB). Dutton Child Bks.
Goss, Marilyn. Maggie Suzanne, Star of Christmas. Goss, Marilyn, illus. 36p. (gr. 3 up). 1988. 15.95 (ISBN 0-9620766-0-0). Art Room Pubns.
Graham, Bob. Where's Sarah. Graham, Bob, illus. LC 88-80591. (ps-1). 1988. 4.95 (ISBN 0-316-32306-3). Little.
Greenberg, Polly. I Know I'm Myself Because... Barrett, Jennifer, illus. 32p. (ps-3). 1986. 16.95 (ISBN 0-89885-045-2); pap. 9.95 (ISBN 0-89885-200-5). Human Sci Pr.
Greene, Bette. Philip Hall Likes Me, I Reckon Maybe. large type ed. (Illus.). 158p. 1989. PLB 15.95 (ISBN 1-55736-106-1, Crnrstn Bks). ABC-CLIO.
Greene, Constance C. Dotty's Suitcase. 144p. (gr. 3-7). 1982. pap. 1.95 (ISBN 0-440-42108-X, YB). Dell.
—A Girl Called Al. 128p. (gr. 5-9). 1977. pap. 2.95 (ISBN 0-440-42810-6, YB). Dell.
—A Girl Called Al. large type ed. 1989. Repr. of 1969 ed. 15.95 (ISBN 1-55736-145-2, Crnrstn Bks). ABC CLIO.
—I Know You, Al. (gr. k-6). 1977. pap. 2.95 (ISBN 0-440-44123-4, YB). Dell.
—I Know You, Al. Barton, Byron, illus. 128p. (gr. 4-8). 1975. pap. 12.95 (ISBN 0-670-39048-8). Viking Child Bks.
—Isabelle Shows Her Stuff. 144p. (gr. 8-12). 1984. pap. 12.95 (ISBN 0-670-41103-5). Viking Child Bks.
—Isabelle Shows Her Stuff. (gr. 4-6). 1986. pap. 2.95 (ISBN 0-440-44152-8, YB). Dell.
—Isabelle the Itch. 128p. (gr. 2-4). 1974. pap. 2.95 (ISBN 0-440-44345-8, YB). Dell.
—Isabelle the Itch. McCully, Emily A., illus. 128p. (gr. 4-6). 1973. pap. 12.95 (ISBN 0-670-40177-3). Viking Child Bks.
Greenwald, Sheila. Give Us a Great Big Smile, Rosy Cole. 80p. (gr. 5-7). 1982. pap. 2.50 (ISBN 0-440-42923-4, YB). Dell.
—The Secret in Miranda's Closet. (gr. k-6). 1989. pap. 2.95 (ISBN 0-440-40128-3, YB). Dell.
—Will the Real Gertrude Hollings Please Stand Up? 176p. (gr. k-6). 1985. pap. 2.95 (ISBN 0-440-49553-9, YB). Dell.
—Write on, Rosy! (Illus.). 112p. 1990. pap. 2.75 (ISBN 0-671-68569-4, Minstrel Bks). PB.
Grifalconi, Ann. Darkness & the Butterfly. Grifalconi, Ann, illus. 32p. (ps-3). 1987. 14.95 (ISBN 0-316-32863-4). Little.
Griffith, Helen. Georgia Music. Stevenson, James, illus. LC 85-24918. 24p. (gr. k-3). 1986. 13.95 (ISBN 0-688-06071-4); PLB 13.88 (ISBN 0-688-06072-2). Greenwillow.
Grollman, Sharon. Shira: A Legacy of Courage. Kushner, Harold S. & Putter, Anne M.intro. by. Epstein, Edward, illus. LC 87-13456. 96p. (gr. 6-12). 1988. pap. 13.95 (ISBN 0-385-24114-3). Doubleday.
Gross, Sukey S. The Golden Gate. Shiman, Hedy, illus. 172p. (gr. 5-8). 1989. 11.95 (ISBN 1-56062-002-1); pap. 8.95 (ISBN 1-56062-003-X). CIS Comm.
—The Secret Diary. Backman, Aidel, illus. (gr. 5-8). 1989. 10.95 (ISBN 0-935063-67-6); pap. 7.95 (ISBN 0-935063-68-4). CIS Comm.
—The Silent Summer. Shiman, Hedy, illus. 139p. (gr. 7-9). 1989. 10.95 (ISBN 1-56062-004-8); pap. 7.95 (ISBN 1-56062-005-6). CIS Comm.
Grossman, Bill. Donna O'Neeshuck Was Chased by Some Cows. Truesdell, Sue, illus. LC 85-45823. 40p. (ps-3). 1991. pap. 4.95 (ISBN 0-06-443255-6, Trophy). HarpC Child Bks.
Guthrie, Donna. Mrs. Gigglebelly is Coming For Tea. 1990. pap. 6.95 (ISBN 0-671-67937-6). S&S Trade.
Haas, Dorothy. Dorothy & the Seven-Leaf Clover. Rose, David, illus. LC 84-16080. 64p. (gr. 2-6). 1985. lib. bdg. 4.99 (ISBN 0-394-97037-3, Random Juv). Random.
—Peanut & Jilly Forever. 64p. (gr. 2-5). 1988. pap. 2.50 (ISBN 0-590-41507-7). Scholastic Inc.
Haas, Irene. The Maggie B. LC 74-18183. (Illus.). 32p. (ps-3). 1984. pap. 4.95 (ISBN 0-689-70764-9, Aladdin). Macmillan Child Grp.
Hahn, Mary D. Daphne's Book. LC 83-20933. 192p. (gr. 4-8). 1983. 13.95 (ISBN 0-89919-183-5, Clarion). HM.
—Daphne's Book. 192p. 1985. pap. 2.50 (ISBN 0-553-15360-9, Skylark). Bantam.
—The Jellyfish Season. LC 85-3759. 192p. (gr. 5-8). 1985. 13.95 (ISBN 0-89919-344-7, Clarion). Ticknor & Fields.
—The Sara Summer. 160p. (gr. 5 up). 1985. pap. 2.75 (ISBN 0-553-15481-8). Bantam.
Haines, Joan. A Banana for Rosie. Barker, Melissa & Logan, Ann, illus. 16p. (Orig.). (ps-1). 1985. pap. 2.65 (ISBN 0-936652-03-9, Pub. by Ed Concern Pubns). Two Ems.
—Meet Rosie Posie. Barker, Melissa & Logan, Ann, illus. 16p. (Orig.). (ps-1). 1985. pap. 2.65 (ISBN 0-936652-00-4, Pub. by Ed Concern Pubns). Two Ems.
—Rosie Posie Has a Bath. Barker, Melissa & Logan, Ann, illus. 16p. (ps-1). 1985. pap. 2.65 (ISBN 0-936652-02-0, Pub. by Ed Concern Pubns). Two Ems.
—Rosie Posie Makes Friends. Berker, Melissa & Logan, Ann, illus. 16p. (Orig.). (ps-1). 1985. pap. 2.65 (ISBN 0-936652-01-2, Pub. by Ed Concern Pubns). Two Ems.
Hall, Lynn. Halsey's Pride. 1990. 12.95 (ISBN 0-684-19155-5, Scribners Young Read). Macmillan Child Grp.
—In Trouble Again, Zelda Hammersmith? (Illus.). 138p. (gr. 3-5). 1987. 13.95 (ISBN 0-15-299964-7, HJ). HarBraceJ.
—In Trouble Again, Zelda Hammersmith. Cruz, Ray, illus. 150p. 1987. 13.95 (ISBN 0-15-238780-3). HarBraceJ.
—In Trouble Again, Zelda Hammersmith? 96p. (gr. 5 up). 1989. pap. 2.50 (ISBN 0-380-70612-1, Camelot). Avon.
—The Leaving. 128p. (gr. 7 up). 1988. pap. 2.95 (ISBN 0-02-043310-7, Collier Young Ad). Macmillan Child Grp.
—The Secret Life of Dagmar Schultz. LC 87-28499. 96p. (gr. 5-8). 1988. 12.95 (ISBN 0-684-18915-1, Scribners Young Read). Macmillan Child Grp.
—The Secret Life of Dagmar Schultz. LC 90-24502. 96p. (gr. 3-7). 1991. pap. 3.95 (ISBN 0-689-71446-7, Aladdin). Macmillan Child Grp.
—The Solitary. LC 86-1546. 128p. (gr. 7 up). 1986. 12.95 (ISBN 0-684-18724-8, Scribners Young Read). Macmillan Child Grp.
—The Solitary. 128p. (gr. 7 up). 1989. pap. 2.95 (ISBN 0-02-043315-8, Collier Young Ad). Macmillan Child Grp.
—Zelda Strikes Again! 144p. (gr. 3 up). 1988. 13.95 (ISBN 0-15-299966-3). HarBraceJ.
Hamilton, Alice S. The Rescue of the Rainbow. LC 87-90113. 89p. 1988. 7.95 (ISBN 0-533-07500-9). Vantage.
Hamilton, Dorothy. Anita's Choice. Moon, Ivan, illus. LC 70-131535. 96p. (gr. 4-9). 1971. pap. 3.95 (ISBN 0-8361-1741-7). Herald Pr.
—Carlie's Pink Room. Graber, Esther Rose, illus. LC 83-26437. 88p. (gr. 7-9). pap. 3.95 (ISBN 0-8361-3354-4). Herald Pr.

—Christmas for Holly. Graber, Esther R., illus. LC 72-141831. 112p. (gr. 4-9). 1971. pap. 3.95 (ISBN 0-8361-1658-5). Herald Pr.
—Gina In-Between. Converse, James, illus. LC 81-13387. 128p. (Orig.). (gr. 5 up). 1982. pap. 3.95 (ISBN 0-8361-1986-X). Herald Pr.
Hamilton, Virginia. Willie Bea & the Time the Martians Landed. 224p. (gr. 4-7). 1989. pap. 3.95 (ISBN 0-689-71328-2, Aladdin). Macmillan Child Grp.
Hamm, Anita M. Lisa & the Raindrops. (gr. 1-4). 1977. 3.50 (ISBN 0-935513-01-9). Samara Pubns.
Hansen, Ron. The Shadowmaker. Tomes, Margot, illus. LC 85-45272. 80p. (gr. 2-6). 1987. PLB 10.89 (ISBN 0-06-022203-4). HarpC Child Bks.
Hardy, Myronn E. Jenni & the Talking Tulip. (Illus.). 110p. (ps-3). 1989. pap. 4.95 (ISBN 0-9621696-3-3). Ezra Pub Inc.
Harler, Anne. New Girl in Town. 112p. (gr. 6-8). 1987. 2.50 (ISBN 0-87406-218-7). Willowisp Pr.
Harrah, Madge. Honey Girl. 128p. 1990. pap. 2.95 (ISBN 0-380-75828-8, Camelot). Avon.
Harris, Robie H. Rosie's Double Dare. De Luna, Tony, illus. LC 79-26907. 128p. (gr. 3-6). 1980. lib. bdg. 5.99 (ISBN 0-394-94459-3). Knopf.
—Rosie's Rock 'n' Roll Riot. MacDonald, Patricia, ed. Tenenbaum, Robert, illus. 128p. (Orig.). (gr. 3-5). 1990. pap. 2.95 (ISBN 0-671-67931-7, Minstrel Bks). PB.
Harvey, Brett. Immigrant Girl: Becky of Eldridge Street. Ray, Deborah K., illus. LC 86-15038. 40p. (gr. 1-4). 1987. reinforced bdg. 12.95 (ISBN 0-8234-0638-5). Holiday.
Hathorn, Libby. Freya's Fantastic Surprise. Thompson, Sharon, illus. (ps-3). 1989. 12.95 (ISBN 0-86896-381-X). Scholastic Inc.
—Freya's Fantastic Surprise. Thompson, Sharon, illus. 32p. (ps-3). 1989. 12.95 (ISBN 0-590-42442-4, Scholastic Hardcover). Scholastic Inc.
Hausman, Gerald. Beth: The Little Girl of Pine Knoll. Totten, Bob, illus. LC 74-82228. 32p. (gr. 6 up). 1974. 15.00 (ISBN 0-912846-08-9). Bookstore Pr.
Hautzig, Esther. The Endless Steppe. LC 68-13582. 256p. (gr. 7 up). 1987. pap. 3.50 (ISBN 0-06-447027-X, Trophy). HarpC Child Bks.
Havill, Juanita. It Always Happens to Leona. McCully, Emily A., illus. LC 88-39534. 96p. (gr. 2-5). 1991. pap. 2.95 (ISBN 0-679-80528-1, Bullseye Bks). Knopf.
Hawes, Louise. Nelson Malone Saves Flight 942. 160p. 1990. pap. 2.95 (ISBN 0-380-70758-6, Camelot). Avon.
Hawks, Robert. The Twenty-Six Minutes. 190p. (Orig.). (gr. 8-12). 1988. pap. 4.95 (ISBN 0-938961-03-9, Stamp Out Sheep Press). Sq One Pubs.
Haynes, Betsy. Taffy Sinclair Goes to Hollywood. (gr. 4 up). 1990. pap. 2.95 (ISBN 0-553-15819-8). Bantam.
Haynes, Mary. Catch the Sea. LC 88-26203. 176p. (gr. 4 up). 1989. 12.95 (ISBN 0-02-743451-6, Bradbury Pr). Macmillan Child Grp.
Haywood, Carolyn. Back to School with Betsy. 192p. (gr. 1-5). 1987. 12.95 (ISBN 0-318-37345-9, HJ); pap. 4.95 (ISBN 0-318-37346-7, HJ). HarBraceJ.
—Betsy & Billy. 156p. 1987. 12.95 (ISBN 0-318-37341-6, HJ); pap. 4.95 (ISBN 0-318-37342-4, HJ). HarBraceJ.
—Betsy & Mr. Killpatrick. (gr. k-6). 1989. pap. 3.25 (ISBN 0-440-40204-2, YB). Dell.
—Betsy & the Boys. LC 45-35133. 192p. (gr. 1-5). 1945. 12.95 (ISBN 0-15-206944-5, HJ); pap. 4.95 (ISBN 0-318-37344-0, HJ). HarBraceJ.
—Betsy's Busy Summer. (gr. k-6). 1989. pap. 3.25 (ISBN 0-440-40171-2, YB). Dell.
—Betsy's Little Star. 160p. (gr. 3-6). 1989. pap. 3.25 (ISBN 0-440-40172-0, YB). Dell.
—Betsy's Play School. (gr. k-6). 1989. pap. 3.25 (ISBN 0-440-40213-1, YB). Dell.
—Betsy's Winterhouse. (gr. k-6). 1989. pap. 3.25 (ISBN 0-440-40227-1, YB). Dell.
—Snowbound with Betsy. (gr. k-6). 1989. pap. 3.25 (ISBN 0-440-40246-8, YB). Dell.
Hedderwick, Mairi. Katie Morag & the Big Boy Cousins. Hedderwick, Mairi, illus. 32p. (ps-3). 1987. 12.95 (ISBN 0-316-35403-1). Little.
Henkel, Virginia. Letters from the Past. Luxford, Bruce, illus. LC 90-10113. 24p. (gr. k-4). 1990. PLB 15.96 (ISBN 0-8114-2698-X). Steck-V.
Henkes, Kevin. Jessica. (Illus.). 32p. (ps-3). 1990. pap. 3.95 (ISBN 0-14-054194-2, Puffin). Puffin Bks.
—Once Around the Block. Chess, Victoria, illus. LC 85-24901. 24p. (gr. k-3). 1987. 11.75 (ISBN 0-688-04954-0); PLB 11.88 (ISBN 0-688-04955-9). Greenwillow.
Henning, Kathy J. Long, Life, & Prosper. (Illus.). 25p. (gr. 3-5). 1988. 4.95 (ISBN 0-533-06956-4). Vantage.
Henry, Marguerite. Misty of Chincoteague. 160p. (gr. 4-6). pap. 1.75 (ISBN 0-590-02388-8). Scholastic Inc.
Her Honor, Katie Shannon. 128p. (gr. 5). 1989. pap. 2.75 (ISBN 0-553-15640-3). Bantam.
Herman, Charlotte. Millie Cooper, Take a Chance. Cogancherry, Helen, illus. LC 88-11081. 112p. (gr. 3 up). 1989. 11.95 (ISBN 0-525-44442-4, DCB). Dutton Child Bks.
Hermes, Patricia. You Shouldn't Have to Say Good-Bye. 128p. (gr. 3-7). 1984. pap. 2.75 (ISBN 0-590-43174-9). Scholastic Inc.
Hest, Amy. Getting Rid of Krista. Rogers, Jacqueline, illus. LC 87-23981. 80p. (gr. 2-5). 1988. 11.95 (ISBN 0-688-07149-X, Morrow Junior Books). Morrow.
—Ring & the Window Seat. (ps-3). 1990. 13.95 (ISBN 0-590-41350-3). Scholastic Inc.
Heyde, Christiane. The Happy Girl. Hawkins, Linda, illus. LC 89-85861. 40p. 1990. 11.95 (ISBN 0-87516-618-0). DeVorss.
Hidaka, Masako. Girl from the Snow Country. Stinchecum, Amanda M., tr. from JPN. LC 86-10584. (Illus.). 32p. (ps-4). 1986. 11.95 (ISBN 0-916291-06-5, Cranky Nell Bk). Kane-Miller Bk.
Hillam, Corbin. Jennifer of the Jungle. Hillam, Corbin, illus. 32p. (ps-2). 1990. text ed. 7.95. Concordia.
Hines, Anna. Boys Are Yucko! (gr. 4-7). 1990. pap. 2.75 (ISBN 0-590-43109-9). Scholastic Inc.
Hines, Anna G. It's Just Me, Emily. 1989. pap. 4.95 (ISBN 0-89919-853-8, Pub. by Clarion). Ticknor & Fields.
Hoban, Russell. Bedtime for Frances. Williams, Garth, illus. LC 60-8347. (ps-2). 1976. pap. 3.95 (ISBN 0-06-443005-7, Trophy). HarpC Child Bks.
Hodge, Lois L. A Season of Change. LC 87-18945. 112p. (gr. 7-12). 1987. pap. 2.95 (ISBN 0-930323-27-0, Kendall Green Pubns). Gallaudet Univ Pr.
Hoffman, Mary. Nancy No-Size. Northway, Jennifer, illus. 32p. (gr. k-3). 1987. 9.95 (ISBN 0-19-520596-0). Oxford U Pr.
Holabird, Katharine. Angelina at the Fair. Craig, Helen, illus. LC 84-28931. 24p. (ps-2). 1988. 11.95 (ISBN 0-517-55744-4, C N Potter Bks). Crown.
—Angelina Ballerina. miniature ed. Craig, Helen, illus. 24p. (ps-2). 1990. 4.95 (ISBN 0-517-57668-6, C N Potter). Crown.
Holcomb, Nan. Sarah's Surprise. Yoder, Dot, illus. 32p. (ps-2). 1990. pap. 5.95 (ISBN 0-944727-07-7). Jason & Nordic Pubs.
Holl, Kristi. Rose Beyond the Wall. 160p. (gr. 2-9). pap. 2.95 (ISBN 0-8167-1309-X). Troll Assocs.
Holl, Kristi D. Hidden in the Fog. LC 88-8178. 128p. (gr. 4-8). 1989. 12.95 (ISBN 0-689-31494-9, Atheneum Child Bk). Macmillan Child Grp.
—Perfect or Not, Here I Come. 160p. (gr. 4-8). 1987. pap. 2.95 (ISBN 0-8167-1048-1). Troll Assocs.
Holland, Isabelle. Dinah & the Green Fat Kingdom. LC 78-8612. 160p. (gr. 5 up). 1988. pap. 3.50 (ISBN 0-06-440221-5, Trophy). HarpC Child Bks.
Hollands, Judith. The Ketchup Sisters: The Deeds of the Desperate Campers. DeRosa, Dee, illus. 80p. (gr. 2-5). 1990. pap. 2.75 (ISBN 0-671-66811-0, Minstrel Bks). PB.
Holliman, Jo Ann G. Julia. 1988. 4.95 (ISBN 0-533-07615-3). Vantage.
Holman, Felice. The Wild Children. LC 83-8974. 160p. (gr. 7 up). 1983. 13.95 (ISBN 0-684-17970-9, Scribners Young Read). Macmillan Child Grp.
Holmes, Barbara W. Charlotte Cheetham: Master of Disaster. Himmelman, John., illus. LC 85-42617. 128p. (gr. 3-6). 1987. pap. 3.50 (ISBN 0-06-440211-8, Trophy). HarpC Child Bks.
Holtze, Sally H. Presenting Norma Fox Mazer. (gr. k-12). 1989. pap. 3.95 (ISBN 0-440-20486-0, LE). Dell.
Honeycutt, Natalie. Josie's Beau. 128p. 1988. pap. 2.50 (ISBN 0-380-70524-9, Camelot). Avon.
Hooks, William H. The Legend of the White Doe. Nolan, Denis, illus. LC 87-11176. 48p. (gr. 3 up). 1988. 13.95 (ISBN 0-02-744350-7, Mcmillan Child Bk). Macmillan Child Grp.
—Moss Gown. Carrick, Donald, illus. (gr. k-4). 1987. 13.95 (ISBN 0-89919-460-5, Pub. by Clarion). Ticknor & Fields.
Hopper, Nancy J. Carrie's Games. 128p. (gr. 7 up). 1989. pap. 2.50 (ISBN 0-380-70538-9, Flare). Avon.
—The Seven & One Half Sins of Stacey Kendall. 112p. (gr. 4-7). 1982. 9.95 (ISBN 0-525-45115-3, Dutton). NAL-Dutton.
Horner, Althea J. Little Big Girl. Rosamilia, Patricia, illus. 32p. (ps-3). 1982. 16.95 (ISBN 0-89885-098-3); pap. 9.95 (ISBN 0-89885-287-0). Human Sci Pr.
Hotze, Sollace. A Circle Unbroken. LC 88-2569. 224p. (gr. 7 up). 1988. 13.95 (ISBN 0-89919-733-7, Pub. by Clarion). Ticknor & Fields.
Howard, Ellen. Edith Herself. Hinter, Ronald, illus. LC 86-10826. 144p. (gr. 3-7). 1987. 12.95 (ISBN 0-689-31314-4, Atheneum Child Bk). Macmillan Child Grp.
Hughes, Shirley. Bathwater's Hot. LC 84-14389. (Illus.). 24p. (gr. k-1). 1985. 4.95 (ISBN 0-688-04202-3). Lothrop.
—Sally's Secret. (Illus.). 32p. (ps-1). 1988. pap. 3.50 (ISBN 0-14-050160-6, Puffin). Puffin Bks.
Hunt, Angela E. Cassie Perkins, No. 1: No More Broken Promises. 1991. PLB 3.95 (ISBN 0-8423-0461-4). Tyndale.
—Cassie Perkins, No. 3: A Basket of Roses. 1991. PLB 3.95 (ISBN 0-8423-0463-0). Tyndale.
—Cassie Perkins Number Two: A Forever Friend. 1991. PLB 3.95 (ISBN 0-685-38697-X). Tyndale.
Hunt, Irene. Up a Road Slowly. 100p. 1987. pap. 2.75 (ISBN 0-425-10003-0, Pub. by Berkley-Pacer). Berkley Pub.
Hurd, Edith T. I Dance in My Red Pajamas. McCully, Emily A., illus. LC 81-47721. 32p. (gr. 1-3). 1982. PLB 13.89 (ISBN 0-06-022700-1). HarpC Child Bks.
Hurmence, Belinda. A Girl Called Boy. (gr. 3-6). 1990. pap. 3.95 (ISBN 0-395-55698-8, Clarion Bks). HM.
Hurwitz, Johanna. Busybody Nora. Hoban, Lillian, illus. LC 89-13649. 64p. (ps up). 1990. Repr. of 1976 ed. 12.95 (ISBN 0-688-09092-3); PLB 12.88 (ISBN 0-688-09093-1, Morrow Jr Bks). Morrow Jr Bks.
—DeDe Takes Charge! De Groat, Diane, illus. LC 84-9085. 128p. (gr. 3-7). 1984. 12.95 (ISBN 0-688-03853-0). Morrow Jr Bks.
—Dede Takes Charge! De Groat, Diane, illus. 128p. (gr. 4-6). 1986. pap. 2.50 (ISBN 0-590-33662-2, Apple Paperbacks). Scholastic Inc.
—Dede Takes Charge! 128p. (gr. 3-7). 1986. pap. 2.75 (ISBN 0-590-43128-5). Scholastic Inc.
—Tough-Luck Karen. De Groat, Diane, illus. 160p. (gr. 4-6). 1984. pap. 2.50 (ISBN 0-590-41118-7, Apple Paperbacks). Scholastic Inc.
—Tough-Luck Karen. 160p. (gr. 3-7). 1984. pap. 2.75 (ISBN 0-590-44046-2). Scholastic Inc.
Hutchins, H. Leanna Builds a Genie Trap. (Illus.). 24p. (ps-8). 1987. 12.95 (ISBN 0-920303-54-4); pap. 4.95 (ISBN 0-920303-55-2). Firefly Bks Ltd.
Impey, Rose. Who's a Bright Girl? Amstutz, Andre, illus. 42p. (gr. 2-4). 1989. 3.95 (ISBN 0-8120-6144-6). Barron.
James, Simon. Sally & the Limpet. James, Simon, illus. LC 90-40088. 32p. (ps-3). 1991. SBE 12.95 (ISBN 0-689-50528-0, M K McElderry). Macmillan Child Grp.
Jane Eyre. (gr. 4 up). 1988. pap. 4.87 (ISBN 0-582-54161-1, 74268). Longman.
Jane Eyre. (gr. 4 up). 1988. Incl. 26 cards. 22.00 (ISBN 0-8172-2182-4). Raintree Pubs.
Jarrow, Gail. If Phyllis Were Here. 140p. (gr. 3-7). 1987. 12.95 (ISBN 0-395-43667-2). HM.
Jensen, Virginia A. Sara & the Door. Strugnell, Ann, illus. LC 84-40775. 32p. (ps-1). 1977. 11.95 (ISBN 0-201-03446-8, Lipp Jr Bks). HarpC Child Bks.
Jeschke, Susan. Lucky's Choice. Jeschke, Susan, illus. (gr. k-3). 1988. pap. 3.95 (ISBN 0-590-40521-7). Scholastic Inc.
Johnston, Norma. Return to Morocco. LC 88-6880. 176p. (gr. 7 up). 1988. 13.95 (ISBN 0-02-747712-6, Four Winds). Macmillan Child Grp.
Jones, Adrienne. Whistle Down a Dark Lane. LC 81-48661. 288p. (gr. 7 up). 1982. 13.95 (ISBN 0-06-023063-0). HarpC Child Bks.
Jones, Robin D. No Shakespeare Allowed. LC 88-33080. 176p. (gr. 6-9). 1989. 12.95 (ISBN 0-689-31488-4, Atheneum Child Bk). Macmillan Child Grp.
Joosse, Barbara M. Anna, the One & Only. Mayo, Gretchen W., illus. LC 88-890. 144p. (gr. 3-7). 1988. 11.95 (ISBN 0-397-32322-0, Lipp Jr Bks); PLB 11.89 (ISBN 0-397-32323-9, Lipp Jr Bks). HarpC Child Bks.
—Anna, the One & Only. Mayo, Gretchen W., illus. LC 88-890. 144p. (gr. 2-6). 1990. pap. 3.50 (ISBN 0-06-440345-9, Trophy). HarpC Child Bks.
Judy Blume. Incl. Are You There, God? It's Me, Margaret; Blubber; Otherwise Known As Sheila the Great; Superfudge; Tales of a Fourth Grade Nothing. 1983. pap. 13.00 boxed set (ISBN 0-440-44348-2). Dell.
Jukes, Mavis. Lights Around the Palm. Schuett, Stacey, illus. LC 86-172. 40p. (gr. 1-5). 1987. 12.95 (ISBN 0-394-88399-3); lib. bdg. 13.99 (ISBN 0-394-98399-8). Knopf.
Kaetler, Sarah. Stories from Grandpa's Rocking Chair. Klassen, Neil, illus. 64p. (Orig.). (gr. 1-5). 1984. pap. 3.95 (ISBN 0-919797-11-3). Kindred Pr.
Kaplow, Robert. Alessandra in Love. LC 87-45883. 160p. (gr. 7 up). 1991. pap. 3.50 (ISBN 0-06-447053-9, Trophy). HarpC Child Bks.
Kassem, Lou. Listen for Rachel. LC 86-8673. 176p. (gr. 7 up). 1986. 13.95 (ISBN 0-689-50396-2, M K McElderry). Macmillan Child Grp.
Kaye, Geraldine. Comfort Herself. Northway, Jenny, illus. 160p. (gr. 6 up). 1985. 10.95 (ISBN 0-233-97614-0). Andre Deutsch.
Kaye, Marilyn. Cassie. LC 87-11944. 144p. (gr. 3-7). 1987. 13.95 (ISBN 0-15-200421-1, Gulliver Bks); pap. 4.95 (ISBN 0-15-200422-X, Gulliver Bks). HarBraceJ.
—Daphne. LC 86-29420. (Illus.). 160p. (gr. 3-7). 1987. 13.95 (ISBN 0-15-200434-3, Gulliver Bks); pap. 3.95 (ISBN 0-317-64881-0). HarBraceJ.
—Erin & the Movie Star. 128p. 1991. pap. 2.95 (ISBN 0-380-76181-5, Camelot). Avon.
—Katie Steals the Show. 128p. 1990. pap. 2.95 (ISBN 0-380-75910-1, Camelot). Avon.
—Lydia. LC 87-12763. 144p. (gr. 2-7). 1987. 13.95 (ISBN 0-15-200510-2, Gulliver Bks); pap. 4.95 (ISBN 0-15-200511-0, Gulliver Bks). HarBraceJ.
—The New & Improved Sarah. 144p. (Orig.). 1990. pap. 2.95 (ISBN 0-380-76180-7, Camelot). Avon.
—New Girl in Cabin Six. 128p. (Orig.). 1989. pap. 2.95 (ISBN 0-380-75703-6, Camelot). Avon.
—Phoebe. (gr. 3-7). 1987. 13.95 (ISBN 0-15-200430-0); pap. 4.95 (ISBN 0-15-200431-9). HarBraceJ.
—A Witch in Cabin Six. 128p. (gr. 3-4). 1990. pap. 2.95 (ISBN 0-380-75912-8, Camelot). Avon.
Keller, Beverly. Desdemona: Twelve Going on Desperate. LC 86-10655. 160p. (gr. 3-7). 1986. 12.95 (ISBN 0-688-06076-5). Lothrop.
—Desdemona: Twelve Going on Desperate. LC 87-45287. 160p. (gr. 3-7). 1988. pap. 2.95 (ISBN 0-06-440226-6, Trophy). HarpC Child Bks.
—Only Fiona. LC 86-45786. 160p. (gr. 3-7). 1988. 11.95 (ISBN 0-06-023269-2); PLB 11.89 (ISBN 0-06-023270-6). HarpC Child Bks.
Keller, Holly. Geraldine's Big Snow. LC 87-14936. (Illus.). 24p. (ps-3). 1988. 11.95 (ISBN 0-688-07513-4); lib. bdg. 11.88 (ISBN 0-688-07514-2). Greenwillow.
—Lizzie's Invitation. LC 86-19380. (ps-3). 1987. 11.75 (ISBN 0-688-06124-9); PLB 11.88 (ISBN 0-688-06125-7). Greenwillow.
Kemp, Gene. The Room with No Windows. 114p. (gr. 3-6). 1989. pap. 4.95 (ISBN 0-571-16117-0). Faber & Faber.

Kennedy, Richard. Amy's Eyes. Egielski, Richard, illus. LC 82-48841. 448p. (gr. 5 up). 1988. pap. 6.95 (ISBN 0-06-440220-7, Trophy). HarpC Child Bks.

Kent, Deborah. One Step at a Time. 208p. (gr. 5-9). 1991. pap. 2.75 (ISBN 0-590-41580-8). Scholastic Inc.

Kerr, M. E. Is That You, Miss Blue? LC 74-2627. 176p. (gr. 7 up). 1987. pap. 2.95 (ISBN 0-06-447033-4, Trophy). HarpC Child Bks.

Kingman, Lee. Luck of the Miss L. (gr. 4-6). 1986. 12.95 (ISBN 0-685-11813-4). HM.

Kitamura, Satoshi. Lily Takes a Walk. (ps-3). 1991. pap. 3.95 (ISBN 0-525-44699-0, Dutton Unicorn). Puffin Bks.

Klein, Norma. Confessions of an Only Child. Cuffari, Richard, illus. LC 73-14750. 112p. (gr. 3-7). 1988. pap. 2.95 (ISBN 0-394-80569-0). Knopf.

—Girls Can Be Anything. Doty, Roy, illus. 32p. (ps-1). 1975. 11.95 (ISBN 0-525-30662-5, DCB); pap. 3.95 (ISBN 0-525-45029-7, DCB). Dutton Child Bks.

—What It's All About. LC 75-10015. 160p. (gr. 3-7). 1989. pap. 2.95 (ISBN 0-394-82302-8, Bullseye Bks). Knopf.

Klein, Robin. Hating Alison Ashley. (gr. 5-9). 1987. pap. 12.95 (ISBN 0-670-80864-4). Viking Child Bks.

Klusmeyer, Joann. Shelly from Rockytop Farm. Taylor, Neil, illus. 65p. (gr. 3-6). 1986. 5.95 (ISBN 1-55523-014-8). Winston-Derek.

Knorr, Dandi D. Allyson J. Cat. Hutton, Kathryn, tr. (Illus.). 32p. (gr. k-2). 1989. pasted 1.99 (ISBN 0-87403-591-0, 3851). Standard Pub.

Komaiko, Leah. Annie Bananie. Cornell, Laura, illus. LC 86-45767. 32p. (ps-3). 1987. 13.95 (ISBN 0-06-023259-5); PLB 13.89 (ISBN 0-06-023261-7). HarpC Child Bks.

—Annie Bananie. Cornell, Laura, illus. LC 86-45767. 32p. (gr. k-3). 1989. pap. 3.95 (ISBN 0-06-443198-3, Trophy). HarpC Child Bks.

Korman, Gordon. This Can't Be Happening at MacDonald Hall. 128p. 1990. pap. 2.75 (ISBN 0-590-44213-9). Scholastic Inc.

Krauss, Ruth & Johnson, Crockett. Is This You? Johnson, Crockett, illus. 32p. (gr. k-3). 1988. pap. 2.95 (ISBN 0-590-41196-9). Scholastic Inc.

Krementz, Jill. A Very Young Rider. (gr. k-6). 1987. pap. 6.95 (ISBN 0-440-49215-7, YB). Dell.

Kroll, Steven. Looking for Daniela: A Romantic Adventure. Lobel, Anita, illus. LC 87-29071. 32p. (gr. k-3). 1988. reinforced bdg. 14.95 (ISBN 0-8234-0695-4). Holiday.

Kunsch de Sokoluk, M. Cristina. Cartas de Ester. (SPA.). 110p. (gr. 10 up). 1988. pap. 3.75 (ISBN 0-311-37027-6). Casa Bautista.

Kurtz, Jane. I'm Calling Molly. Levine, Abby, ed. Trivas, Irene, illus. 32p. (ps-1). 1989. 12.95 (ISBN 0-8075-3468-4). A Whitman.

Lady Lovely Locks & the Pixietails. (Illus.). (gr. k-9). 1988. pap. 1.95 (ISBN 0-318-36476-X). Scholastic Inc.

Lampi, Kathlyn. Lighten Up, Jennifer. (gr. 6 up). 1988. write for info. (ISBN 0-373-98015-9). S&S Trade.

Landon, Lucinda. Meg Mackintosh & the Case of the Curious Whale Watch. Landon, Lucinda, illus. 48p. (gr. 2-5). 1987. 12.95 (ISBN 0-316-51362-8, Joy St Bks). Little.

Langley, Bob. Autumn Tiger. 256p. Date not set. pap. 3.50 (ISBN 0-685-19806-5). Bantam.

Lasky, Kathryn. Pageant. (gr. k-12). 1988. pap. 3.95 (ISBN 0-440-20161-6, LFL). Dell.

L'Engle, Madeleine. A Ring of Endless Light. LC 79-27679. 356p. (gr. 7 up). 1980. 15.95 (ISBN 0-374-36299-8). FS&G.

Leonard, Alison. Tina's Chance. 160p. (gr. 7 up). 1988. pap. 11.95 (ISBN 0-670-82430-5). Viking Child Bks.

Leppard, Lois G. Mandie & the Silent Catacombs. 160p. (gr. 3-8). 1990. 3.95 (ISBN 1-55661-148-X). Bethany Hse.

Lester, Alison. Ruby. Lester, Alison, illus. LC 87-16997. 32p. (ps-3). 1988. 13.95 (ISBN 0-395-46477-3). HM.

Levin, Betty. The Ice Bear. LC 86-254. 192p. (gr. 5 up). 1986. reinforced trade ed. 10.25 (ISBN 0-688-06431-0). Greenwillow.

Levy, Elizabeth. Come Out Smiling: A Novel. LC 80-68734. 192p. (gr. 8-12). 1981. 8.95 (ISBN 0-440-01378-X). Delacorte.

—World Class Gymnast. 112p. 1990. pap. 2.75 (ISBN 0-590-43832-8). Scholastic Inc.

Lewis, Linda. Too Young to Go for Boys. (gr. 2-5). 1990. pap. 2.75 (ISBN 0-671-69560-6, Archway). PB.

—Too Young to Go for Boys. MacDonald, Patricia, ed. 144p. (gr. 4-7). 1990. pap. 2.75 (ISBN 0-671-66603-7, Minstrel). PB.

—We Hate Everything but Boys. (gr. 5-7). 1990. pap. 2.95 (ISBN 0-671-72225-5, Archway). PB.

Lexau, Joan M. Striped Ice Cream. Wilson, John, illus. (gr. 2-6). 1971. pap. 2.50 (ISBN 0-590-41307-4). Scholastic Inc.

—Striped Ice Cream. 128p. (gr. 2-4). 1985. pap. 2.75 (ISBN 0-590-42903-5). Scholastic Inc.

Lillington, Kenneth. Josephine. 148p. (gr. 3-6). 1991. pap. 4.95 (ISBN 0-571-16118-9). Faber & Faber.

Lindbergh, Anne. The People in Pineapple Place. 160p. (gr. 4-5). 1990. pap. 2.95 (ISBN 0-380-70766-7, Camelot). Avon.

Lindbergh, Anne M. Hunky-Dory Dairy. 160p. (gr. 3-7). 1987. pap. 2.75 (ISBN 0-380-70320-3, Camelot). Avon.

Lindgren, Astrid. Lotta on Troublemaker Street. Brinckloe, Julie, illus. Bothmer, Gerry, tr. (Illus.). 64p. (gr. 3-7). 1991. pap. 2.95 (ISBN 0-689-71443-2, Aladdin). Macmillan Child Grp.

—The New Adventures of Pippi Longstocking Activity Book. (Orig.). 1988. pap. 2.95 (ISBN 0-14-050889-9, Puffin). Puffin Bks.

—Pippi Goes on Board. 192p. 1981. Repr. PLB 16.95x (ISBN 0-89966-339-7). Buccaneer Bks.

—Pippi Goes on Board. (Orig.). 1977. pap. 3.95 (ISBN 0-14-032774-6, Puffin); pap. 3.95 (ISBN 0-14-030959-4, Puffin). Puffin Bks.

—Pippi in the South Seas. (Orig.). 1988. pap. 3.95 (ISBN 0-14-032773-8, Puffin). Puffin Bks.

—Pippi in the South Seas. Bothmer, Gerry, tr. Glanzman, Louis S., illus. 128p. (gr. 3-7). 1977. pap. 3.95 (ISBN 0-14-030958-6, Puffin). Puffin Bks.

—Pippi Longstocking. 192p. 1981. Repr. PLB 21.95 (ISBN 0-89966-338-9). Buccaneer Bks.

—Pippi Longstocking. (Orig.). 1988. pap. 3.95 (ISBN 0-14-032772-X, Puffin). Puffin Bks.

—Pippi Longstocking. Lamborn, Florence, tr. Glanzman, Louis S., illus. 158p. (gr. 4-6). 1977. pap. 3.95 (ISBN 0-14-030957-8, Puffin). Puffin Bks.

—Pippi Longstocking. large type ed. 127p. 1987. Repr. of 1945 ed. 13.95 (ISBN 1-55736-152-5, Crnrstn Bks). ABC-CLIO.

Little, Jean. Kate. LC 70-148419. 174p. (gr. 5-8). 1971. PLB 12.89 (ISBN 0-06-023914-X). HarpC Child Bks.

Little Red Riding Hood. (FRE & SPA.). (gr. k-3). sp. ed. 4.95 (ISBN 0-685-28450-6); fr. ed. 4.95 (ISBN 0-685-28451-4). French & Eur.

Little Women. (Illus.). (gr. 3-5). 3.50 (ISBN 0-7214-5005-9). Ladybird Bks.

Lloyd, David. The Sneeze. Wegner, Fritz, illus. LC 85-46022. 32p. (ps-2). 1986. PLB 11.89 (ISBN 0-685-12397-9, Lipp Jr Bks); PLB 11.89 (ISBN 0-397-32196-1). HarpC Child Bks.

Lobel, Arnold. Lucille. LC 64-11616. (Illus.). 64p. (gr. k-3). 1964. PLB 11.89 (ISBN 0-06-023966-2). HarpC Child Bks.

Lorna Doone. (Illus.). (gr. 3-5). 3.50 (ISBN 0-7214-0822-2). Ladybird Bks.

Louie, Al-Ling. Yeh Shen: A Cinderella Story from China. Young, Ed, illus. 32p. (ps-2). 1990. 13.95 (ISBN 0-399-20900-X, Philomel). Putnam Pub Group.

Lovelace, Maud H. Heaven to Betsy. Neville, Vera, illus. LC 45-9806. 268p. (gr. 4-7). 1980. pap. 3.50 (ISBN 0-06-440110-3, Trophy). HarpC Child Bks.

Lowe, George L. B. G., Vol. 1: The Little Drummer Girl Who Drums for the Sun. Montrell, Dan, illus. 21p. (Orig.). (ps). 1988. PLB 5.00x (ISBN 0-685-22681-6). G L Lowe.

Lowry, Lois. Anastasia & Her Chosen Career. 192p. (gr. 3-7). 1987. 13.95 (ISBN 0-395-42506-9). HM.

—Anastasia at Your Service. De Groat, Diane, illus. LC 82-9231. 160p. (gr. 3-6). 1982. 13.95 (ISBN 0-395-32865-9). HM.

—Anastasia at Your Service. large type ed. 224p. 1989. PLB 15.95 (ISBN 1-55736-101-0, Crnrstn Bks). ABC-CLIO.

—Anastasia Has the Answers. (gr. k-6). 1987. pap. 2.95 (ISBN 0-440-40087-2, YB). Dell.

—Anastasia Krupnik. 128p. 1984. pap. 2.95 (ISBN 0-553-15534-2). Bantam.

—Anastasia Krupnik. 160p. (gr. 3-6). 1979. 12.95 (ISBN 0-395-28629-8). HM.

—Anastasia on Her Own. (gr. 2-6). 1986. pap. 2.95 (ISBN 0-440-40291-3, YB). Dell.

—Anastasia on Her Own. large type ed. 184p. 1989. Repr. of 1985 ed. PLB 15.95 (ISBN 1-55736-135-5, Crnrstn Bks). ABC-CLIO.

—Anastasia's Chosen Career. (gr. k-6). 1988. pap. 2.95 (ISBN 0-318-33286-8, YB). Dell.

—The One Hundredth Thing about Caroline. 160p. (gr. 3-6). 1983. 10.95 (ISBN 0-395-34829-3). HM.

—Taking Care of Terrific. large type ed. 208p. 1989. Repr. of 1983 ed. PLB 15.95 (ISBN 1-55736-119-3, Crnrstn Bks). ABC-CLIO.

Luenn, Nancy. Unicorn Crossing. Hanson, Peter E., illus. LC 87-995. 64p. (gr. 2-5). 1987. 11.95 (ISBN 0-689-31384-5, Atheneum). Macmillan Child Grp.

Luger, Harriet. Lauren. 176p. (gr. 9 up). 1981. pap. 1.50 (ISBN 0-440-94700-6, LE). Dell.

Mcbrier, Page. Daphne Takes Charge. 1990. pap. 2.95 (ISBN 0-380-75899-7, Camelot). Avon.

McDaniel, Lurlene. Time to Let Go. (gr. 5 up). 1991. pap. 2.95 (ISBN 0-553-28350-2, Starfire). Bantam.

MacDonald, George. A Daughter's Devotion. rev. ed. Phillips, Michael, ed. LC 88-19256. 320p. (gr. 11 up). 1988. pap. 6.95 (ISBN 0-87123-906-X). Bethany Hse.

—The Princess & the Curdie. (Orig.). (gr. k-6). 1987. pap. 4.95 (ISBN 0-440-47182-6, Pub. by Yearling Clasics). Dell.

Macdonald, Maryann. Fatso Jean, the Ice Cream Queen. (gr. 4 up). 1990. pap. 2.95 (ISBN 0-553-15797-3). Bantam.

McDonnell, Christine. Count Me In. 80p. (Orig.). (gr. 6-9). 1988. pap. 3.95 (ISBN 0-14-031856-9, Puffin). Puffin Bks.

McFann, Jane. One More Chance. 192p. (gr. 6 up). 1988. pap. 2.50 (ISBN 0-380-75466-5, Flare). Avon.

McGrath, Bob. Dog Lies. (Illus.). 48p. (ps-2). 1989. pap. 7.95 incl. audiocassette (ISBN 0-8431-2766-X). Price Stern.

McKean, Thomas. The Search for Sara Sanderson. 160p. (gr. 3-7). 1987. pap. 2.50 (ISBN 0-380-75295-6, Camelot). Avon.

Mckenna, Colleen O. Fifth Grade. 1989. pap. 10.95 (ISBN 0-590-41733-9). Scholastic Inc.

MacLachlan, Patricia. Cassie Binegar. LC 81-48641. 128p. (gr. 3-7). 1982. PLB 11.89 (ISBN 0-06-024034-2). HarpC Child Bks.

—Cassie Binegar. LC 81-48641. 128p. (gr. 3-7). 1987. pap. 3.50 (ISBN 0-06-440195-2, Trophy). HarpC Child Bks.

—Sarah, Plain & Tall. LC 83-49481. 64p. (gr. 3 up). 1987. pap. 3.50 (ISBN 0-06-440205-3, Trophy). HarpC Child Bks.

McNamara, John. Model Behavior. (gr. k-12). 1987. pap. 2.75 (ISBN 0-440-95569-6, LFL). Dell.

Madeline Pop-Up. (Illus.). (ps-3). 13.95 (ISBN 0-317-62531-4). Viking Child Bks.

Martin, Ann M. Baby-Sitters on Board! 240p. (Orig.). (gr. 3-7). 1988. pap. 2.95 (ISBN 0-590-41588-3, Apple Paperbacks). Scholastic Inc.

—Baby-Sitters' Summer Vacation. (gr. 5 up). 1989. pap. 2.95 (ISBN 0-590-42419-X, Apple Paperbacks). Scholastic Inc.

—California Girls! 240p. (gr. 3-7). 1990. pap. 3.50 (ISBN 0-590-43575-2). Scholastic Inc.

—Claudia & Middle School. (gr. 4-7). 1991. pap. 2.95 (ISBN 0-590-44082-9). Scholastic Inc.

—Claudia & the New Girl. 160p. (gr. 3-7). 1988. pap. 2.75 (ISBN 0-590-41126-8, Apple Paperbacks). Scholastic Inc.

—The Ghost at Dawn's House. 144p. (Orig.). (gr. 4-6). 1988. pap. 2.75 (ISBN 0-590-41123-3, Apple Paperbacks). Scholastic Inc.

—Hello, Mallory. 144p. (Orig.). (gr. 3-7). 1988. pap. 2.75 (ISBN 0-590-41128-4, Apple Paperbacks). Scholastic Inc.

—Jessi & the Dance School Phantom. 160p. (gr. 3-7). 1991. pap. 3.25 (ISBN 0-590-44083-7, Apple Paperbacks). Scholastic Inc.

—Jessi & the Superbrat. (gr. 5 up). 1989. pap. 2.95 (ISBN 0-590-42502-1, Apple Paperbacks). Scholastic Inc.

—Karen's Birthday. (gr. 4-7). 1990. pap. 2.75 (ISBN 0-590-44257-0). Scholastic Inc.

—Karen's Ghost. 96p. (gr. 2-4). 1990. pap. 2.75 (ISBN 0-590-43649-X). Scholastic Inc.

—Karen's Goldfish. 112p. (gr. 2-4). 1991. pap. 2.75 (ISBN 0-590-43644-9). Scholastic Inc.

—Karen's in Love. (gr. 4-7). 1991. pap. 2.75 (ISBN 0-590-43645-7). Scholastic Inc.

—Karen's Kittycat Club. 112p. (gr. 2-4). 1989. pap. 2.75 (ISBN 0-590-44264-3). Scholastic Inc.

—Karen's Little Sister. 96p. (gr. 2-4). 1989. pap. 2.75 (ISBN 0-590-44298-8). Scholastic Inc.

—Karen's New Year. (gr. 4-7). 1991. pap. 2.75 (ISBN 0-590-43646-5). Scholastic Inc.

—Karen's Roller Skates. Tang, Susan, illus. 80p. (gr. 2-4). 1988. pap. 2.50 (ISBN 0-590-41781-9). Scholastic Inc.

—Karen's Roller Skates. 64p. (gr. 2-4). 1988. pap. 2.75 (ISBN 0-590-44259-7). Scholastic Inc.

—Karen's School Picture. (gr. 1 up). 1989. pap. 2.50 (ISBN 0-590-42672-9, Apple Paperbacks). Scholastic Inc.

—Karen's School Picture. 112p. (gr. 2-4). 1989. pap. 2.75 (ISBN 0-590-44258-9). Scholastic Inc.

—Karen's Sleepover. (gr. 4-7). 1990. pap. 2.50 (ISBN 0-590-43652-X). Scholastic Inc.

—Karen's Surprise. 112p. (gr. 2-4). 1990. pap. 2.75 (ISBN 0-590-43648-1). Scholastic Inc.

—Karen's Wish. 128p. (gr. 2-4). 1990. pap. 2.95 (ISBN 0-590-43647-3). Scholastic Inc.

—Karen's Witch. 112p. (gr. 2-4). 1988. pap. 2.75 (ISBN 0-590-44300-3). Scholastic Inc.

—Kristy & the Snobs. 160p. (gr. 3-7). 1988. pap. 2.75 (ISBN 0-590-41125-X, Apple Paperbacks). Scholastic Inc.

—Kristy's Big Day. (gr. 4-7). 1987. pap. 2.95 (ISBN 0-590-43899-9). Scholastic Inc.

—Kristy's Great Idea. 160p. (Orig.). (gr. 4-6). 1986. pap. 2.75 (ISBN 0-590-41985-4, Apple Paperbacks). Scholastic Inc.

—Mary Anne vs. Logan. (gr. 4-7). 1991. pap. 2.95 (ISBN 0-590-43570-1). Scholastic Inc.

—Poor Mallory. 160p. 1990. pap. 2.95 (ISBN 0-590-43568-X). Scholastic Inc.

—Slam Book. LC 87-45335. 160p. (gr. 7 up). 1987. 12.95 (ISBN 0-8234-0666-0). Holiday.

—Slam Book. 1989. pap. 2.75 (ISBN 0-590-41838-6). Scholastic Inc.

—Stacey's Mistake. 1988. pap. 2.75 (ISBN 0-590-41584-0). Scholastic Inc.

—Yours Turly, Shirley. LC 88-6460. 144p. (gr. 3-7). 1988. 12.95 (ISBN 0-8234-0719-5). Holiday.

Martin, Guenn. Remember the Eagle Day. Converse, James, illus. LC 83-26376. 128p. (gr. 7-9). 1983. pap. 4.95 (ISBN 0-8361-3351-X). Herald Pr.

Marton, J. Midnight Visit at Molly's House. (Illus.). 24p. (ps-8). 1988. 12.95 (ISBN 0-920303-99-4); pap. 4.95 (ISBN 0-920303-98-6). Firefly Bks Ltd.

Martyn, Harriet. Jenny & the Syndicate. 144p. (gr. 6-9). 1984. 8.95 (ISBN 0-233-97436-9). Andre Deutsch.

Marzollo, Jean. Red Ribbon Rosie. Sims, Blanche, illus. LC 87-29641. 64p. (Orig.). (gr. 2-4). 1988. lib. bdg. 5.99 (ISBN 0-394-99608-9, Random Juv); pap. 2.50 (ISBN 0-394-89608-4). Random.

Mason, Margo. Ready, Alice? (gr. 4 up). 1990. pap. 3.50 (ISBN 0-553-34741-1). Bantam.

Mayper, Monica. After Good-Night. Sis, Peter, illus. LC 86-45766. 32p. (ps-3). 1987. 11.95 (ISBN 0-06-024120-9). HarpC Child Bks.

Mazer, Norma F. A, My Name Is Ami. 160p. (Orig.). (gr. 3-7). 1991. pap. 2.95 (ISBN 0-590-43896-4, Apple Paperbacks). Scholastic Inc.
—Silver. 208p. 1989. pap. 2.95 (ISBN 0-380-75026-0, Flare). Avon.
—Taking Terri Mueller. 192p. (gr. 8 up). 1981. pap. 3.50 (ISBN 0-380-79004-1, 88914-5, Flare). Avon.
Meet Ramona Quimby. Incl. Ramona Quimby, Age Eight; Ramona the Pest; Ramona & Her Father; Ramona & Her Mother. 1983. pap. 11.20 boxed set (ISBN 0-440-45548-0). Dell.
Menzel, Barbara J. Would You Rather? Brahm, Sumishta, illus. LC 81-6810. 32p. (ps-3). 1982. 16.95 (ISBN 0-89885-076-2). Human Sci Pr.
Messenger, Norman. Annabel's House. LC 88-60089. (Illus.). 28p. 1989. 17.95 (ISBN 0-531-05764-X). Orchard Bks Watts.
Meyer, Carolyn. Because of Lissa. (gr. 7 up). 1990. pap. 2.95 (ISBN 0-553-28802-4, Starfire). Bantam.
—Gillian's Choice. 1991. pap. 2.95 (ISBN 0-553-28835-0). Bantam.
Miles, Betty. Looking On. LC 77-15946. 192p. (gr. 5-9). 1989. pap. 3.25 (ISBN 0-394-82597-7, Borzoi Sprinters). Knopf.
—The Real Me. LC 74-160. 128p. (gr. 3-7). 1989. pap. 2.95 (ISBN 0-394-82588-8). Knopf.
Miles, Miska. Annie & the Old One. Parnall, Peter, illus. (gr. 1-3). 1972. lib. bdg. 13.95i (ISBN 0-316-57117-2, Joy St Bks). Little.
Miller, Sandy. Smart Girl. 160p. (gr. 7 up). 1982. pap. 2.25 (ISBN 0-451-11887-1, Sig Vista). NAL-Dutton.
Mills, Claudia. After Fifth Grade, the World! LC 88-26664. 128p. (gr. 3-7). 1989. 12.95 (ISBN 0-02-767041-4, Mcmillan Child Bk). Macmillan Child Grp.
—Cally's Enterprise. LC 87-36471. 128p. (gr. 3-7). 1988. 12.95 (ISBN 0-02-767100-3, Mcmillan Child Bk). Macmillan Child Grp.
—Cally's Enterprise. 128p. (gr. 5 up). 1989. pap. 2.75 (ISBN 0-380-70693-8, Camelot). Avon.
—The One & Only Cynthia Jane Thornton. LC 86-12629. 120p. (gr. 3-7). 1986. 11.95 (ISBN 0-02-767090-2, Mcmillan Child Bk). Macmillan Child Grp.
Mills, Diana. Crazy Hattie. (Illus.). 12p. (gr. 3-7). 1986. pap. 7.95 (ISBN 0-9616555-0-X). Berry Good Child Bks.
Miner, Jane C. Joanna, No. 5. 368p. (gr. 7 up). 1984. pap. 2.95 (ISBN 0-590-33241-4, Sunfire). Scholastic Inc.
—Margaret. 224p. (Orig.). (gr. 7 up). 1988. pap. 2.75 (ISBN 0-590-41191-8). Scholastic Inc.
Montfort, Elizabeth S. That Special Magic. LC 87-71719. (Illus.). 53p. (Orig.). (gr. 2-3). 1988. pap. 5.00 (ISBN 0-916383-37-7). Aegina Pr.
Montgomery, L. M. Anne of Avonlea. (gr. 8 up). 1984. pap. 2.95 (ISBN 0-8049-0219-4). Airmont.
—Anne of Green Gables. Lee, Jody, illus. (gr. 4 up). 1983. deluxe ed. 12.95 (ISBN 0-448-06030-2, G&D). Putnam Pub Group.
—Anne of Green Gables. (gr. 7 up). 1984. pap. 1.95 (ISBN 0-8049-0218-6). Airmont.
—Anne's House of Dreams, No. 5. 240p. (gr. 7-9). 1981. pap. 2.95 (ISBN 0-553-24195-8). Bantam.
—Chronicles of Avonlea. Rubio, Mario, afterword by. 224p. 1988. pap. 2.95 (ISBN 0-451-52233-8, Sig Classics). NAL-Dutton.
—Emily of New Moon. 352p. (Orig.). Date not set. pap. 3.50 (ISBN 0-318-33019-9, Starfire). Bantam.
—Further Chronicles of Avonlea. 208p. (Orig.). 1989. pap. 2.95 (ISBN 0-553-21381-4, Starfire). Bantam.
Montgomery, Lucy M. Anne of Green Gables, Vol. 1. (gr. 4-7). 1984. pap. 2.95 (ISBN 0-553-15327-7). Bantam.
—Emily, 3 vols. (gr. 9-12). 1990. Boxed set. pap. 10.50 (ISBN 0-553-33308-9). Bantam.
—Emily Climbs. 336p. (Orig.). 1983. pap. 3.50 (ISBN 0-553-26214-9, Starfire). Bantam.
Moody, Ralph. Mary Emma & Company. (Illus.). (gr. 8 up). 1961. 11.95 (ISBN 0-393-08382-9). Norton.
Moore, Yvette. Freedom Songs. LC 88-43073. 176p. (gr. 7 up). 1991. 14.95 (ISBN 0-531-05812-3); PLB 14.99 (ISBN 0-531-08412-4). Orchard Bks Watts.
Morgan, Allan. Sadie & the Snowman. Clark, Brenda, illus. 32p. (ps-2). 1987. pap. 2.50 (ISBN 0-590-41826-2). Scholastic Inc.
Morgan, Ken. Pretzels Anyone? 1989. 6.95 (ISBN 0-533-08138-6). Vantage.
Morphew, Sharon. Rachel's Rainbow. Boddy, Joe, illus. 32p. (gr. k-2). 1987. 1.99 (ISBN 0-87403-279-2, 3779). Standard Pub.
Morris, Winifred. The Jell-O Syndrome. LC 85-22939. 168p. (gr. 6 up). 1986. 13.95 (ISBN 0-689-31190-7, Atheneum Child Bk). Macmillan Child Grp.
—The Jell-O Syndrome. LC 90-1437. 176p. (gr. 7 up). 1990. pap. 3.95 (ISBN 0-02-044712-4, Collier Young Ad). Macmillan Child Grp.
Moskin, Marietta D. I Am Rosemarie. (Orig.). (gr. k-12). 1987. pap. 2.95 (ISBN 0-440-94066-4, LFL). Dell.
Munsch, Robert. Millicent & the Wind. Duranceau, Suzanne, illus. 32p. (gr. k-3). 1984. 12.95 (ISBN 0-920236-98-7); pap. 4.95 (ISBN 0-920236-93-6). Firefly Bks Ltd.
Murphy, Elspeth C. Where's My Lamb. LC 87-70608. 1987. 3.95 (ISBN 1-55513-248-0, Chariot Bks). Cook.
—Who Lost a Mitten. LC 87-70615. 1987. 3.95 (ISBN 1-55513-578-1, Chariot Bks). Cook.
Nabb, Magdalen. Josie Smith. Vainio, Pirkko, illus. LC 88-8301. 80p. (gr. 1-4). 1989. 12.95 (ISBN 0-689-50485-3, M K McElderry). Macmillan Child Grp.
Nathan, Robert. Portrait of Jennie. 293p. 1981. Repr. PLB 16.95x (ISBN 0-89966-356-7). Buccaneer Bks.
—Portrait of Jennie. 234p. 1981. Repr. PLB 16.95x (ISBN 0-89967-030-X). Harmony Raine.
Naylor, Phyllis R. Alice in Rapture, Sort Of. 160p. (gr. 3-7). 1989. 12.95 (ISBN 0-689-31466-3, Atheneum Child Bk). Macmillan Child Grp.
Naylor-Reynolds, Phyllis. The Agony of Alice. (gr. k-6). 1988. pap. 2.75 (ISBN 0-440-40051-1, YB). Dell.
Newton, Suzanne. An End to Perfect. 216p. (gr. 3-7). 1986. pap. 3.95 (ISBN 0-14-032229-9, Penguin Bks). Viking Penguin.
—I Will Call It Georgie's Blues. (gr. 7 up). 1986. pap. 2.75 (ISBN 0-440-94090-7, LFL). Dell.
Nicoll, Helen & Pienkowski, Jan. Meg's Veg. 32p. (ps-k). 1985. pap. 3.50 (ISBN 0-14-050356-0, Puffin). Puffin Bks.
Nielsen, Shelly. Just Victoria. 130p. (gr. 5-6). 1986. pap. 3.95 (ISBN 0-89191-609-1). Cook.
Nissen, Henri. Chayna, the Girl No One Wanted. Alex, Ben, ed. (Illus.). 32p. (gr. 3-6). 1987. 7.95 (ISBN 0-8028-5021-9). Eerdmans.
Nixon, Joan L. And Maggie Makes Three. LC 85-16389. (gr. 4-6). 1986. 12.95 (ISBN 0-15-250355-2, HJ). Harbracej.
—And Maggie Makes Three. (gr. k-6). 1987. pap. 2.75 (ISBN 0-440-40127-5, YB). Dell.
—Maggie Forevermore. LC 86-20135. 112p. (gr. 4-7). 1987. 13.95 (ISBN 0-15-250345-5). HarBraceJ.
—Maggie Forevermore. (gr. k-6). 1989. pap. 2.75 (ISBN 0-440-40211-5, YB). Dell.
—Maggie Too. (gr. k-6). 1987. pap. 2.50 (ISBN 0-440-45288-0, YB). Dell.
Noonan, Janet & Calvert, Jacquelyn. Millicent Eats Her Supper. Bartholomew, illus. (ps-2). 1989. 3.49 (ISBN 1-55513-984-1). Cook.
—Millicent Goes to the Shopping Mall. Bartholomew, illus. (ps-2). 1989. 3.49 (ISBN 1-55513-970-1). Cook.
—Millicent Has a Party. Bartholomew, illus. (ps-2). 1989. 3.49 (ISBN 1-55513-983-3). Cook.
—Millicent Plays at the Park. Bartholomew, illus. (ps-2). 1989. 3.49 (ISBN 1-55513-982-5). Cook.
O'Brien, Robert. Z for Zachariah. large type ed. 232p. (gr. 3-8). 1989. Repr. of 1975 ed. PLB 14.95 (ISBN 1-85089-955-X, Pub. by Clio Pr England). ABC-Clio.
O'Dell, Scott. Alexandra. LC 83-26590. 160p. (gr. 7 up). 1984. 12.95 (ISBN 0-395-35571-0, 5-92366). HM.
—Carlotta. 144p. (gr. k-12). 1989. pap. 2.95 (ISBN 0-440-90928-7, LFL). Dell.
—Janey. (gr. 7-12). 1986. write for info. HM.
—My Name Is Not Angelica. 144p. (gr. 5-9). 1989. 14.95 (ISBN 0-395-51061-9). HM.
—Sarah Bishop. 240p. (gr. 7up). 1991. pap. 2.95 (ISBN 0-590-44651-7, Point). Scholastic Inc.
Oke, Janette. Julia's Last Hope. 224p. (Orig.). (gr. 8 up). 1990. pap. 6.95 (ISBN 1-55661-153-6). Bethany Hse.
Orgel, Doris. Starring Becky Suslow. Newsom, Carol, illus. 80p. (gr. 2-5). 1989. pap. 10.95 (ISBN 0-670-82714-2). Viking Child Bks.
Otis, Sharon & Walker, Lois. Tammy's Smile. Porter, Debbie, illus. Goldman, Howard, pref. by. (Illus., Orig.). (ps-7). 1985. wkbk. 6.00 (ISBN 0-9617737-0-7). Total Lrn.
Owen, Annie. Annie's ABC. LC 87-3145. (Illus.). 32p. (gr. 3-9). 1988. Knopf.
Page, Carole G. Kara. LC 81-67317. 159p. (Orig.). (gr. 8-12). 1981. pap. 3.95 (ISBN 0-87123-145-X). Bethany Hse.
Palumbo, Nancy. Meet Penelope P'Nutt: Conoza Penelope P'Nutt. Weaver, Judith, illus. 32p. (gr. k-6). 1989. wkbk. 5.95 (ISBN 0-927024-04-7). Crayons Pubns.
—Meet Penelope P'Nutt: Viens Recontrer Penelope P'Nutt. Weaver, Judith, illus. 32p. (gr. k-6). 1989. wkbk. 5.95 (ISBN 0-927024-05-5). Crayons Pubns.
—Penelope P'Nutt at Play: Los Juegos de Penelope P'Nutt. Weaver, Judith, illus. 32p. (gr. k-6). 1989. wkbk. 5.95 (ISBN 0-927024-16-0). Crayons Pubns.
Parish, Peggy. Good Work, Amelia Bedelia. Sweat, Lynn, illus. LC 75-20360. 56p. (gr. 1-4). 1976. 12.95 (ISBN 0-688-80022-X); PLB 12.88 (ISBN 0-688-84022-1). Greenwillow.
—Teach Us, Amelia Bedelia. Sweat, Lynn, illus. LC 76-22663. 56p. (gr. 1-4). 1977. 12.95 (ISBN 0-688-80069-6); PLB 12.88 (ISBN 0-688-84069-8). Greenwillow.
—Teach Us, Amelia Bedelia. (ps-3). 1980. pap. 2.50 (ISBN 0-590-33362-3). Scholastic Inc.
Park, Barbara. Beanpole. LC 83-111. 160p. (gr. 5 up). 1983. 13.00 (ISBN 0-394-85811-5); lib. bdg. 10.99 (ISBN 0-394-95811-X). Knopf.
Pascal, Francine. Amy's Pen Pal. 1990. pap. 2.99 (ISBN 0-553-15772-8). Bantam.
—Boy Trouble. 1990. pap. 2.95 (ISBN 0-553-28317-0). Bantam.
—Carolyn's Mystery Dolls. (gr. 4-7). 1991. pap. 2.75 (ISBN 0-553-15870-8). Bantam.
—The Case of the Secret Santa. (gr. k-3). 1990. pap. 2.95 (ISBN 0-553-15860-0). Bantam.
—Crybaby Lois. (gr. 4 up). 1990. pap. 2.75 (ISBN 0-553-15818-X). Bantam.
—Dreams of Forever. 208p. (gr. 7 up). 1988. pap. 2.95 (ISBN 0-553-26700-0, Starfire). Bantam.
—Elizabeth's New Hero. 1989. pap. 2.75 (ISBN 0-553-15753-1). Bantam.
—Elizabeth's Super-Selling Lemonade. 1990. pap. 2.75 (ISBN 0-553-15807-4). Bantam.
—Elizabeth's Valentine, No. 4. 1990. pap. 2.75 (ISBN 0-553-15761-2). Bantam.
—Forever & Always. 176p. (gr. 6 up). 1988. pap. 2.95 (ISBN 0-553-26788-4, Starfire). Bantam.
—Jessica & The Money Mix-Up. (gr. 4-7). 1990. pap. 2.95 (ISBN 0-553-15798-1). Bantam.
—Jessica the TV Star. (ps-3). 1991. pap. 2.75 (ISBN 0-553-15850-3). Bantam.
—Jessica's Big Mistake. (ps-3). 1990. pap. 2.75 (ISBN 0-553-15799-X). Bantam.
—Jessica's New Look. (gr. 4-7). 1991. pap. 2.95 (ISBN 0-553-15869-4). Bantam.
—Jessica's Zoo Adventure. (ps-3). 1990. pap. 2.75 (ISBN 0-553-15802-3). Bantam.
—Lila's Story. (gr. 7 up). 1989. pap. 2.95 (ISBN 0-553-28296-4). Bantam.
—Mademoiselle Jessica. (gr. 4-7). 1991. pap. 2.95 (ISBN 0-553-15849-X). Bantam.
—New Elizabeth. 1990. pap. 2.95 (ISBN 0-553-28385-5). Bantam.
—Power Play. 176p. (Orig.). (gr. 7 up). 1985. pap. 2.95 (ISBN 0-553-27493-7). Bantam.
—Second Best. 1988. pap. 2.75 (ISBN 0-553-15665-9). Bantam.
—Together Forever. 176p. (gr. 7 up). 1988. pap. 2.95 (ISBN 0-553-26863-5, Starfire). Bantam.
Pascal, Francine & Stewart, Molly M. Jessica's Cat Trick. (ps-3). 1990. pap. 2.75 (ISBN 0-553-15768-X, Skylark). Bantam.
Pascal, Francine, created by. Promises Broken. 176p. (gr. 7-12). 1986. pap. 2.95 (ISBN 0-553-26156-8). Bantam.
—Tender Promises. 176p. (Orig.). (gr. 7-12). 1986. pap. 2.95 (ISBN 0-553-25812-5, Starfire). Bantam.
Paterson, Katherine. The Great Gilly Hopkins. LC 77-27075. 192p. (gr. 5-9). 1987. pap. 3.50 (ISBN 0-06-440201-0, Trophy). HarpC Child Bks.
Payne, Emmy. Katy No-Pocket. Rey, H. A., illus. (ps-3). 1989. pap. 7.95 incl. cassette (ISBN 0-395-52141-6). HM.
Pearson, Kit. A Handful of Time. (Illus.). 192p. (gr. 3-7). 1991. pap. 3.95 (ISBN 0-14-032268-X, Puffin). Puffin Bks.
Peck, Harry T. The Adventures of Mabel. Rountree, Harry, illus. Cabaniss, Anne M., intro. by. (Illus.). 236p. (gr. k-5). 1986. Repr. of 1896 ed. 19.95 (ISBN 0-9616844-0-2). Greenhouse Pub.
Peck, Richard. Representing Super Doll. 192p. (gr. 7 up). 1989. pap. 2.95 (ISBN 0-440-97362-7, LFL). Dell.
Peek, Merle. Mary Wore Her Red Dress, & Henry Wore His Green Sneakers. 1988. pap. 4.95 (ISBN 0-89919-701-9, Pub. by Clarion). Ticknor & Fields.
Peet, Bill. Encore for Eleanor. Peet, Bill, illus. 48p. (gr. k-3). 1985. 13.95 (ISBN 0-395-29860-1); pap. 3.95 (ISBN 0-317-18520-9). HM.
—Pamela Camel. Peet, Bill, illus. LC 83-18594. 32p. (gr. k-3). 1984. 13.95 (ISBN 0-395-35975-9, 5-93025). HM.
Pendleton, Don. Furia sobre Boston. new ed. Blanco, O., tr. from ENG. (SPA.). 160p. 1974. pap. 0.85 (ISBN 0-88473-312-2). Fiesta Pub.
Perl, Lila. Marleen, the Horror Queen. LC 85-3740. 156p. (gr. 5-8). 1985. 11.95 (ISBN 0-89919-368-4, Clarion). Ticknor & Fields.
—Marleen, the Horror Queen. (gr. 7 up). 1987. pap. 2.50 (ISBN 0-671-62871-2, Archway). PB.
—Me & Fat Glenda. LC 71-179439. 192p. (gr. 3-6). 1979. 13.95 (ISBN 0-395-28871-1, Clarion). HM.
—The Secret Diary of Katie Dinkerhoff. LC 86-31654. 176p. (gr. 7 up). 1987. pap. 11.95 (ISBN 0-590-41131-4). Scholastic Inc.
—The Secret Diary of Katie Dinkerhoff. 176p. (gr. 6-8). 1989. pap. 2.50 (ISBN 0-590-41132-2, Apple Paperbacks). Scholastic Inc.
Peters, Lisa W. Good Morning, River! Ray, Deborah K., illus. 32p. (ps-1). 1990. text ed. 13.95 (ISBN 1-55970-011-4). Arcade Pub Inc.
—Tania's Trolls. Wooding, Sharon, illus. 64p. (gr. 2-4). 1989. 10.95 (ISBN 1-55970-040-8). Arcade Pub Inc.
Pfeffer, Susan B. Fantasy Summer. 208p. (gr. 7 up). 1986. pap. 2.50 (ISBN 0-425-11130-X, Pub. by Berkley-Pacer). Berkley Pub.
—Just Between Us. Tomei, Lorna, illus. LC 79-53606. 128p. (gr. 4-6). 1980. pap. 9.89 (ISBN 0-385-28594-9). Delacorte.
—Kid Power. 121p. (gr. 3-7). 1991. pap. 2.95 (ISBN 0-590-42607-9). Scholastic Inc.
—The Sebastian Sisters: Evvie at Sixteen. (gr. 5 up). 1988. 13.95 (ISBN 0-553-05475-9, Starfire). Bantam.
—Sebastian Sisters: Meg at Sixteen. 1991. pap. 3.50 (ISBN 0-553-28836-9). Bantam.
—Sybil at Sixteen. (gr. 7 up). 1990. pap. 2.95 (ISBN 0-553-28614-5, Starfire). Bantam.
—Truth or Dare. 176p. (gr. 6-8). 1986. pap. 2.75 (ISBN 0-590-43750-X). Scholastic Inc.
—Turning Thirteen. (gr. 6-8). 1989. pap. 2.75 (ISBN 0-590-40765-1, Apple Paperbacks). Scholastic Inc.
Phipson, Joan. Bianca. LC 88-13192. 192p. (gr. 7 up). 1988. 13.95 (ISBN 0-689-50448-9, M K McElderry). Macmillan Child Grp.
Pierce, Tamora. Alanna: The First Adventure. LC 83-2595. 256p. (gr. 5 up). 1989. pap. 3.25 (ISBN 0-679-80114-6, Borzoi Sprinters). Knopf.
Pike, Christopher. Slumber Party. 1985. pap. 2.75 (ISBN 0-590-43014-9). Scholastic Inc.
Pinkwater, Jill. Buffalo Brenda. LC 88-31929. 192p. (gr. 5-9). 1989. 13.95 (ISBN 0-02-774631-3, Mcmillan Child Bk). Macmillan Child Grp.

Pitcher, Valerie. Anya Astern, Come Down from the Sky. LC 90-71860. 44p. (gr. 6). 1991. 6.95 (ISBN 1-55523-412-7). Winston-Derek.

Plantos, T. Heather Hits Her First Home Run. (Illus.). 24p. (ps-8). 1989. pap. 4.95 (ISBN 0-88753-185-7). Firefly Bks Ltd.

Polacco, Patricia. The Keeping Quilt. Polacco, Patricia, illus. 32p. (ps-3). 1988. pap. 14.95 (ISBN 0-671-64963-9). S&S Trade.

Pollinger, Eileen. Stacey. LC 87-71604. 176p. (Orig.). (gr. 9-12). 1987. pap. 3.95 (ISBN 0-87123-943-4). Bethany Hse.

Porter, Eleanor. Pollyanna. (Illus.). (gr. k-9). 1988. pap. 2.50 (ISBN 0-318-36503-0). Scholastic Inc.

Porter, Eleanor H. Pollyanna. (Orig.). (gr. k-6). 1987. pap. 4.95 (ISBN 0-440-45985-0, Pub. by Yearling Classics). Dell.

—Pollyanna. (gr. 4-7). 1987. pap. 2.50 (ISBN 0-590-41269-8, Apple Paperbacks). Scholastic Inc.

—Pollyanna. 1988. pap. 2.25 (ISBN 0-14-035023-3, Puffin). Puffin Bks.

—Pollyanna. 240p. (gr. 4-7). 1987. pap. 2.75 (ISBN 0-590-43405-5). Scholastic Inc.

—Pollyanna Grows Up. 308p. (gr. 4 up). 1980. Repr. of 1915 ed. lib. bdg. 20.95 (ISBN 0-89968-193-X). Lightyear.

—Pollyanna Grows Up. 272p. (gr. 5 up). 1989. pap. 2.25 (ISBN 0-14-035024-1, Puffin). Puffin Bks.

Porter, Gene S. A Girl of the Limberlost. (Orig.). (gr. 3-7). 1986. pap. 4.95 (ISBN 0-440-43090-9, Pub. by Yearling Classics). Dell.

Poulin, Stephane. Could You Stop Josephine? (Illus.). 24p. (ps-3). 1988. 12.95 (ISBN 0-88776-216-6); pap. 6.95 (ISBN 0-88776-227-1). Tundra Bks.

Priebe, Vel. Wendy's Gift. Priebe, Vel, illus. 24p. (Orig.). (ps-2). 1988. pap. 2.50 (ISBN 0-919797-67-9). Kindred Pr.

Prochazkova, Iva. The Season of Secret Wishes. Crawford, Elizabeth D., tr. from GER. LC 89-45291. 208p. (gr. 4-8). 1989. 12.95 (ISBN 0-688-08735-3). Lothrop.

Quin-Harkin, Janet. No Experience Required. 192p. 1990. pap. 3.50 (ISBN 0-449-14530-1, Juniper). Fawcett.

Radlauer, Ruth S. Breakfast by Molly. McCully, Emily A., illus. LC 87-12636. 29p. (ps-1). 1988. pap. 8.95 (ISBN 0-671-66165-5). S&S Trade.

—Molly. McCully, Emily A., illus. LC 86-22566. 32p. (ps-3). 1988. PLB 10.95 (ISBN 0-671-66862-5). S&S Trade.

—Molly at the Library. McCully, Emily A., illus. LC 87-14385. 29p. (ps-2). 1988. pap. 8.95 (ISBN 0-671-66166-3). S&S Trade.

—Molly Goes Hiking. McCully, Emily A., illus. LC 86-18761. 32p. (ps-3). 1987. PLB 10.95 (ISBN 0-671-66860-9). S&S Trade.

Rand, Suzanne. All American Girl. 208p. (Orig.). (gr. 7-12). 1986. pap. 2.50 (ISBN 0-553-25427-8). Bantam.

Randall, Carrie. The Myst. (gr. 4-7). 1991. pap. 2.75 (ISBN 0-590-44022-5). Scholastic Inc.

Ransom, Candice F. Emily, No. 11. 368p. (Orig.). (gr. 7 up). 1985. pap. 2.95 (ISBN 0-590-33410-7, Sunfire). Scholastic Inc.

—Fifteen at Last. 176p. (Orig.). (gr. 6 up). 1987. pap. 2.50 (ISBN 0-590-40849-6, Apple Paperbacks). Scholastic Inc.

—Fifteen at Last. 176p. (Orig.). (gr. 6-8). 1990. pap. 2.75 (ISBN 0-590-43716-X). Scholastic Inc.

—Fourteen & Holding. 1990. pap. 2.95 (ISBN 0-590-43740-2). Scholastic Inc.

—Fourteen & Holding. 176p. (Orig.). (gr. 6-8). 1987. pap. 2.75 (ISBN 0-590-43482-9). Scholastic Inc.

—Millicent the Magnificent. 1989. pap. 2.75 (ISBN 0-590-42516-1). Scholastic Inc.

—Nicole, No. 19. 224p. (Orig.). (gr. 7 up). 1986. pap. 2.25 (ISBN 0-590-40049-5, Sunfire). Scholastic Inc.

—Susannah, No. 2. 368p. (gr. 7 up). 1984. pap. 2.95 (ISBN 0-590-33064-0, Sunfire). Scholastic Inc.

—There's One in Every Family. 176p. (gr. 3-7). 1990. pap. 2.75 (ISBN 0-590-42977-9). Scholastic Inc.

—Thirteen. 192p. (Orig.). (gr. 6-8). 1990. pap. 2.95 (ISBN 0-590-43742-9). Scholastic Inc.

Raskin, Ellen. Spectacles. 2nd ed. Raskin, Ellen, illus. LC 88-10363. 48p. (gr. k-4). 1988. pap. 4.50 (ISBN 0-689-71271-5, Aladdin). Macmillan Child Grp.

Rawlings, Marjorie K. The Secret River. 3rd, facsimile ed. Weisgard, Leonard, illus. Bigham, Julia S., intro. by. (Illus.). 57p. (gr. 3-6). 1987. Repr. of 1955 ed. PLB 12.95 (ISBN 0-935259-02-3). San Marco Bk.

Reed, Ronald F. Rebecca: A Novel for Children. Ham, Lisa K., illus. 37p. (Orig.). (ps-4). Date not set. pap. 8.00 (ISBN 0-924303-00-X). TX Wesleyan Coll.

Reiss, Johanna. The Upstairs Room. LC 77-187940. 192p. (gr. 7 up). 1987. pap. 2.95 (ISBN 0-06-447043-1, Trophy). HarpC Child Bks.

Roberts, Willo D. Caroline, No. 7. 368p. (gr. 7 up). 1984. pap. 2.95 (ISBN 0-590-33239-2, Sunfire). Scholastic Inc.

—The Girl with the Silver Eyes. 208p. (gr. 3-7). 1991. pap. 2.75 (ISBN 0-590-44248-1). Scholastic Inc.

—Victoria, No. 13. 368p. (Orig.). (gr. 7 up). 1985. pap. 2.95 (ISBN 0-590-33615-0, Sunfire). Scholastic Inc.

Robins, Eleanor. Meg Parker, 5 in each set, Sets 1 & 2. (Illus.). 1984. Set. pap. 15.00 (ISBN 0-685-31191-0, High Noon Books). Set 1 (ISBN 0-87879-439-5). Set 2 (ISBN 0-87879-472-7). Acad Therapy.

Robinson, Catherine. Lizzie's Worst Year. (gr. 5-7). 1990. pap. 2.75 (ISBN 0-590-43120-X). Scholastic Inc.

Robinson, Nancy K. Angela, Private Citizen. 160p. 1991. pap. 2.95 (ISBN 0-590-45410-2, Apple Paperbacks). Scholastic Inc.

—Oh Honestly, Angela! Williams, Richard, illus. 128p. (gr. 3-7). 1988. pap. 2.50 (ISBN 0-590-40382-6, Apple Paperbacks). Scholastic Inc.

—Oh Honestly, Angela! 128p. (gr. 4-6). 1985. pap. 10.95 (ISBN 0-590-41287-6). Scholastic Inc.

—Veronica Knows Best. 128p. (gr. 4-6). 1987. pap. 10.95 (ISBN 0-590-40509-8). Scholastic Inc.

—Veronica Meets Her Match. 1990. 12.95 (ISBN 0-590-41512-3, Scholastic Hardcover). Scholastic Inc.

—Veronica the Show-Off. LC 85-4483. (gr. 3-6). 1984. 12.95 (ISBN 0-02-777360-4, Four Winds). Macmillan Child Grp.

—Veronica the Show-Off. Greenwald, Sheila, illus. 128p. (gr. 2-4). 1982. pap. 2.50 (ISBN 0-590-40305-2). Scholastic Inc.

Rock, Gail. Addie & the King of Hearts. (gr. 4-6). 1986. pap. 2.50 (ISBN 0-440-40076-7, YB). Dell.

—A Dream for Addie. (gr. 4-6). 1986. pap. 2.50 (ISBN 0-440-42151-9, YB). Dell.

Rocklin, Joanne. Dear Baby. McKeating, Eileen, illus. LC 87-36468. 112p. (gr. 3-7). 1988. 12.95 (ISBN 0-02-777320-5, Mcmillan Child Bk). Macmillan Child Grp.

—Sonia Begonia. 112p. (gr. 3-7). 1987. pap. 2.50 (ISBN 0-380-70307-6, Camelot). Avon.

Rockwell, Thomas. How to Fight a Girl. 144p. (gr. k-6). 1988. pap. 2.95 (ISBN 0-440-40111-9, YB). Dell.

Rodgers, Mary. Summer Switch. LC 79-2690. 192p. (gr. 5 up). 1984. pap. 3.50 (ISBN 0-06-440140-5, Trophy). HarpC Child Bks.

Rodowsky, Colby. Fitchett's Folly. LC 86-31859. 160p. (gr. 4 up). 1987. 11.95 (ISBN 0-374-32342-9). FS&G.

—Sydney, Herself. 176p. (gr. 7 up). 1989. 12.95 (ISBN 0-374-30649-4). FS&G.

Rody, Lee. The Desperate Search. LC 88-63476. 160p. (gr. 2-6). 1989. pap. 4.95 (ISBN 1-55661-027-0). Bethany Hse.

Rohmer, Harriet & Olivarez, Anna, eds. The Adventures of Connie & Diego Audiocassette. (SPA & ENG.). 1989. 8.95 (ISBN 0-89239-051-4). Childrens Book Pr.

Romer, Ken. Dorothy & the Wooden Soldiers. (Illus.). 52p. (gr. 3-7). 1987. Colorina book with story. pap. 3.95 (ISBN 0-932458-35-1). Star Rover.

Roos, Stephen. And the Winner Is... DeRosa, Dee, illus. LC 88-27519. 128p. (gr. 3-7). 1989. 12.95 (ISBN 0-689-31300-4, Atheneum Child Bk). Macmillan Child Grp.

Rosofsky, Iris. Miriam. LC 87-45859. 192p. (gr. 7 up). 1988. 11.95i (ISBN 0-06-024853-X). HarpC Child Bks.

Ross, Pat. Hannah's Paper Dreams. Dodson, Burt, illus. 64p. (gr. 3-6). 1988. pap. 10.95 (ISBN 0-670-81779-1). Viking Child Bks.

Ross, Tony. I Want My Potty. LC 86-10568. (Illus.). 24p. (ps-k). 1986. 9.95 (ISBN 0-916291-08-1, Cranky Nell Bk). Kane-Miller Bk.

—Super Dooper Jezebel. (Illus.). 32p. (ps up). 1988. 11.95 (ISBN 0-374-33660-1). FS&G.

Rostkowski, Margaret I. After the Dancing Days. LC 85-45810. 240p. (gr. 6-9). 1986. 13.95 (ISBN 0-06-025077-1); PLB 13.89 (ISBN 0-06-025078-X). HarpC Child Bks.

Roth-Hano, Renee. Touch Wood: A Girlhood in Occupied France. LC 87-34326. 304p. (gr. 5-9). 1988. 15.95 (ISBN 0-02-777340-X, Four Winds). Macmillan Child Grp.

Ruckman, Ivy. Melba the Brain. (gr. 4-7). 1991. pap. 3.25 (ISBN 0-440-40423-1). Dell.

Russo, Marisabina. Why Do Grown-Ups Have All the Fun? Russo, Marisabina, illus. LC 86-4644. 24p. (ps-3). 1987. 11.75 (ISBN 0-688-06625-9); PLB 11.88 (ISBN 0-688-06626-7). Greenwillow.

Rylant, Cynthia. A Blue-Eyed Daisy. (gr. k-6). 1987. pap. 2.95 (ISBN 0-440-40927-6, YB). Dell.

Sachar, Louis. Someday Angeline. 160p. (gr. 2-6). 1990. Repr. of 1983 ed. PLB 12.99 (ISBN 0-679-90412-3). McKay.

Sachs, Marilyn. The Fat Girl. (gr. 7 up). 1986. pap. 2.75 (ISBN 0-440-92468-5, LFL). Dell.

—Fourteen. (gr. 4-9). 1988. pap. 2.50 (ISBN 0-318-37107-3). Scholastic Inc.

—Fran Ellen's House. 96p. 1989. pap. 2.75 (ISBN 0-380-70583-4, Camelot). Avon.

—Veronica Ganz. Glanzman, Louis, illus. 160p. (gr. 3-7). 1987. pap. 2.50 (ISBN 0-590-40405-9, Apple Paperbacks). Scholastic Inc.

St. John, Chris. Golden Girl. (gr. 5 up). 1989. pap. 3.50 (ISBN 0-449-13454-7). Fawcett.

Salter, Heidi. Taddy McFinley & the Great Grey Grimly. Thatch, Nancy R., ed. Salter, Heidi, illus. Melton, David, intro. by. LC 89-31820. (Illus.). 26p. (gr. 3-8). 1989. lib. bdg. 12.95 (ISBN 0-933849-21-4). Landmark Edns.

Samuels, Gertrude. Run, Shelley, Run! LC 73-12310. 192p. (gr. 7 up). 1974. 12.95i (ISBN 0-690-00295-5, Crowell Jr Bks). HarpC Child Bks.

Sarasin, Jennifer. Here to Stay. 176p. (gr. 6-10). 1988. pap. 2.50 (ISBN 0-590-41876-9). Scholastic Inc.

Sargent, Sarah. Seeds of Change. 128p. (gr. 3-7). 1989. 12.95 (ISBN 0-02-778031-7, Bradbury Pr). Macmillan Child Grp.

Sauer, Julia. Fog Magic. Ward, Lynd, illus. 128p. (gr. 5-9). 1986. pap. 3.95 (ISBN 0-14-032163-2, Puffin). Puffin Bks.

Saunders, Susan. Dorothy & the Magic Belt. Rose, David, illus. LC 84-17946. 64p. (gr. 2-6). 1985. (Random Juv); pap. 1.95 (ISBN 0-394-87067-0). Random.

—Kate the Boss. (gr. 4-7). 1990. pap. 2.50 (ISBN 0-590-43189-7). Scholastic Inc.

—Kate's Camp-Out. 96p. (Orig.). (gr. 3-7). 1988. pap. 2.50 (ISBN 0-590-41337-6, Apple Paperbacks). Scholastic Inc.

—Kate's Surprise. 96p. (Orig.). (gr. 4-6). 1987. pap. 2.50 (ISBN 0-590-40643-4, Apple Paperbacks). Scholastic Inc.

—Kate's Surprise Visitor. (gr. 5-7). 1990. pap. 2.50 (ISBN 0-590-42819-5). Scholastic Inc.

—Lauren's Afterschool Job. 128p. (gr. 3-7). 1990. pap. 2.75 (ISBN 0-590-43928-6). Scholastic Inc.

—Lauren's Double Disaster. (gr. 4-7). 1991. pap. 2.75 (ISBN 0-590-43926-X). Scholastic Inc.

—Lauren's New Address. 1990. pap. 2.50 (ISBN 0-590-43191-9). Scholastic Inc.

—Lauren's Sleepover Exchange. 112p. (gr. 3-7). 1989. pap. 2.50 (ISBN 0-590-41697-9, Apple Paperbacks). Scholastic Inc.

—Stephanie Strikes Back. 96p. (gr. 3-7). 1988. pap. 2.50 (ISBN 0-590-41694-4, Pub. by Apple Paperbacks). Scholastic Inc.

Schiller, Alexandra. The Raisin Eater. Martin, John J. & Schiller, Alexandra, eds. Schiller, Alexandra, illus. 44p. (gr. 3-4). 1984. 5.00 (ISBN 0-318-18466-4). A Schiller.

Schnur, Steven. Hannah & Cyclops. (gr. 4-7). 1990. pap. 2.75 (ISBN 0-553-15796-5). Bantam.

Schotter, Roni. Northern Fried Chicken. (gr. 6-9). 1983. 10.95 (ISBN 0-399-20920-4, Philomel). Putnam Pub Group.

Schrfranz, Vivian. Overboard. (gr. 7-12). 1988. pap. 2.50 (ISBN 0-590-41875-0). Scholastic Inc.

Schulte, Elaine. Here Comes Ginger. LC 88-38763. (gr. 3-7). 1989. pap. 3.95 (ISBN 1-55513-770-9, Chariot Bks). Cook.

—Here Comes Ginger. 1989. write for info. Prog Bapt Pub.

Schurfranz, Vivian. Josie. 224p. (Orig.). (gr. 6-10). 1988. pap. 2.75 (ISBN 0-590-41207-8). Scholastic Inc.

—Julie, No. 20. 224p. (Orig.). (gr. 7 up). 1986. pap. 2.25 (ISBN 0-590-40268-4, Sunfire). Scholastic Inc.

—Rachel, No. 21. 224p. (Orig.). (gr. 7 up). 1986. pap. 2.50 (ISBN 0-590-40394-X, Sunfire). Scholastic Inc.

Schwartz, Sheila. Growing up Guilty. LC 78-3284. 1978. Pantheon.

Sebestyen, Ouida. The Girl in the Box: The Diary of Anne Frank. 160p. (gr. 7 up). 1988. 12.95 (ISBN 0-316-77935-0, Joy St Bks). Little.

—Words by Heart. LC 78-27847. (gr. 5 up). 1979. 14.95 (ISBN 0-316-77931-8, Joy St Bks). Little.

Service, Pamela F. The Reluctant God. LC 87-16840. 224p. (gr. 5-8). 1988. 14.95 (ISBN 0-689-31404-3, Atheneum Child Bk). Macmillan Child Grp.

Sharmat, Marjorie W. Chasing after Annie. Simont, Marc, illus. LC 80-7906. 80p. (gr. 2-5). 1991. pap. 3.50 (ISBN 0-06-440351-3, Trophy). HarpC Child Bks.

—Getting Closer. (Orig.). (gr. k-12). 1987. pap. 2.50 (ISBN 0-440-92828-1, LFL). Dell.

—Getting Something on Maggie Marmelstein. Shecter, Ben, illus. LC 78-157895. 110p. (gr. 4-6). 1971. PLB 13.89 (ISBN 0-06-025552-8). HarpC Child Bks.

—I Saw Him First. LC 82-14839. 128p. (gr. 7 up). 1983. pap. 12.95 (ISBN 0-385-29243-0). Delacorte.

—Nobody Knows How Scared I Am. (Orig.). (gr. k-12). 1987. pap. 2.50 (ISBN 0-440-96267-6, LFL). Dell.

Sharmat, Mitchell. A Girl of Many Parts. (Orig.). (gr. k-12). 1988. pap. 2.95 (ISBN 0-440-20209-4, LFL). Dell.

Shaw, Janet. Changes for Kirsten: A Winter Story. Graef, Renee, illus. 65p. (Orig.). (gr. 2-5). 1988. 12.95 (ISBN 0-937295-44-2); pap. 5.95 (ISBN 0-937295-45-0). Pleasant Co.

—Changes for Kirsten: A Winter Story. Thieme, Jeanne, ed. Graef, Renee, illus. 72p. (gr. 2-5). 1990. PLB 12.95 (ISBN 0-937295-94-9). Pleasant Co.

—Happy Birthday, Kirsten! A Springtime Story. Graef, Renee, illus. 59p. (Orig.). (gr. 2-5). 1987. 12.95 (ISBN 0-937295-32-9); pap. 5.95 (ISBN 0-937295-33-7). Pleasant Co.

—Kirsten Learns a Lesson: A School Story. Graef, Renee, illus. LC 86-60622. 69p. (Orig.). (gr. 2-5). 1986. 12.95 (ISBN 0-937295-09-4); pap. 5.95 (ISBN 0-937295-10-8). Pleasant Co.

—Kirsten Learns a Lesson: A School Story. Thieme, Jeanne, ed. Graef, Renee, illus. 72p. (gr. 2-5). 1990. PLB 12.95 (ISBN 0-937295-82-5). Pleasant Co.

—Kirsten Saves the Day: A Summer Story. Graef, Renee, illus. 67p. (Orig.). (gr. 2-5). 1988. 12.95 (ISBN 0-937295-38-8); pap. 5.95 (ISBN 0-937295-39-6). Pleasant Co.

—Kirsten Saves the Day: A Summer Story. Thieme, Jeanne, ed. Graef, Renee, illus. 72p. (gr. 2-5). 1990. PLB 12.95 (ISBN 0-937295-91-4). Pleasant Co.

—Kirsten's Boxed Set, 6 bks. (Illus.). 432p. (gr. 2-5). 1990. Boxed set. pap. 34.95 (ISBN 0-937295-76-0). Pleasant Co.

—Kirsten's Surprise: A Christmas Story. Graef, Renee, illus. LC 86-60623. 62p. (Orig.). (gr. 2-5). 1986. 12.95 (ISBN 0-937295-18-3); pap. 5.95 (ISBN 0-937295-19-1). Pleasant Co.

Shaw, Janet B. Meet Kirsten: An American Girl. Graef, Renee, illus. LC 86-60466. 59p. (Orig.). (gr. 2-5). 1986. 12.95 (ISBN 0-937295-00-0); pap. 5.95 (ISBN 0-937295-01-9). Pleasant Co.
—Meet Kirsten: An American Girl. Thieme, Jeanne, ed. Graef, Renee, illus. 72p. (gr. 2-5). 1990. PLB 12.95 (ISBN 0-937295-79-5). Pleasant Co.
Sheldon, Ann. Everybody's Favorite. 128p. (gr. 3-7). 1990. pap. 2.75 (ISBN 0-671-67475-7, Minstrel Bks). PB.
Shreve, Susan. The Bad Dreams of a Good Girl. De Groat, Diane, illus. LC 81-8359. 96p. (gr. 2-5). 1982. 8.95 (ISBN 0-394-84777-6). Knopf.
—The Bad Dreams of a Good Girl. De Groat, Diane, illus. LC 81-8359. 96p. (gr. 3-6). 1990. pap. 2.95 (ISBN 0-394-83199-3). McKay.
—Lily & the Runaway Baby. Truesdell, Sue, illus. LC 87-4684. 64p. (gr. 2-4). 1987. (Random Juv); pap. 1.95 (ISBN 0-394-89104-X, Random Juv). Random.
Shub, Elizabeth. Clever Kate. Lobel, Anita, illus. LC 86-10836. 64p. (gr. 1-4). 1986. pap. 3.95 (ISBN 0-689-71077-1, Aladdin). Macmillan Child Grp.
Shura, Mary F. Gentle Annie. (gr. 4-7). 1991. 12.95 (ISBN 0-590-44367-4). Scholastic Inc.
—Jessica, No. 6. 368p. (gr. 7 up). 1984. pap. 2.95 (ISBN 0-590-33242-2, Sunfire). Scholastic Inc.
—Kate's Book. (gr. 3-7). 1989. pap. 2.75 (ISBN 0-590-42381-9). Scholastic Inc.
Siegal, Aranka. Grace in the Wilderness: After the Liberation, 1945-1948. LC 85-20415. 220p. (gr. 5 up). 1985. 13.95 (ISBN 0-374-32760-2). FS&G.
Simmonds, Posy. Lulu & the Flying Babies. Simmonds, Posy, illus. LC 87-15889. 32p. (gr. k-5). 1989. 9.95 (ISBN 0-394-89597-5). Knopf.
Simpson, Holly. One Step Away. (gr. 6 up). 1989. pap. 2.95 (ISBN 0-449-14593-X). Fawcett.
Singer, Marilyn. Mitzi Meyer, Fearless Warrior Queen. 144p. (Orig.). (gr. 4-6). 1987. pap. 2.50 (ISBN 0-590-40464-4, Apple Paperbacks). Scholastic Inc.
Sirof, Harriet. The Real World. LC 85-13731. 160p. (gr. 7 up). 1985. PLB 11.90 (ISBN 0-531-10080-4). Watts.
Skolsky, Mindy W. Hannah & the Best Father on Route 9W. Weinhaus, Karen A., illus. LC 80-8940. 128p. (gr. 3-6). 1982. PLB 12.89 (ISBN 0-06-025744-X). HarpC Child Bks.
—The Whistling Teakettle & Other Stories about Hannah. LC 76-21395. (Illus.). (gr. 2-5). 1977. 10.89 (ISBN 0-06-025688-5). HarpC Child Bks.
Smith, Anne W. Blue Denim Blues. 128p. (gr. 6 up). 1988. pap. 2.75 (ISBN 0-380-70379-3, Flare). Avon.
Smith, Susan. Angela & the Great Book Battle. MacDonald, Patricia, ed. 112p. (Orig.). (gr. 3-6). 1990. pap. 2.75 (ISBN 0-671-72486-X, Minstrel Bks). PB.
—Sonya Begonia & the Eleventh Birthday Blues. 96p. (Orig.). (gr. 4-5). 1988. pap. 2.50 (ISBN 0-671-64040-2, Minstrel Bks). PB.
—Terri the Great. (Orig.). (gr. 3-6). 1989. pap. 2.50 (ISBN 0-671-66708-4, Minstrel Bks). PB.
Sommer, Susan. And I'm Stuck with Joseph. Moon, Ivan, illus. LC 84-611. 120p. (gr. 7-9). pap. 3.95 (ISBN 0-8361-3356-0). Herald Pr.
Sorensen, Virginia. Plain Girl. Krush, Beth & Krush, joe, illus. 156p. (gr. 3-7). 1988. 5.95 (ISBN 0-318-33251-5, HJ). HarBraceJ.
—Plain Girl. (gr. 3-7). 16.75 (ISBN 0-8446-6398-0). Peter Smith.
Sorenson, Jane. Happy Birth Day. (Illus.). (gr. 2-5). 1988. 3.95 (ISBN 0-87403-488-4, 24-02938). Standard Pub.
—Hi, I'm Katie Hooper. (Illus.). 128p. (gr. 2-5). 1988. 3.95 (ISBN 0-87403-486-8, 24-02936). Standard Pub.
—Home Sweet Haunted Home. (Illus.). 128p. (gr. 2-5). 1988. 3.95 (ISBN 0-87403-487-6, 24-02937). Standard Pub.
—Honor Roll. (Illus.). 128p. (gr. 2-5). 1988. 3.95 (ISBN 0-87403-489-2, 24-02939). Standard Pub.
—Jennifer Says Goodbye. 128p. (Orig.). (gr. 5-9). 1984. pap. 3.95 (ISBN 0-87239-774-2, 3734). Standard Pub.
Southall, Ivan. Rachel. LC 86-45509. 147p. (gr. 5 up). 1986. 11.95 (ISBN 0-374-36163-0). FS&G.
Springer, Nancy. They're All Named Wildfire. LC 88-27497. 128p. (gr. 4 up). 1989. 11.95 (ISBN 0-689-31450-7, Atheneum Child Bk). Macmillan Child Grp.
Springstub, Tricia. Eunice (the Egg Salad) Gottlieb. LC 87-25650. 192p. (gr. 4-6). 1988. pap. 14.95 (ISBN 0-385-29625-8). Delacorte.
Spyri, Johanna. Heidi. LC 85-13292. (gr. 5 up). 1964. pap. 1.95 (ISBN 0-8049-0018-3, CL-18). Airmont.
—Heidi. LC 85-13292. (Illus.). (ps-3). 1985. 1.98 (ISBN 0-517-30779-0). Outlet Bk Co.
—Heidi. Saunders, Susan, adapted by. Rowland, Jada, illus. LC 87-15466. 48p. (gr. 2-5). 1988. PLB 12.89 (ISBN 0-8167-1215-8); pap. 3.95 (ISBN 0-8167-1216-6). Troll Assocs.
—Heidi. (gr. 4 up). 1990. pap. 3.50 (ISBN 0-440-40357-X). Dell.
Stahl, Hilda. Elizabeth Gail & Double Trouble, No. 11. 128p. 1989. pap. 3.95 (ISBN 0-8423-0801-6). Tyndale.
—Elizabeth Gail & the Dangerous Double, No. 4. 128p. (gr. 5 up). 1988. 2.95 (ISBN 0-8423-0742-7). Tyndale.
—Elizabeth Gail & the Great Canoe Conspiracy. 1991. PLB 3.95 (ISBN 0-8423-0815-6). Tyndale.
—Elizabeth Gail & the Holiday Mystery. 128p. 1989. pap. 2.95 (ISBN 0-8423-0802-4). Tyndale.
—Elizabeth Gail & the Music Camp Romance. 128p. 1989. pap. 3.95 (ISBN 0-8423-0808-3). Tyndale.
—Elizabeth Gail & the Secret Love, No. 16. 128p. pap. 3.95 (ISBN 0-8423-0809-1). Tyndale.
—Elizabeth Gail & the Strange Birthday Party. 128p. 1989. pap. 3.95 (ISBN 0-8423-0803-2). Tyndale.
—Elizabeth Gail & the Terrifying News. 128p. 1989. pap. 3.95 (ISBN 0-8423-0812-1). Tyndale.
—Elizabeth Gail & Time for Love. 128p. 1989. pap. 3.95 (ISBN 0-8423-0813-X). Tyndale.
—Elizabeth Gail & Trouble at Sandhill Ranch. 128p. 1989. pap. 3.95 (ISBN 0-8423-0814-8). Tyndale.
—Elizabeth Gail & Trouble from the Past. 128p. 1989. pap. 2.95 (ISBN 0-8423-0804-0). Tyndale.
—Teddy Jo & the Ragged Beggars, No. 8. 128p. (gr. 4-7). 1990. pap. 3.95 (ISBN 0-8423-6980-5). Tyndale.
—Teddy Jo & the Stolen Ring, No. 3. 128p. pap. 3.95 (ISBN 0-8423-6975-9). Tyndale.
—Teddy Jo & the Terrible Secret, No. 1. 128p. pap. 3.95 (ISBN 0-8423-6973-2). Tyndale.
Stapler, Sarah A. Trilby's Trumpet. Stapler, Sarah A., illus. LC 87-397. 16p. (ps-1). 1988. 12.95 (ISBN 0-06-025827-6). HarpC Child Bks.
Starring Sally J. Freedman: As Herself. (gr. 4 up). 1978. pap. 3.25 (ISBN 0-440-98239-1). Dell.
Stauffer, Darlene. Grace Comes Home. LC 83-83119. 128p. (Orig.). (gr. 7-11). 1984. pap. 2.50 (ISBN 0-88243-804-2, 02-0804). Gospel Pub.
Steig, William. Brave Irene. LC 86-80957. (Illus.). 32p. (ps-4). 1986. 15.95 (ISBN 0-374-30947-7). FS&G.
Stephenson, Ruth M. Abigail. (Illus.). 32p. (Orig.). (ps-5). 1988. pap. 7.95 (ISBN 0-945705-00-X). Young Life Pub.
Steptoe, John. Marcia. (Illus.). 80p. (gr. 7 up). 1991. pap. 3.95 (ISBN 0-14-034669-4, Puffin). Puffin Bks.
—Mufaro's Beautiful Daughters: An African Tale. Steptoe, John, illus. LC 84-7158. 32p. (gr. k-3). 1987. 14.95 (ISBN 0-688-04045-4); PLB 14.88 (ISBN 0-688-04046-2). Lothrop.
Stewart, Maureen. Dear Emily. LC 87-62368. 112p. (Orig.). (gr. 3-7). 1988. pap. 3.95 (ISBN 0-14-032059-8, Puffin). Puffin Bks.
Stiles, Martha B. Sarah the Dragon Lady. 96p. (gr. 3-7). 1988. pap. 2.75 (ISBN 0-380-70471-4, Camelot). Avon.
Stine, R. L. The New Girl. (Orig.). (gr. 6-9). 1989. pap. 2.95 (ISBN 0-671-70737-X, Archway). PB.
Stolz, Mary. Ivy Larkin. LC 86-4819. 224p. (gr. 7 up). 1986. 13.95 (ISBN 0-15-239366-8, HJ). HarBraceJ.
—Ivy Larkin. (gr. k-6). 1989. pap. 3.25 (ISBN 0-440-40175-5, YB). Dell.
Stone, Bruce. Half Nelson, Full Nelson. LC 85-42623. 244p. (gr. 7 up). 1985. PLB 12.89 (ISBN 0-06-025922-1). HarpC Child Bks.
Stouffer, Nancy. Lilly. Fitzpatrick, Ann & Stouffer, Nancy, illus. 48p. (gr. k-2). 1989. pap. 2.95 (ISBN 0-927008-26-2). BCI-Bk Cook Inc.
Strauss, Linda L. The Alexandra Ingredient. (Illus.). (gr. 3-6). 1988. 12.95 (ISBN 0-517-57001-7). Crown.
Streatfeild, Noel. Gemma Alone. (Orig.). (gr. k-6). 1987. pap. 3.25 (ISBN 0-440-42865-3, Yearling). Dell.
Stren, Patti. I Was a Fifteen-Year-Old Blimp. LC 85-42624. 192p. (gr. 5-9). 1985. PLB 11.89 (ISBN 0-06-026058-0). HarpC Child Bks.
Strub, Susanne. Lulu Goes Swimming. (ps). 1990. 8.95 (ISBN 0-670-83460-2). Viking Child Bks.
—Lulu on Her Bike. (ps). 1990. 8.95 (ISBN 0-670-83461-0). Viking Child Bks.
Stucky, Naomi R. Sara's Summer. 144p. (Orig.). (gr. 6-12). 1990. pap. 5.95 (ISBN 0-8361-3534-2). Herald Pr.
Sutton, Jane. Definitely Not Sexy. LC 88-18127. 160p. (gr. 7 up). 1988. 12.95 (ISBN 0-316-82325-2). Little.
Suzanne, Jamie. The New Girl. large type ed. Pascal, Francine, created by. 105p. (gr. 7-12). 1990. Repr. of 1987 ed. 9.95 (ISBN 1-55905-069-1). Grey Castle.
Swallow, Pamela C. Leave It to Christy. 160p. (gr. 5-8). 1987. 13.95 (ISBN 0-399-21482-8, Putnam). Putnam Pub Group.
—Leave It to Christy. 144p. (gr. 3-7). 1988. pap. 2.50 (ISBN 0-590-41666-9, Pub. by Apple Paperbacks). Scholastic Inc.
Syder, Zilpha. Janie's Private Eyes. (ps-3). 1989. 14.95 (ISBN 0-385-30146-4). Doubleday.
Sypher, Lucy J. The Edge of Nowhere. Abel, Ray, illus. 211p. (gr. 3-7). 1991. pap. 3.95 (ISBN 0-14-034550-7, Puffin). Puffin Bks.
Tamar, Erika. Blues for Silk Garcia. LC 82-25259. 160p. (gr. 7 up). 1991. pap. 3.50 (ISBN 0-679-80424-2, Borzoi Sprinters). Knopf.
Taylor, Judy. My Dog. Cartwright, Reg, illus. LC 87-15268. 24p. (ps-2). 1988. 11.95 (ISBN 0-02-782472-1, Mcmillan Child Bk). Macmillan Child Grp.
Terris, Susan. Nell's Quilt. LC 87-12961. 192p. (gr. 7-12). 1987. 12.95 (ISBN 0-374-35504-5). FS&G.
Thesman, Jean. The Last April Dancers. 224p. (gr. 7 up). 1987. 13.95 (ISBN 0-395-43024-0). HM.
—Rachel Chance. 180p. (gr. 5-9). 1990. 13.95 (ISBN 0-395-50934-3). HM.
Thompson, Kay. Eloise. Knight, Hilary, illus. LC 55-11039. (gr. k-6). 1969. pap. 15.95 (ISBN 0-671-22350-X). S&S Trade.
Thompson, R. Jenny's Neighbours. (Illus.). 24p. (ps-8). 1987. 12.95 (ISBN 0-920303-73-0); pap. 4.95 (ISBN 0-920303-70-6). Firefly Bks Ltd.
Thompson, Richard. Effie's Bath. Fernandes, Eugenie, illus. 1990. 14.95 (ISBN 1-550370-55-3); pap. 5.95 (ISBN 1-550370-52-9). Firefly Bks Ltd.
Tilly, Nancy. Golden Girl. LC 85-25218. 216p. (gr. 5 up). 1985. 12.95 (ISBN 0-374-32694-0). FS&G.
—The Golden Girl. (gr. k-12). 1988. pap. 2.95 (ISBN 0-440-20095-4, LFL). Dell.
Timm, Carey. The Handy Girls Know How! Gold, Ethel, illus. 64p. (gr. 7-10). 1985. pap. 3.95 (ISBN 0-394-87066-2, Random Juv). Random.
Titherington, Jeanne. Where Are You Going, Emma? (Illus.). 24p. (ps-1). 1988. 11.95 (ISBN 0-688-07081-7); lib. bdg. 11.88 (ISBN 0-688-07082-5). Greenwillow.
Tolles, Martha. Darci in Cabin 13. (gr. 3-7). 1989. pap. 2.75 (ISBN 0-590-41917-X, Apple Paperbacks). Scholastic Inc.
—Who's Reading Darci's Diary? 128p. (gr. 3-7). 1985. pap. 2.75 (ISBN 0-590-42374-6). Scholastic Inc.
Towne, Mary. Wanda the Worrywart. 128p. (gr. 4-7). 1989. 11.95 (ISBN 0-689-31511-2, Atheneum Child Bk). Macmillan Child Grp.
Travers, P. L. Mary Poppins & the House Next Door. Shepard, Mary, illus. (gr. 4 up). 1989. 12.95 (ISBN 0-385-29749-1). Delacorte.
Tripp, Valerie. Changes for Molly: A Winter Story. Backes, Nick, illus. 67p. (Orig.). (gr. 2-5). 1988. 12.95 (ISBN 0-937295-48-5); pap. 5.95 (ISBN 0-937295-49-3). Pleasant Co.
—Changes for Molly: A Winter Story. Thieme, Jeanne, ed. Backes, Nick, illus. 72p. (gr. 2-5). 1990. PLB 12.95 (ISBN 0-937295-96-5). Pleasant Co.
—Changes for Samantha: A Winter Story. Grace, Robert & Niles, N., illus. 67p. (Orig.). (gr. 2-5). 1988. 12.95 (ISBN 0-937295-46-9); pap. 5.95 (ISBN 0-937295-47-7). Pleasant Co.
—Changes for Samantha: A Winter Story. Thieme, Jeanne, ed. Grace, Robert & Niles, Nancy, illus. 72p. (gr. 2-5). 1990. PLB 12.95 (ISBN 0-937295-95-7). Pleasant Co.
—Happy Birthday, Samantha! A Springtime Story. Grace, Robert, illus. 62p. (Orig.). (gr. 2-5). 1987. 12.95 (ISBN 0-937295-34-5); pap. 5.95 (ISBN 0-937295-35-3). Pleasant Co.
—Meet Molly: An American Girl. Payne, C. F., illus. LC 86-60468. 59p. (Orig.). (gr. 2-5). 1986. 12.95 (ISBN 0-937295-06-X); pap. 5.95 (ISBN 0-937295-07-8). Pleasant Co.
—Meet Molly: An American Girl. Thieme, Jeanne, ed. Payne, C. F., illus. 72p. (gr. 2-5). 1990. PLB 12.95 (ISBN 0-937295-81-7). Pleasant Co.
—Molly Learns a Lesson: A School Story. Payne, C. F., illus. LC 86-60626. 67p. (Orig.). (gr. 2-5). 1986. 12.95 (ISBN 0-937295-15-9); pap. 5.95 (ISBN 0-937295-16-7). Pleasant Co.
—Molly Learns a Lesson: A School Story. Thieme, Jeanne, ed. Payne, C. F., illus. 72p. (gr. 2-5). 1990. PLB 12.95 (ISBN 0-937295-84-1). Pleasant Co.
—Molly Saves the Day: A Summer Story. Backes, Nick, illus. 69p. (Orig.). (gr. 2-5). 1988. 12.95 (ISBN 0-937295-42-6); pap. 5.95 (ISBN 0-937295-43-4). Pleasant Co.
—Molly Saves the Day: A Summer Story. Thieme, Jeanne, ed. Backes, Nick, illus. 72p. (gr. 2-5). 1990. PLB 12.95 (ISBN 0-937295-93-0). Pleasant Co.
—Molly's Boxed Set, 6 bks. (Illus.). 432p. (gr. 2-5). 1990. Boxed set. pap. 34.95 (ISBN 0-937295-78-7). Pleasant Co.
—Samantha Saves the Day: A School Adventure. Thieme, Jeanne, ed. Grace, Robert & Niles, Nancy, illus. 72p. (gr. 2-5). 1990. PLB 12.95 (ISBN 0-937295-92-2). Pleasant Co.
—Samantha Saves the Day: A Summer Story. Grace, Robert & Niles, Grace, illus. 65p. (Orig.). (gr. 2-5). 1988. 12.95 (ISBN 0-937295-40-X); pap. 5.95 (ISBN 0-937295-41-8). Pleasant Co.
Tritten, Charles. Heidi Grows Up. (gr. k-6). 1988. pap. 4.95 (ISBN 0-440-40107-0, Pub. by Yearling Classics). Dell.
Turner, Ann. Nettie's Trip South. Himler, Ronald, illus. LC 86-18135. 32p. (gr. 1-5). 1987. 12.95 (ISBN 0-02-789240-9, Mcmillan Child Bk). Macmillan Child Grp.
Tusa, Tricia. Stay Away from the Junkyard! Tusa, Tricia, illus. LC 87-15274. 32p. (gr. k-3). 1988. 14.95 (ISBN 0-02-789541-6, Mcmillan Child Bk). Macmillan Child Grp.
Twohill, Maggie. Bigmouth. LC 86-12889. 128p. (gr. 3-5). 1986. 11.95 (ISBN 0-02-789260-3, Bradbury Pr). Macmillan Child Grp.
Udry, Janice M. What Mary Jo Shared. Sayles, Elizabeth, illus. 32p. (ps-3). 1991. pap. 3.95 (ISBN 0-590-43757-7). Scholastic Inc.
Vail, Virginia. Happy Trails. Bode, Daniel, illus. LC 89-30584. 128p. (gr. 4-5). 1990. PLB 9.89 (ISBN 0-8167-1627-7); pap. text ed. 2.95 (ISBN 0-8167-1628-5). Troll Assocs.
—Riding Home. Bode, Daniel, illus. LC 89-34548. 128p. (gr. 4-6). 1989. PLB 9.89 (ISBN 0-8167-1661-7); pap. text ed. 2.95 (ISBN 0-8167-1662-5). Troll Assocs.
Van der Beek, Deborah. Superbabe! Van der Beek, Deborah, illus. 32p. (ps-1). 1988. 9.95 (ISBN 0-399-21507-7, Putnam). Putnam Pub Group.
VanKempen, Corrigan. Emily Umily. (Illus.). 24p. (ps-8). 1984. 12.95 (ISBN 0-685-38507-8); pap. 4.95 (ISBN 0-920236-99-5). Firefly Bks Ltd.
Van Steenwyk, Elizabeth. Lori for President. 128p. (gr. 5-8). 1988. pap. 2.50 (ISBN 0-87406-322-1). Willowisp Pr.
—Rachel Has a Secret. 128p. (Orig.). (gr. 5-8). 1987. pap. 0.50 (ISBN 0-87406-249-7). Willowisp Pr.
—Sarah's Great Idea. Hickman, Estella, illus. 96p. (Orig.). (gr. 3-5). 1987. pap. 2.25 (ISBN 0-87406-275-6). Willowisp Pr.
Verzuh, Julie W. From the Heart of Lizzie. (gr. 7 up). 1983. pap. 7.50 (ISBN 0-87839-039-1). North Star.

Vitalo, Valerie. Sweet Dreams, Sarah. DeVito, Pam, illus. LC 88-51277. 54p. (ps-4). 1989. 8.95 (ISBN 0-932433-56-1). Windswept Hse.
Voigt, Cynthia. Seventeen Against the Dealer. LC 88-27488. 192p. (gr. 7 up). 1989. 13.95 (ISBN 0-689-31497-3, Atheneum Child Bk). Macmillan Child Grp.
—Stories about Rosie. Kendrick, Dennis, illus. LC 86-3640. 48p. (ps-3). 1986. 12.95 (ISBN 0-689-31296-2, Atheneum Child Bk). Macmillan Child Grp.
Waddell, Martin. Alice the Artist. Langley, Jonathan, illus. 32p. (ps-1). 1988. 10.95 (ISBN 0-525-44385-1, 01063-320, DCB). Dutton Child Bks.
—Amy Said, Vol. 1. (ps-3). 1990. 12.95 (ISBN 0-316-91636-6, Joy St Bks). Little.
Wallace, Barbara B. The Interesting Thing That Happened at Perfect Acres, Inc. Sims, Blanche, illus. LC 87-14547. 144p. (gr. 3-7). 1988. 12.95 (ISBN 0-689-31354-3, Atheneum Child Bk). Macmillan Child Grp.
Wallace, Ian. Morgan the Magnificent. Wallace, Ian, illus. LC 87-15482. 32p. (gr. k-4). 1988. 12.95 (ISBN 0-689-50441-1, M K McElderry). Macmillan Child Grp.
Ward, Cindy. Cookie's Week. De Paola, Tomie, illus. 32p. (ps-1). 1988. 10.95 (ISBN 0-399-21498-4, Putnam). Putnam Pub Group.
Warren, Cathy. Saturday Belongs to Sara. Disalvo-Ryan, Dyanne, illus. LC 87-11783. 48p. (gr. 1-5). 1988. 12.95 (ISBN 0-02-792491-2, Bradbury Pr). Macmillan Child Grp.
Waters, Kate. Sarah Morton's Day: A Day in the Life of a Pilgrim Girl. Kendall, Russ, photos by. (Illus.). 32p. 1991. pap. 4.95 (ISBN 0-590-44871-4, Blue Ribbon Bks). Scholastic Inc.
Weber, Ane, et al. The Girl Who Wanted to Be Beautiful. French, Marty & Christman, Micheal, illus. 26p. (ps up). 1986. Book & Cassette. 7.95 (ISBN 1-55578-109-8). Worlds Wonder.
—The Girl Who Wanted to Be Beautiful. French, Marty & Christman, Michael, illus. 26p. (ps up). 1988. incl. cassette 7.95 (ISBN 1-55578-915-3). Worlds Wonder.
—The Girl With the Pop-Up Garden. French, Marty, et al, illus. 26p. (ps up). 1986. Book & Cassette. 7.95 (ISBN 1-55578-102-0). Worlds Wonder.
Webster, Jean. Daddy-Long-Legs. 256p. (gr. 5 up). 1989. pap. 2.95 (ISBN 0-14-035111-6, Puffin). Puffin Bks.
—Daddy-Long-Legs. 176p. (gr. 5-8). 1988. pap. 2.95 (ISBN 0-590-44094-2). Scholastic Inc.
Wechter, Nell W. Taffy of Torpedo Junction. Sparks, Mary W., illus. LC 57-9312. 134p. (gr. 5-9). 1990. pap. 7.95 (ISBN 0-89587-076-2). Blair.
Weedn, Flavia. Flavia & the Velveteen Rabbit. (Illus.). 52p. 1990. 16.00 (ISBN 0-929632-10-9). Applause Inc.
Wells, Rosemary. Leave Well Enough Alone. LC 76-42586. (gr. 6 up). 1977. 8.95 (ISBN 0-8037-4754-3). Dial Bks Young.
—Noisy Nora. Wells, Rosemary, illus. 40p. (ps-2). 1980. pap. 3.95 (ISBN 0-8037-6193-7). Dial Bks Young.
Wersba, Barbara. Just Be Gorgeous. LC 87-45858. 160p. (gr. 7 up). 1988. 11.95 (ISBN 0-06-026359-8); PLB 11.89 (ISBN 0-06-026360-1). HarpC Child Bks.
Weyland, Jack. Stephanie. LC 88-37541. 212p. (gr. 7 up). 1989. 9.95 (ISBN 0-87579-203-0). Deseret Bk.
Weyn, Suzanne. The Makeover Club. 128p. (gr. 7 up). 1986. pap. 2.50 (ISBN 0-380-75007-4, Flare). Avon.
—Stepping Out. Iskowitz, Joel, illus. LC 89-30586. 96p. (gr. 2-5). 1989. PLB 9.89 (ISBN 0-8167-1619-6); pap. text ed. 2.95 (ISBN 0-8167-1620-X). Troll Assocs.
—A Twist of Fate. Iskowitz, Joel, illus. LC 89-30585. 96p. (gr. 2-5). 1989. PLB 9.89 (ISBN 0-8167-1621-8); pap. text ed. 2.95 (ISBN 0-8167-1622-6). Troll Assocs.
What Katy Did. (Illus.). (gr. 3-5). 3.50 (ISBN 0-7214-1117-7). Ladybird Bks.
Whelan, Gloria. Next Spring an Oriole. Johnson, Pamela, illus. LC 87-4910. 64p. (gr. 2-4). 1987. lib. bdg. 6.99 (ISBN 0-394-99125-7, Random Juv); pap. 1.95 (ISBN 0-394-89125-2, Random Juv). Random.
White, Ruth. Sweet Creek Holler. 168p. (gr. 7 up). 1988. 13.95 (ISBN 0-374-37360-4). FS&G.
Whitmore, Arvella. You're a Real Hero, Amanda. (gr. 5-9). 1985. 12.95 (ISBN 0-395-38950-X). HM.
Whittington, Mary K. Carmina, Come Dance! McDermott, Michael, illus. LC 88-34430. 32p. (gr. k-3). 1989. 12.95 (ISBN 0-689-31554-6, Atheneum Child Bk). Macmillan Child Grp.
Whyte, Jenny B. Adelaide Stores. Prager, Annabelle, illus. LC 72-77767. (gr. 4 up). 1972. 3.95 (ISBN 0-671-65194-3, Little Simon). S&S Trade.
Wiggin, Eric & Wiggin, Kate D. Rebecca of Sunnybrook Farm: The Girl. 256p. (gr. 4-7). 1990. 9.95 (ISBN 1-56121-004-8). Wolgemuth & Hyatt.
Wiggin, Kate D. Rebecca of Sunnybrook Farm. 239p. 1981. Repr. PLB 21.95x (ISBN 0-89966-354-0). Buccaneer Bks.
—Rebecca of Sunnybrook Farm. (gr. k-6). 1986. pap. 4.95 (ISBN 0-440-47533-3, Pub. by Yearling Classics). Dell.
Willard, Nancy. The Highest Hit. McCully, Emily, illus. LC 77-88970. (gr. 4-7). 1978. 6.95 (ISBN 0-15-234278-8, HJ). HarBraceJ.
Willey, Margaret. The Bigger Book of Lydia. LC 82-48842. 256p. (gr. 7 up). 1983. PLB 12.89 (ISBN 0-06-026486-1). HarpC Child Bks.
—The Bigger Book of Lydia. LC 82-48842. 224p. (gr. 7 up). 1988. pap. 3.25 (ISBN 0-06-447049-0, Trophy). HarpC Child Bks.
Williams-Garcia, Rita. Blue Tights. LC 87-17156. 160p. (gr. 7 up). 1988. 12.95 (ISBN 0-525-67234-6, Lodestar Bks). Dutton Child Bks.
Wine, Jeanine. Silly Tillie. LC 87-38311. 32p. (gr. k-3). 1990. 12.95 (ISBN 0-934672-62-8). Good Bks PA.
Winthrop, Elizabeth. Belinda's Hurricane. Watson, Wendy, illus. 64p. (gr. 2-6). 1989. pap. 3.95 (ISBN 0-14-032985-4, Puffin). Puffin Bks.
Wise Woman's Secret. 1991. pap. 14.95 (ISBN 0-671-72603-X). S&S Trade.
Wojciechowski, Susan. Patty Dillman of Hot Dog Fame. LC 88-22565. 192p. (gr. 5 up). 1989. 13.95 (ISBN 0-531-05810-7); PLB 13.99 (ISBN 0-531-08410-8). Orchard Bks Watts.
Wolde, Gunilla. Betsy's Fixing Day. Wolde, Gunilla, illus. LC 78-50056. 24p. (ps). 1990. 4.95 (ISBN 0-394-83781-9, Random Juv). Random.
Wolff, Tobias. The Barracks Thief: And Selected Stories. 1989. pap. 7.95 (ISBN 0-553-34675-X). Bantam.
Wooldridge, Rhoda. Hanah's Mill. LC 83-26515. (Illus.). (gr. 4-6). 1984. pap. 8.00 (ISBN 0-8309-0386-0). Ind Pr MO.
Wooley, Catherine. Cathy Leonard Calling. (gr. 5-7). 1988. pap. 3.95 (ISBN 0-14-032551-4, Puffin). Puffin Bks.
—Ginnie & Geneva. (gr. 5-7). 1988. pap. 3.95 (ISBN 0-317-69651-3, Puffin). Puffin Bks.
Wright, Betty R. The Pike River Phantom. 160p. (gr. 3-7). 1990. pap. 2.75 (ISBN 0-590-42808-X). Scholastic Inc.
—Rosie & the Dance of the Dinosaurs. LC 89-2083. 112p. (gr. 4-7). 1989. 13.95 (ISBN 0-8234-0782-9). Holiday.
Wyeth, Sharon D. Amy's Song. (gr. k-6). 1990. pap. 2.95 (ISBN 0-440-40260-3, YB). Dell.
—Annie K's Theater: The Dinosaur Tooth. (gr. 3-6). 1990. pap. 2.75 (ISBN 0-553-15815-5). Bantam.
Yarbro, Chelsea Q. Four Horses for Tishtry. LC 84-48341. 224p. (gr. 7 up). 1985. HarpC Child Bks.
Yarbrough, Camille. The Shimmershine Queens. 128p. (gr. 5-8). 1989. 13.95 (ISBN 0-399-21465-8, Putnam). Putnam Pub Group.
Yates, Elizabeth. Carolina's Courage. 131p. (Orig.). (gr. 2-4). 1989. pap. 4.95 (ISBN 0-89084-482-8). Bob Jones Univ Pr.
Yeo, Wilma. The Girl in the Window. 128p. (gr. 3-7). 1988. pap. 2.50 (ISBN 0-590-40555-1, Apple Paperbacks). Scholastic Inc.
York, Carol B. Miss Know It All Returns. 96p. 1985. pap. 2.25 (ISBN 0-553-15351-X, Skylark). Bantam.
Young, Alida E. Megan the Klutz. 128p. (gr. 5-8). 1986. 2.95 (ISBN 0-87406-146-6). Willowisp Pr.
Zebrowski, George. The Stars Will Speak. LC 85-42638. 224p. (gr. 7 up). 1985. 12.95i (ISBN 0-06-026886-7). HarpC Child Bks.
Ziefert, Harriet. Come Out, Jessie! Smith, Mavis, illus. LC 87-20484. 32p. (ps-1). 1988. 5.95 (ISBN 0-394-89679-3, Random Juv). Random.
—Dinner's Ready, Jessie! Smith, Mavis, illus. LC 87-20483. 32p. (ps-1). 1988. 5.95 (ISBN 0-394-89680-7, Random Juv). Random.
—Hurry up, Jessie! Smith, Mavis, illus. LC 87-4267. 32p. (ps-1). 1987. 5.95 (ISBN 0-394-89194-5, Random Juv). Random.
—Me Too! Me Too! Gundersheimer, Karen, illus. LC 87-11937. 36p. (ps-1). 1988. 11.95 (ISBN 0-06-026880-8); PLB 11.89 (ISBN 0-06-026893-X). HarpC Child Bks.
—Penny Goes to the Movies. (Illus.). 32p. (ps-2). 1990. pap. 8.95 (ISBN 0-670-83203-0). Viking Child Bks.
—Penny Goes to the Movies. Rader, Laura, illus. 32p. (ps-3). 1990. pap. 3.50 (ISBN 0-14-054225-6, Puffin). Puffin Bks.
Zolotow, Charlotte. I Like to Be Little. Blegvad, Erik, illus. LC 83-45056. 32p. (gr. k-4). 1987. 11.95 (ISBN 0-690-04672-3, Crowell Jr Bks); PLB 12.89 (ISBN 0-690-04674-X, Crowell Jr Bks). HarpC Child Bks.
—It's Not Fair. Reissue. ed. Du Bois, William P., illus. LC 76-3387. 32p. (gr. k-3). 1976. 12.95 (ISBN 0-06-026934-0); PLB 12.89 (ISBN 0-06-026935-9). HarpC Child Bks.
—Not a Little Monkey. Chessare, Michele, illus. LC 88-21457. 32p. (ps-1). 1989. 12.95 (ISBN 0-06-026980-4); PLB 12.89 (ISBN 0-06-026981-2). HarpC Child Bks.

GIRLS–POETRY

Gerber, Merrill J. I'd Rather Think about Robby. LC 88-19849. 160p. (gr. 4-7). 1989. 11.95 (ISBN 0-06-022283-2); PLB 11.89 (ISBN 0-06-022284-0). HarpC Child Bks.

GLACIAL EPOCH

Gallant, Roy A. Ice Ages. (Illus.). 72p. (gr. 4 up). 1985. lib. bdg. 10.40 (ISBN 0-531-04912-4). Watts.
Holman, J. Allan & Gringhuis, Dirk. Mystery Mammals of the Ice Age-Great Lakes Region. Gringhuis, Dirk, illus. LC 72-90919. 45p. (Orig.). (gr. 5-8). 1972. pap. 1.75 (ISBN 0-910726-74-4). Hillsdale Educ.
Ice Age Hunter. (Illus.). (gr. 3-8). lib. bdg. 14.00 (ISBN 0-86592-143-1). Rourke Corp.
Maynard, Christopher. The Great Ice Age. Atkinson, Mike, illus. LC 87-4791. 24p. (gr. 2-5). 1987. lib. bdg. 5.99 (ISBN 0-394-99214-8, Random Juv); (Random Juv). Random.
Stille, Darlene R. Ice Age. LC 90-37681. (Illus.). 48p. (gr. k-4). 1990. PLB 14.60 (ISBN 0-516-01107-3); pap. 4.95 (ISBN 0-516-41107-1). Childrens.
Wyler, Rose & Adams, Gerald. The Story of the Ice Age. Voter, Thomas W., illus. 96p. (Orig.). (gr. 4-6). 1988. pap. 2.50 (ISBN 0-590-41446-1). Scholastic Inc.

GLACIER NATIONAL PARK

Root, Phyllis. Glacier. LC 88-18945. (Illus.). 48p. (gr. 4-5). 1988. 12.95 (ISBN 0-89686-408-1, Crestwood Hse). Macmillan Child Grp.

GLACIERS

Bender, Lionel. Glacier. (Illus.). 32p. (gr. 3-5). 1989. PLB 11.90 (ISBN 0-531-10647-0). Watts.
Bramwell, Martyn. Glaciers & Ice Caps. LC 85-52046. (Illus.). 32p. (gr. 4-9). 1986. PLB 11.40 (ISBN 0-531-10178-9). Watts.
Georges, D. V. Glaciers. LC 85-30884. (Illus.). 48p. (gr. k-4). 1986. PLB 14.60 (ISBN 0-516-01281-9); pap. 4.95 (ISBN 0-516-41281-7). Childrens.
Radlauer, Ruth & Gitkin, Lisa S. The Power of Ice. Gitkin, Lisa S., photos by. LC 85-5714. (Illus.). 48p. (gr. 3-6). 1985. PLB 15.93 (ISBN 0-516-07839-9); pap. 4.95 (ISBN 0-516-47839-7). Childrens.
Simon, Seymour. Icebergs & Glaciers. LC 86-18142. (Illus.). 32p. (ps-3). 1987. 14.95 (ISBN 0-688-06186-9); lib. bdg. 14.88 (ISBN 0-688-06187-7, Morrow Jr Bks). Morrow Jr Bks.
Tangborn, Wendell V. Glaciers. rev. ed. Simont, Marc, illus. LC 87-45306. 32p. (ps-3). 1988. pap. 4.50 (ISBN 0-06-445076-7, Trophy). HarpC Child Bks.
—Glaciers. rev. ed. Simont, Marc, illus. LC 87-47696. 32p. (ps-3). 1988. 13.95 (ISBN 0-690-04682-0, Crowell Jr Bks); PLB 13.89 (ISBN 0-690-04684-7, Crowell Jr Bks). HarpC Child Bks.
Walker, Sally M. Glaciers: Ice on the Move. (Illus.). 48p. (gr. 3-6). 1990. PLB 12.95 (ISBN 0-87614-373-7). Carolrhoda Bks.

GLANDS

Connelly, John P. You're Too Sweet. (gr. 4-9). 1968. 9.95 (ISBN 0-8392-1173-2). Astor-Honor.

GLASS

Kolb, Kenneth & Kolb, Doris. Glass: Its Many Facets. LC 86-32785. 64p. (gr. 6-12). 1988. lib. bdg. 15.95 (ISBN 0-89490-150-8). Enslow Pubs.
Paterson, Alan J. How Glass Is Made. (Illus.). 32p. (gr. 7 up). 1986. 12.95 (ISBN 0-8160-0038-7). Facts on File.

GLASS, STAINED

see Glass Painting and Staining

GLASS MANUFACTURE

Condon, Judith. Recycling Glass. LC 89-70710. 32p. (gr. 5-8). 1991. PLB 11.40 (ISBN 0-531-14077-6). Watts.
Mitgutsch, Ali. From Sand to Glass. Mitgutsch, Ali, illus. LC 80-29572. 24p. (ps-3). 1981. PLB 6.95 (ISBN 0-87614-162-9). Carolrhoda Bks.

GLASS PAINTING AND STAINING

Corning Museum of Glass Staff. Masterpieces of Glass from the Corning Museum: 24 Ready-to-Mail Full-Color. 12p. (Orig.). (gr. 7 up). 1984. pap. 3.95 (ISBN 0-486-24526-8). Dover.

GLIDING AND SOARING

Barrett, Norman. Hang Gliding. Franklin Watts Ltd., ed. (Illus.). 32p. (ps-9). 1988. 10.90 (ISBN 0-531-10350-1). Watts.
Penzler, Otto. Hang Gliding: Riding the Wind. LC 75-21843. (Illus.). 32p. (gr. 5-10). 1976. PLB 10.79 (ISBN 0-89375-008-5); pap. 2.95 (ISBN 0-89375-024-7). Troll Assocs.

GLOBAL SATELLITE COMMUNICATIONS SYSTEMS

see Artificial Satellites in Telecommunication

GLOBES

Broekel, Ray. Maps & Globes. LC 83-7509. (Illus.). 48p. (gr. k-4). 1983. PLB 14.60 (ISBN 0-516-01695-4); pap. 4.95 (ISBN 0-516-41695-2). Childrens.
Edson, Ann & Insel, Eunice. Reading Maps, Globes, Charts, Graphs. (gr. 4-6). 1982. wkbk. 2.69 (ISBN 0-89525-175-2). Ed Activities.
Knowlton, Jack. Maps & Globes. Barton, Harriett, illus. LC 85-47537. 48p. (gr. 2-5). 1985. 14.95 (ISBN 0-690-04457-7, Crowell Jr Bks); PLB 11.89 (ISBN 0-690-04459-3). HarpC Child Bks.
—Maps & Globes. Barton, Harriett, illus. LC 85-47537. 48p. (gr. 2-5). 1986. pap. 4.95 (ISBN 0-06-446049-5, Trophy). HarpC Child Bks.

GLOSSARIES

see also names of language or subject with the subdivision dictionaries, e.g. English Language–Dictionaries; Chemistry–Dictionaries

GNOMES

see Fairies

GO KARTS

see Karts and Karting

GOATS

Burton, Jane. Caper the Kid. Burton, Jane, photos by. LC 89-11566. (Illus.). 32p. (gr. 2-3). 1989. PLB 10.95 (ISBN 0-8368-0203-9). Gareth Stevens Inc.
Edwards, E. Dean. The American Pioneer. (Illus.). 36p. (Orig.). (gr. 1 up). 1988. pap. 2.95. E D Edwards.
Hall, Alice. Dairy Goats: Selecting, Fitting, Showing. Holleran, Betsy, illus. Jackson, Robert A., frwd. by. LC 77-153203. (Illus.). (gr. 7 up). 1975. pap. 4.00x (ISBN 0-932218-02-4). Hall Pr.
Lavine, Sigmund A. Wonders of Goats. 1980. 9.95 (ISBN 0-396-07891-5, Putnam). Putnam Pub Group.
Parkison, Ralph F. The Old Goat. Withrow, Marion O., ed. Bush, William, illus. 112p. (Orig.). (gr. 2-8). 1988. pap. write for info. Little Wood Bks.
Royston, Angela. Goat. (ps-3). 1990. PLB 10.40 (ISBN 0-531-19078-1). Watts.

GOGH, VINCENT VAN, 1853-1890

Lucas, Eileen. Vincent Van Gogh. (Illus.). 64p. (gr. 3-5). 1991. PLB 11.90 (ISBN 0-531-20024-8). Watts.

Raboff, Ernest. Vincent Van Gogh. LC 87-45300. (Illus.). 32p. (gr. 1 up). 1988. pap. 7.95 (ISBN 0-06-446077-0, Trophy). HarpC Child Bks.

GOLD

see also Gold Mines and Mining; Jewelry; Money

Cohen, Daniel. Gold: The Fascinating Study of the Noble Metal Through the Ages. LC 76-18067. (Illus.). 192p. (gr. 7 up). 1976. 10.95 (ISBN 0-87131-218-2). M Evans.

Fodor, R. V. Gold, Copper, Iron: How Metals Are Formed, Found, & Used. LC 87-24464. (Illus.). 96p. (gr. 6-12). 1989. PLB 16.95 (ISBN 0-89490-138-9). Enslow Pubs.

Lye, K. Gold. (Illus.). 48p. (gr. 5 up). Date not set. PLB 15.93 (ISBN 0-86592-272-1). Rourke Corp.

Mitgutsch, Ali. From Gold to Money. Mitgutsch, Ali, illus. LC 84-17488. 24p. (ps-3). 1985. PLB 6.95 (ISBN 0-87614-230-7). Carolrhoda Bks.

GOLD FISH

see Goldfish

GOLD MINES AND MINING

see also Prospecting

Cooper, Michael. Klondike Fever: The Famous Gold Rush of 1898. (gr. 4-7). 1990. pap. 5.95 (ISBN 0-395-54784-9, Clarion Bks). HM.

Stein, R. Conrad. The Story of the Gold at Sutter's Mill. LC 81-6088. (Illus.). 32p. (gr. 3-6). 1981. PLB 13.27 (ISBN 0-516-04617-9). Childrens.

Van Steenwyk, Elizabeth. The California Gold Rush: West with the Forty-Niners. (Illus.). 64p. (gr. 5-8). 1991. PLB 11.90 (ISBN 0-531-20032-9). Watts.

GOLD MINES AND MINING–FICTION

Hollingsworth, Mary. Charlie & the Gold Mine. (Illus.). (ps-3). 1989. 5.95 (ISBN 0-915720-28-0). Brownlow Pub Co.

Miller, Sherry. Snowskate Goes for Gold. Martinez, Jesse, illus. 32p. (Orig.). (gr. k-5). 1984. pap. 1.95 saddle-stitched (ISBN 0-913379-02-6). Double M Pub.

Vandersteen, Willy. A Fool's Gold. Lahey, Nicholas J., tr. from FLE. LC 76-49377. (Illus., Orig.). (gr. 3-8). 1977. pap. 2.50 (ISBN 0-915560-08-9, 08). Hiddigeigei.

Wells, Marian. Colorado Gold. LC 87-35333. 302p. (Orig.). (gr. 9-12). 1988. pap. 6.95 (ISBN 0-87123-966-3). Bethany Hse.

GOLD RUSH

see California–Gold Discoveries

GOLDFISH

Gilbert, Mariana. Your First Goldfish. (Illus.). 36p. (Orig.). 1991. pap. 1.95 (ISBN 0-86622-065-8, YF-108). TFH Pubns.

O'Neal, Zibby. The Language of Goldfish. LC 79-19167. (gr. 6 up). 1980. pap. 14.95 (ISBN 0-670-41785-8). Viking Child Bks.

GOLDMAN, EMMA, 1869-1940

Waldstreicher, David. Emma Goldman. Horner, Matina S., intro. by. (Illus.). 112p. (gr. 5 up). 1990. 17.95 (ISBN 1-55546-655-9). Chelsea Hse.

GOLF

Lerner, Mark. Golf Is for Me. Wolfe, Robert L., illus. LC 81-20927. 48p. (gr. 2-5). 1982. PLB 8.95 (ISBN 0-8225-1143-6). Lerner Pubns.

Schiffman, Roger. Golf Basics. Schoolcraft, Robert, illus. 48p. (gr. 3-7). 1986. 10.95 (ISBN 0-13-357955-7). P-H.

GOLF–BIOGRAPHY

Creighton, Susan. Greg Norman. LC 87-27565. (Illus.). 48p. (gr. 5-6). 1988. PLB 10.95 (ISBN 0-89686-371-9, Crestwood Hse). Macmillan Child Grp.

Gilbert, Tom. Lee Trevino. (Illus.). (gr. 5 up). 1992. PLB 17.95 (ISBN 0-7910-1256-5). Chelsea Hse.

GOLF–FICTION

Walker, David. Rick Tees Off. Wright, Malcolm, ed. Van Zandt, William, illus. Nicklaus, Jack, frwd. by. (Illus.). 112p. (Orig.). (gr. 4-9). 1985. pap. text ed. 3.95 (ISBN 0-9614856-0-4). Pro Golfers.

GOMPERS, SAMUEL, 1850-1924

Kurland, Gerald. Samuel Gompers: Founder of the American Labor Movement. Rahmas, D. Steve, ed. LC 72-190242. 32p. (Orig.). (gr. 7-12). 1972. lib. bdg. 4.20 incl. catalog cards (ISBN 0-87157-524-8). SamHar Pr.

GOOD GROOMING

see Beauty, Personal

GOOSE

see Geese

GORILLAS

Goodall, Jane. Jane Goodall's Animal World: Gorillas. 32p. (gr. 3-7). 1990. pap. 3.95 (ISBN 0-689-71396-7, Aladdin). Macmillan Child Grp.

Schlein, Miriam. Jane Goodall's Animal World: Gorillas. Goodall, Jane, intro. by. LC 89-38550. (Illus.). 32p. (gr. 3-7). 1990. 11.95 (ISBN 0-689-31473-6, Atheneum Child Bk). Macmillan Child Grp.

GORILLAS–FICTION

Aardema, Verna. Princess Gorilla & a New Kind of Water. Chess, Victoria, illus. LC 86-32888. 32p. (ps-3). 1991. pap. 3.95 (ISBN 0-8037-0914-5, Dial Pied Piper). Puffin Bks.

Bailey, Jill. Gorilla Rescue. LC 90-9678. (Illus.). 48p. (gr. 3-7). 1990. PLB 17.28 (ISBN 0-8114-2705-6). Steck-V.

Bornstein, Ruth. Little Gorilla. Bornstein, Ruth, illus. LC 75-25508. 32p. (ps-3). 1979. 13.95 (ISBN 0-395-28773-1, Clarion). HM.

Brown, Anthony. Gorilla. Brown, Anthony, illus. LC 85-13. 32p. (ps-2). 1989. pap. 4.95 (ISBN 0-394-82225-0). Knopf.

Browne, Anthony. Gorilla: Miniature Edition. Browne, Anthony, illus. 32p. (ps-3). 1991. 4.95 (ISBN 0-679-81453-1). Knopf.

Fenner, Carol. Gorilla Gorilla. (gr. 2 up). 1973. (Random Juv). Random.

Hazen, Barbara S. The Gorilla Did It. Cruz, Ray, illus. LC 73-84828. 32p. (ps-1). 1974. 12.95 (ISBN 0-689-30138-3, Atheneum Child Bk). Macmillan Child Grp.

Hoff, Syd. Julius. Hoff, Syd, illus. LC 59-8971. 64p. (gr. k-3). 1959. PLB 11.89 (ISBN 0-06-022491-6). HarpC Child Bks.

Hoffman, Mary. Gorilla. LC 84-24906. (Illus.). 24p. (gr. k-5). 1985. PLB 13.32 (ISBN 0-8172-2413-0). Raintree Pubs.

Mauser, Pat R. Patti's Pet Gorilla. 64p. 1991. pap. 2.95 (ISBN 0-380-71039-0, Camelot). Avon.

Mauser, Patricia R. Patti's Pet Gorilla. Palmisciano, Diane, illus. LC 86-20546. 64p. (gr. 2-4). 1987. 11.95 (ISBN 0-689-31279-2, Atheneum Child Bk). Macmillan Child Grp.

Morozumi, Atsuko. One Gorilla: A Counting Book. Morozumi, Atsuko, illus. 26p. (ps-1). 1990. 13.95 (ISBN 0-374-35644-0). FS&G.

Patterson, Francine. Koko's Story. Cohn, Ronald H., photos by. LC 86-17717. (Illus.). 48p. (ps up). 1987. pap. 10.95 (ISBN 0-590-40272-2, Scholastic Hardcover). Scholastic Inc.

Thorne, Ian. King Kong. LC 76-51147. (Illus.). 48p. (gr. 3 up). 1977. PLB 10.95 (ISBN 0-913940-69-0, Crestwood Hse); pap. 4.95 (ISBN 0-913940-76-3). Macmillan Child Grp.

Wallace, Jim. Search for the Mountain Gorillas. 128p. (gr. 6 up). 1985. pap. 2.25 (ISBN 0-553-26062-6). Bantam.

GOVERNMENT, LOCAL

see Local Government

GOVERNMENT, RESISTANCE TO

Classrooms of Resistance. (Illus.). 168p. (gr. 3-6). 1980. 12.00 (ISBN 0-904613-10-0); pap. 5.95 (ISBN 0-904613-01-1). Writers & Readers.

GOVERNORS

Phillips, Margaret I. Governors of Tennessee. LC 77-26845. (Illus.). 193p. (gr. 6-12). 1978. 14.95 (ISBN 0-88289-169-3). Pelican.

GRAAL

see Grail

GRAHAM, WILLIAM FRANKLIN, 1918-

Wilson, Jean. Crusader for Christ (Billy Graham) (gr. 6-9). 1973. pap. 3.95 (ISBN 0-87508-602-0). Chr Lit.

GRAIL

see also Arthur, King

Pyle, Howard. The Story of the Grail & the Passing of Arthur. Pyle, Howard, illus. LC 85-40302. 340p. (gr. 7 up). 1985. Repr. 18.95 (ISBN 0-684-18483-4, Scribners Young Read). Macmillan Child Grp.

GRAIN

Dineen, Jacqueline. Cereals. 32p. (gr. 3-7). 1988. lib. bdg. 12.95 (ISBN 0-89490-211-3). Enslow Pubs.

Grain. (Illus.). (gr. 5 up). lib. bdg. 15.93 (ISBN 0-86592-263-2). Rourke Corp.

Greenaway, Theresa. Grasses & Grains. LC 90-9563. (Illus.). 48p. (gr. 5-9). 1990. PLB 18.60 (ISBN 0-8114-2729-3). Steck-V.

Moncure, Jane B. What Was It Before It Was Bread? Hygaard, Elizabeth, illus. LC 85-11402. 32p. (ps-2). 1985. PLB 11.97 (ISBN 0-89565-323-0). Childs World.

GRAMMAR

see also Language and Languages

also names of languages with the subdivision Grammar, e.g. English Language–Grammar

Gattegno, Caleb. Words in Color. rev. ed. (Orig.). (gr. k-12). 1977. mini-charts 8.75 (ISBN 0-87825-143-X); Word Charts. 100.00 (ISBN 0-87825-131-6); Phonic Code Charts. 40.00 (ISBN 0-87825-132-4); Book R-0. 0.25 (ISBN 0-87825-127-8); Book R-1. 0.65 (ISBN 0-87825-128-6); Book R-2. 1.50 (ISBN 0-87825-129-4); Book R-3. 1.50 (ISBN 0-87825-130-8); Worksheets 1-7. 3.65 (ISBN 0-87825-178-2); Worksheets 8-14. 1.65 (ISBN 0-87825-059-X). Ed Solutions.

Herman, Ethel & Everett, Karen H. Grammar for Teens. (gr. 5-12). 1989. spiral wkbk. 24.95 (ISBN 1-55999-042-2). LinguiSystems.

—Grammar-Semantics for Teens. (gr. 7-12). 1989. spiral wkbk. 49.90 (ISBN 1-55999-043-0). LinguiSystems.

Webb, Jane C. & Duckett, Barbara. RULES Phonological Evaluation. Seeland, Rene K., illus. 140p. (ps-3). 1990. text ed. 49.95 (ISBN 0-937857-12-2, 1577). Speech Bin.

GRAMMAR SCHOOLS

see Education, Elementary

GRAND CANYON

Henry, Marguerite. Brighty of the Grand Canyon. Dennis, Wesley, illus. LC 53-7233. (gr. 2-9). 1991. 12.95 (ISBN 0-02-743664-0, Mcmillan Child Bk). Macmillan Child Grp.

Mell, Jan. Grand Canyon. LC 88-18707. (Illus.). (gr. 4-8). 1988. PLB 12.95 (ISBN 0-89686-406-5, Crestwood Hse). Macmillan Child Grp.

Radlauer, Ruth S. Grand Canyon National Park. updated ed. LC 76-58525. (Illus.). 48p. (gr. 3 up). 1977. PLB 17.27 (ISBN 0-516-07492-X). Childrens.

Salts, Bobbi. Grand Canyon Discovery: An Activity Book. (Illus.). 32p. (Orig.). (gr. 1-6). 1989. pap. 2.95 (ISBN 0-929526-03-1). Double B Pubns.

Smith, Don. The Grand Canyon: Journey Through Time. new ed. LC 75-23413. (Illus.). 32p. (gr. 5-10). 1976. PLB 10.79 (ISBN 0-89375-007-7); pap. 2.95 (ISBN 0-89375-023-9). Troll Assocs.

GRAND CANYON–FICTION

Henry, Marguerite. Brighty of the Grand Canyon. Dennis, Wesley, illus. LC 90-28636. 224p. (gr. 3-7). 1991. pap. 3.95 (ISBN 0-689-71485-8, Aladdin). Macmillan Child Grp.

Thompson-Hoffman, Susan. Tassel's Mission. Buzzanco, Eileen M., illus. LC 88-64151. 32p. (gr. k-4). 1989. 11.95 (ISBN 0-924483-00-8); bk. & cassette 14.95 (ISBN 0-924483-03-2); bk., cassette & toy 41.95 (ISBN 0-924483-06-7); write for info. cassette (ISBN 0-924483-09-1). Soundprints.

GRAND OPERA

see Opera

GRANDPARENTS–FICTION

Abercrombie, Barbara. Cat-Man's Daughter. LC 79-2676. 160p. (gr. 6-9). 1981. HarpC Child Bks.

Ackerman, Karen. Song & Dance Man. Gammell, Stephen, illus. LC 87-3200. 32p. (ps-2). 1988. 12.95 (ISBN 0-394-89330-1); lib. bdg. 13.99 (ISBN 0-394-99330-6). Knopf.

Aliki. The Two of Them. LC 79-10161. (Illus.). 32p. (gr. k-3). 1979. 12.95 (ISBN 0-688-80225-7); PLB 12.88 (ISBN 0-688-84225-9). Greenwillow.

Allred, Mary. Grandmother Poppy & the Children's Tea Party. LC 84-4933. (Illus.). (gr. k-3). 1984. 5.95 (ISBN 0-8054-4292-8, 4242-92). Broadman.

—Grandmother Poppy & the Funny-Looking Bird. LC 81-65832. (gr. k-3). 1981. bds. 5.95 (ISBN 0-8054-4269-3, 4242-69). Broadman.

Anderson, Lena. Stina's Visit. LC 89-77716. (Illus.). 32p. (ps up). 1991. 13.95 (ISBN 0-688-09665-4); PLB 13.88 (ISBN 0-688-09666-2). Greenwillow.

Ash, Martha C. Grandmother's Visit with Sam. White, Regina, illus. LC 85-71540. 48p. (Orig.). (ps-2). 1985. pap. 4.25 (ISBN 0-933865-00-7). Doris Pubns.

Babbitt, Ellen. Granny's Blackie. Louis-Lucas, Natalie, illus. (gr. 7-9). 1982. pap. 2.50 (ISBN 0-88138-007-5). Green Tiger Pr.

Bacon, Katharine J. Shadow & Light. LC 86-23789. 208p. (gr. 7 up). 1987. 14.95 (ISBN 0-689-50431-4, M K McElderry). Macmillan Child Grp.

Bawden, Nina. The Robbers. LC 79-4152. (Illus.). 160p. (gr. 4-7). 1989. Repr. of 1979 ed. 12.95 (ISBN 0-688-41902-X). Lothrop.

Berenstain, Stan & Berenstain, Janice. The Berenstain Bears & the Week at Grandma's. Berenstain, Stan & Berenstain, Janice, illus. LC 85-25743. (ps-1). 1986. lib. bdg. 5.99 (ISBN 0-394-97335-6, Random Juv); pap. 2.25 (ISBN 0-394-87335-1, Random Juv). Random.

Berridge, Celia. Grandmother's Tales. Berridge, Celia, ed. (Illus.). 32p. (ps-2). 1982. 10.95 (ISBN 0-233-97357-5). Andre Deutsch.

Bobo, Carmen P. Sarah's Growing-up Summer. LC 88-62111. 52p. 1989. 5.95 (ISBN 1-55523-187-X). Winston-Derek.

Bond, Ruskin. Grandfather's Private Zoo. (Illus.). 95p. (gr. 3-5). 1.00 (ISBN 0-88253-345-2). Ind-US Inc.

Bornstein, Ruth L. A Beautiful Seashell. Bornstein, Ruth L., illus. LC 90-4032. 32p. (gr. k-3). 1990. 12.95 (ISBN 0-06-020594-6); PLB 12.89 (ISBN 0-06-020595-4). HarpC Child Bks.

Bourgeois, Paulette. Grandma's Secret, Vol. 1. 1990. 14.95 (ISBN 0-316-10355-1, Joy ST Bks). Little.

Brackett, Rona N. Harry's Grandpa Takes a Mysterious Journey. Johnson, Mackenzie, illus. LC 86-1233. 55p. (Orig.). (gr. 3-6). 1986. text ed. 12.50 (ISBN 0-916955-04-4); pap. 6.75 (ISBN 0-916955-05-2). Arcus Pub.

Brantley, Lucille. Andy's Special Love. 80p. 1990. 9.50 (ISBN 0-8062-3719-8). Carlton.

Bunting, Eve. The Wednesday Surprise. Garrick, Donald, illus. 32p. (gr. k-3). 1989. 13.95 (ISBN 0-89919-721-3, Pub. by Clarion). Ticknor & Fields.

Burningham, John. Granpa. Burningham, John, illus. LC 84-17464. 32p. (ps-1). 1985. 8.95 (ISBN 0-517-55643-X). Crown.

Butterworth, W. E. LeRoy & the Old Man. 168p. (gr. 7 up). 1982. pap. 2.50 (ISBN 0-590-40573-X, Point). Scholastic Inc.

Campbell, Rod. From Gran. (Illus.). 16p. (ps-k). 1987. 9.95 (ISBN 0-87226-035-6, Bedrick Blackie). P Bedrick Bks.

Carlson, Natalie S. A Grandmother for the Orphelines. reissued ed. White, David, illus. LC 80-7769. 96p. (gr. 3-6). 1980. PLB 13.89 (ISBN 0-06-020994-1). HarpC Child Bks.

Carlson-Savage, Natalie. A Grandmother for the Orphelines. (gr. k-6). 1988. pap. 2.75 (ISBN 0-440-40016-3, YB). Dell.

Carlstrom, Nancy W. Grandpappy. Molk, Laurel, illus. (ps-3). 1990. 13.95 (ISBN 0-316-12855-4). Little.

—The Moon Came Too. Ormai, Stella, illus. LC 86-18046. 32p. (ps-1). 1987. 13.95 (ISBN 0-02-717380-1, Mcmillan Child Bk). Macmillan Child Grp.

Caseley, Judith. Apple Pie & Onions. Caseley, Judith, illus. LC 86-9804. 32p. (gr. 1-4). 1987. 11.75 (ISBN 0-688-06762-X); PLB 11.88 (ISBN 0-688-06763-8). Greenwillow.

—Dear Annie. LC 90-39793. (Illus.). 32p. (ps up). 1991. 13.95 (ISBN 0-688-10010-4); PLB 13.88 (ISBN 0-688-10011-2). Greenwillow.

—Grandpa's Garden Lunch. LC 89-23325. (Illus.). 32p. (ps up). 1990. 12.95 (ISBN 0-688-08816-3); PLB 12.88 (ISBN 0-688-08817-1). Greenwillow.
—When Grandpa Came to Stay. Caseley, Judith, illus. LC 85-12616. 32p. (gr. k-2). 1986. 11.75 (ISBN 0-688-06128-1); PLB 11.88 (ISBN 0-688-06129-X). Greenwillow.
Cazet, Denys. Christmas Moon. Cazet, Denys, illus. LC 87-37434. 32p. (ps-2). 1988. pap. 3.95 (ISBN 0-689-71259-6, Aladdin). Macmillan Child Grp.
Chase, Richard. Grandfather Tales. (gr. 4-7). 1990. pap. 4.95 (ISBN 0-395-56150-7). HM.
Christie, Sally & Kavanaugh, Peter. Mean & Mighty Me. (Illus.). 64p. (gr. 4-7). 1991. 10.95 (ISBN 0-525-44700-8, DCB). Dutton Child Bks.
Cole, Norma. The Final Tide. LC 90-6072. 160p. (gr. 5 up). 1990. 13.95 (ISBN 0-689-50510-8, M K McElderry). Macmillan Child Grp.

Conley, Bruce H. Butterflies, Grandpa & Me. (Illus.). 25p. (gr. 4 up). 1976. pap. 2.00 (ISBN 0-685-65885-6). Thum Print.
Butterflies, Grandpa & Me is a simple story about the unexpected death of a grandfather. Written from a child's point of view, twenty-five pages of text & coloring book pictures follow the main character, Richie, from the first time he learns of grandpa's fatal heart attack, through the funeral & into the first week afterward. Shock & numbness, fear, anger, loss of appetite & loneliness are among the many feelings Richie expresses. In search of answers he runs to the creek where the realities of life & death were gently taught by his loving grandfather. Richie's experience includes going to the funeral home, seeing his grandfather's body & asking questions such as, "where are his feet?", "what are the flowers for...?", & "...is he dead or is he just sleeping?" He spends some time with one of grandpa's older friends, attends the funeral & burial & is surprised to find how hungry he is by the end of the day. In the week that follows, as Richie experiences some of the emptiness of his grandfather's absence he also discovers that doing some of the old things in new ways can bring unexpected pleasure & hope.
Publisher Provided Annotation.

Cosgrove, Stephen. Grampa-Lop. James, Robin, illus. LC 84-15078. 32p. (Orig.). (gr. k-4). 1981. pap. 2.95 (ISBN 0-8431-0586-0). Price Stern.
Cross, Verda. Great-Grandma Tells of Threshing Day. Tucker, Kathleen, ed. Owens, Gail, illus. 40p. (gr. 1-6). 1991. 14.95 (ISBN 0-8075-3042-5). A Whitman.
Curtis, Gavin. Grandma's Baseball. Curtis, Gavin, illus. LC 89-22227. 32p. (ps-2). 1990. 12.95 (ISBN 0-517-57389-X); PLB 13.99 (ISBN 0-517-57390-3). Crown.
Cutting, Jillian. Our Grandad. Van der Voo, Jan, illus. 8p. (gr. k-2). 1989. pap. text ed. 15.00 (ISBN 1-55911-271-9). Wright Group.
—Our Grandad, 6 bks. Van der Voo, Jan, illus. 8p. (gr. k-2). 1986. Set. pap. text ed. 12.60 (ISBN 1-55911-327-8). Wright Group.
Dahl, Roald. The Witches. Blake, Quentin, illus. LC 85-519. 200p. (gr. 3-7). 1985. pap. 3.95 (ISBN 0-14-031730-9, Penguin Bks). Viking Penguin.
DeFelice, Cynthia C. When Grampa Kissed His Elbow. Swanson, Karl, illus. LC 90-6696. 32p. (gr. k-3). 1992. RSBE 13.95 (ISBN 0-02-726455-6, Mcmillan Child Bk). Macmillan Child Grp.
Denton, Kady M. Granny Is a Darling. LC 87-22635. (Illus.). 32p. (ps-3). 1988. 12.95 (ISBN 0-689-50452-7, M K McElderry). Macmillan Child Grp.
—Granny Is a Darling. Denton, Kady M., illus. LC 89-18397. 32p. (ps-2). 1990. pap. 4.95 (ISBN 0-689-71207-3, Aladdin). Macmillan Child Grp.
De Paola, Tomie. Nana Upstairs & Nana Downstairs. new ed. De Paola, Tomie, illus. 32p. (ps-3). 1973. 11.95 (ISBN 0-399-21417-8, Putnam). Putnam Pub Group.
—Now One Foot, Now the Other. De Paola, Tomie, illus. 48p. (gr. 3-7). 1981. 11.95 (ISBN 0-399-20774-0, Putnam); pap. 5.95 (ISBN 0-399-20775-9). Putnam Pub Group.
DePaola, Tomie. Watch Out for the Chicken Feet in Your Soup. (Illus.). 32p. (gr. k-4). 1974. PLB 12.95 (ISBN 0-685-35587-X); pap. 5.95 (ISBN 0-685-35588-8). S&S Trade.
Dyjak, Elisabeth. I Should Have Listened to Moon. LC 89-26739. 130p. (gr. 4-6). 1990. 13.95 (ISBN 0-395-52279-X). HM.
Egger, Bettina. Marianne's Grandmother. Jucker, Sita, illus. 32p. (ps-3). 1987. 11.95 (ISBN 0-525-44335-5, 01160-350, DCB). Dutton Child Bks.
Eisenberg, Phyllis R. A Mitzvah Is Something Special. Jeschke, Susan, illus. LC 77-25664. 32p. (gr. k-4). 1978. 12.95 (ISBN 0-06-021807-X); PLB 12.89 (ISBN 0-06-021808-8). HarpC Child Bks.
Feldman, Annette & Leavitt, Nancy. To Grandma & Grandpa with Love. (Illus.). 1990. 7.95 (ISBN 0-8378-2062-6). Gibson.
Fernandes, Kim. Visiting Granny. Fernandes, Kim, illus. Lacroix, Pat, photos by. (Illus.). 24p. (ps-k). 1990. 12.95 (ISBN 1-55037-077-4); pap. 4.95 (ISBN 1-55037-084-7). Firefly Bks Ltd.
Fettig, Art. The Three Robots Find a Grandpa. Carpenter, Joe, illus. LC 84-80378. 96p. (Orig.). (gr. k-7). 1984. pap. 3.95 (ISBN 0-9601334-8-8); cassette incl. Growth Unltd.
Gackenbash, Dick. With Love from Gran. (ps-3). 1990. pap. 4.95 (ISBN 0-395-54775-X, Clarion Bks). HM.
Gaeddert, LouAnn. A Summer Like Turnips. 80p. (gr. 3-6). 1989. 13.95 (ISBN 0-8050-0839-X). H Holt & Co.
Gantschev, Ivan. The Train to Grandma's. LC 87-13899. (Illus.). 36p. (ps up). 1987. 16.95 (ISBN 0-88708-053-7). Picture Bk Studio.
Geller, Norman. I Don't Want to Visit Grandma Anymore. Tomlinson, Albert J., illus. 28p. (gr. 1-4). 1984. pap. 4.95 (ISBN 0-915753-05-7). N Geller Pub.
George, William T. & George, Lindsay B. Fishing at Long Pond. LC 89-77514. (Illus.). 24p. (ps up). 1991. 13.95 (ISBN 0-688-09401-5); PLB 13.88 (ISBN 0-688-09402-3). Greenwillow.
Gilman, Phoebe. Grandma & the Pirates. 1990. 12.95 (ISBN 0-590-43426-8). Scholastic Inc.
Goldman, Susan. Grandma Is Somebody Special. Rubin, Caroline, ed. Golden, Susan, illus. LC 76-18980. 32p. (ps-1). 1976. PLB 9.75 (ISBN 0-8075-3034-4). A Whitman.
Gould, Deborah. Grandpa's Slide Show. Harness, Cheryl, illus. LC 86-20981. 32p. (ps-3). 1987. 13.95 (ISBN 0-688-06972-X); PLB 13.88 (ISBN 0-688-06973-8). Lothrop.
Graham, Bob. Grandad's Magic. Graham, Bob, illus. LC 88-83007. (gr. k-2). 1989. 13.95 (ISBN 0-316-32321-7). Little.
Greenfield, Eloise. Grandmama's Joy. Byard, Carole, illus. LC 79-11403. 32p. (gr. 2-5). 1980. 12.95 (ISBN 0-399-21064-4, Philomel). Putnam Pub Group.
—Grandpa's Face. Cooper, Floyd, illus. LC 87-16729. 32p. (ps-2). 1988. 13.95 (ISBN 0-399-21525-5, Philomel Bks). Putnam Pub Group.
Grender, Iris. Did I Ever Tell You about My Irish Great Grandmother? Ross, Tony, illus. 64p. (gr. 1-3). 1987. 12.95 (ISBN 0-09-146570-2, Pub. by Hutchinson UK). Trafalgar Sq.
Griffin, Peni R. A Dig in Time. LC 90-47388. 192p. (gr. 4-7). 1991. SBE 13.95 (ISBN 0-689-50525-6, M K McElderry). Macmillan Child Grp.
Griffith, Helen V. Grandaddy's Place. Stevenson, James, illus. LC 86-19573. 40p. (gr. 1-4). 1987. 13.95 (ISBN 0-688-06253-9); PLB 13.88 (ISBN 0-688-06254-7). Greenwillow.
Guernsey, JoAnn B. Journey to Almost There. LC 85-2685. 156p. (gr. 5-8). 1985. 11.95 (ISBN 0-89919-338-2, Clarion). Ticknor & Fields.
Hallinan, P. K. We're Very Good Friends, My Grandma & I. Hallinan, P. K., illus. LC 88-35168. 32p. (ps-3). 1989. PLB 13.27 (ISBN 0-516-03652-1). Childrens.
Hamilton, Dorothy. Tony Savala. Ponter, James, illus. LC 75-171537. 104p. (gr. 4-9). 1972. pap. 3.95 (ISBN 0-8361-1674-7). Herald Pr.
Harranth, Wolf. My Old Grandad. Oppermann-Dimow, Christina, illus. Carter, Peter, tr. (Illus.). 30p. (ps-6). 1987. 11.95 (ISBN 0-19-279787-5). Oxford U Pr.
Hartling, Peter. Old John. Crawford, Elizabeth D., tr. from GER. LC 89-12976. 128p. (gr. 4-9). 1990. 11.95 (ISBN 0-688-08734-5). Lothrop.
Haseley, Dennis. Shadows. Bowman, Leslie, illus. 80p. (gr. 2-6). 1991. 12.95 (ISBN 0-374-36761-2). FS&G.
Hedderwick, Mairi. Katie Morag & the Two Grandmothers. Hedderwick, Mairi, illus. 32p. (gr. k-3). 1986. picture bk. 10.95 (ISBN 0-316-35400-7). Little.
Heidi. (Illus.). (gr. 1). 3.50 (ISBN 0-7214-5169-1). Ladybird Bks.
Heidi. (Illus.). (gr. 3-5). 1990. 3.50 (ISBN 0-7214-1210-6). Ladybird Bks.
Herman, Charlotte. Our Snowman Had Olive Eyes. 112p. 1989. pap. 3.95 (ISBN 0-14-034246-X, Puffin). Puffin Bks.
Hest, Amy. The Crack-of-Dawn Walkers. Schwartz, Amy, illus. 32p. (Orig.). (ps-3). 1988. pap. 3.95 (ISBN 0-14-050829-5, Puffin). Puffin Bks.
—The Purple Coat. Schwartz, Amy, illus. LC 85-29186. 32p. (gr. k-3). 1986. 13.95 (ISBN 0-02-743640-3, Four Winds). Macmillan Child Grp.
Hickman, Martha W. When James Allen Whitaker's Grandfather Came to Stay. Hester, Ron, illus. 48p. (gr. 2-4). 1985. 1.00 (ISBN 0-687-45016-0). Abingdon.
Hines, Anna G. Grandma Gets Grumpy. Hines, Anna G., illus. LC 87-17874. (ps-1). 1988. 13.95 (ISBN 0-89919-529-6, Pub. by Clarion). Ticknor & Fields.
—Grandma Gets Grumpy. Hines, Anna G., illus. 32p. (ps). 1990. pap. 4.95 (ISBN 0-395-52595-0). HM.
—Grandpa Gets Grumpy. (Illus.). (ps-1). 1988. 13.95 (ISBN 0-317-68248-2, Pub. by Clarion). Ticknor & Fields.
Hobbie, W. D. Bloodroot. Hobbie, Holly, illus. LC 90-39306. 160p. (gr. 5 up). 1991. 13.95 (ISBN 0-517-58152-3); PLB 14.99 (ISBN 0-517-58153-1). Crown.
Hoffman, Mary. My Grandma Has Black Hair. Burroughes, Joanna, illus. LC 87-24654. 32p. (ps-3). 1988. 9.95 (ISBN 0-8037-0510-7). Dial Bks Young.
Holl, Kristi D. Just Like a Real Family. LC 82-16239. 132p. (gr. 4-6). 1983. 12.95 (ISBN 0-689-30970-8, Atheneum Child Bk). Macmillan Child Grp.
—The Rose Beyond the Wall. LC 85-7948. 180p. (gr. 5-9). 1985. 12.95 (ISBN 0-689-31150-8, Atheneum Child Bk). Macmillan Child Grp.
Hoopes, Lyn L. Half a Button. Watts, Trish P., illus. LC 87-24949. 32p. (ps-2). 1989. 13.95 (ISBN 0-06-024017-2); PLB 13.89 (ISBN 0-06-024018-0). HarpC Child Bks.
Horlacher, Bill & Horlacher, Kathy. I'm Glad I'm Your Grandma. Kathryn, Hutton, illus. 32p. (gr. k-2). 1987. 1.99 (ISBN 0-87403-276-8, 3776). Standard Pub.
Hurd, Edith T. I Dance in My Red Pajamas. McCully, Emily A., illus. LC 81-47721. 32p. (gr. 1-3). 1982. PLB 13.89 (ISBN 0-06-022700-1). HarpC Child Bks.
Johnson, Herschel. A Visit to the Country. Bearden, Romare, illus. LC 87-25083. 32p. (ps-3). 1989. 13.95 (ISBN 0-06-022849-0); PLB 13.89 (ISBN 0-06-022854-7). HarpC Child Bks.
Keller, Holly. The Best Present. LC 87-38086. (Illus.). 32p. (gr. k up). 1989. 11.95 (ISBN 0-688-07319-0); PLB 11.88 (ISBN 0-688-07320-4). Greenwillow.

Kerensky, Elaine. Far Away Gramma. Tremblay, Ruth, illus. 24p. (Orig.). (gr. k-3). 1990. pap. text ed. write for info. (ISBN 0-9627228-0-4). Far Away Fam Playhse.
If you live far away from your grandchildren & wish you could share more in their everyday lives, here's how you can make that wish come true. It's so easy, so much fun, & guaranteed to be a BOX OFFICE SUCCESS. Here's how your FAR AWAY GRAMMA book works. The book is your "stage" & each page is a "scene" from your everyday life. You put yourself "on stage" by snipping yourself out of snapshots you have, or take new snapshots to fit the scene & story. Glue the cutouts on to each page to bring the scene to life. A blank space has been left on the story/script page for you to print the name of your grandchild & your name as well, right into the story. You can even record your voice telling the story on the flip side of the Far Away Gramma Song tape cassette. PRESTO...you are the "director" "producer" & the "star" of your FAR AWAY GRAMMA production in thirteen action-filled, full-color scenes. One trip to the post office & your show is ON-THE-ROAD!
Publisher Provided Annotation.

Khalsa, Dayal K. Tales of a Gambling Grandma. Khalsa, Dayal K., illus. 32p. (gr. 1 up). 1986. 12.95 (ISBN 0-517-56137-9, C N Potter Bks). Crown.
—Tales of a Gambling Grandma. (Illus.). 32p. (gr. 1 up). 1991. 14.95 (ISBN 0-88776-179-8). Tundra Bks.
Kibbey, Marsha. My Grammy. Ritz, Karen, illus. 32p. (gr. 1-4). 1988. PLB 7.95 (ISBN 0-87614-328-1). Carolrhoda Bks.
Klein, Norma. Going Backwards. 92p. (gr. 7 up). 1986. pap. 12.95 (ISBN 0-590-40328-1). Scholastic Inc.
Knox-Wagner, Elaine. My Grandpa Retired Today. Tucker, Kathleen, ed. Robinson, Charles, illus. LC 82-1935. 32p. (gr. 1-3). 1982. PLB 12.95 (ISBN 0-8075-5334-4). A Whitman.
Kroll, Steven. Annie's Four Grannies. Christelow, Eileen, illus. LC 85-27193. 32p. (gr. k-3). 1986. reinforced bdg. 12.95 (ISBN 0-8234-0605-9). Holiday.
Lasky, Kathryn. I Have Four Names for My Grandfather. Knight, Christopher G., illus. (gr. k-3). 1976. lib. bdg. 14.95 (ISBN 0-316-51520-5). Little.
LeShan, Eda J. Grandparents: A Special Kind of Love. Taggart, Tricia, illus. LC 84-5673. 112p. (gr. 3-7). 1984. 13.95 (ISBN 0-02-756380-4, Mcmillan Child Bk). Macmillan Child Grp.
Le Tord, Bijou. My Grandma Leonie. LC 86-32656. (Illus.). 32p. (ps-2). 1987. 11.95 (ISBN 0-02-756490-8, Bradbury Pr). Macmillan Child Grp.

Levinson, Riki. Watch the Stars Come Out. Goode, Diane, illus. LC 84-28672. 32p. (ps-3). 1985. 13.95 (ISBN 0-525-44205-7, DCB). Dutton Child Bks.

Long, Evelyn. Grandma Tellmie about Ant, Wars Snake-Feeders, Blood-Drinking Bugs & Butterfly. Plott, Dave, et al, eds. 31p. 1984. pap. 4.00x (ISBN 0-931881-00-5). Collaborare Pub.

Lorenzo, Carol L. Mama's Ghosts. LC 73-14333. (Illus.). 176p. (gr. 5 up). 1974. 6.95 (ISBN 0-06-024007-5). HarpC Child Bks.

McCully, Emily A. The Grandma Mix-Up. McCully, Emily A., illus. LC 87-29378. 64p. (gr. k-3). 1988. 11.95 (ISBN 0-06-024201-9); PLB 11.89 (ISBN 0-06-024202-7). HarpC Child Bks.

—Grandmas at the Lake. McCully, Emily A., illus. LC 89-26590. 64p. (gr. k-3). 1990. 10.95 (ISBN 0-06-024126-8); PLB 10.89 (ISBN 0-06-024127-6). HarpC Child Bks.

McKee, David. Who's a Clever Baby? Briley, D., ed. McKee, D., illus. LC 88-22966. 32p. (gr. 1-3). 1989. 12.95 (ISBN 0-688-08595-4); PLB 12.88 (ISBN 0-688-08596-2). Lothrop.

MacLachlan, Patricia. Through Grandpa's Eyes. Ray, Deborah, illus. LC 79-2019. 48p. (gr. k-3). 1983. pap. 4.95 (ISBN 0-06-443041-3, Trophy). HarpC Child Bks.

Martin, Ann M. Karen's Grandmother. 1990. pap. 2.50 (ISBN 0-590-43651-1). Scholastic Inc.

Martin, Bill, Jr. & Archambault, John. Knots on a Counting Rope. Rand, Ted, illus. LC 87-14832. 32p. (gr. k-3). 1987. 14.95 (ISBN 0-8050-0571-4). H Holt & Co.

Mazer, Norma F. After the Rain. LC 86-33270. 304p. (gr. 7 up). 1987. 12.95 (ISBN 0-688-06867-7, Morrow Junior Books). Morrow.

—Figure of Speech. 208p. (gr. 5-9). 1975. pap. 3.25 (ISBN 0-440-94374-4, LFL). Dell.

Monjo, F. N. Grand Papa & Ellen Aroon. (gr. k-6). 1990. pap. 2.75 (ISBN 0-440-43004-6, YB). Dell.

Montaufier, Poupa. One Summer at Grandmother's House. Montaufier, Poupa, illus. LC 85-3758. 32p. (gr. 2-5). 1985. PLB 12.95 (ISBN 0-87614-238-2). Carolrhoda Bks.

Moore, Elaine. Grandma's House. Primavera, Elise, illus. LC 84-11233. 32p. (gr. k up). 1985. PLB 14.88 (ISBN 0-688-04116-7); 14.95 (ISBN 0-688-04115-9). Lothrop.

—Grandma's Promise. Primavera, Elise, illus. LC 86-33762. (gr. k-3). 1988. 14.95 (ISBN 0-688-06740-9); lib. bdg. 14.88 (ISBN 0-688-06741-7). Lothrop.

Mower, Nancy A. I Visit My Tutu & Grandma. Wozniak, Patricia A., illus. LC 84-3280. (ps). 1984. 6.95 (ISBN 0-916630-41-2). Pr Pacifica.

Murrow, Liza K. Dancing on the Table. Himler, Ronald, illus. LC 89-46066. 128p. (gr. 3-7). 1990. 13.95 (ISBN 0-8234-0808-6). Holiday.

Neasi, Barbara. Listen to Me. Sharp, Gene, illus. LC 86-10664. 32p. (ps-2). 1986. PLB 11.93 (ISBN 0-516-02072-2); pap. 2.95 (ISBN 0-516-42072-0). Childrens.

Nelson, Vaunda M. Always Gramma. Uhler, Kimanne, illus. 32p. (ps-3). 1988. PLB 13.95 (ISBN 0-399-21542-5, Putnam). Putnam Pub Group.

Nister, Ernest. Visiting Grandma. Nister, Ernest, illus. (gr. k up). 1989. 4.95 (ISBN 0-399-21695-2, Philomel Bks). Putnam Pub Group.

Nixon, Joan L. The Gift. Glass, Andrew, illus. LC 82-17994. 96p. (gr. 4-7). 1983. 12.95 (ISBN 0-02-768160-2, Mcmillan Child Bk). Macmillan Child Grp.

Nobisso, Josephine. Grandpa Loved. Hyde, Maureen, illus. 32p. 1989. 11.95 (ISBN 0-88138-119-5). Green Tiger Pr.

Okimoto, Jean D. Take a Chance, Gramps, Vol. 1. (gr. 4-7). 1990. 13.95 (ISBN 0-316-63812-9, Joy St Bks). Little.

Olson, Arielle N. Hurry Home, Grandma! (ps). 1990. pap. 3.95 (ISBN 0-525-44650-8, DCB). Dutton Child Bks.

Oppenheim, Shulamith L. Waiting for Noah. Hoban, Lillian, illus. LC 89-35561. 32p. (ps-2). 1990. 12.95 (ISBN 0-06-024633-2); PLB 12.89 (ISBN 0-06-024634-0). HarpC Child Bks.

Ortiz, Mamie. My Grandfather & the Boys. Aragon, Sherry, illus. 14p. (Orig.). (ps-7). 1982. pap. 3.75 (ISBN 0-915347-03-2). Pueblo Acoma Pr.

Padoan, Gianni. Remembering Grandad. 1989. 7.99 (ISBN 0-85953-311-5). Childs Play.

Patterson, Nancy R. The Christmas Cup. Bowman, Leslie, illus. LC 88-29112. 80p. (gr. 3-5). 1989. 13.95 (ISBN 0-531-05821-2); PLB 13.99 (ISBN 0-531-08421-3). Orchard Bks Watts.

Paulsen, Gary. The Cookcamp. LC 90-7734. 128p. (gr. 5-7). 1991. 13.95 (ISBN 0-531-05927-8); PLB 13.99 (ISBN 0-531-08527-9). Orchard Bks Watts.

Pearson, Susan. Happy Birthday Grampie. Dillon, Leo & Dillon, Diane, illus. LC 86-31105. 32p. (ps-3). 1987. 10.95 (ISBN 0-8037-3457-3); PLB 10.89 (ISBN 0-8037-3458-1). Dial Bks Young.

Peck, Richard. Those Summer Girls I Never Met. 224p. (gr. 7 up). 1988. 14.95 (ISBN 0-440-50054-0). Delacorte.

Pochocki, Ethel. Grandma Bagley to the Rescue: Adventures with the Brooksville Bunch. LC 89-6690. 112p. (Orig.). (gr. 3-7). 1989. pap. 5.95 (ISBN 0-8066-2414-0, 9-2414). Augsburg Fortress.

Polland, Barbara K. Grandma & Grandpa Are Special People. Reinertson, Barbara, illus. LC 80-66961. 80p. (gr. k-3). 1984. pap. 7.95 (ISBN 0-89087-343-7). Celestial Arts.

Prechtel, Martin. Grandmother Sweat Bath: A Story of the Tzutujil Mana. Prechtel, Martin, illus. Rodney, Janet, ed. (Illus.). 39p. (Orig.). (gr. 6 up). 1990. write for info. Weaselsleeves Pr.

Provost, Gary. Good If It Goes. (gr. 4-7). 1990. pap. 3.95 (ISBN 0-689-71381-9, Aladdin). Macmillan Child Grp.

Pryor, Bonnie. Grandpa Bear. Degen, Bruce, illus. LC 84-25545. 32p. (ps-1). 1985. 12.95 (ISBN 0-688-04551-0, Morrow Junior Books). Morrow.

Rice, Eve. At Grammy's House. LC 89-34617. (Illus.). 32p. (ps up). 1990. 12.95 (ISBN 0-688-08874-0); lib. bdg. 12.88 (ISBN 0-688-08875-9). Greenwillow.

Richardson, Arleta. Still More Stories from Grandma's Attic. (gr. 1-7). 1980. pap. 3.95 (ISBN 0-89191-252-5). Cook.

—Treasures from Grandma's Attic. (gr. 3 up). 1984. pap. 3.95 (ISBN 0-89191-934-1, 59345). Cook.

Riley, Jocelyn. Crazy Quilt. 176p. (gr. 7-12). 1986. pap. 2.50 (ISBN 0-553-25640-8). Bantam.

Roberts, Sarah. I Want to Go Home. Mathieu, Joe, illus. LC 84-11725. 40p. (ps-3). 1985. 4.95 (ISBN 0-394-87027-1, Random Juv); PLB 6.99 (ISBN 0-394-97027-6). Random.

Roberts, Willo D. To Grandmother's House We Go. LC 89-34972. 192p. (gr. 3-7). 1990. 13.95 (ISBN 0-689-31594-5, Atheneum Child Bk). Macmillan Child Grp.

Root, Phyllis & Marron, Carol A. Gretchen's Grandma. Ray, Deborah K., illus. 32p. (gr. k-3). 1983. PLB 14.65 (ISBN 0-940742-16-0). Raintree Pubs.

Schenker, Dona. Throw a Hungry Loop. LC 89-35496. 160p. (gr. 7 up). 1991. 12.95 (ISBN 0-679-80332-7); PLB 13.99 (ISBN 0-679-90332-1). Knopf.

Schertle, Alice. William & Grandpa. Stevenson, D., ed. Dabcovich, Lydia, illus. LC 88-666. 32p. (gr. k-3). 1988. 12.95 (ISBN 0-688-07580-0); PLB 12.88 (ISBN 0-688-07581-9). Lothrop.

Scott, Ann H. Grandmother's Chair. Aubrey, Meg K., illus. 32p. (ps-1). 1990. 13.95 (ISBN 0-395-52001-0, Clarion Bks). HM.

Scott, Blackie. It's Fun at Grandmother's House. LC 85-22021. (Illus.). 48p. (ps-3). 1985. 7.95 (ISBN 0-932419-01-1). Susan Hunter.

Sendak, Philip. In Grandpa's House. Barofsky, Semour, tr. from YID. Sendak, Maurice, illus. LC 85-42625. 48p. (ps up). 1985. 12.95 (ISBN 0-06-025462-9); PLB 10.89 (ISBN 0-06-025463-7). HarpC Child Bks.

Shanjar. Life with Grandfather. 9th ed. Shankar, illus. 54p. (Orig.). (gr. k-3). 1980. pap. 3.50 (ISBN 0-89744-212-1, Pub. by Children's Bk Trust India). Auromere.

Shannon, George. Unlived Affections. LC 88-31470. 144p. (gr. 7 up). 1989. 12.95 (ISBN 0-06-025304-5); PLB 12.89 (ISBN 0-06-025305-3). HarpC Child Bks.

Shecter, Ben. Grandma Remembers. LC 88-31986. (Illus.). 32p. (gr. k-3). 1989. 13.95 (ISBN 0-06-025617-6); PLB 13.89 (ISBN 0-06-025618-4). HarpC Child Bks.

Shpakow, Tanya. Baba. Shpakow, Tanya, illus. LC 88-8223. 40p. (ps-2). 1989. 12.95 (ISBN 0-394-89802-8); lib. bdg. 13.99 (ISBN 0-394-99802-2). Knopf.

Silverman, Erica. On Grandma's Roof. Ray, Deborah K., illus. LC 89-31255. 32p. (ps-2). 1990. 13.95 (ISBN 0-02-782681-3, Mcmillan Child Bk). Macmillan Child Grp.

Skolsky, Mindy W. Carnival & Kopeck & More about Hannah. Weinhaus, Karen A., illus. LC 77-25643. 80p. (gr. 2-5). 1979. PLB 12.89 (ISBN 0-06-025692-3). HarpC Child Bks.

Slote, Alfred. The Trading Game. LC 89-12851. 208p. (gr. 3-7). 1990. 14.95 (ISBN 0-397-32397-2, Lipp Jr Bks); PLB 12.89 (ISBN 0-397-32398-0, Lipp Jr Bks). HarpC Child Bks.

Smith, Robert K. The War with Grandpa. Lauter, Richard, illus. LC 83-14366. 128p. (gr. 4-8). 1984. pap. 12.95 (ISBN 0-385-29314-3). Delacorte.

—The War with Grandpa. Lauter, Richard, illus. 128p. (gr. 5-9). 1984. pap. 3.50 (ISBN 0-440-49276-9, YB). Dell.

Sobel, Barbara. Great-Grandma, Heroine! LC 87-1235. (gr. 3-6). 1987. 7.59 (ISBN 0-87386-049-7); bk. & cassette 16.99 (ISBN 0-317-55324-0); pap. 1.95 (ISBN 0-87386-048-9). Jan Prods.

Spyri, Johanna. Heidi. Sanderson, Ruth, illus. LC 84-47647. (gr. 4-7). 1984. 18.95 (ISBN 0-394-53820-X). Knopf.

Steel, Danielle. Max & Grandma & Grandpa Winky. (ps-3). 1991. 9.95 (ISBN 0-385-30165-0). Doubleday.

Stevens, Carla. Anna, Grandpa, & the Big Storm. Tomes, Margot, illus. 64p. (gr. 1-4). 1986. pap. 3.50 (ISBN 0-14-032119-5, Puffin). Puffin Bks.

Stevens, Margaret. When Grandpa Died. Ualand, Kenneth, illus. LC 78-12360. 32p. (ps-3). 1979. PLB 13.27 (ISBN 0-516-02025-0). Childrens.

Stevenson, James. Brrr! LC 89-34615. (Illus.). 32p. (ps up). 1991. 13.95 (ISBN 0-688-09210-1); PLB 13.88 (ISBN 0-688-09211-X). Greenwillow.

—Could Be Worse! Stevenson, James, illus. LC 76-28534. 32p. (gr. k-3). 1977. 13.95 (ISBN 0-688-80075-0); PLB 13.88 (ISBN 0-688-84075-2). Greenwillow.

—That's Exactly the Way It Wasn't. LC 90-30749. (Illus.). 30p. (ps up). 1991. 13.95 (ISBN 0-688-09868-1); PLB 13.88 (ISBN 0-688-09869-X). Greenwillow.

—There's Nothing to Do! Stevenson, James, illus. LC 85-8104. 32p. (gr. k-3). 1986. 11.75 (ISBN 0-688-04698-3); PLB 11.88 (ISBN 0-688-04699-1). Greenwillow.

—What's under My Bed? Stevenson, James, illus. LC 83-1454. 32p. (gr. k-3). 1983. 13.95 (ISBN 0-688-02325-8); PLB 13.88 (ISBN 0-688-02327-4). Greenwillow.

Stock, Catherine. Emma's Dragon Hunt. Stock, Catherine, illus. LC 83-25109. 32p. (gr. k up). 1984. 11.95 (ISBN 0-688-02696-6); PLB 9.55 (ISBN 0-688-02698-2). Lothrop.

Stolz, Mary. Go Fish. Cummings, Pat, illus. LC 90-4860. 80p. (gr. 2-6). 1991. 12.95 (ISBN 0-06-025820-9); PLB 12.89 (ISBN 0-06-025822-5). HarpC Child Bks.

Stuart, Jesse. The Beatinest Boy. Miller, Jim W., et al, eds. Henneberger, Robert, illus. Zornes, Rocky, contrib. by. (Illus.). 80p. (gr. 3-6). 1989. 10.00 (ISBN 0-945084-12-9); pap. 5.00 (ISBN 0-945084-13-7). J Stuart Found.

Sundvall, Viveca. Mimi Gets a Grandpa. Eriksson, Eva, illus. Fisher, Richard E., tr. (Illus.). 32p. (ps up). 1991. bds. 13.95 (ISBN 91-29-59864-8, Pub. by R&S Bks). FS&G.

Swayne, Sam & Swayne, Zoa. Great-Grandfather in the Honey Tree. LC 81-90738. (Illus.). 53p. (gr. 3-5). 1982. pap. 4.95 perfect bdg. (ISBN 0-9608008-0-8). Legacy Hse.

Tate, Joan. Luke's Garden & Gramp: Two Short Novels. LC 80-8445. 144p. (gr. 5-7). 1981. PLB 11.89 (ISBN 0-06-026144-7). HarpC Child Bks.

Thomas, Jane R. Saying Good-bye to Grandma. Sewall, Marcia, illus. LC 87-20826. 48p. (gr. 1-4). 1988. 14.95 (ISBN 0-89919-645-4, Pub. by Clarion). Ticknor & Fields.

—Saying Good-Bye to Grandma. (ps-3). 1990. pap. 4.95 (ISBN 0-395-54779-2, Clarion Bks). HM.

Thomson, Pat. Can You Hear Me, Grandad? Alborough, Jez, illus. 32p. (gr. k-2). 1988. pap. 8.95 (ISBN 0-385-29599-5). Delacorte.

—Can You Hear Me, Grandad? (gr. k-2). 1988. pap. 2.50 (ISBN 0-440-40025-2, YB). Dell.

—Good Girl Granny. (gr. k-6). 1988. pap. 2.50 (ISBN 0-440-40026-0, YB). Dell.

—Good Girl Granny. Jaques, Faith, illus. LC 87-474. 32p. (gr. k-2). 1988. 8.95 (ISBN 0-385-29602-9). Delacorte.

Thornton, Terence. Grandpa's Chair. Brown, Jane, ed. Thornton, Sandy W., illus. LC 87-7833. (gr. 1-3). 1987. pap. 3.95 (ISBN 0-88070-190-0). Multnomah.

Upham, Elizabeth. Grandmother's Locket. Hall, Maureen K., illus. 38p. (ps-1). 1985. 12.95 (ISBN 0-940696-10-X). Monroe County Lib.

Vance, Joel M. Grandma & the Buck Deer. Colrus, Bill, illus. 173p. 1988. pap. text ed. 11.95 (ISBN 0-87691-322-2). Cedar Glade Pr.

Van Hook, Beverly. Supergranny, No. 1: The Mystery of the Shrunken Heads. Wayson, Catherine, illus. 96p. (gr. 3-7). 1985. lib. bdg. 7.95 (ISBN 0-916761-11-8); pap. 2.95 (ISBN 0-916761-10-X). Holderby & Bierce.

—Supergranny, No. 2: The Case of the Riverboat Riverbelle. Wayson, Catherine, illus. 112p. (gr. 3-7). 1986. lib. bdg. 7.95 (ISBN 0-916761-09-6); pap. 2.95 (ISBN 0-916761-08-8). Holderby & Bierce.

—Supergranny, No. 3: The Ghost of Heidelberg Castle. Wayson, Catherine, illus. 112p. (gr. 3-7). 1987. lib. bdg. 7.95 (ISBN 0-916761-07-X); pap. 2.95 (ISBN 0-916761-06-1). Holderby & Bierce.

—Supergranny, No. 5: Character Who Came to Life. Nelken, Andrea, ed. Wayson, Catherine, illus. 112p. (Orig.). (gr. 3-6). 1989. lib. bdg. 7.95 (ISBN 0-916761-13-4); pap. 2.95 (ISBN 0-916761-12-6). Holderby & Bierce.

—Supergranny: Secret of Devil Mountain. Nelken, Andrea, ed. Wayson, Catherine, illus. 112p. (Orig.). (gr. 3-6). 1988. lib. bdg. 7.95 (ISBN 0-916761-05-3); pap. 2.95 (ISBN 0-916761-04-5). Holderby & Bierce.

—Supergranny 6: The Great College Caper. Nelken, Andrea, ed. Wayson, Catherine, illus. 112p. (gr. 3-6). 1991. pap. 2.95 (ISBN 0-916761-14-2); 8.95 (ISBN 0-916761-15-0). Holderby & Bierce.

SUPERGRANNY 6: The Great College Caper. 112 p. $8.95 (ISBN 0-916761-15-0). $2.95 pap. (ISBN 0-916761-14-2). 1991. Ages 8-12. Holderby & Bierce. Six books in children's mystery series about a gray-haired detective who drives a red Ferrari & fights crime. "Characters are original, the mystery intriguing & the pace fast & furious in SUPERGRANNY 2,"--SLJ, May, 1987. "SUPERGRANNY 3 is fast-paced & entertaining as it works in bits of historical information,"--SLJ, MAY, 1988. "Mystery aficionados fascinated with the way she can spin a tale,"--John Turner, College English Instructor, DES MOINES REGISTER, Mar. 3, 1991.

"Supergranny teaches intergenerational understanding,"--LIFE TIMES, published by Blue Cross/Blue Shield. Author Beverly Van Hook, former Illinois Arts Council Artist in Education. Received Iowa Newspaper Association First Place Award, The Isabel Award for the Arts, The Corneila Meigs Award for Children's Literature. Other Supergranny Titles, 112 p: Mystery of the Shrunken Heads. (ISBN 0-916761-11-8) pap. ***Publisher Provided Annotation.***

Vigna, Judith. Grandma Without Me. Tucker, Kathleen, ed. Vigna, Judith, illus. LC 83-26031. 32p. (gr. k-3). 1984. PLB 12.95 (ISBN 0-8075-3030-1). A Whitman.

Waddell, Martin. Grandma's Bill. Johnson, Jane, illus. LC 90-43014. 32p. (ps-2). 1991. 12.95 (ISBN 0-531-05923-5); PLB 12.99 (ISBN 0-531-08523-6). Orchard Bks Watts.

—My Great Grandpa. Mansell, Dom, illus. 32p. (ps-3). 1990. 14.94 (ISBN 0-399-22155-7, Putnam). Putnam Pub Group.

Wallace, Ian. Chin Chiang & the Dragon's Dance. LC 83-13442. (Illus.). 32p. (gr. k-4). 1984. 12.95 (ISBN 0-689-50299-0, M K McElderry). Macmillan Child Grp.

Walter, Mildred P. Trouble's Child. LC 84-16387. 128p. (gr. 4 up). 1985. 11.95 (ISBN 0-688-04214-7). Lothrop.

What Time Is Grandma Coming? (Illus.). 22p. (ps-1). 1984. 5.95 (ISBN 0-8431-0645-X). Price Stern.

Williams, Barbara. Kevin's Grandma. (ps-1). 1975. 11.95 (ISBN 0-525-33115-8, DCB). Dutton Child Bks.

—Kevin's Grandma. (ps-1). 1978. pap. 3.95 (ISBN 0-525-45039-4, DCB). Dutton Child Bks.

Wilson, Forrest. Super Gran. McKee, David, illus. (gr. 3-7). 1987. pap. 2.95 (ISBN 0-14-031266-8, Puffin). Puffin Bks.

Woodruff, Elvira. The Summer I Shrank My Grandmother. Coville, Katherine, illus. LC 90-55099. 160p. (gr. 3-7). 1990. 13.95 (ISBN 0-8234-0832-9). Holiday.

Yep, Laurence. Child of the Owl. LC 76-24314. 224p. (gr. 7 up). 1977. PLB 12.89 (ISBN 0-06-026743-7). HarpC Child Bks.

Ziefert, Harriet. Happy Easter, Grandma! Levitt, Sidney, illus. LC 87-45001. 32p. (ps). 1988. 4.95 (ISBN 0-694-00225-9). HarpC Child Bks.

—With Love from Grandma. Ray, Deborah K., illus. 40p. (ps-3). 1989. pap. 13.95 (ISBN 0-670-83004-6). Viking Child Bks.

Zolotow, Charlotte. My Grandson Lew. LC 73-14335. (Illus.). 32p. (gr. k-3). 1974. 13.95 (ISBN 0-06-026961-8); PLB 13.89 (ISBN 0-06-026962-6). HarpC Child Bks.

GRANGE, HAROLD EDWARD, 1903-

Spyri, Johanna. Heidi. (gr. k-1). 1986. 8.98 (ISBN 0-685-16841-7, 618141). Outlet Bk Co.

GRANT, ULYSSES SIMPSON, PRESIDENT U. S. 1822-1885

Kent, Zachary. Ulysses S. Grant. LC 88-38056. (Illus.). 100p. (gr. 3 up). 1989. PLB 17.27 (ISBN 0-516-01364-5); pap. 6.95 (ISBN 0-516-41364-3). Childrens.

O'Brian, Steven. Ulysses S. Grant. Schlesinger, Arthur M., intro. by. (Illus.). 112p. (gr. 5 up). 1991. 17.95x (ISBN 1-55546-809-8). Chelsea Hse.

Rickerby, Laura. Ulysses S. Grant & the Strategy of Victory. (Illus.). 160p. (gr. 5 up). 1990. lib. bdg. 16.98 (ISBN 0-382-09944-3); pap. 8.95 (ISBN 0-382-24053-7). Silver Burdett Pr.

Smith, Gene. Lee & Grant. 448p. (gr. 9-12). 1985. pap. 11.95 (ISBN 0-452-01000-4, Mer). NAL-Dutton.

Zadra, Dan. Statesmen in America: Ulysses S. Grant. rev. ed. (gr. 2-4). 1988. PLB 11.50s.p. (ISBN 0-88682-188-6); PLB 16.45 (ISBN 0-318-32956-5). Creative Ed.

GRAPHIC ARTS

see also Drawing; Painting; Printing

Anno, Mitsumasa. The Unique World of Mitsumasa Anno: Selected Works 1968-1977. Morse, Samuel, tr. Anno, Mitsumasa, illus. Gardner, Martin, intro. by. LC 80-12827. (Illus.). 64p. (gr. 7 up). 1980. 19.95 (ISBN 0-399-20743-0, Philomel). Putnam Pub Group.

Belcher, J. A., ed. Sign Language Dot-to-Dot. new ed. 32p. (ps-3). 1979. 2.95 (ISBN 0-917002-40-7). Joyce Media.

Dellosa, Janet & Carson, Patti. Fall Readiness Activities. (Illus.). 32p. (ps-k). 1983. pap. 1.98 (ISBN 0-88724-046-1, CD-8022). CArson-Dellos.

Graphing. (Illus.). 56p. (gr. 7-12). 1990. 8.80 (ISBN 0-941008-73-8). Tops Learning.

Oana, Katherine, et al. Holiday Finger Plays, Worksheets & Paper Plate Art Projects. Carson, Patti & Dellosa, Janet, illus. 32p. (ps-1). 1983. pap. 1.98 (ISBN 0-88724-002-X, CD-7003). Carson-Dellos.

—Finger Fun, Worksheets & Paper Plate Art Project. Dellosa, Janet & Carson, Patti, illus. 32p. (ps-1). 1984. pap. 1.98 (ISBN 0-88724-000-3, CD-7001). Carson-Dellos.

GRAPHIC ARTS–VOCATIONAL GUIDANCE

Roberson, Virginia L. Careers in the Graphic Arts. (Illus.). (gr. 7-12). 1988. lib. bdg. 12.95 (ISBN 0-8239-0803-8). Rosen Group.

GRAPHIC METHODS

Blanchard, Robert. Graphiti, Bk. 1. rev. ed. 24p. (gr. 2-9). 1986. pap. 4.50 (ISBN 0-918932-89-0). Activity Resources.

—Graphiti, Bk. 2. rev. ed. 24p. (gr. 2-9). 1986. wkbk. 4.50 (ISBN 0-918932-90-4). Activity Resources.

Carratello, John & Carratello, Patty. Charts, Graphs, & Diagrams: Beginning. Spence, Paula & Vasconcelles, Keith, illus. 80p. (gr. k up). 1990. wkbk. 7.95 (ISBN 1-55734-168-0). Tchr Create Mat.

Edson, Ann & Insel, Eunice. Reading Maps, Globes, Charts, Graphs. (gr. 4-6). 1982. wkbk. 2.69 (ISBN 0-89525-175-2). Ed Activities.

GRAPHS

see Graphic Methods

GRASSES

Greenaway, Theresa. Grasses & Grains. LC 90-9563. (Illus.). 48p. (gr. 5-9). 1990. PLB 18.60 (ISBN 0-8114-2729-3). Steck-V.

Pearce, Q. L. & Pearce, W. L. In the African Grasslands. Brook, Bonnie, ed. Bettoli, Delana, illus. 24p. (ps-1). 1990. 4.95 (ISBN 0-671-68831-6); PLB 8.98 (ISBN 0-671-68827-8). Silver Pr.

Wyler, Rose. Grass & Grasshoppers. Steltenpohl, Jane, ed. Petruccio, Steven, illus. 32p. (gr. k-2). 1990. lib. bdg. 11.98 (ISBN 0-671-66347-X); pap. 4.95 (ISBN 0-671-66351-8). Messner.

GRASSHOPPERS

see Locusts

GRASSLAND ECOLOGY

Kuhn, Dwight, photos by. The Hidden Life of the Meadow. Schwartz, David M., text by. (Illus.). 40p. (gr. 1 up). 1988. PLB 12.95 (ISBN 0-517-57059-9). Crown.

Lambert, David. Grasslands. Furstinger, Nancy, ed. (Illus.). 48p. (gr. 5-8). 1988. PLB 14.98 (ISBN 0-382-09789-0). Silver Burdett Pr.

Rowan, James P. Prairies & Grasslands. LC 83-7310. (Illus.). 48p. (gr. k-4). 1983. PLB 14.60 (ISBN 0-516-01706-3); pap. 4.95 (ISBN 0-516-41706-1). Childrens.

Sabin, Louis. Grasslands. Watling, James, illus. LC 84-2661. 32p. (gr. 3-6). 1985. PLB 9.49 (ISBN 0-8167-0214-4); pap. text ed. 2.95 (ISBN 0-8167-0215-2). Troll Assocs.

GRAVES

see Cemeteries; Funeral Rites and Ceremonies; Mounds and Mound Builders

GRAVEYARDS

see Cemeteries

GRAVITATION

Branley, Franklyn M. Gravity Is a Mystery. rev. ed. Madden, Don, illus. LC 85-48247. 32p. (ps-3). 1986. 13.95 (ISBN 0-690-04526-3, Crowell Jr Bks); PLB 13.89 (ISBN 0-690-04527-1). HarpC Child Bks.

—Weight & Weightlessness. Booth, Graham, illus. LC 70-132292. 40p. (gr. k-3). 1972. PLB 13.89 (ISBN 0-690-87329-8, Crowell Jr Bks). HarpC Child Bks.

Buegler, Marion E. Discovering Density. Bergman, Lincoln & Fairwell, Kay, eds. Klofkorn, Lisa, illus. Hoyt, Richard, photos by. (Illus.). 49p. (Orig.). (gr. 6-10). 1988. pap. 7.50 (ISBN 0-912511-17-6). Lawrence Science.

Haines, Gail K. Which Way Is Up? Amoroso, Lisa, illus. LC 86-17239. 32p. (gr. 2-5). 1987. 12.95 (ISBN 0-689-31285-7, Atheneum Child Bk). Macmillan Child Grp.

Taylor, Barbara. Weight & Balance. (Illus.). 32p. (gr. 5-8). 1990. PLB 11.40 (ISBN 0-531-14082-2). Watts.

GRAVITY

see Gravitation

GREAT BRITAIN

Anno, Mitsumasa. Annos' Britain. (Illus.). 40p. (gr. 4 up). 1982. Repr. of 1982 ed. 11.95 (ISBN 0-399-20861-5, Philomel Bks). Putnam Pub Group.

Fairclough, Chris. Take a Trip to England. (Illus.). 32p. (gr. 1-3). 1982. PLB 7.99 (ISBN 0-531-04416-5). Watts.

Gantz, David. Let's Visit Britain. Gantz, David, illus. (gr. 1 up). 1989. pap. 4.95 (ISBN 0-671-67213-4). S&S Trade.

Goldstein, Frances. Children's Treasure Hunt Travel Guide to Britain. LC 78-71424. (Illus.). (gr. 1-12). 1979. pap. 6.95 (ISBN 0-933334-00-1, Dist. by Hippocrene). Paper Tiger Pap.

Grant, Neil. United Kingdom. LC 88-18315. (Illus.). 48p. (gr. 4-8). 1988. PLB 14.98 (ISBN 0-382-09513-8). Silver Burdett Pr.

Harris, Sarah. Finding Out about Life in Britain in the 1950's. (Illus.). 48p. (gr. 7-12). 1985. 19.95 (ISBN 0-7134-4424-X, Pub. by Batsford England). Trafalgar Sq.

Langley, Andrew. Passport to Great Britain. LC 85-50171. (Illus.). 48p. (gr. 4-9). 1986. PLB 12.90 (ISBN 0-531-10015-4). Watts.

Sproule, Anna. Great Britain: The Land & Its People. LC 86-17674. (Illus.). 48p. (gr. 5 up). 1987. pap. 6.95 (ISBN 0-382-09460-3); lib. bdg. 15.96 (ISBN 0-382-09254-6). Silver Burdett Pr.

GREAT BRITAIN–BIOGRAPHY

Banks, David. Sarah Ferguson: The Royal Redhead. LC 87-15567. (Illus.). 64p. (gr. 3 up). 1987. PLB 10.95 (ISBN 0-87518-369-7, Dillon). Macmillan Child Grp.

Cooper, John & Morris, Susan. Cromwell Family. 52p. (gr. 6 up). 1987. pap. 7.95 (ISBN 0-685-19634-8, Pub. by S Thornes). Dufour.

Courtney, Julia. Sir Peter Scott: Champion for the Environment & Founder of the World Wildlife Fund. LC 88-2076. (Illus.). 68p. (gr. 5-6). 1989. PLB 12.95 (ISBN 1-55532-819-9). Gareth Stevens Inc.

Gilleo, Alma. Prince Charles. Endres, Helen, illus. LC 78-18938. (gr. k-4). 1978. PLB 10.95 (ISBN 0-89565-029-0). Childs World.

Hole, Dorothy. Margaret Thatcher: Britain's Prime Minister. 128p. (gr. 6 up). 1990. 17.95 (ISBN 0-89490-246-6). Enslow Pubs.

Moskin, Marietta D. Margaret Thatcher. (Illus.). 128p. 1990. lib. bdg. 13.98 (ISBN 0-671-69632-7); pap. 7.95 (ISBN 0-671-69633-5). Messner.

St. John, Jetty. A Family in England. (Illus.). 32p. (gr. 2-5). 1988. lib. bdg. 9.95 (ISBN 0-8225-1679-9). Lerner Pubns.

Wilson, Barbara K. Path Through the Woods. Stewart, Charles, illus. (gr. 7 up). 1958. 18.95 (ISBN 0-685-40040-9). S G Phillips.

GREAT BRITAIN–CIVILIZATION

Binney, Don. Inside Great Britain. FS Staff, ed. (Illus.). 32p. (gr. 1-6). 1988. PLB 11.90 (ISBN 0-531-10612-8). Watts.

GREAT BRITAIN–FICTION

Alcott, Louisa May. Little Men. (Illus.). (gr. 5 up). 1969. pap. 1.95 (ISBN 0-8049-0194-5, CL-194). Airmont.

Austen, Jane. Emma. Duffy, J. D., intro. by. (gr. 9 up). pap. 1.95 (ISBN 0-8049-0102-3, CL-102). Airmont.

—Mansfield Park. Threapleton, M. M., intro. by. (gr. 10 up). pap. 2.95 (ISBN 0-8049-0131-7, CL-131). Airmont.

—Persuasion. Duffy, J. D., intro. by. (gr. 10 up). pap. 2.50 (ISBN 0-8049-0107-4, CL-107). Airmont.

—Pride & Prejudice. (gr. 10 up). pap. 3.50 (ISBN 0-8049-0001-9, CL-1). Airmont.

—Pride & Prejudice. Cogancherry, Helen, illus. Stewart, Diana, adapted by. LC 81-5215. (Illus.). 48p. (gr. 4 up). 1983. PLB 17.32 (ISBN 0-8172-1673-1); pap. 9.27 (ISBN 0-8172-2018-6). Raintree Pubs.

—Pride & Prejudice. Downing, Julie, illus. 384p. (gr. 4 up). 1984. 10.95 (ISBN 0-448-06032-9, G&D). Putnam Pub Group.

—Sense & Sensibility. Spacks, Patricia M., afterword by. 352p. (gr. 9-12). 1983. pap. 3.50 (ISBN 0-553-21334-2, Bantam Classics). Bantam.

Baylis-White, Mary. Sheltering Rebecca. (Illus.). 112p. (gr. 3-8). 1991. 14.95 (ISBN 0-525-67349-0, Lodestar Bks). Dutton Child Bks.

Beni, Ruth. Sir Baldergog the Great. Beni, Ruth, illus. 32p. (gr. 1-3). 1985. 10.95 (ISBN 0-233-97628-0). Andre Deutsch.

Blackmore, R. D. Lorna Doone. 272p. (gr. 4-6). 1984. pap. 2.25 (ISBN 0-14-035021-7, Puffin). Puffin Bks.

Bond, Michael. More about Paddington. Fortnum, Peggy, illus. (gr. 4-6). 1962. 13.95 (ISBN 0-395-06640-9). HM.

—Paddington at Large. (Illus.). (gr. 1-5). 1963. 13.95 (ISBN 0-395-06641-7). HM.

—Paddington at Work. Fortnum, Peggy, illus. LC 67-20372. (gr. 1-5). 1967. 13.95 (ISBN 0-395-06637-9). HM.

—Paddington Goes to Town. 128p. (gr. 2-5). 1972. pap. 2.75 (ISBN 0-440-46793-4, YB). Dell.

—Paddington Goes to Town. Fortnum, Peggy, illus. LC 68-28043. (gr. 1-5). 1977. 13.95 (ISBN 0-395-06635-2). HM.

—Paddington Helps Out. Fortnum, Peggy, illus. (gr. 4-6). 1973. 13.95 (ISBN 0-395-06639-5). HM.

—Paddington Marches On. (Illus.). (gr. 4-6). 1965. 12.95 (ISBN 0-395-06642-5). HM.

—Paddington Takes the Air. Fortnum, Peggy, illus. LC 78-147902. (gr. 3-7). 1971. 14.95 (ISBN 0-395-10909-4). HM.

Boston, Lucy M. Stranger at Green Knowe. Boston, Peter, illus. LC 61-10108. (gr. 4-6). 1961. 9.95 (ISBN 0-15-281752-2, HJ). HarBraceJ.

Bronte, Charlotte. Jane Eyre. (gr. 9 up). 1964. pap. 3.75 (ISBN 0-8049-0017-5, CL-17). Airmont.

—Jane Eyre. Shaw, Charlie, illus. Stewart, Diana, adapted by. LC 80-14426. (Illus.). 48p. (gr. 4 up). 1983. PLB 17.32 (ISBN 0-8172-1661-8); pap. 9.27 (ISBN 0-8172-2012-7). Raintree Pubs.

Bronte, Emily. Wuthering Heights. (gr. 9 up). 1964. pap. 2.95 (ISBN 0-8049-0011-6, CL-11). Airmont.

—Wuthering Heights. Wright, Betty R., adapted by. Cogancherry, Helen, illus. LC 81-15786. 48p. (gr. 4 up). 1982. PLB 17.32 (ISBN 0-8172-1682-0); pap. 9.27 (ISBN 0-8172-2029-1). Raintree Pubs.

Burnett, Frances H. Little Princess. Tudor, Tasha, illus. LC 63-15435. (gr. 4-6). 1963. 12.95 (ISBN 0-397-30693-8, Lipp Jr Bks); PLB 12.89 (ISBN 0-397-31339-X, Lipp Jr Bks). HarpC Child Bks.

—A Little Princess. 224p. (gr. 4-6). 1984. pap. 2.25 (ISBN 0-14-035028-4, Puffin). Puffin Bks.

Butler, Samuel. Way of All Flesh. Rudzik, O. H., intro. by. (gr. 11 up). pap. 2.50 (ISBN 0-8049-0090-6, CL-90). Airmont.

Cooper, Susan. Over Sea, Under Stone. Gill, Margery, illus. LC 66-11199. (gr. 4-6). 1966. 14.95 (ISBN 0-15-259034-X, HJ). HarBraceJ.

David Copperfield. (gr. 4 up). 1988. pap. 4.87 (ISBN 0-582-54160-3, 74267). Longman.

Defoe, Daniel. Moll Flanders. (gr. 11 up). 1969. pap. 2.95 (ISBN 0-8049-0200-3, CL-200). Airmont.

Dickens, Charles. Charles Dickens' A Christmas Carol. Richardson, I. M., ed. Kendall, Jane F., illus. LC 87-11270. 32p. (gr. 2-6). 1988. PLB 9.79 (ISBN 0-8167-1053-8); pap. text ed. 1.95 (ISBN 0-8167-1054-6). Troll Assocs.
—Christmas Carol. LC 85-15815. (gr. 7 up). pap. 2.50 (ISBN 0-8049-0026-4, CL-26). Airmont.
—A Christmas Carol. Hildebrandt, Gregory, illus. LC 85-15815. 128p. 1983. pap. 14.95 (ISBN 0-671-45599-0, Little Simon). S&S Trade.
—A Christmas Carol. (gr. 4-6). 1986. pap. 1.95 (ISBN 0-590-02102-8). Scholastic Inc.
—A Christmas Carol. Beck, Charless, illus. 128p. (gr. 4-6). 1987. pap. 2.50 (ISBN 0-590-41293-0, Pub. by Apple Classics). Scholastic Inc.
—David Copperfield. (gr. 9 up). pap. 3.95 (ISBN 0-8049-0065-5, CL-65). Airmont.
—Great Expectations. Threapleton, M. M., intro. by. (gr. 9 up). pap. 3.95 (ISBN 0-8049-0068-X, CL-68). Airmont.
—The Oxford Illustrated Dickens, 21 vols. Incl. The Old Curiosity Shop. Cattermole, George & Phiz, illus. 1951. 10.95 (ISBN 0-19-254506-X); Our Mutual Friend. Stone, Marcus, illus. 1952. 10.95 (ISBN 0-19-254510-8); The Personal History of David Copperfield. 10.95 (ISBN 0-19-254502-7); The Posthumous Papers of the Pickwick Club. Dickens, Charles. (Illus.). 1947. 10.95 (ISBN 0-19-254501-9); Sketches by Boz: Illustrative of Every-Day Life & Every-Day People. Cruickshank, George, illus. 1957. 10.95 (ISBN 0-19-254518-3); A Tale of Two Cities. 1949. 10.95 (ISBN 0-19-254504-3); The Uncommercial Traveller, & Reprinted Pieces. Dickens, Charles. 1958. 10.95 (ISBN 0-19-254521-3); The Adventures of Oliver Twist. Cruickshank, George, illus. House, Humphy, intro. by. 1949. 10.95 (ISBN 0-19-254505-1); American Notes & Pictures from Italy. Stone, Marcus, et al, illus. Sitwell, Sacheverell, intro. by. 1957. 10.95 (ISBN 0-19-254519-1); Barnaby Rudge: A Tale of the Riots of 'Eighty. Dickens, Charles. 1954. 10.95 (ISBN 0-19-254513-2); Bleak House. Phiz, illus. Sitwell, Osbert, intro. by. 1948. 10.95 (ISBN 0-19-254503-5); Christmas Books. Farjeon, Eleanor, intro. by. (Illus.). 1954. 10.95 (ISBN 0-19-254514-0); Christmas Stories. Dickens, Charles. (Illus.). 774p. 1956. 10.95 (ISBN 0-19-254517-5); Dealings with the Firm of Dombey, & Son, Wholesale, Retail, & for Exploration. Phiz, illus. Garrod, H. W., intro. by. 1950. 10.95 (ISBN 0-19-254507-8); Great Expectations. Dickens, Charles. (Illus.). 460p. 1953. 10.95 (ISBN 0-19-254511-6); Hard Times for These Times. Walker, F. & Greiffenhagen, Maurice, illus. Foot, Dingle, intro. by. 1955. 10.95 (ISBN 0-19-254515-9); The Life & Adventures of Martin Chuzzlewit. Phiz, illus. Russell, Geoffrey, intro. by. 1951. 10.95 (ISBN 0-19-254509-4); The Life & Adventures of Nicholas Nickleby. Phiz, illus. Thorndike, Dame S., intro. by. 1950. 10.95 (ISBN 0-19-254508-6); Little Dorrit. Dickens, Charles. (Illus.). 826p. 1953. 10.95 (ISBN 0-19-254512-4); Master Humphrey's Clock & a Child's History of England. Dickens, Charles. (Illus.). 544p. 1958. 10.95 (ISBN 0-19-254520-5); The Mystery of Edwin Drood. Fildes, Luke & Collins, Charles, illus. Roberts, S. C., intro. by. 294p. 1956. 10.95 (ISBN 0-19-254516-7). 1987. Set. 200.00 (ISBN 0-19-254522-1). Oxford U Pr.
—Pickwick Papers. (gr. 10 up). 1968. pap. 2.95 (ISBN 0-8049-0191-0, CL-191). Airmont.
Eliot, George. Mill on the Floss. (gr. 10 up). 1964. pap. 2.95 (ISBN 0-8049-0043-4, CL-43). Airmont.
—Mill on the Floss. Haight, G. S., ed. LC 62-16032. (gr. 9 up). 1972. pap. 8.36 (ISBN 0-395-05151-7, RivEd). HM.
—Silas Marner. (gr. 9 up). 1964. pap. 2.50 (ISBN 0-8049-0014-0, CL-14). Airmont.
Fielding, Henry. Tom Jones. Rowland, B., intro. by. (gr. 11 up). pap. 2.50 (ISBN 0-8049-0135-X, CL-135). Airmont.
Gardam, Jane. A Long Way from Verona. LC 88-5254. 192p. (gr. 7 up). 1988. 13.95 (ISBN 0-02-735781-3, Mcmillan Child Bk). Macmillan Child Grp.
Goldsmith, Oliver. Vicar of Wakefield. (gr. 10 up). 1964. pap. 1.25 (ISBN 0-8049-0052-3, CL-52). Airmont.
Hardy, Thomas. Far from the Madding Crowd. Gemme, F. R., intro. by. (gr. 11 up). pap. 2.50 (ISBN 0-8049-0136-8, CL-136). Airmont.
—Jude the Obscure. Teitel, N. R., intro. by. (gr. 11 up). pap. 1.95 (ISBN 0-8049-0108-2, CL-108). Airmont.
—Mayor of Casterbridge. Bigoness, J. W., intro. by. (gr. 11 up). pap. 1.95 (ISBN 0-8049-0063-9, CL-63). Airmont.
—Return of the Native. (gr. 10 up). 1964. pap. 3.50 (ISBN 0-8049-0038-8, CL-38). Airmont.
—Tess of the D'Urbervilles. Hogan, A. H., intro. by. (gr. 11 up). pap. 3.50 (ISBN 0-8049-0082-5, CL-82). Airmont.
Hilton, James. Good-Bye, Mr. Chips. (Illus.). (gr. 7 up). 1962. 14.95 (ISBN 0-316-36420-7, Pub. by Atlantic Monthly Pr). Little.
Jane Eyre. (gr. 4 up). 1988. pap. 4.87 (ISBN 0-582-54161-1, 74268). Longman.
Jane Eyre. (gr. 4 up). 1988. Incl. 26 cards. 22.00 (ISBN 0-8172-2182-4). Raintree Pubs.
King-Smith, Dick. Pigs Might Fly. (gr. 4 up). 1990. pap. 3.95 (ISBN 0-14-034537-X, Puffin). Puffin Bks.
—Sophie's Snail. Minter-Kemp, Claire, illus. (gr. k-4). 1989. 11.95 (ISBN 0-385-29824-2). Delacorte.
Kipling, Rudyard. Light That Failed. (gr. 8 up). 1969. pap. 1.50 (ISBN 0-8049-0199-6, CL-199). Airmont.
Morpurgo, Michael. Mr. Nobody's Eyes. 144p. (gr. 5 up). 1990. pap. 12.95 (ISBN 0-670-83022-4). Viking Child Bks.
Nesbit, Edith. Story of the Treasure Seekers. (gr. 4-6). 1987. pap. 2.25 (ISBN 0-685-03990-0, Puffin). Puffin Bks.
Potter, Beatrix. The Tailor of Gloucester. Horden, Michael, read by. (Illus.). (ps-3). 1989. pap. 6.95 bk. & tape (ISBN 0-7232-3668-2). Warne.
The Railway Children. (Illus.). (gr. 3-5). 3.50 (ISBN 0-7214-0824-9). Ladybird Bks.
Sewell, Anna. Black Beauty. (gr. 5 up). pap. 1.50 (ISBN 0-8049-0023-X, CL-23). Airmont.
—Black Beauty. new ed. Farr, Naunerle, ed. Nebres, Rudy, illus. LC 59-12495. 64p. (Orig.). (gr. 5-10). 1973. pap. 2.95 (ISBN 0-88301-094-1). Pendulum Pr.
—Black Beauty. LC 59-12495. (gr. 3-7). 1983. pap. 2.25 (ISBN 0-14-035006-3, Puffin). Puffin Bks.
—Black Beauty. Vance, Eleanor G., ed. Jeffers, Susan, illus. LC 84-27575. 72p. (ps-5). 1986. 12.95 (ISBN 0-394-86575-8, Random Juv); lib. bdg. 12.99 (ISBN 0-394-96575-2, Random Juv). Random.
—Black Beauty. LC 59-12495. (gr. 4-6). 1989. pap. 2.95 (ISBN 0-590-42354-1). Scholastic Inc.
Shaw, Margret. A Wider Tomorrow. LC 90-55096. 144p. 1990. 13.95 (ISBN 0-8234-0837-X). Holiday.
Sohl, Marcia & Dackerman, Gerald. Black Beauty Student Activity Book. (Illus.). 16p. (gr. 4-10). 1976. pap. 1.25 (ISBN 0-88301-183-2). Pendulum Pr.
Sterne, Laurence. Tristram Shandy. (gr. 11 up). 1967. pap. 1.95 (ISBN 0-8049-0152-X, CL-152). Airmont.
Thackeray, William Makepeace. Vanity Fair. Threapleton, M. M., intro. by. (gr. 11 up). pap. 3.95 (ISBN 0-8049-0138-4, CL-138). Airmont.

GREAT BRITAIN–HISTORY

Cunningham, A. & Millard, A. Essential British History. (Illus.). 64p. 1991. lib. bdg. 12.96 (ISBN 0-88110-506-6, Usborne); pap. 5.95 (ISBN 0-7460-0658-6). EDC.
The Georgians. (Illus.). (gr. 5 up). 1990. pap. 3.95. Ladybird Bks.
The Middle Ages. (Illus.). (gr. 5 up). 1990. pap. 3.50. Ladybird Bks.
Sancha, Sheila. Walter Dragun's Town: Crafts & Trade in the Middle Ages. Sancha, Shelia, illus. LC 88-34066. 64p. (gr. 4 up). 1989. 13.95 (ISBN 0-690-04804-1, Crowell Jr Bks); PLB 13.89 (ISBN 0-690-04806-8, Crowell Jr Bks). HarpC Child Bks.
The Spanish Armada. (Illus.). (gr. 5 up). 3.50 (ISBN 0-7214-1093-6). Ladybird Bks.

GREAT BRITAIN–HISTORY–FICTION

Bennett, John. Master Skylark. Hogan, Alice H., intro. by. (gr. 5 up). 1.95 (ISBN 0-8049-0092-2, CL-92). Airmont.
Gerrard, Jean. Matilda Jane. Gerrard, Roy, illus. LC 83-48082. 32p. (ps-3). 1983. 12.95 (ISBN 0-374-34865-0). FS&G.
Konigsburg, E. L. A Proud Taste for Scarlet & Miniver. Konigsburg, E. L., illus. LC 73-76320. 208p. (gr. 5-9). 1973. 13.95 (ISBN 0-689-30111-1, Atheneum Child Bk). Macmillan Child Grp.
Reginald, R. & Menville, Douglas, eds. The Boyhood Days of Guy Fawkes: Or, the Conspirators of Old London. LC 75-46257. (Illus.). (gr. 7 up). 1976. Repr. of 1876 ed. lib. bdg. 18.00x (ISBN 0-405-08116-2). Ayer Co Pubs.
Robin Hood. (FRE.). (gr. 3-8). 9.95 (ISBN 0-685-28453-0). French & Eur.
Rodowsky, Colby. Keeping Time. LC 83-14122. 137p. (gr. 5 up). 1983. 11.95 (ISBN 0-374-34061-7). FS&G.
Tale of Two Cities. 384p. 1989. pap. 2.50 (ISBN 0-8125-0506-9). Tor Bks.
Walsh, Jill P. A Parcel of Patterns. LC 83-48143. 139p. (gr. 7 up). 1983. 11.95 (ISBN 0-374-35750-1). FS&G.

GREAT BRITAIN–HISTORY, NAVAL

James, William. Intelligence & Cryptanalytic Activities of the British Navy in World War I. rev. ed. 230p. (gr. 7). 1984. lib. bdg. 28.80 (ISBN 0-89412-107-3); pap. text ed. 19.80 (ISBN 0-89412-065-4). Aegean Park Pr.

GREAT BRITAIN–HISTORY–TO 1066

Corfe, Tom. The Murder of Archbishop Thomas. LC 76-22419. (Illus.). 52p. (gr. 5 up). 1977. PLB 9.95 (ISBN 0-8225-1202-5). Lerner Pubns.

GREAT BRITAIN–HISTORY–TO 1066–FICTION

Clements, Bruce. Prison Window, Jerusalem Blue. LC 77-10081. 256p. (gr. 7 up). 1977. 12.95 (ISBN 0-374-36126-6). FS&G.

GREAT BRITAIN–HISTORY–MEDIEVAL PERIOD, 1066-1485

De Angeli, Marguerite. The Door in the Wall: Story of Medieval London. De Angeli, Marguerite, illus. LC 64-7025. 111p. (gr. 3-6). 1989. pap. 14.95 (ISBN 0-385-07283-X). Doubleday.

GREAT BRITAIN–HISTORY–NORMAN PERIOD, 1066-1154–FICTION

Chaucer, Geoffrey. The Canterbury Tales. Hastings, Selina, retold by. Cartwright, Reg, illus. LC 88-45163. 80p. (gr. 4 up). 1988. 17.95 (ISBN 0-8050-0904-3). H Holt & Co.
McGraw, Eloise. The Striped Ships. LC 91-7729. 240p. (gr. 7 up). 1991. 14.95 (ISBN 0-689-50532-9, M K McElderry). Macmillan Child Grp.
Scott, Walter. Ivanhoe. (gr. 9 up). 1964. pap. 2.95 (ISBN 0-8049-0034-5, CL-34). Airmont.

GREAT BRITAIN–HISTORY–PLANTAGENETS, 1154-1399

Brooks, Polly S. Queen Eleanor: Independent Spirit of the Medieval World: a Biography of Eleanor of Aquitaine. LC 82-48776. 160p. (gr. 6 up). 1983. PLB 13.89 (ISBN 0-397-31995-9, Lipp Jr Bks). HarpC Child Bks.

GREAT BRITAIN–HISTORY–PLANTAGENETS, 1154-1399–FICTION

Gray, Elizabeth J. Adam of the Road. Lawson, Robert, illus. 320p. (gr. 4-8). 1942. pap. 15.95 (ISBN 0-670-10435-3). Viking Child Bks.
Ivanhoe. (Illus.). 48p. (gr. 4 up). 1988. PLB 17.32 (ISBN 0-8172-2765-2); pap. 9.27 (ISBN 0-8172-2769-5). Raintree Pubs.
Shakespeare, William. Henry IV, Pts. 1 & 2. Young, Archibald, intro. by. (gr. 10 up). pap. 1.25 ea. Pt. 1 (ISBN 0-8049-1018-9, S18). Pt. 2. pap. 0.60 (ISBN 0-685-00150-4, S19). Airmont.
—King John. Rowland, Beryl, intro. by. (gr. 9 up). 1968. pap. 1.95 (ISBN 0-8049-1024-3, S24). Airmont.
—Richard Second. Young, Archibald M., intro. by. (gr. 9 up). pap. 0.60 (ISBN 0-8049-1014-6, S14). Airmont.
Wheeler, Thomas G. All Men Tall. LC 70-77313. (gr. 8 up). 1969. 18.95 (ISBN 0-87599-157-2). S G Phillips.

GREAT BRITAIN–HISTORY–LANCASTER AND YORK, 1399-1485–FICTION

Pyle, Howard. Men of Iron. Bennet, C. L., intro. by. (Illus.). (gr. 6 up). pap. 3.50 (ISBN 0-8049-0093-0, CL-93). Airmont.

GREAT BRITAIN–HISTORY–WARS OF THE ROSES, 1455-1485

Dures, Alan. How & Why: The English Civil War. (Illus.). 64p. (gr. 7-12). 1987. 19.95 (ISBN 0-85219-665-2, Pub. by Batsford England). Trafalgar Sq.

GREAT BRITAIN–HISTORY–WARS OF THE ROSES, 1455-1485–FICTION

Shakespeare, William. Richard Third. Willoughby, John, intro. by. (gr. 9 up). pap. 0.60 (ISBN 0-8049-1015-4, S15). Airmont.
Stevenson, Robert Louis. Black Arrow. (gr. 6 up). 1964. pap. 2.95 (ISBN 0-8049-0020-5, CL-20). Airmont.

GREAT BRITAIN–HISTORY–TUDORS, 1485-1603

Ross, Stewart. Elizabethan Life. (Illus.). 72p. (gr. 7-11). 1991. 19.95 (ISBN 0-7134-6356-2, Pub. by Batsford UK). Trafalgar Sq.
Saraga, Jessica. Tudor Monarchs. (Illus.). 72p. (gr. 7-11). 1991. 19.95 (ISBN 0-7134-6350-3, Pub. by Batsford UK). Trafalgar Sq.
Shakespeare's England. 64p. (gr. 4-8). 1990. 13.95 (ISBN 0-86307-999-7). Marshall Cavendish.
Snellgrove, L. E. Early Modern Age. (Illus.). 256p. (Orig.). (gr. 7-12). 1980. 19.92 (ISBN 0-582-31784-3, 78447). Longman.
The Tudors. (Illus.). (gr. 5 up). 1990. pap. 3.50. Ladybird Bks.

GREAT BRITAIN–HISTORY–TUDORS, 1485-1603–FICTION

Kingsley, Charles. Westward Ho. (gr. 8 up). 1968. pap. 1.25 (ISBN 0-8049-0184-8, CL-184). Airmont.
The Prince & the Pauper. (gr. 4 up). 1988. pap. 4.87 (ISBN 0-582-52284-6, 73812). Longman.
Scott, Walter. Kenilworth. new ed. (gr. 10 up). 1968. pap. 2.95 (ISBN 0-8049-0193-7, CL-193). Airmont.
Twain, Mark. Prince & the Pauper. (gr. 5 up). 1964. pap. 2.50 (ISBN 0-8049-0032-9, 32). Airmont.

GREAT BRITAIN–HISTORY–17TH CENTURY–FICTION

Blackmore, Richard D. Lorna Doone. Threapleton, M. M., intro. by. (gr. 8 up). 1967. pap. 3.50 (ISBN 0-8049-0149-X, CL-149). Airmont.

GREAT BRITAIN–HISTORY–STUARTS, 1603-1714

Jones, Madeline. Growing up in Stuart Times. (gr. 5 up). 1979. 19.95 (ISBN 0-7134-0771-9, Pub. by Batsford England). Trafalgar Sq.
Shakespeare's England. 64p. (gr. 4-8). 1990. 13.95 (ISBN 0-86307-999-7). Marshall Cavendish.
Snellgrove, L. E. Early Modern Age. (Illus.). 256p. (Orig.). (gr. 7-12). 1980. 19.92 (ISBN 0-582-31784-3, 78447). Longman.

GREAT BRITAIN–HISTORY–STUARTS, 1603-1714–FICTION

Wallace, M. Imelda, Sr. Outlaws of Ravenhurst. new ed. Schuster, L. A., illus. (gr. 6-10). 1950. 12.95 (ISBN 0-910334-25-0); pap. 5.95 (ISBN 0-910334-26-9). Cath Authors.

GREAT BRITAIN–HISTORY–CIVIL WAR AND COMMONWEALTH, 1642-1660

Kelly, Rosemary & Kelly, Tony. City at War: Oxford 1642-46. 52p. (gr. 11 up). 1987. pap. 7.95 (ISBN 0-685-19633-X, Pub. by S Thornes). Dufour.
Kelly, Tony. Children in Tudor England. 52p. (gr. 6-9). 1987. pap. 7.95 (ISBN 0-685-19632-1, Pub. by S Thornes). Dufour.

GREAT BRITAIN–HISTORY–CIVIL WAR AND COMMONWEALTH, 1642-1660–FICTION

Gordon, Shirley. Crystal Is My Friend. Frascino, Edward, illus. LC 77-11853. 1978. pap. 7.95 (ISBN 0-06-022112-7). HarpC Child Bks.

GREAT BRITAIN–HISTORY–1714-1837

Garfield, Leon. The House of Hanover England in the Eighteenth Century. LC 75-42422. (Illus.). 128p. (gr. 6 up). 1979. 8.95 (ISBN 0-395-28904-1, Clarion). HM.

GREAT BRITAIN–HISTORY–1714-1837–FICTION

Forester, C. S. Lieutenant Hornblower. (gr. 7 up). 1984. 17.95 (ISBN 0-316-28907-8); pap. 8.95 (ISBN 0-316-28921-3). Little.

—Lord Hornblower, Vol. 1. (gr. 7 up). 1989. 17.95 (ISBN 0-316-28908-6); pap. 8.95 (ISBN 0-316-28943-4). Little.

GREAT BRITAIN–HISTORY–19TH CENTURY

Rawcliffe, Michael. Finding out About: Life in Edwardian Britain. (Illus.). 48p. (gr. 7-10). 1989. 19.95 (ISBN 0-7134-5612-4, Pub. by Batsford England). Trafalgar Sq.

Tames, Richard. Radicals, Reformers & Railways 1815-1851. (Illus.). 72p. (gr. 7-12). 1987. 19.95 (ISBN 0-7134-5264-1, Pub. by Batsford England). Trafalgar Sq.

GREAT BRITAIN–HISTORY–19TH CENTURY–FICTION

Greaves, Margaret. Cat's Magic. LC 80-8451. 192p. (gr. 5 up). 1981. 10.10i (ISBN 0-06-022122-4). HarpC Child Bks.

GREAT BRITAIN–HISTORY–20TH CENTURY

Britain in the 1950's. (Illus.). 72p. (gr. 7-10). 1989. 19.95 (ISBN 0-7134-5838-0, Pub. by Batsford England). Trafalgar Sq.

Gilleo, Alma. Prince Charles. Endres, Helen, illus. LC 78-18938. (gr. k-4). 1978. PLB 10.95 (ISBN 0-89565-029-0). Childs World.

Hodges, Michael. Britain in the 1970's. (Illus.). 72p. (gr. 7-10). 1989. 19.95 (ISBN 0-7134-5913-1, Pub. by Batsford England). Trafalgar Sq.

GREAT BRITAIN–INDUSTRIES–HISTORY

Jones, Madeline. Finding Out about Industrial Britain. (Illus.). 64p. (gr. 7-12). 1984. 19.95 (ISBN 0-7134-4353-7, Pub. by Batsford England). Trafalgar Sq.

GREAT BRITAIN–KINGS AND RULERS

Kings & Queens of England, 2 bks. (Illus.). (gr. 5 up). 3.50 (ISBN 0-317-03014-0). Bk. 1 (ISBN 0-7214-0560-6). Bk. 2 (ISBN 0-7214-0561-4). Ladybird Bks.

Wigner, Annabel. Elizabeth & Akbar: Portraits of Power. 52p. (gr. 11 up). 1987. pap. 7.95 (ISBN 0-85950-541-3, Pub. by S Thornes). Dufour.

GREAT BRITAIN–NOBILITY

Fox, Mary V. Princess Diana. LC 86-4451. (Illus.). 128p. (gr. 4-10). 1986. PLB 17.95 (ISBN 0-89490-129-X). Enslow Pubs.

Greene, Carol. Diana, Princess of Wales. LC 85-12751. (Illus.). 32p. (gr. 2-4). 1985. PLB 13.27 (ISBN 0-516-03538-X); pap. 3.95 (ISBN 0-516-43538-8). Childrens.

Nesnick, Victoria G. Princess Diana: A Book of Questions & Answers for Children. LC 88-30081. (gr. 4 up). 1989. 13.95 (ISBN 0-87131-558-0). M Evans.

GREAT BRITAIN–SOCIAL LIFE AND CUSTOMS

Fairclough, Chris. We Live in Britain. LC 83-72803. 64p. (gr. 4-9). 1984. lib. bdg. 9.49 (ISBN 0-531-04783-0, Pub. by Bookwright Pr). Watts.

James. Lapps - Reindeer Herders of Lapland, Reading Level 5. (Illus.). 48p. (gr. 4-8). Date not set. PLB 15.33 (ISBN 0-86625-263-0). Rourke Corp.

GREAT LAKES

Henderson, Kathy. The Great Lakes. LC 88-34670. (Illus.). 48p. (gr. k-4). 1989. PLB 14.60 (ISBN 0-516-01163-4); pap. 4.95 (ISBN 0-516-41163-2). Childrens.

GREAT LAKES–FICTION

Holling, Holling C. Paddle-to-the-Sea. (Illus.). (gr. 4-6). 1980. 16.95 (ISBN 0-395-15082-5); pap. 7.95 (ISBN 0-395-29203-4). HM.

GREAT PLAINS

Aylesworth, Thomas G. & Aylesworth, Virginia L. The Great Plains (Montana, North Dakota, South Dakota) LC 87-18198. (Illus.). 66p. (gr. 5 up). 1988. lib. bdg. 16.95 (ISBN 1-55546-566-8). Chelsea Hse.

Bullock, Robert. Wilderness Habitat: The Great Plains - A Young Reader's Journal. Bullock, Robert, illus. LC 86-81461. 64p. (Orig.). (gr. k-8). 1987. pap. 5.95 (ISBN 0-943972-10-8). Homestead WY.

Nielsen, Shelly. More Victoria. 130p. (gr. 5-6). 1986. pap. 3.95 (ISBN 0-89191-453-6). Cook.

GREAT SMOKY MOUNTAINS

Radlauer, Ruth. Great Smoky Mountains National Park. updated ed. Zillmer, Rolf, photos by. LC 76-9839. (Illus.). 48p. (gr. 3-12). 1985. PLB 17.27 (ISBN 0-516-07489-X); pap. 4.95 (ISBN 0-516-47489-8). Childrens.

GREECE

Antoniou, Jim. Greece. LC 75-44871. (Illus.). (gr. 6 up). 1976. PLB 16.98 (ISBN 0-382-06104-7). Silver Burdett Pr.

Ardley, Brigette & Ardley, Neil. Greece. (Illus.). 48p. (gr. 4-8). 1989. lib. bdg. 14.98 (ISBN 0-382-09822-6). Silver Burdett Pr.

Buchanan, David. Greek Athletics. McLeish, Kenneth & McLeish, Valerie, eds. (Illus.). 48p. (gr. 7-12). 1976. pap. text ed. 9.00 (ISBN 0-582-20059-8, 70659). Longman.

Green, Roger L. Tales of Greek Heroes. (Orig.). (gr. 5-7). 1989. pap. 2.95 (ISBN 0-14-035099-3, Puffin). Puffin Bks.

Lye, Keith. Take a Trip to Greece. (Illus.). 32p. (gr. k-3). 1983. PLB 7.99 (ISBN 0-531-03759-2). Watts.

Lyle, Garry. Greece. (Illus.). (gr. 5 up). 1988. 14.95 (ISBN 0-7910-1369-3). Chelsea Hse.

Nichols, Roger & Nichols, Sarah. Greek Everyday Life. McLeish, Kenneth & McLeish, Valerie, eds. (Illus.). 48p. (gr. 7-12). 1978. pap. text ed. 9.00 (ISBN 0-582-20672-3, 70819). Longman.

Rutland, Jonathan. An Ancient Greek Town. rev. ed. LC 85-52283. (Illus.). 32p. (gr. 4-9). 1986. PLB 11.90 (ISBN 0-531-19010-2, Pub. by Warwick). Watts.

Spyropulos, Diana. Greece: A Spirited Independence. (Illus.). 128p. (gr. 5 up). 1990. PLB 14.95 (ISBN 0-87518-311-5, Dillon). Macmillan Child Grp.

Stein, R. Conrad. Greece. LC 87-13225. (Illus.). 128p. (gr. 5-9). 1987. PLB 25.27 (ISBN 0-516-02759-X). Childrens.

GREECE–BIOGRAPHY

Hirokawa, Ryuichi. Children of the World: Greece. LC 87-42581. (Illus.). 64p. (gr. 5-6). 1987. PLB 12.95 (ISBN 1-55532-269-7). Gareth Stevens Inc.

Plutarch. Plutarch's Lives. White, John S., ed. LC 66-28487. (Illus.). 468p. (gr. 7 up). 1900. 20.00 (ISBN 0-8196-0174-8). Biblo.

GREECE–CIVILIZATION

see Civilization, Greek

GREECE–FICTION

Colum, Padraic. The Children's Homer: The Adventures of Odysseus & the Tale of Troy. Pogany, Willy, illus. LC 82-12643. 256p. (gr. 5 up). 1982. pap. 7.95 (ISBN 0-02-042520-1, Collier Young Ad). Macmillan Child Grp.

Fenton, Edward. The Refugee Summer. LC 81-12593. 272p. (gr. 7 up). 1982. pap. 10.95 (ISBN 0-385-28854-9). Delacorte.

Fox, Paula. Lily & the Lost Boy. LC 87-5778. 160p. (gr. 6-8). 1987. 12.95 (ISBN 0-531-05720-8); PLB 12.99 (ISBN 0-531-08320-9). Orchard Bks Watts.

Lang, Andrew. Tales of Troy & Greece. Bawden, Edward, illus. 300p. (gr. 5-8). 1978. pap. 2.95 (ISBN 0-571-04984-2). Faber & Faber.

Mara, Pam. The Greeks Pop-up. (Illus.). 32p. (Orig.). (gr. 3 up). 1985. pap. 6.95 (ISBN 0-906212-33-2). Parkwest Pubns.

Mayer, Albert I., Jr. Olympiad. LC 61-12875. (Illus.). (gr. 7 up). 1938. 16.00 (ISBN 0-8196-0115-2). Biblo.

Packard, Edward. Olympus: What Is the Secret of the Oracle. 112p. 1989. pap. text ed. 3.95 (ISBN 0-07-047995-X). McGraw.

Rosen, Billi. Andi's War. LC 88-25786. 144p. (gr. 7 up). 1989. 13.95 (ISBN 0-525-44473-4, DCB). Dutton Child Bks.

—Andi's War. (Illus.). 144p. (gr. 5 up). 1991. pap. 3.95 (ISBN 0-14-034404-7, Puffin). Puffin Bks.

GREECE–HISTORY

Artman, John. Ancient Greece. 64p. (gr. 4-8). 1991. 6.95 (ISBN 0-86653-583-7, GA1310). Good Apple.

Asimov, Isaac. Greeks: A Great Adventure. (Illus.). 320p. (gr. 7 up). 1965. 14.95 (ISBN 0-395-06574-7). HM.

Bains, Rae. Ancient Greece. Frenck, Hal, illus. LC 84-2685. 32p. (gr. 3-6). 1985. PLB 9.49 (ISBN 0-8167-0244-6); pap. text ed. 2.95 (ISBN 0-8167-0245-4). Troll Assocs.

Cohen, Daniel. Ancient Greece. (gr. 4-7). 1990. 11.95 (ISBN 0-385-26064-4); PLB 12.99 (ISBN 0-385-26065-2). Doubleday.

Coolidge, Olivia. The Golden Days of Greece. Arno, Enrico, illus. LC 68-21599. 224p. (gr. 4-7). 1990. PLB 14.89 (ISBN 0-690-04795-9, Crowell Jr Bks). HarpC Child Bks.

Fisher, Leonard E. Olympians: Great Gods & Goddesses of Ancient Greece. Fisher, Leonard E., illus. LC 84-516. 32p. (gr. 1-4). 1984. reinforced bdg. 14.95 (ISBN 0-8234-0522-2); pap. 5.95 (ISBN 0-8234-0740-3). Holiday.

Harris, Nathaniel. Alexander the Great & the Greeks. LC 85-71725. (Illus.). 64p. (gr. k-3). 1986. PLB 12.40 (ISBN 0-531-18030-1, Pub. by Bookwright Pr). Watts.

Household, Geoffrey. The Exploits of Xenophon. Fisher, Leonard E., illus. LC 89-12396. lx, 180p. (gr. 5-12). 1989. Repr. of 1955 ed. lib. bdg. 16.50 (ISBN 0-208-02224-4, Linnet). Shoe String.

Little, Emily. The Trojan Horse: How the Greeks Won the War. Eagle, Michael, illus. LC 87-43118. 48p. (Orig.). (gr. 2-4). 1988. lib. bdg. 6.99 (ISBN 0-394-99674-7, Random Juv); pap. 2.95 (ISBN 0-394-89674-2, Random Juv). Random.

Millard, A. & Peach, S. The Greeks. (Illus.). 96p. 1990. PLB 15.96 (ISBN 0-88110-415-9); pap. 9.95 (ISBN 0-7460-0342-0). EDC.

Odijk, Pamela. The Greeks. (Illus.). 48p. (gr. 5-8). 1989. PLB 16.98 (ISBN 0-382-09884-6). Silver Burdett Pr.

Plutarch. Plutarch's Lives. White, John S., ed. LC 66-28487. (Illus.). 468p. (gr. 7 up). 1900. 20.00 (ISBN 0-8196-0174-8). Biblo.

Polyzoides, G. Ancient Greek History. (Illus.). (gr. 4-6). 3.20 (ISBN 0-686-79636-5). Divry.

Woodford, Susan. The Parthenon. (Illus.). 48p. (gr. 7 up). 1981. pap. 5.95 (ISBN 0-521-22629-5). Cambridge U Pr.

GREECE–SOCIAL LIFE AND CUSTOMS

Steel, Barry. Greek Cities. (ps-3). 1990. PLB 10.40 (ISBN 0-531-18326-2). Watts.

GREECE, MODERN

Burrell, Roy. The Greeks. Connolly, Peter, illus. 128p. (gr. 7 up). 1990. 16.95 (ISBN 0-19-917161-0). Oxford U Pr.

Hollinger, Peggy. Greece. (ps-3). 1990. PLB 12.40 (ISBN 0-531-18305-X). Watts.

GREECE, MODERN–FICTION

Hope, Laura L. Bobbsey Twins & the Greek Hat Mystery. (gr. 1-4). 1964. 3.95 (ISBN 0-448-08057-5, G&D). Putnam Pub Group.

GREECE, MODERN–HISTORY

Polyzoides, G. History of Byzantine & Modern Greece. (Illus.). (gr. 4-6). 3.20 (ISBN 0-686-79635-7). Divry.

GREEK ART

see Art, Greek

GREEK CIVILIZATION

see Civilization, Greek

GREEK DRAMA–COLLECTIONS

Aristophanes. Four Major Plays. new ed. Teitel, N. R., intro. by. Incl. The Acharnians; The Birds; The Clouds; Lysistrata. (gr. 11 up). 1968. pap. 1.95 (ISBN 0-8049-0189-9, CL-189). Airmont.

GREEK LANGUAGE, MODERN–CONVERSATION AND PHRASE BOOKS

Demertzis, Strati. The Power of Modern Greek: Basic Course I. 136p. (Orig.). (gr. 7-12). 1986. pap. text ed. 11.00 (ISBN 0-9618466-0-7). Expressway Pubs.

—The Power of Modern Greek: Basic Course II. 164p. (Orig.). (gr. 7-12). 1986. pap. text ed. 12.00 (ISBN 0-9618466-1-5). Expressway Pubs.

Groten, Frank J., Jr. & Finn, James K. A Basic Course for Reading Attic Greek. LC 85-234367. 284p. (gr. 9-12). 1990. Repr. of 1983 ed. 19.90x (ISBN 0-942573-50-1). Hill School.

GREEK LANGUAGE, MODERN–GRAMMAR

Papantoniou, D. The Greek Children. (Illus.). (gr. 2-3). text ed. 3.20 (ISBN 0-686-79628-4); wkbk. 2.50 (ISBN 0-686-79629-2). Divry.

GREEK LITERATURE

Papantoniou, D. Greek Letters. 158p. (gr. 4-5). 3.20 (ISBN 0-686-79634-9). Divry.

—Greek Stories. (gr. 3-4). 3.20 (ISBN 0-686-79633-0). Divry.

Reeves, James, retold by. The Voyage of Odysseus: Homer's Odyssey. Fraser, Eric, illus. LC 86-10869. 192p. (gr. 4 up). 1986. pap. 6.95 (ISBN 0-87226-092-5, Bedrick Blackie). P Bedrick Bks.

GREEK MYTHOLOGY

see Mythology, Classical

GREEKS IN THE U. S.

Jones, Jayne C. The Greeks in America. rev. ed. LC 68-31504. (Illus.). 80p. (gr. 5 up). PLB 8.95 (ISBN 0-8225-0215-1); pap. 3.95 (ISBN 0-8225-1010-3). Lerner Pubns.

Monos, Dimitri. The Greek Americans. Moynihan, Daniel P., intro. by. 112p. (Orig.). (gr. 5 up). 1988. 17.95 (ISBN 0-87754-880-3); pap. 9.95 (ISBN 0-7910-0266-7). Chelsea Hse.

O'Dell, Scott. Alexandra. 128p. (gr. 7 up). 1985. pap. 2.25 (ISBN 0-449-70135-2, Juniper). Fawcett.

GREEN TURTLE

Cromie, William J. Steven & the Green Turtle. Eaton, Tom, illus. LC 77-85040. 64p. (gr. k-3). 1970. PLB 11.89 (ISBN 0-06-021374-4). HarpC Child Bks.

GREENHOUSES

Kemp, Anthea & Metcalfe, Penny. Mr. Percy's Magic Greenhouse. (Illus.). 32p. (ps-2). 1988. 15.95 (ISBN 0-575-03870-5, Pub. by Gollancz England). Trafalgar Sq.

GREENLAND

Berg, Karin & Berg, Hans. Greenland Through the Year. LC 72-90689. (Illus.). 24p. (gr. k-4). 1973. 7.95 (ISBN 0-87592-023-3). Scroll Pr.

Jacobsen, Peter & Kristensen, Preben. A Family in Greenland. (Illus.). 32p. (gr. 1-6). 1986. PLB 11.90 (ISBN 0-531-18082-4, Pub. by Bookwright). Watts.

Lepthien, Emilie U. Greenland. LC 88-37374. (Illus.). 128p. (gr. 5-9). 1989. PLB 25.27 (ISBN 0-516-02710-7). Childrens.

GREENLAND–FICTION

Hertz, Ole. Tobias Has a Birthday. Tobias, Tobi, tr. from DAN. LC 83-27287. (Illus.). 32p. (gr. k-3). 1984. PLB 7.95 (ISBN 0-87614-261-7). Carolrhoda Bks.

Kortum, Jeanie & Stermer, Dugald. Ghost Vision. LC 82-19410. (Illus.). 144p. (gr. 5-9). o.s.i 10.95; PLB 10.99. Sierra.

GREETING CARDS

Crowther, Robert. Punchout Christmas Cards. 1989. pap. 5.95 (ISBN 0-671-68401-9). S&S Trade.

Folmer, A. P. Fabulous Easter Fun Book. 16p. (gr. k-3). 1986. pap. 3.95 (ISBN 0-590-40207-2). Scholastic Inc.

Kingshead Corporation Staff. Cut, Color & Create: Make Your Own: Christmas Cards. Kingshead Corporation Staff, illus. 24p. (gr. k-4). 1987. pap. 2.97 (ISBN 1-55941-021-3). Kingshead Corp.

Suid, Murray. Greeting Cards. 64p. (gr. 2-6). 1988. 6.95 (ISBN 0-912107-74-X, MM981). Monday Morning Bks.

GROCERY TRADE

Wilks, Shelley. What's It Like to Be a Grocer. Ramsey, Marcy D., illus. LC 89-34394. 32p. (gr. k-3). 1989. lib. bdg. 10.89 (ISBN 0-8167-1805-9); pap. text ed. 2.50 (ISBN 0-8167-1806-7). Troll Assocs.

GROOMING, PERSONAL

see Beauty, Personal

GROOMING FOR WOMEN

see Beauty, Personal

GROTTOES

see Caves

GROUND EFFECT MACHINES

see also Helicopters

GROUNDHOGS–FICTION

Bond, Felicia. Wake up, Vladimir. Bond, Felicia, illus. LC 84-45342. 32p. (ps-3). 1987. 12.95 (ISBN 0-690-04452-6, Crowell Jr Bks). HarpC Child Bks.

Kroll, Steven. It's Groundhog Day! Bassett, Jeni, illus. LC 86-22924. 32p. (ps-3). 1987. reinforced bdg. 14.95 (ISBN 0-8234-0643-1). Holiday.

—It's Groundhog Day. (ps-3). 1991. pap. 2.50 (ISBN 0-590-44669-X). Scholastic Inc.

Moutran, Julia S. The Story of Punxsutawney Phil, "The Fearless Forecaster" Dubnansky, Marsha L., illus. LC 86-82950. 64p. (ps-5). 1987. 14.95 (ISBN 0-9617819-2-0); pap. 8.95 (ISBN 0-9617819-0-4); audiocassette 10.95 (ISBN 0-9617819-3-9). Lit Pubns.

—Will Spring Ever Come to Gobbler's Knob? A Punxsutawney Phil Adventure Story. Sweetland, Marsha L., illus. 64p. (ps-5). 1992. Incl. Phil's Field Guide to Woodland Animals. 15.95 (ISBN 0-9617819-5-5); Incl. Phil's Field Guide to Woodland Animals. pap. 9.95 (ISBN 0-9617819-4-7); audiocass. 10.95. Lit Pubns.

GROUP LIVING
see Collective Settlements

GROUSE–FICTION
Adrian, Mary. American Prairie Chicken. Vaughan-Jackson, Genevieve, illus. LC 68-21353. (gr. 2-6). 1968. 5.95g (ISBN 0-8038-0316-8). Hastings.

GROWTH
For biological and psychological works on the growth and development of animal and human organisms.
see also Children–Growth; Growth (Plants)
Althea. How Do Things Grow? Douglas, Julie, illus. LC 90-10923. 32p. (gr. k-3). 1990. PLB 10.89 (ISBN 0-8167-2118-1); pap. text ed. 2.95 (ISBN 0-8167-2119-X). Troll Assocs.
Bailey, Donna. All about Birth & Growth. LC 90-10134. (Illus.). 48p. (gr. 2-5). 1990. PLB 15.96 (ISBN 0-8114-2777-3). Steck-V.
Bingham, Mindy, et al. Challenges: A Young Man's Journal for Self-Awareness & Personal Planning. Greene, Barbara & Peters, Kathleen, eds. LC 84-70108. (Illus.). 240p. (gr. 7-12). 1987. 18.95 (ISBN 0-911655-26-3, Dist. by Ingram Book Co Bookpeople); pap. 14.95 (ISBN 0-911655-24-7, Dist. by Ingram Book Co Bookpeople); wkbk. 3.95 (ISBN 0-911655-25-5, Dist. by Ingram Book Co Bookpeople). Advocacy Pr.
Birth & Growth. 48p. (gr. 5-8). 1988. PLB 12.98 (ISBN 0-382-09708-4); 9.74s.p. (ISBN 0-685-24615-9). Silver Burdett Pr.
Cameron, Ann. The Seed. Cannon, Beth, illus. LC 74-15296. 36p. (gr. k-4). 1975. Pantheon.
Carola, Robert. How Do I Grow? rev. ed. Crawford, Mel, illus. 32p. (gr. 2-4). 1990. Repr. of 1988 ed. PLB 9.95 (ISBN 1-878363-14-X). Forest Hse.
Eastman, Philip D. Flap Your Wings. Eastman, P. D., illus. 32p. (ps-1). 1985. pap. 4.95 incl. cassette (ISBN 0-394-87655-5). Random.
Gee, R. & Meredith, S. Growing Up: Adolescence, Body Changes & Sex. 48p. 1986. PLB 13.96 (ISBN 0-88110-337-3); pap. 6.95 (ISBN 0-86020-837-0). EDC.
Krauss, Ruth. Growing Story. Rowand, Phyllis, illus. LC 47-30688. (gr. k-3). 1947. 11.95i (ISBN 0-06-023380-X). HarpC Child Bks.
Lovik, Craig J. Things I Can Do Myself. (Illus.). (ps). 1987. pap. 2.25 (ISBN 0-570-09111-X, 56-1586). Concordia.
Nelson, JoAnne. How Tall Are You? Bracken, Carolyn, illus. 16p. (Orig.). (gr. k-2). 1990. pap. 3.95 (ISBN 1-878624-09-1). McClanahan Bk.
Pluckrose, Henry. Growing. Fairclough, Chris, photos by. Franklin Watts Ltd., ed. (Illus.). 32p. (ps-6). 1988. 10. 90 (ISBN 0-531-10454-0). Watts.
Taylor, Kim. Too Slow to See. (gr. 2-5). 1991. 9.95 (ISBN 0-385-30214-2); PLB 10.99 (ISBN 0-385-30215-0). Delacorte.
Whitfield, Philip & Whitfield, Ruth. Why Do Our Bodies Stop Growing? (ps up). 1988. pap. 16.95 (ISBN 0-670-82331-7). Viking Child Bks.
Wilkes, A. Growing Things. (Illus.). 14p. (gr. 2-6). 1986. pap. 4.50 (ISBN 0-7460-0122-3). EDC.

GROWTH (PLANTS)
Taylor, Barbara. Growing Plants. (Illus.). 40p. (gr. k-4). 1991. PLB 11.90 (ISBN 0-531-19128-1, Warwick). Watts.

GUADALCANAL, BATTLE OF, 1942-1943
Tregaskis, Richard. Guadalcanal Diary. (Illus.). (gr. 7-8). 1963. lib. bdg. 8.99 (ISBN 0-394-90355-2). Random.

GUAM
Eustaquio, Roque B. Islas: A Social Studies Workbook. 98p. (gr. 9-12). 1989. write for info wkbk. Marianas Red Pub.
Farrell, Don A. Liberation Nineteen Forty-Four: The Pictorial History of Guam. Koontz, Phyllis, ed. Dimalanta, Ariel, illus. (gr. 8-12). 1984. Repr. 15.95 (ISBN 0-930839-00-5). Micronesian.

GUATEMALA
Cummins, Ronnie. Guatemala. Welch, Rose, illus. LC 89-40246. 64p. (gr. 5-6). 1990. PLB 12.95 (ISBN 0-8368-0120-2). Gareth Stevens Inc.
Haynes, Tricia. Guatemala. (Illus.). (gr. 5 up). 1988. 14. 95 (ISBN 1-55546-175-1). Chelsea Hse.
Lerner Publications, Department of Geography Staff. Guatemala in Pictures. (Illus.). 64p. (gr. 5 up). 1987. PLB 12.95 (ISBN 0-8225-1803-1). Lerner Pubns.

GUATEMALA–FICTION
Martin, Marilyn. Pedro. 152p. (gr. 3 up). 1980. 6.35 (ISBN 0-686-30765-8). Rod & Staff.

GUERRILLA WARFARE
see also World War, 1939-1945–Underground Movements
Coker, Christopher. Terrorism. (Illus.). 32p. (gr. 4-9). 1986. PLB 8.90 (ISBN 0-531-17030-6, Pub. by Gloucester). Watts.

GUEVARA, ERNESTO, 1928-1967
Neimark, Anne. Che! Latin America's Legendary Guerilla Leader. LC 88-23137. 128p. (gr. 6 up). 1989. 13.95 (ISBN 0-397-32308-5, Lipp Jr Bks); PLB 13.89 (ISBN 0-397-32309-3, Lipp Jr Bks). HarpC Child Bks.

GUIDANCE
see Counseling; Vocational Guidance

Tucker, Jeff & Tucker, Ramona. No Artificial Flavors: 100 Per Cent Friendship: Realistic Devotions for Teens. LC 88-34710. 110p. (gr. 7 up). 1989. pap. text ed. 5.95 (ISBN 0-87788-582-6). Shaw Pubs.

GUIDE BOOKS
see names of countries, states, etc. with the subdivision description and travel-guide books (e.g. U. S.–description and Travel etc.) and names of cities with the subdivision Description–Guide Books, e.g. New York–Description, etc.

GUIDE DOGS
Arnold, Caroline. A Guide Dog Puppy Grows Up. Hewett, Richard, photos by. (Illus.). 48p. (gr. 1 up). 1991. 16.95 (ISBN 0-15-232657-X). HarBraceJ.
Curtis, Patricia. Cindy, a Hearing Ear Dog. Cupp, David, illus. LC 80-24487. (gr. 3-5). 1981. 13.95 (ISBN 0-525-27950-4, DCB). Dutton Child Bks.
McPhee, Richard. Tom & Bear: The Training of a Guide Dog Team. McPhee, Richard, photos by. LC 81-43031. (Illus.). 160p. (gr. 5 up). 1981. (Crowell Jr Bks); PLB 9.89 (ISBN 0-690-04137-3). HarpC Child Bks.
Smith, Elizabeth S. A Guide Dog Goes to School: The Story of a Dog Trained to Lead the Blind. Dodson, Bert, illus. LC 87-11056. 64p. (gr. 1-4). 1987. 12.95 (ISBN 0-688-06844-8); lib. bdg. 12.88 (ISBN 0-688-06846-4, Morrow Jr Bks). Morrow Jr Bks.

GUIDE DOGS–FICTION
Garfield, James B. Follow My Leader. Greiner, Robert, illus. LC 57-1611. 192p. (gr. 4-6). 1957. pap. 13.95 (ISBN 0-670-32332-2). Viking Child Bks.
Radlauer, Ed & Radlauer, Ruth. Guide Dog Winners. LC 82-17825. (Illus.). 48p. (gr. 3 up). 1983. PLB 13.27 (ISBN 0-516-07812-7). Childrens.

GUIDE POSTS
see Signs and Signboards

GUIDED MISSILES
Cave, Ron & Cave, Joyce. What about...Missiles. West, David, illus. 32p. (gr. k-3). 1983. PLB 10.90 (ISBN 0-531-03469-0). Watts.
Nicholaus, J. Rockets & Missiles. (Illus.). 48p. (gr. 3-8). 1989. lib. bdg. 18.60 (ISBN 0-86592-418-X). Rourke Corp.

GUILDS
see also Labor and Laboring Classes; Labor Unions

GUINEA PIGS
Barrett, Norman. Guinea Pigs. (Illus.). 32p. (gr. k-4). 1990. PLB 11.40 (ISBN 0-531-14031-8). Watts.
Burton, Jane. Dazy the Guinea Pig. LC 89-11397. (Illus.). 32p. (gr. 2-3). 1989. PLB 10.95 (ISBN 0-8368-0206-3). Gareth Stevens Inc.
—Gipper the Guinea Pig. Burton, Jane, photos by. LC 88-3253. (Illus.). 24p. (Orig.). (ps-3). 1988. lib. bdg. 5.99 (ISBN 0-394-99961-4, Random Juv); pap. 1.95 (ISBN 0-394-89961-X, Random Juv). Random.
Henrie, Fiona. Guinea Pigs. LC 80-50482. (gr. 2-5). 1981. PLB 10.90 (ISBN 0-531-04185-9). Watts.
Petty, Kate. Cobayos. Thompson, George, illus. LC 88-83089. (SPA.). 24p. (gr. k-4). 1991. PLB 10.40 (ISBN 0-531-07914-7). Watts.
Pope, Joyce. Taking Care of Your Guinea Pig. (Illus.). 32p. (gr. 4-9). 1990. PLB 10.90 (ISBN 0-685-13496-2); pap. 3.95 (ISBN 0-531-15169-7). Watts.
Steinkamp, Anja J. Your First Guinea Pig. (Illus.). 36p. (Orig.). 1991. pap. 1.95 (ISBN 0-86622-066-6, YF-109). TFH Pubns.
Vrbova, Zuza. Guinea Pigs. McAulay, Robert, illus. 48p. 1990. PLB 9.95 (ISBN 0-86622-555-2, J-005). TFH Pubns.

GUINEA PIGS–FICTION
Bare, Colleen S. Guinea Pigs Don't Read Books. (gr. k-3). 1985. 11.95 (ISBN 0-399-21910-2, Putnam). Putnam Pub Group.
Duke, Kate. Guinea Pigs Far & Near. Duke, Kate, illus. LC 84-1580. 24p. (ps-1). 1984. 9.95 (ISBN 0-525-44112-3, DCB). Dutton Child Bks.
—What Would a Guinea Pig Do? Duke, Kate, illus. LC 87-22175. 32p. (ps-2). 1988. 12.95 (ISBN 0-525-44378-9, 01258-370, DCB). Dutton Child Bks.
Potter, Beatrix. The Tale of Tuppenny. Angel, Marie, illus. LC 72-89477. 40p. (gr. k-3). 1985. 5.95 (ISBN 0-7232-1724-6). Warne.
Pursell, Margaret S. Polly the Guinea Pig. Hammarberg, Dyan, tr. from FRE. LC 76-29449. (Illus.). 24p. (gr. k-4). 1977. PLB 6.95 (ISBN 0-87614-077-0). Carolrhoda Bks.
Sage, Angie. Monkeys in the Jungle. Sage, Angie, illus. 24p. (ps-k). 1989. 9.95 (ISBN 0-525-44466-1, DCB). Dutton Child Bks.
Smith, Emma. Emily the Traveling Guinea Pig. (gr. 1-5). 1960. 10.95 (ISBN 0-8392-3007-9). Astor-Honor.
Ziefert, Harriet. Where's the Guinea Pig? Lobel, Arnold, illus. LC 86-45950. 14p. (ps). 1987. 3.50 (ISBN 0-694-00182-1). HarpC Child Bks.

GUITAR
Buckingham, Jack. The Accompaniment Guitar: A Beginner's Guide to Song Accompaniment for Individual or Classroom Use. (Illus.). 80p. 1979. pap. 7.00 (ISBN 0-8258-0003-X, 05065). Fischer Inc NY.
Edwards, William H. Fretboard Logic, Vol. 1: The Reasoning Behind the Guitar's Unique Tuning System. rev. ed. (Illus.). 34p. (gr. 7-12). 1983. pap. 9.95 spiral bdg. (ISBN 0-685-29425-0). Edwards Music Pub.
Erbsen, Wayne. The Complete & Painless Guide to the Guitar for Young Beginner. (Illus.). 64p. 1979. pap. 6.95 (ISBN 0-8258-0002-1, PCB 111). Fischer Inc NY.

Isherwood, Millicent. The Guitar. 48p. (gr. 4-7). 1986. pap. 9.95 (ISBN 0-19-321334-6). Oxford U Pr.
Smith, L. Learn to Play Guitar. (Illus.). 64p. (gr. 6-12). 1988. PLB 13.96 (ISBN 0-88110-384-5); pap. 7.95 (ISBN 0-7460-0193-2). EDC.
Traum, Happy. Children's Guitar Guide. (Illus., Orig.). (gr. 4-6). 1969. pap. 6.95 (ISBN 0-8256-2141-0, Amsco Music). Music Sales.
Vahila, Michael. Teaching Guitar to Children: A Complete Guide for Ages 5 to 12. LC 88-63797. (Illus.). 100p. (Orig.). (gr. k-7). Date not set. pap. 9.95 (ISBN 0-942253-01-9); book & cassette pkg. 18.95 (ISBN 0-942253-02-7). PAZ Pub.
Zerbey, Richard J. Jam Plastic: Now You Can Play Lead Guitar with a Live Band. LC 85-754277. (Illus.). 24p. (Orig.). (gr. 7 up). 1986. lib. bdg. 21.95 incl. cassette (ISBN 0-935565-07-8, JPHV-I); pap. 15.95 incl. cassette (ISBN 0-935565-04-3); replacement (tape only) 7.99 (ISBN 0-935565-10-8). Sound Ent.
—Jam Plastic: Now You Can Play Lead Guitar with a Live Band. LC 85-754101. (Illus.). 24p. (Orig.). (gr. 7 up). 1986. lib. bdg. 21.95 incl. cassette (ISBN 0-935565-08-6); pap. 15.95 (ISBN 0-935565-05-1); cassette incl.; replacement tape only 7.99 (ISBN 0-935565-11-6). Sound Ent.
—Jam Plastic: Now You Can Play Lead Guitar with a Live Band. LC 85-754282. (Illus.). 24p. (Orig.). (gr. 7 up). 1986. lib. bdg. 21.95 incl. cassette (ISBN 0-935565-06-X); pap. 15.95 (ISBN 0-935565-03-5); cassette incl.; replacement tape only 7.99 (ISBN 0-935565-09-4). Sound Ent.

GUITAR–FICTION
Bourne, Miriam A. Uncle George Washington & Harriot's Guitar. Primavera, Elise, illus. 64p. (gr. 3-6). 1983. pap. 8.95 (ISBN 0-698-20573-1, Coward). Putnam Pub Group.
Robinson, Jan. The Story of Warple. Jewell, Jack, illus. 32p. (ps). 1990. 12.95 (ISBN 0-89334-137-1). Humanics Ltd.
Rocklin, Joanne. Discovering Martha. 128p. (gr. 3-7). 1991. 13.95 (ISBN 0-02-777444-9, Mcmillan Child Bk). Macmillan Child Grp.

GULLS–FICTION
Bach, Richard. Jonathan Livingston Seagull. 128p. (gr. 7 up). 1976. pap. 3.95 (ISBN 0-380-01286-3). Avon.
—Jonathan Livingston Seagull. LC 75-119617. (Illus.). 93p. (gr. 7 up). 1970. 14.95 (ISBN 0-02-504540-7). Macmillan.
Benchley, Nathaniel. Kilroy & the Gull. Schoenherr, John, illus. LC 76-24309. (gr. 4-6). 1978. pap. 3.50 (ISBN 0-06-440090-5, Trophy). HarpC Child Bks.
Holling, Holling C. Seabird. (Illus.). (gr. 4-6). 1973. 15.95 (ISBN 0-395-18230-1). HM.
Kelley, Rosemary S. Seavy Seagull & the Friendship Sloop Race. 2nd ed. Kelley, Rosemary S., illus. 39p. (ps-k). 1985. pap. 5.95 (ISBN 0-9616905-0-X). R S Kelley.
Pursell, Margaret S. Shelley the Seagull. Hammarberg, Dyan, tr. from FRE. LC 76-29454. (Illus.). 24p. (gr. k-4). 1977. PLB 6.95 (ISBN 0-87614-083-5). Carolrhoda Bks.
Winch, Gordon. Samantha Seagull's Sandals. Sherwood, Rhoda, ed. Olliver, Tony, illus. LC 88-42923. 32p. (gr. 2-3). 1988. PLB 12.95 (ISBN 1-55532-909-8). Gareth Stevens Inc.

GUNNING
see Hunting

GUNS
see Firearms

GUYANA
Gravette, Andy. Guyana. (Illus.). (gr. 5 up). 1989. 14.95 (ISBN 0-333-48504-1). Chelsea Hse.
Lerner Publications, Department of Geography Staff. Guyana in Pictures. (Illus.). 64p. (gr. 5 up). 1988. PLB 12.95 (ISBN 0-8225-1815-5). Lerner Pubns.

GYMNASTICS
see also Physical Education and Training
Barrett, Norman. Gimnasia. (SPA., Illus.). 32p. (gr. k-4). 1990. PLB 11.40 (ISBN 0-531-07906-6). Watts.
—Gymnastics. (Illus.). 32p. (gr. 2 up). 1991. pap. 3.95 (ISBN 0-531-24614-0). Watts.
Berke, Art. Gymnastics. Solomon, Maury, ed. (Illus.). 96p. (gr. 5 up). 1988. PLB 10.40 (ISBN 0-531-10478-8). Watts.
Boy Scouts of America. Cub Scout Sports: Gymnastics. (Illus.). 40p. (gr. 2-5). 1987. pap. 1.35 (ISBN 0-8395-2110-3, 2110). BSA.
Carter, Eneida & Mikalac, Miriam. Break Dance: The Free & Easy Way! Forman, Jan A., illus. 32p. (gr. 7 up). 1984. pap. 9.95 (ISBN 0-916391-00-0). Free & Easy Pubns.
Donovan, Pete. Carol Johnston: The One-Armed Gymnast. LC 82-4449. (Illus.). (gr. 2-8). 1982. PLB 13.27 (ISBN 0-516-04323-4). Childrens.
Levy, Elizabeth. Fear of Falling. 128p. (gr. 3-7). 1991. pap. 2.75 (ISBN 0-590-43834-4, Apple Paperbacks). Scholastic Inc.
McLaughlin, Maria. Gymnastics. (Illus.). 64p. (gr. 7-12). 1984. 22.95 (ISBN 0-7134-4283-2, Pub. by Batsford England). Trafalgar Sq.
Meltzoff, Nancy. A Sense of Balance. LC 77-18508. 160p. (gr. 6-9). 1978. 7.50 (ISBN 0-664-32629-3, Westminster). Westminster John Knox.
Murdock, Tony & Stuart, Nik. Gymnastics. rev. ed. (Illus.). 112p. (gr. 7-9). 1985. PLB 11.90 (ISBN 0-531-10022-7). Watts.
Percefull, Aaron. Gymnastics. 48p. (gr. 1-3). 1982. PLB 7.99 (ISBN 0-531-04377-0). Watts.

Pulley, Maxine. Acrobatics. Austin, Kent, photos by. (Illus.). (gr. 3-7). 1981. 8.95 (ISBN 0-13-003079-1). P-H.
Silverstein, Herma. Mary Lou Retton & the New Gymnasts. LC 85-11471. (Illus.). 83p. (gr. 4-8). 1985. PLB 12.90 (ISBN 0-531-10053-7). Watts.
Sullivan, George. Better Gymnastics for Girls. (Illus.). 64p. (gr. 3-7). 1977. (Putnam); pap. 4.95 (ISBN 0-399-21909-9, Putnam). Putnam Pub Group.
—Mary Lou Retton. Arico, Diane, ed. (Illus.). 64p. (Orig.). 1985. pap. 2.95 (ISBN 0-671-55472-7, Little Simon). S&S Trade.
Traetta, John & Traetta, MaryJean. Gymnastics Basics. Gow, Bill, illus. 64p. (gr. 3-7). 1983. pap. 3.95 (ISBN 0-13-371740-2, Pub. by Treehouse). P-H.
Washington, Rosemary G. Gymnastics Is for Me. Oddie, Alan, photos by. LC 79-4496. (Illus.). 48p. (gr. 2-5). 1979. PLB 8.95 (ISBN 0-8225-1078-2). Lerner Pubns.
Wood, Tim. Gymnastics. Fairclough, Chris, photos by. LC 89-50205. (Illus.). 32p. (gr. k-3). 1989. PLB 10.40 (ISBN 0-531-10826-0). Watts.

GYPSIES

Bemelmans, Ludwig. Madeline & the Gypsies. Bemelmans, Ludwig, illus. 56p. (ps-3). 1977. pap. 3.95 (ISBN 0-14-050261-0, Puffin). Puffin Bks.
Greene, Bette. Them That Glitter & Them That Don't. LC 92-13020. 224p. (gr. 7-12). 1983. Knopf.

GYPSIES–FICTION

Carlson, Natalie S. Family under the Bridge. Williams, Garth, illus. LC 58-5292. 112p. (gr. 3-7). 1958. PLB 13.89 (ISBN 0-06-020991-7). HarpC Child Bks.
Patterson, Geoffrey. Lion & the Gyspy. (ps-3). 1991. 14. 95 (ISBN 0-385-41536-2). Doubleday.
Worth, Valerie. Gypsy Gold. LC 83-20607. 176p. (gr. 12 up). 1983. 10.95 (ISBN 0-374-32828-5); pap. 3.45 (ISBN 0-374-42820-4). FS&G.

GYROSCOPE

Zubrowski, Bernie. Tops: Building & Experimenting with Spinning Toys. Doty, Roy, illus. LC 88-30463. 96p. (gr. 3-7). 1989. PLB 11.88 (ISBN 0-688-08811-2); pap. 6.95 (ISBN 0-688-07561-4, Pub. by Beech Tree Bks). Morrow Jr Bks.

H

HABITATIONS, HUMAN
see Architecture, Domestic; Houses; Housing

HABITATIONS OF ANIMALS
see Animals–Habitations

HABITS OF ANIMALS
see Animals–Habits and Behavior

HAIKU

Atwood, Ann. Haiku: The Mood of the Earth. Atwood, Ann, illus. LC 70-162737. (gr. 3 up). 1971. PLB 9.95 (ISBN 0-684-12494-7, Pub. by Scribner); (Pub. by Scribner). Macmillan.
Henderson, Harold G. Haiku in English. LC 67-16413. (Illus.). (gr. 9 up). 1967. pap. 5.95 (ISBN 0-8048-0228-9). C E Tuttle.
Leivis, Edith M. Haiku Is... a Feeling. King, James B., illus. Leivis, Edith M., intro. by. LC 89-64144. (Illus.). 64p. (Orig.). (gr. 1-3). 1990. pap. 5.95 (ISBN 0-9624993-0-7). Pippin Bks.
Mizumura, Kazue. Flower Moon Snow: A Book of Haiku. Mizumura, Kazue, illus. LC 76-41180. (gr. k-4). 1977. 7.95 (ISBN 0-690-01291-8, Crowell Jr Bks). HarpC Child Bks.

HAILE SELASSIE 1ST, EMPEROR OF ETHIOPIA, 1891-

Negash, Askale. Haile Selassie. Schlesinger, Arthur M., intro. by. (Illus.). 112p. (gr. 5 up). 1989. 17.95x (ISBN 1-55546-850-0). Chelsea Hse.
Obaba, Al-Imam. Emperor Haile Selassie. (Illus.). 43p. (Orig.). 1989. pap. 3.95 (ISBN 0-916157-07-5). African Islam Miss Pubns.

HAIR

Bailey, Donna. All about Skin, Hair & Teeth. LC 90-10050. (Illus.). 48p. (gr. 2-5). 1990. PLB 15.96 (ISBN 0-8114-2783-8). Steck-V.
Goldin, Augusta. Straight Hair, Curly Hair. Emberley, Ed E., illus. LC 66-12669. 40p. (gr. k-3). 1966. PLB 13.89 (ISBN 0-690-77921-6, Crowell Jr Bks). HarpC Child Bks.
Hair. (Illus.). (gr. 5 up). lib. bdg. 14.00 (ISBN 0-86625-278-9). Rourke Corp.
Howse, Cathy. Ultra Black Hair Growth: Six Inches Longer One Year from Now. (Illus.). 92p. (Orig.). (gr. 8 up). 1990. pap. text ed. 10.95 (ISBN 0-9628330-0-2). UBH Pubns.
Punches, Laurie C. How to Simply Cut Children's Hair. Punches, Laurie C., illus. Martinez, Carla, ed. LC 89-90694. (Illus.). 103p. (Orig.). (gr. 11 up). 1989. pap. 7.95 (ISBN 0-929883-10-1); VHS & Beta. video 29.95 (ISBN 0-685-24966-2). Punches Prodns.
—How to Simply Cut Hair. Martinez, Carla, et al, eds. Punches, Laurie C., illus. LC 88-92443. 109p. (Orig.). (gr. 11 up). 1989. pap. 8.95 (ISBN 0-929883-06-3); VHS & Beta. video 29.95 (ISBN 0-929883-07-1). Punches Prodns.
—How to Simply Cut Hair Even Better: Advanced Haircutting. Punches, Laurie C., illus. LC 88-92468. 129p. (Orig.). (gr. 11 up). 1989. pap. 9.95 (ISBN 0-929883-08-X). Punches Prodns.
—How to Simply Highlight Hair. Punches, Laurie C., illus. LC 88-92469. 79p. (Orig.). (gr. 11 up). 1989. pap. 6.95 (ISBN 0-929883-02-0); VHS & Beta. video 19.95 (ISBN 0-929883-03-9). Punches Prodns.
—How to Simply Perm Hair. Punches, Laurie C., illus. LC 88-92467. 74p. (Orig.). (gr. 11 up). 1989. pap. 6.95 (ISBN 0-929883-04-7); VHS & Beta. video 19.95 (ISBN 0-929883-05-5). Punches Prodns.

HAIR–FICTION

Cole, Babette. The Hairy Book. Cole, Babette, illus. LC 84-11496. 40p. (gr. 1-7). 1985. (Random Juv). Random.
Damaris, Gypsy. Pink Hair. 20p. (Orig.). (gr. 1). 1984. pap. 2.35 (ISBN 0-914917-00-5). Folk Life.
De Veaux, Alexis. An Enchanted Hair Tale. Hanna, Cheryl, illus. LC 85-45824. 40p. (gr. k-3). 1987. 12.95 (ISBN 0-06-021623-9); PLB 12.89 (ISBN 0-06-021624-7). HarpC Child Bks.
Frandsen, Karen G. Michael's New Haircut. Frandsen, Karen G., illus. LC 86-11696. 32p. (ps-3). 1986. PLB 13.93 (ISBN 0-516-03545-2); pap. 3.95 (ISBN 0-516-43545-0). Childrens.
Gordon, Sharon. Mike's First Haircut. Fiammenghi, Gioia, illus. LC 87-10911. 32p. (gr. k-2). 1988. PLB 7.06 (ISBN 0-8167-1113-5); pap. text ed. 1.95 (ISBN 0-8167-1114-3). Troll Assocs.
Martin, Ann M. Karen's Haircut. (gr. 4-7). 1990. pap. 2.75 (ISBN 0-590-42670-2). Scholastic Inc.
Yarbrough, Camille. Cornrows. Byard, Carole, illus. LC 78-24010. 48p. (Orig.). (gr. 2-6). 1981. 7.95 (ISBN 0-698-20462-X, Coward); pap. 5.95 (ISBN 0-698-20529-4, Coward). Putnam Pub Group.

HAITI

Anthony, Suzanne. Haiti. (Illus.). 96p. (gr. 5 up). 1989. lib. bdg. 14.95 (ISBN 1-55546-796-2). Chelsea Hse.
Griffiths, John. Take a Trip to Haiti. LC 89-8940. (Illus.). 32p. (gr. 3-5). 1989. PLB 10.90 (ISBN 0-531-10735-3). Watts.
Hanmer, Trudy J. Haiti. Kline, M., ed. (Illus.). 96p. (gr. 7-9). 1988. 10.40 (ISBN 0-531-10479-6). Watts.
Harner, Ruth. Ti-Fam: Witch Doctor's Daughter. (Illus.). 40p. (gr. k-6). 1986. pap. text ed. 8.99 (ISBN 1-55976-051-6). CEF Press.
Lerner Publications, Department of Geography Staff. Haiti in Pictures. (Illus.). 64p. (gr. 5 up). 1987. PLB 12.95 (ISBN 0-8225-1816-3). Lerner Pubns.
Telemaque, Eleanor W. Haiti Through Its Holidays. Hill, Earl, illus. LC 79-52858. 64p. (gr. 4-6). 1980. 8.50x (ISBN 0-685-00779-0). Blyden Pr.

HALLOWEEN

Barkin, Carol & James, Elizabeth. The Scary Halloween Costume Book. Coville, Katherine, illus. LC 81-14249. (gr. 3-6). 1983. 12.95 (ISBN 0-688-00956-5); PLB 12. 88 (ISBN 0-688-00957-3). Lothrop.
Barth, Edna. Witches, Pumpkins & Grinning Ghosts: The Story of the Halloween Symbols. Arndt, Ursula, illus. LC 72-75705. 96p. (gr. 3-6). 1981. pap. 4.95 (ISBN 0-89919-040-5, Pub. by Clarion). Ticknor & Fields.
—Witches, Pumpkins & Grinning Ghosts: The Story of the Halloween Symbols. Arndt, Ursula, illus. LC 72-75705. 96p. (gr. 3-6). 1979. 12.95 (ISBN 0-395-28847-9, Clarion). HM.
Bauer, Caroline F., ed. Halloween: Stories & Poems. LC 88-2675. (Illus.). 96p. (gr. 2-5). 1989. 11.95 (ISBN 0-397-32300-X, Lipp Jr Bks); PLB 12.89 (ISBN 0-397-32301-8, Lipp Jr Bks). HarpC Child Bks.
Brokaw, David. Howl-O-Ween Activity Book. Brokaw, David, illus. 32p. (gr. 3-6). 1982. pap. 1.98 (ISBN 0-88724-039-9, CD-8015). Carson-Dellos.
Brown, Marc. Arthur's Halloween. Brown, Marc, illus. LC 82-14286. 32p. (ps-3). 1983. 14.95 (ISBN 0-316-11116-3, Joy St Bks); pap. 4.95 (ISBN 0-316-11059-0, Joy St Bks). Little.
Carson, Patti & Dellosa, Janet. Halloween Primary Reading & Art Activities. (Illus.). 32p. (gr. 1-3). 1983. pap. 1.98 (ISBN 0-88724-036-4, CD-8027). Carson-Dellos.
—Halloween Readiness Activities. (Illus.). 32p. (ps-k). 1983. pap. 1.98 (ISBN 0-88724-047-X, CD-8023). Carson-Dellos.
Corwin, Judith H. Halloween Fun. Corwin, Judith H., illus. LC 83-8289. 64p. (gr. 3 up). 1983. PLB 10.29 (ISBN 0-671-49421-X); PLB 7.71s.p.; pap. 5.95 (ISBN 0-671-49756-1); pap. 4.46s.p. Messner.
Cracchiolo, Rachelle & Smith, Mary D. Halloween Activities. Crachiolo, Rachelle & Smith, Mary D., illus. 32p. (gr. 1-4). 1980. wkbk. 4.95 (ISBN 1-55734-011-0). Tchr Create Mat.
Cummings, e. e. Hist Whist. Ray, Deborah K., illus. LC 89-596. 24p. (gr. k-4). 1989. 10.95 (ISBN 0-517-57360-1); PLB 11.99 (ISBN 0-517-57258-3). Crown.
Davis, Nancy M, et al. October & Halloween. Davis, Nancy M., illus. 28p. (Orig.). (ps-4). 1986. pap. 4.95 (ISBN 0-937103-01-2). DaNa Pubns.
Fradin, Dennis B. Halloween. LC 89-7681. (Illus.). 48p. (gr. 2-3). 1990. PLB 12.95 (ISBN 0-89490-234-2). Enslow Pubs.
Friedhoffer. How to Haunt a House for Halloween. Brown, Harriet & Kaufman, Richard, illus. IRosoff, ed. 96p. (gr. 4-6). 1988. PLB 11.90 (ISBN 0-531-10501-6). Watts.
Gibbons, Gail. Halloween. Gibbons, Gail, illus. LC 84-519. 32p. (ps-3). 1984. reinforced bdg. 14.95 (ISBN 0-8234-0524-9); pap. 5.95 (ISBN 0-8234-0577-X). Holiday.
—Halloween. Gibbons, Gail, illus. (gr. k-3). 1985. incl. cassette 19.95 (ISBN 0-941078-87-6); pap. 12.95 incl. cassette (ISBN 0-941078-85-X); incl. cassette, 4 paperbacks guide 27.95 (ISBN 0-941078-86-8). Live Oak Media.
Glovach, Linda. The Little Witch's Halloween Book. (Illus.). 32p. (gr. 1-4). 1983. pap. 4.95 (ISBN 0-13-538116-9, Pub. by Treehouse Bks). P-H.
Hart, Rhonda J. You Can Carve Fantastic Jack-O-Lanterns. Foster, Kim, ed. Noyes, Leslie, illus. LC 90-55042. 112p. 1990. pap. 6.95 (ISBN 0-88266-580-4). Storey Comm Inc.
Haywood, Carolyn. Halloween Treats. De Larrea, Victoria, illus. LC 81-3959. 176p. (gr. 4-6). 1981. (Morrow Junior Books); lib. bdg. 12.88 (ISBN 0-688-00709-0). Morrow.
Herda, D. J. Halloween. (Illus.). 72p. (gr. 4 up). 1983. PLB 10.40 (ISBN 0-531-04527-7). Watts.
Hopkins, Lee B., ed. Hey-How for Halloween! McGaffrey, Janet, illus. LC 74-5601. 32p. (gr. 1-5). 1974. 12.95 (ISBN 0-15-233900-0, HJ). HarBraceJ.
Kalman, Bobbie. We Celebrate Halloween. (Illus.). 56p. (gr. 3-4). 1985. 15.95 (ISBN 0-86505-039-2); pap. 7.95 (ISBN 0-86505-049-X). Crabtree Pub Co.
Limburg, Peter R. Weird! The Complete Book of Halloween Words. Lewin, Betsy, illus. LC 88-38678. 128p. (gr. 4-10). 1989. 12.95 (ISBN 0-02-759050-X, Bradbury Pr). Macmillan Child Grp.
Ludwig, Nancy. Halloween Plays & Art Project Puppets. Fowler, Christopher, illus. 32p. (gr. k-3). 1983. pap. 1.98 (ISBN 0-88724-043-7, CD-8019). Carson-Dellos.
Marsh, Carole. Halloween: Silly Trivia. Marsh, Carole, illus. (Orig.). (gr. 2-9). 1986. PLB 19.95 (ISBN 1-55609-169-9); pap. 14.95 (ISBN 0-685-14605-7). Gallopade Pub Group.
May. Halloween, Reading Level 4. (Illus.). 48p. (gr. 3-8). Date not set. PLB 14.60 (ISBN 0-86592-983-1). Rourke Corp.
Moncure, Jane B. Our Halloween Book. rev. ed. Peltier, Pam, illus. LC 85-30868. 32p. (ps-3). 1986. lib. bdg. 11.97 (ISBN 0-89565-348-6). Childs World.
Myra, Harold. Halloween, Is It For Real? Walles, Dwight, illus. LC 82-6323. 32p. (gr. 2-4). 1982. 8.95 (ISBN 0-8407-5268-7). Nelson.
Osborne, Jill E. Make Color & Halloween Decoration. (ps-3). 1989. pap. 1.95 (ISBN 0-89375-644-X). Troll Assocs.
Prelutsky, Jack. It's Halloween. Hafner, Marylin, illus. LC 77-2141. 56p. (gr. 1-4). 1977. 12.95 (ISBN 0-688-80102-1); PLB 12.88 (ISBN 0-688-84102-3). Greenwillow.
—It's Halloween. Hafner, Marilyn, illus. 48p. (gr. k-3). 1986. pap. 2.50 (ISBN 0-590-03275-5). Scholastic Inc.
Reece, Colleen L. My First Halloween Book. Peltier, Pam, illus. LC 84-9431. 32p. (ps-2). 1984. PLB 14.60 (ISBN 0-516-02902-9); pap. 3.95 (ISBN 0-516-42902-7). Childrens.
Sandak, Cass. Halloween. LC 89-25396. (Illus.). 48p. (gr. 5 up). 1990. 10.95 (ISBN 0-89686-500-2, Crestwood Hse). Macmillan Child Grp.
Spooky Fun Activity Book. (Illus.). (ps-2). 1990. 1.95 (ISBN 0-7214-5294-9). Ladybird Bks.
Strand, Julie & Boggs, Juanita. Sing a Song of Halloween: With Communication, Arts & Nutrition Activities. McBride, Molly J., illus. 133p. 1982. pap. text ed. 10. 95 (ISBN 0-910817-00-6). Collaborative Learn.
Strand, Julie, et al. Sing a Song of Halloween: With Communication, Arts & Nutrition Activities. rev. ed. (Illus.). 133p. pap. text ed. write for info. (ISBN 0-910817-03-0). Collaborative Learn.
Supraner, Robyn. Happy Halloween: Things to Make & Do. Barto, Renzo, illus. LC 80-23889. 48p. (gr. 1-5). 1981. lib. bdg. 11.89 (ISBN 0-89375-420-X); pap. 2.95 (ISBN 0-89375-421-8). Troll Assocs.

HALLOWEEN–FICTION

Adams, Adrienne. A Halloween Happening. Adams, Adrienne, illus. LC 81-8969. 32p. (ps-3). 1981. 13.95 (ISBN 0-684-17166-X, Scribners Young Read). Macmillan Child Grp.
—Woggle of Witches. Adams, Adrienne, illus. LC 70-161536. 32p. (ps-3). 1971. 13.95 (ISBN 0-684-12506-4, Scribners Young Read). Macmillan Child Grp.
Aiello, Barbara & Shulman, Jeffrey. Trick or Treat or Trouble: Featuring Brian McDaniel. Barr, Loel, illus. 56p. (gr. 3-6). 1989. PLB 12.95 (ISBN 0-941477-07-X). TFC Bks MD.
Alexander, Sue. Who Goes Out on Halloween-Bank Street. (ps-3). 1990. PLB 9.99 (ISBN 0-553-05891-6, Little Rooster); pap. 3.50 (ISBN 0-553-34922-8). Bantam.
Bacon, Joy. Oliver Bean. Weinberger, Jane, ed. DeVito, Pam, illus. LC 90-70907. 68p. (ps-3). 1991. 12.95 (ISBN 0-932433-71-5); pap. 9.95 (ISBN 0-932433-73-1). Windswept Hse.
Ball, Jacqueline A. Halloween Double Dare. (gr. 4-7). 1990. pap. 2.95 (ISBN 0-06-106006-2, PL). HarperCollins.
Barth, Edna. Jack O'Lantern. Galdone, Paul, illus. LC 73-20194. 48p. (ps-3). 1979. 12.95 (ISBN 0-395-28763-4, Clarion). HM.
Berenstain, Stan & Berenstain, Janice. The Berenstain Bears Trick or Treat. Berenstain, Stan & Berenstain, Janice, illus. LC 89-30884. 32p. (Orig.). (ps-1). 1989. PLB 5.99 (ISBN 0-679-90091-8, Random Juv); pap. 2.25 (ISBN 0-679-80091-3, Random Juv). Random.

Bradbury, Ray. The Halloween Tree. Mugnaini, Joseph, illus. LC 72-2433. 160p. (gr. 6 up). 1972. Repr. of 1972 ed. 12.95 (ISBN 0-394-82409-1); lib. bdg. 13.99 (ISBN 0-394-92409-6). Knopf.
Bridwell, Norman. Clifford's Halloween. Bridwell, Norman, illus. (gr. k-3). 1986. pap. 1.95 (ISBN 0-590-40324-9). Scholastic Inc.
Brook, Ruth. Bitty's Halloween Surprise. Kondo, Vala, illus. LC 86-30730. 32p. (gr. k-3). 1988. PLB 11.89 (ISBN 0-8167-0916-5); pap. text ed. 2.95 (ISBN 0-8167-0917-3). Troll Assocs.
Brown, Ron. The Hag of Halloween. Shand, Jim & Brown, Ron, illus. LC 88-92081. 12p. (Orig.). (gr. 6). 1988. pap. 2.95 (ISBN 0-685-24339-7). Deer Creek NY.
Bunting, Eve. Scary, Scary Halloween. Brett, Jan, illus. LC 86-2642. 32p. (ps-3). 1988. 12.95 (ISBN 0-89919-414-1, Pub. by Clarion); pap. 4.95 (ISBN 0-89919-799-X, Pub. by Clarion). Ticknor & Fields.
Calhoun, Mary. Wobble the Witch Cat. Duvoisin, Roger, illus. LC 58-5018. 32p. (gr. k-3). 1958. PLB 13.88 (ISBN 0-688-31621-2). Morrow Jr Bks.
Carlson, Nancy. Harriet's Halloween Candy. LC 81-18140. (Illus.). 32p. (ps-3). 1982. lib. bdg. 9.95 (ISBN 0-87614-182-3). Carolrhoda Bks.
—Harriet's Halloween Candy. 32p. (gr. k-3). 1984. pap. 3.95 (ISBN 0-14-050465-6, Puffin). Puffin Bks.
—Harriet's Halloween Candy. Carlson, Nancy, illus. (gr. k-3). 1985. bk. & cassette 19.95 (ISBN 0-941078-53-1); pap. 12.95 bk. & cassette (ISBN 0-941078-51-5); cassette, 4 paperbacks & guide 27.95 (ISBN 0-941078-52-3). Live Oak Media.
Carlson, Natalie S. Spooky & the Ghost Cat. Glass, Andrew, illus. LC 84-17146. 32p. (ps-1). 1985. 13.00 (ISBN 0-688-04316-X); lib. bdg. 12.88 (ISBN 0-688-04317-8). Lothrop.
—Spooky Night. Glass, Andrew, illus. LC 82-54. 32p. (ps-3). 1982. 13.95 (ISBN 0-688-00934-4); PLB 13.88 (ISBN 0-688-00935-2). Lothrop.
Carrick, Carol. Old Mother Witch. Carrick, Donald, illus. LC 75-4609. 32p. (ps-4). 1979. 13.95 (ISBN 0-395-28778-2, Clarion). HM.
Cassedy, Sylvia. Best Cat Suit of All. LC 87-24659. (ps-3). 1991. 10.95 (ISBN 0-8037-0516-6); PLB 10.89 (ISBN 0-8037-0517-4). Dial Bks Young.
Charles, Donald. Shaggy Dog's Halloween. Charles, Donald, illus. LC 84-5901. 32p. (ps-3). 1984. lib. bdg. 14.60 (ISBN 0-516-03575-4). Childrens.
Clifford, Eth. Scared Silly. 1989. pap. 2.75 (ISBN 0-590-42382-7). Scholastic Inc.
Coombs, Patricia. Dorrie & the Halloween Plot. LC 76-3643. (Illus.). 48p. (gr. 1-5). 1976. PLB 12.88 (ISBN 0-688-51764-1). Lothrop.
Craig, Janet. Joey the Jack-O'-Lantern. Miller, Susan, illus. LC 87-10845. 32p. (gr. k-2). 1988. PLB 10.89 (ISBN 0-8167-1105-4); pap. text ed. 2.95 (ISBN 0-8167-1106-2). Troll Assocs.
Cusick, Richie T. Trick or Treat. 1989. pap. 2.75 (ISBN 0-590-42456-4). Scholastic Inc.
—Trick or Treat. 208p. (Orig.). (gr. 7 up). 1989. pap. 2.95 (ISBN 0-590-44235-X). Scholastic Inc.
Davis, Jim. Wade's Haunted Halloween. (ps-3). 1990. pap. 2.50 (ISBN 0-553-34931-7). Bantam.
Degen, Bruce. Aunt Possum & the Pumpkin Man. LC 76-58685. (Illus.). (ps-1). 1977. 12.89 (ISBN 0-06-021412-0). HarpC Child Bks.
Devlin, Wende & Devlin, Harry. Cranberry Halloween. LC 81-22134. (Illus.). 32p. (gr. k-3). 1984. 13.95 (ISBN 0-02-729910-4, Four Winds). Macmillan Child Grp.
Donnelly, Liza. Dinosaurs' Halloween. (Illus.). 32p. (gr. k-3). 1987. pap. 12.95 (ISBN 0-590-41025-3, Scholastic Hardcover); pap. 2.50 (ISBN 0-685-18092-1). Scholastic Inc.
Elmore, Patricia. Susannah & the Poison Green Halloween. 112p. (gr. 3-7). 1990. pap. 2.75 (ISBN 0-590-43471-3). Scholastic Inc.
Fass, Bernie & Wolfson, Mack. The Halloween Machine. (gr. k-9). 1984. pap. 15.95, 48 pgs. (ISBN 0-86704-009-2); pap. 2.95 student's ed, 32 pgs. (ISBN 0-86704-010-6). Clarus Music.
Feczko, Kathy. Halloween Party. Sims, Blanche, illus. LC 84-8635. 32p. (gr. k-2). 1985. PLB 10.89 (ISBN 0-8167-0354-X); pap. text ed. 2.95 (ISBN 0-8167-0434-1). Troll Assocs.
Foehl, Jamie L. Trick or Treat Taffy. Foehl, Barbara B., illus. LC 89-92436. 40p. (Orig.). (ps-6). 1989. write for info. (ISBN 0-9625337-0-X); PLB write for info.; pap. write for info. B Bk Pub Co.
Freeman, Don. Tilly Witch. Freeman, Don, illus. (gr. k-3). 1969. pap. 13.95 (ISBN 0-670-71303-1). Viking Child Bks.
Gardner, Beau. Whooo's a Fright On Halloween Night. (ps-1). 1990. 10.95 (ISBN 0-399-22212-X, Putnam). Putnam Pub Group.
Gezi, Kal & Bradford, Ann. The Mystery of the Live Ghosts. McLean, Mina G., illus. LC 78-8142. (gr. k-3). 1978. PLB 9.96 (ISBN 0-89565-026-6). Childs World.
Giff, Patricia R. Beast & the Halloween Horror. Sims, Blanche, illus. (Orig.). (gr. k-6). 1990. pap. 2.75 (ISBN 0-440-40335-9, YB). Dell.
Glovach, Linda. Little Witch's Halloween Book. Glovach, Linda, illus. LC 75-11713. (gr. 1-4). 1975. 7.95 (ISBN 0-13-537985-7). P-H.
Godden, Rumer. Mr. McFadden's Hallowe'en. 128p. (gr. 4-6). 1975. pap. 10.95 (ISBN 0-670-49271-X). Viking Child Bks.
Greene, Carol. The Thirteen Days of Halloween. LC 83-7347. (Illus.). 32p. (ps-2). 1983. PLB 14.60 (ISBN 0-516-08231-0); pap. 3.95 (ISBN 0-516-48231-9). Childrens.
Haywood, Carolyn. Halloween Treats. (gr. 2-4). 1987. pap. 2.95 (ISBN 0-8167-1039-2). Troll Assocs.
Helmrath, M. O. & Bartlett, J. L. Bobby Bear's Halloween. LC 68-56808. (Illus.). 32p. (ps-1). 1968. PLB 9.95 (ISBN 0-87783-004-5); cassette 7.94x (ISBN 0-87783-183-1). Oddo.
Herman, Emily. Hubknuckles. Ray, Deborah K., illus. LC 84-21355. 32p. (gr. 1-4). 1985. 9.95 (ISBN 0-517-55646-4). Crown.
Himmel, Roger J. Lollipop Dragon's First Halloween. Manoni, Mary H., ed. Peters, Luther J. & Ross, Connie, illus. (gr. k-3). 1978. pap. text ed. 29.95 6 bks. & 1 cass. (ISBN 0-89290-040-7); pap. text ed. 10.95 1 bk. & 1 cass. (ISBN 0-685-04660-5). Soc for Visual.
Hoban, Lillian. Arthur's Halloween Costume. LC 83-49465. (Illus.). 64p. (gr. k-3). 1984. 11.95 (ISBN 0-06-022387-1); PLB 11.89 (ISBN 0-06-022391-X). HarpC Child Bks.
Howe, James. Scared Silly: A Halloween Treat. Morrill, Leslie, illus. LC 88-7837. 48p. (gr. k up). 1989. 13.95 (ISBN 0-688-07666-1); PLB 13.88 (ISBN 0-688-07667-X, Morrow Jr Bks). Morrow Jr Bks.
Jasner, W. K. Which Is the Witch? Chess, Victoria, illus. LC 78-11757. (gr. 2-4). 1979. Pantheon.
Johnston, Tony. Soup Bone. (Illus.). 32p. (ps-3). 1990. 12.95 (ISBN 0-15-277255-3). HarbraceJ.
Jones, Michael P. Halloween Bats. (Illus.). 24p. 1984. write for info. (ISBN 0-89904-065-9). Crumb Elbow Pub.
—Halloween Ghosts. (Illus.). 24p. (ps-4). 1983. write for info. (ISBN 0-89904-064-0); pap. text ed. write for info. (ISBN 0-89904-063-2). Crumb Elbow Pub.
—Halloween Pumpkins. (Illus.). 24p. (ps-4). 1984. write for info. (ISBN 0-89904-067-5); pap. text ed. write for info. (ISBN 0-89904-068-3). Crumb Elbow Pub.
—Halloween Witches. (Illus.). 24p. (ps-4). 1983. write for info. (ISBN 0-89904-061-6); pap. text ed. write for info. (ISBN 0-89904-062-4). Crumb Elbow Pub.
Keats, Ezra. The Trip. Keats, Ezra, illus. LC 77-24907. 32p. (gr. k-3). 1978. PLB 12.88 (ISBN 0-688-84123-6). Greenwillow.
Kessel, Joyce K. Halloween. Carlson, Nancy L., illus. LC 80-15890. 48p. (gr. k-4). 1980. PLB 9.95 (ISBN 0-87614-132-7); pap. 3.95 (ISBN 0-87614-475-X). Carolrhoda Bks.
Kraus, Robert. Daddy Long Ears' Halloween. (Illus.). 40p. (ps-1). 1990. bds. 4.95 (ISBN 0-671-70352-8). S&S Trade.
—How Spider Saved Halloween. Kraus, Robert, illus. LC 80-16778. 40p. (ps-3). 1986. (Four Winds); pap. 1.95 (ISBN 0-590-09917-5). Scholastic Inc.
—How Spider Saved Halloween. (Illus.). 32p. (Orig.). (ps-2). 1988. pap. 2.50 (ISBN 0-590-42117-4). Scholastic Inc.
Kunhardt, Edith. Trick or Treat, Danny! LC 87-14963. (Illus.). 24p. (ps-1). 1988. 11.95 (ISBN 0-688-07310-7); lib. bdg. 11.88 (ISBN 0-688-07311-5). Greenwillow.
Laughlin, Florence. The Little Leftover Witch. 2nd ed. Greenwald, Sheila, illus. LC 88-10551. 96p. (gr. 2-6). 1988. pap. 3.50 (ISBN 0-689-71273-1, Aladdin). Macmillan Child Grp.
Leedy, Loreen. The Dragon Halloween Party. Leedy, Loreen, illus. LC 86-286. 32p. (gr. k-3). 1986. 14.95g (ISBN 0-8234-0611-3); pap. 5.95 (ISBN 0-8234-0765-9). Holiday.
Low, Alice. Witches' Holiday. Walton, Tony, illus. (gr. k-3). 1971. lib. bdg. 5.99 (ISBN 0-394-92165-8). Pantheon.
Maestro, Giulio. Halloween Howls: Riddles That Are a Scream. Maestro, Giulio, illus. LC 83-1419. 64p. (gr. 3-7). 1983. 9.95 (ISBN 0-525-44059-3, DCB). Dutton Child Bks.
Mariana. Miss Flora McFlimsey's Halloween. rev. ed. Mariana, illus. LC 86-15270. 40p. (ps-2). 1987. 11.95 (ISBN 0-688-04549-9). Lothrop.
Meyers, Susan. P.J. Clover, Private Eye: The Case of the Halloween Hoot. 1990. 13.95 (ISBN 0-525-67297-4, Lodestar Bks). Dutton Child Bks.
Meyrick, Kathryn. Hazel's Healthy Halloween. 1989. 9.99 (ISBN 0-85953-296-8). Childs Play.
Miller, Jayne. Too Much Trick or Treat. Thatch, Nancy R., ed. Miller, Jayna, illus. Melton, David, intro. by. (Illus.). 26p. (gr. 2-6). 1991. PLB 12.95 (ISBN 0-933849-37-0). Landmark Edns.
Mooser, Stephen. The Ghost with the Halloween Hiccups. DePaola, Tomie, illus. 32p. (gr. k-3). 1978. pap. 2.50 (ISBN 0-380-40287-4, Camelot). Avon.
Nixon, Joan L. The Halloween Mystery. Pacini, Kathy, ed. Cummins, Jim, illus. LC 79-166. (gr. 1-3). 1979. PLB 8.95 (ISBN 0-8075-3136-7). A Whitman.
Pearson, Susan. Porkchop's Halloween. Brown, Rick, illus. LC 88-4427. 32p. (gr. k-3). 1988. pap. 11.95 (ISBN 0-671-66732-7). S&S Trade.
—Porkchop's Halloween. Brown, Rick, illus. 32p. (ps up). 1989. pap. 3.95 (ISBN 0-671-68872-3). S&S Trade.
Peck, Richard. The Dreadful Future of Blossom Culp. (gr. 7 up). 1983. 15.00 (ISBN 0-385-29300-3). Delacorte.
Peck, Robert N. Higbee's Halloween. 101p. (gr. 5-7). 1990. 13.95 (ISBN 0-8027-6968-3); lib. bdg. 14.85 (ISBN 0-8027-6969-1). Walker & Co.
—Trig or Treat. Johnson, Pamela, illus. 96p. (gr. 4-6). 1982. 12.95 (ISBN 0-316-69659-5). Little.
Peterson, John. Tom Little's Great Halloween Scare. Clark, Roberta C., illus. 80p. (gr. 5-8). 1986. pap. 1.95 (ISBN 0-590-04702-7). Scholastic Inc.
—Tom Little's Great Halloween Scare. 1988. pap. 2.50 (ISBN 0-590-42235-9). Scholastic Inc.
Polisar, Barry L. The Haunted House Party: A Halloween Story. (Illus.). 40p. (gr. 3-6). 1987. 9.95 (ISBN 0-938663-02-X); pap. 7.95 (ISBN 0-938663-11-9). Rainbow Morn.
Prager, Annabelle. The Spooky Halloween Party. De Paola, Tomie, illus. LC 81-1945. 48p. (gr. 1-4). 1981. 6.95 (ISBN 0-394-84370-3); lib. bdg. 7.99 (ISBN 0-394-94370-8). Pantheon.
—The Spooky Halloween Party: A Step 2 Book. De Paola, Tomie, illus. LC 88-37571. 48p. (gr. 1-3). 1989. lib. bdg. 6.99 (ISBN 0-394-94961-7, Random Juv); pap. 2.95 (ISBN 0-394-84961-2, Random Juv). Random.
Prelutsky, Jack. It's Halloween. Haffner, Marylin, illus. 48p. (gr. k-3). 1987. Repr. of 1977 ed. Bk. & cassette. 5.95 (ISBN 0-590-63170-5). Scholastic Inc.
—It's Halloween. Hafner, Marylin, illus. 48p. (ps-3). 1987. pap. 2.50 (ISBN 0-590-41536-0); Books & Cassette. 5.95 (ISBN 0-590-63252-3). Scholastic Inc.
Quackenbush, Robert. Detective Mole & Halloween Mystery. 1989. pap. 3.95 (ISBN 0-671-67830-2). S&S Trade.
Rao, Anthony, illus. Halloween Masks. 24p. (ps-3). 1991. pap. 3.99 saddle-stitched (ISBN 0-394-86126-4, Random Juv). Random.
St. George, Judith. The Halloween Pumpkin Smasher. Tomes, Margot, illus. LC 77-26294. 48p. (gr. k-3). 1978. 10.95 (ISBN 0-399-20617-5, Putnam). Putnam Pub Group.
Schulz, Charles M. It's the Great Pumpkin, Charlie Brown. LC 80-10287. (Illus.). 48p. (gr. 3-5). 1980. Random.
Schweninger, Ann. Halloween Surprises. Schweninger, Ann, illus. LC 83-27372. 32p. (ps). 1984. pap. 10.95 (ISBN 0-670-35935-1). Viking Child Bks.
Sears, Yvonne. Amber's Hallowe'en. Sears, Yvonne, illus. LC 87-90131. 36p. (gr. 2-5). 1988. 12.95 (ISBN 0-9618803-0-9). Y-Knot.
Sharmat, Marjorie W. Nate the Great & the Halloween Hunt. (gr. k-6). 1990. pap. 2.95 (ISBN 0-440-40341-3, YB). Dell.
Stain, Dan. Teddy Bears' Halloween Party. (gr. 1-7). 1989. pap. 2.25 (ISBN 0-89954-962-4). Antioch Pub Co.
Stamper, Judith B. Totally Terrific Valentine Party Book. 1990. pap. 1.95 (ISBN 0-590-41713-4). Scholastic Inc.
Stevenson, James. That Terrible Halloween Night. LC 79-27775. (Illus.). 32p. (ps). 1980. PLB 11.88 (ISBN 0-688-84281-X). Greenwillow.
Stock, Catherine. Halloween Monster. Stock, Catherine, illus. LC 89-49530. 32p. (ps-1). 1990. 11.95 (ISBN 0-02-788404-X, Bradbury Pr). Macmillan Child Grp.
Stout, Robert T. The Secret of Halloween. Stout, Robert T., illus. 24p. (Orig.). (ps-6). 1982. pap. 3.50 (ISBN 0-911049-02-9). Yuletide Intl.
Tester, Sylvia R. Magic Monsters Halloween. Bowman, Patricia, illus. LC 79-25183. (gr. k-3). 1980. PLB 11.97 (ISBN 0-89565-121-1). Childs World.
Tudor, Tasha. Pumpkin Moonshine. Tudor, Tasha, illus. LC 89-3543. 40p. (ps-2). 1989. pap. 5.95 (ISBN 0-394-84588-9, Random Juv). Random.
Wiseman, Bernard. Halloween with Morris & Boris. (gr. k-3). 1986. pap. 2.50 (ISBN 0-590-41498-4). Scholastic Inc.
Ziefert, Harriet. Where's the Halloween Treat? Brown, Richard, illus. LC 85-3632. 20p. (ps). 1985. pap. 4.95 (ISBN 0-14-050556-3, Puffin). Puffin Bks.
Zimmer, Dirk. The Trick-or-Treat Trap. LC 81-47113. (Illus.). 32p. (gr. k-3). 1982. 10.95i (ISBN 0-06-026860-3). HarpC Child Bks.

HALLUCINOGENIC DRUGS

Algeo, Phillipa. Acid & Hallucinogens. (ps-3). 1990. PLB 11.90 (ISBN 0-531-10932-1). Watts.

HAMER, FANNIE LOU

Rubel, David. Fannie Lou Hamer: From Sharecropping to Politics. Gallin, Richard, ed. Young, Andrew, intro. by. (Illus.). 128p. (gr. 5 up). 1990. lib. bdg. 16.98 (ISBN 0-382-09923-0); pap. 7.95 (ISBN 0-382-24061-8). Silver Burdett Pr.

HAMILTON, ALEXANDER, 1757-1804

Keller, Mollie. Alexander Hamilton. LC 86-5670. (Illus.). 72p. (gr. 4-9). 1986. lib. bdg. 10.40 (ISBN 0-531-10214-9). Watts.
Kurland, Gerald. Alexander Hamilton: Architect of American Nationalism. Rahmas, D. Steve, ed. LC 73-190245. 32p. (gr. 7-12). 1972. lib. bdg. 4.20 incl. catalog cards (ISBN 0-87157-527-2). SamHar Pr.
O'Brien, Steve. Alexander Hamilton. Schlesinger, Arthur M., Jr., intro. by. (Illus.). 112p. (gr. 5 up). 1989. 17.95 (ISBN 1-55546-810-1). Chelsea Hse.

HAMSTERS

Barrett, Norman. Hamsters. (Illus.). 32p. (gr. k-4). 1990. PLB 11.40 (ISBN 0-531-14032-6). Watts.
Fischer-Nagel, Heiderose & Fischer-Nagel, Andreas. Inside the Burrow: The Life of the Golden Hamster. LC 86-2591. (Illus.). 48p. (gr. 2-5). 1986. PLB 12.95 (ISBN 0-87614-286-2); pap. 6.95 (ISBN 0-87614-478-4). Carolrhoda Bks.
Fritzsche, Helga. Hamsters. (Illus.). 80p. (gr. k-12). 1982. pap. text ed. 4.95 (ISBN 0-8120-2422-2). Barron.
Petty, Kate. Hamsters. Thompson, George, illus. LC 89-50455. 32p. (gr. k-2). 1989. PLB 10.40 (ISBN 0-531-17159-0, Gloucester Pr). Watts.

—Hamsters. Thompson, George, illus. LC 89-50455. (SPA.). 24p. (gr. k-4). 1991. PLB 10.40 (ISBN 0-531-07913-9). Watts.

Pope, Joyce. Taking Care of Your Hamster. (Illus.). 32p. (gr. 2 up). 1990. pap. 3.95 (ISBN 0-531-15170-0). Watts.

Silverstein, Alvin & Silverstein, Virginia. Hamsters: All About Them. LC 74-8863. (Illus.). 128p. (gr. 3-6). 1974. PLB 13.88 (ISBN 0-688-50056-0). Lothrop.

Smith, Peter. Your First Hamster. (Illus.). 36p. (Orig.). 1991. pap. 1.95 (ISBN 0-86622-067-4, YF-110). TFH Pubns.

Sproule, Anna & Sproule, Michael. Hamsters. Caulkins, Janet, ed. (Illus.). 48p. (gr. 1-6). 1988. PLB 11.90 (ISBN 0-531-18216-9, Pub. by Bookwright Pr). Watts.

Vrbova, Zuza. Hamsters. (Illus.). 48p. (gr. 2 up). 1990. PLB 9.95 (ISBN 0-86622-554-4, J-004). TFH Pubns.

Watts, Barrie. Hamster. LC 86-10018. (Illus.). 28p. (gr. 1-5). 1989. 6.95 (ISBN 0-382-09290-2); pap. 3.95 28p. (ISBN 0-382-09957-5); PLB 9.98 (ISBN 0-382-09281-3). Silver Burdett Pr.

HAMSTERS–FICTION

Baker, Alan. Benjamin's Balloon. 32p. 1990. 12.95 (ISBN 0-688-09744-8). Lothrop.

—Benjamin's Dreadful Dream. Baker, Alan, illus. LC 79-5369. (ps-2). 1980. (Lipp Jr Bks). HarpC Child Bks.

—Benjamin's Portrait. Baker, Alan, illus. LC 86-10396. 32p. (ps-2). 1987. PLB 11.88 (ISBN 0-688-06878-2). Lothrop.

Banks, Lynne R. I, Houdini. 128p. (Orig.). 1989. pap. 2.95 (ISBN 0-380-70649-0, Camelot). Avon.

—I, Houdini: The Autobiography of a Self Educated Hamster. Riley, Terry, illus. LC 87-22284. 128p. (gr. 5 up). 1988. pap. 12.95 (ISBN 0-385-24482-7). Doubleday.

Jackson, Neta. The Hamster Who Got Himself Stuck. Babbitt, Anne, illus. 25p. (ps-3). 1991. 3.99 (ISBN 0-88070-416-0). Multnomah.

Mitchell, Janis & Baron, Stanley. The Hamster Ballet Company. LC 85-52135. (Illus.). 64p. (ps up). 1986. 12.95 (ISBN 0-500-01382-9). Thames Hudson.

Pascal, Francine. Runaway Hamster. (ps-3). 1989. pap. 2.75 (ISBN 0-553-15759-0, Skylark). Bantam.

HANCOCK, JOHN, 1737-1793

Fradin, Dennis. John Hancock: First Signer of the Declaration of Independence. LC 88-313332. 48p. (gr. 3-6). 1989. PLB 14.95 (ISBN 0-89490-230-X). Enslow Pubs.

Fritz, Jean. Will You Sign Here, John Hancock? Hyman, Trina S., illus. LC 75-33243. 48p. (gr. 2-6). 1982. 9.95 (ISBN 0-698-20308-9, Coward); pap. 6.95 (ISBN 0-698-20539-1, Coward). Putnam Pub Group.

HAND

Aliki. My Hands. rev. ed. Aliki, illus. LC 89-49158. 32p. (ps-1). 1990. 12.95 (ISBN 0-690-04878-5, Crowell Jr Bks); PLB 12.89 (ISBN 0-690-04880-7, Crowell Jr Bks). HarpC Child Bks.

Damon, Laura. Funny Fingers, Funny Toes. Kennedy, Anne, illus. LC 87-10915. 32p. (gr. k-2). 1988. PLB 10.89 (ISBN 0-8167-1089-9); pap. text ed. 2.95 (ISBN 0-8167-1090-2). Troll Assocs.

Perkins, Al. Hand, Hand, Fingers, Thumb. LC 76-77841. (Illus.). (ps-1). 1969. 6.95 (ISBN 0-394-81076-7, Random Juv); lib. bdg. 7.99 (ISBN 0-394-91076-1). Random.

Silverstein, Alvin & Silverstein, Virginia B. The Story of Your Hand. Wenzel, Greg, illus. LC 85-520. 79p. (gr. 6 up). 1985. lib. bdg. 9.99 (ISBN 0-399-61212-2, Putnam). Putnam Pub Group.

HANDEL, GEORGE FREDERICK, 1685-1759

Great Composers, Bk. 2: Handel, Hayden, Schubert. (Illus.). (gr. 5 up). 3.50 (ISBN 0-7214-0242-9). Ladybird Bks.

Stevens, Bryna. Handel: And the Famous Sword Swallower of Halle. Councell, Ruth T., illus. 32p. (ps-3). 1990. 14.95 (ISBN 0-399-21548-4, Philomel Bks). Putnam Pub Group.

HANDICAPPED

Dwyer, Kathleen M. What Do You Mean I Have a Learning Disability? (Illus.). 32p. (gr. 5-9). 1991. 14.95 (ISBN 0-8027-8102-0); pap. 15.85 (ISBN 0-8027-8103-9). Walker & Co.

Gehret, Jeanne. Learning Disabilities & the Don't-Give-Up Kid. DePauw, Sandra A., illus. Cappella, Kathryn, frwd. by. (Illus.). 32p. (gr. 1-3). 1990. pap. 7.95 (ISBN 0-9625136-0-1). Verbal Images Pr.

Gravelle, Karen. Understanding Birth Defects. LC 90-32658. (Illus.). 126p. (gr. 7-12). 1990. PLB 12.90 (ISBN 0-531-10955-0). Watts.

Stewart, Jeffrey E. Work! A Reading Program. (Illus.). 116p. (Orig.). 1988. pap. 32.50 (ISBN 1-877866-02-4). J E Stewart.

White, Peter. Disabled People. (Illus.). 64p. (gr. 7-9). 1990. 11.90 (ISBN 0-531-17146-9). Watts.

HANDICRAFT

see also Hobbies; Leather Work; Weaving

Adams, Adrienne. The Great Valentine's Day Balloon Race. Adams, Adrienne, illus. LC 80-19527. 32p. (ps-3). 1980. 14.95 (ISBN 0-684-16640-2, Scribners Young Read). Macmillan Child Grp.

Allison, Linda. The Reasons for Seasons: The Great Cosmic Megagalactic Trip Without Moving from Your Chair. Allison, Linda, illus. 128p. (gr. 4 up). 1975. 14.95 (ISBN 0-316-03439-8); pap. 8.95 (ISBN 0-316-03440-1). Little.

—Trash Artists Workshop. LC 80-84184. (gr. 3-8). pap. 8.95 (ISBN 0-8224-9780-8). Fearon Teach Aids.

Araki, Chiyo. Origami in the Classroom, 2 vols. LC 65-13412. (Illus.). (gr. 1 up). 1965-68. bds. 13.95 ea. Vol. 1 (ISBN 0-8048-0452-4). Vol. 2 (ISBN 0-8048-0453-2). C E Tuttle.

Armstrong, Beverly. Build a Doodle Circus. (Illus.). 32p. (gr. k-4). 1986. 2.95 (ISBN 0-88160-133-0, LW138). Learning Wks.

—Build a Doodle Farm. (Illus.). 32p. (gr. k-4). 1986. 2.95 (ISBN 0-88160-130-6, LW135). Learning Wks.

—Build a Doodle Ocean. (Illus.). 32p. (gr. k-4). 1986. 2.95 (ISBN 0-88160-131-4, LW137). Learning Wks.

Arts & Crafts Discovery Units. Incl. Crayon; Mobiles; Paper; Papier Mache; Printing; Puppets; Tempera; Tissue; Watercolor; Weaving (ISBN 0-87628-532-9). (gr. k-7). 1974. 9.95x ea. Ctr Appl Res.

Ashman, I. Make This Model: Haunted House. (Illus.). 32p. (gr. 4 up). 1991. pap. 8.95 (ISBN 0-7460-0647-0, Usborne). EDC.

—Make This Model: Wizards Castle. (Illus.). 32p. (gr. 4 up). 1991. pap. 8.95 (ISBN 0-7460-0607-1, Usborne). EDC.

Barr, Marilynn. Gift Fun. (Illus.). 64p. (ps-1). 1989. 6.95 (ISBN 0-912107-85-5, MM1902). Monday Morning Bks.

—Hang-Ups. (Illus.). 64p. (ps-1). 1989. 6.95 (ISBN 0-912107-84-7, MM1901). Monday Morning Bks.

—Paper Crafts. (Illus.). 64p. (ps-1). 1989. 6.95 (ISBN 0-912107-86-3, MM1903). Monday Morning Bks.

Beard, Daniel C. The American Boy's Handy Book: What to Do & How to Do It. Perrin, Noel, frwd. by. LC 82-3155. (Illus.). 320p. (gr. 4 up). 1983. pap. 11.95 (ISBN 0-87923-449-0, Nonpareil Bks). Godine.

Beaton, Clare. Make & Play: Hats. 1990. pap. 2.95 (ISBN 0-531-15162-X). Watts.

Beegle, Shirley. Craft Fun with Stickers. 64p. (ps-8). 1986. wkbk. 5.95 (ISBN 0-87403-018-8, 2132). Standard Pub.

Beegle, Shirley, ed. Creative Craft Ideas for All Ages. Bartlett, Margaret, intro. by. (Illus., Orig.). (gr. k up). 1966. pap. 7.95 (ISBN 0-87239-321-6, 2795). Standard Pub.

Bernstein, Bonnie & Blair, Leigh. Native American Crafts Workshop. LC 81-82041. (gr. 3-8). 1982. pap. 8.95 (ISBN 0-8224-9784-0). Fearon Teach Aids.

Bonica, Diane. Hand-Shaped Art. Renard, Jan, illus. 112p. (ps-2). 1989. wkbk. 9.95 (ISBN 0-86653-474-1, GA1079). Good Apple.

—Hand-Shaped Gifts. 144p. (ps-4). 1991. 11.95 (ISBN 0-86653-612-4, GA1331). Good Apple.

Borchardt, Lois M. Learning about God's Love: Word-Picture Activities for Children in Grades 1 & 2. 48p. (gr. 1-2). 1986. pap. 2.95 (ISBN 0-570-04354-9, 61-2017). Concordia.

Bottomley, Jim. Paper Projects for Creative Kids of All Ages. 160p. (gr. 5 up). 1983. pap. 12.95 (ISBN 0-316-10349-7). Little.

Brackett, Karen & Manley, Rosie. Beautiful Junk. (gr. 1-6). 1990. pap. 8.95 (ISBN 0-8224-0626-8). Fearon Teach Aids.

Bridgewater, Alan. I Made It Myself: Kids Craft Projects. (Illus.). 192p. 1990. 19.95 (ISBN 0-8306-8339-9, 3339); pap. 11.95 (ISBN 0-8306-3339-1). TAB Bks.

Bridgewater, Alan & Bridgewater, Gill. Holiday Crafts: More Year-Round Crafts Kids Can Make. (Illus.). 256p. 1990. 25.95 (ISBN 0-8306-7409-8, 3409); pap. 16.95 (ISBN 0-8306-3409-6). TAB Bks.

Brown, Ann. Handmade Christmas Gifts That Are Actually Usable. Small, Carol B., illus. LC 87-31993. 75p. (Orig.). (gr. k-6). 1987. pap. 6.95 (ISBN 0-938267-03-5). Bold Prodns.

Brown, Jerome C. Folk Tale PaperCrafts. (gr. k-5). 1989. pap. 7.95 (ISBN 0-8224-3156-4). Fearon Teach Aids.

—Holiday Art Projects. (gr. 3-12). 1984. pap. 4.95 (ISBN 0-8224-5190-5). Fearon Teach Aids.

—Mother Goose PaperCrafts. (gr. k-5). 1989. pap. 7.95 (ISBN 0-8224-3154-8). Fearon Teach Aids.

Burt, Erica. Natural Materials. (Illus.). 32p. (gr. 2-6). 1990. lib. bdg. 13.26 (ISBN 0-86592-486-4); lib. bdg. 9.95s.p. Rourke Corp.

Byrnes, Patricia & Krenz, Nancy. Southwestern Arts & Crafts Projects. Rev. ed. LC 77-18988. (Illus.). (gr. 1-8). 1979. pap. 9.95 (ISBN 0-913270-62-8). Sunstone Pr.

Caney, Steven. Steven Caney's Playbook. LC 75-9816. (Illus.). 240p. (ps-5). 1975. pap. 8.95 (ISBN 0-911104-38-0, 050). Workman Pub.

Carlson, Laurie. Kids Create! Williamson, Susan, ed. Braren, Loretta T., illus. LC 90-33677. 160p. (Orig.). (gr. k-3). 1990. pap. 12.95 (ISBN 0-913589-51-9). Williamson Pub Co.

Carroll, David. Make Your Own Chess Set. Carroll, David, photos by. (Illus.). (gr. 5 up). 1975. (Pub. by Treehouse); pap. 2.95 (ISBN 0-13-547786-7). P-H.

Cheng, Andrea. Let's Make a Present! Easy to Make Gifts for Friends & Relatives of Any Age. Macdonald, Roland B. & Gray, Dan, illus. 128p. (gr. k-5). 1991. pap. 9.95 (ISBN 1-878767-16-X). Murdoch Bks.
"Did you make this? For me!" In an age of mass-produced toys nothing stands out like a present the giver has made especially for a friend. Andrea Cheng presents wonderful projects for you & your child to make, so your child can proudly proclaim, "& I made it for you, all by myself!" Each section of the book describes the right sort of present to make for children of different ages. In learning about what sorts of presents are appropriate for different children, your child will also learn a great deal about herself--why shapes & colors are important for newborns, why intricate patterns will frustrate a preschooler & so on. The presents described in the book are easy to make & generally don't require expensive materials. The book includes full-sized patterns, step-by-step instructions & color illustrations, so making the perfect present is easy--even if you've never been a "craft mom."
Publisher Provided Annotation.

Cheyney, Jeanne & Cheyney, Arnold. Holiday Art Plus. (gr. k-3). 1988. pap. 6.95 (ISBN 0-673-38394-6). Scott F.

Churchill, E. Richard. Paper Science Toys. LC 90-9891. (Illus.). 128p. (gr. 3-10). 1990. 14.95 (ISBN 0-8069-5834-0). Sterling.

Cole, Ann, et al. A Pumpkin in a Pear Tree: Creative Ideas for Twelve Months of Holiday Fun. (Illus.). 112p. (gr. 1 up). 1976. pap. 8.95 (ISBN 0-316-15111-4). Little.

Conaway, Judith. Easy-to-Make Christmas Crafts. Barto, Renzo, illus. LC 85-16475. 48p. (gr. 1-5). 1986. PLB 11.89 (ISBN 0-8167-0674-3); pap. text ed. 2.95 (ISBN 0-8167-0675-1). Troll Assocs.

—Great Gifts to Make. Barto, Renzo, illus. LC 85-16498. 48p. (gr. 1-5). 1986. PLB 11.89 (ISBN 0-8167-0676-X); pap. text ed. 2.95 (ISBN 0-8167-0677-8). Troll Assocs.

Conaway, Judity. Fun-to-Make Nature Crafts. Barto, Renzo, illus. LC 80-23999. 48p. (gr. 1-5). 1981. PLB 11.89 (ISBN 0-89375-440-4); pap. 2.95 (ISBN 0-89375-441-2). Troll Assocs.

Consentino, Phyllis. Teddy Bear Junction: Stop Here for Fine Collector Bears. (Illus.). 104p. (Orig.). 1985. pap. 10.95 (ISBN 0-935855-00-9). T B J Pubns.

Corwin, Judith H. African Crafts. (Illus.). 48p. (gr. k-4). 1990. PLB 11.90 (ISBN 0-531-10846-5). Watts.

Cuyler, Margery. All Around Pumpkin Book. McClintock, Barbara, illus. LC 79-4820. 96p. (gr. 3-7). 1980. pap. 3.95 (ISBN 0-03-056818-8). H Holt & Co.

D'Amato, Janet & D'Amato, Alex. Cardboard Carpentry. D'Amato, Jane & D'Amato, Alex, illus. Thompson, Morton, intro. by. (gr. 2-5). PLB 11.95 (ISBN 0-87460-085-5). Lion Bks.

—Handicrafts for Holidays. D'Amato, Janet & D'Amato, Alex, illus. (gr. 1-4). 1967. PLB 11.95 (ISBN 0-87460-086-3). Lion Bks.

—Indian Crafts. D'Amato, Janet & D'Amato, Alex, illus. (gr. 1-4). PLB 12.95 (ISBN 0-87460-088-X). Lion Bks.

Darling, Kathy. Gift Crafts. (ps-2). 1988. 6.95 (ISBN 0-912107-75-8, MM938). Monday Morning Bks.

Darling, Kathy & Sheridan, Terri. Nature Crafts. 64p. (ps-2). 1988. 6.95 (ISBN 0-912107-76-6, MM939). Monday Morning Bks.

DeBruin, Jerry. Young Scientist Explore: An Encyclopedia of Energy Activities. Czerniak, Charlene, illus. 32p. (gr. 4 up). 1985. wkbk. 4.95 (ISBN 0-86653-270-6, GA 655). Good Apple.

Devonshire, Hilary. Moving Art. (Illus.). 48p. (gr. 5-8). 1990. PLB 11.90 (ISBN 0-531-14076-8). Watts.

Disney, Walt, Productions Staff. The Mickey Mouse Make-It Book. LC 74-5241. (Illus.). 48p. (ps-3). 197.. 3.95 (ISBN 0-394-82555-1, Random Juv); lib. bdg. 4.99 (ISBN 0-394-92555-6). Random.

Edwards, Rosemary & McNall, Margie W. Craft Book for Children. Wallace, Mary H., ed. (Illus.). 64p. (ps-k). 1983. pap. 3.95 wkbk (ISBN 0-912315-03-2). Word Aflame.

Feller, Ron L. & Feller, Marsha Y. Fanciful Faces & Handbound Books: Fairy Tales. Ennes, Phyllis L., ed. Hastings, Kathryn K., illus. Smith, Andrew P., photos by. LC 88-34952. (Illus.). 72p. (Orig.). (gr. 2-9). 1989. pap. 9.95 (ISBN 0-9615873-1-8). Arts Factory.

Filkins, Vanessa. Gifts for Giving. 144p. (gr. k-5). 1991. write for info. (ISBN 0-86653-611-6, GA1330). Good Apple.

Ford, Marianne. Copycats & Artifacts. Pugh, Anna, illus. LC 86-45532. 96p. 1986. pap. 9.95 (ISBN 0-87923-645-0). Godine.

Foreman, Gloria. Busy Hands. (Illus.). (gr. 3-8). 1959. pap. 1.00 (ISBN 0-915198-01-0). G Foreman.

Forte, Imogene. December Patterns, Projects & Plans. 80p. (ps-1). 1989. pap. text ed. 7.95 (ISBN 0-86530-128-X, IP 167-0). Incentive Pubns.

—November Patterns, Projects & Plans. 80p. (ps-1). 1989. pap. text ed. 7.95 (ISBN 0-86530-127-1, IP 166-9). Incentive Pubns.

—October Patterns, Projects & Plans. 80p. (ps-1). 1989. pap. text ed. 7.95 (ISBN 0-86530-126-3, IP 166-8). Incentive Pubns.

—September Patterns, Projects & Plans. 80p. (ps-1). 1989. pap. text ed. 7.95 (ISBN 0-86530-125-5, IP 166-7). Incentive Pubns.

Forte, Imogene & Frank, Marge. Puddles & Wings & Grapevine Swings. LC 81-85014. (Illus.). 304p. (ps-6). 1982. pap. text ed. 16.95 (ISBN 0-86530-004-6, IP-046). Incentive Pubns.

Fowler, Virginie. Paperworks: Colorful Crafts from Picture Eggs to Fish Kites. Fowler, Virginie, illus. 162p. (Orig.). (gr. 5 up). 1982. 10.95 (ISBN 0-13-648543-X). P-H.

Fun Wraps for Tots: Children's Gift Wraps. 1989. 9.99 (ISBN 0-517-68531-0). Outlet Bk Co.

Gakken Co. Ltd. Editors, ed. Things to Do. Time-Life Books Inc. Editors, tr. 90p. (gr. k-3). 1989. write for info. (ISBN 0-8094-4897-1); PLB write for info. (ISBN 0-8094-4898-X). Time-Life.

Gardner, Beau. The Turn about, Think about, Look about Book. Gardner, Beau, illus. LC 80-12885. 32p. (gr. k-6). 1980. 13.95 (ISBN 0-688-41969-0); PLB 13.88 (ISBN 0-688-51969-5). Lothrop.

Gates, Frieda. Easy-to-Make Monster Masks & Disguises. (Illus.). (gr. 1-3). 1981. pap. 3.95 (ISBN 0-13-222794-0, Pub. by Treehouse). P-H.

Gathings, Evelyn. Cut & Make Cat Masks in Full Color. 32p. (gr. 1 up). 1988. pap. 4.95 (ISBN 0-486-25804-1). Dover.

Gendusa, Sam. Carving Jack-O-Lanterns. rev. ed. Ruse, Arnold, ed. Gendusa, Sam, illus. Ruse, Arnold, intro. by. LC 89-92605. (Illus.). 80p. pap. 9.95x (ISBN 0-9621071-1-5). SG Prodns.

Gerson, Trina. Holiday Crafts. Gerson, Janice, illus. 80p. (ps-7). 1983. pap. text ed. write for info. (ISBN 0-9605878-1-0). Anirt Pr.

Giles, Nancy. Creative Food Box Crafts. Petty, Melissa, illus. 64p. (ps-2). 1989. wkbk. 6.95 (ISBN 0-86653-475-X, GA1076). Good Apple.

—Creative Milk Carton Crafts. Petty, Melissa, illus. 64p. (ps-2). 1989. wkbk. 6.95 (ISBN 0-86653-462-8, GA1075). Good Apple.

Goodchild, Peter. The Spark in the Stone: Skills & Projects from the Native American Tradition. LC 90-27324. (Illus.). 144p. (Orig.). (gr. 5 up). 1991. pap. 11.95 (ISBN 1-55652-102-2). Chicago Review.

Green, Mary A. Projects for Christmas. Young, Richard G., ed. Marffy, Janos, illus. LC 89-35285. 32p. (gr. 3-5). 1989. PLB 14.60 (ISBN 0-944483-43-7). Garrett Ed Corp.

Greene, Peggy R. Things to Make. Dugan, Bill, illus. LC 77-91652. 32p. (ps-3). 1981. Random.

Haas, Rudi & Blohm, Hans. The Egg-Carton Zoo, No. 1. Suzuki, David, intro. by. (Illus.). 64p. 1987. pap. 11.95 (ISBN 0-19-540513-7). Oxford U Pr.

Haddad, Helen R. Potato Printing. Haddad, Helen R., illus. LC 80-2458. 64p. (gr. 3-6). 1981. PLB 13.89 (ISBN 0-690-04089-X, Crowell Jr Bks). HarpC Child Bks.

Happy Wraps for Tots: Children's Gift Wraps. 1989. 9.99 (ISBN 0-517-68530-2). Outlet Bk Co.

Hayes, Dympna & Lehman, Melanie. Fun with Things Around the House. Seeman, Tina, illus. 32p. (gr. 2). 1987. PLB 13.85 (ISBN 0-88625-166-4); pap. 2.50 (ISBN 0-88625-155-9). Durkin Hayes Pub.

Heinz, Brian J. Beachcrafts Too. LC 87-35232. (Illus.). 112p. (Orig.). 1988. pap. 9.95 (ISBN 0-936335-01-7). Ballyhoo Bks.

Hershoff, Evelyn G. It's Fun to Make Things from Scrap Materials. (Illus.). (gr. 4 up). 1944. pap. 6.95 (ISBN 0-486-21251-3). Dover.

Highlights Editors. One Hundred Thirty-Two Gift Crafts Kids Can Make. (Illus.). 48p. (Orig.). (gr. 1-6). 1981. pap. 2.95 (ISBN 0-87534-308-2). Highlights.

—One Hundred Twenty-Eight Holiday Crafts Kids Can Make. (Illus.). 48p. (Orig.). (gr. 1-6). 1981. pap. 2.95 (ISBN 0-87534-309-0). Highlights.

—One Hundred Twenty-Five Craft Ideas Kids Can Make from Throw-Aways. (Illus.). 48p. (Orig.). (gr. 1-6). 1981. pap. 2.95 (ISBN 0-87534-306-6, #1730). Highlights.

—One Hundred Twenty-Seven Anytime Crafts Kids Can Make. (Illus.). 48p. (Orig.). (gr. 1-6). 1981. pap. 2.95 (ISBN 0-87534-307-4). Highlights.

Hockenberry, Debra. The Craftmaker's Handbook. (Illus.). 60p. (Orig.). (gr. 12). Date not set. pap. 8.00 (ISBN 1-878056-06-9). D Hockenberry.

Hodgson, Harriet. Contraptions. 64p. (ps-3). 1987. 6.95 (ISBN 0-912107-59-6). Monday Morning Bks.

Holdgate, Charles. Net Making. LC 72-84056. (Illus.). (gr. 7 up). 1972. 12.95 (ISBN 0-87523-180-2). Emerson.

Holzenthaler, Jean. My Hands Can. Tafuri, Nancy, illus. (ps-k). 1978. 12.95 (ISBN 0-525-35490-5, DCB). Dutton Child Bks.

Horn, Donna. Party & Holiday Decorations: A Handbook of Wafer Fun. Horn, Donna, illus. LC 87-50697. 88p. (Orig.). (gr. 4-12). 1988. pap. 14.95 (ISBN 0-935009-97-3). Wafer Mache.

Jayne, Caroline F. String Figures & How to Make Them. (Illus.). 407p. (gr. 7 up). 1906. pap. 5.95 (ISBN 0-486-20152-X). Dover.

Jones. Creative Quickies. (Illus.). 100p. (gr. k-8). 1982. pap. 7.50 (ISBN 0-9607458-0-7). Arts Pubns.

Jones, Joan. Projects for Autumn & Holiday Activities. Young, Richard G., ed. Wheele, Stephen, illus. LC 89-17008. 32p. (gr. 3-5). 1989. PLB 14.60 (ISBN 0-944483-42-9). Garrett Ed Corp.

Kalman, Bobbie. Colonial Crafts. 1991. 14.95 (ISBN 0-86505-490-8); pap. 7.95 (ISBN 0-86505-510-6). Crabtree Pub CO.
In COLONIAL CRAFTS your young readers will take a journey into the 18th century & meet the craftspeople who created useful works of art with handmade tools. They will visit the workshops of the wheelwright, cooper, founder, peruker, shoemaker, milliner, gunsmith, & many more. They will find out how the artisans learned their trades through many years of apprenticeship. They will gain an appreciation for the goods made two hundred years ago that are still beautiful today. They will learn why the craftspeople were an essential part of the colonial community.
Publisher Provided Annotation.

—Home Crafts. (Illus.). 32p. (gr. 3-4). 1990. lib. bdg. 14.95 (ISBN 0-86505-485-1); pap. 7.95 (ISBN 0-86505-505-X). Crabtree Pub Co.
HOME CRAFTS is a colorful potpourri of the domestic industries carried out by settler men & mostly women. It explains how candles & soap were made, wool & flax were cleaned, spun, & woven, & looks at various needle crafts such as sewing quilts & stitching samplers. HOME CRAFTS also explores the transition of crafts from the home to workshop to factory. HOME CRAFTS is part of The Historic Communities Series, fun-to-read books that provide a wealth of information for young readers. The series introduces children to the concept of earlier times in history & looks at community life. The Historic Communities Series is beautifully designed, presenting information in two-page spreads through lively text, a multitude of color photographs, & detailed sketches. The books provide a close-up look at each topic, with step-by-step explanations of how tools & processes work. They are excellent for preparing young children for visits to historic sites & provide good follow-up material.
Publisher Provided Annotation.

Kalter, Joanmarie. The World's Best String Games Ever. LC 89-32404. (Illus.). 128p. (gr. 4-10). 1989. 12.95 (ISBN 0-8069-5738-7). Sterling.

Kingshead Corporation Staff. Cut, Color & Create: Make Your Own: Alphabet Blocks. Kingshead Corporation Staff, illus. 24p. (ps-3). 1987. pap. 2.97 (ISBN 1-55941-005-1). Kingshead Corp.

—Cut, Color & Create: Make Your Own: Alphabet Friends. Kingshead Corporation Staff, illus. 24p. (ps-3). 1987. pap. 2.97 (ISBN 1-55941-003-5). Kingshead Corp.

—Cut, Color & Create: Make Your Own: Beach. Kingshead Corporation Staff, illus. 24p. (ps-4). 1987. pap. 2.97 (ISBN 1-55941-011-6). Kingshead Corp.

—Cut, Color & Create: Make Your Own: Christmas Cards. Kingshead Corporation Staff, illus. 24p. (gr. k-4). 1987. pap. 2.97 (ISBN 1-55941-021-3). Kingshead Corp.

—Cut, Color & Create: Make Your Own: Christmas Garland. Kingshead Corporation Staff, illus. 24p. (ps-2). 1987. pap. 2.97 (ISBN 1-55941-020-5). Kingshead Corp.

—Cut, Color & Create: Make Your Own: Circus. Kingshead Corporation Staff, illus. 24p. (ps-4). 1987. pap. 2.97 (ISBN 1-55941-008-6). Kingshead Corp.

—Cut, Color & Create: Make Your Own: Christmas Ornaments. Kingshead Corporation Staff, illus. 24p. (gr. 2 up). 1987. pap. 2.97 (ISBN 1-55941-018-3). Kingshead Corp.

—Cut, Color & Create: Make Your Own: Christmas Snowflakes. Kingshead Corporation Staff, illus. 24p. (gr. k-3). 1987. pap. 2.97 (ISBN 1-55941-017-5). Kingshead Corp.

—Cut, Color & Create: Make Your Own: Christmas Snowflakes. Kingshead Corporation Staff, illus. 24p. (gr. 3 up). 1987. pap. 2.97 (ISBN 1-55941-019-1). Kingshead Corp.

—Cut, Color & Create: Make Your Own: Doll's Christmas. Kingshead Corporation Staff, illus. 24p. 1987. pap. 2.97 (ISBN 1-55941-013-2). Kingshead Corp.

—Cut-Color-&-Create: Make Your Own: Easter Fun. Kingshead Corporation Staff, illus. 24p. (ps-1). Date not set. pap. 2.97 (ISBN 1-55941-022-1). Kingshead Corp.

—Cut-Color-&-Create: Make Your Own: Easter Fun. Kingshead Corporation Staff, illus. 24p. (ps-1). Date not set. pap. 2.97 (ISBN 1-55941-023-X). Kingshead Corp.

—Cut-Color-&-Create: Make Your Own: Easter Fun. Kingshead Corporation Staff, illus. 24p. (ps-1). Date not set. pap. 2.97 (ISBN 1-55941-024-8). Kingshead Corp.

—Cut, Color & Create: Make Your Own: Easy Christmas Ornaments. Kingshead Corporation Staff, illus. 24p. (ps-2). 1987. pap. 2.97 (ISBN 1-55941-016-7). Kingshead Corp.

—Cut, Color & Create: Make Your Own: Farm. Kingshead Corporation Staff, illus. 24p. (ps-4). 1987. pap. 2.97 (ISBN 1-55941-007-8). Kingshead Corp.

—Cut, Color & Create: Make Your Own: Masks. Kingshead Corporation Staff, illus. 24p. (ps-4). 1988. pap. 2.97 (ISBN 0-685-22520-8). Kingshead Corp.

—Cut, Color & Create: Make Your Own: Number People. Kingshead Corporation Staff, illus. 24p. (ps-3). 1987. pap. 2.97 (ISBN 1-55941-004-3). Kingshead Corp.

—Cut, Color & Create: Make Your Own: Number Blocks. Kingshead Corporation Staff, illus. 24p. (ps-3). 1987. pap. 2.97 (ISBN 1-55941-006-X). Kingshead Corp.

—Cut, Color & Create: Make Your Own: Places to Go. Kingshead Corporation Staff, illus. 24p. (ps-4). 1987. pap. 2.97 (ISBN 1-55941-012-4). Kingshead Corp.

—Cut, Color & Create: Make Your Own: Paperplate Puppets. Kingshead Corporation Staff, illus. 24p. (ps-3). 1987. pap. 2.97 (ISBN 1-55941-002-7). Kingshead Corp.

—Cut, Color & Create: Make Your Own: Paperbag Puppets. Kingshead Corporation Staff, illus. 24p. (ps-3). 1987. pap. 2.97 (ISBN 1-55941-001-9). Kingshead Corp.

—Cut-Color-&-Create: Make Your Own: Pumpkin Magic. Kingshead Corporation Staff, illus. 24p. (ps-1). 1988. pap. 2.97 (ISBN 1-55941-037-X). Kingshead Corp.

—Cut, Color & Create: Make Your Own: Safari. Kingshead Corporation Staff, illus. 24p. (ps-4). 1987. pap. 2.97 (ISBN 1-55941-010-8). Kingshead Corp.

—Cut, Color & Create: Make Your Own: Valentine Fun. Kingshead Corporation Staff, illus. 24p. (gr. k-3). 1987. pap. 2.97 (ISBN 1-55941-015-9). Kingshead Corp.

—Cut, Color & Create: Make Your Own: Valentines. Kingshead Corporation Staff, illus. 24p. (gr. k-3). 1987. pap. 2.97 (ISBN 1-55941-014-0). Kingshead Corp.

—Cut, Color & Create: Make Your Own: Zoo. Kingshead Corporation Staff, illus. 24p. (ps-4). 1987. pap. 2.97 (ISBN 1-55941-009-4). Kingshead Corp.

Kirkman, Will. Nature Crafts Workshop. LC 80-84186. (gr. 3-8). pap. 8.95 (ISBN 0-8224-9781-6). Fearon Teach Aids.

Kohl, MaryAnn F. Mudworks: Creative Clay, Dough, & Modeling Experiences. LC 88-92897. (Illus.). 152p. (Orig.). (ps-6). 1989. pap. 14.95 (ISBN 0-935607-02-1). Bright Ring.

Kohn, Bernice. Beachcomber's Book. Wheatley, Arabelle, illus. (gr. 3-7). 1976. pap. 5.95 (ISBN 0-14-049158-9, Puffin). Puffin Bks.

Lancaster, John. Art with Found Materials. (Illus.). 48p. (gr. 5-8). 1991. PLB 11.90 (ISBN 0-531-14204-3). Watts.

—Paper Sculpture. Fairclough, Chris, photos by. LC 89-8887. (Illus.). 48p. (gr. 3-6). 1989. PLB 11.90 (ISBN 0-531-10758-2). Watts.

Lohf, Sabine. Christmas Crafts. LC 89-22255. 64p. 1989. lib. bdg. 19.93 (ISBN 0-516-09252-9); pap. 8.95 (ISBN 0-516-49252-7). Childrens.

—I Made It Myself. LC 89-22252. 64p. 1989. lib. bdg. 19.93 (ISBN 0-516-09254-5); pap. 8.95 (ISBN 0-516-49254-3). Childrens.

—Things I Can Make with Buttons. (Illus.). 32p. (ps-3). 1990. 6.95 (ISBN 0-87701-687-9). Chronicle Bks.

—Things I Can Make with Cloth. (Illus.). 28p. (ps-3). 1989. 6.95 (ISBN 0-87701-666-6). Chronicle Bks.

—Things I Can Make with Cork. (Illus.). 32p. (ps-3). 1990. 6.95 (ISBN 0-87701-726-3). Chronicle Bks.

—Things I Can Make with Stones. (Illus.). 32p. (ps-2). 1990. 6.95 (ISBN 0-87701-769-7). Chronicle Bks.

Lopshire, Robert. The Beginner Book of Things to Make. Lopshire, Robert, illus. LC 64-22011. (gr. k-3). 1977. lib. bdg. 7.99 (ISBN 0-394-93493-8). Beginner.

Ludwig, Nancy. Scissor Skills. Carson, Patti & Dellosa, Janet, illus. 32p. (ps-1). 1984. pap. 1.98 (ISBN 0-88724-086-0, CD-7025). Carson-Dellos.

McClure, Nancee. Creative Egg Carton Crafts. McClure, Nancee, illus. 64p. (ps-2). 1989. wkbk. 6.95 (ISBN 0-86653-471-7, GA1077). Good Apple.

McCoy, Elin. Secret Spaces, Imaginary Places: Creating Your Own Worlds for Play. Sweat, Lynn, illus. LC 85-23089. 80p. (gr. k-6). 1986. 12.95 (ISBN 0-02-765460-5). Macmillan.

MacKenzie, Joy. The Big Book of Bible Crafts & Projects. Flint, Russ, illus. 212p. (Orig.). (ps-4). 1981. pap. 12.95 (ISBN 0-310-70151-1, 14019P). Zondervan.

McMillan, Dana. Primary Projects. 112p. (gr. k-3). 1984. 9.95 (ISBN 0-912107-20-0). Monday Morning Bks.

McMillan, Mary. Christian Crafts from Hand-Shaped Art. 64p. (ps-5). 1991. 7.95 (ISBN 0-86653-629-9, SS1886). Good Apple.

Martin, Sidney & McMillan, Dana. Calendar Crafts. 64p. (gr. 1-6). 1986. 6.95 (ISBN 0-912107-44-8). Monday Morning Bks.

Morris, Victoria S. String Along with Me: The Math Way. (gr. 4 up). 1976. pap. 3.00 (ISBN 0-914318-05-5). V S Morris.

Murphy, Corinne. Exploring the Hand Arts: For Juniors, Cadettes, Seniors, & Leaders. 112p. (gr. 4-12). 1955. pap. 5.00 (ISBN 0-88441-140-0, 19-994). Girl Scouts USA.

Newsome, Arden. Cork & Wood Crafts. Coner, Nancy, illus. LC 72-112370. 64p. (gr. k-3). 1971. PLB 11.95 (ISBN 0-87460-229-7). Lion Bks.

Nowlin, Susan S. Fall Time Savers. Spence, Paula, et al, illus. 48p. (gr. k-6). 1989. wkbk. 5.95 (ISBN 1-55734-123-0). Tchr Create Mat.

—Spring Time Savers. Spence, Paula, et al, illus. 48p. (gr. k-6). 1989. wkbk. 5.95 (ISBN 1-55734-125-7). Tchr Create Mat.

—Winter Time Savers. Spence, Paula, et al, illus. 48p. (gr. k-6). 1989. wkbk. 5.95 (ISBN 1-55734-124-9). Tchr Create Mat.

—Year-Round Open Worksheets. Spence, Paula, et al, illus. 48p. (gr. k-6). 1989. wkbk. 5.95 (ISBN 1-55734-126-5). Tchr Create Mat.

Orr, Anne. Tatting with Anne Orr. 1989. pap. 2.50 (ISBN 0-486-25982-X). Dover.

Party Wraps for Kids: Children's Gift Wraps. 1989. 9.99 (ISBN 0-517-68533-7). Outlet Bk Co.

Peaslee, Ann & Kille, Jullien. You Can Make It! You Can Do It! 101 E-Z Holiday Craft-Tivities for Children. Ball, Dave, illus. 120p. (Orig.). (gr. 3-6). 1991. pap. 9.95 (ISBN 0-89346-337-X). Heian Intl.

Pettit, Florence H. The Stamp-Pad Printing Book. Pettit, Florence H. & Pettit, Robert N., illus. LC 78-22504. 160p. (gr. 5-9). 1979. 12.95 (ISBN 0-690-03967-0, Crowell Jr Bks). HarpC Child Bks.

Purves, Pamela. Decorating Eggs: In the Style of Faberge. Dace, Rosalind, ed. Search Press Studios Staff, illus. 96p. (Orig.). 1989. pap. 16.95 (ISBN 0-318-41704-9, Pub. by Search Pr UK). A Schwartz & Co.

Ransford, Lynn, et al. ABC Crafts & Cooking. (Illus.). 64p. (ps-2). 1987. wkbk. 6.95 (ISBN 1-55734-090-0). Tchr Create Mat.

Reid, Barbara. Playing with Plasticine. Reid, Barbara, illus. LC 88-39564. 96p. (gr. 3-7). 1989. PLB 11.88 (ISBN 0-688-08415-X); pap. 6.95 (ISBN 0-688-08414-1, Pub. by Beech Tree Bks). Morrow Jr Bks.

Rockwell, Harlow. I Did It. Rockwell, Harlow, illus. LC 86-22146. 64p. (gr. 1-3). 1987. pap. 3.95 (ISBN 0-689-71126-3, Aladdin). Macmillan Child Grp.

—Look at This. Rockwell, Harlow, illus. LC 87-1033. 64p. (gr. 1-4). 1987. pap. 3.95 (ISBN 0-689-71165-4, Aladdin). Macmillan Child Grp.

Rogler, Ingrid. Small Folk Quilters. Moss, Pamela, ed. Cordoba, Ligia, illus. 68p. (gr. 3-10). 1989. pap. text ed. 9.95 (ISBN 0-9622565-0-1). Chitra Pubns.

Roussel, Mike. Scrap Materials. (Illus.). 32p. (gr. 2-6). 1990. lib. bdg. 13.26 (ISBN 0-86592-487-2); lib. bdg. 9.95s.p. (ISBN 0-685-36305-8). Rourke Corp.

Roussel, Mike, et al. Craft Projects, 6 bks. (Illus.). 192p. (gr. 2-6). 1990. Set. lib. bdg. 79.60 (ISBN 0-86592-482-1); Set. lib. bdg. 59.70s.p. (ISBN 0-685-36300-7). Rourke Corp.

Sand Sculptures, Unit 11. (gr. 3). 1991. 7.45 (ISBN 0-88106-784-9). Charlesbridge Pub.

Sand Sculptures Activity Book, Unit 11. (gr. 3). 1991. 3.90 (ISBN 0-88106-787-3). Charlesbridge Pub.

Sand Sculptures Activity Book (EV, Unit 11. (gr. 3). 1991. 3.90 (ISBN 0-88106-786-5). Charlesbridge Pub.

Sattler, Helen R. Recipes for Art & Craft Materials. rev. ed. Shohet, Marti, illus. LC 86-34271. 128p. (gr. 6 up). 1987. 13.95 (ISBN 0-688-07374-3). Lothrop.

Scarry, Richard. Richard Scarry's Best Make-It Book Ever. (Illus.). (gr. k-3). 1977. pap. 8.95 (ISBN 0-394-83492-5, Random Juv). Random.

Sea Castles Activity Book, Unit 9. (gr. 3). 1991. 3.90 (ISBN 0-88106-772-5). Charlesbridge Pub.

Self, Margaret, ed. One Hundred Fifty-Eight Things to Make. LC 70-121625. (Orig.). (gr. 1-6). 1971. pap. 3.95 (ISBN 0-8307-0078-1, 5002605). Regal.

Senterfitt, Marilyn. Christian Crafts with Egg Cartons. 64p. (ps-5). 1991. 7.95 (ISBN 0-86653-574-8). Good Apple.

Shaw, Sheila. Kaleidometrics: The Art of Making Beautiful Patterns from Circles. (Illus.). 32p. (gr. 5-9). 1986. pap. 6.95 (ISBN 0-906212-21-9, Tarquin). Parkwest Pubns.

Smith, A. G. Easy to Make Periscope. 1990. pap. 3.95 (ISBN 0-486-26426-2). Dover.

Smith, A, G. Easy to Make Pinwheels. 1990. pap. 2.95 (ISBN 0-486-26435-1). Dover.

Somerville, L. & Gibson, R. How to Make Pop-Ups. (Illus.). 32p. (gr. 3-7). 1991. lib. bdg. 12.96 (ISBN 0-88110-541-4, Usborne); pap. 4.95 (ISBN 0-7460-0614-4, Usborne). EDC.

Stock, Catherine. A Christmas Angel Collection. Stock, Catherine, illus. 32p. (gr. k up). 1988. pap. 3.95 (ISBN 0-394-80266-7, Random Juv). Random.

Stuart, Sally E. & Young, Woody C. One Hundred Plus Craft & Gift Ideas: Fun & Easy Ideas for Any Occasion. White, Craig, illus. 96p. (Orig.). (gr. 1 up). 1990. pap. 9.95 (ISBN 0-939513-62-5). Joy Pub SJC.

Suid, Anna. Holiday Crafts. 64p. (gr. k-2). 1985. 6.95 (ISBN 0-912107-31-6). Monday Morning Bks.

Suid, Anna & Lieberman, Tanya. Constructions. 64p. (ps-3). 1987. 6.95 (ISBN 0-912107-57-X). Monday Morning Bks.

Suid, Murray. Writing Hangups. 64p. (gr. 2-6). 1988. 6.95 (ISBN 0-912107-73-1, MM980). Monday Morning Bks.

Sullivan, Dianna J. Paper Bag Art Projects. Adkins, Lynda, illus. 32p. (gr. 1-4). 1988. wkbk. 4.95 (ISBN 1-55734-100-1). Tchr Create Mat.

—Paper Plate Art Projects. Adkins, Lynda, illus. 32p. (gr. 1-4). 1988. wkbk. 4.95 (ISBN 1-55734-101-X). Tchr Create Mat.

Super Wraps for Kids: Children's Gift Wraps. 1989. 9.99 (ISBN 0-517-68532-9). Outlet Bk Co.

Supraner, Robyn. Rainy Day Surprises You Can Make. LC 80-19858. (Illus.). 48p. (gr. 1-5). 1981. PLB 11.89 (ISBN 0-89375-428-5); pap. 2.95 (ISBN 0-89375-429-3). Troll Assocs.

Tabibian, Ina. Fearon's Refrigerator Display Rewards. (ps-1). 1989. pap. 6.95 (ISBN 0-8224-3152-1). Fearon Teach Aids.

Things to Make: Arabic. (Illus.). (gr. 5-12). 3.50x (ISBN 0-86685-238-7). Intl Bk Ctr.

Thomson, Ruth. Indians of the Plains. (Illus.). 32p. (gr. k-4). 1991. PLB 11.40 (ISBN 0-531-14157-8). Watts.

—Spring. 1990. PLB 11.90 (ISBN 0-531-14018-0). Watts.

—Summer. 1990. PLB 11.90 (ISBN 0-531-14019-9). Watts.

True, Susan. Nursery Rhyme Crafts. 64p. (gr. k-2). 1985. 6.95 (ISBN 0-912107-33-2). Monday Morning Bks.

Vollmar, Karen & Fischer, Eileen. Kiddie Krafts. 48p. (ps-4). 1982. 5.95 (ISBN 0-86653-059-2, GA 413). Good Apple.

Volpe, Nancee. Good Apple & Seasonal Arts & Crafts. 144p. (gr. 3-7). 1982. 10.95 (ISBN 0-86653-087-8, GA 438). Good Apple.

Vonk, Idalee W. Fifty-Two Elementary Patterns. Karch, Pat, illus. 48p. (Orig.). (gr. 1-6). 1979. pap. 5.95 (ISBN 0-87239-340-2, 3366). Standard Pub.

Waltner, Willard & Waltner, Elma. Hobbycraft for Juniors. (Illus.). (gr. 2-10). 6.70 (ISBN 0-8313-0096-5). Lantern.

—New Look at Old Crafts. LC 70-143700. (Illus.). 142p. (gr. 9 up). 1971. 6.70 (ISBN 0-8313-0098-1). Lantern.

Warren, Jean. Crafts. 80p. (gr. k-2). 1983. 7.95 (ISBN 0-912107-04-9). Monday Morning Bks.

Wilkes, A. & Rosen, C. Simple Things to Make & Do. (Illus.). 72p. (gr. 2-6). Date not set. pap. 8.95 (ISBN 0-7460-0549-0, Usborne). EDC.

Wiseman, Ann. Making Things: The Hand Book of Creative Discovery. Wiseman, Ann, illus. 192p. (gr. 4 up). 1973. pap. 14.95 (ISBN 0-316-94849-7). Little.

Wolfe, Marcia. More Easy Crafts for Children. Briggs, Richard, illus. Lamb, Don, photos by. (Illus.). 96p. (ps-5). 1988. pap. 7.95 (ISBN 0-87403-306-3, 2139). Standard Pub.

Wright, Rachel. Pirates. (Illus.). 32p. (gr. k-4). 1991. PLB 11.40 (ISBN 0-531-14156-X). Watts.

Yawger, Kathleen S. Bible Story Crafts. 96p. (ps-5). 1991. 9.95 (ISBN 0-86653-637-X, SS1895). Good Apple.

Zawadzki, Sandra M. Art Adventures: Basic Crafts, Bk. 4. Zawadski, Sandra M., illus. 48p. (gr. k-6). 1985. wkbk. 5.95 (ISBN 0-86653-301-X, GA 637). Good Apple.

HANDWRITING

see Writing

HANGING

see Capital Punishment

HANNIBAL, 247-183 B.C.

Hannibal. (ARA., Illus.). (gr. 5-12). 3.95x (ISBN 0-86685-254-9). Intl Bk Ctr.

Humphrey, Perla F. Historic People of Color: Hannibal. Spaulding, Ureal, illus. 22p. (Orig.). (gr. 3-8). 1990. pap. write for info. (ISBN 1-878910-02-7). Supplemental Learning.

HANUKKAH (FEAST OF LIGHTS)

Adler, David A. Hanukkah Fun Book: Puzzles, Riddles, Magic & More. LC 76-47459. (Illus.). (gr. 3-7). 1976. pap. 3.95 (ISBN 0-88482-754-2, Bonim Bks). Hebrew Pub.

—Hanukkah Game Book: Games, Riddles, Puzzles & More. (Illus.). (gr. 1-5). 1978. pap. 3.95 (ISBN 0-88482-764-X, Bonim Bks). Hebrew Pub.

—A Picture Book of Hanukkah. Heller, Linda, illus. LC 82-2942. 32p. (gr. k-3). 1982. reinforced bdg. 13.95 (ISBN 0-8234-0458-7); pap. 5.95 (ISBN 0-8234-0574-5). Holiday.

Backman, Aidel. One Night, One Hanukkah Night. (Illus.). 32p. (gr. k-2). 1990. 14.95 (ISBN 0-8276-0368-1). JPS Phila.

Bearman, Jane. The Eight Nights: A Chanukah Counting Book. Bearman, Jane, illus. LC 78-60781. (gr. k-3). 1979. pap. 5.00 (ISBN 0-8074-0237-0, 102562). UAHC.

Behrens, June. Hanukkah. Behrens, Terry, illus. LC 82-17890. 32p. (gr. k-4). 1983. PLB 14.60 (ISBN 0-516-02386-1); pap. 3.95 (ISBN 0-516-42386-X). Childrens.

Block, Linda F. & Dubin, Debbie I. Chanukah on Noah's Ark. 72p. (Orig.). (gr. 1-7). 1987. pap. 6.95 (ISBN 0-9619082-0-3). Noahs Ark.

Burns, Marilyn. The Hanukkah Book. Weston, Martha, illus. LC 80-27935. 128p. (gr. 3-7). 1984. 13.95 (ISBN 0-02-716140-4, Four Winds). Macmillan.

Chaikin, Miriam. Hanukkah. Weiss, Ellen, illus. LC 89-77512. 32p. (ps-3). 1990. reinforced 14.95 (ISBN 0-8234-0816-7). Holiday.

—Light Another Candle: The Story & Meaning of Hanukkah. Demi, illus. LC 80-28137. 80p. (gr. 3-6). 1981. 10.50 (ISBN 0-395-31026-1, Clarion). HM.

—Light Another Candle: The Story & Meaning of Hanukkah. 1987 ed. Demi, illus. (gr. 7 up). 1981. pap. 4.95 (ISBN 0-89919-057-X, Pub. by Clarion). Ticknor & Fields.

Chiel, Kinneret. Complete Book of Hanukah. (Illus.). (gr. 6-8). pap. 6.95x (ISBN 0-87068-367-5). Ktav.

Colen, Kimberly. My Hanukkah Book: Questions, Answers, Activities. Rosenblum, Richard, illus. 24p. (Orig.). (gr. 4-6). 1987. pap. 3.95 (ISBN 0-590-40965-4). Scholastic Inc.

Cooper, Don. Hanukkah Songs & Games. Cook, Donald, illus. 32p. (ps-3). 1989. pap. 6.95 incl. cassette (ISBN 0-679-80041-7). Random.

De Paola, Tomie. My First Chanukah. De PPaola, Tomie, illus. 12p. (ps-k). 1989. 5.95 (ISBN 0-399-21780-0, Putnam). Putnam Pub Group.

Drucker, Malka. Hanukkah: Eight Nights, Eight Lights. Hoban, Brom, illus. LC 80-15852. 96p. (gr. 5 up). 1980. PLB 14.95 (ISBN 0-8234-0377-7). Holiday.

Ehrlich, Amy. Story of Hanukkah. Sherman, Ori, illus. (ps up). 1989. 14.95 (ISBN 0-8037-0615-4); PLB 14.89 (ISBN 0-8037-0616-2). Dial Bks Young.

Fisher, Aileen L. My First Hanukkah Book. Kiedrowski, Priscilla, illus. LC 84-21510. 32p. (ps-2). 1985. lib. bdg. 14.60 (ISBN 0-516-02905-3); pap. 3.95 (ISBN 0-516-42905-1). Childrens.

Fradin, Dennis B. Hannukkah. 48p. (gr. 2-5). 1990. 12.95 (ISBN 0-89490-259-8). Enslow Pubs.

Gellman, Ellie. It's Chanukah. Kahn, Katherine J., illus. LC 85-80782. 12p. (ps). 1985. bds. 4.95 (ISBN 0-930494-51-2). Kar Ben.

Grishaver, Joel L. Building Jewish Life: Hanukkah Activity Book. (Illus.). 31p. 1988. pap. 1.95 (ISBN 0-933873-32-8). Torah Aura.

Groner, Judye & Wikler, Madeline. All about Hanukkah. Schanzer, Rosalyn, illus. LC 88-13435. (gr. k-5). 1988. 10.95 (ISBN 0-930494-81-4); pap. 4.95 (ISBN 0-930494-82-2). Kar Ben.

Hirsh, Marilyn. I Love Hanukkah. Hirsh, Marilyn, illus. (gr. k-3). 1989. incl. cass. 19.95 (ISBN 0-87499-131-5); pap. 12.95 incl. cass. (ISBN 0-87499-130-7); Set; incl. 4 bks., cass., & guide. pap. 27.95 (ISBN 0-87499-132-3). Live Oak Media.

Kalman, Bobbie. We Celebrate Hanukkah. (Illus.). 56p. (gr. 3-4). 1986. 15.95 (ISBN 0-86505-045-7); pap. 7.95 (ISBN 0-86505-055-4). Crabtree Pub Co.

Koralek, Jenny. Hanukkah: The Festival of Lights. Wijngaard, Juan, illus. LC 89-8064. 32p. (gr. k-4). 1990. 13.95 (ISBN 0-688-09329-9); lib. bdg. 13.88 (ISBN 0-688-09330-2). Lothrop.

Poskanzer, Susan. Riddles about Hannukah. Brook, Bonnie, ed. Gray, Rob, illus. 32p. (ps-3). 1990. 5.95 (ISBN 0-671-70555-5); PLB 10.98 (ISBN 0-671-70553-9). Silver Pr.

Scharfstein, Eythe & Scharfstein, Sol. Book of Chanukah. (Illus.). (gr. 2-4). 1959. 5.95x (ISBN 0-87068-357-8). Ktav.

Schotter, Roni. Hanukkah! Hafner, Marylin, illus. (ps-3). 1990. 13.95 (ISBN 0-316-77466-9, Joy St Bks). Little.

Sidi, Smadar S. Chanukah A-Z. Nover, Teri, illus. (ps-2). 1988. 9.95 (ISBN 1-55774-041-0, Dist. by Watts). Adama Pubs Inc.

Silverman, Maida. Festival of Lights: The Story of Hanukkah. Ewing, C. S., illus. LC 87-16076. (gr. 1-5). 1987. 7.95 (ISBN 0-671-65663-5, Little Simon); pap. 2.95 (ISBN 0-671-64376-2). S&S Trade.

Simon, Norma. Hanukah in My House. Gordon, Ayala, illus. (ps-k). 1960. plastic cover 4.50 (ISBN 0-8381-0705-2). United Syn Bk.

Stuhlman, Daniel D. My Own Hanukah Story. Kuppersmith-Krause, Molly B., illus. (Orig.). (ps-5). 1980. pap. 3.95 personalized version (ISBN 0-934402-07-8); decorations 1.00 (ISBN 0-934402-08-6); trade version 2.50 (ISBN 0-934402-12-4). BYLS Pr.

Sussman, Susan. Hanukkah: Eight Lights Around the World. Levine, Abby, ed. (Illus.). 40p. (gr. 2 up). 1988. PLB 10.95 (ISBN 0-8075-3145-6). A Whitman.

—There's No Such Thing As a Chanukah Bush, Sandy Goldstein. Tucker, Kathleen, ed. (Illus.). 40p. (gr. 3-7). 1983. PLB 7.95 (ISBN 0-8075-7862-2). A Whitman.

Vered, Ben. Why Is Hanukkah. (Illus.). (ps-5). 1961. pap. 2.50 (ISBN 0-914080-59-8). Shulsinger Sales.

Wengrov, Charles. The Story of Hanukkah. (Illus.). (gr. k-7). 1965. pap. 2.50 (ISBN 0-914080-52-0). Shulsinger Sales.

Zwebner, Janet. The Animated Menorah Chanukah Activity Book. (Illus.). 48p. (gr. 1-4). 1989. pap. 5.95 (ISBN 0-685-28790-4). Shapolsky Pubs.

HANUKKAH (FEAST OF LIGHTS)–FICTION

Adler, David A. Happy Hanukkah Rebus. Palmer, Jan, illus. 32p. (ps-3). 1989. pap. 11.95 (ISBN 0-670-82419-4). Viking Child Bks.

—Malke's Secret Recipe: A Chanukah Story from Chelm. LC 88-32019. (ps-3). 1989. 10.95 (ISBN 0-930494-88-1); pap. 4.95 (ISBN 0-930494-89-X). Kar Ben.

Armstrong, Beverly. The Hanukkah Happening. (Illus.). 24p. (gr. 2-6). 1987. 4.95 (ISBN 0-88160-150-0, LW263). Learning Wks.

Birenbaum, Barbara. Candle Talk. Birenbaum, Barbara, illus. LC 90-33299. 54p. (gr. 2-5). 1991. PLB 8.95 (ISBN 0-935343-10-5); pap. 5.95g (ISBN 0-935343-15-6). Peartree.

—The Lost Side of the Dreydl. Birenbaum, Barbara, illus. 50p. (gr. 3-5). 1987. pap. 5.95 (ISBN 0-935343-16-4). Peartree.

Burstein, Chaya M. Hanukkah Cat. LC 85-14760. (Illus.). 32p. (ps-3). 1985. pap. 4.95 (ISBN 0-930494-48-2). Kar Ben.

Fox, Terry. A Little Miracle: A Hanukah Story. Fox, David A., illus. LC 85-51615. 52p. (Orig.). (ps up). 1985. pap. 5.95 (ISBN 0-9615397-0-4). Tenderfoot Pr.

Goffstein, M. B. Laughing Latkes. Goffstein, M. B., illus. LC 81-68932. 32p. (ps up). 1980. 6.95 (ISBN 0-374-34364-0). FS&G.

Goldin, Barbara D. Just Enough Is Plenty: A Hannukkah Tale. Chwast, Seymour, illus. (ps-3). 1988. pap. 12.95 (ISBN 0-670-81852-6). Viking Child Bks.

—Just Enough Is Plenty, a Hanukkah Tale. (ps-3). 1990. pap. 3.95 (ISBN 0-14-050787-6, Puffin). Puffin Bks.

Greene, Jacqueline D. The Hanukah Tooth. Ouellet, Pauline A., illus. LC 81-90033. 28p. (ps-2). 1981. pap. 3.00 (ISBN 0-938836-02-1). Pascal Pubs.

—Nathan's Hanukkah Bargain. Rubin, Steffi K., illus. LC 86-20982. 32p. (ps-4). 1986. 10.95 (ISBN 0-930494-62-8); pap. 4.95 (ISBN 0-930494-63-6). Kar Ben.

Hirsh, Marilyn. Potato Pancakes All Around: A Hanukkah Tale. (Illus.). 34p. (gr. 4-8). 1982. pap. 6.95 (ISBN 0-8276-0217-0, 604). JPS Phila.

Kimmel, Eric A. The Chanukkah Guest. Carmi, Giora, illus. LC 89-20073. 32p. (gr. k-3). 1990. reinforced 14.95 (ISBN 0-8234-0788-8). Holiday.

Manushkin, Fran. Latkes & Applesauce: A Hanukkah Story. Spowart, Robin, illus. (ps-3). 1990. 12.95 (ISBN 0-590-42261-8, Scholastic Hardcover). Scholastic Inc.

Miller, Deborah U. & Ostrove, Karen. The Modi'in Motel: An Idol Tale for Hanukkah. LC 86-14611. (Illus.). 32p. (ps-6). 1986. 6.95 (ISBN 0-930494-64-4). Kar Ben.

Scharfstein, Sol. Four Tiny Tot Hanukah Books. Freedman, Arthur, illus. (ps-1). 1987. 5.95 (ISBN 0-88125-226-3). Ktav.

Shostak, Myra. Rainbow Candles: A Chanukah Counting Book. Kahn, Katherine J., illus. LC 86-81718. 12p. (ps). 1986. bds. 4.95 (ISBN 0-930494-59-8). Kar Ben.

Singer, Isaac Bashevis. The Power of Light: Eight Stories for Hanukkah. Lieblich, Irene, illus. LC 80-20263. 87p. (ps-3). 1980. 13.95 (ISBN 0-374-36099-5). FS&G.

Weilerstein, Sadie R. K'tonton in the Circus: A Hanukkah Adventure. Hirsh, Marilyn, illus. LC 81-11765. (gr. 2 up). pap. 8.95 (ISBN 0-8276-0303-7). JPS Phila.

Wolfberg, Carrie. The Happy Dreidles: Hanukhah Adventure. Birenbaum, Barbara, illus. LC 86-12210. 28p. (ps-2). 1986. pap. 2.50 (ISBN 0-935343-00-8). Peartree.

HAPPINESS

Brady, Janeen & Woolley, Diane. Standin' Tall Happiness. Wilson, Grant, illus. 22p. (Orig.). (ps-6). 1982. pap. text ed. 1.50 activity bk. (ISBN 0-944803-46-6); cassette & bk. 8.95 (ISBN 0-944803-47-4). Brite Intl.

Dacquino, V. T. Kiss the Candy Days Good-Bye. (gr. 5-9). 1986. pap. 2.25 (ISBN 0-440-44369-5). Dell.

Vincent, Gabrielle. Smile, Ernest & Celestine. LC 82-1075. (Illus.). 24p. (ps-3). 1982. 10.75 (ISBN 0-688-01247-7); PLB 11.88 (ISBN 0-688-01249-3). Greenwillow.

HARBORS

see also Pilots and Pilotage

Carter, Katherine. Ships & Seaports. LC 82-4463. (Illus.). (gr. k-4). 1982. PLB 14.60 (ISBN 0-516-01656-3); pap. 4.95 (ISBN 0-516-41656-1). Childrens.

Crews, Donald. Harbor. Crews, Donald, illus. LC 81-6607. 32p. (ps-1). 1982. 11.75 (ISBN 0-688-00861-5); PLB 14.88 (ISBN 0-688-00862-3). Greenwillow.

Dupasquier, Philippe. The Harbor. Dupasquier, Philippe, illus. LC 83-16530. 24p. (ps-1). 1984. 3.95 (ISBN 0-448-19053-2, G&D). Putnam Pub Group.

Riegel, Martin P. Ghost Ports of the Pacific, Vol. I: California. LC 89-90772. (Illus.). 52p. (Orig.). 1989. 11.00 (ISBN 0-944871-18-6); pap. 4.95 (ISBN 0-944871-19-4). Riegel Pub.

—Ghost Ports of the Pacific, Vol. II: Oregon. LC 89-90772. (Illus.). 52p. (Orig.). 1989. 11.00 (ISBN 0-944871-20-8); pap. 4.95 (ISBN 0-944871-21-6). Riegel Pub.

HARBORS–FICTION

Harwood, Pearl A. Mrs. Moon's Harbor Trip. Overlie, George, illus. LC 67-15692. 32p. (gr. k-3). 1967. PLB 4.95 (ISBN 0-8225-0116-3). Lerner Pubns.

HARDING, WARREN GAMALIEL, PRESIDENT U. S. 1865-1923

Canadeo, Anne. Warren G. Harding: Twenty-Ninth President of the United States. Young, Richard G., ed. LC 89-39952. (Illus.). 128p. (gr. 5-9). 1990. PLB 17.26 (ISBN 0-944483-64-X). Garrett Ed Corp.

Wade, Linda R. Warren G. Harding. LC 88-38057. (Illus.). 100p. (gr. 3 up). 1989. PLB 17.27 (ISBN 0-516-01368-8). Childrens.

HARES

see Rabbits

HARLEM, NEW YORK (CITY)–FICTION

Mohr, Nicholasa. Nilda. Mohr, Nicholasa, illus. LC 73-8046. 272p. (gr. 5 up). 1973. HarpC Child Bks.

Smalls, Hector I. Irene & the Big, Fine Nickel, Vol. 1. (ps-3). 1991. 14.95 (ISBN 0-316-79871-1). Little.

HARRISON, BENJAMIN, PRESIDENT U. S. 1833-1901

Stevens, Rita. Benjamin Harrison: Twenty-Third President of the United States. Young, Richard G., ed. LC 88-24747. (Illus.). (gr. 5-9). 1989. PLB 17.26 (ISBN 0-944483-15-1). Garrett Ed Corp.

HARRISON, WILLIAM HENRY, PRESIDENT U. S. 1773-1841

Fitz-Gerald, C. William Henry Harrison. LC 87-16842. (Illus.). 100p. (gr. 3 up). 1987. PLB 17.27 (ISBN 0-516-01392-0). Childrens.

Stefoff, Rebecca. William Henry Harrison: Ninth President of the United States. Young, Richard G., ed. LC 89-25652. (Illus.). 128p. (gr. 5-9). 1990. PLB 17.26 (ISBN 0-944483-54-2). Garrett Ed Corp.

HATS

Morris, Ann. Hats, Hats, Hats. Heyman, Ken, photos by. LC 88-26676. (Illus.). 32p. (ps-2). 1989. 13.95 (ISBN 0-688-06338-1); PLB 13.88 (ISBN 0-688-06339-X). Lothrop.

HATS–FICTION

Adams, Pam. Mrs. Honey's Hat. (Illus.). 24p. (ps-2). 1980. 5.50 (ISBN 0-85953-099-X, Pub. by Child's Play England). Childs Play.

Berenstain, Stan & Berenstain, Janice. Old Hat, New Hat. (Illus.). (ps-1). 1970. 6.95 (ISBN 0-394-80669-7, Random Juv); lib. bdg. 6.99 (ISBN 0-394-90669-1). Random.

Blos, Joan W. Martin's Hats. Simont, Marc, illus. LC 83-13389. 32p. (ps-3). 1984. 11.95 (ISBN 0-688-02027-5); PLB 11.88 (ISBN 0-688-02033-X, Morrow Jr Bks). Morrow Jr Bks.

—Martin's Hats. LC 83-13389. (Illus.). 32p. (ps-3). 1984. pap. 3.95 (ISBN 0-688-07039-6, Mulberry). Morrow.

Christelow, Eileen. Olive & the Magic Hat. Christelow, Eileen, illus. LC 87-672. 32p. (gr. k-3). 1987. 12.95 (ISBN 0-89919-513-X, Pub. by Clarion). Ticknor & Fields.

Clark, Emma C. Catch That Hat! LC 89-34881. (Illus.). (ps-2). 1990. 12.95 (ISBN 0-316-14496-7). Little.

Cousins, Lucy. Portly's Hat. Cousins, Lucy, illus. 32p. (ps-1). 1989. 6.95 (ISBN 0-525-44457-2, DCB). Dutton Child Bks.

Cushman, Doug. Uncle Foster's Hat Tree. Cushman, Doug, illus. LC 88-3573. 48p. (ps-3). 1988. 9.95 (ISBN 0-525-44410-6, DCB). Dutton Child Bks.

Dr. Seuss. The Five Hundred Hats of Bartholomew Cubbins. Dr. Seuss, illus. LC 88-38412. 48p. (ps-3). 1989. Repr. of 1938 ed. 9.95 (ISBN 0-394-84484-X); lib. bdg. 8.99 (ISBN 0-394-94484-4). Random.

Harwood, Pearl A. Mrs. Moon's Cement Hat. Overlie, George, illus. LC 67-15696. 32p. (gr. k-3). 1967. PLB 4.95 (ISBN 0-8225-0120-1). Lerner Pubns.

Hines, Anna G. Keep Your Old Hat. 24p. (ps-1). 1987. 8.95 (ISBN 0-525-44299-5, 0869-260, DCB). Dutton Child Bks.

Johnston, Tony. The Witch's Hat. Tomes, Margot, illus. LC 84-9948. 32p. (ps-3). 1984. 9.95 (ISBN 0-399-21010-5, Putnam). Putnam Pub Group.

Keats, Ezra J. Jennie's Hat. Keats, Ezra J., illus. LC 66-15683. 32p. (gr. k-3). 1966. 13.95i (ISBN 0-06-023113-0); PLB 13.89 (ISBN 0-06-023114-9). HarpC Child Bks.

Lear, Edward. The Quangle Wangle's Hat. Stevens, Janet, illus. 32p. (ps-3). 1988. 12.95 (ISBN 0-15-264450-4). HarBraceJ.

Leemis, Ralph. Mister Momboo's Hat. Bassett, Jeni, illus. LC 90-34397. 24p. (ps-k). 1991. 11.95 (ISBN 0-525-65045-8, Cobblehill Bks). Dutton Child Bks.

Mariana. Miss Flora McFlimsey's Easter Bonnet. rev. ed. Mariana, illus. LC 86-15268. 40p. (gr. k-3). 1987. 9.95 (ISBN 0-688-04535-9); PLB 8.88 (ISBN 0-688-04536-7). Lothrop.

Miller, Margaret. Whose Hat? LC 86-18324. (Illus.). 40p. (ps-1). 1988. 13.95 (ISBN 0-688-06906-1); lib. bdg. 13.88 (ISBN 0-688-06907-X). Greenwillow.

Parr, Letitia. A Man & His Hat. (Illus.). 32p. (ps-2). 1991. 13.95 (ISBN 0-399-22255-3, Philomel Bks). Putnam Pub Group.

Reiss, Elayne & Friedman, Rita. Hat Helpers Hullaballoo. (gr. k-1). 10.50 (ISBN 0-89796-868-9). New Dimens Educ.

Roy, Ron. Whose Hat Is That? Hausherr, Rosemarie, photos by. (Illus.). 40p. (ps-3). 1990. pap. 4.95 (ISBN 0-395-54778-4, Clarion Bks). HM.

Scarry, Richard. Be Careful, Mr. Frumble! Scarry, Richard, illus. LC 89-43154. 24p. (Orig.). (ps-2). 1990. pap. 2.25 (ISBN 0-679-80566-4). Random.

Shelly, Walt & Stangl, Jean. Hats, Hats, & More Hats. (gr. 1-5). 1989. pap. 9.95 (ISBN 0-8224-3602-7). Fearon Teach Aids.

Slobodkina, Esphyr. Caps for Sale. Slobodkina, Esphyr, illus. LC 84-43122. 1947. 10.95 (ISBN 0-201-09147-X); PLB 11.89 (ISBN 0-06-025778-4). HarpC Child Bks.

Vicky's New Hat. 1989. 2.99 (ISBN 0-517-69124-8). Outlet Bk Co.

HAUNTED HOUSES

see Ghosts

HAWAII

Bauer, Helen. Hawaii: The Aloha State. rev. ed. Rayson, Ann, rev. by. McCurdy, Bruce S., illus. LC 82-72319. 192p. (gr. 4-7). 1982. 22.95 (ISBN 0-935848-13-4); pap. 15.95 (ISBN 0-935848-15-0); wkbk. 5.95 (ISBN 0-935848-34-7); tchr's. manual 5.00 (ISBN 0-685-06217-1). Bess Pr.

Bellerose, Albert J. Princess Kaiulani: Color Me Hawaii. (Illus.). 128p. (gr. k-6). 1990. pap. 7.95 (ISBN 0-935848-84-3). Bess Pr.

Bisignani, J. D. Big Island Handbook. (Illus.). 347p. (Orig.). 1990. pap. 11.95 (ISBN 0-918373-47-6). Moon Pubns CA.

—Oahu Handbook. (Illus.). 350p. (Orig.). 1990. pap. 11.95 (ISBN 0-918373-49-2). Moon Pubns CA.

Carole Marsh Hawaii Books, 31 bks. Set. 638.45 (ISBN 0-7933-1286-8). Gallopade Pub Group.

Carpenter, Allan. Hawaii. LC 79-9991. (Illus.). 96p. (gr. 4 up). 1979. PLB 19.93 (ISBN 0-516-04111-8). Childrens.

Dunford, Elizabeth P. The Hawaiians of Old. rev. ed. Kudlak, Aimee A., illus. 220p. (gr. 4 up). 1987. text ed. 20.95 (ISBN 0-935848-00-2); pap. text ed. 15.95 (ISBN 0-935848-01-0); wkbk 5.95 (ISBN 0-935848-08-8); tchr's. manual 5.00 (ISBN 0-935848-09-6). Bess Pr.

Durkin, Pat. The Kaua'i Guide to Beaches & Water Activities with Safety Tips. rev. ed. Ida, Gerald, et al, illus. 80p. pap. 2.50 (ISBN 0-942255-08-9, G4-2). Magic Fishes Pr.

—The Kaua'i Guide to Beaches, Water Activities & Safety. Kauai County Planning Dept. Staff, illus. 64p. (Orig.). 1988. pap. 2.50 (ISBN 0-942255-05-4, G4). Magic Fishes Pr.

Feeney, Stephanie. A Is for Aloha. Reese, Jeff, photos by. LC 85-50569. (Illus.). 64p. (ps-3). 1985. 8.95 (ISBN 0-8248-0722-7). UH Pr.

Fradin, Dennis. Hawaii: In Words & Pictures. LC 79-25605. (Illus.). 48p. (gr. 2-5). 1980. PLB 15.93 (ISBN 0-516-03913-X). Childrens.

Ikemoto, Glenn Y. The Kaua'i Guide to Freshwater Sport Fishing. Boynton, David, photos by. (Illus.). 64p. (Orig.). 1989. pap. 2.50 (ISBN 0-942255-07-0, G6). Magic Fishes Pr.

Jacobsen, Peter & Kristensen, Preben. A Family in Hawaii. LC 85-73677. (Illus.). 32p. (gr. 1-6). 1986. PLB 11.90 (ISBN 0-531-18084-0, Pub. by Bookwright). Watts.

Jobson, Joy. The Kaua'i Guide to Kaua'i Products & Speciality Shopping. Stanger, Susan E., illus. 64p. (Orig.). 1988. pap. 2.50 (ISBN 0-942255-03-8, G2). Magic Fishes Pr.

The Kaua'i Guide. 96p. (Orig.). pap. 2.50 (ISBN 0-942255-01-1, G1 & UP). Magic Fishes Pr.

Kikukawa, Cecily H. Ka Mea Ho'ala, the Awakener: The Story of Henry Obookiah. Burningham, Robin, illus. LC 82-70246. 100p. (Orig.). (gr. 7-10). 1982. pap. 6.95 (ISBN 0-935848-10-X). Bess Pr.

Lye, Keith. Take a Trip to Hawaii. Franklin Watts Ltd., ed. (Illus.). 32p. (ps-9). 1988. PLB 7.99 (ISBN 0-531-10466-4). Watts.

McNair, Sylvia. Hawaii. LC 89-35084. 144p. (gr. 4 up). 1989. PLB 25.27 (ISBN 0-516-00457-3). Childrens.

Marsh, Carole. Avast, Ye Slobs! Hawaii Pirate Trivia. (Illus.). (gr. 3-12). 1990. PLB 19.95 (ISBN 0-7933-0352-4); pap. 14.95 (ISBN 0-7933-0351-6); computer disk 29.95 (ISBN 0-7933-0353-2). Gallopade Pub Group.

—The Beast of the Hawaii Bed & Breakfast. (Illus.). (gr. 3-12). 1990. PLB 19.95 (ISBN 0-7933-1531-X); pap. 14.95 (ISBN 0-7933-1532-8); computer disk 29.95 (ISBN 0-7933-1533-6). Gallopade Pub Group.

—The Hard-to-Believe-But-True! Book of Hawaii History, Mystery, Trivia, Legend, Lore, Humor & More. (Illus.). (gr. 3-12). 1990. PLB 19.95 (ISBN 0-7933-0349-4); pap. 14.95 (ISBN 0-7933-0348-6); computer disk 29.95 (ISBN 0-7933-0350-8). Gallopade Pub Group.

—Hawaii & Other State Greats (Biographies) (Illus.). (gr. 3-12). 1990. PLB 19.95 (ISBN 1-55609-577-5); pap. 14.95 (ISBN 1-55609-576-7); computer disk 29.95 (ISBN 0-7933-1539-5). Gallopade Pub Group.

—Hawaii Bandits, Bushwackers, Outlaws, Crooks, Devils, Ghosts, Desperadoes & Other Assorted & Sundry Characters! (Illus.). (gr. 3-12). 1990. PLB 19.95 (ISBN 0-7933-0334-6); pap. 14.95 (ISBN 0-7933-0333-8); computer disk 29.95 (ISBN 0-7933-0335-4). Gallopade Pub Group.

—Hawaii Classic Christmas Trivia: Stories, Recipes, Activities, Legends, Lore & More! (Illus.). (gr. 3-12). 1990. PLB 19.95 (ISBN 0-7933-0337-0); pap. 14.95 (ISBN 0-7933-0336-2); computer disk 29.95 (ISBN 0-7933-0338-9). Gallopade Pub Group.

—Hawaii Coastales. (Illus.). (gr. 3-12). 1990. PLB 19.95 (ISBN 1-55609-573-2); pap. 14.95 (ISBN 1-55609-572-4); computer disk 29.95 (ISBN 0-7933-1535-2). Gallopade Pub Group.

—The Hawaii Hot Air Balloon Mystery. (Illus.). (gr. 2-9). 1990. 19.95 (ISBN 0-7933-2417-3); pap. 14.95 (ISBN 0-7933-2418-1); computer disk 29.95 (ISBN 0-7933-2419-X). Gallopade Pub Group.

—Hawaii "Jography" A Fun Run Thru Our State! (Illus.). (gr. 3-12). 1990. PLB 19.95 (ISBN 1-55609-568-6); pap. 14.95 (ISBN 1-55609-567-8); computer disk 29.95 (ISBN 0-7933-1525-5). Gallopade Pub Group.

—Hawaii Kid's Cookbook: Recipes, How-to, History, Lore & More! (Illus.). (gr. 3-12). 1990. PLB 19.95 (ISBN 0-7933-0346-X); pap. 14.95 (ISBN 0-7933-0345-1); computer disk 29.95 (ISBN 0-7933-0347-8). Gallopade Pub Group.

—Hawaii Quiz Bowl Crash Course! (Illus.). (gr. 3-12). 1990. PLB 19.95 (ISBN 1-55609-575-9); pap. 14.95 (ISBN 1-55609-574-0); computer disk 29.95 (ISBN 0-7933-1534-4). Gallopade Pub Group.

—Hawaii School Trivia: An Amazing & Fascinating Look at Our State's Teachers, Schools & Students! (Illus.). (gr. 3-12). 1990. PLB 19.95 (ISBN 0-7933-0343-5); pap. 14.95 (ISBN 0-7933-0342-7); computer disk 29.95 (ISBN 0-7933-0344-3). Gallopade Pub Group.

—Hawaii Silly Basketball Sports Mysteries. (Illus.). (gr. 3-12). 1990. PLB 19.95 (ISBN 0-7933-1540-9); pap. 14.95 (ISBN 0-7933-1541-7); computer disk 29.95 (ISBN 0-7933-1542-5). Gallopade Pub Group.

—Hawaii: Silly Basketball Sportsmysteries, Vol. I. (Illus.). (gr. 3-12). 1990. PLB 19.95 (ISBN 0-7933-0340-0); pap. 14.95 (ISBN 0-7933-0339-7); computer disk 29.95 (ISBN 0-7933-0341-9). Gallopade Pub Group.

—Hawaii Silly Football Sportsmysteries, Vol. I. (Illus.). (gr. 3-12). 1990. PLB 19.95 (ISBN 1-55609-571-6); pap. 14.95 (ISBN 1-55609-570-8); computer disk 29.95 (ISBN 0-7933-1527-1). Gallopade Pub Group.

—Hawaii Silly Football Sportsmysteries, Vol. II. (Illus.). (gr. 3-12). 1990. PLB 19.95 (ISBN 0-7933-1528-X); pap. 14.95 (ISBN 0-7933-1529-8); computer disk 29.95 (ISBN 0-7933-1530-1). Gallopade Pub Group.

—Hawaii Silly Trivia! (Illus.). (gr. 3-12). 1990. PLB 19.95 (ISBN 1-55609-566-X); pap. 14.95 (ISBN 1-55609-565-1); computer disk 29.95 (ISBN 0-7933-1524-7). Gallopade Pub Group.

—Hawaii's (Most Devastating!) Disasters & (Most Calamitous!) Catastrophies! (Illus.). (gr. 3-12). 1990. PLB 19.95 (ISBN 0-7933-0331-1); pap. 14.95 (ISBN 0-7933-0330-3); computer disk 29.95 (ISBN 0-7933-0332-X). Gallopade Pub Group.

—If My Hawaii Mama Ran the World! (Illus.). (gr. 3-12). 1990. PLB 19.95 (ISBN 0-7933-1536-0); pap. 14.95 (ISBN 0-7933-1537-9); computer disk 29.95 (ISBN 0-7933-1538-7). Gallopade Pub Group.

—Let's Quilt Hawaii & Stuff It Topographically! (Illus.). (gr. 3-12). 1990. PLB 19.95 (ISBN 1-55609-569-4); pap. 14.95 (ISBN 1-55609-093-5); computer disk 29.95 (ISBN 0-7933-1526-3). Gallopade Pub Group.

Missler, Dux. Hawaii Fun Activity Book. (Orig.). (gr. 1-6). 1986. pap. 1.95 (ISBN 0-912180-42-0). Petroglyph.

Nellist, Cassandra L. Child's First Book about Hawaii. Nellist, Cassandra L., illus. 24p. (ps). 1987. 7.95 (ISBN 0-916630-58-7). Pr Pacifica.

Oyama, Kaikilani E. The Kaua'i Guide on Ni'ihau: UniNi'ihau: M-m-m, What a Sweet Potato. Archives of the Kauai Museum Staff & Bernice P. Bishop Museum Staff, illus. (Orig.). 1988. pap. 2.50 (ISBN 0-942255-04-6, G3). Magic Fishes Pr.

Penisten, John. Honolulu. LC 89-11973. (Illus.). 60p. (gr. 3 up). 1989. PLB 12.95 (ISBN 0-87518-416-2, Dillon). Macmillan Child Grp.

Potter, Norris & Kasdon, Lawrence. The Hawaiian Monarchy. LC 82-74176. (Illus.). 256p. (gr. 5-8). 1983. 23.95 (ISBN 0-935848-17-7); pap. 15.95 (ISBN 0-935848-16-9); wkbk. 5.95 (ISBN 0-935848-31-2); Tchr's manual 5.00. Bess Pr.

Radlauer, Ruth. Haleakala National Park. updated ed. Zillmer, Rolf, illus. LC 79-10500. 48p. (gr. 3-12). 1979. PLB 17.27 (ISBN 0-516-07499-7); pap. 4.95 (ISBN 0-516-47499-5). Childrens.

—Hawaii Volcanoes National Park. updated ed. Radlauer, Ed & Radlauer, Ruth, illus. LC 78-19718. 48p. (gr. 3 up). 1979. PLB 17.27 (ISBN 0-516-07498-9, Elk Grove Bks); pap. 4.95 (ISBN 0-516-47498-7). Childrens.

Rizzuto, Shirley O. Hawaii's Pathfinders. Lawrence, Lyn, illus. LC 83-70356. 128p. (gr. 5-8). 1983. pap. 6.95 (ISBN 0-935848-19-3). Bess Pr.

Roes, Carol. Children's Christmas Hulas. (gr. k-1). 1965. pap. 35.00 incl. 4 records (ISBN 0-930932-18-8). M Loke.

—Children's Hulas from Hawaii, Bk. 5. Kaiulani, illus. 13p. (gr. 8). 1966. pap. 5.50 (ISBN 0-930932-10-2); record incl. M Loke.

—Introduction to the Hula. (Illus.). 12p. (gr. 1-3). 1961. pap. 2.50 (ISBN 0-930932-07-2). M Loke.

—Keiki Songs of Hawaii. Stone, Lloyd, illus. 26p. (gr. 6). 1966. pap. 5.50 (ISBN 0-930932-16-1). M Loke.

—Santa's Hawaiian Party. (gr. 1-8). 1966. pap. 35.00 20 minute program (ISBN 0-930932-19-6); record incl. M Loke.

—Song Stories of Hawaii. Stone, Lloyd, illus. 24p. (gr. 1-8). 1959. pap. 5.50 (ISBN 0-930932-17-X). M Loke.

Roes, Carol & Kaiulani. Children's Hulas for Song Stories, Bk. 3. Stone, L., illus. 24p. (gr. 3-4). 1963. pap. 5.50 (ISBN 0-930932-08-0); record incl. M Loke.

—Hulas for 4 Songs. 18p. (gr. 8 up). 1963. pap. 5.50 (ISBN 0-930932-09-9); record incl. M Loke.

Rublowsky, John. Born in Fire: A Geological History of Hawaii. LC 79-2001. (Illus.). 96p. (gr. 5 up). 1981. PLB 12.89 (ISBN 0-06-025089-5). HarpC Child Bks.

Stanley, Fay. The Last Princess: The Story of Princess Kaiulani of Hawaii. Stanley, Diane, illus. LC 89-71445. 40p. (gr. 1-4). 1991. RSBE 15.95 (ISBN 0-02-786785-4, Four Winds). Macmillan Child Grp.

Thompson, Vivian L. Hawaiian Legends of Tricksters & Riddlers. Wozniak, Patricia A., illus. LC 90-44432. 112p. (Orig.). (gr. 4-8). 1990. pap. 8.50 (ISBN 0-8248-1302-2, Kolowalu Bk). UH Pr.

Turner Educational Services, Inc. Staff & Clark, James I. Hawaii. 48p. (gr. 3 up). 1986. PLB 17.32 (ISBN 0-86514-451-6); pap. 9.27 (ISBN 0-86514-526-1); cancelled Beta video (ISBN 0-86514-076-6); cancelled VHS video (ISBN 0-86514-151-7); cancelled 3/4" video (ISBN 0-86514-226-2); cancelled tchr's. study guide (ISBN 0-86514-301-3); cancelled student activity bk. (ISBN 0-86514-376-5); cancelled index. Raintree Pubs.

Twain, Mark. Roughing It. Girling, Z. N., intro. by. (Illus.). (gr. 8 up). pap. 2.95 (ISBN 0-8049-0134-1, CL-134). Airmont.

Valier, Kathy. The Kaua'i Guide to Hiking Trails Less Traveled with Camping Information. (Illus.). 64p. (Orig.). 1989. pap. 2.50 (ISBN 0-942255-06-2, G5). Magic Fishes Pr.

HAWAII–FICTION

Ehlers, Sabine. The Bossy Hawaiian Moon. Kiyabu, Walter H., illus. 32p. (ps-1). 1980. pap. 2.95 (ISBN 0-930492-15-3). Hawaiian Serv.

Feeney, Stephanie. Hawaii Is a Rainbow. Hammid, Hella, illus. LC 80-5462. 64p. (ps-k). 1980. 12.95 (ISBN 0-8248-1007-4). UH Pr.

Goudge, Eileen. Hawaiian Christmas. (gr. 6 up). 1986. pap. 2.95 (ISBN 0-440-93649-7, LFL). Dell.

Hober, David. Kobi the Elf, Magic & Adventure in Hawaii. Pickett, Timothy & Okaze, Kunio, eds. Nagaoki, Kobun, tr. Fontilis, Glen, illus. (ENG & JPN.). 32p. (Orig.). (gr. 1 up). 1990. pap. 4.95 (ISBN 0-9623215-0-8). Moonbeam Magic Pub.

Hope, Laura L. Bobbsey Twins in Volcano Land. (Illus.). (gr. 1-4). 1961. 2.95 (ISBN 0-448-08054-0, G&D). Putnam Pub Group.

Oetting. Keiki of the Islands. LC 71-108728. (Illus.). 96p. (gr. 3 up). 1970. PLB 10.95 (ISBN 0-87783-018-5); pap. 3.94 deluxe ed. (ISBN 0-87783-096-7). Oddo.

Olsen, E. A. Killer in the Trap. Le Blanc, L., illus. LC 68-16399. 48p. (gr. 3 up). 1970. PLB 10.95 (ISBN 0-87783-019-3); pap. 3.94 deluxe ed. (ISBN 0-87783-097-5); cassette 10.60x (ISBN 0-87783-190-4). Oddo.

Pitchford, Gene. Young Folks' Hawaiian Time. (Illus.). (ps). 1965. pap. 2.00 (ISBN 0-87505-275-4). Borden.

Roddy, Lee. The Legend of Fire: A Ladd Family Adventure. rev. ed. Kobobel, Janet, ed. 148p. (gr. 3-6). 1988. pap. 4.99 (ISBN 0-929608-17-8). Focus Family.

Roop, Peter. The Cry of the Conch. Patric, illus. LC 84-4232. (gr. 3-5). 1984. 6.95 (ISBN 0-916630-39-0). Pr Pacifica.

Salter-Mathieson, Nigel. Little Chief Mischief. Gruen, Chuck, illus. (gr. 2-7). 1962. 10.95 (ISBN 0-8392-3020-6). Astor-Honor.

Slepian, Jan. The Broccoli Tapes. (gr. 3-7). 1989. 13.95 (ISBN 0-399-21712-6, Philomel Bks). Putnam Pub Group.

Tabrah, Ruth M. Emily's Hawaii. Hall, Pat, illus. 191p. (gr. 4-6). 1986. pap. 6.95 (ISBN 0-916630-45-5). Pr PaCifica.

HAWAII–HISTORY–FICTION

Gomes, Bernadette. Maile & the Marvelous One. Hall, Pat, illus. LC 84-4715. (gr. 3-6). 1984. 6.95 (ISBN 0-916630-40-4). Pr Pacifica.

Yamashita, Susan. The Menehune & the Nene. O'Connor, Barbara, illus. LC 84-3290. (gr. 3-6). 1984. 6.95 (ISBN 0-916630-42-0). Pr Pacifica.

HAWKS–FICTION

Balaban, John. The Hawk's Tale. Delamare, David, illus. LC 87-14938. 160p. (gr. 8-12). 1988. 14.95 (ISBN 0-15-200462-9, Gulliver Bks). HarBraceJ.

Baylor, Byrd. Hawk, I'm Your Brother. reissued ed. Parnall, Peter, illus. LC 86-10742. 48p. (gr. 1-5). 1986. pap. 3.95 (ISBN 0-689-71102-6, Aladdin). Macmillan Child Grp.

Dickinson, Peter. The Blue Hawk. (gr. 5-9). 1991. 21.50 (ISBN 0-8446-6478-2). Peter Smith.

Le Sueur, Meridel. Sparrow Hawk. DesJarlait, Robert, illus. LC 87-80573. 176p. (gr. 7 up). 1987. Repr. of 1950 ed. 13.95 (ISBN 0-930100-22-0). Holy Cow.

HAYDN, FRANZ JOSEPH, 1732-1809

Great Composers, Bk. 2: Handel, Hayden, Schubert. (Illus.). (gr. 5 up). 3.50 (ISBN 0-7214-0242-9). Ladybird Bks.

HAYES, RUTHERFORD BIRCHARD, PRESIDENT U. S. 1822-1893

Kent, Zachary. Rutherford B. Hayes. LC 88-8679. (Illus.). 100p. (gr. 3 up). 1989. PLB 17.27 (ISBN 0-516-01365-3). Childrens.

Robbins, Neal E. Rutherford B. Hayes: Nineteenth President of the United States. Young, Richard G., ed. LC 88-24565. (Illus.). (gr. 5-9). 1989. PLB 17.26 (ISBN 0-944483-23-2). Garrett Ed Corp.

HEALTH

see Hygiene

Orlandi, Mario, et al. Nutrition. (Illus.). 128p. 1988. 18.95x (ISBN 0-8160-1670-4). Facts on File.

HEALTH, MENTAL

see Mental Health

HEALTH, PUBLIC

see Public Health

HEALTH EDUCATION

Aemmer, Gail. Good Health Fun Book. Rittenour, Gary, illus. 32p. (ps-1). 1984. pap. 1.59 (ISBN 0-88724-062-3, CD-8053). Carson-Dellos.

Arnold, Caroline. Pain: What Is It? How Do We Deal with It? LC 86-29815. (Illus.). 96p. (gr. 3-7). 1986. 12.95 (ISBN 0-688-05710-1); lib. bdg. 12.88 (ISBN 0-688-05711-X, Morrow Jr Bks). Morrow Jr Bks.

Carratello, Patricia. Let's Investigate Health & Safety. Carratello, Patricia, illus. 48p. (gr. 1-4). 1984. wkbk. 5.95 (ISBN 1-55734-214-8). Tchr Create Mat.

Darling, Kathy. Safe Kids, Healthy Kids. (Illus.). 64p. (ps-2). 1989. 6.95 (ISBN 0-912107-92-8, MM1909). Monday Morning Bks.

Groomer, Vera. Growing Stronger: Two - Two. 32p. (ps). 1980. pap. 2.15 (ISBN 0-8127-0271-9). Review & Herald.

Ransford, Lynn. Happy Healthy Bodies. (Illus.). 48p. (gr. 1-4). 1987. wkbk. 5.95 (ISBN 1-55734-223-7). Tchr Create Mat.

Rayner, Claire. The Getting Better Book. King, Tony, illus. 48p. (gr. 1-4). 1989. 11.95 (ISBN 0-233-97750-3). Andre Deutsch.

Skolnick, Georgette B. To Be a Doctor: A Health Education Workbook. Barr, Charlotte & Cook, Tonya, illus. 215p. (Orig.). (gr. 6-9). 1982. student's wkbk. 8.00 (ISBN 0-913855-00-6). GBS CA.

Sullivan, Dianna J. Big & Easy Health. Adkins, Lynda, illus. 48p. (ps-2). 1988. wkbk. 5.95 (ISBN 1-55734-104-4). Tchr Create Mat.

HEALTH OF CHILDREN

see Children–Care and Hygiene

HEARING

see also Ear

Allington, Richard L. & Krull, Kathleen. Hearing. Dober, Wayne, illus. LC 79-28387. 32p. (gr. k-3). 1985. PLB 15.33 (ISBN 0-8172-1291-4); pap. 9.27 (ISBN 0-8172-2479-3). Raintree Pubs.

Berry, Joy W. Teach Me about Listening. Dickey, Kate, ed. LC 85-45087. (Illus.). 36p. (ps). 1986. 4.98 (ISBN 0-685-10726-4). Grolier Inc.

Decker, Nan. The Caption Workbook. Drescher, Joan, illus. 27p. (gr. 5-8). 1984. pap. text ed. 3.50x (ISBN 0-913072-61-3). Natl Assn Deaf.

Gardner, Karen A. My Life As an Ear. rev. ed. (Illus.). 37p. (ps-2). Set of 1-4. PLB 1.70 (ISBN 0-931421-01-2). Hlth Pub SF.

Hearing. (ps). 1976. 2.95 (ISBN 0-900195-57-6, Brimax Bks). Borden.

Moncure, Jane B. Sounds All Around, No. 26-32. Axeman, Lois, illus. LC 82-4516. 32p. (ps-3). 1982. PLB 14.60 (ISBN 0-516-03252-6); pap. 3.95 (ISBN 0-516-43252-4). Childrens.

Parramon, J. M. & Puig, J. J. Hearing. Rius, Maria, illus. 32p. (Orig.). (ps). 1985. pap. 4.95 ea. (ISBN 0-8120-3563-1). Span. ed (ISBN 0-8120-3606-9). Barron.

Pluckrose, Henry. Hearing. Fairclough, Chris, photos by. 32p. (gr. k-3). 1986. lib. bdg. 7.99 (ISBN 0-531-10170-3). Watts.

Pomeroy, Johanna P. Content Area Reading Skills Sound & Hearing: Detecting Sequence. (Illus.). (gr. 4). 1987. pap. text ed. 3.25 (ISBN 0-89525-860-9). Ed Activities.

Richarson, Joy. What Happens When You Listen? LC 86-3729. (Illus.). 32p. (gr. 2-3). 1986. PLB 10.95 (ISBN 1-55532-108-9). Gareth Stevens Inc.

Showers, Paul. Ears Are for Hearing. Keller, Holly, illus. LC 89-17479. 32p. (gr. k-4). 1990. 13.95 (ISBN 0-690-04718-5, Crowell Jr Bks); PLB 13.89 (ISBN 0-690-04720-7, Crowell Jr Bks). HarpC Child Bks.

—Listening Walk. Aliki, illus. LC 61-10495. 40p. (gr. k-3). 1961. PLB 13.89 (ISBN 0-690-49663-X, Crowell Jr Bks). HarpC Child Bks.

Smith, Kathie B. & Crenson, Victoria. Hearing. Storms, Robert S., illus. LC 87-5854. 24p. (gr. k-4). 1988. PLB 9.59 (ISBN 0-8167-1006-6); pap. text ed. 1.95 (ISBN 0-8167-1007-4). Troll Assocs.

Stoker, Richard G. & Gaydos, Janine. Hearing Aids for You & the Zoo. (Illus.). 32p. (gr. k-3). 1984. pap. 4.95 (ISBN 0-317-13888-X). Alexander Graham.

Ward, Brian. The Ear & Hearing. LC 80-54826. (Illus.). 48p. (gr. 4 up). 1981. lib. bdg. 12.40 (ISBN 0-531-04289-8). Watts.

HEART

see also Blood–Circulation

Bailey, Donna. All about Heart & Blood. LC 90-10052. (Illus.). 48p. (gr. 2-5). 1990. PLB 15.96 (ISBN 0-8114-2779-X). Steck-V.

Dunbar, Robert E. Heart & Circulatory System Projects for Young Scientist. 1989. pap. 5.95 (ISBN 0-531-15132-8). Watts.

Heart & Blood. 48p. (gr. 5-8). 1988. PLB 12.98 (ISBN 0-382-09700-9); 9.74s.p. (ISBN 0-685-24608-6). Silver Burdett Pr.

LeMaster, Leslie J. Your Heart & Blood. LC 84-7604. (Illus.). 48p. (gr. k-4). 1984. PLB 14.60 (ISBN 0-516-01933-3); pap. 4.95 (ISBN 0-516-41933-1). Childrens.

Parker, Steve. The Heart & Blood. rev. ed. (Illus.). 48p. (gr. 5 up). 1991. pap. 4.95 (ISBN 0-531-24604-3). Watts.

Saunderson, Jane. Heart & Lungs. Farmer, Andrew & Green, Robina, illus. LC 90-42881. 32p. (gr. 4-6). 1991. PLB 11.89 (ISBN 0-8167-2096-7); pap. text ed. 3.95 (ISBN 0-8167-2097-5). Troll Assocs.

Showers, Paul. Hear Your Heart. Low, Joseph, illus. LC 68-11067. 40p. (gr. k-3). 1968. PLB 12.89 (ISBN 0-690-37379-1, Crowell Jr Bks). HarpC Child Bks.

Silverstein, Alvin & Silverstein, Virginia B. Heartbeats: Your Body, Your Heart. Ormai, Stella, illus. LC 82-48465. 64p. (gr. 3-5). 1983. PLB 13.89 (ISBN 0-397-32038-8, Lipp Jr Bks). HarpC Child Bks.

Ward, Brian. The Heart & Blood. (Illus.). 48p. (gr. 4 up). 1982. PLB 12.40 (ISBN 0-531-04357-6). Watts.

HEART–DISEASES
Arnold, Caroline. Heart Disease. (Illus.). 96p. (gr. 9-12). 1990. PLB 12.40 (ISBN 0-531-10884-8). Watts.

Dunbar, Robert E. Heart & Circulatory System. (Illus.). 128p. (gr. 7-12). 1984. lib. bdg. 12.90 (ISBN 0-531-04766-0). Watts.

Galperin, Anne. Stroke & Heart Disease. (Illus.). (gr. 6-12). 1991. 18.95 (ISBN 0-7910-0077-X). Chelsea Hse.

Re'lem, Dyob & Melger, Boyd A. Hoge Bloeddruk, Myocardiale Infarct, Grafieken. (DUT., Illus.). 69p. (Orig.). (gr. 12 up). 1989. pap. write for info. (ISBN 0-9622463-1-X). B Melger.

Silverstein, Alvin & Silverstein, Virginia B. Heart Disease: America's Number One Killer. rev. ed. LC 83-49495. (Illus.). 160p. (gr. 7 up). 1985. 12.95 (ISBN 0-397-32083-3, Lipp Jr Bks); PLB 12.89 (ISBN 0-397-32084-1, Lipp Jr Bks). HarpC Child Bks.

Tiger, Steven. Heart Disease. LC 85-8949. (Illus.). 72p. (gr. 4-8). 1986. lib. bdg. 11.98 (ISBN 0-671-60021-4). Messner.

HEAT
see also Fire; Temperature; Thermodynamics; Thermometers and Thermometry
Arvetis, Chris. Why Is It Cold? Buckley, James, illus. 32p. (ps-3). 1987. write for info. (ISBN 0-02-689005-4). Checkerboard Pr.

Branley, Franklyn M. Shivers & Goose Bumps: How We Keep Warm. Kelley, True, illus. LC 82-45921. 96p. (gr. 5 up). 1984. (Crowell Jr Bks); PLB 12.89 (ISBN 0-690-04335-X, Crowell Jr Bks). HarpC Child Bks.

Heat. (Illus.). 56p. (gr. 7-10). 1990. 8.80 (ISBN 0-941008-85-1). Tops Learning.

Jennings, Terry. Heat. LC 88-22865. (Illus.). 32p. (gr. 3-6). 1989. PLB 14.60 (ISBN 0-516-08403-8); pap. 4.95 (ISBN 0-516-48403-6). Childrens.

Lafferty, Peter. Burning & Melting: Projects with Heat. (Illus.). 32p. (gr. 5-8). 1990. PLB 11.90 (ISBN 0-531-17235-X). Watts.

Maury, Jean-Pierre. Heat & Cold. 80p. (gr. 8 up). 1989. pap. 4.95 (ISBN 0-8120-4211-5). Barron.

Santrey, Laurence. Heat. Birmingham, Lloyd, illus. LC 84-2711. 32p. (gr. 3-6). 1985. PLB 9.49 (ISBN 0-8167-0306-X); pap. text ed. 2.95 (ISBN 0-8167-0307-8). Troll Assocs.

Whyman, Kathryn. Heat & Energy. (Illus.). 32p. (gr. 1-6). 1986. PLB 11.90 (ISBN 0-531-17022-5, Pub. by Gloucester). Watts.

HEAT–EXPERIMENTS
Gould, Alan. Convection: A Current Event. Bergman, Lincoln & Fairwell, Kay, eds. Klofkorn, Lisa, illus. Hoyt, Richard, photos by. (Illus.). 38p. (Orig.). (gr. 6-9). 1988. pap. 6.50 (ISBN 0-912511-15-X). Lawrence Science.

Oleksy, Walter. Experiments with Heat. LC 85-30860. (Illus.). 48p. (gr. k-4). 1986. PLB 14.60 (ISBN 0-516-01277-0); pap. 4.95 (ISBN 0-516-41277-9). Childrens.

HEAT–FICTION
Fleishman, Seymour. Too Hot in Potzburg. LC 81-11498. (Illus.). 32p. (ps-3). 1981. PLB 11.50 (ISBN 0-8075-8024-4). A Whitman.

HEAVEN
Delp, Debra. Packing for Heaven. Zoglio, Suzanne, ed. Larsen, Rob, illus. 32p. (Orig.). (gr. k-5). 1991. pap. text ed. 8.95 (ISBN 0-941668-03-7). Tower Hill Pr.

Hillis, Don. Heaven Is Out of This World. (Illus.). 47p. 1982. pap. 2.25 (ISBN 0-89323-032-4). Bible Memory.

HEBREW LANGUAGE
Amery & Haron. First Thousand Words in Hebrew. Cartwright, Stephen, illus. 62p. (ps-6). 1985. PLB 11.95 (ISBN 0-86020-863-X, Pub. by Usborne). EDC.

Bachrach, Kalman. Hasefer Alef-Beis Hametzuyar (In Color) Gordon, Ayalah, illus. (HEB.). 67p. (gr. 1). 1960. pap. text ed. 2.50x (ISBN 1-878530-01-1). K Bachrach Co.

—Hasefer Chelek Rishon, Pt. 1: Alef-Beis. Soyer, Yitzhak, illus. (HEB.). 68p. (gr. 1). 1941. pap. text ed. 2.25x (ISBN 1-878530-00-3). K Bachrach Co.

—Hasefer Chelek Sheini, Pt. 2. Krukman, Tsvi, illus. (HEB.). 91p. (gr. 2). 1942. pap. text ed. 2.25x (ISBN 1-878530-09-7). K Bachrach Co.

—Hasefer Chelek Shlishi, Pt. 3. Krukman, Tsvi, illus. (HEB.). 74p. (gr. 3). 1947. pap. text ed. 2.25x (ISBN 1-878530-10-0). K Bachrach Co.

—Me Ah P'Amim V'Echad - Asid (One Thousand Times & One - Future Tense) Dikduk L'Talmidim (Grammar for Students) (HEB.). 46p. (gr. 1-3). 1937. pap. text ed. 1.00x (ISBN 1-878530-21-6). K Bachrach Co.

—Meyah P'Amim V'Echad - Haveh (One Thousand Times & One - Present Tense) Dikduk L'Talmidim (Grammar for Students) (HEB.). 32p. (gr. 1-3). 1937. pap. text ed. 1.00x (ISBN 1-878530-22-4). K Bachrach Co.

—Meyah P'Amim V'Echad - Ovar (One Thousand Times & One - Past Tense) Dikduk L'Talmidim (Grammar for Students) (HEB.). 48p. (gr. 1-3). 1937. pap. text ed. 1.00x (ISBN 1-878530-20-8). K Bachrach Co.

—Targilon Hasefer Chelek Rishon, Pt. 1. (HEB.). 42p. (gr. 1). 1950. wkbk. 2.25x (ISBN 1-878530-11-9). K Bachrach Co.

—Targilon Hasefer Chelek Sheini, Pt. 2. (HEB.). 76p. (gr. 1). 1949. wkbk. 2.25x (ISBN 1-878530-12-7). K Bachrach Co.

—Targilon Hasefer Chelek Shlishi, Pt. 3. (HEB.). 60p. (gr. 3). 1953. wkbk. 2.25x (ISBN 1-878530-13-5). K Bachrach Co.

—Targilon Olami Sefer Rishon, Bk. 1. (HEB.). 54p. (gr. 2). 1936. wkbk. 2.00x (ISBN 1-878530-17-8). K Bachrach Co.

—Targilon Olami Sefer Sheini, Bk. 2. (HEB.). 54p. (gr. 3-4). 1936. wkbk. 2.00x (ISBN 1-878530-18-6). K Bachrach Co.

—Targilon Olami Sefer Shlishi, Bk. 3. (HEB.). 60p. (gr. 4-6). 1939. wkbk. 2.00x (ISBN 1-878530-19-4). K Bachrach Co.

Bachrach, Kalman & Axelrod, Herman. Ketivoni Chelek Chamishi, Pt. 5. Vanner, Vera, illus. (HEB.). 64p. (gr. 6). 1972. pap. text ed. 3.50x (ISBN 1-878530-06-2). K Bachrach Co.

—Ketivoni Chelek Rishon, Pt. 1. Krukman, Tsvi, illus. (HEB.). 72p. (gr. 2). 1957. pap. text ed. 3.50x (ISBN 1-878530-02-X). K Bachrach Co.

—Ketivoni Chelek R'Viyi, Pt. 4. Vanner, Vera, illus. (HEB.). 55p. (gr. 5). 1972. pap. text ed. 3.50x (ISBN 1-878530-05-4). K Bachrach Co.

—Ketivoni Chelek Sheni, Pt. 2. Krukman, Tsvi, illus. (HEB.). 62p. (gr. 3). 1958. pap. text ed. 3.50x (ISBN 1-878530-03-8). K Bachrach Co.

—Ketivoni Chelek Shishi, Pt. 6. Herskowitz, Sarah, illus. (HEB.). 62p. (gr. 7). 1974. pap. text ed. 3.50x (ISBN 1-878530-07-0). K Bachrach Co.

—Ketivoni Chelek Shlishi, Pt. 3. Hershkowitz, Sarah, illus. (HEB.). 64p. (gr. 4). 1959. pap. text ed. 3.50x (ISBN 1-878530-04-6). K Bachrach Co.

—Ketivoni Chelek Sh'Viyi, Pt. 7. Hershkowitz, Sarah, illus. (HEB.). 64p. (gr. 8). 1974. pap. text ed. 3.50x (ISBN 1-878530-08-9). K Bachrach Co.

Coopersmith, Harry, ed. More of the Songs We Sing. Oechsli, K., illus. (ENG & HEB.). 288p. (gr. 4-10). 1970. 9.50x (ISBN 0-8381-0217-4). United Syn Bk.

Ducoff, Helen. How to Learn Hebrew & Love It. 144p. (gr. 3-8). 1990. pap. 8.95 (ISBN 1-56171-030-X). Shapolsky Pubs.

Gaelen, Nina. The Hebrew Primer: Script Writing Workbook. 63p. (gr. 4-7). 1987. pap. text ed. 2.95x (ISBN 0-87441-416-4). Behrman.

Ganz, Yaffa. Alef To Tav. Horen, Michael, illus. 48p. (gr. 1-6). 1989. 11.95 (ISBN 0-89906-962-2); pap. 7.95 (ISBN 0-89906-963-0). Mesorah Pubns.

Goldberg, Nathan. The New Illustrated Hebrew-English Dictionary for Young Readers. (HEB & ENG., Illus.). (gr. 4-7). 1958. pap. 6.95x (ISBN 0-87068-370-5). Ktav.

Goldstein, Rose B. Songs to Share. Schloss, E., illus. (HEB & ENG.). 64p. (ps-5). 2.95x (ISBN 0-8381-0720-6, 10-720). United Syn Bk.

Helfer, Judith. Aleph Bet for You. Helfer, Judith, illus. LC 70-88355. (ps-2). 1969. pap. 3.00 (ISBN 0-88400-024-9). Shengold.

Kahn, Katherine J. Alef Is One: A Hebrew Alphabet & Counting Book. Kahn, Katherine J., illus. LC 89-24428. 48p. (ps-4). 1989. 12.95 (ISBN 0-929371-05-4); pap. 7.95 (ISBN 0-929371-04-6). Kar Ben.

Lapine, Jennifer & Lapine, Susan. My First Hebrew Alphabet Book. (Illus.). 48p. (ps-1). 1977. pap. 3.95 (ISBN 0-8197-0399-0). Bloch.

Nover, Elizabeth Z. Reading Workbook for the Hebrew Primer. 60p. (gr. 4-7). 1987. pap. 2.95 (ISBN 0-317-60046-X). Behrman.

Raban, Zvi & Kipness, Lev. The Hebrew Alphabet. (Illus.). (gr. 4 up). 1986. 9.95 (ISBN 0-915361-38-8, Dist. by Watts). Adama Pubs Inc.

Rossel, Karen T. & Mason, Patrice G. Hebrew Through Prayer, Vol. 1. 65p. (gr. 4-7). 1980. pap. text ed. 3.45x (ISBN 0-87441-313-3); wkbk. 3.25 (ISBN 0-87441-284-6); tchr's ed. 14.95 (ISBN 0-685-18651-2). Behrman.

—Hebrew Through Prayer, Vol. 2. 65p. (gr. 4-7). 1980. pap. text ed. 3.45x (ISBN 0-87441-314-1); wkbk. 3.25 (ISBN 0-87441-285-4); tchr's ed. 14.95 (ISBN 0-317-60048-6). Behrman.

Sheheen, Dennis, ed. A Child's Picture English-Hebrew Dictionary. Meshi, Ita, illus. (gr. 1-3). 1987. 9.95 (ISBN 0-915361-75-2, Dist. by Watts). Adama Pubs Inc.

Sheheen, Dennis, illus. A Child's Picture English-Yiddish Dictionary. LC 85-15659. (gr. k-2). 1985. 9.95 (ISBN 0-915361-29-9, Dist. by Watts). Adama Pubs Inc.

Shumsky, Abraham & Shumsky, Adaia. Alef-Bet: A Hebrew Primer. Bass, Marilyn & Goldman, Marvin, illus. (gr. k-3). 1979. pap. text ed. 6.00 (ISBN 0-8074-0026-2, 405309). UAHC.

Strauss, Ruby, et al. The Hebrew Primer. Brison-Stack, Guy, illus. 128p. (Orig.). (gr. 1-6). 1985. pap. 4.95 (ISBN 0-87441-392-3); tchr's guide 12.50x (ISBN 0-87441-396-6). Behrman.

Strauss, Ruby G. Let's Learn the Alef Bet: Reading Readiness Book for the Hebrew Primer. Stack-Brison, Guy, illus. 94p. (gr. 4-7). 1987. pap. text ed. 4.45x (ISBN 0-87441-439-3); tchr's pamphlet avail. Behrman.

Winter, Magda & Peery, Meira. Heritage Language Program 1-3, 3 wkbks. pap. text ed. 4.25 ea. Behrman.

Yonay, Shahar & Yonay, Rina. Systematic Hebrew, Pt. C. Einat, Tzvi, illus. (gr. 7). 1986. 13.45 (ISBN 0-9616783-0-5). S Yonay.

—Systematic Hebrew, Pt. D. (gr. 8-9). 1987. 14.95 (ISBN 0-9616783-1-3). S Yonay.

—Systematic Hebrew, Pt. B. (gr. 6). 1988. 11.95 (ISBN 0-9616783-3-X). S Yonay.

—Systematic Hebrew, Pt. A. (gr. 5). 1988. 11.95 (ISBN 0-9616783-2-1). S Yonay.

—The Test. (gr. 7-12). 1988. 14.95 (ISBN 0-9616783-4-8). S Yonay.

HEBREW LITERATURE
May use same subdivisions and names of literary forms as for English Literature.
see also Bible; Jewish Literature
Cherney, Ila. My Haggadah. Paiss, Jana, illus. 66p. (gr. 4-7). 1985. pap. text ed. 4.25 (ISBN 0-317-60058-3). Behrman.

Matov, G. Tales of Tzaddikim: Devarim. Weinbach, Shaindel, tr. Bardugo, Miriam, illus. 320p. (gr. 7-12). 1988. 13.95 (ISBN 0-89906-833-2); pap. 10.95 (ISBN 0-89906-834-0). Mesorah Pubns.

—Tales of Tzaddikim: Sh'emos. Weinbach, Shaindel, tr. from HEB. Bardvgo, Miriam, illus. 320p. (gr. 7-12). 1988. 13.95 (ISBN 0-89906-827-8); pap. 10.95 (ISBN 0-89906-828-6). Mesorah Pubns.

Nachman of Breslov. The Fixer. Succot, Miriam & Succot, Eliyah, trs. from HEB. Succot, Miriam & Succot, Eliyah, illus. (gr. 3-12). 1977. pap. 1.50 (ISBN 0-917246-04-7). Maimes.

Saypol, Judyth R. & Wikler, Madeline, illus. My Very Own Simchat Torah. 24p. (gr. k-5). 1981. pap. 2.95 (ISBN 0-930494-11-3). Kar Ben.

Scherman, Nosson. Reb Yitzchak's Jewel: Rashi's Father Gets a Reward. Dershowitz, Yosef & Horen, Michael, illus. 32p. (gr. k-6). 1988. 5.95 (ISBN 0-89906-813-8). Mesorah Pubns.

Sears, David. Tales from Reb Nachman: Parables Told by Rabbi Nachman of Breslov. Sears, David, illus. 32p. (gr. k-6). 1987. 8.95 (ISBN 0-89906-808-1); pap. 5.95 (ISBN 0-89906-809-X). Mesorah Pubns.

Weinbach, Shaindel, tr. from HEB. Tales of Tzaddikim: Bamidbar. Bardugo, Miriam, illus. 320p. (gr. 7-12). 1988. 13.95 (ISBN 0-89906-831-6); pap. 10.95 (ISBN 0-89906-832-4). Mesorah Pubns.

—Tales of Tzaddikim: Vayikra. Bardugo, Miriam, illus. 320p. (gr. 7-12). 1988. 13.95 (ISBN 0-89906-829-4); pap. 10.95 (ISBN 0-89906-830-8). Mesorah Pubns.

HEBREWS
see Jews

HEDGEHOGS–FICTION
Cartwright, Ann. The Winter Hedgehog. Cartwright, Reg, illus. LC 90-5593. 32p. (ps-3). 1990. 12.95 (ISBN 0-02-717775-0, Mcmillan Child Bk). Macmillan Child Grp.

Fredeking, Jean T. The Snuffling Hedgehog. 1987. pap. 20.00x (ISBN 0-317-59264-5, Pub. by A H Stockwell England). State Mutual Bk.

Lawhead, Stephen R. The Tale of Anabelle Hedgehog. (Illus.). 128p. (gr. 4-8). 1990. 9.95 (ISBN 0-7459-1924-3). Lion USA.

Mistress Hedgehog Has an Adventure. (Illus.). (ps-1). 1.98 (ISBN 0-517-45737-7). Outlet Bk Co.

Potter, Beatrix. Meet Mrs. Tiggy-Winkle. (Illus.). 12p. (ps). 1987. bds. 2.95 (ISBN 0-7232-3454-X). Warne.

—The Tale of Mrs. Tiggy-Winkle. Potter, Beatrix, illus. 24p. (ps-2). Date not set. incl. cassette 5.98 (ISBN 1-55886-058-4). Smarty Pants.

HELICOPTERS
Baker, David. Helicopters. (Illus.). 48p. (gr. 3-8). 1987. PLB 18.60 (ISBN 0-317-60509-7). Rourke Corp.

Barrett, N. S. Helicopters. Bryan, Tony, illus. LC 84-50698. 32p. (gr. k-3). 1984. PLB 10.90 (ISBN 0-531-03721-5). Watts.

Barrett, Norman S. Helicopters. 32p. (gr. 3-6). 1989. pap. 3.95 (ISBN 0-531-15140-9). Watts.

Berliner, Don. Helicopters. LC 83-9819. (Illus.). 48p. (gr. 4-9). 1983. PLB 9.95 (ISBN 0-8225-0448-0). Lerner Pubns.

Croome, Angela. Hovercraft. Wilkinson, Gerald, illus. (gr. 5 up). 1962. 14.95 (ISBN 0-8392-3008-7). Astor-Honor.

Graham, Ian. Helicopters. Hayward, Ron & Khan, Aziz, illus. 32p. (gr. 5-6). 1989. PLB 11.90 (ISBN 0-531-17171-X). Watts.

Helicopters. (Illus.). 64p. (gr. 3-9). 1990. PLB 16.95 (ISBN 1-85435-092-7). Marshall Cavendish.

Jefferies, David. Helicopters. (Illus.). 32p. (gr. k-3). 1987. PLB 7.99 (ISBN 0-531-10347-1). Watts.

Jefferis, David. Helicopters. (Illus.). 32p. (gr. 4-6). 1989. PLB 11.90 (ISBN 0-531-10636-5). Watts.

—Helicopters. (ps-3). 1990. PLB 10.90 (ISBN 0-531-19069-2). Watts.

Ladd, James D. Military Helicopters. Gibbons, Tony, et al, illus. 48p. (gr. 5 up). 1987. PLB 9.95 (ISBN 0-8225-1382-X). Lerner Pubns.

Marston, Hope I. Load Lifters. (Illus.). 64p. (gr. 2-5). 1988. 13.95 (ISBN 0-396-09226-8, Putnam). Putnam Pub Group.

Nielsen, Nancy J. Helicopter Pilots. LC 88-12007. (Illus.). 48p. (gr. 5-6). 1988. PLB 10.95 (ISBN 0-89686-399-9, Crestwood Hse). Macmillan Child Grp.

Norman, C. J. Military Helicopters. LC 85-51454. (Illus.). 32p. (gr. 1-6). 1989. PLB 11.40 (ISBN 0-531-10090-1); pap. 3.95 (ISBN 0-531-15141-7). Watts.

Petersen, David. Helicopters. LC 82-23502. (Illus.). 48p. (gr. k-4). 1983. PLB 14.60 (ISBN 0-516-01680-6). Childrens.

Stephen, R. J. The Picture World of Helicopters. (Illus.). 32p. (gr. k-4). 1989. PLB 11.40 (ISBN 0-531-10726-4). Watts.

—Picture World of Military Hellicopters. 1990. PLB 11.40 (ISBN 0-531-14010-5). Watts.

Supermachines. (Illus.). 112p. (gr. 4-9). Date not set. 19.95x (ISBN 1-85435-075-7). Marshall Cavendish.

White, D. Helicopters. (Illus.). 48p. (gr. 3-8). Date not set. PLB 18.60 (ISBN 0-86592-451-1). Rourke Corp.

HEMINGWAY, ERNEST, 1899-1961

Ferrell, Keith. Ernest Hemingway: The Search for Courage. LC 84-10162. 192p. (gr. 7 up). 1984. 10.95 (ISBN 0-87131-431-2). M Evans.

McDowell, N. Hemingway. (Illus.). (gr. 7 up). Date not set. lib. bdg. 18.60 (ISBN 0-86592-298-5). Rourke Corp.

HENRY 8TH, KING OF ENGLAND, 1509-1574

Dwyer, Frank. Henry VIII. Schlesinger, Arthur M., Jr., intro. by. (Illus.). 112p. (gr. 5 up). 1988. lib. bdg. 17.95 (ISBN 0-87754-530-8). Chelsea Hse.

HENRY 8TH, KING OF ENGLAND, 1509-1574–FICTION

Minard, Rosemary. Long Meg. Smith, Philip, illus. LC 81-11103. 64p. (gr. 8-11). 1982. Pantheon.

—Long Meg. Smith, Philip, illus. LC 81-11103. 64p. (gr. 8-11). 1982. Pantheon.

HENRY THE NAVIGATOR, PRINCE OF PORTUGAL, 1394-1460–FICTION

Fisher, Leonard E. Prince Henry the Navigator. Fisher, Leonard E., illus. LC 89-28068. 32p. (gr. 2-6). 1990. 14.95 (ISBN 0-02-735231-5, Mcmillan Child Bk). Macmillan Child Grp.

HENRY, PATRICK, 1736-1799

Fradin, Dennis B. Patrick Henry: "Give Me Liberty or Give Me Death!" LC 88-31330. (Illus.). 48p. (gr. 3-6). 1990. PLB 14.95 (ISBN 0-89490-232-6). Enslow Pubs.

Fritz, Jean. Where Was Patrick Henry on the 29th of May? Tomes, Margot, illus. 48p. (gr. 3-5). 1982. 9.95 (ISBN 0-698-20307-0, Coward); pap. 5.95 (ISBN 0-698-20544-8, Coward). Putnam Pub Group.

Reische, Diana. Patrick Henry. LC 86-23363. (Illus.). (gr. 4-8). 1987. PLB 10.40 (ISBN 0-531-10305-6). Watts.

Sabin, Louis. Patrick Henry: Voice of American Revolution. LC 81-23068. (Illus.). 48p. (gr. 4-6). 1982. PLB 10.79 (ISBN 0-89375-764-0); pap. text ed. 2.95 (ISBN 0-89375-765-9). Troll Assocs.

HENSON, MATTHEW ALEXANDER, 1866-1955

Campling, Elizabeth. Portrait of a Decade: The 1970s. (Illus.). 72p. (gr. 7-10). 1989. 19.95 (ISBN 0-7134-5988-3, Pub. by Batsford England). Trafalgar Sq.

Dolan, Sean. Matthew Henson. (Illus.). 84p. (gr. 3-5). 1991. PLB 12.95 (ISBN 0-7910-1568-8). Chelsea Hse.

Ferris, Jeri. Arctic Explorer: The Story of Matthew Henson. (Illus.). 80p. (gr. 3-6). 1989. PLB 11.95 (ISBN 0-87614-370-2); pap. 5.95 (ISBN 0-87614-507-1). Carolrhoda Bks.

—Arctic Explorer: The Story of Matthew Henson. (Illus.). 80p. (gr. 3-6). 1989. PLB 11.95 (ISBN 0-87614-370-2); pap. 5.95 (ISBN 0-87614-507-1). Carolrhoda Bks.

Gleiter, Jan & Thompson, Kathleen. Matthew Henson. (Illus.). 32p. (Orig.). (gr. 2-5). 1988. PLB 16.67 (ISBN 0-8172-2676-1); pap. text ed. 9.26 (ISBN 0-8172-2680-X). Raintree Pubs.

HERALDRY

see also Chivalry; Decorations of Honor; Flags; Knights And Knighthood

Fradon, Dana. Harold the Herald: A Book about Heraldry. Fradon, Dana, illus. LC 89-49479. (gr. 4-7). 1990. PLB 14.95 (ISBN 0-525-44634-6, DCB). Dutton Child Bks.

Manning, Rosemary. Heraldry. (Illus.). (gr. 7 up). 1966. 14.95 (ISBN 0-7136-0108-6). Dufour.

Parker, James. Glossary of Terms Used in Heraldry. LC 77-94021. (Illus.). (gr. 9 up). 1970. 34.95 (ISBN 0-8048-0715-9). C E Tuttle.

HERBAGE

see Grasses

HERBALS

see Botany

HERCULES

Evslin, Bernard. Hercules. Smith, Joseph A., illus. LC 83-23834. 160p. (gr. 5up). 1984. 14.95 (ISBN 0-688-02748-2). Morrow Jr Bks.

Gates, Doris. Mightiest of Mortals: Heracles. Cuffari, Richard, illus. 96p. (gr. 3-7). 1984. pap. 4.95 (ISBN 0-14-031531-4, Puffin). Puffin Bks.

Richardson, I. M. The Adventures of Hercules. Baxter, Robert, illus. LC 82-16557. 32p. (gr. 4-8). 1983. PLB 11.79 (ISBN 0-89375-865-5); pap. text ed. 2.95 (ISBN 0-89375-866-3). Troll Assocs.

HEREDITY

Conway, Lorraine. Heredity & Embryology. (gr. 5 up). 1980. 6.95 (ISBN 0-916456-90-0, GA 179). Good Apple.

Fradin, Dennis. Heredity. LC 87-831. (Illus.). 48p. (gr. k-4). 1987. PLB 13.27 (ISBN 0-516-01233-9); pap. 4.95 (ISBN 0-516-41233-7). Childrens.

Pomeroy, Johanna P. Content Area Reading skills Reproduction & Heredity: Main Idea. (Illus.). (gr. 4). 1988. pap. text ed. 3.25 (ISBN 1-55737-087-7). Ed Activities.

Showers, Paul. Me & My Family Tree. Madden, Don, illus. LC 77-26595. (gr. k-3). 1978. PLB 13.89 (ISBN 0-690-03887-9, Crowell Jr Bks). HarpC Child Bks.

HERMETIC ART AND PHILOSOPHY

see Astrology; Occult Sciences

HEROES

see also Courage; Explorers; Mythology; Saints

Canon, Jill & Archambault, Alan. Civil War Heroes. Archambault, Alan, illus. 48p. (Orig.). (gr. 7). 1988. pap. 3.95 (ISBN 0-88388-130-6). Bellerophon Bks.

Donev, Mary K. & Donev, Stef. Acts of Courage. Anderian, Kaffi & Johannsen, Rob, illus. 48p. (gr. 5-9). 1985. pap. 5.95 (ISBN 0-88625-091-9). Durkin Hayes Pub.

Hentoff, Nat. American Heroes: In & Out of School. LC 86-29140. 192p. (gr. 7 up). 1987. pap. 14.95 (ISBN 0-385-29565-0). Delacorte.

Saxby, Maurice. The Great Deeds of Superheroes. Ingpen, Robert, illus. 184p. (gr. 7 up). 1990. 24.95 (ISBN 0-87226-342-8). P Bedrick Bks.

Shusterman, Neal. Kid Heroes: True Stories of Rescuers, Survivors & Achievers. 1991. 14.95 (ISBN 0-312-85081-6). Tor Bks.

Wells, Candace & Carroll, Jeri. Legendary Heroes. Foster, Tom, illus. 64p. (gr. k-4). 1987. pap. 6.95 (ISBN 0-86653-380-X, GA1007). Good Apple.

HEROES–FICTION

Ackermann, Jean. A Pride of Heroes: Candid Celebrations. v, 22p. (Orig.). (gr. 8-12). 1984. pap. 6.00 (ISBN 0-9614506-0-6). Box Four Twenty-Four.

Baker, Tim & Heath, Tim. The Dragons at Marshmouldings. (Illus.). 72p. (gr. 10 up). 1987. 7.95 (ISBN 0-8052-8196-7, Pub. by Allison & Busby England). Schocken.

Dehnbostel, Nancy L. & Hartman, Mary E. Superheroes. Sellers, Marci, illus. 48p. (gr. 1-6). 1983. pap. 6.50 (ISBN 0-88047-026-7, 8306). DOK Pubs.

De Regniers, Beatrice S. Everyone One Is Good for Something. LC 79-12223. (Illus.). (gr. k-4). 1980. 13. 95 (ISBN 0-395-28967-X, Clarion). HM.

Estes, Eleanor. The Curious Adventures of Jimmy McGee. O'Brien, John, illus. LC 86-31793. 160p. (gr. 3-7). 1987. 14.95 (ISBN 0-15-221075-X, HJ). HarBraceJ.

Helfer, Andrew. Superman: The Man of Steel. Delbo, Jose, illus. (gr. 3-6). 1987. pap. 2.50 (ISBN 0-671-64332-0, Archway). PB.

Hudson, Eleanor. Teenage Mutant Ninja Turtles Pizza Party: A Step 1 Book - Preschool-Grade 1. Herbert, S. I., illus. LC 90-53243. 32p. (Orig.). (ps-1). 1991. PLB 6.99 (ISBN 0-679-91452-8); pap. 2.95 (ISBN 0-679-81452-3). Random.

Katz, Bobbi. Teenage Mutant Ninja Turtles Don't Do Drugs! A Rap Song. Mones, Isidre, illus. LC 90-53244. 32p. (Orig.). (ps-3). 1991. PLB 5.99 (ISBN 0-679-91485-4); pap. 2.25 (ISBN 0-679-81485-X). Random.

Khalsa, Dayal K. Julian. Khalsa, Dayal K., illus. LC 89-3571. 32p. (gr. 1-3). 1989. 12.95 (ISBN 0-517-57279-6, C N Potter Bks); PLB 13.99 (ISBN 0-517-57410-1). Crown.

McKinley, Robin. The Hero & the Crown. LC 84-4074. 256p. (gr. 7 up). 1984. reinforced 13.95 (ISBN 0-688-02593-5). Greenwillow.

Roop, Peter & Roop, Connie. Keep the Lights Burning, Abbie. Hanson, Peter E., illus. (gr. 2-4). 1989. incl. cass. 19.95 (ISBN 0-87499-135-8); pap. 12.95 incl. cass. (ISBN 0-87499-134-X); Set; incl. 4 bks., guide, & cass. pap. 27.95 (ISBN 0-87499-136-6). Live Oak Media.

Shane, Harold G. Gulliver's Travels. Clark, William, ed. Eckart, Frances, illus. 16p. (gr. 4-8). 1980. pap. 29.95 6 bks. & 1 cass. (ISBN 0-89290-083-0, BC15-6); pap. 10.95 1 bk. & 1 cass. (ISBN 0-685-04648-6, BC15-6). Soc for Visual.

Vigna, Judith. Gregorio y Sus Puntos. Rubin, Caroline, ed. Ada, Alma F., tr. from ENG. Vigna, Judith, illus. LC 76-47528. (SPA.). 32p. (gr. k-3). 1976. PLB 9.75 (ISBN 0-8075-3044-1). A Whitman.

Wagner, Matt, et al. Grendel, No. 4. Wagner, Matt & Rankin, Rich, illus. 48p. (gr. 9-12). 1986. 29.95 (ISBN 0-936211-02-4); pap. 5.95 (ISBN 0-938695-01-0). Graphitti Designs.

Weiss, Ellen & Friedman, Mel. The Adventures of Ratman. Zimmer, Dirk, illus. LC 89-10869. 64p. (Orig.). (gr. 2-4). 1990. PLB 5.99 (ISBN 0-679-90531-6); pap. 1.95 (ISBN 0-679-80531-1). McKay.

Windsor, Patricia. The Hero. LC 87-25658. 192p. (gr. 7 up). 1988. pap. 14.95 (ISBN 0-385-29624-X). Delacorte.

World's Greatest Superheros: Superman. 128p. 1982. pap. 1.95 (ISBN 0-685-04049-6, Dist. by Warner Pub Services & Saint Martin's Press). Tor Bks.

HEROINES

see Heroes; Women in the Bible

HEROISM

see Courage; Heroes

HESSE, HERMAN, 1877-1962

Fleissner, Else M. Herman N. Hesse: Modern German Poet & Writer. Rahmas, D. Steve, ed. LC 70-190244. 32p. (Orig.). (gr. 7-12). 1972. lib. bdg. 4.20 incl. catalog cards (ISBN 0-87157-526-4); pap. 2.95 vinyl laminated covers (ISBN 0-87157-026-2). SamHar Pr.

HIAWATHA, IROQUOIS INDIAN

Bonvillain, Nancy. Hiawatha. (Illus.). 112p. (gr. 5 up). 1992. PLB 18.95 (ISBN 0-7910-1707-9). Chelsea Hse.

Wheeler, Jill. The Story of Hiawatha. Deegan, Paul, ed. Dodson, Liz, illus. 32p. (gr. 4). 1989. PLB 11.95 (ISBN 0-939179-71-7). Abdo & Dghtrs.

HIBERNATION

see Animals–Hibernation

HIDALGO Y COSTILLA, MIGUEL, 1753-1811–FICTION

Father Hidalgo: Mini-Play. (gr. 5 up). 1978. 5.00 (ISBN 0-89550-326-3). Stevens & Shea.

HIEROGLYPHICS

see also Picture Writing

Katan, Norma J. & Mintz, Barbara. Hieroglyphs: The Writing of Ancient Egypt. Katan, Norma J., illus. LC 80-13576. 96p. (gr. 4-7). 1981. 12.95 (ISBN 0-689-50176-5, M K McElderry). Macmillan Child Grp.

Scott, Joseph & Scott, Lenore. Egyptian Hieroglyphs for Everyone: An Introduction to the Writing of Ancient Egypt. reissued ed. Scott, Joseph & Scott, Lenore, illus. LC 68-13080. 96p. (gr. 7 up). 1990. PLB 13.89 (ISBN 0-690-04753-3, Crowell Jr Bks). HarpC Child Bks.

HIGH SCHOOL EDUCATION

see Education, Secondary

HIGH SCHOOLS

Haley, Beverly A. Focus on School: A Reference Handbook. 217p. 1990. lib. bdg. 35.00 (ISBN 0-87436-099-4). ABC-CLIO.

Scott, John I., ed. Getting the Most out of High School. 2nd rev. ed. LC 67-26419. 165p. (gr. 9 up). 1967. 6.50 (ISBN 0-379-00089-X). Oceana.

Souter, John C. Survive! (Orig.). (gr. 9-12). 1983. pap. 4.95 (ISBN 0-8423-6694-6). Tyndale.

Wirths, Claudine G. & Bowman-Kruhm, Mary. I Hate School! How to Hang In & When to Drop Out. Stren, Patti, illus. LC 85-48248. 128p. (gr. 7 up). 1986. 11.95 (ISBN 0-690-04556-5, Crowell Jr Bks); PLB 11.89 (ISBN 0-690-04558-1, Crowell Jr Bks). HarpC Child Bks.

HIGH SPEED AERONAUTICS

see also Rockets (Aeronautics)

HIGHER EDUCATION

see Education, Higher

HIGHWAY ACCIDENTS

see Traffic Accidents

HIGHWAY CONSTRUCTION

see Roads

HIGHWAYMEN

see Robbers and Outlaws

HIGHWAYS

see Roads

HIKING

see also Backpacking; Walking

Fisher, Ron. Mountain Adventure. Crump, Donald J., ed. (Illus.). 1988. 7.95 (ISBN 0-87044-668-1); lib. bdg. 9.50 (ISBN 0-87044-673-8). Natl Geog.

Foster, Lynne. Take a Hike. (gr. 4-7). 1991. pap. 8.95 (ISBN 0-316-28948-5, Joy St Bks). Little.

—Take a Hike! The Sierra Club Beginner's Guide to Hiking & Backpacking. Weston, Martha, illus. (gr. 4-7). 1990. write for info. Sierra.

McVey, Vicki. The Sierra Club Wayfinding Book. Weston, Martha, illus. 96p. (gr. 4-7). 1989. 14.95 (ISBN 0-316-56340-4). Little.

HIMALAYA MOUNTAINS

Reynolds, Jan. Himalaya. Peck, Tim & Ingber, Bonnie V., eds. Reynolds, Jan, illus. 32p. (gr. 2 up). 1990. 14.95. HarBraceJ.

—Himalaya Vanishing Cultures. (gr. 4-7). 1991. write for info. (ISBN 0-15-234465-9). HarBraceJ.

HIMALAYA MOUNTAINS–FICTION

Corbalis, Judy. The Ice Cream Heroes. Parkins, David, illus. LC 89-8069. (gr. 4-7). 1989. 13.95 (ISBN 0-316-15648-5). Little.

HINDUISM

see also Yoga

Bhaktivedanta, Swami A. C. Prahlad, Picture & Story Book. LC 72-2032. (Illus.). (gr. 2-6). 1973. pap. 4.00 (ISBN 0-685-47513-1). Bhaktivedanta.

McLeod, W. H. Way of the Sikh. (gr. 4-8). pap. 7.95 (ISBN 0-7175-0731-9). Dufour.

Madhu Bazaz Wangu. Hinduism. (Illus.). 128p. (gr. 7-12). 1991. 17.95x (ISBN 0-8160-2447-2). Facts on File.

Nivedita, Sr. Cradle Tales of Hinduism. (Illus.). 329p. (gr. 3-12). 1972. pap. 5.95 (ISBN 0-87481-170-8); pap. 5.95 (ISBN 0-87481-131-7). Vedanta Pr.

Ramakrishna, Swami. Tales from Ramakrishna. Chakravarty, Biswarajan, illus. Ray, Irene R. & Gupta, Mallika C.retold by. (Illus.). 54p. (Orig.). (gr. 1-5). 1975. pap. 1.95 (ISBN 0-87481-152-X). Vedanta Pr.

Smarananda, Swami. The Story of Ramakrishna. Chakravarty, Biswaranjan, illus. (Orig.). (gr. k-5). 1976. pap. 1.95 (ISBN 0-87481-168-6). Vedanta Pr.

Srinivasan, A. V. A Hindu Primer: Yaksha Prashna. Satchidananda, Swami, frwd. by. (Illus.). 78p. (gr. 6-12). 1984. pap. 7.70 (ISBN 0-86578-249-0, 6203). Ind-US Inc.

Swami Raghaveshananda. Ramayana for Children. Padmavasan, illus. 44p. (Orig.). (gr. 3-6). 1989. pap. 3.95 (ISBN 81-7120-102-4, Pub. by Ramakrishna Math Madras India). Vedanta Pr.

—Story of Sri Krishna for Children, Pt. I. Padmavasan, illus. 60p. (gr. 4). 1990. 6.95 (ISBN 81-7120-140-7, Pub. by Ramakrishna Math Madras India). Vedanta Pr.

Vishwashrayananda, Swami. Ramakrishna for Children. Chakravarty, Purhachandra, illus. Bagchi, Santosh, tr. from BEN. (Illus.). 40p. (gr. 3-6). 1975. pap. 1.95 (ISBN 0-87481-164-3). Vedanta Pr.

Yogeshananda, Swami. Way of the Hindu. (gr. 3-7). pap. 7.95 (ISBN 0-7175-0626-6). Dufour.

HIPPIES–FICTION

King, Cynthia. Sailing Home. 192p. 1982. 9.95 (ISBN 0-399-20872-0, Putnam). Putnam Pub Group.

HIPPOPOTAMUS

Animal Masks: Gorilla & Hippo. (ps up). 1990. pap. 4.98 (ISBN 0-8317-0358-X). Smithmark.

Arnold, Caroline. Hippo. Hewett, Richard, photos by. LC 88-39794. (Illus.). 48p. (gr. 2 up). 1989. 12.95 (ISBN 0-688-08145-2); PLB 12.88 (ISBN 0-688-08146-0, Morrow Jr Bks). Morrow Jr Bks.

Goodall, Jane, ed. Jane Goodall's Animal World: Hippos. (Illus.). 32p. (gr. 3-7). 1989. pap. 3.95 (ISBN 0-689-71321-5, Aladdin). Macmillan Child Grp.

Green, Carl R. & Sanford, William R. The Hippopotamus. LC 88-1830. (Illus.). 48p. (gr. 5-6). 1988. PLB 10.95 (ISBN 0-89686-383-2, Crestwood Hse). Macmillan Child Grp.
Hoffman, Mary. Hippopotamus. LC 84-24792. (Illus.). 24p. (gr. k-5). 1985. PLB 13.32 (ISBN 0-8172-2412-2). Raintree Pubs.
Pouyanne. Hippo, Reading Level 3-4. (Illus.). 28p. (gr. 2-5). Date not set. PLB 14.60 (ISBN 0-86592-855-X). Rourke Corp.
Schlein, Miriam. Jane Goodall's Animal World: Hippos. Goodall, Jane, ed. (Illus.). 32p. (gr. 3-7). 1989. 11.95 (ISBN 0-689-31469-8, Atheneum Child Bk). Macmillan Child Grp.
Stone, Lynn. Hippopotamus. (Illus.). 24p. (gr. k-5). 1990. lib. bdg. 11.93 (ISBN 0-86593-051-1); lib. bdg. 8. 95s.p. (ISBN 0-685-36347-3). Rourke Corp.
Thaler, Mike. It's Me, Hippo! Chambliss, Maxie, illus. LC 82-48848. 64p. (gr. k-3). 1983. HarpC Child Bks.

HIPPOPOTAMUS–FICTION

Craig, Janet. Thump, Bump: Tiny the Dancing Hippo. Paterson, Diane, illus. LC 87-10933. 32p. (gr. k-2). 1987. PLB 10.89 (ISBN 0-8167-1077-5); pap. text ed. 2.95 (ISBN 0-8167-1078-3). Troll Assocs.
Duvoisin, Roger. Veronica. Duvoisin, Roger, illus. (gr. k-3). 1961. lib. bdg. 13.99 (ISBN 0-394-91792-8). Knopf.
Gaban, Jesus. Harry Presses Himself. Colorado, Nani, illus. 16p. (ps-1). 1991. PLB 10.95 (ISBN 0-8368-0715-4). Gareth Stevens Inc.
Gordon, Sharon. Playground Fun. Karas, G. Brian, illus. LC 86-30854. 32p. (gr. k-2). 1987. lib. bdg. 7.06 (ISBN 0-8167-0990-4); pap. text ed. 1.95 (ISBN 0-8167-0991-2). Troll Assocs.
Grant, Joan. The Blue Faience Hippopotamus. Day, Alexandra, illus. LC 83-83206. 32p. (Orig.). (gr. 7-9). 1984. Repr. of 1942 ed. 11.95 (ISBN 0-88138-020-2, Star & Elephant Bks.). Green Tiger Pr.
Greaves, John. Henrietta the Clumsy Hippo. McLachlan, Edward, illus. (ps-3). 1988. 7.95 (ISBN 0-8120-6090-3). Barron.
Hadithi, Mwenye. Hot Hippo. Kennaway, Adrienne, illus. (ps-3). 1986. lib. bdg. 14.95 (ISBN 0-316-33722-6). Little.
Hunt, Robert. Kiboko the African Hippo. Producciones Ancora, illus. LC 72-736443. (gr. 2-5). 1978. 6 bks. & 1 cass. 29.95 (ISBN 0-89290-028-8); 1 bk. & 1 cass. 10.95 (ISBN 0-685-04652-4). Soc for Visual.
Hurwitz, Johanna. Busybody Nora. Jeschke, Susan, illus. 64p. (gr. 1-5). 1982. pap. 1.50 (ISBN 0-440-41019-3, YB). Dell.
Kessler, Ethel & Kessler, Len. Are There Hippos on the Farm? (Illus.). (ps-k). 1986. 4.95 (ISBN 0-671-62066-5, Little Simon). S&S Trade.
Macdonald, Maryann. Little Hippo Starts School. King, Anna, illus. LC 88-33580. 32p. (ps-3). 1990. 10.95 (ISBN 0-8037-0720-7). Dial Bks Young.
Marshall, James. George & Martha Encore. LC 73-5845. (Illus.). 48p. (gr. k-3). 1977. 13.95 (ISBN 0-395-17512-7); pap. 4.95 (ISBN 0-395-25379-9). HM.
—George & Martha Rise & Shine. Marshall, James, illus. (gr. k-3). 1979. 13.95 (ISBN 0-395-24738-1); pap. 4.95 (ISBN 0-395-28006-0). HM.
—George & Martha Tons of Fun. (Illus.). 48p. (gr. k-3). 1986. 13.95 (ISBN 0-395-29524-6); pap. 3.95 (ISBN 0-395-42646-4). HM.
Martin, Bill, Jr. The Happy Hippopotami. Johnston, Allyn, ed. Everitt, Betsy, illus. 32p. (ps-3). 1991. 12.95 (ISBN 0-15-233380-0). HarBraceJ.
Matsuoka, Kyoko. There's a Hippo in My Bath! Hayashi, Akiko, illus. 1989. 12.95 (ISBN 0-385-26188-8); PLB 12.95 (ISBN 0-385-26189-6). Doubleday.
Mayer, Mercer. Hiccup. LC 76-2284. (Illus.). (ps-2). PLB 9.89 (ISBN 0-8037-3592-8). Dial Bks Young.
Moncure, Jane B. Yes, No, Little Hippo. Gohman, Vera, illus. LC 87-21211. 32p. (ps-2). 1987. PLB 11.97 (ISBN 0-89565-411-3); pap. 6.96 (ISBN 0-89565-451-2). Childs World.
Stadler, John. Three Cheers for Hippo! Stadler, John, illus. LC 87-497. 32p. (ps-3). 1987. 11.95i (ISBN 0-690-04668-5, Crowell Jr Bks); PLB 11.89 (ISBN 0-690-04670-7). HarpC Child Bks.
—Three Cheers for Hippo! Stadler, John, illus. LC 87-497. 32p. (gr. k-3). 1990. pap. 3.95 (ISBN 0-06-443220-3, Trophy). HarpC Child Bks.
Thaler, Mike. Hippo Lemonade. Chambliss, Maxie, illus. LC 85-45257. 64p. (gr. k-3). 1986. PLB 11.89 (ISBN 0-06-026162-5). HarpC Child Bks.
—A Hippopotamus Ate the Teacher. Lee, Jared, illus. 32p. 1981. pap. 2.75 (ISBN 0-380-78048-8, Camelot). Avon.
—There's a Hippopotamus under My Bed. (Illus.). 32p. (gr. k-3). 1978. pap. 2.50 (ISBN 0-380-40238-6, Camelot). Avon.
—What Could a Hippopotamus Be? Grossman, Robert, illus. 40p. (ps-2). 1990. PLB 13.95 (ISBN 0-671-70847-3). S&S Trade.
Waber, Bernard. You Look Ridiculous Said the Rhinoceros to the Hippopotamus. (Illus.). (gr. k-3). 1973. reinforced bdg. 13.95 (ISBN 0-395-07156-9). HM.
Ziefert, Harriet. Harry Takes a Bath. Smith, Mavis, illus. (ps-3). 1987. pap. 8.95 (ISBN 0-670-81721-X, Puffin); pap. 3.50 (ISBN 0-14-050746-9, Puffin). Puffin Bks.

HIROSHIMA

Farris, John. Hiroshima. McGovern, Brian, illus. LC 90-34064. 64p. (gr. 5-8). 1990. PLB 11.95 (ISBN 1-56006-015-8). Lucent Bks.
Hoare, Stephen. Hiroshima. (Illus.). 64p. (gr. 6-8). 1987. 19.95 (ISBN 0-85219-695-4, Pub. by Batsford England). Trafalgar Sq.
McPhillips, Martin. Hiroshima. LC 85-40170. (Illus.). 64p. (gr. 5 up). 1985. PLB 16.98 (ISBN 0-382-06976-5); pap. 7.95. Silver Burdett Pr.
O'Neal, Michael. President Truman & the Atomic Bomb: Opposing Viewpoints. LC 90-35611. (Illus.). 112p. (gr. 3-8). 1990. PLB 13.95 (ISBN 0-89908-079-0). Greenhaven.
Stein, R. Conrad. Hiroshima. LC 82-4538. (Illus.). (gr. 3-8). 1982. PLB 14.60 (ISBN 0-516-04797-3). Childrens.

HIROSHIMA–FICTION

Morimoto, Junko. My Hiroshima. (Illus.). 32p. (ps up). 1990. pap. 12.95 (ISBN 0-670-83181-6). Viking Child Bks.

HISPANO-AMERICAN WAR, 1898
see U. S.–History–War of 1898
HISTOLOGY
see Anatomy; Anatomy, Comparative; Cells
HISTORIANS
see also Archeologists
HISTORICAL ATLASES
see Atlases, Historical
HISTORICAL CHRONOLOGY
see Chronology, Historical
HISTORICAL DICTIONARIES
see History–Dictionaries
HISTORICAL GEOGRAPHY
see Atlases, Historical
HISTORICAL GEOGRAPHY

Crosby, Nina E. & Marten, Elizabeth H. Know Your State. West, James A., illus. 32p. (Orig.). (gr. 4-7). 1984. pap. 5.50 (ISBN 0-88047-036-4, 8401). DOK Pubs.

HISTORIOGRAPHY

Cooper, Kay. Who Put the Cannon in the Courthouse Square: A Guide to Uncovering the Past. Accardo, Anthony, illus. LC 84-17251. (gr. 4 up). 1984. PLB 12.85 (ISBN 0-8027-6561-0). Walker & Co.
Littlefield, Robert S. & Ball, Jane A. Tell Me the Way It Was... Stark, Steve, illus. 32p. (Orig.). (gr. 3-6). 1990. pap. text ed. 8.95 (ISBN 1-879340-07-0, K0108). Kidspeak.

HISTORY, ANCIENT
see also Archeology; Bible; Civilization

Atkins, Sinclair. From Stone Age to Conquest. LC 85-73167. (Illus.). 96p. (gr. 5-8). 1986. pap. 11.95 (ISBN 0-7175-1305-X). Dufour.
Baer, Ruth. Creation to Canaan, Bk. 1. (gr. 7). 1979. 9.50 (ISBN 0-686-30770-4); tchr's. ed. avail. 6.40 (ISBN 0-686-30771-2). Rod & Staff.
Briquebec, John. Ancient World: 30,000 B.C. - A.D. 476. (ps-3). 1990. PLB 13.90 (ISBN 0-531-19073-0). Watts.
British Museum Dept. of Paleontology Staff. The Prehistoric Age. (Illus.). 96p. (gr. 10 up). 1987. pap. 3.95 (ISBN 0-85112-632-4). Sterling.
Cairns, Trevor, ed. People Become Civilized. LC 73-20196. (Illus.). 104p. (gr. 5 up). 1974. PLB 10.95 (ISBN 0-8225-0801-X). Lerner Pubns.
Chisholm. Living in Prehistoric Times. (gr. 2-5). 1983. pap. 4.50 (ISBN 0-86020-623-8); lib. bdg. 11.96 (ISBN 0-88110-104-4). EDC.
Cootes, R. J. & Snellgrove, L. E. The Ancient World. (Illus.). 208p. (gr. 6-12). 1978. pap. text ed. 21.92 (ISBN 0-582-20503-4, 70779). Longman.
De Saint-Beauguat, Henri. The First People. LC 86-42657. (Illus.). 77p. (gr. 7 up). 1987. 15.96 (ISBN 0-382-09212-0); 10.37s.p. (ISBN 0-685-17548-0). Silver Burdett Pr.
De Saint-Beauquet, Henri. The First Settlements. LC 86-42659. (Illus.). 77p. (gr. 7 up). 1987. 15.96 (ISBN 0-382-09213-9); 10.37s.p. (ISBN 0-685-17549-9). Silver Burdett Pr.
Dixon, Dougal. Big Book of Prehistoric Life. 1990. 5.98 (ISBN 0-8317-0862-X). Smithmark.
Magill, Frank N., ed. Great Lives from History, 5 vols. 2500p. (gr. 9-12). 1988. lib. bdg. 350.00 (ISBN 0-89356-545-8). Salem Pr.
Manton, Jo. Gods, Beasts & Men. (gr. 4-8). 12.95 (ISBN 0-7175-0662-2). Dufour.
Milard, A. & Chisholm, J. Early Civilizations. (Illus.). 96p. 1991. PLB 15.96 (ISBN 0-88110-438-8); pap. 9.95 (ISBN 0-7460-0328-5). EDC.
Odijk, Pamela. The Ancient World, 12 bks. (Illus.). (gr. 5-8). 1990. Set, 48p. ea. lib. bdg. 203.76 (ISBN 0-382-09883-8). Silver Burdett Pr.
Schroeder, Mary. Extending U. S. History & Geography. West, James A., illus. 32p. (Orig.). (gr. 3-6). 1984. 5.95 (ISBN 0-88047-041-0, 8404). DOK Pubs.
Verges, Gloria & Verges, Oriol. The Greek & Roman Eras. Rius, Maria & Peris, Carme, illus. (ENG & SPA.). 32p. (gr. 2-4). 1988. pap. 4.50 (ISBN 0-8120-3388-4); La Edad Antigua. pap. 3.95 (ISBN 0-8120-3389-2). Barron.
—Prehistory to Egypt. Rius, Maria, illus. (SPA & ENG.). 32p. (gr. 2-4). 1988. pap. 4.95 (ISBN 0-8120-3390-6); La Prehistoria y el Antiguo Egipto. pap. 3.95 (ISBN 0-8120-3391-4). Barron.

HISTORY, ANCIENT–FICTION

Crow, Donna F. Professor Q's Mysterious Machine. (gr. 3-8). 1983. pap. 3.95 (ISBN 0-89191-562-1). Cook.

HISTORY–ATLASES
see Atlases, Historical
HISTORY, BIBLICAL
see Bible–History of Biblical Events
HISTORY–CHRONOLOGY
see Chronology, Historical
HISTORY, CHURCH
see Church History
HISTORY–CRITICISM
see Historiography
HISTORY–CURIOSA AND MISCELLANY

Carroll, Jeri & Wells, Candance. Pathfinders. Foster, Tom, illus. 64p. (gr. k-4). 1986. wkbk. 6.95 (ISBN 0-86653-357-5, GA 696). Good Apple.
Manley, D. Look & Learn about People, Places & Things. (Illus.). (gr. 2-6). 5.98 (ISBN 0-517-45795-4). Outlet Bk Co.
Manley, Deborah. Long Ago. 1990. 4.99 (ISBN 0-517-69615-0). Outlet Bk Co.
Pringle, Laurence. The Earth Is Flat & Other Great Mistakes. LC 83-7966. 96p. (gr. 3-7). 1983. 12.95 (ISBN 0-688-02466-1); lib. bdg. 12.88 (ISBN 0-688-02467-X, Morrow Jr Bks). Morrow Jr Bks.

HISTORY–DICTIONARIES

Silvani, Harold. Famous Places & Events. 56p. (gr. 3-6). 1975. wkbk. 6.95 (ISBN 1-878669-21-4, 4014). Crea Tea Assocs.

HISTORY–HISTORIOGRAPHY
see Historiography
HISTORY, MILITARY
see Military History
HISTORY, MODERN
Here are entered works covering the period after 1453.
see also Civilization, Modern; Reformation; Renaissance

Arnold, Guy. Book of Dates. (Illus.). 96p. (gr. 7-9). 1990. 13.90 (ISBN 0-531-19049-8). Watts.
Brooman, Josh. The World Since Nineteen Hundred. Date not set. pap. text ed. 8.96 (ISBN 0-582-00989-8, 78443). Longman.
Cairns, Trevor. The Twentieth Century. (Illus.). 168p. (gr. 5 up). 1984. PLB 14.95 (ISBN 0-8225-0810-9). Lerner Pubns.
Campling, Elizabeth. Portrait of a Decade: Nineteen Eighties. (Illus.). 72p. (gr. 7-11). 1990. 19.95 (ISBN 0-7134-6209-4, Pub. by Batsford UK). Trafalgar Sq.
Cannon, Jim, et al. The Contemporary World: Conflict or Co-Operation? 2nd ed. (Illus.). 128p. (Orig.). (gr. 9-12). 1979. pap. text ed. 23.76 (ISBN 0-05-003734-X, 70092). Longman.
Duden, Jane. Nineteen Fifties. LC 89-34400. (Illus.). 48p. (gr. 4-5). 1989. 10.95 (ISBN 0-89686-476-6, Crestwood Hse). Macmillan Child Grp.
—Nineteen Forties. LC 89-34401. (Illus.). 48p. (gr. 4-5). 1989. 10.95 (ISBN 0-89686-475-8, Crestwood Hse). Macmillan Child Grp.
—Nineteen Seventies. LC 89-34630. (Illus.). 48p. (gr. 4-5). 1989. 10.95 (ISBN 0-89686-478-2, Crestwood Hse). Macmillan Child Grp.
—Nineteen Sixties. LC 89-34399. (Illus.). 48p. (gr. 4-5). 1989. 10.95 (ISBN 0-89686-477-4, Crestwood Hse). Macmillan Child Grp.
Dures, Alan & Dures, Katherine. Riots. (Illus.). 72p. (gr. 7-12). 1985. 19.95 (ISBN 0-7134-4350-2, Pub. by Batsford England). Trafalgar Sq.
Felder, Deborah G. The Kids' World Almanac of History. Lane, John, illus. 288p. (Orig.). 1991. 14.95 (ISBN 0-88687-496-3, World Almanac); pap. 6.95 (ISBN 0-88687-495-5, World Almanac). Pharos Bks NY.
Fisher, Trevor. Portrait of a Decade: Nineteen Ten to Nineteen Nineteen. (Illus.). 72p. (gr. 7-11). 1990. 19. 95 (ISBN 0-7134-6071-7, Pub. by Batsford UK). Trafalgar Sq.
Freeman, Charles. Portrait of a Decade: Nineteen Thirties. (Illus.). 72p. (gr. 7-11). 1990. 19.95 (ISBN 0-7134-6073-3, Pub. by Batsford UK). Trafalgar Sq.
Fyson, Nance L. Portrait of a Decade: The 1940s. (Illus.). 72p. (gr. 7-10). 1989. 19.95 (ISBN 0-7134-5628-0, Pub. by Batsford England). Trafalgar Sq.
Goldston, Robert. The Road Between the Wars: 1918-1941. LC 78-51330. (Illus.). (gr. 7 up). 1978. 8.95 (ISBN 0-8037-7467-2). Dial Bks Young.
The Human Story Series, 9 vols. 616p. (gr. 7 up). 1988. Set. 127.68 (ISBN 0-382-09625-8); Set. 82.99s.p. (ISBN 0-685-37323-1). Silver Burdett Pr.
Kramer, Ann. Exploration & Empire: 1450-1760. (ps-3). 1990. PLB 13.90 (ISBN 0-531-19074-9). Watts.
Kuhn, Dwight. More Than Just a...Series, 2 vols. Kuhn, Dwight, photos by. (Illus.). 80p. (gr. 2 up). 1990. Set. 25.90 (ISBN 0-671-94439-8); Set. 19.43s.p.; Set. PLB 31.96 (ISBN 0-671-94438-X); Set. PLB 23.97s.p. Silver Pr.
Leonard, Marcia. How Did That Happen? Series, 4 vols. Chambliss, Maxie & Iosa, Ann, illus. 96p. (ps-1). 1990. Set. 19.80 (ISBN 0-671-31235-9); Set. 14.85s.p. (ISBN 0-685-37312-6); Set. PLB 39.92 (ISBN 0-671-31234-0); Set. PLB 29.94s.p. (ISBN 0-685-37313-4). Silver Pr.
—How Did That Happen? Series, 4 vols. Chambliss, Maxie & Iosa, Ann, illus. 96p. (ps-1). 1990. Set. 19.80 (ISBN 0-671-31235-9); Set. 14.85s.p. (ISBN 0-685-37312-6); Set. PLB 39.92 (ISBN 0-671-31234-0); Set. PLB 29.94s.p. (ISBN 0-685-37313-4). Silver Pr.
Ross, Stewart. The Nineteen Eighties. (Illus.). 72p. (gr. 7-11). 1991. 19.95 (ISBN 0-7134-6361-9, Pub. by Batsford UK). Trafalgar Sq.
Schroeder, Mary. Extending U. S. History & Geography. West, James A., illus. 32p. (Orig.). (gr. 3-6). 1984. 5.95 (ISBN 0-88047-041-0, 8404). DOK Pubs.
Stewart, Gail. Nineteen Hundreds. LC 89-9936. (Illus.). 48p. (gr. 4-5). 1989. 10.95 (ISBN 0-89686-471-5, Crestwood Hse). Macmillan Child Grp.

—Nineteen Tens. LC 89-9946. (Illus.). 48p. (gr. 4-5). 1989. 10.95 (ISBN 0-89686-472-3, Crestwood Hse). Macmillan Child Grp.
—Nineteen Thirties. LC 89-34405. (Illus.). 48p. (gr. 4 up). 1990. 10.95 (ISBN 0-89686-474-X, Crestwood Hse). Macmillan Child Grp.
—Nineteen Twenties. (Illus.). 48p. (gr. 4-5). 1989. 10.95 (ISBN 0-89686-473-1, Crestwood Hse). Macmillan Child Grp.
Tames, Richard. The Nineteen Eighties. (Illus.). 48p. (gr. 5-8). 1990. PLB 12.90 (ISBN 0-531-14079-2). Watts.
—Nineteen Fifties. 1990. PLB 12.90 (ISBN 0-531-14034-2). Watts.
—Nineteen Hundred to Nineteen Nineteen. (Illus.). 48p. (gr. 5-8). 1991. PLB 12.90 (ISBN 0-531-14181-0). Watts.
—The Nineteen Twenties. (Illus.). 48p. (gr. 5-8). 1991. PLB 12.90 (ISBN 0-531-14182-9). Watts.
Townson, W. D., et al. Picture History of the World. (Illus.). 224p. (gr. 5 up). 1986. pap. 19.95 (ISBN 0-448-18988-7, G&D). Putnam Pub Group.
Unstead, R J. Nineteen Forties. 1990. PLB 12.90 (ISBN 0-531-14035-0). Watts.
Ventura, Piero. There Once Was a Time. Ventura, Piero, illus. 160p. (gr. 5 up). 1987. 19.95 (ISBN 0-399-21356-2, Putnam). Putnam Pub Group.
Verges, Gloria & Verges, Oriol. The Contemporary Age (Nineteenth & Twentieth Century) Rius, Maria & Peris, Carme, illus. (ENG & SPA.). 32p. (gr. 2-4). 1988. pap. 4.50 (ISBN 0-8120-3394-9); La Edad Contemporanea. pap. 3.95 (ISBN 0-8120-3395-7). Barron.
—Modern Times (Seventeenth & Eighteenth Century) Rius, Maria & Peris, Carme, illus. 32p. (gr. 2-4). 1988. pap. 4.50 (ISBN 0-8120-3392-2); La Edad Moderna. pap. 3.95 (ISBN 0-8120-3393-0). Barron.
Williams, Betty. Portrait of a Decade: The 1920s. (Illus.). 72p. (gr. 7-10). 1989. 19.95 (ISBN 0-7134-5816-X, Pub. by Batsford England). Trafalgar Sq.
Woodson, Jacqueline, et al. Let's Celebrate Series, 6 vols. Cooper, Floyd, et al, illus. 192p. (gr. k-2). 1990. Set. 35.70 (ISBN 0-671-31231-6); Set. 26.78s.p.; Set. PLB 65.88 (ISBN 0-671-31230-8); Set. PLB 49.41s.p. Silver Pr.

HISTORY, NATURAL
see Natural History

HISTORY, NAVAL
see Naval History;
see names of countries with the subdivision History, Naval e. g. U. S.–History, Naval

HISTORY–PHILOSOPHY
see also Civilization

HISTORY, UNIVERSAL
see World History

HISTRIONICS
see Acting; Theater

HITCHHIKING
see Walking

HITLER, ADOLF, 1889-1945
Bradley, Catherine. Hitler. (ps-3). 1990. PLB 11.90 (ISBN 0-531-17228-7). Watts.
Harris, Nathanial. Hitler. (Illus.). 64p. (gr. 7-10). 1989. 19.95 (ISBN 0-7134-5961-1, Pub. by Batsford England). Trafalgar Sq.
Italia, Bob. Adolf Hitler. Wallner, Rosemary, ed. (Illus.). 32p. (gr. 4). 1990. PLB 11.95 (ISBN 0-939179-79-2). Abdo & Dghtrs.
Kerr, Judith. When Hitler Stole Pink Rabbit. (gr. 3 up). 1987. pap. 3.25 (ISBN 0-440-49017-0, YB). Dell.

HOAXES
see Impostors and Imposture

HOBBIES
see also Collectors and Collecting; Handicraft
Blob Monster-Activity Book. 1989. pap. write for info. (ISBN 0-02-898707-1). Checkerboard Pr.
Dartez, Cecilia C. The Louisiana Plantation Coloring Book. Arrigo, Joseph, illus. 32p. (Orig.). (ps-4). 1985. pap. 2.95 (ISBN 0-88289-473-0). Pelican.
Dolman, Sue, illus. Brambly Hedge Pattern Book. 64p. 1986. 14.95 (ISBN 0-399-21194-2, Philomel). Putnam Pub Group.
Kohn, Eugene. Photography: A Manual for Shutterbugs. Plasencia, Peter P., illus. Noa, Pedro A., photos by. (Illus.). (gr. 3-7). 1965. pap. 1.25 (ISBN 0-685-03891-2). P-H.
Nathan, Beverly & Bizer, Linda. The Huddles Jumbo Activity & Coloring Book. Kong, Emilie, illus. 128p. (ps-8). pap. write for info (ISBN 0-910313-78-4). Parker Bros.
Schulz, Charles M. Charlie Brown's Super Book of Things to Do & Collect. Schulz, Charles M., illus. LC 75-7749. 80p. (gr. 3 up). 1975. (Random Juv). Random.
Ziefert, Harriet. Dress Little Bunny. Ernst, Lisa C., illus. 12p. (ps-1). 1986. pap. 5.95 (ISBN 0-670-80358-8). Viking Child Bks.

HOBBIES–FICTION
Bulla, Clyde R. Daniel's Duck. Sandin, Joan, illus. LC 77-25647. 64p. (gr. k-3). 1979. 11.95 (ISBN 0-06-020908-9); PLB 11.89 (ISBN 0-06-020909-7). HarpC Child Bks.
Harwood, Pearl A. Make-It Room of Mr. & Mrs. Bumba. Overlie, George, illus. LC 74-156357. 32p. (gr. k-3). 1971. PLB 4.95 (ISBN 0-8225-0124-4). Lerner Pubns.

HOCKEY
Aaseng, Nathan. Hockey: You Are the Coach. LC 82-17170. (Illus.). 104p. (gr. 4up). 1983. PLB 8.95 (ISBN 0-8225-1554-7). Lerner Pubns.
—Hockey's Fearless Goalies. LC 83-17512. (Illus.). 80p. (gr. 4 up). 1984. PLB 7.95 (ISBN 0-8225-1341-2). Lerner Pubns.
—Hockey's Super Scorers. LC 83-17511. (Illus.). 80p. (gr. 4up). 1984. PLB 7.95 (ISBN 0-8225-1340-4). Lerner Pubns.
Gemme, Leila B. Hockey Is Our Game. Caliger, Roberta, illus. LC 78-12541. 32p. (gr. 4 up). 1979. PLB 15.93 (ISBN 0-516-03492-8). Childrens.
Gutman, Bill. Go for It: Field Hockey. Brown, Ben, illus. 64p. (gr. 3-7). 1989. PLB 16.50 (ISBN 0-942545-93-1). Grey Castle.
—Go for It: Ice Hockey. Brown, Ben, illus. 64p. (gr. 3-7). 1989. PLB 16.50 (ISBN 0-942545-86-9). Grey Castle.
Hockey All Stars. (Illus.). (gr. k-9). 1988. pap. 2.95 (ISBN 0-318-36491-3). Scholastic Inc.
Kalb, Jonah. The Easy Hockey Book. Morrison, Bill, illus. 64p. (gr. 2-5). 1977. 13.95 (ISBN 0-395-25842-1). HM.
MacLean, Norman. Hockey Basics. Gow, Bill, illus. LC 83-9451. 48p. (gr. 4-6). 1983. 10.95 (ISBN 0-13-392506-4). P-H.
Preston-Mauks, Susan. Field Hockey Is for Me. Preston-Mauks, Susan & Sheehan-Burke, Julia, illus. LC 83-11268. 48p. (gr. 2-5). 1983. PLB 8.95 (ISBN 0-8225-1141-X). Lerner Pubns.
Rainbolt, Richard. Hockey's Top Scorers. LC 74-27471. (Illus.). 72p. (gr. 4 up). 1981. PLB 7.95 (ISBN 0-8225-1056-1). Lerner Pubns.
Rennie, Ross. Boston Bruins. 32p. (gr. 4). 1990. 12.95s.p. (ISBN 0-88682-273-4); 18.50 (ISBN 0-685-28189-2). Creative Ed.
—Buffalo Sabres. 32p. (gr. 4). 1990. 12.95s.p. (ISBN 0-88682-274-2); 18.50 (ISBN 0-685-28190-6). Creative Ed.
—Calgary Flames. 32p. (gr. 4). 1990. 12.95s.p. (ISBN 0-88682-275-0); 18.50 (ISBN 0-685-28191-4). Creative Ed.
—Chicago Blackhawks. 32p. (gr. 4). 1990. 12.95s.p. (ISBN 0-88682-276-9); 18.50 (ISBN 0-685-28192-2). Creative Ed.
—Detroit Red Wings. 32p. (gr. 4). 1990. 12.95s.p. (ISBN 0-88682-277-7); 18.50 (ISBN 0-685-28193-0). Creative Ed.
—Edmonton Oilers. 32p. (gr. 4). 1990. 12.95s.p. (ISBN 0-88682-278-5); 18.50 (ISBN 0-685-28194-9). Creative Ed.
—Hartford Whalers. 32p. (gr. 4). 1990. 12.95s.p. (ISBN 0-88682-279-3); 18.50 (ISBN 0-685-28195-7). Creative Ed.
—Los Angeles Kings. 32p. (gr. 4). 1990. 12.95s.p. (ISBN 0-88682-280-7); 18.50 (ISBN 0-685-28196-5). Creative Ed.
—Minnesota North Stars. 32p. (gr. 4). 1990. 12.95s.p. (ISBN 0-88682-281-5); 18.50 (ISBN 0-685-28197-3). Creative Ed.
—Montreal Canadians. 32p. (gr. 4). 1990. 12.95s.p. (ISBN 0-88682-282-3); 18.50 (ISBN 0-685-28198-1). Creative Ed.
—New Jersey Devils. 32p. (gr. 4). 1990. 12.95s.p. (ISBN 0-88682-283-1); 18.50 (ISBN 0-685-28199-X). Creative Ed.
—New York Islanders. 32p. (gr. 4). 1990. 12.95s.p. (ISBN 0-88682-284-X); 18.50 (ISBN 0-685-28200-7). Creative Ed.
—Philadelphia Flyers. 32p. (gr. 4). 1990. 12.95s.p. (ISBN 0-88682-286-6); 18.50 (ISBN 0-685-28201-5). Creative Ed.
—Pittsburgh Penguins. 32p. (gr. 4). 1990. s.p. 12.95 (ISBN 0-88682-287-4); 18.50 (ISBN 0-685-28202-3). Creative Ed.
—St. Louis Blues. 32p. (gr. 4). 1990. 12.95s.p. (ISBN 0-88682-289-0); 18.50 (ISBN 0-685-28204-X). Creative Ed.
—Toronto Maple Leafs. 32p. (gr. 4). 1990. 12.95s.p. (ISBN 0-88682-290-4); 18.50 (ISBN 0-685-28205-8). Creative Ed.
—Vancouver Canucks. 32p. (gr. 4). 1990. 12.95s.p. (ISBN 0-88682-291-2); 18.50 (ISBN 0-685-28206-6). Creative Ed.
—Washington Capitals. 32p. (gr. 4). 1990. 12.95s.p. (ISBN 0-88682-292-0); 18.50 (ISBN 0-685-28207-4). Creative Ed.
The Stanley Cup. 32p. (gr. 4). 1990. 12.95s.p. (ISBN 0-88682-316-1); 18.50 (ISBN 0-685-28231-7). Creative Ed.

HOCKEY–BIOGRAPHY
Bianchi, J. Champions of Hockey. (Illus.). 24p. (ps-8). 1989. 12.95 (ISBN 0-921285-18-3); pap. 4.95 (ISBN 0-921285-16-7). Firefly Bks Ltd.
Leder, Jane M. Wayne Gretzky. (Illus.). 48p. (gr. 5-6). 1985. PLB 10.95 (ISBN 0-89686-255-0, Crestwood Hse). Macmillan Child Grp.
Wolff, Craig T. Wayne Gretzky: Profil d'un Joueur de Hockey. Curtis, Bruce, photos by. (FRE., Illus.). 64p. (ps-5). 1984. pap. 2.25 (ISBN 0-380-85753-7, Camelot). Avon.

HOCKEY–FICTION
Carrier, Roch. Le Chandail de Hockey. Cohen, Sheldon, illus. (FRE.). 24p. (Orig.). (gr. 1 up). 1985. pap. 6.95 (ISBN 0-88776-176-3, Dist. by U of Toronto Pr); 14. 95 (ISBN 0-88776-171-2). Tundra Bks.
Christopher, Matt. The Hockey Machine. Schroeppel, Richard, illus. (gr. 4 up). 1986. 12.95 (ISBN 0-316-14055-4). Little.
—Ice Magic. Goto, Byron, illus. (gr. 4-6). 1987. PLB 14. 95 (ISBN 0-316-13958-0); pap. 3.95 (ISBN 0-316-13991-2). Little.
Corbett, Scott. The Hockey Girls. 112p. (gr. 5-6). 1976. 8.95 (ISBN 0-525-32065-2, DCB). Dutton Child Bks.
Dickmeyer, Lowell A. Hockey Is for Me. LC 78-54362. (Illus.). 48p. (gr. 2-5). 1978. PLB 8.95 (ISBN 0-8225-1080-4). Lerner Pubns.
Godfrey, Martyn. Ice Hawk. 96p. (gr. 7-12). 1986. pap. text ed. 4.50 (ISBN 0-8219-0235-0, 35361); 1.20 (ISBN 0-8219-0236-9, 35720). EMC.
Halecroft, David. Power Play. (gr. 4 up). 1990. pap. 2.95 (ISBN 0-14-034549-3, Puffin). Puffin Bks.
Harris, Jack C. Ring Raiders: Doom on Ice. (Illus.). 24p. (ps-3). 1989. pap. write for info. (ISBN 0-307-12569-6, Pub. by Golden Bks). Western Pub.
Jenkins, Jerry. The Bizarre Hockey Tournament. (Orig.). (gr. 9-12). 1986. pap. text ed. 3.95 (ISBN 0-8024-8236-8). Moody.
Paulsen, Gary. Dancing Carl. LC 83-2663. 144p. (gr. 6-8). 1983. 12.95 (ISBN 0-02-770210-3, Bradbury Pr). Macmillan Child Grp.
Smith, Alias & Pelkowski, Robert. Hockey: Freddie Face-off & Fanny Falls in Ice Monster. 32p. (ps-3). 1989. pap. 3.95 (ISBN 0-8120-4243-3). Barron.
Swanson, Steven. Brad Benson & the Secret Weapon. LC 83-25206. 127p. (gr. 5-10). 1984. pap. 2.95 (ISBN 0-89191-821-3). Cook.

HOGS
see also Pigs
Hutchings, Tony. Little Pink Piglet. Hutchings, Tony, illus. 12p. (ps-1). 1990. 4.95 (ISBN 1-878624-15-6, 1553800015). McClanahan Bk.
Ross, Dave. A Book of Hugs. Ross, Dave, illus. LC 79-7896. 32p. (gr. 1-6). 1986. 6.95 (ISBN 0-694-00146-5, Crowell Jr Bks). HarpC Child Bks.
Terry, John. Pigs in the Playground. Brewis, Henry, illus. 208p. 1986. pap. 7.95 (ISBN 0-85236-158-0, Pub by Farming Pr UK); pap. text ed. 6.95 (ISBN 0-317-47058-2, Pub. by Farming Pr UK). Diamond Farm Bk.

HOGS–FICTION
Aylesworth, Jim. Hanna's Hog. Rounds, Glen, illus. LC 87-11559. 32p. (gr. k-3). 1988. 13.95 (ISBN 0-689-31367-5, Atheneum Child Bk). Macmillan Child Grp.
Jefferson, David S. Wally the Wart Hog. 1990. 4.95 (ISBN 0-533-08919-0). Vantage.
Sinclair, Tom. Tales of a Wandering Warthog. Levine, Abby, ed. Wallner, John C., illus. LC 84-19621. 134p. (gr. 4 up). 1985. PLB 9.95 (ISBN 0-8075-7754-5). A Whitman.

HOISTING MACHINERY
see also Cranes, Derricks, Etc.; Elevators
Marston, Hope I. Load Lifters. (Illus.). 64p. (gr. 2-5). 1988. 13.95 (ISBN 0-396-09226-8, Putnam). Putnam Pub Group.

HOLIDAYS
see also Fasts and Feasts;
also names of holidays, e.g. Fourth of July
Ainsworth, Catherine H. American Calendar Customs, Vol. I. LC 79-52827. 112p. (Orig.). (ps-12). 1979. pap. 10.00 (ISBN 0-933190-06-9). Clyde Pr.
Alexander, Sue. America's Own Holidays: Mas de Fiesta de los Estados Unidos. FS Staff, ed. Morrill, Leslie, illus. (ENG & SPA.). 48p. 1988. PLB 10.90 (ISBN 0-531-10293-9). Watts.
Baker, James W. Presidents' Day Magic. Overlie, George, illus. 48p. (gr. 2-5). 1989. 8.95 (ISBN 0-8225-2232-2). Lerner Pubns.
Banh Chung Banh Day: The New Year's Rice Cakes. (gr. 2-5). 1972. 2.50 (ISBN 0-686-10279-7). Asia Resource.
Bauman, Toni & Zinkgraf, June. Celebrations. Wunderlin, Linda W., illus. 240p. (gr. k-6). 1985. wkbk. 14.95 (ISBN 0-86653-330-3, GA 666). Good Apple.
Behrens, June. Fiesta! Kratky, Lada, tr. LC 85-23271. (SPA., Illus.). 32p. (ps-3). 1986. PLB 14.60 (ISBN 0-516-38815-0); pap. 3.95 (ISBN 0-516-58815-X). Childrens.
—Fiesta! Ethnic Traditional Holidays. Taylor, Scott, illus. LC 78-8468. 32p. (gr. k-4). 1978. PLB 14.60 (ISBN 0-516-08815-7, Golden Gate); pap. 3.95 (ISBN 0-516-48815-5). Childrens.
Blackwood, Alan. New Year. (Illus.). 48p. (gr. 3-8). 1987. PLB 14.60 (ISBN 0-86592-981-5). Rourke Corp.
Bornstein, Harry. The Holiday Book. 48p. (ps-2). 1974. pap. 6.50 (ISBN 0-913580-30-9, Clerc Bks). Gallaudet Univ Pr.
Bulla, Clyde R. Lincoln's Birthday. Crichlow, Ernest, illus. LC 65-27291. 144p. (gr. 1-3). 1965. PLB 12.89 (ISBN 0-690-49450-5, Crowell Jr Bks). HarpC Child Bks.
—St. Valentine's Day. Angelo, Valenti, illus. LC 65-11643. 40p. (gr. 1-3). 1965. PLB 12.89 (ISBN 0-690-71744-X, Crowell Jr Bks). HarpC Child Bks.
Burnett, Bernice. Holidays. (Illus.). 96p. (gr. 4up). 10.40 (ISBN 0-531-04646-X). Watts.
Carrie, Christopher. Holiday Fun. (Illus.). 32p. (Orig.). (ps up). 1989. 1.99 (ISBN 0-685-27062-9). Binney & Smith.
Carroll, Jeri A. & Wells, Candace B. Learning about Fall & Winter Holidays. 112p. (ps-2). 1988. wkbk. 9.95 (ISBN 0-86653-441-5, GA1048). Good Apple.
Cole, Ann, et al. A Pumpkin in a Pear Tree: Creative Ideas for Twelve Months of Holiday Fun. (Illus.). 112p. (gr. 1 up). 1976. pap. 8.95 (ISBN 0-316-15111-4). Little.
Corrigan, Adeline. Holiday Ring. Rubin, Caroline & Bennett, Rainey, illus. LC 75-15975. 256p. (gr. 3 up). 1975. PLB 12.95 (ISBN 0-8075-3356-4). A Whitman.

Corwin, Judith H. Messner Holiday Library, 9 bks. Corwin, Judith H., illus. (gr. 3 up). 1990. Set, 64p. ea. lib. bdg. 92.61 (ISBN 0-671-92641-1); Set, 64p. ea. pap. 49.55 (ISBN 0-671-92642-X). Messner.

Cracchiolo, Rachelle. Holiday Cards. Darby's Designs, illus. 32p. (gr. 1-6). 1982. wkbk. 4.95 (ISBN 1-55734-031-5). Tchr Create Mat.

Cracchiolo, Rachelle & Smith, Mary D. Holiday Hats. Cracchiolo, Rachelle & Smith, Mary D., illus. 16p. (gr. k-3). 1979. wkbk. 6.50 (ISBN 1-55734-002-1). Tchr Create Mat.

Dalgliesh, Alice. The Fourth of July Story. Nonnast, Marie, illus. LC 86-20662. 32p. (gr. k-4). 1987. pap. 3.95 (ISBN 0-689-71115-8, Aladdin). Macmillan Child Grp.

D'Amato, Janet & D'Amato, Alex. Handicrafts for Holidays. D'Amato, Janet & D'Amato, Alex, illus. (gr. 1-4). 1967. PLB 11.95 (ISBN 0-87460-086-3). Lion Bks.

Dellosa, Janet & Carson, Patti. Year Round Holidays. Dellosa, Janet & Carson, Patti, illus. 32p. (ps-2). 1984. pap. 1.59 (ISBN 0-88724-058-5, CD-8043). Carson-Dellos.

Endersby, Frank. Holidays. (Illus.). 12p. (ps). 1984. 3.50 (ISBN 0-85953-189-9, Child's Play England). Childs Play.

Fox, et al. Holidays & Festivals, 4 bks, Set II, Reading Level 4. (Illus.). 192p. (gr. 3-8). Date not set. Set. PLB 58.40 (ISBN 0-86592-982-3). Rourke Corp.

Fox, Mary V. About Martin Luther King Day. LC 88-23230. (Illus.). 64p. (gr. 4-7). 1989. PLB 15.95 (ISBN 0-89490-200-8). Enslow Pubs.

Frost, Ed & Frost, Roon. The Kids' Holiday Book: Activities Through the Seasons. Leach, Carol, illus. 176p. (Orig.). (ps-7). 1990. pap. 11.95 (ISBN 0-9618806-3-5). Glove Compart Bks.

Garcia, Yolanda. Celebremos. (SPA., Illus.). (gr. 1-6). 10.95 (ISBN 0-935303-03-0). Victory Pub.

Gerson, Trina. Holiday Crafts. Gerson, Janice, illus. 80p. (ps-7). 1983. pap. text ed. write for info. (ISBN 0-9605878-1-0). Anirt Pr.

Glover, Suzanne & Grewe, Georgeann. Holiday Happenings. (gr. 1-4). 1982. pap. 9.95 (ISBN 0-88160-046-6, LW 231). Learning Wks.

Greene, Carol. Holidays Around the World. LC 82-9734. (Illus.). (gr. k-4). 1982. PLB 14.60 (ISBN 0-516-01624-5); pap. 4.95 (ISBN 0-516-41624-3). Childrens.

Grigoli, Valorie. Patriotic Holidays & Celebrations. LC 85-7270. (Illus.). 66p. (gr. 4-7). 1985. PLB 10.40 (ISBN 0-531-10044-8). Watts.

Hand, Phyllis. Celebrate Special Days. Hierstein, Judy, illus. 144p. (gr. k-6). 1985. wkbk. 10.95 (ISBN 0-86653-280-3, SS 841). Good Apple.

Happy Holidays. (Illus.). (ps-5). 3.50 (ISBN 0-7214-0553-3); Series S05, Set 1. flash cards 4.75; Series S05, Set 2. flash cards 4.75. Ladybird Bks.

Holidays Around the World. (Illus.). (ps-7). 1987. 5.95 (ISBN 0-553-05416-3). Bantam.

Ingram, Victoria. Holidays. 64p. (gr. k-3). 1987. 6.95 (ISBN 0-912107-60-X). Monday Morning Bks.

Kalman, Bobbie. We Celebrate Christmas. (Illus.). 56p. (gr. 3-4). 1985. 15.95 (ISBN 0-86505-040-6); pap. 7.95 (ISBN 0-86505-050-3). Crabtree Pub Co.
WE CELEBRATE CHRISTMAS is filled with stories, legends, poems, games, activities & recipes that allow children to experience holiday festivities from around the world. Children can explore the origins & customs of many familiar & colorful festivals & holiday celebrations. They will discover new ways to celebrate holidays & develop an understanding & appreciation of other cultures. WE CELEBRATE CHRISTMAS is part of The Holidays & Festivals Series. Other books in the series are WE CELEBRATE: HANUKKAH, THE HARVEST, HALLOWE'EN, VALENTINE'S DAY, NEW YEAR, FAMILY DAYS, SPRING, WINTER & EASTER. They are all profusely illustrated, fun-filled, multicultural, & easy-to-read.
Publisher Provided Annotation.

—We Celebrate Family Days. (Illus.). 56p. (gr. 3-4). 1986. 15.95 (ISBN 0-86505-048-1); pap. 7.95 (ISBN 0-86505-058-9). Crabtree Pub Co.

—We Celebrate Harvest. (Illus.). 56p. (gr. 3-4). 1986. 15.95 (ISBN 0-86505-044-9); pap. 7.95 (ISBN 0-86505-054-6). Crabtree Pub Co.

Keefe, Betty. Fingerpuppets, Fingerplays & Holidays. (Illus.). 136p. (ps-3). 1984. spiral bdg. 17.95 (ISBN 0-938594-05-2). Spec Lit Pr.

Kollay, Jocelyne. French Holiday Activity Workbook. (FRE & ENG., Illus.). 100p. (Orig.). (gr. 9-12). 1988. wkbk. 16.95 (ISBN 0-9617764-1-2). PS Enterprises.

Kroll, Steven. Happy Mother's Day. Hafner, Marilyn, illus. LC 83-18498. 32p. (ps-3). 1985. 14.95g (ISBN 0-8234-0504-4). Holiday.

LeGros, Lucy C. Instant Centers - Holidays. rev. ed. Legros, Ivor L., illus. 51p. (gr. k-2). 1988. tchr's ed. 5.95 (ISBN 0-317-65724-0). Creat Res NC.

Lemelman, Martin. Chanukah Is... (Illus.). 10p. (ps-k). 1988. bds. 4.95 (ISBN 0-8074-0424-1). UAHC.

Liestman, Vicki. Columbus Day. Hanson, Rick, illus. 56p. (gr. k-4). 1991. PLB 9.95 (ISBN 0-87614-444-X). Carolrhoda Bks.

Lithuanian Photographers Staff. Lithuanian Celebrations: Lietuviu Sventes. Algimantas KEZYS Staff, ed. Bindokiene, Danute, intros. by. (ENG & LIT.). 250p. 1990. pap. text ed. 15.00 (ISBN 0-9617756-4-5). Galerija.

Little People Big Book about Holidays & Celebrations. 64p. (ps-1). 1990. write for info. (ISBN 0-8094-7508-1); PLB write for info. (ISBN 0-8094-7509-X). Time-Life.

Livingston, Myra C. Celebrations. Fisher, Leonard E., illus. LC 84-19216. 32p. (gr. k-3). 1985. reinforced bdg. 14.95 (ISBN 0-8234-0550-8); pap. 5.95 (ISBN 0-8234-0654-7). Holiday.

Lowery, Linda. Martin Luther King Day. Mitchell, Hetty, illus. (gr. 3-5). 1987. incl. cassette 19.95 (ISBN 0-87499-071-8); pap. 12.95 incl. cassette (ISBN 0-87499-070-X); 4 paperbacks, cassette & guide 27.95 (ISBN 0-87499-072-6). Live Oak Media.

MacKenthum, Carole. Holiday Poems, Prayers & Projects. McClure, Nancee, illus. 48p. (gr. 3-7). 1984. wkbk. 6.95 (ISBN 0-86653-234-X, SS 813). Good Apple.

Malnig, Anita. Holidays & Concepts. (gr. k-2). 1985. pap. 5.95 (ISBN 0-8224-3953-0). Fearon Teach Aids.

Packard, Ann & Stafford, Shirley. Holidays. 116p. 1983. write for info. (ISBN 0-9607580-4-6). S Stafford.

Parker, Margot. What Is Veterans Day? Bates, Matt, illus. LC 86-11732. 48p. (ps-3). 1986. PLB 14.60 (ISBN 0-516-03782-X). Childrens.

Perl, Lila & Ada, Alma F. Pinatas & Paper Flowers-Pinatas y Flores de Papel: Holidays of the Americas in English & Spanish. De Larrea, Victoria, illus. LC 82-12211. 96p. (gr. 3-6). 1985. 12.95 (ISBN 0-89919-112-6, Pub. by Clarion); pap. 5.95 (ISBN 0-89919-155-X). Ticknor & Fields.

Poelker, Kathy. Look at the Holidays. Schiller, Juel K., illus. 64p. (ps-4). 1988. Repr. of 1980 ed. tchr's. ed. 7.95 (ISBN 0-317-91200-3). LAM Co.

Reece, Colleen L. Mi Primer Libro de el Dia de las Brujas. Kratky, Lada, tr. Peltier, Pam, illus. LC 85-31396. (SPA.). 32p. (ps-2). 1986. PLB 14.60 (ISBN 0-516-32902-2); pap. 3.95 (ISBN 0-516-52902-1). Childrens.

Renberg, Dalia H. The Complete Family Guide to Jewish Holidays. LC 84-11008. (Illus.). (gr. 4 up). 1985. pap. 15.95 (ISBN 0-915361-09-4, Dist. by Watts). Adama Pubs Inc.

Sandak, Cass. Patriotic Holidays. LC 89-25380. (Illus.). 48p. (gr. 5 up). 1990. 10.95 (ISBN 0-89686-501-0, Crestwood Hse). Macmillan Child Grp.

Scharfstein, Sol. What to Do on a Jewish Holiday? Friedman, Arthur, photos by. (gr. 3-5). 1985. 6.95 (ISBN 0-88125-170-4). Ktav.

Scott, Geoffrey. Memorial Day. Hanson, Peter E., illus. LC 83-1855. 48p. (gr. k-4). 1983. PLB 9.95 (ISBN 0-87614-219-6). Carolrhoda Bks.

Simon, Norma. Passover. Shimin, Symeon, illus. LC 65-11644. (gr. k-3). 1965. PLB 12.89 (ISBN 0-690-61094-7, Crowell Jr Bks). HarpC Child Bks.

Snelling, et al. Holidays & Festivals, 6 bks, Set I, Reading Level 4. (Illus.). 288p. (gr. 3-8). Date not set. Set. PLB 87.60 (ISBN 0-86592-975-0). Rourke Corp.

Sterling, Mary E. Holidays on Parade. Olsen, Shirley, illus. 64p. (gr. k-2). 1988. wkbk. 6.95 (ISBN 1-55734-377-2). Tchr Create Mat.

Sullivan, Dianna J. Patriotic Holidays. Walhood, Darlene, illus. 48p. (gr. 1-5). 1986. wkbk. 5.95 (ISBN 1-55734-115-X). Tchr Create Mat.

Tudor, Tasha. A Time to Keep: The Tasha Tudor Book of Holidays. LC 77-9067. (Illus.). (gr. 4-8). 1988. 13.95 (ISBN 0-02-689091-7, Mcmillan Child Bk). Macmillan Child Grp.

Van Straalen, Alice. The Book of Holidays Around the World. 1986. 14.95 (ISBN 0-525-44270-7, DCB). Dutton Child Bks.

Wells, Candace B. & Carroll, Jeri A. Learning about Spring & Summer Holidays. 112p. (ps-2). 1988. wkbk. 9.95 (ISBN 0-86653-442-3, GA1047). Good Apple.

HOLIDAYS–DRAMA

Gilfond, Henry & Blevins, George. Holiday Plays for Reading. (Illus.). 160p. (gr. 4 up). 1985. PLB 10.85 (ISBN 0-8027-6601-3). Walker & Co.

HOLIDAYS–FICTION

Adler, David. The House on the Roof. Hirsh, Marilyn, illus. LC 84-12555. 32p. (ps-4). pap. 4.95 (ISBN 0-930494-35-0). Kar-Ben.

Bond, Nancy. The Best of Enemies. LC 77-17363. 276p. (gr. 5-8). 1978. 14.95 (ISBN 0-689-50108-0, M K McElderry). Macmillan Child Grp.

Chaikin, Miriam. Make Noise, Make Merry. (gr. 4-7). 1983. 11.95 (ISBN 0-89919-140-1). Ticknor & Fields.

Charles, Freda. The Mystery of Missing Challah. Goldstein, Lil, illus. 40p. (ps). 1981. pap. 5.95 (ISBN 0-8246-0264-1). Jonathan David.

Christian, Mary B. April Fool. Dawson, Diane, illus. LC 86-3508. 48p. (gr. 1-4). 1986. pap. 3.95 (ISBN 0-689-71075-5, Aladdin). Macmillan Child Grp.

Draper, C. G. A Holiday Year. (gr. 5-9). 1988. 12.95 (ISBN 0-316-19203-1). Little.

Foehl, Jamie L. Trick or Treat Taffy. Foehl, Barbara B., illus. LC 89-92436. 40p. (Orig.). (ps-6). 1989. write for info. (ISBN 0-9625337-0-X); PLB write for info.; pap. write for info. B Bk Pub Co.

Johnston, Annie F. The Little Colonel's Holidays. (gr. 5 up). 13.95 (ISBN 0-89201-038-X). Zenger Pub.

Joosse, Barbara M. Fourth of July. McCully, Emily A., illus. LC 82-17301. 48p. (ps-2). 1985. lib. bdg. 11.99 (ISBN 0-394-95195-6); pap. 10.95 (ISBN 0-394-85195-1). Knopf.

Keller, Holly. Henry's Fourth of July. LC 84-13707. (Illus.). 32p. (ps-1). 1985. 10.25 (ISBN 0-688-04012-8); PLB 10.88 (ISBN 0-688-04013-6). Greenwillow.

Manes, Stephen. The Hooples' Horrible Holiday. 128p. (Orig.). (gr. 3-7). 1986. pap. 2.50 (ISBN 0-380-89740-7, Camelot). Avon.

Mariana. Miss Flora McFlimsey's May Day. rev. ed. Mariana, illus. LC 86-15252. 40p. (ps-3). 1987. 9.95 (ISBN 0-688-04545-6). Lothrop.

Moutran, Julia S. Will Spring Ever Come to Gobbler's Knob? A Punxsutawney Phil Adventure Story. Sweetland, Marsha L., illus. 64p. (ps-5). 1992. Incl. Phil's Field Guide to Woodland Animals. 15.95 (ISBN 0-9617819-5-5); Incl. Phil's Field Guide to Woodland Animals. pap. 9.95 (ISBN 0-9617819-4-7); audiocass. 10.95. Lit Pubns.

Pulver, Robin. The Holiday Handwriting School. Karas, G. Brian, illus. LC 89-77085. 32p. (gr. k-3). 1991. RSBE 12.95 (ISBN 0-02-775455-3, Four Winds). Macmillan Child Grp.

Salop, Byrd. The Kiddush Cup Who Hated Wine. Goldstein, Lil, illus. 32p. (gr. 1 up). 1981. pap. 5.95 (ISBN 0-8246-0265-X). Jonathan David.

Schertle, Alice. Jeremy Bean's St. Patrick's Day. Shute, Linda, illus. LC 86-7403. 32p. (ps-2). 1987. 12.95 (ISBN 0-688-04813-7); PLB 12.88 (ISBN 0-688-04814-5). Lothrop.

Sidi, Smadar S. The Dreidle Champ & Other Holiday Stories. Evers, June V., illus. 120p. (gr. 3-9). 1987. 13.95 (ISBN 0-915361-89-2, Dist. by Watts). Adama Pubs Inc.

Treasure Trunk. 1991. pap. 14.95 (ISBN 0-671-69203-8). S&S Trade.

Tudor, Tasha. A Tasha Tudor's Sampler: A Tale for Easter, Pumpkin Moonshine, The Dolls' Christmas. Tudor, Tasha, illus. (gr. k-3). 1977. 9.95 (ISBN 0-679-20412-1). McKay.

Wood, Audrey. The Horrible Holidays. Hoffman, Rosekrans, illus. LC 87-30617. 48p. (ps-3). 1988. 9.95 (ISBN 0-8037-0544-1); PLB 9.89 (ISBN 0-8037-0546-8). Dial Bks Young.

—Horrible Holidays. LC 87-30617. 48p. (ps-3). 1990. pap. 3.95 (ISBN 0-8037-0833-5). Dial Bks Young.

Zolotow, Charlotte. Over & Over. Williams, Garth, illus. LC 56-8149. (gr. k-2). 1957. 11.95i (ISBN 0-06-026955-3). HarpC Child Bks.

HOLIDAYS–POETRY

Parkison, Ralph F. Days. Withrow, Marion O., ed. Bush, William, illus. 60p. (Orig.). (gr. 2-8). 1988. pap. write for info. Little Wood Bks.

HOLLYWOOD, CALIFORNIA

Killingray, David & Yapp, Malcolm. Hollywood. (Illus.). 32p. (gr. 6-11). 1980. pap. text ed. 2.95 (ISBN 0-89908-213-0). Greenhaven.

HOLLYWOOD, CALIFORNIA–FICTION

John, Rob. Club Hollywood. (Illus.). 160p. (gr. 9-12). Date not set. pap. 2.50 (ISBN 0-317-02716-6, Sig Vista). NAL-Dutton.

HOLOCAUST, JEWISH

Abells, Chana B. The Children We Remember. LC 85-24876. (Illus.). 48p. (ps up). 1986. 9.95 (ISBN 0-688-06371-3); PLB 10.88 (ISBN 0-688-06372-1). Greenwillow.

Anne Frank. (gr. 7-12). 1991. PLB 14.95 (ISBN 0-8239-1204-3). Rosen Group.

Atkinson, Linda. In Kindling Flame: The Story of Hannah Senesh 1921-1944. LC 83-24392. 224p. (gr. 9 up). 1985. 14.95 (ISBN 0-688-02714-8). Lothrop.

Bernbaum, Israel. My Brother's Keeper: The Holocaust Through the Eyes of an Artist. LC 84-16100. (Illus.). 64p. (gr. 4-8). 1985. 16.95 (ISBN 0-399-21242-6, Putnam). Putnam Pub Group.

Chaikin, Mirian. A Nightmare in History: The Holocaust 1933-1945. LC 86-17617. 128p. (gr. 5 up). 1987. 14.95 (ISBN 0-89919-461-3, Pub. by Clarion). Ticknor & Fields.

Fersen-Osten, Renee. Don't They Know the World Stopped Breathing? Reminiscences of a Child During the Holocaust Years. 280p. (gr. 5-8). 1990. 16.95 (ISBN 1-56171-019-9). Shapolsky Pubs.

Finkelstein, Norman. Remember Not to Forget: A Memory of the Holocaust. Hokanson, Lars & Hokanson, Lois, illus. LC 84-17315. 32p. (gr. 1-3). 1985. PLB 10.90 (ISBN 0-531-04892-6). Watts.

Friedman, Ina R. The Other Victims: First-Person Stories of Non-Jews Persecuted by the Nazis. 224p. (gr. 5-9). 1990. 14.95 (ISBN 0-395-50212-8). HM.

Isaacman, Clara & Grossman, Joan A. Clara's Story. LC 84-14339. 180p. (gr. 5-9). 1984. 11.95 (ISBN 0-8276-0243-X). JPS Phila.

Landau, Elaine. We Survived the Holocaust. (Illus.). 144p. (gr. 9-12). 1991. 13.95 (ISBN 0-531-15229-4); PLB 13.90 (ISBN 0-531-11115-6). Watts.
Meltzer, Milton. Never to Forget: The Jews of the Holocaust. LC 75-25409. (gr. 7 up). 1976. PLB 13.89 (ISBN 0-06-024175-6). HarpC Child Bks.
—Rescue: The Story of How Gentiles Saved Jews in the Holocaust. LC 87-47816. (Illus.). 224p. (gr. 7 up). 1988. 13.95 (ISBN 0-06-024209-4); PLB 13.89 (ISBN 0-06-024210-8). HarpC Child Bks.
Neimark, Anne E. One Man's Valor: Leo Baeck & the Holocaust. LC 85-27366. (Illus.). 128p. (gr. 5-9). 1986. 14.95 (ISBN 0-525-67175-7, Lodestar Bks). Dutton Child Bks.
Rogasky, Barbara. Smoke & Ashes: The Story of the Holocaust. LC 87-28617. (Illus.). 192p. (gr. 5 up). 1988. 16.95 (ISBN 0-8234-0697-0). Holiday.
—Smoke & Ashes: The Story of the Holocaust. (Illus.). 1991. pap. 9.95 (ISBN 0-8234-0878-7). Holiday.
Rossell, Seymour. The Holocaust. (Illus.). 128p. (gr. 10-12). 1990. 12.40 (ISBN 0-531-10674-8). Watts.
Roth-Hano, Renee. Touch Wood: A Girlhood Occupied In France. 304p. (gr. 5 up). 1989. pap. 4.95 (ISBN 0-14-034085-8, Puffin). Puffin Bks.
Sender, Ruth M. The Cage. LC 86-8562. 252p. (gr. 7 up). 1986. 14.95 (ISBN 0-02-781830-6, Mcmillan Child Bk). Macmillan Child Grp.
—To Life. 240p. (gr. 6 up). 1990. pap. 4.95 (ISBN 0-14-034367-9, Puffin). Puffin Bks.
Stadtler, Bea. The Holocaust: A History of Courage & Resistance. Bial, Morrison D., ed. Martin, David S., illus. Bauer, Yehuda, intro. by. LC 74-11469. (Illus.). 210p. (gr. 5-7). 1975. pap. text ed. 5.95x (ISBN 0-87441-231-5); Discussion Guide: By Nancy Karkowsky. pap. text ed. 6.95 (ISBN 0-87441-257-9). Behrman.
Stein, R. Conrad. The Holocaust. LC 85-31415. (Illus.). 48p. (gr. 4-8). 1986. PLB 14.60 (ISBN 0-516-04767-1). Childrens.
Tames, Richard. Anne Frank. (Illus.). 32p. (gr. 7-9). 1990. 11.90 (ISBN 0-531-10763-9). Watts.
Tyler, Laura & Renna, Giani. Anne Frank. (Illus.). 104p. (gr. 5-8). 1990. lib. bdg. 16.98 (ISBN 0-382-09975-3); pap. 8.95 (ISBN 0-382-24002-2). Silver Burdett Pr.
Walshaw, Rachela & Walshaw, Sam. From Out of the Firestorm: A Memoir of the Holocaust. 260p. (gr. 5-8). 1990. pap. 10.95 (ISBN 1-56171-021-0). Shapolsky Pubs.
Zyskind, Sara. Stolen Years. LC 81-1953. 288p. (gr. 6 up). 1981. 11.95 (ISBN 0-8225-0766-8). Lerner Pubns.

HOLOCAUST, JEWISH–FICTION

Treseder, Terry W. Hear O Israel: A Story of the Warsaw Ghetto. Bloom, Lloyd, illus. LC 89-7029. 48p. (gr. 3 up). 1990. 13.95 (ISBN 0-689-31456-6, Atheneum Child Bk). Macmillan Child Grp.

HOLOGRAPHY

Graham, Ian. Lasers & Holograms. (Illus.). 32p. (gr. 5-8). 1991. PLB 11.90 (ISBN 0-531-17264-3, Gloucester Pr). Watts.
Heckman, Philip. The Magic of Holography. LC 85-27489. (Illus.). 256p. (gr. 7 up). 1986. 19.95 (ISBN 0-689-31168-0, Atheneum Child Bk). Macmillan Child Grp.

HOLY GRAIL

see Grail

HOLY SCRIPTURES

see Bible

HOLY SEE

see Catholic Church; Popes

HOLY SHROUD

Scavone, Daniel. The Shroud of Turin: Opposing Viewpoints. LC 88-24355. (Illus.). 112p. (gr. 3-8). 1988. PLB 13.95 (ISBN 0-89908-061-8). Greenhaven.

HOME

see also Home Economics; Marriage

Ask about the Home. 64p. (gr. 4-5). 1987. PLB 18.25 (ISBN 0-8172-2882-9); pap. 13.27 (ISBN 0-8172-2894-2). Raintree Pubs.
Klingel, Fitterer. Home Safety. (Illus.). 32p. (ps up). 1986. PLB 10.95s.p. (ISBN 0-88682-081-2); 15.65 (ISBN 0-685-09468-5). Creative Ed.
Larsson, Carl & Rudstrom, Lennart. A Home. (Illus.). 32p. (gr. 3-5). 1974. 13.95 (ISBN 0-399-20400-8, Sandcastle Bks); pap. 9.95 (ISBN 0-685-04192-1, Sandcastle Bks). Putnam Pub Group.
Talkabout the Home. (ARA., Illus.). (gr. 1-3). 3.50x (ISBN 0-86685-233-6). Intl Bk Ctr.
Walker, Mort & Browne, Dik. Hi & Lois: Good Housekeeping. 128p. 1986. pap. 1.95 (ISBN 0-8125-6906-7, Dist. by Warner Pub Services). Tor Bks.

HOME–FICTION

Asch, Frank. Goodbye House. Asch, Frank, illus. LC 85-19263. (ps-2). 1989. 12.95 (ISBN 0-671-67054-9); pap. 4.95 (ISBN 0-671-67927-9). S&S Trade.
Bellairs, John. The House with a Clock in Its Walls. 192p. (gr. 3 up). 1974. pap. 3.50 (ISBN 0-440-43742-3, YB). Dell.
Betancourt, Jeanne. Home Sweet Home. (gr. 7 up). 1989. pap. 2.95 (ISBN 0-553-27857-6, Starfire). Bantam.
Cole, Joanna. The Clown-Arounds Have a Party. Smath, Jerry, illus. LC 82-2128. 48p. (ps-3). 1982. 5.95 (ISBN 0-8193-1085-9); PLB 5.95 (ISBN 0-8193-1086-7). Parents.
—This Is the Place for Me. Van Horn, William, illus. 32p. (Orig.). (gr. k-3). 1986. pap. 1.95 (ISBN 0-590-33996-6). Scholastic Inc.
Fritz, Jean. Homesick: My Own Story. (gr. k-6). 1984. pap. 3.50 (ISBN 0-440-43683-4, YB). Dell.
Hague, Kathleen. The Man Who Kept House. Hague, Michael, illus. LC 80-26258. 32p. (ps-3). 1988. pap. 3.95 (ISBN 0-15-251699-9, VoyB). HarBraceJ.
Hannah, Valerie. Little Jollys Find a Home. Herrick, George H., ed. Kokino, Olga, illus. 36p. (Orig.). (gr. k-3). 1991. pap. 6.95 (ISBN 0-941281-79-5). V H Pub.
Kemp, Gene. No Place Like. LC 83-8901. 120p. (gr. 6-10). 1983. 13.95 (ISBN 0-571-13063-1). Faber & Faber.
Lindbergh, Anne. Tidy Lady. Hoguet, Susan, illus. LC 88-10905. (gr. k-3). 1989. 13.95 (ISBN 0-15-287150-0). HarBraceJ.
Malone, Nola L. A Home. LC 87-17849. (Illus.). 24p. (ps-2). 1988. 12.95 (ISBN 0-02-751440-4, Bradbury Pr). Macmillan Child Grp.
Monfried, Lucia. Dishes All Done. Agee, Jon, illus. 16p. (ps-k). 1989. 7.95 (ISBN 0-525-44433-5, DCB). Dutton Child Bks.
Ormerod, Jan. Sunshine. LC 80-84971. (Illus.). 32p. (ps-1). 1981. PLB 13.88 (ISBN 0-688-00553-5). Lothrop.
—Sunshine. LC 80-84971. (Illus.). (ps-3). 1990. pap. 3.95 (ISBN 0-688-09353-1, Mulberry). Morrow.
Parker, Ann N. Home Is Where the Shade Tree Is. Vickery, Diane, illus. 18p. (gr. k-4). 1988. pap. 3.95 (ISBN 0-943487-13-7). Sevgo Pr.
Rockwell, Anne. Our Garage Sale. Rockwell, Harlow, illus. LC 80-16704. 24p. (ps-1). 1984. 10.25 (ISBN 0-688-80278-8); PLB 10.88 (ISBN 0-688-84278-X). Greenwillow.
Tubby, I. M. I'm a Little House. Kraus, Robert, ed. Tubby, I. M., illus. 10p. (ps). 1982. pap. 2.95 (ISBN 0-671-45566-4, Little Simon). S&S Trade.
Ziefert, Harriet. In My Kitchen. Rader, Laura, illus. LC 89-3720. 24p. (Orig.). (ps-1). 1989. pap. 2.25 (ISBN 0-394-84894-2, Random Juv). Random.
—When the TV Broke. LC 88-82404. (Illus.). 32p. (ps-3). 1989. pap. 8.95 (ISBN 0-670-82668-5). Viking Child Bks.

HOME DECORATION

see Interior Decoration

HOME ECONOMICS

see also Consumer Education; Cookery; Dairying; Entertaining; Food; Fuel; Furniture; House Cleaning; Interior Decoration; Sewing; Shopping

Allen, Eleanor. Home Sweet Home: A History of Housework. (Illus.). 64p. (gr. 6 up). 1979. 14.95 (ISBN 0-7136-1927-9). Dufour.
Alvarez del Real, Maria E., ed. Como Reparar 500 Problemas De la Casa. (SPA., Illus.). 352p. (Orig.). 1988. pap. 4.50x (ISBN 0-944499-33-3). Editorial Amer.
Chaback, Elaine & Fortunato, Pat. The Official Kids' Survival Kit: How to Do Things on Your Own. (gr. 4 up). 1981. pap. 10.95 (ISBN 0-316-13531-3). Little.
Chamberlain, Valerie M. & Buddinger, Peyton B. Teen Guide. 6th ed. O'Neill, Martha, ed. Evelyne Johnson Associates Staff, illus. 528p. 1985. text ed. 30.00 (ISBN 0-07-007842-4); pap. text ed. 11.68 (ISBN 0-07-007831-9). McGraw.
Sanders, Pete. At Home. (Illus.). 32p. (gr. 3-6). 1989. PLB 11.90 (ISBN 0-531-17148-5). Watts.

HOME ECONOMICS–EQUIPMENT AND SUPPLIES

see also Household Equipment and Supplies

HOME EDUCATION

see Self-Culture

HOME MISSIONS

see Missions

HOME REPAIRING

see Houses–Repairing

HOME STUDY COURSES

see Self-Culture

HOMER–ADAPTATIONS

Homer. Odyssey. (gr. 9 up). pap. 2.95 (ISBN 0-8049-0057-4, CL-57). Airmont.

HOMES

see Houses

HOMOSEXUALITY

Cohen, Daniel & Cohen, Susan. When Someone You Know Is Gay. LC 89-1260. (gr. 12 up). 1989. 13.95 (ISBN 0-87131-567-X). M Evans.
Hunt, Morton. Gay: What You Should Know about Homosexuality. rev. ed. LC 87-23626. 224p. (gr. 6 up). 1988. 15.95 (ISBN 0-374-32525-1); pap. 6.95 (ISBN 0-374-42524-8). FS&G.
Landau, Elaine. Different Drummer: Homosexuality in America. LC 85-21679. 112p. (gr. 7 up). 1986. lib. bdg. 12.98 (ISBN 0-671-55497-2). Messner.

HOMOSEXUALITY–FICTION

Chambers, Aidan. Dance on My Grave. LC 82-48258. 256p. (gr. 7 up). 1983. PLB 13.89 (ISBN 0-06-021254-3). HarpC Child Bks.
Childress, Alice. Those Other People. 144p. (gr. 8 up). 1989. 13.95 (ISBN 0-399-21510-7, Putnam). Putnam Pub Group.
Donovan, John. I'll Get There: It Better Be Worth the Trip. LC 69-15539. (gr. 7 up). 1969. PLB 12.89 (ISBN 0-06-021718-9). HarpC Child Bks.
Heron, Ann & Maran, Meredith. How Would You Feel If Your Dad Was Gay? Martins, George, illus. 32p. (gr. 1-5). 1991. text ed. 9.95 (ISBN 1-55583-188-5). Alyson Pubns.
Holland, Isabelle. The Man Without a Face. Reissue. ed. LC 71-37736. 144p. (gr. 7 up). 1972. Repr. of 1972 ed. 12.95 (ISBN 0-397-31211-3, Lipp Jr Bks); PLB 12.89 (ISBN 0-397-32264-X, Lipp Jr Bks). HarpC Child Bks.
Meyer, Carolyn. Elliott & Win. LC 89-70868. 208p. (gr. 7 up). 1990. pap. 3.95 (ISBN 0-02-044702-7, Collier Young Ad). Macmillan Child Grp.
Mosca, Frank. All American Boys. 116p. (Orig.). (gr. 7-12). pap. 5.95 (ISBN 0-932870-44-9). Alyson Pubns.
Newman, Leslea. Gloria Goes to Gay Pride. Crocker, Russell, illus. 48p. (Orig.). (ps-2). 1991. pap. 7.95 (ISBN 1-55583-185-0). Alyson Pubns.
Willhoite, Michael. Daddy's Roommate. Willhoite, Michael, illus. 32p. (ps). 1990. 14.95 (ISBN 1-55583-178-8). Alyson Pubns.
Woodson, Jacqueline. Dear One. (gr. 4-7). 1991. 14.00 (ISBN 0-385-30416-1). Delacorte.

HONDURAS

Haynes, Tricia. Honduras. (Illus.). (gr. 5 up). 1988. 14.95 (ISBN 0-222-00959-4). Chelsea Hse.
Lerner Publications, Department of Geography Staff. Honduras in Pictures. (Illus.). 64p. (gr. 5 up). 1987. PLB 12.95 (ISBN 0-8225-1804-X). Lerner Pubns.

HONEY

see also Bees

Hogan, Paula Z. The Honeybee. LC 78-21165. (Illus.). 32p. (gr. 1-4). 1984. PLB 27.99 incl. cassette (ISBN 0-8172-2229-4) (ISBN 0-685-09511-8). Raintree Pubs.

HONG KONG

Fairclough, Chris. We Live in Hong Kong. (Illus.). 64p. (gr. 4-8). 1986. lib. bdg. 9.49 (ISBN 0-531-18027-1, Pub. by Bookwright Pr). Watts.
Fyson, Nance L. Hong Kong. LC 89-26247. (Illus.). 96p. (gr. 6-11). 1990. PLB 18.60 (ISBN 0-8114-2433-2). Steck-V.
Jacobsen & Kristensen. A Family in Hong Kong. LC 84-73580. (Illus.). 32p. (gr. 3-5). 1985. 11.90 (ISBN 0-531-18001-8, Pub. by Bookwright Pr). Watts.
Lyle, Garry. Hong Kong. (Illus.). (gr. 5 up). 1988. 14.95 (ISBN 0-222-00800-8). Chelsea Hse.
McKenna, Nancy D. A Family in Hong Kong. (Illus.). 32p. (gr. 2-5). 1987. 9.95 (ISBN 0-8225-1676-4). Lerner Pubns.
Stein, R. Conrad. Hong Kong. LC 84-23199. (Illus.). 128p. (gr. 5-9). 1985. lib. bdg. 25.27 (ISBN 0-516-02765-4). Childrens.
Wright, David K. Hong Kong. LC 90-9669. (Illus.). 64p. (gr. 5-6). 1991. PLB 12.95 (ISBN 0-8368-0382-5). Gareth Stevens Inc.

HOOVER, HERBERT CLARK, PRESIDENT U. S. 1874-1964

Clinton, Susan. Herbert Hoover. LC 87-35711. (Illus.). 100p. (gr. 3 up). 1988. PLB 17.27 (ISBN 0-516-01355-6); pap. 6.95 (ISBN 0-516-41355-4). Childrens.
Hilton, Suzanne. The World of Young Herbert Hoover. Steins, Deborah, illus. (gr. 5-8). 1987. 12.95 (ISBN 0-8027-6708-7); PLB 13.85 (ISBN 0-8027-6709-5). Walker & Co.
Polikof, Barbara G. Herbert C. Hoover: Thirty-First President of the United States. Young, Richard G., ed. LC 89-39946. (Illus.). 128p. (gr. 5-9). 1990. PLB 17.26 (ISBN 0-944483-58-5). Garrett Ed Corp.

HORMONES

Villee, Claude A., Jr. Human Hormones. Head, J. J., ed. Johnson, Patricia & Steffen, Ann T., illus. LC 86-72197. 16p. (Orig.). (gr. 10 up). 1987. pap. text ed. 2.15 (ISBN 0-89278-371-0, 45-9771). Carolina Biological.

HOROLOGY

see Clocks and Watches; Sundials

HOROSCOPE

see Astrology

HORROR STORIES

Aiken, Joan. Give Yourself a Fright. (gr. 7 up). 1989. 14.95 (ISBN 0-440-50120-2). Delacorte.
—A Touch of Chill. LC 79-3331. 124p. (gr. 7 up). 1980. 9.95 (ISBN 0-385-29310-0). Delacorte.
Albright, Molly. Fright Night. Connor, Eulala, illus. LC 88-12388. 96p. (gr. 3-6). 1989. PLB 9.89 (ISBN 0-8167-1486-X); pap. text ed. 2.95 (ISBN 0-8167-1487-8). Troll Assocs.
—Meet Miss Dracula. DeRosa, Dee, illus. LC 87-13871. 96p. (gr. 3-6). 1988. PLB 9.89 (ISBN 0-8167-1157-7); pap. text ed. 2.95 (ISBN 0-8167-1158-5). Troll Assocs.
Alcock, Vivien. The Haunting of Cassie Palmer. (gr. k-6). 1990. pap. 2.95 (ISBN 0-440-43370-3, YB). Dell.
Alexander, Sue. More Witch, Goblin & Ghost Stories. Winter, Jeanette, illus. LC 78-3280. (gr. 1-4). 1978. 6.95 (ISBN 0-394-83933-1); lib. bdg. 7.99 (ISBN 0-394-93933-6). Pantheon.
—Witch, Goblin, & Ghost Are Back. Winter, Jeanette, illus. LC 83-22157. 62p. (gr. 1-4). 1985. 6.95 (ISBN 0-394-86296-1, Pant Bks Young); lib. bdg. 9.99 (ISBN 0-394-96296-6). Pantheon.
Allen, Derek, retold by. Blood from the Mummy's Tomb. 160p. (gr. 6 up). 1988. pap. 2.95 (ISBN 0-8120-4074-0). Barron.
The Bank Street Book of Scary Tales. (Orig.). (gr. 4 up). 1989. pap. 3.50 (ISBN 0-318-41225-X, Minstrel Bks). PB.
Bedard, Michael. A Darker Magic. 192p. 1989. pap. 2.95 (ISBN 0-380-70611-3, Flare). Avon.
Bellairs, John. The Figure in the Shadows. 192p. (gr. 4-7). 1977. pap. 3.50 (ISBN 0-440-42551-4, YB). Dell.
Bennett, Jay. The Haunted One. (gr. 7 up). 1989. pap. 2.95 (ISBN 0-449-70314-2, Juniper). Fawcett.
Beresford, Elisabeth. Emily & the Haunted Castle. (Illus.). 124p. (gr. 4-6). 1988. 13.95 (ISBN 0-09-170460-X, Pub. by Hutchinson UK). Trafalgar Sq.
Brennan, J. H. Kingdom of Horror. (gr. 6-12). 1987. pap. 2.50 (ISBN 0-440-94540-2). Dell.

—The Vampire in Love. Glienke, Amelie, illus. 128p. (gr. 2-6). 1991. 12.95 (ISBN 0-8037-0905-6); lib. bdg. 12. 89 (ISBN 0-8037-0906-4). Dial Bks Young.
—The Vampire on the Farm. Glienke, Amelie, illus. LC 87-2153. 144p. (gr. 2-6). 1989. 10.95 (ISBN 0-8037-0326-0); PLB 10.89 (ISBN 0-8037-0327-9). Dial Bks Young.
—The Vampire Takes a Trip. Glienke, Amelie, illus. LC 84-22995. 160p. (gr. 2-6). 1985. 9.95 (ISBN 0-8037-0199-3); PLB 9.89 (ISBN 0-8037-0201-9). Dial Bks Young.
Steiner, Barbara. The Photographer. 144p. 1989. pap. 2.95 (ISBN 0-380-75758-3, Flare). Avon.
Stevenson, Drew. The Case of the Visiting Vampire. (Illus.). 128p. (gr. 3-7). 1986. 10.95 (ISBN 0-396-08856-2, Putnam). Putnam Pub Group.
Stevenson, Robert Louis. Dr. Jekyll & Mr. Hyde. (gr. 5 up). 1978. 6.95 (ISBN 0-448-41110-5, G&D). Putnam Pub Group.
—Dr. Jekyll & Mr. Hyde. new ed. Platt, Kin, ed. Redondo, Nestor, illus. LC 73-75457. 64p. (Orig.). (gr. 5-10). 1973. pap. 2.95 (ISBN 0-88301-096-8); student activity bk. 1.25 (ISBN 0-88301-176-X). Pendulum Pr.
—Dr. Jekyll & Mr. Hyde. McMullan, Kate, adapted by. Van Munching, Paul, illus. LC 87-23542. 96p. (gr. 3-7). 1988. pap. 1.95 (ISBN 0-317-66886-2, Random Juv). Random.
—Dr. Jekyll & Mr. Hyde. 1990. pap. 2.50 (ISBN 0-8125-0448-8). Tor Bks.
Stoker, Bram. Dracula. Lowndes, R. A., intro. by. LC 83-5471. (gr. 7 up). pap. 2.25 (ISBN 0-8049-0072-8, CL-72). Airmont.
—Dracula. (gr. 4-6). 1986. pap. 2.95 (ISBN 0-14-035048-9, Puffin). Puffin Bks.
—Dracula. (gr. 4 up). 1989. pap. 4.87 (ISBN 0-582-52282-X, 73810). Longman.
—Dracula. Spinner, Stephanie, ed. Spence, Jim, illus. LC 87-23541. 96p. (gr. 3-7). 1988. pap. 1.95 (ISBN 0-317-66897-8, Random Juv). Random.
—Dracula. 1990. 3.98 (ISBN 0-8317-1483-2). Smithmark.
Stoker, Bram, et al. Dracula, Frankenstein, Dr. Jekyll & Mr. Hyde. King, Stephen, intro. by. 672p. (RL 7). 1978. pap. 5.95 (ISBN 0-451-52363-6, Sig Classics). NAL-Dutton.
Tallis, Robyn. Horrorvid. (gr. 6 up). 1989. pap. 2.95 (ISBN 0-8041-0461-1). Ivy Books.
Thorne, Ian. The Deadly Mantis. LC 81-22074. (Illus.). 48p. (gr. 3 up). 1982. PLB 10.95 (ISBN 0-89686-214-3, Crestwood Hse); pap. 4.95 (ISBN 0-89686-217-8). Macmillan Child Grp.
—Dracula. LC 76-51145. (Illus.). 48p. (gr. 3 up). 1977. PLB 9.95 (ISBN 0-913940-67-4, Crestwood Hse); pap. 4.95 (ISBN 0-913940-74-7); cass. 7.95 (ISBN 0-89686-485-5). Macmillan Child Grp.
—Frankenstein. Schroeder, Howard, ed. LC 76-51144. (Illus.). 48p. (gr. 3 up). 1977. PLB 10.95 (ISBN 0-913940-66-6, Crestwood Hse); pap. 4.95 (ISBN 0-913940-73-9); cass. 7.95 (ISBN 0-685-01269-7). Macmillan Child Grp.
—Mad Scientists. LC 76-51149. (Illus.). 48p. (gr. 3 up). 1977. PLB 10.95 (ISBN 0-913940-70-4, Crestwood Hse); pap. 4.95 (ISBN 0-913940-77-1); cass. 7.95 (ISBN 0-89686-487-1). Macmillan Child Grp.
Villa, Mickie, ed. The Comics That Ate My Brains. Wooley, John, intro. by. (Illus.). 140p. 1991. pap. 9.95 (ISBN 0-944735-77-0). Malibu Graphics.
Warren, William E. & Frascino, Edward. The Thing in the Swamp & More Not-So-Scary. LC 84-6769. (Illus.). 96p. (gr. 3-7). 1984. 10.95 (ISBN 0-13-917196-7). P-H.
Westwood, Chris. He Came from the Shadows. LC 90-38005. 224p. (gr. 7 up). 1991. 14.95 (ISBN 0-06-021658-1); PLB 14.89 (ISBN 0-06-021659-X). HarpC Child Bks.
Wierd & Spooky Tales. (Illus.). 192p. (gr. 3-8). Date not set. pap. 10.95 (ISBN 0-87460-391-9). Lion Bks.
Williamson, J. N. The Black School. (Orig.). 1989. pap. 3.50 (ISBN 0-440-20265-5). Dell.
Yolen, Jane & Greenberg, Martin H., eds. Werewolves: A Collection of Original Stories. LC 87-45863. 288p. (gr. 5-9). 1988. 13.95 (ISBN 0-06-026798-4); PLB 13.89 (ISBN 0-06-026799-2). HarpC Child Bks.
Young, Richard & Young, Judy D. Favorite Scary Stories of American Children. Hall, Wendell E., illus. 112p. (Orig.). (ps-5). 1990. pap. 8.95 (ISBN 0-87483-119-9). August Hse.

HORSE

see Horses

HORSE RACING

Cosgrove, Stephen. Derby Downs. Edelson, Wendy, illus. LC 88-25526. (gr. 6). 1988. 9.95 (ISBN 0-88070-240-0); deluxe ed. 10.95 (ISBN 0-88070-257-5). Multnomah.
Farley, Walter. Man O' War. (Illus.). (gr. 4-6). 1962. lib. bdg. 6.99 (ISBN 0-394-90616-0, Random Juv). Random.
Henry, Marguerite. Born to Trot. Dennis, Wesley, illus. LC 50-10271. 224p. (gr. 3 up). 1987. 8.95 (ISBN 0-528-82135-0); pap. 3.95 (ISBN 0-02-688755-X, Aladdin). Macmillan Child Grp.
The Kentucky Derby. 32p. (gr. 4). 1990. 12.95s.p. (ISBN 0-88682-312-9); 18.50 (ISBN 0-685-28227-9). Creative Ed.
Phillips, Louis. Willie Shoemaker. LC 88-14966. (Illus.). 48p. (gr. 5-6). 1988. PLB 10.95 (ISBN 0-89686-381-6, Crestwood Hse). Macmillan Child Grp.
Roth, Harold. A Day at the Races. LC 83-2345. (Illus.). 64p. (gr. 3-6). 1983. 10.95 (ISBN 0-394-85814-X, Pant Bks Young). Pantheon.

HORSE RACING–FICTION

Farley, Walter. Black Stallion. Ward, Keith, illus. LC 85-19927. (gr. 3-7). 1977. 3.95 (ISBN 0-394-80601-8, Random Juv); lib. bdg. 10.99 (ISBN 0-394-90601-2); pap. 3.95 (ISBN 0-394-83609-X). Random.
—Black Stallion & Satan. (Illus.). (gr. 4-6). 1978. 3.95 (ISBN 0-394-80605-0, Random Juv); lib. bdg. 8.99 (ISBN 0-394-90605-5); pap. 2.95 (ISBN 0-394-83914-5). Random.
—Black Stallion Challenged. LC 64-15094. (Illus.). (gr. 5-9). 1980. 3.95 (ISBN 0-394-80617-4, Random Juv); lib. bdg. 10.99 (ISBN 0-394-90617-9); pap. 2.95 (ISBN 0-394-84371-1). Random.
—Black Stallion's Courage. LC 56-5471. (Illus.). (gr. 4-6). 1978. 3.95 (ISBN 0-394-80612-3, Random Juv); lib. bdg. 6.99 (ISBN 0-394-90612-8); pap. 2.95 (ISBN 0-394-83918-8). Random.
—Black Stallion's Filly. LC 52-7216. (Illus.). (gr. 4-6). 1978. lib. bdg. 8.99 (ISBN 0-394-90608-X, Random Juv); PLB 8.99 (ISBN 0-685-04257-X); pap. 3.95 (ISBN 0-394-83916-1). Random.
—Black Stallion's Sulky Colt. (Illus.). (gr. 4-6). 1978. (Random Juv); lib. bdg. 10.99 (ISBN 0-394-90610-1); pap. 2.95 (ISBN 0-394-83917-X). Random.
—Blood Bay Colt. (Illus.). (gr. 4-6). 1978. 3.95 (ISBN 0-394-80606-9, Random Juv); lib. bdg. 8.99 (ISBN 0-394-90606-3); pap. 2.95 (ISBN 0-394-83915-3). Random.
—Island Stallion Races. (Illus.). (gr. 4-6). 1980. 3.95 (ISBN 0-394-80611-5, Random Juv); lib. bdg. 6.99 (ISBN 0-394-90611-X); pap. 2.95 (ISBN 0-394-84375-4). Random.
—Son of the Black Stallion. (Illus.). (gr. 4-6). 1977. 3.95 (ISBN 0-394-80603-4, Random Juv); lib. bdg. 10.99 (ISBN 0-394-90603-9); pap. 3.95 (ISBN 0-394-83612-X). Random.
Hardcastle, Michael. Kickback. 128p. (gr. 7-12). 1990. 10. 95 (ISBN 0-571-14951-0). Faber & Faber.
Henry, Marguerite. Black Gold. Dennis, Wesley, illus. LC 57-14557. 176p. (gr. 2-9). 1987. 8.95 (ISBN 0-528-82130-X); pap. 3.95 (ISBN 0-02-688754-1, Aladdin). Macmillan Child Grp.
—Gaudenzia Pride of the Palio. 1989. 12.95 (ISBN 0-02-689416-5). Macmillan Child Grp.
Hoppe, Joanne. Pretty Penny Farm. LC 86-1516. 224p. (gr. 7 up). 1987. 12.95 (ISBN 0-688-07201-1, Morrow Junior Books). Morrow.
Peyton, K. M. Free Rein. LC 83-8151. (gr. 8 up). 1983. 10.95 (ISBN 0-399-20995-6, Philomel). Putnam Pub Group.
Reed, Kevin J. The Saratoga Yearling. Herold, Meri G., ed. Corrigan, Wendy O., illus. 110p. (Orig.). (gr. 5-9). 1985. pap. 3.95 (ISBN 0-9614546-0-1). Chowder Pr.

HORSEBREAKING

see Horses–Training

HORSEMANSHIP

see also Rodeos

Asch, Connie. Horsemen of the World Coloring Book. Asch, Connie, illus. 32p. (gr. k-6). 1987. pap. 2.50 (ISBN 0-918080-30-4). Treasure Chest.
Biggs, Johnathan. Riding in Motion: A Three-Dimensional Guide to Horses for Young People. Horwood, Janet & Clifton-Dey, Richard, illus. LC 87-45765. 14p. (gr. 3-6). 1988. pop-up bk. 15.95 (ISBN 0-397-32258-5, Lipp Jr Bks). HarpC Child Bks.
Boy Scouts of America. Horsemanship. (Illus.). 64p. (gr. 6-12). 1986. pap. 1.85 (ISBN 0-8395-3298-9, 3298). BSA.
Callahan, Dorothy M. Julie Krone: A Winning Jockey. LC 89-26061. (Illus.). (gr. 3 up). 1990. 10.95 (ISBN 0-87518-425-1, Dillon); PLB 9.95 (ISBN 0-685-31386-7). Macmillan Child Grp.
Damrell, Liz. With the Wind. Marchesi, Stephen, illus. LC 89-48942. 32p. (ps-2). 1991. 14.95 (ISBN 0-531-05882-4); PLB 14.99 (ISBN 0-531-08482-5). Orchard Bks Watts.
Dumas, Philippe. The Lippizaners: And the Spanish Riding School of Vienna. (gr. 3-7). 1981. 10.95 (ISBN 0-13-537068-X). P-H.
Pervier, Evelyn. Horsemanship: Basics for Beginners. LC 83-10004. (Illus.). 96p. (Orig.). (gr. 6 up). 1984. pap. 7.95 (ISBN 0-668-05935-4). Prentice Hall Pr.
—Horsemanship: Basics for Intermediate Riders. LC 83-10003. (Illus.). 94p. (gr. 6 up). 1984. pap. 6.95 (ISBN 0-668-05942-7). Prentice Hall Pr.
—Horsemanship: Basics for More Advanced Riders. LC 83-10002. (Illus.). 94p. (gr. 6 up). 1984. pap. 6.95 (ISBN 0-668-05950-8). Prentice Hall Pr.
Sayer, Angela. The Young Rider's Handbook. Whitcomb, Gerald, illus. LC 83-19734. 224p. (gr. 5 up). 1984. 9.95 (ISBN 0-668-06044-1). Prentice Hall Pr.
Spataro, Lucian. Ride Across America: An Environmental Commitment. Baird, Tate, ed. Goodall, Jane, frwd. by. LC 90-72061. (Illus.). 183p. (gr. 9 up). 1991. 15.95 (ISBN 0-914127-44-6, 1R-1). Univ Class.
Watson, Mary G. Fields & Fencing. Vincer, Carole, illus. 24p. (Orig.). (gr. 3 up). 1988. pap. 7.95 (ISBN 0-901366-66-8, Pub. by Threshold Bks). Half Halt Pr.
Winter, Ginny L. Riding Book. Winter, Ginny L., illus. (gr. k-3). 1963. 8.95 (ISBN 0-8392-3031-1). Astor-Honor.

HORSEMANSHIP–FICTION

Berry, Barbara. His Majesty's Mark. LC 76-11631. (gr. 4 up). 1976. 6.95 (ISBN 0-672-52182-2, Bobbs). Macmillan.
Callan, Elizabeth K. Good Luck Pony. LC 90-50366. 40p. (ps-3). 1990. 12.95 (ISBN 0-89480-859-1, 1859). Workman Pub.
Doty, Jean S. Dark Horse. Chhuy, Dorothy H., illus. LC 82-21651. 122p. (gr. 4-6). 1983. 12.95 (ISBN 0-688-01703-7). Morrow Jr Bks.
Hewett, Joan. Laura Loves Horses. Hewett, Richard, photos by. (Illus.). 48p. (gr. 2-5). 1990. 14.95 (ISBN 0-89919-844-9). HM.
Rounds, Glen. Once We Had a Horse. LC 76-151758. (Illus.). 64p. (ps-3). 1971. 6.95 (ISBN 0-8234-0193-6). Holiday.
Vail, Virginia. Happy Trails. Bode, Daniel, illus. LC 89-30584. 128p. (gr. 4-5). 1990. PLB 9.89 (ISBN 0-8167-1627-7); pap. text ed. 2.95 (ISBN 0-8167-1628-5). Troll Assocs.

HORSES

see also Ponies

Baby Horses. 8p. (ps-k). 1.95; incl. cassette 4.95 (ISBN 0-8431-1550-5). Price Stern.
Berry, Barbara. The Thoroughbreds. LC 73-16809. 1974. 6.95 (ISBN 0-672-51829-5, Bobbs). Macmillan.
Brady, Irene. America's Horses & Ponies. Brady, Irene, illus. 202p. (gr. 4 up). 1976. pap. 9.95 (ISBN 0-395-24050-6, Sandpiper). HM.
Brown, Fern. Behind the Scenes at the Horse Hospital. Tucker, Kathleen, ed. LC 81-94. (Illus.). 48p. (gr. 3-9). 1981. PLB 12.95 (ISBN 0-8075-0610-9). A Whitman.
Brown, Fern G. Horses & Foals. (Illus.). 72p. (gr. 4-9). 1986. lib. bdg. 10.40 (ISBN 0-531-10118-5). Watts.
Carleton-Lausten, Esther. Summer of the Wild Horses. Wheeler, Penny E., ed. 96p. (Orig.). 1989. pap. 6.95 (ISBN 0-8280-0422-6). Review & Herald.
Chapple, Judy. Your Horse: A Step-by-Step Guide to Horse Ownership. LC 84-22280. (Illus.). 144p. (gr. 8 up). 1984. (Garden Way Pub); pap. 9.95 (ISBN 0-88266-353-4, Graden Way Pub). Storey Comm Inc.
Cole, Joanna. A Horse's Body. Wexler, Jerome, photos by. LC 80-28147. (Illus.). 48p. (gr. k-3). 1981. 13.95 (ISBN 0-688-00362-1); PLB 13.88 (ISBN 0-688-00363-X, Morrow Jr Bks). Morrow Jr Bks.
Davidson, Margaret. Five True Horse Stories. 1989. pap. 2.50 (ISBN 0-590-42400-9). Scholastic Inc.
Dell, Catherine. Horses & Ponies. Bissex, Thelma & Turner, Elizabeth, illus. LC 88-17652. 24p. (Orig.). (gr. 2-5). 1989. PLB 5.99 (ISBN 0-394-99987-8). Random.
Forbis, Judith E. Hoofbeats along the Tigris. Forbis, Judith E., illus. Forbis, Donald L., intro. by. (Illus.). 146p. (gr. 8 up). 1990. Repr. 34.95 (ISBN 0-9625644-1-9). Ansata Pubns.
Fry, Fiona S. Horses. (Illus.). (gr. 6up). 1981. 14.95 (ISBN 0-7136-2114-1). Dufour.
Gise, Joanne. A Picture Book of Horses. Pistolesi, Roseanna, illus. LC 90-40437. 24p. (gr. 1-4). 1991. lib. bdg. 9.59 (ISBN 0-8167-2152-1); pap. text ed. 2.50 (ISBN 0-8167-2153-X). Troll Assocs.
Green, Carl R. & Sanford, William R. The Wild Horses. LC 85-13276. (Illus.). 48p. (gr. 5-6). 1986. PLB 10.95 (ISBN 0-89686-291-7, Crestwood Hse). Macmillan Child Grp.
Greydanus, Rose. Horses. Snyder, Joel, illus. LC 82-20296. 32p. (gr. k-2). 1983. lib. bdg. 10.89 (ISBN 0-89375-900-7); pap. 2.95 (ISBN 0-8167-1479-7). Troll Assocs.
Harris, Richard. I Can Read About Horses. LC 72-96960. (Illus.). (gr. 2-4). 1973. pap. 1.95 (ISBN 0-89375-054-9). Troll Assocs.
Henry, Marguerite. Album of Horses. Dennis, Wesley, illus. LC 51-14002. 112p. (gr. 3-7). 1951. 11.95 (ISBN 0-528-82050-8). Checkerboard Pr.
—Marguerite Henry's All About Horses. Osborne, M., illus. (gr. 4-8). 1967. (Random Juv). Random.
Herriot, James. Bonny's Big Day. Brown, Ruth, illus. 32p. (gr. k up). 1987. 10.95 (ISBN 0-312-01000-1). St Martin.
—Bonny's Big Day. Brown, Ruth, illus. 32p. 1991. pap. 6.95 (ISBN 0-312-06571-X). St Martin.
Hirschi, Ron. Where Do Horses Live? 1989. 11.95 (ISBN 0-8027-6878-4); lib. bdg. 12.85 (ISBN 0-8027-6879-2). Walker & Co.
Horses. (Illus.). (ps-2). pap. write for info. (ISBN 0-528-87115-3). Checkerboard Pr.
Horses. (gr. 4-6). 1984. 2.95 (ISBN 0-8431-4271-5). Price Stern.
Isenbart, Hans-Heinrich. Birth of a Foal. David, Thomas, illus. LC 85-17406. 48p. (gr. 2-5). 1986. lib. bdg. 12.95 (ISBN 0-87614-239-0). Carolrhoda Bks.
James, Shirley K. Going to a Horse Farm. (Illus.). 32p. (ps-8). 1992. 14.95 (ISBN 0-88106-477-7). Charlesbridge Pub.
Jurmain, Suzanne. One upon a Horse: A History of Horses--& How They Shaped Our History. LC 88-17522. (Illus.). 176p. (gr. 4 up). 1989. 15.95 (ISBN 0-688-05550-8). Lothrop.
Kalas, Sybille. The Wild Horse Family Book. Crampton, Patricia, tr. Kalas, Sybille, illus. LC 89-3929. (ps up). 1989. 15.95 (ISBN 0-88708-110-X). Picture Bk Studio.
Kidd, Jane. Fact Finders: Horses & Ponies. 1989. 6.99 (ISBN 0-517-69206-6). Outlet Bk Co.
LaBonte, Gail. The Miniature Horse. LC 89-26046. (Illus.). 60p. (gr. 3 up). 1990. PLB 12.95 (ISBN 0-87518-424-3, Dillon). Macmillan Child Grp.
Lavine, Sigmund A. & Casey, Brigid. Wonders of Draft Horses. 1983. 10.95 (ISBN 0-396-08138-X, Putnam). Putnam Pub Group.

Locker, Thomas. The Mare on the Hill. Locker, Thomas, illus. LC 85-1684. 32p. (gr. k-12). 1985. 15.95 (ISBN 0-8037-0207-8); PLB 14.89 (ISBN 0-8037-0208-6). Dial Bks Young.

Lundell, Margo. Harold Roth's Big Book of Horses. Roth, Harold, photos by. (Illus.). 48p. (gr. 2-5). 1987. 7.95 (ISBN 0-448-19203-9, G&D). Putnam Pub Group.

McGowan, E. M. Horses & Ponies, A Photo-Fact Book. (Illus., Orig.). 1988. pap. 1.95 (ISBN 0-942025-26-1). Kidsbks.

Morris, Dean. Horses. rev. ed. LC 87-16690. (Illus.). 48p. (Orig.). (gr. 2-6). 1987. PLB 17.32 (ISBN 0-8172-3209-5). Raintree PUbs.

Nentl, Jerolyn. Draft Horses. LC 83-7831. (Illus.). 48p. (gr. 4 up). 1983. PLB 9.95 (ISBN 0-89686-233-X, Crestwood Hse). Macmillan Child Grp.

Patent, Dorothy H. Appaloosa Horses. Munoz, William, photos by. LC 88-4470. (Illus.). 80p. (gr. 3-7). 1988. reinforced bdg. 14.95 (ISBN 0-8234-0706-3). Holiday.

—Horses of America. LC 81-4165. (Illus.). 80p. (gr. 3-7). 1981. reinforced bdg. 14.95 (ISBN 0-8234-0399-8). Holiday.

—Miniature Horses. Munoz, William, photos by. (Illus.). 48p. (gr. 3-7). 1991. 14.95 (ISBN 0-525-65049-0, Cobblehill Bks). Dutton Child Bks.

—Quarter Horses. Munoz, William, photos by. LC 85-904. (Illus.). 96p. (gr. 3-7). 1985. reinforced bdg. 12.95 (ISBN 0-8234-0573-7). Holiday.

Philp, Candace T. Rodeo Horses. LC 83-11732. (Illus.). 48p. (gr. 4 up). 1983. PLB 9.95 (ISBN 0-89686-230-5, Crestwood Hse). Macmillan Child Grp.

Ponies & Horses. 32p. (Orig.). 1984. pap. 1.25 (ISBN 0-8431-1509-2). Price Stern.

Posell, Elsa. Horses. LC 81-7741. (Illus.). 48p. (gr. k-4). 1981. PLB 14.60 (ISBN 0-516-01623-7); pap. 4.95 (ISBN 0-516-41623-5). Childrens.

Robison, Nancy. Hunters & Jumpers. LC 83-7832. (Illus.). 48p. (gr. 4 up). 1983. PLB 9.95 (ISBN 0-89686-227-5, Crestwood Hse). Macmillan Child Grp.

Rodenas, Paula. The Random House Book of Horses & Horsemanship. Cassels, Jean, illus. Farley, Walter, frwd. by. LC 86-42934. (Illus.). 192p. (gr. 3-7). 1991. 17.95 (ISBN 0-394-88705-0); PLB 18.99 (ISBN 0-394-98705-5). Random.

Rounds, Glen. Once We Had a Horse. LC 76-151758. (Illus.). 64p. (ps-3). 1971. 6.95 (ISBN 0-8234-0193-6). Holiday.

Stephens, Nancy. Horse Tails: A Look at Life with Horses. (Illus.). 220p. (Orig.). (gr. 7-12). 1990. pap. 9.95 (ISBN 0-685-29151-0). Squared Away.

Stone, Lynn. Horses. (Illus.). 24p. (gr. k-5). 1990. lib. bdg. 11.93 (ISBN 0-86593-035-X); lib. bdg. 8.95s.p. (ISBN 0-685-36311-2). Rourke Corp.

Thompson, Neil. A Closer Look at Horses. Barrett, Peter, illus. LC 78-4834. 32p. (gr. 4 up). 1978. PLB 5.99 (ISBN 0-531-01428-2, Gloucester Pr). Watts.

Warner, Rita. Wonderful World of Horses Color & Story Album. (Illus.). 32p. (Orig.). (gr. 3 up). 1976. pap. 3.95 (ISBN 0-685-04958-2). Troubador Pr.

Watson, Mary G. Feeds & Feeding. Vincer, Carole, illus. 24p. (Orig.). (gr. 3 up). 1988. pap. 7.95 (ISBN 0-901366-37-4, Pub. by Threshold Bks). Half Halt Pr.

Wildlife Education, Ltd. Staff. Wild Horses. Hoopes, Barbara, illus. 20p. (Orig.). (gr. 5 up). 1982. pap. 2.25 (ISBN 0-937934-08-9). Wildlife Educ.

HORSES–FICTION

Alter, Judy. Maggie & a Horse Named Devildust. Shaw, Charles, illus. LC 88-22815. 160p. (gr. 4-9). 1989. pap. 5.95 (ISBN 0-936650-08-7). E C Temple.

—Maggie & the Search for Devildust. Shaw, Charles, illus. LC 88-8019. 160p. (gr. 4-9). 1989. pap. 5.95 (ISBN 0-936650-09-5). E C Temple.

Anderson, Clarence W. Billy & Blaze Book Bag, 3 bks. Anderson, Clarence W., illus. Incl. Billy & Blaze. 48p. 1971; Blaze Finds the Trail. 48p. 1972; Blaze & the Forest Fire. 48p. 3.95 (ISBN 0-685-03274-4). (Illus.). (gr. k-3). 1973. (Collier Young Ad); pap. 1.95 ea. Macmillan Child Grp.

Anderson, Ella. Jo-Jo. (gr. 2-7). 1975. pap. 1.95 (ISBN 0-87508-693-4). Chr Lit.

Anderson, Marilyn D. The Wild Arabian. (Illus.). 96p. (gr. 4-7). 1987. 2.25 (ISBN 0-87406-207-1). Willowisp Pr.

Bagnold, Enid. National Velvet. 293p. 1981. Repr. PLB 16.95x (ISBN 0-89966-359-1). Buccaneer Bks.

—National Velvet. 339p. 1981. Repr. PLB 18.95 (ISBN 0-89967-033-4). Harmony Raine.

—National Velvet. Lewin, Ted, illus. LC 85-2982. 207p. (gr. 3 up). 1985. 15.95 (ISBN 0-688-05788-8). Morrow Jr Bks.

Balch, Glenn. Christmas Horse. Crowell, Pers, illus. Woodward, Tim, intro. by. (Illus.). 1990. pap. 9.95 (ISBN 0-931659-10-8). Limberlost Pr.

Bashful Bard. Cricket & the Flying Horse. Bashful Bard, illus. LC 89-84946. 28p. (Orig.). (ps-1). 1989. pap. 2.99 (ISBN 1-877906-06-9). Kenney Pubns.

Bauer, Marion Dane. Touch the Moon. Berenzy, Alix, illus. LC 87-663. 96p. (gr. 4-7). 1987. 12.95 (ISBN 0-89919-526-1, Pub. by Clarion). Ticknor & Fields.

Berg, Jean H. Mr. Koonan's Bargain. LC 70-158559. (gr. 1-4). 1971. 7.95 (ISBN 0-87874-002-3, Nautilus). Galloway.

Berst, Barbara. We Are Farmers. Berst, Barbara, illus. 24p. (Orig.). (ps-2). Date not set. acid-free cotton paper 25.00, (ISBN 0-9614126-3-1); pap. 9.95 (ISBN 0-9614126-2-3). Natl Lilac Pub.

Black Beauty. (gr. 4 up). 1989. pap. 4.88 (ISBN 0-582-54145-X, 74255). Longman.

Black Beauty. (Illus.). (gr. 3-5). 3.50 (ISBN 0-7214-0956-3). Ladybird Bks.

Blanc, Esther S. Berchick, My Mother's Horse. Dixon, Tennessee, illus. 36p. (gr. k-5). 1989. 14.95 (ISBN 0-912078-81-2). Volcano Pr.

Blumberg, Leda. Breezy. 96p. (gr. 3-7). 1988. pap. 2.50 (ISBN 0-380-89942-6, Camelot). Avon.

Braun, P. C., ed. The Big Book of Favorite Horse Stories. Savitt, Sam, illus. 336p. (gr. 7 up). 1982. 9.95 (ISBN 0-448-42641-2, G&D). Putnam Pub Group.

Brett, Jan. Fritz & the Beautiful Horses. Brett, Jan, illus. 32p. (gr. k-3). 1987. 13.95 (ISBN 0-395-30850-X); pap. 3.95 (ISBN 0-395-45356-9). HM.

Bryant, Bonnie. Horse Shy, Bk. No. 2. (gr. 3-7). 1988. pap. 2.75 (ISBN 0-317-69287-9). Bantam.

Bullaty, Sonja. Little Wild Ponies. (ps-3). 1987. pap. 7.95 (ISBN 0-671-64115-8). S&S Trade.

Bullaty, Sonja & Lomeo, Angelo. The Little Wild Ponies. (Illus.). (ps-5). 1987. 7.95 (ISBN 0-317-62449-0, Little Simon). S&S Trade.

Byars, Betsy. The Winged Colt of Casa Mia. Cuffari, Richard, illus. 132p. (gr. 3-7). 1981. pap. 2.95 (ISBN 0-380-00201-9, Camelot). Avon.

Calvert, Patricia. The Snowbird. LC 80-19139. 160p. (gr. 7 up). 1989. 12.95 (ISBN 0-684-19120-2, Scribners Young Read). Macmillan Child Grp.

—The Stone Pony. 160p. (gr. 7-9). 1983. pap. 2.99 (ISBN 0-451-13729-9, Sig). NAL-Dutton.

Campbell, Barbara. A Girl Called Bob & a Horse Called Yoki. LC 81-68780. 170p. (gr. 3-7). 1982. 11.95 (ISBN 0-8037-3149-3); PLB 11.89 (ISBN 0-8037-3150-7). Dial Bks Young.

—Taking Care of Yoki. LC 85-46040. 160p. (gr. 3-7). 1986. pap. 3.50 (ISBN 0-06-440173-1, Trophy). HarpC Child Bks.

Campbell, Joanna. The Wild Mustang. (gr. 3-5). 1989. pap. 2.75 (ISBN 0-553-15698-5, Skylark). Bantam.

Cavanna, Betty. Banner Year. LC 87-23692. 224p. (gr. 7 up). 1987. 12.95 (ISBN 0-688-05779-9). Morrow Jr Bks.

Christman, Ernest H. & Christman, Catherine. Darby's Stable: Cartoons & Stories, Level Two, Progressive Phonics. LC 84-50859. (Illus.). 88p. (Orig.). (gr. k-12). 1984. pap. text ed. 7.50 (ISBN 0-912329-04-1). Tutorial Press.

Cleaver, Vera. Belle Pruitt. LC 87-45879. 176p. (gr. 4-7). 1990. pap. 3.50 (ISBN 0-06-440249-5, Trophy). HarpC Child Bks.

Clymer, Eleanor. The Horse in the Attic. Lewin, Ted, illus. LC 83-6377. 96p. (gr. 3-6). 1983. 11.95 (ISBN 0-02-719040-4, Bradbury Pr). Macmillan Child Grp.

Cockerill, Pamela. Winter Ponies. (Illus.). 144p. (gr. 5-7). 1988. 17.95 (ISBN 0-340-40547-3, Pub. by Hodder & Stoughton UK). Trafalgar Sq.

Coerr, Eleanor. Chang's Paper Pony. Ray, Deborah K., illus. LC 87-45679. 64p. (gr. k-3). 1988. 11.95 (ISBN 0-06-021328-0); PLB 11.89 (ISBN 0-06-021329-9). HarpC Child Bks.

Corcoran, Barbara. A Horse Named Sky. LC 85-20060. 204p. (gr. 3-7). 1986. 12.95 (ISBN 0-689-31193-1, Atheneum Child Bk). Macmillan Child Grp.

Cosgrove, Stephen. Glitterby Baby. James, Robin, illus. LC 85-14354. 32p. (Orig.). (gr. 1-4). 1978. pap. 2.95 (ISBN 0-8431-1166-6). Price Stern.

—Mumkin. James, Robin, illus. 32p. (gr. 5-9). 1986. pap. 2.95 (ISBN 0-8431-1431-2). Price Stern.

—Nitter Pitter. James, Robin, illus. 32p. (gr. 1-4). 1978. pap. 2.95 (ISBN 0-8431-0570-4). Price Stern.

Coughlin, Joseph W. Jack Dawn & the Vanishing Horses. 140p. (Orig.). (gr. 5-8). 1980. pap. 2.95 (ISBN 0-89323-009-X). Bible Memory.

Coville, Bruce. Herds of Thunder: Manes of Gold. (gr. 4-7). 1991. pap. 9.00 (ISBN 0-385-41905-8). Doubleday.

—Herds of Thunder Manes of Gold: A Collection of Horse Stories & Poems. Lewin, Ted, illus. LC 88-34651. 176p. (gr. 5-10). 1989. 15.95 (ISBN 0-385-24642-0). Doubleday.

Currie, Quinn. Black Beauty. rev. ed. Ryan, Donna, illus. 126p. (gr. k-8). 1990. pap. 9.95 (ISBN 0-9623072-2-X). S Ink WA.

Denton, Terry. Janet's Horses. (ps-3). 1991. 12.95 (ISBN 0-395-51601-3). HM.

Doren, Marion. A Pony in the Field. 160p. (gr. 3-7). 1991. pap. 2.75 (ISBN 0-590-43663-5, Apple Paperbacks). Scholastic Inc.

Dryden, Pamela. Riding Home. 144p. (gr. 3-7). 1988. pap. 2.95 (ISBN 0-553-15591-1). Bantam.

Duncan, Lois. Horses of Dreamland. Diamond, Donna, illus. 32p. (ps-3). 1986. 12.95 (ISBN 0-316-19554-5). Little.

Easton, Patricia H. Rebel's Choice. (gr. 7 up). 1989. 14.95 (ISBN 0-15-200571-4, Gulliver Bks). HarBraceJ.

Endersby, Frank. The Boy & the Horse. Endersby, Frank, illus. 16p. (ps-2). 1980. 5.50 (ISBN 0-85953-098-1, Pub. by Child's Play England). Childs Play.

Escoula, Yvonne. Six Blue Horses. LC 70-103044. (gr. 5-9). 1970. 18.95 (ISBN 0-87599-162-9). S G Phillips.

Eytcheson, Pat. Catch a Winner. Eakin, Edwin M., ed. Peacock, Joe, illus. 48p. (gr. 2-3). 1989. 10.95 (ISBN 0-89015-704-9, Pub. by Panda Bks). Eakin Pr.

Farley, Walter. Black Stallion. Ward, Keith, illus. LC 85-19927. (gr. 3-7). 1977. 3.95 (ISBN 0-394-80601-8, Random Juv); lib. bdg. 10.99 (ISBN 0-394-90601-2); pap. 3.95 (ISBN 0-394-83609-X). Random.

—The Black Stallion, No. 1. reissue ed. LC 41-21882. 192p. (gr. 3-7). 1991. pap. 3.95 (ISBN 0-679-81343-8, Bullseye Bks). Knopf.

—The Black Stallion: An Easy-to-Read Adaptation. Rabinowitz, Sandy, illus. LC 85-19927. 48p. (ps-3). 1986. 6.95 (ISBN 0-394-86876-5, Random Juv); lib. bdg. 7.99 (ISBN 0-394-96876-X). Beginner.

—Black Stallion & Flame. LC 60-10029. (Illus.). (gr. 5 up). 1980. 3.95 (ISBN 0-394-80615-8, Random Juv); lib. bdg. 10.99 (ISBN 0-394-90615-2); pap. 3.95 (ISBN 0-394-84372-X). Random.

—Black Stallion & Satan. (Illus.). (gr. 4-6). 1978. 3.95 (ISBN 0-394-80605-0, Random Juv); lib. bdg. 8.99 (ISBN 0-394-90605-5); pap. 2.95 (ISBN 0-394-83914-5). Random.

—The Black Stallion & the Girl. (gr. 4 up). 1977. 3.95 (ISBN 0-394-82145-9, Random Juv); lib. bdg. 10.99 (ISBN 0-394-92145-3); pap. 3.95 (ISBN 0-394-83614-6). Random.

—Black Stallion Challenged. LC 64-15094. (Illus.). (gr. 5-9). 1980. 3.95 (ISBN 0-394-80617-4, Random Juv); lib. bdg. 10.99 (ISBN 0-394-90617-9); pap. 2.95 (ISBN 0-394-84371-1). Random.

—The Black Stallion: Golden Anniversary Edition. large type ed. D'Andrea, Domenick, illus. LC 90-53670. 224p. (gr. 4 up). 1991. Repr. of 1941 ed. gift ed. 15.00 (ISBN 0-679-81349-7, Random Juv); lib. bdg. 15.99 gift ed. (ISBN 0-679-91349-1). Random.

—The Black Stallion Legend. LC 83-1870. (Illus.). 224p. (gr. 5-9). 1983. lib. bdg. 10.99 (ISBN 0-394-96026-2). Random.

—The Black Stallion Legend. LC 83-1870. (Illus.). 192p. (gr. 5-8). 1985. pap. 3.95 (ISBN 0-394-87500-1, Random Juv). Random.

—The Black Stallion Returns. LC 45-8763. (Illus.). 208p. (gr. 5 up). 1977. 9.95 (ISBN 0-394-85509-4); pap. 2.95 (ISBN 0-394-83610-3). Random.

—The Black Stallion Returns, No. 2. reissue ed. LC 45-8763. 208p. (gr. 3-7). 1991. pap. 3.95 (ISBN 0-679-81344-6, Bullseye Bks). Knopf.

—The Black Stallion Returns: Movie Storybooks. Spinner, Stephanie, ed. Farley, Tim, photos by. LC 82-3861. (Illus.). 64p. (gr. 2-7). 1983. lib. bdg. 6.99 (ISBN 0-394-95412-2). Random.

—The Black Stallion Revolts. LC 53-6284. (gr. 4-9). 1977. 3.95 (ISBN 0-394-80609-3, Random Juv); lib. bdg. 6.99 (ISBN 0-394-90609-8); pap. 3.95 (ISBN 0-394-83613-8). Random.

—Black Stallion's Courage. LC 56-5471. (Illus.). (gr. 4-6). 1978. 3.95 (ISBN 0-394-80612-3, Random Juv); lib. bdg. 6.99 (ISBN 0-394-90612-8); pap. 2.95 (ISBN 0-394-83918-8). Random.

—Black Stallion's Filly. LC 52-7216. (Illus.). (gr. 4-6). 1978. lib. bdg. 8.99 (ISBN 0-394-90608-X, Random Juv); PLB 8.99 (ISBN 0-685-04257-X); pap. 3.95 (ISBN 0-394-83916-1). Random.

—Black Stallion's Ghost. Draper, Angie, illus. (gr. 5-9). 1978. lib. bdg. 10.99 (ISBN 0-394-90618-7, Random Juv); PLB 7.99 (ISBN 0-685-04258-8); pap. 3.95 (ISBN 0-394-83919-6). Random.

—Black Stallion's Sulky Colt. (Illus.). (gr. 4-6). 1978. (Random Juv); lib. bdg. 10.99 (ISBN 0-394-90610-1); pap. 2.95 (ISBN 0-394-83917-X). Random.

—Blood Bay Colt. (Illus.). (gr. 4-6). 1978. 3.95 (ISBN 0-394-80606-9, Random Juv); lib. bdg. 8.99 (ISBN 0-394-90606-3); pap. 2.95 (ISBN 0-394-83915-3). Random.

—The Horse-Tamer. LC 58-9030. 160p. (gr. 5-8). 1980. 3.95 (ISBN 0-394-80614-X, Random Juv); lib. bdg. 6.99 (ISBN 0-394-90614-4); pap. 2.95 (ISBN 0-394-84374-6). Random.

—Island Stallion. (Illus.). (gr. 5-6). 1980. 3.95 (ISBN 0-394-80604-2, Random Juv); lib. bdg. 6.99 (ISBN 0-394-90604-7); pap. 3.95 (ISBN 0-394-84376-2). Random.

—Island Stallion Races. (Illus.). (gr. 4-6). 1980. 3.95 (ISBN 0-394-80611-5, Random Juv); lib. bdg. 6.99 (ISBN 0-394-90611-X); pap. 2.95 (ISBN 0-394-84375-4). Random.

—Island Stallion's Fury. (Illus.). (gr. 5-6). 1980. 3.95 (ISBN 0-394-80607-7, Random Juv); lib. bdg. 6.99 (ISBN 0-394-90607-1); pap. 2.95 (ISBN 0-394-84373-8). Random.

—Little Black, a Pony. LC 61-7789. (Illus.). 62p. (gr. 1-2). 1961. 6.95 (ISBN 0-394-80021-4); lib. bdg. 7.99 (ISBN 0-394-90021-9). Beginner.

—Little Black Goes to the Circus. LC 63-13866. (Illus.). (gr. k-3). 1963. 3.95 (ISBN 0-394-80033-8). Beginner.

—Man O' War. LC 62-9000. (Illus.). 352p. (gr. 5-9). 1983. pap. 3.95 (ISBN 0-394-86015-2). Random.

—Son of the Black Stallion. (Illus.). (gr. 4-6). 1977. 3.95 (ISBN 0-394-80603-4, Random Juv); lib. bdg. 10.99 (ISBN 0-394-90603-9); pap. 3.95 (ISBN 0-394-83612-X). Random.

—Son of the Black Stallion, No. 3. reissue ed. LC 47-3369. 288p. (gr. 3-7). 1991. pap. 3.95 (ISBN 0-679-81345-4, Bullseye Bks). Knopf.

Farley, Walter & Farley, Steven. The Young Black Stallion. LC 89-42763. 192p. (gr. 5-9). 1989. 10.95 (ISBN 0-394-84562-5); lib. bdg. 11.99 (ISBN 0-394-94562-X). Random.

—The Young Black Stallion, No. 20. LC 89-42763. 176p. (gr. 3-7). 1991. pap. 3.95 (ISBN 0-679-81348-9, Bullseye Bks). Knopf.

Feagles, Anita. Casey, the Utterly Impossible Horse. Wilson, Dagmar, illus. LC 88-13871. 96p. (gr. 3-7). 1989. Repr. of 1960 ed. lib. bdg. 15.00 (ISBN 0-208-02239-2, Linnet). Shoe String.

Fleischman, Paul. Path of the Pale Horse. LC 82-48611. 160p. (gr. 6 up). 1983. PLB 12.89 (ISBN 0-06-021905-X). HarpC Child Bks.

Fleischman, Sid. Me & the Man on the Moon-Eyed Horse. (Illus.). (gr. 3 up). 1977. 14.95 (ISBN 0-316-28571-4, Joy St Bks). Little.
Fletcher, Dorothy. Week of Dream Horses. Borelli, Theresa, illus. (gr. 7-9). 1984. pap. 2.50 (ISBN 0-88138-017-2). Green Tiger Pr.
Gates, Doris. A Filly for Melinda. LC 83-14617. 180p. (gr. 3-7). 1984. pap. 11.95 (ISBN 0-670-31328-9). Viking Child Bks.
Gauch, Patricia L. This Time, Tempe Wick? Tomes, Margot, illus. LC 86-61791. 48p. (gr. 2-5). 1987. 11.95 (ISBN 0-936915-04-8, Shoe Tree Pr). Betterway Pubns.
Gibson, Sylvia S. Latawnya, the Naughty Horse, Learns to Say "No" to Drugs. 1990. 6.95 (ISBN 0-533-09102-0). Vantage.
Gilbert, Miriam. Rosie: The Oldest Horse in St. Augustine. Roch, J., illus. LC 67-30409. (FRE, SPA & ENG.). (gr. k-6). 1974. 5.95 (ISBN 0-87208-105-2); pap. 6.95 (ISBN 0-87208-007-2). Island Pr Pubs.
Gipson, Fred. Little Arliss. Himler, Ronald, illus. LC 77-17643. (gr. 4-6). 1978. 12.95i (ISBN 0-06-022008-2); PLB 12.89 (ISBN 0-06-022009-0). HarpC Child Bks.
Goble, Paul. The Girl Who Loved Wild Horses. Goble, Paul, illus. LC 77-20500. 32p. (gr. k-3). 1982. 13.95 (ISBN 0-02-736570-0, Bradbury Pr). Macmillan Child Grp.
Goudge, Elizabeth. The Little White Horse. 15.95 (ISBN 0-89966-474-1). Buccaneer Bks.
Griffiths, Helen. The Dancing Horses. LC 81-6762. 160p. (gr. 5 up). 1982. 9.95 (ISBN 0-8234-0437-4). Holiday.
Gruenberg, Linda. Hummer. 192p. (gr. 5-9). 1990. 13.95 (ISBN 0-395-51080-5). HM.
Gwynne, Fred. The Sixteen-Hand Horse. Gwynne, Fred, illus. LC 79-13284. (gr. 1-5). 1987. 11.95 (ISBN 0-13-811522-2). Prentice Hall Pr.
—The Sixteen Hand Horse. Gwynne, Fred, illus. LC 79-13284. (gr. 1-6). 1987. pap. 11.95 (ISBN 0-671-66291-0); pap. 5.95 (ISBN 0-671-66968-0). S&S Trade.
Hall, Lynn. Danza! LC 81-8992. 186p. (gr. 4-8). 1981. 12.95 (ISBN 0-684-17158-9, Scribners Young Read). Macmillan Child Grp.
—Ride a Dark Horse. LC 87-12310. 176p. (gr. 7 up). 1987. 12.95 (ISBN 0-688-07471-5, Morrow Junior Books). Morrow.
—The Something-Special Horse. Rabinowitz, Sandy, illus. LC 84-23636. 112p. (gr. 4-7). 1985. 12.95 (ISBN 0-684-18343-9, Scribners Young Read). Macmillan Child Grp.
Hanson, Andrea. The Adventures of Black Beauty: Beauty Finds a Home. LC 83-3006. (Illus.). 160p. (gr. 3-7). 1983. Random.
Harris, Aurand. Ride a Blue Horse. 44p. (Orig.). (gr. k-3). 1986. pap. 4.50 playscript (ISBN 0-87602-264-6). Anchorage.
Hart, Sharon M. The Stolen Horse: Animal Rescue Farm, No. 1. 112p. (gr. 2-5). 1988. pap. 2.50 (ISBN 0-590-41501-8). Scholastic Inc.
Haynes, Betsy. Taffy Sinclair, Queen of the Soaps. (ps-7). 1985. pap. 2.75 (ISBN 0-553-15647-0, Skylark). Bantam.
Heilbroner, Joan. Robert the Rose Horse. LC 62-9218. (Illus.). 72p. (gr. 1-2). 1962. 6.95 (ISBN 0-394-80025-7); lib. bdg. 7.99 (ISBN 0-394-90025-1). Beginner.
Henry, Marguerite. An Innkeeper's Horse. Dennis, Wesley, illus. 24p. (ps-3). 1988. pap. 1.95 (ISBN 0-02-688805-X). Checkerboard Pr.
—Justin Morgan Had a Horse. Dennis, Wesley, illus. LC 54-8903. 176p. (gr. 2-9). 1954. write for info. (ISBN 0-528-82255-1); pap. write for info. (ISBN 0-528-87682-1). Macmillan Child Grp.
—Justin Morgan Had a Horse. Dennis, Wesley, illus. 176p. (Orig.). (gr. 2-9). 1989. 12.95 (ISBN 0-02-689322-3); pap. 3.95 (ISBN 0-02-688757-6, Aladdin). Macmillan Child Grp.
—Justin Morgan Had a Horse. 2nd ed. Dennis, Wesley, illus. 176p. (gr. 3-7). 1991. pap. 3.95 (ISBN 0-689-71534-X, Aladdin). Macmillan Child Grp.
—Misty of Chincoteague. Dennis, Wesley, illus. LC 47-11404. 176p. (gr. 2-9). 1990. 12.95 (ISBN 0-02-743622-5, Mcmillan Child Bk); pap. 3.95 (ISBN 0-02-688759-2). Macmillan Child Grp.
—Misty of Chincoteague. Dennis, Wesley, illus. LC 90-27237. 176p. (gr. 3-7). 1991. pap. 3.95 (ISBN 0-689-71492-0, Aladdin). Macmillan Child Grp.
—Mustang, Wild Spirit of the West. Lougheed, Robert, illus. LC 66-10876. 224p. (gr. 4 up). 1987. 8.95 (ISBN 0-528-82327-2); pap. 3.95 (ISBN 0-02-688760-6, Aladdin). Macmillan Child Grp.
—Our First Pony. Rudish, Rich, illus. LC 84-13409. 64p. (gr. 1-5). write for info. (ISBN 0-02-743625-X). Macmillan Child Grp.
—A Pictorial Life Story of Misty. LC 76-41864. (Illus.). 112p. (gr. 3 up). 1976. write for info. (ISBN 0-02-743626-8). Macmillan Child Grp.
—San Domingo: The Medicine Hat Stallion. Longheed, Robert, illus. LC 72-7416. 224p. (gr. 2-9). 1986. 8.95 (ISBN 0-528-82443-0). Macmillan Child Grp.
—Sea Star: Orphan of Chincoteague. Dennis, Wesley, illus. LC 49-11474. 176p. (gr. 2-9). 1987. 8.95 (ISBN 0-02-743627-6); pap. 3.95 (ISBN 0-02-688761-4). Macmillan Child Grp.
—Stormy: Misty's Foal. Dennis, Wesley, illus. LC 63-13334. 224p. (gr. 2-9). 1987. 8.95 (ISBN 0-528-82083-4, Aladdin Bks); pap. 3.95 (ISBN 0-02-688762-2, Aladdin Bks). Macmillan Child Grp.
—Stormy, Misty's Foal. Dennis, Wesley, illus. LC 90-27306. 224p. (gr. 3-7). 1991. pap. 3.95 (ISBN 0-689-71487-4, Aladdin). Macmillan Child Grp.
—White Stallion of Lipizza. Dennis, Wesley, illus. LC 64-17445. 112p. (gr. 3-8). write for info. (ISBN 0-02-743628-4, Mcmillan Child Bk). Macmillan Child Grp.
Hiller, B. B. Horse Crazy, No. 1. 144p. (Orig.). 1988. pap. 2.75 (ISBN 0-553-15594-6, Skylark). Bantam.
—The Saddle Club, Bk. 2. 144p. (Orig.). 1988. pap. 2.99 (ISBN 0-553-15611-X, Skylark). Bantam.
Hodges, Margaret. The Little Humpbacked Horse. Conover, Chris, illus. 32p. (ps up). 1987. pap. 3.95 (ISBN 0-374-44495-1). FS&G.
Hoff, Syd. Barney's Horse. Hoff, Syd, illus. LC 87-66. 32p. (ps-3). 1987. 10.95 (ISBN 0-06-022449-5); PLB 10.89 (ISBN 0-06-022450-9). HarpC Child Bks.
—Barney's Horse. Hoff, Syd, illus. LC 87-66. 32p. (ps-2). 1990. pap. 2.95 (ISBN 0-06-444142-3, Trophy). HarpC Child Bks.
—Chester. Hoff, Syd, illus. LC 61-5768. 64p. (gr. k-3). 1961. PLB 11.89 (ISBN 0-06-022456-8). HarpC Child Bks.
—Chester. Hoff, Syd, illus. LC 61-5768. 64p. (gr. k-3). 1986. pap. 3.50 (ISBN 0-06-444095-8, Trophy). HarpC Child Bks.
—Horse in Harry's Room. Hoff, Syd, illus. LC 71-104753. 32p. (gr. k-3). 1970. PLB 10.89 (ISBN 0-06-022483-5). HarpC Child Bks.
—The Horse in Harry's Room. Hoff, Syd, illus. LC 71-104753. 32p. (ps-2). 1985. pap. 2.95 (ISBN 0-06-444073-7, Trophy). HarpC Child Bks.
—Thunderhoof. Hoff, Syd, illus. LC 75-129855. (gr. k-3). 1971. PLB 9.89 (ISBN 0-685-02069-X). HarpC Child Bks.
Holland, Isabelle. Toby the Splendid. LC 86-24681. 160p. (gr. 5 up). 1987. 13.95 (ISBN 0-8027-6674-9); PLB 14.85 (ISBN 0-8027-6675-7). Walker & Co.
Hope, Laura L. Bobbsey Twins: The Missing Pony Mystery. Sanderson, Ruth, illus. 112p. (gr. 2-5). 1981. 7.95 (ISBN 0-671-42295-2, Little Simon); pap. 3.50 (ISBN 0-671-42296-0). S&S Trade.
Hoppe, Joanne. Pretty Penny Farm. LC 86-1516. 224p. (gr. 7 up). 1987. 12.95 (ISBN 0-688-07201-1, Morrow Junior Books). Morrow.
Hovde, Jeanne. A Horse for Cassie. LC 88-7355. 132p. (gr. 3-6). 1988. pap. 3.95 (ISBN 1-55513-587-0, Chariot Bks). Cook.
James, Will. Smoky the Cow Horse. James, Will, illus. LC 87-1129. 324p. (gr. 7 up). 1987. pap. 3.95 (ISBN 0-689-71171-9, Aladdin). Macmillan Child Grp.
Jeffers, Susan. If Wishes Were Horses. (Illus.). (ps-3). 1987. pap. 3.95 (ISBN 0-525-44325-8, 0383-120, DCB). Dutton Child Bks.
Johnson, Robin. Horse Stories. (Illus.). 96p. (Orig.). (gr. 5-9). 1988. pap. 1.95 (ISBN 0-942025-18-0). Kidsbks.
Klusmeyer, Joann. Shelly from Rockytop Farm. Taylor, Neil, illus. 65p. (gr. 3-6). 1986. 5.95 (ISBN 1-55523-014-8). Winston-Derek.
Knowles, Anne. Under the Shadow. LC 82-48857. 128p. (gr. 5 up). 1983. PLB 11.89 (ISBN 0-06-023222-6). HarpC Child Bks.
Koertge, Ron. The Arizona Kid. 224p. (gr. 7 up). 1989. pap. 3.50 (ISBN 0-380-70776-4, Flare). Avon.
Krauss, Ruth. Charlotte & the White Horse. LC 55-8819. (Illus.). 24p. (gr. k-3). 1969. PLB 11.89 (ISBN 0-06-023361-3). HarpC Child Bks.
Laundrie, Amy C. Whinny of the Wild Horses. Helmer, Jean C., illus. LC 88-21460. 128p. (gr. 3-6). 1990. 13.95 (ISBN 0-02-754542-3, Four Winds Press). Macmillan Child Grp.
Lawson, Robert. Mr. Revere & I. Lawson, Robert, illus. (gr. 7-10). 1953. 14.95 (ISBN 0-316-51739-9). Little.
—Mr. Revere & I. Lawson, Robert, illus. 152p. (gr. 3-6). 1988. pap. 5.95 (ISBN 0-316-51729-1). Little.

Leib, Mani. Yingl Tsingl Khvat. Lissitzky, El, illus. 32p. (ps-5). 11.95 (ISBN 0-918825-52-0); lib. bdg. 11.75x (ISBN 0-918825-54-7). Moyer Bell Limited.
The delightful nursery rhymes tell of an adventurous soul who dreams of riding off on a magic horse to find a better life, & does. A dual language book, the Yiddish facsimile of the 1991 Russian edition features startling fresh black-&-white drawings by the pre-eminent Constructivist artist, El Lisssitzky. The English version reproduces the illustrations, & is the first translation of this beloved story by the poet who sucessfully revived the Yiddish ballad.
Publisher Provided Annotation.

Lewis, C. S. The Horse & His Boy. Baynes, Pauline, illus. LC 54-12817. 202p. (gr. 4 up). 1988. 12.95 (ISBN 0-02-757650-7, Mcmillan Child Bk); pap. 3.50 (ISBN 0-02-044200-9, Collier). Macmillan Child Grp.
Lobel, Arnold. Lucille. Lobel, Arnold, illus. LC 64-11616. 64p. (gr. k-3). 1986. pap. 3.50 (ISBN 0-06-444096-6, Trophy). HarpC Child Bks.
Luenn, Nancy, ed. A Horse's Tale: Ten Adventures in One Hundred Years. Megale, Marina & Schumacher, Sharon, illus. LC 88-61152. 96p. (Orig.). (gr. 2-6). 1988. lib. bdg. 15.95 (ISBN 0-943990-51-3); pap. 7.95 (ISBN 0-943990-50-5). Parenting Pr.

MacDougall, Mary-Katherine. Black Jupiter. Gruver, Kate E., ed. Moyers, William, illus. 181p. (gr. 5 up). 8.95 (ISBN 0-940175-01-0). Now Comns.
"It was late for the horses to be so high in the mountains. By this time in other years they had already found winter quarters in a lower area. But this fall they were waiting for a colt." That colt was Black Jupiter. Snow came. The horses had to leave through the rock gateway the black mare could not yet get through. The stallion stayed with her. The next dawn the colt came but did not move or make a sound. The horses left the newborn colt alone in the snow. Jim Peters, a prospector, living alone in his cabin, was sensitive to wildlife. He felt something was wrong when he heard two horses leaving a day after the herd. He found Black Jupiter alive but not strong. He took him to his cabin. There are Gregg & Jenine Jordan, children of a mining engineer, a threat to Jim & his mining plans. In turn, Jim is suspected of stealing from the surveying crew. Black Jupiter, set in the Rocky Mountains with a factual copper mining background, is a mystery story of distrust & misunderstanding, healed by love & a colt. There is a happy Christmas chapter. Black & white illustrations.
Publisher Provided Annotation.

McHargue, Georgess. The Horseman's Word. LC 80-68736. 272p. (gr. 7 up). 1981. pap. 9.95 (ISBN 0-385-28472-1). Delacorte.
McLane, Gretel B. Kailia & the King's Horse. Kenyon, Tony, illus. 96p. (gr. 4-6). 1982. 7.95 (ISBN 0-916630-28-5). Pr Pacifica.
Martin, Ann M. Good-Bye Stacey, Good-Bye. 160p. (gr. 3-7). 1988. pap. 2.75 (ISBN 0-590-41127-6, Apple Paperbacks). Scholastic Inc.
Mayer, Marianna. Black Horse. Thamer, Katie, illus. LC 83-25271. 42p. (ps-3). 1987. pap. 4.95 (ISBN 0-8037-0181-0). Dial Bks Young.
Moore, Ruth N. Mystery of the Missing Stallions. Converse, James, illus. LC 84-19. 136p. (Orig.). (gr. 3-8). pap. 4.95 (ISBN 0-8361-3376-5). Herald Pr.
Morpurgo, Michael. War Horse. large type ed. 162p. (gr. 3-8). 1989. Repr. of 1982 ed. PLB 14.95 (ISBN 1-85089-943-6, Pub. by Clio Pr England). ABC-CLIO.
Morrison, Dorothy N. Somebody's Horse. LC 86-3641. 224p. (gr. 4-8). 1986. 14.95 (ISBN 0-689-31290-3, Atheneum Child Bk). Macmillan Child Grp.
—Somebody's Horse. (gr. 4-8). 1987. pap. 2.95 (ISBN 0-8167-1046-5). Troll Assocs.
O'Hara, Mary. The Catch Colt. LC 85-42737. 160p. (gr. 5 up). 1985. pap. 2.95 (ISBN 0-06-440157-X, Trophy). HarpC Child Bks.
—My Friend Flicka. LC 87-45654. 272p. (gr. 7 up). 1988. pap. 3.95 (ISBN 0-06-080902-7, P-902, PL). HarperCollins.
—Thunderhead. 320p. (gr. 5-9). 1967. pap. 1.75 (ISBN 0-440-98875-6, LFL). Dell.
Osborne, Mary P. Moonhorse. Saelig, S. M., illus. LC 87-3818. 40p. (ps-3). 1991. 14.95 (ISBN 0-394-88960-6); lib. bdg. 15.99 (ISBN 0-394-98960-0). Knopf.
Parker, Cam. A Horse in New York. 144p. (Orig.). (gr. 5 up). 1989. pap. 2.75 (ISBN 0-380-75704-4, Camelot). Avon.
Patent, Dorothy H. Draft Horses. Munoz, William, photos by. LC 85-21998. (Illus.). 96p. (gr. 3-7). 1986. reinforced bdg 12.95 (ISBN 0-8234-0597-4). Holiday.
—A Horse of a Different Color. Munoz, William, photos by. (Illus.). 64p. (gr. 3-7). 1988. 13.95 (ISBN 0-396-08836-8, Putnam). Putnam Pub Group.
Paterson, Katherine. Jacob Have I Loved. large type ed. 251p. (gr. k-6). 1990. Repr. PLB 15.95 (ISBN 1-55736-167-3, Crnrstn Bks). ABC-CLIO.
Peck, Robert N. Spanish Hoof. LC 84-21776. 192p. (gr. 5-9). 1985. lib. bdg. 9.99 (ISBN 0-394-97261-9). Knopf.
Peterson, Jeanne W. Sometimes I Dream Horses. Schick, Eleanor, illus. LC 83-47710. 32p. (ps-3). 1987. PLB 11.89 (ISBN 0-06-024713-4). HarpC Child Bks.
Peyton, K. M. Darkling. 1990. 14.95 (ISBN 0-385-30086-7). Doubleday.

Rabinowitz, Sandy. How I Trained My Colt. (ps). 1991. pap. 2.75 (ISBN 0-553-15848-1). Bantam.
Rappaport, Doreen. The Boston Coffee Party. McCully, Emily A., illus. LC 87-45301. 64p. (gr. k-3). 1990. pap. 3.50 (ISBN 0-06-444141-5, Trophy). HarpC Child Bks.
Rawlings, Marjorie K. The Yearling. Wyeth, N. C., illus. LC 85-40301. 416p. 1985. 24.95 (ISBN 0-684-18461-3, Scribners Young Read); 75.00 (ISBN 0-684-18508-3, Scribners). Macmillan Child Grp.
Ray, Lou. The Burros of Mavrick Gulch. (Illus.). 44p. (Orig.). (gr. k-5). 1983. pap. 7.95 (ISBN 0-9612346-0-1, 83-090410). Ray-Foster.
Richardson, Gale T. The Wings. (gr. 9-12). 1989. write for info. (ISBN 0-9614337-4-4). Poetry Unltd.
Rockwood, Joyce. Groundhog's Horse. Kalin, Victor, illus. LC 77-22676. 128p. (gr. 2-4). 1978. reinforced ed. 12.95 (ISBN 0-8050-1173-0). H Holt & Co.
Ross, Harriet, compiled by. Great Stories about Horses. Bolle, Frank, illus. LC 63-18759. 160p. (gr. 3-9). 1991. PLB 9.95 (ISBN 0-87460-202-5). Lion Bks.
Rounds, Glen. Once We Had a Horse. LC 76-151758. (Illus.). 64p. (ps-3). 1971. 6.95 (ISBN 0-8234-0193-6). Holiday.
—Wild Appaloosa. Rounds, Glen, illus. LC 82-48751. 96p. (gr. 3-7). 1983. 13.95 (ISBN 0-8234-0482-X). Holiday.
Rounds, Glen, adapted by. & illus. The Blind Colt. LC 89-1779. 84p. (gr. 3-5). 1989. 14.95 (ISBN 0-8234-0010-7); pap. 4.95 (ISBN 0-8234-0758-6). Holiday.
Sachar, Louis. There's a Boy in the Girls Bathroom. large type ed. 1990. Repr. PLB 15.95 (ISBN 1-55736-174-6, Crnrstn Bks). ABC-CLIO.
St. John, Chris. A Horse of Her Own. (gr. 5 up). 1989. pap. 2.95 (ISBN 0-449-13451-2). Fawcett.
—Kate's Challenge. (gr. 5 up). 1989. pap. 2.95 (ISBN 0-449-13453-9). Fawcett.
Sewall, Marcia. Riding That Strawberry Roan. LC 84-21904. (Illus.). 32p. (ps-2). 1985. pap. 9.95 (ISBN 0-670-80623-4). Viking Child Bks.
Sewell, Anna. Black Beauty. (gr. 5 up). pap. 1.50 (ISBN 0-8049-0023-X, CL-23). Airmont.
—Black Beauty. (Illus.). 320p. (gr. 4 up). 1945. 12.95 (ISBN 0-448-11007-5, G&D); pap. 7.95 (ISBN 0-685-01831-8, G&D). Putnam Pub Group.
—Black Beauty. (Illus.). (gr. 6-9). 1978. 2.95 (ISBN 0-448-14940-0, G&D). Putnam Pub Group.
—Black Beauty. new ed. Farr, Naunerle, ed. Nebres, Rudy, illus. LC 59-12495. 64p. (Orig.). (gr. 5-10). 1973. pap. 2.95 (ISBN 0-88301-094-1). Pendulum Pr.
—Black Beauty. LC 59-12495. (gr. 3-7). 1983. pap. 2.25 (ISBN 0-14-035006-3, Puffin). Puffin Bks.
—Black Beauty. Vance, Eleanor G., ed. Jeffers, Susan, illus. LC 84-27575. 72p. (ps-5). 1986. 12.95 (ISBN 0-394-86575-8, Random Juv); lib. bdg. 12.99 (ISBN 0-394-96575-2, Random Juv). Random.
—Black Beauty. LC 59-12495. (gr. 4-6). 1989. pap. 2.95 (ISBN 0-590-42354-1). Scholastic Inc.
—Black Beauty. Barish, Wendy, ed. Speirs, John, illus. LC 59-12495. 240p. 1982. pap. 15.95 (ISBN 0-671-43789-5, Little Simon). S&S Trade.
—Black Beauty. (gr. 2-6). 1986. 7.98 (ISBN 0-685-16851-4). Outlet Bk Co.
—Black Beauty. McKinley, Robin, adapted by. Jeffers, Susan, illus. Kingsley, Ben, contrib. by. (Illus.). 72p. (ps-5). 1987. incl. cass. 17.95 (ISBN 0-394-89228-3, Random Juv). Random.
—Black Beauty. 96p. (gr. 2-6). 1989. pap. 2.95 (ISBN 0-448-11077-6, G&D). Putnam Pub Group.
—Black Beauty. 240p. (ps-8). Date not set. pap. 2.50 (ISBN 0-451-52056-4, Sig Classics). NAL-Dutton.
—Black Beauty. Dubowski, Cathy, adapted by. D'Andrea, Domenick, illus. LC 89-62772. 96p. (Orig.). (gr. 2-6). 1990. lib. bdg. 5.99 (ISBN 0-679-90370-4, Random Juv); pap. 2.95 (ISBN 0-679-80370-X, Random Juv). Random.
—Black Beauty. (gr. 4 up). 1990. pap. 3.50 (ISBN 0-440-40355-3, Pub. by Yearling Classics). Dell.
—Black Beauty. 75p. 1986. pap. 2.95 (ISBN 0-451-52295-8, Sig Classics). NAL-Dutton.
—Black Beauty. Keeping, Charles, illus. 216p. (gr. 5 up). 1990. 19.95 (ISBN 0-374-30776-8). FS&G.
—Black Beauty & the Runaway Horse. Richardson, I. M., adapted by. Milone, Karen, illus. LC 82-7029. 32p. (gr. 3-5). 1983. PLB 10.79 (ISBN 0-89375-812-4); pap. 2.95 (ISBN 0-89375-813-2). Troll Assocs.
—Black Beauty Finds a Home. Richardson, I. M., adapted by. Milone, Karen, illus. LC 82-7024. 32p. (gr. 3-5). 1983. PLB 10.79 (ISBN 0-89375-816-7); pap. 2.95 (ISBN 0-89375-817-5). Troll Assocs.
—Black Beauty Grows Up. Richardson, I. M., ed. Milone, Karen, illus. LC 82-7075. 32p. (gr. 3-5). 1983. PLB 10.79 (ISBN 0-89375-810-8); pap. 2.95 (ISBN 0-89375-811-6). Troll Assocs.
—The Courage of Black Beauty. Richardson, I. M., adapted by. Milone, Karen, illus. LC 82-7090. 32p. (gr. 3-5). 1983. PLB 10.79 (ISBN 0-89375-814-0); pap. 2.95 (ISBN 0-89375-815-9). Troll Assocs.
Shaffer, Ann. The Camel Express. LC 88-20268. (Illus.). 40p. (gr. 3-6). 1989. PLB 10.95 (ISBN 0-87518-400-6, Dillon). Macmillan Child Grp.
Sheldon, Ann. A Horse for Jackie. (gr. 3-6). 1989. pap. 2.75 (ISBN 0-671-67471-4, Minstrel Bks). PB.
—A Star in the Saddle. (Orig.). (gr. 3-6). 1989. pap. 2.75 (ISBN 0-318-41208-X, Minstrel Bks). PB.
Shub, Elizabeth. The White Stallion. Isadora, Rachel, illus. 64p. (gr. 1-4). 1984. pap. 2.50 (ISBN 0-553-15244-0, Skylark). Bantam.
Singer, Marilyn. Horsemaster. LC 84-21522. 180p. (gr. 7up). 1985. 13.95 (ISBN 0-689-31102-8, Atheneum Child Bk). Macmillan Child Grp.
Snyder, Zilpha K. A Season of Ponies. (gr. k-6). 1988. pap. 2.95 (ISBN 0-440-40006-6). Dell.
—Season of Ponies. (gr. 4-6). 16.00 (ISBN 0-8446-6376-X). Peter Smith.
Sohl, Marcia & Dackerman, Gerald. Black Beauty Student Activity Book. (Illus.). 16p. (gr. 4-10). 1976. pap. 1.25 (ISBN 0-88301-183-2). Pendulum Pr.
Spiller, Burton L. Thorough Bred. 2nd ed. Hunt, Lynn B., illus. 200p. (gr. 10 up). Repr. of 1936 ed. 35.00 (ISBN 0-685-37782-2). Derrydale Pr.
Spinka, Penina K. White Hare's Horses. LC 90-42777. 160p. (gr. 5-9). 1991. SBE 12.95 (ISBN 0-689-31654-2, Atheneum Child Bk). Macmillan Child Grp.
Spray, Carole. The Mare's Egg. La Fave, Kim, illus. 56p. (Orig.). (gr. k-7). 1981. 11.95 (ISBN 0-920656-07-2); pap. 9.95 (ISBN 0-685-35607-8). Camden Hse Pub.
Springer, Nancy. Colt. (gr. 4-7). 1991. 13.95 (ISBN 0-8037-1022-4). Dial Bks Young.
—A Horse to Love. LC 86-45487. 192p. (gr. 3-7). 1987. 11.95 (ISBN 0-06-025824-1); PLB 12.89 (ISBN 0-06-025825-X). HarpC Child Bks.
—Not on a White Horse. LC 87-3477. 192p. (gr. 4-8). 1989. pap. 2.95 (ISBN 0-394-82965-4, Bullseye Bks). Knopf.
Steinbeck, John. The Red Pony. Dennis, Wesley, illus. 128p. (ps-5). 1989. pap. 15.95 (ISBN 0-670-82990-0). Viking Child Bks.
Stone, Bruce. Been Clever Forever. LC 86-45774. 384p. (gr. 7 up). 1990. pap. 3.25 (ISBN 0-06-447013-X, JK013, Trophy). HarpC Child Bks.
Swortzell, Lowell. The Little Humpback Horse. (Orig.). (gr. 1 up). 1984. pap. 5.00 (ISBN 0-87602-244-1). Anchorage.
Thomas, Joyce C. The Golden Pasture. LC 85-27910. 144p. (gr. 7 up). 1986. pap. 11.95 (ISBN 0-590-33681-9, Scholastic Hardcover). Scholastic Inc.
—The Golden Pasture. 144p. (gr. 7 up). 1987. pap. 2.50 (ISBN 0-590-33638-X). Scholastic Inc.
Towne, Mary. Boxed In. LC 81-43875. 160p. (gr. 4-6). 1982. PLB 11.89 (ISBN 0-690-04239-6, Crowell Jr Bks). HarpC Child Bks.
Troll. Black Beauty Activity Book. 64p. (ps-3). 1991. pap. 1.95 (ISBN 0-8167-2290-0). Troll Assocs.
Vail, Virginia. Gift Horse. 128p. (gr. 3-7). 1991. pap. 2.75 (ISBN 0-590-42803-9, Apple Paperbacks). Scholastic Inc.
—Horseback Summer. Bode, Daniel, illus. LC 89-30583. 128p. (gr. 4-6). 1990. lib. bdg. 9.49 (ISBN 0-8167-1625-0); pap. text ed. 2.95 (ISBN 0-8167-1626-9). Troll Assocs.
Washburn, JoAnn. Maude the Mare. LC 87-51039. (Illus.). 44p. (gr. k-3). 1988. 6.95 (ISBN 1-55523-123-3). Winston-Derek.
Wayland, April H. Night Horse. 1991. 12.95 (ISBN 0-590-42629-X, Scholastic Hardcover). Scholastic Inc.
Wood, Elizabeth L. Many Horses. Pollock, Dean, illus. (gr. 5-11). 1953. 7.95 (ISBN 0-8323-0175-2). Binford Mort.
Worcester, Donald E. War Pony. Pauley, Paige, illus. LC 83-40486. 96p. (gr. 4 up). 1984. Repr. of 1961 ed. 10.95 (ISBN 0-912646-85-3). Tex Christian.
Zolotow, Charlotte. A Rose, a Bridge, & a Wild Black Horse. Spowart, Robin, illus. LC 86-25840. 32p. (ps-1). 1987. 12.95 (ISBN 0-06-026938-3); PLB 12.89 (ISBN 0-685-18178-2, C Zolotow Bks). HarpC Child Bks.

HORSES–HISTORY

Anderson, John K. Horses & Riding. Conkle, Nancy, illus. 48p. (gr. 7-9). 1979. pap. 2.50 (ISBN 0-88388-066-0). Bellerophon Bks.
Henry, Marguerite. King of the Wind. Dennis, Wesley, illus. LC 48-8773. 176p. (gr. 2-9). 1990. 12.95 (ISBN 0-02-743629-2, Mcmillan Child Bk); pap. 3.95 (ISBN 0-02-688758-4). Macmillan Child Grp.
—King of the Wind. Dennis, Wesley, illus. 176p. (gr. 3-7). 1991. pap. 3.95 (ISBN 0-689-71486-6, Aladdin). Macmillan Child Grp.
—Marguerite Henry's All About Horses. Osborne, M., illus. (gr. 4-8). 1967. (Random Juv). Random.

HORSES–LEGENDS

Green Tiger Press Staff, ed. Flying Horses. 12p. (Orig.). (gr. 7-9). 1982. pap. 2.50 (ISBN 0-88138-005-9). Green Tiger Pr.
Small, Howard I. Monty's Pal. Hengen, Nona, illus. LC 78-73621. viii, 120p. (gr. 3-8). 1979. 6.95 (ISBN 0-931474-08-6). TBW Bks.

HORSES–PICTURES, ILLUSTRATIONS, ETC.

Featherly, Jay. Mustangs: Wild Horses of the American West. (Illus.). 48p. (gr. 2-5). 1986. lib. bdg. 12.95 (ISBN 0-87614-293-5). Carolrhoda Bks.
Henry, Marguerite. A Pictorial Life Story of Misty. LC 76-41864. (Illus.). 112p. (gr. 3 up). 1976. write for info. (ISBN 0-02-743626-8). Macmillan Child Grp.
Jeffers, Susan. All the Pretty Horses. Jeffers, Susan, illus. 32p. (ps-2). 1985. pap. 2.95 (ISBN 0-590-40353-2, Blue Ribbon Bks.). Scholastic Inc.
Knight, Dodo. Crazy about Horses Poster Book. (gr. 4-7). 1990. pap. 2.95 (ISBN 0-590-42826-8). Scholastic Inc.
Longstreet, Stephen, ed. Horse in Art. (Illus., Orig.). (ps). 1965. treasure trove bdg. 10.95x (ISBN 0-87505-045-X); pap. 4.95 (ISBN 0-87505-198-7). Borden.
Sonberg, Lynn. A Horse Named Paris. Robbins, Ken, illus. LC 86-6886. 48p. (gr. 2-4). 1986. 14.95 (ISBN 0-02-786260-7, Bradbury Pr). Macmillan Child Grp.
Spizzirri Publishing Co. Staff. Horses: An Educational Coloring Book. Spizzirri, Linda, ed. (Illus.). 32p. (gr. k-5). 1985. pap. 1.95 (ISBN 0-86545-068-4). Spizzirri.

HORSES–POETRY

Hubbell, Patricia. A Grass Green Gallop. Himler, Ronald, illus. LC 89-36354. 48p. (gr. 4-8). 1990. 14.95 (ISBN 0-689-31604-6, Atheneum Child Bk). Macmillan Child Grp.
Jeffers, Susan. If Wishes Were Horses: Mother Goose Rhymes. Jeffers, Susan, illus. LC 79-9986. (ps-3). 1979. 13.95 (ISBN 0-525-32531-X, DCB). Dutton Child Bks.

HORSES–TRAINING

Clay, Patrice. We Work with Horses: Trainer, Groom, Jockey, Hotwalker, Instructor, Blacksmith, Veterinarian, Show Rider, Breeder. (gr. 12up). 9.95 (ISBN 0-399-20735-X). Brown Bk.
Freeman, Charlotte M. A Day in the Life of a Horse Trainer. Jann, Gayle, illus. LC 87-10681. 32p. (gr. 4-8). 1988. PLB 11.79 (ISBN 0-8167-1111-9); pap. text ed. 2.95 (ISBN 0-8167-1112-7). Troll Assocs.
Henry, Marguerite. Born to Trot. Dennis, Wesley, illus. LC 50-10271. 224p. (gr. 3 up). 1987. 8.95 (ISBN 0-528-82135-0); pap. 3.95 (ISBN 0-02-688755-X, Aladdin). Macmillan Child Grp.
Holderness-Roddam, Jane. Preparing for a Show. Vincer, Carole, illus. 24p. (gr. 3 up). 1989. pap. 7.95 (ISBN 0-901366-09-9, Pub. by Threshold Bks). Half Halt Pr.
Ricci, A. James. Understanding & Training Horses. Wormer, J. Van, photos by. LC 64-14466. (Illus.). (gr. 10 up). 1964. 15.95 (ISBN 0-397-00356-0). HarpC Child Bks.
Saville, Lynn. Horses in the Circus Ring. Saville, Lynn, photos by. LC 88-18931. (Illus.). 32p. (gr. k-4). 1989. 13.95 (ISBN 0-525-44417-3, DCB). Dutton Child Bks.

HORSES IN MOVING-PICTURES

Amaral, Anthony. Movie Horses: Their Treatment & Training. (gr. 5-7). 5.50 (ISBN 0-672-50388-3, Bobbs). Macmillan.

HORTICULTURE

see Gardening

HOSPITALITY

see Entertaining

HOSPITALS

see also Children–Hospitals; Nurses and Nursing

Banks, Ann. Hospital Journal: A Kid's Guide to a Strange Place. Bobak, Cathy, illus. 64p. (gr. 2-5). 1989. pap. 7.95 (ISBN 0-14-032688-X, Puffin). Puffin Bks.
Butler, Daphne. First Look in the Hospital. LC 90-10245. (Illus.). 32p. (gr. 1-2). 1991. lib. bdg. 10.95 (ISBN 0-8368-0563-1). Gareth Stevens Inc.
Carter, Sharon & Monnig, Judith. Coping with a Hospital Stay. Rosen, Ruth, ed. 128p. (gr. 7 up). 1987. PLB 12.95 (ISBN 0-8239-0682-5). Rosen Group.
Coleman, William L. My Hospital Book. Walles, Dwight, illus. LC 81-10094. 96p. (Orig.). (gr. 2-7). 1981. pap. 5.95 (ISBN 0-87123-354-1). Bethany Hse.
Elliott, Ingrid G. Hospital Roadmap: A Book to Help Explain the Hospital Experience to Young children. LC 82-80226. (Illus.). 36p. (Orig.). (gr. k-2). 1984. pap. 8.95 (ISBN 0-9608150-0-7). Resources Children.
—Hospital Roadmap Manual: A Curriculum Guide to Explain the Hospital Experience to Young Children. 100p. (Orig.). (gr. k-2). 1986. pap. 11.95 (ISBN 0-9608150-1-5). Resources Children.
Going into Hospital. (Illus.). (ps). 3.50 (ISBN 0-7214-0849-4). Ladybird Bks.
Howe, James. The Hospital Book. Warshaw, Mal, photos by. LC 80-27747. (Illus.). 96p. (gr. 2-4). 1983. pap. 4.95 (ISBN 0-517-54235-8). Crown.
Sauer, Sue, et al. Stevie Has His Heart Examined. Goldstein, Nancy, ed. Albury, Mary, illus. (ps-7). 1983. pap. text ed. 4.25 (ISBN 0-937423-00-9). U M H & C.
—Stevie Has His Heart Repaired. Goldstein, Nancy, ed. Albury, Mary, illus. (ps-7). 1979. pap. text ed. 4.25 (ISBN 0-937423-01-7). U M H & C.
Shepherd, Sue, et al. Color Me Special. Albury, Mary, illus. (ps-3). 1982. pap. text ed. 4.00 (ISBN 0-937423-02-5). U M H & C.
Sigel, Lois S. New Careers in Hospitals. rev. ed. (Illus.). (gr. 7-12). 1990. PLB 12.95 (ISBN 0-8239-1172-1). Rosen Group.
Stein, Sara B. A Hospital Story. LC 73-15269. (Illus.). 48p. (ps-8). 1984. pap. 7.95 (ISBN 0-8027-7222-6). Walker & Co.
—A Hospital Story. LC 73-15269. (Illus.). 48p. (gr. 1 up). 1974. 10.95 (ISBN 0-8027-6173-9). Walker & Co.

HOSPITALS–FICTION

Balter, Lawrence. Alfred Goes to the Hospital. Schanzer, Roz, illus. 40p. (gr. 3-7). 1990. 5.95 (ISBN 0-8120-6150-0). Barron.
Civardi, Anne & Cartwright, Stephen. Going to the Hospital. 16p. (ps up). 1987. 2.95 (ISBN 0-7460-0073-1). EDC.
Coles, Allison. Mandy & the Hospital. Charlton, Michael, illus. 28p. (ps up). 1985. 3.95 (ISBN 0-88110-269-5). EDC.
Degens, T. On the Third Ward. LC 89-77451. 256p. (gr. 6 up). 1990. 14.95 (ISBN 0-06-021428-7); PLB 14.89 (ISBN 0-06-021429-5). HarpC Child Bks.
Godfrey, Jan. Me in the Hospital. (ps-3). 1989. pap. 1.95 (ISBN 0-7459-1733-X). Lion USA.
Hantzig, Deborah. A Visit to the Sesame Street Hospital. Mathieu, Joe, illus. LC 84-17852. 32p. (ps-4). 1985. lib. bdg. 5.99 (ISBN 0-394-97062-4, Random Juv); pap. 2.25 (ISBN 0-394-87062-X). Random.

Hogan, Paula Z. & Hogan, Kirk. The Hospital Scares Me. Thelen, Mary, illus. Wilson, Jerrian M., intro. by. LC 79-23886. (Illus.). 32p. (gr. k-6). 1980. PLB 16.67 (ISBN 0-8172-1351-1). Raintree Pubs.
Howe, James. A Night Without Stars. LC 82-16278. 192p. (gr. 4-7). 1983. 13.95 (ISBN 0-689-30957-0, Atheneum Child Bk). Macmillan Child Grp.
Jones, Rebecca C. Angie & Me. LC 81-4367. 132p. (gr. 5-9). 1981. 11.95 (ISBN 0-02-747980-3, Mcmillan Child Bk). Macmillan Child Grp.
Keller, Holly. The Best Present. LC 87-38086. (Illus.). 32p. (gr. k up). 1989. 11.95 (ISBN 0-688-07319-0); PLB 11.88 (ISBN 0-688-07320-4). Greenwillow.
Martin, Charles E. Island Rescue. Martin, Charles E., illus. LC 84-13672. 32p. (gr. k-3). 1985. 11.75 (ISBN 0-688-04257-0); PLB 11.88 (ISBN 0-688-04258-9). Greenwillow.
Rockwell, Anne. The Emergency Room. Rockwell, Harlow, illus. LC 84-20161. 24p. (ps-2). 1985. 13.95 (ISBN 0-02-777300-0, Mcmillan Child Bk). Macmillan Child Grp.
Roy, Ron. Move over, Wheelchairs Coming Through. Hausherr, Rosemarie, illus. LC 84-14314. 96p. (gr. 4-7). 1985. 13.95 (ISBN 0-89919-249-1, Clarion). HM.
Sachs, Elizabeth A. Just Like Always. (gr. 4-7). 1990. pap. 3.95 (ISBN 0-689-71389-4, Aladdin). Macmillan Child Grp.
Steel, Danielle. Max's Daddy Goes to the Hospital. Rogers, Jacqueline, illus. (ps-2). 1989. 8.95 (ISBN 0-385-29797-1). Delacorte.

HOSPITALS–STAFF

John, Hughes. Janet the Hospital Helper. (Illus.). 40p. (gr. 7-12). 1975. pap. 2.65 (ISBN 0-915510-02-2). Janus Bks.

HOT RODS

see Automobile Racing; Automobiles

HOTELS, MOTELS, ETC.–FICTION

De Segur, Comtesse. The Angel Inn. Aiken, Joan, tr. from FRE. Marriott, Pat, illus. LC 78-12784. 240p. (gr. 3 up). 1978. pap. 6.95 (ISBN 0-916144-29-1). Stemmer Hse.
Fleischman, Paul. The Half-a-Moon Inn. Jacobi, Kathy, illus. LC 79-2010. 96p. (gr. 3-7). 1991. pap. 3.50 (ISBN 0-06-440364-5, Trophy). HarpC Child Bks.
Graham, Alastair. Full Moon Soup: Or Fall of the Hotel Splendile. (ps-3). 1991. 14.95 (ISBN 0-8037-1045-3). Dial Bks Young.
Hoban, Julia. Buzby. Himmelman, John, illus. LC 89-29408. 64p. (gr. k-3). 1990. 11.95 (ISBN 0-06-022399-5); PLB 11.89 (ISBN 0-06-022398-7). HarpC Child Bks.
Ruby, Lois. Pig-Out Inn. LC 86-21433. 180p. (gr. 5 up). 1987. 12.95 (ISBN 0-395-42714-2). HM.
Wyllie, Stephen. Monkey's Crazy Hotel. Roffey, Maureen, illus. LC 87-45149. 24p. (ps-k). 1987. 8.95 (ISBN 0-694-00224-0). HarpC Child Bks.
Wyss, Thelma H. Here at the Scenic-Vu Motel. LC 87-45308. 192p. (gr. 7 up). 1988. 13.95 (ISBN 0-06-022250-6); PLB 12.89 (ISBN 0-06-022251-4). HarpC Child Bks.

HOTELS, MOTELS, ETC.–VOCATIONAL GUIDANCE

John, Hughes. Jester the Bellhop. (Illus.). 40p. (gr. 7-12). 1975. pap. 2.65 (ISBN 0-915510-05-7). Janus Bks.

HOUDINI, HARRY, 1874-1926

Borland, Kathryn K. & Speicher, Helen R. Harry Houdini: Young Magician. LC 90-23321. (Illus.). 192p. (gr. 3-7). 1991. pap. 3.95 (ISBN 0-689-71476-9, Aladdin). Macmillan Child Grp.
Fago, John N. & Toan, Debbie. Houdini - Walt Disney. Cruz, E. R. & Henson, Tenny, illus. (gr. 4-12). 1979. pap. text ed. 2.95 (ISBN 0-88301-350-9); wkbk 1.25 (ISBN 0-88301-374-6). Pendulum Pr.
Kraske, Robert. Harry Houdini: Master of Magic. (gr. 2-6). 1989. pap. 2.50 (ISBN 0-590-42402-5). Scholastic Inc.
Levy, Elizabeth. Running Out of Magic with Houdini. Sims, Blanche & Rutherford, Jenny, illus. LC 80-28427. 128p. (gr. 3-6). 1981. lib. bdg. 4.99 (ISBN 0-394-94685-5); pap. 1.95 (ISBN 0-394-84685-0). Knopf.
Sabin, Louis. The Great Houdini, Daring Escape Artist. Eitzen, Allan, illus. LC 89-5170. 48p. (gr. 4-6). 1990. PLB 10.79 (ISBN 0-8167-1769-9); pap. text ed. 2.95 (ISBN 0-8167-1770-2). Troll Assocs.

HOUSE BOATS

see Houseboats

HOUSE CLEANING

Pluckrose, Henry. Clean It! Fairclough, Chris, photos by. (Illus.). 32p. (gr. k-4). 1990. PLB 10.40 (ISBN 0-531-14063-6). Watts.

HOUSE DECORATION

see Interior Decoration

HOUSE FLIES

see Flies

HOUSE FURNISHING

see Interior Decoration

HOUSE PAINTING

Painting. (Illus.). 32p. (gr. 6-12). 1983. pap. 1.85 (ISBN 0-8395-3372-1, 3372). BSA.

HOUSE PLANTS

Gattis, L. S., III. Houseplants for Pathfinders: A Basic Youth Enrichment Skill Honor Packet. (Illus.). 24p. (Orig.). (gr. 5 up). 1989. pap. 5.00 tchr's. ed. (ISBN 0-936241-50-0). Cheetah Pub.

HOUSE REPAIRING

see Houses–Repairing

HOUSEBOATS

Rickard, Graham. Mobile Homes. (Illus.). 32p. (gr. 2-5). 1989. 9.95 (ISBN 0-8225-2130-X). Lerner Pubns.

HOUSEBOATS–FICTION

Warner, Gertrude C. Houseboat Mystery. Cunningham, David, illus. LC 67-26521. 128p. (gr. 3-8). 1967. PLB 9.95 (ISBN 0-8075-3412-9). A Whitman.

HOUSEHOLD APPLIANCES

see Household Equipment and Supplies

HOUSEHOLD EMPLOYEES–FICTION

Parish, Peggy. Amelia Bedelia. Siebel, Fritz, illus. LC 63-14367. 32p. (gr. k-3). 1963. 10.95 (ISBN 0-06-024640-5); PLB 11.89 (ISBN 0-06-024641-3). HarpC Child Bks.
—Amelia Bedelia & the Baby. Sweat, Lynn, illus. 64p. (gr. k-3). 1982. pap. 3.50 (ISBN 0-380-57067-X, Camelot). Avon.
—Amelia Bedelia & the Surprise Shower. Siebel, Fritz, illus. LC 66-18655. 64p. (gr. k-3). 1979. pap. 3.50 (ISBN 0-06-444019-2, Trophy). HarpC Child Bks.
—Amelia Bedelia Helps Out. Sweat, Lynn, illus. 64p. (gr. k-3). 1981. pap. 3.50 (ISBN 0-380-53405-3, Camelot). Avon.
—Good Work, Amelia Bedelia. Sweat, Lynn, illus. LC 75-20360. 56p. (gr. 1-4). 1976. 12.95 (ISBN 0-688-80022-X); PLB 12.88 (ISBN 0-688-84022-1). Greenwillow.
—Good Work, Amelia Bedelia. Sweat, Lynn, illus. 164p. (gr. k-5). 1980. pap. 3.50 (ISBN 0-380-49171-0, Camelot). Avon.
—Thank You, Amelia Bedelia. Siebel, Fritz, illus. LC 64-11835. (gr. k-3). 1964. 11.95 (ISBN 0-06-024665-0); PLB 10.89 (ISBN 0-06-024652-9). HarpC Child Bks.

HOUSEHOLD EQUIPMENT AND SUPPLIES

Cohen, Daniel. The Last Hundred Years: Household Technology. LC 82-15442. (Illus.). 192p. (gr. 5 up). 1982. 8.95 (ISBN 0-87131-386-3). M Evans.
Scarry, Richard. Richard Scarry Huckle's Book. Scarry, Richard, illus. (ps). 1979. 2.95 (ISBN 0-394-84130-1, Random Juv). Random.
Wilkins, Mary-Jane. Everyday Things & How They Work. Bull, Peter, illus. 40p. (gr. 4-5). 1991. PLB 11.40 (ISBN 0-531-19109-5). Watts.

HOUSEHOLD MANAGEMENT

see Home Economics

HOUSEKEEPING

see Home Economics

HOUSES

Here are entered general works on houses.
see also Building; Building–Repair and Reconstruction

Adkins, Jan. How a House Happens. (Illus.). 32p. (gr. 5 up). 1983. pap. 3.95 (ISBN 0-8027-7206-4). Walker & Co.
Althea. Building a House. (Illus.). 26p. (gr. 2-5). 1983. pap. 2.50 (ISBN 0-521-27152-5). Cambridge U Pr.
Barton, Byron. Building a House. LC 80-22674. (Illus.). 32p. (ps-1). 1981. PLB 13.88 (ISBN 0-688-84291-7). Greenwillow.
Bowyer. Houses & Homes. (gr. 4-9). 1978. (Usborne-Hayes); PLB 13.96 (ISBN 0-88110-117-6); pap. 6.95 (ISBN 0-86020-191-0). EDC.
Brown, Richard, illus. Muchas Palabras Sobre Mi Casa. (SPA.). (ps-1). 1989. pap. 3.95 (ISBN 0-15-200532-3, Gulliver Bks). HarBraceJ.
—One Hundred Words about My House. (ps-1). 1989. pap. 3.95 (ISBN 0-15-200556-0, Voy B). HarBraceJ.
Carter, Katherine. Houses. LC 82-4431. (Illus.). (gr. k-4). 1982. PLB 14.60 (ISBN 0-516-01672-5). Childrens.
Emberley, Rebecca. My House, Mi Casa: A Book in Two Languages. Emberley, Rebecca, illus. LC 89-12893. (ps-2). 1990. 14.95 (ISBN 0-316-23637-3). Little.
Flint, Russ. Let's Build a House. LC 89-29425. (Illus.). (ps-2). 1990. 11.95 (ISBN 0-8249-8432-3). Ideals.
Gibbons, Gail. How a House Is Built. Gibbons, Gail, illus. LC 90-55107. 32p. (ps-3). 1990. reinforced 13.95 (ISBN 0-8234-0841-8). Holiday.
Hogner, Franz. From Blueprint to House. Lerner, Mark, tr. from GER. (Illus.). 24p. (ps-3). 1986. lib. bdg. 6.95 (ISBN 0-87614-295-1). Carolrhoda Bks.
Humberstone. Things at Home. (gr. 2-5). 1981. (Usborne-Hayes); PLB 11.96 (ISBN 0-88110-021-8); pap. 3.95 (ISBN 0-86020-501-0). EDC.
James, Alan. Homes in Cold Places. (Illus.). 32p. (gr. 2-5). 1989. 9.95 (ISBN 0-8225-2131-8). Lerner Pubns.
—Homes in Hot Places. (Illus.). 32p. (gr. 2-5). 1989. 9.95 (ISBN 0-8225-2132-6). Lerner Pubns.
—Homes on Water. (Illus.). 32p. (gr. 2-5). 1989. 9.95 (ISBN 0-8225-2127-X). Lerner Pubns.
Lambert, Mark. Homes in the Future. (Illus.). 32p. (gr. 2-5). 1989. 9.95 (ISBN 0-8225-2126-1). Lerner Pubns.
Moving Day. 1990. 2.99 (ISBN 0-517-69195-7). Outlet Bk Co.
People & Homes. (Illus.). 32p. (gr. 3-6). 1986. 10.95 (ISBN 0-86020-901-6). EDC.
Rickard, Graham. Building Homes. (Illus.). 32p. (gr. 2-5). 1989. 9.95 (ISBN 0-8225-2129-6). Lerner Pubns.
—Homes in Space. (Illus.). 32p. (gr. 2-5). 1989. 9.95 (ISBN 0-8225-2125-3). Lerner Pubns.
—Mobile Homes. (Illus.). 32p. (gr. 2-5). 1989. 9.95 (ISBN 0-8225-2130-X). Lerner Pubns.
Robbins, Ken. Building a House. LC 83-16513. (Illus.). 48p. (gr. 3-5). 1984. 14.95 (ISBN 0-02-777400-7, Four Winds). Macmillan Child Grp.
Rogers, Fred. Moving. (Illus.). 32p. (ps-4). 1987. 12.95 (ISBN 0-399-21383-X, Putnam); pap. 5.95 (ISBN 0-399-21384-8, Putnam). Putnam Pub Group.
Watson. The House. (gr. k-2). 1980. 6.95 (ISBN 0-86020-389-1, Usborne-Hayes); PLB 11.95 (ISBN 0-88110-068-4); pap. 2.95 (ISBN 0-86020-388-3). EDC.
Weiss, Harvey. Shelters: From Tepee to Igloo. Weiss, Harvey, illus. LC 87-47698. 80p. (gr. 5-8). 1988. 10.95 (ISBN 0-690-04553-0, Crowell Jr Bks); PLB 12.89 (ISBN 0-690-04555-7, Crowell Jr Bks). HarpC Child Bks.
Whiting, Charles. The Home Front: Germany. LC 81-21406. (Illus.). 208p. (gr. 7 up). 1982. lib. bdg. 25.93 (ISBN 0-8094-3420-2, 0-8094-257-6); pap. 19.93 (ISBN 0-8094-2508-4). Time-Life.

HOUSES–FICTION

Adams, Pam, illus. The House That Jack Built. 16p. (ps-2). 1978. 8.00 (ISBN 0-85953-076-0, Pub. by Child's Play England). Childs Play.
Banks, Ann & Evans, Nancy. Goodbye, House. Russo, Marisabina, illus. 64p. (gr. 2-6). 1988. pap. 7.95 (ISBN 0-517-53907-1, Harmony). Crown.
Blume, Judy. Iggie's House. 128p. (gr. 3-6). 1986. pap. 3.25 (ISBN 0-440-44062-9, YB). Dell.
Bour, Daniele. The House from Morning to Night. LC 84-21873. (Illus.). 16p. (ps-3). 1985. 9.95 (ISBN 0-916291-01-4). Kane Miller Bk.
Brown, Beth. House Without a Home. Hill, Dorothy, illus. LC 70-112367. 48p. (gr. k-3). 1971. PLB 10.95 (ISBN 0-87460-221-1). Lion Bks.
Brown, Marc. There's No Place Like Home. Brown, Marc, illus. LC 84-4229. 48p. (ps-3). 1984. 5.95 (ISBN 0-8193-1125-1). Parents.
Burton, Virginia L. Little House. (Illus.). (gr. k-3). 1978. 13.95 (ISBN 0-395-18156-9); pap. 4.95 (ISBN 0-395-25938-X). HM.
Calhoun, Mary. Depend on Katie John. Frame, Paul, illus. LC 61-7328. 208p. (gr. 3-6). 1961. PLB 12.89 (ISBN 0-06-020926-7). HarpC Child Bks.
—Katie John. Frame, Paul, illus. LC 60-5775. (gr. 3-6). 1960. PLB 12.89 (ISBN 0-06-020951-8). HarpC Child Bks.
Cameron, Ann. The Stories Julian Tells. Strugness, Ann, illus. LC 80-18023. 96p. (gr. k-5). 1981. 8.95 (ISBN 0-394-84301-0); lib. bdg. 8.99 (ISBN 0-394-94301-5). Pantheon.
Cassedy, Sylvia. Behind the Attic Wall. LC 82-45922. 320p. (gr. 3-7). 1983. (Crowell Jr Bks); PLB 13.89 (ISBN 0-690-04337-6, Crowell Jr Bks). HarpC Child Bks.
Christopher, John. Beyond the Burning Lands: The Sword of the Spirits Trilogy. LC 78-152288. 224p. (gr. 7 up). 1989. pap. 3.95 (ISBN 0-02-042572-4, Collier Young Ad). Macmillan Child Grp.
Cowley, Joy. My Home. Moxley, Susan, illus. 8p. (gr. k-2). 1989. pap. text ed. 15.00 (ISBN 1-55911-280-8). Wright Group.
—My Home, 6 bks. Moxley, Susan, illus. 8p. (gr. k-2). 1986. Set. pap. text ed. 12.60 (ISBN 1-55911-351-0). Wright Group.
De Brunhoff, Laurent. Chateau du Roi Babar. (FRE.). (gr. 3-8). 15.95 (ISBN 0-685-11078-8). French & Eur.
Dragonwagon, Crescent. Home Place. Pinkney, Jerry, illus. LC 89-32911. 40p. (ps-3). 1990. 14.95 (ISBN 0-02-733190-3, Mcmillan Child Bk). Macmillan Child Grp.
Dupasquier, Philippe. Our House on the Hill. (ps-3). 1988. pap. 11.95 (ISBN 0-670-81971-9). Viking Child Bks.
Firmin, Peter. Pinney Finds a House. Firmin, Peter, illus. 32p. (ps-3). 1986. pap. 4.95 (ISBN 0-670-80956-X). Viking Child Bks.
George, Jean C. One Day in the Desert. Brenner, Fred, illus. LC 82-45924. 48p. (gr. 5-7). 1983. PLB 13.89 (ISBN 0-690-04341-4, Crowell Jr Bks). HarpC Child Bks.
Goffstein, Brooke. A House, a Home. Goffstein, Brooke, illus. LC 88-37376. 32p. (ps up). 1989. 13.95 (ISBN 0-06-022436-3); PLB 13.89 (ISBN 0-06-022437-1). HarpC Child Bks.
Green, Wendy. The New House. (ps-3). 1989. pap. 1.95 (ISBN 0-7459-1737-2). Lion USA.
Harwood, Pearl A. Mr. Bumba's New Home. Folger, Joseph, illus. LC 64-19775. 32p. (gr. k-3). 1964. PLB 4.95 (ISBN 0-8225-0101-5). Lerner Pubns.
—Mrs. Moon & the Dark Stairs. Overlie, George, illus. LC 67-15693. 32p. (gr. k-3). 1967. PLB 4.95 (ISBN 0-8225-0117-1). Lerner Pubns.
Hoberman, Mary A. A House Is a House for Me. Fraser, Betty, illus. 48p. (ps-3). 1982. pap. 3.95 (ISBN 0-14-050394-3, Puffin). Puffin Bks.
Hoberman, Mary Ann. A House Is a House for Me. Fraser, Betty, illus. (gr. k-3). 1984. incl. cassette 19.95 (ISBN 0-941078-33-7); pap. 12.95 incl. cassette (ISBN 0-941078-31-0); incl. 4 bks., cassette, & guide 27.95 (ISBN 0-317-07117-3). Live Oak Media.
Holland, Isabelle. The Empty House. LC 82-48464. 128p. (gr. 6 up). 1983. PLB 12.89 (ISBN 0-397-32006-X, Lipp Jr Bks). HarpC Child Bks.
A House Is a House for Me. (ps-3). 1988. pap. 6.95 incl. cassette (ISBN 0-14-095065-6, Puffin). Puffin Bks.
Hutchins, Pat. The House That Sailed Away. Hutchins, Lawrence, illus. LC 74-9823. 192p. (gr. 2-6). 1975. PLB 11.88 (ISBN 0-688-84013-2). Greenwillow.
Kellogg, Steven, retold by. & illus. There Was an Old Woman. 48p. (ps-3). 1984. 13.95 (ISBN 0-02-749780-1, Four Winds). Macmillan.
Krahn, Fernando. Arthur's Adventure in the Abandoned House. Krahn, Fernando, illus. LC 80-22249. (ps-1). 1981. 8.25 (ISBN 0-525-25945-7, 0801-240, DCB). Dutton Child Bks.

Krauss, Ruth. Very Special House. Sendak, Maurice, illus. LC 53-7115. (ps-1). 1953. 12.89 (ISBN 0-685-02070-3). HarpC Child Bks.

L'Engle, Madeleine. A House Like a Lotus. (gr. 6-12). 1985. pap. 3.50 (ISBN 0-440-93685-3, LFL). Dell.

Le Sieg, Theodore. In a People House. (Illus.). (ps-1). 1972. 6.95 (ISBN 0-394-82395-8, Random Juv); lib. bdg. 7.99 (ISBN 0-394-92395-2). Random.

Lionni, Leo. Biggest House in the World. Lionni, Leo, illus. LC 68-12646. (gr. k-3). 1968. lib. bdg. 12.99 (ISBN 0-394-90944-5). Pantheon.

—The Biggest House in the World. LC 68-12646. (Illus.). 32p. (ps-6). 1987. pap. 2.95 (ISBN 0-317-53625-7). Knopf.

Lively, Penelope. A House Inside Out. Parkins, David, illus. LC 87-19946. 144p. (gr. 4-7). 1988. 12.95 (ISBN 0-525-44332-0, 01258-370, DCB). Dutton Child Bks.

Loelling, Carol. Whose House Is This? (Illus.). 22p. (ps-4). 1978. 5.95 (ISBN 0-8431-0444-9). Price Stern.

Lord, Bette B. In the Year of the Boar & Jackie Robinson. Simont, Marc, illus. LC 83-48440. 176p. (gr. 3-7). 1984. 12.95 (ISBN 0-06-024003-2); PLB 12.89 (ISBN 0-06-024004-0). HarpC Child Bks.

Lunn, Janet. The Root Cellar. LC 83-3246. 256p. (gr. 5 up). 1983. 14.95 (ISBN 0-684-17855-9, Scribners Young Read). Macmillan Child Grp.

McGraw, S. This Old New House. (Illus.). 32p. (ps-8). 1989. 12.95 (ISBN 1-55037-035-9); pap. 4.95 (ISBN 1-55037-034-0). Firefly Bks Ltd.

McKillip, Patricia. The House on Parchment Street. Robinson, Charles, illus. 192p. (gr. 3-7). 1991. pap. 3.95 (ISBN 0-689-71471-8, Aladdin). Macmillan Child Grp.

Nixon, Joan L. House On Hackmans Hill (R) 1986. pap. 2.75 (ISBN 0-590-42370-3). Scholastic Inc.

Norton, Andre & Miller, Phyllis. House of Shadows. LC 83-16197. 216p. (gr. 5-9). 1984. 14.95 (ISBN 0-689-50298-2, M K McElderry). Macmillan Child Grp.

Oechsli, Kelly. Home Sweet Home. LC 83-8607. (Illus.). 32p. (gr. 3-6). 1983. PLB 14.65 (ISBN 0-940742-34-9). Raintree Pubs.

Pfanner, Louise. Louise Builds a House. LC 88-23415. (Illus.). 32p. (ps-1). 1989. 12.95 (ISBN 0-531-05796-8); PLB 12.99 (ISBN 0-531-08396-9). Orchard Bks Watts.

Pryor, Bonnie. The House on Maple Street. Peck, Beth, illus. LC 86-12648. 32p. (gr. k-3). 1987. (Morrow Junior Books); lib. bdg. 13.88 (ISBN 0-688-06381-0, Morrow Junior Books). Morrow.

Rockwell, Anne. In Our House. Rockwell, Anne, illus. LC 85-47535. 32p. (ps-1). 1991. pap. 4.95 (ISBN 0-06-107413-6). HarpC Child Bks.

Roundabout Cozy Cottage. (ps-1). 1987. 5.95 (ISBN 0-448-11328-7, G&D). Putnam Pub Group.

Rusty's House. 1989. 2.99 (ISBN 0-517-69122-1). Outlet Bk Co.

Skiff, Andrea. Blueberry & the Victorian House. Peterson, Elizabeth J., ed. (Illus.). 27p. (gr. 2-5). 1986. pap. 4.95 (ISBN 0-938911-03-1). Indiv Educ Syst.

Stahl, Hilda. Teddy Jo & the Abandoned House. LC 83-50991. 128p. (Orig.). (gr. 2-8). 1984. pap. 2.95 (ISBN 0-8423-6949-X). Tyndale.

Taylor, Dorothy L. Abigail's New Home. Schimmel, Beth, illus. LC 82-238196. 20p. (gr. k-3). 7.50 (ISBN 0-9610640-0-5). D L Taylor.

Taylor, E. J. Ivy Cottage. Taylor, E. J., illus. LC 84-900. 32p. (ps-4). 1985. 7.95 (ISBN 0-394-86831-5). Knopf.

Yue, Charlotte & Yue, David. The Igloo. LC 88-6154. (Illus.). 128p. (gr. 3-7). 1988. 13.95 (ISBN 0-395-44613-9). HM.

Zelinsky, Paul O. The Maid & the Mouse & the Odd-Shaped House: A Story in Rhyme. (Illus.). 32p. (gr. k-3). 1981. 12.95 (ISBN 0-396-07938-5, Putnam). Putnam Pub Group.

HOUSES–REPAIRING

Boy Scouts of America. Home Repairs. (Illus.). 42p. (gr. 6-12). 1961. pap. 1.85 (ISBN 0-8395-3329-2, 3329). BSA.

HOUSES OF ANIMALS

see Animals–Habitations

HOUSING

Davis, Bertha. America's Housing Crisis. (gr. 9-12). 1990. PLB 12.90 (ISBN 0-531-10917-8). Watts.

HOUSING–FICTION

Holman, Felice. Secret City, U. S. A. LC 89-39841. 208p. (gr. 5-9). 1990. 13.95 (ISBN 0-684-19168-7, Scribners Young Read). Macmillan Child Grp.

Mendoza, George. Need a House? Call Ms. Mouse! Smith, Doris S., illus. LC 81-80884. 48p. (ps-3). 1981. 5.95 (ISBN 0-448-16575-9, G&D). Putnam Pub Group.

Snyder, Carol. The Great Condominium Rebellion. Kramer, Anthony, illus. LC 81-65491. 128p. (gr. 4-6). 1981. PLB 11.95 (ISBN 0-385-28352-0). Delacorte.

HOUSTON, SAMUEL, 1793-1863

Gleiter, Jan & Thompson, Kathleen. Sam Houston. LC 87-24161. (Illus.). 32p. (Orig.). (gr. 2-5). 1987. PLB 16.67 (ISBN 0-8172-2660-5); pap. text ed. 9.27 (ISBN 0-8172-2664-8). Raintree Pubs.

James, Marquis. The Raven: A Biography of Sam Houston. (Illus.). 527p. (gr. 10-12). 1988. pap. 10.95 (ISBN 0-292-77040-5). U of Tex Pr.

Latham, Jean L. Sam Houston: Hero of Texas. (Illus.). 80p. (gr. 2-6). 1991. Repr. of 1965 ed. PLB 12.95 (ISBN 0-7910-1441-X). Chelsea Hse.

Zadra, Dan. Statesmen in America: Sam Houston. rev. ed. (gr. 2-4). 1988. PLB 11.50s.p. (ISBN 0-88682-187-8); PLB 16.45 (ISBN 0-318-32959-X). Creative Ed.

HOUSTON, SAMUEL, 1793-1863–FICTION

James, Bessie R. & James, Marquis. Six Feet Six. (gr. 7-9). 1931. 5.95 (ISBN 0-672-50499-5, Bobbs). Macmillan.

HUDSON, HENRY, d. 1611

Harley, Ruth. Henry Hudson. new ed. LC 78-18053. (Illus.). 48p. (gr. 4-7). 1979. PLB 9.89 (ISBN 0-89375-171-5); pap. 2.95 (ISBN 0-89375-163-4). Troll Assocs.

HUGHES, JAMES LANGSTON, 1902-1967

Meltzer, Milton. Langston Hughes: A Biography. LC 68-21925. 296p. (gr. 7 up). 1988. PLB 13.89 (ISBN 0-690-04762-2, Crowell Jr Bks). HarpC Child Bks.

Rummel, Jack. Langston Hughes. King, Coretta Scott, intro. by. (Illus.). 112p. (Orig.). (gr. 5 up). 1989. 17.95 (ISBN 1-55546-595-1); pap. 9.95 (ISBN 0-7910-0201-2). Chelsea Hse.

Walker, Alice. Langston Hughes, American Poet. LC 73-9565. (Illus.). 40p. (gr. 2-5). 1974. PLB 14.89 (ISBN 0-690-00219-X, Crowell Jr Bks). HarpC Child Bks.

HUMAN BODY

see Anatomy

HUMAN FIGURE IN ART

see Anatomy

HUMAN RACE

see Anthropology; Man

HUMAN RELATIONS

Here are entered works that deal with the integration of people so that they can live and work together with psychological, social and economic satisfaction.

see also Behavior; Intercultural Education; Prejudices and Antipathies; Psychology, Applied; Social Adjustment; Toleration;

also interpersonal relations between individuals or group of individuals, e.g. Parent and Child

Ancona, George. Team Work. Ancona, George, illus. LC 82-45579. 48p. (gr. 3-6). 1983. (Crowell Jr Bks). HarpC Child Bks.

Carney, Mary L. Too Tough to Hurt. 128p. 1991. pap. 5.95 (ISBN 0-310-28621-2, Youth Bks). Zondervan.

Carroll, Jeri A. Let's Learn about Getting Along with Others. 64p. (ps-2). 1988. wkbk 7.95 (ISBN 0-86653-439-3, GA1042). Good Apple.

Crum, Thomas F. Magic of Conflict Workshop for Young People. Heffernan, Cheryl, illus. (gr. 6-12). 1989. multi-media kit 49.95 (ISBN 1-877803-04-9). AIKI Works.

Davis, Duane. Being a Friend Manual, No. 1. rev. ed. 1988. tchr's. ed. 2.00 (ISBN 0-88671-329-3). Am Guidance.

—My Friends & Me Story Book. rev. ed. (ps-k). 1988. pap. text ed. 59.00 (ISBN 0-88671-326-9). Am Guidance.

Davis, Duane E. Being a Friend Manual, No. 2. rev. ed. 1988. tchr's. ed. 2.00 (ISBN 0-88671-330-7). Am Guidance.

—Being a Friend, No. 1: Story Activities for Personal Growth. (Illus.). (ps). 1988. pap. text ed. 35.00 (ISBN 0-88671-327-7). Am Guidance.

—Being a Friend, No. 2: Story Activities for Social Growth. (Illus.). (ps). 1988. pap. text ed. 35.00 (ISBN 0-88671-328-5). Am Guidance.

Educational Assessment Publishing Company Staff. Parent - Child Learning Library: Healthy Relationships. (Illus.). 32p. (gr. k-3). Date not set. text ed. 9.95 (ISBN 0-942277-55-4). Educ Assess Pub.

—Parent - Child Learning Library: Healthy Relationships English Big Book. (Illus.). 32p. (gr. k-3). Date not set. text ed. 28.50 (ISBN 0-942277-73-2). Educ Assess Pub.

—Parent - Child Learning Library: Health Relationships Spanish Big Book. (SPA., Illus.). 32p. (gr. k-3). Date not set. text ed. 28.50 (ISBN 0-942277-74-0). Educ Assess Pub.

—Parent - Child Learning Library: Healthy Relationships Spanish Edition. (SPA.). 32p. (ps). Date not set. text ed. 9.95 (ISBN 0-942277-91-0). Educ Assess Pub.

Elchoness, Monte. Why Can't Anyone Hear Me? A Guide for Surviving Adolescence. 2nd, rev. ed. Elchoness, Monte, illus. LC 86-737. 200p. (gr. 6-12). 1989. pap. 10.95 (ISBN 0-936781-06-8, Dist. by Publishers Group West). Monroe Pr.

Fellows, Bob. Easily Fooled: New Insights & Techniques for Resisting Manipulation. Gray, Steve, illus. 36p. (Orig.). (gr. 7 up). 1989. pap. 5.95 (ISBN 0-9622879-0-3). MindMatters.

Gelman, Jan. Marci's Secret Book of Flirting: (Don't Go Out Without It) LC 89-2439. 96p. (Orig.). (gr. 4-8). 1990. lib. bdg. 6.99 (ISBN 0-394-91931-9, Bullseye Bks); pap. 2.95 (ISBN 0-394-81931-4, Bullseye Bks). Knopf.

Hensel, Lila. Who Is My Neighbor? A Primer for Group Discussion. 32p. (Orig.). 1989. pap. 2.95 (ISBN 0-932727-29-8). Hope Pub Hse.

Hermes, Patricia. Be Still My Heart. 160p. (gr. 5-9). 1990. 14.95 (ISBN 0-399-21917-X, Putnam). Putnam Pub Group.

Johnson, Ward. Caring Is What Counts. Cooke, Tom, illus. 40p. (ps-3). 1983. 5.95 (ISBN 0-685-06604-5, 7004). Parker Bros.

Kramer, Patricia. The Dynamics of Relationships. rev. ed. (Illus.). 430p. (Orig.). (gr. 8-12). 1990. pap. text ed. 34.95 tchr's. manual (ISBN 0-317-90984-3). Equal Partners.

—The Dynamics of Relationships: A Guide to Developing Self-Esteem & Social Skills for Teens & Young Adults, Bk. 1. rev. ed. (Illus.). 331p. (Orig.). (gr. 8-12). 1990. pap. text ed. 16.95 student manual (ISBN 0-317-90983-5). Equal Partners.

—The Dynamics of Relationships: A Guide to Developing Self-Esteem & Social Skills for Teens & Young Adults, Bk. 2. rev. ed. (Illus.). 49p. (gr. 8-12). 1990. pap. text ed. 8.95 student manual (sexuality) (ISBN 0-317-90981-9). Equal Partners.

Kramer, Patricia & Frazer, Linda. The Dynamics of Relationships. rev. ed. (Illus.). 125p. (gr. 4-7). 1990. pap. text ed. 13.95 student manual (ISBN 0-317-90982-7). Equal Partners.

Lucas, Betty. For Children's Sake. 1989. 7.95 (ISBN 0-533-08080-0). Vantage.

Moncure, Jane B. You & Me. Bolt, John, illus. LC 81-17009. 112p. (gr. 2-6). 1980. lib. bdg. 11.97 (ISBN 0-89565-212-9). Childs World.

Ottens, Allen J. Coping with Romantic Breakup. 147p. (gr. 7-12). 1987. PLB 12.95 (ISBN 0-8239-0649-3). Rosen Group.

Pincus, Debbie. Interactions. 96p. (gr. 4-9). 1988. wkbk. 9.95 (ISBN 0-86653-448-2, GA1057). Good Apple.

Schwartz, L. Feelings about Friends. (gr. 3-6). 1988. 4.95 (ISBN 0-88160-168-3, LW 281). Learning Wks.

Scott, Sharon. Too Smart for Trouble. Phillips, George, illus. 112p. (Orig.). (gr. k-5). 1990. pap. 7.95 (ISBN 0-87425-121-4). Human Res Dev Pr.

Smock, Jerri. The Swan: A Storybook for Adults & Other Children. Poppler, Susan, illus. 21p. (gr. 7 up). 1989. incl. cassette 13.95g (ISBN 0-944586-00-7). WIN Pub.

THE SWAN: A STORYBOOK FOR ADULTS & OTHER CHILDREN is a four color fairytale book with accompanying seven minute cassette. It is a teaching tool for therapists, school teachers & families to learn about commitment, separation & individuality. It is a metaphor of two swans on puddle pond who meet & fall in love. Thomas the Toad narrates the love story with other characters such as Bucky Beaver & the guppy fish sharing their thoughts & ideas about Crystal, the female swan & her love for the male swan, & for herself. In the back of the book are questions & activities for therapy groups, classes & families to work together on & to learn about each other & their own strengths in living their lives, separately & collectively. The illustrations are beautifully done & the tape recorded voices weave a magical story of symbols & meaningful messages. *Publisher Provided Annotation.*

Stanish, Bob. The Giving Book. 112p. (gr. 3-8). 1988. 9.95 (ISBN 0-86653-459-8, GA1065). Good Apple.

Watson, Jane W., et al. Sometimes I'm Jealous. Trivas, Irene, illus. 32p. (ps up). 1986. pap. 2.95 (ISBN 0-517-56062-3). Crown.

Webster-Doyle, Terrence. Why Is Everybody Always Picking on Me? A Guide to Handling Bullies. (Illus.). (gr. 5-12). 1991. 14.95 (ISBN 0-942941-23-3); pap. 9.95 (ISBN 0-942941-22-5). Atrium Pubns.

White, Joe. Looking for Love in All the Wrong Places. (gr. 7 up). 1983. pap. 3.95 (ISBN 0-8423-3825-X). Tyndale.

Worth, Bonnie. Fraggles Book of Cooperation. 1989. write for info. (ISBN 0-02-689263-4). Checkerboard Pr.

Ziegler, Sandra. Fairness. Endres, Helen, illus. LC 88-18976. 32p. (gr. k-3). 1989. PLB 11.97 (ISBN 0-89565-390-7); pap. 6.96 (ISBN 0-89565-526-8). Childs World.

—Understanding. Williams, Jenny, illus. LC 88-23745. 32p. (gr. k-3). 1989. PLB 11.97 (ISBN 0-89565-452-0); pap. 6.96 (ISBN 0-89565-528-4). Childs World.

HUMAN RELATIONS–FICTION

Adler, C. S. A Tribe for Lexi. LC 90-6322. 160p. (gr. 3-7). 1991. SBE 12.95 (ISBN 0-02-700361-2, Mcmillan Child Bk). Macmillan Child Grp.

Coombs, Karen M. Beating Bully O'Brien. (gr. 3-7). 1991. pap. 2.95 (ISBN 0-380-75935-7, Camelot). Avon.

Cornwell, Anita. The Girls of Summer. Caines, Kelly, illus. LC 88-64051. 100p. (Orig.). (gr. 6 up). 1989. pap. 12.95 (ISBN 0-938678-11-6). New Seed.

Galvin, Matthew R. Robby Really Transforms: A Story About Grown-ups Helping Children. Ferraro, Sandra, illus. LC 87-34883. 48p. (ps-6). 1988. lib. bdg. 14.95 (ISBN 0-945354-05-3); pap. 4.95 (ISBN 0-945354-02-9). Magination Pr.

Gauch, Patricia L. Night Talks. 160p. (gr. 5 up). 1983. pap. 10.95 (ISBN 0-399-20911-5, Putnam). Putnam Pub Group.

Gerber, Merrill J. I'd Rather Think about Robbie. LC 88-19849. 160p. (gr. 4-7). 1990. pap. 3.50 (ISBN 0-06-440381-5, Trophy). HarpC Child Bks.

Greene, Constance C. I & Sproggy. McCully, Emily A., illus. 144p. (gr. 5 up). 1981. pap. 1.95 (ISBN 0-440-43986-8, YB). Dell.

Guccione, Leslie D. Nobody Listens to Me. 176p. (gr. 3-7). 1991. pap. 2.75 (ISBN 0-590-43106-4, Apple Paperbacks). Scholastic Inc.

Gunn, Robin J. Surprise Endings. Kobobel, Janet, ed. 160p. (Orig.). (gr. 7-11). 1991. pap. 4.99 (ISBN 1-56179-024-9). Focus Family.

Hamilton, Dorothy. Kerry. Graber, Esther R., illus. LC 72-4073. 114p. (gr. 4-10). 1973. pap. 3.95 (ISBN 0-8361-1690-9). Herald Pr.

Holland, Isabelle. Now Is Not Too Late. LC 79-22610. (gr. 5-8). 1980. 12.95 (ISBN 0-688-41937-2). Lothrop.

Hurwitz, Johanna. New Neighbors for Nora. reissued ed. Hoban, Lillian, illus. LC 90-47882. 80p. (ps). 1991. Repr. of 1979 ed. 12.95 (ISBN 0-688-09947-5); PLB 12.88 (ISBN 0-688-09948-3, Morrow Jr Bks). Morrow Jr Bks.

Killien, Christi. Putting on an Act. (gr. 5 up). 1986. 12.95 (ISBN 0-395-41027-4). HM.

Lowry, Lois. Your Move, J. P.! 128p. (gr. 3-7). 1990. 13.95 (ISBN 0-395-53639-1). HM.

McCullers, Carson. Sucker. Hayes, James, illus. LC 85-29114. 40p. (gr. 4 up). 1986. PLB 10.95s.p. (ISBN 0-88682-053-7); PLB 15.65 (ISBN 0-685-12418-5). Creative Ed.

Pascal, Francine. The Hand-Me-Down Kid. LC 79-5462. (gr. 5-9). 1980. pap. 12.95 (ISBN 0-670-35969-6). Viking Child Bks.

Pevsner, Stella. And You Give Me a Pain, Elaine. (gr. 7-9). 1989. pap. 2.75 (ISBN 0-671-68838-3, Archway). PB.

Posner, Richard. Goodnight, Cinderella. LC 89-17091. 242p. 1989. 13.95 (ISBN 0-87131-587-4). M Evans.

Roos, Stephen. My Secret Admirer. Newsom, Carol, illus. LC 84-5010. 112p. (gr. 4-6). 1984. 14.95 (ISBN 0-385-29342-9); PLB 13.95 (ISBN 0-385-29343-7). Delacorte.

Silver, Norman. No Tigers in Africa. (Illus.). 100p. (gr. 7 up). 1991. 13.95 (ISBN 0-525-44733-4, DCB). Dutton Child Bks.

Springstubb, Tricia. With a Name Like Lulu, Who Needs More Trouble? Kastner, Jill, illus. (gr. 5-9). 1989. 14.95 (ISBN 0-385-29823-4). Delacorte.

Stokes, Jack. Wiley & the Hairy-Man. (gr. k-12). 1970. pap. 2.00x (ISBN 0-88020-004-9). Dramatic Pub.

Voigt, Cynthia. The Runner. LC 84-21663. 192p. (gr. 8 up). 1985. 14.95 (ISBN 0-689-31069-2, Atheneum Child Bk). Macmillan Child Grp.

Wilkinson, Brenda. Ludell & Willie. 144p. (gr. 6 up). 1985. pap. 2.25 (ISBN 0-553-24995-9). Bantam.

HUMAN RIGHTS

see Civil Rights

HUMANISM

Here are entered works on culture founded on the study of the classics.

see also Learning and Scholarship; Renaissance

HUMBOLDT, ALEXANDER, FREIHERR VON, 1769-1859

Gaines, Ann. Alexander von Humboldt, Colossus of Exploration. Goetzmann, William H., ed. Collins, Michael, intro. by. (Illus.). 112p. (gr. 5 up). 1991. PLB 18.95 (ISBN 0-7910-1313-8). Chelsea Hse.

HUMMING-BIRDS

Foster, Susan Q. The Humming Bird among the Flowers. Oxford Scientific Films Ser., photos by. LC 89-31912. (Illus.). 32p. (gr. 4-6). 1989. PLB 10.95 (ISBN 0-8368-0115-6). Gareth Stevens Inc.

Greenewalt, Crawford H. Hummingbirds. 1990. pap. 15.95 (ISBN 0-486-26431-9). Dover.

Harrison, Virginia. The World of Humming Birds. Oxford Scientific Films Staff, photos by. LC 89-31913. (Illus.). 32p. (gr. 2-3). 1989. PLB 10.95 (ISBN 0-8368-0140-7). Gareth Stevens Inc.

HUMOROUS PICTURES

see Cartoons and Caricatures; Comic Books, Strips, Etc.

HUMOROUS POETRY

see also Limericks; Nonsense Verses

Amery, H., compiled by. The Usborne Book of Funny Poems. (Illus.). 32p. (gr. 2-6). 1990. lib. bdg. 13.96 (ISBN 0-88110-416-7, Usborne); pap. 5.95 (ISBN 0-7460-0444-3, Usborne). EDC.

Cohen, Shari. Prime Time Rhyme. (gr. k-6). 1990. 10.95 (ISBN 0-9620467-4-4). Forward March.
Grandmas, babysitters, strange people, neighbors, teachers, roller coasters, frogs, clothes, dogs, toothfairies, chickenpox, food, treehouses, romance (romance?), & a guy named "Stu" are all taken on in this light-hearted look at growing up. Share these & many more secret thoughts & feelings about school, friends, family, & life in general with "Prime Time Rhyme's seventy-three humorous poems about the joys & struggles of childhood. HIDE ME: My grandmother dressed me today/She sent me to school/In loud checkered shorts/And a Mickey Mouse belt/And a wide striped shirt/ With a collar of felt/A polka dot vest/ With buttons that shine/Gray flannel socks/That are one of a kind/High leather boots/With buckles up the side/Even grandmothers should know/ That a kid has his pride!
Publisher Provided Annotation.

Cole, William. Oh, How Silly! Ungerer, Tomi, illus. 80p. (gr. 2 up). 1990. pap. 3.95 (ISBN 0-14-034441-1, Puffin). Puffin Bks.

—Oh, What Nonsense. Ungerer, Tomi, illus. 80p. (gr. 2 up). 1990. pap. 3.95 (ISBN 0-14-034442-X, Puffin). Puffin Bks.

Cole, William, ed. Oh, Such Foolishness! De Paola, Tomie, illus. LC 78-1622. 96p. (gr. 3-6). 1978. 11.95 (ISBN 0-397-31807-3, Lipp Jr Bks). HarpC Child Bks.

Dahl, Roald. Roald Dahl's Revolting Rhymes. Blake, Quentin, illus. LC 82-15263. 48p. (gr. 3-6). 1983. 14.00 (ISBN 0-394-85422-5); lib. bdg. 14.99 (ISBN 0-394-95422-X). Knopf.

Prelutsky, Jack. The New Kid on the Block. Stevenson, James, illus. LC 83-20621. 160p. (gr. 1 up). 1984. 14.95 (ISBN 0-688-02271-5); PLB 14.88 (ISBN 0-688-02272-3). Greenwillow.

Prelutsky, Jack, compiled by. For Laughing Out Loud: Poems to Tickle Your Funnybone. Priceman, Marjorie, illus. LC 90-33010. 96p. (gr. 2-7). 1991. 14.95 (ISBN 0-394-82144-0); PLB 15.99 (ISBN 0-394-92144-5). Knopf.

HUMOROUS STORIES

see Wit and Humor

HUNDRED YEARS' WAR, 1339-1453–FICTION

Wheeler, Thomas G. All Men Tall. LC 70-77313. (gr. 8 up). 1969. 18.95 (ISBN 0-87599-157-2). S G Phillips.

HUNGARIANS IN THE U. S.

Gracza, Rezsoe & Gracza, Margaret. The Hungarians in America. LC 68-31503. (Illus.). 80p. (gr. 5 up). 1969. PLB 11.95 (ISBN 0-8225-0216-X); pap. 3.95 (ISBN 0-8225-1011-1). Lerner Pubns.

Vardy, Steven B. The Hungarian Americans. Moynihan, Daniel P., intro. by. (Illus.). 112p. (gr. 5 up). 1990. lib. bdg. 17.95 (ISBN 0-87754-884-6). Chelsea Hse.

HUNGARY

Hintz, Martin. Hungary. LC 88-10899. (Illus.). 128p. (gr. 5-9). 1988. PLB 25.27 (ISBN 0-516-02707-7). Childrens.

Popescu, Julian. Hungary. (Illus.). (gr. 5 up). 1988. 14.95 (ISBN 0-222-00945-4). Chelsea Hse.

St. John, Jetty. A Family in Hungary. (Illus.). 32p. (gr. 2-5). 1988. lib. bdg. 9.95 (ISBN 0-8225-1683-7). Lerner Pubns.

HUNGARY–FICTION

Seredy, Kate. Good Master. Seredy, Kate, illus. LC 85-43043. (gr. 4-6). 1935. pap. 13.95 (ISBN 0-670-34592-X). Viking Child Bks.

—The Good Master. (Illus.). 196p. (gr. 5-9). 1986. pap. 4.95 (ISBN 0-14-030133-X, Puffin). Puffin Bks.

—Singing Tree. (gr. 4 up). 1990. pap. 4.95 (ISBN 0-14-034543-4, Puffin). Puffin Bks.

—White Stag. Seredy, Kate, illus. (gr. 7 up). 1937. pap. 12.95 (ISBN 0-670-76375-6). Viking Child Bks.

HUNGARY–HISTORY

Blackwood. Hungarian Uprising, Reading Level 8. (Illus.). 80p. (gr. 7 up). Date not set. PLB 17.26 (ISBN 0-86592-032-X). Rourke Corp.

Siegal, Aranka. Upon the Head of the Goat: A Childhood in Hungary, 1939-1944. LC 81-12642. 214p. (gr. 7 up). 1981. 14.95 (ISBN 0-374-38059-7). FS&G.

HUNGARY–HISTORY–REVOLUTION, 1956

Blackwood, Alan. Hungarian Uprising. LC 86-20341. (Illus.). 77p. (gr. 7 up). 1987. 17.26 (ISBN 0-318-32641-8). Rourke Corp.

Michener, James A. Bridge at Andau. (gr. 10 up). 1957. 19.95 (ISBN 0-394-41778-X). Random.

HUNS

Bombarde, Odile. The Barbarians. Grant, Donald, illus. LC 87-34092. 38p. (gr. k-5). 1988. 4.95 (ISBN 0-944589-10-3, 103). Young Discovery Lib.

HUNS–FICTION

Gardonyi, Geza. Slave of the Huns. Ambrus, Victor C., illus. LC 70-84166. (gr. 8 up). 1969. 5.95 (ISBN 0-672-50500-2, Bobbs). Macmillan.

HUNTING

see also Game Preserves; Tracking and Trailing; Trapping

Bulpin, Tom V. The Hunter Is Death. Astley-Maberly, C. T., illus. 348p. (gr. 10 up). 1987. Repr. of 1962 ed. 30.00 (ISBN 0-940143-08-9). Safari Pr.

Fleckenstein, Henry A., Jr. Decoys of the Mid-Atlantic Region. LC 79-52438. (Illus.). 256p. (gr. 9-12). 1989. pap. 19.95 (ISBN 0-88740-174-0). Schiffer.

Parker, Eric. Colonel Hawker's Shooting Diaries. 2nd ed. Northcote, James, illus. 300p. (gr. 10 up). 1990. Repr. of 1931 ed. 35.00. Derrydale Pr.

Sobol, Donald J. Encyclopedia Brown's Book of the Wacky Outdoors. (Orig.). (gr. 5 up). 1988. pap. 2.50 (ISBN 0-553-15598-9). Bantam.

Stelson, Caren B. Safari. Stelson, Kim A., illus. 40p. (gr. k-4). 1989. pap. 5.95 (ISBN 0-685-25642-1, First Ave Edns). Lerner Pubns.

HUNTING–FICTION

Christian, Mary B. Linc. 128p. (gr. 7 up). 1991. 12.95 (ISBN 0-02-718580-X, Mcmillan Child Bk). Macmillan Child Grp.

Cosgrove, Stephen. Trapper. James, Robin, illus. 32p. (gr. k-4). 1982. pap. 2.95 (ISBN 0-8431-0587-9). Price Stern.

De Paola, Tomie. The Hunter & the Animals: A Wordless Picture Book. LC 81-2875. (Illus.). 32p. (ps-3). 1981. reinforced bdg. 14.95 (ISBN 0-8234-0397-1); pap. 5.95 (ISBN 0-8234-0428-5). Holiday.

Hughes, Monica. Hunter in the Dark. LC 82-13807. 144p. (gr. 5-9). 1983. 13.95 (ISBN 0-689-30959-7, Atheneum Child Bk). Macmillan Child Grp.

—Hunter in the Dark. 144p. (gr. 7 up). 1984. pap. 2.95 (ISBN 0-380-67702-4, 60063-3, Flare). Avon.

Hutchins, Pat. One Hunter. Hutchins, Pat, illus. LC 81-6352. 24p. (ps-1). 1982. 13.95 (ISBN 0-688-00614-0); PLB 13.88 (ISBN 0-688-00615-9). Greenwillow.

—One Hunter. LC 81-6352. (Illus.). 24p. (ps-3). pap. 3.95 (ISBN 0-688-06522-8, Mulberry). Morrow.

Kilroy, Sally. The Baron's Hunting Party. (ps-3). 1988. 9.95 (ISBN 0-670-81313-3). Viking Child Bks.

Leedy, Loreen. The Dragon ABC Hunt. Leedy, Loreen, illus. LC 85-21907. 36p. (ps-1). 1986. 14.95g (ISBN 0-8234-0596-6). Holiday.

Mendoza, George. The Hunter I Might Have Been. (Illus.). 48p. (gr. 3-6). 1989. pap. 6.95 (ISBN 0-89815-333-6). Ten Speed Pr.

Nordqvist, Sven. The Fox Hunt. Nordqvist, Sven, illus. LC 87-28197. 32p. (ps-2). 1988. 12.95 (ISBN 0-688-06881-2); PLB 12.88 (ISBN 0-688-06882-0, Morrow Jr Bks). Morrow Jr Bks.

Paulsen, Gary. Tracker. LC 83-22447. 96p. (gr. 6-8). 1984. 12.95 (ISBN 0-02-770220-0, Bradbury Pr). Macmillan Child Grp.

Peet, Bill. The Gnats of Knotty Pine. Peet, Bill, illus. LC 75-17024. 48p. (gr. k-3). 1984. 13.95 (ISBN 0-395-21405-X); pap. 3.95 (ISBN 0-395-36612-7). HM.

Standish, Burt L. Frank Merriwell's Hunting Tour. Rudman, Jack, ed. (gr. 9 up). Date not set. 9.95 (ISBN 0-8373-9307-8); pap. 3.95 (ISBN 0-8373-9007-9). F Merriwell.

Troy, John. Ben at Large. 1990. pap. 12.50 (ISBN 1-55971-048-9). Northword.

Turnbull, Ann. Rob Goes A-Hunting. Teasdale, Denise, illus. LC 90-30626. 32p. (ps-1). 1990. 13.95 (ISBN 0-531-05877-8); PLB 13.99 (ISBN 0-531-08477-9). Orchard Bks Watts.

HURRICANES

Archer, Jules. Hurricane! LC 90-45369. (Illus.). 48p. (gr. 5-6). 1991. RSBE 10.95 (ISBN 0-89686-597-5, Crestwood Hse). Macmillan Child Grp.

Branley, Franklyn M. Hurricane Watch. Maestro, Giulio, illus. LC 85-47534. 32p. (ps-3). 1985. PLB 13.89 (ISBN 0-690-04471-2, Crowell Jr Bks). HarpC Child Bks.

—Hurricane Watch. Maestro, Giulio, illus. LC 85-47534. 32p. (gr. k-3). 1987. pap. 4.50 (ISBN 0-06-445062-7, Trophy). HarpC Child Bks.

Fradin, Dennis. Disaster! Hurricanes. LC 81-38553. (Illus.). (gr. 3 up). 1982. PLB 17.27 (ISBN 0-516-00852-8). Childrens.

Hamilton, Sue. Hurricane Hugo. Hamilton, John, ed. (Illus.). 32p. (gr. 4). 1990. PLB 11.95 (ISBN 0-939179-85-7). Abdo & Dghtrs.

Lampton, Christopher. Hurricane. (Illus.). 64p. (gr. 3-6). 1991. PLB 17.25 (ISBN 1-56294-030-9). Millbrook Pr.

Lane, Rose W. Let the Hurricane Roar. LC 85-42742. 128p. (gr. 5-9). 1985. pap. 3.50 (ISBN 0-06-440158-8, Trophy). HarpC Child Bks.

McNulty, Faith. Hurricane. Owens, Gail, illus. LC 79-2672. 64p. (gr. 3-5). 1983. 11.95i (ISBN 0-06-024142-X). HarpC Child Bks.

HURRICANES–FICTION

Hurwitz, Johanna. Hurricane Elaine. De Groat, Diane, illus. LC 86-12409. 112p. (gr. 5-8). 1986. 12.95 (ISBN 0-688-06461-2). Morrow Jr Bks.

Mahy, Margaret. Blood & Thunder Adventures on Hurricanes. (gr. 4-7). 1991. pap. 3.25 (ISBN 0-440-40422-3). Dell.

Winthrop, Elizabeth. Belinda's Hurricane. Watson, Wendy, illus. LC 84-8028. (gr. 1-4). 1984. 10.95 (ISBN 0-525-44106-9, DCB). Dutton Child Bks.

HUTCHINSON, ANNE (MARBURY), 1590-1643

Fradin, Dennis B. Anne Hutchinson: Fighter for Religious Freedom. LC 88-31329. (Illus.). 48p. (gr. 3-6). 1989. PLB 14.95 (ISBN 0-89490-229-6). Enslow Pubs.

HYDRAULIC ENGINEERING

see also Irrigation; Rivers; Water

HYDROELECTRIC POWER

see Water Power

HYDROFOIL BOATS

Stone, Jane. Challenge! The Big Thunderboats. new ed. LC 75-23408. (Illus.). 32p. (gr. 5-10). 1976. PLB 10.79 (ISBN 0-89375-003-4); pap. 2.95 (ISBN 0-89375-019-0). Troll Assocs.

HYDROLOGY

see Water

HYENAS–FICTION

McKissack, Patricia. Monkey-Monkey's Trick. Meisel, Paul, illus. LC 88-3072. 48p. (Orig.). (gr. 1-3). 1988. lib. bdg. 6.99 (ISBN 0-394-99173-7, Random Juv); pap. 2.95 (ISBN 0-394-89173-2, Random Juv). Random.

HYGIENE

see also Air; Children–Care and Hygiene; Clothing and Dress; Diet; Exercise; Food; Gymnastics; Mental Health; Narcotics; Physical Education and Training; Physiology; Sanitation; Sleep; Water–Pollution

Allen, Eleanor. Wash & Brush up. (Illus.). 64p. (gr. 7 up). 1977. 14.95 (ISBN 0-7136-1639-3). Dufour.

Bains, Rae. Health & Hygiene. Zink-White, Nancy, illus. LC 84-2627. 32p. (gr. 3-6). 1985. PLB 9.49 (ISBN 0-8167-0180-6); pap. text ed. 2.95 (ISBN 0-8167-0181-4). Troll Assocs.

Baldwin, Dorothy. Health & Drugs. (Illus.). 32p. 1987. PLB 15.93 (ISBN 0-86592-292-6). Rourke Corp.

—Health & Exercise. (Illus.). 32p. (gr. 3-8). 1987. PLB 15.93 (ISBN 0-86592-293-4). Rourke Corp.

—Health & Feelings. (Illus.). 32p. (gr. 3-8). 1987. PLB 15.93 (ISBN 0-86592-290-X). Rourke Corp.

—Health & Food. (Illus.). 32p. (gr. 3-8). 1987. PLB 15.93 (ISBN 0-86592-294-2). Rourke Corp.

—Health & Friends. (Illus.). 32p. (gr. 3-8). 1987. PLB 15.93 (ISBN 0-86592-289-6). Rourke Corp.

—Health & Hygiene. (Illus.). 32p. (gr. 3-8). 1987. PLB 15.93 (ISBN 0-86592-291-8). Rourke Corp.

Berry, Joy W. What to Do When Your Mom or Dad Says..."Clean Your Room!" Bartholomew, illus. Berry, Joy W., intro. by. LC 82-81200. (Illus.). 48p. (gr. 3-7). 1982. 4.98 (ISBN 0-941510-00-X). Living Skills.

—What to Do When Your Mom or Dad Says..."Clean Yourself Up!" Bartholomew, illus. Berry, Joy W., intro. by. (Illus.). 48p. (gr. 3-7). 1981. 3.95 (ISBN 0-941510-04-2). Living Skills.

—What to Do When Your Mom or Dad Says..."Clean Yourself Up!" LC 82-81200. (gr. 3 up). 1982. 14.60 (ISBN 0-516-02572-4). Childrens.

Bleich, Alan R. Coping with Health Risks & Risky Behavior. Rosen, Roger, ed. (gr. 7-12). 1990. lib. bdg. 12.95 (ISBN 0-8239-1072-5). Rosen Group.

Brady, Janeen. Standin' Tall Cleanliness. Galloway, Neil, illus. 22p. (Orig.). (ps-6). 1984. pap. text ed. 1.50 activity bk. (ISBN 0-944803-54-7); cassette & bk. 8.95 (ISBN 0-944803-55-5). Brite Intl.

Brown, Laurie K. & Brown, Marc. Dinosaurs Alive & Well! A Guide to Good Health. (ps-3). 1990. 14.95 (ISBN 0-316-10998-3, Joy St Bks). Little.

Cobb, Vicki. Keeping Clean. Hafner, Marylin, illus. LC 88-2930. 32p. (gr. k-3). 1989. 11.95 (ISBN 0-397-32312-3, Lipp Jr Bks); PLB 11.89 (ISBN 0-397-32313-1). HarpC Child Bks.

Davies, Leah G. Kelly Bear Health. Davies, Joy D., illus. LC 89-85159. 28p. (Orig.). (ps-3). 1989. pap. 4.50 (ISBN 0-9621054-2-2). Kelly Bear Bks.

Diehl, Harold S., et al. Health & Safety for You. 5th ed. 1980. text ed. 29.52 (ISBN 0-07-016863-6). McGraw.

Donahue, Parnell & Capellaro, Helen. Germs Make Me Sick: A Health Handbook for Kids. Oechsli, Kelly, illus. LC 74-15309. 96p. (gr. 4 up). 1975. Knopf.

Elgin, Kathleen & Osterritter, John F. Twenty-Eight Days. LC 73-77779. (Illus.). 64p. (gr. 5 up). 1973. pap. 5.95 (ISBN 0-679-51382-5). McKay.

Fraser, K. & Tatchell, J. You & Your Fitness & Health. (Illus.). 48p. (gr. 6-10). 1987. PLB 13.96 (ISBN 0-88110-234-2); pap. 6.95 (ISBN 0-7460-0004-9). EDC.

Gay, Kathlyn. They Don't Wash Their Socks! (Illus.). (gr. 4-7). 1990. 13.95 (ISBN 0-8027-6916-0); lib. bdg. 14.85 (ISBN 0-8027-6917-9). Walker & Co.

Goodbody, Slim. The Healthy Habits Handbook. Curtis, Bruce, photos by. (Illus.). (gr. 4-7). 1983. 9.95 (ISBN 0-698-20590-1, Coward); pap. 4.95 (ISBN 0-698-20592-8). Putnam Pub Group.

Greenbaum, David & Wasser, Edward. My First Health & Nutrition Coloring Book: Mr. Carrots Coloring Book. Puglisi, Lou, illus. 40p. (Orig.). (gr. 2). 1988. pap. 0.99 (ISBN 0-9621833-0-X). D Greenbaum.

Hammer, Arnold. The Rosen Photo Guide to a Career in Health & Fitness. (Illus.). (gr. 7-12). 1988. lib. bdg. 12.95 (ISBN 0-8239-0820-8). Rosen Group.

Hayes, Marilyn. Jumbo Health Yearbook: Grade 3. 96p. (gr. 3). 1978. 18.00 (ISBN 0-8209-0063-X, JHY 3). ESP.

—Jumbo Health Yearbook: Grade 4. 96p. (gr. 4). 1979. 18.00 (ISBN 0-8209-0064-8, JHY 4). ESP.

Houston, Jack. Jumbo Health Yearbook: Grade 5. 96p. (gr. 5). 1979. 18.00 (ISBN 0-8209-0065-6, JHY 5). ESP.

—Jumbo Health Yearbook: Grade 6. 96p. (gr. 6). 1979. 18.00 (ISBN 0-8209-0066-4, JHY 6). ESP.

—Jumbo Health Yearbook: Grade 7. 96p. (gr. 7). 1979. 18.00 (ISBN 0-8209-0067-2, JHY 7). ESP.

—Jumbo Health Yearbook: Grade 8. 96p. (gr. 8). 1979. 18.00 (ISBN 0-8209-0068-0, JHY 8). ESP.

Jacobsen, Karen. Health. LC 81-6193. (Illus.). 48p. (gr. k-4). 1981. PLB 14.60 (ISBN 0-516-01622-9). Childrens.

Jones, Lorraine H. & Tsumura, Ted K. Health & Safety for You. 7th ed. 480p. 1987. text ed. 29.96 (ISBN 0-07-065386-0). McGraw.

Lobb, Nancy. Basic Health. (gr. 1 up). Date not set. pap. 4.25 (ISBN 0-88323-224-3, 244). Pendergrass Pub.

McDonnell, Janet. Good Health: A Visit from Droopy. Dunnington, Tom, illus. LC 90-1871. 32p. (ps-2). 1990. lib. bdg. 11.97 (ISBN 0-89565-582-9). Childs World.

Moncure, Jane B. Healthkins Help. Axeman, Lois, illus. LC 82-14713. 32p. (ps-2). 1982. lib. bdg. 10.95 (ISBN 0-89565-242-0). Childs World.

—Magic Monsters Learn about Health. Endres, Helen, illus. LC 79-24240. (ps-3). 1980. PLB 11.97 (ISBN 0-89565-117-3). Childs World.

Neff, Fred. Keeping Fit Handbook for Physical Conditioning & Better Health. Reid, James, illus. LC 75-38478. 56p. (gr. 5 up). 1977. PLB 8.95 (ISBN 0-8225-1157-6). Lerner Pubns.

Odor, Ruth S. What's a Body to Do? Letwenko, Ed, illus. LC 81-17031. 112p. (gr. 2-6). 1980. PLB 11.97 (ISBN 0-89565-209-9). Childs World.

Orlandi, Mario, et al. Maintaining Good Health. 128p. (gr. 5 up). 1989. 18.95 (ISBN 0-8160-1667-4). Facts On File.

Petty, Kate. Going to the Doctor. Kopper, Lisa, illus. 24p. (gr. 1-3). 1987. PLB 5.29 (ISBN 0-531-17069-1, Gloucester Pr). Watts.

Rayner, Claire. The Don't Spoil Your Body Book. King, Tony, tr. Lansdown, Richard, intro. by. (Illus.). 48p. (gr. 3 up). 1989. pap. 4.95 (ISBN 0-8120-6098-9). Barron.

Salter, Charles A. Looking Good, Eating Right: A Sensible Guide to Proper Nutrition & Weight Loss for Teens. (Illus.). 144p. (gr. 7 up). 1991. PLB 13.90 (ISBN 1-56294-047-3). Millbrook Pr.

Simon, Nissa. Don't Worry, You're Normal. LC 81-43324. 192p. (gr. 7 up). 1982. (Crowell Jr Bks); PLB 12.89 (ISBN 0-690-04139-X, Crowell Jr Bks). HarpC Child Bks.

—Don't Worry, You're Normal: A Teenager's Guide to Self-Health. LC 81-43324. 192p. (gr. 6 up). 1986. pap. 4.95 (ISBN 0-06-446020-7, Trophy). HarpC Child Bks.

Spizman, Robyn. Bulletin Boards: Ideas for Science & Health. Pesiri, Evelyn, illus. 48p. (gr. k-6). 1984. wkbk. 5.95 (ISBN 0-86653-253-6, GA 570). Good Apple.

Springate, Kay W. Let's Learn about Good Health. 64p. (ps-2). 1988. wkbk. 6.95 (ISBN 0-86653-438-5, GA1041). Good Apple.

Tsumura, Ted K. & Jones, Lorraine H. Health & Safety for You. 6th ed. O'Neill, Martha, ed. (Illus.). 288p. (gr. 7-12). 1984. 30.32 (ISBN 0-07-065378-X). McGraw.

Ward, Brian R. Health & Hygiene. (Illus.). 48p. (gr. 4-12). 1988. PLB 12.40 (ISBN 0-531-10561-X). Watts.

Wathen, Judy & Sussman, Ellen. Teach Me Health & Safety. Burris, Priscilla, illus. 40p. (Orig.). (ps-k). 1989. pap. 4.95 (ISBN 0-933606-75-3); tchr's. guide avail. Monkey Sisters.

HYGIENE–FICTION

Alexander, Liza. The World According to Elmo: A Story about Health & Hygiene. (Illus.). 32p. (ps-k). 1989. pap. write for info. (ISBN 0-307-13111-4, Pub. by Golden Bks). Western Pub.

Berenstain, Stan & Berenstain, Janice. The Berenstain Bears & the Messy Room. Berenstain, Janice & Berenstain, Stan, illus. Lerner, Sharon, ed. 32p. (ps-2). 1983. lib. bdg. 5.99 (ISBN 0-394-95639-7); pap. 2.25 (ISBN 0-394-85639-2). Random.

Bottner, Barbara. Messy. Bottner, Barbara, illus. LC 78-50420. (gr. k-2). 1979. 6.95 (ISBN 0-440-05492-3); pap. 6.46 (ISBN 0-440-05493-1). Delacorte.

Bowling, David L. & Bowling, Patricia H. Dirty Dingy Daryl. Martz, John, ed. Bowling, Patricia H., illus. LC 81-83120. 24p. (ps-4). 1981. 6.00 (ISBN 0-939700-00-X); pap. 3.00 (ISBN 0-939700-01-8). I D I C P.

Buchanan, J. Taking Care of My Cold. (Illus.). 24p. (ps-8). 1990. pap. 4.95 (ISBN 0-88753-197-0). Firefly Bks Ltd.

Burningham, John. Time to Get out of the Bath, Shirley. Burningham, John, illus. LC 76-58503. 32p. (gr. k-2). 1978. 13.95 (ISBN 0-690-01378-7, Crowell Jr Bks); PLB 13.89 (ISBN 0-690-01379-5). HarpC Child Bks.

Clean Team Staff & Campbell, Jeff. Spring Cleaning. (Orig.). (gr. 7 up). 1989. pap. 5.95 (ISBN 0-440-50162-8, Dell Trade Pbks). Dell.

Dutton, Cheryl. Not in Here, Dad! Smith, Wendy, illus. 32p. (ps-2). 1989. 10.95 (ISBN 0-8120-6105-5). Barron.

Frankel, Alona. Once upon a Potty: His. LC 79-53769. (Illus.). (ps-3). 1980. 4.95 (ISBN 0-8120-5371-0); pkg., 1987 12.95 (ISBN 0-8120-7457-2). Barron.

Guymon, Maurine B. The Adventures of Micki Microbe. Zagone, Arlene T., illus. 88p. (gr. 2-5). 1987. 15.00 (ISBN 0-9618650-0-8). MoDel Pubs.
An imaginative & whimsical way of introducing children to various functions of the body while emphasizing good health. A lactic acid microbe, Micki, travels down Maggie's Throat Street when she takes a drink of milk. While visiting Tonsil Park & meeting the Pneumo Twins the microbes are detected by Watch Dog Cough & as he barks they are sent flying through the air landing on Jamie's ball. Now Jamie is the recipient & upon licking his fingers the microbes travel past his White Teeth Hills & find long chains of the streptococcus family in his Throat Street. In like manner Micki & other microbes travel from one child to another via apples, popsicles, pencils & spoons. Subsequent visits through the body introduces Lung House, Nose Cave, Tear Duct Waterfall, Windpipe Lane, etc. The White Corpuscle Policemen enter the story to destroy bad microbes & prevent infection in Blood River. Seventy three beautiful illustrations enhance the 88 page book. It has a sewn, hard bound laminated cover. Order from: MoDel Publishers, Box 645, Byron, CA 94514 or Baker Taylor; Select Books, Evanston, IL; Monroe Press, Sepulveda, CA.
Publisher Provided Annotation.

Hall, Carol M. A Bath for Willie. (Illus.). 32p. (ps-2). 1987. 5.95 (ISBN 0-8059-3068-X). Dorrance.

Hamsa, Bobbie. Dirty Larry. LC 83-10079. (Illus.). 32p. (ps-2). 1983. PLB 11.93 (ISBN 0-516-02040-4); pap. 2.95 (ISBN 0-516-42040-2). Childrens.

Hayes, Geoffrey. Patrick Takes a Bath. Hayes, Geoffrey, illus. LC 84-1658. 32p. (ps-1). 1989. pap. 2.95 (ISBN 0-679-80164-2, Dragonfly Bks). Knopf.

Henkes, Kevin. Clean Enough. Henkes, Kevin, illus. LC 81-6386. 24p. (gr. k-3). 1982. PLB 10.88 (ISBN 0-688-00829-1). Greenwillow.

Howard, Neva. Tommy & James Cell. 32p. Date not set. write for info. N Howard.

Hutchins, Pat. Tidy Titch. LC 90-38483. (Illus.). 32p. (ps up). 1991. 13.95 (ISBN 0-688-09963-7); PLB 13.88 (ISBN 0-688-09964-5). Greenwillow.

Jacobs, Don. Happy Exercise: An Adventure into a Fit World. Speidel, Sandy, illus. LC 80-23547. 48p. (Orig.). (ps-5). 1980. pap. 4.95 (ISBN 0-89037-170-9). Anderson World.

McPhail, David. Andrew's Bath. McPhail, David, illus. (ps-3). 1984. 13.95 (ISBN 0-316-56319-6, Joy St Bks). Little.

Mahy, Margaret. Keeping House. Smith, Wendy, illus. LC 90-37591. 32p. (gr. k-4). 1991. SBE 13.95 (ISBN 0-689-50515-9, M K McElderry). Macmillan Child Grp.

Moncure, Jane B. Caring for My Body. McCallum, Jodie, illus. 32p. (ps-2). 1990. lib. bdg. 9.96 (ISBN 0-89565-668-X). Childs World.

Munsch, Robert. Jonathan Cleaned-up: Then He Heard a Sound. Martchenko, Michael, illus. 32p. (gr. 4-7). 1981. 12.95 (ISBN 0-920236-22-7); pap. 4.95 (ISBN 0-920236-20-0). Firefly Bks Ltd.

Nelson, Ray, Jr. The Internal Adventures of Donovan Willoughby. LC 91-18810. (Illus.). 48p. (ps-7). 1991. 12.95 (ISBN 0-89802-572-9). Beautiful Am.

Nerlove, Miriam. I Meant to Clean My Room Today. LC 87-16968. (Illus.). 32p. (ps-3). 1988. 12.95 (ISBN 0-689-50438-1, M K McElderry). Macmillan Child Grp.

Rockwell, Anne & Rockwell, Harlow. Nice & Clean. Rockwell, Anne & Rockwell, Harlow, illus. LC 84-3945. 24p. (ps-1). 1984. 12.95 (ISBN 0-02-777290-X, Mcmillan Child Bk). Macmillan Child Grp.

Sustendal, Pat, illus. The Care Bear Bath Book. 10p. (ps). 1983. 2.95 (ISBN 0-394-86071-3). Random.

HYGIENE, MENTAL

see Mental Health

HYGIENE, PUBLIC

see Public Health

HYGIENE, SOCIAL

see Hygiene; Public Health

HYMENOPTERA

see Ants; Bees; Wasps

HYMNOLOGY

see Hymns

HYMNS

see also Carols; Church Music

Beautiful Ways Songs. (gr. k-6). pap. 0.50 (ISBN 0-686-29099-2). Faith Pub Hse.

Curry, W. Lawrence, ed. Songs & Hymns for Primary Children. (gr. 1-3). 1978. softcover 3.95 (ISBN 0-664-10117-8, Westminster). Westminster John Knox.

Griffin, Steve. Children's Guitar Hymnal. 32p. (gr. 4-10). 1978. wkbk. 2.95 (ISBN 0-89228-052-2). Impact Bks MO.

Hartzler, Arlene & Gaeddert, John, eds. Children's Hymnary. LC 67-24327. (gr. k-7). 1967. 5.95 (ISBN 0-87303-095-8). Faith & Life.

Hymns & Songs. (Illus.). (gr. 2-4). 3.50 (ISBN 0-7214-0522-3). Ladybird Bks.

Montgomery, Dorothy. Knowing Christ Song. Lautermilch, John, illus. 19p. (gr. k-6). 1981. visualized song 2.99 (ISBN 3-90117-025-1). CEF Press.

More Songs to Play. (gr. k-4). 1988. 6.95 (ISBN 0-8054-4706-7). Broadman.

Overholtzer, Ruth. Salvation Songs, Vol. I. 100p. (gr. k-6). 1975. pap. text ed. 2.99 (ISBN 3-90117-100-2). CEF Press.
—Salvation Songs, Vol. II. 105p. (gr. k-4). 1979. pap. text ed. 2.99 (ISBN 1-55976-201-2). CEF Press.
—Salvation Songs, Vol. III. 100p. (gr. k-6). 1975. pap. text ed. 2.99 (ISBN 1-55976-202-0). CEF Press.
—Salvation Songs, Vol. IV. (Illus.). 96p. (gr. k-6). 1979. pap. text ed. 2.99 (ISBN 1-55976-203-9). CEF Press.

HYPNOTISM
see also Mind and Body; Psychoanalysis
Ansari, Masud. Modern Hypnosis: Theory & Practice. Ansari, Said S., illus. 232p. (gr. 5). 1982. pap. 6.95 (ISBN 0-685-05553-1). MAS-Pr.

I

IBM PERSONAL COMPUTER
Taitt, Jennifer. IBM, Vol. 1. 55p. (gr. 4-12). 1983. pap. text ed. 11.95 (ISBN 0-88193-031-8). Create Learn.
—IBM, Vol. 2. 54p. (gr. 4-12). 1983. pap. text ed. 11.95 (ISBN 0-88193-032-6). Create Learn.
—IBM, Vol. 3. 51p. (gr. 5-12). 1983. pap. text ed. 11.95 (ISBN 0-88193-033-4). Create Learn.
—IBM, Vol. 4. 66p. (gr. 5-12). 1983. pap. text ed. 11.95 (ISBN 0-88193-034-2). Create Learn.

ICE
see also Glaciers; Icebergs
Dolan, Edward F., Jr. Great Mysteries of the Ice & Snow. (Illus.). 128p. (gr. 9-12). 1985. 8.95 (ISBN 0-396-08642-X, Putnam). Putnam Pub Group.

ICE AGE
see Glacial Epoch

ICE CREAM, ICES, ETC.
Cobb, Vicki. The Scoop on Ice Cream. Karas, Brian, illus. 48p. (gr. 4 up). 1985. 11.95 (ISBN 0-316-14895-4). Little.
Jaspersohn, William. Ice Cream. LC 87-38331. (Illus.). 48p. (gr. 3-7). 1988. 13.95 (ISBN 0-02-747821-1, Mcmillan Child Bk). Macmillan Child Grp.
Keller, Stella. Ice Cream. (Illus.). 32p. (gr. 1-4). 1989. PLB 13.32 (ISBN 0-8172-3523-X). Raintree Pubs.
Mitgutsch, Ali. From Milk to Ice Cream. Mitgutsch, Ali, illus. LC 81-81. 24p. (ps-3). 1981. PLB 6.95 (ISBN 0-87614-158-0). Carolrhoda Bks.
Neimark, Jill. Ice Cream. Milone, Karen, illus. LC 84-10915. (gr. 2-6). 1986. 11.95 (ISBN 0-8038-3440-3); pap. 11.95 (ISBN 0-8038-9290-X). Hastings.
Reece, Colleen L. What Was It Before It Was Ice Cream? Axeman, Lois, illus. LC 85-13262. 32p. (ps-2). 1985. PLB 11.97 (ISBN 0-89565-325-7). Childs World.
Willard, Dennis. The Incredible Ice Cream Book. 64p. (gr. 3-8). 1987. pap. 3.95 (ISBN 0-87406-392-2). Willowisp Pr.

ICE HOCKEY
see Hockey

ICE SKATING
see Skating

ICE SPORTS
see Winter Sports

ICEBERGS
Arvetis, Chris. What Is an Iceberg? Buckley, James, illus. 32p. (ps-3). 1987. write for info. (ISBN 0-02-689009-7). Checkerboard Pr.
Gans, Roma. Danger--Icebergs! Revised Edition of Icebergs. Rosenblum, Richard, illus. LC 87-531. 32p. (ps-3). 1987. 13.95 (ISBN 0-690-04627-8, Crowell Jr Bks); PLB 13.89 (ISBN 0-690-04629-4, Crowell Jr Bks). HarpC Child Bks.
—Danger--Icebergs! Revised Edition of Icebergs. Rosenblum, Richard, illus. LC 87-531. 32p. (ps-3). 1987. pap. 4.50 (ISBN 0-06-445066-X, Trophy). HarpC Child Bks.
Poole, Lynn & Poole, Gray. Danger, Iceberg Ahead. (Illus.). (gr. 1-4). 1961. lib. bdg. 4.39 (ISBN 0-394-90121-5). Random.
Simon, Seymour. Icebergs & Glaciers. LC 86-18142. (Illus.). 32p. (ps-3). 1987. 14.95 (ISBN 0-688-06186-9); lib. bdg. 14.88 (ISBN 0-688-06187-7, Morrow Jr Bks). Morrow Jr Bks.
Wood, Jenny. Icebergs: Titans of the Oceans. LC 90-55462. (Illus.). 32p. (gr. 3-4). 1990. PLB 11.95 (ISBN 0-8368-0470-8). Gareth Stevens Inc.

ICELAND
Evans, J. O. Iceland. (Illus.). (gr. 5 up). 1988. 14.95 (ISBN 0-222-00926-8). Chelsea Hse.
Jacobsen, P & Kristensen, P. A Family in Iceland. LC 85-62086. (Illus.). 32p. (gr. k-6). 1986. lib. bdg. 11.90 (ISBN 0-531-18036-0, Pub. by Bookwright Pr). Watts.
Lepthien, Emilie U. Iceland. LC 86-29966. (Illus.). 128p. (gr. 5-9). 1987. PLB 25.27 (ISBN 0-516-02775-1). Childrens.
Porter, Eliot, photos by. Iceland. Porter, Jonathan, text by. (Illus.). 1989. 50.00 (ISBN 0-8212-1731-3, Bulfinch Pr). Little.

ICHTHYOLOGY
see Fishes

ICONOGRAPHY
see Art; Christian Art and Symbolism; Portraits

IDAHO
Bair, Elmer O. Elmer Bair's Story: 1899-1987, Vol. 1. Mangan, Velda B., ed. Chaffin, Maureen A., illus. LC 87-80294. 484p. (gr. 9 up). 1987. 20.00 (ISBN 0-9618269-0-8). Elmer Bair.
Carole Marsh Idaho Books, 31 bks. Set. 638.45 (ISBN 0-7933-1287-6). Gallopade Pub Group.
Carpenter, Allan. Idaho. new ed. LC 79-9804. (Illus.). 96p. (gr. 4 up). 1979. PLB 19.93 (ISBN 0-516-04112-6). Childrens.
Fisher, Ronald K. Beyond the Rockies: A Narrative History of Idaho. LC 89-83506. (Illus.). (gr. 4-9). 1989. text ed. 14.85 (ISBN 0-941734-00-5); write for info. tchr's. ed. Alpha & Omega.
Fradin, Dennis. Idaho: In Words & Pictures. LC 80-14660. (Illus.). 48p. (gr. 2-5). 1980. PLB 15.93 (ISBN 0-516-03914-8). Childrens.
Marsh, Carole. Avast, Ye Slobs! Idaho Pirate Trivia. (Illus.). (gr. 3-12). 1990. PLB 19.95 (ISBN 0-7933-0376-1); pap. 14.95 (ISBN 0-7933-0375-3); computer disk 29.95 (ISBN 0-7933-0377-X). Gallopade Pub Group.
—The Beast of the Idaho Bed & Breakfast. (Illus.). (gr. 3-12). 1990. PLB 19.95 (ISBN 0-7933-1550-6); pap. 14.95 (ISBN 0-7933-1551-4); computer disk 29.95 (ISBN 0-7933-1552-2). Gallopade Pub Group.
—The Hard-to-Believe-But-True! Book of Idaho History, Mystery, Trivia, Legend, Lore, Humor & More. (Illus.). (gr. 3-12). 1990. PLB 19.95 (ISBN 0-7933-0373-7); pap. 14.95 (ISBN 0-7933-0372-9); computer disk 29.95 (ISBN 0-7933-0374-5). Gallopade Pub Group.
—Idaho & Other State Greats (Biographies) (Illus.). (gr. 3-12). 1990. PLB 19.95 (ISBN 1-55609-592-9); pap. 14.95 (ISBN 1-55609-591-0); computer disk 29.95 (ISBN 0-7933-1558-1). Gallopade Pub Group.
—Idaho Bandits, Bushwackers, Outlaws, Crooks, Devils, Ghosts, Desperadoes & Other Assorted & Sundry Characters! (Illus.). (gr. 3-12). 1990. PLB 19.95 (ISBN 0-7933-0358-3); pap. 14.95 (ISBN 0-7933-0357-5); computer disk 29.95 (ISBN 0-7933-0359-1). Gallopade Pub Group.
—Idaho Classic Christmas Trivia: Stories, Recipes, Activities, Legends, Lore & More! (Illus.). (gr. 3-12). 1990. PLB 19.95 (ISBN 0-7933-0361-3); pap. 14.95 (ISBN 0-7933-0360-5); computer disk 29.95 (ISBN 0-7933-0362-1). Gallopade Pub Group.
—Idaho Coastales. (Illus.). (gr. 3-12). 1990. PLB 19.95 (ISBN 1-55609-588-0); pap. 14.95 (ISBN 1-55609-587-2); computer disk 29.95 (ISBN 0-7933-1554-9). Gallopade Pub Group.
—The Idaho Hot Air Balloon Mystery. (Illus.). (gr. 2-9). 1990. 19.95 (ISBN 0-7933-2426-2); pap. 14.95 (ISBN 0-7933-2427-0); computer disk 29.95 (ISBN 0-7933-2428-9). Gallopade Pub Group.
—Idaho "Jography" A Fun Run Thru Our State! (Illus.). (gr. 3-12). 1990. PLB 19.95 (ISBN 1-55609-583-X); pap. 14.95 (ISBN 1-55609-582-1); computer disk 29.95 (ISBN 0-7933-1544-1). Gallopade Pub Group.
—Idaho Kid's Cookbook: Recipes, How-to, History, Lore & More! (Illus.). (gr. 3-12). 1990. PLB 19.95 (ISBN 0-7933-0370-2); pap. 14.95 (ISBN 0-7933-0369-9); computer disk 29.95 (ISBN 0-7933-0371-0). Gallopade Pub Group.
—Idaho Quiz Bowl Crash Course! (Illus.). (gr. 3-12). 1990. PLB 19.95 (ISBN 1-55609-590-2); pap. 14.95 (ISBN 1-55609-589-9); computer disk 29.95. Gallopade Pub Group.
—Idaho School Trivia: An Amazing & Fascinating Look at Our State's Teachers, School & Students! (Illus.). (gr. 3-12). 1990. PLB 19.95 (ISBN 0-7933-0367-2); pap. 14.95 (ISBN 0-7933-0366-4); computer disk 29.95 (ISBN 0-7933-0368-0). Gallopade Pub Group.
—Idaho Silly Basketball Sportsmysteries, Vol. I. (Illus.). (gr. 3-12). 1990. PLB 19.95 (ISBN 0-7933-0364-8); pap. 14.95 (ISBN 0-7933-0363-X); computer disk 29.95 (ISBN 0-7933-0365-6). Gallopade Pub Group.
—Idaho Silly Basketball Sportsmysteries. (Illus.). (gr. 3-12). 1990. PLB 19.95 (ISBN 0-7933-1559-X); pap. 14.95 (ISBN 0-7933-1560-3); computer disk 29.95 (ISBN 0-7933-1561-1). Gallopade Pub Group.
—Idaho Silly Football Sportsmysteries, Vol. I. (Illus.). (gr. 3-12). 1990. PLB 19.95 (ISBN 1-55609-586-4); pap. 14.95 (ISBN 1-55609-585-6); computer disk 29.95 (ISBN 0-7933-1546-8). Gallopade Pub Group.
—Idaho Silly Football Sportsmysteries, Vol. II. (Illus.). (gr. 3-12). 1990. PLB 19.95 (ISBN 0-7933-1547-6); pap. 14.95 (ISBN 0-7933-1548-4); computer disk 29.95 (ISBN 0-7933-1549-2). Gallopade Pub Group.
—Idaho Silly Trivia! (Illus.). (gr. 3-12). 1990. PLB 19.95 (ISBN 1-55609-581-3); pap. 14.95 (ISBN 1-55609-580-5); computer disk 29.95 (ISBN 0-7933-1543-3). Gallopade Pub Group.
—Idaho's (Most Devastating!) Disasters & (Most Calamitous!) Catastrophies! (Illus.). (gr. 3-12). 1990. PLB 19.95 (ISBN 0-7933-0355-9); pap. 14.95 (ISBN 0-7933-0354-0); computer disk 29.95 (ISBN 0-7933-0356-7). Gallopade Pub Group.
—If My Idaho Mama Ran the World! (Illus.). (gr. 3-12). 1990. PLB 19.95 (ISBN 0-7933-1555-7); pap. 14.95 (ISBN 0-7933-1556-5); computer disk 29.95 (ISBN 0-7933-1557-3). Gallopade Pub Group.
—Let's Quilt Idaho & Stuff It Topographically! (Illus.). (gr. 3-12). 1990. PLB 19.95 (ISBN 1-55609-584-8); pap. 14.95 (ISBN 1-55609-139-7); computer disk 29.95 (ISBN 0-7933-1545-X). Gallopade Pub Group.
Turner Program Services, Inc. Staff & Clark, James I. Idaho. LC 85-12151. 48p. (gr. 3 up). 1985. PLB 17.32 (ISBN 0-86514-429-X); pap. 9.27 (ISBN 0-86514-504-0); cancelled Beta video (ISBN 0-86514-054-5); cancelled VHS video (ISBN 0-86514-129-0); cancelled 3/4" video (ISBN 0-86514-204-1); cancelled tchr's. guide (ISBN 0-86514-279-3); cancelled student activity bk. (ISBN 0-86514-354-4); cancelled index. Raintree Pubs.
Walgamott, Charles S. Six Decades Back. Arrington, Leonard J., intro. by. LC 90-33649. (Illus.). 368p. 1990. pap. 18.95 (ISBN 0-89301-137-1). U of Idaho Pr.
Young, Virgil M. Story of Idaho: Centennial Edition. LC 89-36899. (Illus.). 304p. (ps-4). 1990. 22.95 (ISBN 0-89301-131-2). U of Idaho Pr.

IDENTITY, PERSONAL
see Personality

IDIOCY
see Mentally Handicapped

IDIOMS
see names of languages with the subdivision Idioms, e.g. English Language–Idioms

ILLINOIS
Aylesworth, Thomas G. & Aylesworth, Virginia L. Western Great Lakes (Illinois, Iowa, Wisconsin, Minnesota) (Illus.). 64p. (gr. 3 up). 1992. PLB 16.95 (ISBN 0-7910-1046-5). Chelsea Hse.
Carole Marsh Illinois Books, 31 bks. Set. 638.45 (ISBN 0-7933-1288-4). Gallopade Pub Group.
Carpenter, Allan. Illinois. new ed. LC 78-32064. (Illus.). 96p. (gr. 4 up). 1979. PLB 19.93 (ISBN 0-516-04113-4). Childrens.
Carter, Alden R. Illinois. (Illus.). 96p. (gr. 4-9). 1987. PLB 10.40 (ISBN 0-531-10387-0). Watts.
Fradin, Dennis. Illinois: In Words & Pictures. LC 76-7389. (Illus.). 48p. (gr. 2-5). 1976. PLB 15.93 (ISBN 0-516-03911-3); pap. 4.95 (ISBN 0-516-43911-1). Childrens.
Frazier, Carl & Frazier, Rosalie. The Lincoln Country-In Pictures. LC 63-19173. (Illus.). (gr. 4-6). 1963. 6.95 (ISBN 0-8038-4238-4). Hastings.
Marsh, Carole. Avast, Ye Slobs! Illinois Pirate Trivia. (Illus.). (gr. 3-12). 1990. PLB 19.95 (ISBN 0-7933-0400-8); pap. 14.95 (ISBN 0-7933-0399-0); computer disk 29.95 (ISBN 0-7933-0401-6). Gallopade Pub Group.
—The Beast of the Illinois Bed & Breakfast. (Illus.). (gr. 3-12). 1990. PLB 19.95 (ISBN 0-7933-1590-5); pap. 14.95 (ISBN 0-7933-1591-3); computer disk 29.95 (ISBN 0-7933-1592-1). Gallopade Pub Group.
—The Hard-to-Believe-But-True! Book of Illinois History, Mystery, Trivia, Legend, Lore, Humor & More. (Illus.). (gr. 3-12). 1990. PLB 19.95 (ISBN 0-7933-0397-4); pap. 14.95 (ISBN 0-7933-0396-6); computer disk 29.95 (ISBN 0-7933-0398-2). Gallopade Pub Group.
—If My Illinois Mama Ran the World! (Illus.). (gr. 3-12). 1990. PLB 19.95 (ISBN 0-7933-1595-6); pap. 14.95 (ISBN 0-7933-1596-4); computer disk 29.95 (ISBN 0-7933-1597-2). Gallopade Pub Group.
—Illinois & Other State Greats (Biographies) (Illus.). (gr. 3-12). 1990. PLB 19.95 (ISBN 1-55609-416-7); pap. 14.95 (ISBN 1-55609-415-9); computer disk 29.95 (ISBN 0-7933-1598-0). Gallopade Pub Group.
—Illinois Bandits, Bushwackers, Outlaws, Crooks, Devils, Ghosts, Desperadoes & Other Assorted & Sundry Characters! (Illus.). (gr. 3-12). 1990. PLB 19.95 (ISBN 0-7933-0382-6); pap. 14.95 (ISBN 0-7933-0381-8); computer disk 29.95 (ISBN 0-7933-0383-4). Gallopade Pub Group.
—Illinois Classic Christmas Trivia: Stories, Recipes, Activities, Legends, Lore & More! (Illus.). (gr. 3-12). 1990. PLB 19.95 (ISBN 0-7933-0385-0); pap. 14.95 (ISBN 0-7933-0384-2); computer disk 29.95 (ISBN 0-7933-0386-9). Gallopade Pub Group.
—Illinois Coastales. (Illus.). (gr. 3-12). 1990. PLB 19.95 (ISBN 1-55609-412-4); pap. 14.95 (ISBN 1-55609-411-6); computer disk 29.95 (ISBN 0-7933-1594-8). Gallopade Pub Group.
—The Illinois Hot Air Balloon Mystery. (Illus.). (gr. 2-9). 1990. 19.95 (ISBN 0-7933-2435-1); pap. 14.95 (ISBN 0-7933-2436-X); computer disk 29.95 (ISBN 0-7933-2437-8). Gallopade Pub Group.
—Illinois "Jography" A Fun Run Thru Our State! (Illus.). (gr. 3-12). 1990. PLB 19.95 (ISBN 1-55609-407-8); pap. 14.95 (ISBN 1-55609-406-X); computer disk 29.95 (ISBN 0-7933-1584-0). Gallopade Pub Group.
—Illinois Kid's Cookbook: Recipes, How-to, History, Lore & More! (Illus.). (gr. 3-12). 1990. PLB 19.95 (ISBN 0-7933-0394-X); pap. 14.95 (ISBN 0-7933-0393-1); computer disk 29.95 (ISBN 0-7933-0395-8). Gallopade Pub Group.
—Illinois Quiz Bowl Crash Course! (Illus.). (gr. 3-12). 1990. PLB 19.95 (ISBN 1-55609-414-0); pap. 14.95 (ISBN 1-55609-413-2); computer disk 29.95 (ISBN 0-7933-1593-X). Gallopade Pub Group.
—Illinois School Trivia: An Amazing & Fascinating Look at Our State's Teachers, Schools & Students! (Illus.). (gr. 3-12). 1990. PLB 19.95 (ISBN 0-7933-0391-5); pap. 14.95 (ISBN 0-7933-0390-7); computer disk 29.95 (ISBN 0-7933-0392-3). Gallopade Pub Group.
—Illinois Silly Basketball Sportsmysteries, Vol. I. (Illus.). (gr. 3-12). 1990. PLB 19.95 (ISBN 0-7933-0388-5); pap. 14.95 (ISBN 0-7933-0387-7); computer disk 29.95 (ISBN 0-7933-0389-3). Gallopade Pub Group.

—Illinois Silly Basketball Sportsmysteries, Vol. II. (Illus.). (gr. 3-12). 1990. PLB 19.95 (ISBN 0-7933-1599-9); pap. 14.95 (ISBN 0-7933-1600-6); computer disk 29. 95 (ISBN 0-7933-1601-4). Gallopade Pub Group.

—Illinois Silly Football Sportsmysteries, Vol. I. (Illus.). (gr. 3-12). 1990. PLB 19.95 (ISBN 1-55609-410-8); pap. 14.95 (ISBN 1-55609-409-4); computer disk 29. 95 (ISBN 0-7933-1586-7). Gallopade Pub Group.

—Illinois Silly Football Sportsmysteries. (Illus.). (gr. 3-12). 1990. PLB 19.95 (ISBN 0-7933-1587-5); pap. 14. 95 (ISBN 0-7933-1588-3); computer disk 29.95 (ISBN 0-7933-1589-1). Gallopade Pub Group.

—Illinois Silly Trivia! (Illus.). (gr. 3-12). 1990. PLB 19.95 (ISBN 1-55609-405-1); pap. 14.95 (ISBN 1-55609-113-3); computer disk 29.95 (ISBN 0-7933-1583-2). Gallopade Pub Group.

—Illinois's (Most Devastating!) Disasters & (Most Calamitous!) Catastrophies! (Illus.). (gr. 3-12). 1990. PLB 19.95 (ISBN 0-7933-0379-6); pap. 14.95 (ISBN 0-7933-0378-8); computer disk 29.95 (ISBN 0-7933-0380-X). Gallopade Pub Group.

—Let's Quilt Illinois & Stuff It Topographically! (Illus.). (gr. 3-12). 1990. PLB 19.95 (ISBN 1-55609-408-6); pap. 14.95 (ISBN 1-55609-097-8); computer disk 29. 95 (ISBN 0-7933-1585-9). Gallopade Pub Group.

Stein, R. Conrad. Illinois. (Illus.). 144p. (gr. 4 up). 1987. 25.27 (ISBN 0-516-00459-X). Childrens.

Stepien, William, et al. Discovering Illinois. (Illus.). 184p. (gr. 4). 1986. 20.00 (ISBN 0-685-24528-4, Peregrine Smith). Gibbs Smith Pub.

Turner Educational Services, Inc. Staff & Clark, James I. Illinois. 48p. (gr. 3 up). 1986. PLB 17.32 (ISBN 0-86514-452-4); pap. 9.27 (ISBN 0-86514-527-X); cancelled Beta video (ISBN 0-86514-077-4); cancelled VHS video (ISBN 0-86514-152-5); cancelled 3/4" video (ISBN 0-86514-227-0); cancelled tchr's. study guide (ISBN 0-86514-302-1); cancelled student activity bk. (ISBN 0-86514-377-3); cancelled index. Raintree Pubs.

ILLUSIONS

see Optical Illusions

ILLUSTRATION OF BOOKS

see also Drawing

Mitgutsch, Ali. From Picture to Picture Book. (Illus.). 24p. (ps-3). 1988. PLB 6.95 (ISBN 0-87614-353-2). Carolrhoda Bks.

ILLUSTRATIONS, HUMOROUS

see Cartoons and Caricatures

Thaler, Mike. Oinkers Away! Pig Riddles, Cartoons & Jokes. (gr. 3-6). 1989. pap. 2.50 (ISBN 0-671-67456-0, Minstrel Bks). PB.

IMAGINARY ANIMALS

see Animals, Mythical

IMAGINATION

see also Creation (Literary, Artistic, etc.)

Adler, C. S. Help, Pink Pig. LC 85-6329. 176p. (gr. 5-7). 1985. 14.95 (ISBN 0-399-21282-5, Putnam). Putnam Pub Group.

Anno, Mitsumasa. Topsy-Turvies: Pictures to Stretch the Imagination. Anno, Mitsumasa, illus. LC 71-96054. 28p. (gr. k-5). 1970. 6.50 (ISBN 0-8348-2004-8). Weatherhill.

—Upside-Downers: More Pictures to Stretch the Imagination. Weatherby, Meredith & Trumbull, Suzanne, trs. from JPN. Anno, Mitsumasa, illus. LC 71-157269. 28p. (gr. k-3). 1971. 6.50 (ISBN 0-8348-2005-6). Weatherhill.

Berry, Joy W. Teach Me about Pretending. Dickey, Kate, ed. LC 85-45091. (Illus.). 36p. (ps). 1986. 4.98 (ISBN 0-685-10731-0). Grolier Inc.

Eberle, Bob. Scamper On. Weber, June K., illus. 64p. (Orig.). (gr. k-12). 1984. 6.95 (ISBN 0-88047-047-X, 8413). DOK Pubs.

Jane, Pamela. Just Plain Penny. 160p. (gr. 3-7). 1990. 13. 95 (ISBN 0-395-52807-0). HM.

Little People Big Book about Imagination. 64p. (ps-1). 1990. write for info. (ISBN 0-8094-7479-4); PLB write for info. (ISBN 0-8094-7480-8). Time-Life.

Neuberger, Phyllis J. Suppose You Were a Kitten. LC 82-91105. (Illus.). (gr. 1-3). 1982. pap. 2.95 (ISBN 0-9610050-0-9). P J Neuberger.

Oram, Hiawyn. In the Attic. Kitamura, Satoshi, illus. LC 84-15570. (ps-2). 1985. 11.95 (ISBN 0-8050-0779-2). H Holt & Co.

Short, David & Short, Pat. Entice Their Imaginations. Breviek, Phil, illus. 64p. (gr. k-6). 1985. wkbk. 6.95 (ISBN 0-86653-324-9, GA 658). Good Apple.

Wakayama, Shizuko. Out for a Walk. (Illus.). 22p. (ps-1). 1981. 3.50 (ISBN 0-89346-196-2). Heian Intl.

IMAGINATION–FICTION

Alexander, Martha. And My Mean Old Mother Will Be Sorry, Blackboard Bear. Alexander, Martha, illus. LC 72-707. 32p. (ps-2). 1985. PLB 10.89 (ISBN 0-8037-0593-X). Dial Bks Young.

Alexander, Sue. Lila on the Landing. Eagle, Ellen, illus. LC 87-301. 64p. (gr. 2-5). 1987. 13.95 (ISBN 0-89919-340-4, Pub. by Clarion). Ticknor & Fields.

Berger, Barbara H. When the Sun Rose. Berger, Barbara H., illus. LC 86-2484. 32p. (ps-2). 1986. 13.95 (ISBN 0-399-21360-0, Philomel). Putnam Pub Group.

Breitmeyer, Lois & Leithauser, Gladys. Who Should I Be? 1991. pap. 2.95 (ISBN 0-8091-6599-6). Paulist Pr.

Brown, Margaret W. David's Little Indian. Charlip, Remy, illus. 48p. (gr. 2-5). 1989. Repr. of 1954 ed. 10. 95 (ISBN 0-929077-02-4, Hopscotch Bks); PLB 10.95 (ISBN 0-317-92547-4, Hopscotch Bks). Watermark Inc.

Browne, Anthony. Changes. Browne, Anthony, illus. LC 90-4283. 32p. (ps-3). 1991. Repr. of 1990 ed. 14.95 (ISBN 0-679-81029-3); PLB 15.99 (ISBN 0-679-91029-8). Knopf.

Burningham, John. Where's Julius? (ps-1). 1986. pap. 9.95 (ISBN 0-517-56476-9). Crown.

Butler, Susan. A Trip to the Jungle. (Illus.). 40p. (Orig.). (ps-2). 1978. pap. 3.95 (ISBN 0-931416-00-0). Open Books.

Cain, Barbara S. Double-Dip Feelings: A Book to Help Children Understand Emotions. O'Brien, Ann S., illus. LC 89-49382. 32p. 1990. 15.95 (ISBN 0-945354-23-1); pap. 5.95 (ISBN 0-945354-20-7). Magination Pr.

Cleary, Beverly. Beezus & Ramona. Darling, Louis, illus. LC 55-7623. 192p. (gr. 3-7). 1955. 12.95 (ISBN 0-688-21076-7); PLB 12.88 (ISBN 0-688-31076-1, Morrow Jr Bks). Morrow Jr Bks.

—Emily's Runaway Imagination. 224p. (gr. k-6). 1980. pap. 3.25 (ISBN 0-440-42215-9, YB). Dell.

—Emily's Runaway Imagination. 224p. 1990. pap. 3.50 (ISBN 0-380-70923-6, Camelot). Avon.

Cummings, Pat. Jimmy Lee Did It. LC 84-21322. (Illus.). (ps-1). 1985. 13.95 (ISBN 0-688-04632-0); PLB 12.88 (ISBN 0-688-04633-9). Lothrop.

Dobrin, Arnold. Josephine's 'Magination. Dobrin, Arnold, illus. 48p. (gr. k-3). 1975. pap. 2.25 (ISBN 0-590-40175-0). Scholastic Inc.

Dr. Seuss. Oh! the Thinks You Can Think! Dr. Seuss, illus. LC 75-1602. 48p. (ps-1). 1975. 6.95 (ISBN 0-394-83129-2); lib. bdg. 7.99 (ISBN 0-394-93129-7). Beginner.

Fitzgerald, John D. Great Brain. (gr. k-6). 1972. pap. 3.50 (ISBN 0-440-43071-2, YB). Dell.

Franklin, Jonathan. Don't Wake the Baby. (Illus.). 32p. (ps-1). 1991. bds. 13.95 jacketed (ISBN 0-374-31826-3). FS&G.

Greenfield, Eloise. Me & Neesie. Barnett, Moneta, illus. LC 74-23078. 40p. (gr. 1-4). 1975. PLB 13.89 (ISBN 0-690-00715-9, Crowell Jr Bks). HarpC Child Bks.

Henkes, Kevin. Jessica. LC 87-38087. (Illus.). 24p. (gr. k up). 1989. 11.95 (ISBN 0-688-07829-X); PLB 11.88 (ISBN 0-688-07830-3). Greenwillow.

Hoff, Syd. Horse in Harry's Room. Hoff, Syd, illus. LC 71-104753. 32p. (gr. k-3). 1970. PLB 10.89 (ISBN 0-06-022483-5). HarpC Child Bks.

Hollands, Judith. Mrs. Mudgie & Mr. James. Delaney, Molly, illus. LC 87-35143. 32p. (gr. k-2). 1988. 13.95 (ISBN 0-689-31389-6, Atheneum Child Bk). Macmillan Child Grp.

I Thought I Saw. (Orig.). (ps-2). 1974. 5.50 (ISBN 0-85953-074-4, Pub. by Child's Play England); pap. 4.00 (ISBN 0-85953-029-9). Childs Play.

Kroll, Steven. I'd Like to Be. Appleby, Ellen, illus. LC 86-25215. 48p. (ps-3). 1987. 5.95 (ISBN 0-8193-1141-3). Parents.

Laurencin, Genevieve. I Wish I Were. Wensell, Ulises, illus. 32p. (gr. k-3). 1987. 7.95 (ISBN 0-399-21416-X, Putnam). Putnam Pub Group.

Leach, Maria. The Thing at the Foot of the Bed. 112p. (gr. 4-5). 1981. pap. 3.25 (ISBN 0-440-48773-0, YB). Dell.

Lester, Alison. Imagine. Lester, Alison, illus. 32p. (gr. k-3). 1990. 13.95 (ISBN 0-395-53753-3). HM.

Lewis, Hilda. Ship That Flew. Levrin, Nora, illus. LC 58-5903. (gr. 3-7). 1958. 22.95 (ISBN 0-87599-067-3). S G Phillips.

Miller, Albert G. Captain Whopper. Komisarow, Donald, illus. (gr. 3-7). 1968. 10.95 (ISBN 0-8392-3058-3). Astor-Honor.

Morgan, Lenore. Dragons & Stuff. LC 70-108725. (Illus.). 32p. (gr. 2-4). 1970. PLB 9.95 (ISBN 0-87783-012-6); pap. 3.94 deluxe ed. (ISBN 0-87783-091-6). Oddo.

O'Leary, Daniel J. & Dalton, Kathleen. Where Is God? Sabatte, Frank, illus. 1991. pap. 2.95 (ISBN 0-8091-6598-8). Paulist Pr.

Paterson, Katherine. Un Puente Hasta Therabithia. (SPA.). (gr. 1-6). 8.50 (ISBN 84-204-3633-X). Santillana.

Peet, Bill. Wump World. Peet, Bill, illus. LC 72-124999. (gr. 3-5). 1981. 13.95 (ISBN 0-395-19841-0); pap. 3.95 (ISBN 0-395-31129-2). HM.

Pfanner, Louise. Louise Builds a House. LC 88-23415. (Illus.). 32p. (ps-1). 1989. 12.95 (ISBN 0-531-05796-8); PLB 12.99 (ISBN 0-531-08396-9). Orchard Bks Watts.

Townsend, John R. Rob's Place. LC 86-27373. (gr. 4-9). 1988. PLB 12.95 (ISBN 0-688-07258-5). Lothrop.

Townson, Hazel. What on Earth...? (ps-3). 1991. 13.95 (ISBN 0-316-85138-8). Little.

White, E. B. Trumpet of the Swan. Frascino, Edward, illus. LC 72-112484. (gr. 3-6). 1970. 10.95 (ISBN 0-06-026397-0); PLB 11.89 (ISBN 0-06-026398-9). HarpC Child Bks.

Zolotow, Charlotte. I Have a Horse of My Own. Mitsuhashi, Yoko, illus. LC 64-22344. 32p. (ps-2). 1980. 11.95 (ISBN 0-690-04046-6, Crowell Jr Bks). HarpC Child Bks.

IMBECILITY

see Mentally Handicapped

IMMERSION, BAPTISMAL

see Baptism

IMMIGRANTS

see Immigration and Emigration

IMMIGRATION AND EMIGRATION

Here are entered works on migration from one country to another. Works on the movement of population within a country for permanent settlements are entered under Migration, internal.

see also Refugees

also names of countries with the subdivision Immigration And Emigration (e.g. U. S.–Immigration And Emigration, etc.); names of countries, cities, etc. with the subdivision Foreign Population (e.g. U. S.–Foreign Population, etc.); and names of nationalities, e.g. Italians In The U. S., etc.

Crosby, Nina E. & Marten, Elizabeth H. Don't Teach Let Me Learn about Presidents, of the U. S. People, Genealogy, Immigrants. (Illus.). 80p. (Orig.). (gr. 3-9). 1979. pap. 8.95 tchr's. enrichment manual (ISBN 0-914634-67-4, 7912). DOK Pubs.

Dudley, William, ed. Immigration: Opposing Viewpoints. LC 90-13854. (Illus.). 240p. (gr. 10 up). 1990. PLB 15. 95 (ISBN 0-89908-485-0); pap. text ed. 8.95 (ISBN 0-89908-460-5). Greenhaven.

Evitts, William J. Early Immigration in the United States. (Illus.). 64p. (gr. 3-5). 1989. PLB 11.90 (ISBN 0-531-10744-2). Watts.

Freedman, Russell. Immigrant Kids. LC 79-20060. 64p. (gr. 3-7). 1980. 13.95 (ISBN 0-525-32538-7, DCB). Dutton Child Bks.

Hartmann, Edward G. American Immigration. LC 79-12998. (Illus.). 120p. (gr. 5 up). 1979. PLB 11.95 (ISBN 0-8225-0232-1); pap. 3.95 (ISBN 0-8225-1030-8). Lerner Pubns.

Hillbrand, Percie V. The Norwegians in America. rev. ed. LC 67-15683. (Illus.). 80p. (gr. 5 up). PLB 11.95 (ISBN 0-8225-0243-7); pap. 3.95 (ISBN 0-8225-1041-3). Lerner Pubns.

Jacobson, Gloria. Two for America: The True Story of a Swiss Immigrant. Cliff, Don, illus. 36p. (gr. 4). 1989. pap. 8.50 (ISBN 0-9618399-1-0). G Jacobson.

Kurelek, William & Engelhart, Margaret S. They Sought a New World: The Story of European Immigration to North America. (Illus.). 48p. (gr. 4 up). 1985. 14.95 (ISBN 0-88776-172-0, Dist. by U of Toronto Pr); pap. 7.95 (ISBN 0-88776-213-1). Tundra Bks.

Mageli, Paul. The Immigrant Experience: An Annotated Bibliography. 200p. 1991. PLB 40.00x (ISBN 0-89356-671-3, Magill Bks). Salem Pr.

Mayberry, Jodine. Filipinos. Daniels, Roger, contrib. by. (Illus.). 64p. (gr. 5-8). 1990. PLB 12.40 (ISBN 0-531-10978-X). Watts.

—Mexicans. Daniels, Roger, contrib. by. (Illus.). 64p. (gr. 5-8). 1990. PLB 12.40 (ISBN 0-531-10979-8). Watts.

Mizumura, Kazue. If I Were a Cricket... Mizumura, Kazue, illus. LC 73-3495. 32p. (ps-3). 1973. PLB 13. 89 (ISBN 0-690-00076-6, Crowell Jr Bks). HarpC Child Bks.

Perrin, Linda. Immigrants from the Far East. LC 80-65840. 192p. 1980. 12.95 (ISBN 0-385-28115-3). Delacorte.

Reimers, David. The Immigrant Experience. Moynihan, Daniel P., intro. by. (Illus.). 112p. (gr. 5 up). 1989. 17. 95x (ISBN 0-87754-881-1). Chelsea Hse.

Robbins, Albert. Immigrants from Northern Europe. LC 80-68741. 224p. 1982. 9.95 (ISBN 0-385-28138-2). Delacorte.

Schreiner, Nikki B., et al. The Whole World Kit: American Dream Activity Cards. Weathers, Susan, et al, illus. 60p. (gr. 4-8). 1990. pap. text ed. 215.00 (ISBN 1-879218-29-1). Touch & See Educ.

Steidl, Kim S. Portraits of Asian-Pacific Americans. 96p. (gr. 4-8). 1991. 9.95 (ISBN 0-86653-598-5, GA1323). Good Apple.

Szumski, Bonnie. Immigration: Identifying Propaganda Techniques. (Illus.). 32p. (gr. 3-6). 1990. PLB 8.95 (ISBN 0-89908-639-X). Greenhaven.

Wytrwal, Joseph. The Poles in America. LC 68-31506. (Illus.). 88p. (gr. 5 up). 1969. PLB 11.95 (ISBN 0-8225-0218-6); pap. 3.95 (ISBN 0-8225-1019-7). Lerner Pubns.

IMMIGRATION AND EMIGRATION–FICTION

Angell, Judie. One-Way to Ansonia. LC 85-5652. 192p. (gr. 6-8). 1985. 11.95 (ISBN 0-02-705860-3, Bradbury Pr). Macmillan Child Grp.

—One Way to Ansonia. 192p. 1986. pap. 2.50 (ISBN 0-425-08880-4, Pub. by Berkley-Pacer). Berkley Pub.

Gross, Virginia T. It's Only Goodbye. 1990. 11.95 (ISBN 0-670-83289-8). Viking Child Bks.

Levine, Ellen. I Hate English! Bjorkman, Steve, illus. (gr. k-2). 1989. pap. 12.95 (ISBN 0-590-42305-3). Scholastic Inc.

Sandin, Joan. The Long Way to a New Land. Sandin, Joan, illus. LC 80-8942. 64p. (gr. k-3). 1981. 11.95i (ISBN 0-06-025193-X); PLB 11.89 (ISBN 0-06-025194-8). HarpC Child Bks.

Shapiro, Irwin. Joe Magarac & His U. S. A. Citizen Papers. Daugherty, James, illus. LC 78-66070. 58p. (gr. 1-8). 1979. pap. 3.95 (ISBN 0-8229-5305-6). U of Pittsburgh Pr.

Taylor, Sydney. All-of-a-Kind Family. John, Helen, illus. 189p. (gr. 3-6). 1988. Repr. of 1951 ed. 11.95 (ISBN 0-929093-00-3). Taylor Prodns. ALL-OF-A-KIND FAMILY by Sydney Taylor, was first published in 1951, after winning the Follett Children's Book Contest, & has been in

print continuously since then. It was highly acclaimed & adored by readers from its first appearance & has become a classic, as have the other titles in this series, described below. It was followed over the years by four other books about this immigrant family growing up on New York's Lower East Side in the years immediately before & during the First World War, & each in turn, received the same enthusiastic reception. They are: ALL-OF-A-KIND FAMILY DOWNTOWN (ISBN 0-929093-01-1); MORE ALL-OF-A-KIND FAMILY (ISBN 0-929093-02-X); ALL-OF-A-KIND FAMILY UPTOWN (ISBN 0-929093-03-8); ELLA OF ALL-OF-A-KIND FAMILY (ISBN 0-929093-04-6). Over the years, each new book was greeted with glowing reviews from the children's major media. More importantly, perhaps, is the fact that readers welcomed each...& that these readers continue to remember the books fondly & order them for their own children & grandchildren. This family of five girls, later joined by a baby brother, has been taken to the heart of America & has created a firmly entrenched place in its children's literature. Distributed by the Talman Company, 150 Fifth Avenue, New York, NY 10011. Each book is hardcovered & is $11.95.
Publisher Provided Annotation.

IMMUNITY
see also Allergy; Communicable Diseases
Gutnik, Martin J. Immunology. (Illus.). 128p. (gr. 10-12). 1990. 12.40 (ISBN 0-531-10672-1). Watts.
Nourse, Alan E. Your Immune System. (Illus.). 72p. (gr. 4). 1983. PLB 10.40 (ISBN 0-531-04462-9). Watts.
—Your Immune System. rev. ed. (Illus.). 128p. (gr. 7-12). 1989. PLB 12.40 (ISBN 0-531-10817-1). Watts.
IMPLEMENTS, UTENSILS, ETC.
see Agricultural Machinery; Household Equipment and Supplies; Tools
IMPORTS
see Commerce
IMPOSTORS AND IMPOSTURE
Stewart, Gail B. Famous Hoaxes. LC 89-25422. (Illus.). 48p. (gr. 5 up). 1990. 10.95 (ISBN 0-89686-507-X, Crestwood Hse). Macmillan Child Grp.
IMPRESSIONISM (ART)
Reyero, Carlos. The Key to Art from Romanticism to Impressionism. (Illus.). 80p. (gr. 8 up). 1990. PLB 15. 95 (ISBN 0-8225-2058-3). Lerner Pubns.
IMPRISONMENT
see Prisons
INCAS
Appel, Benjamin. Shepherd of the Sun. Bryson, Bernarda, illus. (gr. 5 up). 1961. 10.95 (ISBN 0-8392-3033-8). Astor-Honor.
Bateman, Penny. Aztecs & Incas. FS-Aladdin Staff, ed. Shone, Rob, illus. LC 88-50497. 32p. (gr. 6 up). 1988. PLB 11.90 (ISBN 0-531-10622-5). Watts.
Bierhorst, John, ed. & tr. Black Rainbow: Legends of the Incas & Myths of Ancient Peru. LC 76-19092. 160p. (gr. 5 up). 1976. 9.95 (ISBN 0-374-30829-2). FS&G.
Harkonen, Reijo. The Grandchildren of the Incas. Pitkanen, Matti A., photos by. (Illus.). 40p. (gr. 3-6). 1991. PLB 14.95 (ISBN 0-87614-397-4). Carolrhoda Bks.
McKissack, Patricia. Tne Inca. LC 85-6712. (Illus.). 45p. (gr. 2-3). 1985. PLB 14.60 (ISBN 0-516-01268-1); pap. 4.95 (ISBN 0-516-41268-X). Childrens.
—Los Incas. LC 85-6712. (SPA.). 48p. (gr. k-4). 1987. PLB 14.60 (ISBN 0-516-31268-5); pap. 4.95 (ISBN 0-516-51268-4). Childrens.
Marrin, Albert. Inca & Spaniard: Pizarro & the Conquest of Peru. LC 88-29372. (Illus.). 224p. (gr. 5 up). 1989. 13.95 (ISBN 0-689-31481-7, Atheneum Child Bk). Macmillan Child Grp.
Morrison, M. An Inca Farmer. (Illus.). 32p. (gr. 3-8). Date not set. PLB 14.00 (ISBN 0-86592-144-X). Rourke Corp.
Morrison, Marion. Atahuallpa & the Incas. LC 85-73680. (Illus.). 64p. (gr. 4-9). 1986. PLB 12.40 (ISBN 0-531-18080-8, Pub. by Bookwright). Watts.
Odijk, Pamela. The Incas. (Illus.). 48p. (gr. 5-8). 1990. PLB 16.98 (ISBN 0-382-09889-7). Silver Burdett Pr.

INCAS–FICTION
Clark, Ann N. Secret of the Andes. Charlot, Jean, illus. (gr. 3-7). 1976. pap. 3.95 (ISBN 0-14-030926-8, Puffin). Puffin Bks.
—Secret of the Andes. Charlot, Jean, illus. (gr. 4-8). 1952. pap. 14.95 (ISBN 0-670-62975-8). Viking Child Bks.
INCINERATION
see Refuse and Refuse Disposal
INDEPENDENCE DAY (U. S.)
see Fourth of July
INDEX LIBORUM PROHIBITORUM
see Catholic Literature
INDIA
Ardley, Brigette & Ardley, Neil. India. (Illus.). 48p. (gr. 4-8). 1989. lib. bdg. 14.98 (ISBN 0-382-09795-5). Silver Burdett Pr.
Ashton, Stephen. Indian Independence. (Illus.). 72p. (gr. 7-12). 1986. 19.95 (ISBN 0-7134-4774-5, Pub. by Batsford England). Trafalgar Sq.
Caldwell, John C. India. (Illus.). (gr. 5 up). 1990. 14.95 (ISBN 0-7910-1371-5). Chelsea Hse.
Constitution of India for the Younger Reader. 1971. pap. 1.75 (ISBN 0-88253-410-6). Ind-US Inc.
Cumming, David. India. (Illus.). 32p. (gr. k-4). 1991. RLB 11.90 (ISBN 0-531-18391-2, Pub. by Boatwright Pr). Watts.
Das, Prodeepta. India. (Illus.). 32p. (gr. 5-8). 1990. PLB 11.90 (ISBN 0-531-14045-8). Watts.
Galbraith, Catherine A. & Mehta, Rama. India Now & Through Time. 160p. (gr. 6 up). 1980. 14.95 (ISBN 0-395-29207-7). HM.
Haskins, Jim. Count Your Way Through India. Dodson, Liz B., illus. 24p. (gr. 1-4). 1990. PLB 11.95 (ISBN 0-87614-414-8). Carolrhoda Bks.
Kalman, Bobbie. India - the Land. (Illus.). 32p. (gr. 4-5). 1990. lib. bdg. 14.95 (ISBN 0-86505-210-7); pap. 7.95 (ISBN 0-86505-290-5). Crabtree Pub Co.
—India - the People. (Illus.). 32p. (gr. 4-5). 1990. lib. bdg. 14.95 (ISBN 0-86505-211-5); pap. 7.95 (ISBN 0-86505-291-3). Crabtree Pub Co.

—India: The Culture. (Illus.). 32p. (gr. 4-5). 1990. lib. bdg. 14.95 (ISBN 0-86505-212-3); pap. 7.95 (ISBN 0-86505-292-1). Crabtree Pub Co.
INDIA: THE CULTURE & its accompanying volumes INDIA: THE LAND & INDIA: THE PEOPLE acquaint children with this intriguing, ancient country. The whole world has been influenced by the rich & colorful culture of India. India's art, architecture, music, festivals, food & dancing all have their roots in India's three major religions. Explore this fascinating culture through stunning photographs & easy-to-read text. Learn about special aspects of India, such as its geography, history, development, family life, & religions.
Publisher Provided Annotation.

Kanitkar, V. P. Indian Food & Drink. (Illus.). 48p. (gr. 4-8). 1987. lib. bdg. 12.40 (ISBN 0-531-18119-7, Pub. by Bookwright Pr). Watts.
Kaur, Sharon. Food in India. LC 88-31294. (Illus.). 32p. (gr. 3-6). 1989. lib. bdg. 13.26 (ISBN 0-86625-339-4). Rourke Corp.
Kublin, Hyman. India: Regional Study. rev. ed. (Illus.). 228p. (gr. 9-12). 1973. pap. 19.20 (ISBN 0-395-13928-7). HM.
Lerner Publications, Department of Geography Staff, ed. India in Pictures. (Illus.). 64p. (gr. 5 up). 1989. 12.95 (ISBN 0-8225-1852-X). Lerner Pubns.
Lye, Keith. Take a Trip to India. 32p. (gr. 1-3). 1982. PLB 7.99 (ISBN 0-531-04347-9). Watts.
Sandal, Veenu. We Live in India. LC 83-72802. 64p. (gr. 4-8). 1984. lib. bdg. 9.49 (ISBN 0-531-04784-9, Pub. by Bookwright Pr). Watts.
Singh, Anne. Living in India. Matthews, Sarah, tr. from FRE. Riquier, Aline, illus. LC 87-31803. 38p. (gr. k-5). 1988. 4.95 (ISBN 0-944589-14-6, 146). Young Discovery Lib.
The Taj Mahal. 48p. (gr. 4-5). 1989. PLB 10.95 (ISBN 0-685-26413-0). Capstone Pr.
INDIA–BIOGRAPHY
Allison, Carol. Ringu of India's Forest. Espe, Marvin, illus. 52p. (gr. k-6). 1987. pap. text ed. 8.99 (ISBN 1-55976-050-8). CEF Press.
Ghosh, A. Chanakya. Vilas, Anil, illus. (gr. 1-8). 1979. pap. 3.00 (ISBN 0-89744-152-4). Auromere.
Giff, Patricia R. Mother Teresa: A Sister to the Poor. Lewin, Ted, illus. LC 85-40885. 64p. (gr. 2-6). 1986. pap. 10.95 (ISBN 0-670-81096-7). Viking Child Bks.
Haskins, James. India under Indira & Rajiv Gandhi. LC 88-21209. (Illus.). 104p. (gr. 6 up). 1989. PLB 17.95 (ISBN 0-89490-146-X). Enslow Pubs.
Singh, Mala. The Story of Guru Nanak. (Illus.). (gr. 2-9). 1979. 6.50 (ISBN 0-89744-138-9). Auromere.

INDIA–DESCRIPTION AND TRAVEL
Khanna, K. As They Saw India. Khanna, Krishna, illus. (gr. 1-9). 1979. pap. 2.50 (ISBN 0-89744-172-9). Auromere.
Singh, Mala. Kashmir. Sharma, P. N., photos by. (Illus.). (gr. 1-10). 1979. pap. 2.50 (ISBN 0-89744-177-X). Auromere.
Valiappa, Al. Story of Our Rivers: Book II. Chakravarty, Pranab, illus. (gr. 1-9). 1979. pap. 2.50 (ISBN 0-89744-184-2). Auromere.
INDIA–FICTION
Anand, Mulk R. Maya of Mohenjo-Daro. 3rd ed. Biswas, Pulak, illus. 24p. (Orig.). (gr. k-3). 1980. pap. 2.50 (ISBN 0-89744-214-8, Pub. by Children's Bk Trust India). Auromere.
Bonnici, Peter. The Festival. Kopper, Lisa, illus. LC 84-15597. 32p. (ps-3). 1985. PLB 9.95 (ISBN 0-87614-229-3). Carolrhoda Bks.
Bosse, Malcolm J. Ganesh. LC 80-2453. 192p. (gr. 7 up). 1981. 11.06i (ISBN 0-690-04102-0, Crowell Jr Bks). HarpC Child Bks.
Dasa, Yogesvara & Dasi, Jyotirmayi-Devi. A Gift of Love: The Story of Sudama Brahmin. Dasa, Puskar, illus. LC 82-8874. 32p. (gr. 5-8). 1982. PLB 7.00 (ISBN 0-89647-015-6). Bala Bks.
Dutta, S. & Hemalata. Harishchandra. Wheaton, Jaya, illus. (gr. 1-8). 1979. pap. 2.00 (ISBN 0-89744-155-9). Auromere.
Furchgott, Terry. Nanda in India. Furchgott, Terry, illus. 32p. (ps-3). 1983. 9.95 (ISBN 0-233-97480-6). Andre Deutsch.
Guillot, Rene. The Three Hundred Ninety-Seventh White Elephant. Leatham, Moyra, illus. (gr. 3-7). 1957. 18.95 (ISBN 0-87599-043-6). S G Phillips.
Jekel, Pamela. The Third Jungle Book. Malick, Nancy, illus. LC 90-36410. 276p. (Orig.). 1990. 19.95 (ISBN 0-917665-47-3). Bookmakers Guild.
The Jungle Book. Date not set. 9.98 (ISBN 0-517-67902-7). Outlet Bk Co.
Kamal, Aleph. The Bird Who Was an Elephant. Lessac, Frane, illus. LC 89-14536. 32p. (gr. k-4). 1990. 14.95 (ISBN 0-397-32445-6, Lipp Jr Bks); PLB 14.89 (ISBN 0-397-32446-4, Lipp Jr Bks). HarpC Child Bks.
Kipling, Rudyard. Jungle Books. (gr. 5 up). pap. 1.95 (ISBN 0-8049-0109-0, CL-109). Airmont.
—The Jungle Books. 336p. 1961. pap. 3.95 (ISBN 0-451-52340-7, Sig Classics). NAL-Dutton.
—The Miracle of Purun Bhagat. LC 85-26956. 40p. (gr. 6 up). 1986. PLB 10.95s.p. (ISBN 0-88682-052-9); 15.65 (ISBN 0-685-12409-6). Creative Ed.
Shivkumar. Krishna & Sudama. Gupta, M. L. Dutta, illus. (gr. 1-8). 1979. pap. 2.00 (ISBN 0-89744-156-7). Auromere.
Smarananada. Story of Sarada Devi. Chakravarty, Biswaranjan, illus. 36p. (Orig.). (gr. k-4). 1987. pap. 2.50 (ISBN 0-87481-229-1, Pub. by Advaita Ashram India). Vedanta Pr.
Tales from the Jungle Book. (Illus.). (gr. 3-5). 3.50 (ISBN 0-7214-0997-0). Ladybird Bks.
Wright, Meg, illus. Three Stories from India. (gr. 1-8). 1984. pap. text ed. 9.50 (ISBN 0-86508-166-2). BCM Pubn.
INDIA–HISTORY
Ashton, Stephen. The British in India. (Illus.). 86p. (gr. 7-9). 1988. 19.95 (ISBN 0-7134-5475-X, Pub. by Batsford England). Trafalgar Sq.
Prabhakar, Vishnu. Story of Swarajya: Part I. (Illus.). (gr. 1-10). 1979. pap. 2.50 (ISBN 0-89744-185-0). Auromere.
Prakash, Sumangal. Story of Swarajya: Part II. Khemraj, P., illus. (gr. 1-10). 1979. pap. 2.50 (ISBN 0-89744-186-9). Auromere.
Rawding, F. W. The Rebellion in India, 1857. (Illus.). 48p. (gr. 7 up). 1977. pap. 5.95 (ISBN 0-521-20683-9). Cambridge U Pr.
INDIA RUBBER
see Rubber
INDIANA
Berry, S. L. Indianapolis. (Illus.). 60p. (gr. 3 up). 1990. 12.95 (ISBN 0-87518-426-X, Dillon); PLB 12.95 (ISBN 0-685-33006-0). Macmillan Child Grp.
Carole Marsh Indiana Books, 31 bks. Set. 638.45 (ISBN 0-7933-1289-2). Gallopade Pub Group.
Carpenter, Allan. Indiana. new ed. LC 78-12459. (Illus.). 96p. (gr. 4 up). 1979. PLB 19.93 (ISBN 0-516-04114-2). Childrens.
Fradin, Dennis. Indiana: In Words & Pictures. LC 79-21383. (Illus.). 48p. (gr. 2-5). 1980. PLB 15.93 (ISBN 0-516-03912-1). Childrens.
Marsh, Carole. Avast, Ye Slobs! Indiana Pirate Trivia. (Illus.). (gr. 3-12). 1990. PLB 19.95 (ISBN 0-7933-0424-5); pap. 14.95 (ISBN 0-7933-0423-7); computer disk 29.95. Gallopade Pub Group.
—The Beast of the Indiana Bed & Breakfast. (Illus.). (gr. 3-12). 1990. PLB 19.95 (ISBN 0-7933-1609-X); pap. 14.95 (ISBN 0-7933-1610-3); computer disk 29.95 (ISBN 0-7933-1611-1). Gallopade Pub Group.
—The Hard-to-Believe-But-True! Book of Indiana History, Mystery, Trivia, Legend, Lore, Humor & More. (Illus.). (gr. 3-12). 1990. PLB 19.95 (ISBN 0-7933-0421-0); pap. 14.95 (ISBN 0-7933-0420-2); computer disk 29.95 (ISBN 0-7933-0422-9). Gallopade Pub Group.
—If My Indiana Mama Ran the World! (Illus.). (gr. 3-12). 1990. PLB 19.95 (ISBN 0-7933-1613-8); pap. 14. 95 (ISBN 0-7933-1614-6); computer disk 29.95 (ISBN 0-7933-1615-4). Gallopade Pub Group.

Henry Tall Bull & Weist, Tom. Grandfather & the Popping Machine. (gr. 2-12). 1970. 2.95 (ISBN 0-89992-004-7). Coun India Ed.
—The Spotted Horse. (gr. 2-10). 1970. 2.95 (ISBN 0-89992-002-0). Coun India Ed.
—Veho. (gr. 2-6). 1971. 1.95 (ISBN 0-89992-007-1). Coun India Ed.
—The Winter Hunt. 32p. (gr. 3-9). 1971. 2.95 (ISBN 0-89992-006-3). Coun India Ed.
Hirschfelder, Arlene. Happily May I Walk: American Indians & Alaska Natives Today. LC 85-43349. 160p. (gr. 5 up). 1986. 13.95 (ISBN 0-684-18624-1, Scribners Young Read). Macmillan Child Grp.
Hoxie, Fred & Markowitz, Harvey. Native Americans: North America--An Annotated Bibliography. 200p. 1991. PLB 40.00x (ISBN 0-89356-670-5, Magill Bks). Salem Pr.
Indian Canoeing. (Illus.). (gr. 6-12). 1976. 3.95 (ISBN 0-686-22273-3). Coun India Ed.
Indian Lore. (Illus.). 90p. (gr. 6-12). 1959. pap. 1.85 (ISBN 0-8395-3358-6, 3358). BSA.
Indians. 24p. (ps-2). 1989. pap. 1.29 (ISBN 0-02-898255-X). Checkerboard Pr.
Jacobson, Daniel. Indians of North America. (Illus.). 96p. (gr. 4up). PLB 10.40 (ISBN 0-531-04647-8). Watts.
Job, Kenneth. Indians in New York State. Whitman, Bernard, ed. Whitman, Shirley, illus. 48p. (Orig.). (gr. 4-7). 1989. pap. text ed. 5.00 (ISBN 0-918433-01-0). In Educ.
Johnson, Gail E. Phantom Horse of Collister's Fields. (gr. 4-12). 1974. 2.95 (ISBN 0-89992-062-4). Coun India Ed.
Jones, Jayne C. The American Indian in America, Vol. II. LC 73-13378. (Illus.). 96p. (gr. 5 up). 1973. PLB 11.95 (ISBN 0-8225-0227-5); pap. 3.95 (ISBN 0-8225-1002-2). Lerner Pubns.
—The American Indian in America, Vol. I. LC 72-3591. (Illus.). 104p. (gr. 5 up). 1973. PLB 11.95 (ISBN 0-8225-0224-0); pap. 3.95 (ISBN 0-8225-1001-4). Lerner Pubns.
Kennedy, John G. The Tarahumara. (Illus.). (gr. 5 up). 1990. 17.95 (ISBN 1-55546-730-X). Chelsea Hse.
Keyworth, C. L. California Indians. (Illus.). 96p. (gr. 5-8). 1990. 18.95x (ISBN 0-8160-2386-7). Facts on File.
Kindle, Patricia & Finney, Susan. American Indians. McKay, Ardis, illus. 64p. (gr. 4-8). 1985. wkbk. 6.95 (ISBN 0-86653-290-0, GA 673). Good Apple.
Kniffen, Fred. Indians of Louisiana. (Illus.). 108p. (gr. 6-12). 1976. 12.50 (ISBN 0-911116-97-4). Pelican.
Knobloch, Madge. Havasupai Years. (gr. 9 up). 1988. pap. 5.95 (ISBN 0-89992-117-5, NO. 117-5); PLB 11.95 (ISBN 0-685-25221-3). Coun India Ed.
Layman, Paul E. Seal for a Pal. (gr. 4-9). 1972. pap. 2.95 (ISBN 0-89992-029-2). Coun India Ed.
Liptak, Karen. Indians of the Pacific Northwest. (Illus.). 96p. (gr. 5-8). 1990. 18.95x (ISBN 0-8160-2384-0). Facts on File.
—Indians of the Southwest. (Illus.). 96p. (gr. 5-8). 1990. 18.95x (ISBN 0-8160-2385-9). Facts on File.
—North American Indian Medicine People. (Illus.). 64p. (gr. 5-8). 1990. PLB 11.90 (ISBN 0-531-10868-6). Watts.
—North American Indian Sign Language. Berry, Don, illus. 64p. (gr. 5-8). 1990. PLB 11.90 (ISBN 0-531-10869-4). Watts.
—North American Indian Survival Skills. (Illus.). 64p. (gr. 5-8). 1990. PLB 11.90 (ISBN 0-531-10870-8). Watts.
McCall, Barbara, et al. Native American People, 6 bks, Reading Level 4. (Illus.). 192p. (gr. 5-8). Date not set. Set. PLB 79.60 (ISBN 0-86625-375-0). Rourke Corp.
Magorian, James. Keeper of Fire. Hardgrove, Tanya, illus. 78p. (Orig.). (gr. 4-12). 1984. lib. bdg. 10.95 (ISBN 0-89992-388-7); pap. 4.95 (ISBN 0-89992-088-8). Coun India Ed.
Marsh, Jessie. Chinook. 32p. (ps-9). 1976. 2.95 (ISBN 0-89992-041-1). Coun India Ed.
Martini, Teri. Indians. LC 81-15442. (Illus.). 48p. (gr. k-4). 1982. PLB 14.60 (ISBN 0-516-01628-8); pap. 4.95 (ISBN 0-516-41628-6). Childrens.
Matthews, L. Indians. (Illus.). 32p. (gr. 3-8). Date not set. PLB 17.26 (ISBN 0-86625-364-5). Rourke Corp.
May, Robin. Plains Indians of North America. (Illus.). 48p. (gr. 4-8). 1987. PLB 15.33 (ISBN 0-317-60597-6). Rourke Corp.
Merrell, James H. The Catawbas. Porter, Frank W., III, intro. by. (Illus.). 112p. (gr. 5 up). 1989. 17.95 (ISBN 1-55546-694-X). Chelsea Hse.
Morgan, Buford. Quest for Quivera: Coronado's Exploration into Southern U. S. 189p. (gr. 10 up). 1990. 15.95 (ISBN 0-89992-425-5); pap. 9.95 (ISBN 0-89992-125-6). Coun India Ed.
Muller, Carrel & Muller, Brenda. Louisiana Indians. Muller, Carrel & Muller, Brenda, illus. 64p. (gr. 3 up). 1985. 7.50 (ISBN 0-915785-01-3). Bonjour Books.
Native Americans. (Illus.). 32p. (ps-8). pap. 29.50 (ISBN 0-87474-347-8). Smithsonian.
North American Indian. (gr. 4-6). pap. 2.95 (ISBN 0-8431-4254-5). Price Stern.
Ourada, Patricia. The Menominee. (Illus.). (gr. 5 up). 1990. 17.95 (ISBN 1-55546-715-6). Chelsea Hse.
The Plains Indian Book. (gr. 1-6). 1974. pap. 3.95 (ISBN 0-918858-02-X). Fun Pub AZ.
Porter, Frank W. The Coast Salish Peoples. (Illus.). (gr. 5 up). 1989. 17.95 (ISBN 1-55546-701-6). Chelsea Hse.
The Potawatomi: Great Lakes. 112p. (gr. 7-12). PLB 16.95 (ISBN 0-685-21873-2, 201240). Know Unltd.
Reyhner, Jon. Heart Butte: A Blackfeet Indian Community. (Illus.). 24p. (gr. k-4). 1984. pap. 1.95 (ISBN 0-89992-097-7). Coun India Ed.
Roop, Peter. Little Blaze & the Buffalo Jump. Wells, Jesse, illus. 28p. (Orig.). (gr. 3-8). 1984. lib. bdg. 6.45 (ISBN 0-89992-389-5); pap. 1.95 (ISBN 0-89992-089-6). Coun India Ed.
Ruskin, Thelma. Indians of the Tidewater Country: Of Maryland, Virginia, Delaware & North Carolina. Buchanan, Carol & Ruskin, Robert, eds. Ruskin, Robert, illus. & intro. by. LC 85-73263. 132p. (gr. 4-5). 1986. casebound 15.00 (ISBN 0-317-46003-X). MD Hist Pr.
Schneider, Mary J. The Hidatsa. Porter, Frank W., III, intro. by. (Illus.). 112p. (gr. 5 up). 1989. 17.95 (ISBN 1-55546-707-5). Chelsea Hse.
Schultz, John W. Famine Winter. (gr. 4-10). 1984. pap. 2.95 (ISBN 0-89992-094-2). Coun India Ed.
Schuster, Helen H. The Yakima. (Illus.). (gr. 5 up). 1990. 17.95 (ISBN 1-55546-735-0). Chelsea Hse.
Shaffer, Susan L., ed. Anasazi, the Ancient Villagers. Harper-Marinick, Maria & Kinzie, Mable L., illus. (gr. 4). 1987. incl. 30 student bklts. & 1 tchr's. resource binder which contains poster, lesson plans, overhead transparencies, 1 realia, color slides & audio-cassette 294.43 (ISBN 0-934351-13-9); tchr's. resource binder only 197.95 (ISBN 0-934351-24-4); student's bklt. only 4.95 (ISBN 0-934351-29-5). Heard Mus.
—Native Peoples of the Southwest. (Illus., Orig.). (gr. 2-6). 1987. incl. 5 tchr. resource binders & 150 student bklts. Each binder contains lesson plans, slides, audio-cassette, overhead transparencies, realias, artifact, poster & 30 student bklts. 1472.15 (ISBN 0-934351-00-7). Heard Mus.
—O'odham, Indians of the Sonoran Desert. Harper-Marinick, Maria & Kinzie, Mable B., illus. (gr. 5). 1987. incl. 30 student bklts. & 1 tchr's. resource binder which contains poster, lesson plans, overhead transparencies, 1 realia, color slides & audio-cassette 294.43 (ISBN 0-934351-14-7); tchr's. resource binder only 197.95 (ISBN 0-934351-25-2); student bklt. only 4.95 (ISBN 0-934351-30-9). Heard Mus.
Shemie, Bonnie. Houses of Bark: Tipi, Wigwam, & Longhouse. Shemie, Bonnie, illus. 24p. (gr. 3-7). 1990. 12.95 (ISBN 0-88776-246-8). Tundra Bks.
—Maisons D'Ecorce: Tipi, Wigwam et Longue Maison. Shemie, Bonnie, illus. 24p. (gr. 3-7). 1990. 12.95 (ISBN 0-88776-256-5). Tundra Bks.
Shields, Allan. Tragedy of Tenaya. (gr. 6). 1974. 3.95 (ISBN 0-89992-043-8). Coun India Ed.
Silverberg, Robert. The Moundbuilders. LC 85-25953. 276p. 1986. pap. 7.95 (ISBN 0-8214-0839-9). Ohio U Pr.
Simmons, William S. The Narragansett. Porter, Frank W., III, intro. by. (Illus.). 112p. (gr. 5 up). 1989. 17.95 (ISBN 1-55546-718-0). Chelsea Hse.
Spizzirri Publishing Co. Staff. California Indians: An Educational Coloring Book. Spizzirri, Linda, ed. (Illus.). 32p. (gr. 1-8). 1986. pap. 1.95 (ISBN 0-86545-080-3). Spizzirri.
—Plains Indians: An Educational Coloring Book. Spizzirri, Linda, ed. Spizzirri, Peter M., illus. 32p. (gr. 1-8). 1981. pap. 1.95 (ISBN 0-86545-025-0). Spizzirri.
—Southeast Indians: An Educational Coloring Book. Spizzirri, Linda, ed. (Illus.). 32p. (gr. k-5). 1985. pap. 1.95 (ISBN 0-86545-065-X). Spizzirri.
—Southwest Indians: An Educational Coloring Book. Spizzirri, Linda, ed. (Illus.). 32p. (gr. 1-8). 1986. pap. 1.95 (ISBN 0-86545-075-7). Spizzirri.
Stan, S. The Ojibwe. (Illus.). 32p. (gr. 5-8). 1989. lib. bdg. 13.26 (ISBN 0-86625-381-5). Rourke Corp.
Stanley, Samuel & Oberg, Pearl. The Hunt. 32p. (gr. 5-9). 1976. pap. 2.95 (ISBN 0-89992-047-0). Coun India Ed.
Tanner, Helen H. The Ojibwa. (Illus.). (gr. 5 up). 1992. 17.95 (ISBN 1-55546-721-0). Chelsea Hse.
Throssel, Richard. Blue Thunder. 32p. (gr. 6-12). 1976. 2.95 (ISBN 0-89992-046-2). Coun India Ed.
Trafzer, Clifford. The Chinook. Porter, Frank W., III, intro. by. (Illus.). 112p. (gr. 5 up). 1990. 17.95 (ISBN 1-55546-698-2). Chelsea Hse.
Trafzer, Clifford E. California's Indians & the Gold Rush. LC 89-64434. (Illus.). 61p. (Orig.). (gr. 4-7). 1990. pap. 10.95 (ISBN 0-940113-21-X). Sierra Oaks Pub.
Tunis, Edwin. Indians. rev. ed. Tunis, Edwin, illus. LC 78-60175. 160p. (gr. 5 up). 1979. Repr. of 1959 ed. PLB 24.89 (ISBN 0-690-01283-7, Crowell Jr Bks). HarpC Child Bks.
Upton, Richard. The Indian As a Soldier at Fort Custer, Montana 1890-1895: Lieutenant Samuel C. Robertson's First Cavalry Crow Indian Contingent. Remington, Frederic & Goff, O. S., illus. LC 83-80826. 147p. (gr. 7-12). 1983. 27.50 (ISBN 0-912783-00-1). Upton Sons.
Vallejo, Mariano, et al. Great Indians of California. Knill, Harry, ed. (Illus.). 48p. (gr. 6). 1981. pap. 3.95 (ISBN 0-88388-087-3). Bellerophon Bks.
Vandervelde, Marjorie. Across the Tundra. (gr. 4-12). 1972. 2.95 (ISBN 0-89992-053-5). Coun India Ed.
—Could It Be Old Hiari. (gr. 5-9). 1975. 2.95 (ISBN 0-89992-040-3). Coun India Ed.
—Sam & the Golden People. (gr. 4-9). 1972. 1.95 (ISBN 0-89992-027-6). Coun India Ed.
Waldman, Carl. Encyclopedia of Native American Tribes. Braun, Molly, illus. 308p. 1987. 40.00x (ISBN 0-8160-1421-3). Facts on File.
Walens, Stanley. The Kwakiutl. (Illus.). (gr. 5 up). 1992. 17.95 (ISBN 1-55546-711-3). Chelsea Hse.
Warner, Rita, illus. North American Indians Color & Story Album. 32p. (Orig.). 1978. pap. 4.50 (ISBN 0-8431-1727-3). Price Stern.
Warren, Betsy. Indians Who Lived in Texas. Warren, Betsy, illus. LC 71-76607. 48p. (gr. 2 up). 1981. Repr. of 1970 ed. lib. bdg. 10.95 (ISBN 0-937460-02-8). Hendrick-Long.
—Let's Remember...Indians of Texas. Warren, Betsy, illus. 32p. (gr. 3-7). 1981. pap. 4.50 (ISBN 0-937460-03-6). Hendrick-Long.
Warren, Elizabeth. I Can Read About Indians. LC 74-24880. (Illus.). (gr. 2-4). 1975. pap. 1.95 (ISBN 0-89375-061-1). Troll Assocs.
Watson, Jane W. The First Americans: Tribes of North America. Howell, Troy, illus. (gr. 1-4). 1980. Pantheon.
Weinstein-Farson, Laurie. The Wampanoag. Porter, Frank, intro. by. (Illus.). 104p. (gr. 5 up). 1988. lib. bdg. 17.95x (ISBN 1-55546-733-4); pap. 9.95 (ISBN 0-7910-0368-X). Chelsea Hse.
Weiss, Malcolm E. Sky Watchers of Ages Past. McFadden, Eliza, illus. (gr. 5-9). 1982. 7.95 (ISBN 0-395-29525-4). HM.
Wheeler, M. J. First Came the Indians. Houston, James, illus. LC 82-13916. 32p. (gr. 1-5). 1983. 11.95 (ISBN 0-689-50258-3, M K McElderry). Macmillan Child Grp.
Wilson, Terry P. The Osage. Porter, Frank, intro. by. (Illus.). 104p. (gr. 5 up). 1988. lib. bdg. 17.95x (ISBN 1-55546-722-9). Chelsea Hse.
Wolfson, Evelyn. American Indian Tools & Ornaments. 1981. 8.95 (ISBN 0-679-20509-8). McKay.
—From Abenaki to Zuni: A Dictionary of Native American Tribes. Bock, William S., photos by. (gr. 5 up). 1988. 17.95 (ISBN 0-8027-6789-3); PLB 18.85 (ISBN 0-8027-6790-7). Walker & Co.
Wood, J. Walter. Son of the Dine'. (gr. 5-9). 1972. 2.95 (ISBN 0-89992-023-3). Coun India Ed.
Wunder, John R. The Kiowa. (Illus.). (gr. 5 up). 1989. 17.95 (ISBN 1-55546-710-5). Chelsea Hse.

INDIANS OF NORTH AMERICA–ALGONKIN INDIANS–FICTION

Cohlene, Terri. Little Firefly: An Algonquian Legend. (gr. 4-7). 1990. pap. 3.95 (ISBN 0-8167-2363-X). Troll Assocs.

INDIANS OF NORTH AMERICA–ALGONQUIAN INDIANS

D'Apice, Rita & D'Apice, Mary. Algonquian. (Illus.). 32p. (gr. 5-8). 1990. lib. bdg. 13.26 (ISBN 0-86625-388-2); lib. bdg. 9.95s.p. (ISBN 0-685-36386-4). Rourke Corp.
Thompson, Dorothea M. The Sokokis: Native Americans of New Hampshire. Thompson, Brownlow L., illus. 150p. (Orig.). (gr. 4). 1986. pap. 9.95x (ISBN 0-931947-50-2). Thompson Pr.

INDIANS OF NORTH AMERICA–AMUSEMENTS

see Indians of North America–Games; Indians of North America–Social Life and Customs

INDIANS OF NORTH AMERICA–ANTIQUITIES

see also Mounds and Mound Builders

Johnson, Elden. The Prehistoric Peoples of Minnesota. rev. ed. LC 87-32663. (Illus.). 35p. (gr. 9-12). 1988. pap. 3.95 (ISBN 0-87351-223-5). Minn Hist.
Smith, Howard E., Jr. All about Arrowheads & Spear Points. Dewey, Jennifer O., illus. 80p. (gr. 4-7). 1989. 14.95 (ISBN 0-8050-0892-6). H Holt & Co.
Snow, Dean R. The Archaeology of North America. Porter, Frank W., III, intro. by. (Illus.). 128p. (gr. 5 up). 1989. 17.95 (ISBN 1-55546-691-5). Chelsea Hse.
Wheat, Pam & Whorton, Brenda, eds. Clues from the Past: A Resource Book on Archeology. Thompson, Eileen, illus. 200p. (gr. 3 up). 1990. pap. 17.95 (ISBN 0-937460-65-6). Hendrick-Long.
Wood, Marian. Ancient America. 1990. 17.95 (ISBN 0-8160-2210-0). Facts on File.

INDIANS OF NORTH AMERICA–APACHE INDIANS

Doherty, Craig A. & Doherty, Katherine M. The Apaches & Navajos. (Illus.). 64p. (gr. 3-5). 1989. PLB 11.90 (ISBN 0-531-10743-4). Watts.
—The Apaches & Navajos. (Illus.). 64p. (gr. 3 up). 1991. pap. 4.95 (ISBN 0-531-15602-8). Watts.
Levin, Beatrice & Vanderveld, Marjorie. Me Run Fast Good: Biographies of Tewanima (Hopi), Carlos Montezuma (Apache) & John Horse (Seminole) 32p. (gr. 5-9). 1983. pap. 2.95 (ISBN 0-89992-087-X). Coun India Ed.
McCall, Barbara. Apache. (Illus.). 32p. (gr. 5-8). 1990. lib. bdg. 13.26 (ISBN 0-86625-384-X); lib. bdg. 9.95s.p. (ISBN 0-685-36387-2). Rourke Corp.
McKissack, Patricia. The Apache. LC 84-7803. (Illus.). 48p. (gr. k-4). 1984. lib. bdg. 14.60 (ISBN 0-516-01925-2); pap. 4.95 (ISBN 0-516-41925-0). Childrens.
Melody, Michael E. The Apache. Porter, Frank, intro. by. (Illus.). 104p. (gr. 5 up). 1988. 17.95 (ISBN 1-55546-689-3); pap. 9.95 (ISBN 0-7910-0352-3). Chelsea Hse.
Shaffer, Susan L., ed. Inde, the Western Apache. Harper-Marinick, Maria & Kinzie, Mable B., illus. (gr. 2). 1987. incl. 30 student bklts. & 1 tchr's. resource binder which contains poster, lesson plans, overhead transparencies, 1 realia, color slides & audio-cassette 294.43 (ISBN 0-934351-11-2); tchr's. resource binder only 197.95 (ISBN 0-934351-22-8); student bklt. only 4.95 (ISBN 0-934351-27-9). Heard Mus.
Shorto, Russell. Geronimo. (Illus.). 144p. (gr. 5-7). 1989. PLB 12.98 (ISBN 0-382-09571-5); pap. 7.95 (ISBN 0-382-09760-2). Silver Burdett Pr.

INDIANS OF NORTH AMERICA–APACHE INDIANS–FICTION

Martinello, Marian, et al. Hopes, Prayers & Promises. Shelton, Caroline, illus. 48p. (gr. k-8). 1986. 12.95 (ISBN 0-935857-05-2); pap. write for info. (ISBN 0-935857-06-0). Texart.

INDIANS OF NORTH AMERICA–ART

Baylor, Byrd. When Clay Sings. Bahti, Tom, illus. LC 70-180758. 32p. (ps-3). 1987. Repr. of 1977 ed. 12.95 (ISBN 0-684-18829-5, Scribners Young Read). Macmillan Child Grp.

—When Clay Sings. Bahti, Tom, illus. LC 86-20587. 32p. (gr. 1-4). 1987. pap. 3.95 (ISBN 0-689-71106-9, Aladdin). Macmillan Child Grp.

Gates, Frieda. North American Indian Masks. Gates, Frieda, illus. 64p. (gr. 5 up). 1982. 8.95 (ISBN 0-8027-6462-2); lib. bdg. 9.85 (ISBN 0-8027-6463-0). Walker & Co.

Highwater, Jamake. Many Smokes, Many Moons: A Chronology of American Indian History Through Indian Art. LC 77-17475. 128p. 1978. 15.95 (ISBN 0-685-35100-9, Lipp Jr Bks). HarpC Child Bks.

McNutt, Nan. The Bentwood Box. 3rd ed. Osawa, Yasu & Jackson, Nathan, illus. 36p. (Orig.). (gr. 3-8). 1989. pap. text ed. 9.95 (ISBN 0-9614534-0-0). N McNutt Assocs.

—The Button Blanket. 2nd ed. Osawa, Yasu & Dawson, Nancy, illus. 44p. (gr. k-3). 1989. pap. 7.95 (ISBN 0-9614534-1-9). N McNutt Assocs.

—The Button Blanket. 2nd ed. (Illus.). 44p. (gr. k-3). 1989. pap. 7.95 (ISBN 0-9614534-3-5). Workshop Pubns.

—The Cedar Plank Mask. (Illus.). 34p. (gr. 3-6). 1991. pap. 9.95 (ISBN 0-9614534-2-7). N McNutt Assocs.

—The Northwest Coast Indian Art Series, 3 bks. Osawa, Yasu, et al, illus. 118p. (gr. 2-9). 1991. Set. pap. 29.85 (ISBN 0-9614534-4-3). N McNutt Assocs.

Three activity books for children, ages 7 through 14, presenting the art of the Northwest Coast Indians as seen on boxes, ceremonial blankets & masks. Through the use of puzzles, games, designs, & illustrated stories by Yasu Osawa, children will explore the traditional & contemporary art & culture. Each book is packed with Northwest Coast Indian designs. These designs have been created by one of the following well known Indian artists, Nathon Jackson (Tlingit), Nancy Dawson (Kwakiutl), George David (Nuu-chah-nulth), & Greg Colfax (Makah). A special treat for the adults is the adult teaching guide with that "something extra." You will find this book an invaluable resource providing background information & ideas to use with groups of children in scouting or the classroom. The series includes three colored activity sheets for making a model bentwood box, button blanket, & cedar plank mask.
Publisher Provided Annotation.

Villasenor, David. Tapestries in Sand: The Spirit of Indian Sandpainting. rev. ed. (Illus.). 112p. (gr. 4 up). 1966. 14.95 (ISBN 0-911010-23-8); pap. 7.95 (ISBN 0-911010-22-X). Naturegraph.

Wesche, Alice. Wild Brothers of the Indians: As Pictured by the Ancient Americans. LC 77-79064. (Illus.). (gr. 3-8). 1977. pap. 4.95 (ISBN 0-918080-21-5). Treasure Chest.

INDIANS OF NORTH AMERICA–BIOGRAPHY

Bulla, Clyde R. Squanto, Friend of the Pilgrims. 112p. 1990. pap. 2.75 (ISBN 0-590-44055-1). Scholastic Inc.

Capps, Benjamin. The Great Chiefs. LC 75-744. (Illus.). (gr. 7 up). 1975. 19.93 (ISBN 0-8094-1494-5, Pub. by Time-Life). Silver Burdett Pr.

Chief Joseph's Own Story As Told by Chief Joseph in 1879. (gr. 4 up). 1972. 2.95 (ISBN 0-89992-019-5). Coun India Ed.

D'Aulaire, Ingri & D'Aulaire, Edgar P. Pocahontas. D'Aulaire, Ingri & D'Aulaire, Edgar P., illus. 48p. (gr. 1-4). 1985. pap. 13.95 (ISBN 0-385-07454-9). Doubleday.

Eastman, Charles A. Indian Boyhood. Blumenschein, E. L., illus. LC 68-58282. (gr. 3-7). pap. 4.95 (ISBN 0-486-22037-0). Dover.

Eckert, Allan W. Blue Jacket: War Chief of Shawnees. LC 69-10656. 177p. (gr. 7 up). 1983. pap. 5.95 (ISBN 0-913428-36-1). Landfall Pr.

Fellers, Charles. Blue Stone: An Anasazi Indian Boy. Hughes, Maxine W., ed. Kyar, Shirley E., illus. LC 89-92548. 61p. (Orig.). (ps-k). 1989. pap. 6.95 (ISBN 0-9625214-7-7). Laughing Fox.

Fellers, Charles L. Red Frog Man: A Hohokam Leader. Hughes, Maxine W., ed. Kyar, Shirley E., illus. 64p. (Orig.). (gr. 1-6). 1990. pap. write for info. (ISBN 0-9625214-4-2). Laughing Fox.

Hatheway, Flora. Chief Plenty Coups: Life of the Crow Indian Chief. (gr. 4). 1971. 2.95 (ISBN 0-89992-005-5). Coun India Ed.

Levin, Beatrice & Vanderveld, Marjorie. Me Run Fast Good: Biographies of Tewanima (Hopi), Carlos Montezuma (Apache) & John Horse (Seminole) 32p. (gr. 5-9). 1983. pap. 2.95 (ISBN 0-89992-087-X). Coun India Ed.

McGovern, Ann. The Defenders. (Illus.). 128p. (Orig.). (gr. 3-7). 1987. pap. 2.50 (ISBN 0-590-40512-8). Scholastic Inc.

Morrison, Dorothy N. Chief Sarah: Sarah Winnemucca's Fight for Indian Rights. (Illus.). 192p. (gr. 4 up). 1990. pap. 5.95 (ISBN 0-87595-204-6). Oregon Hist.

Richards, Dorothy F. Pocahontas, Child-Princess. Nelson, John, illus. LC 78-7719. (gr. k-4). 1978. PLB 10.95 (ISBN 0-89565-035-5). Childs World.

Trenholm, Virginia C. Omen of the Hawks. LC 89-63585. (Illus.). 312p. (gr. 9-12). 1989. 18.95 (ISBN 0-943255-26-0); pap. 9.95 (ISBN 0-943255-35-X). Portfolio Pub.

Upton, H. Indian Chiefs. (Illus.). 32p. (gr. 3-8). 1990. lib. bdg. 17.26 (ISBN 0-86625-400-5). Rourke Corp.

INDIANS OF NORTH AMERICA–CANADA–FICTION

Robinson, Margaret A. A Woman of Her Tribe. LC 90-31534. 144p. (gr. 7 up). 1990. 12.95 (ISBN 0-684-19223-3, Scribners Young Read). Macmillan Child Grp.

INDIANS OF NORTH AMERICA–CAPTIVITIES

Seaver, James E. A Narrative of the Life of Mrs. Mary Jemison. Abrams, George, intro. by. 196p. 1990. pap. text ed. 12.95x (ISBN 0-8156-2491-3). Syracuse U Pr.

INDIANS OF NORTH AMERICA–CAPTIVITIES–FICTION

Richter, Conrad. Light in the Forest. Chappell, Warren, illus. (gr. 6 up). 1966. 17.95 (ISBN 0-394-43314-9). Knopf.

Smith, Mary P. Boy Captive of Old Deerfield. (Illus.). (gr. 5-6). Repr. of 1904 ed. lib. bdg. 17.95x (ISBN 0-89190-961-3, Pub. by River City Pr). Amereon Ltd.

Speare, Elizabeth G. Calico Captive. Mars, Witold T., illus. 288p. (gr. 7-9). 1957. 13.95 (ISBN 0-395-07112-7). HM.

Wisler, G. Clifton. The Raid. LC 85-10152. 128p. (gr. 5-9). 1985. 11.95 (ISBN 0-525-67169-2, Lodestar Bks). Dutton Child Bks.

INDIANS OF NORTH AMERICA–CHEROKEE INDIANS

Bealer, Alex. Only the Names Remain: The Cherokees & the Trail of Tears. Bock, William S., illus. (gr. 4-6). 1972. lib. bdg. 14.95 (ISBN 0-316-08520-0). Little.

Lepthien, Emilie U. The Cherokee. LC 84-27476. (Illus.). 48p. (gr. k-4). 1985. lib. bdg. 14.60 (ISBN 0-516-01938-4); pap. 4.95 (ISBN 0-516-41938-2). Childrens.

—The Mandans. LC 89-22235. 48p. (gr. k-4). 1989. PLB 14.60 (ISBN 0-516-01180-4); pap. 4.95 (ISBN 0-516-41180-2). Childrens.

McCall, B. The Cherokee. (Illus.). 32p. (gr. 5-8). 1989. lib. bdg. 13.26 (ISBN 0-86625-376-9). Rourke Corp.

Perdue, Thea. The Cherokee. Porter, Frank W., III, intro. by. (Illus.). 112p. (Orig.). (gr. 5 up). 1989. 17.95 (ISBN 1-55546-695-8); pap. 9.95 (ISBN 0-7910-0357-4). Chelsea Hse.

Steele, Phillip. The Last of the Cherokee Warriors. 2nd ed. (Illus.). 111p. (gr. 6-12). 1978. 7.95 (ISBN 0-911116-99-0); pap. 5.95 (ISBN 0-88289-203-7). Pelican.

Stein, R. Conrad. The Story of the Trail of Tears. Catrow, David, III, illus. LC 84-28507. 32p. (gr. 3-6). 1985. lib. bdg. 13.27 (ISBN 0-516-04683-7); pap. 3.95 (ISBN 0-516-44683-5). Childrens.

Underwood, Tom. Cherokee Legends & the Trail of Tears. Crowe, Amanda, illus. 32p. (gr. 4-12). 1956. 3.00 (ISBN 0-935741-00-3). Cherokee Pubns.

Underwood, Tom B. The Magic Lake: A Mystical Healing Lake of the Cherokee. Simmons, Shirley, illus. 20p. (gr. 1-3). 1982. 3.00 (ISBN 0-935741-08-9). Cherokee Pubns.

INDIANS OF NORTH AMERICA–CHEROKEE INDIANS–FICTION

Cohlene, Terri. Dancing Drum: A Cherokee Legend. 48p. (gr. 4-7). 1990. pap. 3.95 (ISBN 0-8167-2362-1). Troll Assocs.

Rockwood, Joyce. Groundhog's Horse. Kalin, Victor, illus. LC 77-22676. 128p. (gr. 2-4). 1978. reinforced ed. 12.95 (ISBN 0-8050-1173-0). H Holt & Co.

INDIANS OF NORTH AMERICA–CHEYENNE INDIANS

Fradin, Dennis B. The Cheyenne. LC 87-33792. (Illus.). 48p. (gr. k-4). 1988. PLB 14.60 (ISBN 0-516-01211-8); pap. 4.95 (ISBN 0-516-41211-6). Childrens.

Gilliland, Hap. O'kohome: The Coyote Dog. Hardgrove, Tanya, illus. 47p. (Orig.). (gr. 4-9). 1989. PLB 3.95 (ISBN 0-89992-402-6); pap. 9.95 (ISBN 0-89992-102-7). Coun India Ed.

Henry Tall Bull & Weist, Tom. Cheyenne Legends of Creation. (gr. 4-9). 1972. 2.95 (ISBN 0-89992-025-X). Coun India Ed.

—Cheyenne Warriors. (gr. 4-12). 1976. pap. 2.95 (ISBN 0-89992-015-2). Coun India Ed.

Hoig, Stan. The Cheyenne. Porter, Frank W., III, intro. by. (Illus.). 112p. (gr. 5 up). 1989. 17.95 (ISBN 1-55546-696-6); pap. 9.95 (ISBN 0-7910-0358-2). Chelsea Hse.

Lodge, Sally. Cheyenne. (Illus.). 32p. (gr. 5-8). 1990. lib. bdg. 13.26 (ISBN 0-86625-387-4); lib. bdg. 9.95s.p. (ISBN 0-685-36388-0). Rourke Corp.

Sonneborn, Liz. Cheyenne. (Illus.). 80p. (gr. 2-5). 1992. PLB 12.95 (ISBN 0-7910-1654-4). Chelsea Hse.

INDIANS OF NORTH AMERICA–CHEYENNE INDIANS–FICTION

Cohlene, Terri. Quillworker: A Cheyenne Legend. 48p. (gr. 4-7). 1990. pap. 3.95 (ISBN 0-8167-2358-3). Troll Assocs.

Goble, Paul. Death of the Iron Horse. Goble, Paul, illus. LC 85-28011. 32p. (gr. k-3). 1987. 13.95 (ISBN 0-02-737830-6, Bradbury Pr). Macmillan Child Grp.

INDIANS OF NORTH AMERICA–CHILDREN

Armstrong, Nancy. Navajo Children. (gr. 2-6). 1975. 2.95 (ISBN 0-89992-037-3). Coun India Ed.

Ashabranner, Brent. To Live in Two Worlds: American Indian Youth Today. Conklin, Paul, photos by. (Illus.). (gr. 7-11). Date not set. 13.95 (ISBN 0-396-08321-8, Putnam). Putnam Pub Group.

Chandonnet, Ann. Chief Stephen's Parky: One Year in the Life of an Athapascan Girl. Gilliland, Hap, ed. (Illus.). 72p. (Orig.). (gr. 4-12). 1989. PLB 12.95 (ISBN 0-89992-419-0); pap. 6.95 (ISBN 0-89992-119-1). Coun India Ed.

The Children, Always the Children. 48p. (gr. 4-5). 1989. PLB 10.95. Capstone Pr.

INDIANS OF NORTH AMERICA–CHIPPEWA INDIANS

Osinski, Alice. The Chippewa. LC 86-32687. (Illus.). 48p. (gr. k-4). 1987. PLB 14.60 (ISBN 0-516-01230-4); pap. 4.95 (ISBN 0-516-41230-2). Childrens.

INDIANS OF NORTH AMERICA–CHIPPEWA INDIANS–FICTION

Dietrich, Wilson G. The Adventures of a Chippewa Indian Boy Muckwa. Graves, Helen, ed. LC 89-52120. (Illus.). 71p. (gr. 3-10). 1990. pap. 5.95 (ISBN 1-55523-304-X). Winston-Derek.

Wosmek, Frances. A Brown Bird Singing. Lewin, Ted, illus. LC 85-24002. 160p. (gr. 5-10). 1985. 11.95 (ISBN 0-688-06251-2). Lothrop.

INDIANS OF NORTH AMERICA–CHOCTAW INDIANS

Lepthien, Emilie U. The Choctaw. LC 87-14583. (Illus.). 48p. (gr. k-4). 1987. PLB 14.60 (ISBN 0-516-01240-1); pap. 4.95 (ISBN 0-516-41240-X). Childrens.

McKee, Jesse O. The Choctaw. (Illus.). (gr. 5 up). 1989. 17.95 (ISBN 1-55546-699-0). Chelsea Hse.

INDIANS OF NORTH AMERICA–CHUMASHAN INDIANS

Gibson, Robert O. The Chumash. (Illus.). (gr. 5 up). 1989. 17.95 (ISBN 1-55546-700-8). Chelsea Hse.

Santa Barbara Museum of Natural History. California's Chumash Indians. rev. ed. Powell, Ann, et al, illus. 72p. (ps-4). 1988. pap. 5.95 (ISBN 0-945092-00-8). EZ Nature.

INDIANS OF NORTH AMERICA–COMANCHE INDIANS

Rollings, Willard H. The Comanche. Porter, Frank W., III, intro. by. (Illus.). 112p. (gr. 5 up). 1989. 17.95 (ISBN 1-55546-702-4); pap. 9.95 (ISBN 0-7910-0359-0). Chelsea Hse.

INDIANS OF NORTH AMERICA–COMANCHE INDIANS–FICTION

Harper, Preston F. Warlords of the West: A Story of the Comanche. (Illus.). 150p. (Orig.). (gr. 6-12). 1989. 14.95 (ISBN 0-685-24277-3); pap. 4.95. Borderlands Pr.

INDIANS OF NORTH AMERICA–COSTUME AND ADORNMENT

Authentic North American Arctic Circle Indian Clothing for Special Times. (ps-3). write for info. (ISBN 0-931363-10-1). Celia Totus Enter.

Authentic North American California Indian Clothing for Special Times. (ps-3). write for info. (ISBN 0-931363-09-8). Celia Totus Enter.

Authentic North American Columbia River Plateau & California Indian Cradleboards. (ps-5). write for info. (ISBN 0-931363-15-2). Celia Totus Enter.

Authentic North American Columbia River Plateau Indian Clothing for Special Times. (ps-3). write for info. (ISBN 0-931363-01-2). Celia Totus Enter.

Authentic North American Columbia River Plateau Yakima Indian Clothing for Special Times. (ps-3). write for info. (ISBN 0-931363-00-4). Celia Totus Enter.

Authentic North American Great Basin Indian Clothing for Special Times. (ps-3). write for info. (ISBN 0-931363-06-3). Celia Totus Enter.

Authentic North American Great Basin, Southwest, & Southeast Cradleboards. (ps-5). write for info. (ISBN 0-931363-13-6). Celia Totus Enter.

Authentic North American Indian Baby Cradles. (ps-5). write for info. (ISBN 0-931363-16-0). Celia Totus Enter.

Authentic North American Oregon Indian Clothing for Special Times. (ps-3). write for info. (ISBN 0-931363-11-X). Celia Totus Enter.

Authentic North American Pacific Northwest Coast Indian Clothing for Special Times. (ps-3). write for info. (ISBN 0-931363-02-0). Celia Totus Enter.

Authentic North American Pacific Northwest Coast, Woodlands & Arctic Circle Indian Cradles & Cradleboards. (ps-5). write for info. (ISBN 0-931363-14-4). Celia Totus Enter.

Authentic North American Plains Indian Cradle Boards. (ps-3). write for info. (ISBN 0-931363-12-8). Celia Totus Enter.

Authentic North American Plains Indian Clothing for Special Times. (ps-3). write for info. (ISBN 0-931363-03-9). Celia Totus Enter.

Authentic North American Plains Indian Clothing for Special Times. (ps-3). write for info. (ISBN 0-931363-05-5). Celia Totus Enter.

Authentic North American Southeast Indian Clothing for Special Times. (ps-3). write for info. (ISBN 0-931363-07-1). Celia Totus Enter.

Authentic North American Southwest Indian Clothing for Special Times. (ps-3). write for info. (ISBN 0-931363-04-7). Celia Totus Enter.

Authentic North American Woodland Indian Clothing for Special Times. (ps-3). write for info. (ISBN 0-931363-08-X). Celia Totus Enter.

D'Amato, Janet & D'Amato, Alex. Indian Crafts. D'Amato, Janet & D'Amato, Alex, illus. (gr. 1-4). PLB 12.95 (ISBN 0-87460-088-X). Lion Bks.

Hofsinde, Robert. Indian Costumes. Hofsinde, Robert, illus. LC 68-11895. (gr. 3-7). 1968. PLB 12.88 (ISBN 0-688-31614-X, Morrow Junior Books). Morrow.

—Indian Warriors & Their Weapons. Hofsinde, Robert, illus. LC 65-11041. (gr. 4-7). 1965. PLB 11.88 (ISBN 0-688-31613-1, Morrow Junior Books). Morrow.

INDIANS OF NORTH AMERICA–CREE INDIANS–FICTION

Mowat, Farley. Lost in the Barrens. (Illus.). (gr. 7 up). 1956. 15.95 (ISBN 0-316-58638-2, Joy St Bks). Little.

INDIANS OF NORTH AMERICA–CREEK INDIANS

Green, Michael D. The Creeks. Porter, Frank, intro. by. (Illus.). 104p. (gr. 5 up). 1990. lib. bdg. 17.95x (ISBN 1-55546-703-2). Chelsea Hse.

INDIANS OF NORTH AMERICA–CROW INDIANS

Hagman, Ruth. The Crow. LC 90-37679. (Illus.). 48p. (gr. k-4). 1990. PLB 14.60 (ISBN 0-516-01103-0); pap. 4.95. Childrens.

Hatheway, Flora. Chief Plenty Coups: Life of the Crow Indian Chief. (gr. 4). 1971. 2.95 (ISBN 0-89992-005-5). Coun India Ed.

Hoxie, Frederick E. The Crow. (Illus.). (gr. 5 up). 1989. 17.95 (ISBN 1-55546-704-0); pap. 9.95 (ISBN 0-7910-0379-5). Chelsea Hse.

INDIANS OF NORTH AMERICA–CROW INDIANS–FICTION

McGraw, Eloise J. Moccasin Trail. 256p. (gr. 5-9). 1986. pap. 4.95 (ISBN 0-14-032170-5, Puffin). Puffin Bks.

Sobol, Rose. Woman Chief. 112p. (gr. 5-9). 1979. pap. 1.25 (ISBN 0-440-99657-0, LFL). Dell.

INDIANS OF NORTH AMERICA–CUSTOMS

see Indians of North America–Social Life and Customs

INDIANS OF NORTH AMERICA–DAKOTA INDIANS

Bleeker, Sonia. The Sioux Indians: Hunters & Warriors of the Plains. Sasaki, Kisa N., illus. (gr. 3-6). 1962. PLB 11.88 (ISBN 0-688-31457-0). Morrow Jr Bks.

Hook, John. Sitting Bull & the Plains Indians. (Illus.). 64p. (gr. 4-8). 1987. PLB 12.40 (ISBN 0-531-18102-2, Pub. by Bookwright Pr). Watts.

Stein, R. Conrad. The Story of Wounded Knee. LC 83-6584. (Illus.). 32p. (gr. 3-6). 1983. PLB 13.27 (ISBN 0-516-04665-9); pap. 3.95 (ISBN 0-516-44665-7). Childrens.

INDIANS OF NORTH AMERICA–DAKOTA INDIANS–FICTION

Sandoz, Mari. The Story Catcher. LC 85-31810. (Illus.). 175p. (gr. 7-10). 1986. 5.95 (ISBN 0-8032-9163-9, Bison). U of Nebr Pr.

INDIANS OF NORTH AMERICA–DANCES

DeCesare, Ruth. Myth, Music & Dance of the American Indian. Feldstein, Sandy, et al, eds. Seckler, Judy & Shelly, Walt, illus. 80p. (gr. 4-12). 1988. tchr's. ed. 12.95 (ISBN 0-88284-371-0, 3518); student, 16p 3.95 (ISBN 0-88284-372-9, 3520); Student Songbk., 24p 4.95 (ISBN 0-88284-373-7, 3519); tchr's ed. with cassette 19.95 (ISBN 0-88284-383-4, 3534). Alfred Pub.

INDIANS OF NORTH AMERICA–DELAWARE INDIANS

Myers, Albert C., ed. William Penn's Own Account of Lenni Lenape or Delaware Indians. (Illus.). 96p. (gr. 7 up). 1986. pap. 6.95 (ISBN 0-912608-13-7). Mid Atlantic.

INDIANS OF NORTH AMERICA–DELAWARE INDIANS–FICTION

Harrington, M. R. The Indians of New Jersey: Dickon Among the Lenapes. LC 63-15519. (Illus.). (gr. 4-6). 1963. pap. 8.95x (ISBN 0-685-04412-2); pap. 8.95x (ISBN 0-8135-0425-2). Rutgers U Pr.

INDIANS OF NORTH AMERICA–DWELLINGS

Brandt, Keith. Indian Homes. Guzzi, George, illus. LC 84-2650. 32p. (gr. 3-6). 1985. PLB 9.49 (ISBN 0-8167-0126-1); pap. text ed. 2.95 (ISBN 0-8167-0127-X). Troll Assocs.

Nashone. Where Indians Live: American Indian Houses. Smith, Louise, illus. 37p. (Orig.). (gr. k-6). 1989. pap. 6.95 (ISBN 0-940113-16-3). Sierra Oaks Pub.

INDIANS OF NORTH AMERICA–FICTION

Adams, Patricia. Pocahontas, Indian Princess. (Orig.). (gr. k-6). 1987. pap. 2.95 (ISBN 0-440-47067-6, YB). Dell.

Armstrong, Nancy. Navajo Long Walk. (gr. 4-9). 1983. pap. 4.95 (ISBN 0-89992-083-7). Coun India Ed.

Asch, Connie. Tohono O'Odham Indian Coloring Book. rev. ed. (Illus.). 32p. (gr. 2-6). 1990. pap. 2.50 (ISBN 0-918080-60-6). Treasure Chest.

Banks, Lynne R. The Indian in the Cupboard. Cole, Brock, illus. 192p. (gr. 4-7). 1982. pap. 3.50 (ISBN 0-380-60012-9, Camelot). Avon.

—Return of the Indian. Geldart, William, illus. LC 85-31119. 192p. (gr. 4-6). 1986. pap. 13.95 (ISBN 0-385-23497-X). Doubleday.

—The Return of the Indian. (gr. 3-7). 1987. pap. 3.50 (ISBN 0-380-70284-3, Camelot). Avon.

—The Return of the Indian. (Illus.). (gr. k-9). 1988. pap. 2.95 (ISBN 0-318-36505-7). Scholastic Inc.

—The Return of the Indian. large type ed. (Illus.). 227p. 1989. PLB 15.95 (ISBN 1-55736-104-5, Crnrstn Bks). ABC-CLIO.

—The Secret of the Indian. 160p. 1990. pap. 3.50 (ISBN 0-380-71040-4, Camelot). Avon.

Batdorf, Carol. Seawolf: Building a Canoe. Clark, Patricia, illus. 24p. (Orig.). (gr. 1-6). 1990. pap. 4.95 (ISBN 0-88839-247-8). Hancock House.

—Tinka: A Day in a Little Girl's Life. Batdorf, Carol, illus. 32p. (Orig.). (gr. 1-6). 1990. pap. 5.95 (ISBN 0-88839-249-4). Hancock House.

Baylor, Byrd. Hawk, I'm Your Brother. Parnall, Peter, illus. LC 75-39296. 48p. (ps-3). 1976. 13.95 (ISBN 0-684-14571-5, Scribners Young Read). Macmillan Child Grp.

Benchley, Nathaniel. Red Fox & His Canoe. Lobel, Arnold, illus. LC 64-16650. 64p. (gr. k-3). 1964. PLB 11.89 (ISBN 0-06-020476-1). HarpC Child Bks.

Blood, Charles L. & Link, Martin. The Goat in the Rug. Parker, Nancy W., illus. LC 80-17315. 40p. (ps-3). 1984. Repr. of 1976 ed. 14.95 (ISBN 0-02-710920-8, Four Winds). Macmillan Child Grp.

Borland, Hal. When the Legends Die. 224p. (gr. 6-12). 1984. pap. 3.50 (ISBN 0-553-25738-2). Bantam.

Bowne, Elizabeth. Cocha: The Story of a Uru Indian Boy Who Lives on a Floating Island. Morrison, Cathy, illus. LC 89-15062. 116p. (gr. 4-10). 1990. 14.95 (ISBN 0-917665-40-6); pap. 9.95 (ISBN 0-917665-41-4). Bookmakers Guild.

Brown, Towana J. Raglagger. Brown, Becky, illus. LC 89-90647. 168p. (Orig.). (gr. 5-7). 1989. pap. 3.50 (ISBN 0-9622060-2-4). T J Brown.

Brown, Vinson. Return of the Indian Spirit. Johnson, W. Cameron, illus. LC 81-65887. 64p. (gr. 5 up). 1982. pap. 5.95 (ISBN 0-89087-401-8). Celestial Arts.

Coerr, Eleanor. The Bell Ringer & the Pirates. Sandin, Joan, illus. LC 82-47700. 64p. (gr. k-3). 1983. PLB 10.89 (ISBN 0-06-021355-8). HarpC Child Bks.

Cohlene, Terri. Clamshell Boy: A Makah Legend. 48p. (gr. 4-7). 1990. pap. 3.95 (ISBN 0-8167-2361-3). Troll Assocs.

Connolly, Thomas E. A Coeur D'Alene Indian Story. 85p. Date not set. pap. 4.50 (ISBN 0-685-38689-9). Ye Galleon.

Cooper, James Fenimore. Deerslayer. (gr. 6 up). 1964. pap. 1.25 (ISBN 0-8049-0031-0, CL31). Airmont.

—The Deerslayer. 528p. (gr. 9-12). 1991. pap. 3.50 (ISBN 0-553-21085-8, Bantam Classics). Bantam.

—The Deerslayer: or The First War-Path. Wyeth, N. C., illus. LC 90-34326. 480p. 1990. 22.95 (ISBN 0-684-19224-1, Scribners Young Read); deluxe ed. 75.00 (ISBN 0-684-19234-9, Scribner). Macmillan Child Grp.

—Last of the Mohicans. (gr. 6 up). 1964. pap. 3.50 (ISBN 0-8049-0005-1, CL-5). Airmont.

—The Last of the Mohicans. new & abr. ed. Farr, Naunerle, ed. Carrillo, Fred, illus. (gr. 4-12). 1977. pap. text ed. 2.95 (ISBN 0-88301-267-7). Pendulum Pr.

—The Last of the Mohicans. Wyeth, N. C., illus. LC 86-17694. 376p. 1986. 24.95 (ISBN 0-684-18711-6, Scribners Young Read); deluxe ed. 75.00 (ISBN 0-684-18716-7, Scribner). Macmillan Child Grp.

—The Last of the Mohicans. 24.95 (ISBN 0-89968-254-5). Buccaneer Bks.

—Pathfinder. (gr. 6 up). 1964. pap. 2.95 (ISBN 0-8049-0035-3, CL-35). Airmont.

Curry, Jane L., ed. Back in the Beforetime: Tales of the California Indians. Watts, James, illus. LC 86-21339. 144p. (gr. 3-7). 1987. 13.95 (ISBN 0-689-50410-1, M K McElderry). Macmillan Child Grp.

Cutler, Ebbitt. I Once Knew an Indian Woman. Johnson, Bruce, illus. 72p. (gr. 5 up). 1985. (Dist. by U of Toronto Pr); pap. 5.95 (ISBN 0-88776-068-6). Tundra Bks.

Dalgliesh, Alice. The Courage of Sarah Noble. Weisgard, Leonard, illus. LC 54-5922. 64p. (gr. 1-5). 1987. Repr. of 1954 ed. 12.95 (ISBN 0-684-18830-9, Scribners Young Read). Macmillan Child Grp.

Davis, R. Dell. Ashes & Sparks. LC 89-81718. (Illus.). 184p. 1989. Set. incl. audiotape & slipcase 24.95 (ISBN 0-9616736-1-3). J Franklin.

De Paola, Tomie, ed. & illus. The Legend of the Indian Paintbrush. LC 87-20160. 40p. (ps-2). 1988. 13.95 (ISBN 0-399-21534-4, Putnam). Putnam Pub Group.

Desai, Anita. The Village by the Sea: An Indian Family Story. large type ed. 320p. (gr. 5 up). 1988. lib. bdg. 16.95 (ISBN 0-7451-0655-2, Pub. by Chivers Pr UK). G K Hall.

Dygert, Janice. Red Horse & the Buffalo Robe Man. Gilliland, Hap, ed. (Illus.). (gr. 4-8). 1978. 2.95 (ISBN 0-89992-074-8). Coun India Ed.

Fleischman, Paul. Saturnalia. LC 89-36380. 128p. (gr. 7 up). 1990. 12.95 (ISBN 0-06-021912-2); PLB 12.89 (ISBN 0-06-021913-0). HarpC Child Bks.

Friskey, Margaret. Indian Two Feet & His Eagle Feather. Hawkinson, John & Hawkinson, Lucy, illus. LC 67-20101. 64p. (gr. k-3). 1967. PLB 15.93 (ISBN 0-516-03503-7). Childrens.

—Indian Two Feet & His Horse. (Illus.). 64p. (gr. k-3). 1959. 15.93 (ISBN 0-516-03501-0). Childrens.

—Indian Two Feet & the ABC Moose Hunt. Hawkinson, John, illus. LC 77-4467. 32p. (gr. k-2). 1977. PLB 14.60 (ISBN 0-516-03500-2). Childrens.

—Indian Two Feet & the Wolf Cubs. Hawkinson, John, illus. 64p. (gr. k-3). 1971. PLB 15.93 (ISBN 0-516-03506-1). Childrens.

—Indian Two Feet Rides Alone. Hankinson, John, illus. LC 80-12688. 32p. (gr. k-3). 1980. PLB 14.60 (ISBN 0-516-03523-1). Childrens.

Fritz, Jean. The Good Giants & The Bad Pukwudgies. De Paola, Tomie, illus. 40p. (gr. 3-7). 1982. (Sandcastle Bks); pap. 5.95 (ISBN 0-399-21732-0, Sandcastle Bks). Putnam Pub Group.

Garaway, Margaret K. Dezbah & the Dancing Tumbleweeds. Lowmiller, Cathie, illus. 175p. (Orig.). (gr. 3-5). 1990. pap. 7.95 (ISBN 0-918080-50-9). Treasure Chest.

George, Jean C. The Talking Earth. LC 82-48850. 160p. (gr. 5 up). 1987. pap. 3.95 (ISBN 0-06-440212-6, Trophy). HarpC Child Bks.

Girion, Barbara. Indian Summer. 1990. pap. 11.95 (ISBN 0-590-42636-2). Scholastic Inc.

Goble, Paul, retold by. & illus. Iktomi & the Boulder: A Plains Indian Story. LC 87-35789. 32p. (ps-2). 1988. 14.95 (ISBN 0-531-05760-7); PLB 14.99 (ISBN 0-531-08360-8). Orchard Bks Watts.

Godden, Rumer. The Valiant Chatti-Maker. Roy, Jeroo, illus. LC 83-7000. 64p. (gr. 3-7). 1983. pap. 9.95 (ISBN 0-670-74236-8). Viking Child Bks.

Gregory, Kristiana. Jenny of the Tetons. 144p. (gr. 5-7). 1989. 13.95 (ISBN 0-15-200480-7). HarBraceJ.

—Legend of Jimmy Spoon. 1990. 15.95 (ISBN 0-15-200506-4). HarbraceJ.

Gregory, Kristina. Jenny of the Tetons. 162p. (gr. 4-7). 1991. pap. 4.95 (ISBN 0-15-200481-5, HJ). HarBraceJ.

Hale, Janet C. The Owl's Song. 144p. (gr. 7 up). 1976. pap. 2.50 (ISBN 0-380-00605-7, 60212-1, Flare). Avon.

Highwater, Jamake. The Ceremony of Innocence. LC 84-48334. 192p. (gr. 7 up). 1985. 12.95 (ISBN 0-06-022301-4); PLB 12.89 (ISBN 0-06-022302-2). HarpC Child Bks.

—I Wear the Morning Star. LC 85-45258. 160p. (gr. 7 up). 1986. 12.95 (ISBN 0-06-022355-3); PLB 12.89 (ISBN 0-06-022356-1). HarpC Child Bks.

Hill, Gerald N. The Year of the Indians. Hill, Gerald, Jr., illus. 54p. (Orig.). (gr. 4-7). 1985. pap. 4.95 (ISBN 0-912133-06-6). Hilltop Pub Co.

Hobbs, Will. Bearstone. 144p. (gr. 6-9). 1989. 12.95 (ISBN 0-689-31496-5, Atheneum Child Bk). Macmillan Child Grp.

Hoff, Syd. Little Chief. Hoff, Syd, illus. LC 61-12098. 64p. (gr. k-3). 1961. PLB 10.89 (ISBN 0-685-02062-2). HarpC Child Bks.

The Horsecatcher. LC 86-4360. 192p. (gr. 5-8). 1986. 17.95x (ISBN 0-8032-4166-6); pap. 6.95 (ISBN 0-8032-9160-4, Bison). U of Nebr Pr.

Houston, James. The Falcon Bow: An Arctic Legend. LC 86-5378. 96p. (gr. 3-7). 1986. 12.95 (ISBN 0-689-50411-X, M K McElderry). Macmillan Child Grp.

Hudson, Jan. Dawn Rider. 192p. (gr. 6 up). 1990. 14.95 (ISBN 0-399-22178-6, Philomel Bks). Putnam Pub Group.

Huff, Gary. Indian Tales That Teach. 80p. (gr. k-4). 1987. saddle stitch 8.50x (ISBN 0-87322-129-X, 4919, YMCA USA). Human Kinetics.

Irwin, Hadley. We Are Mesquakie, We Are One. LC 80-19000. 128p. (gr. 5 up). 1980. 7.95 (ISBN 0-912670-85-1). Feminist Pr.

Jackson, Helen H. Ramona: Wyeth Edition. Wyeth, N. C., illus. (gr. 6 up). 1939. Repr. of 1884 ed. 17.95 (ISBN 0-316-45467-2). Little.

James, J. Alison. Sing for a Gentle Rain. LC 90-639. 224p. (gr. 7 up). 1990. 14.95 (ISBN 0-689-31561-9, Atheneum Child Bk). Macmillan Child Grp.

Kachel, Limana. Homer Littlebird's Rabbit: Cheyenne Indian Story for Children. 32p. (ps-2). 1983. pap. 2.95 (ISBN 0-89992-084-5). Coun India Ed.

Katz, Welwyn W. False Face. LC 88-12847. 176p. (gr. 5-9). 1988. 13.95 (ISBN 0-689-50456-X, M K McElderry). Macmillan Child Grp.

Kissinger, Rosemary. Quanah Parker: Comanche Chief. (Illus.). 96p. (ps-8). 1991. 12.95 (ISBN 0-88289-785-3). Pelican.

Lampman, Evelyn S. Treasure Mountain. (Illus.). 207p. (gr. 4). 1990. pap. 6.95 (ISBN 0-87595-231-3). Oregon Hist.

The Last of the Mohicans. (Illus.). (gr. 3-5). 3.50. Ladybird Bks.

Levin, Betty. Brother Moose. LC 89-34437. (gr. 5 up). 1990. 12.95 (ISBN 0-688-09266-7). Greenwillow.

Levitt, Paul M. & Guralnick, Elissa. The Stolen Appaloosa & Other Indian Stories. LC 88-6133. (Illus.). 88p. (Orig.). (gr. 3-8). 1988. 12.95 (ISBN 0-917665-19-8). Bookmakers Guild.

Longfellow, Henry Wadsworth. Hiawatha. LC 83-26972. (Illus.). (gr. 2-5). 1984. PLB 16.67 (ISBN 0-8172-2106-9); PLB 27.99 incl. cassette (ISBN 0-8172-2237-5); pap. 9.27 (ISBN 0-8172-2250-2); pap. 23.95 incl. cassette (ISBN 0-8172-2265-0); cassette 14.00 (ISBN 0-685-09531-2). Raintree Pubs.

McNickle, D'Arcy. Runner in the Sun. Houser, Allan C., illus. LC 87-5986. 260p. 1987. pap. 10.95 (ISBN 0-8263-0974-7). U of NM Pr.

Marsh, Carole. Those Whose Names Were Terrible. Rhodes, Priscilla, illus. (Orig.). (gr. 4-8). 1983. pap. 14.95 (ISBN 0-935326-48-0). Gallopade Pub Group.

Martin, Bill, Jr. & Archambault, John. Knots on a Counting Rope. Rand, Ted, illus. LC 87-14832. 32p. (gr. k-3). 1987. 14.95 (ISBN 0-8050-0571-4). H Holt & Co.

Mayo, Gretchen W. North American Indian Stories, 4 vols. Mayo, Gretchen W., illus. 256p. (gr. 5 up). 1991. Set. pap. 23.80 (ISBN 0-8027-7341-9). Walker & Co.

Monjo, F. N. Indian Summer. Lobel, Anita, illus. LC 78-20264. 192p. (gr. k-3). 1968. PLB 11.89 (ISBN 0-06-024328-7). HarpC Child Bks.

Morris, Oradel N. I Hear the Song of the Houmas: J'Entends La Chanson des Houmas. LC 88-92449. (Illus.). (gr. 4-10). 1991. write for info. (ISBN 0-944064-04-3). Paupieres Pub.

O'Dell, Scott. Island of the Blue Dolphins. Lewin, Ted, illus. 192p. (gr. 5 up). 1990. 17.95 (ISBN 0-395-53680-4). HM.

—The Serpent Never Sleeps: A Novel of Jamestown & Pocahontas. Lewin, Ted, illus. 240p. (gr. 5 up). 1987. 15.95 (ISBN 0-395-44242-7). HM.

—Streams to the River, River to the Sea: A Novel of Sacagawea. 1986. 14.95 (ISBN 0-395-40430-4). HM.

—Streams to the River, River to the Sea: A Novel of Sacagawea. large type ed. 312p. (gr. 7 up). 1989. lib. bdg. 14.95 (ISBN 0-8161-4811-2, Large Print Bks). G K Hall.

Parish, Peggy. Good Hunting, Blue Sky. Watts, James, illus. LC 84-43143. 64p. (gr. k-3). 1988. 11.95 (ISBN 0-06-024661-8); PLB 11.89 (ISBN 0-06-024662-6). HarpC Child Bks.

—Good Hunting, Blue Sky. Watts, James, illus. LC 84-43143. 64p. (gr. k-3). 1991. pap. 3.50 (ISBN 0-06-444148-2, Trophy). HarpC Child Bks.

Passey, Helen K. Speak to the Rain. 160p. (gr. 7 up). 1989. 12.95 (ISBN 0-689-31489-2, Atheneum Child Bk). Macmillan Child Grp.

Peck, Robert. Jo Silver. LC 85-3720. 144p. (gr. 8-12). 1985. 9.95 (ISBN 0-910923-20-5). Pineapple Pr.

Peyton, John L. Voices from the Ice. Peyton, John L., illus. 56p. (gr. k-4). 1990. pap. 5.95 (ISBN 0-939923-15-7). M & W Pub Co.

Pomerantz, Charlotte. Timothy Tall Feather. Stock, Catherine, illus. LC 85-24819. 32p. (gr. k-3). 1986. 11.75 (ISBN 0-688-04246-5); PLB 11.88 (ISBN 0-688-04247-3). Greenwillow.

Rodolph, Stormy. Quest for Courage. Lucero, Ruth, illus. 102p. (Orig.). (gr. 5-12). 1984. lib. bdg. 12.95 (ISBN 0-89992-392-5); pap. 6.95 (ISBN 0-89992-092-6). Coun India Ed.

Roop, Peter. Natosi: Strong Medicine. 32p. (gr. 3-8). 1984. 8.45 (ISBN 0-89992-390-9); pap. 2.95 (ISBN 0-89992-090-X). Coun India Ed.

—Sik-Ki-Mi. 32p. (gr. 3-6). 1984. 7.95 (ISBN 0-89992-391-7); pap. 2.95 (ISBN 0-89992-091-8). Coun India Ed.

Sandoz, Mari. The Story Catcher. LC 85-31810. (Illus.). 175p. (gr. 7-10). 1986. 5.95 (ISBN 0-8032-9163-9, Bison). U of Nebr Pr.

San Souci, Robert. Legend of Scarface. San Souci, Daniel, illus. LC 77-15170. 40p. (gr. k-3). 1987. pap. 5.95 (ISBN 0-385-15874-2, Pub. by Zephyr-BFYR). Doubleday.

Schultz, James W. The Loud Mouthed Gun. (gr. 4-8). 1984. pap. 1.95 (ISBN 0-89992-095-0). Coun India Ed.

—Running Eagle. (gr. 2-10). 1984. pap. 1.95 (ISBN 0-89992-093-4). Coun India Ed.

Searcy, Margaret Z. The Charm of the Bear Claw Necklace. Brough, Hazel, illus. LC 89-78044. 80p. (gr. 3-7). 1990. 10.95 (ISBN 0-88289-821-3); pap. 5.95 (ISBN 0-88289-777-2). Pelican.

—Wolf Dog of the Woodland Indians. Brough, Hazel, illus. 112p. (Orig.). (ps-8). 1991. pap. 5.95 (ISBN 0-88289-778-0). Pelican.

Shetterly, Susan H. Raven's Light: A Myth from the People of the Northwest Coast. Shetterly, Robert, illus. LC 89-78183. 32p. (gr. 1-5). 1991. SBE 13.95 (ISBN 0-689-31629-1, Atheneum Child Bk). Macmillan Child Grp.

Siberell, Anne. Whale in the Sky. Siberell, Anne, illus. LC 82-2483. 32p. (ps-3). 1985. 12.95 (ISBN 0-525-44021-6, DCB); pap. 3.95 (ISBN 0-525-44197-2, DCB). Dutton Child Bks.

Spinka, Penina K. White Hare's Horses. LC 90-42777. 160p. (gr. 5-9). 1991. SBE 12.95 (ISBN 0-689-31654-2, Atheneum Child Bk). Macmillan Child Grp.

Taylor, C. J. Deux Plumes et la Solitude Disparue. Taylor, C. J., illus. 24p. (gr. 1-5). 1990. 12.95 (ISBN 0-88776-255-7). Tundra Bks.

—How Two-Feather Was Saved from Loneliness. Taylor, C. J., illus. 24p. (gr. 1-5). 1990. 12.95 (ISBN 0-88776-254-9). Tundra Bks.

Taylor, Morris. Top of the Hill. 64p. 1988. pap. 4.95 (ISBN 0-87961-183-9). Naturegraph.

Thomasma, Kenneth. Kunu: Escape on the Missouri. Fleuter, Craig, illus. (ps-8). 1989. 9.95 (ISBN 0-8010-8891-7); pap. 6.95 (ISBN 0-8010-8892-5). Baker Bk.

Weechees. Sun Boy & His Hunter's Bow. 32p. (gr. 4-8). 1988. pap. 2.95 (ISBN 0-89992-115-9, NO. 115-9); PLB 8.45 (ISBN 0-685-25219-1). Coun India Ed.

—Sun Boy & the Angry Panther. 32p. (gr. 4-8). 1988. pap. 2.95 (ISBN 0-89992-114-0, NO. 114-0); PLB 8.45 (ISBN 0-685-25218-3). Coun India Ed.

—Sun Boy & the Monster of To-Oh-Pah. 32p. (gr. 4-8). 1988. pap. 2.95 (ISBN 0-89992-113-2); PLB 8.45 (ISBN 0-685-25217-5). Coun India Ed.

—Sun Boy: Cou-Yan-Nai: Comanchee Indian Story for Children. 32p. (gr. 4-9). 1983. pap. 2.95 (ISBN 0-686-44422-1). Coun India Ed.

Wesche, Alice M. Runs Far, Son of the Chichimecs. (gr. 3-7). 1982. pap. 7.95 (ISBN 0-89013-133-3). Museum NM Pr.

White Deer of Autumn. Ceremony-In the Circle of Life. San Souci, Daniel, illus. LC 83-7353. 32p. (gr. 3-6). 1983. PLB 14.65 (ISBN 0-940742-24-1). Raintree Pubs.

Worcester, Donald. Lone Hunter's Gray Pony. Pauley, Paige, illus. LC 84-16157. 70p. (gr. 4 up). 1985. 10.95 (ISBN 0-87565-001-5). Tex Christian.

Worcester, Donald E. War Pony. Pauley, Paige, illus. LC 83-40486. 96p. (gr. 4 up). 1984. Repr. of 1961 ed. 10.95 (ISBN 0-912646-85-3). Tex Christian.

INDIANS OF NORTH AMERICA–FOLKLORE

see Folklore, Indian

INDIANS OF NORTH AMERICA–GAMES

Whitney, Alex. Sports & Games the Indians Gave Us. Ostberg, Marie & Ostberg, Nils, illus. (gr. 7 up). 1977. 7.95 (ISBN 0-679-20391-5). McKay.

INDIANS OF NORTH AMERICA–GOVERNMENT RELATIONS

Bealer, Alex. Only the Names Remain: The Cherokees & the Trail of Tears. Bock, William S., illus. (gr. 4-6). 1972. lib. bdg. 14.95 (ISBN 0-316-08520-0). Little.

Kelly, Lawrence C. Federal Indian Policy. (Illus.). (gr. 5 up). 1990. 17.95 (ISBN 1-55546-706-7). Chelsea Hse.

McCiard, Megan & Ypsilantis, George. Hiawatha. Furstinger, Nancy, ed. (Illus.). 138p. (gr. 5-7). 1989. PLB 12.98 (ISBN 0-382-09568-5); pap. 7.95 (ISBN 0-382-09757-2). Silver Burdett Pr.

Nabokov, Peter, ed. Native American Testimony: An Anthology of Indian & White Relations. Deloria, Vine, Jr., pref. by. LC 77-11558. (Illus.). 242p. 1984. pap. text ed. 8.95x (ISBN 0-06-131993-7, TB 1993, Torch). HarperCollins.

INDIANS OF NORTH AMERICA–HAIDA INDIANS

Beck, Mary L. Heroes & Heroines in Tlingit-Haida Legend. DeWitt, Nancy, illus. LC 89-14931. 113p. (Orig.). (gr. 8 up). 1989. pap. 12.95 (ISBN 0-88240-334-6). Alaska Northwest.

INDIANS OF NORTH AMERICA–HISTORY

see also Indians of North America–Wars

Aragon, Hilda, illus. A Pueblo Village. 8p. (Orig.). (ps-7). 1982. pap. 4.00 (ISBN 0-915347-17-2). Pueblo Acoma Pr.

Armstrong, Nancy, et al. The Heritage. (gr. 3-6). 1977. 2.95 (ISBN 0-89992-065-9). Coun India Ed.

As Long As the Grass Grows... 48p. (gr. 4-5). 1989. PLB 10.95. Capstone Pr.

Beyer, Don E. The Totem Pole Indians of the Northwest. (Illus.). 64p. (gr. 3 up). 1991. pap. 4.95 (ISBN 0-531-15607-9). Watts.

Black, Sheila. Sitting Bull. Furstinger, Nancy, ed. (Illus.). 144p. (gr. 5-7). 1989. PLB 12.98 (ISBN 0-382-09572-3); pap. 7.95 (ISBN 0-382-09761-0). Silver Burdett Pr.

Boss-Ribs, Mary C. & Running-Crane, Jenny. Stories of Our Blackfeet Grandmothers. (Orig.). (gr. 1-6). 1984. pap. 1.95 (ISBN 0-89992-096-9). Coun India Ed.

Brian, J. & Freeman, Jodi L. The Old Ones: A Children's Book about the Anasazi Indians. Flanagan, Terry, illus. LC 86-50383. 64p. (Orig.). (gr. k-4). 1986. pap. 2.95 (ISBN 0-937871-27-3). Think Shop.

Cwiklik, Robert. King Philip. Furstinger, Nancy, ed. (Illus.). 144p. (gr. 5-7). 1989. PLB 12.98 (ISBN 0-382-09573-1); pap. 7.95 (ISBN 0-382-09762-9). Silver Burdett Pr.

—Sequoia. Furstinger, Nancy, ed. (Illus.). 142p. (gr. 5-7). 1989. PLB 12.98 (ISBN 0-382-09570-7); pap. 7.95 (ISBN 0-382-09759-9). Silver Burdett Pr.

Dream Catchers. 48p. (gr. 4-5). 1989. PLB 10.95 (ISBN 0-685-26403-3). Capstone Pr.

Engel, Lorenz. Among the Plains Indians. Catlin, George & Bodmer, Karl, illus. LC 74-102895. 108p. (gr. 5 up). 1970. PLB 10.95 (ISBN 0-8225-0564-9). Lerner Pubns.

Hardgrove, Tanya. Alaska in the Days That Were Before. (gr. 2-10). 1985. pap. 2.95 (ISBN 0-89992-098-5). Coun India Ed.

Highwater, Jamake. Many Smokes, Many Moons: A Chronology of American Indian History Through Indian Art. LC 77-17475. 128p. 1978. 15.95 (ISBN 0-685-35100-9, Lipp Jr Bks). HarpC Child Bks.

Josephy, Alvin M., Jr. Alvin Josephy's History of the Native Americans Series, 6 bks. (Illus.). 864p. (gr. 5-7). 1989. Set. PLB 77.88 (ISBN 0-382-09808-0); Set. pap. 47.70 (ISBN 0-382-09809-9). Silver Burdett Pr.

Katz, William. Black Indians: A Hidden Heritage. LC 85-28770. (Illus.). 208p. (gr. 5 up). 1986. 15.95 (ISBN 0-689-31196-6, Atheneum Child Bk). Macmillan Child Grp.

Nabokov, Peter, ed. Native American Testimony: An Anthology of Indian & White Relations. Deloria, Vine, Jr., pref. by. LC 77-11558. (Illus.). 242p. 1984. pap. text ed. 8.95x (ISBN 0-06-131993-7, TB 1993, Torch). HarperCollins.

—Native American Testimony: An Anthology of Indian & White Relations. First Encounter to Dispossession. LC 77-11558. (Illus.). (gr. 7 up). 1978. write for info. (ISBN 0-690-01313-2, Crowell Jr Bks). HarpC Child Bks.

Ruppel, Maxine. Vostaas: The Story of Montana's Indian Nations. (gr. 3-11). 1970. 3.95 (ISBN 0-89992-001-2). Coun India Ed.

Sansom-Flood, Renee & Bernie, Shirley A. Remember Your Relatives, Vol. 1: Yankton Sioux Images, 1851 to 1904. Bruguier, Leonard R., ed. Flood, William J., et al, illus. Hoover, Herbert T., intro. by. 55p. (Orig.). (gr. 12). 1985. pap. 8.50 (ISBN 0-9621936-0-7). Yankton Sioux Tribe.

We Have Always Been Here. 48p. (gr. 4-5). 1989. PLB 10.95 (ISBN 0-685-26408-4). Capstone Pr.

Yue, Charlotte. The Tipi: A Center of Native American Life. Yue, David, illus. LC 83-19529. 96p. (gr. 4-7). 1984. lib. bdg. 10.99 (ISBN 0-394-96177-3); pap. 10.95 (ISBN 0-394-86177-9). Knopf.

INDIANS OF NORTH AMERICA–HISTORY–FICTION

Thomasma, Kenneth. Amazing Indian Children. (gr. 3-8). 1991. 9.95 (ISBN 1-880114-12-7); pap. 6.95. Grandview. "Amazing Indian Children" is a series of five books, historic fiction written for a third grade read-ability. They are packed with Indian lore, history, geography & high adventure. Each book has a child as the central character who lives during a key time in that tribe's history. Through the Indian child's eyes the reader re-lives dramatic historic events. These books are accurately researched & are in use in over 1000 schools. They have been translated into Danish, Dutch, Eskimo & Spanish. Over 300,000 have been sold. NAYA NUKI: GIRL WHO RAN-ISBN 1-880114-01-1 cloth; 1-880114-00-3 pkb. With her friend, Sacagewea, a Shoshoni Indian Girl is taken prisoner, escapes & makes a 1000 mile wilderness journey back to her people. SOUN TETOKEN: NEZ PERCE BOY-ISBN 1-880114-08-9 cloth; 1-880114-07-0 pkb. Although mute since the death of his parents in a forest fire a young boy in Chief Joseph's band lives a happy adventurous life until the War of 1877 changes his life forever. OM-KAS-TOE OF THE BLACKFEET-ISBN 1-880114-06-2 cloth; 1-800114-05-4 pkb. Life changes dramatically for the Blackfeet people in the early 1700's when a twin brother & sister discover a strange animal & succeed in capturing it & returning it to their tribe. KUNU: ESCAPE ON THE MISSOURI-ISBN 1-880114-04-6 cloth; 1-880114-03-8 pkb. Following the forced removal of his people from Minnesota to South Dakota, a Winnebago Indian boy & his dying grandfather embark on a dangerous river journey back to their homeland. PATHKI NANA: KOOTENAI GIRL-ISBN 1-800114-10-0 cloth; 1-800114-09-7 pkb. A 9 year old Kootenai girl with a very poor self image leaves her village to seek her guardian spirit & finds herself in a life & death struggle with an evil man who seeks to end her life before she can return to her people. To order call 1-800-525-7344.
Publisher Provided Annotation.

INDIANS OF NORTH AMERICA–HOPI INDIANS

Levin, Beatrice & Vanderveld, Marjorie. Me Run Fast Good: Biographies of Tewanima (Hopi), Carlos Montezuma (Apache) & John Horse (Seminole) 32p. (gr. 5-9). 1983. pap. 2.95 (ISBN 0-89992-087-X). Coun India Ed.

Shaffer, Susan L., ed. Hopi, the Desert Farmers. Harper-Marinick, Maria & Kinzie, Mable B., illus. (gr. 3). 1987. incl. 30 student bklts. & 1 tchr's. resource binder which contains poster, lesson plans, overhead transparencies, 1 realia, color slides & audio-cassette 294.43 (ISBN 0-934351-12-0); tchr's. resource binder only 197.95 (ISBN 0-934351-23-6); student bklt. only 4.95 (ISBN 0-934351-28-7). Heard Mus.

Tomchek, Ann. The Hopi. LC 87-8037. (Illus.). 48p. (gr. k-4). 1987. PLB 13.27 (ISBN 0-516-01234-7); pap. 4.95 (ISBN 0-516-41234-5). Childrens.

INDIANS OF NORTH AMERICA–HOPI INDIANS–FICTION

Latterman, Terry. Little Joe, a Hopi Indian Boy, Learns a Hopi Indian Secret. Hawkins, Mary E., ed. Latterman, Terry, illus. LC 85-61836. 32p. (gr. 4-12). 1985. 12.95 (ISBN 0-934739-01-3). Pussywillow Pub.

Mike, Jan M. Kachi; a Hopi Girl: Historical Paper Doll Book to Read, Color & Cut. Lowmiller, Cathie, illus. 32p. (gr. k-6). 1989. pap. 3.95 (ISBN 0-918080-47-9). Treasure Chest.

Wolkstein, Diane. Squirrel's Song. Hoban, Lillian, illus. LC 76-5483. (ps-2). 1976. Knopf.

INDIANS OF NORTH AMERICA–HUPA INDIANS–FICTION

Oakley, Don. The Adventure of Christian Fast. Wiggins, D. Kevin, illus. LC 88-8001. 279p. (Orig.). (gr. 9 up). 1989. 12.95 (ISBN 0-9619465-1-2); pap. 8.95 (ISBN 0-9619465-2-0). Eyrie Pr.

INDIANS OF NORTH AMERICA–HURON INDIANS

Bonvillain, Nancy. The Huron. (Illus.). (gr. 5 up). 1989. 17.95 (ISBN 1-55546-708-3). Chelsea Hse.

INDIANS OF NORTH AMERICA–INDUSTRIES

Meiczinger, John. How to Draw Indian Arts & Crafts. Meiczinger, John, illus. LC 88-50807. 32p. (gr. 2-6). 1988. lib. bdg. 10.65 (ISBN 0-8167-1537-8, Pub. by Watermill Pr); pap. text ed. 1.95 (ISBN 0-8167-1515-7, Pub. by Watermill Pr). Troll Assocs.

Wilbur, C. Keith. Indian Handcrafts. LC 90-3522. (Illus.). 144p. (gr. 5 up). 1990. pap. 13.95 (ISBN 0-87106-496-0). Globe Pequot.

INDIANS OF NORTH AMERICA–IROQUOIS INDIANS

Doherty, Craig A. & Doherty, Katherine M. The Iroquois. (Illus.). 64p. (gr. 3-5). 1989. PLB 11.90 (ISBN 0-531-10747-7). Watts.

—The Iroquois. (Illus.). 64p. (gr. 3 up). 1991. pap. 4.95 (ISBN 0-531-15603-6). Watts.

Graymont, Barbara. The Iroquois. Porter, Frank, intro. by. (Illus.). 104p. (Orig.). (gr. 5 up). 1989. 17.95 (ISBN 1-55546-709-1); pap. 9.95 (ISBN 0-7910-0361-2). Chelsea Hse.

McCall, B. The Iroquois. (Illus.). 32p. (gr. 5-8). 1989. lib. bdg. 13.26 (ISBN 0-86625-378-5). Rourke Corp.

INDIANS OF NORTH AMERICA–IROQUOIS INDIANS–FICTION

Baker, Betty. Little Runner of the Longhouse. Lobel, Arnold, illus. LC 62-8040. 64p. (gr. k-3). 1962. PLB 11.89 (ISBN 0-06-020341-2). HarpC Child Bks.

—Little Runner of the Longhouse. Lobel, Arnold, illus. LC 62-8040. 64p. (gr. k-3). 1989. pap. 3.50 (ISBN 0-06-444122-9, Trophy). HarpC Child Bks.

Bruchac, Joseph. Iroquois Stories: Heroes & Heroines, Monsters & Magic. Burgevin, Daniel, illus. LC 85-5705. 198p. (gr. 3-7). 1985. pap. 8.95 (ISBN 0-89594-234-8). Crossing Pr.

INDIANS OF NORTH AMERICA–KIOWA INDIANS–LEGENDS

Bullshows, Harry & Gilliland, Hap. Legends of Chief Bald Eagle. (gr. 2-10). 1977. 2.95 (ISBN 0-89992-034-9). Coun India Ed.

Clark, Ella, ed. In the Beginning. (gr. 5 up). 1977. 2.95 (ISBN 0-89992-055-1). Coun India Ed.

Gingras, Louie & Rainboldt, Jo. Coyote & Kootenai. (gr. 2-6). 1977. 2.95 (ISBN 0-89992-067-5). Coun India Ed.

Morss, Willard N. & Herren, Janet M. Stolen Princess: A Northwest Indian Legend. Millard, Carolyn, illus. LC 83-82920. 79p. (Orig.). (gr. 4-8). 1983. pap. 8.95 (ISBN 0-9613025-0-X). J M Herren.

INDIANS OF NORTH AMERICA–LEGENDS

see also Folklore, Indian

Bass, Althea. Grandfather Grey Owl Told Me. (gr. 4 up). 1973. 2.95 (ISBN 0-89992-051-9). Coun India Ed.

—Nightwalker & the Buffalo. (gr. 4-9). 1972. 2.95 (ISBN 0-89992-032-2). Coun India Ed.

Bierhorst, John, ed. In the Trail of the Wind: American Indian Poems & Ritual Orations. Bierhorst, Jane B., illus. LC 71-144822. 224p. (gr. 7 up). 1971. 6.95 (ISBN 0-374-33640-7). FS&G.

Bishop, James, Jr., et al. Experience Jerome & the Verde Valley Legends & Legacies, No. II. Henry, Ron, illus. LC 90-71606. 356p. (Orig.). (gr. 8-12). 1990. pap. 12.95 (ISBN 0-9628329-1-X). Thorne Enterprises.

Caduto, Michael J. & Bruchac, Joseph. Keepers of the Earth: Native American Stories, & Environmental Activities for Children. Fadden, John K. & Wood, Carol, illus. Momaday, N. Scott, intro. by. LC 88-3620. 209p. (gr. 1-6). 1988. indexed 19.95 (ISBN 1-55591-027-0). Fulcrum Pub.

Cheyenne Short Stories: A Collection of Ten Traditional Stores of the Cheyenne. (CHY & ENG.). (gr. 2 up). 1977. 2.95 (ISBN 0-89992-057-8). Coun India Ed.

Cohlene, Terri. Clamshell Boy. (Illus.). 48p. (gr. 4-8). 1990. lib. bdg. 19.93 (ISBN 0-86593-001-5); lib. bdg. 14.95s.p. Rourke Corp.

—Dancing Drum. (Illus.). 48p. (gr. 4-8). 1990. lib. bdg. 19.93 (ISBN 0-86593-007-4); lib. bdg. 14.95s.p. Rourke Corp.

—Ka-Ha-Si & the Loon. (Illus.). 48p. (gr. 4-8). 1990. lib. bdg. 19.93 (ISBN 0-86593-002-3); lib. bdg. 14.95s.p. Rourke Corp.

—Little Firefly. (Illus.). 48p. (gr. 4-8). 1990. lib. bdg. 19.93 (ISBN 0-86593-005-8); lib. bdg. 14.95s.p. (ISBN 0-685-36333-3). Rourke Corp.

—Native American Legends, 6 bks. (Illus.). 288p. (gr. 4-8). 1990. Set. lib. bdg. 119.60 (ISBN 0-86593-000-7); Set. lib. bdg. 89.70s.p. Rourke Corp.

—Quillworker. (Illus.). 48p. (gr. 4-8). 1990. lib. bdg. 19.93 (ISBN 0-86593-004-X); lib. bdg. 14.95s.p. (ISBN 0-685-36334-1). Rourke Corp.

—Turquoise Boy. (Illus.). 48p. (gr. 4-8). 1990. lib. bdg. 19.93 (ISBN 0-86593-003-1); lib. bdg. 14.95s.p. (ISBN 0-685-36335-X). Rourke Corp.

Connolly, James E., ed. Why the Possum's Tail Is Bare: And Other North American Indian Nature Tales. Adams, Andrea, illus. LC 84-26871. 56p. (gr. 3 up). 1985. PLB 13.95 (ISBN 0-88045-069-X). Stemmer Hse.

Crow, Moses N. Hoksila & the Red Buffalo. Provincial, Bernard W., illus. 40p. (Orig.). (gr. 3 up). 1991. pap. 5.95 (ISBN 1-877976-02-4, 4B6ZO017). Tipi Pr.
Among the Lakota, this legend is called, Enya-hoksei. It is told differently by every story-teller of every clan. The outline of the legend remains the same as it travels with time. The whole story changes with the changing of times. The significance of it, as it goes through the ages, is that it has no horses in it. The story has to be very old. But like all legends, it keeps in tune with the passing of time. When Hoksila the young warrior begins his long journey, his hunt to rescue his wife & to rid his tribe of the red buffalo with the ugly black spots. Then he could free all the young maidens. This is a story of the battle of good & evil, & how it's been handed down by the Lakota. An engaging story for the young & those not so young.
Publisher Provided Annotation.

—A Legend from Crazy Horse Clan. Flood, Renee S., ed. Soldier, Daniel L., illus. 36p. (Orig.). (gr. 3 up). 1987. pap. 4.95 (ISBN 1-877976-03-2, 4B6ZO010). Tipi Pr.
"A Legend from Crazy Horse Clan" is a story for children of all ages. Beautiful illustrations by Daniel Long Soldier keep the legend alive in the reader's eye. The historian or student of Indian ways will enjoy the book as much as the child of seven, in whose imagination the baby raccoon Mesu embodies all that is faithful & loving in a small furry pet. Listen carefully to the words of Tashia. The symbolic role of man & woman is evident throughout the legend. Although the story essentially describes the life of a girl, the narrator is male. Clearly, the legend describes the male viewpoint of manhood, religion, courtship, aging & death. The characters are gentle, yet there is a strong underlying theme of tribal identity. Without a doubt, we are looking at life through the eyes of a warrior. Indian oral narration is spoken American literature in its finest form. When Lakota children of the 1990s become grandparents themselves, they will tell the legends again. Thanks

to Moses Big Crow, one of those legends may well be "A Legend from Crazy Horse Clan."
Publisher Provided Annotation.

Crowder, Jack L. & Hill, Faith. Tonibah & the Rainbow. Tohtsonie, Clara & Wilson, Joe, trs. Crowder, Jack L., photos by. (ENG & NAV., Illus.). 32p. (Orig.). (gr. 7 up). 1986. pap. 6.95 (ISBN 0-9616589-1-6). Upper Strata.

Crowl, Christine. The Hunter & the Woodpecker. (Illus.). 12p. (Orig.). (ps-6). 1990. pap. 2.50 (ISBN 1-877976-09-1, 4B6ZO015). Tipi Pr.
This children's book describes how the Sioux first discovered the flute, which makes magical music. The Red Headed Woodpecker tells a young brave of its powers to win over a beautiful maiden. A charming story, delightfully illustrated in four color. A story for children of all ages.
Publisher Provided Annotation.

—White Buffalo Women. (Illus.). 18p. (Orig.). (gr. 6). 1991. pap. 2.50 (ISBN 1-877976-10-5, 4B6ZO014). Tipi Pr.
This story is a core legend of the Sioux & how the Sioux received the Sacred Prayer Pipe. The pipe was an important religious symbol among the Sioux. It was a "moveable" altar which was used in prayer & ceremony. It was the most cherished thing a man could own. The legend of "White Buffalo Women" & the pipe, originated with the Brule Sioux & is a story that has been handed down through the centuries. Beautifully told & illustrated in four color, a charming story for children young & old.
Publisher Provided Annotation.

De Angulo, Jaime. Indian Tales. De Angulo, Jaime, illus. 256p. (gr. 5 up). 1984. 8.95 (ISBN 0-374-52163-8, Am Century). FS&G.

DeArmond, Dale. The Seal Oil Lamp. DeArmond, Dale, illus. 48p. (gr. k-4). 1988. 14.95 (ISBN 0-316-17786-5). Little.

DeCesare, Ruth. Myth, Music & Dance of the American Indian. Feldstein, Sandy, et al, eds. Seckler, Judy & Shelly, Walt, illus. 80p. (gr. 4-12). 1988. tchr's. ed. 12.95 (ISBN 0-88284-371-0, 3518); student, 16p 3.95 (ISBN 0-88284-372-9, 3520); Student Songbk., 24p 4.95 (ISBN 0-88284-373-7, 3519); tchr's ed. with cassette 19.95 (ISBN 0-88284-383-4, 3534). Alfred Pub.

Earring, Monica F., et al. Prairie Legends. Robinson, Pat, illus. (gr. 6-9). 1978. 2.95 (ISBN 0-89992-069-1). Coun India Ed.

Egbert, Rebecca A. The Vision of the Spokane Prophet. Gilliland, Hap, ed. Hardgrove, Tanya, illus. 36p. (Orig.). (gr. 5-10). 1989. PLB 9.95 (ISBN 0-89992-418-2); pap. 3.95 (ISBN 0-89992-118-3). Coun India Ed.

From the Great Mystery. 48p. (gr. 4-5). 1989. PLB 10.95 (ISBN 0-685-26406-8). Capstone Pr.

Gerber, Will, et al. The Rings on Woot-Kew's Tail: Indian Legends of the Origin of the Sun, Moon & Stars. (gr. 3-9). 1973. 2.95 (ISBN 0-89992-059-4). Coun India Ed.

Goble, Paul. Buffalo Woman. LC 83-15704. (Illus.). 32p. (gr. k up). 1984. 13.95 (ISBN 0-02-737720-2, Bradbury Pr). Macmillan Child Grp.

—Buffalo Woman. Goble, Paul, illus. LC 86-20573. 32p. (gr. k up). 1987. pap. 4.95 (ISBN 0-689-71109-3, Aladdin). Macmillan Child Grp.

—The Great Race: Of the Birds & Animals. LC 90-39983. (Illus.). 32p. (gr. k-3). 1991. pap. 4.95 (ISBN 0-689-71452-1, Aladdin). Macmillan Child Grp.

Goble, Paul, retold by. & illus. Iktomi & the Berries: A Plains Indian Story. LC 88-23353. 32p. (ps-2). 1989. 14.95 (ISBN 0-531-05819-0); PLB 14.99 (ISBN 0-531-08419-1). Orchard Bks Watts.

Goble, Paul, as told by. & illus. Iktomi & the Buffalo Skull: A Plains Indian Story. LC 90-7716. 32p. (ps-2). 1991. 14.95 (ISBN 0-531-05911-1); PLB 14.99 (ISBN 0-531-08511-2). Orchard Bks Watts.

Griffin, Arthur E., ed. Ah Mo: Indian Legends from Washington State. Malin, Edward, illus. 75p. (Orig.). (gr. 2-5). 1989. pap. write for info. Bainbridge Pr.

—The Legend of Tom Pepper & Other Stories. Malin, Edward, illus. 100p. (Orig.). (gr. 2-5). 1989. pap. write for info. Bainbridge Pr.

—Spelyi & Other Indian Legends. Malin, Edward, illus. (gr. 2-5). 1989. write for info. Bainbridge Pr.

Henry Tall Bull & Weist, Tom. Cheyenne Legends of Creation. (gr. 4-9). 1972. 2.95 (ISBN 0-89992-025-X). Coun India Ed.

Highwater, Jamake. ANPAO: An American Indian Odyssey. Scholder, Fritz, illus. LC 77-9264. 256p. (gr. 5-9). 1977. 13.95 (ISBN 0-397-31750-6, Lipp Jr Bks). HarpC Child Bks.

Holthaus, Mary. The Hunter & the Ravens. 32p. (gr. 1-6). 1976. 2.95 (ISBN 0-89992-049-7). Coun India Ed.

Hurmence, Belinda. The Nightwalker. LC 88-2827. 144p. (gr. 4-7). 1988. 12.95 (ISBN 0-89919-732-9, Pub. by Clarion). Ticknor & Fields.

Keeper, Berry. The Old Ones Told Me: American Indian Stories for Children. (Illus.). 36p. (Orig.). 1989. pap. 4.95 (ISBN 0-8323-0473-5). Binford Mort.

Kerven, Rosalind. Earth Magic, Sky Magic: North American Indian Tales. (Illus.). 96p. 1991. 12.95 (ISBN 0-521-36235-0); pap. 7.95 (ISBN 0-521-36806-5). Cambridge U Pr.

Lacapa, Michael. The Flute Player: An Apache Folktale. Lacapa, Michael, illus. LC 89-63749. 64p. (gr. 1-3). 1990. 14.95 (ISBN 0-87358-500-3). Northland AZ.

Levin, Beatrice. Indian Myths from the Southeast. (gr. 4-12). 1974. 2.95 (ISBN 0-89992-071-3). Coun India Ed.

McGovern, Ann. The Defenders. 128p. (Orig.). (gr. 3-7). 1987. pap. 2.75 (ISBN 0-590-43866-2). Scholastic Inc.

Marsh, Jessie. Indian Folk Tales from Coast to Coast. Cunningham, Tanya, illus. (gr. 3-6). 1978. 2.95 (ISBN 0-89992-068-3). Coun India Ed.

Masson, Marcelle. A Bag of Bones: Legends of the Wintu Indians of Northern California. LC 66-23398. 130p. (gr. 4 up). 1966. 14.95 (ISBN 0-911010-27-0); pap. 7.95 (ISBN 0-911010-26-2). Naturegraph.

Matson, Emerson N. Legends of the Great Chiefs. (Illus.). 144p. (gr. 8-12). pap. 5.95 (ISBN 0-9609940-0-9). Storypole.

Mayo, Gretchen W. Star Tales: North American Indian Stories about the Stars. 96p. (gr. 5 up). 1987. 11.95 (ISBN 0-8027-6672-2); PLB 12.85 (ISBN 0-8027-6673-0). Walker & Co.

Moore, Elizabeth B. & Couvillon, Alice W. Louisiana Indian Tales. 112p. 1990. 10.95 (ISBN 0-88289-756-X). Pelican.

Nashone. Grandmother Stories: Northwestern Indian Tales. (Illus.). (gr. 5-12). 1987. pap. 7.95 (ISBN 0-940113-06-6). Sierra Oaks Pub.

Norman, Howard. How Glooskap Outwits the Ice Giants: And Other Tales of the Maritime Indians, Vol. 1. 1989. 14.95 (ISBN 0-316-61181-6, Joy St Bks). Little.

Olin, Caroline & Dutton, Bertha P. Myths & Legends of the Indian Southwest, Bk. 1. (Illus.). (gr. 5). 1978. pap. 3.95 (ISBN 0-88388-049-0). Bellerophon Bks.

Redhawk, Richard. Grandfather Origin Story: The Navajo Indian Begining. (Orig.). (gr. 3-6). 1988. pap. 6.95 (ISBN 0-940113-07-4). Sierra Oaks Pub.

Red Hawk, Richard. Grandfather's Story of Navajo Monsters. Whitehorse, David, illus. (Orig.). (ps-7). 1988. pap. 6.95 (ISBN 0-940113-11-2). Sierra Oaks Pub.

—A Trip to a Pow Wow. Brook, Anne C., illus. 45p. (Orig.). (gr. k-3). 1988. pap. 6.95 (ISBN 0-940113-14-7). Sierra Oaks Pub.

Sally Old Coyote & Joy Yellow Tail Toineeta. Indian Tales of the Northern Plains. (gr. 2-5). 1972. 2.95 (ISBN 0-89992-018-7). Coun India Ed.

Simms, Thomas E. Otokahekagapi (First Beginnings) Sioux Creation Story. (Illus.). 36p. (Orig.). 1987. pap. 3.50 (ISBN 1-877976-06-7, 4B6ZO005). Tipi Pr.

The first in a series of Lakota legends, is written & illustrated to foster greater respect for a proud people's tradition. This account in English & Lakota presents the profundity of the creation mystery. The pictures are Indian pictures, because this is the beginning of the Sioux Creation account. But it is for all children everywhere, because everyone asks about how things got started & how the World began. "So this picture book is like a little ball game. We shall learn that the book is a ball. Wakantanka will throw this ball to us, which is this book, & we shall catch it. Then we shall understand it. And we shall enjoy ourselves. Bring the ball -- this book -- to the Center, which is your Heart, then you will receive a present. The present is invisible, like a little secret. Good. That's all. Now I shall throw the ball to you. Catch it!"
Publisher Provided Annotation.

Troughton, Joanna, retold by. & illus. How Rabbit Stole the Fire: A North American Indian Folk Tale. LC 85-15629. 28p. (ps-2). 1986. 14.95 (ISBN 0-87226-040-2, Bedrick Blackie). P Bedrick Bks.

INDIANS OF NORTH AMERICA–MOHAWK INDIANS

Bonvillain, Nancy. Mohawk. (Illus.). (gr. 5 up). 1992. PLB 17.95 (ISBN 0-7910-1636-6); pap. 9.95 (ISBN 0-7910-1679-X). Chelsea Hse.

INDIANS OF NORTH AMERICA–MUSIC

DeCesare, Ruth. Myth, Music & Dance of the American Indian. Feldstein, Sandy, et al, eds. Seckler, Judy & Shelly, Walt, illus. 80p. (gr. 4-12). 1988. tchr's. ed. 12.95 (ISBN 0-88284-371-0, 3518); student, 16p 3.95 (ISBN 0-88284-372-9, 3520); Student Songbk., 24p 4.95 (ISBN 0-88284-373-7, 3519); tchr's ed. with cassette 19.95 (ISBN 0-88284-383-4, 3534). Alfred Pub.

Fichter, George S. American Indian Music & Musical Instruments. (gr. 5-10). 1978. 8.95 (ISBN 0-679-20443-1). McKay.

INDIANS OF NORTH AMERICA–MYTHOLOGY

see Folklore, Indian; Indians of North America–Legends; Indians of North America–Religion and Mythology

INDIANS OF NORTH AMERICA–NAVAHO INDIANS

Armer, Laura A. Waterless Mountain. Armer, Laura A., illus. (gr. 5-8). 1931. 11.95 (ISBN 0-679-20233-1). McKay.

Armstrong, Nancy. Navajo Children. (gr. 2-6). 1975. 2.95 (ISBN 0-89992-037-3). Coun India Ed.

Doherty, Craig A. & Doherty, Katherine M. The Apaches & Navajos. (Illus.). 64p. (gr. 3-5). 1989. PLB 11.90 (ISBN 0-531-10743-4). Watts.

—The Apaches & Navajos. (Illus.). 64p. (gr. 3 up). 1991. pap. 4.95 (ISBN 0-531-15602-8). Watts.

Hoffman, Virginia. Lucy Learns to Weave: Gathering Plants. Denetsosie, Hoke, illus. LC 74-4894. 46p. (gr. 1-4). 1974. pap. 7.00 (ISBN 0-89019-009-7). Rough Rock Pr.

Iverson, Peter J. The Navajos. (Illus.). (gr. 5 up). 1990. 17.95 (ISBN 1-55546-719-9); pap. 9.95 (ISBN 0-7910-0390-6). Chelsea Hse.

Jayant, Amber. Silas & the Mad-Sad People. LC 80-83882. (Illus.). (gr. 1-5). 1981. 6.95 (ISBN 0-938678-08-6). New Seed.

Kreischer, Elsie. Navaho Magic of Hunting. 32p. (gr. 4-10). 1988. pap. 2.95 (ISBN 0-89992-099-3, NO. 099-3); PLB 8.45 (ISBN 0-685-25216-7). Coun India Ed.

Lagerquist, Syble. Philip Johnston & the Navajo Code Talkers. (gr. 4-12). 1975. 2.95 (ISBN 0-89992-038-1). Coun India Ed.

New Mexico People & Energy Collective Staff, et al. Red Ribbons for Emma. LC 80-83883. (Illus.). 48p. (Orig.). (gr. 3 up). 1981. limited ed. 12.00 (ISBN 0-938678-07-8). New Seed.

Osinski, Alice. The Navajo. (Illus.). (gr. k-4). PLB 14.60 (ISBN 0-516-01236-3); pap. 4.95 (ISBN 0-516-41236-1). Childrens.

Shaffer, Susan L., ed. Dine, the Navajo. Harper-Marinick & Kinzie, Mable B., illus. (gr. 6). 1987. incl. 30 student bklts. & 1 tchr's. resource binder which contains poster, lesson plans, overhead transparencies, 1 realia, color slides & audio-cassette 294.43 (ISBN 0-934351-15-5); tchr's. resource binder only 197.95 (ISBN 0-934351-26-0); student's bklt. only 4.95 (ISBN 0-934351-31-7). Heard Mus.

Stan, S. The Navajo. (Illus.). 32p. (gr. 5-8). 1989. lib. bdg. 13.26 (ISBN 0-86625-380-7). Rourke Corp.

INDIANS OF NORTH AMERICA–NAVAHO INDIANS–FICTION

Blood, Charles L. & Link, Martin. The Goat in the Rug. Parker, Nancy W., illus. LC 89-77701. 40p. (ps-3). 1990. pap. 3.95 (ISBN 0-689-71418-1, Aladdin). Macmillan Child Grp.

Clark, Ann N. Little Herder in Autumn. Harrington, John P., ed. Young, Robert W., tr. Denetsosie, Hoke, illus. LC 88-70848. (ENG & NAV.). 96p. (gr. 1-5). 1988. 19.95 (ISBN 0-941270-47-5); pap. 8.95 (ISBN 0-941270-46-7). Ancient City Pr.

Cohlene, Terri. Turquoise Boy: A Navajo Legend. 48p. (gr. 4-7). 1990. pap. 3.95 (ISBN 0-8167-2360-5). Troll Assocs.

Crowder, Jack L. & Hill, Faith. Stephanie & the Coyote. 3rd, rev. ed. Morgan, William, tr. Holm, Wayne, intro. by. (NAV & ENG., Illus.). 32p. (gr. 3 up). pap. 4.95 (ISBN 0-9616589-0-8). Upper Strata.

Garaway, Margaret K. Ashkii & His Grandfather. Warren, Harry, illus. LC 89-50604. 32p. (Orig.). (gr. k-6). 1989. pap. 5.95 (ISBN 0-918080-41-X). Treasure Chest.

Mike, Jan M. Dolii; a Navajo Girl: Historical Paper Doll Book to Read, Color & Cut. Lowmiller, Cathie, illus. 32p. (gr. k-6). 1990. pap. 3.95 (ISBN 0-918080-54-1). Treasure Chest.

Moon, Sheila. Deepest Roots. Renfrew, Susan, illus. LC 86-19578. 240p. (gr. 8-12). 1986. pap. 8.95 (ISBN 0-917479-10-6). Guild Psy.

—Knee-Deep in Thunder. Parnell, Peter, illus. LC 86-19534. 307p. (gr. 8-12). 1986. pap. 8.95 (ISBN 0-917479-08-4). Guild Psy.

Pitts, Paul. Racing the Sun. 160p. 1988. pap. 2.95 (ISBN 0-380-75496-7, Camelot). Avon.

Wilson, Bennett. The Magic Feather: An Adventure in Navajo Land. Wilson, Bennett, illus. 42p. (Orig.). (gr. 1-6). 1989. pap. 5.00 (ISBN 0-918080-48-7). Treasure Chest.

Yazzie, Earl. More Monster Stories from the Navajo Country, Vol. 3. (Illus.). 43p. (Orig.). (gr. k-5). Date not set. pap. 6.95 (ISBN 0-940113-12-0). Sierra Oaks Pub.

INDIANS OF NORTH AMERICA–NAVAHO INDIANS–LEGENDS

Morgan, William. Navajo Coyote Tales. Thompson, Hildegard, ed. & tr. Lind, Jenny, illus. LC 88-72048. 50p. (gr. 1-3). 1988. pap. 7.95 (ISBN 0-941270-52-1). Ancient City Pr.

INDIANS OF NORTH AMERICA–NEZ PERCE INDIANS

Howes, Kathi. Nez Perce. (Illus.). 32p. (gr. 5-8). 1990. lib. bdg. 13.26 (ISBN 0-86625-379-3); lib. bdg. 9.95s.p. (ISBN 0-685-36389-9). Rourke Corp.

Osinski, Alice. The Nez Perce. LC 88-11822. (Illus.). 48p. (gr. k-4). 1988. PLB 14.60 (ISBN 0-516-01154-5); pap. 4.95 (ISBN 0-516-41154-3). Childrens.

Schneider, Bill. Flight of the Nez Perce. White, Dan, illus. LC 88-80227. 32p. 1988. pap. 4.95 (ISBN 0-937959-39-1). Falcon Pr MT.

Tutzer, Clifford. The Nez Perce. (Illus.). (gr. 5 up). 1992. 17.95 (ISBN 1-55546-720-2). Chelsea Hse.

INDIANS OF NORTH AMERICA–OGLALA INDIANS

Greene, Carol. Black Elk: A Man with a Vision. LC 90-39480. (Illus.). 48p. (gr. k-3). 1990. PLB 15.27 (ISBN 0-516-04213-0). Childrens.

INDIANS OF NORTH AMERICA–PAIUTE INDIANS

Bunte, Pamela A. & Franklin, Robert J. The Paiute. (Illus.). (gr. 5 up). 1990. 17.95 (ISBN 1-55546-723-7). Chelsea Hse.

INDIANS OF NORTH AMERICA–PAPAGO INDIANS

Baylor, Byrd. The Desert Is Theirs. Parnall, Peter, illus. LC 74-24417. 32p. (ps-3). 1975. 13.95 (ISBN 0-684-14266-X, Scribners Young Read). Macmillan Child Grp.

INDIANS OF NORTH AMERICA–PAWNEE INDIANS–FICTION

Cohen, Caron L. Mud Pony. 1989. pap. 3.95 (ISBN 0-590-41526-3). Scholastic Inc.

Cohen, Caron Lee, adapted by. The Mud Pony: A Traditional Skidi Pawnee Tale. Begay, Shonto, illus. LC 87-23451. 32p. (gr. k-4). 1988. pap. 12.95 (ISBN 0-590-41525-5). Scholastic Inc.

Fradin, Dennis B. The Pawnee. LC 88-11820. (Illus.). 48p. (gr. k-4). 1988. PLB 14.60 (ISBN 0-516-01155-3); pap. 4.95 (ISBN 0-516-41155-1). Childrens.

Howell, War Cry. Gramma Curlychief's Pawnee Indian Stories. Burns, Kathy, illus. LC 82-71948. 88p. (Orig.). (gr. 5-12). 1985. pap. 4.50x (ISBN 0-943864-22-4). Davenport.

INDIANS OF NORTH AMERICA–POETRY

Bierhorst, John, ed. In the Trail of the Wind: American Indian Poems & Ritual Orations. Bierhorst, Jane B., illus. (gr. 8 up). 1987. pap. 4.95 (ISBN 0-374-43576-6). FS&G.

Longfellow, Henry Wadsworth. Hiawatha's Childhood. Le Cain, Errol, illus. 32p. (gr. k up). 1984. 14.95 (ISBN 0-374-33065-4). FS&G.

Sneve, Virginia H., selected by. Dancing Teepees: Poems of American Indian Youth. Gammell, Stephen, illus. 1991. pap. 5.95 (ISBN 0-8234-0879-5). Holiday.

Wood, Nancy. Many Winters. Howell, Frank, illus. LC 74-3554. 80p. (gr. 6 up). 1974. pap. 14.95 (ISBN 0-385-02226-3). Doubleday.

INDIANS OF NORTH AMERICA–POMO INDIANS

Brown, Vinson. Pomo Indians of California & Their Neighbors. Elsasser, Albert B., ed. Andrews, Douglas, illus. LC 78-13946. 64p. (Orig.). (gr. 4 up). 1969. 13.95 (ISBN 0-911010-31-9); pap. 6.95 (ISBN 0-911010-30-0). Naturegraph.

INDIANS OF NORTH AMERICA–PUEBLO INDIANS

Clark, Ann N. Sun Journey: A Story of Zuni Pueblo. reissued ed. Sandy, Percy T., illus. LC 88-70955. 96p. (gr. 3 up). 1988. 19.95 (ISBN 0-941270-49-1); pap. 8.95 (ISBN 0-941270-48-3). Ancient City Pr.

D'Apice, Mary. Pueblo. (Illus.). 32p. (gr. 5-8). 1990. lib. bdg. 13.26 (ISBN 0-86625-385-8); lib. bdg. 9.95s.p. (ISBN 0-685-36390-2). Rourke Corp.

Folsom, Franklin. Red Power on the Rio Grande. Ortiz, Alfonso, intro. by. 144p. (gr. 4 up). 1989. 12.95 (ISBN 0-89992-421-2); pap. 8.95 (ISBN 0-89992-121-3). Coun India Ed.

McDermott, Gerald. Flecha al Sol: Un Cuento do Los Indios Pueblo. McDermott, Gerald, illus. (SPA.). 48p. (ps-3). 1991. pap. 3.95 (ISBN 0-14-054364-3, Puffin). Puffin Bks.

Ortiz, Alfonso. The Pueblo. (Illus.). (gr. 5 up). 1992. 17.95 (ISBN 1-55546-727-X). Chelsea Hse.

Trimble, Stephen. The Village of Blue Stone. Dewey, Jennifer O. & Reade, Deborah, illus. LC 88-34194. 64p. (gr. 3-7). 1990. 13.95 (ISBN 0-02-789501-7, Mcmillan Child Bk). Macmillan Child Grp.

Yue, Charlotte. The Pueblo. (gr. 4-7). 1990. pap. 4.95 (ISBN 0-395-54961-2). HM.

INDIANS OF NORTH AMERICA–PUEBLO INDIANS–ANTIQUITIES

Radlauer, Ruth. Mesa Verde National Park. updated ed. Zillmer, Rolf, photos by. LC 76-27350. (Illus.). 48p. (gr. 3 up). 1984. PLB 17.27 (ISBN 0-516-07490-3); pap. 4.95 (ISBN 0-516-47490-1). Childrens.

INDIANS OF NORTH AMERICA-PUEBLO INDIANS-FICTION
Vallo, Lawrence. Tales of a Pueblo Boy. LC 86-5876. (Illus.). 48p. (Orig.). 1987. pap. 5.95 (ISBN 0-86534-089-7). Sunstone Pr.

INDIANS OF NORTH AMERICA-RECREATIONS
see Indians of North America-Games

INDIANS OF NORTH AMERICA-RELIGION AND MYTHOLOGY
see also Indians of North America-Dances; Totems and Totemism
Clark, Ella. Guardian Spirit Quest. (gr. 5-12). 1974. pap. 2.95 (ISBN 0-89992-045-4). Coun India Ed.
Hildreth, Dolly, et al. The Money God. (gr. 6). 1972. 2.95 (ISBN 0-89992-031-4). Coun India Ed.
McDonald, W. H. Creation Tales from the Salish. (gr. 3-9). 1973. 2.95 (ISBN 0-89992-061-6). Coun India Ed.
Olin, Caroline & Dutton, Bertha P. Myths & Legends of the Indian Southwest, Bk. 1. (Illus.). (gr. 5). 1978. pap. 3.95 (ISBN 0-88388-049-0). Bellerophon Bks.
Villasenor, David. Tapestries in Sand: The Spirit of Indian Sandpainting. rev. ed. (Illus.). 112p. (gr. 4 up). 1966. 14.95 (ISBN 0-911010-23-8); pap. 7.95 (ISBN 0-911010-22-X). Naturegraph.
Willoya, William & Brown, Vinson. Warriors of the Rainbow: Strange & Prophetic Dreams of the Indian Peoples. (Illus.). 94p. (gr. 4 up). 1962. 13.95 (ISBN 0-911010-25-4); pap. 6.95 (ISBN 0-911010-24-6). Naturegraph.

INDIANS OF NORTH AMERICA-SALISH INDIANS-FICTION
Law, Katheryn. Salish Folk Tales. (gr. 2-8). 1972. 2.95 (ISBN 0-89992-028-4). Coun India Ed.
McDonald, W. H. Creation Tales from the Salish. (gr. 3-9). 1973. 2.95 (ISBN 0-89992-061-6). Coun India Ed.

INDIANS OF NORTH AMERICA-SEMINOLE INDIANS
Brooks, B. The Seminole. (Illus.). 32p. (gr. 5-8). 1989. lib. bdg. 13.26 (ISBN 0-86625-377-7). Rourke Corp.
Clark, Electa. Osceola: Young Seminole Indian. (Illus.). (gr. 3-7). 5.95 (ISBN 0-672-50144-9, Bobbs). Macmillan.
Garbarino, Merwyn S. The Seminole. Potter, Frank W., intro. by. (Illus.). 112p. (Orig.). (gr. 5 up). 1989. 17.95 (ISBN 1-55546-729-6); pap. 9.95 (ISBN 0-7910-0367-1). Chelsea Hse.
Lee, Martin. The Seminoles. (Illus.). 64p. (gr. 3 up). 1991. pap. 4.95 (ISBN 0-531-15604-4). Watts.
Lepthien, Emilie U. The Seminole. LC 84-23141. (Illus.). 45p. (gr. 2-4). 1985. lib. bdg. 14.60 (ISBN 0-516-01941-4); pap. 4.95 (ISBN 0-516-41941-2). Childrens.
Levin, Beatrice & Vanderveld, Marjorie. Me Run Fast Good: Biographies of Tewanima (Hopi), Carlos Montezuma (Apache) & John Horse (Seminole) 32p. (gr. 5-9). 1983. pap. 2.95 (ISBN 0-89992-087-X). Coun India Ed.
The Seminole: Southeast. 112p. (gr. 7-12). PLB 16.95 (ISBN 0-685-21874-0, 201244). Know Unltd.

INDIANS OF NORTH AMERICA-SHAWNEE INDIANS
Eckert, Allan W. Blue Jacket: War Chief of the Shawnees. LC 69-10656. (Illus.). (gr. 7 up). 1969. 14.95 (ISBN 0-316-20863-9). Little.

INDIANS OF NORTH AMERICA-SIGN LANGUAGE
Cody, Iron Eyes. Indian Talk: Hand Signals of the North American Indians. Cody, Iron Eyes, illus. LC 73-16246. 112p. (gr. 1 up). 1970. 12.95 (ISBN 0-911010-83-1); pap. 5.95 (ISBN 0-911010-82-3). Naturegraph.
Hofsinde, Robert. Indian Sign Language. Hofsinde, Robert, illus. LC 56-5178. (gr. 5 up). 1956. PLB 12.88 (ISBN 0-688-31610-7, Morrow Junior Books). Morrow.

INDIANS OF NORTH AMERICA-SIKSIKA INDIANS-FICTION
Yolen, Jane. Sky Dogs. Moser, Barry, illus. LC 89-26960. 32p. (ps-3). 1990. 15.95 (ISBN 0-15-275480-6); limited ed., numbered & s 100.00 (ISBN 0-15-275481-4). HarBraceJ.

INDIANS OF NORTH AMERICA-SIOUX INDIANS
Brooks, B. The Sioux. (Illus.). 32p. (gr. 5-8). 1989. lib. bdg. 12.67 (ISBN 0-86625-382-3). Rourke Corp.

Crow, Moses N. Hoksila & the Red Buffalo. Provincial, Bernard W., illus. 40p. (Orig.). (gr. 3 up). 1991. pap. 5.95 (ISBN 1-877976-02-4, 4B6ZO017). Tipi Pr.
Among the Lakota, this legend is called, Enya-hoksei. It is told differently by every story-teller of every clan. The outline of the legend remains the same as it travels with time. The whole story changes with the changing of times. The significance of it, as it goes through the ages, is that it has no horses in it. The story has to be very old. But like all legends, it keeps in tune with the passing of time. When Hoksila the young warrior begins his long journey, his hunt to rescue his wife & to rid his tribe of the red buffalo with the ugly black spots. Then he could free all the young maidens. This is a story of the battle of good & evil, & how it's been handed down by the Lakota. An engaging story for the young & those not so young.
Publisher Provided Annotation.

—A Legend from Crazy Horse Clan. Flood, Renee S., ed. Soldier, Daniel L., illus. 36p. (Orig.). (gr. 3 up). 1987. pap. 4.95 (ISBN 1-877976-03-2, 4B6ZO010). Tipi Pr.
"A Legend from Crazy Horse Clan" is a story for children of all ages. Beautiful illustrations by Daniel Long Soldier keep the legend alive in the reader's eye. The historian or student of Indian ways will enjoy the book as much as the child of seven, in whose imagination the baby raccoon Mesu embodies all that is faithful & loving in a small furry pet. Listen carefully to the words of Tashia. The symbolic role of man & woman is evident throughout the legend. Although the story essentially describes the life of a girl, the narrator is male. Clearly, the legend describes the male viewpoint of manhood, religion, courtship, aging & death. The characters are gentle, yet there is a strong underlying theme of tribal identity. Without a doubt, we are looking at life through the eyes of a warrior. Indian oral narration is spoken American literature in its finest form. When Lakota children of the 1990s become grandparents themselves, they will tell the legends again. Thanks to Moses Big Crow, one of those legends may well be "A Legend from Crazy Horse Clan."
Publisher Provided Annotation.

Crowl, Christine. The Hunter & the Woodpecker. (Illus.). 12p. (Orig.). (ps-6). 1990. pap. 2.50 (ISBN 1-877976-09-1, 4B6ZO015). Tipi Pr.
This children's book describes how the Sioux first discovered the flute, which makes magical music. The Red Headed Woodpecker tells a young brave of its powers to win over a beautiful maiden. A charming story, delightfully illustrated in four color. A story for children of all ages.
Publisher Provided Annotation.

—White Buffalo Women. (Illus.). 18p. (Orig.). (gr. 6). 1991. pap. 2.50 (ISBN 1-877976-10-5, 4B6ZO014). Tipi Pr.
This story is a core legend of the Sioux & how the Sioux received the Sacred Prayer Pipe. The pipe was an important religious symbol among the Sioux. It was a "moveable" altar which was used in prayer & ceremony. It was the most cherished thing a man could own. The legend of "White Buffalo Women" & the pipe, originated with the Brule Sioux & is a story that has been handed down through the centuries. Beautifully told & illustrated in four color, a charming story for children young & old.
Publisher Provided Annotation.

Hoover, Herbert T. The Yankton Sioux. Porter, Frank, intro. by. (Illus.). 104p. (gr. 5 up). 1988. lib. bdg. 17.95 (ISBN 1-55546-736-9); pap. 9.95 (ISBN 0-7910-0369-8). Chelsea Hse.
Landau, Elaine. The Sioux. (Illus.). 64p. (gr. 3 up). 1991. pap. 4.95 (ISBN 0-531-15606-0). Watts.
McGovern, Ann. If You Lived with the Sioux Indians. (gr. k-3). 1976. pap. 2.95 (ISBN 0-590-40533-0). Scholastic Inc.
Osinski, Alice. The Sioux. LC 84-7629. (Illus.). 48p. (gr. k-4). 1984. lib. bdg. 14.60 (ISBN 0-516-01929-5); pap. 4.95 (ISBN 0-516-41929-3). Childrens.
Sandoz, Mari. These Were the Sioux. Kills Two & Amos Bad Heart Bull, illus. LC 85-8914. 118p. (gr. 6-12). 1985. pap. 4.95 (ISBN 0-8032-9151-5, Bison). U of Nebr Pr.

Simms, Thomas E. Otokahekagapi (First Beginnings) Sioux Creation Story. (Illus.). 36p. (Orig.). 1987. pap. 3.50 (ISBN 1-877976-06-7, 4B6ZO005). Tipi Pr.
The first in a series of Lakota legends, is written & illustrated to foster greater respect for a proud people's tradition. This account in English & Lakota presents the profundity of the creation mystery. The pictures are Indian pictures, because this is the beginning of the Sioux Creation account. But it is for all children everywhere, because everyone asks about how things got started & how the World began. "So this picture book is like a little ball game. We shall learn that the book is a ball. Wakantanka will throw this ball to us, which is this book, & we shall catch it. Then we shall understand it. And we shall enjoy ourselves. Bring the ball -- this book -- to the Center, which is your Heart, then you will receive a present. The present is invisible, like a little secret. Good. That's all. Now I shall throw the ball to you. Catch it!"
Publisher Provided Annotation.

INDIANS OF NORTH AMERICA-SIOUX INDIANS-FICTION
Shubert, J. Lansing. The Legacy of George Partridgeberry. Steele, Robert, ed. Shubert, Christiane, illus. 381p. (Orig.). (gr. 9-12). 1990. pap. 12.95 (ISBN 0-9627015-0-5). J L Shubert.

INDIANS OF NORTH AMERICA-SOCIAL LIFE AND CUSTOMS
see also Indians of North America-Dances; Indians of North America-Games
Batdorf, Carol. Gifts of the Season: Life among the Northwest Indians. Graves, Katheryn, illus. 24p. (Orig.). (gr. 1-6). 1990. pap. 5.95 (ISBN 0-88839-246-X). Hancock House.
Behrens, June. Powwow. LC 83-7274. (Illus.). 32p. (gr. k-4). 1983. PLB 14.60 (ISBN 0-516-02387-X); pap. 3.95 (ISBN 0-516-42387-8). Childrens.
Boss-Ribs, Mary C. & Running-Crane, Jenny. Stories of Our Blackfeet Grandmothers. (Orig.). (gr. 1-6). 1984. pap. 1.95 (ISBN 0-89992-096-9). Coun India Ed.
Boule, Mary N. The California Native American Tribes. Liddell, Dan, illus. (gr. 1-8). 1991. pap. 68.95 boxed ed. (ISBN 1-877599-23-9). Merryant Pubs.
Brandt, Keith. Indian Festivals. Guzzi, George, illus. LC 84-2644. 32p. (gr. 3-6). 1985. PLB 9.49 (ISBN 0-8167-0182-2); pap. text ed. 2.95 (ISBN 0-8167-0183-0). Troll Assocs.
Carter, Alden R. The Shoshoni. (Illus.). 64p. (gr. 3-5). 1989. PLB 11.90 (ISBN 0-531-10753-1). Watts.
Family, Clan, Nation. 48p. (gr. 4-5). 1989. PLB 10.95 (ISBN 0-685-26404-1). Capstone Pr.
A Feast for Everyone. 48p. (gr. 4-5). 1989. PLB 10.95 (ISBN 0-685-26405-X). Capstone Pr.
Gilliland, Hap. Coyote's Pow-Wow. (gr. 1-6). 1972. 2.95 (ISBN 0-89992-022-5). Coun India Ed.
Goodchild, Peter. The Spark in the Stone: Skills & Projects from the Native American Tradition. LC 90-27324. (Illus.). 144p. (Orig.). (gr. 5 up). 1991. pap. 11.95 (ISBN 1-55652-102-2). Chicago Review.
Hofsinde, Robert. Indian Warriors & Their Weapons. Hofsinde, Robert, illus. LC 65-11041. (gr. 4-7). 1965. PLB 11.88 (ISBN 0-688-31613-1, Morrow Junior Books). Morrow.
Hoyt-Goldsmith, Diane. Pueblo Storyteller. Migdale, Lawrence, illus. LC 90-46405. 32p. (gr. 3-7). 1991. PLB 14.95 reinforced (ISBN 0-8234-0864-7). Holiday.
McGaw, Jessie B. Chief Red Horse Tells About Custer. LC 81-1392. (Illus.). 40p. (gr. 4 up). 1981. 9.95 (ISBN 0-525-66713-X, Lodestar Bks). Dutton Child Bks.

McKeown, Martha F. Come to Our Salmon Feast. LC 59-9823. (Illus.). (gr. 4-9). 1959. 7.95 (ISBN 0-8323-0157-4). Binford Mort.
May, R. A Plains Indian Warrior. (Illus.). 32p. (gr. 3-8). Date not set. PLB 14.00 (ISBN 0-86592-147-4). Rourke Corp.
Medicine Man. 48p. (gr. 4-5). 1989. PLB 10.95 (ISBN 0-685-26407-6). Capstone Pr.
Payne, Elizabeth. Meet the North American Indians. (Illus.). (gr. 2-6). 1965. 5.95 (ISBN 0-394-80060-5, Random Juv); lib. bdg. 8.99 (ISBN 0-394-90060-X, Random Juv). Random.
Thomson, Ruth. Indians of the Plains. (Illus.). 32p. (gr. k-4). 1991. PLB 11.40 (ISBN 0-531-14157-8). Watts.
Trimble, Stephen. The Village of Blue Stone. Dewey, Jennifer O. & Reade, Deborah, illus. LC 88-34194. 64p. (gr. 3-7). 1990. 13.95 (ISBN 0-02-789501-7, Mcmillan Child Bk). Macmillan Child Grp.
Wolfson, Evelyn. Growing up Indian. Bock, William S., illus. LC 86-9053. 96p. (gr. 10 up). 1986. 10.95 (ISBN 0-8027-6643-9); PLB 11.85 (ISBN 0-8027-6644-7). Walker & Co.

INDIANS OF NORTH AMERICA–SPORTS
see Indians of North America–Games

INDIANS OF NORTH AMERICA–WARS
see also U. S.–History–French and Indian War, 1755-1763

Henry Tall Bull & Weist, Tom. Cheyenne Warriors. (gr. 4-12). 1976. pap. 2.95 (ISBN 0-89992-015-2). Coun India Ed.
McGaw, Jessie B. Chief Red Horse Tells About Custer. LC 81-1392. (Illus.). 40p. (gr. 4 up). 1981. 9.95 (ISBN 0-525-66713-X, Lodestar Bks). Dutton Child Bks.
Marrin, Albert. War Clouds in the West: Indians & Cavalrymen, 1860-1890. LC 84-4621. (Illus.). 224p. (gr. 4 up). 1984. 14.95 (ISBN 0-689-31066-8, Atheneum Child Bk). Macmillan Child Grp.

INDIANS OF NORTH AMERICA–WYAM INDIANS

McKeown, Martha F. Come to Our Salmon Feast. LC 59-9823. (Illus.). (gr. 4-9). 1959. 7.95 (ISBN 0-8323-0157-4). Binford Mort.
—Linda's Indian Home. LC 56-8826. (Illus.). (gr. 3-7). 1969. 7.95 (ISBN 0-8323-0151-5). Binford Mort.

INDIANS OF NORTH AMERICA–YUMA INDIANS

Bee, Robert L. The Yuma. (Illus.). (gr. 5 up). 1989. 17.95 (ISBN 1-55546-737-7). Chelsea Hse.

INDIANS OF NORTH AMERICA–ZUNI INDIANS–FICTION

Hillerman, Tony. The Boy Who Made Dragonfly: A Zuni Myth. Grado, Janet, illus. LC 86-6996. 85p. (gr. 5 up). 1986. pap. 8.95 (ISBN 0-8263-0910-0). U of NM Pr.

INDIANS OF SOUTH AMERICA

Beck, Barbara L. The Incas. rev. ed. Greenberg, Lorna, rev. by. (Illus.). 72p. (gr. 4 up). 1983. PLB 10.40 (ISBN 0-531-04528-5). Watts.
A Day with Tupi. (gr. 4). pap. 2.00 (ISBN 0-915266-01-6). Awani Pr.
Flora. Feathers Like a Rainbow: An Amazon Indian Tale. Flora, illus. LC 88-26788. 32p. (gr. k-3). 1989. 13.95 (ISBN 0-06-021837-1); PLB 13.89 (ISBN 0-06-021838-X). HarpC Child Bks.
Morrison. Indians of the Amazon, Reading Level 5. (Illus.). 48p. (gr. 4-8). Date not set. PLB 15.33 (ISBN 0-86625-266-5). Rourke Corp.
Morrison, Marion. Indians of the Andes. (Illus.). 48p. (gr. 4-8). 1987. PLB 15.33 (ISBN 0-86625-260-6). Rourke Corp.
Redhawk, Richard. Grandmother's Christmas Story: A True Tale of the Quechan Indians. (Illus.). (ps-5). 1987. pap. 6.95 (ISBN 0-940113-08-2). Sierra Oaks Pub.

INDIANS OF SOUTH AMERICA–FICTION

O'Dell, Scott. The Amethyst Ring. LC 82-23388. 224p. (gr. 7 up). 1983. 12.95 (ISBN 0-395-33886-7). HM.
Ritch, Ronald. Bones of Molech. Graves, Helen, ed. LC 86-51078. 240p. 1987. pap. 9.95 (ISBN 1-55523-061-X). Winston-Derek.

INDIANS OF SOUTH AMERICA–LEGENDS

Bierhorst, John, ed. & tr. Black Rainbow: Legends of the Incas & Myths of Ancient Peru. LC 76-19092. 160p. (gr. 5 up). 1976. 9.95 (ISBN 0-374-30829-2). FS&G.
Bierhorst, John, ed. In the Trail of the Wind: American Indian Poems & Ritual Orations. Bierhorst, Jane B., illus. LC 71-144822. 224p. (gr. 7 up). 1971. 6.95 (ISBN 0-374-33640-7). FS&G.
McDermott, Gerald. Arrow to the Sun: A Pueblo Indian Tale. LC 73-16172. (Illus.). 48p. (gr. 1 up). 1974. pap. 14.95 (ISBN 0-670-13369-8). Viking Child Bks.

INDIC LITERATURE–COLLECTIONS

Das, Manoj. Books Forever. Chatterji, Sukumar, illus. (gr. 2-8). 1979. pap. 2.50 (ISBN 0-89744-175-3). Auromere.

INDIVIDUALISM
see also Communism

Simon, Norma. Why Am I Different? Rubin, Caroline, ed. Leder, Dora, illus. LC 76-41172. 32p. (gr. k-2). 1976. PLB 10.95 (ISBN 0-8075-9074-6). A Whitman.

INDIVIDUALITY
see also Personality

Barclay, Shinan N. Who Am I? What Am I? Where Do I Belong? The Storytale about the Search for Meaning, Identity & Purpose. (Illus.). 40p. (ps-4). 1990. 5.95 (ISBN 0-317-89505-2); pap. write for info. (ISBN 0-945086-08-3). Sunlight Prodns.
Barker, Shane R. Finding a Friend in the Mirror. LC 88-21743. viii, 113p. (gr. 7-12). 1988. 8.95 (ISBN 0-87579-178-6). Deseret Bk.
Danziger, Paula. Can You Sue Your Parents for Malpractice? LC 78-72856. 266p. (gr. 7 up). 1979. 14.95 (ISBN 0-385-28112-9). Delacorte.
DePaola, Tomie. The Art Lesson. DePaola, Tomie, illus. 32p. (ps-3). 1989. 13.95 (ISBN 0-399-21688-X, Putnam). Putnam Pub Group.
Gaston, Blanche P. I Like Me, Vol. I. Kerns, Aaron, illus. 24p. (Orig.). (gr. k-3). 1982. 6.95x (ISBN 0-9608516-0-7); pap. 4.95x (ISBN 0-9608516-1-5). I Like Me Pubs.
Konczal, Dee & Pesetski, Loretta. We All Come in Different Packages. 88p. (gr. 3-6). 1983. 8.95 (ISBN 0-88160-099-7, LW 243). Learning Wks.
Pinkwater, Manus. The Big Orange Splot. (Illus.). (gr. k-2). 1977. 9.95g (ISBN 0-8038-0777-5). Hastings.
Schwartz, Linda. I Am Special. 24p. (gr. 1-4). 1978. 3.95 (ISBN 0-88160-053-9, LW 601). Learning Wks.
Spier, Peter. People. Spier, Peter, illus. LC 78-19832. 48p. (gr. 1-3). 1980. PLB 13.95 (ISBN 0-385-13181-X); pap. 14.99 (ISBN 0-385-13182-8). Doubleday.
Starkman, Neal. Personal Views. Gellos, Nancy, illus. LC 89-22302. 43p. (Orig.). (gr. 6-12). 1989. pap. 5.95 (ISBN 0-935529-12-8). Comprehen Health Educ.
Thomasson, Merry. Hey Look at Me! Here We Go. Havens, Greg, illus. (ps-2). 1987. 9.95 (ISBN 0-9615407-0-2). Thomasson-Grant.
—Hey Look at Me! I Can Be. Poole, Valerie, illus. (ps-2). 1987. 9.95 (ISBN 0-9615407-1-0). Thomasson-Grant.
—Hey Look at Me! I Like to Dream. Poole, Valerie, illus. (ps-2). 1987. 9.95 (ISBN 0-9615407-2-9). Thomasson-Grant.

INDOCHINA
see Asia, Southeastern

INDONESIA

Hassal, S. & Hassal, P. Brunei. (Illus.). (gr. 5 up). 1988. 14.95 (ISBN 0-7910-0158-X). Chelsea Hse.
Jacobs, Judy. Indonesia: A Nation of Islands. (Illus.). 128p. (gr. 5 up). 1990. PLB 14.95 (ISBN 0-87518-423-5, Dillon). Macmillan Child Grp.
Lerner Publications, Department of Geography Staff, ed. Indonesia in Pictures. (Illus.). 64p. (gr. 5 up). 1990. PLB 12.95 (ISBN 0-8225-1860-0). Lerner Pubns.
Lye, Keith. Take a Trip to Indonesia. Payne, Tony, illus. LC 84-51076. 32p. (gr. k-3). 1985. PLB 7.99 (ISBN 0-531-04940-X). Watts.
Lyle, Garry. Indonesia. (Illus.). (gr. 5 up). 1988. 14.95 (ISBN 0-222-01035-5). Chelsea Hse.
Williams, Jeff T. Macao. (Illus.). 96p. (gr. 5 up). 1988. lib. bdg. 14.95 (ISBN 1-55546-786-5). Chelsea Hse.

INDUCTION (LOGIC)
see Logic

INDUSTRIAL DRAWING
see Mechanical Drawing

INDUSTRIAL MANAGEMENT
see also Business; Machinery; Marketing

INDUSTRIAL MATERIALS
see Materials

INDUSTRIAL PSYCHOLOGY
see Psychology, Applied

INDUSTRIAL REVOLUTION
see Great Britain–History–19th Century; Industry–History

INDUSTRIAL WASTES
see Waste Products

INDUSTRIES
see Industry

INDUSTRY
For general works on manufacturing and mechanical activities. Names of all individual industries are not included in this list but are to be added as needed, e.g. Steel Industry And Trade, etc.
see also Machinery in Industry; Manufactures

Grigoli, Valorie. Service Industries. 72p. (gr. 4-8). 1984. PLB 10.40 (ISBN 0-531-04832-2). Watts.
Sproule, Anna. New Ideas in Industry. MacDonald, Ed, ed. (Illus.). 48p. (gr. 4 up). 1988. PLB 11.90 (ISBN 0-531-19502-3, Hampstead Pr). Watts.

INDUSTRY–HISTORY

Brownstone, David M. & Franck, Irene. Manufacturers & Miners. (Illus.). 176p. 1988. 17.95x (ISBN 0-8160-1447-7). Facts on File.
Tunis, Edwin. Colonial Craftsmen: The Beginnings of American Industry. Tunis, Edwin, illus. LC 75-29612. 160p. (gr. 7 up). 1976. 24.95 (ISBN 0-690-01062-1, Crowell Jr Bks). HarpC Child Bks.
Vialls, Christine. The Industrial Revolution Begins. LC 81-13714. (Illus.). 52p. (gr. 5 up). 1982. PLB 9.95 (ISBN 0-8225-1223-8). Lerner Pubns.
Weitzman, David. Windmills, Bridges, & Old Machines Discovering Our Industrial Past. LC 82-3231. (Illus.). 128p. (gr. 5 up). 1982. 15.95 (ISBN 0-684-17456-1, Scribner). Macmillan.

INDUSTRY AND ART
see Art Industries and Trade

INEBRIATES
see Alcoholism

INEQUALITY
see Equality

INFANTS
For works about children in the earliest period of life, usually the first two years only.

Ahlberg, Janet & Ahlberg, Allan. The Baby's Catalogue. LC 82-9928. (Illus.). 32p. (gr. k up). 1983. 14.95i (ISBN 0-316-02037-0, Joy St Bks). Little.
Asmann, Lynn & Sprague, Jane. Baby Basics. Asmann, Lynn, illus. (gr. 5 up). 1980. pap. 4.95 (ISBN 0-938416-00-6). BCS Educ Aids.
Banish, Roslyn. Let Me Tell You about My Baby. rev. ed. Banish, Rosyln, illus. LC 87-31890. 64p. (ps-1). 1988. Repr. of 1982 ed. 12.95 (ISBN 0-06-020382-X); PLB 12.89 (ISBN 0-06-020383-8). HarpC Child Bks.
—Let Me Tell You about My Baby. Banish, Roslyn, illus. LC 87-31890. 64p. (ps-1). 1988. pap. 3.95 (ISBN 0-06-446084-3, Trophy). HarpC Child Bks.
Berenstain, Stan & Berenstain, Janice. The New Baby. Berenstain, Stan & Berenstain, Janice, illus. LC 74-2535. 32p. (Orig.). (ps-1). 1974. pap. 2.25 (ISBN 0-394-82908-5, Random Juv). Random.
Brown, Laurie K. Baby Time: A Grownup's Handbook to Use with Baby. Brown, Marc, illus. LC 88-34901. 48p. 1989. 12.95 (ISBN 0-394-89462-6); lib. bdg. 13.99 (ISBN 0-394-99462-0). Knopf.
Cartwright, Stephen, illus. The New Baby. 16p. (ps up). 1986. 2.95 (ISBN 0-86020-966-0). EDC.
Cole, Joanna. The New Baby at Your House. Hammid, Hella, photos by. LC 85-10653. (Illus.). 48p. (ps-3). 1985. 11.95 (ISBN 0-688-05806-X); lib. bdg. 11.88 (ISBN 0-688-05807-8, Morrow Jr Bks); pap. 5.95 (ISBN 0-688-07418-9, Mulberry Bks). Morrow Jr Bks.
Foord, Jo, photos by. The Book of Babies: A First Picture Book of All the Things That Babies Do. LC 90-39490. (Illus.). 32p. (ps). 1991. 10.95 (ISBN 0-679-80955-4); PLB 12.99 (ISBN 0-679-90955-9). Random.
Gee, R. Babies: Understanding Conception, Birth & the First Years. 48p. (gr. 5-10). 1986. PLB 13.96 (ISBN 0-88110-336-5); pap. 6.95 (ISBN 0-86020-839-7). EDC.
Henderson, Kathy. The Baby's Book of Babies. Sieveking, Anthea, photos by. LC 88-20428. (Illus.). 24p. (ps-k). 1989. 9.95 (ISBN 0-8037-0634-0). Dial Bks Young.
Hendrickson, Karen. Baby & I Can Play & Fun with Toddlers. rev. ed. Steelsmith, Shari, ed. LC 89-64200. (Illus.). 56p. (ps-3). 1990. lib. bdg. 16.95 (ISBN 0-943990-57-2); pap. 6.95 (ISBN 0-943990-56-4). Parenting Pr.
Howard, Lin, illus. Hello Baby. 14p. (ps). 1984. padded cotton percale 4.95 (ISBN 0-448-41200-4, G&D). Putnam Pub Group.
Jacobsen, Mark & Kozlovski, Jane. Baby's Book. Jacobsen, Judith, ed. La Belle, Susan, illus. 1989. 24.95 (ISBN 0-9623800-0-8). Me Two Pubns.
—Baby's First Year. Jacobsen, Judith, ed. La Belle, Susan, illus. 1989. pap. 9.95 (ISBN 0-9623800-1-6). Me Two Pubns.
Jonas, Ann. When You Were a Baby. Jonas, Ann, illus. LC 81-12800. 24p. (ps-1). 1982. 14.95 (ISBN 0-688-00863-1); PLB 14.88 (ISBN 0-688-00864-X). Greenwillow.
Kugler, Lisa. A New Baby for Us: Sibling Preparation & Activity Book for Big Brothers & Sisters. Kugler, Lisa, illus. 32p. (Orig.). (ps-1). 1990. pap. 5.95 (ISBN 0-944782-03-5). Glover Pr.
Lawrence, John. Good Babies, Bad Babies: A Primer for Expectant Parents. (ps). 1990. 10.95 (ISBN 0-87923-823-2). Godine.
Ormerod, Jan. One Hundred One Things to Do with a Baby. LC 84-4401. (Illus.). 32p. (ps-2). 1984. lib. bdg. 13.88 (ISBN 0-688-03802-6). Lothrop.
Oxenbury, Helen. Family. (Illus.). 14p. (ps-k). 1981. 3.50 (ISBN 0-671-42110-7, Little Simon). S&S Trade.
Pankow, Valerie. No Bigger Than My Teddy Bear. 12/1987 ed. Connelly, Gwen, illus. (ps-2). pap. 0.50 (ISBN 0-687-28028-1). Abingdon.
Patent, Dorothy H. Babies! LC 87-26663. (Illus.). 40p. (gr. k-3). 1988. reinforced bdg. 14.95 (ISBN 0-8234-0685-7); pap. 5.95 (ISBN 0-8234-0701-2). Holiday.
Petty, Kate. The New Baby. Kopper, Lisa, illus. 24p. (gr. 1-3). 1987. PLB 5.29 (ISBN 0-531-17071-3, Gloucester Pr). Watts.
Rogers, Fred. The New Baby. Judkis, Jim, photos by. LC 84-26210. (Illus.). 32p. (gr. k-2). 1985. 12.95 (ISBN 0-399-21236-1, Putnam); pap. 5.95 (ISBN 0-399-21238-8, Putnam). Putnam Pub Group.
Rowland, Pleasant T. Our New Baby. Thieme, Jeanne, ed. Backes, Nick, illus. (ps). 1990. White Version. 19.95 ea. (ISBN 0-937295-64-7); African-American Version. 19.95 (ISBN 0-937295-65-5). Pleasant Co.
Schaffer, Patricia. How Babies & Family Are Made-There Is More Than One Way! Corbett, Susanne, illus. LC 86-23087. 64p. (gr. k-4). 1988. pap. 6.95 (ISBN 0-935079-17-3). Tabor Sarah Bks.
See What Baby Can Do. (ps). 2.50 (ISBN 0-448-03047-0, G&D). Putnam Pub Group.
Stein, Sara B. That New Baby. LC 73-15271. (Illus.). 48p. 1984. pap. 8.95 (ISBN 0-8027-7227-7). Walker & Co.
Stodden, Norma J. & McCormick, Linda. The All Gone Book. Levy, Gail, ed. Loui, Jill, illus. 18p. (ps). 1988. bds. 3.95 (ISBN 0-943693-05-5). TRI Pubns.
—The Love Book. Levy, Gail, ed. Loui, Jill, illus. 18p. (ps). 1988. bds. 3.95 (ISBN 0-943693-04-7). TRI Pubns.
—The More Book. Levy, Gail, ed. Loui, Jill, illus. 18p. (ps). 1988. bds. 3.95 (ISBN 0-943693-03-9). TRI Pubns.
Stortz, Diane M. What Are Babies Like? Hutton, Kathryn, illus. 20p. (ps). 1987. 1.59 (ISBN 0-87403-312-8, 2012). Standard Pub.
Tannenbaum, D. Leb. Getting Ready for Baby. Bahr, Amy C., ed. Rao, Tony, illus. 64p. 1982. pap. 3.95 (ISBN 0-671-45324-6, Little Simon). S&S Trade.
Twinn, Michael, illus. My Baby Brother. 8p. (ps-2). 1977. 2.00 (ISBN 0-85953-068-X, Pub. by Child's Play England). Childs Play.
Wilburn, Kathy, illus. The Pudgy Book of Babies. 16p. (gr. k). 1984. pap. 2.95 (ISBN 0-448-10207-2, G&D). Putnam Pub Group.

Young, Mary M., illus. Bear with Me: Story & Coloring Book Adjusting to Life with a New Baby. 16p. (ps-3). 1989. pap. 7.95 (ISBN 0-943114-20-9, CB100). Childbirth Graphics.

INFANTS–DISEASES

see Children–Diseases

INFANTS–FICTION

Alexander, Martha. When the New Baby Comes, I'm Moving Out. Alexander, Martha, illus. LC 79-4275. 32p. (gr. k-3). 1981. pap. 3.95 (ISBN 0-8037-9563-7). Dial Bks Young.

Aliki. Welcome, Little Baby. LC 86-7648. (Illus.). 24p. (ps up). 1987. 13.95 (ISBN 0-688-06810-3); PLB 13.88 (ISBN 0-688-06811-1). Greenwillow.

Anderson, Norma R. An Elfindale Story. Gonzales, Joe, illus. LC 81-5977. 36p. (Orig.). (gr. 1-6). 1981. pap. 5.95 (ISBN 0-913504-64-5). Lowell Pr.

Anholt, Catherine. Aren't You Lucky! 1991. 13.95 (ISBN 0-316-04264-1). Little.

Asch, Frank. Baby in the Box. Gibbons, Gail, illus. LC 88-16452. 32p. (ps-3). 1989. PLB 12.95 (ISBN 0-8234-0725-X). Holiday.

—Baby in the Box. (Illus.). (ps). 1990. Repr. 5.95 (ISBN 0-8234-0844-2). Holiday.

Bradman, Tony. This Little Baby. Williams, Jenny, illus. 32p. (ps-k). 1990. 13.95 (ISBN 0-399-22202-2, Putnam). Putnam Pub Group.

Brook, Ruth. Happy Birthday, Baby. Kondo, Vala, illus. LC 86-30750. 32p. (gr. k-3). 1988. PLB 11.89 (ISBN 0-8167-0912-2); pap. text ed. 2.95 (ISBN 0-8167-0913-0). Troll Assocs.

Brown, Marc. Arthur's Baby, Vol. 1. 1987. 13.95 (ISBN 0-316-11123-6). Little.

Burningham, John. The Baby. LC 75-4564. (Illus.). (ps-1). 1975. PLB 11.89 (ISBN 0-690-00901-1, Crowell Jr Bks). HarpC Child Bks.

Byrne, David. Stay up Late. Kalman, Maira, illus. LC 87-10399. (ps up). 1987. pap. 14.95 (ISBN 0-670-81895-X). Viking Child Bks.

Caseley, Judith. Annie's Potty. LC 89-34717. (Illus.). 24p. (ps up). 1990. 12.95 (ISBN 0-688-09065-6); lib. bdg. 12.88 (ISBN 0-688-09066-4). Greenwillow.

Chorao, Kay. The Cherry Pie Baby. Chorao, Kay, illus. LC 88-2630. 32p. (ps-3). 1989. 12.95 (ISBN 0-525-44435-1, DCB). Dutton Child Bks.

—Kate's Box. Chorao, Kay, illus. LC 82-2403. 24p. (ps). 1982. 3.95 (ISBN 0-525-44010-0, DCB). Dutton Child Bks.

Cook, Jean T. Hugs for Our New Baby. (Illus.). (ps-2). 1987. 5.95 (ISBN 0-570-04165-1, 56-1622). Concordia.

Cowley, Joy. Baby Gets Dressed. Belton, Robyn, illus. 8p. (gr. k-2). 1989. pap. text ed. 15.00 (ISBN 1-55911-274-3). Wright Group.

—Baby Gets Dressed, 6 bks. Belton, Robyn, illus. 8p. (gr. k-2). 1986. Set. pap. text ed. 12.60 (ISBN 1-55911-335-9). Wright Group.

Drawbaugh, Susan M. What Pet Will I Get? LC 77-83881. (gr. 1-3). 1977. 7.95 (ISBN 0-89430-017-2). Palos Verdes.

France, Melissa D. Ten Little Babies. (ps). 1990. 9.95 (ISBN 0-525-44643-5, DCB). Dutton Child Bks.

Franklin, Jonathan. Don't Wake the Baby. (Illus.). 32p. (ps-1). 1991. bds. 13.95 jacketed (ISBN 0-374-31826-3). FS&G.

Gerstein, Mordicai. Arnold of the Ducks. Gerstein, Mordicai, illus. LC 82-47735. 64p. (gr. k-3). 1983. 12.95 (ISBN 0-06-022002-3); PLB 12.89 (ISBN 0-06-022003-1). HarpC Child Bks.

Goodall, Jane & Van Lawick-Goodall, Hugo. Grub the Bush Baby. 80p. (ps up). 1988. 13.95 (ISBN 0-395-48696-3, Sandpiper); pap. 5.95 (ISBN 0-395-48695-5, Sandpiper). HM.

Harper, Anita. It's Not Fair. Hellard, Susan, illus. LC 86-4950. 24p. (ps-k). 1986. 10.95 (ISBN 0-399-21365-1, Philomel). Putnam Pub Group.

Hedderwick, Mairi. Katie Morag & the Tiresome Ted. Hedderwick, Mairi, illus. LC 85-23786. (gr. k-3). 1986. 12.95 (ISBN 0-316-35401-5). Little.

Henkes, Kevin. Julius, the Baby of the World. LC 88-34904. (Illus.). 32p. (ps up). 1990. 12.95 (ISBN 0-688-08943-7); PLB 12.88 (ISBN 0-688-08944-5). Greenwillow.

Hennessy, B. G. A, B, C, D, Tummy, Toes, Hands, Knee. Watson, Wendy, illus. 32p. (ps-1). 1989. pap. 12.95 (ISBN 0-670-81703-1). Viking Child Bks.

Hoban, Russell. A Baby Sister for Frances. Hoban, Lillian, illus. LC 64-15154. (gr. k-3). 1976. pap. 3.95 (ISBN 0-06-443006-5, Trophy). HarpC Child Bks.

Howard, Lin, illus. Baby Talk. 14p. (ps). 1984. padded cotton percale 4.95 (ISBN 0-448-41201-2, G&D). Putnam Pub Group.

Hutchins, Pat. Where's The Baby? Hutchins, Pat, illus. LC 86-33566. 32p. (ps-3). 1988. 11.95 (ISBN 0-688-05933-3); lib. bdg. 11.88 (ISBN 0-688-05934-1). Greenwillow.

Isadora, Rachel. Babies. LC 88-18782. (Illus.). (ps up). 1990. 13.95 (ISBN 0-688-08031-6); PLB 13.88 (ISBN 0-688-08032-4). Greenwillow.

—I Hear. Isadora, Rachel, illus. LC 84-6103. 32p. (ps). 1985. 11.75 (ISBN 0-688-04061-6); PLB 11.88 (ISBN 0-688-04062-4). Greenwillow.

—I See. Isadora, Rachel, illus. LC 84-6104. 32p. (ps). 1985. PLB 13.88 (ISBN 0-688-04060-8). Greenwillow.

—I See. LC 90-48254. (Illus.). 24p. (ps up). Date not set. bds. 6.95 (ISBN 0-688-10523-8). Greenwillow.

Jam, Teddy. Night Cars. LC 88-37230. (Illus.). 32p. (ps-1). 1989. 13.95 (ISBN 0-531-05793-3); PLB 13.99 (ISBN 0-531-08393-4). Orchard Bks Watts.

Jarrell, Mary. The Knee-Baby. Shimin, Symeon, illus. 32p. (ps up). 1988. pap. 4.95 (ISBN 0-374-44244-4). FS&G.

Jonas, Ann. When You Were a Baby. Jonas, Ann, illus. 32p. (ps-1). 1986. pap. 3.95 (ISBN 0-14-050574-1, Puffin). Puffin Bks.

—When You Were a Baby. LC 90-47799. (Illus.). 24p. (ps up). 1991. bds. 6.95 (ISBN 0-688-10525-4). Greenwillow.

Keller, Holly. What Alvin Wanted. LC 88-34917. (Illus.). 32p. (ps up). 1990. 12.95 (ISBN 0-688-08933-X); lib. bdg. 12.88 (ISBN 0-688-08934-8). Greenwillow.

Kingsley, Charles. Water Babies. Adam, G. Mercer, ed. Childers, Norman, illus. (gr. k-4). Repr. of 1905 ed. 12.95 (ISBN 0-940561-09-3). White Rose Pr.

Koehler, Phoebe. The Day We Met You. LC 89-35344. 48p. (ps-k). 1990. 12.95 (ISBN 0-02-750901-X, Bradbury Pr). Macmillan Child Grp.

Kramer, Robin. Where's Baby? (Illus.). 20p. (ps). 1990. 10.95 (ISBN 0-8249-8362-9). Ideals.

Lakin, Patricia. Don't Touch My Room. Brewster, Patience, illus. 32p. (ps-3). 1988. 12.95 (ISBN 0-316-51230-3); pap. 5.95 (ISBN 0-316-51228-1). Little.

Lasky, Kathryn & Knight, Maxwell B. A Baby for Max. Knight, Christopher G., photos by. LC 84-5307. (Illus.). 48p. (gr. k-3). 1984. 12.95 (ISBN 0-684-18064-2, Scribners Young Read). Macmillan Child Grp.

Lindgren, Barbro. The Wild Baby. Prelutsky, Jack, tr. from SWE. Erikkson, Eva, illus. LC 81-2151. (gr. k-3). 1981. PLB 13.88 (ISBN 0-688-00601-9). Greenwillow.

MacCombie, Turi, illus. Hush, Little Baby. 1989. pap. 5.95 (ISBN 0-553-45907-4). Bantam.

McKee, David. Who's a Clever Baby? Briley, D., ed. McKee, D., illus. LC 88-22966. 32p. (gr. 1-3). 1989. 12.95 (ISBN 0-688-08595-4); PLB 12.88 (ISBN 0-688-08596-2). Lothrop.

Marron, Carol A. No Trouble for Grandpa. Burstein, Chaya, illus. LC 83-7977. 32p. (gr. 3-6). 1983. PLB 14.65 (ISBN 0-940742-27-6). Raintree Pubs.

Oppenheim, Joanne. Wake up, Baby! Sweat, Lynn, illus. (ps-3). 1990. PLB 9.99 (ISBN 0-553-05907-6); pap. 3.50 (ISBN 0-553-34914-7). Bantam.

Ormerod, Jan. Just Like Me. LC 85-18056. (Illus.). 24p. (ps). 1986. 4.95 (ISBN 0-688-04211-2). Lothrop.

—Messy Baby. LC 84-12610. (Illus.). 24p. (ps). 1985. 4.95 (ISBN 0-688-04128-0). Lothrop.

—Reading. LC 84-12628. (Illus.). 24p. (ps). 1985. 4.95 (ISBN 0-688-04127-2). Lothrop.

—The Saucepan Game. Briley, D., ed. Ormerod, Jan, illus. LC 88-12893. 32p. (ps). 1989. 10.95 (ISBN 0-688-08518-0); PLB 10.88 (ISBN 0-688-08519-9). Lothrop.

—This Little Nose. Ormerod, Jan, illus. LC 87-2605. 24p. (ps). 1987. 5.95 (ISBN 0-688-07276-3). Lothrop.

Parish, Peggy. Amelia Bedelia & the Baby. Sweat, Lynn, illus. LC 80-22263. 64p. (gr. 1-3). 1981. 13.95 (ISBN 0-688-00316-8); PLB 13.88 (ISBN 0-688-00321-4). Greenwillow.

Paterson, Diane. Smile for Auntie. LC 76-2285. (Illus.). (gr. k-2). 1976. 7.95 (ISBN 0-8037-8066-4); PLB 7.89 (ISBN 0-8037-8067-2); Pied Piper Bk. pap. 3.50 (ISBN 0-8037-7981-X). Dial Bks Young.

Sage, Chris. Happy Baby. LC 89-78045. (Illus.). 12p. (ps). 1990. 5.95 (ISBN 0-8037-0883-1). Dial Bks Young.

—Sleepy Baby. LC 89-78339. (Illus.). 12p. (ps). 1990. 5.95 (ISBN 0-8037-0888-2). Dial Bks Young.

Schaffer, Barbara. Hush, Little Baby. Schaffer, Barbara, illus. 10p. (ps). 1982. 3.50 (ISBN 0-448-46829-8, G&D). Putnam Pub Group.

Skorpen, Liesel M. His Mother's Dog. Mullin, M. E., illus. LC 76-58707. (ps-3). 1978. HarpC Child Bks.

Smith, Wendy. The Witch Baby. Smith, Wendy, illus. LC 85-40590. 32p. (ps-3). 1986. pap. 7.95 (ISBN 0-670-80953-5). Viking Child Bks.

Stevenson, James. Worse Than Willy! Stevenson, James, illus. LC 83-14201. 32p. (gr. k-3). 1984. 10.25 (ISBN 0-688-02596-X); PLB 10.88 (ISBN 0-688-02597-8). Greenwillow.

Szekeres, Cyndy. The New Baby. (Illus.). (ps-k). 1989. pap. write for info. (ISBN 0-307-11998-X). Western Pub.

Taylor, Mark A. One Tiny Baby. Hutton, Kathryn, illus. 32p. (gr. k-2). 1989. 1.99 (ISBN 0-87403-599-6, 3859). Standard Pub.

Terris, Susan. Baby-Snatcher. 240p. (gr. 6-8). 1986. pap. 2.50 (ISBN 0-590-40241-2, Apple Paperbacks). Scholastic Inc.

—Baby-Snatcher. 240p. (gr. 6-8). 1986. pap. 2.95 (ISBN 0-590-43756-9). Scholastic Inc.

Van Der Beek, Deborah. Superbabe at the Park. Van Der Beek, Deborah, illus. 32p. (ps-1). 1989. 11.95 (ISBN 0-399-21750-9, Putnam). Putnam Pub Group.

Waterton, Betty. Baby Boat. Fitzgerald, Joanne, illus. LC 89-11173. 32p. (ps-1). 1990. 10.95 (ISBN 0-679-80368-8); PLB 11.99 (ISBN 0-679-90368-2). McKay.

Willis, Jeanne. Earthlets, As Explained by Professor Xargle. Ross, Tony, illus. LC 88-23692. 32p. (ps-2). 1989. 13.95 (ISBN 0-525-44465-3, DCB). Dutton Child Bks.

Yabuuchi, Masayuki. Whose Baby? Yabuuchi, Masayuki, illus. LC 84-1088. 32p. (gr. k-1). 1985. 8.95 (ISBN 0-399-21210-8, Philomel). Putnam Pub Group.

Ziefert, Harriet. Before I Was Born. Coes, Rufus, illus. LC 88-37255. 40p. (ps-1). 1989. 11.95 (ISBN 0-394-85128-5); lib. bdg. 12.99 (ISBN 0-394-95128-X). Knopf.

INFECTION AND INFECTIOUS DISEASES

see Communicable Diseases

INFIRMARIES

see Hospitals

INFORMATION SERVICES

Lambert, Mark. Information Technology. (Illus.). 48p. (gr. 5-8). 1991. PLB 12.40 (ISBN 0-531-18386-6). Watts.

INFORMATION STORAGE AND RETRIEVAL SYSTEMS

Luehrmann, Arthur & Peckham, Herbert. Appleworks Date Bases: A Hands-On Guide. (Illus.). 168p. (Orig.). (gr. 7-12). 1987. pap. text ed. 9.25 (ISBN 0-941681-03-3); tchr's. set 18.50 (ISBN 0-941681-11-4). Computer Lit Pr.

—Hands-on Appleworks: A Guide to Word Processing, Data Bases & Spreadsheets. LC 87-836. (Illus.). 478p. (Orig.). (gr. 7-12). 1987. pap. text ed. 19.95 (ISBN 0-941681-07-6); tchr's. set 29.95 (ISBN 0-941681-13-0). Computer Lit Pr.

INITIAL TEACHING ALPHABET

Lenski, Lois. Little Farm. Lenski, Lois, illus. LC 58-12902. (gr. k-3). 1980. 5.25 (ISBN 0-8098-1009-3). McKay.

McConnell, Keith. The AnimAlphabet Encyclopedia. McConnell, Keith A., illus. 48p. (gr. 4 up). 1982. pap. 5.95 (ISBN 0-916144-97-6). Stemmer Hse.

INJURIES

see First Aid

INJURIOUS INSECTS

see Insects, Injurious and Beneficial

INLAND NAVIGATION

see also Canals; Lakes

INQUISITION–FICTION

Von Canon, Claudia. The Inheritance. LC 82-23418. 224p. (gr. 7 up). 1983. 10.95 (ISBN 0-395-33891-3). HM.

INSANE

see Mental Illness

INSECTICIDES

see also Insects, Injurious and Beneficial

Waldrop, Victor H., et al. The Unhuggables: The Truth about Snakes, Slugs, Skunks, Spiders, & Other Animals That Are Hard to Love. Pidgeon, Jean, illus. LC 88-19531. 96p. (gr. 2-7). 1988. 14.95 (ISBN 0-912186-91-7, 19419); PLB 17.95 (ISBN 0-912186-96-8, 19419). Natl Wildlife.

INSECTS

see also names of insects, e.g. Bees; Butterflies; Wasps

Ants & Insects. (ARA., Illus.). (gr. 8-12). 3.50x (ISBN 0-86685-185-2). Intl Bk Ctr.

Arneson, D. J. Incredible Insects. (Illus.). 24p. (Orig.). 1990. pap. 2.50 (ISBN 0-942025-20-2). Kidsbks.

Bailes, Edith G. But Will It Bite Me? A Reference Book of Insects for Children & Their Grownups. 112p. (Orig.). (gr. 1-6). 1985. pap. 9.95 (ISBN 0-9611118-1-X). Cardamom.

Barrett, Norman. Poisonous Insects. (Illus.). 32p. (gr. k-4). 1991. PLB 11.40 (ISBN 0-531-14152-7). Watts.

Batulla, Barbara. Insects. (Illus.). 40p. (Orig.). (gr. 2-6). 1990. pap. 4.95 (ISBN 0-920534-21-X, Pub. by Hyperion Pr Ltd CN). Sterling.

Better Homes & Gardens Editors. Bugs, Bugs, Bugs. (Illus.). 32p. 1989. 4.95 (ISBN 0-696-01884-5). Meredith Bks.

Boy Scouts of America. Insect Study. (Illus.). 64p. (gr. 6-12). 1985. pap. 1.85 (ISBN 0-8395-3353-5, 3353). BSA.

Braithwaite, Althea. Ladybugs. (ps-6). 1989. PLB 8.95 (ISBN 0-88462-190-1). Dearborn Finan.

Brandt, Keith. Insects. Brickman, Robin, illus. LC 84-2659. 32p. (gr. 2-6). 1985. PLB 9.49 (ISBN 0-8167-0184-9); pap. text ed. 2.95 (ISBN 0-8167-0185-7). Troll Assocs.

Burton, Maurice. Insects & Their Relatives. (Illus.). 64p. 1984. 15.95 (ISBN 0-87196-986-6). Facts on File.

Colbery, Katie. Find the Mistakes Science: Incredible Insects. (gr. 4-7). 1991. pap. 2.95 (ISBN 0-8431-2814-3). Price Stern.

Cooper, Don. Boogie-Woogie Bugs. Forrest, Sandra, illus. (ps-3). 1989. bk. & cassette 5.95 (ISBN 0-394-82950-6). Random.

Cottam, Clarence & Zim, Herbert S. Insects. Irving, James G., illus. 160p. 1987. pap. write for info. (ISBN 0-307-24055-X, Pub. by Golden Bks). Western Pub.

Cutting, Brian & Cutting, Jillian. Are You a Ladybug? Male, Alan, illus. 16p. (Orig.). (gr. k-2). 1988. pap. text ed. 23.00 (ISBN 1-55911-029-5). Wright Group.

—Are You a Ladybug, 6 bks. Male, Alan, illus. 16p. (Orig.). (gr. k-2). 1988. Set. pap. text ed. 19.80 (ISBN 1-55911-030-9). Wright Group.

Day, O. M. ABC's of Bugs & Beasts. Day, O. M., illus. 31p. (Orig.). (gr. 3-12). 1991. pap. 11.95 (ISBN 0-9629795-1-1). Klar-Iden Pub.
ABC's of Bugs & Beasts is primarily a picture book with colorful & comical illustrations of insects & animals. Critics have called O. M. Day's book a work of art with depth & value above

mere "read-to-me" entertainment. The book is meant to instill in children the concern for an interest in all living creatures, & to stimulate a desire for reading. O. M. Day specifically chose the insect to show that even they have a design in nature's plan, be it for good or for bad. Although focused to the younger child, older children also should have an interest. Various zoos find this publication appealing as well & are ordering. With the combination of the amusing illustrations & alphabet limericks, ABC's of Bugs & Beasts informs & entertains children. Klar-Iden, the publisher of ABC's of Bugs & Beasts is committed to publish only a small number of books each year, because it is their desire to produce quality rather than quantity. O. M. Day's book met their criteria. To order please contact Klar-Iden Publishing, 6963 Douglas Boulevard, Box #115, Granite Bay, CA 95661 or call (415) 856-1059.
Publisher Provided Annotation.

Embry, Lynn. Scientific Encounters of the Insect World. 64p. (gr. 4-7). 1988. wkbk. 6.95 (ISBN 0-86653-424-5, GA 1039). Good Apple.

Fine, Edith & Josephson, Judith. Big on Bugs. 24p. (ps). 1982. 2.95 (ISBN 0-88160-089-X, LW 128). Learning Wks.

Fischer-Nagel, Andreas & Fischer-Nagel, Heiderose. Life of the Ladybug. Fischer-Nagel, Andreas & Fischer-Nagel, Heiderose, illus. LC 85-25467. 48p. (gr. 2-5). 1986. lib. bdg. 12.95 (ISBN 0-87614-240-4). Carolrhoda Bks.

Fisher, Aileen. When It Comes to Bugs. Degen, Chris & Degen, Bruce, illus. LC 85-45248. 32p. (gr. k-3). 1986. PLB 12.89 (ISBN 0-06-021822-3). HarpC Child Bks.

Fitzsimons, Cecilia. My First Insects, Spiders & Crawlers: Pop-Up Field Guide. Fitzsimons, Cecilia, illus. LC 86-45490. 12p. (gr. k-4). 1987. 8.95 (ISBN 0-06-021889-4). HarpC Child Bks.

Fowler, Allan. It's a Good Thing There Are Insects. LC 90-2205. (Illus.). 32p. (ps-2). 1990. PLB 12.60; pap. 30.60 big bk. (ISBN 0-516-49465-1). Childrens.

Gattis, L. S., III. Insects for Pathfinders: A Basic Youth Enrichment Skill Honor Packet. (Illus.). 24p. (Orig.). (gr. 5 up). 1987. pap. 5.00 tchr's. ed. (ISBN 0-936241-30-6). Cheetah Pub.

Goor, Ron & Goor, Nancy. Insect Metamorphosis: From Egg to Adult. LC 89-15144. (Illus.). 32p. (gr. 2-6). 1990. 13.95 (ISBN 0-689-31445-0, Atheneum Child Bk). Macmillan Child Grp.

Gorey, Edward. The Bug Book. (Illus.). (gr. 4 up). 1987. 8.95 (ISBN 0-915361-69-8, Dist. by Watts). Adama Pubs Inc.

Hickman, Pamela M. Bugwise. 1991. pap. 8.95 (ISBN 0-201-57074-2). Addison-Wesley.

Holly, Brian. Bugs & Critters. Gruettner, Diane & Black, Diane, illus. 32p. (gr. 3-7). 1985. pap. 3.50 (ISBN 0-88625-118-4). Durkin Hayes Pub.

Hornblow, Leonora & Hornblow, Arthur. Insects Do the Strangest Things. Frith, Michael K., illus. LC 68-10046. (gr. 2-9). 1968. 5.95 (ISBN 0-394-80072-9, Random Juv); lib. bdg. 8.99 (ISBN 0-394-90072-3). Random.

Horton, Casey. Insects. 40p. (gr. 4up). 1984. lib. bdg. 12.40 (ISBN 0-531-03476-3). Watts.

Insect World. (Illus.). 88p. (ps-3). 1989. 15.93 (ISBN 0-8094-4841-6); lib. bdg. 21.27 (ISBN 0-8094-4842-4). Time-Life.

Insects. (gr. 4-6). 1960. pap. 2.95 (ISBN 0-8431-4272-3). Wonder.

Insects. (Illus.). 20p. (gr. k up). 1990. laminated, wipe clean surface 3.95 (ISBN 0-88679-590-7). Educ Insights.

Insects & Small Animals. (Illus.). (gr. 4 up). 3.50 (ISBN 0-7214-0320-4). Ladybird Bks.

Insects of Arizona. (Illus.). 32p. (gr. 3 up). 1984. pap. 1.00 (ISBN 0-935810-14-5). Primer Pubs.

Johnson, Sylvia A. Chirping Insects. Sato, Yuko, illus. LC 86-15380. 48p. (gr. 4 up). 1986. PLB 14.95 (ISBN 0-8225-1486-9). Lerner Pubns.

—Chirping Insects. 1990. pap. 5.95 (ISBN 0-8225-9562-1). Lerner Pubns.

—Ladybugs. Sato, Yuko, illus. LC 83-18777. 48p. (gr. 4 up). 1983. PLB 14.95 (ISBN 0-8225-1481-8). Lerner Pubns.

—Water Insects. Masuda, Modoki, illus. 48p. (gr. 4 up). 1989. PLB 14.95 (ISBN 0-8225-1489-3). Lerner Pubns.

Kirkpatrick, Rena K. Look at Insects. rev. ed. Farmer, Andrew, illus. LC 84-26228. 32p. (gr. 2-4). 1985. PLB 15.99 (ISBN 0-8172-2351-7); pap. text ed. 9.27 (ISBN 0-8172-2376-2). Raintree Pubs.

Losito, Linda, et al. Insects & Spiders. (Illus.). 96p. 1989. 17.95x (ISBN 0-8160-1967-3). Facts on File.

McKissack, Patricia & McKissack, Fredrick. Bugs! Martin, Clovis, illus. LC 88-22875. 32p. (ps-2). 1988. PLB 11.93 (ISBN 0-516-02088-9); pap. 2.95 (ISBN 0-516-42088-7). Childrens.

Mattern, Joanne. A Picture Book of Insects. Kinnealy, Janice, illus. LC 90-11211. 24p. (gr. 1-4). 1991. PLB 9.59 (ISBN 0-8167-2154-8); pap. 2.50 (ISBN 0-8167-2155-6). Troll Assocs.

Merrians, Deborah. I Can Read About Insects. Nodel, Norman, illus. LC 76-54493. (gr. 2-5). 1977. pap. 1.95 (ISBN 0-89375-040-9). Troll Assocs.

Morris, Dean. Insects That Live in Families. (ps-3). 1990. pap. 11.99 (ISBN 0-8172-3235-4). Raintree Pubs.

Mound, Laurence. Insect. Keates, Colin, et al, photos by. LC 89-15603. (Illus.). 64p. (gr. 5 up). 1990. 15.00 (ISBN 0-679-80441-2); PLB 14.99 (ISBN 0-679-90441-7). McKay.

Naden, C. J. I Can Read About Creepy Crawly Creatures. LC 78-68469. (Illus.). (gr. 3-6). 1979. pap. 1.95 (ISBN 0-89375-207-X). Troll Assocs.

Oda, Hidetomo. Insects & Their Homes. Pohl, Kathleen, ed. LC 85-28226. (Illus.). 32p. (gr. 3-7). 1986. PLB 16.67 (ISBN 0-8172-2528-5); pap. 9.27 (ISBN 0-8172-2553-6). Raintree Pubs.

Owen, Jennifer. Insect Life. Jackson, Ian & Harris, Alan, illus. 32p. (gr. 4-7). 1985. PLB 13.96 (ISBN 0-88110-173-7, Pub. by Usborne); pap. 5.95 (ISBN 0-86020-843-5). EDC.

Parker, Nancy W. & Wright, Joan R. Bugs. LC 86-29387. (Illus.). 40p. (gr. 1-4). 1987. 11.95 (ISBN 0-688-06623-2); lib. bdg. 11.88 (ISBN 0-688-06624-0). Greenwillow.

Penn, Linda. Young Scientists Explore: Insects, Bk. 1. 32p. (gr. k-3). 1982. 4.95 (ISBN 0-86653-070-3, GA 403). Good Apple.

Podendorf, Illa. Insects. LC 81-7689. (Illus.). 48p. (gr. k-4). 1981. PLB 13.27 (ISBN 0-516-01627-X); pap. 4.95 (ISBN 0-516-41627-8). Childrens.

Pohl, Kathleen. Giant Water Bugs. (Illus.). 32p. (gr. 3-7). 1986. pap. text ed. 16.67 (ISBN 0-8172-2714-8); pap. 9.27 (ISBN 0-8172-2732-6). Raintree Pubs.

Preston-Mafham, Ken. Discovering Centipedes & Millipedes. (ps-3). 1990. PLB 11.90 (ISBN 0-531-18313-0). Watts.

Quinn, Kaye. Book of Bugs & Other Insects. (Illus.). 80p. (Orig.). (gr. 2-4). 1989. pap. 2.50 (ISBN 0-8431-2375-3). Price Stern.

Reidel, Marlene. From Egg to Butterfly. Reidel, Marlene, illus. LC 81-204. 24p. (ps-3). 1981. PLB 6.95 (ISBN 0-87614-153-X). Carolrhoda Bks.

Selsam, Millicent E. Backyard Insects. Goor, Ronald, photos by. 40p. (ps-3). 1988. pap. 2.95 (ISBN 0-590-42256-1). Scholastic Inc.

Selsam, Millicent E. & Hunt, Joyce. A First Look at Insects. Springer, Harriett, illus. LC 73-92451. 32p. (gr. 2-4). 1974. PLB 12.85 (ISBN 0-8027-6182-8). Walker & Co.

Settel, Joanne & Baggett, Nancy. How Do Ants Know When You're Having A Picnic? And Other Questions Kids Ask about Insects & Other Crawly Things. Tunney, Linda, illus. LC 86-3353. 112p. (gr. 3-7). 1986. 12.95 (ISBN 0-689-31268-7, Atheneum Childrens Bk). Macmillan Child Grp.

Seymour, Peter. Insects: A Close-Up Look. Helmer, Jean C., illus. (gr. 2-5). 1985. 8.95 (ISBN 0-02-782120-X, Mcmillan Child Bk). Macmillan Child Grp.

Souza, Dorothy. Eight Legs. (Illus.). 40p. (gr. 1-4). 1991. PLB 12.95 (ISBN 0-87614-441-5). Carolrhoda Bks.

—Insects Around the House. (Illus.). 40p. (gr. 1-4). 1991. PLB 12.95 (ISBN 0-87614-438-5). Carolrhoda Bks.

—Insects in the Garden. (Illus.). 40p. (gr. 1-4). 1991. PLB 12.95 (ISBN 0-87614-439-3). Carolrhoda Bks.

—What Bit Me? (Illus.). 40p. (gr. 1-4). 1991. PLB 12.95 (ISBN 0-87614-440-7). Carolrhoda Bks.

Steele, Philip. Insects. LC 90-42016. (Illus.). 32p. (gr. 5-6). 1991. SBE 9.95 (ISBN 0-89686-581-9, Crestwood Hse). Macmillan Child Grp.

Stidworthy, John. Insects. (Illus.). 32p. (gr. 5-6). 1989. PLB 11.90 (ISBN 0-531-17184-1). Watts.

Whayne, Susanne S. The World of Insects. Dudley, Ebet, illus. 48p. (gr. 3-7). 1990. PLB 9.95 (ISBN 0-671-69018-3). S&S Trade.

Williams, Geoffrey T. Giants of the Insects World. (gr. 4-7). 1991. pap. 9.95 (ISBN 0-8431-2832-1). Price Stern.

The World in Your Backyard: And Other Stories of Insects & Spiders. (Illus.). 63p. (gr. 3-5). 1989. 10.95 (ISBN 0-88309-132-1). Zaner-Bloser.

INSECTS–COLLECTION AND PRESERVATION

Danks, Hugh. The Bug Book & Bug Bottle. LC 86-40541. (Illus.). 64p. (Orig.). (gr. k-5). 1987. pap. 8.95 (ISBN 0-89480-314-X, 1314). Workman Pub.

The Official Insect Collector's Kit. (gr. 3-6). incl. bug viewer 3.95 (ISBN 0-87406-479-1, 42-20316-3). Willowisp Pr.

INSECTS–FICTION

Barrett, Ethel. Smarty the Adventurous Fly. Blankenbaker, Frances, ed. Gaddy, David, illus. LC 89-37544. 24p. (gr. 3-7). 1989. 4.95 (ISBN 0-8307-1380-8, 5111863). Regal.

Brown, Ruth. Ladybug, Ladybug. Brown, Ruth, illus. 32p. (ps-1). 1988. 12.95 (ISBN 0-525-44423-8, DCB). Dutton Child Bks.

Carle, Eric. The Grouchy Ladybug. Carle, Eric, illus. LC 77-3170. 48p. (ps-1). 1977. 14.95i (ISBN 0-690-01391-4, Crowell Jr Bks); PLB 14.89 (ISBN 0-690-01392-2). HarpC Child Bks.

Cole, Joanna. Golly Gump Swallowed a Fly. Weissman, Bari, illus. LC 81-11072. 48p. (ps-3). 1982. 5.95 (ISBN 0-8193-1069-7); lib. bdg. 5.95 (ISBN 0-8193-1070-0). Parents.

Duffy, William G., Jr. The Adventures of Grubber Bug. LC 82-71946. 45p. (ps-3). 1984. 3.50x (ISBN 0-943864-33-X). Davenport.

Gackenbach, Dick. Little Bug. (Illus.). 32p. (ps-2). 1981. 13.95 (ISBN 0-395-30080-0, Clarion). HM.

Gangloff, Deborah. Albert & Victoria. Woodman, Bill, illus. 64p. (gr. 2 up). 1988. 10.95 (ISBN 0-517-57044-0). Crown.

Hass, E. A. Incognito Mosquito Flies Again. Madden, Don, illus. LC 84-15889. 112p. (gr. 3-6). 1985. lib. bdg. 4.99 (ISBN 0-394-96728-3, Random Juv); pap. 1.95 (ISBN 0-394-86728-9). Random.

—Incognito Mosquito Makes History. Madden, Don, illus. LC 86-20417. 128p. (gr. 3-6). 1987. lib. bdg. 5.99 (ISBN 0-394-97055-1, Random Juv); (BYR). Random.

—Incognito Mosquito, Private Insective. Madden, Don, illus. LC 84-6827. 112p. (gr. 3-6). 1985. pap. 1.95 (ISBN 0-394-86729-7, Random Juv). Random.

—Incognito Mosquito Takes to the Air. Fanelli, Jenny, ed. Madden, Don, illus. LC 85-2240. 112p. (gr. 3-6). 1986. lib. bdg. 4.99 (ISBN 0-394-97054-3); pap. 2.95 (ISBN 0-394-87054-9). Random.

Heller, Ruth. How to Hide a Butterfly. Heller, Ruth, illus. LC 85-70287. 32p. (ps-2). 1986. pap. 4.95 (ISBN 0-448-10478-4, G&D). Putnam Pub Group.

Hucklebug. (gr. 1-6). 1978. pap. 2.95 (ISBN 0-8431-0556-9). Price Stern.

Ipcar, Dahlov. Bug City. (gr. 2-5). 1985. pap. 6.95 (ISBN 0-930096-67-3). G Gannett.

James, Mary. Shoebag. (gr. 5-7). 1990. pap. 12.95 (ISBN 0-590-43029-7). Scholastic Inc.

Jones, Michael P., ed. Andorff the Energy Ant's Coloring Book. abr. ed. (Illus.). 34p. 1984. text ed. 11.00 (ISBN 0-89904-071-3); pap. text ed. 6.00 (ISBN 0-89904-072-1). Crumb Elbow Pub.

Jones, Renata. The Little White Ladybug. De Tuerk, Lif, illus. 54p. (ps-3). 1990. 8.95 (ISBN 0-932433-67-7). Windswept Hse.

Kent, Jack. The Caterpillar & the Polliwog. LC 82-7533. (Illus.). 32p. (gr. k-4). 1985. PLB 12.95 (ISBN 0-671-66280-5); pap. 5.95 (ISBN 0-671-66281-3). S&S Trade.

Kotzwinkle, William. Trouble in Bugland. Servello, Joe, illus. LC 82-49338. 160p. 1986. pap. 9.95 (ISBN 0-87923-555-1). Godine.

—Trouble in Bugland: A Collection of Inspector Mantis Mysteries. Servello, Joe, illus. LC 82-49338. 160p. (gr. 5 up). 1983. 9.95 (ISBN 0-87923-472-5). Godine.

McLaughlin, Molly. Dragonflies. (gr. 1-5). 1989. 14.95 (ISBN 0-8027-6846-6); PLB 15.85 (ISBN 0-8027-6847-4). Walker & Co.

Marcroft, Karen. Fulbert Firefly. Marcroft, Renee, illus. LC 85-90463. 48p. (gr. 3-8). 1986. 14.95 (ISBN 0-935849-00-9). Marcroft Prods.

Maxner, Joyce. Lady Bugatti. Hawkes, Kevin, illus. LC 90-19127. 32p. (gr. k up). 1991. 13.95 (ISBN 0-688-10340-5); PLB 13.88 (ISBN 0-688-10341-3). Lothrop.

Peet, Bill. The Gnats of Knotty Pine. Peet, Bill, illus. LC 75-17024. 48p. (gr. k-3). 1984. 13.95 (ISBN 0-395-21405-X); pap. 3.95 (ISBN 0-395-36612-7). HM.

Poulet, Virginia. Blue Bug & the Bullies. Meighan, Don, illus. LC 79-159789. 32p. (gr. k-3). 1971. PLB 14.60 (ISBN 0-516-03418-9); pap. 3.95 (ISBN 0-516-43418-7). Childrens.

—Blue Bug Finds a Friend. Maloney, Mary & Fleming, Stan, illus. LC 76-30369. 32p. (gr. k-3). 1977. PLB 14.60 (ISBN 0-516-03426-X). Childrens.

—Blue Bug Goes to Paris. Anderson, Peggy P., illus. LC 85-31390. 32p. (ps-3). 1986. PLB 14.60 (ISBN 0-516-03480-4). Childrens.

—Blue Bug to the Rescue. LC 76-8547. (Illus.). 32p. (ps-3). 1976. PLB 14.60 (ISBN 0-516-03425-1). Childrens.

—Blue Bug's Beach Party. Fleming, Stan & Maloney, Mary, illus. LC 74-31224. 32p. (gr. k-3). 1975. PLB 14.60 (ISBN 0-516-03423-5). Childrens.

—Blue Bug's Treasure. Maloney, Mary & Fleming, Stan, illus. LC 75-40352. 32p. (gr. k-2). 1976. PLB 14.60 (ISBN 0-516-03424-3). Childrens.

Reese, Bob. Scary Larry the Very Very Hairy Tarantula. LC 81-3871. (Illus.). 24p. (ps-2). 1981. 11.27 (ISBN 0-516-02306-3); pap. 2.95 (ISBN 0-516-42306-1). Childrens.

Reynolds-Naylor, Phyllis. Beetles Lightly Toasted. (gr. k-6). 1989. pap. 2.95 (ISBN 0-440-40143-7, YB). Dell.

Ryder, Joanne. When the Woods Hum. LC 90-37879. (Illus.). 32p. (gr. 1 up). 1991. 13.95 (ISBN 0-688-07057-4); PLB 13.88 (ISBN 0-688-07058-2, Morrow Jr Bks). Morrow Jr Bks.

Stone, Rosetta. Because a Little Bug Went Ka-Choo! Frith, Michael, illus. LC 75-1605. 48p. (gr. k-3). 1975. 6.95 (ISBN 0-394-83130-6); lib. bdg. 7.99 (ISBN 0-394-93130-0). Beginner.

Turin, Adela & Selig, Syvie. Of Cannons & Caterpillars. (Illus.). 32p. (gr. 3-6). 1980. 4.95 (ISBN 0-904613-62-3). Writers & Readers.

Webster, Jean. Daddy-Long-Legs. (Orig.). (gr. k-6). 1987. pap. 4.95 (ISBN 0-440-41673-6, Pub. by Yearling Classics). Dell.

Wickstrom, Lois. Ladybugs for Loretta. Mion, Francie & Johnson, Priscilla M., illus. (gr. k-6). 1978. pap. 2.00 (ISBN 0-916176-04-5). Sproing.
Wood, Leslie. The Frog & the Fly. (Illus.). 16p. 1987. pap. 2.95 (ISBN 0-19-272154-2). Oxford U Pr.

INSECTS–HABITS AND BEHAVIOR

Harrison, Virginia. The World of Honeybees. Oxford Scientific Films Staff, photos by. LC 89-33936. (Illus.). 32p. (gr. 2-3). 1989. PLB 10.95 (ISBN 0-8368-0142-3). Gareth Stevens Inc.
Hornblow, Leonora & Hornblow, Arthur. Insects Do the Strangest Things. Barlowe, Dorothy, illus. LC 88-30201. 64p. (gr. 2-4). 1990. lib. bdg. 6.99 (ISBN 0-394-94306-6); pap. 3.95 (ISBN 0-394-84306-1). Random.
Horton, et al. Amazing Fact Book of Insects. (Illus.). 32p. 1987. 11.95 (ISBN 0-685-23227-1). Creative Ed.
Mimicry & Camouflage. 64p. (gr. 5 up). 1988. 14.95 (ISBN 0-8160-1657-7). Facts On File.
Morris, Dean. Insects That Live in Families. rev. ed. LC 87-16696. (Illus.). 48p. (gr. 2-6). 1987. PLB 17.32 (ISBN 0-8172-3210-9). Raintree Pubs.
Nelson, JoAnne. Backyard Bugs. Collier, Roberta, illus. 16p. (Orig.). (gr. k-2). 1990. pap. 3.95 (ISBN 1-878624-08-3). McClanahan Bk.
Oda, Hidetomo. Insect Hibernation. Pohl, Kathy, ed. LC 85-2892. (Illus.). 32p. (Orig.). (gr. 3-7). 1986. text ed. 16.67 (ISBN 0-8172-2526-9); pap. text ed. 9.27 (ISBN 0-8172-2551-X). Raintree Pubs.
—Insects & Flowers. Pohl, Kathy, ed. LC 85-28206. (Illus.). 32p. (gr. 3-7). 1986. text ed. 16.67 (ISBN 0-8172-2527-7); pap. text ed. 9.27 (ISBN 0-8172-2552-8). Raintree Pubs.
—Insects in the Pond. Pohl, Kathy, ed. LC 85-28227. (Illus.). 32p. (gr. 3-7). 1986. text ed. 16.67 (ISBN 0-8172-2529-3); pap. text ed. 9.27 (ISBN 0-8172-2554-4). Raintree Pubs.
—The Ladybug. Pohl, Kathy, ed. LC 85-28199. (Illus.). 32p. (gr. 3-7). 1986. text ed. 16.67 (ISBN 0-8172-2538-2); pap. text ed. 9.27 (ISBN 0-8172-2563-3). Raintree Pubs.
O'Toole, Christopher. The Honeybee in the Meadow. Oxford Scientific Films Staff, photos by. LC 89-33935. (Illus.). 32p. (gr. 4-6). 1989. PLB 10.95 (ISBN 0-8368-0117-2). Gareth Stevens Inc.
Selsam, Millicent E. Where Do They Go? Insects in Winter. Wheatley, Arabelle, illus. LC 82-70976. 32p. (gr. k-3). 1984. 9.95 (ISBN 0-685-07285-1). Scholastic Inc.
Wyler, Rose. Grass & Grasshoppers. Steltenpohl, Jane, ed. Petruccio, Steven, illus. 32p. (gr. k-2). 1990. lib. bdg. 11.98 (ISBN 0-671-66347-X); pap. 4.95 (ISBN 0-671-66351-8). Messner.

INSECTS, INJURIOUS AND BENEFICIAL

see also Insecticides
also names of insects, e.g. locusts; silkworms, etc.
Bender, Lionel. Poisonous Insects. FS-Aladdin Staff, ed. LC 88-50510. (Illus.). 32p. (gr. 1-6). 1988. PLB 11.90 (ISBN 0-531-17103-5, Gloucester Pr). Watts.
Berger, Melvin. Stranger Than Fiction: Killer Bugs. 128p. (Orig.). 1990. pap. 2.95 (ISBN 0-380-76036-3, Camelot). Avon.
Heymann, Georgianne. Aphids. (Illus.). 32p. (gr. 3-7). 1986. PLB 16.67 (ISBN 0-8172-2717-2). Raintree Pubs.

INSECTS AS CARRIERS OF DISEASE

see also Flies; Mosquitoes

INSPECTION OF SCHOOLS

see School Administration and Organization

INSPIRATION

see Creation (Literary, Artistic, etc.)

INSTRUCTION

see Education; Teaching

INSTRUMENTS, MUSICAL

see Musical Instruments

INSURANCE

Park, Jae S. Now What? Auto Accident Claims Guide. 100p. (Orig.). Date not set. pap. text ed. 3.95 (ISBN 0-685-28055-1). Park Pub Co.

INTEGRATED CIRCUITS

Davies. Inside the Chip. Round, Grahm, illus. (gr. 6 up). 1984. pap. 3.95 (ISBN 0-86020-729-3). EDC.

INTEGRATION, RACIAL

see Race Problems

INTELLECT

see also Creation (Literary, Artistic, etc.); Imagination; Knowledge, Theory of; Logic; Perception; Reasoning; Senses and Sensation; Thought and Thinking
Sanford, Doris. Don't Look at Me: A Child's Book about Feeling Different. Evans, Graci, illus. LC 86-185484. 27p. (ps-5). 1986. 7.95 (ISBN 0-88070-150-1). Multnomah.
Wenger, Win. A Method for Personal Growth & Development. (Illus.). 135p. (Orig.). (gr. 7-12). 1986. pap. 20.00 (ISBN 0-931865-09-3). Psychegenics.

INTELLECTUAL LIFE

see Culture; Learning and Scholarship

INTELLIGENCE

see Intellect

INTELLIGENCE OF ANIMALS

see Animal Intelligence

INTELLIGENCE SERVICE–U. S.

Kronenwetter, Michael. Covert Action. (Illus.). (gr. 9-12). 1991. PLB 12.90 (ISBN 0-531-13018-5). Watts.

INTEMPERANCE

see Alcoholism

INTERCOLLEGIATE ATHLETICS

see Athletics

INTERCULTURAL EDUCATION

For works dealing with the eradication of racial and religious prejudices by showing the nature and effects of race, creed and immigrant cultures.
Cole, Ann, et al. Children Are Children Are Children: An Activity Approach to Exploring Brazil, France, Iran, Japan, Nigeria, & the U. S. S. R. (Illus.). (gr. 3-7). 1978. pap. 15.95 (ISBN 0-316-15113-0). Little.

INTERCULTURAL EDUCATION–FICTION

Jackson, Jesse. Call Me Charley. Spiegel, Doris, illus. LC 45-9807. 156p. (gr. 5 up). 1945. PLB 13.89 (ISBN 0-06-022786-9). HarpC Child Bks.

INTERIOR DECORATION

see also Coverlets; Furniture; Tapestry
Everett, F. & Woods, P., eds. Design & Decorate Your Room. (Illus.). 48p. (gr. 6 up). 1989. lib. bdg. 13.96 (ISBN 0-88110-392-6, Usborne); pap. 7.95 (ISBN 0-7460-0438-9). EDC.
James, Elizabeth & Barkin, Carol. A Place of Your Own. Jacobs, Lou, Jr., illus. 96p. (gr. 9 up). 1981. (Dutton); pap. o.p. (ISBN 0-525-37099-4). NAL-Dutton.
Rourke, A. Decorating Your Room. (Illus.). 32p. (gr. 5 up). 1989. lib. bdg. 14.00 (ISBN 0-86625-286-X). Rourke Corp.
Sherrow, Victoria. Dream Rooms, Decorating with Flair. Magnuson, Diana, illus. LC 90-48241. 128p. (gr. 5-9). 1990. lib. bdg. 10.89 (ISBN 0-8167-2293-5); pap. text ed. 2.95 (ISBN 0-8167-2294-3). Troll Assocs.
Storm, Betsy. I Can Be an Interior Designer. LC 89-15758. 32p. (gr. k-3). 1989. PLB 13.93 (ISBN 0-516-01958-9); pap. 3.95 (ISBN 0-516-41958-7). Childrens.
Wood, Leslie. My House. (Illus.). 16p. (ps up). 1988. pap. 2.95 (ISBN 0-19-272186-0). Oxford U Pr.

INTERNAL-COMBUSTION ENGINES

see Gas and Oil Engines

INTERNATIONAL COOPERATION

For general works on international cooperative activities, with or without the participation of governments.
see also United Nations

INTERNATIONAL ECONOMIC RELATIONS

Fisher, Barbara & Spiegel, Richard, eds. Streams Four. (Illus.). 150p. (Orig.). (gr. 9-12). 1990. pap. 5.00 (ISBN 0-934830-44-4). Ten Penny.
Snow, Robbie & Milder, John. Year of Birth: A Month by Month Companion to Pregnancy, Birth & the First Three Months of Infancy. (Illus.). 124p. (Orig.). (gr. 12). 1991. pap. 14.95 (ISBN 0-9623321-2-7). Crystal Press.

INTERNATIONAL EDUCATION

For works on education for international understanding, world citizenship, etc.
see also Intercultural Education

INTERNATIONAL EXHIBITIONS

see Exhibitions

INTERNATIONAL LAW

see also International Relations; Pirates; Salvage; Slave Trade; War
Weiss, Malcolm E. One Sea, One Law? LC 81-47535. (Illus.). 120p. (gr. 4-6). 1982. 10.95 (ISBN 0-15-258690-3, HJ). HarBraceJ.

INTERNATIONAL ORGANIZATION

For works on plans leading towards political organizations of nations.
see also International Law; World Politics
also names of specific organizations, e.g. United Nations, etc.

INTERNATIONAL RELATIONS

see also Diplomacy; Disarmament; International Economic Relations; International Law; Peace
also names of countries with the subdivision Foreign Relations, e.g. U. S.–Foreign Relations, etc.
Arnold, Terrell E. & Kennedy, Moorhead. Think about Terrorism: The New Warfare. LC 87-21158. (Illus.). 153p. (gr. 9-12). 1988. lib. bdg. 14.85 (ISBN 0-8027-6757-5); pap. 5.95 (ISBN 0-8027-6758-3). Walker & Co.
Edwards, R. International Terrorism. (Illus.). 48p. (gr. 5 up). Date not set. PLB 18.00 (ISBN 0-86592-285-3). Rourke Corp.
Galicich, Anne. Samantha Smith: A Journey for Peace. LC 87-13614. (Illus.). 64p. (gr. 3 up). 1987. PLB 10.95 (ISBN 0-87518-367-0, Dillon). Macmillan Child Grp.
Kronenwetter, Michael. The War Against Terrorism. Steltenpohl, Jane, ed. (Illus.). 138p. (gr. 7-10). 1989. lib. bdg. 12.98 (ISBN 0-671-69050-7). Messner.
Nabhan, Martin, et al. World Partners, 6 bks. (Illus.). 384p. (gr. 7 up). 1990. Set. lib. bdg. 95.60 (ISBN 0-86593-087-2); Set. lib. bdg. 71.70s.p. (ISBN 0-685-36361-9). Rourke Corp.
Pringle, Laurence. Living in a Risky World. LC 88-31686. (Illus.). 112p. (gr. 5 up). 1989. 12.95 (ISBN 0-688-04326-7). Morrow Jr Bks.
Reynolds, Tony, et al. World Issues, 7 bks, Set III. (Illus.). 336p. (gr. 5 up). 1990. Set. lib. bdg. 126.00 (ISBN 0-86592-095-8); Set. lib. bdg. 94.50s.p. (ISBN 0-685-36375-9). Rourke Corp.
Swisher, Karin, ed. The Superpowers: A New Detente: Opposing Viewpoints. LC 89-36525. (Illus.). 264p. (gr. 10 up). 1989. PLB 15.95 (ISBN 0-89908-443-5); pap. 8.95 (ISBN 0-89908-418-4). Greenhaven.

INTERNATIONAL RELATIONS–FICTION

Blume, Judy. Iggie's House. large type, unabr. ed. 158p. (gr. 3-6). 1989. lib. bdg. 13.95 (ISBN 0-8161-4449-4). G K Hall.
Wibberley, Leonard. Mouse That Roared. (gr. 6-12). 1971. pap. 3.50 (ISBN 0-553-24969-X). Bantam.

INTERNATIONAL TRADE

see Commerce

INTERPERSONAL RELATIONS

see Human Relations

INTERPLANETARY COMMUNICATION

see Interstellar Communication

INTERPLANETARY VOYAGES

see also Outer Space–Exploration; Rockets (Aeronautics); Space Flight
Cameron, Eleanor. Mr. Bass's Planetoid. Darling, Louis, illus. (gr. 3-7). 1958. 14.95 (ISBN 0-316-12525-3, Joy St Bks). Little.
—The Wonderful Flight to the Mushroom Planet. Henneberger, Robert, illus. (gr. 4-6). 1988. 14.95 (ISBN 0-316-12537-7, Joy St Bks); pap. 4.95 (ISBN 0-316-12540-7, Joy St Bks). Little.
Elam, Richard M. Young Visitor to Mars. (Illus.). (gr. 4-7). PLB 6.70 (ISBN 0-8313-0031-0). Lantern.
Farrow, Peter & Lampert, Diane. Twyllyp. (Illus.). (gr. 3-7). 1963. 10.95 (ISBN 0-8392-3040-0). Astor-Honor.
Helmrath, M. O. & Bartlett, J. L. Bobby Bear's Rocket Ride. LC 68-56809. (Illus.). 32p. (ps-1). 1968. PLB 12.35 prebound (ISBN 0-87783-008-8); cassette 7.94x (ISBN 0-87783-186-6). Oddo.
Yolen, Jane. Commander Toad & the Dis-Asteroid. Degen, Bruce, illus. LC 84-1897. 64p. (gr. 4). 1985. lib. bdg. 8.99 (ISBN 0-698-30744-5, Coward); pap. 5.95 (ISBN 0-698-20620-7, Coward). Putnam Pub Group.

INTERSTELLAR COMMUNICATION

Marsh, Carole. The Backyard Searcher's Extra Terrestrial Log Book. (Illus.). (gr. 4-9). 1983. PLB 19.95 (ISBN 1-55609-282-2); pap. 14.95 (ISBN 0-935326-27-8). Gallopade Pub Group.
—How to Find an Extra Terrestrial in Your Own Backyard. (Illus.). 1983. 14.95 (ISBN 0-935326-09-X). Gallopade Pub Group.

INSTELLAR VOYAGES

see Interplanetary Voyages

INTERVIEWING (JOURNALISM)

see Reporters and Reporting

INTOLERANCE

see Toleration

INTOXICATION

see Alcoholism; Narcotic Habit

INVALIDS

see Physically Handicapped

INVASION OF PRIVACY

see Privacy, Right of

INVENTIONS

see also Creation (Literary, Artistic, etc.); Inventors
Bender, Lionel. Invention. King, Dave, photos by. LC 90-4888. (Illus.). 64p. (gr. 5 up). 1991. 15.00 (ISBN 0-679-80782-9); PLB 15.99 (ISBN 0-679-90782-3). Knopf.
Brown, Julie & Hott, Michael. Inventing Things. LC 89-11506. (Illus.). 64p. (gr. 2-3). 1990. PLB 12.95 (ISBN 0-8368-0035-4). Gareth Stevens Inc.
Crump, Donald J., ed. Small Inventions That Make a Big Difference. LC 83-23770. 104p. (gr. 3-8). 1984. 6.95 (ISBN 0-87044-498-0); PLB 8.50 (ISBN 0-87044-503-0). Natl Geog.
Dempsey, Michael, ed. Growing up with Science: The Illustrated Encyclopedia of Invention, 26 vols. rev. ed. LC 82-63047. (Illus.). (gr. 5-10). 1987. Set. 181.48 (ISBN 0-87475-841-6). Stuttman.
Elting, Mary. The Answer Book about Robots & Other Inventions. Barnes-Murphy, Rowan, illus. 80p. (gr. 3-7). 1984. pap. 2.95 (ISBN 0-448-13802-6, G&D). Putnam Pub Group.
Filson, Brent. Superconductors & Other New Breakthroughs in Science. (Illus.). 128p. (gr. 5-9). 1989. PLB 12.98 (ISBN 0-671-65857-3); PLB 9.74s.p. (ISBN 0-685-24680-9). Messner.
Friddle, Sue. Jake Art. Friddle, Jacob, illus. (Orig.). (gr. k-7). 1989. pap. 5.00 (ISBN 0-9623308-1-7). Anyones Pub.
Gardner, Robert. Experimenting with Inventions. (gr. 4-7). 1990. PLB 12.40 (ISBN 0-531-10910-0). Watts.
Groves, Seli & Buchman, Dian D. What If? Fifty Discoveries That Changed the World. 96p. (gr. 5-9). 1988. pap. 1.95 (ISBN 0-590-41009-1). Scholastic Inc.
Holt, Michael. Inventions. (Illus.). 64p. (gr. 4-6). 1990. PLB 12.95 (ISBN 0-8368-0010-9). Gareth Stevens Inc.
Jacobs, Daniel. What Does It Do? Inventions Then & Now. (Illus.). 24p. (ps-2). 1990. PLB 12.33 (ISBN 0-8172-3586-8); PLB 9.25 (ISBN 0-685-33581-X). Raintree Pubs.
Kinghorn, Harriet & Morberg, Mary. Research Shapes: Inventions. (Illus.). 64p. (gr. 2-5). 1989. 6.95 (ISBN 1-878279-01-7, MM1918). Monday Morning Bks.
Lets Discover Index. LC 86-646. (gr. 4-7). 1990. 13.27 (ISBN 0-8172-2596-X). Raintree Pubs.
McCormack, Alan. Inventors Workshop. LC 80-84185. (gr. 3-8). 1981. pap. 8.95 (ISBN 0-8224-9783-2). Fearon Teach Aids.
Murphy, Jim. Guess Again: More Weird & Wacky Inventions. LC 85-24320. (Illus.). 64p. (gr. 3-6). 1986. 13.95 (ISBN 0-02-767720-6, Bradbury Pr). Macmillan Child Grp.
Peterson, Patricia R. The Know It All: Resource Book for Kids & Grown-Ups, Too! (Illus.). 112p. (gr. 2 up). 1989. pap. 15.95 (ISBN 0-913705-45-4, ZB14-B). Zephyr Pr AZ.
Quinn, Kaye. Inventive Inventions. Quinn, Kaye, illus. 40p. (gr. 2-6). 1986. pap. 2.50 (ISBN 0-8431-1893-8). Price Stern.

Reid, S. Invention & Discovery: The Facts You Need to Know at a Glance. (Illus.). 128p. (gr. 6 up). 1987. PLB 15.96 (ISBN 0-88110-231-8); pap. 9.95 (ISBN 0-86020-956-3). EDC.

Schneider, Herman & Schneider, Nina. Quick Science: Science Experiments You Can Do in a Minute. Kessler, Leonard, illus. 64p. (Orig.). (gr. 4-6). 1987. pap. 2.95 activity bk. (ISBN 0-590-41354-6). Scholastic Inc.

Smith, David & Cassin, Sue. The Amazing Book of Firsts: Great Ideas. (ps up). 1990. PLB 5.98 (ISBN 0-7924-5400-6, Mallard Pr). BDD Promo Bk.

—The Amazing Book of Firsts: Record Makers. (ps up). 1990. PLB 5.98 (ISBN 0-7924-5399-9, Mallard Pr). BDD Promo Bk.

Stanish, Bob. The Unconventional Invention Book. (gr. 3-12). 1981. 8.95 (ISBN 0-86653-035-5, GA 263). Good Apple.

Stanish, Bob & Singletary, Carol. Inventioneering. Skiles, Janet, illus. 64p. (gr. 3-9). 1987. pap. 7.95 (ISBN 0-86653-402-4, GA 1019). Good Apple.

Sylvester, Diane. Inventions, Robots, Future. 112p. (gr. 4-6). 1984. 9.95 (ISBN 0-88160-108-X, LW 905). Learning Wks.

Tanner, Joey. Futuristics: A Zephyr Learning Packet. 73p. (gr. k-8). 1981. pap. 16.95 spiral bdg. (ISBN 0-913705-16-0, ZM03-V). Zephyr Pr AZ.

Taylor, Barbara. Be an Inventor. Weekly Reader Staff, illus. 64p. (gr. 4-6). 1987. 11.95 (ISBN 0-15-205950-4, VoyB); pap. 7.95 (ISBN 0-15-205951-2, VoyB). HarBraceJ.

Weiss, Harvey. How to Be an Inventor. LC 79-7823. (Illus.). 96p. (gr. 5 up). 1980. (Crowell Jr Bks); lib. bdg. 14.89 (ISBN 0-685-02096-7). HarpC Child Bks.

Wulffson, Don L. The Invention of Ordinary Things. Doty, Roy, illus. LC 80-17498. 96p. (gr. 3 up). 1981. PLB 12.88 (ISBN 0-688-51978-4). Lothrop.

Wyatt, Valerie. Amazing Investigations: Inventions. Kolacz, Jerzy, illus. 96p. (gr. 3-7). 1988. 12.95 (ISBN 0-13-023706-X, Little Simon). S&S Trade.

INVENTIONS–FICTION

Brightfield, Richard. U. S. A. What Is the Great American Invention. 112p. (gr. 4-6). 1989. pap. text ed. 3.95 (ISBN 0-07-048000-1). McGraw.

Cartwright, Pauline. Mr. Butterby's Amazing Machines. LC 90-10072. (Illus.). 16p. (gr. 1-4). 1990. PLB 14.64 (ISBN 0-8114-2690-4). Steck-V.

Haas, Dorothy. Burton's Zoom Zoom Va-Rooom Machine. Bobak, Cathy, illus. LC 89-77426. 144p. (gr. 5-8). 1990. 12.95 (ISBN 0-02-738201-X, Bradbury Pr). Macmillan Child Grp.

Johnson, Arvis M. The Bubble Machine. (Illus.). 26p. (Orig.). 1991. pap. write for info. (ISBN 1-55618-070-5). Brunswick Pub.

INVENTORS

see also Inventions

Aaseng, Nathan. The Inventors: Nobel Prizes in Chemistry, Physics, & Medicine. (Illus.). 80p. (gr. 5 up). 1988. PLB 12.95 (ISBN 0-8225-0651-3). Lerner Pubns.

Akinsheye, Dexter. African American Inventor Adolphus Samms, Vol. I. Akinsheye, Dayo, ed. Gibbs, C. R., intro. by. (Illus., Orig.). (gr. 1-12). Date not set. pap. 3.00 (ISBN 0-685-26241-3); Set of 39 titles. pap. 78.00 (ISBN 0-685-26242-1). TD Pub.

—African American Inventor Adolphus Samms, Vol. III. Akinsheye, Dayo, ed. Gibbs, C. R., intro. by. (Illus., Orig.). (gr. 1-12). Date not set. pap. 3.00 (ISBN 0-685-26243-X); Set of 39 titles. pap. 78.00 (ISBN 0-685-26244-8). TD Pub.

—African American Inventor Adolphus Samms, Vol. II. Akinsheye, Dayo, ed. Gibbs, C. R., intro. by. (Illus., Orig.). (gr. 1-12). Date not set. pap. 3.00 (ISBN 0-685-26245-6); Set of 39 titles. pap. 78.00 (ISBN 0-685-26246-4). TD Pub.

—African American Inventor Alice H. Parker. Akinsheye, Dayo, ed. Gibbs, C. R., intro. by. (Illus., Orig.). (gr. 1-12). Date not set. pap. 3.00 (ISBN 0-685-26189-1); Set of 39 titles. pap. 78.00 (ISBN 0-685-26190-5). TD Pub.

—African American Inventor Andrew J. Beard. Akinsheye, Dayo, ed. Gibbs, C. R., intro. by. (Illus., Orig.). (gr. 1-12). Date not set. pap. 3.00 (ISBN 0-685-26239-1); Set of 39 titles. pap. 78.00 (ISBN 0-685-26240-5). TD Pub.

—African American Inventor Benjamin F. Jackson. Akinsheye, Dayo, ed. Gibbs, C. R., intro. by. (Illus., Orig.). (gr. 1-12). Date not set. pap. 3.00 (ISBN 0-685-26205-7); Set of 39 titles. pap. 78.00 (ISBN 0-685-26206-5). TD Pub.

—African American Inventor Charles C. Brooks, Vol. II. Akinsheye, Dayo, ed. Gibbs, C. R., intro. by. (Illus., Orig.). (gr. 1-12). Date not set. pap. 3.00 (ISBN 0-685-26207-3); Set of 39 titles. pap. 78.00 (ISBN 0-685-26208-1). TD Pub.

—African American Inventor Charles C. Brooks, Vol. I. Akinsheye, Dayo, ed. Gibbs, C. R., intro. by. (Illus., Orig.). (gr. 1-12). Date not set. pap. 3.00 (ISBN 0-685-26209-X); Set of 39 titles. pap. 78.00 (ISBN 0-685-26210-3). TD Pub.

—African American Inventor Edward R. Lewis. Akinsheye, Dayo, ed. Gibbs, C. R., intro. by. (Illus., Orig.). (gr. 1-12). Date not set. pap. 3.00 (ISBN 0-685-26225-1); Set of 39 titles. pap. 78.00 (ISBN 0-685-26226-X). TD Pub.

—African American Inventor Elijah McCoy. Akinsheye, Dayo, ed. Gibbs, C. R., intro. by. (Illus., Orig.). (gr. 1-12). Date not set. pap. 3.00 (ISBN 0-685-26237-5); Set of 39 titles. pap. 78.00 (ISBN 0-685-26238-3). TD Pub.

—African American Inventor Frederick Jones, Vol. I. Akinsheye, Dayo, ed. Gibbs, C. R., intro. by. (Illus., Orig.). (gr. 1-12). Date not set. pap. 3.00 (ISBN 0-685-26173-5); Set of 39 titles. pap. 78.00 (ISBN 0-685-26174-3). TD Pub.

—African American Inventor Frederick Jones, Vol. II. Akinsheye, Dayo, ed. Gibbs, C. R., intro. by. (Illus., Orig.). (gr. 1-12). Date not set. pap. 3.00 (ISBN 0-685-26177-8); Set of 39 titles. pap. 78.00 (ISBN 0-685-26178-6). TD Pub.

—African American Inventor Garrett T. Morgan, Vol. II. Akinsheye, Dayo, ed. Gibbs, C. R., intro. by. (Illus., Orig.). (gr. 1-12). Date not set. pap. 3.00 (ISBN 0-685-26217-0); Set of 39 titles. pap. 78.00 (ISBN 0-685-26218-9). TD Pub.

—African American Inventor Garrett T. Morgan, Vol. I. Akinsheye, Dayo, ed. Gibbs, C. R., intro. by. (Illus., Orig.). (gr. 1-12). Date not set. pap. 3.00 (ISBN 0-685-26219-7); Set of 39 titles. pap. 78.00 (ISBN 0-685-26220-0). TD Pub.

—African American Inventor George F. Grant. Akinsheye, Dayo, ed. Gibbs, C. R., intro. by. (Illus., Orig.). (gr. 1-12). Date not set. pap. 3.00 (ISBN 0-685-26183-2); Set of 39 titles. pap. 78.00 (ISBN 0-685-26184-0). TD Pub.

—African American Inventor George R. Carruthes. Akinsheye, Dayo, ed. Gibbs, C. R., intro. by. (Illus., Orig.). (gr. 1-12). Date not set. pap. 3.00 (ISBN 0-685-26191-3); Set of 39 titles. pap. 78.00 (ISBN 0-685-26192-1). TD Pub.

—African American Inventor George Toliver. Akinsheye, Dayo, ed. Gibbs, C. R., intro. by. (Illus., Orig.). (gr. 1-12). Date not set. pap. 3.00 (ISBN 0-685-26227-8); Set of 39 titles. pap. 78.00 (ISBN 0-685-26228-6). TD Pub.

—African American Inventor George W. Murray. Akinsheye, Dayo, ed. Gibbs, C. R., intro. by. (Illus., Orig.). (gr. 1-12). Date not set. pap. 3.00 (ISBN 0-685-26199-9); Set of 39 titles. pap. 78.00 (ISBN 0-685-26200-6). TD Pub.

—African American Inventor Gertrude Downing. Akinsheye, Dayo, ed. Gibbs, C. R., intro. by. (Illus., Orig.). (gr. 1-12). Date not set. pap. 3.00 (ISBN 0-685-26213-8); Set of 39 titles. pap. 78.00. TD Pub.

—African American Inventor Granville T. Woods, Vol. II. Akinsheye, Dayo, ed. Gibbs, C. R., intro. by. (Illus., Orig.). (gr. 1-12). Date not set. pap. 3.00 (ISBN 0-685-26231-6); Set of 39 titles. pap. 78.00 (ISBN 0-685-26232-4). TD Pub.

—African American Inventor Granville T. Woods, Vol. I. Akinsheye, Dayo, ed. Gibbs, C. R., intro. by. (Illus., Orig.). (gr. 1-12). Date not set. pap. 3.00 (ISBN 0-685-26233-2); Set of 39 titles. pap. 78.00 (ISBN 0-685-26234-0). TD Pub.

—African American Inventor Harold Linden. Akinsheye, Dayo, ed. Gibbs, C. R., intro. by. (Illus., Orig.). (gr. 1-12). Date not set. pap. 3.00 (ISBN 0-685-26195-6); Set of 39 titles. pap. 78.00 (ISBN 0-685-26196-4). TD Pub.

—African American Inventor Henrietta Bradberry. Akinsheye, Dayo, ed. Gibbs, C. R., intro. by. (Illus., Orig.). (gr. 1-12). Date not set. pap. 3.00 (ISBN 0-685-26175-1); Set of 39 titles. pap. 78.00 (ISBN 0-685-26176-X). TD Pub.

—African American Inventor Henry Blair. Akinsheye, Dayo, ed. Gibbs, C. R., intro. by. (Illus., Orig.). (gr. 1-12). Date not set. pap. 3.00 (ISBN 0-685-26179-4); Set of 39 titles. pap. 78.00 (ISBN 0-685-26180-8). TD Pub.

—African American Inventor Hubert Julian. Akinsheye, Dayo, ed. Gibbs, C. R., intro. by. (Illus., Orig.). (gr. 1-12). Date not set. pap. 3.00 (ISBN 0-685-26181-6); Set of 39 titles. pap. 78.00 (ISBN 0-685-26182-4). TD Pub.

—African American Inventor Jack A. Johnson. Akinsheye, Dayo, ed. Gibbs, C. R., intro. by. (Illus., Orig.). (gr. 1-12). Date not set. pap. 3.00 (ISBN 0-685-26169-7); Set of 39 titles. pap. 78.00 (ISBN 0-685-26170-0). TD Pub.

—African American Inventor James T. Redding. Akinsheye, Dayo, ed. Gibbs, C. R., intro. by. (Illus., Orig.). (gr. 1-12). Date not set. pap. 3.00 (ISBN 0-685-26211-1); Set of 39 titles. pap. 78.00 (ISBN 0-685-26212-X). TD Pub.

—African American Inventor Jan E. Matzeliger. Akinsheye, Dayo, ed. Gibbs, C. R., intro. by. (Illus., Orig.). (gr. 1-12). Date not set. pap. 3.00 (ISBN 0-685-26215-4); Set of 39 titles. pap. 78.00 (ISBN 0-685-26216-2). TD Pub.

—African American Inventor John Pickering. Akinsheye, Dayo, ed. Gibbs, C. R., intro. by. (Illus., Orig.). (gr. 1-12). Date not set. pap. 3.00 (ISBN 0-685-26193-X); Set of 39 titles. pap. 78.00 (ISBN 0-685-26194-8). TD Pub.

—African American Inventor Joseph H. Smith. Akinsheye, Dayo, ed. Gibbs, C. R., intro. by. (Illus., Orig.). (gr. 1-12). Date not set. pap. 3.00 (ISBN 0-685-26235-9); Set of 39 titles. pap. 78.00 (ISBN 0-685-26236-7). TD Pub.

—African American Inventor Lewis H. Latimer, Vol. I. Akinsheye, Dayo, ed. Gibbs, C. R., intro. by. (Illus., Orig.). (gr. 1-12). Date not set. pap. 3.00 (ISBN 0-685-26185-9); Set of 39 titles. pap. 78.00 (ISBN 0-685-26186-7). TD Pub.

—African American Inventor Lewis H. Latimer, Vol. II. Akinsheye, Dayo, ed. Gibbs, C. R., intro. by. (Illus., Orig.). (gr. 1-12). Date not set. pap. 3.00 (ISBN 0-685-26187-5); Set of 39 titles. pap. 78.00 (ISBN 0-685-26188-3). TD Pub.

—African American Inventor Lewis Latimer. Akinsheye, Dayo, ed. Gibbs, C. R., intro. by. (Illus., Orig.). (gr. 1-12). Date not set. pap. 3.00 (ISBN 0-685-26201-4); Set of 39 titles. pap. 78.00 (ISBN 0-685-26202-2). TD Pub.

—African American Inventor Miriam E. Benjamin. Akinsheye, Dayo, ed. Gibbs, C. R., intro. by. (Illus., Orig.). (gr. 1-12). Date not set. pap. 3.00 (ISBN 0-685-26221-9); Set of 39 titles. pap. 78.00 (ISBN 0-685-26222-7). TD Pub.

—African American Inventor Norbert Rillieux. Akinsheye, Dayo, ed. Gibbs, C. R., intro. by. (Illus., Orig.). (gr. 1-12). Date not set. pap. 3.00 (ISBN 0-685-26223-5); Set of 39 titles. pap. 78.00 (ISBN 0-685-26224-3). TD Pub.

—African American Inventor Richard Spikes. Akinsheye, Dayo, ed. Gibbs, C. R., intro. by. (Illus., Orig.). (gr. 1-12). Date not set. pap. 3.00 (ISBN 0-685-26171-9); Set of 39 titles. pap. 78.00 (ISBN 0-685-26172-7). TD Pub.

—African American Inventor Richard Toomey. Akinsheye, Dayo, ed. Gibbs, C. R., intro. by. (Illus., Orig.). (gr. 1-12). Date not set. pap. 3.00 (ISBN 0-685-26229-4); Set of 39 titles. pap. 78.00 (ISBN 0-685-26230-8). TD Pub.

—African American Inventor Sara E. Goode. Akinsheye, Dayo, ed. Gibbs, C. R., intro. by. (Illus., Orig.). (gr. 1-12). Date not set. pap. 3.00 (ISBN 0-685-26203-0); Set of 39 titles. pap. 78.00 (ISBN 0-685-26204-9). TD Pub.

—African American Inventor William B. Purvis. Akinsheye, Dayo, ed. Gibbs, C. R., intro. by. (Illus., Orig.). (gr. 1-12). Date not set. pap. 3.00 (ISBN 0-685-26197-2); Set of 39 titles. pap. 78.00 (ISBN 0-685-26198-0). TD Pub.

Brophy, Ann. John Ericson & the Inventions of War. Gallin, Richard, ed. Steele, Henry, intro. by. (Illus.). 160p. (gr. 5 up). 1990. PLB 16.98 (ISBN 0-382-09943-5); pap. 8.95 (ISBN 0-382-24052-9). pap. 8.95. Silver Burdett Pr.

Carroll, Jeri & Wells, Candace. Inventors. Foster, Tom, illus. 64p. (gr. k-4). 1987. pap. 6.95 (ISBN 0-86653-381-8, GA1006). Good Apple.

Cousins, Margaret. Thomas Alva Edison. (Illus.). (gr. 4-8). 1965. lib. bdg. 8.99 (ISBN 0-394-90410-9, Random Juv). Random.

Dunn, Andrew. Alexander Graham Bell. (Illus.). 48p. (gr. 5-7). 1991. PLB 12.40 (ISBN 0-531-18418-8, Pub. by Bookwright Pr). Watts.

Lomask, Milton. Great Lives: Invention & Technology. (Illus.). 288p. (gr. 4-6). 1991. 22.95 (ISBN 0-684-19106-7, Scribners Young Read). Macmillan Child Grp.

Mitchell, Barbara. Shoes for Everyone: A Story about Jan Matzeliger. Mitchell, Hetty, illus. 64p. (gr. 3-6). 1986. PLB 9.95 (ISBN 0-87614-290-0); pap. 4.95 (ISBN 0-87614-473-3). Carolrhoda Bks.

Noonan, Geoffrey J. Nineteenth-Century Inventors. 128p. (gr. 6-9). 1992. lib. bdg. 16.95x (ISBN 0-8160-2480-4). Facts on File.

Ott, Virginia & Swanson, Gloria. Man with a Million Ideas: Fred Jones, Genius Inventor. LC 76-22444. (Illus.). 112p. (gr. 5 up). 1977. PLB 9.95 (ISBN 0-8225-0761-7). Lerner Pubns.

Patton, Sally & Maletis, Margaret. Inventors. rev. ed. 72p. (gr. 2-6). 1989. pap. text ed. 12.95 (ISBN 0-913705-35-7, ZS01). Zephyr Pr AZ.

Quiri, Patricia R. Alexander Graham Bell. (Illus.). 64p. (gr. 3-5). 1991. PLB 11.90 (ISBN 0-531-20022-1). Watts.

Richards, Norman. Dreamers & Doers: Inventors Who Changed the World. LC 81-21029. (Illus.). 156p. (gr. 5 up). 1984. 13.95 (ISBN 0-689-30914-7, Atheneum Child Bk). Macmillan Child Grp.

Sweet, Dovie D. Red Light, Green Light: The Life of Garrett Morgan & His Invention of the Stop Light. 4th ed. (Orig.). (gr. 1-6). 1988. pap. 5.00 (ISBN 0-682-49088-1). Kitwardo Pubs.

Van Steenwyk, Elizabeth. Levi Strauss: The Blue Jeans Man. (gr. 6-9). 1988. 13.95 (ISBN 0-8027-6795-8); PLB 14.85 (ISBN 0-8027-6796-6). Walker & Co.

Williams, Brian. Karl Benz. (Illus.). 48p. (gr. 5-8). 1991. RLB 12.40 (ISBN 0-531-18404-8, Pub. by Boatwright Pr). Watts.

INVENTORS–FICTION

Baker, Keith. The Magic Fan. (ps-3). 1989. 14.95 (ISBN 0-15-250750-7). HarBraceJ.

Fenner, Carol. A Summer of Horses. LC 88-45878. 144p. (Orig.). (gr. 3-6). 1989. lib. bdg. 7.99 (ISBN 0-394-90480-X); pap. 2.95 (ISBN 0-394-80480-5). Knopf.

Haas, Dorothy. Burton's Zoom Zoom Va-Rooom Machine. Bobak, Cathy, illus. LC 89-77426. 144p. (gr. 5-8). 1990. 12.95 (ISBN 0-02-738201-X, Bradbury Pr). Macmillan Child Grp.

Quin-Harkin, Janet. Septimus Bean & His Amazing Machine. Cumings, Art, illus. LC 79-163. 48p. (ps-3). 1980. 5.95 (ISBN 0-8193-0999-0). Parents.

INVERTEBRATES

see also Insects; Mollusks; Worms

Batulla, Barbara. Intervertebrates. Osen, Arlene, illus. 40p. (Orig.). (gr. 2-6). 1990. pap. 4.95 (ISBN 0-920534-57-0, Pub. by Hyperion Pr Ltd CN). Sterling.

Bender, Lionel. Invertebrates. Khan, Aziz, illus. 40p. (gr. 1). 1988. 12.40 (ISBN 0-318-37441-2). Watts.

Harlow, Rosie & Morgan, Gareth. Observing Minibeasts. Kuo Kang Chen, illus. 40p. (gr. 5-8). 1991. PLB 12.90 (ISBN 0-531-19125-7, Warwick). Watts.

Hemsley, William. Jellyfish to Insects: Projects with Biology. (Illus.). 32p. (gr. 5-9). 1991. PLB 11.90 (ISBN 0-531-17293-7, Gloucester Pr). Watts.

Illustrated Encyclopedia of Wildlife, Vol. 11: The Invertebrates, Pt. I. 240p. (gr. 7 up). 1990. lib. bdg. write for info. (ISBN 1-55905-047-0). Grey Castle.

Illustrated Encyclopedia of Wildlife, Vol. 12: The Invertebrates, Pt. II. 184p. (gr. 7 up). 1990. lib. bdg. write for info. (ISBN 1-55905-048-9). Grey Castle.

Illustrated Encyclopedia of Wildlife, Vol. 13: The Invertebrates, Pt. III. 184p. (gr. 7 up). 1990. lib. bdg. write for info. (ISBN 1-55905-049-7). Grey Castle.

Illustrated Encyclopedia of Wildlife, Vol. 14: The Invertebrates, Pt. IV. 184p. (gr. 7 up). 1990. lib. bdg. write for info. (ISBN 1-55905-050-0). Grey Castle.

Illustrated Encyclopedia of Wildlife, Vol. 15: The Invertebrates, Pt. V & Index. 192p. (gr. 7 up). 1990. lib. bdg. write for info. (ISBN 1-55905-051-9). Grey Castle.

Landau, Elaine. Interesting Invertebrates: A Look at Some Animals Without Backbones. (Illus.). 64p. (gr. 5-8). 1991. PLB 11.90 (ISBN 0-531-20036-1). Watts.

Loewer, Peter. The Inside-Out Stomach: An Introduction to Animals without Backbones. Jenkins, Jean, illus. LC 89-6499. 64p. (gr. 2 up). 1990. 13.95 (ISBN 0-689-31432-9, Atheneum Child Bk). Macmillan Child Grp.

Losito, Linda, et al. Simple Animals. (Illus.). 96p. 1989. 17.95x (ISBN 0-8160-1968-1). Facts on File.

Selsam, Millicent E. & Hunt, Joyce. A First Look at Animals Without Backbones. Springer, Harriett, illus. LC 76-12056. (gr. 2-4). 1976. PLB 9.85 (ISBN 0-8027-6269-7). Walker & Co.

Shepherd, Elizabeth. No Bones: A Key to Bugs & Slugs, Worms, & Ticks, Spiders & Centipedes, & Other Creepy Crawlies. Patterson, Ippy, illus. LC 87-1549. 96p. (gr. 2-5). 1988. 13.95 (ISBN 0-02-782880-8, Mcmillan Child Bk). Macmillan Child Grp.

Wiessinger, John. Bugs, Slugs, & Crayfish - Right Before Your Eyes. LC 89-1143. (Illus.). 64p. (gr. 4-10). 1989. PLB 15.95 (ISBN 0-89490-264-4). Enslow Pubs.

INVESTIGATIONS

Spellman, Linda. Creative Investigations. 48p. (gr. 4-8). 1982. 5.95 (ISBN 0-88160-045-8, LW 230). Learning Wks.

INVESTMENTS

see also Stock Exchange; Stocks

Young, Robin. The Stock Market. (Illus.). 80p. (gr. 5 up). 1991. PLB 14.95 (ISBN 0-8225-1780-9). Lerner Pubns.

IOWA

Aylesworth, Thomas G. & Aylesworth, Virginia L. Western Great Lakes (Illinois, Iowa, Wisconsin, Minnesota) (Illus.). 64p. (gr. 3 up). 1992. PLB 16.95 (ISBN 0-7910-1046-5). Chelsea Hse.

Canady, Robert & Annis, Scott. Color in Iowa Coloring Album. (Illus.). 32p. (Orig.). (gr. 1-5). 1984. pap. 3.95 (ISBN 0-9615584-0-7). Little Gnome.

Carole Marsh Iowa Books, 31 bks. Set. 638.45 (ISBN 0-7933-1290-6). Gallopade Pub Group.

Carpenter, Allan. Iowa. LC 79-11802. (Illus.). 96p. (gr. 4 up). 1979. PLB 19.93 (ISBN 0-516-04115-0). Childrens.

Carter, Brian. State Government in Iowa. 5th ed. Institute of Public Affairs Staff, ed. (Illus.). (gr. 10). 1990. pap. text ed. 7.00 (ISBN 0-317-02886-3). U Iowa IPA.

Fradin, Dennis. Iowa: In Words & Pictures. LC 79-19399. (Illus.). 48p. (gr. 2-5). 1980. PLB 15.93 (ISBN 0-516-03915-6); pap. 4.95 (ISBN 0-516-43915-4). Childrens.

Jenison, Norma J. & Benjamin, Starr J. The Eyes of the Storm: Belmond, Iowa Recalls the 1966 Homecoming Day Tornado. LC 89-84423. (Illus.). 256p. (Orig.). 1989. pap. 8.95 (ISBN 0-9623288-0-4). T Lydia Pr.

Marsh, Carole. Avast, Ye Slobs! Iowa Private Trivia. (Illus.). (gr. 3-12). 1990. PLB 19.95 (ISBN 0-7933-0448-2); pap. 14.95 (ISBN 0-7933-0447-4); computer disk 29.95 (ISBN 0-7933-0449-0). Gallopade Pub Group.

—The Beast of the Iowa Bed & Breakfast. (Illus.). (gr. 3-12). 1990. PLB 19.95 (ISBN 0-7933-1628-6); pap. 14.95 (ISBN 0-7933-1629-4); computer disk 29.95 (ISBN 0-7933-1630-8). Gallopade Pub Group.

—The Hard-to-Believe-But-True! Book of Iowa History, Mystery, Trivia, Legend, Lore, Humor & More. (Illus.). (gr. 3-12). 1990. PLB 19.95 (ISBN 0-7933-0445-8); pap. 14.95 (ISBN 0-7933-0444-X); computer disk 29.95 (ISBN 0-7933-0446-6). Gallopade Pub Group.

—If My Iowa Mama Ran the World! (Illus.). (gr. 3-12). 1990. PLB 19.95 (ISBN 0-7933-1633-2); pap. 14.95 (ISBN 0-7933-1634-0); computer disk 29.95 (ISBN 0-7933-1635-9). Gallopade Pub Group.

—Iowa & Other State Greats (Biographies) (Illus.). (gr. 3-12). 1990. PLB 19.95 (ISBN 1-55609-459-0); pap. 14.95 (ISBN 1-55609-458-2); computer disk 29.95 (ISBN 0-7933-1636-7). Gallopade Pub Group.

—Iowa Bandits, Bushwackers, Outlaws, Crooks, Devils, Ghosts, Desperadoes & Other Assorted & Sundry Characters! (Illus.). (gr. 3-12). 1990. PLB 19.95 (ISBN 0-7933-0430-X); pap. 14.95 (ISBN 0-7933-0429-6); computer disk 29.95 (ISBN 0-7933-0431-8). Gallopade Pub Group.

—Iowa Classic Christmas Trivia: Stories, Recipes, Activities, Legends, Lore & More! (Illus.). (gr. 3-12). 1990. PLB 19.95 (ISBN 0-7933-0433-4); pap. 14.95 (ISBN 0-7933-0432-6); computer disk 29.95 (ISBN 0-7933-0434-2). Gallopade Pub Group.

—Iowa Coastales. (Illus.). (gr. 3-12). 1990. PLB 19.95 (ISBN 1-55609-455-8); pap. 14.95 (ISBN 1-55609-454-X); computer disk 29.95 (ISBN 0-7933-1632-4). Gallopade Pub Group.

—The Iowa Hot Air Balloon Mystery. (Illus.). (gr. 2-9). 1990. 19.95 (ISBN 0-7933-2453-X); pap. 14.95 (ISBN 0-7933-2454-8); computer disk 29.95 (ISBN 0-7933-2455-6). Gallopade Pub Group.

—Iowa "Jography" A Fun Run Thru Our State! (Illus.). (gr. 3-12). 1990. PLB 19.95 (ISBN 1-55609-450-7); pap. 14.95 (ISBN 1-55609-085-4); computer disk 29.95 (ISBN 0-7933-1622-7). Gallopade Pub Group.

—Iowa Kid's Cookbook: Recipes, How-to, History, Lore & More! (Illus.). (gr. 3-12). 1990. PLB 19.95 (ISBN 0-7933-0442-3); pap. 14.95 (ISBN 0-7933-0441-5); computer disk 29.95 (ISBN 0-7933-0443-1). Gallopade Pub Group.

—Iowa Quiz Bowl Crash Course! (Illus.). (gr. 3-12). 1990. PLB 19.95 (ISBN 1-55609-457-4); pap. 14.95 (ISBN 1-55609-456-6); computer disk 29.95 (ISBN 0-7933-1631-6). Gallopade Pub Group.

—Iowa School Trivia: An Amazing & Fascinating Look at Our State's Teachers, Schools & Students! (Illus.). (gr. 3-12). 1990. PLB 19.95 (ISBN 0-7933-0439-3); pap. 14.95 (ISBN 0-7933-0438-5); computer disk 29.95 (ISBN 0-7933-0440-7). Gallopade Pub Group.

—Iowa Silly Basketball Sportsmysteries, Vol. I. (Illus.). (gr. 3-12). 1990. PLB 19.95 (ISBN 0-7933-0436-9); pap. 14.95 (ISBN 0-7933-0435-0); computer disk 29.95 (ISBN 0-7933-0437-7). Gallopade Pub Group.

—Iowa Silly Basketball Sportsmysteries, Vol. II. (Illus.). (gr. 3-12). 1990. PLB 19.95 (ISBN 0-7933-1637-5); pap. 14.95 (ISBN 0-7933-1638-3); computer disk 29.95 (ISBN 0-7933-1639-1). Gallopade Pub Group.

—Iowa Silly Football Sportsmysteries, Vol. I. (Illus.). (gr. 3-12). 1990. PLB 19.95 (ISBN 1-55609-453-1); pap. 14.95 (ISBN 1-55609-452-3); computer disk 29.95 (ISBN 0-7933-1624-3). Gallopade Pub Group.

—Iowa Silly Football Sportsmysteries, Vol. II. (Illus.). (gr. 3-12). 1990. PLB 19.95 (ISBN 0-7933-1625-1); pap. 14.95 (ISBN 0-7933-1626-X); computer disk 29.95 (ISBN 0-7933-1627-8). Gallopade Pub Group.

—Iowa Silly Trivia! (Illus.). (gr. 3-12). 1990. PLB 19.95 (ISBN 1-55609-449-3); pap. 14.95 (ISBN 1-55609-084-6); computer disk 29.95 (ISBN 0-7933-1621-9). Gallopade Pub Group.

—Iowa's (Most Devastating!) Disasters & (Most Calamitous!) Catastrophies! (Illus.). (gr. 3-12). 1990. PLB 19.95 (ISBN 0-7933-0426-1); pap. 14.95 (ISBN 0-7933-0427-X); computer disk 29.95 (ISBN 0-7933-0428-8). Gallopade Pub Group.

—Let's Quilt Iowa & Stuff It Topographically! (Illus.). (gr. 3-12). 1990. PLB 19.95 (ISBN 1-55609-451-5); pap. 14.95 (ISBN 1-55609-072-2); computer disk 29.95 (ISBN 0-7933-1623-5). Gallopade Pub Group.

Turner Program Services, Inc. Staff & Clark, James I. Iowa. 48p. (gr. 3 up). 1985. PLB 17.32 (ISBN 0-86514-431-1); pap. 9.27 (ISBN 0-86514-506-7); cancelled Beta video (ISBN 0-86514-056-1); cancelled VHS video (ISBN 0-86514-131-2); cancelled 3/4" video (ISBN 0-86514-206-8); cancelled tchr's. guide (ISBN 0-86514-281-5); cancelled student activity bk. (ISBN 0-86514-356-0); cancelled index. Raintree Pubs.

IRAN

Azerbaijan. (Illus.). (gr. 5 up). Date not set. write for info. (ISBN 0-7910-0165-2). Chelsea Hse.

Husain, A. Revolution in Iran. (Illus.). 80p. (gr. 7 up). Date not set. PLB 17.26 (ISBN 0-86592-038-9). Rourke Corp.

Lawson, Don. America Held Hostage: From the Teheran Embassy Takeover to the Iran-Contra Affair. (Illus.). 144p. (gr. 7-12). 1991. PLB 12.90 (ISBN 0-531-11009-5). Watts.

Lerner Publications, Department of Geography Staff, ed. Iran in Pictures. (Illus.). 64p. (gr. 5 up). 1989. 12.95 (ISBN 0-8225-1848-1). Lerner Pubns.

Mannetti, Lisa. Iran & Iraq: Nations at War. 96p. (gr. 7-12). 1986. lib. bdg. 12.90 (ISBN 0-531-10155-X). Watts.

Miller, William M. Tales of Persia: A Book for Children. Melton, Lily, illus. 145p. (gr. 1-6). 1988. pap. 5.95 (ISBN 0-87552-292-0). Presby & Reformed.

Sanders, Renfield. Iran. (Illus.). (gr. 5 up). 1990. 14.95 (ISBN 0-7910-1104-6). Chelsea Hse.

IRAN–FICTION

Wolkstein, Diane. The Red Lion: A Persian Story. LC 77-3963. (gr. k-3). 1977. 8.61 (ISBN 0-690-01346-9, Crowell Jr Bks). HarpC Child Bks.

IRAN–HISTORY

Childs, N. The Gulf War, Reading Level 8. (Illus.). 80p. (gr. 7 up). Date not set. PLB 17.26 (ISBN 0-86592-048-6). Rourke Corp.

IRAQ

Bratman, Fred. War in the Persian Gulf. (Illus.). 64p. (gr. 7 up). 1991. PLB 19.25 (ISBN 1-56294-051-1); pap. 4.95 (ISBN 1-878841-61-0). Millbrook Pr.

Childs, N. The Gulf War, Reading Level 8. (Illus.). 80p. (gr. 7 up). Date not set. PLB 17.26 (ISBN 0-86592-048-6). Rourke Corp.

Foster, Leila M. Iraq. LC 90-2174. (Illus.). 128p. (gr. 5-9). 1990. PLB 25.27 (ISBN 0-516-02723-9). Childrens.

Iraq. (Illus.). (gr. 5 up). 1988. 14.95 (ISBN 0-7910-0094-X). Chelsea Hse.

Lerner Publications, Department of Geography Staff. Iraq in Pictures. (Illus.). 64p. (gr. 5 up). 1990. PLB 12.95 (ISBN 0-8225-1847-3). Lerner Pubns.

Mannetti, Lisa. Iran & Iraq: Nations at War. 96p. (gr. 7-12). 1986. lib. bdg. 12.90 (ISBN 0-531-10155-X). Watts.

IRELAND

Bailey, Donna & Sproule, Anna. Ireland. LC 90-9645. (Illus.). 32p. (gr. 2-5). 1990. PLB 14.64 (ISBN 0-8114-2562-2). Steck-V.

Byrne, Art & McMahon, Sean. Lives: One Hundred Thirteen Great Irishwomen & Irishmen. Short, John, illus. 230p. (Orig.). (gr. 9-12). 1991. pap. 16.95 (ISBN 1-85371-094-6, Pub. by Poolbeg Pr). Dufour.

Fairclough, Chris. We Live in Ireland. (Illus.). 64p. (gr. 4-9). 1986. PLB 9.49 (ISBN 0-531-18070-0, Pub. by Bookwright). Watts.

Fradin, Dennis. The Republic of Ireland. LC 83-20960. (Illus.). 128p. (gr. 5-9). 1984. lib. bdg. 23.93 (ISBN 0-516-02767-0). Childrens.

Grant, Neil. Ireland. (Illus.). 48p. (gr. 4-8). 1989. lib. bdg. 14.98 (ISBN 0-382-09819-6). Silver Burdett Pr.

Irish Question. (Illus.). (gr. 7 up). lib. bdg. 17.26 (ISBN 0-86592-027-3). Rourke Corp.

Irvine, John. Treasury of Irish Saints. (gr. 1 up). 1984. 9.95 (ISBN 0-85105-902-3, Pub. by Colin Smythe Ltd Britain). Dufour.

Kronenwetter, Michael. Northern Ireland. (Illus.). 160p. (gr. 9-12). 1990. PLB 13.90 (ISBN 0-531-10942-9). Watts.

Lewis, John. Ireland: A Divided Country. (Illus.). 32p. (gr. 5-9). 1989. PLB 11.90 (ISBN 0-531-17169-8). Watts.

Lye, Keith. Take a Trip to Ireland. (Illus.). 32p. (gr. 1-3). 1984. lib. bdg. 7.99 (ISBN 0-531-04741-5). Watts.

Meyer, Carolyn. Voices of Northern Ireland: Growing up in a Troubled Land. LC 87-199. (Illus.). 212p. (gr. 7 up). 1987. 15.95 (ISBN 0-15-200635-4, Gulliver Bks). HarBraceJ.

Moriarty, Mary & Sweeney, Catherine. Theobald Wolfe Tone. (Illus.). 64p. 1989. pap. 8.95 (ISBN 0-86278-160-4, Pub. by O'Brien Press Ltd Eire). Dufour.

Peplow, Mary & Shipley, Debra. Ireland. LC 90-32821. (Illus.). 96p. (gr. 6-11). 1990. PLB 18.60 (ISBN 0-8114-2430-8). Steck-V.

Pomeray, J. K. Ireland. (Illus.). 96p. (gr. 5 up). 1988. lib. bdg. 14.95x (ISBN 1-55546-794-6). Chelsea Hse.

Wagner, Annabel. Timeline: Ireland. (Illus.). 64p. (gr. 7-9). 1988. 19.95 (ISBN 0-85219-716-0, Pub. by Batsford England). Trafalgar Sq.

IRELAND–FICTION

Bell, Sam H. The Hollow Ball. 256p. (Orig.). (gr. 10-12). 1991. pap. 11.95 (ISBN 0-85640-452-7, Pub. by Blackstaff Pr Belfast). Dufour.

Conlon-McKenna, Marita. Under the Hawthorn Tree. Teskey, Donald, illus. LC 90-55097. 160p. (gr. 3-7). 1990. 13.95 (ISBN 0-8234-0838-8). Holiday.

El Flautista De Hamelin. (SPA.). (gr. 2). 1990. casebound 3.50 (ISBN 0-7214-1413-3). Ladybird Bks.

Joyce, James. The Encounter. 32p. (gr. 6 up). 1982. PLB 10.95s.p. (ISBN 0-87191-896-X); 15.65 (ISBN 0-685-06211-2). Creative Ed.

McCaughren, Tom. The Silent Sea. Myler, Terry, illus. 111p. (Orig.). 1988. pap. 7.95 (ISBN 0-947962-20-4, Pub. by Children's Pr). Irish Bks Media.

Malterre, Elona. The Last Wolf of Ireland. (gr. 4-9). 1990. 13.95 (ISBN 0-395-54381-9, Clarion Bks). HM.

Nixon, Joan L. The Gift. Glass, Andrew, illus. LC 82-17994. 96p. (gr. 4-7). 1983. 12.95 (ISBN 0-02-768160-2, Mcmillan Child Bk). Macmillan Child Grp.

Ryan, Joan & Snell, Gordon, eds. Land of Tales: Stories of Ireland for Children. 2nd ed. (Illus.). 160p. (gr. 4-8). 1983. 10.95 (ISBN 0-907606-15-6, Pub. by Glendale Pr). Irish Bks Media.

Stevens, Kathleen. Molly, McCullough, & Tom the Rogue. Zemach, Margot, illus. LC 82-45584. 32p. (gr. 1-5). 1991. pap. 4.95 (ISBN 0-06-443261-0, Trophy). HarpC Child Bks.

Tannen, Mary. The Wizard Children of Finn. Borgoyne, illus. LC 80-20955. 256p. (gr. 3 up). 1981. Knopf.

Willard, Nancy. The Ballad of Biddy Early. Moser, Barry, illus. LC 88-29187. 48p. (gr. 5 up). 1989. 13.95 (ISBN 0-394-88414-0); lib. bdg. 14.99 (ISBN 0-394-98414-5). Knopf.

IRELAND–HISTORY

Furlong, Nicholas. A Foster Son for a King. (Illus.). 128p. (Orig.). (gr. 5-8). 1986. 9.95 (ISBN 0-947962-03-4, Pub. by Childrens Pr); pap. 5.95 (ISBN 0-947962-04-2, Pub. by Childrens Pr). Irish Bks Media.

Ingram, Cecil B. Ulsterheart: An Ancient Irish Habitation. LC 88-72366. (Illus.). 350p. (gr. 12). 1988. 60.00x (ISBN 0-9621544-0-7). All Ireland Inc.

Joyce, P. W. A Child's History of Ireland. Harrison, Hank, ed. (Illus.). 225p. (gr. 8-12). 14.95 (ISBN 0-918501-24-5); pap. write for info. (ISBN 0-918501-26-1). Archives Pr.

McMahon, Sean. The Poolbeg Book of Irish Placenames. 113p. (Orig.). (gr. 10-12). 1991. pap. 8.95 (ISBN 1-85371-087-3, Pub. by Poolbeg Pr). Dufour.

Newman, Roger C. Murtagh & the Vikings. (Illus.). 96p. (Orig.). (gr. 5-8). 1986. 9.95 (ISBN 0-947962-05-0, Pub. by Childrens Pr); pap. 5.95 (ISBN 0-947962-06-9, Pub. by Childrens Pr). Irish Bks Media.

Roche, Richard. The Call of the Wood Pigeon - Glaoch an Choluir Choille: A Day in the Life of a Monk in Pre-Viking Ireland. (Illus., Orig.). (gr. 1-8). 1990. pap. 5.95 (ISBN 1-85390-047-8, Pub. by Veritas Pubns Eire). Irish Bks Media.

Stein, Wendy. A Book of Ancient Ireland. Swanberg, Nancy & Anderson, L., illus. (gr. k). 1978. pap. text ed. 3.50 (ISBN 0-88388-060-1). Bellerophon Bks.

Stewart, Gail B. Northern Ireland. LC 90-36291. (Illus.). 48p. (gr. 5-6). 1990. RSBE 10.95 (ISBN 0-89686-551-7, Crestwood Hse). Macmillan Child Grp.

IRISH IN THE U. S.

Franck, Irene M. Irish-American Heritage. (Illus.). 160p. (gr. 5 up). 1989. 16.95x (ISBN 0-8160-1630-5). Facts on File.

Johnson, James E. Irish in America. rev. ed. LC 66-10148. (Illus.). 80p. (gr. 5 up). 1981. PLB 11.95 (ISBN 0-8225-0203-8); pap. 3.95 (ISBN 0-8225-1012-X). Lerner Pubns.

Watts, James. The Irish Americans. Moynihan, Daniel P., intro. by. 112p. (Orig.). (gr. 5 up). 1988. 17.95 (ISBN 0-87754-855-2); pap. 9.95 (ISBN 0-7910-0267-5). Chelsea Hse.

IRISH IN THE U. S.–FICTION

Giff, Patricia R. The Gift of the Pirate Queen. Rutherford, Jenny, illus. LC 82-70310. 160p. (gr. 4-6). 1982. 11.95 (ISBN 0-385-28338-5); PLB 11.95 (ISBN 0-385-28339-3). Delacorte.

Lasky, Kathryn. Prank. (gr. 6 up). 1986. pap. 2.75 (ISBN 0-440-97144-6, LFL). Dell.

IRISH LITERATURE–COLLECTIONS

Brinn, Ross. To the Woods & Waters Wild: A Collection of Irish Writings. O'Mahony, Kieran, ed. LC 90-80516. 150p. (Orig.). 1990. pap. 9.95 (ISBN 0-944638-02-3). Educare Pr.

IRISH POETRY–COLLECTIONS

Quinn, Bridie & Cashman, S., eds. Wolfhound Book of Irish Poems for Young People. (Illus.). 192p. (ps-8). 1975. pap. 9.95 (ISBN 0-86327-002-6, Pub. by Wolfhound Press Eire). Dufour.

IRON

Fodor, R. V. Gold, Copper, Iron: How Metals Are Formed, Found, & Used. LC 87-24464. (Illus.). 96p. (gr. 6-12). 1989. PLB 16.95 (ISBN 0-89490-138-9). Enslow Pubs.

Lambert, M. Iron & Steel. (Illus.). 48p. (gr. 5 up). Date not set. PLB 15.93 (ISBN 0-86592-268-3). Rourke Corp.

IRON CURTAIN COUNTRIES

see Communist Countries

IRON INDUSTRY AND TRADE

Martin, John H. A Day in the Life of a High-Iron Worker. Jann, Gayle, illus. LC 84-2449. 32p. (gr. 4-8). 1985. PLB 11.79 (ISBN 0-8167-0107-5); pap. text ed. 2.95 (ISBN 0-8167-0108-3). Troll Assocs.

IRRIGATION

see also Dams; Windmills

Kourik, Robert. Gray Water Use in the Landscape: How to Use Gray Water to Save Your Landscape During Droughts. Schmidt, Heidi, illus. Hill, Amie, ed. (Illus.). 28p. (Orig.). 1988. pap. text ed. 6.00 (ISBN 0-9615848-1-5). Metamorphic Pr.

ISABEL 1ST, LA CATOLICA, QUEEN OF SPAIN, 1451-1504

Burch, Joann J. Isabella of Castile: Queen on Horseback. (Illus.). 64p. (gr. 5-8). 1991. PLB 11.90 (ISBN 0-531-20033-7). Watts.

Stevens, Paul. Ferdinand & Isabella. Schlesinger, Arthur M., Jr., intro. by. (Illus.). 112p. (gr. 5 up). 1988. lib. bdg. 17.95 (ISBN 0-87754-523-5). Chelsea Hse.

ISAIAH, THE PROPHET

Head, Constance. Isaiah: The Prophet Prince. 384p. (Orig.). (ps-6). 1988. pap. 4.95 (ISBN 0-8423-1751-1). Tyndale.

Heifner, Fred. Isaiah: Messenger for God. Johnston, Cliff, illus. (gr. 1-6). 1978. 5.95 (ISBN 0-8054-4243-X, 4242-43). Broadman.

ISLAM

Ahmad, P. Color & Learn Salat. pap. 3.00 (ISBN 0-317-43013-0). Kazi Pubns.

Ahsan, M. M. Muslim Festivals. (Illus.). 48p. (gr. 3-8). 1987. PLB 14.60 (ISBN 0-86592-979-3). Rourke Corp.

Al-Islam, Da'i. Prophet Sulaiman. 32p. (gr. 1-5). 1985. pap. 3.95 (ISBN 0-940368-53-6). Tahrike Tarsile Quran.

Ashraf. Lessons in Islam, 5. 8.50 (ISBN 0-686-18391-6). Kazi Pubns.

Chaudhry, Saida. Call to Prophethood. (Illus.). (gr. 2-5). pap. 4.00 (ISBN 0-89259-046-7). Am Trust Pubns.

—We Are Muslim Children. (gr. 4). pap. 4.00 (ISBN 0-89259-050-5). Am Trust Pubns.

Doray, S. J. Gateway to Islam, 4. pap. 10.00 (ISBN 0-686-18395-9). Kazi Pubns.

Hamid, J. Islamic Activity Book, Nos. I, II & III. 1988. pap. 3.00 ea. (ISBN 0-317-43011-4). Kazi Pubns.

Hashim, A. S. Eleven Surahs Explained. pap. 5.95 (ISBN 0-686-18412-2); Complete series. pap. 49.50 (ISBN 0-686-18413-0). Kazi Pubns.

—Ibadat. pap. 5.95 (ISBN 0-686-18414-9); pap. 49.50 entire ser. (ISBN 0-686-18415-7). Kazi Pubns.

—Iman, Basic Beliefs. pap. 5.95 (ISBN 0-686-18416-5); pap. 49.50 entire ser. (ISBN 0-686-18417-3). Kazi Pubns.

—Islamic Arabic. pap. 5.95 (ISBN 0-686-18398-3); pap. 49.50 entire ser. (ISBN 0-686-18399-1). Kazi Pubns.

Hayes, K. H. Stories of Great Muslims. 5.95 (ISBN 0-686-18389-4). Kazi Pubns.

Hood, Abdul Latif Al. Islam. (Illus.). 48p. (gr. 4-6). 1987. lib. bdg. 12.40 (ISBN 0-531-18063-8, Pub. by Bookwright Pr). Watts.

Iqbal, Muhammad. Way of the Muslim. (gr. 3-7). pap. 7.95 (ISBN 0-7175-0632-0). Dufour.

Keene, Michael. Being a Muslim. (Illus.). 64p. (gr. 7-12). 1987. 19.95 (ISBN 0-7134-4667-6, Pub. by Batsford England). Trafalgar Sq.

Obaba, Al-Imam & Abdullah. The Why & How of Burial & Death of a Muslim. (Illus.). 24p. (Orig.). 1985. pap. 1.50 (ISBN 0-916157-03-2). African Islam Miss Pubns.

Qaderi, M. Taleem-Ul-Islam, 4. pap. 7.50 (ISBN 0-686-18387-8). Kazi Pubns.

Siddiqui, A. A. Elementary Teachings of Islam. pap. 4.95 (ISBN 0-686-18397-5). Kazi Pubns.

ISLAM–HISTORY

Karim, F. Heroes of Islam. Incl. Bk. 1. Muhammad; Bk. 2. Abu Bakr; Bk. 3. Umar; Bk. 4. Othman; Bk. 5. Ali; Bk. 6. Khalid Bin Walid; Bk. 7. Mohammad Bin Qasim; Bk. 8. Mahmood of Ghazni; Bk. 9. Mohyuddin; Bk. 10. Sultan Tipu; Bk. 11. Aisha the Truthful; Bk. 12. Hussain the Martyr; Bk. 13. Some Companions of the Prophet-I; Bk. 14. Some Companions of the Prophet-II; Bk. 15. Some Companions of the Prophet-III. Set. pap. 45.00 (ISBN 0-686-18393-2); pap. 3.00 ea. Kazi Pubns.

ISLANDS

see also Coral Reefs and Islands;
also names of islands and groups of islands, e.g. Cuba

Bender, Lionel. Island. (Illus.). 32p. (gr. k-6). 1989. PLB 11.90 (ISBN 0-531-10820-1). Watts.

Cape Verde. (Illus.). (gr. 5 up). 1989. 14.95 (ISBN 0-7910-0145-8). Chelsea Hse.

Dicks, Brian. Lanzarote: Fire Island of the Canaries. (Illus.). 62p. (gr. 7-9). 1988. 17.95 (ISBN 0-85219-727-6, Pub. by Batsford England). Trafalgar Sq.

Fyson, Nance L. Sri Lanka. (Illus.). 64p. (gr. 7-9). 1988. 19.95 (ISBN 0-318-32901-8, Pub. by Batsford England). Trafalgar Sq.

Gibbons, Gail. Surrounded by Sea: Life on a New England Fishing Island. (ps-3). 1991. 14.95 (ISBN 0-316-30961-3). Little.

Gould, Dennis E. Comores (Comoro Islands) (Illus.). (gr. 5 up). 1988. 14.95 (ISBN 0-222-01119-X). Chelsea Hse.

Hassall, S. & Hassall, P. J. Seychelles. (Illus.). (gr. 5 up). 1988. 14.95 (ISBN 0-7910-0104-0). Chelsea Hse.

Norgrove, Ross. Blueprint for Paradise. 2nd ed. (Illus.). 202p. 1989. pap. 14.95 (ISBN 0-918373-38-7). Moon Pubns CA.

Ogg, Diana. Coll: Island of the Hebrides. (Illus.). 63p. (gr. 7-9). 1988. 17.95 (ISBN 0-85219-728-4, Pub. by Batsford England). Trafalgar Sq.

Rydell, Wendy. All about Islands. Burns, Ray, illus. LC 83-4833. 32p. (gr. 3-6). 1984. lib. bdg. 10.59 (ISBN 0-89375-975-9); pap. text ed. 2.95 (ISBN 0-89375-976-7). Troll Assocs.

Solomon Islands. (Illus.). (gr. 5 up). 1989. 13.95 (ISBN 0-7910-0163-6). Chelsea Hse.

Strange, Ian J. The Falklands. (Illus.). 160p. (gr. 7-11). 1985. 15.95 (ISBN 0-396-08616-0, Putnam). Putnam Pub Group.

Wildsmith, Brian. The Island. (Illus.). 16p. 1987. pap. 2.95 (ISBN 0-19-272137-2). Oxford U Pr.

ISLANDS–FICTION

Abolafia, Yossi. Yanosh's Island. LC 86-19462. 32p. (gr. k-3). 1987. 11.75 (ISBN 0-688-06816-2); PLB 11.88 (ISBN 0-688-06817-0). Greenwillow.

Anderson, Margaret J. Light in the Mountain. Marcellino, Fred, illus. LC 81-14266. 192p. (gr. 5-9). 1982. 9.95 (ISBN 0-394-84791-1); lib. bdg. 9.99 (ISBN 0-394-94791-6). Knopf.

Ballantyne, Robert M. The Coral Island. (gr. 4-6). 1986. pap. 2.25 (ISBN 0-14-035040-3, Puffin). Puffin Bks.

Chetin, Helen. Angel Island Prisoner. Harvey, Catherine, tr. Lee, Jan, illus. LC 82-51170. (CHI & ENG.). (gr. 3 up). 1982. 7.95 (ISBN 0-938678-09-4). New Seed.

Dillon, Ellis. The Island of Ghosts. LC 89-31265. 160p. (gr. 5-7). 1989. 12.95 (ISBN 0-684-19107-5, Scribners Young Read). Macmillan Child Grp.

Harris, Aurand. Treasure Island. (gr. 4 up). 1983. pap. 4.50 (ISBN 0-87602-253-0). Anchorage.

Kinsey-Warnock, Natalie. Wild Horses of Sweetbriar. (ps-3). 1990. 13.95 (ISBN 0-525-65015-6, Cobblehill Bks). Dutton Child Bks.

Koci, Marta. Sarah's Bear. LC 86-30241. (Illus.). 28p. (ps). 1987. 14.95 (ISBN 0-88708-038-3). Picture Bk Studio.

Macdonald, Golden. The Little Island. Weisgard, Leonard, illus. 42p. (ps-3). 1946. pap. 14.95 (ISBN 0-385-07381-X). Doubleday.

Martin, Charles E. For Rent. Martin, Charles E., illus. LC 85-864. 32p. (gr. k-3). 1986. 11.75 (ISBN 0-688-05716-0); PLB 11.88 (ISBN 0-688-05717-9). Greenwillow.

—Island Winter. Marten, Charles E., illus. LC 83-14098. 32p. (gr. k-3). 1984. 10.25 (ISBN 0-688-02590-0); PLB 10.88 (ISBN 0-688-02592-7). Greenwillow.

—Summer Business. Martin, Charles E., illus. LC 83-25422. 32p. (gr. k-3). 1984. PLB 14.88 (ISBN 0-688-03864-6). Greenwillow.

Mazer, Harry. The Island Keeper. 176p. (gr. k-12). 1982. pap. 3.25 (ISBN 0-440-94774-X, LFL). Dell.

Mitchell, Adrian, ed. Baron on the Island of Cheese. Benson, Patrick, illus. 32p. (gr. 3 up). 1986. 12.95 (ISBN 0-399-21309-0, Philomel Bks). Putnam Pub Group.

The Mysterious Island. (gr. 4 up). 1988. pap. 4.87 (ISBN 0-582-54143-3, 74253). Longman.

Ness, Evaline. Sam, Bangs & Moonshine. Ness, Evaline, illus. LC 66-10113. 48p. (ps-2). 1966. 14.95 (ISBN 0-8050-0314-2); pap. 4.95 (ISBN 0-8050-0315-0). H Holt & Co.

Nixon, Joan L. Haunted Island. 128p. (Orig.). (gr. 3-7). 1987. pap. 2.50 (ISBN 0-590-40203-X, Apple Paperbacks). Scholastic Inc.

O'Dell, Scott. Island of the Blue Dolphins. 192p. (gr. k-6). 1987. pap. 3.50 (ISBN 0-440-43988-4, YB). Dell.

—Island of the Blue Dolphins. large type ed. 161p. (gr. 2-6). 1987. Repr. of 1960 ed. lib. bdg. 14.95 (ISBN 1-55736-002-2). ABC-CLIO.

Paulsen, Gary. The Island. LC 87-24761. (Illus.). 224p. (gr. 6-9). 1988. 13.95 (ISBN 0-531-05749-6); PLB 13.99 (ISBN 0-531-08349-7). Orchard Bks Watts.

Peet, Bill. The Kweeks of Kookatumdee. Peet, Bill, illus. LC 84-22379. 32p. (gr. k-3). 1985. 12.95 (ISBN 0-395-37902-4). HM.

Roddy, Lee. Mystery of the Island Jungle. Weedon, Larry, ed. 160p. (Orig.). (gr. 3-7). 1989. pap. 4.99 (ISBN 0-929608-19-4). Focus Family.

Rodgers, Raboo. Island of Peril. (gr. 5 up). 1987. 12.95 (ISBN 0-395-43082-8). HM.

Stouffer, Nancy. The Myn & Memory Mountain: Circle Island. Fitzpatrick, Ann, illus. 48p. (gr. 1-5). 1989. pap. 2.95 (ISBN 0-927008-52-1). BCI-Bk Cook Inc.

Townsend, John R. The Islanders. LC 81-47105. 256p. (gr. 7 up). 1981. 11.95 (ISBN 0-397-31940-1, Lipp Jr Bks). HarpC Child Bks.

Van Raven, Pieter. Harpoon Island. LC 88-32763. 160p. (gr. 6-9). 1989. 12.95 (ISBN 0-684-19092-3, Scribners Young Read). Macmillan Child Grp.

Vere-Hodge, Gwenda. Teddy Bear Island. 43p. (gr. 7-10). 1986. 15.00X (ISBN 0-7223-2006-X, Pub. by A H Stockwell England). State Mutual Bk.

Verne, Jules. Mysterious Island. (gr. 8 up). pap. 1.95 (ISBN 0-8049-0077-9, CL-77). Airmont.

Wilkes. Treasure Island. (gr. 3-6). 1982. (Usborne-Hayes); PLB 11.96 (ISBN 0-88110-063-3). EDC.

ISLANDS OF THE PACIFIC

Crump, Donald J., ed. America's Pacific Isles. (Illus.). 1990. 8.95 (ISBN 0-318-42778-8); lib. bdg. 9.50 (ISBN 0-318-42779-6). Natl Geog.

Deverell, Gweneth. Follow the Sun...to Tahiti, to Western Samoa, to Fiji, to Melanesia, to Micronesia. (gr. 1-3). 1982. 3.95 (ISBN 0-377-00120-1). Friendship Pr.

Fairfield, Sheila. People & Nations of the Far East & the Pacific. Sherwood, Rhoda, ed. LC 88-42918. (Illus.). 64p. (gr. 5-6). 1988. PLB 13.95 (ISBN 1-55532-907-1). Gareth Stevens Inc.

Lyle, Garry. Pacific Islands. (Illus.). (gr. 5 up). 1988. 14.95 (ISBN 0-222-01034-7). Chelsea Hse.

Phillips, Douglas & Levi, Steven C. The Pacific Rim Region: Emerging Giant. (Illus.). 160p. (gr. 6-12). 1988. lib. bdg. 18.95 (ISBN 0-89490-191-5). Enslow Pubs.

Vilsoni, Patricia H. South Pacific Islanders. (Illus.). 48p. (gr. 4-8). 1987. PLB 15.33 (ISBN 0-86625-259-2). Rourke Corp.

ISLANDS OF THE PACIFIC–FICTION

Gittins, Anne. Tales from the South Pacific Islands. LC 76-5411. (Illus.). 96p. (gr. 3 up). 1977. 7.95 (ISBN 0-916144-02-X). Stemmer Hse.

Keeping, Charles. Adam & Paradise Island. (Illus.). 32p. (gr. 3-6). 1989. 13.95 (ISBN 0-19-279842-1). Oxford U Pr.

Lang, W. Harold. Islands of the Pacific. Kubat, Frank J., Jr., ed. LC 87-83228. (Illus.). 168p. 1988. 44.95 (ISBN 0-945201-00-1). Gannam-Kubat.

ISRAEL

Bamberger, David. A Young Person's History of Israel. Mandelkern, Nicholas, ed. (Illus.). 150p. (Orig.). (gr. 5-7). 1985. pap. 6.95 (ISBN 0-87441-393-1); By Sara M. Schacheer & Priscilla Fishman. tchr's guide 12.50x (ISBN 0-87441-419-9); student's activity bk. 4.25 (ISBN 0-87441-429-6). Behrman.

Burstein, Chaya M. A Kid's Catalog of Israel. Burstein, Chaya, illus. 288p. (gr. 7 up). 1988. 12.95 (ISBN 0-8276-0263-4). JPS Phila.

Cahill, Mary J. Israel. (Illus.). 96p. (gr. 5 up). 1988. lib. bdg. 14.95 (ISBN 1-55546-791-1). Chelsea Hse.

Clayton-Felt, Josh. To Be Seventeen In Israel: Through the Eyes of an American Teenager. LC 86-24723. (Illus.). 96p. (gr. 7-12). 1987. lib. bdg. 12.90 (ISBN 0-531-10249-1). Watts.

Department of Geography, Lerner Publications. Israel in Pictures. (Illus.). 64p. (gr. 5 up). 1988. PLB 12.95 (ISBN 0-8225-1833-3). Lerner Pubns.

Fisher, Leonard E. The Wailing Wall. Fisher, Leonard E., illus. LC 88-27192. 32p. (gr. 1-5). 1989. 14.95 (ISBN 0-02-735310-9, Mcmillan Child Bk). Macmillan Child Grp.

Frankel, Max & Hoffman, Judy. I Live in Israel. Fishman, Priscilla, ed. LC 79-12833. (Illus.). (gr. 3-4). 1979. pap. text ed. 5.95x (ISBN 0-87441-317-6). Behrman.

Haskins, Jim. Count Your Way Through Israel. Hanson, Rick, illus. 24p. (gr. 1-4). 1990. PLB 11.95 (ISBN 0-87614-415-6). Carolrhoda Bks.

James, Ian. Israel. (ps-3). 1990. PLB 11.90 (ISBN 0-531-14028-8). Watts.

Jones, Helen H. Israel. LC 85-5740. (Illus.). 128p. (gr. 5-9). 1986. PLB 25.27 (ISBN 0-516-02766-2). Childrens.
Lange, Suzanne. The Year. LC 78-120787. (gr. 8 up). 1970. 18.95 (ISBN 0-87599-173-4). S G Phillips.
Lawton, Clive A. Passport to Israel. Franklin Watts Ltd., ed. (Illus.). 48p. (gr. 7 up). 1988. 12.90 (ISBN 0-531-10494-X). Watts.
Rogoff, Mike. Israel. LC 90-10027. (Illus.). 96p. (gr. 6-11). 1990. PLB 18.60 (ISBN 0-8114-2432-4). Steck-V.
Rohr, Janelle & Anderson, Robert, eds. Israel: Opposing Viewpoints. LC 88-24432. (Illus.). 250p. (gr. 10 up). 1988. PLB 15.95 (ISBN 0-89908-435-4); pap. text ed. 8.95 (ISBN 0-89908-410-9). Greenhaven.
Rutland, Jonathan. Take a Trip to Israel. (Illus.). 32p. (gr. 1-3). 1981. lib. bdg. 7.99 (ISBN 0-531-04318-5). Watts.
Sidon, et al. The Animated Israel. 54p. 1987. 14.95 (ISBN 0-8246-0326-5). Jonathan David.
Taylor, Allegra. A Kibbutz in Israel. (Illus.). 32p. (gr. 2-5). 1987. 9.95 (ISBN 0-8225-1678-0). Lerner Pubns.
Tolhurst, Marilyn. Israel. (Illus.). 48p. (gr. 4-8). 1989. lib. bdg. 14.98 (ISBN 0-382-09830-7). Silver Burdett Pr.
Topek, Susan R. Israel Is... Kahn, Katherine J., illus. LC 88-83569. 12p. (ps). 1989. bds. 4.95 (ISBN 0-930494-92-X). Kar Ben.

ISRAEL–FICTION

Meir, Mira. Alina: A Russian Girl Comes to Israel. Shapiro, Zeva, tr. from HEB. Rozen, Yael, illus. 48p. (gr. 2-4). 1982. 7.95 (ISBN 0-8276-0208-1, 495). JPS Phila.
Semel, Nava. Becoming Gershona. Simckes, Seymour, tr. 128p. (gr. 4 up). 1990. 12.95 (ISBN 0-670-83105-0). Viking Child Bks.
Steiner, Connie C. On Eagles Wings & Other Things. 32p. (gr. k-4). 1987. 12.95 (ISBN 0-8276-0274-X). JPS Phila.

ISRAEL–HISTORY

Lehman, Emil. Israel: Idea & Reality. (Illus.). (gr. 8 up). 3.95x (ISBN 0-8381-0205-0, 10-205). United Syn Bk.
Nover, Elizabeth Z. My Land of Israel. Rosenblum, Richard, illus. 35p. (Orig.). (gr. 1-2). 1987. pap. text ed. 4.25 (ISBN 0-87441-447-4). Behrman.

ISRAEL–HISTORY–FICTION

Weilerstein, Sadie R. K'tonton in Israel, 3 bks. Safian, Elizabeth & Chernak, Judy, illus. (ps-6). 1988. Set of 3 bks. in zip loc bag. pap. 6.95 (ISBN 0-944633-32-3); Set of 3 bks. & cassettes. pap. 29.95; pap. 2.95 ea. Bk. 1: A Visit with K'tonton & K'tonton on Kibbutz, 40p. Bk. 2: K'tonton in Jerusalem-I: Adventure on Yom Ha'atzma'ut, Israel's Independence Day, 32p. Bk. 3: K'tonton in Jerusalem-II: Adventure in the Old City, 36p. pap. 10.95 ea. bk. & cassette; cassette 8.95 ea. J Chernak.

ISRAEL–POLITICS AND GOVERNMENT

Morris, Ann. When Will the Fighting Stop? A Child's View of Jerusalem. Rivlin, Lilly, illus. LC 88-34181. 64p. (gr. 3-7). 1990. 13.95 (ISBN 0-689-31508-2, Atheneum Child Bk). Macmillan Child Grp.

ISRAEL-ARAB BORDER CONFLICTS

see Jewish-Arab Relations

ISRAEL-ARAB WAR, 1967-

Lawless, Richard & Bleaney, C. H. The First Day of the Six Day War. (Illus.). 64p. (gr. 7-11). 1990. 19.95 (ISBN 0-85219-820-5, Pub. by Batsford England). Trafalgar Sq.

ISRAEL-ARAB WAR, 1967--FICTION

Reboul, Antoine. Thou Shalt Not Kill. Craig, Stephanie, tr. LC 77-77312. (gr. 5-8). 1969. 18.95 (ISBN 0-87599-161-0). S G Phillips.

ISRAELITES

see Jews

ITALIAN LANGUAGE

Amery, H. & DiBello, P. The First Thousand Words in Italian. Cartwright, Stephen, illus. 64p. (gr. 1-6). 1983. 11.95 (ISBN 0-86020-768-4). EDC.
Davies, H. Beginner's Italian Dictionary. (Illus.). 128p. (gr. 6 up). 1991. lib. bdg. 15.96 (ISBN 0-88110-423-X, Usborne); pap. 9.95 (ISBN 0-7460-0764-7). EDC.
De Brunhoff, Laurent. Je Parle Italien avec Babar. (FRE.). (gr. 4-6). 7.95 (ISBN 0-685-11274-8). French & Eur.
Sheheen, Dennis, illus. A Child's Picture English-Italian Dictionary. LC 86-14052. (gr. k-2). 1986. 9.95 (ISBN 0-915361-57-4, Dist. by Watts). Adama Pubs Inc.

ITALIAN LANGUAGE–STUDY AND TEACHING

Hazzan, Anne-Francoise. Let's Learn Italian Coloring Book. (Illus.). 64p. (gr. 4 up). 1988. pap. 3.95 (ISBN 0-8442-8060-7, Passport Bks). Natl Textbk.
Wilkes, Angela. Italian for Beginners. 48p. (ps-1). 1988. 7.95 (ISBN 0-8442-8059-3, Passport Bks). Natl Textbk.

ITALIANS IN THE U. S.

Di Franco, J. Philip. The Italian Americans. Moynihan, Daniel P., intro. by. 112p. (Orig.). (gr. 5 up). 1988. 17.95 (ISBN 0-87754-886-2); pap. 9.95 (ISBN 0-7910-0268-3). Chelsea Hse.
Grossman, Ronald. The Italians in America. rev. ed. LC 66-10149. (Illus.). 64p. (gr. 5 up). 1979. PLB 11.95 (ISBN 0-8225-0202-X); pap. 3.95 (ISBN 0-8225-1013-8). Lerner Pubns.

ITALY

Angilillo, Barbara W. Italy. LC 90-10191. (Illus.). 96p. (gr. 6-11). 1990. PLB 18.60 (ISBN 0-8114-2438-3). Steck-V.
Anno, Mitsumasa, illus. Anno's Italy. 48p. (gr. 4 up). 1984. 10.95 (ISBN 0-399-20770-8, Philomel); pap. 5.95 (ISBN 0-399-21032-6, Philomel). Putnam Pub Group.
Bonomi, Kathryn. Italy. (Illus.). (gr. 5 up). 1991. 14.95 (ISBN 1-55546-752-0). Chelsea Hse.
Brubaker, David. Court & Commedia. (Illus.). (gr. 7-12). 1975. PLB 14.95 (ISBN 0-8239-0317-6). Rosen Group.
Carricle, Noel. San Marino. (Illus.). (gr. 5 up). 1988. 14.95 (ISBN 0-7910-0101-6). Chelsea Hse.
Fairclough, Chris. Take a Trip to Italy. (Illus.). 32p. (gr. 1-3). 1981. lib. bdg. 7.99 (ISBN 0-531-04319-3). Watts.
Getting to Know Italy. 48p. 1989. 7.95 (ISBN 0-8442-8066-6, Passport Bks). Natl Textbk.
Goldstein, Frances. Children's Treasure Hunt Travel Guide to Italy. Goldstein, Frances, illus. LC 79-67280. (Orig.). (gr. k-12). 1980. pap. 6.95 (ISBN 0-933334-01-X, Dist. by Hippocrene). Paper Tiger Pap.
Mariella, Cinzia. Passport to Italy. LC 85-50172. (Illus.). 48p. (gr. 4-9). 1986. PLB 12.90 (ISBN 0-531-10016-2). Watts.
Sproule, Anna. Italy. (Illus.). 48p. (gr. 5-10). 1987. PLB 16.98 (ISBN 0-382-09473-5); pap. 6.95 (ISBN 0-382-09480-8). Silver Burdett Pr.
Stein, R. Conrad. Italy. LC 83-14259. (Illus.). 128p. (gr. 5-9). 1983. PLB 25.27 (ISBN 0-516-02768-9). Childrens.

ITALY–ANTIQUITIES

The Leaning Tower of Pisa. 48p. (gr. 4-5). 1989. PLB 10.95 (ISBN 0-685-26411-4). Capstone Pr.

ITALY–CIVILIZATION

Binney, Don. Inside Italy. FS Staff, ed. (Illus.). 32p. (gr. 1-6). 1988. PLB 11.90 (ISBN 0-531-10613-6). Watts.

ITALY–FICTION

Boccaccio, Giovanni. Chichibo & the Crane. Luzatti, Lele, illus. (gr. 1-6). 1961. 8.95 (ISBN 0-8392-3004-4). Astor-Honor.
Brown, Regina. Little Brother. Bornschlegel, Ruth, illus. (gr. 3-7). 1962. 8.95 (ISBN 0-8392-3019-2). Astor-Honor.
Caselli, Giovanni. A Roman Soldier. Sergio, illus. LC 86-4366. 30p. (gr. 4-6). 1986. 12.95 (ISBN 0-87226-106-9). P Bedrick Bks.
Henry, Marguerite. Gaudenzia Pride of the Palio. 1989. 12.95 (ISBN 0-02-689416-5). Macmillan Child Grp.
Hope, Laura L. Bobbsey Twins' Mystery of the King's Puppet. (gr. 1-4). 1967. 4.50 (ISBN 0-448-08060-5, G&D). Putnam Pub Group.
Moravia. Sette Racconti. (gr. 7-12). pap. 5.95 (ISBN 0-88436-060-1, 55258). EMC.
Ventura, Piero & Ventura, Marisa. The Painter's Trick. Ventura, Piero & Ventura, Marisa, illus. LC 76-54411. (gr. k-2). 1977. (Random Juv); lib. bdg. 6.99 (ISBN 0-394-93320-6). Random.

ITALY–HISTORY

The Italian Renaissance. 64p. (gr. 4-8). 1990. 13.95 (ISBN 0-86307-998-9). Marshall Cavendish.

ITALY–HISTORY–FICTION

Boccaccio. Andreuccio de Perugia. (gr. 7-12). pap. 4.95 (ISBN 0-88436-049-0, 55250). EMC.

ITALY–SOCIAL LIFE AND CUSTOMS

Buicchi, Edwina. Italian Food & Drink. (Illus.). 48p. (gr. 4-8). 1987. PLB 12.40 (ISBN 0-531-18120-0, Pub. by Bookwright Pr). Watts.
Hubley, John & Hubley, Penny. A Family in Italy. (Illus.). 32p. (gr. 2-5). 1987. PLB 9.95 (ISBN 0-8225-1673-X). Lerner Pubns.

IVORY COAST

Ivory Coast. (Illus.). (gr. 5 up). 1989. 14.95 (ISBN 0-7910-0125-3). Chelsea Hse.

IWO JIMA, BATTLE OF, 1945

Stein, R. Conrad. The Story of the Battle for Iwo Jima. Meents, Len W., illus. LC 77-5088. 32p. (gr. 3-5). 1977. PLB 13.27 (ISBN 0-516-04607-1). Childrens.

J

JACKSON, ANDREW, PRESIDENT U. S. 1767-1845

Coit, Margaret L. Andrew Jackson. large type ed. (Illus.). 176p. (gr. 4-8). 1991. Repr. of 1965 ed. PLB 17.95 (ISBN 1-55905-082-9). Grey Castle.
Csinski, Alice. Andrew Jackson. LC 86-29983. (Illus.). 100p. (gr. 3 up). 1987. PLB 17.27 (ISBN 0-516-01387-4); pap. 6.95 (ISBN 0-516-41387-2). Childrens.
Gutman, William. Andrew Jackson & the New Populism. (Illus.). 144p. (gr. 3-6). 1987. pap. 4.95 (ISBN 0-8120-3917-3). Barron.
Hilton, Suzanne. The World of Young Andrew Jackson. Lynn, Patricia, illus. (gr. 5-8). 1988. 12.95 (ISBN 0-8027-6814-8); PLB 13.85 (ISBN 0-8027-6815-6). Walker & Co.
Quackenbush, Robert. Who Let Muddy Boots into the White House? A Story of Andrew Jackson. LC 86-4989. (Illus.). 40p. (gr. 2-6). 1986. PLB 11.95 (ISBN 0-671-66970-2). S&S Trade.
Remini, Robert V. The Revolutionary Age of Andrew Jackson. LC 74-2623. (gr. 7 up). 1976. 10.95i (ISBN 0-06-024856-4). HarpC Child Bks.
Sabin, Louis. Andrew Jackson, Frontier Patriot. Smolinski, Dick, illus. LC 85-1094. 48p. (gr. 4-6). 1986. lib. bdg. 10.79 (ISBN 0-8167-0547-X); pap. text ed. 2.95 (ISBN 0-8167-0548-8). Troll Assocs.
Stefoff, Rebecca. Andrew Jackson: 7th President of the United States. Young, Richard G., ed. LC 87-32878. (Illus.). (gr. 5-9). 1988. PLB 17.26 (ISBN 0-944483-08-9). Garrett Ed Corp.

JACKSON, JESSE, 1941-

Celsi, Teresa. Jesse Jackson & Political Power. (Illus.). 32p. (gr. 2-4). 1991. PLB 11.50 (ISBN 1-56294-040-6); pap. 3.95 (ISBN 1-878841-70-X). Millbrook Pr.
Kosof, Anna. Jesse Jackson. (Illus.). 128p. (gr. 7-12). 1987. PLB 11.90 (ISBN 0-531-10413-3). Watts.
McKissack, Patricia C. Jesse Jackson: A Biography. 112p. (gr. 3-7). 1989. 11.95 (ISBN 0-590-43181-1, Scholastic Hardcover). Scholastic Inc.
McKissak, Patricia. Jesse Jackson: A Biography. 112p. (gr. 3-7). 1990. 2.75 (ISBN 0-590-42395-9). Scholastic Inc.
Martin, Patricia S. Jesse Jackson: A Black Leader. (Illus.). 24p. (gr. 1-4). 1987. PLB 12.33 (ISBN 0-86592-170-9). Rourke Corp.
Stone, Eddie. Jesse Jackson. rev. ed. (ps-10). 1988. pap. 2.75 (ISBN 0-87067-840-X). Holloway.
Wilkinson, Brenda. Jesse Jackson: Still Fighting for the Dream. Gallin, Richard, ed. Young, Andrew, intro. by. (Illus.). 128p. (gr. 5 up). 1990. lib. bdg. 16.98 (ISBN 0-382-09926-5); pap. 7.95 (ISBN 0-382-24064-2). Silver Burdett Pr.

JACKSON, MAHALIA, 1911-1972

Wolfe, Charles. Mahalia Jackson. Horner, Matina S., intro. by. 112p. (gr. 5 up). 1990. 17.95 (ISBN 1-55546-661-3). Chelsea Hse.

JACKSON, THOMAS JONATHAN, 1824-1863

Bennett, Barbara J. Stonewall Jackson: Lee's Greatest Lieutenant. (Illus.). 160p. (gr. 5 up). 1990. lib. bdg. 16.98 (ISBN 0-382-09939-7); pap. 8.95 (ISBN 0-382-24048-0). Silver Burdett Pr.
Carpenter. Thomas Jonathan "Stonewall" Jackson, Reading Level 6. (Illus.). 112p. (gr. 4 up). 1987. PLB 18.60 (ISBN 0-86625-326-2). Rourke Corp.
Fritz, Jean. Stonewall. (Illus.). (gr. 3-7). 1979. 14.95 (ISBN 0-399-20698-1, Putnam). Putnam Pub Group.
Ludwig, Charles. Stonewall Jackson: Loved in the South Admired in the North. (Illus.). (gr. 3-6). 1989. pap. 6.95 (ISBN 0-88062-157-5). Mott Media.

JACOB, THE PATRIARCH

Jacob. (Illus.). (gr. 2-4). 3.50 (ISBN 0-7214-1111-8). Ladybird Bks.
Paamoni, Zev. The Adventures of Jacob. (Illus.). (gr. 5-10). 1970. 3.00 (ISBN 0-914080-26-1). Shulsinger Sales.

JAILS

see Prisons

JAM

Mitgutsch, Ali. From Fruit to Jam. Mitgutsch, Ali, illus. LC 81-58. 24p. (ps-3). 1981. PLB 6.95 (ISBN 0-87614-154-8). Carolrhoda Bks.

JAMAICA

Hubley, John & Hubley, Penny. A Family in Jamaica. LC 85-6887. (Illus.). 32p. (gr. 2-5). 1985. PLB 9.95 (ISBN 0-8225-1657-8). Lerner Pubns.
Lerner Publications, Department of Geography Staff. Jamaica in Pictures. (Illus.). 64p. (gr. 5 up). 1987. PLB 12.95 (ISBN 0-8225-1814-7). Lerner Pubns.
Maxwell, Ken. How to Speak Jamaican. McLaren, Livingston, illus. 46p. (Orig.). (gr. 7 up). 1981. pap. 2.50 (ISBN 976-8001-21-6, Jamrite Pubns). Humor Us Pubns Inc.
Robinson, Kim & Walcott, Harclyde. The How to Be Jamaican Handbook. Fearon, Trevor, ed. McLaren, Livingston & Robinson, Kim, illus. 79p. (Orig.). (gr. 7 up). 1987. pap. 5.95 (ISBN 976-8001-24-0, Jamrite Pubns). Humor Us Pubns Inc.
Wilkins, Frances. Jamaica. (Illus.). (gr. 5 up). 1988. 14.95 (ISBN 1-55546-176-X). Chelsea Hse.

JAMAICA–FICTION

Berry, James. A Thief in the Village: And Other Stories of Jamaica. 156p. (gr. 4 up). 1990. pap. 3.95 (ISBN 0-14-034357-1, Puffin). Puffin Bks.
Havill, Juanita. Jamaica Tag-Along. O'Brien, Anne S., illus. 1990. pap. 4.95 (ISBN 0-395-54949-3). HM.
Hope, Laura L. Bobbsey Twins' Mystery on the Deep Blue Sea. (gr. 1-4). 1930. 3.95 (ISBN 0-448-08011-7, G&D). Putnam Pub Group.

JAMES, JESSE WOODSON, 1847-1882

Ernst, John. Jesse James. Miller, Ted, illus. LC 76-10206. (gr. 4-7). 1976. 9.95 (ISBN 0-13-509695-2). P-H.
Love, Robertus. The Rise & Fall of Jesse James. Fellman, Michael, intro. by. LC 89-24965. xxiv, 446p. 1990. pap. 11.95 (ISBN 0-8032-7932-9, Bison). U of Nebr Pr.

JAMESTOWN, VIRGINIA–FICTION

O'Dell, Scott. The Serpent Never Sleeps: A Novel of Jamestown & Pocahontas. (gr. 8 up). 1988. pap. 3.50 (ISBN 0-449-70328-2, Juniper). Fawcett.

JAMESTOWN, VIRGINIA–HISTORY

Campbell, Elizabeth A. Jamestown: The Beginning. Bock, William S., illus. 96p. (gr. 4-6). 1974. lib. bdg. 15.95 (ISBN 0-316-12599-7). Little.

JAMESTOWN, VIRGINIA–HISTORY–FICTION

Knight, James E. Jamestown, New World Adventure. Wenzel, David, illus. LC 81-23086. 32p. (gr. 5-9). 1982. PLB 10.79 (ISBN 0-89375-724-1); pap. text ed. 2.95 (ISBN 0-89375-725-X). Troll Assocs.

JAPAN

Ashby, Gwynneth. Take a Trip to Japan. LC 80-52719. (gr. 1-3). 1981. PLB 7.99 (ISBN 0-531-00990-4). Watts.

Coates, Bryan E. Japan. (Illus.). 32p. (gr. k-4). 1991. RLB 11.90 (ISBN 0-531-18392-0, Pub. by Boatwright Pr). Watts.

Downer, Lesley. Japan. (ps-3). 1990. PLB 12.40 (ISBN 0-531-18306-8). Watts.

Dudley, William, ed. Japan: Opposing Viewpoints. LC 89-36620. (Illus.). 240p. (gr. 10 up). 1989. PLB 15.95 (ISBN 0-89908-444-3); pap. 8.95 (ISBN 0-89908-419-2). Greenhaven.

Gantz, David. Let's Visit Japan. Gantz, David, illus. (gr. 1 up). 1989. pap. 4.95 (ISBN 0-671-67215-0). S&S Trade.

Greene, Carol. Japan. LC 83-7603. (Illus.). 128p. (gr. 5-9). 1983. PLB 25.27 (ISBN 0-516-02769-7). Childrens.

Haskins, Jim. Count Your Way Through Japan. (Illus.). 24p. (gr. 1-4). 1987. lib. bdg. 11.95 (ISBN 0-87614-301-X); pap. 4.95 (ISBN 0-87614-485-7). Carolrhoda Bks.

Jacobsen, Karen. Japan. LC 82-4445. (Illus.). (gr. k-4). 1982. PLB 14.60 (ISBN 0-516-01630-X); pap. 4.95 (ISBN 0-516-41630-8). Childrens.

James, Ian. Japan. (Illus.). 32p. (gr. k-6). 1989. PLB 11.90 (ISBN 0-531-10760-4). Watts.

James, Richard. Japan: The Land & Its People. rev. ed. LC 86-15565. (Illus.). (gr. 6 up). 1987. PLB 15.96 (ISBN 0-382-09256-2); pap. 6.95 (ISBN 0-382-09463-8). Silver Burdett Pr.

Kalman, Bobbie. Japan: The Land. (Illus.). 32p. (gr. 4-5). 1989. lib. bdg. 14.95 (ISBN 0-86505-204-2); pap. 7.95 (ISBN 0-86505-284-0). Crabtree Pub Co.
JAPAN: THE LAND & its two accompanying volumes, JAPAN: THE PEOPLE, & JAPAN: THE CULTURE make up a mini-series of books introducing children to the fascinating "land of the rising sun." Filled with an interesting array of topics, each book concentrates on one aspect of life in Japan. The books are profusely illustrated with more than 35 color photographs & drawings & present easy-to-read information in two-page spreads. Your young readers will get a close-up look at the daily lives of the people as well as an overview of the history, geography, & culture of Japan. The three books on Japan are part of the Lands, People, & Culture Series.
Publisher Provided Annotation.

Kraft, Kinuko. Journey to Japan. LC 86-40011. (Illus.). 1986. pap. 12.95 (ISBN 0-670-80119-4). Viking Child Bks.

Lerner Publications, Department of Geography Staff. Japan in Pictures. (Illus.). 64p. (gr. 5 up). 1989. PLB 12.95 (ISBN 0-8225-1861-9). Lerner Pubns.

Meeks, Christopher. Japan. (Illus.). 64p. (gr. 7 up). 1990. lib. bdg. 15.93 (ISBN 0-86593-089-9); lib. bdg. 11.95s.p. (ISBN 0-685-36366-X). Rourke Corp.

Meyer, Carolyn. A Voice from Japan: An Outsider Looks In. (Illus.). 240p. (gr. 5 up). 1988. 14.95 (ISBN 0-15-200633-8, Gulliver Bks). HarBraceJ.

—Voices of Japan. 240p. (gr. 7 up). 1988. 14.95 (ISBN 0-318-32785-6, Gulliver Bks). HarBraceJ.

Ottenheimer, Laurence. Japan: Land of Samurai & Robots. Nikly, Michelle, illus. LC 87-34524. 38p. (gr. k-5). 1988. 4.95 (ISBN 0-944589-11-1, 111). Young Discovery Lib.

Parker, Steve. Japan. Kossmann, Walter & Fink, Joanne, eds. (Illus.). 48p. (gr. 4-8). 1988. PLB 14.98 (ISBN 0-382-09504-9). Silver Burdett Pr.

Stefoff, Rebecca. Japan. (Illus.). 112p. (gr. 5 up). 1988. lib. bdg. 14.95 (ISBN 1-55546-199-9). Chelsea Hse.

Takeshita, Jiro. Food in Japan. LC 88-31465. (Illus.). 32p. (gr. 3-6). 1989. lib. bdg. 13.26 (ISBN 0-86625-340-8). Rourke Corp.

Thurley, Elizabeth F. Through the Year in Japan. (Illus.). 72p. (gr. 7-12). 1985. 19.95 (ISBN 0-7134-4819-9, Pub. by Batsford England). Trafalgar Sq.

Uchida, Yoshiko. Samurai of Gold Hill. rev. ed. Forberg, Ati, illus. LC 84-20424. 128p. (gr. 4-12). 1985. pap. 5.95 (ISBN 0-916870-86-3). Creative Arts Bk.

JAPAN-BIOGRAPHY

Honda, Maasaki. Shinichi Suzuki: Man of Love. Selden, Kyoko, tr. from JPN. 72p. (Orig.). (gr. 7-12). 1984. pap. text ed. 7.95 (ISBN 0-87487-199-9, Suzuki Method). Summy-Birchard.

Hoobler, Dorothy & Hoobler, Thomas. Showa: The Age of Hirohito. 228p. (gr. 7 up). 1990. 15.95 (ISBN 0-8027-6966-7); lib. bdg. 16.85 (ISBN 0-8027-6967-5). Walker & Co.

Hyman, Mark. Black Shogun of Japan - Sophonisa: Wife of Two Warring Kings & Other Stories from Antiquity. Massed, Cal, illus. 120p. (Orig.). (gr. 9-12). 1989. pap. 11.00 (ISBN 0-915515-01-6). M Hyman Assocs.

Italia, Bob. Emperor Hirohito. Walner, Rosemary, ed. (Illus.). 32p. (gr. 4). 1990. PLB 11.95 (ISBN 0-939179-80-6). Abdo & Dghtrs.

JAPAN-CIVILIZATION

Gaskin, Carol. Camelot World: Secrets of the Samurai. 128p. (Orig.). 1990. pap. 2.95 (ISBN 0-380-76040-1, Camelot). Avon.

Kalman, Bobbie. Japan - the Culture. (Illus.). 32p. (gr. 4-5). 1989. lib. bdg. 14.95 (ISBN 0-86505-206-9); pap. 7.95 (ISBN 0-86505-286-7). Crabtree Pub Co.

—Japan - the People. (Illus.). 32p. (gr. 4-5). 1989. lib. bdg. 14.95 (ISBN 0-86505-205-0); pap. 7.95 (ISBN 0-86505-285-9). Crabtree Pub Co.

Pilbeam, Mavis. Japan. FS-Aladdin Staff, ed. Shone, Rob, illus. 32p. (gr. 4-9). 1988. PLB 11.90 (ISBN 0-531-10623-3). Watts.

Tames, Richard. Passport to Japan. FS-Watts Staff, ed. (Illus.). 48p. (gr. 4-9). 1988. PLB 12.90 (ISBN 0-531-10535-0). Watts.

JAPAN-FICTION

Baker, Keith. The Magic Fan. (ps-3). 1989. 14.95 (ISBN 0-15-250750-7). HarBraceJ.

Friedman, Ina R. How My Parents Learned to Eat. Say, Allen, illus. LC 84-18553. 32p. (gr. k-3). 1987. 13.95 (ISBN 0-395-35379-3); pap. 3.95 (ISBN 0-395-44235-4). HM.

Haugaard, Erik C. Samurai's Tale. 1990. pap. 4.95 (ISBN 0-395-54970-1). HM.

Hope, Laura L. Bobbsey Twins & the Goldfish Mystery. (Illus.). (gr. 1-4). 1962. 2.95 (ISBN 0-448-08055-9, G&D). Putnam Pub Group.

Hughes, Dean. Nutty & the Case of the Ski-Slope Spy. LC 90-176. 128p. (gr. 3-7). 1990. pap. 3.95 (ISBN 0-689-71438-6, Aladdin). Macmillan Child Grp.

Kalman, Maira. Sayonara, Mrs. Kackleman. Kalman, Maira, illus. 40p. (ps-5). 1989. pap. 14.95 (ISBN 0-670-82945-5). Viking Child Bks.

Lifton, Betty J. Joji & the Dragon. Mitsui, Eiichi, illus. LC 88-8434. 64p. (gr. 1-3). 1989. Repr. of 1957 ed. lib. bdg. 15.00 (ISBN 0-208-02245-7, Pub. by Linnet). Shoe String.

Lolling, Atsuko G. Aki & the Banner of Names: And Other Stories from Japan. (Orig.). (gr. 1-6). 1991. pap. 4.95 (ISBN 0-377-00218-6). Friendship Pr.
This book introduces young readers to children in Japan like Masaki, who watches anxiously as his once playful brother becomes frustrated by declining test marks; & Mariko who envies her friends' special celebration of a Shinto holiday. Young readers will be introduced to Japanese culture & society--they will recognize some familiar problems such as the pressure to do well in school & tensions within the family. A Teacher's Guide is also available.
Publisher Provided Annotation.

Mosel, Arlene. The Funny Little Woman. Lent, Blair, illus. (ps-4). 1972. 15.95 (ISBN 0-525-30265-4, 01258-370, DCB); pap. 4.95 (ISBN 0-525-45036-X, DCB). Dutton Child Bks.

Namioka, Lensey. Island of Ogres. LC 88-22058. 208p. (gr. 7 up). 1989. 13.95 (ISBN 0-06-024372-4); PLB 13.89 (ISBN 0-06-024373-2). HarpC Child Bks.

—Valley of the Broken Cherry Trees. LC 79-53605. (gr. 7 up). 1980. 8.95 (ISBN 0-440-09325-2). Delacorte.

Paterson, Katherine. The Master Puppeteer. Wells, Haru, illus. LC 75-8614. 192p. (gr. 6 up). 1976. 14.95 (ISBN 0-690-00913-5, Crowell Jr Bks). HarpC Child Bks.

—Of Nightingales That Weep. LC 74-8294. (Illus.). (gr. 5 up). 1974. 13.95 (ISBN 0-690-00485-0, Crowell Jr Bks). HarpC Child Bks.

—Of Nightingales That Weep. Wells, Haru, illus. LC 74-8294. 192p. (gr. 4 up). 1989. pap. 3.50 (ISBN 0-06-440282-7, Trophy). HarpC Child Bks.

Sakade, Florence. Kintaro's Adventures & Other Stories. Hayashi, Yoshio, illus. (gr. 1-5). 1958. pap. 8.95 (ISBN 0-8048-0343-9). C E Tuttle.

—Little One-Inch & Other Japanese Children's Favorite Stories. (Illus.). (gr. 1-5). 1958. pap. 8.95 (ISBN 0-8048-0384-6). C E Tuttle.

—Peach Boy & Other Japanese Children's Favorite Stories. Kurosaki, Yoshisuke, illus. (gr. 1-5). 1958. pap. 8.95 (ISBN 0-8048-0469-9). C E Tuttle.

Sakade, Florence, ed. Urashima Taro & Other Japanese Children's Stories. (Illus.). (gr. 1-6). 1958. pap. 8.95 (ISBN 0-8048-0609-8). C E Tuttle.

Say, Allen. The Ink-Keeper's Apprentice. LC 78-20264. (gr. 7 up). 1979. PLB 12.89 (ISBN 0-06-025209-X). HarpC Child Bks.

Yashima, Taro. Crow Boy. (Illus.). (gr. k-3). 1976. pap. 3.95 (ISBN 0-14-050172-X, Puffin). Puffin Bks.

—Crow Boy. Yashima, T., illus. (gr. k-3). 1955. pap. 13.95 (ISBN 0-670-24931-9). Viking Child Bks.

JAPAN-FOREIGN RELATIONS- U. S.

Blumberg, Rhoda. Commodore Perry in the Land of the Shogun. LC 84-21800. (Illus.). 128p. (gr. 4 up). 1985. 14.95 (ISBN 0-688-03723-2). Lothrop.

JAPAN-HISTORY

Hyman, Mark. Black Shogun of Japan - Sophonisa: Wife of Two Warring Kings & Other Stories from Antiquity. Massed, Cal, illus. 120p. (Orig.). (gr. 9-12). 1989. pap. 11.00 (ISBN 0-915515-01-6). M Hyman Assocs.

Roberson, John R. Japan: From Shogun to Sony. LC 84-21622. (Illus.). 208p. (gr. 6 up). 1985. 13.95 (ISBN 0-689-31076-5, Atheneum Child Bk). Macmillan Child Grp.

Roberts, Jenny. Samurai Warriors. 1990. PLB 11.90 (ISBN 0-531-17202-3). Watts.

Tames, Richard. Japan since Nineteen Forty-Five. (Illus.). 72p. (gr. 7-10). 1989. 19.95 (ISBN 0-7134-5930-1, Pub. by Batsford England). Trafalgar Sq.

JAPAN-SOCIAL LIFE AND CUSTOMS

Elkin, Judith. A Family in Japan. (Illus.). 32p. (gr. 2-5). 1987. PLB 9.95 (ISBN 0-8225-1672-1). Lerner Pubns.

Hearn, Lafcadio. In Ghostly Japan. LC 79-138068. (Illus.). (gr. 9 up). 1971. pap. 10.95 (ISBN 0-8048-0965-8). C E Tuttle.

Jacobsen, P. & Kristensen, P. A Family in Japan. (Illus.). 32p. (gr. k-6). 1984. lib. bdg. 11.90 (ISBN 0-531-03825-4). Watts.

Steele, A. A Samurai Warrior. (Illus.). 32p. (gr. 3-8). Date not set. PLB 14.00 (ISBN 0-86592-145-8). Rourke Corp.

Sugimoto, Etsu I. Daughter of the Samurai. LC 66-15849. (gr. 9 up). 1966. pap. 13.95 (ISBN 0-8048-1655-7). C E Tuttle.

JAPANESE IN THE U. S.

Davis, Daniel S. Behind Barbed Wire: The Imprisonment of Japanese Americans During World War II. (Illus.). (gr. 7 up). 1982. 15.95 (ISBN 0-525-26320-9, DCB). Dutton Child Bks.

Hamanaka, Sheila. The Journey: Japanese Americans, Racism, & Renewal. LC 89-22877. (Illus.). 40p. (gr. 5 up). 1990. 18.95 (ISBN 0-531-05849-2); PLB 18.99 (ISBN 0-531-08449-3). Orchard Bks Watts.

Japanese American Curriculum Project, Inc. Staff. Japanese American Journey: The Story of a People. Hongo, Florence M. & Burton, Miyo, eds. LC 85-80521. (Illus.). 181p. (Orig.). (gr. 5-8). 1985. 22.50x (ISBN 0-934609-00-4); pap. 12.95x (ISBN 0-934609-01-2). JACP Inc.

Moynihan, Daniel P., ed. Japanese Americans. (Illus.). 112p. (gr. 7-12). PLB 16.95 (047831). Know Unltd.

Tajiri, Vincent, ed. Through Innocent Eyes: Teen-agers' Impressions of WW2 Internment Camp Life. Kurushima, Eddie & Nakayama, Mike, illus. Ichioka, Yuji, intros. by. 120p. (Orig.). 1990. 49.50 (ISBN 0-9624450-0-2); pap. 29.50 (ISBN 0-9624450-1-0); audio tape 15.00 (ISBN 1-878385-00-3). Keiro Services.
In 1942, some 120,000 Japanese Americans, without benefit of due process, were removed from their homes & confined to stark internment centers in desolate areas of the United States. Of the Japanese Americans interned, 30,000 were school age children. For the first time, the writing & artwork of these young people have been compiled into a single volume to bring us their voices & visions. In this return to a historical time of racial stereotyping & hatred; war hysteria & paranoia, one finds the voices surprisingly restrained. There is little anger here--no bitterness or despair. Here are pages that are key to the young-vibrant with optimism & hope. Ray Franchi, a teacher at Poston (one of the ten internment camps) & Paul Takeda, a Red Cross worker compiled the original scrapbook of sketches & writings so that other school-aged children could become familiar with the plight of the Japanese Americans during the war. However, the scrapbook remained submerged until 45 years later. Keiro Services, a non-profit organization providing long-term care to the Japanese American elderly decided to make the collection

available to increase awareness & education among the general public. Edited by Vincent Tajiri, the book contains the illustrations & sketches of fifty children along with contributing works by other known authors of the camp experience. Also included is a brief interview with the schoolteacher, Franchi. The audio version of Through Innocent Eyes was produced by Family Media with an introduction by George Takei (of Star Trek fame).
Publisher Provided Annotation.

Uchida, Yoshiko. Journey to Topaz. rev. ed. Carrick, Donald, illus. LC 84-70422. 160p. (gr. 4-12). 1985. pap. 7.95 (ISBN 0-916870-85-5). Creative Arts Bk.

JAPANESE IN THE U. S.-FICTION

Poynter, Margaret. A Time Too Swift. LC 89-30896. 192p. (gr. 5 up). 1990. 13.95 (ISBN 0-689-31146-X, Atheneum Child Bk). Macmillan Child Grp.

Uchida, Yoshiko. The Best Bad Thing. LC 85-26790. 136p. (gr. 4-7). 1986. pap. 3.95 (ISBN 0-689-71069-0, Aladdin). Macmillan Child Grp.

—A Jar of Dreams. LC 81-3480. 144p. (gr. 5-7). 1981. 12.95 (ISBN 0-689-50210-9, M K McElderry). Macmillan Child Grp.

—Journey Home. Robinson, Charles, illus. LC 78-8792. 144p. (gr. 5-7). 1978. 13.95 (ISBN 0-689-50126-9, M K McElderry). Macmillan Child Grp.

Yashima, Taro. Umbrella. Yashima, Taro, illus. (ps-1). 1977. pap. 3.95 (ISBN 0-14-050240-8, Puffin). Puffin Bks.

—Umbrella. Yashima, T., illus. (ps-1). 1958. pap. 13.95 (ISBN 0-670-73858-1). Viking Child Bks.

JAPANESE LANGUAGE-CONVERSATION AND PHRASE BOOKS

Hirate, Susan H. & Kawaura, Noriko. Nihongo Daisuki! Japanese Language Activities for Children. LC 89-81822. (JPN & ENG., Illus.). 208p. (gr. k-6). 1990. tchr's ed. 19.95 (ISBN 0-935848-82-7). Bess Pr.

Huntington, Seiko. Japanese "ABCs" Hiragana Learning Cards. Huntington, Seiko, illus. 128p. (Orig.). (gr. 1 up). 1988. pap. 16.95 (ISBN 0-936845-05-8). Sakura Press.

Maeda, Jun. Let's Study Japanese. LC 64-24949. (Illus.). (gr. 9 up). 1965. pap. 6.95 (ISBN 0-8048-0362-5). C E Tuttle.

Mahoney, Judy. Teach Me Japanese. Satoh, Naomi, tr. from FRE, SPA & GER. Bennett, Charlotte, illus. 20p. (ps-5). 1990. pap. 11.95 incl. 25 min. cass. (ISBN 0-934633-17-7). Teach Me.

—Teach Me More Japanese. Satoh, Naomi, tr. from FRE. Kamstra, Angela, illus. (JPN.). 20p. (ps-5). 1991. pap. 13.95 incl. 45 min. cass. (ISBN 0-934633-20-7). Teach Me.

Murray, D. M. & Wong, T. W. Noodle Words: An Introduction to Chinese & Japanese Characters. LC 79-147179. (Illus.). (gr. 9 up). 1971. pap. 6.95 (ISBN 0-8048-0948-8). C E Tuttle.

Sheheen, Dennis, illus. A Child's Picture English-Japanese Dictionary. (gr. k-6). 1987. 9.95 (ISBN 1-55774-000-3, Dist. by Watts). Adama Pubs Inc.

JAPANESE LANGUAGE-GRAMMAR

Huntington, Seiko. Untangling Nihongo III: A Japanese Workbook, Vol. III. (Illus.). 135p. (Orig.). 1986. pap. 14.95 (ISBN 0-936845-02-3). Sakura Press.

Huntington, Seiko & Huntington, Andrew S. Japanese "ABCs" II: Katakana Learning Cards. (Illus.). 128p. (Orig.). 1990. pap. 16.95 (ISBN 0-936845-06-6). Sakura Press.

Stacy, Selmarie. Ganbatte: (How to Read Japanese) (Illus.). 58p. (Orig.). (gr. 7 up). 1990. pap. 6.95 wkbk. (ISBN 0-935984-09-7). Spheric Hse.

JAPANESE POETRY-COLLECTIONS

Lewis, Richard, ed. In a Spring Garden. Keats, Ezra J., illus. LC 65-23965. 32p. (ps up). 1989. Repr. of 1965 ed. 13.95 (ISBN 0-8037-4024-7). Dial Bks Young.

JAZZ MUSIC

Blocher, Arlo. Jazz. new ed. LC 75-39816. (Illus.). 32p. (gr. 5-10). 1976. PLB 10.79 (ISBN 0-89375-014-X); pap. 2.95 (ISBN 0-89375-030-1). Troll Assocs.

Carlin, Richard. Jazz. (Illus.). 128p. (gr. 7-12). 1991. 17. 95x (ISBN 0-8160-2229-1). Facts on File.

Griffin, Clive D. Jazz. (Illus.). 69p. (gr. 7-9). 1988. 19.95 (ISBN 0-85219-754-3, Pub. by Batsford England). Trafalgar Sq.

Terkel, Studs. Giants of Jazz. rev. ed. LC 75-20024. (Illus.). 192p. (gr. 5 up). 1975. 15.95 (ISBN 0-690-00998-4, Crowell Jr Bks). HarpC Child Bks.

JAZZ MUSIC-FICTION

Hentoff, Nat. Jazz Country. LC 65-15557. 160p. (gr. 7 up). 1965. PLB 12.89 (ISBN 0-06-022306-5). HarpC Child Bks.

Hurd, Thacher. Mama Don't Allow. LC 83-47703. (Illus.). 40p. (ps-3). 1984. 13.95 (ISBN 0-06-022689-7); PLB 13.89 (ISBN 0-06-022690-0). HarpC Child Bks.

JAZZ MUSIC-HISTORY

Longstreet, Stephen. Magic Trumpets: A Young People's Story of Jazz. Scott, Allen, ed. Longstreet, Stephen, illus. (Orig.). (gr. 6-12). 1989. pap. write for info. (ISBN 0-913705-42-X). Zephyr Pr AZ.

JEEPS

see Automobiles; Trucks

JEFFERSON, THOMAS, PRESIDENT U. S. 1743-1826

Adler, David A. A Picture Book of Thomas Jefferson. Wallner, John & Wallner, Alexandra, illus. LC 89-20076. 32p. (gr. k-3). 1990. 14.95 (ISBN 0-8234-0791-8). Holiday.

—A Picture Book of Thomas Jefferson. Wallner, John & Wallner, Alexandra, illus. 1991. pap. 5.95 (ISBN 0-8234-0881-7). Holiday.

—Thomas Jefferson: Father of Our Democracy. Garrick, Jacqueline, illus. LC 87-45336. 48p. (gr. 1-4). 1987. reinforced bdg. 12.95 (ISBN 0-8234-0667-9). Holiday.

Barrett, Marvin. Meet Thomas Jefferson. Torres, Angelo, illus. (gr. 2-6). 1967. (Random Juv); lib. bdg. 8.99 (ISBN 0-394-90067-7). Random.

—Meet Thomas Jefferson. Fogarty, Pat, illus. LC 88-19069. 72p. (gr. 2-4). 1989. PLB 6.99 (ISBN 0-394-91964-5); pap. 2.95 (ISBN 0-394-81964-0). Random.

Bober, Natalie. Thomas Jefferson: Man on a Mountain. LC 87-37462. (Illus.). 288p. (gr. 7 up). 1988. 15.95 (ISBN 0-689-31154-0, Atheneum Child Bk). Macmillan Child Grp.

Colver, Anne. Thomas Jefferson: Author of Independence. (Illus.). 80p. (gr. 2-6). 1992. Repr. of 1963 ed. PLB 12.95 (ISBN 0-7910-1443-6). Chelsea Hse.

Farr, Naunerle C. George Washington-Thomas Jefferson. Carrillo, Fred & Cruz, E. R., illus. (gr. 4-12). 1979. pap. text ed. 2.95 (ISBN 0-88301-355-X); wkbk. 1.25 (ISBN 0-88301-379-7). Pendulum Pr.

Hargrove, Jim. Thomas Jefferson. LC 86-9658. (Illus.). 100p. (gr. 3 up). 1986. PLB 17.27 (ISBN 0-516-01385-8); pap. 6.95 (ISBN 0-516-41385-6). Childrens.

Hilton, Suzanne. The World of Young Tom Jefferson. Bock, William S., illus. 96p. (gr. 3-6). 1986. 12.95 (ISBN 0-8027-6621-8); lib. bdg. 12.85 (ISBN 0-8027-6622-6). Walker & Co.

Johnson, Ann D. Value of Foresight: The Story of Thomas Jefferson. Pileggi, Steve, illus. LC 79-19548. (gr. k-6). 1979. 9.95 (ISBN 0-916392-42-2, Pub. by Value Communications). Oak Tree Pubns.

Komroff, Manuel. Thomas Jefferson. large type ed. (Illus.). 160p. (gr. 4-8). 1991. Repr. of 1961 ed. PLB 17.95 (ISBN 1-55905-083-7). Grey Castle.

Meltzer, Milton. Thomas Jefferson: The Revolutionary Aristocrat. (Illus.). 256p. (gr. 9-12). 1991. 15.95 (ISBN 0-531-15227-8); PLB 15.90 (ISBN 0-531-11069-9). Watts.

Milton, Joyce. The Story of Thomas Jefferson. (gr. k-6). 1990. 2.95 (ISBN 0-440-40265-4, YB). Dell.

Monsell, Helen A. Thomas Jefferson. (Illus.). 192p. (gr. 2-6). 1989. pap. 3.95 (ISBN 0-689-71347-9, Aladdin). Macmillan Child Grp.

Patterson, Charles. Thomas Jefferson. LC 86-23361. (Illus.). 96p. (gr. 4-8). 1987. PLB 10.40 (ISBN 0-531-10306-4). Watts.

Quackenbush, Robert. Pass the Quill; I'll Write a Draft: A Story of Thomas Jefferson. Quackenbush, Robert, illus. 32p. (gr. 2-6). 1989. PLB 13.95 (ISBN 0-945912-07-2). Pippin Pr.

Richards, Norman. The Story of Monticello. Mitchell, Chuck, illus. LC 70-100699. 32p. (gr. 4-8). 1970. PLB 13.27 (ISBN 0-516-04627-6). Childrens.

Sabin, Francene. Young Thomas Jefferson. Baxter, Robert, illus. LC 85-1093. 48p. (gr. 4-6). 1985. lib. bdg. 10.79 (ISBN 0-8167-0561-5); pap. text ed. 2.95 (ISBN 0-8167-0562-3). Troll Assocs.

Santrey, Laurence. Thomas Jefferson. Eitzen, Allan, illus. LC 84-2579. 32p. (gr. 3-6). 1985. PLB 9.49 (ISBN 0-8167-0176-8); pap. text ed. 2.95 (ISBN 0-8167-0177-6). Troll Assocs.

Shorto, Russell. Thomas Jefferson & the American Ideal. (Illus.). 144p. (gr. 3-6). 1987. pap. 4.95 (ISBN 0-8120-3918-1). Barron.

Smith, Kathie B. Thomas Jefferson. Steltenpohl, Jane, ed. Seward, James, illus. 24p. (gr. 4-6). 1989. lib. bdg. 7.98 (ISBN 0-671-67512-5); PLB 5.99s.p. (ISBN 0-685-25428-3). Messner.

Smith, Kathie B. & Bradbury, Pamela Z. Thomas Jefferson. (Illus.). (ps up). 1989. pap. 2.25 (ISBN 0-671-64768-7, Little Simon). S&S Trade.

Stefoff, Rebecca. Thomas Jefferson: 3rd President of the United States. Young, Richard G., ed. LC 87-32818. (Illus.). (gr. 5-9). 1988. PLB 17.26 (ISBN 0-944483-07-0). Garrett Ed Corp.

JELLYFISHES

Shale, David & Coldrey, Jennifer. The World of a Jellyfish. LC 86-5704. (Illus.). 32p. (gr. 2-3). 1986. 10. 95 (ISBN 1-55532-073-2). Gareth Stevens Inc.

Waters, John F. A Jellyfish Is Not a Fish. Mizumura, Kazue, illus. LC 77-26594. (gr. k-3). 1979. (Crowell Jr Bks); PLB 11.89 (ISBN 0-690-03889-5). HarpC Child Bks.

JENGHIS KHAN, 1162-1227

Demi. Chingis Khan. Demi, illus. LC 90-28807. 64p. (gr. 3-5). 1991. 19.95 (ISBN 0-8050-1708-9). H Holt & Co.

Lamb, Harold. Genghis Khan & the Mongol Horde. Fax, Elton, illus. viii, 182p. (gr. 5 up). 1990. Repr. of 1954 ed. lib. bdg. 16.50 (ISBN 0-208-02287-2, Linnet). Shoe String.

JERUSALEM

Hostetler, Marian. Journey to Jerusalem. Eitzen, Allan, illus. LC 77-19347. 128p. (gr. 4-8). 1978. pap. 3.95 (ISBN 0-8361-1848-0). Herald Pr.

Kuskin, Karla. Jerusalem, Shining Still. Frampton, David, illus. LC 86-25841. 32p. (ps up). 1987. 13.95 (ISBN 0-06-023548-9); PLB 13.89 (ISBN 0-06-023549-7). HarpC Child Bks.

Shaw, Lee H., Jr. How to Live Forever in the New Jerusalem. 56p. (Orig.). (gr. 9-12). 1985. pap. 3.00x (ISBN 0-9614311-0-5). Elijah-John.

JERUSALEM-FICTION

Parker, Lois. Return to Jerusalem. Wheeler, Gerald, ed. 160p. (Orig.). 1988. pap. 6.95 (ISBN 0-8280-0426-9). Review & Herald.

JESUS CHRIST

see also Christianity

Aprendamos de Jesus: Learning about Jesus. (SPA.). 32p. 1987. pap. 1.50 (ISBN 0-311-26610-X). Casa Bautista.

Ball, Ann. Holy Names of Jesus: Devotions, Litanies, Meditations. LC 90-60646. 192p. (Orig.). 1990. pap. 7.95 (ISBN 0-87973-428-0, 428). Our Sunday Visitor.

Beegle, Shirley. Jesus Quizzes. 1985. pap. 0.69 (ISBN 0-87239-824-2, 2814). Standard Pub.

Bennett, Marian. Jesus, God's Son. Williams, Abigail, illus. 14p. (Orig.). (ps-3). 1982. pap. 4.95 (ISBN 0-87239-564-2, 2705). Standard Pub.

Berthier, Rene. Jesus, Friend of Children. (Illus.). 80p. (gr. 2-8). 1990. 9.95 (ISBN 0-85648-053-3); pap. 6.95 (ISBN 0-85648-316-8). Lion USA.

Brennan-Nichols, Patricia. Getting to Know Jesus. Haberson, Lydia, illus. 68p. (Orig.). (gr. k-3). 1984. pap. 4.95 (ISBN 0-89505-130-3). Tabor Pub.

—Getting to Know Jesus: Teacher's Guide. (Illus.). 80p. (gr. k-3). 1984. 11.95 (ISBN 0-89505-131-1). Tabor Pub.

—Learning to Love Jesus. (Illus.). 80p. (Orig.). (gr. 4-6). 1985. tchr's. guide 15.95 (ISBN 0-89505-329-2); pap. 4.95 72p. (ISBN 0-89505-328-4). Tabor Pub.

Buerger, Jane. Growing As Jesus Grew. Hook, Francis, illus. (ps-2). 1985. PLB 5.95 (R4924). Standard Pub.

Caffrey, Stephanie & Kenslea, Timothy. The Shepherds Find a King. 16p. (ps-1). 1978. pap. 1.95 (ISBN 0-8192-1232-6). Morehouse Pub.

Churchwell, Kay. Baby Jesus. LC 85-24335. (Illus.). (ps). 1986. 4.95 (ISBN 0-8054-4170-0). Broadman.

Coleman, William. Jesus, My Forever Friend. Hanna, Wayne, illus. (gr. 4-8). 1981. 14.95 (ISBN 0-89191-370-X, 53702). Cook.

Colina, Tessa, ed. Jesus, My Teacher: (Pupil Activities Book Two) (Illus.). 16p. (gr. 1-5). 1978. pap. 1.95 (ISBN 0-87239-269-4, 2441). Standard Pub.

D. C. Cook Editors. The Big Picture Book about Jesus. Hook, Richard & Hook, Frances, illus. LC 77-72722. (gr. k-3). 1977. 12.95 (ISBN 0-89191-077-8, 08292). Cook.

Daniel, Rebecca. Book II-His Boyhood. McClure, Nancee, illus. 32p. (gr. 2-7). 1984. wkbk. 5.95 (ISBN 0-86653-223-4, SS 825). Good Apple.

—Book IV-the Teacher. McClure, Nancee, illus. 32p. (gr. 2-7). 1984. wkbk. 5.95 (ISBN 0-86653-225-0, SS 827). Good Apple.

—Book V-The Healer. McClure, Nancee, illus. 32p. (gr. 2-7). wkbk. 5.95 (ISBN 0-86653-226-9, SS 828). Good Apple.

—Book VI-His Miracles. McClure, Nancee, illus. 32p. (gr. 2-7). 1984. wkbk. 5.95 (ISBN 0-86653-227-7, SS 829). Good Apple.

—Book VII-His Parables. McClure, Nancee, illus. 32p. (gr. 2-7). 1984. wkbk. 5.95 (ISBN 0-86653-228-5, SS 830). Good Apple.

—Book VIII-More Parables. McClure, Nancee, illus. 32p. (gr. 2-7). 1984. wkbk. 5.95 (ISBN 0-86653-229-3, SS 831). Good Apple.

—Book X-His Last Days. McClure, Nancee, illus. 32p. (gr. 2-7). 1984. wkbk. 5.95 (ISBN 0-86653-231-5, SS 833). Good Apple.

—Book XI-His Last Hours. McClure, Nancee, illus. 32p. (gr. 2-7). 1984. wkbk. 5.95 (ISBN 0-86653-232-3, SS 834). Good Apple.

—Book XII-His Resurection. McClure, Nancee, illus. 32p. (gr. 2-7). 1984. wkbk. 5.95 (ISBN 0-86653-233-1, SS 835). Good Apple.

—Jesus & His Miracles. 16p. (ps-3). 1991. 16.95 (ISBN 0-86653-634-5, SS1879). Good Apple.

Daughters of St. Paul. Always with Jesus. 1973. pap. 2.95 (ISBN 0-8198-0714-1). Dghtrs St Paul.

Davis, Susan. Password to Heaven. 32p. (gr. k-3). 1980. pap. 2.50 (ISBN 0-8127-0298-0). Review & Herald.

Dean, Bessie. Let's Learn about Jesus: A Child's Coloring Book of the Life of Christ. (Illus.). 72p. (ps-6). 1988. pap. 5.95 (ISBN 0-88290-131-1). Horizon Utah.

Dede, Vivian. Jesus' First Miracle. LC 59-1445. (Illus.). 24p. (ps-4). 1990. pap. 1.39 (ISBN 0-570-09022-9). Concordia.

DePaola, Tomie. The Miracles of Jesus. DePaola, Tomie, illus. LC 86-18297. 32p. (gr. 1-4). 1987. reinforced bdg. 14.95 (ISBN 0-8234-0635-0). Holiday.

Eager, George B. Wake up World! Jesus Is Coming Soon! 40p. (Orig.). (gr. 7-12). 1980. pap. 1.00 (ISBN 0-9603752-3-6). Mailbox.

Enns, Peter & Forsberg, Glen. Jesus Is Alive! & Five Other Stories. Friesen, John H., illus. 24p. (ps-5). 1985. book & cassette 4.95 (ISBN 0-936215-06-2). STL Intl.

Evans, Helen K. Jesus, My Friend. 64p. (ps-3). 1988. 7.95 (ISBN 0-86653-428-8, SS1856). Good Apple.

Fahs, Sophia L. Jesus - the Carpenter's Son. rev. ed. Baldridge, Cyrus L., illus. 160p. pap. 14.95 (ISBN 1-55896-090-2). Unitarian Univ.

Fogle, Jeanne S. Symbols of God's Love: Codes & Passwords. Ducket, Mary Jean & Lane, W. Ben, eds. Weidner, Bea, illus. LC 86-12014. 32p. (Orig.). (gr. k-3). 1986. pap. 6.95 (ISBN 0-664-24050-X, Westminster). Westminster John Knox.
Frank, Penny. Secrets Jesus Told. (Illus.). 24p. (ps-4). 3.95 (ISBN 0-85648-762-7). Lion USA.
Garlow, Willa R. Jesus Is a Special Person. LC 85-24361. (Illus.). (ps). 1986. 4.95 (ISBN 0-8054-4166-2). Broadman.
Gray, Ronald D. Christopher Wren & St. Paul's Cathedral. LC 81-13696. (Illus.). 48p. (gr. 7 up). 1980. pap. 5.95 (ISBN 0-521-21666-4). Cambridge U Pr.
Griffin, Henry W. Jesus for Children. Swisher, Elizabeth, illus. 132p. 1986. 12.95; pap. 7.95 (ISBN 0-86683-866-X). Harper SF.
Groth, Lynn. Jesus Loves Children. 16p. (Orig.). (ps). 1985. pap. 1.25 (ISBN 0-938272-78-0). Wels Board.
—Reaching Tender Hearts, Vol. 1. Grunze, Richard, ed. May, Lawrence & Steele, Loren, illus. 157p. (ps-k). 1987. pap. 7.95 (ISBN 0-938272-42-X). WELS Board.
—Reaching Tender Hearts, Vol. 2. Grunze, Richard, ed. May, Lawrence & Steele, Loren, illus. 176p. (ps-k). 1988. pap. 8.95 (ISBN 0-938272-43-8). WELS Board.
—A Very Special Baby-Jesus. 8p. (Orig.). (ps). 1985. pap. 1.25 (ISBN 0-938272-76-4). Wels Board.
Hornsby, Sarah. Getting to Know Jesus from A to Z. 1989. 9.95 (ISBN 0-8007-1624-8). Revell.
Jacobs, Paul S. Born into Light. LC 87-20792. 144p. (gr. 7 up). 1988. pap. 11.95 (ISBN 0-590-40710-4, Scholastic Hardcover). Scholastic Inc.
Jesus Shows Us How to Live. 12p. (gr. k-3). 1982. 8.95 (ISBN 0-89191-522-2). Cook.
Jesus Was a Child Like You. 12p. (gr. k-3). 1982. 8.95 (ISBN 0-89191-525-7, 55251). Cook.
Johnson, Joy, et al. Where's Jesus? Bornum, Shari, illus. 24p. (Orig.). (ps). 1980. pap. 3.00. Centering Corp.
Kaufman, Margie. A, B, See How Jesus Loves Me. Davis, Deena, ed. Kaufman, Rick, illus. LC 88-34258. 29p. (ps). 1989. 7.95 (ISBN 0-88070-277-X). Multnomah.
Klug, Ron & Klug, Lyn. Jesus Lives. LC 82-72848. 32p. (Orig.). (ps). 1982. pap. 4.95 (ISBN 0-8066-1952-X, 10-3527, Augsburg). Augsburg Fortress.
—Jesus Loves: Stories about Jesus for Children. Konsterile, Paul, illus. LC 86-81807. 32p. (Orig.). (gr. 3-8). 1986. pap. 4.95 saddlestitch (ISBN 0-8066-2235-0, 10-3526, Augsburg). Augsburg Fortress.
Lashbrook, Marilyn. The Best Day Ever: The Story of Jesus. Sharp, Chris, illus. LC 90-63764. (gr. k-3). 1991. 5.95 (ISBN 0-86606-444-3, 875). Roper Pr.
Leone, Dee. The Miracles of Jesus. 48p. (ps-1). 1990. 6.95 (ISBN 0-86653-554-3, SS1874). Good Apple.
Lewis, Lorna. Jesus Is Risen! Baker, Arthur, illus. 32p. (gr. k-3). 1990. saddle-stitched 1.25 (ISBN 0-8028-5054-5). Eerdmans.
Lindvall, Ella K. My Friend Jesus. Walles, Dwight, illus. 32p. (Orig.). (gr. 1-3). 1989. pap. 2.95 (ISBN 0-8024-5949-8). Moody.
The Lord Is My Shepherd. (Illus.). (gr. k-6). 1963. 4.99 (ISBN 3-90117-004-9). CEF Press.
Lost & Found Kit. (gr. k-6). 1978. 19.99 (ISBN 1-55976-105-9). CEF Press.
McAllister, Dawson. A Walk with Christ Through the Resurrection. Whitney, Roger, illus. (gr. 5-12). 1981. pap. 8.95 (ISBN 0-923417-14-1). Shepherd Minst.
—A Walk with Christ to the Cross. Whitney, Roger, illus. (gr. 5-12). 1980. pap. 8.95 (ISBN 0-923417-09-5). Shepherd Minst.
—Who Are You, Jesus? Lewis, Paul, illus. (gr. 5-12). 1986. pap. 7.95 (ISBN 0-923417-05-2). Shepherd Minst.
McAllister, Dawson & Kimmel, Tim. Walk with Christ to the Cross. (gr. 5-12). 1981. pap. 5.95 tchr's. guide (ISBN 0-923417-20-6). Shepherd Minst.
McAllister, Dawson & May, Tom. Who Are You Jesus? (gr. 5-12). 1986. pap. 7.95 tchr's. guide (ISBN 0-923417-03-6). Shepherd Minst.
McFadzean, Anita. One Special Star. Jaspers, Kate, illus. 32p. (ps-1). 1991. bds. 3.95 jacketed (ISBN 0-671-74024-5, Little Simon). S&S Trade.
Marchand, Roger. Meeting Jesus in Holy Communion. 32p. (gr. 1-3). 1984. pap. 2.50 (ISBN 0-89243-202-0). Liguori Pubns.
Marquart, M. Jesus' Second Family. (gr. k-2). 1977. pap. 1.39 (ISBN 0-570-06111-3, 59-1229). Concordia.
Mullen, Sharon. When Jesus Was Born. LC 86-17558. (ps). 1987. 5.95 (ISBN 0-8054-4177-8). Broadman.
My Book about Jesus. (Illus.). 32p. (ps-2). 1985. 1.95 (ISBN 0-225-66388-0). Harper SF.
Nargi, Ben J. Are You He Who Is to Come. LC 88-51027. 138p. 1989. pap. 6.95 (ISBN 1-55523-177-2). Winston-Derek.
Nystrom, Carolyn. Who Is Jesus? 32p. (ps-2). 1980. pap. 3.95 (ISBN 0-8024-6159-X). Moody.
Oetting, R. When Jesus Was a Lad. LC 68-56816. (Illus.). 32p. (gr. 2-3). 1968. PLB 9.95x (ISBN 0-87783-047-9). Oddo.
Pankow, Eleanor. Let's Talk about Jesus. (Illus.). (gr. k-6). 1963. 3.99 (ISBN 3-90117-015-4). CEF Press.
Parry, Alan & Parry, Linda. Jesus is Alive! Parry, Alan, illus. 24p. (ps). 1990. pap. 0.99 (ISBN 0-8066-2479-5, 9-2479). Augsburg Fortress.
—Paul Meets Jesus. Parry, Alan, illus. 24p. (ps). 1990. pap. 0.99 (ISBN 0-8066-2480-9, 9-2480). Augsburg Fortress.
Podhaizer, Mary E. Following Christ: Activity Book. Puccetti, Patricia I., ed. 41p. (Orig.). (gr. 6). 1985. pap. 3.00 (ISBN 0-89870-066-3). Ignatius Pr.
Rosen, Ruth, ed. Jesus for Jews. Owens, Nate, illus. LC 87-20343. 336p. (Orig.). (gr. 12). 1987. 13.95 (ISBN 0-9616148-3-8); pap. 7.95 (ISBN 0-9616148-4-6); pap. 4.95 mass market (ISBN 0-9616148-2-X). Messianic Jewish.
Royer, Katherine. Nursery Stories of Jesus. (Illus.). 48p. (ps). 1957. pap. 2.95 (ISBN 0-8361-1276-8). Herald Pr.
Sayers, Susan. Jesus on a Donkey. Baker, Arthur, illus. 32p. (gr. k-3). 1990. saddle-stitched 1.25 (ISBN 0-8028-5056-1). Eerdmans.
—The Road to the Cross. Baker, Arthur, illus. 32p. (gr. k-3). 1990. saddle stitched 1.25 (ISBN 0-8028-5058-8). Eerdmans.
Senterfitt, Marilyn. Celebrate Jesus. 144p. (gr. 1-6). 1988. 10.95 (ISBN 0-86653-425-3, SS845). Good Apple.
Sieg, Robert C. What John Says about Jesus: An Interpretation for the Very Young. LC 89-61304. (Illus.). 104p. (Orig.). 1989. pap. 7.95 (ISBN 1-55618-072-1). Brunswick Pub.
—What Matthew Says about Jesus: An Interpretation for the Very Young. LC 89-61306. (Illus.). 132p. (Orig.). 1989. pap. 7.95 (ISBN 1-55618-073-X). Brunswick Pub.
Simon, Mary M. Little Visits with Jesus. (Illus.). 256p. (ps-3). 1987. 9.95 (ISBN 0-570-03076-5, 6-1191); pap. 7.95 (ISBN 0-570-03075-7, 06-1190). Concordia.
Sparks, Judy, ed. Yes! Jesus Loves Me. Woggon, Bill, illus. 24p. (ps-2). 1985. 1.99 (ISBN 0-87239-882-X, 3682). Standard Pub.
Stewart, Frances T. & Stewart, Charles P. The Birth of Jesus. (Orig.). (gr. 3 up). 1985. pap. 6.95 (ISBN 0-8054-4171-9). Broadman.
Stewart, Pat, illus. Jesus' Bethlehem Birthday. (ps-2). 1989. 9.95 (ISBN 1-55513-814-4). Cook.
Stirrup Associates, Inc. Staff. My Jesus Pocketbook of the Beginning. Harvey, Bonnie C. & Phillips, Cheryl M., eds. Burnett, Lindy, illus. LC 84-50918. 32p. (Orig.). (ps-3). 1984. pap. 0.69 (ISBN 0-937420-14-X). Stirrup Assoc.
Stoner, Laura M. Jesus: A Story Color Book. (Illus.). 80p. (Orig.). (gr. 1-8). 1985. pap. 3.95 wkbk. (ISBN 0-934426-07-4). Napsac Reprods.
Sumrall, Lester. Adventuring with Christ. 2nd ed. 161p. 1988. Repr. of 1938 ed. text ed. 11.95 (ISBN 0-937580-13-9). LeSEA Pub Co.
Sutherland, E. A. Studies in Christian Education: Christ's Education Was Gained from Heaven-Appointed Sources, from Useful Work, from the Study of the Scriptures, from Nature, & from the Experiences of Life - God's Lesson Books. 160p. (gr. 9 up). 1989. pap. 6.95 (ISBN 0-945460-04-X). Upward Way.
Svensson, Borje. Great Miracles of Jesus. Mitchell, Vic, illus. 10p. (ps-2). 1985. 8.95 (ISBN 0-89191-940-6, 59402, Chariot Bks). Cook.
Tangvald, Christine. Jesus Is for Me. 24p. (ps-2). 1989. pap. 2.95 (ISBN 1-55513-740-7, Chariot Bks). Cook.

Taylor, Ken. Good News for Little People. 1991. 10.95 (ISBN 0-8423-6628-8). Tyndale.
In simple language & colorful illustrations especially for children, Dr. Kenneth N. Taylor tells stories about the life of Jesus in the book Good News for Little People. Read about the wondrous birth of Jesus, the marvelous miracles he performed during his life, the sadness of his death on the cross, & the glory of his resurrection. Each story & illustration is followed by simple questions, a short prayer, & a Bible verse. Good News for Little People is the fourth book in Dr. Kenneth Taylor's best-selling Little People series which consists of Big Thoughts for Little People, Giant Steps for Little People & Wise Words for Little People. Other children's books by Dr. Taylor include The Bible in Pictures for Little Eyes, The Living Bible Story Book, Stories for the Children's Hour & My First Bible in Pictures. Dr. Taylor is the father of ten children & the grandfather of twenty-seven grandchildren! He is a graduate of Wheaton College & Northern Baptist Seminary. Presently the chairman & founder of Tyndale House Publishers, Dr. Taylor & his wife Margaret live in Wheaton, Illinois.
Publisher Provided Annotation.

Thomas, Mack. What Would Jesus Do? Mortenson, Denis, illus. 256p. (ps-3). 1991. 12.95 (ISBN 0-945564-05-8). Questar Pubs.
Almost a century ago, a new novel revolutionized the concept of Christian discipleship. The book was Charles M. Sheldon's In His Steps. Conservative estimates place the book's sales at more than 25 million copies--ranking it behind only the Bible in popularity among Christian readers in this century. And now, In His Steps has been retold for children, with its timeless message as clear & powerful as ever. As both a book & audio cassette, What Would Jesus Do? presents the stirring call of following Christ in a way that young children can easily understand & embrace. The delightful text is written in short, simple sentences, & is set in a clear typeface especially recommended for early readers. Each short chapter focuses in a fresh way on the book's core concept--learning to ask throughout the day, What would Jesus do? Discussion questions for each chapter help parents & teachers highlight this truth for children. Enhancing the text are full-color illustrations on more than 200 pages. Detailed & charming, they capture the book's flavor as a work that transcends time & cultures.
Publisher Provided Annotation.

Tiner, John H. Jesus the Teacher Word Search. 48p. 1986. pap. 2.95 (ISBN 0-87403-049-8, 2693). Standard Pub.
Waggoner, E. J. Christ & His Righteousness. 96p. (gr. 9 up). 1988. pap. 3.95 (ISBN 0-945460-01-5). Upward Way.
Watson, Elizabeth E. Tell Me about Jesus. (gr. 1 up). 1980. pap. 4.95 (ISBN 0-570-03484-1, 56-1705). Concordia.
Wezeman, Phyllis & Weissner, Colleen. Seaside with the Savior. (Illus.). 144p. (gr. 1-6). 1989. 24.95 (ISBN 1-55513-186-7, 68718). Cook.
White, E. G. Christ Our Savior. (Illus.). 160p. (gr. 5 up). 1989. pap. 7.95 (ISBN 0-945460-05-8). Upward Way.
—Christ Our Savior. (SPA., Illus.). 176p. (gr. 5 up). 1990. pap. 7.95 (ISBN 0-945460-10-4). Upward Way.
Willis, Doris. Jesus Grew. (ps). 1990. 3.95 (ISBN 0-687-03124-9). Abingdon.
Would You Like to Know Jesus? (gr. 3-7). 1989. pap. 0.99 (ISBN 1-55513-935-3, Chariot Bks). Cook.
Wyatt, Margaret. My Friend Jesus. Wyatt, Tracey, illus. LC 86-90051. 20p. (Orig.). (ps-12). 1986. pap. 2.25 (ISBN 0-9616117-0-7). M Wyatt.
Wyly, Louise B. Quiet Moments Preschoolers. Wigginton, Shirley, ed. Hand, Judy, illus. 128p. (Orig.). (ps-k). 1988. pap. 3.95 (ISBN 0-87403-471-X, 2803). Standard Pub.
Young, Barbara. Jesus Is My Very Best Friend. (ps-k). 1984. 5.95 (ISBN 0-570-04097-3, 56-1465). Concordia.
Yzermans, Vencent A. Jesus & Caesar Augustus: A Legend. Yell, Vonett & Bergmann, Melvin, illus. LC 89-50566. 180p. (Orig.). (gr. 7-12). 1989. pap. 7.95 (ISBN 0-89622-396-5). Twenty-Third.

JESUS CHRIST–ART

see also Bible–Pictorial Works; Christian Art and Symbolism

Johnson, Stephen & Johnson, Renae. Around the World with Jesus. (Illus.). 144p. (gr. 1-6). 1989. 24.95 (ISBN 1-55513-872-1, 68726). Cook.

JESUS CHRIST–BIOGRAPHY

see also Jesus Christ–Nativity

Baby Jesus. (Illus.). (gr. 2-4). 3.50 (ISBN 0-7214-1313-7). Ladybird Bks.
Brittain, Grady B. Platy: The Child in Us. McBoon, Linda, illus. LC 81-6503. 53p. (Orig.). (ps-8). 1981. pap. 0.50 (ISBN 0-86663-761-3). Ide Hse.
Brown, Alice & Kirk, Pat. Jesus: God's Champion for Today's Children. (Illus.). (ps-3). 1986. 8.95 (ISBN 0-915720-21-3). Brownlow Pub Co.
Bull, Norman. Jesus the Nazarene. (gr. 2-7). pap. 10.95 (ISBN 0-7175-0981-8). Dufour.
Burns, Jim. Radical for the King. 64p. (Orig.). (gr. 9-12). 1989. pap. 4.99 (ISBN 0-89081-721-9). Harvest Hse.
Carr, Dan. Our Savior Is Born. (gr. 1 up). 1984. 7.95 (ISBN 0-570-04092-2, 56-1460). Concordia.
Daniel, Rebecca. Book V-The Healer. McClure, Nancee, illus. 32p. (gr. 2-7). wkbk. 5.95 (ISBN 0-86653-226-9, SS 828). Good Apple.

—Book VI-His Miracles. McClure, Nancee, illus. 32p. (gr. 2-7). 1984. wkbk. 5.95 (ISBN 0-86653-227-7, SS 829). Good Apple.
—Book XI-His Last Hours. McClure, Nancee, illus. 32p. (gr. 2-7). 1984. wkbk. 5.95 (ISBN 0-86653-232-3, SS 834). Good Apple.
—Book XII-His Resurection. McClure, Nancee, illus. 32p. (gr. 2-7). 1984. wkbk. 5.95 (ISBN 0-86653-233-1, SS 835). Good Apple.
—Jesus' Life. 48p. (ps-6). 1988. 6.95 (ISBN 0-86653-460-1, SS855). Good Apple.
De Graaf, Anne. The Early Years of Jesus. (Illus.). 32p. 1989. 4.95 (ISBN 0-310-52720-1). Zondervan.
Doney, Meryl. Jesus: The Man Who Changed History. (Illus.). 48p. (gr. 4 up). 1988. text ed. 13.95 (ISBN 0-7459-1050-5). Lion USA.
The Early Life of Jesus. (gr. 4-6). 1990. 1.55 (ISBN 0-89636-116-0, JB 1C). Accent Bks.
Egermeier, Elsie E. Egermeier's Picture-Story Life of Jesus. Inns, Kenneth, illus. (gr. k-6). 1969. 7.95 (ISBN 0-87162-008-1, D2015). Warner Pr.
Henry, Kay V. Jesus Was a Helper. LC 86-17540. (ps). 1987. pap. 5.95 (ISBN 0-8054-4176-X). Broadman.
Hershey, Katherine. Life of Christ, Vol. I. Banse, Charles & Chappell, David, illus. 54p. (gr. k-6). 1987. pap. text ed. 9.45 (ISBN 1-55976-000-1). CEF Press.
—Life of Christ, Vol. III. Banse, Charles, illus. 51p. (gr. k-6). 1978. pap. text ed. 9.45 (ISBN 1-55976-002-8). CEF Press.
—Life of Christ, Vol. IV. Banse, Charles, illus. 49p. (gr. k-6). 1978. pap. text ed. 9.45 (ISBN 1-55976-003-6). CEF Press.
—Life of Christ, Vol. II. (Illus.). 55p. (gr. k-6). 1987. pap. 9.45 (ISBN 1-55976-001-X). CEF Press.
Hill, Dave. Most Wonderful King. Wind, B., illus. (gr. 3-4). 1968. laminated bdg. 1.39 (ISBN 0-570-06032-X, 59-1145). Concordia.
Hilliard, Dick & Valenti-Hilliard, Beverly. Happenings! Collopy, George F., illus. 48p. (gr. 1 up). 1981. pap. text ed. 4.95 (ISBN 0-89390-033-8). Resource Pubns.
Huffaker, Alice. Resurrection Day. (ps-3). 1990. pap. 3.95 (ISBN 0-8024-2638-7). Moody.
Kageyama, Akiko. Journey to Bethlehem. 26p. (ps-3). 1983. 9.95 (ISBN 0-8170-1012-2). Judson.
Kanaar, Barbara. A Child's Story of Jesus. Hutton, Kathryn, illus. 24p. (ps-2). 1986. 1.99 (ISBN 0-87403-023-4, 3483). Standard Pub.
Larsen, Dan. Jesus. Bohl, Al, illus. 224p. (gr. 4-8). 1989. pap. text ed. 2.50 (ISBN 1-55748-100-8). Barbour & Co.
L'Engle, Madeleine. The Glorious Impossible. Giotto, illus. 64p. (gr. 3 up). 1990. PLB 19.95 (ISBN 0-671-68690-9). S&S Trade.
Lynn, Claire. No Crib for a Bed. Lautermilch, John, illus. (Orig.). (ps-1). 1983. pap. 2.25 (ISBN 0-89323-029-4). Bible Memory.
McMillan, Mary. The Story of Jesus. 48p. (ps-1). 1988. 6.95 (ISBN 0-86653-454-7, SS1804). Good Apple.
Maschke, Ruby. Teachings of Christ Story-N-Puzzle Book. 48p. (Orig.). (gr. 4 up). 1981. pap. 2.95 (ISBN 0-87239-451-4, 2842). Standard Pub.
Osborne, John T. Miracles. Osborne, John T., illus. 90p. 1988. pap. text ed. 5.75 (ISBN 0-929918-00-2). Midstates Pub.
Otting, Rae. When Jesus Was a Lad. Marilue, illus. (gr. 1-2). 1978. pap. 1.25 (ISBN 0-89508-055-9). Rainbow Bks.
Peterson, Esther A. A Child's Life of Christ. Lee, Nancy, illus. 44p. (gr. 3-8). 1987. 6.95 (ISBN 1-55523-045-8). Winston-Derek.
Podhaizer, Mary E. Jesus Our Life: Activity Book. Puccetti, Patricia I., ed. 76p. (Orig.). (gr. 2). 1984. pap. 3.00 (ISBN 0-89870-063-9). Ignatius Pr.
Ralph, Margaret. Jesus: Historias de su Vida. King, Gordon, illus. LaValle, Teresa, tr. (Illus.). 28p. (gr. 4). 1979. 2.75 (ISBN 0-311-38536-2, Edit Mundo). Casa Bautista.
Savary, Louis. The Life of Jesus. Goodwill, Rita, illus. 43p. (ps-4). 1989. 5.59 (ISBN 0-88271-099-0). Regina Pr.
Schrage, Alice. The King Who Lives Forever. LC 81-50590. 128p. (gr. 1-7). 1981. pap. text ed. 3.95 (ISBN 0-8307-0766-2, 5810604). Regal.
Sieg, Robert C. What Luke Says about Jesus: An Interpretation for the Very Young. LC 89-61303. (Illus.). 118p. (Orig.). 1990. pap. 7.95 (ISBN 1-55618-074-8). Brunswick Pub.
Sockey, Daria M. Jesus Our Life. Puccetti, Patricia I., ed. (Illus.). 151p. (Orig.). (gr. 2). 1984. pap. 5.55 (ISBN 0-89870-061-2). Ignatius Pr.
Stewart, Frances T. & Stewart, Charles P., III. When Jesus Was a Boy. (Orig.). (gr. k-3). 1987. pap. 6.95 (ISBN 0-8054-4188-3). Broadman.
Stirrup Associates, Inc. Staff. My Jesus Pocketbook of Scripture Pictures. Sherman, Erin, illus. LC 82-80351. 32p. (Orig.). (ps-3). 1982. pap. 0.69 (ISBN 0-937420-02-6). Stirrup Assoc.
Storr, Catherine, as told by. Jesus & John the Baptist. (Illus.). 32p. (gr. k-4). 1985. PLB 14.65 (ISBN 0-8172-2037-2). Raintree Pubs.
—Jesus the Healer. (Illus.). 32p. (gr. k-4). 1985. PLB 14.65 (ISBN 0-8172-2041-0). Raintree Pubs.
Story of Jesus Pop-Up Book. (Illus.). (ps-1). 1.98 (ISBN 0-517-43888-7). Outlet Bk Co.
Tallach, Isobel. Life of Jesus. (Orig.). (ps-3). 1984. pap. 1.75 (ISBN 0-85151-345-X). Banner of Truth.
Who Is Jesus? (gr. 4-6). 1990. 1.55 (ISBN 0-89636-117-9, JB 2C). Accent Bks.
Wolf, Bob. Just Like Jesus. (Illus.). 24p. (Orig.). (gr. 1-4). 1982. pap. 1.00 (ISBN 0-89323-034-0). Bible Memory.

JESUS CHRIST–BIRTH

see Jesus Christ–Nativity

JESUS CHRIST–FICTION

Ahern, Denise. Bread & the Wine, No. Sixteen. (Illus.). (gr. k-4). 1979. 1.39 (ISBN 0-570-06127-X, 59-1245). Concordia.
Animals Gift. 1991. pap. 13.95 (ISBN 0-671-72962-4). S&S Trade.
Aoki, Hisako. Santa's Favorite Story. 2nd ed. Gantschev, Ivan, illus. LC 82-60895. 28p. (gr. k up). 1990. Repr. of 1982 ed. 4.95 (ISBN 0-88708-153-3). Picture Bk Studio.
Barnes, Joyce B. Patches, the Blessed Beast of Burden. Ramirez-Walker, Linda J., illus. 36p. 1990. 15.00 (ISBN 0-9628493-0-8). J B Barnes.
Black, Auguste R. Miracles at the Inn. Sherentz, Michael K., illus. 24p. (Orig.). (gr. 1-12). 1990. pap. 4.95 (ISBN 0-9628010-1-1). A R Black.
Briscoe, Jill. Caleb's Colt: A Heartwarming Adventure of Hope & Change. rev. ed. Cragg, Sheila, ed. Flint, Russ, illus. 48p. (gr. k-3). 1989. Repr. of 1986 ed. 7.99 (ISBN 0-929608-24-0). Focus Family.
—The Innkeeper's Daughter: A Delightful Discovery of a Wonderful Miracle. rev. ed. Cragg, Sheila, ed. Flint, Russ, illus. 48p. (gr. 2 up). Repr. of 1984 ed. 7.99 (ISBN 0-929608-18-6). Focus Family.
De Santis, Zerlina. A Child's Story of the Baby Who Changed the World. LC 74-232. (Illus.). (ps-3). 1.75 (ISBN 0-8198-0191-7). Dghtrs St Paul.

Fryar, Jane. Lost at the Mall: Morris the Mouse Adventure Ser. Wilson, Deborah, illus. 32p. (ps-1). 1991. 7.95 (ISBN 0-570-04196-1, 56-1655). Concordia.
Lost at the Mall is one of two titles in the new Morris The Mouse Adventure Series, which features Morris the Mouse, a well-loved Sunday School character. When 5-year-old Broderick slips Morris into his pocket for a trip to the mall, the two get lost. Amid the confusion & fear of being all alone in a strange place, Morris reminds Broderick that Jesus will help & take care of him in any situation. The Morris books are a great way to assist parents & teachers in helping their 3- to 6-year old children identify the unique talents God has given them & be assured of God's constant care. For children ages 3 to 6. 32 pp. 4-color hardcover. $7.95. Concordia Publishing House. Item no. 56-1655. ISBN 0-570-04196-1. To order -- Call Toll Free 1-800-325-3040.
Publisher Provided Annotation.

Geier, Marguerite E. Rama, the Holy Family Dog. 1991. 11.95 (ISBN 0-533-09441-0). Vantage.
Head, Constance. The Man Who Carried the Cross for Jesus. (Illus.). (gr. k-4). 1979. 1.39 (ISBN 0-570-06124-5, 59-1242). Concordia.
Heise, Robert F. The Night Before Jesus. Wade, John, illus. 28p. (gr. 3-6). 1990. 12.95 (ISBN 0-9627049-0-3). Dogwood NC.
Helldorfer, M. C. Daniel's Gift. Downing, Julie, illus. LC 90-186. 32p. (gr. k-3). 1990. pap. 4.95 (ISBN 0-689-71440-8, Aladdin). Macmillan Child Grp.
Herold, Ann B. The Mysterious Passover Visitors. (Illus.). 112p. (Orig.). (gr. 8-12). 1989. pap. 4.95 (ISBN 0-8361-3494-X). Herald Pr.
Nystrom, Carolyn. Growing Jesus' Way. (gr. 2). 1982. 3.95 (ISBN 0-8024-6151-4). Moody.
One Special Star. 1991. pap. 11.95 (ISBN 0-671-74023-7). S&S Trade.
Sanchez-Silva, Jose M. The Miracle of Marcelino. (SPA., Illus.). 122p. (Orig.). (gr. 1-6). 1963. pap. 3.95 (ISBN 0-933932-28-6). Scepter Pubs.
Savitz, Harriet M. & Syring, K. Michael. The Pail of Nails. Shaw, Charles, illus. (gr. 3 up). 1990. 10.95 (ISBN 0-687-29974-8). Abingdon.
Smith, Sally Ann. Candle, a Story of Love & Faith. Luther, Luana, ed. Jung, Mary, illus. 42p. 1991. pap. write for info. (ISBN 0-944875-22-X). Doral Pub.
Speare, Elizabeth G. Bronze Bow. 256p. (gr. 6 up). 1961. 13.95 (ISBN 0-395-07113-5). HM.
Van Horn, Brian & Van Horn, Chris. Lordy Lamb & the Twelve Lisciples. Mowdy, Sharon, ed. Scott, Rita & Van Horn, Brian, illus. 40p. (gr. k-5). 1989. 8.95 (ISBN 1-877765-00-7). Lambgel Family.
Wallace, Lew. Ben Hur. Bennet, C. L., intro. by. (gr. 9 up). pap. 2.95 (ISBN 0-8049-0074-4, CL-74). Airmont.
Wedeven, Carol S. The Christmas Crib That Zack Built. Fisher, Nell F., illus. 1989. casebound 9.95 (ISBN 0-687-07816-4). Abingdon.

JESUS CHRIST–ICONOGRAPHY

see Jesus Christ–Art

JESUS CHRIST–NATIVITY

see also Christmas

Away in a Manger. 1989. 6.95 (ISBN 0-02-689338-X). Checkerboard Pr.
Bennett, Marian, ed. Baby Jesus. Karch, Paul, illus. 10p. (ps). 1985. 3.95 (ISBN 0-87239-907-9, 2747). Standard Pub.
Billington, Rachel. The First Christmas. Brown, Barbara, illus. LC 87-20383. 32p. (gr. k-5). 1987. 12.95 (ISBN 0-8192-1415-9); pap. 6.95 (ISBN 0-8192-1410-8). Morehouse Pub.
Brandt, Catharine. The Story of Christmas for Children. LC 74-79366. (Illus.). 20p. (Orig.). (gr. 1 up). 1974. pap. 7.95 (ISBN 0-8066-2030-7, 10-6041, Augsburg). Augsburg Fortress.
Brown, Margaret W. Christmas in the Barn. Cooney, Barbara, illus. LC 52-7858. 32p. (gr. k-3). 1961. PLB 13.89 (ISBN 0-690-19272-X, Crowell Jr Bks); PLB 12.89 (ISBN 0-685-04855-1). HarpC Child Bks.
The Christmas Story. (gr. k-4). 1990. 3.50 (ISBN 0-7214-1190-8). Ladybird Bks.
Daniel, Rebecca. Book I-His Birth. McClure, Nancee, illus. 32p. (gr. 2-7). 1984. wkbk. 5.95 (ISBN 0-86653-213-7, SS 824). Good Apple.
Evans, Helen K. Jesus Is Born. 64p. (ps-3). 1990. 7.95 (ISBN 0-86653-551-9, SS894). Good Apple.
Forell, Betty & Wind, Betty. Little Benjamin & the First Christmas. (Illus.). (ps-3). 1964. laminated bdg. 1.39 (ISBN 0-570-06005-2, 59-1113). Concordia.
Frank, Penny. The First Christmas. (Illus.). 24p. (gr. 1 up). 1986. 3.95 (ISBN 0-85648-757-0). Lion USA.
Galusha, David. The First Christmas. McIlrath, James, illus. LC 81-82147. 32p. (ps up). 1981. wkbk. 3.95 (ISBN 0-87973-662-3, 662). Our Sunday Visitor.
Hayes, Sarah. Away in a Manger. Moore, Inga, illus. (gr. 1-7). 1987. pap. 10.95 (ISBN 0-671-64311-8, Little Simon). S&S Trade.
Hillert, Margaret. The Birth of Jesus. Endres, Helen, illus. 24p. (gr. k-1). 1988. 4.99 (ISBN 0-87403-458-2, 24-03697). Standard Pub.
Johnson, Pamela, illus. The Story of the First Christmas. LC 90-23154. 24p. (ps up). 1991. 2.95 (ISBN 0-694-00364-6). HarpC Child Bks.
Klug, Ron & Klug, Lyn. Jesus Comes: the Story of Jesus' Birth for Children. Konsterile, Paul, illus. LC 86-81808. 32p. (Orig.). (gr. 3-8). 1986. pap. 4.95 saddlestitch (ISBN 0-8066-2234-2, 10-3497, Augsburg). Augsburg Fortress.
LaFortune, Claude. Greeting Jesus: Let's Make the Nativity Scene. (Illus.). 24p. (Orig.). 1988. wkbk. 5.95 (ISBN 0-318-39855-9). Twenty-Third.
Laird, Elizabeth, adapted by. The Road to Bethlehem: An Ethiopian Nativity. Waite, Terry, frwd. by. LC 87-45112. (Illus.). 32p. (gr. 1-5). 1987. 12.95 (ISBN 0-8050-0539-0). H Holt & Co.
Lashbrook, Marilyn. No Tree for Christmas: The Story of Jesus' Birth. Britt, Stephanie M., illus. LC 88-62025. 32p. (ps). 1989. 5.95 (ISBN 0-86606-434-6, 866). Roper Pr.
Lesch, Christiane. In Bethlehem Long Ago. Lawson, Polly, tr. from GER. Lesch, Christiane, illus. 28p. (ps-2). Repr. of 1988 ed. 14.95 (ISBN 0-86315-076-4, Pub. by Floris Bks UK). Gryphon Hse.
McKissack, Patricia & McKissack, Frederick. All Paths Lead to Bethlehem. Shoemaker, Kathryn E., illus. LC 87-70472. 32p. (Orig.). (ps-3). 1987. pap. 4.95 (ISBN 0-8066-2265-2, 10-0220, Augsburg). Augsburg Fortress.
McMillan, Mary. Baby Jesus. Grossmann, Dan, illus. 48p. (ps-1). 1986. wkbk. 6.95 (ISBN 0-86653-369-9, SS 1800). Good Apple.
Mee, Charles L., Jr. Happy Birthday, Baby Jesus. Munowitz, Ken, illus. LC 76-3831. 32p. (ps-3). 1976. 12.95 (ISBN 0-06-024162-4). HarpC Child Bks.
Murphy, Mary. Mary Had a Baby. Amen! 16p. (Orig.). (ps-8). 1991. pap. text ed. 14.95 (ISBN 0-89243-339-6); pap. text ed. 1.00 coloring bk. (ISBN 0-89243-340-X). Liguori Pubns.
The Nativity. (Illus.). 24p. 4.95 (ISBN 0-687-15736-6). Abingdon.
Parry, Alan & Parry, Linda. Baby Jesus. Parry, Alan, illus. 24p. (ps). 1990. pap. 0.99 (ISBN 0-8066-2478-7, 9-2478). Augsburg Fortress.
Shely, Patricia. El Nino Jesus. Granberry, Nola, tr. Karch, Pat, illus. (SPA.). 16p. (gr. 1-3). 1987. pap. 1.40 (ISBN 0-311-38563-X). Casa Bautista.
Stirrup Associates, Inc. Staff. My Jesus Pocketbook of a Very Special Birth Day. Harvey, Bonnie C. & Phillips, Cheryl M., eds. Burnett, Lindy, illus. LC 84-50919. 32p. (ps). 1984. pap. 0.69 (ISBN 0-937420-15-8). Stirrup Assoc.
Storr, Catherine, retold by. The Birth of Jesus. Rowe, Gavin, illus. LC 82-9048. 32p. (gr. k-4). 1982. PLB 14.65 (ISBN 0-8172-1977-3). Raintree Pubs.
Trent, Robbie. The First Christmas. rev. ed. Simont, Marc, illus. LC 89-29729. 32p. (ps-2). 1990. pap. 3.50 (ISBN 0-06-443249-1, Trophy). HarpC Child Bks.
Vivas, Julie. The Nativity. Vivas, Julia, illus. (ps up). 1988. 13.95 (ISBN 0-15-200535-8, Gulliver Bks). HarBraceJ.
Walton, John & Walton, Kim. Jesus, God's Son, Is Born. LC 87-70612. 1987. pap. 3.49 (ISBN 1-55513-230-8, Chariot Bks). Cook.
Wijngaard, Juan, illus. The Nativity. LC 90-5309. 29p. (gr. k up). 1990. write for info. (ISBN 0-7445-1260-3). Lothrop.

Winthrop, Elizabeth. Story of the Nativity. 1986. pap. 2.25 (ISBN 0-671-63019-9). S&S Trade.
Woggon, Guillermo. Alla en el Pesebre. Cranberry, Nola, tr. from ENG. (SPA., Illus.). 16p. (ps-2). 1987. pap. 1.40 (ISBN 0-311-38562-1). Casa Bautista.

JESUS CHRIST–NATIVITY–DRAMA

Butterworth, Nick & Inkpen, Mick. The Nativity Play. Butterworth, Nick & Inkpen, Mick, illus. 32p. (gr. k-3). 1985. 11.95 (ISBN 0-316-11903-2). Little.
Irsch, Ed. As It Was Told: A Play for Christmas. 16p. (Orig.). (gr. k-4). 1980. pap. text ed. 3.95 (ISBN 0-89536-439-5, 0146). CSS of Ohio.

JESUS CHRIST–PARABLES

Castagnola, Larry. More Parables for Little People. Muren, Nancy L., illus. LC 87-62532. 82p. (Orig.). (gr. 4-5). 1987. pap. 7.95 (ISBN 0-89390-095-8). Resource Pubns.
Dale, Alan T. God Cares for Everybody, Everywhere. (Orig.). (gr. 3-5). 1978. pap. 1.95 (ISBN 0-8192-1237-7). Morehouse Pub.
Daniel, Rebecca. Book VII-His Parables. McClure, Nancee, illus. 32p. (gr. 2-7). 1984. wkbk. 5.95 (ISBN 0-86653-228-5, SS 830). Good Apple.
—Book VIII-More Parables. McClure, Nancee, illus. 32p. (gr. 2-7). 1984. wkbk. 5.95 (ISBN 0-86653-229-3, SS 831). Good Apple.
DePaola, Tomie. The Parables of Jesus. DePaola, Tomie, illus. LC 86-18323. 32p. (gr. 1-4). 1987. reinforced bdg. 14.95 (ISBN 0-8234-0636-9). Holiday.
Glavich, Kathleen. Acting Out the Miracles & Parables: 52 Five-Minute Plays for Education & Worship. LC 88-50330. (Illus., Orig.). (gr. 4-6). 1988. pap. 12.95 (ISBN 0-89622-363-9). Twenty-Third.
The Good Samaritan. 1989. text ed. 3.95 cased (ISBN 0-7214-5246-9). Ladybird Bks.
Grimes, Bobbie M. The Parable of Jesus & Santa. Cooley, Nance, illus. LC 84-90331. 40p. (ps-5). 1984. 14.95 (ISBN 0-9613328-0-8). B & D Pub.
Hilliard, Dick & Valenti-Hilliard, Beverly. Wonders! Collopy, George F., illus. 45p. (Orig.). (gr. 1 up). 1981. pap. text ed. 4.95 (ISBN 0-89390-032-X). Resource Pubns.
Jesus & the Donkey. (ps). 1991. Set of 6. pap. 3.95 (ISBN 0-8007-7118-4). Revell.
Jones, Mary A. Favorite Stories of Jesus. LC 81-50278. (Illus.). 112p. (ps-2). 1981. write for info. (ISBN 0-02-689035-6). Macmillan.
Kramer, Janice & Mathews. Good Samaritan. LC 63-23369. (Illus.). (ps-k). 1964. laminated bdg. 1.39 (ISBN 0-570-06000-1, 59-1102). Concordia.
Kratavil, Helen S. Parables of Christ. Butcher, Sam, illus. 64p. (gr. k-6). 1974. pap. text ed. 11.50 (ISBN 1-55976-015-X). CEF Press.
Powers, Isaias. Father Ike's Stories for Children: Teaching Christian Values Through Animal Stories. LC 88-50332. (Illus.). 64p. (Orig.). 1988. pap. 4.95 (ISBN 0-89622-370-1). Twenty-Third.
The Prodigal Son. 1989. text ed. 3.95 cased (ISBN 0-7214-5247-7). Ladybird Bks.
Reid, John C. Parables from Nature: Earthly Stories with Heavenly Meanings. 2nd ed. Foley, Timothy, illus. 96p. (gr. k-4). 1991. pap. 8.95 (ISBN 0-8028-4052-3). Eerdmans.
Schindler, Regine. The Lost Sheep. Heyduck-Huth, Hilde, illus. LC 80-68546. 32p. (gr. k-3). 1982. Repr. 0.80 (ISBN 0-687-22780-1). Abingdon.
Singleton, Kathy. The Good Samaritan. Baker, Arthur, illus. 32p. (gr. k-3). 1990. saddle-stitched 1.25 (ISBN 0-8028-5052-9). Eerdmans.
Taylor, Kenneth N. The Prodigal Son. (Illus.). 1989. bds. 3.95 (ISBN 0-8423-5040-3, 755040-3). Tyndale.

JESUS CHRIST–POETRY

Thomas, Joan G. If Jesus Came to My House. Thomas, Joan G., illus. 24p. (gr. k-3). 1951. 12.95 (ISBN 0-688-40981-4). Lothrop.

JESUS CHRIST–SERMON ON THE MOUNT

see Sermon on the Mount

JESUS CHRIST–TEACHINGS

Dean, Bessie. Lessons Jesus Taught. Dean, Bessie, illus. 72p. (Orig.). (gr. k-5). 1980. pap. 5.95 (ISBN 0-88290-146-X). Horizon Utah.
Kendrick, Rosalyn. In the Steps of Jesus. 128p. (gr. 8-10). 1985. pap. 10.95 (ISBN 0-7175-1309-2). Dufour.
Lang, June & Carl, Angela. Twenty-Six Children's Church Programs: Getting to Know Jesus. Ostendorf, Edward, illus. 112p. (gr. 1-6). 1983. pap. 7.95 (ISBN 0-87239-608-8, 3378). Standard Pub.
The Magpie's Story. 28p. 1988. 4.95 (ISBN 0-310-55820-4, 19091). Zondervan.
Willis, Doris. Jesus, My Friend & Teacher. (ps). 1990. 3.95 (ISBN 0-687-03123-0). Abingdon.

JESUS CHRIST IN ART

see Jesus Christ–Art

JET PLANES

Chant, Chris. Jetliner: From Takeoff to Touchdown. Bishop, Denis & Holt, Peter, illus. LC 82-81164. 40p. (gr. 4-8). 1982. PLB 12.40 (ISBN 0-531-03461-5). Watts.
Jacobs, Lou, Jr. Jumbo Jets. LC 73-78280. (Illus.). (gr. 5-9). 1969. 7.50 (ISBN 0-672-52280-2, Bobbs). Macmillan.
Jefferis, David. Jet Age. Franklin Watts Ltd., ed. (Illus.). 32p. (gr. 7-9). 1988. PLB 11.90 (ISBN 0-531-10508-3). Watts.

JEWELRY

see also Gems

Everett, F. Make Your Own Jewelry. (Illus.). (gr. 6 up). 1987. PLB 13.96 (ISBN 0-88110-243-1); pap. 5.95 (ISBN 0-7460-0077-4). EDC.
Zechlin, Katharina. Creative Enameling & Jewelry-Making. Kuttner, Paul, tr. LC 65-20877. (gr. 10 up). 1965. 6.95 (ISBN 0-8069-5062-5); PLB 6.69 (ISBN 0-8069-5063-3). Sterling.

JEWELS

see Gems; Jewelry; Precious Stones

JEWISH-ARAB RELATIONS

Abodaher, David J. Youth in the Middle East: Voices of Despair. (Illus.). 128p. (gr. 9-12). 1990. PLB 12.40 (ISBN 0-531-10961-5). Watts.
Bernards, Neal. The Palestinian Conflict: Identifying Propaganda Techniques. (Illus.). 32p. (gr. 3-6). 1990. PLB 8.95 (ISBN 0-89908-602-0). Greenhaven.
Carroll, Raymond. The Palestine Question. 96p. (gr. 7 up). 1983. PLB 12.90 (ISBN 0-531-04549-8). Watts.
Harper, Paul. Arab-Israeli Conflict. (gr. 4-7). 1990. PLB 12.90 (ISBN 0-531-18294-0). Watts.
Pimlott, John. Middle East: A Background to the Conflicts. (Illus.). 40p. (gr. 5-8). 1991. PLB 11.90 (ISBN 0-531-17329-1, Gloucester Pr). Watts.
Regan, Geoffry. Israel & the Arabs. (Illus.). 52p. (gr. 5 up). 1986. PLB 8.95 (ISBN 0-8225-1234-3). Lerner Pubns.
Reische, Diana. Arafat & the Palestine Liberation Organization. (Illus.). 160p. (gr. 9-12). 1991. PLB 13.90 (ISBN 0-531-11000-1). Watts.

JEWISH-ARAB RELATIONS–FICTION

Ofek, Uriel. Smoke over Golan: A Novel of the 1973 Yom Kippur War in Israel. Taslitt, Israel I., tr. from HEB. Bloom, Lloyd, illus. LC 78-22488. 192p. (gr. 4-7). 1979. PLB 12.89 (ISBN 0-06-024614-6). HarpC Child Bks.

JEWISH HOLIDAYS

see Fasts and Feasts–Judaism

JEWISH LANGUAGE

see Hebrew Language

JEWISH LITERATURE

see also Bible; Hebrew Literature

Atkin, Abraham. Chelkeinu. 200p. text ed. 6.50 (ISBN 0-914131-09-5, A120). Torah Umesorah.
—Darkeinu Daled. text ed. 4.00 (ISBN 0-914131-13-3, A102). Torah Umesorah.
Atkins, Abraham. Darkeinu Gimel. (gr. 4 up). text ed. 3.85 (ISBN 0-914131-14-1, A101). Torah Umesorah.
Ginsburg, Marvell. Tattooed Torah. (Illus.). 32p. (gr. k-3). 1983. 6.95 (ISBN 0-8074-0252-4, 104030). UAHC.
Grossman, Cheryl S. & Engman, Suzy. Jewish Literature for Children: A Teaching Guide. 230p. (Orig.). (gr. 4 up). 1985. text ed. 19.00 (ISBN 0-86705-018-7); pap. text ed. 15.00 (ISBN 0-685-10172-X). AIRE.
Haskelevich, B., ed. & tr. from ENG & HEB. My First Siddur: A Selection of Prayers for Jewish Boys & Girls. LC 90-82127. (RUS., Illus.). 32p. (Orig.). (gr. k-8). 1990. pap. 1.50 (ISBN 1-878860-01-1). Noviysvet.
Hautzig, Esther, tr. from YID. The Seven Good Years & Other Stories of I. L. Peretz. Kogan, Deborah, illus. 96p. (gr. 3-6). 1984. 10.95 (ISBN 0-8276-0244-8). JPS Phila.
Karkowsky, Nancy. The Ten Commandments: Text & Activity Book. (gr. 3-4). 5.95 (ISBN 0-317-70145-2). Behrman.
Plaut, W. Gunther, ed. Deluxe Torah Commentary. 1835p. 1988. deluxe ed. 55.00 (ISBN 0-8074-0333-4, 381630). UAHC.
Schur, Maxine. Hannah Szenes: A Song of Light. LC 85-5794. (Illus.). 104p. (gr. 5-9). 1985. 10.95 (ISBN 0-8276-0251-0). JPS Phila.
Silbermann, A. M., ed. The Children's Haggadah. Singer, Erwin, illus. Wartski, Isidore & Super, Arthur S., trs. (Illus.). 100p. (gr. 2-5). 1972. 16.95 (ISBN 0-87306-984-6). Feldheim.
Weilerstein, Sadie R. Ten & a Kid. Domanska, Janina, illus. LC 61-12600. 186p. (gr. 6-10). 1973. Repr. of 1961 ed. 8.95 (ISBN 0-8276-0009-7). JPS Phila.
Zar, Rose. In the Mouth of the Wolf. 224p. (gr. 6 up). 1983. 10.95 (ISBN 0-8276-0225-1); pap. 8.95 (ISBN 0-8276-0382-7). JPS Phila.

JEWISH RELIGION

see Judaism

JEWS

see also Discrimination

Burstein, Chaya M. The Jewish Kids Catalog. Burstein, Chaya M., illus. 224p. (gr. 3-7). 1983. pap. 12.95 (ISBN 0-8276-0215-4). JPS Phila.
Ganz, Yaffa. The Jewish Fact-Finder: A Bookful of Important Jewish Facts & Handy Information. (gr. 5-9). 1988. 12.95 (ISBN 0-87306-447-X); pap. 9.95 (ISBN 0-87306-470-4). Feldheim.
Gittelsohn, Roland B. How Do I Decide? (Orig.). (gr. 7-9). 1989. pap. text ed. 8.95x (ISBN 0-87441-488-1). Behrman.
Goldstein, Andrew & Wikler, Madeline. My Very Own Jewish Home. LC 83-4357. (Illus.). 40p. (ps-3). 1979. 6.95 (ISBN 0-930494-24-5); pap. 4.95 (ISBN 0-930494-08-3). Kar Ben.
Jacobs, Louis. Way of the Jews. (gr. 3-7). pap. 7.95 (ISBN 0-7175-0875-7). Dufour.
Lemelman, Martin. My Jewish Home: Sinchah Ba'ambatyah - Fun in the Bathtub. (Illus.). 10p. (ps). 1987. polyvinyl 3.95 (ISBN 0-8074-0327-X, 102001). UAHC.
Provost, Gary & Levine-Provost, Gail. David & Max. 196p. (gr. 5-9). 1988. pap. 8.95 (ISBN 0-8276-0315-0). JPS Phila.
Roseman, Kenneth. All in My Jewish Family. Leipzig, Arthur, photos by. (Illus.). 32p. (gr. k-3). 1984. pap. 5.00 wkbk. (ISBN 0-8074-0266-4, 103800). UAHC.
Rosenberg, Amye. Tzedakah. (Illus.). (gr. k-1). 1979. pap. text ed. 4.25 (ISBN 0-87441-279-X). Behrman.
Saypol, Judyth R. & Wikler, Madeline. My Very Own Rosh Hashanah. (Illus.). 32p. (gr. k-6). 1978. pap. 2.95 (ISBN 0-930494-06-7). Kar Ben.
Syme, Daniel & Bogot, Howard. I'm Growing. Compere, Janet, illus. 32p. (ps-1). 1982. pap. 4.00 (ISBN 0-8074-0167-6, 101095). UAHC.
Synge, Ursula. The People & the Promise. LC 74-10661. 192p. (gr. 7-10). 1974. 18.95 (ISBN 0-87599-208-0). S G Phillips.
Thum, Robert & Dworski, Susan. My Jewish World. (Illus., Orig.). (gr. 3-4). 1989. pap. text ed. 7.95 (ISBN 0-87441-478-4); tchr's. guide 14.95 (ISBN 0-87441-489-X). Behrman.
Weilerstein, Sadie R. What the Moon Brought. (Illus.). 159p. (gr. 1-3). 1942. pap. 7.95 (ISBN 0-8276-0265-0). JPS Phila.

JEWS–BIOGRAPHY

see also Rabbis

Abrahams, Robert D. Sound of Bow Bells: Sir David Salomons. LC 62-12320. 158p. (gr. 6-10). 1962. 3.50 (ISBN 0-8276-0159-X). JPS Phila.
Anne Frank. (gr. 7-12). 1991. PLB 14.95 (ISBN 0-8239-1204-3). Rosen Group.
Arem, Tzvi Z. The Story of Reb Baruch Ber: The Kamenitzer Rosh Yeshiba - Rabbi Baruch Ber Leibowitz & His Successor, Rabbi Reuven Grozovsky. (Illus.). 128p. (gr. 6-12). 1987. 10.95 (ISBN 0-89906-804-9); pap. 7.95 (ISBN 0-89906-805-7). Mesorah Pubns.
Auerbacher, Inge. I Am a Star: Child of the Holocaust. Bernbaum, Israel, illus. LC 86-16410. 96p. (gr. 5 up). 1987. PLB 9.95 (ISBN 0-671-66643-6). S&S Trade.
Bernheim, Mark. Father of the Orphans: The Story of Janusz Korczak. Paterson, Katherine, frwd. by. LC 88-16138. (Illus.). 176p. (gr. 5-9). 1989. 15.95 (ISBN 0-525-67265-6, Lodestar Bks). Dutton Child Bks.
Drucker, Malka. Eliezer Ben-Yehuda: The Father of Modern Hebrew. LC 86-15213. (Illus.). 128p. (gr. 5-9). 1987. 13.95 (ISBN 0-525-67184-6, Lodestar Bks). Dutton Child Bks.
Eisenberg, Azriel. Fill a Blank Page: A Biography of Solomon Schechter. (Illus.). (gr. 6-11). 3.75 (ISBN 0-8381-0730-3, 10-730). United Syn Bk.
Feder, Harriet K. Judah Who Always Said, "No!" Kahn, Katherine J., illus. LC 90-4854. 32p. (ps-2). 1990. 12.95 (ISBN 0-929371-13-5); pap. 4.95 (ISBN 0-929371-14-3). Kar Ben.
Finkelman, S. The Story of Reb Yosef Chaim: The Life & Times of Rabbi Yosef Chaim Sonnefield, the Guardian of Jerusalem. Dershowitz, Y., illus. 160p. (gr. 6-12). 1984. 10.95 (ISBN 0-89906-779-4); pap. 7.95 (ISBN 0-89906-780-8). Mesorah Pubns.
Finkelman, Shimon. The Story of Reb Elchonon: The Life of Rabbi Elchonon Wasserman. Dershowitz, Yosef, illus. 160p. (gr. 6-12). 1984. 10.95 (ISBN 0-89906-770-0); pap. 7.95 (ISBN 0-89906-771-9). Mesorah Pubns.
—The Story of Reb Nachum'ke: The Nineteen Century Tzaddik - A Legend in His Time. Dershowitz, Yosef, illus. 144p. (gr. 6-12). 1985. 10.95 (ISBN 0-89906-781-6); pap. 7.95 (ISBN 0-89906-782-4). Mesorah Pubns.
—The Story of Reb Yisrael Salanter: The Legendary Founder of the Mussar Movement. Dershowitz, Y., illus. 96p. (gr. 6-12). 1986. 10.95 (ISBN 0-89906-797-2); pap. 7.95 (ISBN 0-89906-798-0). Mesorah Pubns.
Gurko, Miriam. Theodor Herzl: The Road to Israel. Weihs, Erika, illus. 96p. (gr. 3-7). 1988. 12.95 (ISBN 0-8276-0312-6). JPS Phila.
Hurwitz, Johanna. Anne Frank: Life in Hiding. Rosenberry, Vera, illus. 64p. (gr. 2-5). 1988. 10.95 (ISBN 0-8276-0311-8). JPS Phila.
Karp, Deborah. Heroes of American Jew History. (Illus.). (gr. 6-7). 1966. pap. 6.95x (ISBN 0-87068-539-2). Ktav.
—Heroes of American Jewish History. (gr. 5). 1972. pap. 6.95x (ISBN 0-87068-394-2). Ktav.
—Heroes of Jewish Thought. (Illus.). (gr. 5-7). 1965. pap. 6.95x (ISBN 0-87068-538-4). Ktav.
Koehn, Ilse. Mischling, Second Degree: My Childhood in Nazi Germany. 240p. (gr. 6 up). 1990. pap. 4.95 (ISBN 0-14-034290-7, Puffin). Puffin Bks.
Kustanowitz, Shulamit E. Henrietta Szold: Israel's Helping Hand. Masheris, Robert, illus. 64p. (gr. 2-6). 1990. pap. 10.95 (ISBN 0-670-82518-2). Viking Child Bks.
Matov, G. Tales of Tzaddikim: Bereishis. Weinbach, Shaindel, tr. from HEB. Bardugo, Miriam, illus. 320p. (gr. 7-12). 1987. 13.95 (ISBN 0-89906-825-1); pap. 10.95 (ISBN 0-89906-826-X). Mesorah Pubns.
Scherman, Nosson & Gevirtz, Eliezer. The Story of the Chofetz Chaim. Dershowitz, Yosef, illus. 160p. (gr. 6-12). 1987. 10.95 (ISBN 0-89906-766-2); pap. 7.95 (ISBN 0-89906-767-0). Mesorah Pubns.
Shapolsky, Ian. The Jewish Trivia & Information Book. 400p. (gr. 6-12). 1985. pap. 5.95 (ISBN 0-933503-08-3). Shapolsky Pubs.
Strom, Yale. A Tree Still Stands: Jewish Youth in Eastern Europe Today. Levitin, Sonia, intro. by. (Illus.). 112p. (gr. 3 up). 1990. 16.95 (ISBN 0-399-22154-9, Philomel Bks). Putnam Pub Group.

Teller, Hanoch. The Story of the Steipler Gaon: The Life & Times of Rabbi Yaakov Yisrael Kanievsky. Dershowitz, Y., illus. 96p. (gr. 6-12). 1986. 10.95 (ISBN 0-89906-795-6); pap. 7.95 (ISBN 0-89906-796-4). Mesorah Pubns.
—Sunset. 2nd ed. (Illus.). 288p. (gr. 12). 1988. Repr. of 1987 ed. 9.95 (ISBN 0-317-68545-7). NYC Pub Co.

JEWS–FESTIVALS

see Fasts and Feasts–Judaism

JEWS–FICTION

Abramson, Ruth. The Cresta Adventure. (gr. 4-7). 1989. 8.95 (ISBN 0-87306-493-3). Feldheim.
Adler, David A. A Children's Treasure of Chassidic Tales. Haas, Arie, illus. 64p. (gr. 4-12). 1981. 8.95 (ISBN 0-89906-785-9); pap. 5.95 (ISBN 0-89906-786-7). Mesorah Pubns.
—The Number on My Grandfather's Arm. 28p. (gr. 1-3). 1987. 7.95 (ISBN 0-8074-0328-8, 103641). UAHC.
Appleman, Harlene & Shapiro, Jane. A Seder for Tu B'Shevat. McLean, Chari R., illus. 32p. (ps up). pap. 2.95 (ISBN 0-930494-39-3). Kar Ben.
Barrie, Barbara. Lone Star. (gr. 5 up). 1990. 13.95 (ISBN 0-385-30156-1). Delacorte.
Baylis-White, Mary. Sheltering Rebecca. (Illus.). 112p. (gr. 3-8). 1991. 14.95 (ISBN 0-525-67349-0, Lodestar Bks). Dutton Child Bks.
Birnhack, Sarah. Happy Is the Heart: A Year in the Life of a Jewish Girl. Birnhack, Sarah, illus. (gr. 5-8). 1976. 7.95 (ISBN 0-87306-131-4); pap. 5.95 (ISBN 0-685-01629-3). Feldheim.
Bush, Lawrence. Emma Ansky-Levine & Her Mitzvah Machine. Iskowitz, Joel, illus. (Orig.). (gr. 4-6). 1991. pap. 7.95 (ISBN 0-8074-0458-6, 123933). UAHC.
—Rooftop Secrets & Other Stories of Anti-Semitism. Vorspan, Albert, commentary by. LC 86-1362. (Illus.). 144p. (Orig.). (gr. 7 up). 1986. pap. text ed. 7.95 (ISBN 0-8074-0314-8, 121720). UAHC.
Chaikin, Miriam. Feathers in the Wind. Saldutti, Denise, illus. LC 88-10978. 64p. (gr. 3-5). 1989. 10.95 (ISBN 0-06-021162-8); PLB 10.89 (ISBN 0-06-021163-6). HarpC Child Bks.
—How Yossi Beat the Evil Urge. Mathers, Petra, illus. LC 82-47705. 64p. (gr. 3-5). 1983. 9.57i (ISBN 0-06-021184-9). HarpC Child Bks.
—Yossi Tries to Help God. Saldutti, Denise, illus. LC 85-45848. 80p. (gr. 3-5). 1987. 11.95 (ISBN 0-06-021197-0); PLB 11.89 (ISBN 0-06-021198-9). HarpC Child Bks.
Chapman, Carol. The Tale of Meshka the Kvetch. Lobel, Arnold, illus. LC 80-11225. 32p. (gr. k-3). 1980. 13.95 (ISBN 0-525-40745-6, DCB). Dutton Child Bks.
Charles, Freda. The Mystery of Missing Challah. Goldstein, Lil, illus. 40p. (ps). 1981. pap. 5.95 (ISBN 0-8246-0264-1). Jonathan David.
Feder, Harriet. It Happened in Shushan: A Purim Story. Schanzer, Roz, illus. LC 88-2676. (Orig.). (ps-3). 1988. pap. 3.95 (ISBN 0-930494-75-X). Kar Ben.
Feder, Harriet K. Not Yet, Elijah! Halpern, Joan, illus. LC 89-1744. 32p. (gr. k-3). 1989. pap. 4.95 (ISBN 0-930494-95-4). Kar Ben.
Feund, Chanie. Read Me Berashis. Leff, Tora, illus. LC 90-83948. 32p. (ps-2). 1990. 9.95. CIS Comm.
Firer, Benzion. Saadiah Weissman. 140p. (gr. 5-12). 1982. 9.95 (ISBN 0-87306-294-9); pap. 6.95 (ISBN 0-685-07830-2). Feldheim.
—The Twins. Scae, Bracha, tr. from HEB. 230p. (gr. 4-8). 1983. 9.95 (ISBN 0-87306-279-5); pap. 6.95 (ISBN 0-87306-340-6). Feldheim.
Fruchter, Yaakov. The Best of Olmeinu - Book Three: Chanukah & Other Stories, Bk. 3. Scherman, Nosson, ed. Dershowitz, Yosef, illus. 160p. (gr. 5-12). 1982. 10.95 (ISBN 0-89906-754-9); pap. 7.95 (ISBN 0-89906-755-7). Mesorah Pubns.
—The Best of Olomeinu: Pesach & Other Stories, Bk. 5. Scherman, Nosson, ed. Dershowitz, Yosef, illus. 160p. (gr. 5-12). 1984. 10.95 (ISBN 0-89906-758-1); pap. 7.95 (ISBN 0-317-65876-X). Mesorah Pubns.
—The Best of Olomeinu: Sefirah, Shavuos & Summer Stories, Bk. 4. Scherman, Nosson, ed. Dershowitz, Yosef, illus. 160p. (gr. 5-12). 1983. 10.95 (ISBN 0-317-65874-3); pap. 7.95 (ISBN 0-317-65875-1). Mesorah Pubns.
—The Best of Olomeinu: Shabos & Other Stories, Bk. 2. Scherman, Nosson, ed. Dershowitz, Yosef, illus. 160p. (gr. 5-12). 1982. 10.95 (ISBN 0-89906-752-2); pap. 7.95 (ISBN 0-89906-753-0). Mesorah Pubns.
—The Best of Olomeinu: Stories for All Year Round, Bk. 1. Scherman, Nosson, ed. Dershowitz, Yosef, illus. 160p. (gr. 5-12). 1981. 10.95 (ISBN 0-89906-750-6); pap. 7.95 (ISBN 0-89906-751-4). Mesorah Pubns.
—The Best of Olomeinu: Succos & Other Stories, Bk. 6. Scherman, Nosson, ed. Dershowitz, Yosef, illus. 160p. (gr. 5-12). 1984. 10.95 (ISBN 0-89906-760-3); pap. 7.95 (ISBN 0-89906-761-1). Mesorah Pubns.
Fructer, Yaakov. The Best of Olomeinu: Purim & Other Stories, Bk. 7. Scherman, Nosson, ed. (Illus.). 160p. (gr. 5-12). 1986. 10.95 (ISBN 0-89906-762-X); pap. 7.95 (ISBN 0-89906-763-8). Mesorah Pubns.
Fuchs, Yitzchak Y. Halichos Bas Yisroel, Vol. 1. Dombey, Moshe, tr. from HEB. (gr. 7-12). 1986. 13. 95 (ISBN 0-87306-397-X). Feldheim.
Ganz, Yaffa. Hello Heddy Levi. (gr. 4-7). 1989. 8.95 (ISBN 0-87306-480-1). Feldheim.
—Shukis Upsidedown Dream. Gewirtz, Bina, illus. (gr. k-3). 1986. 5.95 (ISBN 0-87306-384-8). Feldheim.
Gellman, Ellie. Justin's Hebrew Name. Gellner, Barbara, illus. LC 88-6825. 32p. (gr. k-3). 1988. pap. 4.95 (ISBN 0-930494-78-4). Kar Ben.
Gold, Auner. The Purple Ring. Hinlicky, Gregg, illus. 191p. (gr. 9-12). 1986. 10.95 (ISBN 0-935063-16-1); pap. 8.95 (ISBN 0-935063-15-3). CIS Comm.
Gottesman, Meir U. Chaimkel the Dreamer. Scheinberg, Shepsil, illus. 157p. (gr. 3-5). 1987. 9.95 (ISBN 0-935063-26-9); pap. 7.95 (ISBN 0-935063-27-7). CIS Comm.
Grode, Phyllis A. Sophie's Name. Haas, Shelly O., illus. LC 90-4833. 32p. (gr. k-3). 1990. 12.95 (ISBN 0-929371-18-6); pap. 4.95 (ISBN 0-929371-19-4). Kar Ben.
Halpern, Chaiky. The Dink That Stopped the Clock. 24p. (Orig.). (ps-3). 1985. pap. 2.95 (ISBN 0-87306-379-1). Feldheim.
Heller, Linda. The Castle on Hester Street. Heller, Linda, illus. 32p. (gr. k-3). 1990. pap. 6.95t (ISBN 0-8276-0323-1, 496). JPS Phila.
Hirsh, Marilyn. I Love Hanukkah. Hirsh, Marilyn, illus. LC 84-497. 32p. (ps-3). 1984. reinforced 12.95 (ISBN 0-8234-0525-7); pap. 5.95 (ISBN 0-8234-0622-9). Holiday.
Hubner, Carol K. Silent Shofar. Forst, Sigmund, illus. (gr. 3 up). 6.95 (ISBN 0-910818-53-3); pap. 5.95 (ISBN 0-910818-54-1). Judaica Pr.
—The Tattered Tallis. Kramer, Devorah, illus. 128p. (gr. 3-8). 1979. 6.95 (ISBN 0-910818-19-3). Judaica Pr.
Hurwitz, Johanna. The Rabbi's Girls. Johnson, Pamela, illus. 160p. (gr. 3-7). 1989. pap. 3.95 (ISBN 0-14-032951-X, Puffin). Puffin Bks.
Karkowsky, Nancy. Grandma's Soup. Haas, Shelly O., illus. LC 89-30875. 32p. (gr. k-5). 1989. 10.95 (ISBN 0-930494-98-9); pap. 4.95 (ISBN 0-930494-99-7). Kar Ben.
Kaye, Marilyn. The Atonement of Mindy Wise. Van Doren, Liz, ed. 160p. (gr. 7 up). 1991. 15.95 (ISBN 0-15-200402-5, Gulliver Bks). HarBraceJ.
Kerr, Judith. When Hitler Stole Pink Rabbit. Kerr, Judith, illus. (gr. 6 up). 1972. 8.95 (ISBN 0-698-20182-5, Coward). Putnam Pub Group.
Kimmel, Eric A. The Chanukkah Tree. Carmi, Giora, illus. LC 88-4510. 32p. (gr. k-3). 1988. reinforced bdg. 13.95 (ISBN 0-8234-0705-5). Holiday.
Klein-Ehlich, Tzvia. A Children's Treasure of Sephardic Tales. Galitzer, Channa, illus. 64p. (gr. 4-10). 1985. 9.95 (ISBN 0-89906-787-5); pap. 6.95 (ISBN 0-89906-788-3). Mesorah Pubns.
Kogan, Mark. Archivist, Vol. 1. Khotianovsky, Olga, ed. (RUS., Illus.). 300p. (Orig.). (gr. 9-12). 1990. pap. text ed. write for info. (ISBN 0-9624922-0-5). Hazar NY.
Kranzler, Gershon. Golden Shoes: And Other Stories. (Illus.). (gr. 4-9). 8.95 (ISBN 0-87306-123-3); pap. 6.95 (ISBN 0-685-01628-5). Feldheim.
—Yoshko the Dumbbell. (gr. 4-9). pap. 5.95 (ISBN 0-87306-246-9). Feldheim.
Laird, Christa. Shadow of the Wall. LC 89-34469. (gr. 7 up). 1990. 12.95 (ISBN 0-688-09336-1). Greenwillow.
Lasky, Kathryn. The Night Journey. Hyman, Trina S., illus. 152p. (gr. 5-9). 1986. pap. 4.95 (ISBN 0-14-032048-2, Puffin). Puffin Bks.
—Night Journey. 1986. pap. 12.95 (ISBN 0-670-80935-7). Viking Child Bks.
Leader, R. L. Faithful Soldiers. (gr. 7 up). 1989. 12.95 (ISBN 0-944070-12-4). Targum Pr.
Lehmann, Marcus. Family y Aguilar. Breuer, Jacob, adapted by. (gr. 7 up). 8.95 (ISBN 0-87306-122-5). Feldheim.
Levitin, Sonia. Journey to America. Robinson, Charles, illus. LC 86-22234. 160p. (gr. 3-6). 1987. pap. 3.95 (ISBN 0-689-71130-1, Aladdin). Macmillan Child Grp.
—The Return. LC 86-25891. 224p. (gr. 5 up). 1987. 13. 95 (ISBN 0-689-31309-8, Atheneum Child Bk). Macmillan Child Grp.
Lewis, Shari, adapted by. One-Minute Jewish Stories. Collier, Roberta, illus. (ps-3). 1989. 7.95 (ISBN 0-385-24447-9). Doubleday.
Marcus, Audrey F. & Zwerin, Raymond A. Like a Maccabee. Carmi, Giora, illus. (gr. k-3). 1991. 11.95 (ISBN 0-8074-0445-4, 102564). UAHC.
Matas, Carol. Lisa's War. LC 88-29525. 128p. (gr. 7 up). 1989. 12.95 (ISBN 0-684-19010-9, Scribners Young Read). Macmillan Child Grp.
Mazer, Harry. The Last Mission. 192p. (gr. 7 up). 1981. pap. 3.25 (ISBN 0-440-94797-9, LE). Dell.
Medoff, Francine. The Mouse in the Matzah Factory. Goldstein, David, illus. LC 82-23349. 40p. (ps-3). 1983. pap. 4.95 (ISBN 0-930494-19-9). Kar Ben.
Merling, Beryl. Olomeinu Gems: Stories for All Year Round. Dershowitz, Yosef. (Illus.). 128p. (gr. 5-12). 1987. 10.95 (ISBN 0-89906-764-6); pap. 7.95 (ISBN 0-89906-765-4). Mesorah Pubns.
Neville, Emily C. Berries Goodman. LC 65-19485. (gr. 5-9). 1975. pap. 3.50 (ISBN 0-06-440072-7, Trophy). HarpC Child Bks.
Oppenheim, Shulamith L. Appleblossom. Yolen, Jane, ed. Yardley, Joanna, illus. 40p. (gr. 1-7). 1991. 14.95 (ISBN 0-15-203750-0, HJ). HarBraceJ.
Reiss, Johanna. The Upstairs Room. LC 77-187940. 208p. (gr. 7 up). 1990. pap. 3.50 (ISBN 0-06-440370-X, Trophy). HarpC Child Bks.
Richter, Hans P. Friedrich. (gr. 5-9). 1987. pap. 4.95 (ISBN 0-14-032205-1, Puffin). Puffin Bks.
Roseman, Kenneth. The Melting Pot. (Illus.). 144p. (Orig.). (gr. 4-6). 1984. pap. 6.95 (ISBN 0-8074-0269-9, 146065). UAHC.
Rothstein, Chaya L. The Mentchkins Make Shabbos. Perlstein, Rivky, illus. (ps-2). 1986. pap. 2.95 (ISBN 0-317-42728-8). Feldheim.
Safran, Faigy. Uncle Moishy Visits Torah Island. Snowdone, Linda, illus. 32p. (gr. 2-8). 1987. bk. & cassette 13.95 (ISBN 0-318-32597-7); pap. 7.95 (ISBN 0-89906-807-3). Mesorah Pubns.
Salop, Byrd. The Kiddush Cup Who Hated Wine. Goldstein, Lil, illus. 32p. (gr. 1 up). 1981. pap. 5.95 (ISBN 0-8246-0265-X). Jonathan David.
Saypol, Judyth R. & Wikler, Madeline. My Very Own Shavuot Book. Wikler, Madeline & Fishman, Tamar, illus. 28p. (gr. k-6). 1982. pap. 2.95 (ISBN 0-930494-15-6). Kar Ben.
Schachnowitz, Selig. Light from the West. Leftwich, Joseph, tr. (gr. 7 up). 8.95 (ISBN 0-87306-124-1). Feldheim.
Scherman, Nosson. Tales From the Rebbe's Table. Sears, David, illus. 32p. 1986. 8.95 (ISBN 0-89906-789-1); pap. 5.95 (ISBN 0-89906-790-5). Mesorah Pubns.
—Tales from the Yeshiva World. Sears, Dovid, illus. 32p. 1986. 8.95 (ISBN 0-89906-791-3); pap. 5.95 (ISBN 0-89906-792-1). Mesorah Pubns.
Schilder, Rosalind. Dayenu - Enough! How Uncle Murray Saved the Seder. Kahn, Katherine J., photos by. LC 88-1238. (Illus., Orig.). (ps-3). 1988. pap. 4.95 (ISBN 0-930494-76-8). Kar Ben.
Schnur, Steven. The Narrowest Bar Mitzvah. Lazzaro, Victor, illus. 48p. (Orig.). (gr. 4-6). 1986. pap. text ed. 5.95 (ISBN 0-8074-0316-4, 123923). UAHC.
—The Return of Morris Schumsky. Lazzaro, Victor, illus. 48p. (gr. 4-6). 1987. pap. 6.95 (ISBN 0-8074-0358-X, 123927). UAHC.
Schwartz, Amy. Mrs. Moskowitz & the Sabbath Candlesticks. Schwartz, Amy, illus. 32p. (gr. 5-9). 1983. pap. 6.95t (ISBN 0-8276-0231-6). JPS Phila.
Segal, Jerry. The Place Where Nobody Stopped. Pilkey, Dav, illus. LC 90-43016. 160p. (gr. 6-8). 1991. 14.95 (ISBN 0-531-05897-2); PLB 14.99 (ISBN 0-531-08497-3). Orchard Bks Watts.
Sevela, Ephraim. We Were Not Like Other People. Bouis, Antonina, tr. from RUS. LC 89-11015. 224p. (gr. 7 up). 1989. 13.95 (ISBN 0-06-025507-2); PLB 14.89 (ISBN 0-06-025508-0). HarpC Child Bks.
Sherman, Eileen B. Independence Avenue. 164p. (gr. 5-8). 1990. 13.95 (ISBN 0-8276-0367-3). JPS Phila.
—Monday in Odessa. (gr. 9-12). 1986. 10.95 (ISBN 0-8276-0262-6). JPS Phila.
Sidi, Smadar S. Little Daniel & the Jewish Delicacies. Schaer, Miriam, illus. (ps-5). 1988. 9.95 (ISBN 1-55774-028-3, Dist. by Watts). Adama Pubs Inc.
Singer, Isaac Bashevis. Naftali the Storyteller & His Horse, Sus. Zemach, Margot, illus. LC 76-26917. 144p. (gr. 4 up). 1976. 13.95 (ISBN 0-374-35490-1). FS&G.
—A Tale of Three Wishes. Lieblich, Irene, illus. LC 75-43632. 32p. (ps-3). 1976. 11.95 (ISBN 0-374-37370-1). FS&G.
Sokoloff, David. Jewish Stories of Fun & Adventure. (Illus.). 96p. (gr. 1-3). 1990. pap. 5.95 (ISBN 0-685-35727-9). Shapolsky Pubs.
Steiner, Connie C. On Eagles Wings & Other Things. 32p. (gr. k-4). 1987. 12.95 (ISBN 0-8276-0274-X). JPS Phila.
Stern, Steve. Mickey & the Golem: A Child's Hanukkah in the South, 1912. Seagle, Jeanne, illus. LC 85-26244. 48p. (gr. 5 up). 1986. 9.95 (ISBN 0-918518-40-7). St Lukes Pr.
Topek, Susan R. A Holiday for Noah. Springer, Sally, illus. LC 89-48189. 24p. (ps). 1990. 10.95 (ISBN 0-929371-07-0); pap. 4.95 (ISBN 0-929371-08-9). Kar Ben.
Treseder, Terry W. Hear O Israel: A Story of the Warsaw Ghetto. Bloom, Lloyd, illus. LC 89-7029. 48p. (gr. 3 up). 1990. 13.95 (ISBN 0-689-31456-6, Atheneum Child Bk). Macmillan Child Grp.
Vineberg, Ethel. Grandmother Came from Dworitz: A Jewish Love Story. Briansky, Rita, illus. 44p. (gr. 4 up). 1987. Repr. of 1978 ed. text ed. 3.95 (ISBN 0-88776-195-X). Tundra Bks.
Weilerstein, Sadie R. Best of K'tonton. Hirsh, Marilyn, illus. LC 80-20177. 96p. (gr. 1 up). 1980. pap. 9.95 (ISBN 0-8276-0187-5, 467). JPS Phila.
—K'tonton in the Circus: A Hanukkah Adventure. Hirsh, Marilyn, illus. LC 81-11765. (gr. 2 up). pap. 8.95 (ISBN 0-8276-0303-7). JPS Phila.
Weinbach, Shaindel. The Three Merchants: And Other Stories. Dershowitz, Y., illus. 160p. (gr. 6-12). 1983. 10.95 (ISBN 0-89906-768-9); pap. 7.95 (ISBN 0-89906-769-7). Mesorah Pubns.
Weissenberg, Fran. The Streets Are Paved with Gold. LC 89-24413. (Illus.). 160p. (Orig.). (gr. 5 up). 1990. pap. 5.95 (ISBN 0-943173-51-5). Harbinger AZ.
Winkler, Gershon. The Hostage Torah. Jones, Yochanan, illus. (gr. 7 up). 1981. pap. 5.95 (ISBN 0-910818-34-7). Judaica Pr.
Yolen, Jane. Devil's Arithmetic. 1990. pap. 3.95 (ISBN 0-14-034535-3, Puffin). Puffin Bks.
Zakon, Miriam S. The Egyptian Star. Gaelen, Nina, illus. 114p. (gr. 3-9). 1983. o. p. 6.95 (ISBN 0-910818-47-9); pap. 5.95 (ISBN 0-910818-48-7). Judaica Pr.
Zusman, Evelyn. The Passover Parrot. Kahn, Katherine J., illus. LC 83-22182. 40p. (ps-3). 1984. pap. 4.95 (ISBN 0-930494-30-X). Kar Ben.

JEWS–FOLKLORE

see Folklore, Jewish

JEWS–HISTORY

Abells, Chana B. The Children We Remember. LC 85-24876. (Illus.). 48p. (ps up). 1986. 9.95 (ISBN 0-688-06371-3); PLB 10.88 (ISBN 0-688-06372-1). Greenwillow.

Bernheim, Mark. Father of the Orphans: The Story of Janusz Korczak. Paterson, Katherine, frwd. by. LC 88-16138. (Illus.). 176p. (gr. 5-9). 1989. 15.95 (ISBN 0-525-67265-6, Lodestar Bks). Dutton Child Bks.

Bull, Norman. Church of the Jews. (gr. 2-7). 10.95 (ISBN 0-7175-0450-6). Dufour.

—Founders of the Jews. (gr. 2-7). pap. 10.95 (ISBN 0-7175-0977-X). Dufour.

Charry, Elias & Segal, Abraham. The Eternal People. (Illus.). 448p. (gr. 9-11). 7.50x (ISBN 0-8381-0206-9, 10-206). United Syn Bk.

Dimont, Max I. The Amazing Adventures of the Jewish People. LC 84-16806. 175p. (gr. 8 up). 1984. pap. 5.95 (ISBN 0-87441-391-5). Behrman.

Drew, Margaret, ed. Holocaust & Human Behavior: Annotated Bibliography. 124p. 1989. lib. bdg. 15.85 (ISBN 0-8027-9411-4). Walker & Co.

Eisenberg, Azriel. Fill a Blank Page: A Biography of Solomon Schechter. (Illus.). (gr. 6-11). 3.75 (ISBN 0-8381-0730-3, 10-730). United Syn Bk.

Fishman, Isidore. Remember the Days of Old. (Illus.). (gr. 4-9). 1970. 4.95 (ISBN 0-685-04135-2). Prayer Bk.

Goldwurm, Hersh. History of the Jewish People: The Second Temple Era. (Illus.). 226p. (gr. 7-8). 1982. 16.95 (ISBN 0-89906-454-X); pap. 12.95 (ISBN 0-89906-455-8). Mesorah Pubns.

Holder, Meir. History of the Jewish People: From Yavneh to Pumbedisa. Goldwurm, Hersh, ed. (Illus.). 332p. (gr. 7-8). 1986. 16.95 (ISBN 0-89906-499-X); pap. 12.95 (ISBN 0-89906-475-2). Mesorah Pubns.

Karp, Deborah. Heroes of American Jew History. (Illus.). (gr. 6-7). 1966. pap. 6.95x (ISBN 0-87068-539-2). Ktav.

Lipson, Ruth. Modeh Ani Means Thank You. (Illus.). (ps-2). 1986. 6.95 (ISBN 0-317-42732-6). Feldheim.

Meltzer, Milton. The Jews in America: A Picture Album. LC 84-14344. (Illus.). (gr. 5-9). 1985. 12.95 (ISBN 0-8276-0246-4). JPS Phila.

—Never to Forget: The Jews of the Holocaust. LC 75-25409. (gr. 7 up). 1976. PLB 13.89 (ISBN 0-06-024175-6). HarpC Child Bks.

Odijk, Pamela. Israelites. (Illus.). 48p. (gr. 5-8). 1990. PLB 16.98 (ISBN 0-382-09888-9). Silver Burdett Pr.

Rosenfield, Geraldine. The Heroes of Masada. Sugarman, S. Allan, illus. 38p. (gr. 6-10). pap. 1.50 (ISBN 0-8381-0733-8, 10-732). United Syn Bk.

Rossel, Seymour. Introduction to Jewish History. Kozodoy, Neil, ed. Kahn, Katherine, illus. 128p. (gr. 4-5). 1981. pap. text ed. 6.95 (ISBN 0-87441-335-4); By Lenore C. Kipper. tchr's guide 12.50x (ISBN 0-87441-378-8); Malkah L. Avrami. student's activity bk. 4.25 (ISBN 0-87441-363-X). Behrman.

Sachar, A. L. History of the Jews. rev. ed. (gr. 6 up). 1967. pap. text ed. 26.36 (ISBN 0-07-553559-9); pap. text ed. 20.95 (ISBN 0-685-02836-4). McGraw.

Samuels, Ruth. Pathways Through Jewish History. rev ed. (Illus.). (gr. 7-10). 1977. pap. 9.00x (ISBN 0-87068-520-1). Ktav.

Stadtler, Bea. The Adventures of Gluckel of Hameln. LC 67-18814. (gr. 6-10). 3.75 (ISBN 0-8381-0731-1, 10-731). United Syn Bk.

Synge, Ursula. The People & the Promise. LC 74-10661. 192p. (gr. 7-10). 1974. 18.95 (ISBN 0-87599-208-0). S G Phillips.

Tepp, Leo. A History of the Jewish Experience: Eternal Faith, Eternal People. (gr. 9 up). 12.95 (ISBN 0-317-70167-3). Behrman.

Weilerstein, Sadie R. Jewish Heroes, 2 bks. Cassel, Lili, illus. 208p. (gr. 2-3). pap. 4.25x ea. Bk. 1 (ISBN 0-8381-0180-1). Bk. 2 (ISBN 0-8381-0177-1). United Syn Bk.

JEWS–HISTORY–FICTION

Atlas, Susan. Passover Passage. 5.95 (ISBN 0-933873-46-8). Torah Aura. Rebecca Able learns about Jewish history & culture while spending a Passover holiday on-board her grandparents sailboat in the Caribbean. This adolescent novel explores the meaning of family, traditional Jewish values & growing up. Through Becca's eyes, the reader sees, feels, hears & smells what it's like to be an adolescent a-sail for the first time.
Publisher Provided Annotation.

Cohen, Barbara. Yussel's Prayer. Deraney, Michael J., illus. LC 80-25377. 32p. (gr. k-4). 1981. PLB 12.88 (ISBN 0-688-00461-X). Lothrop.

Gold, Avner. Envoy from Vienna. Hinlicky, Gregg, contrib. by. 185p. (gr. 9-12). 1986. 10.95 (ISBN 0-935063-22-6); pap. 8.95 (ISBN 0-935063-21-8). CIS Comm.

Margolin, Miriam. Little Stories for Little Children. Ryback, Issachar, illus. 32p. (gr. k-3). 1986. Repr. of 1922 ed. 11.75x (ISBN 0-918825-55-5); 11.95 (ISBN 0-918825-53-9). Moyer Bell Limited.
These are simple stories of shtetl life that attain an astonishing immediacy throughout the Picassoesque black-&-white drawings of Issachar Ryback, a Russian artist often compared with Marc Chagall. First published in 1922 by the Jewish Section of Comissariat for Folk Education, USSR.
Publisher Provided Annotation.

Narell, Irena. Joshua: Fighter for Bar Kochba. LC 78-55959. (gr. 6-12). 1979. pap. 5.95 (ISBN 0-934764-01-8). Akiba Pr.

Orgel, Doris. A Certain Magic. LC 75-9204. 192p. (gr. 5 up). 1976. 7.95 (ISBN 0-8037-5405-1). Dial Bks Young.

Roseman, Kenneth. Escape from the Holocaust. 192p. (Orig.). (gr. 4-6). 1985. pap. 6.95 (ISBN 0-8074-0307-5, 140070). UAHC.

Schachnowitz, Selig. Avrohom ben Avrohom: The Famous Historical Novel About the Ger Tzedek of Vilna. (gr. 7 up). 9.95 (ISBN 0-87306-134-9); pap. 6.95 (ISBN 0-685-01625-0). Feldheim.

Sender, Ruth M. To Life. LC 88-9312. 240p. (gr. 7 up). 1988. 14.95 (ISBN 0-02-781831-4, Mcmillan Child Bk). Macmillan Child Grp.

Thoene, Bodie. Light in Zion. LC 88-4578. 352p. (Orig.). (gr. 11-12). 1988. pap. 7.95 (ISBN 0-87123-990-6). Bethany Hse.

JEWS–LANGUAGE
see Hebrew Language

JEWS–LITERATURE
see Hebrew Literature; Jewish Literature

JEWS–PERSECUTIONS

Adler, David. We Remember the Holocaust. LC 87-21139. (Illus.). 144p. (gr. 6-9). 1989. 16.95 (ISBN 0-8050-0434-3). H Holt & Co.

Leitner, Isabella & Leitner, Irving A. Saving the Fragments: From Auschwitz to New York. 128p. (gr. 9-12). Date not set. pap. 6.95 (ISBN 0-317-02718-2, Plume). NAL-Dutton.

Meltzer, Milton. Never to Forget: The Jews of the Holocaust. LC 75-25409. (gr. 7 up). 1976. PLB 13.89 (ISBN 0-06-024175-6). HarpC Child Bks.

Patterson, Charles. Anti-Semitism: The Road to the Holocaust & Beyond. 160p. (gr. 8). 1988. pap. 9.95 (ISBN 0-8027-7318-4). Walker & Co.

Stein, R. Conrad. The Holocaust. LC 85-31415. (Illus.). 48p. (gr. 4-8). 1986. PLB 14.60 (ISBN 0-516-04767-1). Childrens.

JEWS–RELIGION
see Judaism

JEWS–RITES AND CEREMONIES

Chanover, Hyman & Zusman, Evelyn. A Book of Prayer for Junior Congregations: Sabbath & Festivals. (ENG & HEB.). 256p. (gr. 4-7). 4.50x (ISBN 0-8381-0174-7, 10-174). United Syn Bk.

Chanover, Hyman, adapted by. Service for the High Holy Days Adapted for Youth. LC 72-2058. 192p. (gr. 8 up). 1972. pap. 4.95x (ISBN 0-87441-123-8). Behrman.

Eisenberg, Azriel & Robinson, Jessie B. My Jewish Holidays. 208p. (gr. 5-6). 3.95x (ISBN 0-8381-0176-3, 10-176). United Syn Bk.

Epstein, Morris. All about Jewish Holidays & Customs. rev. ed. (gr. 5-6). 1969. pap. 7.95x (ISBN 0-87068-500-7). Ktav.

Gersh, Harry. When a Jew Celebrates. Weihs, Erika, illus. LC 70-116678. 256p. (gr. 5-6). 1971. pap. text ed. 7.95x (ISBN 0-87441-091-6); tchr's guide 14.95; student activity bk. 3.95; tchr's cassette 5.95 (ISBN 0-685-00740-5). Behrman.

Grossman, Miriam. The Wonder of Becoming You: How a Jewish Girl Grows Up. (gr. 6-8). 1988. 8.95 (ISBN 0-87306-438-0). Feldheim.

Metter, Bert. Bar Mitzvah, Bat Mitzvah: How Jewish Boys & Girls Come of Age. Friedman, Marvin, illus. LC 83-23230. 64p. (Orig.). (gr. 4 up). 1984. (Clarion); pap. 4.95 (ISBN 0-89919-292-0). HM.

Neusner, Jacob. Mitzvah. (gr. 6-8). 5.95 (ISBN 0-317-70156-8); tchr's guide 14.95 (ISBN 0-317-70157-6). Behrman.

Oren, Rony. The Animated Haggadah (1990 Edition) (Illus.). 54p. 1990. 14.95 (ISBN 0-944007-43-0). Shapolsky Pubs.

Syme, Daniel B. Jewish Mourning. 1989. pap. 3.00 (ISBN 0-8074-0332-6, 388494). UAHC.

Zlotowitz, M. My Blessings for Food: Birchas Hamozon. Horen, Michael, illus. 32p. (gr. 1-6). 7.95 (ISBN 0-89906-799-9). Mesorah Pubns.

Zwebner, Janet. The Animated Haggadah Activity Book. 48p. (ps-8). 1990. pap. 5.95 (ISBN 0-944007-46-5). Shapolsky Pubs.

JEWS IN CHINA

Patent, Gregory. Shanghai Passage. Lewin, Ted, illus. 128p. (gr. 5-9). 1990. 13.95 (ISBN 0-89919-743-4, Clarion Bks). HM.

JEWS IN GERMANY

Koehn, Ilse. Mischling, Second Degree: My Childhood in Nazi Germany. LC 77-6189. 240p. (gr. 7 up). 1977. PLB 12.88 (ISBN 0-688-84110-4). Greenwillow.

—Mischling, Second Degree: My Childhood in Nazi Germany. 240p. (gr. 6 up). 1990. pap. 4.95 (ISBN 0-14-034290-7, Puffin). Puffin Bks.

JEWS IN POLAND

Sender, Ruth M. The Cage. LC 86-8562. 252p. (gr. 7 up). 1986. 14.95 (ISBN 0-02-781830-6, Mcmillan Child Bk). Macmillan Child Grp.

JEWS IN THE NETHERLANDS

Frank, Anne. Anne Frank: The Diary of a Young Girl. rev. ed. Mooyaart, B. M., tr. Roosevelt, Eleanor, intro. by. LC 52-6355. 312p. (gr. 7 up). 1967. 21.95 (ISBN 0-385-04019-9). Doubleday.

Isaacman, Clara & Grossman, Joan A. Clara's Story. LC 84-14339. 180p. (gr. 5-9). 1984. 11.95 (ISBN 0-8276-0243-X). JPS Phila.

JEWS IN THE SOVIET UNION

Bayar, Steven & Bayar, Ilene. Rachel & Mischa. Ruthen, Marlene L., illus. LC 88-9450. 32p. (ps-3). 1988. pap. 4.95 (ISBN 0-930494-77-6). Kar Ben.

JEWS IN THE SOVIET UNION–FICTION

Lasky, Kathryn. Night Journey. 1986. pap. 12.95 (ISBN 0-670-80935-7). Viking Child Bks.

JEWS IN THE U. S.

Bayar, Steven & Bayar, Ilene. Rachel & Mischa. Ruthen, Marlene L., illus. LC 88-9450. 32p. (ps-3). 1988. pap. 4.95 (ISBN 0-930494-77-6). Kar Ben.

Brownstone, David M. The Jewish-American Heritage. LC 87-19905. (Illus.). 128p. (gr. 7 up). 1988. 16.95 (ISBN 0-8160-1628-3). Facts on File.

Finkelstein, Norman H. The Other Fourteen Ninety-Two: Jewish Settlement in the New World. LC 89-6253. (Illus.). 96p. (gr. 5-9). 1989. 12.95 (ISBN 0-684-18913-5, Scribners Young Read). Macmillan Child Grp.

Huttenbach, Henry. The Jewish Americans. Moynihan, Daniel P., intro. by. 112p. (Orig.). (gr. 5 up). 1989. 17.95 (ISBN 0-87754-887-0); pap. 9.95 (ISBN 0-7910-0270-5). Chelsea Hse.

Kenvin, Helene. This Land of Liberty: A History of America's Jews. 216p. (gr. 7-9). 1986. pap. text ed. 8.95x (ISBN 0-87441-421-0). Behrman.

Kustanowitz, Shulamit E. Henrietta Szold: Israel's Helping Hand. Masheris, Robert, illus. 64p. (gr. 2-6). 1990. pap. 10.95 (ISBN 0-670-82518-2). Viking Child Bks.

Prophet, Elizabeth C. Ascended Masters on Soul Mates & Twin Flames Bks I & II. 340p. 19.95, (ISBN 0-916766-85-3); 317p. 19.95, (ISBN 0-916766-86-1). Summit Univ.

JEWS IN THE U. S.–FICTION

Blume, Judy. Starring Sally J. Freedman As Herself. LC 76-57805. 296p. (gr. 4-7). 1982. 14.95 (ISBN 0-02-711070-2, Bradbury Pr). Macmillan Child Grp.

Chaikin, Miriam. Finders Weepers. Egielski, Richard, illus. LC 79-9608. 128p. (gr. 3-6). 1980. PLB 12.89. HarpC Child Bks.

—I Should Worry, I Should Care. Egielski, Richard, illus. LC 78-19480. (gr. 3-6). 1979. 12.89 (ISBN 0-06-021174-1). HarpC Child Bks.

Feldman, Eva B. Seymour, the Formerly Fearful. LC 89-35668. 160p. (gr. 3-6). 1990. 12.95 (ISBN 0-02-734371-5, Four Winds Press). Macmillan Child Grp.

Hurwitz, Johanna. Once I Was a Plum Tree. Fetz, Ingrid, illus. LC 79-23518. 160p. (gr. 4-6). 1980. PLB 12.88 (ISBN 0-688-32223-9). Morrow Jr Bks.

Lasky, Kathryn. Pageant. LC 86-12087. 228p. (gr. 7 up). 1986. 14.95 (ISBN 0-02-751720-9, Four Winds). Macmillan Child Grp.

Little, Jean. Kate. LC 70-148419. 174p. (gr. 5-8). 1971. PLB 12.89 (ISBN 0-06-023914-X). HarpC Child Bks.

—Kate. LC 20-148419. 174p. (gr. 5-8). 1973. pap. 3.95 (ISBN 0-06-440037-9, Trophy). HarpC Child Bks.

Snyder, Carol. Ike & Mama & the Block Wedding. Robinson, Charles, illus. LC 78-11702. (gr. 2-6). 1979. 7.95 (ISBN 0-698-20461-1, Coward). Putnam Pub Group.

JIUJITSU
see Judo

JOAN OF ARC, SAINT, 1412-1431

Banfield, Susan. Joan of Arc. (Illus.). 112p. (gr. 5 up). 1985. lib. bdg. 17.95 (ISBN 0-87754-556-1). Chelsea Hse.

Brooks, Polly S. Beyond the Myth: The Story of Joan of Arc. LC 89-37327. (Illus.). 192p. (gr. 7 up). 1990. 14.95 (ISBN 0-397-32422-7, Lipp Jr Bks); PLB 14.89 (ISBN 0-397-32423-5, Lipp Jr Bks). HarpC Child Bks.

Daughters Of St. Paul. Wind & Shadows. (gr. 4-7). 3.00 (ISBN 0-8198-0174-7). Dghtrs St Paul.

Smith, Dorothy. Saint Joan: The Girl in Armour. Broomfield, Robert, illus. 1990. 2.95 (ISBN 0-8091-6594-5). Paulist Pr.

Storr, Catherine. Joan of Arc. Taylor, Robert, illus. LC 84-18346. 32p. (gr. 2-5). 1985. PLB 16.67 (ISBN 0-8172-2111-5); pap. 9.27 (ISBN 0-8172-2254-5). Raintree Pubs.

Windeatt, Mary F. St. Joan of Arc. Harmon, Gedge, illus. 32p. (gr. 1-5). 1989. Repr. of 1954 ed. wkbk. 3.00 (ISBN 0-89555-367-8). TAN Bks Pubs.

JOAN OF ARC, SAINT, 1412-1431–FICTION

Dana, Barbara. Young Joan. LC 90-39494. 384p. (gr. 7 up). 1991. 17.95 (ISBN 0-06-021422-8); PLB 17.89 (ISBN 0-06-021423-6). HarpC Child Bks.

Goodwin, Marie. Where the Towers Pierce the Sky. LC 88-37497. 192p. (gr. 7 up). 1989. 13.95 (ISBN 0-02-736871-8, Four Winds). Macmillan Child Grp.

JOBS
see Occupations; Professions

JOHN, SAINT, APOSTLE

Laux, Dorothy. John: Beloved Apostle. McPheeters, William, illus. (gr. 1-6). 1977. bds. 5.95 (ISBN 0-8054-4234-0, 4242-34). Broadman.

JOHN THE BAPTIST–FICTION

Human, Johnnie. John the Baptist: Forerunner of Jesus. Padgett, James, illus. (gr. 1-6). 1978. 5.95 (ISBN 0-8054-4240-5, 4242-40). Broadman.

Storr, Catherine, as told by. Jesus & John the Baptist. (Illus.). 32p. (gr. k-4). 1985. PLB 14.65 (ISBN 0-8172-2037-2). Raintree Pubs.

JOHNSON, ANDREW, PRESIDENT U. S. 1808-1875

Durwood, Thomas A. Andrew Johnson: Rebuilding the Union. Gallin, Richard, ed. Steele, Henry, intro. by. (Illus.). 160p. (gr. 5 up). 1990. PLB 16.98 (ISBN 0-382-09945-1); PLB 12.74s.p.; pap. 8.95 (ISBN 0-382-24054-5); pap. 5.96s.p. Silver Burdett Pr.

Kent, Zachary. Andrew Johnson. LC 88-39115. (Illus.). 100p. (gr. 3 up). 1989. PLB 17.27 (ISBN 0-516-01363-7). Childrens.

Paley, Alan L. Andrew Johnson: The President Impeached. Rahmas, D. Steve, ed. LC 74-190248. 32p. (gr. 7-12). 1972. lib. bdg. 4.20 incl. catalog cards (ISBN 0-87157-531-0); pap. 2.95 (ISBN 0-87157-031-9). SamHar Pr.

Stevens, Rita. Andrew Johnson: Seventeenth President of the United States. Young, Richard G., ed. LC 88-28487. (Illus.). (gr. 5-9). 1989. PLB 17.26 (ISBN 0-944483-16-X). Garrett Ed Corp.

JOHNSON, JAMES WELDON, 1871-1938

Tolbert-Rouchaleau, Jane. James Weldon Johnson. King, Coretta Scott, intro. by. (Illus.). 112p. (Orig.). (gr. 5 up). 1988. 17.95 (ISBN 1-55546-596-X); pap. 9.95 (ISBN 0-7910-0211-X). Chelsea Hse.

JOHNSON, LYNDON BAINES, PRESIDENT U. S. 1908-1973

Devaney, John. Lyndon Baines Johnson, President. LC 85-31751. 128p. (gr. 5 up). 1986. 12.95 (ISBN 0-8027-6638-2); PLB 12.85 (ISBN 0-8027-6639-0). Walker & Co.

Falkof, Lucille. Lyndon B. Johnson: Thirty-Sixth President of the United States. Young, Richard G., ed. LC 88-31003. (Illus.). (gr. 5-9). 1989. PLB 17.26 (ISBN 0-944483-20-8). Garrett Ed Corp.

Hargrove, Jim. Lyndon B. Johnson. LC 87-15890. (Illus.). 100p. (gr. 3 up). 1987. 17.27 (ISBN 0-516-01396-3). Childrens.

Kaye, Tony. Lyndon B. Johnson. Schlesinger, Arthur M., Jr., intro. by. (Illus.). 112p. (gr. 5 up). 1988. lib. bdg. 17.95 (ISBN 0-87754-536-7). Chelsea Hse.

Kurland, Gerald. Lyndon Baines Johnson: President Caught in an Ordeal of Power. Rahmas, D. Steve, ed. LC 76-190243. 32p. (Orig.). (gr. 7-12). 1972. lib. bdg. 4.20 incl. catalog cards (ISBN 0-87157-525-6); pap. 2.95 vinyl laminated covers (ISBN 0-87157-025-4). SamHar Pr.

Lynch, Dudley. The President from Texas: Lyndon Baines Johnson. LC 74-26817. (Illus.). 192p. (gr. 6 up). 1975. 12.95 (ISBN 0-690-00627-6, Crowell Jr Bks). HarpC Child Bks.

Lyndon B. Johnson: Mini-Play. (gr. 8 up). 1978. 6.50 (ISBN 0-89550-318-2). Stevens & Shea.

JOKES

see Wit and Humor

JOLIET, LOUIS, 1645-1700

Stein, R. Conrad. The Story of Marquette & Jolliet. LC 81-5036. (Illus.). 32p. (gr. 3-6). 1981. PLB 13.27 (ISBN 0-516-04630-6). Childrens.

JONAH, THE PROPHET

Amoss, Berthe. Jonah. (Illus.). 10p. (ps-7). 1989. pap. 2.95 (ISBN 0-922589-09-7). More Than Card.

Briscoe, Jill. Jonah & the Worm. Armstrong, Tom & Davis, Florence, illus. 143p. (gr. 6). 1989. pap. write for info. Jilcoe.

Jonah. 1989. text ed. 3.95 cased (ISBN 0-7214-5260-4). Ladybird Bks.

Jonah & the Whale. 1991. Set of 6. pap. 3.95 (ISBN 0-8007-7119-2). Revell.

Lashbrook, Marilyn. I Don't Want to: The Story of Jonah. Britt, Stephanie M., illus. LC 87-60264. 32p. (ps). 1987. 5.95 (ISBN 0-86606-428-1, 844). Roper Pr.

Sant Bani School Children, illus. Book of Jonah. LC 84-50924. (gr. 1-6). 1984. pap. 6.95 (ISBN 0-89142-044-4). Sant Bani Ash.

Stirrup Associates, Inc. Staff. My Jesus Pocketbook of Jonah & the Big Fish. Harvey, Bonnie C. & Phillips, Cheryl M., eds. Fulton, Ginger A., illus. LC 83-51679. 32p. (ps-3). 1984. pap. 0.69 (ISBN 0-937420-09-3). Stirrup Assoc.

Storr, Catherine, retold by. Jonah & the Whale. Wilkinson, Barry, illus. LC 82-23023. 32p. (gr. k-4). 1983. PLB 14.65 (ISBN 0-8172-1984-6). Raintree Pubs.

JONATHAN (BIBLICAL CHARACTER)

Bearman, Jane. Jonathan. Bearman, Jane, illus. LC 65-21754. (gr. 3 up). 1975. 3.95 (ISBN 0-8246-0089-4). Jonathan David.

JONES, JOHN PAUL, 1747-1792

Brandt, Keith. John Paul Jones: Hero of the Seas. Swan, Susan, illus. LC 82-16045. 48p. (gr. 4-6). 1983. PLB 10.79 (ISBN 0-89375-849-3); pap. text ed. 2.95 (ISBN 0-89375-850-7). Troll Assocs.

Worcester, Donald E. John Paul Jones. (gr. 4-6). 1961. 4.36 (ISBN 0-395-01755-6, Piper). HM.

Zadra, Dan. Statesmen in America: John Paul Jones. rev. ed. (gr. 2-4). 1988. PLB 11.50s.p. (ISBN 0-88682-193-2); PLB 16.45 (ISBN 0-318-32957-3). Creative Ed.

JORDAN

Department of Geography, Lerner Publications. Jordan in Pictures. (Illus.). 64p. (gr. 5 up). 1988. PLB 12.95 (ISBN 0-8225-1834-1). Lerner Pubns.

Jordan. (Illus.). (gr. 5 up). 1988. 14.95 (ISBN 0-7910-0096-6). Chelsea Hse.

JOSEPH, NEZ PERCE CHIEF, 1840-1904

Grant, Matthew G. & Zadra, Dan. Chief Joseph. LC 73-9816. 1987. PLB 11.50s.p. (ISBN 0-88682-158-4); 16.45 (ISBN 0-685-01251-4). Creative Ed.

Jassem, Kate. Chief Joseph, Leader of Destiny. new ed. LC 78-18048. (Illus.). 48p. (gr. 4-6). 1979. PLB 9.89 (ISBN 0-89375-155-3); pap. 2.95 (ISBN 0-89375-145-6). Troll Assocs.

Pollock, Dean. Joseph: Chief of the Nez Perce. 5th ed. (Illus.). 64p. (gr. 5 up). 1990. pap. 7.95g (ISBN 0-8323-0482-4). Binford Mort.

Yates, Diana. Chief Joseph: Thunder Coming up from the Water. (Illus.). 104p. (gr. 4-9). 1991. pap. 9.95 (ISBN 0-9623380-8-7). Ward Hill Pr.

JOSEPH, SAINT

Hershey, Katherine. Joseph. (Illus.). 40p. (gr. k-6). 1979. pap. text ed. 9.45 (ISBN 1-55976-006-0). CEF Press.

Lashbrook, Marilyn. Get Lost, Little Brother: The Story of Joseph. Britt, Stephanie M., illus. LC 87-62503. 32p. (ps). 1988. 5.95 (ISBN 0-86606-432-X, 863). Roper Pr.

Patrignani. A Manual of Practical Devotion to St. Joseph. LC 82-50594. 328p. 1982. pap. 12.50 (ISBN 0-89555-175-6). TAN Bks Pubs.

JOSEPH THE PATRIARCH

Barrett, Ethel. Joseph. LC 79-65232. 128p. (gr. 1-6). 1979. pap. 3.95 (ISBN 0-8307-0715-8, 5607701). Regal.

Joseph. (ps-2). 3.95 (ISBN 0-7214-5067-9). Ladybird Bks.

McMillan, Mary. Joseph & His Brothers. 48p. (ps-1). 1988. 6.95 (ISBN 0-86653-451-2, SS1803). Good Apple.

Storr, Catherine, as told by. Joseph & the Famine. (Illus.). 32p. (gr. k-4). 1985. PLB 14.65 (ISBN 0-8172-2038-0). Raintree Pubs.

The Story of Joseph. (Illus.). (gr. 4). 3.50 (ISBN 0-7214-0152-X). Ladybird Bks.

Summers, Jester. Joseph: the Forgiver. (Illus.). (gr. 1-6). 1976. bds. 5.95 (ISBN 0-8054-4224-3, 4242-24). Broadman.

White, J. Edson. The Story of Joseph: From Shepherd Boy to a Ruler of Egypt. (Illus.). (gr. 3 up). 1990. pap. 4.95 (ISBN 0-945460-07-4). Upward Way.

Williams, Rex. Joseph. (Illus.). 224p. (gr. 3 up). 1990. pap. 2.50 (ISBN 1-55748-116-4). Barbour & Co.

JOURNALISM

Berger, Gilda. Violence & the Media. (Illus.). 176p. (gr. 7-12). 1989. PLB 12.90 (ISBN 0-531-10808-2). Watts.

Craig, Janet. What's It Like to Be a Newspaper Reporter. Kolding, Richard M., illus. LC 89-34384. 32p. (gr. k-3). 1989. lib. bdg. 10.89 (ISBN 0-8167-1807-5); pap. text ed. 2.50 (ISBN 0-8167-1808-3). Troll Assocs.

Dahlstrom, Lorraine M. Writing down the Days: Three Hundred Sixty-Five Creative Journaling Ideas for Young People. 176p. 1990. pap. 12.95 (ISBN 0-915793-19-9). Free Spirit Pub.

Harwood, William N. Writing & Editing School News. 3rd, rev. ed. 364p. (gr. 11-12). 1990. pap. text ed. 12.27 (ISBN 0-931054-21-4). Clark Pub.

Jaspersohn, William. A Day in the Life of a Television News Reporter. Jaspersohn, William, illus. 96p. (gr. 5 up). 1981. 15.95 (ISBN 0-316-45813-9). Little.

Journalism. (Illus.). 40p. (gr. 6-12). 1983. pap. 1.85 (ISBN 0-8395-3350-0, 3350). BSA.

Kronenwetter, Michael. Journalism Ethics. Rasof, Henry, ed. (Illus.). 128p. (gr. 7-12). 1988. PLB 12.90 (ISBN 0-531-10589-X). Watts.

Mabery, D. L. Tell Me about Yourself: How to Interview Anyone from Your Friends to Famous People. LC 85-7001. 80p. (gr. 4 up). 1985. PLB 10.95 (ISBN 0-8225-1604-7). Lerner Pubns.

Rogers, Donald J. Press vs. Government: Constitutional Issues. LC 86-8369. (Illus.). 160p. (gr. 5-9). 1986. lib. bdg. 10.29 (ISBN 0-671-61105-4). Messner.

Rothstein, Evelyn, et al. Editing Writes, Red Edition. Gompper, Gail, illus. 110p. (gr. 4-6). 1989. pap. 7.95 (ISBN 0-913935-45-X). ERA-CCR.

Sansevere, Carol Q. The Real Scoop. 160p. (Orig.). (gr. 5-9). Date not set. pap. 2.95 (ISBN 1-55802-205-8). Lynx Bks.

Suid, Murray, et al. For the Love of Editing. 112p. (gr. 2-6). 1983. 9.95 (ISBN 0-912107-00-6). Monday Morning Bks.

JOURNALISM–FICTION

Conford, Ellen. Dear Lovey Hart: I Am Desperate. 224p. (gr. 4-6). 1975. 14.95 (ISBN 0-316-15306-0). Little.

Jaspersohn, William. Magazine: Behind the Scenes at Sports Illustrated. (Illus.). 128p. (gr. 7 up). 1983. 14.95 (ISBN 0-316-45815-5). Little.

JOURNALISM–U. S.

Cormier, Robert. I Have Words to Spend: Reflections of a Small Town Editor. 1991. pap. 15.95 (ISBN 0-385-30289-4). Doubleday.

JOURNALISTS

Brown, Marzella. Newspaper Reporters. Coan, Sharon, ed. Apodaca, Blanqui, illus. 48p. (gr. 3-6). 1990. wkbk. 5.95 (ISBN 1-55734-137-0). Tchr Create Mat.

Carlson, Judy. Nothing Is Impossible, Said Nelly Bly. (Illus.). 32p. (gr. 1-4). 1989. PLB 13.32 (ISBN 0-8172-3521-3). Raintree Pubs.

Vonier, Sprague. Edward R. Murrow. LC 89-4344. (Illus.). 64p. (gr. 5-6). 1989. PLB 12.95 (ISBN 0-8368-0100-8). Gareth Stevens Inc.

JOURNEYS

see Voyages around the World

JUAREZ, BENITO PABLO, 1806-1872

Benito Juarez: Mini-Play. (gr. 5 up). 1978. 5.00 (ISBN 0-89550-374-3). Stevens & Shea.

Davis, Linda. A Purim Story. (Illus.). (ps-3). 1988. 7.95 (ISBN 0-317-68087-0). Feldheim.

Gleiter, Jan. Benito Juarez. De Varona, Frank, intro. by. (SPA & ENG., Illus.). 32p. (gr. 3-6). 1990. PLB 16.67 (ISBN 0-8172-3381-4). Raintree Pubs.

JUDAISM

see also Jews; Sabbath; Synagogues

Abrams, Judith Z. Rosh Hashanah - A Family Service. Kahn, Katherine J., illus. LC 90-4855. 32p. (Orig.). (ps-4). 1990. pap. 3.95 (ISBN 0-929371-16-X). Kar Ben.

—Selichot - A Family Service. Kahn, Katherine J., illus. LC 90-4863. 24p. (ps-4). 1990. pap. 3.95 (ISBN 0-929371-15-1). Kar Ben.

—Yom Kippur - A Family Service. Kahn, Katherine J., illus. LC 90-4862. 22p. (Orig.). (ps-4). 1990. pap. 3.95 (ISBN 0-929371-17-8). Kar Ben.

Antokol, Avraham Z. A Life of Mitzvos. 156p. (gr. 10up). 12.95 (ISBN 0-9618174-1-0). Machon Historia.

Bamberger, David. Judaism & the World's Religions. (gr. 7-8). 7.95 (ISBN 0-317-70158-4); tchr's guide 14.95. Behrman.

Beiner, Stan J. Sedra Scenes: Skits for Every Torah Portion. LC 82-71282. 225p. (Orig.). (gr. 6-12). 1982. pap. text ed. 9.50 (ISBN 0-86705-007-1). AIRE.

Bennett, Alan D., ed. Journey Through Judaism: The Best of Keeping Posted. (gr. 10 up). 1991. pap. 12.00 (ISBN 0-8074-0311-3, 160500). UAHC.

Bogot, Howard. Yoni. (ps). 1982. pap. 4.00 (ISBN 0-8074-0166-8, 101980). UAHC.

Borovetz, Fran. Ha Motzi Bracha Kit. (Illus.). 32p. (Orig.). (gr. 3-4). 1985. pap. text ed. 4.95 (ISBN 0-933873-03-4). Torah Aura.

Borowitz, Eugene & Patz, Naomi. Explaining Reform Judaism. 183p. (gr. 6-8). 1985. pap. text ed. 7.95 (ISBN 0-87441-394-X); By Kerry Olitzky. tchr's. ed., 96pps. 14.95x (ISBN 0-87441-436-9); wkbk., 90pps. 4.25 (ISBN 0-317-60043-5). Behrman.

Cedarbaum, Sophia. A First Book of Jewish Holidays. Ruthen, Marlene L., illus. LC 85-105348. 80p. (gr. 1-3). 1984. pap. text ed. 6.00 (ISBN 0-8074-0274-5, 301500). UAHC.

Chaikin, Miriam. Menorahs, Mezuzas, & Other Jewish Symbols. Weihs, Erika, illus. 96p. (gr. 5 up). 1990. 14.95 (ISBN 0-89919-856-2, Clarion Bks). HM.

Cohen, Annie N. A Jewish Child's Book of Memories: The First Seven Years. Yerman, Neil, illus. (ps-2). Date not set. 14.95 (ISBN 0-933503-24-5). Shapolsky Pubs.

Einstein, Stephen J. & Kukoff, Lydia. Every Person's Guide to Judaism. 196p. 1989. pap. 8.95 (ISBN 0-8074-0434-9, 142610). UAHC.

Elias, Miriam. Goodbye, My Friends. (gr. 6-9). 1989. 10.95 (ISBN 0-87306-491-7); pap. 8.95 (ISBN 0-87306-492-5). Feldheim.

Fields, Harvey J. A Torah Commentary for Our Times, Vol. 2: Exodus & Leviticus. Carmi, Giora, illus. (gr. 7-9). 1991. pap. text ed. 12.00x (ISBN 0-8074-0334-2, 164010). UAHC.

Fishman, Priscilla. Learn Mishnah Notebook. 128p. (gr. 7-8). 1983. pap. 3.50x (ISBN 0-87441-369-9). Behrman.

Freund, Chavie. Read Me the Haggadah. Ieff, Tova, illus. (ps-2). 1990. 10.95 (ISBN 1-56062-021-8). CIS Comm.

Ganz, Yaffa. Follow the Moon: A Journey Through the Jewish Year. Klineman, Harvey, illus. (gr. k-4). 1984. 8.95 (ISBN 0-87306-369-4). Feldheim.

—The Jewish Fact-Finder: A Bookful of Important Jewish Facts & Handy Information. (gr. 5-9). 1988. 12.95 (ISBN 0-87306-447-X); pap. 9.95 (ISBN 0-87306-470-4). Feldheim.

—Who Knows One? A Book of Jewish Numbers. Klineman, Harvey, illus. (gr. k-4). 1981. 8.95 (ISBN 0-87306-285-X). Feldheim.

Gates, Fay C. Judaism. (Illus.). 128p. (gr. 7-12). 1991. 17.95x (ISBN 0-8160-2444-8). Facts on File.

Gates of Awe. 64p. (ps-8). 1991. 12.95 (ISBN 0-88123-014-6). Central Conf.

Geller, Norman. It's Not the Jewish Christmas. Gruchow, Jane C., illus. 20p. (gr. 3-6). 1985. pap. 4.95 (ISBN 0-915753-09-X). N Geller Pub.

Gittelsohn, Roland B. Love in Your Life: A Jewish View of Teenage Sexuality. (gr. 7-9). 1991. pap. 9.95 (ISBN 0-8074-0460-8, 142685). UAHC.

Gold, Yeshara. Hurry, Friday's a Short Day: One Boy's Erev Shabbat in Jerusalem's Old City. (Illus.). 32p. (gr. 3-8). 1986. 8.95 (ISBN 0-89906-800-6); pap. 5.95 (ISBN 0-89906-801-4). Mesorah Pubns.

—Just a Week to Go: One Boy's Pesach Preparations in Jerusalem's Old City. (Illus.). 32p. (gr. 3-8). 1987. 8.95 (ISBN 0-89906-802-2); pap. 5.95 (ISBN 0-89906-803-0). Mesorah Pubns.

Golomb, Morris. Know Jewish Living & Enjoy It. LC 78-54569. (Illus.). (gr. 5-9). 1981. 14.95 (ISBN 0-88400-054-0). Shengold.

Gottesman, Meir U. Shpeter: Book One. (Illus.). (gr. 1-3). 1981. 5.95 (ISBN 0-910818-35-5); pap. 4.95 (ISBN 0-910818-36-3). Judaica Pr.

—Shpeter: Book Two. (Illus.). (gr. 1-3). 1981. 5.95 (ISBN 0-910818-39-8); pap. 4.95 (ISBN 0-910818-40-1). Judaica Pr.
Greenberg, Sidney & Silverman, Morris. Siddurenu. (gr. 3-7). 8.95x (ISBN 0-87677-099-5). Prayer Bk.
Grishaver, Joel L. Being Torah Student Commentary, 2 Vols. (Illus.). 72p. (Orig.). (gr. 2-4). 1986. pap. text ed. 4.50 ea. Vol. 1 (ISBN 0-933873-09-3). Vol. 2 (ISBN 0-933873-10-7). Torah Aura.
—Torah Toons I. (Illus.). 115p. (Orig.). (gr. 4 up). 1985. pap. text ed. 5.50 (ISBN 0-933873-01-8). Torah Aura.
—Torah Toons II. (Illus.). 114p. (Orig.). (gr. 6 up). 1985. pap. text ed. 5.50 (ISBN 0-933873-02-6). Torah Aura.
Grossman, Roz & Gewirtz, Gladys. Let's Play Dreidel. Springer, Sally, illus. LC 89-34892. 16p. (ps-3). 1989. incl. tape & dreidel 8.95 (ISBN 0-929371-00-3). Kar Ben.
Jacobs, Louis. The Book of Jewish Practice. (gr. 9 up). 8.95 (ISBN 0-317-70168-1). Behrman.
—Hasidic Thought. (gr. 8-10). 8.95 (ISBN 0-317-70162-2). Behrman.
Karlinsky, Isaiah & Karlinsky, Ruth. My First Book of Mitzvos. (Illus.). (gr. k-3). 1986. 7.95 (ISBN 0-87306-388-0). Feldheim.
Keene, Michael & Wood, Angela. Being a Jew. (Illus.). 64p. (gr. 7-12). 1987. 19.95 (ISBN 0-7134-4668-4, Pub. by Batsford England). Trafalgar Sq.
Kipper, Lenore & Bogot, Howard. Alef-Bet of Jewish Values: Code Words of Jewish Life. Paiss, Jana, illus. 64p. (gr. 4-6). 1985. pap. text ed. 6.00 (ISBN 0-8074-0267-2, 101087). UAHC.
Kitman, Carol & Hurwitz, Ann. One Mezuzah: A Jewish Counting Book. (gr. k). 6.95 (ISBN 0-317-70144-4). Behrman.

Kobre, Faige. A Sense of Shabbat. LC 89-40361. (Illus.). 32p. 1990. 11.95 (ISBN 0-933873-44-1). Torah Aura.
In the sensuous photographs & simple text which make up this picture book, the taste, feel, sound, look & touch of Shabbat all make themselves manifest. The Shabbat presented here is at once holy & wonderous, & simultaneously, comfortable & familiar. It is a book the reader will go back to over & over. This book is a treasure.
Publisher Provided Annotation.

Kripke, Dorothy K. & Levin, Meyer. God & the Story of Judaism. LC 62-17078. (gr. 4-6). 1962. By Toby K. Kurzband. 6.95x (ISBN 0-87441-000-2). Behrman.
Kushner, Lawrence. The Book of Miracles: A Young Person's Guide to Jewish Spirituality. (Illus.). 96p. (Orig.). (gr. 4-6). 1987. pap. text ed. 7.95 (ISBN 0-8074-0323-7, 123926). UAHC.
Learsi, Rufus. Prince of Judah & Other Stories of a Great Journey. 1962 ed. LC 62-21985. (Illus.). (gr. 6-10). 8.95 (ISBN 0-88400-031-1). Shengold.
Lemelman, Martin. My Jewish Home. Lemelman, Martin, illus. 10p. (ps-k). 1988. pap. 3.95 boardbk. (ISBN 0-8074-0415-2, 102002). UAHC.
Levin, Meyer & Kurzband, Toby. Story of the Jewish Way of Life. LC 59-13487. (gr. 4-6). 1959. 6.95 (ISBN 0-87441-003-7). Behrman.
Liebermann, M. Coloring Books on Events of the Jewish Months: Nisan. (ps-2). 1987. 2.50 (ISBN 0-914131-86-9, D712). Torah Umesorah.
—Coloring Books on Events of the Jewish Months: Tishrei, Cheshvan. (ps-2). 1987. 2.50 (ISBN 0-914131-84-2, D710). Torah Umesorah.
—Coloring Books on the Parshas Hashavua: Bereishis. (ps-2). 1987. 2.50 (ISBN 0-914131-79-6, D700). Torah Umesorah.
—Coloring Books on the Parshas Hashavua: Devorim. (ps-2). 1987. 2.50 (ISBN 0-914131-83-4, D704). Torah Umesorah.
—Coloring Books on the Parshas Hashavua: Shemos. (ps-2). 1987. 2.50 (ISBN 0-914131-80-X, D701). Torah Umesorah.
—Coloring Books on the Parshas Hashavua: Vayikrah. (ps-2). 1987. 2.50 (ISBN 0-914131-81-8, D702). Torah Umesorah.
—Learn as You Color Series III: Brachos. (ps-2). 1987. 2.50 (ISBN 0-914131-88-5, D720). Torah Umesorah.
Lion The Printer. Seven Days a Week. (Illus.). (gr. k-5). 1977. spiral 2.00 (ISBN 0-914080-62-8). Shulsinger Sales.
Meyer, Henye. The Exiles of Crocodile Island. Dershowitz, Yosef, illus. 224p. (gr. 6-12). 1984. 10.95 (ISBN 0-89906-772-7); pap. 7.95 (ISBN 0-89906-773-5). Mesorah Pubns.
Moskowitz, Nachama S. Bridge to Prayer: The Jewish Worship Workbook, Vol. II. (Illus.). 144p. (gr. 6-7). 1989. pap. text ed. 6.00 (ISBN 0-8074-0432-2, 123596). UAHC.
Olomeinu: Our World Alphabetical Index of Themes & Personalities. 1987. 3.00 (ISBN 0-914131-72-9, D050). Torah Umesorah.
Orovitz, Norma A. Puzzled! The Jewish Word Search. LC 77-83177. (gr. 3 up). 1977. pap. 3.95 (ISBN 0-8197-0022-3). Bloch.
Pasachoff, Naomi. Basic Judaism for Young People, Vol. 1: Israel. 150p. (gr. 4-5). 1987. pap. text ed. 7.95 (ISBN 0-87441-423-7); By Lesley Silverstone. student activity bk., 90pgs. 4.25x (ISBN 0-87441-440-7). Behrman.
—Basic Judaism for Young People, Vol 2: Torah. 150p. (gr. 5-6). 1986. pap. text ed. 7.95 (ISBN 0-87441-424-5); By Lois M. Cohn. student activity bk., 92pps. 4.25x (ISBN 0-87441-442-3). Behrman.
—Basic Judaism for Young People, Vol. 3: God. (gr. 6-7). 7.95 (ISBN 0-317-70146-0); tchr's guide & dupl. masters 12.50 (ISBN 0-317-70147-9); student activity bk. 4.25 (ISBN 0-317-70148-7). Behrman.
Polish, Daniel F., et al. Drug, Sex, & Integrity: What Does Judaism Say? Diaz, Jose, illus. (gr. 7-9). 1991. pap. 10.00 (ISBN 0-8074-0459-4, 168505). UAHC.
Portnoy, Mindy A. Mommy Never Went to Hebrew School. Haas, Shelly O., illus. LC 89-30874. 32p. (gr. k-5). 1989. 10.95 (ISBN 0-930494-96-2); pap. 4.95 (ISBN 0-930494-97-0). Kar Ben.
Prager, Janice & LePoff, Arlene. Why Be Different: A Look into Judasim. 118p. (gr. 6-8). 1986. pap. text ed. 7.95 (ISBN 0-87441-427-X). Behrman.
Rabinowitz, Jan. The Tzedakah Workbook. Golub, Jane & Grishaver, Joelrev. by. (Illus.). 32p. (Orig.). (gr. 4-5). 1986. pap. text ed. 3.95 (ISBN 0-933873-07-7). Torah Aura.

Ray, Eric. Sofer: The Story of a Torah Scroll. LC 85-52420. (Illus.). 32p. (Orig.). (ps-4). 1986. pap. 4.95 (ISBN 0-933873-04-2). Torah Aura.
Writing a Torah takes love & patience, knowledge & skill. Eric Ray is a gentle, wise man, a skilled artist & a learned Jew. In this read-aloud text & photo essay, both his craft & his passions are shared. Sitting by Eric's side, we learn how a Sofer makes a mezuzot, tefillin & Sefer Torah, & we learn to love the Torah a little bit more.
Publisher Provided Annotation.

Roseman, Kenneth D. The Tenth of Av. 96p. (Orig.). (gr. 4-6). 1988. pap. text ed. 6.95 (ISBN 0-8074-0359-8, 123928). UAHC.
Rosen, Ruth, ed. Jesus for Jews. Owens, Nate, illus. LC 87-20343. 336p. (Orig.). (gr. 12). 1987. 13.95 (ISBN 0-9616148-3-8); pap. 7.95 (ISBN 0-9616148-4-6); pap. 4.95 mass market (ISBN 0-9616148-2-X). Messianic Jewish.
Rosenberg, Amye. Mitzvot. (Illus.). 30p. (gr. 1-5). pap. text ed. 4.25 (ISBN 0-87441-387-7). Behrman.
Rosenthal, Yaffa. Mitzvos We Can Do. Kunda, Shmuel, illus. 32p. (gr. 1-8). 1982. 9.95 (ISBN 0-89906-775-1); pap. 6.95 (ISBN 0-89906-776-X). Mesorah Pubns.
—Thank You Hashem. Kunda, Shmuel, illus. 32p. (gr. 1-8). 1983. 9.95 (ISBN 0-89906-777-8); pap. 6.95 (ISBN 0-89906-778-6). Mesorah Pubns.
Rossel, Seymour. When a Jew Seeks Wisdom: The Sayings of the Fathers. LC 75-14119. (gr. 7). pap. 7.95 (ISBN 0-87441-089-4); student's encounter bk. 3.95 (ISBN 0-685-00741-3); tchr's guide 14.95. Behrman.
Sagarin, James & Sagarin, Lori. Oseh Shalom. (Illus.). (gr. 4-6). 1990. wkbk. 6.00x (ISBN 0-8074-0351-2, 123703). UAHC.
Saypol, Judyth R. & Wikler, Madeline. My Very Own Haggadah. Rev. ed. Burstein, Chaya, illus. LC 83-6. 32p. (ps-3). pap. text ed. 2.95 (ISBN 0-930494-23-7). Kar Ben.
Shamir, Ilana & Shavit, Shlomo, eds. The Young Reader's Encyclopedia of Jewish History. LC 87-10599. (gr. 7 up). 1987. pap. 17.95 (ISBN 0-670-81738-4). Viking Child Bks.
Shapolsky, Ian. The Beginner's Jewish Book of Why & What. 292p. (gr. 9-12). Date not set. 11.95 (ISBN 0-933503-99-7). Shapolsky Pubs.
Simms, Laura & Kozodoy, Ruth. Exploring Our Living Past. Harlow, Jules, ed. Rosenberg, Amye & Weihs, Erika, illus. (gr. k-2). 1978. pap. 7.95 (ISBN 0-87441-309-5); tchr's guide 19.95x (ISBN 0-87441-276-5). Behrman.
Simon, Solomon & Bial, Morrison D. The Rabbis' Bible, Vol. 1: Torah, 2 pts. (gr. 5-6). 6.95 (ISBN 0-317-70149-5); tchr's guide 12.50 (ISBN 0-317-70150-9); tchr's resource bk. 14.95 (ISBN 0-317-70151-7); student activity bk. 3.50 (ISBN 0-317-70152-5). Behrman.
—The Rabbis' Bible, Vol. 2: Early Prophets. (gr. 6-7). 6.95 (ISBN 0-317-70153-3); tchr's guide 12.50 (ISBN 0-317-70154-1); tchr's resource bk. 14.95 (ISBN 0-317-70155-X). Behrman.
Simon, Solomon & Rothberg, Abraham. The Rabbis' Bible, Vol. 3: Later Prophets. (gr. 7-8). 6.95 (ISBN 0-317-70159-2); tchr's guide 12.50 (ISBN 0-317-70160-6); tchr's resource bk. 14.95 (ISBN 0-317-70161-4). Behrman.
Singer, Howard. With Mind & Heart. (gr. 8 up). 3.95x (ISBN 0-8381-0203-4, 10-203). United Syn Bk.
Teich, Shmuel. The Rishonim: Biographical Sketches of the Prominent Early Rabbinic Sages & Leaders from the Tenth-Fifteenth Centuries. Goldwurm, Hersh, ed. & intro. by. (Illus.). 224p. (gr. 7-8). 1982. 13.95 (ISBN 0-89906-452-3); pap. 10.95 (ISBN 0-89906-453-1). Mesorah Pubns.
Touger, Malka. Sefer Hamitzvot for Youth, Vols. 1 & 2. (gr. 7-10). 1988. 18.00 (ISBN 0-940118-26-2). Vol. 1, 248 Positive Commandments, 95p. Vol. 2, 365 Negative Commandments, 144p. Maznaim.
Wolff, Ferida. Pink Slippers, Bat Mitzvah Blues. (gr. 3-7). 1989. 13.95 (ISBN 0-8276-0332-0). JPS Phila.
Yedwab, Paul M. The Alef-Bet of Blessing. (Illus.). 80p. (Orig.). (gr. k-3). 1989. pap. text ed. 6.00x (ISBN 0-8074-0436-5, 101094). 5.00 (ISBN 0-8074-0461-6, 208029). UAHC.

JUDGES
see also Lawyers
Greene, Carol. Sandra Day O'Connor: First Woman on the Supreme Court. LC 81-18038. (Illus.). 32p. (gr. 1-4). 1982. PLB 13.27 (ISBN 0-516-03618-1). Childrens.
Woods, Harold & Woods, Geraldine. Equal Justice: A Biography of Sandra Day O'Connor. LC 84-23042. (Illus.). 128p. (gr. 6 up). 1985. PLB 12.95 (ISBN 0-87518-292-5, Dillon). Macmillan Child Grp.

JUDO
see also Karate
Barrett, Norman. Artes Marciales. LC 88-50361. (SPA., Illus.). 32p. (gr. k-4). 1990. PLB 11.40 (ISBN 0-531-07902-3). Watts.
—Martial Arts. (Illus.). 32p. (gr. 2 up). 1991. pap. 3.95 (ISBN 0-531-24617-5). Watts.
Gadd, Stephen & Smith, Tony. My First Judo Book. (Illus.). 80p. (gr. 4-7). 1991. pap. 11.95 (ISBN 1-85223-248-X, Pub. by Crowood UK). Trafalgar Sq.
Harman, Lori & Holm, John R. Judo Is for Me. (Illus.). 48p. (gr. 2-5). 1986. lib. bdg. 8.95 (ISBN 0-8225-1149-5). Lerner Pubns.
Harrington, Anthony P. Every Boy's Judo. (Illus.). (gr. 7 up). 11.95 (ISBN 0-87523-125-X). Emerson.
—Every Girl's Judo. (Illus.). (gr. 7 up). 11.95 (ISBN 0-87523-127-6). Emerson.
Kobayashi, Kiyoshi & Sharp, Harold E. Sport of Judo. LC 57-75. (Illus.). (gr. 9 up). 1957. pap. 9.95 (ISBN 0-8048-0542-3). C E Tuttle.
Neff, Fred. Basic Jujitsu Handbook. Reid, James, illus. LC 75-38472. 56p. (gr. 5 up). 1976. PLB 8.95 (ISBN 0-8225-1151-7). Lerner Pubns.
—Manual of Throws for Sport Judo & Self-Defense. Reid, James, illus. LC 75-38476. 56p. (gr. 5 up). 1976. PLB 8.95 (ISBN 0-8225-1155-X). Lerner Pubns.
Wood, Tim. Judo. Fairclough, Chris, photos by. (Illus.). 32p. (gr. k-4). 1990. PLB 10.40 (ISBN 0-531-14052-0). Watts.

JUGGLERS AND JUGGLING
Cooney, Barbara. The Little Juggler. Cooney, Barbara, illus. LC 61-10576. 48p. (gr. 5 up). Repr. of 1961 ed. 10.95 (ISBN 0-8038-4239-2). Hastings.
DePaola, Tomie. The Clown of God. De Paola, Tomie, illus. LC 78-3845. (gr. k up). 1978. 13.95 (ISBN 0-15-219175-5, HJ). HarBraceJ.
Humphrey, Ron. Juggling for Fun & Entertainment. LC 67-14278. (Illus.). (gr. 6 up). 1967. pap. 4.95 (ISBN 0-8048-1133-4). C E Tuttle.
Lehrman, Robert. Juggling. LC 81-48654. 256p. (gr. 7 up). 1982. HarpC Child Bks.
Meyer, Charles R. How to Be a Juggler. (Illus.). (gr. 4-7). 1977. 6.95 (ISBN 0-679-20407-5). McKay.
Pack, Robert. The Octopus Who Wanted to Juggle. Willard, Nancy, illus. (Orig.). (ps-7). 1990. text ed. 13. 95 (ISBN 0-913123-26-9). Galileo.
Temple, Nancy M. & Aronson, Rande. Juggling Is for Me. (Illus.). 48p. (gr. 2-5). 1986. lib. bdg. 8.95 (ISBN 0-8225-1146-0). Lerner Pubns.

JUNIPERUS OF ASSISI, BROTHER, 13TH CENTURY
Benedict, Rex. Oh, Brother Juniper. Berg, Joan, illus. (gr. 5-6). 1963. lib. bdg. 4.99 (ISBN 0-394-91457-0). Pantheon.

JUNK
see Waste Products

JURISPRUDENCE
see Law

JURISTS
see Lawyers

JURY
Kolanda, Jo & Curley, Patricia. Trial by Jury. Solomon, Maury, ed. (Illus.). 96p. (gr. 5 up). 1988. PLB 10.40 (ISBN 0-531-10610-1). Watts.

JUSTICE, ADMINISTRATION OF
see also Crime and Criminals
Alberton, Kathleen. The ABC's of Family Court: A Children's Guide. Clarke, Dorothy J., illus. LC 88-120423. 54p. (gr. 1-12). 1987. pap. 1.50 (ISBN 0-9619599-0-8). NYC Law Dept.
Green, Carl & Sanford, William. Judiciary. (Illus.). 96p. (gr. 7 up). 1990. lib. bdg. 18.60 (ISBN 0-86593-086-4); lib. bdg. 13.95s.p. Rourke Corp.

JUVENILE DELINQUENCY
see also Child Welfare
Alberton, Kathleen. The ABC's of Family Court: A Children's Guide. Clarke, Dorothy J., illus. LC 88-120423. 54p. (gr. 1-12). 1987. pap. 1.50 (ISBN 0-9619599-0-8). NYC Law Dept.
Barden, Renardo. Gangs. LC 89-1413. (Illus.). 48p. (gr. 4 up). 1989. 10.95 (ISBN 0-89686-440-5, Crestwood Hse). Macmillan Child Grp.

—Gangs. (Illus.). 64p. (gr. 7 up). 1990. lib. bdg. 15.93 (ISBN 0-86593-073-2); lib. bdg. 11.95s.p. (ISBN 0-685-36324-4). Rourke Corp.

Cruz, Nicky & Buckingham, Jamie. Run Baby Run. (gr. 9-12). 1984. pap. 3.50 (ISBN 0-515-09105-7). Jove Pubns.

Haskins, James. Street Gangs: Yesterday & Today. (Illus.). (gr. 6 up). 1977. pap. 4.95 (ISBN 0-8038-2662-1). Hastings.

Hyde, Margaret O. Juvenile Justice & Injustice. rev. ed. LC 82-20150. 128p. (gr. 7 up). 1983. PLB 12.90 (ISBN 0-531-04594-3). Watts.

Landau, Elaine. Teenage Violence. Steltenpohl, Jane, ed. (Illus.). 128p. (gr. 7 up). 1990. lib. bdg. 12.98 (ISBN 0-671-70153-3); pap. 5.95 (ISBN 0-671-70154-1). Messner.

Lang, Susan S. Teen Violence. (Illus.). 176p. (gr. 9-12). 1991. PLB 13.90 (ISBN 0-531-11057-5). Watts.

Riekes, Linda & Ackerly, Sally M. Juvenile Problems & Law. 2nd ed. (Illus.). 133p. (gr. 4-6). 1980. pap. text ed. 13.00 (ISBN 0-8299-1026-3). West Pub.

Street Gangs: Gaining Turf, Losing Ground. 176p. (gr. 7-12). 1991. PLB 16.95 (ISBN 0-8239-1332-5); pap. 8.95 (ISBN 0-8239-1333-3). Rosen Group.

Webb, Margot. Coping with Street Gangs. Rosen, Roger, ed. 64p. (gr. 7-12). 1990. lib. bdg. 12.95 (ISBN 0-8239-1071-7). Rosen Group.

JUVENILE DELINQUENCY–FICTION

Caldwell, E. S. She's Gone. Quigley, Ed, illus. LC 75-43158. 128p. (Orig.). (gr. 8-11). 1976. pap. 2.95 (ISBN 0-88243-893-X, 02-0893); tchr's. guide 4.50 (ISBN 0-88243-167-6, 32-0167). Gospel Pub.

Dana, Barbara. Crazy Eights. LC 77-25645. 208p. (gr. 7 up). 1978. PLB 12.89 (ISBN 0-06-021389-2). HarpC Child Bks.

Fox, Paula. How Many Miles to Babylon? Giovanopoulos, Paul, illus. LC 79-25802. 128p. (gr. 5-7). 1982. 12.95 (ISBN 0-02-735590-X, Bradbury Pr). Macmillan Child Grp.

Grey, Harry. The Hoods. 1987. Repr. lib. bdg. 21.95x (ISBN 0-89966-549-7). Buccaneer Bks.

Hinton, S. E. Rumble Fish. LC 75-8004. 112p. (gr. 7 up). 1975. pap. 13.95 (ISBN 0-385-28675-9). Delacorte.

Tunis, John R. City for Lincoln. 1989. pap. 3.95 (ISBN 0-15-218580-1). HarbraceJ.

JUVENILE LITERATURE

see Children'S Literature

K

K. K. K.

see Ku Klux Klan

KANGAROOS

Arnold, Caroline. Kangaroo. Hewett, Richard, illus. LC 86-18103. 48p. (gr. 2-5). 1987. 12.95 (ISBN 0-688-06480-9); lib. bdg. 12.88 (ISBN 0-688-06481-7, Morrow Jr Bks). Morrow Jr Bks.

Bender, Lionel. Kangaroos & Other Marsupials. FS-Aladdin Staff, ed. (Illus.). 32p. (gr. 1-6). 1988. PLB 11.90 (ISBN 0-531-17102-7, Gloucester Pr). Watts.

Dalmais. Kangaroo, Reading Level 3-4. (Illus.). 28p. (gr. 2-5). Date not set. PLB 14.60 (ISBN 0-86592-864-9). Rourke Corp.

Eugene, Toni. Koalas & Kangaroos: Strange Animals of Australia. Crump, Donald J., ed. LC 81-607859. 32p. (ps-3). 1981. lib. bdg. 10.95 (ISBN 0-87044-403-4); PLB 12.95 (ISBN 0-87044-408-5). Natl Geog.

Hogan, Paula Z. The Kangaroo. Mayo, Gretchen, illus. LC 79-13660. (gr. 1-4). 1979. PLB 16.67 (ISBN 0-8172-1504-2). Raintree Pubs.

—The Kangaroo. LC 79-13660. (Illus.). 32p. (gr. 1-4). 1981. PLB 27.99g incl. cassette (ISBN 0-8172-1843-2); cassette 14.00 (ISBN 0-685-09539-8). Raintree Pubs.

Petty, Kate. Kangaroos. (ps-3). 1990. PLB 10.40 (ISBN 0-531-17195-7). Watts.

Rau, Margaret. The Gray Kangaroo at Home. Hulsmann, Eva, illus. LC 77-14942. (gr. 5-8). 1978. lib. bdg. 6.99 (ISBN 0-394-93451-2). Knopf.

Sanford, William R. & Green, Carl R. The Kangaroo. (Illus.). 48p. (gr. 4-5). 1987. PLB 10.95 (ISBN 0-89686-322-0, Crestwood Hse). Macmillan Child Grp.

Saunier, Nadine. The Kangaroo. Wirth, Pascale, illus. 20p. (ps). 1989. 5.95 (ISBN 0-8120-5982-4). Barron.

Selsam, Millicent E. & Hunt, Joyce. A First Look at Kangaroos, Kaolas & Other Animals with Pouches. Springer, Harriet, illus. LC 85-3126. 32p. (gr. k-3). 1985. 9.95 (ISBN 0-8027-6600-5); PLB 12.85 (ISBN 0-8027-6579-3). Walker & Co.

Serventy, Vincent. Kangaroo. LC 84-17994. (Illus.). 24p. (gr. k-5). 1985. PLB 13.32 (ISBN 0-8172-2418-1). Raintree Pubs.

Stone, Lynn. Kangaroos. (Illus.). 24p. (gr. k-5). 1990. lib. bdg. 11.93 (ISBN 0-86593-058-9); lib. bdg. 8.95s.p. (ISBN 0-685-36371-6). Rourke Corp.

Wax, Wendy & Rowland, Della. Ten Things I Know about Kangaroos. Payne, Thomas, illus. 24p. 1989. 6.95 (ISBN 0-8092-4350-4, Calico Bks). Contemp Bks.

—Ten Things I Know about Penguins. Payne, Thomas, illus. 24p. 1989. 6.95 (ISBN 0-8092-4349-0, Calico Bks). Contemp Bks.

KANGAROOS–FICTION

Blume, Judy. The One in the Middle Is the Green Kangaroo. Aitken, Amy, illus. 48p. (gr. k-2). 1982. pap. 2.95 (ISBN 0-440-46731-4, YB). Dell.

Dahl, Roald. Matilda. Blake, Quentin, illus. 224p. (gr. 3-7). 1988. pap. 14.95 (ISBN 0-670-82439-9). Viking Child Bks.

Harper, Anita. It's Not Fair. Hellard, Susan, illus. LC 86-4950. 24p. (ps-k). 1986. 10.95 (ISBN 0-399-21365-1, Philomel). Putnam Pub Group.

—What Feels Best? Hellard, Susan, illus. LC 88-4173. 32p. (ps-1). 1988. 11.95 (ISBN 0-399-21567-0, Putnam). Putnam Pub Group.

Hunt, Robert. Marsu the Red Kangaroo. Producciones Ancora, illus. LC 72-736444. (gr. 2-5). 1978. pap. 29.95 6 bks. & 1 cass. (ISBN 0-89290-029-6); pap. 10.95 1 bk. & 1 cass. Soc for Visual.

Kipling, Rudyard. The Sing-Song of Old Man Kangaroo. Taylor, Michael C., illus. LC 85-22920. 32p. (gr. 1-5). 1986. 10.95 (ISBN 0-87226-073-9, Dist. by Har-Row). P Bedrick Bks.

—The Sing-Song of Old Man Kangaroo. Rowe, John A., illus. LC 90-7382. 32p. (gr. k up). 1990. 14.95 (ISBN 0-88708-152-5). Picture Bk Studio.

Leonard, Marcia & Duell. Little Kangaroo's Bad Day. (ps-7). 1987. pap. 2.75 (ISBN 0-553-15461-3). Bantam.

Mayer, Mercer. What Do You Do with a Kangaroo? Mayer, Mercer, illus. 48p. (ps-2). 1987. 2.95 (ISBN 0-590-40655-8, Blue Ribbon Bks). Scholastic Inc.

Payne, Emmy. Katy No-Pocket. (gr. 1-3). 1973. reinforced bdg. 13.95 (ISBN 0-395-17104-0). HM.

—Katy No-Pocket. Rey, H. A., illus. 32p. (gr. k-3). 1973. pap. 5.95 (ISBN 0-395-13717-9, Sandpiper). HM.

Roberts, Thom. Atlantic Free Balloon Race. (gr. 3-7). 1986. pap. 2.50 (ISBN 0-380-89868-3, Camelot). Avon.

KANSAS

Aylesworth, Thomas G. & Aylesworth, Virginia L. South Central (Louisiana, Arkansas, Missouri, Kansas, Oklahoma) (Illus.). 64p. (gr. 3 up). 1992. PLB 16.95 (ISBN 0-7910-1047-3). Chelsea Hse.

Carole Marsh Kansas Books, 31 bks. Set. 638.45 (ISBN 0-7933-1291-4). Gallopade Pub Group.

Carpenter, Allan. Kansas. new ed. LC 79-12433. (Illus.). 96p. (gr. 4 up). 1979. PLB 19.93 (ISBN 0-516-04116-9). Childrens.

Desmond, J. Kansas Boy. MacLennan, Kathy, ed. LC 79-67031. 140p. (gr. 4-12). 1979. pap. 4.95x perfect bound (ISBN 0-934044-02-3). Roush Bks.

Fradin, Dennis. Kansas: In Words & Pictures. Wahl, Richard, illus. LC 80-12576. 48p. (gr. 2-5). 1980. PLB 15.93 (ISBN 0-516-03916-4). Childrens.

Isern, Thomas & Wilson, Raymond. Kansas Land. (Illus.). 237p. (gr. 7). 1987. 22.00 (ISBN 0-685-24529-2, Peregrine Smith). Gibbs Smith Pub.

Kent, Zachary. Kansas. LC 90-35385. (Illus.). 144p. (gr. 4 up). 1990. PLB 25.27 (ISBN 0-516-00462-X). Childrens.

Marsh, Carole. Avast, Ye Slobs! Kansas Pirate Trivia. (Illus.). (gr. 3-12). 1990. PLB 19.95 (ISBN 0-7933-0472-5); pap. 14.95 (ISBN 0-7933-0471-7); computer disk 29.95 (ISBN 0-7933-0473-3). Gallopade Pub Group.

—The Beast & the Kansas Bed & Breakfast. (gr. 3-12). 1989. 19.95 (ISBN 1-55609-371-3); pap. 14.95 (ISBN 1-55609-372-1); bk. on computer disk 29.95 (ISBN 1-55609-373-X). Gallopade Pub Group.

—The Hard-to-Believe-But-True! Book of Kansas History, Mystery, Trivia, Legend, Lore, Humor & More. (Illus.). (gr. 3-12). 1990. PLB 19.95 (ISBN 0-7933-0469-5); pap. 14.95 (ISBN 0-7933-0468-7); computer disk 29.95 (ISBN 0-7933-0470-9). Gallopade Pub Group.

—If My Kansas Mama Ran the World. (gr. 3-12). 1989. 19.95 (ISBN 1-55609-374-8); pap. 14.95 (ISBN 1-55609-375-6); bk. on computer disk 29.95 (ISBN 1-55609-376-4). Gallopade Pub Group.

—Kansas & Other State Greats (Biographies) (gr. 3-12). 1989. 19.95 (ISBN 1-55609-362-4); pap. 14.95 (ISBN 1-55609-363-2); bk. on computer disk 29.95 (ISBN 1-55609-364-0). Gallopade Pub Group.

—Kansas Bandits, Bushwackers, Outlaws, Crooks, Devils, Ghosts, Desperadoes & Other Assorted & Sundry Characters! (Illus.). (gr. 3-12). 1990. PLB 19.95 (ISBN 0-7933-0454-7); pap. 14.95 (ISBN 0-7933-0453-9); computer disk 29.95 (ISBN 0-7933-0455-5). Gallopade Pub Group.

—Kansas Classic Christmas Trivia: Stories, Recipes, Activities, Legends, Lore & More! (Illus.). (gr. 3-12). 1990. PLB 19.95 (ISBN 0-7933-0457-1); pap. 14.95 (ISBN 0-7933-0456-3); computer disk 29.95 (ISBN 0-7933-0458-X). Gallopade Pub Group.

—Kansas Coastales. 1989. PLB 19.95 (ISBN 1-55609-365-9); pap. 14.95 (ISBN 1-55609-366-7); bk. on computer disk 29.95 (ISBN 1-55609-367-5). Gallopade Pub Group.

—The Kansas Hot Air Balloon Mystery. (Illus.). (gr. 2-9). 1990. 19.95 (ISBN 0-7933-2462-9); pap. 14.95 (ISBN 0-7933-2463-7); computer disk 29.95 (ISBN 0-7933-2464-5). Gallopade Pub Group.

—Kansas "Jography" A Fun Run Thru Your State. (gr. 3-12). 1989. PLB 19.95 (ISBN 1-55609-353-5); pap. 14.95 (ISBN 1-55609-354-3); bk. on computer disk 29.95 (ISBN 1-55609-355-1). Gallopade Pub Group.

—Kansas Kid's Cookbook: Recipes, How-to, History, Lore & More! (Illus.). (gr. 3-12). 1990. PLB 19.95 (ISBN 0-7933-0466-0); pap. 14.95 (ISBN 0-7933-0465-2); computer disk 29.95 (ISBN 0-7933-0467-9). Gallopade Pub Group.

—Kansas Quiz Bowl Crash Course. (gr. 3-12). 1989. PLB 19.95 (ISBN 1-55609-359-4); pap. 14.95 (ISBN 1-55609-360-8); bk. on computer disk 29.95 (ISBN 1-55609-361-6). Gallopade Pub Group.

—Kansas School Trivia: An Amazing & Fascinating Look at Our State's Teachers, Schools & Students! (Illus.). (gr. 3-12). 1990. PLB 19.95 (ISBN 0-7933-0463-6); pap. 14.95 (ISBN 0-7933-0462-8); computer disk 29.95 (ISBN 0-7933-0464-4). Gallopade Pub Group.

—Kansas Silly Basketball Sportsmysteries, Vol. I. (Illus.). (gr. 3-12). 1990. PLB 19.95 (ISBN 0-7933-0460-1); pap. 14.95 (ISBN 0-7933-0459-8); computer disk 29.95 (ISBN 0-7933-0461-X). Gallopade Pub Group.

—Kansas Silly Basketball Sportsmysteries, Vol. II. (Illus.). (gr. 3-12). 1990. PLB 19.95 (ISBN 0-7933-1640-5); pap. 14.95 (ISBN 0-7933-1641-3); computer disk 29.95 (ISBN 0-7933-1642-1). Gallopade Pub Group.

—Kansas Silly Football Mystery, Vol. I. (gr. 3-12). 1989. PLB 19.95 (ISBN 1-55609-368-3); pap. 14.95 (ISBN 1-55609-369-1); bk. on computer disk 29.95 (ISBN 1-55609-370-5). Gallopade Pub Group.

—Kansas Silly Football Mystery, Vol. II. (gr. 3-12). 1989. PLB 19.95 (ISBN 1-55609-377-2); pap. 14.95 (ISBN 0-318-41972-6); bk. on computer disk 29.95 (ISBN 1-55609-379-9). Gallopade Pub Group.

—Kansas Silly Trivia. (gr. 3-12). 1989. PLB 19.95 (ISBN 0-318-41973-4); pap. 14.95 (ISBN 1-55609-351-9); bk. on computer disk 29.95 (ISBN 1-55609-352-7). Gallopade Pub Group.

—Kansas's (Most Devastating!) Disasters & (Most Calamitous!) Catastrophies! (Illus.). (gr. 3-12). 1990. PLB 19.95 (ISBN 0-7933-0451-2); pap. 14.95 (ISBN 0-7933-0450-4); computer disk 29.95 (ISBN 0-7933-0452-0). Gallopade Pub Group.

—Lets Quilt Kansas. (gr. 3-12). 1989. PLB 19.95 (ISBN 1-55609-356-X); pap. 14.95 (ISBN 1-55609-357-8); bk. on computer disk 29.95 (ISBN 1-55609-358-6). Gallopade Pub Group.

Thompson, Kathleen. Kansas. LC 87-16406. 48p. (gr. 4 up). 1987. 17.32 (ISBN 0-86514-464-8); cancelled tchr's. study guide (ISBN 0-86514-604-7); cancelled Beta video (ISBN 0-86514-091-X); cancelled VHS video (ISBN 0-317-67075-1); cancelled 3/4" video (ISBN 0-86514-241-6). Raintree Pubs.

KANSAS–FICTION

Rossiter, Phyllis. Moxie. LC 90-30027. 192p. (gr. 5 up). 1990. 13.95 (ISBN 0-02-777831-2, Four Winds). Macmillan Child Grp.

Schlein, Miriam. Big Talk. rev. ed. Auclair, Joan, illus. LC 89-35343. 32p. (ps-1). 1990. 12.95 (ISBN 0-02-781231-6, Bradbury Pr). Macmillan Child Grp.

Wilder, Laura I. Little House on the Prairie. rev. ed. Williams, Garth, illus. LC 52-7526. 238p. (gr. 3-7). 1953. 14.95i (ISBN 0-06-026445-4); PLB 14.89 (ISBN 0-06-026446-2). HarpC Child Bks.

KARATE

Brightfield, Richard. Master of Karate. (gr. 9-12). 1990. pap. 2.95 (ISBN 0-553-28202-6). Bantam.

Brimner, Larry D. Karate. Rakos, Jennie, ed. (Illus.). 72p. (gr. 7-9). 1988. PLB 10.40 (ISBN 0-531-10480-X). Watts.

Cho, Sihak H. Better Karate for Boys. (Illus.). 64p. (gr. 3-7). 1972. 9.95 (ISBN 0-396-06568-6, Putnam). Putnam Pub Group.

Hiller, B. B. & Kamen, Robert M. The Karate Kid II. (Illus.). 144p. (Orig.). (gr. 4 up). 1986. pap. 2.50 (ISBN 0-590-40292-7, Point). Scholastic Inc.

Kozuki, Russell. Junior Karate. (Illus.). (gr. 4-6). 1986. pap. 2.50 (ISBN 0-671-62489-X, Archway). PB.

—Junior Karate. LC 71-167665. (Illus.). 128p. (gr. 11 up). 1971. 12.95 (ISBN 0-8069-4446-3); PLB 15.69 (ISBN 0-8069-4447-1). Sterling.

—Karate for Young People. LC 73-93590. (Illus.). 128p. (gr. 11 up). 1982. pap. 5.95 (ISBN 0-8069-7560-1). Sterling.

Lawrence, Robb. Karatesaurus. 1989. pap. 1.50 (ISBN 0-590-42308-8). Scholastic Inc.

Lewis, Tom G. Karate for Kids. 120p. (Orig.). (gr. 2-10). 1980. pap. 3.95 (ISBN 0-89826-005-1). Natl Paperback.

Nardi, Thomas J. Karate Basics. Petronella, Mike, illus. LC 84-6929. 48p. (gr. 3-7). 1989. PLB 11.95 (ISBN 0-671-66288-0). S&S Trade.

Neff, Fred. Basic Karate Handbook. Reid, James, illus. LC 75-38471. 56p. (gr. 5 up). 1976. PLB 8.95 (ISBN 0-8225-1150-9). Lerner Pubns.

—Karate Is for Me. Reid, James E., photos by. LC 79-16900. (Illus.). 48p. (gr. 2-5). 1980. PLB 8.95 (ISBN 0-8225-1090-1). Lerner Pubns.

Nishiyama, Hidetaka & Brown, Richard C. Karate: Art of Empty-Hand Fighting. (Illus.). (gr. 9 up). 1991. pap. 16.95 (ISBN 0-8048-1668-9). C E Tuttle.

Parulski, George R., Jr. Action Karate. LC 85-26257. (Illus.). 128p. (gr. 2 up). 1987. 13.95 (ISBN 0-8069-6268-2). Sterling.

Pfluger, A. Karate: Basic Principles. Kuttner, Paul & Cunningham, Dale S., trs. LC 67-27760. (Illus.). (gr. 8 up). 1969. Repr. of 1967 ed. 6.95 (ISBN 0-8069-4432-3); PLB 7.49 (ISBN 0-8069-4433-1). Sterling.

Queen, J. Allen. Fighting Karate. LC 88-22087. (Illus.). 128p. (gr. 5-9). 1989. 14.95 (ISBN 0-8069-6838-9). Sterling.

—Fighting Karate. LC 88-22087. (Illus.). 128p. (gr. 3-10). 1990. pap. 6.95 (ISBN 0-8069-6839-7). Sterling.

—Karate Handbook. LC 85-28096. (Illus.). 128p. (gr. 8 up). 1986. 14.95 (ISBN 0-8069-6286-0). Sterling.

—Karate Handbook. LC 85-28096. (Illus.). 128p. (gr. 2 up). 1987. pap. 7.95 (ISBN 0-8069-6288-7). Sterling.

—Karate to Win. LC 87-36572. (Illus.). 128p. (Orig.). (gr. 7 up). 1989. pap. 7.95 (ISBN 0-8069-6685-8). Sterling.

—Total Karate. LC 89-49313. (Illus.). 128p. 1990. 14.95 (ISBN 0-8069-6714-5). Sterling.

Sewalson, Don. Street Self-Defense. Sewalson, Don, illus. 81p. (gr. 6-12). 1986. pap. 6.75 (ISBN 0-938419-01-3). DM Pub.

—Street Self-Defense. Sewalson, Don, illus. 63p. (gr. 6-12). 1986. pap. 6.75 (ISBN 0-938419-03-X). DM Pub.

—Street Self-Defense. Sewalson, Don, illus. 58p. (gr. 6-12). 1986. pap. 6.75 (ISBN 0-938419-02-1). DM Pub.

—Street Self-Defense: Complete Edition. Sewalson, Don, illus. 193p. (gr. 6-12). 1986. 27.00 (ISBN 0-938419-04-8); pap. 16.95 (ISBN 0-938419-00-5). DM Pub.

Teitelbaum, Michael. Jr. Karate, A Photo-Fact Book. (Illus.). 24p. (Orig.). 1988. pap. 1.95 (ISBN 0-942025-47-4). Kidsbks.

—Tae Kwon Do. (Illus.). 24p. (Orig.). 1990. pap. 2.50 (ISBN 0-942025-88-1). Kidsbks.

Webster-Doyle, Terrence. Facing the Double Edged Sword: The Art of Karate for Young People. Cameron, Rod, illus. LC 73-83919. 90p. (Orig.). (gr. 5-9). 1988. 14.95 (ISBN 0-942941-17-9); pap. 9.95 (ISBN 0-942941-16-0). Atrium Pubns.

Yates, Keith D. & Robbins, H. Bryan. Korean Karate. LC 86-23150. (Illus.). 128p. (gr. 4-12). 1987. 12.95 (ISBN 0-8069-6458-8). Sterling.

—Korean Karate. LC 86-23150. (Illus.). 128p. (Orig.). (gr. 4-12). 1988. pap. 5.95 (ISBN 0-8069-6836-2). Sterling.

KARTS AND KARTING

Fichter, George S. Karts & Karting. (Illus.). 72p. (gr. 4 up). 1982. PLB 10.40 (ISBN 0-531-04394-0). Watts.

Radlauer, Ed. Karting Winners. LC 82-1129. (Illus.). (gr. 3-6). 1982. PLB 13.27 (ISBN 0-516-07811-9). Childrens.

Washington, Rosemary G. Karting: Racing's Fast Little Cars. LC 80-12385. (Illus.). 48p. (gr. 4-9). 1980. PLB 9.95 (ISBN 0-8225-0435-9). Lerner Pubns.

KELLER, HELEN ADAMS, 1880-1968

Adler, David A. A Picture Book of Helen Keller. Wallner, John & Wallner, Alexandra, illus. LC 89-77510. 32p. (gr. k-3). 1990. reinforced 14.95 (ISBN 0-8234-0818-3). Holiday.

Davidson, Margaret. Helen Keller. Watson, Wendy, illus. 64p. (gr. k-3). 1973. pap. 2.50 (ISBN 0-590-41745-2). Scholastic Inc.

—Helen Keller. 1989. pap. 2.50 (ISBN 0-590-42404-1). Scholastic Inc.

Gibson, William. The Miracle Worker. (gr. 6-9). 1984. pap. 3.50 (ISBN 0-553-24778-6). Bantam.

Graff, Stewart. Helen Keller. (ps-3). 1991. pap. 2.95 (ISBN 0-440-40439-8). Dell.

Graff, Stewart & Graff, Polly A. Helen Keller. Frame, Paul, illus. 80p. (gr. 2-7). 1980. pap. 2.95 (ISBN 0-440-43566-8, YB). Dell.

—Helen Keller: Toward the Light. (Illus.). 80p. (gr. 2-6). 1992. Repr. of 1965 ed. PLB 12.95 (ISBN 0-7910-1412-6). Chelsea Hse.

Hunter, Nigel. Helen Keller. LC 85-71721. (Illus.). 32p. (gr. 4-8). 1986. PLB 11.90 (ISBN 0-531-18031-X, Pub. by Bookwright Pr). Watts.

Johnson, Ann D. The Value of Determination: The Story of Helen Keller. 2nd ed. Pileggi, Steven, illus. LC 76-54762. 64p. (gr. k-6). 1976. 9.95 (ISBN 0-916392-07-4, Pub. by Value Communications). Oak Tree Pubns.

Keller, Helen. Story of My Life. Barnett, M. R., intro. by. (gr. 8 up). pap. 2.95 (ISBN 0-8049-0070-1, CL-70). Airmont.

—The Story of My Life. 160p. (gr. 7 up). Teaching Guide. 1.25 (ISBN 0-590-40982-4). Scholastic Inc.

Kudlinski, Kathleen V. Helen Keller: A Light for the Blind. Diamond, Donna, illus. 64p. (gr. 2-6). 1989. pap. 10.95 (ISBN 0-670-82460-7). Viking Child Bks.

Peare, Catherine O. The Helen Keller Story. LC 59-10979. 192p. (gr. 4-6). 1990. PLB 13.89 (ISBN 0-690-04793-2, Crowell Jr Bks). HarpC Child Bks.

—The Helen Keller Story. large type ed. (Illus.). 176p. (gr. 4-8). 1991. Repr. of 1959 ed. PLB 17.95 (ISBN 1-55905-084-5). Grey Castle.

Sabin, Francene. Courage of Helen Keller. LC 81-23109. (Illus.). 48p. (gr. 4-6). 1982. PLB 10.79 (ISBN 0-89375-754-3); pap. text ed. 2.95 (ISBN 0-89375-755-1). Troll Assocs.

Santrey, Laurence. Helen Keller. Frenck, Hal, illus. LC 84-2682. 32p. (gr. 3-6). 1985. PLB 9.49 (ISBN 0-8167-0156-3); pap. text ed. 2.95 (ISBN 0-8167-0157-1). Troll Assocs.

Tames, Richard. Helen Keller. (Illus.). 32p. (gr. 5-6). 1989. PLB 11.90 (ISBN 0-531-10764-7). Watts.

—Helen Keller. (Illus.). 32p. (gr. 5 up). 1991. pap. 3.95 (ISBN 0-531-24609-4). Watts.

Wepman, Dennis. Helen Keller. Horner, Matina, intro. by. (Illus.). 112p. (Orig.). (gr. 5 up). 1988. 17.95 (ISBN 1-55546-662-1); pap. 9.95 (ISBN 0-7910-0417-1). Chelsea Hse.

Wilkie, Katharine E. Helen Keller: From Tragedy to Triumph. Doremus, Robert, illus. LC 86-10719. 192p. (gr. 2-6). 1986. pap. 3.95 (ISBN 0-02-041980-5, Aladdin). Macmillan Child Grp.

Wilkie, Katherine E. Helen Keller: From Tragedy to Triumph. new ed. LC 82-17859. (Illus.). 196p. (Orig.). (gr. 2 up). 1983. pap. write for info. (ISBN 0-672-52749-9). Macmillan Child Grp.

KENNEDY, JOHN FITZGERALD, PRESIDENT U. S. 1917-1963

Anderson, Catherine C. John F. Kennedy. (Illus.). 112p. (gr. 5 up). 1991. PLB 15.95 (ISBN 0-8225-4904-2). Lerner Pubns.

Denenberg, Barry. John Fitzgerald Kennedy: America's 35th President. 128p. (gr. 5-8). 1988. pap. 2.75 (ISBN 0-590-41344-9). Scholastic Inc.

Falkof, Lucille. John F. Kennedy: 35th President of the United States. Young, Richard G., ed. LC 87-35954. (Illus.). (gr. 5-9). 1988. PLB 17.26 (ISBN 0-944483-03-8). Garrett Ed Corp.

Frisbee, Lucy P. John Fitzgerald Kennedy: America's Youngest President. Fiorentinl, Al, illus. 192p. (gr. 2-6). 1986. pap. 3.95 (ISBN 0-02-041990-2, Aladdin). Macmillan Child Grp.

Frolick, S. J. Once There Was a President. rev. ed. LC 80-69972. 64p. (gr. 3-7). 1980. pap. 6.95 (ISBN 0-9605426-0-4). Black Star Pub.

Graves, Charles P. John F. Kennedy. Frame, Paul, illus. 80p. (gr. 1-7). 1981. pap. 2.95 (ISBN 0-440-44242-7, YB). Dell.

John F. Kennedy: Mini Play. (gr. 8 up). 1977. 6.50 (ISBN 0-89550-372-7). Stevens & Shea.

Kent, Zachary. John F. Kennedy. (Illus.). (gr. 3 up). 1989. PLB 17.27 (ISBN 0-516-41390-2); pap. 6.95 (ISBN 0-318-41757-X). Childrens.

Levine, I. E. John Kennedy: Young Man in the White House. large type ed. (Illus.). 176p. (gr. 4-8). 1991. Repr. of 1964 ed. PLB 17.95 (ISBN 1-55905-085-3). Grey Castle.

Mills, Judie. John F. Kennedy. Kline, M., ed. LC 87-29470. (Illus.). 384p. (gr. 7-12). 1988. PLB 16.90 (ISBN 0-531-10520-2). Watts.

—John F. Kennedy. 1988. 14.95 (ISBN 0-531-15086-0). Watts.

Smith, Kathie B. John F. Kennedy. Seward, James, illus. LC 86-33863. 24p. (gr. 4-6). 1987. lib. bdg. 7.98 (ISBN 0-671-64602-8); PLB 5.99s.p. (ISBN 0-685-18831-0). Messner.

—John F. Kennedy. (gr. k-5). 1987. pap. 2.25 (ISBN 0-671-64025-9, Little Simon). S&S Trade.

White, Nancy B. Meet John F. Kennedy. (Illus.). (gr. 2-5). 1965. 6.95 (ISBN 0-394-80059-1, Random Juv); lib. bdg. 8.99 (ISBN 0-394-90059-6). Random.

KENNEDY, JOHN FITZGERALD, PRESIDENT U. S. 1917-1963–ASSASSINATION

Donnelly, Judy. Who Shot the President? The Death of John F. Kennedy. LC 88-4418. (Illus.). 48p. (Orig.). (gr. 2-4). 1988. lib. bdg. 6.99 (ISBN 0-394-99944-4, Random Juv); pap. 2.95 (ISBN 0-394-89944-X). Random.

Hamilton, Sue. The Assassination of a President: John F. Kennedy. Hamilton, John, ed. (Illus.). 32p. (gr. 4). 1990. PLB 11.95 (ISBN 0-939179-55-5). Abdo & Dghtrs.

Hoare, Stephen. The Assassination of John F. Kennedy. (gr. 7 up). 1989. 19.95 (ISBN 0-85219-766-7, Pub. by Batsford England). Trafalgar Sq.

Waggoner, Jeffrey. The Assassination of President Kennedy: Opposing Viewpoints. LC 89-37442. (Illus.). 112p. (gr. 3-10). 1989. PLB 13.95 (ISBN 0-89908-068-5). Greenhaven.

KENNEDY, ROBERT FRANCIS, 1925-1968

Petrillo, Daniel J. Robert Kennedy. Schlesinger, Arthur M., Jr., intro. by. (Illus.). 112p. (Orig.). (gr. 5 up). 1989. 17.95 (ISBN 1-55546-840-3); pap. 9.95 (ISBN 0-7910-0581-X). Chelsea Hse.

KENNEDY, ROBERT FRANCIS, 1925-1968–ASSASSINATION

Hamilton, Sue. The Killing of a Candidate: Robert F. Kennedy. Hamilton, John, ed. (Illus.). 32p. (gr. 4). 1989. PLB 11.95 (ISBN 0-939179-57-1). Abdo & Dghtrs.

Stein, R. Conrad. The Story of the Assassination of John F. Kennedy. Neely, Keith, illus. LC 85-10936. 31p. (gr. 3-4). 1985. PLB 13.27 (ISBN 0-516-04693-4). Childrens.

KENNY, ELIZABETH, 1886-1952

Crofford, Emily. Healing Warrior: A Story about Sister Elizabeth Kenny. Ritz, Karen, illus. 64p. (gr. 3-6). 1989. PLB 9.95 (ISBN 0-87614-382-6). Carolrhoda Bks.

KENTUCKY

Carpenter, Allan. Kentucky. new ed. LC 79-12696. (Illus.). 96p. (gr. 4 up). 1979. PLB 19.93 (ISBN 0-516-04117-7). Childrens.

Fradin, Dennis. Kentucky: In Words & Pictures. Wahl, Richard, illus. LC 80-25810. 48p. (gr. 2-5). 1981. PLB 15.93 (ISBN 0-516-03917-2). Childrens.

Marsh, Carole. Avast, Ye Slobs! Kentucky Pirate Trivia. (Illus.). (gr. 3-8). 1990. PLB 19.95 (ISBN 0-7933-0496-2); pap. 14.95 (ISBN 0-7933-0495-4); disk 29.95. Gallopade Pub Group.

—The Beast of the Kentucky Bed & Breakfast. (Illus.). (gr. 3-8). 1990. PLB 19.95 (ISBN 0-7933-1650-2); pap. 14.95 (ISBN 0-7933-1651-0); disk 29.95 (ISBN 0-7933-1652-9). Gallopade Pub Group.

—Carole Marsh Kentucky Books, 31 bks. (Illus.). (gr. 3-8). 1990. Set. PLB 638.45 (ISBN 0-7933-1292-2). Gallopade Pub Group.

—The Hard-to-Believe-But-True! Book of Kentucky History, Mystery, Trivia, Legend, Lore, Humor & More. (Illus.). (gr. 3-8). 1990. PLB 19.95 (ISBN 0-7933-0493-8); pap. 14.95 (ISBN 0-7933-0492-X); disk 29.95 (ISBN 0-7933-0494-6). Gallopade Pub Group.

—If My Kentucky Mama Ran the World! (Illus.). (gr. 3-8). 1990. lib. bdg. 19.95 (ISBN 0-7933-1655-3); pap. 14.95 (ISBN 0-7933-1656-1); disk 29.95 (ISBN 0-7933-1657-X). Gallopade Pub Group.

—Kentucky & Other State Greats (Biographies) (Illus.). (gr. 3-8). 1990. PLB 19.95 (ISBN 1-55609-448-5); pap. 14.95 (ISBN 1-55609-447-7); disk 29.95 (ISBN 0-7933-1658-8). Gallopade Pub Group.

—Kentucky Bandits, Bushwackers, Outlaws, Crooks, Devils, Ghosts, Desperadoes & Other Assorted & Sundry Characters! (Illus.). (gr. 3-8). 1990. PLB 19.95 (ISBN 0-7933-0478-4); pap. 14.95 (ISBN 0-7933-0477-6); disk 29.95 (ISBN 0-7933-0479-2). Gallopade Pub Group.

—Kentucky Classic Christmas Trivia: Stories, Recipes, Activities, Legends, Lore & More! (Illus.). (gr. 3-8). 1990. PLB 19.95 (ISBN 0-7933-0481-4); pap. 14.95 (ISBN 0-7933-0480-6); disk 29.95 (ISBN 0-7933-0482-2). Gallopade Pub Group.

—Kentucky Coastales. (Illus.). (gr. 3-8). 1990. PLB 19.95 (ISBN 1-55609-444-2); pap. 14.95 (ISBN 1-55609-443-4); disk 29.95 (ISBN 0-7933-1654-5). Gallopade Pub Group.

—The Kentucky Hot Air Balloon Mystery. (Illus.). (gr. 2-9). 1990. 19.95 (ISBN 0-7933-2471-8); pap. 14.95 (ISBN 0-7933-2472-6); computer disk 29.95 (ISBN 0-7933-2473-4). Gallopade Pub Group.

—Kentucky "Jography" A Fun Run Thru Our State! (Illus.). (gr. 3-8). 1990. PLB 19.95 (ISBN 1-55609-439-6); pap. 14.95 (ISBN 1-55609-109-5); disk 29.95 (ISBN 0-7933-1644-8). Gallopade Pub Group.

—Kentucky Kid's Cookbook: Recipes, How-To, History, Lore & More! (Illus.). (gr. 3-8). 1990. PLB 19.95 (ISBN 0-7933-0490-3); pap. 14.95 (ISBN 0-7933-0489-X); disk 29.95 (ISBN 0-7933-0491-1). Gallopade Pub Group.

—Kentucky Quiz Bowl Crash Course! (Illus.). (gr. 3-8). 1990. PLB 19.95 (ISBN 1-55609-446-9); pap. 14.95 (ISBN 1-55609-445-0); disk 29.95 (ISBN 0-7933-1653-7). Gallopade Pub Group.

—Kentucky School Trivia: An Amazing & Fascinating Look at Our State's Teachers, Schools & Students! (Illus.). (gr. 3-8). 1990. PLB 19.95 (ISBN 0-7933-0487-3); pap. 14.95 (ISBN 0-7933-0486-5); disk 29.95 (ISBN 0-7933-0488-1). Gallopade Pub Group.

—Kentucky Silly Basketball Sportsmysteries, Vol. I. (Illus.). (gr. 3-8). 1990. PLB 19.95 (ISBN 0-7933-0484-9); pap. 14.95 (ISBN 0-7933-0483-0); disk 29.95 (ISBN 0-7933-0485-7). Gallopade Pub Group.

—Kentucky Silly Basketball Sportsmysteries, Vol. II. (Illus.). (gr. 3-8). 1990. PLB 19.95 (ISBN 0-7933-1659-6); pap. 14.95 (ISBN 0-7933-1660-X); disk 29.95 (ISBN 0-7933-1661-8). Gallopade Pub Group.

—Kentucky Silly Football Sportsmysteries, Vol. I. (Illus.). (gr. 3-8). 1990. PLB 19.95 (ISBN 1-55609-442-6); pap. 14.95 (ISBN 1-55609-441-8); disk 29.95 (ISBN 0-7933-1646-4). Gallopade Pub Group.

—Kentucky Silly Football Sportsmysteries, Vol. II. (Illus.). (gr. 3-8). 1990. PLB 19.95 (ISBN 0-7933-1647-2); pap. 14.95 (ISBN 0-7933-1648-0); disk 29.95 (ISBN 0-7933-1649-9). Gallopade Pub Group.

—Kentucky Silly Trivia! (gr. 3-8). 1990. PLB 19.95 (ISBN 1-55609-438-8); pap. 14.95 (ISBN 1-55609-040-4); disk 29.95 (ISBN 0-7933-1643-X). Gallopade Pub Group.

—Kentucky's (Most Devastating!) Disasters & (Most Calamitous!) Catastrophies! LC 7933000476000008. (Illus.). (gr. 3-8). 1990. PLB 19.95 (ISBN 0-7933-0475-X); pap. 14.95 (ISBN 0-7933-0474-1); disk 29.95. Gallopade Pub Group.

Ryen, Dag. Traces: The Story of Lexington's Past. Crow, James L. & Finkel, Becky, illus. 177p. (gr. 4 up). 1987. text ed. 13.95 (ISBN 0-912839-08-2). Lexington-Fayette.

Stuart, Jesse. Kentucky Is My Land. Miller, Jim W., afterword by. 107p. (gr. 10 up). 1987. Repr. of 1952 ed. 10.95 (ISBN 0-945084-01-3). J Stuart Found.

—The Thread That Runs So True. 1977. lib. bdg. 30.00 (ISBN 0-684-15160-X, Scribner); pap. 8.95 (ISBN 0-684-71904-5, Scribner). Macmillan.

Turner Educational Services, Inc. Staff, et al. Kentucky. 48p. (gr. 3 up). 1986. PLB 17.32 (ISBN 0-86514-453-2); pap. 9.27 (ISBN 0-86514-528-8); cancelled Beta video (ISBN 0-86514-078-2); cancelled VHS video (ISBN 0-86514-153-3); cancelled 3/4" video (ISBN 0-86514-228-9); cancelled tchr's. study guide; cancelled student activity bk. (ISBN 0-86514-378-1); cancelled index. Raintree Pubs.

KENTUCKY–FICTION

Cannon, Bettie. A Bellsong for Sarah Raines. LC 87-4299. 192p. (gr. 7 up). 1987. 13.95 (ISBN 0-684-18839-2, Scribners Young Read). Macmillan Child Grp.

Green, Michelle Y. Willie Pearl. Date not set. write for info (ISBN 0-9627697-0-3). W Ruth Co.

Hines, Jane B. Kentucky Boy. Graves, Helen, ed. Taylor, Neil, illus. LC 86-40281. 155p. (Orig.). (gr. 4-8). 1986. pap. 7.95 (ISBN 1-55523-033-4). Winston-Derek.

Stiles, Martha B. Kate of Still Waters. LC 90-5546. 240p. (gr. 4-7). 1990. 14.95 (ISBN 0-02-788395-7, Mcmillan Child Bk). Macmillan Child Grp.

Stuart, Jesse. Hie to the Hunters. 5th ed. Herndon, Jerry A. & Zornes, Rockyintro. by. 270p. (gr. 8 up). 1988. 20.00 (ISBN 0-945084-06-4). J Stuart Found.
—Plowshare in Heaven. 2nd ed. Herndon, Jerry A., et al, eds. LC 90-62718. (Illus.). 288p. (gr. 7 up). 1991. Repr. of 1958 ed. 20.00 (ISBN 0-945084-21-8). J Stuart Found.

KENYA

Adamson, Joy. Born Free: A Lioness of Two Worlds. (Illus.). (gr. 9 up). 1970. Pantheon.
Bailey, Donna & Sproule, Anna. Kenya. LC 90-9644. (Illus.). 32p. (gr. 2-5). 1990. PLB 14.64 (ISBN 0-8114-2563-0). Steck-V.
Lerner Publications, Department of Geography Staff. Kenya in Pictures. (Illus.). 64p. (gr. 5 up). 1988. 12.95 (ISBN 0-8225-1830-9). Lerner Pubns.
Lye, Keith. Take a Trip to Kenya. LC 85-50163. (Illus.). 32p. (gr. 1-6). 1985. PLB 7.99 (ISBN 0-531-10011-1). Watts.
McLean, Virginia O. & Klyce, Katherine P. Kenya, Jambo! LC 88-63987. (Illus.). 36p. (gr. k-6). 1989. 15.95 (ISBN 0-9606046-4-2); Incl. cassette. pap. 11.95 (ISBN 0-9606046-5-0). Redbird.
Maren, Michael. The Land & People of Kenya. LC 88-22959. (Illus.). 208p. (gr. 6 up). 1989. 14.95 (ISBN 0-397-32334-4, Lipp Jr Bks); PLB 14.89 (ISBN 0-397-32335-2, Lipp Jr Bks). HarpC Child Bks.
Stein, R. Conrad. Kenya. LC 85-14949. (Illus.). 127p. (gr. 4-6). 1985. PLB 25.27 (ISBN 0-516-02770-0). Childrens.

KEPLER, JOHANNES, 1571-1630

Tiner, John H. Johannes Kepler: Giant of Faith & Science. Burke, Rod, illus. LC 77-558. (gr. 3-6). 1977. pap. 6.95 (ISBN 0-915134-11-X). Mott Media.

KEROSENE

see Petroleum

KEY, FRANCIS SCOTT, 1779-1843

Collins, David. Francis Scott Key. Van Seversen, Joe, illus. 113p. (gr. 3-6). 1982. pap. 6.95 (ISBN 0-915134-91-8). Mott Media.

KEYNES, JOHN MAYNARD, 1883-1946

Victor, R. F. John Maynard Keynes: Father of Modern Economics. Rahmas, D. Steve, ed. 32p. (Orig.). (gr. 7-12). 1972. lib. bdg. 4.20 incl. catalog cards (ISBN 0-87157-517-5); pap. 2.95 vinyl laminated covers (ISBN 0-87157-017-3). SamHar Pr.

KEYS

see Locks and Keys

KIBBUTZ

see Collective Settlements

KINDERGARTEN

Carson, Patti & DEllosa, Janet. Pre-School & Kindergarten Skills. Carson, Patti & Dellosa, Janet, illus. 24p. (ps-k). 1984. pap. 1.98 (ISBN 0-88724-072-0, CD7015). Carson-Dellos.
Forte, Imogene. Think about It! Kindergarten. (Illus.). 80p. (ps-k). 1981. pap. text ed. 7.95 (ISBN 0-913916-96-X, IP-96X). Incentive Pubn.
Gagnon, Constance. Help! for Preschoolers. 64p. (ps). 1982. 4.95 (ISBN 0-86653-061-4, GA 412). Good Apple.
Howe, James. When You Go to Kindergarten. Imershein, Betsy, photos by. LC 85-18055. (Illus.). 48p. (ps-k). 1986. lib. bdg. 10.99 (ISBN 0-394-97303-8); pap. 1.48 (ISBN 0-394-87303-3). Knopf.
Kindergarten, Bk. 2. (Illus.). 48p. (ps-k). 1983. wkbk. 4.98 (ISBN 0-86734-025-8, FS-2654). Schaffer Pubns.
Kindergarten Vocabulary. (Illus.). 24p. (ps-k). 1986. 3.98 (ISBN 0-86734-069-X, FS-3059). Schaffer Pubns.
Lamarche, Beth A. Classification: Kindergarten - Grade 1. Rittenour, Gary, illus. 64p. (Orig.). (gr. k-1). 1987. pap. 4.95 (ISBN 0-88724-243-X). Carson-Dellos.
—Classification: Preschool - Kindergarten. Rittenour, Gary, illus. 64p. (Orig.). (ps-k). 1987. pap. text ed. 4.95 (ISBN 0-88724-242-1, CO-0938). Carson-Dellos.
Schaffer, Frank, Publications Staff. Kindergarten, Bk. 1. (Illus.). 48p. (gr. k). 1983. wkbk. 4.98 (ISBN 0-86734-024-X, FS-2653). Schaffer Pubns.
—Kindergarten Skills. (Illus.). 24p. (ps-k). 1980. wkbk. 3.98 (ISBN 0-86734-012-6, PS-3025). Schaffer Pubns.
Sussman, Ellen & Johnson, Helen. A Sunny Start: Getting Ready for Kindergarten. Rundell, Wendi S., illus. 44p. (Orig.). (ps). 1983. pap. 5.95 (ISBN 0-933606-20-6, MS-611). Monkey Sisters.
Taulbee, Annette. Kindergarten Activities. (Illus.). 24p. (ps-k). 1986. 3.98 (ISBN 0-86734-065-7, FS-3057). Schaffer Pubns.
—Kindergarten Math. (Illus.). 24p. (ps-k). 1986. 3.98 (ISBN 0-86734-070-3, FS-3062). Schaffer Pubns.
—Kindergarten Thinking Skills. (Illus.). 24p. (ps-k). 1986. 3.98 (ISBN 0-86734-067-3, FS-3060). Schaffer Pubns.

KINDERGARTEN–FICTION

Cleary, Beverly. Ramona the Pest. Darling, Louis, illus. LC 68-12981. (gr. 3-7). 1968. 13.95 (ISBN 0-688-21721-4); PLB 13.88 (ISBN 0-688-31721-9). Morrow.
Cohen, Miriam. Will I Have a Friend? Hoban, Lillian, illus. LC 86-17454. (ps-k). 1986. pap. 4.95 (ISBN 0-689-71141-7, Aladdin Bks). Macmillan Child Grp.
My Mom Made Me Go to School. 1991. 13.00 (ISBN 0-385-30041-7). Doubleday.

KINDNESS TO ANIMALS

see Animals–Treatment

KINETICS

see Motion

KING, BILLIE JEAN (MOFFITT), 1943-

Hahn, James & Hahn, Lynn. King! The Sports Career of Billie Jean King. LC 81-9822. (Illus.). 48p. (gr. 3 up). 1981. PLB 9.95 (ISBN 0-89686-134-1, Crestwood Hse). Macmillan Child Grp.

KING, CORETTA SCOTT, 1927-

Patrick, Diane. Coretta Scott King. (Illus.). 144p. (gr. 9-12). 1991. PLB 13.90 (ISBN 0-531-13005-3). Watts.

KING, MARTIN LUTHER, 1929-1968

Adler, David A. Martin Luther King, Jr. Free at Last. Casilla, Robert, illus. LC 86-4670. 48p. (gr. 1-4). 1986. reinforced bdg. 12.95 (ISBN 0-8234-0618-0); pap. 4.95 (ISBN 0-8234-0619-9). Holiday.
—A Picture Book of Martin Luther King, Jr. Casilla, Robert, illus. LC 89-1930. 32p. (gr. k-3). 1989. reinforced bdg. 14.95 (ISBN 0-8234-0770-5); pap. 5.95 (ISBN 0-8234-0847-7). Holiday.
Alico, Stella H. Benjamin Franklin-Martin Luther King Jr. Cruz, E. R., illus. (gr. 4-12). 1979. pap. text ed. 2.95 (ISBN 0-88301-353-3); wkbk 1.25 (ISBN 0-88301-377-0). Pendulum Pr.
Bains, Rae. Martin Luther King. Frenck, Hal, illus. LC 84-2666. 32p. (gr. 3-6). 1985. PLB 9.49 (ISBN 0-8167-0160-1); pap. text ed. 2.95 (ISBN 0-8167-0161-X). Troll Assocs.
Behrens, June. Martin Luther King, Jr. The Story of a Dream. Siberell, Anne, illus. LC 78-23873. 32p. (gr. k-4). 1979. PLB 15.93 (ISBN 0-516-08879-3, Golden Gate). Childrens.
Clayton, Ed. Martin Luther King: The Peaceful Warrior. Hodges, David, illus. 128p. (gr. 3-6). 1986. pap. 2.50 (ISBN 0-671-63119-5, Minstrel Bks). PB.
Darby, Jean. Martin Luther King, Jr. (Illus.). 112p. (gr. 5 up). 1990. PLB 15.95 (ISBN 0-8225-4902-6). Lerner Pubns.
Davidson, Margaret. I Have a Dream: The Story of Martin Luther King. (Illus.). 128p. (Orig.). (gr. 2-5). 1986. pap. 2.50 (ISBN 0-590-41291-4, Lucky Star); tchr's. guide 1.25 (ISBN 0-590-40675-2). Scholastic Inc.
—I Have a Dream: The Story of Martin Luther King. 128p. (Orig.). (gr. 2-5). 1986. pap. 2.75 (ISBN 0-590-43825-5). Scholastic Inc.
—I Have a Dream: The Story of Martin Luther King. (gr. 4-7). 1991. pap. 2.75 (ISBN 0-590-44230-9). Scholastic Inc.
De Kay, James T. Meet Martin Luther King Jr. LC 78-79789. (gr. 3-6). 1969. 5.95 (ISBN 0-394-80055-9, Random Juv); lib. bdg. 8.99 (ISBN 0-394-90055-3). Random.
—Meet Martin Luther King, Jr. LC 88-26383. (Illus.). 72p. (gr. 2-4). 1989. PLB 6.99 (ISBN 0-394-91962-9); pap. 2.95 (ISBN 0-394-81962-4). Random.
Faber, Doris & Faber, Donald. Martin Luther King, Jr. large type ed. (Illus.). 128p. (gr. 4-8). 1991. Repr. of 1986 ed. PLB 17.95 (ISBN 1-55905-086-1). Grey Castle.
Faber, Doris & Faber, Harold. Martin Luther King, Jr. LC 85-21678. (Illus.). 128p. (gr. 7 up). 1986. lib. bdg. 9.98 (ISBN 0-671-60175-X). Messner.
Fox, Mary V. About Martin Luther King Day. LC 88-23230. (Illus.). 64p. (gr. 4-7). 1989. PLB 15.95 (ISBN 0-89490-200-8). Enslow Pubs.
Greene, Carol. Martin Luther King, Jr. A Man Who Changed Things. Dobson, Steven, illus. LC 88-37714. 48p. (gr. k-3). 1989. PLB 15.27 (ISBN 0-516-04205-X); pap. 4.95 (ISBN 0-516-44205-8). Childrens.
Hakim, Rita. Martin Luther King, Jr. And the March Toward Freedom. (Illus.). 32p. (gr. 2-4). 1991. PLB 15.25 (ISBN 1-878841-13-0); pap. 3.95 (ISBN 1-878841-33-5). Millbrook Pr.
Hamilton, Sue. The Killing of a Leader: Dr. Martin Luther King. Hamilton, John, ed. (Illus.). 32p. (gr. 4). 1989. PLB 11.95 (ISBN 0-939179-56-3). Abdo & Dghtrs.
Haskins, James. The Life & Death of Martin Luther King, Jr. LC 77-3157. (Illus.). (gr. 5 up). 1977. PLB 13.88 (ISBN 0-688-51802-8). Lothrop.
Hunter, Nigel. Martin Luther King, Jr. Hook, Richard, illus. LC 84-73575. 32p. (gr. 2-4). 1985. PLB 11.90 (ISBN 0-531-18019-0, Pub. by Bookwright Pr). Watts.
Jakoubek, Robert. Martin Luther King, Jr. (gr. 5 up). 1990. pap. 9.95 (ISBN 0-7910-0243-8). Chelsea Hse.
Jones, Margaret. Martin Luther King, Jr. Scott, R., illus. LC 68-9483. 36p. (gr. 1-4). 1968. PLB 13.27 (ISBN 0-516-03524-X); pap. 3.95 (ISBN 0-516-43524-8). Childrens.
Kent, Zachary. The Story of Admiral Peary at the North Pole. LC 88-11824. (Illus.). 32p. (gr. 3-6). 1988. PLB 13.27 (ISBN 0-516-04738-8); pap. 3.95 (ISBN 0-516-44738-6). Childrens.
Levine, Ellen. If You Lived At the Time of Martin Luther King. 1990. pap. 2.95 (ISBN 0-590-42582-X). Scholastic Inc.
Lillegard, Dee. My First Martin Luther King Book. Endres, Helen, illus. LC 86-31670. 32p. (ps-2). 1987. PLB 14.60 (ISBN 0-516-02908-8); pap. 3.95 (ISBN 0-516-42908-6). Childrens.
Lowery, Linda. Martin Luther King Day. Mitchell, Hetty, illus. 56p. (gr. k-4). 1987. lib. bdg. 9.95 (ISBN 0-87614-299-4); pap. 4.95 (ISBN 0-87614-468-7). Carolrhoda Bks.
—Martin Luther King Day. Mitchell, Hetty, illus. (gr. 3-5). 1987. incl. cassette 19.95 (ISBN 0-87499-071-8); pap. 12.95 incl. cassette (ISBN 0-87499-070-X); 4 paperbacks, cassette & guide 27.95 (ISBN 0-87499-072-6). Live Oak Media.
—Martin Luther King Day. Mitchell, Hetty, illus. 56p. (gr. k-4). 1987. pap. 4.95 (ISBN 0-685-25639-1, First Ave Edns). Lerner Pubns.
McKissack, Patricia. Martin Luther King, Jr. A Man to Remember. LC 83-23933. (Illus.). 128p. (gr. 4 up). 1984. lib. bdg. 17.27 (ISBN 0-516-03206-2). Childrens.
—Our Martin Luther King Book. Endres, Helen, illus. LC 86-6785. 32p. (ps-3). 1986. PLB 11.97 (ISBN 0-89565-342-7). Childs World.
McKissack, Patricia & McKissack, Fredrick. Martin Luther King, Jr. Man of Peace. Ostendorf, Ned, illus. LC 90-19156. 32p. (gr. 1-4). 1991. PLB 12.95 (ISBN 0-89490-302-0). Enslow Pubs.
Martin Luther King, Jr. (Illus.). (gr. 5-6). 1990. pap. 7.95 (ISBN 0-8192-1524-4). Morehouse Pub.
Martin Luther King Jr: Mini Play. (gr. 5 up). 1977. 6.50 (ISBN 0-89550-363-8). Stevens & Shea.
Millender, Dharathula H. Martin Luther King, Jr. Young Man with a Dream. Fiorentino, Al, illus. LC 86-10739. 192p. (gr. 2-6). 1986. pap. 3.95 (ISBN 0-02-042010-2, Aladdin). Macmillan Child Grp.
Milton, Joyce. Marching to Freedom: The Story of Martin Luther King Jr. (Orig.). (gr. k-6). 1987. pap. 2.95 (ISBN 0-440-45433-6, YB). Dell.
Obaba, Al-Imam. Dr. Martin Luther King, Jr. (Illus.). 43p. (Orig.). 1989. pap. 3.95 (ISBN 0-916157-14-8). African Islam Miss Pubns.
Ottenheimer. Martin Luther King, Jr. (gr. 2-5). 1987. pap. 2.25 (ISBN 0-671-63632-4, Little Simon). S&S Trade.
Parker, Margot. What Is Martin Luther King, Jr. Day? Bates, Matt, illus. LC 89-29254. 48p. (ps-3). 1990. 14.60 (ISBN 0-685-34687-0); pap. 4.95 (ISBN 0-516-03784-6); PLB 13.27 (ISBN 0-685-34688-9). Childrens.
Patrick, Diane. Martin Luther King, Jr. 1990. PLB 11.90 (ISBN 0-531-10892-9). Watts.
Patterson, Lillie. Martin Luther King, Jr. & the Montgomery Bus Boycott. 1989. 15.95x (ISBN 0-8160-1605-4). Facts On File.
Peck, Ira. The Life & Words of Martin Luther King Jr. (Illus.). 96p. (Orig.). (gr. 3-7). 1986. pap. 2.50 (ISBN 0-590-41309-0); tchr's. guide 1.25 (ISBN 0-590-40934-4). Scholastic Inc.
Philosophy of Non-Violence: Martin Luther King Mini-Play. (gr. 8 up). 1978. 6.50 (ISBN 0-89550-313-1). Stevens & Shea.
Rowland, Della. Martin Luther King, Jr. The Dream of Peaceful Revolution. Gallin, Richard, ed. Young, Andrew, intro. by. (Illus.). 128p. (gr. 5 up). 1990. lib. bdg. 16.98 (ISBN 0-382-09924-9); pap. 7.95 (ISBN 0-382-24062-6). Silver Burdett Pr.
Schlank, Carol H. & Metzger, Barbara. Martin Luther King, Jr. A Biography for Young Children. Kastner, John, illus. 24p. (ps-3). 1989. pap. 3.95 (ISBN 0-9613271-2-X). RAEYC.
—Martin Luther King, Jr. A Biography for Young Children. rev. ed. Kastner, John, illus. 32p. (ps-k). 1990. PLB 14.95 (ISBN 0-87659-123-3); pap. 6.95 (ISBN 0-87659-122-5). Gryphon Hse.
Schloredt, Valeri. Martin Luther King, Jr: America's Great Nonviolent Leader in the Struggle for Human Rights. Sherwood, Rhoda, ed. LC 88-2211. (Illus.). 68p. (gr. 5-6). 1988. PLB 12.95 (ISBN 1-55532-817-2). Gareth Stevens Inc.
Schloredt, Valerie. Martin Luther King, Jr. Leader in the Struggle for Civil Rights. Birch, Beverley, adapted by. LC 89-77587. (Illus.). 64p. (gr. 3-4). 1990. PLB 12.95 (ISBN 0-8368-0392-2). Gareth Stevens Inc.
Schmidt, Fran & Friedman, Alice. Fighting Fair: Dr. Martin Luther King Jr. for Kids. Heyne, Chris, illus. 40p. (Orig.). (gr. 4-9). 1986. pap. text ed. 13.95 (ISBN 1-878227-01-7). GCAPEF.
—Fighting Fair: Dr. Martin Luther King Jr. for Kids. rev. ed. Heyne, Chris, illus. (gr. 4-9). 1990. Set. pap. text ed. 74.95 69 p., incl. poster, video (ISBN 1-878227-02-5); tchr's. ed., incl. poster 19.95 (ISBN 1-878227-07-6); Set of 5. wkbk., 48p. 11.95 (ISBN 1-878227-08-4). GCAPEF.
Schulke, Flip, ed. Martin Luther King, Jr. A Documentary...Montgomery to Memphis. King, Coretta Scott, intro. by. (Illus.). 224p. (gr. 8 up). 1976. 24.95 (ISBN 0-393-07487-0); limited ed. o.p. 100.00 (ISBN 0-685-62030-1); pap. 14.95 (ISBN 0-393-07492-7). Norton.
Smith, Kathie B. Martin Luther King, Jr. Seward, James, illus. LC 86-28059. 24p. (gr. 4-6). 1987. PLB 7.98 (ISBN 0-671-64149-2); PLB 5.99s.p. (ISBN 0-685-18830-2). Messner.
Tate, Eleanora E. Thank You, Dr. Martin Luther King, Jr. 1990. 12.95 (ISBN 0-531-15151-4). Watts.
Thompson, Margurite. Martin Luther King Jr. A Story For Children. 24p. (gr. k-3). 1983. 3.00 (ISBN 0-912444-25-8). Gaus.
Woodson, Jacqueline. Martin Luther King, Jr. Brook, Bonnie, ed. Cooper, Floyd, illus. 32p. (gr. k-2). 1990. 5.95 (ISBN 0-671-69112-0); PLB 10.98 (ISBN 0-671-69106-6). Silver Pr.

Yette, Samuel F. & Yette, Frederick W. Washington & Two Marches: 1963 & 1983. (Illus.). 1984. 25.00 (ISBN 0-911253-02-5); pap. 16.95 (ISBN 0-911253-03-3); deluxe ed. 50.00 deluxe ltd. ed (ISBN 0-317-11590-1). Cottage Bks.

This is a beautiful, moving pictorial commemorative of two of the greatest demonstrations for human & civil rights in U.S. history. The 1963 March, led by the late Dr. Martin Luther King, Jr., & the 1983 March dedicated to him, are both recorded here with 150 spectacular full color photographs. Also presented is much that took place between the two marches. This is the first visualization of the "Third American Revolution," the extraordinary transformation of the nation's African-American leadership into national leadership & international influence. It is a prized supplement to social studies in scores of public school systems. As a teacher in Delaware put it: "Every school in the country needs a copy of this book. The pictures are so good, the students won't have to read the book. But because the pictures are so good, the kids will want to read it." Jointly recommended by Dr. King's widow, Coretta Scott King, & Dr. Joseph Lowery, president of the Southern Christian Leadership Conference, the book is a testament to the efficacy of democracy, a constitutional primer. Said Dr. Lowery, it documents "the great strides in the struggle for civil rights & the accomplishments that Black people have made...since the signing of the Civil Rights Act in 1964." Wrote the Washington Afro-American: "It is a work of camera art which should be in every library in the country & in every home...The book not only depicts, in photo-essays, the tremendous & momentous significance of the two marches...but provides an added dimension with its timely, well-researched & brilliant comments about the events covered. It is a classic."
Publisher Provided Annotation.

KING PHILIP'S WAR, 1675-1676

Cwiklik, Robert. King Philip. Furstinger, Nancy, ed. (Illus.). 144p. (gr. 5-7). 1989. PLB 12.98 (ISBN 0-382-09573-1); pap. 7.95 (ISBN 0-382-09762-9). Silver Burdett Pr.

KINGS AND RULERS

see also Dictators
also names of countries with the subdivision Kings and Rulers, e.g. Great Britain–Kings and Rulers; etc.; also names of individual kings and rulers, e.g. Elizabeth 2nd, Queen of Great Britain; etc.

Aliki. A Medieval Feast. LC 82-45923. (Illus.). 32p. (gr. 2-6). 1986. pap. 5.95 (ISBN 0-06-446050-9, Trophy). HarpC Child Bks.

Andersen, Hans Christian. The Snow Queen. Le Gallienne, Eva, tr. from DAN. Zeldich, Arieh, illus. LC 83-47711. 128p. (gr. 2-5). 1985. 13.95 (ISBN 0-06-023694-9); PLB 13.89 (ISBN 0-06-023695-7). HarpC Child Bks.

Babbitt, Lucy C. The Oval Amulet. LC 83-49479. 224p. (gr. 7 up). 1985. PLB 13.89 (ISBN 0-06-020301-3). HarpC Child Bks.

Barrett, Kevin. Imperial Crisis: House Devon in Turmoil. (Illus.). 56p. (gr. 10-12). 1985. pap. 12.00 (ISBN 0-915795-37-X, 9300). Iron Crown Ent Inc.

Coen, Rena N. Kings & Queens in Art. LC 64-8042. (Illus.). (gr. 5 up). 1965. PLB 5.95 (ISBN 0-8225-0155-4). Lerner Pubns.

King-Smith, Dick. The Queen's Nose. Bennett, Jill, illus. LC 83-49480. 160p. (gr. 3-7). 1985. PLB 11.89 (ISBN 0-06-023246-3). HarpC Child Bks.

KINGS AND RULERS–FICTION

Adams, Michael, illus. The Emperor's New Clothes. Ingram, John, ed. Adams, Michael, illus. 48p. (gr. 1-4). 1990. 5.95 (ISBN 0-88101-106-1). Unicorn Pub.

Alexander, Lloyd. The Beggar Queen. (gr. 6-12). 1985. pap. 3.25 (ISBN 0-440-90548-6, LFL). Dell.

—The High King. LC 68-11833. (gr. 4-6). 1968. 16.95 (ISBN 0-8050-1114-5). H Holt & Co.

—The High King. 288p. (gr. k-6). 1969. pap. 3.50 (ISBN 0-440-43574-9, YB). Dell.

Baum, L. Frank. Queen Zixi of Ix: Or, the Story of the Magic Cloak. Richardson, Frederick, illus. Gardner, M., intro. by. (Illus.). 231p. (gr. 1-3). 1971. pap. 4.95 (ISBN 0-486-22691-3). Dover.

Bentheim, Rozelle. King Kid. LC 91-2058. (Illus.). 128p. (gr. 4-7). 1991. 13.95 (ISBN 0-8050-1633-3). H Holt & Co.

Brenner, Peter. King for One Day. Wyss, Manspeter, illus. LC 74-151271. 36p. (ps-3). 7.95 (ISBN 0-87592-027-6). Scroll Pr.

Brittain, Bill. My Buddy, the King. LC 88-35704. 144p. (gr. 5-8). 1989. 12.95 (ISBN 0-06-020724-8); PLB 12.89 (ISBN 0-06-020725-6). HarpC Child Bks.

—The Wish Giver: Three Tales of Coven Tree. Glass, Andrew, illus. LC 82-48264. 192p. (gr. 3-7). 1986. pap. 3.50 (ISBN 0-06-440168-5, Trophy). HarpC Child Bks.

Burnett, Frances H. Little Lord Fauntleroy. 190p. (gr. 7 up). 1985. pap. 2.25 (ISBN 0-14-035025-X, Puffin). Puffin Bks.

Charnas, Suzy M. The Bronze King. 208p. 1987. pap. 2.95 (ISBN 0-553-15493-1, Skylark). Bantam.

Christian, Mary B. Penrod Again. Dyer, Jane, illus. LC 86-21846. 56p. (gr. 1-4). 1987. 9.95 (ISBN 0-02-718550-8, Mcmillan Child Bk). Macmillan Child Grp.

Cleaver, Vera & Cleaver, Bill. Queen of Hearts. LC 77-18252. 160p. (gr. 5 up). 1987. pap. 3.50 (ISBN 0-06-440196-0, Trophy). HarpC Child Bks.

Cooper, Susan. The Grey King. (Illus.). (gr. 7 up). 1978. pap. 3.95 (ISBN 0-689-70448-8, Aladdin). Macmillan Child Grp.

Gwynne, Fred. The King Who Rained. (gr. 1-5). 11.95 (ISBN 0-317-62057-6); pap. 5.95 (ISBN 0-317-62058-4). P-H.

Harris, Geraldine. Prince of the Godborn. (gr. k-12). 1987. pap. 2.50 (ISBN 0-440-95407-X, LFL). Dell.

Haugaard, Erik C. Prince Boghole. Downing, Julie, illus. LC 86-61. 32p. (gr. k-3). 1987. 13.95 (ISBN 0-02-743440-0, Mcmillan Child Bk). Macmillan Child Grp.

Hennessy, B. G. The Missing Tarts. Pearson, Tracey C., illus. 32p. (ps-3). 1991. pap. 3.95 (ISBN 0-14-050815-5, Puffin). Puffin Bks.

Herge. King Ottokar's Sceptre. (Illus., Orig.). (gr. k up). 1974. pap. 6.95 (ISBN 0-316-35831-2, Joy St Bks). Little.

Hillig, Chuck. The Magic King. Hesik, Blue, illus. LC 84-50928. 32p. (Orig.). (ps-2). 1984. 12.95 (ISBN 0-913299-07-3, Dist. by PGW). Stillpoint.

Hoelscher, Gwen. Prince Skippy's Quest. (Illus.). 64p. (Orig.). (gr. 6 up). 1986. pap. 7.95 (ISBN 0-9617597-0-4). Wright Monday Pr.

Jay, Ruth J. Mary Slessor: White Queen of the Cannibals. (Orig.). 1985. pap. 3.95 (ISBN 0-8024-0464-2). Moody.

Jwing-Ming, Yang. The Mask of the King. Dougall, Alan, ed. Xieu-Lin, Li, illus. 52p. (gr. 4 up). 1990. 9.95 (ISBN 0-940871-11-4). Yangs Martial Arts.

Kahn, Peggy. The Popples & King Most. Beylon, Cathy, illus. LC 85-19414. 32p. (gr. k-5). 1986. 4.95 (ISBN 0-394-88148-6). Random.

Kase, Judith B. The Emperor's New Clothes. (gr. k up). 1978. 4.50 (ISBN 0-87602-125-9). Anchorage.

Korczak, Janusz. King Matt the First. Lourie, Richard, tr. from POL. Bettelheim, Bruno, intro. by. LC 84-80504. 332p. (gr. 1 up). 1986. 15.95 (ISBN 0-374-34139-7). FS&G.

Lewis, C. S. The Chronicles of Narnia: The Lion, The Witch & the Wardrobe; Prince Caspian; The Voyage of the "Dawn Treader"; The Silver Chair; The Horse & His Boy; The Magician's Nephew; The Last Battle. Baynes, Pauline, illus. (gr. 4 up). 1986. Set. pap. 39.95 (ISBN 0-02-044500-8, Collier Young Ad). Macmillan Child Grp.

Liberati, Bruce D. The King Who Only Loved. Liberati, Zona, ed. (Illus.). (gr. 1-6). 1989. write for info. Word Dist Intl.

Littledale, Freya. King Midas & the Golden Touch. Horne, Daniel, illus. (gr. k-3). 1989. pap. 2.50 (ISBN 0-590-42262-6). Scholastic Inc.

McAllister, Angela. The King Who Sneezed. Henwood, Simon, illus. LC 88-6858. 32p. (gr. k-3). 1988. 12.95 (ISBN 0-688-08327-7); PLB 12.88 (ISBN 0-688-08328-5, Morrow Jr Bks). Morrow Jr Bks.

McKee, David. King Rollo's Spring. (ps). 2.95 (ISBN 0-317-62529-2). Viking Child Bks.

—King Rollo's Winter. (ps). 2.95 (ISBN 0-317-62528-4). Viking Child Bks.

McMullen, Eunice & McMullen, Nigel. Dragon for Breakfast. (Illus.). 28p. (ps-3). 1990. PLB 12.95 (ISBN 0-87614-650-7). Carolrhoda Bks.

Mahy, Margaret. Seventeen Kings & Forty-Two Elephants. Fogelman, Phyllis J., ed. MacCarthy, Patricia, illus. LC 87-5311. 32p. (ps-3). 1990. pap. 4.95 (ISBN 0-8037-0781-9). Dial Bks Young.

Mayne, William. All the King's Men. LC 87-25659. 192p. (gr. 3-7). 1988. pap. 14.95 (ISBN 0-385-29626-6). Delacorte.

Mitchell, Adrian, adapted by. The Baron All at Sea. Benson, Patrick, illus. 32p. (gr. 3 up). 1987. 12.95 (ISBN 0-399-21387-2, Philomel Bks). Putnam Pub Group.

Neale, J. M. Good King Wenceslas. Henterly, Jamichael, illus. LC 88-3633. 24p. (ps up). 1988. 11.95 (ISBN 0-525-44420-3, DCB). Dutton Child Bks.

Newby, Robert. King Midas. Majewski, Dawn & Cozzolino, Sandra, illus. 64p. (gr. 1-6). 1990. PLB 14.95 (ISBN 1-878363-25-5). Forest Hse.

Newman, Matt H., ed. Thanksgiving for King. LC 66-3461. (Illus.). (gr. k-3). 1980. 6 bks. & 1 cass. 29.95 (ISBN 0-89290-087-3, BC13-4); 1 bk. & 1 cass. 10.95 (ISBN 0-318-42851-2). Soc for Visual.

Oppenheim, Joanne. The Story Book Prince. Litzinger, Rosanne, illus. LC 85-31745. 32p. (ps-3). 1987. 12.95 (ISBN 0-15-200590-0, Gulliver Bks). HarBraceJ.

Orczy, Emmuska. Lord Tony's Wife. 1986. Repr. lib. bdg. 19.95x (ISBN 0-89966-553-5). Buccaneer Bks.

Peck, Richard. Princess Ashley. LC 86-29064. 208p. (gr. 7 up). 1987. pap. 14.95 (ISBN 0-385-29561-8). Delacorte.

Robbins, Ruth. Baboushka & the Three Kings. Sidjakov, Nicholas, illus. LC 60-15036. 32p. (ps-3). 1986. pap. 3.95 (ISBN 0-395-42647-2). HM.

Robison, Nancy. Ten Tall Soldiers. Knight, Hilary, illus. LC 87-32090. 32p. (ps-2). 1991. 13.95 (ISBN 0-8050-0768-7). H Holt & Co.

Ruskin, John. The King of the Golden River or the Black Brother. Doyle, Richard, illus. LC 74-82199. viii, 56p. (gr. 1 up). 1974. pap. 2.95 (ISBN 0-486-20066-3). Dover.

Service, Pamela F. Being of Two Minds. LC 90-24097. 192p. (gr. 3-7). 1991. 13.95 (ISBN 0-689-31524-4, Atheneum Child Bk). Macmillan Child Grp.

Shankar, Alaka. The Seven Queens. Vyas, Anil, illus. 16p. (Orig.). (gr. k-3). 1980. pap. 2.50 (ISBN 0-89744-217-2, Pub. by Children's Bk Trust India). Auromere.

Siekkinen, Raija. Mister King. Steffa, Tim, tr. Taina, Hannu, illus. 32p. (gr. k-4). 1987. lib. bdg. 12.95 (ISBN 0-87614-315-X). Carolrhoda Bks.

Singer, Isaac Bashevis. Naftali, the Storyteller & His Horse, Sus. Zemach, Margot, illus. (gr. 3 up). 1987. pap. 3.50 (ISBN 0-374-45487-6). FS&G.

Utz. The King, the Queen, & the Lima Bean. LC 73-93020. (Illus.). 32p. (gr. k-3). 1974. PLB 9.95 (ISBN 0-87783-121-1); pap. 3.94 deluxe ed. (ISBN 0-87783-122-X). Oddo.

Vandersteen, Willy. The King Drinks. Lahey, Nicholas J., tr. from FLE. LC 77-78696. (Illus., Orig.). (gr. 3-8). 1977. pap. 2.50 (ISBN 0-915560-04-6). Hiddigeigei.

West, Colin. The King's Toothache. Dalton, Anne, illus. LC 87-8416. 24p. (ps-2). 1990. pap. 3.95 (ISBN 0-06-443168-1, Trophy). HarpC Child Bks.

Wilkes, Larry. The King's Egg Dance. Wilkes, Larry, illus. 32p. (gr. k-4). 1990. PLB 12.95 (ISBN 0-87614-446-6). Carolrhoda Bks.

KIPLING, RUDYARD, 1865-1936

Kamen, Gloria. Kipling: Storyteller of East & West. LC 85-7945. (Illus.). 80p. (gr. 3 up). 1985. 13.95 (ISBN 0-689-31195-8, Atheneum Child Bk). Macmillan Child Grp.

Rudyard Kipling. (Illus.). 700p. 8.98 (ISBN 0-517-34798-9). Outlet Bk Co.

KITCHEN GARDENS

see Vegetable Gardening

KITCHEN UTENSILS

see Household Equipment and Supplies

KITCHENS

Kalman, Bobbie. The Kitchen. (Illus.). 32p. (gr. 3-4). 1990. lib. bdg. 14.95 (ISBN 0-86505-484-3); pap. 7.95 (ISBN 0-86505-504-1). Crabtree Pub Co.
In THE KITCHEN, young readers enter a settler home. They take a close look at the early fireplace, the tools & utensils surrounding it, & the domestic chores that were carried out there such as baking bread & making butter. Comparing an early kitchen with a kitchen of today will allow children to realize the difficulties settlers had just getting food on their tables. Your young readers will gain an understanding of how the settlers made do in a world without refrigerators, toasters, & food processors. THE KITCHEN is part of The Historic Communities Series, fun-to-read books that provide a wealth of information for young readers. The series introduces children to the concept of earlier times in history & looks at community life. The Historic Communities Series is beautifully designed, presenting information in two-page spreads through lively text, a multitude of color photographs, & detailed sketches. The books provide a close-up look at each topic, with step-by-step explanations of how tools & processes work. They are excellent for preparing young children for visits to historic sites & provide good follow-up material.
Publisher Provided Annotation.

Sendak, Maurice. In the Night Kitchen. Sendak, Maurice, illus. LC 70-105483. 48p. (ps-3). 1970. 14.95 (ISBN 0-06-025489-0); PLB 14.89 (ISBN 0-06-025490-4). HarpC Child Bks.

KITES

Gattis, L. S., III. Kites for Pathfinders: A Basic Youth Enrichment Skill Honor Packet. Gattis, L. S., III, illus. 18p. (Orig.). (gr. 5 up). 1986. pap. 5.00 tchr's. ed. (ISBN 0-936241-07-1). Cheetah Pub.

Gibbons, Gail. Catch the Wind! All about Kites. Gibbons, Gail, illus. LC 88-28820. (gr. k-3). 1989. 14.95 (ISBN 0-316-30955-9). Little.

Heller, Ruth. Kites Sail High: A Book about Verbs. (Illus.). 48p. (ps-3). 1991. pap. 5.95 (ISBN 0-448-40074-X, G&D). Putnam Pub Group.

Jue, David F. Chinese Kites: How to Make & Fly Them. LC 67-16412. (Illus.). (gr. 6 up). 1967. 10.95 (ISBN 0-8048-0101-0). C E Tuttle.

The Kite. (Illus.). (ps-5). 3.50 (ISBN 0-7214-8002-0); 1.95 (ISBN 0-7214-8008-X). Ladybird Bks.

Webber, Helen. My Kite Is the Magic Me. Webber, Helen, illus. (gr. k-6). 1968. 8.95 (ISBN 0-8392-3055-9). Astor-Honor.

KITES–FICTION

Brock, Ray. Go Fly a Kite. (Illus.). (gr. 4 up). 1976. pap. 5.00 (ISBN 0-912846-17-8). Bookstore Pr.

Caraway, Jane. One Windy Day. Smath, Jerry, illus. 24p. (ps-2). 1990. PLB 12.33 (ISBN 0-8172-3579-5); PLB 9.25 (ISBN 0-685-33576-3). Raintree Pubs.

MacDonald, Elizabeth. Mike's Kite. Kendall, Robert, illus. LC 90-6912. 32p. (ps-3). 1990. 13.95 (ISBN 0-531-05876-X); PLB 13.99 (ISBN 0-531-08476-0). Orchard Bks Watts.

Rey, Margaret & Rey, H. A. Curious George Flies a Kite. (Illus.). 80p. (gr. k-3). 1973. 12.95 (ISBN 0-395-16965-8). HM.

—Curious George Flies a Kite. Rey, H. A., illus. (gr. k-3). 1977. pap. 3.95 (ISBN 0-395-25937-1). HM.

Ross, Katharine. Grover, Grover, Come on Over: A Step 1 Book - Preschool-Grade 1. Cooke, Tom, illus. LC 90-33947. 32p. (Orig.). (ps-1). 1991. PLB 6.99 (ISBN 0-679-91117-0); pap. 2.95 (ISBN 0-679-81117-6). Random.

Ruthstrom, Dorotha. The Big Kite Contest. Hoban, Lillian, illus. LC 79-26903. 48p. (gr. 1-3). 1980. bds 6.95 (ISBN 0-394-84430-0). Pantheon.

Spirn, Michele. The Kite Race. (ps-1). 1988. 8.49; incl. cassette 16.99 (ISBN 0-685-25198-5); pap. 1.95 (ISBN 0-87386-051-9); pap. 9.95 incl. cassette (ISBN 0-685-25199-3). Jan Prods.

Wise, Francis H. & Wise, Joyce M. Kites. (Illus.). (gr. 1). 1977. pap. 1.50 (ISBN 0-915766-38-8). Wise Pub.

KLONDIKE GOLD FIELDS

Cooper, Michael. Klondike Fever: The Famous Gold Rush of 1898. LC 89-+013. (Illus.). 80p. (gr. 4 up). 1989. 14.95 (ISBN 0-89919-803-1, Clarion Bks). HM.

Ray, Delia. Gold! the Klondike Adventure. (gr. 5-9). 1989. 14.95 (ISBN 0-525-67288-5, Lodestar Bks). Dutton Child Bks.

KNIGHTHOOD

see Knights and Knighthood

KNIGHTS AND KNIGHTHOOD

see also Heraldry

Cairns, Trevor. Medieval Knights. (Illus.). 64p. 1991. pap. write for info. (ISBN 0-521-38953-4). Cambridge U Pr.

Corbin, Carole L. Kinghts. 64p. (gr. 3-5). 1989. PLB 11.90 (ISBN 0-531-10692-6). Watts.

A Crusading Knight. (Illus.). (gr. 3-8). lib. bdg. 14.00 (ISBN 0-86592-142-3). Rourke Corp.

Dines, Glen. Sir Cecil & the Bad Blue Beast. Dines, Glen, illus. LC 70-125868. (gr. k-2). 1970. 18.95 (ISBN 0-87599-175-0). S G Phillips.

Fall of Camelot. (gr. 7 up). 1986. lib. bdg. 22.60 (ISBN 0-685-10870-8, Pub. by Time-Life). Silver.

The Fall of Camelot. (Illus.). 144p. (gr. 7 up). 1986. 19.93 (ISBN 0-8094-5257-X); lib. bdg. 25.93 (ISBN 0-8094-5258-8). Time-Life.

Hindley. Knights & Castles. (gr. 4-6). 1976. (Usborne-Hayes); PLB 13.96 (ISBN 0-88110-100-1); pap. 6.95 (ISBN 0-86020-068-X). EDC.

Lang, Andrew, ed. King Arthur: Tales of the Round Table. Ford, H. J., illus. LC 67-26996. (gr. 5 up). 1987. pap. 7.95 (ISBN 0-8052-0196-3). Schocken.

Pyle, Howard. The Story of King Arthur & His Knights. Pyle, Howard, illus. xviii, 313p. (gr. 7 up). pap. 6.95 (ISBN 0-486-21445-1). Dover.

Windrow, Martin. The Medieval Knight. LC 84-52569. (Illus.). 32p. (gr. 4-9). 1986. lib. bdg. 11.90 (ISBN 0-531-03834-3). Watts.

KNIGHTS AND KNIGHTHOOD–FICTION

Brett, Simon. The Three Detectives & the Knight in Armor. LC 87-16566. 176p. (gr. 5-9). 1987. 13.95 (ISBN 0-684-18895-3, Scribners Young Read). Macmillan Child Grp.

Bulla, Clyde R. The Sword in the Tree. Galdone, Paul, illus. LC 56-5699. 128p. (gr. 2-5). 1962. PLB 12.89 (ISBN 0-690-79909-8, Crowell Jr Bks). HarpC Child Bks.

Cain, Michael. The Legend of Sir Miguel. Thatch, Nancy R., ed. Melton, David, intro. by. LC 90-5927. (Illus.). 26p. (gr. 3-6). 1990. lib. bdg. 12.95 (ISBN 0-933849-26-5). Landmark Edns.

Craig, Helen. The Knight, the Princess & the Dragon. Craig, Helen, illus. LC 84-19419. 32p. (ps-2). 1985. lib. bdg. 8.99 (ISBN 0-394-97212-0). Knopf.

De Paola, Tomie. The Knight & the Dragon. (Illus.). 32p. (gr. k-2). 1980. 10.95 (ISBN 0-399-20707-4, Putnam); pap. 5.95 (ISBN 0-399-20708-2, Putnam). Putnam Pub Group.

Eager, Edward. Knight's Castle. Bodecker, N. M., illus. (gr. 4-6). 16.75 (ISBN 0-8446-6232-1). Peter Smith.

—Knight's Castle. Treherne, Katie T. & Bodecker, N. M., illus. 208p. (gr. 3-7). 1989. pap. 3.95 (ISBN 0-15-243105-5). HarBraceJ.

Evrard, Gaetan. How I Cured Don Quixote by Doctor Sancho Panza. LC 86-60963. (ps-3). 10.45 (ISBN 0-382-09305-4). Silver.

Faulkner, William. Knight's Gambit. Blotner, Joseph, ed. 256p. (gr. 9 up). 1978. pap. 4.95 (ISBN 0-394-72729-0, Vin). Random.

Garrick, Liz. Quest for King Arthur, No. 23. Best, Charles, illus. 144p. (ps-6). 1988. pap. 2.50 (ISBN 0-553-27126-1). Bantam.

Gerrard, Roy. Sir Cedric. LC 84-6111. (Illus.). 32p. (ps up). 1984. 12.95 (ISBN 0-374-36959-3). FS&G.

—Sir Cedric. (Illus.). 32p. (gr. k up). 1986. pap. 3.95 (ISBN 0-374-46659-9). FS&G.

Gross, Gwen. Knights of the Round Table. Green, Norman, illus. LC 85-2176. 112p. (gr. 2-5). 1991. lib. bdg. 6.99 (ISBN 0-394-97579-0, Random Juv); pap. 2.95 (ISBN 0-394-87579-6, Random Juv). Random.

Hazen, Barbara S. The Knight Who Was Afraid of the Dark. Ross, Tony, illus. LC 88-18149. 32p. (ps-3). 1989. 12.95 (ISBN 0-8037-0667-7); PLB 12.89 (ISBN 0-8037-0668-5). Dial Bks Young.

Hodges, Margaret, retold by. The Kitchen Knight. Hyman, Trina S., illus. LC 89-11215. 32p. (gr. 1-4). 1990. reinforced 14.95 (ISBN 0-8234-0787-X). Holiday.

Hunter, Mollie. Knight of the Golden Plain. Simont, Marc, illus. LC 82-48747. 48p. (gr. k-4). 1983. 12.95 (ISBN 0-06-022685-4); PLB 12.89 (ISBN 0-06-022686-2). HarpC Child Bks.

Lasker, Joe. Tournament of Knights. Lasker, Joe, illus. LC 85-48075. 32p. (gr. 3 up). 1986. (Crowell Jr Bks); PLB 12.89 (ISBN 0-690-04542-5, Crowell Jr Bks). HarpC Child Bks.

Lively, Penelope. The Whispering Knights. large type ed. 248p. (gr. 3 up). 1990. lib. bdg. 16.95x (ISBN 0-7451-1153-X, Lythway Large Print). G K Hall.

McKinley, Robin. The Blue Sword. LC 82-2895. 288p. (gr. 7 up). 1982. reinforced 13.95 (ISBN 0-688-00938-7). Greenwillow.

Oakeshott, R. Ewart. Knight & His Castle. Oakeshott, R. Ewart, illus. 108p. 1991. 15.95 (ISBN 0-8023-1294-2). Dufour.

Peet, Bill. Cowardly Clyde. (Illus.). 48p. (gr. k-3). 1984. 13.95 (ISBN 0-395-27802-3); pap. 4.95 (ISBN 0-395-36171-0). HM.

Pierce, Tamora. In the Hand of the Goddess. LC 84-2946. 240p. (gr. 5 up). 1990. pap. 3.50 (ISBN 0-679-80111-1). McKay.

—In the Hand of the Goddess: Song of the Lioness, Bk. Two. LC 84-2946. 240p. (gr. 7 up). 1984. 14.95 (ISBN 0-689-31054-4, Atheneum Child Bk). Macmillan Child Grp.

—The Woman Who Rides Like a Man: Song of the Lioness, Book Three. LC 85-20054. 276p. (gr. 7-9). 1986. 14.95 (ISBN 0-689-31117-6, Atheneum Child Bk). Macmillan Child Grp.

Preiss, Byron & Gasperini, Jim. Secret of the Knights. Hescox, Richard, illus. 144p. (gr. 4 up). 1984. pap. 2.25 (ISBN 0-553-25368-9). Bantam.

Pyle, Howard. Men of Iron. Hitchner, Earle, adapted by. Geehan, Wayne, illus. LC 89-33926. 48p. (gr. 3-6). 1990. PLB 12.89 (ISBN 0-8167-1871-7); pap. text ed. 3.95 (ISBN 0-8167-1872-5). Troll Assocs.

—The Story of the Champions of the Round Table. Pyle, Howard, illus. xviii, 329p. (ps-4). 1968. pap. 7.95 (ISBN 0-486-21883-X). Dover.

Reeves, James, retold by. Exploits of Don Quixote. Ardizzone, Edward, illus. LC 85-11170. (gr. 5 up). 1985. 12.95 (ISBN 0-87226-025-9, Bedrick Blackie); (Bedrick Blackie). P Bedrick Bks.

Rutland, Jonathan. Knights & Castles. Berry, John, et al, illus. LC 86-26182. 24p. (gr. 2-5). 1987. (Random Juv). Random.

Ryan, John. Bad Year for Dragons. LC 89-37279. 28p. (gr. 1-4). 1989. 7.95 (ISBN 0-8192-1512-0). Morehouse Pub.

Scieszka, Jon. Knights of the Kitchen Table. Smith, Lane, illus. 64p. (gr. 3-7). 1991. 10.95 (ISBN 0-670-83622-2). Viking Child Bks.

Scott, Dennis. Sir Gawain & the Green Knight. (gr. k up). 1978. 5.50 (ISBN 0-87602-202-6). Anchorage.

Sutcliff, Rosemary. The Light Beyond the Forest. Felts, Shirley, illus. LC 79-23396. 144p. (gr. 4-7). 1980. 13.95 (ISBN 0-525-33665-6, 01258-370, DCB). Dutton Child Bks.

—The Road to Camlann: The Death of King Arthur. Felts, Shirley, illus. 144p. (gr. 4-7). 1982. 14.95 (ISBN 0-525-44018-6, DCB). Dutton Child Bks.

—The Sword & the Circle. 256p. (gr. 4-7). 1981. 14.95 (ISBN 0-525-40585-2, DCB). Dutton Child Bks.

Twain, Mark. Connecticut Yankee in King Arthur's Court. LC 83-9162. (gr. 5 up). 1964. pap. 3.25 (ISBN 0-8049-0029-9, CL-29). Airmont.

—A Connecticut Yankee in King Arthur's Court. Hyman, Trina S., illus. LC 87-62879. 384p. (gr. 5 up). 1988. 19.95 (ISBN 0-688-06346-2); signed ltd. ed. 100.00 (ISBN 0-688-08258-0, Morrow Jr Bks). Morrow Jr Bks.

Wilde, Nicholas. Sir Bertie & the Wyvern: A Tale of Heraldry. LC 84-7779. (Illus.). 64p. (gr. 2-6). 1984. PLB 8.95 (ISBN 0-87614-273-0). Carolrhoda Bks.

Winthrop, Elizabeth. The Castle in the Attic. Hyman, Trina S., illus. LC 85-5607. 192p. (gr. 4-7). 1985. 13.95 (ISBN 0-8234-0579-6). Holiday.

KNIGHTS OF THE ROUND TABLE

see Arthur, King

KNITTING

Coleman, Anne. Fabrics & Yarns. (Illus.). 32p. (gr. 2-6). 1990. lib. bdg. 13.26 (ISBN 0-86592-483-X); lib. bdg. 9.95s.p. Rourke Corp.

Hansen, Robin. Sunny's Mittens: Learn to Knit - Lovikka Mittens. Stock, Lois L., illus. LC 90-61410. 48p. (gr. 3-6). 1990. pap. 12.95 wire-o bdg. (ISBN 0-89272-290-8). Down East.

Lawler, T. Sewing & Knitting. (Illus.). 64p. (gr. 5 up). Date not set. pap. 2.95 (ISBN 0-86020-311-5, Usborne). EDC.

Von Wartburg, Ursula. The Workshop Book of Knitting. Von Wartburg, Ursula, illus. LC 71-157313. 160p. (gr. 3 up). 1978. (Atheneum). Macmillan.

Wilkes, A. & Garbera, C. Knitting. (Illus.). 48p. (gr. 6 up). 1986. PLB 13.96 (ISBN 0-88110-320-9); pap. 5.95 (ISBN 0-86020-983-0). EDC.

KNOTS AND SPLICES

Budworth, Geoffrey. The Knot Book. LC 84-26843. (Illus.). 160p. (gr. 7 up). 1985. 8.95 (ISBN 0-8069-5714-X); pap. 7.95 (ISBN 0-8069-7944-5). Sterling.

Gibson, Charles E. Handbook of Knots & Splices: & Other Work with Hempen & Wire Rope. (Illus.). (gr. 7 up). 11.95 (ISBN 0-87523-146-2). Emerson.

MacFarlan, Allan & MacFarlan, Paulette. Knotcraft: The Practical & Entertaining Art of Tying Knots. 186p. (gr. 6up). 1983. pap. 4.50 (ISBN 0-486-24515-2). Dover.

Pioneering. (Illus.). 48p. (gr. 6-12). 1974. pap. 1.85 (ISBN 0-8395-3382-9, 3382). BSA.

KNOWLEDGE, THEORY OF

Here are entered works that treat the origin, nature, methods and limits of human knowledge.

see also Belief and Doubt; Intellect; Perception; Senses and Sensation

Daniel, Becky & Daniel, Charlie. Comprehension Zoo. 64p. (gr. 2-4). 1979. 6.95 (ISBN 0-916456-40-4, GA113). Good Apple.

—Thinker Sheets. 64p. (gr. 2-6). 1978. 7.95 (ISBN 0-916456-23-4, GA78). Good Apple.

—What's Next? 64p. (gr. k-6). 1979. 6.95 (ISBN 0-916456-41-2, GA116). Good Apple.

Krewer, John. Future Think. 64p. (gr. k-3). 1979. 6.95 (ISBN 0-916456-56-0, GA108). Good Apple.

Tyler, Sydney B. Young Think Program Two. 90p. (Orig.). (gr. k-1). 1988. pap. text ed. 25.00 report cover (ISBN 0-912781-13-0). Thomas Geale.

KOALAS

Arnold, Caroline. Koala. Hewett, Richard, illus. LC 86-18092. 48p. (gr. 2-5). 1987. 13.95 (ISBN 0-688-06478-7); lib. bdg. 13.88 (ISBN 0-688-06479-5, Morrow Jr Bks). Morrow Jr Bks.

Bright, Michael. Koalas. (Illus.). 32p. (gr. 5-8). 1990. PLB 11.90 (ISBN 0-531-17246-5). Watts.

Burt, Denise. Birth of a Koala. LC 88-14578. (Illus.). 40p. (gr. 3-7). 1988. Repr. of 1986 ed. 12.95 (ISBN 0-944176-02-X). Terra Nova.

Eugene, Toni. Koalas & Kangaroos: Strange Animals of Australia. Crump, Donald J., ed. LC 81-607859. 32p. (ps-3). 1981. lib. bdg. 10.95 (ISBN 0-87044-403-4); PLB 12.95 (ISBN 0-87044-408-5). Natl Geog.

Green, Carl R. & Sanford, William R. The Koala. (Illus.). 48p. (gr. 5-6). 1987. PLB 10.95 (ISBN 0-89686-334-4, Crestwood Hse). Macmillan Child Grp.

Lepthien, Emilie U. Koalas. LC 90-2219. (Illus.). 48p. (gr. k-4). 1990. PLB 14.60 (ISBN 0-516-01108-1); pap. 4.950 (ISBN 0-516-41108-X). Childrens.

Rothaus, Jim. Koala Bears. 24p. (gr. 3). 1988. 17.10 (ISBN 0-88682-227-0); PLB 11.95s.p. (ISBN 0-318-37910-4). Creative Ed.

Selsam, Millicent E. & Hunt, Joyce. A First Look at Kangaroos, Kaolas & Other Animals with Pouches. Springer, Harriet, illus. LC 85-3126. 32p. (gr. k-3). 1985. 9.95 (ISBN 0-8027-6600-5); PLB 12.85 (ISBN 0-8027-6579-3). Walker & Co.

Serventy, Vincent. Koala. LC 84-17995. (Illus.). 24p. (gr. k-5). 1985. PLB 13.32 (ISBN 0-8172-2416-5). Raintree Pubs.

Stone, Lynn. Koalas. (Illus.). 24p. (gr. k-5). 1990. lib. bdg. 11.93 (ISBN 0-86593-055-4); lib. bdg. 8.95s.p. (ISBN 0-685-36372-4). Rourke Corp.

Wildlife Education, Ltd. Staff. Koalas. Havlicek, Karel & Stuart, Walter, illus. 20p. (gr. 5 up). 1983. pap. 2.25 (ISBN 0-937934-13-5). Wildlife Educ.

KOALAS–FICTION

Broome, Errol. The Smallest Koala. Mason, Gwen, illus. (ps-1). 1988. 11.95 (ISBN 0-949447-65-X). Terra Nova.

Case, Mary. Katie Koala Bear, Vol. 1: What Will Katie Wear to School? Shaffer, Dianna, illus. LC 89-83279. 28p. (gr. 2-4). 1989. pap. text ed. 4.95 (ISBN 0-685-28857-9). Koala Pub Co.

—Katie Koala Bear, Vol. 2: Katie's Tree of Designs. Shaffer, Dianna, illus. 28p. (gr. 2-4). Date not set. pap. text ed. 4.95 (ISBN 1-877995-00-2). Koala Pub Co.

—Katie Koala Bear, Vol. 3: Katie & Karla Make Pizza. Shaffer, Dianna, illus. 28p. (gr. 2-4). Date not set. pap. text ed. 4.95 (ISBN 1-877995-05-3). Koala Pub Co.

—Katie Koala Bear, Vol. 4: Katie Loves Math. Shaffer, Dianna, illus. 28p. (gr. 2-4). Date not set. pap. text ed. 4.95 (ISBN 1-877995-13-4). Koala Pub Co.
—Katie Koala Bear, Vol. 5: Katie Learns to Read. Shaffer, Dianna, illus. 28p. (gr. 2-4). Date not set. pap. text ed. 4.95 (ISBN 1-877995-04-5). Koala Pub Co.

Case, Mary & Shaffer, Dianna. Katie Koala Bear in What Will Katie Wear to School? (Illus.). 20p. (Orig.). 1989. pap. 4.95 (ISBN 1-877995-06-1). Koala Pub Co.
Katie Koala in What Will Katie Wear To School? is the first of a series of story books for primary students. It is designed for whole language strategies in the classroom. Katie is a charming Koala bear. In this book, she gets ready for school & dresses for cold weather. What Katie wears to school each day is carefully recorded on the Koala's family calendar. A paper reproducible cutout is available with each book, so the add-on story can be told using the feltboard. A blank calendar & graphing strategies are included also.
Publisher Provided Annotation.

Fox, Mem. Koala Lou. 1989. 13.95 (ISBN 0-15-200502-1). HarbraceJ.
Gelman, Rita G. A Koala Grows Up. Fiammenghi, Gioia, illus. 32p. (Orig.). (gr. k-3). 1986. pap. 3.95 (ISBN 0-590-41869-6). Scholastic Inc.
Hunt, Robert. Koolah: The White Koala. Teason, James, illus. LC 74-735895. (gr. 2-5). 1978. 6 bks. & 1 cass. 29.95 (ISBN 0-89290-036-9); 1 bk. & 1 cass. 10.95 (ISBN 0-685-04656-7). Soc for Visual.
Oana, Katherine. Kippy Koala. Cooper, William, ed. Butrick, Lyn M., illus. LC 85-51823. 16p. (Orig.). (ps up). 1985. pap. text ed. 3.72x (ISBN 0-914127-21-7). Univ Class.

KOREA
Cho, Byung K. Korean Culture Tourism & Language: For Everything You Need to Know about Korea. 357p. (gr. 7 up). 1988. 29.00 (ISBN 0-685-30452-3). B K Cho.
Farley, Carol. Korea: A Country Divided. (Illus.). 128p. (gr. 5 up). 1991. PLB 14.95 (ISBN 0-87518-465-0, Dillon). Macmillan Child Grp.
Han, Suzanne C. Let's Color Korea: Traditional Lifestyles. 24p. (gr. k-3). 1989. 6.95 (ISBN 0-930878-94-9). Hollym Intl.
Haskins, Jim. Count Your Way Through Korea. Hockerman, Dennis, illus. 24p. (gr. 1-4). 1989. 11.95 (ISBN 0-87614-348-6); pap. 4.95 (ISBN 0-87614-516-0). Carolrhoda Bks.
Jacobsen, Karen. Korea. LC 89-10043. 48p. (gr. k-4). 1989. PLB 14.60 (ISBN 0-516-01174-X); pap. 4.95 (ISBN 0-516-41174-8). Childrens.
Kim, Richard E. Lost Names: Scenes from a Boyhood in Japanese-Occupied Korea. 224p. 1988. 14.95 (ISBN 0-87663-678-4). Universe.
Lerner Publications, Department of Geography Staff, ed. South Korea in Pictures. (Illus.). 64p. (gr. 5 up). 1989. PLB 12.95 (ISBN 0-8225-1868-6). Lerner Pubns.
Lye, Keith. Take a Trip to South Korea. (Illus.). 32p. (gr. 1-6). 1985. PLB 7.99 (ISBN 0-531-10012-X). Watts.
McNair, Sylvia. Korea. LC 85-23273. (Illus.). 127p. (gr. 5-6). 1986. PLB 25.27 (ISBN 0-516-02771-9). Childrens.
Mayberry, Jodine. Koreans. (Illus.). 64p. (gr. 5-10). 1991. PLB 12.40 (ISBN 0-531-11106-7). Watts.
Moffett, Eileen. Korean Ways. Moffett, Eileen, illus. 55p. (gr. k up). 1986. 10.95 (ISBN 0-8048-7013-6, Pub. by Seoul Intl Tourist Korea). C E Tuttle.
Mueller, M. Let's Color Korea: Traditional Games. 24p. (gr. k-3). 1989. 6.95x (ISBN 0-930878-95-7). Hollym Intl.

KOREA–FICTION
Adams, Edward B. Herdboy & Weaver. Choi, Dong-Ho, illus. 32p. (gr. 3). 1981. 8.95 (ISBN 0-8048-1470-8, Pub by Seoul Intl Publishing House). C E Tuttle.
—Woodcutter & Nymph. Choi, Dong-Ho, illus. 32p. (gr. 3). 1982. 8.95 (ISBN 0-8048-1471-6, Pub by Seoul Intl Publishing House). C E Tuttle.
Burkholder, Ruth C. Mi Jun's Difficult Decision. O'Dwyer, Chung S. & Fwhang, Duk S., illus. LC 83-20494. 14p. (Orig.). (gr. 4-6). 1984. pap. 4.95 (ISBN 0-377-00139-2). Friendship Pr.
Ilyon. The Birth of Tangun: The Legend of Korea's First King. Adams, Edward B., tr. from KOR. Yoon, Hak-Jung, illus. 28p. (gr. 5). 1986. 7.50 (ISBN 0-685-17153-1, Pub. by Seoul Intl Pub Hse Korea). C E Tuttle.
—The Death of Echadon. Adams, Edward B., tr. Yoon, Hak-Jung, illus. 28p. (gr. 5). 1986. 7.50 (ISBN 0-685-17155-8, Pub. by Seoul Intl Pub Hse Korea). C E Tuttle.
—King Munmu of Silia. Adams, Edward B., tr. Yoon, Hak-Jung, illus. 28p. (gr. 5). 1986. 7.50 (ISBN 0-685-17157-4, Pub. by Seoul Intl Pub Hse Korea). C E Tuttle.
—The Three Good Events. Adams, Edward B., tr. from KOR. Yoon, Hak-Jung, illus. 28p. (gr. 5). 1986. 7.50 (ISBN 0-685-17156-6, Pub. by Seoul Intl Pub Hse Korea). C E Tuttle.
—The Three Prophecies of Queen Sondok. Adams, Edward B., tr. from KOR. Yoon, Hak-Jung, illus. 28p. (gr. 5). 1986. 7.50 (ISBN 0-685-17154-X, Pub. by Seoul Intl Pub Hse Korea). C E Tuttle.

KOREA, PEOPLE'S DEMOCRATIC REPUBLIC OF
Ashby, Gwynneth. A Family in South Korea. (Illus.). 32p. (gr. 2-5). 1987. 9.95 (ISBN 0-8225-1675-6). Lerner Pubns.
Nash, Amy. North Korea. (Illus.). (gr. 5 up). 1990. 14.95 (ISBN 0-7910-0157-1). Chelsea Hse.

KOREA, REPUBLIC OF
Shepheard, Patricia. South Korea. (Illus.). (gr. 5 up). 1988. 14.95 (ISBN 0-7910-0118-0). Chelsea Hse.

KOREAN WAR, 1950-1953
Edwards, R. Korean War. (Illus.). 80p. (gr. 7 up). Date not set. PLB 17.26 (ISBN 0-86592-036-2). Rourke Corp.
The Korean War Soldier at Heartbreak Ridge. 48p. (gr. 5-6). 1989. PLB 10.95 (ISBN 0-685-26358-4). Capstone Pr.
Smith, Carter. The Korean War. (Illus.). 64p. (gr. 5 up). 1990. lib. bdg. 16.98 (ISBN 0-382-09953-2); pap. 7.95 (ISBN 0-382-09949-4). Silver Burdett Pr.

KOREANS IN THE U. S.–FICTION
Griffiths, Ann H. Korean Americans. (Illus.). 128p. (gr. 6-10). 1991. lib. bdg. 17.95x (ISBN 0-8160-2300-X). Facts on File.
Rhie, Schi-Zhin. Soon-Hee in America. Rhie, Schi-Zhin, illus. LC 77-81780. 36p. (gr. k-3). 1977. PLB 6.50x (ISBN 0-930878-00-0). Hollym Intl.

KU KLUX KLAN
Cook, Fred J. The Ku Klux Klan: America's Recurring Nightmare. rev. ed. Steltenpohl, Jane, ed. (Illus.). 176p. (gr. 7 up). 1989. lib. bdg. 12.98 (ISBN 0-671-68421-3). Messner.
Meltzer, Milson. The Truth about the Ku Klux Klan. (Illus.). 129p. (gr. 7 up). 1982. PLB 12.90 (ISBN 0-531-04498-X). Watts.
Moore, Robert B. Violence, the KKK & the Struggle for Equality. 72p. (Orig.). (gr. 9 up). 1981. pap. 5.95 (ISBN 0-930040-38-4). CIBC.

KUBLAI KHAN, EMPEROR OF CHINA, 1216-1294
Dramer, Kim. Kublai Khan. (Illus.). (gr. 5 up). 1990. 17.95 (ISBN 1-55546-812-8). Chelsea Hse.

KUWAIT
Bratman, Fred. War in the Persian Gulf. (Illus.). 64p. (gr. 7 up). 1991. PLB 19.25 (ISBN 1-56294-051-1); pap. 4.95 (ISBN 1-878841-61-0). Millbrook Pr.
Lerner Publications, Department of Geography Staff, ed. Kuwait in Pictures. (Illus.). 64p. (gr. 5 up). 1989. 12.95 (ISBN 0-8225-1846-5). Lerner Pubns.
Mulloy, Martin. Kuwait. (Illus.). (gr. 5 up). 1988. 14.95 (ISBN 0-7910-0154-7). Chelsea Hse.

L

LABOR (OBSTETRICS)
see Childbirth

LABOR AND LABORING CLASSES
see also Child Labor; Communism; Labor Unions; Machinery in Industry; Occupations
also names of classes of laborers e.g. Agricultural Laborers; Miners; etc.; and names of countries, cities, etc. with the subdivisions Economic Conditions and Social Conditions, e.g. U. S.–Economic Conditions; U. S.–Social Conditions
Boy Scouts of America. American Labor. (Illus.). 48p. (Orig.). (gr. 6-12). 1987. pap. 1.85 (ISBN 0-8395-3326-8, 3326). BSA.
Claypool, Jane. Unemployment. 96p. (gr. 7 up). 1983. PLB 12.90 (ISBN 0-531-04586-2). Watts.
—The Worker in America. LC 84-27152. (Illus.). 128p. (gr. 7 up). 1985. PLB 12.90 (ISBN 0-531-04933-7). Watts.
Flagler, John J. The Labor Movement in the United States. (Illus.). 96p. (gr. 5 up). 1990. PLB 15.95 (ISBN 0-8225-1778-7). Lerner Pubns.
Gelder, L. van, et al. Enciclopedia Juvenil Labor, 3 vols. (SPA.). 592p. 1977. Set. leatherette 99.50 (ISBN 84-335-0333-2, S-50474). French & Eur.
The Ludlow Massacre: Mini-Play. (gr. 5 up). 1978. 6.50 (ISBN 0-89550-321-2). Stevens & Shea.
Lynd, Alice & Lynd, Staughton, eds. Rank & File: Personal Histories by Working-Class Organizers. Lynd, Alice, intro. by. 320p. (gr. 9-12). 1988. pap. 10.00 (ISBN 0-85345-752-2). Monthly Rev.
McCombs, Barbara L. & Brannan, Linda. Consideration for Co-Worker Rights. (Illus.). 32p. (Orig.). (gr. 7-12). 1990. Set. 10 wkbks. & tchr's. guide 44.95 (ISBN 1-56119-063-2); tchr's. guide 1.95 (ISBN 1-56119-010-1); software 39.95 (ISBN 1-56119-105-1). Educ Pr MD.
The Pullman Strike: Mini-Play. (gr. 5 up). 1978. 6.50 (ISBN 0-89550-322-0). Stevens & Shea.

LABOR AND LABORING CLASSES–FICTION
Getzel. The Stone Cutter Who Wanted to Be Rich. LC 90-82859. (Illus.). 48p. (gr. 1-5). 1990. 9.95. CIS Comm.
Harry Bridges: Mini-Play. (gr. 5 up). 1978. 6.50 (ISBN 0-89550-327-1). Stevens & Shea.
Hayford, James. Gridley Firing. Azarian, Mary, illus. LC 87-61473. 160p. (Orig.). (gr. 4 up). 1987. pap. 9.95 (ISBN 0-933050-49-6). New Eng Pr VT.
Kessler, Leonard. Here Comes the Strikeout. Kessler, Leonard, illus. LC 65-10728. 64p. (gr. k-3). 1987. incl. cassette 5.98 (ISBN 0-694-00174-0, Trophy). HarpC Child Bks.
Sebestyen, Ouida. On Fire. 192p. 1987. pap. 2.95 (ISBN 0-553-26862-7, Starfire). Bantam.

LABOR AND LABORING CLASSES–HOUSING
see Housing

LABOR AND LABORING CLASSES–U. S.
The Flint Sit-Down Strike: Mini-Play. (gr. 5 up). 1978. 6.50 (ISBN 0-89550-320-4). Stevens & Shea.
The Haymarket Affair: Mini-Play. (gr. 5 up). 1978. 6.50 (ISBN 0-89550-323-9). Stevens & Shea.
Issues in American History: The Worker in America. Claypool, Jane. 120p. (gr. 5 up). 1985. PLB 12.90 (ISBN 0-531-06556-1). Watts.

LABOR DAY
Scott, Geoffrey. Labor Day. Wyman, Cherie R., illus. LC 81-15485. 48p. (gr. k-4). 1982. PLB 9.95 (ISBN 0-87614-178-5). Carolrhoda Bks.

LABOR ORGANIZATIONS
see Labor Unions

LABOR SAVING DEVICES, HOUSEHOLD
see also Household Equipment and Supplies

LABOR UNIONS
Lens, Sidney. Strikemakers & Strikebreakers. LC 84-28618. (Illus.). 192p. (gr. 7 up). 1985. 14.95 (ISBN 0-525-67165-X, Lodestar Bks). Dutton Child Bks.
Meltzer, Milton. Bread & Roses: The Struggle of American Labor, 1865-1915. Scott, John A., ed. (Illus.). 160p. 1990. 17.95x (ISBN 0-8160-2371-9). Facts on File.

LABORERS
see Labor and Laboring Classes

LADYBIRDS
Cutting, Brian & Cutting, Jillian. Are You a Ladybug? Male, Alan, illus. 16p. (Orig.). (gr. k-2). 1988. pap. text ed. 23.00 (ISBN 1-55911-029-5). Wright Group.
—Are You a Ladybug, 6 bks. Male, Alan, illus. 16p. (Orig.). (gr. k-2). 1988. Set. pap. text ed. 19.80 (ISBN 1-55911-030-9). Wright Group.
Pouyanne. Ladybug, Reading Level 3-4. (Illus.). 28p. (gr. 2-5). Date not set. PLB 14.60 (ISBN 0-86592-863-0). Rourke Corp.
Watts, Barrie. Ladybug. (Illus.). 28p. (gr. 1-5). 1989. 6.95 (ISBN 0-382-09441-7); PLB 9.98 (ISBN 0-382-09437-9); pap. 3.95 28p. (ISBN 0-382-09960-5). Silver Burdett Pr.
—Ladybugs. Watts, Barrie, photos by. (Illus.). 32p. (gr. k-4). 1990. PLB 10.40 (ISBN 0-531-14043-1); pap. 3.95 (ISBN 0-531-15616-8). Watts.

LAFAYETTE, MARIE ADRIENNE FRANCOIS (DE NOAILLES) MARQUISE DE, 1759-1802
Zadra, Dan. Statesmen in America: Lafayette. (gr. 2-4). 1988. PLB 11.50s.p. (ISBN 0-88682-190-8); PLB 16.45 (ISBN 0-318-32960-3). Creative Ed.

LAFAYETTE, MARIE JOSEPH PAUL YVES ROCH GILBERT DU MOTIER, MARQUIS DE, 1757-1834
Brandt, Keith. Lafayette, Hero of Two Nations. Snow, Scott, illus. LC 89-33981. 48p. (gr. 4-6). 1990. PLB 10.79 (ISBN 0-8167-1771-0); pap. text ed. 2.95 (ISBN 0-8167-1772-9). Troll Assocs.

LAGUARDIA, FIORELLO HENRY, 1882-1947
Kurland, Gerald. Fiorello LaGuardia: The People's Mayor of New York. Rahmas, D. Steve, ed. LC 77-190238. 32p. (Orig.). (gr. 7-12). 1972. lib. bdg. 4.20 incl. catalog cards (ISBN 0-87157-520-5); pap. 2.95 vinyl laminated covers (ISBN 0-87157-020-3). SamHar Pr.

LAKES
Bender, Lionel. Lake. (Illus.). 32p. (gr. 3-5). 1989. PLB 11.90 (ISBN 0-531-10708-6, Gloucester Pr). Watts.
Crump, Donald J., ed. The World's Wild Shores. (Illus.). 1990. 7.95 (ISBN 0-87044-716-5); lib. bdg. 9.50 (ISBN 0-318-42775-3). Natl Geog.
Mulherin, Jenny. Rivers & Lakes. LC 84-51228. (Illus.). 38p. (gr. 4-6). 1984. PLB 12.40 (ISBN 0-531-04836-5). Watts.
Nichols, James. Boundary Waters. LC 86-378. 176p. (gr. 7 up). 1986. 12.95 (ISBN 0-8234-0616-4). Holiday.
Santrey, Laurence. Lakes & Ponds. Moylan, Holly, illus. LC 84-2653. 32p. (gr. 3-6). 1985. PLB 9.49 (ISBN 0-8167-0206-3); pap. text ed. 2.95 (ISBN 0-8167-0207-1). Troll Assocs.
Snow, John. Secrets of Ponds & Lakes. Jack, Susan, ed. Dowling, Jak, intro. by. (Illus.). 96p. (Orig.). (gr. 4-10). 1982. pap. 3.95 (ISBN 0-930096-30-4). G Gannett.

LAMPS–FICTION
Lang, Andrew. Aladdin. Le Cain, Errol, illus. 32p. (gr. k-3). 1983. pap. 4.95 (ISBN 0-14-050389-7, Puffin). Puffin Bks.

LAND
Here are entered general works which cover such topics as types of land, the utilization, distribution and development of land and the economic factors which affect the value of land. Works which treat only of ownership of land are entered under Real Estate.
see also Agriculture; Farms; Feudalism

Greene, Carol. Caring for Our Land. (Illus.). 32p. (gr. 1-4). 1991. PLB 12.95 (ISBN 0-89490-354-3). Enslow Pubs.
Herda, D. J. & Madden, Margaret L. Land Use & Abuse. (Illus.). 144p. (gr. 9-12). 1990. PLB 12.90 (ISBN 0-531-10953-4). Watts.

LAND SURVEYING
see Surveying

LAND USE
see Land

LANDSCAPE ARCHITECTURE
see also Cemeteries
Landscape Architecture. (Illus.). 48p. (gr. 6-12). 1969. pap. 1.85 (ISBN 0-8395-3355-1, 3355). BSA.

LANDSCAPE DESIGN
see Landscape Architecture

LANDSCAPE DRAWING
see also Landscape Painting
Arnosky, Jim. Sketching Outdoors in Summer. LC 87-29728. (gr. 5 up). 1988. PLB 12.95 (ISBN 0-688-06286-5). Lothrop.
—Sketching Outdoors in Winter. LC 88-2202. (Illus.). 48p. (gr. 5 up). 1988. 12.95 (ISBN 0-688-06290-3). Lothrop.
Baxter, Leon. Landscapes. Baxter, Leon, illus. 24p. (gr. 2-7). 1989. pap. 2.95 (ISBN 0-8249-8325-4). Ideals.
Zaidenberg, Arthur. How to Draw Landscapes, Seascapes & Cityscapes. Zaidenberg, Arthur, illus. LC 63-10467. (gr. 5-10). 1963. PLB 12.89 (ISBN 0-200-00074-8, B38431, Crowell Jr Books). HarpC Child Bks.

LANDSCAPE GARDENING
see also Landscape Architecture; Shrubs; Trees

LANDSCAPE PAINTING
see also Landscape Drawing
Larsson, Carl & Rudstrom, Lennart. A Farm. LC 76-2130. (Illus.). 32p. (gr. 3 up). 1976. 13.95 (ISBN 0-399-20541-1, Putnam). Putnam Pub Group.

LANGUAGE AND LANGUAGES
Here are entered general works on the history, philosophy, origin, etc. of language. Comparative studies of languages are entered under Philology, Comparative.
see also Grammar; Phonetics; Rhetoric; Semantics; Speech; Voice; Writing
also names of languages or groups of cognate languages, e.g. English Language; etc.; also classes of people with the subdivision Language, e.g. Children–Language; etc.
Blonigen, Julie A. Concepts for Learning. Kammeyer-Seeland, Rene, illus. 172p. (ps-2). 1989. tchr's. ed. 29.95 (ISBN 0-937857-08-4, 1565). Speech Bin.
Buddle, Jackie. Fun with Words. Davis, Annelies, illus. 32p. (gr. 2). 1988. PLB 13.85 (ISBN 0-88625-164-8); pap. 2.50 (ISBN 0-88625-161-3). Durkin Hayes Pub.
Collins, Linda B. & Spangler, Carol S. The Communication Program Planning Book: A Plan Book for Speech-Language Pathologists. 200p. (gr. k-12). 1989. 21.95 (ISBN 0-937857-10-6, 1567). Speech Bin.
Doray, Maya. J Is for Jump: Moving into Language Skills. (ps-2). 1982. pap. 7.95 (ISBN 0-8224-4004-0). Fearon Teach Aids.
Forte, Imogene & MacKenzie, Joy. The Kids' Stuff: Book of Reading & Language Arts for the Primary Grades. (Illus.). 240p. (gr. 1-3). 1989. pap. text ed. 14.95 (ISBN 0-86530-121-2, IP 01-3). Incentive Pubns.
Gelhay, Patrick & Marcantel, David E. Notre Langue Louisianaise: Our Louisiana Language, Bk. 1. Graeff, Benny, et al, illus. LC 85-81018. (ENG & FRE.). 180p. (gr. 4). 1985. text ed. 14.95 (ISBN 0-935085-00-9); Tchr's ed. 14.95 (ISBN 0-935085-01-7); write for info. Dialogue Booklet (ISBN 0-935085-03-3); Cassette Tape Set 49.95 (ISBN 0-935085-02-5). Ed Francaises.
Greene, Carol. Language. LC 83-7421. (Illus.). 48p. (gr. k-4). 1983. PLB 14.60 (ISBN 0-516-01694-6). Childrens.
Hazelton, Cathy A. Communication Cartoons. (Illus.). 160p. (ps-5). 1989. tchr's. ed. 29.95 (ISBN 0-937857-09-2, 1566). Speech Bin.
Hough, Belva L. Here's Help! For Primary Reading & Language Arts. (gr. 1-3). 1987. pap. 5.95 (ISBN 0-8224-3617-5). Fearon Teach Aids.
Moldenhauer, Janice. Developing Dictionary Skills. 64p. (gr. 3-8). 1979. 6.95 (ISBN 0-916456-48-X, GA120). Good Apple.
Schwartz, Alvin. The Cat's Elbow: & Other Secret Languages. Zemach, Margot, illus. LC 81-5513. 96p. (gr. 3 up). 1982. 12.95 (ISBN 0-374-31224-9). FS&G.
Shah, Bharat S. A Programmed Text to Learn Gujarati. Kapadia, Madhusudan, frwd. by. 300p. (Orig.). (gr. 6 up). Date not set. pap. text ed. 15.00 (ISBN 0-685-26969-8). Setubandh Pubns.
Sorensen, Ginny & Hierstein, Judy. WOW (We're on Our Way)! 1986. 9.95 (ISBN 1-55999-086-4). LinguiSystems.
Sussman, Ellen. Language Arts Library. Burris, Priscilla, illus. 44p. (Orig.). (gr. 3-6). 1984. pap. text ed. 5.95 (ISBN 0-933606-27-3, MS-627). Monkey Sisters.
Swisher, Clarice. The Beginning of Language: Opposing Viewpoints. LC 89-7940. (Illus.). 112p. (gr. 3-10). 1989. PLB 13.95 (ISBN 0-89908-064-2). Greenhaven.
Talley, Gene W. How to Learn a Foreign Language: Easy-to-Use, Diagrammed Study Techniques That Will Help You Learn a New Language. LC 89-91138. 52p. (Orig.). (gr. 11-12). 1989. pap. 6.75 (ISBN 0-9622222-0-8). G Talley.
Tavzel, Carolyn. Blooming Holidays. (ps-5). 1989. pap. 13.95 (ISBN 1-55999-025-2). LinguiSystems.
Wayman, Joe. Breaking Language Barriers. Wayman, Joe, illus. 96p. (gr. k-8). 1985. wkbk. 8.95 (ISBN 0-86653-329-X, GA 641). Good Apple.
Zachman, Linda, et al. Thinking to Go: Ready to Go, Ready to Teach Worksheets for Critical Thinking Skills. booklets 27.95 (ISBN 1-55999-078-3). LinguiSystems.

LANGUAGE ARTS
see Communication; English Language; Reading; Speech
Beechick, Ruth. A Strong Start in Language: Grades K-3. 32p. (Orig.). (gr. k-3). 1986. pap. 3.95 (ISBN 0-940319-02-0). Arrow Press.
Opie, Brenda & McAvinn, Douglas. Effective Language Arts Techniques for Middle Grades (4-8) An Integrated Approach. McAvinn, Douglas, illus. 84p. (Orig.). (gr. 4-8). 1989. pap. text ed. 7.95 (ISBN 0-685-26803-9). Masterminds Pubns.
Thurston, Cheryl M. Cottonwood Game Book. 55p. (Orig.). (gr. 5-12). 1986. pap. text ed. 14.95 (ISBN 1-877673-01-3). Cottonwood Pr.

LANGUAGES AND VOCATIONAL OPPORTUNITIES
Kaplan, Andrew. Careers for Wordsmiths. (Illus.). 64p. (gr. 7 up). 1991. PLB 12.90 (ISBN 1-56294-024-4). Millbrook Pr.

LAOS
Diamond, Judith. Laos. LC 89-34279. 128p. (gr. 5-9). 1989. PLB 25.27 (ISBN 0-516-02713-1). Childrens.
Zickgraf, Ralph. Laos. (Illus.). (gr. 5 up). 1991. 14.95 (ISBN 0-7910-0159-8). Chelsea Hse.

LARGE TYPE BOOKS
Banks, Lynne R. The Fairy Rebel. large type ed. (Illus.). 227p. 1989. PLB 15.95 (ISBN 1-55736-124-X, Crnrstn Bks). ABC-CLIO.
Fitzgerald, John D. The Great Brain. large type ed. (Illus.). 219p. 1989. PLB 15.95 (ISBN 1-55736-102-9, Crnrstn Bks). ABC-CLIO.
Jones, Ron. B-Ball: The Team that Never Lost a Game. (gr. 5 up). 1990. 14.95 (ISBN 0-553-05867-3). Bantam.
Maney, D. C. Our Changing Landscape. LC 89-11340. (Illus.). 64p. (gr. 4-6). 1990. PLB 12.95 (ISBN 0-8368-0008-7). Gareth Stevens Inc.
Mayberry, Anne. The Terracotta Place. large type ed. LC 89-27151. 475p. 1989. lib. bdg. 16.95 (ISBN 0-89621-898-8). Thorndike Pr.
Oke, Janette. Love Finds a Home. large type ed. 224p. (Orig.). 1989. pap. 7.95 (ISBN 1-55661-093-9); pap. 5.95 (ISBN 1-55661-086-6). Bethany Hse.
Oneal, Zibby. The Language of Goldfish. large type ed. PLB 15.95 (ISBN 0-685-29758-6, Crnrstn Bks). ABC-CLIO.
Peck, Robert N. Soup & Me. large type ed. 139p. 1990. Repr. PLB 15.95 (ISBN 1-55736-162-2, Crnrstn Bks). ABC-CLIO.
Taylor, Theodore. The Cay. large type ed. 154p. (gr. k-6). 1990. Repr. PLB 15.95 (ISBN 1-55736-163-0, Crnrstn Bks). ABC-CLIO.
Wilder, Laura I. By the Shores of Silver Lake. large type ed. 1990. Repr. PLB 15.95 (ISBN 1-55736-176-2, Crnrstn Bks). ABC-CLIO.

LA SALLE, ROBERT CAVELIER, SIEUR DE, 1643-1687
Coulter, Tony. La Salle & the Explorers of the Mississippi. Goetzmann, William H., ed. Collins, Michael, intro. by. (Illus.). 112p. (gr. 5 up). 1991. PLB 18.95 (ISBN 0-7910-1304-9). Chelsea Hse.
Nolan, Jeannette C. La Salle & the Grand Enterprise. large type ed. (Illus.). 176p. (gr. 4-8). 1991. Repr. of 1951 ed. PLB 17.95 (ISBN 1-55905-087-X). Grey Castle.

LASERS
Barrett, N. S. Lasers & Holograms. LC 84-52000. (Illus.). 32p. (gr. 1-6). 1985. PLB 11.40 (ISBN 0-531-04946-9). Watts.
Burroughs, William. Lasers. (Illus.). 64p. (gr. 7-12). 1982. lib. bdg. 10.90 (ISBN 0-531-09196-1, Warwick). Watts.
DeVere, Charles. Lasers. LC 84-80510. (Illus.). 40p. (gr. 4 up). 1984. PLB 12.40 (ISBN 0-531-04869-1). Watts.
French, P. M. & Taylor, J. W. How Lasers Are Made. (Illus.). 32p. (gr. 5-12). 1987. 12.95x (ISBN 0-8160-1690-9). Facts on File.
Graham, Ian. Lasers & Holograms. (Illus.). 32p. (gr. 5-8). 1991. PLB 11.90 (ISBN 0-531-17264-3, Gloucester Pr). Watts.
Johnson, Jim. Lasers. Mille, Mark & Blair, Jay, illus. LC 80-17871. 48p. (gr. 4-12). 1985. PLB 15.99g (ISBN 0-8172-1400-3); pap. 9.27 (ISBN 0-8172-1431-3). Raintree Pubs.
Lasers: What They Can Do & How They Work. 48p. (gr. 6 up). 1984. PLB 13.96 (ISBN 0-88110-165-6); pap. 6.95 (ISBN 0-86020-722-6). EDC.
Nardo, Don. Lasers: Humanity's Magic Light. LC 90-6269. (Illus.). 96p. (gr. 5-8). 1990. PLB 15.95 (ISBN 1-56006-200-2). Lucent Bks.
Oleksy, Walter. Lasers. LC 85-30894. (Illus.). 48p. (gr. k-4). 1986. PLB 14.60 (ISBN 0-516-01282-7); pap. 4.95 (ISBN 0-516-41282-5). Childrens.
Stevens, Lawrence. Laser Basics. Seiden, Art, illus. 48p. (gr. 3-7). 1985. 10.95 (ISBN 0-13-523606-1). P-H.
Whyman, Kathryn. Light & Lasers. (Illus.). 32p. (gr. 1-6). 1986. PLB 11.90 (ISBN 0-531-17033-0, Pub. by Gloucester). Watts.
Woods, et al. Lasers: Activities for the Classroom. (Illus.). 85p. (Orig.). 1990. pap. text ed. 12.95 (ISBN 0-87192-216-9). Davis Mass.

LATIMER, LEWIS
Turner, Glennette. Lewis Howard Latimer. (Illus.). 144p. (gr. 5-7). 1990. PLB 13.98 (ISBN 0-382-09524-3); pap. 7.95 (ISBN 0-382-24162-2). Silver Burdett Pr.

LATIN AMERICA
see also South America
Lamb, Ruth S. Latin America: Sites & Insights. (gr. 9-12). 1963. pap. 4.00 (ISBN 0-912434-02-3). Ocelot Pr.

LATIN AMERICA–BIOGRAPHY
Jose Duarte. (Illus.). 112p. (gr. 6-12). 1991. PLB 17.95 (ISBN 0-7910-1241-7). Chelsea Hse.

LATIN AMERICA–FICTION
Carle, Eric. What's for Lunch? 10p. (ps-1). 1982. 4.95 (ISBN 0-399-20897-6, Philomel). Putnam Pub Group.

LATIN-AMERICANS IN THE U. S.
Cullison, Alan. The South Americans. Moynihan, Daniel P., intro. by. (Illus.). 112p. (gr. 5 up). 1991. lib. bdg. 17.95 (ISBN 0-87754-863-3). Chelsea Hse.
Thomas, Piri. Down These Mean Streets. LC 78-3287. (gr. 7 up). 1967. pap. 5.95 (ISBN 0-685-02840-2). Knopf.

LATIN LANGUAGE
Anderson, John A. & Groten, Frank J., Jr. Latin: A Course for Schools & Colleges. rev. ed. LC 71-102077. (Illus.). 357p. (gr. 7-12). 1988. Repr. of 1970 ed. 17.50 (ISBN 0-942573-00-5). Hill School.
DaParma, Charles W., et al. Latin Study Aid. 1987. pap. 2.75 (ISBN 0-87738-035-X). Youth Ed.
Marsh, Carole. Latin for Kids: Of All the Gaul. (Illus.). (gr. 2-10). 1983. 14.95 (ISBN 0-935326-17-0). Gallopade Pub Group.

LATIN LITERATURE
Lind, Levi R., ed. Latin Poetry in Verse Translation. LC 57-59176. (gr. 9 up). 1957. pap. 8.36 (ISBN 0-395-05118-5, RivEd). HM.

LATTER-DAY SAINTS
see Mormons and Mormonism

LAW
see also Judges; Jury; Lawyers; Police
also special branches of law, e.g. International Law; For laws on special subjects see names of subjects with the subdivision Laws and Regulations, e.g. Automobiles–Laws and Regulations
Dolan, Edward F., Jr. Protect Your Legal Rights: A Handbook for Teenagers. LC 83-8162. 128p. (gr. 7 up). 1983. lib. bdg. 11.29 (ISBN 0-671-46121-4). Messner.
Fox, Ken. Everything You Need to Know about Your Legal Rights. (gr. 7-12). 1991. PLB 12.95 (ISBN 0-8239-1322-8). Rosen Group.
Law. (Illus.). 64p. (gr. 6-12). 1975. pap. 1.85 (ISBN 0-8395-3389-6, 3389). BSA.
Lipson, Greta & Lipson, Eric. Everyday Law for Young Citizens. 160p. (gr. 5 up). 1988. wkbk. 11.95 (ISBN 0-86653-447-4, GA1056). Good Apple.
Miller, Marvin. You Be the Jury: Courtroom II. 96p. (gr. 4 up). 1989. pap. 2.50 (ISBN 0-590-41885-8). Scholastic Inc.
Olney, Ross R. & Olney, Patricia J. Up Against the Law: Your Rights As a Minor. LC 84-10209. 192p. (gr. 7 up). 1985. 12.95 (ISBN 0-525-66781-4, Lodestar Bks). Dutton Child Bks.
Sgarlata, Joseph. Law & Public Policy. 162p. (Orig.). (gr. 11-12). 1990. pap. text ed. 13.75x (ISBN 0-936826-34-7). PS Assocs Croton.
Shuster, Albert H. & Miller, Russell R. The Young Citizen Observes the Law. Cooper, William H., ed. Butrick, Lyn M., illus. LC 83-80867. 93p. (gr. 4-8). 1983. pap. text ed. 5.27 (ISBN 0-914127-03-9); tchr's. ed. 4.88 (ISBN 0-685-07834-5). Univ Class.
Shuster, Albert H., et al. The Young Christian Observes the Law. Cooper, William H., ed. Butrick, Lyn M., illus. LC 83-80868. 106p. (gr. 4-8). 1983. pap. text ed. 5.27 (ISBN 0-914127-02-0). Univ Class.

LAW, INTERNATIONAL
see International Law

LAW–U. S.
Burns, Steven L. & Nickens, Wayne. Not Guilty, Not Crazy. 150p. (Orig.). (gr. 11 up). 1985. pap. 6.00 (ISBN 0-933131-00-3). I-Med Pr.
Riekes, Linda & Ackerly, Salley M. Lawmaking. 2nd ed. (Illus.). 142p. (gr. 5-9). 1980. pap. text ed. 13.00 (ISBN 0-8299-1023-9); tchrs.' ed. 13.00 (ISBN 0-8299-1024-7). West Pub.
Zerman, Melvyn B. Beyond a Reasonable Doubt: Inside the American Jury System. Caldwell, John, illus. LC 80-2451. 224p. (gr. 7 up). 1981. PLB 12.89 (ISBN 0-690-04095-4, Crowell Jr Bks). HarpC Child Bks.

LAW–VOCATIONAL GUIDANCE
Fenten, D. X. Ms. Attorney. LC 74-4492. (Illus.). 160p. (gr. 9 up). 1974. 7.50 (ISBN 0-664-32552-1, Westminster). Westminster John Knox.

LAW ENFORCEMENT
see also Police

LAW ENFORCEMENT–VOCATIONAL GUIDANCE
Cohen, Paul & Cohen, Shari. Careers in Law Enforcement & Security. Rosen, Ruth, ed. (gr. 7-12). 1990. PLB 12.95 (ISBN 0-8239-1026-1). Rosen Group.
Fry, William R. & Hoopes, Roy. Paralegal Careers. LC 85-20443. (Illus.). 64p. (gr. 6-12). 1986. PLB 15.95 (ISBN 0-89490-105-2). Enslow Pubs.

LAW OF NATIONS
see International Law

LAWN TENNIS
see Tennis

LAWS
see Law

LAWSON FAMILY

Lawson, Robert. They Were Strong & Good. Lawson, Robert, illus. (gr. 4-6). 1940. pap. 13.95 (ISBN 0-670-69949-7). Viking Child Bks.

LAWYERS

see also Judges; Law–Vocational Guidance

Anderson, LaVere. Robert Todd Lincoln: President's Boy. (Illus.). (gr. 3-7). 1967. 3.95 (ISBN 0-672-50161-9, Bobbs). Macmillan.

Brownell, David. Great Lawyers. Conkle, Nancy, illus. 48p. (Orig.). (gr. 8). 1988. pap. 3.50 (ISBN 0-88388-133-0). Bellerophon Bks.

Davie, John L. His Honor, the Buckaroo: The Autobiography of John L. Davie. rev. ed. LC 87-91072. (Illus.). 239p. (gr. 9-12). 1988. pap. 9.95 (ISBN 0-943077-12-5). J Herzberg.

Fry, William R. & Hoopes, Roy. Legal Careers & the Legal System. (Illus.). 64p. (gr. 6-12). 1988. lib. bdg. 14.95 (ISBN 0-89490-142-7). Enslow Pubs.

Hewett, Joan. Public Defender: Lawyer for the People. Hewett, Richard, photos by. (Illus.). 48p. (gr. 4-8). 1991. 14.95 (ISBN 0-525-67340-7, Lodestar Bks). Dutton Child Bks.

LAWYERS–FICTION

Brown, Drollene. Belva Lockwood Wins Her Case. Levine, Abby, ed. (Illus.). 48p. (gr. 3-7). 1987. PLB 10.50 (ISBN 0-8075-0630-3). A Whitman.

LAYOUT AND TYPOGRAPHY

see Printing

LEADERSHIP

Bartlett, Jaye. Freddy the Elephant: The Story of a Sensitive Leader. Dubina, Alan, illus. 45p. (Orig.). (ps up). 1991. pap. 11.95 incl. cassette (ISBN 1-878064-01-0). New Age CT.
Freddy doesn't like himself. He is chubby & can't move very fast. His mentor, Gran-Fada, King of all the Elephants, recognizes Freddy's potential, & encourages Freddy with his majestic understanding. As Freddy grows & learns to accept himself, hope triumphs over low self-esteem. Every child & adult will identify with Freddy's many trials & tribulations, & will cherish the memory of their own "sensitive leader."
Publisher Provided Annotation.

Bly, Leon. An Analysis of Leadership & How to Be a Better Leader. 117p. (Orig.). (gr. 9). 1988. text & wkbk. 24.95 (ISBN 0-9621505-0-9). Cnsltnts Unlimited.

LEAR, EDWARD, 1812-1888

Kamen, Gloria. Edward Lear: King of Nonsense. Lear, Edward, illus. LC 89-28023. 80p. (gr. 2-7). 1990. 12.95 (ISBN 0-689-31419-1, Atheneum Child Bk). Macmillan Child Grp.

LEARNING, ART OF

see Study, Method of

LEARNING AND SCHOLARSHIP

see also Culture; Education; Research

Berry, Joy. Every Kid's Guide to Thinking & Learning. (Illus.). 48p. (gr. 3-7). 1987. 4.95 (ISBN 0-516-21424-1); PLB 14.60 (ISBN 0-516-01424-2). Childrens.

Berry, Joy W. What to Do When Your Mom or Dad Says..."Get Good Grades!" LC 81-83789. (Illus.). 48p. (gr. 3 up). 1982. lib. bdg. 14.60 (ISBN 0-516-02569-4). Childrens.

Berry, Marilyn. Help Is on the Way for Listening Skills. (Illus.). 48p. (gr. 4-6). 1987. PLB 14.60 (ISBN 0-516-03285-2); pap. 4.95 (ISBN 0-516-43285-0). Childrens.

—Help Is on the Way for Thinking Skills. (Illus.). 48p. (gr. 4-6). 1987. PLB 13.93 (ISBN 0-516-03284-4); pap. 4.95 (ISBN 0-516-43284-2). Childrens.

BrainBusters. 24p. (Orig.). (gr. 1-5). 1989. pap. 5.95 (ISBN 0-8431-3151-9); Super Q wand 11.00 (ISBN 0-8431-3115-2). Price Stern.

Cosgrove, Stephen. Ming Ling: Serendipity Books - En Espanol. James, Robin, illus. (SPA.). 32p. (Orig.). (gr. k-4). 1989. pap. 2.95 (ISBN 0-8431-2403-2). Price Stern.

—Morgan y Yo: Serendipity Books - En Espanol. James, Robin, illus. (SPA.). 32p. (Orig.). (gr. k-4). 1989. pap. 2.95 (ISBN 0-8431-2405-9). Price Stern.

—Pegasita: Serendipity Books - En Espanol. James, Robin, illus. (SPA.). 32p. (Orig.). (gr. k-4). 1989. pap. 2.95 (ISBN 0-8431-2407-5). Price Stern.

—Rabito Orejas Gachas, No. 1: Serendipity Books - En Espanol. James, Robin, illus. (SPA.). 32p. (Orig.). (gr. k-4). 1989. pap. 2.95 (ISBN 0-8431-2402-4). Price Stern.

Dickinson, Lavona & Watts, Ramona. Come Learn with Me. (ps). 1989. pap. 9.95 (ISBN 0-8224-1377-9). Fearon Teach Aids.

Get It Right. (Illus.). 24p. (Orig.). (gr. 1-5). 1989. pap. 5.95 (ISBN 0-8431-3162-4); Super Q Wand 11.00 (ISBN 0-318-39947-4). Price Stern.

Get the Message. (Illus.). 24p. (Orig.). (gr. 1-5). 1989. pap. 5.95 (ISBN 0-8431-3150-0); Super Q Wand 11.00 (ISBN 0-318-39949-0). Price Stern.

Getting Ready for Kindergarten. 24p. (Orig.). (ps). pap. 3.95 (ISBN 0-8431-3142-X); Little Q Answer Wand 7.00 (ISBN 0-318-39954-7). Price Stern.

Getting Ready for Preschool. 24p. (Orig.). (ps). pap. 3.95 (ISBN 0-8431-3141-1); Little Q Answer Wand 7.00 (ISBN 0-318-39956-3). Price Stern.

In the Know. 24p. (Orig.). (gr. 1-5). 1989. pap. 5.95 (ISBN 0-8431-3159-4); Super Q Wand 11.00 (ISBN 0-318-39944-X). Price Stern.

Janover, Caroline. Josh: A Boy with Dyslexia. LC 88-10661. (Illus.). 100p. (gr. 3-6). 1988. pap. 7.95 (ISBN 0-914525-10-7); 11.95 (ISBN 0-914525-18-2). Waterfront Bks.

Kindergarten Skills. 32p. (Orig.). (ps). wkbk. 4.95 (ISBN 0-8431-3105-5). Price Stern.

Learning ABCs - A-M. 24p. (Orig.). (ps). 1988. pap. 3.95 (ISBN 0-8431-3132-2); Little Q Electronic Answer Wand 7.00 (ISBN 0-8431-3114-4). Price Stern.

Learning 1-10. 24p. (Orig.). (ps). 1988. pap. 3.95 (ISBN 0-8431-3133-0); Little Q Answer Wand 7.00 (ISBN 0-318-39957-1). Price Stern.

Learning 1-20. 24p. (Orig.). (ps). 1988. pap. 3.95 (ISBN 0-8431-3134-9); Little Q Answer Wand 7.00 (ISBN 0-318-39958-X). Price Stern.

Magos, Eunice & Hornnes, Esther. London Bridge Learning Games. Sussman, Ellen, ed. (Illus.). 48p. (Orig.). (ps-1). 1985. 5.95 (ISBN 0-933606-39-7, 638). Monkey Sisters.

Nevins, Dan. More Three-D Mouse Mazes. (Illus.). 48p. (Orig.). (gr. 2-5). 1989. pap. 2.95 (ISBN 0-8431-2337-0). Price Stern.

Number Fun. 32p. (Orig.). (gr. 2-5). wkbk. 4.95 (ISBN 0-8431-3109-8). Price Stern.

Preschool Skills. 32p. (Orig.). (ps). wkbk. 4.95 (ISBN 0-8431-3103-9). Price Stern.

Reading Readiness. 32p. (Orig.). (gr. 2-5). wkbk. 4.95 (ISBN 0-8431-3112-8). Price Stern.

Scholarship. (Illus.). 80p. (gr. 6-12). 1988. pap. 1.85 (ISBN 0-8395-3384-5, 3384). BSA.

Schulz, Mary K. & Zelvis, Dorothy A. Preschool to Go: Ready to Go, Ready to Teach Worksheets for Learning Readiness. 1988. booklets 27.95 (ISBN 1-55999-064-3). LinguiSystems.

Super Set, No. 1: First Number Skills, 4 wkbks. (Orig.). (ps). Set, 32 pgs. ea. 4.00 (ISBN 0-8431-3118-7). Price Stern.

Super Set, No. 2: First Word Skills, 4 wkbks. (Orig.). (gr. k-2). Set, 32 pgs. ea. 4.00 (ISBN 0-8431-3119-5). Price Stern.

Super Set, No. 3: PreSchool Skills, 4 wkbks. (Orig.). (ps-2). Set, 32 pgs. ea. 4.00 (ISBN 0-8431-3120-9). Price Stern.

Super Set, No. 4: Kindergarten Skills, 4 wkbks. (Orig.). (gr. k-1). Set, 32 pgs. ea. 4.00 (ISBN 0-8431-3121-7). Price Stern.

Super Set, No. 5: Early Grade Skills, 4 wkbks. (Orig.). (gr. 1-3). Set, 32 pgs. ea. 4.00 (ISBN 0-8431-3122-5). Price Stern.

Super Set, No. 6: Grades 2-5 Skills, 4 wkbks. (Orig.). (gr. 1-3). Set, 32 pgs. ea. 4.00 (ISBN 0-8431-3123-3). Price Stern.

Walt Disney Fun to Learn Library. 1985. write for info. Bantam.

Word Fun. 32p. (Orig.). (gr. 2-5). wkbk. 4.95 (ISBN 0-8431-3111-X). Price Stern.

Zachman, Linda, et al. Thinking to Go: Ready to Go, Ready to Teach Worksheets for Critical Thinking Skills. booklets 27.95 (ISBN 1-55999-078-3). LinguiSystems.

LEATHER WORK

Leatherwork. (Illus.). 48p. (gr. 6-12). 1983. pap. 1.85 (ISBN 0-8395-3310-1, 3310). BSA.

LEAVES

Bellegarde, Ida R. Lisping Leaves. (gr. 9 up). 1976. 8.95 (ISBN 0-918340-03-9). Bell Ent.

Harlow, Rosie & Morgan, Gareth. Trees & Leaves. Peperell, Liz, illus. 40p. (gr. 5-8). 1991. PLB 12.90 (ISBN 0-531-19126-5, Warwick). Watts.

Johnson, Sylvia A. How Leaves Change. Sato, Yuko, illus. 48p. (gr. 4 up). 1986. PLB 12.95 (ISBN 0-8225-1483-4, First Ave Edns); pap. 5.95 (ISBN 0-8225-9513-3, First Ave Edns). Lerner Pubns.

Kirkpatrick, Rena K. Look at Leaves. rev. ed. Milne, Annabel & Stebbing, Peter, illus. LC 84-26360. 32p. (gr. 2-4). 1985. PLB 15.99 (ISBN 0-8172-2353-3); pap. text ed. 9.27 (ISBN 0-8172-2378-9). Raintree Pubs.

Lerner, Sharon. I Found a Leaf. Lerner, Sharon, illus. LC 64-25679. 40p. (gr. 3-6). 1964. PLB 6.95 (ISBN 0-8225-0251-8). Lerner Pubns.

Orange, Anne. The Leaf Book. Lerner, Sharon, illus. LC 74-12745. 32p. (gr. k-3). 1975. PLB 7.95 (ISBN 0-8225-0296-8). Lerner Pubns.

Selsam, Millicent E. A First Look at Leaves. Selsam, Millicent E. & Hunt, Joyce, eds. Springer, Harriett, illus. LC 72-81376. 32p. (gr. 2-4). 1972. PLB 11.85 (ISBN 0-8027-6118-6). Walker & Co.

Wheeler, Cindy. Marmalade's Yellow Leaf. Wheeler, Cindy, illus. LC 81-20793. 24p. (ps-1). 1982. lib. bdg. 12.99 (ISBN 0-394-95024-0). Knopf.

Wiggers, Raymond. Picture Guide to Tree Leaves. (Illus.). 64p. (gr. 3-5). 1991. PLB 11.90 (ISBN 0-531-20025-6). Watts.

LEBANON

Abood, Doris M. Lebanon: Bridge Between East & West. Art, Eve, illus. Thomas, Danny, intro. by. LC 73-84565. (Illus.). 40p. (gr. 5-10). 1973. 3.50 (ISBN 0-913228-07-9). Dillon-Liederbach.

Lerner Publications, Department of Geography Staff, ed. Lebanon in Pictures. (Illus.). 64p. (gr. 5 up). 1988. 12.95 (ISBN 0-8225-1832-5). Lerner Pubns.

Stewart, Gail B. Lebanon. LC 90-35499. (Illus.). 48p. (gr. 5-6). 1990. RSBE 10.95 (ISBN 0-89686-550-9, Crestwood Hse). Macmillan Child Grp.

LEE, ROBERT EDWARD, 1807-1870

Bains, Rae. Robert E. Lee, Brave Leader. Smolinski, Dick, illus. LC 85-1092. 48p. (gr. 4-6). 1985. lib. bdg. 10.79 (ISBN 0-8167-0545-3); pap. text ed. 2.95 (ISBN 0-8167-0546-1). Troll Assocs.

Brandt, Keith. Robert E. Lee. Lawn, John, illus. LC 84-2687. 32p. (gr. 3-6). 1985. PLB 9.49 (ISBN 0-8167-0278-0); pap. text ed. 2.95 (ISBN 0-8167-0279-9). Troll Assocs.

Buchanan, Patricia. Robert E Lee: A Hero for Young Americans. LC 90-70314. 142p. (gr. 5-8). 1990. pap. 6.95 (ISBN 1-55523-334-1). Winston-Derek.

Commager, Henry S. America's Robert E. Lee. large type ed. (Illus.). 128p. (gr. 4-8). 1991. Repr. of 1951 ed. PLB 17.95 (ISBN 1-55905-088-8). Grey Castle.

Dubowski, Cathy E. Robert E. Lee & the Rise of the South. (Illus.). 160p. (gr. 5 up). 1990. lib. bdg. 16.98 (ISBN 0-382-09942-7); pap. 8.95 (ISBN 0-382-24051-0). Silver Burdett Pr.

Greene, Carol. Robert E. Lee: Leader in War & Peace. Dobson, Steven, illus. LC 89-33749. 48p. (gr. k-3). 1989. PLB 15.27 (ISBN 0-516-04209-2); pap. 4.95 (ISBN 0-516-44209-0). Childrens.

Monsell, Helen A. Robert E. Lee: Young Confederate. Arthur, James & Morrow, Gray, illus. LC 86-10736. 192p. (gr. 2-6). 1986. pap. 3.95 (ISBN 0-02-042020-X, Aladdin). Macmillan Child Grp.

Morrison, Ellen E. Gentle Man of Destiny: A Portrait of Robert E. Lee. 2nd, rev. ed. LC 80-201289. (Illus.). 16p. (gr. 6). 1984. saddle-stitched 1.75 (ISBN 0-9622537-1-5). Morielle Pr.

Robert E. Lee. (Illus.). (gr. 5 up). 1992. 17.95 (ISBN 1-55546-814-4). Chelsea Hse.

Smith, Gene. Lee & Grant. 448p. (gr. 9-12). 1985. pap. 11.95 (ISBN 0-452-01000-4, Mer). NAL-Dutton.

Weidhorn, Manfred. Robert E. Lee. LC 87-14500. (Illus.). 160p. (gr. 5 up). 1988. 13.95 (ISBN 0-689-31340-3, Atheneum Child Bk). Macmillan Child Grp.

Zadra, Dan. Statesmen in America: Robert E. Lee. rev. ed. (gr. 2-4). 1988. PLB 11.50s.p. (ISBN 0-88682-192-4); PLB 16.45 (ISBN 0-318-32958-1). Creative Ed.

LEFT- AND RIGHT-HANDEDNESS

Lerner, Marguerite R. Lefty: The Story of Left-Handedness. Andre, Rov, illus. LC 60-14007. (gr. k-5). 1960. PLB 5.95 (ISBN 0-8225-0005-1). Lerner Pubns.

LEFT- AND RIGHT-HANDEDNESS–FICTION

McKee, Craig & Holland, Margaret. The Turned-Around Taxi. Kersell, James L., illus. (gr. k-4). 1985. 1.95 (ISBN 0-87406-025-7). Willowisp Pr.

LEGAL HOLIDAYS

see Holidays

LEGAL PROFESSION

see Lawyers

LEGENDS

see also Fables; Fairy Tales; Folklore; Mythology

Asolon, Karel B., ed. The Phantom of Devil's Bridge & the Tale of Buffalo Castle. (Illus.). 41p. (Orig.). (gr. 4). 1985. pap. 12.00 (ISBN 0-930329-04-X). Kabel Pubs.

De Coster, Charles T. Flemish Legends. Taylor, Harold, tr. Delstanche, Albert, illus. LC 78-74513. (gr. 7 up). 1979. Repr. of 1920 ed. 18.75x (ISBN 0-8486-0217-X). Roth Pub Inc.

De Paola, Tomie, retold by. & illus. The Legend of the Bluebonnet: An Old Tale of Texas. LC 82-12391. 32p. (ps-3). 1983. 13.95 (ISBN 0-399-20937-9, Putnam); pap. 5.95 (ISBN 0-399-20938-7, Putnam). Putnam Pub Group.

Dever, Joe. The Tides of Treachery. 1991. pap. 3.50 (ISBN 0-425-12551-3). Berkley Pub.

Ellis, Terry. The Legend of Willow Wood Springs. LC 85-63828. (Illus.). 180p. (Orig.). (gr. 4 up). 1989. pap. 3.75 (ISBN 0-915677-30-X). Roundtable Pub.

Lines, Kathleen, ed. The Faber Book of Greek Legends. Jacques, Faith, illus. 272p. (gr. 4 up). 1986. pap. 11.95 (ISBN 0-571-13920-5). Faber & Faber.

Revich, S. J. Ibrahim the Magician. Hinlicky, Gregg, illus. 126p. (gr. 4-7). 1987. 9.95 (ISBN 0-935063-33-1); pap. 7.95 (ISBN 0-935063-34-X). CIS Comm.

Ross, Harriet, compiled by. Heroes & Heroines of Many Lands. 160p. (gr. 3-9). 1990. PLB 12.95 (ISBN 0-87460-214-9). Lion Bks.

Ruskin, John. The King of the Golden River or the Black Brother. Doyle, Richard, illus. LC 74-82199. viii, 56p. (gr. 1 up). 1974. pap. 2.95 (ISBN 0-486-20066-3). Dover.

Tannen, Mary. The Lost Legend of Finn. Hostovich, Michael, illus. LC 81-15599. 160p. (gr. 5-8). 1982. Knopf.

Westphal, Patricia R. The Legend of Ice Breaker. LC 89-40245. 32p. (gr. 1-2). 1990. PLB 12.95 (ISBN 0-8368-0119-9). Gareth Stevens Inc.

LEGENDS–AFRICA

Courlander, Harold. The Crest & the Hide & Other African Stories. Vachula, Monica, illus. 144p. 1982. 11.95 (ISBN 0-698-20536-7, Coward). Putnam Pub Group.

LEGENDS–CHINA

Chang, Florence C. Believe It or Not: An Anthology of Ancient Tales Retold. Chang, Shou-Jen, illus. LC 80-68258. 80p. (gr. 10-12). 1980. pap. 6.25x (wkbk. incl.) (ISBN 0-936620-02-1). Ginkgo Hut.

Lee, Jeanne M. Legend of the Li River: An Ancient Chinese Tale. Lee, Jeanne M., illus. LC 83-79. 32p. (gr. k-3). 1983. 11.95 (ISBN 0-03-063523-3). H Holt & Co.

Mui, Shan. The Seven Magic Orders. Tabrah, Ruth, ed. Mui, Y. T., illus. LC 72-86743. (gr. 1-7). 1973. 5.95 (ISBN 0-89610-011-1). Island Heritage.

LEGENDS–GERMANY

Browning, Robert. The Pied Piper of Hamelin: A Classic Tale. Jose, Eduard, adapted by. Suire, Diane D., tr. from SPA. Rovira, Francesc, illus. LC 88-35313. 32p. (gr. 1-4). 1988. PLB 10.95 (ISBN 0-89565-471-7). Childs World.

Pied Piper. (Illus.). (ps-1). 1985. 1.98 (ISBN 0-517-47105-1). Outlet Bk Co.

The Pied Piper of Hamelin. (Illus.). (ps-3). 1985. 2.98 (ISBN 0-517-28805-2). Outlet Bk Co.

Storr, Catherine, retold by. The Pied Piper of Hamelin. LC 84-26971. (Illus.). 32p. (gr. k-5). 1984. PLB 16.67 (ISBN 0-8172-2107-7); PLB 27.99 incl. cassette (ISBN 0-8172-2238-3); cassette 14.00 (ISBN 0-685-09502-9). Raintree Pubs.

LEGENDS–GREAT BRITAIN

Merrill, John N. Legends of Derbyshire. 2nd ed. Merrill, John N., illus. 71p. (Orig.). (gr. 6 up). 1975. pap. 3.00 (ISBN 0-913714-15-1). Legacy Bks.

Pyle, Howard. The Story of King Arthur & His Knights. (Illus.). (gr. 7 up). 1978. Repr. of 1903 ed. lib. bdg. 12.00 luxury ed. (ISBN 0-932106-01-3, Pub by Marathon Pr). S J Durst.

LEGENDS–HAWAII

Colum, Padriac. Legends of Hawaii. (Illus.). (gr. 8 up). 1937. text ed. 30.00x (ISBN 0-300-00376-5). Yale U Pr.

Guard, David. Hale-Mano: A Legend of Hawaii. Sumile, Caridad, illus. LC 80-69773. 118p. (gr. 6). 1990. 9.95 (ISBN 0-89742-048-9). Celestial Arts.

LEGENDS–INDIA

Awasthy, Rajendra. Stories of Valour. Roy, Sharadindu Sen, illus. (gr. 1-9). 1979. pap. 2.50 (ISBN 0-89744-182-6). Auromere.

Choudhary, Bani R. The Story of Krishna. (Illus.). (gr. 3-10). 1979. 7.25 (ISBN 0-89744-134-6). Auromere.

—The Story of Ramayan. (Illus.). (gr. 3-10). 1979. 7.50 (ISBN 0-89744-133-8). Auromere.

Ghosh, A. Legends from Indian History. Mukerji, Debrabrata, illus. (gr. 1-8). 1979. pap. 3.00 (ISBN 0-89744-157-5); 4.50 (ISBN 0-685-00594-1). Auromere.

Hemalata. Dhruva. Chakravorty, Saila, illus. (gr. 1-8). 1979. pap. 2.50 (ISBN 0-89744-153-2). Auromere.

Mehta, Hansa. Prince of Ayodhya. (Illus.). (gr. 1-9). 1979. pap. 2.50 (ISBN 0-89744-178-8). Auromere.

Narayana, T. R. Bheesma. Sharma, Mukesh, illus. (gr. 1-8). 1979. pap. 3.00 (ISBN 0-89744-151-6). Auromere.

Savitri. Savitri & Satyavan. Wheaton, Jaya, illus. (gr. 1-9). 1979. pap. 2.75 (ISBN 0-89744-160-5). Auromere.

Savitri & Dutta, S. Shakuntala. Varma, B. G., illus. (gr. 1-9). 1979. pap. 2.75 (ISBN 0-89744-161-3). Auromere.

Singh, Kartar & Dhillon, Gurdial S. Stories from Sikh History, 10 vols. Anand, illus. (gr. 1 up). 1971. Vol. I. pap. text ed. 2.25 (ISBN 0-89744-075-7); Vol. II. pap. text ed. 2.25 (ISBN 0-89744-076-5); Vol. III. pap. text ed. 2.25 (ISBN 0-89744-077-3); Vol. IV. pap. text ed. 2.50 (ISBN 0-89744-078-1); Vol. V. pap. text ed. 2.50 (ISBN 0-89744-079-X); Vol. VI. pap. text ed. 2.50 (ISBN 0-89744-080-3); Vol. VII. pap. text ed. 3.00 (ISBN 0-89744-081-1); Vol. VIII. pap. text ed. 4.00 (ISBN 0-89744-082-X); Vol. X. pap. text ed. 4.25 (ISBN 0-87944-083-8), Vol. IX, pap. text ed. 3.50 (ISBN 0-89744-084-6). Auromere.

LEGENDS, INDIAN

see Indians of North America–Legends

LEGENDS–IRELAND

Guard, David. Deirdre: A Celtic Legend. Guard, Gretchen, illus. LC 80-69774. 120p. (gr. 6). 1990. Repr. of 1977 ed. 9.95 (ISBN 0-89742-047-0). Celestial Arts.

LEGENDS–ITALY

DePaola, Tomie. The Clown of God. De Paola, Tomie, illus. LC 78-3845. (gr. k up). 1978. 13.95 (ISBN 0-15-219175-5, HJ). HarBraceJ.

—The Clown of God. DePaola, Tomie, illus. LC 78-3845. (ps-3). 1978. pap. 4.95 (ISBN 0-15-618192-4, VoyB). HarBraceJ.

LEGENDS–JAPAN

Harris, Rosemary. Child in the Bamboo Grove. Le Cain, Errol, illus. LC 72-4064. (gr. 1-3). 1972. 18.95 (ISBN 0-87599-194-7). S G Phillips.

Pratt, Davis. Magic Animals of Japan. Kula, Elsa, illus. LC 67-17483. (gr. 1-4). 1967. (Pub. by Parnassus); PLB 5.88 (ISBN 0-87466-020-3). HM.

Quayle, Eric, retold by. The Shining Princess & Other Japanese Legends. Foreman, Michael, illus. 112p. (gr. k-5). 1989. 15.95 (ISBN 1-55970-039-4). Arcade Pub Inc.

LEGENDS, JEWISH

Freehof, Lillian S. Bible Legends: An Introduction to Midrash, Vol. 1: Genesis. Schwartz, Howard, ed. (gr. 4-6). 1987. pap. text ed. 6.95 (ISBN 0-8074-0357-1, 123050). UAHC.

LEGENDS–MEXICO

Shetterly, Susan. Dwarf-Wizard of Uxmal. Shettly, Robert, illus. LC 89-32864. 32p. (gr. k-5). 1990. 13.95 (ISBN 0-689-31455-8, Atheneum Child Bk). Macmillan Child Grp.

LEGENDS–NORWAY

Barth, Edna. Balder & the Mistletoe: A Story for the Winter Holidays. Cuffari, Richard, illus. LC 78-4523. 64p. (gr. 3). 1979. 10.95 (ISBN 0-395-28956-4, Clarion). HM.

LEGENDS–POLYNESIA

Sperry, Armstrong. Call It Courage. Sperry, Armstrong, illus. LC 40-4229. 96p. (gr. 5-7). 1968. 12.95 (ISBN 0-02-786030-2, Mcmillan Child Bk). Macmillan Child Grp.

LEGENDS–SCANDINAVIA

Evans, C. & Millard, A. Greek & Norse Legends. (Illus.). 112p. (gr. 6-10). 1987. pap. 11.95 (ISBN 0-7460-0240-8). EDC.

LEGENDS–SOVIET UNION

Crouch, Marcus. Ivan: Stories of Old Russia. Dewar, Bob, illus. 80p. (gr. 3-7). 1989. jacketed 17.95 (ISBN 0-19-274135-7). Oxford U Pr.

LEGENDS–U. S.

Glazer, Tom. Eye Winker, Tom Tinker, Chin Chopper. Himler, Ron, illus. LC 72-97497. 64p. (ps-3). 1978. pap. 6.95 (ISBN 0-385-13344-8, Zephyr-BFYR). Doubleday.

Haviland, Virginia, ed. North American Legends. (gr. 4 up). 1979. 9.95 (ISBN 0-399-20810-0, Philomel). Putnam Pub Group.

Irving, Washington. Legend of Sleepy Hollow. Hitchner, Earle, adapted by. Van Buuren, John, illus. LC 89-33942. 48p. (gr. 3-6). 1990. PLB 12.89 (ISBN 0-8167-1869-5); pap. text ed. 3.95 (ISBN 0-8167-1870-9). Troll Assocs.

Kellogg, Steven. Johnny Appleseed. Kellogg, Steven, illus. LC 87-27317. 48p. (gr. 2 up). 1988. 14.95 (ISBN 0-688-06417-5); PLB 14.88 (ISBN 0-688-06418-3, Morrow Jr Bks). Morrow Jr Bks.

Rohmer, Harriet, adapted by. The Legend of Food Mountain: La Montana del Alimento. Carrillo, Graciela, illus. LC 81-71634. 24p. (gr. k-8). 1982. 12.95 (ISBN 0-89239-022-0). Childrens Book Pr.

LEGENDS–WALES

Alexander, Lloyd. Black Cauldron. LC 65-13868. (gr. 5-9). 1965. 15.95 (ISBN 0-8050-0992-2). H Holt & Co.

—Book of Three. LC 64-18250. 224p. (gr. 4-6). 1964. 15.95 (ISBN 0-8050-0874-8, HR&W). H Holt & Co.

LEGENDS AND STORIES OF ANIMALS

see Animals–Fiction; Fables

LEGERDEMAIN

see Magic

LEIF ERICSSON, d. ca. 1020

Janeway, Elizabeth. Vikings. (Illus.). (gr. 7-9). 1964. lib. bdg. 8.99 (ISBN 0-394-90312-9, Random Juv). Random.

Zadra, Dan. Explorers of America: Leif Erickson. (gr. 2-4). 1988. PLB 11.50s.p. (ISBN 0-88682-180-0); 16.45 (ISBN 0-318-32945-X). Creative Ed.

LEISURE

see also Hobbies; Recreation

LEMMINGS–FICTION

Arkin, Alan. The Lemming Condition. Sandin, Joan, illus. LC 75-6296. 64p. (gr. 4 up). 1976. 12.95 (ISBN 0-06-020133-9). HarpC Child Bks.

LENIN, VLADIMIR ILYICH, 1870-1924

Rawcliffe, Michael. Lenin. (Illus.). 64p. (gr. 6-9). 1989. 19.95 (ISBN 0-7134-5611-6, Pub. by Batsford England). Trafalgar Sq.

LENSES

Aust, Siegfried. Lenses! Take a Closer Look. Nyncke, Helge, illus. 32p. (gr. 2-5). 1991. PLB 13.95 (ISBN 0-8225-2151-2). Lerner Pubns.

LEONARDO DA VINCI, 1452-1519

Harris, Nathaniel. Leonardo & the Renaissance. (Illus.). (gr. 1-9). 1987. PLB 12.40 (ISBN 0-531-18137-5, Pub. by Bookwright Pr). Watts.

Leonardo Da Vinci. (ARA., Illus.). (gr. 5-12). 3.50x (ISBN 0-685-02574-8). Intl Bk Ctr.

Marshall, Norman F. & Ripamonti, Aldo. Leonardo da Vinci. (Illus.). 104p. (gr. 5-8). 1990. 16.98 (ISBN 0-382-09982-6); pap. 8.95 (ISBN 0-382-24007-3). Silver Burdett Pr.

Provensen, Alice & Provensen, Martin. Leonardo da Vinci: The Artist, Inventor, Scientist in Three-Dimensional Movable Pictures. LC 83-26005. (Illus.). 12p. 1984. pap. 16.95 (ISBN 0-670-42384-X). Viking Child Bks.

Raboff, Ernest. Leonardo da Vinci. Da Vinci, Leonardo, illus. LC 87-45155. 32p. (gr. 1 up). 1987. 11.95 (ISBN 0-397-32218-6, Lipp Jr Bks). HarpC Child Bks.

—Leonardo da Vinci. Da Vinci, Leonardo, illus. LC 87-45146. 32p. (gr. 1 up). 1987. pap. 7.95 (ISBN 0-06-446076-2, Trophy). HarpC Child Bks.

Venezia, Mike. Da Vinci. Venezia, Mike, illus. LC 88-37715. 32p. (gr. 2-5). 1989. PLB 14.60 (ISBN 0-516-02275-X); pap. 4.95 (ISBN 0-516-42275-8). Childrens.

LEONOWENS, ANNA HARRIETTE CRAWFORD

Landon, Margaret. Anna & the King of Siam. Ayer, M., illus. 1944. 16.95 (ISBN 0-381-98135-5, A05201); 16.45i (ISBN 0-685-02093-2). HarpC Child Bks.

LEOPARDS

Bailey, Jill. Save the Snow Leopard. Green, John, illus. LC 90-45917. 48p. (gr. 3-7). 1991. PLB 17.28 (ISBN 0-8114-2709-9). Steck-V.

Braithwaite, Althea. Leopards. (ps-6). 1988. PLB 7.95 (ISBN 0-88462-172-3); pap. 2.95 (ISBN 0-88462-173-1). Dearborn Finan.

Crump, Donald J., ed. Lions & Tigers & Leopards: The Big Cats. (Illus.). (gr. k-4). 1990. Set. 13.95 (ISBN 0-87044-820-X); Set. PLB write for info. (ISBN 0-87044-825-0). Natl Geog.

Stone, L. Leopards. (Illus.). 24p. (gr. k-5). 1989. lib. bdg. 11.93 (ISBN 0-86592-502-X). Rourke Corp.

LEOPARDS–FICTION

Achebe, Chinua & Iroaganachi, John. How the Leopard Got His Claws. Christiansen, Per, illus. LC 72-93382. 32p. (gr. 6 up). 1973. 5.95 (ISBN 0-89388-056-6). Okpaku Communications.

Cherry, Lynne, illus. Snow Leopard. LC 86-24033. (ps). 1987. bds. 3.50 (ISBN 0-525-44305-3, DCB); book & toy package 13.95 (ISBN 0-685-14571-9, DCB). Dutton Child Bks.

LEPIDOPTERA

see Butterflies; Moths

LETTER WRITING

Lincoln, Wanda & Suid, Murray. For the Love of Letter Writing. 112p. (gr. 2-6). 1983. 9.95 (ISBN 0-912107-01-4). Monday Morning Bks.

Mischel, Florence. How to Write a Letter. rev. ed. Greenberg, Lorna, ed. Green, Anne C., illus. LC 88-10263. 72p. (gr. 5-9). 1988. PLB 10.40 (ISBN 0-531-10587-3). Watts.

Oana, Katherine. How to Write Notes. Carson, Patti & Dellosa, Janet, illus. 32p. (gr. 2-5). 1984. pap. 1.98 (ISBN 0-88724-096-8, CD-7035). Carson-Dellos.

LETTER WRITING–FICTION

Brisson, Pat. Kate Heads West. Brown, Rick, illus. LC 89-27590. 40p. (gr. 2-5). 1990. 12.95 (ISBN 0-02-714345-7, Bradbury Pr). Macmillan Child Grp.

Caseley, Judith. Dear Annie. LC 90-39793. (Illus.). 32p. (ps up). 1991. 13.95 (ISBN 0-688-10010-4); PLB 13.88 (ISBN 0-688-10011-2). Greenwillow.

Cleary, Beverly. Dear Mr. Henshaw. large type ed. Zelinsky, Paul O., illus. 141p. (gr. 2-6). 1987. Repr. of 1983 ed. lib. bdg. 14.95 (ISBN 1-55736-001-4). ABC-CLIO.

Corbett, Scott. The Mailbox Trick. Galdone, Paul, illus. 112p. (gr. 4-6). 1987. pap. 2.50 (ISBN 0-590-32196-X, Apple Paperbacks). Scholastic Inc.

Dearest Grand-Ma. 1991. pap. 13.95 (ISBN 0-385-41843-4). Doubleday.

Hoban, Lillian. Arthur's Pen Pal. LC 75-6289. (Illus.). 64p. (gr. k-3). 1982. pap. 3.50 (ISBN 0-06-444032-X, Trophy). HarpC Child Bks.

Keats, Ezra J. A Letter to Amy. LC 68-24329. (Illus.). 32p. (gr. k-3). 1984. pap. 5.95 (ISBN 0-06-443063-4, Trophy). HarpC Child Bks.

Klein, Robin. Penny Pollard in Print. James, Ann, illus. 64p. (gr. 4 up). 1988. bds. 10.95 (ISBN 0-19-554638-5). Oxford U Pr.

—Penny Pollard's Diary. James, Ann, illus. 56p. (ps-6). 1987. 10.95 (ISBN 0-19-554415-3); pap. 5.95 (ISBN 0-19-554649-0). Oxford U Pr.

—Penny Pollard's Letters. James, Ann, illus. 64p. (ps-6). 1987. 10.95 (ISBN 0-19-554575-3). Oxford U Pr.

LETTERING

Lancaster, John. Lettering. FS-Ltd Staff, ed. (Illus.). 32p. (gr. 1-6). 1988. PLB 11.90 (ISBN 0-531-10624-1). Watts.

LETTERS

Lewis, C. S. Letters to Children. Dorsett, Lyle W., ed. & compiled by. LC 84-25025. 160p. (gr. 5 up). 1985. SBE 9.95 (ISBN 0-02-570830-9). Macmillan.

Zimelman, Nathan. Please Excuse Jasper. Cruz, Ray, illus. 32p. (gr. k-4). 1987. 1.00 (ISBN 0-687-31643-X). Abingdon.

LETTERS OF CREDIT

see Credit

LETTERS OF THE ALPHABET

see Alphabet

LEVANT

see Near East

LEWIS, CLIVE STAPLES, 1898-1963

Sibley, Brian. Land of Narnia: Brian Sibley Explores the World of C. S. Lewis. Baynes, Pauline, illus. LC 90-4192. 96p. (gr. 5 up). 1990. 19.95 (ISBN 0-06-025625-7); PLB 19.89 (ISBN 0-06-025626-5). HarpC Child Bks.

LEWIS, JOHN LLEWELLYN, 1880-

John L. Lewis: Mini-Play. (gr. 5 up). 1978. 6.50 (ISBN 0-89550-311-5). Stevens & Shea.

LEWIS, MERIWETHER, 1774-1809

Stefoff, Rebecca. Lewis & Clark. (Illus.). (gr. 3-5). 1992. PLB 12.95 (ISBN 0-7910-1750-8). Chelsea Hse.

Zadra, Dan. Explorers of America: Lewis & Clark. rev. ed. (gr. 2-4). 1988. PLB 11.50s.p. (ISBN 0-88682-183-5); 16.45 (ISBN 0-318-32947-6). Creative Ed.

LEWIS AND CLARK EXPEDITION

Blumberg, Rhoda. The Incredible Journey of Lewis & Clark. LC 87-4235. (Illus.). 144p. (gr. 4 up). 1987. 17.95 (ISBN 0-688-06512-0). Lothrop.

Brown, Marion M. Sacagawea: Indian Interpreter to Lewis & Clark. LC 87-33810. (Illus.). 119p. (gr. 4 up). 1988. PLB 17.27 (ISBN 0-516-03262-3). Childrens.

Daugherty, James. Of Courage Undaunted: Across the Continent with Lewis & Clark. large type ed. (Illus.). 168p. (gr. 4-8). 1991. Repr. of 1951 ed. PLB 17.95 (ISBN 1-55905-089-6). Grey Castle.

McGrath, Patrick. The Lewis & Clark Expedition. LC 84-40381. (Illus.). 64p. (gr. 5 up). 1989. PLB 16.98 (ISBN 0-382-06828-9); pap. 7.95 (ISBN 0-382-09899-4). Silver Burdett Pr.

Petersen, David & Coburn, Mark. Meriwether Lewis & William Clark: Soldiers, Explorers, & Partners in History. LC 88-14040. (Illus.). 152p. (gr. 4 up). 1988. PLB 17.27 (ISBN 0-516-03264-X). Childrens.

Sabin, Francene. Lewis & Clark. Lawn, John, illus. LC 84-2642. 32p. (gr. 3-6). 1985. PLB 9.49 (ISBN 0-8167-0224-1); pap. text ed. 2.95 (ISBN 0-8167-0225-X). Troll Assocs.

Stein, R. Conrad. The Story of the Lewis & Clark Expedition. Aronson, Lou, illus. LC 78-4648. 32p. (gr. 3-6). 1978. PLB 13.27 (ISBN 0-516-04620-9); pap. 3.95 (ISBN 0-516-44620-7). Childrens.

LEWIS AND CLARK EXPEDITION–FICTION

Bohner, Charles. Bold Journey: West with Lewis & Clark. LC 84-19328. (Illus.). 171p. (gr. 5 up). 1985. 11.95 (ISBN 0-395-36691-7); pap. 4.95 (ISBN 0-395-54978-7). HM.

LIBERIA

Department of Geography, Lerner Publications. Liberia in Pictures. (Illus.). 64p. (gr. 5 up). 1988. PLB 12.95 (ISBN 0-8225-1837-6). Lerner Pubns.

Humphrey, Sally. A Family in Liberia. (Illus.). 32p. (gr. 2-5). 1987. PLB 9.95 (ISBN 0-8225-1674-8). Lerner Pubns.

LIBERTY

see also Civil Rights; Equality; Religious Liberty

Deegan, Paul. Rights over Rights. Abbott, Phyllis, et al, eds. Wadsworth, Elaine, illus. 48p. (gr. 4). 1987. lib. bdg. 10.95 (ISBN 0-939179-21-0). Abdo & Dghtrs.

—Right to Bear Arms. Abbott, Phyllis, et al, eds. Wadsworth, Elaine, illus. 32p. (gr. 4). 1987. lib. bdg. 10.95 (ISBN 0-939179-24-5). Abdo & Dghtrs.

—Search & Seizure. Abbott, Phyllis, et al, eds. Wadsworth, Elaine, illus. 32p. (gr. 4). 1987. lib. bdg. 10.95 (ISBN 0-939179-23-7). Abdo & Dghtrs.

Monroe, Judy. Censorship. LC 89-25407. (Illus.). 48p. (gr. 4 up). 1990. 10.95 (ISBN 0-89686-490-1, Crestwood Hse). Macmillan Child Grp.

Moore, Ruth N. In Search of Liberty, Vol. 1. Converse, James, illus. LC 83-10827. 168p. (Orig.). (gr. 7-10). 1983. pap. 4.95 (ISBN 0-8361-3340-4). Herald Pr.

Sabin, Francene. Freedom Documents. Dole, Bob, illus. LC 84-8596. 32p. (gr. 3-6). 1985. PLB 9.49 (ISBN 0-8167-0238-1); pap. text ed. 2.95 (ISBN 0-8167-0239-X). Troll Assocs.

LIBERTY BELL

Boland, Charles M. Ring in the Jubilee: The Story of America's Liberty Bell. LC 72-80407. (Illus.). 96p. (gr. 6 up). 1973. pap. 5.95 (ISBN 0-85699-055-8). Chatham Pr.

Miller, Natalie. Story of the Liberty Bell. Warren, B., illus. LC 65-12215. 32p. (gr. 2-5). 1965. PLB 13.27 (ISBN 0-516-04622-5). Childrens.

LIBERTY OF SPEECH

see Free Speech

LIBRARIANS

Johnson, Jean. Librarians A to Z. Johnson, Jean, photos by & illus. 48p. (gr. 1-3). 1989. 11.95 (ISBN 0-8027-6841-5); lib. bdg. 12.85 (ISBN 0-8027-6842-3). Walker & Co.

Paige, David. A Day in the Life of a Librarian. Ruhlin, Roger, illus. LC 84-8552. 32p. (gr. 4-8). 1985. PLB 11.79 (ISBN 0-8167-0101-6); pap. text ed. 2.95 (ISBN 0-8167-0102-4). Troll Assocs.

LIBRARIANS–FICTION

Pinkwater, Daniel. Aunt Lulu. Pinkwater, Daniel, illus. LC 88-1736. 32p. (gr. k-3). 1988. 12.95 (ISBN 0-02-774661-5, Mcmillan Child Bk). Macmillan Child Grp.

LIBRARIANSHIP

see Library Science

LIBRARIES

see also School Libraries

Berry, Marilyn. Help Is on the Way for Library Skills. Bartholomew, illus. 48p. (gr. 4-6). 1985. PLB 14.60 (ISBN 0-516-03235-6). Childrens.

Cleary, Florence D. Discovering Books & Libraries: A Handbook for Students in the Middle & Upper Grades. 2nd ed. LC 76-55368. 196p. (gr. 7-12). 1977. pap. 10.00 (ISBN 0-8242-0594-4). Wilson.

De Ponce, Blanca N. La Aventura de Estudiar: Programa para Desarrollar Destrezas de Estudio e Informacion en el nivel Elemental e Intermedio. Figueroa, Ivelisse, illus. (SPA.). 100p. (Orig.). (gr. 5-9). 1984. write for info. B Ponce.

Fujimoto, Patricia. Libraries. LC 83-26252. (Illus.). 48p. (gr. k-4). 1984. lib. bdg. 14.60 (ISBN 0-516-01725-X). Childrens.

Gibbons, Gail. Check It Out! The Book about Libraries. Gibbons, Gail, illus. 32p. (ps up). 1988. pap. 3.95 (ISBN 0-15-216401-4, VoyB). HarBraceJ.

Gilchrist, Cherry. A Visit to the Library. (gr. 2-5). 1985. pap. 2.50 (ISBN 0-521-31931-5). Cambridge U Pr.

Hoffman, Jeanne & Prizzi, Elaine. Big Fearon Dictionary & Library Skills Kit. (gr. 4-8). 1989. pap. 19.95 (ISBN 0-8224-3055-X). Fearon Teach Aids.

Knowlton, Jack. Books & Libraries. Barton, Harriet, illus. LC 89-70804. 48p. (gr. 2-5). 1991. 14.95 (ISBN 0-06-021609-3); PLB 14.89 (ISBN 0-06-021610-7). HarpC Child Bks.

Lakritz, Esther. Developing Library Skills. 112p. (gr. 4-8). 1989. 9.95 (ISBN 0-86653-481-4, GA1081). Good Apple.

McCutcheon, Randall. Can You Find It? 25 Library Scavenger Hunts to Sharpen Your Research Skills: Twenty-Five Library Scavenger Hunts to Sharpen Your Research Skills. LC 88-19020. (Illus.). 208p. (Orig.). (gr. 9 up). 1989. pap. 10.95x (ISBN 0-915793-14-8). Free Spirit Pub.

McInerney, Claire. Find It! The Inside Story at Your Library. Pulver, Harry, illus. 56p. (gr. 4-6). 1989. PLB 9.95 (ISBN 0-8225-2425-2). Lerner Pubns.

Murtha, Philly. Library: Your Teammate. Redpath, Ann, ed. 32p. (gr. 4 up). 1984. PLB 9.95 (ISBN 0-87191-999-0); 14.25 (ISBN 0-685-10399-4). Creative Ed.

Santrey, Laurence. Using the Library. Dole, Bob, illus. LC 84-2590. 32p. (gr. 3-6). 1985. PLB 9.49 (ISBN 0-8167-0122-9); pap. text ed. 2.95 (ISBN 0-8167-0123-7). Troll Assocs.

Shapiro, Lillian L. Teaching Yourself in Libraries: A Guide to the High School Media Center & Other Libraries. LC 78-16616. 180p. (gr. 7-12). 1978. 10.00 (ISBN 0-8242-0628-2). Wilson.

Vreeken, Elizabeth. Ramon's Adventures in the Library. Hershenson, Roberta, illus. LC 67-31108. 48p. (gr. 1-3). 1967. 3.95 (ISBN 0-379-00243-4). Oceana.

Weil, Lisl. Let's Go to the Library. Weil, Lisl, illus. LC 90-55105. 32p. (gr. k-3). 1990. reinforced 13.95 (ISBN 0-8234-0829-9). Holiday.

LIBRARIES, CHILDREN'S

see also Children–Books and Reading; Children's Literature

Rockwell, Anne. I Like the Library. LC 77-6365. (ps-4). 1977. 11.95 (ISBN 0-525-32528-X, DCB). Dutton Child Bks.

Tuma-Church, Deb. The Storytime Handbook. Tuma-Church, Deb, illus. 73p. (ps-5). 1988. wkbk. spiral bdg. 7.95 (ISBN 0-939644-37-1). Media Pub.

LIBRARIES, CHILDREN'S–FICTION

Bonsall, Crosby N. Tell Me Some More. Siebel, Fritz, illus. LC 61-5773. 64p. (gr. k-3). 1961. PLB 11.89 (ISBN 0-06-020601-2). HarpC Child Bks.

Freeman, Don. Quiet! There's a Canary in the Library. Freeman, Dan, illus. LC 69-15398. 48p. (gr. k-3). 1969. 14.60 (ISBN 0-516-08737-1); pap. 3.95 (ISBN 0-516-48737-X). Childrens.

LIBRARIES–FICTION

Alexander, Martha. How My Library Grew, By Dinah. Alexander, Martha, illus. 32p. (gr. k-5). 1983. 18.00 (ISBN 0-8242-0679-7). Wilson.

Charles, Donald. Calico Cat Meets Bookworm. LC 78-6557. (Illus.). 32p. (gr. 3). 1978. PLB 14.60 (ISBN 0-516-03441-3). Childrens.

Clifford, Eth. Help! I'm a Prisoner in the Library. (Illus.). 112p. (gr. 2-5). 1979. 13.95 (ISBN 0-395-28478-3). HM.

—Help! I'm a Prisoner in the Library. 96p. (gr. 4-6). 1991. pap. 2.75 (ISBN 0-590-44351-8, Apple Paperbacks). Scholastic Inc.

Crow, Sherry R. Library Lightning. (Illus.). 128p. (gr. 3-6). 1990. pap. 12.95 (ISBN 0-913839-72-8). Bk Lures.

Enerson, Laura. Our Library Lives in a Bus. Robin, illus. LC 77-71462. (gr. 3-5). 1977. 3.50 (ISBN 0-930480-01-5). R H Barnes.

Greenwald, Sheila. The Mariah Delaney Lending Library Disaster. (Illus.). (gr. 4-6). 1977. 14.95 (ISBN 0-395-25836-7). HM.

—The Mariah Delany Lending Library Disaster. (gr. k-6). 1986. pap. 2.75 (ISBN 0-440-45327-5, YB). Dell.

Haas, Dorothy. Alcott Library Is Falling Down. (gr. 4-7). 1991. pap. 2.50 (ISBN 0-590-43558-2). Scholastic Inc.

Houghton, Eric. Walter's Magic Wand. Teasdale, Denise, illus. LC 89-35400. 32p. (ps-1). 1990. 13.95 (ISBN 0-531-05851-4); PLB 13.99 (ISBN 0-531-08451-5). Orchard Bks Watts.

Hutchins, Hazel. Nicholas at the Library. Ohi, Ruth, illus. 32p. (ps-2). 1990. 14.95 (ISBN 1-55037-134-7); pap. 5.95 (ISBN 1-55037-132-0). Firefly Bks Ltd.

Nesbit, Edith. The Town in the Library. Tourret, Shirley, illus. LC 87-8971. 32p. (gr. 1 up). 1988. 10.95 (ISBN 0-8037-0477-1). Dial Bks Young.

Pellowski, Michael J. Ghost in the Library. Durham, Robert, illus. LC 88-1236. 48p. (Orig.). (gr. 1-4). 1989. PLB 9.89 (ISBN 0-8167-1337-5); pap. text ed. 2.95 (ISBN 0-8167-1338-3). Troll Assocs.

Poulet, Virginia. Blue Bug Goes to the Library. Anderson, Peggy P., illus. LC 79-15219. 32p. (ps-3). 1979. PLB 14.60 (ISBN 0-516-03430-8). Childrens.

LIBRARIES, SCHOOL

see School Libraries

LIBRARY SCIENCE

Here are entered general works on the organization and administration of libraries. Works about services offered by libraries to patrons are entered under Library Service.

Cook, Sybilla. Library Flipper: A Dewey Decimal System Guide. 49p. (gr. 1 up). 1988. trade edition 5.95 (ISBN 1-878383-08-6). C Lee Pubns.

Daniels, Lolee & Pollard, Rita. The Library Experience: Sharing the Responsibility. Sullivan-Szarek, Mary, illus. (gr. 6-8). 1987. Teacher's manual, 130pp. 64.95 (ISBN 0-935637-08-7); Student workbook, 120pp. 11.99 (ISBN 0-935637-09-5); Transparency Set. 85.00 (ISBN 0-935637-10-9). Cambridge Strat.

How to Use Your Library. 1972. pap. 1.95 (ISBN 0-87738-030-9). Youth Ed.

LIBRARY SCIENCE–VOCATIONAL GUIDANCE

Puedo Ser Bibliotecaria: (I Can Be a Librarian) LC 87-35537. (SPA & ENG.). 32p. (gr. k-3). 1989. 13.93 (ISBN 0-516-31913-2); pap. 3.95 (ISBN 0-516-51913-1). Childrens.

LIBRARY SERVICE

Mallett, Jerry & Bartch, Marian. Booker's Bunch, Bk. 1. 80p. (gr. 3-4). 1988. PLB 9.14 (ISBN 0-8000-4735-4, 036417). Perma Bound.

—Booker's Bunch, Bk. 2. 88p. (gr. 3-4). 1988. PLB 9.14 (ISBN 0-8000-4736-2, 036418). Perma Bound.

LIBYA

Brill, Marlene T. Libya. LC 87-13192. (Illus.). 128p. (gr. 5-9). 1987. PLB 25.27 (ISBN 0-516-02776-X). Childrens.

LIFE

Alexander, Lloyd. The First Two Lives of Lukas-Kasha. 224p. (gr. 7 up). 1982. pap. 2.25 (ISBN 0-440-42784-3, YB). Dell.

Aten, Jerry. Prime Time Life Skills. Filkins, Vanessa, illus. 64p. (gr. 2-5). 1983. wkbk. 6.95 (ISBN 0-86653-126-2, GA 487). Good Apple.

Pfeffer, Susan B. About David: A Novel. LC 80-65837. 176p. (gr. 7 up). 1980. 11.95 (ISBN 0-385-28013-0). Delacorte.

Warburg, Sandol S. Growing Time. Weisgard, Leonard, illus. 48p. (gr. k-3). 1975. pap. 1.50 (ISBN 0-395-19971-9, Sandpiper). HM.

LIFE (BIOLOGY)

see also Biology; Genetics; Old Age; Reproduction

Dahl, Tessa. Babies, Babies, Babies. Dodds, Siobhan, illus. 32p. (ps-2). 1991. 12.95 (ISBN 0-670-83921-3). Viking Child Bks.

Gamlin, Linda. Life on Earth. FS-Aladdin Staff, ed. Hayward, Ron, illus. 40p. (gr. 4-9). 1988. PLB 12.40 (ISBN 0-531-17120-5, Gloucester Pr). Watts.

Living Things. (Illus.). 32p. (Orig.). (gr. 3-6). 1989. pap. 2.95 (ISBN 0-8431-2371-0). Price Stern.

Raffi. Everything Grows. McMillan, Bruce, illus. LC 88-37162. 32p. (ps-2). 1989. 9.95 (ISBN 0-517-57387-3); PLB 10.99 (ISBN 0-517-57275-3). Crown.

LIFE, CHRISTIAN

see Christian Life

LIFE–ORIGIN

Asimov, Isaac. How Did We Find Out about the Beginning of Life? Wool, David, illus. LC 81-71196. 64p. (gr. 4-7). 1982. PLB 10.85 (ISBN 0-8027-6448-7). Walker & Co.

Doney, Malcolm & Doney, Meryl. Who Made Me? Butterworth, Nick & Inkpen, Mick, illus. 38p. (ps-3). 1987. 9.95 (ISBN 0-310-55660-0, 19064). Zondervan.

Gamlin, Linda. Origins of Life. FS-Aladdin Staff, ed. Hayward, Ron, illus. 40p. (gr. 4-9). 1988. PLB 12.40 (ISBN 0-531-17119-1, Gloucester Pr). Watts.

Jaspersohn, William. How Life on Earth Began. LC 85-10557. (Illus.). 48p. (gr. 2-4). 1985. PLB 10.90 (ISBN 0-531-10030-8). Watts.

Lasky, Kathryn. Traces of Life: The Origins of Humankind. Powell, Whitney, illus. LC 89-12092. 144p. (gr. 5 up). 1990. 16.95 (ISBN 0-688-07237-2). Morrow Jr Bks.

Matthews, Rupert. How Life Began. Newman, Colin, illus. LC 88-23779. 32p. (gr. 3-6). 1989. PLB 11.40 (ISBN 0-531-18267-3, Pub. by Bookwright Pr). Watts.

LIFE, SPIRITUAL

see Spiritual Life

LIFE ON OTHER PLANETS

see also Interstellar Communication

Asimov, Isaac. Is There Life on Other Planets? 1991. pap. 4.95 (ISBN 0-440-40348-0, YB). Dell.

Asimov, Isaac, et al, eds. Extraterrestrials. LC 83-49489. 256p. (gr. 7 up). 1988. pap. 3.25 (ISBN 0-06-447018-0, Trophy). HarpC Child Bks.

Berger, Melvin. If You Lived on Mars. LC 88-9105. (Illus.). 80p. (gr. 3-5). 1989. 13.95 (ISBN 0-525-67260-5, Lodestar Bks). Dutton Child Bks.

Branley, Franklyn M. Is There Life in Outer Space? Madden, Don, illus. LC 83-45057. 32p. (ps-3). 1984. (Crowell Jr Bks); PLB 13.89 (ISBN 0-690-04375-9). HarpC Child Bks.

—Mysteries of Life on Earth & Beyond. LC 86-19928. 80p. (gr. 5-9). 1987. 11.95 (ISBN 0-525-67195-1, Lodestar Bks). Dutton Child Bks.

Crum, Wesley S. UFO Crash at Aztec: The Aztec Recovery, 25 March 1948. Stevens, Wendelle C., ed. (Illus.). 1p. (gr. 9-12). 1989. poster 3.95 (ISBN 0-934269-16-5). UFO Photo.

Darling, David. Could You Ever Meet an Alien? (Illus.). (gr. 4 up). 1990. 14.95 (ISBN 0-87518-447-2, Dillon). Macmillan Child Grp.

Darling, David J. Other Worlds: Is There Life Out There? Swofford, Jeanette, illus. LC 84-23069. 64p. (gr. 4 up). 1985. PLB 10.95 (ISBN 0-87518-287-9, Dillon). Macmillan Child Grp.

Dwiggins, Don. Hello? Who's Out There? The Search for Extraterrestrial Life. (Illus.). 112p. (ps-8). 1987. 11.95 (ISBN 0-399-61228-9, Putnam). Putnam Pub Group.

Fradin, Dennis. Search for Extraterrestrial Intelligence. LC 87-14618. (Illus.). 48p. (gr. k-4). 1987. PLB 14.60 (ISBN 0-516-01242-8); pap. 4.95 (ISBN 0-516-41242-6). Childrens.

Marsh, Carole. The Backyard Searcher's Extra Terrestrial Log Book. (Illus.). (gr. 4-9). 1983. PLB 19.95 (ISBN 1-55609-282-2); pap. 14.95 (ISBN 0-935326-27-8). Gallopade Pub Group.

—How to Find an Extra Terrestrial in Your Own Backyard. (Illus.). 1983. 14.95 (ISBN 0-935326-09-X). Gallopade Pub Group.

Stevens, Wendelle C. UFO Calendar 1990. (Illus.). 26p. (gr. 9-12). 1989. wkbk. 9.95 (ISBN 0-934269-19-X). UFO Photo.

Who Are You. 24p. (ps-2). 1989. pap. 1.29 (ISBN 0-02-898252-5). Checkerboard Pr.

LIFE SUPPORT SYSTEMS (SPACE ENVIRONMENT)
see also Apollo Project

LIFESAVING
Landau, Elaine. Why Are They Starving Themselves? Understanding Anorexia Nervosa & Bulimia. Schor, Ellen, intro. by. LC 82-24913. 160p. (gr. 7 up). 1983. PLB 13.98 (ISBN 0-671-45582-6); pap. 4.95 (ISBN 0-671-49492-9). Messner.

Lifesaving. (Illus.). 64p. (gr. 6-12). 1980. pap. 1.85 (ISBN 0-8395-3278-4, 3278). BSA.

LIFTS
see Elevators; Hoisting Machinery

LIGHT
see also Color; Lasers; Optics; Radiation; Radioactivity

Anderson, L. W. Light & Color. rev. ed. LC 87-23225. (Illus.). 48p. (gr. 2-6). 1987. PLB 17.32 (ISBN 0-8172-3257-5); pap. 9.27 (ISBN 0-8172-3282-6). Raintree Pubs.

Ardley, Neil. The Science Book of Light. Van Doren, Liz, ed. (Illus.). 28p. (gr. 2-5). 1991. 9.95 (Gulliver Bks). HarBraceJ.

Asimov, Isaac. How Did We Find Out about the Speed of Light. Wool, David, illus. LC 86-4085. 64p. (gr. 5 up). 1986. 10.95 (ISBN 0-8027-6637-4); lib. bdg. 11.85 (ISBN 0-8027-6613-7). Walker & Co.

Bains, Rae. Light. Harriton, Chuck, illus. LC 84-2719. 32p. (gr. 3-6). 1985. PLB 9.49 (ISBN 0-8167-0202-0); pap. text ed. 2.95 (ISBN 0-8167-0203-9). Troll Assocs.

Crews, Donald. Light. LC 80-20273. (Illus.). 32p. (ps-1). 1981. PLB 13.88 (ISBN 0-688-00310-9). Greenwillow.

Hill, Julie & Hill, Julian. Looking at Light & Color. (Illus.). 48p. (gr. 5-8). 1986. 18.95 (ISBN 0-7134-5153-X, Pub. by Batsford England). Trafalgar Sq.

Pomeroy, Johanna P. Content Area Reading Skills Light: Main Idea. (Illus.). (gr. 3). 1989. pap. text ed. 3.25 (ISBN 1-55737-687-5). Ed Activities

Walpole, Brenda. Light. (Illus.). 40p. (gr. 4-6). 1987. PLB 12.90 (ISBN 0-531-19026-9, Pub. by Warwick Pr). Watts.

Watson, Philip. Light Fantastic. Scruton, Clive & Fenton, Ronald, illus. LC 82-80989. 48p. (gr. 3-6). 1983. PLB 11.88 (ISBN 0-688-00969-7). Lothrop.

Webb, Angela. Light. Fairclough, Chris, photos by. Franklin Watts Ltd., ed. (Illus.). 32p. (ps-6). 1988. 7.99 (ISBN 0-531-10455-9). Watts.

Whyman, Kathryn. Light & Lasers. (Illus.). 32p. (gr. 1-6). 1986. PLB 11.90 (ISBN 0-531-17033-0, Pub. by Gloucester). Watts.

Wilkins, Mary-Jane. Air, Light & Water. Bull, Peter, illus. LC 90-42620. 40p. (Orig.). (gr. 2-5). 1991. pap. 3.95 (ISBN 0-679-80859-0). Random.

LIGHT-EXPERIMENTS
Ardley, Neil. Science Book of Light. (gr. 4-7). 1991. 9.95 (ISBN 0-15-200577-3). HarBraceJ.

Broekel, Ray. Experiments with Light. LC 85-30888. (Illus.). 48p. (gr. k-4). 1986. PLB 14.60 (ISBN 0-516-01278-9); pap. 4.95 (ISBN 0-516-41278-7). Childrens.

Gardner, Robert. Light. (Illus.). 136p. (gr. 7 up). 1991. lib. bdg. 14.98 (ISBN 0-671-69037-X); pap. 9.95 (ISBN 0-671-69042-6). Messner.

Taylor, Barbara. Bouncing & Bending Light. (ps-3). 1990. PLB 11.40 (ISBN 0-531-14014-8). Watts.

—Color & Light. (ps-3). 1990. PLB 11.40 (ISBN 0-531-14015-6). Watts.

—Color & Light. (Illus.). 40p. (gr. k-4). 1991. PLB 11.90 (ISBN 0-531-19127-3, Warwick). Watts.

Ward, Alan. Experimenting with Light & Illusions. Flax, Zena, illus. 48p. (gr. 2-7). 1991. PLB 12.95 (ISBN 0-7910-1514-9). Chelsea Hse.

LIGHT AMPLIFICATION BY STIMULATED EMISSION OF RADIATION
see Lasers

LIGHT AND SHADE
see Shades and Shadows

LIGHTHOUSES
Gibbons, Gail. Beacons of Light: Lighthouses. Gibbons, Gail, illus. LC 89-33884. 32p. (gr. 1 up). 1990. 12.95 (ISBN 0-688-07379-4); PLB 12.88 (ISBN 0-688-07380-8, Morrow Jr Bks). Morrow Jr Bks.

Schaper, Sue. The Seashore & Our Lighthouse. Mackler, Carole B., ed. Vanderwalten, Kate, illus. 24p. (gr. k-8). 1989. pap. 3.95 (ISBN 0-317-94103-8). SSGI Pr.

LIGHTHOUSES-FICTION
Ardizzone, Edward. Tim to the Lighthouse. (Illus.). 48p. (gr. 1-4). 1987. pap. 6.95 (ISBN 0-19-272107-0). Oxford U Pr.

Armitage, Ronda. The Lighthouse Keeper's Catastrophe. Armitage, David, illus. 32p. (ps-3). 1986. 10.95 (ISBN 0-233-97891-7). Andre Deutsch.

—Lighthouse Keeper's Rescue. 1989. 11.95 (ISBN 0-233-98428-3). Andre Deutsch.

Farrell, Vivian. Robert's Tall Friend: A Story of the Fire Island Lighthouse. Edwards, Christy, illus. LC 87-35246. 64p. (gr. 4-7). 1988. write for info. (ISBN 0-9619832-0-5). Island-Metro Pubns.

Roop, Peter & Roop, Connie. Keep the Lights Burning, Abbie. Hanson, Peter E., illus. (gr. 2-4). 1989. incl. cass. 19.95 (ISBN 0-87499-135-8); pap. 12.95 incl. cass. (ISBN 0-87499-134-X); Set; incl. 4 bks., guide, & cass. pap. 27.95 (ISBN 0-87499-136-6). Live Oak Media.

Sargent, Ruth. The Littlest Lighthouse. Litchfield, Marion, illus. LC 81-66268. 32p. (Orig.). (ps-1). 1981. pap. 4.50 (ISBN 0-89272-119-7). Down East.

Thiele, Colin. The Hammerhead Light. LC 76-24311. (gr. 5 up). 1977. PLB 6.89 (ISBN 0-06-026117-X). HarpC Child Bks.

LIGHTING
see also Candles

LIGHTNING
Cutts, David. I Can Read About Thunder & Lightning. LC 78-66273. (Illus.). (gr. 2-6). 1979. pap. 1.95 (ISBN 0-89375-217-7). Troll Assocs.

Pearce, Q. L. Lightning & Other Wonders of the Sky. Steltenpohl, Jane, ed. Fraser, Mary A., illus. 64p. (gr. 4-6). 1989. PLB 12.98 (ISBN 0-671-68534-1); pap. 5.95 (ISBN 0-671-68648-8). Messner.

LIMERICKS
see also Nonsense Verses

Brewton, John E. & Blackburn, Lorraine A., eds. They've Discovered a Head in the Box for the Bread & Other Laughable Limericks. Krahn, Fernando, illus. LC 77-26598. 144p. (gr. 3-7). 1978. PLB 12.89 (ISBN 0-690-03883-6, Crowell Jr Bks). HarpC Child Bks.

Brewton, Sara & Brewton, John E. Laughable Limericks. Fetz, Ingrid, illus. LC 65-16179. 160p. (gr. 3-6). 1990. PLB 12.89 (ISBN 0-690-04887-4, Crowell Jr Bks). HarpC Child Bks.

Brown, Marc, compiled by. & illus. Party Rhymes. 48p. (ps-3). 1988. 13.95 (ISBN 0-525-44402-5, DCB). Dutton Child Bks.

Ciardi, John. The Hopeful Trout & Other Limericks. LC 87-23587. 1989. 13.95 (ISBN 0-395-43606-0). HM.

Cole, Joanna & Calmenson, Stephanie. Miss Mary Mack: And Other Children's Street Rhymes. Tiegreen, Alan, illus. LC 89-37266. 64p. (gr. 2 up). 1990. PLB 11.88 (ISBN 0-688-08330-7); pap. 6.95 (ISBN 0-688-09749-9, Pub. by Beech Tree Bks). Morrow Jr Bks.

Corbett, Scott. Jokes to Read in the Dark. Gusman, Annie, illus. LC 79-23129. 80p. (gr. 5-9). 1980. 12.95 (ISBN 0-525-32796-7, 01063-320, DCB); (DCB). Dutton Child Bks.

Disston, Harry. Riding Rhymes for Young Riders. Brown, Paul, illus. (gr. 1-6). 1951. pap. 1.95 (ISBN 0-87027-100-8). Cumberland Pr.

Gawron, Marlene. Busy Bodies: Finger Plays & Action Rhymes. rev. ed. (Illus.). 72p. (ps-1). 1988. pap. 5.50 (ISBN 0-913545-12-0). Moonlight FL.

Lear, Edward. Lear's Nonsense ABCs. LC 90-53464. (Illus.). 120p. (ps-8). 1991. 4.95 (ISBN 0-89471-985-8). Running Pr.

Lobel, Arnold. The Book of Pigericks. Lobel, Arnold, illus. LC 82-47730. 48p. (gr. k-3). 1983. 14.95 (ISBN 0-06-023982-4); PLB 14.89 (ISBN 0-06-023983-2). HarpC Child Bks.

Palmer, Michele, ed. Rainy Day Rhymes: A Collection of Chants, Forecasts & Tales. Guerin, Penny, illus. LC 84-60412. 24p. (Orig.). (gr. k up). 1984. pap. 2.95 (ISBN 0-932306-02-0). Rocking Horse.

Roehl, Harvey N. A Carousel of Limericks. Hyman, Pat, illus. LC 85-22538. 60p. (Orig.). (gr. 4-8). 1986. pap. 7.95 (ISBN 0-911572-47-3, A-313). Vestal.

Simms, Susan R. Rhyme Time with the Rymons: Kitchen Magician. Dallgas-Frey, Paul, illus. 36p. (ps-3). 1990. pap. 15.95 incl. audiocassette (ISBN 1-55999-136-4). LinguiSystems.

—Rhyme Time with the Rymons: My Think 'n' Do Book. Basso, Bill, illus. 100p. (ps-3). 1990. pap. 10.95 spiral bdg., wkbk. (ISBN 1-55999-139-9). LinguiSystems.

—Rhyme Time with the Rymons: Squeeze for the Keys. Dallgas-Frey, Paul, illus. 36p. (ps-3). 1990. pap. 15.95 incl. audiocassette (ISBN 1-55999-138-0). LinguiSystems.

—Rhyme Time with the Rymons: Wakin' to the Bacon. Dallgas-Frey, Paul, illus. 36p. (ps-3). 1990. pap. 15.95 incl. audiocassette (ISBN 1-55999-137-2). LinguiSystems.

Thompson, Jonathan, Jr. ABC Limericks. (Illus.). 40p. (gr. 3-6). 3.95 (ISBN 0-933479-04-2). Thompson.

Ziegler, Sandra K. Knock-Knocks, Limericks, & Other Silly Sayings. Magnuson, Diana, illus. LC 82-19764. 48p. (gr. 1-5). 1983. PLB 13.27 (ISBN 0-516-01872-8); pap. 3.95 (ISBN 0-516-41872-6). Childrens.

LIMITATION OF ARMAMENT
see Disarmament

LINCOLN, ABRAHAM, PRESIDENT U. S. 1809-1865
Abraham Lincoln. (gr. 2-5). 1987. pap. 2.25 (ISBN 0-671-62982-4, Little Simon). S&S Trade.

Adler, David A. Picture Book of Abraham Lincoln. LC 88-16393. (gr. k-3). 1989. 14.95g (ISBN 0-8234-0731-4); pap. 5.95 (ISBN 0-8234-0801-9). Holiday.

Bains, Rae. Abraham Lincoln. Smolinski, Dick, illus. LC 84-2581. 32p. (gr. 3-6). 1985. PLB 9.49 (ISBN 0-8167-0146-6); pap. text ed. 2.95 (ISBN 0-8167-0147-4). Troll Assocs.

Barkan, Joanne. Abraham Lincoln. Brook, Bonnie, ed. Miller, Lyle, illus. 32p. (gr. k-2). 1990. 5.95 (ISBN 0-671-69113-9); PLB 10.98 (ISBN 0-671-69107-4). Silver Pr.

Brandt, Keith. Abe Lincoln: The Young Years. LC 81-23172. (Illus.). 48p. (gr. 4-6). 1982. PLB 10.79 (ISBN 0-89375-750-0); pap. text ed. 2.95 (ISBN 0-89375-751-9). Troll Assocs.

Bulla, Clyde R. Lincoln's Birthday. Crichlow, Ernest, illus. LC 65-27291. 144p. (gr. 1-3). 1965. PLB 12.89 (ISBN 0-690-49450-5, Crowell Jr Bks). HarpC Child Bks.

Cary, Barbara. Meet Abraham Lincoln. Davis, J., illus. (gr. 2-6). 1965. 5.95 (ISBN 0-394-80057-5, Random Juv); lib. bdg. 8.99 (ISBN 0-394-90057-X). Random.

—Meet Abraham Lincoln. Marchesi, Stephen, illus. LC 88-19066. 72p. (gr. 2-4). 1989. PLB 6.99 (ISBN 0-394-91966-1); pap. 2.99 (ISBN 0-394-81966-7). Random.

Collins, David R. Abraham Lincoln. Quinton, Myron, illus. LC 76-2456. (gr. 3-6). 1976. pap. 6.95 (ISBN 0-915134-93-4). Mott Media.

Colver, Anne. Abraham Lincoln. Moyers, William, illus. 76p. (gr. 1-7). 1981. pap. 2.95 (ISBN 0-440-40001-5, YB). Dell.

—Abraham Lincoln: For the People. (Illus.). 80p. (gr. 2-6). 1992. Repr. of 1960 ed. PLB 12.95 (ISBN 0-7910-1414-2). Chelsea Hse.

D'Aulaire, Ingri & D'Aulaire, Edgar P. Abraham Lincoln. rev. ed. (gr. k-4). 1957. pap. 10.95 (ISBN 0-385-07669-X). Doubleday.

D'Aulaire, Ingri & Parin, Edgar P. Abraham Lincoln. LC 86-24403. (Illus.). 64p. (gr. 4-6). 1987. pap. 9.95 (ISBN 0-385-24108-9, Pub. by Zephyr-BFYR). Doubleday.

Farr, Naunerle C. Abraham Lincoln - Franklin D. Roosevelt. Redondo, Nestor & LoFamia, Jun, illus. (gr. 4-12). 1979. pap. text ed. 2.95 (ISBN 0-88301-354-1); wkbk. 1.25 (ISBN 0-88301-378-9). Pendulum Pr.

Fradin, Dennis B. Lincoln's Birthday. 48p. (gr. 2-5). 1990. 12.95 (ISBN 0-89490-250-4). Enslow Pubs.

Frazier, Carl & Frazier, Rosalie. The Lincoln Country-In Pictures. LC 63-19173. (Illus.). (gr. 4-6). 1963. 6.95 (ISBN 0-8038-4238-4). Hastings.

Freedman, Russell. Lincoln: A Photobiography. 160p. (gr. 4 up). 1987. 16.95 (ISBN 0-89919-380-3, Pub. by Clarion). Ticknor & Fields.

Gibbons, Ted. Lincoln & the Lady. 21p. 1989. pap. text ed. 2.50 (ISBN 0-929985-11-7). Sonos.

Goodman, Ailene S. Abe Lincoln in Song & Story. LC 88-753827. (gr. 4-12). 1988. incl. cassette 11.98 (ISBN 0-9620704-0-8). A S Goodman.

Greene, Carol. Abraham Lincoln: President of a Divided Country. Dobson, Steven, illus. LC 89-33845. 48p. (gr. k-3). 1989. PLB 15.27 (ISBN 0-516-04206-8); pap. 4.95 (ISBN 0-516-44206-6). Childrens.

Gross, Ruth B. If You Grew Up with Abraham Lincoln. 80p. (gr. 2-4). 1985. 2.50 (ISBN 0-590-40727-9). Scholastic Inc.

—True Stories about Abraham Lincoln. Turzak, Charles, illus. 48p. (gr. 2-7). 1988. pap. 1.95 (ISBN 0-590-40976-X). Scholastic Inc.

Hargrove, Jim. Abraham Lincoln: Sixteenth President of the United States. (Illus.). 100p. (gr. 4-7). 1988. 17.27 (ISBN 0-516-01359-9); pap. 6.95 (ISBN 0-516-41359-7). Childrens.

Holland, Margaret. Abraham Lincoln. (Illus.). 48p. (Orig.). (gr. 3-8). 1990. pap. text ed. 2.99 (ISBN 0-87406-563-1). Willowisp Pr.

Jacobs, William J. Lincoln. LC 90-8815. (Illus.). 48p. (gr. 4-6). 1991. SBE 12.95 (ISBN 0-684-19274-8, Scribners Young Read). Macmillan Child Grp.

Johnson, Ann D. The Value of Respect: The Story of Abraham Lincoln. LC 77-12455. (Illus.). (gr. k-6). 1977. 9.95 (ISBN 0-916392-14-7, Pub. by Value Communications). Oak Tree Pubns.

Kent, Zachary. The Story of the Election of Abraham Lincoln. Canaday, Ralph, illus. LC 85-23277. 32p. (gr. 3-6). 1986. PLB 13.27 (ISBN 0-516-04669-1); pap. 3.95 (ISBN 0-516-44669-X). Childrens.

Lee, Andrew. Lincoln. (Illus.). 64p. (gr. 6-9). 1989. 19.95 (ISBN 0-7134-5662-0, Pub. by Batsford England). Trafalgar Sq.

McGovern, Ann. If You Grew up With Abraham Lincoln. Turkle, Brinton, illus. (gr. 2-4). 1985. pap. 2.25 (ISBN 0-590-33631-2). Scholastic Inc.

McNeer, May. America's Abraham Lincoln. large type ed. (Illus.). 128p. (gr. 4-8). 1991. Repr. of 1957 ed. PLB 17.95 (ISBN 1-55905-090-X). Grey Castle.

Metzger, Larry. Abraham Lincoln. LC 86-22455. (Illus.). 96p. (gr. 4-8). 1987. PLB 10.40 (ISBN 0-531-10307-2). Watts.

Morgan, Lee & Cattaneo, Pietro. Abraham Lincoln. (Illus.). 104p. (gr. 5-8). 1990. 16.98 (ISBN 0-382-09973-7); pap. 8.95 (ISBN 0-382-24000-6). Silver Burdett Pr.

North, Sterling. Abe Lincoln: Log Cabin to White House. LC 87-4654. (Illus.). 160p. (gr. 5-9). 1987. lib. bdg. 8.99 (ISBN 0-394-90361-7, Random Juv); pap. 3.95 (ISBN 0-394-89179-1). Random.

Richards, Kenneth. The Story of the Gettysburg Address. Dunnington, Tom, illus. LC 70-82962. 32p. (gr. 3-5). 1969. 13.27 (ISBN 0-516-04615-2); pap. 3.95 (ISBN 0-516-44615-0). Childrens.

Sandburg, Carl. Abe Lincoln Grows Up. Daugherty, James, illus. LC 74-17180. 224p. (gr. 6 up). 1975. 19.95 (ISBN 0-15-201037-8, HJ); pap. 5.95 (ISBN 0-15-602615-5). HarBraceJ.

Shorto, Russell. Abraham Lincoln & the End of Slavery. (Illus.). 32p. (gr. 2-4). 1991. PLB 11.50 (ISBN 1-878841-12-2); pap. 3.95 (ISBN 1-878841-36-X). Millbrook Pr.

—Abraham Lincoln: To Preserve the Union. (Illus.). 160p. (gr. 5 up). 1990. lib. bdg. 16.98 (ISBN 0-382-09937-0); pap. 8.95 (ISBN 0-382-24046-4). Silver Burdett Pr.

Smith, Kathie B. Abraham Lincoln. Seward, James, illus. LC 86-28060. 24p. (gr. 4-6). 1987. PLB 7.98 (ISBN 0-671-64148-4); PLB 5.99s.p. (ISBN 0-685-18829-9). Messner.

Sproule, Anna. Abraham Lincoln: Leader of a Nation in Crisis. LC 90-10374. (Illus.). 68p. (gr. 5-6). 1991. PLB 13.95 (ISBN 0-8368-0216-0). Gareth Stevens Inc.

Stefoff, Rebecca. Abraham Lincoln: Sixteenth President of the United States. Young, Richard G., ed. LC 88-28488. (Illus.). (gr. 5-9). 1989. PLB 17.26 (ISBN 0-944483-14-3). Garrett Ed Corp.

Stevenson, Augusta. Abraham Lincoln: The Great Emancipator. Robinson, Jerry, illus. 192p. (gr. 2-6). 1986. pap. 3.95 (ISBN 0-02-042030-7, Aladdin). Macmillan Child Grp.

Wallower, Lucille. My Book about Abraham Lincoln. Gump, Patricia L., ed. (gr. 2-4). 1967. pap. 1.95 (ISBN 0-931992-10-9). Penns Valley.

Weinberg, Larry. Story of Abraham Lincoln. (gr. 4-7). 1991. pap. 2.95 (ISBN 0-440-40411-8). Dell.

LINCOLN, ABRAHAM, PRESIDENT U. S. 1809-1865–ASSASSINATION

Hamilton, Sue. The Assassination of Abraham Lincoln. Hamilton, John, ed. (Illus.). 32p. (gr. 4). 1990. PLB 11.95 (ISBN 0-939179-54-7). Abdo & Dghtrs.

Hayman, Leroy. The Death of Lincoln: A Picture History of the Assassination. (Illus.). 128p. (gr. 3 up). 1987. pap. 2.50 (ISBN 0-590-40639-6). Scholastic Inc.

—The Death of Lincoln: A Picture History of the Assassination. 128p. (gr. 4 up). 1987. pap. 2.95 (ISBN 0-590-44570-7). Scholastic Inc.

Kent, Zachary. The Story of Ford's Theatre & the Death of Lincoln. LC 87-17662. (Illus.). 32p. (gr. 3-6). 1987. PLB 13.27 (ISBN 0-516-04729-9); pap. 3.95 (ISBN 0-516-33729-7). Childrens.

LINCOLN, ABRAHAM, PRESIDENT U. S. 1809-1865–DRAMA

Abraham Lincoln: Mini-Play, 2 pts. (gr. 5 up). 1978. 6.50 ea.; Pt. 1. (ISBN 0-89550-317-4); Pt. 2. (ISBN 0-89550-325-5). Stevens & Shea.

LINCOLN, ABRAHAM, PRESIDENT U. S. 1809-1865–MONUMENTS, ETC.

Miller, Natalie. Story of the Lincoln Memorial. Dunnington, Tom, illus. LC 66-10304. 32p. (gr. 2-5). 1966. PLB 13.27 (ISBN 0-516-04623-3). Childrens.

LINCOLN, MARY (TODD) 1818-1882

Anderson, LaVere. Mary Todd Lincoln: President's Wife. Cary, illus. 80p. (gr. 2-6). 1991. Repr. of 1975 ed. PLB 12.95 (ISBN 0-7910-1415-0). Chelsea Hse.

LINCOLN, ROBERT TODD, 1843-1926

Anderson, LaVere. Robert Todd Lincoln: President's Boy. (Illus.). (gr. 3-7). 1967. 3.95 (ISBN 0-672-50161-9, Bobbs). Macmillan.

LINCOLN MEMORIAL, WASHINGTON, D. C.

Miller, Natalie. Story of the Lincoln Memorial. Dunnington, Tom, illus. LC 66-10304. 32p. (gr. 2-5). 1966. PLB 13.27 (ISBN 0-516-04623-3). Childrens.

LINDBERGH, CHARLES AUGUSTUS, 1902-

Collins, David R. Charles Lindbergh: Hero Pilot. Mays, Victor, illus. 80p. (gr. 2-6). 1991. Repr. PLB 12.95 (ISBN 0-7910-1417-7). Chelsea Hse.

Farr, Naunerle C. & Fago, John N. Amelia Earhart - Charles Lindbergh. Vicatan, illus. (gr. 4-12). 1979. pap. text ed. 2.95 (ISBN 0-88301-349-5); wkbk. 1.25 (ISBN 0-88301-373-8). Pendulum Pr.

Lindbergh, Charles A. Boyhood on the Upper Mississippi: A Reminiscent Letter. LC 72-75804. (Illus.). 50p. (gr. 4-12). 1987. pap. 7.95 (ISBN 0-87351-217-0). Minn Hist.

Randolph, Blythe. Charles Lindbergh. 1990. 12.95 (ISBN 0-531-15150-6). Watts.

—Charles Lindbergh. (gr. 4-7). 1990. PLB 13.90 (ISBN 0-531-10918-6). Watts.

Stein, R. Conrad. The Story of the Spirit of St. Louis. Meents, Len W., illus. LC 83-23174. 32p. (gr. 3-6). 1984. lib. bdg. 13.27 (ISBN 0-516-04667-5); pap. 3.95 (ISBN 0-516-44667-3). Childrens.

LINGUISTICS

see Language and Languages

LIONS

Adamson, Joy. Born Free: A Lioness of Two Worlds. (Illus.). (gr. 9 up). 1970. Pantheon.

Bender, Lionel. Lions & Tigers. FS-Aladdin Staff, ed. (Illus.). 32p. (gr. 1-6). 1988. PLB 11.90 (ISBN 0-531-17101-9, Gloucester Pr). Watts.

Cartwright, Anne & Cartwright, Reg. Proud & Fearless Lion. 32p. (ps-1). 1987. 8.95 (ISBN 0-8120-5800-3). Barron.

Crump, Donald J., ed. Lions & Tigers & Leopards: The Big Cats. (Illus.). (gr. k-4). 1990. Set. 13.95 (ISBN 0-87044-820-X); Set. PLB write for info. (ISBN 0-87044-825-0). Natl Geog.

Goodall, Jane, ed. Jane Goodall's Animal World: Lions. (Illus.). 32p. (gr. 3-7). 1989. pap. 3.95 (ISBN 0-689-71322-3, Aladdin). Macmillan Child Grp.

Green, Carl R. & Sanford, William R. African Lion. LC 87-13648. (Illus.). 48p. (gr. 5-6). 1987. PLB 10.95 (ISBN 0-89686-328-X, Crestwood Hse). Macmillan Child Grp.

Hoffman, Mary. Lion. LC 84-24794. (Illus.). 24p. (gr. k-5). 1985. PLB 13.32 (ISBN 0-8172-2411-4). Raintree Pubs.

Hurd, Edith T. Johnny Lion's Rubber Boots. Hurd, Clement, illus. LC 70-183165. 64p. (gr. k-3). 1972. PLB 11.89 (ISBN 0-06-022710-9). HarpC Child Bks.

Johnson, Sylvia A. The Lions of Africa. Hammarberg, Dyan, tr. from FRE. LC 76-29474. (Illus.). 24p. (gr. k-4). 1977. PLB 6.95 (ISBN 0-87614-081-9). Carolrhoda Bks.

Lions & Tigers. 32p. (Orig.). (ps-1). 1984. pap. 1.25 (ISBN 0-8431-1511-4). Price Stern.

MacGuire, Leslie. Jane Goodall's Animal World: Lions. Goodall, Jane, ed. (Illus.). 32p. (gr. 3-7). 1989. 11.95 (ISBN 0-689-31470-1, Atheneum Child Bk). Macmillan Child Grp.

Petty, Kate. Finding Out about Lions & Tigers. Barwick, Tessa, illus. 32p. (gr. k-3). 1989. 2.50 (ISBN 0-87406-410-4, 42-18343-1). Willowisp Pr.

—Lions. (ps-3). 1990. PLB 10.40 (ISBN 0-531-17196-5). Watts.

Stone, L. Lions. (Illus.). 24p. (gr. k-5). 1989. lib. bdg. 11.93 (ISBN 0-86592-501-1). Rourke Corp.

Yoshida, Toshi. Young Lions. Yoshida, Toshi, illus. 40p. (gr. 1-5). 1989. 14.95 (ISBN 0-399-21546-8, Philomel Bks). Putnam Pub Group.

LIONS–FICTION

Aardema, Verna. Rabbit Makes a Monkey of Lion. Pinkney, Jerry, illus. LC 86-11523. 32p. (ps-3). 1989. 11.95 (ISBN 0-8037-0297-3); PLB 11.89 (ISBN 0-8037-0298-1). Dial Bks Young.

Allen, Pamela. A Lion in the Night. Allen, Pamela, illus. LC 85-12346. 32p. (ps-2). 1986. 11.95 (ISBN 0-399-21203-5, Putnam). Putnam Pub Group.

Angeli, Marguerite de. The Lion in the Box. 1975. 12.95 (ISBN 0-385-03317-6). Doubleday.

Beittel, Kenneth R. & Beittel, Joan N. Ralph & Deno in Vermont. Beittel, Kenneth R., illus. LC 90-86028. 32p. (Orig.). (gr. 5 up). 1990. pap. 6.00 (ISBN 0-9628511-0-8). HVHA.

Blagowidow, George. In Search of the Lady Lion Tamer. 1987. 15.95 (ISBN 0-15-144500-1). HarBraceJ.

Bulla, Clyde R. Lion to Guard Us. LC 80-2455. (Illus.). 128p. (gr. 3-5). 1989. pap. 3.50 (ISBN 0-06-440333-5, Trophy). HarpC Child Bks.

Bussard, Paula. Words Can Hurt. Goodridge, Larry, illus. 28p. (gr. k-3). 1985. 1.39 (ISBN 0-87239-965-6, 3385). Standard Pub.

Daugherty, James. Andy & the Lion. Daugherty, James, illus. LC 38-27390. 80p. (gr. 1-4). 1938. pap. 13.95 (ISBN 0-670-12433-8). Viking Child Bks.

—Andy & the Lion. (Illus.). 72p. (ps-3). 1989. pap. 3.95 (ISBN 0-14-050277-7, Puffin). Puffin Bks.

Desaix, Frank. Hilary & the Lions. (gr. 4-8). 1990. 13.95 (ISBN 0-374-33237-1). FS&G.

Fatio, Louise. The Happy Lion. Duvoisin, Roger, illus. 32p. (ps-3). 1986. pap. 4.95 (ISBN 0-590-41936-6, Blue Ribbon Bks). Scholastic Inc.

Freeman, Don. Dandelion. Freeman, Don, illus. LC 64-21472. 48p. (ps-2). 1964. pap. 12.95 (ISBN 0-670-25532-7). Viking Child Bks.

Frost, Erica. Mr. Lion Goes to Lunch. Epstein, Len, illus. LC 85-14012. 48p. (Orig.). (gr. 1-3). 1986. PLB 9.89 (ISBN 0-8167-0638-7); pap. text ed. 2.95 (ISBN 0-8167-0639-5). Troll Assocs.

Guillot, Rene. Sirga. Kiddell-Monroe, Joan, illus. LC 59-12198. (gr. 6-9). 1959. 18.95 (ISBN 0-87599-046-0). S G Phillips.

Hadithi, Mwenye. Lazy Lion. (ps-4). 1990. 14.95 (ISBN 0-316-33725-0). Little.

Hammond, Jane. Lester the Lion. (ps-k). 1983. pap. 1.50 (ISBN 0-87162-291-2, D5605). Warner Pr.

Hancock, Joy E. The Loudest Little Lion. Fay, Ann, ed. (Illus.). 24p. (ps-k). 1988. PLB 10.95 (ISBN 0-8075-4773-5). A Whitman.

Hunt, Robert. Curly & Simba: Twin African Lions. McBarron, H. Charles, illus. LC 74-735890. (gr. 2-5). 1978. 6 bks. & 1 cass. 29.95 (ISBN 0-89290-031-8); 1 bk. & 1 cass. 10.95 (ISBN 0-685-04638-9). Soc for Visual.

Hurd, Edith T. Johnny Lion's Bad Day. LC 78-85035. (Illus.). 64p. (gr. k-3). 1970. PLB 11.89 (ISBN 0-06-022708-7). HarpC Child Bks.

—Johnny Lion's Book. Hurd, Clement, illus. LC 65-14490. 64p. (gr. k-3). 1965. PLB 11.89 (ISBN 0-06-022706-0). HarpC Child Bks.

Kessel. Le Lion. (gr. 7-12). pap. 5.95 (ISBN 0-88436-112-8, 40277). EMC.

Kimba the Lion. (ps). 1976. 2.50 (ISBN 0-904494-30-6, Brimax Bks). Borden.

Koram, Gamal. When Lions Could Fly. (Illus.). 42p. (gr. 4-12). 1989. pap. 5.00 (ISBN 1-877610-01-1). Sea Island.

La Fontaine. The Lion & the Rat. Wildsmith, Brian, illus. 32p. 1987. 12.95 (ISBN 0-19-279607-0); pap. 5.95 (ISBN 0-19-272167-4). Oxford U Pr.

Lewis, C. S. The Lion, the Witch & the Wardrobe. Baynes, Pauline, illus. LC 50-10611. 160p. (gr. 4 up). 1988. 12.95 (ISBN 0-02-758120-9, Mcmillan Child Bk). Macmillan Child Grp.

The Lion Who Couldn't Say No. (ps-3). 1988. pap. 2.50 (ISBN 0-318-36472-7). Scholastic Inc.

Lyne, Sandy. The Lion & the Boy. Reilly, Kathy, illus. 48p. (gr. 4-7). 1988. 12.95 (ISBN 0-933905-04-1); pap. 9.95 (ISBN 0-933905-15-7). Claycomb Pr.

McIntire, Donald. The Pemaquid Loon from Temple. Bull, Kris F., illus. 1988. pap. 5.99 (ISBN 0-317-92307-2). Herit Print Co.

McPhail, David. Snow Lion. McPhail, David, illus. LC 82-8119. 48p. (ps-3). 1987. 5.95 (ISBN 0-8193-1097-2); PLB 5.95 (ISBN 0-8193-1098-0). Parents.

—Snow Lion. McPhail, David, illus. 48p. (gr. 3-7). 1990. pap. 2.95 (ISBN 0-448-04335-1, G&D). Putnam Pub Group.

Michael, Emory H. Androcles & the Lion. Hatchem, Mia, illus. LC 87-51492. 44p. (gr. k-4). 1988. 6.95 (ISBN 1-55523-132-2). Winston-Derek.

Mora, Emma. Cyril the Lion. 30p. (ps-1). 1987. 3.95 (ISBN 0-8120-5811-9). Barron.

Peet, Bill. Eli. Peet, Bill, illus. LC 77-17500. 48p. (gr. k-3). 1978. 13.95 (ISBN 0-395-26454-5). HM.

—Randy's Dandy Lions. (Illus.). (gr. k-3). 1980. 13.95 (ISBN 0-395-18507-6); pap. 3.95 (ISBN 0-395-27498-2). HM.

Pene du Bois, William. Lion. (Illus.). 32p. (ps-3). 1983. pap. 4.95 (ISBN 0-14-050417-6, Penguin Bks). Viking Penguin.

Pierce, Tamora. Lioness Rampant. LC 88-6213. 336p. (gr. 6 up). 1990. pap. 3.50 (ISBN 0-679-80113-8, Borzoi Sprinters). Knopf.

Pryor, Bonnie. Seth of the Lion People. LC 88-18747. 128p. (gr. 3-6). 1988. 11.95 (ISBN 0-688-07327-1). Morrow Jr Bks.

Rogers, Paul. Forget-Me-Not. Berridge, Celia, illus. LC 83-5969. 32p. (gr. k-1). 1984. pap. 8.95 (ISBN 0-670-32365-9). Viking Child Bks.

Rogers, Paul T. Forget-Me-Not. Berridge, Celia, illus. 32p. (ps-k). 1986. pap. 3.50 (Puffin). Puffin Bks.

Shaw, George Bernard. Androcles & the Lion. Storr, Catherine, ed. Hood, Philip, illus. LC 86-6665. 32p. (gr. 2-5). 1986. PLB 16.67 (ISBN 0-8172-2625-7). Raintree Pubs.

Silverstein, Shel. Lafcadio, the Lion Who Shot Back. Silverstein, Shel, illus. LC 62-13320. 112p. (gr. 3-6). 1963. 13.95 (ISBN 0-06-025675-3); PLB 13.89 (ISBN 0-06-025676-1). HarpC Child Bks.

Stone, Elaine M. Tekla & the Lion. LC 90-71366. (Illus.). 44p. (gr. 3-6). 1991. pap. 7.95 (ISBN 1-55523-388-0). Winston-Derek.

The Tawny Scrawny Lion & the Clever Monkey. (ps-3). 1989. Incl. cass. write for info. incl. cass. (13681, Pub. by Golden Bks). Western Pub.

Wagener, Gerda. Leo the Lion. Ignatowicz, Nina, tr. from GER. Michl, Reinhard, illus. LC 90-46272. 32p. (gr. k-3). 1991. 14.95 (ISBN 0-06-021656-5); PLB 14.89 (ISBN 0-06-021657-3). HarpC Child Bks.

—Leo the Lion. Ignatowicz, Nina, tr. from GER. Michl, Reinhard, illus. LC 90-46272. 32p. (gr. k-3). 1991. 14.95 (ISBN 0-06-021656-5); PLB 14.89 (ISBN 0-06-021657-3). HarpC Child Bks.

Wells, Rosemary. A Lion for Lewis. Wells, Rosemary, illus. LC 82-70197. 32p. (ps-2). 1982. 9.95 (ISBN 0-8037-4683-0); PLB 9.89 (ISBN 0-8037-4686-5). Dial Bks Young.
—A Lion for Lewis. Wells, Rosemary, illus. 32p. (ps-2). 1984. pap. 3.95 (ISBN 0-8037-0096-2, Dial Pied Piper). Puffin Bks.
Zelinsky, Paul O. The Lion & the Stoat. Zelinsky, Paul O., illus. LC 83-16326. 40p. (gr. 1-3). 1984. PLB 10.88 (ISBN 0-688-02563-3). Greenwillow.
Zimelman, Nathan. Treed by a Pride of Irate Lions. Goffe, Toni, illus. LC 89-30344. (gr. k-3). 1990. 14.95 (ISBN 0-316-98802-2). Little.

LIONS-HABITS AND BEHAVIOR

Michel, Anna. Little Wild Lion Cub. Chen, Tony, illus. LC 79-17509. 48p. (gr. 1-4). 1980. Pantheon.

Taylor, Dave. The Lion & the Savannah. (Illus.). 32p. (gr. 3-4). 1990. lib. bdg. 14.95 (ISBN 0-86505-364-2); pap. 7.95 (ISBN 0-86505-394-4). Crabtree Pub Co.
Life in a lion pride is the subject of LION & THE SAVANNAH. The various roles of the female lion, from mother to hunter, are explored. The book also explains lion territories, the lives of lion cubs, & weaves the King of Beasts into the tapestry of the grassland ecosystem, highlighting the animals of prey, the scavengers, & the decomposers. A section on predators guides children away from applying human values to the animal world. The dynamic, complex relationship between an animal & its habitat is the focus of The Animals & Their Ecosystems Series. Dramatic photographs & lively text portray the exciting daily struggle for survival. Each book takes an intimate look at the adventures of a single animal, following it through the important stages of life. The other animals that share the same ecosystem are also highlighted. Other books in the series include ELEPHANT & THE SCRUB FOREST, BISON & THE GREAT PLAINS, & ALLIGATOR & THE EVERGLADES.
Publisher Provided Annotation.

LIONS-POETRY

Peet, Bill. Hubert's Hair-Raising Adventure. (Illus.). 36p. (gr. k-3). 1959. 13.95 (ISBN 0-395-15083-3). HM.

LIQUIDS

Agler, Leigh. Liquid Explorations. Bergman, Lincoln & Fairwell, Kay, eds. Klofkorn, Lisa, illus. Hoyt, Richard, photos by. (Illus.). 67p. (Orig.). (gr. 1-3). 1987. pap. 7.50 (ISBN 0-912511-51-6). Lawrence Science.
Barber, Jacqueline. Solids, Liquids, & Gases. Bergman, Lincoln & Fairwell, Kay, eds. Baker, Lisa H. & Peterson, Adria, illus. Barber, Jacqueline, et al, photos by. 56p. (Orig.). (gr. 3-6). 1986. pap. 10.00 (ISBN 0-912511-69-9). Lawrence Science.
Berger, Melvin. Solids, Liquids & Gases: From Superconductors to the Ozone Layer. (Illus.). 80p. (gr. 5 up). 1989. 11.99 (ISBN 0-399-21731-2, Putnam). Putnam Pub Group.
Durant, Penny R. Make A Splash! Science Activities with Liquids. Huehnergarth, John, illus. LC 90-34063. 32p. (gr. 1-4). 1991. PLB 12.90 (ISBN 0-531-10971-2). Watts.
Watson, Philip. Liquid Magic. Wood, Elizabeth & Fenton, Ronald, illus. LC 82-80988. 48p. (gr. 3-6). 1983. PLB 11.88 (ISBN 0-688-00967-0). Lothrop.

LITERARY CRITICISM

see Criticism; Literature–History and Criticism

LITERATURE-BIO-BIBLIOGRAPHY

see also Authors

LITERATURE-BIOGRAPHY

see Authors

LITERATURE-CRITICISM

see Literature–History and Criticism

LITERATURE-EVALUATION

see Book Reviews; Books and Reading; Books and Reading-Best Books; Criticism; Literature–History and Criticism

LITERATURE-HISTORY AND CRITICISM

see also Authors; Criticism

Cahn, Julie. Holiday Romance. Schnedier, Meg & Schwartz, Betty, eds. 128p. (Orig.). (gr. 4-5). 1983. pap. 2.85 (ISBN 0-671-46450-7, Little Simon). S&S Trade.
Magill, Frank N., ed. Masterplots II, 4 vols. 1745p. (gr. 9-12). 1989. Set. PLB 350.00 (ISBN 0-89356-478-8, Magill Bks). Salem Pr.
—Masterplots II, 4 vols. 1695p. 1991. Set. PLB 350.00 (ISBN 0-89356-579-2, Magill Bks). Salem Pr.
Rowbotham, Judith. Good Girls Make Good Wives: Guidance for Girls in Victorian Fiction. (Illus.). 256p. (gr. 9-12). 1989. text ed. 45.00 (ISBN 0-631-16395-6); pap. text ed. 15.95 (ISBN 0-631-16396-4). Basil Blackwell.
Williams, Brian. Literature. LC 90-36113. (Illus.). 48p. (gr. 6-11). 1990. PLB 18.60 (ISBN 0-8114-2365-4). Steck-V.
World Book, Inc. Staff, ed. Stories of Freedom: The 1988 Childcraft Annual. LC 65-25105. (Illus.). 288p. (gr. 8-12). 1988. lib. bdg. write for info. (ISBN 0-7166-0688-7). World Bk.

LITERATURE-STORIES, PLOTS, ETC.

Preston-Foster, Mary. Fun With Fiction. (gr. 2-5). 1988. pap. 6.95 (ISBN 0-8224-3173-4). Fearon Teach Aids.

LITERATURE AS A PROFESSION

see Authors; Authorship; Journalism; Journalists

LITTERING

see Refuse and Refuse Disposal

LITTLE, MALCOLM, 1925-1965

Adoff, Arnold. Malcolm X. Wilson, John, illus. LC 85-42974. 40p. (gr. 2-5). 1985. pap. 5.95 (ISBN 0-06-446015-0, Trophy). HarpC Child Bks.
Cwiklik, Robert. Malcolm X & Black Pride. (Illus.). 32p. (gr. 2-4). 1991. PLB 11.50 (ISBN 1-56294-042-2); pap. 3.95 (ISBN 1-878841-73-4). Millbrook Pr.
Davies, Mark. Malcolm X: Another Side of the Movement. Gallin, Richard, ed. Young, Andrew, intro. by. (Illus.). 128p. (gr. 5 up). 1990. lib. bdg. 16.98 (ISBN 0-382-09925-7); pap. 7.95 (ISBN 0-382-24063-4). Silver Burdett Pr.
Obaba, Al-Imam. Malcolm X Great Nubian Quiz. (Illus.). 43p. (Orig.). 1988. pap. 3.95 (ISBN 0-916157-16-4). African Islam Miss Pubns.
Rummel, Jack. Malcolm X. King, Coretta Scott, intro. by. (Illus.). 112p. (gr. 5 up). 1989. lib. bdg. 17.95x (ISBN 1-55546-600-1); pap. 9.95 (ISBN 0-7910-0227-6). Chelsea Hse.

LITTLE BIG HORN, BATTLE OF THE, 1876

Henckel, Mark. Battle of the Little Bighorn. Potter, John, illus. 32p. (Orig.). (gr. 3-7). 1991. pap. 5.95 (ISBN 1-56044-042-2). Falcon Pr MT.
Stein, R. Conrad. The Story of Little Bighorn. LC 83-6594. (Illus.). 32p. (gr. 3-6). 1983. PLB 13.27 (ISBN 0-516-04663-2); pap. 3.95 (ISBN 0-516-44663-0). Childrens.
Willis, Charles. Battle of Little Big Horn. (Illus.). 64p. 1990. lib. bdg. 16.98 (ISBN 0-382-09952-4); pap. 7.95 (ISBN 0-382-09948-6). Silver Burdett Pr.

LITTLE LEAGUE BASEBALL

Kruetzer, Peter. Little League's Official How-to-Play Baseball Book. 1990. 19.95 (ISBN 0-385-41227-4); pap. 12.95 (ISBN 0-385-41278-9). Doubleday.
—Little League's Official How-to-Play Baseball Handbook. 1990. pap. 9.95 (ISBN 0-385-24700-1). Doubleday.
Newman, Gerald. Happy Birthday, Little League. 64p. (gr. 3-6). 1989. PLB 11.90 (ISBN 0-531-10687-X). Watts.

LITTLE LEAGUE BASEBALL-FICTION

Benchley, Nathaniel. Only Earth & Sky Last Forever. LC 72-82891. 204p. (gr. 7 up). 1974. pap. 4.95 (ISBN 0-06-440049-2, Trophy). HarpC Child Bks.
Konigsburg, E. L. About the B'nai Bagels. Konigsburg, E. L., illus. LC 69-13529. 176p. (gr. 4-6). 1971. 13.95 (ISBN 0-689-20631-3, Atheneum Child Bk). Macmillan Child Grp.

LIVESTOCK

see also Cattle; Cows; Dairying; Domestic Animals; Hogs; Horses; Sheep; Veterinary Medicine

Whyte, Malcolm. Farm Animals. (Illus.). 32p. (Orig.). (gr. 1-4). 1989. pap. 3.50 (ISBN 0-8431-1960-8). Price Stern.

LIVINGSTONE, DAVID, 1813-1873

Clinton, Susan. Henry Stanley & David Livingstone. LC 90-2172. (Illus.). 128p. (gr. 3 up). 1990. PLB 25.27 (ISBN 0-516-03055-8). Childrens.
Stocker, Fern N. Growing up with David Livingstone. 128p. (Orig.). 1987. pap. 2.99 (ISBN 0-8163-0679-6). Pacific Pr Pub Assn.

LIZARDS

Barrett, Norman. Dragons & Lizards. (Illus.). 32p. (gr. k-4). 1991. PLB 11.40 (ISBN 0-531-14111-X). Watts.
Bender, Lionel. First Sight: Lizards & Dragons. 1990. pap. 3.95 (ISBN 0-531-17259-7). Watts.
—Lizards & Dragons. Franklin Watts Ltd., ed. (Illus.). 32p. (gr. k-9). 1988. PLB 11.90 (ISBN 0-531-17075-6, Gloucester Pr). Watts.
Creighton, Susan. The Giant Lizard. LC 88-16128. (Illus.). 48p. (gr. 5-6). 1988. PLB 10.95 (ISBN 0-89686-394-8, Crestwood Hse). Macmillan Child Grp.
Curtis, Neil. Discovering Snakes & Lizards. LC 85-72248. (Illus.). 48p. (gr. k-6). 1986. lib. bdg. 11.90 (ISBN 0-531-18048-4, Pub. by Bookwright Pr). Watts.
Gravelle, Karen. Lizards. (Illus.). 64p. (gr. 5-8). 1991. PLB 11.90 (ISBN 0-531-20026-4). Watts.
Harrison, Virginia. The World of Lizards. Oxford Scientific Films Staff, photos by. LC 87-42608. (Illus.). 32p. (gr. 2-3). 1988. PLB 10.95 (ISBN 1-55532-307-3). Gareth Stevens Inc.
Linley, Mike. The Lizard in the Jungle. Oxford Scientific Films, photos by. LC 87-42612. (Illus.). 32p. (gr. 4-6). 1988. PLB 10.95 (ISBN 1-55532-303-0). Gareth Stevens Inc.
Martin, L. Chameleons. (Illus.). 24p. (gr. k-5). 1989. lib. bdg. 11.94 (ISBN 0-86592-576-3). Rourke Corp.
—Iguanas. (Illus.). 24p. (gr. k-5). 1989. lib. bdg. 11.93 (ISBN 0-86592-575-5). Rourke Corp.
—Komodo Dragons. (Illus.). 24p. (gr. k-5). 1989. lib. bdg. 11.93 (ISBN 0-86592-574-7). Rourke Corp.
—Lizards. (Illus.). 24p. (gr. k-5). 1989. lib. bdg. 11.93 (ISBN 0-86592-577-1). Rourke Corp.
Mattison, Chris. Lizards of the World. (Illus.). 192p. 1989. 24.95x (ISBN 0-8160-1900-2). Facts on File.
Morris, Dean. Snakes & Lizards. rev. ed. LC 87-16697. (Illus.). 48p. (gr. 2-6). 1987. PLB 17.32 (ISBN 0-8172-3212-5). Raintree Pubs.
Pettit, Jayne. Amazing Lizards. (Illus.). 72p. (gr. 3-7). 1990. pap. 2.50 (ISBN 0-590-43682-1). Scholastic Inc.
Scherrow, Victoria. The Gecko. (Illus.). 60p. (gr. 3 up). 1990. PLB 12.95 (ISBN 0-87518-441-3, Dillon). Macmillan Child Grp.
Serventy, Vincent. Lizard. (Illus.). 24p. (gr. k-5). 1986. PLB 13.32 (ISBN 0-8172-2706-7). Raintree Pubs.
Smith, Trevor. Amazing Lizards. Young, Jerry, photos by. LC 90-31884. (Illus.). 32p. (Orig.). (gr. 1-5). 1991. lib. bdg. 9.99 (ISBN 0-679-90819-6); pap. 6.95 (ISBN 0-679-80819-1). Knopf.

LIZARDS-FICTION

Bush, Don. Magic Smith the Chameleon. 62p. (gr. 3). text ed. 6.50 (ISBN 0-943978-02-5). Rolling Hills Pr.
Carle, Eric. The Mixed-Up Chameleon. 2nd ed. Carle, Eric, illus. LC 83-45950. 32p. (ps-3). 1984. 14.95 (ISBN 0-690-04396-1, Crowell Jr Bks); PLB 14.89 (ISBN 0-690-04397-X). HarpC Child Bks.
Gardner, Richard A. Dorothy & the Lizard of Oz. Richmond, Frank, illus. LC 80-12787. 108p. (gr. 1-6). 1980. 14.95 (ISBN 0-933812-03-5). Creative Therapeutics.
Hale, Bruce. The Legend of the Laughing Gecko: A Hawaiian Fantasy. Hale, Bruce, illus. Brown, Susana, concept by. (Illus.). 32p. (Orig.). (ps-3). 1989. pap. write for info. Geckostufs.
Kemvichanuvat, Cherdchai. The Poor Lizard. Rodriguez, Gloria F., ed. Chang, Phillip, illus. Pinta, Thanom, tr. (Illus.). (gr. k-3). 1979. pap. 3.50 (ISBN 0-686-26621-8, Pub. by New Day Pub Philippines). Cellar.
Lopshire, Robert. I Am Better Than You. Lopshire, Robert, illus. LC 68-24325. 64p. (gr. k-3). 1968. PLB 11.89 (ISBN 0-06-023997-2). HarpC Child Bks.
Magellan, Mauro. Cambio Chameleon. Magellan, Mauro, illus. LC 89-19995. 32p. 1990. 12.95 (ISBN 0-89334-118-5). Humanics Ltd.
Massie, Diane R. Chameleon Was a Spy. Massie, Diane R., illus. LC 78-19510. (gr. 2-6). 1979. (Crowell Jr Bks). HarpC Child Bks.

Rowan, Barbara. Igor & Mom. Powell, Michelle, illus. LC 90-84009. 43p. (Orig.). (gr. k-4). 1991. pap. 7.50 (ISBN 0-9622863-2-X). Bristlecone Pubns.
In preparation for the fifth-grade science fair, ten-year-old Jason trains his large green iguana, Igor, to run to his food dish at the sound of a bell. While Jason is showing his experiment to Mom, who is frightened of the green creature, Igor escapes. Mom ends up finding & capturing Igor while Jason is at school & gets the iguana to the science room in time for the judging. However, Igor doesn't answer the bell & fails to win the blue ribbon that Jason has been coveting. At three o'clock, the school bell rings & Igor runs to his dish. Jason laughs & decides the green honorable mention ribbon matches his pet better anyway.
Publisher Provided Annotation.

Ryder, Joanne. Lizard in the Sun. Rothman, Michael, illus. LC 89-33886. 32p. (gr. k up). 1990. 13.95 (ISBN 0-688-07172-4); PLB 13.88 (ISBN 0-688-07173-2, Morrow Jr Bks). Morrow Jr Bks.
Shannon, George. Lizard's Song. Aruego, Jose & Dewey, Ariane, illus. LC 80-21432. 32p. (gr. k-3). 1981. 13.95 (ISBN 0-688-80310-5); PLB 13.88 (ISBN 0-688-84310-7). Greenwillow.
Wallace, Bill. Ferret in the Bedroom, Lizards in the Fridge. LC 85-21996. 144p. (gr. 3-7). 1986. 13.95 (ISBN 0-8234-0600-8). Holiday.

LLAMAS

Arnold, Caroline. Llama. Hewett, Richard, photos by. LC 87-27130. (Illus.). 48p. (gr. 2-5). 1988. 12.95 (ISBN 0-688-07540-1); PLB 12.88 (ISBN 0-688-07541-X). Morrow.

Barkman, Betty. Llamas in Their Formative Years: Behavior & Socialization. LC 88-70547. (Illus.). 60p. (Orig.). (gr. 11 up). 1991. pap. text ed. 25.00 (ISBN 0-945860-00-5). Birch Bark Pr.

Barkman, Betty & Barkman, Paul. A Well Trained Llama: A Trainers Guide. rev. ed. LC 88-93027. (Illus.). 95p. (Orig.). (gr. 9 up). 1989. pap. text ed. 25.00 (ISBN 0-945860-01-3). Birch Bark Pr.

Hart, Rosana. Living with Llamas: Tales from Juniper Ridge. rev. ed. (Illus.). 192p. 1991. pap. 11.95 (ISBN 0-916289-13-3). Juniper Ridge.

Kienlen, Helen & Sandercock, Lois. Llamas. Bower, J. R., illus. 16p. (Orig.). (gr. k-4). 1989. pap. text ed. 4.00 (ISBN 0-9626864-0-9). Holistic Learning.

LaBonte, Gail. The Llama. LC 88-16407. (Illus.). 60p. (gr. 3 up). 1989. PLB 12.95 (ISBN 0-87518-393-X, Dillon). Macmillan Child Grp.

LLAMAS–FICTION

Cosgrove, Stephen. Pish-Posh. James, Robin, illus. 32p. (gr. 5-9). 1986. pap. 2.95 (ISBN 0-8431-1449-5). Price Stern.

—Pish-Posh. James, Robin, illus. LC 86-15616. (gr. k-2). 1986. 12.66 (ISBN 0-86592-240-3). Rourke Corp.

Guarino, Deborah. Is Your Mama a Llama? Kellogg, Steven, illus. 1991. pap. 3.95 (ISBN 0-590-44725-4, Blue Ribbon Bks). Scholastic Inc.

Massi, Jeri. The Myth of the Llama. Thompson, Del & Thompson, Dana, illus. 118p. (Orig.). (gr. 6). 1989. pap. 5.95 (ISBN 1-877778-00-1). Llama Bks.

LOAN FUNDS, STUDENT

see Student Loan Funds

LOBSTERS

Bailey, Jill. Discovering Crabs & Lobsters. (Illus.). 48p. (gr. 1 up). 1987. lib. bdg. 11.90 (ISBN 0-531-18125-1, Pub. by Bookwright Pr). Watts.

LOBSTERS–FICTION

Harriman, Edward. Leroy the Lobster & Crabby Crab. (Illus.). (ps-1). 1967. pap. 6.95 (ISBN 0-89272-000-X). Down East.

Olsen, E. A. Lobster King. LC 68-16400. (Illus.). 48p. (gr. 3 up). 1970. PLB 10.95 (ISBN 0-87783-024-X); pap. 3.94 deluxe ed. (ISBN 0-87783-099-1); cassette 10.60x (ISBN 0-87783-192-0). Oddo.

Ziefert, Harriet. Bob & Shirley: A Tale of Two Lobsters. Smith, Mavis, illus. LC 90-43150. 32p. (gr. k-3). 1991. PLB 11.89 (ISBN 0-06-026908-1); pap. 3.95 (ISBN 0-06-107427-6). HarpC Child Bks.

LOCAL GOVERNMENT

see also Cities and Towns

Eichner, James. First Book of Local Government. rev ed. (gr. 5-9). 1983. PLB 10.40 (ISBN 0-531-04642-7). Watts.

Santrey, Laurence. State & Local Government. Dole, Bob, illus. LC 84-8440. 32p. (gr. 3-6). 1985. PLB 9.49 (ISBN 0-8167-0270-5); pap. text ed. 2.95 (ISBN 0-8167-0271-3). Troll Assocs.

LOCH NESS, SCOTLAND

Abels, Harriette S. Loch Ness Monster. LC 87-9027. (Illus.). 48p. (gr. 5-6). 1987. PLB 10.95 (ISBN 0-89686-343-3, Crestwood Hse). Macmillan Child Grp.

Berke, Sally. Monster at Loch Ness. LC 77-24715. (Illus.). 48p. (gr. 4 up). 1983. PLB 17.32 (ISBN 0-8172-1054-7); pap. 9.27 (ISBN 0-8172-2160-3). Raintree Pubs.

Hezlep, William. Nessie. (gr. 3-12). 1980. pap. text ed. 5.00 (ISBN 0-88734-401-1). Players Pr.

San Souci, Robert. The Loch Ness Monster: Opposing Viewpoints. LC 89-12026. (Illus.). 112p. (gr. 3-10). 1989. PLB 13.95 (ISBN 0-89908-072-3). Greenhaven.

—The Loch Ness Monster: Opposing Viewpoints. LC 89-12026. (Illus.). 112p. (gr. 3-10). 1989. PLB 13.95 (ISBN 0-89908-072-3). Greenhaven.

LOCKS AND KEYS

Gibbons, Gail. Locks & Keys. LC 79-7825. (Illus.). 32p. (gr. 1-4). 1980. PLB 13.89 (ISBN 0-690-04059-8, Crowell Jr Bks). HarpC Child Bks.

Hughes, Shirley. Alfie Gets in First. Hughes, Shirley, illus. LC 81-8427. 32p. (ps-1). 1982. 13.95 (ISBN 0-688-00848-8); PLB 13.88 (ISBN 0-688-00849-6). Lothrop.

Sharmat, Marjorie W. Nate the Great & the Missing Key. Simont, Marc, illus. 48p. (gr. 1-4). 1982. pap. 2.99 (ISBN 0-440-46191-X, YB). Dell.

LOCOMOTION

see Aeronautics; Automobiles; Boats and Boating; Flight; Navigation; Transportation; Walking

LOCOMOTIVES

Chant, Chris. Steam Locomotives. Batchelor, John, illus. LC 88-28763. 63p. (gr. 3 up). 1989. PLB 16.95 (ISBN 1-85435-087-0). Marshall Cavendish.

Scarry, Huck. Aboard a Steam Locomotive. LC 86-16957. (Illus.). (gr. 4-12). 1987. 12.95 (ISBN 0-13-000373-5). P-H.

LOCOMOTIVES–FICTION

Burton, Virginia L. Choo Choo. (Illus.). 48p. (gr. k-3). 1973. 14.95 (ISBN 0-395-17684-0). HM.

Fleming, Ian. Chitty Chitty Bang Bang. 159p. (gr. 5-6). Repr. of 1964 ed. lib. bdg. 15.95 (ISBN 0-88411-983-1, Pub. by Aeonian Pr). Amereon Ltd.

Peet, Bill. Smokey. (Illus.). (gr. k-3). 1962. 12.95 (ISBN 0-395-15992-X). HM.

LOCUSTS

Bailey, Jill. Life Cycle of a Grasshopper. (ps-3). 1990. PLB 8.99 (ISBN 0-531-18314-9). Watts.

Dallinger, Jane. Grasshoppers. LC 80-27806. (Illus.). (gr. 4 up). 1981. PLB 14.95 (ISBN 0-8225-1455-9). Lerner Pubns.

—Grasshoppers. Sato, Yuko, photos by. (Illus.). 48p. (gr. 4 up). pap. 5.95 (ISBN 0-8225-9568-0). Lerner Pubns.

Hasegawa, Yo. The Grasshopper. Pohl, Kathy, ed. LC 85-28228. (Illus.). 32p. (gr. 3-7). 1986. text ed. 16.67 (ISBN 0-8172-2536-6); pap. text ed. 9.27 (ISBN 0-8172-2561-7). Raintree Pubs.

Watts, Barrie. Grasshoppers & Crickets. (Illus.). 32p. (gr. k-4). 1991. PLB 10.40 (ISBN 0-531-14161-6); pap. 3.95 (ISBN 0-531-15618-4). Watts.

LOCUSTS–FICTION

Davidson, Anne A. WordBach Willie. Jacque, Carol A., illus. 42p. (Orig.). (gr. k-2). 1984. pap. 5.95 (ISBN 0-9613763-0-9). Neuse Pr.

Fontenot, Mary A. Clovis Crawfish & the Singing Cigales. Vincent, Eric, illus. LC 81-5608. 32p. (ps-4). 1981. 11.95 (ISBN 0-88289-270-3). Pelican.

Kherdian, David. Song in the Walnut Grove. Zelisky, Paul, illus. LC 82-6596. 112p. (gr. 3-7). 1982. lib. bdg. 8.99 (ISBN 0-394-95519-6). Knopf.

Reese, Bob. Scary Larry Meets Big Willie. LC 83-7553. (Illus.). 32p. (ps-2). 1983. PLB 11.93 (ISBN 0-516-02323-3); pap. 3.95 (ISBN 0-516-42323-1). Childrens.

Sushiela. The Ant & the Grasshopper: A Love Story. Sushiela, illus. LC 89-92067. 129p. (Orig.). (gr. 5 up). 1990. pap. 15.95 (ISBN 0-9623363-1-9). Running Water.

Turner, Ann. Grasshopper Summer. LC 88-13847. 144p. (gr. 3-7). 1989. 13.95 (ISBN 0-02-789511-4, Mcmillan Child Bk). Macmillan Child Grp.

—Grasshopper Summer. 166p. (gr. 5-9). 1990. pap. 2.95 (ISBN 0-8167-2262-5). Troll Assocs.

LOG CABINS

Danforth, Helen H. A Tale of Two Cabins. (Illus.). 36p. (Orig.). (gr. 7 up). 1985. pap. 4.95 (ISBN 0-9614899-0-1). Pioneer Farm.

LOGGING

see Lumber and Lumbering

LOGIC

see also Knowledge, Theory of; Reasoning; Thought and Thinking

Butrick, Lyn M. Logic for Space Age Kids, Vol. II. Cooper, William H., ed. Butrick, Lyn M., illus. LC 84-50892. 32p. (gr. 3-6). 1984. pap. 5.27 (ISBN 0-914127-16-0). Univ Class.

Daniel, Becky. Logic Thinker Sheets. 64p. (gr. 4-8). 1989. 7.95 (ISBN 0-86653-505-5, GA1099). Good Apple.

Eads, Sandra & Post, Beverly. Logic in the Round. (gr. 5 up). 1989. pap. 7.95 (ISBN 0-8224-4206-X). Fearon Teach Aids.

Lieberman, Lillian. Making Inferences. 64p. (gr. 2-5). 1989. 6.95 (ISBN 0-912107-88-X, MM1905). Monday Morning Bks.

Post, Beverly & Eads, Sandra. Logic, Anyone? One Hundred Sixty-Five Brain-Stretching Problems. (gr. 5-12). 1982. pap. 11.95 (ISBN 0-8224-4326-0); wrk bk 3.95 (ISBN 0-8224-4327-9). Fearon Teach Aids.

Risby, Bonnie. Connections, Beginning. Franklin, Jean, illus. 32p. (gr. 3-4). 1982. 5.00 (ISBN 0-931724-16-3). Dandy Lion.

—Connections, Intermediate. Draze, Dianne, ed. Franklin, Jean, illus. 32p. (gr. 5-6). 1981. 5.00 (ISBN 0-931724-15-5). Dandy Lion.

—Connections, Introductory. Draze, Dianne, ed. Franklin, Jean, illus. 32p. (gr. 2-4). 1982. 5.00 (ISBN 0-931724-17-1). Dandy Lion.

Rothstein, Erica L. & Renineke, eds. Dell Book of Logic Problems, No. 3. (Orig.). 1988. pap. 9.95 (ISBN 0-440-50068-0, Dell Trade Pbks). Dell.

Schoenfield, Mark & Rosenblatt, Jeanette. Adventures with Logic. (gr. 5-7). 1985. pap. 7.95 (ISBN 0-8224-0285-8). Fearon Teach Aids.

—Discovering Logic. (gr. 4-6). 1985. pap. 7.95 (ISBN 0-8224-1915-7). Fearon Teach Aids.

—Playing with Logic. (gr. 3-5). 1985. pap. 7.95 (ISBN 0-8224-5310-X). Fearon Teach Aids.

Tilkin, Sheldon L. & Conoway, Judith. Predicting Outcomes. (Illus.). 24p. (gr. 3-4). 1980. wkbk. 2.95 (ISBN 0-89403-575-4). EDC.

—Predicting Outcomes. (Illus.). 24p. (gr. 4-5). 1980. wkbk. 2.95 (ISBN 0-89403-585-1). EDC.

LONDON, JACK, 1876-1916

Gleiter, Jan & Thompson, Kathleen. Jack London. LC 87-23578. (Illus.). 32p. (Orig.). (gr. 2-5). 1987. PLB 16.67 (ISBN 0-8172-2661-3); pap. 9.26 (ISBN 0-8172-2665-6). Raintree Pubs.

Jack London. (Illus.). (gr. 2-5). 1989. PLB 27.99 incl. cassette (ISBN 0-8172-2952-3); pap. 23.95 incl. cassette (ISBN 0-8172-2960-4). Raintree Pubs.

LONDON

Book of London: A Guide to the Story of London. (Illus.). 64p. (gr. 5 up). 1987. PLB 13.96 (ISBN 0-88110-260-1); pap. 8.95 (ISBN 0-7460-0050-2). EDC.

Davis, James E. & Hawke, Sharryl D. London. (Illus.). 64p. (gr. 4-9). 1990. PLB 18.00 (ISBN 0-8172-3027-0). Raintree Pubs.

Hughes, Richard. Lost in London. Wheeler, Jill, ed. Lowery, Carol, illus. 48p. (gr. 4). 1988. lib. bdg. 10.95 (ISBN 0-939179-47-4). Abdo & Dghtrs.

Lovett, Sarah. Kidding Around London: A Young Person's Guide to the City. Taylor, Michael, illus. 64p. (Orig.). (gr. 3 up). 1989. pap. 9.95 (ISBN 0-945465-24-6). John Muir.

Munro, Roxie. The Inside-Outside Book of London. LC 89-12023. (Illus.). (ps up). 1989. 13.95 (ISBN 0-525-44522-6, DCB). Dutton Child Bks.

Natural History Museum (London) (Illus.). (gr. 5 up). 3.50 (ISBN 0-7214-1181-9). Ladybird Bks.

Wild, Anne. Pop-Up London. (Illus.). 32p. (gr. 3 up). 1985. pap. 6.95 (ISBN 0-906212-30-8). Parkwest Pubns.

Wittich, John. Discovering London Street Names. 96p. (Orig.). (gr. 6 up). 1977. pap. 3.00 (ISBN 0-913714-09-7). Legacy Bks.

LONDON–FICTION

Alcock, Vivien. The Cuckoo Sister. LC 85-20648. 158p. (gr. 4-6). 1986. pap. 14.95 (ISBN 0-385-29467-0). Delacorte.

Ashley, Bernard. Terry on the Fence. Keeping, Charles, illus. LC 76-39898. (gr. 5-9). 1977. 18.95 (ISBN 0-87599-222-6). S G Phillips.

Bangs, Edward. Yankee Doodle. Kellogg, Steven, illus. 40p. (ps-3). 1984. 13.95 (ISBN 0-02-749800-X, Four Winds). Macmillan Child Grp.

Bawden, Nina. The Robbers. LC 79-4152. (Illus.). 160p. (gr. 4-7). 1989. Repr. of 1979 ed. 12.95 (ISBN 0-688-41902-X). Lothrop.

Bemelmans, Ludwig. Madeline in London. Bemelmans, Ludwig, illus. 56p. (ps-3). 1977. pap. 3.95 (ISBN 0-14-050199-1, Puffin). Puffin Bks.

Dickens, Charles. Dombey & Son. (ps-8). 1990. Repr. lib. bdg. 29.95x (ISBN 0-89966-678-7). Buccaneer Bks.

—Little Dorrit. (ps-8). 1990. Repr. lib. bdg. 39.95x (ISBN 0-89966-680-9). Buccaneer Bks.

—Oliver Twist. (gr. 9 up). 1964. pap. 3.50 (ISBN 0-8049-0009-4, CL-9). Airmont.

—Oliver Twist. (gr. 4 up). 1989. pap. 4.87 (ISBN 0-582-52279-X, 73808). Longman.

—Oliver Twist. 496p. (gr. 9-12). Date not set. pap. 2.50 (ISBN 0-451-51685-0, Sig Classics). NAL-Dutton.

—Oliver Twist. abridged ed. Martin, Les, adapted by. Zallinger, Jean, illus. LC 89-24279. 96p. (Orig.). (gr. 2-6). 1990. PLB 5.99 (ISBN 0-679-90391-7); pap. 2.95 (ISBN 0-679-80391-2). Random.

Godden, Rumer. An Episode of Sparrows. 208p. (gr. 7 up). 1989. pap. 4.95 (ISBN 0-14-034024-6, Puffin). Puffin Bks.

Hope, Laura L. Bobbsey Twins at London Tower. (Illus.). (gr. 1-4). 1959. 4.50 (ISBN 0-448-08052-4, G&D). Putnam Pub Group.

Joy, Margaret. Allotment Lane in London. Hillard, Sue, illus. 96p. (gr. 3-7). 1990. bds. 10.95 laminated (ISBN 0-571-15403-4). Faber & Faber.

Oliver Twist. (Illus.). (gr. 3-5). 3.50 (ISBN 0-7214-0823-0). Ladybird Bks.

Wolff, Ashley. The Bells of London. (gr. k-3). 1984. 12.95 (ISBN 0-396-08485-0, Putnam). Putnam Pub Group.

LONDON–HISTORY

London. (Illus.). (gr. 5 up). 3.50 (ISBN 0-7214-0976-8). Ladybird Bks.

Rawcliffe, Michael. Finding Out about Victorian London. (Illus.). 48p. (gr. 7-12). 1985. 19.95 (ISBN 0-7134-4745-1, Pub. by Batsford England). Trafalgar Sq.

Tolan, Stephanie S. Plague Year. LC 89-13605. (Illus.). 208p. (gr. 7 up). 1990. 12.95 (ISBN 0-688-08801-5). Morrow Jr Bks.

LONDON–HISTORY–FICTION

De Angeli, Marguerite. The Door in the Wall: Story of Medieval London. De Angeli, Marguerite, illus. LC 64-7025. 111p. (gr. 3-6). 1989. pap. 14.95 (ISBN 0-385-07283-X). Doubleday.

Paton-Walsh, Jill. Fireweed. LC 73-109554. 144p. (gr. 6 up). 1970. 14.95 (ISBN 0-374-32310-0, Sunburst). FS&G.

LONDON–POETRY

Bemmelmans, Ludwig. Madeline in London. Bemelmans, Ludwig, illus. (gr. k-3). 1961. pap. 14.95 (ISBN 0-670-44648-3). Viking Child Bks.

LONDON–POLICE

Wilkes, J. The London Police in the Nineteenth Century. LC 76-57247. (Illus.). 48p. (gr. 7 up). 1977. pap. 5.95 (ISBN 0-521-21406-8). Cambridge U Pr.

LONDON. TOWER

Fisher, Leonard E. The Tower of London. Fisher, Leonard E., illus. LC 87-1629. 32p. (gr. 1-5). 1987. PLB 13.95 (ISBN 0-02-735370-2, Mcmillan Child Bk). Macmillan Child Grp.

Saunders, Susan. The Tower of London. (gr. 2-4). 1984. pap. 2.25 (ISBN 0-553-15490-7, Skylark). Bantam.

The Tower of London. 48p. (gr. 4-5). 1989. PLB 10.95 (ISBN 0-685-26414-9). Capstone Pr.

The Tower of London. (Illus.). (gr. 5 up). 3.50 (ISBN 0-7214-1002-2). Ladybird Bks.

LONELINESS–FICTION

Conford, Ellen. Dear Lovey Hart, I Am Desperate. 154p. (gr. 7 up). 1977. pap. 2.50 (ISBN 0-590-40721-X, Point). Scholastic Inc.

Crompton, Anne E. The Snow Pony. 128p. (gr. 4-7). Date not set. 14.95 (ISBN 0-8050-1573-6). H Holt & Co.

Fritz, Jean. Homesick: My Own Story. Tomes, Margot, illus. 160p. (gr. 3-7). 1982. 13.95 (ISBN 0-399-20933-6, Putnam). Putnam Pub Group.

Grimes, Frances H. Stages of Love. 160p. (Orig.). (gr. 8-12). 1989. pap. 2.95 (ISBN 1-55802-080-2). Lynx Bks.

Hall, Donald. The Man Who Lived Alone. Azarian, Mary, illus. LC 84-47655. 36p. (gr. 2 up). 1984. 12.50 (ISBN 0-87923-538-1). Godine.

Peck, Richard. Close Enough to Touch. LC 81-65498. 192p. (gr. 7 up). 1981. 15.00 (ISBN 0-385-28145-5). Delacorte.

Roberts, Sarah & Mathieu, Joe. Nobody Cares About Me! LC 81-15913. (Illus.). 40p. (ps-2). 1982. lib. bdg. 6.99 (ISBN 0-394-95177-8); pap. 4.95 (ISBN 0-394-85177-3). Random.

Wagener, Gerda. Leo the Lion. Ignatowicz, Nina, tr. from GER. Michl, Reinhard, illus. LC 90-46272. 32p. (gr. k-3). 1991. 14.95 (ISBN 0-06-021656-5); PLB 14.89 (ISBN 0-06-021657-3). HarpC Child Bks.

LONG ISLAND–FICTION

Fitzhugh, Louise. Long Secret. Fitzhugh, Louise, illus. LC 65-23370. (gr. 5 up). 1965. 13.95i (ISBN 0-06-021410-4); PLB 13.89 (ISBN 0-06-021411-2). HarpC Child Bks.

LONGEVITY

see Old Age

LOOKING GLASSES

see Mirrors

LOONS

Billings, Charlene W. The Loon. (Illus.). 48p. (gr. 2-5). 1988. 10.95 (ISBN 0-396-09244-6, Putnam). Putnam Pub Group.

Green, Ivah J. Loon. LC 65-22310. (Illus.). 32p. (gr. 4 up). 1968. PLB 9.95 (ISBN 0-87783-025-8). Oddo.

Josephson, Judith P. The Loon. LC 88-9599. (Illus.). 48p. (gr. 5-6). 1988. PLB 10.95 (ISBN 0-89686-390-5, Crestwood Hse). Macmillan Child Grp.

Klein, Tom. Loon Magic for Kids. 48p. 1990. 14.95 (ISBN 1-55971-047-0); pap. 6.95 (ISBN 1-55971-121-3). Northword.

—Loon Magic for Kids. LC 90-9860. (Illus.). 48p. (gr. 3-4). 1990. PLB 12.95 (ISBN 0-8368-0402-3). Gareth Stevens Inc.

LOONS–FICTION

Krupinsky, Jacquelyn S. Look Out for Loons. Krupinsky, Lisa A., ed. Arbuckle, Jane & Krupinsky, Lisa, illus. 28p. (Orig.). (gr. k-3). 1983. pap. 5.95 (ISBN 0-912123-01-X). Woodbury Pr.

LORD'S DAY

see Sabbath

LORD'S PRAYER

Dumelle, Grace. The Lord's Prayer: Explained for Little Ones. Williams, Abbie, illus. 24p. (Orig.). Date not set. pap. text ed. 4.95 (ISBN 0-937739-08-1). Roman IL.

The Lord's Prayer. (ps-2). 3.95 (ISBN 0-7214-5015-6). Ladybird Bks.

The Lord's Prayer & Other Prayers. (Illus.). (gr. 2-4). 3.50 (ISBN 0-7214-0809-5). Ladybird Bks.

Lucy, Reda, pseud. The Lord's Prayer for Children. Nannie, illus., pseud. 24p. (Orig.). (ps-3). 1981. pap. 2.25 (ISBN 0-87516-437-4). DeVorss.

Tudor, Tasha. Give Us This Day, the Lord's Prayer. (Illus.). (ps up). 1989. 8.95 (ISBN 0-399-21442-9, Philomel Bks). Putnam Pub Group.

Webb, Barbara O. The Lord's Prayer: The Prayer Jesus Taught. (Illus.). 24p. (Orig.). (gr. k-4). 1986. saddle stitch 3.95 (ISBN 0-570-08529-2, 56-1556). Concordia.

LOS ANGELES

Davis, James E. & Hawke, Sharryl D. Los Angeles. (Illus.). 64p. (gr. 4-9). 1990. PLB 18.00 (ISBN 0-8172-3028-9). Raintree Pubs.

Lee, Greg. Los Angeles, California. LC 89-7723. (Illus.). 48p. (gr. 4-5). 1989. 12.95 (ISBN 0-89686-466-9, Crestwood Hse). Macmillan Child Grp.

Los Angeles Children's Museum Staff. Color Your Way Through L. A. Polsky, Carol, ed. U. S.-Japan Cross Culture Center & Opinion Editors, trs. Rubin, Marvin, illus. (ENG, SPA & JPN.). 56p. (Orig.). (gr. k up). 1983. 3.95 (ISBN 0-914953-00-1). Los Angeles.

St. George, Mark. Los Angeles: City of Dreams II. rev. ed. (Illus.). 160p. Date not set. 16.95 (ISBN 0-9620541-4-3); pap. 9.95 (ISBN 0-9620541-5-1). Proteus LA.

Stewart, G. Los Angeles. (Illus.). 48p. (gr. 5 up). 1989. lib. bdg. 14.60 (ISBN 0-86592-540-2). Rourke Corp.

Zach, Cheryl. Los Angeles. (Illus.). 60p. (gr. 3 up). 1989. PLB 12.95 (ISBN 0-87518-415-4, Dillon). Macmillan Child Grp.

LOS ANGELES–FICTION

Block, Francesca L. Weetzie Bat. LC 88-6214. 96p. (gr. 7 up). 1989. 12.95 (ISBN 0-06-020534-2); PLB 12.89 (ISBN 0-06-020536-9). HarpC Child Bks.

Rocklin, Joanne. Jace the Ace. De Groat, Diane, illus. LC 90-34095. 112p. (gr. 2-6). 1990. 11.95 (ISBN 0-02-777445-7, Mcmillan Child Bk). Macmillan Child Grp.

Weisberg, Valerie H. Three Jolly Stories Include: Three Jollys, Jollys Visit L. A., Jolly Gets Mugged: An ESL Adult-Child Reader. Kolino, Olga, illus. 76p. (Orig.). 1985. pap. text ed. 6.95x (ISBN 0-9610912-4-X). V H Pub. "Hands across the-sea" tell realistic & humorous situations in three separate stories with questions after each to promote understanding, comprehension & sharing of ideas. The glossary gives definitions for British & American idioms. Earthquakes, mistaken identity & mugging are just a few of the mishaps confronting the British triplets when they visit L.A.--Reviewed by Carol Cunningham, Santa Barbara News Press & Goelta Sun. Its sequel (the genesis of the Jollys) is Little Jollys Find A Home, which is printed on recycled paper & is a timely, delightful story. Found in Farmers Jolly & Dolly's truck, the answer to how they came to be there is a big mystery. However, with good food & loving attention the Jollys grow strong & happy. This sympathetic mystery "will give solace & reassurance to homeless or orphaned children & empathy for others."--Independent Small Press Review, Spring 1991. "The writing & graphics in this story are endearing & in these troubled times, they bring a message of love & hope." ***Publisher Provided Annotation.***

LOUIS 14TH, KING OF FRANCE, 1638-1715

Aliki. King's Day: Louis XIV of France. LC 88-38179. (Illus.). 32p. (gr. 2-6). 1989. 13.95 (ISBN 0-690-04588-3, Crowell Jr Bks); PLB 13.89 (ISBN 0-690-04590-5, Crowell Jr Bks). HarpC Child Bks.

LOUISIANA

Aylesworth, Thomas G. & Aylesworth, Virginia L. South Central (Louisiana, Arkansas, Missouri, Kansas, Oklahoma) (Illus.). 64p. (gr. 3 up). 1992. PLB 16.95 (ISBN 0-7910-1047-3). Chelsea Hse.

Carpenter, Allan. Louisiana. LC 78-3390. (Illus.). 96p. (gr. 4 up). 1978. PLB 19.93 (ISBN 0-516-04118-5). Childrens.

Dartez, Cecilia C. The Louisiana Plantation Coloring Book. Arrigo, Joseph, illus. 32p. (Orig.). (ps-4). 1985. pap. 2.95 (ISBN 0-88289-473-0). Pelican.

Fradin, Dennis. Louisiana: In Words & Pictures. Wahl, Richard, illus. LC 80-28609. 48p. (gr. 2-5). 1981. PLB 15.93 (ISBN 0-516-03918-0). Childrens.

Gelhay, Patrick & Marcantel, David E. Notre Langue Louisianaise: Our Louisiana Language, Bk. 1. Graeff, Benny, et al, illus. LC 85-81018. (ENG & FRE.). 180p. (gr. 4). 1985. text ed. 14.95 (ISBN 0-935085-00-9); Tchr's ed. 14.95 (ISBN 0-935085-01-7); write for info. Dialogue Booklet (ISBN 0-935085-03-3); Cassette Tape Set 49.95 (ISBN 0-935085-02-5). Ed Francaises.

Marsh, Carole. Avast, Ye Slobs! Louisiana Pirate Trivia. (Illus.). (gr. 3-8). 1990. PLB 19.95 (ISBN 0-7933-0520-9); pap. 14.95 (ISBN 0-7933-0519-5); disk 29.95 (ISBN 0-7933-0521-7). Gallopade Pub Group.

—The Beast of the Louisiana Bed & Breakfast. (Illus.). (gr. 3-8). 1990. PLB 19.95 (ISBN 0-7933-1669-3); pap. 14.95 (ISBN 0-7933-1670-7); disk 29.95 (ISBN 0-7933-1671-5). Gallopade Pub Group.

—Carole Marsh Louisiana Books, 31 bks. (Illus.). (gr. 3-8). 1990. Set. PLB 638.45 (ISBN 0-7933-1293-0). Gallopade Pub Group.

—The Hard-to-Believe-But-True! Book of Louisiana History, Mystery, Trivia, Legend, Lore, Humor & More. (Illus.). (gr. 3-8). 1990. PLB 19.95 (ISBN 0-7933-0517-9); pap. 14.95 (ISBN 0-7933-0516-0); disk 29.95 (ISBN 0-7933-0518-7). Gallopade Pub Group.

—If My Louisiana Mama Ran the World! (Illus.). (gr. 3-8). 1990. lib. bdg. 19.95 (ISBN 0-7933-1674-X); pap. 14.95 (ISBN 0-7933-1675-8); disk 29.95 (ISBN 0-7933-1676-6). Gallopade Pub Group.

—Let's Quilt Louisiana & Stuff It Topographically! (Illus.). (gr. 3-8). 1990. PLB 19.95 (ISBN 1-55609-397-7); pap. 14.95 (ISBN 1-55609-075-7); disk 29.95 (ISBN 0-7933-1664-2). Gallopade Pub Group.

—Louisiana & Other State Greats (Biographies) LC 7933001677000004. (Illus.). (gr. 3-8). 1990. lib. bdg. 19.95 (ISBN 1-55609-404-3); pap. 14.95 (ISBN 1-55609-403-5); disk 29.95. Gallopade Pub Group.

—Louisiana Bandits, Bushwackers, Outlaws, Crooks, Devils, Ghosts, Desperadoes & Other Assorted & Sundry Characters! (Illus.). (gr. 3-8). 1990. PLB 19.95 (ISBN 0-7933-0502-0); pap. 14.95 (ISBN 0-7933-0501-2); disk 29.95 (ISBN 0-7933-0503-9). Gallopade Pub Group.

—Louisiana Classic Christmas Trivia: Stories, Recipes, Activities, Legends, Lore & More! (Illus.). (gr. 3-8). 1990. PLB 19.95 (ISBN 0-7933-0505-5); pap. 14.95 (ISBN 0-7933-0504-7); disk 29.95 (ISBN 0-7933-0506-3). Gallopade Pub Group.

—Louisiana Coastales. (Illus.). (gr. 3-8). 1990. PLB 19.95 (ISBN 1-55609-400-0); pap. 14.95 (ISBN 1-55609-119-2); disk 29.95 (ISBN 0-7933-1673-1). Gallopade Pub Group.

—The Louisiana Hot Air Balloon Mystery. (Illus.). (gr. 2-9). 1990. 19.95 (ISBN 0-685-37850-0); pap. 14.95 (ISBN 0-7933-2481-5); computer disk 29.95 (ISBN 0-7933-2482-3). Gallopade Pub Group.

—Louisiana "Jography" A Fun Run Thru Our State! (Illus.). (gr. 3-8). 1990. lib. bdg. 19.95 (ISBN 1-55609-396-9); pap. 14.95 (ISBN 1-55609-108-7); disk 29.95 (ISBN 0-7933-1663-4). Gallopade Pub Group.

—Louisiana Kid's Cookbook: Recipes, How-to, History, Lore & More! (Illus.). (gr. 3-8). 1990. PLB 19.95 (ISBN 0-7933-0514-4); pap. 14.95 (ISBN 0-7933-0513-6); disk 29.95 (ISBN 0-7933-0515-2). Gallopade Pub Group.

—Louisiana Quiz Bowl Crash Course! (Illus.). (gr. 3-8). 1990. PLB 19.95 (ISBN 1-55609-402-7); pap. 14.95 (ISBN 1-55609-401-9); disk 29.95 (ISBN 0-7933-1672-3). Gallopade Pub Group.

—Louisiana School Trivia: An Amazing & Fascinating Look at Our State's Teachers, Schools & Students! (Illus.). (gr. 3-8). 1990. PLB 19.95 (ISBN 0-7933-0511-X); pap. 14.95 (ISBN 0-7933-0510-1); disk 29.95 (ISBN 0-7933-0512-8). Gallopade Pub Group.

—Louisiana Silly Basketball Sportsmysteries, Vol. I. (Illus.). (gr. 3-8). 1990. PLB 19.95 (ISBN 0-7933-0508-X); pap. 14.95 (ISBN 0-7933-0507-1); disk 29.95 (ISBN 0-7933-0509-8). Gallopade Pub Group.

—Louisiana Silly Basketball Sportsmysteries, Vol. II. (Illus.). (gr. 3-8). 1990. PLB 19.95 (ISBN 0-7933-1678-2); pap. 14.95 (ISBN 0-7933-1679-0); disk 29.95 (ISBN 0-7933-1680-4). Gallopade Pub Group.

—Louisiana Silly Football Sportsmysteries, Vol. I. (Illus.). (gr. 3-8). 1990. PLB 19.95 (ISBN 1-55609-399-3); pap. 14.95 (ISBN 1-55609-398-5); disk 29.95 (ISBN 0-7933-1665-0). Gallopade Pub Group.

—Louisiana Silly Football Sportsmysteries, Vol. II. (Illus.). (gr. 3-8). 1990. PLB 19.95 (ISBN 0-7933-1666-9); pap. 14.95 (ISBN 0-7933-1667-7); disk 29.95 (ISBN 0-7933-1668-5). Gallopade Pub Group.

—Louisiana Silly Trivia! (Illus.). (gr. 3-8). 1990. PLB 19.95 (ISBN 1-55609-395-0); pap. 14.95 (ISBN 1-55609-041-2); disk 29.95 (ISBN 0-7933-0522-5). Gallopade Pub Group.

—Louisiana's (Most Devastating!) Disasters & (Most Calamitous!) Catastrophies! (Illus.). (gr. 3-8). 1990. PLB 19.95 (ISBN 0-7933-0499-7); pap. 14.95 (ISBN 0-7933-0498-9); disk 29.95. Gallopade Pub Group.

Muller, Carrel & Muller, Brenda. Explore Louisiana. (Illus.). 32p. (gr. 4 up). 1984. 5.50 (ISBN 0-915785-00-5). Bonjour Books.

Norwood, David, et al, illus. Children's Tour of Red Stick City. 32p. (gr. 1-6). 1980. pap. text ed. 2.00 (ISBN 0-9608282-2-2). YWCO.

Turner Program Services, Inc. Staff & Clark, James I. Louisiana. LC 85-9976. 48p. (gr. 3 up). 1985. PLB 17.32 (ISBN 0-86514-432-X); pap. text ed. 9.27 (ISBN 0-86514-507-5); cancelled Beta video (ISBN 0-86514-057-X); cancelled VHS video (ISBN 0-86514-132-0); cancelled 3/4" video (ISBN 0-86514-207-6); cancelled tchr's. guide (ISBN 0-86514-282-3); cancelled student activity bk. (ISBN 0-86514-357-9); cancelled index. Raintree Pubs.

Word, Christine. Ghosts Along the Bayou: Tales of Haunted Places in Southwestern Louisiana. Fuchs, Jeff, illus. 160p. (gr. 6-12). 1988. 12.95 (ISBN 0-937614-09-2). Acadiana Pr.

LOUISIANA–FICTION

Edler, Timothy. Crawfish-Man Rescues Ron Guidry. (Illus.). (gr. k-8). 1980. lea. 6.00 (ISBN 0-931108-05-5). Little Cajun Bks.

Fontenot, Mary A. Clovis Crawfish & Bertile's Bon Voyage. Blazek, Scott R., illus. 32p. (ps-8). 1991. 11.95 (ISBN 0-88289-825-6). Pelican.

—Clovis Crawfish & Simeon Suce-Fleur. Blazek, Scott R., illus. LC 89-35370. 32p. (gr. k-5). 1990. 11.95 (ISBN 0-88289-751-9). Pelican.

Johnson, Zenobia M. & Broussard, Lucretia-del J. Louisiana Reading Adventures. (Illus.). 32p. (Orig.). (gr. 4-7). 1984. 3.50 (ISBN 0-9617411-0-4). Z M Johnson.

Landry, Tom. The Ballad of Tont Lala. (Illus.). 32p. (gr. k-8). leather 6.00 (ISBN 0-931108-11-X). Little Cajun Bks.

Raphael, Morris. Maria: Goddess of the Teche. Ferry, Kate, illus. 48p. 1991. 13.95 (ISBN 0-9608866-8-0). M Raphael.

Snellings, M. L. Jessie Strikes Louisiana Gold. (gr. 3-7). 1969. 3.95 (ISBN 0-87511-116-5). Claitors.

LOUISIANA–HISTORY

Amoss, Berthe. The Loup Garou. Amoss, Berthe, illus. LC 79-20536. 48p. (ps-4). 1979. 8.95 (ISBN 0-88289-189-8). Pelican.

Bridges, L. T. Flags of Louisiana. (ps-8). 1971. 3.95 (ISBN 0-87511-010-X). Claitors.

Phares, Ross. Cavalier in the Wilderness. Hastings, Jack, illus. LC 76-1409. 290p. (gr. 6-12). 1976. 14.95 (ISBN 0-88289-128-6); pap. 8.95 (ISBN 0-88289-127-8). Pelican.

Raphael, Morris. The Battle in the Bayou Country. Minvielle, Chestee H., illus. 199p. (gr. 5-12). 1976. 12.95 (ISBN 0-9608866-0-5). M Raphael.

LOUISIANA PURCHASE

Phelan, Mary K. The Story of the Louisiana Purchase. Aloise, Frank, illus. LC 78-22505. (gr. 4-6). 1979. 13.95 (ISBN 0-690-03955-7, Crowell Jr Bks). HarpC Child Bks.

LOVE

see also Dating (Social Customs); Friendship; Marriage

Alvarez del Real, Maria E., ed. Como Escribir Cartas De Amor. (SPA., Illus.). 288p. (Orig.). 1988. pap. 4.00x (ISBN 0-944499-38-4). Editorial Amer.

Bacher, June M. Love Is a Gentle Stranger. LC 82-83839. 160p. (gr. 10 up). 1983. pap. 5.99 (ISBN 0-89081-374-4). Harvest Hse.

Barth, Edna. Hearts, Cupids & Red Roses. Arndt, Ursula, illus. LC 73-7128. 64p. (gr. 3-6). 1979. 13.95 (ISBN 0-395-28841-X, Clarion). HM.

Deiros, Pablo A. El Amor Es Cosa Seria: Love Is Serious Business. (SPA.). 64p. 1988. pap. 2.50 (ISBN 0-311-12339-2). Casa Bautista.

Dickenson, Celia. Too Many Boys. 160p. (Orig.). (gr. 5-6). 1984. pap. 2.50 (ISBN 0-553-26615-2). Bantam.

Edmark, Tomima. Kissing: Everything You Ever Wanted to Know. (Illus.). 144p. (Orig.). 1991. pap. 6.95 (ISBN 0-671-70883-X, Fireside). S&S Trade.

Everly, Kathleen & Gordon, Sol. How Can You Tell If You're Really in Love? Cohen, Vivien, illus. 20p. (gr. 7-12). 1983. pap. 1.95 (ISBN 0-934978-06-9). Ed-U Pr.

Field, Mary & Field, Elliot. A Loving Guide to the World As a Two Year-Old Says It. Taklender, Sharon, illus. 14p. (Orig.). (ps up). 1983. pap. 5.95 (ISBN 0-914445-00-6). Palm Springs Pub.

Girion, Barbara. A Tangle of Roots. 160p. (Orig.). (gr. 5 up). 1985. pap. 2.25 (ISBN 0-448-47747-5, G&D). Putnam Pub Group.

Goley, Elaine. Love. (Illus.). 32p. (gr. 1-4). 1987. PLB 132.66 10 bk. set (ISBN 0-317-60399-X); PLB 13.26 (ISBN 0-86592-380-9). Rourke Corp.

Hostvedt, Jan. Loving Somebody. 32p. (gr. k-2). 1986. comb bdg. 3.95 (ISBN 0-89191-270-3, Chariot Bks). Cook.

Hunt, Morton. The Young Person's Guide to Love. LC 75-28371. 181p. (gr. 5 up). 1975. 12.95 (ISBN 0-374-38757-5). FS&G.

Hurst, Hugo. A Search for Meaning in Love, Sex, & Marriage. rev. ed. LC 75-9961. 234p. (gr. 11-12). 1975. pap. text ed. 6.50x (ISBN 0-88489-063-5); teaching manual 3.00x (ISBN 0-88489-119-4). St. Marys.

Johnson, Helen M. How Do I Love Me? 2nd ed. 105p. (gr. 10 up). 1986. pap. text ed. 9.50 (ISBN 0-88133-224-0). Sheffield WI.

Lewis, Linda. Loving Two Is Hard to Do. 160p. (gr. 6-9). 1990. pap. 2.95 (ISBN 0-671-70587-3, Archway). PB.

Loving. 64p. (gr. 3-8). 7.95 (ISBN 0-86653-180-7, GA 540, Dist. by Ingram). Good Apple.

Makris, Kathryn. Mission: Love. 192p. (Orig.). (gr. 7-12). 1986. pap. 2.25 (ISBN 0-553-25470-7). Bantam.

Miles, Betty. Around & Around-Love. Jeyman, Ken, et al, photos by. LC 75-2539. (Illus.). 48p. (ps up). 1975. Knopf.

Moncure, Jane B. Caring. rev. ed. Endes, Helen, illus. LC 80-27506. (gr. k-3). 1981. PLB 11.97 (ISBN 0-89565-201-3). Childs World.

Morris, Ann. Loving. 32p. 1990. 13.95 (ISBN 0-688-06340-3); PLB 13.88 (ISBN 0-688-06341-1). Lothrop.

RanDelle, B. J. & Marshbum, Sandra. Lessons in Love. Dodd, John & Taylor, Leigh, illus. LC 24-476. 64p. (gr. k-4). 1982. text ed. 5.95 (ISBN 0-910445-00-1). Randelle Pubns.

Rennert, Maggie. I Love You. Frankel, Alona, illus. (ps up). 1987. 9.95 (ISBN 0-915361-71-X, Dist. by Watts). Adama Pubs Inc.

Reynolds, Elizabeth. The Perfect Boy. 176p. (Orig.). (gr. 7-12). 1986. pap. 2.25 (ISBN 0-553-25469-3). Bantam.

Stefoff, Rebecca. Friendship & Love. (Illus.). (gr. 6-12). 1989. 18.95 (ISBN 0-7910-0039-7). Chelsea Hse.

Tudor, Tasha, ed. & illus. All for Love. LC 83-21959. 96p. (gr. 6-8). 1984. 15.95 (ISBN 0-399-21012-1, Philomel). Putnam Pub Group.

Wyatt, Molly. Kim's Winter. (gr. 7 up). 1982. pap. 1.75 (ISBN 0-317-00342-9, Sig Vista). NAL-Dutton.

LOVE–FICTION

Adler, C. S. Roadside Valentine. LC 83-9394. 180p. (gr. 7 up). 1983. 13.95 (ISBN 0-02-700350-7, Mcmillan Child Bk). Macmillan Child Grp.

Aiken, Joan. Black Hearts in Battersea. 224p. (gr. 5 up). 1981. pap. 1.75 (ISBN 0-440-90648-2, LFL). Dell.

Aks, Patricia. Impossible Love. 144p. (Orig.). (gr. 9-12). 1991. pap. 3.50 (ISBN 0-449-70297-9, Juniper). Fawcett.

Alborough, Jez H. The Grass Is Always Greener. (Illus.). 32p. (ps-3). 1987. 9.95 (ISBN 0-8037-0468-2). Dial Bks Young.

All Night Long. 128p. (Orig.). (gr. 7-12). 1984. pap. 2.95 (ISBN 0-553-27568-2). Bantam.

Althoff, Victoria. Key to My Heart. 176p. (gr. 5-8). 1989. pap. 1.25 (ISBN 0-87406-384-1). Willowisp Pr.

Anderson, Janet S. The Happy Birthday Hug. Ewers, Joe, illus. LC 85-9476. 32p. (ps-3). 1985. pap. 0.99 (ISBN 0-87372-006-7); 3.50 (ISBN 0-910313-90-3). Parker Bros.

Anderson, Mary. Catch Me, I'm Falling in Love. (gr. k-12). 1987. pap. 2.50 (ISBN 0-440-91122-2, LFL). Dell.

—Do You Call That a Dream Date? LC 86-908. 176p. (gr. 7 up). 1987. pap. 14.95 (ISBN 0-385-29488-3). Delacorte.

Andrews, Kristi. Upstaged, No. 7. 176p. (Orig.). (gr. 6 up). 1988. pap. 2.50 (ISBN 0-553-26704-3). Bantam.

Asher, Sandy. Everything Is Not Enough. (gr. k-12). 1988. pap. 2.75 (ISBN 0-440-20002-4, LFL). Dell.

Avi. Romeo & Juliet - Together (& Alive!) at Last. LC 87-7680. 128p. (gr. 6-8). 1987. 11.95 (ISBN 0-531-05721-6); PLB 11.99 (ISBN 0-531-08321-7). Orchard Bks Watts.

Bacher, June M. With All My Heart. 192p. (gr. 9 up). pap. 5.99, 1989 (ISBN 0-89081-707-3); pap. 2.95, 1984 (ISBN 0-89081-410-4). Harvest Hse.

Baer, Judy. Riddles of Love-Sweet Dreams No. 63: Kiss Me Creep. 1991. pap. 2.50 (ISBN 0-553-30233-7). Bantam.

Bates, Betty. The Great Male Conspiracy. LC 86-45389. 176p. (gr. 3-7). 1986. 12.95 (ISBN 0-8234-0629-6). Holiday.

Becker, Eve. The Love Potion. (gr. 4-7). 1989. pap. 2.75 (ISBN 0-553-15731-0, Skylark). Bantam.

Beecham, Jahnna. Dance With Me. 192p. 1987. pap. 2.50 (ISBN 0-317-65473-X, Sweet Dreams). Bantam.

—The Right Combination, No. 139. 192p. (Orig.). (gr. 5 up). 1988. pap. 2.50 (ISBN 0-553-27005-2, Sweet Dreams). Bantam.

Bellairs, John. Trolley to Yesterday. (gr. 4-7). 1990. pap. 3.50 (ISBN 0-553-15795-7). Bantam.

Bennett, Paul. Follow the River. LC 87-7911. 192p. (gr. 6 up). 1987. 12.95 (ISBN 0-531-05714-3); PLB 12.99 (ISBN 0-531-08314-4). Orchard Bks Watts.

Bernard, Elizabeth. Changing Partners. (gr. 6 up). 1988. pap. 2.95 (ISBN 0-449-13303-6, Juniper). Fawcett.

—Second Best. (gr. 6 up). 1988. pap. 2.95 (ISBN 0-449-13308-7). Fawcett.

Bischoff, David. Some Kind of Wonderful: Movie Tie-In. (gr. 9 up). 1987. pap. 2.50 (ISBN 0-440-98042-9). Dell.

Blair, Alison. Love by the Book. (gr. 10 up). 1989. pap. 2.95 (ISBN 0-8041-0331-3). Ivy Books.

Blake, Susan. A Change of Heart. 224p. (Orig.). (gr. 7-12). 1986. pap. 2.95 (ISBN 0-553-26168-1). Bantam.

Bloss, Janet. If Only Love Could Last. 144p. (gr. 6-8). 1985. 2.50 (ISBN 0-87406-014-1). Willowisp Pr.

Blume, Judy. It's Not the End of the World. (gr. k-6). 1982. pap. 3.50 (ISBN 0-440-94140-7). Dell.

—Just As Long As We're Together. 304p. (gr. k-6). 1988. pap. 3.50 (ISBN 0-440-40075-9, YB). Dell.

—The Pain & the Great One. (gr. k-12). 1985. pap. 3.95 (ISBN 0-440-46819-1, YB). Dell.

—Then Again, Maybe I Won't. large type ed. (gr. 5-7). 1988. lib. bdg. 13.95x (ISBN 0-8161-4417-6, Large Print Bks). G K Hall.

Boies, Janice. Heart & Soul. 192p. (gr. 7 up). 1988. pap. 2.50 (ISBN 0-553-26949-6). Bantam.

—Just the Way You Are. 176p. (Orig.). (gr. 7-12). 1986. pap. 2.50 (ISBN 0-553-25815-X). Bantam.

—Love on Strike. (gr. 9-12). 1990. pap. 2.75 (ISBN 0-553-28633-1). Bantam.

—Wright Boy, Wrong Girl. LC 88-91249. 186p. (gr. 6 up). 1989. pap. 2.95 (ISBN 0-8041-0239-2). Ivy Books.

Boulding, J. Russell. Thora's Saga: A Tale of Old Iceland. LC 85-73124. (Illus.). 184p. (Orig.). (gr. 6-12). 1986. pap. 4.95 (ISBN 0-936001-00-3). Peaceable Pr.

Bracale, Carla. Fair-Weather Love. (gr. 5 up). 1989. pap. 2.95 (ISBN 0-8041-0240-6). Ivy Books.

—Puppy Love. (gr. 9-12). 1991. pap. 2.95 (ISBN 0-553-28830-X). Bantam.

Branscum, Robbie. Johnny May Grows Up. Marstall, Bob, illus. LC 86-45780. 128p. (gr. 4-8). 1987. 11.95 (ISBN 0-06-020606-3); PLB 12.89 (ISBN 0-06-020607-1). HarpC Child Bks.

Bridgers, Sue E. Permanent Connections. LC 86-45491. 288p. (gr. 7 up). 1988. pap. 3.50 (ISBN 0-06-447020-2, Trophy). HarpC Child Bks.

Bronte, Charlotte. Jane Eyre. Mitchell, Kathy, illus. (gr. 4 up). 1983. deluxe ed. 13.95 (ISBN 0-448-06031-0, G&D). Putnam Pub Group.

Bronte, Emily. Wuthering Heights. Wright, Betty R., adapted by. Cogancherry, Helen, illus. LC 81-15786. 48p. (gr. 4 up). 1982. PLB 17.32 (ISBN 0-8172-1682-0); pap. 9.27 (ISBN 0-8172-2029-1). Raintree Pubs.

—Wuthering Heights. 224p. 1990. pap. 2.50 (ISBN 0-8125-0516-6). Tor Bks.

Brown, Charlotte, adapted by. The Taming of the Shrew. (Illus.). 32p. (gr. 5 up). 1987. pap. 1.50 (ISBN 0-88680-276-8). I E Clark.

Brown, Irene B. I Loved You, Logan McGee! 144p. (gr. 5-9). 1988. pap. 3.95 (ISBN 0-14-032701-0, Puffin). Puffin Bks.

Brown, Joan W. Another Love. 192p. (gr. 9 up). 1989. pap. 5.99 (ISBN 0-89081-708-1). Harvest Hse.

Bryan, Ashley. Sh-Ko & His Eight Wicked Brothers. Yoshimura, Fumio, illus. LC 88-892. 32p. (ps-3). 1988. 12.95 (ISBN 0-689-31446-9, Atheneum Child Bk). Macmillan Child Grp.

Buckley, Kate. Love Notes. Levine, Abby, ed. Buckley, Kate, illus. LC 88-212. 32p. (gr. k-3). 1989. PLB 13.95 (ISBN 0-8075-4780-8). A Whitman.

Buffet, Pam & Buffet, Guy. Kahala: Where the Rainbow Ends. Tabrah, Ruth, ed. LC 72-76459. (Illus.). (gr. 1-7). 1973. pap. 5.95 (ISBN 0-89610-006-5). Island Heritage.

Bunting, Eve. Karen Kepplewhite Is the World's Best Kisser. (gr. 5-7). 1986. pap. 2.50 (ISBN 0-671-63327-9, Archway). PB.

—Will You Be My POSSLQ. LC 87-322. (gr. 7-12). 1987. 12.95 (ISBN 0-15-297399-0, HJ). HarBraceJ.

Byars, Betsy. Bingo Brown & the Language of Love. large type ed. 152p. 1989. PLB 15.95 (ISBN 1-55736-146-0, Crnrstn Bks). ABC-CLIO.

—A Blossom Promise. Rogers, Jacqueline, illus. LC 87-5367. 160p. (gr. 4-6). 1987. pap. 14.95 (ISBN 0-385-29578-2). Delacorte.

Cadwallader, Sharon. Star-Crossed Love. 176p. (Orig.). (gr. 7-12). 1987. pap. 2.50 (ISBN 0-553-26339-0). Bantam.

Cahn, Julie. Spotlight on Love. (gr. 2-7). 1984. pap. 2.95 (ISBN 0-671-52625-1, Little Simon). S&S Trade.

Calhoun, Mary. Katie John & Heathcliff. LC 80-7770. 160p. (gr. 3-6). 1981. pap. 3.50 (ISBN 0-06-440120-0, Trophy). HarpC Child Bks.

Cameron, Ann. The Most Beautiful Place in the World. Allen, Thomas B., illus. LC 88-4228. 64p. (ps-3). 1988. 11.95 (ISBN 0-394-89463-4); lib. bdg. 11.99 (ISBN 0-394-99463-9). Knopf.

Castillo, Steve. Maximum Happiness: Jack & Jill Discover True Love. Castillo, Steve, illus. 58p. (Orig.). (gr. 9). 1989. 5.95 (ISBN 0-317-93187-3). Paisley Bks.

Caudell, Marian. Listen to Your Heart. 176p. (Orig.). (gr. 7-12). 1986. pap. 2.50 (ISBN 0-553-25727-7). Bantam.

Caudill, Rebecca. Did You Carry the Flag Today, Charley? (gr. k-6). 1988. pap. 2.95 (ISBN 0-440-40092-9). Dell.

Cavanna, Betty. Romance on Trial. LC 84-10415. 96p. (gr. 6-9). 1984. 10.95 (ISBN 0-664-32715-X, Westminster). Westminster John Knox.

—Storm in Her Heart. LC 82-20237. 94p. (gr. 7-10). 1983. 9.95 (ISBN 0-664-32700-1, Westminster). Westminster John Knox.

Chisholm, Gloria. Andrea. LC 83-71614. 160p. (Orig.). (gr. 9 up). 1983. pap. 3.95 (ISBN 0-87123-297-9). Bethany Hse.

Claypool, Jane. A Love for Violet. LC 82-10980. 76p. (gr. 7-10). 1982. 8.95 (ISBN 0-664-32697-8, Westminster). Westminster John Knox.

Cloverdale Press Staff. Trust in Love. 176p. (Orig.). 1988. pap. 2.50 (ISBN 0-553-27229-2, Sweet Dreams). Bantam.

Cohen, Daniel. Hollywood Dinosaur. (Illus.). (gr. 7 up). 1987. pap. 2.50 (ISBN 0-671-64598-6, Archway). PB.

Coleman, Nancy, et al. Hugs, Kisses, & Smiles, 3 bks. Duris, Ellen, illus. 72p. (ps-k). 1990. Set. pap. 7.95 (ISBN 0-8249-7395-X). Ideals.

Conford, Ellen. Dear Lovey Heart I Am Desperate. 1990. pap. 2.95 (ISBN 0-590-43820-4). Scholastic Inc.

—If This Is Love, I'll Take Spaghetti. 1990. pap. 2.95 (ISBN 0-590-43819-0). Scholastic Inc.

—If This Is Love, I'll Take Spaghetti. 166p. (gr. 7 up). 1984. pap. 2.75 (ISBN 0-590-42754-7). Scholastic Inc.

—The Things I Did for Love. 144p. 1988. pap. 2.95 (ISBN 0-553-27374-4, Starfire). Bantam.

Conrad, Barnaby. Time Is All We Have. 1989. pap. 4.95 (ISBN 0-440-20245-0). Dell.

Conrad, Pam. Holding Me Here. 160p. (gr. 7 up). 1987. pap. 2.95 (ISBN 0-553-26525-3, Starfire). Bantam.

Cooney, Caroline B. Summer Nights. 76p. (gr. 7 up). 1988. pap. 2.50 (ISBN 0-590-41548-4, Point). Scholastic Inc.

Cooper, M. E. Break Away. 192p. (gr. 7 up). 1988. pap. 2.50 (ISBN 0-590-41688-X). Scholastic Inc.

—Don't Get Close. 192p. (Orig.). (gr. 7 up). 1988. pap. 2.50 (ISBN 0-590-41687-1). Scholastic Inc.

—Mean to Me. 192p. (Orig.). (gr. 7 up). 1988. pap. 2.50 (ISBN 0-590-41686-3). Scholastic Inc.

Corcoran, Barbara. The Sky Is Falling. LC 87-33358. 192p. (gr. 3-7). 1988. 13.95 (ISBN 0-689-31388-8, Atheneum Child Bk). Macmillan Child Grp.

Creighton, Susan. Hugs from the Heart. Ewers, Joe, illus. 32p. (ps-3). 1985. pap. 0.99 (ISBN 0-87372-005-9). Parker Bros.

Curry, Jane L. The Lotus Cup. LC 85-21467. 164p. (gr. 7 up). 1986. 13.95 (ISBN 0-689-50384-9, M K McElderry). Macmillan Child Grp.

Cutburth, Ronald W. Love from the Sea. Naumann, Cynthia E., ed. Persels, Beth, illus. Tostado, Rocio G., tr. (SPA., Illus.). 27p. (gr. 5-8). 1990. pap. write for info. (ISBN 1-878291-09-2). Love From Sea.

—Love from the Sea. Naumann, Cynthia E., ed. West, Bobbie, tr. Persels, Beth, illus. (CHI.). 27p. (gr. 5-8). 1990. pap. write for info. (ISBN 1-878291-11-4). Love From Sea.

—Love from the Sea. Naumann, Cynthia E., ed. Percels, Beth, illus. 27p. (Orig.). (gr. 4-7). 1990. pap. 3.50 (ISBN 1-878291-01-7). Love From Sea.

Daley, Dan. A Song for Linda, No. 122. 144p. (Orig.). (gr. 7-12). 1987. pap. 2.50 (ISBN 0-553-26419-2). Bantam.

Daly, Maureen. Act of Love. LC 86-1863. 176p. (gr. 7 up). 1986. pap. 12.95 (ISBN 0-590-33873-0). Scholastic Inc.

—Acts of Love. 192p. (gr. 7 up). 1987. pap. 2.95 (ISBN 0-590-40708-2, Point). Scholastic Inc.

—Acts of Love. 192p. (gr. 7 up). 1987. pap. 2.75 (ISBN 0-590-43631-7). Scholastic Inc.

—Seventeenth Summer. (gr. 7-9). 1985. pap. 2.95 (ISBN 0-671-61931-4, Archway). PB.

DeClements, Barthe. How Do You Lose Those Ninth Grade Blues? 144p. (gr. 7 up). 1984. pap. 2.50 (ISBN 0-590-40969-7, Point). Scholastic Inc.

De Gale, Ann. Island Encounter. (Orig.). (gr. 6 up). 1986. pap. 2.50 (ISBN 0-440-94026-5, LFL). Dell.

Dickinson, Peter. The Changes: A Trilogy, 3 vols. Incl. The Devil's Children. 192p. 1986. pap. 14.95 (ISBN 0-385-29449-2); Heartsease. 192p. 1986. pap. 14.95 (ISBN 0-385-29451-4); The Weathermonger. 244p. 1986. pap. 14.95 (ISBN 0-385-29450-6). (gr. 7 up). 1986. pap. Delacorte.

Donahue, Marilyn. Somebody Special to Love. LC 88-14809. (gr. 3-7). 1988. pap. 4.49 (ISBN 0-89191-360-2, Chariot Bks). Cook.

Double Love. (gr. 7-12). 1984. pap. 2.99 (ISBN 0-553-27567-4). Bantam.

Duane, Diane. So You Want to Be a Wizard. (gr. 5-8). 1986. pap. 2.75 (ISBN 0-440-98252-9, LFL). Dell.

DuKore, Jesse. Long Distance Love. (gr. 7-12). 1983. pap. 2.25 (ISBN 0-553-17853-9). Bantam.

Eires, Anita. Summer Awakening. (gr. 6 up). 1986. pap. 2.50 (ISBN 0-440-98369-X, LFL). Dell.

Ellis, Lucy. Pink Parrots, No. 3: Mixed Signals. (gr. 4-7). 1991. pap. 3.50 (ISBN 0-316-18566-3). Little.

Falk, Bonnie H. Forget-Me-Not. Huber, Nancy D., illus. LC 84-90501. 192p. (gr. 4-8). 1984. pap. 7.95 (ISBN 0-9614108-0-9). BHF Memories.

Fields, Terri. The Other Me. 160p. (Orig.). (gr. 7-12). 1987. pap. 2.50 (ISBN 0-553-26196-7). Bantam.

Finney, Shan. Geared for Romance. 192p. (Orig.). (gr. 7-12). 1987. pap. 2.50 (ISBN 0-553-26902-X). Bantam.
Foley, June. Falling in Love Is No Snap. LC 86-1990. 144p. (gr. 7 up). 1986. pap. 14.95 (ISBN 0-385-29490-5). Delacorte.
—Falling in Love Is No Snap. 144p. (gr. 6 up). 1989. pap. 2.95 (ISBN 0-440-20349-X, LFL). Dell.
—It's No Crush, I'm in Love. LC 81-15214. 224p. (gr. 7 up). 1982. 12.95 (ISBN 0-385-28465-9). Delacorte.
—Love by Any Other Name. LC 82-72752. 224p. (gr. 7 up). 1983. pap. 13.95 (ISBN 0-385-29245-7). Delacorte.
Foslien, Dagmar. A Garden of Love to Share. Paris, Pat & Williams, Karin, illus. 1984. incl. cassette 7.95 (ISBN 0-910313-63-6). Parker Bros.
Foster, Sharon. Stormy Leigh. 368p. (Orig.). (gr. 9 up). 1988. pap. 6.95 (ISBN 1-56292-535-0). Honor Bks Ok.
Foster, Stephanie. A Chance at Love, No. 6. 192p. (gr. 5 up). 1988. pap. 2.95 (ISBN 0-553-27017-6, Sweet Dreams). Bantam.
Fowler, Ruth. Lights! Camera! Love in Action! Smothers, Mark, illus. 64p. (Orig.). (gr. 4-6). 1989. pap. text ed. 3.95 (ISBN 0-936625-68-6). Womans Mission Union.
Fox, Paula. A Place Apart. LC 80-36717. 184p. (gr. 6 up). 1980. 12.95 (ISBN 0-374-35985-7). FS&G.
Freeman, Lory. Loving Touches. Deach, Carol, illus. LC 85-62434. 32p. (Orig.). (ps). 1985. PLB 12.95 (ISBN 0-943990-21-1); pap. 3.95 (ISBN 0-943990-20-3). Parenting Pr.
From the Heart. 1988. 6.95 (ISBN 0-89954-776-1). Antioch Pub Co.
Garden, Nancy. Annie on My Mind. LC 82-9189. 232p. (gr. 7 up). 1982. 12.95 (ISBN 0-374-30366-5); pap. 3.50 (ISBN 0-374-40413-5). FS&G.
Gardiner, Judy. Come Back Soon. LC 85-40385. 139p. (gr. 6-8). 1985. pap. 11.95 (ISBN 0-670-80150-X). Viking Child Bks.
Garfield, Leon. The Night of the Comet. LC 79-50670. (gr. 7 up). 1979. 8.95 (ISBN 0-685-01396-0); pap. 7.45 (ISBN 0-385-28753-4). Delacorte.
Geringer, Laura. A Three Hat Day. Lobel, Arnold, illus. LC 85-42640. 32p. (ps-3). 1985. 12.95 (ISBN 0-06-021988-2); PLB 12.89 (ISBN 0-06-021989-0). HarpC Child Bks.
Giff, Patricia R. Love, from the Fifth-Grade Celebrity. Morrill, Leslie, illus. LC 85-46075. 144p. (gr. 4-6). 1986. 13.95 (ISBN 0-385-29486-7). Delacorte.
—Tootsie Tanner, Why Don't You Talk? An Abby Jones, Junior Detective, Mystery. Kramer, Anthony, illus. LC 86-32910. 144p. (gr. 4-6). 1987. pap. 13.95 (ISBN 0-385-29579-0). Delacorte.
Gorman, Susan. The Game of Love. (gr. 6 up). 1988. pap. 2.50 (ISBN 0-553-27476-7). Bantam.
—This Time for Real. 192p. (Orig.). (gr. 7 up). 1988. pap. 2.50 (ISBN 0-553-27175-X). Bantam.
Goudge, Eileen. Against the Rules. (Orig.). (gr. 6 up). 1986. pap. 2.25 (ISBN 0-440-90096-4, LFL). Dell.
—Deep-Sea Summer. (Orig.). (gr. k-12). 1988. pap. 2.95 (ISBN 0-440-20123-3). Dell.
—Heart for Sale. (Orig.). (gr. 7-12). 1986. pap. 2.25 (ISBN 0-440-93382-X, LFL). Dell.
—Kiss & Make Up. 154p. (Orig.). (gr. 6-12). 1986. pap. 2.25 (ISBN 0-440-94514-3, LFL). Dell.
—Presenting Superhunk. (Orig.). (gr. 6-12). 1985. pap. 2.25 (ISBN 0-440-97172-1, LFL). Dell.
—Something Borrowed, Something Blue. (Orig.). (gr. k-12). 1988. pap. 2.95 (ISBN 0-440-20055-5, LFL). Dell.
—Sweet Talk. (Orig.). (gr. k-12). 1986. pap. 2.25 (ISBN 0-440-98411-4, LFL). Dell.
—Sweet Talk. 160p. 1986. pap. 2.95 (ISBN 0-553-17220-4). Bantam.
—A Touch of Ginger. (Orig.). (gr. 7-12). 1985. pap. 2.25 (ISBN 0-440-98816-0, LFL). Dell.
—Treat Me Right. (Orig.). (gr. 6 up). 1986. pap. 2.25 (ISBN 0-440-98845-4, LFL). Dell.
Graham, Heather X. Sweet Savage Eden. (Orig.). 1989. pap. 3.95 (ISBN 0-440-20235-3). Dell.
Greenberg, Jan. Exercises of the Heart. LC 86-11977. 160p. (gr. 6 up). 1986. 11.95 (ISBN 0-374-32237-6). FS&G.
Greene, Bette. Philip Hall Likes Me, I Reckon, Maybe. Lilly, Charles, illus. 144p. 1975. pap. 3.25 (ISBN 0-440-45755-6, YB). Dell.
—Philip Hall Likes Me. I Reckon Maybe. Lilly, Charles, illus. LC 74-2887. 160p. (gr. 3-6). 1974. 13.95 (ISBN 0-8037-6098-1); PLB 13.89 (ISBN 0-8037-6096-5). Dial Bks Young.
Greene, Constance C. The Love Letters of J. Timothy Owen. LC 85-45846. 192p. (gr. 7 up). 1986. 11.95 (ISBN 0-06-022156-9); PLB 11.89 (ISBN 0-06-022157-7). HarpC Child Bks.
—The Love Letters of J. Timothy Owen. LC 85-45846. 192p. (gr. 7 up). 1988. pap. 2.75 (ISBN 0-06-447026-1, Trophy). HarpC Child Bks.
—Monday I Love You. LC 87-27084. 160p. (gr. 7 up). 1988. 11.95 (ISBN 0-06-022183-6); PLB 11.89 (ISBN 0-06-022205-0). HarpC Child Bks.
Greene, Yvonne. Little Sister. (gr. 11 up). 1981. pap. 2.50 (ISBN 0-553-26613-6). Bantam.
—The Love Hunt. 192p. (Orig.). (gr. 5 up). 1985. pap. 2.25 (ISBN 0-553-25070-1). Bantam.
Greenwald, Sheila. Valentine Rosy. (gr. 3-7). 1986. pap. 2.50 (ISBN 0-440-49203-3, YB). Dell.
Gregory, Diana. Two's a Crowd. 144p. (Orig.). (gr. 6 up). 1985. pap. 2.25 (ISBN 0-553-24992-4). Bantam.
Grimes, Frances H. Sweet Dreams: Love Lines, No. 154. (gr. 6 up). 1988. pap. 2.50 (ISBN 0-318-37112-X). Bantam.
Grove, Vicki. Good-bye, My Wishing Star. 128p. (gr. 3-7). 1988. 12.95 (ISBN 0-399-21532-8, Putnam). Putnam Pub Group.
—Goodbye My Wishing Star. 1989. pap. 2.75 (ISBN 0-590-42152-2). Scholastic Inc.
Guccione, Leslie D. Tell Me How the Wind Sounds. 1989. 12.95 (ISBN 0-590-42615-X, Scholastic Hardcover). Scholastic Inc.
Guest, Elissa H. The Handsome Man. 160p. (gr. 7 up). 1981. pap. 1.95 (ISBN 0-440-93437-0, LFL). Dell.
—The Handsome Man. 192p. (gr. 7 up). 1989. pap. 2.95 (ISBN 0-02-043282-8, Collier Young Ad). Macmillan Child Grp.
Hahn, Mary D. Jellyfish Season. 176p. (gr. 7 up). 1987. pap. 2.50 (ISBN 0-380-70254-1, Flare). Avon.
Hallinan, P. K. How Do I Love You? (Illus.). 24p. (ps-k). 1990. pap. 3.95 (ISBN 0-8249-8415-3). Ideals.
Hamilton, Virginia. A White Romance. 200p. (gr. 8 up). 1987. 14.95 (ISBN 0-399-21213-2, Philomel Bks). Putnam Pub Group.
Hanes, Betsy. Taffy Sinclair & the Romance Machine Disaster. 128p. (Orig.). 1987. pap. 2.75 (ISBN 0-553-15644-6, Skylark). Bantam.
Harper, Elaine. Homecoming. 157p. 1986. 1.95 (ISBN 0-373-06181-1). Silhouette.
Hart, Bruce & Hart, Carole. Cross Your Heart. 256p. (Orig.). (gr. 6 up). 1988. pap. 3.50 (ISBN 0-380-89971-X, Flare). Avon.
Hartling, Peter. Ben Loves Anna. (gr. 4-7). 1990. 12.95 (ISBN 0-87951-407-8). Overlook Pr.
Hatonn & L-L Research Staff. What Is Love? A Coloring Book for Kids. (Illus.). 34p. (ps-2). 1984. pap. 6.95 (ISBN 0-945007-05-1). L-L Resrch.
Hawley, Richard. Shining Still. (Illus.). 192p. Date not set. 12.95 (ISBN 0-374-36811-2). FS&G.
Hayes, Sheila. You've Been Away All Summer. 160p. (gr. 4-8). 1988. pap. 2.50 (ISBN 0-590-40791-0, Apple Paperbacks). Scholastic Inc.
Heart to Heart. 176p. (Orig.). (gr. 7-12). 1987. pap. 2.50 (ISBN 0-553-26293-9). Bantam.
Hermes, Patricia. You Shouldn't Have to Say Good-Bye. LC 82-47933. 120p. (gr. 4-6). 1982. 11.95 (ISBN 0-15-299944-2, HJ). HarBraceJ.
—You Shouldn't Have to Say Good-Bye. 128p. (gr. 4-6). pap. 2.50 (ISBN 0-590-41355-4, Apple Paperbacks). Scholastic Inc.
Herrick, Ann. The Perfect Guy. (gr. 5 up). 1989. pap. 2.95 (ISBN 0-553-27927-0). Bantam.
Hill, Eric. Puppy Love. (Illus.). 32p. (ps-k). 1982. 3.95 (ISBN 0-399-20935-2, Putnam). Putnam Pub Group.
Hold Me Tight, No. 36. (gr. 7-12). 1988. pap. 2.50 (ISBN 0-590-41689-8). Scholastic Inc.
Holland, Isabelle. After the First Love. (gr. 7 up). 1983. pap. 2.25 (ISBN 0-449-70064-X, Juniper). Fawcett.
—Search. 1991. pap. 3.95 (ISBN 0-449-70342-8). Fawcett.
—Summer of My First Love. (gr. 7 up). 1983. pap. 2.95 (ISBN 0-449-70079-8, Juniper). Fawcett.
Honeycutt, Natalie. Josie's Beau. LC 87-5732. 160p. (gr. 6-8). 1987. 11.95 (ISBN 0-531-05718-6); PLB 11.99 (ISBN 0-531-08318-7). Orchard Bks Watts.
Hooper, Mary. Follow That Dream. (Orig.). (gr. 6 up). 1986. pap. 2.50 (ISBN 0-440-92644-0, LFL). Dell.
—Friends & Rivals. (Orig.). (gr. 6 up). 1986. pap. 2.50 (ISBN 0-440-92660-2, LFL). Dell.
Hope in Darkness. 1988. 6.95 (ISBN 0-89954-775-3). Antioch Pub Co.
Hopkins, Lee B. I Loved Rose Ann. Fetz, Ingrid, illus. LC 75-26824. 48p. (gr. 1-4). 1976. Knopf.
Hudson, Anne & Daniels, Neil. Ozzie: An Odyssey of Love. Daniels, Neil, illus. LC 83-81305. 72p. (Orig.). (gr. 1-6). 1983. pap. 3.95 (ISBN 0-940258-10-2). Kripalu Pubns.
Hunter, Mollie. The Three-Day Enchantment. Simont, Marc, illus. LC 84-48350. 64p. (gr. k-4). 1985. PLB 12.89 (ISBN 0-06-022693-5). HarpC Child Bks.
Jacobs, Barbara. Stolen Kisses. (Orig.). (gr. 6 up). 1986. pap. 2.50 (ISBN 0-440-97734-7, LFL). Dell.
Jarnow, Jill. Lifeguard Summer, No. 142. 192p. (Orig.). (gr. 7-9). 1988. pap. 2.50 (ISBN 0-553-27124-5, Sweet Dreams). Bantam.
Johnston, Norma. The Watcher in the Mist. 208p. 1986. pap. 2.95 (ISBN 0-553-26032-4, Starfire). Bantam.
Jordan, June. His Own Where. LC 71-146283. 1971. 11.95 (ISBN 0-690-38133-6, Crowell Jr Bks). HarpC Child Bks.
The Judy Blume Memory Book. (gr. k-6). 1988. pap. 8.95 (ISBN 0-440-40120-8, YB). Dell.
Kaplow, Robert. Alessandra in Love. LC 88-23141. 160p. (gr. 7 up). 1989. 11.95 (ISBN 0-397-32281-X, Lipp Jr Bks); PLB 12.89 (ISBN 0-397-32282-8, Lipp Jr Bks). HarpC Child Bks.
Keene, Carolyn. Going to Far. 160p. 1990. pap. 2.95 (ISBN 0-671-67761-6, Archway). PB.
—Heart of Danger. (gr. 7 up). 1989. pap. 2.95 (ISBN 0-671-68728-X, Archway). PB.
—Hit & Run Holiday. (gr. 7 up). 1989. pap. 2.95 (ISBN 0-671-70289-0, Archway). PB.
—Love Times Three. (Orig.). (gr. 9-12). 1989. pap. 2.95 (ISBN 0-671-67759-4, Archway). PB.
—Stolen Kisses. 160p. 1990. pap. 2.95 (ISBN 0-671-67762-4, Archway). PB.
Kent, Deborah. Talk to Me, My Love. (Orig.). (gr. k-12). 1987. pap. 2.75 (ISBN 0-440-97810-6, LFL). Dell.
Kenyon, Kate. Who's the Junior High Hunk? 160p. (gr. 5-9). 1988. pap. 2.50 (ISBN 0-590-41388-0). Scholastic Inc.
Kerr, M. E. Him She Loves? LC 83-48818. 224p. (gr. 7 up). 1984. PLB 12.89 (ISBN 0-06-023239-0). HarpC Child Bks.
—I Stay Near You. 192p. 1986. pap. 2.50 (ISBN 0-425-08870-7, Pub. by Berkley-Pacer). Berkley Pub.
—If I Love You, Am I Trapped Forever? 192p. (gr. 7 up). 1974. pap. 2.25 (ISBN 0-440-94320-5, LFL). Dell.
—If I Love You, Am I Trapped Forever? LC 72-9860. 176p. (gr. 7 up). 1973. PLB 12.89 (ISBN 0-06-023149-1). HarpC Child Bks.
—If I Love You, Am I Trapped Forever? LC 72-9860. 192p. (gr. 7 up). 1988. pap. 2.95 (ISBN 0-06-447032-6, Trophy). HarpC Child Bks.
—Love Is a Missing Person. LC 75-6299. 176p. (gr. 7 up). 1988. pap. 2.95 (ISBN 0-06-447034-2, Trophy). HarpC Child Bks.
Keyes, Daniel. Flowers for Algernon: A Classic Story of Struggle. (Illus.). (gr. 4 up). 1987. PLB 10.95s.p. (ISBN 0-88682-007-3); 15.65. Creative Ed.
Killien, Christi. All of the Above. LC 86-27872. (gr. 5-9). 1987. 12.95 (ISBN 0-395-43023-2). HM.
Klein, Norma. Older Men. 192p. 1988. pap. 2.95 (ISBN 0-449-70261-8, Juniper). Fawcett.
—Snapshots. 128p. 1986. pap. 2.50 (ISBN 0-449-70157-3, Juniper). Fawcett.
Klein, Robin. Laurie Loved Me Best. 160p. (gr. 5-9). 1988. pap. 11.95 (ISBN 0-670-82211-6). Viking Child Bks.
Knudson, R. R. Just Another Love Story. (gr. 7 up). 1984. pap. 2.50 (ISBN 0-380-65532-2, 60172-9, Flare). Avon.
Koertge, Ron. Where the Kissing Never Stops. (gr. k-12). 1988. pap. 2.95 (ISBN 0-440-20167-5). Dell.
Lamb, Jane M. Sharing with Thumpy: My Story of Love & Grief. Dodge, Nancy C., illus. 48p. (gr. k-12). 1985. pap. 8.95 workbook (ISBN 0-918533-10-4). Prairie Lark.
Landis, J. D. Looks Aren't Everything. 1991. pap. 3.50 (ISBN 0-553-28860-1). Bantam.
Lantz, Francess. Truth about Making Out. (gr. 4 up). 1990. pap. 2.95 (ISBN 0-553-15813-9). Bantam.
Lawrence, Amy. Color It Love. 1983. pap. 1.95 (ISBN 0-448-13576-0, Pub. by Tempo). Ace Bks.
Lawrence, D. H. You Touched Me. 48p. (gr. 6 up). 1982. PLB 10.95s.p. (ISBN 0-87191-894-3); PLB 15.65 (ISBN 0-685-06209-0). Creative Ed.
Leroe, Ellen. Have a Heart, Cupid Delaney. 160p. (gr. 5 up). 1988. pap. 2.95 (ISBN 0-553-27002-8, Starfire). Bantam.
—Personal Business. 144p. (gr. 6 up). 1987. pap. 2.95 (ISBN 0-553-26652-7, Starfire). Bantam.
Levy, Elizabeth. First Date. 1990. pap. 2.75 (ISBN 0-590-42825-X). Scholastic Inc.
Levy, Marilyn. Touching. (gr. 6 up). 1988. pap. 3.50 (ISBN 0-449-70267-7, Juniper). Fawcett.
Lewis, Linda. All for the Love of That Boy. 224p. (gr. 7-9). 1989. pap. 2.95 (ISBN 0-671-68243-1, Archway). PB.
—Dedicated to That Boy I Love. 168p. (gr. 6-9). 1990. pap. 2.75 (ISBN 0-671-68244-X, Archway). PB.
—My Heart Belongs to That Boy. (Orig.). (gr. 7 up). 1990. pap. 2.95 (ISBN 0-671-70353-6, Archway). PB.
—We Love only Older Boys. 176p. (Orig.). (gr. 7 up). 1990. pap. 2.95 (ISBN 0-671-69558-4, Archway). PB.
Lexau, Joan. Don't Be My Valentine. Hoff, Syd, illus. LC 85-42621. 64p. (gr. k-3). 1985. PLB 11.89 (ISBN 0-06-023873-9). HarpC Child Bks.
Likken, Laurie. Winner Takes All. 192p. 1987. pap. 2.50 (ISBN 0-317-65474-8, Sweet Dreams). Bantam.
Lipsyte, Robert. Jock & Jill. LC 81-47723. 160p. (gr. 7 up). 1982. PLB 13.89 (ISBN 0-06-023900-X). HarpC Child Bks.
Littke, Lael. Loydene in Love. LC 86-12000. 160p. (gr. 6 up). 1986. 13.95 (ISBN 0-15-249888-5, HJ). HarBraceJ.
Lowry, Lois. Autumn Street. 192p. (gr. 4-7). 1986. pap. 3.25 (ISBN 0-440-40344-8, YB). Dell.
Lykken, Laurie. Priceless Love. 192p. (Orig.). (gr. 7 up). 1988. pap. 2.50 (ISBN 0-553-27174-1). Bantam.
—The Truth about Love. 1991. pap. 2.95 (ISBN 0-553-28862-8). Bantam.
Lyons, Pam. Danny's Girl. (Orig.). (gr. 6 up). 1986. pap. 2.50 (ISBN 0-440-91830-8, LFL). Dell.
—Love Around the Corner. (Orig.). (gr. k-12). 1987. pap. 2.50 (ISBN 0-440-94726-X, LFL). Dell.
—Tug of Love. (Orig.). (gr. 6 up). 1986. pap. 2.50 (ISBN 0-440-98818-7, LFL). Dell.
MacBain, Carol. Heartbreak Hill. 192p. (Orig.). (gr. 7-12). 1987. pap. 2.50 (ISBN 0-553-26195-9). Bantam.
—Stand By for Love. 192p. (Orig.). (gr. 7-12). 1987. pap. 2.50 (ISBN 0-553-26903-8). Bantam.
MacDonald, George. The Landlady's Master. Phillips, Michael R., ed. 208p. (Orig.). (gr. 11 up). 1989. pap. 6.95 (ISBN 0-87123-904-3). Bethany Hse.
McDonnell, Christine. Just for the Summer. De Groat, Diane, illus. LC 87-8201. (gr. 2-5). 1987. pap. 11.95 (ISBN 0-670-80059-7). Viking Child Bks.
McGill, Joyce. Here We Go Again. 155p. 1986. 1.95 (ISBN 0-373-06184-6). Silhouette.
MacLachlan, Patricia. Seven Kisses in a Row. Marrella, Maria P., illus. LC 82-47718. 64p. (gr. 2-5). 1988. pap. 2.95 (ISBN 0-06-440231-2, Trophy). HarpC Child Bks.
Marigold Beach. 155p. 1986. 1.95 (ISBN 0-373-06183-8). Silhouette.

Mark, Jan. Handles. LC 86-43076. 160p. (gr. 5-9). 1987. pap. 3.95 (ISBN 0-14-031587-X, Puffin). Puffin Bks.
Marshall, Andrea. Handle with Care. 157p. 1984. pap. 1.95 (ISBN 0-671-53407-6). Silhouette.
Marshall, Mollie. Ready for Romance. 192p. (Orig.). (gr. 6-12). 1982. pap. 1.95 (ISBN 0-8439-1129-8). Dorchester Pub Co.
Martin, Ann M. Dawn & the Older Boy. (gr. 4-7). 1990. pap. 3.25 (ISBN 0-590-43566-3). Scholastic Inc.
—Just a Summer Romance. LC 86-46201. 176p. (gr. 7 up). 1987. 13.95 (ISBN 0-8234-0649-0). Holiday.
—Just a Summer Romance. 1988. 2.50 (ISBN 0-590-41432-1, Point). Scholastic Inc.
—Just a Summer Romance. 1988. pap. 2.75 (ISBN 0-590-43999-5, NAL). Scholastic Inc.
Martin, LaJoyce. Heart-Shaped Pieces. Bernard, David, ed. Agnew, Tim, illus. LC 90-22517. 160p. (Orig.). (gr. 9 up). 1991. pap. 6.95 (ISBN 0-932581-78-1). Word Aflame.
Mazer, Harry. The Girl of His Dreams. LC 86-47749. 192p. (gr. 7 up). 1987. 12.95 (ISBN 0-690-04640-5, Crowell Jr Bks); PLB 12.89 (ISBN 0-690-04642-1, Crowell Jr Bks). HarpC Child Bks.
—I Love You, Stupid! LC 81-43033. 192p. (gr. 7 up). 1981. PLB 12.89 (ISBN 0-690-04121-7, Crowell Jr Bks). HarpC Child Bks.
Mazer, Norma F. Someone to Love. LC 82-72755. 256p. (gr. 7 up). 1983. 13.95 (ISBN 0-685-06446-8). Delacorte.
—Someone to Love. 256p. (gr. k-12). 1985. pap. 3.25 (ISBN 0-440-98062-3, LFL). Dell.
—Summer Girls, Love Boys & Other Short Stories. LC 82-70320. 192p. (gr. 7 up). 1982. pap. 11.95 (ISBN 0-385-28930-8). Delacorte.
—Summer Girls, Love Boys: And Other Short Stories. 256p. (gr. 7 up). 1989. pap. 3.25 (ISBN 0-440-98375-4, LFL). Dell.
—When We First Met. 192p. (gr. 7 up). 1984. pap. 2.50 (ISBN 0-590-40359-1, Point). Scholastic Inc.
—When We First Met. 1991. pap. 2.95 (ISBN 0-590-43823-9). Scholastic Inc.
Michaels, Fran. Mr. Wonderful. 192p. (Orig.). (gr. 7-12). 1987. pap. 2.50 (ISBN 0-553-26340-4). Bantam.
Miklowitz, Gloria D. Goodbye Tomorrow. LC 86-23948. 192p. (gr. 7 up). 1987. 13.95 (ISBN 0-385-29562-6). Delacorte.
—Goodbye Tomorrow. (gr. k-12). 1988. pap. 3.25 (ISBN 0-440-20081-4, LFL). Dell.
—Love Story, Take Three. (gr. k-12). 1987. pap. 2.75 (ISBN 0-440-95084-8, LFL). Dell.
—The War Between the Classes. (gr. 6 up). 1986. pap. 3.25 (ISBN 0-440-99406-3, LFL). Dell.
Miner, Jane C. Roxanne, Vol. 15. 368p. (Orig.). (gr. 11 up). 1985. pap. 2.95 (ISBN 0-590-33686-X, Sunfire). Scholastic Inc.
—Veronica, No. 18. 224p. (Orig.). (gr. 7 up). 1986. pap. 2.25 (ISBN 0-590-33933-8, Sunfire). Scholastic Inc.
Montgomery, L. M. Anne of Avonlea: An Anne of Green Gables Story. Sieffert, Clare, illus. 320p. 1990. 13.95 (ISBN 0-448-40063-4, G&D). Putnam Pub Group.
Moore, Inga. Rose & the Nightingale. Moore, Inga, illus. LC 89-24429. 32p. (ps-2). 1990. pap. 3.95 (ISBN 0-679-80197-9, Dragonfly Bks). Knopf.
Morris, Ann. Kiss Time. Roffey, Maureen, illus. LC 85-45334. 16p. (ps). 1986. 3.50 (ISBN 0-694-00073-6). HarpC Child Bks.
Morrison, Dorothy N. Whisper Again. 208p. (gr. 2-9). pap. 2.95 (ISBN 0-8167-1307-3). Troll Assocs.
Murphy, Barbara B. One Another. 160p. (gr. 7 up). 1991. pap. 3.95 (ISBN 0-02-042015-3, Collier Young Ad). Macmillan Child Grp.
Murrow, Liza K. Fire in the Heart. 255p. (gr. 5-9). 1990. pap. 2.95 (ISBN 0-8167-2261-7). Troll Assocs.
Myers, Walter D. Motown & Didi: A Love Story. LC 84-3632. 192p. (gr. 7 up). 1984. pap. 12.95 (ISBN 0-670-49062-8). Viking Child Bks.
Nesbit, Edith. Long Ago When I Was Young. Ardizzone, Edward & Buchanan, George, illus. LC 87-8974. 136p. (ps up). 1988. 14.95 (ISBN 0-8037-0476-3). Dial Bks Young.
Newman, Nanette & Foreman, Michael. A Cat & Mouse Love Story. Foreman, Michael, illus. 32p. (gr. k-3). 1985. 14.95 (ISBN 0-434-98045-5, Pub. by W Heinemann Ltd). Trafalgar Sq.
Nielsen, Virginia. La Sauvage. (Orig.). 1988. pap. 3.95 (ISBN 0-440-20190-X). Dell.
Nimmo, Jenny. Orchard of the Crescent Moon. 170p. (gr. 5-9). 1990. pap. 2.95 (ISBN 0-8167-2265-X). Troll Assocs.
Nixon, Joan L. A Family Apart. 176p. (gr. 5 up). 1988. pap. 3.50 (ISBN 0-553-27478-3, Starfire). Bantam.
No More Boys. 176p. (gr. 5-6). 1986. pap. 2.25 (ISBN 0-553-25643-2). Bantam.
Nobile, Jeanett. Portrait of Love. 166p. (gr. 6-8). 1983. pap. 2.25 (ISBN 0-553-17846-6). Bantam.
O'Connor, Jane. Yours till Niagara Falls, Abby. 128p. (Orig.). (gr. 3-7). 1991. pap. 2.75 (ISBN 0-590-42854-3). Scholastic Inc.
O'Donnell, Thomas. The Journal of Malt Witty. 1989. 10.00 (ISBN 0-533-08038-X). Vantage.
Ogilvie, Elisabeth. My Summer Love. 192p. (Orig.). (gr. 7 up). 1985. pap. 2.25 (ISBN 0-590-33266-X, Wildfire). Scholastic Inc.
Oke, Janette. Love Takes Wing. LC 88-19276. 224p. (Orig.). (gr. 8 up). 1988. pap. 5.95 (ISBN 1-55661-035-1). Bethany Hse.
—Love Takes Wing. large type ed. LC 88-19276. 224p. (gr. 4 up). 1988. pap. 7.95 (ISBN 1-55661-045-9). Bethany Hse.
Okimoto, Jean D. Jason's Women. LC 85-28655. 210p. (gr. 7up). 1986. 14.95 (ISBN 0-316-63809-9, 638099, Joy St Bks). Little.
Older, Jules. Hank Prank in Love. (Illus.). 64p. (gr. 1-3). 1987. 14.95 (ISBN 0-434-95555-8, Pub. by W Heinemann Ltd). Trafalgar Sq.
Oldham, June. Grow Up Cupid. (gr. k-12). 1989. pap. 2.95 (ISBN 0-440-20256-6, LFL). Dell.
O'Neal, Zibby. In Summer Light. LC 85-50806. 180p. (gr. 7 up). 1985. pap. 12.95 (ISBN 0-670-80784-2). Viking Child Bks.
Ormondroyd, Edward. Theodore's Rival. Larrecq, John M., illus. (gr. 4-8). 1986. pap. 3.95 (ISBN 0-395-41669-8, Sandpiper). HM.
Overton, Jenny. The Ship from Simnel Street. LC 85-21965. 224p. (gr. 5 up). 1986. reinforced trade ed. 10.25 (ISBN 0-688-06182-6). Greenwillow.
Park, Ruth. Playing Beatie Bow. LC 81-8097. 204p. (gr. 5-9). 1982. 13.95 (ISBN 0-689-30889-2, Atheneum Child Bk). Macmillan Child Grp.
Parkison, Ralph F. Eovl. Withrow, Marion O., ed. Bush, William, illus. 36p. (Orig.). (gr. 2-8). 1988. pap. write for info. Little Wood Bks.
Pascal, Francine. All Night Long. large type ed. 134p. (gr. 5-8). 1989. Repr. of 1984 ed. PLB 10.50 (ISBN 1-55905-014-4, Dist. by Gareth Stevens); 9.50 (ISBN 1-55905-004-7). Grey Castle.
—Dangerous Love. (gr. 7 up). 1984. pap. 2.95 (ISBN 0-553-27741-3). Bantam.
—Dear Sister. (gr. 7 up). 1984. pap. 2.95 (ISBN 0-553-27672-7). Bantam.
—Head over Heels. (Orig.). (gr. 5). 1985. pap. 2.95 (ISBN 0-553-27444-9). Bantam.
—Heartbreaker. 176p. (gr. 7 up). 1984. pap. 2.95 (ISBN 0-553-27569-0). Bantam.
—In Love Again. (gr. 7 up). 1989. pap. 2.95 (ISBN 0-553-28193-3). Bantam.
—Jessica the Rock Star. (gr. 5 up). 1989. pap. 2.99 (ISBN 0-553-15766-3). Bantam.
—Love & Betrayal & Hold the Mayo! (gr. 5-9). 1986. pap. 2.95 (ISBN 0-440-94735-9, LFL). Dell.
—Love Letters. 160p. (gr. 6 up). 1985. pap. 2.75 (ISBN 0-553-26883-X). Bantam.
—My First Love & Other Disasters. 176p. (gr. 7 up). 1986. pap. 2.95 (ISBN 0-440-95447-9, LFL). Dell.
—My First Love & Other Disasters. LC 78-25720. (gr. 7 up). 1979. pap. 14.95 (ISBN 0-670-49952-8). Viking Child Bks.
—The Perfect Girl. 1991. pap. 2.95 (ISBN 0-553-28901-2). Bantam.
—Perfect Summer. 256p. (Orig.). (gr. 6 up). 1985. pap. 3.50 (ISBN 0-553-25072-8). Bantam.
—Regina's Legacy. 1991. pap. 2.95 (ISBN 0-553-28863-6). Bantam.
—Showdown. 160p. (gr. 6). 1985. pap. 2.95 (ISBN 0-553-27589-5). Bantam.
—Too Good to Be True. 592p. (Orig.). (gr. 7 up). 1984. pap. 2.75 (ISBN 0-553-26824-4). Bantam.
—Wrong Kind of Girl. (gr. 7 up). 1984. pap. 2.95 (ISBN 0-553-27668-9). Bantam.
Pascal, Francine, created by. Loving. 208p. (Orig.). (gr. 7-12). 1991. pap. 3.50 (ISBN 0-553-24716-6). Bantam.
—The Older Boy. (gr. 3-7). 1988. pap. 2.99 (ISBN 0-553-15664-0, Skylark). Bantam.
Past Perfect. 192p. (Orig.). (gr. 7-12). 1987. pap. 2.50 (ISBN 0-553-26789-2). Bantam.
Paton Walsh, Jill. Torch. LC 87-45995. 176p. 1988. 12.95 (ISBN 0-374-37684-0). FS&G.
Perl, Lila. Fat Glenda's Summer Romance. 176p. (Orig.). (gr. 5-8). 1988. pap. 2.50 (ISBN 0-671-64857-8, Archway). PB.
Petersen, P. J. The Boll Weevil Express. 92p. (gr. 6 up). 1984. pap. 2.95 (ISBN 0-440-91040-4, LFL). Dell.
Pevsner, Stella. I'll Always Remember You... Maybe. 192p. (gr. 6 up). 1981. 12.95 (ISBN 0-395-31024-5, Clarion). HM.
Peyton, K. M. The Edge of the Cloud. 192p. (gr. 7 up). 1989. pap. 3.95 (ISBN 0-14-030905-5, Puffin). Puffin Bks.
—Flambards. 224p. (gr. 7 up). 1989. pap. 3.95 (ISBN 0-14-034153-6, Puffin). Puffin Bks.
—Flambards in Summer. 208p. (gr. 7 up). 1989. pap. 3.95 (ISBN 0-14-034154-4, Puffin). Puffin Bks.
Phillips, Erin. Research for Romance. 186p. (gr. 7 up). 1984. pap. 1.95 (ISBN 0-671-53396-7). PB.
Pitt, Jane. Secret Hearts. (Orig.). (gr. 6 up). 1986. pap. 2.50 (ISBN 0-440-97722-3, LFL). Dell.
Playing Games. 176p. (gr. 5-6). 1986. pap. 2.25 (ISBN 0-553-25642-4). Bantam.
Playing with Fire. 149p. (gr. 7-12). 1984. pap. 2.99 (ISBN 0-553-27669-7). Bantam.
Polcovar, Jane. Hey, Good Looking! 144p. (gr. 6 up). 1985. pap. 2.25 (ISBN 0-553-24383-7). Bantam.
Posner, Richard. Sweet Pain. LC 87-8930. 224p. (gr. 8 up). 1987. 11.95 (ISBN 0-685-17452-2). M Evans.
Provensen, Alice & Provensen, Martin. Shaker Lane. (ps up). 14.95 (ISBN 0-317-62524-1). Viking Child Bks.
Pryor, Bonnie. Rats, Spiders & Love. Higgenbottom, J. Winslow, illus. LC 85-25831. 128p. (gr. 4-6). 1986. 13.95 (ISBN 0-688-05867-1). Morrow Jr Bks.
Quin-Harkin, Janet. Best Friends Forever, No. 6. 176p. (Orig.). (gr. 7-12). 1986. pap. 2.50 (ISBN 0-553-26111-8). Bantam.
—Dream Come True. (gr. 6 up). 1988. pap. 2.95 (ISBN 0-8041-0334-8). Ivy Books.
—Growing Pains. 176p. (Orig.). (gr. 6 up). 1986. pap. 2.50 (ISBN 0-553-26034-0). Bantam.
—Home Sweet Home. (gr. 6 up). 1988. pap. 2.95 (ISBN 0-8041-0333-X). Ivy Books.
—My Secret Love. 224p. (Orig.). (gr. 7-12). 1986. pap. 2.95 (ISBN 0-553-25884-2). Bantam.
—One Hundred One Ways to Meet Mr. Right. 176p. (Orig.). (gr. 6 up). 1985. pap. 2.25 (ISBN 0-553-24946-0). Bantam.
—Out of Love. 208p. (Orig.). (gr. 6 up). 1986. pap. 2.50 (ISBN 0-553-25937-7). Bantam.
—The Trouble with Toni. 192p. (Orig.). (gr. 6 up). 1986. pap. 2.50 (ISBN 0-553-25724-2). Bantam.
—Wanted: Date for Saturday Night. 160p. 1986. pap. 2.50 (ISBN 0-425-08448-5, Pub. by Berkley-Pacer). Berkley Pub.
Rand, Suzanne. The Boy She Left Behind. 192p. (Orig.). (gr. 6). 1985. pap. 2.25 (ISBN 0-553-24890-1). Bantam.
Ransom, Candice. The Love Charm: Romance Novel. 128p. (Orig.). (gr. 4-8). 1990. pap. 2.95 (ISBN 0-87406-522-4). Willowisp Pr.
Ransom, Candice F. Amanda, No. 1. 368p. (gr. 7 up). 1984. pap. 2.95 (ISBN 0-590-32774-7, Sunfire). Scholastic Inc.
Raymond, Patrick. Daniel & Esther. LC 89-49588. 176p. (gr. 7 up). 1990. 12.95 (ISBN 0-689-50504-3, M K McElderry). Macmillan Child Grp.
Redish, Jane. Promise Me Love. 176p. (Orig.). (gr. 7-12). 1986. pap. 2.50 (ISBN 0-553-26158-4). Bantam.
Reit, Ann. The First Time. (Orig.). (gr. 5 up). 1986. pap. 2.50 (ISBN 0-440-92560-6, LFL). Dell.
Reynolds, Elizabeth. Stolen Kisses. 144p. (Orig.). (gr. 7-12). 1986. pap. 2.50 (ISBN 0-553-25726-9). Bantam.
Robinson, Barbara. Temporary Times, Temporary Places. LC 81-47732. 128p. (gr. 7 up). 1982. 9.95i (ISBN 0-06-025039-9). HarpC Child Bks.
Rock, Gail. Addie & the King of Hearts. McVicker, Charles, illus. LC 75-35776. 96p. (gr. 4-6). 1976. Knopf.
Roos, Stephen. Confessions of a Wayward Preppie. LC 85-16241. 144p. (gr. 7 up). 1986. 13.95 (ISBN 0-385-29454-9). Delacorte.
—My Secret Admirer. (gr. k-12). 1991. pap. 3.25 (ISBN 0-440-45950-8, YB). Dell.

Rowe, Jeanine C. Eyes of Desire. Hannan, R., ed. 370p. 1991. pap. 5.99 (ISBN 0-9626415-0-2). Intl Info NY. Set against the beauty of Normandy, France, here is an unforgettable love story that takes us into kinder times. Desiree Achain is stolen by Gypsies at the age of three & is now a young woman who captivates us with her fierce courage & tender heart. Fate brings her to Bart Aubry who searches & finds her family - a search that leads to strange findings. She's reunited with her mother, a wealthy but bitter woman whose mind is like the worm-eaten apple on a perfect tree that reveals disturbing secrets. Our heroine is appalled by shattering confrontations with her mother's demands for her to marry the evil Gaspar. Then she awakened one night to hear her mother argue with a mysterious stranger. Hate & love, murder & sorrow, even though these are entwined in the story, we leave it with a warm heart. Time period 1947.
Publisher Provided Annotation.

Rue, Nancy. Stop in the Name of Love. Rosen, Roger, ed. (gr. 7 up). 1988. lib. bdg. 12.95 (ISBN 0-8239-0794-5). Rosen Group.
Ryan, Mary E. Dance a Step Closer. 1988. pap. 2.95 (ISBN 0-440-20127-6, LFL). Dell.
Rylant, Cynthia. A Couple of Kooks: And Other Stories about Love. LC 90-30646. 112p. (gr. 7 up). 1990. 13.95 (ISBN 0-531-05900-6); PLB 13.99 (ISBN 0-531-08500-7). Orchard Bks Watts.
—A Kindness. LC 88-1454. 128p. (gr. 7 up). 1988. 13.95 (ISBN 0-531-05767-4); PLB 13.99 (ISBN 0-531-08367-5). Orchard Bks Watts.
Saal, Jocelyn & Burman, Margaret. On Thin Ice. 181p. (gr. 6 up). 1983. pap. 1.95 (ISBN 0-553-17070-8). Bantam.
Sachs, Marilyn. Almost Fifteen. LC 86-29209. (gr. 4-9). 1987. 12.95 (ISBN 0-525-44285-5, DCB). Dutton Child Bks.
—Baby Sister. LC 85-16171. (gr. 7-11). 1986. 13.95 (ISBN 0-525-44213-8, DCB). Dutton Child Bks.
—Fourteen. 128p. (gr. 7 up). 1985. pap. 2.95 (ISBN 0-380-69842-0, Flare). Avon.
—Hello... Wrong Number. 96p. (gr. 7 up). 1984. pap. 2.50 (ISBN 0-590-41570-0, Point). Scholastic Inc.

St. Pierre, Stephanie. Project Boyfriend. 1991. pap. 2.95 (ISBN 0-553-28900-4). Bantam.
Sallis, Susan. Only Love. LC 79-2686. 256p. (gr. 7 up). 1980. PLB 12.89 (ISBN 0-06-025175-1). HarpC Child Bks.
Schulz, Charles M. Love Is Walking Hand in Hand. (Illus.). 64p. (ps up). 1987. pap. 5.95 (ISBN 0-345-34873-7). Pharos Bks NY.
—Someday You'll Find Her, Charlie Brown. Schulz, Charles M., illus. LC 82-3666. 48p. (gr. 1-6). 1982. lib. bdg. 6.99 (ISBN 0-394-95429-7). Random.
Schurfranz, Vivian. Cassie, No. 14. 368p. (Orig.). (gr. 7 up). 1985. pap. 2.95 (ISBN 0-590-33688-6, Sunfire). Scholastic Inc.
—Danielle, No. 4. 368p. (gr. 7 up). 1984. pap. 2.95 (ISBN 0-590-33156-6, Sunfire). Scholastic Inc.
—Megan, No. 16. 224p. (Orig.). (gr. 7 up). 1986. pap. 2.75 (ISBN 0-590-41468-2, Sunfire). Scholastic Inc.
Scoppettone, Sandra. Long Time Between Kisses. LC 81-47853. 224p. (gr. 7 up). 1982. HarpC Child Bks.
Secrets. 118p. (gr. 6 up). 1984. pap. 2.99 (ISBN 0-553-27578-X). Bantam.
Service, Pamela F. Tomorrow's Magic. (gr. 5 up). 1988. pap. 3.95 (ISBN 0-449-70305-3, Juniper). Fawcett.
Shakespeare, William. Romeo & Juliet. Shaw, Charles, illus. Stewart, Diana, adapted by. LC 79-24465. (Illus.). 48p. (gr. 4 up). 1983. PLB 17.32 (ISBN 0-8172-1653-7); pap. 9.27 (ISBN 0-8172-2020-8). Raintree Pubs.
Shannon, Jacqueline. Big Guy, Little Women. (gr. 6-8). 1989. pap. 2.75 (ISBN 0-590-41685-5, Apple Paperbacks). Scholastic Inc.
—Class Crush. 176p. (Orig.). (gr. 5-9). 1987. pap. 2.25 (ISBN 0-590-40407-5). Scholastic Inc.
Sharmat, Marjorie W. Fighting over Me. (Orig.). (gr. 6 up). 1986. pap. 2.50 (ISBN 0-440-92530-4, LFL). Dell.
—He Noticed I'm Alive & Other Hopeful Signs. (Orig.). (gr. k-12). 1989. pap. 2.95 (ISBN 0-440-93809-0, LFL). Dell.
—Here Comes Mr. Right. (gr. 5 up). 1987. pap. 2.50 (ISBN 0-440-93841-4). Dell.
—I Think I'm Falling in Love. (Orig.). (gr. 6 up). 1986. pap. 2.50 (ISBN 0-440-94011-7, LFL). Dell.
—I'm Going to Get Your Boyfriend. (Orig.). (gr. k-12). 1987. pap. 2.50 (ISBN 0-440-94004-4, LFL). Dell.
—Snobs Beware. (Orig.). (gr. 6 up). 1986. pap. 2.50 (ISBN 0-440-98092-5, LFL). Dell.
—Two Guys Noticed Me...& Other Miracles. (gr. k up). 1989. pap. 2.95 (ISBN 0-440-98846-2, LFL). Dell.
Shura, Mary F. Diana. 224p. (gr. 6-10). 1988. pap. 2.75 (ISBN 0-590-41416-X). Scholastic Inc.
—Marilee, No. 9. 368p. (Orig.). (gr. 7 up). 1985. pap. 2.95 (ISBN 0-590-33433-6, Sunfire). Scholastic Inc.
Silsbee, Peter. Love among the Hiccups. 224p. (gr. 7 up). 1989. pap. 3.95 (ISBN 0-02-044983-6, Collier Young Ad). Macmillan Child Grp.
Simbal, Joanne. Gifts from the Heart, No. 146. 176p. (Orig.). 1988. pap. 2.50 (ISBN 0-553-27228-4, Sweet Dreams). Bantam.
Singer, Marilyn. The Course of True Love Never Did Run Smooth. LC 82-48630. 256p. (gr. 7 up). 1983. 12. 95 (ISBN 0-06-025753-9); PLB 12.89 (ISBN 0-06-025754-7). HarpC Child Bks.
—Storm Rising. 1989. pap. 12.95 (ISBN 0-590-42173-5). Scholastic Inc.
Singleton, Koni. Bearhugs. LC 87-80827. (Illus.). 32p. (Orig.). (gr. k-3). 1987. pap. 5.95 (ISBN 0-942411-00-5). Heartprint Pr.
Sloate, Susan. Racing Hearts. (gr. 7 up). 1991. pap. 2.99 (ISBN 0-553-28962-4). Bantam.
Smith, Doris B. Dreams & Drummers. LC 77-26590. 192p. (gr. 6 up). 1978. PLB 12.89 (ISBN 0-690-03843-7, Crowell Jr Bks). HarpC Child Bks.
Snyder, Zilpha K. The Headless Cupid. Raible, Alton, illus. (gr. 3-7). 1985. pap. 3.25 (ISBN 0-440-43507-2, YB). Dell.
Spector, Debra. Secret Admirer. 160p. (gr. 6 up). 1985. pap. 2.25 (ISBN 0-553-24688-7). Bantam.
Spinelli, Jerry. Jason & Marceline. (gr. k-12). 1988. pap. 3.50 (ISBN 0-440-20166-7, LFL). Dell.
Springstubb, Tricia. Lulu vs. Love. 1990. 13.95 (ISBN 0-385-30036-0). Doubleday.
Stahl, Hilda. Elizabeth Gail & the Missing Love Letters, No. 13. 128p. 1989. pap. 3.95 (ISBN 0-8423-0807-5). Tyndale.
Stanek, Lou W. Gleanings. LC 85-42622. 192p. (gr. 6 up). 1985. PLB 12.89 (ISBN 0-06-025809-8). HarpC Child Bks.
Steiner, Barbara. Puppy Love. 112p. (Orig.). (gr. 4-6). 1990. pap. text ed. 2.75 (ISBN 0-87406-463-5). Willowisp Pr.
Stewart, A. C. Elizabeth's Tower. LC 72-4063. 220p. (gr. 6-9). 1972. 18.95 (ISBN 0-87599-193-9). S G Phillips.
Stine, R. L. Blind Date. 208p. (Orig.). (gr. 7 up). 1986. pap. 2.25 (ISBN 0-590-40326-5, Point). Scholastic Inc.
—Blind Date. 1986. pap. 2.75 (ISBN 0-590-43125-0). Scholastic Inc.
—The Boyfriend. 176p. (gr. 7 up). 1990. pap. 2.95 (ISBN 0-590-43279-6). Scholastic Inc.
Stowe, Aurelia, ed. Love Will Come: Stories of Romance. 1963. lib. bdg. 4.99 (ISBN 0-394-91363-9). Random.
—Love Will Come: Stories of Romance. 1963. lib. bdg. 4.99 (ISBN 0-394-91363-9). Random.
Strasser, Todd. Workin' for Peanuts. LC 82-14070. 192p. (gr. 7 up). 1983. pap. 12.95 (ISBN 0-385-29236-8). Delacorte.
Sunshine, Tina. An X-Rated Romance. 142p. (gr. 7 up). 1988. pap. 2.50 (ISBN 0-380-87817-8, Flare). Avon.
Taylor, Mildred D. Let the Circle Be Unbroken. (gr. 7-12). 1983. pap. 3.50 (ISBN 0-553-23436-6). Bantam.
Taylor, Theodore. Waking up a Rainbow. LC 85-16239. 224p. (gr. 7 up). 1986. pap. 14.95 (ISBN 0-385-29435-2). Delacorte.
Taylor, William. Paradise Lane. LC 87-9434. 176p. (gr. 7 up). 1987. pap. 12.95 (ISBN 0-590-41013-X). Scholastic Inc.
—Paradise Lane. 176p. (gr. 7 up). 1989. pap. 2.75 (ISBN 0-590-41014-8). Scholastic Inc.
Thesman, Jean. Couldn't I Start Over? 176p. (Orig.). (gr. 7 up). 1989. pap. 2.95 (ISBN 0-380-75717-6, Flare). Avon.
Ullman, James R. Banner in the Sky. LC 54-7296. 256p. (gr. 7 up). 1988. pap. 3.25 (ISBN 0-06-447048-2, Trophy). HarpC Child Bks.
Ure, Jean. See You Thursday. LC 83-5217. 224p. (gr. 7 up). 1983. pap. 12.95 (ISBN 0-385-29303-8). Delacorte.
Vail, Linda. My Wicked Valentine. (Orig.). 1989. pap. 3.95 (ISBN 0-440-20233-7). Dell.
Voigt, Cynthia. Dicey's Song. LC 82-3882. 204p. (gr. 6 up). 1982. 14.95 (ISBN 0-689-30944-9, Atheneum Child Bk). Macmillan Child Grp.
—The Runner. 1986. pap. 2.50 (ISBN 0-449-70154-9, Juniper). Fawcett.
Wallace, Bill. Beauty. 128p. (gr. 4-7). 1989. pap. 2.95 (ISBN 0-671-68272-5, Minstrel Bks). PB.
Ward, James M. & Hong, Jane C. Pool of Radiance. LC 88-51726. 352p. (Orig.). 1989. pap. 3.95 (ISBN 0-88038-735-1). TSR Inc.
Warren, Andrea. Searching for Love. 240p. (Orig.). (gr. 7-12). 1987. pap. 2.95 (ISBN 0-553-26292-0). Bantam.
Weisinger, Steve. The Little Book of Hugs. Davies, Sumiko, illus. LC 90-60083. 28p. (ps). 1991. bds. 2.95 (ISBN 0-679-80755-1). Random.
—The Little Book of Kisses. Davies, Sumiko, illus. LC 90-60082. 28p. (ps). 1991. bds. 2.95 (ISBN 0-679-80754-3). Random.
Wersba, Barbara. Beautiful Losers. LC 87-7590. 192p. (gr. 7 up). 1988. 11.95 (ISBN 0-06-026363-6); PLB 11.89 (ISBN 0-06-026364-4). HarpC Child Bks.
—Fat: A Love Story. LC 86-45485. 128p. (gr. 7 up). 1987. 11.95 (ISBN 0-06-026400-4); PLB 11.89 (ISBN 0-06-026415-2). HarpC Child Bks.
—Fat: A Love Story. (gr. k-8). 1990. pap. 3.50 (ISBN 0-440-20537-9, LFL). Dell.
—Love Is the Crooked Thing. LC 87-171. 160p. (gr. 7 up). 1987. 11.95 (ISBN 0-06-026366-0); PLB 11.89 (ISBN 0-06-026367-9). HarpC Child Bks.
—Love Is the Crooked Thing. 1990. 3.50 (ISBN 0-440-20542-5, LFL). Dell.
—Tunes for a Small Harmonica. LC 75-25411. 192p. (gr. 7 up). 1976. PLB 8.79 (ISBN 0-06-026373-3). HarpC Child Bks.
White, Joe. Looking for Love in All the Wrong Places. rev. & updated ed. 1991. pap. 3.95 (ISBN 0-8423-3829-2). Tyndale.
Wilde, Oscar. The Nightingale & the Rose. Wright, Freire & Foreman, Michael, illus. (gr. 4 up). 1981. 14.95 (ISBN 0-19-520231-7). Oxford U Pr.
Willard, Barbara. The Iron Lily. (gr. k-12). 1989. pap. 3.25 (ISBN 0-440-20434-8, LFL). Dell.
Wine, Jeanine. Mrs. Tibbles & the Special Someone. LC 87-14966. 32p. (ps-3). 12.95 (ISBN 0-934672-54-7). Good Bks PA.
Winfield, Julia. Only Make-Believe. 176p. (Orig.). (gr. 7-12). 1987. pap. 2.50 (ISBN 0-553-26418-4). Bantam.
—Private Eyes. 160p. (Orig.). (gr. 7-12). 1989. pap. 2.75 (ISBN 0-553-25814-1). Bantam.
Winthrop, Elizabeth. Sloppy Kisses. Burgess, Anne, illus. LC 90-105. 32p. (gr. k-3). 1990. pap. 4.95 (ISBN 0-689-71410-6, Aladdin). Macmillan Child Grp.
Wittman, Sally. The Wonderful Mrs. Trumbly. Apple, Margot, illus. LC 81-47737. 40p. (gr. k-3). 1982. PLB 9.89g (ISBN 0-06-026512-4). HarpC Child Bks.
Wolitzer, Hilma. Out of Love. LC 76-40983. (Illus.). 160p. (gr. 5 up). 1976. 11.95 (ISBN 0-374-35675-0). FS&G.
Wolitzer, Hilmer. Wish You Were Here. 180p. (gr. 5 up). 1986. pap. 3.45 (ISBN 0-374-48412-0, Sunburst). FS&G.
Wunsch, Josephine. The Perfect Ten. 156p. 1986. 1.95 (ISBN 0-373-06182-X). Silhouette.
Wyeth, Sharon D. Boy Crazy. (gr. 4-7). 1991. pap. 2.95 (ISBN 0-440-40426-6, YB). Dell.
—Rocky Romance, No. 137. 192p. (Orig.). (gr. 7-12). 1988. pap. 2.50 (ISBN 0-553-26948-8, Sweet Dreams). Bantam.
Zable, Rona S. Love at the Laundromat. 160p. (gr. 7 up). 1992. pap. 2.99 (ISBN 0-553-27225-X, Starfire). Bantam.
Zach, Cheryl. The Frog Princess. 186p. 1984. pap. 1.95 (ISBN 0-671-53404-1). Silhouette.
Zadra, Dan. Talk Like an Eagle. (Illus.). 32p. (gr. 6 up). 1986. PLB 10.95s.p. (ISBN 0-88682-021-9); PLB 15. 65. Creative Ed.
—There Will Never Be Another You. (Illus.). 32p. (gr. 6 up). 1986. PLB 10.95s.p. (ISBN 0-88682-015-4); PLB 15.65 (ISBN 0-685-11041-9). Creative Ed.
Zolotow, Charlotte. If You Listen. Reissue. ed. Simont, Marc, illus. LC 79-2688. 32p. (gr. k-3). 1980. 13.95 (ISBN 0-06-027049-7); PLB 12.89 (ISBN 0-06-027050-0). HarpC Child Bks.
—Some Things Go Together. Gundersheimer, Karen, illus. LC 82-48694. 24p. (ps-3). 1983. 12.95 (ISBN 0-690-04327-9, Crowell Jr Bks); PLB 11.89 (ISBN 0-690-04328-7, Crowell Jr Bks). HarpC Child Bks.

LOVE (THEOLOGY)

Baden. The Greatest Gift Is Love. LC 59-1314. 24p. (gr. k-4). 1985. pap. 1.39 (ISBN 0-570-06196-2). Concordia.
Crook, Carol. Overflowing with Love. 19p. (Orig.). (gr. 7 up). 1989. pap. 0.95x (ISBN 0-939399-06-7). Bks of Truth.
Deiros, Pablo A. El Amor Es Cosa Seria: Love Is Serious Business. (SPA.). 64p. 1988. pap. 2.50 (ISBN 0-311-12339-2). Casa Bautista.
Herbert, Janet. Love Is Kind. Herbert, Janet, illus. 32p. (ps up). 1986. plastic comb bdg. 3.95 (ISBN 0-89191-928-7, 59287, Chariot Bks). Cook.
Hutchcroft, Vera. Give What You Can. Butcher, Sam, illus. 20p. (gr. k-6). 1984. pap. text ed. 4.25 (ISBN 1-55976-142-3). CEF Press.
McCaw, Mabel. What Is Loving? Todd, Barbara, illus. 12p. (ps). 1987. 3.25 (ISBN 0-8378-5208-0). Gibson.
Moncure, Jane B. Love. rev. ed. Hohag, Linda, illus. LC 80-27479. 32p. (gr. k-3). 1981. PLB 11.97 (ISBN 0-89565-205-6). Childs World.
Nighswander, Ada. The Little Martins Learn to Love. (ps-4). 6.75 (ISBN 0-686-30775-5). Rod & Staff.

LOVE POETRY

Greenfield, Eloise. Honey, I Love: And Other Love Poems. Dillon, Diane & Dillon, Leo, illus. LC 77-2845. 48p. (gr. 1-3). 1978. 11.95 (ISBN 0-690-01334-5, Crowell Jr Bks); PLB 12.89 (ISBN 0-690-03845-3). HarpC Child Bks.

LOW, JULIETTE (GORDON) 1860-1927

Behrens, June. Juliette Low: Founder of the Girl Scouts of America. LC 88-11976. (Illus.). 32p. (gr. 2-5). 1988. PLB 13.27 (ISBN 0-516-04171-1); pap. 3.95 (ISBN 0-516-44171-X). Childrens.
Kudlinski, Kathleen V. Juliette Gordon Low: America's First Girl Scout. Hamanaka, Sheila, illus. 64p. (gr. 2-6). 1989. pap. 3.95 (ISBN 0-14-032691-X, Puffin). Puffin Bks.
Steelsmith, Shari. Juliette Gordon Low: Founder of the Girl Scouts. Pope, Connie J., illus. LC 89-62673. 32p. (Orig.). (ps-4). 1990. lib. bdg. 15.95 (ISBN 0-943990-37-8); pap. 5.95 (ISBN 0-943990-36-X). Parenting Pr.

LUKE, SAINT–FICTION

Brown, Robert. Luke: Doctor-Writer. Hester, Ron, illus. (gr. 1-6). 1977. bds. 5.95 (ISBN 0-8054-4233-2, 4242-33). Broadman.

LULLABIES

Aliki. Hush Little Baby: A Folk Lullaby. (Illus.). 32p. (gr. k-4). 1968. PLB 11.95 (ISBN 0-671-66299-6); pap. 4.95 (ISBN 0-671-66742-4). S&S Trade.
Amoss, Berthe. Lullaby & Good Night. (Illus.). 10p. (ps-7). 1989. pap. 2.95 (ISBN 0-922589-13-5). More Than Card.
Aragon, Jane Chelsea. Lullaby. Radzinski, Kandy, illus. 32p. (ps-1). 1989. 11.95 (ISBN 0-87701-576-7). Chronicle Bks.
Bang, Molly. Ten, Nine, Eight. Bang, Molly, illus. LC 81-20106. 24p. (ps-1). 1983. 13.95 (ISBN 0-688-00906-9); PLB 13.88 (ISBN 0-688-00907-7). Greenwillow.
Brown, J. Aaron, ed. A Child's Gift of Lullabyes. Vienneau, Jim, illus. 14p. (ps). 1987. Book packaged with cassette. 12.95 (ISBN 0-927945-01-0). Someday Baby.
—Un Regalo de Arrullos Para Ninos. Vienneau, Jim, illus. Pineda, Sysy, tr. (SPA., Illus.). 14p. (ps). 1988. Book with cassette. 12.95 (ISBN 0-927945-02-9). Someday Baby.
Carlson. A Christmas Lullaby. 24p. (gr. k-4). 1985. pap. 1.39 (ISBN 0-570-06195-4, 59-1296). Concordia.
Cassatt, Mary, illus. Lullabies & Good Night. 32p. 1989. 12.95 (ISBN 0-8249-8441-2); incl. 60-min. cassette 16. 95 (ISBN 0-8249-7351-8). Ideals.
Chusid, Nancy. Favorite Lullabies. Chusid, Nancy, illus. 32p. (Orig.). (gr. 2-6). 1990. pap. 6.95 incl. cassette (ISBN 1-878624-06-7). McClanahan Bk.
Favorite Lullabies. (Illus.). 32p. (gr. k-2). 1988. 4.95 (ISBN 0-87449-413-3). Modern Pub NYC.
Gutmann, Bessie P. Nursery Songs & Lullabies. (Illus.). 32p. 1990. 9.95x (ISBN 0-448-23457-2, G&D). Putnam Pub Group.
Headington, Christopher. Sweet Sleep: A Collection of Lullabies & Cradle Songs. LC 88-26898. (Illus.). 96p. 1990. 14.95 (ISBN 0-517-57321-0); PLB 15.99 (ISBN 0-517-57820-4). Crown.
Highwater, Jamake. Moonsong Lullaby. Keegan, Marcia, illus. LC 81-1909. 32p. (ps-3). 1981. 14.95 (ISBN 0-688-00427-X). Lothrop.
Hughes, Margaret A. Mother Goose Favorite Lullabies. HIcks, Russell, et al, illus. 26p. (ps). 1987. 9.95 (ISBN 0-934323-51-8); pre-programmed audio cass. tapes avail. Alchemy Comms.
Marzollo, Jean. Close Your Eyes. Jeffers, Susan, illus. LC 76-42935. (ps-2). 1978. 12.95 (ISBN 0-8037-1609-5); PLB 12.89 (ISBN 0-8037-1610-9). Dial Bks Young.
Plotz, Helen. A Week of Lullabies. Russo, Marisabina, illus. LC 86-18458. 32p. (ps-3). 1988. 11.95 (ISBN 0-688-06652-6); lib. bdg. 11.88 (ISBN 0-688-06653-4). Greenwillow.
Pomerantz, Charlotte. All Asleep. Tafuri, Nancy, illus. 32p. (ps-1). 1986. pap. 3.95 (ISBN 0-14-050548-2, Puffin). Puffin Bks.

Stanley, Diane. Birdsong Lullaby. Stanley, Diane, illus. LC 85-5654. (ps-2). 1985. 12.95 (ISBN 0-688-05804-3). Morrow Jr Bks.

Sweet Dreams: A Lullaby Tape, Vol. I. 12p. (ps-6). 1989. cassette & book 13.95 (ISBN 0-938971-16-6). JTG Nashville.

Sweet Dreams: A Lullaby Tape, Vol. II. 12p. (ps-6). 1989. cassette & book 13.95 (ISBN 0-938971-17-4). JTG Nashville.

LUMBER AND LUMBERING

see also Forests and Forestry; Trees; Wood

Adams, Peter D. Early Loggers & the Sawmill. (Illus.). 64p. (gr. 4-5). 1981. 14.95 (ISBN 0-86505-005-8); pap. 5.95 (ISBN 0-86505-006-6). Crabtree Pub Co.

John, Hughes. Larry the Logger. (Illus.). 40p. (gr. 7-12). 1975. pap. 2.65 (ISBN 0-915510-04-9). Janus Bks.

Newton, James R. Forest Log. Brady, Irene, illus. LC 78-22515. 32p. (gr. 2-5). 1980. 11.95 (ISBN 0-690-04007-5, Crowell Jr Bks). HarpC Child Bks.

Timber. (Illus.). (gr. 5 up). lib. bdg. 15.93 (ISBN 0-86592-267-5). Rourke Corp.

LUMBER AND LUMBERING–FICTION

Paulsen, Gary. The Winter Room. LC 89-42541. 128p. (gr. 6-9). 1989. 11.95 (ISBN 0-531-05839-5); PLB 11.99 (ISBN 0-531-08439-6). Orchard Bks Watts.

LUMBER AND LUMBERING–LEGENDS

Kellogg, Steven. Paul Bunyan. Kellogg, Steven, illus. LC 83-26684. 1988. pap. 7.95 incl. cassette (ISBN 0-688-08397-8). Morrow.

Kurelek, William. Lumberjack. (Illus.). 48p. (gr. 5 up). text ed. 17.95 (ISBN 0-88776-052-X, Dist. by U of Toronto Pr). Tundra Bks.

McCormick, Dell J. Paul Bunyan Swings His Axe. McCormick, Dell J., illus. LC 36-33409. (gr. 4-6). 1936. 8.95 (ISBN 0-87004-093-6). Caxton.

—Tall Timber Tales: More Paul Bunyan Stories. Livesley, Lorna, illus. LC 39-20778. (gr. 4-6). 1939. 7.95 (ISBN 0-87004-094-4). Caxton.

Shephard, Esther. Paul Bunyan. Kent, Rockwell, illus. LC 85-5448. 284p. (gr. 7 up). 1985. 12.95 (ISBN 0-15-259749-2, HJ); pap. 6.95 (ISBN 0-15-259755-7). HarBraceJ.

Turney, Ida V. Paul Bunyan, the Work Giant. (Illus.). (gr. 3 up). 1969. 7.95 (ISBN 0-8323-0163-9). Binford Mort.

LUMINESCENCE, ANIMAL

see Bioluminescence

LUNAR EXPEDITIONS

see Space Flight to the Moon

LUNAR EXPLORATION

see Moon–Exploration

LUNAR PROBES

see also names of space projects, e.g. Mariner Project; etc.

LUNCH ROOMS

see Restaurants, Bars, etc.

LUNCHEONS

Watanabe, Shigeo. What a Good Lunch! Ohtomo, Yasuo, illus. 32p. (gr. k). 1981. 8.95 (ISBN 0-399-20811-9, Philomel); pap. 3.95 (ISBN 0-399-21048-2, Philomel). Putnam Pub Group.

LUTHER, MARTIN, 1483-1546

Fehlauer, Adolph. Life & Faith of Martin Luther. (gr. 6-9). 1981. pap. 6.95 (ISBN 0-8100-0125-X, 15N0376). Northwest Pub.

Nohl, Frederick. Martin Luther: Hero of Faith. LC 62-14146. (Illus.). (gr. 4-6). 1962. pap. 5.95 (ISBN 0-570-03727-1, 12-2629). Concordia.

Schwiebert, Ernest G. Luther & His Times: The Reformation from a New Perspective. (Illus.). (gr. 9 up). 1950. 26.95 (ISBN 0-570-03246-6, 15-1164). Concordia.

LUXEMBOURG

Carrick, Noel. Luxembourg. (Illus.). (gr. 5 up). 1988. 14.95 (ISBN 0-222-01144-0). Chelsea Hse.

Lepthien, Emilie U. Luxembourg. LC 89-34664. 128p. (gr. 5-9). 1989. PLB 25.27 (ISBN 0-516-02714-X). Childrens.

LYING

see Truthfulness and Falsehood

LYME DISEASE

Landau, Elaine. Lyme Disease. 1990. PLB 11.90 (ISBN 0-531-10931-3). Watts.

Silverstein, Alvin, et al. Lyme Disease, the Great Imitator: How to Prevent & Cure It. Sigal, Leonard H., pref. by. LC 90-81250. (Illus.). 126p. (gr. 5 up). 1990. 12.95 (ISBN 0-9623653-8-6); pap. 5.95 (ISBN 0-9623653-9-4). Avstar Pub.

Lyme Disease, The Great Imitator "does a good job of presenting a simplified overview of the biology of Lyme disease." (Starred review) - AAAS Science Books & Films. "The Silversteins survey the history of Lyme disease, describe its course, & present the tick's life cycle....well researched & well organized, serving not only to inform but to exemplify how the medical & research communities address a peculiarly knotty problem. A question-&-answer chapter serves as an excellent summary."--Kirkus Reviews. "The book tells common sense rules to help prevent tick bites, lists symptoms, & explains the course of the disease in easy to understand terms."--Book Nook. "...previewed by nine authorities who provided additional insights. The useful information here will especially interest outdoor enthusiasts. Highly Recommended."--The Book Report. "'Lyme Disease & Your Pets' is a chapter that will interest many readers. "--Small Press Book Review. "...in-depth insights...numerous black & white illustrations of ticks & hosts, as well as close-up shots of common Lyme symptoms....the best, latest advice for prevention & treatment."--Midwest Book Review.

Publisher Provided Annotation.

LYNX

Savarin, Julian J. Lynx. 240p. 1986. 15.95 (ISBN 0-8027-0890-0). Walker & Co.

LYSERGIC ACID DIETHYLAMIDE

Gunn, Jeffrey. Pen Pals, Vol. 8: Facts about Acid. Wolfe, Debra, illus. (Orig.). (gr. 3). 1990. pap. write for info. (ISBN 1-879146-08-8). Knowldg Pub.

M

MACARTHUR, DOUGLAS, 1880-1964

Darby, Jean. Douglas MacArthur. (Illus.). 112p. (gr. 5 up). 1989. 15.95 (ISBN 0-8225-4901-8). Lerner Pubns.

Finkelstein, Norman. The Emperor General: A Biography of Douglas MacArthur. LC 88-22863. (Illus.). 128p. (gr. 5 up). 1989. PLB 12.95 (ISBN 0-87518-396-4, Dillon). Macmillan Child Grp.

Skipper, G. C. MacArthur & the Philippines. LC 81-38520. (Illus.). 48p. (gr. 3-8). 1982. PLB 14.60 (ISBN 0-516-04794-9). Childrens.

MACHINE TOOLS

Cohen, Lynn. Energy & Machines. 64p. (ps-2). 1988. 6.95 (ISBN 0-912107-78-2, MM982). Monday Morning Bks.

MACHINERY

see also Agricultural Machinery; Engines; Inventions; Locomotives; Machine Tools; Mechanical Drawing; Mechanics; Steam Engines

Adkins, Jan. Moving Heavy Things. (Illus.). (gr. 5 up). 1980. 13.95 (ISBN 0-395-29206-9). HM.

Bains, Rae. Simples Machines. Veno, Joseph, illus. LC 84-2607. 32p. (gr. 3-6). 1985. PLB 9.49 (ISBN 0-8167-0166-0); pap. text ed. 2.95 (ISBN 0-8167-0167-9). Troll Assocs.

Barton, Byron. Machines at Work. Barton, Byron, illus. LC 86-24221. 32p. (ps-1). 1987. 7.95 (ISBN 0-694-00190-2, Crowell Jr Bks); PLB 12.89 (ISBN 0-690-04573-5). HarpC Child Bks.

Baxter, Leon. Baxter's Book of Machines. (Illus.). 24p. (gr. 2-5). 1990. pap. 3.95 (ISBN 0-8249-8376-9). Ideals.

Boy Scouts of America. Machinery. (Illus.). 58p. (gr. 6-12). 1983. pap. 1.85 (ISBN 0-8395-3337-3, 3337). BSA.

Carratello, John & Carratello, Patty. Hands on Science: Simple Machines. Wright, Terry & Spence, Paula, illus. 32p. (gr. 2-5). 1988. wkbk. 4.95 (ISBN 1-55734-227-X). Tchr Create Mat.

Dixon, Malcolm. In the Factory. Norris, Roger, illus. LC 83-71638. 32p. (gr. 3-6). 1983. PLB 10.90 (ISBN 0-531-04701-6). Watts.

Echaore & Wentz. Machines. rev. ed. (Illus.). 48p. (gr. 7-12). 1987. pap. text ed. 2.95 (ISBN 0-88102-090-7); tchr's. guide avail. Janus Bks.

Fleisher, Paul & Keeler, Patricia. Looking Inside: Machines & Constructions. (Illus.). 40p. (gr. 2-7). 1991. RSBE 13.95 (ISBN 0-689-31483-3, Atheneum Child Bk). Macmillan Child Grp.

Horton, et al. Amazing Fact Book of Machines. (Illus.). 32p. 1987. 11.95 (ISBN 0-87191-846-3). Creative Ed.

Horvatic, Anne. Simple Machines. Bruner, Stephen, photos by. (Illus.). 32p. (gr. 1-4). 1989. 13.95 (ISBN 0-525-44492-0, DCB). Dutton Child Bks.

How It Works. 1991. pap. 3.95 (ISBN 0-7214-5325-2). Ladybird Bks.

Illustrated Guides Series, 8 vols. LC 88-28764. (Illus.). 512p. (gr. 3-9). 1990. Set. 135.60 (ISBN 1-85435-085-4). Marshall Cavendish.

Lafferty, Peter. Big Book of How Things Work. 1990. 5.98 (ISBN 0-8317-0859-X). Smithmark.

Lambert, Mark & Hamilton-MacLaren, Alistair. Machines. (Illus.). 48p. (gr. 5-8). 1991. RLB 12.40 (ISBN 0-531-18413-7, Pub. by Boatwright Pr). Watts.

Machines. (Illus.). 48p. (gr. 7-12). 1989. pap. 6.95 (ISBN 0-941008-99-1). Tops Learning.

Machines, Cars, Boats, & Airplanes. Date not set. 5.98 (ISBN 0-517-68232-X). Outlet Bk Co.

Malam, John. Pop-Up Machines. Everitt-Stewart, Andy & Mutimer, Ray, illus. LC 90-60819. 10p. (gr. 1 up). 1991. 7.95 (ISBN 0-679-80872-8). Random.

Nash, Paul. Monster Machines. Harris, Peter, ed. LC 89-12010. (Illus.). 32p. (gr. 2-4). 1989. PLB 11.93 (ISBN 0-944483-36-4). Garrett Ed Corp.

Pape, Donna L. The Book of Foolish Machinery. Winkowski, Frederic, illus. 32p. (gr. 2-5). 1988. pap. 2.50 (ISBN 0-590-40907-7). Scholastic Inc.

Pomeroy, Johanna P. Content Area Reading Skills Machines: Detecting Sequence. (Illus.). (gr. 3). 1989. pap. text ed. 3.25 (ISBN 1-55737-690-5). Ed Activities.

Potter, Tony. See How It Works: Earth Movers. Lawrie, Robin, illus. 28p. (ps-3). 1989. pap. 7.95 (ISBN 0-689-71302-9, Aladdin). Macmillan Child Grp.

Rawson. How Machines Work. (gr. 2-5). 1976. PLB 13.96 (ISBN 0-88110-115-X); pap. 6.95 (ISBN 0-86020-197-X). EDC.

Rockwell, Anne. Machines. Rockwell, Harlow, illus. LC 72-185149. 24p. (ps-2). 1972. 12.95 (ISBN 0-02-777520-8, Mcmillan Child Bk). Macmillan Child Grp.

Rockwell, Anne & Rockwell, Harlow. Machines. Rockwell, Anne & Rockwell, Harlow, illus. LC 85-42744. 24p. (ps-2). 1985. pap. 3.95 (ISBN 0-06-446009-6, Trophy). HarpC Child Bks.

Stephen, R. J. Undersea Machines. LC 85-52093. (Illus.). 32p. (gr. k-6). 1987. lib. bdg. 10.90 (ISBN 0-531-10187-8). Watts.

Stickland, Paul. Machines As Tall As Giants. Stickland, Paul, illus. LC 88-34695. (gr. k-3). 1989. (Random Juv); PLB 10.99 (ISBN 0-394-95375-4). Random.

Strickland, Paul. All about Diggers. LC 90-9820. (Illus.). 16p. (ps-2). 1990. PLB 9.95 (ISBN 0-8368-0422-8). Gareth Stevens Inc.

Thompson, Graham. Diggers & Loaders. LC 86-5680. (Illus.). 24p. (gr. 1-2). 1986. PLB 10.95 (ISBN 1-55532-101-1). Gareth Stevens Inc.

Weiss, Harvey. Machines & How They Work. LC 82-45925. (Illus.). 96p. (gr. 5-8). 1983. PLB 12.89 (ISBN 0-690-04300-7, Crowell Jr Bks). HarpC Child Bks.

Wilkin, Fred. Machines. LC 85-30936. (Illus.). 48p. (gr. k-4). 1986. PLB 14.60 (ISBN 0-516-01283-5). Childrens.

The World of Machines. (Illus.). 80p. (gr. k-6). 1986. pap. 13.27 (ISBN 0-8172-2591-9). Raintree Pubs.

MACHINERY, AUTOMATIC

see Automation

MACHINERY–MODELS

see also Airplanes–Models; Automobiles–Models; Railroads–Models

MACHINERY IN INDUSTRY

Hoban, Tana. Dig, Drill, Dump, Fill. LC 75-11987. (Illus.). 32p. (ps-3). 1975. PLB 13.88 (ISBN 0-688-84016-7). Greenwillow.

MACHINES

see Machinery

MACKINAC ISLAND

Penrod, John S. Straits of Mackinac & Mackinac Island. rev. ed. (gr. 7 up). 1989. pap. 4.49 (ISBN 0-942618-20-3). Penrod-Hiawatha.

MCKINLEY, WILLIAM, PRESIDENT U. S. 1843-1901

Collins, David R. William McKinley: Twenty-Fifth President of the United States. Young, Richard G., ed. LC 89-39954. (Illus.). 128p. (gr. 5-9). 1990. PLB 17.26 (ISBN 0-944483-55-0). Garrett Ed Corp.

Kent, Zachary. William McKinley: Twenty-Fifth President of the United States. LC 88-10881. (Illus.). 100p. (gr. 3 up). 1988. PLB 17.27 (ISBN 0-516-01361-0). Childrens.

MACY, ANNE SULLIVAN, 1866-1936

Davidson, Margaret. Helen Keller's Teacher. 160p. (Orig.). (gr. 3-7). 1972. pap. 2.50 (ISBN 0-590-02224-5). Scholastic Inc.

MADAGASCAR

Department of Geography, Lerner Publications. Madagascar in Pictures. (Illus.). 64p. (gr. 5 up). 1988. PLB 12.95 (ISBN 0-8225-1841-4). Lerner Pubns.

Stevens, Rita. Madagascar. (Illus.). 112p. (gr. 5 up). 1988. lib. bdg. 14.95 (ISBN 1-55546-195-6). Chelsea Hse.

MADISON, DOROTHY (PAYNE) TODD, 1768-1849

Klingel, Cindy. Women of America: Dolly Madison. (gr. 2-4). 1987. PLB 11.50s.p. (ISBN 0-88682-167-3); PLB 16.45 (ISBN 0-318-32938-7). Creative Ed.

Waldrop, Ruth. Dolly Madison. LC 89-61360. (Illus.). 112p. (gr. 3 up). 1989. PLB 10.95 (ISBN 0-318-50084-1); pap. 6.95 (ISBN 0-9616894-3-9). Rusk Inc.

MADISON, JAMES PRESIDENT U. S. 1751-1836

Banfield, Susan. James Madison. LC 86-11080. 72p. (gr. 4-9). 1986. lib. bdg. 10.40 (ISBN 0-531-10217-3). Watts.

Clinton, Susan. James Madison. LC 86-13630. (Illus.). 100p. (gr. 3 up). 1986. PLB 17.27 (ISBN 0-516-01382-3); pap. 6.95 (ISBN 0-516-41382-1). Childrens.

Fritz, Jean. The Great Little Madison. (Illus.). 160p. (gr. 5 up). 1989. 15.95 (ISBN 0-399-21768-1, Putnam). Putnam Pub Group.

Kelly, Regina Z. James Madison: Statesman & President. large type ed. (Illus.). 144p. (gr. 4-8). 1991. Repr. of 1966 ed. PLB 17.95 (ISBN 1-55905-091-8). Grey Castle.

Leavell, Perry. James Madison. Schlesinger, Arthur M., intro. by. (Illus.). 112p. (gr. 5 up). 1988. 17.95 (ISBN 1-55546-815-2). Chelsea Hse.

Polikof, Barbara G. James Madison: Fourth President of the United States. Young, Richard G., ed. LC 88-24537. (Illus.). (gr. 5-9). 1989. PLB 17.26 (ISBN 0-944483-22-4). Garrett Ed Corp.

MADONNA

see Mary, Virgin

MAGAZINES

see Periodicals

MAGELLAN, FERDINAND, d. 1521

Asimov, Isaac. Ferdinand Magellan. LC 91-9207. (Illus.). 64p. (gr. 3-4). 1991. PLB 14.95 (ISBN 0-8368-0560-7). Gareth Stevens Inc.

Blackwood, Alan. Ferdinand Magellan. LC 85-71722. (Illus.). 32p. (gr. 4-8). 1986. lib. bdg. 11.90 (ISBN 0-531-18032-8, Pub. by Bookwright Pr). Watts.

Brewster, Scott & Baraldi, Giani. Ferdinand Magellan. (Illus.). 104p. (gr. 5-8). 1990. lib. bdg. 16.98 (ISBN 0-382-09979-6); pap. 8.95 (ISBN 0-382-24005-7). Silver Burdett Pr.

Brownlee, Walter. The First Ships Round the World. LC 73-91815. (Illus.). 48p. (gr. 7 up). 1974. pap. 5.95 (ISBN 0-521-20438-0). Cambridge U Pr.

Harley, Ruth. Ferdinand Magellan. new ed. LC 78-18058. (Illus.). 48p. (gr. 4-7). 1979. PLB 9.89 (ISBN 0-89375-176-6); pap. 2.95 (ISBN 0-89375-168-5). Troll Assocs.

Humble, Richard & Hook, Richard. The Voyage of Magellan. (Illus.). 32p. (gr. 4-7). 1989. PLB 11.90 (ISBN 0-531-10638-1). Watts.

Schecter, Darrow. I Can Read About Magellan. LC 78-73713. (Illus.). (gr. 3-6). 1979. pap. 1.95 (ISBN 0-89375-209-6). Troll Assocs.

Stefoff, Rebecca. Ferdinand Magellan & the Discovery of the World Ocean. Goetzmann, William H., ed. Collins, Michael, intro. by. (Illus.). 128p. (gr. 5 up). 1990. lib. bdg. 18.95 (ISBN 0-7910-1291-3). Chelsea Hse.

Wilkie, Katherine. Ferdinand Magellan: Noble Captain. Coyle, P., illus. (gr. 4-6). 1963. pap. 2.44 (ISBN 0-395-01751-3, Piper). HM.

MAGIC

see also Card Tricks; Occult Sciences

Adams, Pam, illus. Magic. 32p. (Orig.). (ps-2). 1978. 5.50 (ISBN 0-85953-104-X, Pub. by Child's Play England); pap. 4.00 (ISBN 0-85953-081-7). Childs Play.

Alexander, Martha. Three Magic Flip Books. Incl. The Magic Hat; The Magic Picture; The Magic Box. (Illus.). (ps-k). 1984. Three bks. in a shrink-wrapped slipcase. 5.95 (ISBN 0-8037-0051-2, 0578-170). Dial Bks Young.

Ames, Gerald & Wyler, Rose. Magic Secrets. Stubis, Talivaldis, illus. LC 67-4229. 64p. (gr. k-3). 1967. PLB 10.89 (ISBN 0-06-020069-3). HarpC Child Bks.

Bailey, Vanessa. Magic Tricks: Games & Projects for Children. (Illus.). 32p. (gr. k-4). 1990. PLB 11.40 (ISBN 0-531-17256-2). Watts.

Baker, James W. April Fools' Day Magic. Overlie, George, illus. 48p. (gr. 2-5). 1989. 7.95 (ISBN 0-8225-2230-6). Lerner Pubns.

—Arbor Day Magic. Overlie, George, illus. 48p. (gr. 2-5). 1989. 8.95 (ISBN 0-8225-2235-7). Lerner Pubns.

—Columbus Day Magic. Overlie, George, illus. 48p. (gr. 2-5). 1989. 8.95 (ISBN 0-8225-2237-3). Lerner Pubns.

—Illusions Illustrated: A Professional Magic Show for Young Performers. Ayres, Carter M., photos by. Swofford, Jeanette, illus. LC 83-19549. 120p. (gr. 6 up). 1984. PLB 10.95 (ISBN 0-8225-0768-4, First Ave Edns); pap. 4.95 (ISBN 0-8225-9512-5, First Ave Edns). Lerner Pubns.

—New Year's Magic. Overlie, Goerge, illus. 48p. (gr. 2-5). 1989. 8.95 (ISBN 0-8225-2231-4). Lerner Pubns.

—Presidents' Day Magic. Overlie, George, illus. 48p. (gr. 2-5). 1989. 8.95 (ISBN 0-8225-2232-2). Lerner Pubns.

—St. Patrick's Day Magic. Overlie, George, illus. 48p. (gr. 2-5). 1989. 8.95 (ISBN 0-8225-2234-9). Lerner Pubns.

—Thanksgiving Magic. Overlie, George, illus. 48p. (gr. 2-5). 1989. 8.95 (ISBN 0-8225-2233-0). Lerner Pubns.

Beisner, Monika. Secret Spells & Curious Charms. Beisner, Monika, illus. LC 85-45323. 32p. (ps up). 1986. 12.95 (ISBN 0-374-36692-6). FS&G.

Bernstein, Bob. Monday Morning Magic. 64p. (gr. k-6). 1982. 6.95 (ISBN 0-86653-080-0, GA 425). Good Apple.

Blackstone, Harry, Jr., et al. The Blackstone Book of Magic & Illusion. Bradbury, Ray, frwd. by. Mason, Eric, illus. LC 84-29486. 248p. (gr. 7 up). 1985. 22.95 (ISBN 0-937858-45-5). Newmarket.

Boy Scouts of America. Cub Scout Magic. (Illus.). 146p. (gr. 3-5). 1960. pap. 5.95x (ISBN 0-8395-3219-9, 3219). BSA.

Brandreth, Gyles. Quick & Easy Magic Tricks. (Illus.). 96p. (Orig.). 1988. pap. 1.95 (ISBN 0-942025-33-4). Kidsbks.

Broekel, Ray & White, Laurence. Now You See It: Easy Magic for Beginners. Morrison, William, illus. (gr. 1-3). 1979. 13.95 (ISBN 0-316-93595-6). Little.

Chew, Ruth. Mostly Magic. (gr. 2-4). 1982. pap. 1.95 (ISBN 0-590-32331-8). Scholastic Inc.

Churchill, E. Richard. Optical Illusion Tricks & Toys. Michaels, Mames, illus. LC 88-34379. 128p. (gr. 5-10). 1989. 12.95. Sterling.

Collis, Len. Magic Tricks for Children. Carter, Terry & George, Bob, illus. 96p. (gr. 3 up). 1989. pap. 4.95 (ISBN 0-8120-4289-1). Barron.

Conaway, Judith. More Magic Tricks You Can Do. LC 86-11351. (Illus.). 48p. (gr. 1-5). 1987. PLB 11.89 (ISBN 0-8167-0864-9); pap. text ed. 2.95 (ISBN 0-8167-0865-7). Troll Assocs.

Crosby, Nina E. & Marten, Elizabeth H. Don't Teach! Let Me Learn about Fantasy, Magic, Monkeys & Monsters. Rossi, Richard, illus. 72p. (Orig.). (gr. 3-10). 1984. 8.95 (ISBN 0-88047-045-3, 8410). DOK Pubs.

Disney, Walt, Productions Staff. The Mickey Mouse Magic Book. LC 74-16420. (Illus.). 48p. (gr. 1-2). 1975. 5.95 (ISBN 0-394-82567-5, Random Juv); lib. bdg. 4.99 (ISBN 0-394-92567-X). Random.

Duncan, Lois. A Gift of Magic. Stewart, Arvis, illus. (gr. 4-6). 1971. 14.95 (ISBN 0-316-19545-6). Little.

Eldin, Peter. The Magic Handbook. Colville, Jeane, et al, illus. LC 85-171061. 192p. (gr. 4 up). 1985. lib. bdg. 9.79 (ISBN 0-671-55040-3); pap. 6.95. Messner.

Evans, C. & Keable-Elliott, I. Usborne Complete Book of Magic. (Illus.). 64p. 1989. PLB 13.96 (ISBN 0-88110-383-7); pap. 7.95 (ISBN 0-7460-0300-5). EDC.

Fabian, Stella. A Handful of Magic. Mejia, Roger, illus. 125p. (gr. 2-6). 1988. pap. 3.25 (ISBN 0-922434-36-0). Brighton & Lloyd.

Fields, Keith & Holland, Charlie. Magic for All. (Illus.). 96p. (Orig.). (gr. 6-12). 1990. pap. 9.95 (ISBN 0-7153-9272-7, Pub. by David & Charles Pub UK). Sterling.

Firestone, Allan L. Mr. Luckypennys Magic Book. Katz, Deborah, illus. LC 77-71450. (gr. 2-7). 1977. pap. 4.95 (ISBN 0-934682-01-1). Emmett.

Fisher, John. John Fisher's Magic Book. De Paola, Tomie, illus. (gr. 5-8). 1975. pap. 1.95 (ISBN 0-13-510222-7, Pub. by Treehouse). P-H.

Forte, Imogene. Magic & Make-Believe. LC 84-62930. (Illus.). 80p. (gr. k-6). 1985. 3.95 (ISBN 0-86530-099-2, IP 91-3). Incentive Pubns.

—Rainy Day: Magic for Wonderful Wet Weather. LC 83-82332. (Illus.). 80p. (gr. k-6). 1983. pap. text ed. 3.95 (ISBN 0-86530-094-1, IP94-1). Incentive Pubns.

Friedhoffer. Magic Tricks, Science Facts. 1990. pap. 5.95 (ISBN 0-531-15186-7). Watts.

Friedhoffer, Bob. Magic Tricks, Science Facts. 1990. PLB 12.90 (ISBN 0-531-10902-X). Watts.

Fulves, Karl. The Children's Magic Kit: Sixteen Easy-to-Do Tricks Complete with Cardboard Cutouts. Schmidt, Joseph K., illus. 32p. (Orig.). (gr. 3-6). 1981. pap. 3.95 (ISBN 0-486-24019-3). Dover.

—Self-Working Table Magic: Ninety-Seven Foolproof Tricks with Everyday Objects. Schmidt, Joseph K., illus. 128p. (Orig.). 1981. pap. 3.95 (ISBN 0-486-24116-5). Dover.

Gill, Shelley R. Mammoth Magic. Cartwright, Shannon, illus. 36p. (Orig.). (gr. k-6). 1986. pap. 7.95 (ISBN 0-934007-01-2). Paws Four Pub.

Gormley, Beatrice. The Magic Mean Machine. McCully, Emily A., illus. 128p. (Orig.). (gr. 5 up). 1989. pap. 2.75 (ISBN 0-380-75519-X, Camelot). Avon.

Hoyt, Marie A. Work-Game Sheets for Magnet Magic Etc. Bye, C. J., et al, illus. 28p. (Orig.). (gr. 2-8). 1984. pap. text ed. 2.50 (ISBN 0-914911-03-1). Educ Serv Pr.

Kettelkamp, Larry. Magic Made Easy. rev. ed. Eutemey, Loring, illus. Klotzbeacher, Donovan, photos by. LC 80-22947. (Illus.). (gr. 3-7). 1981. 13.95 (ISBN 0-688-00458-X); PLB 13.88 (ISBN 0-688-00377-X, Morrow Jr Bks). Morrow Jr Bks.

Klein, Tom & Wolpert, Tom. Animal Magic for Kids Series, 4 vols. (Illus.). 1991. Set. lib. bdg. 51.80 (ISBN 0-8368-0659-X). Gareth Stevens Inc.

Levy, Robert & Joseph, Joan. Robert Levy's Magic Book. LC 76-16016. (Illus.). 216p. (gr. 5 up). 1976. 10.95 (ISBN 0-87131-219-0). M Evans.

Lewis, Shari & Zimmerman, Dick. Shari Lewis Presents One Hundred-One Magic Tricks for Kids to Do. Buller, Jon, illus. LC 89-10360. 96p. (Orig.). 1990. PLB 9.99 (ISBN 0-394-92059-7); pap. 6.95 (ISBN 0-394-82059-2). Random.

Lipson, Greta & Bolkosky, Sidney. Mighty Myth. 152p. (gr. 5-12). 1982. 11.95 (ISBN 0-86653-064-9, GA 419). Good Apple.

McGill, Ormond. Balancing Magic & Other Tricks. Green, Anne C., illus. LC 86-7841. 96p. (gr. 4-8). 1986. PLB 10.40 (ISBN 0-531-10208-4). Watts.

Magic & Magicians. (Illus.). (gr. 8-12). 1982. 7.95 (ISBN 0-698-20562-6, Coward). Putnam Pub Group.

Magic & Migicians. 48p. (gr. 4-5). 1989. PLB 10.95 (ISBN 0-685-26164-6). Capstone Pr.

Moche, Dinah. Magic Science Tricks. (gr. 4-6). 1977. pap. 1.95 (ISBN 0-590-40200-5). Scholastic Inc.

Nozaki, Akihiro & Anno, Mitsumasa. Anno's Hat Tricks. LC 84-18900. (Illus.). 44p. (gr. 3 up). 1985. 15.95 (ISBN 0-399-21212-4, Philomel). Putnam Pub Group.

Rigney, Francis J. A Beginner's Book of Magic. (Illus.). (gr. 6 up). 1963. 9.95 (ISBN 0-8159-5103-5). Devin.

Seuling, Barbara. Abracadabra! Creating Your Own Magic Show from Beginning to End. (gr. 3-6). 1975. (Archway); pap. 1.25 (ISBN 0-671-29805-4). PB.

Severn, Bill. Magic with Rope, Ribbon, & String. 224p. (gr. 6 up). 1981. 9.95 (ISBN 0-679-20813-5). McKay.

Shalit, Nathan. Science Magic Tricks: Over 50 Fun Tricks That Mystify & Dazzle. Ulan, Helen C., illus. LC 79-18645. 128p. (gr. 4-9). 1981. o.s.i 9.95 (ISBN 0-03-047116-8); pap. 5.95 (ISBN 0-8050-0234-0). H Holt & Co.

Snyder, Zilpha K. Black & Blue Magic. (gr. 4-6). 15.00 (ISBN 0-8446-6418-9). Peter Smith.

Stoddard, Edward. The First Book of Magic. (Illus.). 80p. (gr. 4-7). 1982. pap. 2.75 (ISBN 0-380-49221-0, Camelot). Avon.

Stoddart, Edward. First Book of Magic. rev. ed. (Illus.). 72p. (gr. 3up). PLB 10.40 (ISBN 0-531-04643-5). Watts.

Sundquist, Nancy & Brin, Susannah. Fifty Magic Tricks I Can Do. (Illus.). 48p. (gr. 1-5). 1988. pap. 2.95 (ISBN 0-8431-1868-7). Price Stern.

Supraner, Robyn. Magic Tricks You Can Do! Barto, Renzo, illus. LC 80-19780. 48p. (gr. 1-5). 1981. PLB 11.89 (ISBN 0-89375-418-8); pap. text ed. 2.95 (ISBN 0-89375-419-6). Troll Assocs.

Van der Meer, Ron. The Pop-Up Book of Magic Tricks. LC 83-80210. (Illus.). (gr. 1-5). 1983. pap. 12.95 (ISBN 0-670-56508-3). Viking Child Bks.

Van Rensselaer, Alexander. Your Book of Magic. (gr. 9 up). 1968. 7.95 (ISBN 0-571-06939-8). Transatl Arts.

Walter, Marion. Magic Mirror Tricks. Haber-Schaim, Navah, illus. 32p. (gr. k-3). pap. 1.95 incl. mirror (ISBN 0-590-40875-5). Scholastic Inc.

White, Larry & Broekel, Ray. Razzle Dazzle! Magic Tricks for You. Fay, Ann, ed. Seltzer, Meyer, illus. 48p. (gr. 3-8). 1987. PLB 10.95 (ISBN 0-8075-6857-0). A Whitman.

Williams, Randall. The Rosen Photo Guide to a Career in Magic. (Illus.). (gr. 7-12). 1988. lib. bdg. 12.95 (ISBN 0-8239-0817-8). Rosen Group.

Wilson, Mark. Mark Wilson's Complete Course in Magic. LC 87-73058. (Illus.). 472p. 1988. Repr. of 1975 ed. 17.98 (ISBN 0-89471-623-9, Pub. by Courage Bks.). Running Pr.

Wolpert, Tom. Whale Magic for Kids. Nicklin, Flip, illus. LC 90-50718. 48p. (gr. 3-4). 1991. lib. bdg. 12.95. Gareth Stevens Inc.

Wyler, Rose & Ames, Gerald. Magic Secrets. rev. ed. Dorros, Arthur, illus. LC 89-35841. 64p. (gr. k-3). 1990. 10.95 (ISBN 0-06-026646-5); PLB 10.89 (ISBN 0-06-026647-3). HarpC Child Bks.

Zalewski, Pat. Golden Dawn Enochian Magic. LC 90-36697. (Illus.). 224p. 1990. pap. 12.95 (ISBN 0-87542-898-3). Llewellyn Pubns.

MAGIC–FICTION

Alexander, Lloyd. The Wizard in the Tree. 144p. (gr. 5 up). 1981. pap. 3.25 (ISBN 0-440-49556-3, Pub. by Yearling Classics). Dell.

Anderson, Joy. Juma & the Magic Jinn. Mikolaycak, Charles, illus. LC 85-23815. 40p. (gr. 1-3). 1986. 12.95 (ISBN 0-688-05443-9); PLB 12.88 (ISBN 0-688-05444-7). Lothrop.

Andrews, Kristi. All That Glitters, No. 2: Take Two. 176p. (Orig.). 1987. pap. 2.50 (ISBN 0-553-26417-6). Bantam.

Arnold, Tim. The Winter Mittens. LC 88-2736. (Illus.). 32p. (gr. 3-6). 1988. PLB 12.95 (ISBN 0-689-50449-7, M K McElderry). Macmillan Child Grp.

Avi. No More Magic. LC 74-15299. 144p. (gr. 3-7). 1990. pap. 3.25 (ISBN 0-394-85001-7, Bullseye Bks). Knopf.

Ayres, Becky. Victoria Flies High. Koontz, Robin M., illus. LC 89-694. 32p. (ps-3). 1990. 12.95 (ISBN 0-525-65014-8, Cobblehill Bks). Dutton Child Bks.

Ballard, Robin. Cat & Alex & the Magic Flying Carpet. Ballard, Robin, illus. LC 90-33229. 32p. (ps-1). 1991. 14.95 (ISBN 0-06-020389-7); PLB 14.89 (ISBN 0-06-020390-0). HarpC Child Bks.

Bauer, Marion Dane. Touch the Moon. Berenzy, Alix, illus. LC 87-663. 96p. (gr. 4-7). 1987. 12.95 (ISBN 0-89919-526-1, Pub. by Clarion). Ticknor & Fields.

Becker, Eve. The Magic Mix-Up. (gr. 4-7). 1989. pap. 2.75 (ISBN 0-553-15770-1, Skylark). Bantam.

—The Sneezing Spell. (gr. 4-7). 1990. pap. 2.75 (ISBN 0-553-15774-4, Skylark). Bantam.

—Thirteen Means Magic. (gr. 4-7). 1989. pap. 2.75 (ISBN 0-553-15730-2, Skylark). Bantam.

—Too Much Magic. (gr. 4-7). 1990. pap. 2.75 (ISBN 0-553-15785-X). Bantam.

Bedard, Michael. A Darker Magic. LC 86-28829. 192p. (gr. 5-9). 1987. 14.95 (ISBN 0-689-31342-X, Atheneum Child Bk). Macmillan Child Grp.

Beisert, Heide H. My Magic Cloth: A Story for a Whole Week. Beisert, Heide H., illus. Lewis, Naomi, tr. LC 86-60490. (Illus.). 32p. (gr. k-3). 1986. 14.95 (ISBN 1-55858-069-7). North-South Bks NYC.

Bellairs, John. The Dark Secret of Weatherend. Gorey, Edward, illus. 208p. (gr. 5 up). 1984. 13.95 (ISBN 0-8037-0072-5); PLB 13.89 (ISBN 0-8037-0074-1). Dial Bks Young.

—The Figure in the Shadows. Mayer, Mercer, illus. LC 74-2885. 168p. (gr. 4-7). 1975. PLB 13.89 (ISBN 0-8037-4917-1). Dial Bks Young.

—The Spell of the Sorcerer's Skull. 176p. 1985. pap. 2.75 (ISBN 0-553-15357-9, Skylark). Bantam.

Berry, James R. Magicians of Erianne. LC 85-45833. 256p. (gr. 7 up). 1988. 13.95 (ISBN 0-06-020556-3); PLB 13.89 (ISBN 0-06-020557-1). HarpC Child Bks.

Blacker, Terence. In Control, Ms. Wiz? Goffe, Toni, illus. 64p. (gr. 2-5). 1990. pap. 2.95 (ISBN 0-8120-4500-9). Barron.

Bolton, Elizabeth. Secret of the Magic Potion. Sims, Blanche, illus. LC 84-8881. 48p. (gr. 2-4). 1985. PLB 10.89 (ISBN 0-8167-0420-1); pap. text ed. 2.95 (ISBN 0-8167-0421-X). Troll Assocs.

Brittain, Bill. Devil's Donkey. Glass, Andrew, illus. LC 80-7907. 128p. (gr. 3-7). 1981. PLB 13.89 (ISBN 0-06-020683-7). HarpC Child Bks.

—The Wish Giver: Three Tales of Coven Tree. Glass, Andrew, illus. LC 82-48264. 192p. (gr. 3-7). 1983. 12.95i (ISBN 0-06-020686-1); PLB 12.89 (ISBN 0-06-020687-X). HarpC Child Bks.

Broekel, Ray & White, Laurence B., Jr. Hocus Pocus: Magic You Can Do. Fay, Anne, ed. Thelen, Mary, illus. LC 83-26096. 48p. (gr. 3 up). 1984. PLB 10.95 (ISBN 0-8075-3350-5). A Whitman.

Brown, Marc. Arthur's April Fool. LC 82-20368. (Illus.). 32p. (ps-3). 1985. 13.95 (ISBN 0-316-11196-1, Joy St Bks); pap. 4.95 (ISBN 0-316-11234-8, Joy St Bks). Little.

Buffett, Jimmy & Buffett, Savannah J. Trouble Dolls. Ingber, Bonnie V., intro. by. Davis, Lambert, illus. 32p. (ps). 1991. 14.95 (ISBN 0-15-290790-4). HarBraceJ.

Carter, Anne. The Fisherwoman. Brierley, Louise, illus. 32p. (gr. 1-4). 1991. 14.95 (ISBN 0-688-09872-X); PLB 14.88 (ISBN 0-688-09873-8). Lothrop.

Charnas, Suzy M. The Golden Thread. 1989. 13.95 (ISBN 0-553-05821-5, Starfire). Bantam.

Chew, Ruth. Magic Cave. Chew, Ruth, illus. LC 79-12972. (gr. 2-6). 1978. pap. 8.95 (ISBN 0-8038-4711-4). Hastings.

—Second-Hand Magic. 128p. (gr. 2-5). 1986. pap. 2.25 (ISBN 0-590-40118-1, Lucky Star). Scholastic Inc.

—The Trouble with Magic. Chew, Ruth, illus. 112p. (gr. 2-5). 1985. pap. 2.50 (ISBN 0-590-41085-7, Lucky Star). Scholastic Inc.

Chitwood, Deb. The Magic Ring. Fraydas, Stan, illus. LC 82-62432. 32p. (ps-3). 1983. 9.95 (ISBN 0-942044-01-0). Polestar.

Christelow, Eileen. Olive & the Magic Hat. Christelow, Eileen, illus. LC 87-672. 32p. (gr. k-3). 1987. 12.95 (ISBN 0-89919-513-X, Pub. by Clarion). Ticknor & Fields.

Clifton, Lucille. The Lucky Stone. Payson, Dale, illus. LC 78-72862. 64p. (gr. 4-6). 1979. pap. 6.46 (ISBN 0-385-28600-7). Delacorte.

Cole, Joanna. Mixed-Up Magic. Kelly, True, illus. 32p. (Orig.). (gr. k-3). 1987. pap. 2.50 (ISBN 0-590-40789-9). Scholastic Inc.

—Mixed-Up Magic. Donnelly, Judy, ed. Kelley, True, illus. LC 87-14965. 32p. (gr. k-3). 1987. 8.95 (ISBN 0-8038-9298-5). Hastings.

Colum, Padraic. The Boy Apprenticed to an Enchanter. Leight, Edward, illus. (gr. 3-7). 1991. 20.00 (ISBN 0-8446-6482-0). Peter Smith.

Conrad, Pam. Prairie Songs. Zudeck, Darryl S., illus. LC 85-42633. 176p. (gr. 5 up). 1987. pap. 3.50 (ISBN 0-06-440206-1, Trophy). HarpC Child Bks.

Corbett, Scott. The Hairy Horror Trick. Galdone, Paul, illus. 112p. (gr. 4-6). 1985. pap. 2.50 (ISBN 0-590-32195-1, Apple Paperbacks). Scholastic Inc.

Degen, Bruce. The Little Witch & the Riddle. Degen, Bruce, illus. LC 78-19475. 64p. (gr. k-3). 1980. PLB 11.89 (ISBN 0-06-021415-5). HarpC Child Bks.

Degroat, Florence. A Fairy's Workday. Wilson, Patricia, illus. 65p. (gr. 1-6). 1983. pap. 2.25 (ISBN 0-87516-508-7). DeVorss.

De Paola, Tomie. Strega Nona's Magic Lessons. De Paola, Tomie, illus. LC 80-28260. (ps-3). 1982. 13.95 (ISBN 0-15-281785-9, HJ). HarBraceJ.

DePaola, Tomie. Strega Nona's Magic Lessons. DePaola, Tomie, illus. (gr. 1-4). 1984. pap. 4.95 (ISBN 0-15-281786-7, VoyB). HarBraceJ.

Dillon, Barbara. A Mom by Magic. Lindberg, Jeffrey, illus. LC 89-29410. 144p. (gr. 3-7). 1990. 13.95 (ISBN 0-397-32450-2, Lipp Jr Bks); PLB 13.89 (ISBN 0-397-32449-9, Lipp Jr Bks). HarpC Child Bks.

Dixon, Franklin W. Hardy Boys: Billion Dollar Ransom. Barish, Wendy, ed. Morrill, Leslie, illus. 192p. (gr. 3-7). 1982. 8.50 (ISBN 0-671-42352-5, Little Simon); pap. 3.50 (ISBN 0-671-42355-X). S&S Trade.

Doors in Time Book, No. 1. 1991. pap. 12.95 (ISBN 0-671-72997-7). S&S Trade.

Duane, Diane. Deep Wizardry. LC 84-15566. 288p. (gr. 7 up). 1985. 15.95 (ISBN 0-385-29373-9). Delacorte.

Dubowski, Cathy E. Pretty Good Magic. Dubowski, Mark, illus. LC 87-4784. 48p. (gr. 1-3). 1987. lib. bdg. 6.99 (ISBN 0-394-99068-4, Random Juv); pap. 2.95 (ISBN 0-394-89068-X, Random Juv). Random.

Duncan, Lois. A Gift of Magic. (gr. 5-7). 1989. pap. 3.50 (ISBN 0-671-72649-8, Archway). PB.

Dutton, Sandra. The Magic of Myrna C. Waxweather. Clark, Matthew, illus. LC 86-20579. 96p. (gr. 2-5). 1987. 12.95 (ISBN 0-689-31273-3, Atheneum Child Bk). Macmillan Child Grp.

—The Magic of Myrna C. Waxweather. (gr. 2-6). 1990. pap. 2.75 (ISBN 0-553-15788-4, Skylark). Bantam.

Eager, Edward. Half Magic. Bodecker, N. M., illus. LC 54-5153. (gr. 4-6). 1954. 12.95 (ISBN 0-15-233078-X, HJ). HarBraceJ.

—Half Magic. Treherne, Katie T. & Bodecker, N. M., illus. 208p. (gr. 3-7). 1989. pap. 3.95 (ISBN 0-15-233081-X). HarBraceJ.

—Magic by the Lake. Treherne, Katie T. & Bodecker, N. M., illus. 208p. (gr. 3-7). 1989. pap. 3.95 (ISBN 0-15-250444-3). HarBraceJ.

—Magic or Not? Bodecker, N. M., illus. (gr. 4-6). 1984. 16.75 (ISBN 0-8446-6154-6). Peter Smith.

—Magic or Not? Treherne, Katie T. & Bodecker, N. M., illus. 208p. (gr. 3-7). 1989. pap. 3.95 (ISBN 0-15-251160-1). HarBraceJ.

—Seven-Day Magic. (gr. 4-6). 15.75 (ISBN 0-8446-6381-6). Peter Smith.

—Seven-Day Magic. Treherne, Katie T. & Bodecker, N. M., illus. 208p. (gr. 3-7). 1989. pap. 3.95 (ISBN 0-15-272916-X). HarBraceJ.

Eastman, David. The Sorcerer's Apprentice. Jones, John, illus. LC 87-13767. 32p. (gr. k-4). 1987. PLB 9.79 (ISBN 0-8167-1067-8); pap. text ed. 1.95 (ISBN 0-8167-1068-6). Troll Assocs.

Eastman, David, adapted by. Aladdin & the Wonderful Lamp. Waldman, Bryna, illus. LC 87-13756. 32p. (gr. 1-4). 1988. PLB 9.79 (ISBN 0-8167-1073-2); pap. text ed. 1.95 (ISBN 0-8167-1074-0). Troll Assocs.

Ernst, Lisa C. & Ernst, Lee. The Tangram Magician. (Illus.). 24p. 1990. 16.95 (ISBN 0-8109-3851-0). Abrams.

Everitt, Betsy. Frida the Wondercat. 1990. 13.95 (ISBN 0-15-229540-2). HarbraceJ.

Fleischman, Sid. Mr. Mysterious & Company. Von Schmidt, Eric, illus. (gr. 4-6). 1962. 14.95 (ISBN 0-316-28578-1, Joy St Bks). Little.

Galdone, Paul. The Magic Porridge Pot. Galdone, Paul, illus. LC 76-3531. 32p. (ps-3). 1979. 13.95 (ISBN 0-395-28805-3, Clarion). HM.

Gaskin, Carol. The War of the Wizards. Price, T. Alexander, illus. LC 84-2663. 128p. (gr. 3-7). 1985. PLB 9.49 (ISBN 0-8167-0318-3); pap. text ed. 2.95 (ISBN 0-8167-0319-1). Troll Assocs.

Gathorne-Hardy, Jonathan. Jane's Adventures In & Out of the Book. Hill, Nicholas, illus. LC 80-29185. 192p. (gr. 5 up). 1981. 13.95 (ISBN 0-87951-122-2). Overlook Pr.

Gono & the Magic Hat. 36p. (ps-4). 1985. 8.95 (ISBN 0-88684-179-8); cassette tape avail. Listen USA.

Gormley, Beatrice. Fifth Grade Magic. McCully, Emily A., illus. 144p. (gr. 3-6). 1982. 12.95 (ISBN 0-525-44007-0, DCB). Dutton Child Bks.

—Fifth Grade Magic. McCully, Emily A., illus. 128p. (gr. 3-7). 1984. pap. 2.95 (ISBN 0-380-67439-4, 60216-4, Camelot). Avon.

—The Ghastly Glasses. McCully, Emily A., illus. LC 85-10112. 128p. (gr. 2-6). 1985. 12.95 (ISBN 0-525-44215-4, DCB). Dutton Child Bks.

—More Fifth Grade Magic. McCully, Emily A., illus. LC 88-25683. 112p. (gr. 3-6). 1989. 11.95 (ISBN 0-525-44486-6, DCB). Dutton Child Bks.

Graham, Bob. Grandad's Magic. Graham, Bob, illus. LC 88-83007. (gr. k-2). 1989. 13.95 (ISBN 0-316-32321-7). Little.

Green, Phyllis. Eating Ice Cream with a Werewolf. Stern, Patti, illus. LC 82-47727. 128p. (gr. 3-7). 1983. PLB 11.89 (ISBN 0-06-022141-0). HarpC Child Bks.

Greydanus, Rose. Hocus Pocus, Magic Show! Goodman, Joan, illus. LC 81-2637. 32p. (gr. k-2). 1981. PLB 10.89 (ISBN 0-89375-539-7); pap. text ed. 2.95 (ISBN 0-89375-540-0). Troll Assocs.

Grimm, Jacob & Grimm, Wilhelm K. The Magic Ring. Winter, Jeanette, illus. & retold by. LC 86-21042. 40p. (ps-3). 1987. Knopf.

Hamilton, Virginia. The Magical Adventures of the Pretty Pearl. LC 82-48629. 320p. (gr. 6 up). 1983. 12.95 (ISBN 0-06-022186-0). HarpC Child Bks.

Hastings. Rufus & Christopher & the Magic Bubble. LC 73-87799. (Illus.). 32p. (gr. k-2). 1974. PLB 9.95 (ISBN 0-87783-127-0); pap. 3.94 deluxe ed. (ISBN 0-87783-128-9); cassette 7.94x (ISBN 0-87783-197-1). Oddo.

Heuvel, Karen. The Magic Crystal. (Illus.). 32p. (ps-8). 1990. pap. 5.95 (ISBN 0-317-93237-3). Blue Water Pub.

Hill, Douglas. Penelope's Pendant. (gr. 5-7). 1991. 12.95 (ISBN 0-385-41641-5). Doubleday.

Hillert, Margaret. Magic Beans. (ps-3). 1989. pap. 3.50 (ISBN 0-8136-5553-6). Modern Curr.

Himmelman, John. Amanda & the Magic Garden. (ps-3). 1987. pap. 10.95 (ISBN 0-670-80823-7). Viking Child Bks.

Hiser, Constance. No Bean Sprouts, Please! Ewing, Carolyn, illus. LC 89-1817. 64p. (gr. 2-5). 1989. 13.95 (ISBN 0-8234-0760-8). Holiday.

Horn, Myrna. Krista's Magic Hat. LC 90-71359. (Illus.). 44p. (gr. k-3). 1991. 5.95 (ISBN 1-55523-397-X). Winston-Derek.

Hurd, Inis I. The Magic Lamp. Gesner, Ethel & Irvine, Bonnie, illus. LC 87-30728. 140p. (gr. 4-7). 1989. PLB 14.50 (ISBN 0-944517-00-5). Christian Center.

Jacobs, W. W. The Monkey's Paw. LC 86-2329. 48p. (gr. 6 up). 1986. PLB 10.45s.p. (ISBN 0-88682-060-X); PLB 14.95 (ISBN 0-685-12411-8). Creative Ed.

Jensen, Helen Z. Uncle Ivan's Magic Box. LC 86-32903. (Illus.). 32p. (ps-4). 1987. 11.95 (ISBN 0-8037-0095-4, 01160-350). Dial Bks Young.

Jones, Diana W. The Ogre Downstairs. LC 89-11741. 192p. (gr. 5 up). 1990. 12.95 (ISBN 0-688-09195-4). Greenwillow.

—Witch Week. LC 82-6074. 256p. (gr. 3-7). 1988. pap. 2.95 (ISBN 0-394-80600-X). Knopf.

Koda-Callan, Elizabeth. The Magic Locket. Koda-Callan, Elizabeth, illus. LC 88-5508. (ps-3). 1988. 12.95 (ISBN 0-89480-602-5, 1602). Workman Pub.

Krakoff, S. B. The Magick Cave. 175p. (Orig.). (gr. 6-7). 1989. pap. write for info. Charcoal St Pr.

Krensky, Stephen. Ghostly Business. (gr. 4-7). 1990. pap. 3.95 (ISBN 0-689-71364-9, Aladdin). Macmillan Child Grp.

Kroll, Steven. The Big Bunny & the Magic Show. Stevens, Janet, illus. 32p. (ps-2). 1987. pap. 3.95 (ISBN 0-590-44633-9). Scholastic Inc.

Lee, Tanith. Black Unicorn. Cooper, Heather, illus. 144p. (gr. 7 up). 1991. 14.95 (ISBN 0-689-31575-9, Atheneum Child Bk). Macmillan Child Grp.

Le Landgren. A Touch of Magic: A Fantasy Adventure. LC 90-8183. (Orig.). (gr. 2-7). 1990. pap. 7.95 (ISBN 0-943367-03-4). Princess Pub.

Lester, Helen. The Revenge of the Magic Chicken. Munsinger, Lynn, illus. 32p. (gr. k-3). 1990. 13.95 (ISBN 0-395-50929-7). HM.

—The Wizard, the Fairy, & the Magic Chicken. Munsinger, Lynn, illus. LC 82-21302. 32p. (gr. k-3). 1988. pap. 4.95 (ISBN 0-395-47945-2). HM.

Levoy, Myron. The Magic Hat of Mortimer Wintergreen. Glass, Andrew, illus. LC 87-45292. 224p. (gr. 3-7). 1988. 11.95 (ISBN 0-06-023841-0); PLB 11.89 (ISBN 0-06-023842-9). HarpC Child Bks.

—The Magic Hat of Mortimer Wintergreen. LC 87-45292. 224p. (gr. 3-7). 1990. pap. 3.95 (ISBN 0-06-440335-1, Trophy). HarpC Child Bks.

Levy, Elizabeth. Running Out of Magic with Houdini. Sims, Blanche & Rutherford, Jenny, illus. LC 80-28427. 128p. (gr. 3-6). 1981. lib. bdg. 4.99 (ISBN 0-394-94685-5); pap. 1.95 (ISBN 0-394-84685-0). Knopf.

McDermott, Gerald. Tim O'Toole & the Little People. (ps-3). 1990. pap. 13.95 (ISBN 0-670-80393-6). Viking Child Bks.

MacDonald, Betty. Hello, Mrs. Piggle-Wiggle. LC 57-5613. (Illus.). (gr. 1-3). 1985. pap. 3.50 (ISBN 0-06-440149-9, Trophy). HarpC Child Bks.

—Mrs. Piggle-Wiggle. rev. ed. LC 47-1876. (Illus.). 120p. (gr. 1-3). 1985. pap. 3.50 (ISBN 0-06-440148-0, Trophy). HarpC Child Bks.

—Mrs. Piggle-Wiggle's Farm. LC 54-7299. (Illus.). 132p. (gr. 1-3). 1985. pap. 3.50 (ISBN 0-06-440150-2, Trophy). HarpC Child Bks.

—Mrs. Piggle-Wiggle's Magic. LC 49-11124. (Illus.). 144p. (gr. 1-3). 1985. pap. 3.50 (ISBN 0-06-440151-0, Trophy). HarpC Child Bks.

Madsen, Ross M. PerryWinkle & the Book of Magic Spells. Zimmer, Dirk, illus. LC 85-15932. 48p. (ps-3). 1988. pap. 4.95 (ISBN 0-8037-0501-8). Dial Bks Young.

Magorian, James. The Magic Pretzel. LC 88-71603. 32p. (gr. 2-5). 1988. pap. 3.00 (ISBN 0-930674-28-6). Black Oak.

Major, Beverly. The Magic Pizza. Shortall, Leonard, illus. LC 77-26993. (gr. 2-5). 1978. 5.95 (ISBN 0-13-545202-3). P-H.

Marilue. Bobby Bear's Magic Show. Marilue, illus. LC 89-62707. 32p. (ps-2). 1990. PLB 12.95 (ISBN 0-87783-253-6). Oddo.

Martin, Bill, Jr. & Archambault, John. The Magic Pumpkin. Lee, Robert J., illus. 32p. (ps-2). 1989. 14.95 (ISBN 0-8050-1134-X). H Holt & Co.

Matthews, Morgan. Houdini, the Vanishing Hare. Gustafson, Dana, illus. LC 88-1286. 48p. (Orig.). (gr. 1-4). 1989. PLB 9.89 (ISBN 0-8167-1343-X); pap. text ed. 2.95 (ISBN 0-8167-1344-8). Troll Assocs.

Mayer, Mercer. A Special Trick. LC 69-18220. (Illus.). (gr. k-3). 1976. pap. 4.95 (ISBN 0-8037-8103-2). Dial Bks Young.

Moffit, Linda L. The Magic Mirror. LC 89-50125. (Illus.). 80p. (Orig.). (gr. k-7). 1989. pap. 8.95 (ISBN 0-87516-615-6). DeVorss.

Moncure, Jane B. Word Bird's Magic Wand. Hohag, Linda, illus. LC 90-1645. 32p. (ps-2). 1990. lib. bdg. 11.97 (ISBN 0-89565-580-2); pap. text ed. 6.96 (ISBN 0-89565-611-6). Childs World.

Montgomery, L. M. Jane of Lantern, Magic for Marigold. (gr. 7 up). 1989. pap. 2.95 (ISBN 0-318-41644-1, Starfire). Bantam.

Morrison, Dorothy N. Vanishing Act. LC 88-36026. 208p. (gr. 4-8). 1989. 13.95 (ISBN 0-689-31513-9, Atheneum Child Bk). Macmillan Child Grp.

Murad, Maria B. The Magic Words. Margodo, Dick, illus. 40p. (ps-3). 1984. 5.95 (ISBN 0-910313-17-2). Parker Bros.

Naylor, Phyllis R. Beetles, Lightly Toasted. LC 87-911. 144p. (gr. 3-7). 1987. 12.95 (ISBN 0-689-31355-1, Atheneum Child Bk). Macmillan Child Grp.

Nesbit, Edith. Enchanted Castle. 231p. 1981. Repr. PLB 10.95x (ISBN 0-89966-361-3). Buccaneer Bks.

—Five Children & It. 188p. 1981. Repr. PLB 19.95 (ISBN 0-89966-362-1). Buccaneer Bks.

Newman, Robert. The Case of the Watching Boy. LC 86-28859. 192p. (gr. 3-7). 1987. 13.95 (ISBN 0-689-31317-9, Atheneum Child Bk). Macmillan Child Grp.

Nimmo, Jenny. Orchard of the Crescent Moon. LC 88-36806. 176p. (gr. 5 up). 1989. 13.95 (ISBN 0-525-44438-6, DCB). Dutton Child Bks.

Nister, Ernest. Merry Magic-Go-Round. (Illus.). (gr. k up). 1983. PLB 10.95 (ISBN 0-399-20946-8, Philomel). Putnam Pub Group.

Nixon, Jean L. A Deadly Game of Magic. LC 83-8379. 148p. (gr. 8 up). 1983. 13.95 (ISBN 0-15-222954-X, HJ). HarBraceJ.

—A Deadly Game of Magic. (gr. 6-12). 1985. pap. 3.25 (ISBN 0-440-92102-3, LFL). Dell.

Ostheeren, Ingrid. Jonathan Mouse & the Magic Box. Mathieu, Agnes, illus. Lanning, Rosemary, tr. from GER. LC 89-43248. (Illus.). 32p. (gr. k-3). 1990. 13.95t (ISBN 1-55858-087-5). North-South Bks NYC.

Pearson, Carol L. I Believe in Make Believe. (Orig.). (gr. k up). 1984. pap. 4.50 (ISBN 0-87602-255-7). Anchorage.

Pellowski, Michael J. Magic Broom. Garry-McCord, Kathi, illus. LC 85-14054. 48p. (Orig.). (gr. 1-3). 1986. PLB 9.89 (ISBN 0-8167-0636-0); pap. text ed. 2.95 (ISBN 0-8167-0637-9). Troll Assocs.

—Mixed-up Magic. Cushman, Doug, illus. LC 88-1312. 48p. (Orig.). (gr. 1-3). 1989. PLB 9.89 (ISBN 0-8167-1327-8); pap. text ed. 2.95 (ISBN 0-8167-1328-6). Troll Assocs.

Poskitt, Kjartan. Mystery of the Magic Toy. Higham, David, illus. 32p. (gr. k-3). 1989. 7.95 (ISBN 0-8249-8406-4). Ideals.

Quin-Harkin, Janet. Magic Growing Powder. Cumings, Art, illus. LC 80-18019. 48p. (ps-3). 1981. 5.95 (ISBN 0-8193-1037-9); PLB 5.95 (ISBN 0-8193-1038-7). Parents.

—Magic Growing Powder. (Illus.). 48p. (ps-2). 1991. pap. 2.95 (ISBN 0-448-40104-5, G&D). Putnam Pub Group.

Reuter, Bjarne. Buster's World. (Illus.). 154p. (gr. 5-9). 1991. pap. 3.95 (ISBN 0-14-034471-3, Puffin). Puffin Bks.

Roberts, Jane. Emir's Education in the Proper Use of Magical Powers. Cherry, Lynne, illus. 138p. (gr. 3 up). 1984. pap. 8.95 (ISBN 0-913299-08-1, Dist. by PGW). Stillpoint.

Roberts, Willo D. The Magic Book. LC 85-20056. 146p. (gr. 4-6). 1986. 12.95 (ISBN 0-689-31120-6, Atheneum Child Bk). Macmillan Child Grp.

—The Magic Book. LC 88-19360. 160p. (gr. 2-6). 1988. pap. 3.95 (ISBN 0-689-71284-7, Aladdin). Macmillan Child Grp.

Sabin, Francene. The Magic String. Snyder, Joel, illus. LC 81-4076. 32p. (gr. k-2). 1981. PLB 10.89 (ISBN 0-89375-547-8); pap. 2.95 (ISBN 0-89375-548-6). Troll Assocs.

Schwartz, Alvin, ed. Tales of Trickery from the Land of Spoof. Christiana, David, illus. LC 85-16004. 87p. (gr. 4 up). 1985. 11.95 (ISBN 0-374-37378-7). FS&G.

Selden, George. The Genie of Sutton Place. LC 72-90531. 192p. (gr. 3 up). 1973. 12.95 (ISBN 0-374-32527-8). FS&G.

Service, Pamela F. Tomorrow's Magic. LC 86-32123. 208p. (gr. 4-8). 1987. 14.95 (ISBN 0-689-31320-9, Atheneum Child Bk). Macmillan Child Grp.

Sewell, Doug. Antoine & the Magic Coin. Alex, Ben, ed. (Illus.). 32p. (gr. 3-6). 1987. 7.95 (ISBN 0-8028-5022-7). Eerdmans.

Smith, Wendy. The Witch Baby. Smith, Wendy, illus. LC 85-40590. 32p. (ps-3). 1986. pap. 7.95 (ISBN 0-670-80953-5). Viking Child Bks.

Snyder, Zilpha K. Black & Blue Magic. Holtan, Gene, illus. LC 66-12850. 192p. (gr. 3-7). 1972. Spartan ed. 5.95 (ISBN 0-689-30075-1, Atheneum). Macmillan Child Grp.

—Black & Blue Magic. (gr. k-6). 1988. pap. 3.25 (ISBN 0-440-40053-8, YB). Dell.

—The Changing Maze. Mikolaycak, Charles, illus. LC 85-5009. 96p. (gr. k-4). 1985. SBE 12.95 (ISBN 0-02-785900-2, Mcmillan Child Bk). Macmillan Child Grp.

—The Headless Cupid. Raible, Alton, illus. LC 78-154763. 208p. (gr. 4-6). 1971. 14.95 (ISBN 0-689-20687-9, Atheneum Child Bk). Macmillan Child Grp.

Sobol, Donald J. The Amazing Power of Ashur Fine. (gr. 4-8). 1987. pap. 2.95 (ISBN 0-8167-1049-X). Troll Assocs.

Sorensen, LaDawn. Magical Mr. E. (Illus.). 44p. (gr. k-2). 1991. pap. 5.95 (ISBN 1-55523-360-0). Winston-Derek.

Steele, Mary Q. Because of the Sand Witches There. Galdone, Paul, illus. LC 75-5932. 192p. (gr. 3-7). 1975. 11.75 (ISBN 0-688-80001-7); PLB 11.88 (ISBN 0-688-84001-9). Greenwillow.

Steig, William. Silvestre y la Piedrecita Magica. Mlawer, Teresa, tr. from ENG. Steig, William, illus. 32p. (gr. 1-3). 1990. PLB 12.95 (ISBN 0-9625162-0-1). Lectorum Pubns.

Sutton, Scott E. The Secret of GorBee Grotto. (Illus.). 60p. (gr. 2-4). 1987. 12.95 (ISBN 0-9617199-3-1). Sutton Pubns.

Talbert, Marc. Double Or Nothing. (gr. 3-7). 1990. 14.95 (ISBN 0-8037-0832-7). Dial Bks Young.

Tapp, Kathy K. Moth-Kin Magic. Chessare, Michele, illus. LC 83-2782. 128p. (gr. 3-6). 1983. 12.95 (ISBN 0-689-50288-5, M K McElderry). Macmillan Child Grp.

Theriot, David. Leola et la pirogue. Easterling, Mae L., illus. (FRE.). 39p. (gr. 3). 1979. pap. text ed. 1.25 (ISBN 0-911409-03-3). Natl Mat Dev.

Travers, P. L. Mary Poppins. rev. ed. (gr. 4-7). 1991. pap. 3.50 (ISBN 0-440-40406-1). Dell.

—Mary Poppins Comes Back. (gr. 4-7). 1991. pap. 3.50 (ISBN 0-440-40418-5). Dell.

—Mary Poppins in the Park. (gr. 4-7). 1991. pap. 3.50 (ISBN 0-440-40452-5). Dell.

—Mary Poppins Opens the Door. (gr. 4-7). 1991. pap. 3.50 (ISBN 0-440-40432-0). Dell.

Trotman, Felicity, as told by. The Sorcerer's Apprentice. (Illus.). 32p. (gr. k-5). 1985. PLB 16.67 (ISBN 0-8172-2505-6); pap. 9.27 (ISBN 0-8172-2513-7). Raintree Pubs.

Turkle, Brinton. Do Not Open. Turkle, Brinton, illus. LC 80-10289. 32p. (ps-2). 1981. pap. 13.95 (ISBN 0-525-28785-X, 01258-370, DCB). Dutton Child Bks.

Twohill, Maggie. Jeeter, Mason & the Magic Headset. LC 84-21538. 112p. (gr. 4-6). 1985. 10.95 (ISBN 0-02-789530-0, Bradbury Pr). Macmillan Child Grp.

—Jeeter, Mason & the Magic Headset. (gr. 3-6). 1986. pap. 2.75 (ISBN 0-440-44220-6, YB). Dell.

Wallace, Barbara B. Miss Switch to the Rescue. McCord, Kathleen G., illus. LC 81-10916. 144p. (gr. 4-6). 1983. 1.00 (ISBN 0-687-27077-4). Abingdon.

Ward, Nick. A Bag of Tricks. (Illus.). 16p. 1987. pap. 2.95 (ISBN 0-19-272143-7). Oxford U Pr.

Welch, Fay. The Magic Swap Shop. rev. ed. (gr. 3-12). 1985. pap. text ed. 6.00 (ISBN 0-88734-509-3). Players Pr.

Wellin Magic. 36p. (ps-4). 1985. 8.95 (ISBN 0-88684-180-1); cassette tape avail. Listen USA.

Willard, Nancy. The Marzipan Moon. Sewall, Marcia, illus. LC 80-24221. 48p. (ps-3). 1981. 9.95 (ISBN 0-15-252962-4, HJ). HarBraceJ.

Wolkstein, Diane. The Banza. Brown, Marc, illus. LC 81-65845. 32p. (ps-3). 1981. PLB 12.89 (ISBN 0-8037-0429-1). Dial Bks Young.

—The Magic Wings: A Tale from China. Parker, Robert A., illus. LC 83-1611. 32p. (gr. 2-4). 1986. 10.95 (ISBN 0-525-44062-3, 01063-320, DCB); pap. 4.95 (ISBN 0-525-44275-8, DCB). Dutton Child Bks.

Woods, Audrey. Magic Shoelaces. Woods, Audrey, illus. 32p. (ps-2). 1981. 5.50 (ISBN 0-85953-109-0, Pub. by Child's Play England). Childs Play.

Yolen, Jane. The Magic Three of Solatia. Noonan, Julia, illus. LC 74-5010. 256p. (gr. 4-10). 1974. 12.95 (ISBN 0-690-00532-6, Crowell Jr Bks). HarpC Child Bks.

—Wizard's Hall. Ingber, Bonnie V., ed. 144p. (gr. 4-7). 1991. 13.95 (ISBN 0-15-298132-2). HarBraceJ.

York, Carol B. Miss Know-It-All & the Magic House. Stock, Catherine, illus. (gr. 3-7). 1989. pap. 2.75 (ISBN 0-318-41641-7, Skylark). Bantam.

Young, Tommy S. Tommy Scott Young Spins Magical Tales, 2 vols. Irvin, Nathanial, Jr., ed. Incl. Vol. I. Barney McCabe. LC 85-61698. 44p. 7.95 (ISBN 0-685-10585-7); Vol. II. Tiny Hooty & the Percher. LC 85-61699. 36p. PLB 10.00 (ISBN 0-685-10586-5). LC 85-6198. (gr. 1-8). 1985. PLB 13.95 Barney McCabe, vol. I, 44pgs. (ISBN 0-934721-01-7); PLB 13.95 Tiny Hooty & the Percher, Vol. II, 36 pgs. (ISBN 0-934721-02-5); PLB 29.95 Cassette & Book Package (ISBN 0-934721-07-6); Cassette Tape Vol. I, 17 min. 30 sec. 11.95, Vol. II 18 min. 22 sec. (ISBN 0-934721-00-9). Raspberry Rec.

Zambreno, M. A Plague of Sorcerers. 1991. 16.95 (ISBN 0-15-262430-9, HJ). HarBraceJ.

Zeplin, Zeno. Secret Magic. Jones, Judy, illus. 56p. (gr. 3-6). 1990. lib. bdg. 8.95 casebound (ISBN 1-877740-03-9); pap. text ed. 4.95g (ISBN 1-877740-04-7). Nel-Mar Pub.

Ziefert, Harriet. The Small Potatoes & the Magic Show. Brown, Richard, illus. (Orig.). (gr. k-6). 1984. pap. 2.75 (ISBN 0-440-48114-7, YB). Dell.

—The Small Potatoes Club & the Small Potatoes & the Magic Show. Brown, Richard, illus. 64p. (Orig.). (gr. k-6). 1984. pap. 2.99 (ISBN 0-440-48034-5, YB). Dell.

MAGICIANS

Borland, Kathryn K. & Speicher, Helen R. Harry Houdini: Young Magician. LC 90-23321. (Illus.). 192p. (gr. 3-7). 1991. pap. 3.95 (ISBN 0-689-71476-9, Aladdin). Macmillan Child Grp.

Fortman, Jan. Houdini & Other Masters of Magic. LC 77-12638. (Illus.). 48p. (gr. 4-5). 1977. PLB 14.65g (ISBN 0-8172-1032-6). Raintree Pubs.

Lawrence, Ann. Merlin the Wizard. Hunter, Susan, illus. 32p. (gr. 2-5). 1986. PLB 16.67 (ISBN 0-8172-2628-1); pap. text ed. 9.27 (ISBN 0-8172-2636-2). Raintree Pubs.

MAGICIANS–FICTION

Alexander, Lloyd. The Wizard in the Tree. Kubinyi, Laszlo, illus. 144p. (gr. 4-7). 1974. 14.95 (ISBN 0-525-43128-4, DCB). Dutton Child Bks.

Coombs, Patricia. Dorrie & the Witches' Camp. Coombs, Patricia, illus. LC 82-9986. 48p. (gr. 1-5). 1983. PLB 12.88 (ISBN 0-688-01508-5). Lothrop.

—The Magician & McTree. Coombs, Patricia, illus. LC 83-11984. (gr. 1-4). 1984. 11.95 (ISBN 0-688-02109-3). Lothrop.

Fujikawa, Gyo. The Magic Show. LC 81-80651. (Illus.). 32p. (ps-1). 1981. 3.95 (ISBN 0-448-11750-9, G&D). Putnam Pub Group.

Jones, Diana W. Archer's Goon. LC 83-17199. 256p. (gr. 7 up). 1984. reinforced 10.25 (ISBN 0-688-02582-X). Greenwillow.

Koste, Virginia. The Wonderful Wizard of Oz. 60p. (gr. 3-7). 1982. saddle stitch 2.50x (ISBN 0-88020-106-1). Dramatic Pub.

Lacome, Julie. Hocus Pocus. Lacome, Julie, illus. LC 90-36257. (ps). 1991. 11.95 (ISBN 0-688-10158-5, Tambourine Bks). Morrow.

Laurin, Anne. Perfect Crane. Mikolaycak, Charles, illus. LC 80-7912. 32p. (gr. 1-4). 1981. PLB 12.89 (ISBN 0-06-023744-9). HarpC Child Bks.

Lewis, C. S. The Magician's Nephew. 192p. (gr. 4 up). 1970. pap. 3.50 (ISBN 0-02-044230-0, Collier Young Ad). Macmillan Child Grp.

McGowen, Tom. Magician's Apprentice. LC 86-19743. 128p. (gr. 5-9). 1987. 12.95 (ISBN 0-525-67189-7, Lodestar Bks). Dutton Child Bks.

—The Magicians' Challenge. LC 89-32333. 144p. (gr. 5-9). 1989. 13.95 (ISBN 0-525-67289-3, Lodestar Bks). Dutton Child Bks.

—The Magician's Company. LC 88-11107. 128p. (gr. 5 up). 1988. 13.95 (ISBN 0-525-67261-3, Lodestar Bks). Dutton Child Bks.

McGraw, Eloise J. Joel & the Great Merlini. Arnosky, Jim, illus. LC 79-4580. (gr. 3-5). 1979. Pantheon.

Le Magicien d'Oz. (FRE., Illus.). (gr. 2). 3.50 (ISBN 0-7214-1292-0). Ladybird Bks.

Peretz, I. L. & Shulevitz, Uri. The Magician. LC 85-42955. (Illus.). 32p. (gr. k-6). 1985. PLB 11.95 (ISBN 0-02-782770-4, Mcmillan Child Bk). Macmillan Child Grp.

Selznick, Brian. The Houdini Box. Selznick, Brian, illus. LC 90-5387. 64p. (gr. 1-6). 1991. 13.00 (ISBN 0-679-81429-9); PLB 13.99 (ISBN 0-679-91429-3). Knopf.

MAGNETISM

see also Electricity; Electromagnetism; Magnets

Branley, Franklyn M. & Vaughn, Eleanor K. Mickey's Magnet. Johnson, Crockett, illus. (gr. k-3). pap. 1.50 (ISBN 0-590-02334-9). Scholastic Inc.

Challand, Helen. Experiments with Magnets. LC 85-30851. (Illus.). 48p. (gr. k-4). 1986. PLB 14.60 (ISBN 0-516-01279-7); pap. 4.95 (ISBN 0-516-41279-5). Childrens.

DeBruin, Jerry. Young Scientist Explore: Electricity & Magnetism. Czerniak, Charlene, illus. 32p. (gr. 4 up). 1985. wkbk. 4.95 (ISBN 0-86653-269-2, GA 654). Good Apple.

Fitzpatrick, Julie. Magnets. LC 84-40838. (Illus.). 32p. (gr. 2-5). PLB 9.96 (ISBN 0-382-09061-6). Silver Burdett Pr.

Jennings, Terry. Magnets. (Illus.). 24p. (gr. k-4). 1990. PLB 10.40 (ISBN 0-531-17211-2). Watts.

Pomeroy, Johanna P. Content Area Reading Skills Electricity & Magnetism. (Illus.). (gr. 4). 1987. pap. text ed. 3.25 (ISBN 0-89525-859-5). Ed Activities.

Taylor, Barbara. Batteries & Magnets. (Illus.). 40p. (gr. k-4). 1991. PLB 11.90 (ISBN 0-531-19130-3, Warwick). Watts.

—Electricity & Magnets. (Illus.). 32p. (gr. 5-8). 1990. PLB 11.40 (ISBN 0-531-14083-0). Watts.

Vogt, Gregory. Electricity & Magnetism. LC 85-10565. (Illus.). 84p. (gr. 5-8). 1985. PLB 10.40 (ISBN 0-531-10038-3). Watts.

Ward, ALan. Experimenting with Magnetism. Flax, Zena, illus. 48p. (gr. 2-7). 1991. PLB 12.95 (ISBN 0-7910-1509-2). Chelsea Hse.

Whyman, Kathryn. Electricity & Magnetism. (Illus.). 32p. (gr. k-6). 1986. PLB 8.99 (ISBN 0-531-17020-9, Gloucester Pr). Watts.

Zubrowski, Bernie. Blinkers & Buzzers: Building & Experimenting with Electricity & Magnetism. Doty, Roy, illus. LC 90-44519. 112p. (gr. 3 up). 1991. PLB 12.88 (ISBN 0-688-09966-1). Morrow Jr Bks.

MAGNETS

Adler, David. Amazing Magnets. Lawler, Dan, illus. LC 82-17377. 32p. (gr. 3-6). 1983. PLB 10.59 (ISBN 0-89375-894-9); pap. text ed. 2.95 (ISBN 0-89375-895-7). Troll Assocs.

Amery, H. & Littler, A. The KnowHow Book of Batteries & Magnets: Safe & Simple Experiments, Models & Games. (Illus.). 32p. (gr. 3-6). 1977. pap. 5.95 (ISBN 0-86020-008-6). EDC.

Branley, Franklyn M. & Vaughn, Eleanor K. Mickey's Magnet. Johnson, Crockett, illus. (gr. k-3). pap. 1.50 (ISBN 0-590-02334-9). Scholastic Inc.

Cash, Terry. Electricity & Magnets. Chen, Kuo K. & Bull, Peter, illus. 40p. (gr. 5-6). 1989. PLB 12.90 (ISBN 0-531-19063-3). Watts.

Fitzpatrick, Julie. Magnets. LC 84-40838. (Illus.). 32p. (gr. 2-5). PLB 9.96 (ISBN 0-382-09061-6). Silver Burdett Pr.

Freeman, Mae. The Real Magnet Book. (gr. k-3). 1970. pap. 1.75 (ISBN 0-590-01660-1, Schol Pap). Scholastic Inc.

Jennings, Terry. Magnets. (Illus.). 24p. (gr. k-4). 1990. PLB 10.40 (ISBN 0-531-17211-2). Watts.

Kirkpatrick, Rena K. Look at Magnets. rev. ed. Knight, Ann, illus. LC 84-26252. 32p. (gr. 2-4). 1985. PLB 15.99 (ISBN 0-8172-2354-1); pap. text ed. 9.27 (ISBN 0-8172-2379-7). Raintree Pubs.

Santrey, Laurence. Magnets. Veno, Joseph, illus. LC 84-2597. 32p. (gr. 3-6). 1985. PLB 9.49 (ISBN 0-8167-0140-7); pap. text ed. 2.95 (ISBN 0-8167-0141-5). Troll Assocs.

MAINE

Carpenter, Allan. Maine. new ed. LC 79-10804. (Illus.). 96p. (gr. 4 up). 1979. PLB 19.93 (ISBN 0-516-04119-3). Childrens.

Cayford, John E. Maine Firsts. 3rd, rev. & enl. ed. LC 79-56551. 68p. (Orig.). pap. text ed. 18.50 (pack of 10) (ISBN 0-941216-11-X); tchrs. ed 20.00 (ISBN 0-941216-12-8). Cay-Bel.

Engfer, LeeAnne. Maine. (Illus.). 72p. (gr. 3-6). 1991. PLB 12.95 (ISBN 0-8225-2701-4). Lerner Pubns.

Fradin, Dennis. Maine: In Words & Pictures. LC 79-25122. (Illus.). 48p. (gr. 2-5). 1980. PLB 15.93 (ISBN 0-516-03919-9). Childrens.

Gibbons, Gail. Surrounded by Sea: Life on a New England Fishing Island. (ps-3). 1991. 14.95 (ISBN 0-316-30961-3). Little.

Harrington, Ty. Maine. LC 88-38399. (Illus.). 144p. (gr. 4 up). 1989. PLB 25.27 (ISBN 0-516-00465-4). Childrens.

McMillan, Bruce. Finestkind O'Day, Lobstering in Maine. (Illus.). 48p. (gr. 3-8). 1990. 15.00 (ISBN 0-685-35117-3). Apple Isl Bks.

Marsh, Carole. Avast, Ye Slobs! Maine Pirate Trivia. (Illus.). (gr. 3-8). 1990. PLB 19.95 (ISBN 0-7933-0545-4); pap. 14.95 (ISBN 0-7933-0544-6); disk 29.95 (ISBN 0-7933-0546-2). Gallopade Pub Group.

—The Beast of the Maine Bed & Breakfast. (Illus.). (gr. 3-8). 1990. PLB 19.95 (ISBN 0-7933-1681-2); pap. 14.95 (ISBN 0-7933-1682-0) (ISBN 0-7933-1683-9). Gallopade Pub Group.

—Carole Marsh Maine Books, 31 bks. (Illus.). (gr. 3-8). 1990. Set. PLB 638.45 (ISBN 0-7933-1294-9). Gallopade Pub Group.
—The Hard-to-Believe-But-True! Book of Maine History, Mystery, Trivia, Legend, Lore, Humor & More. (Illus.). (gr. 3-8). 1990. PLB 19.95 (ISBN 0-7933-0542-X); pap. 14.95 (ISBN 0-7933-0541-1); disk 29.95 (ISBN 0-7933-0543-8). Gallopade Pub Group.
—If My Maine Mama Ran the World! (Illus.). (gr. 3-8). 1990. lib. bdg. 19.95 (ISBN 0-7933-1687-1); pap. 14. 95 (ISBN 0-7933-1688-X); disk 29.95 (ISBN 0-7933-1689-8). Gallopade Pub Group.
—Let's Quilt Maine & Stuff It Topographically! (Illus.). (gr. 3-8). 1990. PLB 19.95 (ISBN 1-55609-599-6); pap. 14.95 (ISBN 1-55609-068-4); disk 29.95 (ISBN 1-55609-601-1). Gallopade Pub Group.
—Maine & Other State Greats (Biographies) (Illus.). (gr. 3-8). 1990. PLB 19.95 (ISBN 1-55609-614-3); pap. 14. 95 (ISBN 1-55609-615-1); disk 29.95 (ISBN 1-55609-616-X). Gallopade Pub Group.
—Maine Bandits, Bushwackers, Outlaws, Crooks, Devils, Ghosts, Desperadoes & Other Assorted & Sundry Characters! (Illus.). (gr. 3-8). 1990. PLB 19.95 (ISBN 0-7933-0527-6); pap. 14.95 (ISBN 0-7933-0526-8); disk 29.95 (ISBN 0-7933-0528-4). Gallopade Pub Group.
—Maine Classic Christmas Trivia: Stories, Recipes, Activities, Legends, Lore & More! (Illus.). (gr. 3-8). 1990. PLB 19.95 (ISBN 0-7933-0530-6); pap. 14.95 (ISBN 0-7933-0529-2); disk 29.95 (ISBN 0-7933-0531-4). Gallopade Pub Group.
—Maine Coastales. (Illus.). (gr. 3-8). 1990. PLB 19.95 (ISBN 1-55609-608-9); pap. 14.95 (ISBN 1-55609-609-7); disk 29.95 (ISBN 1-55609-610-0). Gallopade Pub Group.
—The Maine Hot Air Balloon Mystery. (Illus.). (gr. 2-9). 1990. 19.95 (ISBN 0-7933-2489-0); pap. 14.95 (ISBN 0-7933-2490-4); computer disk 29.95 (ISBN 0-7933-2491-2). Gallopade Pub Group.
—Maine "Jography" A Fun Run Thru Our State! (Illus.). (gr. 3-8). 1990. PLB 19.95 (ISBN 1-55609-596-1); pap. 14.95 (ISBN 1-55609-597-X); disk 29.95 (ISBN 1-55609-598-8). Gallopade Pub Group.
—Maine Kid's Cookbook: Recipes, How-to, History, Lore & More! (Illus.). (gr. 3-8). 1990. PLB 19.95 (ISBN 0-7933-0539-X); pap. 14.95 (ISBN 0-7933-0538-1); disk 29.95 (ISBN 0-7933-0540-3). Gallopade Pub Group.
—Maine Quiz Bowl Crash Course! (Illus.). (gr. 3-8). 1990. PLB 19.95 (ISBN 1-55609-611-9); pap. 14.95 (ISBN 1-55609-612-7); disk 29.95 (ISBN 1-55609-613-5). Gallopade Pub Group.
—Maine School Trivia: An Amazing & Fascinating Look at Our State's Teachers, Schools & Students! (Illus.). (gr. 3-8). 1990. PLB 19.95 (ISBN 0-7933-0536-5); pap. 14.95 (ISBN 0-7933-0535-7); disk 29.95 (ISBN 0-7933-0537-3). Gallopade Pub Group.
—Maine Silly Basketball Sportsmysteries, Vol. I. (Illus.). (gr. 3-8). 1990. PLB 19.95 (ISBN 0-7933-0533-0); pap. 14.95 (ISBN 0-7933-0532-2); disk 29.95 (ISBN 0-7933-0534-9). Gallopade Pub Group.
—Maine Silly Basketball Sportsmysteries, Vol. II. (Illus.). (gr. 3-8). 1990. PLB 19.95 (ISBN 0-7933-1684-7); pap. 14.95 (ISBN 0-7933-1685-5); disk 29.95 (ISBN 0-7933-1686-3). Gallopade Pub Group.
—Maine Silly Football Sportsmysteries, Vol. I. (Illus.). (gr. 3-8). 1990. PLB 19.95 (ISBN 1-55609-602-X); pap. 14.95 (ISBN 1-55609-604-6); disk 29.95 (ISBN 1-55609-606-2). Gallopade Pub Group.
—Maine Silly Football Sportsmysteries, Vol. II. (Illus.). (gr. 3-8). 1990. PLB 19.95 (ISBN 1-55609-603-8); pap. 14.95 (ISBN 1-55609-605-4); disk 29.95 (ISBN 1-55609-607-0). Gallopade Pub Group.
—Maine Silly Trivia! (Illus.). (gr. 3-8). 1990. PLB 19.95 (ISBN 1-55609-593-7); pap. 14.95 (ISBN 1-55609-594-5); disk 29.95 (ISBN 1-55609-595-3). Gallopade Pub Group.
—Maine's (Most Devastating!) Disasters & (Most Calamitous!) Catastrophies! (Illus.). (gr. 3-8). 1990. PLB 19.95 (ISBN 0-7933-0524-1, 0-7933-0525-X); pap. 14.95 (ISBN 0-7933-0523-3); disk 29.95. Gallopade Pub Group.
Turner Program Services, Inc. Staff & Clark, James I. Maine. LC 85-9975. 48p. (gr. 3 up). 1985. PLB 17.32 (ISBN 0-86514-433-8); pap. text ed. 9.27 (ISBN 0-86514-508-3); cancelled Beta video (ISBN 0-86514-058-8); cancelled VHS video; cancelled 3/4" video (ISBN 0-86514-208-4); cancelled tchr's. guide (ISBN 0-86514-283-1); cancelled student activity bk. (ISBN 0-86514-358-7); cancelled index. Raintree Pubs.

MAINE–FICTION

Campbell, Louise A. & Bowers, Grace A. Muffin, The Maine Puffin. Mason, MacAdam L., illus. 40p. (Orig.). (gr. k-3). 1988. pap. 9.95 (ISBN 0-9621949-0-5). Muffin Enter.
There's a lovable, colorful bird that lives off the coast of Maine. He learns to swim, learns to take a bath & learns to eat by himself. He catches a cold & meets a new friend. He's Muffin, an Atlantic Puffin growing up on the islands off the Maine coast. With his mother & father, his friends & the wide open ocean he learns everything a young person would...well, almost everything. Muffin learns to fly, too. MUFFIN, THE MAINE PUFFIN is a children's book written by first-time authors Louise Campbell & Grace Bowers. The colorful illustrations by MacAdam Lee Mason are perfectly matched to these seven stories of the triumphs & obstacles of growing & learning. MUFFIN, THE MAINE PUFFIN is a wonderful idea for children (or grandchildren) 4 to 8 years old.
Publisher Provided Annotation.

McCloskey, Robert. Burt Dow: Deep-Water Man. McCloskey, Robert, illus. LC 68-364. 64p. (gr. 4-6). 1963. pap. 15.95 (ISBN 0-670-19748-3). Viking Child Bks.
—One Morning in Maine. (ps-3). 1976. pap. 3.95 (ISBN 0-14-050174-6, Puffin). Puffin Bks.
—One Morning in Maine. McCloskey, Robert, illus. (gr. k-3). 1952. pap. 13.95 (ISBN 0-670-52627-4). Viking Child Bks.
—Time of Wonder. McCloskey, Robert, illus. (gr. k-3). 1957. pap. 15.95 (ISBN 0-670-71512-3). Viking Child Bks.
—Time of Wonder. (Illus.). 64p. (ps-3). 1989. pap. 4.95. Warne.

MAINE–HISTORY

Kuller, Alison M. An Outward Bound School. Stewart, Thomas R. & Kuller, Alison M., illus. LC 89-5169. 32p. (gr. 3-6). 1990. PLB 10.79 (ISBN 0-8167-1731-1); pap. text ed. 2.95 (ISBN 0-8167-1732-X). Troll Assocs.
Rolde, Neil. Maine: A Narrative History. (Illus.). 356p. (Orig.). 1990. pap. 19.95 (ISBN 0-88448-069-0). Tilbury Hse.
Smith, Marion J. Pokey & Timothy of Stonehouse Farm. LC 73-80612. 72p. (gr. 4-6). 1973. pap. 3.95 (ISBN 0-87027-129-6). Cumberland Pr.

MAIZE

see Corn

MAKE-UP (COSMETICS)

see Cosmetics

MAKE-UP, THEATRICAL

Freeman, Ron. Makeup Art. LC 90-38305. (Illus.). 48p. (gr. 5-8). 1991. PLB 11.90 (ISBN 0-531-14133-0). Watts.
Terry, Ellen & Anderson, Lynne. Makeup & Masks. rev. ed. LC 78-139744. 112p. (gr. 7 up). 1982. PLB 14.95 (ISBN 0-8239-0232-3). Rosen Group.

MALADJUSTED CHILDREN

see Problem Children

MALAWI

Department of Geography, Lerner Publications. Malawi in Pictures. (Illus.). 64p. (gr. 5 up). 1988. PLB 12.95 (ISBN 0-8225-1842-2). Lerner Pubns.
Sanders, Renfield. Malawi. (Illus.). 104p. (gr. 5 up). 1988. lib. bdg. 14.95 (ISBN 1-55546-193-X). Chelsea Hse.

MALAYA

Lim, John. At Grandmother's House. LC 77-79548. (Illus.). (gr. 1-6). 1977. pap. 2.95 (ISBN 0-88776-099-6). Tundra Bks.

MALAYA–FICTION

Conrad, Joseph. Lord Jim. Gemme, F. R., intro. by. (gr. 10 up). pap. 1.95 (ISBN 0-8049-0054-X, CL-54). Airmont.
—Outcast of the Islands. Teitel, N. R., intro. by. (gr. 9 up). pap. 1.50 (ISBN 0-8049-0113-9, CL-113). Airmont.

MALAYSIA, FEDERATION OF

Elder, Bruce. Take a Trip to Malaysia. Payne, Tony, illus. LC 84-51807. 32p. (gr. k-3). 1985. PLB 7.99 (ISBN 0-531-04941-8). Watts.
Lerner Publications, Department of Geography Staff, ed. Malaysia in Pictures. (Illus.). 64p. (gr. 5 up). 1989. 12. 95 (ISBN 0-8225-1854-6). Lerner Pubns.
Major, John S. The Land & People of Malaysia & Brunei. LC 90-20124. (Illus.). 272p. (gr. 6 up). 1991. 17.95 (ISBN 0-06-022488-6); PLB 17.89 (ISBN 0-06-022489-4). HarpC Child Bks.
Newman, Bernard. Malaysia. (Illus.). (gr. 5 up). 1988. 14. 95 (ISBN 0-222-01024-X). Chelsea Hse.
Wee, Jessie. We Live in Malaysia & Singapore. LC 84-73585. (Illus.). 60p. (gr. 1-6). 1985. 9.49 (ISBN 0-531-18007-7, Pub. by Bookwright Pr). Watts.
Wright, David K. Malaysia. LC 87-33784. (Illus.). 128p. (gr. 4-8). 1988. PLB 25.27 (ISBN 0-516-02702-6). Childrens.

MALCOLM X

see Little, Malcolm, 1925-1965

MAMMALS

see also Primates;
also names of mammals, e.g. Bats

Anderson, Lucia. Mammals & Their Milk. (Illus.). 48p. (gr. 3-7). 1984. 11.95 (ISBN 0-396-08315-3, Putnam). Putnam Pub Group.
Bender, Lionel. Birds & Mammals. Franklin Watts Ltd., ed. Khan, Aziz, illus. 40p. (gr. 7-9). 1988. PLB 12.40 (ISBN 0-531-17091-8, Gloucester Pr). Watts.
Board, Tessa. Mammals. (Illus.). 40p. (gr. 4 up). 1983. PLB 12.40 (ISBN 0-531-03473-9). Watts.
Book of Mammals, 2 vols. (Illus.). 304p. (gr. 3-8). 1981. 22.95 (ISBN 0-87044-376-3); lib. bdg. 25.95 (ISBN 0-87044-379-8). Natl Geog.
Book of Sea Mammals-Coloring Book. 1985. pap. 3.50 (ISBN 0-88388-067-9). Bellerophon Bks.
Crump, Donald J. Creatures Small & Furry. LC 83-13456. 32p. (ps-3). 1983. of 4 10.95 set (ISBN 0-87044-486-7); lib. bdg. 12.95 (ISBN 0-87044-491-3). Natl Geog.
Crump, Donald J., ed. Giants from the Past. LC 81-47893. 104p. (gr. 3-8). 1983. 6.95 (ISBN 0-87044-424-7); PLB 8.50 (ISBN 0-87044-429-8). Natl Geog.
Fowler, Allan. It Could Still Be a Mammal. LC 90-2161. (Illus.). 32p. (ps-2). 1990. PLB 12.60 (ISBN 0-516-04903-8); pap. 30.60 big bk. (ISBN 0-516-49463-5). Childrens.
Grace, Theresa. A Picture Book of Underwater Life. Pistolesi, Roseanna, illus. LC 89-37330. 24p. (gr. 1-4). 1990. lib. bdg. 9.59 (ISBN 0-8167-1906-3); pap. text ed. 2.50 (ISBN 0-8167-1907-1). Troll Assocs.
Heller, Ruth. How to Hide a Polar Bear. Heller, Ruth, illus. LC 85-70286. 32p. (ps-2). 1986. pap. 4.95 (ISBN 0-448-10477-6, G&D). Putnam Pub Group.
Hiller, Ilo. Introducing Mammals to Young Naturalists. LC 89-35523. (Illus.). 112p. (gr. 6). 1990. lib. bdg. 21. 50x (ISBN 0-89096-427-0); pap. 12.95 (ISBN 0-89096-428-9). Tex A&M Univ Pr.
Kalman, Bobbie. Forest Mammals. Loates, Glen, illus. 56p. (gr. 3-4). 1987. 15.95 (ISBN 0-86505-165-8); pap. 7.95 (ISBN 0-86505-185-2). Crabtree Pub Co.
Kaufman, Joe. Joe Kaufman's Big Book about Mammals & Birds. (gr. 1-7). 1989. write for info. (ISBN 0-307-15813-6, Pub. by Golden Bks). Western Pub.
McCord. Prehistoric Mammals. (gr. 4-6). 1977. PLB 13. 96 (ISBN 0-86020-129-5, Usborne-Hayes); pap. 6.95 (ISBN 0-88110-120-6); pap. 5.95 (ISBN 0-86020-128-7). EDC.
Mammals. (Illus.). 32p. (ps-8). pap. 29.50 (ISBN 0-87474-335-4). Smithsonian.
Mammals of Arizona. (Illus.). 32p. (gr. 3 up). 1984. pap. 1.00 (ISBN 0-935810-16-1). Primer Pubs.
Matthews, Downs. Polar Bear Cubs. Guravich, Dan, photos by. (Illus.). (gr. 2 up). 1989. pap. 13.95 (ISBN 0-671-66757-2). S&S Trade.
Minelli, Giuseppe. Mammals. (Illus.). 64p. 1988. 15.95 (ISBN 0-8160-1560-0). Facts on File.
Nentl, Jerolyn. The Wild Cats. LC 83-22506. (Illus.). 48p. (gr. 4-5). 1984. PLB 10.95 (ISBN 0-89686-249-6, Crestwood Hse). Macmillan Child Grp.
Neuman, Pearl. When Winter Comes. (Illus.). 32p. (gr. 1-4). 1989. PLB 13.32 (ISBN 0-8172-3519-1). Raintree Pubs.
O'Neill, Mary. Life after the Dinosaurs. Bindon, John, illus. LC 89-31164. 32p. (gr. 3-7). 1989. lib. bdg. 12.89 (ISBN 0-8167-1639-0); pap. text ed. 3.95 (ISBN 0-8167-1640-4). Troll Assocs.
Palmer, S. Manatees. (Illus.). 24p. (gr. k-5). 1989. lib. bdg. 11.93 (ISBN 0-86592-359-0). Rourke Corp.
Parker, Steve. Mammal. Burton, Jane & King, Dave, photos by. LC 88-22656. (Illus.). 64p. (gr. 5 up). 1989. 15.00 (ISBN 0-394-82258-7); lib. bdg. 14.99 (ISBN 0-394-92258-1). Knopf.
Parsons, Alexandra. Amazing Mammals. Young, Jerry, photos by. LC 89-38831. (Illus.). 32p. (gr. 1-5). 1990. 6.95 (ISBN 0-679-80224-X); PLB 9.99 (ISBN 0-679-90224-4). McKay.
Sabin, Francene. Mammals. Veno, Joseph, illus. LC 84-2658. 32p. (gr. 3-6). 1985. PLB 9.49 (ISBN 0-8167-0208-X); pap. text ed. 2.95 (ISBN 0-8167-0209-8). Troll Assocs.
Schneider, Jeff. My Friend the Manatee: An Ocean Magic Book. Spoon, Wilfred, illus. LC 90-61576. 12p. (ps). 1991. 4.95g (ISBN 1-877779-08-3). Schneider Educational.
Spizzirri Publishing Co. Staff. Mammals: An Educational Coloring Book. Spizzirri, Linda, ed. Spizzirri, Peter M., et al, illus. 32p. (gr. 1-8). 1981. pap. 1.95 (ISBN 0-86545-027-7). Spizzirri.
Steele, Philip. Wild Animals. LC 90-42014. (Illus.). 32p. (gr. 5-6). 1991. SBE 9.95 (ISBN 0-89686-584-3, Crestwood Hse). Macmillan Child Grp.
Stone, Lynn. Hyenas. (Illus.). 24p. (gr. k-5). 1990. lib. bdg. 11.93 (ISBN 0-86593-049-X); lib. bdg. 8.95s.p. (ISBN 0-685-36348-1). Rourke Corp.
—Wombats. (Illus.). 24p. (gr. k-5). 1990. lib. bdg. 11.93 (ISBN 0-86593-059-7); lib. bdg. 8.95s.p. (ISBN 0-685-36374-0). Rourke Corp.
Tee-Van, Helen D. Small Mammals Are Where You Find Them. (Illus.). (gr. 3-7). 1967. lib. bdg. 5.99 (ISBN 0-394-91643-3). Knopf.
Torbit, Stephen C. Large Mammals of the Central Rockies: A Guide to Their Locations & Ecology. Torbit, Stephen C., illus. 72p. (gr. 12). 1987. pap. 7.95 (ISBN 0-9618450-0-7). Bennet Creek.
Whyte, Malcolm. Prehistoric Mammals Action Set, No. 4. Smith, Dan, illus. 24p. (gr. 1 up). 1988. pap. 5.95 (ISBN 0-8431-1955-1). Price Stern.
Wiessinger, John. Flowers, Ferns, & Funguses - Right Before Your Eyes. LC 89-1437. (Illus.). 64p. (gr. 4-10). 1989. PLB 15.95 (ISBN 0-89490-267-9). Enslow Pubs.
Wrigley, Robert E. Small Mammals. Olson, Arlene, illus. 40p. (Orig.). (gr. 2-7). 1990. pap. 4.95 (ISBN 0-920534-56-2, Pub. by Hyperion Pr Ltd CN). Sterling.

MAMMALS, FOSSIL

see also names of extinct animals, e.g. Mastodon; etc.

Holman, J. Allan & Gringhuis, Dirk. Mystery Mammals of the Ice Age-Great Lakes Region. Gringhuis, Dirk, illus. LC 72-90919. 45p. (Orig.). (gr. 5-8). 1972. pap. 1.75 (ISBN 0-910726-74-4). Hillsdale Educ.

Kerrod, Robin. Primates, Insect Eaters & Baleen Whales. (Illus.). 96p. 1988. 17.95x (ISBN 0-8160-1961-4). Facts on File.

Losito, Linda, et al. Mammals: The Small Plant-Eaters. (Illus.). 96p. 1988. 17.95x (ISBN 0-8160-1958-4). Facts on File.

Mcgowen, Tom. Album of Prehistoric Animals. 1989. pap. 4.95 (ISBN 0-02-689418-1). Checkerboard Pr.

Matthews, Rupert. Age of Mammals. (ps-3). 1990. PLB 11.40 (ISBN 0-531-18311-4). Watts.

—Ice Age Animals. (ps-3). 1990. PLB 11.40 (ISBN 0-531-18300-9). Watts.

O'Toole, Christopher & Stidworthy, John. Mammals: The Hunters. (Illus.). 96p. 1988. 17.95x (ISBN 0-8160-1959-2). Facts on File.

Ricciuti, Edward. Older Than the Dinosaurs: The Origin & Rise of the Mammals. Malsberg, Edward, illus. LC 77-26606. 96p. (gr. 5-12). 1980. (Crowell Jr Bks). HarpC Child Bks.

Stidworthy, John, et al. Mammals: Large Plant-Eaters. (Illus.). 96p. 1988. 17.95x (ISBN 0-8160-1960-6). Facts on File.

MAN

Disney, Walt, Productions Staff. All about People. LC 85-43075. 80p. (Orig.). 1985. pap. 5.95 (ISBN 0-553-05536-4). Bantam.

Hall, Donald. Oxcart Man. Cooney, Barbara, tr. (gr. 1-5). 1984. incl. cassette 19.95 (ISBN 0-941078-41-8); pap. 12.95 incl. cassette (ISBN 0-941078-40-X); pap. 27.95 4 bks, cassette & guide (ISBN 0-941078-42-6). Live Oak Media.

Ingram, Victoria. People. 64p. (gr. k-3). 1987. 6.95 (ISBN 0-912107-62-6). Monday Morning Bks.

MAN–ANTIQUITY

see Man–Origin and Antiquity

MAN–COLOR

see Color of Man

MAN–INFLUENCE OF ENVIRONMENT

see also Color of Man

Anderson, Modelyn K. Environmental Diseases. (Illus.). 72p. (gr. 4-9). 1987. PLB 10.40 (ISBN 0-531-10382-X). Watts.

Group for Environmental Education, Inc. Staff. Our Man-Made Environment, Book 7. (gr. 7). 1973. pap. 7.95x (ISBN 0-262-07050-2). MIT Pr.

Money, D. C. The Changing Face of the Earth. LC 89-11339. (Illus.). 64p. (gr. 2-3). 1990. PLB 12.95 (ISBN 0-8368-0033-8). Gareth Stevens Inc.

MAN–INFLUENCE ON NATURE

Duggleby, John. Pesticides. LC 90-35496. (Illus.). 48p. (gr. 5-6). 1990. RSBE 10.95 (ISBN 0-89686-540-1, Crestwood Hse). Macmillan Child Grp.

Hare, Tony. Habitat Destruction. (Illus.). 32p. (gr. 5-8). 1991. PLB 11.90 (ISBN 0-531-17307-0, Gloucester Pr). Watts.

MAN–ORIGIN AND ANTIQUITY

see also Anatomy, Comparative; Evolution; Man, Prehistoric

Asimov, Isaac. How Did We Find Out about Our Human Roots? Wool, David, illus. (gr. 4-8). 1979. PLB 10.85 (ISBN 0-8027-6361-8). Walker & Co.

Kalmenoff, Matthew. Primitive Man. (Illus.). (gr. 4-6). 1984. pap. 2.95 (ISBN 0-8431-4256-1). Price Stern.

Lampton, Christopher. New Theories on the Origin of the Human Race. (Illus.). 160p. (gr. 7-12). 1989. PLB 13.40 (ISBN 0-531-10783-3). Watts.

McCaughrean, Geraldine. A Little Lower than the Angels. 144p. (gr. 6-9). 1987. 13.95 (ISBN 0-19-271561-5). Oxford U Pr.

MAN, PREHISTORIC

see also Cave Dwellers; Man–Origin and Antiquity; also names of countries, cities, etc. with the subdivision Antiquities, e.g. U. S–Antiquities; etc.

Coville, Bruce. Prehistoric People. (gr. 4-7). 1990. 11.95 (ISBN 0-385-24922-5); PLB 12.99 (ISBN 0-385-24923-3). Doubleday.

Hart, Angela. Prehistoric Man. (Illus.). 32p. (gr. 2-4). 1983. PLB 7.99 (ISBN 0-531-04511-0). Watts.

Jaspersohn, William. How People First Lived. Accardo, Anthony, illus. LC 85-10554. 48p. (gr. 2-4). 1985. PLB 10.90 (ISBN 0-531-10031-6). Watts.

Lambert, Mark. Rainbow Encyclopedia of Prehistoric Life. Sington, Adrian, ed. LC 82-80987. (Illus.). 144p. (gr. 4 up). 1982. write for info. (ISBN 0-528-82388-4). Macmillan.

McCord. Early Man. (gr. 4-6). 1977. (Usborne-Hayes); PLB 13.96 (ISBN 0-88110-121-4); pap. 6.95 (ISBN 0-86020-130-9). EDC.

McGowen, Tom. Album of Prehistoric Man. Ruth, Rod, illus. (gr. 5 up). 1979. pap. write for info. (ISBN 0-528-87051-3). Checkerboard Pr.

—Album of Prehistoric Man. Ruth, Rod, illus. 64p. (gr. 3-7). 1987. pap. 4.95 (ISBN 0-02-688514-X). Checkerboard Pr.

People of Long Ago. (Illus.). 80p. (gr. k-6). 1986. pap. 13.27 (ISBN 0-8172-2587-0). Raintree Pubs.

Santrey, Laurence. Prehistoric People. Smolinski, Dick, illus. LC 84-8464. 32p. (gr. 3-6). 1985. PLB 9.49 (ISBN 0-8167-0242-X); pap. text ed. 2.95 (ISBN 0-8167-0243-8). Troll Assocs.

MAN, PREHISTORIC–FICTION

Brennan, J. H. Shiva: An Adventure of the Ice Age. LC 89-77654. 192p. (gr. 5 up). 1990. 13.95 (ISBN 0-397-32453-7, Lipp Jr Bks); PLB 13.89 (ISBN 0-397-32454-5, Lipp Jr Bks). HarpC Child Bks.

Evarts, Hal. Jay-Jay & the Peking Monster. (gr. 5-9). 1984. 15.25 (ISBN 0-8446-6166-X). Peter Smith.

Hoff, Syd. Stanley. Hoff, Syd, illus. LC 62-8873. 64p. (gr. k-3). 1962. PLB 11.89 (ISBN 0-06-022536-X). HarpC Child Bks.

Turnbull, Ann. Maroo of the Winter Caves. LC 84-4327. 144p. (gr. 4-7). 1984. 13.95 (ISBN 0-89919-304-8, Clarion). HM.

Turner, Ann. Time of the Bison. Peck, Beth, illus. LC 86-23476. 64p. (gr. 2-6). 1987. 12.95 (ISBN 0-02-789300-6, Mcmillan Child Bk). Macmillan Child Grp.

MAN IN SPACE

see Manned Space Flight

MAN O' WAR (RACE HORSE)

Farley, Walter. Man O' War. (Illus.). (gr. 4-6). 1962. lib. bdg. 6.99 (ISBN 0-394-90616-0, Random Juv). Random.

MANAGEMENT OF CHILDREN

see Children–Management

MANNED SPACE FLIGHT

see also Astronauts; Outer Space–Exploration; Space Medicine; also names of projects, e.g. Gemini Project; etc.

Asimov, Isaac. Piloted Space Flights. LC 89-11303. (Illus.). (gr. 3-4). 1990. PLB 12.95 (ISBN 1-55532-371-5). Gareth Stevens Inc.

MANNERS

see Courtesy; Etiquette

MANNERS AND CUSTOMS

see also Chivalry; Clothing and Dress; Costume; Etiquette; Funeral Rites and Ceremonies; Holidays; Marriage Customs and Rites; Travel

Allen, Thomas B. Where the Children Live. (Illus.). 27p. 1980. 10.95 (ISBN 0-13-957126-4). P-H.

Branson, Mary K. A Carousel of Countries: Games, Songs, Recipes & Customs from Around the World. (Illus.). 96p. (Orig.). (gr. 1-6). 1986. pap. 5.95 (ISBN 0-936625-53-8, New Hope AL). Womans Mission Union.

Brown, Marc & Krensky, Stephen. Perfect Pigs: An Introduction to Manners. LC 83-746. (Illus.). 32p. (ps-3). 1983. 14.95 (ISBN 0-316-11079-5, Joy St Bks); pap. 6.95 (ISBN 0-316-11080-9, Joy St Bks). Little.

Countries & Customs. 96p. (gr. 3-8). 1987. PLB 240.00 set (ISBN 0-685-18920-1); pap. 13.27 (ISBN 0-8172-3059-9). Raintree Pubs.

Hallinan, P. K. I'm Thankful Each Day. Hallinan, P. K., illus. 24p. (gr. k-6). 1985. pap. 3.95 (ISBN 0-8249-8008-5). Ideals.

Hoving, Walter. Tiffany's Table Manners for Teenagers. Eula, Joe, illus. LC 88-23964. 96p. (gr. 5 up). 1989. Repr. of 1962 ed. 11.95 (ISBN 0-394-82877-1). Random.

Leaf, Munro. Manners Can Be Fun. 2nd, rev. ed. Leaf, Munro, illus. LC 84-48459. 48p. (gr. k-3). 1985. pap. 3.95 (ISBN 0-06-443053-7, Trophy). HarpC Child Bks.

Le Sieg, Theodore. Come Over to My House. Erdoes, R., illus. LC 66-10686. 72p. (gr. k-3). 1966. 3.95 (ISBN 0-394-80044-3); lib. bdg. 7.99 (ISBN 0-394-90044-8). Beginner.

MANNERS AND CUSTOMS–FICTION

Bridwell, Norman. Clifford's Manners. Bridwell, Norman, illus. 32p. (gr. k-3). 1987. pap. 1.95 (ISBN 0-590-40564-0). Scholastic Inc.

Gray, Nigel. A Country Far Away. LC 88-22360. (Illus.). 32p. (ps-1). 1989. 13.95 (ISBN 0-531-05792-5); PLB 13.99 (ISBN 0-531-08392-6). Orchard Bks Watts.

MANTLE, MICKEY CHARLES, 1931-

Wolff, Rick. Mickey Mantle. Murray, Jim, illus. 64p. (gr. 3 up). 1991. PLB 14.95 (ISBN 0-7910-1181-X). Chelsea Hse.

MANUFACTURES

see also Machinery; Waste Products

Crump, Donald J., ed. How Things Are Made. LC 79-3242. (Illus.). 104p. (gr. 3-8). 1981. 6.95 (ISBN 0-87044-334-8); PLB 8.50 (ISBN 0-87044-339-9). Natl Geog.

MAO, TSE-TUNG, 1893-

Garza, Hedda. Mao Zedong. (Illus.). 112p. (gr. 5 up). 1988. lib. bdg. 17.95 (ISBN 0-87754-564-2). Chelsea Hse.

Kurland, Gerald. Mao Tse-Tung: Founder of Communist China. Rahmas, D. Steve, ed. LC 75-190232. 32p. (Orig.). (gr. 7-12). 1972. lib. bdg. 4.20 incl. catalog cards (ISBN 0-87157-514-0); pap. 2.95 vinyl laminated covers (ISBN 0-87157-014-9). SamHar Pr.

Lawson, Don. The Long March: Red China under Chairman Mao. LC 82-45580. (Illus.). 160p. (gr. 7 up). 1983. PLB 12.89 (ISBN 0-690-04272-8, Crowell Jr Bks). HarpC Child Bks.

Marrin, Albert. Mao Tse-Tung & His China. (Illus.). 284p. (gr. 7 up). 1989. pap. 14.95 (ISBN 0-670-82940-4). Viking Child Bks.

MAORIS

Higham, Charles. The Maoris. LC 83-1856. (Illus.). 52p. (gr. 5 up). 1983. PLB 9.95 (ISBN 0-8225-1229-7). Lerner Pubns.

MAORIS–FICTION

Anderson, Margaret J. Light in the Mountain. Marcellino, Fred, illus. LC 81-14266. 192p. (gr. 5-9). 1982. 9.95 (ISBN 0-394-84791-1); lib. bdg. 9.99 (ISBN 0-394-94791-6). Knopf.

MAP DRAWING

see also Atlases

Cartwright, Sally. What's in a Map? Gackenbach, Dick, illus. LC 76-10694. (gr. k-3). 1976. PLB 6.99 (ISBN 0-698-30635-X, Coward). Putnam Pub Group.

Mango, Karin N. Mapmaking. Corwin, Judith H., illus. LC 83-25084. 112p. (gr. 4 up). 1984. lib. bdg. 9.29 (ISBN 0-671-45518-4). Messner.

Ryan, Peter. Explorers & Mapmakers. Molan, Chris, illus. LC 89-31824. 48p. (gr. 4-7). 1990. 14.95 (ISBN 0-525-67285-0, Lodestar Bks). Dutton Child Bks.

MAPLE

Metcalf, Rosamond S. The Sugar Maple. Hearn, James, photos by. LC 82-595. (Illus.). 40p. (gr. 3-5). 1982. pap. 3.50x (ISBN 0-914016-87-3). Phoenix Pub.

MAPS

Arnold, Carolyn. Maps & Globes: Fun, Facts, & Activities. Sweat, Lynn, illus. LC 84-7595. 32p. (gr. k-4). 1984. PLB 11.90 (ISBN 0-531-04720-2). Watts.

Aten, Jerry. Maptime... U. S. A. 64p. (gr. 4 up). 1982. 7.95 (ISBN 0-86653-093-2, GA 422). Good Apple.

—Prime Time Maps. Filkins, Vanessa, illus. 64p. (gr. 2-5). 1983. wkbk. 7.95 (ISBN 0-86653-108-4, GA 470). Good Apple.

Baynes, John. How Maps Are Made. LC 86-20342. (Illus.). 32p. (gr. 5-12). 1987. 12.95x (ISBN 0-8160-1691-7). Facts on File.

Broekel, Ray. Maps & Globes. LC 83-7509. (Illus.). 48p. (gr. k-4). 1983. PLB 14.60 (ISBN 0-516-01695-4); pap. 4.95 (ISBN 0-516-41695-2). Childrens.

Cartwright, Sally. What's in a Map? Gackenbach, Dick, illus. LC 76-10694. (gr. k-3). 1976. PLB 6.99 (ISBN 0-698-30635-X, Coward). Putnam Pub Group.

Cobb, Annie. Squirrel's Treasure Hunt. Wilburn, Kathy, illus. 32p. (gr. k-3). 1991. PLB 10.98 (ISBN 0-671-70391-9); 5.95 (ISBN 0-671-70395-1). Silver Pr.

Edson, Ann & Insel, Eunice. Reading Maps, Globes, Charts, Graphs. (gr. 4-6). 1982. wkbk. 2.69 (ISBN 0-89525-175-2). Ed Activities.

Hartman, Gail. As the Crow Flies: A First Book of Maps. Stevenson, Harvey, illus. (ps-1). 1991. 12.95 (ISBN 0-02-743005-7, Bradbury Pr). Macmillan Child Grp.

Knowlton, Jack. Maps & Globes. Barton, Harriett, illus. LC 85-47537. 48p. (gr. 2-5). 1985. 14.95 (ISBN 0-690-04457-7, Crowell Jr Bks); PLB 11.89 (ISBN 0-690-04459-3). HarpC Child Bks.

—Maps & Globes. Barton, Harriett, illus. LC 85-47537. 48p. (gr. 2-5). 1986. pap. 4.95 (ISBN 0-06-446049-5, Trophy). HarpC Child Bks.

Lye, Keith. Measuring & Maps: Projects with Geography. (Illus.). 32p. (gr. 5-8). 1991. PLB 11.90 (ISBN 0-531-17325-9, Gloucester Pr). Watts.

Riffel, Paul. Reading Maps. LC 79-13628. (Illus.). (gr. 7 up). 1973. pap. 6.95 plastic comb bdg. (ISBN 0-8331-1300-3). Hubbard Sci.

Rushdoony, Haig A. Language of Maps: A Map Skills Program for Grades 4-6. (gr. 4-6). 1983. pap. 11.95 (ISBN 0-8224-4242-6). Fearon Teach Aids.

Wentrcek, Ginger. Marvelous Maps & Graphs. (gr. 1-3). pap. 4.95 (ISBN 0-8224-6332-6). Fearon Teach Aids.

MAPS, HISTORICAL

see Atlases, Historical

MARCHES FOR NEGRO CIVIL RIGHTS

see Blacks–Civil Rights

MARCONI, GUGLIELMO, MARCHESE, 1874-1937

Morgan, Nina. Guglielmo Marconi. (Illus.). 48p. (gr. 5-7). 1991. PLB 12.40 (ISBN 0-531-18417-X, Pub. by Bookwright Pr.). Watts.

Tames, Richard. Guglielmo Marconi. (Illus.). 32p. (gr. 5-8). 1990. PLB 11.90 (ISBN 0-531-14024-5). Watts.

MARFAN'S SYNDROME

Bernhardt, Barbara A., et al. The Marfan Syndrome: A Booklet for Teenagers. LeHew, Ronald, illus. 20p. 1988. pap. 1.00 (ISBN 0-918335-03-5). Natl Marfan Foun.

MARIHUANA

Booher, Albert R. Marijuana. 11p. (gr. 5-9). 1988. pap. text ed. 5.95 (ISBN 0-685-28978-8). Madonna Edu Syst.

Godfrey, Martin. Marijuana. (Illus.). 64p. (gr. 4-9). 1987. PLB 11.90 (ISBN 0-531-10437-0). Watts.

Gunn, Jeffrey. Pen Pals, Vol. 4: Facts about Pot. Wolfe, Debra, illus. (Orig.). (gr. 3). 1990. pap. write for info. (ISBN 1-879146-04-5). Knowldg Pub.

Leahy, Barbara H. Marijuana: A Dangerous "High" Way. rev. ed. Farrell, Lee & Jensen, Rosemary D., eds. Moles, Danna, illus. LC 82-62440. 173p. (Orig.). (gr. 4-9). 1983. pap. 6.95 (ISBN 0-9610312-1-2). B Leahy.

Stronck, David. Marijuana - The Real Story. Nelson, Mary & Clark, Kay, eds. Ransom, Robert D., illus. 30p. (gr. 5-8). 1987. pap. text ed. 2.95 (ISBN 0-941816-36-2). Network Pubns.

Stwertka, Eve & Stwertka, Albert. Marijuana. rev. ed. LC 85-22526. (Illus.). 72p. (gr. 4-9). 1986. PLB 10.40 (ISBN 0-531-10122-3). Watts.

Tobias, Ann. Pot: What It Is, What It Does. Huffman, Tom, illus. LC 78-10817. 48p. (gr. 3-4). 1979. PLB 12.88 (ISBN 0-688-84200-3). Greenwillow.

MARINE ANIMALS

see also Fishes; Fresh-Water Animals

Althea. Undersea Homes. 24p. (gr. 2 up). 1986. 5.95 (ISBN 0-521-30297-8); pap. 2.95 (ISBN 0-685-10901-1). Cambridge U Pr.

Barrett, Norman. Monsters of the Deep. (Illus.). 32p. (gr. k-4). 1991. PLB 11.40 (ISBN 0-531-14150-0). Watts.

Bender, Lionel. Creatures of the Deep. (Illus.). 32p. (gr. 3-6). 1989. PLB 11.90 (ISBN 0-531-17162-0, Gloucester Pr). Watts.

Berger, Melvin. Stranger Than Fiction: Sea Monsters. 96p. 1991. pap. 2.95 (ISBN 0-380-76054-1, Camelot). Avon.

Carwardine, Mark. Water Animals. Young, Richard G., ed. Camm, Martin, illus. LC 89-7879. 45p. (gr. 3-5). 1989. PLB 13.26 (ISBN 0-944483-31-3). Garrett Ed Corp.

Coldrey, Jennifer. Life in the Sea. LC 90-38113. (Illus.). 32p. (gr. 4-7). 1991. PLB 11.90 (ISBN 0-531-18360-2). Watts.

Colin, Patrick L. Marine Invertebrates & Plants of the Living Reef. (Illus.). 512p. (gr. 7 up). 1988. lib. bdg. 29.95 (ISBN 0-86622-875-6, H-971). TFH Pubns.

Cook, David. Ocean Life. Cook, David, illus. LC 84-12065. 32p. (gr. 3-7). 1985. bds. 5.95 (ISBN 0-517-55429-1). Crown.

Doubilet, Anne. Under the Sea from A to Z. Doubilet, David, photos by. LC 90-1355. (Illus.). 32p. (gr. k-6). 1991. 14.95 (ISBN 0-517-57836-0); PLB 15.99 (ISBN 0-517-57837-9). Crown.

Fine, John C. Creatures of the Sea. (Illus.). 32p. (ps-4). 1989. 13.95 (ISBN 0-689-31420-5, Atheneum Child Bk). Macmillan Child Grp.

Fitzsimons, Cecilia. My First Fishes & Other Waterlife: Pop-Up Field Guide. Fitzsimons, Cecilia, illus. LC 86-45489. 12p. (gr. k-4). 1987. 8.95 (ISBN 0-06-021873-8). HarpC Child Bks.

Geistdoefer, Patrick. Undersea Giants. Boucher, Joelle, illus. LC 87-34531. 38p. (gr. k-5). 1988. 4.95 (ISBN 0-944589-02-2, 022). Young Discovery Lib.

Gelman, Rita G. Monsters of the Sea, Vol. 1. (ps-3). 1990. 12.95 (ISBN 0-316-30738-6, Joy St Bks). Little.

Hogner, Dorothy C. Sea Mammals. Collins, Patricia, illus. LC 78-22503. (gr. 4 up). 1979. 8.61i (ISBN 0-690-03949-2, Crowell Jr Bks). HarpC Child Bks.

Holling, Holling C. Pagoo. Holling, L. W., illus. (gr. 3-9). 1957. 15.95 (ISBN 0-395-06826-6). HM.

Mallory, Kenneth. The Red Sea. (Illus.). 48p. (gr. 5-7). 1991. 12.95 (ISBN 0-531-15213-8); PLB 13.90 (ISBN 0-531-10993-3). Watts.

Myers, Arthur. Sea Creatures Do Amazing Things. Zallinger, Jean D., illus. LC 80-20089. 72p. (gr. 2-5). 1981. 7.95 (ISBN 0-394-84487-4); lib. bdg. 8.99 (ISBN 0-394-94487-9). Random.

Palmer, Sarah. Sea Mammal Discovery Library, 6 bks, Reading Level 2. (Illus.). 144p. (gr. k-5). Date not set. Set. PLB 71.60 (ISBN 0-86592-357-4). Rourke Corp.

Penny, Malcolm. Exploiting the Sea. LC 90-38112. (Illus.). 32p. (gr. 4-7). 1991. PLB 11.90 (ISBN 0-531-18359-9). Watts.

Pick, C. Undersea. (Illus.). 32p. 1976. PLB 13.96 (ISBN 0-88110-437-X); pap. 6.95 (ISBN 0-86020-092-2). EDC.

Podendorf, Illa. Animals of Sea & Shore. LC 81-38453. (Illus.). 48p. (gr. k-4). 1982. PLB 14.60 (ISBN 0-516-01615-6); pap. 4.95 (ISBN 0-516-41615-4). Childrens.

Posell, Elsa. Whales & Other Sea Mammals. LC 82-4451. (gr. k-4). 1982. 14.60 (ISBN 0-516-01663-6); pap. 4.95 (ISBN 0-516-41663-4). Childrens.

Quinn, Kaye. Creatures of the Deep. (Illus.). 48p. (Orig.). (ps-2). 1989. pap. 2.95 (ISBN 0-8431-2726-0). Price Stern.

Reinstedt, Randall A. Otters, Octopuses, & Odd Creatures of the Deep. Bergez, John, ed. LC 87-82106. (Illus.). 64p. (gr. 3-6). 1987. lib. bdg. 9.95 (ISBN 0-933818-21-1). Ghost Town.

Rinard, Judy. Amazing Animals of the Sea. Crump, Donald J., ed. LC 80-8796. (Illus.). 104p. (gr. 3-8). 1981. 6.95 (ISBN 0-87044-382-8); PLB 8.50 (ISBN 0-87044-387-9). Natl Geog.

Sea Animals. 32p. (Orig.). 1984. pap. 1.25 (ISBN 0-8431-1517-3). Price Stern.

Shale, David & Coldrey, Jennifer. Man-of-War at Sea. LC 86-5703. (Illus.). 32p. (gr. 4-6). 1987. 10.95 (ISBN 1-55532-069-4). Gareth Stevens Inc.

Sibbald, Jean H. Sea Mammals: The Warm-Blooded Ocean Explorers. LC 87-33291. (Illus.). 128p. (gr. 4 up). 1988. PLB 11.95 (ISBN 0-87518-372-7, Dillon). Macmillan Child Grp.

Spizzirri Publishing Co. Staff. Prehistoric Sea Life: An Educational Coloring Book. Spizzirri, Linda, ed. Kohn, Arnie, illus. 32p. (gr. 1-8). 1981. pap. 1.95 (ISBN 0-86545-020-X). Spizzirri.

Waldrop, Victor H., ed. Amazing Creatures of the Sea. LC 87-20413. (Illus.). 96p. (gr. 1-6). 1987. PLB 15.95 (ISBN 0-912186-83-6, 19416). Natl Wildlife.

Waters, John F. Marine Animal Collectors: How Creatures of the Sea Contribute to Science & Our Knowledge of Man. LC 69-15053. (Illus.). (gr. 6-9). 1969. PLB 6.95 (ISBN 0-8038-4648-7). Hastings.

Westerkov, Kim. Playmates of the Sea. LC 90-10555. (Illus.). 24p. (gr. 1-4). 1990. PLB 15.96 (ISBN 0-8114-2693-9). Steck-V.

Whyte, Malcolm. Sea Life. (Illus.). 32p. (Orig.). (gr. 1-4). pap. 3.50 (ISBN 0-8431-1959-4). Price Stern.

Wyler, Rose. Seashore Surprises. (Illus.). 32p. (gr. k-3). 1991. PLB 11.98 (ISBN 0-671-69165-1); pap. 4.95 (ISBN 0-671-69167-8). Messner.

MARINE ANIMALS–FICTION

Allen, Laura J. Ottie & the Star. Allen, Laura J., illus. LC 78-22485. 32p. (ps-3). 1979. HarpC Child Bks.

Coatsworth, Elizabeth. Under the Green Willow. Domanska, Janina, illus. LC 84-1471. 24p. (gr. k-3). 1984. 9.25 (ISBN 0-688-03845-X); PLB 8.59 (ISBN 0-688-03846-8). Greenwillow.

Fontenot, Mary A. Clovis Crawfish & the Spinning Spider. (Illus.). 32p. 1987. 11.95 (ISBN 0-88289-644-X). Pelican.

Heller, Ruth. How to Hide an Octopus. Heller, Ruth, illus. LC 85-70288. 32p. (ps-2). 1986. pap. 4.95 (ISBN 0-448-10476-8, G&D). Putnam Pub Group.

Lee, A. Laney. Island Eyes: The Adventures of a Shell. Dowd, Ken, illus. LC 85-8972. 112p. (gr. 2-5). 1987. 12.95 (ISBN 0-688-06094-3). Lothrop.

Limmer, Milly J. Where Will You Swim Tonight? Fay, Ann, ed. Pittman, Helena C., illus. 32p. (ps-1). 1990. 13.95 (ISBN 0-8075-8949-7). A Whitman.

Marshall, Janet P. My Camera: At the Aquarium: At the Aquarium, Vol. 1. 1989. 12.95 (ISBN 0-316-54713-1). Little.

Tate, Suzanne. Mary Manatee: A Tale of Sea Cows. Melvin, James, illus. LC 90-60102. 28p. (Orig.). (gr. k-3). 1990. pap. 3.95 (ISBN 0-9616344-9-9). Nags Head Art.

MARINE ARCHITECTURE
see Shipbuilding

MARINE BIOLOGY
see also Fresh-Water Biology; Marine Animals; Marine Ecology; Marine Plants; Marine Resources

Anson, August. Marine Biology & Ocean Science. (Illus.). 340p. (gr. 9-12). 1990. text ed. 24.95 (ISBN 0-9624094-0-5); pap. text ed. 18.95 (ISBN 0-9624094-1-3). Balaena Bks.

Arnold, Caroline. A Walk on the Great Barrier Reef. Arnold, Arthur, illus. 48p. (gr. 2-5). 1988. pap. 6.95 (ISBN 0-685-25645-6, First Ave Edns). Lerner Pubns.

Be an Underwater Detective. (gr. 2 up). 1989. 3.99 (ISBN 0-517-68913-8). Outlet Bk Co.

Center for Marine Conservation Staff. The Ocean Book: Aquarium & Seaside Activities & Ideas for All Ages. (gr. k-6). 1989. pap. text ed. 12.95 (ISBN 0-471-62078-5). Wiley.

Cole, Joanna. Nighttime Animals. Lilly, Kenneth, illus. LC 85-7593. 32p. (ps-2). 1985. 9.95 (ISBN 0-394-87189-8); lib. bdg. 12.99 (ISBN 0-394-97189-2). Knopf.

Conway, Lorraine. Marine Biology. 64p. (gr. 5 up). 1982. 6.95 (ISBN 0-86653-056-8, GA 400). Good Apple.

Craig, Janet. What's under the Ocean. Harvey, Paul, illus. LC 81-11425. 32p. (gr. k-2). 1982. PLB 10.89 (ISBN 0-89375-652-0); pap. 2.95 (ISBN 0-89375-653-9). Troll Assocs.

Curran, Eileen. Life in the Sea. Snyder, Joel, illus. LC 84-16190. 32p. (gr. k-2). 1985. lib. bdg. 10.89 (ISBN 0-8167-0448-1); pap. text ed. 2.95 (ISBN 0-8167-0449-X). Troll Assocs.

Feeney, Stephanie & Fielding, Ann. Sand to Sea: Marine Life of Hawaii. LC 88-38669. 1989. 12.95 (ISBN 0-8248-1180-1, Kolowalu Bk). UH Pr.

Jaspersohn, William. A Day in the Life of a Marine Biologist. (Illus.). 96p. (gr. 5 up). 1982. 15.95 (ISBN 0-316-45814-7). Little.

Maidoff, Ilka. Let's Explore the Shore. (Illus.). (gr. 5 up). 1962. 9.95 (ISBN 0-8392-3017-6). Astor-Honor.

Mallory, Kenneth. The Red Sea. (Illus.). 48p. (gr. 5-7). 1991. 12.95 (ISBN 0-531-15213-8); PLB 13.90 (ISBN 0-531-10993-3). Watts.

Mills, Dick. Encyclopedia of the Marine Aquarium. 1988. 12.99 (ISBN 0-517-63378-7). Outlet Bk Co.

Morris, Dean. Underwater Life. rev. ed. LC 87-16693. (Illus.). 48p. (gr. 2-6). 1987. PLB 17.32 (ISBN 0-8172-3214-1). Raintree Pubs.

Paige, David. A Day in the Life of a Marine Biologist. Ruhlin, Roger, photos by. LC 80-54097. (Illus.). 32p. (gr. 4-8). 1981. PLB 11.79 (ISBN 0-89375-446-3); pap. 2.95 (ISBN 0-89375-447-1); cassette avail. Troll Assocs.

Parker, Steve. Seashore. King, Dave, illus. LC 88-27173. 64p. (gr. 5 up). 1989. 15.00 (ISBN 0-394-82254-4); PLB 14.99 (ISBN 0-394-92254-9). Knopf.

Sea Life. (Illus.). 20p. (gr. k up). 1990. laminated, wipe clean surface 3.95 (ISBN 0-88679-818-3). Educ Insights.

Sea Life. (Illus.). 16p. (gr. k up). 1990. laminated, wipe clean surface 9.95 (ISBN 0-88679-662-8). Educ Insights.

Selberg, Ingrid. Secrets of the Deep. Fogelman, Phyllis J., ed. McGuiness, Doreen, illus. 12p. (gr. 1-5). 1990. 12. 95 (ISBN 0-8037-0766-5). Dial Bks Young.

Seymour, Peter, et al. What Lives in the Sea. Johnson, Pam, illus. Carter, David A. & Strejan, John designed by. (Illus.). 10p. (gr. 2-5). 1985. 8.95 (ISBN 0-02-782170-6, Mcmillan Child Bk). Macmillan Child Grp.

Shannon, George. Sea Gifts. Azarian, illus. LC 88-45429. (gr. 2-4). 1989. 11.95 (ISBN 0-87923-770-8). Godine.

Sibbald, Jean. Sea Creatures on the Move. LC 89-12027. (Illus.). 128p. (gr. 4 up). 1989. PLB 11.95 (ISBN 0-87518-412-X, Dillon). Macmillan Child Grp.

Thompson, Brenda & Overbeck, Cynthia. Under the Sea. Beisner, Monica, illus. LC 76-22470. 24p. (gr. k-3). 1977. PLB 5.95 (ISBN 0-8225-1363-3). Lerner Pubns.

Williams, Brian. Under the Sea. Allen, Graham, et al, illus. LC 88-17654. 24p. (Orig.). (gr. 2-5). 1989. PLB 5.99 (ISBN 0-394-99990-8); pap. 2.95 (ISBN 0-394-89990-3). Random.

Wood, John N. Nature Hide & Seek: Oceans. Harrison, Mark, illus. LC 85-73. 24p. (gr. 1-4). 1985. 11.95 (ISBN 0-394-87583-4). Knopf.

Zim, Herbert S. & Ingle, Lester. Seashores. Barlowe, Dorothea & Barlowe, Sy, illus. (gr. 5 up). 1955. pap. write for info. (ISBN 0-307-24496-2, Golden Pr). Western Pub.

MARINE BIOLOGY–FICTION

Montgomery, Raymond A. Journey under the Sea. large type ed. Granger, Paul, illus. 117p. (gr. 3-7). 1987. Repr. of 1977 ed. 8.95 (ISBN 0-942545-04-4); PLB 9.95 (ISBN 0-942545-10-9, Dist. by Grolier). Grey Castle.

Olsen, E. A. Mystery at Salvage Rock. LC 68-16401. (Illus.). 48p. (gr. 3 up). 1970. PLB 10.95 (ISBN 0-87783-027-4); pap. 3.94 deluxe ed. (ISBN 0-87783-101-7); cassette 10.60x (ISBN 0-87783-195-5). Oddo.

O'Niel, Lily. Manatee Lagoon. (Illus.). 44p. PLB 14.95 (ISBN 0-9629414-0-9). Harbor City Pubns.
The small group of manatees left Blue Springs to head out to sea, with the St. John's River as it spilled out into the Atlantic Ocean. The aquatic mammals drifted with an easy flowing Southern current that brought them to the Indian River Lagoon & also very far from home for the first time. They couldn't have known the dangers that awaited them. This is a story of the Florida manatee & the vast richness of Florida's wildlife. It is environmentally educational & will stimulate the reader's imagination into a learning experience, with the beautiful full-color illustrations, entertaining children as well as adults. This 44 page book has a 2 page glossary which teaches children valuable reading skills. MANATEE LAGOON is geared for the elementary grade reading levels & is written in a simple easy-to-read style. (This book is library bound & the pages are acid resistant, for lasting quality).
Publisher Provided Annotation.

Tate, Suzanne. Pearlie Oyster: A Tale of an Amazing Oyster. Melvin, James, illus. LC 89-92226. 28p. (Orig.). (gr. k-3). 1989. pap. 3.95 (ISBN 0-9616344-7-2). Nags Head Art.

MARINE ECOLOGY

Hare, Tony. Polluting the Sea. (Illus.). 32p. (gr. 4-8). 1991. PLB 11.90 (ISBN 0-531-17290-2). Watts.

Hogan, Paula. Dying Oceans. LC 91-10216. (Illus.). 32p. (gr. 3-4). 1991. PLB 12.95 (ISBN 0-8368-0476-7). Gareth Stevens Inc.

MARINE FAUNA
see Marine Animals

MARINE FLORA
see Marine Plants

MARINE GEOLOGY
see Submarine Geology

MARINE PLANTS
see also Algae

Doubilet, Anne. Under the Sea from A to Z. Doubilet, David, photos by. LC 90-1355. (Illus.). 32p. (gr. k-6). 1991. 14.95 (ISBN 0-517-57836-0); PLB 15.99 (ISBN 0-517-57837-9). Crown.

Hall, Howard. The Kelp Forest. Leon, Vicki, ed. (Illus.). 40p. (Orig.). 1990. pap. 5.95 (ISBN 0-918303-21-4). Blake Pub.

MARINE RESOURCES
see also Fisheries

Baker, Susan. First Look under the Sea. (Illus.). 32p. (gr. 1-2). 1991. PLB 10.95 (ISBN 0-8368-0702-2). Gareth Stevens Inc.

MARINE ZOOLOGY
see Marine Animals

MARINERS
see Seamen

MARIONETTES
see Puppets and Puppet Plays

MARITIME DISCOVERIES
see Discoveries (In Geography)

MARKET GARDENING
see Vegetable Gardening

MARKETING

Vrana, Ronald, ed. The Nature of the Private Enterprise Market System. rev. ed. 76p. (gr. 9-12). 1988. Repr. of 1977 ed. tchr's. ed. 8.00 (ISBN 0-943447-03-8). Ent & Educ Found.

—Who Sets Prices? rev. ed. (Illus.). 70p. (gr. 9-12). 1987. Repr. of 1977 ed. tchr's. ed. 8.00 (ISBN 0-943447-00-3). Ent & Educ Found.

MARKETING (HOME ECONOMICS)
see Shopping

MARKETING OF FARM PRODUCE
see Farm Produce–Marketing

MARKETS
see also Fairs

MARKETS–FICTION

Anno, Mitsumasa, illus. Anno's Flea Market. LC 83-21954. 44p. 1984. 11.95 (ISBN 0-399-21031-8, Philomel). Putnam Pub Group.

Haseley, Dennis. The Thieves' Market. Desimini, Lisa, illus. LC 90-38440. 32p. (gr. 1-5). 1991. 14.95 (ISBN 0-06-022492-4); PLB 14.89 (ISBN 0-06-022493-2). HarpC Child Bks.

MARMOTS–FICTION

Johnson, Crockett. Will Spring Be Early or Will Spring Be Late? Johnson, Crockett, illus. LC 59-9424. 48p. (gr. k-3). 1961. PLB 12.89 (ISBN 0-690-89423-6, Crowell Jr Bks). HarpC Child Bks.

MARQUETTE, JACQUES, 1637-1675

Stein, R. Conrad. The Story of Marquette & Jolliet. LC 81-5036. (Illus.). 32p. (gr. 3-6). 1981. PLB 13.27 (ISBN 0-516-04630-6). Childrens.

MARRIAGE

see also Dating (Social Customs); Domestic Relations; Family; Family Life; Family Life Education; Sex; Sexual Ethics

Buhay, Debra. Black & White of Marriage. 30p. (gr. 12). Date not set. pap. 2.00 (ISBN 1-878056-04-2). D Hockenberry.

Friedrich, Liz. Teen Guide to Married Life. 1990. pap. 4.95 (ISBN 0-531-15209-X). Watts.

Hurst, Hugo. A Search for Meaning in Love, Sex, & Marriage. rev. ed. LC 75-9961. 234p. (gr. 11-12). 1975. pap. text ed. 6.50x (ISBN 0-88489-063-5); teaching manual 3.00x (ISBN 0-88489-119-4). St. Marys.

Hurth, Robert. How to Videotape Weddings. (gr. 4-7). 1991. pap. 16.95 (ISBN 1-55788-008-5, HP Books). Price Stern.

Miller, Cynthia P. Challenges of the Heart. Bernard, David, ed. Agnew, Tim, illus. LC 90-21432. 144p. (Orig.). 1991. pap. 6.95 (ISBN 0-932581-79-X). Word Aflame.

Saperstein, M. J. First Wife Second Wife. rev. ed. 64p. (Orig.). 1985. pap. 2.95 (ISBN 0-8431-1016-3). Price Stern.

MARRIAGE–FICTION

Balter, Lawrence. The Wedding: Adjusting to a Parent's Remarriage. Schanzer, Roz, illus. 40p. (ps-2). 1989. 5.95 (ISBN 0-8120-6118-7). Barron.

Bosley, Judith A. Bride in Pink. Billups, Annie, ed. D'Allaird, John, illus. 95p. (Orig.). 1989. pap. text ed. 3.50 (ISBN 0-88336-761-0). New Readers.

Crane, Stephen. Bride Comes to Yellow Sky. Johnson, V. C., illus. 40p. (gr. 6 up). 1982. PLB 10.95s.p. (ISBN 0-87191-827-7); 15.65 (ISBN 0-685-05632-5). Creative Ed.

Delton, Judy. Angel's Mother's Wedding. 128p. (gr. 3-7). 1987. 12.95 (ISBN 0-395-44470-5). HM.

Emecheta, Buchi. The Moonlight Bride. LC 82-17816. 77p. (gr. 6-10). 1983. pap. 6.95 (ISBN 0-8076-1063-1). Braziller.

Emery, Anne. Stepfamily. LC 79-26908. 140p. (gr. 5-7). 1980. 9.50 (ISBN 0-664-32660-9, Westminster). Westminster John Knox.

Green, Wendy. The Wedding. (ps-3). 1989. pap. 1.95 (ISBN 0-7459-1736-4). Lion USA.

Hall, Amanda, illus. & adapted by. The Foolish Husbands. LC 86-28887. 26p. (gr. k-3). 1987. 12.95 (ISBN 0-87226-154-9, Bedrick Blackie). P Bedrick Bks.

Howard, Pearl A. A Special Guest for Mr. & Mrs. Bumba. 32p. (gr. k-3). 1983. Repr. of 1971 ed. 4.95 (ISBN 0-8225-0123-6). Lerner Pubns.

Leonard, Laura. Saving Damaris. 192p. (gr. 3-7). 1989. 13.95 (ISBN 0-689-31553-8, Atheneum Child Bk). Macmillan Child Grp.

Lyle, Letcher L. Dark but Full of Diamonds. (gr. 12 up). 1981. 9.95 (ISBN 0-698-20517-0, Coward). Putnam Pub Group.

Miklowitz, Gloria D. The Day the Senior Class Got Married. 160p. (gr. 6 up). 1985. pap. 2.75 (ISBN 0-440-92096-5, LFL). Dell.

Pevsner, Stella. Me, My Goat, & My Sister's Wedding. LC 84-12734. 192p. (gr. 4-7). 1985. 13.95 (ISBN 0-89919-305-6, Clarion). HM.

Porte, Barbara A. Harry Gets an Uncle. Abolafia, Yossi, illus. LC 90-39562. 48p. (gr. k up). 1991. 13.95 (ISBN 0-688-09389-2); PLB 13.88 (ISBN 0-688-09390-6). Greenwillow.

Rubel, Nicole. Uncle Henry & Aunt Henrietta's Honeymoon. Rubel, Nicole, illus. LC 85-15944. 32p. (ps-2). 1988. pap. 3.95 (ISBN 0-8037-0498-4). Dial Bks Young.

Sharmat, Marjorie W. How to Have a Gorgeous Wedding. 144p. (gr. k-12). 1989. pap. 2.95 (ISBN 0-440-93794-9, LFL). Dell.

Smith, Barry. Minnie & Ginger: A Twentieth-Century Romance. Smith, Barry, illus. LC 90-40330. 32p. (ps-3). 1991. 13.95 (ISBN 0-517-58253-8, C N Potter Bks). Crown.

Tolles, Martha. Marrying Off Mom. 1990. pap. 2.75 (ISBN 0-590-42843-8). Scholastic Inc.

Turner, Ann. Third Girl from the Left. LC 85-30028. 180p. (gr. 7 up). 1986. 13.95 (ISBN 0-02-789510-6, Mcmillan Child Bk). Macmillan Child Grp.

Williams, Barbara. Mitzi & the Terrible Tyrannosaurus Rex. McCully, Emily A., illus. LC 81-12665. 112p. (gr. 2-4). 1982. 10.95 (ISBN 0-525-45105-6, 0966-290, Dutton). NAL-Dutton.

Wolkoff, Judie. Happily Ever after...Almost. 224p. (gr. 5-9). 1984. pap. 2.95 (ISBN 0-440-43366-5, YB). Dell.

Wood, Phyllis A. Meet Me in the Park, Angie. LC 83-16937. 118p. (gr. 7-10). 1983. 11.95 (ISBN 0-664-32710-9, Westminster). Westminster John Knox.

MARRIAGE COUNSELING

Lindsay, Jeanne W. Teenage Marriage: Coping with Reality. rev. ed. (Illus.). 208p. 1988. 15.95 (ISBN 0-930934-31-8); pap. 9.95 (ISBN 0-930934-30-X). Morning Glory.

MARRIAGE CUSTOMS AND RITES

Snyder, Carol. Ike & Mama & the Block Wedding. Robinson, Charles, illus. LC 78-11702. (gr. 2-6). 1979. 7.95 (ISBN 0-698-20461-1, Coward). Putnam Pub Group.

MARRIAGE CUSTOMS AND RITES–FICTION

Lewin, Hugh. Jafta & the Wedding. Kopper, Lisa, illus. LC 82-12836. 24p. (ps-3). 1983. PLB 9.95 (ISBN 0-87614-210-2); pap. 3.95 (ISBN 0-87614-497-0). Carolrhoda Bks.

—Jafta & the Wedding. Kopper, Lisa, illus. 24p. (ps-3). 1989. pap. 3.95 (ISBN 0-685-24884-4, First Ave Edns). Lerner Pubns.

McCullers, Carson. Member of the Wedding. (gr. 9-12). 1985. pap. 3.50 (ISBN 0-553-25051-5). Bantam.

Peterson, John. The Littles Have a Wedding. Clark, Roberta C., illus. (gr. 4-6). 1972. pap. 2.25 (ISBN 0-590-32009-2). Scholastic Inc.

MARS (PLANET)

Asimov, Isaac. Mars: Our Mysterious Neighbor. LC 87-42599. (Illus.). (gr. 3-4). 1988. PLB 11.95 (ISBN 1-55532-354-5). Gareth Stevens Inc.

Baker, David. Exploring Mars. (Illus.). 48p. (gr. 3-8). 1987. PLB 18.60 (ISBN 0-86592-404-X). Rourke Corp.

British Museum, Geological Department Staff. Moon, Mars & Meteorites. (Illus.). 36p. (gr. 7 up). 1986. pap. 4.50 (ISBN 0-521-32414-9). Cambridge U Pr.

Corrick, James A. Mars. (Illus.). 128p. (gr. 7-12). 1991. PLB 12.40 (ISBN 0-531-12528-9). Watts.

Fradin, Dennis B. Mars. LC 88-39122. (Illus.). 48p. (gr. k-4). 1989. PLB 14.60 (ISBN 0-516-01164-2); pap. 4.95 (ISBN 0-516-41164-0). Childrens.

Landau, Elaine. Mars. (Illus.). 64p. (gr. 3-5). 1991. PLB 11.90 (ISBN 0-531-20012-4). Watts.

Selsam, Millicent E. & Hunt, Joyce. A First Look at Mars. 32p. (gr. 1-3). 1991. 11.95 (ISBN 0-8027-8135-7); PLB 12.85 (ISBN 0-8027-8136-5). Walker & Co.

Simon, Seymour. Mars. LC 86-31106. (Illus.). 32p. (ps-3). 1987. 13.00 (ISBN 0-688-06584-8); lib. bdg. 12.88 (ISBN 0-688-06585-6, Morrow Jr Bks). Morrow Jr Bks.

Vogt, Gregory. Mars & the Inner Planets. (Illus.). 72p. (gr. 4 up). 1982. PLB 10.40 (ISBN 0-531-04384-3). Watts.

Young, Ruth. A Trip to Mars. Cocca-Leffler, Maryann, illus. LC 89-70936. 32p. (ps-1). 1990. 14.95 (ISBN 0-531-05892-1); PLB 14.99 (ISBN 0-531-08492-2). Orchard Bks Watts.

MARS (PLANET)–FICTION

Hamilton, Virginia. Willie Bea & the Time the Martians Landed. LC 83-1659. 224p. (gr. 5-9). 1983. reinforced 14.00 (ISBN 0-688-02390-8). Greenwillow.

Pinkwater, Daniel. Alan Mendelsohn, the Boy from Mars. LC 78-12052. (gr. 4-7). 1979. 14.95 (ISBN 0-525-25360-2, DCB). Dutton Child Bks.

Williams, Geoff. Hello, Mars! (Illus.). 64p. (gr. 2-7). 1989. 10.95 (ISBN 0-8431-2733-3); incl. cassette 13.95 (ISBN 0-8431-2745-7). Price Stern.

MARSHALL, GEORGE CATLETT, 1880-1959

Lubetkin, Wendy. George Marshall. (Illus.). (gr. 5 up). 1990. 17.95 (ISBN 1-55546-843-8). Chelsea Hse.

MARSHALL, THURGOOD, 1908-

Hess, Debra. Thurgood Marshall: The Fight for Equal Justice. Gallin, Richard, ed. Young, Andrew, intro. by. (Illus.). 128p. (gr. 5 up). 1990. lib. bdg. 16.98 (ISBN 0-382-09921-4); pap. 7.95 (ISBN 0-382-24058-8). Silver Burdett Pr.

MARSHES

Caitlin, Stephen. Wonders of Swamps & Marshes. Watling, James, illus. LC 89-4967. 32p. (gr. 2-4). 1989. PLB 10.89 (ISBN 0-8167-1765-6); pap. text ed. 2.95 (ISBN 0-8167-1766-4). Troll Assocs.

Knowles, Eve. Amazing Marsh. Goldberg, Grace, illus. 48p. (gr. 3-5). 1988. 8.95 (ISBN 0-89272-259-2). Down East.

Liptak, Karen. Saving Our Wetlands & Their Wildlife. (Illus.). 64p. (gr. 5-8). 1991. PLB 11.90 (ISBN 0-531-20092-2). Watts.

Sabin, Francene. Swamps & Marshes. Flynn, Barbara, illus. LC 84-2717. 32p. (gr. 3-6). 1985. PLB 9.49 (ISBN 0-8167-0280-2); pap. text ed. 2.95 (ISBN 0-8167-0281-0). Troll Assocs.

MARSHES–FICTION

Dominick, Bayard. Joe, a Porpoise. (Illus.). (gr. 3-5). 1968. 10.95 (ISBN 0-8392-3067-2). Astor-Honor.

Edler, Timothy J. Coocan: Boy of the Swamp. (Illus.). 40p. (gr. k-8). 1983. pap. 6.00 (ISBN 0-931108-09-8). Little Cajun Bks.

—Dark Gator. (Illus.). 48p. (gr. k-8). 1980. pap. 6.00 (ISBN 0-931108-06-3). Little Cajun Bks.

MARSUPIALIA

Barrett, Norman. Kangaroos & Other Marsupials. (Illus.). 32p. (gr. k-4). 1991. PLB 11.40 (ISBN 0-531-14113-6). Watts.

MARTHA'S VINEYARD, MASSACHUSETTS–FICTION

Cross, Gilbert B. A Witch Across Time. LC 89-38474. 224p. (gr. 6-9). 1990. 14.95 (ISBN 0-689-31602-X, Atheneum Child Bk). Macmillan Child Grp.

MARTINIQUE–FICTION

Zobel, Joseph. Black Shack Alley. Warner, Keith Q., tr. from FRE. LC 78-13852. (Illus., Orig.). (gr. 9 up). 1980. case 18.00 (ISBN 0-914478-67-2); pap. 10.50 (ISBN 0-914478-68-0). Three Continents.

MARX, HEINRICH KARL, 1818-1883

Feinberg, Barbara S. Marx & Marxism. LC 85-11474. (Illus.). 128p. (gr. 7 up). 1985. PLB 12.90 (ISBN 0-531-10065-0). Watts.

Karl Marx. LC 86-73117. (Illus.). 32p. (gr. 1-6). 1987. lib. bdg. 11.90 (ISBN 0-531-18133-2, Pub. by Bookwright Pr). Watts.

MARXISM

see Communism

MARY, VIRGIN

Bodker, Cecil. Mary of Nazareth. 1989. 14.95 (ISBN 9-129-59178-3, Pub. by R & S Bks). FS&G.

Cutting, Edith. Mary, in Bethlehem. Hierstein, Judy, illus. 48p. (gr. 2-6). 1986. wkbk. 5.95 (ISBN 0-86653-370-2, SS 1812). Good Apple.

Hintze, Barbara. Mary: Mother of Jesus. Padgett, James R., illus. (gr. 1-6). 1977. bds. 5.95 (ISBN 0-8054-4232-4, 4242-32). Broadman.

Hronas, G. H. The Illustrated Life of the Theotokos for Children. 1990. pap. 4.95 (ISBN 0-937032-73-5). Light&Life Pub Co MN.

Mulqueen, Jack & Chatton, Ray. God's Mother Is My Mother. Chatton, Ray, illus. 28p. (Orig.). (gr. 1-3). 1978. pap. 2.50 (ISBN 0-913382-49-3, 103-13). Prow Bks-Franciscan.

Windeatt, Mary F. Our Lady of Banneux. Harmon, Gedge, illus. 32p. (gr. 1-5). 1989. Repr. of 1954 ed. wkbk. 3.00 (ISBN 0-89555-364-3). TAN Bks Pubs.

—Our Lady of Beauraing. Harmon, Gedge, illus. 32p. (gr. 1-5). 1989. Repr. of 1954 ed. wkbk. 3.00 (ISBN 0-89555-363-5). TAN Bks Pubs.

—Our Lady of Fatima. Harmon, Gedge, illus. 32p. (gr. 1-5). 1989. Repr. of 1954 ed. wkbk. 3.00 (ISBN 0-89555-357-0). TAN Bks Pubs.

—Our Lady of Guadalupe. Harmon, Gedge, illus. 32p. (gr. 1-5). 1989. Repr. of 1954 ed. wkbk. 3.00 (ISBN 0-89555-359-7). TAN Bks Pubs.

—Our Lady of Knock. Harmon, Gedge, illus. 32p. (gr. 1-5). 1989. Repr. of 1954 ed. wkbk. 3.00 (ISBN 0-89555-362-7). TAN Bks Pubs.

—Our Lady of la Salette. Harmon, Gedge, illus. 32p. (gr. 1-5). 1989. Repr. of 1954 ed. wkbk. 3.00 (ISBN 0-89555-361-9). TAN Bks Pubs.

—Our Lady of Lourdes. Harmon, Gedge, illus. 32p. (gr. 1-5). 1989. Repr. of 1954 ed. wkbk. 3.00 (ISBN 0-89555-358-9). TAN Bks Pubs.

—Our Lady of Pellevoisin. Harmon, Gedge, illus. 32p. (gr. 1-5). 1989. Repr. of 1954 ed. wkbk. 3.00 (ISBN 0-89555-366-X). TAN Bks Pubs.

—Our Lady of Pontmain. Harmon, Gedge, illus. 32p. (gr. 1-5). 1989. Repr. of 1954 ed. wkbk. 3.00 (ISBN 0-89555-365-1). TAN Bks Pubs.

—Our Lady of the Miraculous Medal. Harmon, Gedge, illus. 32p. (gr. 1-5). 1989. Repr. of 1954 ed. wkbk. 3.00 (ISBN 0-89555-360-0). TAN Bks Pubs.

MARY STUART, QUEEN OF THE SCOTS, 1542-1587–FICTION

Hunter, Mollie. You Never Knew Her As I Did! LC 81-47114. 224p. (gr. 7 up). 1981. 13.95 (ISBN 0-06-022678-1). HarpC Child Bks.

MARYLAND

Carpenter, Allan. Maryland. new ed. LC 78-14892. (Illus.). 96p. (gr. 4 up). 1979. PLB 19.93 (ISBN 0-516-04120-7). Childrens.

Eagen, Jane & McGinnis, Jeanne. Our Maryland. (Illus.). 288p. (gr. 4). 1987. 22.00 (ISBN 0-685-24530-6, Peregrine Smith). Gibbs Smith Pub.

Fradin, Dennis. Maryland: In Words & Pictures. LC 80-15185. (Illus.). 48p. (gr. 2-5). 1980. PLB 15.93 (ISBN 0-516-03920-2). Childrens.

Marsh, Carole. Avast, Ye Slobs! Maryland Pirate Trivia. (Illus.). (gr. 3-8). 1990. PLB 19.95 (ISBN 0-7933-0569-1); pap. 14.95 (ISBN 0-7933-0568-3); disk 29.95 (ISBN 0-7933-0570-5). Gallopade Pub Group.

—The Beast of the Maryland Bed & Breakfast. (Illus.). (gr. 3-8). 1990. PLB 19.95 (ISBN 0-7933-1690-1); pap. 14.95 (ISBN 0-7933-1691-X); disk 29.95 (ISBN 0-7933-1692-8). Gallopade Pub Group.

—The Hard-to-Believe-But-True! Book of Maryland History, Mystery, Trivia, Legend, Lore, Humor & More. (Illus.). (gr. 3-8). 1990. PLB 19.95 (ISBN 0-7933-0566-7); pap. 14.95 (ISBN 0-7933-0565-9); disk 29.95 (ISBN 0-7933-0567-5). Gallopade Pub Group.

—If My Maryland Mama Ran the World! (Illus.). (gr. 3-8). 1990. lib. bdg. 19.95 (ISBN 0-7933-1693-6); pap. 14.95 (ISBN 0-7933-1694-4); disk 29.95 (ISBN 0-7933-1695-2). Gallopade Pub Group.

—Let's Quilt Maryland & Stuff It Topographically! (Illus.). (gr. 3-8). 1990. PLB 19.95 (ISBN 1-55609-622-4); pap. 14.95 (ISBN 1-55609-058-7); disk 29.95 (ISBN 1-55609-623-2). Gallopade Pub Group.

—Maryland & Other State Greats (Biographies) (Illus.). (gr. 3-8). 1990. PLB 19.95 (ISBN 1-55609-636-4); pap. 14.95 (ISBN 1-55609-637-2); disk 29.95 (ISBN 1-55609-638-0). Gallopade Pub Group.

—Maryland Bandits, Bushwackers, Outlaws, Crooks, Devils, Ghosts, Desperadoes & Other Assorted & Sundry Characters! (Illus.). (gr. 3-8). 1990. PLB 19.95 (ISBN 0-7933-0551-9); pap. 14.95 (ISBN 0-7933-0550-0); disk 29.95 (ISBN 0-7933-0552-7). Gallopade Pub Group.

—Maryland Books, 19 bks. (Illus.). (gr. 3-8). 1990. Set. PLB 379.00 (ISBN 0-7933-1295-7). Gallopade Pub Group.

—Maryland Classic Christmas Trivia: Stories, Recipes, Activities, Legends, Lore & More! (Illus.). (gr. 3-8). 1990. PLB 19.95 (ISBN 0-7933-0554-3); pap. 14.95 (ISBN 0-7933-0553-5); disk 29.95 (ISBN 0-7933-0555-1). Gallopade Pub Group.

—Maryland Coastales. (Illus.). (gr. 3-8). 1990. PLB 19.95 (ISBN 1-55609-630-5); pap. 14.95 (ISBN 1-55609-631-3); disk 29.95 (ISBN 1-55609-632-1). Gallopade Pub Group.

—The Maryland Hot Air Balloon Mystery. (Illus.). (gr. 2-9). 1990. 19.95 (ISBN 0-7933-2498-X); pap. 14.95 (ISBN 0-7933-2499-8); computer disk 29.95 (ISBN 0-7933-2500-5). Gallopade Pub Group.

—Maryland "Jography" A Fun Run Thru Our State! (Illus.). (gr. 3-8). 1990. PLB 19.95 (ISBN 1-55609-619-4); pap. 14.95 (ISBN 1-55609-620-8); disk 29.95 (ISBN 1-55609-621-6). Gallopade Pub Group.

—Maryland Kid's Cookbook: Recipes, How-to, History, Lore & More! (Illus.). (gr. 3-8). 1990. PLB 19.95 (ISBN 0-7933-0563-2); pap. 14.95 (ISBN 0-7933-0562-4); disk 29.95 (ISBN 0-7933-0564-0). Gallopade Pub Group.

—Maryland Quiz Bowl Crash Course! (Illus.). (gr. 3-8). 1990. PLB 19.95 (ISBN 1-55609-633-X); pap. 14.95 (ISBN 1-55609-634-8); disk 29.95 (ISBN 1-55609-635-6). Gallopade Pub Group.

—Maryland School Trivia: An Amazing & Fascinating Look at Our State's Teachers, Schools & Students! (Illus.). (gr. 3-8). 1990. PLB 19.95 (ISBN 0-7933-0560-8); pap. 14.95 (ISBN 0-7933-0559-4); disk 29.95 (ISBN 0-7933-0561-6). Gallopade Pub Group.

—Maryland Silly Basketball Sportsmysteries, Vol. I. (Illus.). (gr. 3-8). 1990. PLB 19.95 (ISBN 0-7933-0557-8); pap. 14.95 (ISBN 0-7933-0556-X); disk 29.95 (ISBN 0-7933-0558-6). Gallopade Pub Group.

—Maryland Silly Basketball Sportsmysteries, Vol. II. (Illus.). (gr. 3-8). 1990. PLB 19.95 (ISBN 0-7933-1696-0); pap. 14.95 (ISBN 0-7933-1697-9); disk 29.95 (ISBN 0-7933-1698-7). Gallopade Pub Group.

—Maryland Silly Football Sportsmysteries, Vol. I. (Illus.). (gr. 3-8). 1990. PLB 19.95 (ISBN 1-55609-624-0); pap. 14.95 (ISBN 1-55609-625-9); disk 29.95 (ISBN 1-55609-626-7). Gallopade Pub Group.

—Maryland Silly Football Sportsmysteries, Vol. II. (Illus.). (gr. 3-8). 1990. PLB 19.95 (ISBN 1-55609-627-5); pap. 14.95 (ISBN 1-55609-628-3); disk 29.95 (ISBN 1-55609-629-1). Gallopade Pub Group.

—Maryland Silly Trivia! (Illus.). (gr. 3-8). 1990. PLB 19.95 (ISBN 1-55609-617-8); pap. 14.95 (ISBN 1-55609-042-0); disk 29.95 (ISBN 1-55609-618-6). Gallopade Pub Group.

Reef, Catherine. Baltimore. LC 89-25695. (Illus.). 60p. (gr. 3 up). 1990. 12.95 (ISBN 0-87518-427-8, Dillon); PLB 12.95 (ISBN 0-685-31388-3). Macmillan Child Grp.

Rollo, Vera F. A Geography of Maryland: Ask Me! (About Maryland) 188p. (gr. k-6). 1983. casebound 14.95 (ISBN 0-917882-10-5); tchrs. handbk. 8.00 (ISBN 0-686-96786-0). MD Hist Pr.

Seiden, Art. Michael Shows off Baltimore. Seiden, Art, illus 32p. (gr. 1-5). 1982. 5.95 (ISBN 0-942806-01-8). Outdoor Bks.

Turner Program Services, Inc. Staff & Clark, James I. Maryland. 48p. (gr. 3 up). 1985. PLB 17.32 (ISBN 0-86514-434-6); pap. text ed. 9.27 (ISBN 0-86514-509-1); cancelled Beta video (ISBN 0-86514-059-6); cancelled VHS video (ISBN 0-86514-134-7); cancelled 3/4" video (ISBN 0-86514-209-2); cancelled tchr's. guide (ISBN 0-86514-284-X); cancelled student activity bk. (ISBN 0-86514-359-5); cancelled index. Raintree Pubs.

Wilson, Richard & Bridner, E. L., Jr. Maryland: Its Past & Present. 234p. (gr. 4). 1987. casebound 16.75 (ISBN 0-917882-13-X). MD Hist Pr.

MARYLAND–HISTORY

Boyce-Ballweber, Hettie. The First People of Maryland. LC 87-61066. 110p. (gr. 1-6). 1987. casebound 15.00 (ISBN 0-917882-24-5). MD Hist Pr.

Fradin, Dennis B. The Maryland Colony. LC 90-2210. (Illus.). 160p. (gr. 4 up). 1990. PLB 22.60 (ISBN 0-516-00394-1). Childrens.

Marsh, Carole. Maryland's (Most Devastating!) Disasters & (Most Calamitous!) Catastrophies! (Illus.). (gr. 3-8). 1990. PLB 19.95 (ISBN 0-7933-0548-9); pap. 14.95 (ISBN 0-7933-0547-0); disk 29.95 (ISBN 0-7933-0549-7). Gallopade Pub Group.

Schaun, George & Schaun, Virginia. Everyday Life in Colonial Maryland. 130p. (gr. k-12). 1982. casebound 14.75 (ISBN 0-917882-11-3). MD Hist Pr.

Weinberg, Alyce T. Spirits of Frederick. LC 79-54039. (Illus.). 73p. (Orig.). 1979. pap. 3.95x (ISBN 0-9604552-0-5). A T Weinberg.

MASERS, OPTICAL

see Lasers

MASKS (FOR THE FACE)

Beaton, Clare. Make & Play: Masks. 1990. pap. 2.95 (ISBN 0-531-15163-8). Watts.

Gates, Frieda. Easy-to-Make Monster Masks & Disguises. (Illus.). (gr. 1-3). 1981. pap. 3.95 (ISBN 0-13-222794-0, Pub. by Treehouse). P-H.

Holroyd, Angela. The Big Book of Animal Masks. Anstey, David, illus 32p. (gr. k-4). 1990. heavy card 8.95 (ISBN 0-671-72580-7). S&S Trade.

—The Big Book of Monster Masks. Anstey, David, illus. 32p. (gr. k-4). 1990. heavy card 8.95 (ISBN 0-671-72579-3). S&S Trade.

Mah, Ronald. North America Animal Masks & Hats. Werges, Rosanne, ed. (Illus.). 48p. (Orig.). (gr. k-4). 1988. pap. 4.95 (ISBN 0-9615903-2-7). Symbiosis Bks.

Supraner, Robyn. Great Masks to Make. Barto, Renzo, illus. LC 80-24077. 48p. (gr. 1-5). 1981. PLB 11.89 (ISBN 0-89375-436-6); pap. 2.95 (ISBN 0-89375-437-4). Troll Assocs.

Terry, Ellen & Anderson, Lynne. Makeup & Masks. rev. ed. LC 78-139744. 112p. (gr. 7 up). 1982. PLB 14.95 (ISBN 0-8239-0232-3). Rosen Group.

Valat, Pierre-Marie. Animal Faces: Fifteen Punch-Out Masks. (Illus.). 32p. (ps up). 1988. pap. 14.95 (ISBN 0-525-44440-8, DCB). Dutton Child Bks.

MASONRY

Boy Scouts of America. Masonry. (Illus.). 64p. (gr. 6-12). 1980. pap. 1.85 (ISBN 0-8395-3339-X, 3339). BSA.

MASS COMMUNICATION

see Communication

MASSACHUSETTS

Carpenter, Allan. Massachusetts. new ed. LC 78-3785. (Illus.). 96p. (gr. 4 up). 1978. PLB 19.93 (ISBN 0-516-04121-5). Childrens.

Fradin, Dennis. Massachusetts: In Words & Pictures. Wahl, Richard, illus. LC 80-26161. 48p. (gr. 2-5). 1981. PLB 15.93 (ISBN 0-516-03921-0); pap. 4.95 (ISBN 0-516-43921-9). Childrens.

Kent, Deborah. Massachusetts. LC 87-9402. (Illus.). 144p. (gr. 4 up). 1987. PLB 25.27 (ISBN 0-516-00467-0). Childrens.

Marsh, Carole. Avast, Ye Slobs! Massachusetts Pirate Trivia. (Illus.). (gr. 3-8). 1990. PLB 19.95 (ISBN 0-7933-0593-4); pap. 14.95 (ISBN 0-7933-0592-6); disk 29.95 (ISBN 0-7933-0594-2). Gallopade Pub Group.

—The Beast of the Massachusetts Bed & Breakfast. (Illus.). (gr. 3-8). 1990. PLB 19.95 (ISBN 0-7933-1699-5); pap. 14.95 (ISBN 0-7933-1700-2); disk 29.95 (ISBN 0-7933-1701-0). Gallopade Pub Group.

—Carole Marsh Massachusetts Books, 31 bks. (Illus.). (gr. 3-8). 1990. Set. PLB 638.45 (ISBN 0-7933-1296-5). Gallopade Pub Group.

—The Hard-to-Believe-But-True! Book of Massachusetts History, Mystery, Trivia, Legend, Lore, Humor & More. (Illus.). (gr. 3-8). 1990. PLB 19.95 (ISBN 0-7933-0590-X); pap. 14.95 (ISBN 0-7933-0589-6); disk 29.95 (ISBN 0-7933-0591-8). Gallopade Pub Group.

—If My Massachusetts Mama Ran the World! (Illus.). (gr. 3-8). 1990. lib. bdg. 19.95 (ISBN 0-7933-1702-9); pap. 14.95 (ISBN 0-7933-1703-7); disk 29.95 (ISBN 0-7933-1704-5). Gallopade Pub Group.

—Let's Quilt Massachusetts & Stuff It Topographically! (Illus.). (gr. 3-8). 1990. PLB 19.95 (ISBN 1-55609-684-4); pap. 14.95 (ISBN 1-55609-685-2); disk 29.95 (ISBN 1-55609-686-0). Gallopade Pub Group.

—Massachusetts & Other State Greats (Biographies) (Illus.). (gr. 3-8). 1990. PLB 19.95 (ISBN 1-55609-699-2); pap. 14.95 (ISBN 1-55609-700-X); disk 29.95 (ISBN 1-55609-701-8). Gallopade Pub Group.

—Massachusetts Bandits, Bushwackers, Outlaws, Crooks, Devils, Ghosts, Desperadoes & Other Assorted & Sundry Characters! (Illus.). (gr. 3-8). 1990. PLB 19.95 (ISBN 0-7933-0575-6); pap. 14.95 (ISBN 0-7933-0574-8); disk 29.95 (ISBN 0-7933-0576-4). Gallopade Pub Group.

—Massachusetts Classic Christmas Trivia: Stories, Recipes, Activities, Legends, Lore & More! (Illus.). (gr. 3-8). 1990. PLB 19.95 (ISBN 0-7933-0578-0); pap. 14.95 (ISBN 0-7933-0577-2); disk 29.95 (ISBN 0-7933-0579-9). Gallopade Pub Group.

—Massachusetts Coastales. (Illus.). (gr. 3-8). 1990. PLB 19.95 (ISBN 1-55609-693-3); pap. 14.95 (ISBN 1-55609-694-1); disk 29.95 (ISBN 1-55609-695-X). Gallopade Pub Group.

—The Massachusetts Hot Air Balloon Mystery. (Illus.). (gr. 2-9). 1990. 19.95 (ISBN 0-7933-2507-2); pap. 14.95 (ISBN 0-7933-2508-0); computer disk 29.95 (ISBN 0-7933-2509-9). Gallopade Pub Group.

—Massachusetts "Jography" A Fun Run Thru Our State! (Illus.). (gr. 3-8). 1990. PLB 19.95 (ISBN 1-55609-682-8); pap. 14.95 (ISBN 1-55609-111-7); disk 29.95 (ISBN 1-55609-683-6). Gallopade Pub Group.

—Massachusetts Kid's Cookbook: Recipes, How-to, History, Lore & More! (Illus.). (gr. 3-8). 1990. PLB 19.95 (ISBN 0-7933-0587-X); pap. 14.95 (ISBN 0-7933-0586-1); disk 29.95 (ISBN 0-7933-0588-8). Gallopade Pub Group.

—Massachusetts' (Most Devastating!) Disasters & (Most Calamitous!) Catastrophies! (Illus.). (gr. 3-8). 1990. PLB 19.95 (ISBN 0-7933-0572-1); pap. 14.95 (ISBN 0-7933-0571-3); disk 29.95 (ISBN 0-7933-0573-X). Gallopade Pub Group.

—Massachusetts Quiz Bowl Crash Course! (Illus.). (gr. 3-8). 1990. PLB 19.95 (ISBN 1-55609-696-8); pap. 14.95 (ISBN 1-55609-697-6); disk 29.95 (ISBN 1-55609-698-4). Gallopade Pub Group.

—Massachusetts School Trivia: An Amazing & Fascinating Look at Our State's Teachers, Schools & Students! (Illus.). (gr. 3-8). 1990. PLB 19.95 (ISBN 0-7933-0584-5); pap. 14.95 (ISBN 0-7933-0583-7); disk 29.95 (ISBN 0-7933-0585-3). Gallopade Pub Group.

—Massachusetts Silly Basketball Sportsmysteries, Vol. I. (Illus.). (gr. 3-8). 1990. PLB 19.95 (ISBN 0-7933-0581-0); pap. 14.95 (ISBN 0-7933-0580-2); disk 29.95 (ISBN 0-7933-0582-9). Gallopade Pub Group.

—Massachusetts Silly Basketball Sportsmysteries, Vol. II. (Illus.). (gr. 3-8). 1990. PLB 19.95 (ISBN 0-7933-1705-3); pap. 14.95 (ISBN 0-7933-1706-1); disk 29.95 (ISBN 0-7933-1707-X). Gallopade Pub Group.

—Massachusetts Silly Football Sportsmysteries, Vol. I. (Illus.). (gr. 3-8). 1990. PLB 19.95 (ISBN 1-55609-687-9); pap. 14.95 (ISBN 1-55609-688-7); disk 29.95 (ISBN 1-55609-689-5). Gallopade Pub Group.

—Massachusetts Silly Football Sportsmysteries, Vol. II. (Illus.). (gr. 3-8). 1990. PLB 19.95 (ISBN 1-55609-690-9); pap. 14.95 (ISBN 1-55609-691-7); disk 29.95 (ISBN 1-55609-692-5). Gallopade Pub Group.

—Massachusetts Silly Trivia! (Illus.). (gr. 3-8). 1990. PLB 19.95 (ISBN 1-55609-680-1); pap. 14.95 (ISBN 1-55609-110-9); disk 29.95 (ISBN 1-55609-681-X). Gallopade Pub Group.

Norton, Bettina A. Neighborhood Trivia Hunt for Concord, Massachusetts. (Illus.). 20p. (gr. 7-12). 1985. pap. 4.95 (ISBN 0-938357-02-6). BAN Pub Boston.

Turner Program Services, Inc. Staff & Clark, James I. Massachusetts. LC 85-11915. 48p. (gr. 3 up). 1985. PLB 17.32 (ISBN 0-86514-435-4); pap. text ed. 9.27 (ISBN 0-86514-510-5); cancelled Beta video (ISBN 0-86514-060-X); cancelled VHS video (ISBN 0-86514-135-5); cancelled 3/4" video (ISBN 0-86514-210-6); cancelled tchr's. guide (ISBN 0-86514-285-8); cancelled student activity bk. (ISBN 0-86514-360-9); cancelled index. Raintree Pubs.

MASSACHUSETTS–FICTION

Christian, Mary B. Goody Sherman's Pig. Zimmer, Dirk, illus. LC 90-35181. 48p. (gr. 2-6). 1991. RSBE 12.95 (ISBN 0-02-718251-7, Mcmillan Child Bk). Macmillan Child Grp.

Corcoran, Barbara. The Hideaway. LC 86-28849. 128p. (gr. 5-9). 1987. 12.95 (ISBN 0-689-31353-5, Atheneum Child Bk). Macmillan Child Grp.

MASSACHUSETTS–HISTORY

Anderson, Joan. The First Thanksgiving Feast. Ancona, George, photos by. LC 84-5803. (Illus.). 48p. (gr. 2-6). 1984. 14.95 (ISBN 0-89919-287-4, Clarion). HM.

MASSACHUSETTS–HISTORY–COLONIAL PERIOD

Fradin, Dennis B. The Massachusetts Colony. LC 86-9753. (Illus.). 160p. (gr. 4 up). 1986. PLB 22.60 (ISBN 0-516-00386-0). Childrens.

Payne, Elizabeth. Meet the Pilgrim Fathers. Vestal, H. B., illus. (gr. 4 up). 1966. lib. bdg. 8.99 (ISBN 0-394-90063-4, Random Juv). Random.

MASSACHUSETTS–HISTORY–FICTION

Daugherty, James. The Landing of the Pilgrims. LC 80-21430. (Illus.). 160p. (gr. 5-9). 1981. PLB 7.99 (ISBN 0-685-04232-4, Random Juv); pap. 3.95 (ISBN 0-394-84697-4). Random.

Fritz, Jean. Early Thunder. Ward, Lynd, illus. LC 67-24217. (gr. 7-11). 1967. 9.95 (ISBN 0-698-20036-5, Coward). Putnam Pub Group.

Smith, Mary P. Boy Captive of Old Deerfield. (Illus.). (gr. 5-6). Repr. of 1904 ed. lib. bdg. 17.95x (ISBN 0-89190-961-3, Pub. by River City Pr). Amereon Ltd.

—Boys & Girls of Seventy-Seven. 2nd ed. Silvester, Susan B., ed. Grunwald, C., illus. LC 86-30607. 333p. (gr. 5 up). 1987. Repr. of 1909 ed. 14.00 (ISBN 0-913993-08-5). Paideia MA.

MATERIA MEDICA

see also Poisons

MATERIALS

Jennings, Terry. Materials. LC 88-22884. (Illus.). 32p. (gr. 3-6). 1989. PLB 14.60 (ISBN 0-516-08405-4); pap. 4.95 (ISBN 0-516-48405-2). Childrens.

Laithwaite, Eric. Using Materials. Franklin Watts Ltd., ed. (Illus.). 32p. (gr. 4-9). 1988. 11.90 (ISBN 0-531-10264-5). Watts.

Riley, Peter D. Materials. (Illus.). 48p. (gr. 7-12). 1986. 17.95 (ISBN 0-85219-628-8, Pub. by Batsford England). Trafalgar Sq.

Taylor, Barbara. Structures & Materials. (Illus.). 32p. (gr. 5-8). 1991. PLB 11.40 (ISBN 0-531-14186-1). Watts.

MATERNITY

see Mothers

MATHEMATICAL DRAWING

see Geometrical Drawing; Mechanical Drawing

MATHEMATICAL RECREATIONS

Arnold, Carolyn. Measurements: Fun, Facts & Activities. Johnson, Pamela, illus. LC 84-7555. 32p. (gr. k-4). 1984. lib. bdg. 11.90 (ISBN 0-531-04721-0). Watts.

Aten, Jerry. Good Apple & Math Fun. 144p. (gr. 3-7). 1981. 10.95 (ISBN 0-86653-023-1, GA 279). Good Apple.

Bernstein, Bob. Math Thinking Motivators. 96p. (gr. 2-7). 1988. wkbk. 9.95 (ISBN 0-86653-431-8, GA1049). Good Apple.

Blum, Raymond. Mathemagic. Sinclair, Jeff, illus. 128p. (gr. 4-11). 1991. 12.95 (ISBN 0-8069-8354-X). Sterling.

Bureloff, Morris & Johnson, Connie. Calculators, Number Patterns, & Magic. Roes, Ruth, illus. (gr. 4-12). 1977. pap. text ed. 6.95 (ISBN 0-918932-49-1). Activity Resources.

Burns, Marilyn. The I Hate Mathematics! Book. Hairston, Martha, illus. 128p. (gr. 5 up). 1975. 14.95 (ISBN 0-316-11740-4); pap. 8.95 (ISBN 0-316-11741-2). Little.

Carroll, Lewis. A Tangled Tale. LC 74-82735. 1975. 4.95 (ISBN 0-89388-181-3). Okpaku Communications.

—A Tangled Tale. Frost, Arthur B., illus. LC 87-50437. 208p. (gr. 5-12). 1987. pap. 7.95 (ISBN 0-940561-06-9). White Rose Pr.

Daniel, Becky. Math Thinker Sheets. 64p. (gr. 4-8). 1988. wkbk. 7.95 (ISBN 0-86653-429-6, GA1036). Good Apple.
Dobson, Eileen. The First Maths Games File. 40p. (ps-4). 1986. pap. 7.25 (ISBN 0-906212-42-1, Tarquin). Parkwest Pubns.
Edmiston, Margaret. Merlin Book of Logic Puzzles. (Illus.). 128p. (gr. 4-11). 1991. 12.95 (ISBN 0-8069-8220-9). Sterling.
Egsgard, John, et al. Making Connections: With Mathematics. (Illus.). 102p. (gr. 9-12). 1989. pap. 19.95 (ISBN 0-939765-27-6, G116). Janson Pubns.
Friedhoffer. More Magic Tricks, Science Facts. Kaufman, Richard, illus. White, Timothy, photos by. (Illus.). 128p. (gr. 5-8). 1990. PLB 12.90 (ISBN 0-531-10969-0). Watts.
Giblin, Peter, ed. Mathematical Challenges: Puzzles & Problems in Secondary School Mathematics. (Illus.). 59p. (gr. 9-12). 1989. pap. 17.50 (ISBN 0-939765-28-4, G118). Janson Pubns.
Hewavisenti, Latshmi. Counting. (Illus.). 32p. (gr. k-4). 1991. PLB 11.40 (ISBN 0-531-17266-X, Gloucester Pr). Watts.
McCarthy, Donald. Fun with Math-E-Magic. Cooper, William H., ed. McCarthy, Donald W., illus. 65p. (gr. 4-9). pap. 2.60 (ISBN 0-914127-01-2). Univ Class.
Sachar, Louis. Sideways Arithmetic from Wayside School. 1989. pap. 2.75 (ISBN 0-590-42416-5). Scholastic Inc.
Spizman, Robyn. Bulletin Boards: To Reinforce Basic Math Skills. Pesiri, Evelyn, illus. 64p. (gr. k-6). 1984. wkbk. 6.95 (ISBN 0-86653-208-0, GA 573). Good Apple.

MATHEMATICAL SETS
see Set Theory

MATHEMATICS
see also Algebra; Arithmetic; Binary System (Mathematics); Calculus; Geometry; Mechanics; Mensuration; Numbers Theory; Set Theory

Addition. (Illus.). (gr. 1-3). 3.50 (ISBN 0-7214-0704-8). Ladybird Bks.
Adler, Irving. Mathematics. (gr. 4-7). 1990. 11.95 (ISBN 0-385-26142-X); PLB 12.99 (ISBN 0-385-26143-8). Doubleday.
Alberti, Delbert & Mason, George. Laboratory Laughter. Firmhand, Zelda, illus. (Orig.). (gr. 2-9). 1974. pap. 6.95 (ISBN 0-918932-25-4). Activity Resources.
Allasio, John, et al. Sequential Math 2: A Workbook. 141p. (gr. 9-12). 1990. pap. 6.95 (ISBN 0-937820-65-2); answer key 2.74 (ISBN 0-937820-66-0). Westsea Pub.
Anno, Mitsumasa. Anno's Math Games. 104p. (ps-3). 1987. 18.95 (ISBN 0-399-21151-9, Philomel Bks). Putnam Pub Group.
—Anno's Math Games II. Anno, Mitsumasa, illus. 104p. (gr. 1-4). 1989. 19.95 (ISBN 0-399-21615-4, Philomel Bks). Putnam Pub Group.
Armstrong, Bev. Math a la Mode. (gr. 3-4). 1979. pap. 3.95 (ISBN 0-88160-064-4, LW 704). Learning Wks.
—The Subtraction Submarine. (gr. 1-2). 1979. pap. 3.95 (ISBN 0-88160-062-8, LW 702). Learning Wks.
Aten, Jerry. Prime Time Math Skills. Filkins, Vanessa, illus. 64p. (gr. 2-5). 1984. wkbk 6.95 (ISBN 0-86653-155-6, GA 524). Good Apple.
Aydelott, Jimmie. Art & Math Throughout the Year. (gr. 1-6). 1989. pap. 6.95 (ISBN 0-8224-0104-5). Fearon Teach Aids.
Azzolino, Agnes. Math Games for the Young Child. Vinik, Michael, illus. (Orig.). (ps-2). 1987. pap. text ed. 8.40 (ISBN 0-9623593-1-9). Mathematical.
Bank Street College of Education Editors. Let's Do Math. (gr. 1-2). 1986. pap. 3.95 (ISBN 0-8120-3627-1). Barron.
Bartch, Marian R. & Mallett, Jerry J. Math Motivators: Puzzles, Games, Bulletin Boards & Special Motivators, 2 vols. (gr. 1-6). 1986. pap. 7.95 ea. Vol. I, Gr. 1-3 (ISBN 0-673-18264-9). Vol. II, Gr. 4-6 (ISBN 0-673-18265-7). Scott F.
Becker, Jan, et al. Enhance Chance. (Illus., Orig.). (gr. k-9). 1973. pap. 6.95 (ISBN 0-918932-10-6). Activity Resources.
Bernstein, Bob. Mathemactivities. 112p. (gr. 2-7). 1991. 9.95 (ISBN 0-86653-617-5, GA1336). Good Apple.
Bogad, Carolyn. Fraction Fantasy. (gr. 5-7). 1979. pap. 3.95 (ISBN 0-88160-067-9, LW 707). Learning Wks.
Book of Tables (Multiplication) (Illus.). (gr. 1-3). 3.50 (ISBN 0-7214-0663-7). Ladybird Bks.
Booth, Eugene. In the Garden. LC 77-7628. (Illus.). 24p. (gr. k-3). 1977. PLB 13.32 (ISBN 0-8393-0115-4). Raintree Pubs.
Broekel, Ray. Word Problems: Grades 5-6 Math. Hoffman, Joan, ed. Cook, Chris, illus. 32p. (gr. 5-6). 1981. wkbk. 1.99 (ISBN 0-938256-42-4). Sch Zone Pub Co.
Brooks, L., et al. Business Mathematics. 10th ed. 576p. (gr. 9-12). 1987. text ed. 24.96 (ISBN 0-07-008166-2). McGraw.
Burma, Marcay & Schroeder, Mary A. Math in Bloom (Addition & Subtraction) (gr. 1-4). 1989. spiral wkbk. 39.95 (ISBN 1-55999-058-9). LinguiSystems.
—Math in Bloom (Multiplication & Division) (gr. 2-6). 1989. spiral wkbk. 39.95 (ISBN 1-55999-059-7). LinguiSystems.
Burns, Marilyn. Math for Smarty Pants: Or Who Says Mathematicians Have Little Pig Eyes. Weston, Martha, illus. 140p. (gr. 7 up). 1982. 14.95 (ISBN 0-316-11738-2); pap. 8.95 (ISBN 0-316-11739-0). Little.
Capretta, Laura. Beginning Math Skills 1-10. Carson, Patti & Dellosa, Janet, illus. 32p. (ps-1). 1984. pap. 1.98 (ISBN 0-88724-089-5, CD-7028). Carson-Dellos.
Clark, Clara E. A Tangram Diary. (Illus.). 64p. (Orig.). (gr. 3-6). 1980. pap. 6.95 (ISBN 0-934734-05-4). Construct Educ.
Clark, Clara E. & Sternberg, Betty J. Math in Stride, Bk. 1. (Illus.). 166p. (Orig.). (gr. k-2). 1980. pap. 5.95 (ISBN 0-934734-06-2); tchr's. manual 19.95 (ISBN 0-934734-12-7). Construct Educ.
—Math in Stride, Bk. 2. (Illus.). 203p. (Orig.). (gr. 1-3). 1980. pap. 6.50 (ISBN 0-934734-07-0); tchr's. manual 19.95 (ISBN 0-934734-13-5). Construct Educ.
—Math in Stride, Bk. 3. (Illus.). 219p. (Orig.). (gr. 2-4). 1980. pap. 6.95 (ISBN 0-934734-08-9). Construct Educ.
CMSP Projects. Applied Math Concepts: Lines & Perimeters Area & Volume. rev. ed. (Illus.). 91p. pap. text ed. write for info. (ISBN 0-942851-01-3). CMSP Projects.
Cook, Sue C. The Numbers Book: Student Syllabus, 2 vols. (gr. k-2). 1974. Vol. 1. pap. text ed. 11.85 ea. packs of 10 (ISBN 0-89420-081-X, 193050); Vol. 2. pap. text ed. 11.85 ea. packs of 10 (ISBN 0-89420-082-8, 193051); cass. recordings 17.38 (ISBN 0-89420-208-1, 193000). Natl Book.
Cornwall, Susan. Mathematical Manka. Firmhand, Zelda, illus. (gr. 1-9). 1974. pap. 6.95 (ISBN 0-918932-29-7). Activity Resources.
Cotter, Joan A. Worksheets for the Abacus, Complete Volume. (Illus.). 320p. (gr. k-4). 1990. 24.95 (ISBN 0-9609636-6-9). Activities Learning.
Craig, Linda & Praytor, Phyllis. Criterion Referenced Test Kit: Math. Reed, Tom, illus. 54p. (gr. 4). 1978. write for info. (ISBN 0-936394-01-3). Education Serv.
Crary, Elizabeth. My Name Is Not Dummy. Horosko, Marina M., illus. LC 83-24983. 32p. (Orig.). (ps-2). 1983. PLB 14.95 (ISBN 0-9602862-9-2); pap. 4.95 (ISBN 0-9602862-8-4). Parenting Pr.
Cutting, Brian & Cutting, Jillian. Fact & Fantasy Math - Emergent Level: Captain B's Ark; Math Is Everywhere & Sunshine Street, 3 bks. (Illus.). 48p. (gr. k-1). Set. pap. text ed. 8.20 (ISBN 1-55911-026-0). Wright Group.
Daniel, Becky. Hooray for the Big Book of Math Facts! 288p. (gr. 1-4). 1990. 24.95 (ISBN 0-86653-533-0, GA1148). Good Apple.
—Math Brainstorms. 80p. (gr. 1-4). 1990. 7.95 (ISBN 0-86653-565-9, GA1170). Good Apple.
Daniel, Becky & Daniel, Charlie. Big Addition Book. 64p. (gr. k-3). 1979. 6.95 (ISBN 0-916456-44-7, GA118). Good Apple.
—Big Subtraction Book. 64p. (gr. k-3). 1979. 6.95 (ISBN 0-916456-43-9, GA117). Good Apple.
—The Division Book. 64p. (gr. 3-6). 1980. 6.95 (ISBN 0-916456-77-3, GA 190). Good Apple.
—The Multiplication Book. 64p. (gr. 2-6). 1980. 6.95 (ISBN 0-916456-76-5, GA 191). Good Apple.
Davis, Richard C., et al. Rational Numbers Study Aid. 1976. pap. 3.00 (ISBN 0-87738-039-2). Youth Ed.
Dellosa, Janet & Carson, Patti. Matching: Similarities & Differences. Dellosa, Janet & Carson, Patti, illus. 32p. (ps-1). 1983. pap 1.98 (ISBN 0-88724-010-0, CD-7011). Carson-Dellos.
Dirkes, M. Ann. Math Through Creative Thinking. Zilliox, Elaine, ed. (Illus.). 44p. (Orig.). (gr. 4-12). 1984. 5.95 (ISBN 0-88047-034-8, 7707). DOK Pubs.
Division. (Illus.). (gr. 1-3). 3.50 (ISBN 0-7214-0707-2). Ladybird Bks.
Duncan, Jim. Practical Math Skills - Intermediate Level. Tom, Darcy, illus. 64p. (gr. 4-6). 1989. wkbk. 6.95 (ISBN 0-86653-465-2, GA1070). Good Apple.
—Practical Math Skills - Junior High Level. Tom, Darcy, illus. 64p. (gr. 7-9). 1989. wkbk. 6.95 (ISBN 0-86653-466-0, GA1071). Good Apple.
—Practical Math Skills - Primary Level. Tom, Darcy, illus. 64p. (gr. 1-3). 1989. wkbk. 6.95 (ISBN 0-86653-464-4, GA1069). Good Apple.
Dunn, Patricia. Math Trivial Pursuit - Intermediate Level. Dunn, Patricia, illus. 64p. (gr. 4-6). 1989. wkbk. 9.95 (ISBN 0-86653-468-7, GA1073). Good Apple.
—Math Trivial Pursuit - Junior High Level. Dunn, Patricia, illus. 64p. (gr. 7-9). 1989. wkbk. 9.95 (ISBN 0-86653-469-5, GA1074). Good Apple.
—Math Trivial Pursuit - Primary Level. Dunn, Patricia, illus. 64p. (gr. 1-3). 1989. wkbk. 9.95 (ISBN 0-86653-492-X, GA1072). Good Apple.
Ecker, Michael W. Getting Started in Problem Solving & Math Contests. 128p. (gr. 7-12). 1987. PLB 11.90 (ISBN 0-531-10342-0). Watts.
Eicholz, Robert, et al. Extending the Ideas Enrichment Workbook. 2nd ed. (gr. 4). 1980. pap. text ed. write for info. (ISBN 0-201-16035-8); pap. text ed. write for info. (ISBN 0-201-16045-5); Grade 4. write for info. tchr's ed. (ISBN 0-201-16046-3). Addison-Wesley.
—Extending the Ideas Enrichment Workbook. 2nd ed. (gr. 5-6). 1980. pap. text ed. write for info. (ISBN 0-201-16055-2); Grade 5. write for info. tchr's ed. (ISBN 0-201-16056-0); pap. text ed. write for info. (ISBN 0-201-16065-X); Grade 6. write for info. tchr's ed. (201-16066). Addison-Wesley.
Erdtmann, Greta. The Path to Math. Erdtmann, Greta, illus. Doman, Glenn, intro. by. (Illus.). 60p. (ps). 1981. 8.95 (ISBN 0-936676-11-6). Better Baby.
Erickson, Tim. Get It Together: Math Problems for Groups Grades 4-12. Craig, Rose & Noll, Sally, illus. 180p. (Orig.). 1989. pap. 15.00 (ISBN 0-912511-53-2). Lawrence Science.
Fekete, Irene & Denyer, Jamine. Mathematics. (Illus.). 64p. (gr. 7 up). 15.95 (ISBN 0-87196-990-4). Facts on File.
Figure It Out. (Illus.). 24p. (Orig.). (gr. 1-5). 1989. 4.95 (ISBN 0-8431-3161-6); Super Q Wand 11.00 (ISBN 0-318-39946-6). Price Stern.
Finnegan, Thomas J., et al. Mathematics Study Aid. 1975. pap. 2.50 (ISBN 0-87738-036-8). Youth Ed.
Forsthoefel, John. Utilizing Problem Solving in Math. Zilliox, Elaine, illus. 40p. (Orig.). (gr. 3-8). 1984. 5.95 (ISBN 0-88047-039-9, 8405). DOK Pubs.
Frank, Marjorie. The Kids' Stuff: Book of Math for the Middle Grades. (Illus.). 240p. (gr. 4-6). 1988. pap. text ed. 14.95 (ISBN 0-86530-012-7, IP 13-1). Incentive Pubns.
—The Kids' Stuff: Book of Math for the Primary Grades. (Illus.). 240p. (gr. 1-3). 1988. pap. text ed. 14.95 (ISBN 0-86530-040-2, IP 13-0). Incentive Pubns.
Gillham, Bill & Hulme, Susan. Let's Look for Numbers. Siegieda, Jan, illus. & photos by LC 83-24066. 24p. (ps-1). 1984. 4.95 (ISBN 0-698-20613-4, Putnam). Putnam Pub Group.
Glover, Suzanne & Grewe, Georgeann. Math Magic. (gr. 3-6). 1982. pap. 9.95 (ISBN 0-88160-047-4, LW 232). Learning Wks.
Goodwin, Irene & Silvers, Ruth. Polka Dotted Pencil Pushers: Math. Goodwin, Irene, illus. LC 79-63129. 156p. (Orig.). 1979. pap. 8.95 tchr's. guide (ISBN 0-932970-08-7). Prinit Pr.
Greenes, Carole, et al. Mathletics: Gold Medal Problems. (Illus.). 149p. (gr. 8-10). 1989. pap. 19.95 (ISBN 0-939765-31-4, G119). Janson Pubns.
Gregorich, Barbara. Basic Math. Hoffman, Joan, ed. Koontz, Robin M., illus. 32p. (gr. 1). 1988. wkbk. 1.49 (ISBN 0-88743-162-3). Sch Zone Pub Co.
—Basic Math. Hoffman, Joan, ed. Koontz, Robin M., illus. 32p. (gr. 2). 1988. wkbk. 1.49 (ISBN 0-88743-168-2). Sch Zone Pub Co.
—Basic Math: First Grade. Hoffman, Joan, ed. Koontz, Robin M., illus. 32p. (gr. 1). 1990. wkbk. 3.49 (ISBN 0-88743-181-X). Sch Zone Pub Co.
—Basic Math: Second Grade. Hoffman, Joan, ed. Koontz, Robin M., illus. 32p. (gr. 2). 1990. wkbk. 3.49 (ISBN 0-88743-187-9). Sch Zone Pub Co.
—Word Problems: Grades 1-2 Math. Hoffman, Joan, ed. Cook, Chris, illus. 32p. (gr. 1-2). 1982. wkbk. 1.99 (ISBN 0-938256-45-9). Sch Zone Pub Co.
—Word Problems: Grades 3-4 Math. Hoffman, Joan, ed. Cook, Chris, illus. 32p. (gr. 3-4). 1982. wkbk. 1.99 (ISBN 0-938256-46-7). Sch Zone Pub Co.
Griesbach, Ellen & Taylor, Jerry. The Prentice-Hall Encyclopedia of Mathematics. Taylor, Louis, ed. (Illus., Orig.). (gr. 6 up). 1982. 39.50 (ISBN 0-13-696013-8). P-H.
Grimm, Gary & Mitchell, Don. Good Apple Math Book. 220p. (gr. 3-8). 1975. 13.95 (ISBN 0-916456-00-5, GA59). Good Apple.
Guy, Richard K. Fair Game: How to Play Impartial Combinatorial Games. Malkevitch, Joseph, ed. Joliffe, Dale, illus. 113p. (Orig.). (gr. 9-12). 1989. pap. text ed. 12.95 (ISBN 0-912843-16-0). COMAP Inc.
Hamilton, Sally & Fenelon, Robert. Math Manor. 48p. (gr. 4-6). 1982. 5.95 (ISBN 0-88160-050-4, LW 236). Learning Wks.
Haugo, John E. Math Regrouping Games: Apple Set. 32p. (gr. 4-6). 1982. Set. 71.92 (ISBN 0-07-079118-X). McGraw.
—Math Regrouping Games: TRS-80 Model III Set. (Illus.). 32p. (gr. 4-6). 1982. Set. 71.92 (ISBN 0-07-079224-0). McGraw.
—Math Skill Games: Apple Set. (Illus.). 40p. (gr. 4-6). 1982. Set. 71.92 (ISBN 0-07-079116-3). McGraw.
—Math Skill Games: TRS-80 Model III Set. Kovaleik, Terry, illus. 40p. (gr. 4-6). 1982. Set. 71.92 (ISBN 0-07-079222-4). McGraw.
Hawkins, Colin. Adding Animals. (Illus.). 12p. (ps-1). 1983. 9.95 (ISBN 0-399-20940-9, Putnam). Putnam Pub Group.
Heath, Royal V. Mathemagic: Magic, Puzzles & Games with Numbers. (Illus.). 128p. (gr. 2 up). pap. 3.95 (ISBN 0-486-20110-4). Dover.
Henrich, Stephen & Henrich, Jean. Adventure Math, No. 1: Addition & Subtraction. (Illus.). 80p. (Orig.). 1988. pap. write for info. wkbk. (HE 600). Henrich Enter.
—Adventure Math, No. 2: Multiplication & Division. Henrich, Jean, illus. 80p. (Orig.). (gr. 4-12). 1988. pap. write for info. (HE 700). Henrich Enter.
—Story Starters on Colonial-Revolutionary America. rev. ed. (Illus.). 80p. (gr. 4-12). 1988. write for info. wkbk. (HE 200). Henrich Enter.
Hewavisenti, Latshmi. Problem Solving. (Illus.). 32p. (gr. k-4). 1991. PLB 11.40 (ISBN 0-531-17318-6, Gloucester Pr). Watts.
Hodges, et al. Basic Studies: Understanding Mathematics. rev. ed. 165p. (gr. 4-8). 1988. pap. text ed. 15.00 (ISBN 0-913310-30-1). PAR Inc.
Holbrook, Joe. Basic Competency in Secondary Mathematics. (gr. 7-12). 1979. 69.00 (ISBN 0-89525-198-1). Ed Activities.
Hough, Belva L. Here's Help! For Primary Math. (gr. 1-3). 1987. pap. 5.95 (ISBN 0-8224-3616-7). Fearon Teach Aids.
Isaak, Betty. Math Mobile. 48p. (gr. 1-4). 1982. 5.95 (ISBN 0-88160-016-4, LW 119). Learning Wks.
Jenkins, Gerald & Wild, Anne. Make Shapes One. (Illus.). 24p. (Orig.). (gr. 4 up). 1985. pap. 4.95 (ISBN 0-906212-00-6). Parkwest Pubns.

—Make Shapes Three. 24p. (Orig.). (gr. 4 up). 1985. pap. 4.95 (ISBN 0-906212-02-2). Parkwest Pubns.

—Make Shapes Two. (Illus.). 24p. (Orig.). (gr. 4 up). 1985. pap. 4.95 (ISBN 0-906212-01-4). Parkwest Pubns.

—Mathematical Curiosities Three. (Illus.). 60p. (gr. 5-9). 1986. pap. 5.95 (ISBN 0-906212-25-1, Tarquin). Parkwest Pubns.

Jenkins, Lee. The Balance Book. (Illus., Orig.). (gr. 2-8). 1974. pap. 6.50 (ISBN 0-918932-02-5). Activity Resources.

Jenkins, Lee & McLean, Peggy. It's a Tangram World. rev. ed. Laycock, Mary, ed. 48p. (gr. 3-6). 1981. pap. 6.95 (ISBN 0-918932-70-X). Activity Resources.

Johnson, Donovan A. Mathmagic with Flexagons. Kaz, Diane, ed. (Orig.). (gr. 4-12). 1974. pap. 6.95 (ISBN 0-918932-30-0). Activity Resources.

Joseph, Andre. The Psycho-Mathematical Basic Skills Learning Workbooklet. 67p. (gr. 6-7). 1980. 8.00 (ISBN 0-936264-00-4); write for info. (ISBN 0-936264-01-2). Andres & Co.

Justus, Fred. Jumbo Math Yearbook: Grade 1. 96p. (gr. 1). 1980. 18.00 (ISBN 0-8209-0030-3, JMY 1). ESP.

Keston, Louise, ed. Math Skills by Objectives. 240p. (gr. 7-9). 1985. pap. text ed. 5.25 (ISBN 0-317-46527-9). Cambridge Bk.

Kumbaraci, Turkan & Gardenier, George H. Fun with Numbers: Statistical Methods: Games & Song. Gardenier, Turhan K., illus. LC 89-90944. 15p. (gr. 1-8). 1989. 20.00x (ISBN 0-685-29038-7, 0002). Teka Trends.

—Time: Statistical Methods: Games & Songs. Gardenier, Turhan K., illus. LC 89-90944. 19p. (gr. 1-8). 1989. 20.00 (ISBN 0-685-29041-7, 0005). Teka Trends.

—Two-by-Two: Statistical Methods: Games & Songs. Gardenier, Turhan K., illus. LC 89-90944. 19p. (gr. 1-8). 1989. 20.00 (ISBN 0-685-29042-5, 0006). Teka Trends.

Lacret-Subirat, Fabian. Lacret Mathematics Basic Skills. (Illus.). 467p. (gr. 7-12). 1986. text ed. 15.00 softcover (ISBN 0-943144-17-5). Lacret Pub.

—Mastering HSPT-Math Skills. (Illus.). 250p. (gr. 7-12). 1986. pap. 15.00 (ISBN 0-943144-19-1); answer key school use only avail. Lacret Pub.

—Mastering Math Basic Skills Workbook. (Illus.). 251p. (gr. 7). 1987. pap. 8.48 (ISBN 0-943144-21-3). Lacret Pub.

Lafferty, Peter. Archimedes. (Illus.). 48p. (gr. 5-8). 1991. RLB 12.40 (ISBN 0-531-18403-X, Pub. by Boatwright Pr). Watts.

Laycock, Mary. Base Ten Mathematics. Jung, Tom, photos by. Moray, Joe, intro. by. (gr. 1-9). 1976. pap. 6.95 (ISBN 0-918932-03-3). Activity Resources.

—Bucky for Beginners. Kyzer, Martha, illus. 64p. (Orig.). (gr. 4-12). 1984. pap. text ed. 6.95 (ISBN 0-918932-82-3). Activity Resources.

Laycock, Mary & Smart, Margaret. Solid Sense of Mathematics, 3 vols. (Illus.). 64p. (Orig.). (gr. 4-9). 1981. pap. text ed. 6.95 ea. (ISBN 0-918932-74-2). Activity Resources.

Laycock, Mary, et al. Geoblocks & Geojackets: Metric Version. rev., 2nd ed. Laycock, Mary, et al, illus. 96p. (Orig.). (gr. 3-10). 1988. pap. 8.95 (ISBN 0-918932-91-2). Activity Resources.

Learning Forum Staff. Success Through Math Mastery. (gr. 8-12). 1989. 24.95 (ISBN 0-945525-11-7). Supercamp.

Lenchner, George. Mathematical Olympiad Contest Problems for Children (Also for Teachers, Parents, & Other Adults) Lenchner, George, illus. LC 90-83825. 176p. (Orig.). (gr. 3-8). 1990. pap. 18.95 (ISBN 0-9626662-0-3). Glenwood Pubns.
A unique collection of 250 mathematical problems to stimulate & challenge children. The introduction describes the problem solving process & various strategies. Other sections provide answers, hints to get the reader started, & different methods of solution. The concepts serve as an extension & enrichment of the mathematics curriculum for elementary & middle schools. The problems offer opportunities for children to experience the fun, pleasure, & thrill of discovery associated with creative problem solving.
Publisher Provided Annotation.

Lindberg, Karen. Addition One. Ryan, Shirley, ed. Beckes, Shirley, illus. (gr. 1). write for info. wkbk. (ISBN 0-307-23539-4, Golden Bks). Western Pub.

Lund, Charles & Smart, Margaret. Focus on Calculator Math. Kyzer, Martha, illus. Laycock, Mary, intro. by. (Illus.). (gr. 4-12). 1979. pap. text ed. 6.95 (ISBN 0-918932-66-1). Activity Resources.

McCabe, J. L. Everyday Mathematics: A Study Guide. (Illus.). 168p. (Orig.). 1988. pap. text ed. 13.95 (ISBN 0-942465-11-3). Everyday Bks.

McCoy, Leah P. Elementary Math Flipper, Vol. I. 39p. (gr. 3-6). Date not set. trade edition 5.95 (ISBN 1-878383-13-2). C Lee Pubns.

McGreevey, Carla & Kelinson, Roberta M. Blooming Math: Fun Activities for Beginning Math Based on Benjamin Bloom's Taxonomy. (ps-3). 1988. pap. 13.95 (ISBN 1-55999-027-9). LinguiSystems.

McLaughlin, Jack. People Piece Puzzles. (Illus.). (gr. 2-8). 1973. pap. 6.95 (ISBN 0-918932-38-6). Activity Resources.

McLean, P., et al. Building Understanding (Primary) (gr. 1-3). 1990. 7.50 (ISBN 0-918932-96-3). Activity Resources.

McLean, Peggy & Sternberg, Betty. People Piece Primer. (Orig.). (gr. k-3). 1975. pap. 6.95 (ISBN 0-918932-37-8). Activity Resources.

McLean, Peggy, et al. Let's Pattern Block It. (Illus., Orig.). (gr. k-8). 1973. pap. 12.50 (ISBN 0-918932-26-2). Activity Resources.

McNichols, Joan & McNichols, Larry. Sports. Meyers, Barbara, illus. (Orig.). (gr. 1-9). 1974. pap. 6.95 (ISBN 0-918932-41-6). Activity Resources.

Magos, Eunice & Hornnes, Esther. First Lessons in... Reading, Writing, Math, Science. Sussman, Ellen, intro. by. Burris, Priscilla, illus. 40p. (Orig.). (ps-1). 1987. Reading. pap. 4.95 (ISBN 0-933606-47-8, MS-647); Writing. pap. 4.95 (ISBN 0-933606-48-6, MS-648); Math. pap. 4.95 (ISBN 0-933606-49-4, MS-649); Science. pap. 4.95 (ISBN 0-933606-50-8, MS-650). Monkey Sisters.

Marsh, Carole. Math for Boys: A Book with the Number or Getting Boys to Love & Excel in Math! (Illus.). (gr. 4-12). 1989. PLB 19.95 (ISBN 1-55609-806-5); pap. 14.95 (ISBN 1-55609-830-8); computer disk 29.95 (ISBN 1-55609-878-2). Gallopade Pub Group.

—Math for Girls: The Book with the Number to Get Girls to Love & Excel in Math! (Illus.). 60p. (gr. 3-9). 1989. PLB 19.95 (ISBN 1-55609-343-8); pap. 14.95 (ISBN 1-55609-344-6); computer disk 29.95 (ISBN 1-55609-345-4). Gallopade Pub Group.

Martinez, Eliseo R. & Martinez, Irma C. Supplemental Studies in Math, Vol. 1. (Illus.). 73p. (ps-1). 1985. wkbk. 8.75 (ISBN 1-878300-00-8). Childrens Work.

Math Help. 32p. (ps-1). 1984. 2.95 (ISBN 0-86653-240-4, GA 588). Good Apple.

Math Help. 32p. (gr. k-2). 1984. 2.95 (ISBN 0-86653-241-2, GA 587). Good Apple.

Math Help. 32p. (gr. 1-3). 1984. 2.95 (ISBN 0-86653-242-0, GA 589). Good Apple.

Math Help. 32p. (gr. 2-4). 1984. 2.95 (ISBN 0-86653-243-9, GA 590). Good Apple.

Math Yellow Pages for Students & Teachers. LC 87-82071. 64p. (gr. k-6). 1988. pap. text ed. 6.95 (ISBN 0-86530-008-9). Incentive Pubns.

Mathews, Louise. Bunches & Bunches of Bunnies. Bassett, Jeni, illus. 32p. (gr. k-3). 1991. pap. 3.95 (ISBN 0-590-44766-1). Scholastic Inc.

May, Lola. Modern Math Grade by Grade, 9 bks. (gr. k-8). pap. write for info. gr. k (ISBN 0-685-47095-4); pap. write for info. ea. gr. 1-8. Macmillan.

Morabe-Murphy, Lock. Decimals & Percents. (Illus.). 80p. (gr. 7-12). 1986. pap. text ed. 4.95 (ISBN 0-88102-053-2); tchr's ed. 12.95 (ISBN 0-88102-054-0). Janus Bks.

Moreno, Anthony. HSPT Mathematics: A Workbook. 133p. (gr. 8-12). 1988. pap. 6.95 (ISBN 0-937820-56-3); answer key 2.25 (ISBN 0-937820-57-1). Westsea Pub.

Multiplication. (Illus.). (gr. 1-3). 3.50 (ISBN 0-7214-0706-4). Ladybird Bks.

Musical Math. (ps-3). 1987. bk. & cassette 14.95 (ISBN 0-8431-2548-9). Price Stern.

My First Book of Addition. (Illus.). 32p. (gr. 1-2). 1985. 3.95 (ISBN 0-394-87705-5). Random.

My First Book of Multiplication. (Illus.). 32p. (gr. 2-5). 1985. 3.95 (ISBN 0-394-87706-3). Random.

My First Counting Book. (Illus.). 32p. (ps). 1985. 3.95 (ISBN 0-394-87703-9). Random.

My First Math Book. 24p. (Orig.). (ps). pap. 3.95 (ISBN 0-8431-3140-3); Little Q Answer Wand 7.00 (ISBN 0-318-39952-0). Price Stern.

My First Numbers. (Illus.). 32p. (ps). 1985. 3.95 (ISBN 0-394-87686-5). Random.

Number Fun. (Illus.). 32p. (gr. 2-5). 1985. 3.95 (ISBN 0-394-87692-X). Random.

O'Brien, Thomas C. Odds & Evens. Eitzen, Allan, illus. (gr. 1-4). 1973. (Crowell Jr Bks); filmstrip with record 12.85 (ISBN 0-690-59071-7); filmstrip with cassette 15.85 (ISBN 0-690-59073-3). HarpC Child Bks.

Palmer, Martha. Transition Math. Hoffman, Joan, ed. Cook, Chris, illus. 32p. (gr. k-1). 1979. wkbk. 1.99 (ISBN 0-938256-27-0). Sch Zone Pub Co.

Perry, Cheryl & Faulkner, Hal. Holiday Mathemagic. (Illus.). (gr. 4-10). 1977. pap. text ed. 6.95 (ISBN 0-918932-50-5). Activity Resources.

Peterson, Elizabeth J. Beginning Math at Home. Dewagian, Jeanette, illus. 75p. (ps-1). 4 sets 10.95, (ISBN 0-938911-01-5). Indiv Educ Syst.

Sachs, Leroy, ed. Projects to Enrich School Mathematics: Level 2. LC 88-5259. (Illus.). 96p. (Orig.). (gr. 7-9). 1988. pap. 7.00 (ISBN 0-87353-260-0). NCTM.

—Projects to Enrich School Mathematics: Level 3. LC 88-5129. (Illus.). 128p. (Orig.). (gr. 10-12). 1988. pap. 10.00 (ISBN 0-87353-261-9). NCTM.

Scarry, Richard. Getting Ready for Numbers. Scarry, Richard, illus. 32p. (ps-k). 1987. pap. 1.95 (ISBN 0-394-89039-6, Random Juv). Random.

Schwartz, Linda. The Addition Magician. Armstrong, Bev, intro. by. (gr. 1-2). 1979. pap. 3.95 (ISBN 0-88160-061-X, LW 701). Learning Wks.

—Hot Fudge Fractions. (gr. 3-4). 1979. pap. 3.95 (ISBN 0-88160-065-2, LW 705). Learning Wks.

—Math Marathon. (gr. 5-7). 1979. pap. 3.95 (ISBN 0-88160-066-0, LW 706). Learning Wks.

—Mighty Math. Armstrong, Bev, illus. (gr. k-3). 1979. pap. 3.95 (ISBN 0-88160-076-8, LW 809). Learning Wks.

Sharp, Richard M. & Metzner, Seymour. The Sneaky Square & 113 Other Math Activities For Kids. (Illus.). 126p. (ps up). 1990. 15.95 (ISBN 0-8306-8474-3, 3474); pap. 8.95 (ISBN 0-8306-3474-6). TAB Bks.

Smart, M., et al. Building Understanding (Middle) (gr. 4-8). 1990. 8.95 (ISBN 0-918932-97-1). Activity Resources.

Smart, Margaret. Focus on Percent. Laycock, Mary, ed. (Illus.). (gr. 5-9). 1978. pap. text ed. 6.95 (ISBN 0-918932-54-8). Activity Resources.

Smart, Margaret A. Focus on Pre-Algebra. Laycock, Mark, intro. by. (Illus.). 48p. (Orig.). (gr. 6-9). 1983. pap. text ed. 6.95 (ISBN 0-918932-81-5). Activity Resources.

Solutions. (Illus.). 72p. (gr. 7-12). 1990. 12.30 (ISBN 0-941008-82-7). Tops Learning.

Speiser, E. & Weiser, M., eds. Math Skills by Objectives. 352p. (gr. 7-9). 1988. pap. text ed. 6.00 (ISBN 0-8428-0202-9). Cambridge Bk.

Sternberg, Betty. Attribute Acrobatics. (Illus., Orig.). (gr. 1-9). 1974. pap. 8.50 (ISBN 0-918932-01-7). Activity Resources.

—Colored Cubes Activity Cards. (Illus., Orig.). (gr. 2-8). 1973. pap. 4.95 (ISBN 0-918932-06-8). Activity Resources.

Stwertka, Albert. Recent Revolution in Mathematics. Green, Anne, illus. 128p. (gr. 7-12). 1987. PLB 12.90 (ISBN 0-531-10418-4). Watts.

Taulbee, Annette. Kindergarten Math. (Illus.). 24p. (ps-k). 1986. 3.98 (ISBN 0-86734-070-3, FS-3062). Schaffer Pubns.

Taylor, Anne. Math in Art. Taylor, Anne, illus. (Orig.). (gr. 1-9). 1974. pap. 6.95 (ISBN 0-918932-28-9). Activity Resources.

Thomas, David. Math Projects for Young Scientists. 1989. pap. 5.95 (ISBN 0-531-15133-6). Watts.

Thompson, Denisse & Van Loy, Merrie. Fundamental Skills of Mathematics. Howland, Joe & Savige, Katherine, eds. Howland, Thomas, illus. LC 87-50098. 536p. (gr. 9-12). 1987. text ed. 19.95 (ISBN 0-943202-16-7). H & H Pub.

Treff, August V. & Jacobs, Donald H. Life Skills Mathematics. (Illus.). 288p. (gr. 7-12). 1983. text ed. 18.49 (ISBN 0-86601-064-5); tchr's. guide 11.99 (ISBN 0-86601-068-8); wkbk. 4.99 (ISBN 0-86601-116-1). Media Materials.

Trinkle, Timothy, et al. Practice, Practice, Practice, Plus, Bk. II: Proportions, Percents, Integers, Rationals, Equations, Area, Volume, Problem Solving, Combinations. 2nd ed. 224p. 1990. pap. 10.75 (ISBN 0-685-35051-7); answer book 2.50 (ISBN 0-685-35052-5). ST Two.

Usher, Michael A. & Bormuth, Robert. Experiencing Life Through Mathematics, Vol. 1. rev. ed. (Illus.). 128p. (Orig.). (gr. 8-12). 1978. pap. text ed. 4.92 (ISBN 0-913688-18-5); tchrs. ed. 8.00x (ISBN 0-913688-19-3). Pawnee Pub.

Vaughn, JIm. Jumbo Math Yearbook: Grade 3. 96p. (gr. 3). 1978. 18.00 (ISBN 0-8209-0032-X, JMY 3). ESP.

Vervoort & Mason. Calculator Math, 3 vols. (gr. 7-12). 1980. pap. 9.95 ea. Beginning Grades 5-7 (ISBN 0-8224-1200-4). Intermediate Grades 6-8 (ISBN 0-8224-1201-2). Advanced Grades 8-10 (ISBN 0-8224-1202-0). Fearon Teach Aids.

Wardlaw, Lee. Me Plus Math Equals Headache. Hoy, Joanne H., illus. (Orig.). (gr. 1-3). 1986. pap. 2.95 (ISBN 0-931093-07-4). Red Hen Pr.

Watson. One, Two, Three. Higham, illus. 28p. (ps-2). 1985. 2.95 (ISBN 0-86020-850-8). EDC.

—Simple Sums. Higham, illus. 28p. (ps-2). 1985. 2.95 (ISBN 0-86020-779-X). EDC.

Wells, David. Can You Solve These?, No. 2: Mathematical Problems to Test Your Thinking Powers. (Illus.). 80p. (Orig.). (gr. 5 up). 1985. pap. 6.95 (ISBN 0-906212-34-0). Parkwest Pubns.

White, Laurence B., Jr. & Broekel, Ray. Math-a-Magic: Number Tricks for Magicians. Mathews, Judith, ed. Seltzer, Meyer, illus. 48p. (gr. 3-8). 1990. 10.95 (ISBN 0-8075-4994-0). A Whitman.

Wiebe, Arthur. Domino Math, 2 bks. Creative Teaching Assocs. Staff, illus. 60p. Bks. A & B. write for info. set (ISBN 1-878669-18-4, 4145); wkbk. 6.95 ea. Bk. A, Grades 1-4, 1973 (ISBN 1-878669-19-2, 4145). Bk. B, Grades 2-6, 1974 (4146). Crea Tea Assocs.

Zaslavsky, Claudia. Count on Your Fingers African Style. Pinkney, Jerry, illus. LC 77-26586. 32p. (gr. k-3). 1980. (Crowell Jr Bks); PLB 12.89 (ISBN 0-690-03865-8, Crowell Jr Bks). HarpC Child Bks.

MATHEMATICS–DATA PROCESSING

Petty, Kate. Numbers. LC 85-70952. (Illus.). 32p. (gr. k-6). 1986. lib. bdg. 10.40 (ISBN 0-531-17009-8, Gloucester Pr). Watts.

Thomas, David A. The Math-Computer Connection. LC 86-10992. (Illus.). 128p. (gr. 7-12). 1986. PLB 11.90 (ISBN 0-531-10231-9). Watts.

MATHEMATICS–DICTIONARIES

Abdelnoor, R. E. The Silver Burdett Mathematical Dictionary. LC 86-45568. 126p. (gr. 5-12). pap. 7.95 (ISBN 0-382-09309-7); 12.98 (ISBN 0-382-09485-9). Silver Burdett Pr.

Dyches, Richard W. & Shaw, Jean M. First Math Dictionary. Sornat, Czeslaw, illus. 104p. (gr. k-4). 1991. 14.95 (ISBN 0-531-15238-3); PLB 14.90 (ISBN 0-531-11111-3). Watts.

Mathematics Encyclopedia. (Illus.). 144p. (gr. 4 up). 1989. 14.95 (ISBN 0-02-689202-2). Checkerboard Pr.

MATHEMATICS–STUDY AND TEACHING

Adler, David A. Base Five. Ross, illus. LC 74-18325. (gr. k-3). 1975. 10.53 (ISBN 0-690-00668-3, Crowell Jr Bks). HarpC Child Bks.

Beckmann, Beverly. Numbers in God's World. (ps). 1983. 6.95 (ISBN 0-570-04083-3, 56-1438). Concordia.

Carson-Dellosa Publishing Staff. Beat It Math Drills: Addition & Subtraction (Grade 1) Carson, Patti & Dellosa, Janet, illus. 64p. (gr. 1). 1986. pap. write for info. (ISBN 0-88724-171-9, CD-0924). Carson-Dellos.

—Beat It Math Drills: Addition & Subtraction (Grades 1-3) Carson, Patti & Dellosa, Janet, illus. 64p. (gr. 1-3). 1986. pap. write for info. (ISBN 0-88724-172-7, CD-0925). Carson-Dellos.

—Beat It Math Drills: Multiplication & Division (Grades 3-6) Carson, Patti & Dellosa, Janet, illus. 64p. (gr. 3-6). 1986. pap. write for info. (ISBN 0-88724-174-3, CD-0926). Carson-Dellos.

Embry, Lynn & Bobo, Betty. Math America. Skiles, Janet, illus. 128p. (gr. 4-6). 1987. pap. 10.95 (ISBN 0-86653-378-8, GA1015). Good Apple.

—Math Around the World. 144p. (gr. 4-6). 1991. 11.95 (ISBN 0-86653-600-0, GA1319). Good Apple.

Geoffrion, Sondra. Power Study to up Your Grades in Math. LC 88-61284. 60p. (gr. 11 up). 1989. pap. text ed. 3.95 (ISBN 0-88247-783-8). R & E Pubs.

Hoban, Tana. Count & See. Hoban, Tana, illus. LC 72-175597. 40p. (ps-2). 1972. 13.95 (ISBN 0-02-744800-2, Mcmillan Child Bk). Macmillan Child Grp.

Kumbaraci, Turkan & Gardenier, George H. Branching Trees: Statistical Methods: Games & Songs. Gardenier, Turhan K., illus. LC 89-90944. 27p. (gr. 1-8). 1989. 30.00x (ISBN 0-685-29039-5, 0003). Teka Trends. BRANCHING TREES provides a unique approach to teaching math without fear by combining poetry, music, & 3-D games. It simplifies complicated concepts used by scientists & industrial engineers & presents them using media familiar to children. It's sub-components are: a) FUN WITH NUMBERS presents an overview of terms such as "matrix", "run", & "factor". b) BRANCHES makes children use the "factorial" design & introduces them to Latin Square. c) COMPUTER MODELS designs a "metamodel" equation & plots it in 3-D form. d) TIME traces changes over time & relates it to quality control concepts with examples in environmental monitoring. e) TWO-by-TWO provides templates for "stem & leaf" charts, an innovation in statistical presentation, & presents methods to compare two sets of data. Provides a bridge between mathematics & science by illustrating how to design experiments with minimal cost. Methods for reducing sample size are illustrated & several such statistical plans, usually taught at college level (or post graduate level) are incorporated. Orientation is through use of poetry, music, & dexterity-oriented 3-D games. Music theory knowledge is not essential, because notes are presented in text form. Teamwork is emphasized by presenting dexterity tasks for groups of 4. Central theme of the examples is a planting exercise which can be tried out at school or home. The series have been pilot-tested at grades 2-3. Class exercise component (which can be duplicated by teacher) is incorporated. _Publisher Provided Annotation._

North Carolina School of Science & Mathematics, Department of Mathematics & Computer Science Staff. Data Analysis. LC 88-5305. (Illus.). 132p. (Orig.). (gr. 11-12). 1988. pap. 10.00 (ISBN 0-87353-263-5). NCTM.

—Geometric Probability. LC 88-5305. (Illus.). 40p. (Orig.). (gr. 11-12). 1988. pap. 9.00 (ISBN 0-87353-259-7). NCTM.

Schaffer, Frank, Publications Staff. Multiplication. (Illus.). 24p. (gr. 3-5). 1978. wkbk. 3.98 (ISBN 0-86734-010-X, FS 3011). Schaffer Pubns.

Spizman, Robyn. Bulletin Boards: To Reinforce Basic Math Skills. Pesiri, Evelyn, illus. 64p. (gr. k-6). 1984. wkbk. 6.95 (ISBN 0-86653-208-0, GA 573). Good Apple.

Trowell, Judith M., ed. Projects to Enrich School Mathematics: Level I. LC 89-14017. (Illus.). 168p. (gr. 4-6). 1989. pap. 14.50 (ISBN 0-87353-280-5). NCTM.

MATHEWSON, CHRISTOPHER, 1880-1925

Macht, Norm. Christy Mathewson. Murray, Jim, intro. by. (Illus.). 64p. (gr. 3 up). 1991. PLB 14.95 (ISBN 0-7910-1182-8). Chelsea Hse.

MATISSE, HENRI, 1869-1954

Munthe, Nelly. Meet Matisse. Munthe, Nelly, illus. 48p. (gr. 4 up). 1983. 17.95 (ISBN 0-316-58960-8). Little.

Raboff, Ernest. Henri Matisse. Matisse, Henri, illus. LC 87-16866. 32p. (gr. 1 up). 1988. 11.95 (ISBN 0-397-32238-0, Lipp Jr Bks). HarpC Child Bks.

—Henri Matisse. Matisse, Henri, illus. LC 87-17701. 32p. (gr. 1 up). 1988. pap. 5.95 (ISBN 0-06-446080-0, Trophy). HarpC Child Bks.

MATRIMONY

see Marriage

MATTER

Kerrod, Robin. Changing Things. (Illus.). 56p. (gr. 3-5). 1987. 14.95 (ISBN 0-382-09421-2). Silver Burdett Pr.

Pomeroy, Johanna P. Content Area Reading Skills Matter: Locating Details. (Illus.). (gr. 4). 1988. pap. text ed. 3.25 (ISBN 1-55737-086-9). Ed Activities.

Wilkin, Fred. Matter. LC 85-30882. (Illus.). 48p. (gr. k-4). 1986. PLB 14.60 (ISBN 0-516-01284-3). Childrens.

MATTER–PROPERTIES

Cobb, Vicki. Why Can't You Unscramble an Egg? 1990. 12.95 (ISBN 0-525-67293-1, Lodestar). Dutton Child Bks.

MAXIMS

see Proverbs

MAY DAY–FICTION

Uttley, Alison. The May Queen. Percy, Graham, illus. 32p. (ps-2). 1989. bds. 4.95 laminated (ISBN 0-571-15296-1). Faber & Faber.

MAYAS

see Indians of Mexico–Mayas

MAYFLOWER (SHIP)

McGovern, Ann. If You Sailed on the Mayflower. Handelsman, J. B., illus. (gr. k-3). 1985. pap. 2.95 (ISBN 0-590-41801-7). Scholastic Inc.

MAYFLOWER (SHIP)–FICTION

Gay, David. Voyage to Freedom: Story of the Pilgrim Fathers. 149p. 1984. pap. 7.95 (ISBN 0-85151-384-0). Banner of Truth. "You are standing on a narrow quay-side waiting to board a small sailing ship. You are about to make an exciting but dangerous & uncomfortable voyage..." So begins the racy & imaginative account of the voyage of the Mayflower which David Gay has written specially for young people. His exciting historical narrative follows the nine week passage of the Pilgrims through the eyes of an imaginary family, Matthew & Martha Lovelace, with their typical children, Justice & Prudence. They encounter such fascinating characters as Master Reynolds, John Howland & William Butten - all of whom really took The Mayflower's historic voyage. Here are three thousand miles of adventure, written with a sensitive appreciation of God's care for his people, & young people's love for adventure. _Publisher Provided Annotation._

MAYO, CHARLES HORACE, 1865-1939

Crofford, Emily. Frontier Surgeons: A Story about the Mayo Brothers. Ritz, Karen, illus. 64p. (gr. 3-6). 1989. PLB 9.95 (ISBN 0-87614-381-8). Carolrhoda Bks.

MAYO, WILLIAM JAMES, 1861-1939

Crofford, Emily. Frontier Surgeons: A Story about the Mayo Brothers. Ritz, Karen, illus. 64p. (gr. 3-6). 1989. PLB 9.95 (ISBN 0-87614-381-8). Carolrhoda Bks.

MAYO FAMILY

Johnson, Spencer. The Value of Sharing: The Story of the Mayo Brothers. Pileggi, Steve, illus. LC 78-10578. (gr. k-6). 1978. PLB 9.95 (ISBN 0-916392-28-7, Pub. by Value Communications). Oak Tree Pubns.

MAYORS

Kurland, Gerald. Fiorello LaGuardia: The People's Mayor of New York. Rahmas, D. Steve, ed. LC 77-190238. 32p. (Orig.). (gr. 7-12). 1972. lib. bdg. 4.20 incl. catalog cards (ISBN 0-87157-520-5); pap. 2.95 vinyl laminated covers (ISBN 0-87157-020-3). SamHar Pr.

—Richard Daley: The Strong Willed Mayor of Chicago. Rahmas, D. Steve, ed. LC 70-190236. 32p. (Orig.). (gr. 7-12). lib. bdg. 4.20 incl. catalog cards (ISBN 0-87157-518-3); pap. 2.95 vinyl laminated covers (ISBN 0-87157-018-1). SamHar Pr.

Roberts, Maurice. Henry Cisneros: Mexican-American Mayor. LC 85-29057. (Illus.). 30p. (gr. 3-5). 1986. PLB 13.27 (ISBN 0-516-03485-5). Childrens.

Roberts, Naurice. Henry Cisneros: Alcalde Mexico-Americano. LC 85-29057. 32p. (gr. 2-5). 1988. PLB 13.27 (ISBN 0-516-33485-9); pap. 3.95 (ISBN 0-516-53485-8). Childrens.

MAYS, WILLIE HOWARD, 1931-

Sabin, Louis. Willie Mays, Young Superstar. Jones, John R., illus. LC 89-33979. 48p. (gr. 4-6). 1989. PLB 10.79 (ISBN 0-8167-1775-3); pap. text ed. 2.95 (ISBN 0-8167-1776-1). Troll Assocs.

MAZE PUZZLES

Gamiello, Elvira. Haunted Mazes. (Illus.). 96p. (Orig.). 1988. pap. 1.95 (ISBN 0-942025-29-6). Kidsbks.

—Maze Madness. (Illus.). 64p. (Orig.). (gr. 4-6). 1988. pap. 1.95 (ISBN 0-942025-93-8). Kidsbks.

—Space Age Mazes. (Illus., Orig.). (gr. 4-6). 1989. pap. 1.95 (ISBN 0-942025-94-6). Kidsbks.

Nevins, Dan. Three-D Mouse Mazes. (Illus.). 48p. (gr. 8-11). 1987. pap. 2.93 (ISBN 0-8431-1883-0). Price Stern.

Sullivan, Scott. Tough Mazes. (Illus.). 48p. (Orig.). (gr. 6 up). 1989. pap. 3.50 (ISBN 0-8431-2332-X). Price Stern.

Tallarico, Anthony. Stop & Find Maze Madness. Tallarico, Anthony, illus. 12p. (Orig.). (gr. 4-7). 1990. pap. 1.95 (ISBN 1-878890-00-X). Palisades Prodns.

MEAD, MARGARET, 1901-

Castiglia, Julie. Margaret Mead. (Illus.). 144p. (gr. 5-7). 1989. PLB 13.98 (ISBN 0-382-09525-1). Silver Burdett Pr.

Johnson, Spencer. The Value of Understanding: The Story of Margaret Mead. Pileggi, Stephen, illus. LC 79-9800. (gr. k-6). 1979. 9.95 (ISBN 0-916392-37-6, Pub. by Value Communications). Oak Tree Pubns.

Ludle, Jacqueline. Margaret Mead. (Illus.). 118p. (gr. 7 up). 1983. PLB 12.90 (ISBN 0-531-04590-0). Watts.

Rice, Edward. Margaret Mead: A Portrait. LC 76-3827. (Illus.). 256p. (gr. 7 up). 1979. PLB 13.89 (ISBN 0-06-025002-X). HarpC Child Bks.

Saunders, Susan. Margaret Mead: The World Was Her Family. Lewin, Ted, illus. (gr. 2-6). 1987. pap. 10.95 (ISBN 0-670-81051-7). Viking Child Bks.

—Margaret Mead: The World Was Her Family. Lewin, Ted, illus. (Orig.). (gr. 2-6). 1988. pap. 3.95 (ISBN 0-14-032063-6, Puffin). Puffin Bks.

—Margaret Mead: The World Was Her Family. Lewin, Ted, illus. (gr. 2 up). 1988. pap. 3.50 (ISBN 0-318-33446-1). Viking Penguin.

Ziesk, Edra. Margaret Mead. Horner, Matina S., intro. by. (Illus.). 112p. (gr. 7-12). 1990. pap. 17.95 (ISBN 1-55546-667-2). Chelsea Hse.

MEAL PLANNING

see Nutrition

MEASURES

see Weights and Measures

MEASURING

see Mensuration

MECHANICAL BRAINS

see Computers

MECHANICAL DRAWING

see also Geometrical Drawing; Graphic Methods; Lettering

Boy Scouts of America. Drafting. (Illus.). 32p. (gr. 6-12). 1965. pap. 1.85 (ISBN 0-8395-3273-3, 3273). BSA.

Peach, S. Technical Drawing: Design, Illustration & Model Making. (Illus.). 48p. (gr. 6 up). 1987. PLB 13.96 (ISBN 0-88110-247-4); pap. 6.95 (ISBN 0-7460-0094-4). EDC.

MECHANICAL ENGINEERING

see also Engines; Machinery; Power (Mechanics)

MECHANICS

see also Force and Energy; Liquids; Machinery; Motion; Power (Mechanics); Steam Engines

Ardley, Neil. Making Things Move. (Illus.). 32p. (gr. 4-6). 1984. PLB 11.90 (ISBN 0-531-03711-1). Watts.

How Things Work. 1984. pap. 10.95 (ISBN 0-671-49898-3, Little Simon). S&S Trade.

Hoye, David. What Is a Lever: Is It a Seesaw? McEntee, Steve, illus. 20p. (gr. 3). 1989. pap. 2.95 plastic paper (ISBN 0-317-94123-2). Kidzco Pub.

Humberstone. Things That Go. (gr. 2-5). 1981. 6.95 (ISBN 0-86020-500-2, Usborne-Hayes); PLB 11.96 (ISBN 0-88110-020-X); pap. 3.95 (ISBN 0-86020-493-6). EDC.

Macaulay, David. The Way Things Work. Macaulay, David, illus. 400p. (ps up). 1988. 29.95 (ISBN 0-395-42857-2). HM.

Pomeroy, Johanna P. Content Area Reading Skills Mechanics: Cause & Effect. (Illus.). (gr. 4). 1988. pap. text ed. 3.25 (ISBN 1-55737-088-5). Ed Activities.

Potter, Tony. See How It Works: Trucks. Lawrie, Robin, illus. 28p. (ps-3). 1989. pap. 7.95 (ISBN 0-689-71301-0, Aladdin). Macmillan Child Grp.

Simple Mechanics. (Illus.). (gr. 3-5). 3.50 (ISBN 0-7214-0659-9). Ladybird Bks.

MECHANICS (PERSONS)

Florian, Douglas. An Auto Mechanic. LC 90-48809. (Illus.). 24p. (ps up). 1991. 13.95 (ISBN 0-688-10635-8); PLB 13.88 (ISBN 0-688-10636-6). Greenwillow.

Gaskin, Carol. A Day in the Life of a Racing Car Mechanic. Klein, John F., illus. LC 84-2430. 32p. (gr. 4-8). 1985. PLB 11.79 (ISBN 0-8167-0091-5); pap. 2.95 (ISBN 0-8167-0092-3). Troll Assocs.

Imershein, Betsy. Auto Mechanic. Steltenpohl, Jane, ed. Imershein, Betsy, illus. 32p. (gr. k-3). 1989. lib. bdg. 9.98 (ISBN 0-671-68184-2); pap. 4.95 (ISBN 0-671-68187-7). Messner.

MEDICAL CENTERS

see also Hospitals

MEDICAL PROFESSION

see Medicine; Physicians

MEDICAL RESEARCH

see Medicine–Research

MEDICAL TECHNOLOGY–VOCATIONAL GUIDANCE

Bryan, Jenny. Medical Technology. (Illus.). 48p. (gr. 5-8). 1991. RLB 12.40 (ISBN 0-531-18398-X, Pub. by Boatwright Pr). Watts.

Garell, Dale C. & Snyder, Solomon H., eds. Medical Technology. (Illus.). (gr. 6-12). 1989. 18.95 (ISBN 0-7910-0087-7). Chelsea Hse.

MEDICINE

see also Anatomy; Bacteriology; Hospitals; Hygiene; Hypnotism; Mind and Body; Pathology; Pharmacy; Physiology

also headings beginning with the word Medical

Aaseng, Nathan. The Disease Fighters: The Nobel Prize in Medicine. (Illus.). 80p. (gr. 5 up). 1987. PLB 12.95 (ISBN 0-8225-0652-1). Lerner Pubns.

Ardley, Neil. Health & Medicine. LC 82-50060. (Illus.). 40p. (gr. 4 up). 1982. PLB 12.40 (ISBN 0-531-04474-2). Watts.

Baron, Connie. The Physically Disabled. LC 88-21554. (Illus.). 48p. (gr. 5-6). 1988. PLB 10.95 (ISBN 0-89686-417-0, Crestwood Hse). Macmillan Child Grp.

Barrett, Norman. Picture World of Ambulances. LC 90-31223. (Illus.). 32p. (gr. k-4). 1991. PLB 11.40 (ISBN 0-531-14090-3). Watts.

Beasant. Medicine Doctors & Health: How Illness Can Be Prevented & Cured. (Illus.). 32p. (gr. 4-8). 1986. PLB 13.96 (ISBN 0-88110-221-0); pap. 6.95 (ISBN 0-86020-948-2). EDC.

Benziger, John. The Corpuscles Meet the Virus Invaders. Benziger, John & Benziger, Mary, illus. LC 90-80327. 30p. (gr. 3-6). 1990. 14.95 (ISBN 0-9620961-1-3). Corpuscles Intergalactica.

Berger, Melvin. Sports Medicine. LC 81-43891. (Illus.). 128p. (gr. 5 up). 1982. 12.95 (ISBN 0-690-04209-4, Crowell Jr Bks); PLB 12.89 (ISBN 0-690-04210-8, Crowell Jr Bks). HarpC Child Bks.

Bernards, Neal, ed. Euthanasia: Opposing Viewpoints. LC 89-2181. (Illus.). 235p. (gr. 10 up). 1989. PLB 15.95 (ISBN 0-89908-442-7); pap. 8.95 (ISBN 0-89908-417-6). Greenhaven.

Center for Attitudinal Healing Staff. Advice to Doctors & Other Big People...from Kids. Jampolsky, Gerald, intro. by. (Illus.). 164p. (Orig.). (gr. 8-12). 1990. pap. 8.95 (ISBN 0-89087-618-5). Celestial Arts.

Coen, Rena N. Medicine in Art. LC 79-84408. (Illus.). 64p. (gr. 5 up). 1970. PLB 5.95 (ISBN 0-8225-0166-X). Lerner Pubns.

Finn, Jeffrey. Health Care Delivery. (Illus.). (gr. 6-12). Date not set. 18.95 (ISBN 0-7910-0084-2). Chelsea Hse.

Fradin, Dennis B. Medicine: Yesterday, Today, & Tomorrow. LC 88-15336. 194p. (gr. 4 up). 1989. PLB 34.60 (ISBN 0-516-00538-3). Childrens.

Galperin, Ann. Gynecological Disorders. (Illus.). (gr. 6-12). 1991. 18.95 (ISBN 0-7910-0075-3). Chelsea Hse.

Garell, Dale C. & Snyder, Solomon H., eds. Arthritis. (Illus.). (gr. 6-12). 1992. 18.95 (ISBN 0-7910-0057-5). Chelsea Hse.

Gordon, James S. Holistic Medicine. (Illus.). 116p. (gr. 6-12). 1988. lib. bdg. 18.95x (ISBN 0-7910-0085-0). Chelsea Hse.

Grauer, Neil. Medicine & the Law. (Illus.). (gr. 6-12). 1990. 18.95 (ISBN 0-7910-0088-5). Chelsea Hse.

Heintze, Carl. Medical Ethics. (Illus.). 128p. (gr. 7-12). 1987. PLB 12.90 (ISBN 0-531-10414-1). Watts.

Hyde, Margaret O. & Forsyth, Elizabeth H. Medical Dilemmas. 112p. 1990. 14.95 (ISBN 0-399-21902-1, Putnam). Putnam Pub Group.

Jussim, Daniel. Medical Ethics. (Illus.). 144p. (gr. 7 up). 1990. lib. bdg. 12.98 (ISBN 0-671-70015-4). Messner.

Kittredge, Mary. The Common Cold. (Illus.). (gr. 6-12). 1990. 18.95 (ISBN 0-7910-0060-5). Chelsea Hse.

—Headaches. (Illus.). (gr. 6-12). 1989. 18.95 (ISBN 0-7910-0064-8). Chelsea Hse.

Kusinitz, Mark. Folk Medicine. (Illus.). (gr. 6-12). 1992. 18.95 (ISBN 0-7910-0083-4). Chelsea Hse.

Lappin, Myra & Feinglass, Sanford. Need a Doctor? (Illus.). 64p. (gr. 7-12). 1981. pap. text ed. 3.95 (ISBN 0-915510-58-8). Janus Bks.

Levine, Saul V. & Wilcox, Kathleen. Dear Doctor. LC 86-21335. 256p. (gr. 7 up). 1987. PLB 12.88 (ISBN 0-688-07094-9); pap. 6.95 (ISBN 0-688-07095-7). Lothrop.

Marshall, Eliot & Finn, Jeffrey. Medical Ethics. (Illus.). (gr. 6-12). 1990. 18.95 (ISBN 0-7910-0086-9). Chelsea Hse.

Martin, M. W. Let's Talk about the New World of Medicine. LC 72-91738. (Illus.). 76p. (gr. 3-6). 1973. PLB 4.95 (ISBN 0-8246-0149-1). Jonathan David.

Medicine: The Body & Healing. LC 84-50608. 40p. (gr. 4 up). 1984. PLB 11.90 (ISBN 0-531-04837-3). Watts.

Silverstein, Alvin & Silverstein, Virginia B. Headaches: All about Them. LC 83-43140. 160p. (gr. 7 up). 1984. 12.95 (ISBN 0-397-32077-9, Lipp Jr Bks); PLB 12.89 (ISBN 0-397-32078-7, Lipp Jr Bks). HarpC Child Bks.

Stewart, Gail B. Alternative Healing: Opposing Viewpoints. LC 90-3807. (Illus.). 112p. (gr. 3-8). 1990. PLB 13.95 (ISBN 0-89908-083-9). Greenhaven.

Sully, Nina. Looking at Medicine. (Illus.). 72p. (gr. 7-12). 1984. 19.95 (ISBN 0-7134-3847-9, Pub. by Batsford England). Trafalgar Sq.

Szumski, Bonnie, ed. The Health Crisis: Opposing Viewpoints. LC 88-24317. (Illus.). 250p. (gr. 10 up). 1988. PLB 15.95 (ISBN 0-89908-438-9); pap. text ed. 8.95 (ISBN 0-89908-413-3). Greenhaven.

MEDICINE–BIOGRAPHY

see also Nurses and Nursing; Physicians

MEDICINE, DENTAL

see Dentistry; Teeth

MEDICINE–DICTIONARIES

Alstetter, Billy. Speech & Hearing. (Illus.). (gr. 6-12). 1991. 18.95 (ISBN 0-7910-0029-X). Chelsea Hse.

Edelson, Edward. Sports Medicine. (Illus.). (gr. 6-12). 1988. 18.95 (ISBN 0-7910-0030-3); pap. 9.95 (ISBN 0-7910-0470-8). Chelsea Hse.

Garell, Dale C. & Snyder, Solomon H., eds. The Encyclopedia of Health, 79 vols. (Illus.). 8848p. (gr. 5 up). 1988. Set. lib. bdg. 1497.05 (ISBN 0-7910-0007-9). Chelsea Hse.

—Nuclear Medicine. (Illus.). (gr. 7-12). 1989. 18.95 (ISBN 0-7910-0070-2). Chelsea Hse.

—Occupational Health. (Illus.). (gr. 6-12). 1989. 18.95 (ISBN 0-7910-0089-3). Chelsea Hse.

Kittredge, Mary. Pain. (Illus.). (gr. 6-12). 1992. 18.95 (ISBN 0-7910-0072-9). Chelsea Hse.

Kusinitz, Marc. Tropical Medicine. (Illus.). (gr. 6-12). 1990. 18.95 (ISBN 0-7910-0079-6). Chelsea Hse.

Miller, Martha. Kidney Disorders. (Illus.). (gr. 6-12). 1992. 18.95 (ISBN 0-7910-0066-4). Chelsea Hse.

Nardo, Don. Medical Diagnosis. (Illus.). (gr. 6-12). 1993. 18.95 (ISBN 0-7910-0067-2). Chelsea Hse.

Zonderman, John & Shader, Laurel. Mononucleosis & Other Infectious Diseases. (Illus.). (gr. 6-12). 1989. 18.95 (ISBN 0-7910-0069-9). Chelsea Hse.

MEDICINE–FICTION

Bach, Alice. Waiting for Johnny Miracle. LC 79-2813. 256p. (gr. 7 up). 1980. 10.53i (ISBN 0-06-020348-X). HarpC Child Bks.

Brandenberg, Franz. I Wish I Was Sick, Too! Aliki, illus. LC 75-46610. 32p. (gr. k-3). 1976. PLB 12.88 (ISBN 0-688-84047-7). Greenwillow.

Chalmers, Mary. Come to the Doctor, Harry. Chalmers, Mary, illus. LC 80-7910. 32p. (ps-1). 1981. 10.95 (ISBN 0-06-021178-4). HarpC Child Bks.

Cherry, Lynne. Who's Sick Today? Cherry, Lynne, illus. LC 87-22185. 24p. (ps-1). 1988. 11.95 (ISBN 0-525-44380-0, 01160-350, DCB). Dutton Child Bks.

Cole, Joanna. Get Well, Clown-Arounds! Smath, Jerry, illus. LC 82-8148. 48p. (ps-3). 1983. 5.95 (ISBN 0-8193-1095-6); PLB 5.95 (ISBN 0-8193-1096-4). Parents.

Dahl, Roald. George's Marvelous Medicine. Blake, Quentin, illus. LC 81-11811. 96p. (gr. 3-7). 1982. 12.00 (ISBN 0-394-84600-1, Bullseye Bks); lib. bdg. 12.99 (ISBN 0-394-94600-6, Bullseye Bks). Knopf.

—George's Marvelous Medicine. large type ed. 152p. 1990. Repr. PLB 14.95 (ISBN 1-85089-985-1, Windrush). ABC-CLIO.

Epstein, Beryl & Epstein, Samuel. Dr. Beaumont & the Man with the Hole in His Stomach. Scrofani, Joseph, illus. LC 77-8236. (gr. 3-5). 1978. PLB 6.99 (ISBN 0-698-30680-5, Coward). Putnam Pub Group.

Kennedy, Shannon. There's No Cure. 96p. (gr. 5-8). 1989. pap. 1.00 (ISBN 0-87406-386-8). Willowisp Pr.

Killien, Christi. Fickle Fever. 128p. (gr. 5-9). 1988. 13.95 (ISBN 0-395-48159-7). HM.

Mayhar, Ardath. Medicine Walk. LC 85-7469. 96p. (gr. 4-8). 1985. 11.95 (ISBN 0-689-31135-4, Atheneum Child Bk). Macmillan Child Grp.

Robison, Deborah & Perez, Carla. Your Turn, Doctor. Robison, Deborah, illus. LC 81-68778. 32p. (ps-2). 1982. PLB 7.89 (ISBN 0-8037-9788-5). Dial Bks Young.

Rockwell, Anne & Rockwell, Harlow. Sick in Bed. Rockwell, Anne & Rockwell, Harlow, illus. LC 81-15637. 24p. (ps-k). 1982. 8.95 (ISBN 0-02-777730-8, Mcmillan Child Bk). Macmillan Child Grp.

MEDICINE–HISTORY

Behm, Barbara. The Story of Medicine. LC 91-11739. (Illus.). 64p. (gr. 2-3). 1991. PLB 12.95 (ISBN 0-8368-0049-4). Gareth Stevens Inc.

Bender, Lionel. Frontiers of Medicine. (Illus.). 32p. (gr. 5-8). 1991. PLB 11.90 (ISBN 0-531-17298-8, Gloucester Pr). Watts.

Brownstone, David M. & Franck, Irene. Healers. (Illus.). 240p. (gr. 6-10). 1989. 17.95 (ISBN 0-8160-1446-9). Facts on File.

Cohen, Daniel. The Last Hundred Years: Medicine. LC 81-14357. (Illus.). 192p. (gr. 5 up). 1981. 8.95 (ISBN 0-87131-356-1). M Evans.

Kalman, Bobbie. Early Health & Medicine. (Illus.). 64p. (gr. 4-5). 1983. 14.95 (ISBN 0-86505-031-7); pap. 7.95 (ISBN 0-86505-030-9). Crabtree Pub Co.

Parker, Steve. The History of Medicine. LC 90-23744. (Illus.). 64p. (gr. 4-6). 1991. PLB 12.95 (ISBN 0-8368-0024-9). Gareth Stevens Inc.

MEDICINE, POPULAR

Here are entered medical books for the layman.

Reid, Ace. Cowpokes Home Remedies. 7th ed. Reid, Ace, illus. 56p. (gr. k-5). pap. 5.00 (ISBN 0-917207-07-6). Reid Ent.

MEDICINE, PEDIATRIC

see Children–Diseases

MEDICINE, PREVENTIVE

see Bacteriology; Hygiene; Immunity; Public Health

MEDICINE–RESEARCH

Berger, Melvin. Disease Detectives. LC 77-26589. (Illus.). (gr. 4 up). 1978. 9.57i (ISBN 0-690-03907-7, Crowell Jr Bks). HarpC Child Bks.

MEDICINE, VETERINARY

see Veterinary Medicine

MEDICINE–VOCATIONAL GUIDANCE

Carter, Adam. A Day in the Life of a Medical Detective. Duncan, Bob, illus. LC 84-8851. 32p. (gr. 4-8). 1985. PLB 11.79 (ISBN 0-8167-0097-4); pap. text ed. 2.95 (ISBN 0-8167-0098-2). Troll Assocs.

Epstein, Rachel. Careers in Health Care. Koop, C. Everett, intro. by. (Illus.). 112p. (gr. 6-12). 1989. 18.95 (ISBN 0-7910-0081-8). Chelsea Hse.

Medicine. 1990. 12.95 (ISBN 0-8239-1152-7). Rosen Group.

MEDICINE AND ART

Coen, Rena N. Medicine in Art. LC 79-84408. (Illus.). 64p. (gr. 5 up). 1970. PLB 5.95 (ISBN 0-8225-0166-X). Lerner Pubns.

MEDIEVAL CIVILIZATION

see Civilization, Medieval

MEDITATIONS

Christian, S. Rickly. Alive: Daily Devotions for Young People. (Illus.). 1990. pap. 8.95 (ISBN 0-310-71031-6, Campus Life). Zondervan.

—Alive Two. (Illus.). 1990. pap. 8.95 (ISBN 0-310-71041-3, Campus Life). Zondervan.

Cristo Vive en Me. (SPA & ENG.). (gr. 2). pap. text ed. 2.00 (ISBN 0-8198-1426-1); 1.00 (ISBN 0-8198-1427-X). Dghtrs St Paul.

Edgerton, Jean & Rolff, Ray. The Year of Our Lord: A Primer. Edgerton, Jean, illus. 102p. (Orig.). 1989. pap. 15.95 wkbk. (ISBN 0-9624794-0-3). Lilium Pr.

Hodgson, Joan. Our Father. Ripper, Peter, illus. (ps-3). 1977. pap. 2.95 (ISBN 0-85487-040-7). DeVorss.

Hornsby, Sarah. At the Name of Jesus. Hornsby, Sarah, illus. 256p. 1986. 10.95 (ISBN 0-8007-9078-2, Chosen Bks). Revell.

Jacobs, Mildred Spires. Come unto Me. (Illus.). 56p. (Orig.). (gr. 5-6). 1982. pap. 2.95 (ISBN 0-9609612-0-8). Enrich Enter.

Kelly, Robert. How Do I Make up My Mind, Lord? LC 82-70948. (Orig.). (gr. 3-7). 1982. pap. 4.95 (ISBN 0-8066-1923-6, 10-3168, Augsburg). Augsburg Fortress.

Kerl, Mary A. Where Are You, Lord? LC 82-70949. 112p. (Orig.). (gr. 3-6). 1982. pap. 4.95 (ISBN 0-8066-1924-4, 10-7069, Augsburg). Augsburg Fortress.

Langford, Anne. Meditation for Little People. Bethards, David, illus. LC 75-46191. 40p. (gr. k-4). 1976. pap. 5.50 (ISBN 0-87516-211-8). DeVorss.

Lawhead, Stephen R. In the Hall of the Dragon King, Bk. I. LC 82-71942. 348p. (gr. 7-12). 1982. pap. 9.95t (ISBN 0-89107-257-8, Crossway Bks). Good News.

Mandeville. Sower. (gr. 1-2). 1979. 3.50 (ISBN 0-7214-0451-0). Chr Lit.

—Two New Houses. (gr. 2-7). 1977. 3.50 (ISBN 0-7214-0450-2). Chr Lit.

Richter, Betts. Something Special Within. 2nd ed. Jacobsen, Alice, illus. 48p. (ps-5). 1982. pap. 5.50 (ISBN 0-87516-488-9). DeVorss.

Sanders, Bill. Outtakes: Devotions for Girls. 160p. (gr. 7-12). 1988. pap. 6.95 (ISBN 0-8007-5284-8). Revell.

MEDITERRANEAN REGION

Lyle, Garry. Cyprus. (Illus.). (gr. 5 up). 1988. 14.95 (ISBN 0-222-00942-X). Chelsea Hse.

MEIR, GOLDA (MABOVITZ), 1898-

Adler, David A. Our Golda: The Story of Golda Meir. Ruff, Donna, illus. LC 83-16798. 64p. (gr. 3-7). 1984. pap. 11.95 (ISBN 0-670-53107-3). Viking Child Bks.

—Our Golda: The Story of Golda Meir. Ruff, Donna, illus. 64p. (gr. 2-6). 1986. pap. 3.95 (ISBN 0-14-032104-7, Puffin). Puffin Bks.

Keller, Mollie. Golda Meir. LC 82-20203. (Illus.). 128p. (gr. 7 up). 1983. PLB 13.90 (ISBN 0-531-04591-9). Watts.

MEMOIRS

see Autobiographies; Biography

MEMORY

Gallant, Roy A. Memory: How It Works & How to Improve It. LC 85-4471. (Illus.). 128p. (gr. 7 up). 1984. Repr. of 1980 ed. SBE 12.95 (ISBN 0-02-736850-5, Four Winds). Macmillan Child Grp.

Meltzer, Milton. The Landscape of Memory. LC 86-32406. 132p. (gr. 7 up). 1987. pap. 12.95 (ISBN 0-670-80821-0). Viking Child Bks.

Reid, S. Memory Skills. (Illus.). 48p. (gr. 6-10). 1988. PLB 12.96 (ISBN 0-88110-305-5); pap. 5.95 (ISBN 0-7460-0163-0). EDC.

Wartik, Nancy. Memory & Learning. (Illus.). (gr. 5-12). 1992. 18.95 (ISBN 0-7910-0022-2). Chelsea Hse.

MEN

see Man

MENDESIA, GRACIA, 1510-1569

Stadtler, Bea. Story of Dona Gracia Mendes. Shevo, Aharon, illus. LC 70-83166. (gr. 6-9). 1969. 4.50 (ISBN 0-8381-0734-6). United Syn Bk.

MENNONITES

Guenther, Gloria M. Gift of Love. Penner, Kathy, illus. (Orig.). (gr. 5-8). 1989. pap. 6.95 (ISBN 0-919797-58-X, Pub. by Kindred Pr). Herald Pr.

Vernon, Louise A. Night Preacher. LC 73-94378. (Illus.). 134p. (gr. 3-8). 1969. pap. 4.95 (ISBN 0-8361-1774-3). Herald Pr.

MENNONITES–FICTION

Tallarico, Beatrice & Stone, S. C. Tindel's Blue Door. 2nd ed. (Illus.). 19p. (gr. 2-8). 1986. pap. 2.95 (ISBN 0-936191-14-7). Tallstone Pub.

Vernon, Louise A. Beggars Bible: An Illustrated Historical Fiction of John Wycliffe for the 9-14 Age-Group. LC 77-131534. (Illus.). 128p. (gr. 4-9). 1971. 4.95 (ISBN 0-8361-1732-8). Herald Pr.

—Secret Church. LC 67-15988. (Illus.). 128p. (gr. 3-8). 1967. pap. 4.50 (ISBN 0-8361-1783-2). Herald Pr.

MENSURATION

see also Geodesy; Surveying; Weights and Measures

Allington, Richard L. & Krull, Kathleen. Measuring. Spangler, Noel, illus. LC 82-9840. 32p. (gr. k-3). 1985. PLB 15.33 (ISBN 0-8172-1389-9); pap. 9.27 (ISBN 0-8172-2482-3). Raintree Pubs.

Hewavisenti, Latshmi. Measuring. (Illus.). 32p. (gr. k-4). 1991. PLB 11.40 (ISBN 0-531-17319-4, Gloucester Pr). Watts.

Hoban, Tana. Over, Under & Through & Other Special Concepts. Hoban, Tana, photos by. LC 72-81055. (Illus.). 32p. (ps-2). 1973. 13.95 (ISBN 0-02-744820-7, Mcmillan Child Bk). Macmillan Child Grp.

Laithwaite, Eric. Size: The Measure of Things. FRanklin Watts Ltd., ed. (Illus.). 32p. (gr. 4-9). 1988. 8.99 (ISBN 0-531-10263-7). Watts.

Sneider, Cary & Gould, Alan. Height-O-Meters. Bergman, Lincoln & Fairwell, Kay, eds. Klofkorn, Lisa, illus. Hoyt, Richard. (Illus.). 60p. (gr. 6-10). 1989. pap. 7.50 (ISBN 0-912511-22-2). Lawrence Science.

Westcott, Alvin & Schluep, J. Fun with Timothy Triangle. LC 66-11445. (Illus.). 64p. (gr. 4 up). 1970. pap. 3.94 deluxe ed. (ISBN 0-87783-014-2); answer key 0.39x (ISBN 0-87783-164-5). Oddo.

MENTAL DEFICIENCY

see Mentally Handicapped

MENTAL DISEASES

see Mental Illness; Psychology, Pathological

MENTAL HEALTH

see also Mental Illness; Mind and Body; Psychology, Pathological

Hales, Dianne. Depression. LC 88-34176. (Illus.). 101p. (gr. 6-12). 1989. 18.95 (ISBN 0-7910-0046-X). Chelsea Hse.

Kunz, Roxane B. & Swenson, Judy H. Feeling Down: The Way Back Up. McKee, Mary, illus. LC 85-24604. 48p. (gr. 2-6). 1986. lib. bdg. 8.95 (ISBN 0-87518-326-3, Dillon). Macmillan Child Grp.

Mallick, Joan. Anorexia. Head, J. J., ed. Steffen, Ann T. & Slifko, Fran, illus. LC 86-72198. 16p. (Orig.). (gr. 10 up). 1987. pap. text ed. 2.15 (ISBN 0-89278-373-7, 45-9773). Carolina Biological.

Maloney, Michael & Kranz, Rachel. Straight Talk about Anxiety & Depression. Ryan, Elizabeth A., ed. 128p. (gr. 5-12). 1991. lib. bdg. 16.95x (ISBN 0-8160-2434-0). Facts on File.

Silverstein, Herma. Teenage Depression. (Illus.). 128p. (gr. 9-12). 1990. 11.95 (ISBN 0-531-15183-2); PLB 12.90 (ISBN 0-531-10960-7). Watts.

MENTAL HYGIENE

see Mental Health

MENTAL ILLNESS

see also Mental Health

Bergman, Thomas. We Laugh, We Love, We Cry: Children Living with Mental Retardation. LC 88-42971. (Illus.). 48p. (gr. 4-5). 1989. PLB 10.95 (ISBN 1-55532-914-4). Gareth Stevens Inc.

Byck, Robert. Treating Mental Illness. (Illus.). (gr. 5 up). 1986. 18.95 (ISBN 0-87754-774-2). Chelsea Hse.

Dinner, Sherry H. Nothing to Be Ashamed Of: Growing up with Mental Illness in Your Family. LC 88-13244. 160p. (gr. 5 up). 1991. pap. 7.95 (ISBN 0-688-08493-1, Pub. by Beech Tree Bks). Morrow.

—Nothing to Be Ashamed Of: Growing up with Mental Illness in Your Family. 160p. (ps-3). 1989. PLB 12.88 (ISBN 0-688-08482-6). Lothrop.

Greenberg, Harvey R. Emotional Illness in Your Family: Helping Your Relatives, Helping Yourself. 304p. (gr. 6 up). 1989. 16.95 (ISBN 0-02-736921-8, Mcmillan Child Bk). Macmillan Child Grp.

Johnson, Julie T. Understanding Mental Illness: For Teens Who Care about Someone with Mental Illness. 70p. (gr. 6 up). Repr. of 1989 ed. 4.95g (ISBN 0-8225-9574-5). Lerner Pubns.

Lundy, Alan. Diagnosing & Treating Mental Illness. (Illus.). (gr. 6-12). 1990. 18.95 (ISBN 0-7910-0047-8). Chelsea Hse.

Ruth, Eric. Aunt Dodie Has Alzheimers. Okoren, Christine, ed. Ruth, Eric & Okoren, Christine, illus. 11p. (Orig.). (gr. 1-6). 1988. pap. text ed. 3.95 (ISBN 0-685-22513-5). Paraclete MI.

Vonnegut, Mark. The Eden Express. (gr. 6 up). 1988. pap. 4.95 (ISBN 0-440-20205-1, LE). Dell.

MENTAL ILLNESS–FICTION

Bennett, James. I Can Hear the Mourning Dove. 224p. (gr. 7 up). 1990. 14.95 (ISBN 0-395-53623-5). HM.

Hamilton-Paterson, James. House in the Waves. LC 76-103043. (gr. 8 up). 1970. 18.95 (ISBN 0-87599-171-8). S G Phillips.

Milton, Joyce. Save the Loonies. LC 82-18393. 160p. (gr. 7 up). 1984. 11.95 (ISBN 0-02-766950-5, Four Winds Pr). Macmillan Child Grp.

Moeri, Louise. The Girl Who Lived on the Ferris Wheel. LC 79-11359. (gr. 5-9). 1979. 8.95 (ISBN 0-525-30659-5, DCB). Dutton Child Bks.

Neufeld, John. Lisa, Bright & Dark. (gr. 7 up). 1969. 18.95 (ISBN 0-87599-153-X). S G Phillips.

Riley, Jocelyn. Crazy Quilt. 176p. (gr. 7-12). 1986. pap. 2.50 (ISBN 0-553-25640-8). Bantam.

Rowan, Barbara. Denial of Rights. Powell, Michelle, illus. LC 90-84008. 153p. (Orig.). (gr. 8 up). 1991. pap. 8.00 (ISBN 0-9622863-4-6). Bristlecone Pubns.

Fifteen-year-old Lindsey Crawford spent two months at Springhill Home, a small, short-term community institution for teenage girls who suffer emotional & behavioral problems. Lindsey hated it. "The kids in here are totally dinged out," she said. "There's a bunch of freaks in this place." So Lindsey ran away. Upon Lindsey's return, Janet Wayne, a counselor, seeks to uncover the emotional trauma she is sure Lindsey is suffering. However, Lindsey's case manager, Rhonda Newhy, wants her committed to a correctional institution instead. Only one week remains to uncover the real reasons behind Lindsey's inappropriate behavior. Has Lindsey been abused or is she a delinquent? She has never revealed her past to anyone. What happened during the three weeks that Lindsey was on the run which finally prompts her to reveal her secrets to Janet? Although DENIAL OF RIGHTS is fiction, the events & many of the conversations were taken from actual accounts of teenagers who were confined to a mental health facility. The author spent a year with the teenagers doing research for her master's thesis. DENIAL OF RIGHTS was born of the pain & suffering of those young people.

Publisher Provided Annotation.

Streatfeild, Noel. Thursday's Child. (Orig.). (gr. 5 up). 1986. pap. 3.50 (ISBN 0-440-48687-4, YB). Dell.

Zindel, Paul. Harry & Hortense at Hormone High. 160p. (gr. 7-12). 1985. pap. 2.95 (ISBN 0-553-25175-9, Starfire). Bantam.

MENTAL PHILOSOPHY

see Philosophy; Psychology

MENTAL TELEPATHY

see Thought Transference

MENTALLY HANDICAPPED

see also Mental Illness

Anders, Rebecca. A Look at Mental Retardation. Forrai, Maria, illus. LC 75-38466. 36p. (gr. 3-6). 1976. PLB 6.95 (ISBN 0-8225-1303-X). Lerner Pubns.

Dick, Jean. Mental & Emotional Disabilities. LC 88-21555. (Illus.). 48p. (gr. 5-6). 1988. PLB 10.95 (ISBN 0-89686-418-9, Crestwood Hse). Macmillan Child Grp.

Dolce, Laura. Mental Retardation. (Illus.). (gr. 6-12). 1992. 18.95 (ISBN 0-7910-0050-8). Chelsea Hse.

Dunbar, Robert E. Mental Retardation. (Illus.). 96p. (gr. 9-12). 1991. PLB 12.40 (ISBN 0-531-12502-5). Watts.

Exley, Helen. What It's Like to Be Me. 2nd ed. (Illus.). 127p. (gr. 4-11). 1984. pap. 10.95 (ISBN 0-377-00144-9). Friendship Pr.

Sobol, Harriet L. My Brother Steven Is Retarded. Agre, Patricia, illus. LC 76-46996. 32p. (gr. 3-6). 1977. 12.95 (ISBN 0-02-785990-8, Mcmillan Child Bk). Macmillan Child Grp.

MENTALLY HANDICAPPED–EDUCATION

Crowther, Jean D. What Do I Do Now, Mom? Growing-up Guidance for Young Teen-age Girls. Bagley, Val C., illus. LC 80-82257. 86p. (gr. 9-12). 1980. 6.95 (ISBN 0-88290-134-6). Horizon Utah.

Fisher, Gary & Cummings, Rhoda. The Survival Guide for Kids with LD (Learning Differences) 104p. 1990. pap. 9.95 (ISBN 0-915793-18-0). Free Spirit Pub.

Howard, Diane W. Swimming Upstream: A Complete Guide to the College Application Process for the Learning Disabled Student. Lord, J. R., intro. by. (Illus.). 140p. (Orig.). (gr. 8-12). 1989. pap. write for info. wkbk. Hunt Hse Pub.

MENTALLY HANDICAPPED–FICTION

Booth, Zilpha M. Finding a Friend. Breeden, Teisha, illus. LC 86-50987. 54p. (gr. 1-5). 1987. pap. 3.95 (ISBN 0-932433-22-7). Windswept Hse.

Brown, Towana J. Leave, Retard, Leave! Brown, Becky, illus. 127p. (Orig.). (gr. 8-12). 1988. pap. 3.50 (ISBN 0-9622060-0-8). T J Brown.

Cleaver, Vera & Cleaver, Bill. Me Too. 160p. (gr. 7-9). 1973. 13.95 (ISBN 0-397-31485-X, Lipp Jr Bks). HarpC Child Bks.

Fassler, Joan. One Little Girl. Smyth, M. Jane, illus. LC 76-80120. 32p. (ps-3). 1969. 16.95 (ISBN 0-87705-008-2). Human Sci Pr.

Hall, Lynn. Just One Friend. LC 85-40294. 112p. (gr. 7 up). 1985. 12.95 (ISBN 0-684-18471-0, Scribners Young Read). Macmillan Child Grp.

Hasler, Evaline. Martin Is Our Friend. Besmarowitz, Dorothea, illus. LC 81-4853. 24p. (gr. 2-4). 1981. 0.50 (ISBN 0-687-23650-9). Abingdon.

Jasmine, Cairo. Our Brother Has Down's Syndrome. (Illus.). 24p. (ps-8). 1985. 12.95 (ISBN 0-920303-30-7); pap. 4.95 (ISBN 0-920303-31-5). Firefly Bks Ltd.

Keyes, Daniel. Flowers for Algernon. (gr. 8 up). 1970. pap. 3.50 (ISBN 0-553-25665-3). Bantam.

Nystrom, Carolyn. The Trouble with Josh. Rees, Gary, illus. 48p. (gr. 6-12). 1989. text ed. 7.95 (ISBN 0-7459-1621-X). Lion USA.

Wright, Betty R. My Sister Is Different. Cogancherry, Helen, illus. Nietupski, John, intro. by. LC 80-25508. (Illus.). 32p. (gr. k-6). 1981. PLB 16.67 (ISBN 0-8172-1369-4). Raintree Pubs Ltd.

MENTALLY RETARDED

see Mentally Handicapped

MERCHANDISE

see Commercial Products

MERCHANDISING

see Marketing

MERCURY (PLANET)

Asimov, Isaac. Mercury: The Quick Planet. LC 87-42605. (Illus.). 32p. (gr. 3-4). 1989. PLB 11.95 (ISBN 1-55532-360-X). Gareth Stevens Inc.

—Mercury: The Spotted Giant. LC 87-42605. (Illus.). 32p. (gr. 2-5). 1989. PLB 9.95. Gareth Stevens Inc.

Baker, David. Exploring Venus & Mercury. LC 88-33707. (Illus.). 48p. (gr. 4-6). 1989. PLB 18.60 (ISBN 0-86592-371-X). Rourke Corp.

MERMAIDS–FICTION

Andersen, Hans Christian. The Little Mermaid. Treherne, Katie T., adapted by. & illus. LC 89-31602. (gr. 3-4). 1989. 15.95 (ISBN 0-15-246320-8). HarBraceJ.

—The Little Mermaid. Iwasaki, Chihiro, illus. 1991. pap. 3.95 (ISBN 0-590-44456-5). Scholastic Inc.

Balducci, Rita. Disney's The Little Mermaid: Tales from under the Sea. LC 90-85427. (Illus.). 80p. (gr. 2-7). 1991. 10.95 (ISBN 1-56282-014-1, Disney Pr). W Disney Pub.

Calmenson, Stephanie, adapted by. Walt Disney Pictures Presents the Little Mermaid. Maten, Frenc, illus. (ps-k). 1991. pap. write for info. (ISBN 0-307-10027-8, Golden Pr). Western Pub.

Carpenter, Mimi G. Mermaid in a Tidal Pool. Carpenter, Mimi G., illus. 32p. (Orig.). (ps-6). 1985. pap. 8.95 (ISBN 0-9614628-0-9). Beachcomber Pr.

Carr, Jan. Little Mermaid M-TV. 1989. pap. 2.50 (ISBN 0-590-42988-4, SHLS). Scholastic Inc.

Colmenson, Stephanie. Walt Disney Pictures Presents the Little Mermaid: Ariel above the Sea. Mateu, Franc, illus. (gr. k-2). 1991. 4.25 (ISBN 0-307-11697-2, Golden Pr). Western Pub.

Dale, Nora. Nan & the Sea Monster. (Illus.). 32p. (gr. 1-4). 1989. PLB 13.32 (ISBN 0-8172-3526-4). Raintree Pubs.

Littledale, Freya, as told by. The Little Mermaid. San Souci, Daniel, illus. 40p. (Orig.). (gr. k-3). 1986. pap. 3.95 (ISBN 0-590-44358-5). Scholastic Inc.

Noble, Trinka H. Hansy's Mermaid. Noble, Trinka H., illus. LC 82-45509. 32p. (ps-2). 1983. 10.95 (ISBN 0-8037-3605-3, 01063-320); PLB 10.89 (ISBN 0-8037-3606-1). Dial Bks Young.

Nwapa, Flora. Mammywater. (gr. 3-5). pap. 7.00 (ISBN 0-317-38704-9, Pub. by Tana Pr Nigeria). Three Continents.

La Petite Sirene. (FRE., Illus.). (gr. 3). 3.50 (ISBN 0-7214-1289-0). Ladybird Bks.

Walt Disney's the Little Mermaid. (ps-3). Date not set. write for info. (ISBN 0-307-12345-6, Golden Pr). Western Pub.

MERRY-GO-ROUNDS–FICTION

Bergeon, JoAnne M. Lions, Tigers & Bears Go 'Round. Morrison, Cathy, illus. LC 89-15046. 24p. (gr. 1-6). 1989. 13.95 (ISBN 0-917665-34-1). Bookmakers Guild.

Bolton, Mimi D. Merry-Go-Round Family. 2nd ed. (Illus.). 225p. (gr. 3-7). 1990. Repr. of 1954 ed. 14.95x (ISBN 0-9614274-2-6). Wisla Pubs.

Foster, Elizabeth. Gigi in America: The Further Adventures of a Merry-Go-Round Horse. Cote, Phyllis N., illus. 130p. (gr. 4-8). pap. 9.95 (ISBN 0-913028-69-X). North Atlantic.

—Gigi: The Story of a Merry-Go-Round Horse. Birchoff, Ilse, illus. 124p. (gr. 4-8). pap. 9.95 (ISBN 0-913028-55-X). North Atlantic.

Hegarty, Sue & Geoghegan, Judy. Carousel Coloring Book. Hennigh, Susan, illus. 32p. (Orig.). (gr. k-8). 1989. pap. 4.50 (ISBN 0-9622526-1-1). Freels Fndtn.

Samstag, Nicholas. Kay Kay Comes Home. Shahn, Ben, illus. (gr. 5-7). 1962. 10.95 (ISBN 0-8392-3015-X). Astor-Honor.

Sargent, Ruth. The Island Merry Go Round. Weinberger, Jane, ed. DeVito, Pamela, illus. LC 88-50277. 46p. (Orig.). (gr. 1-4). 1988. pap. 7.95 (ISBN 0-932433-46-4). Windswept Hse.

MESMERISM

see Hypnotism

METABOLISM

see also Nutrition

Balestrino, Philip. Fat & Skinny. Makie, Pam, illus. LC 74-12306. (gr. k-3). 1975. 8.95 (ISBN 0-690-00454-0, Crowell Jr Bks). HarpC Child Bks.

METAL WORK

see Metalwork

METALLURGY

see also Mineralogy

also names of metals, e.g. Gold; etc.

Mitgutsch, Ali. From Ore to Spoon. Mitgutsch, Ali, illus. LC 80-28862. 24p. (ps-3). 1981. PLB 6.95 (ISBN 0-87614-161-0). Carolrhoda Bks.

METALS

Dineen, Jacqueline. Metals & Minerals. 32p. (gr. 4-8). 1988. lib. bdg. 12.95 (ISBN 0-89490-218-0). Enslow Pubs.

Radford, Don. Looking at Metals. (Illus.). 48p. (gr. 5-8). 1985. 19.95 (ISBN 0-7134-4772-9, Pub. by Batsford England). Trafalgar Sq.

Reymond, Jean-Pierre. Metals: Born of Earth & Fire. Prunier, James, illus. LC 87-34596. 38p. (gr. k-5). 1988. 4.95 (ISBN 0-944589-19-7, 197). Young Discovery Lib.

Story of Metals. (ARA., Illus.). (gr. 5-12). 3.50x (ISBN 0-86685-227-1). Intl Bk Ctr.

Whyman, Kathryn. Metals & Alloys. Franklin Wattts Ltd., ed. (Illus.). 32p. (gr. k-9). 1988. PLB 8.99 (ISBN 0-531-17083-7, Gloucester Pr). Watts.

METALWORK

see also Jewelry; Steel

Boy Scouts of America. Metalwork. (Illus.). 36p. (gr. 6-12). 1969. pap. 1.85 (ISBN 0-8395-3312-8, 3312). BSA.

Groneman, Chris H. & Feirer, John L. Getting Started in Metalworking. (Illus.). 1979. text ed. 9.52 (ISBN 0-07-024998-9). McGraw.

Hawkins, Leslie V. Art Metal & Enameling. 234p. (gr. 9-12). 1974. text ed. 17.60 (ISBN 0-02-662240-8). Bennett IL.

Mitgutsch, Ali. From Ore to Spoon. Mitgutsch, Ali, illus. LC 80-28862. 24p. (ps-3). 1981. PLB 6.95 (ISBN 0-87614-161-0). Carolrhoda Bks.

Walker, John R. Metal Projects, Bk. 3. LC 77-21602. (Illus.). 96p. (gr. 9 up). pap. 8.00 (ISBN 0-87006-238-7); pap. 6.00 (ISBN 0-685-01929-2). Goodheart.

METAMORPHIC ROCKS

see Rocks

METEORITES

Branley, Franklyn M. Shooting Stars. Keller, Holly, illus. LC 88-14190. 32p. (ps-1). 1989. 13.95 (ISBN 0-690-04701-0, Crowell Jr Bks); PLB 13.89 (ISBN 0-690-04703-7, Crowell Jr Bks). HarpC Child Bks.

British Museum, Geological Department Staff. Moon, Mars & Meteorites. (Illus.). 36p. (gr. 7 up). 1986. pap. 4.50 (ISBN 0-521-32414-9). Cambridge U Pr.

Lauber, Patricia. Voyagers from Space: Meteors & Meteorites. Eagle, Mike, illus. LC 86-47745. 80p. (gr. 5 up). 1989. 14.95 (ISBN 0-690-04632-4, Crowell Jr Bks); PLB 14.89 (ISBN 0-690-04634-0, Crowell Jr Bks). HarpC Child Bks.

METEOROLOGICAL INSTRUMENTS

see also Thermometers and Thermometry

METEOROLOGISTS

Witty, Margot & Witty, Ken. A Day in the Life of a Meteorologist. Sanacore, Stephen, photos by. LC 80-54098. (Illus.). 32p. (gr. 4-8). 1981. PLB 11.79 (ISBN 0-89375-450-1); pap. 2.95 (ISBN 0-89375-451-X); cassettes avail. Troll Assocs.

METEOROLOGY

see also Air; Atmosphere; Climate; Clouds; Floods; Hurricanes; Lightning; Rain and Rainfall; Seasons; Snow; Storms; Thunderstorms; Tornadoes; Weather; Weather Forecasting; Winds

Gakken Co. Ltd. Staff, ed. Wind & Weather. Time-Life Books Inc. Editors, tr. (Illus.). 90p. (gr. k-3). 1989. 15.93 (ISBN 0-8094-4829-7); PLB 21.27 (ISBN 0-8094-4830-0). Time-Life.

Graf, Mike. The Weather Report. (gr. 3-6). 1989. pap. 13.95 (ISBN 0-8224-7511-1). Fearon Teach Aids.

Green, Ivah. Splash & Trickle. Connor, Bil, illus. (gr. 2-3). 1978. pap. 1.25 (ISBN 0-89508-062-1). Rainbow Bks.

McVey, Vicki. Sierra Club Book of Weatherwisdom. (gr. 4-7). 1991. 15.95 (ISBN 0-316-56341-2). Little.

Pettigrew, Mark. Weather. Nevett, Louise, illus. 32p. (gr. 1-6). 1987. PLB 11.90 (ISBN 0-531-17060-8, Gloucester Pr). Watts.

Steele, Philip. Heatwave: Causes & Effects. (Illus.). 32p. (gr. 5-8). 1991. PLB 11.90 (ISBN 0-531-11023-0). Watts.

Tannenbaum, Beulah. Making & Using Your Own Weather Station. 1989. PLB 12.40 (ISBN 0-531-10675-6). Watts.

Taylor, Michael. Aircraft Carriers. 1989. pap. 3.95 (ISBN 0-590-41997-8). Scholastic Inc.

METEORS

see also Meteorites

Asimov, Isaac. Comets & Meteors. LC 89-4632. 32p. (gr. 3-4). 1989. PLB 11.95 (ISBN 1-55532-400-2). Gareth Stevens Inc.

—What is a Shooting Star? (Illus.). 24p. (gr. 2-3). 1991. PLB 11.95 (ISBN 0-8368-0436-8). Gareth Stevens Inc.

Bendick, Jeanne. Comets & Meteors: Visitors from Space. (Illus.). 32p. (gr. k-2). 1991. PLB 11.90 (ISBN 1-56294-001-5); pap. 3.95 (ISBN 1-878841-55-6). Millbrook Pr.

Berger, Melvin. Comets, Meteors & Asteroids. (Illus.). 80p. (gr. 7 up). 1981. 9.99 (ISBN 0-399-61148-7, Putnam). Putnam Pub Group.

Branley, Franklyn M. Shooting Stars. Keller, Holly, illus. LC 88-14190. 32p. (ps-1). 1991. pap. 4.50 (ISBN 0-06-445103-8, Trophy). HarpC Child Bks.

Couper, Heather. Comets & Meteors. LC 84-52570. (Illus.). 32p. (gr. 5-9). 1985. PLB 11.90 (ISBN 0-531-10000-6). Watts.

Fichter, George S. Comets & Meteors. (Illus.). 72p. (gr. 4 up). 1982. PLB 10.40 (ISBN 0-531-04382-7). Watts.

Levinson, Riki. Mira Como Salen Las Estrellas. Goode, Diane, illus. (SPA.). (gr. 1-6). 14.95 (ISBN 84-372-6607-6). Santillana.

METER

see Versification

METHOD OF STUDY

see Study, Method of

METHODOLOGY

see special subjects with the subdivision Methodology, e.g. Science–Methodology; etc.

METRIC SYSTEM

Ardley, Neil. Making Metric Measurements. 32p. (gr. 4-6). 1984. lib. bdg. 11.90 (ISBN 0-531-04615-X). Watts.

Brady, Janeen. The Metrics Are Coming! (gr. k-4). 1980. cassette 7.95 (ISBN 0-944803-14-8). Brite Intl.

Branley, Franklyn M. Think Metric! Booth, Graham, illus. LC 72-78279. (gr. 3-6). 1972. 12.89 (ISBN 0-690-81861-0, Crowell Jr Bks). HarpC Child Bks.

Brownlee, Juanita. Tangram Geometry in Metric. Merrick, Paul, illus. (Orig.). (gr. 5-10). 1976. pap. 6.95 (ISBN 0-918932-43-2, 0140701407). Activity Resources.

DeBruin, Jerry & Sherperak, Rita. Touching & Teaching Metrics. (gr. k-8). 1977. 14.95 (ISBN 0-916456-08-0). JED.

DeBruin, Jerry, et al. Touching & Teaching Metrics: Duplicating Masters for the Primary Grades. (gr. k-3). 1978. 9.95 (ISBN 0-916456-26-9). JED.

Donovan, Frank. Let's Go Metric. (Illus.). 192p. 1974. 6.95 (ISBN 0-679-40057-5, Weybright). McKay.

Finnegan, Thomas J., et al. Metric System Study Aid. 1976. pap. 2.50 (ISBN 0-87738-042-2). Youth Ed.

Leaf, Munro. Metric Can Be Fun. Leaf, Munro, illus. LC 75-29223. (gr. 1-3). 1976. (Lipp Jr Bks); pap. 1.95 (ISBN 0-397-31680-1). HarpC Child Bks.

Miller, Mary & Richardson, Toni. The Merry Metric Cookbook. Miller, Mary, illus. (Orig.). (gr. k-3). 1974. pap. 4.50 (ISBN 0-918932-32-7). Activity Resources.

Richardson, Toni & Miller, Mary. Making Metric Maneuvers. Miller, Mary, illus. (Orig.). (gr. 2-7). 1973. pap. 8.50 (ISBN 0-918932-27-0). Activity Resources.

Ross, Frank, Jr. The Metric System: Measures for All Mankind. Galster, Robert, illus. LC 74-14503. 128p. (gr. 7-10). 1974. 23.95 (ISBN 0-87599-198-X). S G Phillips.

—The Metric System: Measures for All Mankind. Galster, Robert, illus. LC 74-14503. 128p. (gr. 7-10). 1974. 23.95 (ISBN 0-87599-198-X). S G Phillips.

METROLOGY

see Mensuration; Weights and Measures

METROPOLITAN AREAS

see also Cities and Towns; Urban Renewal

METTERNICH-WINNEBURG, CLEMENS LOTHAR WENZEL, FURST VON, 1773-1859

Von der Heide, John. Klemens von Metternich. Schlesinger, Arthur M., Jr., intro. by. (Illus.). 112p. (gr. 5 up). 1988. lib. bdg. 17.95 (ISBN 0-87754-541-3). Chelsea Hse.

MEXICAN WAR, 1845-1848

see U. S.–History–War with Mexico, 1845-1848

MEXICAN AMERICANS

see also Mexicans in the U. S.

Brown, Tricia. Hello, Amigos! Ortiz, Fran, photos by. LC 86-9882. (Illus.). 48p. (gr. 1-4). 1986. 13.95 (ISBN 0-8050-0090-9). H Holt & Co.

Catalano, Julie. Mexican Americans. Moynihan, Daniel P., intro. by. 112p. (Orig.). (gr. 5 up). 1988. 17.95 (ISBN 0-87754-857-9); pap. 9.95 (ISBN 0-7910-0272-1). Chelsea Hse.

Emiliano Zapata: Mini Play. (gr. 5 up). 1977. 5.00 (ISBN 0-89550-357-3). Stevens & Shea.

Garcia, Ruperto. Cesar Chavez. (Illus.). 112p. (gr. 5 up). 1991. PLB 17.95 (ISBN 0-7910-1232-8). Chelsea Hse.

Hewett, Joan. Hector Lives in the United States Now: The Story of a Mexican-American Child. Hewett, Richard R., illus. LC 89-36572. 48p. (gr. 2-5). 1990. 13.95 (ISBN 0-397-32295-X, Lipp Jr Bks); PLB 13.89 (ISBN 0-397-32278-X, Lipp Jr Bks). HarpC Child Bks.

Marquez, Nancy & Perez, Theresa. Portraits of Mexican Americans. 96p. (gr. 4-8). 1991. 9.95 (ISBN 0-86653-605-1, GA1324). Good Apple.

Morey, Janet & Dunn, Wendy. Famous Mexican Americans. LC 89-7218. (Illus.). (gr. 5 up). 1989. 14.95 (ISBN 0-525-65012-1, Cobblehill Bks). Dutton Child Bks.

Nicholson, Loren. Romualdo Pacheco's California! The Mexican-American Who Won. (Illus.). 112p. (Orig.). (gr. 10-12). 1991. pap. text ed. 12.95 (ISBN 0-9623233-2-2). CA HPA.

Wolf, Bernard. In This Proud Land: The Story of a Mexican American Family. reissue (1978) ed. LC 78-9680. (Illus.). 96p. (gr. 4 up). 1987. PLB 12.89 (ISBN 0-397-32268-2, Lipp Jr Bks). HarpC Child Bks.

MEXICAN AMERICANS–FICTION

Ludwig & Santibanez. Mexican American Coloring Book. (Illus.). 32p. (gr. 4 up). pap. 2.50 (ISBN 0-930504-00-3). Polaris Pr.

Martini, Teri. Feliz Navidad, Pablo. McNichols, William H., illus. 1990. 2.95 (ISBN 0-8091-6597-X). Paulist Pr.

Soto, Gary. Baseball in April: And Other Stories. (gr. 7 up). 1990. 14.95 (ISBN 0-15-205720-X). HarbraceJ.

MEXICANS IN THE U. S.

Pinchot, Jane. The Mexicans in America. rev. ed. LC 72-3587. (Illus.). 104p. (gr. 5 up). 1989. PLB 11.95 (ISBN 0-8225-0222-4); pap. 3.95 (ISBN 0-8225-1016-2). Lerner Pubns.

MEXICO

Benitez, Mirna. How Spider Tricked Snake. (Illus.). 32p. (gr. 1-4). 1989. PLB 13.32 (ISBN 0-8172-3524-8). Raintree Pubs.

Brandt, Keith. Mexico & Central America. Eitzen, Allan, illus. LC 84-2668. 32p. (gr. 3-6). 1985. PLB 9.49 (ISBN 0-8167-0264-0); pap. text ed. 2.95 (ISBN 0-8167-0265-9). Troll Assocs.

Department of Geography, Lerner Publications Company Staff. Mexico in Pictures. (Illus.). 64p. (gr. 5 up). 1988. PLB 12.95 (ISBN 0-8225-1801-5). Lerner Pubns.

Epstein, Sam & Epstein, Beryl. Mexico. rev. ed. (Illus.). 72p. (gr. 4 up). 1983. PLB 10.40 (ISBN 0-531-04530-7). Watts.

Fincher, E. B. Mexico & the United States: Their Linked Destinies. LC 82-45581. (Illus.). 224p. (gr. 7 up). 1983. 12.95 (ISBN 0-690-04310-4, Crowell Jr Bks); (Crowell Jr Bks). HarpC Child Bks.

Garver, Susan & McGuire, Paula. From Mexico, Cuba, & Puerto Rico. (gr. 7-11). pap. 2.50 (ISBN 0-317-13311-X, LFL). Dell.

Getting to Know Mexico. 48p. 1990. 7.95 (ISBN 0-8442-7623-5). Natl Textbk.

Haskins, Jim. Count Your Way Through Mexico. Byers, Helen, illus. 24p. (gr. 1-4). 1989. 11.95 (ISBN 0-87614-349-4); pap. 4.95 (ISBN 0-87614-517-9). Carolrhoda Bks.

Iuzarry, Carmen. Passport to Mexico. LC 86-50571. (Illus.). 48p. (gr. 4-8). 1987. PLB 12.90 (ISBN 0-531-10271-8). Watts.

Jacobsen, Karen. Mexico. Kratky, Lada, tr. from ENG. LC 82-4437. (SPA., Illus.). 48p. (gr. k-4). 1984. lib. bdg. 14.60 (ISBN 0-516-31632-X); pap. 4.95 (ISBN 0-516-51632-9). Childrens.

Jacobson, Karen. Mexico. LC 82-4437. (Illus.). (gr. k-4). 1982. PLB 14.60 (ISBN 0-516-01632-6); pap. 4.95 (ISBN 0-516-41632-4). Childrens.

James, Ian. Mexico. (Illus.). 32p. (gr. k-6). 1989. PLB 11.90 (ISBN 0-531-10761-2). Watts.

Lye, Keith. Take a Trip to Mexico. LC 82-50061. 32p. (gr. 1-3). 1982. PLB 7.99 (ISBN 0-531-04471-8). Watts.

Paltrowitz, Stuart & Paltrowitz, Donna. Content Area Reading Skills-Competency Mexico: Locating Details. (Illus.). (gr. 4). 1987. pap. text ed. 3.25 (ISBN 0-89525-854-4). Ed Activities.

Poulet, Virginia. Azulin Visita a Mexico: Blue Bug Visits Mexico. Anderson, Peggy P., illus. LC 89-25420. (SPA.). 32p. (ps-2). 1990. PLB 14.60 (ISBN 0-516-33429-8). Childrens.

Rummel, Jack. Mexico. (Illus.). (gr. 5 up). 1990. 14.95 (ISBN 0-7910-1110-0). Chelsea Hse.

Somonte, Carlos. We Live in Mexico. (Illus.). 60p. (gr. 4-8). 1984. PLB 9.49 (ISBN 0-531-03820-3). Watts.

Stein, R. Conrad. Mexico. LC 83-21049. (Illus.). 128p. (gr. 5-9). 1984. lib. bdg. 25.27 (ISBN 0-516-02772-7). Childrens.

Widdows, Richard. Mexico. (Illus.). 48p. (gr. 4-8). 1988. PLB 14.98 (ISBN 0-382-09506-5). Silver Burdett Pr.

MEXICO (CITY)

Davis, James E. & Hawke, Sharryl D. Mexico City. (Illus.). 64p. (gr. 4-9). 1990. PLB 18.00 (ISBN 0-8172-3029-7). Raintree Pubs.

MEXICO–FICTION

Brandel, Marc. An Ear for Danger. LC 88-26823. 144p. (gr. 5 up). 1989. lib. bdg. 6.99 (ISBN 0-394-99943-6). Random.

Ets, Marie H. Gilberto & the Wind. Ets, Marie H., illus. LC 63-8527. (gr. k-3). 1978. pap. 3.95 (ISBN 0-14-050276-9, Puffin). Puffin Bks.

Ets, Marie H. & Labastida, Aurora. Nine Days to Christmas. Ets, Marie H., illus. (ps-2). 1959. pap. 13.95 (ISBN 0-670-51350-4). Viking Child Bks.

George, Jean C. Shark Beneath the Reef. LC 88-25194. 192p. (gr. 7 up). 1989. 11.95 (ISBN 0-06-021992-0); PLB 11.89 (ISBN 0-06-021993-9). HarpC Child Bks.

Gordon, Alvin J. Tortillas. DeGrazia, Ted, illus. 20p. (Orig.). (gr. 1-3). 1971. pap. 6.95 (ISBN 0-916955-06-0). ARCUS Pub.
Lewis, Thomas P. Hill of Fire. Sandin, Joan, illus. LC 70-121802. 64p. (gr. k-3). 1971. PLB 10.89. HarpC Child Bks.
Matthews, Billie P. & Chichester, A. Lee. Secret of the Cibolo. Roberts, Melissa, ed. (Illus.). 104p. (gr. 4-7). 1988. 8.95 (ISBN 0-89015-638-7, Pub. by Panda Bks). Eakin Pr.
Toepperwein, Emilie & Toepperwein, Fritz A. Jose & the Mexican Jumping Bean. (Illus.). (gr. 4-7). 1965. PLB 2.95 (ISBN 0-910722-05-6). Highland Pr.
Villicana, Eugenio. Viva Morelia. Manriquez, Elisa, illus. LC 72-159842. 64p. (gr. 4-6). 1972. 6.95 (ISBN 0-87131-098-8). M Evans.
Williams, Jeanne. Tame the Wild Stallion. Conoly, Walle, illus. LC 84-16257. 182p. (gr. 4 up). 1985. 14.95 (ISBN 0-87565-002-3); pap. 8.95 (ISBN 0-87565-009-0). Tex Christian.

MEXICO–HISTORY

Department of Geography, Lerner Publications Company Staff. Mexico in Pictures. (Illus.). 64p. (gr. 5 up). 1988. PLB 12.95 (ISBN 0-8225-1801-5). Lerner Pubns.
Fisher, Leonard E. Pyramid of the Sun - Pyramid of the Moon. Fisher, Leonard E., illus. LC 88-1410. 32p. (gr. 1-5). 1988. 13.95 (ISBN 0-02-735300-1). Macmillan Child Grp.
Grier, Paula. The Early Mexicans. (Illus.). 47p. (Orig.). (gr. 6-8). 1982. pap. text ed. 14.95 (ISBN 1-878550-03-9). Inter Dev Res Assn.
Killingray, David. The Mexican Revolution. Yapp, Malcolm, et al, eds. (Illus.). 32p. (gr. 6-11). 1980. pap. text ed. 2.95 (ISBN 0-89908-112-6). Greenhaven.
Miguel Hidalgo y Costilla. (Illus.). 32p. (gr. 3-6). 1988. PLB 16.67 (ISBN 0-8172-2905-1); pap. 9.27 (ISBN 0-685-28501-4). Raintree Pubs.
Ochoa, George. The Fall of Mexico City. (Illus.). 64p. (gr. 5 up). 1989. PLB 16.98 (ISBN 0-382-09836-6); pap. 7.95 (ISBN 0-382-09853-6). Silver Burdett Pr.

MEXICO–HISTORY–SPANISH COLONY, 1540-1810–FICTION

Gray, Genevieve. How Far, Felipe? Grifalconi, Ann, illus. LC 77-11846. 64p. (gr. k-3). 1978. PLB 11.89 (ISBN 0-06-022108-9). HarpC Child Bks.

MEXICO–PRESIDENTS

Lazaro Cardenas: Mini Play. (gr. 5 up). 1977. 5.00 (ISBN 0-89550-358-1). Stevens & Shea.

MEXICO–SOCIAL LIFE AND CUSTOMS

Casagrande, Louis B. & Johnson, Sylvia A. Focus on Mexico: Modern Life in an Ancient Land. (Illus.). 96p. (gr. 5up). 1986. lib. bdg. 15.95 (ISBN 0-8225-0645-9). Lerner Pubns.
Moran, Tom. A Family in Mexico. (Illus.). 32p. (gr. 2-5). 1987. 9.95 (ISBN 0-8225-1677-2). Lerner Pubns.
Somonte, Carlos. We Live in Mexico. (Illus.). 60p. (gr. 4-8). 1984. PLB 9.49 (ISBN 0-531-03820-3). Watts.

MICE

Burton, Robert. The Mouse in the Barn. Oxford Scientific Films, photos by. LC 87-42614. (Illus.). 32p. (gr. 4-6). 1988. PLB 10.95 (ISBN 1-55532-305-7). Gareth Stevens Inc.
Fischer-Nagel, Heiderose & Fischer-Nagel, Andreas. A Look Through the Mouse Hole. Fischer-Nagel, Heiderose & Fischer-Nagel, Andreas, illus. 48p. (gr. 2-5). 1989. lib. bdg. 12.95 (ISBN 0-87614-326-5). Carolrhoda Bks.
Harrison, Virginia. The World of Mice. Oxford Scientific Films Staff, photos by. LC 87-42609. (Illus.). 32p. (gr. 2-3). 1988. PLB 10.95 (ISBN 1-55532-309-X). Gareth Stevens Inc.
Kirby, Mansfield. The Secret of Thut-Mouse III: or Basil Beaudesert's Revenge. Post, Mance, illus. LC 85-47588. 64p. (ps up). 1985. 11.95 (ISBN 0-374-36677-2). FS&G.
Mezek, Karen. A Picnic with the Barleys. Mezek, Karen, illus. LC 88-80360. 36p. (Orig.). 1989. pap. 9.99 (ISBN 0-89081-658-1). Harvest Hse.
Royston, Angela. Mouse. Pledger, Maurice, illus. 24p. (gr. k-3). 1989. pap. 2.95 (ISBN 0-8249-8369-6). Ideals.
Wexler, Jerome. Pet Mice. Tucker, Kathleen, ed. (Illus.). 48p. (gr. 2-8). 1989. PLB 13.95 (ISBN 0-8075-6524-5). A Whitman.
Wood, John N. Survival: Could You Be a Mouse? Bown, Derick, illus. 32p. (gr. 2-6). 1990. 10.95 (ISBN 0-8249-8445-5). Ideals.

MICE–FICTION

Aesop. The City Mouse & the Country Mouse. Wheeler, Jody, illus. LC 85-70290. 18p. (ps). 1985. 3.95 (ISBN 0-448-10226-9, G&D). Putnam Pub Group.
—The Country Mouse & the City Mouse. Lydecker, Laura, illus. LC 86-27238. 32p. (ps-1). 1987. Knopf.
Aliki. At Mary Bloom's. Aliki, illus. LC 75-45482. 32p. (gr. k-3). 1983. 11.25 (ISBN 0-688-02480-7); PLB 14.88 (ISBN 0-688-02481-5). Greenwillow.
Allen, Laura J. Rollo & Tweedy & the Case of the Missing Cheese. Allen, Laura J., illus. LC 82-47731. 48p. (gr. k-3). 1983. HarpC Child Bks.
Aragon, Jane Chelsea. Major & the Mousehole Mice. (ps-3). 1990. pap. 13.95 (ISBN 0-671-68853-7). S&S Trade.
Asch, Frank. Pearl's Promise. Asch, Frank, illus. LC 83-17153. 160p. (gr. 4-6). 1984. PLB 12.95 (ISBN 0-385-29321-6); pap. 12.95 (ISBN 0-385-29325-9). Delacorte.
Barklem, Jill. Autumn Story. Barklem, Jill, illus. LC 80-15433. 32p. (gr. 1 up). 1986. pap. 9.95 (ISBN 0-399-20745-7, Philomel Bks). Putnam Pub Group.
—The High Hills. Barklem, Jill, illus. LC 86-8177. 32p. (ps-3). 1986. 12.95 (ISBN 0-399-21361-9, Philomel). Putnam Pub Group.
—The Secret Staircase. LC 83-6270. (Illus.). (ps-3). 1986. pap. 13.95 (ISBN 0-399-20994-8, Philomel). Putnam Pub Group.
—Spring Story. Barklem, Jill, illus. LC 80-15300. 32p. (gr. 1 up). 1986. pap. 8.95 (ISBN 0-399-20746-5, Philomel); PLB 6.99 (ISBN 0-399-61156-8). Putnam Pub Group.
—Summer Story. Barklem, Jill, illus. LC 80-15423. 32p. (gr. 1 up). 1986. pap. 9.95 (ISBN 0-399-20747-3, Philomel); PLB 6.99 (ISBN 0-399-61157-6). Putnam Pub Group.
—Winter Story. Barklem, Jill, illus. LC 80-15422. 32p. (gr. 1 up). 1986. 9.95 (ISBN 0-399-20748-1, Philomel). Putnam Pub Group.
Bishop & Leechman. The Adventures of Jozedek. Nudd, Stacy, illus. LC 86-72946. 62p. (Orig.). (gr. 4-5). 1987. pap. 6.00 (ISBN 0-916383-23-7). Aegina Pr.
Boegehold, Betty. Here's Pippa! Szekeres, Cyndy, illus. LC 88-27256. 128p. (gr. k-3). 1989. pap. 2.95 (ISBN 0-394-82702-3). Knopf.
—Hurray for Pippa! Szekeres, Cyndy, illus. LC 79-19105. 64p. (gr. k-3). 1980. Knopf.
—Pippa Pops Out! Szekeres, Cyndy, illus. LC 78-12491. (ps-3). 1979. 4.95 (ISBN 0-394-84057-7). Knopf.
—Pippa Pops Out! Szekeres, Cyndy, illus. 64p. (ps-3). 1980. pap. 0.95 (ISBN 0-440-46865-5, YB). Dell.
Boegehold, Betty & Szekeres, Cyndy. Here's Pippa Again. LC 74-15303. (Illus.). 64p. (ps-2). 1975. Knopf.
Brandenberg, Franz. Nice New Neighbors. Aliki, illus. LC 77-1651. 56p. (gr. 1-4). 1977. PLB 13.88 (ISBN 0-688-84105-8). Greenwillow.
—Nice New Neighbors. Aliki, illus. 32p. (ps-2). 1990. pap. 2.75 (ISBN 0-590-44117-5). Scholastic Inc.
Brown, Frances R. The Tales of Minerva & Tickfeld Mouse: A Tre Fantasy. 74p. 1990. 7.95 (ISBN 0-533-08611-6). Vantage.
Brown, Marcia. Once a Mouse. LC 61-14769. (Illus.). 32p. (ps-5). 1982. pap. 3.95 (ISBN 0-689-70751-7, Aladdin). Macmillan Child Grp.
Brown, Michael. Santa Mouse. De Witt, Elfrieda, illus. (gr. k-3). 1966. 4.95 (ISBN 0-448-04213-4, G&D); PLB 3.09 (ISBN 0-448-13914-6). Putnam Pub Group.
—Santa Mouse. Barbaresi, Nina, illus. 16p. (ps). 1984. 3.95 (ISBN 0-448-10215-3, G&D). Putnam Pub Group.
—Santa Mouse Meets Marmaduke. DeSantis, George, illus. LC 74-92384. (gr. k-7). 1978. pap. 2.50 (ISBN 0-448-14749-1, G&D). Putnam Pub Group.
Buchanan, Heather S. George & Matilda Mouse & the Doll's House. Buchanan, Heather S., illus. 40p. (ps-3). 1988. pap. 12.95 (ISBN 0-671-66844-7). S&S Trade.
—George & Matilda Mouse & the Floating School. LC 89-22036. (Illus.). 40p. (ps-3). 1990. PLB 13.95 (ISBN 0-671-70613-6). S&S Trade.
Bullock, Kathleen. A Friend for Mitzi Mouse. LC 90-31559. (Illus.). 40p. (ps-1). 1990. PLB 13.95 (ISBN 0-671-68867-7). S&S Trade.
Burgess, Thornton W. Adventures of Whitefoot the Woodmouse. Cady, Harrison & Kerr, George, illus. (gr. k-3). 1944. (G&D). Putnam Pub Group.
Burningham, John. Trubloff: The Mouse Who Wanted to Play the Balalaika. (ps). 1965. lib. bdg. write for info. (ISBN 0-394-97316-X, Random Juv). Random.
Bussard, Paula J. Grandmother Mouse's Secret. Goodridge, Lawrence, illus. 32p. (gr. k-6). 1986. 1.39 (ISBN 0-87403-102-8, 3432). Standard Pub.
—A Loving Touch. Goodridge, Lawrence, illus. 32p. (gr. k-6). 1986. 1.39 (ISBN 0-87403-106-0, 3436). Standard Pub.
—Rascal's Choice. Goodridge, Lawrence, illus. 32p. (gr. k-6). 1986. 1.39 (ISBN 0-87403-103-6, 3433). Standard Pub.
—A Surprise for Lunchbox. Goodridge, Lawrence, illus. 32p. (gr. k-6). 1986. 1.39 (ISBN 0-87403-104-4, 3434). Standard Pub.
—Sydney's Soup-Can Message. Goodridge, Lawrence, illus. 32p. (gr. k-6). 1986. 1.39 (ISBN 0-87403-101-X, 3431). Standard Pub.
—Where Should the Money Go? Goodridge, Lawrence, illus. 32p. (gr. k-6). 1986. 1.39 (ISBN 0-87403-105-2, 3435). Standard Pub.
Butler, M. Christina. Stanley in the Dark. Rutherford, Meg, illus. 32p. (ps-1). 1990. with dust jacket 12.95 (ISBN 0-8120-6158-6). Barron.
Carle, Eric. Do You Want to Be My Friend? Carle, Eric, illus. LC 70-140643. 32p. (ps-2). 1971. 13.95 (ISBN 0-690-24276-X, Crowell Jr Bks); PLB 13.89 (ISBN 0-690-01137-7, Crowell Jr Bks). HarpC Child Bks.
Carratello, Patty. Mice on Ice. Spivak, Darlene, ed. Smythe, Linda, illus. 16p. (gr. k-2). 1988. wkbk. 1.95 (ISBN 1-55734-382-9). Tchr Create Mat.
Cartlidge, Michelle. Bear's Room: No Peeking. (Illus.). 24p. (gr. k-2). 1986. 3.95 (ISBN 0-87406-124-5, 15-11820-5). Willowisp Pr.
—A House for Lily Mouse. (gr. 1-5). 1987. 10.95 (ISBN 0-13-395849-3). P-H.
—Mouse House. (ps). 1990. 3.95 (ISBN 0-525-44638-9, DCB). Dutton Child Bks.
Cauley, Lorinda B. The Town Mouse & the Country Mouse. Cauley, Lorinda B., illus. LC 84-11532. 32p. (ps-3). 1984. 11.95 (ISBN 0-399-21123-3, Putnam); pap. 5.95 (ISBN 0-399-21126-8). Putnam Pub Group.
Cauley, Lorinda B., retold by. The Town Mouse & the Country Mouse. (Illus.). 32p. (ps-3). 1990. pap. 5.95 (ISBN 0-399-22009-7, Putnam). Putnam Pub Group.
Chorao, Kay. Cathedral Mouse. Chorao, Kay, illus. LC 87-33398. 32p. (ps-2). 1988. 12.95 (ISBN 0-525-44400-9, DCB). Dutton Child Bks.
The City Mouse & the Country Mouse, Unit 7. (gr. 2). 1991. 5-pack 21.25 (ISBN 0-88106-758-X). Charlesbridge Pub.
Cleary, Beverly. Lucky Chuck. Higginbottom, J. Winslow, illus. LC 83-13386. 40p. (gr. k-3). 1984. 13.95 (ISBN 0-688-02736-9); PLB 13.88 (ISBN 0-688-02738-5, Morrow Jr Bks). Morrow Jr Bks.
—The Mouse & the Motorcycle. Darling, Louis, illus. LC 65-20956. (gr. 2-6). 1965. 13.95 (ISBN 0-688-21698-6); PLB 13.88 (ISBN 0-688-31698-0). Morrow.
—The Mouse & the Motorcycle. large type ed. 1989. Repr. of 1965 ed. PLB 15.95 (ISBN 1-55736-137-1, Crnrstn Bks). ABC-CLIO.
—The Mouse & the Motorcycle. 160p. 1990. pap. 3.50 (ISBN 0-380-70924-4, Camelot). Avon.
—Mouse House Trio, 3 vols. (gr. 4-7). 1990. pap. 9.75 (ISBN 0-440-36016-1). Dell.
—Ralph S. Mouse. Zelinsky, Paul O., illus. LC 82-3516. 160p. (gr. 4-6). 1982. 14.95 (ISBN 0-688-01452-6); lib. bdg. 14.88 (ISBN 0-688-01455-0). Morrow.
—Ralph S. Mouse. large type ed. 160p. 1989. Repr. of 1982 ed. PLB 15.95 (ISBN 1-55736-136-3, Crnrstn Bks). ABC-CLIO.
—Ramona, Mouse, 4 vols. (gr. 4-7). 1990. Boxed Set. pap. 14.00 (ISBN 0-380-71483-3). Avon.
Clohe. Fairyland Favorites: Town Mouse & Country Mouse. 1989. 2.98 (ISBN 0-671-06188-7). S&S Trade.
Conly, Jane L. Racso & the Rats of NIMH. Lubin, Leonard, illus. LC 85-42634. 288p. (gr. 4-7). 1988. pap. 3.50 (ISBN 0-06-440245-2, Trophy). HarpC Child Bks.
Coon, Alma S. The Mouse & the Mill & the Bottle Babies. Shoemaker, Kathryn, illus. 44p. (ps-1). 1982. 4.95 (ISBN 0-87935-061-X). Williamsburg.
Cormier, Robert. I Am the Cheese. LC 76-55948. 224p. (gr. 7-12). 1977. 18.95 (ISBN 0-394-83462-3). Pantheon.
Cosgrove, Stephen. Little Mouse on the Prairie. James, Robin, illus. 32p. (gr. 1-4). 1978. pap. 2.95 (ISBN 0-8431-0569-0). Price Stern.
Cowley, Joy. Ratty-Tatty. Matijasevic, Astrid, illus. 16p. (Orig.). (gr. k-2). 1987. pap. text ed. 23.00 (ISBN 1-55624-164-X). Wright Group.
Craig, Janet. Windy Day. Durrell, Julie, illus. LC 87-10909. 32p. (gr. k-2). 1987. PLB 6.11 (ISBN 0-8167-0982-3); pap. text ed. 1.95 (ISBN 0-8167-0983-1). Troll Assocs.
Crust, Linda. Melvin's Cold Feet. Brindle, John, illus. LC 90-47201. 32p. (gr. 2-3). 1991. lib. bdg. 12.95 (ISBN 0-8368-0356-6). Gareth Stevens Inc.
Dickens, Charles. Mickey's Christmas Carol. Disney Studio Staff, ed. LC 84-9491. (Illus.). (gr. k up). 1984. pap. 5.95 (ISBN 0-517-55525-5). Crown.
DiFiori, Larry. Muffin Mouse's New House. DiFiori, Larry, illus. (ps-k). 1991. pap. write for info. (ISBN 0-307-10028-6, Golden Pr). Western Pub.
Disney. Rescuers. 1990. 5.98 (ISBN 0-8317-2474-9). Smithmark.
Disney Animated Shorts. Mickey Mouse Movie Stories. Sendak, Maurice, intro. by. (Illus.). 208p. (gr. 2 up). 1988. 19.95 (ISBN 0-8109-1529-4). Abrams.
Disney, Walt, Productions Staff. The Great Mouse Detective. LC 86-42608. (Illus.). 48p. (ps-3). 1986. (Random Juv); (BYR). Random.
—Walt Disney Productions Presents "The Rescuers" LC 76-54412. (Illus.). (ps-2). 1977. 6.95 (ISBN 0-394-83456-9, Random Juv); lib. bdg. 4.99 (ISBN 0-394-93456-3). Random.
Dominquez, Angel. Diary of a Victorian Mouse. Dominquez, Angel, illus. 32p. (ps up). 1991. 14.95 (ISBN 1-55970-121-8). Arcade Pub Inc.
Dubanevich, Arlene. Tom's Tail. (ps-3). 1990. 13.95 (ISBN 0-670-83021-6). Viking Child Bks.
Dunbar, Joyce. Ten Little Mice. 1990. 13.95 (ISBN 0-15-200601-X). HarbraceJ.
Durrell, Julie. Mouse Tails. Durrell, Julie, illus. LC 84-12638. 32p. (ps-1). 1985. 6.95 (ISBN 0-517-55592-1). Crown.
Edwards, Richard. A Mouse in My Roof. Venice, illus. (ps up). 1990. write for info. Delacorte.
Emberley, Michael. Ruby, Vol. 1. (ps-3). 1990. 14.95 (ISBN 0-316-23643-8). Little.
Ernst, Lisa C. Rescue of Aunt Pansy. (ps-2). 1987. pap. 8.95 (ISBN 0-670-81716-3). Viking Child Bks.
Fidge, Louis. Bubble & Squeak: The Car; Bubble Plays a Trick; A Parcel for Squeak; The Party; The Hot Air Balloon & The Lost Ball, 6 bks. Masters, Chris, illus. 96p. (Orig.). (gr. k-1). 1988. Set. pap. text ed. 28.90 (ISBN 1-55624-488-6). Wright Group.
Field, Rachel. Road Might Lead to Anywhere, Vol. 1. LC 89-32815. (ps-3). 1990. 14.95 (ISBN 0-316-28178-6). Little.
Fowler, Richard. There's a Mouse about the House. (Illus.). 24p. (ps-1). 1984. 9.95 (ISBN 0-88110-154-0). EDC.
Frankel, Julie E. Mice! Venezia, Mike, illus. LC 86-1008. 32p. (ps-2). 1986. PLB 11.93 (ISBN 0-516-02070-6); pap. 2.95 (ISBN 0-516-42070-4). Childrens.
Freeman, Don. Norman the Doorman. Freeman, Don, illus. (ps-2). 1959. pap. 15.95 (ISBN 0-670-51515-9). Viking Child Bks.

Fryar, Jane. Lost at the Mall: Morris the Mouse Adventure Ser. Wilson, Deborah, illus. 32p. (ps-1). 1991. 7.95 (ISBN 0-570-04196-1, 56-1655). Concordia.
Lost at the Mall is one of two titles in the new Morris The Mouse Adventure Series, which features Morris the Mouse, a well-loved Sunday School character. When 5-year-old Broderick slips Morris into his pocket for a trip to the mall, the two get lost. Amid the confusion & fear of being all alone in a strange place, Morris reminds Broderick that Jesus will help & take care of him in any situation. The Morris books are a great way to assist parents & teachers in helping their 3- to 6-year old children identify the unique talents God has given them & be assured of God's constant care. For children ages 3 to 6. 32 pp. 4-color hardcover. $7.95. Concordia Publishing House. Item no. 56-1655. ISBN 0-570-04196-1. To order -- Call Toll Free 1-800-325-3040.
Publisher Provided Annotation.

Fuchshuber, Annegert. Giant Story - Mouse Tale: A Half Picture Book. (Illus.). 32p. (ps-3). 1988. lib. bdg. 12.95 (ISBN 0-87614-319-2); pap. 5.95 (ISBN 0-87614-500-4). Carolrhoda Bks.
—Giant Story Mouse Tale. (Illus.). 32p. (ps-3). 1989. pap. 5.95 (ISBN 0-685-24888-7, First Ave Edns). Lerner Pubns.
Gaudreau, Carmen. Bernard et Bridget: a la cabane a sucre. LeBlanc, Lorraine, illus. (FRE.). 40p. (gr. k-1). 1979. pap. text ed. 1.50 (ISBN 0-911409-47-5); of 53 2x2 slides 13.25 set (ISBN 0-686-42727-0). Natl Mat Dev.
Gentile, Gennaro L. The Mouse in the Manger. McKissack, Vernon, illus. LC 78-72944. 80p. (gr. k-4). 1978. pap. 5.95 (ISBN 0-87793-165-8). Ave Maria.
Geraghty, Paul. Look Out, Patrick! Geraghty, Paul, illus. LC 89-77850. 32p. (ps-1). 1990. 12.95 (ISBN 0-02-735822-4, Mcmillan Child Bk). Macmillan Child Grp.
Ginsburg, Mirra. Four Brave Sailors. Tafuri, Lynn, illus. LC 86-7555. 24p. (ps-1). 1987. 11.75 (ISBN 0-688-06514-7); PLB 11.88 (ISBN 0-688-06515-5). Greenwillow.
Gomi, Taro. Hide & Seek. Young, Richard G., ed. Kaisei-sha, tr. LC 89-12049. (Illus.). 32p. (gr. 1-3). 1989. PLB 13.26 (ISBN 0-944483-45-3). Garrett Ed Corp.
Gordon, Sharon. Maxwell Mouse. Rosenberg, Amye, illus. LC 81-4653. 32p. (gr. k-2). 1981. PLB 10.89 (ISBN 0-89375-501-X); pap. 2.95 (ISBN 0-89375-502-8). Troll Assocs.
Graham, John. I Love You, Mouse. De Paola, Tomie, illus. LC 78-6214. 32p. (ps-3). 1990. pap. 3.95 (ISBN 0-15-644106-3, VoyB). HarBraceJ.
Grambling, Lois G. Elephant & Mouse Get Ready for Christmas. Maze, Deborah, illus. 32p. 1990. with dust jacket 12.95 (ISBN 0-8120-6185-3). Barron.
Hargreaves, Roger. Sam Squeak. Jolliffe, Gray, illus. LC 89-60412. 32p. (Orig.). (ps-3). 1989. pap. 1.95 (ISBN 0-679-80120-0). Random.
Himmelman, John. Montigue on the High Seas. (Illus.). 32p. (ps-3). 1990. pap. 3.95 (ISBN 0-14-050789-2, Puffin). Puffin Bks.
Hirashima, Jean, illus. Wee Mouse's Peekaboo House. LC 89-64279. 14p. (ps). 1991. bds. 2.95 (ISBN 0-679-80786-1). Random.
Hoban, Russell. The Mouse & His Child. (gr. k-6). 1990. pap. 3.50 (ISBN 0-440-40293-X, YB). Dell.
—The Mouse & His Child. large type ed. 312p. (gr. 3-7). 1990. lib. bdg. 17.95x (ISBN 0-7451-1104-1, Lythway Large Print). G K Hall.
Hoff, Syd. Mrs. Brice's Mice. Hoff, Syd, illus. LC 87-45680. 32p. (ps-2). 1988. 10.95 (ISBN 0-06-022451-7); PLB 10.89 (ISBN 0-06-022452-5). HarpC Child Bks.
—Mrs. Brice's Mice. Hoff, Syd, illus. LC 87-45680. 32p. (ps-2). 1991. pap. 2.95 (ISBN 0-06-444145-8, Trophy). HarpC Child Bks.
Holabird, Katharine. Angelina Ballerina. Craig, Helen, illus. LC 83-8233. (ps-2). 1988. pap. 13.00 (ISBN 0-517-55083-0, C N Potter Bks). Crown.
—Angelina Book & Doll Package. Craig, Helen, illus. LC 83-8233. 32p. (ps-2). 1989. book & doll 20.00 (ISBN 0-517-57089-0, C N Potter Bks). Crown.
—Angelina on Stage. Craig, Helen, illus. 24p. (ps-2). 1988. 11.95 (ISBN 0-517-56073-9, C N Potter Bks). Crown.
—Angelina's Birthday Surprise. Craig, Helen, illus. LC 89-3513. 32p. (ps-2). 1989. 11.95 (ISBN 0-517-57325-3, C N Potter Bks). Crown.
Holland, Barbara. Creepy-Mouse Coming to Get You. LC 84-14202. 120p. (gr. 4-7). 1985. 10.95 (ISBN 0-89919-329-3, Clarion). HM.
Hollier, Jo. Charlie Churchmouse Finds a Home. Kichejian, Janet, ed. Pullig, Louis, illus. 16p. 1989. 14.95 (ISBN 0-685-29440-4). Silver Pubns.
Hollingsworth, Mary. Charlie & the Jinglemouse. (Illus.). (ps-3). 1989. 5.95 (ISBN 0-915720-25-6). Brownlow Pub Co.
Hopkins, Margaret. Sleepytime for Baby Mouse. Schmidt, Karen L., illus. 12p. (ps-3). 1985. 3.95 (ISBN 0-448-40875-9, G&D). Putnam Pub Group.
Hoppe, Matthias. Mouse & Elephant. (ps-3). 1991. 14.95 (ISBN 0-316-37284-6). Little.
Hurd, Thacher. Blackberry Ramble. Hurd, Thacher, illus. LC 88-14188. 32p. (ps-3). 1989. 12.95 (ISBN 0-517-57349-0); PLB 13.99 (ISBN 0-517-57105-6). Crown.
—Little Mouse's Big Valentine. Hurd, Thacher, illus. LC 89-34515. 32p. (ps-1). 1990. 12.95 (ISBN 0-06-026192-7); PLB 10.89 (ISBN 0-06-026193-5). HarpC Child Bks.
—The Pea Patch Jig. LC 86-2693. (Illus.). (ps-2). 1988. 11.95 (ISBN 0-517-56307-X). Crown.
If You Give a Mouse a Cookie. (gr. k-9). 1988. pap. 2.50 (ISBN 0-318-36470-0). Scholastic Inc.
Ireland, Vicky. The Town Mouse, & the Country Mouse. 38p. (Orig.). (gr. k-3). 1987. pap. 4.50 playscript (ISBN 0-87602-266-2). Anchorage.
Ivimey, John W. Three Blind Mice, Vol. 1. LC 88-1302. (ps-3). 1990. 13.95 (ISBN 0-316-13867-3, Joy St Bks). Little.
Iwamura, Kazuo. The Fourteen Forest Mice & the Harvest Moon Watch. Knowlton, Mary L., tr. from JPN. Iwamura, Kazuo, illus. LC 90-50706. 32p. (gr. k-3). 1991. PLB 11.95 (ISBN 0-8368-0497-X). Gareth Stevens Inc.
—The Fourteen Forest Mice & the Spring Meadow Picnic. Knowlton, Mary L., tr. from JPN. Iwamura, Kazuo, illus. LC 90-50704. 32p. (gr. k-3). 1991. PLB 11.95 (ISBN 0-8368-0498-8). Gareth Stevens Inc.
—The Fourteen Forest Mice & the Summer Laundry Day. Knoulton, Mary L., tr. from JPN. Iwamura, Kazuo, illus. LC 90-50705. 32p. (gr. k-3). 1991. PLB 11.95 (ISBN 0-8368-0576-3). Gareth Stevens Inc.
—The Fourteen Forest Mice & the Winter Sledding Day. Knowlton, Mary L., tr. from JPN. Iwamura, Kazuo, illus. LC 90-50707. 32p. (gr. k-3). 1991. PLB 11.95 (ISBN 0-8368-0499-6). Gareth Stevens Inc.
Janice. Little Bear Marches in the Saint Patrick's Day Parade. Mariana, illus. LC 67-15712. 40p. (gr. k-3). PLB 11.88 (ISBN 0-688-51075-2). Lothrop.
Johnson, Pamela. A Mouse's Tale. D'Andrade, Diane, ed. (Illus.). 32p. (gr. k-4). 1991. 11.95 (ISBN 0-15-256032-7). HarBraceJ.
Jose, Eduard, adapted by. The Vain Little Mouse: A Classic Tale. Riehecky, Janet, tr. from SPA. Asensio, Augusti, illus. LC 88-35214. 32p. (gr. 1-4). 1988. PLB 10.95 (ISBN 0-89565-464-4). Childs World.
Joubert, Jean. White Owl & Blue Mouse. Levertov, Denise, tr. from FRE. Gay, Michel, illus. LC 90-70710. 64p. (gr. 1-3). 1990. 13.95 (ISBN 0-944072-13-5). Zoland Bks.
Kahalewai, Marilyn. Maui Mouse's Supper. LC 87-92276. (Illus.). 16p. (Orig.). (ps-3). 1989. 9.95 (ISBN 0-935848-57-6). Bess Pr.
Keller, Holly. The New Boy. LC 90-41757. (Illus.). 24p. (ps up). 1991. 13.95 (ISBN 0-688-09827-4); PLB 13.88 (ISBN 0-688-09828-2). Greenwillow.
Kellogg, Steven. The Island of the Skog. LC 73-6019. (Illus.). (gr. k-3). 1976. pap. 4.95 (ISBN 0-8037-4122-7). Dial Bks Young.
—The Island of the Skog. Kellogg, Steven, illus. LC 73-6019. 32p. (ps-3). 1973. 13.95 (ISBN 0-8037-3842-0); PLB 13.89 (ISBN 0-8037-3840-4). Dial Bks Young.
Kerr, Phyllis F. I Tricked You! (Illus.). 40p. (ps-k). 1990. PLB 13.95 (ISBN 0-685-35586-1). S&S Trade.
Kingsley, Emily P., adapted by. An American Tail: The Storybook. Kirschner, David, et al, illus. 64p. (gr. 1-5). 1986. pap. 5.95 (ISBN 0-448-48612-1, Platt & Munk). Putnam Pub Group.
King-Smith, Dick. Martin's Mice. Alborough, Jez, illus. LC 88-20359. 128p. (gr. 3 up). 1988. 12.95 (ISBN 0-517-57113-7). Crown.
—Martin's Mice. large print ed. (gr. 4-7). 1989. lib. bdg. 16.50 (ISBN 0-7451-0956-X, Lythway Large Print). G K Hall.
—Martin's Mice. 1990. pap. 2.95 (ISBN 0-440-40380-4, Pub. by Yearling Classics). Dell.
Kraus, Robert. Another Mouse to Feed. Aruego, Jose & Dewey, Ariane, illus. 32p. (ps-1). 1988. bk. & cassette 6.95 (ISBN 0-671-67146-4). S&S Trade.
—Another Mouse to Feed. Aruego, Jose & Dewey, Ariane, illus. LC 78-21259. (ps). 1987. pap. 10.95 (ISBN 0-671-66522-7); pap. 5.95 (ISBN 0-671-66688-6). S&S Trade.
—Noel the Coward. Aruego, Jose & Dewey, Ariane, illus. 32p. (ps-3). 1988. pap. 12.95 (ISBN 0-671-66845-5); pap. 5.95 (ISBN 0-671-66846-3). S&S Trade.
—Where Are You Going, Little Mouse? Aruego, Jose & Dewey, Ariane, illus. LC 84-25868. 32p. (ps-1). 1986. 13.95 (ISBN 0-688-04294-5); PLB 13.95 (ISBN 0-688-04295-3). Greenwillow.
—Where Are You Going, Little Mouse? Dewey, Jose & Dewey, Ariane, illus. LC 84-25868. (ps up). 1989. 4.95 (ISBN 0-688-08747-7, Mulberry). Morrow.
—Whose Mouse Are You? Aruego, Jose, illus. LC 70-89931. 32p. (ps-k). 1986. pap. 4.95 (ISBN 0-689-71142-5, Aladdin). Macmillan Child Grp.
—Whose Mouse Are You? Aruego, Jose, illus. LC 70-89931. 32p. (ps-2). 1970. 13.95 (ISBN 0-02-751190-1, Mcmillan Child Bk). Macmillan Child Grp.
Kroll, Steven. The Biggest Pumpkin Ever. Bassett, Jeni, illus. LC 83-18492. 32p. (ps-3). 1984. reinforced bdg. 14.95 (ISBN 0-8234-0505-2). Holiday.
Kwitz, Mary D. & Ornai, Stella. Shadow over Mousehaven Manor. 160p. (gr. 3-7). 1990. pap. 2.75 (ISBN 0-590-42033-X). Scholastic Inc.
Leonard, Marcia & Schmidt, Karen. Little Mouse Makes a Mess. 32p. (Orig.). (gr. 1). 1985. pap. 2.50 (ISBN 0-553-15301-3). Bantam.
Lionni, Leo. Alexander & the Wind-up Mouse. reissue ed. Lionni, Leo, illus. LC 76-77423. 32p. (ps-2). 1991. 15.00 (ISBN 0-394-80914-9); lib. bdg. 15.99 (ISBN 0-394-90914-3). Knopf.
—Frederick. Lionni, Leo, illus. (gr. k-3). 1973. pap. 2.95 (ISBN 0-394-82614-0). Pantheon.
—Geraldine the Music Mouse. Lionni, Leo, illus. LC 79-932. (ps-3). 1979. 6.95 (ISBN 0-394-84238-3). Pantheon.
—Matthew's Dream. Lionni, Leo, illus. LC 90-34243. 32p. (ps-3). 1991. 15.00 (ISBN 0-679-81075-7); PLB 15.99 (ISBN 0-679-91075-1). Knopf.
—Nicolas, Where Have You Been? Foster, Frances, ed. Rosenthal, Eileen, designed by. LC 86-18574. (Illus.). 32p. (ps-3). 1987. lib. bdg. 11.99 (ISBN 0-394-98370-X). Knopf.
—Tillie & the Wall. Lionni, Leo, illus. LC 88-9316. 32p. (ps-2). 1989. 11.95 (ISBN 0-394-82155-6); lib. bdg. 12.99 (ISBN 0-394-92155-0). Knopf.
Lobel, Arnold. Martha the Movie Mouse. Lobel, Arnold, illus. 32p. (gr. k-3). 1966. PLB 12.89 (ISBN 0-06-023970-0). HarpC Child Bks.
—Mouse Soup. Lobel, Arnold, illus. LC 76-41517. 64p. (gr. k-3). 1977. 11.95 (ISBN 0-06-023967-0); PLB 11.89 (ISBN 0-06-023968-9). HarpC Child Bks.
—Mouse Tales. Lobel, Arnold, illus. LC 72-76511. 64p. (ps-3). 1978. pap. 3.50 (ISBN 0-06-444013-3, Trophy). HarpC Child Bks.
—Mouse Tales. Lobel, Arnold, illus. LC 72-76511. 64p. (ps-3). 1985. pap. 5.98 incl. cassette (ISBN 0-694-00030-2, Trophy). HarpC Child Bks.
Lubin, Leonard B. Christmas Gift-Bringers. Lubin, Leonard B., illus. LC 89-2292. 32p. (gr. k-4). 1989. 12.95 (ISBN 0-688-07019-1); PLB 12.88 (ISBN 0-688-07020-5). Lothrop.
Lundell, Margo. The Wee Mouse Who Was Afraid of the Dark. McQueen, Lucinda, illus. 32p. 1991. pap. 1.95 (ISBN 0-448-40060-X, Platt & Munk Pubs). Putnam Pub Group.
McCully, Emily A. The Christmas Gift. McCully, Emily A., illus. LC 87-45758. 32p. (ps-1). 1988. 12.95 (ISBN 0-06-024211-6); PLB 12.89 (ISBN 0-06-024212-4). HarpC Child Bks.
McKissack, Patricia & McKissack, Frederick. Country Mouse & City Mouse. Sikorski, Anne, illus. LC 85-12759. (gr. 1-2). 1985. PLB 11.93 (ISBN 0-516-02362-4); pap. 3.95 (ISBN 0-516-42362-2). Childrens.
Majewski, Joe. A Friend for Oscar Mouse. Majewski, Maria, illus. LC 87-5365. 32p. (ps-2). 1991. pap. 3.95 (ISBN 0-8037-0913-7, Dial Pied Piper). Puffin Bks.
Malotki, Ekkehart, retold by. The Mouse Couple. Lacapa, Michael, illus. LC 88-60916. 64p. (gr. 1-4). 1988. 14.95 (ISBN 0-87358-473-2). Northland AZ.
Mark, Jan. Hairs in the Palm of the Hand. large type ed. (Illus.). (gr. 3-8). 1989. Repr. of 1981 ed. PLB 14.95 (ISBN 1-85089-968-1, Pub. by Clio Pr England). ABC-CLIO.
Martin, Jacqueline B. Bizzy Bones & Uncle Ezra. Ormai, Stella, illus. LC 83-25618. 32p. (ps-2). 1984. PLB 12.88 (ISBN 0-688-03782-8). Lothrop.
Martin, Melanie. Madison Moves to the Country. Karas, G. Brian, illus. LC 88-1313. 48p. (Orig.). (gr. 1-4). 1989. PLB 9.89 (ISBN 0-8167-1345-6); pap. text ed. 2.95 (ISBN 0-8167-1346-4). Troll Assocs.
Martin, Melanie & Karas, G. Brian. Morris, the Millionaire Mouse. LC 88-1235. (Illus.). 48p. (Orig.). (gr. 1-4). 1988. PLB 9.89 (ISBN 0-8167-1339-1); pap. text ed. 2.95 (ISBN 0-8167-1340-5). Troll Assocs.
Matijasevic, Astrid, illus. Ratty-Tatty, 6 bks. 16p. (Orig.). (gr. k-2). 1987. Set. pap. text ed. 19.80 (ISBN 1-55624-740-0). Wright Group.
Mayne, William. Mousewing. Baynton, Martin, illus. 32p. (ps-3). 1988. 9.95 (ISBN 0-13-604240-6). P-H.
Mendoza, George. Henri Mouse. Boucher, Joelle, illus. 32p. (ps-3). 1986. pap. 3.95 (ISBN 0-14-050636-5, Puffin). Puffin Bks.
—Need a House? Call Ms. Mouse! Smith, Doris S., illus. LC 81-80884. 48p. (ps-3). 1981. 5.95 (ISBN 0-448-16575-9, G&D). Putnam Pub Group.
Mezek, Karen. Christmas at the Rumpole Mansion. LC 89-31537. (Illus., Orig.). (ps-3). 1989. 9.99 (ISBN 0-89081-710-3). Harvest Hse.
—The Rumpoles & the Barleys. Mezek, Karen, illus. LC 88-80376. 40p. (Orig.). (ps-2). 1988. 9.99 (ISBN 0-89081-657-3). Harvest Hse.
Michaels, Ski. The Big Surprise. Paterson, Diane, illus. LC 85-14017. 48p. (gr. 1-3). 1986. PLB 9.89 (ISBN 0-8167-0576-3); pap. text ed. 2.95 (ISBN 0-8167-0577-1). Troll Assocs.
Mickey & the Beanstalk. (Illus.). (ps-3). 1974. 6.95 (ISBN 0-394-82550-0); lib. bdg. 4.99 (ISBN 0-394-92550-5). Random.
Mickey Mouse & Friends. 1990. write for info. (ISBN 0-307-15535-8, Golden Pr). Western Pub.
Miller, Edna. Mousekin Finds a Friend. Miller, Edna, illus. (ps-3). 1971. (Pub. by Treehouse). P-H.

—Mousekin Finds a Friend. 1987. pap. 5.95 (ISBN 0-13-604216-3). P-H.

—Mousekin Finds a Friend. LC 67-18924. (Illus.). 32p. (gr. k-4). 1967. PLB 11.95 (ISBN 0-13-604224-4). P-H.

—Mousekin Finds a Friend. LC 67-18924. (Illus.). 32p. (gr. k-4). 1987. pap. 5.95 (ISBN 0-671-66973-7). S&S Trade.

—Mousekin Takes a Trip. (Illus.). (ps-3). 1976. 9.95x (ISBN 0-13-604363-1, Pub. by Treehouse). P-H.

—Mousekin's ABC. LC 72-176159. (Illus.). 32p. (gr. k-4). 1972. PLB 11.95 (ISBN 0-13-604125-6). P-H.

—Mousekin's ABC. LC 72-176159. (Illus.). 32p. (gr. k-4). 1974. pap. 5.95 (ISBN 0-671-66473-5). S&S Trade.

—Mousekin's Birth. Miller, Edna, illus. 32p. (gr. k-3). 1982. pap. 2.50 (ISBN 0-13-604132-9, Pub. by Treehouse). P-H.

—Mousekin's Christmas Eve. Miller, Edna, illus. (gr. k-3). 1972. 11.95 (ISBN 0-13-604454-9, Pub. by Treehouse). P-H.

—Mousekin's Christmas Eve. LC 65-25244. (Illus.). 32p. (gr. k-4). 1972. pap. 5.95 (ISBN 0-671-66479-4). S&S Trade.

—Mousekin's Close Call. Miller, Edna, illus. LC 77-27571. (gr. k-3). 1980. 9.95x (ISBN 0-13-604207-4, Pub. by Treehouse); pap. 3.95 (ISBN 0-13-604199-X). P-H.

—Mousekin's Family. Miller, Edna, illus. (gr. k-3). 1972. PLB 9.95x (ISBN 0-13-604462-X, Pub. by Treehouse); pap. 5.95 (ISBN 0-13-604157-4). P-H.

—Mousekins Family. (ps up). 1987. 11.95 (ISBN 0-13-604182-5). P-H.

—Mousekin's Family. LC 69-12673. (Illus.). 32p. (gr. k-4). 1972. pap. 5.95 (ISBN 0-671-66477-8). S&S Trade.

—Mousekin's Frosty Friend. LC 89-29892. (Illus.). 32p. (gr. k-4). 1990. PLB 12.95 (ISBN 0-671-70445-1). S&S Trade.

—Mousekin's Golden House. Miller, Edna, illus. (gr. k-3). 1971. PLB 9.95x (ISBN 0-13-604421-2, Pub. by Treehouse). P-H.

—Mousekin's Golden House. 1987. 11.95 (ISBN 0-13-604232-5). P-H.

—Mousekin's Golden House. LC 64-16429. (Illus.). 32p. (gr. k-4). 1971. pap. 5.95 (ISBN 0-671-66972-9). S&S Trade.

—Mousekin's Golden House. LC 87-32111. (ps-3). 1987. 12.95 (ISBN 0-671-66282-1). S&S Trade.

—Mousekin's Thanksgiving. Miller, Edna, illus. 32p. (ps-3). 1988. pap. 5.95 (ISBN 0-671-66859-5). S&S Trade.

—Mousekin's Woodland Sleepers. (Illus.). (gr. k-3). 1977. (Pub. by Treehouse); pap. 3.95 (ISBN 0-13-604561-8). P-H.

—Mousekin's Woodland Sleepers. 1987. 11.95 (ISBN 0-13-604505-7). P-H.

—Mousekins Woodland Sleepers. (ps-3). 1988. pap. 5.95 (ISBN 0-13-604497-2). P-H.

Miller, Moira. Oscar Mouse Finds a Home. Majewska, Maria, illus. LC 85-1655. 32p. (ps-2). 1985. 11.95 (ISBN 0-8037-0229-9). Dial Bks Young.

—Oscar Mouse Finds a Home. 1990. pap. 3.95 (ISBN 0-8037-0740-1, Dial Pied Piper). Puffin Bks.

—Proverbial Mouse. Deuchar, Ian, illus. LC 86-16737. 32p. (ps-3). 1987. 11.95 (ISBN 0-8037-0195-0). Dial Bks Young.

Moore, Lilian. I'll Meet You at the Cucumbers. Wooding, Sharon, illus. LC 87-15195. 72p. (gr. 2-6). 1988. 12.95 (ISBN 0-689-31243-1, Atheneum Child Bk). Macmillan Child Grp.

Morimoto, Junko. Mouse's Marriage. (Illus.). 32p. (Orig.). (ps-1). 1988. pap. 3.95 (ISBN 0-14-050678-0, Puffin). Puffin Bks.

Mousekins Fables. 1986. pap. 5.95 (ISBN 0-671-66475-1). S&S Trade.

Naylor, Phyllis R. Maudie in the Middle. 1990. pap. 3.25 (ISBN 0-440-40324-3, Pub. by Yearling Classics). Dell.

Noll, Sally. Watch Where You Go. LC 88-35591. (Illus.). 32p. (ps up). 1990. 12.95 (ISBN 0-688-08498-2); lib. bdg. 12.88 (ISBN 0-688-08499-0). Greenwillow.

Numeroff, Laura J. If You Give a Mouse a Cookie. Bond, Felicia, illus. LC 84-48343. 32p. (ps-2). 1985. 10.95 (ISBN 0-06-024586-7); PLB 11.89 (ISBN 0-06-024587-5). HarpC Child Bks.

Oakley, Graham. The Church Mice Adrift. LC 76-25705. (Illus.). 40p. (gr. k-4). 1977. SBE 12.95 (ISBN 0-689-30562-1, Atheneum Child Bk). Macmillan Child Grp.

—The Church Mice at Bay. Oakley, Graham, illus. LC 78-62260. 40p. (gr. k-3). 1979. 13.95 (ISBN 0-689-30629-6, Atheneum Child Bk). Macmillan Child Grp.

—The Church Mice in Action. LC 82-11394. (Illus.). 32p. (gr. k-3). 1983. 13.95 (ISBN 0-689-30949-X, Atheneum Child Bk). Macmillan Child Grp.

—The Church Mice in Action. LC 82-11394. (Illus.). 32p. (ps up). 1985. pap. 4.95 (ISBN 0-689-71038-0, Aladdin). Macmillan Child Grp.

—The Church Mice Spread Their Wings. Oakley, Graham, illus. LC 75-15102. 40p. (gr. k-3). 1976. 12.95 (ISBN 0-689-30496-X, Atheneum Child Bk). Macmillan Child Grp.

—The Church Mouse. Oakley, Graham, illus. LC 72-75276. 40p. (gr. k-3). 1972. 13.95 (ISBN 0-689-30058-1, Atheneum Child Bk). Macmillan Child Grp.

—The Church Mouse. (Illus.). 40p. (gr. k-4). 1980. pap. 4.95 (ISBN 0-689-70475-5, Aladdin). Macmillan Child Grp.

—The Diary of a Church Mouse. Oakley, Graham, illus. 32p. (gr. k-3). 1987. 13.95 (ISBN 0-689-31334-9, Atheneum Child Bk). Macmillan Child Grp.

O'Brien, Robert C. Mrs. Frisby & the Rats of Nimh. Bernstein, Zena, illus. LC 74-134818. 240p. (gr. 3-7). 1971. 14.95 (ISBN 0-689-20651-8, Atheneum Child Bk). Macmillan Child Grp.

Oechsli, Kelly. Mice at Bat. Oechsli, Kelly, illus. LC 85-45266. 64p. (gr. 1-3). 1986. PLB 11.89 (ISBN 0-06-024624-3). HarpC Child Bks.

—Mice at Bat. Oechsli, Kelly, illus. LC 85-45266. 64p. (gr. k-3). 1990. pap. 3.50 (ISBN 0-06-444139-3, Trophy). HarpC Child Bks.

Ormondroyd, Edward. Broderick. Larrecq, John M., illus. LC 77-83752. (gr. k-3). 1969. (Pub. by Parnassus); PLB 4.77 (ISBN 0-686-86580-4). HM.

Ostheeren, Ingrid. Jonathan Mouse. Lanning, Rosemary, tr. from GER. LC 85-10501. (Illus.). 32p. (gr. k-3). 1986. 13.95 (ISBN 1-55858-064-6). North-South Bks NYC.

—Jonathan Mouse & the Magic Box. Mathieu, Agnes, illus. Lanning, Rosemary, tr. from GER. LC 89-43248. (Illus.). 32p. (gr. k-3). 1990. 13.95t (ISBN 1-55858-087-5). North-South Bks NYC.

Parish, Peggy. Play Ball, Amelia Bedelia. Tripp, Wallace, illus. LC 71-85028. 64p. (ps-3). 1985. (Trophy); pap. 3.50 (ISBN 0-06-444005-2, Trophy). HarpC Child Bks.

Parkison, Ralph F. The Twig & the Mouse, Bk. 2. Withrow, Marion O., ed. Bush, William, illus. 17p. (Orig.). (gr. 2-6). 1988. pap. 4.25 (ISBN 0-929949-01-3). Little Wood Bks.

Parry, Marian, illus. City Mouse - Country Mouse & Two More Mouse Tales from Aesop. (gr. 2-3). 1971. pap. 2.25 (ISBN 0-590-40260-9). Scholastic Inc.

Phillips, Joan. Mickey Mouse & the Pet Show. (Illus.). 40p. (gr. k-2). 1989. write for info. (ISBN 0-307-11684-0, Pub. by Golden Bks). Western Pub.

Pia, Jacklyn M. Woops & Friends. 1989. 6.95 (ISBN 0-533-08155-6). Vantage.

Pizer, Abigail. Nosey Gilbert. Pizer, Abigail, illus. LC 86-13504. 32p. (ps-3). 1987. 11.95 (ISBN 0-8037-0081-4). Dial Bks Young.

Pochocki, Ethel. The Attic Mice. Catrow, David, illus. LC 90-32064. 128p. (gr. 2-5). 1990. 13.95 (ISBN 0-8050-1298-2). H Holt & Co.

Potter, Beatrix. El Cuento de Juanito Raton de Ciudad. (SPA., Illus.). 64p. 1988. 5.95 (ISBN 0-7232-3560-0). Warne.

—El Cuento de los Dos Malvados Ratones. (SPA., Illus.). 64p. 1988. 5.95 (ISBN 0-7232-3559-7). Warne.

—Mouse Tales. (Illus.). 128p. 1989. 8.95 (ISBN 0-7232-3543-0). Warne.

—Scenes from the Tale of Two Bad Mice. 1990. 6.95 (ISBN 0-7232-3713-1). Warne.

—The Tailor of Gloucester. (Illus.). 57p. (gr. k-3). 1973. pap. 1.75 (ISBN 0-486-20176-7). Dover.

—The Tailor of Gloucester. Atkinson, Allen, illus. 1984. pap. 2.25 (ISBN 0-553-15220-3). Bantam.

—The Tale of Johnny Town-Mouse. (ps-3). 1987. 5.95 (ISBN 0-7232-3472-8); pap. 2.25 (ISBN 0-7232-3497-3). Warne.

—The Tale of Mrs. Tittlemouse. 1987. 5.95 (ISBN 0-7232-3470-1); pap. 2.25 (ISBN 0-7232-3495-7). Warne.

—The Tale of Mrs. Tittlemouse & Other Mouse Stories. LC 85-40386. (Illus.). 80p. (ps-3). 1985. 10.95 (ISBN 0-7232-3324-1). Warne.

—Tale of Mrs. Tittlemouse & Other Mouse Stories. (gr. 3 up). 1988. pap. 5.95 (ISBN 0-14-050525-3, Puffin). Puffin Bks.

—The Tale of Pigling Bland. 1987. 5.95 (ISBN 0-7232-3474-4); pap. 2.25 (ISBN 0-7232-3499-X). Warne.

—The Tale of the Tailor of Gloucester. (Illus.). 64p. (ps-3). 1987. 3.95 (ISBN 0-671-63234-5, Little Simon). S&S Trade.

—The Tale of Two Bad Mice. LC 74-75268. (Illus.). 59p. (gr. 2-4). 1974. pap. 1.75 (ISBN 0-486-23065-1). Dover.

—The Tale of Two Bad Mice. 64p. (Orig.). (ps). 1984. pap. 2.25 (ISBN 0-553-15219-X). Bantam.

—The Tale of Two Bad Mice. (Illus.). (ps-3). 1987. 5.95 (ISBN 0-7232-3464-7). Warne.

—The Tale of Two Bad Mice. 1987. pap. 2.25 (ISBN 0-7232-3489-2). Warne.

—Tale of Two Bad Mice. (Illus.). 1991. pap. 1.99 (ISBN 0-7232-3769-7). Warne.

Pryor, Bonnie. The Porcupine Mouse. Begin, Maryjane, illus. LC 87-12305. (ps-2). 1988. 13.95 (ISBN 0-688-07153-8); PLB 13.88 (ISBN 0-688-07154-6, Morrow Jr Bks). Morrow Jr Bks.

Le Rat des Villes et le Rat des Champs. (FRE., Illus.). (gr. 1). 3.50 (ISBN 0-7214-1275-0). Ladybird Bks.

Roche, P. K. Webster & Arnold Go Camping. (Illus.). 32p. (ps-3). 1991. pap. 3.95 (ISBN 0-14-050806-6, Puffin). Puffin Bks.

Rosen, Michael. A Cat & Mouse Story. (Illus.). 32p. (gr. k-3). 1983. 9.95 (ISBN 0-233-97484-9). Andre Deutsch.

Rosenblatt, Arthur S. Noah's Park. Ewers, Joe, illus. (ps-3). 1986. 7.95 (ISBN 0-316-75723-3). Little.

Ross, Dave. Little Mouse's Valentine. LC 85-15357. (Illus.). 32p. (ps-k). 1986. 11.95 (ISBN 0-688-06224-5); (Morrow Jr Bks). Morrow Jr Bks.

Rowe, Amy & Rowe, Philip. Ernest the Fierce Mouse. rev. ed. Norton, Andrea, illus. 32p. (gr. k-2). 1990. Repr. of 1985 ed. PLB 9.45 (ISBN 1-878363-08-5). Forest Hse.

Rusling, Albert. The Mouse & Mrs. Proudfoot. Rusling, Albert, illus. LC 84-17871. 32p. (gr. k-3). 1985. 12.95 (ISBN 0-13-604265-1). P-H.

Schmidt, Bernd. Our Friend the Musician. Young, Richard G., ed. Mangold, Paul, illus. LC 89-16771. 24p. (gr. 1-3). 1989. PLB 13.26 (ISBN 0-944483-48-8). Garrett Ed Corp.

—Our Friend the Writer. Young, Richard G., ed. Mangold, Paul, illus. LC 89-16770. 24p. (gr. 1-3). 1989. PLB 13.26 (ISBN 0-944483-49-6). Garrett Ed Corp.

Schories, Pat. Mouse Around. (ps-3). 1991. bds. 11.95 (ISBN 0-374-35080-9). FS&G.

Schwartz, Roslyn. Rose & Dorothy. LC 90-43013. (Illus.). 32p. (ps-2). 1991. 13.95 (ISBN 0-531-05918-9); PLB 13.99 (ISBN 0-531-08518-X). Orchard Bks Watts.

Severn, Jeffrey. George & His Giant Shadow. Severn, Jeffrey, illus. 32p. (ps-1). 1990. 12.95 (ISBN 0-87701-634-8). Chronicle Bks.

Sharp, Margery. Miss Bianca. Williams, Garth, illus. (gr. 2-4). 1923. 0.95 (ISBN 0-440-45761-0, YB). Dell.

—Miss Bianca in the Salt Mines. 1978. pap. 1.25 (ISBN 0-440-45717-3, YB). Dell.

Singer, A. L. Rescuers Down Under. 1990. pap. 2.75 (ISBN 0-590-44365-8). Scholastic Inc.

Smith, Wendy. The Lonely, Only Mouse. Smith, Wendy, illus. LC 86-40013. 32p. (ps-3). 1986. pap. 8.95 (ISBN 0-670-81251-X). Viking Child Bks.

—The Lonely, Only Mouse. (Illus.). 32p. 1988. pap. 3.50 (ISBN 0-14-050651-9, Puffin). Puffin Bks.

Solomon, Hannah. Mouse Days: A Book of Seasons. Lionni, Leo, illus. (ps-2). 1981. lib. bdg. 8.99 (ISBN 0-394-94548-4). Pantheon.

Spring, Grace J. The Fabulous House of Marcella Mouse. Spring, Grace J., illus. LC 85-7518. 24p. (gr. 1-6). 1985. pap. 3.95 (ISBN 0-317-39846-6). Andrew Mtn Pr.

Standiford, Natalie. Dollhouse Mouse: Just Right for 4's & 5's. Fleming, Denise, illus. LC 87-43201. 32p. (ps-k). 1989. PLB 5.99 (ISBN 0-394-99935-5). Random.

Stanley, Diane. The Conversation Club. Stanley, Diane, illus. LC 83-739. 32p. (ps-2). 1983. 10.95 (ISBN 0-02-786740-4, Mcmillan Child Bk). Macmillan Child Grp.

Steig, William. Abel's Island. Steig, William, illus. LC 75-35916. 119p. (gr. 1 up). 1985. pap. 3.95 (ISBN 0-374-40016-4, Sunburst). FS&G.

—Amos & Boris. Steig, William, illus. LC 72-165403. 32p. (ps-3). 1971. 16.95 (ISBN 0-374-30278-2). FS&G.

Steptoe, John. The Story of Jumping Mouse. Steptoe, John, illus. LC 82-14848. 40p. (gr. k-3). 1984. 13.95 (ISBN 0-688-01902-1); PLB 13.88 (ISBN 0-688-01903-X). Lothrop.

—The Story of the Jumping Mouse. LC 82-14848. (Illus.). (gr. 1 up). 1989. pap. 4.95 (ISBN 0-688-08740-X, Mulberry). Morrow.

Stern, Peter. Max the Dragon. LC 89-48310. (Illus.). 32p. (ps-2). 1990. 12.95 (ISBN 0-517-57587-6); PLB 13.99 (ISBN 0-517-57588-4). Crown.

Stevens, Janet, adapted by. & illus. The Town Mouse & the Country Mouse. LC 86-14276. 32p. (ps-3). 1987. reinforced bdg. 14.95 (ISBN 0-8234-0633-4); pap. 5.95 (ISBN 0-8234-0733-0). Holiday.

Stolz, Mary. Belling the Tiger. Montresor, Beni, illus. LC 61-5776. 64p. (gr. 2-5). 1990. PLB 12.89 (ISBN 0-06-025863-2). HarpC Child Bks.

Stone, Bernard. Quasimodo Mouse. Steadman, Ralph, illus. 32p. (gr. 1-4). 1987. 13.95 (ISBN 0-86264-072-5, Pub. by Anderson Pr UK). Trafalgar Sq.

Szekeres, Cyndy. Good Night, Sweet Mouse: Book & Doll. 1989. Incl. book & doll. write for info. (ISBN 0-307-14003-2, Pub. by Golden Bks). Western Pub.

Tallon, Robert. Latouse My Moose. Tallon, Robert, illus. LC 82-23397. 48p. (ps-2). 1983. 9.95 (ISBN 0-394-86017-9). Knopf.

Teitelbaum, Michael. An American Tail: Little Lost Fievel. (Illus.). (ps-3). 1986. pap. 2.25 (ISBN 0-448-48621-0, Platt & Munk); bk. & audio cassette 5.95 (ISBN 0-448-48615-6). Putnam Pub Group.

Teitelbaum, Michael, adapted by. An American Tail: Escape from the Catsacks. (Illus.). 24p. (ps-3). 1986. pap. 2.25 (ISBN 0-448-48614-8, G&D); bk & audio cassette 5.95 (ISBN 0-448-48616-4, G&D). Putnam Pub Group.

—An American Tail: Fievel's New York Adventure. (Illus.). 24p. 1986. pap. 2.25 (ISBN 0-448-48613-X, G&D). Putnam Pub Group.

—An American Tail: The Mott Street Maulers. (Illus.). 24p. (ps-3). 1986. pap. 2.25 (ISBN 0-448-48618-0, G&D). Putnam Pub Group.

Timm, Stephen A. The Dragon & the Mouse: Together Again. Lalo, illus. LC 81-90230. 46p. (ps-8). 1981. 12.95 (ISBN 0-939728-03-6); pap. 4.95 (ISBN 0-939728-04-4). Steppingstone Ent.

Titus, Eve. Anatole. 1990. pap. 4.95 (ISBN 0-553-34870-1). Bantam.

—Anatole & the Cat. (ps-3). 1990. pap. 4.95 (ISBN 0-553-34871-X). Bantam.

—Anatole & the Piano. (ps-3). 1990. pap. 4.95 (ISBN 0-553-34888-4). Bantam.

—Anatole & the Thirty Thieves. (ps-3). 1990. pap. 4.95 (ISBN 0-553-34889-2). Bantam.

—Anatole & the Toy Shop. Galdone, Paul, illus. (ps-8). 1991. pap. 4.99 (ISBN 0-553-35239-3). Bantam.

—Anatole over Paris. Galdone, Paul, illus. (ps-8). 1991. pap. 4.99 (ISBN 0-553-35240-7). Bantam.

Tom Kitten Mittens & Moppet: A Beatrix Potter Bath Book. 1989. 2.95 (ISBN 0-7232-3585-6). Warne.

Town Mouse & Country Mouse. (Illus.). 24p. (ps-k). 1989. 1.29 (ISBN 0-02-898168-5). Checkerboard Pr.

Tudor, Tasha. Mouse Mills Catalogue for Spring. Tudor, Tasha, illus. Mouse, Timothy D., tr. LC 89-50061. (Illus.). 40p. (gr. k up). 1989. pap. text ed. 6.95 (ISBN 0-9621753-2-3). Jenny Wren Pr.

Ure, Jean. Hi There, Supermouse. LC 84-18042. 124p. (gr. 3-7). 1985. pap. 3.50 (ISBN 0-14-031716-3, Puffin). Puffin Bks.

Van Laan, Nancy. A Mouse in My House. Priceman, Marjorie, illus. LC 89-15591. 32p. (ps-3). 1990. 9.95 (ISBN 0-679-80043-3); PLB 10.99 (ISBN 0-679-90043-8). Knopf.

Van Leeuwen, Jean. The Great Christmas Kidnapping Caper. Kellogg, Steven, illus. LC 75-9201. 144p. (gr. 2-6). 1975. 12.95 (ISBN 0-685-01454-1). Dial Bks Young.

—The Great Rescue Operation. Apple, Margot, illus. LC 81-65851. 176p. (gr. 2-6). 1982. 10.95 (ISBN 0-685-01455-X); PLB 10.89 (ISBN 0-685-01456-8). Dial Bks Young.

—The Great Rescue Operation. Apple, Margot, illus. 144p. (gr. 3 up). 1990. pap. 3.95 (ISBN 0-14-034288-5, Puffin). Puffin Bks.

Waddell, Martin & Miller, Virginia. Squeak-a-Lot. LC 90-3568. (Illus.). 32p. (ps up). 1991. 13.95 (ISBN 0-688-10244-1); PLB 13.88 (ISBN 0-688-10245-X). Greenwillow.

Waggoner, Sara M. Cheekie. (Illus.). 96p. (ps-3). 1988. 12.95 (ISBN 0-8059-3114-7). Dorrance.

Wahl, Jan. Pleasant Fieldmouse. Sendak, Maurice, illus. LC 64-14684. 80p. (gr. k-3). 1964. PLB 11.89 (ISBN 0-06-026331-8). HarpC Child Bks.

Wallner, John. City Mouse - Country Mouse & Two More Tales from Aesop. Wallner, John, illus. 32p. (Orig.). (gr. k-3). 1987. pap. 2.50 (ISBN 0-590-41155-1). Scholastic Inc.

Walsh, Ellen S. Mouse Paint. Walsh, Ellen S., illus. 32p. (ps-1). 1989. 11.95 (ISBN 0-15-256025-4). HarBraceJ.

Walt Disney Productions. Rescuers Down Under. 1990. 5.98 (ISBN 0-8317-7389-8). Smithmark.

Walt Disney's Mickey's Christmas Carol. (ps-3). 1990. write for info. (ISBN 0-307-12179-8). Western Pub.

Waters, Tony. Sailor's Bride. (ps-3). 1991. 14.99 (ISBN 0-385-41441-2); pap. 13.95 (ISBN 0-385-41440-4). Doubleday.

Weinberger, Jane. Vim, a Very Important Mouse. 8th ed. Allen, Rosemary, illus. LC 84-50872. 40p. (ps-4). 1989. 4.95 (ISBN 0-932433-01-4). Windswept Hse.

Wells, Claudia E. Whiskers, the Bank Mouse. Shardin, Arthur, illus. LC 77-10823. (gr. 1-4). 1981. 4.50 (ISBN 0-930506-00-6); pap. write for info. (ISBN 0-930506-01-4). Popcorn Pubs.

West, Cindy. Mickey Mouse & the Bicycle Race. Ross, Sharon, illus. LC 87-83496. 40p. (gr. k-2). 1988. write for info. (ISBN 0-307-11690-5, Pub. by Golden Bks). Western Pub.

White, E. B. E. B. White Boxed Set. Incl. Charlotte's Web; The Trumpet of the Swan; Stuart Little. (Illus.). (gr. 3 up). 27.60i (ISBN 0-686-77171-0). HarpC Child Bks.

—E. B. White Boxed Set. Incl. Charlotte's Web; The Trumpet of the Swan; Stuart Little. (Illus.). (gr. 3 up). 1974. pap. 10.50 (ISBN 0-06-440061-1, Trophy). HarpC Child Bks.

—Stuart Little. Williams, Garth, illus. LC 45-9585. 132p. (gr. 3-6). 1945. 10.95 (ISBN 0-06-026395-4); PLB 11.89 (ISBN 0-06-026396-2). HarpC Child Bks.

—Stuart Little. LC 45-9585. (Illus.). 132p. (gr. 3-7). 1974. pap. 3.50 (ISBN 0-06-440056-5, Trophy). HarpC Child Bks.

—Stuart Little. large type, unabr. ed. (Illus.). 176p. (gr. 3-7). 1988. lib. bdg. 13.95x (ISBN 0-8161-4490-7). G K Hall.

The Wideawake Mice. (Illus.). (ps-2). 3.50 (ISBN 0-7214-0919-9). Ladybird Bks.

Wood, Audrey & Wood, Audrey. Tugford Wanted to Be Bad. LC 83-318. (Illus.). 32p. (ps-3). 1983. 9.95 (ISBN 0-15-291083-2, HJ). HarBraceJ.

Wood, David. Happy Birthday, Mouse! Fowler, Richard, illus. 24p. (ps-1). 1990. 11.95 (ISBN 0-448-19023-0, G&D). Putnam Pub Group.

Yolen, Jane. Mice on Ice. DiFiori, Lawrence, illus. LC 79-19342. 80p. (gr. k-3). 1980. 7.95 (ISBN 0-525-34872-7, Dutton). NAL-Dutton.

York, Carol B. The Good Day Mice. De Larrea, Victoria, illus. 112p. (gr. 3-7). 1989. pap. 2.75 (ISBN 0-553-15373-0, Skylark). Bantam.

Zeldin, Florence. A Mouse in Our Jewish House. Rauchwerger, Lisa, illus. LC 89-40362. 32p. (ps). 1990. 11.95 (ISBN 0-933873-43-3). Torah Aura.
This imaginative counting book, by noted children's author Florence Zeldin, combines the mastery of counting from one to twelve with the introduction of the basic celebrations of the Jewish year. A mouse named Archie Akhbar inhabits this book. Brought to life by the imaginative paper sculptures of Lisa Rauchwerger, Archie eats an escalating number of pieces of food on each subsequent Jewish holiday.
Publisher Provided Annotation.

Zelinsky, Paul O. The Maid & the Mouse & the Odd-Shaped House: A Story in Rhyme. (Illus.). 32p. (gr. k-3). 1981. 12.95 (ISBN 0-396-07938-5, Putnam). Putnam Pub Group.

Ziefert, Harriet. A Clean House for Mole & Mouse. Prebenna, David, illus. (Orig.). (ps-3). 1988. pap. 3.50 (ISBN 0-14-050810-4, Puffin). Puffin Bks.

—New House for Mouse & Mole. Prebenna, David, illus. (ps-3). 1987. pap. 8.95 (ISBN 0-670-81720-1). Viking Child Bks.

Zimelman, Nathan. Shaughnessy. Davenport, May, ed. Bd. with Humanization of Freddie Mouse. Blake, Richard. LC 81-71551. 64p. (Orig.). (gr. 3-5). 1984. pap. 3.50x (ISBN 0-943864-38-0). Davenport.

MICE–POETRY

Fisher, Aileen. The House of a Mouse. Sandin, Joan, illus. LC 87-24947. 32p. (ps-3). 1988. 11.95 (ISBN 0-06-021848-7); PLB 11.89 (ISBN 0-06-021849-5). HarpC Child Bks.

Howard, Jean G. Of Mice & Mice. limited ed. Howard, Jean G., illus. LC 78-50486. (gr. k-4). 1978. 3.50 (ISBN 0-930954-03-3); deluxe ed. 50.00 (ISBN 0-930954-04-1). Tidal Pr.

MICHELANGELO BUONARROTI, 1475-1564–FICTION

Ventura, Piero. Michelangelo's World. Ventura, Piero, illus. 48p. (gr. 9-12). 1989. 13.95 (ISBN 0-399-21593-X, Putnam). Putnam Pub Group.

MICHIGAN

Carole Marsh Michigan Books, 31 bks. Set. 638.45 (ISBN 0-7933-1297-3). Gallopade Pub Group.

Carpenter, Allan. Michigan. LC 78-8001. (Illus.). 96p. (gr. 4 up). 1978. PLB 19.93 (ISBN 0-516-04122-3). Childrens.

Fradin, Dennis. Michigan: In Words & Pictures. LC 79-225356. (Illus.). 48p. (gr. 2-5). 1980. PLB 15.93 (ISBN 0-516-03922-9). Childrens.

Hall, Betty L. Michigan Survival. rev. ed. 160p. (gr. 10-12). 1986. pap. text ed. 5.84 (ISBN 0-936159-02-2). Westwood Pr.

Hildebrand, Janice. Sheboygan County: One Hundred Fifty Years of Progress: An Illustrated History. (Illus.). 208p. (gr. 7 up). 1988. 29.95 (ISBN 0-89781-252-2). Windsor Pubns Inc.

Hintz, Martin. Michigan. (Illus.). 96p. (gr. 4-9). 1987. PLB 10.40 (ISBN 0-531-10362-5). Watts.

Kachaturoff, Grace. Michigan! (Illus.). 298p. (gr. 4). 1987. 23.00 (ISBN 0-685-24531-4, Peregrine Smith). Gibbs Smith Pub.

McConnell, David B. Discover Michigan. Rasmussen, George L., illus. LC 81-6722. 144p. (gr. 4). 1981. tchrs. guide 5.30x (ISBN 0-910726-08-6). Hillsdale Educ.

Marsh, Carole. Avast, Ye Slobs!: Michigan Pirate Trivia. (Illus.). (gr. 3 up). 1990. PLB 19.95 (ISBN 0-7933-0617-5); pap. 14.95 (ISBN 0-7933-0616-7); computer disk 29.95 (ISBN 0-7933-0618-3). Gallopade Pub Group.

—The Beast of the Michigan Bed & Breakfast. (Illus.). (gr. 3 up). 1990. PLB 19.95 (ISBN 0-7933-1708-8); pap. 14.95 (ISBN 0-7933-1709-6); computer disk 29.95 (ISBN 0-7933-1710-X). Gallopade Pub Group.

—The Hard-to-Believe-But-True! Book of Michigan History, Mystery, Trivia, Legend, Lore, Humor & More. (Illus.). (gr. 3 up). 1990. PLB 19.95 (ISBN 0-7933-0614-0); pap. 14.95 (ISBN 0-7933-0613-2); computer disk 29.95 (ISBN 0-7933-0615-9). Gallopade Pub Group.

—If My Michigan Mama Ran the World! (Illus.). (gr. 3 up). 1990. lib. bdg. 19.95 (ISBN 0-7933-1723-1); pap. 14.95 (ISBN 0-7933-1724-X); computer disk 29.95 (ISBN 0-7933-1725-8). Gallopade Pub Group.

—Let's Quilt Michigan & Stuff It Topographically! (Illus.). (gr. 3 up). 1990. PLB 19.95 (ISBN 1-55609-669-0); pap. 14.95 (ISBN 1-55609-138-9); computer disk 29.95 (ISBN 1-55609-670-4). Gallopade Pub Group.

—Michigan & Other State Greats (Biographies) (Illus.). (gr. 3 up). 1990. PLB 19.95 (ISBN 1-55609-677-1); pap. 14.95 (ISBN 1-55609-678-X); computer disk 29.95 (ISBN 1-55609-679-8). Gallopade Pub Group.

—Michigan Bandits, Bushwackers, Outlaws, Crooks, Devils, Ghosts, Desperadoes & Other Assorted & Sundry Characters! (Illus.). (gr. 3 up). 1990. PLB 19.95 (ISBN 0-7933-0599-3); pap. 14.95 (ISBN 0-7933-0598-5); computer disk 29.95 (ISBN 0-7933-0600-0). Gallopade Pub Group.

—Michigan Classic Christmas Trivia: Stories, Recipes, Activities, Legends, Lore & More! (Illus.). (gr. 3 up). 1990. PLB 19.95; pap. 14.95 (ISBN 0-7933-0601-9); computer disk 29.95 (ISBN 0-7933-0603-5). Gallopade Pub Group.

—Michigan Coastales. (Illus.). (gr. 3 up). 1990. PLB 19.95 (ISBN 1-55609-671-2); pap. 14.95 (ISBN 1-55609-672-0); computer disk 29.95 (ISBN 1-55609-673-9). Gallopade Pub Group.

—The Michigan Hot Air Balloon Mystery. (Illus.). (gr. 2-9). 1990. 19.95 (ISBN 0-7933-2516-1); pap. 14.95 (ISBN 0-7933-2517-X); computer disk 29.95 (ISBN 0-7933-2518-8). Gallopade Pub Group.

—Michigan "Jography" A Fun Run Thru Our State. (Illus.). (gr. 3 up). 1990. PLB 19.95 (ISBN 1-55609-666-6); pap. 14.95 (ISBN 1-55609-667-4); computer disk 29.95 (ISBN 1-55609-668-2). Gallopade Pub Group.

—Michigan Kid's Cookbook: Recipes, How-To, History, Lore & More! (Illus.). (gr. 3 up). 1990. PLB 19.95 (ISBN 0-7933-0611-6); pap. 14.95 (ISBN 0-7933-0610-8); computer disk 29.95 (ISBN 0-7933-0612-4). Gallopade Pub Group.

—Michigan Quiz Bowl Crash Course! (Illus.). (gr. 3 up). 1990. PLB 19.95 (ISBN 1-55609-674-7); pap. 14.95 (ISBN 1-55609-675-5); computer disk 29.95 (ISBN 1-55609-676-3). Gallopade Pub Group.

—Michigan School Trivia: An Amazing & Fascinating Look at Our State's Teachers, Schools & Students! (Illus.). (gr. 3 up). 1990. PLB 19.95 (ISBN 0-7933-0608-6); pap. 14.95 (ISBN 0-7933-0607-8); computer disk 29.95 (ISBN 0-7933-0609-4). Gallopade Pub Group.

—Michigan Silly Basketball Sportsmysteries, Vol. I. (Illus.). (gr. 3 up). 1990. PLB 19.95 (ISBN 0-7933-0605-1); pap. 14.95 (ISBN 0-7933-0604-3); computer disk 29.95 (ISBN 0-7933-0606-X). Gallopade Pub Group.

—Michigan Silly Basketball Sportsmysteries, Vol. II. (Illus.). (gr. 3 up). 1990. PLB 19.95 (ISBN 0-7933-1711-8); pap. 14.95 (ISBN 0-7933-1712-6); computer disk 29.95 (ISBN 0-7933-1713-4). Gallopade Pub Group.

—Michigan Silly Football Sportsmysteries, Vol. I. (Illus.). (gr. 3 up). 1990. PLB 19.95 (ISBN 1-55609-702-6); pap. 14.95 (ISBN 1-55609-703-4); computer disk 29.95 (ISBN 1-55609-704-2). Gallopade Pub Group.

—Michigan Silly Football Sportsmysteries, Vol. II. (Illus.). (gr. 3 up). 1990. PLB 19.95 (ISBN 1-55609-705-0); pap. 14.95 (ISBN 1-55609-706-9); computer disk 29.95 (ISBN 1-55609-707-7). Gallopade Pub Group.

—Michigan Silly Trivia! (Illus.). (gr. 3 up). 1990. PLB 19.95 (ISBN 1-55609-663-1); pap. 14.95 (ISBN 1-55609-664-X); computer disk 29.95 (ISBN 1-55609-665-8). Gallopade Pub Group.

—Michigan's (Most Devastating!) Disasters & (Most Calamitous!) Catastrophies! (Illus.). (gr. 3 up). 1990. PLB 19.95 (ISBN 0-7933-0596-9); pap. 14.95 (ISBN 0-7933-0595-0); computer disk 29.95 (ISBN 0-7933-0597-7). Gallopade Pub Group.

Mitchell, John C. Michigan: An Illustrated History for Children. 2nd ed. Woodrutt, Thomas R., illus. 52p. (gr. 1-6). 1987. Repr. 14.95 (ISBN 0-9621466-0-9). Suttons Bay Pubns.

Parker, Lois & McConnell, David. A Little Peoples' Beginning on Michigan. Deeter, Theresa, illus. 32p. (Orig.). (gr. 1-2). 1981. pap. 4.95 (ISBN 0-910726-06-X). Hillsdale Educ.

Stein, R. Conrad. Michigan. LC 87-9383. (Illus.). 144p. (gr. 4 up). 1987. PLB 25.27 (ISBN 0-516-00468-9). Childrens.

Thompson, Kathleen. Michigan. LC 87-16373. 48p. (gr. 3 up). 1987. 17.32 (ISBN 0-86514-465-6); cancelled tchr's. study guide (ISBN 0-86514-605-5); cancelled Beta video (ISBN 0-86514-092-8); cancelled VHS video (ISBN 0-86514-167-3); cancelled 3/4" video (ISBN 0-86514-242-4). Raintree Pubs.

Zimmerman, Chanda K. Detroit. LC 88-35914. (Illus.). 60p. (gr. 3 up). 1989. lib. bdg. 12.95 (ISBN 0-87518-409-X, Dillon). Macmillan Child Grp.

MICHIGAN–ANTIQUITIES

Penrod, John S. Tahquamenon in Michigan's Upper Peninsula. (gr. 7 up). 1988. pap. 4.49 (ISBN 0-942618-12-2). Penrod-Hiawatha.

—The Upper Peninsula of Michigan. rev. ed. (gr. 7 up). 1988. pap. 4.49 (ISBN 0-942618-11-4). Penrod-Hiawatha.

MICROBES

see Bacteriology; Microorganisms; Viruses

MICROBIOLOGY

see also Bacteriology; Microorganisms; Microscope and Microscopy

MICROCOMPUTERS

Ault, Rosalie S. BASIC Programming for Kids. LC 83-12773. (Illus.). 192p. (gr. 5 up). 1983. 10.95 (ISBN 0-685-06975-3); pap. 9.95 (ISBN 0-395-34920-6). HM.

Bailey, Harold J., et al. Commodore LOGO: Activities for Exploring Turtle Graphics. (Illus.). 320p. (gr. 5-8). 1984. pap. 14.95 (ISBN 0-89303-376-6). Brady Bks.

Baldwin, Margaret & Pack, Gary. Computer Graphics. 96p. (gr. 6-8). 1984. lib. bdg. 10.40 (ISBN 0-531-04704-0). Watts.

BASIC for Elementary Grades. (gr. 4 up). 1982. write for info. tchr's. guide (ISBN 0-89525-273-2); write for info. 5 filmstrips; Incl. filmstrips & 5 cassettes. tchr's. guide 149.00 (ISBN 0-685-08664-X). Ed Activities.

Bitter, Gary G. & Camuse, Ruth A. Using a Microcomputer in the Classroom. (gr. k-12). 1983. pap. text ed. 25.00 (ISBN 0-8359-8144-4, Reston). P-H.

Duck, Mike. Using Computer Graphics: Hangman. (gr. 4 up). 1984. 12.40 (ISBN 0-531-03483-6). Watts.

Kemnitz, T. M. & Mass, Lynne. Kids Working with Computers: Acorn BASIC. (gr. 2-6). 1984. 4.99 (ISBN 0-89824-086-7). Trillium Pr.

Kemnitz, Thomas M. & Mass, Lynne. Kids Working with Computers: The Apple BASIC Manual. Schlendorf, Lori, illus. 42p. (gr. 4-7). 1983. pap. 4.99 (ISBN 0-89824-092-1). Trillium Pr.

—Kids Working with Computers: The Atari BASIC Manual. Schlendorf, Lori, illus. 48p. (gr. 4-7). 1983. pap. 4.99 (ISBN 0-89824-062-X). Trillium Pr.

Lewis, Bruce. Meet the Computer. (Illus.). 48p. (gr. 2-5). 1977. 8.95 (ISBN 0-396-07456-1, Putnam). Putnam Pub Group.

Liebowitz, Jay & Zelde, Janet S. Kids & Computers. 2nd ed. Rogers, Nip, illus. 70p. (gr. 3-6). 1989. write for info. (ISBN 0-9623252-0-1); pap. write for info. (ISBN 0-9623252-2-8). J Liebowitz.

Pantiel, Mindy & Petersen, Becky. Kids, Teachers, & Computers: A Guide to Computers in the Elementary School. (Illus.). 176p. 1984. pap. text ed. 25.00 (ISBN 0-13-515420-0); pap. text ed. 16.95 (ISBN 0-13-515396-4). P-H.

Petty, Kate. Pictures. West, C. & Barwick, T., illus. LC 85-81979. 32p. (gr. k-6). 1986. lib. bdg. 10.40 (ISBN 0-531-17018-7, Gloucester Pr). Watts.

—Puzzles. West, C. & Barwick, T., illus. LC 85-81980. 32p. (gr. k-6). 1986. lib. bdg. 10.40 (ISBN 0-531-17019-5, Gloucester Pr). Watts.

Sterchele, Norman. Beginning at the Beginning with Your MS-DOS Microcomputer: An Introduction to: The Machine, DOS & Procedures. (Illus.). 96p. (Orig.). (gr. 10). 1989. pap. 11.95 (ISBN 0-9624107-0-5). Compu-Aid.

Taitt, Jennifer. IBM, Vol. 1. 55p. (gr. 4-12). 1983. pap. text ed. 11.95 (ISBN 0-88193-031-8). Create Learn.

—IBM, Vol. 2. 54p. (gr. 4-12). 1983. pap. text ed. 11.95 (ISBN 0-88193-032-6). Create Learn.

—IBM, Vol. 3. 51p. (gr. 5-12). 1983. pap. text ed. 11.95 (ISBN 0-88193-033-4). Create Learn.

—IBM, Vol. 4. 66p. (gr. 5-12). 1983. pap. text ed. 11.95 (ISBN 0-88193-034-2). Create Learn.

Taitt, Kathy. Apple, Vol. 1. 59p. (gr. 4-12). 1983. pap. text ed. 11.95 (ISBN 0-88193-001-6). Create Learn.

—Apple, Vol. 2. 61p. (gr. 4-12). 1983. pap. text ed. 11.95 (ISBN 0-88193-002-4). Create Learn.

—Apple, Vol. 3. 55p. (gr. 5-12). 1983. pap. text ed. 11.95 (ISBN 0-88193-003-2). Create Learn.

—Apple, Vol. 4. 57p. (gr. 5-12). 1983. pap. text ed. 11.95 (ISBN 0-88193-004-0). Create Learn.

—Apple, Vol. 5. 57p. (gr. 6-12). 1983. pap. text ed. 11.95 (ISBN 0-88193-005-9). Create Learn.

—Apple, Vol. 6. 68p. (gr. 6-12). 1984. pap. text ed. 11.95 (ISBN 0-88193-006-7). Create Learn.

Thomas, David A. The Math-Computer Connection. LC 86-10992. (Illus.). 128p. (gr. 7-12). 1986. PLB 11.90 (ISBN 0-531-10231-9). Watts.

Wert, Debra. Mac's Choice Workbook. Anfenson-Vance, Deborah, et al, eds. Wilson, Miriam J., intro. by. (Illus.). 36p. (gr. 2-6). 1989. pap. 5.00 (ISBN 0-944576-03-6). Rocky River Pubs.

White, Jack R. How Computers Really Work. (Illus.). 128p. (gr. 3-7). 1986. 10.95 (ISBN 0-396-08768-X, Putnam). Putnam Pub Group.

MICROCOMPUTERS–PROGRAMMING

Nance, Douglas W. Pascal: Introduction to Programming & Problem Solving. (Illus.). 630p. (gr. 9-12). 1986. text ed. 34.25 (ISBN 0-314-93206-2). West Pub.

MICROELECTRONICS

Billings, Charlene W. Microchip: Small Wonder. (Illus.). 64p. (gr. 2-5). 1984. 8.95 (ISBN 0-396-08452-4, Putnam). Putnam Pub Group.

Levine, Janice R. Microcomputers in Elementary & Secondary Education: A Guide to Resources. 64p. (gr. k-12). 1983. 3.75 (ISBN 0-937597-06-6, IR-65). ERIC Clear.

MICROGRAPHIC ANALYSIS

see Microscope and Microscopy

MICROMINIATURE ELECTRONIC EQUIPMENT

see Microelectronics

MICROMINIATURIZATION (ELECTRONICS)

see Microelectronics

MICRONESIA

Edmonds, I. G. Micronesia: Pebbles in the Sea. LC 73-22689. 1974. 6.95 (ISBN 0-672-51815-5, Bobbs). Macmillan.

MICROORGANISMS

see also Bacteriology; Microscope and Microscopy; Viruses

Anderson, Lucia. The Smallest Life Around Us. Grant, Leigh, illus. LC 77-15858. (gr. 2-4). 1987. PLB 12.95 (ISBN 0-517-53227-1). Crown.

Bender, Lionel. Around the Home. (Illus.). 32p. (gr. 5-8). 1991. PLB 11.90 (ISBN 0-531-17348-8, Gloucester Pr). Watts.

Sabin, Francene. Microbes & Bacteria. Acosta, Andres, illus. LC 84-2749. 32p. (gr. 3-6). 1985. PLB 9.49 (ISBN 0-8167-0232-2); pap. text ed. 2.95 (ISBN 0-8167-0233-0). Troll Assocs.

MICROPROCESSORS

CES Industries, Inc. Staff. Ed-Lab Experiment Manual: CES 380-85 Microprocessors. (Illus., Orig.). (gr. 9-12). 1984. pap. write for info. (ISBN 0-86711-076-7). CES Industries.

Kerbo, Ronal C. Caves. LC 81-4514. (Illus.). 48p. (gr. 3 up). 1981. PLB 15.93 (ISBN 0-516-07638-8); pap. 4.95 (ISBN 0-516-47638-6). Childrens.

MICROSCOPE AND MICROSCOPY

Bender, Lionel. Around the Home. (Illus.). 32p. (gr. 5-8). 1991. PLB 11.90 (ISBN 0-531-17348-8, Gloucester Pr). Watts.

—Frontiers of Medicine. (Illus.). 32p. (gr. 5-8). 1991. PLB 11.90 (ISBN 0-531-17298-8, Gloucester Pr). Watts.

Bleifeld, Maurice. Experimenting with a Microscope. Rasof, Henry, ed. (Illus.). 112p. (gr. 7-12). 1988. PLB 12.40 (ISBN 0-531-10580-6). Watts.

Kumin, Maxine. The Microscope. Lobel, Arnold, illus. LC 82-47728. 32p. (ps-3). 1984. 11.95 (ISBN 0-06-023523-3); PLB 11.89 (ISBN 0-06-023524-1). HarpC Child Bks.

Oxlade, C. & Stockley, C. The World of the Microscope. (Illus.). 48p. 1989. PLB 13.96 (ISBN 0-88110-364-0); pap. 7.95 (ISBN 0-7460-0289-0). EDC.

Riley, Peter. Looking at Microscopes. (Illus.). 48p. (gr. 5-8). 1985. 19.95 (ISBN 0-7134-4632-3, Pub. by Batsford England). Trafalgar Sq.

Selsam, Millicent E. Greg's Microscope. Lobel, Arnold, illus. LC 63-8002. 64p. (gr. k-3). 1963. PLB 11.89 (ISBN 0-06-025296-0). HarpC Child Bks.

Sneider, Cary I. More Than Magnifiers. Bergman, Lincoln & Fairwell, Kay, eds. Bevilacqua, Carol, illus. Hoyt, Richard, photos by. (Illus.). 47p. (Orig.). (gr. 6-9). 1988. pap. 6.50 (ISBN 0-912511-62-1). Lawrence Science.

Stwertka, Eve & Stwertka, Albert. Microscope: How to Use It & Enjoy It. LC 88-23127. (Illus.). (gr. 4-7). 1988. lib. bdg. 9.98 (ISBN 0-671-63705-3); pap. 4.95 (ISBN 0-671-67060-3). Messner.

Taylor, Ron. Through the Microscope. (Illus.). 64p. (gr. 4-7). 1985. 15.95 (ISBN 0-8160-1075-7). Facts on File.

Wilkin, Fred. Microscopes & Telescopes. LC 83-7592. (Illus.). 48p. (gr. k-4). 1983. PLB 14.60 (ISBN 0-516-01696-2); pap. 4.95 (ISBN 0-516-41696-0). Childrens.

MICROSCOPIC ANALYSIS

see Microscope and Microscopy

MICROSCOPIC ORGANISMS

see Microorganisms

MICROWAVE COOKERY

Morris, Sally M. The Kid's Microwave Cookbook. Patterson-Estes, Kathleen, illus. 144p. (Orig.). 1991. pap. 6.95 (ISBN 1-55867-018-1). Bristol Pub Ent CA.

Stancil, Rosemary D. & Wilkins, Lorela N. Kids' Simply Scrumptious Microwaving. 1987. pap. 7.95 (ISBN 0-449-90226-9, Columbine). Fawcett.

MIDDLE AGES

see also Chivalry; Civilization, Medieval; Knights and Knighthood; Renaissance

Adams, Brian. Medieval Castles. LC 88-83092. (Illus.). 32p. (gr. 5-7). 1989. PLB 11.90 (ISBN 0-531-17155-8, Gloucester Pr). Watts.

Cairns, Trevor, ed. Barbarians, Christians, & Muslims. LC 73-20213. (Illus.). 104p. (gr. 5 up). 1975. PLB 10.95 (ISBN 0-8225-0803-6). Lerner Pubns.

Caselli, Giovanni. The Middle Ages. LC 87-27105. 48p. (gr. 7 up). 1988. 16.95 (ISBN 0-87226-176-X). P Bedrick Bks.

Chamberlain, E. R. Florence in the Time of the Medici. Reeves, Marjorie, ed. (Illus.). 96p. (Orig.). (gr. 7-12). 1982. pap. 8.76 (ISBN 0-582-20489-5, 70771). Longman.

Conway, Lorraine. The Middle Ages. Akins, Linda, illus. 64p. (gr. 4-8). 1987. pap. 6.95 (ISBN 0-86653-400-8, GA 1022). Good Apple.

Cootes, R. J. Middle Ages. 2nd ed. 208p. (gr. 6-12). 1989. pap. text ed. 21.52 (ISBN 0-582-31783-5, 78446). Longman.

Early Middle Ages. (gr. 4-7). 1990. 20.67 (ISBN 0-8172-3307-5). Raintree Pubs.

Farre, Marie. Long Ago in a Castle. Matthews, Sarah, tr. from FRE. Thibault, Dominique, illus. LC 87-33996. 38p. (gr. k-5). 1988. 4.95 (ISBN 0-944589-06-5, 065). Young Discovery Lib.

Late Middle Ages. (gr. 4-7). 1990. 20.67 (ISBN 0-8172-3308-3). Raintree Pubs.

Lyttle, Richard B. Land Beyond the River: Europe in the Age of Migration. LC 85-28758. (Illus.). 192p. (gr. 5 up). 1986. 14.95 (ISBN 0-689-31199-0, Atheneum Child Bk). Macmillan Child Grp.

The Middle Ages. 64p. (gr. 4-8). 1990. 13.95 (ISBN 0-86307-995-4). Marshall Cavendish.

The Middle Ages. (Illus.). (gr. 5 up). 1990. pap. 3.50. Ladybird Bks.

Oakes, Catherine. The Middle Ages. Biesty, Stephen, illus. (gr. 3-7). 1989. 13.95 (ISBN 0-15-200451-3, Gulliver Bks). HarBraceJ.

Sabin, Louis. Middle Ages. Frenck, Hal, illus. LC 84-2670. 32p. (gr. 3-6). 1985. PLB 9.49 (ISBN 0-8167-0174-1); pap. text ed. 2.95 (ISBN 0-8167-0175-X). Troll Assocs.

Sauvain, Philip. Castles & Crusaders. Robins, Jim, illus. 32p. (gr. 1-6). 1986. PLB 11.90 (ISBN 0-531-19015-3, Pub. by Warwick). Watts.

Verges, Gloria & Verges, Oriol. The Middle Ages. Rius, Maria & Peris, Carme, illus. 32p. (gr. 2-4). 1988. pap. 4.50 (ISBN 0-8120-3386-8); La Edad Media. pap. 3.95 (ISBN 0-8120-3387-6). Barron.

Weber, Sally & Glasscock, Paula. Castles, Pirates, Knights & Other Learning Delights. 104p. (gr. 5-8). 1980. 8.95 (ISBN 0-916456-92-7, GA 158). Good Apple.

MIDDLE AGES–FICTION

Anno, Mitsumasa. Anno's Medieval World. Anno, Mitsumasa, illus. LC 79-28367. 56p. (gr. 3 up). 1990. 16.95 (ISBN 0-399-20742-2, Philomel); PLB 12.99 (ISBN 0-399-61153-3). Putnam Pub Group.

Cosman, Madeleine P. The Medieval Baker's Daughter: A Bilingual Adventure in Medieval Life with Costumes, Banners, Music, Food, & a Mystery Play. LC 84-71590. (ENG & SPA., Illus.). 112p. (gr. 3-12). 1984. pap. 7.95 (ISBN 0-916491-18-8). Bard Hall Pr.

Intelligent young people desiring to know what life was like in medieval England will love this story of Johanna Baxter of Bread Street in the year 1412. This book also recreates medieval clothes, food, talk, song & theater by instructions for creating authentic banners, costumes, recipes, & music, as well as by the script for the amusing newly translated medieval play called Noah's Flood. A useful glossary briefly explains unfamiliar words of Johanna's world. On facing pages, this bilingual book has the Spanish & English texts. The Medieval Baker's Daughter or La Hija de la Panadera Medieval is a successful experiment in cultural unity; students reading & creating together a beautiful medieval feast or festival appreciate one another's talents, interests & languages. Dr. Cosman, an expert in medical law, directs the Medieval & Renaissance Institute at City College, City University of New York. A vivid public lecturer & TV personality, she is the author of many successful books such as Fabulous Feasts: Medieval Cookery & Ceremony (Braziller) & Medieval Holidays & Festivals: A Calendar of Celebrations (Scribner's), she makes glories of the Middle Ages accessible to readers of all ages.

Publisher Provided Annotation.

Gerrard, Roy. Sir Cedric. LC 84-6111. (Illus.). 32p. (ps up). 1984. 12.95 (ISBN 0-374-36959-3). FS&G.

Gray, Elizabeth J. Adam of the Road. Lawson, Robert, illus. 320p. (gr. 4-8). 1942. pap. 15.95 (ISBN 0-670-10435-3). Viking Child Bks.

Kemp, Gene. Jason Bodger & the Priory Ghost. Turney, Elaine M., illus. LC 85-4444. 144p. (gr. 5-8). 1985. 12.95 (ISBN 0-571-13645-1). Faber & Faber.

Scarry, Huck. Looking into the Middle Ages. Scarry, Huck, illus. LC 84-47626. 12p. (gr. 2 up). 1985. 12.50 (ISBN 0-06-025224-3). HarpC Child Bks.

Wilde, Nicholas. Sir Bertie & the Wyvern: A Tale of Heraldry. LC 84-7779. (Illus.). 64p. (gr. 2-6). 1984. PLB 8.95 (ISBN 0-87614-273-0). Carolrhoda Bks.

MIDDLE ATLANTIC STATES

see Atlantic States

MIDDLE EAST

see Asia; Near East

MIDDLE STATES

see Atlantic States

MIDDLE WEST

Herda, D. J. Environmental America: The North Central States. (Illus.). 64p. (gr. 5-8). 1991. PLB 13.90 (ISBN 1-878841-08-4). Millbrook Pr.

Jacobson, Daniel. The North Central States. 96p. (gr. 4 up). 1984. lib. bdg. 10.40 (ISBN 0-531-04731-8). Watts.

Siebert, Diane. Heartland. Minor, Wendell, illus. LC 87-29380. 32p. (ps-3). 1989. 13.95 (ISBN 0-690-04730-4, Crowell Jr Bks); PLB 13.89 (ISBN 0-690-04732-0). HarpC Child Bks.

MIDGETS

see Dwarfs

MIDWAY, BATTLE OF, 1942

Skipper, G. C. Battle of Midway. LC 80-17495. (Illus.). 48p. (gr. 3 up). 1980. PLB 14.60 (ISBN 0-516-04782-5). Childrens.

MIDWEST

see Middle West

MIDWIFERY

see Childbirth

MIGRANT LABOR–FICTION

Gates, Doris. Blue Willow. Lantz, Paul, illus. LC 40-32435. 176p. (gr. 4-7). 1940. pap. 13.95 (ISBN 0-670-17557-9). Viking Child Bks.

Papagapitos, Karen. Jose's Basket. 1990. 6.95 (ISBN 0-533-09066-0). Vantage.

MIGRATION

see Immigration and Emigration

MIGRATION OF ANIMALS

see Animals–Migration

MILITARY AERONAUTICS

see Aeronautics, Military

MILITARY AIRPLANES

see Airplanes, Military

MILITARY ART AND SCIENCE
see also Aeronautics, Military; Arms and Armor; Battles; Disarmament; Fortification; Guerrilla Warfare; Signals and Signaling; Soldiers; Spies; War
also headings beginning with the word Military
Baker. Soviet Air Force. LC 88-12121. (Illus.). 48p. (gr. 3-8). Date not set. PLB 18.60 (ISBN 0-86625-331-9). Rourke Corp.
—Soviet Forces in Space. LC 88-14050. (Illus.). 48p. (gr. 3-8). Date not set. PLB 18.60 (ISBN 0-86625-335-1). Rourke Corp.
Cross, Robin. Modern Military Weapons. (Illus.). 32p. (gr. 5-8). 1991. PLB 11.90 (ISBN 0-531-11174-1); pap. 7.95 (ISBN 0-531-15627-3). Watts.
Gander, Terry. Artillery. Gibbons, Tony, et al, illus. 48p. (gr. 5 up). 1987. PLB 9.95 (ISBN 0-8225-1380-3). Lerner Pubns.
Ladd, James D. Amphibious Techniques. Sarson, Peter & Bryan, Tony, illus. LC 84-10003. 48p. (gr. 5 up). 1985. PLB 9.95 (ISBN 0-8225-1379-X, First Ave Edns); pap. 4.95 (ISBN 0-8225-9505-2, First Ave Edns). Lerner Pubns.
Lowe, Malcolm V. Bombers. Gibbons, Tony, et al, illus. 48p. (gr. 5 up). 1987. PLB 9.95 (ISBN 0-8225-1381-1, First Ave Edns); pap. 4.95 (ISBN 0-8225-9541-9, First Ave Edns). Lerner Pubns.
Miller. Soviet Navy. LC 88-11327. (Illus.). 48p. (gr. 3-8). 1988. PLB 18.60 (ISBN 0-86625-336-X). Rourke Corp.
—Soviet Rocket Forces. LC 88-11367. (Illus.). 48p. (gr. 3-8). 1988. PLB 18.60 (ISBN 0-86625-333-5). Rourke Corp.
—Soviet Submarines. (Illus.). 48p. (gr. 3-8). Date not set. PLB 18.60 (ISBN 0-86625-332-7). Rourke Corp.
Smith, Chris & Harbor, Bernard. Military Technology. (Illus.). 48p. (gr. 5-8). 1991. RLB 12.40 (ISBN 0-531-18456-0, Pub. by Boatwright Pr). Watts.
Wood. Soviet Army. (Illus.). 48p. (gr. 3-8). Date not set. PLB 18.60 (ISBN 0-86625-334-3). Rourke Corp.

MILITARY ART AND SCIENCE–STUDY AND TEACHING
see Military Education

MILITARY BIOGRAPHY
see Generals

MILITARY EDUCATION
see also names of military schools, e.g. U. S. Military Academy, West Point; etc.
Collins, Robert F. Qualifying for Admission to the Service Academies: A Student's Guide. Rosen, Ruth, ed. (Illus.). 154p. (gr. 7 up). 1987. lib. bdg. 14.95 (ISBN 0-8239-0696-5). Rosen Group.

MILITARY ENGINEERING
see also Fortification

MILITARY HISTORY
see also Battles; Naval History;
also names of countries with the subdivision Army or History, Military
Wars That Changed the World, 6 vols. LC 87-36748. (Illus.). 192p. (gr. 4-10). 1988. Set. 61.95 (ISBN 0-86307-929-6). Marshall Cavendish.

MILITARY LIFE
see Soldiers

MILITARY POWER
see Disarmament; Military Art and Science; Sea Power

MILITARY SCHOOLS
see Military Education

MILITARY SCIENCE
see Military Art and Science

MILITARY SERVICE–VOCATIONAL GUIDANCE
Macdonald, Robert W. Exploring Careers in the Military Services. rev. ed. Rosen, Ruth, ed. (Illus.). 190p. (gr. 7 up). 1991. 14.95 (ISBN 0-8239-1358-9). Rosen Group.
Slappey, Mary M. Exploring Military Service for Women. rev. ed. (Illus.). 168p. (gr. 9-12). 1989. PLB 14.95 (ISBN 0-8239-0996-4). Rosen Group.

MILITARY SIGNALING
see Signals and Signaling

MILITARY TRAINING
see Military Education

MILITARY VEHICLES
see Vehicles, Military

MILK
Carrick, Donald. Milk. Carrick, Donald, illus. LC 84-25879. 24p. (ps-1). 1985. lib. bdg. 12.88 (ISBN 0-688-04823-4). Greenwillow.
Giblin, James C. Milk: The Fight for Purity. LC 85-48252. (Illus.). 128p. (gr. 3-7). 1986. 12.95 (ISBN 0-690-04572-7, Crowell Jr Bks); PLB 12.89 (ISBN 0-690-04574-3, Crowell Jr Bks). HarpC Child Bks.
Ross, Catherine. Amazing Milk Book. 1991. pap. 6.68 (ISBN 0-201-57087-4). Addison-Wesley.
Turner, Dorothy. Milk. Yates, John, illus. 32p. (gr. 1-4). 1989. PLB 9.95 (ISBN 0-87614-361-3). Carolrhoda Bks.

MILL AND FACTORY BUILDINGS
see Factories

MILLAY, EDNA ST. VINCENT, 1892-1950
Daffron, Carolyn. Edna St. Vincent Millay. Horner, Matina S., intro. by. (Illus.). 112p. (gr. 5 up). 1990. 17.95 (ISBN 1-55546-668-0). Chelsea Hse.

MIND
see Intellect; Psychology

MIND AND BODY
see also Dreams; Hypnotism; Nervous System; Psychoanalysis; Psychology, Pathological; Sleep
Brandreth, Gyles. Amazing Facts about Your Body. Craig, Bobby, illus. LC 80-1088. 32p. (gr. 5-8). 1981. pap. 2.95 (ISBN 0-385-17018-1, Zephyr-BFYR). Doubleday.
Check, William. The Mind-Body Connection. (Illus.). (gr. 6-12). 1990. 18.95 (ISBN 0-7910-0068-0). Chelsea Hse.
Kettelkamp, Larry. A Partnership of Mind & Body: Biofeedback. LC 76-24818. (Illus.). (gr. 5-9). 1976. PLB 12.88 (ISBN 0-688-32088-0). Morrow.
—Your Marvelous Mind. Kettlekamp, Larry, illus. LC 80-18614. 80p. (gr. 5-8). 1980. 9.95 (ISBN 0-664-32670-6, Westminster). Westminster John Knox.
Youngs, Bettie B. A Stress Management Guide for Young People. 6th ed. Nelson, Trish, illus. 88p. (gr. 6-12). 1986. pap. text ed. 9.95x (ISBN 0-940221-00-4). Lrng Tools-Bilicki Pubns.

MIND CURE
see Christian Science; Mind and Body

MINERAL INDUSTRIES
see Mines and Mineral Resources

MINERAL LANDS
see Mines and Mineral Resources

MINERAL OIL
see Petroleum

MINERAL RESOURCES
see Mines and Mineral Resources

MINERALOGY
see also Gems; Precious Stones
Arneson, D. J. Rocks & Minerals. Friedman, Howard, illus. 32p. (Orig.). 1990. pap. 2.50 (ISBN 0-942025-90-3). Kidsbks.
Bains, Rae. Rocks & Minerals. Maccabe, Richard, illus. LC 84-8644. 32p. (gr. 3-6). 1985. PLB 9.49 (ISBN 0-8167-0186-5); pap. text ed. 2.95 (ISBN 0-8167-0187-3). Troll Assocs.
Brown, Vinson, et al. Rocks & Minerals of California. 3rd. rev. ed. LC 72-13423. (Illus.). 200p. (gr. 4 up). 1972. 15.95 (ISBN 0-911010-59-9); pap. 8.95 (ISBN 0-911010-58-0). Naturegraph.
Dineen, Jacqueline. Metals & Minerals. 32p. (gr. 4-8). 1988. lib. bdg. 12.95 (ISBN 0-89490-218-0). Enslow Pubs.
Fichter, George S. Rocks & Minerals. Wynne, Patricia, illus. LC 81-17847. 96p. (gr. 2 up). 1982. pap. 5.95 (ISBN 0-394-84772-5). Random.
Gattis, L. S., III. Rocks & Minerals for Pathfinders: A Basic Youth Enrichment Skill Honor Packet. (Illus.). 22p. (Orig.). (gr. 5 up). 1987. pap. 5.00 tchr's. ed. (ISBN 0-936241-29-2). Cheetah Pub.
Hyler, Nelson W. Rocks & Minerals. Shannon, Kenyon, illus. (gr. 4-6). pap. 2.95 (ISBN 0-8431-4274-X). Wonder.
Lampert, David. Rocks & Minerals. (Illus.). 32p. (gr. 4-9). 1986. PLB 7.99 (ISBN 0-531-10165-7). Watts.
McGowen, Tom. Album of Rocks & Minerals. Ruth, Rod, illus. 64p. (gr. 3 up). 1981. write for info. (ISBN 0-528-82400-7). Checkerboard Pr.
—Album of Rocks & Minerals. Ruth, Rod, illus. 64p. (gr. 3-7). 1987. pap. 4.95 (ISBN 0-02-688504-2). Checkerboard Pr.
Marcus, Elizabeth. Rocks & Minerals. Lawler, Dan, illus. LC 82-17424. 32p. (gr. 3-6). 1983. PLB 10.59 (ISBN 0-89375-876-0); pap. text ed. 2.95 (ISBN 0-89375-877-9). Troll Assocs.
Podendorf, Illa. Rocks & Minerals. LC 81-38494. (Illus.). 48p. (gr. k-4). 1982. PLB 14.60 (ISBN 0-516-01648-2); pap. 4.95 (ISBN 0-516-41648-0). Childrens.
Rocks & Minerals. (Illus.). 32p. (gr. 1-4). 1987. pap. 2.95 (ISBN 0-8431-4296-0). Price Stern.
Zim, Herbert S. & Shaffer, Paul R. Rocks & Minerals. Perlman, Raymond, illus. (gr. 6 up). 1957. pap. write for info. (ISBN 0-307-24499-7, Golden Pr). Western Pub.

MINERALS
see Mineralogy

MINERS–FICTION
Leppard, Lois G. Mandie & the Abandoned Mine, Bk. 8. LC 87-70883. 144p. (Orig.). (gr. 5-8). 1987. pap. 3.95 (ISBN 0-87123-932-9). Bethany Hse.
Rappaport, Doreen. Trouble at the Mines. Sandin, Joan, illus. LC 84-45339. 96p. (gr. 3-7). 1987. 11.95 (ISBN 0-690-04445-3, Crowell Jr Bks); PLB 11.89 (ISBN 0-690-04446-1, Crowell Jr Bks). HarpC Child Bks.
Weber, Kathryn. Molly Moonshine & Timothy. Downey, Jane, illus. 44p. (gr. 2-4). 1990. pap. 2.95 (ISBN 1-878438-01-8). Ranch House Pr.

MINES AND MINERAL RESOURCES
see also Mineralogy; Mining Engineering; Prospecting
also specific types of mines and mining, e.g. Coal Mines and Mining; etc.
Bates, Robert L. Industrial Minerals: How They Are Found & Used. LC 87-36537. 64p. (gr. 6-12). 1988. lib. bdg. 15.95 (ISBN 0-89490-174-5). Enslow Pubs.
Brownstone, David M. & Franck, Irene. Manufacturers & Miners. (Illus.). 176p. 1988. 17.95x (ISBN 0-8160-1447-7). Facts on File.
Makela, Constance E. Iron Mining Fun Book for Children: Featuring Orville Ore. Makela, Constance E., illus. 44p. (Orig.). (gr. k-6). 1982. pap. 2.00x (ISBN 0-9608686-0-7). Happy Thoughts & Rainbow.
Metcalf, Doris & Marson, Ron. Rocks & Minerals. Marson, Peg, illus. 88p. 1989. tchr's. ed. 15.70 (ISBN 0-941008-23-1). Tops Learning.
Mitgutsch, Ali. From Ore to Spoon. Mitgutsch, Ali, illus. LC 80-28862. 24p. (ps-3). 1981. PLB 6.95 (ISBN 0-87614-161-0). Carolrhoda Bks.
Natural History Museum Staff. Rocks & Minerals. Keates, Colin & Einsiedel, Andreas, photos by. LC 87-26514. (Illus.). 64p. (gr. 5 up). 1988. 15.00 (ISBN 0-394-89621-1); lib. bdg. 14.99 (ISBN 0-394-99621-6). Knopf.

MINES AND MINERAL RESOURCES–FICTION
Clymer, Eleanor. Santiago's Silver Mine. 80p. (Orig.). (gr. k-6). 1989. pap. 2.75 (ISBN 0-440-40157-7, YB). Dell.
Edwards, Page. Scarface Joe. LC 83-20667. 128p. (gr. 7 up). 1984. 12.95 (ISBN 0-02-733270-5, Four Winds). Macmillan Child Grp.
Fink, Dale B. Mr. Silver & Mrs. Gold. Chan, Shirley, illus. LC 79-15924. 32p. (ps-3). 1980. 16.95 (ISBN 0-87705-447-9). Human Sci Pr.
Ghost Mines of Yosemite. (gr. 6 up). pap. 2.00 (ISBN 0-915266-02-4). Awani Pr.

MINIATURE CAMERAS
see Cameras

MINIATURE OBJECTS
see Dollhouses; Models and Model Making; Toys;
see names of objects with the subdivision Models, e.g. Airplanes–Models

MINING
see Mines and Mineral Resources; Mining Engineering

MINING ENGINEERING
Brownstone, David M. & Franck, Irene. Manufacturers & Miners. (Illus.). 176p. 1988. 17.95x (ISBN 0-8160-1447-7). Facts on File.

MINISTERS OF THE GOSPEL
see Clergy

MINKS–FICTION
Burgess, Thornton. Billy Mink. 91p. 1981. Repr. PLB 17.95x (ISBN 0-89966-352-4). Buccaneer Bks.
—Billy Mink. 178p. 1981. Repr. PLB 17.95 (ISBN 0-89967-026-1). Harmony Raine.
Liers, Emil E. A Mink's Story. LC 78-10374. (gr. 6-9). 1979. pap. 4.50 (ISBN 0-8127-0205-0). Review & Herald.

MINNESOTA
Aylesworth, Thomas G. & Aylesworth, Virginia L. Western Great Lakes (Illinois, Iowa, Wisconsin, Minnesota) (Illus.). 64p. (gr. 3 up). 1992. PLB 16.95 (ISBN 0-7910-1046-5). Chelsea Hse.
Carole Marsh Minnesota Books, 31 bks. Set. 638.45 (ISBN 0-7933-1298-1). Gallopade Pub Group.
Carpenter, Allan. Minnesota. new ed. LC 78-8000. (Illus.). 96p. (gr. 4 up). 1978. PLB 19.93 (ISBN 0-516-04123-1). Childrens.
Finsand, Mary J. The Town That Moved. Sandland, Reg, illus. LC 82-9703. 48p. (gr. k-4). 1983. PLB 9.95 (ISBN 0-87614-200-5). Carolrhoda Bks.
Fradin, Dennis. Minnesota: In Words & Pictures. LC 79-21543. (Illus.). 48p. (gr. 2-5). 1980. PLB 15.93 (ISBN 0-516-03923-7). Childrens.
Gelbach, Deborah. From This Land: A History of Minnesota's Empires, Enterprises & Entrepreneurs. (Illus.). 384p. (gr. 7 up). 1988. 34.95 (ISBN 0-89781-231-X). Windsor Pubns Inc.
Johnson, Elden. The Prehistoric Peoples of Minnesota. rev. ed. LC 87-32663. (Illus.). 35p. (gr. 9-12). 1988. pap. 3.95 (ISBN 0-87351-223-5). Minn Hist.
Marsh, Carole. Avast, Ye Slobs!: Minnesota Pirate Trivia. (Illus.). (gr. 3 up). 1990. PLB 19.95 (ISBN 0-7933-0641-8); pap. 14.95 (ISBN 0-7933-0640-X); computer disk 29.95 (ISBN 0-7933-0642-6). Gallopade Pub Group.
—The Beast of the Minnesota Bed & Breakfast. (Illus.). (gr. 3 up). 1990. PLB 19.95 (ISBN 0-7933-1714-2); pap. 14.95 (ISBN 0-7933-1715-0); computer disk 29.95 (ISBN 0-7933-1716-9). Gallopade Pub Group.
—The Hard-to-Believe-But-True! Book of Minnesota History, Mystery, Trivia, Legend, Lore, Humor & More. (Illus.). (gr. 3 up). 1990. PLB 19.95 (ISBN 0-7933-0638-8); pap. 14.95 (ISBN 0-7933-0637-X); computer disk 29.95 (ISBN 0-7933-0639-6). Gallopade Pub Group.
—If My Minnesota Mama Ran the World! (Illus.). (gr. 3 up). 1990. lib. bdg. 19.95 (ISBN 0-7933-1717-7); pap. 14.95 (ISBN 0-7933-1718-5); computer disk 29.95 (ISBN 0-7933-1719-3). Gallopade Pub Group.
—Let's Quilt Minnesota & Stuff It Topographically! (Illus.). (gr. 3 up). 1990. PLB 19.95 (ISBN 1-55609-645-3); pap. 14.95 (ISBN 1-55609-099-4); computer disk 29.95 (ISBN 1-55609-647-X). Gallopade Pub Group.
—Minnesota & Other State Greats (Biographies) (Illus.). (gr. 3 up). 1990. PLB 19.95 (ISBN 1-55609-660-7); pap. 14.95 (ISBN 1-55609-661-5); computer disk 29.95 (ISBN 1-55609-662-3). Gallopade Pub Group.
—Minnesota Bandits, Bushwackers, Outlaws, Crooks, Devils, Ghosts, Desperadoes & Other Assorted & Sundry Characters! (Illus.). (gr. 3 up). 1990. PLB 19.95 (ISBN 0-7933-0623-X); pap. 14.95 (ISBN 0-7933-0622-1); computer disk 29.95 (ISBN 0-7933-0624-8). Gallopade Pub Group.
—Minnesota Classic Christmas Trivia: Stories, Recipes, Activities, Legends, Lore & More! (Illus.). (gr. 3 up). 1990. PLB 19.95 (ISBN 0-7933-0626-4); pap. 14.95 (ISBN 0-7933-0625-6); computer disk 29.95 (ISBN 0-7933-0627-2). Gallopade Pub Group.
—Minnesota Coastales. (Illus.). (gr. 3 up). 1990. PLB 19.95 (ISBN 1-55609-654-2); pap. 14.95 (ISBN 1-55609-655-0); computer disk 29.95 (ISBN 1-55609-656-9). Gallopade Pub Group.
—The Minnesota Hot Air Balloon Mystery. (Illus.). (gr. 2-9). 1990. 19.95 (ISBN 0-7933-2525-0); pap. 14.95 (ISBN 0-7933-2526-9); computer disk 29.95 (ISBN 0-7933-2527-7). Gallopade Pub Group.

—Minnesota "Jography" A Fun Run Thru Our State. (Illus.). (gr. 3 up). 1990. PLB 19.95 (ISBN 1-55609-642-9); pap. 14.95 (ISBN 1-55609-643-7); computer disk 29.95 (ISBN 1-55609-644-5). Gallopade Pub Group.

—Minnesota Kid's Cookbook: Recipes, How-To, History, Lore & More. (Illus.). (gr. 3 up). 1990. PLB 19.95 (ISBN 0-7933-0635-3); pap. 14.95 (ISBN 0-7933-0634-5); computer disk 29.95 (ISBN 0-7933-0636-1). Gallopade Pub Group.

—Minnesota Quiz Bowl Crash Course! (Illus.). (gr. 3 up). 1990. PLB 19.95 (ISBN 1-55609-657-7); pap. 14.95 (ISBN 1-55609-658-5); computer disk 29.95 (ISBN 1-55609-659-3). Gallopade Pub Group.

—Minnesota School Trivia: An Amazing & Fascinating Look at Our State's Teachers, Schools & Students! (Illus.). (gr. 3 up). 1990. PLB 19.95 (ISBN 0-7933-0632-9); pap. 14.95 (ISBN 0-7933-0631-0); computer disk 29.95 (ISBN 0-7933-0633-7). Gallopade Pub Group.

—Minnesota Silly Basketball Sportsmysteries, Vol. I. (Illus.). (gr. 3 up). 1990. PLB 19.95 (ISBN 0-7933-0629-9); pap. 14.95 (ISBN 0-7933-0628-0); computer disk 29.95 (ISBN 0-7933-0630-2). Gallopade Pub Group.

—Minnesota Silly Basketball Sportsmysteries, Vol. II. (Illus.). (gr. 3 up). 1990. PLB 19.95 (ISBN 0-7933-1720-7); pap. 14.95 (ISBN 0-7933-1721-5); computer disk 29.95 (ISBN 0-7933-1722-3). Gallopade Pub Group.

—Minnesota Silly Football Sportsmysteries, Vol. I. (Illus.). (gr. 3 up). 1990. PLB 19.95 (ISBN 1-55609-648-8); pap. 14.95 (ISBN 1-55609-649-6); computer disk 29.95 (ISBN 1-55609-650-X). Gallopade Pub Group.

—Minnesota Silly Football Sportsmysteries, Vol. II. (Illus.). (gr. 3 up). 1990. PLB 19.95 (ISBN 1-55609-651-8); pap. 14.95 (ISBN 1-55609-652-6); computer disk 29.95 (ISBN 1-55609-653-4). Gallopade Pub Group.

—Minnesota Silly Trivia! (Illus.). (gr. 3 up). 1990. PLB 19.95 (ISBN 1-55609-639-9); pap. 14.95 (ISBN 1-55609-640-2); computer disk 29.95 (ISBN 1-55609-641-0). Gallopade Pub Group.

—Minnesota's (Most Devastating!) Disasters & (Most Calamitous!) Catastrophies! (Illus.). (gr. 3 up). 1990. PLB 19.95 (ISBN 0-7933-0620-5); pap. 14.95 (ISBN 0-7933-0619-1); computer disk 29.95 (ISBN 0-7933-0621-3). Gallopade Pub Group.

Nielsen, Nancy. Boundary Waters Canoe Area, Minnesota. LC 89-7688. (Illus.). 48p. (gr. 4-5). 1989. 12.95 (ISBN 0-89686-465-0, Crestwood Hse). Macmillan Child Grp.

Paulsen, Gary. Woodsong. Paulsen, Ruth W., illus. LC 89-70835. 144p. (gr. 7 up). 1990. 12.95 (ISBN 0-02-770221-9, Bradbury Pr). Macmillan Child Grp.

Sansome, Constance J. Minnesota in Maps: A Trailblazer Atlas. Sansome, Constance J. & Jefferson, Lisa E., illus. 32p. (gr. 4-8). 1990. 17.95 (ISBN 0-9626025-0-7); pap. 12.95 (ISBN 0-9626025-1-5). Trailblazer Bks.

Thompson, Kathleen. Minnesota. LC 87-16405. 48p. (gr. 3 up). 1988. 17.32 (ISBN 0-86514-466-4); cancelled tchr's. study guide (ISBN 0-86514-606-3); cancelled Beta video (ISBN 0-86514-093-6); cancelled VHS video (ISBN 0-86514-168-1); cancelled 3/4" video (ISBN 0-86514-243-2). Raintree Pubs.

MINNESOTA–FICTION

Kresel, Maryann. Thoughts of Yesterday. (Illus.). 106p. (Orig.). 1989. pap. 9.95 (ISBN 0-944958-37-0). Elfin Cove Pr.

Lovelace, Maud H. Betsy & Joe. Neville, Vera, illus. LC 48-8096. 256p. (gr. 5 up). 1948. 14.95 (ISBN 0-690-13378-2, Crowell Jr Bks). HarpC Child Bks.

—Betsy & Tacy Go Downtown. Lenski, Lois, illus. LC 43-51264. 180p. (gr. 2-5). 1966. PLB 13.89 (ISBN 0-690-13450-9, Crowell Jr Bks). HarpC Child Bks.

—Betsy & Tacy Go over the Big Hill. Lenski, Lois, illus. LC 42-23557. 171p. (gr. 2-5). 1966. PLB 12.89i (ISBN 0-690-13521-1, Crowell Jr Bks); PLB 12.89 (ISBN 0-686-82912-3, Crowell Jr Bks). HarpC Child Bks.

—Betsy-Tacy. Lenski, Lois, illus. LC 40-30965. 113p. (gr. 2-5). 1966. PLB 13.89 (ISBN 0-690-13805-9, Crowell Jr Bks). HarpC Child Bks.

—Betsy-Tacy & Tib. Lenski, Lois, illus. LC 41-18714. 128p. (gr. 2-5). 1966. PLB 13.89 (ISBN 0-690-13876-8, Crowell Jr Bks). HarpC Child Bks.

—Betsy's Wedding. Neville, Vera, illus. LC 55-11108. 241p. (gr. 5 up). 1955. 14.95 (ISBN 0-690-13733-8, Crowell Jr Bks). HarpC Child Bks.

Paulsen, Gary. The Winter Room. LC 89-42541. 128p. (gr. 6-9). 1989. 11.95 (ISBN 0-531-05839-5); PLB 11.99 (ISBN 0-531-08439-6). Orchard Bks Watts.

Thomas, Jane R. Courage at Indian Deep. LC 83-14404. (Illus.). 128p. (gr. 3-7). 1984. 13.95 (ISBN 0-89919-181-9, Clarion). HM.

Wilder, Laura I. On the Banks of Plum Creek. rev. ed. Williams, Garth, illus. LC 52-7528. 340p. (gr. 3-7). 1953. 14.95 (ISBN 0-06-026470-5); PLB 14.89 (ISBN 0-06-026471-3). HarpC Child Bks.

MINORITIES

see also Discrimination; Race Problems

Behrens, June. Samoans! Behrens, T. L., photos by. LC 85-32529. (Illus.). 31p. (gr. 2-4). 1986. PLB 14.60 (ISBN 0-516-02388-8). Childrens.

Stanek, Muriel. We Came from Vietnam. Fay, Ann, ed. McMahon, W. Franklin, illus. 48p. (gr. 1-6). 1985. PLB 10.50 (ISBN 0-8075-8699-4). A Whitman.

MIRACLE PLAYS

see Mysteries and Miracle Plays

MIRRORS

Davies, Kay. My Mirror. 1990. 6.95 (ISBN 0-385-41128-6); PLB 7.99 (ISBN 0-385-41196-0). Doubleday.

Fitzpatrick, Julie. Mirrors. LC 84-40837. (Illus.). 32p. (gr. 2-5). PLB 9.96 (ISBN 0-382-09059-4). Silver Burdett Pr.

McDonough, Jerome. Mirrors. (Illus.). 32p. (gr. 7 up). 1987. pap. 2.50 (ISBN 0-88680-278-4). I E Clark.

Taylor, Barbara. Bouncing & Bending Light. (ps-3). 1990. PLB 11.40 (ISBN 0-531-14014-8). Watts.

MISDEMEANORS (LAW)

see Criminal Law

MISSILES, GUIDED

see Guided Missiles

MISSING PERSONS

Bren Guernsey, JoAnn. Missing Children. LC 89-25210. (Illus.). 48p. (gr. 4 up). 1990. 10.95 (ISBN 0-89686-494-4, Crestwood Hse). Macmillan Child Grp.

Christensen, Loren. Missing Children. (Illus.). 64p. (gr. 7 up). 1990. lib. bdg. 15.93 (ISBN 0-86593-076-7); lib. bdg. 11.95s.p. Rourke Corp.

MISSIONARIES

Barrett, Marsha. Vena Aguillard: Woman of Faith. LC 82-73664. (gr. 4-6). 1983. 5.95 (ISBN 0-8054-4281-2, 4242-81). Broadman.

Beck, Margaret. Madugu. Whitney, Dick, illus. 26p. (gr. k-6). 1987. pap. text ed. 5.50 (ISBN 1-55976-052-4). CEF Press.

Bostrom, Alice. David Livingstone, Missionary to Africa. Lautermilch, John, illus. 32p. (Orig.). 1982. pap. 1.95 (ISBN 0-89323-027-8). Bible Memory.

Brown, Pam. It Was Always Africa. LC 86-2240. (gr. 7-10). 1986. pap. 4.95 (ISBN 0-8054-4335-5). Broadman.

Chamberlain, Eugene. Loyd Corder: Traveler for God. LC 82-73663. (gr. 4-6). 1983. 5.95 (ISBN 0-8054-4284-7, 4242-84). Broadman.

Cutts, William A. Weak Thing in Moni Land: The Story of Bill & Gracie Cutts. Richardson, Don, frwd. by. LC 90-80454. (Illus.). 168p. (Orig.). 1990. pap. 7.99 (ISBN 0-87509-429-5). Chr Pubns.

Davis, Rebecca H. With Daring Faith. 187p. (Orig.). 1987. pap. 4.95 (ISBN 0-89084-414-3). Bob Jones Univ Pr.

Dick, Lois H. I Dare. Lombard, Lynette, illus. 42p. (gr. k-6). 1971. pap. text ed. 9.45 (ISBN 1-55976-034-6). CEF Press.

—Run Ma Run. Butcher, Sam, illus. 57p. (gr. k-6). 1978. pap. text ed. 8.99 (ISBN 1-55976-055-9). CEF Press.

Harner, Ruth. Rejoicing with Joy. Butcher, Sam, illus. 21p. (gr. k-6). 1988. pap. text ed. 4.25 (ISBN 1-55976-145-8). CEF Press.

Heath, Lou. Ed Taylor: Father of Migrant Missions. LC 81-70911. (gr. k-3). 1982. 5.95 (ISBN 0-8054-4278-2, 4242-78). Broadman.

Hibschman, Barbara. I Want to Be a Missionary. Wulf, Barbara L., illus. 24p. (Orig.). (gr. 1-6). 1990. pap. 2.99 (ISBN 0-87509-436-8). Chr Pubns.

Hillam, Corbin. Jennifer of the City. Hillam, Corbin, illus. 32p. (ps-2). 1990. text ed. 7.95 (ISBN 0-570-04183-X). Concordia.

Hockett, Betty M. Whistling Bombs & Bumpy Trains: The Life-Story of Anna Nixon. Loewen, Janelle, illus. LC 89-84572. 80p. (Orig.). (gr. 3-6). 1989. pap. 3.50 (ISBN 0-943701-15-5). George Fox Pr.

Hoffman, Janet T. The Pattersons: Missionary Publishers. LC 83-71836. (gr. 4-6). 1984. 5.95 (ISBN 0-8054-4288-X, 4242-88). Broadman.

Hollaway, Lee. The Donald Orrs: Missionary Duet. LC 82-732666. (gr. 4-6). 1983. 5.95 (ISBN 0-8054-4283-9, 4242-83). Broadman.

—Los Orr: Duo Misionero. 64p. 1987. pap. 2.75 (ISBN 0-311-01073-3). Casa Bautista.

Howard, Mildred T. These Are My People. (Illus.). 152p. (Orig.). (gr. 3). 1984. pap. 6.94 (ISBN 0-89084-242-6). Bob Jones Univ Pr.

Human, Johnnie. Finlay & Julia Graham: Missionary Partners. LC 86-4148. (gr. 4-6). 1986. 5.95 (ISBN 0-8054-4327-4). Broadman.

Jacobs, William J. Mother Teresa: Helping the Poor. (Illus.). 48p. (gr. 2-4). 1991. PLB 11.90 (ISBN 1-56294-020-1). Millbrook Pr.

Johnston, Sammie. The Dream Builders. 192p. (Orig.). (gr. 7-12). 1989. pap. text ed. 4.95 (ISBN 0-936625-64-3, New Hope AL). Womans Mission Union.

Kent, Renee. You Can Be a Musician & a Missionary, Too. McClain, Cindy, ed. Sealy, Kathy, illus. 64p. (Orig.). (gr. 4-6). 1988. pap. 3.95 (ISBN 0-936625-37-6, PZ7.K419Y). Womans Mission Union.

Kiefer, James. Hudson Taylor. Beerhorst, Adrian, illus. 53p. (gr. k-6). 1973. pap. text ed. 8.99 (ISBN 1-55976-054-0). CEF Press.

Kizer, Kathryn W. The Harley Shields: Alaskan Missionaries. LC 84-5821. (gr. k-3). 1984. 5.95 (ISBN 0-8054-4285-5, 4242-85). Broadman.

Lathem, Judy. Hattie Gardner: Determined Adventurer. LC 81-70909. (gr. 4-6). 1982. 5.95 (ISBN 0-8054-4280-4, 4242-80). Broadman.

McElrath, William N. Oz & Mary Quick: Taiwan Teammates. LC 84-2962. (gr. 4-6). 1984. pap. 5.95 (ISBN 0-8054-4287-1, 4242-87). Broadman.

McMinn, Tom. The Caudills: Courageous Missionaries. LC 81-70474. (gr. 4-6). 1982. 5.95 (ISBN 0-8054-4277-4, 4242-77). Broadman.

Marxhausen, Joanne. Some of My Best Friends Are Trees. LC 56-1640. (Illus., Orig.). (ps-4). 1990. pap. 6.95 (ISBN 0-570-04182-1, 56-1640). Concordia.

Massey, Barbara. Virginia Wingo: Teacher & Friend. LC 82-73665. (gr. k-3). 1983. 5.95 (ISBN 0-8054-4282-0, 4242-82). Broadman.

Miller, S. My Book about Hudson. 1989. 5.95 (ISBN 9971-972-69-7). OMF Bks.

Mouillesseaux, Claire & Seger, Doris. Devil-Kings & Cannibals. (Illus.). 52p. (gr. k-4). 1962. pap. text ed. 8.99 (ISBN 1-55976-053-2). CEF Press.

Ryan, Roberta. The George Lozuks: Doers of the Word. LC 85-6615. (gr. 4-6). 1985. 5.95 (ISBN 0-8054-4293-6, 4242-93). Broadman.

Strawn, Kathy. Matthew's Dad Is a Missionary. Sealy, Kathy, illus. 32p. (Orig.). (gr. 1-3). 1988. pap. 2.95 (ISBN 0-936625-38-4). Womans Mission Union.

Swift, Catherine. Gladys Aylward. LC 89-61792. 128p. 1989. pap. 3.95 (ISBN 1-55661-090-4). Bethany Hse.

Timyan, Janis, illus. A Happy Day for Ramona & Other Missionary Stories for Children. LC 87-71018. (Orig.). (gr. 1-5). 1987. pap. 3.99 (ISBN 0-87509-392-2). Chr Pubns.

—The Pink & Green Church & Other Missionary Stories for Children. LC 87-71019. (gr. 1-5). 1988. pap. 3.99 (ISBN 0-87509-393-0). Chr Pubns.

Wallace, Mary H. Profiles of Pentecostal Missionaries. Agnew, Tim, contrib. by. LC 86-15919. (Illus.). 352p. (Orig.). 1986. pap. 6.95 (ISBN 0-932581-00-5). Word Aflame.

Walsh, Vincent M. Prepare My People. 100p. (Orig.). 1986. pap. text ed. 5.00 (ISBN 0-943374-13-8). Key of David.

Wendell, Belew M. Ken Prickett: Man of Joy. LC 85-6208. (gr. 4-6). 1985. 5.95 (ISBN 0-8054-4296-0, 4242-96). Broadman.

Whittlesey, Marjorie T. The Dragon Will Survive. LC 89-17585. 1991. 13.95 (ISBN 0-87949-315-1). Ashley Bks.

Zook, Mary R. Little Missionaries. 184p. (ps-5). 1979. 6.75 (ISBN 0-686-30764-X). Rod & Staff.

MISSIONARIES–FICTION

Ross, Uta O. The Boy Who Wanted to Be a Missionary. Dieneman, Debbie, illus. 48p. (Orig.). (gr. 1-3). 1984. pap. 0.70 (ISBN 0-687-03910-X). Abingdon.

Wilkinson, Barbara. Apples for the Missionaries. Dillard, Karen, illus. 32p. (Orig.). (gr. 1-3). 1989. pap. text ed. 2.95 (ISBN 0-936625-67-8). Womans Mission Union.

MISSIONS

see also Missionaries;

also names of churches, denominations, religious orders, etc. with the subdivision Missions, e.g. Catholic Church–Missions; etc.

Beasley, Mrs. Jim. Missions Studies: Brazil. (Illus.). 32p. (Orig.). (ps). 1985. pap. 2.25 (ISBN 0-89114-155-3). Baptist Pub Hse.

Douglass, Herbert E. Why Jesus Waits: How the Sanctuary Message Explains the Mission of the Seventh-Day Adventist Church. rev. ed. LC 76-10925. 96p. (gr. 10 up). 1987. pap. 3.95 (ISBN 0-945460-00-7). Upward Way.

Durham, Jackie. In Search of Energy. Pennington, Celeste, ed. Stevens, Bill, illus. (Orig.). (gr. 4-6). 1984. pap. 1.75 (ISBN 0-937170-27-5). Home Mission.

Newberry, Tina T. Kelli Tyler Extraordinaire. 120p. (Orig.). (gr. 4-6). 1990. pap. text ed. 3.50 (ISBN 0-936625-91-0, New Hope AL). Womans Mission Union.

Pratt, Anne H. Junior Missionary Handbook. 64p. (Orig.). (gr. 3-6). 1987. pap. 5.95 (ISBN 0-88290-318-7). Horizon Utah.

Richardson, Freida. Madagascar's Miracle Story. Bernard, David, ed. Richardson, Jerry, intro. by. LC 89-32335. (Illus.). 156p. (Orig.). 1989. pap. 6.95 (ISBN 0-932581-47-1). Word Aflame.

Smith, Anne. Get into the Action: An Activity Book for Children on Mission Action. 31p. (Orig.). (gr. 1-6). 1990. pap. text ed. 2.95 (ISBN 0-936625-84-8). Womans Mission Union.

Spizzirri Publishing Co. Staff & Spizzirri, Linda. California Missions: An Educational Coloring Book. (Illus.). 32p. (gr. k-5). 1985. pap. 1.95 (ISBN 0-86545-062-5). Spizzirri.

Steere, D'Ann. Choice Adventures, No. 4: The Rain Forest Mission. (gr. 3-7). 1991. PLB 3.95 (ISBN 0-8423-5028-4). Tyndale.

Sutton, Jan. One Giant Step: Putting Feet to Missions. 80p. (Orig.). (gr. 7-12). 1990. pap. text ed. 3.95 (ISBN 0-936625-85-6). Womans Mission Union.

MISSISSIPPI

Braynard, Frank O. U. S. Steamships: A Picture Postcard History. Cronkite, Walter, intro. by. (Illus.). 144p. (Orig.). Date not set. pap. write for info. (ISBN 0-930256-20-4). Almar.

Carole Marsh Mississippi Books, 31 bks. Set. 638.45 (ISBN 0-7933-1299-X). Gallopade Pub Group.

Carpenter, Allan. Mississippi. LC 78-3400. (Illus.). 96p. (gr. 4 up). 1978. PLB 19.93 (ISBN 0-516-04124-X). Childrens.

Carson, Robert. Mississippi. LC 88-11747. (Illus.). 144p. (gr. 4 up). 1988. PLB 25.27 (ISBN 0-516-00470-0). Childrens.

Fradin, Dennis. Mississippi: In Words & Pictures. Wahl, Richard, illus. LC 80-36855. 48p. (gr. 2-5). 1980. PLB 15.93 (ISBN 0-516-03924-5). Childrens.

Marsh, Carole. Avast, Ye Slobs!: Mississippi Pirate Trivia. (Illus.). (gr. 3 up). 1990. PLB 19.95 (ISBN 0-7933-0666-3); pap. 14.95 (ISBN 0-7933-0665-5); computer disk 29.95 (ISBN 0-7933-0667-1). Gallopade Pub Group.

—The Beast of the Mississippi Bed & Breakfast. (Illus.). (gr. 3 up). 1990. PLB 19.95 (ISBN 0-7933-0644-2); pap. 14.95 (ISBN 0-7933-1726-6); computer disk 29.95 (ISBN 0-7933-1727-4). Gallopade Pub Group.

—The Hard-to-Believe-But-True! Book of Mississippi History, Mystery, Trivia, Legend, Lore, Humor & More. (Illus.). (gr. 3 up). 1990. PLB 19.95 (ISBN 0-7933-0663-9); pap. 14.95 (ISBN 0-7933-0662-0); computer disk 29.95 (ISBN 0-7933-0664-7). Gallopade Pub Group.

—If My Mississippi Mama Ran the World! (Illus.). (gr. 3 up). 1990. lib. bdg. 19.95 (ISBN 0-7933-1728-2); pap. 14.95 (ISBN 0-7933-1729-0); computer disk 29.95 (ISBN 0-7933-1730-4). Gallopade Pub Group.

—Let's Quilt Mississippi & Stuff It Topographically! (Illus.). (gr. 3 up). 1990. PLB 19.95 (ISBN 1-55609-710-7); pap. 14.95 (ISBN 1-55609-074-9); computer disk 29.95 (ISBN 1-55609-716-6). Gallopade Pub Group.

—Mississippi & Other State Greats (Biographies) (Illus.). (gr. 3 up). 1990. PLB 19.95 (ISBN 1-55609-725-5); pap. 14.95 (ISBN 1-55609-726-3); computer disk 29.95 (ISBN 1-55609-727-1). Gallopade Pub Group.

—Mississippi Bandits, Bushwackers, Outlaws, Crooks, Devils, Ghosts, Desperadoes & Other Assorted & Sundry Characters! (Illus.). (gr. 3 up). 1990. PLB 19.95 (ISBN 0-7933-0648-5); pap. 14.95 (ISBN 0-7933-0647-7); computer disk 29.95 (ISBN 0-7933-0649-3). Gallopade Pub Group.

—Mississippi Classic Christmas Trivia: Stories, Recipes, Activities, Legends, Lore & More. (Illus.). (gr. 3 up). 1990. PLB 19.95 (ISBN 0-7933-0651-5); pap. 14.95 (ISBN 0-7933-0650-7); computer disk 29.95 (ISBN 0-7933-0652-3). Gallopade Pub Group.

—Mississippi Coastales. (Illus.). (gr. 3 up). 1990. PLB 19.95 (ISBN 1-55609-720-4); pap. 14.95 (ISBN 1-55609-122-2); computer disk 29.95 (ISBN 1-55609-721-2). Gallopade Pub Group.

—The Mississippi Hot Air Balloon Mystery. (Illus.). (gr. 2-9). 1990. 19.95 (ISBN 0-7933-2534-X); pap. 14.95 (ISBN 0-7933-2535-8); computer disk 29.95 (ISBN 0-7933-2536-6). Gallopade Pub Group.

—Mississippi "Jography" A Fun Run Thru Our State. (Illus.). (gr. 3 up). 1990. PLB 19.95 (ISBN 1-55609-709-3); pap. 14.95 (ISBN 1-55609-091-9); computer disk 29.95 (ISBN 1-55609-715-8). Gallopade Pub Group.

—Mississippi Kid's Cookbook: Recipes, How-To, History, Lore & More. (Illus.). (gr. 3 up). 1990. PLB 19.95 (ISBN 0-7933-0660-4); pap. 14.95 (ISBN 0-7933-0659-0); computer disk 29.95 (ISBN 0-7933-0661-2). Gallopade Pub Group.

—Mississippi Quiz Bowl Crash Course! (Illus.). (gr. 3 up). 1990. PLB 19.95 (ISBN 1-55609-722-0); pap. 14.95 (ISBN 1-55609-723-9); computer disk 29.95 (ISBN 1-55609-724-7). Gallopade Pub Group.

—Mississippi School Trivia: An Amazing & Fascinating Look at Our State's Teachers, Schools & Students! (Illus.). (gr. 3 up). 1990. PLB 19.95 (ISBN 0-7933-0657-4); pap. 14.95 (ISBN 0-7933-0656-6); computer disk 29.95 (ISBN 0-7933-0658-2). Gallopade Pub Group.

—Mississippi Silly Basketball Sports Mysteries, Vol. II. (Illus.). (gr. 3 up). 1990. PLB 19.95 (ISBN 0-7933-1731-2); pap. 14.95 (ISBN 0-7933-1732-0); computer disk 29.95. Gallopade Pub Group.

—Mississippi Silly Basketball Sportsmysteries, Vol. I. (Illus.). (gr. 3 up). 1990. PLB 19.95 (ISBN 0-7933-0654-X); pap. 14.95 (ISBN 0-7933-0653-1); computer disk 29.95 (ISBN 0-7933-0655-8). Gallopade Pub Group.

—Mississippi Silly Football Sportsmysteries, Vol. I. (Illus.). (gr. 3 up). 1990. PLB 19.95 (ISBN 1-55609-711-5); pap. 14.95 (ISBN 1-55609-712-3); computer disk 29.95 (ISBN 1-55609-713-1). Gallopade Pub Group.

—Mississippi Silly Football Sportsmysteries, Vol. II. (Illus.). (gr. 3 up). 1990. PLB 19.95 (ISBN 1-55609-717-4); pap. 14.95 (ISBN 1-55609-718-2); computer disk 29.95 (ISBN 1-55609-719-0). Gallopade Pub Group.

—Mississippi Silly Trivia! (Illus.). (gr. 3 up). 1990. PLB 19.95 (ISBN 1-55609-708-5); pap. 14.95 (ISBN 1-55609-039-0); computer disk 29.95 (ISBN 1-55609-714-X). Gallopade Pub Group.

—Mississippi's (Most Devastating!) Disasters & (Most Calamitous!) Catastrophies! (Illus.). (gr. 3 up). 1990. PLB 19.95 (ISBN 0-7933-0645-0); pap. 14.95 (ISBN 0-7933-0643-4); computer disk 29.95 (ISBN 0-7933-0646-9). Gallopade Pub Group.

Thompson, Kathleen. Mississippi. LC 87-16440. 48p. (gr. 3 up). 1987. 17.32 (ISBN 0-86514-467-2); cancelled tchr's. study guide (ISBN 0-86514-607-1); cancelled Beta video (ISBN 0-86514-094-4); cancelled VHS video (ISBN 0-86514-169-X); cancelled 3/4" video (ISBN 0-86514-244-0). Raintree Pubs.

MISSISSIPPI–FICTION

Butterworth, W. E. LeRoy & the Old Man. 168p. (gr. 7 up). 1982. pap. 2.50 (ISBN 0-590-40573-X, Point). Scholastic Inc.

Naylor, Phyllis R. Night Cry. LC 83-15569. 168p. 1984. 13.95 (ISBN 0-689-31017-X, Atheneum Child Bk). Macmillan Child Grp.

Twain, Mark. The Adventures of Tom Sawyer. Moser, Barry, illus. Glassman, Peter, afterword by. LC 89-60838. (Illus.). 272p. (ps up). 1989. 21.95 (ISBN 0-688-07510-X). Morrow Jr Bks.

MISSISSIPPI RIVER

Crisman, Ruth. The Mississippi. (Illus.). 72p. (gr. 4-8). 1984. lib. bdg. 10.40 (ISBN 0-531-04826-8). Watts.

Holling, Holling C. Minn of the Mississippi. (Illus.). (gr. 4-6). 1951. 16.95 (ISBN 0-395-17578-X). HM.

McCall, Edith. Biography of a River: The Mississippi. (Illus.). (gr. 7 up). 1990. 16.95 (ISBN 0-8027-6914-4); lib. bdg. 17.85 (ISBN 0-8027-6915-2). Walker & Co.

—Mississippi Steamboatman: The Story of Henry Miller Shreve. LC 85-13795. (Illus.). 115p. (gr. 5-8). 1986. 11.95 (ISBN 0-8027-6597-1). Walker & Co.

Zeck, Pam & Zeck, Gerry. Mississippi Sternwheelers. LC 81-15553. (Illus.). 32p. (gr. k-4). 1982. PLB 9.95 (ISBN 0-87614-180-7). Carolrhoda Bks.

MISSISSIPPI RIVER–FICTION

Clemens, Samuel. Huckleberry Finn. Farr, Naunerle, ed. Redondo, Francisco, illus. LC 73-75468. 64p. (Orig.). (gr. 5-10). 1973. pap. 2.95 (ISBN 0-88301-098-4). Pendulum Pr.

—Tom Sawyer. new ed. Shapiro, Irwin, ed. Cruz, E. R., illus. LC 73-75465. 64p. (Orig.). (gr. 5-10). 1973. pap. 2.95 (ISBN 0-88301-103-4); student activity bk. 1.25 (ISBN 0-88301-179-4). Pendulum Pr.

Clements, Bruce. I Tell a Lie Every So Often. LC 73-22356. 160p. (gr. 5 up). 1984. pap. 3.50 (ISBN 0-374-43539-1). FS&G.

Fichter, George S. First Steamboat down the Mississippi. Boddy, Joe, illus. 112p. (gr. 4-6). 1989. 8.95 (ISBN 0-88289-715-2). Pelican.

Holling, Holling C. Minn of the Mississippi. Holling, Holling C., illus. (gr. 4-6). 1978. pap. 7.95 (ISBN 0-395-27399-4). HM.

Koste, Virginia G. The Trial of Tom Sawyer. (gr. 4 up). 1978. 4.50 (ISBN 0-87602-213-1). Anchorage.

Tom Sawyer. 320p. (gr. 3-9). 1981. pap. 7.95 (ISBN 0-448-11002-4, G&D). Putnam Pub Group.

Tom Sawyer. (Illus.). (gr. 3-5). 3.50 (ISBN 0-7214-0977-6). Ladybird Bks.

Twain, Mark. The Adventures of Huckleberry Finn. LC 85-9576. (gr. 5 up). pap. 2.75 (ISBN 0-8049-0004-3, CL-4). Airmont.

—Adventures of Huckleberry Finn. McKay, Donald & Polseno, Jo, illus. LC 85-9576. 448p. (gr. 4-6). 12.95 (ISBN 0-448-06000-0, G&D); pap. 7.95 (ISBN 0-448-11000-8, G&D). Putnam Pub Group.

—Adventures of Huckleberry Finn. LC 85-9576. (gr. 3-7). 1983. pap. 2.95 (ISBN 0-14-035007-1, Puffin Bks). Puffin Bks.

—The Adventures of Huckleberry Finn. 384p. (Orig.). (gr. 4-6). 1987. pap. 2.50 (ISBN 0-590-40801-1, Pub. by Apple Classics); tchr's. guide 1.25 (ISBN 0-590-40662-0). Scholastic Inc.

—The Adventures of Tom Sawyer. LC 63-19420. (gr. 5 up). 1964. pap. 2.50 (ISBN 0-8049-0006-X, CL-6). Airmont.

—The Adventures of Tom Sawyer. LC 62-19420. 224p. (gr. 3-7). 1983. pap. 2.25 (ISBN 0-14-035003-9, Puffin). Puffin Bks.

—The Adventures of Tom Sawyer. 320p. (Orig.). (gr. 4-6). 1987. pap. 2.50 (ISBN 0-590-40800-3, Pub. by Apple Classics); tchr's. guide 1.25 (ISBN 0-590-40663-9). Scholastic Inc.

Twain, Mark, pseud. Adventures of Tom Sawyer. Gise, Joanne, adapted by. James, Raymond, illus. LC 89-20559. 48p. (gr. 3-6). 1989. lib. bdg. 12.89 (ISBN 0-8167-1859-8); pap. text ed. 3.95 (ISBN 0-8167-1860-1). Troll Assocs.

Twain, Mark. Adventures of Tom Sawyer. 1989. 9.99 (ISBN 0-517-68813-1). Outlet Bk Co.

—Adventures of Tom Sawyer & Adventures of Huckleberry Finn. Dickey, James, intro. by. 1979. pap. 3.95 (ISBN 0-451-52272-9). NAL-Dutton.

—Huckleberry Finn. Stewart, Diana, adapted by. Neidigh, Sherry, illus. LC 79-24312. 48p. (gr. 4 up). 1983. PLB 17.32 (ISBN 0-8172-1651-0); pap. 9.27 (ISBN 0-8172-2009-7). Raintree Pubs.

—Life on the Mississippi. Willoughby, J., intro. by. (gr. 9 up). pap. 1.95 (ISBN 0-8049-0055-8, CL-55). Airmont.

—Reader's Digest Best Loved Books for Young Readers: The Adventures of Huckleberry Finn. Ogburn, Jackie, ed. Falter, John, illus. 192p. (gr. 4-12). 1989. 3.99 (ISBN 0-945260-30-X). Choice Pub NY.

—Reader's Digest Best Loved Books for Young Readers: The Adventures of Tom Sawyer. Ogburn, Jackie, ed. Falter, John, illus. 136p. (gr. 4-12). 1989. 3.99 (ISBN 0-945260-19-9). Choice Pub NY.

—Tom Sawyer. rev. ed. (Illus.). (gr. 7-12). 1982. pap. 3.50 (ISBN 0-671-44135-3, RE). PB.

—Tom Sawyer Abroad. Rowland, B., intro. by. Bd. with Tom Sawyer Detective. (gr. 5up). pap. 1.50 (ISBN 0-8049-0126-0, CL-126). Airmont.

MISSISSIPPI VALLEY

see also Middle West

MISSOURI

Aylesworth, Thomas G. & Aylesworth, Virginia L. South Central (Louisiana, Arkansas, Missouri, Kansas, Oklahoma) (Illus.). 64p. (gr. 3 up). 1992. PLB 16.95 (ISBN 0-7910-1047-3). Chelsea Hse.

Carole Marsh Missouri Books, 31 bks. Set. 638.45 (ISBN 0-7933-1300-7). Gallopade Pub Group.

Carpenter, Allan. Missouri. LC 78-3551. (Illus.). 96p. (gr. 4 up). 1978. PLB 19.93 (ISBN 0-516-04125-8). Childrens.

Fradin, Dennis. Missouri: In Words & Pictures. Wahl, Richard, illus. LC 80-12249. 48p. (gr. 2-5). 1980. PLB 15.93 (ISBN 0-516-03925-3). Childrens.

McCandless, Perry & Foley, William E. Missouri: Then & Now. LC 90-32545. (Illus.). 240p. 1990. text ed. 12.95 (ISBN 0-8262-0747-2). U of Mo Pr.

Marsh, Carole. Avast, Ye Slobs!: Missouri Pirate Trivia. (Illus.). (gr. 3 up). 1990. PLB 19.95 (ISBN 0-7933-0690-6); pap. 14.95 (ISBN 0-7933-0689-2); computer disk 29.95 (ISBN 0-7933-0691-4). Gallopade Pub Group.

—The Beast of the Missouri Bed & Breakfast. (Illus.). (gr. 3 up). 1990. PLB 19.95 (ISBN 0-7933-1734-7); pap. 14.95 (ISBN 0-7933-1735-5); computer disk 29.95. Gallopade Pub Group.

—The Hard-to-Believe-But-True! Book of Missouri History, Mystery, Trivia, Legend, Lore, Humor & More. (Illus.). (gr. 3 up). 1990. PLB 19.95 (ISBN 0-7933-0687-6); pap. 14.95 (ISBN 0-7933-0686-8); computer disk 29.95 (ISBN 0-7933-0688-4). Gallopade Pub Group.

—If My Missouri Mama Ran the World! (Illus.). (gr. 3 up). 1990. lib. bdg. 19.95 (ISBN 0-7933-1737-1); pap. 14.95 (ISBN 0-7933-1738-X); computer disk 29.95 (ISBN 0-7933-1739-8). Gallopade Pub Group.

—Let's Quilt Missouri & Stuff It Topographically! (Illus.). (gr. 3 up). 1990. PLB 19.95 (ISBN 1-55609-733-6); pap. 14.95 (ISBN 1-55609-734-4); computer disk 29.95 (ISBN 1-55609-735-2). Gallopade Pub Group.

—Missouri & Other State Greats (Biographies) (Illus.). (gr. 3 up). 1990. PLB 19.95 (ISBN 1-55609-748-4); pap. 14.95 (ISBN 1-55609-749-2); computer disk 29.95 (ISBN 1-55609-750-6). Gallopade Pub Group.

—Missouri Bandits, Bushwackers, Outlaws, Crooks, Devils, Ghosts, Desperadoes & Other Assorted & Sundry Characters! (Illus.). (gr. 3 up). 1990. PLB 19.95 (ISBN 0-7933-0672-8); pap. 14.95 (ISBN 0-7933-0671-X); computer disk 29.95 (ISBN 0-7933-0673-6). Gallopade Pub Group.

—Missouri Classic Christmas Trivia: Stories, Recipes, Activities, Legends, Lore & More. (Illus.). (gr. 3 up). 1990. PLB 19.95 (ISBN 0-7933-0675-2); pap. 14.95 (ISBN 0-7933-0674-4); computer disk 29.95 (ISBN 0-7933-0676-0). Gallopade Pub Group.

—Missouri Coastales. (Illus.). (gr. 3 up). 1990. PLB 19.95 (ISBN 1-55609-742-5); pap. 14.95 (ISBN 1-55609-743-3); computer disk 29.95 (ISBN 1-55609-744-1). Gallopade Pub Group.

—The Missouri Hot Air Balloon Mystery. (Illus.). (gr. 2-9). 1990. 19.95 (ISBN 0-7933-2543-9); pap. 14.95 (ISBN 0-7933-2544-7); computer disk 29.95 (ISBN 0-7933-2545-5). Gallopade Pub Group.

—Missouri "Jography" A Fun Run Thru Our State. (Illus.). (gr. 3 up). 1990. PLB 19.95 (ISBN 1-55609-730-1); pap. 14.95 (ISBN 1-55609-731-X); computer disk 29.95 (ISBN 1-55609-732-8). Gallopade Pub Group.

—Missouri Kid's Cookbook: Recipes, How-To, History, Lore & More. (Illus.). (gr. 3 up). 1990. PLB 19.95 (ISBN 0-7933-0684-1); pap. 14.95 (ISBN 0-7933-0683-3); computer disk 29.95 (ISBN 0-7933-0685-X). Gallopade Pub Group.

—Missouri Quiz Bowl Crash Course! (Illus.). (gr. 3 up). 1990. PLB 19.95 (ISBN 1-55609-745-X); pap. 14.95 (ISBN 1-55609-746-8); computer disk 29.95 (ISBN 1-55609-747-6). Gallopade Pub Group.

—Missouri School Trivia: An Amazing & Fascinating Look at Our State's Teachers, Schools & Students! (Illus.). (gr. 3 up). 1990. PLB 19.95 (ISBN 0-7933-0681-7); pap. 14.95 (ISBN 0-7933-0680-9); computer disk 29.95 (ISBN 0-7933-0682-5). Gallopade Pub Group.

—Missouri Silly Basketball Sportsmysteries, Vol. I. (Illus.). (gr. 3 up). 1990. PLB 19.95 (ISBN 0-7933-0678-7); pap. 14.95 (ISBN 0-7933-0677-9); computer disk 29.95. Gallopade Pub Group.

—Missouri Silly Basketball Sportsmysteries, Vol. II. (Illus.). (gr. 3 up). 1990. PLB 19.95 (ISBN 0-7933-1740-1); pap. 14.95 (ISBN 0-7933-1741-X); computer disk 29.95 (ISBN 0-7933-1742-8). Gallopade Pub Group.

—Missouri Silly Football Sportsmysteries, Vol. I. (Illus.). (gr. 3 up). 1990. PLB 19.95 (ISBN 1-55609-736-0); pap. 14.95 (ISBN 1-55609-737-9); computer disk 29.95. Gallopade Pub Group.

—Missouri Silly Football Sportsmysteries, Vol. II. (Illus.). (gr. 3 up). 1990. PLB 19.95 (ISBN 1-55609-739-5); pap. 14.95 (ISBN 1-55609-740-9); computer disk 29.95 (ISBN 1-55609-741-7). Gallopade Pub Group.

—Missouri Silly Trivia! (Illus.). (gr. 3 up). 1990. PLB 19.95 (ISBN 1-55609-728-X); pap. 14.95 (ISBN 1-55609-100-1); computer disk 29.95 (ISBN 1-55609-729-8). Gallopade Pub Group.

—Missouri's (Most Devastating!) Disasters & (Most Calamitous!) Catastrophies! (Illus.). (gr. 3 up). 1990. PLB 19.95 (ISBN 0-7933-0669-8); pap. 14.95 (ISBN 0-7933-0668-X); computer disk 29.95 (ISBN 0-7933-0670-1). Gallopade Pub Group.

Sanford, William R. & Green, Carl R. Missouri. LC 89-35082. 144p. (gr. 4 up). 1989. PLB 25.27 (ISBN 0-516-00471-9). Childrens.

Sturman, Susan. Kansas City. LC 90-25614. (Illus.). 60p. (gr. 3 up). 1990. 12.95 (ISBN 0-87518-432-4, Dillon); PLB 12.95 (ISBN 0-685-31387-5). Macmillan Child Grp.

Turner Program Services, Inc. Staff & Clark, James I. Missouri. LC 85-9979. 48p. (gr. 3 up). 1985. PLB 17.32 (ISBN 0-86514-436-2); pap. text ed. 9.27 (ISBN 0-86514-511-3); cancelled Beta video (ISBN 0-86514-061-8); cancelled VHS video (ISBN 0-86514-136-3); cancelled 3/4" video (ISBN 0-86514-211-4); cancelled tchr's. guide (ISBN 0-86514-286-6); cancelled student activity bk. (ISBN 0-86514-361-7); cancelled index. Raintree Pubs.

MISSOURI–FICTION

Clemens, Samuel. Huckleberry Finn. Farr, Naunerle, ed. Redondo, Francisco, illus. LC 73-75468. 64p. (Orig.). (gr. 5-10). 1973. pap. 2.95 (ISBN 0-88301-098-4). Pendulum Pr.

—Tom Sawyer. new ed. Shapiro, Irwin, ed. Cruz, E. R., illus. LC 73-75465. 64p. (Orig.). (gr. 5-10). 1973. pap. 2.95 (ISBN 0-88301-103-4); student activity bk. 1.25 (ISBN 0-88301-179-4). Pendulum Pr.

Clemens, Samuel L. Huckleberry Finn. 1988. Repr. of 1899 ed. lib. bdg. 59.00x (ISBN 0-317-90076-5). Reprint Servs.

Clements, Bruce. I Tell a Lie Every So Often. LC 73-22356. 160p. (gr. 5 up). 1984. pap. 3.50 (ISBN 0-374-43539-1). FS&G.

Tom Sawyer. 320p. (gr. 3-9). 1981. pap. 7.95 (ISBN 0-448-11002-4, G&D). Putnam Pub Group.

Tom Sawyer. (Illus.). (gr. 3-5). 3.50 (ISBN 0-7214-0977-6). Ladybird Bks.

Twain, Mark. The Adventures of Huckleberry Finn. LC 85-9576. (gr. 5 up). pap. 2.75 (ISBN 0-8049-0004-3, CL-4). Airmont.

—Adventures of Huckleberry Finn. McKay, Donald & Polseno, Jo, illus. LC 85-9576. 448p. (gr. 4-6). 12.95 (ISBN 0-448-06000-0, G&D); pap. 7.95 (ISBN 0-448-11000-8, G&D). Putnam Pub Group.

—Adventures of Huckleberry Finn. LC 85-9576. (gr. 3-7). 1983. pap. 2.95 (ISBN 0-14-035007-1, Puffin Bks). Puffin Bks.

—The Adventures of Huckleberry Finn. LC 85-9576. 384p. (gr. 4-6). 1986. pap. 2.25 (ISBN 0-14-039046-4, Penguin Classics). Viking Penguin.

—The Adventures of Huckleberry Finn. 384p. (Orig.). (gr. 4-6). 1987. pap. 2.50 (ISBN 0-590-40801-1, Pub. by Apple Classics); tchr's. guide 1.25 (ISBN 0-590-40662-0). Scholastic Inc.

—The Adventures of Tom Sawyer. LC 63-19420. (gr. 5 up). 1964. pap. 2.50 (ISBN 0-8049-0006-X, CL-6). Airmont.

—The Adventures of Tom Sawyer. LC 62-19420. 224p. (gr. 3-7). 1983. pap. 2.25 (ISBN 0-14-035003-9, Puffin). Puffin Bks.

—The Adventures of Tom Sawyer. 320p. (Orig.). (gr. 4-6). 1987. pap. 2.50 (ISBN 0-590-40800-3, Pub. by Apple Classics); tchr's. guide 1.25 (ISBN 0-590-40663-9). Scholastic Inc.

Twain, Mark, pseud. Adventures of Tom Sawyer. Gise, Joanne, adapted by. James, Raymond, illus. LC 89-20559. 48p. (gr. 3-6). 1989. lib. bdg. 12.89 (ISBN 0-8167-1859-8); pap. text ed. 3.95 (ISBN 0-8167-1860-1). Troll Assocs.

Twain, Mark. Adventures of Tom Sawyer. 1989. 9.99 (ISBN 0-517-68813-1). Outlet Bk Co.

—Adventures of Tom Sawyer & Adventures of Huckleberry Finn. Dickey, James, intro. by. 1979. pap. 3.95 (ISBN 0-451-52272-9). NAL-Dutton.

—Huckleberry Finn. Stewart, Diana, adapted by. Neidigh, Sherry, illus. LC 79-24312. 48p. (gr. 4 up). 1983. PLB 17.32 (ISBN 0-8172-1651-0); pap. 9.27 (ISBN 0-8172-2009-7). Raintree Pubs.

—Life on the Mississippi. Willoughby, J., intro. by. (gr. 9 up). pap. 1.95 (ISBN 0-8049-0055-8, CL-55). Airmont.

—Tom Sawyer. rev. ed. (Illus.). (gr. 7-12). 1982. pap. 3.50 (ISBN 0-671-44135-3, RE). PB.

—Tom Sawyer Abroad. Rowland, B., intro. by. Bd. with Tom Sawyer Detective. (gr. 5up). pap. 1.50 (ISBN 0-8049-0126-0, CL-126). Airmont.

MISSOURI VALLEY

Wilder, Laura I. On the Way Home. Lane, Rose W., ed. LC 62-17966. (Illus.). 112p. (gr. 7 up). 1962. 12.95 (ISBN 0-06-026489-6); PLB 12.89 (ISBN 0-06-026490-X). HarpC Child Bks.

MOBILES (SCULPTURE)

Birmingham, Duncan. Fantasy Mobiles. (Illus.). 24p. (Orig.). (gr. 4-7). 1986. pap. 4.95 (ISBN 0-906212-52-9, Tarquin). Parkwest Pubns.

Morris, Victoria S. More Mobiles: Math Shapes & Forms. (gr. 1-8). 1977. pap. 3.00 (ISBN 0-914318-03-9). V S Morris.

Williams, Guy R. Making Mobiles. (Illus.). (gr. 7 up). 1969. 11.95 (ISBN 0-87523-167-5). Emerson.

MOCKINGBIRDS

Doughty, Robin W. The Mockingbird. (Illus.). 80p. (gr. 10-12). 1988. 12.95 (ISBN 0-292-75099-4). U of Tex Pr.

MODEL CAR RACING

Murphy, Fred. Radio-Controlled Action Cars. (Illus.). 24p. (Orig.). 1990. pap. 2.50 (ISBN 0-942025-87-3). Kidsbks.

MODELING

see also Sculpture–Technique

Brown, Charlene & Davis, Carolyn. Clay Fun. (Illus.). 64p. (Orig.). 1989. pap. 5.95 (ISBN 0-929261-28-3, BA03). W Foster Pub.

Gibson, R. & Tyler, J. Playdough. (Illus.). 32p. (ps-3). 1989. lib. bdg. 13.96 (ISBN 0-88110-413-2, Usborne); pap. 5.95 (ISBN 0-7460-0465-6). EDC.

Hull, Jeannie. Clay. Fairclough, Chris, photos by. LC 89-9959. (Illus.). 48p. (gr. 3-6). 1989. PLB 11.90 (ISBN 0-531-10757-4). Watts.

Slade, Richard. Your Book of Modelling. (gr. 4 up). 1968. 7.95 (ISBN 0-571-08387-0). Transatl Arts.

MODELS, FASHION

Basford, Teri M. Ten Steps to Becoming a Model. (Illus.). 50p. (Orig.). (gr. 9). 1989. pap. write for info.; pap. text ed. write for info. T Mack Glamour.

Beirne, Barbara. Under the Lights: A Child Model at Work. (Illus.). 56p. (gr. 2-5). 1988. PLB 12.95 (ISBN 0-87614-316-8). Carolrhoda Bks.

Colquitt, Ken. Modeling Made Easy: Getting Started Without Getting Taken. Rae, Debra, ed. (Illus.). 96p. (Orig.). (gr. 6-12). 1988. pap. 7.95x (ISBN 0-9619773-0-2). Starmakers.

Moss, Miriam. Fashion Model. LC 90-15082. (Illus.). 32p. (gr. 5-6). 1991. RSBE 11.95 (ISBN 0-89686-609-2, Crestwood Hse). Macmillan Child Grp.

MODELS, FASHION–FICTION

Green, Yvonne. Rising Star: Kelly Blake, Teen Model, No. 2. 176p. (gr. 7-12). 1986. pap. 2.50 (ISBN 0-553-25639-4). Bantam.

Greene, Yvonne. Double Trouble. 160p. (Orig.). (gr. 7-12). 1986. pap. 2.50 (ISBN 0-553-26154-1). Bantam.

—Hard to Get-Kelly Blake. 176p. (Orig.). (gr. 7-12). 1986. pap. 2.50 (ISBN 0-553-26037-5). Bantam.

—Headliners-Kelly Blake. 160p. (Orig.). (gr. 7-12). 1986. pap. 2.50 (ISBN 0-553-26112-6). Bantam.

—Paris Nights, No. 6. 160p. (Orig.). (gr. 7-12). 1987. pap. 2.50 (ISBN 0-553-26199-1). Bantam.

MODELS AND MODEL MAKING

see also names of objects with the subdivision Models, e.g. Airplanes–Models

Ashman, Iain. Make This Model Castle. Stitt, Sue & McCaig, Ron, illus. (gr. 4-9). 1983. pap. 5.95 (ISBN 0-13-545947-8, Pub. by Treehouse). P-H.

—Make This Model Village. Stitt, Sue & McCaig, Ron, illus. (gr. 4-9). 1983. pap. 5.95 (ISBN 0-13-545954-0, Pub. by Treehouse). P-H.

Boy Scouts of America. Model Design & Building. (Illus.). 44p. (gr. 6-12). 1964. pap. 1.85 (ISBN 0-8395-3280-6, 3280). BSA.

Caket, Colin. Model a Monster: Making Dinosaurs from Everyday Materials. (Illus.). 160p. (gr. 4 up). 1986. 12.95 (ISBN 0-7137-1671-1, Pub. by Blandford Pr UK); pap. 10.95 (ISBN 0-7137-1672-X). Sterling.

Cummings, Richard. Make Your Own Model Forts & Castles. Cummings, Richard, illus. (gr. 6 up). 1977. 8.95 (ISBN 0-679-20400-8). McKay.

Herda, D. J. Model Boats & Ships. (Illus.). 72p. (gr. 4 up). 1982. PLB 10.40 (ISBN 0-531-04463-7). Watts.

Picther, Caroline. Build Your Own Airport. Nevett, Louise, illus. LC 85-50509. 32p. (gr. 1-6). 1985. PLB 11.90 (ISBN 0-531-10028-6). Watts.

Pitcher, Caroline. Build Your Own Farmyard. LC 85-50510. (Illus.). 30p. (gr. 1-3). 1985. PLB 11.90 (ISBN 0-531-10029-4). Watts.

Purdy, Susan & Sandak, Cass R. Ancient Egypt. LC 82-6962. (Illus.). 32p. (gr. 4-6). 1982. PLB 9.90 (ISBN 0-531-04452-1). Watts.

Zubrowski, Bernie. Raceways: Having Fun with Balls & Tracks. LC 84-20600. (Illus.). 80p. (gr. 3-7). 1985. PLB 11.95 (ISBN 0-688-04159-0); pap. 6.95 (ISBN 0-688-04160-4, Pub. by Beech Tree Bks). Morrow Jr Bks.

MODERN CIVILIZATION

see Civilization, Modern

MODERN HISTORY

see History, Modern

MOHAMMED, 570?-632

Alladin, Bilzik. Story of Mohammad the Prophet. Anand, B. M., illus. (gr. 3-10). 1979. 7.25 (ISBN 0-89744-139-7). Auromere.

Hashim, A. S. Life of Prophet Muhammad-I. pap. 7.50 (ISBN 0-686-18410-6); pap. 49.50 entire ser. (ISBN 0-686-18411-4). Kazi Pubns.

—Life of Prophet Muhammad-II. pap. 6.50 (ISBN 0-686-18408-4); pap. 49.50 entire ser. (ISBN 0-686-18409-2). Kazi Pubns.

MOLECULES

Bains, Rae. Molecules & Atoms. Harriton, Chuck, illus. LC 84-2712. 32p. (gr. 3-6). 1985. PLB 9.49 (ISBN 0-8167-0284-5); pap. text ed. 2.95 (ISBN 0-8167-0285-3). Troll Assocs.

Mebane, Robert C. & Rybolt, Thomas R. Adventures with Atoms & Molecules Bk. II: More Chemistry Experiments for Young People. Perkins, Ronald I., intro. by. LC 85-10177. (Illus.). 96p. (gr. 4-9). 1987. lib. bdg. 16.95 (ISBN 0-89490-164-8). Enslow Pubs.

MOLES (ANIMALS)–FICTION

Billiet, Daniel. The Great Invasion of the Stone Moles. Becker, Jane R., tr. from FRE. Rutten, Nicole, illus. LC 89-26371. 32p. 1990. 13.95 (ISBN 1-55670-153-5). Stewart Tabori & Chang.

Chouinard, Roger & Chouinard, Mariko. One Magic Box: A Book about Numbers. (Illus.). 32p. (ps-3). 1989. PLB 13.99 (ISBN 0-385-26204-3, Zephyr-BFYR). Doubleday.

Finger, Charles J. Tales from Silver Lands. (Illus.). 225p. (gr. 4-6). 1965. 16.95 (ISBN 0-385-07513-8, Zephyr-BFYR). Doubleday.

—Tales from Silver Lands. 1989. pap. 2.95 (ISBN 0-590-42447-5). Scholastic Inc.

Himmelman, John. Montigue on the High Seas. (Illus.). 32p. (ps-3). 1990. pap. 3.95 (ISBN 0-14-050789-2, Puffin). Puffin Bks.

Hunt, Rod. Mole Wins a Prize: Little Stories Ser. Gordon, Mike, illus. 32p. (ps-k). 1987. 6.95 (ISBN 0-09-167520-0, Pub. by Hutchinson UK). Trafalgar Sq.

Johnston, Tony. Happy Birthday Mole & Troll. (gr. k-6). 1989. pap. 2.95 (ISBN 0-440-40217-4, YB). Dell.

Mole & His New Red Hat. (gr. 3-7). 1974. 9.50 (ISBN 0-686-23317-4). Rochester Folk Art.

Townsend, Sue. The Secret Diary of Adrian Mole, Aged 13 3-4. 208p. (gr. 8 up). 1984. pap. 3.95 (ISBN 0-380-86876-8, Flare). Avon.

Tripp, C. J. Just Mole. Hudd, Stacy, illus. LC 87-71721. 137p. (Orig.). (gr. 4-6). 1989. pap. 7.00 (ISBN 0-916383-39-3). Aegina Pr.

Ziefert, Harriet. New House for Mouse & Mole. Prebenna, David, illus. (ps-3). 1987. pap. 8.95 (ISBN 0-670-81720-1). Viking Child Bks.

MOLLUSKS

see also Shells

Oda, Hidetomo. Snails. LC 85-28211. (Illus.). 32p. (gr. 3-7). 1986. PLB 16.67 (ISBN 0-8172-2544-7); pap. text ed. 9.27 (ISBN 0-8172-2569-2). Raintree Pubs.

MONARCHS

see Kings and Rulers

MONASTERIES

see also Monasticism and Religious Orders

MONASTIC ORDERS

see Monasticism and Religious Orders

MONASTICISM AND RELIGIOUS ORDERS

Boyd, Anne. Life in a Fifteenth Century Monastery. LC 76-22452. (Illus.). 52p. (gr. 5 up). 1979. PLB 9.95 (ISBN 0-8225-1208-4). Lerner Pubns.

Greene, Carol. Mother Teresa: Friend of the Friendless. LC 83-7386. (Illus.). 32p. (gr. 2-5). 1983. PLB 13.27 (ISBN 0-516-03559-2). Childrens.

MONASTICISM AND RELIGIOUS ORDERS–FICTION

Stolz, Mary. Pangur Ban. Johnson, Pamela, illus. LC 87-35049. 196p. (gr. 7 up). 1988. 13.95 (ISBN 0-06-025861-6); PLB 13.89 (ISBN 0-06-025862-4). HarpC Child Bks.

MONASTICISM AND RELIGIOUS ORDERS FOR WOMEN

Gray, Charlotte. Mother Teresa: Servant to the World's Suffering People. Ullstein, Susan, adapted by. LC 89-49750. (Illus.). 64p. (gr. 3-4). 1990. PLB 12.95 (ISBN 0-8368-0393-0). Gareth Stevens Inc.

Mohan, Claire J. Mother Teresa's Someday: The Young Life of Mother Teresa of Calcutta. Gallagher, Patricia C., ed. Thomes, Susannah H., illus. 60p. (Orig.). (gr. k-6). 1990. PLB 14.95 (ISBN 0-9621500-6-1); pap. 6.95 (ISBN 0-9621500-7-X). Young Sparrow Pr.

Mother Teresa. (Illus.). (gr. 5-6). 1990. pap. 7.95 (ISBN 0-8192-1523-6). Morehouse Pub.

MONETARY QUESTION

see Money

MONEY

see also Banks and Banking; Coins; Credit; Gold

Bank Street College of Education Editors. Let's Learn about Money. (gr. 1-2). 1986. pap. 3.95 (ISBN 0-8120-3626-3). Barron.

Bungum, Jane. Money & Financial Institutions. (Illus.). 88p. (gr. 5 up). 1991. PLB 15.95 (ISBN 0-8225-1781-7). Lerner Pubns.

Byers, Patricia & Preston, Julia. The Kids' Money Book. LC 82-184275. (Illus.). 144p. (gr. 2-6). 1983. pap. 4.95 (ISBN 0-89709-041-1). Liberty Pub.

Cantwell, Lois. Money & Banking. (Illus.). 72p. (gr. 4-8). 1984. lib. bdg. 10.40 (ISBN 0-531-04827-6). Watts.

Carson, Patti & Dellosa, Janet. Basics about Money. Clapsadle, Mark, illus. 32p. (gr. 1-2). 1984. pap. 1.98 (ISBN 0-88724-094-1, CD-7033). Carson-Dellos.

—Beginning Money Skills. Clapsadle, Mark, illus. 32p. (ps-k). 1984. pap. 1.98 (ISBN 0-88724-087-9, CD-7026). Carson-Dellos.

Cribb, Joe. Money. British Museum, illus. LC 89-15589. 64p. (gr. 5 up). 1990. 13.95 (ISBN 0-679-80438-2); PLB 14.99 (ISBN 0-679-90438-7). McKay.

Elkin, Benjamin. Money. LC 83-7436. (Illus.). 48p. (gr. k-4). 1983. PLB 14.60 (ISBN 0-516-01697-0). Childrens.

Jones, David. Your Book of Money. (gr. 7 up). 1971. 7.95 (ISBN 0-571-09341-8). Transatl Arts.

Knowledge Unlimited Staff, ed. What Is Money: From Barter to Banking. (Illus.). 21p. (gr. 4-12). incl. 2 filmstrips, 2 cass., 2 guides 66.00 (ISBN 0-915291-34-7). Know Unltd.

—What Is Money: The Ups & Downs of the Money Supply. (Illus.). 27p. (gr. 4-12). 1984. incl. 2 filmstrips, 2 cass., 2 guides 66.00 (ISBN 0-915291-27-4). Know Unltd.

Kyte, Kathy S. The Kids' Complete Guide to Money. Brown, Richard, illus. LC 84-3962. 96p. (gr. 5 up). 1984. lib. bdg. 10.99 (ISBN 0-394-96672-4); pap. 4.95 (ISBN 0-394-86672-X). Knopf.

Lee, Mary P. Coping with Money. Rosen, Ruth, ed. (gr. 7 up). 1988. lib. bdg. 12.95 (ISBN 0-8239-0783-X). Rosen Group.

Mitgutsch, Ali. From Gold to Money. Mitgutsch, Ali, illus. LC 84-17488. 24p. (ps-3). 1985. PLB 6.95 (ISBN 0-87614-230-7). Carolrhoda Bks.

Money Matters. (gr. 7-12). 3.95 (ISBN 0-317-42455-6). Learning Well.

Ockenga, Earl & Rucker, Walt. Money. Dawson, Dave, illus. 16p. (gr. 1). 1990. pap. text ed. 1.25 (ISBN 1-56281-125-8, M125). Extra Eds.

Pellowski, Michael J. Moosey Saves Money. Harvey, Paul, illus. LC 85-14053. 48p. (Orig.). (gr. 1-3). 1986. PLB 9.89 (ISBN 0-8167-0628-X); pap. text ed. 2.95 (ISBN 0-8167-0629-8). Troll Assocs.

Price, Ray B. & Cox, Gale R. How to Acquire Wealth: One Man's Odyssey. LC 90-61189. 87p. (Orig.). 1990. pap. text ed. 8.95 (ISBN 0-9626318-0-9). Price Pub SC.

Silver, A. David. A Young Person's First Book of Wealth. (Illus.). 300p. (gr. 7-12). 1987. wkbk. 15.95x (ISBN 0-945214-00-6). Silver Prescrip Pr.

Smith, Allan H., ed. Teenage Money Making Guide. Trachsler, Don, illus. LC 84-90126. 281p. (Orig.). (gr. 6-12). 1984. pap. 10.00 (ISBN 0-931113-00-8). Success Publ.

Spiselman, David. A Teenagers Guide to Money, Banking & Finance. LC 87-11059. 128p. (gr. 6 up). 1988. lib. bdg. 11.29 (ISBN 0-671-64345-2); pap. 5.95 (ISBN 0-671-65979-0). Messner.

Wallace, David. Money Basics: An Introduction for Young People. D'Amato, Janet, illus. 48p. 1984. 9.95 (ISBN 0-13-600479-2). P-H.

Wilkinson, Elizabeth. Making Cents: Every Kid's Guide to Money, Vol. 1. 1989. 14.95 (ISBN 0-316-94101-8); pap. 8.95 (ISBN 0-316-94102-6). Little.

Wool, John D. Counting My Money, Bk. I. 80p. (gr. 1 up). 1987. pap. text ed. 3.75 (ISBN 0-88323-229-4, 171); tchr's. key 1.50 (ISBN 0-318-33409-7, 224). Pendergrass Pub.

Young, Woody. Moneywise. White, Craig, illus. 48p. (Orig.). (gr. 1-5). 1986. pap. text ed. 4.95 (ISBN 0-939513-30-7). Joy Pub SJC.

MONEY–FICTION

Brancato, Robin F. Uneasy Money. Hendrix, Bryan, designed by. LC 86-45296. (Illus.). 256p. (gr. 7-10). 1986. 11.95 (ISBN 0-394-86954-0); lib. bdg. 11.99 (ISBN 0-394-96954-5). Knopf.

—Uneasy Money. LC 86-45296. 256p. (gr. 7 up). 1989. pap. 2.95 (ISBN 0-394-82055-X). Knopf.

Brittain, Bill. All the Money in the World. LC 77-25635. (Illus.). 160p. (gr. 3-7). 1979. PLB 14.89 (ISBN 0-06-020676-4). HarpC Child Bks.

—All the Money in the World. Robinson, Charles, illus. LC 77-25635. 160p. (gr. 4-7). 1982. pap. 3.50 (ISBN 0-06-440128-6, Trophy). HarpC Child Bks.

Carris, Joan. Rusty Timmons' First Million. Mulkey, Kim, illus. LC 85-40096. 192p. (gr. 5-9). 1985. (Lipp Jr Bks); PLB 11.89 (ISBN 0-397-32155-4). HarpC Child Bks.

Ellis, Jana. Sweet Success. LC 89-36348. 160p. (gr. 7 up). 1989. pap. text ed. 2.50 (ISBN 0-8167-1673-0). Troll Assocs.

German, Don. Mattie's Money Tree. Chauncy, Lisa, illus. LC 84-11849. 94p. (gr. 2-4). 1984. 10.95 (ISBN 0-664-32716-8, Westminster). Westminster John Knox.

Haywood, Carolyn. Here's a Penny. Rev. ed. Haywood, Carolyn & Yakovetic, Joe, illus. LC 44-7329. 156p. (gr. 1-4). 1986. pap. 4.95 (ISBN 0-15-640062-6, VoyB). HarBraceJ.

Heide, Florence P. Treehorn's Treasure. Gorey, Edward, illus. LC 81-4043. 64p. (gr. 3-6). 1981. 11.95 (ISBN 0-8234-0425-0). Holiday.

Hoban, Lillian. Arthur's Funny Money. Hoban, Lillian, illus. LC 80-7903. 64p. (gr. k-3). 1981. 11.95 (ISBN 0-06-022343-X); PLB 11.89 (ISBN 0-06-022344-8). HarpC Child Bks.

Hunt, Dave. The Money Tree. Mezek, Karen, illus. 32p. (Orig.). (ps-3). 1989. 9.99 (ISBN 0-89081-753-7). Harvest Hse.

Korman, Gordon. No Coins, Please! (gr. 4-7). 1985. pap. 2.95 (ISBN 0-590-43709-7). Scholastic Inc.

Maestro, Betsy & Maestro, Giulio. Dollars & Cents for Harriet. (ps-1). 1988. PLB 12.95 (ISBN 0-517-56958-2). Crown.

Manes, Stephen. Make Four Million Dollars. (gr. 4-7). 1991. 14.95 (ISBN 0-553-07050-9). Bantam.

Pfeffer, Susan B. Kid Power. (Illus.). 121p. (gr. 4-6). 1982. pap. 2.50 (ISBN 0-590-41003-2, Apple Paperbacks); tchr's. guide 1.25 (ISBN 0-590-40987-5). Scholastic Inc.

Rockwell, Thomas. How to Get Fabulously Rich. Frammenghi, Gioia, illus. 128p. (gr. 5-8). 1990. 12.95 (ISBN 0-531-15180-8); PLB 12.90 (ISBN 0-531-10877-5). Watts.

Sharmat, Marjorie W. Rich Mitch. Lustig, Loretta, illus. 144p. (gr. 4-6). 1985. pap. 2.50 (ISBN 0-590-40576-4, Apple Paperbacks). Scholastic Inc.

Silverstein, Herma. Mad, Mad Monday. (gr. 7-9). 1989. pap. 2.50 (ISBN 0-671-67403-X, Archway). PB.

Viorst, Judith. Alexander Who Used to Be Rich, Vol. 1. 1978. 13.95 (ISBN 0-689-30602-4, Atheneum Child Bk). Macmillan Child Grp.

Vosper, Alice. Rags to Riches. 222p. (gr. 7 up). 1983. pap. 2.25 (ISBN 0-380-83873-7, Flare). Avon.

Weyn, Suzanne. Three for the Show. Iskowitz, Joel, illus. LC 89-34547. 96p. (gr. 3-5). 1989. PLB 9.89 (ISBN 0-8167-1655-2); pap. text ed. 2.95 (ISBN 0-8167-1656-0). Troll Assocs.

White, Cristine A. Matthew's Allowance. LC 89-51091. 44p. (gr. k-3). 1989. 5.95 (ISBN 1-55523-249-3). Winston-Derek.

Williams, Vera B. A Chair for My Mother. Williams, Vera B., illus. LC 81-7010. 32p. (gr. k-3). 1982. 13.95 (ISBN 0-688-00914-X); PLB 12.88 (ISBN 0-688-00915-8). Greenwillow.

MONEY RAISING

see Fund Raising

MONGOOSES–FICTION

Minagawa, Toshio. The Mongoose & the Mynas. 32p. (ps-3). 1991. 6.95 (ISBN 0-8062-3931-X). Carlton.

Montgomery, H. Mongoose Magoo. LC 68-56822. (Illus.). 64p. (gr. 2-5). 1968. PLB 10.95 (ISBN 0-87783-026-6); pap. 3.94 deluxe ed. (ISBN 0-87783-100-9). Oddo.

Wilson, Willie. Up Mountain One Time. Bertrand, Karen, illus. LC 87-7624. 144p. (gr. 3-6). 1987. 12.95 (ISBN 0-531-05725-9); PLB 12.99 (ISBN 0-531-08325-X). Orchard Bks Watts.

MONKEYS

Anderson, Norman D. & Brown, Walter R. Lemurs. (Illus.). 64p. (gr. 2-5). 1984. 9.95 (ISBN 0-396-08454-0, Putnam). Putnam Pub Group.

Barrett, Norman. Monos y Simios. LC 87-50849. (SPA., Illus.). 32p. (gr. k-4). 1991. PLB 11.40 (ISBN 0-531-07918-X). Watts.

—Picture Library: Monkey & Apes. 1990. pap. 3.95 (ISBN 0-531-15205-7). Watts.

Carwardine, Mark. Monkeys & Apes. Young, Richard G., ed. Camm, Martin, illus. LC 89-32808. 45p. (gr. 3-5). 1989. PLB 13.26 (ISBN 0-944483-28-3). Garrett Ed Corp.

Crosby, Nina E. & Marten, Elizabeth H. Don't Teach! Let Me Learn about Fantasy, Magic, Monkeys & Monsters. Rossi, Richard, illus. 72p. (Orig.). (gr. 3-10). 1984. 8.95 (ISBN 0-88047-045-3, 8410). DOK Pubs.

Haldane, Suzanne. Helping Hands: How Monkeys Assist People Who Are Disabled. Haldane, Suzanne, photos by. (Illus.). 48p. (gr. 3-7). 1991. 14.95 (ISBN 0-525-44723-7, DCB). Dutton Child Bks.

Hoffman, Mary. Monkey. LC 84-15117. (Illus.). 24p. (gr. k-5). 1985. PLB 13.32 (ISBN 0-8172-2406-8). Raintree Pubs.

Lumley, Kathryn W. Monkeys & Apes. LC 82-12779. (Illus.). (gr. k-4). 1982. PLB 14.60 (ISBN 0-516-01633-4); pap. 4.95 (ISBN 0-516-41633-2). Childrens.

Monkeys & Apes. 32p. (Orig.). (ps-1). 1984. pap. 1.25 (ISBN 0-8431-1518-1). Price Stern.

Morris, Dean. Monkeys & Apes. rev. ed. LC 87-16688. (Illus.). 48p. (gr. 3). 1987. PLB 15.99 (ISBN 0-8172-3211-7). Raintree Pubs.

—Monkeys & Apes. (gr. 2-6). 1990. pap. 17.32 (ISBN 0-8172-3236-2). Raintree Pubs.

Overbeck, Cynthia. Monkeys. LC 81-1961. (Illus.). 48p. (gr. 4 up). 1981. PLB 14.95 (ISBN 0-8225-1464-8). Lerner Pubns.

Rau, Margaret. The Snow Monkey at Home. Hulsmann, Eva, illus. LC 78-31550. (gr. 4-7). 1979. lib. bdg. 6.99 (ISBN 0-394-93976-X). Knopf.

Richmond, Gary. Zookeeper Looks at Monkeys. 1991. pap. 3.99 (ISBN 0-8499-0861-2). Word Bks.

Sheffer, H. R. Moto-Cross Monkey. LC 80-28762. (Illus.). 48p. (gr. 3 up). 1980. PLB 9.95 (ISBN 0-89686-106-6, Crestwood Hse). Macmillan Child Grp.

Silverman, Maida. The Golden Book of Monkeys, Apes, & Other Primates. Spence, James, illus. (gr. 3-6). 1991. 6.95 (ISBN 0-307-15858-6, Golden Pr). Western Pub.

Steedman, Scott. Amazing Monkeys. Young, Jerry, photos by. LC 90-19238. (Illus.). 32p. (Orig.). (gr. 1-5). 1991. PLB 9.99 (ISBN 0-679-91517-6); pap. 6.95 (ISBN 0-679-81517-1). Knopf.

Stone, Lynn. Gibbons. (Illus.). 24p. (gr. k-5). 1990. lib. bdg. 11.93 (ISBN 0-86593-062-7); lib. bdg. 8.95s.p. (ISBN 0-685-36317-1). Rourke Corp.

—Monkey Discovery Library, 6 bks. (Illus.). 144p. (gr. k-5). 1990. Set. lib. bdg. 71.60 (ISBN 0-86593-061-9); Set. lib. bdg. 53.70s.p. (ISBN 0-685-36314-7). Rourke Corp.

—Orangutans. (Illus.). 24p. (gr. k-5). 1990. lib. bdg. 11.93 (ISBN 0-86593-065-1); lib. bdg. 8.95s.p. (ISBN 0-685-36319-8). Rourke Corp.

—Snow Monkeys. (Illus.). 24p. (gr. k-5). 1990. lib. bdg. 11.93 (ISBN 0-86593-066-X); lib. bdg. 8.95s.p. (ISBN 0-685-36320-1). Rourke Corp.

Whitehead, Patricia. Monkeys. Dodson, Bert, illus. LC 81-11439. 32p. (gr. k-2). 1982. PLB 10.89 (ISBN 0-89375-670-9); pap. text ed. 2.95 (ISBN 0-89375-671-7). Troll Assocs.

MONKEYS–FICTION

Bierhorst, John, ed. The Monkey's Haircut: And Other Stories Told by the Maya. Parker, Robert A., illus. LC 85-28471. 160p. (gr. 5 up). 1986. 13.00 (ISBN 0-688-04269-4). Morrow Jr Bks.

Brown, Marc. Two Little Monkeys. 1989. 5.95 (ISBN 0-525-44533-1, DCB). Dutton Child Bks.

Calmenson, Stephanie. One Little Monkey. Appleby, Ellen, illus. LC 82-7958. 48p. (ps-3). 1982. pap. 5.95 (ISBN 0-8193-1091-3); PLB 5.95 (ISBN 0-8193-1092-1). Parents.

Carr, Jan. I Am Curious about Me. Campana, Manny, illus. 48p. (ps-2). 1990. pap. 1.95 (ISBN 0-590-44032-2). Scholastic Inc.

Christelow, Eileen. Five Little Monkeys Jumping on the Bed. (ps-3). 1990. pap. 4.95 (ISBN 0-395-55701-1, Clarion Bks). HM.

Clifford, Eth. Harvey's Marvelous Monkey Mystery. LC 86-20837. (gr. 3-6). 1987. 13.95 (ISBN 0-395-42622-7). HM.

Crozat, Francois. I Am a Little Monkey. (Illus.). (ps-3). 1991. large 7.95 (ISBN 0-8120-6149-7); miniature 2.95 (ISBN 0-8120-6221-3). Barron.

De Brunhoff, Jean. Babar & Zephir. Haas, Merle, tr. (Illus.). (ps). 1969. 9.95 (ISBN 0-394-80579-8, Random Juv); lib. bdg. 5.99 (ISBN 0-394-90579-2). Random.

Frazer, Benjamin. Copper the Cat & the Mystery of Maroopa the Monkey. Faulkner, Matt, illus. 32p. 1990. 9.95 (ISBN 0-8092-4269-9). Contemp Bks.

Fuentes, Vilma M. The Monkey & the Crocodile. Inis, Ninabeth R., illus. 31p. (Orig.). (gr. k-2). 1984. pap. 3.50 (ISBN 971-10-0127-6, Pub. by New Day Philippines). Cellar.

Galdone, Paul. The Monkey & the Crocodile: A Jakata Tale from India. Galdone, Paul, illus. LC 78-79939. 32p. (ps-3). 1987. pap. 4.95 (ISBN 0-89919-524-5, Pub. by Clarion). Ticknor & Fields.

—The Turtle & the Monkey. Galdone, Paul, illus. 32p. (ps-3). 1990. pap. 4.95 (ISBN 0-395-54425-4, Clarion Bks). HM.

Gantos, Jack. Rotten Ralph's Show & Tell. Rubel, Nicole, illus. 32p. (ps-3). 1989. 13.95 (ISBN 0-395-44312-1). HM.

Gao, R. L., tr. from CHI. The Adventures of Monkey King. Allen, Rita, illus. 132p. (Orig.). (gr. 2-5). 1989. pap. 6.95 (ISBN 0-9620765-1-1). Victory Press.

Gelman, Rita G. More Spaghetti, I Say. Kent, Jack, illus. 32p. (Orig.). (gr. k-3). 1987. pap. 2.50 (ISBN 0-590-41199-3). Scholastic Inc.

—Why Can't I Fly? Kent, Jack, illus. 48p. (ps-3). 1986. pap. 1.95 (ISBN 0-590-71581-X, Hello Reader). Scholastic Inc.

Jacobs, W. W. The Monkey's Paw. Richardson, I. M., adapted by. Lawn, John, illus. LC 81-19824. 32p. (gr. 5-10). 1982. PLB 10.79 (ISBN 0-89375-628-8); pap. text ed. 2.95 (ISBN 0-89375-629-6). Troll Assocs.

—The Monkey's Paw. rev. ed. (gr. 9-12). 1989. Repr. of 1905 ed. multi-media kit 35.00 (ISBN 0-685-31128-7). Balance Pub.

Jones, Charles. Monkey, Monkey. 25p. (Orig.). (gr. k-3). 1986. pap. 4.50 playscript (ISBN 0-87602-265-4). Anchorage.

Kraus, Robert. Klunky Monkey, New Kid in Class. Brook, Bonnie, ed. Kraus, Robert, illus. 48p. (ps-3). 1990. lib. bdg. 8.98 (ISBN 0-671-70853-8); pap. 3.50 (ISBN 0-671-70854-6). Silver Pr.

LaFleur, Tom & Brennan, Gale. Spunky the Monkey. Murtagh, Betty, illus. 16p. (Orig.). (gr. k-6). 1981. pap. 1.25 (ISBN 0-685-02457-1). Brennan Bks.

Leos, Frances. I Am Curious about Animals. Campana, Manny, illus. 48p. (gr. k-2). 1988. pap. 1.95 (ISBN 0-590-41874-2). Scholastic Inc.

Little, Karen E. Monkey Match. (ps-1). 1981. 4.50 (ISBN 0-913545-03-1). Moonlight FL.

McKissack, Patricia. Who Is Coming? Martin, Clovis, illus. LC 86-11805. 32p. (ps-2). 1986. PLB 11.93 (ISBN 0-516-02073-0); pap. 2.95 (ISBN 0-516-42073-9). Childrens.

Marshall, James. George & Martha One Fine Day. Marshall, James, illus. 48p. (gr. k-3). 1982. 13.95 (ISBN 0-395-27154-1); pap. 4.95 (ISBN 0-395-32921-3). HM.

Mathiesen, Egon. Oswald the Monkey. (Illus.). (gr. k-3). 1959. 9.95 (ISBN 0-8392-3025-7). Astor-Honor.

Mayhar, Ardath & Fortier, Ron. Monkey Station. LC 88-51729. 320p. (Orig.). 1989. pap. 3.95 (ISBN 0-88038-743-2). TSR Inc.

Morris, Jill. Monkey & the White Bone Demon. Sheng, Lin, et al, illus. LC 83-17670. 32p. 1984. pap. 10.95 (ISBN 0-670-48574-8). Viking Child Bks.

Namjoshi, Suniti. Aditi & the One-Eyed Monkey. Hassan, Hanife, illus. LC 88-19058. 96p. (gr. 2-5). 1989. lib. bdg. 10.95 (ISBN 0-8070-8314-3); pap. 3.95 (ISBN 0-8070-8315-1). Beacon Pr.

One Hundred Monkeys. 1991. pap. 13.95 (ISBN 0-671-73564-0). S&S Trade.

Pen Cai Ying, adapted by. Monkey Creates Havoc in Heaven. Ye Pin Kwei & Morris, Jill, trs. Xin Kuan Liang, et al, illus. 32p. (ps-3). 1989. pap. 9.95 (ISBN 0-670-81805-4). Viking Child Bks.

Rawls, Wilson. Summer of the Monkeys. 288p. (gr. 7 up). 1977. pap. 3.50 (ISBN 0-440-98175-1, LFL). Dell.

Rey, H. A. Cecily G. & the Nine Monkeys. Rey, H. A., illus. (ps-3). 1989. pap. 3.95 (ISBN 0-395-50651-4, Sandpiper). HM.

—Curious George. (Illus.). 56p. (gr. k-3). 1973. 12.95 (ISBN 0-395-15993-8). HM.

—Curious George. Rey, H. A., illus. 48p. (gr. k-3). 1973. pap. 3.95 (ISBN 0-395-15023-X, Sandpiper). HM.

—Curious George Gets a Medal. (Illus.). 48p. (gr. k-3). 1957. 12.95 (ISBN 0-395-16973-9). HM.

—Curious George Learns the Alphabet. (Illus.). 72p. (gr. k-3). 1963. 12.95 (ISBN 0-395-16031-6). HM.

—Curious George Learns the Alphabet. Rey, H. A., illus. LC 62-12261. 72p. (gr. k-3). 1973. pap. 3.95 (ISBN 0-395-13718-7, Sandpiper). HM.

—Curious George Rides a Bike. (Illus.). 48p. (gr. k-3). 1952. 12.95 (ISBN 0-395-16964-X). HM.

—Curious George Rides a Bike. new ed. (Illus.). 48p. (gr. k-3). 1973. pap. 3.95 (ISBN 0-395-17444-9, Sandpiper). HM.

—Curious George Rides a Bike. 48p. (gr. k-3). pap. 1.95 (ISBN 0-590-02045-5). Scholastic Inc.

—Curious George Takes a Job. (Illus.). 48p. (gr. k-3). 1973. 12.95 (ISBN 0-395-15086-8). HM.

—Curious George Takes a Job. Rey, H. A., illus. 48p. (gr. k-3). 1974. pap. 3.95 (ISBN 0-395-18649-8, Sandpiper). HM.

—Jorge el Curioso. (SPA., Illus.). (gr. k-3). 1961. 13.95 (ISBN 0-395-17075-3). HM.

Rey, H. A. & Rey, Margaret. Curious George Goes to the Hospital. (Illus.). 48p. (gr. 1-5). 1973. 12.95 (ISBN 0-395-18158-5); pap. 3.95 (ISBN 0-395-07062-7). HM.

Rey, Margaret. Curious George & the Pizza. LC 85-2434. 32p. (ps-2). 1985. 8.95 (ISBN 0-395-39039-7); pap. 2.95 (ISBN 0-395-39033-8). HM.

Rey, Margaret & Rey, H. A. Curious George Flies a Kite. Rey, H. A., illus. (gr. k-3). 1977. pap. 3.95 (ISBN 0-395-25937-1). HM.

Rey, Margaret & Shalleck, Alan J. Curious George at the Beach. (Illus.). 32p. (ps-2). 1988. 9.95 (ISBN 0-395-48666-1); pap. 2.95 (ISBN 0-395-48660-2). HM.

—Curious George at the Railroad Station. (Illus.). 32p. (ps-2). 1988. 9.95 (ISBN 0-395-48667-X); pap. 2.95 (ISBN 0-395-48657-2). HM.

—Curious George Bakes a Cake. (Illus.). 32p. (ps-2). 1990. 9.95 (ISBN 0-395-55725-9); pap. 2.95 (ISBN 0-395-55716-X). HM.

—Curious George Bakes a Cake. (Illus.). 32p. (ps-2). 1990. 9.95 (ISBN 0-395-55725-9); pap. 2.95 (ISBN 0-395-55716-X). HM.

—Curious George Goes Camping. (Illus.). 32p. (ps-2). 1990. 9.95 (ISBN 0-395-55726-7); pap. 2.95 (ISBN 0-395-55715-1). HM.

—Curious George Goes Camping. (Illus.). 32p. (ps-2). 1990. 9.95 (ISBN 0-395-55726-7); pap. 2.95 (ISBN 0-395-55715-1). HM.

—Curious George Goes to a Restaurant. (Illus.). 32p. (ps-2). 1988. 9.95 (ISBN 0-395-48664-5); pap. 2.95 (ISBN 0-395-48658-0). HM.

—Curious George Goes to a Toy Store. (Illus.). 32p. (ps-2). 1990. 9.95 (ISBN 0-395-55724-0); pap. 2.95 (ISBN 0-395-55714-3). HM.

—Curious George Goes to an Air Show. (Illus.). 32p. (ps-2). 1990. 9.95 (ISBN 0-395-55991-X); pap. 2.95 (ISBN 0-395-55989-8). HM.

—Curious George Goes to an Air Show. (Illus.). 32p. (ps-2). 1990. 9.95 (ISBN 0-395-55991-X); pap. 2.95 (ISBN 0-395-55989-8). HM.

—Curious George Goes to School. (Illus.). (ps-3). 1990. Bk. & cass. pap. 6.95 (ISBN 0-395-56483-2). HM.

—Curious George Visits an Amusement Park. (Illus.). 32p. (ps-2). 1988. 9.95 (ISBN 0-395-48665-3); pap. 2.95 (ISBN 0-395-48659-9). HM.

Rey, Margaret & Shalleck, Allan J. Curious George & the Pizza. 1988. pap. 6.95 incl. cass. (ISBN 0-395-48874-5). HM.

—Curious George at the Airport. 1988. pap. 6.95 incl. cass. (ISBN 0-395-48877-X). HM.

—Curious George at the Fire Station. 1988. pap. 6.95 incl. cass. (ISBN 0-395-48875-3). HM.

Rey, Margaret, ed. Curious George & the Dump Truck. (Illus.). 32p. (ps-2). 1984. 8.95 (ISBN 0-395-36635-6); pap. 2.95 (ISBN 0-395-36629-1). HM.

—Curious George at the Fire Station. LC 85-2471. 32p. (ps-2). 1985. 8.95 (ISBN 0-395-39037-0); pap. 2.95 (ISBN 0-395-39031-1). HM.

—Curious George Goes Hiking. LC 85-2433. 32p. (ps-2). 1985. 8.95 (ISBN 0-395-39038-9); pap. 2.95 (ISBN 0-395-39032-X). HM.

—Curious George Goes Sledding. (Illus.). 32p. (ps-2). 1984. 9.95 (ISBN 0-395-36637-2); pap. 2.95 (ISBN 0-395-36631-3). HM.

—Curious George Goes to the Aquarium. (Illus.). 32p. (ps-2). 1984. 9.95 (ISBN 0-395-36634-8); pap. 2.95 (ISBN 0-395-36628-3). HM.

—Curious George Goes to the Circus. (Illus.). 32p. (ps-2). 1984. 9.95 (ISBN 0-395-36636-4); pap. 2.95 (ISBN 0-395-36630-5). HM.

—Curious George Visits the Zoo. LC 85-2415. 32p. (ps-2). 1985. 8.95 (ISBN 0-395-39036-2); pap. 2.95 (ISBN 0-395-39030-3). HM.

Rey, Margaret & Shalleck, Allan J., eds. Curious George at the Airport. (Illus.). 32p. (ps-2). 1987. 8.95 (ISBN 0-395-45355-0); pap. 2.95 (ISBN 0-395-45368-2). HM.

—Curious George at the Ballet. LC 86-7469. (Illus.). 32p. (ps-2). 1986. 8.95 (ISBN 0-395-42477-1); pap. 2.95 (ISBN 0-395-42474-7). HM.

—Curious George at the Laundromat. (Illus.). 32p. (ps-2). 1987. 8.95 (ISBN 0-395-45353-4); pap. 2.95 (ISBN 0-395-45367-4). HM.

—Curious George Goes Fishing. (Illus.). 32p. (ps-2). 1987. 8.95 (ISBN 0-395-45351-8); pap. 2.95 (ISBN 0-395-45405-0). HM.

—Curious George Plays Baseball. LC 86-10609. (Illus.). 32p. (ps-2). 1986. 8.95 (ISBN 0-395-39041-9); pap. 2.95 (ISBN 0-395-39035-4). HM.

—Curious George Visits the Police Station. (Illus.). 32p. (ps-2). 1987. 8.95 (ISBN 0-395-45349-6); pap. 2.95 (ISBN 0-395-45366-6). HM.

—Curious George Walks the Pets. LC 86-7470. (Illus.). 32p. (ps-2). 1986. 8.95 (ISBN 0-395-39040-0); pap. 2.95 (ISBN 0-395-39034-6). HM.

Rey, Margret. Curious George & the Dinosaur. (ps-3). 1989. 9.95 (ISBN 0-395-51942-X). HM.

—Curious George Goes to a Costume Party. (gr. 4-7). 1986. 8.95 (ISBN 0-395-42478-X). HM.

Rey, Margret & Shalleck, Alan J. Curious George & the Dinosaur. (Illus.). (ps-3). 1990. pap. 6.95 incl. cassette (ISBN 0-395-56484-0, Clarion Bks). HM.

Reynolds, Sandra L. Marky the Monkey. 1990. 6.95 (ISBN 0-533-08873-9). Vantage.

Slobodkina, Esphyr. Caps for Sale. 32p. (gr. k-3). Big Book. 19.50 (ISBN 0-590-71742-1); pap. 2.95 (ISBN 0-590-71775-8). Scholastic Inc.

Spacone, Carl. No Monkey Too Big. Hoffman, John, ed. Brophy, Paul, illus. 224p. (Orig.). (gr. 9 up). 1987. 8.95 (ISBN 0-944712-00-2); pap. text ed. 8.95 (ISBN 0-318-23727-X). Spacone Pub.

The Tawny Scrawny Lion & the Clever Monkey. (ps-3). 1989. Incl. cass. write for info. incl. cass. (13681, Pub. by Golden Bks). Western Pub.

Travers, Pamela L. Friend Monkey. Keeping, Charles, illus. LC 70-161389. (gr. k-3). 1971. 6.95 (ISBN 0-15-229555-0, HJ). HarBraceJ.

—Friend Monkey. (Orig.). (gr. k-6). 1987. pap. 4.95 (ISBN 0-440-42817-3, Pub. by Yearling Classics). Dell.

Vail, Virginia. Monkey Business. 128p. (gr. 3-7). 1987. pap. 2.50 (ISBN 0-590-40183-1). Scholastic Inc.

West, Colin. The "Not Me" Said the Monkey. LC 87-8417. (Illus.). 24p. (ps-2). 1989. pap. 3.95 (ISBN 0-06-443167-3, Trophy). HarpC Child Bks.

Woodruff, Elvira. Mrs. McClosky's Monkeys. LC 87-16359. (ps-3). 1991. 12.95 (ISBN 0-590-41233-7). Scholastic Inc.

Wriggins, Sally. White Monkey King: A Chinese Fable. Solbert, Ronni, illus. LC 76-44281. (gr. 1-5). 1977. Pantheon.

MONKS

see Monasticism and Religious Orders

MONOLOGS

Majeski, Bill. Fifty Great Monologs for Student Actors. Zapel, Arthur L., ed. LC 87-14103. 144p. (Orig.). (gr. 10 up). 1987. pap. 9.95 (ISBN 0-916260-43-7, B-197). Meriwether Pub.

Murray, John. Modern Monologues for Young People. rev. ed. 150p. (gr. 7-12). 1982. pap. 10.95 (ISBN 0-8238-0255-8). Plays.

MONOPLANES

see Airplanes

MONROE, JAMES, PRESIDENT U. S. 1758-1831

Bains, Rae. James Monroe, Young Patriot. Frenck, Hal, illus. LC 85-1071. 48p. (gr. 4-6). 1986. lib. bdg. 10.79 (ISBN 0-8167-0557-7); pap. text ed. 2.95 (ISBN 0-8167-0558-5). Troll Assocs.

Fitz-Gerald, Christine M. James Monroe. LC 86-33436. (Illus.). 100p. (gr. 3 up). 1987. PLB 17.27 (ISBN 0-516-01383-1); pap. 6.95 (ISBN 0-516-41383-X). Childrens.

Stefoff, Rebecca. James Monroe: 5th President of the United States. Young, Richard G., ed. LC 87-32845. (Illus.). (gr. 5-9). 1988. PLB 17.26 (ISBN 0-944483-11-9). Garrett Ed Corp.

Wetzel, Charles. James Monroe. (Illus.). (gr. 5 up). 1989. 17.95 (ISBN 1-55546-817-9). Chelsea Hse.

MONSTERS

see also Dwarfs; Giants

Abels, Harriette S. Loch Ness Monster. LC 87-9027. (Illus.). 48p. (gr. 5-6). 1987. PLB 10.95 (ISBN 0-89686-343-3, Crestwood Hse). Macmillan Child Grp.

Ames, Lee J. Draw Fifty Beasties: And Yugglies & Turnover Uglies & Things That Go Bump in the Night. Ames, Lee J., illus. 64p. (gr. 3 up). 1988. PLB 12.95 (ISBN 0-385-24625-0); pap. 13.99 (ISBN 0-385-24626-9). Doubleday.

Antonopulos, Barbara. The Abominable Snowman. LC 77-21387. (Illus.). 48p. (gr. 4 up). 1983. PLB 17.32 (ISBN 0-8172-1053-9); pap. 12.99 (ISBN 0-8172-2151-4). Raintree Pubs.

Bendick, Jeanne. Scare a Ghost, Tame a Monster. Bendick, Jeanne, illus. LC 82-23696. 120p. (gr. 3-6). 1983. 11.95 (ISBN 0-664-32701-X, Westminster). Westminster John Knox.

Berger, Melvin. Monsters. 128p. 1991. pap. 2.95 (ISBN 0-380-76053-3, Camelot). Avon.

Cameron, Ann. Harry (The Monster) Winter, Jeanette, illus. 48p. 1980. Pantheon.

Carmichael, Carrie. Bigfoot: Man, Monster, or Myth? LC 77-13297. (Illus.). 48p. (gr. 4up). 1983. pap. 9.27 (ISBN 0-8172-2154-9). Raintree Pubs.

Cohen, Daniel. America's Very Own Monsters. (Illus.). 48p. (gr. 3-7). 1982. 9.95 (ISBN 0-396-08069-3, Putnam). Putnam Pub Group.

—The Greatest Monsters in the World. (Illus.). 96p. (gr. 4 up). 1986. pap. 2.50 (ISBN 0-671-62672-8, Archway). PB.

—Monster Hunting Today. (Illus.). 128p. (gr. 9-12). 1983. 8.95 (ISBN 0-396-08184-3, Putnam). Putnam Pub Group.

—Monsters You Never Heard Of. (gr. k up). 1986. pap. 2.50 (ISBN 0-671-44484-0, Archway). PB.

—Monsters You Never Heard Of. (gr. 9-12). 1980. 8.95 (ISBN 0-396-07789-7, Putnam). Putnam Pub Group.

Dynamite Monster Hall of Fame. (gr. 3-5). pap. 1.50 (ISBN 0-590-11806-4, Schol Pap). Scholastic Inc.

Garden, Nancy. Vampires. LC 72-13830. (gr. 7 up). 1973. (Lipp Jr Bks); pap. 2.95 (ISBN 0-397-31457-4). HarpC Child Bks.

Hawkins, Colin. Take Away Monsters. Hawkins, Colin, illus. 12p. (ps-2). 1984. 9.95 (ISBN 0-399-20962-X, Putnam). Putnam Pub Group.

Horton, et al. Amazing Fact Book of Monsters. (Illus.). 32p. 1987. 11.95 (ISBN 0-87191-847-1). Creative Ed.

Howell, Michael & Ford, Peter. The Elephant Man: Retold for Children. Geary, Robert, illus. (gr. 2-8). 1987. 9.95 (ISBN 0-8052-8160-6, Pub. by Allison & Busby England). Schocken.

Hughes, Ted. Nessie the Monster. LC 73-13231. (ps-3). 1974. 6.50 (ISBN 0-672-51798-1, Bobbs). Macmillan.

Ideals Childrens Book Editors. Funny Monsters. (Illus.). 16p. (ps-3). 1989. pap. 2.95 (ISBN 0-8249-8367-X). Ideals.

Miller. Monsters. Francis, John, illus. 32p. (gr. k-6). 1977. pap. 5.95 (ISBN 0-86020-146-5). EDC.

Most, Bernard. Boo! LC 80-18984. (Illus.). 31p. 1980. 7.95 (ISBN 0-13-079780-4). P-H.

Rawson. Dragons. (gr. k-4). 1980. 6.95 (ISBN 0-86020-337-9, Usborne-Hayes); PLB 11.96 (ISBN 0-88110-055-2); pap. 2.95 (ISBN 0-86020-336-0). EDC.

—Dragons, Giants & Witches. (gr. k-4). 1979. 10.95 (ISBN 0-86020-342-5, Usborne-Hayes). EDC.

Ross, David. How to Prevent Monster Attacks. Ross, David, illus. (gr. 2-6). 1986. pap. 2.50 (ISBN 0-671-55832-3, Minstrel Bks). PB.

Selsam, Millicent E. Strange Creatures That Really Lived. Dewey, Jennifer, illus. 32p. (ps-4). 1989. pap. 3.95 (ISBN 0-590-44430-1). Scholastic Inc.

Seltzer, Meyer. Hide-&-Go Shriek Monster Riddles. Levine, Abby, ed. Seltzer, Meyer, illus. 32p. (gr. 1-5). 1990. PLB 8.95 (ISBN 0-8075-3273-8). A Whitman.

Simon, Seymour. Space Monsters: From Movies, TV & Books. LC 77-3566. 80p. (gr. 4 up). 1977. 12.95 (ISBN 0-397-31765-4, Lipp Jr Bks). HarpC Child Bks.

Spellman, Linda. Monsters, Mysteries, UFOs. 112p. (gr. 4-6). 1984. 9.95 (ISBN 0-88160-095-4, LW 903). Learning Wks.

Stallman, Birdie. Learning about Dragons. Halverson, Lydia, illus. LC 81-4746. 48p. (gr. 2-6). 1981. 17.27 (ISBN 0-516-06531-9); pap. 4.95 (ISBN 0-516-46531-7). Childrens.

Tallarico, Tony. Things You Always Wanted to Know about Monsters: But Were Afraid to Ask. (Illus.). 64p. (Orig.). Date not set. pap. 1.95 (ISBN 0-942025-59-8). Kidsbks.

Taylor, David. Animal Monsters: Fantasies & Facts of the Animal World. (Illus.). 48p. (gr. 4 up). Repr. of 1989 ed. 5.95g (ISBN 0-8225-9575-3). Lerner Pubns.

MONSTERS–FICTION

Adler, David A. Cam Jansen & the Mystery of the Monster. (gr. k-3). 1986. pap. 2.75 (ISBN 0-440-41022-3, YB). Dell.

Alcock, Vivien. The Monster Garden. LC 88-6900. 160p. (gr. 5-9). 1988. 13.95 (ISBN 0-440-50053-2). Delacorte.

—The Monster Garden. (gr. k-6). 1990. pap. 2.95 (ISBN 0-440-40257-3, YB). Dell.

Ancona, George. Monster Movers. Ancona, George, photos by. LC 83-5504. (Illus.). 48p. (gr. 2-5). 1983. 15.95 (ISBN 0-525-44063-1, DCB). Dutton Child Bks.

Anderson, Marilyn D. The Bubble Gum Monster. Hickman, Estella, illus. 64p. (Orig.). (gr. k-2). 1987. pap. text ed. 2.50 (ISBN 0-87406-299-3). Willowisp Pr.

Anderson, Mary. The Curse of the Demon. (gr. k-6). 1989. pap. 2.95 (ISBN 0-440-40203-4, YB). Dell.

—The Hairy Beast in the Woods. (gr. 8-12). 1989. pap. 2.75 (ISBN 0-318-42743-5, Pub. by Yearling Classics). Dell.

—Mostly Monsters, No. 1. (gr. k-6). 1989. pap. 2.95 (ISBN 0-440-40178-X, YB). Dell.

—Mostly Monsters, No. 2. (Orig.). (gr. k-6). 1989. pap. 2.95 (ISBN 0-440-40181-X, YB). Dell.

Asimov, Isaac, et al, eds. Young Monsters. LC 84-48352. 224p. (gr. 6-9). 1985. PLB 12.89 (ISBN 0-06-020170-3). HarpC Child Bks.

Avery, Lorraine. Secret in the Lake. Thomas, Linda, illus. LC 89-5119. 96p. (gr. 4-6). 1989. PLB 9.89 (ISBN 0-8167-1710-9); pap. text ed. 2.95 (ISBN 0-8167-1711-7). Troll Assocs.

Bad Ben & the Monster. (gr. k-2). 1990. text ed. 3.95 cased (ISBN 0-7214-5266-3). Ladybird Bks.

Barden, Rosalind. TV Monster. (Illus.). 32p. (ps-2). 1988. 12.95 (ISBN 0-517-56934-5). Crown.

Barr, Ken, illus. Frankenstein. Weinberg, Larry, adapted by. LC 81-15703. (Illus.). 96p. (gr. 2-5). 1982. lib. bdg. 4.99 (ISBN 0-394-94827-0); pap. 1.95 (ISBN 0-394-84827-6). Random.

Bennett, Jack. The Voyage of the Lucky Dragon. 156p. (gr. 7 up). 1982. 9.95 (ISBN 0-13-944165-4). P-H.

Berenstain, Michael. The Creature Catalog: A Monster Watcher's Guide. Berenstain, Michael, illus. LC 82-5365. 64p. (gr. 3-7). 1982. Random.

Better Homes & Gardens Editors. Dandy Dragon Day. 32p. Date not set. 4.95 (ISBN 0-696-01902-7). Meredith Bks.

—There's a Monster in My Soup. 32p. 1990. 4.95 (ISBN 0-696-01903-5). Meredith Bks.

Briggs, Raymond. Fungus the Bogeyman. 1990. pap. 4.95 (ISBN 0-14-054235-3, Puffin). Puffin Bks.

Broun, Heywood. The Fifty-First Dragon. Redpath, Ann, ed. Delessert, Etienne, illus. 32p. (gr. 4 up). 1985. PLB 10.95s.p. (ISBN 0-88682-005-7); 15.65 (ISBN 0-685-10397-8). Creative Ed.

Bulla, Clyde R. My Friend the Monster. Chessare, Michele, illus. LC 79-7826. 96p. (gr. 2-5). 1981. PLB 11.89 (ISBN 0-690-04087-3, Crowell Jr Bks). HarpC Child Bks.

—My Friend the Monster. Chessare, Michele, illus. LC 79-7826. 96p. (gr. 2-5). 1990. pap. 3.50 (ISBN 0-06-440378-5, Trophy). HarpC Child Bks.

Byars, Betsy. The Blossoms & the Green Phantom. Rogers, Jacqueline, illus. 160p. (gr. k-6). 1988. pap. 2.95 (ISBN 0-440-40069-4). Dell.

Carey, Valerie S. Harriet & William & the Terrible Creature. (ps). 1990. pap. 3.95 (ISBN 0-525-44652-4, DCB). Dutton Child Bks.

Chevalier, Christa. Spence & the Sleepytime Monster. Tucker, Kathleen, ed. Chevalier, Christa, illus. LC 83-25988. 32p. (ps-1). 1984. PLB 10.95 (ISBN 0-8075-7574-7). A Whitman.

Christian, Mary B. Go West, Swamp Monsters. Brown, Marc, illus. LC 84-12686. 48p. (ps-3). 1985. 8.95 (ISBN 0-8037-0091-1); PLB 8.89 (ISBN 0-8037-0144-6). Dial Bks Young.

Robison, Nancy. Ten Tall Soldiers. Knight, Hilary, illus. LC 87-32090. 32p. (ps-2). 1991. 13.95 (ISBN 0-8050-0768-7). H Holt & Co.

Ross, Dave. How to Prevent Monster Attacks. LC 83-26536. (Illus.). 64p. (gr. 4 up). 1984. 7.00 (ISBN 0-688-03790-9). Morrow Jr Bks.

Ross, Tony. I'm Coming to Get You! Ross, Tony, illus. LC 84-5831. (ps-2). 1984. 11.95 (ISBN 0-8037-0119-5). Dial Bks Young.

Sabraw, John. I Wouldn't Be Scared. LC 88-23352. (Illus.). 32p. (ps-1). 1989. 13.95 (ISBN 0-531-05818-2); PLB 13.99 (ISBN 0-531-08418-3). Orchard Bks Watts.

Sanford, William & Green, Carl. Bride of Frankenstein. LC 84-17539. (Illus.). 48p. (gr. 3-5). 1985. PLB 9.95 (ISBN 0-89686-259-3, Crestwood Hse). Macmillan Child Grp.

—Dracula's Daughter. LC 84-27462. (Illus.). 48p. (gr. 3-5). 1985. PLB 9.95 (ISBN 0-89686-260-7, Crestwood Hse). Macmillan Child Grp.

—Ghost of Frankenstein. LC 84-29231. (Illus.). 48p. (gr. 3-5). 1985. PLB 9.95 (ISBN 0-89686-261-5, Crestwood Hse). Macmillan Child Grp.

—The Mole People. LC 84-23913. (Illus.). 48p. (gr. 3-5). 1985. PLB 9.95 (ISBN 0-89686-262-3, Crestwood Hse). Macmillan Child Grp.

—The Raven. LC 84-19866. (Illus.). 48p. (gr. 3-5). 1985. PLB 9.95 (ISBN 0-89686-263-1, Crestwood Hse). Macmillan Child Grp.

Saunders, Susan. Attack of the Monster Plants. 64p. (gr. 4). 1986. pap. 2.25 (ISBN 0-553-15399-4). Bantam.

Schick, Joel & Schick, Alice. Mary Shelley's Frankenstein. Schick, Joel & Schick, Alice, illus. LC 80-385. 48p. (gr. 4-6). 1981. PLB 11.95 (ISBN 0-385-28302-4). Delacorte.

Sendak, Maurice. Donde Viven Los Monstrous. Sendak, Maurice, illus. (SPA.). (gr. 1-6). 14.95 (ISBN 84-204-3022-6). Santillana.

—Seven Little Monsters. Sendak, Maurice, illus. LC 76-18400. (gr. 1 up). 1977. PLB 12.89 (ISBN 0-06-025478-5). HarpC Child Bks.

Sesame Street & Kingsley, Emily P. Cookie Monster's Storybook. Cooke, Tom, illus. LC 79-3914. (ps-2). 1979. (Random Juv). Random.

Seymour, Miranda. Vampire of Verdonia. (Illus.). 100p. (gr. 3-6). 1988. 10.95 (ISBN 0-233-97867-4). Andre Deutsch.

Sharmat, Marjorie W. Scarlet Monster Lives Here. Kendrick, Dennis, illus. LC 78-19484. 64p. (gr. k-3). 1979. PLB 11.89 (ISBN 0-06-025527-7). HarpC Child Bks.

—Scarlet Monster Lives Here. Kendrick, Dennis, illus. LC 78-19484. 64p. (gr. k-3). 1986. pap. 3.50 (ISBN 0-06-444098-2, Trophy). HarpC Child Bks.

Sharmat, Marjorie W. & Sharmat, Mitchell. The Pizza Monster. Bruncus, Denise, illus. (ps up). 1989. 12.95 (ISBN 0-385-29722-X). Delacorte.

—The Pizza Monster: Olivia Sharp, Agent for Secrets. (gr. k-6). 1990. pap. 2.75 (ISBN 0-440-40286-7, YB). Dell.

Shelley, Mary Wollstonecraft. Frankenstein. Schick, Alice & Schick, Joel, eds. LC 80-385. (Illus.). 48p. (gr. 3 up). 1980. PLB 10.89 (ISBN 0-440-02693-8); pap. 4.95 (ISBN 0-440-02692-X). Delacorte.

—Frankenstein. Binder, Otto, ed. Cruz, Nardo, illus. LC 73-75462. 64p. (Orig.). (gr. 5-10). 1973. pap. 2.95 (ISBN 0-88301-097-6); student activity bk. 1.25 (ISBN 0-88301-177-8). Pendulum Pr.

—Frankenstein. Kelley, Gary, illus. Stewart, Diana, adapted by. LC 81-5216. (Illus.). 48p. (gr. 4 up). 1983. PLB 17.32 (ISBN 0-8172-1674-X); pap. 9.27 (ISBN 0-8172-2008-9). Raintree Pubs.

Slater, Jim. Big Snowy. Slater, Christopher, illus. LC 80-53066. (ps-3). 1981. pap. 1.25 (ISBN 0-394-84736-9). Random.

Smith, Alison. Come Away Home. Haeffele, Deborah, illus. LC 90-41534. 112p. (gr. 3-5). 1991. SBE 11.95 (ISBN 0-684-19283-7, Scribners Young Read). Macmillan Child Grp.

Smith, Janice L. The Monster in the Third Dresser Drawer. Gackenbach, Dick, illus. LC 81-47109. 96p. (gr. 1-4). 1981. 12.95 (ISBN 0-06-025734-2); PLB 12.89 (ISBN 0-06-025739-3). HarpC Child Bks.

—The Monster in the Third Dresser Drawer: And Other Stories about Adam Joshua. Gackenbach, Dick, illus. LC 81-47109. 96p. (gr. 1-4). 1988. pap. 3.50 (ISBN 0-06-440223-1, Trophy). HarpC Child Bks.

Sommer-Bodenburg, Angela. The Vampire Takes a Trip. Glienke, Amelia, illus. (gr. 3-7). 1987. pap. 2.50 (ISBN 0-671-64822-5, Minstrel Bks). PB.

Spence, Jim, illus. Dracula. Spinner, Stephanie, adapted by. LC 81-15867. (Illus.). 96p. (gr. 2-5). 1982. lib. bdg. 4.99 (ISBN 0-394-94828-9); pap. 1.95 (ISBN 0-394-84828-4). Random.

Stanish, Bob. A Monster's Shoe & the Cat. Stanish, Bob, illus. 44p. (gr. 1-4). 1983. pap. 8.95 tchr's. enrichment bk. (ISBN 0-88047-018-6, 8303). DOK Pubs.

Stern, Steve. Hershel & the Beast. Gills, K. King, illus. LC 86-27789. 64p. (Orig.). (gr. 1-5). 1987. text ed. 13.95 (ISBN 0-938507-05-2). Ion Books.

Stevens, Kathleen. The Beast in the Bathtub. Bowler, Ray, illus. LC 85-12691. 32p. (gr. 2-3). 1985. PLB 12.95 (ISBN 0-918831-15-6). Gareth Stevens Inc.

—Bully for the Beast! Bowler, Ray, illus. LC 88-33090. 32p. (gr. 2-3). 1990. PLB 12.95 (ISBN 0-8368-0020-6). Gareth Stevens Inc.

Stevenson, Drew. The Case of the Horrible Swamp Monster. (Illus.). 96p. (gr. 3-7). 1984. 10.95 (ISBN 0-318-40991-7, Putnam). Putnam Pub Group.

—The Case of the Wandering Werewolf. (Illus.). 128p. (gr. 3-7). 1987. 11.95 (ISBN 0-396-09154-7, Putnam). Putnam Pub Group.

Stoker, Bram. Dracula. Schick, Alice & Schick, Joel, eds. LC 83-5471. (Illus.). 48p. (gr. 3 up). 1980. PLB 10.89 (ISBN 0-440-01349-6); pap. 6.95 (ISBN 0-440-01348-8). Delacorte.

—Dracula. Farr, Naunerle, ed. Redondo, Nestor, illus. LC 83-5471. 64p. (Orig.). (gr. 5-10). 1973. pap. 2.95 (ISBN 0-88301-100-X); student activity bk. 1.25 (ISBN 0-88301-175-1). Pendulum Pr.

Sutcliff, Rosemary. Beowulf. Keeping, Charles, illus. (gr. 5-9). 1984. 14.75 (ISBN 0-8446-6165-1). Peter Smith.

Tester, Sylvia R. Magic Monsters Around the Year. LC 78-23800. (Illus.). (ps-3). 1979. PLB 11.97 (ISBN 0-89565-059-2). Childs World.

—Magic Monsters Learn about Safety. Magine, John, illus. LC 78-24365. (ps-3). 1979. PLB 11.97 (ISBN 0-89565-060-6). Childs World.

—What Is a Monster? Magnuson, Diana, illus. LC 78-23642. (ps-3). 1979. PLB 11.97 (ISBN 0-89565-055-X). Childs World.

Thaler, Mike. King Kong's Underwear. 96p. (Orig.). (gr. 7 up). 1986. pap. 2.50 (ISBN 0-380-89823-3, Camelot). Avon.

Things That Go. (Illus.). 8p. (ps). 1978. 2.50 (ISBN 0-448-46809-3, G&D). Putnam Pub Group.

Thorne, Ian. The Deadly Mantis. LC 81-22074. (Illus.). 48p. (gr. 3 up). 1982. PLB 10.95 (ISBN 0-89686-214-3, Crestwood Hse); pap. 4.95 (ISBN 0-89686-217-8). Macmillan Child Grp.

—Dracula. LC 76-51145. (Illus.). 48p. (gr. 3 up). 1977. PLB 9.95 (ISBN 0-913940-67-4, Crestwood Hse); pap. 4.95 (ISBN 0-913940-74-7); cass. 7.95 (ISBN 0-89686-485-5). Macmillan Child Grp.

—Frankenstein. Schroeder, Howard, ed. LC 76-51144. (Illus.). 48p. (gr. 3 up). 1977. PLB 10.95 (ISBN 0-913940-66-6, Crestwood Hse); pap. 4.95 (ISBN 0-913940-73-9); cass. 7.95 (ISBN 0-685-01269-7). Macmillan Child Grp.

—Godzilla. LC 76-51148. (Illus.). 48p. (gr. 3 up). 1977. PLB 10.95 (ISBN 0-913940-68-2, Crestwood Hse); pap. 4.95 (ISBN 0-913940-75-5); cass. 7.95 (ISBN 0-89686-486-3). Macmillan Child Grp.

—It Came from Outer Space. LC 81-1419. (Illus.). 48p. (Orig.). (gr. 3 up). 1982. PLB 9.95 (ISBN 0-89686-213-5, Crestwood Hse); pap. 4.95 (ISBN 0-89686-216-X). Macmillan Child Grp.

—King Kong. LC 76-51147. (Illus.). 48p. (gr. 3 up). 1977. PLB 10.95 (ISBN 0-913940-69-0, Crestwood Hse); pap. 4.95 (ISBN 0-913940-76-3). Macmillan Child Grp.

—Mad Scientists. LC 76-51149. (Illus.). 48p. (gr. 3 up). 1977. PLB 10.95 (ISBN 0-913940-70-4, Crestwood Hse); pap. 4.95 (ISBN 0-913940-77-1); cass. 7.95 (ISBN 0-89686-487-1). Macmillan Child Grp.

—The Wolf Man. LC 76-51146. (Illus.). 48p. (gr. 3 up). 1977. PLB 9.95 (ISBN 0-913940-71-2, Crestwood Hse); pap. 4.95 (ISBN 0-913940-78-X); cass. 7.95 (ISBN 0-89686-488-X). Macmillan Child Grp.

Timm, Stephen A. The Dragon & the Mouse: The Dream. Lalo, illus. 45p. 1982. 12.95 (ISBN 0-939728-05-2); pap. 4.95 (ISBN 0-939728-06-0). Steppingstone Ent.

The Vanishing Monster. (Illus.). (ps-2). 3.50 (ISBN 0-7214-0914-8). Ladybird Bks.

Waddell, Martin. Little Dracula's Christmas. Wright, Joseph, illus. 32p. (gr. k up). 1986. pap. 3.95 (ISBN 0-14-050658-6, Penguin Bks). Viking Penguin.

—Little Dracula's First Bite. Wright, Joseph, illus. 32p. (gr. k up). 1986. pap. 3.95 (ISBN 0-14-050657-8, Penguin Bks). Viking Penguin.

Wahl, Jan. Dracula's Cat. LC 77-27051. (Illus.). (ps-3). 1981. 6.95 (ISBN 0-685-03842-4); pap. 2.50 (ISBN 0-685-03843-2). P-H.

Wallace, Daisy, ed. Monster Poems. Chorao, Kay, illus. LC 75-17680. 32p. (gr. k-3). 1990. reinforced 12.95 (ISBN 0-8234-0268-1); pap. 4.95 (ISBN 0-8234-0848-5). Holiday.

Weinberg, Michael A. The Horrible Terrible Dragon: A Folktale. Weinberg, Kay, illus. 10p. (gr. 1-3). 1949. pap. 1.00 (ISBN 0-9601014-3-8). Weinberg.

Whitlock, Susan L. Donovan Scares the Monsters. Abolafia, Yossi, illus. LC 86-4783. 24p. (gr. k-3). 1987. 11.75 (ISBN 0-688-06438-8); PLB 11.88 (ISBN 0-688-06439-6). Greenwillow.

Williams, Jeffery W. The Adventures of the Little Whimpo's, No. 1. Williams, Jeffery W., illus. 34p. (gr. 3 up). 1990. 4.00 (ISBN 1-878392-03-4); pap. 2.95 (ISBN 0-685-30134-6). R Kids Pub.

—The Four Wheels of Justice Fighting Force: The Chemical Creatures. Williams, Jeffery W., illus. 28p. (gr. 3 up). 1990. pap. 2.95 (ISBN 1-878392-01-8). R Kids Pub.

Willis, Jeanne. The Monster Bed. Varley, Jeanne, illus. LC 86-10366. 32p. (ps-2). 1987. 12.95 (ISBN 0-688-06804-9); PLB 12.88 (ISBN 0-688-06805-7). Lothrop.

Willoughby, Elaine M. Boris & the Monsters. Munsinger, Lynn, illus. 32p. (gr. k-3). 1980. pap. 4.95 (ISBN 0-395-42649-9). HM.

Winthrop, Elizabeth. Maggie & the Monster. DePaola, Tomie, illus. LC 86-19593. 32p. (ps-2). 1988. reinforced bdg. 14.95 (ISBN 0-8234-0639-3); pap. 5.95 (ISBN 0-8234-0698-9). Holiday.

Wolak, Camilla H. Squire Gullible & the Dragon. rev. ed. LC 89-43530. (gr. 3-12). 1985. pap. text ed. 6.00 (ISBN 0-88734-508-5). Players Pr.

Wylie, Joann. Have You Hugged Your Monster Today? A Manners's Story. Wylie, David, illus. LC 84-12132. 32p. (ps-2). 1984. 14.60 (ISBN 0-516-04493-1); pap. 3.95 (ISBN 0-516-44493-X). Childrens.

Wylie, Joanne. Do You Know Where Your Monster Is Tonight: A Time Story. Wylie, David, illus. LC 84-12122. 32p. (ps-2). 1984. 14.60 (ISBN 0-516-04491-5). Childrens.

—Sabes Donde Esta Tu Monstruo Esta Noche? Kratky, Lada, tr. Wylie, David, illus. LC 85-31423. (SPA.). 32p. (ps-2). 1986. PLB 14.60 (ISBN 0-516-34491-9); pap. 3.95 (ISBN 0-516-54491-8). Childrens.

Wylie, Joanne & Wylie, David. The Gumdrop Monster: A Color Story. LC 84-12133. (Illus.). 32p. (ps-2). 1985. 14.60 (ISBN 0-516-04492-3). Childrens.

Yep, Laurence. Dragon of the Lost Sea. LC 81-48644. 224p. (gr. 7 up). 1982. 10.53i (ISBN 0-06-026746-1). HarpC Child Bks.

Yolen, Jane. Commander Toad in Space. Degen, Bruce, illus. 64p. (gr. 3-5). 1980. PLB 8.99 (ISBN 0-698-30724-0, Coward); pap. 5.95 (ISBN 0-698-20522-7). Putnam Pub Group.

—Dragon's Blood. LC 81-69668. 256p. (gr. 7 up). 1982. 14.95 (ISBN 0-385-28226-5). Delacorte.

—Dragon's Blood. (gr. 7 up). 1984. pap. 3.50 (ISBN 0-440-91802-2, LFL). Dell.

Zemach, Harve. The Judge: An Untrue Tale. Zemach, Margot, illus. LC 79-87209. 48p. (ps-3). 1969. 14.95 (ISBN 0-374-33960-0). FS&G.

Zimelman, Nathan. If I Were Strong Enough. Paterson, Diane, illus. LC 81-19076. 32p. (gr. k-3). 1982. 0.50 (ISBN 0-687-18670-6). Abingdon.

MONSTROSITIES

see Monsters

MONTANA

Carole Marsh Montana Books, 31 bks. Set. 638.45 (ISBN 0-7933-1301-5). Gallopade Pub Group.

Carpenter, Allan. Montana. new ed. LC 79-683. (Illus.). 96p. (gr. 4 up). 1979. PLB 19.93 (ISBN 0-516-04126-6). Childrens.

Cooper, Myrtle E. From Tent Town to City: A Chronological History of Billings, Montana 1882-1935. Von Vogt, Janice, ed. Hulteng, Lee, illus. Wright, Kathryn, intro. by. (Illus.). 79p. (Orig.). (gr. 6-8). 1982. pap. 5.95 (ISBN 0-9613224-0-3). Parmly Lib.

Fradin, Dennis. Montana: In Words & Pictures. Wahl, Richard, illus. LC 80-25023. 48p. (gr. 2-5). 1981. PLB 15.93 (ISBN 0-516-03926-1); pap. 4.95 (ISBN 0-516-43926-X). Childrens.

Larson, Paul. Nothing Ventured, Nothing Gained: The Montana Entrepreneur's Guide. (Illus.). 300p. (Orig.). (gr. 12). 1989. pap. 19.95 (ISBN 0-685-29454-4). University MT.

Marsh, Carole. Avast, Ye Slobs!: Montana Pirate Trivia. (Illus.). (gr. 3 up). 1990. PLB 19.95 (ISBN 0-7933-0715-5); pap. 14.95 (ISBN 0-7933-0714-7); computer disk 29.95 (ISBN 0-7933-0716-3). Gallopade Pub Group.

—The Beast of the Montana Bed & Breakfast. (Illus.). (gr. 3 up). 1990. PLB 19.95 (ISBN 0-7933-1743-6); pap. 14.95 (ISBN 0-7933-1744-4); computer disk 29.95 (ISBN 0-7933-1745-2). Gallopade Pub Group.

—The Hard-to-Believe-But-True! Book of Montana History, Mystery, Trivia, Legend, Lore, Humor & More. (Illus.). (gr. 3 up). 1990. PLB 19.95 (ISBN 0-7933-0712-0); pap. 14.95 (ISBN 0-7933-0711-2); computer disk 29.95 (ISBN 0-7933-0713-9). Gallopade Pub Group.

—If My Montana Mama Ran the World! (Illus.). (gr. 3 up). 1990. lib. bdg. 19.95 (ISBN 0-7933-1746-0); pap. 14.95 (ISBN 0-7933-1747-9); computer disk 29.95 (ISBN 0-7933-1748-7). Gallopade Pub Group.

—Let's Quilt Montana & Stuff It Topographically! (Illus.). (gr. 3 up). 1990. PLB 19.95 (ISBN 1-55609-757-3); pap. 14.95 (ISBN 1-55609-131-1); computer disk 29.95 (ISBN 1-55609-759-X). Gallopade Pub Group.

—Montana & Other State Greats (Biographies) (Illus.). (gr. 3 up). 1990. PLB 19.95 (ISBN 1-55609-772-7); pap. 14.95 (ISBN 1-55609-773-5); computer disk 29.95 (ISBN 1-55609-774-3). Gallopade Pub Group.

—Montana Bandits, Bushwackers, Outlaws, Crooks, Devils, Ghosts, Desperadoes & Other Assorted & Sundry Characters! (Illus.). (gr. 3 up). 1990. PLB 19.95 (ISBN 0-7933-0697-3); pap. 14.95 (ISBN 0-7933-0696-5); computer disk 29.95 (ISBN 0-7933-0698-1). Gallopade Pub Group.

—Montana Classic Christmas Trivia. (gr. 3 up). 1990. PLB 19.95 (ISBN 0-7933-0700-7); pap. 14.95 (ISBN 0-7933-0699-X); computer disk 29.95 (ISBN 0-7933-0701-5). Gallopade Pub Group.

—Montana Coastales. (Illus.). (gr. 3 up). 1990. PLB 19.95 (ISBN 1-55609-766-2); pap. 14.95 (ISBN 1-55609-767-0); computer disk 29.95 (ISBN 1-55609-768-9). Gallopade Pub Group.

—The Montana Hot Air Balloon Mystery. (Illus.). (gr. 2-9). 1990. 19.95 (ISBN 0-7933-2552-8); pap. 14.95 (ISBN 0-7933-2553-6); computer disk 29.95 (ISBN 0-7933-2554-4). Gallopade Pub Group.

—Montana "Jography" A Fun Run Thru Our State. (Illus.). (gr. 3 up). 1990. PLB 19.95 (ISBN 1-55609-754-9); pap. 14.95 (ISBN 1-55609-755-7); computer disk 29.95 (ISBN 1-55609-756-5). Gallopade Pub Group.

—Montana Kid's Cookbook: Recipes, How-To, History, Lore & More. (Illus.). (gr. 3 up). 1990. PLB 19.95 (ISBN 0-7933-0709-0); pap. 14.95 (ISBN 0-7933-0708-2); computer disk 29.95 (ISBN 0-7933-0710-4). Gallopade Pub Group.

—Montana Quiz Bowl Crash Course! (Illus.). (gr. 3 up). 1990. PLB 19.95 (ISBN 1-55609-769-7); pap. 14.95 (ISBN 1-55609-770-0); computer disk 29.95 (ISBN 1-55609-771-9). Gallopade Pub Group.

—Montana School Trivia: An Amazing & Fascinating Look at Our State's Teachers, Schools & Students! (Illus.). (gr. 3 up). 1990. PLB 19.95 (ISBN 0-7933-0706-6); pap. 14.95 (ISBN 0-7933-0705-8); computer disk 29.95 (ISBN 0-7933-0707-4). Gallopade Pub Group.

—Montana Silly Basketball Sportsmysteries, Vol. I. (Illus.). (gr. 3 up). 1990. PLB 19.95 (ISBN 0-7933-0703-1); pap. 14.95 (ISBN 0-7933-0702-3); computer disk 29.95 (ISBN 0-7933-0704-X). Gallopade Pub Group.

—Montana Silly Basketball Sportsmysteries, Vol. II. (Illus.). (gr. 3 up). 1990. PLB 19.95 (ISBN 0-7933-1749-5); pap. 14.95 (ISBN 0-7933-1750-9); computer disk 29.95 (ISBN 0-7933-1751-7). Gallopade Pub Group.

—Montana Silly Football Sportsmysteries, Vol. I. (Illus.). (gr. 3 up). 1990. PLB 19.95 (ISBN 1-55609-760-3); pap. 14.95 (ISBN 1-55609-761-1); computer disk 29.95 (ISBN 1-55609-762-X). Gallopade Pub Group.

—Montana Silly Football Sportsmysteries, Vol. II. (Illus.). (gr. 3 up). 1990. PLB 19.95 (ISBN 1-55609-763-8); pap. 14.95 (ISBN 1-55609-764-6); computer disk 29.95 (ISBN 1-55609-765-4). Gallopade Pub Group.

—Montana Silly Trivia! (Illus.). (gr. 3 up). 1990. PLB 19.95 (ISBN 1-55609-751-4); pap. 14.95 (ISBN 1-55609-752-2); computer disk 29.95 (ISBN 1-55609-753-0). Gallopade Pub Group.

—Montana's (Most Devastating!) Disasters & (Most Calamitous!) Catastrophies! (Illus.). (gr. 3 up). 1990. PLB 19.95; pap. 14.95 (ISBN 0-7933-0692-2); computer disk 29.95 (ISBN 0-7933-0695-7). Gallopade Pub Group.

—The Nebraska Hot Air Balloon Mystery. (Illus.). (gr. 2-9). 1990. 19.95 (ISBN 0-7933-2561-7); pap. 14.95 (ISBN 0-7933-2562-5); computer disk 29.95 (ISBN 0-7933-2563-3). Gallopade Pub Group.

Shirley, Gayle. M Is for Montana. Bergum, Constance, illus. LC 87-73310. 32p. (Orig.). 1988. pap. 7.95 (ISBN 0-937959-32-4, ABC Press). Falcon Pr MT.

Thompson, Kathleen. Montana. LC 87-26465. 48p. (gr. 3 up). 1988. 17.32 (ISBN 0-86514-468-0); cancelled tchr's. study guide (ISBN 0-86514-610-1); cancelled Beta video (ISBN 0-86514-095-2); cancelled VHS video (ISBN 0-86514-170-3); cancelled 3/4" video (ISBN 0-86514-245-9). Raintree Pubs.

MONTANA–FICTION

Bly, Stephen & Bly, Janet. Crystal's Blizzard Trek. LC 86-16721. (gr. 7-10). 1986. pap. 3.95 (ISBN 1-55513-055-0, Chariot Bks). Cook.

Lasky, Kathryn. The Bone Wars. LC 88-13426. 378p. (gr. 7 up). 1988. 12.95 (ISBN 0-688-07433-2, Morrow Junior Books). Morrow.

Stein, Charlotte M. The Stained Glass Window. Sakurai, Jennifer, ed. Stein, Michele P., illus. LC 88-70883. 150p. (Orig.). 1991. incl. wkbk. 16.95 (ISBN 0-916634-13-2); pap. 11.95 incl. wkbk. (ISBN 0-916634-12-4). Double M Pr.

MONTESSORI, MARIA, 1870-1952

MacDonald, Fiona. A Chance to Learn. (Illus.). 48p. (gr. 7-9). 1990. 8.99 (ISBN 0-531-19512-0). Watts.

Standing, E. M. Maria Montessori: Her Life & Work. McDermott, John J., intro. by. (Illus.). 382p. (gr. 9-12). 1989. pap. 9.95 (ISBN 0-452-26090-6, Plume). NAL-Dutton.

MONTHS

Brown, Marzella. Cooperative Learning: Activities for Cooperative Learning. Rivera, Doreen, et al, illus. 48p. (gr. 2-5). 1990. wkbk. 5.95 (ISBN 1-55734-109-5). Tchr Create Mat.

—Cooperative Learning: All about Cooperative Learning. Wright, Theresa, illus. 48p. (gr. 2-5). 1990. wkbk. 5.95 (ISBN 1-55734-107-9). Tchr Create Mat.

Carson, Patti, et al. Days, Months, Seasons. (Illus.). 20p. (gr. 2-4). 1984. pap. 5.95 (ISBN 0-88724-098-4, CD-0568). Carson-Dellos.

Cracchiolo, Rachelle & Smith, Mary D. Calendar Activities. Crachiolo, Rachelle & Smith, Mary D., illus. 32p. (gr. 1-3). 1980. wkbk 5.95 (ISBN 1-55734-030-7). Tchr Create Mat.

Hale, Janet. April Monthly Activities. Apodaca, Blanqui, illus. 80p. (gr. 1-5). 1990. wkbk. 7.95 (ISBN 1-55734-158-3). Tchr Create Mat.

—February Monthly Activities. Apodaca, Blanqui & Spence, Paula, illus. 80p. (gr. 1-5). 1989. wkbk. 7.95 (ISBN 1-55734-156-7). Tchr Create Mat.

—January Monthly Activities. Apodaca, Blanqui & Spence, Paula, illus. 80p. (gr. 1-5). 1989. wkbk. 7.95 (ISBN 1-55734-155-9). Tchr Create Mat.

—July Monthly Activities. Apodaca, Blanqui, et al, illus. 80p. (gr. 1-5). 1990. wkbk. 7.95 (ISBN 1-55734-165-6). Tchr Create Mat.

—June Monthly Activities. Apodaca, Blanqui & Spence, Paula, illus. 80p. (gr. 1-5). 1990. wkbk. 7.95 (ISBN 1-55734-164-8). Tchr Create Mat.

—March Monthly Activities. Apodaca, Blanqui, et al, illus. 80p. (gr. 1-5). 1990. wkbk. 7.95 (ISBN 1-55734-157-5). Tchr Create Mat.

—May Monthly Activities. Apodaca, Blanqui, et al, illus. 80p. (gr. 1-5). 1990. wkbk. 7.95 (ISBN 1-55734-159-1). Tchr Create Mat.

Hughes, Paul. The Months of the Year. Harris, Peter, ed. Burn, Jeffery, illus. LC 89-11759. 63p. (gr. 4-7). 1989. PLB 15.93 (ISBN 0-944483-33-X). Garrett Ed Corp.

Leslie, Clare W. Nature All Year Long. LC 90-47866. (Illus.). 56p. (gr. 2 up). Date not set. 16.95 (ISBN 0-688-09183-0). Greenwillow.

Maestro, Betsy & Maestro, Giulio. Through the Year with Harriet. Maestro, Betsy & Maestro, Giulio, illus. LC 84-29339. 32p. (ps-1). 1986. PLB 12.95 (ISBN 0-517-55613-8). Crown.

Sterling, Mary E. & Nowlin, Susan S. Monthly Activities: November Monthly Activities. Spence, Paula, et al, illus. 80p. (gr. 1-5). 1989. wkbk. 7.95 (ISBN 1-55734-153-2). Tchr Create Mat.

—October Monthly Activities. Spence, Paula, et al, illus. 80p. (gr. 1-5). 1989. wkbk. 7.95 (ISBN 1-55734-152-4). Tchr Create Mat.

—September Monthly Activities. Spence, Paula, et al, illus. 80p. (gr. 1-5). 1989. wkbk. 7.95 (ISBN 1-55734-151-6). Tchr Create Mat.

Thomas, Jennifer. Masterpiece of the Month. Apodaca, Blanqui & Wright, Theresa, illus. 96p. (gr. k-5). 1990. wkbk. 9.95 (ISBN 1-55734-018-8). Tchr Create Mat.

MONTHS–POETRY

Sendak, Maurice. Chicken Soup with Rice. Sendak, Maurice, illus. 48p. (ps-3). 1962. PLB 12.89 (ISBN 0-06-025535-8). HarpC Child Bks.

MONTREAL–FICTION

Poulin, Stephane. Ah Belle Cite-A Beautiful City ABC. Poulin, Stephane, illus. (ENG & FRE.). 28p. (gr. k-3). 14.95 (ISBN 0-88776-175-5, Dist. by U of Toronto Pr). Tundra Bks.

MONUMENTS

see also Pyramids

The Eiffel Tower. 48p. (gr. 4-5). 1989. PLB 10.95 (ISBN 0-685-26409-2). Capstone Pr.

Hallett, Bill & Hallett, Jane. Look up Look down Look All Around Bandelier National Monument. (Illus.). 32p. (Orig.). (gr. 3-8). 1990. pap. 3.95 activity bk. (ISBN 1-877827-02-9). Look & See.

Sharp, Margery. The Turret. 144p. (gr. 3 up). 1974. pap. 1.25 (ISBN 0-440-48630-0, YB). Dell.

MOON

see also Tides

Adler, David. All about the Moon. Burns, Raymond, illus. LC 82-17422. 32p. (gr. 3-6). 1983. PLB 10.59 (ISBN 0-89375-886-8); pap. text ed. 2.95 (ISBN 0-89375-887-6). Troll Assocs.

Arvetis, Chris. What Is the Moon? Buckley, James, illus. 32p. (ps-3). 1987. write for info. (ISBN 0-02-689007-0). Checkerboard Pr.

Asimov, Isaac. Why Does the Moon Change Its Shape? (Illus.). 24p. (gr. 2-3). 1991. PLB 11.95 (ISBN 0-8368-0438-4). Gareth Stevens Inc.

Baker, David. Living on the Moon. (Illus.). 48p. (gr. 3-8). 1989. lib. bdg. 18.60 (ISBN 0-86592-374-4). Rourke Corp.

Barrett, Norman. The Moon. Jobson, Ron, illus. LC 85-50157. 32p. (gr. 3-5). 1985. PLB 11.40 (ISBN 0-531-10003-0). Watts.

Branley, Franklyn M. The Moon Seems to Change. rev. ed. Emberley, Barbara & Emberley, Ed E., illus. LC 86-47747. 32p. (ps-3). 1987. 13.95 (ISBN 0-690-04583-2, Crowell Jr Bks); PLB 13.89 (ISBN 0-690-04585-9). HarpC Child Bks.

—The Moon Seems to Change. rev. ed. Emberley, Barbara & Emberley, Ed E., illus. LC 86-27097. 32p. (ps-3). 1987. pap. 4.50 (ISBN 0-06-445065-1, Trophy). HarpC Child Bks.

—What the Moon Is Like. rev. ed. Kelley, True, illus. LC 85-47904. 32p. (ps-3). 1986. PLB 13.89 (ISBN 0-690-04512-3, Crowell Jr Bks). HarpC Child Bks.

—What the Moon Is Like. Kelley, True, illus. LC 85-45400. 32p. (gr. k-3). 1986. Book & Cassette Set. 7.95 (ISBN 0-694-00205-4, Trophy); pap. 4.50 (ISBN 0-06-445052-X, Trophy). HarpC Child Bks.

British Museum, Geological Department Staff. Moon, Mars & Meteorites. (Illus.). 36p. (gr. 7 up). 1986. pap. 4.50 (ISBN 0-521-32414-9). Cambridge U Pr.

DeBruin, Jerry. Young Scientists Explore: The Moon, Bk. 3. 32p. (gr. 4 up). 1982. 4.95 (ISBN 0-86653-074-6, GA 407). Good Apple.

Goldish, Meish. Does the Moon Change Shape? (Illus.). 32p. (gr. 1-4). 1989. PLB 13.32 (ISBN 0-8172-3518-3). Raintree Pubs.

Greenberg, Judith E. & Carey, Helen H. The Moon. Corvi, Donna, illus. 32p. (gr. 2-4). 1990. PLB 16.67 (ISBN 0-8172-3752-6). Raintree Pubs.

Kerrod, Robin. Race for the Moon. LC 79-2347. (Illus.). 36p. (gr. 3-6). 1980. PLB 9.95 (ISBN 0-8225-1183-5). Lerner Pubns.

A Kid's Guide to Living on the Moon. 48p. (gr. 4-5). 1989. PLB 10.95 (ISBN 0-685-26420-3). Capstone Pr.

Nicoll, Helen & Pienkowski, Jan. Meg on the Moon. (Illus.). 32p. (ps). 1980. 15.95 (ISBN 0-434-95424-1, Pub. by W Heinemann Ltd). Trafalgar Sq.

Santrey, Laurence. Moon. Schindler, S. D., illus. LC 84-8441. 32p. (gr. 3-6). 1985. PLB 9.49 (ISBN 0-8167-0252-7); pap. text ed. 2.95 (ISBN 0-8167-0253-5). Troll Assocs.

Simon, Seymour. The Moon. LC 84-28753. (Illus.). 32p. (gr. k-3). 1984. 13.95 (ISBN 0-02-782840-9, Four Winds). Macmillan Child Grp.

Sneider, Cary I. Earth, Moon, & Stars. Bergman, Lincoln & Fairwell, Kay, eds. Baker, Lisa H. & Bevilacqua, Carol, illus. Sneider, Cary I., photos by. 50p. (Orig.). (gr. 5-9). 1986. pap. 9.00 (ISBN 0-912511-18-4). Lawrence Science.

Stevenson, Robert Louis. The Moon. Saldutti, Denise, illus. LC 83-47704. 32p. (ps-2). 1984. PLB 13.89 (ISBN 0-06-025789-X). HarpC Child Bks.

Witcomb, Gerald, illus. The Moon. 32p. (gr. 3-5). 1985. 5.95x (ISBN 0-86685-448-7). Intl Bk Ctr.

MOON–EXPLORATION

Cosner, Shaaron. Lunar Bases. 1990. PLB 11.90 (ISBN 0-531-10894-5). Watts.

Furniss, Tim. The First Men on the Moon. Bull, Peter, illus. LC 88-24166. 32p. (gr. 4-6). 1989. PLB 11.40 (ISBN 0-531-18240-1). Watts.

Muirden, James. Going to the Moon. Code, Nigel, illus. LC 87-4560. 32p. (ps-1). 1987. 3.95 (ISBN 0-394-89186-4, Random Juv); lib. bdg. 7.99 (ISBN 0-394-99186-9). Random.

MOON–EXPLORATION–FICTION

Herge. Explorers on the Moon. (gr. k up). 1976. pap. 7.95 (ISBN 0-316-35846-0, Joy St Bks). Little.

—Objectif Lune. (FRE., Illus.). (gr. 7-9). looseleaf bdg. 19.95 (ISBN 0-685-28409-3). French & Eur.

—On a Marche Sur la Lune. (FRE., Illus.). (gr. 7-9). looseleaf bdg. 19.95 (ISBN 0-685-28410-7). French & Eur.

MOON–FICTION

Addison-Wesley Staff. How the Moon Got in the Sky Little Book. (Illus.). 16p. (gr. k-3). 1989. pap. text ed. 4.50 (ISBN 0-201-19359-0). Addison-Wesley.

Aiken, Joan. The Moon's Revenge. Lee, Alan, illus. LC 87-2863. 32p. (gr. 3-7). 1988. 12.95 (ISBN 0-394-89380-8); lib. bdg. 13.99 (ISBN 0-394-99380-2). Knopf.

Alexander, Martha. Maggie's Moon. Alexander, Martha, illus. LC 82-1575. 32p. (ps-2). 1982. PLB 7.89 (ISBN 0-8037-5721-2). Dial Bks Young.

Asch, Frank. Happy Birthday Mood. Asch, Frank, illus. 32p. (ps-1). 1988. Bk. & cassette. pap. 6.95 (ISBN 0-671-67145-6). S&S Trade.

—Happy Birthday, Moon. (Illus.). 32p. (gr. k-4). 1985. PLB 12.95 (ISBN 0-671-66454-9); pap. 4.95 (ISBN 0-671-66455-7). S&S Trade.

Balzola, Asun. Munia & the Moon. (Illus.). 1989. 11.95 (ISBN 0-521-37143-0). Cambridge U Pr.

Bates, Betty. The Great Male Conspiracy. (gr. k-6). 1990. pap. 2.95 (ISBN 0-440-40247-6, YB). Dell.

Bess, Clayton. The Truth about the Moon. Hoffman, Rosekrans, illus. 48p. (gr. k-3). 1983. 13.95 (ISBN 0-395-34551-0). HM.

Carle, Eric. Papa, Please Get the Moon for Me. LC 85-29785. (Illus.). 32p. (ps up). 1986. 16.95 (ISBN 0-88708-026-X). Picture Bk Studio.

Coats, Laura J. Marcella & the Moon. Coats, Laura J., illus. LC 85-15309. 32p. (gr. k-3). 1986. 12.95 (ISBN 0-02-719050-1, Mcmillan Child Bk). Macmillan Child Grp.

Danziger, Paula. This Place Has No Atmosphere. LC 85-46070. 128p. (gr. 7 up). 1986. pap. 14.95 (ISBN 0-385-29489-1). Delacorte.

Duncan, Lois. Birthday Moon. Davis, Susan, illus. 32p. (ps-3). 1989. 13.95 (ISBN 0-670-82238-8). Viking Child Bks.

Edens, Cooper. Now Is the Moon's Eyebrow. (Orig.). (gr. 7-12). 1987. pap. 8.95 (ISBN 0-88138-070-9). Green Tiger Pr.

Elzbieta. Dikou & the Mysterious Moon Sheep. Elzbieta, illus. LC 87-13587. 32p. (ps-3). 1988. 11.95i (ISBN 0-690-04692-8, Crowell Jr Bks). HarpC Child Bks.

Galt, Denham. Pierrot's Moon. 1990. 8.95 (ISBN 0-533-08711-2). Vantage.

Guest, Elissa H. Over the Moon. LC 85-28505. 160p. (gr. 7 up). 1986. 12.95 (ISBN 0-688-04148-5). Morrow Jr Bks.

Hadley, Eric & Hadley, Tessa. Legends of the Sun & Moon. LC 82-17720. (Illus.). 32p. (gr. 3-7). 1989. 11.95 (ISBN 0-521-25227-X); pap. 7.95 (ISBN 0-521-37912-1). Cambridge U Pr.

Heckman, Philip. The Moon Is Following Me. Young, Mary O., illus. LC 89-14921. 32p. (ps-1). 1991. SBE 13.95 (ISBN 0-689-31565-1, Atheneum Child Bk). Macmillan Child Grp.

L'Engle, Madeleine. The Moon by Night. 256p. (gr. 6 up). 1981. pap. 3.25 (ISBN 0-440-95776-1, LE). Dell.

Linklater, Eric. The Wind on the Moon. 302p. (gr. 5-7). 1989. pap. 5.95 (ISBN 0-86241-131-9, Pub. by Cnngt Pub Ltd). Trafalgar Sq.

O'Dell, Scott. Sing down the Moon. large type ed. 176p. (gr. 9-12). 1989. Repr. of 1970 ed. lib. bdg. 15.95 (ISBN 1-55736-142-8, Crnrstn Bks). ABC-CLIO.

Ormerod, Jan. Moonlight. Ormerod, Jan, illus. LC 81-8290. 32p. (ps-1). 1982. 14.95 (ISBN 0-688-00846-1); PLB 14.88 (ISBN 0-688-00847-X). Lothrop.

Pyle, Howard. The Garden Behind the Moon. (Illus.). 192p. (gr. 4-6). 1988. Repr. of 1895 ed. 14.95 (ISBN 0-930407-06-7, Dist. by Kampmann). Parabola Bks.

Salter, Mary J. The Moon Comes Home. Schuett, Stacey, illus. LC 88-31735. 40p. (ps-2). 1989. 12.95 (ISBN 0-394-89983-0); lib. bdg. 13.99 (ISBN 0-394-99983-5). Knopf.

Ungerer, Tomi. Moon Man. (ps-3). 1991. 16.00 (ISBN 0-385-30429-3). Delacorte.

Vander Els, Betty. The Bombers Moon. LC 85-47591. 129p. (gr. 4 up). 1985. 11.95 (ISBN 0-374-30864-0). FS&G.

Wildsmith, Brian. What the Moon Saw. Wildsmith, Brian, illus. 32p. (ps-3). 1978. 14.95 (ISBN 0-19-279724-7); pap. 6.95 (ISBN 0-19-272157-7). Oxford U Pr.

Willard, Nancy. The Nightgown of the Sullen Moon. McPhail, David, illus. LC 83-8472. (ps-3). 1983. 14.95 (ISBN 0-15-257429-8, HJ). HarBraceJ.

Wynne-Jones, Tim. Builder of the Moon. Wallace, Ian, illus. 1989. 14.95 (ISBN 0-689-50472-1, M K McElderry). Macmillan Child Grp.

Zalben, Jane B. Water from the Moon. LC 86-46439. 160p. (gr. 8 up). 1987. 12.95 (ISBN 0-374-38238-7). FS&G.

MOON, VOYAGES TO

see Space Flight to the Moon

MOORS–FICTION

Rogers, Jean. The Secret Moose. LC 84-12897. (Illus.). 64p. (gr. 3-5). 1985. 13.95 (ISBN 0-688-04248-1); PLB 13.88 (ISBN 0-688-04249-X). Greenwillow.

MOOSE

Ahlstrom, Mark E. The Moose. LC 85-26931. (Illus.). 48p. (gr. 4-5). 1985. 10.95 (ISBN 0-89686-279-8, Crestwood Hse). Macmillan Child Grp.

Hassett, Ann & Hassett, John. Moose on the Loose. Hassett, John, illus. 48p. (Orig.). (ps-4). 1987. pap. 7.95 (ISBN 0-89272-245-2). Down East.

Rue, Leonard L., III & Owen, William. Meet the Moose. (Illus.). 64p. (gr. 3-7). 1985. 9.95 (ISBN 0-396-08605-5, Putnam). Putnam Pub Group.

MOOSE–FICTION

Allen, Jonathan. Mucky Moose. Allen, Jonathan, illus. LC 90-6363. 32p. (ps-3). 1991. 12.95 (ISBN 0-02-700251-9, Mcmillan Child Bk). Macmillan Child Grp.

Bernier, Evariste. Baxter Bear & Moses Moose. Peterson, Dawn, illus. LC 90-61408. 48p. (gr. 1-4). 1990. 12.95 (ISBN 0-89272-287-8). Down East.

Brennan, Gale. Toulouse the Mouse. Flint, Russ, illus. 16p. (Orig.). (gr. k-6). 1981. pap. 1.25 (ISBN 0-685-02458-X). Brennan Bks.

Butterworth, William E. Moose, the Thing, & Me. (gr. 5 up). 1982. 9.95 (ISBN 0-395-32077-1). HM.

Carlstrom, Nancy W. Moose in the Garden. Desimini, Lisa, illus. LC 89-29407. 32p. (ps-2). 1990. 13.95 (ISBN 0-06-021015-X); PLB 13.89 (ISBN 0-06-021014-1). HarpC Child Bks.

DeVries, Douglas. Muscles, the Moose Calf. Parker, Patricia, illus. LC 89-84651. 32p. (Orig.). (ps-3). 1989. 8.00 (ISBN 1-877721-00-X). Jade Ram Pub.

—Muscles Visits Anchorage. Parker, Patricia, illus. LC 90-61154. 32p. (Orig.). (ps-3). 1990. pap. text ed. 8.00 (ISBN 1-877721-01-8). Jade Ram Pub.

Dr. Seuss. Thidwick, the Big-Hearted Moose. Dr. Seuss, illus. (gr. k-3). 1962. 10.00 (ISBN 0-394-80086-9, Random Juv); lib. bdg. 10.99 (ISBN 0-394-90086-3). Random.

Hoff, Syd. Santa's Moose. LC 78-22483. (Illus.). 32p. (ps-3). 1986. pap. 2.95 (ISBN 0-06-444102-4, Trophy). HarpC Child Bks.

Latimer, Jim. When Moose Was Young. Carrick, Donald, illus. LC 89-10059. 32p. (gr. 1-3). 1990. 13.95 (ISBN 0-684-18932-1, Scribners Young Read). Macmillan Child Grp.

Matthews, Morgan. The Big Race. Schindler, S. D., illus. LC 88-1287. 48p. (Orig.). (gr. 1-4). 1989. PLB 9.89 (ISBN 0-8167-1329-4); pap. text ed. 2.95 (ISBN 0-8167-1330-8). Troll Assocs.

Ochs, Carol P. Moose on the Loose. Mitchell, Anastasia, illus. 32p. (ps-4). 1991. PLB 12.95 (ISBN 0-87614-448-2). Carolrhoda Bks.

Pinkwater, Daniel M. Return of the Moose. (Illus.). 64p. (gr. 3-7). 1979. 9.95 (ISBN 0-396-07674-2, Putnam). Putnam Pub Group.

Pinkwater, Manus. Blue Moose. (Illus.). 48p. (gr. k-3). 1975. 10.95 (ISBN 0-396-07151-1, Putnam). Putnam Pub Group.

Wakefield, Pat & Carrara, Larry. A Moose for Jessica. Carrara, Larry, photos by. LC 87-13663. (Illus.). 32p. (gr. k up). 1987. 14.95 (ISBN 0-525-44342-8, DCB). Dutton Child Bks.

Wiseman, B. Morris the Moose. rev. ed. Wiseman, B., illus. LC 87-33485. 32p. (ps-2). 1989. 10.95 (ISBN 0-06-026475-6); PLB 10.89 (ISBN 0-06-026476-4). HarpC Child Bks.

—Morris the Moose. rev. ed. Wiseman, B., illus. LC 87-33485. 32p. (ps-2). 1991. pap. 3.50 (ISBN 0-06-444146-6, Trophy). HarpC Child Bks.

Wiseman, Bernard. Morris & Boris. (gr. k-3). Date not set. 15.95 (ISBN 0-399-21905-6, Putnam). Putnam Pub Group.

—Morris Goes to School. Wiseman, Bernard, illus. LC 75-77944. 64p. (gr. k-3). 1970. PLB 11.89 (ISBN 0-06-026548-5). HarpC Child Bks.

—Morris Has a Cold. 1990. pap. 2.95 (ISBN 0-590-43429-2). Scholastic Inc.

—Morris Tells Boris Mother Moose Stories & Rhymes. (Illus.). 48p. (gr. k-3). 1975. 5.95 (ISBN 0-396-07693-9, Putnam). Putnam Pub Group.

MORAL EDUCATION

see Character Education

MORAL PHILOSOPHY

see Ethics

MORALITY

see Ethics

MORALS

see Behavior; Ethics

MORE, SIR THOMAS, SAINT, 1478-1535

Smith, Dorothy. Thomas More: The King's Good Servant. Broomfield, Robert, illus. 1990. 2.95 (ISBN 0-8091-6595-3). Paulist Pr.

MORMONS AND MORMONISM

Crowther, Jean D. Book of Mormon Puzzles & Pictures for Young Latter-Day Saints. LC 77-74495. (Illus.). 56p. (gr. 3 up). 1977. pap. 5.50 (ISBN 0-88290-080-3). Horizon Utah.

Dean, Bessie. Let's Learn of God's Love. LC 79-89367. (Illus.). 64p. (ps-3). 1979. pap. 3.95 (ISBN 0-88290-124-9). Horizon Utah.

—Living the Articles of Faith. Dean, Bessie, illus. 88p. (gr. k-4). 1988. pap. 5.95 (ISBN 0-88290-336-5). Horizon Utah.

England, Kathleen. Why We Are Baptized. LC 78-19180. (Illus.). (gr. 2-5). 1978. pap. 5.95 (ISBN 0-87747-893-7). Deseret Bk.

Featherstone, Vaughn J. The Aaronic Priesthood & You. LC 87-15731. 140p. (gr. 7-12). 1987. 9.95 (ISBN 0-87579-085-2). Deseret Bk.

Halverson, Sandy. Book of Mormon Activity Book: Creative Scripture Learning Experiences for Children 4-12. Halverson, Sandy, illus. 80p. (gr. 3-8). 1982. pap. 9.95 (ISBN 0-88290-188-5, 4521). Horizon Utah.

Madsen, Susan A. The Lord Needed a Prophet. LC 90-81829. (Illus.). 190p. (gr. 3-6). 1990. 10.95 (ISBN 0-87579-276-6). Deseret Bk.

Neeley, Deta P. A Child's Story of the Book of Mormon. LC 87-19903. 382p. (gr. 1-6). 1987. 12.95 (ISBN 0-87579-101-8). Deseret Bk.

Oviatt, Joan. The One Game. LC 82-19817. 185p. (gr. 10 up). 1988. pap. 4.95 (ISBN 0-87579-162-X). Deseret Bk.

Pettit, Ray. My Excellent Adventure: Achievement Activities for Young Latter-Day Saints. LC 90-37121. 138p. (gr. 3-6). 1990. pap. 6.95 (ISBN 0-87579-358-4). Deseret Bk.

Sing with Me. (gr. 1-6). 1974. 5.50 (ISBN 0-87747-362-5). Deseret Bk.

Wyss, Thelma H. Show Me Your Rocky Mountains! LC 82-9471. 133p. (gr. 3-6). 1989. pap. 4.95 (ISBN 0-87579-234-0). Deseret Bk.

MORMONS AND MORMONISM–FICTION

Brigham Young & the Robin Soup. 12p. (Orig.). 1988. pap. text ed. 1.95 (ISBN 0-929985-01-X). Sonos.

Hughes, Dean. Cornbread & Prayer. LC 88-18853. 143p. (gr. 7-12). 1988. 8.95 (ISBN 0-87579-135-2). Deseret Bk.

—Facing the Enemy. LC 82-12810. 143p. (gr. 3-9). 1991. pap. 4.95 (ISBN 0-87579-498-X). Deseret Bk.

—Lucky's Gold Mine. LC 90-31072. 132p. (Orig.). (gr. 3-6). 1990. pap. 4.95 (ISBN 0-87579-350-9). Deseret Bk.

Johnson, Marjorie. Book of Mormon Stories for Little Children. LC 76-3991. (Illus.). 96p. (Orig.). (ps-7). 1976. pap. 6.95 (ISBN 0-88290-063-3). Horizon Utah.

Robison, Pamela. Alma. 90p. (gr. 5-10). 1985. pap. 6.25 (ISBN 0-8309-0409-3). Herald Hse.

MOROCCO

Hintz, Martin. Morocco. LC 84-23269. (Illus.). 128p. (gr. 5-9). 1985. lib. bdg. 25.27 (ISBN 0-516-02774-3). Childrens.

Lerner Publications, Department of Geography Staff, ed. Morocco in Pictures. (Illus.). 64p. (gr. 5 up). 1988. 12.95 (ISBN 0-8225-1843-0). Lerner Pubns.

Lye, Keith. Take a Trip to Morocco. Franklin Watts Ltd., ed. (Illus.). 32p. (ps-9). 1988. PLB 7.99 (ISBN 0-531-10467-2). Watts.

Nelson, Harold D., ed. Morocco: A Country Study. LC 85-600265. (Illus.). 476p. (gr. 9-12). 1986. 15.00 (ISBN 0-16-001640-1, S/N 008-020-01072-3). USGPO.

Wilkins, Frances. Morocco. (Illus.). (gr. 5 up). 1988. 14.95 (ISBN 1-55546-186-7). Chelsea Hse.

MOROCCO–FICTION

Johnston, Norma. Return to Morocco. LC 88-6880. 176p. (gr. 7 up). 1988. 13.95 (ISBN 0-02-747712-6, Four Winds). Macmillan Child Grp.

Sales, Francesc. Ibrahim. Simont, Marc, tr. from CAT. Sariola, Eulalia, illus. LC 87-29382. 32p. (gr. k-3). 1989. 11.95 (ISBN 0-397-32146-5, Lipp Jr Bks); PLB 11.89 (ISBN 0-397-32147-3). HarpC Child Bks.

MORONS

see Mentally Handicapped

MORPHOLOGY

see Anatomy; Anatomy, Comparative; Biology

MORSE, SAMUEL FINLEY BREESE, 1791-1872

Kerby, Mona. Samuel Morse. (Illus.). 64p. (gr. 3-5). 1991. PLB 11.90 (ISBN 0-531-20023-X). Watts.

Tiner, John H. Samuel F. B. Morse: Artist with a Message. (Illus.). (gr. 3-6). 1987. pap. 6.95 (ISBN 0-88062-137-0). Mott Media.

MORTUARY CUSTOMS

see Funeral Rites and Ceremonies

MOSCOW

Davis, James E. & Hawke, Sharryl D. Moscow. (Illus.). 64p. (gr. 4-9). 1990. PLB 18.00 (ISBN 0-8172-3030-0). Raintree Pubs.

MOSES

Barrett, Ethel. Moses. LC 82-16521. (gr. 1-7). 1982. pap. text ed. 3.95 (ISBN 0-8307-0772-7, 5811201). Regal.

De Graaf, Anne. Moses: God's Chosen Leader. Montero, Jose P., illus. 32p. (gr. k-4). 1991. 7.95 (ISBN 0-8028-5035-9). Eerdmans.

Hall, Rachel. Baby in a Basket. Baker, Arthur, illus. 32p. (gr. k-3). 1990. saddle stitched 1.25 (ISBN 0-8028-5063-4). Eerdmans.

Hodges. Moses & the Ten Plagues. 24p. (Orig.). (gr. k-4). 1985. pap. 1.39 (ISBN 0-570-06190-3, 59-1291). Concordia.

Johnson, Sylvia A. Mosses. Izawa, Masana, illus. LC 83-17488. 48p. (gr. 4 up). 1983. PLB 14.95 (ISBN 0-8225-1482-6). Lerner Pubns.

Lashbrook, Marilyn. Who Needs a Boat? The Story of Moses. Britt, Stephanie M., illus. LC 87-83295. 32p. (ps). 1988. 5.95 (ISBN 0-86606-431-1, 862). Roper Pr.

Lehmann, Asher. Young Moses, Crown Prince of Egypt. Goldman, Bonnie & Goldstein-Alpern, Neva, eds. Hirschler, Gertrude, tr. Forst, Siegmund, illus. 150p. (gr. 9-12). 1987. 8.95 (ISBN 0-910818-64-9); pap. 7.95 (ISBN 0-685-18059-X). Judaica Pr.

Moses. (ps-2). 3.95 (ISBN 0-7214-5066-0). Ladybird Bks.

Mumma, Win. Moses: The Man Who Talked to Bushes. (Illus.). 32p. Package of 6. pap. 5.34 (ISBN 0-8423-4543-4). Tyndale.

Overholtzer, Ruth. Moses, Vol. II. Andreasen, Norma, illus. 50p. (gr. k-6). 1967. pap. text ed. 9.45 (ISBN 1-55976-008-7). CEF Press.

Parry, Alan & Parry, Linda. Baby Moses. Parry, Alan, illus. 24p. (ps). 1990. pap. 0.99 (ISBN 0-8066-2477-9, 9-2477). Augsburg Fortress.

Parry, Linda & Parry, Alan. Miriam & Moses. Parry, Linda & Parry, Alan, illus. LC 90-80556. 24p. (Orig.). (ps-2). Date not set. pap. 1.49 (ISBN 0-8066-2489-2, 9-2489, Augsburg). Augsburg Fortress.

Russell, Jim, illus. Moses of the Bullrushes: Retold by Catherine Storr. 32p. (gr. k-4). 1984. 14.65 (ISBN 0-8172-1990-0, Raintree Children's Books Belitha Press Ltd. - London). Raintree Pubs.

Stewart, Frances T. & Stewart, Charles P., III. Moses: God's Chosen Leader. LC 88-12814. (Orig.). (gr. k-3). 1988. pap. 6.95 (ISBN 0-8054-4189-1). Broadman.

Storr, Catherine, ed. Moses in the Wilderness. (Illus.). 32p. (gr. k-4). 1985. PLB 14.65 (ISBN 0-8172-2039-9). Raintree Pubs.

Truitt, Gloria A. Noah & God's Promise. 24p. (Orig.). (gr. k-4). 1985. pap. 1.39 (ISBN 0-570-06193-8, 59-1294). Concordia.

Vos Wezeman, Phyllis & Wiessner, Colleen A. On the Move with Moses. 33p. (Orig.). (gr. 1-6). 1988. pap. 5.95 (ISBN 0-940754-60-6). Ed Ministries.

MOSES, GRANDMA (MRS. ANNA MARY ROBERTSON MOSES) 1860-1961

Laing, Martha. Grandma Moses: The Grand Old Lady of American Art. Rahmas, D. Steve, ed. LC 71-190231. 32p. (Orig.). (gr. 7-9). 1972. lib. bdg. 4.20 incl. catalog cards (ISBN 0-87157-513-2); pap. 2.95 vinyl laminated covers (ISBN 0-87157-013-0). SamHar Pr.

O'Neal, Zibby. Grandma Moses: Painter of Rural. Ruff, Donna & Moses, Grandma, illus. LC 86-4071. 64p. (gr. 2-6). 1986. pap. 10.95 (ISBN 0-670-80664-1). Viking Child Bks.

MOSQUITOES

Patent, Dorothy H. Mosquitoes. LC 86-45387. (Illus.). 40p. (gr. 3-7). 1986. reinforced bdg. 12.95 (ISBN 0-8234-0627-X). Holiday.

MOSSES

Johnson, Sylvia. Mosses. Izawa, Masana, photos by. (Illus.). 48p. (gr. 4 up). pap. 5.95g (ISBN 0-8225-9563-X). Lerner Pubns.

MOTHER GOOSE

Atkinson, Allen. Old King Cole & Other Favorites. (Illus.). 64p. (Orig.). 1986. pap. 2.50 (ISBN 0-553-15355-2). Bantam.

Baby's Mother Goose. (Illus.). (ps). 1978. 2.50 (ISBN 0-448-46804-2, G&D). Putnam Pub Group.

Baron, Michelle. Hector Nursery Rhyme: Little Boy Blue. Mazurek, Theresa, et al, illus. 26p. (ps). 1987. Packaged with pre-programmed audio cass. tape. 9.95 (ISBN 0-934323-47-X). Alchemy Comms.

—Hector Nursery Rhyme: The Three Little Kittens. Mazurek, Theresa, et al, illus. 26p. (ps). 1987. Packaged with pre-programmed audio cass. tape. 9.95 (ISBN 0-934323-46-1). Alchemy Comms.

Barrett, John E. & View-Master International, photos by. Big Bird's Mother Goose. LC 83-63404. (Illus.). 28p. (ps). 1984. bds. 2.95 (ISBN 0-394-86745-9, Pub. by BYR). Random.

Battaglia, Aurelius, ed. Mother Goose. (ps-1). 1973. pap. 2.25 (ISBN 0-394-82661-2, Random Juv). Random.

Bracken, Carolyn, illus. Humpty Dumpty & Other Rhymes. (ps-k). 3.95 (ISBN 0-7214-5194-2). Ladybird Bks.

—Jack & Jill & Other Rhymes. (ps-k). 3.95 (ISBN 0-7214-5193-4). Ladybird Bks.

—Little Bo-Peep & Other Rhymes. (ps-k). 3.95 (ISBN 0-7214-5195-0). Ladybird Bks.

—Old Mother Hubbard & Other Rhymes. (ps-k). 3.95 (ISBN 0-7214-5196-9). Ladybird Bks.

Children's Treasury: Mother Goose Nursery Rhymes. 1990. 7.98 (ISBN 0-8317-1361-5). Smithmark.

Decker, Marjorie A. Christian Mother Goose Tales. (gr. 1-2). 1987. 10.95 (ISBN 1-55748-009-5); pap. text ed. 6.95 (ISBN 1-55748-008-7). Barbour & Co.

De Paola, Tomie. Mother Goose Story Streamers. De Paola, Tomie, illus. 28p. (ps-3). 1984. 4.95 (ISBN 0-399-21004-0, Putnam). Putnam Pub Group.

Edens, Cooper, compiled by. The Glorious Mother Goose. LC 87-35491. (Illus.). 96p. 1988. 15.95 (ISBN 0-689-31434-5, Atheneum Child Bk). Macmillan Child Grp.

Favorite Mother Goose Rhymes. LC 62-15042. (ps-2). 1978. write for info. (ISBN 0-528-82215-2). Checkerboard Pr.

Forsse, Ken & Hughes, Margaret. The Little Red Hen. Becker, Mary, ed. (Illus.). 26p. (ps). 1986. packaged with pre-programmed audio cass. tape 9.95 (ISBN 0-934323-22-4). Alchemy Comms.

—The Tortoise & the Hare. Becker, Mary, ed. (Illus.). 26p. (ps). 1986. incl. pre-programmed audio cass. tape 9.95 (ISBN 0-934323-21-6). Alchemy Comms.
Greenaway, Kate. Mother Goose: Or, the Old Nursery Rhymes. Greenaway, Kate, illus. (gr. k-3). 1901. 5.95 (ISBN 0-7232-0591-4). Warne.
Greenaway, Kate, illus. Mother Goose. 12p. (ps-5). 1973. pap. 3.25 (ISBN 0-914510-04-5). Evergreen.
Harris Fair, Martha & Ragsdale, Karl S., eds. Mother Goose Bustin' Loose. Pigford, Barbara, illus. 18p. (Orig.). (gr. k-8). 1982. pap. 5.00 (ISBN 0-911181-02-4). Harris Academy.
Hennessy, B. G. The Missing Tarts. Pearson, Tracey C., illus. 32p. (ps-3). 1989. pap. 12.95 (ISBN 0-670-82039-3). Viking Child Bks.
Hickey. Mother Goose & More: Classic Nursery Rhymes with Added Lines. Moss, Marissa, illus. 48p. (ps-3). 1990. 7.77 (ISBN 0-9623940-0-9); lib. bdg. 7.00; text ed. 12.95; tchr's. ed. 9.00. Additions Pr.
Hopkins, Lee B. Animals from Mother Goose. 1989. 6.95 (ISBN 0-15-200406-8). HarbraceJ.
—People from Mother Goose. 1989. 6.95 (ISBN 0-15-200558-7). HarbraceJ.
Hughes, Margaret. The Ugly Duckling. Forsse, Ken & Becker, Mary, eds. (Illus.). 26p. (ps). 1986. 9.95 (ISBN 0-934323-24-0). Alchemy Comms.
Hughes, Margaret & Forsse, Ken, eds. Cinderella. Hicks, Russell, et al, illus. 26p. (ps). 1986. incl. pre-programmed audio cass. tape 9.95 (ISBN 0-934323-23-2). Alchemy Comms.
Lobel, Arnold, illus. The Just Right Mother Goose: Just Right for 3's & 4's. LC 88-43156. 32p. (ps). 1989. 4.95 (ISBN 0-394-82860-7); PLB 5.99 (ISBN 0-394-92860-1). Random.
Loomans, Diane, et al. Positively Mother Goose. Kramer, Linda, ed. Henrichson, Ronda, illus. LC 90-52634. 32p. 1991. 14.95 (ISBN 0-915811-24-3). H J Kramer Inc.
Marcus, Leonard S. & Schwartz, Amy, eds. Mother Goose's Little Misfortunes. Schwartz, Amy, illus. LC 89-77425. 32p. 1990. 15.95 (ISBN 0-02-781431-9, Bradbury Pr). Macmillan Child Grp.
Marshall, James, illus. James Marshall's Mother Goose. LC 79-2574. 40p. (ps-3). 1979. 14.95 (ISBN 0-374-33653-9). FS&G.
Mother Goose Board Book. (ps). 1959. bds. 3.95 (ISBN 0-448-03077-2, G&D). Putnam Pub Group.
Mother Goose Book. 1987. 11.79 (ISBN 0-671-63659-6). S&S Trade.
Mother Goose-Coloring Book. 1985. pap. 3.50 (ISBN 0-88388-012-1). Bellerophon Bks.
Mother Goose Staff. Little Red Riding Hood. Facsimile ed. LC 86-11772. (Illus.). 56p. (gr. k-5). 1986. Repr. of 1924 ed. 11.95 (ISBN 0-916410-35-8). A D Bragdon.
Mountain, Lee, et al. Mother Goose Tea Party. (Illus.). 16p. (gr. k-1). 1991. pap. 18.75 (ISBN 0-89061-944-1). Jamestown Pubs.
Nudelman, Edward D., frwd. by. The Jessie Willcox Smith Mother Goose. enhanced ed. (Illus.). 192p. 1991. 24.95 (ISBN 0-88289-844-2); deluxe ed. 75.00 (ISBN 0-88289-830-2). Pelican.
Provensen, Alice & Provensen, Martin. The Mother Goose Book. LC 76-8548. (Illus.). (gr. 1 up). 1976. (Random Juv). Random.
Richardson, Frederick, illus. Mother Goose. Classic Volland ed. Grover, Eulalie O., intro. by. LC 72-161577. (Illus.). 160p. (ps-4). 1915. 12.95 (ISBN 0-02-689094-1). Checkerboard Pr.
Scarry, Richard, illus. Richard Scarry's Best Mother Goose Ever. (ps-1). 1970. write for info. (ISBN 0-307-15578-1, Golden Bks). Western Pub.
Sesame Street Staff. The Sesame Street Mother Goose. Jones, Randy, illus. LC 75-39341. (ps-3). 1976. 7.95 (ISBN 0-394-83256-6, Random Juv). Random.
Tripp, Wallace. Granfa' Grig Had a Pig & Other Rhymes Without Reason from Mother Goose. Tripp, Wallace, illus. 96p. (gr. 4-12). 1976. 17.95 (ISBN 0-316-85282-1); pap. 10.95 (ISBN 0-316-85284-8). Little.
Tudor, Tasha. Mother Goose. Tudor, Tasha, illus. LC 58-58523. (gr. k-3). 1980. 9.95 (ISBN 0-8098-1901-5). McKay.
—Mother Goose. LC 88-30674. (Illus.). 96p. (ps-2). 1989. 8.95 (ISBN 0-394-84407-6). Random.
Walz, Richard, illus. The Pudgy Book of Mother Goose. 16p. (gr. k). 1984. 2.95 (ISBN 0-448-10212-9, G&D). Putnam Pub Group.

MOTHER GOOSE–SONGS AND MUSIC

Lancaster, Francine. Mother Goose & Other Nursery Songs: From the Collection of the Museum of Fine Arts, Boston. (ps up). 1987. incl. cassette 16.95 (ISBN 0-930647-03-3). Lancaster Prodns.

MOTHERS

Alvarez del Real, Maria E., ed. Guia Practica para la Mujer. (SPA., Illus.). 320p. (Orig.). 1989. pap. 4.00x (ISBN 0-944499-37-6). Editorial Amer.

Duggan, Maureen H. Mommy Doesn't Live Here Anymore. Liberman, Jane, illus. 48p. (Orig.). (ps-7). 1987. pap. 8.95 (ISBN 0-944453-01-5). B Brae. "Mommy Doesn't Live Here Anymore" - a sensitive chronicle of a mother's alcoholism & how it affected her children. It has successfully captured the essence of life within an alcoholic family: the stresses, tensions, pressures & pains. Most importantly, it has done so from the vantage point of the child, as the child reflects upon the total experience. No other work has presented such a realistic portrayal of the magnitude of suffering, emotional pain & psychic turmoil of young children within alcoholic families. It reveals the thoughts, reasoning, feelings & behaviors of children in alcoholic homes, & yet, accomplishes such spirit of understanding & sympathy within an overall message of hope & help for our children. "Mommy Doesn't Live Here Anymore" is an inspirational work, revealing that the tragedies of familial alcoholism & tragic consequences for our youth need to be dealt with in a personal & delicate manner." Maureen Duggan has always been regarded highly for her thoughtful & gentle manner, compassionate understanding, & her acute sensitivity towards alcoholics & family needs. Her own serenity & spirituality are guides for many seeking their own honesty & fulfillment."--Nelson C. Acquilano, Executive Director, Council on Alcoholism of The Finger Lakes, N.Y. *Publisher Provided Annotation.*

English, Jennifer. My Mommy's Special. LC 85-12836. 32p. (gr. k-3). 1985. PLB 14.60 (ISBN 0-516-03861-3). Childrens.
Horlacher, Bill & Horlacher, Kathy. I'm Glad I'm Your Mother. Hutton, Kathryn, illus. 24p. (ps-2). 1985. 1.99 (ISBN 0-87239-876-5, 3676). Standard Pub.
Landau, Elaine. Surrogate Mothers. Rosoff, Iris, ed. (Illus.). 144p. (gr. 7 up). 1988. PLB 12.90 (ISBN 0-531-10603-9). Watts.
Lasker, Joe. Mothers Can Do Anything. Lasker, Joe, illus. LC 72-83684. 40p. (gr. k-3). 1972. PLB 12.95 (ISBN 0-8075-5287-9). A Whitman.
Polisar, Barry L. Juggling Babies & a Career. (ps-6). 1989. incl. cassette 9.95 (ISBN 0-9615696-2-X). Rainbow Morn.
Reimold, Mary G. My Mom Is a Runner. Dorris, Sid, illus. 32p. (ps-2). 1987. 1.00 (ISBN 0-687-27545-8). Abingdon.

MOTHERS–FICTION

Auch, Mary J. Kidnapping Kevin Kowalski. LC 89-46065. 128p. (gr. 3-7). 1990. 13.95 (ISBN 0-8234-0815-9). Holiday.
Balter, Lawrence. A. J.'s Mom Gets a New Job. Schanzer, Roz, illus. 40p. (gr. 3-7). 1990. 5.95 (ISBN 0-8120-6151-9). Barron.
Bauer, Caroline Feller. My Mom Travels a Lot. Parker, Nancy W., illus. (gr. k-3). 1982. incl. cassette 19.95 (ISBN 0-941078-23-X); pap. 12.95 incl. cassette (ISBN 0-941078-21-3); pap. 27.95 4 bks., cassette & guide (ISBN 0-941078-22-1); sound filmstrip 22.95 (ISBN 0-941078-24-8). Live Oak Media.
Bauer, Marion D. Like Mother, Like Daughter. LC 85-479. 156p. (gr. 5-9). 1985. 12.95 (ISBN 0-89919-356-0, Clarion). Ticknor & Fields.
Baum, Louis. After Dark. Varley, Susan, illus. LC 89-16123. 32p. (ps-3). 1990. 11.95 (ISBN 0-87951-382-9). Overlook Pr.
Berry, Christine. Mama Went Walking. Brusca, Maria C., illus. LC 89-39789. 32p. (ps-3). 1990. 14.95 (ISBN 0-8050-1261-3). H Holt & Co.
Blaine, Mary. Terrible Thing That Happened at Our House. Wallner, John C., illus. 32p. (gr. k-3). 1983. pap. 2.95 (ISBN 0-590-40355-9). Scholastic Inc.
Calvert, Patricia. Yesterday's Daughter. LC 86-13753. 144p. (gr. 7 up). 1986. 12.95 (ISBN 0-684-18746-9, Scribners Young Read). Macmillan Child Grp.
Chaffin, Lillie D. Tommy's Big Problem. Petie, Haris, illus. (ps-2). PLB 6.70 (ISBN 0-8313-0016-7). Lantern.
Chevalier, Christa. Spence Isn't Spence Anymore. Levine, Abby, ed. Chevalier, Christa, illus. 32p. (ps-1). 1985. 10.95 (ISBN 0-8075-7565-8). A Whitman.
Cleary, Beverly. Ramona & Her Mother. LC 79-10323. (Illus.). 208p. (gr. 4-6). 1979. 13.95 (ISBN 0-688-22195-5); PLB 13.88 (ISBN 0-688-32195-X). Morrow.
Clymer, Eleanor. My Mother Is the Smartest Woman in the World. Kincade, Nancy, illus. LC 82-1685. 96p. (gr. 4-6). 1982. 11.95 (ISBN 0-689-30916-3, Atheneum Child Bk). Macmillan Child Grp.
Cole, Babette. The Trouble with Mom. Cole, Babette, illus. 32p. (gr. 5-8). 1984. 12.95 (ISBN 0-698-20624-X, Coward); pap. 5.95 (Coward). Putnam Pub Group.
Daly, Niki. Ben's Gingerbread Man. LC 85-3327. (Illus.). 24p. (ps-1). 1985. 4.95 (ISBN 0-670-80806-7). Viking Child Bks.
Delton, Judy. Angel's Mother's Boyfriend. Apple, Margot, illus. LC 82-27054. 176p. (gr. 2-5). 1986. 12.95 (ISBN 0-395-39968-8). HM.
—Angel's Mother's Boyfriend. (gr. k-6). 1990. pap. 2.95 (ISBN 0-440-40275-1, YB). Dell.
—Angel's Mother's Wedding. (gr. k-6). 1990. pap. 2.95 (ISBN 0-440-40281-6, YB). Dell.
—Bad, Bad Bunnies. (gr. k-6). 1990. pap. 2.75 (ISBN 0-440-40278-6, YB). Dell.
De Regniers, Beatrice S. Waiting for Mama. De Larrea, Victoria, illus. LC 83-14982. 32p. (ps-2). 1984. 9.95 (ISBN 0-89919-222-X, Clarion). HM.
Doman, Bruce K. Goodbye, Mommy. Melton, David, illus. LC 77-79632. 86p. (ps-2). 1982. 8.95 (ISBN 0-936676-00-0). Better Baby.
Dorer, Ann. Mother Makes a Mistake. LC 89-42638. 32p. (gr. 1-2). 1990. PLB 12.95 (ISBN 0-8368-0109-1). Gareth Stevens Inc.
Drescher, Joan. My Mother's Getting Married. Drescher, Joan, illus. LC 84-18642. 32p. (ps-3). 1989. pap. 3.95 (ISBN 0-8037-0642-1). Dial Bks Young.
Ehrlich, Amy. Where It Stops, Nobody Knows. 224p. (gr. 6 up). 1990. pap. 3.95 (ISBN 0-14-034266-4, Puffin). Puffin Bks.
Filichia, Peter. The Most Embarrassing Mother in the World. 192p. 1991. pap. 2.95 (ISBN 0-380-76084-3, Flare). Avon.
Finley, Martha. Elsie's Motherhood. 243p. 1981. Repr. PLB 21.95x (ISBN 0-89966-335-4). Buccaneer Bks.
Fox, Mem. Koala Lou. 1989. 13.95 (ISBN 0-15-200502-1). HarbraceJ.
Gilden, Mel. Harry Newberry & the Raiders of the Red Drink. LC 88-28402. 144p. (gr. 4-8). 1989. 14.95 (ISBN 0-8050-0698-2). H Holt & Co.
Greene, Constance C. Star Shine. (gr. k-6). 1987. pap. 2.75 (ISBN 0-440-47920-7, YB). Dell.
Griffin, Sandra U. Earth Circles. Griffin, Sandra U., illus. 32p. (ps-3). 1989. 12.95 (ISBN 0-8027-6843-1); PLB 13.85 (ISBN 0-8027-6845-8). Walker & Co.
Hall, Lynn. Letting Go. LC 86-31483. 112p. (gr. 6-9). 1987. 12.95 (ISBN 0-684-18781-7, Scribners Young Read). Macmillan Child Grp.
Hallinan, P. K. We're Very Good Friends, My Mother & I. Hallinan, P. K., illus. LC 88-26880. 32p. (ps-3). 1989. PLB 13.27 (ISBN 0-516-03654-8). Childrens.
Hamilton, Dorothy. Joel's Other Mother. Graber, Esther R., illus. 120p. (gr. 3-7). 1984. pap. 3.95 (ISBN 0-8361-3355-2). Herald Pr.
Hay, John. Mama, Were You Ever Young? (Illus.). 32p. (gr. k-4). 1989. 12.95 (ISBN 0-88138-134-9). Green Tiger Pr.
Haynes, Betsy. Great Mom Swap. 160p. (Orig.). 1986. pap. 2.50 (ISBN 0-553-15398-6, Skylark). Bantam.
Hazen, Barbara S. Even If I Did Something Awful? Kincade, Nancy, illus. LC 81-1907. 32p. (ps-2). 1981. 12.95 (ISBN 0-689-30843-4, Atheneum Child Bk). Macmillan Child Grp.
Help for Mom. 24p. (ps-2). 1989. pap. 1.29 (ISBN 0-02-898249-5). Checkerboard Pr.
Hest, Amy. The Mommy Exchange. DiSalvo-Ryan, Dyanne, illus. LC 90-40596. 32p. (ps-2). 1991. pap. 3.95 (ISBN 0-689-71450-5, Aladdin). Macmillan Child Grp.
Himmel, Roger J. Mother's Day Surprise. new ed. Manoni, Mary H., ed. Peters, Luther J. & Ross, Connie, illus. LC 73-739485. (gr. k-3). 1978. pap. text ed. 29.95 6 bks. & 1 cass. (ISBN 0-89290-042-3); pap. text ed. 10.95 1 bk. & 1 cass. Soc for Visual.
Hines, Anna G. It's Just Me, Emily. Hines, Anna G., illus. (ps-1). 1987. 12.95 (ISBN 0-89919-487-7, Pub. by Clarion). Ticknor & Fields.
Holabird, Katharine. Alexander & the Magic Boat. Craig, Helen, illus. 24p. (ps-2). 1990. 11.95 (ISBN 0-517-58142-6); PLB 12.99 (ISBN 0-517-58149-3). Crown.
Jacoby, Alice. My Mother's Boyfriend & Me. (gr. 9 up). 1988. pap. 2.95 (ISBN 0-449-70311-8, Juniper). Fawcett.
Johnson, Dolores. What Will Mommy Do When I'm at School? Johnson, Dolores, illus. LC 90-5559. 32p. (ps-k). 1990. 12.95 (ISBN 0-02-747845-9, Mcmillan Child Bk). Macmillan Child Grp.
Jones, Rebecca C. The Believers. LC 89-84223. 192p. (gr. 3-7). 1991. pap. 3.95 (ISBN 0-679-80594-X, Bullseye Bks). Knopf.
Joosse, Barbara M. Dinah's Mad, Bad Wishes. McCully, Emily A., illus. LC 88-884. 32p. (gr. k-3). 1989. 12.95 (ISBN 0-06-023098-3); PLB 12.89 (ISBN 0-06-023099-1). HarpC Child Bks.
—Pieces of the Picture. LC 88-28151. 144p. (gr. 5-7). 1989. 12.95 (ISBN 0-397-32342-5, Lipp Jr Bks); PLB 12.89 (ISBN 0-397-32343-3, Lipp Jr Bks). HarpC Child Bks.
Kandoian, Ellen. Maybe She Forgot. (ps). 1990. 12.95 (ISBN 0-525-65031-8, Cobblehill Bks). Dutton Child Bks.
Kennaley, Lucinda H. My Mom Is Pregnant! Kennaley, Lucinda H., illus. 60p. (Orig.). (ps). 1990. pap. text ed. 9.95 (ISBN 0-9628067-0-6). Thoth MO.
Klevin, Jill R. Turtles Together Forever! Edwards, Linda S., illus. LC 82-70313. 160p. (gr. 4-6). 1982. pap. 9.95 (ISBN 0-385-29045-4); pap. 9.89 (ISBN 0-385-29046-2). Delacorte.
Levine, Abby. What Did Mommy Do Before You? (ps-3). 1990. pap. 3.95 (ISBN 0-14-054215-9, Puffin). Puffin Bks.
Levy, Elizabeth. The Case of the Mind-Reading Mommies. Eagle, Ellen, illus. 1990. pap. 2.95 (ISBN 0-671-69435-9). S&S Trade.

Lewin, Hugh. Jafta's Mother. Kopper, Lisa, illus. LC 82-12863. 24p. (ps-3). 1983. PLB 9.95 (ISBN 0-87614-208-0); pap. 3.95 (ISBN 0-87614-495-4). Carolrhoda Bks.
—Jafta's Mother. Kopper, Lisa, illus. LC 82-12863. 24p. (ps-3). 1983. PLB 9.95 (ISBN 0-87614-208-0); pap. 3.95 (ISBN 0-87614-495-4). Carolrhoda Bks.
—Jafta's Mother. Kopper, Lisa, illus. 24p. (ps-3). 1989. pap. 3.95 (ISBN 0-685-24885-2, First Ave Edns). Lerner Pubns.
McDaniel, Lurlene. Mother, Please Don't Die. 144p. (Orig.). (gr. 6-8). 1988. pap. 2.95 (ISBN 0-87406-288-8). Willowisp Pr.
Marriott, Janice. Letters to Lesley. LC 90-41406. 144p. (gr. 4-9). PLB 7.99 (ISBN 0-679-91595-8, Bullseye Bks); pap. 3.50 (ISBN 0-679-81595-3, Bullseye Bks). Knopf.
Marron, Carol A. Mother Told Me So. Karn, George, illus. LC 83-7271. 32p. (gr. k-3). 1983. PLB 14.65g (ISBN 0-940742-26-8). Raintree Pubs.
Marsh, Carole. If My Mama Ran the World. 1989. 19.95 (ISBN 1-55609-287-3); pap. 14.95 (ISBN 0-318-37385-8). Gallopade Pub Group.
Martin, Ann M. Kristy & the Mother's Day Surprise. 1989. pap. 2.75 (ISBN 0-590-42002-X). Scholastic Inc.
May, Robert E. Poppa & Elizabeth: A Bobtail Romance. McQueen, Don, illus. 32p. (Orig.). (ps-3). 1988. PLB 11.89 (ISBN 0-87397-314-3); pap. 5.95 (ISBN 0-87397-313-5). Strode.
Mazer, Harry. Someone's Mother Is Missing. 1990. 14.95 (ISBN 0-385-30161-8). Delacorte.
Merriam, Eve. Mommies At Work. (ps-3). 1991. pap. 2.25 (ISBN 0-671-73275-7). S&S Trade.
Mire, Betty. It's Funny How Things Change. LC 84-1164. 155p. (gr. 5-10). 1985. 11.95 (ISBN 0-88289-431-5). Pelican.
Moms Are Special. 1988. bds. 3.95 (ISBN 1-55513-999-X, Chariot Bks). Cook.
My Mother. 22p. (gr. k-3). 1980. pap. 3.00 (ISBN 0-89744-215-6, Pub. by Children's Bk India). Auromere.
Nixon, Joan L. Star Baby. (gr. 7 up). 1989. 14.95 (ISBN 0-553-05838-X, Starfire). Bantam.
O'Connor, Frank. My Oedipus Complex. Delessert, Etienne, illus. LC 85-32526. 40p. (gr. 4 up). 1986. PLB 10.95s.p. (ISBN 0-88682-062-6); PLB 15.65 (ISBN 0-685-12413-4). Creative Ed.
O'Neal, Zibby. A Formal Feeling. LC 82-2018. (Illus.). 168p. (gr. 7 up). 1982. pap. 12.95 (ISBN 0-670-32488-4). Viking Child Bks.
Ormerod, Jan. Mom's Home. Ormerod, Jan, illus. LC 87-2712. 24p. (ps). 1987. 5.95 (ISBN 0-688-07274-7). Lothrop.
Oxenbury, Helen. Mother's Helper. LC 81-68773. 14p. (ps-k). 1982. bds. 3.50 (ISBN 0-8037-5425-6). Dial Bks Young.
Paris, Lena. Mom Is Single. Christianson, Mark, illus. LC 79-22585. 32p. (gr. k-3). 1980. PLB 13.27 (ISBN 0-516-01477-3). Childrens.
Porte, Barbara A. Harry's Mom. Abolafia, Yossi, illus. LC 84-25955. 48p. (gr. 1-4). 1985. 10.25 (ISBN 0-688-04817-X); lib. bdg. 10.88 (ISBN 0-688-04818-8). Greenwillow.
Porter-Gaylord, Laurel. I Love My Mommy Because... Wolff, Ashley, illus. LC 90-2792. 24p. (ps). 1991. 5.95 (ISBN 0-525-44625-7, DCB). Dutton Child Bks.
Poulin, Stephane. My Mother's Love. Poulin, Stephane, illus. 32p. (ps-1). 1990. 15.95 (ISBN 1-55037-149-5); pap. 5.95 (ISBN 1-55037-148-7). Firefly Bks Ltd.
Reuter, Margaret. My Mother Is Blind. Lanier, Philip, illus. LC 78-12645. 32p. (ps-3). 1979. PLB 13.27 (ISBN 0-516-02021-8). Childrens.
Rinaldi, Ann. But in the Fall I'm Leaving. LC 84-48740. 224p. (gr. 7 up). 1985. 12.95 (ISBN 0-8234-0560-5). Holiday.
Riskind, Mary. Follow That Mom. LC 86-20049. (gr. 4-6). 1987. 12.95 (ISBN 0-395-41553-5). HM.
Robinson, Mary. Give It up, Mom. (gr. 5-9). 1989. 13.95 (ISBN 0-395-49700-0). HM.
Robinson, Nancy K. Mom, You're Fired! Arno, Ed, illus. 112p. (Orig.). (gr. 4-6). 1983. pap. 2.50 (ISBN 0-590-40294-3, Apple Paperbacks). Scholastic Inc.
—Mom, You're Fired! 144p. (gr. 4-6). pap. 2.50 (ISBN 0-590-41058-X, Apple Paperbacks). Scholastic Inc.
—Mom, You're Fired! 112p. (gr. 3-7). 1991. pap. 2.75 (ISBN 0-590-42335-5). Scholastic Inc.
Rose, Deborah L. Meredith's Mother Takes the Train. Levine, Abby, ed. Trivas, Irene, illus. 24p. (ps-k). 1990. 10.95 (ISBN 0-8075-5061-2). A Whitman.
Ruckman, Ivy. Who Invited the Undertaker? LC 89-1865. 192p. (gr. 3-7). 1989. 13.95 (ISBN 0-690-04832-7, Crowell Jr Bks); PLB 13.89 (ISBN 0-690-04834-3, Crowell Jr Bks). HarpC Child Bks.
Sachs, Marilyn. Fourteen. LC 82-18209. 128p. (gr. 4-9). 1983. 10.95 (ISBN 0-525-44044-5, DCB). Dutton Child Bks.
Sawicki, Norma J. Something for Mom. Weston, Martha, illus. LC 86-34421. 32p. (ps-1). 1987. PLB 12.88 (ISBN 0-688-05590-7). Lothrop.
Shahan, Sherry. Operation Dump the Boyfriend. (Illus.). 96p. (gr. 3-6). 1988. 1.00 (ISBN 0-87406-287-X, 22-15397-9). Willowisp Pr.
Shannon, George. The Surprise. Aruego, Jose & Dewey, Ariane, illus. LC 83-1434. 32p. (gr. k-3). 1983. 13.95 (ISBN 0-688-02313-4). Greenwillow.
Sharmat, Marjorie W. Hooray for Mother's Day! Wallner, John, illus. LC 85-14146. 32p. (gr. k-3). 1986. 14.95g (ISBN 0-8234-0588-5). Holiday.
Sheppherd, Joseph. Mama Buzurg Is Coming. Reed, Susan, illus. 32p. 1986. pap. 4.50 (ISBN 0-85398-219-8). G Ronald Pub.
Shine, Michael. Mama Llama's Pajamas. Villegas, Carene, illus. 45p. (Orig.). (ps-3). 1990. pap. 8.95 (ISBN 0-945265-32-8). Romar Bks.
Shreve, Susan. The Revolution of Mary Leary. LC 82-185. 192p. (gr. 5-9). 1982. Knopf.
Smith, Marya. Across the Creek. 164p. (gr. 5 up). 1989. 13.95 (ISBN 1-55970-041-6). Arcade Pub Inc.
Snyder, Zilpha K. The Birds of Summer. LC 82-13756. 204p. (gr. 7 up). 1983. 10.95 (ISBN 0-689-30967-8, Atheneum Childrens Bks). Macmillan Child Grp.
Stanek, Muriel. I Speak English for My Mom. Tucker, Kathleen, ed. Friedman, Judith, illus. 32p. (gr. 2-5). 1989. 10.95 (ISBN 0-8075-3659-8). A Whitman.
Steiner, Michael P., Sr. Not a Wicked Stepmother. (Orig.). (gr. 4 up). 1990. pap. 7.95 (ISBN 1-879417-00-6). Stern & Stern.
Tobias, Tobi. The Dawdlewalk. Swofford, Jeanette, illus. LC 81-21666. 32p. (ps-2). 1983. PLB 9.95 (ISBN 0-87614-190-4). Carolrhoda Bks.
Tolan, Stephanie S. The Great Skinner Strike. LC 82-17992. 120p. (gr. 7 up). 1983. 12.95 (ISBN 0-02-789360-X, Mcmillan Child Bk). Macmillan Child Grp.
Tolles, Martha. Marrying Off Mom. 1990. pap. 2.75 (ISBN 0-590-42843-8). Scholastic Inc.
Ungerer, Tomi. No Kiss for Mother. (gr. 4-7). 1991. 13.00 (ISBN 0-385-30384-X); PLB 13.99 (ISBN 0-385-30385-8). Delacorte.
Van Leeuwen, Jean. Dear Mom You're Ruining My Life. (gr. 4 up). 1990. pap. 3.95 (ISBN 0-14-034386-5, Puffin). Puffin Bks.
Waber, Bernard. Lyle Finds His Mother. LC 74-5336. (Illus.). 48p. (gr. k-3). 1974. 13.95 (ISBN 0-395-19489-X). HM.
Wells, Rosemary. Hazel's Amazing Mother. Wells, Rosemary, illus. LC 85-1447. (ps-2). 1989. 3.95 (ISBN 0-8037-0703-7). Dial Bks Young.
Weyland, Jack. Sara, Whenever I Hear Your Name. LC 86-29071. 152p. 1987. 9.95 (ISBN 0-87579-070-4). Deseret Bk.
Williams, Suzanne. Mommy Doesn't Know My Name. Shachat, Andrew, illus. 48p. (ps). 1990. 13.95 (ISBN 0-395-54228-6). HM.
Williams, Vera B. A Chair for My Mother. LC 81-7010. (ps-3). 1988. pap. 7.95 incl. cassette (ISBN 0-688-08400-1, Mulberry). Morrow.
Winthrop, Elizabeth. A Very Noisy Girl. LC 90-39175. (Illus.). 32p. (ps-3). 1991. PLB 14.95 (ISBN 0-8234-0858-2). Holiday.
Wynot, Jillian. The Mother's Day Sandwich. Chambliss, Maxie, illus. LC 89-35649. 32p. (ps-2). 1990. 14.95 (ISBN 0-531-05857-3); PLB 14.99 (ISBN 0-531-08457-4). Orchard Bks Watts.
Zeder, Suzan. Mother Hicks. 68p. (Orig.). (gr. k-3). 1986. pap. 5.50 playscript (ISBN 0-87602-263-8). Anchorage.
Ziefert, Harriet. Surprise! Morgan, Mary, illus. (Orig.). (ps-3). 1988. pap. 3.50 (ISBN 0-14-050814-7, Puffin). Puffin Bks.
Zindel, Bonnie & Zindel, Paul. A Star for the Latecomer. LC 79-1786. 192p. (gr. 7 up). 1980. 12.95 (ISBN 0-06-026847-6). HarpC Child Bks.
Zindel, Paul. I Love My Mother. Melo, John, illus. LC 74-20389. 32p. (gr. k-3). 1975. PLB 13.89 (ISBN 0-06-026836-0). HarpC Child Bks.
Zindel, Paul & Zindel, Bonnie. A Star for the Latecomer. 160p. (gr. 6 up). 1985. pap. 2.50 (ISBN 0-553-25578-9). Bantam.
Zolotow, Charlotte. Say It! Stevenson, James, illus. LC 79-25115. 24p. (gr. k-3). 1980. PLB 14.88 (ISBN 0-688-84276-3). Greenwillow.

MOTHERS–POETRY

Schlein, Miriam. Way Mothers Are. Lasker, Joe, illus. LC 63-13332. (ps-2). 1963. PLB 12.95 (ISBN 0-8075-8692-7). A Whitman.

MOTHER'S DAY

Moncure, Jane B. Our Mother's Day Book. Rev. ed. Lexa, Susan, illus. LC 86-29980. (ps-3). 1987. PLB 11.97 (ISBN 0-89565-346-X). Childs World.

MOTHS

see also Butterflies; Caterpillars; Silkworms

Butterflies & Moths. (Illus.). 32p. (ps-1). 1986. pap. 1.25 (ISBN 0-8431-1523-8). Price Stern.
Cook, David. Small World of Butterflies & Moths. LC 80-85051. (gr. k-3). 1981. PLB 10.40 (ISBN 0-531-03454-2). Watts.
Cox & Cork. Butterflies & Moths. (gr. 2-5). 1980. PLB 11.96 (ISBN 0-88110-073-0); pap. 3.95 (ISBN 0-86020-477-4). EDC.
Gattis, L. S., III. Butterflies & Moths for Pathfinders: A Basic Youth Enrichment Skill Honor Packet. (Illus.). 20p. (Orig.). (gr. 5 up). 1987. pap. 5.00 tchr's. ed. (ISBN 0-936241-31-4). Cheetah Pub.
Jourdan, Eveline. Butterflies & Moths Around the World. LC 80-20086. (Illus.). 108p. (gr. 5 up). 1981. PLB 10.95 (ISBN 0-8225-0567-3). Lerner Pubns.
Mitchell, Robert & Zim, Herbert S. Butterflies & Moths. Durenceau, Andre, illus. (gr. 5 up). 1964. PLB write for info. (ISBN 0-307-24052-5); pap. write for info. (Golden Pr). Western Pub.
Morris, Dean. Butterflies & Moths. rev. ed. LC 87-16666. (Illus.). 48p. (gr. 2-6). 1987. PLB 17.32 (ISBN 0-8172-3204-4). Raintree Pubs.
Porter, Keith. Discovering Butterflies & Moths. LC 85-73664. (Illus.). 48p. (gr. 4-9). 1986. PLB 11.90 (ISBN 0-531-18055-7, Pub. by Bookwright). Watts.
—Discovering Butterflies & Moths. (Illus.). 48p. (gr. 2 up). 1990. pap. 4.95 (ISBN 0-531-18364-5). Watts.
Rowan, James P. Butterflies & Moths. LC 83-7216. (Illus.). 48p. (gr. k-4). 1983. PLB 14.60 (ISBN 0-516-01692-X); pap. 4.95 (ISBN 0-516-41692-8). Childrens.
Sabin, Louis. Amazing World of Butterflies & Moths. Helmer, Jean C., illus. LC 81-7504. 32p. (gr. 2-4). 1982. PLB 10.89 (ISBN 0-89375-560-5); pap. text ed. 2.95 (ISBN 0-89375-561-3); cassette 9.95 (ISBN 0-685-04943-4). Troll Assocs.
Still, John. Amazing Butterflies & Moths. Young, Jerry, photos by. LC 90-19234. (Illus.). 32p. (Orig.). (gr. 1-5). 1991. PLB 9.99 (ISBN 0-679-91515-X); pap. 6.95 (ISBN 0-679-81515-5). Knopf.
Watts, Barrie. Moth. (Illus.). 25p. (gr. k-4). 1991. PLB 9.98 (ISBN 0-382-24218-1); 6.95 (ISBN 0-382-24220-3). Silver Pr.

MOTION

see also Force and Energy; Mechanics; Speed

Althea. What Makes Things Move? Green, Robina, illus. LC 90-10924. 32p. (gr. k-3). 1990. PLB 10.89 (ISBN 0-8167-2124-6); pap. text ed. 2.95 (ISBN 0-8167-2125-4). Troll Assocs.
Ardley, Neil. Making Things Move. (Illus.). 32p. (gr. 4-6). 1984. PLB 11.90 (ISBN 0-531-03771-1). Watts.
—Muscles to Machines: Projects with Movement. 1990. PLB 11.90 (ISBN 0-531-17200-7). Watts.
Cobb, Vicki. Why Doesn't the Earth Fall Up? And Other Not Such Dumb Questions about Motion. Enik, Ted, illus. LC 88-11108. 40p. (gr. 2-5). 1989. 12.95 (ISBN 0-525-67253-2, Lodestar Bks). Dutton Child Bks.
Jennings, Terry. Bouncing & Rolling. Franklin Watts Ltd., ed. Anstey, David, illus. 24p. (gr. k-3). 1988. PLB 10.40 (ISBN 0-531-17085-3, Gloucester Pr). Watts.
—Floating & Sinking. Franklin Watts Ltd., ed. Anstey, David, illus. 24p. (gr. k-3). 1988. PLB 10.40 (ISBN 0-531-17086-1, Gloucester Pr). Watts.
Kerrod, Robin. Moving Things. (Illus.). 56p. (gr. 3-5). 1987. 14.95 (ISBN 0-382-09422-0). Silver Burdett Pr.
Motion. (Illus.). 88p. (gr. 7-12). 1990. 15.70 (ISBN 0-941008-98-3). Tops Learning.
Ross, Michael E. What Makes Everything Go? 94p. (gr. k-2). 1979. pap. 3.95 (ISBN 0-939666-19-7). Yosemite Assn.
Walpole, Brenda. Movement. (Illus.). 40p. (gr. 4-6). 1987. lib. bdg. 12.90 (ISBN 0-531-19027-7, Gloucester Pr). Watts.
Watson, Philip. Super Motion. Scruton, Clive & Falconer, Elizabeth, illus. LC 82-80990. 48p. (gr. 3-6). 1983. PLB 11.88 (ISBN 0-688-00971-9). Lothrop.

MOTION–POETRY

McCracken, Elizabeth, ed. To Mother: An Anthology of Mother Verse. Wiggin, Kate D., intro. by. LC 17-13752. (Illus.). (gr. 7-12). 1976. Repr. of 1917 ed. 17.50x (ISBN 0-89609-051-5). Roth Pub Inc.

MOTION PICTURE CARTOONS

Disney, Walt, Productions Staff. The Aristocats. LC 73-15626. (Illus.). 48p. (ps-2). 1974. 5.95 (ISBN 0-394-82553-5, Random Juv); lib. bdg. 4.99 (ISBN 0-394-92553-X). Random.
—The Sorcerer's Apprentice. LC 73-9891. (Illus.). 48p. (ps-2). 1974. 6.95 (ISBN 0-394-82551-9, Random Juv); lib. bdg. 4.99 (ISBN 0-394-92551-3). Random.
—Walt Disney Productions Presents "The Rescuers" LC 76-54412. (Illus.). (ps-2). 1977. 6.95 (ISBN 0-394-83456-9, Random Juv); lib. bdg. 4.99 (ISBN 0-394-93456-3). Random.
Geis, Darlene, ed. Walt Disney's Treasury of Children's Classics. (Illus.). (gr. 5 up). 1978. 29.95 (ISBN 0-8109-0812-3). Abrams.

MOTION PICTURE INDUSTRY

Belgrano, Giovanni. Let's Make a Movie. LC 72-90235. (Illus.). 48p. (gr. 4-9). 1973. 9.95 (ISBN 0-87592-028-4). Scroll Pr.
Borie, Marcia & Wilkerson, Tichi. Hollywood Legends: The Golden Years of the Hollywood Reporter. 2nd ed. (Illus.). 350p. (gr. 7 up). 1988. pap. 14.95 (ISBN 0-942139-03-8). Tale Weaver.
Ruth, Marianne & Locke, Raymond F. Cruel City. LC 90-52813. (Illus.). 1991. 19.95 (ISBN 0-915677-48-2). Roundtable Pub.
Schwartz, Perry. Making Movies. (Illus.). 80p. (gr. 5 up). 1989. 13.95 (ISBN 0-8225-1635-7). Lerner Pubns.
Vendetti, James. The Theatre Student & FilmMaking. (Illus.). (gr. 7-12). PLB 14.95 (ISBN 0-8239-0386-9). Rosen Group.

MOTION PICTURE PLAYS

Leaflets of the White Rose: A Filmplay. 125p. (Orig.). 1991. pap. 8.95 (ISBN 1-879710-02-1). Riverside FL.
Ross, Katharine. Movie Storybook. (ps-3). 1990. pap. 69.50 (ISBN 0-679-80705-5, Fodor). McKay.
Rupert & the Frog Song. (Illus.). (ps-2). 3.50 (ISBN 0-7214-1028-6). Ladybird Bks.
Walt Disney's Classic Movie Treasury. (ps-3). Date not set. write for info. (ISBN 0-307-15508-0, Golden Pr). Western Pub.

MOTION PICTURES

Aylesworth, Thomas G. Movie Monsters. LC 75-12997. (Illus.). 80p. (gr. 4-7). 1975. (Lipp Jr Bks); (Lipp Jr Bks). HarpC Child Bks.
—Movie Monsters. LC 75-12997. (Illus.). 80p. (gr. 4-8). 1990. PLB 12.89 (ISBN 0-397-32467-7, Lipp Jr Bks). HarpC Child Bks.
Balcziak, B. Movies. (Illus.). 48p. (gr. 4-8). 1989. lib. bdg. 14.00 (ISBN 0-86592-058-3). Rourke Corp.

Bliss, Sands & Co. Staff. The Magic Moving Picture Book. 32p. (gr. 4 up). 1975. pap. 3.95 (ISBN 0-486-23224-7). Dover.

Bonifer, Michael. The Making of Tron. Ellenshaw, Harrison, illus. 96p. (Orig.). (gr. 1-4). 1982. pap. 7.95 (ISBN 0-671-45575-3, Little Simon). S&S Trade.

Brode, Douglas. Lost Films of the Fifties. (Illus.). 288p. (Orig.). 1988. pap. 15.95 (ISBN 0-8065-1092-7, Citadel Pr). Carol Pub Group.

Cherrell, Gwen. How Movies Are Made. (Illus.). 32p. 1989. 12.95x (ISBN 0-8160-2039-6). Facts on File.

Cohen, Daniel. Masters of Horror. LC 83-14402. (Illus.). 128p. (gr. 6up). 1984. 12.95 (ISBN 0-89919-221-1, Clarion). HM.

Coynik, David. Film: Real to Reel. (Illus.). 273p. (Orig.). (gr. 10-12). 1976. pap. text ed. 11.73 (ISBN 0-88343-304-4); tchr's. manual o.p. 3.40 (ISBN 0-88343-305-2). McDougal-Littell.

Dowd, Ned. That's a Wrap: How Movies Are Made. Horenstein, Henry, photos by. Mamet, David, frwd. by. LC 91-6435. (Illus.). 64p. (gr. 3-7). 1991. PLB 15.00 jacketed (ISBN 0-671-70972-0, S&S BYR). S&S Trade.

Earley, Steven C. An Introduction to American Movies. (Illus.). 337p. (gr. 9-12). 1978. pap. 5.95 (ISBN 0-451-62725-3, Ment). NAL-Dutton.

Fradin, Dennis B. Movies. LC 83-7261. (Illus.). 48p. (gr. k-4). 1983. PLB 14.60 (ISBN 0-516-01699-7). Childrens.

Gibbons, Gail. Lights! Camera! Action!: How a Movie Is Made. Gibbons, Gail, illus. LC 85-47536. 32p. (gr. 1-4). 1985. 13.95 (ISBN 0-690-04476-3, Crowell Jr Bks); PLB 13.89 (ISBN 0-690-04477-1). HarpC Child Bks.

—Lights! Camera! Action! How a Movie Is Made. Gibbons, Gail, illus. LC 85-47536. 32p. (gr. 1-4). 1989. pap. 3.95 (ISBN 0-06-446088-6, Trophy). HarpC Child Bks.

Gleasner, Diana. The Movies. (Illus.). (gr. 4-6). 1983. lib. bdg. 8.85 (ISBN 0-8027-6483-5). Walker & Co.

Hunter, Nigel. The Movies. LC 90-9937. (Illus.). 48p. (gr. 6-11). 1990. PLB 18.60 (ISBN 0-8114-2363-8). Steck-V.

Knight, Arthur. The Liveliest Art: A Panoramic History of the Movies. rev. ed. (Illus.). 384p. (gr. 9-12). 1979. pap. 4.95 (ISBN 0-451-62652-4, Ment). NAL-Dutton.

Magill, Frank N., ed. Magill's Cinema Annual, 1989. 600p. (gr. 9-12). 1989. PLB 50.00x (ISBN 0-89356-408-7, Magill Bks). Salem Pr.

Meredith. Films & Special Effects. 32p. (gr. 6up). PLB 13.96 (ISBN 0-88110-164-8); pap. 5.95 (ISBN 0-86020-749-8). EDC.

Merrison, Tim. Movies. Stefoff, Rebecca, ed. LC 90-3964. (Illus.). 32p. (gr. 4-8). 1991. PLB 17.26 (ISBN 0-944483-94-1). Garrett Ed Corp.

Meyer, Nicholas E. Magic in the Dark: A Young Viewer's History of the Movies. (Illus.). 292p. (gr. 3-11). 1985. 17.95 (ISBN 0-8160-1256-3). Facts on File.

Moore, Douglas. Entertainment: Movies. Baker, Syd, illus. 50p. (Orig.). (gr. 7 up). 1986. pap. text ed. 8.00 (ISBN 0-939990-48-2); incl. cassette 19.00 (ISBN 0-939990-62-8). Intl Linguistics.

Powers, Tom. Horror Movies. (Illus.). 80p. (gr. 5 up). pap. 7.95 (ISBN 0-8225-9570-2). Lerner Pubns.

—Movie Monsters. (Illus.). 80p. (gr. 5 up). Repr. of 1989 ed. 7.95 (ISBN 0-8225-9571-0). Lerner Pubns.

Waskey, Leah. Monster Gallery Color & Story Album. Savee, Mark, illus. 32p. 1973. pap. 3.95 (ISBN 0-8431-1728-1). Price Stern.

MOTION PICTURES–BIOGRAPHY

see also Actors and Actresses

Collins, Tom. Steven Spielberg: Creator of E. T. LC 83-21068. (Illus.). 64p. (gr. 3 up). 1983. PLB 10.95 (ISBN 0-87518-249-6, Dillon). Macmillan Child Grp.

Erlanger, Ellen. Jane Fonda: More Than a Movie Star. LC 83-27542. (Illus.). 56p. (gr. 4 up). 1984. PLB 9.95 (ISBN 0-8225-0485-5). Lerner Pubns.

Hargrove, Jim. Steven Spielberg: Amazing Filmmaker. LC 87-13249. (Illus.). 128p. (gr. 4-8). 1988. PLB 17.27 (ISBN 0-516-03263-1). Childrens.

McAllister. Steven Spielberg, Reading Level 2. (Illus.). 24p. (gr. 1-4). Date not set. PLB 12.33 (ISBN 0-86592-427-9). Rourke Corp.

MOTION PICTURES–FICTION

Bond, Michael. Paddington on Screen. Macey, Barry, illus. (gr. 2-5). 1982. 13.95 (ISBN 0-395-32950-7). HM.

Bradman, Tony. Dilly & the Horror Movie. Hellard, Susan, illus. 25p. (gr. 2-5). 1989. pap. 9.95 (ISBN 0-670-82351-1). Viking Child Bks.

Byars, Betsy. The Two-Thousand-Pound Goldfish. LC 81-48652. 160p. (gr. 5 up). 1982. 14.95 (ISBN 0-06-020889-9); PLB 14.89 (ISBN 0-06-020890-2). HarpC Child Bks.

Conaway, Judith, adapted by. King Kong. Berenstain, Michael, illus. LC 82-15078. 96p. (gr. 2-5). 1983. 3.95 (ISBN 0-394-85617-1); lib. bdg. 4.99 (ISBN 0-394-95617-6). Random.

Eller, Scott. Twenty-First Century Fox. (Illus.). (gr. 12 up). 1989. pap. 12.95 (ISBN 0-590-41939-0). Scholastic Inc.

Hughes, Dean. Nutty, the Movie Star. LC 88-36614. 144p. (gr. 3-7). 1989. 12.95 (ISBN 0-689-31509-0, Atheneum Child Bk). Macmillan Child Grp.

Kendall, Jane. Miranda & the Movies. Kendall, Jane, illus. LC 89-1515. 224p. (gr. 6 up). 1989. 14.95 (ISBN 0-517-57301-6); PLB 14.99 (ISBN 0-517-57357-1). Crown.

Pfeffer, Susan B. Take Two & Rolling. 192p. (Orig.). (gr. 5 up). 1985. pap. 2.50 (ISBN 0-448-47737-8, G&D). Putnam Pub Group.

Streatfeild, Noel. Movie Shoes. 288p. (Orig.). (gr. 4-7). pap. 3.25 (ISBN 0-440-45815-3, YB). Dell.

Wolfe, Elle. Palm Beach Prep, No. 4: Screen Test. (gr. 4-7). 1990. pap. 2.95 (ISBN 0-8125-1062-3). Tor Bks.

MOTION PICTURES–PLAY WRITING

see Motion Picture Plays

MOTOR BOATS

see Motorboats

MOTOR CARS

see Automobiles

MOTOR CYCLES

see Motorcycles

MOTOR TRUCKS

see Trucks

MOTORBOATS

Andersen, T. J. Power Boat Racing. LC 87-30502. (Illus.). 48p. (gr. 5-6). 1988. PLB 10.95 (ISBN 0-89686-359-X, Crestwood Hse). Macmillan Child Grp.

Jackson, Al & Tardy, Gene. Drag Boat Racing: The National Championships. (Illus.). 48p. (gr. 3-7). 1973. PLB 6.89x (ISBN 0-914844-05-9); pap. 3.95 (ISBN 0-914844-06-7). J Alden.

MOTORCYCLES

Armitage, Barry. Motorcycles. LC 88-16964. (Illus.). 32p. (gr. 2-8). 1988. 12.95 (ISBN 0-8069-6892-3). Sterling.

—Motorcycles! (Illus.). 32p. (Orig.). (gr. 3-8). 1988. pap. 3.95 (ISBN 0-87406-306-X). Willowisp Pr.

Barrett, N. S. Trail Bikes. 1990. pap. 3.95 (ISBN 0-531-15173-5). Watts.

Barrett, Norman. Bicicross. (SPA., Illus.). 32p. (gr. k-4). 1990. PLB 11.40 (ISBN 0-531-07904-X). Watts.

—Motorcycles. (Illus.). 32p. (gr. 2 up). 1991. pap. 3.95 (ISBN 0-531-15142-5). Watts.

Barrett, Norman S. BMX Bikes. (Illus.). (gr. 3-6). 1989. pap. 3.95 (ISBN 0-531-15138-7). Watts.

BMX Photo Fact Book. (Illus.). (gr. k-9). 1989. pap. 1.95 (ISBN 0-318-36480-8). Scholastic Inc.

Chirinian, Alain. Motorcycles. (Illus.). 64p. (gr. 5-9). 1989. PLB 10.98 (ISBN 0-671-68029-3); PLB 8.24s.p.; pap. 4.95 (ISBN 0-671-68034-X); pap. 3.71s.p. Messner.

Coombs, Charles I. BMX: A Guide to Bicycle Motocross. LC 82-20904. (Illus.). 144p. (gr. 4-6). 1983. 13.95 (ISBN 0-688-01867-X). Morrow Jr Bks.

Estrem, Paul. ATV's. LC 87-19900. (Illus.). 48p. (gr. 5-6). 1987. PLB 10.95 (ISBN 0-89686-348-4, Crestwood Hse). Macmillan Child Grp.

—BMX's. LC 87-15554. (Illus.). 48p. (gr. 5-6). 1987. PLB 10.95 (ISBN 0-89686-349-2, Crestwood Hse). Macmillan Child Grp.

—Motocross Cycles. LC 87-16115. (Illus.). 48p. (gr. 5-6). PLB 10.95 (ISBN 0-89686-354-9, Crestwood Hse). Macmillan Child Grp.

Flint, Russ. All about Motorcycles. LC 90-9826. (Illus.). 16p. (ps-2). 1990. PLB 9.95 (ISBN 0-8368-0424-4). Gareth Stevens Inc.

Griffin, John Q. Motorcycles on the Move. LC 75-17435. (Illus.). 52p. (gr. 4-9). 1976. PLB 9.95 (ISBN 0-8225-0414-6). Lerner Pubns.

Holder, William G. Monster 4-Wheelers. LC 87-15733. (Illus.). 48p. (gr. 5-6). 1987. PLB 10.95 (ISBN 0-89686-353-0, Crestwood Hse). Macmillan Child Grp.

Jaspersohn, William. Motorcycle: The Making of a Harley-Davidson. 127p. (gr. 10-12). 1984. 14.95 (ISBN 0-316-45817-1). Little.

Jefferis, David. Trailbikes. (Illus.). 32p. (gr. k-3). 1984. lib. bdg. 7.99 (ISBN 0-531-04709-1). Watts.

Jeffries, David. Trail Bikes & Motorcross. 1990. PLB 12.90 (ISBN 0-531-19076-5). Watts.

Kerrod, Robin. Motorcycles. (Illus.). 32p. (gr. 5-6). 1989. PLB 11.90 (ISBN 0-531-17152-3). Watts.

Motorcross Cycles. 48p. (gr. 3-4). 1989. PLB 10.95 (ISBN 0-685-26377-0). Capstone Pr.

Motorcycles. 48p. (gr. 3-4). 1989. PLB 10.95 (ISBN 0-685-26378-9). Capstone Pr.

Mundale, Susan. Mopeds: The Go-Everywhere Bikes. LC 79-165511. (Illus.). 48p. (gr. 4-9). 1979. PLB 9.95 (ISBN 0-8225-0428-6). Lerner Pubns.

Naden, C. J. Cycle Chase. LC 79-64638. (Illus.). 32p. (gr. 4-9). 1980. PLB 10.79 (ISBN 0-89375-249-5); pap. 2.95 (ISBN 0-89375-263-0). Troll Assocs.

—High Gear. LC 79-64637. (Illus.). 32p. (gr. 4-9). 1980. PLB 10.79 (ISBN 0-89375-248-7); pap. 2.95 (ISBN 0-89375-262-2). Troll Assocs.

—I Can Read About Motorcycles. LC 78-74657. (Illus.). (gr. 3-6). 1979. pap. 1.95 (ISBN 0-89375-212-6). Troll Assocs.

—Motorcycle Challenge, Trials & Races. LC 79-52178. (Illus.). 32p. (gr. 4-9). 1980. PLB 10.79 (ISBN 0-89375-252-5); pap. 2.95 (ISBN 0-89375-253-3). Troll Assocs.

—Rough Rider. LC 79-52177. (Illus.). 32p. (gr. 4-9). 1980. PLB 10.79 (ISBN 0-89375-250-9); pap. 2.95 (ISBN 0-89375-251-7). Troll Assocs.

Norman, C. J. The Picture World of Motorcycles. (Illus.). 32p. (gr. k-4). 1989. PLB 11.40 (ISBN 0-531-10727-2). Watts.

Price, Stern & Sloan Staff. Motorcycles. (Illus.). 32p. (gr. 7-12). 1987. pap. 2.95 (ISBN 0-8431-4287-1). Price Stern.

Rae, Rusty. The World's Biggest Motorcycle Race: The Daytona 200. LC 77-92297. (Illus.). 56p. (gr. 4-9). 1978. PLB 9.95 (ISBN 0-8225-0422-7). Lerner Pubns.

Smith, Don. The Baja Run: Racing Fury. LC 75-23412. (Illus.). 32p. (gr. 5-10). 1976. PLB 10.79 (ISBN 0-89375-000-X); pap. 2.95 (ISBN 0-89375-016-6). Troll Assocs.

Spencer, Jeffrey E. Total Training for Motocross. Reese, Rex W., ed. (Illus.). 250p. (Orig.). 1983. lib. bdg. 19.95 (ISBN 0-317-05978-5). Total Pub.

Stambler, Irwin. Off-Roading: Racing & Riding. (Illus.). 128p. (gr. 7 up). 1984. 10.95 (ISBN 0-399-21144-6, Putnam). Putnam Pub Group.

Stewart, Gail. Motorcycle Racing. LC 87-33198. (Illus.). 48p. (gr. 5-6). 1988. PLB 10.95 (ISBN 0-89686-360-3, Crestwood Hse). Macmillan Child Grp.

Tardy, Gene & Jackson, Al. Motorcycle: Cross-Country Racing. (Illus.). (gr. 3-7). 1974. PLB 6.89x (ISBN 0-914844-00-8). J Alden.

—Motorcycle: Grand Prix Racing. (Illus.). (gr. 3-7). 1974. PLB 6.89x (ISBN 0-914844-01-6). J Alden.

Wood, Tim. Motorcycling. Fairclough, Chris, photos by. LC 89-50200. (Illus.). 32p. (gr. k-3). 1989. PLB 10.40 (ISBN 0-531-10827-9). Watts.

Yaw, John & Rae, Rusty. Grand National Championship Races. LC 77-92293. (Illus.). 48p. (gr. 4-9). 1978. PLB 9.95 (ISBN 0-8225-0424-3). Lerner Pubns.

MOTORCYCLES–FICTION

Christopher, Matt. Dirt Bike Racer. Bomzer, Barry, illus. LC 79-745. (gr. 4-6). 1986. 13.95 (ISBN 0-316-13977-7); pap. 3.95 (ISBN 0-316-14053-8). Little.

Frances, Marian. Witch on a Motorcycle. new ed. (Illus.). (gr. 3-4). 1972. pap. 1.95 (ISBN 0-89375-047-6). Troll Assocs.

Hewett, Joan. Motorcycle on Patrol. (gr. 4-7). 1990. pap. 5.95 (ISBN 0-395-54789-X, Clarion Bks). HM.

Moran, Tom. Bicycle Motocross Racing. (Illus.). 48p. (gr. 4-9). 1985. PLB 9.95 (ISBN 0-8225-0510-X). Lerner Pubns.

St. George, Mark. The Wolfpack. 210p. (Orig.). 1990. 14.95 (ISBN 0-9620541-2-7); pap. 4.95 (ISBN 0-9620541-3-5). Proteus LA.

Schulz, Charles M. You're a Good Sport, Charlie Brown. LC 76-8128. (Illus.). (gr. 1 up). 1976. 4.95 (ISBN 0-394-83297-3, Random Juv). Random.

MOTORING

see Automobiles–Touring

MOTORS

see Engines

MOTT, LUCRETIA (COFFIN) 1793-1880

Sawyer, Kem K. Lucretia Mott: Friend of Justice. Carter, Rosalynn & Carter, Rosalynncontrib. by. LC 91-70822. (Illus.). 48p. (gr. 4-8). 1991. 17.95g (ISBN 1-878668-04-8); pap. 7.95 (ISBN 1-878668-08-0). Disc Enter Ltd.

MOUNDS AND MOUND BUILDERS

Silverberg, Robert. The Moundbuilders. LC 85-25953. 276p. 1986. pap. 7.95 (ISBN 0-8214-0839-9). Ohio U Pr.

MOUNT RUSHMORE, SOUTH DAKOTA

St. George, Judith. The Mount Rushmore Story. LC 84-24963. (Illus.). 128p. (gr. 5 up). 1985. 13.95 (ISBN 0-399-21117-9, Putnam). Putnam Pub Group.

MOUNT VERNON, VIRGINIA

Miller, Natalie. The Story of Mount Vernon. LC 82-12217. (Illus.). 32p. (gr. 2-5). 1965. PLB 13.27 (ISBN 0-516-04624-1). Childrens.

MOUNTAIN CLIMBING

see Mountaineering

MOUNTAIN LIFE–SOUTHERN STATES

Althea. Mountain Homes. (Illus.). 24p. (gr. 1 up). 1985. pap. 3.95 (ISBN 0-521-31620-0). Cambridge U Pr.

MOUNTAIN LIFE–SOUTHERN STATES–FICTION

Dragonwagon, Crescent. The Itch Book. Mahler, Joseph, illus. LC 89-2695. 32p. (gr. k-3). 1990. 13.95 (ISBN 0-02-733121-0, Mcmillan Child Bk). Macmillan Child Grp.

Smyers, Jacquelyn. The Time a Cloud Came into the Cabin (A Mountain Tale for Boys) Smyers, Carrie M., illus. LC 86-50627. 12p. (Orig.). (ps-6). 1986. pap. 3.98 (ISBN 0-9615130-3-9). Very Idea.

—The Time a Cloud Came into the Cabin (A Mountain Tale for Girls) Smyers, Carrie M., illus. LC 86-50626. 12p. (Orig.). (ps-6). 1986. pap. 3.98 (ISBN 0-9615130-4-7). Very Idea.

White, Alana. Come Next Spring. 176p. (gr. 4-8). 1990. 13.95 (ISBN 0-395-52593-4). HM.

MOUNTAINEERING

Allen, Linda B. High Mountain Challenge: A Guide for Young Mountaineers. Trafton, Mary, illus. LC 89-16. 224p. (Orig.). (gr. 6-12). 1989. pap. 9.95 (ISBN 0-910146-98-5). AMC Books.

Gleasner. Rock Climbing. 1980. 7.95 (ISBN 0-679-20925-5). McKay.

Hargrove, Jim & Johnson, S. A. Mountain Climbing. LC 82-21690. (Illus.). 48p. (gr. 4-9). 1983. PLB 9.95 (ISBN 0-8225-0505-3). Lerner Pubns.

Hyden, Tom & Anderson, Tim. Rock Climbing Is for Me. Wolfe, Bob & Wolfe, Diane, illus. LC 84-2906. 48p. (gr. 2-5). 1984. PLB 8.95 (ISBN 0-8225-1147-9). Lerner Pubns.

Jones, Michael P. & Boldt, Jeanine, eds. The Mountaineer, Vol. 1, No. 1. (Illus.). 42p. 1984. pap. text ed. 4.00 (ISBN 0-89904-017-9). Crumb Elbow Pub.

Rock Climbing. 48p. (gr. 3-4). 1989. PLB 10.95 (ISBN 0-685-26391-6). Capstone Pr.

Updegraff, Imelda & Updegraff, Robert. Mountains & Valleys. (Illus.). (gr. 4 up). 1981. PLB 9.95s.p. (ISBN 0-89813-042-5); PLB 14.25 (ISBN 0-685-11050-8). Creative Ed.

MOUNTAINEERING–FICTION

Ahlbom, Jens. Jonathan of Gull Mountain. Lucas, Barbara, tr. from SWE. Ahlbom, Jens, illus. 32p. (ps up). 1987. 12.95 (ISBN 9-12-957590-7, Pub. by R & S Bks). FS&G.

Branscum, Robbie. Old Blue Tilley. LC 90-6348. 96p. (gr. 5-9). 1991. SBE 11.95 (ISBN 0-02-711931-9, Mcmillan Child Bk). Macmillan Child Grp.

Burch, Robert. Ida Early Comes over the Mountain. 152p. (gr. 3-7). 1982. pap. 2.50 (ISBN 0-380-57091-2, Camelot). Avon.

Catchpole, Clive. Mountains. McIntyre, Brian, illus. LC 83-25273. 32p. (gr. k-4). 1985. pap. 4.95 (ISBN 0-8037-0087-3, 0481-140). Dial Bks Young.

Chetwin, Grace. Gom on Windy Mountain. 1990. pap. 3.50 (ISBN 0-440-20543-3, LFL). Dell.

George, Jean C. My Side of the Mountain. George, Jean C., illus. LC 87-27556. 176p. (gr. 3-7). 1988. 13.95 (ISBN 0-525-44392-4, 01258-370, DCB); pap. 4.95 (ISBN 0-525-44395-9, 0481-140, DCB). Dutton Child Bks.

Gerstein, Mordicai. The Mountains of Tibet. Gerstein, Mordicai, illus. LC 85-45684. 32p. (gr. 2 up). 1987. 13.95 (ISBN 0-06-022144-5); PLB 12.89 (ISBN 0-06-022149-6). HarpC Child Bks.

Gouffe, Marie A. Treasures Beyond the Snows. Sellon, Michael B., illus. LC 77-95392. (gr. 3-9). 1970. 3.75 (ISBN 0-8356-0026-2, Quest). Theos Pub Hse.

Grimm, Jacob, et al. The Glass Mountain. Hogrogian, Nonny, illus. & retold by. LC 84-7848. 40p. (ps-3). 1985. lib. bdg. 12.99 (ISBN 0-394-96724-0). Knopf.

Harwood, Pearl A. Climbing a Mountain with Mr. & Mrs. Bumba. Overlie, George, illus. LC 70-156353. 32p. (gr. k-3). 1971. PLB 4.95 (ISBN 0-8225-0129-5). Lerner Pubns.

Haswell, Peter. Pog Climbs Mount Everest. LC 89-26530. (Illus.). 32p. (ps-1). 1990. 13.95 (ISBN 0-531-05873-5); PLB 13.99 (ISBN 0-531-08473-6). Orchard Bks Watts.

Herz, Roger J. The Old Man of the Mountain. Aldworth, Susan, illus. 1989. pap. text ed. 3.95 (ISBN 0-9619560-1-1). TGNW Pr.

Lobel, Arnold. Ming Lo Moves the Mountain. Lobel, Arnold, illus. LC 81-13327. 32p. (gr. k-3). 1982. PLB 13.88 (ISBN 0-688-00611-6). Greenwillow.

—Ming Lo Moves the Mountain. (ps-3). 1986. pap. 3.95 (ISBN 0-590-42902-7). Scholastic Inc.

Mountain Adventure. (Illus.). (ps-5). 3.50 (ISBN 0-7214-0024-8). Ladybird Bks.

Ramsay, Marjorie B. Nyra. Ramsay, Marjorie B., illus. (gr. 4-7). 1979. 4.95 (ISBN 0-917182-10-3). Triumph Pub.

Roper, Robert. In Caverns of Blue Ice. (gr. 4-7). 1991. 14.95 (ISBN 0-316-75606-7). Little.

Rylant, Cynthia. When I Was Young in the Mountains. LC 81-5359. (Illus.). 32p. (ps-3). 1985. 13.95 (ISBN 0-525-42525-X, 0966-290, DCB); pap. 3.95 (ISBN 0-525-44198-0, DCB). Dutton Child Bks.

Tomkins, Jasper. The Catalog. LC 84-144717. (Illus.). 56p. (gr. k up). 1981. pap. 5.95 (ISBN 0-914676-54-7, Star & Elephant Bks.). Green Tiger Pr.

—Mountains Crack Up! (Illus.). 60p. (gr. k-6). 1987. pap. 5.95 (ISBN 0-88138-093-8). Green Tiger Pr.

Ullman, James R. Banner in the Sky. LC 54-7296. 256p. (gr. 7 up). 1988. 12.95 (ISBN 0-397-32141-4, Lipp Jr Bks); PLB 12.89 (ISBN 0-397-30264-9, Lipp Jr Bks). HarpC Child Bks.

Warner, Gertrude C. Mountain Top Mystery. Cunningham, David, illus. LC 64-7722. 128p. (gr. 3-7). 1990. PLB 9.95 (ISBN 0-8075-5292-5); pap. 3.50 (ISBN 0-8075-5293-3). A Whitman.

MOUNTAINEERS OF THE SOUTH

see Mountain Life–Southern States

MOUNTAINS

see also Mountaineering; Volcanoes;
also names of mountain ranges, e.g. Rocky Mountains; etc.

Arnold, Caroline. A Walk up a Mountain. Brook, Bonnie, ed. Tanz, Freya, illus. 32p. (ps-1). 1990. 4.95 (ISBN 0-671-68667-4); lib. bdg. 9.98 (ISBN 0-671-68663-1). Silver Pr.

Arvetis, Chris. What Is a Mountain? 32p. (ps-3). 1987. 3.95 (ISBN 0-02-689004-6). Checkerboard Pr.

Ask about the Mountains & the Sea. 64p. (gr. 4-5). 1987. PLB 18.25 (ISBN 0-8172-2877-2); pap. 13.27 (ISBN 0-8172-2889-6). Raintree Pubs.

Baker, Susan. First Look at Mountains. LC 91-9420. (Illus.). 32p. (gr. 1-2). 1991. PLB 10.95 (ISBN 0-8368-0703-0). Gareth Stevens Inc.

Barrett, Norman. Montanas. (SPA., Illus.). 32p. (gr. k-4). 1991. PLB 11.40 (ISBN 0-531-07923-6). Watts.

—Mountains. (Illus.). 32p. (gr. 2 up). 1991. pap. 3.95 (ISBN 0-531-24616-7). Watts.

Bender, Lionel. Mountain. (Illus.). 32p. (gr. 3-5). 1989. PLB 11.90 (ISBN 0-531-10646-2). Watts.

Berger, Melvin. As Old As the Hills. Schindler, Stephen D., illus. 32p. (gr. k-4). 1989. PLB 12.90 (ISBN 0-531-10699-3). Watts.

Brandt, Keith. Mountains. Cumings, Art, illus. LC 84-2577. 32p. (gr. 3-6). 1985. PLB 9.49 (ISBN 0-8167-0154-7); pap. text ed. 2.95 (ISBN 0-8167-0155-5). Troll Assocs.

Carlson, Natalie S. The Surprise in the Mountains. Primavera, Elise, illus. LC 82-47716. 32p. (gr. 1-3). 1983. HarpC Child Bks.

Catchpole, Clive. Mountains. McIntyre, Brian, illus. LC 83-25273. 32p. (gr. k-4). 1985. pap. 4.95 (ISBN 0-8037-0087-3, 0481-140). Dial Bks Young.

Curran, Eileen. Mountains & Volcanoes. Watling, James, illus. LC 84-8638. 32p. (gr. k-2). 1985. PLB 10.89 (ISBN 0-8167-0347-7); pap. text ed. 2.95 (ISBN 0-8167-0348-5). Troll Assocs.

George, Jean C. One Day in the Alpine Tundra. Gaffney-Kessel, Walter, illus. LC 82-45590. 48p. (gr. 5-7). 1984. 13.95 (ISBN 0-690-04325-2, Crowell Jr Bks); PLB 13.89 (ISBN 0-690-04326-0, Crowell Jr Bks). HarpC Child Bks.

Hogan, Paula. Fragile Mountains. LC 91-2019. (Illus.). 32p. (gr. 3-4). 1991. PLB 12.95 (ISBN 0-8368-0475-9). Gareth Stevens Inc.

Lobel, Arnold. Ming Lo Moves the Mountain. Lobel, Arnold, illus. 32p. (ps-3). 1986. pap. 2.95 (ISBN 0-590-33994-X, Blue Ribbon Bks); Bk. & Cassette Set. 6.95 (ISBN 0-590-63097-0). Scholastic Inc.

Lye, Keith. Mountains. (Illus.). 48p. (gr. 5-8). 1987. PLB 14.98 (ISBN 0-382-09498-0). Silver Burdett Pr.

Magley, Beverly. The Fire Mountains: The Story of the Cascade Volcanos. Dowden, D. D., illus. LC 88-83884. 32p. (Orig.). (gr. 3-6). 1989. pap. 4.95 (ISBN 0-937959-57-X). Falcon Pr MT.

Marcus, Elizabeth. All about Mountains & Volcanoes. Veno, Joseph, illus. LC 83-4834. 32p. (gr. 3-6). 1984. lib. bdg. 10.59 (ISBN 0-89375-969-4); pap. text ed. 2.95 (ISBN 0-89375-970-8). Troll Assocs.

Morgan, Patricia G. A Mountain Adventure. Herde, Tom, illus. LC 87-3486. 32p. (gr. 3-6). 1988. PLB 10.79 (ISBN 0-8167-1173-9); pap. text ed. 2.95 (ISBN 0-8167-1174-7). Troll Assocs.

Mountains. 32p. (gr. 3-5). 5.95x (ISBN 0-86685-455-X). Intl Bk Ctr.

Rius, Maria & Parramon, J. M. The Mountains. (ps). 1986. 6.95 (ISBN 0-8120-5746-5); pap. 3.95 (ISBN 0-8120-3698-0). Barron.

Stewart, G. In the Mountains. (Illus.). 32p. (gr. 3-8). 1989. lib. bdg. 13.26 (ISBN 0-86592-107-5). Rourke Corp.

Stone, L. Mountains. (Illus.). 48p. (gr. 4-8). 1989. lib. bdg. 14.00 (ISBN 0-86592-448-1). Rourke Corp.

Stone, Lynn M. Mountains. LC 83-7276. (Illus.). 48p. (gr. k-4). 1983. PLB 14.60 (ISBN 0-516-01698-9); pap. 4.95 (ISBN 0-516-41698-7). Childrens.

Uba, Gregory. Is a Mountain Just a Rock. Mitchell, Joanie, illus. LC 83-61882. 260p. (gr. 6-9). 1984. pap. 3.95 (ISBN 0-942610-03-2). Mina Pr.

Wilkes. Mountains. 24p. (gr. 4-6). 1980. (Usborne-Hayes); PLB 11.96 (ISBN 0-88110-079-X); pap. 3.95 (ISBN 0-86020-468-5). EDC.

MOUNTAINS–POETRY

Curtis, Donald A. Fantasy on Sunset Mountain. LC 82-74122. 44p. (Orig.). (gr. 3-12). 1982. pap. 3.50 (ISBN 0-9610284-0-8). D A Curtis.

MOURNING CUSTOMS

see Funeral Rites and Ceremonies

MOUSE

see Mice

MOUTH-ORGAN–FICTION

McCloskey, Robert. Lentil. McCloskey, Robert, illus. (gr. k-3). 1940. pap. 14.95 (ISBN 0-670-42357-2). Viking Child Bks.

MOVIES

see Motion Pictures

MOVING, HOUSEHOLD–FICTION

Amdur, Nikki. One of Us. Sanderson, Ruth, illus. LC 81-65847. (gr. 3-6). 1981. 8.95 (ISBN 0-8037-6742-0); PLB 8.89 (ISBN 0-8037-6743-9). Dial Bks Young.

Balter, Lawrence. Sue Lee's New Neighborhood: Adjusting to a New Move. Schanzer, Roz, illus. 40p. (ps-2). 1989. 5.95 (ISBN 0-8120-6116-0). Barron.

Bulla, Clyde R. A Lion to Guard Us. Chessare, Michele, illus. LC 80-2455. (gr. 2-5). 1981. 12.95 (ISBN 0-690-04096-2, Crowell Jr Bks); PLB 12.89 (ISBN 0-690-04097-0, Crowell Jr Bks). HarpC Child Bks.

Carlstrom, Nancy W. I'm Not Moving, Mama! Wickstrom, Thor, illus. LC 89-38151. 32p. (ps-1). 1990. 13.95 (ISBN 0-02-717286-4, Mcmillan Child Bk). Macmillan Child Grp.

Cartwright, Stephen, illus. Moving House. 16p. (ps up). 1986. 2.95 (ISBN 0-86020-967-9). EDC.

Caseley, Judith. Hurricane Harry. LC 90-13809. (Illus.). 128p. (gr. 1 up). 1991. 13.95 (ISBN 0-688-10027-9). Greenwillow.

Dowling, Paul. Meg & Jack Are Moving. Dowling, Paul, illus. 32p. (ps-3). 1990. 10.95 (ISBN 0-395-53514-X). HM.

—Meg & Jack's New Friends. Dowling, Paul, illus. 32p. (ps-3). 1990. 10.95 (ISBN 0-395-53513-1). HM.

Duncan, Lois. Wonder Kid Meets the Evil Lunch Snatcher. Sanfilippo, Margaret, illus. LC 87-26490. 76p. (gr. 7-10). 1988. 9.95 (ISBN 0-316-19558-8). Little.

Fleming, Alice. Welcome to Grossville. LC 84-23664. 112p. (gr. 5-7). 1985. 12.95 (ISBN 0-684-18289-0, Scribners Young Read). Macmillan Child Grp.

Giff, Patricia R. Matthew Jackson Meets the Wall. 1990. 13.95 (ISBN 0-385-29972-9). Doubleday.

Greenwald, Dorothy. Coping with Moving. Rosen, Ruth, ed. 128p. (gr. 7 up). 1987. PLB 12.95 (ISBN 0-8239-0683-3). Rosen Group.

Haynes, Mary. The Great Pretenders. LC 90-32162. 144p. (gr. 4-7). 1990. 12.95 (ISBN 0-02-743452-4, Bradbury Pr). Macmillan Child Grp.

Haywood, Carolyn. Eddie's Valuable Property. Haywood, Carolyn, illus. LC 74-17499. 192p. (gr. 3-7). 1975. PLB 12.88 (ISBN 0-688-32014-7). Morrow Jr Bks.

Hughes, Shirley. Moving Molly. Hughes, Shirley, illus. 32p. (ps-2). 1982. pap. 3.95 (ISBN 0-13-604579-0, Pub. by Treehouse). P-H.

Jacobson, Jane. City, Sing, for Me: A Country Child Moves to the City. Rowen, Amy, illus. LC 77-11130. 32p. (gr. 1-5). 1978. 16.95 (ISBN 0-87705-358-8). Human Sci Pr.

Kaplan, Marjorie. The Fifteenth Peanut Butter Sandwich. McKeating, Eileen, illus. LC 89-32784. 64p. (gr. 2-4). 1990. 12.95 (ISBN 0-02-749350-4, Four Winds Press). Macmillan Child Grp.

Lowry, Lois. Anastasia Again! De Groat, Diane, illus. 160p. (gr. 3-6). 1981. 13.95 (ISBN 0-395-31147-0). HM.

McKend, H. Moving Gives Me a Stomach Ache. (Illus.). 32p. (ps-8). 1988. pap. 4.95 (ISBN 0-88753-178-4). Firefly Bks Ltd.

Moving Day. 1990. 2.99 (ISBN 0-517-69195-7). Outlet Bk Co.

Mulford, Philippa G. The World Is My Eggshell. LC 85-16198. (gr. 7 up). 1986. pap. 14.95 (ISBN 0-385-29432-8). Delacorte.

Nida, Patricia C. & Heller, Wendy M. The Teenager's Survival Guide to Moving. LC 87-1134. 148p. 1987. pap. 2.95 (ISBN 0-02-044510-5, Collier Young Ad). Macmillan Child Grp.

Park, Barbara. The Kid in the Red Jacket. Schwartz, Anne, ed. Rosenthal, Eileen, designed by. LC 86-20113. 96p. (gr. 3-6). 1987. 9.95 (ISBN 0-394-88189-3); lib. bdg. 9.99 (ISBN 0-394-98189-8). Knopf.

Pearson, Gayle. Fish Friday. LC 85-22922. 192p. (gr. 5-9). 1986. 13.95 (ISBN 0-689-31200-8, Atheneum Child Bk). Macmillan Child Grp.

Petty, Kate. Moving House. Kopper, Lisa, illus. 24p. (gr. 1-3). 1987. PLB 5.29 (ISBN 0-531-17070-5, Gloucester). Watts.

Rocklin, Joanne. Jace the Ace. De Groat, Diane, illus. LC 90-34095. 112p. (gr. 2-6). 1990. 11.95 (ISBN 0-02-777445-7, Mcmillan Child Bk). Macmillan Child Grp.

Scherer, Bonnie. Benjy's New Home. McCracken, Bill, illus. LC 89-60806. 7p. 1989. pap. 1.50 (ISBN 0-9622421-0-1). B Scherer.
Written & published in Billings, MT, BENJY'S NEW HOME is a story about a Cottontail rabbit who discovered that moving can be an exciting new experience. Children of all ages will delight in following Benjy's adventures. About the Author, Benjy's New Home is the first published effort of author Bonnie Scherer, stemming from her own close encounter of a personal kind with a rabbit who took up residence in her front yard. A registered nurse & multi-talented mother of two sons, Bonnie & her husband Jered are residents of Billings, Montana. She has inspired & encouraged many people across the nation with her unpublished (as yet) writings on the trials, tribulations & victories of a cancer patient, also stemming from personal experience. A sequel to Benjy's New Home is already in first draft. About the Illustrator, Bill McCracken has "strewn" his work across America in the form of portraits, illustrations & advertising art. A native of South Dakota & a resident of Florida for many years, Bill & his wife Mony now live in Mobile, Alabama where he is employed as a media minister with Alabama's largest church. Look for The Rescue of Rusty Rabbit by B. Scherer (Easter 1992) dealing with children obeying their parents.
Publisher Provided Annotation.

Schulz, Charles M. Is This Good-Bye, Charlie Brown? Schulz, Charles M., illus. LC 83-17801. 48p. (gr. 1 up). 1984. 4.95 (ISBN 0-394-85953-7, Random Juv); lib. bdg. 6.99 (ISBN 0-394-95953-1). Random.

Silsbee, Peter. The Temptation of Kate. LC 90-1351. 160p. (gr. 6-9). 1990. 13.95 (ISBN 0-02-782761-5, Bradbury Pr). Macmillan Child Grp.

Stolz, Mary. King Emmett the Second. Williams, Garth, illus. LC 89-77506. 56p. (gr. 2 up). 1991. 12.95 (ISBN 0-688-09520-8). Greenwillow.

Szekeres, Cyndy. Moving Day. (Illus.). 24p. (ps-k). 1989. pap. write for info. (ISBN 0-307-11997-1, Pub. by Golden Bks). Western Pub.

Thomas, Jane R. Courage at Indian Deep. LC 83-14404. (Illus.). 128p. (gr. 3-7). 1984. 13.95 (ISBN 0-89919-181-9, Clarion). HM.

Tobias, Tobi. Moving Day. Du Bois, William P., illus. LC 75-22275. 36p. (gr. k-2). 1976. Knopf.

Towne, Mary. Their House. LC 89-34969. 208p. (gr. 5 up). 1990. 13.95 (ISBN 0-689-31562-7, Atheneum Child Bk). Macmillan Child Grp.

Wood, Phyllis A. Pass Me a Pine Cone. LC 82-1870. 160p. (gr. 7-9). 1982. 11.95 (ISBN 0-664-32692-7, Westminster). Westminster John Knox.

Yep, Laurence. The Star Fisher. 160p. (gr. 3 up). 1991. 12.95 (ISBN 0-688-09365-5). Morrow Jr Bks.

MOZART, JOHANN CHRYSOSTROM WOLFGANG AMADEUS, 1756-1791

Brighton, Catherine. Mozart: Scenes from the Childhood of the Great Composer. (ps-3). 1990. 14.95 (ISBN 0-385-41537-0); PLB 15.99 (ISBN 0-385-41538-9). Doubleday.

Downing, Julie. Mozart Tonight. Downing, Julie, illus. LC 90-34479. 40p. 1991. RSBE 15.95 (ISBN 0-02-732881-3, Bradbury Pr). Macmillan Child Grp.

Gallez, Christophe. Mozart. 32p. (gr. 4). 1990. 11.95s.p. (ISBN 0-88682-322-6); 17.10 (ISBN 0-685-28237-6). Creative Ed.

Great Composers, Bk. 1: Bach, Mozart, Beethoven. (Illus.). (gr. 5 up). 3.50 (ISBN 0-7214-0230-5). Ladybird Bks.

Greene, Carol. Wolfgang Amadeus Mozart: Musician. LC 87-13824. (Illus.). 152p. (gr. 4 up). 1987. PLB 17.27 (ISBN 0-516-03261-5). Childrens.

Loewen, L. Mozart. (Illus.). 112p. (gr. 5 up). 1989. lib. bdg. 17.26 (ISBN 0-86592-605-0). Rourke Corp.

Neidorf, Mary. Operantics with Wolfgang Amadeus Mozart. LC 86-14435. 32p. (Orig.). (gr. 3-6). 1987. pap. 4.95 (ISBN 0-86534-092-7). Sunstone Pr.

Patton, Barbara W. Introducing Wolfgang Amadeus Mozart. (Illus.). 48p. (Orig.). (gr. 3-9). 1991. pap. 6.95 (ISBN 1-878636-03-0). Soundboard Bks.

Sabin, Francene. Mozart, Young Music Genius. Miyake, Yoshi, illus. LC 89-33980. 48p. (gr. 4-6). 1990. lib. bdg. 10.79 (ISBN 0-8167-1773-7); pap. text ed. 2.95 (ISBN 0-8167-1774-5). Troll Assocs.

Sage, Alison. Play Mozart. Gabby, Terry, illus. Bunting, Janet, contrib. by. (Illus.). 32p. (gr. 1-4). 1988. Incl. built-in 22-note electronic keyboard. 13.95 (ISBN 0-8120-5924-7). Barron.

Tames, Richard. Mozart. LC 90-32378. (Illus.). 32p. 1991. PLB 11.90 (ISBN 0-531-14107-1). Watts.

Thompson, Wendy. Wolfgang Amadeus Mozart. (Illus.). 48p. (gr. 7up). 1991. 16.95 (ISBN 0-670-83679-6). Viking Child Bks.

MUHAMMAD ALI, 1942-

Denenberg, Barry. The Story of Muhammad Ali, Heavyweight Champion of the World. (Illus.). 96p. (gr. 3-5). 1990. pap. 2.95 (ISBN 0-440-40259-X, YB). Dell.

Rummel, Jack. Muhammad Ali. King, Coretta Scott, intro. by. (Illus.). 112p. (Orig.). (gr. 5 up). 1988. 17.95 (ISBN 1-55546-569-2); pap. 9.95 (ISBN 0-7910-0210-1). Chelsea Hse.

MUIR, JOHN, 1838-1914

Force, Eden. John Muir. Gallin, Richard, ed. (Illus.). 144p. (gr. 5-9). 1990. lib. bdg. 13.98 (ISBN 0-382-09965-6); pap. 7.95 (ISBN 0-382-09970-2). Silver Burdett Pr.

Tolan, Sally. John Muir: Naturalist, Writer & Guardian of the North American Wilderness. LC 89-4367. (Illus.). 64p. (gr. 5-6). 1989. PLB 12.95 (ISBN 0-8368-0099-0). Gareth Stevens Inc.

MULTIMATE (COMPUTER PROGRAM)

Guerriero, Diane. How to Use MultiMate Advantage II. Jensen, Gayle, ed. (Illus.). 80p. (gr. 6 up). 1988. bk. & 4 tapes 99.00 (ISBN 0-917792-56-4). FlipTrack.

MUMMIES

Alden, Laura. Learning about Mummies. Stasiak, Krystyna, illus. LC 87-24294. 46p. (gr. 3-6). 1988. PLB 17.27 (ISBN 0-516-06567-X); pap. 4.95 (ISBN 0-516-46567-8). Childrens.

Aliki. Mummies Made in Egypt. Aliki, illus. LC 77-26603. 32p. (gr. 2-6). 1979. 12.95 (ISBN 0-690-03858-5, Crowell Jr Bks); PLB 13.89 (ISBN 0-690-03859-3, Crowell Jr Bks). HarpC Child Bks.

—Mummies Made in Egypt. Aliki, illus. LC 85-42746. 32p. (gr. 2-6). 1985. pap. 5.95 (ISBN 0-06-446011-8, Trophy). HarpC Child Bks.

Bellairs, John. The Mummy, the Will, & the Crypt. Gorey, Edward, illus. 192p. (gr. 5 up). 1983. 12.95 (ISBN 0-8037-0029-6); PLB 12.89 (ISBN 0-8037-0030-X). Dial Bks Young.

Glubok, Shirley & Tamarin, Alfred. The Mummy of Ramose. LC 76-21392. (Illus.). 1978. PLB 11.89 (ISBN 0-06-022042-2). HarpC Child Bks.

Hutchins, Pat. The Curse of the Egyptian Mummy. Hutchins, Laurence, illus. LC 83-1713. 160p. (gr. 3-5). 1983. PLB 10.88 (ISBN 0-688-01762-2). Greenwillow.

Lauber, Patricia. Tales Mummies Tell. LC 83-46172. (Illus.). 128p. (gr. 5-9). 1985. 12.95 (ISBN 0-690-04388-0, Crowell Jr Bks); PLB 12.89 (ISBN 0-690-04389-9, Crowell Jr Bks). HarpC Child Bks.

Perl, Lila. Mummies, Tombs, & Treasure: Secrets of Ancient Egypt. Weihs, Erika, illus. LC 86-17646. 128p. (gr. 4 up). 1987. 14.95 (ISBN 0-89919-407-9, Pub. by Clarion). Ticknor & Fields.

Ross, Pat. M & M & the Mummy Mess. LC 84-20847. 48p. (ps-3). 1985. pap. 9.95 (ISBN 0-670-80548-3). Viking Child Bks.

Spinner, Stephanie. The Mummy's Tomb. 64p. (gr. 2 up). 1985. pap. 2.25 (ISBN 0-553-15439-7). Bantam.

Wright, Bob. The Mummy's Crown. bilingual ed. Bourne, Phyllis & Tusquets, Eugenia, trs. from ENG. Heidinger, Herb, illus. (SPA & ENG.). 96p. (gr. 1-5). 1989. pap. text ed. 4.95 (ISBN 0-87879-660-6, High Noon Books). Acad Therapy.

MUMPS

Lerner, Marguerite R. Dear Little Mumps Child. Overlie, George, illus. LC 59-15145. (gr. k-5). 1959. PLB 5.95 (ISBN 0-8225-0003-5). Lerner Pubns.

MUNICIPAL ENGINEERING

see also Refuse and Refuse Disposal; Water Supply

MUNICIPAL GOVERNMENT

see also Cities and Towns

also names of cities with the subdivision Politics and Government, e.g. New York (City)–Politics and Government; etc.

MUNICIPALITIES

see Cities and Towns

MURDER–FICTION

Duncan, Lois. Killing Mr. Griffin. (gr. 7 up). 1978. 14.95 (ISBN 0-316-19549-9). Little.

Fowler, Zinita. The Last Innocent Summer. LC 89-20417. 145p. (gr. 6-9). 1990. pap. 11.95 (ISBN 0-87565-045-7). Tex Christian.
THE LAST INNOCENT SUMMER is a story about a small town with a swimming pool, the Ritz Theater, a city park, a town square & a J.C. Penney store. It's a story about slumber parties, small-town funerals, community picnics & local intrigues. It's also a story about honor & caring & the way we live. Skeeter, the ten-year-old narrator, tells about the murder of two little girls that rocked the small Texas town in which she lived, & of how her close-knit family's involvement in events beyond their control changed their lives in that troubled summer of 1931. Skeeter learns some disturbing lessons: people can do bad things & then make them worse trying to keep from being found out; not all mothers love their children, nor all children love their mothers; it's hard to say "I love you" to those you love. "Fowler's deftly crafted story has depth & pace & a picture of a community that may remind some readers of Harper Lee's TO KILL A MOCKINGBIRD."--Bulletin of the Center for Children's Books, Univ. of Chicago. "The emotion of small town joys & sorrows & the prejudices of different groups as they struggle to coexist are brought together with good clear dialogue & colorful description to make (a) most enjoyable story."--VOYA. Chosen best Juvenile of 1991 by the Texas Institute of Letters.
Publisher Provided Annotation.

Hall, Lynn. A Killing Freeze. LC 88-5143. 128p. (gr. 7 up). 1988. 12.95 (ISBN 0-688-07867-2). Morrow Jr Bks.

Newman, Robert. The Case of the Vanishing Corpse. LC 79-22078. 228p. (gr. 4-6). 1985. pap. 4.95 (ISBN 0-689-71037-2, Aladdin). Macmillan Child Grp.

Nixon, Joan L. Whispers from the Dead. (gr. 7 up). 1989. 14.95 (ISBN 0-385-29809-9). Delacorte.

Poe, Edgar Allan. Los Asesinatos de la Calle Morgue. (SPA.). 4.95 (ISBN 0-685-31011-6). Santillana.

Thorburn, James W. Murder at Sun Valley. Witte, Sue, illus. LC 86-50305. 304p. (Orig.). (gr. 6). 1986. 8.99 (ISBN 0-938191-00-4). Woodside Pr ID.

Waters, Gaby & Round, Graham. Murder on the Midnight Plane. (Illus.). 48p. (gr. 4-9). 1987. PLB 10.96 (ISBN 0-88110-389-6); pap. 4.50 (ISBN 0-86020-952-0). EDC.

Whelan, Gloria. The Secret Keeper. LC 89-39125. 192p. 1990. 12.95 (ISBN 0-679-80572-9); PLB 13.99 (ISBN 0-679-90572-3). McKay.

MURROW, EDWARD ROSCOE, 1908-1965

Vonier, Sprague. Edward R. Murrow. LC 89-4344. (Illus.). 64p. (gr. 5-6). 1989. PLB 12.95 (ISBN 0-8368-0100-8). Gareth Stevens Inc.

MUSCLES

Ardley, Neil. Muscles to Machines: Projects with Movement. 1990. PLB 11.90 (ISBN 0-531-17200-7). Watts.

Harrington, William F. Theories of Muscle Contraction. Head, J. J., ed. LC 77-94953. (Illus.). 32p. (gr. 10 up). 1981. pap. 2.70 (ISBN 0-89278-314-1, 45-9714). Carolina Biological.

Saunderson, Jane. Muscles & Bones. Farmer, Andrew & Green, Robina, illus. LC 90-42882. 32p. (gr. 4-6). 1991. lib. bdg. 11.89 (ISBN 0-8167-2088-6); pap. text ed. 3.95 (ISBN 0-8167-2089-4). Troll Assocs.

Skeleton & Movement. 48p. (gr. 5-8). 1988. PLB 12.98 (ISBN 0-382-09702-5); 9.74s.p. (ISBN 0-685-24610-8). Silver Burdett Pr.

MUSEUMS

see also Art–Galleries and Museums;

also names of countries, cities, etc. with the subdivision Galleries and Museums (e.g. U. S.–Galleries and Museums; etc.); and names of galleries and museums, e.g. New York Metropolitan Museum of Art

Adams, P., illus. The Child's Play Museum. (ps-2). 1977. 5.50 (ISBN 0-85953-094-9, Pub. by Childs's Play England). Childs Play.

Althea. Visiting a Museum. 26p. (gr. 2-5). 1983. pap. 3.95 (ISBN 0-521-27160-6). Cambridge U Pr.

Amos, Janine. Let's Go to the Museum. Roberts, Peter, illus. LC 89-17339. 32p. (gr. 1-3). 1990. PLB 9.95 (ISBN 1-85435-241-5). Marshall Cavendish.

Natural History Museum (London) (Illus.). (gr. 5 up). 3.50 (ISBN 0-7214-1181-9). Ladybird Bks.

Papajani, Janet. Museums. LC 82-23621. (Illus.). 48p. (gr. k-4). 1989. PLB 14.60 (ISBN 0-516-01682-2); pap. 4.95 (ISBN 0-516-41682-0). Childrens.

Reist, Linnaeus L. The Colorful Landis Brothers: Founders of the Landis Valley Museum. Severs, Susan B., ed. & illus. LC 87-90447. 100p. (Orig.). (gr. 11-12). 1987. pap. write for info. (ISBN 0-9618501-0-8). S R Severs.

The Story of Madame Tussaud. (Illus.). (gr. 5 up). 1990. 3.50 (ISBN 0-7214-1091-X). Ladybird Bks.

Suarez, Diana. Color & Discover: A Children's Guide to the North Carolina Museum of Art. Fender, Susan, illus. LC 87-62986. 40p. (Orig.). (ps-6). 1987. pap. 3.50 (ISBN 0-88259-956-9). NCMA.

Weil, Lisl. Let's Go to the Museum. Weil, Lisl, illus. LC 89-2078. 32p. (gr. k-3). 1989. reinforced 13.95 (ISBN 0-8234-0784-5). Holiday.

MUSEUMS–FICTION

Butterworth, Nick. School Trip. 1990. 13.95 (ISBN 0-385-30242-8). Delacorte.

Cameron, Eleanor. The Court of the Stone Children. 208p. (gr. 5 up). 1973. 13.95 (ISBN 0-525-28350-1, DCB). Dutton Child Bks.

Freeman, Don. Norman the Doorman. Freeman, Don, illus. (ps-2). 1959. pap. 15.95 (ISBN 0-670-51515-9). Viking Child Bks.

Greenwald, Sheila. The Secret Museum. Greenwald, Sheila, illus. 128p. (gr. k-6). 1989. pap. 2.95 (ISBN 0-440-40148-8, YB). Dell.

Morrow, Barbara. Help for Mr. Peale. Morrow, Barbara, illus. LC 89-39273. 32p. (gr. 1-3). 1990. 13.95 (ISBN 0-02-767590-4, Mcmillan Child Bk). Macmillan Child Grp.

Ross, Pat. M & M & the Mummy Mess. Hafner, Marylin, illus. 48p. (gr. 1-4). 1986. pap. 3.95 (ISBN 0-14-032084-9, Puffin). Puffin Bks.

Wandelmaier, Roy. Secret of the Old Museum. Smolinski, Dick, illus. LC 85-2533. 112p. (gr. 3-6). 1985. lib. bdg. 9.49 (ISBN 0-8167-0531-3); pap. text ed. 2.95 (ISBN 0-8167-0532-1). Troll Assocs.

MUSHROOMS

see also Fungi

Johnson, Sylvia A. Mushrooms. Izawa, Masana, illus. LC 82-212. 48p. (gr. 4 up). 1982. PLB 14.95 (ISBN 0-8225-1473-7). Lerner Pubns.

Selsam, Millicent E. Mushrooms. Wexler, Jerome, photos by. LC 85-18953. (Illus.). 48p. (gr. 2-5). 1986. 12.95 (ISBN 0-688-06248-2); (Morrow Jr Bks). Morrow Jr Bks.

Watts, Barrie. Mushroom. LC 86-6659. (Illus.). 25p. (gr. 2-5). 1986. 6.95 (ISBN 0-382-09301-1); PLB 9.98 (ISBN 0-382-09287-2); pap. 3.95 (ISBN 0-382-24017-0). Silver Burdett Pr.

MUSIC

see also Church Music; Jazz Music; Musicians; Sound

also Orchestral Music; Organ Music; Piano music; etc. and headings beginning with the words Music and Musical

Bailey, Eva. Music & Musicians. (Illus.). 72p. (gr. 7-12). 1983. 19.95 (ISBN 0-7134-1310-7, Pub. by Batsford England). Trafalgar Sq.

Boy Scouts of America. Cub Scout Songbook. (Illus.). 80p. (gr. 3-5). 1969. pap. 2.40x (ISBN 0-8395-3222-9, 3222A). BSA.

Clark, Frances & Goss, Louise. Music Maker, Pt. A. (Illus.). 56p. (gr. 2 up). 1986. pap. text ed. 6.95 wkbk. (ISBN 0-913277-20-7). New Schl Mus Study.

De Paola, Tomie. The Friendly Beasts: An Old English Christmas Carol. De Paola, Tomie, illus. 32p. (ps-2). 1981. 13.95 (ISBN 0-399-20739-2, Putnam); pap. 5.95 (ISBN 0-399-20777-5, Putnam). Putnam Pub Group.

Douillard, Jeanne, ed. Chasons de Chez-Nous. Snow, Suzanne. Blais, Lise M. Albert, Julie D., illus. (FRE.). 61p. (gr. k-6). 1978. pap. text ed. 1.00 (ISBN 0-911409-01-7). Natl Mat Dev.

Feierabend, John M. Music for Very Little People. Kramer, Gary M., illus. 74p. (ps). 1986. pap. 14.95 (ISBN 0-685-14607-3); pap. write for info. incl. tape (ISBN 0-913932-13-2); cassette avail. Boosey & Hawkes.

Ferguson, Kathleen M. Musical Mysteries. Melton, Gerald, illus. 144p. (gr. 4-8). 1985. wkbk. 10.95 (ISBN 0-86653-282-X, GA 684). Good Apple.

Francis, Carolyn. Music Reading & Theory Skills, Level 1 & 2: A Sequential Method for Practice & Mastery. 226p. (gr. 4-12). 1986. incl. reproducible curriculum pkg. 179.95 (ISBN 0-931303-04-4); 3-ring binder, black line masters avail. (ISBN 0-931303-02-8). Innovative Learn.

Friou, Deborah. Rodgers & Hammerstein for the Harp. 48p. (Orig.). 1990. pap. 15.95 (ISBN 0-9628120-0-5). Friou Music.

Grasmick, Alta C. U'n I Read a Note. Rust, Thomas O., illus. 68p. (gr. k-1). 1989. pap. 15.95 (ISBN 0-9621909-0-X). A C Grasmick.

Greene, Carol. Music. LC 83-7255. (Illus.). 48p. (gr. k-4). 1983. PLB 14.60 (ISBN 0-516-01701-2). Childrens.

Kaplan, Don. See with Your Ears: The Creative Music Book. Hoburg, Maryanne R., illus. LC 82-81463. 128p. (Orig.). (gr. 1-7). 1982. pap. 6.95 (ISBN 0-938530-09-7, 09-7); tchr's guide cancelled 2.00 (ISBN 0-938530-20-8, 20-8). Lexikos.

Keener, Joseph. Music Series. (gr. 1-7). 1982. pap. write for info. (ISBN 0-686-37780-X). Rod & Staff.

Kobialka, Daniel & Hanser, Suzanne. When You Wish upon a Star: Relaxation Music for Children. Kulberg, Andy. 12p. (Orig.). (ps-3). 1988. musical cassette & booklet 10.98 (ISBN 0-929909-00-3). Li-Sem Enter.

Laurencin, Genevieve. Music! Bogard, Vicki, tr. from FRE. Millet, Claude & Millet, Denise, illus. LC 89-8892. (gr. k-5). 1989. 4.95 (ISBN 0-944589-25-1, 025). Young Discovery Lib.

Menotti, Gian-Carlo. Amahl & the Night Visitors. Lemieux, Michele, illus. LC 84-27196. 64p. (ps up). 1986. 15.00 (ISBN 0-688-05426-9); lib. bdg. 14.88 (ISBN 0-688-05427-7, Morrow Jr Bks). Morrow Jr Bks.

Music & Bugling. (Illus.). 56p. (gr. 6-12). 1990. pap. 1.85 (ISBN 0-8395-3336-5, 3336A). BSA.

Nelson, Lisa M. Bright Smiles & Blue Skies: Positive Music for Today's Kids. (Illus.). 16p. (Orig.). (gr. k-6). pap. 9.95 incl. audio tape (ISBN 0-9627863-0-6). Brght Ideas CA.

Patella, Chris & Oddo, Eileen. Makin Music! Schoonover, Kevin, illus. 75p. (Orig.). (gr. k-2). 1989. write for info. tchrs. ed. (ISBN 0-944333-02-8); LP or Cassette avail. Musical Munchkins.

Pearce, Elvina T. Solo Flight. Clark, Frances & Goss, Louise, eds. (gr. 2 up). 1986. pap. text ed. 3.50 (ISBN 0-913277-18-5). New Schl Mus Study.

Reynolds, Malvina. There's Music in the Air. Simmons, Elly, illus. LC 76-19261. 96p. (gr. 1-12). 1976. pap. 5.00 (ISBN 0-915620-05-7). Schroder Music.

Rhoton, Jessian L. The Magic Treble Tree. Erickson, Cindy R., illus. 48p. 1989. PLB write for info. Happy Music Pub.

—The Magic Treble Tree. Erickson, Cindy R., illus. 48p. 1990. write for info. (ISBN 0-9624162-9-0). Happy Music Pub.

Rusch, Harold W. The Beat Goes On, Bk. 1. (gr. 7 up). 1980. pap. 14.95 (ISBN 0-8497-4148-3, V67). Kjos.

Santrey, Laurence. Music. Croll, Carolyn, illus. LC 84-2648. 32p. (gr. 3-6). 1985. PLB 9.49 (ISBN 0-8167-0218-7); pap. text ed. 2.95 (ISBN 0-8167-0219-5). Troll Assocs.

Swan, Susan E., illus. The Twelve Days of Christmas. LC 80-28097. 32p. (gr. k-4). 1981. PLB 9.79 (ISBN 0-89375-474-9); pap. text ed. 1.95 (ISBN 0-89375-475-7). Troll Assocs.

Taylor, Ann. Chamber Music Primer: Four Piano Trio Pieces. Bryant, Larkin, illus. (Orig.). (gr. 1-6). 1983. pap. 6.75 (ISBN 0-943644-01-1); cassette 5.98 (ISBN 0-685-06794-7). Ivory Pal.

Taylor, Barbara. Sound & Music. (Illus.). 32p. (gr. 5-8). 1991. PLB 11.40 (ISBN 0-531-14185-3). Watts.

Townsend, Jennifer A. Burst into Music: Teaching Music to Young Children. Woll, Anna, illus. (ps-3). Date not set. pap. write for info. (ISBN 1-877969-25-7). J & S Pub.

Weil, Lisl. The Magic of Music. Weil, Lisl, illus. LC 88-21362. 32p. (gr. k-3). 1989. reinforced bdg. 13.95 (ISBN 0-8234-0735-7). Holiday.

Wojcio, Michael D. & Gustason, Gerilee. Music in Motion: Twenty Two Songs in Signing Exact English, for Children. Norris, Carolyn, illus. 112p. (Orig.). 1982. 9.95 (ISBN 0-916708-07-1). Modern Signs.

MUSIC–ACOUSTICS AND PHYSICS

see also Sound

Ardley, Neil. Sound & Music. LC 83-51441. (Illus.). 32p. (gr. 4-8). 1984. PLB 11.90 (ISBN 0-531-03776-2). Watts.

—Sound Waves to Music: Projects with Sound. (Illus.). 32p. (gr. 5-8). 1990. PLB 11.90 (ISBN 0-531-17236-8). Watts.

Balcziak, B. Music. (Illus.). 48p. (gr. 4-8). 1989. lib. bdg. 14.00 (ISBN 0-86592-056-7). Rourke Corp.

Berger, Melvin. The Science of Music. Buchanan, Yvonne, illus. LC 87-24921. 160p. (gr. 5-9). 1989. (Crowell Jr Bks); PLB 13.89 (ISBN 0-690-04647-2, Crowell Jr Bks). HarpC Child Bks.

MUSIC, AMERICAN

Krishef, Robert K. Grand Ole Opry. LC 77-90151. (Illus.). 72p. (gr. 5 up). 1978. PLB 5.95 (ISBN 0-8225-1405-2). Lerner Pubns.

—The New Breed. LC 77-90153. (Illus.). 72p. (gr. 5 up). 1978. PLB 7.95 (ISBN 0-8225-1406-0). Lerner Pubns.

Saunders, Susan. Dolly Parton: Country Goin' to Town. Pate, Rodney, illus. 64p. (gr. 2-6). 1986. pap. 3.95 (ISBN 0-14-032162-4, Puffin). Puffin Bks.

Waring, Diana. History Alive Through Music America: The Heart of a New Land. (Illus.). 78p. (Orig.). (gr. 3-8). 1991. pap. 17.95 incl. cassette (ISBN 1-879459-01-9); pap. 9.95 (ISBN 1-879459-00-0); cassette 9.95 (ISBN 1-879459-02-7). Hear & Learn Pubns.

—History Alive Through Music Westward Ho! The Heart of the Old West. (Illus.). 66p. (Orig.). (gr. 6-10). 1991. pap. 17.95 incl. cassette (ISBN 1-879459-03-5); pap. 9.95 (ISBN 1-879459-04-3); cassette 9.95 (ISBN 1-879459-05-1). Hear & Learn Pubns.

MUSIC–ANALYSIS, APPRECIATION

Copland, Aaron. What to Listen for in Music. rev. ed. 192p. (gr. 9-12). 1989. pap. 4.95 (ISBN 0-451-62687-7, Ment). NAL-Dutton.

Ensor, Wendy-Ann. Heroes & Heroines in Music. (Illus.). (gr. 1-4). 1981. cassette 18.00x (ISBN 0-685-06116-7). Oxford U Pr.

Griffin, Clive. Classical Music. (Illus.). 64p. (gr. 7-9). 1988. 19.95 (ISBN 0-85219-756-X, Pub. by Batsford England). Trafalgar Sq.

Luck, Oliver W. Music Is Math. Luck, Oliver W., illus. (Orig.). (gr. 4-12). 1987. pap. 7.00 (ISBN 0-9626686-0-5). Owl Pub CA.

Tatchell, J. Understanding Music. (Illus.). 64p. (gr. 4 up). 1990. lib. bdg. 13.96 (ISBN 0-88110-382-9, Usborne); pap. 7.95 (ISBN 0-7460-0302-1, Usborne). EDC.

MUSIC–APPRECIATION

see Music–Analysis, Appreciation

Sharp, Vera. Little Princess' Symphony Adventures. Armstrong, M. J., illus. 76p. (ps-6). 1985. incl. 2 cassettes 49.00 (ISBN 0-9616987-0-5). V Sharp.

MUSIC–BIOGRAPHY

see Musicians

MUSIC, DRAMATIC

see Opera

MUSIC–FICTION

Angell, Judie. The Buffalo Nickel Blues Band. 192p. (gr. 3-7). 1991. pap. 3.95 (ISBN 0-689-71448-3, Aladdin). Macmillan Child Grp.

Bozung, Dick. The Magical Musical Spiraled Seashell, & Friends. Bozung, Dick, et al, illus. 160p. (Orig.). 1989. pap. 20.00 (ISBN 0-9622341-1-7); write for info. audio tape (ISBN 0-9622341-5-X). Seven Arrows.

Brook, Ruth. Play It Again, Rosie. Kondo, Vala, illus. LC 86-30749. 32p. (gr. k-3). 1987. PLB 11.89 (ISBN 0-8167-0904-1); pap. text ed. 2.95 (ISBN 0-8167-0905-X). Troll Assocs.

Carlson, Nancy. Harriet's Recital. LC 81-18135. (Illus.). 32p. (ps-3). 1982. lib. bdg. 9.95 (ISBN 0-87614-181-5). Carolrhoda Bks.

—Loudmouth George & the Cornet. LC 82-22171. (Illus.). 32p. (ps-3). 1983. PLB 9.95 (ISBN 0-87614-214-5). Carolrhoda Bks.

Clement, Claude. The Voice of the Wood. Clement, Frederic, photos by. LC 88-22892. (Illus.). 32p. (gr. k up). 1989. 14.95 (ISBN 0-8037-0635-9). Dial Bks Young.

Clymer, Eleanor. The Horse in the Attic. 96p. (gr. 4-6). 1985. pap. 2.50 (ISBN 0-440-43798-9, YB). Dell.

Cooney, Caroline B. Don't Blame the Music. LC 85-21727. 172p. (gr. 8 up). 1986. 14.95 (ISBN 0-448-47778-5, G&D). Putnam Pub Group.

Corbett, W. J. The Song Pentecost. (gr. k-6). 1985. pap. 3.25 (ISBN 0-440-48092-2, YB). Dell.

Distler, Bette. Timothy Tuneful. Ohlsson, Ib, illus. LC 68-11270. (ps-3). 1968. 3.50g (ISBN 0-685-16349-0, CCPr). Macmillan.

Escovito, Pete. Viva la Musica. (gr. 4-7). 1991. pap. 9.95 (ISBN 0-930647-09-2). Lancaster Prodns.

Fleischman, Paul. Rondo in C. Wentworth, Janet, illus. LC 87-29375. 32p. (gr. k-3). 1988. 13.95 (ISBN 0-06-021856-8); PLB 13.89 (ISBN 0-06-021857-6). HarpC Child Bks.

Frank, Elizabeth B. Cooder Cutlas. LC 85-45822. 320p. (gr. 7 up). 1987. 13.95i (ISBN 0-685-17655-X); PLB 13.89 (ISBN 0-06-021860-6). HarpC Child Bks.

Friesel, Uwe. Tim, the Peacemaker. Wilkon, Jozef, illus. LC 72-145822. 32p. (ps-3). 8.95 (ISBN 0-87592-052-7). Scroll Pr.

Gehrt, Vicky E. A Matter of Music. Paris, Pat & Thornley, Jean, illus. 1984. incl. cassette 7.95 (ISBN 0-910313-64-4). Parker Bros.

Greenfield, Eloise. I Make Music. Gilchrist, Jan S., illus. 12p. (ps-1). 1991. bds. 4.95 (ISBN 0-86316-205-3). Writers & Readers.

Griffith, Helen. Georgia Music. Stevenson, James, illus. LC 85-24918. 24p. (gr. k-3). 1986. 13.95 (ISBN 0-688-06071-4); PLB 13.88 (ISBN 0-688-06072-2). Greenwillow.

Haseley, Dennis. The Old Banjo. Gammell, Stephen, illus. 32p. (gr. 1-5). 1990. pap. 3.95 (ISBN 0-689-71380-0, Aladdin). Macmillan Child Grp.

Hopper, Nancy. Wake Me When the Band Starts Playing. LC 87-22898. 160p. (gr. 7 up). 1988. 13.95 (ISBN 0-525-67244-3, Lodestar Bks). Dutton Child Bks.

Johnston, Tony. Pages of Music. DePaola, Tomie, illus. 32p. (gr. k-3). 1988. PLB 13.95 (ISBN 0-399-21436-4, Putnam). Putnam Pub Group.

Kaplan, Carol & Becker, Sandi. Stone Soup - A "Rock" Opera. Mitter, Kathy, illus. 29p. (ps). 1989. tchr's. ed. 16.95 (ISBN 0-88734-408-9). Players Pr.

Keats, Ezra J. Louie's Search. Keats, Ezra J., illus. 32p. (gr. k-3). 1989. pap. 4.95 (ISBN 0-689-71354-1, Aladdin). Macmillan Child Grp.

Komaiko, Leah. I Like the Music. Westman, Barbara, illus. LC 87-170. 32p. (ps-3). 1987. 12.95i (ISBN 0-06-023271-4); PLB 13.89 (ISBN 0-06-023272-2). HarpC Child Bks.

—I Like the Music. Westman, Barbara, illus. LC 87-170. 32p. (ps-3). 1989. pap. 4.50 (ISBN 0-06-443189-4, Trophy). HarpC Child Bks.

Kraus, Robert. Musical Max. Aruego, Jose & Dewey, Ariane, illus. LC 89-77079. 40p. 1990. PLB 13.95 (ISBN 0-671-68681-X). S&S Trade.

L'Engle, Madeleine. The Small Rain: A Novel. LC 84-47839. 371p. (gr. 7 up). 1984. 14.95 (ISBN 0-374-26637-9); pap. 8.95 (ISBN 0-374-51912-9). FS&G.

Levy, Elizabeth. Something Queer in Rock N' Roll. Gerstein, Mordicai, illus. LC 86-19772. 48p. (gr. k-3). 1987. pap. 12.95 (ISBN 0-385-29547-2). Delacorte.

Lewis, Richard. All of You Was Singing. Young, Ed, illus. LC 89-18263. 32p. 1991. SBE 13.95 (ISBN 0-689-31596-1, Atheneum Child Bk). Macmillan Child Grp.

Lionni, Leo. Geraldine the Music Mouse. Lionni, Leo, illus. LC 79-932. (ps-3). 1979. 6.95 (ISBN 0-394-84238-3). Pantheon.

Livingston, Alan W. & Schallert, William. Sparky's Magic Piano. (Illus.). 48p. (ps-2). Date not set. bk. & cassette 7.98 (ISBN 1-55886-066-5). Smarty Pants.

Locke, Robert. Tracks. (gr. 5 up). 1986. 12.95 (ISBN 0-395-40571-8). HM.

Lynch, Patricia. Brogeen Follows the Magic Flute. 191p. (ps-8). 1988. pap. 5.95 (ISBN 1-85371-022-9, Pub. by Poolbeg Press Ltd Eire). Dufour.

McMillion, Mac. Who'll Sing For Me. LC 87-91267. 130p. (Orig.). 1987. pap. 10.00 (ISBN 0-9619399-0-7). M McMillion Pub.

Magorian, James. The Beautiful Music. LC 88-71142. 12p. (gr. 2-5). 1988. pap. 3.00 (ISBN 0-930674-25-1). Black Oak.

Micucci, Charles. A Little Night Music. Micucci, Charles, illus. LC 88-505. 32p. (ps-3). 1989. 10.95 (ISBN 0-688-07900-8); PLB 10.88 (ISBN 0-688-07901-6, Morrow Jr Bks). Morrow Jr Bks.

Sage, James. The Little Band. Narahashi, Keiko, illus. LC 90-40089. 32p. (ps-3). 1991. SBE 13.95 (ISBN 0-689-50516-7, M K McElderry). Macmillan Child Grp.

Sargent, Sarah. Watermusic. LC 85-22396. (gr. 6-9). 1986. 11.95 (ISBN 0-89919-436-2, Pub. by Clarion). Ticknor & Fields.

Strasser, Todd. Rock 'n Roll Nights. 224p. (gr. 7 up). 1983. pap. 2.95 (ISBN 0-440-97318-X, LFL). Dell.

Tusa, Tricia. Miranda. LC 85-26769. (Illus.). 32p. (gr. 7 up). 1986. pap. 3.95 (ISBN 0-689-71064-X, Aladdin). Macmillan Child Grp.

Walter, Mildred P. Ty's One-Man Band. Tomes, Margot, illus. 48p. (gr. k-3). 1984. pap. 3.95 (ISBN 0-590-40178-5). Scholastic Inc.

Weber, Ane. Return to the Land of the Music Machine. Pendergrass, Mark, illus. (gr. 1-4). 1984. 4.95 (ISBN 0-89191-836-1); pap. 3.95x (ISBN 0-89191-785-3). Cook.

Weber, Ane & Pendergrass, Mark. In the Land of the Music Machine. (Illus., Orig.). (gr. 1-4). 1984. 5.95 (ISBN 0-89191-835-3); pap. 4.95 (ISBN 0-89191-784-5). Cook.

Zolotow, Charlotte. Everything Glistens & Everything Sings. Tomes, Margot, illus. LC 86-31917. 96p. (ps-3). 1987. 11.95 (ISBN 0-15-226488-4, HJ). HarBraceJ.

MUSIC–HISTORY AND CRITICISM

Adair, Audrey J. Great Composers & Their Music History, Unit 5: Fifty Ready to Use Activities. 112p. (gr. 3-9). 1987. pap. text ed. 18.95 (ISBN 0-13-363797-2, Parker Publishing Co.). P-H.

—Special Days Throughout the Year: Fifty Ready-to-Use Activities, Unit 6. 112p. (gr. 3-9). 1987. pap. 12.95 (ISBN 0-13-826421-X, Parker Publishing Co). P-H.

Carlin, Richard. European Classical Music, 1600-1855. (Illus.). 144p. 1988. 17.95x (ISBN 0-8160-1382-9). Facts on File.

Kennedy, Rosemary G. Bach to Rock: An Introduction to Famous Composers & Their Music. 6th, rev. ed. Ronniger, Mary S., illus. 161p. (gr. 4-9). 1989. pap. 14.95; audio cassette 16.95. Rosemary Corp.

Lang, Paul H. & Bettmann, Otto L. Pictorial History of Music. (Illus.). (gr. 9 up). 1960. 19.95 (ISBN 0-393-02107-6). Norton.

Mundy. Story of Music. (gr. 6-9). 1980. (Usborne-Hayes); PLB 13.96 (ISBN 0-88110-031-5); pap. 6.95 (ISBN 0-86020-443-X). EDC.

Starr, Constance. The Music Road, Bk. 3. 96p. 1985. pap. 7.95 (ISBN 0-914425-02-1). Kingston Ellis.

The Story of Music. (Illus.). (gr. 5 up). 3.50 (ISBN 0-7214-0217-8). Ladybird Bks.

Waring, Diana. History Alive Through Music America: The Heart of a New Land. (Illus.). 78p. (Orig.). (gr. 3-8). 1991. pap. 17.95 incl. cassette (ISBN 1-879459-01-9); pap. 9.95 (ISBN 1-879459-00-0); cassette 9.95 (ISBN 1-879459-02-7). Hear & Learn Pubns.

—History Alive Through Music Westward Ho! The Heart of the Old West. (Illus.). 66p. (Orig.). (gr. 6-10). 1991. pap. 17.95 incl. cassette (ISBN 1-879459-03-5); pap. 9.95 (ISBN 1-879459-04-3); cassette 9.95 (ISBN 1-879459-05-1). Hear & Learn Pubns.

MUSIC, INDIAN

see Indians of North America–Music

MUSIC–INSTRUCTION AND STUDY
see Music–Study and Teaching
MUSIC–NOTATION
see Musical Notation
MUSIC, POPULAR (SONGS, ETC.)
Blocher, Arlo. Country. LC 75-39817. (Illus.). 32p. (gr. 5-10). 1976. PLB 10.79 (ISBN 0-89375-012-3); pap. 2.95 (ISBN 0-89375-028-X). Troll Assocs.
Feierabend, John. Music for Little People. Kramer, Gary, illus. 74p. (Orig.). (ps). 1989. pap. 11.95 (ISBN 0-913932-46-9); pap. 14.95 incl. tape (ISBN 0-913932-48-5). Boosey & Hawkes.
Ramsey, Marjorie E., ed. It's Music! LC 84-435. (Illus.). 56p. (ps-9). 1984. 7.50 (ISBN 0-87173-104-5). ACEI.
Warner, Laverne & Craycraft, Kenneth. Fun with Familiar Tunes. Filkins, Vanessa, illus. 128p. (ps-3). 1987. pap. 10.95 (ISBN 0-86653-414-8, GA1014). Good Apple.
MUSIC, POPULAR (SONGS, ETC.)–FICTION
Provost, Gary & Levine-Provost, Gail. Popcorn. 160p. 1989. pap. 2.75 (ISBN 0-425-08884-7, Pub. by Berkley-Pacer). Berkley Pub.
MUSIC, SACRED
see Church Music
MUSIC–STUDY AND TEACHING
see also Musical Form
Duna, Bill & Duna, Lois. Let's Play--Right Away with Play-Along Tape, Bk. 1. Guthrie, Ruth, illus. 32p. (Orig.). (gr. k up). 1981. pap. 12.95 (ISBN 0-942928-00-8). Duna Studios.
Harp, David. Make Me Musical: Instant Harmonica Education for Kids. 2nd, rev. ed. (Illus.). (ps-4). 1989. pap. 19.95 (ISBN 0-918321-15-8); cassette & harmonica incl. Musical Idiot.
Hellden, Daniel. Hi! Said the Blackbird: And Twelve Other American Folk Songs to Sing & Play. 24p. (gr. 1-4). 1981. pap. 6.00 (ISBN 0-918812-17-8). MMB Music.
Landon, Joseph W. Music Lab. (Illus.). 182p. (Orig.). (gr. 3-8). 1982. pap. 10.95x packet & guide (ISBN 0-943988-00-4). Music Educ Pubns.
Leanza, Frank. Music Book for Kids of Any Age, Vol. 1. rev. ed. (Illus.). 56p. (gr. 1-4). 1988. pap. 9.95 (ISBN 0-934687-02-1). Crystal Pubs.
—Music Book for Kids of Any Age, Vol. 2. rev. ed. (Illus.). 60p. (gr. 1-4). 1988. text ed. 10.95 (ISBN 0-934687-03-X). Crystal Pubs.
Preucil, Doris. Suzuki Viola School: Piano Accompaniments, Vol. 3. Suzuki, Shinichi, ed. 32p. (gr. k-12). 1983. pap. text ed. 6.50 (ISBN 0-87487-246-4, Suzuki Method). Summy-Birchard.
Ronnholm, Ursula O. Mi Libro de Palabras: Oraciones y Cuemtos. rev. ed. Rabell, Edda, ed. & tr. Montero, Miguel, illus. (SPA.). 100p. (gr. k-6). 1989. pap. 7.00 (ISBN 0-941911-08-X). Two Way Bilingual.
—Writing Through Music. rev. ed. Ronnholm, Paul, ed. Montero, Miguel, tr. from SPA. (Illus.). 74p. (gr. k-3). 1989. pap. text ed. 4.00 (ISBN 0-941911-09-8). Two Way Bilingual.
Spieler, Benjamin D. The Student Clarinetist: A Method for Class Instruction, 3 bks. rev. ed. (Illus.). (gr. 4-9). Date not set. pap. 2.80 ea. Bk. I, 56p. Bk. II, 64p. Bk. III, 36 p. Player Pr.
Suzuki, Shinichi. Note Reading for Violin. Selden, Kyoko, tr. from JPN. 112p. (gr. 1-6). 1985. pap. text ed. 14.95 (ISBN 0-87487-213-8, Suzuki Method). Summy-Birchard.
—Suzuki Cello School, Vol. 1: Piano Accompaniment. 24p. (gr. k-12). 1982. pap. text ed. 6.50 (ISBN 0-87487-263-4, Suzuki Method). Summy-Birchard.
—Suzuki Cello School, Vol. 2: Piano Accompaniment. 24p. (gr. k-12). 1982. pap. text ed. 6.50 (ISBN 0-87487-264-2, Suzuki Method). Summy-Birchard.
—Suzuki Viola School: Viola Part, Vol. 3. Preucil, Doris, ed. 24p. (gr. k-12). 1983. pap. text ed. 6.50 (ISBN 0-87487-243-X, Suzuki Method). Summy-Birchard.
—Suzuki Viola School: Viola Part, Vol. 4. Preucil, Doris, ed. 32p. (gr. k-12). 1983. pap. text ed. 6.50 (ISBN 0-87487-244-8, Suzuki Method). Summy-Birchard.
Vahila, Michael. Teaching Guitar to Children: A Complete Guide for Ages 5 to 12. LC 88-63797. (Illus.). 100p. (Orig.). (gr. k-7). Date not set. pap. 9.95 (ISBN 0-942253-01-9); book & cassette pkg. 18.95 (ISBN 0-942253-02-7). PAZ Pub.
MUSIC–THEORY
see also Musical Form
MUSIC–VOCATIONAL GUIDANCE
Hayward, Phillip. The Pop Music Business. LC 88-29287. (Illus.). 48p. (gr. 6-12). 1989. PLB 12.95 (ISBN 0-86307-978-4). Marshall Cavendish.
MUSIC APPRECIATION
see Music–Analysis, Appreciation
MUSICAL APPRECIATION
see Music–Analysis, Appreciation
MUSICAL COMEDIES
see Musical Revues, Comedies, Etc.
MUSICAL CRITICISM
see Music–History and Criticism
MUSICAL EDUCATION
see Music–Study and Teaching
MUSICAL FORM
see also Opera
Meyer, Carolyn & Pickens, Kel. Sing & Learn. Hayes, Steve, illus. 144p. (ps-3). 1989. wkbk. 11.95 (ISBN 0-86653-476-8, GA1078). Good Apple.
MUSICAL INSTRUCTION
see Music–Study and Teaching

MUSICAL INSTRUMENTS
see also Orchestra;
also groups of instruments, e.g. Percussion Instruments; Stringed Instruments; Wind Instruments; etc.; also names of musical instruments, e.g. Drum; etc.
ABC: Musical Instruments from the Metropolitan Museum of Art. 32p. (gr. 2 up). 1988. 10.95 (ISBN 0-8109-1878-1). Abrams.
Ardley, Neil. Music. King, Dave, et al, photos by. LC 88-13394. (Illus.). 64p. (gr. 5 up). 1989. 13.95 (ISBN 0-394-82259-5); lib. bdg. 14.99 (ISBN 0-394-92259-X). Knopf.
Blackwood, Alan. Musical Instruments. (Illus.). 32p. (gr. 1-6). 1987. lib. bdg. 8.99 (ISBN 0-531-18146-4, Pub. by Bookwright Pr). Watts.
Bouchard, Robert. Let's Play the Recorder. (gr. 6 up). 9.95 (ISBN 0-8283-1471-3). Branden Pub Co.
Darlow, Denys. Musical Instruments. (Illus.). (gr. 6 up). 1980. 14.95 (ISBN 0-7136-2043-9). Dufour.
Elliott, Donald. Alligators & Music. Arrowood, Clinton, illus. LC 84-13862. (gr. 8). 1984. (Pub. by Gambit); pap. 8.95 (ISBN 0-87645-118-0, Pub. by Gambit). Harvard Common Pr.
Fichter, George S. American Indian Music & Musical Instruments. (gr. 5-10). 1978. 8.95 (ISBN 0-679-20443-1). McKay.
Hawthorn, P. First Book of the Recorder. (Illus.). 64p. (gr. 2-6). 1987. PLB 12.96 (ISBN 0-88110-471-X); pap. 7.95 (ISBN 0-7460-0069-3). EDC.
Isadora, Rachel. Ben's Trumpet. Isadora, Rachel, illus. LC 78-12885. 32p. (gr. k-3). 1979. 13.00 (ISBN 0-688-80194-3). Greenwillow.
Kettelkamp, Larry. Electronic Musical Instruments: What They Do, How They Work. Deutsch, Herbert, frwd. by. LC 83-23819. (Illus.). 128p. (gr. 7up). 1984. 11.95 (ISBN 0-688-02781-4). Morrow Jr Bks.
Lillegard, Dee. Brass. LC 87-32990. (Illus.). 32p. (ps-3). 1988. PLB 14.60 (ISBN 0-516-02218-0); pap. 3.95 (ISBN 0-516-42218-9). Childrens.
—An Introduction to Musical Instruments: Woodwinds. LC 87-18232. (Illus.). 32p. (ps-3). 1987. PLB 14.60 (ISBN 0-516-02217-2); pap. 3.95 (ISBN 0-516-42217-0). Childrens.
—Strings. LC 87-32994. (Illus.). 32p. (ps-3). 1988. PLB 14.60 (ISBN 0-516-02219-9); pap. 3.95 (ISBN 0-516-42219-7). Childrens.
McLean, Margaret. Make Your Own Musical Instruments. Stott, Ken, illus. 32p. (gr. 4-7). 1988. PLB 9.95 (ISBN 0-8225-0895-8, First Ave Edns); pap. 4.95 (ISBN 0-8225-9558-3, First Ave Edns). Lerner Pubns.
May, Dorothy. Dulcimer Classicks. May, Charles, illus. 48p. (Orig.). (gr. 6 up). 1980. pap. 2.95 (ISBN 0-941126-02-1). Meadowlark.
—Dulcimer Songbag for Christmas. May, Charles, illus. 48p. (gr. 3 up). 1978. pap. 2.95 (ISBN 0-941126-01-3). Meadowlark.
Moniot, Janet. Clay Whistles...the Voice of Clay. Rey, Mary L., ed. LC 89-51777. (Illus.). 56p. (Orig.). 1990. pap. 11.95 spiral bdg. (ISBN 0-9624893-0-1); video & book 34.95 (ISBN 0-9624893-1-X). Whistle Pr.
Music & Bugling. (Illus.). 56p. (gr. 6-12). 1990. pap. 1.85 (ISBN 0-8395-3336-5, 3336A). BSA.
Poffenberger, Nancy. Instant Recorder Fun: Book One. 32p. (gr. 4). 1986. pap. 4.95 (ISBN 0-938293-14-1). Fun Pub OH.
—Instant Recorder Fun Package 1 (recorder & book) 32p. (gr. 3). 1986. Repr. of 1983 ed. blister-pak pkg. 10.95 (ISBN 0-938293-15-X). Fun Pub OH.
Starr, Greg R. What's a Sequencer: A Basic Guide to Their Features & Use. Eiche, Jon, ed. LC 90-53369. 64p. (Orig.). 1991. 5.95 (ISBN 0-7935-0083-4, HL00330045). H Leonard Pub Corp.
The Story of Musical Instruments. (Illus.). (gr. 5 up). 3.50 (ISBN 0-7214-0142-2). Ladybird Bks.
Suzuki, Shinichi. Suzuki Cello School: Piano Accompaniment, Vol. 5. 24p. (gr. k-12). 1983. pap. text ed. 6.50 (ISBN 0-87487-270-7, Suzuki Method). Summy-Birchard.
—Suzuki Cello School, Vol. 4: Cello Part. 16p. (gr. k-12). 1983. pap. text ed. 6.50 (ISBN 0-87487-266-9, Suzuki Method). Summy-Birchard.
—Suzuki Cello School, Vol. 4: Piano Accompaniment. 24p. (gr. k-12). 1983. pap. text ed. 6.50 (ISBN 0-87487-269-3, Suzuki Method). Summy-Birchard.
—Suzuki Cello School, Vol. 5: Cello Part. 24p. (gr. k-12). pap. text ed. 6.50 (ISBN 0-87487-267-7, Suzuki Method). Summy-Birchard.
—Suzuki Cello School, Vol 6: Cello Part. 16p. (gr. k-12). 1984. pap. text ed. 6.50 (ISBN 0-87487-268-5, Suzuki Method). Summy-Birchard.
—Suzuki Cello School, Vol. 6: Piano Accompaniments. 24p. (Orig.). (gr. 6-12). 1984. pap. text ed. 6.50 (ISBN 0-87487-271-5, Suzuki Method). Summy-Birchard.
—Suzuki Viola School: Piano Accompaniments, Vol. 4. Preucil, Doris, ed. 64p. (gr. k-12). 1983. pap. text ed. 10.95 (ISBN 0-87487-275-8, Suzuki Method). Summy-Birchard.
Walther, Tom. Make Mine Music. Walther, Tom, illus. 128p. (Orig.). (gr. 3 up). 1981. 14.95 (ISBN 0-316-92111-4); pap. 7.95 (ISBN 0-316-92112-2). Little.
Wiseman, Ann. Making Musical Things: Improvised Instruments. Wiseman, Ann, illus. LC 79-4474. 64p. (gr. 3 up). 1979. 13.95 (ISBN 0-684-16114-1, Scribners Young Read). Macmillan Child Grp.

MUSICAL NOTATION
Feeman, Jeff & Feeman, Maryellen. Key in on Keyboarding. Fowler, Christopher, illus. (gr. 3-8). 1984. pap. 7.95 spiral bd.-typing-stand-up base (ISBN 0-88724-029-1, CD-9041). Carson-Dellos.
—Keyboarding Activities Workbook. Fowler, Christopher, illus. 32p. (gr. 2-5). 1984. pap. 1.98 (ISBN 0-88724-030-5, CD-9042). Carson-Dellos.
MUSICAL REVUES, COMEDIES, ETC.
Brooks, Hindi. Captain Noah. (Illus.). 36p. (Orig.). 1989. pap. 3.00 bk. (ISBN 0-88680-317-9); Piano-Vocal Score 15.00 (ISBN 0-685-34521-1). I E Clark.

Carey, Karla. Julie & Jackie at the Circus: The Play & Musical Play (with Music Book, Story-&-Song Cassette & Piano Cassette) Nolan, Dennis, illus. LC 88-12910. 44p. 1990. pap. 35.00 complete pkg. (ISBN 1-55768-152-X); pap. 25.00 book only (ISBN 1-55768-177-5); story-&-song or piano cass. 8.00 (ISBN 1-55768-027-2). LC Pub.
The talent behind the Julie & Jackie Children's Series: Karla Carey, well-known California author-composer. "Outstanding composer," said Frederick Jagel (former Metropolitan Opera & teacher in San Francisco). "Up-&-coming San Francisco composer's brilliant music brings inspiration in song" (Army of Stars coast-to-coast broadcast, USA & Canada). In speaking of another work, R. Frederick Henry (prominent artist & teacher in Berkeley, California) said, "These etudes, Poems for Piano, are a treasure belonging in the active repertoire of every pianist." Karla Carey now brings remarkable descriptive music & fascinating stories to each of these five children's books. Dennis Nolan, now-renowned award-winning illustrator, at an early age on his first professional assignment, provided the 71 charming colorful pictures in the five Julie & Jackie books - which will bring encouragement to all budding artists. The Series (" Christmastime," "Calendar," "Circus," "Journeying," "Ranch") brings fun while teaching. A child reads & listens to cassette, while watching colorful pictures & learning from storytellers & songs that bring the many characters to life. Each production includes: Children's Book, Music Book & Musical Play (complete instructions, explicit detail, laymen's terms, dialogue hints, directions, gestures, song-presentation, costuming, choreography, stage-settings, property, lighting) each book with cassette.
Publisher Provided Annotation.

Church, Jeff. Dick Whittington & His Cat: A Musical Play Based on an English Folk Tale. (Illus.). 56p. (Orig.). (ps-7). 1990. pap. 3.75 (ISBN 0-88680-340-3); piano/vocal score 10.00 (ISBN 0-88680-341-1). I E Clark.
Crabtree, Paul. I Sincerely Doubt That This Old House Is Very Haunted: Musical. 1968. 4.50 (ISBN 0-87602-142-9). Anchorage.
Egner, Thorbjorn. People & Robbers of Cardemon Town: Musical. 1968. 4.50 (ISBN 0-87602-172-0). Anchorage.
Graczyk, Ed. Aesop's Falables: Musical. 1969. 4.50 (ISBN 0-87602-100-3). Anchorage.
—Runaway: Musical. 1973. 4.50 (ISBN 0-87602-196-8). Anchorage.
Harder, Eleanor & Harder, Ray. Good Grief, a Griffin: Musical. 1968. 4.50 (ISBN 0-87602-131-3). Anchorage.
Harris, Aurand. Just So Stories: Musical. 1971. 4.50 (ISBN 0-87602-145-3). Anchorage.
—The Plain Princess: Musical. 1955. 4.50 (ISBN 0-87602-176-3). Anchorage.
—Steal Away Home: Musical. 1972. 4.50 (ISBN 0-87602-206-9). Anchorage.
—Yankee Doodle: Musical. 1975. 4.50 (ISBN 0-87602-223-9). Anchorage.

Mueller, Tobin J. Danger, Dinosaurs! A Musical Comedy about the Evolution & Extinction of the Dinosaurs. Heller, Joe, illus. (ps-8). 1990. Audio tape incl. pap. 14.95 (ISBN 1-56213-003-X). Ctr Stage Prodns.
—Music of the Planet: A Musical Journey about the World & Wonders of Our Solar System. (ps-8). 1990. pap. 14.95 (ISBN 1-56213-017-X). Ctr Stage Prodns.
—Say Yes! to Life: A Musical Drama about the Dangers Drugs Pose to the joys of Living. Patros, Ann & Patros, Dan, photos by. (Illus.). (gr. 4-9). 1990. Audio tape incl. pap. 14.95 (ISBN 1-56213-045-5). Ctr Stage Prodns.
—The Sound of Money: A Musical Adventure about Economics & the Building of Community. Vanderlinden, Kathy, illus. (ps-8). Audio tape incl. pap. 14.95 (ISBN 1-56213-031-5). Ctr Stage Prodns.
—To Save the Planet: A Musical Fable about the Environment & What We Can Do to Help. Heller, Joe, illus. 54p. (gr. 4-9). 1991. Audio tape Incl. pap. 14.95 (ISBN 1-56213-078-1). Ctr Stage Prodns.
Wright, Carol L. Pegora the Witch: Musical. 1966. 4.50 (ISBN 0-87602-171-2). Anchorage.

MUSICIANS

see also Black Musicians; Composers; Pianists; Singers; Violinists, Violoncellists, Etc.

Bailey, Eva. Music & Musicians. (Illus.). 72p. (gr. 7-12). 1983. 19.95 (ISBN 0-7134-1310-7, Pub. by Batsford England). Trafalgar Sq.
Barboza, Ronald, ed. A Salute to Cape Verdean Musicians & Their Music. (Illus.). 48p. (gr. 9-12). 1989. pap. 10.00 (ISBN 0-9627637-0-5). D&C Cape Verdeans.
Corbin, Carol L. John Lennon. (Illus.). 128p. (gr. 7 up). 1982. PLB 12.90 (ISBN 0-531-04478-5). Watts.
Green, Carl R. & Sanford, William R. Alabama. LC 86-13530. (Illus.). 32p. (gr. 4-5). PLB 9.95 (ISBN 0-89686-294-1, Crestwood Hse). Macmillan Child Grp.
Grey, Charlotte. Bob Geldof: Champion of Africa's Hungry People. Adrian-Vallance, D'Arcy, adapted by. LC 89-77588. (Illus.). 64p. (gr. 3-4). 1990. PLB 12.95 (ISBN 0-8368-0391-4). Gareth Stevens Inc.
Hamilton, Sue. The Killing of a Rock Star: John Lennon. Hamilton, John, ed. (Illus.). 32p. (gr. 4). 1989. PLB 11.95 (ISBN 0-939179-59-8). Abdo & Dghtrs.
Hankin, Rebecca. I Can Be a Musician. LC 84-12136. (Illus.). 32p. (gr. k-3). 1984. lib. bdg. 13.93 (ISBN 0-516-01844-2). Childrens.
Lake, Bonnie & Krishef, Robert. Western Stars of Country Music. LC 77-90149. (Illus.). 72p. (gr. 5 up). 1978. PLB 5.95 (ISBN 0-8225-1407-9). Lerner Pubns.
Loewen, Nancy. Profiles in Music, 6 bks, Reading Level 6. (Illus.). 602p. (gr. 5 up). Date not set. Set. PLB 103.60 (ISBN 0-86592-604-2). Rourke Corp.
Mabery, D L. Prince. (Illus.). 48p. (gr. 4-9). 1985. PLB 8.95 (ISBN 0-8225-1603-9). Lerner Pubns.
Moriarty, Mary & Sweeney, Catherine. Bob Geldof. LC 89-50965. (Illus.). 80p. (Orig.). (gr. 9-12). 1990. pap. 8.95 (ISBN 0-86278-163-9, Pub. by O'Brien Press Ltd Eire). Dufour.
New Kids on the Block Trivia Quiz Book. 64p. (gr. 4-7). 1990. pap. 1.95 (ISBN 0-8167-2227-7). Troll Assocs.
O'Regan, Susan K. Neil Diamond. (Illus.). (gr. 4 up). 1975. PLB 9.75s.p. (ISBN 0-89813-107-3); PLB 13.95 (ISBN 0-685-01262-X). Creative Ed.
Paige, David. A Day in the Life of a Rock Musician. Ruhlin, Roger, photos by. LC 78-68808. (Illus.). 32p. (gr. 4-8). 1980. PLB 11.79 (ISBN 0-89375-225-8); pap. 2.95 (ISBN 0-89375-229-0). Troll Assocs.
Patton, Sally. Musicians. 145p. (gr. 2-6). 1976. pap. text ed. 12.95 (ISBN 0-913705-37-3, ZS03). Zephyr Pr AZ.
Raso, Anne. New Kids On the Block Scrapbook. (Illus.). 64p. (gr. 2-6). 1990. pap. 4.95 (ISBN 0-87449-962-3). Modern Pub NYC.
Riese, Randall & Hitchens, Neal. Nashville Babylon: The Uncensored Truth & Private Lives of Country Music's Greatest Stars. (Illus.). 304p. (Orig.). 1988. pap. 12.95 (ISBN 0-86553-166-8). Congdon & Weed.
Rodino, A. Music Master. (Illus.). (gr. 3-7). 1968. 3.00 (ISBN 0-8198-0105-4). Dghtrs St Paul.
Saunders, Susan. Dolly Parton: Country Goin' to Town. LC 85-40440. (Illus.). 56p. (gr. 2-6). 1985. pap. 10.95 (ISBN 0-670-80787-7). Viking Child Bks.

MUSICIANS, AMERICAN

Buddy Holly. 48p. (gr. 5-6). 1989. PLB 10.95 (ISBN 0-685-26349-5). Capstone Pr.
Crocker, Chris. Cyndi Lauper. Arico, Diane, ed. (Illus.). 64p. (gr. 3-7). 1985. pap. 3.50 (ISBN 0-671-55475-1, Little Simon); 9.29 (ISBN 0-685-09958-X). S&S Trade.
Currie, Cherie & Schusterman, Neal. Neon Angel: The Cherie Currie Story. (Illus.). 192p. 1989. pap. 4.95 (ISBN 0-8431-2348-6). Price Stern.
Elvis Presley. 48p. (gr. 5-6). 1989. PLB 10.95 (ISBN 0-685-26353-3). Capstone Pr.
Greenberg, Keith E. Madonna. LC 85-18030. (Illus.). 40p. (gr. 4-9). 1986. lib. bdg. 9.95 (ISBN 0-8225-1606-3). Lerner Pubns.
Koenig, Terry. Bruce Springsteen. Schoeder, Howard, ed. LC 86-8961. (Illus.). 32p. (gr. 4-5). PLB 9.95 (ISBN 0-89686-303-4, Crestwood Hse). Macmillan Child Grp.
—Lionel Richie. LC 86-13588. (Illus.). 32p. (gr. 4-5). PLB 9.95 (ISBN 0-89686-302-6, Crestwood Hse). Macmillan Child Grp.

MUSICIANS, BLACK

see Black Musicians

MUSICIANS–FICTION

Carlson, Nancy. Harriet's Recital. Carlson, Nancy, illus. (gr. k-3). 1985. bk. & cassette 19.95 (ISBN 0-941078-69-8); pap. 12.95 bk. & cassette (ISBN 0-941078-67-1); cassette, 4 paperbacks & guide 27.95 (ISBN 0-941078-68-X). Live Oak Media.
Christian, Mary B. Singin' Somebody Else's Song. 192p. (gr. 5 up). 1990. pap. 3.95 (ISBN 0-14-034169-2, Puffin). Puffin Bks.
Coco, Eugene B. The Fiddler's Son. Sabuda, Robert, illus. 32p. 1988. 9.95 (ISBN 0-88138-111-X). Green Tiger Pr.
Cosgrove, Stephen. Fiddler. Brown, Jane, ed. Edelson, Wendy, illus. LC 87-20989. (gr. 1-3). 1988. 9.95 (ISBN 0-88070-211-7); deluxe ed. 10.95 (ISBN 0-88070-235-4). Multnomah.
De Mejo, Oscar. Journey to Boc Boc: The Kidnapping of a Rock Star. De Mejo, Oscar, illus. LC 85-45261. 48p. (gr. 3-7). 1987. 12.95 (ISBN 0-06-021579-8); PLB 12.89 (ISBN 0-06-021580-1). HarpC Child Bks.
Griffith, Helen V. Alex & the Cat. Low, Joseph, illus. LC 81-11608. 64p. (gr. 1-3). 1982. 13.95 (ISBN 0-688-00420-2); PLB 13.88 (ISBN 0-688-00421-0). Greenwillow.
Gross, Ruth B. The Bremen-Town Musicians. Kent, Jack, illus. 32p. (gr. k-2). 1985. pap. 1.95 (ISBN 0-590-33835-8). Scholastic Inc.
—The Bremen-Town Musicians. Kent, Jack, illus. 32p. (Orig.). (ps-2). 1985. pap. 2.50 (ISBN 0-590-42364-9). Scholastic Inc.
Haas, Jessie. Keeping Barney. LC 81-7029. 160p. (gr. 5-9). 1982. reinforced bdg. 11.75 (ISBN 0-688-00859-3). Greenwillow.
Hoban, Brom. Skunk Lane. Hoban, Brom, illus. LC 81-47729. 64p. (gr. 2-4). 1983. 8.61i (ISBN 0-06-022347-2). HarpC Child Bks.
Keller, Holly. Cromwell's Glasses. Keller, Holly, illus. LC 81-6644. 32p. (gr. k-3). 1982. 14.95 (ISBN 0-688-00834-8). Greenwillow.
Kuskin, Karla. The Philharmonic Gets Dressed. LC 81-48658. (Illus.). 48p. (gr. k-3). 1982. 12.95 (ISBN 0-06-023622-1); PLB 11.89 (ISBN 0-06-023623-X). HarpC Child Bks.
Landis, J. D. The Band Never Dances. LC 88-28401. 288p. (gr. 7 up). 1989. 13.95 (ISBN 0-06-023721-X); PLB 13.89 (ISBN 0-06-023722-8). HarpC Child Bks.
Major, Kevin. Dear Bruce Springsteen. (gr. k-12). 1989. pap. 3.25 (ISBN 0-440-20410-0). Dell.
Poole, Valerie. Obadiah Coffee & the Music Contest. Poole, Valerie, illus. LC 89-49548. 32p. (ps-3). 1991. 14.95 (ISBN 0-06-021619-0); PLB 14.89 (ISBN 0-06-021620-4). HarpC Child Bks.
Salerno-Sonnenberg, Nadja. Nadja on My Way. LC 89-7661. (Illus.). (gr. 5-9). 1989. 13.95 (ISBN 0-517-57392-X); PLB 13.99 (ISBN 0-517-57391-1). Crown.
Shyer, Marlene F. Me & Joey Pinstripe, the King of Rock. LC 88-15841. 224p. (gr. 7 up). 1988. 13.95 (ISBN 0-684-18941-0, Scribners Young Read). Macmillan Child Grp.
Thomas, Ianthe. Willie Blows a Mean Horn. Toulmin-Rothe, Ann, illus. LC 74-2637. 24p. (gr. k-3). 1981. PLB 11.89 (ISBN 0-06-026107-2). HarpC Child Bks.
Vincent, Gabrielle. Bravo, Ernest & Celestine! Vincent, Gabrielle, illus. LC 81-6423. 24p. (gr. k-3). 1982. 10.75 (ISBN 0-688-00857-7); PLB 10.88 (ISBN 0-688-00858-5). Greenwillow.

MUSICIANS, NEGRO

see Black Musicians

MUSKRATS

Arnosky, Jim. Come out, Muskrats. Arnosky, Jim, illus. LC 88-26611. 40p. (ps-3). 1989. 12.95 (ISBN 0-688-05457-9); PLB 12.88 (ISBN 0-688-05458-7). Lothrop.

MUSKRATS–FICTION

Burgess, Thornton. Jerry Muskrat at Home. 1986. Repr. lib. bdg. 17.95 (ISBN 0-89966-527-6). Buccaneer Bks.
Oana, Katherine. Minnie Muskrat. Baird, Tate, ed. Butrick, Lyn M., illus. LC 88-51856. 16p. (Orig.). (ps-k). 1989. pap. 4.52 (ISBN 0-914127-10-1). Univ Class.

MUSLIMS, BLACK

see Black Muslims

MUSLIMS–FICTION

Clyde, Ahmad. Cheng Ho's Voyage. Durkee, Noura, illus. LC 81-66951. 32p. (Orig.). (gr. 3-7). 1981. pap. 2.00 (ISBN 0-89259-021-1). Am Trust Pubns.

MUSSOLINI, BENITO, 1883-1945

Italia, Bob. Benito Mussolini. Walner, Rosemary, ed. (Illus.). 32p. (gr. 4). 1990. PLB 11.95 (ISBN 0-939179-81-4). Abdo & Dghtrs.
Lyttle, Richard B. Il Duce: The Rise & Fall of Benito Mussolini. LC 86-28851. 256p. (gr. 7 up). 1987. 15.95 (ISBN 0-689-31213-X, Atheneum Child Bk). Macmillan Child Grp.
Mulvihill, Margaret. Mussolini: And Italian Fascism. (Illus.). 64p. (gr. 5-8). 1990. PLB 11.90 (ISBN 0-531-17253-8). Watts.

MUTATION (BIOLOGY)

see Evolution

MYCOLOGY

see Fungi

MYSTERIES AND MIRACLE PLAYS

Bonica, Diane. Biblical Easter & Spring Performances. (Illus.). 96p. (ps-2). 1989. 9.95 (ISBN 0-86653-478-4, SS1869). Good Apple.
Daniel, Rebecca. Three-Minute Bible Skits & Songs. 96p. (gr. 1-7). 1991. 9.95 (ISBN 0-86653-628-0, SS1885). Good Apple.
Daniel, Rebecca, compiled by. Biblical Christmas Performances. 96p. (ps-8). 1988. 9.95 (ISBN 0-86653-461-X, SS1868). Good Apple.
—Biblical Christmas Plays & Musicals. 96p. (ps-8). 1989. 9.95 (ISBN 0-86653-513-6, SS1871). Good Apple.
—Biblical Performances for Early Childhood. 96p. (ps-1). 1990. 9.95 (ISBN 0-86653-548-9, SS1872). Good Apple.
Gamm, David. Child's Play. LC 78-51069. (Illus.). 96p. (gr. 3-8). 1978. pap. 4.95 (ISBN 0-87793-150-X). Ave Maria.
Glavich, Mary K. Gospel Plays for Students: Thirty-Six Scripts for Education & Worship. LC 89-50562. (Illus.). x, 102p. 1989. 12.95 (ISBN 0-89622-407-4). Twenty-Third.
Hayes, Theresa. Getting Your Act Together. LC 85-16548. 112p. (gr. 7-12). 1986. pap. 4.95 (ISBN 0-87239-998-2, 3358). Standard Pub.
Ison, Colleen. Goliath's Last Stand. LC 85-17315. 112p. (gr. k-6). 1986. pap. 4.95 (ISBN 0-87239-997-4, 3357). Standard Pub.
Jones, Kathy. Acting for God. Henson, Grace, illus. 48p. (gr. 4-8). 1984. wkbk. 6.95 (ISBN 0-86653-236-6, SS 818). Good Apple.
Keene, Carolyn. Deadly Intent. 155p. (gr. 5-8). 1989. pap. 2.95 (ISBN 0-671-68727-1, Archway). PB.
Schera, Judith, et al. Biblical Performances for Vacation Bible School. 96p. (gr. 1-8). 1991. 9.95 (ISBN 0-86653-578-0). Good Apple.
Scherra, J., et al. Biblical Puppet Performances. 96p. (ps-8). 1990. 9.95 (ISBN 0-86653-549-7, SS1873). Good Apple.

MYSTERY AND DETECTIVE STORIES

Ables. Mystery on the Delta. (gr. 7 up). PLB 6.70 (ISBN 0-8313-0001-9). Lantern.
Adams & Coudert, Allison. Alice Whipple, Fifth Grade Detective. (ps-7). 1987. pap. 2.25 (ISBN 0-317-64197-2, Skylark). Bantam.
Adams, Laurie & Coudert, Allison. Alice Investigates. 96p. (Orig.). 1987. pap. 2.75 (ISBN 0-553-15485-0, Skylark). Bantam.
Adkins, Jan. Solstice: A Mystery of the Season. Adkins, Jan, illus. 128p. 1990. 12.95 (ISBN 0-8027-6970-5); lib. bdg. 13.85 reinforced (ISBN 0-8027-6971-3). Walker & Co.
Adler, C. S. Footsteps on the Stairs. LC 81-15146. 160p. (gr. 4-6). 1982. pap. 12.95 (ISBN 0-385-28303-2). Delacorte.
—Footsteps on the Stairs. 160p. (gr. 5-9). 1984. pap. 2.25 (ISBN 0-440-42654-5, YB). Dell.
Adler, David A. Cam Jansen & the Mystery at the Monkey House. Natti, Susanna, illus. LC 85-40443. 56p. (gr. 2-4). 1985. pap. 10.95 (ISBN 0-670-80782-6). Viking Child Bks.
—Cam Jansen & the Mystery at The Monkey House. (gr. k-6). 1988. pap. 2.95 (ISBN 0-440-40047-3, YB). Dell.
—Cam Jansen & the Mystery Corn Popper. Natti, Susanna, illus. 64p. (gr. 2-5). 1986. pap. 10.95 (ISBN 0-670-81118-1). Viking Child Bks.
—Cam Jansen & the Mystery Monster Movie. Natti, Susanna, illus. LC 83-16693. 64p. (gr. 2-5). 1984. pap. 10.95 (ISBN 0-670-20035-2). Viking Child Bks.
—Cam Jansen & the Mystery of Flight 54. Natti, Susanna, illus. 64p. (gr. 2-5). 1989. pap. 10.95 (ISBN 0-670-81841-0). Viking Child Bks.
—Cam Jansen & the Mystery of the Babe Ruth Baseball. Natti, Susanna, illus. LC 82-2621. 64p. (gr. 2-5). 1982. pap. 10.95 (ISBN 0-670-20037-9). Viking Child Bks.
—Cam Jansen & the Mystery of the Carnival Prize. (gr. k-6). 1987. pap. 2.75 (ISBN 0-440-41202-1, YB). Dell.
—Cam Jansen & the Mystery of the Circus Clown. Natti, Susanna, illus. LC 82-50363. 64p. (gr. 2-4). 1983. pap. 10.95 (ISBN 0-670-20036-0). Viking Child Bks.
—Cam Jansen & the Mystery of the Circus Clown. Natti, Susanna, illus. 64p. (gr. 1-4). 1985. pap. 2.75 (ISBN 0-440-41021-5, YB). Dell.
—Cam Jansen & the Mystery of the Dinosaur Bones. Natti, Susanna, illus. LC 80-25132. 64p. (gr. 2-5). 1981. pap. 10.95 (ISBN 0-670-20040-9). Viking Child Bks.
—Cam Jansen & the Mystery of the Dinosaur Bones. Natti, Susanna, illus. (gr. 1-4). 1983. pap. 2.75 (ISBN 0-440-41199-8, YB). Dell.
—Cam Jansen & the Mystery of the Dinosaur Bones. Natti, Susanna, illus. 64p. (gr. 2-5). 1991. pap. 3.95 (ISBN 0-14-034674-0, Puffin). Puffin Bks.
—Cam Jansen & the Mystery of the Gold Coins. Natti, Susanna, illus. LC 81-16158. 64p. (gr. 2-5). 1982. pap. 10.95 (ISBN 0-670-20038-7). Viking Child Bks.
—Cam Jansen & the Mystery of the Stolen Diamonds. Natti, Susanna, illus. LC 79-20695. 64p. (gr. 2-5). 1980. pap. 10.95 (ISBN 0-670-20039-5). Viking Child Bks.
—Cam Jansen & the Mystery of the Stolen Diamonds. Natti, Susanna, illus. (gr. 1-4). 1982. pap. 2.75 (ISBN 0-440-41111-4, YB). Dell.
—Cam Jansen & the Mystery of the Stolen Diamonds. Natti, Susanna, illus. 64p. (gr. 2-5). 1991. pap. 3.95 (ISBN 0-14-034670-8, Puffin). Puffin Bks.
—Cam Jansen & the Mystery of the Television Dog. Natti, Susanna, illus. LC 81-2207. 64p. (gr. 2-5). 1981. pap. 10.95 (ISBN 0-670-20042-5). Viking Child Bks.
—Cam Jansen & the Mystery of the Television Dog. Natti, Susanna, illus. 64p. (gr. 1-4). 1983. pap. 2.75 (ISBN 0-440-41196-3, YB). Dell.
—Cam Jansen & the Mystery of the Television Dog. Natti, Susanna, illus. 64p. (gr. 2-5). 1991. pap. 3.95 (ISBN 0-14-034676-7, Puffin). Puffin Bks.

—Cam Jansen & the Mystery of the U. F. O. Natti, Susanna, illus. LC 80-15580. 64p. (gr. 7-10). 1980. pap. 10.95 (ISBN 0-670-20041-7). Viking Child Bks.
—Cam Jansen & the Mystery of the U. F. O. Natti, Susanna, illus. (gr. 1-4). 1982. pap. 2.75 (ISBN 0-440-41142-4, YB). Dell.
—Cam Jansen & the Mystery of the U. F. O. Natti, Susanna, illus. 64p. (gr. 2-5). 1991. pap. 3.95 (ISBN 0-14-034672-4, Puffin). Puffin Bks.
—The Fourth Floor Twins & Disappearing Parrot Trick, No. 3. Trivas, Irene, illus. LC 85-40833. 64p. (gr. 2-5). 1986. pap. 10.95 (ISBN 0-670-80926-8). Viking Child Bks.
—The Fourth Floor Twins & the Fish Snitch Mystery. Trivas, Irene, illus. 64p. (gr. 1-4). 1986. pap. 3.95 (ISBN 0-14-032082-2, Puffin). Puffin Bks.
—The Fourth Floor Twins & the Fortune Cookie Chase. Trivas, Irene, illus. 64p. (gr. 1-4). 1986. pap. 3.95 (ISBN 0-14-032083-0, Puffin). Puffin Bks.
—Fourth Floor Twins & the Sand Castle Contest. (gr. 4 up). 1990. pap. 3.95 (ISBN 0-14-032654-5, Puffin). Puffin Bks.
—The Fourth Floor Twins & the Silver Ghost Express. Trivas, Irene, illus. (gr. 2-5). 1987. pap. 3.95 (ISBN 0-14-032215-9, Puffin). Puffin Bks.
—Fourth Floor Twins & the Skyscraper Parade. Trivas, Irene, illus. LC 86-28961. (gr. 2-5). 1987. pap. 10.95 (ISBN 0-670-81603-5). Viking Child Bks.
Adorjan, Carol. The Copy Cat Mystery. 128p. 1990. pap. 2.95 (ISBN 0-380-75743-5, Camelot). Avon.
Adrian, Mary. The Fireball Mystery. Lonette, Reisie, illus. LC 77-17151. (gr. 2-6). 1977. 8.95 (ISBN 0-8038-2325-8). Hastings.
—The Mystery of the Dinosaur Graveyard. Hannans, Nancy, illus. LC 82-2951. 128p. (gr. 4-7). 1982. PLB 9.95 (ISBN 0-8038-4738-6). Hastings.
Ahlberg, Allan. Mystery Tour. LC 90-2942. (Illus.). 24p. (ps up). 1991. 12.95 (ISBN 0-688-09957-2); PLB 12.88 (ISBN 0-688-09958-0). Greenwillow.
Aiken, Joan. Died on a Rainy Sunday. (gr. k-12). 1988. pap. 2.95 (ISBN 0-440-20097-0, LFL). Dell.
—Night Fall. (gr. 5 up). 1988. pap. 2.95 (ISBN 0-440-20054-7, LFL). Dell.
—The Stolen Lake. (gr. 4-6). 15.00 (ISBN 0-8446-6417-0). Peter Smith.
—A Whisper in the Night. (gr. 5 up). 14.75 (ISBN 0-8446-6420-0). Peter Smith.
—A Whisper in the Night: Tales of Terror & Suspense. (gr. k-12). 1988. pap. 3.25 (ISBN 0-440-20185-3, LE). Dell.
Albrecht, Peggy. Secret of the Old House, No. 1. (gr. 6-8). 1983. pap. 2.95 (ISBN 0-87508-653-5). Chr Lit.
Alcock, Vivien. The Mysterious Mr. Ross. LC 87-5455. 160p. (gr. 5-9). 1987. pap. 14.95 (ISBN 0-385-29581-2). Delacorte.
—The Mysterious Mr. Ross. (gr. k-6). 1990. pap. 2.95 (ISBN 0-440-40282-4, YB). Dell.
—The Stonewalkers. LC 82-13956. 192p. (gr. 4-6). 1983. pap. 12.95 (ISBN 0-385-29233-3). Delacorte.
Alexander, Judy. James Bond Story Book. (Illus.). 64p. (gr. 3 up). 1985. 6.95 (ISBN 0-448-18972-0, G&D). Putnam Pub Group.
Alexander, Lloyd. Castle of Llyr. 192p. (gr. k-6). 1969. pap. 3.50 (ISBN 0-440-41125-4, YB). Dell.
—Westmark. LC 80-22242. (gr. 5 up). 1981. 15.95 (ISBN 0-525-42335-4, DCB). Dutton Child Bks.
Alexander, Sue. World Famous Muriel & the Magic Mystery. Frazee, Marla, illus. LC 89-22396. 32p. (gr. k-3). 1990. 12.95 (ISBN 0-690-04787-8, Crowell Jr Bks); PLB 12.89 (ISBN 0-690-04789-4, Crowell Jr Bks). HarpC Child Bks.
Alexander, William. The Case of the Funny Money Man. Ewers, Joe, illus. LC 89-36358. 96p. (gr. 4-7). 1990. PLB 9.89 (ISBN 0-8167-1692-7); pap. text ed. 2.95 (ISBN 0-8167-1693-5). Troll Assocs.
—The Case of the Gumball Bandits. Ewers, Joe, illus. LC 89-36558. 96p. (gr. 4-7). 1990. PLB 9.89 (ISBN 0-8167-1696-X); pap. text ed. 2.95 (ISBN 0-8167-1697-8). Troll Assocs.
—The Ghost of Shockly Manor. Ewers, Joe, illus. LC 89-36544. 96p. (gr. 4-7). 1990. PLB 9.89 (ISBN 0-8167-1694-3); pap. text ed. 2.95 (ISBN 0-8167-1695-1). Troll Assocs.
Alfred Hitchcock's Witch's Brew. Hitchcock, Alfred, selected by. 192p. (gr. 5 up). 1983. pap. 2.95 (ISBN 0-394-85911-1). Random.
Allard, Harry. Miss Nelson Is Missing. (ps-3). 1987. pap. 7.95 incl. cass. (ISBN 0-395-45737-8). HM.
Alman, Mickey. Scene of the Crime. 1990. pap. 3.50 (ISBN 0-8041-0600-2). Ivy Books.
Amoss, Berthe. Secret Lives. 192p. (gr. 1-9). 1981. pap. 2.95 (ISBN 0-440-47904-5, YB). Dell.
Anderson, Sanna. The Stormy Night. (Illus.). (ps-2). 1991. 12.95 (ISBN 0-8423-6772-1). Tyndale.
Angell, Judie. The Weird Disappearance of Jordan Hall. LC 87-7781. 128p. (gr. 6-8). 1987. 11.95 (ISBN 0-531-05727-5); PLB 11.99 (ISBN 0-531-08327-6). Orchard Bks Watts.
Appleton, Victor. Tom Swift: Ark Two. (Illus.). 192p. (gr. 3-7). 1982. 8.95 (ISBN 0-671-43952-9, Little Simon); pap. 2.75 (ISBN 0-671-43953-7). S&S Trade.
—Tom Swift: Crater of Mystery. Barish, Wendy, ed. 192p. (gr. 3-7). 1983. 8.95 (ISBN 0-671-43954-5, Little Simon); pap. 3.95 (ISBN 0-671-43955-3). S&S Trade.
—Tom Swift: The War in Outer Space. 192p. (Orig.). (gr. 3-7). 1981. 8.95 (ISBN 0-671-42539-0, Little Simon); pap. 3.95 (ISBN 0-671-42579-X). S&S Trade.
Arden, William. Alfred Hitchcock & the Three Investigators in the Mystery of the Dancing Devil. LC 76-8134. (Illus.). (gr. 4-7). 1984. pap. 2.95 (ISBN 0-394-86425-5, Random Juv). Random.
—Alfred Hitchcock & the Three Investigators in the Mystery of the Dead Man's Riddle. Hearne, William, illus. LC 74-4934. 160p. (gr. 4-7). 1984. (Random Juv); lib. bdg. 5.39 (ISBN 0-394-92927-6); pap. 2.95 (ISBN 0-394-86422-0). Random.
—Alfred Hitchcock & the Three Investigators in the Mystery of the Moaning Cave. Hitchcock, Alfred, ed. Kane, Harry, illus. LC 68-23677. (gr. 4-7). 1978. 2.95 (ISBN 0-394-81423-1, Random Juv); pap. 1.95 (ISBN 0-394-83773-8); pap. 1.95 (ISBN 0-685-04247-2). Random.
—Alfred Hitchcock & the Three Investigators in the Mystery of the Shrinking House. Hitchcock, Alfred, ed. (Illus.). (gr. 4-7). 1985. (Random Juv); lib. bdg. 6.99 (ISBN 0-394-92482-7); pap. 1.95 (ISBN 0-394-83777-0); pap. 2.95 (ISBN 0-394-86418-2). Random.
—Alfred Hitchcock & the Three Investigators in the Mystery of the Deadly Double. Mott, Herb, illus. LC 78-55960. (gr. 4-7). 1978. (Random Juv); lib. bdg. 5.39 (ISBN 0-394-93902-6). Random.
—Alfred Hitchcock & the Three Investigators in the Mystery of the Headless Horse, No. 26. Hearne, Jack, illus. LC 77-74458. (gr. 4-8). 1977. 2.95 (ISBN 0-394-83569-7, Random Juv); lib. bdg. 5.39 (ISBN 0-394-93569-1). Random.
—Alfred Hitchcock & the Three Investigators in the Secret of the Crooked Cat. Hitchcock, Alfred, ed. (Illus.). (gr. 4-9). 1985. 2.95 (ISBN 0-394-81188-7); lib. bdg. 6.99 (ISBN 0-394-91188-1); pap. 2.95 (ISBN 0-394-86413-1). Random.
—Alfred Hitchcock & the Three Investigators in the Secret of Shark Reef. Hitchcock, Alfred, ed. (Illus.). (gr. 4-7). 1985. pap. 2.95 (ISBN 0-394-86430-1). Random.
—Alfred Hitchcock & the Three Investigators in the Secret of Phantom Lake. Hitchcock, Alfred, ed. (Illus.). (gr. 4-7). 1984. 2.95 (ISBN 0-394-82651-5, Random Juv); lib. bdg. 6.99 (ISBN 0-394-92651-X); pap. 1.95 (ISBN 0-394-84257-X); pap. 2.95 (ISBN 0-394-86419-0). Random.
—Hot Wheels. LC 88-29695. 144p. (gr. 5 up). 1989. PLB 6.99 (ISBN 0-394-99959-2). Random.
—Hot Wheels. LC 88-9338. 144p. (Orig.). (gr. 5 up). 1989. pap. 2.95 (ISBN 0-394-89959-8). Knopf.
—Hot Wheels: Crimebusters, No. 1. reissue ed. LC 88-9338. 144p. (gr. 4-8). 1991. pap. 3.50 (ISBN 0-679-81380-2, Bullseye Bks). Knopf.
—The Mystery of the Dancing Devil. Hitchcock, Alfred, ed. LC 80-29350. 144p. (gr. 4-7). 1981. pap. 1.95 (ISBN 0-685-04219-7). Random.
—The Mystery of the Deadly Double. LC 79-29638. 160p. (gr. 4-7). 1985. pap. 2.95 (ISBN 0-394-86428-X). Random.
—The Mystery of the Headless Horse. Hitchcock, Alfred, ed. LC 80-29259. 160p. (gr. 4-7). 1985. pap. 3.95 (ISBN 0-394-86426-3). Random.
—The Mystery of the Moaning Cave, No. 10. LC 83-26985. 176p. (gr. 4-8). 1991. pap. 3.50 (ISBN 0-679-81172-9, Bullseye Bks). Knopf.
—The Mystery of the Purple Pirate, No. 33. reissue ed. LC 82-372. 192p. (gr. 4-8). 1991. pap. 3.50 (ISBN 0-679-81174-5, Bullseye Bks). Knopf.
—The Mystery of the Smashing Glass. LC 83-26984. (Illus.). 192p. (gr. 4-7). 1984. (Pub. by BYR); pap. 2.95 (ISBN 0-394-86550-2). Random.
—The Mystery of Wrecker's Rock. LC 85-28155. (Illus.). 192p. (gr. 4-6). 1986. lib. bdg. 6.99 (ISBN 0-394-97375-5, Random Juv); pap. 2.95 (ISBN 0-394-87375-0, BYR). Random.
Arizzi, Mavis. It's a Mystery. (Illus.). 32p. (gr. 4-8). 1985. pap. 3.95 (ISBN 0-913839-45-0). Bk Lures.
Artes, Dorothy B. Rick & Po: Village Detectives, Bk. 2. LC 86-50878. (Illus.). 98p. (Orig.). (gr. 4-6). 1987. pap. 4.00 (ISBN 0-932433-28-6). Windswept Hse.
Arthur, Robert. Alfred Hitchcock & the Three Investigators in the Mystery of the Green Ghost. Hitchcock, Alfred, ed. (Illus.). (gr. 4-8). 1985. 2.95 (ISBN 0-394-81228-X, Random Juv); lib. bdg. 6.99 (ISBN 0-394-91228-4); pap. 1.95 (ISBN 0-394-84258-8); pap. 3.95 (ISBN 0-394-86404-2). Random.
—Alfred Hitchcock & the Three Investigators in the Mystery of the Screaming Clock. Hitchcock, Alfred, ed. Kane, Harry, illus. LC 68-23676. (gr. 4-7). 1984. 2.95 (ISBN 0-394-81288-3, Random Juv); pap. 2.95 (ISBN 0-394-86409-3). Random.
—Alfred Hitchcock & the Three Investigators in the Mystery of the Stuttering Parrot. Hitchcock, Alfred, ed. (Illus.). (gr. 4-8). 1985. (Random Juv); lib. bdg. 5.39 (ISBN 0-394-91243-8); pap. 1.95 (ISBN 0-394-83767-3); pap. 2.95 (ISBN 0-394-86402-6). Random.
—Alfred Hitchcock & the Three Investigators in the Mystery of the Talking Skull. Hitchcock, Alfred, ed. Kane, Harry, illus. LC 69-20274. (gr. 4-7). 1984. (Random Juv); lib. bdg. 5.39 (ISBN 0-394-91380-9); pap. 3.95 (ISBN 0-394-86411-5). Random.
—Alfred Hitchcock & the Three Investigators in the Mystery of the Vanishing Treasure. Hitchcock, Alfred, ed. Kane, Harry, illus. (gr. 4-8). 1985. 2.95 (ISBN 0-394-81550-5, Random Juv); lib. bdg. 6.99 (ISBN 0-394-91550-X); pap. 2.95 (ISBN 0-394-86405-0). Random.
—Alfred Hitchcock & the Three Investigators in the Mystery of the Whispering Mummy. Hitchcock, Alfred, ed. (Illus.). (gr. 4-8). 1978. (Random Juv); pap. 1.95 (ISBN 0-394-83768-1). Random.
—Alfred Hitchcock & the Three Investigators in the Mystery of the Fiery Eye. Kane, Harry, illus. LC 77-28860. (gr. 4-8). 1984. 2.95 (ISBN 0-394-81661-7, Random Juv); lib. bdg. 6.99 (ISBN 0-394-91661-1); pap. 2.95 (ISBN 0-394-86407-7). Random.
—Alfred Hitchcock & the Three Investigators in the Mystery of the Silver Spider. Kane, Harry, illus. (gr. 4-8). 1985. (Random Juv); lib. bdg. 5.39 (ISBN 0-394-91663-8); pap. 1.95 (ISBN 0-394-83771-1); pap. 2.95 (ISBN 0-394-86408-5). Random.
—Alfred Hitchcock & the Three Investigators in the Secret of Skeleton Island. Hitchcock, Alfred, ed. Kane, Harry, illus. (gr. 4-9). 1985. 2.95 (ISBN 0-394-81552-1, Random Juv); lib. bdg. 5.39 (ISBN 0-394-91552-6); pap. 1.95 (ISBN 0-394-83769-X); pap. 3.95 (ISBN 0-394-86406-9). Random.
—Alfred Hitchcock & the Three Investigators in the Secret of Terror Castle. Hitchcock, Alfred, ed. (Illus.). (gr. 4-8). 1985. (Random Juv); lib. bdg. 5.39 (ISBN 0-394-91241-1); pap. 1.95 (ISBN 0-394-83766-5); pap. 2.95 (ISBN 0-394-86401-8). Random.
—Mystery & More Mystery. Lambert, Saul, illus. (gr. 7-11). 1972. 2.95 (ISBN 0-685-04261-8, Random Juv). Random.
—Mystery & More Mystery. Lambert, Saul, illus. (gr. 7-11). 1972. 2.95 (ISBN 0-685-04261-8, Random Juv). Random.
—The Mystery of the Stuttering Parrot, No. 2. reissue ed. LC 83-26983. 192p. (gr. 4-8). 1991. pap. 3.50 (ISBN 0-679-81171-0, Bullseye Bks). Knopf.
—The Secret of Terror Castle, No. 1. reissue ed. LC 83-26987. 176p. (gr. 4-8). 1991. pap. 3.50 (ISBN 0-679-81176-1, Bullseye Bks). Knopf.
Ashabranner, Brent. Dark Harvest. (Illus.). 192p. (gr. 7-11). 1985. 14.95 (ISBN 0-396-08624-1, Putnam). Putnam Pub Group.
Asimov, Janet & Asimov, Isaac. Norby & the Court Jester. 128p. (gr. 3-7). 1991. 12.95 (ISBN 0-8027-8131-4); PLB 13.85 (ISBN 0-8027-8132-2). Walker & Co.
—Norby Down to Earth. (Illus.). (gr. 4-9). 1989. 12.95 (ISBN 0-8027-6866-0); PLB 13.85 (ISBN 0-8027-6867-9). Walker & Co.
Austin, Jennifer. Mystery in Hollywood. Meisel, Ann, illus. 168p. (gr. 3-7). 1990. pap. 4.95 (ISBN 0-448-37702-0, G&D). Putnam Pub Group.
—Race Against Time. Meisel, Ann, illus. 168p. (gr. 3-7). 1990. pap. 4.95 (ISBN 0-448-37701-2, G&D). Putnam Pub Group.
—Ticket to Danger. Meisel, Ann, illus. 168p. (gr. 3-7). 1990. pap. 4.95 (ISBN 0-448-37700-4, G&D). Putnam Pub Group.
—Treasure Beach. Meisel, Ann, illus. 168p. (gr. 3-7). 1990. pap. 4.95 (ISBN 0-448-37703-9, G&D). Putnam Pub Group.
Avery, Louisia. The Risks of RO - Episode 4: Child's Play. Wimberly, Potice & Andrews, Dianne, eds. Smith, Pauline, illus. 110p. (Orig.). 1988. pap. text ed. 5.95 (ISBN 0-945779-03-8). Ethnic Role Model.
Avi. Who Stole the Wizard of Oz? James, Derek, illus. LC 81-884. 128p. (gr. 3-6). 1981. lib. bdg. 7.99 (ISBN 0-394-94644-8). Knopf.
—Windcatcher. LC 90-40574. 128p. (gr. 3-7). 1991. SBE 12.95 (ISBN 0-02-707761-6, Bradbury Pr). Macmillan Child Grp.
—Wolf Rider: A Tale of Terror. LC 86-13607. 224p. (gr. 7 up). 1986. 14.95 (ISBN 0-02-707760-8, Bradbury Pr). Macmillan Child Grp.
Babbitt, Natalie. The Eyes of the Amaryllis. LC 77-11862. 160p. (gr. 3 up). 1977. 13.95 (ISBN 0-374-32241-4). FS&G.
—Goody Hall. (Illus.). 176p. (gr. 4 up). 1986. pap. 3.50 (ISBN 0-374-42767-4). FS&G.
Babisch, Donald. Who Is That Peeking in My Windows. Caroland, Mary, ed. LC 90-83590. (Illus.). 44p. 1991. pap. 4.95 (ISBN 1-55523-374-0). Winston-Derek.
Bach, Alice. Parrot Woman. (Orig.). (gr. k-6). 1987. pap. 2.95 (ISBN 0-440-46987-2, YB). Dell.
Baer, Judy. Paige. LC 86-70912. 160p. (Orig.). (gr. 7-9). 1986. pap. 3.95 (ISBN 0-87123-894-2). Bethany Hse.
Baker, Eugene. At the Scene of the Crime. Axeman, Lois, illus. LC 80-14091. 32p. (gr. 2-5). 1980. PLB 9.48 (ISBN 0-89565-151-3). Childs World.
—In the Detective's Lab. Axeman, Linda, illus. LC 80-17787. 32p. (gr. 2-5). 1980. PLB 9.48 (ISBN 0-89565-154-8). Childs World.
—Master of Disguise. Axeman, Lois, illus. LC 80-11297. 32p. (gr. 2-5). 1980. PLB 9.48 (ISBN 0-89565-149-1). Childs World.
Baker, Tom. High School Highways, 5 novels in ea. set, Sets 1 & 2. (Illus.). (gr. 4-12). 1988. pap. 12.50 ea. set (Pub. by High Noon Books). Set 1, 240p (ISBN 0-87879-536-7, Pub. by High Noon Books). Set 2, 240p (ISBN 0-87879-582-0, Pub. by High Noon Books). Acad Therapy.
The Bank Street Book of Mysteries. (Illus., Orig.). (gr. 4 up). 1989. pap. 3.95 (ISBN 0-671-63148-9, Minstrel Bks). PB.
Bannister, Ned. Cadets: Code Name: Snowball, No. 1. (gr. 3 up). 1988. pap. 2.95 (ISBN 0-345-35115-0). Ballantine.
Barklem, Jill. The Secret Staircase. Barklem, Jill, illus. 32p. (ps-3). 1989. pap. 5.95 (ISBN 0-399-21726-6, Sandcastle Bks). Putnam Pub Group.

Barr, Mike. Murder Can Be Comic. McLaughlin, Frank, illus. 5p. 1988. incl. puzzle 15.95 (ISBN 0-922242-05-4). Lombard Mktg.

Barret, Ethel. Muffy & the Mystery of the Stolen Eggs: Sylvester the Three Spined Stickle Back. (gr. 2-6). 1980. pap. 5.95 incl. cass. (ISBN 0-8307-0689-5, 5606691). Regal.

Barzun, Jacques & Taylor, Wendell H. A Catalogue of Crime: A Reader's Guide to the Literature of Mystery, Detection, & Related Genres. LC 88-45884. 864p. (gr. 7 up). 1989. 50.00 (ISBN 0-06-010263-2, HarpT). HarperCollins.

Base, Graeme. The Eleventh Hour: A Curious Mystery. (Illus.). 32p. 1990. 14.95 (ISBN 0-8109-0851-4). Abrams.

Bates, Betty. Call Me Friday the Thirteenth. Edwards, Linda S., illus. 112p. (gr. 3-7). 1985. pap. 2.50 (ISBN 0-440-40984-5, LFL). Dell.

Bellairs, John. The Curse of the Blue Figurine. Gorey, Edward, illus. LC 82-73217. 224p. (gr. 5 up). 1983. 11.95 (ISBN 0-8037-1119-0); PLB 11.89 (ISBN 0-8037-1265-0). Dial Bks Young.

—The Curse of the Blue Figurine. 208p. (gr. 4-6). 1984. pap. 3.50 (ISBN 0-553-15540-7, RL6IL4, Skylark). Bantam.

—The Dark Secret of Weatherend. 192p. 1986. pap. 2.50 (ISBN 0-553-15375-7, Skylark). Bantam.

—The Letter, the Witch & the Ring. 192p. (gr. 3-6). 1977. pap. 3.25 (ISBN 0-440-44722-4, YB). Dell.

—The Mummy, the Will & the Crypt. 176p. (gr. 6). 1985. pap. 2.75 (ISBN 0-553-15498-2). Bantam.

—Secret of the Underground Room. (Illus.). 160p. (ps-3). 1990. 13.95 (ISBN 0-8037-0863-7); PLB 13.89 (ISBN 0-8037-0864-5). Dial Bks Young.

—The Spell of the Sorcerer's Skull. LC 84-7114. (gr. 5 up). 1985. 11.95 (ISBN 0-8037-0120-9); PLB 11.89 (ISBN 0-8037-0122-5). Dial Bks Young.

Bellem, Robert L. Dan Turner, Hollywood Detective. Mason, Tom, ed. Wilber, Ron, illus. 64p. 1990. pap. 7.95 (ISBN 0-944735-65-7). Malibu Graphics.

Bennett, Jay. The Birthday Murderer. 160p. (gr. 7 up). 1980. pap. 1.50 (ISBN 0-440-90576-1, LFL). Dell.

—Coverup. 144p. (gr. 9-12). 1991. 13.95 (ISBN 0-531-15224-3); PLB 13.90 (ISBN 0-531-11091-5). Watts.

—The Dark Corridor. (gr. 6 up). 1990. pap. 3.50 (ISBN 0-449-70337-1, Juniper). Fawcett.

—The Dark Corridor: A Novel of Suspense for Young Adults. 176p. (gr. 7 up). 1988. 12.95 (ISBN 0-531-15090-9). Watts.

—Deathman, Do Not Follow Me. 144p. (gr. 7 up). 1986. pap. 2.50 (ISBN 0-590-40525-X, Point). Scholastic Inc.

—Say Hello to the Hit Man. 144p. (gr. 7 up). 1981. pap. 1.95 (ISBN 0-440-97618-9, LFL). Dell.

—Sing Me a Death Song. 144p. (gr. 12 up). 1990. pap. 3.50 (ISBN 0-449-70369-X, Juniper). Fawcett.

—Skinhead. 128p. (gr. 7-12). 1991. 13.95 (ISBN 0-531-15218-9); PLB 13.90 (ISBN 0-531-11001-X). Watts.

Ben-Uri, Galila. The Missing Crown. Hinlicky, Gregg, illus. 223p. (gr. 5-7). 1988. 11.95 (ISBN 0-935063-41-2); pap. 8.95 (ISBN 0-935063-42-0). CIS Comm.

—The Mysterious Cargo. Hinlicky, Gregg, illus. 285p. (gr. 5-7). 1989. 13.95 (ISBN 1-56062-006-4); pap. 10.95 (ISBN 1-56062-007-2). CIS Comm.

Bilezikian, Gary. While I Slept. Bilezikian, Gary, illus. LC 90-52514. 32p. (ps-1). 1990. 12.95 (ISBN 0-531-05875-1); PLB 12.99 (ISBN 0-531-08475-2). Orchard Bks Watts.

Binnamin, Vivian. The Case of the Anteater's Missing Lunch. Brook, Bonnie, ed. Nelsen, Jeffrey S., illus. 32p. (gr. k-3). 1990. PLB 6.98 (ISBN 0-671-68816-2); pap. 2.50 (ISBN 0-671-68820-0). Silver Pr.

—The Case of the Planetarium Puzzle. Brook, Bonnie, ed. Nelsen, Jeffrey S., illus. 32p. (gr. k-3). 1990. PLB 6.98 (ISBN 0-671-68819-7); pap. 2.50 (ISBN 0-671-68823-5). Silver Pr.

Black, Auguste R. The Shelby Avenue Gang. Black, Candice N., illus. 66p. (Orig.). (gr. 2-5). 1990. pap. 3.95 (ISBN 0-9628010-0-3). A R Black.

Blaine, John. The Magic Talisman. Frolich, Dany, illus. Goodwin, Hal, afterword by. (Illus.). 213p. (gr. 8-12). 1989. 25.00 (ISBN 0-936414-06-5). Manuscript Pr.

Blair, Cynthia. The Hot Fudge Sunday Affair. 1985. pap. 2.95 (ISBN 0-449-70158-1, Juniper). Fawcett.

Blake, Olive. The Grape Jelly Mystery. Goodman, Joan E., illus. LC 78-18040. 48p. (gr. 2-4). 1979. PLB 10.89 (ISBN 0-89375-096-4); pap. 2.95 (ISBN 0-89375-084-0). Troll Assocs.

—Mystery of the Lost Letter. Kossin, Sanford, illus. LC 78-18037. 48p. (gr. 2-4). 1979. PLB 10.89 (ISBN 0-89375-093-X); pap. 2.95 (ISBN 0-89375-081-6). Troll Assocs.

—Mystery of the Lost Pearl. Parker, Ed, illus. LC 78-60121. 48p. (gr. 2-4). 1979. PLB 10.89 (ISBN 0-89375-086-7); pap. 2.95 (ISBN 0-89375-074-3). Troll Assocs.

Bloch, Mary H. Footprints in the Swamp. Shetterly, Robert, illus. LC 84-21553. 80p. (gr. 4-6). 1985. 12.95 (ISBN 0-689-31085-4, Atheneum Child Bk). Macmillan Child Grp.

Blount, Mary C. Sebastian (Super Sleuth) & the Stars-in-His-Eyes Mystery. McCue, Lisa, illus. 64p. (gr. 3-5). 1990. pap. 2.75 (ISBN 0-671-63254-X, Minstrel Bks). PB.

Bly & Stephen. Crystal's Perious Ride. LC 85-27983. 144p. (gr. 5-7). 1986. pap. 3.95 (ISBN 0-89191-603-2). Cook.

—Crystal's Solid Gold Discovery. LC 85-27966. 144p. (gr. 5-7). 1986. pap. 3.95 (ISBN 0-89191-604-0). Cook.

Bly, Stephen & Bly, Janet. Crystal's Grand Entry. LC 86-18402. (gr. 7-10). 1986. pap. 3.95 (ISBN 1-55513-056-9, Chariot Bks). Cook.

—Crystal's Mill Town Mystery. LC 86-11591. (gr. 7-10). pap. 3.95 (ISBN 1-55513-054-2, Chariot Bks). Cook.

Bobbsey Twins & the Coral Turtle Mystery. 196p. (gr. k-5). 4.50 (ISBN 0-448-08072-9, G&D). Putnam Pub Group.

Bodecker, N. M. Carrot Holes & Frisbee Trees. Winters, Nina, illus. LC 83-2799. 48p. (gr. 3-5). 1983. 12.95 (ISBN 0-689-50097-1, M K McElderry). Macmillan Child Grp.

Bodie, Idella. The Secret of Telfair Inn. Yancy, Louise, illus. LC 79-177909. 98p. (gr. 5-9). 1983. pap. 6.95 (ISBN 0-87844-050-X). Sandlapper Pub Co.

Bolton, Elizabeth. Case of the Wacky Cat. Harvey, Paul, illus. LC 84-8725. 48p. (gr. 2-4). 1985. PLB 10.89 (ISBN 0-8167-0400-7); pap. text ed. 2.95 (ISBN 0-8167-0401-5). Troll Assocs.

—Ghost in the House. Burns, Ray, illus. LC 84-20530. 48p. (gr. 2-4). 1985. PLB 10.89 (ISBN 0-8167-0418-X); pap. 2.95 (ISBN 0-8167-0419-8). Troll Assocs.

—Secret of the Ghost Piano. Fiammenghi, Gioia, illus. LC 84-8745. 48p. (gr. 2-4). 1985. PLB 10.89 (ISBN 0-8167-0410-4); pap. text ed. 2.95 (ISBN 0-8167-0411-2). Troll Assocs.

—The Tree House Detective Club. Schindler, S. D., illus. LC 84-8762. 48p. (gr. 2-4). 1985. PLB 10.89 (ISBN 0-8167-0404-X); pap. text ed. 2.95 (ISBN 0-8167-0405-8). Troll Assocs.

Bond, Ann S. Adam & Noah & the Cops. Shortall, Leonard, illus. LC 82-21181. 160p. (gr. 3-6). 1983. 8.95 (ISBN 0-395-33225-7). HM.

Bones on Black Spruce Mountain. 128p. (gr. 4-6). 1984. pap. text ed. 2.50 (ISBN 0-553-15443-5, Skylark). Bantam.

Bonsall, Crosby. The Case of the Cat's Meow. Bonsall, Crosby, illus. LC 65-11451. 64p. (gr. k-3). 1978. pap. 3.50 (ISBN 0-06-444017-6, Trophy). HarpC Child Bks.

—The Case of the Double Cross. LC 80-7768. (Illus.). 64p. (gr. k-3). 1982. pap. 3.50 (ISBN 0-06-444029-X, Trophy). HarpC Child Bks.

—The Case of the Dumb Bells. LC 66-8267. (Illus.). 64p. (gr. k-3). 1982. pap. 3.50 (ISBN 0-06-444030-3, Trophy). HarpC Child Bks.

—The Case of the Hungry Stranger. Bonsall, Crosby, illus. LC 63-17947. 64p. (ps-3). 1980. incl. cassette 5.98 (ISBN 0-694-00001-9, Trophy); pap. 3.50 (ISBN 0-06-444026-5, Trophy). HarpC Child Bks.

Bonsall, Crosby N. Case of the Cat's Meow. Bonsall, Crosby N., illus. LC 65-11451. 64p. (gr. k-3). 1965. PLB 11.89 (ISBN 0-06-020561-X). HarpC Child Bks.

—The Case of the Double Cross. LC 80-7768. (Illus.). 64p. (gr. k-3). 1980. 11.89 (ISBN 0-06-020602-0); PLB 11.89 (ISBN 0-06-020603-9). HarpC Child Bks.

—Case of the Dumb Bells. Bonsall, Crosby N., illus. LC 66-8267. 64p. (gr. k-3). 1966. PLB 11.89 (ISBN 0-06-020624-1). HarpC Child Bks.

—Case of the Hungry Stranger. Bonsall, Crosby N., illus. LC 63-17947. 64p. (gr. k-3). 1963. PLB 11.89 (ISBN 0-06-020571-7). HarpC Child Bks.

—Case of the Scaredy Cats. LC 75-159039. (Illus.). 64p. (gr. k-3). 1971. PLB 10.89 (ISBN 0-685-02058-4). HarpC Child Bks.

—Caso del Forastero Hambriento. Belpre, Pura, tr. Bonsall, Crosby N., illus. LC 69-14449. (SPA.). 64p. (gr. k-3). 1969. PLB 10.89 (ISBN 0-06-020574-1). HarpC Child Bks.

Bottner, Barbara. Let Me Tell You Everything. MacDonald, Patricia, ed. 160p. 1991. pap. 2.95 (ISBN 0-671-72323-5, Archway). PB.

Boyd, Candy D. Circle of Gold. 128p. (Orig.). (gr. 4-6). 1948. pap. 2.50 (ISBN 0-590-40754-6, Apple Paperbacks). Scholastic Inc.

Bradford, Ann & Gezi, Kal. The Mystery of the Midget Clown. McLean, Mina G., illus. LC 80-72513. 32p. (gr. k-4). 1980. PLB 9.96 (ISBN 0-89565-146-7). Childs World.

—The Mystery of the Missing Dogs. McLean, Mina G., illus. LC 80-10436. 32p. (gr. k-4). 1980. PLB 9.96 (ISBN 0-89565-143-2). Childs World.

Bradman, Tony. The Bluebeards: Mystery at Musket Bay. Murphy, Rowan B., illus. 64p. (gr. 3-6). 1990. pap. 2.95 (ISBN 0-8120-4422-3). Barron.

Brandel, Marc. An Ear for Danger. LC 88-45880. 144p. (Orig.). (gr. 5 up). 1989. pap. 2.95 (ISBN 0-394-89943-1). Knopf.

—The Mystery of the Kidnapped Whale. LC 83-3008. (Illus.). 192p. (gr. 4-7). 1983. pap. 2.95 (ISBN 0-394-85841-7). Random.

—The Mystery of the Kidnapped Whale, No. 35. reissue ed. LC 83-3008. 176p. (gr. 4-8). 1991. pap. 3.50 (ISBN 0-679-81175-3, Bullseye Bks). Knopf.

—The Mystery of the Rogues Reunion. LC 84-13395. (Illus.). 192p. (gr. 4-7). 1985. lib. bdg. 6.99 (ISBN 0-394-96920-0, Random Juv). Random.

—The Mystery of the Two-Toed Pigeon. LC 83-21174. (Illus.). 160p. (gr. 4-7). 1984. (Random Juv); pap. 2.95 (ISBN 0-394-85976-6). Random.

Brander, Gary & Marlow, Dan I. Gumshoes. 1989. 12.96 (ISBN 0-8224-3338-9, Fearon Educ). Fearon Teach Aids.

Branscum, Robbie. Cameo Rose. LC 88-21546. 96p. (gr. 6-9). 1989. 11.95i (ISBN 0-06-020558-X); PLB 11.89 (ISBN 0-06-020559-8). HarpC Child Bks.

—Cameo Rose. LC 88-21546. 96p. (gr. 6-9). 1989. 11.95i (ISBN 0-06-020558-X); PLB 11.89 (ISBN 0-06-020559-8). HarpC Child Bks.

Breckler, Rosemary. Where Are the Twins? LC 79-10390. 96p. (gr. 7 up). 1979. hardcover 8.95 (ISBN 0-664-32651-X, Westminster). Westminster John Knox.

Brenford, Dana. A Case of Poison. Schaeppi, Kristi, illus. LC 88-22071. 64p. (gr. 4-5). 1988. PLB 10.95 (ISBN 0-89686-426-X, Crestwood Hse). Macmillan Child Grp.

—Danger in the Endless Cave. Schaeppi, Kristi, illus. LC 88-22847. 64p. (gr. 5-6). 1988. PLB 10.95 (ISBN 0-89686-421-9, Crestwood Hse). Macmillan Child Grp.

—The Guardian of the Hopewell Treasure. Schaeppi, Kristi, illus. LC 88-22907. 64p. (gr. 5-6). 1988. PLB 10.95 (ISBN 0-89686-423-5, Crestwood Hse). Macmillan Child Grp.

—The Kidnapped Falcon. Schaeppi, Kristi, illus. LC 88-22846. 64p. (gr. 5-6). 1988. PLB 10.95 (ISBN 0-89686-419-7, Crestwood Hse). Macmillan Child Grp.

—The Vanishing Stream. LC 88-22072. (Illus.). 64p. (gr. 5-6). 1988. PLB 10.95 (ISBN 0-89686-425-1, Crestwood Hse). Macmillan Child Grp.

Brennan, J. H. The Castle of Darkness. 192p. (Orig.). (gr. 6 up). 1986. pap. 2.50 (ISBN 0-440-91120-6, LFL). Dell.

—Voyage of Terror. (Orig.). (gr. k-12). 1987. pap. 2.50 (ISBN 0-440-99324-5, LFL). Dell.

Brenner, Barbara. The Falcon Sting. LC 88-14567. 176p. (gr. 7 up). 1988. 13.95 (ISBN 0-02-712320-0, Bradbury Pr). Macmillan Child Grp.

—A Killing Season. LC 80-69995. 192p. (gr. 7 up). 1984. 12.95 (ISBN 0-02-712310-3, Four Winds). Macmillan Child Grp.

—The Mystery of the Plumed Serpent. Sims, Blanche, illus. LC 80-17316. 128p. (gr. 3-6). 1981. lib. bdg. 4.99 (ISBN 0-394-94531-X). Knopf.

—The Mystery of the Plumed Serpent. Sims, Blanche, illus. LC 80-17316. 128p. (gr. 3-6). 1989. pap. 2.95 (ISBN 0-394-82590-X). Knopf.

Brett, Simon. The Three Detectives & the Missing Superstar. LC 86-15556. 192p. (gr. 5-9). 1986. 13.95 (ISBN 0-684-18708-6, Scribners Young Read). Macmillan Child Grp.

Bridges, Laurie. The Ashton Horror. 160p. (gr. 7 up). 1984. pap. 2.50 (ISBN 0-553-26609-8). Bantam.

Brightfield, Richard. Murder Comes to Life. LC 89-36329. 96p. (gr. 7 up). 1990. PLB 9.89 (ISBN 0-8167-1686-2); pap. text ed. 2.95 (ISBN 0-8167-1687-0). Troll Assocs.

Brod, Alexandra. Who Stole Travada? Lucke, Peggy, ed. Stotz, Gunther, illus. 128p. (gr. 3-6). 1987. pap. 4.95 (ISBN 0-940589-00-1). Adventure Pr.

Brookins, Dana. Who Killed Sack Annie? 160p. (gr. 4-7). 1983. 10.95 (ISBN 0-89919-137-1, Clarion). HM.

Brooks, Bruce. Midnight Hour Encores. LC 86-45035. 288p. (gr. 7 up). 1988. pap. 3.50 (ISBN 0-06-447021-0, Trophy). HarpC Child Bks.

Bunting, Eve. The Ghost Children. LC 88-20356. 160p. (gr. 6-9). 1989. 13.95 (ISBN 0-89919-843-0, Pub. by Clarion). Ticknor & Fields.

—The Ghosts of Departure Point. LC 81-48602. 113p. (gr. 6 up). 1982. 12.95i (ISBN 0-397-31997-5, Lipp Jr Bks); (Lipp Jr Bks). HarpC Child Bks.

—The Haunting of SafeKeep. LC 84-48354. 160p. (gr. 7 up). 1985. PLB 12.89 (ISBN 0-397-32113-9, Lipp Jr Bks). HarpC Child Bks.

—Is Anybody There? LC 87-45881. 176p. (gr. 4-7). 1990. 13.95x (ISBN 0-397-32302-6, Trophy); PLB 13.89x (ISBN 0-397-32303-4, Trophy); pap. 3.50 (ISBN 0-06-440347-5, Trophy). HarpC Child Bks.

—The Skate Patrol. Tucker, Kathleen, ed. LC 80-18640. (Illus.). 40p. (gr. 2-5). 1980. PLB 8.95 (ISBN 0-8075-7393-0). A Whitman.

—The Skate Patrol Rides Again. Madden, Don, illus. LC 81-11504. 48p. (gr. 2-5). 1981. PLB 8.95 (ISBN 0-8075-7395-7). A Whitman.

—Someone Is Hiding on Alcatraz Island. 144p. 1986. pap. 2.75 (ISBN 0-425-10294-7, Pub. by Berkley-Pacer). Berkley Pub.

Buss, Nancy. Rose-Petal & the Evil Weeds. Paris, Pat, illus. 1984. incl. cassette 7.95 (ISBN 0-685-08159-1). Parker Bros.

Cameron, Eleanor. The Court of the Stone Children. 192p. (gr. 4 up). 1990. pap. 3.95 (ISBN 0-14-034289-3, Puffin). Puffin Bks.

Campfire Stories. (gr. 2-7). 1984. 3.50 (ISBN 0-671-50198-4, Little Simon). S&S Trade.

Carey, M. V. The Case of the Savage Statue. Leonard, Tom, illus. LC 86-62639. 128p. (gr. 4-7). 1987. lib. bdg. 5.99 (ISBN 0-394-98225-8, Random Juv); pap. 2.95 (ISBN 0-394-88225-3). Random.

—Mystery of the Cranky Collector. LC 87-4723. 192p. (gr. 4-7). 1987. lib. bdg. 6.99 (ISBN 0-394-99153-2, Random Juv); pap. 2.95 (ISBN 0-394-89153-8, Random Juv). Random.

Carey, Mary V. Alfred Hitchcock & the Three Investigators in the Mystery of the Magic Circle. Hearne, Jack, illus. LC 78-55915. (gr. 4-7). 1978. (Random Juv); lib. bdg. 6.99 (ISBN 0-394-93607-8). Random.

—Alfred Hitchcock & the Three Investigators in the Mystery of the Invisible Dog. Hearne, Jack, illus. LC 75-8073. 160p. (gr. 4-7). 1975. (Random Juv); lib. bdg. 5.39 (ISBN 0-394-93105-X); pap. 1.95 (ISBN 0-685-04249-9). Random.

—Alfred Hitchcock & the Three Investigators in the Mystery of Death Trap Mine. Hearne, Jack, illus. LC 76-8135. (gr. 4-7). 1985. (Random Juv); lib. bdg. 5.99 (ISBN 0-394-93321-4); pap. 1.95 (ISBN 0-394-84449-1); pap. 2.95 (ISBN 0-394-86424-7). Random.

—Alfred Hitchcock & the Three Investigators in the Mystery of the Flaming Footprints. Hitchcock, Alfred, ed. (Illus.). (gr. 4-7). 1984. 1.95 (ISBN 0-394-83776-2, Random Juv); lib. bdg. 5.39 (ISBN 0-394-92296-4). Random.

—Alfred Hitchcock & the Three Investigators in the Mystery of the Singing Serpent. Hitchcock, Alfred, ed. (Illus.). (gr. 4-7). 1972. (Random Juv); lib. bdg. 6.99 (ISBN 0-394-92408-8); pap. 1.95 (ISBN 0-685-04251-0). Random.

—Alfred Hitchcock & the Three Investigators in the Mystery of Monster Mountain. Hitchcock, Alfred, ed. (Illus.). (gr. 4-7). 1985. (Random Juv); lib. bdg. 5.39 (ISBN 0-394-92664-1); pap. 3.95 (ISBN 0-394-86420-4). Random.

—Alfred Hitchcock & the Three Investigators in the Secret of the Haunted Mirror. Hearne, Jack, illus. LC 74-5750. 160p. (gr. 4-7). 1984. (Random Juv); lib. bdg. 5.39 (ISBN 0-394-92820-2); pap. 1.95 (ISBN 0-394-84450-5); pap. 2.95 (ISBN 0-394-86421-2). Random.

—The Mystery of the Blazing Cliffs. Hitchcock, Alfred, ed. LC 80-10954. 192p. (gr. 4-7). 1981. lib. bdg. 6.99 (ISBN 0-394-94504-2); pap. 2.95 (ISBN 0-394-84504-8). Random.

—The Mystery of the Creep-Show Crooks. LC 85-2237. (Illus.). 192p. (gr. 4-7). 1985. lib. bdg. 6.99 (ISBN 0-394-97382-8, Random Juv); pap. 2.95 (ISBN 0-394-87382-3). Random.

—The Mystery of the Invisible Dog. LC 79-27778. 160p. (gr. 4-7). 1984. pap. 2.95 (ISBN 0-394-86423-9). Random.

—The Mystery of the Magic Circle. LC 79-27657. 160p. (gr. 4-7). 1985. pap. 2.95 (ISBN 0-394-86427-1). Random.

—The Mystery of the Missing Mermaid. LC 83-3030. (Illus.). 192p. (gr. 4-7). 1983. lib. bdg. 6.99 (ISBN 0-394-95875-6); pap. 3.95 (ISBN 0-394-85875-1). Random.

—The Mystery of the Scar-Faced Beggar. LC 81-4040. 192p. (gr. 4-7). 1981. pap. 2.95 (ISBN 0-394-84903-5). Random.

—The Mystery of the Trail of Terror. LC 84-1952. (Illus.). 192p. (gr. 4-7). 1984. lib. bdg. 6.99 (ISBN 0-394-96609-0, Pub. by BYR); pap. 2.95 (ISBN 0-394-86609-6). Random.

Carlson, Dale. The Mystery of the Shining Children. (Illus.). (gr. 3-7). 1983. 2.95 (ISBN 0-448-19001-X, G&D). Putnam Pub Group.

Cassedy, Sylvia. Behind the Attic Wall. 320p. (gr. 4 up). 1985. pap. 3.95 (ISBN 0-380-69843-9, Camelot). Avon.

Cates, Emily. The Ghost Ferry. (gr. 4-7). 1991. pap. 2.95 (ISBN 0-553-15863-5). Bantam.

—The Mystery of Misty Island Inn. 1990. pap. 2.95 (ISBN 0-553-15858-9). Bantam.

Cebulash, Mel. Hot Like the Sun: A Terry Tyndale Mystery. LC 85-18180. 112p. (gr. 5 up). 1986. 10.95 (ISBN 0-8225-0729-3). Lerner Pubns.

Cesari, Aura. Night Journeys. (Illus.). 12p. (gr. 7-9). 1985. pap. 2.50 (ISBN 0-88138-053-9, Pub. by Envelope Bks). Green Tiger Pr.

Chant, Barry. Spindles & the Mystery of the Missing Numbat. 1991. PLB 3.95 (ISBN 0-8423-6213-4). Tyndale.

Chirian, Helene. Crossword Mysteries: Who Dunnit Challenge. (gr. 4-7). 1991. pap. 2.95 (ISBN 0-8431-2788-0). Price Stern.

Christian, Mary B. Dead Man in Catfish Bay. Tucker, Kathleen, ed. LC 84-19616. (Illus.). 128p. (gr. 4-9). 1985. 9.95 (ISBN 0-8075-1522-1). A Whitman.

—Deadline for Danger. Tucker, Kathy, ed. LC 82-17470. (Illus.). 128p. (gr. 4-9). 1982. PLB 9.95 (ISBN 0-8075-1518-3). A Whitman.

—Determined Detectives. (gr. 2-4). pap. 2.50 ea. Maltese Feline, 64p (ISBN 0-8167-1369-3). Merger on the Orient Expressway, 48p (ISBN 0-8167-1313-8). Mysterious Case Case, 64p (ISBN 0-8167-1311-1). Phantom of the Operetta, 64p (ISBN 0-8167-1312-X). Troll Assocs.

—The Doggone Mystery. Fay, Ann, ed. LC 80-10448. (Illus.). (gr. 1-3). 1980. PLB 8.95 (ISBN 0-8075-1656-2). A Whitman.

—The Maltese Feline. Howell, Kathleen C., illus. LC 87-24367. 64p. (gr. 2-5). 1988. 10.95 (ISBN 0-525-44334-7, 01063-320, DCB). Dutton Child Bks.

—Merger on the Orient Expressway. Howell, Kathleen C., illus. 64p. (gr. 2-6). 1986. 10.95 (ISBN 0-525-44231-6, 0966-290, DCB). Dutton Child Bks.

—The Mysterious Case Case. Eagle, Ellen, illus. LC 85-6948. 64p. (gr. 2-6). 1985. 9.95 (ISBN 0-525-44217-0, DCB). Dutton Child Bks.

—Mystery at Camp Triumph. Fay, Ann, ed. (Illus.). 128p. (gr. 4-9). 1986. 9.95 (ISBN 0-8075-5366-2). A Whitman.

—The Mystery of the Fallen Tree. Boddy, Joe, illus. (ps-8). 1991. 8.95 (ISBN 0-88335-274-5, AH56); pap. 4.95 (ISBN 0-88335-288-5, AS56). Milliken Pub Co.

—The Mystery of the Message from the Sky. Boddy, Joe, illus. (ps-8). 1991. 8.95 (ISBN 0-88335-298-2, AH57); pap. 4.95 (ISBN 0-88335-289-3, AS57). Milliken Pub Co.

—The Mystery of the Midnight Raider. Boddy, Joe, illus. (ps-8). 1991. 8.95 (ISBN 0-88335-271-0, AH53); pap. 4.95 (ISBN 0-88335-285-0, AS53). Milliken Pub Co.

—The Mystery of the Missing Red Wagon. Boddy, Joe, illus. (ps-8). 8.95 (ISBN 0-88335-286-9, AH54); pap. 4.95 (ISBN 0-88335-272-9, AS54). Milliken Pub Co.

—The Mystery of the Missing Scarf. Bolinske, Janet L., ed. Boddy, Joe, illus. LC 88-60630. 32p. (Orig.). (gr. 1-3). 1989. text ed. 8.95 (ISBN 0-88335-596-5); pap. text ed. 4.95 (ISBN 0-88335-549-3). Milliken Pub Co.

—The Mystery of the Polluted Stream. Boddy, Joe, illus. (ps-8). 1991. 8.95 (ISBN 0-88335-299-0, AH58); pap. 4.95 (ISBN 0-88335-290-7, AS58). Milliken Pub Co.

—The Mystery of the Unsigned Valentine. Boddy, Joe, illus. (ps-8). 1991. 8.95 (ISBN 0-88335-273-7, AH55); pap. 4.95 (ISBN 0-88335-287-7, AS55). Milliken Pub Co.

—The North Pole Mystery. Bolinske, Janet L., ed. Boddy, Joe, illus. LC 88-60633. 32p. (Orig.). (gr. 1-3). 1989. text ed. 8.95 (ISBN 0-88335-593-0); pap. text ed. 4.95 (ISBN 0-88335-597-3). Milliken Pub Co.

—The Pet Day Mystery. Bolinske, Janet L., ed. Boddy, Joe, illus. LC 88-60631. 32p. (Orig.). (gr. 1-3). 1989. text ed. 8.95 (ISBN 0-88335-595-7); pap. text ed. 4.95 (ISBN 0-88335-599-X). Milliken Pub Co.

—Sebastian & the Bone to Pick Mystery. 64p. 1986. pap. 2.25 (ISBN 0-553-15385-4, Skylark). Bantam.

—Sebastian (Super Sleuth) & the Baffling Bigfoot. McCue, Lisa, illus. LC 89-13049. 64p. (gr. 2-6). 1990. 10.95 (ISBN 0-02-718215-0, Mcmillan Child Bk). Macmillan Child Grp.

—Sebastian (Super Sleuth) & the Bone to Pick Mystery. McCue, Lisa, illus. LC 83-5406. 64p. (gr. 2-5). 1983. 10.95 (ISBN 0-02-718440-4, Mcmillan Child Bk). Macmillan Child Grp.

—Sebastian (Super Sleuth) & the Clumsy Cowboy. McCue, Lisa, illus. LC 84-21758. 64p. (gr. 2-5). 1985. 10.95 (ISBN 0-02-718480-3, Mcmillan Child Bk). Macmillan Child Grp.

—Sebastian (Super Sleuth) & the Clumsy Cowboy. McCue, Lisa, illus. (gr. 3-5). 1988. pap. 2.50 (ISBN 0-671-63251-5, Minstrel Bks). PB.

—Sebastian (Super Sleuth) & the Crummy Yummies Caper. McCue, Lisa, illus. LC 82-20861. 64p. (gr. 2-5). 1983. 10.95 (ISBN 0-02-718430-7, Mcmillan Child Bk). Macmillan Child Grp.

—Sebastian (Super Sleuth) & the Egyptian Connection. McCue, Lisa, illus. LC 87-34986. 64p. (gr. 2-5). 1988. 10.95 (ISBN 0-02-718560-5, Mcmillan Child Bk). Macmillan Child Grp.

—Sebastian (Super Sleuth) & the Egyptian Connection. McCue, Lisa, illus. 64p. (gr. 3-7). 1991. pap. 3.95 (ISBN 0-689-71514-5, Aladdin). Macmillan Child Grp.

—Sebastian (Super Sleuth) & the Hair of the Dog Mystery. McCue, Lisa, illus. LC 82-10066. 64p. (gr. 2-5). 1982. 10.95 (ISBN 0-02-718260-6, Mcmillan Child Bk). Macmillan Child Grp.

—Sebastian (Super Sleuth) & the Mystery Patient. McCue, Lisa, illus. 64p. (gr. 2-6). 1991. SBE 10.95 (ISBN 0-02-718571-0, Mcmillan Child Bk). Macmillan Child Grp.

—Sebastian (Super Sleuth) & the Purloined Sirloin. McCue, Lisa, illus. 64p. (ps). 1988. pap. 2.50 (ISBN 0-671-63253-1, Minstrel Bks). PB.

—Sebastian (Super Sleuth) & the Santa Claus Caper. (Illus.). (gr. 3-5). 1988. pap. 2.50 (ISBN 0-671-63252-3, Minstrel Bks). PB.

—Sebastian (Super Sleuth) & the Secret of the Skewered Skier. McCue, Lisa, illus. LC 83-19569. 64p. (gr. 2-5). 1984. 10.95 (ISBN 0-02-718450-1, Mcmillan Child Bk). Macmillan Child Grp.

—Sebastian (Super Sleuth) & the Time Capsule Caper. McCue, Lisa, illus. LC 88-29295. 64p. (gr. 2-6). 1989. 10.95 (ISBN 0-02-718570-2, Mcmillan Child Bk). Macmillan Child Grp.

—Sebastian (SuperSleuth) & the Crummy Yummies Caper. 64p. (gr. 6 up). 1985. pap. 2.25 (ISBN 0-553-15293-9). Bantam.

—The Sherlock Street Detectives Package. Bolinske, Janet L., ed. Boddy, Joe, illus. (Orig.). (gr. 1-3). 1989. text ed. 32.00 (ISBN 0-88335-591-4); pap. text ed. 18.00 (ISBN 0-88335-592-2). Set of 4 books, 32 pp. each. Milliken Pub Co.

—The UFO Mystery. Bolinske, Janet L., ed. Boddy, Joe, illus. LC 88-60632. 32p. (Orig.). (gr. 1-3). 1989. text ed. 8.95 (ISBN 0-88335-594-9); pap. text ed. 4.95 (ISBN 0-88335-598-1). Milliken Pub Co.

Christopher, Matt. Secret of Rock Island. 9p. (gr. 3-7). 1988. incl. puzzle 9.95 (ISBN 0-922242-06-2). Lombard Mktg.

—Skateboard Tough. (gr. 4-7). 1991. 14.95 (ISBN 0-316-14247-6). Little.

Civardi. Clues & Suspects. (gr. 2-5). 1979. (Usborne-Hayes); PLB 11.96 (ISBN 0-88110-039-0); pap. 4.50 (ISBN 0-86020-229-1). EDC.

Clapp, Patricia. Jane-Emily. 160p. (gr. 5 up). 1971. pap. 1.75 (ISBN 0-440-94185-7, LFL). Dell.

Clark, Margaret G. Mystery in the Flooded Museum. (gr. 3-7). Date not set. 8.95 (ISBN 0-396-07550-9, Putnam). Putnam Pub Group.

Cleary, Beverly. Ralph S. Mouse. Zelinsky, Paul O., illus. 144p. (gr. 2-6). 1983. pap. 3.25 (ISBN 0-440-47582-1, YB). Dell.

Clifford, Eth. The Dastardly Murder of Dirty Pete. Hughes, George, illus. 128p. (gr. 2-5). 1981. 13.95 (ISBN 0-395-31671-5). HM.

—Dastardly Murder of Dirty Pete. 1986. pap. 2.75 (ISBN 0-671-68859-6). S&S Trade.

—Harvey's Marvelous Monkey Mystery. (gr. 3-7). 1988. pap. 2.75 (ISBN 0-317-68550-3). PB.

Climo, Shirley. Gopher, Tanker, & the Admiral. McKeating, Eileen, illus. LC 83-45240. 128p. (gr. 2-6). 1984. 12.95 (ISBN 0-690-04382-1, Crowell Jr Bks); (Crowell Jr Bks). HarpC Child Bks.

Clymer, Eleanor. The Get-Away Car. (gr. 4-7). 1978. 8.95 (ISBN 0-525-30470-3, DCB). Dutton Child Bks.

Cobb, Vicki. Inspector Bodyguard Patrols the Land of U. Sandford, John, illus. 128p. (gr. 4). 1987. pap. 8.95 (ISBN 0-685-18030-1, Little Simon). S&S Trade.

—Inspector Bodyguard Patrols the Land of U. Sandford, John, illus. LC 86-8334. 128p. (gr. 4 up). 1987. lib. bdg. 13.79 (ISBN 0-671-60306-X); pap. 8.95 (ISBN 0-671-63260-4). Messner.

Cohen, Dan. The Case of the Battling Ball Clubs. Overlie, George, illus. LC 79-84356. 32p. (gr. 1-4). 1979. PLB 5.95 (ISBN 0-87614-101-7). Carolrhoda Bks.

—The Case of the Long Lost Twin. Overlie, George, illus. LC 79-84357. 32p. (gr. 1-4). 1979. PLB 5.95 (ISBN 0-87614-094-0). Carolrhoda Bks.

—The Mystery of the Faded Footprint. Overlie, George, illus. LC 79-84360. 32p. (gr. 1-4). 1979. PLB 5.95 (ISBN 0-87614-097-5). Carolrhoda Bks.

—The Mystery of the Marked Money. Overlie, George, illus. LC 79-50788. 32p. (gr. 1-4). 1979. PLB 5.95 (ISBN 0-87614-100-9). Carolrhoda Bks.

Cohen, Daniel. Horror in the Movies. (Illus.). 128p. (gr. 5 up). 1986. pap. 2.50 (ISBN 0-671-62671-X, Archway). PB.

Cole, Bruce. The Pumpkinville Mystery. Gwynne, Fred, narrated by. (Illus.). 32p. (gr. 1-4). 1988. Incl. cassettes. 6.95 (ISBN 0-671-67147-2). S&S Trade.

Coleman, Mary A. Secret Passageway. Nix, Harriet, illus. 48p. (Orig.). (gr. 1-6). 1989. pap. 8.50 (ISBN 0-685-28398-4). Agee Pub.

Coleman, William. Chesapeake Charlie & the Bay Bank Robbers. LC 80-66638. 112p. (Orig.). (gr. 2-6). 1980. pap. 3.95 (ISBN 0-87123-113-1). Bethany Hse.

Coleman, William L. Chesapeake Charlie & the Haunted Ship. LC 82-73912. 112p. (Orig.). (gr. 2-6). 1983. pap. 3.95 (ISBN 0-87123-282-0). Bethany Hse.

—Chesapeake Charlie & the Stolen Diamonds. LC 81-68077. 112p. (Orig.). (gr. 5-8). 1981. pap. 3.95 (ISBN 0-87123-170-0). Bethany Hse.

Collier, James L. & Collier, Christopher. War Comes to Willy Freeman. LC 82-70317. 192p. (gr. 4-6). 1983. pap. 13.95 (ISBN 0-385-29235-X). Delacorte.

Collins, William W. Moonstone. Lane, L., Jr., intro. by. (gr. 10 up). pap. 2.95 (ISBN 0-8049-0076-0, CL-76). Airmont.

Conaway, Judith. Detective Tricks You Can Do. Barto, Renzo, illus. LC 85-28881. 48p. (gr. 1-5). 1986. PLB 11.89 (ISBN 0-8167-0672-7); pap. text ed. 2.95 (ISBN 0-8167-0673-5). Troll Assocs.

Conford, Ellen. A Case for Jenny Archer. Palmisciano, Diane, illus. LC 88-14169. (gr. 2-4). 1988. 10.95 (ISBN 0-316-15266-8). Little.

—A Case For Jenny Archer. (ps-3). 1990. pap. 2.95 (ISBN 0-316-15352-4). Little.

—Me & the Terrible Two. Carroll, Charles, illus. 128p. (gr. 4-6). 1974. 14.95 (ISBN 0-316-15303-6). Little.

—To All My Fans, with Love from Sylvie. (gr. 7 up). 1987. pap. 2.50 (ISBN 0-671-63763-0, Archway). PB.

Conrad, Joseph. Children's Illustrated Secret Agent. (gr. k up). 1991. pap. 3.95 (ISBN 0-425-12524-6). Berkley Pub.

Cook, Bernadine. Looking for Susie. Scull, Marie-Louise, illus. 32p. (gr. 1-3). 1991. lib. bdg. 14.50 (ISBN 0-208-02241-4, Pub. by Linnet). Shoe String.

Coombs, Charles. Young Atom Detective. (Illus.). (gr. 4-7). PLB 6.70 (ISBN 0-8313-0021-3). Lantern.

Coontz, Otto. Mystery Madness. (gr. 4-9). 1982. 8.95 (ISBN 0-395-32079-8). HM.

Cooper, John R. Mel Martin: First Base Jinx. 208p. (gr. 3-7). 1982. 8.95 (ISBN 0-671-44539-1, Little Simon); pap. 2.95 (ISBN 0-671-44548-0). S&S Trade.

Cooper, Susan. The Dark Is Rising. (gr. 7 up). 1976. pap. 3.95 (ISBN 0-689-70420-8, Aladdin). Macmillan Child Grp.

—Greenwitch. Heslop, Michael, illus. LC 73-85319. 148p. (gr. 4-7). 1985. 14.95 (ISBN 0-689-30426-9, M K McElderry). Macmillan Child Grp.

—Over Sea, Under Stone. Gill, Margery, illus. LC 66-11199. (gr. 4-6). 1966. 14.95 (ISBN 0-15-259034-X, HJ). HarBraceJ.

Corbett, Scott. Grave Doubts. LC 82-47916. 144p. (gr. 3-7). 1982. 14.95 (ISBN 0-316-15659-0, Joy St Bks). Little.

—Here Lies the Body. (gr. 4-7). 1990. pap. 4.95 (ISBN 0-316-15753-8, Joy St Bks). Little.

—Red Room Riddle. (gr. 4-7). 1990. pap. 4.95 (ISBN 0-316-15754-6, Joy St Bks). Little.

—The Trouble with Diamonds. Dodson, Bert, illus. LC 84-18762. (gr. 3-7). 1985. 11.95 (ISBN 0-525-44190-5, DCB). Dutton Child Bks.

Corcoran, Barbara. Mystery on Ice. LC 84-21559. 156p. (gr. 4-7). 1985. 12.95 (ISBN 0-689-31089-7, Atheneum Child Bk). Macmillan Child Grp.

Cormier, Robert. After the First Death. 1991. pap. 3.95 (ISBN 0-440-20835-1, LFL). Dell.

—Now & at the Hour. 1991. pap. 3.99 (ISBN 0-440-20882-3). Dell.

Costikyan, Greg. Another Day, Another Dungeon. 1990. pap. 3.95 (ISBN 0-8125-0140-3). Tor Bks.
Courtney, Dayle. The Great UFO Chase. rev. ed. 160p. (gr. 6-9). 1991. pap. 4.99 (ISBN 0-87403-833-2, 24-03883). Standard Pub.
—Jaws of Terror. rev. ed. 160p. (gr. 6-9). 1991. pap. 4.99 (ISBN 0-87403-831-6, 24-03881). Standard Pub.
Coville, Bruce. Waiting Spirits. 160p. (Orig.). (gr. 8-10). 1984. pap. text ed. 2.25 (ISBN 0-553-26004-9). Bantam.
Craig, Helen. The Night of the Paper Bag Monsters. Craig, Helen, illus. LC 84-25045. 32p. (ps-3). 1985. lib. bdg. 11.99 (ISBN 0-394-97307-0). Knopf.
Cresswell, Helen. The Night Watchmen. Floyd, Gareth, illus. 128p. (gr. 2-7). 1989. pap. 3.95 (ISBN 0-689-71292-8, Aladdin). Macmillan Child Grp.
Cross, Gillian. The Dark Behind the Curtain. 160p. (Orig.). (gr. k-12). 1988. pap. 2.95 (ISBN 0-440-20207-8, LFL). Dell.
—The Dark Behind the Curtain. (Illus.). 160p. (gr. 1-5). 1987. 12.95 (ISBN 0-19-271457-0). Oxford U Pr.
—The Demon Headmaster. Rees, Gary, illus. 174p. (ps up). 1987. 9.95 (ISBN 0-19-271460-0). Oxford U Pr.
—On the Edge. LC 84-48741. 176p. (gr. 7 up). 1985. 13.95 (ISBN 0-8234-0559-1). Holiday.
Cunningham, Marilyn. A Place of Power. Kratoville, Betty L., ed. Lucey, Jack, illus. 64p. (gr. 3-9). 1989. lib. bdg. 4.95 (ISBN 0-87879-651-7, High Noon Books). Acad Therapy.
Curry, Jane L. Mindy's Mysterious Miniature. (gr. 4-7). 19.75 (ISBN 0-8446-6433-2). Peter Smith.
Cushman, Doug. Aunt Eater Loves a Mystery. Cushman, Doug, illus. LC 87-73. 64p. (gr. k-3). 1987. 11.95 (ISBN 0-06-021326-4); PLB 11.89 (ISBN 0-06-021327-2). HarpC Child Bks.
—Aunt Eater Loves a Mystery. Cushman, Doug, illus. LC 87-73. 64p. (ps-3). 1989. pap. 3.50 (ISBN 0-06-444126-1, Trophy). HarpC Child Bks.
Czerkas, Stephen & Czerkas, Sylvia J. My Life with the Dinosaurs. (Orig.). (gr. 4-6). 1989. pap. 2.75 (ISBN 0-671-63454-2, Minstrel Bks). PB.
Dalby, Richard. Mysteries For Christmas. 1990. 5.98 (ISBN 0-8317-6294-2). Smithmark.
Damon, Laura. Secret Valentine. Kennedy, Anne, illus. LC 87-13736. 32p. (gr. k-2). 1987. PLB 10.89 (ISBN 0-8167-1101-1); pap. text ed. 2.95 (ISBN 0-8167-1102-X). Troll Assocs.
Daniel, Jennifer. Spin-a-Story, the Haunted Banana & Other Wacky Mysteries. Brown, Jean, illus. 24p. (Orig.). (gr. 4-7). 1990. pap. 2.95 (ISBN 1-878890-02-6). Palisades Prodns.
Danziger, Paula. The Pistachio Prescription. 160p. (gr. 5 up). 1978. pap. 3.50 (ISBN 0-440-96895-X, LFL). Dell.
The Dark & Deadly Pool. 192p. (gr. 6 up). 1989. pap. 3.25 (ISBN 0-440-20348-1, LFL). Dell.
Davis, Doris. The Mystery of Briar Rose Manor. LC 89-82583. (Illus.). 208p. (Orig.). 1990. pap. 3.95 (ISBN 0-88243-652-X, 02-0652). Gospel Pub.
DeClements, Barthe & Greimes, Christopher. Double Trouble. 144p. (gr. 7 up). 1988. pap. 2.75 (ISBN 0-590-41248-5, Point). Scholastic Inc.
Deleon, Eric. Pitch & Hasty Check It Out. LC 88-1483. 96p. (gr. 3-5). 1988. 11.95 (ISBN 0-531-05768-2); PLB 11.99 (ISBN 0-531-08368-3). Orchard Bks Watts.
Delton, Judy. The Mystery of the Haunted Cabin. O'Brien, Anne S., illus. LC 86-7723. 128p. (gr. 2-5). 1986. 13.95 (ISBN 0-395-41917-4). HM.
De Maupassant, Guy. The Necklace. rev. ed. Weissenhorn, Mathilde, tr. from FRE. (gr. 9-12). 1989. Repr. of 1907 ed. multi-media kit 35.00 (ISBN 0-685-31124-4). Balance Pub.
Devlin, Wende & Devlin, Harry. Cranberry Halloween. Devlin, Wende & Devlin, Harry, illus. LC 89-18666. 40p. (gr. k-3). 1990. pap. 3.95 (ISBN 0-689-71428-9, Aladdin). Macmillan Child Grp.
—Cranberry Mystery. LC 85-16015. (Illus.). 40p. (ps-3). 1984. Repr. of 1978 ed. PLB 13.95 (ISBN 0-02-729920-1, Four Winds). Macmillan Child Grp.
De Weese, Gene. The Dandelion Caper. (gr. k-6). 1989. pap. 2.95 (ISBN 0-440-40202-6, YB). Dell.
Dickens, Charles. Mystery of Edwin Drood. Budgey, N. F., intro. by. (gr. 10 up). pap. 1.50 (ISBN 0-8049-0114-7, CL-114). Airmont.
Dickinson, Peter. Annerton Pit. (gr. 7 up). 1977. 14.95 (ISBN 0-316-18430-6, Joy St Bks). Little.
—Seventh Raven. 1991. pap. 3.50 (ISBN 0-440-20836-X, LFL). Dell.
Dicks, Terrance. Goliath & the Cub Scouts. Littlewood, Valerie, illus. 64p. (gr. 2-4). 1990. pap. 2.95 (ISBN 0-8120-4493-2). Barron.
D'Ignazio, Fred. Chip Mitchell: The Case of the Chocolate-Covered Bugs. Pearson, Larry, illus. LC 85-6882. 128p. (gr. 5-9). 1985. 10.95 (ISBN 0-525-67168-4, Lodestar Bks). Dutton Child Bks.
—Chip Mitchell: The Case of the Stolen Computer Brains. (Illus.). 128p. (gr. 5-9). 1983. 8.95 (ISBN 0-525-66790-3, 0869-260, Lodestar Bks). Dutton Child Bks.
Disney, Walt, Productions Staff. The Great Mouse Detective. LC 86-42608. (Illus.). 48p. (ps-3). 1986. (Random Juv); (BYR). Random.
—Walt Disney Productions Presents "The Mystery of the Missing Peanuts" LC 75-1088. (Illus.). 48p. (gr. 1-2). 1975. (Random Juv); lib. bdg. 4.99 (ISBN 0-394-92572-6). Random.
Dixon, Franklin. Hardy Boys Digest. 1987. Boxed. pap. 14.00 (ISBN 0-671-91514-2, Minstrel Bks). PB.
Dixon, Franklin W. Apeman's Secret. 1989. pap. 3.50 (ISBN 0-671-69068-X). S&S Trade.
—Arctic Patrol Mystery. LC 69-12166. (Illus.). (gr. 4-7). 1969. 4.50 (ISBN 0-448-08948-3, G&D). Putnam Pub Group.
—The Billion Dollar Ransom. 192p. (gr. 5-6). 1988. pap. 3.50 (ISBN 0-671-66228-7, Minstrel Bks). PB.
—The Blackwing Puzzle. 208p. 1990. pap. 3.50 (ISBN 0-671-70472-9, Minstrel). PB.
—Blood Money. 160p. (Orig.). 1989. pap. 2.95 (ISBN 0-671-67480-3, Archway). PB.
—Blood Relations. (gr. 7 up). 1989. pap. 2.95 (ISBN 0-671-68779-4, Archway). PB.
—Bombay Boomerang. Wilson, George, illus. LC 70-100116. (gr. 5-9). 1970. 4.50 (ISBN 0-448-08949-1, G&D). Putnam Pub Group.
—The Borderline Case. (gr. 7 up). 1989. pap. 2.95 (ISBN 0-671-72452-5, Archway). PB.
—The Borgia Dagger. 160p. (Orig.). (gr. 7 up). 1988. pap. 2.95 (ISBN 0-671-67956-2, Archway). PB.
—Breakdown in Axeblade. (Orig.). (gr. 3-7). 1989. pap. 3.50 (ISBN 0-671-66311-9, Minstrel Bks). PB.
—Cast of Criminals. (Orig.). (gr. 7 up). 1989. pap. 3.50 (ISBN 0-671-66307-0, Minstrel Bks). PB.
—Castle Fear. Greenberg, Ann, ed. 160p. (Orig.). (gr. 7 up). 1990. pap. 2.95 (ISBN 0-671-70041-3, Archway). PB.
—Cave-In! 192p. 1990. pap. 3.50 (ISBN 0-671-69486-3, Minstrel Bks). PB.
—Clue of the Broken Blade. LC 73-119043. (Illus.). (gr. 5-9). 1942. 4.50 (ISBN 0-448-08921-1, G&D). Putnam Pub Group.
—The Clue of the Hissing Serpent. new ed. (Illus.). 196p. (gr. 5-9). 1974. 4.50 (ISBN 0-448-08953-X, G&D). Putnam Pub Group.
—Clue of the Screeching Owl. (Illus.). (gr. 5-9). 1962. 4.50 (ISBN 0-448-08941-6, G&D). Putnam Pub Group.
—Collision Course. 160p. 1989. pap. 2.95 (ISBN 0-671-67481-1, Archway). PB.
—Countdown to Terror. (Orig.). (gr. 7 up). 1989. pap. 2.95 (ISBN 0-671-64691-5, Archway). PB.
—The Crimson Flame. Barish, Wendy, ed. 192p. (gr. 3-7). 1983. 8.50 (ISBN 0-671-42366-5, Little Simon); pap. 3.50 (ISBN 0-671-42367-3). S&S Trade.
—The Crowning Terror. 160p. (Orig.). (gr. 7 up). 1989. pap. 2.95 (ISBN 0-671-70713-2, Archway). PB.
—The Crowning Terror: Casefiles Six. large type ed. 154p. (gr. 5-10). 1988. Repr. of 1987 ed. 9.50 (ISBN 0-942545-47-8); PLB 10.50 (ISBN 0-942545-57-5, Dist. by Gareth Stevens). Grey Castle.
—Cult of Crime. (gr. 7 up). 1989. pap. 2.95 (ISBN 0-671-68726-3, Archway). PB.
—Cult of Crime: Casefiles Three. large type ed. LC 88-21493. 151p. (gr. 5-10). 1988. Repr. of 1987 ed. 9.50 (ISBN 0-942545-44-3); PLB 10.50 (ISBN 0-942545-54-0, Dist. by Gareth Stevens). Grey Castle.
—Danger on the Air. (Orig.). (gr. 3-7). 1989. pap. 3.50 (ISBN 0-671-66305-4, Minstrel Bks). PB.
—Danger on Vampire Trail. Wilson, George, illus. LC 70-130337. (gr. 5-9). 1971. 4.50 (ISBN 0-448-08950-5, G&D). Putnam Pub Group.
—Danger Zone. 160p. 1990. pap. 2.95 (ISBN 0-671-67485-4, Archway). PB.
—Dead on Target: Casefiles One. large type ed. 153p. (gr. 5-10). 1988. Repr. of 1987 ed. 9.50 (ISBN 0-942545-42-7); PLB 10.50 (ISBN 0-942545-52-4, Dist. by Gareth Stevens). Grey Castle.
—The Dead Season. 160p. 1990. pap. 2.95 (ISBN 0-671-67483-8, Archway). PB.
—The Deadliest Dare. (Orig.). (gr. 7 up). 1989. pap. 2.95 (ISBN 0-671-67478-1, Archway). PB.
—Deadly Chase. (gr. 7 up). 1986. pap. 3.50 (ISBN 0-671-62477-6, Minstrel Bks). PB.
—Deathgame. 160p. (Orig.). (gr. 7 up). 1987. pap. 3.50 (ISBN 0-671-73672-8, Archway). PB.
—Deathgame: Casefiles Seven. large type ed. 151p. (gr. 7-10). 1988. Repr. of 1987 ed. 9.50 (ISBN 0-942545-48-6); PLB 10.50 (ISBN 0-942545-58-3, Dist. by Gareth Stevens). Grey Castle.
—Diplomatic Deceit. 160p. 1990. pap. 2.95 (ISBN 0-671-67486-2, Archway). PB.
—Disappearing Floor. (gr. 5-9). 1940. 4.50 (ISBN 0-448-08919-X, G&D). Putnam Pub Group.
—Disaster for Hire. (gr. 7 up). 1989. pap. 2.95 (ISBN 0-671-70491-5, Archway). PB.
—Double Exposure. (Orig.). (gr. 7 up). 1989. pap. 2.95 (ISBN 0-671-69376-X, Archway). PB.
—Edge of Destruction. 160p. (Orig.). (gr. 7 up). 1989. pap. 3.50 (ISBN 0-671-73669-8, Archway). PB.
—Edge of Destruction: Casefiles Five. large type ed. LC 88-21492. 153p. (gr. 5-10). 1988. Repr. 9.50 (ISBN 0-942545-46-X); PLB 10.50 (ISBN 0-942545-56-7, Dist. by Gareth Stevens). Grey Castle.
—Evil, Inc. (gr. 7 up). 1989. pap. 2.95 (ISBN 0-671-70359-5, Archway). PB.
—Evil, Inc. Casefiles Two. large type ed. 153p. (gr. 5-10). 1988. Repr. of 1987 ed. 9.50 (ISBN 0-942545-43-5); PLB 10.50 (ISBN 0-942545-53-2, Dist. by Gareth Stevens). Grey Castle.
—The Firebird Rocket. LC 77-76131. (Illus.). (gr. 5-9). 1978. 4.50 (ISBN 0-448-08957-2, G&D). Putnam Pub Group.
—Flesh & Blood. 160p. (Orig.). (gr. 7 up). 1990. pap. 2.95 (ISBN 0-671-67487-0, Archway). PB.
—Flickering Torch Mystery. (gr. 5-9). 1943. 4.50 (ISBN 0-448-08922-X, G&D); PLB 3.29 (ISBN 0-448-18922-4, G&D). Putnam Pub Group.
—Foul Play. Greenberg, Ann, ed. 160p. (Orig.). (gr. 7 up). 1990. pap. 2.95 (ISBN 0-671-70043-X, Archway). PB.
—Fright Wave. 160p. (Orig.). 1990. pap. 2.95 (ISBN 0-671-67488-9, Archway). PB.
—Game Plan for Disaster. 1987. pap. 3.50 (ISBN 0-671-64288-X, Minstrel Bks). PB.
—The Genius Thieves. 1988. pap. 2.95 (ISBN 0-671-68047-1, Archway). PB.
—The Genius Thieves: Casefiles Nine. large type ed. 153p. (gr. 5-10). 1988. Repr. of 1987 ed. 9.50 (ISBN 0-942545-50-8); PLB 10.50 (ISBN 0-942545-60-5, Dist. by Gareth Stevens). Grey Castle.
—Great Airport Mystery. (gr. 5-9). 1930. 4.50 (ISBN 0-448-08909-2, G&D). Putnam Pub Group.
—The Hardy Boys - The Four-Headed Dragon: Mystery Stories, Vol. 69. 176p. (ps). 1988. pap. 3.50 (ISBN 0-671-65797-6, Minstrel Bks). PB.
—Hardy Boys: Billion Dollar Ransom. Barish, Wendy, ed. Morrill, Leslie, illus. 192p. (gr. 3-7). 1982. 8.50 (ISBN 0-671-42352-5, Little Simon); pap. 3.50 (ISBN 0-671-42355-X). S&S Trade.
—Hardy Boys Case File No. 71: Track of the Zombie. 1986. pap. 3.50 (ISBN 0-671-62623-X). PB.
—Hardy Boys Case File No. 79: Sky Sabotage. 1986. pap. 3.50 (ISBN 0-671-62625-6). S&S Trade.
—Hardy Boys Case File No. 81: Demon's Den. 1986. pap. 3.50 (ISBN 0-671-62622-1, Wallaby). S&S Trade.
—Hardy Boys Casefiles, No. 47: Flight into Danger. Greenberg, Ann, ed. 160p. (Orig.). 1991. pap. 3.50 (ISBN 0-671-70044-8, Archway). PB.
—Hardy Boys Casefiles, No. 59: Night of the Werewolf. Greenberg, Ann, ed. 192p. 1990. pap. 3.50 (ISBN 0-671-70993-3, Minstrel Bks). PB.
—The Hardy Boys: Demon's Den. Barish, Wendy, ed. Frame, Paul, illus. 208p. (gr. 3 up). 1984. 9.95 (ISBN 0-685-09177-5, Little Simon). S&S Trade.
—The Hardy Boys: Game Plan for Disaster, No. 76. Schneider, Meg, ed. (Illus.). 208p. (gr. 3-7). 1982. 9.95 (ISBN 0-671-42364-9, Little Simon); pap. 3.50 (ISBN 0-671-42365-7). S&S Trade.
—The Hardy Boys: Ghost Stories. Schwartz, Betty, ed. (Illus.). 160p. (Orig.). (gr. 3-7). 1984. pap. 3.50 (ISBN 0-671-50808-3, Little Simon). S&S Trade.
—The Hardy Boys Gift Set, 3 vols. Boxed Set. pap. 8.55 (ISBN 0-317-12424-2, Little Simon). S&S Trade.
—Hardy Boys: Mystery of Smugglers Cove. Morrill, Leslie, illus. 192p. (gr. 3-7). 1980. PLB 7.95 (ISBN 0-671-41117-9, Little Simon); pap. 3.50 (ISBN 0-671-41112-8). S&S Trade.
—The Hardy Boys Mystery Stories, No. 64: Mystery of Smugglers Cove. 176p. (Orig.). (gr. 3-6). 1988. pap. 3.50 (ISBN 0-671-66229-5, Minstrel Bks). PB.
—The Hardy Boys No. 75: Trapped at Sea. Schneider, Meg, ed. (Illus.). 192p. (gr. 3-7). 1982. 9.95 (ISBN 0-671-42362-2, Little Simon); pap. 3.50 (ISBN 0-671-42363-0). S&S Trade.
—The Hardy Boys, No. 90: Danger on the Diamond. 160p. (Orig.). (gr. 3-6). 1988. pap. 3.50 (ISBN 0-671-63425-9, Minstrel Bks). PB.
—Hardy Boys: The Apeman's Secret. (Illus.). 192p. (Orig.). (gr. 3-7). 1980. 7.95 (ISBN 0-671-95530-6, Little Simon). S&S Trade.
—The Hardy Boys: The Blackwing Puzzle. 1984. 8.95 (ISBN 0-671-49726-X, Little Simon); pap. 3.50 (ISBN 0-671-49725-1). S&S Trade.
—Hardy Boys: The Demon's Den. 1984. 8.95 (ISBN 0-685-08794-8, Little Simon); pap. 2.95 (ISBN 0-685-08795-6). S&S Trade.
—Hardy Boys: The Infinity Clue. Morrill, Leslie, illus. 192p. (Orig.). (gr. 3-7). 1981. (Little Simon). S&S Trade.
—Hardy Boys: The Mummy Case. Morrill, Leslie, illus. 192p. (gr. 3-7). 1980. PLB 7.95 (ISBN 0-671-41116-0, Little Simon); pap. 3.50 (ISBN 0-671-41111-X). S&S Trade.
—Hardy Boys: The Outlaw's Silver. Morrill, Leslie, illus. 192p. (Orig.). (gr. 3-7). 1981. (Little Simon); pap. 3.50 (ISBN 0-671-42337-1). S&S Trade.
—Hardy Boys: The Pentagon Spy. (Illus.). (gr. 3-7). 1980. lib. bdg. 7.95 (ISBN 0-671-95562-4, Little Simon); pap. 3.50 (ISBN 0-671-95570-5). S&S Trade.
—The Hardy Boys: The Skyfire Puzzle. Arico, Diane, ed. 160p. (gr. 3-7). 1985. 9.95 (ISBN 0-671-49732-4, Little Simon); pap. 3.50 (ISBN 0-671-49731-6). S&S Trade.
—Hardy Boys: The Stone Idol. Morrill, Leslie, illus. 192p. (gr. 3-7). 1981. 8.50 (ISBN 0-671-42289-8, Little Simon); pap. 2.75 (ISBN 0-671-42290-1). S&S Trade.
—Hardy Boys: The Submarine Caper. Morrill, Leslie, illus. 192p. (Orig.). (gr. 3-7). 1981. 9.95 (ISBN 0-671-42338-X, Little Simon). S&S Trade.
—The Hardy Boys: The Swamp Monster. Arico, Diane, ed. 192p. (gr. 8-12). 1985. 9.95 (ISBN 0-671-55054-3, Little Simon); pap. 3.50 (ISBN 0-671-55048-9). S&S Trade.
—Hardy Boys: The Vanishing Thieves. Morrill, Leslie, illus. 176p. (Orig.). (gr. 3-7). 9.95 (ISBN 0-671-42291-X, Little Simon); pap. 3.50 (ISBN 0-671-42292-8). S&S Trade.
—Hardy Boys: Tic-Tac Terror. Morril, Leslie, illus. 192p. (gr. 3-7). 1982. 8.50 (ISBN 0-671-42356-8, Little Simon); pap. 3.50 (ISBN 0-671-42357-6). S&S Trade.
—Hardy Boys: Track of the Zombie. Morrill, Leslie, illus. 192p. (gr. 3-7). 1982. 8.50 (ISBN 0-671-42348-7, Little Simon). S&S Trade.

—Hardy Boys: Voodoo Plot. Morrill, Lesie, illus. 192p. (gr. 3-7). 1982. 8.50 (ISBN 0-671-42350-9, Little Simon); pap. 3.50 (ISBN 0-671-42351-7). S&S Trade.
—Haunted Fort. (gr. 5-9). 1964. 4.50 (ISBN 0-448-08944-0, G&D). Putnam Pub Group.
—Hidden Harbor Mystery. (gr. 5-9). 1935. 4.50 (ISBN 0-448-08914-9, G&D). Putnam Pub Group.
—Highway Robbery. Greenberg, Ann, ed. 160p. (Orig.). 1990. pap. 2.95 (ISBN 0-671-70038-3, Archway). PB.
—Hooded Hawk Mystery. rev. ed. Wilson, George, illus. (gr. 5-9). 1955. 4.50 (ISBN 0-448-08934-3, G&D); PLB 3.29 (ISBN 0-448-18934-8, G&D). Putnam Pub Group.
—Hostage of Hate: Casefiles Ten. large type ed. 153p. (gr. 5-10). 1988. Repr. of 1987 ed. 9.50 (ISBN 0-942545-51-6); PLB 10.50 (ISBN 0-942545-61-3, Dist. by Gareth Stevens). Grey Castle.
—Hostages of Hate. 160p. (Orig.). (gr. 7 up). 1989. pap. 2.95 (ISBN 0-671-69579-7, Archway). PB.
—House on the Cliff. (gr. 5-9). 1927. 4.50 (ISBN 0-448-08902-5, G&D). Putnam Pub Group.
—In Self-Defense. Greenberg, Ann, ed. 160p. (Orig.). (gr. 7 up). 1990. pap. 2.95 (ISBN 0-671-70042-1, Archway). PB.
—The Infinity Clue. 192p. 1989. pap. 3.50 (ISBN 0-671-69154-6, Minstrel Bks). PB.
—The Jungle Pyramid. LC 76-14297. (Illus.). (gr. 5-9). 1977. 4.50 (ISBN 0-448-08956-4, G&D). Putnam Pub Group.
—A Killing in the Market. (gr. 7 up). 1989. pap. 2.95 (ISBN 0-671-68472-8, Archway). PB.
—Last Laugh. Greenberg, Ann, ed. 160p. (gr. 7 up). 1990. pap. 3.50 (ISBN 0-671-74614-6, Archway). PB.
—The Lazarus Plot. (gr. 7 up). 1988. pap. 2.95 (ISBN 0-671-68048-X, Archway). PB.
—The Lazarus Plot: Casefiles Four. large type ed. 152p. (gr. 5-10). 1988. Repr. of 1987 ed. 9.50 (ISBN 0-942545-45-1); PLB 10.50 (ISBN 0-942545-55-9, Dist. by Gareth Stevens). Grey Castle.
—Line of Fire. 160p. (Orig.). (gr. 7 up). 1989. pap. 2.95 (ISBN 0-671-68805-7, Archway). PB.
—Mark on the Door. rev. ed. (gr. 5-9). 1934. 4.50 (ISBN 0-448-08913-0, G&D). Putnam Pub Group.
—Melted Coins. rev. ed. LC 78-86722. (Illus.). (gr. 5-9). 1944. 2.95 (ISBN 0-448-18923-2, G&D). Putnam Pub Group.
—The Million Dollar Nightmare. Greenberg, Ann, ed. 160p. (Orig.). (gr. 4-7). 1990. pap. 3.50 (ISBN 0-671-69272-0, Minstrel Bks). PB.
—The Money Hunt. 160p. 1990. pap. 3.50 (ISBN 0-671-69451-0, Minstrel Bks). PB.
—The Mummy Case. 192p. (gr. 3-6). 1987. pap. 3.50 (ISBN 0-671-64289-8, Minstrel Bks). PB.
—The Mysterious Caravan. new ed. LC 74-10463. (Illus.). 196p. (gr. 5-9). 1975. 4.50 (ISBN 0-448-08954-8, G&D). Putnam Pub Group.
—Mystery of Cabin Island. (gr. 5-9). 1929. 4.50 (ISBN 0-448-08908-4, G&D). Putnam Pub Group.
—Mystery of the Chinese Junk. (gr. 5-9). 1959. 3.29 (ISBN 0-448-18939-9, G&D). Putnam Pub Group.
—Mystery of the Desert Giant. (Illus.). (gr. 5-9). 1960. PLB 3.29 (ISBN 0-448-18940-2, G&D). Putnam Pub Group.
—The Mystery of the Samurai Sword. (Illus.). (gr. 3-6). 1979. 7.95 (ISBN 0-671-95506-3, Little Simon); pap. 3.50 (ISBN 0-671-95497-0). S&S Trade.
—Mystery of the Samurai Sword. (gr. 2-7). 1984. 8.85 (ISBN 0-685-09393-X, Little Simon). S&S Trade.
—Mystery of the Samurai Sword. (gr. 3-7). 1988. pap. 3.50 (ISBN 0-671-67302-5, Minstrel Bks). PB.
—The Mystery of the Silver Star. (gr. 3-6). 1987. pap. 3.50 (ISBN 0-671-64374-6, Minstrel Bks). PB.
—Mystery of the Spiral Bridge. (Illus.). (gr. 5-9). 1966. 4.50 (ISBN 0-448-08945-9, G&D). Putnam Pub Group.
—Mystery of the Whale Tattoo. (gr. 5-9). 1967. 4.50 (ISBN 0-448-08947-5, G&D). Putnam Pub Group.
—Night of the Werewolf. (Illus.). (gr. 3-6). 1979. 9.95 (ISBN 0-671-95498-9, Little Simon). S&S Trade.
—Night of the Werewolf. (gr. 2-7). 1984. 8.85 (ISBN 0-685-09390-5, Little Simon). S&S Trade.
—Nightmare in Angel City. (Orig.). (gr. 7 up). 1989. pap. 2.95 (ISBN 0-671-69185-6, Archway). PB.
—Nowhere to Run. (Orig.). (gr. 7 up). 1989. pap. 2.95 (ISBN 0-671-64690-7, Archway). PB.
—The Number File. (Orig.). (gr. 7 up). 1989. pap. 2.95 (ISBN 0-671-68806-5, Archway). PB.
—The Pentagon Spy. (gr. 2-7). 1984. 8.85 (Little Simon). S&S Trade.
—The Pentagon Spy. (gr. 3-7). 1988. pap. 3.50 (ISBN 0-671-67221-5, Minstrel Bks). PB.
—Perfect Getaway. 160p. (Orig.). (gr. 7 up). 1988. pap. 2.95 (ISBN 0-671-68049-8, Archway). PB.
—Phantom Freighter. rev. ed. Wilson, George, illus. LC 75-115957. (gr. 5-9). 1947. 4.50 (ISBN 0-448-08926-2, G&D); PLB 3.29 (ISBN 0-448-18926-7). Putnam Pub Group.
—Program for Destruction. (gr. 3-6). 1987. pap. 3.50 (ISBN 0-671-64895-0, Minstrel Bks). PB.
—Revenge of the Desert Phantom. (gr. 7 up). 1985. pap. 3.50 (ISBN 0-671-49729-4, Minstrel Bks). PB.
—The Roaring River Mystery. Schwartz, Betty, ed. (Orig.). (gr. 3-7). 1984. 9.95 (ISBN 0-671-49722-7, Little Simon); pap. 3.50 (ISBN 0-671-73004-5). S&S Trade.
—Running on Empty. 160p. 1990. pap. 2.95 (ISBN 0-671-67484-6, Archway). PB.
—Scene of the Crime. (gr. 7 up). 1989. pap. 2.95 (ISBN 0-671-69377-8, Archway). PB.
—Secret Agent on Flight 101. (gr. 5-9). 1967. 4.50 (ISBN 0-448-08946-7, G&D). Putnam Pub Group.
—The Secret of Pirates' Hill. rev. ed. (Illus.). 196p. (gr. 5-9). 1957. 4.50 (ISBN 0-448-08936-X, G&D). Putnam Pub Group.
—Secret of Skull Mountain. (gr. 5-9). 1948. 4.50 (ISBN 0-448-08927-0, G&D). Putnam Pub Group.
—Secret of the Caves. rev. ed. (gr. 5-9). 1929. 4.50 (ISBN 0-448-08907-6, G&D). Putnam Pub Group.
—Secret of the Old Mill. (gr. 5-9). 1927. 4.50 (ISBN 0-448-08903-3, G&D). Putnam Pub Group.
—Secret Panel. rev. ed. LC 74-86693. (Illus.). (gr. 5-9). 1946. 4.50 (ISBN 0-448-08925-4, G&D). Putnam Pub Group.
—Secret Warning. (gr. 5-9). 1938. 4.50 (ISBN 0-448-08917-3, G&D). Putnam Pub Group.
—See No Evil: Casefiles Eight. large type ed. 152p. (gr. 5-10). 1988. Repr. of 1987 ed. 9.50 (ISBN 0-942545-49-4); PLB 10.50 (ISBN 0-942545-59-1, Dist. by Gareth Stevens). Grey Castle.
—The Serpent's Tooth Mystery. (Orig.). (gr. 3-7). 1988. pap. 3.50 (ISBN 0-671-66310-0, Minstrel Bks). PB.
—The Shadow Killers. 1988. pap. 3.50 (ISBN 0-671-66309-7, Minstrel Bks). PB.
—The Shattered Helmet. LC 72-90825. (Illus.). 196p. (gr. 5-9). 1973. 4.50 (ISBN 0-448-08952-1, G&D); PLB 3.29 (ISBN 0-448-18952-6). Putnam Pub Group.
—Shield of Fear. 1988. pap. 3.50 (ISBN 0-671-66308-9, Minstrel Bks). PB.
—Sign of the Crooked Arrow. rev ed. Wilson, George, illus. LC 71-100119. (gr. 5-9). 1949. 4.50 (ISBN 0-448-08928-9, G&D); (Putnam). Putnam Pub Group.
—The Sky Blue Frame. 160p. (Orig.). (gr. 3-6). 1988. pap. 3.50 (ISBN 0-671-64974-4, Minstrel Bks). PB.
—The Skyfire Puzzle. (gr. 3-7). 1989. pap. 3.50 (ISBN 0-671-67458-7, Minstrel Bks). PB.
—The Smoke Screen Mystery. Greenberg, Ann, ed. 160p. (Orig.). (gr. 3-6). 1990. pap. 3.50 (ISBN 0-671-69274-7, Minstrel Bks). PB.
—Spark of Suspicion. 160p. (Orig.). 1989. pap. 3.50 (ISBN 0-671-66304-6, Minstrel Bks). PB.
—The Sting of the Scorpion. LC 78-57930. (Illus.). (gr. 3-7). 1979. 4.50 (ISBN 0-448-08958-0, G&D). Putnam Pub Group.
—The Stone Idol. 192p. 1990. pap. 3.50 (ISBN 0-671-69402-2, Minstrel Bks). PB.
—Strategic Moves. Greenberg, Ann, ed. 160p. (Orig.). (gr. 7 up). 1990. pap. 2.95 (ISBN 0-671-70040-5, Archway). PB.
—Street Spies. (gr. 7 up). 1989. pap. 2.95 (ISBN 0-671-69186-4, Archway). PB.
—The Swamp Monster. (gr. 3-7). 1989. pap. 3.50 (ISBN 0-671-62681-7, Minstrel Bks). PB.
—Terminal Shock. 160p. 1990. pap. 3.50 (ISBN 0-671-69288-7, Minstrel). PB.
—Thick As Thieves. (Orig.). (gr. 7 up). 1989. pap. 2.95 (ISBN 0-671-67477-3, Archway). PB.
—Tic-Tac Terror. 1988. pap. 3.50 (ISBN 0-671-66858-7, Minstrel Bks). PB.
—Too Many Traitors. 160p. (Orig.). (gr. 7 up). 1989. pap. 2.95 (ISBN 0-671-68804-9, Archway). PB.
—Tower Treasure. (gr. 5-9). 1927. 4.50 (ISBN 0-448-08901-7, G&D). Putnam Pub Group.
—Tower Treasure. 1991. 12.95 (ISBN 1-55709-144-7). Applewood.
—Tricky Business. 160p. (gr. 3-6). 1988. pap. 3.50 (ISBN 0-671-64973-6, Minstrel Bks). PB.
—Trouble in the Pipeline. (gr. 7 up). 1989. pap. 2.95 (ISBN 0-671-64689-3, Archway). PB.
—Twisted Claw. rev. ed. LC 77-86667. (Illus.). (gr. 5-9). 1939. 4.50 (ISBN 0-448-08918-1, G&D). Putnam Pub Group.
—Wailing Siren Mystery. rev. ed. (Illus.). (gr. 5-9). 1951. 4.50 (ISBN 0-448-08930-0, G&D); PLB 3.29 (ISBN 0-448-18930-5). Putnam Pub Group.
—What Happened at Midnight. (gr. 5-9). 1931. 4.50 (ISBN 0-448-08910-6, G&D). Putnam Pub Group.
—While the Clock Ticked. (gr. 5-9). 1932. 4.50 (ISBN 0-448-08911-4, G&D). Putnam Pub Group.
—Wipeout. (Orig.). (gr. 7 up). 1989. pap. 3.50 (ISBN 0-671-66306-2, Minstrel Bks). PB.
—The Witchmaster's Key. LC 75-17392. (Illus.). 196p. (gr. 5-9). 1976. 4.50 (ISBN 0-448-08955-6, G&D). Putnam Pub Group.
—Without a Trace. (Orig.). (gr. 7 up). 1989. pap. 2.95 (ISBN 0-671-67479-X, Archway). PB.
—Yellow Feather Mystery. (gr. 5-9). 1954. 4.50 (ISBN 0-448-08933-5, G&D); PLB 3.29 (ISBN 0-448-18933-X). Putnam Pub Group.

Dixon, Franklin W. & Barish, Wendy. Cave-In. Frame, Paul, illus. 192p. (Orig.). (gr. 3-7). 1983. 9.95 (ISBN 0-671-42368-1, Little Simon); 3.50 (ISBN 0-671-62621-3); pap. 3.50 (ISBN 0-671-42369-X). S&S Trade.
—Sky Sabotage. Frame, Paul, illus. 192p. (Orig.). (gr. 3-7). 1983. 9.95 (ISBN 0-671-47556-8, Little Simon). S&S Trade.

Dixon, Franklin W. & Keene, Carolyn. The Secret of the Knight's Sword. Schwartz, Betty, ed. Frame, Paul, illus. 128p. (Orig.). (gr. 3-7). 1984. pap. 3.50 (ISBN 0-671-49919-X, Little Simon). S&S Trade.

Dixon, Franklin W. & Spina, D. A. Hardy Boys Detective Handbook. rev. ed. (Illus.). 224p. (gr. 4-7). 1972. 4.50 (ISBN 0-448-01990-6, G&D); PLB 3.29 (ISBN 0-448-03227-9, G&D). Putnam Pub Group.

Dixon, S. The Vanishing Village. (Illus.). 48p. 1990. lib. bdg. 10.96 (ISBN 0-88110-405-1); pap. 4.50 (ISBN 0-7460-0330-7). EDC.

Docekal, Eileen M. Nature Detective: How to Solve Outdoor Mysteries. LC 89-31387. (Illus.). 128p. (gr. 4-12). 1989. 14.95 (ISBN 0-8069-6844-3). Sterling.

Dolby, K. The Ghost in the Mirror. (Illus.). 48p. 1989. lib. bdg. 10.96 (ISBN 0-88110-369-1); pap. 4.50 (ISBN 0-7460-0334-X). EDC.

Donev, Mary K. Mysteries. Rowden, Rick, illus. 48p. (gr. 5-9). 1985. PLB 10.69 (ISBN 0-87617-024-6, Pub. by C Hayes Pr). Penworthy Pub.

Donovan, Donna. The Missing Mascot. 8p. (gr. 3-7). 1988. incl. puzzle 9.95 (ISBN 0-922242-08-9). Lombard Mktg.

Doyle, Arthur Conan. The Adventure of the Speckled Band. 64p. (gr. 6). 1990. 10.95 (ISBN 0-88682-301-3). Creative Ed.
—Adventures of Sherlock Holmes. 272p. (gr. 9-12). 1989. pap. 2.50 (ISBN 0-8125-0424-0). Tor Bks.
—The Adventures of Sherlock Holmes, Bk. 1. Glass, Andrew, illus. Sadler, Catherine E., adapted by. (Illus.). 140p. (Orig.). (gr. 4-7). 1981. pap. 2.95 (ISBN 0-380-78089-5, 85589-5, Camelot). Avon.
—The Adventures of Sherlock Holmes, Bk. 2. Glass, Andrew, illus. Sadler, Catherine E., adapted by. (Illus.). 156p. (Orig.). (gr. 4-7). 1981. pap. 2.95 (ISBN 0-380-78097-6, 85597-6, Camelot). Avon.
—The Adventures of Sherlock Holmes, Bk. 3. Glass, Andrew, illus. Sadler, Catherine E., frwd. by. (Illus.). 112p. (Orig.). (gr. 4-7). 1981. pap. 2.95 (ISBN 0-380-78105-0, 60233-4, Camelot). Avon.
—The Adventures of Sherlock Holmes, Bk. 4. Glass, Andrew, illus. Sadler, Catherine E., adapted by. (Illus.). 112p. (Orig.). (gr. 4-7). 1981. pap. 2.95 (ISBN 0-380-78113-1, 60234-2, Camelot). Avon.
—Case Book of Sherlock Holmes. (gr. 10 up). 1984. pap. 2.50 (ISBN 0-425-10194-0). Berkley Pub.
—Complete Sherlock Holmes. LC 65-6074. 1960. Two vols. 19.95 (ISBN 0-385-04591-3); pap. 22.50 (ISBN 0-385-00689-6). Doubleday.
—The Great Adventures of Sherlock Holmes. (Illus.). 256p. (gr. 5 up). 1991. pap. 2.95 (ISBN 0-14-035116-7, Puffin). Puffin Bks.
—Great Stories of Sherlock Holmes. 287p. (gr. 5 up). 1962. pap. 1.75 (ISBN 0-440-93190-8, LFL). Dell.
—His Last Bow. (gr. 10 up). 1984. pap. 2.50 (ISBN 0-425-10491-5). Berkley Pub.
—Hound of the Baskervilles. (gr. 8 up). pap. 1.75 (ISBN 0-8049-0062-0, CL-62). Airmont.
—The Hound of the Baskervilles. (Illus.). (gr. k-6). 1979. pap. text ed. 4.25x (ISBN 0-19-581211-5). Oxford U Pr.
—Hound of the Baskervilles. new & abr. ed. Fago, John N., ed. Cruz, E. R., illus. (gr. 4-12). 1977. pap. text ed. 2.95 (ISBN 0-88301-264-2). Pendulum Pr.
—The Hound of the Baskervilles. 104p. (gr. 7-8). 1983. pap. text ed. 6.95x (ISBN 0-7069-2470-3, Pub by Vikas India); text ed. 6.95x (ISBN 0-685-08261-X). Advent NY.
—The Hound of the Baskervilles. (gr. 10 up). 1983. pap. 2.75 (ISBN 0-425-10405-2). Berkley Pub.
—The Hound of the Baskervilles. (gr. 4-6). 1986. pap. 2.25 (ISBN 0-14-035064-0, Puffin). Puffin Bks.
—Memoirs of Sherlock Holmes. (gr. 10 up). 1984. pap. 2.75 (ISBN 0-425-10402-8). Berkley Pub.
—Mysteries of Sherlock Holmes. Conaway, Judith, ed. Miller, Lyle, illus. LC 87-23540. 96p. (gr. 3-7). 1988. pap. 1.95 (ISBN 0-317-66929-X, Random Juv). Random.
—Reader's Digest Best Loved Books for Young Readers: Great Cases of Sherlock Holmes. Ogburn, Jackie, ed. Deel, Guy, illus. 184p. (gr. 4-12). 1989. 3.99 (ISBN 0-945260-22-9). Choice Pub NY.
—The Red-Headed League. 64p. (gr. 6). 1990. 10.95s.p. (ISBN 0-88682-300-5); 15.65 (ISBN 0-685-28215-5). Creative Ed.
—Sherlock Holmes. Toht, Don, illus. Stewart, Diana, adapted by. LC 79-24106. (Illus.). 48p. (gr. 4 up). 1983. PLB 17.32 (ISBN 0-8172-1657-X); pap. 9.27 (ISBN 0-8172-2021-6). Raintree Pubs.
—Silver Blaze. 64p. (gr. 6). 1990. 10.95s.p. (ISBN 0-88682-302-1); 15.65 (ISBN 0-685-28217-1). Creative Ed.
—Six Notable Adventures of Sherlock Holmes. 512p. (gr. 3 up). 1982. pap. 6.95 (ISBN 0-448-41101-6, G&D). Putnam Pub Group.

Drobot, Eve. Amazing Investigations: Money. Weissmann, Joe, illus. 96p. (gr. 3-7). 1988. 12.95 (ISBN 0-13-023714-0, Little Simon). S&S Trade.

Duffy, James. The Christmas Gang. McClintock, Barbara, illus. LC 88-32762. 80p. (gr. 3-6). 1989. 11.95 (ISBN 0-684-19008-7, Scribners Young Read). Macmillan Child Grp.
—Cleaver of the Good Luck Diner. 112p. 1991. pap. 2.95 (ISBN 0-380-71073-0, Camelot). Avon.
—The Man in the River. LC 89-10200. 176p. (gr. 5-7). 1990. 13.95 (ISBN 0-684-19161-X, Scribners Young Read). Macmillan Child Grp.

Duncan, Lois. Down a Dark Hall. 192p. (gr. 7 up). 1974. 13.95 (ISBN 0-316-19547-2). Little.
—Down a Dark Hall. 192p. (gr. 5-9). 1990. pap. 3.50 (ISBN 0-440-91805-7, LFL). Dell.
—I Know What You Did Last Summer. (gr. 7 up). 1973. 14.95 (ISBN 0-316-19546-4). Little.
—Killing Mr. Griffin. 224p. (gr. 7 up). 1990. pap. 3.50 (ISBN 0-440-94515-1, LFL). Dell.

—Ransom. 144p. (gr. 7-12). 1990. pap. 3.50 (ISBN 0-440-97292-2, LFL). Dell.
—The Twisted Window. LC 86-29054. 192p. (gr. 7 up). 1987. pap. 14.95 (ISBN 0-385-29566-9). Delacorte.
—The Twisted Window. 192p. (gr. k-12). 1988. pap. 3.50 (ISBN 0-440-20184-5, LFL). Dell.
Dunlop, Eileen. The House on the Hill. LC 87-388. 160p. (gr. 4 up). 1987. 13.95 (ISBN 0-8234-0658-X). Holiday.
Dunmire, Marj. Not Even Footprints. Dunmire, Marj, illus. 72p. (Orig.). (gr. 2-7). 1987. pap. 4.95 (ISBN 0-942559-04-5). Pegasus Graphics.
Eastman, David, adapted by. Sherlock Holmes: The Adventure of the Empty House. Eitzen, Allan, illus. LC 81-11673. 32p. (gr. 5-9). 1982. PLB 10.79 (ISBN 0-89375-616-4); pap. 2.95 (ISBN 0-89375-617-2). Troll Assocs.
—Sherlock Holmes: The Adventure of the Speckled Band. Eitzen, David, illus. LC 81-11694. 32p. (gr. 5-9). 1982. PLB 10.79 (ISBN 0-89375-618-0); pap. 2.95 (ISBN 0-89375-619-9); cassettes avail. Troll Assocs.
—Sherlock Holmes: The Final Problem. Eitzen, Allan, illus. LC 81-11609. 32p. (gr. 5-9). 1982. PLB 10.79 (ISBN 0-89375-612-1); pap. 2.95 (ISBN 0-89375-613-X). Troll Assocs.
—Sherlock Holmes: The Red-Headed League. Eitzen, Allan, illus. LC 81-11619. 32p. (gr. 5-9). 1982. PLB 10.79 (ISBN 0-89375-614-8); pap. 2.95 (ISBN 0-89375-615-6). Troll Assocs.
Ecke, Wolfgang. The Castle of the Red Gorillas. Rettich, Rolf, illus. LC 82-23122. 120p. (gr. 5-9). 1983. 9.95 (ISBN 0-13-120360-6). P-H.
—The Face at the Window. Ecke, Wolfgang, illus. LC 79-15628. (gr. 5-9). 1979. 9.95 (ISBN 0-13-299115-2). P-H.
—The Midnight Chess Game. Rettich, Rolf, illus. LC 84-26564. 144p. (gr. 5 up). 1985. 10.95 (ISBN 0-13-582826-0). P-H.
Ehrlich, Amy. The Dark Card. 1991. 13.95 (ISBN 0-670-83733-4). Viking Child Bks.
Eisenberg, Lisa. Mystery at Snowshoe Mountain Lodge. LC 86-11535. 176p. (gr. 5 up). 1987. 12.95 (ISBN 0-8037-0359-7). Dial Bks Young.
—Mystery at Snowshoe Mountain Lodge. 176p. (gr. 2-9). pap. 2.95 (ISBN 0-8167-1322-7). Troll Assocs.
Elam, Richard M., ed. Teen-Age Suspense Stories. (gr. 6-10). 1963. PLB 6.70 (ISBN 0-8313-0047-7). Lantern.
Elfman, Blossom. The Ghost-Sitter. 112p. 1990. pap. 3.50 (ISBN 0-449-70358-4, Juniper). Fawcett.
Elmore, Patricia. Susannah & the Blue House Mystery. Wallner, John, illus. LC 79-20491. 176p. (gr. 4-7). 1980. 10.25 (ISBN 0-525-40525-9, DCB). Dutton Child Bks.
—Susannah & the Poison Green Halloween. Schick, Joel, illus. LC 82-2493. 128p. (gr. 4-7). 1982. 9.95 (ISBN 0-525-44019-4, DCB). Dutton Child Bks.
Enright, Elizabeth. Spiderweb for Two. (gr. k-6). 1987. pap. 2.95 (ISBN 0-440-48203-8, YB). Dell.
Erickson, John R. Hank the Cowdog: Faded Love. (gr. 3 up). 1985. 9.95 (ISBN 0-916941-11-6); pap. 6.95 (ISBN 0-916941-10-8); 13.95 (ISBN 0-916941-12-4). Maverick Bks.
—Hank the Cowdog: Murder in the Middle Pasture. Holmes, Gerald L., illus. 91p. (Orig.). (gr. 3 up). 1985. 9.95 (ISBN 0-916941-08-6); pap. 6.95 (ISBN 0-916941-07-8); talking book 13.95 (ISBN 0-916941-09-4). Maverick Bks.
Escoula, Yvonne. Six Blue Horses. LC 70-103044. (gr. 5-9). 1970. 18.95 (ISBN 0-87599-162-9). S G Phillips.
Estes, Rose. The Case of the Dancing Dinosaur. Vincente, illus. LC 83-63444. 128p. (gr. 4-7). 1985. (Random Juv); pap. 2.95 (ISBN 0-394-86431-X, BYR). Random.
—The Mystery of the Turkish Tattoo. Fanelli, Jenny, ed. Gowing, Toby, illus. LC 85-62805. 128p. (gr. 4-7). 1986. pap. 2.95 (ISBN 0-394-86434-4). Random.
Eustis, Helen. The Redheaded Woman. Reinhard, Michl, illus. LC 84-145828. 36p. (Orig.). (gr. 7 up). 1983. pap. 6.95 (ISBN 0-88138-013-X). Green Tiger Pr.
Eyerly, Jeannette. Angel Baker, Thief. LC 84-47634. 224p. (gr. 7 up). 1984. 12.02i (ISBN 0-397-32096-5, Lipp Jr Bks); PLB 12.89 (ISBN 0-397-32097-3). HarpC Child Bks.
Eyles, Heather. Into the Night House. Gon, Adriano, illus. 64p. (gr. 4-7). 1990. pap. 2.95 (ISBN 0-8120-4423-1). Barron.
Falconer, Lois C. To Kim with Love. 80p. (gr. 7-10). 1987. 6.95 (ISBN 0-8059-3056-6). Dorrance.
False Moves: The Nancy Drew Files, Case 9. large type ed. 149p. (gr. 5-10). 1988. Repr. of 1987 ed. 9.50 (ISBN 0-942545-40-0); PLB 10.50 (ISBN 0-942545-35-4, Dist. by Grolier). Grey Castle.
Farley, Carol. The Case of the Haunted Health Club. 112p. 1991. pap. 2.95 (ISBN 0-380-75918-7, Camelot). Avon.
—The Case of the Lost Lookalike. 112p. 1988. pap. 2.50 (ISBN 0-380-75450-9, Camelot). Avon.
Farley, Walter. Black Stallion & Flame. LC 60-10029. (Illus.). (gr. 5 up). 1980. 3.95 (ISBN 0-394-80615-8, Random Juv); lib. bdg. 10.99 (ISBN 0-394-90615-2); pap. 3.95 (ISBN 0-394-84372-X). Random.
—The Black Stallion Mystery. (gr. 4-6). 1977. 3.95 (ISBN 0-394-80613-1, Random Juv); lib. bdg. 10.99 (ISBN 0-394-90613-6); pap. 2.95 (ISBN 0-394-83611-1). Random.
—Black Stallion's Ghost. Draper, Angie, illus. (gr. 5-9). 1978. lib. bdg. 10.99 (ISBN 0-394-90618-7, Random Juv); PLB 7.99 (ISBN 0-685-04258-8); pap. 3.95 (ISBN 0-394-83919-6). Random.
Figarsky, Irene F. Kadookie Head. 1990. 6.95 (ISBN 0-533-08982-4). Vantage.
Fish, Helen D. When the Root Children Wake Up. Von Olfers, Sibylle, illus. 24p. 1988. Repr. of 1906 ed. 12.95 (ISBN 0-88138-103-9). Green Tiger Pr.
Fitzgerald, John D. The Return of the Great Brain. Mayer, Mercer, illus. LC 73-15443. 176p. (gr. 4-7). 1985. 12.95 (ISBN 0-8037-7403-6). Dial Bks Young.
Fitzhugh, Louise. Long Secret. Fitzhugh, Louise, illus. LC 65-23370. (gr. 5 up). 1965. 13.95i (ISBN 0-06-021410-4); PLB 13.89 (ISBN 0-06-021411-2). HarpC Child Bks.
—Sport. LC 78-72861. 250p. (gr. 4-6). 1979. pap. 8.95 (ISBN 0-385-28908-1). Delacorte.
Fleischman, Paul. Graven Images. Glass, Andrew, illus. LC 81-48649. 96p. (gr. 6 up). 1987. pap. 3.50 (ISBN 0-06-440186-3, Trophy). HarpC Child Bks.
—The Half-a-Moon Inn. Jacobi, Kathy, illus. LC 79-2010. 96p. (gr. 5 up). 1980. PLB 12.89 (ISBN 0-06-021918-1). HarpC Child Bks.
Fleischman, Sid. The Bloodhound Gang in The Case of the Secret Message. Harmuth, William, illus. LC 80-28469. 64p. (gr. 2-4). 1981. Random.
—The Bloodhound Gang in the Case of the 264-Pound Burglar. Morrison, Bill, illus. LC 81-12066. 64p. (gr. 2-5). 1982. pap. 1.50 (ISBN 0-394-85108-0). Random.
—The Case of the Flying Clock. Harmuth, William, illus. LC 80-28056. 64p. (gr. 2-4). 1981. Random.
—Mr. Mysterious & Company, Vol. 1. (gr. 4-7). 1990. pap. 4.95 (ISBN 0-316-28614-1). Little.
Foley, Louise M. The Mardi Gras Mystery. 128p. (Orig.). (gr. 4). 1987. pap. 2.25 (ISBN 0-553-26291-2). Bantam.
—The Mystery of Echo Lodge. 128p. (gr. 4 up). 1985. pap. 2.25 (ISBN 0-553-26313-7). Bantam.
—The Mystery of the Highland Crest. (gr. 4 up). 1984. pap. 1.95 (ISBN 0-553-24344-6). Bantam.
—Mystery of the Sacred Stones: Choose Your Own Adventure, No. 79. 128p. (Orig.). (gr. 7 up). 1988. pap. 2.50 (ISBN 0-553-26950-X). Bantam.
Follett, Ken. The Mystery Hideout. Marchesi, Stephen, illus. LC 89-39961. 96p. (gr. 5 up). 1990. Repr. of 1976 ed. 12.95 (ISBN 0-688-08721-3). Morrow Jr Bks.
The Foolish Mystery. (Illus.). 26p. (Orig.). (gr. k-6). 1990. pap. 4.00 (ISBN 0-9625059-4-3). Fountain Light Pr.
Foreman, Marcey G. The Russian in the Attic. LC 88-50755. 119p. (gr. 5-8). 1988. 7.95 (ISBN 1-55523-160-8). Winston-Derek.
Fox, Paula. The Moonlight Man. LC 85-26907. 192p. (gr. 7 up). 1986. 13.95 (ISBN 0-02-735480-6, Bradbury Pr). Macmillan Child Grp.
French, Dorothy K. Pioneer Saddle Mystery. LC 75-12428. 192p. (gr. 5-10). 1975. PLB 6.70 (ISBN 0-8313-0113-9). Lantern.
French, Michael. Pursuit. LC 82-70319. 192p. (gr. 7 up). 1982. 9.95 (ISBN 0-385-28781-X). Delacorte.
Friedland, Joyce & Kessler, Rikki. Charlotte's Web: A Study Guide. (gr. 2-5). 1983. tchr's. ed. & wkbk. 14.95 (ISBN 0-88122-015-9). LRN Links.
Frost, Erica. Case of the Missing Chick. new ed. Harvey, Paul, illus. LC 78-18036. 48p. (gr. 2-4). 1979. PLB 10.89 (ISBN 0-89375-092-1); pap. 2.95 (ISBN 0-89375-080-8). Troll Assocs.
—Harold & the Dinosaur Mystery. new ed. Sims, Deborah, illus. LC 78-60123. 48p. (gr. 2-4). 1979. PLB 10.89 (ISBN 0-89375-088-3); pap. 2.95 (ISBN 0-89375-076-X). Troll Assocs.
—Mystery of the Midnight Visitors. Gamache, Ann, illus. LC 78-18038. 48p. (gr. 2-4). 1979. PLB 10.89 (ISBN 0-89375-094-8); pap. 2.95 (ISBN 0-89375-082-4). Troll Assocs.
—Mystery of the Runaway Sled. Grant, Leigh, illus. LC 78-60124. 48p. (gr. 2-4). 1979. PLB 10.89 (ISBN 0-89375-089-1); pap. 2.95 (ISBN 0-89375-077-8). Troll Assocs.
Fujikawa, Gyo. Millie's Secret. Duenewald, Doris, ed. (Illus.). (gr. k-3). 1978. PLB 3.50 (ISBN 0-448-14726-2, G&D). Putnam Pub Group.
Furman, Abraham L., ed. Everygirls Detective Stories. (Illus.). (gr. 6-10). PLB 6.70 (ISBN 0-8313-0060-4). Lantern.
—More Teen-Age Haunted Stories. (gr. 5-10). 1967. PLB 6.70 (ISBN 0-8313-0057-4). Lantern.
—Teen-Age Detective Stories. LC 68-23983. (gr. 6-10). 1968. 6.70 (ISBN 0-8313-0044-2). Lantern.
Galbraith, Kathryn O. Something Suspicious. LC 85-4003. 168p. (gr. 3-7). 1985. 11.95 (ISBN 0-689-50322-9, M K McElderry). Macmillan Child Grp.
—Something Suspicious. 128p. (gr. 3 up). 1987. pap. 2.50 (ISBN 0-380-70253-3, Camelot). Avon.
Gantz, David. Ms. Agatha in the Return of the Children. Gantz, David, illus. 26p. (ps-3). 1988. Incl. full-color stickers. pap. 2.95 (ISBN 0-671-64206-5). S&S Trade.
Gardiner, John R. General Butterfingers. Smith, Catherine B., illus. 96p. (gr. 3-7). 1986. 12.95 (ISBN 0-395-41853-4). HM.
Garfield, Leon. Devil in the Fog. (gr. k-6). 1988. pap. 3.25 (ISBN 0-440-40095-3, YB). Dell.
Gasperini, Jim. Sail with Pirates. Pierard, John & Nino, Alex, illus. 144p. (gr. 4 up). 1984. pap. 2.50 (ISBN 0-553-26497-4). Bantam.
Gehrts, Barbara. Don't Say a Word. Crawford, Elizabeth D., tr. LC 86-7248. 192p. (gr. 7 up). 1986. 13.95 (ISBN 0-689-50412-8, M K McElderry). Macmillan Child Grp.
Gersbach, Jo R. The Case of the Buried Money Bags. (gr. 5-8). 1978. 6.50 (ISBN 0-87881-065-X). Mojave Bks.
Gevirtz, Eliezer. The Mystery of the Missing Bar Mitzvah Gift. (gr. 4-7). 1987. 9.95 (ISBN 0-317-57109-5); pap. 7.95 (ISBN 0-317-57110-9). Feldheim.
—The Mystery of the Missing Pushke. Mazal, Chanan, illus. 200p. (gr. 5-7). 1982. 8.95 (ISBN 0-87306-291-4); pap. 6.95 (ISBN 0-685-07004-2). Feldheim.
Gezi, Kal & Bradford, Ann. The Mystery at Misty Falls. McLean, Mina G., illus. LC 80-15708. 32p. (gr. k-4). 1980. PLB 9.96 (ISBN 0-89565-147-5). Childs World.
—The Mystery in the Secret Club House. McLean, Mina G., illus. LC 78-6418. (gr. k-3). 1978. PLB 9.96 (ISBN 0-89565-027-4). Childs World.
—The Mystery of the Blind Writer. McLean, Mina G., illus. LC 80-12395. 32p. (gr. k-4). 1980. PLB 9.96 (ISBN 0-89565-145-9). Childs World.
—The Mystery of the Square Footprints. McLean, Mina G., illus. LC 80-10437. 32p. (gr. k-4). 1980. PLB 9.96 (ISBN 0-89565-144-0). Childs World.
Gibson, Eva. Marty. LC 86-72529. 176p. (Orig.). (gr. 6-9). 1987. pap. 3.95 (ISBN 0-87123-915-9). Bethany Hse.
Giff, Patricia R. Have You Seen Hyacinth Macaw: A Mystery. Kramer, Anthony, illus. LC 80-68729. 128p. (gr. 4-7). 1981. 9.95 (ISBN 0-440-03467-1); PLB 9.89 (ISBN 0-440-03472-8). Delacorte.
—Loretta P. Sweeny, Where Are You? Kramer, Anthony, illus. 144p. (gr. 4-8). 1990. pap. 3.25 (ISBN 0-440-44926-X, YB). Dell.
—The Mystery of the Blue Ring. (Orig.). (gr. k-6). 1987. pap. 3.25 (ISBN 0-440-45998-2, YB). Dell.
—The Mystery of the Blue Ring. (gr. 1-4). 15.00 (ISBN 0-8446-6375-1). Peter Smith.
—The Powder Puff Puzzle. (Orig.). (gr. k-6). 1987. pap. 2.75 (ISBN 0-440-47180-X, YB). Dell.
—The Riddle of the Red Purse. (Orig.). (gr. k-6). 1987. pap. 2.75 (ISBN 0-440-47534-1, YB). Dell.
—The Riddle of the Red Purse. (gr. 1-4). 14.75 (ISBN 0-8446-6374-3). Peter Smith.
—The Secret at the Polk Street School. (Orig.). (gr. k-6). 1987. pap. 2.75 (ISBN 0-440-47696-8, YB). Dell.
Giff, Patricia R. & Kramer, Anthony. Loretta P. Sweeny, Where Are You? LC 83-5164. (Illus.). 144p. (gr. 4-6). 1983. 11.95 (ISBN 0-385-29298-8); PLB 11.95 (ISBN 0-385-29299-6). Delacorte.
Gilleo, Alma. The Easter Basket Mystery. Bargielski, Pat, illus. (gr. 1-3). 6 bks. & 1 cass. 29.95 (ISBN 0-89290-011-3); 1 bk. & 1 cass. 10.95 (ISBN 0-685-04639-7). Soc for Visual.
Gillet, David. Mystery Rider at Thunder Ridge. LC 87-27846. 1988. pap. 4.49 (ISBN 1-55513-398-3, Chariot Bks). Cook.
Gillham, Bill. A Place to Hide. Majewska, Maria, illus. 112p. (gr. 2-6). 1983. 9.95 (ISBN 0-233-97496-2). Andre Deutsch.
Gilligan, Shannon. The Case of the Missing Formula. (gr. 4-7). 1991. pap. 2.95 (ISBN 0-553-15864-3). Bantam.
—The Clue in the Clock Tower. (gr. 4-7). 1991. pap. 2.95 (ISBN 0-553-15855-4). Bantam.
—Mona Is Missing. 64p. (Orig.). 1984. pap. 2.25 (ISBN 0-553-15441-9). Bantam.
—The Mystery of Ura Senke. 128p. (Orig.). (gr. 5). 1985. pap. 2.25 (ISBN 0-553-25499-5). Bantam.
Gleeson, Libby. I Am Susannah. LC 88-24568. 128p. (gr. 4-7). 1989. 12.95 (ISBN 0-8234-0742-X). Holiday.
Gold, Avner. The Impostor. Reinman, Y. Y., ed. LC 85-72405. 192p. (gr. 5 up). 1985. 9.95 (ISBN 0-935063-14-5); pap. 7.95 (ISBN 0-935063-13-7). CIS Comm.
Goldman, Kelly & Davidson, Ronnie. Sherlick Hound & the Valentine Mystery. Levine, Abby, ed. Madden, Don, illus. 32p. (gr. 1-4). 1989. 8.95 (ISBN 0-8075-7335-3). A Whitman.
Gondosch, Linda. The Witches of Hopper Street. (Illus.). (gr. 3-6). 1988. pap. 2.50 (ISBN 0-671-64066-6, Minstrel Bks). PB.
Gonzalez, Gloria. A Deadly Rhyme. (Orig.). (gr. 5-8). 1986. pap. 2.50 (ISBN 0-440-91866-9, LFL). Dell.
Gorey, Edward. The Tunnel Calamity. Gorey, Edmund, illus. 9p. (Orig.). (ps-1). 1984. pap. 4.95 (ISBN 0-399-21055-5, Putnam). Putnam Pub Group.
Gorog, Judith. No Swimming in Dark Pond & Other Stories. LC 86-22586. 1987. 13.95 (ISBN 0-399-21418-6, Philomel). Putnam Pub Group.
The Great Brain Does It Again. (gr. 3-7). 1976. pap. 3.25 (ISBN 0-440-42983-8, YB). Dell.
Greene, Constance C. Double-Dare O'Toole. 176p. (gr. 4-7). 1983. pap. 3.25 (ISBN 0-440-41982-4, YB). Dell.
Griffin, Peni R. Otto from Otherwhere. LC 89-38026. (gr. 4-7). 1990. 13.95 (ISBN 0-689-50500-0, M K McElderry). Macmillan Child Grp.
Gunning, Thomas. Strange Mysteries. 96p. (gr. 2-9). pap. 2.95 (ISBN 0-318-37427-7). Troll Assocs.
Guy, Rosa. And I Heard a Bird Sing. LC 86-19907. 240p. (gr. 7 up). 1987. pap. 14.95 (ISBN 0-385-29563-4). Delacorte.
—The Disappearance. 256p. (gr. 7 up). 1986. pap. 3.25 (ISBN 0-440-92064-7, LFL). Dell.
—New Guys Around the Block. LC 82-72818. 192p. (gr. 7 up). 1983. pap. 11.95 (ISBN 0-385-29247-3). Delacorte.
Haas, Dorothy. To Catch a Crook. (gr. 4-6). 1989. pap. 2.75 (ISBN 0-671-67240-1, Minstrel Bks). PB.

Haggard, H. Rider. King Solomon's Mines. Gemme, F. R., intro. by. (gr. 8 up). pap. 1.95 (ISBN 0-8049-0140-6, CL-140). Airmont.
—She. Wollheim, D., intro. by. (gr. 8 up). pap. 1.95 (ISBN 0-8049-0146-5, CL-146). Airmont.
Hahn, Mary D. Following the Mystery Man. LC 87-17896. 192p. (gr. 4-8). 1988. 12.95 (ISBN 0-89919-680-2, Pub. by Clarion). Ticknor & Fields.
—Following the Mystery Man. 192p. (gr. 4 up). 1989. pap. 2.95 (ISBN 0-380-70677-6, Camelot). Avon.
Hahn, Mary Downing. The Dead Man in Indian Creek. 160p. (gr. 4-8). 1990. 13.95 (ISBN 0-395-52397-4). HM.
Hale, Anna. Mystery on Mackinac Island. McLane, Lois, illus. LC 89-35484. 184p. (Orig.). (gr. 3-5). 1989. pap. 8.95 (ISBN 0-943173-34-5). Harbinger AZ.
Hall, Lynn. Murder at the Spaniel Show. LC 88-18244. 128p. (gr. 7 up). 1988. 12.95 (ISBN 0-684-18961-5, Scribners Young Read). Macmillan Child Grp.
—Murder in a Pig's Eye. 1990. 14.95 (ISBN 0-15-256268-0). HarbraceJ.
—The Tormentors. 128p. (gr. 3-7). 1990. 14.95 (ISBN 0-15-289470-5). HarBraceJ.
Hamilton, Virginia. The House of Dies Drear. Keith, Eros, illus. LC 68-23059. 256p. (gr. 6-9). 1984. 14.95 (ISBN 0-02-742500-2, Mcmillan Child Bk); pap. 3.95 (ISBN 0-02-043520-7, Collier). Macmillan Child Grp.
—The Mystery of Drear House. reinforced ed. LC 86-9829. 224p. (gr. 5 up). 1987. 11.75 (ISBN 0-688-04026-8). Greenwillow.
Hamley, Dennis. Pageants of Despair. LC 74-10841. 180p. (gr. 7-10). 1974. 18.95 (ISBN 0-87599-205-6). S G Phillips.
Hansen, Joyce. Home Boy. 160p. (gr. 6 up). 1982. 13.95 (ISBN 0-89919-114-2, Clarion). HM.
Harnett, Cynthia. Cargo of the Madalena. Harnett, Cynthia, illus. LC 83-24874. 240p. (gr. 5 up). 1984. 9.95 (ISBN 0-8225-0890-7). Lerner Pubns.
—The Great House. Harnett, Cynthia, illus. LC 83-24880. 180p. (gr. 5 up). 1984. 9.95 (ISBN 0-8225-0893-1). Lerner Pubns.
—The Merchant's Mark. Harnett, Cynthia, illus. LC 83-24879. 192p. (gr. 5 up). 1984. 9.95 (ISBN 0-8225-0891-5). Lerner Pubns.
—The Sign of the Green Falcon. Harnett, Cynthia, illus. LC 83-24831. 288p. (gr. 5 up). 1984. 9.95 (ISBN 0-8225-0888-5). Lerner Pubns.
—Stars of Fortune. Harnett, Cynthia, illus. LC 83-24836. 288p. (gr. 5 up). 1984. 9.95 (ISBN 0-8225-0892-3). Lerner Pubns.
—The Writing on the Hearth. Floyd, Gareth, illus. LC 83-23904. 300p. (gr. 5 up). 1984. PLB 9.95 (ISBN 0-8225-0889-3). Lerner Pubns.
Harris, Betsy. Here in My Heart. LC 89-20419. 128p. (gr. 5-9). 1989. pap. text ed. 2.50 (ISBN 0-8167-1911-X). Troll Assocs.
—Only Friends. LC 89-20371. 128p. (gr. 5-9). 1990. pap. text ed. 2.50 (ISBN 0-685-29562-1). Troll Assocs.
Hartson, Eleanore & Taylor, Mark. Maxie's Mystery Files: The Stalled Mall & Other Crazy Cases. Vasconcellos, Daniel, illus. (gr. 3-5). 1987. 10.95 (ISBN 0-316-61423-8). Little.
Hass, E. A. Incognito Mosquito Flies Again! Madden, Don, illus. LC 84-6827. 112p. (gr. 2-6). 1989. pap. 2.95 (ISBN 0-394-82893-3, Bullseye Bks). Knopf.
—Incognito Mosquito, Private Insective. Hass, E. A., illus. LC 82-205. 96p. (gr. 2-5). 1982. PLB 13.88 (ISBN 0-688-01434-8). Lothrop.
—Incognito Mosquito, Private Insective. Madden, Don, illus. LC 84-15889. 112p. (gr. 2-6). 1989. pap. 2.95 (ISBN 0-394-82891-7, Bullseye Bks). Knopf.
—Incognito Mosquito Takes to the Air. Fanelli, Jenny, ed. Madden, Don, illus. LC 85-2240. 112p. (gr. 3-6). 1986. lib. bdg. 4.99 (ISBN 0-394-97054-3); pap. 2.95 (ISBN 0-394-87054-9). Random.
Hastings, Beverly. Watcher in the Dark. 160p. 1986. pap. 2.75 (ISBN 0-425-10131-2, Pub. by Berkley-Pacer). Berkley Pub.
Haven, Susan. Maybe I'll Move to the Lost & Found. (gr. 7-9). 1989. pap. 2.75 (ISBN 0-671-67402-1, Archway). PB.
Hawthorne, Nathaniel. The House of the Seven Gables. abr. ed. Farr, Naunerle, ed. Trinidad, Angel & Guitierez, Domy, illus. (gr. 4-12). 1977. pap. text ed. 2.95 (ISBN 0-88301-265-0). Pendulum Pr.
Haycraft, Howard, ed. Boys' Second Book of Great Detective Stories. LC 40-7099. (gr. 7 up). 1940. HarpC Child Bks.
Hayes, Geoffrey. The Mystery of the Pirate Ghost: An Otto & Uncle Tooth Adventure. Hayes, Geoffrey, illus. LC 84-18228. 48p. (gr. 2-3). 1985. (Random Juv); pap. 2.95 (ISBN 0-394-87220-7). Random.
—The Secret of Foghorn Island. Hayes, Geoffrey, illus. LC 87-16095. 48p. (Orig.). (gr. 2-3). 1988. lib. bdg. 6.99 (ISBN 0-394-99614-3, Random Juv); pap. 2.95 (ISBN 0-394-89614-9). Random.
Healey, Larry. The Town Is on Fire. (gr. 6 up). 1979. PLB 12.90 s&l (ISBN 0-531-02898-4). Watts.
Heide, Florence P. The Day of Ahmed's Secret. 32p. 1990. 13.95 (ISBN 0-688-08894-5); PLB 13.88 (ISBN 0-688-08895-3). Lothrop.
Heide, Florence P. & Heide, Roxanne. Body in the Brillstone Garage. Anne, Fay, ed. Krush, Joseph, illus. LC 79-18368. (gr. 4-9). 1980. PLB 9.95 (ISBN 0-8075-0825-X). A Whitman.
—Mystery at Southport Cinema. Pacini, Kathy, ed. Fleishman, Seymour, illus. LC 78-1300. (gr. 3-8). 1978. PLB 9.95 (ISBN 0-8075-5363-8). A Whitman.
—Time Bomb at Brillstone. Fay, Ann, ed. Krush, Joe, illus. LC 82-10863. 128p. (gr. 4-9). 1982. PLB 9.95 (ISBN 0-8075-7942-4). A Whitman.
Heimann, Rolf. For Eagle Eyes Only. (gr. 4-7). 1990. pap. 3.95 (ISBN 0-8167-2202-1). Troll Assocs.
Helldorfer, M. C. Almost Home. Harness, Cheryl, illus. LC 87-10371. 224p. (gr. 4-8). 1987. 14.95 (ISBN 0-02-743512-1, Bradbury Pr). Macmillan Child Grp.
Herberman, Ethan. The Great Butterfly Hunt: The Mystery of the Migrating Monarchs. (Illus.). (gr. 5 up). 1990. PLB 14.95 (ISBN 0-671-69427-8); pap. 5.95 (ISBN 0-671-69428-6). S&S Trade.
Herge. Affaire Tournesol. (FRE., Illus.). (gr. 7-9). looseleaf bdg. 19.95 (ISBN 0-685-28405-0). French & Eur.
—Bijoux de la Castafiore. (FRE., Illus.). 62p. (gr. 7-9). looseleaf bdg. 19.95 (ISBN 0-685-28406-9). French & Eur.
—Coke En Stock. (FRE., Illus.). (gr. 7-9). looseleaf bdg. 19.95 (ISBN 0-685-28407-7). French & Eur.
—The Crab with the Golden Claws. LC 73-21249. (Illus.). 64p. (Orig.). (gr. k up). 1974. pap. 6.95 (ISBN 0-316-35833-9, Joy St Bks). Little.
—Etoile Mysterieuse. (FRE., Illus.). (gr. 7-9). looseleaf bdg. 19.95 (ISBN 0-685-28417-4). French & Eur.
—Ile Noire. (FRE., Illus.). (gr. 7-9). looseleaf bdg. 19.95 (ISBN 0-685-01731-1). French & Eur.
—Objectif Lune. (FRE., Illus.). (gr. 7-9). looseleaf bdg. 19.95 (ISBN 0-685-28409-3). French & Eur.
—Red Rackham's Treasure. LC 73-21253. (Illus.). 64p. (Orig.). (gr. k up). 1974. pap. 6.95 (ISBN 0-316-35834-7, Joy St Bks). Little.
—The Secret of the Unicorn. LC 73-21250. (Illus.). 64p. (Orig.). (gr. k up). 1974. pap. 7.95 (ISBN 0-316-35832-0, Joy St Bks). Little.
—Sept Boules de Cristal. (FRE., Illus.). (gr. 7-9). 19.95 (ISBN 0-685-28416-6). French & Eur.
Hermes, Patricia. Nobody's Fault. 112p. (gr. 5 up). 1983. pap. 2.75 (ISBN 0-440-46523-0, YB). Dell.
Herold, Ann B. Aaron's Dark Secret. (gr. 3 up). 1985. pap. 3.95 (ISBN 0-934998-21-3). Bethel Pub.
Heuck, Sigrid. The Hideout. Lesser, Rika, tr. from GER. LC 87-20169. (Illus.). (gr. 6 up). 1988. 13.95 (ISBN 0-525-44343-6, 01354-410, DCB). Dutton Child Bks.
Heyer, Marilee. The Forbidden Door. 32p. (ps-3). 1988. pap. 14.95 (ISBN 0-670-81740-6). Viking Child Bks.
Hildick, E. W. The Case of the Muttering Mummy: A McGurk Mystery. LC 85-23747. (Illus.). 160p. (gr. 3-7). 1986. 12.95 (ISBN 0-02-743960-7, Mcmillan Child Bk). Macmillan Child Grp.
—The Case of the Purloined Parrot: A McGurk Mystery. LC 89-37924. 160p. (gr. 3-5). 1990. 12.95 (ISBN 0-02-743965-8, Mcmillan Child Bk). Macmillan Child Grp.
—The Case of the Wandering Weathervanes. Brunkus, Denise, illus. LC 87-13171. 160p. (gr. 3-7). 1988. 12.95 (ISBN 0-02-743970-4, Mcmillan Child Bk). Macmillan Child Grp.
Hilgartner, Beth. A Murder for Her Majesty. 256p. (gr. 5 up). 1986. 13.95 (ISBN 0-395-41451-2). HM.
Hitchcock, Alfred. Alfred Hitchcock's Spellbinders in Suspense. Isen, Harold, illus. (gr. 7-11). 1982. lib. bdg. 6.99 (ISBN 0-394-91665-4, Random Juv); pap. 3.95 (ISBN 0-394-84900-0). Random.
Hitchcock, Alfred, ed. Alfred Hitchcock & the Three Investigators in the Mystery of the Laughing Shadow. (Illus.). (gr. 4-7). 1985. 2.95 (ISBN 0-394-81492-4, Random Juv); pap. 1.95 (ISBN 0-394-83775-4); pap. 2.95 (ISBN 0-394-86412-3). Random.
—Alfred Hitchcock's Daring Detectives. Shilstone, Arthur, illus. LC 76-79077. (gr. 5 up). 1982. 6.95 (ISBN 0-394-81490-8, Random Juv); pap. 3.95 (ISBN 0-394-84902-7). Random.
—Alfred Hitchcock's Daring Detectives. Shilstone, Arthur, illus. LC 76-79077. (gr. 5 up). 1982. 6.95 (ISBN 0-394-81490-8, Random Juv); pap. 3.95 (ISBN 0-394-84902-7). Random.
—Alfred Hitchcock's Ghostly Gallery. (Illus.). (gr. 5-8). 1962. 6.95 (ISBN 0-394-81226-3, Random Juv). Random.
—Alfred Hitchcock's Haunted Houseful. LC 84-15949. (Illus.). 272p. (gr. 4-9). 1985. lib. bdg. 6.99 (ISBN 0-394-91224-1, Random Juv); pap. 3.95 (ISBN 0-394-87041-7, Random Juv). Random.
—Alfred Hitchcock's Monster Museum. LC 81-13883. (Illus.). 224p. (gr. 5 up). 1982. pap. 3.95 (ISBN 0-394-84899-3). Random.
—Alfred Hitchcock's Solve-Them-Yourself Mysteries. LC 63-7818. (Illus.). 256p. (gr. 6-9). 1986. 8.95 (ISBN 0-394-81242-5, Random Juv); lib. bdg. 6.99 (ISBN 0-394-91242-X, Random Juv); pap. 3.95 (ISBN 0-394-88240-7, Random Juv). Random.
Hoban, Lillian. The Case of the Two Masked Robbers. Hoban, Lillian, illus. LC 85-45819. 64p. (gr. k-3). 1988. pap. 3.50 (ISBN 0-06-444121-0, Trophy). HarpC Child Bks.
Holiday Camp Mystery. (Illus.). (ps-5). 3.50 (ISBN 0-7214-0012-4); Series S05, Set 1. flash cards 4.75; Series S05, Set 2. flash cards 4.75. Ladybird Bks.
Holl, Kristi. Trusting in the Dark. Skivington, Janice, illus. 128p. (Orig.). (gr. 3-6). 1990. pap. 4.99 (ISBN 0-87403-749-2, 24-03969). Standard Pub.
Holland, Isabelle. The Unfrightened Dark. LC 89-31570. 128p. (gr. 6-8). 1990. 13.95 (ISBN 0-316-37173-4). Little.
Hollands, Judith. The Ketchup Sisters, No. 1: The Rescue of the Red-Blooded Librarian. DeRosa, Dee, illus. 80p. (gr. 2-5). 1989. pap. 2.75 (ISBN 0-671-66810-2, Minstrel Bks). PB.
—The Secret of the Haunted Doghouse. DeRosa, Dee, illus. 80p. (Orig.). (gr. 2-5). 1990. pap. 2.75 (ISBN 0-671-66812-9, Minstrel). PB.
Hope, Laura L. Big Adventure at Home. Gonzalez, Pepe, illus. 120p. 1990. 4.50 (ISBN 0-448-09134-8, G&D). Putnam Pub Group.
—Bobbsey Twins' Adventures with Baby May. LC 68-12753. (Illus.). (gr. 1-4). 1968. 4.50 (ISBN 0-448-08017-6, G&D). Putnam Pub Group.
—Bobbsey Twins & the Big River Mystery. (gr. 1-4). 1963. 4.50 (ISBN 0-448-08056-7, G&D). Putnam Pub Group.
—Bobbsey Twins & the Doodlebug Mystery. (Illus.). (gr. 1-4). 1969. 4.50 (ISBN 0-448-08062-1, G&D). Putnam Pub Group.
—Bobbsey Twins & the Flying Clown. 196p. (gr. k-5). 4.50 (ISBN 0-448-08067-2, G&D). Putnam Pub Group.
—Bobbsey Twins & the Freedom Bell Mystery. 196p. (gr. k-5). 4.50 (ISBN 0-448-08069-9, G&D). Putnam Pub Group.
—Bobbsey Twins & the Goldfish Mystery. (Illus.). (gr. 1-4). 1962. 2.95 (ISBN 0-448-08055-9, G&D). Putnam Pub Group.
—Bobbsey Twins & the Greek Hat Mystery. (gr. 1-4). 1964. 3.95 (ISBN 0-448-08057-5, G&D). Putnam Pub Group.
—Bobbsey Twins & the Mystery at Snow Lodge. (gr. 1-4). 1930. 4.50 (ISBN 0-448-08005-2, G&D). Putnam Pub Group.
—Bobbsey Twins & the Play House Secret. rev. ed. (Illus.). (gr. 1-4). 1968. 4.50 (ISBN 0-448-08018-4, G&D). Putnam Pub Group.
—Bobbsey Twins & the Secret of Candy Castle. (Illus.). (gr. 1-4). 1968. 4.50 (ISBN 0-448-08061-3, G&D). Putnam Pub Group.
—The Bobbsey Twins & the Smoky Mountain Mystery. (Illus.). (gr. 1-4). 1977. 4.50 (ISBN 0-448-08070-2, G&D). Putnam Pub Group.
—Bobbsey Twins & the Tagalong Giraffe. (gr. 1-4). 4.50 (ISBN 0-448-08066-4, G&D). Putnam Pub Group.
—Bobbsey Twins & the Talking Fox Mystery. (Illus.). (gr. 1-4). 1970. 4.50 (ISBN 0-448-08063-X, G&D). Putnam Pub Group.
—Bobbsey Twins at London Tower. (Illus.). (gr. 1-4). 1959. 4.50 (ISBN 0-448-08052-4, G&D). Putnam Pub Group.
—Bobbsey Twins at Pilgrim Rock. (gr. 1-4). 1957. 4.50 (ISBN 0-448-08050-8, G&D). Putnam Pub Group.
—Bobbsey Twins: Camp Fire Mystery. Speirs, John, illus. 128p. (gr. 3-8). 1982. 8.95 (ISBN 0-671-43374-1, Little Simon); pap. 3.50 (ISBN 0-671-43373-3). S&S Trade.
—Bobbsey Twins: Dune Buggy Mystery. Sanderson, Ruth, illus. 112p. (gr. 2-5). 1981. 7.95 (ISBN 0-671-42293-6, Little Simon); pap. 3.50 (ISBN 0-671-42294-4). S&S Trade.
—Bobbsey Twins' Forest Adventure. (gr. 1-4). 1958. 3.95 (ISBN 0-448-08051-6, G&D). Putnam Pub Group.
—The Bobbsey Twins in a TV Mystery Show, Vol. 71. LC 77-76127. (Illus.). (gr. 1-4). 1978. 4.50 (ISBN 0-448-08071-0, G&D). Putnam Pub Group.
—Bobbsey Twins in the Mystery Cave. (Illus.). (gr. 1-4). 1960. 2.95 (ISBN 0-448-08053-2, G&D). Putnam Pub Group.
—Bobbsey Twins' Mystery at Meadowbrook. rev. ed. (gr. 1-4). 1963. 2.95 (ISBN 0-448-08007-9, G&D). Putnam Pub Group.
—Bobbsey Twins' Mystery at School. (gr. 1-4). 1930. 4.50 (ISBN 0-448-08004-4, G&D). Putnam Pub Group.
—Bobbsey Twins' Mystery of the King's Puppet. (gr. 1-4). 1967. 4.50 (ISBN 0-448-08060-5, G&D). Putnam Pub Group.
—Bobbsey Twins' Mystery on the Deep Blue Sea. (gr. 1-4). 1930. 3.95 (ISBN 0-448-08011-7, G&D). Putnam Pub Group.
—Bobbsey Twins of Lakeport. (gr. 1-4). 1936. 4.50 (ISBN 0-448-08001-X, G&D). Putnam Pub Group.
—Bobbsey Twins on a Bicycle Trip. (gr. 1-4). 1955. 4.50 (ISBN 0-448-08048-6, G&D). Putnam Pub Group.
—The Bobbsey Twins on a Houseboat. Gonzalez, Pepe, illus. 120p. 1990. 4.50 (ISBN 0-448-09099-6, G&D). Putnam Pub Group.
—Bobbsey Twins on Blueberry Island. (gr. 1-4). 1930. 4.50 (ISBN 0-448-08010-9, G&D). Putnam Pub Group.
—Bobbsey Twins' Search for the Green Rooster. (gr. 1-4). 1965. 4.50 (ISBN 0-448-08058-3, G&D). Putnam Pub Group.
—Bobbsey Twins' Search in the Great City. (gr. 1-4). 1930. 4.50 (ISBN 0-448-08009-5, G&D). Putnam Pub Group.
—Bobbsey Twins' Secret at the Seashore. rev. ed. (gr. 1-4). 1936. 4.50 (ISBN 0-448-08003-6, G&D). Putnam Pub Group.
—The Bobbsey Twins: Secret in the Pirate's Cave. Sanderson, Ruth, illus. 128p. (gr. 2-5). 1980. PLB 7.95 (ISBN 0-671-41118-7, Little Simon); pap. 3.50 (ISBN 0-671-41113-6). S&S Trade.
—Bobbsey Twins Solve a Mystery. (gr. 1-4). 1934. 4.50 (ISBN 0-448-08027-3, G&D). Putnam Pub Group.

—The Bobbsey Twins: The Blue Poodle Mystery. (Illus.). 128p. (gr. 2-5). 1980. 8.95 (ISBN 0-671-95546-2, Little Simon); pap. 3.50 (ISBN 0-671-95554-3). S&S Trade.
—The Bobbsey Twins: The Ghost in the Computer. Barish, Wendy, ed. Speirs, John, illus. 128p. 1984. pap. 3.50 (ISBN 0-671-43590-6, Little Simon). S&S Trade.
—The Bobbsey Twins: The Haunted House Mystery. Arico, Diane, ed. Speirs, John, illus. 128p. (gr. 7-10). 1985. pap. 3.50 (ISBN 0-671-54996-0, Little Simon). S&S Trade.
—The Bobbsey Twins: The Music Box Mystery. Barish, Wendy, ed. Speirs, John, illus. 128p. (gr. 2-5). 1983. 8.95 (ISBN 0-671-43588-4, Little Simon); pap. 3.50 (ISBN 0-671-43589-2). S&S Trade.
—Bobbsey Twins: The Mystery at Cherry Corners. rev. ed. (Illus.). (gr. 1-4). 1971. 2.95 (ISBN 0-448-08020-6, G&D). Putnam Pub Group.
—The Bobbsey Twins: The Mystery of the Hindu Temple. Barish, Wendy, ed. (Illus.). 128p. (Orig.). (gr. 7-10). 1985. pap. 3.50 (ISBN 0-671-55499-9, Little Simon). S&S Trade.
—Bobbsey Twins: The Red, White & Blue Mystery. (Illus.). (gr. 1-4). 1971. 2.95 (ISBN 0-448-08064-8, G&D). Putnam Pub Group.
—Bobbsey Twins: The Rose Parade Mystery. (Illus.). 112p. (Orig.). (gr. 2-5). 1981. 8.95 (ISBN 0-671-43372-5, Little Simon); pap. 3.50 (ISBN 0-671-43371-7). S&S Trade.
—The Bobbsey Twins: The Scarecrow Mystery. Barish, Wendy, ed. Speirs, John, illus. 128p. (gr. 2-5). 1984. pap. 3.50 (ISBN 0-671-53238-3, Little Simon). S&S Trade.
—Bobbsey Twins Visit to the Great West. rev. ed. (gr. 1-4). 1966. 4.50 (ISBN 0-448-08013-3, G&D). Putnam Pub Group.
—The Case at Creepy Castle. Jennis, Paul, illus. 96p. 1990. pap. 2.95 (ISBN 0-671-69289-5, Minstrel Bks). PB.
—The Case of the Close Encounter. Jennis, Paul, illus. 96p. (gr. 2-3). 1988. pap. 2.95 (ISBN 0-671-62656-6, Minstrel Bks). PB.
—The Case of the Crooked Contest. (Illus., Orig.). (gr. 2-4). 1989. pap. 2.95 (ISBN 0-671-63074-1, Minstrel Bks). PB.
—The Case of the Crying Clown. (Illus., Orig.). (gr. 2-4). 1989. pap. 2.95 (ISBN 0-671-55501-4, Minstrel Bks). PB.
—The Case of the Missing Dinosaur. Jennis, Paul, illus. 96p. 1990. pap. 2.95 (ISBN 0-671-67597-4, Minstrel Bks). PB.
—The Case of the Runaway Money. (gr. 2-4). 1987. pap. 2.95 (ISBN 0-671-62652-3, Minstrel Bks). PB.
—The Chocolate Covered Clue. (Illus., Orig.). (gr. 2-4). 1989. pap. 2.95 (ISBN 0-671-63073-3, Minstrel Bks). PB.
—The Clue in the Classroom. (Illus., Orig.). (gr. 2-4). 1988. pap. 2.95 (ISBN 0-671-63072-5, Minstrel Bks). PB.
—The Clue That Flew Away. Tsui, George, illus. (gr. 2-4). 1987. pap. 2.95 (ISBN 0-671-62653-1, Minstrel Bks). PB.
—The Great Skate Mystery. Greenberg, Ann, ed. Barrett, Randy, illus. 96p. (Orig.). (gr. 2-4). 1990. pap. 2.95 (ISBN 0-671-69293-3, Minstrel Bks). PB.
—Mystery at Meadowbrook. Gonzalez, Pepe, illus. 120p. 1990. 4.50 (ISBN 0-448-09100-3, G&D). Putnam Pub Group.
—Mystery at School. Gonzalez, Pepe, illus. 120p. (gr. 2-5). 1989. 5.95 (ISBN 0-448-09074-0, G&D). Putnam Pub Group.
—The Mystery at Snow Lodge. Gonzalez, Pepe, illus. 120p. 1990. 4.50 (ISBN 0-448-09098-8, G&D). Putnam Pub Group.
—The Mystery of the Missing Mummy. Jennis, Paul, illus. 160p. (Orig.). 1989. pap. 2.95 (ISBN 0-671-67595-8, Minstrel Bks). PB.
—The New Bobbsey Twins, Vol. 4. Jennis, Paul, illus. 96p. (Orig.). (ps). 1988. pap. 2.95 (ISBN 0-671-62654-X, Minstrel Bks). PB.
—The New Bobbsey Twins, No. 6: Mystery on the Mississippi. Jennis, Paul, illus. 96p. (Orig.). (gr. 2-4). 1988. pap. 2.95 (ISBN 0-671-62657-4, Minstrel Bks). PB.
—The Secret at Sleepaway Camp. Berrett, Randy, illus. 96p. (Orig.). (gr. 2-4). 1990. pap. 2.95 (ISBN 0-671-69290-9, Minstrel). PB.
—The Secret of Jungle Park. Tsui, George, illus. (gr. 2-4). 1987. pap. 2.95 (ISBN 0-671-62651-5, Minstrel Bks). PB.
—Secret of the Stolen Clue. 1989. pap. 2.95 (ISBN 0-671-67596-6, Little Simon). S&S Trade.
—The Secret of the Stolen Puppies. (Orig.). (gr. 2-4). 1988. pap. 2.95 (ISBN 0-671-62659-0, Minstrel Bks). PB.
—The Show & Tell Mystery. Greenberg, Ann, ed. Berrett, Randy, illus. 96p. (gr. 2-4). 1990. pap. 2.95 (ISBN 0-671-69291-7, Minstrel Bks). PB.
—Trouble in Toyland. Jennis, Paul, illus. (gr. 2-4). 1988. pap. 2.95 (ISBN 0-671-62658-2, Minstrel Bks). PB.
—The Weird Science Mystery. Berrett, Randy & Barrett, Randy, illus. 96p. (Orig.). (gr. 2-4). 1990. pap. 2.95 (ISBN 0-671-69292-5, Minstrel Bks). PB.
Hostetler, Kay. Bushytail & the Case of the Missing Nuts. Pressler, Susan, illus. 68p. (Orig.). (gr. k-3). 1989. pap. 4.95 (ISBN 1-878329-00-6). Spec Creations.
Hostetler, Mirian. Mystery at the Mall. Stamm, Gwen, illus. LC 85-13951. 88p. (Orig.). (gr. 5-6). 1985. pap. 3.95 (ISBN 0-8361-3401-X). Herald Pr.
Hound of the Baskervilles. (Illus.). (gr. 4 up). 3.50 (ISBN 0-7214-0719-6). Ladybird Bks.
Howard, Elizabeth. A Scent of Murder. Kaluta, Michael W., illus. LC 87-4583. 144p. (gr. 5 up). 1987. (Random Juv); pap. 5.99 (ISBN 0-394-97548-0, BYR). Random.
Howard, John. Backyard Mystery. (Illus.). (gr. 2-3). 1972. pap. 1.95 (ISBN 0-89375-046-8). Troll Assocs.
Howard, Milly. The Treasure of Pelican Cove. (Illus.). 112p. (Orig.). 1988. pap. 4.95 (ISBN 0-89084-464-X). Bob Jones Univ Pr.
Howe, James. The Case of the Missing Mother. Cleaver, William, illus. LC 82-13287. 32p. (gr. 1-6). 1983. pap. 1.95 (ISBN 0-394-85729-1). Random.
—Dew Drop Dead: A Sebastian Barth Mystery. LC 89-34697. 160p. (gr. 3-7). 1990. 12.95 (ISBN 0-689-31425-6, Atheneum Child Bk). Macmillan Child Grp.
—Eat Your Poison, Dear. LC 86-3582. 144p. (gr. 4-7). 1986. 12.95 (ISBN 0-689-31206-7, Atheneum Child Bk). Macmillan Child Grp.
—Howliday Inn. Munsinger, Lynn, illus. LC 81-10886. 208p. (gr. 4-6). 1982. 13.95 (ISBN 0-689-30846-9, Atheneum Child Bk). Macmillan Child Grp.
—Stage Fright. 144p. 1991. pap. 2.95 (ISBN 0-380-71331-4, Camelot). Avon.
—What Eric Knew: A Sebastian Barth Mystery. 156p. (gr. 4-6). 1990. 12.95 (ISBN 0-689-31702-6, Atheneum Child Bk). Macmillan Child Grp.
Hughes, Dean. Nutty & the Case of the Mastermind Thief. 128p. 1986. pap. 2.75 (ISBN 0-553-15414-1, Skylark). Bantam.
—Nutty & the Case of the Ski-Slope Spy. LC 85-7962. 144p. (gr. 4-6). 1985. 12.95 (ISBN 0-689-31126-5, Atheneum Child Bk). Macmillan Child Grp.
Hunter, Mollie. The Haunted Mountain. Kubinyi, Laszlo, illus. LC 77-183164. 140p. (gr. 5-8). 1972. PLB 12.89 (ISBN 0-06-022667-6). HarpC Child Bks.
—A Stranger Came Ashore. LC 75-10814. 176p. (gr. 5-8). 1975. PLB 13.89 (ISBN 0-06-022652-8). HarpC Child Bks.
Hurd, Thacher. Mystery on the Docks. Hurd, Thacher, illus. LC 82-48261. 32p. (ps-3). 1983. 12.95 (ISBN 0-06-022701-X); PLB 12.89 (ISBN 0-06-022702-8). HarpC Child Bks.
Hutchens, Paul. The Case of the Missing Calf. (gr. 3-9). 1988. pap. text ed. 3.50 (ISBN 0-8024-4837-2). Moody.
—Locked in the Attic. 128p. (gr. 3-7). 1973. pap. 3.50 (ISBN 0-8024-4831-3). Moody.
—The Sugar Creek Gang & Blue Cow. (Illus.). 128p. (gr. 3-7). 1971. pap. 3.50 (ISBN 0-8024-4822-4). Moody.
—Sugar Creek Gang & Screams in the Night. (gr. 3-7). 1967. pap. 3.50 (ISBN 0-8024-4812-7). Moody.
—Sugar Creek Gang & the Brown Box Mystery. (gr. 3-7). 1970. pap. 3.50 (ISBN 0-8024-4834-8). Moody.
—The Sugar Creek Gang & the Bull Fighter. (gr. 3-7). pap. 3.50 (ISBN 0-8024-4820-8). Moody.
—Sugar Creek Gang & the Ghost Dog. (gr. 3-7). 1968. pap. 3.50 (ISBN 0-8024-4832-1). Moody.
—The Sugar Creek Gang & the Green Tent Mystery. (gr. 3-7). pap. 3.50 (ISBN 0-8024-4819-4). Moody.
—Sugar Creek Gang & the Haunted House. (gr. 3-7). 1967. pap. 3.50 (ISBN 0-8024-4816-X). Moody.
—The Sugar Creek Gang & the Killer Bear. (gr. 3-7). pap. 3.50 (ISBN 0-8024-4802-X). Moody.
—Sugar Creek Gang & the Killer Cat. (gr. 3-7). 1966. pap. 3.50 (ISBN 0-8024-4825-9). Moody.
—Sugar Creek Gang & the Lost Campers. (gr. 3-7). 1968. pap. 3.50 (ISBN 0-8024-4804-6). Moody.
—Sugar Creek Gang & the Mystery Cave. (gr. 3-7). 1966. pap. 3.50 (ISBN 0-8024-4807-0). Moody.
—The Sugar Creek Gang & the Mystery Thief. (gr. 3-7). pap. 3.50 (ISBN 0-8024-4809-7). Moody.
—Sugar Creek Gang & the Palm Tree Manhunt. (gr. 3-7). 1969. pap. 3.50 (ISBN 0-8024-4808-9). Moody.
—Sugar Creek Gang & the Runaway Rescue. 96p. (gr. 3-7). 1973. pap. 3.50 (ISBN 0-8024-4828-3). Moody.
—Sugar Creek Gang & the Secret Hideout. (gr. 3-7). 1968. pap. 3.50 (ISBN 0-8024-4806-2). Moody.
—The Swamp Robber. (gr. 3-7). 1966. pap. 3.50 (ISBN 0-8024-4801-1). Moody.
—The Timber Wolf. (gr. 3-7). 1965. pap. 3.50 (ISBN 0-8024-4823-2). Moody.
—The Trapline Thief. 128p. (gr. 3-7). 1971. pap. 3.50 (ISBN 0-8024-4821-6). Moody.
—The Treasure Hunt. (gr. 3-7). 1967. pap. 3.50 (ISBN 0-8024-4814-3). Moody.
—The Tree House Mystery. (gr. 3-7). 1972. pap. 3.50 (ISBN 0-8024-4835-6). Moody.
—The Watermelon Mystery. (Illus.). 128p. (gr. 3-7). 1971. pap. 3.50 (ISBN 0-8024-4826-7). Moody.
The Invisible Man. (Illus.). (gr. 3-5). 3.50 (ISBN 0-7214-1079-0). Ladybird Bks.
Irving, Washington. Legend of Sleepy Hollow. 1991. pap. 2.50 (ISBN 0-8125-0475-5). Tor Bks.
Jack B. Quick, Sports Detective: The Case of the Basketball Joker & Other Mysteries. (gr. 3-7). 1990. pap. 3.50 (ISBN 0-316-72910-8). Little.
Jamie & the Mystery Quilt. 160p. (gr. 4-6). 1987. pap. 2.50 (ISBN 0-590-40122-X, Apple Paperworks). Scholastic Inc.
Jenkins, Jerry B. Daniel's Big Surprise. (gr. 4-7). 1990. pap. 4.50 (ISBN 0-8024-0805-2). Moody.
—Mystery At the Ballpark. (gr. 4-7). 1990. pap. 4.50 (ISBN 0-8024-0811-7). Moody.
—Mystery of the Golden Palomino. (Orig.). 1989. pap. 4.50 (ISBN 0-8024-8386-0). Moody.
—Mystery of the Kidnapped Kid. (gr. 9-12). 1988. pap. 3.95 (ISBN 0-8024-8376-3). Moody.
—Mystery of the Missing Sister. (gr. 9-12). 1988. pap. 3.95 (ISBN 0-8024-8378-X). Moody.
—Mystery of the Mixed-Up Teacher. (Orig.). (gr. 9-12). 1988. pap. 3.95 (ISBN 0-8024-8377-1). Moody.
—Mystery of the Phony Murder. 1989. pap. 4.50 (ISBN 0-8024-8388-7). Moody.
—Mystery of the Scorpion Threat. (gr. 9-12). 1988. pap. 3.95 (ISBN 0-8024-8379-8). Moody.
—Mystery of the Skinny Sophomore. (Orig.). 1989. pap. 4.50 (ISBN 0-8024-8387-9). Moody.
—Mystery on the Midway. (Orig.). 1989. pap. 4.50 (ISBN 0-8024-8385-2). Moody.
Johnson, Lois W. The Creeping Shadows. 144p. (Orig.). (gr. 2-8). pap. 4.95 (ISBN 1-55661-102-1). Bethany Hse.
Jones, Adrienne. The Beckoner. LC 79-1715. 256p. (gr. 7 up). 1980. HarpC Child Bks.
Jones, Martha T. The Ghost at the Old Stone Fort. LaFreniere, Annette, ed. Loughran, Donna, illus. 104p. (gr. 4 up). 1990. lib. bdg. 11.95 (ISBN 0-937460-61-3). Hendrick-Long.
Jordan, Cathleen & Manson, Cynthia, eds. Tales from Alfred Hitchcock's Mystery Magazine. Jordan, Cathleen, intro. by. LC 88-9013. 320p. (gr. 7 up). 1988. 12.95 (ISBN 0-688-08176-2). Morrow Jr Bks.
Jukes, Mavis. Blackberries in the Dark. (gr. k-6). 1987. pap. 2.75 (ISBN 0-440-40647-1, YB). Dell.
Karl, Jean. Strange Tomorrow. (gr. 7 up). 1988. pap. 2.95 (ISBN 0-440-20052-0, LFL). Dell.
Keele, Luqman & Pinkwater, Daniel. Java Jack. LC 79-7892. (Illus.). 160p. (gr. 5-12). 1980. 7.95 (ISBN 0-690-03995-6, Crowell Jr Bks). HarpC Child Bks.
Keene, Carolyn. Bad Medicine. (Orig.). (gr. 7 up). 1989. pap. 2.95 (ISBN 0-671-64702-4, Archway). PB.
—The Black Widow. (gr. 7 up). 1989. pap. 2.95 (ISBN 0-671-70357-9, Archway). PB.
—The Bluebeard Room. 1988. pap. 3.50 (ISBN 0-671-66857-9, Minstrel Bks). PB.
—The Broken Anchor. Frame, Paul, illus. 192p. (gr. 3-7). 1983. 8.95 (ISBN 0-671-46462-0, Little Simon); pap. 3.50 (ISBN 0-671-46461-2). S&S Trade.
—Bungalow Mystery. (gr. 4-7). 1930. 4.50 (ISBN 0-448-09503-3, G&D). Putnam Pub Group.
—Buried In Time. Greenberg, Ann, ed. 224p. (gr. 7 up). 1990. pap. 2.95 (ISBN 0-671-67463-3, Archway). PB.
—Buried Secrets. (gr. 7 up). 1989. pap. 2.95 (ISBN 0-671-68520-1, Archway). PB.
—Buried Secrets: The Nancy Drew Files, Case 10. large type ed. 151p. (gr. 7-10). 1988. Repr. of 1987 ed. 9.50 (ISBN 0-942545-41-9); PLB 10.50 (ISBN 0-942545-36-2, Dist. by Grolier). Grey Castle.
—Captive Witness. 192p. (Orig.). 1990. pap. 3.50 (ISBN 0-671-70471-0, Minstrel). PB.
—The Case of the Disappearing Deejay. (Orig.). (gr. 7 up). 1989. pap. 3.50 (ISBN 0-671-66314-3, Minstrel Bks). PB.
—The Case of the Disappearing Diamonds. (gr. 3-6). 1987. pap. 3.50 (ISBN 0-671-64896-9, Minstrel Bks). PB.
—The Case of the Photo Finish. Greenberg, Ann, ed. 160p. (Orig.). (gr. 3-6). 1990. pap. 3.50 (ISBN 0-671-69281-X, Minstrel Bks). PB.
—The Case of the Rising Stars. (Orig.). (gr. 3-7). 1989. pap. 3.50 (ISBN 0-671-66312-7, Minstrel Bks). PB.
—The Case of the Safecracker's Secret. 160p. 1990. pap. 3.50 (ISBN 0-671-66318-6, Minstrel Bks). PB.
—Circle of Evil. 160p. (Orig.). (gr. 7 up). 1988. pap. 2.95 (ISBN 0-671-68050-1, Archway). PB.
—Clue in the Ancient Disguise. Frame, Paul, illus. 192p. (gr. 8-12). 1982. 9.95 (ISBN 0-671-45553-2, Little Simon); pap. 3.50 (ISBN 0-671-45552-4). S&S Trade.
—Clue in the Ancient Disguise. (gr. 7 up). 1987. pap. 3.50 (ISBN 0-671-64279-0, Minstrel Bks). PB.
—The Clue in the Camera. 160p. (gr. 3-6). 1988. pap. 3.50 (ISBN 0-671-64962-0, Minstrel Bks). PB.
—The Clue in the Crossword Cipher. (gr. 4-7). 1967. 4.50 (ISBN 0-448-09544-0, G&D); (G&D). Putnam Pub Group.
—The Clue in the Crumbling Wall. (Illus.). 192p. (gr. 4-7). 1945. 4.50 (ISBN 0-448-09522-X, G&D). Putnam Pub Group.
—Clue in the Diary. (gr. 4-7). 1932. 4.50 (ISBN 0-448-09507-6, G&D). Putnam Pub Group.
—The Clue in the Jewel Box. (Illus.). 196p. (gr. 4-7). 1943. 4.50 (ISBN 0-448-09520-3, G&D). Putnam Pub Group.
—Clue in the Old Stagecoach. (gr. 4-7). 1960. 4.50 (ISBN 0-448-09537-8, G&D). Putnam Pub Group.
—Clue of the Black Keys. rev. ed. LC 68-21715. (Illus.). (gr. 4-7). 1951. 4.50 (ISBN 0-448-09528-9, G&D); (G&D). Putnam Pub Group.
—Clue of the Broken Locket. (gr. 4-7). 1943. 4.50 (ISBN 0-448-09511-4, G&D). Putnam Pub Group.
—Clue of the Dancing Puppet. (Illus.). (gr. 4-7). 1962. 4.50 (ISBN 0-448-09539-4, G&D); (G&D). Putnam Pub Group.
—Clue of the Tapping Heels. LC 71-86679. (Illus.). (gr. 4-7). 1939. 4.50 (ISBN 0-448-09516-5, G&D); (G&D). Putnam Pub Group.
—Cold As Ice. Greenberg, Ann, ed. 160p. (Orig.). (gr. 7 up). 1990. pap. 2.95 (ISBN 0-671-70031-6, Archway). PB.
—A Crime for Christmas. (gr. 7 up). 1988. pap. 2.95 (ISBN 0-318-37404-8). PB.

—A Crime for Christmas. (gr. 7 up). 1988. pap. 2.95 (ISBN 0-671-64918-3, Archway). PB.
—The Crooked Banister. Dolwick, Bill, illus. LC 77-130336. (gr. 4-7). 1971. 4.50 (ISBN 0-448-09548-3, G&D). Putnam Pub Group.
—The Curious Coronation. LC 75-1581. (Illus.). 196p. (gr. 4-7). 1976. 2.95 (ISBN 0-448-09094-5, G&D). Putnam Pub Group.
—Danger for Hire. Greenberg, Ann, ed. 160p. (Orig.). (gr. 7 up). 1990. pap. 2.95 (ISBN 0-671-70029-4, Archway). PB.
—Danger in Disguise. (gr. 7 up). 1989. pap. 2.95 (ISBN 0-671-64700-8, Archway). PB.
—Dangerous Games. (Orig.). (gr. 7 up). 1989. pap. 2.95 (ISBN 0-671-64920-5, Archway). PB.
—A Date with Deception. 160p. (Orig.). 1990. pap. 2.95 (ISBN 0-671-67500-1, Archway). PB.
—Deadly Doubles. (gr. 7 up). 1987. pap. 2.75 (ISBN 0-671-62643-4, Archway). PB.
—Deadly Doubles: The Nancy Drew Files, Case 7. large type ed. 147p. (gr. 5-10). 1988. Repr. of 1987 ed. 9.50 (ISBN 0-942545-38-9); PLB 10.50 (ISBN 0-942545-33-8, Dist. by Grolier). Grey Castle.
—Deadly Intent. large type ed. (gr. 5-10). 1988. 9.50 (ISBN 0-942545-23-0); PLB 10.50 (ISBN 0-942545-28-1, Dist. by Grolier). Grey Castle.
—Death by Design. (gr. 7 up). 1989. pap. 2.95 (ISBN 0-671-70358-7, Archway). PB.
—Deep Secrets. Greenberg, Ann, ed. 160p. (gr. 7 up). 1990. pap. 3.50 (ISBN 0-671-74525-5, Archway). PB.
—Double Crossing. (gr. 7 up). 1988. pap. 2.95 (ISBN 0-317-69579-7). PB.
—The Double Horror of Fenley Place. (gr. 3-6). 1987. pap. 3.50 (ISBN 0-671-64387-8, Minstrel Bks). PB.
—The Double Jinx Mystery. LC 72-90826. (Illus.). 196p. (gr. 4-7). 1973. 4.50 (ISBN 0-448-09550-5, G&D). Putnam Pub Group.
—Enemy Match. Barish, Wendy, ed. Frame, Paul, illus. 192p. 1984. 8.95 (ISBN 0-671-49736-7, Little Simon); pap. 3.50 (ISBN 0-671-49735-9). S&S Trade.
—Enemy Match. 192p. (gr. 3-6). 1987. pap. 3.50 (ISBN 0-671-64283-9, Minstrel Bks). PB.
—False Impressions. 160p. 1990. pap. 2.95 (ISBN 0-671-67495-1, Archway). PB.
—False Moves. (gr. 7 up). 1989. pap. 2.95 (ISBN 0-671-70493-1, Archway). PB.
—Fatal Attraction. 160p. (gr. 7 up). 1989. pap. 2.95 (ISBN 0-671-68730-1, Archway). PB.
—Fatal Ransom (R) 1989. pap. 2.95 (ISBN 0-671-68860-X, Archway). PB.
—The Final Scene. (Orig.). (gr. 7 up). 1989. pap. 2.95 (ISBN 0-671-67490-0, Archway). PB.
—Flirting with Danger. 160p. (Orig.). (gr. 7 up). 1990. pap. 2.95 (ISBN 0-671-67499-4, Archway). PB.
—Ghost of Blackwood Hall. LC 67-20844. (gr. 4-7). 1948. 4.50 (ISBN 0-448-09525-4, G&D). Putnam Pub Group.
—Ghost of Craven Cove. 1989. pap. 3.50 (ISBN 0-671-66317-8, Little Simon). S&S Trade.
—The Girl Who Couldn't Remember. 160p. (Orig.). 1989. pap. 3.50 (ISBN 0-671-66316-X, Minstrel Bks). PB.
—The Greek Symbol Mystery. (gr. 2-7). 1984. 8.50 (ISBN 0-685-09397-2, Little Simon). S&S Trade.
—The Greek Symbol Mystery. (gr. 3-7). 1989. pap. 3.50 (ISBN 0-671-67457-9, Minstrel Bks). PB.
—Guilty Secrets. 160p. (gr. 6 up). 1989. pap. 2.95 (ISBN 0-671-67760-8, Archway). PB.
—The Haunted Bridge. (Illus.). 196p. (gr. 4-7). 1938. 4.50 (ISBN 0-448-09515-7, G&D). Putnam Pub Group.
—The Haunted Carousel. Barish, Wendy, ed. Frame, Paul, illus. 192p. (Orig.). (gr. 8-12). 1983. (Little Simon); pap. 3.50 (ISBN 0-671-47555-X). S&S Trade.
—The Haunted Carousel. 192p. (gr. 7). 1988. pap. 3.50 (ISBN 0-671-66227-9, Minstrel Bks). PB.
—The Haunted Lagoon. rev ed. LC 72-90828. (Illus.). 196p. (gr. 4-7). 1973. 2.95 (ISBN 0-448-09088-0, G&D). Putnam Pub Group.
—The Haunted Showboat. (gr. 4-7). 1958. 4.50 (ISBN 0-448-09535-1, G&D); PLB 3.29 (ISBN 0-448-19535-6, G&D). Putnam Pub Group.
—The Haunting of Horse Island. Greenberg, Ann, ed. 160p. (Orig.). (gr. 3-6). 1990. pap. 3.50 (ISBN 0-671-69284-4, Minstrel Bks). PB.
—High Marks for Malice. (gr. 7 up). 1989. pap. 2.95 (ISBN 0-671-64699-0, Archway). PB.
—Hit & Run Holiday. large type ed. (gr. 5-10). 1989. 9.50 (ISBN 0-942545-25-7); lib. bdg. 10.50 (ISBN 0-942545-31-1, Dist. by Grolier). Grey Castle.
—The Joker's Revenge. (Orig.). (gr. 7 up). 1988. pap. 3.50 (ISBN 0-671-63426-7, Minstrel Bks). PB.
—The Kachina Doll Mystery. (gr. 3-7). 1988. pap. 3.50 (ISBN 0-671-67220-7, Minstrel Bks). PB.
—Last Dance. (Orig.). (gr. 7 up). 1989. pap. 2.95 (ISBN 0-671-67489-7, Archway). PB.
—The Last Resort: A Nancy Drew & Hardy Boys Supermystery. 224p. (gr. 7 up). 1990. pap. 2.95 (ISBN 0-671-67461-7, Archway). PB.
—The Mardi Gras Mystery. 160p. (gr. 3-6). 1988. pap. 3.50 (ISBN 0-671-64961-2, Minstrel Bks). PB.
—A Model Crime. Greenberg, Ann, ed. 160p. (Orig.). (gr. 7 up). 1990. pap. 2.95 (ISBN 0-671-70028-6, Archway). PB.
—Most Likely to Die. (gr. 7 up). 1989. pap. 2.95 (ISBN 0-671-69184-8, Archway). PB.
—The Mountain-Peak Mystery. LC 77-76133. (Illus.). (gr. 4-7). 1978. 2.95 (ISBN 0-448-09096-1, G&D). Putnam Pub Group.
—Murder on Ice. (gr. 7 up). 1989. pap. 2.95 (ISBN 0-671-68729-8, Archway). PB.
—Murder on Ice. large type ed. (gr. 5-10). 1988. 9.50 (ISBN 0-942545-24-9); PLB 10.50 (ISBN 0-942545-29-X, Dist. by Grolier). Grey Castle.
—The Mysterious Image. Barish, Wendy, ed. Frame, Paul, illus. 192p. (gr. 4-7). 1984. 8.95 (ISBN 0-671-49738-3, Little Simon); pap. 3.50 (ISBN 0-671-49737-5). S&S Trade.
—The Mysterious Image. 208p. 1990. pap. 3.50 (ISBN 0-671-69401-4, Minstrel Bks). PB.
—Mysterious Mannequin. Johnson, Ray, illus. LC 77-100115. (gr. 4-7). 1970. 4.50 (ISBN 0-448-09547-5, G&D). Putnam Pub Group.
—Mystery at Lilac Inn. (gr. 4-7). 1930. 4.50 (ISBN 0-448-09504-1, G&D). Putnam Pub Group.
—The Mystery at Magnolia Mansion. Greenberg, Ann, ed. 160p. (Orig.). (gr. 3-6). 1990. pap. 3.50 (ISBN 0-671-69282-8, Minstrel Bks). PB.
—Mystery at the Moss-Covered Mansion. (Illus.). (gr. 4-7). 1971. 4.50 (ISBN 0-448-09518-1, G&D). Putnam Pub Group.
—Mystery at the Ski Jump. rev. ed. (Illus.). (gr. 4-7). 1968. 4.50 (ISBN 0-448-09529-7, G&D). Putnam Pub Group.
—Mystery of Crocodile Island. LC 77-76128. (Illus.). (gr. 4-7). 1978. 4.50 (ISBN 0-448-09555-6, G&D). Putnam Pub Group.
—The Mystery of Misty Canyon. (gr. 3-7). 1988. pap. 3.50 (ISBN 0-671-63417-8, Minstrel Bks). PB.
—Mystery of the Bamboo Bird. new ed. (Illus.). 192p. (gr. 4-7). 1973. 2.95 (ISBN 0-448-09089-9, G&D). Putnam Pub Group.
—Mystery of the Fire Dragon. (gr. 4-7). 1961. 4.50 (ISBN 0-448-09538-6, G&D). Putnam Pub Group.
—The Mystery of the Glowing Eye. (Illus.). 192p. (gr. 4-7). 1974. 4.50 (ISBN 0-448-09551-3, G&D). Putnam Pub Group.
—Mystery of the Ivory Charm. LC 74-3868. (Illus.). 196p. (gr. 4-7). 1974. Repr. of 1936 ed. 4.50 (ISBN 0-448-09513-0, G&D). Putnam Pub Group.
—Mystery of the Ninety-Nine Steps. (gr. 4-7). 1965. 4.50 (ISBN 0-448-09543-2, G&D). Putnam Pub Group.
—Mystery of the Stone Tiger. (Illus.). 192p. (gr. 4-7). 1972. 2.95 (ISBN 0-448-09081-3, G&D). Putnam Pub Group.
—Mystery of the Wax Queen. (Illus.). 192p. (gr. 4-7). 1972. 2.95 (ISBN 0-448-09084-8, G&D). Putnam Pub Group.
—Mystery of the Winged Lion. (gr. 7 up). 1989. pap. 3.50 (ISBN 0-318-41224-1, Minstrel Bks). PB.
—Mystery Train. Greenberg, Ann, ed. 224p. (Orig.). (gr. 7 up). 1990. pap. 2.95 (ISBN 0-671-67464-1, Archway). PB.
—A Nancy Drew & Hardy Boys Super Mystery: Double Crossing. 224p. (Orig.). (gr. 7 up). 1988. pap. 2.95 (ISBN 0-671-64917-5, Archway). PB.
—Nancy Drew & Hardy Boys Super Sleuths, No. 2. 1984. pap. 3.50 (ISBN 0-671-50194-1). S&S Trade.
—Nancy Drew & the Flying Saucer Mystery, No. 58. (gr. 4-7). 1988. pap. 3.50 (ISBN 0-671-72320-0). S&S Trade.
—Nancy Drew Digest. 1987. Boxed. pap. 14.00 (ISBN 0-671-91515-0, Minstrel Bks). PB.
—Nancy Drew Files: Don't Look Twice, No. 55. Greenberg, Ann, ed. 160p. (Orig.). 1991. pap. 3.50 (ISBN 0-671-70032-4, Archway). PB.
—The Nancy Drew Files, No. 24: Till Death Do Us Part. 160p. (Orig.). (gr. 7-12). 1989. pap. 2.95 (ISBN 0-671-68378-0, Archway). PB.
—Nancy Drew Files, No. 70: Broken Anchor. 1987. pap. 3.50 (ISBN 0-671-74228-0). PB.
—Nancy Drew Files, No. 75: The Emerald Eyed Cat Mystery. 1987. pap. 3.50 (ISBN 0-671-64282-0). PB.
—Nancy Drew Files, No. 76: Eskimos Secret. 1986. pap. 3.50 (ISBN 0-671-73003-7). PB.
—Nancy Drew Files, No. 78: The Phantom of Venice. 1985. pap. 3.50 (ISBN 0-671-49745-6). S&S Trade.
—Nancy Drew Files, No. 83: The Case of the Vanishing Veil. 160p. (Orig.). (gr. 3-6). 1988. pap. 3.50 (ISBN 0-671-63413-5, Minstrel Bks). PB.
—The Nancy Drew Files, No. 84: The Joker's Revenge. 1988. pap. 3.50 (ISBN 0-671-63414-3). PB.
—Nancy Drew Files, No.1: Ghost Stories. 1983. pap. 3.50 (ISBN 0-671-46468-X). S&S Trade.
—The Nancy Drew Ghost Stories. Schneider, Meg, ed. Frame, Paul, illus. (gr. 3-7). 1983. 8.95 (ISBN 0-685-06733-5, Little Simon); pap. 3.50. S&S Trade.
—Nancy Drew Ghost Stories. Frame, Paul, illus. 160p. 1983. 8.50 (ISBN 0-685-06755-6); pap. 2.85 (ISBN 0-685-06756-4). S&S Trade.
—Nancy Drew Ghost Stories II. Arico, Diane, ed. Frame, Paul, illus. 160p. (Orig.). (gr. 8-12). 9.95 (ISBN 0-671-55075-6, Little Simon); pap. text ed. 3.50 (ISBN 0-671-55070-5). S&S Trade.
—Nancy Drew Gift Set, 3 vols. Boxed Set. pap. 8.55 (ISBN 0-317-12425-0, Little Simon). S&S Trade.
—Nancy Drew: Mystery of the Winged Lion. (Illus.). 192p. (gr. 3-7). 1977. 8.95 (ISBN 0-671-42370-3, Little Simon); pap. 3.50 (ISBN 0-671-42371-1). S&S Trade.
—Nancy Drew Mystery Stories: Back-to-Back Edition. (gr. 3-7). 1987. 7.95 (ISBN 0-448-09570-X, G&D). Putnam Pub Group.
—Nancy Drew Mystery Stories, No. 78: The Phantom of Venice. 160p. (Orig.). (gr. 3-6). 1988. pap. 3.50 (ISBN 0-671-66230-9, Minstrel Bks). PB.
—Nancy Drew: Race Against Time. (Illus.). 208p. (gr. 3-7). 1982. 8.95 (ISBN 0-671-42372-X, Little Simon); pap. 3.50 (ISBN 0-671-42373-8). S&S Trade.
—Nancy Drew: The Bluebeard Room. Barish, Wendy & LeVert, Suzanne, eds. 160p. (Orig.). (gr. 3-7). 1985. write for info. (Little Simon). S&S Trade.
—Nancy Drew: The Captive Witness. (Illus.). 192p. (gr. 3-7). 1981. 8.95 (ISBN 0-671-42360-6, Little Simon); pap. 3.50 (ISBN 0-671-42361-4). S&S Trade.
—Nancy Drew: The Elusive Heiress. Frame, Paul, illus. 192p. (gr. 3-7). 1982. 8.95 (ISBN 0-671-44555-3, Little Simon); pap. 2.95 (ISBN 0-671-44553-7). S&S Trade.
—Nancy Drew: The Emerald-Eyed Cat. 1984. 9.90 (ISBN 0-671-49740-5, Little Simon); pap. 3.50 (ISBN 0-671-49739-1). S&S Trade.
—Nancy Drew: The Ghost in the Gondola. Barish, Wendy & LeVert, Suzanne, eds. 160p. (Orig.). (gr. 3-7). 1985. write for info. (Little Simon). S&S Trade.
—Nancy Drew: The Greek Symbol Mystery. Sanderson, Ruth, illus. 192p. (gr. 3-7). 1981. lib. bdg. 8.95 (ISBN 0-671-42297-9, Little Simon); pap. 2.95 (ISBN 0-671-42298-7). S&S Trade.
—Nancy Drew: The Kachina Doll Mystery. (Illus.). 192p. (gr. 3-7). 1981. 8.95 (ISBN 0-671-42346-0, Little Simon); pap. 3.50 (ISBN 0-671-42347-9). S&S Trade.
—Nancy Drew: The Secret in the Old Lace. 192p. (gr. 3-7). 1980. PLB 8.95 (ISBN 0-671-41119-5, Little Simon); pap. 3.50 (ISBN 0-671-41114-4). S&S Trade.
—Nancy Drew: The Silver Cobweb, No. 71. Greenberg, Ann, ed. 208p. 1990. pap. 3.50 (ISBN 0-671-70992-5, Minstrel Bks). PB.
—Nancy Drew: The Sinister Omen. Frame, Paul, illus. 192p. (gr. 3-7). 1982. 8.95 (ISBN 0-671-44554-5, Little Simon); pap. 3.50 (ISBN 0-671-44552-9). S&S Trade.
—Nancy Drew: The Swami's Ring. (Illus.). 192p. (gr. 3-7). 1981. (Little Simon); pap. 2.75 (ISBN 0-671-42345-2). S&S Trade.
—Nancy Drew: The Twin Dilemma. (Illus.). 192p. (gr. 3-7). 1981. 8.95 (ISBN 0-671-42358-4, Little Simon); pap. 2.95 (ISBN 0-671-42359-2). S&S Trade.
—Nancy's Mysterious Letter. (gr. 4-7). 1963. 4.50 (ISBN 0-448-09508-4, G&D). Putnam Pub Group.
—Never Say Die. (gr. 7 up). 1988. pap. 2.95 (ISBN 0-671-68051-X, Archway). PB.
—The One Hundred Year Mystery. (gr. 4-7). 2.95 (ISBN 0-448-09095-3, G&D). Putnam Pub Group.
—Out of Bounds. 160p. 1990. pap. 2.95 (ISBN 0-671-67497-8, Archway). PB.
—Over the Edge. (Orig.). (gr. 7 up). 1989. pap. 2.95 (ISBN 0-671-64703-2, Archway). PB.
—The Paris Connection: A Nancy Drew & Hardy Boys Supermystery. 224p. 1990. pap. 2.95 (ISBN 0-671-67462-5, Archway). PB.
—The Phantom Surfer. (Illus.). 192p. (gr. 4-7). 1972. 2.95 (ISBN 0-448-09086-4, G&D). Putnam Pub Group.
—The Picture Perfect Mystery. 160p. 1990. pap. 3.50 (ISBN 0-671-66319-4, Minstrel Bks). PB.
—Playing with Fire. (gr. 7 up). 1989. pap. 2.95 (ISBN 0-671-70356-0, Archway). PB.
—Portrait in Crime. Greenberg, Ann, ed. 160p. (Orig.). 1990. pap. 2.95 (ISBN 0-671-70026-X, Archway). PB.
—Pure Poison. (gr. 7 up). 1990. pap. 2.95 (ISBN 0-671-72226-3, Archway). PB.
—The Puzzle at Pineview School. (Orig.). (gr. 7 up). 1989. pap. 3.50 (ISBN 0-671-66315-1, Minstrel Bks). PB.
—Quest of the Missing Map. LC 70-86692. (Illus.). (gr. 4-7). 1942. 4.50 (ISBN 0-448-09519-X, G&D); PLB 3.29 (ISBN 0-448-19519-4). Putnam Pub Group.
—Race Against Time. 208p. 1990. pap. 3.50 (ISBN 0-671-69485-5, Minstrel Bks). PB.
—Recipe for Murder. 160p. (Orig.). (gr. 7 up). 1989. pap. 2.95 (ISBN 0-671-68802-2, Archway). PB.
—Rich & Dangerous. (gr. 7 up). 1989. pap. 2.95 (ISBN 0-671-70139-8, Archway). PB.
—The Riddle of the Frozen Fountain. (Illus.). 192p. (gr. 4-7). 1972. 2.95 (ISBN 0-448-09082-1, G&D). Putnam Pub Group.
—The Ringmaster's Secret. rev. ed. LC 74-3867. (Illus.). 196p. (gr. 4-7). 1974. Repr. of 1954 ed. 4.50 (ISBN 0-448-09531-9, G&D). Putnam Pub Group.
—The Scarlet Slipper Mystery. rev. ed. LC 74-3869. (Illus.). 196p. (gr. 4-7). 1955. 4.50 (ISBN 0-448-09532-7, G&D); PLB 3.29 (ISBN 0-448-19532-1). Putnam Pub Group.
—Scent of Danger. 160p. 1990. pap. 2.95 (ISBN 0-671-67496-X, Archway). PB.
—The Search for Cindy Austin. (Orig.). (gr. 3-7). 1989. pap. 3.50 (ISBN 0-671-66313-5, Minstrel Bks). PB.
—Secret at Shadow Ranch. (gr. 4-7). 1931. 4.50 (ISBN 0-448-09505-X, G&D). Putnam Pub Group.
—The Secret in the Old Attic. rev. ed. Johnson, Ray, illus. LC 78-100118. (gr. 4-7). 1955. 4.50 (ISBN 0-448-09521-1, G&D). Putnam Pub Group.
—The Secret of Mirror Bay. (Illus.). 196p. (gr. 4-7). 1972. 4.50 (ISBN 0-448-09549-1, G&D). Putnam Pub Group.
—Secret of Red Gate Farm. (gr. 4-7). 1931. 4.50 (ISBN 0-448-09506-8, G&D). Putnam Pub Group.
—The Secret of Shady Glen. 1988. pap. 3.50 (ISBN 0-671-63416-X, Minstrel Bks). PB.
—The Secret of the Forgotten City. new ed. LC 74-10461. (Illus.). 196p. (gr. 4-7). 1975. 4.50 (ISBN 0-448-09552-1, G&D). Putnam Pub Group.

—Secret of the Golden Pavilion. (Illus.). (gr. 4-7). 1959. 4.50 (ISBN 0-448-09536-X, G&D). Putnam Pub Group.
—Secret of the Old Clock. (gr. 4-7). 1930. 4.50 (ISBN 0-448-09501-7, G&D). Putnam Pub Group.
—The Secret of the Silver Dolphin. (Illus.). 192p. (gr. 4-7). 1972. 2.95 (ISBN 0-448-09083-X, G&D). Putnam Pub Group.
—The Secret of the Swiss Chalet. rev ed. LC 72-90827. (Illus.). 196p. (gr. 4-7). 1973. 2.95 (ISBN 0-448-09087-2, G&D). Putnam Pub Group.
—Secret of the Wooden Lady. (gr. 4-7). 1950. 4.50 (ISBN 0-448-09527-0, G&D). Putnam Pub Group.
—Secrets Can Kill. (gr. 7 up). 1989. pap. 2.95 (ISBN 0-671-68523-6, Archway). PB.
—Secrets Can Kill. large type ed. (gr. 5-10). 1988. 9.50 (ISBN 0-942545-22-2); PLB 10.50 (ISBN 0-942545-27-3, Dist. by Grolier). Grey Castle.
—Shadow of a Doubt. 160p. (Orig.). 1989. pap. 2.95 (ISBN 0-671-67492-7, Archway). PB.
—Shock Waves. (gr. 7 up). 1989. pap. 2.95 (ISBN 0-671-64919-1, Archway). PB.
—The Silent Suspect. 160p. (Orig.). 1990. pap. 3.50 (ISBN 0-671-69280-1, Minstrel). PB.
—The Silver Cobweb. Schneider, Meg, ed. Frame, Paul, illus. 192p. (Orig.). (gr. 3-7). 1983. 9.95 (ISBN 0-685-06731-9, Little Simon). S&S Trade.
—The Silver Cobweb. Frame, Paul, illus. 192p. 1983. 8.95 (ISBN 0-685-06757-2); pap. 3.50. S&S Trade.
—Sinister Paradise. (gr. 7 up). 1989. pap. 2.95 (ISBN 0-671-68803-0, Archway). PB.
—Sisters in Crime. 160p. (Orig.). (gr. 7 up). 1988. pap. 2.95 (ISBN 0-671-67957-0, Archway). PB.
—Smile & Say Murder. (gr. 7 up). 1988. pap. 2.95 (ISBN 0-671-68053-6, Archway). PB.
—Smile & Say Murder. large type ed. (gr. 5-10). 1988. 9.50 (ISBN 0-942545-26-5); PLB 10.50 (ISBN 0-942545-30-3, Dist. by Grolier). Grey Castle.
—Something to Hide. 160p. 1989. pap. 2.95 (ISBN 0-671-67493-5, Archway). PB.
—Spider Sapphire Mystery. (Illus.). (gr. 4-7). 1968. 4.50 (ISBN 0-448-09545-9, G&D). Putnam Pub Group.
—Strange Message in the Parchment. (gr. 4-7). 1977. 4.50 (ISBN 0-448-09554-8, G&D). Putnam Pub Group.
—The Suspect Next Door. (Orig.). (gr. 7 up). 1989. pap. 2.95 (ISBN 0-671-67491-9, Archway). PB.
—The Swami's Ring. (gr. 7 up). 1986. pap. 3.50 (ISBN 0-671-62467-9, Minstrel Bks). PB.
—The Thirteenth Pearl. LC 78-57931. (Illus.). (gr. 3-7). 1979. 4.50 (ISBN 0-448-09556-4, G&D). Putnam Pub Group.
—This Side of Evil. 160p. (Orig.). (gr. 7 up). 1987. pap. 2.95 (ISBN 0-671-72227-1, Archway). PB.
—Till Death Do Us Part. 1988. pap. 2.95 (ISBN 0-318-35168-4). PB.
—Trail of Lies. Greenberg, Ann, ed. 160p. (Orig.). (gr. 7 up). 1990. pap. 2.95 (ISBN 0-671-70030-8, Archway). PB.
—Trial by Fire. 160p. (Orig.). (gr. 7 up). 1987. pap. 2.75 (ISBN 0-671-64138-7, Archway). PB.
—The Triple Hoax. (gr. 2-7). 1984. 8.85 (ISBN 0-685-09396-4, Little Simon). S&S Trade.
—Trouble in Tahiti. (gr. 7 up). 1989. pap. 2.95 (ISBN 0-671-64698-2, Archway). PB.
—The Trouble with Love. Greenberg, Ann, ed. 160p. (Orig.). (gr. 6 up). 1990. pap. 2.95 (ISBN 0-671-67766-7, Archway). PB.
—The Twin Dilemma. (gr. 3-7). 1988. pap. 3.50 (ISBN 0-671-67301-7, Minstrel Bks). PB.
—Two Points to Murder. (gr. 7 up). 1987. pap. 2.75 (ISBN 0-671-63079-2, Archway). PB.
—Two Points to Murder: The Nancy Drew Files, Case 8. large type ed. 151p. (gr. 5-10). 1988. Repr. of 1987 ed. 9.50 (ISBN 0-942545-39-7); PLB 10.50 (ISBN 0-942545-34-6, Dist. by Grolier). Grey Castle.
—Vanishing Act. (gr. 7 up). 1989. pap. 2.95 (ISBN 0-671-64701-6, Archway). PB.
—Very Deadly Yours. 160p. (Orig.). (gr. 7 up). 1988. pap. 2.95 (ISBN 0-671-68061-7, Archway). PB.
—White Water Terror: The Nancy Drew Files, Case 6. large type ed. 149p. (gr. 5-10). 1988. Repr. of 1986 ed. 9.50 (ISBN 0-942545-37-0); PLB 10.50 (ISBN 0-942545-32-X, Dist. by Grolier). Grey Castle.
—Win, Place or Die. 160p. 1990. pap. 2.95 (ISBN 0-671-67498-6, Archway). PB.
—Wings of Fear. 160p. (Orig.). (gr. 7 up). 1989. pap. 2.95 (ISBN 0-671-70140-1, Archway). PB.
—The Winking Ruby Mystery. (Illus.). 192p. (gr. 4-7). 1974. 2.95 (ISBN 0-448-09092-9, G&D). Putnam Pub Group.
Keene, Carolyn & Dixon, Franklin W. Danger on Ice. Schwartz, Betty, ed. Frame, Paul, illus. 128p. (Orig.). (gr. 3-7). 1984. pap. 2.95 (ISBN 0-671-49920-3, Little Simon). S&S Trade.
—The Feathered Serpent. Schwartz, Betty, ed. Frame, Paul, illus. 128p. (Orig.). (gr. 3-7). 1984. pap. 3.50 (ISBN 0-671-49921-1, Little Simon). S&S Trade.
—Nancy Drew & the Hardy Boys. Barish, Wendy, ed. Frame, Paul, illus. 192p. (Orig.). (gr. 3 up). 1984. pap. 2.95 (ISBN 0-685-09176-7, Little Simon). S&S Trade.
—Nancy Drew & the Hardy Boys Be a Detective Mystery Stories: Ticket to Intrigue. Arico, Diane, ed. Frame, Paul, illus. 128p. (Orig.). (gr. 3-7). 1985. pap. 2.95 (ISBN 0-671-55735-1, Little Simon). S&S Trade.
—Nancy Drew & the Hardy Boys Be a Detective: The Alaskan Mystery. Arico, Diane, ed. Frame, Paul, illus. 128p. (Orig.). 1985. pap. 3.50 (ISBN 0-671-54550-7, Little Simon). S&S Trade.
—Nancy Drew & the Hardy Boys Be a Detective: The Missing Money Mystery. Arico, Diane, ed. Frame, Paul, illus. 128p. (gr. 8-12). 1985. pap. 2.95 (ISBN 0-671-54551-5, Little Simon). S&S Trade.
—Nancy Drew & the Hardy Boys: Jungle of Evil. Arico, Diane, ed. Frame, Paul, illus. 128p. (Orig.). (gr. 3-7). 1985. pap. 2.95 (ISBN 0-671-55734-3, Little Simon). S&S Trade.
—Secret Cargo. Schwartz, Betty, ed. Frame, Paul, illus. 128p. (Orig.). 1984. pap. 2.95 (ISBN 0-671-49922-X, Little Simon). S&S Trade.
—Super Sleuths, No. 2. Frame, Paul, illus. (gr. 2-7). 1984. 3.50 (ISBN 0-685-09395-6, Little Simon). S&S Trade.
Kehret, Peg. Deadly Stranger. 176p. (gr. 2-9). pap. 2.95 (ISBN 0-8167-1308-1). Troll Assocs.
—Deadly Stranger. 144p. (ps-8). 1987. 13.95 (ISBN 0-399-21701-0, Putnam). Putnam Pub Group.
Keller, Rosanne. Stormy Night Stories, 10 bks. Kempster, Teddy, ed. (Illus.). 160p. (gr. 8-12). 1988. Boxed Set. 14.95 (ISBN 0-88336-992-3). New Readers.
Kelley, True. The Mystery of the Stranger in the Barn. (Illus.). 32p. (gr. k-3). 1986. 10.95 (ISBN 0-396-08779-5, Putnam). Putnam Pub Group.
Kellogg, Steven. The Mystery of the Flying Orange Pumpkin. Kellogg, Steven, illus. LC 80-11748. 32p. (ps-2). 1983. pap. 3.50 (ISBN 0-8037-0019-9). Dial Bks Young.
—The Mystery of the Missing Red Mitten. LC 73-15439. (Illus.). 32p. (ps-2). 1974. 8.95 (ISBN 0-8037-6195-3); PLB 8.89 (ISBN 0-8037-6194-5). Dial Bks Young.
—The Mystery of the Missing Red Mitten. LC 73-15439. (Illus.). (gr. k-2). 1977. pap. 3.50 (ISBN 0-8037-5749-2). Dial Bks Young.
—The Mystery of the Stolen Blue Paint. Kellogg, Steven, illus. LC 81-15314. 32p. (ps-2). 1982. PLB 8.89 (ISBN 0-8037-5659-3). Dial Bks Young.
—Mystery of the Stolen Blue Paint. Kellogg, Steven, illus. LC 81-15314. 32p. (ps-2). 1986. pap. 3.95 (ISBN 0-8037-0285-X). Dial Bks Young.
—Prehistoric Pinkerton. Kellogg, Steven, illus. LC 86-2201. 32p. (ps-3). 1987. 12.95 (ISBN 0-8037-0322-8); PLB 12.89 (ISBN 0-8037-0323-6). Dial Bks Young.
Kelso, Mary J. Abducted! Kelso, Mary J., illus. (Orig.). (gr. 6 up). 1988. pap. 6.95 (ISBN 0-9621406-0-0). MarKel Pr.
Kemp, Gene. Juniper: A Mystery. (gr. 5-7). 1986. 10.95 (ISBN 0-571-13902-7). Faber & Faber.
Keown, Don. Scoop Doogan Mysteries, 5 novels in ea. set, Sets 1 & 2. (Illus.). 1984. Set. pap. 15.00 (ISBN 0-685-31194-5, High Noon Books). Set 1, 48p (ISBN 0-87879-433-6). Set 2, 48p (ISBN 0-87879-466-2). Acad Therapy.
Kerr, M. E. Fell Back. LC 88-35762. 192p. (gr. 7 up). 1991. pap. 3.50 (ISBN 0-06-447057-1, Trophy). HarpC Child Bks.
—Fell Down. LC 90-49921. 208p. (gr. 7 up). 1991. 14.95 (ISBN 0-06-021763-4); PLB 14.89 (ISBN 0-06-021764-2). HarpC Child Bks.
Kesteven, G. R. The Awakening Water. LC 78-27186. (gr. 4-8). 1979. 9.95g (ISBN 0-8038-0471-7). Hastings.
Kherdian, David. The Mystery of the Diamond in the Wood. Geiger, Paul, illus. LC 83-272. 128p. (gr. 3 up). 1983. lib. bdg. 9.99 (ISBN 0-394-95603-6). Knopf.
Kidd, Ronald. Second Fiddle: A Sizzle & Splat Mystery. LC 88-3592. 160p. (gr. 7 up). 1988. 12.95 (ISBN 0-525-67252-4, Lodestar Bks). Dutton Child Bks.
Kidney, Dorothy. The Mystery of the Old Clock Shop. (Orig.). (gr. 4-6). 1981. pap. 4.95 (ISBN 0-8341-0728-7). Beacon Hill.
Killien, Christi. Putting on an Act. (gr. 4-9). 1988. pap. 2.95 (ISBN 0-440-20186-1, LFL). Dell.
Kittredge, William & Krauzer, Steven M., eds. The Great American Detective. 432p. (gr. 9-12). Date not set. pap. 4.95 (ISBN 0-317-02723-9, Ment). NAL-Dutton.
Klein, Norma. Mom, the Wolfman & Me. (gr. 5 up). 1972. lib. bdg. 9.99 (ISBN 0-394-92470-3). Pantheon.
Kline, Suzy. Herbie Jones & the Class Gift. Williams, Richard, illus. 96p. (gr. 2-6). 1987. 12.95 (ISBN 0-399-21452-6, Putnam). Putnam Pub Group.
—Horrible Harry's Secret. LC 90-32482. (gr. 4-7). 1990. 10.95 (ISBN 0-670-82470-4). Viking Child Bks.
Kohls, Tom. The Missing Hair Net. 31p. 1987. pap. 3.25 (ISBN 0-8163-0713-X). Pacific Pr Pub Assn.
Konigsburg, E. L. The Dragon in the Ghetto Caper. 128p. (gr. 5-6). 1985. pap. 2.75 (ISBN 0-440-42148-9, YB). Dell.
—Father's Arcane Daughter. LC 76-5495. 128p. (gr. 4-8). 1976. SBE 12.95 (ISBN 0-689-30524-9, Atheneum Child Bk). Macmillan Child Grp.
—From the Mixed-up Files of Mrs. Basil E. Frankweiler. (Illus.). (gr. 3-7). 1972. pap. 3.95 (ISBN 0-689-70308-2, Aladdin). Macmillan Child Grp.
Kotzwinkle, William. Trouble in Bugland: A Collection of Inspector Mantis Mysteries. Servello, Joe, illus. LC 82-49338. 160p. (gr. 5 up). 1983. 9.95 (ISBN 0-87923-472-5). Godine.
Kwitz, Mary D. Gumshoe Goose, Private Eye. (ps-3). 1991. pap. 3.95 (ISBN 0-8037-0923-4, Dial Easy to Read). Puffin Bks.
Landis, Mary M. The Missing Popcorn & Other Stories. (gr. 3-6). 1976. 6.35 (ISBN 0-686-15480-0). Rod & Staff.
Landon, Lucinda. Meg MacKintosh & the Case of the Missing Babe Ruth Baseball: A Solve-It-Yourself Mystery. Landon, Lucinda, illus. LC 85-20055. 48p. (gr. 2-5). 1986. 13.95 (ISBN 0-316-51318-0, 513180, Joy St Bks). Little.
Langton, Jane. The Diamond in the Window. Blegvad, Erik, illus. LC 62-7312. 256p. (gr. 5 up). 1973. pap. 3.50 (ISBN 0-06-440042-5, Trophy). HarpC Child Bks.
Larkin, Barbara. The Secret of the Stolen Mandolin. 160p. (Orig.). 1987. pap. 3.75 (ISBN 1-85168-003-9, Pub. by Oneworld UK). Pub Service.
Lasky, K. Double Trouble Squared. 1991. 12.95 (ISBN 0-15-224126-4, HJ). HarBraceJ.
Lavelle, Sheila. The Disappearing Granny. Kopper, Lisa, illus. 42p. (gr. 2-4). 1989. 3.95 (ISBN 0-8120-6134-9). Barron.
Law, Carol R. The Case of the Weird Street Firebug. Morrison, Bill, illus. LC 79-26906. 128p. (gr. 3-6). 1980. pap. 1.95 (ISBN 0-394-84480-7). Knopf.
Lawrence, James. Binky Brothers & the Fearless Four. Kessler, Leonard, illus. LC 75-77936. 64p. (gr. k-3). 1970. 4.95 (ISBN 0-06-023760-0). HarpC Child Bks.
—Binky Brothers, Detectives. Kessler, Leonard, illus. LC 68-10374. 64p. (gr. k-3). 1968. PLB 11.89 (ISBN 0-06-023759-7). HarpC Child Bks.
—Binky Brothers, Detectives. Kessler, Leonard, illus. LC 68-10374. 64p. (ps-3). 1985. pap. 5.98 incl. cassette (ISBN 0-694-00018-3, Trophy). HarpC Child Bks.
Lawson, Robert. Captain Kidd's Cat. (Illus.). (gr. 2-4). 1984. pap. 7.95 (ISBN 0-316-51735-6). Little.
Leigh, S. Journey to the Lost Temple. (Illus.). 48p. 1989. lib. bdg. 10.96 (ISBN 0-88110-406-X); pap. 4.50 (ISBN 0-7460-0308-0). EDC.
L'Engle, Madeleine. Dragons in the Waters. LC 76-2477. 304p. (gr. 7 up). 1976. 16.95 (ISBN 0-374-31868-9). FS&G.
—The Young Unicorns. LC 68-13682. 256p. (gr. 7 up). 1968. 16.95 (ISBN 0-374-38778-8). FS&G.
Leppard, Lois G. Mandie & the Cherokee Legend, Bk. 2. LC 83-70894. 144p. (Orig.). (gr. 4-7). 1983. pap. 3.95 (ISBN 0-87123-321-5). Bethany Hse.
—Mandie & the Forbidden Attic, Bk. 4. LC 84-72710. 144p. (Orig.). (gr. 4-7). 1985. pap. 3.95 (ISBN 0-87123-822-5). Bethany Hse.
—Mandie & the Secret Tunnel, Bk. 1. LC 82-74053. 144p. (Orig.). (gr. 4-7). 1983. pap. 3.95 (ISBN 0-87123-320-7). Bethany Hse.
—Mandie & the Trunk's Secret, Bk. 5. LC 85-71474. 144p. (Orig.). (gr. 3-7). 1985. pap. 3.95 (ISBN 0-87123-839-X). Bethany Hse.
—Mandie & the Washington Nightmare, Bk. 12. LC 88-63464. 160p. (Orig.). (gr. 4-8). 1989. pap. 3.95 (ISBN 1-55661-065-3). Bethany Hse.
Lerangis, Peter. Foul Play. LC 89-39459. 144p. (Orig.). (gr. 5 up). 1990. pap. 2.95 (ISBN 0-679-80090-5). McKay.
—Foul Play. LC 89-37138. 144p. (gr. 5 up). 1990. PLB 6.99 (ISBN 0-679-90090-X). McKay.
Levin, Betty. The Keeping Room. LC 80-23931. (Illus.). 248p. 1989. Repr. of 1981 ed. 11.95 (ISBN 0-688-80300-8). Greenwillow.
Levy, Elizabeth. The Case of the Gobbling Squash. Eagle, Ellen, illus. (gr. 2-4). 1989. 10.95 (ISBN 0-671-63655-3); pap. 2.95 (ISBN 0-671-68873-1). S&S Trade.
—The Case of the Mind-Reading Mommies. Eagle, Ellen, illus. (gr. 2-4). 1989. pap. 10.95 (ISBN 0-671-63656-1). S&S Trade.
—Cold As Ice. LC 88-12898. 176p. (gr. 7 up). 1988. 12. 95 (ISBN 0-688-06579-1). Morrow Jr Bks.
—Nasty Competition. (gr. 4-7). 1991. pap. 2.75 (ISBN 0-590-43833-6). Scholastic Inc.
—Something Queer at the Ball Park. Gerstein, Mordicai, illus. 48p. (gr. 1-4). 1984. pap. 2.75 (ISBN 0-440-48116-3, YB). Dell.
—Something Queer at the Haunted School. Gerstein, Mordicai, illus. LC 81-1940. 48p. (gr. 1-3). 1982. 8.95 (ISBN 0-440-08349-4); pap. 9.95 (ISBN 0-385-28992-8). Delacorte.
—Something Queer at the Haunted School. Gerstein, Mordicai, illus. 48p. (gr. 1-4). 1983. pap. 2.75 (ISBN 0-440-48461-8, YB). Dell.
—Something Queer at the Lemonade Stand. Gerstein, Mordicai, tr. LC 81-69666. (Illus.). 48p. (gr. 1-3). 1982. 7.95 (ISBN 0-440-07859-8); pap. 10.95 (ISBN 0-385-28901-4). Delacorte.
—Something Queer at the Lemonade Stand. Gerstein, Mordicai, illus. 48p. (gr. k-6). 1983. pap. 2.99 (ISBN 0-440-48495-2, YB). Dell.
—Something Queer at the Library. Gerstein, Mordicai, illus. 48p. (gr. 1-4). 1989. pap. 2.75 (ISBN 0-440-48120-1, YB). Dell.
Lexau, Joan M. The Dog Food Caper. Hafner, Marylin, illus. LC 84-1904. 48p. (ps-3). 1985. 8.95 (ISBN 0-8037-0107-1); PLB 8.89 (ISBN 0-8037-0108-X). Dial Bks Young.
—Homework Caper. Hoff, Syd, illus. LC 66-11493. 62p. (gr. k-3). 1966. PLB 11.89 (ISBN 0-06-023856-9). HarpC Child Bks.
—Rooftop Mystery. Hoff, Syd, illus. LC 68-16821. 64p. (gr. k-3). 1968. PLB 11.89 (ISBN 0-06-023865-8). HarpC Child Bks.
Liebman, Arthur, ed. Classic Crime Stories: The Criminal in Literature. 239p. (gr. 7-12). 1975. PLB 10.97 (ISBN 0-8239-0310-9). Rosen Group.

Lindbergh, Anne M. The Shadow on the Dial. (gr. 3-7). 1988. pap. 2.75 (ISBN 0-380-70545-1, Camelot). Avon.

Lipman, Michel & Furniss, Cathy. Legal Eagle Series, 5 novels. Kratoville, Betty L., ed. (Illus.). 240p. (Orig.). (gr. 4-12). 1988. Set. pap. 15.00 (ISBN 0-87879-594-4, Pub. by High Noon Books). Acad Therapy.

Lisle, Janet T. Sirens & Spies. LC 90-185. 176p. (gr. 7 up). 1990. pap. 3.95 (ISBN 0-02-044341-2, Collier Young Ad). Macmillan Child Grp.

Little, Jack. Moon of Isis. LC 76-8728. (gr. 5 up). 1976. pap. 4.00 (ISBN 0-934768-00-5). Altair Pr.

Longmeyer, Carole M. Clemson Football Mystery. Rhodes, Priscilla, illus. (Orig.). (gr. 3 up). 1983. PLB 19.95 (ISBN 1-55609-164-8); pap. 14.95 (ISBN 0-935326-28-6). Gallopade Pub Group.

—Deadly Duke Football Mystery. Rhodes, Priscilla, illus. (Orig.). (gr. 3 up). pap. 14.95 (ISBN 0-935326-31-6). Gallopade Pub Group.

—Georgia Tech Football Mystery. Rhodes, Priscilla, illus. (Orig.). (gr. 3 up). 1983. pap. 14.95 (ISBN 0-935326-30-8). Gallopade Pub Group.

—Maryland Football Mystery. Rhodes, Priscilla, illus. 80p. (Orig.). (gr. 3 up). pap. 14.95 (ISBN 0-935326-32-4). Gallopade Pub Group.

—NC State Football Mystery. Rhodes, Priscilla, illus. (Orig.). (gr. 3 up). pap. 14.95 (ISBN 0-935326-33-2). Gallopade Pub Group.

—Virginia Football Mystery. Rhodes, Priscilla, illus. 80p. (Orig.). (gr. 3 up). pap. 14.95 (ISBN 0-935326-35-9). Gallopade Pub Group.

—Wake Forest Football Mystery. Rhodes, Priscilla, illus. (Orig.). (gr. 3 up). pap. 14.95 (ISBN 0-935326-34-0). Gallopade Pub Group.

Lorimer, Janet. The Mystery of the Missing Treasure. 112p. (Orig.). (gr. 4-6). 1987. pap. 2.50 (ISBN 0-590-40490-3, Apple Paperbacks). Scholastic Inc.

Lunn, Janet. Shadow in Hawthorn Bay. 192p. (gr. 5-9). 1988. pap. 3.95 (ISBN 0-14-032436-4, Puffin). Puffin Bks.

McBrier, Page. Secret of the Old Garage. Sims, Blanche, illus. LC 85-16505. 96p. (gr. 3-6). 1986. PLB 9.89 (ISBN 0-8167-0543-7); pap. text ed. 2.95 (ISBN 0-8167-0544-5). Troll Assocs.

McCall, Barbara. The Three Investigator's Book of Mystery Puzzles. Rao, Anthony, illus. 64p. (gr. 3-7). 1982. pap. 1.50 (ISBN 0-394-85107-2). Random.

McCay, William. Shoot the Works. LC 89-37749. 144p. (gr. 5 up). 1990. PLB 6.99 (ISBN 0-679-90157-4); pap. 2.95 (ISBN 0-679-80157-X). McKay.

McCoy, Lois, et al. The Byte Brothers Input an Investigation. Morrill, Leslie H., illus. 1983. pap. 2.25 (ISBN 0-380-85571-2, 85571, Camelot). Avon.

McCusker, Paul. High Flyer with a Flat Tire: An Adventure in Odyssey. Craig, Sheila, ed. Loccisano, Karen, illus. 85p. (Orig.). (gr. 3-6). 1991. pap. 3.99 (ISBN 1-56179-022-2). Focus Family.

MacDonald, Reby E. The Ghosts of Austwick Manor. 160p. (gr. 3-7). 1991. pap. 3.95 (ISBN 0-689-71533-1, Aladdin). Macmillan Child Grp.

McEvoy, Seth. Mission to Microworld. 1984. pap. 1.95 (ISBN 0-553-24521-X). Bantam.

McGraw, Eloise. The Seventeenth Swap. (gr. 4-8). 1987. pap. 2.95 (ISBN 0-8167-1050-3). Troll Assocs.

McGraw, Eloise J. The Golden Goblet. 248p. (gr. 5-9). 1986. pap. 4.95 (ISBN 0-14-030335-9, Puffin). Puffin Bks.

—The Money Room. 192p. (gr. 7 up). 1991. pap. 3.95 (ISBN 0-02-044484-2, Collier Young Ad). Macmillan Child Grp.

McHargue, Georgess. The Horseman's Word. (gr. k-12). 1988. pap. 2.95 (ISBN 0-440-20126-8, LFL). Dell.

—The Turquoise Toad Mystery. LC 81-69664. 160p. (gr. 4-6). 1982. 9.95 (ISBN 0-385-29057-8). Delacorte.

McKay, William. Funny Business. LC 88-45879. 144p. (Orig.). (gr. 5 up). 1989. pap. 2.95 (ISBN 0-394-89981-4). Knopf.

McKee, Chuck & McKee, David. The Mystery of the Blue Arrows. (Illus.). 32p. (ps-1). 1991. 15.95 (ISBN 0-86264-267-1, Pub. by Andersen Pr UK). Trafalgar Sq.

McNear, Robert & Glassman, Bruce. The Marathon Race Mystery. Rogers, Jackie, illus. LC 84-16395. 128p. (gr. 3-7). 1985. lib. bdg. 9.49 (ISBN 0-8167-0444-9); pap. text ed. 2.95 (ISBN 0-8167-0445-7). Troll Assocs.

McVey, R. Parker. The Missing Rock Star Caper. Rogers, Jackie, illus. LC 84-8721. 128p. (gr. 3-7). 1985. lib. bdg. 9.49 (ISBN 0-8167-0398-1); pap. text ed. 2.95 (ISBN 0-8167-0399-X). Troll Assocs.

—Mystery at the Ball Game. Rogers, Jackie, illus. LC 84-8486. 128p. (gr. 3-7). 1985. lib. bdg. 9.49 (ISBN 0-8167-0336-1); pap. text ed. 2.95 (ISBN 0-8167-0337-X). Troll Assocs.

Maguire, Gregory. Lights on the Lake. LC 81-12478. 262p. (gr. 5 up). 1981. 13.95 (ISBN 0-374-34463-9). FS&G.

Maguire, Jack. Trouble & More Trouble. Ashby, Ruth, ed. (Illus.). 64p. (Orig.). (gr. 2-5). 1990. pap. 2.75 (ISBN 0-671-64042-9, Minstrel Bks). PB.

Majors, G. Who Would Want to Kill Hallie Panky's Cat? 160p. (gr. 4-7). 1981. 8.95g (ISBN 0-8038-8094-4). Hastings.

Mallett, Jerry & Bartch, Marian. The Mystery at Chung's Chinese Restaurant. Smith, Mark D., illus. 61p. (gr. 4-7). 1987. PLB 7.35 (ISBN 0-8000-1699-8, 207909). Perma Bound.

—Mystery at Madame Darkle's Wax Museum. Smith, Mark D., illus. 57p. (gr. 4-7). 1987. PLB 7.35 (ISBN 0-8000-0506-6, 207916). Perma Bound.

—Mystery at the Hollender Hotel. Smith, Mark D., illus. 57p. (gr. 4-7). 1987. PLB 7.35 (ISBN 0-8000-0507-4, 207918). Perma Bound.

—Mystery at the Laff-a-Lott Amusement Park. Smith, Mark D., illus. 59p. (gr. 4-7). 1987. PLB 7.35 (ISBN 0-8000-0509-0, 207923). Perma Bound.

—Mystery at the Seesaw Cinema Company. Smith, Mark D., illus. 60p. (gr. 4-7). 1987. PLB 7.35 (ISBN 0-8000-0508-2, 207922). Perma Bound.

Manes, Stephen. The Hooples' Haunted House. Weston, Martha, illus. 112p. (gr. 3-7). 1983. pap. 2.25 (ISBN 0-440-43794-6, YB). Dell.

Markham, Marion M. The Birthday Party Mystery. Estrada, Pau, illus. (gr. 2 up). 1989. 13.95 (ISBN 0-395-49698-5). HM.

—The Birthday Party Mystery. 64p. (gr. 1-4). 1990. pap. 2.95 (ISBN 0-380-70968-6, Camelot Young). Avon.

—The Christmas Present Mystery. McCully, Emily A., illus. LC 84-4557. 48p. (gr. 2-5). 13.95 (ISBN 0-395-36383-7). HM.

—The Halloween Candy Mystery. McCully, Emily A., illus. LC 82-6059. 48p. (gr. 2-5). 1982. 9.95 (ISBN 0-395-32437-8). HM.

—The Halloween Candy Mystery. 64p. (gr. 1-4). 1990. pap. 2.95 (ISBN 0-380-70965-1, Camelot Young). Avon.

—The Thanksgiving Day Parade Mystery. Cassidy, Dianne, illus. LC 86-4618. 48p. (gr. 2-5). 1986. 10.95 (ISBN 0-395-41855-0). HM.

Marsh, Carole. Bat Cave Mystery. (Orig.). (gr. 3-8). 1986. PLB 19.95 (ISBN 1-55609-154-0); pap. 14.95 (ISBN 0-935326-72-3). Gallopade Pub Group.

—Blackbeard the Pirate's Missing Head Mystery Spook Kit. (Illus.). (ps-6). 1986. PLB 24.95 (ISBN 0-935326-19-7). Gallopade Pub Group.

—The Haunt of Hope Plantation. Marsh, Carole, illus. (Orig.). (gr. 3-9). 1982. 19.95 (ISBN 1-55609-170-2); pap. 14.95 (ISBN 0-935326-03-0). Gallopade Pub Group.

—Mystery of Old Salem Activity Book. 12p. (Orig.). (gr. 4-8). 1986. pap. 12.00 (ISBN 0-935326-67-7). Gallopade Pub Group.

—Mystery of Old Salem Gamebook. (Orig.). (gr. 4-8). 1986. pap. 19.95 (ISBN 0-935326-66-9). Gallopade Pub Group.

—Mystery of Old Salem S. P. A. R. K. Kit. (Illus., Orig.). (gr. 3-9). 1986. pap. 24.95 (ISBN 0-935326-74-X). Gallopade Pub Group.

—Mystery of Stone Mountain. (Orig.). (gr. 3-7). 1983. PLB 19.95 (ISBN 1-55609-180-X); pap. 14.95 (ISBN 0-935326-25-1). Gallopade Pub Group.

—Mystery of the Lost Colony. (Illus.). (gr. 4-9). 1983. PLB 19.95 (ISBN 1-55609-182-6); pap. 14.95 (ISBN 0-935326-05-7). Gallopade Pub Group.

—Mystery of Tryon Palace Activity Book. (Orig.). (gr. 3-6). 1986. pap. 14.95 (ISBN 0-935326-69-3). Gallopade Pub Group.

—Mystery of Tryon Palace Gamebook. (Orig.). (gr. 2-6). 1986. pap. 14.95 (ISBN 0-935326-70-7). Gallopade Pub Group.

—Mystery of Tryon Palace S. P. A. R. K. Kit. (Illus., Orig.). (gr. 3-8). 1986. pap. 24.95 (ISBN 0-317-44654-1). Gallopade Pub Group.

—Old Salem Mystery. (Orig.). (gr. 3-12). 1986. 19.95 (ISBN 1-55609-184-2); pap. 14.95 (ISBN 0-935326-59-6). Gallopade Pub Group.

—Tryon Palace Mystery. (Orig.). (gr. 3-12). 1986. 19.95 (ISBN 1-55609-193-1); pap. 14.95 (ISBN 0-935326-58-8). Gallopade Pub Group.

Martin, Ann M. Mary Anne's Bad Luck Mystery, No. 17. 144p. (gr. 3-7). 1988. pap. 2.75 (ISBN 0-590-41585-9). Scholastic Inc.

—Missing since Monday. 176p. (gr. 7 up). 1987. pap. 2.75 (ISBN 0-590-43136-6). Scholastic Inc.

—Stacey & the Mystery of Stoneybrook. 1990. pap. 2.95. Scholastic Inc.

Martin, Les. Raiders of the Lost Ark Storybook. (Illus.). 64p. (gr. 5-9). 1981. lib. bdg. 6.99 (ISBN 0-394-94802-5). Random.

Masefield, John. The Midnight Folk. (gr. k-6). 1985. pap. 4.95 (ISBN 0-440-45631-2, Pub. by Yearling Classics). Dell.

Massie, Diane R. Chameleon the Spy & the Terrible Toaster Trap. LC 81-43877. (Illus.). 40p. (gr. 2-6). 1982. (Crowell Jr Bks). HarpC Child Bks.

Masters, M. The Secret of the Video Game Scores & Other Mysteries. Hanrahan, Mariellen, et al, eds. Gadbois, Brett, illus. LC 83-26554. 108p. (gr. 2-6). 1984. pap. 1.95 (ISBN 0-671-54466-7). Meadowbrook.

Matas, Carol. Code Name Kris. LC 90-32656. 160p. (gr. 7 up). 1990. 12.95 (ISBN 0-684-19208-X, Scribners Young Read). Macmillan Child Grp.

Maxwell, Edith. Just Dial a Number. (gr. 7-9). 1988. pap. 2.75 (ISBN 0-671-67422-6, Archway). PB.

Mayer, Albert I. Mystery at Seabreeze. (gr. 6-10). 1965. PLB 6.70 (ISBN 0-8313-0077-9). Lantern.

—Mystery at the Pitchers Mound. LC 74-112672. (gr. 5-10). 1970. 6.70 (ISBN 0-8313-0078-7). Lantern.

Mayne, William. The Red Book of Hob Stories. Benson, Patrick, illus. LC 83-15125. 32p. (gr. k-4). 1984. 7.95 (ISBN 0-399-21047-4, Philomel). Putnam Pub Group.

Mazer, Harry. When the Phone Rang. 240p. (gr. 7 up). 1986. pap. 2.50 (ISBN 0-590-40383-4, Point). Scholastic Inc.

Meacham, Margaret. The Secret of Heron Creek. LC 90-50373. 136p. (Orig.). (gr. 5-8). 1991. pap. 7.95 (ISBN 0-87033-414-X). Tidewater.

Meyers, Susan. P. J. Clover, Private Eye: The Case of the Missing Mouse. Fiammenghi, Gloria, illus. LC 84-25892. 128p. (gr. 4-6). 1985. 11.95 (ISBN 0-525-67162-5, Lodestar Bks). Dutton Child Bks.

Mezek, Karen. Katie Sails the Nile. Mezek, Karen, illus. LC 90-33471. 64p. (Orig.). (ps-8). 1990. pap. 4.99 (ISBN 0-89081-814-2). Harvest Hse.

—Katie's Russian Holiday. (Illus.). 58p. (Orig.). (gr. 2-6). 1991. pap. 4.99 (ISBN 0-89081-861-4). Harvest Hse.

—Katie's Swiss Adventure. Mezek, Karen, illus. LC 90-33472. 64p. (Orig.). (ps-8). 1990. pap. 4.99 (ISBN 0-89081-815-0). Harvest Hse.

Michaels, Ski. Mystery of the Missing Fuzzy. Smolinski, Dick, illus. LC 85-14084. 48p. (Orig.). (gr. 1-3). 1986. PLB 9.89 (ISBN 0-8167-0646-8); pap. text ed. 2.95 (ISBN 0-8167-0647-6). Troll Assocs.

—Mystery of the Windy Meadow. Atkinson, Allen, illus. LC 85-14019. 48p. (Orig.). (gr. 1-3). 1986. PLB 9.89 (ISBN 0-8167-0630-1); pap. text ed. 2.95 (ISBN 0-8167-0631-X). Troll Assocs.

Miller, Lyle, illus. Mysteries of Sherlock Holmes. Conaway, Judith, adapted by. LC 81-15751. (Illus.). 96p. (gr. 2-5). 1982. lib. bdg. 4.99 (ISBN 0-394-95086-0); pap. 1.95 (ISBN 0-394-85086-6). Random.

Miller, Marvin. You Be the Detective. (gr. 4-7). 1991. pap. 2.50 (ISBN 0-590-42731-8). Scholastic Inc.

Miller, Marvin & Robinson, Nancy K. TACK Against Time. Tiegreen, Alan, illus. 128p. (Orig.). (gr. 3-6). 1983. pap. 2.25 (ISBN 0-590-32406-3). Scholastic Inc.

—TACK to the Rescue. Tiegreen, Alan, illus. 128p. (Orig.). (gr. 3-6). 1982. pap. 2.50 (ISBN 0-590-41935-8). Scholastic Inc.

Miller, Marvin, ed. You Be the Jury. Roper, Bob, illus. 80p. (Orig.). (gr. 4-6). 1987. pap. 2.50 (ISBN 0-590-40193-9). Scholastic Inc.

Miller, W. Wesley. Blain's Woods. Kratoville, Betty L., ed. Lucey, Jack, illus. 64p. (gr. 3-9). 1989. lib. bdg. 4.95 (ISBN 0-87879-618-5, High Noon Books). Acad Therapy.

—Connections, 5 novels. Kratoville, Betty L., ed. Heidinger, Herbert H., illus. 240p. (Orig.). (gr. 4-12). 1988. Set. pap. 15.00 (ISBN 0-87879-556-1, Pub. by High Noon Books). Acad Therapy.

—The Dark Secret. Kratoville, Betty L., ed. Lucey, Jack, illus. 64p. (gr. 3-9). 1989. lib. bdg. 4.95 (ISBN 0-87879-620-7, High Noon Books). Acad Therapy.

Mills. Secret Carousel. (ps-7). 1987. pap. 2.50 (ISBN 0-553-15499-0, Skylark). Bantam.

Mills, Adam. Mystery of Maguire's Farm. (gr. 3 up). 1988. pap. 2.95 (ISBN 0-318-37384-X). Ballantine.

Milne, Teddy. The Candy Puzzle: An Alexa Powell Mystery. LC 89-60248. 172p. (gr. 6-8). 1988. pap. 8.95 (ISBN 0-938875-16-7). Pittenbruach Pr.

Mini Mysteries Featuring Mickey Mouse & Friends. (Illus.). 24p. (ps-3). 1989. pap. write for info. (ISBN 0-307-11719-7, Pub. by Golden Bks). Western Pub.

Monjo, F. N. The Secret of the Sachem's Tree. Tomes, Margot, illus. 64p. (gr. 1-5). 1973. pap. 0.75 (ISBN 0-440-47634-8, Yearling). Dell.

Monsell, Mary E. Crackle Creek. McCord, Kathleen G., illus. LC 89-15105. 64p. (gr. 2-4). 1990. 12.95 (ISBN 0-689-31564-3, Atheneum Child Bk). Macmillan Child Grp.

—Mr. Pin: The Chocolate Files. Christelow, Eileen, illus. LC 89-78228. 64p. (gr. 2-5). 1990. 11.95 (ISBN 0-689-31639-9, Atheneum Child Bk). Macmillan Child Grp.

Montgomery, Raymond A. Mystery of the Maya. large type ed. Anderson, Richard, illus. 134p. (gr. 3-7). 1987. Repr. of 1977 ed. 8.95 (ISBN 0-942545-00-1); PLB 9.95 (ISBN 0-942545-06-0, Dist. by Grolier). Grey Castle.

Moore, Peggy S. The Case of the Missing Bike & Other Things. Adome, Afua, illus. 40p. (Orig.). (gr. 4-6). 1987. pap. 3.00 (ISBN 0-9613078-1-1). Detroit Black.

Moore, Ruth N. Danger in the Pines. LC 82-15770. 160p. (gr. 4-9). 1983. text ed. 7.95 (ISBN 0-8361-3313-7); pap. 4.95 (ISBN 0-8361-3314-5). Herald Pr.

—Mystery at Camp Ichthus. Gerig, Sibyl G., illus. LC 86-25637. 128p. (Orig.). (gr. 3-9). 1986. pap. 4.95 (ISBN 0-8361-3421-4). Herald Pr.

—Mystery at Indian Rocks. Bond, Magi, illus. LC 80-25803. 192p. (gr. 5-10). 1981. pap. 4.95 (ISBN 0-8361-1944-4). Herald Pr.

—Mystery at the Spanish Castle. 112p. (Orig.). (gr. 4-8). 1990. pap. 4.95 (ISBN 0-8361-3515-6). Herald Pr.

—Mystery of the Lost Heirloom. Converse, James, illus. LC 85-27334. 152p. (Orig.). (gr. 6-9). 1985. pap. 4.95 (ISBN 0-8361-3408-7). Herald Pr.

—Mystery of the Secret Code. Converse, James, illus. LC 85-5441. 128p. (Orig.). (gr. 7-9). 1985. pap. 4.95 (ISBN 0-8361-3394-3). Herald Pr.

Mooser, Stephen. The Case of the Slippery Sharks. Morrill, Leslie, illus. LC 87-3490. 96p. (gr. 3-6). 1988. PLB 9.89 (ISBN 0-8167-1177-1); pap. text ed. 2.95 (ISBN 0-8167-1178-X). Troll Assocs.

—Into the Unknown: Nine Astounding Stories. Stevenson, Dinah, ed. LC 79-3336. (Illus.). (gr. 5 up). 1980. (Lipp Jr Bks); PLB 9.89 (ISBN 0-397-31904-5). HarpC Child Bks.

—The Secret Gold Mine. Morrill, Leslie, illus. LC 87-16151. 96p. (gr. 3-6). 1987. PLB 9.89 (ISBN 0-8167-1179-8); pap. text ed. 2.95 (ISBN 0-8167-1180-1). Troll Assocs.

—Secret in the Old Mansion. Morrill, Leslie, illus. LC 87-15456. 96p. (gr. 3-6). 1987. PLB 9.89 (ISBN 0-8167-1175-5); pap. text ed. 2.95 (ISBN 0-8167-1176-3). Troll Assocs.

Mott, Michael. Master Entrick. (gr. 3-6). 1986. pap. 2.95 (ISBN 0-440-45818-8, YB). Dell.

Murphy, Elspeth C. Becky Garcia. Kenyon, Tony, illus. LC 86-8877. 108p. (gr. 3-5). 1986. pap. 3.95 (ISBN 1-55513-029-1). Cook.

—The Mystery of the Carousel Horse. LC 87-16722. (gr. 4-8). 1988. pap. 2.49 (ISBN 1-55513-163-8, Chariot Bks). Cook.

—The Mystery of the Double Trouble. LC 87-26461. 1988. pap. 2.49 (ISBN 1-55513-545-5, Chariot Bks). Cook.

—The Mystery of the Gravestone Riddle. LC 87-16721. 1988. pap. 2.49 (ISBN 1-55513-800-4, Chariot Bks). Cook.

—The Mystery of the Laughing Cat. LC 87-16719. 1988. pap. 2.49 (ISBN 1-55513-649-4, Chariot Bks). Cook.

—Mystery of the Messed-Up Wedding. LC 87-16720. 1988. pap. 2.49 (ISBN 1-55513-687-7, Chariot Bks). Cook.

—The Mystery of the Second Map. LC 87-24919. 1988. pap. 2.49 (ISBN 1-55513-526-9, Chariot Bks). Cook.

—The Mystery of the Silent Idol. LC 87-24285. 1988. pap. 2.49 (ISBN 1-55513-527-7, Chariot Bks). Cook.

—The Mystery of the Silver Dolphin. LC 87-24285. 1988. pap. 2.49 (ISBN 1-55513-515-3, Chariot Bks). Cook.

—Mystery of the Tattletale Parrot. LC 87-26460. 1988. pap. 2.49 (ISBN 1-55513-528-5, Chariot Bks). Cook.

—The Mystery of the Vanishing Present. LC 87-20852. 1988. pap. 2.49 (ISBN 1-55513-364-9, Chariot Bks). Cook.

Murrow, Liza K. Fire in the Heart. LC 88-45864. 264p. 1989. 14.95 (ISBN 0-8234-0750-0). Holiday.

The Mystery of the Railroad Bell. (gr. 4-6). 1990. 1.55 (ISBN 0-89636-115-2, JB 4B). Accent Bks.

The Mystery of the Singing Serpent. LC 80-18947. 160p. (gr. 4-7). 1985. pap. 2.95 (ISBN 0-394-86417-4). Random.

Mystery on the Island. (Illus.). (ps-5). 3.50 (ISBN 0-7214-0011-6); Series S05, Set 1. flash cards 4.75; Series S05, Set 2. flash cards 4.75. Ladybird Bks.

Naylor, Phyllis R. Bernie & the Bessledorf Ghost. LC 88-29389. 144p. (gr. 3-7). 1990. 12.95 (ISBN 0-689-31499-X, Atheneum Child Bk). Macmillan Child Grp.

—The Bodies in the Bessledorf Hotel. LC 86-3602. 144p. (gr. 3-7). 1986. 12.95 (ISBN 0-689-31304-7, Atheneum Child Bk). Macmillan Child Grp.

Nevfield, Len. Skystalker. Rivoche, Paul & Humphrey, Brian, illus. 128p. (Orig.). 1985. pap. 1.95 (ISBN 0-553-24894-4). Bantam.

Newman, Robert. Case of the Murdered Players. LC 85-7956. 224p. (gr. 4-6). 1985. 13.95 (ISBN 0-689-31155-9, Atheneum Child Bk). Macmillan Child Grp.

Nickell, Joe. The Magic Detectives: Join Them in Solving Strange Mysteries. (Illus.). 115p. (gr. 4-9). 1989. 8.95 (ISBN 0-87975-547-4). Prometheus Bks.

Nixon, Joan L. Candidate for Murder. 1991. 14.95 (ISBN 0-385-30257-6). Delacorte.

—The Dark & Deadly Pool. LC 87-6723. 192p. (gr. 7 up). 1987. 14.95 (ISBN 0-385-29585-5). Delacorte.

—The Easter Mystery. Fuhs, Pat, ed. Cummins, Jim, illus. LC 81-13011. 32p. (gr. 1-3). 1981. PLB 8.95 (ISBN 0-8075-1874-3). A Whitman.

—The Halloween Mystery. Pacini, Kathy, ed. Cummins, Jim, illus. LC 79-166. (gr. 1-3). 1979. PLB 8.95 (ISBN 0-8075-3136-7). A Whitman.

—The Happy Birthday Mystery. Ann, Fay, ed. Cummins, Jim, illus. LC 79-18362. (gr. 1-3). 1980. PLB 8.95 (ISBN 0-8075-3150-2). A Whitman.

—The House on Hackman's Hill. 128p. (Orig.). (gr. 4-6). 1986. pap. 2.50 (ISBN 0-590-33804-8, Apple Paperbacks). Scholastic Inc.

—The Kidnapping of Christina Lattimore. 196p. (gr. 7 up). 1980. pap. 3.25 (ISBN 0-440-94520-8, LFL). Dell.

—The New Year's Mystery. Pacini, Kathy, ed. Cummins, Jim, illus. LC 79-172. (gr. 1-3). 1979. PLB 8.95 (ISBN 0-8075-5592-4). A Whitman.

—The Other Side of Dark. 1987. pap. 3.25 (ISBN 0-440-96638-8, LFL). Dell.

—The Other Side of Dark. LC 85-46074. 144p. (gr. 7 up). 1986. 14.95 (ISBN 0-385-29481-6). Delacorte.

—The Seance. 160p. (gr. 7 up). 1981. pap. 2.95 (ISBN 0-440-97937-4, LE). Dell.

—Secret Silent Screams. (gr. k-8). 1990. pap. 3.25 (ISBN 0-440-20539-5, LFL). Dell.

—The Stalker. LC 84-16962. (gr. 7 up). 1985. 14.95 (ISBN 0-385-29376-3). Delacorte.

—The Thanksgiving Mystery. Fay, Ann, ed. Cummins, Jim, illus. LC 79-27346. (gr. 1-3). 1980. PLB 8.95 (ISBN 0-8075-7820-7). A Whitman.

—The Valentine Mystery. Tucker, Kathleen, ed. Cummins, Jim, illus. LC 79-7055. (gr. 1-3). 1979. PLB 8.95 (ISBN 0-8075-8450-9). A Whitman.

O'Brien, Robert C. The Silver Crown. LC 88-2837. 272p. (gr. 7 up). 1988. pap. 3.95 (ISBN 0-02-044651-9, Collier Young Ad). Macmillan Child Grp.

O'Connell, Jean S. The Dollhouse Caper. Blegvad, Erik, illus. LC 75-25501. 96p. (gr. 3-6). 1988. pap. 2.95 (ISBN 0-06-440236-3, Trophy). HarpC Child Bks.

O'Dell, Scott. Dark Canoe. LC 68-29334. (Illus.). 160p. (gr. 7 up). 1968. 13.95 (ISBN 0-395-06960-2). HM.

Okimoto, Jean D. Who Did It, Jenny Lake? 143p. (gr. 6-10). 1984. pap. 2.25 (ISBN 0-399-21104-7, Putnam). Putnam Pub Group.

Oliver, M. Search for the Sunken City. (Illus.). 48p. 1989. lib. bdg. 10.96 (ISBN 0-88110-409-4); pap. 4.50 (ISBN 0-7460-0304-8). EDC.

Oliver, M. & Waters, G. Agent Arthur's Puzzle Adventures. (Illus.). 1990. pap. 9.95 (ISBN 0-7460-0147-9). EDC.

Oram, Hiawyn. In the Attic. Kitamura, Satoshi, illus. LC 84-15570. (Orig.). (gr. k-3). 1988. pap. 4.95 (ISBN 0-8050-0780-6). H Holt & Co.

Oxenbury, Helen. Curious Creatures. Oxenbury, Helen, illus. LC 79-2980. 9p. (ps-3). 1985. 4.95 (ISBN 0-694-00033-7). HarpC Child Bks.

Packard, Edward. Who Killed Harlowe Thrombey, No. 9. large type ed. Granger, Paul, illus. 121p. (gr. 3-7). 1987. Repr. of 1981 ed. 8.95 (ISBN 0-942545-13-3); PLB 9.95 (ISBN 0-942545-18-4, Dist. by Grolier). Grey Castle.

Pageler, Elaine. Numero Uno Gang Mysteries, 5 novels. (Illus.). 240p. (Orig.). (gr. 4-12). 1988. Set. pap. 15.00 (ISBN 0-87879-550-2, Pub. by High Noon Books). Acad Therapy.

—Runaway Magic. Kratoville, Betty L., ed. Lucey, Jack, illus. 64p. (gr. 3-9). 1989. lib. bdg. 4.95 (ISBN 0-87879-652-5, High Noon Books). Acad Therapy.

Palazzo-Craig, Janet. Mystery of the Missing Wigs. Harvey, Paul, illus. LC 81-7615. 48p. (gr. 2-4). 1982. PLB 10.89 (ISBN 0-89375-592-3); pap. text ed. 2.95 (ISBN 0-89375-593-1). Troll Assocs.

Palmer, Bernard. Danny Orlis & the Angle Inlet Mystery. large type ed. Date not set. 2.95 (ISBN 0-8474-6100-9). Back to Bible.

—Danny Orlis & the Mystery at Smuggler's Point. large type ed. Date not set. 2.95 (ISBN 0-8474-6105-X). Back to Bible.

—Danny Orlis & the Mystery of the Wrecked Plane. large type ed. Date not set. 2.95 (ISBN 0-8474-6103-3). Back to Bible.

—Danny Orlis & the Point Barrow Mystery. large type ed. Date not set. 2.95 (ISBN 0-8474-6108-4). Back to Bible.

—Danny Orlis Resists the Witch Doctor. large type ed. Date not set. 2.95 (ISBN 0-8474-6104-1). Back to Bible.

Parish, Peggy. Hermit Dan. 160p. (gr. k-6). 1981. pap. 3.25 (ISBN 0-440-43501-3, YB). Dell.

Park, Barbara. Maxie, Rosie, & Earl--Partners in Grime. Strogart, Alexander, illus. LC 89-28027. 128p. (gr. 3-7). 1991. pap. 3.50 (ISBN 0-679-80643-1, Bullseye Bks). Knopf.

Pascal, Francine. The Case of the Secret Santa. (gr. k-3). 1990. pap. 2.95 (ISBN 0-553-15860-0). Bantam.

—Deadly Summer. 1989. pap. 2.95 (ISBN 0-553-28010-4). Bantam.

—Jessica's Christmas Carol. (gr. 4-6). 1989. pap. 3.50 (ISBN 0-553-15767-1). Bantam.

Paterson, Cynthia. The Foxwood Kidnap. Paterson, Brian, illus. 32p. (ps-3). 1986. 6.95 (ISBN 0-8120-5771-6). Barron.

Paterson, Katherine. The Sign of the Chrysanthemum. Landa, Peter, illus. LC 72-7553. (gr. 5-9). 1976. 13.95 (ISBN 0-690-73625-8, Crowell Jr Bks). HarpC Child Bks.

Patterson, Geoffrey. The Story of Hay. (Illus.). 32p. (gr. k-3). 1983. 10.95 (ISBN 0-233-97356-7). Andre Deutsch.

Paul, Paula. Sarah, Sissy Weed, & the Ships of the Desert. (Illus.). 112p. (gr. 5-6). 1985. 8.95 (ISBN 0-89015-504-6); pap. 4.95 (ISBN 0-89015-552-6). Eakin Pr.

Pearson, Susan. The Bogeyman Caper. Fiammenghi, Giola, illus. 80p. (gr. 1-3). 1990. PLB 11.95 (ISBN 0-671-70565-2); pap. 2.95 (ISBN 0-671-70569-5). S&S Trade.

—The Campfire Ghosts. Fiammenghi, Giola, illus. 96p. (gr. 1-3). 1990. PLB 11.95 (ISBN 0-671-70567-9); pap. 2.95 (ISBN 0-671-70571-7). S&S Trade.

—Eagle-Eye Ernie Comes to Town. Fiammenghi, Gioia, illus. 80p. (gr. 1-3). 1990. PLB 11.95 (ISBN 0-671-70564-4); pap. 2.95 (ISBN 0-671-70568-7). S&S Trade.

—The Tap Dance Mystery. Fiammenghi, Giola, illus. 96p. (gr. 1-3). 1990. PLB 11.95 (ISBN 0-671-70566-0); pap. 2.95 (ISBN 0-671-70570-9). S&S Trade.

Peck, Richard. Blossom Culp & the Sleep of Death. (gr. k-6). 1987. pap. 3.25 (ISBN 0-440-40676-5, YB). Dell.

—The Dreadful Future of Blossom Culp. (gr. k-6). 1987. pap. 3.25 (ISBN 0-440-42154-3, YB). Dell.

Peck, Robert N. A Day No Pigs Would Die. (gr. 7 up). 1972. 19.00 (ISBN 0-394-48235-2). Knopf.

Pelta, Kathy. The Parrot Man Mystery. Ritz, Karen, illus. 164p. (gr. 3-7). 1989. 14.95 (ISBN 0-8050-1130-7). H Holt & Co.

Perl, Lila. Blue Monday & Friday the Thirteenth: The Stories Behind the Days of the Week. Weihs, Erika, illus. LC 85-13051. (gr. 3-6). 1986. 12.95 (ISBN 0-89919-327-7, Pub. by Clarion). Ticknor & Fields.

Peters, Sharon. The Marching Band Mystery. Trivas, Irene, illus. LC 84-8783. 48p. (gr. 2-4). 1985. PLB 10.89 (ISBN 0-8167-0406-6); pap. text ed. 2.95 (ISBN 0-8167-0407-4). Troll Assocs.

Petersen, P. J. The Freshman Detective Blues. LC 87-5380. 192p. (gr. 4-6). 1987. 14.95 (ISBN 0-385-29586-3). Delacorte.

Phantom from the Past. (Illus.). (gr. 5 up). 1990. pap. 3.50. Ladybird Bks.

Pike, Christopher. Scavenger Hunt. (Orig.). (gr. 8 up). 1989. pap. 2.95 (ISBN 0-671-67656-3, Archway). PB.

—Slumber Party. LC 84-20238. 170p. (Orig.). (gr. 7 up). 1985. pap. 2.50 (ISBN 0-590-40927-1, Point). Scholastic Inc.

—Spellbound. 224p. (Orig.). (gr. 8 up). 1989. pap. 2.95 (ISBN 0-671-68793-X, Archway). PB.

Pilling, Ann. The Big Pink. LC 87-50988. 154p. (gr. 3-7). 1988. 11.95 (ISBN 0-670-81156-4). Viking Child Bks.

—Henry's Leg. Clifford, Rowan, illus. 160p. (gr. 4 up). 1990. pap. 3.95 (ISBN 0-14-032978-1, Puffin). Puffin Bks.

Pinkwater, Daniel. The Muffin Fiend. LC 85-10944. (Illus.). 48p. (gr. 3-7). 1986. 12.95 (ISBN 0-688-04274-0); PLB 12.88 (ISBN 0-688-04275-9). Lothrop.

Pinkwater, Jill. The Disappearance of Sister Perfect. LC 86-16676. (gr. 5-9). 1987. 13.95 (ISBN 0-525-44278-2, DCB). Dutton Child Bks.

Platt, Kin. Big Max. Lopshire, Robert, illus. LC 65-14488. 64p. (gr. k-3). 1965. PLB 11.89 (ISBN 0-06-024751-7). HarpC Child Bks.

—Big Max in the Mystery of the Missing Moose. Lopshire, Robert, illus. LC 76-58727. 64p. (gr. k-3). 1977. PLB 11.89 (ISBN 0-06-024757-6). HarpC Child Bks.

—Dracula, Go Home. Mayo, Frank, illus. 96p. (gr. 7 up). 1981. pap. 1.25 (ISBN 0-440-92022-1, LE). Dell.

—The Ghost of Hellsfire Street. LC 80-10446. 256p. (gr. 4-6). 1980. 12.95 (ISBN 0-385-28317-2). Delacorte.

Poe, Edgar Allan. The Gold-Bug. 80p. (gr. 6). 1990. 10.95s.p. (ISBN 0-88682-303-X); 15.65 (ISBN 0-685-28218-X). Creative Ed.

—The Purloined Letter. LC 86-4156. 48p. (gr. 9 up). 1986. PLB 10.95s.p. (ISBN 0-88682-061-8); PLB 15.65 (ISBN 0-685-12424-X). Creative Ed.

—Tales of Mystery & Imagination. (ps-6). 1989. pap. 4.87 (ISBN 0-582-54159-X, 74266). Longman.

—Tales of Mystery & Imagination, Retold by Henniker-Major. Owen, C., illus. (gr. 3 up). 1975. pap. text ed. 4.25x (ISBN 0-19-580511-9). Oxford U Pr.

—The Tell-Tale Heart. rev. ed. (gr. 9-12). 1989. Repr. of 1902 ed. multi-media kit 35.00 (ISBN 0-685-31131-7). Balance Pub.

—Ten Great Mysteries by Edgar Allan Poe. Conklin, Groff, ed. 218p. (gr. 7 up). 1968. pap. 2.25 (ISBN 0-590-08595-6, Schol Pap). Scholastic Inc.

Porte, Barbara A. Fat Fanny, Beanpole Bertha, & the Boys. Chambliss, Maxie, illus. LC 90-7686. 112p. (gr. 3-5). 1991. 14.95 (ISBN 0-531-05928-6); PLB 14.99 (ISBN 0-531-08528-7). Orchard Bks Watts.

Pryor, Bonnie. Mr. Z & the Time Clock. LC 85-25353. 120p. (gr. 4 up). 1986. lib. bdg. 9.95 (ISBN 0-87518-328-X, Dillon). Macmillan Child Grp.

—The Twenty-Four Hour Lipstick Mystery. Hamanaka, Sheila, illus. LC 89-34483. 128p. (gr. 3 up). 1989. 11.95 (ISBN 0-688-08198-3). Morrow Jr Bks.

Pryor, Bonnie & Baird, Anne. Belly Buttons. Bracken, Carolyn & Fernandes, Eugenie, illus. (ps). 1987. 3.95 (ISBN 0-671-63640-5, Little Simon). S&S Trade.

Pullman, Philip. Shadow in the North. LC 87-29846. 336p. (gr. 7 up). 1989. pap. 3.25 (ISBN 0-394-82599-3, Borzoi Sprinters). Knopf.

Quackenbush, Robert. Bicycle to Treachery. 48p. (gr. 1-5). 1991. pap. 2.95 (ISBN 0-671-73346-X, S&S BYR). S&S Trade.

—Cable Car to Catastrophe. Quackenbush, Robert, illus. 48p. (gr. 1-5). 1985. pap. 4.95 (ISBN 0-13-110032-7). P-H.

—Danger in Tibet: A Miss Mallard Mystery. Quackenbush, Robert, illus. 32p. (gr. 1-4). 1989. 14.95 (ISBN 0-945912-03-X). Pippin Pr.

—Dig to Disaster: A Miss Mallard Mystery. (Illus.). 48p. (gr. 1-5). 1982. 9.95 (ISBN 0-13-211870-X). P-H.

—Dogsled to Dread. LC 86-25394. (Illus.). 48p. (gr. 2-6). 1988. PLB 12.95 (ISBN 0-671-66518-9). S&S Trade.

—Express Train to Trouble: A Miss Mallard Mystery. (Illus.). (gr. 1-4). 1981. 9.95 (ISBN 0-13-298067-3). P-H.

—Gondola to Danger: A Miss Mallard Mystery. LC 83-9473. (Illus.). 48p. (gr. 2-4). 1983. 9.95 (ISBN 0-13-360180-3). P-H.

—Oh, What an Awful Mess: The Story of Charles Goodyear. (Illus.). 40p. (gr. k-3). 1983. pap. 3.95 (ISBN 0-13-633396-6, Pub. by Treehouse Bks). P-H.

—Rickshaw to Horror. LC 83-19083. (Illus.). 48p. 1984. 11.95 (ISBN 0-13-781014-8). P-H.

—Sherlock Chick & the Peekaboo Mystery. Quackenbush, Robert, illus. 48p. (gr. 3-7). 1990. pap. 2.95 (ISBN 0-448-04334-3, G&D). Putnam Pub Group.

—Sherlock Chick's First Case. Quackenbush, Robert, illus. LC 86-9398. 48p. (ps-3). 1986. 5.95 (ISBN 0-8193-1148-0). Parents.

—Stage Door to Terror. 48p. (gr. 1-5). 1991. pap. 2.95 (ISBN 0-671-73347-8, S&S BYR). S&S Trade.

—Stairway to Doom. LC 82-21484. (Illus.). 48p. (gr. 2-6). 1986. pap. 5.95 (ISBN 0-671-67053-0). S&S Trade.

—Surfboard to Peril: A Miss Mallard Mystery. Quackenbush, Robert, illus. 48p. (gr. 1-5). 1986. 11.95 (ISBN 0-13-877986-4). P-H.

—Taxi to Intrigue. 48p. (gr. 1-5). 1991. pap. 2.95 (ISBN 0-671-73345-1, S&S BYR). S&S Trade.

Radford, Ken. House in the Shadows. LC 87-45351. 184p. (gr. 4 up). 1987. 12.95 (ISBN 0-8234-0673-3). Holiday.

Raskin, Ellen. The Mysterious Disappearance of Leon: (I Mean Noel) (Illus.). 160p. (gr. 5-9). 1989. pap. 4.95 (ISBN 0-14-032945-5, Puffin). Puffin Bks.
—The Tatooed Potato & Other Clues. 176p. (gr. 5-9). 1989. pap. 3.95 (ISBN 0-14-032980-3, Puffin). Puffin Bks.
—Tattooed Potato & Other Clues. (gr. 4-7). 1975. 15.95 (ISBN 0-525-40805-3, 01451-440, DCB). Dutton Child Bks.
—The Westing Game. Raskin, Ellen, illus. 192p. (gr. 7 up). 1984. pap. 3.50 (ISBN 0-380-67991-4, Flare). Avon.
—The Westing Game. (gr. 5-9). 1978. 14.95 (ISBN 0-525-42320-6, DCB). Dutton Child Bks.
Rathjen, Carl H. Mystery at Smoke River. LC 68-23986. (gr. 6-10). 1968. PLB 6.70 (ISBN 0-8313-0083-3). Lantern.
Razzi, Jim. The Plant Monster. (Orig.). (gr. 1-3). 1987. pap. 2.50 (ISBN 0-671-62094-0, Minstrel Bks). PB.
Razzi, Jim & Razzi, Mary. The Search for King Pup's Tomb. 64p. (gr. 3). 1985. pap. 2.25 (ISBN 0-553-15312-9). Bantam.
—Sherluck Bones Mystery, No. 3. (gr. 2-4). 1987. pap. 2.25 (ISBN 0-553-15440-0, Skylark). Bantam.
—The Sherluck Bones Mystery-Detective Book, No. 6. 64p. (Orig.). (gr. 1-3). 1984. pap. text ed. 2.25 (ISBN 0-553-15412-5, Skylark). Bantam.
Razzi, Mary & Razzi, Jim. Sherluck Bones Mystery, No. 2. (gr. 2-4). 1987. pap. 1.95 (ISBN 0-685-19144-3, Skylark). Dell.
Reaves, Michael. Sword of the Samurai. Perry, Steve, illus. 144p. (gr. 4 up). 1984. pap. 2.75 (ISBN 0-553-26427-3). Bantam.
Repp, Gloria. Secret of the Golden Cowrie. (Illus.). 199p. (Orig.). (gr. 4-6). 1988. pap. 4.95 (ISBN 0-89084-459-3). Bob Jones Univ Pr.
The Return of Sherlock Holmes. (gr. 4 up). 1988. pap. 4.87 (ISBN 0-582-54155-7, 74262). Longman.
Robert, Adrian. The Awful Mess Mystery. Harvey, Paul, illus. LC 84-8724. 48p. (gr. 2-4). 1985. PLB 10.89 (ISBN 0-8167-0402-3); pap. text ed. 2.95 (ISBN 0-8167-0403-1). Troll Assocs.
—Ellen Ross, Private Detective. Garcia, T. R., illus. LC 84-8744. 48p. (gr. 2-4). 1985. PLB 10.89 (ISBN 0-8167-0414-7); pap. text ed. 2.95 (ISBN 0-8167-0415-5). Troll Assocs.
—Secret of the Haunted Chimney. Trivas, Irene, illus. LC 84-8763. 48p. (gr. 2-4). 1985. PLB 10.89 (ISBN 0-8167-0408-2); pap. text ed. 2.95 (ISBN 0-8167-0409-0). Troll Assocs.
—Secret of the Old Barn. Carter, Penny, illus. LC 84-8743. 48p. (gr. 2-4). 1985. PLB 10.89 (ISBN 0-8167-0412-0); pap. text ed. 2.95 (ISBN 0-8167-0413-9). Troll Assocs.
Roberts, Willo D. Dark Secrets. 1991. pap. 3.50 (ISBN 0-449-70395-9). Fawcett.
—Megan's Island. (gr. 4-7). 1990. pap. 3.95 (ISBN 0-689-71387-8, Aladdin). Macmillan Child Grp.
—The Minden Curse. (gr. 4-7). 1990. pap. 3.95 (ISBN 0-689-71378-9, Aladdin). Macmillan Child Grp.
—More Minden Curses. LC 90-31674. 240p. (gr. 3-7). 1990. pap. 3.95 (ISBN 0-689-71412-2, Aladdin). Macmillan Child Grp.
—The Pet-Sitting Peril. LC 89-77696. 176p. (gr. 3-7). 1990. pap. 3.95 (ISBN 0-689-71427-0, Aladdin). Macmillan Child Grp.
—Scared Stiff. LC 90-37732. 192p. (gr. 3-7). 1991. SBE 13.95 (ISBN 0-689-31692-5, Atheneum Child Bk). Macmillan Child Grp.
—To Grandmother's House We Go. LC 89-34972. 192p. (gr. 3-7). 1990. 13.95 (ISBN 0-689-31594-5, Atheneum Child Bk). Macmillan Child Grp.
—The View from the Cherry Tree. LC 75-6759. 192p. (gr. 5 up). 1975. 14.95 (ISBN 0-689-30483-8, Atheneum Child Bk). Macmillan Child Grp.
Robinson, Mary. The Amazing Valvano & the Mystery of the Hooded Rat. LC 87-26179. 168p. (gr. 3-7). 1988. 12.95 (ISBN 0-395-44314-8). HM.
—The Amazing Valvano & the Mystery of the Hooded Rat. 160p. (gr. 5). 1990. pap. 2.75 (ISBN 0-380-70713-6, Camelot). Avon.
Roddy, Lee. D J Dillon & the Mystery of the Black Hole Mine. 132p. (gr. 3-7). 1987. pap. 4.99 (ISBN 0-89693-320-2). Victor Bks.
Rosen, Michael. The Deadman Tapes. 160p. (gr. 7-9). 1989. pap. 7.95 (ISBN 0-233-98443-7, Pub. by A Deutsch England). Trafalgar Sq.
Ross, Harriet, compiled by. Great Mystery Stories. Bolle, Frank, illus. 160p. (gr. 3-9). pap. 10.95 (ISBN 0-87460-194-0). Lion Bks.
Rotsler, William. The A-Team, No. 1: Defense Against Terror. Barish, Wendy, ed. 128p. (Orig.). 1983. pap. 3.95 (ISBN 0-671-49608-5, Little Simon). S&S Trade.
Ruckman, Ivy. What's an Average Kid Like Me Doing Way up Here? 144p. (gr. k-6). 1984. pap. 2.75 (ISBN 0-440-49448-6, YB). Dell.
Ryan, Mary C. The Voice from the Mendelsohns Maple. Roman, Irena, illus. LC 89-31569. 132p. (gr. 5-7). 1990. 13.95 (ISBN 0-316-76360-8). Little.
Sabin, Fran & Sabin, Lou. The Great Santa Claus Mystery. Trivas, Irene, illus. LC 81-7530. 48p. (gr. 2-4). 1982. PLB 10.89 (ISBN 0-89375-602-4); pap. text ed. 2.95 (ISBN 0-89375-603-2). Troll Assocs.
—Mystery at the Jellybean Factory. Trivas, Irene, illus. LC 81-10388. 48p. (gr. 2-4). 1982. PLB 10.89 (ISBN 0-89375-600-8); pap. text ed. 2.95 (ISBN 0-89375-601-6); cassette 9.95 (ISBN 0-685-04950-7). Troll Assocs.
St. John, Patricia M. The Tanglewood's Secret. (gr. 5-8). 1951. pap. 4.50 (ISBN 0-8024-0007-8). Moody.
St. Laurent, Fred. The Heavy House. Soule, Jean, et al, eds. (Illus.). 250p. (Orig.). (gr. 8 up). 1987. pap. 4.95 perfect bdg (ISBN 0-938447-02-5). Rendezvous Pubns.
Sanborn, Laura & Sanborn, Jane. The Mystery of Horseshoe Mountain. Wallace, Joan, illus. 108p. (Orig.). (gr. 4-12). 1983. pap. 4.95x (ISBN 0-910715-01-7). Search Public.
Sanders, Scott R. Bad Man Ballad. LC 86-2695. 224p. (gr. 6-8). 1986. 14.95 (ISBN 0-02-778230-1, Bradbury Pr). Macmillan Child Grp.
Sands, AnnaMaria. Annie Wilkins Mystery Series, 5 novels. Heidinger, Herbert, illus. 240p. (Orig.). (gr. 4-12). 1988. Set. pap. 15.00 (ISBN 0-87879-571-5, Pub. by High Noon Books). Acad Therapy.
Santos, Elsie S. The Mystery at Shawme Pond. Alvaro, Albert M., ed. Santos, Duarte, illus. 20p. (Orig.). (ps-1). 1983. pap. 3.95 (ISBN 0-914151-01-0). Shawme Ent.
Saunders, Susan. The Creature from Miller's Pond. (Illus.). (gr. 4-8). 1983. pap. 2.25 (ISBN 0-553-15424-9). Bantam.
—Mystery Cat & the Monkey Business. 96p. (Orig.). 1986. pap. 2.25 (ISBN 0-553-15452-4). Bantam.
—The Mystery of the Hard Luck Rodeo. Rosales, Melodye, illus. LC 88-37896. 64p. (Orig.). (gr. 2-4). 1989. PLB 6.99 (ISBN 0-394-92344-8); pap. 1.95 (ISBN 0-394-82344-3). Random.
Savage, Cindy. Cave of the Living Skeletons. 124p. (Orig.). (gr. 5-8). 1989. pap. text ed. 1.25 (ISBN 0-87406-398-1). Willowisp Pr.
Schlee, Ann. The Vandal. large type ed. 296p. (gr. 5 up). 1988. lib. bdg. 16.95x (ISBN 0-7451-0658-7, Pub. by Chivers Pr UK). G K Hall.
Schoch, Tim. Flash Fry, Private Eye. 96p. (Orig.). (gr. 3-7). 1986. pap. 2.50 (ISBN 0-380-75108-9, Camelot). Avon.
Schultz, Irene. The Woodland Gang & the Dark Old House. (Illus.). 128p. (gr. 3 up). 1984. pap. 4.95 (ISBN 0-318-40971-2). Addison-Wesley.
—The Woodland Gang & the Dinosaur Bones. Cahoun, Cindy, illus. 128p. (gr. 3 up). 1988. pap. 4.95 (ISBN 0-201-50056-6). Addison-Wesley.
—The Woodland Gang & the Ghost Cat. Kahoun, Cindy, illus. 128p. (gr. 3 up) 1988. pap. 4.95 (ISBN 0-201-50054-X). Addison-Wesley.
—The Woodland Gang & the Indian Cave. Kahoun, Cindy, illus. 128p. (gr. 3 up). 1988. pap. 4.95 (ISBN 0-201-50055-8). Addison-Wesley.
—The Woodland Gang & the Museum Robbery. Kahoun, Cindy, illus. 128p. (Orig.). (gr. 3 up). 1988. pap. 4.95 (ISBN 0-201-50053-1). Addison-Wesley.
—The Woodland Gang & the Mystery Quilt. Kahoun, Cindy, illus. 128p. (gr. 3 up). 1988. pap. 4.95 (ISBN 0-201-50051-5). Addison-Wesley.
—The Woodland Gang & the Secret Spy Code. Cahoun, Cindy, illus. 128p. (Orig.). (gr. 3 up). 1988. pap. 4.95 (ISBN 0-201-50052-3). Addison-Wesley.
Schuyler, Royce. Jessie J: Red Rock Ranch Detective: A Literary Adventure for Gifted Students. Kester, Ellen S., ed. Turner, Joseph R., III, illus. 190p. (Orig.). (gr. 3-6). 1989. pap. 6.95 (ISBN 0-685-26280-4); tchr's. manual 35.00 (ISBN 0-685-26281-2). Pickwick Pubs.
Schwandt, Stephen. Guilt Trip. LC 89-15106. 192p. (gr. 7 up). 1990. 13.95 (ISBN 0-689-31557-0, Atheneum Child Bk). Macmillan Child Grp.
—The Last Goodie. LC 85-5641. 176p. (gr. 5 up). 1985. 11.95 (ISBN 0-8050-0550-1). H Holt & Co.
Schwartz, Alvin. In a Dark, Dark Room & Other Scary Stories. Zimmer, Dirk, illus. LC 83-47699. 64p. (gr. k-3). 1984. 11.95 (ISBN 0-06-025271-5); PLB 11.89 (ISBN 0-06-025274-X). HarpC Child Bks.
Scoppettone, Sandra. Playing Murder. LC 83-47707. 224p. (gr. 7 up). 1985. PLB 12.89 (ISBN 0-06-025284-7). HarpC Child Bks.
—Playing Murder. LC 83-47707. 224p. (gr. 7 up). 1987. pap. 2.75 (ISBN 0-06-447046-6, Trophy). HarpC Child Bks.
Scott, Bill. Many Kinds of Magic: Tales of Mystery, Myth & Enchantment. (gr. 4-7). 1990. 14.95 (ISBN 0-670-82971-4). Viking Child Bks.
Scott, Elaine. Choices. MacDonald, Patricia, ed. 192p. (gr. 7 up). 1990. pap. 2.95 (ISBN 0-671-70294-7, Archway). PB.
Scott, R. C. Blood Sport. (gr. 7 up). 1984. pap. 2.25 (ISBN 0-553-23866-3). Bantam.
Senn, Steve. The Double Disappearance of Walter Fozbek. new ed. 128p. (gr. 2-4). 1980. 9.95 (ISBN 0-8038-1571-9). Hastings.
Sharmat, Marjorie W. Mysteriously Yours, Maggie Marmelstein. Shecter, Ben, illus. LC 81-48656. 160p. (gr. 3-6). 1982. 12.95 (ISBN 0-06-025516-1). HarpC Child Bks.
—Mysteriously Yours, Maggie Marmelstein. Shecter, Ben, illus. LC 81-48656. 160p. (gr. 3-6). 1984. pap. 3.50 (ISBN 0-06-440145-6, Trophy). HarpC Child Bks.
—Nate the Great. Simont, Marc, illus. 64p. (gr. 1-3). 1972. PLB 6.99 (ISBN 0-698-30444-6, Coward). Putnam Pub Group.
—Nate the Great. 64p. (gr. 1-4). 1977. pap. 2.95 (ISBN 0-440-46126-X, YB). Dell.
—Nate the Great & the Boring Beach Bag. Simont, Marc, illus. 48p. (gr. 1-4). 1987. 11.95 (ISBN 0-698-20631-2, Coward). Putnam Pub Group.
—Nate the Great & the Fishy Prize. Simont, Marc, illus. 48p. (gr. 1-4). 1988. 10.95 (ISBN 0-698-20639-8, Coward). Putnam Pub Group.
—Nate the Great & the Halloween Hunt. (Illus.). 48p. (gr. 1-4). 1989. 11.95 (ISBN 0-698-20635-5, Coward). Putnam Pub Group.
—Nate the Great & the Lost List. Simont, Marc, illus. (gr. k-2). 1975. PLB 9.99 (ISBN 0-698-30593-0, Coward). Putnam Pub Group.
—Nate the Great & the Lost List. Simont, Marc, illus. 48p. 1981. pap. 2.50 (ISBN 0-440-46282-7, YB). Dell.
—Nate the Great & The Missing Key. Simont, Marc, illus. 48p. (gr. 7-10). 1981. PLB 6.99 (ISBN 0-698-30726-7, Coward). Putnam Pub Group.
—Nate the Great & the Missing Key. Simont, Marc, illus. 48p. (gr. 1-4). 1981. 10.95 (ISBN 0-698-20630-4, Coward). Putnam Pub Group.
—Nate the Great & the Phony Clue. Simont, Marc, illus. 48p. (gr. k-6). 1981. pap. 2.95 (ISBN 0-440-46300-9, YB). Dell.
—Nate the Great & the Phony Clue. Simont, Marc, illus. 48p. (gr. 1-4). 1988. 11.95 (ISBN 0-698-20638-X, Coward). Putnam Pub Group.
—Nate the Great & the Sticky Case. Simont, Marc, illus. (gr. k-6). 1981. pap. 2.95 (ISBN 0-440-46289-4). Dell.
—Nate the Great & the Sticky Case. Simont, Marc, illus. (gr. 1-4). 1987. 10.95 (ISBN 0-698-20629-0, Coward). Putnam Pub Group.
—Nate the Great Goes Down in the Dumps. Simont, Marc, illus. 48p. (gr. 1-4). 1989. 11.95 (ISBN 0-698-20636-3, Coward). Putnam Pub Group.
—Nate the Great Goes Undercover. 48p. 1978. pap. 2.95 (ISBN 0-440-46302-5, YB). Dell.
—Nate the Great Goes Undercover. Simont, Marc, illus. 48p. (gr. 1-4). 1989. 11.95 (ISBN 0-698-20643-6, Coward); PLB 9.99 (ISBN 0-698-30547-7, Coward). Putnam Pub Group.
Sharmat, Marjorie W. & Sharmat, Craig. Nate the Great & the Musical Note. Simont, Marc, illus. 48p. (gr. 1-4). 1990. 11.95 (ISBN 0-698-20645-2, Coward). Putnam Pub Group.
Shaw, Diana. Gone Hollywood: A Carter Colborn Mystery. (gr. 7 up). 1988. 12.95 (ISBN 0-316-78343-9, Joy St Bks). Little.
—Lessons in Fear: A Carter Colborn Mystery. (gr. 7 up). 1987. 12.95 (ISBN 0-316-78341-2, Joy St Bks). Little.
—What You Don't Know Can Hurt You, Vol. 1. 1990. 13.95 (ISBN 0-316-78344-7, Joy St Bks). Little.
Shaw, Murray, adapted by. The Adventures of Black Peter & The 'Gloria Scott, Vol. I. Overlie, George, illus. (gr. 4-6). 1990. PLB 9.95 (ISBN 0-87614-385-0). Carolrhoda Bks.
—The Adventures of the Cardboard Box & Scandal in Bohemia, Vol. II. Overlie, George, illus. (gr. 4-6). 1990. PLB 9.95 (ISBN 0-87614-386-9). Carolrhoda Bks.
—Adventures of the Copper Beeches & The Redheaded League, Vol. IV. Overlie, George, illus. (gr. 4-6). 1990. PLB 9.95 (ISBN 0-87614-388-5). Carolrhoda Bks.
—Adventures of the Six Napoleons & the Blue Carbuncle, Vol. III. Overlie, George, illus. (gr. 4-6). 1990. PLB 9.95 (ISBN 0-87614-387-7). Carolrhoda Bks.
Sheldon, Ann. The Crystal Trail. (Orig.). (gr. 3-6). 1988. pap. 2.75 (ISBN 0-671-64037-2, Minstrel Bks). PB.
—The Emperor's Pony. Barish, Wendy, ed. 192p. (Orig.). (gr. 3-8). 1983. pap. 3.95 (ISBN 0-671-47558-4, Little Simon). S&S Trade.
—The Glimmering Ghost. (Orig.). (gr. 3-6). 1989. pap. 2.75 (ISBN 0-671-64038-0, Minstrel Bks). PB.
—Linda Craig: Search for Scorpio. Barish, Wendy, ed. 160p. (Orig.). (gr. 3 up). 1984. pap. 3.95 (ISBN 0-671-53237-5, Little Simon). S&S Trade.
—Linda Craig: Secret of the Old Sleigh. Schneider, Meg, ed. 192p. (gr. 3-7). 1983. pap. 3.95 (ISBN 0-671-46459-0, Little Simon). S&S Trade.
—Linda Craig: The Clue on the Desert Trail. 192p. (gr. 3-7). 1981. (Little Simon); pap. 3.95 (ISBN 0-671-42652-4). S&S Trade.
—Linda Craig: The Ghost Town Treasure. 192p. (gr. 3-7). 1982. (Little Simon); pap. 2.75 (ISBN 0-671-44526-X). S&S Trade.
—Linda Craig: The Mystery in Mexico. rev. ed. 192p. (Orig.). (gr. 3-7). 1981. (Little Simon); pap. 3.95 (ISBN 0-671-42703-2). S&S Trade.
—Linda Craig: The Mystery of Horseshoe Canyon. 192p. (gr. 3-7). 1981. (Little Simon); pap. 3.95 (ISBN 0-671-42654-0). S&S Trade.
—Linda Craig: The Palomino Mystery. (gr. 3-7). 1981. (Little Simon); pap. 3.50 (ISBN 0-671-42650-8). S&S Trade.
—Linda Craig: The Secret of Rancho Del Sol. 192p. (gr. 3-7). 1981. (Little Simon); pap. 3.95 (ISBN 0-671-42648-6). S&S Trade.
—The Silver Stallion. (gr. 3-6). 1988. pap. 2.75 (ISBN 0-671-64036-4, Minstrel Bks). PB.
Shire, Ellen. The Mystery at Number Seven, Rue Petite. LC 77-79854. (ps-3). 1978. (Random Juv). Random.
Shura, Mary F. Don't Call Me Toad! (Illus.). 128p. (ps-8). 1987. 12.95 (ISBN 0-399-21706-1, Putnam). Putnam Pub Group.
—The Josie Gambit. 128p. (gr. 3-7). 1988. pap. 2.50 (ISBN 0-380-70497-8, Camelot). Avon.
—The Mystery at Wolf River. (gr. 3-7). 1989. pap. 2.50 (ISBN 0-590-42266-9, Apple Paperbacks). Scholastic Inc.

Siegel, Barbara & Siegel, Scott. Shockwaves, Vol. 4. 160p. (Orig.). (gr. 7 up). 1988. pap. 2.50 (ISBN 0-671-60682-4, Archway). PB.

Silsbee, Peter. Love among the Hiccups. LC 86-26883. 224p. (gr. 7 up). 1987. 13.95 (ISBN 0-02-782760-7, Bradbury Pr). Macmillan Child Grp.

Singer, Marilyn. The Case of the Cackling Car. Glasser, Judith, illus. LC 84-48333. 64p. (gr. 3-7). 1985. 10.95 (ISBN 0-06-025632-X). HarpC Child Bks.

—The Case of the Cackling Car: A Sam & Dave Mystery. Glasser, Judy, illus. LC 84-48333. 64p. (gr. 3-7). 1988. pap. 2.95 (ISBN 0-06-440243-6, Trophy). HarpC Child Bks.

—The Case of the Fixed Election: A Sam & Dave Mystery. Williams, Richard, illus. LC 88-21178. 80p. (gr. 3-7). 1989. 10.95 (ISBN 0-06-025844-6); PLB 10.89 (ISBN 0-06-025845-4). HarpC Child Bks.

—A Clue in Code. Glasser, Judith, illus. LC 84-48335. 64p. (gr. 3-7). 1985. PLB 10.89 (ISBN 0-06-025637-0). HarpC Child Bks.

—A Clue in Code: A Sam & Dave Mystery. Glasser, Judy, illus. LC 84-48335. 64p. (gr. 3-7). 1988. pap. 2.95 (ISBN 0-06-440244-4, Trophy). HarpC Child Bks.

—The Hoax on You: A Sam & Dave Mystery. Williams, Richard, illus. LC 88-22004. 64p. (gr. 3-7). 1989. 10.95 (ISBN 0-06-025850-0); PLB 10.89 (ISBN 0-06-025851-9). HarpC Child Bks.

—Leroy Is Missing. Glasser, Judy, illus. LC 83-48441. 64p. (gr. 3-7). 1984. PLB 10.89 (ISBN 0-06-025797-0). HarpC Child Bks.

—Where There's a Will, There's a Wag. Glass, Andrew, illus. LC 85-24837. 96p. (gr. 2-4). 1986. 11.95 (ISBN 0-03-005747-7). H Holt & Co.

Skulavik, Mary A. Bert. Kostrko, Zofia, illus. 32p. (ps-3). 1990. 13.95 (ISBN 0-8027-6962-4); lib. bdg. 14.85 (ISBN 0-8027-6963-2). Walker & Co.

Sleator, William. Into the Dream. Sanderson, Ruth, illus. LC 78-11825. 144p. (gr. 3-7). pap. 3.50 (ISBN 0-679-80348-3, Bullseye Bks). Knopf.

—Spirit House. 192p. (gr. 5 up). 1991. 13.95 (ISBN 0-525-44814-4, DCB). Dutton Child Bks.

Slote, Alfred. C.O.L.A.R. Kramer, Anthony, illus. LC 80-8723. 96p. (gr. 3-5). 1981. PLB 12.89 (ISBN 0-397-31937-1, Lipp Jr Bks). HarpC Child Bks.

Smaridge, Norah. The Mysteries in the Commune. (Illus.). 192p. (gr. 6-12). 1982. 10.95 (ISBN 0-396-08076-6, Putnam). Putnam Pub Group.

—The Mystery in the Old Mansions. Handville, Robert, illus. 176p. (gr. 6-9). 1981. 8.95 (ISBN 0-396-07980-6, Putnam). Putnam Pub Group.

Smith, Carole. Stealing Isn't Easy. Tucker, Kathleen, ed. LC 84-2388. (Illus.). 128p. (gr. 4-9). 1984. PLB 9.95 (ISBN 0-8075-7621-2). A Whitman.

—Who Burned the Hartley House? Levine, Abby, ed. Dickson, Glenn, illus. 128p. (gr. 3-9). 1985. 9.95 (ISBN 0-8075-8993-4). A Whitman.

Smith, Doris B. A Taste of Blackberries. Robinson, Charles, illus. LC 72-7558. 64p. (gr. 3-6). 1973. PLB 12.89 (ISBN 0-690-80512-8, Crowell Jr Bks). HarpC Child Bks.

Smith, T. H. Cry to the Night Wind. 168p. (gr. 5-9). 1986. pap. 11.95 (ISBN 0-670-80750-8). Viking Child Bks.

—Cry to the Night Wind. (gr. 5-9). 1988. pap. 4.95 (ISBN 0-14-031931-X, Puffin). Puffin Bks.

Snyder, Zilpha K. The Famous Stanley Kidnapping Case. (gr. 4-6). 1985. pap. 3.50 (ISBN 0-440-42485-2, YB). Dell.

—Janie's Private Eyes. (gr. 5-7). 1989. 14.95 (ISBN 0-440-50123-7). Delacorte.

—Janie's Private Eyes. (gr. k-6). 1990. pap. 3.50 (ISBN 0-440-40279-4, YB). Dell.

—The Truth About Stone Hollow. (gr. k-6). 1986. pap. 3.25 (ISBN 0-440-48846-X, YB). Dell.

—The Velvet Room. (gr. k-6). 1988. pap. 3.25 (ISBN 0-440-40042-2, YB). Dell.

—The Velvet Room. (gr. 4-6). 15.00 (ISBN 0-8446-6419-7). Peter Smith.

Sobol, Donald. Finds The Clues. (gr. 4-7). 1987. pap. 2.50 (ISBN 0-553-15570-9). Bantam.

Sobol, Donald J. The Amazing Power of Ashur Fine: A Fine Mystery. LC 86-12407. 144p. (gr. 5-9). 1986. 12.95 (ISBN 0-02-786270-4, Mcmillan Child Bk). Macmillan Child Grp.

—The Best of Encyclopedia Brown, 4 vols. Ohlsson, Ib & Shortall, Leonard, illus. (gr. 4-6). Boxed Set. pap. 7.80 (ISBN 0-590-00662-2, Apple Paperbacks). Scholastic Inc.

—Encyclopedia Brown & the Case of the Dead Eagles. Shortall, Leonard & Brandi, Lillian, illus. LC 75-15911. 96p. (gr. 3-5). 1979. 11.95 (ISBN 0-525-67220-6, Lodestar Bks). Dutton Child Bks.

—Encyclopedia Brown & the Case of the Dead Eagles. (gr. 4-6). 1977. pap. 2.25 (ISBN 0-590-41466-6, Apple Paperbacks). Scholastic Inc.

—Encyclopedia Brown & the Case of the Exploding Plumbing. Shortall, Leonard, illus. 80p. (gr. 4-6). 1984. pap. 2.25 (ISBN 0-590-40531-4, Apple Paperbacks). Scholastic Inc.

—Encyclopedia Brown & the Case of the Mysterious Handprints. Owens, Gail, illus. LC 85-8798. 96p. (gr. 3-7). 1985. 12.95 (ISBN 0-688-04626-6). Morrow Jr Bks.

—Encyclopedia Brown & the Case of the Midnight Visitor. Shortall, Leonard & Brandi, Lillian, illus. LC 77-22159. 96p. (gr. 3-5). 1979. 11.95 (ISBN 0-525-67221-4, Lodestar Bks). Dutton Child Bks.

—Encyclopedia Brown & the Case of the Secret Pitch. (gr. 4-8). 1978. pap. 2.25 (ISBN 0-553-15587-3, Skylark Bks). Bantam.

—Encyclopedia Brown & the Case of the Secret Pitch. Shortall, Leonard & Brandi, Lillian, illus. LC 65-199640. 96p. (gr. 3-5). 1979. 11.95 (ISBN 0-525-67202-8, Lodestar Bks). Dutton Child Bks.

—Encyclopedia Brown Boy Detective. (gr. 4-8). 1985. pap. 2.95 (ISBN 0-553-15724-8). Bantam.

—Encyclopedia Brown, Boy Detective. Shortall, Leonard & Brandi, Lillian, illus. LC 63-9632. 96p. (gr. 3-5). 1979. 11.95 (ISBN 0-525-67200-1, Lodestar Bks). Dutton Child Bks.

—Encyclopedia Brown Carries On. Ohlsson, Ib, illus. LC 79-6340. 80p. (gr. 3-7). 1984. 12.95 (ISBN 0-02-786190-2, Four Winds). Macmillan Child Grp.

—Encyclopedia Brown Carries On. 80p. (gr. 4-6). 1981. pap. 2.25 (ISBN 0-590-40530-6, Apple Paperbacks). Scholastic Inc.

—Encyclopedia Brown Carries On. (gr. 3-7). 1990. pap. 2.50 (ISBN 0-590-44109-4). Scholastic Inc.

—Encyclopedia Brown Finds the Clues. (gr. 4-8). 1982. pap. 2.95 (ISBN 0-553-15725-6). Bantam.

—Encyclopedia Brown Finds the Clues. Shortall, Leonard & Brandi, Lillian, illus. LC 66-10230. 96p. (gr. 3-5). 1979. 11.95 (ISBN 0-525-67204-4, Lodestar Bks). Dutton Child Bks.

—Encyclopedia Brown Gets His Man. Shortall, Leonard & Brandi, Lillian, illus. LC 67-24666. 96p. (gr. 3-5). 1979. 11.95 (ISBN 0-525-67206-0, Lodestar Bks). Dutton Child Bks.

—Encyclopedia Brown Gets His Man, No. 4. LC 67-24666. (gr. 4-8). 1982. pap. 2.50 (ISBN 0-553-15526-1, Skylark Bks). Bantam.

—Encyclopedia Brown Keeps the Peace. Shortall, Leonard & Brandi, Lillian, illus. LC 73-82912. 96p. (gr. 3-5). 1979. 11.95 (ISBN 0-525-67208-7, Lodestar Bks). Dutton Child Bks.

—Encyclopedia Brown Keeps the Peace, No. 6. 1982. pap. 2.95 (ISBN 0-553-15735-3, Skylark Bks). Bantam.

—Encyclopedia Brown Lends a Hand. Shortall, Leonard & Brandi, Lillian, illus. LC 74-10281. 96p. (gr. 3-5). 1979. 11.95 (ISBN 0-525-67218-4, Lodestar Bks). Dutton Child Bks.

—Encyclopedia Brown Saves the Day. Shortall, Leonard & Brandi, Lillian, illus. LC 71-117149. 96p. (gr. 3-5). 1979. 11.95 (ISBN 0-525-67210-9, Lodestar Bks). Dutton Child Bks.

—Encyclopedia Brown Saves the Day, No. 7. (gr. 4-8). 1982. pap. 2.50 (ISBN 0-553-15539-3, Skylark Bks). Bantam.

—Encyclopedia Brown Sets the Pace. Ohlsson, Ib, illus. LC 81-69511. 96p. (gr. 3-7). 1984. 12.95 (ISBN 0-02-786200-3, Four Winds). Macmillan Child Grp.

—Encyclopedia Brown Sets the Pace. 96p. (gr. 3-7). 1991. pap. 2.95 (ISBN 0-590-44577-4, Apple Paperbacks). Scholastic Inc.

—Encyclopedia Brown Shows the Way. Shortall, Leonard & Brandi, Shortall, illus. LC 72-2911. 96p. (gr. 3-5). 1979. 11.95 (ISBN 0-525-67216-8, Lodestar Bks). Dutton Child Bks.

—Encyclopedia Brown Shows the Way, No. 9. 96p. (gr. 3-6). 1982. pap. 2.75 (ISBN 0-553-15737-X). Bantam.

—Encyclopedia Brown Solves Them All. Shortall, Leonard & Brandi, Lillian, illus. LC 68-22746. 96p. (gr. 3-5). 1979. 11.95 (ISBN 0-525-67212-5, Lodestar Bks). Dutton Child Bks.

—Encyclopedia Brown Solves Them All. LC 68-22746. 96p. (gr. 4-6). 1977. pap. 2.25 (ISBN 0-590-40470-9, Apple Paperbacks). Scholastic Inc.

—Encyclopedia Brown Takes the Case. Shortall, Leonard & Brandi, Leonard, illus. LC 73-6443. 96p. (gr. 3-5). 1979. 11.95 (ISBN 0-525-66318-5, Lodestar Bks). Dutton Child Bks.

—Encyclopedia Brown Takes the Case, No. 10. (gr. 8-12). 1982. pap. 2.50 (ISBN 0-553-15528-8). Bantam.

—Encyclopedia Brown Tracks Them Down. Shortall, Leonard & Brandi, Lillian, illus. LC 77-160147. 96p. (gr. 3-5). 1979. 11.95 (ISBN 0-525-67214-1, Lodestar Bks). Dutton Child Bks.

—Encyclopedia Brown's Book of Wacky Crimes. LC 82-9683. (Illus.). 128p. (gr. 3-5). 1982. 12.95 (ISBN 0-525-66786-5, Lodestar Bks). Dutton Child Bks.

—Encyclopedia Brown's Book of Wacky Crimes. Enik, Ted, illus. 1983. pap. 2.25 (ISBN 0-553-15358-7). Bantam.

—Encyclopedia Brown's Book of Wacky Spies. Enik, Ted, illus. LC 83-17179. 128p. (gr. 3-7). 1984. 13.95 (ISBN 0-688-02744-X). Morrow Jr Bks.

—Encyclopedia Brown's Third Record Book of Weird & Wonderful Facts. Murdocca, Sal, illus. LC 85-11613. 144p. (gr. 3-7). 1985. 11.95 (ISBN 0-688-05705-5). Morrow Jr Bks.

—More Two-Minute Mysteries. 160p. (gr. 5-9). 1986. pap. 2.50 (ISBN 0-590-40129-7, Apple Paperbacks). Scholastic Inc.

—Still More Two-Minute Mysteries. 128p. (gr. 6 up). 1986. pap. 2.50 (ISBN 0-590-41137-3, Apple Paperbacks). Scholastic Inc.

—Still More Two Minute Mysteries. (gr. 4-7). 1986. pap. 2.75 (ISBN 0-590-44424-7). Scholastic Inc.

—Two-Minute Mysteries. 160p. (Orig.). (gr. 5-8). 1986. pap. 2.50 (ISBN 0-590-41292-2, Apple Paperbacks). Scholastic Inc.

—Two-Minute Mysteries. 160p. (Orig.). (gr. 6-8). 1986. pap. 2.75 (ISBN 0-590-42856-X). Scholastic Inc.

Sobol, Donald J. & Andrews, Glenn. Encyclopedia Brown Takes the Cake! Ohlsson, Ib, illus. 128p. (gr. 4-6). 1984. pap. 2.25 (ISBN 0-590-40220-X, Apple Paperbacks). Scholastic Inc.

—Encyclopedia Brown Takes the Cake! A Cook & Case Book. Ohlsson, Ib, illus. LC 82-84250. 128p. (gr. 3-7). 1984. 12.95 (ISBN 0-02-786210-0, Four Winds). Macmillan Child Grp.

Southall, Ivan. The Long Night Watch. LC 83-48702. 160p. (gr. 7 up). 1984. 11.95 (ISBN 0-374-34644-5). FS&G.

Spicer, Dorothy. Humming Top. LC 68-31176. (gr. 7-11). 1968. 18.95 (ISBN 0-87599-147-5). S G Phillips.

Spirn, Michele. What's in the Trunk? (ps-1). 1988. 8.49 (ISBN 0-87386-057-8); incl. cassette 16.99 (ISBN 0-685-25202-7); pap. 1.95 (ISBN 0-87386-053-5); pap. 9.95 incl. cassette (ISBN 0-685-25203-5). Jan Prods.

Stahl, Hilda. Elizabeth Gail & the Mystery at the Johnson Farm, No. 1. 128p. (gr. 5 up). 1988. 3.95 (ISBN 0-8423-0739-7). Tyndale.

—Elizabeth Gail & the Secret Box, No. 2. 128p. (gr. 5 up). 1988. 2.95 (ISBN 0-8423-0740-0). Tyndale.

—Elizabeth Gail & the Teddy Bear Mystery. (gr. 3-9). 1979. pap. 2.95 (ISBN 0-8423-0722-2). Tyndale.

—Elizabeth Gail & the Teddy Bear Mystery, No. 3. 128p. (gr. 5 up). 1988. 3.95 (ISBN 0-8423-0811-3). Tyndale.

—The Missing Newspaper Caper. LC 86-71178. 128p. (gr. 4-6). 1987. pap. 3.95 (ISBN 0-89636-221-3). Accent Bks.

—The Mystery at the Wheeler Place. LC 85-73456. 128p. (Orig.). (gr. 4-6). 1986. pap. 3.95 (ISBN 0-89636-203-5). Accent Bks.

—Teddy Jo & the Broken Locket Mystery. (gr. 3-9). 1986. pap. 2.95 (ISBN 0-8423-6968-6). Tyndale.

—Teddy Jo & the Missing Portrait. (gr. 3-9). 1986. pap. 2.95 (ISBN 0-8423-6969-4). Tyndale.

—Teddy Jo & the Strangers in the Pink House, No. 4. 128p. (gr. 4-7). 1990. pap. 3.95 (ISBN 0-8423-6976-7). Tyndale.

—Teddy Jo & the Yellow Room Mystery, No. 2. 128p. (gr. 4-7). 1990. pap. 3.95 (ISBN 0-8423-6974-0). Tyndale.

—Tim Avery's Secret. LC 85-70271. 128p. (gr. 4-6). 1986. pap. 3.95 (ISBN 0-89636-213-2). Accent Bks.

Stanley, George E. Codebreaker Kids. 112p. (gr. 3-7). 1987. pap. 2.95 (ISBN 0-380-75228-X, Camelot). Avon.

—The Codebreaker Kids Return. 128p. (gr. 3-7). 1989. pap. 2.50 (ISBN 0-380-75608-0, Camelot). Avon.

—The Italian Spaghetti Mystery. LC 86-20681. 112p. (gr. 3 up). 1987. pap. 2.50 (ISBN 0-380-75166-6, Camelot). Avon.

Star, Leonard & Drake, Stan. The Go Between. (Illus.). 48p. pap. 4.95 (ISBN 2-205-06574-2). Dargaud Pub.

Starr, Leonard & Drake, Stan. The Blood Tapes. (Illus.). 48p. pap. 4.95 (ISBN 2-205-06956-X). Dargaud Pub.

—The Million-Dollar Hit. (Illus.). 48p. pap. 4.95 (ISBN 2-205-06576-9). Dargaud Pub.

—One-Two-Three Die. (Illus.). 48p. pap. 4.95 (ISBN 2-205-06952-7). Dargaud Pub.

Steffens, J. & Carr, J. Mystery & Suspense. (gr. 7-12). 1983. 9.95 (ISBN 0-88160-096-2, LW 1006). Learning Wks.

Stegeman, Janet A. Last Seen on Hopper's Lane. 240p. (gr. 7 up). 1985. pap. 2.25 (ISBN 0-590-33108-6, Point). Scholastic Inc.

Steiner, Barbara. Oliver Dibbs to the Rescue! Christelow, Eileen, illus. 128p. 1988. pap. 2.50 (ISBN 0-685-19349-7, Camelot). Avon.

Stevenson, Drew. The Case of the Visiting Vampire. (Illus.). (gr. 3-6). 1988. pap. 2.50 (ISBN 0-671-65732-1, Minstrel Bks). PB.

Stevenson, Robert Louis. Dr. Jekyll & Mr. Hyde. (gr. 5 up). 1978. 6.95 (ISBN 0-448-41110-5, G&D). Putnam Pub Group.

—Dr. Jekyll & Mr. Hyde. new ed. Platt, Kin, ed. Redondo, Nestor, illus. LC 73-75457. 64p. (Orig.). (gr. 5-10). 1973. pap. 2.95 (ISBN 0-88301-096-8); student activity bk. 1.25 (ISBN 0-88301-176-X). Pendulum Pr.

—Dr. Jekyll & Mr. Hyde. McMullan, Kate, ed. Van Munching, Paul, illus. LC 83-15972. 94p. (gr. 5 up). 1984. lib. bdg. 4.99 (ISBN 0-394-96365-2, Random Juv); pap. 2.95 (ISBN 0-394-86365-8). Random.

—Kidnapped. 1991. pap. 2.50 (ISBN 0-8125-0473-9). Tor Bks.

Stine, Megan & Stine, H. William. The Case of the House of Horrors: A Find Your Fate Mystery. LC 86-60228. (Illus.). 128p. (gr. 4-8). 1986. lib. bdg. 4.99 (ISBN 0-394-98226-6, Random Juv). Random.

—The Case of the Weeping Coffin. Hulsey, John, illus. LC 84-63443. 128p. (gr. 4-7). 1985. (Random Juv); pap. 1.95 (ISBN 0-685-09734-X, BYR). Random.

—Long Shot, Bk. 10. LC 89-24355. 144p. (gr. 5 up). 1990. lib. bdg. 7.99 (ISBN 0-679-90526-X). Random.

—Murder to Go. LC 88-14693. 144p. (gr. 5 up). 1989. PLB 6.99 (ISBN 0-394-99980-0). Random.

—Murder to Go. LC 88-14693. 144p. (Orig.). (gr. 5 up). 1989. pap. 2.95 (ISBN 0-394-89980-6). Knopf.

—Murder to Go: Crimebusters, No. 2. reissue ed. LC 88-14693. 144p. (gr. 4-8). 1991. pap. 3.50 (ISBN 0-679-81381-0, Bullseye Bks). Knopf.

—Thriller Diller. LC 88-45881. (Illus.). 144p. (Orig.). (gr. 5 up). 1989. pap. 2.95 (ISBN 0-394-82936-0). Knopf.

Stine, R. L. Curtains. MacDonald, Patricia, ed. 160p. (Orig.). (gr. 7 up). 1990. pap. 2.95 (ISBN 0-671-69498-7, Archway). PB.

—Fear Street: Ski Weekend. MacDonald, Patricia, ed. 160p. 1991. pap. 2.95 (ISBN 0-671-72480-0, Archway). PB.

Stine, R, L. Fear Street the Overnight (R) 1989. pap. 2.95 (ISBN 0-671-73207-2, ARCHWAY). S&S Trade.

Stine, R. L. Missing. 224p. (gr. 6-9). 1990. pap. 2.95 (ISBN 0-671-69410-3, Archway). PB.

—The Sleepwalker. 160p. (Orig.). (gr. 6-9). 1990. pap. 2.95 (ISBN 0-671-69412-X, Archway). PB.

—The Stepsister. MacDonald, Patricia, ed. 176p. (Orig.). (gr. 7 up). 1990. pap. 2.95 (ISBN 0-671-70244-0, Archway). PB.

Stone, G. H. Fatal Error. LC 90-52580. 144p. (gr. 5 up). 1991. lib. bdg. 7.99 (ISBN 0-679-90587-1). Random.

—Fatal Error. LC 89-43717. 144p. (Orig.). (gr. 5 up). 1990. pap. 2.95 (ISBN 0-679-80587-7, Borzoi Sprinters). Knopf.

—Reel Trouble. LC 89-2691. 144p. (Orig.). (gr. 5 up). 1989. pap. 2.95 (ISBN 0-394-84350-9, Borzoi Sprinters). Knopf.

—Reel Trouble. LC 89-3852. 144p. (gr. 5 up). 1990. lib. bdg. 6.99 (ISBN 0-394-94350-3). Random.

—Rough Stuff. LC 88-26689. 144p. (gr. 5 up). 1989. PLB 6.99 (ISBN 0-394-90178-9). Random.

Stover, Marjorie F. When the Dolls Woke. Loccisano, Karen, illus. 144p. (gr. 4-6). 1987. pap. 2.50 (ISBN 0-590-40419-9, Apple Paperbacks). Scholastic Inc.

Striker, Susan. The Mystery-Anti-Coloring Book. (Illus.). 96p. (Orig.). (gr. 1 up). 1991. pap. 5.95 (ISBN 0-8050-1600-7). H Holt & Co.

Sullivan, Eleanor & Manson, Cynthia, eds. Tales from Ellery Queen's Mystery Magazine: Short Stories for Young Adults. Nixon, Joan L., intro. by. LC 86-7634. 256p. (gr. 7 up). 1986. 13.95 (ISBN 0-15-284205-5, HJ). HarBraceJ.

Super Beach Mystery. 176p. (gr. 3-7). 1991. pap. 2.95 (ISBN 0-590-43923-5). Scholastic Inc.

Supraner, Robyn. Case of the Missing Canary. new ed. Stillerman, Robbie, illus. LC 78-60122. 48p. (gr. 2-4). 1979. PLB 10.89 (ISBN 0-89375-087-5); pap. 2.95 (ISBN 0-89375-075-1). Troll Assocs.

—Case of the Missing Rattles. Goodman, Joan E., illus. LC 81-10378. 48p. (gr. 2-4). 1982. PLB 10.89 (ISBN 0-89375-590-7); pap. text ed. 2.95 (ISBN 0-89375-591-5). Troll Assocs.

—Mystery at the Zoo. new ed. Dodson, Bert, illus. LC 78-60126. (gr. 2-4). 1979. PLB 10.89 (ISBN 0-89375-091-3); pap. 2.95 (ISBN 0-89375-079-4). Troll Assocs.

—Mystery of the Lost Ring (with Two Hearts) Winborn, Marsha, illus. LC 81-7520. 48p. (gr. 2-4). 1982. PLB 10.89 (ISBN 0-89375-596-6); pap. text ed. 2.95 (ISBN 0-89375-597-4); cassette 9.95 (ISBN 0-685-04951-5). Troll Assocs.

—Mystery of the Witch's Shoes. new ed. Apple, Margot, illus. LC 78-60125. 48p. (gr. 2-4). 1979. PLB 10.89 (ISBN 0-89375-090-5); pap. 2.95 (ISBN 0-89375-078-6). Troll Assocs.

Suter, Joanne. Hidden Bay. 116p. (Orig.). (gr. 3-8). 1986. pap. text ed. 3.15 (ISBN 0-88120-742-X, 742). SRA.

Svedberg, Ulf. Nicky the Nature Detective. Anderson, Lena, illus. Selberg, Ingrid, tr. (Illus.). 52p. (gr. 5 up). 1988. 12.95 (ISBN 9-12-958786-7, R & S Bks). FS&G.

Swift, Carolyn. Bugsy Goes to Limerick. 170p. 1990. pap. 6.95 (ISBN 1-85371-014-8, Pub. by Poolbeg Press Ltd., Eire). Dufour.

Swinford, Betty. Mystery at Pier Fourteen. LC 87-82753. (Illus.). 144p. (gr. 7-11). 1988. 3.50 (ISBN 0-88243-654-6, 02-0654). Gospel Pub.

Tallent, Mary M. The Secret at Robert's Roost. 168p. (Orig.). (gr. 4-8). 1988. pap. 3.95 (ISBN 0-941711-05-6). Wyrick & Co.

Tate, Eleanora E. The Secret of Gumbo Grove. LC 86-26742. (Illus.). 256p. (gr. 7-12). 1987. 12.95 (ISBN 0-531-15051-8); lib. bdg. 12.90 (ISBN 0-531-10298-X). Watts.

—The Secret of Gumbo Grove. (Orig.). (gr. 7 up). 1988. pap. 3.50 (ISBN 0-553-27226-8, Pub. by Starfire). Bantam.

Taylor, John R. Hairline Cracks. 128p. (gr. 5-9). 1990. 14.95 (ISBN 0-525-67304-0, Lodestar Bks). Dutton Child Bks.

Taylor, Theodore. Teetoncey. Cuffari, Richard, illus. (gr. 3-7). 1991. pap. 3.50 (ISBN 0-380-71024-2, 52118-0). Avon.

Thompson, Julian F. Discontinued. 304p. (gr. 7 up). 1986. pap. 2.75 (ISBN 0-590-40116-5, Point). Scholastic Inc.

—Discontinued. 304p. (gr. 7 up). 1986. 12.95 (ISBN 0-590-33321-6); pap. 3.50 (ISBN 0-590-42464-5). Scholastic Inc.

Three Adventures of Sherlock Holmes. (gr. 4 up). 1988. pap. 4.87 (ISBN 0-582-52286-2, 73814). Longman.

Tintin et la Mystere de la Toison d'Or. (gr. 7-9). 15.95 (ISBN 0-685-33970-X). French & Eur.

Titus, Eve. Basil & the Lost Colony. (Illus.). (gr. 3-6). 1989. pap. 2.50 (ISBN 0-671-64120-4, Minstrel Bks). PB.

—Basil & the Pygmy Cats: A Basil of Baker Street Mystery. (Illus.). (gr. 3-6). 1989. pap. 2.75 (ISBN 0-671-64119-0, Minstrel Bks). PB.

—Basil in Mexico: A Basil of Baker Street Mystery. Galdone, Paul, illus. 96p. (gr. 3-6). 1990. pap. 2.75 (ISBN 0-671-64117-4, Minstrel Bks). PB.

Titus, Eve & Galdone, Paul. Basil of Baker Street. (gr. 3-6). 1958. PLB 8.95 (ISBN 0-07-064907-3). McGraw.

Topper, Frank. Mystery at the Bike Race. Rogers, Jackie, illus. LC 84-16452. 128p. (gr. 3-7). 1985. lib. bdg. 9.49 (ISBN 0-8167-0454-6); pap. text ed. 2.95 (ISBN 0-8167-0455-4). Troll Assocs.

Townsend, John R. The Hidden Treasure. 176p. (gr. 3-7). 1988. pap. 2.50 (ISBN 0-590-41840-8, Apple Paperbacks). Scholastic Inc.

Travis, Falcon. Super Sleuth: Mini-Mysteries for You to Solve. LC 84-26814. (Illus.). 128p. (gr. 5 up). 1985. 12.95 (ISBN 0-8069-4700-4). Sterling.

—Super Sleuth: Mini-Mysteries for You to Solve. LC 84-26814. (Illus.). 128p. (gr. 3 up). 1987. pap. 4.95 (ISBN 0-8069-6490-1). Sterling.

Trease, Geoffrey. A Flight of Angels. 120p. (gr. 4-8). 1989. PLB 9.95 (ISBN 0-8225-0731-5). Lerner Pubns.

Treat, Lawrence. You're the Detective! Twenty-Four Solve-Them-Yourself Picture Mysteries. Borowik, Kathleen, illus. LC 82-49346. 80p. (Orig.). (gr. 3-6). 1983. pap. 7.95 (ISBN 0-87923-478-4). Godine.

The Triple Hoax. 192p. 1989. pap. 3.50 (ISBN 0-671-69153-8, Minstrel Bks). PB.

Twain, Mark. Tom Sawyer, Abroad & Tom Sawyer, Detective. Busch, Frederick, afterword by. 224p. (ps-8). 1985. pap. 1.95 (ISBN 0-451-51961-2, Sig Classics). NAL-Dutton.

Uchida, Yoshiko. The Best Bad Thing. LC 83-2833. 132p. (gr. 4-7). 1983. 12.95 (ISBN 0-689-50290-7, M K McElderry). Macmillan Child Grp.

Ure, Jean. One Green Leaf. (gr. 7 up). 1989. 14.95 (ISBN 0-385-29751-3). Delacorte.

Utz. The Houndstooth Check. LC 79-190268. (Illus.). 32p. (gr. 2-3). 1972. PLB 9.95 (ISBN 0-87783-057-6); pap. 3.94 deluxe ed. (ISBN 0-87783-095-9). Oddo.

Valin, Jonathan. Fire Lake. 1989. pap. 3.50 (ISBN 0-440-20145-4). Dell.

Van Allsburg, Chris. The Mysteries of Harris Burdick. LC 84-9006. (Illus.). 32p. (gr. 5 up). 1984. 15.95 (ISBN 0-395-35393-9). HM.

—The Stranger. Van Allsburg, Chris, illus. LC 86-15235. 32p. (gr. 2-4). 1986. 16.95 (ISBN 0-395-42331-7). HM.

Vandersteen, Willy. The Zincshrinker. Lahey, Nicholas J., tr. from FLE. LC 76-49379. (Illus., Orig.). (gr. 3-8). 1977. pap. 2.50 (ISBN 0-915560-03-8, 03). Hiddigeigei.

Van Hook, Beverly. Supergranny, No. 1: The Mystery of the Shrunken Heads. Wayson, Catherine, illus. 96p. (gr. 3-7). 1985. lib. bdg. 7.95 (ISBN 0-916761-11-8); pap. 2.95 (ISBN 0-916761-10-X). Holderby & Bierce.

—Supergranny, No. 2: The Case of the Riverboat Riverbelle. Wayson, Catherine, illus. 112p. (gr. 3-7). 1986. lib. bdg. 7.95 (ISBN 0-916761-09-6); pap. 2.95 (ISBN 0-916761-08-8). Holderby & Bierce.

—Supergranny, No. 3: The Ghost of Heidelberg Castle. Wayson, Catherine, illus. 112p. (gr. 3-7). 1987. lib. bdg. 7.95 (ISBN 0-916761-07-X); pap. 2.95 (ISBN 0-916761-06-1). Holderby & Bierce.

—Supergranny, No. 5: Character Who Came to Life. Nelken, Andrea, ed. Wayson, Catherine, illus. 112p. (Orig.). (gr. 3-6). 1989. lib. bdg. 7.95 (ISBN 0-916761-13-4); pap. 2.95 (ISBN 0-916761-12-6). Holderby & Bierce.

—Supergranny: Secret of Devil Mountain. Nelken, Andrea, ed. Wayson, Catherine, illus. 112p. (Orig.). (gr. 3-6). 1988. lib. bdg. 7.95 (ISBN 0-916761-05-3); pap. 2.95 (ISBN 0-916761-04-5). Holderby & Bierce.

—**Supergranny 6: The Great College Caper. Nelken, Andrea, ed. Wayson, Catherine, illus. 112p. (gr. 3-6). 1991. pap. 2.95 (ISBN 0-916761-14-2); 8.95 (ISBN 0-916761-15-0). Holderby & Bierce.**
SUPERGRANNY 6: The Great College Caper. 112 p. $8.95 (ISBN 0-916761-15-0). $2.95 pap. (ISBN 0-916761-14-2). 1991. Ages 8-12. Holderby & Bierce. Six books in children's mystery series about a gray-haired detective who drives a red Ferrari & fights crime. "Characters are original, the mystery intriguing & the pace fast & furious in SUPERGRANNY 2,"--SLJ, May, 1987. "SUPERGRANNY 3 is fast-paced & entertaining as it works in bits of historical information,"--SLJ, MAY, 1988. "Mystery aficionados fascinated with the way she can spin a tale,"-- John Turner, College English Instructor, DES MOINES REGISTER, Mar. 3, 1991. "Supergranny teaches intergenerational understanding,"--LIFE TIMES, published by Blue Cross/Blue Shield. Author Beverly Van Hook, former Illinois Arts Council Artist in

Education. Received Iowa Newspaper Association First Place Award, The Isabel Award for the Arts, The Corneila Meigs Award for Children's Literature. Other Supergranny Titles, 112 p: Mystery of the Shrunken Heads. (ISBN 0-916761-11-8) pap. *Publisher Provided Annotation.*

Vivelo, Jackie. Super Sleuth & the Bare Bones: Super Sleuth III. 112p. (gr. 4-7). 1988. 12.95 (ISBN 0-399-21536-0, Putnam). Putnam Pub Group.

—Supersleuth: Twelve Solve-It-Yourself Mysteries. LC 84-22297. 64p. (gr. 3-8). 10.95 (ISBN 0-399-21220-5, Putnam). Putnam Pub Group.

Voigt, Cynthia. The Callender Papers. LC 82-13797. 224p. (gr. 4-8). 1983. 14.95 (ISBN 0-689-30971-6, Atheneum Child Bk). Macmillan Child Grp.

—The Callender Papers. (gr. 6 up). 1985. pap. 3.50 (ISBN 0-449-70184-0, Juniper). Fawcett.

—Come a Stranger. LC 86-3610. 208p. (gr. 6 up). 1986. 14.95 (ISBN 0-689-31289-X, Atheneum Child Bk). Macmillan Child Grp.

Wallace, Barbara B. The Barrel in the Basement. Wooding, Sharon L., illus. LC 84-21521. 144p. (gr. 4-6). 1985. 11.95 (ISBN 0-689-31105-2, Atheneum Child Bk). Macmillan Child Grp.

Wallace, Bill. Trapped in Death Cave. LC 83-48962. 176p. (gr. 4-7). 1984. 13.95 (ISBN 0-8234-0516-8). Holiday.

Wallace, Pamela. Partners in Crime. 1990. pap. 4.50 (ISBN 0-553-28472-X). Bantam.

Walter, Mildred P. Mariah Loves Rock. (gr. 3-9). 1989. pap. 2.95 (ISBN 0-8167-1838-5). Troll Assocs.

Wandelmaier, Roy. The Great Rock 'n' Roll Mystery. Burns, Raymond, illus. LC 84-8753. 48p. (gr. 2-4). 1985. PLB 10.89 (ISBN 0-8167-0416-3); pap. text ed. 2.95 (ISBN 0-8167-0417-1). Troll Assocs.

Warhola, James, illus. The Pumpkinville Mystery. LC 87-2533. 32p. (gr. 1-4). 1987. PLB 10.95 (ISBN 0-671-66905-2); pap. 5.95 (ISBN 0-671-66906-0). S&S Trade.

Warner, Gertrude C. Benny Uncovers a Mystery. (gr. 3-8). 1991. pap. 3.50 (ISBN 0-8075-0645-1). A Whitman.

—Bicycle Mystery. Cunningham, David, illus. LC 79-126428. 128p. (gr. 3-7). 1970. PLB 9.95 (ISBN 0-8075-0708-3). A Whitman.

—Bicycle Mystery. (gr. 3-8). 1990. pap. 3.50 (ISBN 0-8075-0709-1). A Whitman.

—Blue Bay Mystery. LC 61-15230. (Illus.). (gr. 3-7). PLB 9.95 (ISBN 0-8075-0793-8). A Whitman.

—Blue Bay Mystery. 1990. pap. 3.50 (ISBN 0-8075-0794-6). A Whitman.

—The Boxcar Children Mysteries, 4 titles. 1990. Set. pap. 14.00 boxed (ISBN 0-8075-0854-3). A Whitman.

—Bus Station Mystery. Cunningham, David, illus. LC 74-8293. 128p. (gr. 3-8). 1974. PLB 9.95 (ISBN 0-8075-0975-2). A Whitman.

—Bus Station Mystery. (gr. 3-8). 1991. pap. 3.50 (ISBN 0-8075-0976-0). A Whitman.

—Caboose Mystery. LC 66-10791. (Illus.). 128p. (gr. 3-7). 1966. PLB 9.95 (ISBN 0-8075-1008-4). A Whitman.

—Caboose Mystery. (gr. 3-8). 1990. pap. 3.50 (ISBN 0-8075-1009-2). A Whitman.

—Houseboat Mystery. Cunningham, David, illus. LC 67-26521. 128p. (gr. 3-8). 1967. PLB 9.95 (ISBN 0-8075-3412-9). A Whitman.

—Houseboat Mystery. (gr. 3-8). 1990. pap. 3.50 (ISBN 0-8075-3413-7). A Whitman.

—Lighthouse Mystery. Cunningham, David, illus. LC 63-20354. 128p. (gr. 3-7). 1990. PLB 9.95 (ISBN 0-8075-4545-7); pap. 3.50 (ISBN 0-8075-4546-5). A Whitman.

—Mike's Mystery. LC 60-8428. (Illus.). 128p. (gr. 3-7). 1960. PLB 9.95 (ISBN 0-8075-5140-6). A Whitman.

—Mike's Mystery. 1990. pap. 3.50 (ISBN 0-8075-5141-4). A Whitman.

—Mountain Top Mystery. Cunningham, David, illus. LC 64-7722. 128p. (gr. 3-7). 1990. PLB 9.95 (ISBN 0-8075-5292-5); pap. 3.50 (ISBN 0-8075-5293-3). A Whitman.

—Mystery Behind the Wall. Cunningham, David, illus. LC 72-13356. 128p. (gr. 3-7). 1973. PLB 9.95 (ISBN 0-8075-5364-6). A Whitman.

—Mystery Behind the Wall. (gr. 3-8). 1991. pap. 3.50 (ISBN 0-8075-5367-0). A Whitman.

—Mystery in the Sand. Cunningham, David, illus. LC 70-165823. 128p. (gr. 3-7). 1971. PLB 9.95 (ISBN 0-8075-5373-5). A Whitman.

—Mystery in the Sand. (gr. 3-8). 1990. pap. 3.50 (ISBN 0-8075-5372-7). A Whitman.

—Mystery Ranch. Gringhuis, Dirk, illus. LC 58-9953. 128p. (gr. 3-7). 1989. PLB 9.95 (ISBN 0-8075-5390-5); pap. 3.50 (ISBN 0-8075-5391-3). A Whitman.

—Schoolhouse Mystery. Cunningham, David, illus. LC 65-23889. 128p. (gr. 3-7). 1990. PLB 9.95 (ISBN 0-8075-7262-4); pap. 3.50 (ISBN 0-8075-7263-2). A Whitman.

—Snowbound Mystery. Cunningham, David, illus. LC 68-9124. (gr. 3-7). 1990. PLB 9.95 (ISBN 0-8075-7517-8); pap. 3.50 (ISBN 0-8075-7516-X). A Whitman.

—Surprise Island. Gehr, Mary, illus. LC 49-49618. (gr. 3-7). 1989. PLB 9.95 (ISBN 0-8075-7673-5); pap. 3.50 (ISBN 0-8075-7674-3). A Whitman.
—Tree House Mystery. Cunningham, David, illus. LC 77-91744. 128p. (gr. 3-7). 1969. PLB 9.95 (ISBN 0-8075-8086-4). A Whitman.
—Tree House Mystery. (gr. 4-7). 1990. pap. 3.50 (ISBN 0-8075-8087-2). A Whitman.
—Woodshed Mystery. LC 62-19726. (Illus.). 128p. (gr. 3-7). 1990. PLB 9.95 (ISBN 0-8075-9206-4); pap. 3.50 (ISBN 0-8075-9207-2). A Whitman.
—The Woodshed Mystery. (gr. 2-6). 1990. pap. 3.50 (ISBN 0-685-34874-1). A Whitman.
—Yellow House Mystery. LC 53-13243. (Illus.). 128p. (gr. 3-7). PLB 9.95 (ISBN 0-8075-9365-6). A Whitman.
—The Yellow House Mystery. (gr. 2-7). 1989. pap. 3.50 (ISBN 0-8075-9366-4). A Whitman.
Warren, Mary P. The Haunted Kitchen. LC 75-31941. (Illus.). 124p. (gr. 4-6). 1976. 6.95 (ISBN 0-664-32584-X, Westminster). Westminster John Knox.
Warren, William E. Footsteps in the Fog. Frascino, Edward, illus. 112p. (gr. 3-7). 1985. 11.95 (ISBN 0-13-324807-0). P-H.
Waters, G. Agent Arthur on the Stormy Seas. (Illus.). 48p. 1990. lib. bdg. 10.96 (ISBN 0-88110-407-8); pap. 4.50 (ISBN 0-7460-0143-6). EDC.
Wathen, Judy. The Hide & Seek Mystery. Hartelius, Margaret A., illus. 24p. (Orig.). (ps-2). 1985. pap. 2.95 (ISBN 0-590-33428-X). Scholastic Inc.
Weinberg, Larry. The Curse. (gr. 7 up). 1984. pap. 2.50 (ISBN 0-553-26549-0). Bantam.
Wells, Rosemary. The Man in the Woods. 192p. (gr. 6 up). 1984. 12.95 (ISBN 0-8037-0071-7). Dial Bks Young.
—The Man in the Woods. 232p. (gr. 7up). 1985. pap. 2.75 (ISBN 0-590-41114-4, Point). Scholastic Inc.
—The Man in the Woods. 232p. (gr. 7 up). 1991. pap. 2.95 (ISBN 0-590-43826-3). Scholastic Inc.
—Through the Hidden Door. LC 86-24273. 256p. (gr. 5 up). 1987. 14.95 (ISBN 0-8037-0276-0). Dial Bks Young.
West, Cindy. The Superkids & the Singing Dog. Mathieu, Joe, illus. LC 81-50042. 48p. (gr. 1-4). 1982. lib. bdg. 4.99 (ISBN 0-394-94924-2). Random.
West, Nick. Alfred Hitchcock & the Three Investigators in the Mystery of the Nervous Lion. Hitchcock, Alfred, ed. (Illus.). (gr. 4-7). 1985. 2.95 (ISBN 0-394-82308-7, Random Juv); lib. bdg. 6.99 (ISBN 0-394-92308-1). Random.
—Alfred Hitchcock & the Three Investigators in the Mystery of the Coughing Dragon. Kane, Harry, illus. LC 74-117549. (gr. 4-7). 1970. 2.95 (ISBN 0-394-81411-8, Random Juv); lib. bdg. 6.99 (ISBN 0-394-91411-2); pap. 1.95 (ISBN 0-685-04253-7). Random.
—The Mystery of the Coughing Dragon. LC 80-18982. 176p. (gr. 4-7). 1984. pap. 2.95 (ISBN 0-394-86414-X). Random.
West, Pamela. Yours Truly, Jack the Ripper. 1989. pap. 3.50 (ISBN 0-440-20259-0). Dell.
Whelan, Gloria. The Secret Keeper. LC 89-39125. 192p. (gr. 7 up). 1991. pap. 3.95 (ISBN 0-679-80702-0, Borzoi Sprinters). Knopf.
White, Ellen E. Friends for Life. 176p. (gr. 7 up). 1983. pap. 2.95 (ISBN 0-380-82578-3, Flare). Avon.
Whitney, Phyllis A. Mystery of the Black Diamonds. Gretzer, John, illus. LC 53-8355. 222p. (gr. 4-8). 1954. 7.50 (ISBN 0-664-32099-6, Westminster). Westminster John Knox.
Wilkes. Catching Crooks. (gr. 2-5). 1979. (Usborne-Hayes); PLB 11.96 (ISBN 0-88110-040-4); pap. 4.50 (ISBN 0-86020-227-5). EDC.
Wilkes, Marilyn Z. C.L.U.T.Z. (gr. 2-3). 1983. pap. 2.50 (ISBN 0-553-15515-6). Bantam.
Willard, Nancy. Night Story. Plume, Ilse, illus. LC 85-17677. 32p. (ps-3). 1986. 13.95 (ISBN 0-15-257348-8, HJ). Harbracej.
Windsor, Patricia. The Sandman's Eyes. LC 84-19888. 280p. (gr. 7 up). 1985. 15.95 (ISBN 0-385-29381-X). Delacorte.
Winfield, Arthur. The Rover Boys at College. 312p. 1980. Repr. PLB 12.95x (ISBN 0-89967-008-3). Harmony Raine.
—The Rover Boys at School. 302p. 1980. Repr. PLB 12.95x (ISBN 0-89967-009-1). Harmony Raine.
Winkler, Gershon. The Secret of Sambatyon. Goldman, Bonnie, ed. Bloom, Lloyd, illus. 132p. (gr. 4 up). 1987. 6.95 (ISBN 0-910818-68-1); pap. 5.95 (ISBN 0-910818-69-X). Judaica Pr.
Winterfeld, Henry. Detectives in Togas. 1990. pap. 3.95 (ISBN 0-15-223415-2). HarbraceJ.
—Mystery of the Roman Ransom. 1990. pap. 3.95 (ISBN 0-15-256614-7). HarbraceJ.
Wolf, Jill. Teddy Bear's Are Special Friends: Little Treasure Book. Wilson-Heaney, Kathyrn, illus. 24p. (gr. 3-7). 1985. pap. 2.25 (ISBN 0-89954-466-5). Antioch Pub Co.
Wolfe, L. E. Case of the Sneaker Snatcher & Other Mysteries. (gr. 4-7). 1991. pap. 3.50 (ISBN 0-316-95097-1). Little.
Wood, Audrey. Detective Valentine. Wood, Audrey, illus. LC 86-45784. 40p. (gr. k-3). 1987. 12.95 (ISBN 0-06-026599-X); PLB 12.89 (ISBN 0-06-026600-7). HarpC Child Bks.
Woolgar, Jack. Missing Gold Mystery. (gr. 7 up). 1977. PLB 6.70 (ISBN 0-8313-0111-2). Lantern.
—Mystery in the Desert. (gr. 6-8). 1967. 6.70 (ISBN 0-8313-0107-4); PLB 6.19 (ISBN 0-685-13778-3). Lantern.
Wosmek, Frances. Never Mind Murder. LC 77-7950. 138p. (gr. 6-10). 1977. 7.95 (ISBN 0-664-32620-X, Westminster). Westminster John Knox.
Wright, Betty R. Christina's Ghost. LC 85-42880. 128p. (gr. 3-7). 1985. 13.95 (ISBN 0-8234-0581-8). Holiday.
—The Dollhouse Murders. LC 83-6147. 160p. (gr. 3-7). 1983. 13.95 (ISBN 0-8234-0497-8). Holiday.
—Dollhouse Murders. 160p. (gr. 3-7). 1985. pap. 2.75 (ISBN 0-590-43461-6). Scholastic Inc.
—The Midnight Mystery. 144p. (gr. 4-7). 1991. pap. 2.95 (ISBN 0-590-43758-5, Apple Paperbacks). Scholastic Inc.
—The Secret Window. 176p. (gr. 4-6). 1984. pap. 2.50 (ISBN 0-590-40561-6, Apple Paperbacks). Scholastic Inc.
Wright, Bob. The Falling Star Mystery. bilingual ed. Bourne, Phyllis & Tusquets, Eugenia, trs. from ENG. Heidinger, Herb, illus. (SPA & ENG.). 96p. (gr. 1-5). 1989. pap. text ed. 4.95 (ISBN 0-87879-663-0, High Noon Books). Acad Therapy.
—The Gold Coin Robbery. bilingual ed. Bourne, Phyllis & Tusquets, Eugenia, trs. from ENG. Heidinger, Herb, illus. (SPA & ENG.). 96p. (gr. 1-5). 1989. pap. text ed. 4.95 (ISBN 0-87879-667-3, High Noon Books). Acad Therapy.
—On the Air, 5 plays in ea. set, 3 sets. (gr. 1-5). 1988. Missing Diamons, 16p. 6.50 (ISBN 0-87879-578-2, High Noon Books); Zebra Mystery, 16p. 6.50 (ISBN 0-87879-579-0, High Noon Books); Mad Scientist, 16p. 6.50 (ISBN 0-87879-580-4, High Noon Books). Acad Therapy.
—The Secret Staircase. bilingual ed. Bourne, Phyllis & Tusquets, Eugenia, trs. from ENG. Heidinger, Herb, illus. (SPA & ENG.). 96p. (gr. 1-5). 1989. pap. text ed. 4.95 (ISBN 0-87879-659-2, High Noon Books). Acad Therapy.
—The Siamese Turtle Mystery. bilingual ed. Bourne, Phyllis & Tusquets, Eugenia, trs. from ENG. Heidinger, Herb, illus. (SPA & ENG.). 96p. (gr. 1-5). 1989. pap. text ed. 4.95 (ISBN 0-87879-658-4, High Noon Books). Acad Therapy.
—The Silver Buckle Mystery. bilingual ed. Bourne, Phyllis & Tusquets, Eugenia, trs. from ENG. Heidinger, Herb, illus. (SPA & ENG.). 96p. (gr. 1-5). 1989. pap. text ed. 4.95 (ISBN 0-87879-664-9, High Noon Books). Acad Therapy.
—The Thief in the Green Van. bilingual ed. Bourne, Phyllis & Tusquets, Eugenia, trs. from ENG. Heidinger, Herb, illus. (ENG & SPA.). 96p. (gr. 1-5). 1989. pap. text ed. 4.95 (ISBN 0-87879-666-5, High Noon Books). Acad Therapy.
—The Tom & Ricky Map. Heidinger, Herb, illus. (gr. 1-9). 1983. 2.00 (ISBN 0-87879-375-5, High Noon Books). Acad Therapy.
—Tom & Ricky Mystery Series, 9 sets, 5 different novels per set. Heidinger, Herb, illus. (gr. 1-9). 1983. pap. 15.00 ea., 48p. ea. (High Noon Books). Set 1 (ISBN 0-87879-326-7). Set 2 (ISBN 0-87879-336-4, High Noon Books). Set 3 (ISBN 0-87879-357-7, High Noon Books). Set 4 (ISBN 0-87879-363-1, High Noon Books). Set 5 (ISBN 0-87879-390-9, High Noon Books). Set 6 (ISBN 0-87879-396-8, High Noon Books). Set 7 (ISBN 0-87879-419-0, High Noon Books). Set 8 (ISBN 0-87879-425-5, High Noon Books). Acad Therapy.
—The Tree House Mystery. bilingual ed. Bourne, Phyllis & Tusquets, Eugenia, trs. from ENG. Heidinger, Herb, illus. (ENG & SPA.). 96p. (gr. 1-5). 1989. pap. text ed. 4.95 (ISBN 0-87879-665-7, High Noon Books). Acad Therapy.
—The Video Game Spy. bilingual ed. Bourne, Phyllis & Tusquets, Eugenia, trs. from ENG. Heidinger, Herb, illus. (ENG & SPA.). 96p. (gr. 1-5). 1989. pap. text ed. 4.95 (ISBN 0-87879-662-2, High Noon Books). Acad Therapy.
Wrightson, Patricia. A Little Fear. LC 83-2784. 120p. (gr. 3-7). 1983. 12.95 (ISBN 0-689-50291-5, M K McElderry). Macmillan Child Grp.
Yep, Laurence. The Mark Twain Murders. LC 81-69510. 160p. (gr. 7 up). 1984. 13.95 (ISBN 0-02-793670-8, Four Winds). Macmillan Child Grp.
—The Mark Twain Murders. LC 81-69510. 160p. (gr. 7 up). 1984. 13.95 (ISBN 0-02-793670-8, Four Winds). Macmillan Child Grp.
Yolen, Jane. Heart's Blood. (Orig.). (gr. 6 up). 1986. pap. 3.25 (ISBN 0-440-93385-4, LFL). Dell.
—Piggins & the Royal Wedding. Dyer, Jane, illus. 32p. (gr. 5-8). 1989. 13.95 (ISBN 0-15-261687-X). HarBraceJ.
—The Robot & Rebecca the Missing Owser. McCrady, Lady, illus. LC 81-4870. 96p. (gr. 3-6). 1981. lib. bdg. 4.99 (ISBN 0-394-94832-7). Knopf.
—The Robot & Rebecca: The Mystery of the Code-Carrying Kids. Obrist, Jurg, illus. LC 79-27391. 96p. (gr. 3-6). 1980. Knopf.
—Shirlick Holmes & the Case of the Wandering Wardrobe. Rao, Anthony, illus. 80p. (gr. 9-12). 1981. 8.95 (ISBN 0-698-20498-0, Coward). Putnam Pub Group.
York, Carol B. Once upon a Dark November. LC 89-2021. 112p. (gr. 5-9). 1989. 13.95 (ISBN 0-8234-0780-2). Holiday.
—Secrets in the Attic. 112p. (Orig.). (gr. 4-6). 1988. pap. 2.50 (ISBN 0-590-40607-8, Apple Paperbacks). Scholastic Inc.
—Secrets in the Attic. 112p. (Orig.). (gr. 3-7). 1991. pap. 2.75 (ISBN 0-590-42605-2). Scholastic Inc.
Young, Alida E. Terror in the Tomb of Death. 112p. (Orig.). (gr. 6-9). 1988. pap. 1.25 (ISBN 0-87406-321-3). Willowisp Pr.
Zeplin, Zeno. Popcorn Is Missing: A Katy & Beth Mystery. Jones, Judy, illus. 48p. (gr. 2-4). 1990. lib. bdg. 6.95 casebound (ISBN 1-877740-01-2); pap. text ed. 3.95 (ISBN 1-877740-02-0). Nel-Mar Pub.
Ziefert, Harriet. Mr. Rose's Class: Mystery Day. Brown, Rihard, illus. 64p. (gr. 1-3). 1988. 8.95 (ISBN 0-316-98769-7). Little.
Zimmerman, R. D. Bomb. 4p. 1987. incl. puzzle 16.95 (ISBN 0-922242-01-1). Lombard Mktg.
Zindel, Paul. The Undertaker's Gone Bananas. LC 78-54606. 256p. (gr. 7 up). 1978. PLB 13.89 (ISBN 0-06-026846-8). HarpC Child Bks.

MYTHICAL ANIMALS
see Animals, Mythical

MYTHOLOGY
see also Animals, Mythical; Folklore; Heroes; Indians of North America–Religion and Mythology; Totems and Totemism

Asimov, Isaac. Mythology & the Universe. LC 89-11360. (Illus.). 32p. (gr. 3-4). 1989. PLB 11.95 (ISBN 1-55532-403-7). Gareth Stevens Inc.
Colum, Padraic. The Children of Odin: The Book of Northern Myths. reissued ed. Pogany, Willy, illus. LC 83-20368. 280p. (gr. 5up). 1984. 14.95 (ISBN 0-02-722890-8); pap. 7.95 (ISBN 0-02-042100-1, Collier Young Ad). Macmillan Child Grp.
Coomaraswamy, Ananda K. & Nivedita, Sr. Myths of the Hindus & Buddhists. (Illus.). 400p. (gr. 4-8). pap. 7.95 (ISBN 0-486-21759-0). Dover.
Espeland, Pamela. The Story of Baucis & Philemon. Overlie, George, illus. LC 80-27674. 32p. (gr. 1-4). 1981. PLB 7.95 (ISBN 0-87614-140-8). Carolrhoda Bks.
—The Story of Cadmus. Sandland, Reg, illus. LC 80-66795. 32p. (gr. 1-4). 1980. PLB 7.95 (ISBN 0-87614-128-9). Carolrhoda Bks.
—The Story of King Midas. Overlie, George, illus. LC 80-66794. 32p. (gr. 1-4). 1980. PLB 7.95 (ISBN 0-87614-129-7). Carolrhoda Bks.
—Theseus & the Road to Athens. Sandland, Reg, illus. LC 80-27713. 32p. (gr. 1-4). 1981. PLB 7.95 (ISBN 0-87614-141-6). Carolrhoda Bks.
Evslin, Bernard. Heroes, Gods & Monsters of Greek Myths. (ps-7). 1984. pap. 4.50 (ISBN 0-553-25920-2). Bantam.
Evslin, Bernard, et al. The Greek Gods. (gr. 7-12). 1972. pap. 2.25 (ISBN 0-590-06350-2, Schol Pap). Scholastic Inc.
Fisher, Leonard E. Jason & the Golden Fleece. Fisher, Leonard E., illus. LC 89-20074. 32p. (gr. 1-4). 1990. 14.95 (ISBN 0-8234-0794-2). Holiday.
Fisher, Leonard E., retold by. & illus. Theseus & the Minotaur. LC 88-1970. 32p. (gr. 1-4). 1988. reinforced bdg. 14.95 (ISBN 0-8234-0703-9). Holiday.
Graves, Robert. Greek Gods & Heroes. 125p. 1965. pap. 3.25 (ISBN 0-440-93221-1, LFL). Dell.
Green, R. L. The Tale of Thebes. LC 76-22979. (Illus.). 1977. Cambridge U Pr.
Green, Roger L. Tales of Greek Heroes. (Orig.). (gr. 5-7). 1989. pap. 2.95 (ISBN 0-14-035099-3, Puffin). Puffin Bks.
Hadley, Eric & Hadley, Tessa. Legends of Earth, Air, Fire & Water. (Illus.). 32p. 1985. 11.95 (ISBN 0-521-26311-5). Cambridge U Pr.
Harrison, Michael. The Curse of the Ring. (gr. 5-8). 1987. 17.95 (ISBN 0-19-274131-4). Oxford U Pr.
—Doom of the Gods. Humphries, Tudor, illus. 80p. (gr. 3 up). 1987. 17.95 (ISBN 0-19-274128-4). Oxford U Pr.
Hawthorne, Nathaniel. Wonder Book. Hogan, A. H., intro. by. (gr. 5 up). pap. 2.50 (ISBN 0-8049-0118-X, CL-118). Airmont.
Homer. Odysseus & the Giants. Richardson, I. M., adapted by. Frenck, Hal, illus. LC 83-14233. 32p. (gr. 4-8). 1984. PLB 11.79 (ISBN 0-8167-0009-5); pap. text ed. 2.95 (ISBN 0-8167-0010-9). Troll Assocs.
Karl, Nancy. Activities with Myths. (Illus.). 32p. (gr. 4-7). 1983. pap. 4.95 (ISBN 0-913839-01-9). Bk Lures.
Lattimore, Deborah N. The Prince & the Golden Ax: A Minoan Tale. Lattimore, Deborah N., illus. LC 87-21193. 40p. (gr. k-3). 1988. 12.95 (ISBN 0-06-023715-5); PLB 12.89 (ISBN 0-06-023716-3). HarpC Child Bks.

Li, Xiao M., tr. from CHI. The Mending of the Sky & Other Chinese Myths. Wu, Shan M., illus. Buckley, Cicely, intro. by. (Illus.). 54p. (Orig.). (gr. 5 up). 1989. pap. 9.00 (ISBN 0-9617481-3-3). Oyster River Pr.
Beautifully illustrated with calligraphy & halftones from watercolors by Shan Ming Wu. Brief bibliography & a note on Chinese names. "Young & old will marvel at how the ingenuity of gods & humans helped people survive natural disasters, political strife, & how pottery, silk, cooking, herbal medicine & the written language came to be

invented for the benefit of humankind. Provides a window on ancient & present-day China."--A. Shipman, UNH Dept. Classics. "Straightforward renderings with colorful, dramatic phrases, enhanced by Shan Ming Wu's fine illustrations with the charm of traditional Chinese paintings."--Small Press Book Review. On the invention of the writing system: Cang Xie had a broad dragon-like face with four shining eyes. As a child...he spent hours observing celestial bodies & earthly creatures...When his characters were first brought to light,...the whole world was shocked, & ghosts cried at night. It was feared people might give up farming & become interested in playing with the other characters... *Publisher Provided Annotation.*

Lindgren, Astrid. Brothers Lionheart. Tate, Joan, tr. Lambert, J. K., illus. LC 85-573. 184p. (gr. 4-6). 1985. pap. 4.95 (ISBN 0-14-031955-7, Puffin). Puffin Bks.

McKissack, Patricia & McKissack, Fredrick. King Midas & His Gold. Dunnington, Tom, illus. LC 86-11744. 32p. (ps-2). 1986. PLB 11.93 (ISBN 0-516-03984-9); pap. 3.95 (ISBN 0-516-43984-7). Childrens.

Middleton, Haydn. Island of the Mighty. 80p. (gr. 5-8). 1987. 17.95 (ISBN 0-19-274133-0). Oxford U Pr.

Mystic Jhamon Publishers Staff, ed. Is Man a Free Agent? (Illus.). 128p. (gr. 6 up). 1985. pap. 9.95 (ISBN 0-933961-01-4). Mystic Jhamom.

Osborne, Mary P. Favorite Greek Myths. Howell, Troy, illus. (gr. 2-6). 1989. pap. 15.95 (ISBN 0-590-41338-4). Scholastic Inc.

Richardson, I. M. The Adventures of Eros & Psyche. Baxter, Robert, illus. LC 82-16057. 32p. (gr. 4-8). 1983. PLB 11.79 (ISBN 0-89375-861-2); pap. text ed. 2.95 (ISBN 0-89375-862-0). Troll Assocs.

Rungachary, Santha. Tales for All Times. Khemraj, P., illus. (gr. 1-9). 1979. pap. 2.50 (ISBN 0-89744-187-7). Auromere.

Simon, Seymour. Hidden Worlds: Pictures of the Invisible. LC 83-5407. (Illus.). 48p. (gr. 3up). 1983. 13.95 (ISBN 0-688-02464-5); lib. bdg. 13.88 (ISBN 0-688-02465-3, Morrow Jr Bks). Morrow Jr Bks.

Steffens, J. & Carr, J. Myths & Fables. (gr. 7-12). 1984. 9.95 (ISBN 0-88160-113-6, LW 1008). Learning Wks.

Stephanides Brothers Staff. Greek Mythology, 6 Vols. (gr. 5-10). Set. 60.00 (ISBN 0-916634-26-4). Double M Pr.

Sylvester, Diane & Wiemann, Mary. Mythology, Archeology, Architecture. 112p. (gr. 4-6). 1982. 9.95 (ISBN 0-88160-081-4, LW 901). Learning Wks.

Tchudi, Stephen. Probing the Unknown: From Myth to Science. LC 89-35938. (Illus.). 160p. 1990. 14.95 (ISBN 0-684-19086-9, Scribners Young Read). Macmillan Child Grp.

Trezise, Percy. The Flying Fox Warriors. Keller, Kathy, intro. by. Trezise, Percy, illus. LC 88-20123. 32p. (gr. 2-3). 1988. PLB 12.95 (ISBN 1-55532-946-2). Gareth Stevens Inc.

—Gidja the Moon. Keller, Kathy, intro. by. Trezise, Percy, illus. LC 88-20120. 32p. (gr. 2-3). 1988. PLB 12.95 (ISBN 1-55532-948-9). Gareth Stevens Inc.

—Turramulli the Giant Quinkin. Keller, Kathy, intro. by. Trezise, Percy, illus. LC 88-20119. 32p. (gr. 2-3). 1988. PLB 12.95 (ISBN 1-55532-947-0). Gareth Stevens Inc.

Trezise, Percy & Haginikitas, Mary. Black Duck & Water Rat. LC 88-20121. (Illus.). 32p. (gr. 2-3). 1988. PLB 12.95 (ISBN 1-55532-945-4). Gareth Stevens Inc.

Yolen, Jane. Touch Magic: Fantasy, Faerie & Folklore in the Literature of Childhood. 128p. (gr. 6 up). 1981. 12.95 (ISBN 0-399-20830-5, Philomel). Putnam Pub Group.

Zimmerman. Dictionary of Classical Mythology. (gr. 9 up). 1983. pap. 4.95 (ISBN 0-553-25776-5). Bantam.

MYTHOLOGY, CLASSICAL

Asimov, Isaac. Words from the Myths. Barss, William, illus. 224p. (gr. 5-10). 1961. 14.95 (ISBN 0-395-06568-2). HM.

Barth, Edna. Cupid & Psyche: A Love Story. Forberg, Ati, illus. LC 76-8821. 64p. (gr. 3-6). 1979. 14.95 (ISBN 0-395-28840-1, Clarion). HM.

Benson, Sally. Stories of the Gods & Heroes. Savage, Steele, illus. (gr. 4-6). 1940. 15.95 (ISBN 0-8037-8291-8). Dial Bks Young.

Billout, Guy. Thunderbolt & Rainbow: A Look at Greek Mythology. (Illus.). 1981. 9.95 (ISBN 0-13-920637-X). P-H.

Britt, Helen. Ye Gods. 1987. pap. text ed. 14.88 (ISBN 0-88334-196-4, 76161). Longman.

Connolly, Peter. The Legend of Odysseus. (Illus.). 80p. (gr. 7-12). 1988. 17.95 (ISBN 0-19-917065-7). Oxford U Pr.

Coolidge, Olivia. Greek Myths. Sandoz, E., illus. 256p. (gr. 7 up). 1949. 13.95 (ISBN 0-395-06721-9). HM.

D'Aulaire, Ingri & D'Aulaire, Edgar P. D'Aulaires' Book of Greek Myths. D'Aulaire, Ingri & D'Aulaire, Edgar P., illus. LC 62-15877. 1980. 18.95 (ISBN 0-385-01583-6, Zephyr-BFYR); PLB 19.99 (ISBN 0-385-07108-6); pap. 12.95 (ISBN 0-385-15787-8, Zephyr-BFYR). Doubleday.

Evans & Millard. Greek Myths & Legends. (Illus.). 64p. (gr. 6-10). 1986. PLB 13.96 (ISBN 0-88110-224-5); pap. 7.96 (ISBN 0-86020-946-6). EDC.

Evans, C. & Millard, A. Greek & Norse Legends. (Illus.). 112p. (gr. 6-10). 1987. pap. 11.95 (ISBN 0-7460-0240-8). EDC.

Evlsin, Bernard. Greek Gods. (gr. 4-7). 1984. pap. 2.95 (ISBN 0-590-44110-8). Scholastic Inc.

Evslin, Bernard. Gods, Demigods & Demons: An Encyclopedia of Greek Mythology. 240p. (gr. 7 up). 1988. pap. 2.95 (ISBN 0-590-41448-8, Point). Scholastic Inc.

Evslin, Bernard, et al. The Greek Gods. Hunter, William, illus. 120p. (gr. 7 up). 1988. pap. 2.50 (ISBN 0-590-41396-1, Point). Scholastic Inc.

—Heroes & Monsters of Greek Myth. Hunter, William, illus. 112p. (gr. 7 up). 1988. pap. 2.50 (ISBN 0-590-41072-5, Point); tchr's. guide 1.25 (ISBN 0-590-40670-1). Scholastic Inc.

Gerstein, Mordicai. Tales of Pan. LC 83-49484. (Illus.). 64p. (gr. 2-5). 1986. 12.95i (ISBN 0-06-021996-3); PLB 12.89 (ISBN 0-06-021997-1). HarpC Child Bks.

Goennel, Heidi. Sometimes I Like to Be Alone. Goennel, Heidi, illus. LC 88-30780. (gr. k-2). 1989. 14.95 (ISBN 0-316-31842-6). Little.

Gottlieb, Gerald. The Adventures of Ulysses. Savage, Steele, illus. LC 88-19232. xii, 170p. (gr. 6-12). 1988. Repr. of 1959 ed. lib. bdg. 16.50 (ISBN 0-208-02222-8, Linnet). Shoe String.

Hamilton, Edith. Mythology. Savage, Steele, illus. (gr. 7 up). 1942. 19.95 (ISBN 0-316-34114-2). Little.

Hawthorne, Nathaniel. Tanglewood Tales. (Illus.). (gr. 7 up). 1968. pap. 2.50 (ISBN 0-8049-0175-9, CL-175). Airmont.

—A Wonder Book & Tanglewood Tales. Charvat, William, et al, eds. LC 77-150221. (Illus.). 476p. (gr. 5 up). 1972. 47.75 (ISBN 0-8142-0158-X). Ohio St U Pr.

—A Wonder Book for Girls & Boys. LC 87-50436. 362p. (gr. 3-7). 1987. pap. 7.95 (ISBN 0-940561-07-7). White Rose Pr.

Hewitt, Kathryn. King Midas & the Golden Touch. Hewitt, Kathryn, illus. LC 86-7681. (ps-3). 1987. 12.95 (ISBN 0-15-242800-3). HarBraceJ.

Hodges, Margaret. The Arrow & the Lamp: The Story of Psyche. Diamond, Donna, illus. LC 86-2728. (gr. 4-8). 1989. 14.95 (ISBN 0-316-36790-7). Little.

Homer. Odysseus & the Cyclops. Richardson, I. M., adapted by. Frenck, Hal, illus. LC 83-14236. 32p. (gr. 4-8). 1984. lib. bdg. 11.79 (ISBN 0-8167-0007-9); pap. text ed. 2.95 (ISBN 0-8167-0008-7). Troll Assocs.

—Odysseus & the Great Challenge. Richardson, I. M., adapted by. Frenck, Hal, illus. LC 83-14232. 32p. (gr. 4-8). 1984. lib. bdg. 11.79 (ISBN 0-8167-0013-3); pap. text ed. 2.95 (ISBN 0-8167-0014-1). Troll Assocs.

—Odysseus & the Magic of Circe. Richardson, I. M., adapted by. Frenck, Hal, illus. LC 83-14237. 32p. (gr. 4-8). 1984. lib. bdg. 11.79 (ISBN 0-8167-0011-7); pap. text ed. 2.95 (ISBN 0-8167-0012-5). Troll Assocs.

—The Voyage of Odysseus. Richardson, I. M., adapted by. Frenck, Hal, illus. LC 83-14235. 32p. (gr. 4-8). 1984. lib. bdg. 11.79 (ISBN 0-8167-0005-2); pap. text ed. 2.95 (ISBN 0-8167-0006-0). Troll Assocs.

—The Wooden Horse. Richardson, I. M., adapted by. Frenck, Hal, illus. LC 83-18061. 32p. (gr. 4-8). 1984. PLB 11.79 (ISBN 0-8167-0057-5); pap. text ed. 2.95 (ISBN 0-8167-0058-3). Troll Assocs.

McDermott, Gerald. Daughter of Earth: A Roman Myth. McDermott, Gerald, illus. LC 82-23585. 32p. (ps-3). 1984. pap. 15.00 (ISBN 0-385-29294-5). Delacorte.

McLean, Mollie & Wiseman, Anne. The Adventures of Greek Heroes. Mars, Witold T., illus. LC 61-10628. 192p. (ps-3). 1973. 13.95 (ISBN 0-395-06913-0, Sandpiper); pap. 5.95. HM.

Naden, C. J., adapted by. Jason & the Golden Fleece. Baxter, Robert, illus. LC 80-50068. 32p. (gr. 4-8). 1980. PLB 11.79 (ISBN 0-89375-360-2); pap. 2.95 (ISBN 0-89375-364-5). Troll Assocs.

—Pegasus, the Winged Horse. new ed. LC 80-50069. (Illus.). 32p. (gr. 4-8). 1980. PLB 11.79 (ISBN 0-89375-361-0); pap. 2.95 (ISBN 0-89375-365-3). Troll Assocs.

—Perseus & Medusa. Baxter, Robert, illus. LC 80-50083. 32p. (gr. 4-8). 1980. PLB 11.79 (ISBN 0-89375-362-9); pap. 2.95 (ISBN 0-89375-366-1). Troll Assocs.

—Theseus & the Minotaur. Baxter, Robert, illus. LC 80-50067. 32p. (gr. 4-8). 1980. PLB 11.79 (ISBN 0-89375-363-7); pap. 2.95 (ISBN 0-89375-367-X). Troll Assocs.

Newby, Robert. King Midas: With Selected Sentences in American Sign Language. Majewski, Dawn & Cozzolino, Sandy, illus. LC 90-4908. 64p. (gr. 1-5). 13.95 (ISBN 0-930323-75-0, Pub. by K Green Pubns). Gallaudet Univ Pr.

Oldfield, Pamela, retold by. Tales from Ancient Greece. Harris, Nick, illus. 64p. (gr. 5-9). 1989. 14.95 (ISBN 0-385-26224-8, Zephyr-BFYR). Doubleday.

Richardson, I. M. Demeter & Persephone: The Seasons of Time. Baxter, Robert, illus. LC 82-16023. 32p. (gr. 4-8). 1983. PLB 11.79 (ISBN 0-89375-863-9); pap. text ed. 2.95 (ISBN 0-89375-864-7). Troll Assocs.

—Prometheus & the Story of Fire. Baxter, Robert, illus. LC 82-15979. 32p. (gr. 4-8). 1983. PLB 11.79 (ISBN 0-89375-859-0); pap. text ed. 2.95 (ISBN 0-89375-860-4). Troll Assocs.

Start Exploring Bulfinch's Mythology: Classic Tales of Heroes, Gods, & Magic. (Illus.). 128p. (Orig.). (gr. 2 up). 1989. pap. 7.95 (ISBN 0-89471-710-3). Running Pr.

Stephanides Brothers Staff. Greek Mythology, 6 vols. (gr. 5-10). Set. 60.00x (ISBN 0-916634-25-6). Double M Pr.

Stevens, Janet. Androcles & the Lion. Stevens, Janet, illus. LC 89-1953. 32p. (ps-3). 1989. PLB 14.95 (ISBN 0-8234-0768-3). Holiday.

Storr, Catherine. King Midas. Codd, Mike, illus. LC 84-18307. 32p. (gr. 2-5). 1985. PLB 16.67 (ISBN 0-8172-2112-3); pap. 9.27 (ISBN 0-8172-2255-3). Raintree Pubs.

Storr, Catherine, as told by. Theseus & the Minotaur. (Illus.). 32p. (gr. k-5). 1985. PLB 16.67 (ISBN 0-8172-2506-4); pap. 9.27 (ISBN 0-8172-2514-5). Raintree Pubs.

Switzer, Ellen & Costas. Greek Myths: Gods, Heroes & Monsters - Their Sources, Their Stories & Their Meanings. LC 87-22690. (Illus.). 224p. (gr. 6 up). 1988. PLB 16.95 (ISBN 0-689-31253-9, Atheneum Child Bk). Macmillan Child Grp.

Woodbridge, F. J. The Son of Apollo: Themes of Plato. 272p. (gr. 7 up). 1972. Repr. of 1929 ed. 20.00 (ISBN 0-8196-0278-7). Biblo.

Yolen, J. & Nolan, D. Wings. 1991. 15.95 (ISBN 0-15-297850-X, HJ). HarBraceJ.

MYTHOLOGY, INDIAN

see Indians of North America–Religion and Mythology

MYTHOLOGY, NORSE

Crossley-Holland, Kevin. Axe-Age, Wolf-Age: A Selection for Children from the Norse Myths. Firmin, Hannah, illus. 128p. (gr. 6 up). 1985. 11.95 (ISBN 0-233-97688-4). Andre Deutsch.

Daly, Kathleen N. Norse Mythology A to Z. (Illus.). 144p. 1990. 24.95x (ISBN 0-8160-2150-3). Facts on File.

Green, Richard L. Myths of the Norsemen. Wildsmith, Brian, illus. (gr. 4-6). 1970. pap. 3.50 (ISBN 0-14-030464-9, Penguin Bks). Viking Penguin.

Mayer, Marianna. Iduna & the Magic Apples. Gal, Laszlo, illus. LC 88-2494. 40p. (gr. k-4). 1988. 16.95 (ISBN 0-02-765120-7, Mcmillan Child Bk). Macmillan Child Grp.

Norse Myths & Legends. (Illus.). 48p. (gr. 6-10). 1986. PLB 13.96 (ISBN 0-88110-249-0); pap. 6.95 (ISBN 0-7460-0010-3). EDC.

MYTHS

see Mythology

N

N A T O

see North Atlantic Treaty Organization

NADER, RALPH, 1934-

Celsi, Teresa. Ralph Nader: The Consumer Revolution. (Illus.). 104p. (gr. 7 up). 1991. PLB 19.95 (ISBN 1-56294-044-9). Millbrook Pr.

NAMES–FICTION

De Paola, Tomie. Andy: That's My Name. (ps-2). 1988. 10.95x (ISBN 0-685-03770-3, Little Simon); pap. 4.95 (ISBN 0-685-03771-1). S&S Trade.

Filichia, Peter. What's in a Name? 224p. (gr. 7 up). 1988. pap. 2.75 (ISBN 0-380-75536-X, Flare). Avon.

Mazer, Norma F. B, My Name Is Bunny. LC 86-22039. 160p. (Orig.). (gr. 6 up). 1987. pap. 12.95 (ISBN 0-590-40930-1, Scholastic Hardcover); pap. 2.50 (ISBN 0-590-40055-X). Scholastic Inc.

NAMES, GEOGRAPHICAL

Rickard, Graham. How Places Got Their Names. Harris, Peter, ed. LC 89-12022. (Illus.). 46p. (gr. 4-7). 1989. PLB 15.93 (ISBN 0-944483-34-8). Garrett Ed Corp.

NAMES, PERSONAL

Freeman, J. W. Discovering Surnames: Their Origins & Meanings. 4th ed. 72p. (gr. 6 up). 1979. pap. 2.50 (ISBN 0-913714-36-4). Legacy Bks.

Hazen, Barbara S. Last, First, Middle & Nick: All About Names. Weissman, Sam Q., illus. (gr. 1-4). 1979. 7.95 (ISBN 0-13-523944-3). P-H.

The Ladybird Baby Names Book. (Illus.). 1990. 3.95 (ISBN 0-7214-5284-1). Ladybird Bks.

Lee, Mary P. Your Name - All about It. LC 79-22145. (Illus.). 128p. (gr. 3-7). 1980. 9.95 (ISBN 0-664-32656-0, Westminster). Westminster John Knox.

Lee, Mary P. & Lee, Richard S. Last Names First..& Some First Names too. Weber, Debora, illus. LC 84-20860. 119p. (gr. 5-9). 1985. 11.95 (ISBN 0-664-32719-2, Westminster). Westminster John Knox.

Meltzer, Milton. A Book about Names. Richter, Mischa, illus. LC 83-45241. 128p. (gr. 7 up). 1984. 13.95 (ISBN 0-690-04380-5, Crowell Jr Bks); PLB 13.89 (ISBN 0-690-04381-3, Crowell Jr Bks). HarpC Child Bks.

Les Nombres. (FRE., Illus.). 3.50 (ISBN 0-7214-0798-6). Ladybird Bks.

NAMES, PERSONAL–FICTION

Engel, Diana. Josephina Hates Her Name. Engel, Diana, illus. LC 88-1500. 32p. (ps-2). 1989. 13.95 (ISBN 0-688-07795-1); PLB 13.88 (ISBN 0-688-07796-X, Morrow Jr Bks). Morrow Jr Bks.

Greene, Constance C. A Girl Called Al. large type ed. 1989. Repr. of 1969 ed. 15.95 (ISBN 1-55736-145-2, Crnrstn Bks). ABC CLIO.

Henkes, Kevin. Chrysanthemum. LC 90-39803. (Illus.). 32p. (ps up). 1991. 13.95 (ISBN 0-688-09699-9); PLB 13.88 (ISBN 0-688-09700-6). Greenwillow.

Waber, Bernard. But Names Will Never Hurt Me. Waber, Bernard, illus. LC 75-40473. 32p. (gr. k-3). 1976. 14.95 (ISBN 0-395-24383-1). HM.

NANTUCKET, MASSACHUSETTS–FICTION

Finley, Martha. Elsie at Nantucket. 301p. 1981. Repr. PLB 21.95x (ISBN 0-89966-333-8). Buccaneer Bks.

—Elsie at Nantucket. 302p. 1980. Repr. PLB 17.95x (ISBN 0-89967-011-3). Harmony Raine.

Turkle, Brinton. Rachel & Obadiah. Turkle, Brinton, illus. LC 77-15661. (gr. k-3). 1978. 12.95 (ISBN 0-525-38020-5, DCB). Dutton Child Bks.

—Rachel & Obadiah. Turkle, Brinton, illus. (gr. 1-3). 1987. pap. 3.95 (ISBN 0-525-44303-7, DCB). Dutton Child Bks.

NAPOLEON 1ST, EMPEROR OF THE FRENCH, 1769-1821

Harris, Nathaniel. Napoleon. (Illus.). 64p. (gr. 6-9). 1989. 19.95 (ISBN 0-7134-5730-9, Pub. by Batsford England). Trafalgar Sq.

Marrin, Albert. Napoleon & the Napoleonic Wars. 1991. 14.95 (ISBN 0-670-83480-7). Viking Child Bks.

Weidhorn, Manfred. Napoleon. LC 86-3352. (Illus.). 224p. (gr. 7 up). 1986. 16.95 (ISBN 0-689-31163-X, Atheneum Child Bk). Macmillan Child Grp.

NAPOLEONIC WARS

see France–History–Revolution, 1789-1799

NARCOTIC HABIT

Ball, Jacquiline A. Everything You Need to Know about Drug Abuse. Rosen, Roger, ed. Glassman, Richard, photos by. (Illus.). 64p. (gr. 7 up). 1988. PLB 12.95 (ISBN 0-8239-0811-9). Rosen Group.

Berger, Gilda. Crack-The New Drug Epidemic. (Illus.). 128p. (gr. 7-12). 1987. PLB 12.90 (ISBN 0-531-10410-9). Watts.

—Drug Testing: A New Weapon to Fight the Drug Crisis. (Illus.). 128p. (gr. 7-12). 1987. PLB 12.90 (ISBN 0-531-10411-7). Watts.

—Joey's Story: Straight Talk about Drugs. Kirk, Barbara, photos by. (Illus.). 64p. (gr. 7 up). 1991. PLB 17.25 (ISBN 1-56294-003-1). Millbrook Pr.

Berry, Joy. About Substance Abuse. Bartholomew, illus. 48p. (gr. 3 up). 1990. PLB 14.60 (ISBN 0-516-02956-8); 6.95 (ISBN 0-516-22956-7). Childrens.

Booher, Albert R. A Guide to Drugs & Their Effects, Pt. II. 9p. (gr. 5-9). 1988. pap. text ed. 5.95 (ISBN 0-685-28980-X). Madonna Edu Syst.

—A Guide to Drugs & Their Effects, Pt. I. 9p. (gr. 5-9). 1988. pap. text ed. 5.95 (ISBN 0-685-28981-8). Madonna Edu Syst.

Brady, Janeen. Safety Kids Play It Smart, Vol. 2: Stay Safe from Drugs. Twede, Evan, illus. (Orig.). (gr. k-6). 1985. pap. text ed. 5.95 songbook (ISBN 0-944803-21-0); pap. text ed. 1.25 dialogue bk., 1985, 16pgs. (ISBN 0-944803-24-5); act. bk. 2.25 (ISBN 0-944803-22-9); cassette & bk. 9.95 (ISBN 0-944803-23-7); video avail. (ISBN 0-944803-72-5). Brite Intl.

Community Intervention, Inc. Staff. Saying Yes, Saying No: You & Drugs--A Positive Approach to Staying Drug Free. 24p. (Orig.). (gr. 8-12). 1986. pap. 3.95 (ISBN 0-9613416-4-5). Comm Intervention.

De la Martre, Audrey, ed. Chemical Abuse Assessment Workbook for Adolescents. rev. ed. Payne, William J., intro. by. 34p. (gr. 6-12). 1989. Repr. of 1981 ed. wkbk. 7.00 (ISBN 0-317-92294-7). New Connect Pub.

Di Silvestro, Frank. Kid Wise Talks to Kids about Drugs. Berlin, Rosemary, illus. 22p. (gr. 1-8). 1990. pap. write for info. (ISBN 0-934591-02-4). Songs & Stories.

Drugs & Drinking. 48p. (gr. 6-8). 1990. pap. 6.95 (ISBN 1-55945-118-1). Group Pub.

Edwards, Gabrielle I. Coping with Drug Abuse. rev. ed. Rosen, Roger, ed. (gr. 7 up). 1990. lib. bdg. 12.95 (ISBN 0-8239-1144-6). Rosen Group.

Fradin, Dennis B. Drug Abuse. LC 87-33789. (Illus.). 48p. (gr. k-4). 1988. PLB 14.60 (ISBN 0-516-01212-6); pap. 4.95 (ISBN 0-516-41212-4). Childrens.

Gaetano, Ronald J. & Masterson, James J. Teenage Drug Abusers: One Hundred Most Commonly Asked Questions about Adolescent Substance Abuse. 128p. (gr. 9 up). 1988. write for info. Union Hosp Found.

Gibson, Christine R. & Hargrave, J. Michael. The Tator Tales: A Guide to Substance Abuse Prevention for Youth & Adults. Majewski, Chuck, illus. (Orig.). (gr. 4-8). Date not set. pap. write for info. Tator Enterprises.

Harris, Jonathan. Drugged Athletes: The Crisis in American Sports. LC 86-29396. 204p. (gr. 5-9). 1987. 14.95 (ISBN 0-02-742740-4, Four Winds). Macmillan Child Grp.

Hawley, Richard. Drugs & Society. 160p. (gr. 7 up). 1991. PLB 15.85 (ISBN 0-8027-8114-4); pap. 8.95 (ISBN 0-8027-7366-4). Walker & Co.

Hawley, Richard A. Think about Drugs & Society: Responding to an Epidemic. LC 87-21681. 157p. 1988. 14.85 (ISBN 0-8027-6749-4); pap. 5.95 (ISBN 0-8027-6750-8). Walker & Co.

Hazen, Barbara S. Just Say No. Friedman, Joy, illus. (ps-3). Date not set. pap. write for info. (ISBN 0-307-12612-9, Golden Pr). Western Pub.

Hurwitz, Sue & Shniderman, Nancy. Drugs & Your Friends. (gr. 7-12). 1991. PLB 14.95 (ISBN 0-8239-1264-7). Rosen Group.

Jones, Penny. The Brown Bottle. 40p. (gr. 4 up). 1983. text ed. 3.50 (ISBN 0-89486-170-0). Hazelden.

Kronenwetter, Michael. Drugs in America. (Illus.). 144p. (gr. 7 up). 1990. lib. bdg. 12.98 (ISBN 0-671-70557-1). Messner.

Lee, Essie E. Breaking the Connection: How Young People Achieve Drug-Free Lives. LC 87-18586. (Illus.). 160p. (gr. 7 up). 1988. lib. bdg. 13.98 (ISBN 0-671-63637-5); pap. 5.95 (ISBN 0-671-67059-X). Messner.

Leone, Bruno, et al, eds. Chemical Dependency: Opposing Viewpoints. 460p. 1989. lib. bdg. 19.95 (ISBN 0-89908-543-1). Greenhaven.

Lukas, Scott E. Amphetamines: Danger in the Fast Lane. (Illus.). (gr. 5 up). 1985. PLB 18.95 (ISBN 0-87754-755-6). Chelsea Hse.

McCormick, Michele. Designer-Drug Abuse. (Illus.). 128p. (gr. 10-12). 1990. 12.90 (ISBN 0-531-10660-8). Watts.

McFarland, Rhoda. Coping with Substance Abuse. rev. ed. Rosen, Ruth, ed. 144p. (gr. 7 up). 1990. lib. bdg. 12.95 (ISBN 0-8239-1135-7). Rosen Group.

—Drugs & Your Brothers & Sisters. (gr. 7-12). 1991. PLB 14.95 (ISBN 0-8239-1266-3). Rosen Group.

McMillan, Daniel. Winning the Battle Against Drugs: Rehabilitation Programs. (Illus.). 160p. (gr. 9-12). 1991. PLB 13.90 (ISBN 0-531-11063-X). Watts.

Makela, Chuck. After You've Tried Everything Else: A "More Excellent Way" to Freedom from Addictions. 32p. (Orig.). (gr. 7 up). 1987. pap. 1.00 (ISBN 0-9618532-0-4). Just Pub Hse.

Malerba-Foran, Joan. When You Look in the Mirror, What Do You See? 24p. (Orig.). (gr. 7 up). 1985. pap. 1.95 (ISBN 0-89486-262-6). Hazelden.

Morris-Vann, Artie M. My Parents Are Drug Abusers. 40p. (Orig.). (ps-5). pap. 6.50 (ISBN 0-317-02490-6). Aid-U Pub.

Nardo, Don. Drugs & Sports. LC 90-6686. (Illus.). 112p. (gr. 5-8). 1990. PLB 11.95 (ISBN 1-56006-112-X). Lucent Bks.

Newton, David E. Particle Accelerations. (Illus.). 128p. (gr. 10-12). 1990. 12.40 (ISBN 0-531-10671-3). Watts.

Orlandi, Mario & Prue, Donald. Substance Abuse. (gr. 5 up). 1989. 18.95 (ISBN 0-8160-1669-0). Facts On File.

Parker, Steve. The Drug War. (Illus.). 32p. (gr. 5-8). 1990. PLB 8.90 (ISBN 0-531-17241-4). Watts.

Pringle, Mary L. & Ellis, Joseph. Sis & Chris & the Knowbots in "We Don't Need Drugs to Be O. K." Educational Coloring Book. (gr. k-5). 1987. pap. 1.95 (ISBN 0-935847-03-0). Inst Subs Abuse Res.

Reiners, Kenneth G. Addicted to the Addict: From Codependency to Recovery. LC 87-50843. 64p. (Orig.). (gr. 9-12). 1987. pap. 4.95 (ISBN 0-934104-06-9). Woodland.

Rico, Armando B. There's a Rock in Your Coke. 47p. (Orig.). 1987. pap. 2.50 (ISBN 1-879219-02-6). Veracruz Pubs.

Rosenberg, Maxine B. On the Mend. Steinhoff, Sharon, ed. LC 91-11202. (Illus.). 128p. (gr. 4 up). 1991. 14.95 (ISBN 0-02-777914-9, Bradbury Pr). Macmillan Child Grp.

Rundquist, Thomas J. & Parent, Frederick. Horse Is Boss: Drug Culture Education & Prevention Game. 2nd ed. Randquist, Thomas J, illus. 42p. (Orig.). (gr. 7-12). 1988. pap. text ed. 30.50x (ISBN 0-9618567-1-8). Nova Media.

Ryan, Elizabeth A. Straight Talk about Drugs & Alcohol. 160p. 1989. 16.95x (ISBN 0-8160-1525-2). Facts on File.

Seixas, Judith S. Living with a Parent Who Takes Drugs. LC 89-1995. 96p. 1989. 12.95 (ISBN 0-688-08627-6). Greenwillow.

Shoker, Nancy. Substance Abuse. Koop, C. Everett, intro. by. (Illus.). 112p. (gr. 6-12). 1993. 18.95 (ISBN 0-7910-0078-8). Chelsea Hse.

Smith, Sandra L. Heroin. (gr. 7-12). 1991. PLB 14.95 (ISBN 0-8239-1268-X). Rosen Group.

Super, Gretchen. Drugs & Our World. (Illus.). 48p. (gr. k-3). 1990. PLB 14.95 (ISBN 0-941477-88-6). TFC Bks MD.

—What Are Drugs? (Illus.). 48p. (gr. k-3). 1990. PLB 14.95 (ISBN 0-941477-87-8). TFC Bks MD.

—You Can Say "No" to Drugs! (Illus.). 48p. (gr. k-3). 1990. PLB 14.95 (ISBN 0-941477-89-4). TFC Bks MD.

Ward, Brian R. Drugs & Drug Abuse. Franklin Watts Ltd., ed. (Illus.). 32p. (gr. 7-12). 1988. PLB 12.40 (ISBN 0-531-10358-7). Watts.

Westfall, Tanja & Miles, Patrick. Decisions, 5 Vols. Karch, Cheri, ed. Tully, Carol & Rizzuto, Joe, illus. 160p. (gr. 4-7). 1989. Set. text ed. 38.95 (ISBN 1-877618-00-4). APIX Intl.

—Decisions: Building Bricks - Crystal, Vol 3. Karch, Cherl, ed. Tully, Carol & Rizzuto, Joe, illus. 32p. (gr. 4-7). 1989. text ed. 7.79 (ISBN 1-877618-03-9). APIX Intl.

—Decisions: Struggle in the Willow Tree, Vol. 1. Karch, Cheri, ed. Tully, Carol & Rizzuto, Joe, illus. 32p. (gr. 4-7). 1989. text ed. 7.79 (ISBN 1-877618-01-2). APIX Intl.

—Decisions: The Edge - LSD, Vol. 5. Karch, Cheri, ed. Tully, Carol & Rizzuto, Joe, illus. 32p. (gr. 4-7). 1989. text ed. 7.79 ea. (ISBN 1-877618-05-5). APIX Intl.

—Decisions: The Pit, Vol. 2. Karch, Cheri, ed. Tully, Carol & Rizzuto, Joe, illus. 32p. (gr. 4-7). 1989. text ed. 7.79 (ISBN 1-877618-02-0). APIX Intl.

—Decisions: The Survivor, Vol. 4. Karch, Cheri, ed. Tully, Carol & Rizzuto, Joe, illus. 32p. (gr. 4-7). 1989. text ed. 7.84 (ISBN 1-877618-04-7). APIX Intl.

Williams, Richard N. Handbook of Substance Abuse. 2nd ed. LC 91-60152. (Illus.). 120p. (gr. 6-12). 1991. text ed. 39.50 (ISBN 1-879278-00-6). Pharmaco-Video Pubns.

Wise, Francis H. Youth & Drugs. Wise, Joyce M., illus. (gr. 10 up). Date not set. 4.95 (ISBN 0-686-86911-7). Wise Pub.

Wood, Judy, et al. Sunakorn Drug Prevention Teaching Curriculum. LC 89-50139. 184p. (gr. k-5). 1989. 22.95 (ISBN 0-938021-42-7). Turner Pub KY.

Woolley, Merle E. Say No to Drugs Color & Learn Book. Frising, Nic, illus. 20p. (gr. k-6). 1988. wkbk. 1.50 (ISBN 0-9623773-0-9). Mapakam Inc.

NARCOTIC HABIT–FICTION

Bank Street College of Education Staff, et al. No Way, Slippery Slick! LC 90-45163. (Illus.). 32p. (gr. k-3). 1991. pap. 3.50 (ISBN 0-06-107438-1). HarpC Child Bks.

Childress, Alice. A Hero Ain't Nothin but a Sandwich. 128p. (gr. 7 up). 1977. pap. 2.95 (ISBN 0-380-00132-2, Flare). Avon.

Cook, John M. Inside Four Ninety-Five. Haye, Caroline, ed. (Illus.). 128p. 1989. write for info. J M Cook Pub.

Go Ask Alice. LC 74-159446. 160p. (gr. 6 up). 1971. PLB 11.95 (ISBN 0-671-66458-1). S&S Trade.

Irwin, Hadley. Can't Hear You Listening. LC 90-32675. 208p. (gr. 7 up). 1990. 13.95 (ISBN 0-689-50513-2, M K McElderry). Macmillan Child Grp.

Katz, Bobbi. Teenage Mutant Ninja Turtles Don't Do Drugs! A Rap Song. Mones, Isidre, illus. LC 90-53244. 32p. (Orig.). (ps-3). 1991. PLB 5.99 (ISBN 0-679-91485-4); pap. 2.25 (ISBN 0-679-81485-X). Random.

Morey, Walt. The Lemon Meringue Dog. LC 80-171. 176p. (gr. 4-7). 1980. 13.95 (ISBN 0-525-33455-6, DCB). Dutton Child Bks.

NARCOTICS

Appalachee Center for Human Services Staff. Choosing for Yourself 6-8. (Illus.). 208p. (gr. 6-8). 1988. Repr. of 1984 ed. 3-ring binder 200.00 (ISBN 1-8776670-2-1). Shared Learning.

—Choosing for Yourself 9-12. (Illus.). 222p. 1988. Repr. of 1984 ed. 3-ring binder 200.00 (ISBN 1-8776670-3-X). Shared Learning.

Booher, Albert R. Barbiturates. 11p. (gr. 5-9). 1988. pap. text ed. 5.95 (ISBN 0-685-28974-5). Madonna Edu Syst.

—Cocaine. 11p. (gr. 5-9). 1988. pap. text ed. 5.95 (ISBN 0-685-28979-6). Madonna Edu Syst.

—Drug & Alcohol Review. 13p. (gr. 5-9). 1988. pap. text ed. 5.95 (ISBN 0-685-28970-2). Madonna Edu Syst.

—Drug & Alcohol Terms. 9p. (gr. 5-9). 1988. pap. text ed. 5.95 (ISBN 0-685-28975-3). Madonna Edu Syst.

—Psychoactive Drugs I. 11p. (gr. 5-9). 1988. pap. text ed. 5.95 (ISBN 0-685-28972-9). Madonna Edu Syst.

—Psychoactive Drugs II. 9p. (gr. 5-9). 1988. pap. text ed. 5.95 (ISBN 0-685-28971-0). Madonna Edu Syst.

—Stimulants. 11p. (gr. 5-9). 1988. pap. text ed. 5.95 (ISBN 0-685-28973-7). Madonna Edu Syst.

Chapman, Dorothy. My Body Is Where I Live. (gr. k-4). 1989. text ed. 19.95 (ISBN 0-88671-297-1, 5102). Am Guidance.

Hafford, Jeannette N. Run Children Run: Tiny Warns Children about the Dangers of Drugs. (Illus.). (ps-8). 1989. pap. text ed. write for info. (ISBN 0-9616549-2-9). Tinys Self Help Bks.

Harris, Jonathan. Drugged America. LC 90-47649. 208p. (gr. 6 up). 1991. SBE 13.95 (ISBN 0-02-742745-5, Four Winds). Macmillan Child Grp.

Hawkes, N. International Drug Trade. (Illus.). 48p. (gr. 5 up). Date not set. PLB 18.00 (ISBN 0-86592-280-2). Rourke Corp.

Hyde, Margaret O. Drug Wars. (Illus.). 112p. (gr. 6 up). 1990. 11.95 (ISBN 0-8027-6900-4); lib. bdg. 12.85 (ISBN 0-8027-6901-2). Walker & Co.

Johnson, Joan J. America's War on Drugs. (Illus.). 160p. (gr. 9-12). 1990. 12.95 (ISBN 0-531-15179-4); PLB 13.90 (ISBN 0-531-10954-2). Watts.

King, Jesse J., Sr. You Can Say No to Drugs. King, Linda L., ed. King, Jesse J., Sr., illus. 24p. (Orig.). (gr. k-5). 1989. pap. text ed. 1.25 (ISBN 0-685-25956-0). J Lynn Pub.

—You Can Say No to Drugs: For Fifth Grade. King, Linda L., ed. King, Jesse J., Sr., illus. 24p. (Orig.). (gr. 5). 1990. pap. text ed. 1.25 (ISBN 0-685-25962-5). J Lynn Pub.

—You Can Say No to Drugs: For First Grade. King, Linda L., ed. King, Jesse J., Sr., illus. 24p. (Orig.). (gr. 1). 1989. pap. text ed. 1.25 (ISBN 0-685-25958-7). J Lynn Pub.

—You Can Say No to Drugs: For Fourth Grade. King, Linda L., ed. King, Jesse J., Sr., illus. 24p. (Orig.). (gr. 4). 1990. pap. text ed. 1.25 (ISBN 0-685-25961-7). J Lynn Pub.

—You Can Say No to Drugs: For Kindergarten. King, Linda L., ed. King, Jesse J., Sr., illus. 24p. (Orig.). (gr. k). 1989. pap. text ed. 1.25 (ISBN 0-685-25957-9). J Lynn Pub.

—You Can Say No to Drugs: For Second Grade. King, Linda L., ed. King, Jesse J., Sr., illus. 24p. (Orig.). (gr. 2). 1989. pap. text ed. 1.25 (ISBN 0-685-25959-5). J Lynn Pub.

—You Can Say No to Drugs: For Third Grade. King, Linda L., ed. King, Jesse J., Sr., illus. 24p. (Orig.). (gr. 3). 1990. pap. text ed. 1.25 (ISBN 0-685-25960-9). J Lynn Pub.

Klass, David. Wrestling with Honor. LC 88-16147. 208p. (gr. 7 up). 1989. 14.95 (ISBN 0-525-67268-0, Lodestar Bks). Dutton Child Bks.

Lutes, Chris. What Teenagers Are Saying about Drugs & Alcohol. 1990. pap. 7.95 (ISBN 0-310-71051-0, Campus Life). Zondervan.

Madison, Arnold. Drugs & You. rev. ed. Steltenpohl, Jane, ed. (Illus.). 128p. (gr. 4-6). 1990. PLB 12.98 (ISBN 0-671-69147-3); pap. 4.95 (ISBN 0-671-69148-1). Messner.

Pearce, Jenny. Colombia: The Drug War. (Illus.). 40p. (gr. 5-8). 1990. PLB 11.90 (ISBN 0-531-17237-6). Watts.

Rico, Armando B. A Sound Mind in a Sound Body. 23p. (Orig.). 1990. pap. 16.00 (ISBN 1-879219-03-4). Veracruz Pubs.

Terkel, Susan N. Should Drugs Be Legalized? (Illus.). 160p. (gr. 9-12). 1990. 12.95 (ISBN 0-531-15182-4); PLB 13.90 (ISBN 0-531-10944-5). Watts.

Washton, Arnold & Boundy, Donna. Cocaine & Crack: What You Need to Know. LC 88-16814. 96p. (gr. 5-10). 1989. lib. bdg. 16.95 (ISBN 0-89490-162-1). Enslow Pubs.

NATION OF ISLAM
see Black Muslims

NATIONAL ANTHEMS
see National Songs

NATIONAL DANCES
see Folk Dancing

NATIONAL DEFENSES
see names of countries with the subdivision Defenses, e.g. U. S.–Defenses

NATIONAL FOOTBALL LEAGUE
Kaplan, Richard. Great Linebackers of the NFL. (Illus.). (gr. 5-9). 1970. (Random Juv). Random.

Rothaus, James R. Atlanta Falcons. 48p. (gr. 4 up). 1991. PLB 10.45 (ISBN 0-88682-359-5). Creative Ed.

—Detroit Lions. 48p. (gr. 4 up). 1986. PLB 12.95 (ISBN 0-88682-366-8); 18.50 (ISBN 0-685-14310-4). Creative Ed.

NATIONAL GUARD (U. S.)
see U. S.–National Guard

NATIONAL HOLIDAYS
see Holidays;
see names of national holidays, e. g. Fourth of July

NATIONAL HYMNS
see National Songs

NATIONAL MONUMENTS
see National Parks and Reserves

NATIONAL PARKS AND RESERVES
Brown, Richard, illus. A Kid's Guide to National Parks. 160p. (gr. 1 up). 1989. pap. 6.95 (ISBN 0-318-37140-5, Gulliver Bks). HarBraceJ.

Crump, Donald J., ed. Adventures in Your National Parks. (gr. 3-8). 1989. 6.95 (ISBN 0-685-24968-9); PLB 8.50 (ISBN 0-87044-702-5). Natl Geog.

—Pathways to Discovery: Exploring America's National Trails. (Illus.). 1991. 8.95 (ISBN 0-87044-792-0). Natl Geog.

Diamond, Lynnell. Let's Discover Capitol Reef, Arches, & Canyonlands National Parks: A Children's Activity Book for Ages 6-11. (Illus.). 32p. (gr. 1-6). 1991. pap. 4.95 (ISBN 0-89886-286-8). Mountaineers.

—Let's Discover Petrified Forest National Park: A Children's Activity Book for Ages 6-11. (Illus.). 32p. (gr. 1-6). 1991. pap. 4.95 (ISBN 0-89886-285-X). Mountaineers.

Fischer, Christy, et al. National Parks: A Kid's-Eye View: The Rocky Mountains. (Illus.). 24p. (Orig.). (gr. 4-6). 1988. pap. 5.95 (ISBN 0-945710-00-3). Starword Bks.

Peters, Lisa W. Serengeti. LC 89-7859. (Illus.). 48p. (gr. 4-5). 1989. 12.95 (ISBN 0-89686-433-2, Crestwood Hse). Macmillan Child Grp.

Radlauer, Ruth. Acadia National Park. Radlauer, Ed & Radlauer, Ruth, illus. LC 77-18056. 48p. (gr. 3 up). 1978. PLB 17.27 (ISBN 0-516-07495-4, Elk Grove Bks). Childrens.

—Denali National Park & Preserve. Rev. ed. LC 81-3876. (Illus.). 48p. (gr. 3 up). 1981. PLB 17.27 (ISBN 0-516-07743-0). Childrens.

—Shenandoah National Park. Radlauer, Ed & Radlauer, Ruth, illus. LC 81-15521. 48p. (gr. 3 up). 1982. PLB 15.93 (ISBN 0-516-07744-9). Childrens.

—Zion National Park. updated ed. Radlauer, Ed, illus. LC 78-4028. 48p. (gr. 3 up). 1978. PLB 17.27 (ISBN 0-516-07497-0, Elk Grove Bks). Childrens.

Radlauer, Ruth S. Rocky Mountain National Park. updated ed. LC 77-2585. (Illus.). 48p. (gr. 3 up). 1977. PLB 17.27 (ISBN 0-516-07493-8). Childrens.

Rudig, Doug. Zion Adventure Guide. LC 77-78309. (Illus.). 32p. (gr. 2-7). 1978. pap. 1.95 (ISBN 0-915630-07-9). Zion.

Sateren, Shelley S. Banff. LC 89-33152. (Illus.). 48p. (gr. 4-5). 1989. 12.95 (ISBN 0-89686-431-6, Crestwood Hse). Macmillan Child Grp.

Sotnak, Lewann. Carlsbad Caverns. LC 88-17707. (Illus.). 48p. (gr. 4-8). 1989. PLB 12.95 (ISBN 0-89686-403-0, Crestwood Hse). Macmillan Child Grp.

NATIONAL PARKS AND RESERVES–U. S.
Lovett, Sarah. Kidding Around the National Parks of the Southwest: A Young Person's Guide. Strock, Glen, illus. 108p. (Orig.). (gr. 3 up). 1990. pap. 12.95 (ISBN 0-945465-72-6). John Muir.

Melbo, Irving R. Our Country's National Parks, 2 Vols. (gr. 4-8). 1973. 7.95 (ISBN 0-672-51825-2, Bobbs); 7.95 (ISBN 0-672-51826-0). Macmillan.

Radlauer, Ruth. Bryce Canyon National Park. updated ed. Radlauer, Ed & Radlauer, Ruth, illus. LC 79-22722. 48p. (gr. 3 up). 1980. PLB 17.27 (ISBN 0-516-07484-9, Elk Grove Bks.); pap. 4.95 (ISBN 0-516-47484-7). Childrens.

—Grand Teton National Park. Rev. ed. LC 80-12257. (Illus.). 48p. (gr. 3 up). 1980. PLB 17.27 (ISBN 0-516-07740-6). Childrens.

—Haleakala National Park. updated ed. Zillmer, Rolf, illus. LC 79-10500. 48p. (gr. 3-12). 1979. PLB 17.27 (ISBN 0-516-07499-7); pap. 4.95 (ISBN 0-516-47499-5). Childrens.

—Mammoth Cave National Park. updated ed. Radlauer, Ed, illus. LC 77-26764. 48p. (gr. 3 up). 1978. PLB 17.27 (ISBN 0-516-07496-2, Elk Grove Bks); pap. 4.95 (ISBN 0-516-47496-0). Childrens.

—Mesa Verde National Park. updated ed. Zillmer, Rolf, photos by. LC 76-27350. (Illus.). 48p. (gr. 3 up). 1984. PLB 17.27 (ISBN 0-516-07490-3); pap. 4.95 (ISBN 0-516-47490-1). Childrens.

—Olympic National Park. updated ed. Zillmer, Rolf, photos by. LC 77-5836. (Illus.). 48p. (gr. 3 up). 1978. PLB 17.27 (ISBN 0-685-01060-0) (ISBN 0-516-07494-6). Childrens.

Root, Phyllis & McCormick, Maxine. Great Basin. LC 88-18645. (Illus.). 48p. (gr. 4-5). 1988. 12.95 (ISBN 0-89686-410-3, Crestwood Hse). Macmillan Child Grp.

NATIONAL PLANNING
see names of countries with the subdivision Economic Policy; Social Policy; e.g. U. S.–Economic Policy; U. S. –Social Policy

NATIONAL RESOURCES
see Natural Resources;
see names of countries with the subdivision Economic Conditions, e.g. U.S.–Economic Conditions

NATIONAL SOCIALISM
Bornstein, Jerry. The Neo-Nazis. LC 85-5363. (Illus.). 192p. (gr. 7 up). 1986. lib. bdg. 11.98 (ISBN 0-671-50238-7). Messner.

NATIONAL SOCIALISM–FICTION
Kerr, M. E. Gentlehands. LC 77-11860. (gr. 7-9). 1978. PLB 16.89 (ISBN 0-06-023177-7). HarpC Child Bks.

Sevela, Ephraim. Why There Is No Heaven on Earth. Lourie, Richard, tr. LC 81-47736. (RUS.). 224p. (gr. 7 up). 1982. 11.06i (ISBN 0-06-025502-1). HarpC Child Bks.

Wuorio, Eva-Lis. Detour to Danger: A Novel. LC 81-65501. 192p. (gr. 7 up). 1981. 12.95 (ISBN 0-385-28206-0). Delacorte.

NATIONAL SONGS
see also Folk Songs
Spier, Peter. The Star-Spangled Banner. Spier, Peter, illus. LC 73-79112. 48p. (gr. 1 up). 1973. 12.95 (ISBN 0-385-09458-2); pap. 11.95 (ISBN 0-385-07746-7). Doubleday.

—The Star-Spangled Banner. Spier, Peter, illus. LC 73-79112. 48p. (gr. 1 up). 1973. 12.95 (ISBN 0-385-09458-2); pap. 11.95 (ISBN 0-385-07746-7). Doubleday.

Young, Woody. Song Wise, Three: Battle Hymn of the Republic. White, Craig, illus. 24p. (Orig.). 1986. pap. text ed. 2.95 (ISBN 0-939513-13-7). Joy Pub SJC.

—Song Wise, Vol. Four: America. White, Craig, illus. 24p. (Orig.). 1986. pap. text ed. 2.95 (ISBN 0-939513-14-5). Joy Pub SJC.

—Song Wise, Vol. One: The Star Spangled Banner. White, Craig, illus. 24p. (Orig.). 1986. pap. text ed. 2.95 (ISBN 0-939513-11-0). Joy Pub SJC.

—Song Wise, Vol. Two: America the Beautiful. White, Craig, illus. 24p. (Orig.). 1986. pap. text ed. 2.95 (ISBN 0-939513-12-9). Joy Pub SJC.

NATIONALITY (CITIZENSHIP)
see Citizenship

NATIONS, LAW OF
see International Law

NATIVITY OF CHRIST
see Jesus Christ–Nativity

NATURAL DISASTERS
see Disasters

NATURAL HISTORY
Here are entered popular works describing animals, plants, minerals and nature in general. Handbooks on the detailed study of birds, flowers, etc. are entered under Nature Study.
see also Aquariums; Biology; Botany; Fossils; Fresh-Water Biology; Geographical Distribution of Animals and Plants; Geology; Marine Biology; Mineralogy; Zoology
Allen, Eugenie. The Best Ever Kids' Book of Lists. 128p. (Orig.). 1991. pap. 2.95 (ISBN 0-380-76357-5, Camelot). Avon.

Arnosky, Jim. Secrets of a Wildlife Watcher. LC 82-24920. (Illus.). 64p. (gr. 5 up). 1983. 13.95 (ISBN 0-688-02079-8); lib. bdg. 13.88 (ISBN 0-688-02081-X). Lothrop.

Borland, Hal. The Golden Circle: A Book of Months. Dowden, Anne O., illus. LC 77-23560. 64p. (gr. 5 up). 1977. 13.95 (ISBN 0-690-03803-8, Crowell Jr Bks). HarpC Child Bks.

Brownstone, David & Franck, Irene. Natural Wonders of America. (Illus.). 64p. (gr. 3-7). 1989. pap. 7.95 (ISBN 0-689-71229-4, Aladdin). Macmillan Child Grp.

Burton, Virginia L. Life Story. (Illus.). (gr. k-3). 1989. 15.95 (ISBN 0-395-16030-8); pap. 6.95 (ISBN 0-395-52017-7). HM.

Dean, Anabel. Strange Partners: The Story of Symbiosis. Matte, L'Enc, illus. LC 75-38479. 96p. (gr. 3-6). 1976. lib. bdg. 6.95 (ISBN 0-8225-1100-2). Lerner Pubns.

Dixon, Douglas. Be a Fossil Detective. (gr. 2 up). 1989. 3.99 (ISBN 0-517-68022-X). Outlet Bk Co.

Ganeri, Anita & Butterfield, Maira. Natural World. Bull, Peter & Johnson, Paul, illus. LC 89-11349. 48p. (gr. 4-5). 1989. PLB 11.95 (ISBN 0-8368-0133-4). Gareth Stevens Inc.

Hall, Derek. Sierra Club's Growing Up Books. Butler, John, illus. Incl. Otter Swims. LC 83-22004. 4.95 (ISBN 0-685-08469-8); PLB 6.99; Panda Climbs. LC 83-17462. 4.95 (ISBN 0-685-08471-X); PLB 6.99; Tiger Runs. LC 84-793. 1984. 24p. (ps up). 1984. Knopf.

Magley, Beverly. The Fire Mountains: The Story of the Cascade Volcanos. Dowden, D. D., illus. LC 88-83884. 32p. (Orig.). (gr. 3-6). 1989. pap. 4.95 (ISBN 0-937959-57-X). Falcon Pr MT.

Martin, Bill, Jr. Little Nature Books. Incl. Poppies Afield; Frogs in a Pond; Butterflies Becoming; Germination; Ants Underground; A Mushroom Is Growing; A Hydra Goes Walking; Moon Cycle; Messenger Bee; June Bugs. (Illus.). (gr. 1-6). 1975. 149.00 (ISBN 0-87827-196-1); tchr's. guide incl. (ISBN 0-685-55948-3); cassettes incl. Ency Brit Ed.

Middleton, Nick. Atlas of the Natural World. (Illus.). 64p. 1990. 16.95x (ISBN 0-8160-2131-7). Facts on File.

National Geographical Society Staff, ed. Books for Young Explorers, 4 vols, Set 1. Incl. Dinosaurs. LC 72-91418; Treasures in the Sea. LC 72-91421; Dogs Working for People. LC 72-91419; Lion Cubs. LC 72-91420. (ps-3). 1972. PLB 12.95 avail. only from Natl. Geog. (ISBN 0-87044-300-3). Natl Geog.

Nature. (Illus.). 112p. (gr. 4-9). Date not set. 19.95x (ISBN 1-85435-074-9). Marshall Cavendish.

Richards, John. Hidden Country: Nature on Your Doorstep. LC 72-12745. (Illus.). 144p. (gr. 5-8). 1973. PLB 18.95 (ISBN 0-87599-195-5). S G Phillips.

Ross, Michael E. Cycles, Cycles, Cycles. (Illus.). 88p. (gr. 1-3). 1979. pap. 3.95 (ISBN 0-939666-01-4). Yosemite Assn.

Stidworthy, John. Naturalist. (Illus.). 32p. (gr. 5-8). 1991. PLB 11.90 (ISBN 0-531-17356-9, Gloucester Pr). Watts.

Wyler, Rose. Wonderful Woods. Petruccio, Steven, illus. 32p. (gr. k-3). 1990. PLB 11.98 (ISBN 0-671-69164-3); pap. 4.95 (ISBN 0-671-69166-X). Messner.

NATURAL HISTORY–AUSTRALIA
Crump, Donald J., ed. Wonderful Animals of Australia, Bk. 1. (Illus.). (ps-3). 1990. Set. 21.95 (ISBN 0-87044-809-9). Natl Geog.

NATURAL HISTORY, BIBLICAL
see Bible–Natural History

NATURAL HISTORY–DICTIONARIES
Silver, Donald. Checkerboard Nature Encyclopedia. (gr. 4-7). 1990. 9.95 (ISBN 0-02-689307-X). Checkerboard Pr.

NATURAL HISTORY–FICTION
Carlstrom, Nancy W. Wild Wild Sunflower Child Anna. Pinkney, Jerry, illus. LC 90-40679. 32p. (ps-1). 1991. pap. 4.95 (ISBN 0-689-71445-9, Aladdin). Macmillan Child Grp.

Doucet, Daisy J. Can You Imagine. 1991. 7.95 (ISBN 0-533-08961-1). Vantage.

Goffstein, M. B. Natural History. Goffstein, M. B., illus. LC 79-7318. 32p. (ps-3). 1979. 8.95 (ISBN 0-374-35498-7). FS&G.

Morrow, Barbara. Help for Mr. Peale. Morrow, Barbara, illus. LC 89-39273. 32p. (gr. 1-3). 1990. 13.95 (ISBN 0-02-767590-4, Mcmillan Child Bk). Macmillan Child Grp.

NATURAL HISTORY–NORTH AMERICA
Hamerstrom, Frances. Walk When the Moon Is Full. Katona, Robert, illus. LC 75-33878. 64p. (gr. 3-8). 1975. 15.95 (ISBN 0-912278-69-2); pap. 6.95 (ISBN 0-912278-84-6). Crossing Pr.

NATURAL HISTORY–OUTDOOR BOOKS
see Nature Study

NATURAL HISTORY–SOUTHWEST, NEW
Baylor, Byrd. I'm in Charge of Celebrations. Parnall, Peter, illus. LC 85-19633. 32p. (gr. 1-4). 1986. 13.95 (ISBN 0-684-18579-2, Scribners Young Read). Macmillan Child Grp.

NATURAL HISTORY–U. S.
Brownstone, David M. & Franck, Irene M. Natural Wonders of America. LC 88-27487. (Illus.). 64p. (gr. 3-7). 1989. 14.95 (ISBN 0-689-31430-2, Atheneum Child Bk). Macmillan Child Grp.

Freeman, Marie E. & Davis, Maria H. Alpine to Alkali. Delany, Dan & Walker, Jan, illus. LC 83-80807. 150p. (Orig.). (gr. 7-12). 1983. pap. text ed. 7.95 (ISBN 0-913205-01-X); special price 3.98 (ISBN 0-913205-06-0). Grace Dangberg.

NATURAL HISTORY MUSEUMS
Gibbons, Gail. Dinosaurs, Dragonflies & Diamonds: All About Natural History Museums. Gibbons, Gail, illus. LC 88-388. 32p. (gr. k-3). 1988. PLB 13.95 (ISBN 0-02-737240-5, Four Winds). Macmillan Child Grp.

NATURAL LAW
see Civil Rights; Ethics; International Law; Liberty

NATURAL RESOURCES

see also Conservation of Natural Resources; Fisheries; Forests and Forestry; Marine Resources; Mines and Mineral Resources; Power Resources; Soil Conservation; Water Power; Water Supply

Arnold, Caroline. Natural Resources: Fun, Facts, & Activities. Carter, Penny, tr. LC 84-19598. (Illus.). 32p. (gr. 1-3). 1985. lib. bdg. 10.90 (ISBN 0-531-04898-5). Watts.

Bittinger, Gayle. Our World. McKinnon, Elizabeth, ed. Jones, Kathy, illus. LC 89-52145. 80p. (Orig.). 1990. pap. 7.95 (ISBN 0-911019-30-8). Warren Pub Hse.

Green, I. Conservation from A to Z. LC 66-11443. (Illus.). 64p. (gr. 4 up). 1968. PLB 10.95 (ISBN 0-87783-009-6); pap. 3.94 deluxe ed. (ISBN 0-87783-088-6). Oddo.

Kalman, Bobbie. Natural Resources. (Illus.). 32p. (gr. 2-3). 1987. 14.95 (ISBN 0-86505-077-5); pap. 5.95 (ISBN 0-86505-099-6). Crabtree Pub Co.

Peckham, Alex. Resources Control. (Illus.). 40p. (gr. 5-8). 1990. PLB 11.90 (ISBN 0-531-17234-1). Watts.

Peckham, Alexander. Changing Landscapes. (Illus.). 40p. (gr. 6-9). 1991. PLB 11.90 (ISBN 0-531-17289-9, Gloucester Pr). Watts.

Wood, John N. Nature Hide & Seek: Jungles. Schulman, Janet, ed. Dean, Kevin, illus. LC 86-21450. 24p. (ps-4). 1987. 9.95 (ISBN 0-394-87802-7). Knopf.

NATURAL RESOURCES–U. S.

see also U. S.–Economic Conditions

NATURAL SELECTION

see also Evolution

NATURALISTS

Mitchell, A. The Young Naturalist. (Illus.). 32p. (gr. 5-10). 1984. PLB 13.96 (ISBN 0-88110-235-0); pap. 6.95 (ISBN 0-86020-653-X). EDC.

Tolan, Sally. John Muir: Naturalist, Writer & Guardian of the North American Wilderness. LC 89-4367. (Illus.). 64p. (gr. 5-6). 1989. PLB 12.95 (ISBN 0-8368-0099-0). Gareth Stevens Inc.

Ward, Peter. The Adventures of Charles Darwin: A Story of the Beagle Voyage. LC 81-21751. (Illus.). 96p. (gr. 4-7). 1986. 12.95 (ISBN 0-521-24510-9); pap. 5.95 (ISBN 0-521-31074-1). Cambridge U Pr.

Warren, Betsy. Wilderness Walkers: Naturalists in Early Texas. La Freniere, Annette, ed. Warren, Betsy, illus. LC 55-7501. 112p. (gr. 4-8). 1987. PLB 12.95 (ISBN 0-937460-26-5). Hendrick-Long.

NATURE

Booth, Eugene. In the Air. LC 77-7984. (Illus.). 24p. (gr. k-3). 1977. PLB 13.32 (ISBN 0-8393-0105-7). Raintree Pubs.

British Museum Staff. Nature at Work. LC 78-66795. (Illus.). (gr. 7 up). 1978. pap. 12.95 (ISBN 0-521-29469-X). Cambridge U Pr.

Childrens First Nature Encyclopedia. 1987. 6.98 (ISBN 0-671-08189-6). S&S Trade.

Chinery, Michael. Illustrated World of Nature. Warwick Press, ed. Streek, Tony, illus. 64p. (gr. 4-9). 13.90 (ISBN 0-531-19034-X, Warwick). Watts.

Cox & Cork. First Book of Nature. (gr. 2-5). 1980. 12.95 (ISBN 0-86020-483-9, Usborne-Hayes). EDC.

—Flowers. (gr. 2-5). 1980. (Usborne-Hayes); PLB 11.96 (ISBN 0-88110-074-9); pap. 3.95 (ISBN 0-86020-479-0). EDC.

DeBruin, Jerry. Nature. Swemba, Jeane, illus. 32p. (gr. 4 up). 1986. wkbk 4.95 (ISBN 0-86653-339-7, GA 688). Good Apple.

Faber, Doris & Faber, Harold. Great Lives: Nature & the Environment. LC 90-8847. (Illus.). 304p. (gr. 4-6). 1991. SBE 22.95 (ISBN 0-684-19047-8, Scribners Young Read). Macmillan Child Grp.

Field, Nancy & Machlis, Sally. Discovering Endangered Species. (Illus.). 40p. (Orig.). (gr. 3-7). 1990. pap. 3.95 (ISBN 0-941042-09-X). Dog Eared Pubns.

Hamerstrom, Frances. Walk When the Moon Is Full. Katona, Robert, illus. LC 75-33878. 64p. (gr. 3-8). 1975. 15.95 (ISBN 0-912278-69-2); pap. 6.95 (ISBN 0-912278-84-6). Crossing Pr.

Hayes, Dympna & Lehman, Melanie. Fun with Nature. Kelly, Teri, ed. Davis, Annelies, illus. 32p. (gr. 2). 1987. PLB 13.85 (ISBN 0-88625-154-0); pap. 2.50 (ISBN 0-685-30766-2). Durkin Hayes Pub.

Henry, Lucia K. Nature Study Mini-Units: Ducks, Otters, Whales, Rabbits, Pandas. (Illus.). 48p. (gr. k-2). 1987. wkbk. 5.95 (ISBN 1-55734-219-9). Tchr Create Mat.

Hess, Lilo. Secrets in the Meadow. Hess, Lilo, photos by. LC 85-43350. (Illus.). 64p. (gr. 3-6). 1986. SBE 13.95 (ISBN 0-684-18525-3, Scribners Young Read). Macmillan Child Grp.

Hiller, Ilo. Young Naturalist: From Texas Parks & Wildlife Magazine. LC 83-45107. (Illus.). 176p. (gr. 2-8). 1983. 15.95 (ISBN 0-89096-163-8). Tex A&M Univ Pr.

Hoy, Ken. Land Life. (Illus.). 12p. 1990. 11.95 (ISBN 0-8249-8472-2). Ideals.

Jones, Michael P., ed. Oregon River Watch: A Contemporary History of Oregon's Waterways, Vol. 1. Bachmann, Mark, et al, illus. 48p. (Orig.). 1985. text ed. 9.95 (ISBN 0-89904-143-4); pap. text ed. 5.00 (ISBN 0-89904-144-2); composition 8.00 (ISBN 0-89904-145-0). Crumb Elbow Pub.

—Oregon River Watch: A Contemporary History of Oregon's Waterways, Vol. 2. Bachmann, Mark, et al, illus. 50p. (Orig.). 1985. text ed. 9.95 (ISBN 0-89904-146-9); pap. text ed. 5.00 (ISBN 0-89904-147-7); composition 8.00 (ISBN 0-89904-148-5). Crumb Elbow Pub.

Kelley, Colleen. Kids' Stuff: Simple Science & Nature Projects for Children. Kelley, Colleen, illus. 96p. (gr. k-6). 1989. pap. text ed. 4.95 (ISBN 0-9618052-2-6). Daily Hampshire.

Kilpatrick. Creepy Crawlies. (gr. 2-5). 1982. (Usborne-Hayes); PLB 11.96 (ISBN 0-88110-076-5); pap. 3.95 (ISBN 0-86020-630-0). EDC.

Kirkman, Will. Nature Crafts Workshop. LC 80-84186. (gr. 3-8). pap. 8.95 (ISBN 0-8224-9781-6). Fearon Teach Aids.

Liptak, Karen. Out in the Night. Fuller, Sandy F., illus. LC 89-1833. 32p. (Orig.). (gr. 3-5). 1989. PLB 15.95 (ISBN 0-943173-19-1); pap. 8.95 (ISBN 0-943173-31-0). Harbinger AZ.

Little People Big Book about Nature. 64p. (ps-1). 1990. write for info. (ISBN 0-8094-7512-X); PLB write for info. (ISBN 0-8094-7513-8). Time-Life.

Lohf, Sabine. Things I Can Make with Leaves. (Illus.). 32p. (ps-2). 1990. 6.95 (ISBN 0-87701-763-8). Chronicle Bks.

Milne, Lorus J. & Milne, Margery. Nature's Clean-up Crew. (Illus.). 64p. (gr. 3-7). 1982. 8.95 (ISBN 0-396-08038-3, Putnam). Putnam Pub Group.

Nature Close-Ups. (Illus.). (gr. 3-7). 1986. Set of 40 titles, 32 pp. ea. PLB 613.20 (ISBN 0-8172-2724-5); Set of 40 titles, 32 pp. ea. pap. 370.80 (ISBN 0-8172-2725-3). Raintree Pubs.

Oliver, Stephen, photos by. Nature. LC 90-23568. (Illus.). 24p. (ps-k). 1991. 7.00 (ISBN 0-679-81805-7, Random Juv). Random.

Pearce, Q. L. Quicksand & Other Earthly Wonders. Steltenpohl, Jane, ed. Fraser, Mary A., illus. 64p. (gr. 4-6). 1989. PLB 12.98 (ISBN 0-671-68530-9); pap. 5.95 (ISBN 0-671-68646-1). Messner.

Podendorf, Illa. Jungles. LC 82-4454. (gr. k-4). 1982. 14.60 (ISBN 0-516-01631-8). Childrens.

Rainis, Genneth. Nature Projects for Young Scientists. 1989. pap. 5.95 (ISBN 0-531-15135-2). Watts.

Rankin, William. Come Hibernate with Me. Camphouse, Marylyn J., frwd. by. (Illus.). 214p. (Orig.). (gr. 9 up). 1989. 30.00 (ISBN 0-9623948-0-7). M Camphouse.

Ruth Heller's World of Nature. (Illus.). (ps up). 1988. 3.95 (ISBN 0-448-09826-1, G&D). Putnam Pub Group.

Schnieper, Claudia. On the Trail of the Fox. Scherer, Elise, tr. (GER., Illus.). 48p. (gr. 2-5). 1986. lib. bdg. 12.95 (ISBN 0-87614-287-0); pap. 6.95 (ISBN 0-87614-480-6). Carolrhoda Bks.

Selberg, Ingrid. Nature's Hidden World. Miller, Andrew, illus. 14p. (gr. k-2). 1984. 12.95 (ISBN 0-399-20973-5, Philomel). Putnam Pub Group.

Thoreau, Henry David. Walden. Langmack, F., intro. by. Bd. with On Civil Disobedience. (gr. 10up). pap. 1.50 (ISBN 0-8049-0083-3, CL-83). Airmont.

—Walden. Sherman, Paul, ed. Bd. with Civil Disobedience. LC 60-16148. (gr. 9 up). 1960. pap. 8.76 (ISBN 0-395-05113-4, RivEd). HM.

Veith, Jan T. Natural Wonders. 64p. (gr. 3-6). 1987. 9.95 (ISBN 0-912107-56-1). Monday Morning Bks.

Wheeler. Fishes. (gr. 2-5). 1982. (Usborne-Hayes); PLB 11.96 (ISBN 0-88110-075-7); pap. 3.95 (ISBN 0-86020-626-2). EDC.

Wilkes, Angela. My First Nature Book. (Illus.). (gr. 1-5). 1990. write for info. Knopf.

Wood, Jenny. Wonderworks of Nature, 4 vols. (Illus.). 32p. (gr. 3-4). 1990. Set. PLB 47.80 (ISBN 0-8368-0468-6). Gareth Stevens Inc.

NATURE, EFFECT OF MAN ON

see Man–Influence on Nature

NATURE IN LITERATURE

see also Nature in Poetry

NATURE IN ORNAMENT

see Design, Decorative

NATURE IN POETRY

Larrick, Nancy, selected by. Room for Me & a Mountain Lion: Poetry of Open Spaces. (Illus.). 192p. (gr. 5 up). 1989. pap. 6.95 (ISBN 0-87131-569-6). M Evans.

Lewis, Richard, ed. In a Spring Garden. Keats, Ezra J., illus. LC 65-23965. 32p. (ps up). 1989. Repr. of 1965 ed. 13.95 (ISBN 0-8037-4024-7). Dial Bks Young.

Mizumura, Kazue. Flower Moon Snow: A Book of Haiku. Mizumura, Kazue, illus. LC 76-41180. (gr. k-4). 1977. 7.95 (ISBN 0-690-01291-8, Crowell Jr Bks). HarpC Child Bks.

Ryder, Joanne. Under Your Feet. Nolan, Dennis, illus. 32p. (ps-3). 1990. 13.95 (ISBN 0-02-777955-6, Four Winds). Macmillan Child Grp.

NATURE PHOTOGRAPHY

see also Photography of Animals

NATURE POETRY

see Nature in Poetry

NATURE STUDY

see also Animals–Habits and Behavior; Botany; Zoology

Allison, Linda. The Reasons for Seasons: The Great Cosmic Megagalactic Trip Without Moving from Your Chair. Allison, Linda, illus. 128p. (gr. 4 up). 1975. 14.95 (ISBN 0-316-03439-8); pap. 8.95 (ISBN 0-316-03440-1). Little.

Arnosky, Jim. Crinkleroot's Book of Animal Tracking. rev. ed. Arnosky, Jim, illus. LC 88-15353. 48p. (gr. 2-6). 1989. 13.95 (ISBN 0-02-705851-4, Bradbury Pr). Macmillan Child Grp.

—I Was Born in a Tree & Raised by Bees. Arnosky, Jim, illus. LC 88-6121. 48p. (gr. 2-6). 1988. Repr. of 1977 ed. 13.95 (ISBN 0-02-705841-7, Bradbury Pr). Macmillan Child Grp.

Arvetis, Chris & Palmer, Carole. Why Does It Float? Buckley, James, illus. 32p. (ps-3). 1984. Repr. 3.95 (ISBN 0-528-82399-X). Checkerboard Pr.

—Why Does It Fly? Buckley, James, illus. 32p. (ps-3). 1984. Repr. 3.95 (ISBN 0-528-82074-5). Checkerboard Pr.

—Why Does It Rain? Buckley, James, illus. 32p. (ps-3). 1984. Repr. 3.95 (ISBN 0-528-82073-7, Checkerbord Pr). Macmillan.

—Why Does It Snow? Buckley, James, illus. 32p. (ps-3). 1984. 3.95 (ISBN 0-528-82823-1). Checkerboard Pr.

—Why Is It Dark? Buckley, James, illus. 32p. (ps-3). 1984. 3.95 (ISBN 0-528-82075-3). Checkerboard Pr.

Bank Street College of Education Editors. Let's Explore Land, Water, Air. (gr. 1-2). 1986. pap. 2.95 (ISBN 0-8120-3624-7). Barron.

Barlowe, Dot & Barlowe, Sy. Who Lives Here? Barlowe, Dot & Barlowe, Sy, illus. LC 79-27494. 32p. (ps-3). 1980. pap. 2.25 (ISBN 0-394-83740-1). Random.

Benton, Allen H. & Bunting, Richard L. Young People's Nature Guide. De Santo, Rita, et al, illus. 177p. (gr. 2-4). 1978. pap. text ed. 3.00 (ISBN 0-942788-05-2). Marginal Med.

Berenstain, Stan & Berenstain, Janice. The Bears' Nature Guide. Berenstain, Stan & Berenstain, Janice, illus. LC 75-8070. 72p. (ps-3). 1975. 6.95 (ISBN 0-394-83125-X, Random Juv); lib. bdg. 6.99 (ISBN 0-394-93125-4). Random.

Binnamin, Vivian. Field Trip Mysteries Series, 4 vols. Nelsen, Jeffrey S., illus. 128p. (gr. k-3). 1990. Set. PLB 27.92 (ISBN 0-671-94436-3); Set. PLB 20.94s.p.; Set. pap. 10.00 (ISBN 0-671-94437-1); Set. pap. 7.50s.p. Silver Pr.

Bowden, Marcia. Nature for the Very Young: A Handbook of Indoor & Outdoor Activities. Rishel, Marilyn, illus. (ps-2). 1989. pap. 10.95 (ISBN 0-318-41683-2). Wiley.

Boy Scouts of America. Nature. (Illus.). 48p. (gr. 6-12). 1973. pap. 1.85 (ISBN 0-8395-3285-7, 3285). BSA.

Brown, Tom, Jr. Tom Brown's Field Guide to Nature & Survival for Children. 1989. pap. 8.95 (ISBN 0-425-11106-7). Berkley Pub.

Carpenter, Mimi G. What the Sea Left Behind. Carpenter, Mimi G., illus. LC 81-66251. 32p. (gr. 1-4). 1981. pap. 7.95 (ISBN 0-89272-123-5). Down East.

Cooper, Ursula. Mini Walks on the Mesa. Harroun, Dorothy, illus. LC 89-4448. 32p. (Orig.). (gr. 3-6). 1989. pap. 6.95 (ISBN 0-86534-133-8). Sunstone Pr.

Crump, Donald J., ed. Adventures in Your National Parks. (gr. 3-8). 1989. 6.95 (ISBN 0-685-24968-9); PLB 8.50 (ISBN 0-87044-702-5). Natl Geog.

—Books for Young Explorers, 4 bks, Set 16. (gr. k-4). 1989. Set. 10.95 (ISBN 0-685-24969-7); Set. PLB 12.95 (ISBN 0-685-24970-0). No. 1: Cottontails - Little Rabbits of Field & Forest. No. 2: Amazing Otters. No. 3: Animals of the High Mountains. No. 4: Animal Clowns. Natl Geog.

Dekkers, Midas. The Nature Book: Discovering, Exploring, Observing, Experimenting with Plants & Animals at Home & Outdoors. DeVrede, Angelo, illus. Michael, Jan, tr. from DUT. LC 87-5696. (Illus.). 96p. (gr. 3-7). 1988. 12.95 (ISBN 0-02-726690-7, Mcmillan Child Bk). Macmillan Child Grp.

Delon-Boltz, Mireille, et al. First Nature Watch, 6 bks, Set 2. (Illus.). 12p. (Orig.). (gr. k-1). 1986. pap. text ed. 14.80 (ISBN 1-55624-067-8, WGO678). Wright Group.

Diamond, Lynnell. Let's Discover Capitol Reef, Arches, & Canyonlands National Parks: A Children's Activity Book for Ages 6-11. (Illus.). 32p. (gr. 1-6). 1991. pap. 4.95 (ISBN 0-89886-286-8). Mountaineers.

—Let's Discover Petrified Forest National Park: A Children's Activity Book for Ages 6-11. (Illus.). 32p. (gr. 1-6). 1991. pap. 4.95 (ISBN 0-89886-285-X). Mountaineers.

Evelyn-Marie. Pick Your Own Strawberries. rev. ed. Evelyn-Marie, illus. 32p. (gr. k-3). pap. 3.00 (ISBN 0-9614746-3-7). Berry Bks.

Field, Nancy & Machlis, Sally. Discovering Crater Lake. Machlis, Sally, illus. 32p. (Orig.). (gr. 1-6). 1989. pap. 3.50 (ISBN 0-941042-08-1). Dog Eared Pubns.

Florian, Douglas. Nature Walk. LC 88-39430. (Illus.). 32p. (ps up). 1989. 12.95 (ISBN 0-688-08266-1); PLB 12.88 (ISBN 0-688-08269-6). Greenwillow.

Hamerstrom, Frances. Walk When the Moon Is Full. Katona, Robert, illus. LC 75-33878. 64p. (gr. 3-8). 1975. 15.95 (ISBN 0-912278-69-2); pap. 6.95 (ISBN 0-912278-84-6). Crossing Pr.

Herridge, Douglas & Hughes, Susan. The Environmental Detective Kit. LC 90-48247. (Illus.). 80p. (gr. 3 up). 1991. 12.95 (ISBN 0-06-107408-X). HarpC Child Bks.

Holing, Dwight. EarthTrips: A Guide to Nature Travel on a Fragile Planet. (Illus.). 180p. (Orig.). 1991. pap. 12.95 (ISBN 1-879326-05-1). Living Planet Pr.

Holmes, Jean E. Sea Island Sanctuary. Woolsey, Raymond H., ed. 128p. (Orig.). (gr. 6-8). 1988. pap. 6.95 (ISBN 0-8280-0436-6). Review & Herald.

Janssen, Lawrence H. Earth Care a Mandate: Nature Study Guide Keyed to the Black Hills. Janssen, Lawrence H., illus. LC 85-73644. 80p. (Orig.). (gr. 7-12). 1985. pap. 3.95 (ISBN 0-917575-03-2). Cedars WI.

—Horsethief Lake Old Baldy Trail Guides. Janssen, Lawrence H., illus. (Orig.). (gr. 7-12). 1986. pap. 1.00 (ISBN 0-917575-04-0). Cedars WI.

Jenkins, Christine. Loving Our Neighbor the Earth: Faith-Filled Science Activities for 9-11 Years Olds. LC 91-10968. (Illus.). 160p. (Orig.). (gr. 4-6). 1990. pap. 21.95 (ISBN 0-89390-204-7). Resource Pubns.

Jorgensen, Eric, et al. Manure, Meadows & Milkshakes. Hone, Elizabeth, ed. Hendrick, Andrea, illus. 132p. (Orig.). (ps-8). 1986. pap. text ed. 9.95 tchrs. ed. (ISBN 0-318-20228-X). Trust Hidden Villa.

Junek, Jaroslav, et al. First Nature Watch, 12 bks. (Illus., Orig.). (gr. k-1). 1986. Set. pap. text ed. 25.40 (ISBN 1-55624-000-7). Wright Group.

Leslie, Clare W. Nature All Year Long. LC 90-47866. (Illus.). 56p. (gr. 2 up). Date not set. 16.95 (ISBN 0-688-09183-0). Greenwillow.

Milord, Susan. The Kids' Nature Book: Three Hundred Sixty-Five Indoor - Outdoor Activities & Experiences. Williamson, Susan, ed. LC 89-14724. 160p. (Orig.). (ps-3). 1989. pap. 12.95 (ISBN 0-913589-42-X). Williamson Pub Co.

National Geographic Society Staff. Books for Young Explorers, 4 vols., set 8. Incl. Wild Cats. Winston, Peggy D. LC 81-47742; Amazing Animal Groups. LC 81-47743; Koalas & Kangaroos: Strange Animals of Australia. Eugene, Toni. LC 81-607859; Life in Ponds & Streams. Amos, William H. LC 81-47745. (Illus.). (ps-3). 1981. Set. lib. bdg. 12.95 (ISBN 0-87044-405-0); Set. PLB 10.95 (ISBN 0-87044-410-7). Natl Geog.

—Books for Young Explorers, 4 vols, set 9. Incl. Animals That Travel. Urquhart, Jennifer C. LC 82-47856; Puppies. Rinard, Judith E. LC 82-47857; Animals in Winter. Fisher, Ronald M. LC 82-47859; What Happens in the Autumn. Venino, Suzanne. LC 82-47858. 1982. lib. bdg. write for info. Natl Geog.

Pearce, Q. L. & Pearce, W. J. Nature's Footprints Series, 4 vols. Bettoli, Delana, illus. 96p. (ps-1). 1990. Set. 19.80 (ISBN 0-671-94431-2); Set. 14.85s.p.; Set. PLB 35.92 (ISBN 0-671-94430-4); Set. PLB 29.94s.p. Silver Pr.

Rights, Mollie. Beastly Neighbors: All About Wild Things in the City or Why Earwigs Make Good Mothers. (Illus.). 128p. (Orig.). (gr. 3 up). 1981. 14.95 (ISBN 0-316-74576-6); pap. 7.95 (ISBN 0-316-74577-4). Little.

Scheid, Margaret. Discovering Acadia: A Guide for Young Naturalists. Scheid, Margaret, illus. LC 86-71350. 80p. (ps-12). 1988. pap. 11.95 (ISBN 0-934745-04-8). Acadia Pub Co.

Schnieper, Claudia. An Apple Tree Through the Year. Baumli, Othmar, photos by. (Illus.). 48p. (gr. 2-5). 1987. PLB 12.95 (ISBN 0-87614-248-X); pap. 6.95 (ISBN 0-87614-483-0). Carolrhoda Bks.

Smith, Gina. Blooming Mother Nature: Fun Language Activities to Unfold the Wonders of Nature Based on Bloom's Taxonomy. (Illus.). 80p. (ps-4). 1990. pap. 13.95 perfect-bound (ISBN 1-55999-119-4). LinguiSystems.

Sterry, Paul. Big Book of Nature. 1990. 5.98 (ISBN 0-8317-0864-6). Smithmark.

Stidworthy, John. Naturalist. (Illus.). 32p. (gr. 5-8). 1991. PLB 11.90 (ISBN 0-531-17356-9, Gloucester Pr). Watts.

Ward, Alan. Experimenting with Nature Study. Flax, Zena, illus. 48p. (gr. 2-7). 1991. PLB 12.95 (ISBN 0-7910-1515-7). Chelsea Hse.

Webster, David. Exploring Nature Around the Year Series, 4 bks. (Illus.). 96p. (gr. 2-4). 1989. Set. PLB 43.92 (ISBN 0-671-94109-7); Set. pap. 19.80 (ISBN 0-671-94110-0). Messner.

—Spring. Steadman, Barbara, illus. 48p. (gr. 2-4). 1990. lib. bdg. 10.98 (ISBN 0-671-65858-1); pap. 4.95 (ISBN 0-671-65983-9). Messner.

Wilkes, Angela. My First Activity Book. LC 89-2640. (Illus.). 48p. (gr. 1-5). 1990. 11.95 (ISBN 0-394-86583-9); lib. bdg. 13.99 (ISBN 0-394-96583-3). McKay.

—My First Nature Book. LC 89-8019. (Illus.). 48p. (gr. 1-5). 1990. 11.95 (ISBN 0-394-86610-X); lib. bdg. 12.99 (ISBN 0-394-96610-4). McKay.

Williams, H. Crazy Creatures. (Illus.). 32p. (gr. 1-4). 1989. pap. 2.95 (ISBN 0-88625-222-9). Durkin Hayes Pub.

Wyler, Rose. Outdoor Science Series, 6 Bks. (Illus.). 64p. (gr. k-2). 1989. Set. PLB 71.88 (ISBN 0-671-94099-6); Set. pap. 29.70 (ISBN 0-671-94100-3). Messner.

Zim, Herbert S. & Ingle, Lester. Seashores. Barlowe, Dorothea & Barlowe, Sy, illus. (gr. 5 up). 1955. pap. write for info. (ISBN 0-307-24496-2, Golden Pr). Western Pub.

NATURE STUDY–DICTIONARIES

Moore, Leonard. Enciclopedia Juvenil De la Naturaleza. (SPA.). 256p. 1976. 59.95 (ISBN 84-272-5930-1, S-50476). French & Eur.

NATURE STUDY–FICTION

Allen, Marjorie N. & Rotner, Shelley. Changes. Rotner, Shelley, photos by. LC 90-6601. (Illus.). 32p. (ps-1). 1991. RSBE 13.95 (ISBN 0-02-700252-7, Mcmillan Child Bk). Macmillan Child Grp.

Babar's Little Library: Stories About Earth, About Fire, About Air, About Water, 4 bks. (ps-2). 1980. Set. 8.95 (ISBN 0-394-84365-7). Random.

Bastin, Marjolein. Vera's Special Hobbies. (Illus.). 28p. (ps-2). 1985. 2.95 (ISBN 0-8120-5692-2). Barron.

Bodsworth, Nan. A Nice Walk in the Jungle. (Illus.). 32p. (ps-2). 1990. pap. 12.95 (ISBN 0-670-82476-3). Viking Child Bks.

Canfield, Dorothy. The Bent Twig. 340p. 1981. Repr. PLB 13.95x (ISBN 0-89967-018-0). Harmony Raine.

Devine, Bob. Uncle Bob's Kangaroo & Flying Squirrel Book. VanSeveran, Joe, illus. (Orig.). 1989. pap. 3.25 (ISBN 0-8024-9062-X). Moody.

—Uncle Bob's Owl & Elephant Book. VanSeveran, Joe, illus. (Orig.). 1989. pap. 3.25 (ISBN 0-8024-9060-3). Moody.

—Uncle Bob's Raccoon & Woodchuck Book. VanSeveran, Joe, illus. (Orig.). 1989. pap. 3.25 (ISBN 0-8024-9059-X). Moody.

—Uncle Bob's Seal & Polar Bear Book. VanSeveran, Joe, illus. (Orig.). 1989. pap. 3.25 (ISBN 0-8024-9061-1). Moody.

Duston, Nettie M. Some Tales of Mother Earth & Her Children, 3 vols. Musso, Laurie D., illus. LC 83-60494. 412p. (gr. 2-5). 1983. Set. 29.95 (ISBN 0-9610150-0-4) (ISBN 0-9610150-1-2, VOL. I) (ISBN 0-9610150-2-0, VOL. II) (ISBN 0-9610150-3-9, VOL. III). Megans Wld.

Fife, Dale H. Empty Lot, Vol. 1. (ps-3). 1991. 14.95 (ISBN 0-316-28167-0). Little.

Hudson, Jan. Sweetgrass. 160p. (gr. 3-7). 1989. 13.95 (ISBN 0-399-21721-5, Philomel Bks). Putnam Pub Group.

Iverson, Diane. I Celebrate the World. (Illus.). 32p. (Orig.). 1989. pap. 5.95 (ISBN 0-9623349-0-1). MS Pub.

Kitchen, Bert. Tenrec's Twigs. Kitchen, Bert, illus. 32p. (gr. k-4). 1989. 14.95 (ISBN 0-399-21720-7, Philomel Bks). Putnam Pub Group.

Lockwood, Barbara & McAuley, Marilyn. Good Gifts from God. LC 87-71383. 1988. bds. 4.95 (ISBN 1-55513-366-5, Chariot Bks). Cook.

The Old Meadow. (gr. k-6). 1989. pap. 3.25 (ISBN 0-440-40238-7, YB). Dell.

Parnall, Peter. Apple Tree. Parnall, Peter, illus. LC 86-23730. 32p. (gr. k-3). 1988. 13.95 (ISBN 0-02-770160-3, Mcmillan Child Bk). Macmillan Child Grp.

Pizzo, Joan E. Little Crumb: Tales of the Back Bay. Geronimi, Clyde, illus. 29p. (Orig.). (gr. k-6). 1980. PLB 10.95 (ISBN 0-939126-00-1); pap. 7.95 (ISBN 0-939126-01-X); tchr's manual, 35p 8.95 (ISBN 0-939126-03-6). Back Bay.

Plum, Carol T. The Butterfly Secret: I Am Special Childrens Story Books. 32p. (ps-3). 1989. lib. bdg. 9.95 (ISBN 0-87973-017-X, 17); pap. text ed. 5.95 (ISBN 0-87973-014-5, 14). Our Sunday Visitor.

—The Swinging Tree: I Am Special Childrens Story Books. 32p. (gr. 3-8). 1989. lib. bdg. 9.95 (ISBN 0-87973-016-1, 16); pap. text ed. 5.95 (ISBN 0-87973-013-7, 13). Our Sunday Visitor.

Shulevitz, Uri. Dawn. Shulevitz, Uri, illus. LC 74-9761. 32p. (ps up). 1974. 14.95 (ISBN 0-374-31707-0). FS&G.

Wood, Jeanne. The Last Leaf. 1992. 6.95 (ISBN 0-8062-4107-1). Carlton.

Yep, Laurence. Sweetwater. Noonan, Julia, illus. LC 72-9867. 224p. (gr. 5 up). 1983. pap. 3.50 (ISBN 0-06-440135-9, Trophy). HarpC Child Bks.

Zolotow, Charlotte. When the Wind Stops. Reissue. ed. Knotts, Howard, illus. LC 74-2635. 32p. (gr. k-3). 1975. PLB 12.89 (ISBN 0-06-026972-3). HarpC Child Bks.

NAVAL ADMINISTRATION

see names of countries with the subhead Navy, e.g. U. S. Navy

NAVAL AERONAUTICS

see Aeronautics, Military

NAVAL AIRPLANES

see Airplanes, Military

NAVAL ARCHITECTURE

see also Boatbuilding; Shipbuilding; Ships; Steamboats; Warships

NAVAL ART AND SCIENCE

see also Military Art and Science; Navigation; Sea Power; Seamen; Shipbuilding; Signals and Signaling; Submarine Warfare; Submarines; Warships

NAVAL BATTLES

see also Battles; Naval History;

also names of countries with the subdivision History, Naval, e.g. U. S.–History, Naval, etc.; and names of battles

NAVAL BIOGRAPHY

see also Seamen

also names of navies with the subdivision Biography, e.g. U. S. Navy–Biography

NAVAL HISTORY

see also Military History; Pirates

also names of countries with the subhead Navy or the subdivision History, naval, e.g. U. S. Navy; U. S.–History, Naval

Van Orden, M. D. U. S. Navy Ships & Coast Guard Cutters: A Naval Institute Book for Young Readers. Burke, Arleigh, frwd. by. LC 89-13539. (Illus.). 96p. (gr. 5-11). 1990. PLB 17.95 (ISBN 0-87021-212-5). Naval Inst Pr.

NAVAL SIGNALING

see Signals and Signaling

NAVAL WARFARE

see Submarine Warfare

NAVIGATION

see also Harbors; Knots and Splices; Lighthouses; Pilots and Pilotage; Radar; Shipwrecks; Signals and Signaling; Tides; Winds

Berenstain, Michael. The Ship Book. (Illus.). (gr. k-3). 1978. 6.95 (ISBN 0-679-20449-0). McKay.

NAVIGATORS

see Discoveries (In Geography); Explorers; Seamen

NAVY

see Sea Power

see names of countries with the subhead Navy, e.g. U. S. Navy

NAZI MOVEMENT

see National Socialism

NEAR EAST

Ali, Maureen. The Middle East. (Illus.). 48p. (gr. 5-10). 1988. PLB 16.98 (ISBN 0-382-09472-7). Silver Burdett Pr.

Benin. (Illus.). (gr. 5 up). 1989. 14.95 (ISBN 0-7910-0143-1). Chelsea Hse.

Hassall, S. Bahrain. (Illus.). (gr. 5 up). 1988. 14.95 (ISBN 0-222-01093-2). Chelsea Hse.

Jacobsen, Peter & Kristensen, Preben. A Family in the Persian Gulf. LC 84-73579. (Illus.). 32p. (gr. 2-5). 1985. PLB 11.90 s&l (ISBN 0-531-18003-4, Pub. by Bookwright Pr). Watts.

Johnson, Julia. United Arab Emirates. (Illus.). (gr. 5 up). 1988. 14.95 (ISBN 1-55546-178-6). Chelsea Hse.

Kublin, Hyman. The Middle East: Regional Study. rev. ed. LC 72-6696. (Illus.). 258p. (gr. 9-12). 1973. pap. 19.20 (ISBN 0-395-13931-7). HM.

—The Middle East: Selected Readings. rev ed. LC 72-12182. (Illus.). 246p. (gr. 9-12). 1973. pap. 19.20 (ISBN 0-395-13932-5). HM.

Mason, Antony. Middle East. LC 88-18312. (Illus.). 48p. (gr. 4-8). 1988. PLB 14.98 (ISBN 0-382-09514-6). Silver Burdett pr.

Osborne, Christine. People at Work in the Middle East. (gr. 6 up). 1988. 19.95 (ISBN 0-7134-5571-3, Pub. by Batsford England). Trafalgar Sq.

Stefoff, Rebecca. West Bank-Gaza Strip. (Illus.). 104p. (gr. 5 up). 1988. lib. bdg. 14.95 (ISBN 1-55546-782-2). Chelsea Hse.

Tarasar, Constance J. New Friends-New Places. (Orig.). (gr. 1-3). 1979. pap. 2.50 (ISBN 0-377-00088-4). Friendship Pr.

NEAR EAST–ANTIQUITIES

Tubb, Jonathan. Bible Lands. Hills, Alan, photos by. LC 91-2388. (Illus.). 64p. (gr. 5 up). 1991. 15.00 (ISBN 0-679-81457-4); lib. bdg. 15.99 (ISBN 0-679-91457-9). Knopf.

NEAR EAST–DESCRIPTION AND TRAVEL

Rickman, Marueen. Qatar. (Illus.). (gr. 5 up). 1988. 14.95 (ISBN 1-55546-173-5). Chelsea Hse.

NEAR EAST–FICTION

Schami, Rafik. A Hand Full of Stars. Lesser, Rika, tr. from ARA. (gr. 7 up). 1990. 14.95 (ISBN 0-525-44535-8, DCB). Dutton Child Bks.

NEAR EAST–HISTORY

Civilizations of the Middle East. (Illus.). 80p. (gr. 4 up). 1988. PLB 22.00 (ISBN 0-8172-3303-2). Raintree Pubs.

Lawless, Richard. The Middle East since 1945. (Illus.). 72p. (gr. 7-10). 1989. 19.95 (ISBN 0-7134-5991-3, Pub. by Batsford England). Trafalgar Sq.

NEAR EAST–POLITICS

Abodaher, David J. Youth in the Middle East: Voices of Despair. (Illus.). 128p. (gr. 9-12). 1990. PLB 12.40 (ISBN 0-531-10961-5). Watts.

Evans, Michael. The Gulf Crisis. FS-Aladdin Staff, ed. LC 88-50525. (Illus.). 32p. (gr. 4-9). 1988. PLB 8.90 (ISBN 0-531-17110-8, Gloucester Pr). Watts.

Messenger, Charles. The Middle East. Franklin Watts Ltd., ed. (Illus.). 64p. (gr. k up). 1988. 10.29 (ISBN 0-531-10539-3). Watts.

Salzman, Marian & O'Reilly, Ann. War & Peace in the Persian Gulf: What Teenagers Want to Know. LC 91-2569. 123p. (Orig.). (gr. 8 up). 1991. pap. 5.95 (ISBN 1-56079-135-7). Petersons Guides.

NEBRASKA

Carole Marsh Nebraska Books, 31 bks. Set. 638.45 (ISBN 0-7933-1302-3). Gallopade Pub Group.

Carpenter, Allan. Nebraska. LC 78-10480. (Illus.). 96p. (gr. 4 up). 1979. PLB 19.93 (ISBN 0-516-04127-4). Childrens.

Fradin, Dennis. Nebraska: In Words & Pictures. LC 79-19456. (Illus.). 48p. (gr. 2-5). 1980. PLB 15.93 (ISBN 0-516-03927-X). Childrens.

Hargrove, Jim. Nebraska. LC 88-11746. (Illus.). 144p. (gr. 4 up). 1988. PLB 25.27 (ISBN 0-516-00473-5). Childrens.

Hutchinson, Duane. A Storyteller's Hometown. LC 88-82706. (Illus.). 316p. (Orig.). (gr. 7 up). 1989. pap. 9.95 (ISBN 0-934988-19-6). Foun Bks.

Manley, Robert N. Nebraska: Our Pioneer Heritage. Warp, Eric & Elley, Charles, illus. 197p. (gr. 4-6). 1981. text ed. 7.50 (ISBN 0-939644-00-2); tchr's. guide 50 pgs. 4.00 (ISBN 0-939644-01-0). Media Pub.

Marsh, Carole. Avast, Ye Slobs!: Nebraska Pirate Trivia. (Illus.). (gr. 3 up). 1990. PLB 19.95 (ISBN 0-7933-0739-2); pap. 14.95 (ISBN 0-7933-0738-4); computer disk 29.95 (ISBN 0-7933-0740-6). Gallopade Pub Group.

—The Beast of the Nebraska Bed & Breakfast. (Illus.). (gr. 3 up). 1990. PLB 19.95 (ISBN 0-7933-1752-5); pap. 14.95 (ISBN 0-7933-1753-3); computer disk 29.95 (ISBN 0-7933-1754-1). Gallopade Pub Group.

—The Hard-to-Believe-But-True! Book of Nebraska History, Mystery, Trivia, Legend, Lore, Humor & More. (Illus.). (gr. 3 up). 1990. PLB 19.95 (ISBN 0-7933-0736-8); pap. 14.95 (ISBN 0-7933-0735-X); computer disk 29.95 (ISBN 0-7933-0737-6). Gallopade Pub Group.

—If My Nebraska Mama Ran the World! (Illus.). (gr. 3 up). 1990. PLB 19.95 (ISBN 0-7933-1755-X); pap. 14.95 (ISBN 0-7933-1756-8); computer disk 29.95 (ISBN 0-7933-1757-6). Gallopade Pub Group.
—Let's Quilt Nebraska & Stuff It Topographically! (Illus.). (gr. 3 up). 1990. PLB 19.95 (ISBN 1-55609-781-6); pap. 14.95 (ISBN 1-55609-779-4); computer disk 29.95 (ISBN 1-55609-783-2). Gallopade Pub Group.
—Nebraska & Other State Greats (Biographies) (Illus.). (gr. 3 up). 1990. PLB 19.95 (ISBN 1-55609-796-4); pap. 14.95 (ISBN 1-55609-797-2); computer disk 29.95 (ISBN 1-55609-798-0). Gallopade Pub Group.
—Nebraska Bandits, Bushwackers, Outlaws, Crooks, Devils, Ghosts, Desperadoes & Other Assorted & Sundry Characters! (Illus.). (gr. 3 up). 1990. PLB 19.95 (ISBN 0-7933-0721-X); pap. 14.95 (ISBN 0-7933-0720-1); computer disk 29.95 (ISBN 0-7933-0722-8). Gallopade Pub Group.
—Nebraska Classic Christmas Trivia: Stories, Recipes, Activities, Legends, Lore & More! (Illus.). (gr. 3 up). 1990. PLB 19.95 (ISBN 0-7933-0724-4); pap. 14.95 (ISBN 0-7933-0723-6); computer disk 29.95 (ISBN 0-7933-0725-2). Gallopade Pub Group.
—Nebraska Coastales. (Illus.). (gr. 3 up). 1990. PLB 19.95 (ISBN 1-55609-790-5); pap. 14.95 (ISBN 1-55609-791-3); computer disk 29.95 (ISBN 1-55609-792-1). Gallopade Pub Group.
—Nebraska "Jography" A Fun Run Thru Our State. (Illus.). (gr. 3 up). 1990. PLB 19.95 (ISBN 1-55609-778-6); pap. 14.95; computer disk 29.95 (ISBN 1-55609-780-8). Gallopade Pub Group.
—Nebraska Kid's Cookbook: Recipes, How-To, History, Lore & More! (Illus.). (gr. 3 up). 1990. PLB 19.95 (ISBN 0-7933-0733-3); pap. 14.95 (ISBN 0-7933-0732-5); computer disk 29.95 (ISBN 0-7933-0734-1). Gallopade Pub Group.
—Nebraska Quiz Bowl Crash Course! (Illus.). (gr. 3 up). 1990. PLB 19.95 (ISBN 1-55609-793-X); pap. 14.95 (ISBN 1-55609-794-8); computer disk 29.95 (ISBN 1-55609-795-6). Gallopade Pub Group.
—Nebraska School Trivia: An Amazing & Fascinating Look at Our State's Teachers, Schools & Students! (Illus.). (gr. 3 up). 1990. PLB 19.95 (ISBN 0-7933-0730-9); pap. 14.95 (ISBN 0-7933-0729-5); computer disk 29.95 (ISBN 0-7933-0731-7). Gallopade Pub Group.
—Nebraska Silly Basketball Sportsmysteries, Vol. I. (Illus.). (gr. 3 up). 1990. PLB 19.95 (ISBN 0-7933-0727-9); pap. 14.95 (ISBN 0-7933-0726-0); computer disk 29.95 (ISBN 0-7933-0728-7). Gallopade Pub Group.
—Nebraska Silly Basketball Sportsmysteries, Vol. II. (Illus.). (gr. 3 up). 1990. PLB 19.95 (ISBN 0-7933-1758-4); pap. 14.95 (ISBN 0-7933-1759-2); computer disk 29.95 (ISBN 0-7933-1760-6). Gallopade Pub Group.
—Nebraska Silly Football Sportsmysteries, Vol. I. (Illus.). (gr. 3 up). 1990. PLB 19.95 (ISBN 1-55609-784-0); pap. 14.95 (ISBN 1-55609-785-9); computer disk 29.95 (ISBN 1-55609-786-7). Gallopade Pub Group.
—Nebraska Silly Football Sportsmysteries, Vol. II. (Illus.). (gr. 3 up). 1990. PLB 19.95 (ISBN 1-55609-787-5); pap. 14.95 (ISBN 1-55609-788-3); computer disk 29.95 (ISBN 1-55609-789-1). Gallopade Pub Group.
—Nebraska Silly Trivia! (Illus.). (gr. 3 up). 1990. PLB 19.95 (ISBN 1-55609-775-1); pap. 14.95 (ISBN 1-55609-776-X); computer disk 29.95 (ISBN 1-55609-777-8). Gallopade Pub Group.
—Nebraska's (Most Devastating!) Disasters & (Most Calamitous!) Catastrophies! (Illus.). (gr. 3 up). 1990. PLB 19.95 (ISBN 0-7933-0718-X); pap. 14.95 (ISBN 0-7933-0717-1) (ISBN 0-7933-0719-8). Gallopade Pub Group.
Prairie-Plains Resource Institute Staff & Whitney, William S. Microcosm of the Platte: A Guide to Bader Memorial Park Natural Area. Whitney, Jan & Twedt, Curt, eds. Whitney, William S., illus. 140p. (Orig.). (gr. 10-12). 1988. pap. text ed. 10.00 (ISBN 0-945614-00-4). Prairie Plains Res Inst.
Thompson, Kathleen. Nebraska. LC 87-264855. 48p. (gr. 3 up). 1988. 17.32 (ISBN 0-86514-473-7); cancelled tchr's. study guide (ISBN 0-86514-611-X); cancelled Beta video (ISBN 0-86514-101-0); cancelled VHS video (ISBN 0-86514-176-2); cancelled 3/4" video (ISBN 0-86514-251-3). Raintree Pubs.

NEBRASKA–FICTION

Ott, Margaret U. Sterling's Carrie. LC 89-62351. (Illus., Orig.). 1989. pap. text ed. 9.95 (ISBN 0-939644-64-9). Media Pub.

Saban, Vera. Right Now Forever. Mills, Janie, illus. LC 90-39763. 130p. (Orig.). (gr. 4-6). 1990. pap. write for info. (ISBN 0-914565-34-6). Capstan Pubns.
Ten seemed a magic number to Jennie Barnes, & she had become ten years old January of that year of 1915. Surely, she thought, this must be the best age of all, & she wished she could stay ten forever. So the story begins of a little girl on a tenant farm in old Nebraska. The book was critiqued by fourth & fifth graders: Jeff commented, "I think the story was similar to the story WHERE THE RED FERN GROWS. I wouldn't mind reading it over & over again." And Greg said he "Liked this book, because I like people who are poor & still get the things they want." The teacher's comment: "This book captivated the students & kept their interest. Even when I had reached the end of a chapter with just a few minutes of class left, they wanted me to keep reading!"--Douglas Walton of Nelson, Nebraska. Illustrations by Janie Mills add interest & value. To order this book & for additional information on other TimberTrails Books, call (307) 568-2604.
Publisher Provided Annotation.

NECROMANCY
see Divination; Witchcraft

NEEDLEWORK
see also names of needlework; e.g. Dressmaking; Embroidery; Sewing; Tapestry
Messent, Jan. Wool 'n Magic: Creative Uses of Yarn... Knitting, Crochet, Embroidery. Dawson, Pam, ed. Search Press Studios Staff, illus. 144p. 1989. 32.95 (ISBN 0-85532-614-X). A Schwartz & Co.
Moore, Marsha. The Teddy Bear Book. (Illus.). 165p. (ps up). 1984. 24.95 (ISBN 0-916410-09-9). A D Bragdon.

NEFERTITI, QUEEN OF EGYPT, 14TH CENTURY B.C.
Holmes, Burnham. Nefertiti: The Mystery Queen. LC 77-10445. (Illus.). 48p. (gr. 4-5). 1983. PLB 15.99 (ISBN 0-8172-1056-3); pap. 9.27 (ISBN 0-8172-2165-4). Raintree Pubs.

NEGRO ARTISTS
see Black Artists
NEGRO ATHLETES
see Black Athletes
NEGRO AUTHORS
see Black Authors
NEGRO FOLKLORE
see Black Folklore
NEGRO MUSICIANS
see Black Musicians
NEGRO NATIONALISM
see Black Muslims
NEGRO POETRY
see Black Poetry
NEGROES
see Blacks
NEGROES IN ART
see Blacks in Literature and Art
NEGRO RACE
see Blacks
NEGRO SPIRITUALS
see Spirituals
NEGROES IN BUSINESS
see Blacks–Employment

NEHRU, JAWAHARLAL, 1889-1964
Rau, M. Nehru for Children. (Illus.). (gr. 4-12). 1979. 5.50 (ISBN 0-89744-159-1). Auromere.

NEIGHBORHOOD
see Community Life
NEIGHBORHOOD SCHOOLS
see Schools
NEO-IMPRESSIONISM (ART)
see Impressionism (Art)
NEOLITHIC PERIOD
see Stone Age

NEPAL
Lerner Publications, Department of Geography Staff, ed. Nepal in Pictures. (Illus.). 64p. (gr. 5 up). 1989. 12.95 (ISBN 0-8225-1851-1). Lerner Pubns.
San Suu Kyi Sung. Nepal. (Illus.). (gr. 5 up). 1988. 14.95 (ISBN 0-222-00981-0). Chelsea Hse.

NERVOUS SYSTEM
see also Brain; Psychology, Pathological
The Brain & Nervous System. (Illus.). 48p. (gr. 4up). 1981. PLB 12.40 (ISBN 0-531-04288-X). Watts.
Brain & Nervous System. 48p. (gr. 5-8). 1988. PLB 12.98 (ISBN 0-382-09703-3); 9.74s.p. (ISBN 0-685-24611-6). Silver Burdett Pr.
Edelson, Edward. The Neurological System. (Illus.). (gr. 7-12). 1989. 18.95 (ISBN 0-7910-0023-0). Chelsea Hse.
LeMaster, Leslie J. Your Brain & Nervous System. LC 84-7635. (Illus.). 48p. (gr. k-4). 1984. PLB 14.60 (ISBN 0-516-01931-7); pap. 4.95 (ISBN 0-516-41931-5). Childrens.
Parker, Steve. Brain & Nervous System. (ps-3). 1990. PLB 12.90 (ISBN 0-531-14026-1). Watts.
—The Brain & Nervous System. rev. ed. (Illus.). 48p. (gr. 5 up). 1991. pap. 4.95 (ISBN 0-531-24600-0). Watts.
—Nerves to Senses: Projects with Biology. (Illus.). 32p. (gr. 5-8). 1991. PLB 11.90 (ISBN 0-531-17295-3, Gloucester Pr). Watts.
Ralston, Diane D. & Ralston, Henry J., III. The Nerve Cell. Head, J. J., ed. Imrick, Ann T., illus. LC 84-45836. 16p. (Orig.). (gr. 10 up). 1988. pap. text ed. 2.15 (ISBN 0-89278-357-5, 45-9757). Carolina Biological.

NESTS
see Birds–Eggs and Nests

NETHERLANDS
Fradin, Dennis B. The Netherlands. LC 82-17896. (Illus.). 128p. (gr. 5-9). 1983. PLB 25.27 (ISBN 0-516-02779-4). Childrens.
James, Ian. The Netherlands. (Illus.). 32p. (gr. 5-8). 1990. PLB 11.90 (ISBN 0-531-14044-X). Watts.
Ozer, Steven. Netherlands. (Illus.). (gr. 5 up). 1990. 14.95 (ISBN 0-7910-1107-0). Chelsea Hse.
—The Netherlands. (Illus.). (gr. 5 up). 1988. 13.95. Chelsea Hse.
Reiss, Johanna. The Journey Back. LC 76-12615. 128p. (gr. 5 up). 1976. 12.95 (ISBN 0-690-01252-7, Crowell Jr Bks). HarpC Child Bks.
Van Stegeren, Theo. The Land & People of The Netherlands. LC 90-47650. (Illus.). 256p. (gr. 6 up). 1991. 17.95 (ISBN 0-06-022537-8); PLB 17.89 (ISBN 0-06-022538-6). HarpC Child Bks.

NETHERLANDS–FICTION
Andersen, Hans Christian. The Tinderbox. Moser, Barry, adapted by. Hutton, Warwick, illus. LC 88-9206. 32p. (gr. 1 up). 1988. 13.95 (ISBN 0-689-50458-6, M K McElderry). Macmillan Child Grp.
—Tinderbox, Vol. 1. (ps-9). 1990. 14.95 (ISBN 0-316-03938-1). Little.
Ardizzone, Edward, illus. Ardizzone's English Fairy Tales: Twelve Fairy Tales from the Collection of Joseph Jacobs. LC 85-71251. 78p. (gr. 2-7). 1986. 10.95 (ISBN 0-233-97306-0). Andre Deutsch.
DeJong, Meindert. Shadrach. Sendak, Maurice, illus. LC 53-5250. 192p. (gr. 3-6). 1953. PLB 14.89 (ISBN 0-06-021546-1). HarpC Child Bks.
—Wheel on the School. Sendak, Maurice, illus. LC 54-8945. 256p. (gr. 4-7). 1954. 14.95 (ISBN 0-06-021585-2); PLB 14.89 (ISBN 0-06-021586-0). HarpC Child Bks.
Dodge, Mary M. Hans Brinker. Baldridge, C. L., illus. (gr. 4-6). 1945-63. deluxe ed. 11.95 (ISBN 0-448-06011-6, G&D); Companion Lib. Ed. o.p. 2.95 (ISBN 0-448-05462-0). Putnam Pub Group.
—Hans Brinker: The Silver Skates. LC 54-14472. (gr. 5 up). pap. 2.50 (ISBN 0-8049-0099-X, CL-99). Airmont.
Green, Norma. The Hole in the Dike. Carle, Eric, illus. LC 74-23562. 32p. (gr. k-3). 1975. 14.95 (ISBN 0-690-00734-5, Crowell Jr Bks); PLB 14.89 (ISBN 0-690-00676-4). HarpC Child Bks.
Krasilovsky, Phyllis. Cow Who Fell in the Canal. Spier, Peter, illus. LC 56-8236. 38p. (gr. k-1). 1985. pap. 11.95 (ISBN 0-385-07585-5). Doubleday.
Noble, Trinka H. Hansy's Mermaid. Noble, Trinka H., illus. LC 82-45509. 32p. (ps-2). 1983. 10.95 (ISBN 0-8037-3605-3, 01063-320); PLB 10.89 (ISBN 0-8037-3606-1). Dial Bks Young.

NETHERLANDS–HISTORY–GERMAN OCCUPATION, 1940-1945
Tames, Richard. Anne Frank. (Illus.). 32p. (gr. 5 up). 1991. pap. 3.95 (ISBN 0-531-24608-6). Watts.

NEUROLOGY
see Nervous System

NEVADA
Aylesworth, Thomas G. & Aylesworth, Virginia L. The West (Arizona, Nevada, Utah) (Illus.). 64p. (gr. 3 up). 1992. PLB 16.95 (ISBN 0-7910-1049-X). Chelsea Hse.
Carole Marsh Nevada Books, 31 bks. Set. 638.45 (ISBN 0-7933-1303-1). Gallopade Pub Group.
Carpenter, Allan. Nevada. LC 79-4355. (Illus.). 96p. (gr. 4 up). 1979. PLB 19.93 (ISBN 0-516-04128-2). Childrens.
Fradin, Dennis. Nevada: In Words & Pictures. Wahl, Richard, illus. LC 80-24179. 48p. (gr. 2-6). 1981. PLB 15.93 (ISBN 0-516-03928-8). Childrens.
Lillegard, Dee & Stoker, Wayne. Nevada. LC 90-34665. (Illus.). 144p. (gr. 4 up). 1990. PLB 25.27 (ISBN 0-516-00474-3). Childrens.
Marsh, Carole. Avast, Ye Slobs! Nevada Pirate Trivia. (Illus.). 1990. PLB 19.95 (ISBN 0-7933-0763-5); pap. 14.95 (ISBN 0-7933-0762-7); computer disk 29.95 (ISBN 0-7933-0764-3). Gallopade Pub Group.
—The Beast of the Nevada Bed & Breakfast. (Illus.). 1990. PLB 19.95 (ISBN 0-7933-1761-4); pap. 14.95 (ISBN 0-7933-1762-2); computer disk 29.95 (ISBN 0-7933-1763-0). Gallopade Pub Group.
—The Hard-to-Believe-But-True! Book of Nevada History, Mystery, Trivia, Legend, Lore, Humor & More. (Illus.). 1990. PLB 19.95 (ISBN 0-7933-0760-0); pap. 14.95 (ISBN 0-7933-0759-7); computer disk 29.95 (ISBN 0-7933-0761-9). Gallopade Pub Group.
—If My Nevada Mama Ran the World! (Illus.). 1990. lib. bdg. 19.95 (ISBN 0-7933-1764-9); pap. 14.95 (ISBN 0-7933-1765-7); computer disk 29.95 (ISBN 0-7933-1766-5). Gallopade Pub Group.
—Let's Quilt Nevada & Stuff It Topographically! (Illus.). 1990. PLB 19.95 (ISBN 1-55609-805-7); pap. 14.95 (ISBN 1-55609-130-3); computer disk 29.95 (ISBN 1-55609-807-3). Gallopade Pub Group.
—Nevada & Other State Greats (Biographies) (Illus.). 1990. PLB 19.95 (ISBN 1-55609-820-0); pap. 14.95 (ISBN 1-55609-821-9); computer disk 29.95 (ISBN 1-55609-822-7). Gallopade Pub Group.

—Nevada Bandits, Bushwackers, Outlaws, Crooks, Devils, Ghosts, Desperadoes & Other Assorted & Sundry Characters! (Illus.). 1990. PLB 19.95 (ISBN 0-7933-0745-7); pap. 14.95 (ISBN 0-7933-0744-9); computer disk 29.95 (ISBN 0-7933-0746-5). Gallopade Pub Group.

—Nevada Classic Christmas Trivia: Stories, Recipes, Activities, Legends, Lore & More! (Illus.). 1990. PLB 19.95 (ISBN 0-7933-0748-1); pap. 14.95 (ISBN 0-7933-0747-3); computer disk 29.95 (ISBN 0-7933-0749-X). Gallopade Pub Group.

—Nevada Coastales. (Illus.). 1990. PLB 19.95 (ISBN 1-55609-814-6); pap. 14.95 (ISBN 1-55609-815-4); computer disk 29.95 (ISBN 1-55609-816-2). Gallopade Pub Group.

—The Nevada Hot Air Balloon Mystery. (Illus.). (gr. 2-9). 1990. 19.95 (ISBN 0-7933-2570-6); pap. 14.95 (ISBN 0-7933-2571-4); computer disk 29.95 (ISBN 0-7933-2572-2). Gallopade Pub Group.

—Nevada "Jography" A Fun Run Thru Our State! (Illus.). 1990. PLB 19.95 (ISBN 1-55609-802-2); pap. 14.95 (ISBN 1-55609-803-0); computer disk 29.95 (ISBN 1-55609-804-9). Gallopade Pub Group.

—Nevada Kid's Cookbook: Recipes, How-to, History, Lore & More! (Illus.). 1990. PLB 19.95 (ISBN 0-7933-0757-0); pap. 14.95 (ISBN 0-7933-0756-2); computer disk 29.95 (ISBN 0-7933-0758-9). Gallopade Pub Group.

—Nevada Quiz Bowl Crash Course! (Illus.). 1990. PLB 19.95 (ISBN 1-55609-817-0); pap. 14.95 (ISBN 1-55609-818-9); computer disk 29.95 (ISBN 1-55609-819-7). Gallopade Pub Group.

—Nevada School Trivia: An Amazing & Fascinating Look at Our State's Teachers, Schools & Students! (Illus.). 1990. PLB 19.95 (ISBN 0-7933-0754-6); pap. 14.95 (ISBN 0-7933-0753-8); computer disk 29.95 (ISBN 0-7933-0755-4). Gallopade Pub Group.

—Nevada Silly Basketball Sportsmystereis, Vol. 2. (Illus.). 1990. PLB 19.95 (ISBN 0-7933-1767-3); pap. 14.95 (ISBN 0-7933-1768-1); computer disk 29.95 (ISBN 0-7933-1769-X). Gallopade Pub Group.

—Nevada Silly Basketball Sportsmysteries, Vol. 1. (Illus.). 1990. PLB 19.95 (ISBN 0-7933-0751-1); pap. 14.95 (ISBN 0-7933-0750-3); computer disk 29.95 (ISBN 0-7933-0752-X). Gallopade Pub Group.

—Nevada Silly Football Sportsmysteries, Vol. 1. (Illus.). 1990. PLB 19.95 (ISBN 1-55609-808-1); pap. 14.95 (ISBN 1-55609-809-X); computer disk 29.95 (ISBN 1-55609-810-3). Gallopade Pub Group.

—Nevada Silly Football Sportsmysteries, Vol. 2. (Illus.). 1990. PLB 19.95 (ISBN 1-55609-811-1); pap. 14.95 (ISBN 1-55609-812-X); computer disk 29.95 (ISBN 1-55609-813-8). Gallopade Pub Group.

—Nevada Silly Trivia! (Illus.). 1990. PLB 19.95 (ISBN 1-55609-799-9); pap. 14.95 (ISBN 1-55609-800-6); computer disk 29.95 (ISBN 1-55609-801-4). Gallopade Pub Group.

—Nevada's (Most Devastating!) Disasters & (Most Calamitous!) Castastrophies! (Illus.). 1990. PLB 19.95 (ISBN 0-7933-0742-2); pap. 14.95 (ISBN 0-7933-0741-4); computer disk 29.95 (ISBN 0-7933-0743-0). Gallopade Pub Group.

Root, Phyllis & McCormick, Maxine. Great Basin. LC 88-18645. (Illus.). 48p. (gr. 4-5). 1988. 12.95 (ISBN 0-89686-410-3, Crestwood Hse). Macmillan Child Grp.

Turner Program Services, Inc. Staff. Nevada. 48p. (gr. 3 up). 1985. PLB 17.32 (ISBN 0-86514-437-0); pap. text ed. 9.27 (ISBN 0-86514-512-1); cancelled Beta video (ISBN 0-86514-062-6); cancelled VHS video (ISBN 0-86514-137-1); cancelled 3/4" video (ISBN 0-86514-212-2); cancelled tchr's. guide (ISBN 0-86514-287-4); cancelled student activity bk. (ISBN 0-86514-362-5); cancelled index. Raintree Pubs.

NEW ENGLAND

Aylesworth, Thomas G. & Aylesworth, Virginia L. Southern New England (Connecticut, Massachusetts, Rhode Island) LC 87-17880. (Illus.). 66p. (Orig.). (gr. 3 up). 1988. PLB 16.95 (ISBN 1-55546-552-8); pap. 6.95 (ISBN 0-7910-0544-5). Chelsea Hse.

Crump, Donald J., ed. New England: Land of Scenic Splendor. (Illus.). 1989. 7.95 (ISBN 0-318-42773-7); lib. bdg. 9.50 (ISBN 0-87044-715-7). Natl Geog.

Frost, Ed & Frost, Roon. Just for Kids: The New England Guide & Activity Book for Young Travelers. Leach, Carol, illus. 150p. (Orig.). (ps-5). 1989. pap. 7.95 (ISBN 0-9618806-2-7). Glove Compart Bks.

Mathieu, Joe. The Olden Days. Mathieu, Joe, illus. 32p. (ps-3). 1981. lib. bdg. 4.99 (ISBN 0-394-94085-7). Random.

NEW ENGLAND—FICTION

Alcott, Louisa May. Eight Cousins. (gr. 7 up). 1974. 17.95 (ISBN 0-316-03091-0). Little.

—Jack & Jill. (gr. 5 up). 1979. 17.95 (ISBN 0-316-03092-9). Little.

—Jo's Boys & How They Turned Out. (gr. 7 up). 1986. 17.95 (ISBN 0-316-03093-7). Little.

—Little Men. Brich, Reginald, illus. (gr. 7 up). 1971. 17.95 (ISBN 0-316-03094-5). Little.

—Little Women. (Illus.). (gr. 6 up). pap. 2.95 (ISBN 0-8049-0106-6, CL-106). Airmont.

—Little Women. Magagna, Anna M. & Jambor, Louis, illus. (gr. 4-6). 1981. Illustrated Junior Library. pap. 9.95 (ISBN 0-448-11019-9, G&D); deluxe ed. 14.95 (ISBN 0-448-06019-1); Companion Library 3.95 (ISBN 0-448-05466-3). Putnam Pub Group.

—Little Women. 59.95 (ISBN 0-8490-0547-7). Gordon Pr.

—Little Women. Smith, Jessie W., illus. (gr. 7 up). 1968. 17.95 (ISBN 0-316-03095-3). Little.

—Little Women. 320p. (gr. 3-7). 1983. pap. 2.25 (ISBN 0-14-035008-X, Puffin). Puffin Bks.

—Little Women. 1963. 37.50 (ISBN 0-685-20188-0, 144-7). Saphrograph.

—Little Women. Barish, Wendy, ed. Cheng, Judith, illus. 576p. 1982. 15.95 (ISBN 0-671-44447-6, Little Simon). S&S Trade.

—Little Women. 1983. Repr. lib. bdg. 18.95x (ISBN 0-89966-408-3). Buccaneer Bks.

—Little Women. Bedall, Madelon, intro. by. 1981. pap. 6.00 (ISBN 0-685-06605-3, Modern Lib). Random.

—Little Women. Douglas, Ann, intro. by. 480p. (gr. 3 up). 1983. pap. 3.95 (ISBN 0-451-52341-5, Sig Classic). NAL-Dutton.

—Little Women. Edwards, Gunvor, illus. Gliberry, Lysbeth, retold by. (Illus.). 48p. (gr. 7-12). 1975. pap. text ed. 2.25x (ISBN 0-19-421804-X). Oxford U Pr.

—Little Women. LC 62-20197. (gr. 4 up). 1986. pap. 3.95 (ISBN 0-02-041240-1, Collier). Macmillan.

—Little Women. (gr. 2 up). 8.98 (ISBN 0-517-63489-9). Outlet Bk Co.

—Little Women. (Orig.). (gr. k-6). 1987. pap. 6.95 (ISBN 0-440-44768-2, Pub. by Yearling Classics). Dell.

—Little Women. 256p. (gr. 3-7). 1986. pap. 2.50 (ISBN 0-590-40498-9, Pub. by Apple Classics). Scholastic Inc.

—Little Women. James, Derek, illus. LC 87-45450. 512p. 1988. 18.95 (ISBN 0-394-56279-8). Knopf.

—Little Women. Showalter, Elaine, intro. by. 608p. 1989. pap. 5.95 (ISBN 0-14-039069-3, Penguin Classics). Viking Penguin.

—Little Women. 1989. Repr. of 1867 ed. lib. bdg. 79.00 (ISBN 0-685-27395-4). Reprint Servs.

—Little Women. Auerbach, Nina, afterword by. 480p. 1983. pap. 3.95 (ISBN 0-553-21275-3, Bantam Classics Spectra). Bantam.

—Little Women, 4 vols. large type ed. (gr. 7 up). Repr. of 1946 ed. Set. write for info. NAVH.

—Little Women. large type ed. 336p. 1987. 15.95 (ISBN 0-7089-8384-7, Charnwood). Ulverscroft.

—Little Women. 1986. pap. 2.95 (ISBN 0-590-43797-6). Scholastic Inc.

—Little Women. 1988. 2.98 (ISBN 0-671-09222-7). S&S Trade.

—Little Women. Smith, Jessie W., illus. 388p. (gr. 4 up). 1986. 12.95 (ISBN 0-681-40055-2). Longmeadow Pr.

—Little Women, Vol. 2: The Sisters Grow Up. Lindskoog, Kathryn, ed. (Illus.). (gr. 3-7). 1991. pap. 6.99 (ISBN 0-88070-463-2). Multnomah.

—Old-Fashioned Girl. Abbot, Elenore, illus. (gr. 7 up). 1969. 17.95 (ISBN 0-316-03096-1). Little.

—Reader's Digest Best Loved Books for Young Readers: Little Women. Ogburn, Jackie, ed. English, Mark, illus. 176p. (gr. 4-12). 1989. 3.99 (ISBN 0-945260-25-3). Choice Pub NY.

—Rose in Bloom. (gr. 5-9). 1971. Repr. 5.95 (ISBN 0-448-02366-0, G&D). Putnam Pub Group.

—Rose in Bloom. Price, Hattie L., illus. (gr. 7 up). 1976. 16.95 (ISBN 0-316-03098-8). Little.

—Under the Lilacs. Davis, Marguerite, illus. (gr. 7 up). 1977. 17.95 (ISBN 0-316-03099-6). Little.

Blos, Joan W. A Gathering of Days: A New England Girl's Journal, 1830-32. LC 79-16898. 144p. (gr. 4-7). 1979. 12.95 (ISBN 0-684-16340-3, Scribners Young Read). Macmillan Child Grp.

Brady, Philip. Reluctant Hero: A Snowy Road to Salem in 1802. 144p. (gr. 7 up). 1990. 16.95 (ISBN 0-8027-6972-1); lib. bdg. 17.85 (ISBN 0-8027-6974-8). Walker & Co.

Drake, Samuel A. Book of New England Legends & Folk Lore. LC 76-157254. (Illus.). (gr. 9 up). 1971. pap. 14.95 (ISBN 0-8048-0990-9). C E Tuttle.

Garden, Nancy. Fours Crossing. LC 80-21854. 199p. (gr. 5 up). 1981. 13.95 (ISBN 0-374-32451-4). FS&G.

Hale, Edward E. Man Without a Country & Other Stories. (gr. 5 up). 1968. pap. 1.95 (ISBN 0-8049-0185-6, CL-185). Airmont.

Hall, Donald. Ox-Cart Man. Cooney, Barbara, illus. LC 79-14466. (gr. k-3). 1979. pap. 14.95 (ISBN 0-670-53328-9). Viking Child Bks.

—Ox-Cart Man. Cooney, Barbara, illus. 40p. (ps-3). 1983. pap. 4.95 (ISBN 0-14-050441-9, Puffin). Puffin Bks.

Hawthorne, Nathaniel. House of the Seven Gables. (gr. 9 up). 1964. pap. 2.95 (ISBN 0-8049-0016-7, CL-16). Airmont.

—Scarlet Letter. (gr. 9 up). 1964. pap. 2.75 (ISBN 0-8049-0007-8, CL-7). Airmont.

—Scarlet Letter. Levin, Harry, ed. LC 60-2662. (gr. 9 up). 1960. pap. 7.56 (ISBN 0-395-05142-8, RivEd). HM.

Little Women. (gr. 4 up). 1988. pap. 4.87 (ISBN 0-582-54162-X, 74269). Longman.

Little Women. Centennial ed. (Illus.). (gr. 3-7). 1968. 17.95. Little.

Lorimer, Janet. Trouble with Buster: A Day in the Life of a Pilgrim Girl. 1990. pap. 2.50 (ISBN 0-590-42641-9). Scholastic Inc.

Richardson, Judith B. David's Landing. Bang, Molly, illus. LC 84-22084. 150p. (gr. 3-7). write for info. (ISBN 0-9611374-1-X). Woods Hole Hist.

Wiggin, Eric & Wiggin, Kate D. Rebecca of Sunnybrook Farm: The Girl. 256p. (gr. 4-7). 1990. 9.95 (ISBN 1-56121-004-8). Wolgemuth & Hyatt.

Wiggin, Kate D. Rebecca of Sunnybrook Farm. (gr. 5 up). pap. 1.50 (ISBN 0-8049-0144-9, CL-144). Airmont.

NEW ENGLAND—HISTORY

Blos, Joan W. A Gathering of Days: A New England Girl's Journal, 1830-32. LC 79-16898. 145p. (gr. 5 up). 1982. pap. 3.95 (ISBN 0-689-70750-9, Aladdin). Macmillan Child Grp.

Vaughn, Evelyn. Norwood & Eloise Waterhouse: Starters of Churches. LC 85-6718. (gr. k-3). 1985. 5.95 (ISBN 0-8054-4294-4, 4242-94). Broadman.

NEW GUINEA—FICTION

Tabrah, Ruth. The Old Man & the Astronauts. LC 75-16524. (Illus.). (gr. 1-7). 1975. 5.95 (ISBN 0-89610-015-4). Island Heritage.

NEW HAMPSHIRE

Carole Marsh New Hampshire Books, 31 bks. Set. 638.45 (ISBN 0-7933-1304-X). Gallopade Pub Group.

Carpenter, Allan. New Hampshire. LC 79-11454. (Illus.). 96p. (gr. 4 up). 1979. PLB 19.93 (ISBN 0-516-04129-0). Childrens.

Fradin, Dennis. New Hampshire: In Words & Pictures. Wahl, Richard, illus. LC 80-25421. 48p. (gr. 2-5). 1981. PLB 15.93 (ISBN 0-516-03929-6). Childrens.

Fradin, Dennis B. The New Hampshire Colony. LC 87-14619. (Illus.). 190p. (gr. 4 up). 1987. PLB 22.60 (ISBN 0-516-00388-7). Childrens.

Marsh, Carole. Avast, Ye Slobs! New Hampshire Pirate Trivia. (Illus.). 1990. PLB 19.95 (ISBN 0-7933-0787-2); pap. 14.95 (ISBN 0-7933-0786-4); computer disk 29.95 (ISBN 0-7933-0788-0). Gallopade Pub Group.

—The Beast of the New Hampshire Bed & Breakfast. (Illus.). 1990. PLB 19.95 (ISBN 0-7933-1770-3); pap. 14.95 (ISBN 0-7933-1771-1); computer disk 29.95 (ISBN 0-7933-1772-X). Gallopade Pub Group.

—The Hard-to-Believe-But-True! Book of New Hampshire History, Mystery, Trivia, Legend, Lore, Humor & More. (Illus.). 1990. PLB 19.95 (ISBN 0-7933-0784-8); pap. 14.95 (ISBN 0-7933-0783-X); computer disk 29.95 (ISBN 0-7933-0785-6). Gallopade Pub Group.

—If My New Hampshire Mama Ran the World! (Illus.). 1990. lib. bdg. 19.95 (ISBN 0-7933-1773-8); pap. 14.95 (ISBN 0-7933-1774-6); computer disk 29.95 (ISBN 0-7933-1775-4). Gallopade Pub Group.

—Let's Quilt New Hampshire & Stuff It Topographically! (Illus.). 1990. PLB 19.95 (ISBN 1-55609-829-4); pap. 14.95 (ISBN 1-55609-067-6); computer disk 29.95 (ISBN 1-55609-831-6). Gallopade Pub Group.

—New Hampshire & Other State Greats (Biographies) (Illus.). 1990. PLB 19.95; pap. 14.95 (ISBN 1-55609-845-6); computer disk 29.95 (ISBN 1-55609-846-4). Gallopade Pub Group.

—New Hampshire Bandits, Bushwackers, Outlaws, Crooks, Devils, Ghosts, Desperadoes & Other Assorted & Sundry Characters! (Illus.). 1990. PLB 19.95 (ISBN 0-7933-0769-4); pap. 14.95 (ISBN 0-7933-0768-6); computer disk 29.95 (ISBN 0-7933-0770-8). Gallopade Pub Group.

—New Hampshire Classic Christmas Trivia: Stories, Recipes, Activities, Legends, Lore & More! (Illus.). 1990. PLB 19.95 (ISBN 0-7933-0772-4); pap. 14.95 (ISBN 0-7933-0771-6); computer disk 29.95 (ISBN 0-7933-0773-2). Gallopade Pub Group.

—New Hampshire Coastales. (Illus.). 1990. PLB 19.95 (ISBN 1-55609-838-3); pap. 14.95 (ISBN 1-55609-839-1); computer disk 29.95 (ISBN 1-55609-840-5). Gallopade Pub Group.

—The New Hampshire Hot Air Balloon Mystery. (Illus.). (gr. 2-9). 1990. 19.95 (ISBN 0-7933-2579-X); pap. 14.95 (ISBN 0-7933-2580-3); computer disk 29.95 (ISBN 0-7933-2581-1). Gallopade Pub Group.

—New Hampshire "Jography" A Fun Run Thru Our State! (Illus.). 1990. PLB 19.95 (ISBN 1-55609-826-X); pap. 14.95 (ISBN 1-55609-827-8); computer disk 29.95 (ISBN 1-55609-828-6). Gallopade Pub Group.

—New Hampshire Kid's Cookbook: Recipes, How-to, History, Lore & More! (Illus.). 1990. PLB 19.95 (ISBN 0-7933-0781-3); pap. 14.95 (ISBN 0-7933-0780-5); computer disk 29.95 (ISBN 0-7933-0782-1). Gallopade Pub Group.

—New Hampshire Quiz Bowl Crash Course! (Illus.). 1990. PLB 19.95 (ISBN 1-55609-841-3); pap. 14.95 (ISBN 1-55609-842-1); computer disk 29.95 (ISBN 1-55609-843-X). Gallopade Pub Group.

—New Hampshire School Trivia: An Amazing & Fascinating Look at Our State's Teachers, Schools & Students! (Illus.). 1990. PLB 19.95 (ISBN 0-7933-0778-3); pap. 14.95 (ISBN 0-7933-0777-5); computer disk 29.95 (ISBN 0-7933-0779-1). Gallopade Pub Group.

—New Hampshire Silly Basketball Sportsmysteries, Vol. I. (Illus.). 1990. PLB 19.95 (ISBN 0-7933-0775-9); pap. 14.95 (ISBN 0-7933-0774-0); computer disk 29.95 (ISBN 0-7933-0776-7). Gallopade Pub Group.

—New Hampshire Silly Basketball Sportsmysteries, Vol. II. (Illus.). 1990. PLB 19.95 (ISBN 0-7933-1776-2); pap. 14.95 (ISBN 0-7933-1777-0); computer disk 29.95 (ISBN 0-7933-1778-9). Gallopade Pub Group.

—New Hampshire Silly Football Sportsmysteries, Vol. 1. (Illus.). 1990. PLB 19.95 (ISBN 1-55609-832-4); pap. 14.95 (ISBN 1-55609-833-2); computer disk 29.95 (ISBN 1-55609-834-0). Gallopade Pub Group.

—New Hampshire Silly Football Sportsmysteries, Vol. 2. (Illus.). 1990. PLB 19.95 (ISBN 1-55609-835-9); pap. 14.95 (ISBN 1-55609-836-7); computer disk 29.95 (ISBN 1-55609-837-5). Gallopade Pub Group.

—New Hampshire Silly Trivia! (Illus.). 1990. PLB 19.95 (ISBN 1-55609-823-5); pap. 14.95 (ISBN 1-55609-824-3); computer disk 29.95 (ISBN 1-55609-825-1). Gallopade Pub Group.

—New Hampshire's (Most Devastating!) Disasters & (Most Calamitous!) Catastrophies! (Illus.). 1990. PLB 19.95 (ISBN 0-7933-0766-X); pap. 14.95 (ISBN 0-7933-0765-1); computer disk 29.95 (ISBN 0-7933-0767-8). Gallopade Pub Group.

Thompson, Kathleen. New Hampshire. LC 87-26480. 48p. (gr. 3 up). 1988. 17.32 (ISBN 0-86514-469-9); cancelled tchr's. study guide (ISBN 0-86514-612-8); cancelled Beta video (ISBN 0-86514-096-0); cancelled VHS video (ISBN 0-86514-171-1); cancelled (ISBN 0-86514-246-7). Raintree Pubs.

NEW HAMPSHIRE–FICTION

Bailey, Carolyn S. Miss Hickory. Gannett, Ruth, illus. LC 46-7275. (gr. 4-7). 1977. pap. 3.95 (ISBN 0-14-030956-X, Puffin). Puffin Bks.

—Miss Hickory. Gannett, Ruth, illus. (gr. 4-7). 1946. pap. 13.95 (ISBN 0-670-47940-3). Viking Child Bks.

Corcoran, Barbara. Stay Tuned. LC 90-1017. 208p. (gr. 3-7). 1991. SBE 13.95 (ISBN 0-689-31673-9, Atheneum Child Bk). Macmillan Child Grp.

Fleischman, Paul. Rear-View Mirrors. LC 85-45387. 128p. (gr. 7 up). 1986. 12.95 (ISBN 0-06-021866-5); PLB 12.89 (ISBN 0-06-021867-3). HarpC Child Bks.

Hoppe, Joanne. Pretty Penny Farm. LC 86-1516. 224p. (gr. 7 up). 1987. 12.95 (ISBN 0-688-07201-1, Morrow Junior Books). Morrow.

NEW HAMPSHIRE–HISTORY

Rosal, Lorenca. The Liberty Key: The Story of the N.H. Constitution. (Illus.). 300p. 1987. 12.95 (ISBN 0-685-19456-6). Equity Pub NH.

Thompson, Dorothea M. Will Stark & Boobear: Ranger Scouts, Vol. 2. 2nd ed. Thompson, Brownlow L., illus. 150p. (gr. 5-10). pap. text ed. 9.95 (ISBN 0-931947-52-9). Thompson Pr.

NEW JERSEY

Aylesworth, Thomas G. & Aylesworth, Virginia L. Upper Atlantic: New Jersey - New York. (Illus.). 64p. (gr. 3 up). 1987. PLB 16.95 (ISBN 1-55546-553-6); pap. 6.95 (ISBN 0-685-35556-X). Chelsea Hse.

Bain, Geri. New Jersey. (Illus.). 72p. (gr. 4-9). 1987. PLB 10.40 (ISBN 0-531-10389-7). Watts.

Carole Marsh New Jersey Books, 31 bks. Set. 638.45 (ISBN 0-7933-1305-8). Gallopade Pub Group.

Carpenter, Allan. New Jersey. LC 78-14891. (Illus.). 96p. (gr. 4 up). 1979. PLB 19.93 (ISBN 0-516-04130-4). Childrens.

Fradin, Dennis. New Jersey: In Words & Pictures. Wahl, Richard, illus. LC 80-19688. 48p. (gr. 2-5). 1980. PLB 15.93 (ISBN 0-516-03930-X). Childrens.

Kent, Deborah. New Jersey. LC 87-9401. (Illus.). 144p. (gr. 4 up). 1987. PLB 25.27 (ISBN 0-516-00476-X). Childrens.

Marsh, Carole. Avast, Ye Slobs! New Jersey Pirate Trivia. (Illus.). 1990. PLB 19.95 (ISBN 0-7933-1809-2); pap. 14.95 (ISBN 0-7933-1810-6); computer disk 29.95 (ISBN 0-7933-1811-4). Gallopade Pub Group.

—The Beast of the New Jersey Bed & Breakfast. (Illus.). 1990. PLB 19.95 (ISBN 0-7933-1779-7); pap. 14.95 (ISBN 0-7933-1780-0); computer disk 29.95 (ISBN 0-7933-1781-9). Gallopade Pub Group.

—The Hard-to-Believe-But-True! Book of New Jersey History, Mystery, Trivia, Legend, Lore, Humor & More. (Illus.). 1990. PLB 19.95 (ISBN 0-7933-1806-8); pap. 14.95 (ISBN 0-7933-1807-6); computer disk 29.95 (ISBN 0-7933-1808-4). Gallopade Pub Group.

—If My New Jersey Mama Ran the World! (Illus.). 1990. lib. bdg. 19.95 (ISBN 0-7933-1782-7); pap. 14.95 (ISBN 0-7933-1783-5); computer disk 29.95 (ISBN 0-7933-1784-3). Gallopade Pub Group.

—Let's Quilt New Jersey & Stuff It Topographically! (Illus.). 1990. PLB 19.95 (ISBN 1-55609-853-7); pap. 14.95 (ISBN 1-55609-069-2); computer disk 29.95 (ISBN 1-55609-855-3). Gallopade Pub Group.

—New Jersey & Other State Greats (Biographies) (Illus.). 1990. PLB 19.95 (ISBN 1-55609-868-5); pap. 14.95 (ISBN 1-55609-869-3); computer disk 29.95 (ISBN 1-55609-870-7). Gallopade Pub Group.

—New Jersey Bandits, Bushwackers, Outlaws, Crooks, Devils, Ghosts, Desperadoes & Other Assorted & Sundry Characters! (Illus.). 1990. PLB 19.95 (ISBN 0-7933-1788-6); pap. 14.95 (ISBN 0-7933-1789-4); computer disk 29.95 (ISBN 0-7933-1790-8). Gallopade Pub Group.

—New Jersey Classic Christmas Trivia: Stories, Recipes, Activities, Legends, Lore & More! (Illus.). 1990. PLB 19.95 (ISBN 0-7933-1791-6); pap. 14.95 (ISBN 0-7933-1792-4); computer disk 29.95 (ISBN 0-7933-1793-2). Gallopade Pub Group.

—New Jersey Coastales. (Illus.). 1990. PLB 19.95 (ISBN 1-55609-862-6); pap. 14.95 (ISBN 1-55609-863-4); computer disk 29.95 (ISBN 1-55609-864-2). Gallopade Pub Group.

—The New Jersey Hot Air Balloon Mystery. (Illus.). (gr. 2-9). 1990. 19.95 (ISBN 0-7933-2588-9); pap. 14.95 (ISBN 0-7933-2589-7); computer disk 29.95 (ISBN 0-7933-2590-0). Gallopade Pub Group.

—New Jersey "Jography" A Fun Run Thru Our State! (Illus.). 1990. PLB 19.95 (ISBN 1-55609-850-2); pap. 14.95 (ISBN 1-55609-851-0); computer disk 29.95 (ISBN 1-55609-852-9). Gallopade Pub Group.

—New Jersey Kid's Cookbook: Recipes, How-to, History, Lore & More. (Illus.). 1990. PLB 19.95 (ISBN 0-7933-1803-3); pap. 14.95 (ISBN 0-7933-1804-1); computer disk 29.95 (ISBN 0-7933-1805-X). Gallopade Pub Group.

—New Jersey Quiz Bowl Crash Course! (Illus.). 1990. PLB 19.95 (ISBN 1-55609-865-0); pap. 14.95 (ISBN 1-55609-866-9); computer disk 29.95 (ISBN 1-55609-867-7). Gallopade Pub Group.

—New Jersey School Trivia: An Amazing & Fascinating Look at Our State's Teachers, Schools & Students! (Illus.). 1990. PLB 19.95 (ISBN 0-7933-1800-9); pap. 14.95 (ISBN 0-7933-1801-7); computer disk 29.95 (ISBN 0-7933-1802-5). Gallopade Pub Group.

—New Jersey Silly Basketball Sportsmysteries, Vol. 1. (Illus.). 1990. PLB 19.95 (ISBN 0-7933-1794-0); pap. 14.95 (ISBN 0-7933-1795-9); computer disk 29.95 (ISBN 0-7933-1796-7). Gallopade Pub Group.

—New Jersey Silly Basketball Sportsmysteries, Vol. 2. (Illus.). 1990. PLB 19.95 (ISBN 0-7933-1797-5); pap. 14.95 (ISBN 0-7933-1798-3); computer disk 29.95 (ISBN 0-7933-1799-1). Gallopade Pub Group.

—New Jersey Silly Football Sportsmysteries, Vol. 1. (Illus.). 1990. PLB 19.95 (ISBN 1-55609-856-1); pap. 14.95 (ISBN 1-55609-857-X); computer disk 29.95 (ISBN 1-55609-858-8). Gallopade Pub Group.

—New Jersey Silly Football Sportsmysteries, Vol. 2. (Illus.). 1990. PLB 19.95 (ISBN 1-55609-859-6); pap. 14.95 (ISBN 1-55609-860-X); computer disk 29.95 (ISBN 1-55609-861-8). Gallopade Pub Group.

—New Jersey Silly Trivia! (Illus.). 1990. PLB 19.95 (ISBN 1-55609-847-2); pap. 14.95 (ISBN 1-55609-848-0); computer disk 29.95 (ISBN 1-55609-849-9). Gallopade Pub Group.

—New Jersey's (Most Devastating!) Disasters & (Most Calamitous!) Catastrophies! (Illus.). 1990. PLB 19.95; pap. 14.95 (ISBN 0-7933-1786-X); computer disk 29.95 (ISBN 0-7933-1787-8). Gallopade Pub Group.

Murray, Thomas C. & Barnes, Valerie. The Seven Wonders of New Jersey--& Then Some. LC 80-16424. (Illus.). 128p. (gr. 7-12). 1981. pap. 11.95 (ISBN 0-89490-017-X). Enslow Pubs.

Turner Program Services, Inc. Staff & Clark, James I. New Jersey. LC 85-9981. 48p. (gr. 3 up). 1985. PLB 17.32 (ISBN 0-86514-438-9); pap. text ed. 9.27 (ISBN 0-86514-513-X); cancelled Beta video (ISBN 0-86514-063-4); cancelled VHS video (ISBN 0-86514-138-X); cancelled 3/4" video (ISBN 0-86514-213-0); cancelled tchr's. guide (ISBN 0-86514-288-2); cancelled student activity bk. (ISBN 0-86514-363-3); cancelled index. Raintree Pubs.

You New Jersey & the World. 256p. 1990. 15.95 (ISBN 0-89359-000-2); write for info. tchr's. ed. 1986 (ISBN 0-89359-001-0). Afton Pub.
The story of New Jersey is written to capture & hold children's interest. Appealing full-color illustrations include photographs, paintings, historic prints, maps, charts & graphs. Thirteen chapters, organized by topic, include Mapping, Geography, Colonial Times, Revolution, Indians, Environment & Government. NJEA Review says, "The book offers an in-depth, well-presented picture of our state, as well as interesting reading. School & public libraries will want to include it on their shelves." Complete, correlating line includes comprehensive teacher's guide, evaluation & review sheets, filmstrips, map skills program, posters, activities text, map charts, resource books (including NJ: A Mirror on America, 1988 edition, which is also used as a high school text), a play, a choral reading & computer discs. Order through Afton Publishing Co. Inc., PO Box 1399, Andover, NJ 07821; (201) 579-2442; FAX (201) 579-2842.
Publisher Provided Annotation.

NEW JERSEY–FICTION

Robertson, Keith. Henry Reed's Baby-Sitting Service. McCloskey, Robert, illus. (gr. 5-8). 1966. pap. 14.95 (ISBN 0-670-36825-3). Viking Child Bks.

NEW JERSEY–HISTORY

Brown, Edward. Just Around the Corner in New Jersey. (Illus.). 112p. (gr. 6 up). 1987. pap. 5.95 (ISBN 0-912608-17-X). Mid Atlantic.

McCloy, James F. & Miller, Ray, Jr. The Jersey Devil. (Illus.). 121p. (gr. 5 up). 1987. pap. 6.95 (ISBN 0-912608-11-0). Mid Atlantic.

McMahon, William. Pine Barrens Legends, Lore & Lies. (Illus.). 149p. (gr. 6 up). 1986. pap. 6.95 (ISBN 0-912608-19-6). Mid Atlantic.

Rabold, Ted & Fair, Phillip. New Jersey: Yesterday & Today. Ferguson, Laurie, illus. 110p. (Orig.). (gr. 4). 1982. 9.95 (ISBN 0-931992-41-9); pap. text ed. 4.95 (ISBN 0-931992-43-5). Penns Valley.

NEW MEXICO

Ashabranner, Brent. Born to the Land: An American Portrait. Conklin, Paul, photos by. (Illus.). 144p. (gr. 5 up). 1989. 14.95 (ISBN 0-399-21716-9, Putnam). Putnam Pub Group.

Aylesworth, Thomas G. & Aylesworth, Virginia L. The Southwest (Texas, New Mexico, Colorado) (Illus.). 64p. (gr. 3 up). 1992. PLB 16.95 (ISBN 0-7910-1048-1). Chelsea Hse.

Carole Marsh New Mexico Books, 31 bks. Set. 638.45 (ISBN 0-7933-1306-6). Gallopade Pub Group.

Carpenter, Allan. New Mexico. LC 78-2695. (Illus.). 96p. (gr. 4 up). 1978. PLB 19.93 (ISBN 0-516-04131-2). Childrens.

Chapman, Al. Coloring Book of New Mexico Santos. Ortega, Pedro R., tr. Chapman, Al, illus. (SPA & ENG.). 32p. (gr. 1-8). 1982. pap. 3.00 (ISBN 0-913270-19-9). Sunstone Pr.

Fradin, Dennis. New Mexico: In Words & Pictures. Wahl, Richard, illus. LC 81-298. 48p. (gr. 2-5). 1981. PLB 15.93 (ISBN 0-516-03931-8); pap. 4.95 (ISBN 0-516-43931-6). Childrens.

Hallett, Bill & Hallett, Jane. Look up Look Down Look All Around Chaco Culture National Historical Park. Jackson, Lori, illus. 32p. (Orig.). (gr. 3-8). 1989. pap. 3.45 activity bk. (ISBN 0-685-26277-4). Look & See.

—Look up Look Down Look All Around El Morro National Monument. Chaffee, Dan, illus. 32p. (Orig.). (gr. 3-8). 1988. pap. 3.45 activity bk. (ISBN 0-943087-04-X). Look & See.

Marsh, Carole. Avast, Ye Slobs! New Mexico Pirate Trivia. (Illus.). 1990. PLB 19.95 (ISBN 0-7933-0811-9); pap. 14.95 (ISBN 0-7933-0810-0); computer disk 29.95 (ISBN 0-7933-0812-7). Gallopade Pub Group.

—The Beast of the New Mexico Bed & Breakfast. (Illus.). 1990. PLB 19.95 (ISBN 0-7933-1812-2); pap. 14.95 (ISBN 0-7933-1813-0); computer disk 29.95 (ISBN 0-7933-1814-9). Gallopade Pub Group.

—The Hard-to-Believe-But-True! Book of New Mexico History, Mystery, Trivia, Legend, Lore, Humor & More. (Illus.). 1990. PLB 19.95 (ISBN 0-7933-0808-9); pap. 14.95 (ISBN 0-7933-0807-0); computer disk 29.95 (ISBN 0-7933-0809-7). Gallopade Pub Group.

—If My New Mexico Mama Ran The World! (Illus.). 1990. lib. bdg. 19.95 (ISBN 0-7933-1815-7); pap. 14.95 (ISBN 0-7933-1816-5); computer disk 29.95 (ISBN 0-7933-1817-3). Gallopade Pub Group.

—Let's Quilt New Mexico & Stuff It Topographically! (Illus.). 1990. PLB 19.95 (ISBN 1-55609-877-4); pap. 14.95 (ISBN 1-55609-127-3); computer disk 29.95 (ISBN 1-55609-879-0). Gallopade Pub Group.

—New Mexico & Other State Greats (Biographies) (Illus.). 1990. PLB 19.95 (ISBN 1-55609-892-8); pap. 14.95 (ISBN 1-55609-893-6); computer disk 29.95 (ISBN 1-55609-894-4). Gallopade Pub Group.

—New Mexico Bandits, Bushwackers, Outlaws, Crooks, Devils, Ghosts, Desperadoes & Other Assorted & Sundry Characters! (Illus.). 1990. PLB 19.95 (ISBN 0-7933-0793-7); pap. 14.95 (ISBN 0-7933-0792-9); computer disk 29.95 (ISBN 0-7933-0794-5). Gallopade Pub Group.

—New Mexico Classic Christmas Trivia: Stories, Recipes, Activities, Legends, Lore & More! (Illus.). 1990. PLB 19.95 (ISBN 0-7933-0796-1); pap. 14.95 (ISBN 0-7933-0795-3); computer disk 29.95 (ISBN 0-7933-0797-X). Gallopade Pub Group.

—New Mexico Coastales. (Illus.). 1990. PLB 19.95 (ISBN 1-55609-886-3); pap. 14.95 (ISBN 1-55609-887-1); computer disk 29.95 (ISBN 1-55609-888-X). Gallopade Pub Group.

—The New Mexico Hot Air Balloon Mystery. (Illus.). (gr. 2-9). 1990. 19.95 (ISBN 0-7933-2597-8); pap. 14.95 (ISBN 0-7933-2598-6); computer disk 29.95 (ISBN 0-7933-2599-4). Gallopade Pub Group.

—New Mexico "Jography" A Fun Run Thru Our State! (Illus.). 1990. PLB 19.95 (ISBN 1-55609-874-X); pap. 14.95 (ISBN 1-55609-875-8); computer disk 29.95 (ISBN 1-55609-876-6). Gallopade Pub Group.

—New Mexico Kid's Cookbook: Recipes, How-to, History, Lore & More! (Illus.). 1990. PLB 19.95 (ISBN 0-7933-0805-4); pap. 14.95 (ISBN 0-7933-0804-6); computer disk 29.95 (ISBN 0-7933-0806-2). Gallopade Pub Group.

—New Mexico Quiz Bowl Crash Course! (Illus.). 1990. PLB 19.95 (ISBN 1-55609-889-8); pap. 14.95 (ISBN 1-55609-890-1); computer disk 29.95 (ISBN 1-55609-891-X). Gallopade Pub Group.

—New Mexico School Trivia: An Amazing & Fascinating Look at Our State's Teachers, Schools & Students! (Illus.). 1990. PLB 19.95 (ISBN 0-7933-0802-X); pap. 14.95 (ISBN 0-7933-0801-1); computer disk 29.95 (ISBN 0-7933-0803-8). Gallopade Pub Group.

—New Mexico Silly Basketball Sportsmystereis, Vol. 1. (Illus.). 1990. PLB 19.95 (ISBN 0-7933-0799-6); pap. 14.95 (ISBN 0-7933-0798-8); computer disk 29.95 (ISBN 0-7933-0800-3). Gallopade Pub Group.

—New Mexico Silly Basketball Sportsmysteries, Vol. 2. (Illus.). 1990. PLB 19.95 (ISBN 0-7933-1818-1); pap. 14.95 (ISBN 0-7933-1819-X); computer disk 29.95 (ISBN 0-7933-1820-3). Gallopade Pub Group.

—New Mexico Silly Football Sportsmysteries. (Illus.). 1990. PLB 19.95 (ISBN 1-55609-880-4); pap. 14.95 (ISBN 1-55609-881-2); computer disk 29.95 (ISBN 1-55609-882-0). Gallopade Pub Group.
—New Mexico Silly Football Sportsmysteries. (Illus.). 1990. pap. 14.95 (ISBN 1-55609-884-7); computer disk 29.95 (ISBN 1-55609-885-5). Gallopade Pub Group.
—New Mexico Silly Trivia! (Illus.). 1990. PLB 19.95 (ISBN 1-55609-871-5); pap. 14.95 (ISBN 1-55609-872-3); computer disk 29.95 (ISBN 1-55609-873-1). Gallopade Pub Group.
—New Mexico's (Most Devastating!) Disasters & (Most Calamitous!) Catastrophies! (Illus.). 1990. PLB 19.95 (ISBN 0-7933-0790-2); pap. 14.95 (ISBN 0-7933-0789-9); computer disk 29.95 (ISBN 0-7933-0791-0). Gallopade Pub Group.
Roberts, Susan & Roberts, Calvin. A History of New Mexico. rev. ed. (Illus.). 400p. (gr. 6-9). 1991. text ed. 45.00 (ISBN 0-8263-1264-0). U of NM Pr.
Salts, Bobbi. New Mexico Is for Kids! An Activity Book. Parker, Steve, illus. 32p. (gr. 1-6). 1989. pap. 2.95 (ISBN 0-929526-02-3). Double B Pubns.
Simmons, Marc. New Mexico. (Illus.). 328p. (gr. 4). 1983. text ed. 17.25x (ISBN 0-87905-135-3, Peregrine Smith). Gibbs Smith Pub.
—New Mexico! rev. ed. (Illus.). 313p. (gr. 4). 1991. text ed. 45.00 (ISBN 0-8263-1265-9). U of NM Pr.
Turner Program Services, Inc. Staff & Clark, James I. New Mexico. LC 85-10832. 48p. (gr. 3 up). 1985. PLB 17.32 (ISBN 0-86514-439-7); pap. text ed. 9.27 (ISBN 0-86514-514-8); cancelled Beta video (ISBN 0-86514-064-2); cancelled VHS video (ISBN 0-86514-139-8); cancelled 3/4" video (ISBN 0-86514-214-9); cancelled tchr's. guide (ISBN 0-86514-289-0); cancelled student activity bk. (ISBN 0-86514-364-1); cancelled index. Raintree Pubs.

NEW MEXICO–ANTIQUITIES

Dressman, John. On the Cliffs of Acoma. Ortega, Pedro R., tr. from SPA. LC 83-20177. (Illus.). 32p. (gr. 2-4). 1984. pap. 5.95 (ISBN 0-86534-021-8). Sunstone Pr.

NEW MEXICO–FICTION

Atwood, Marjorie, Jr. Galisteo Legend. Smith, James C., ed. Yamashita, Mina, illus. 48p. (Orig.). 1991. pap. 6.95 (ISBN 0-86534-154-0). Sunstone Pr.
Elster, Alayne. Julio & His New Amigo. 1988. 4.95 (ISBN 0-533-07646-3). Vantage.
Krumgold, Joseph. And Now Miguel. Charlot, Jean, illus. LC 53-8415. 245p. (gr. 5 up). 1987. 12.95 (ISBN 0-690-09118-4, Crowell Jr Bks); PLB 12.89 (ISBN 0-690-04696-0, Crowell Jr Bks). HarpC Child Bks.

NEW ORLEANS

Carvin, Ruth. A Visit to New Orleans: With Pictures to Color & Verses to Read. rev. ed. Dolobowsky, Mena, illus. 32p. (gr. k-4). 1988. coloring bk. 3.50 (ISBN 0-9616390-2-4). Carvin Pub.
Nichols, Joan K. New Orleans. LC 88-35915. (Illus.). 60p. (gr. 3 up). 1989. lib. bdg. 12.95 (ISBN 0-87518-403-0, Dillon). Macmillan Child Grp.

NEW ORLEANS–FICTION

Dartez, Cecilia C. Jenny Giraffe Discovers the French Quarter. Wilson, Shelby, illus. 32p. (ps-8). 1991. 11.95 (ISBN 0-88289-819-1). Pelican.
Flettrich, Terry. House in the Bend of Bourbon Street. Lo-An, illus. (gr. 1-6). 1974. pap. 2.95 (ISBN 0-88289-015-8). Pelican.
Rice, James. Gaston Goes to Mardi Gras. LC 77-13302. (Illus.). 40p. (gr. 1-6). 1977. 11.95 (ISBN 0-88289-158-8). Pelican.

NEW ORLEANS–HISTORY

Historic Santa Fe Association Staff, ed. We're So Lucky to Live in Santa Fe: An Activities Book in Historical Preservation. (Illus.). 26p. (gr. 4 up). pap. 4.95 (ISBN 0-89013-196-1). Museum NM Pr.

NEW TESTAMENT

see Bible. New Testament

NEW WORDS

see Words, New

NEW YEAR

Baker, James W. New Year's Magic. Overlie, Goerge, illus. 48p. (gr. 2-5). 1989. 8.95 (ISBN 0-8225-2231-4). Lerner Pubns.
Blackwood, Alan. New Year. (Illus.). 48p. (gr. 3-8). 1987. PLB 14.60 (ISBN 0-86592-981-5). Rourke Corp.
Kalman, Bobbie. We Celebrate New Year. (Illus.). 56p. (gr. 3-4). 1985. 15.95 (ISBN 0-86505-041-4); pap. 7.95 (ISBN 0-86505-051-1). Crabtree Pub Co.
Kelley, Emily. Happy New Year. Kiedrowski, Priscilla, illus. 48p. (gr. k-4). 1984. PLB 9.95 (ISBN 0-87614-269-2); pap. 3.95 (ISBN 0-87614-469-5). Carolrhoda Bks.
—Happy New Year. Kiedrowski, Priscilla, illus. (gr. k-4). 1987. pap. 3.95 (ISBN 0-685-18661-X, First Ave Edns). Lerner Pubns.

NEW YEAR–FICTION

Harwood, Pearl A. New Year's Day with Mr. & Mrs. Bumba. Overlie, George, illus. LC 77-156355. 32p. (gr. k-3). 1971. PLB 4.95 (ISBN 0-8225-0127-9). Lerner Pubns.
Schulz, Charles M. Happy New Year, Charlie Brown. Schulz, Charles M., illus. LC 86-42566. 48p. (gr. 3-6). 1986. (Random Juv); lib. bdg. 7.99 (ISBN 0-394-98467-6). Random.
Stevenson, James. Un-Happy New Year, Emma! LC 88-18802. (Illus.). 32p. (ps up). 1989. 12.95 (ISBN 0-688-08342-0); PLB 12.88 (ISBN 0-688-08343-9). Greenwillow.

NEW YORK (CITY)

Adams, Barbara Johnston. New York. LC 88-20245. (Illus.). 60p. (gr. 3 up). 1988. PLB 12.95 (ISBN 0-87518-384-0, Dillon). Macmillan Child Grp.
Biemer, Linda. New York City: Our Community. (Illus.). 100p. (gr. 4). 1986. 9.30 (ISBN 0-685-24532-2, Peregrine Smith). Gibbs Smith Pub.
Climo, Shirley. City! New York. Ancona, George, illus. LC 89-13482. 64p. (gr. 3-7). 1990. 15.95 (ISBN 0-02-719020-X, Mcmillan Child Bk). Macmillan Child Grp.
Davis, Jim & Hawke, Sherryl D. New York. (Illus.). 64p. (gr. 4-9). 1990. PLB 17.32 (ISBN 0-8172-3031-9). Raintree Pubs.
McGowan, E. M. A Look Around New York City. (Illus.). 32p. (Orig.). (gr. 1-4). 1988. pap. 1.25 (ISBN 0-87406-142-3). Willowisp Pr.
Stewart, G. New York. (Illus.). 48p. (gr. 5 up). 1989. lib. bdg. 14.60 (ISBN 0-86592-541-0). Rourke Corp.

NEW YORK (CITY)–DESCRIPTION

Brown, Richard, illus. A Kid's Guide to New York City. 160p. (gr. 1 up). 1988. pap. 6.95 (ISBN 0-15-200458-0, Gulliver Bks). HarBraceJ.
Clinton, Patrick. The Story of the Empire State Building. LC 87-25687. (Illus.). 32p. (gr. 3-6). 1987. PLB 13.27 (ISBN 0-516-04730-2); pap. 3.95 (ISBN 0-516-44730-0). Childrens.
Deegan, Paul. New York, New York. LC 89-32945. (Illus.). 48p. (gr. 4-5). 1989. 12.95 (ISBN 0-89686-467-7, Crestwood Hse). Macmillan Child Grp.
Fisher, Bubbles. Candy Apple New York for Kids. 2nd ed. 1989. pap. 12.95 (ISBN 0-13-114976-8). P-H.
Munro, Roxie. The Inside-Outside Book of New York City. (Illus.). 48p. (gr. k-3). 1985. 13.95 (ISBN 0-396-08513-X, Putnam). Putnam Pub Group.

NEW YORK (CITY)–FICTION

Buchan, Stuart. Guys Like Us. (gr. 7 up). 1986. 14.95 (ISBN 0-385-29448-4). Delacorte.
Charnas, Suzy M. The Bronze King. 208p. 1988. pap. 2.95 (ISBN 0-553-27104-0, Starfire). Bantam.
Cooney, Barbara. Hattie & the Wild Waves. Cooney, Barbara, illus. (ps-3). 1990. 14.95 (ISBN 0-670-83056-9). Viking Child Bks.
Cummings, Pat. C.L.O.U.D.S. LC 85-9719. (Illus.). 32p. (ps-3). 1986. 12.95 (ISBN 0-688-04682-7); PLB 12.88 (ISBN 0-688-04683-5). Lothrop.
Danziger, Paula. Remember Me to Harold Square. LC 87-6844. 168p. (gr. 7 up). 1987. pap. 14.95 (ISBN 0-385-29610-X). Delacorte.
—Remember Me to Harold Square. 144p. (gr. k-12). 1988. pap. 3.25 (ISBN 0-440-20153-5, LFL). Dell.
Davis, Edward E. Bruno the Pretzel Man. Simont, Marc, illus. LC 84-47630. 64p. (gr. 2-5). 1984. HarpC Child Bks.
De Brunhoff, Laurent. Babar a New York. (Illus.). (gr. 4-6). bds. 15.95 (ISBN 0-685-11024-9). French & Eur.
Decker, Dorothy. Stripe Visits New York. Decker, Dorothy, illus. LC 85-6768. 48p. (gr. k-3). 1986. PLB 10.95 (ISBN 0-87518-267-4, Dillon). Macmillan Child Grp.
Donovan, John. I'll Get There: It Better Be Worth the Trip. LC 69-15539. (gr. 7 up). 1969. PLB 12.89 (ISBN 0-06-021718-9). HarpC Child Bks.
Ehrlich, Amy. Annie: The Storybook Based on the Movie. LC 81-15416. (Illus.). 64p. (gr. 5 up). 1982. Random.
Fitzhugh, Louise. Sport. 224p. (gr. 7 up). 1980. pap. 1.75 (ISBN 0-440-98350-9, LFL). Dell.
Ford, Barbara. The Eagles' Child. LC 90-5633. 160p. (gr. 3-7). 1990. 12.95 (ISBN 0-02-735405-9, Mcmillan Child Bk). Macmillan Child Grp.
French, Fiona. Snow White in New York. 32p. 1990. pap. 6.95 (ISBN 0-19-272210-7). Oxford U Pr.
Greene, Constance C. Al(exandra) the Great. 144p. (gr. 5-9). 1983. pap. 2.95 (ISBN 0-440-40350-2, YB). Dell.
Greenwald, Sheila. Valentine Rosy. Greenwald, Sheila, illus. LC 84-9694. 89p. (gr. 4 up). 1984. 11.95 (ISBN 0-316-32708-5, Joy St Bks). Little.
Hamilton, Virginia. Planet of Junior Brown. LC 71-155264. 240p. (gr. 5-9). 1971. 14.95 (ISBN 0-02-742510-X, Mcmillan Child Bk). Macmillan Child Grp.
Hope, Laura L. Bobbsey Twins' Search in the Great City. (gr. 1-4). 1930. 4.50 (ISBN 0-448-08009-5, G&D). Putnam Pub Group.
James, Henry. Washington Square. Tate, E., intro. by. (gr. 10 up). 1969. pap. 1.50 (ISBN 0-8049-0210-0, CL-210). Airmont.
Konigsburg, E. L. From the Mixed-Up Files of Mrs. Basil E. Frankweiler. 1987. pap. 3.95 (ISBN 0-689-71181-6, Aladdin). Macmillan Child Grp.
Kovalski, Maryann. Jingle Bells. Kovalski, Maryann, illus. 32p. (ps-2). 1988. 12.95 (ISBN 0-316-50258-8). Little.
L'Engle, Madeleine. The Young Unicorns. LC 68-13682. 256p. (gr. 7 up). 1968. 16.95 (ISBN 0-374-38778-8). FS&G.
Marsh, Fabienne. The Moralist of the Alphabet Streets. 252p. (gr. 10 up). 1991. 15.95 (ISBN 0-945575-47-5). Algonquin Bks.
Mazer, Harry. Cave under the City. LC 86-45008. 160p. (gr. 3-7). 1986. 13.95 (ISBN 0-690-04557-3, Crowell Jr Bks); PLB 13.89 (ISBN 0-690-04559-X, Crowell Jr Bks). HarpC Child Bks.
Mezek, Karen. Katie Goes to New York. (Illus.). 58p. (Orig.). (gr. 2-6). 1991. pap. 4.99 (ISBN 0-89081-864-9). Harvest Hse.
Miller-Lachmann, Lyn. Hiding Places. 206p. (Orig.). (gr. 9-12). 1987. pap. 4.95 (ISBN 0-938961-00-4, Stamp Out Sheep Pr). Sq One Pubs.
Orden, J. Hannah. In Real Life. 224p. (gr. 7 up). 1990. pap. 12.95 (ISBN 0-670-82679-0). Viking Child Bks.
Pinkwater, Jill. Tails of the Bronx: A Tale of the Bronx. 208p. (gr. 3-7). 1991. SBE 13.95 (ISBN 0-02-774652-6, Mcmillan Child Bk). Macmillan Child Grp.
Sawyer, Ruth. Roller Skates. Angelo, Valenti, illus. 184p. (gr. 5-9). 1986. pap. 3.95 (ISBN 0-14-030358-8, Puffin). Puffin Bks.
Selden, George. Chester Cricket's Pigeon Ride. Williams, Garth, illus. LC 80-20326. 64p. (ps-3). 1981. 14.95 (ISBN 0-374-31239-7). FS&G.
—Cricket in Times Square. Williams, Garth, illus. (gr. 2-7). 1970. pap. 3.50 (ISBN 0-440-41563-2, YB). Dell.
—The Genie of Sutton Place. LC 72-90531. 192p. (gr. 3 up). 1973. 12.95 (ISBN 0-374-32527-8). FS&G.
Skolsky, Mindy W. The Whistling Teakettle & Other Stories about Hannah. LC 76-21395. (Illus.). (gr. 2-5). 1977. 10.89 (ISBN 0-06-025688-5). HarpC Child Bks.
Snyder, Carol. Ike & Mama & Trouble at School. Robinson, Charles, illus. LC 82-12557. (gr. 4-7). 1983. 9.95 (ISBN 0-698-20570-7, Coward). Putnam Pub Group.
Swift, Hildegarde H. & Ward, Lynd. Little Red Lighthouse & the Great Gray Bridge. Ward, Lynd, illus. LC 42-36286. (gr. k-3). 1942. 15.95 (ISBN 0-15-247040-9, HJ). HarBraceJ.

Taylor, Sydney. All-of-a-Kind Family. John, Helen, illus. 189p. (gr. 3-6). 1988. Repr. of 1951 ed. 11.95 (ISBN 0-929093-00-3). Taylor Prodns. ALL-OF-A-KIND FAMILY by Sydney Taylor, was first published in 1951, after winning the Follett Children's Book Contest, & has been in print continuously since then. It was highly acclaimed & adored by readers from its first appearence & has become a classic, as have the other titles in this series, described below. It was followed over the years by four other books about this immigrant family growing up on New York's Lower East Side in the years immediately before & during the First World War, & each in turn, received the same enthusiastic reception. They are: ALL-OF-A-KIND FAMILY DOWNTOWN (ISBN 0-929093-01-1); MORE ALL-OF-A-KIND FAMILY (ISBN 0-929093-02-X); ALL-OF-A-KIND FAMILY UPTOWN (ISBN 0-929093-03-8); ELLA OF ALL-OF-A-KIND FAMILY (ISBN 0-929093-04-6). Over the years, each new book was greeted with glowing reviews from the children's major media. More importantly, perhaps, is the fact that readers welcomed each...& that these readers continue to remember the books fondly & order them for their own children & grandchildren. This family of five girls, later joined by a baby brother, has been taken to the heart of America & has created a firmly entrenched place in its children's literature. Distributed by the Talman Company, 150 Fifth Avenue, New York, NY 10011. Each book is hardcovered & is $11.95.
Publisher Provided Annotation.

Wibberley, Leonard. Mouse That Roared. (gr. 6-12). 1971. pap. 3.50 (ISBN 0-553-24969-X). Bantam.

NEW YORK (CITY)–HISTORY

Climo, Shirley. City! New York. Ancona, George, illus. LC 89-13482. 64p. (gr. 3-7). 1990. 15.95 (ISBN 0-02-719020-X, Mcmillan Child Bk). Macmillan Child Grp.
Costabel, Eva D. Jews of New Amsterdam. Costabel, Eva D., illus. LC 87-27873. 32p. (gr. 2-6). 1988. 13.95 (ISBN 0-689-31351-9, Atheneum Child Bk). Macmillan Child Grp.
Quackenbush, Robert. Pop! Goes the Weasel & Yankee Doodle: New York in 1776 & Today, with Songs & Pictures. reissue (1976) ed. Quackenbush, Robert, illus. LC 75-28312. 40p. (ps up). 1988. PLB 13.89 (ISBN 0-397-32265-8, Lipp Jr Bks). HarpC Child Bks.

NEW YORK. METROPOLITAN MUSEUM OF ART–FICTION

Konigsburg, E. L. From the Mixed-Up Files of Mrs. Basil E. Frankweiler. Konigsburg, E. L., illus. LC 67-18988. 168p. (gr. 3-7). 1970. 13.95 (ISBN 0-689-20586-4, Atheneum Child Bk). Macmillan Child Grp.

—From the Mixed-Up Files of Mrs. Basil E. Frankweiler. 160p. (gr. 5 up). 1977. pap. 3.50 (ISBN 0-440-43180-8, YB). Dell.

NEW YORK (STATE)

Aylesworth, Thomas G. & Aylesworth, Virginia L. Upper Atlantic: New Jersey - New York. (Illus.). 64p. (gr. 3 up). 1987. PLB 16.95 (ISBN 1-55546-553-6); pap. 6.95 (ISBN 0-685-35556-X). Chelsea Hse.

Biemer, Linda. New York: Our Communities. (Illus.). 328p. (gr. 4). 1983. text ed. 18.60x (ISBN 0-87905-111-6, Peregrine Smith). Gibbs Smith Pub.

Carole Marsh New York Books, 31 bks. Set. 638.45 (ISBN 0-7933-1307-4). Gallopade Pub Group.

Carpenter, Allan. New York. new ed. LC 78-3395. (Illus.). 96p. (gr. 4 up). 1978. PLB 19.93 (ISBN 0-516-04132-0). Childrens.

Fradin, Dennis. New York: In Words & Pictures. Wahl, Richard, illus. LC 81-28366. 48p. (gr. 2-5). 1981. PLB 15.93 (ISBN 0-516-03932-6); pap. 4.95 (ISBN 0-516-43932-4). Childrens.

Higby, Roy C. A Man from the Past. 2nd ed. Lux, Don, illus. McLoughlin, William G., intro. by. (Illus.). (gr. 5-12). pap. 4.25 (ISBN 0-914692-02-X). Big Moose.

LeVert, Suzanne. New York. (Illus.). 96p. (gr. 4-9). 1987. PLB 10.40 (ISBN 0-531-10390-0). Watts.

Marsh, Carole. Avast, Ye Slobs! New York Pirate Trivia. (Illus.). 1990. PLB 19.95 (ISBN 0-7933-0835-6); pap. 14.95 (ISBN 0-7933-0834-8); computer disk 29.95 (ISBN 0-7933-0836-4). Gallopade Pub Group.

—The Beast of the New York Bed & Breakfast. (Illus.). 1990. PLB 19.95 (ISBN 0-7933-1821-1); pap. 14.95 (ISBN 0-7933-1822-X); computer disk 29.95 (ISBN 0-7933-1823-8). Gallopade Pub Group.

—The Hard-to-Believe-But-True! Book of New York History, Mystery, Trivia, Legend, Lore, Humor & More. (Illus.). 1990. PLB 19.95 (ISBN 0-7933-0832-1); pap. 14.95 (ISBN 0-7933-0831-3); computer disk 29.95 (ISBN 0-7933-0833-X). Gallopade Pub Group.

—If My New York Mama Ran the World! (Illus.). 1990. lib. bdg. 19.95 (ISBN 0-7933-1827-0); pap. 14.95 (ISBN 0-7933-1828-9); computer disk 29.95 (ISBN 0-7933-1829-7). Gallopade Pub Group.

—Let's Quilt New York & Stuff It Topographically! (Illus.). 1990. PLB 19.95 (ISBN 1-55609-904-5); pap. 14.95 (ISBN 1-55609-060-9); computer disk 29.95 (ISBN 1-55609-905-3). Gallopade Pub Group.

—New York & Other State Greats (Biographies) (Illus.). 1990. PLB 19.95 (ISBN 1-55609-918-5); pap. 14.95 (ISBN 1-55609-919-3); computer disk 29.95 (ISBN 1-55609-920-7). Gallopade Pub Group.

—New York Bandits, Bushwackers, Outlaws, Crooks, Devils, Ghosts, Desperadoes & Other Assorted & Sundry Characters! (Illus.). 1990. PLB 19.95 (ISBN 0-7933-0817-8); pap. 14.95 (ISBN 0-7933-0816-X); computer disk 29.95 (ISBN 0-7933-0818-6). Gallopade Pub Group.

—New York Classic Christmas Trivia: Stories, Recipes, Activies, Legends, Lore & More! (Illus.). 1990. PLB 19.95 (ISBN 0-7933-0820-8); pap. 14.95; computer disk 29.95 (ISBN 0-7933-0821-6). Gallopade Pub Group.

—New York Coastales. (Illus.). 1990. PLB 19.95 (ISBN 1-55609-912-6); pap. 14.95 (ISBN 1-55609-913-4); computer disk 29.95 (ISBN 1-55609-914-2). Gallopade Pub Group.

—The New York Hot Air Balloon Mystery. (Illus.). (gr. 2-9). 1990. 19.95 (ISBN 0-7933-2606-0); pap. 14.95 (ISBN 0-7933-2607-9); computer disk 29.95 (ISBN 0-7933-2608-7). Gallopade Pub Group.

—New York "Jography" A Fun Run Thru Our State! (Illus.). 1990. PLB 19.95 (ISBN 1-55609-897-9); pap. 14.95 (ISBN 1-55609-898-7); computer disk 29.95 (ISBN 1-55609-899-5). Gallopade Pub Group.

—New York Kid's Cookbook: Recipes, How-to, History, Lore & More! (Illus.). 1990. PLB 19.95 (ISBN 0-7933-0829-1); pap. 14.95 (ISBN 0-7933-0828-3); computer disk 29.95 (ISBN 0-7933-0830-5). Gallopade Pub Group.

—New York Quiz Bowl Crash Course! (Illus.). 1990. PLB 19.95 (ISBN 1-55609-915-0); pap. 14.95 (ISBN 1-55609-916-9); computer disk 29.95 (ISBN 1-55609-917-7). Gallopade Pub Group.

—New York School Trivia: An Amazing & Fascinating Look at Our State's Teachers, Schools & Students! (Illus.). 1990. PLB 19.95 (ISBN 0-7933-0826-7); pap. 14.95 (ISBN 0-7933-0825-9); computer disk 29.95 (ISBN 0-7933-0827-5). Gallopade Pub Group.

—New York Silly Basketball Sportsmysteries, Vol. 1. (Illus.). 1990. PLB 19.95 (ISBN 0-7933-0823-2); pap. 14.95 (ISBN 0-7933-0822-4); computer disk 29.95 (ISBN 0-7933-0824-0). Gallopade Pub Group.

—New York Silly Basketball Sportsmysteries, Vol. 2. (Illus.). 1990. PLB 19.95; pap. 14.95 (ISBN 0-7933-1825-4); computer disk 29.95 (ISBN 0-7933-1826-2). Gallopade Pub Group.

—New York Silly Football Sportsmysteries, Vol. 1. (Illus.). 1990. PLB 19.95 (ISBN 1-55609-906-1); pap. 14.95 (ISBN 1-55609-907-X); computer disk 29.95 (ISBN 1-55609-908-8). Gallopade Pub Group.

—New York Silly Football Sportsmysteries, Vol. 2. (Illus.). 1990. PLB 19.95 (ISBN 1-55609-909-6); pap. 14.95 (ISBN 1-55609-910-X); computer disk 29.95 (ISBN 1-55609-911-8). Gallopade Pub Group.

—New York Silly Trivia! (Illus.). 1990. PLB 19.95 (ISBN 1-55609-895-2); pap. 14.95 (ISBN 1-55609-103-6); computer disk 29.95 (ISBN 1-55609-896-0). Gallopade Pub Group.

—New York's (Most Devasting!) Disasters & (Most Calamitous!) Catastrophies! (Illus.). 1990. PLB 19.95 (ISBN 0-7933-0814-3); pap. 14.95 (ISBN 0-7933-0813-5); computer disk 29.95 (ISBN 0-7933-0815-1). Gallopade Pub Group.

Reed, Harold A. Memories of Days in the Life of a Small Boy. (Illus.). 125p. (Orig.). (gr. 3-5). 1988. pap. 9.95 (ISBN 0-931485-06-1). Scriptorium Pr.

Stein, R. Conrad. New York. LC 88-11748. (Illus.). 144p. (gr. 4 up). 1988. PLB 25.27 (ISBN 0-516-00478-6). Childrens.

Thompson, Kathleen. New York. LC 87-26481. 48p. (gr. 3 up). 1988. 17.32 (ISBN 0-86514-474-5); cancelled tchr's. study guide (ISBN 0-86514-614-4); cancelled Beta video (ISBN 0-86514-102-9); cancelled VHS video (ISBN 0-86514-177-0); cancelled (ISBN 0-86514-252-1). Raintree Pubs.

NEW YORK (STATE)–FICTION

Gleiter, Jan, retold by. The Legend of Sleepy Hollow. Thompson, Kathleen, retold by. LC 84-9931. (Illus.). (gr. 2-5). 1984. PLB 16.67 (ISBN 0-8172-2117-4); PLB 27.99g incl. cassette (ISBN 0-8172-2239-1); pap. 9.27 (ISBN 0-8172-2260-X); pap. 23.95 incl. cassette (ISBN 0-8172-2270-7); cassette 14.00 (ISBN 0-685-09505-3). Raintree Pubs.

Irving, Washington. Legend of Sleepy Hollow & Other Stories. (gr. 6 up). 1964. pap. 2.75 (ISBN 0-8049-0050-7, CL-50). Airmont.

—Rip Van Winkle. Howe, John, retold by. & illus. (ps-3). 1988. 14.95 (ISBN 0-316-37578-0). Little.

—Rip Van Winkle: The Mountain Top Edition. rev. ed. Oakes, Donald T., ed. Wyeth, N. C. & Murtagh, Mark, illus. Hommel, Justine L., contrib. by. LC 89-62869. 92p. (gr. 9). 1989. pap. write for info. (ISBN 0-9624216-0-X). MTH Soc Inc.

The Legend of Sleepy Hollow. 1989. 5.98 (ISBN 0-685-28323-2, Mallard Pr). BDD Promo Bk.

Storr, Catherine, retold by. Rip Van Winkle. LC 83-26996. (Illus.). 32p. (gr. k-5). 1984. PLB 16.67 (ISBN 0-8172-2108-5); pap. 9.27 (ISBN 0-8172-2252-9); PLB 27.99 incl. cassette (ISBN 0-8172-2236-7); pap. 23.95 incl. cassette (ISBN 0-8172-2267-7); cassette only 14.00 (ISBN 0-685-09499-5). Raintree Pubs.

Wilder, Laura I. Farmer Boy. rev. ed. Williams, Garth, illus. LC 52-7527. (gr. 2-7). 1961. 14.95 (ISBN 0-06-026425-X); PLB 14.89 (ISBN 0-06-026421-7). HarpC Child Bks.

York, Carol B., ed. Ichabod Crane & the Headless Horseman. Irving, Washington. LC 79-66323. (Illus.). 48p. (gr. 3-6). 1980. lib. bdg. 9.89 (ISBN 0-89375-316-5); pap. 2.95 (ISBN 0-89375-315-7). Troll Assocs.

—Rip Van Winkle. new ed. Washington, Irving. LC 79-66314. (Illus.). 48p. (gr. 3-6). 1980. lib. bdg. 9.89 (ISBN 0-89375-300-9); pap. 2.95 (ISBN 0-89375-299-1). Troll Assocs.

NEW YORK (STATE)–HISTORY

Ellis, David M. New York State: Gateway to America. (Illus.). 400p. (gr. 7 up). 1988. 24.95 (ISBN 0-89781-246-8). Windsor Pubns Inc.

Ray, Frederic. Old Fort Niagara: An Illustrated History. rev. ed. (Illus.). 16p. pap. 1.25 (ISBN 0-941967-06-9). Old Fort Niagara Assn.

Whitman, Bernard. New York State Map Skills Resource Guide. Whitman, Shirley, illus. 85p. (Orig.). (gr. 4-7). 1984. tchr's. ed. 18.00 (ISBN 0-918433-00-2). In Educ.

NEW YORK (STATE)–HISTORY–FICTION

Collier, James L. & Collier, Christopher. Who Is Carrie? LC 83-23947. 192p. (gr. 4-6). 1984. 14.95 (ISBN 0-385-29295-3). Delacorte.

Giff, Patricia R. Columbus Circle. (Orig.). (gr. k-6). 1988. pap. 2.75 (ISBN 0-440-40036-8, YB). Dell.

Lonergan, Carroll V. Brave Boys of Old Fort Ticonderoga. LC 87-22144. (gr. 6 up). 1987. write for info., 192 p. (ISBN 0-932334-57-1, Empire State Bks); pap. 7.95, 144 p. (ISBN 1-55787-018-7, NY16028, Empire State Bks). Heart of the Lakes.

NEW YORK (STATE)–POLITICS AND GOVERNMENT

New York State League of Women Voters Staff. A Guide to New York State Government. 6th ed. Fairbanks, Mary Jo, ed. 191p. (gr. 12). 1989. text ed. 14.95x (ISBN 0-936826-33-9). PS Assocs Croton.

NEW YORK METS (BASEBALL TEAM)

Jennings, Jay. Long Shots. 64p. (gr. 5-7). 1990. 14.98 (ISBN 0-382-24105-3); pap. 8.95 (ISBN 0-382-24112-6). Silver Burdett Pr.

NEW ZEALAND

Armitage, Ronda. New Zealand. Caulkins, Janet, ed. Fairclough, Chris, photos by. (Illus.). 48p. (gr. 1-6). 1988. PLB 12.40 (ISBN 0-531-18158-8, Pub. by Bookwright Pr). Watts.

Ball, John. We Live in New Zealand. LC 83-72805. 64p. (gr. 4-8). 1984. text ed. 9.49 (ISBN 0-531-04781-4, Pub. by Bookwright Pr). Watts.

Caldwell, John C. New Zealand. (Illus.). (gr. 5 up). 1988. 14.95 (ISBN 0-7910-1363-4). Chelsea Hse.

Keyworth, Valerie. New Zealand: Land of the Long White Cloud. LC 89-11716. (Illus.). 128p. (gr. 5 up). 1990. PLB 14.95 (ISBN 0-87518-414-6, Dillon). Macmillan Child Grp.

Lerner Publications, Department of Geography Staff. New Zealand in Pictures. (Illus.). 64p. (gr. 5 up). 1990. PLB 12.95 (ISBN 0-8225-1862-7). Lerner Pubns.

Mahy, Margaret. The Changeover: A Supernatural Romance. 264p. (gr. 7 up). 1985. pap. 2.50 (ISBN 0-590-41289-2, Point). Scholastic Inc.

Wiremu. The Maoris of New Zealand, Reading Level 5. (Illus.). 48p. (gr. 4-8). Date not set. PLB 15.33 (ISBN 0-86625-264-9). Rourke Corp.

NEW ZEALAND–FICTION

Anderson, Margaret J. Light in the Mountain. Marcellino, Fred, illus. LC 81-14266. 192p. (gr. 5-9). 1982. 9.95 (ISBN 0-394-84791-1); lib. bdg. 9.99 (ISBN 0-394-94791-6). Knopf.

Marriott, Janice. Letters to Lesley. LC 90-41406. 144p. (gr. 4-9). PLB 7.99 (ISBN 0-679-91595-8, Bullseye Bks); pap. 3.50 (ISBN 0-679-81595-3, Bullseye Bks). Knopf.

NEWBERY MEDAL BOOKS

Newberry Award Treasures, 5 vols, No. 2. (gr. 4-7). 1990. pap. 16.25 boxed set (ISBN 0-440-36002-1). Dell.

Newbery Awards, 5 vols, No. 1. (gr. 4-7). 1990. pap. 16.75 boxed set (ISBN 0-440-45963-X). Dell.

NEWFOUNDLAND–FICTION

Major, Kevin. Thirty-Six Exposures. LC 84-4995. (gr. 7 up). 1984. 14.95 (ISBN 0-385-29347-X). Delacorte.

NEWS BROADCASTS

see Radio Broadcasting; Television Broadcasting

NEWSBOYS

Sant, Thomas. The Amazing Adventures of Albert & His Flying Machine. DeRosa, Dee, illus. 160p. (gr. 4-7). 1990. 13.95 (ISBN 0-525-67302-4, Lodestar Bks). Dutton Child Bks.

NEWSPAPER WORK

see Journalism; Reporters and Reporting

NEWSPAPERS

see also Periodicals; Reporters and Reporting

Allen, Karen K. & Miller, Margery S. Reading the Newspaper: Advanced Level. 190p. (Orig.). (gr. 9-12). 1988. pap. text ed. 9.60 (ISBN 0-89061-500-4). Jamestown Pubs.

Arnold, Caroline & Silverstein, Herma. Hoaxes That Made Headlines. LC 86-17986. (Illus.). 160p. (gr. 5 up). 1986. 9.79 (ISBN 0-671-63259-0). Messner.

Balcziak, B. Newspapers. (Illus.). 48p. (gr. 4-8). 1989. lib. bdg. 14.00 (ISBN 0-86592-069-9). Rourke Corp.

Crisman, Ruth. Hot Off the Press: Getting the News into Print. (Illus.). 80p. (gr. 4 up). 1990. PLB 12.95 (ISBN 0-8225-1625-X). Lerner Pubns.

Debnam, Betty & Avery, Lois. The Mini Page & Your Newspaper Activity Book. 128p. (gr. k-6). 1980. pap. 7.95 (ISBN 0-8362-4209-2). Andrews & McMeel.

Fleming, Thomas. Behind the Headlines. (gr. 5 up). 1989. 14.95 (ISBN 0-8027-6890-3); PLB 15.85 (ISBN 0-8027-6891-1). Walker & Co.

Gibbons, Gail. Deadline! From News to Newspaper. Gibbons, Gail, illus. LC 86-47654. 32p. (gr. 1-4). 1987. PLB 12.89 (ISBN 0-690-04602-2, Crowell Jr Bks). HarpC Child Bks.

Jagger, Chris, ed. Making the Most of News For You. (Illus.). 32p. (gr. 5-12). 1989. tchr's. ed. 3.25 (ISBN 0-88336-180-9). New Readers.

Larned, Phyllis & Randall, Nick. Reading a Newspaper. (Illus.). 64p. (gr. 7-12). 1978. pap. text ed. 3.95 (ISBN 0-915510-26-X). Janus Bks.

Leedy, Loreen. The Furry News: How to Make a Newspaper. Leedy, Loreen, illus. LC 89-20094. 32p. (gr. k-3). 1990. PLB 13.95 (ISBN 0-8234-0793-4). Holiday.

Mann, Brenda. Newspapers. LC 88-29286. (Illus.). 48p. (gr. 6-12). 1989. PLB 12.95 (ISBN 0-86307-975-X). Marshall Cavendish.

Petersen, David. Newspapers. LC 83-10069. (Illus.). 48p. (gr. k-4). 1983. PLB 14.60 (ISBN 0-516-01702-0). Childrens.

Walters, Sarah. How Newspapers Are Made. (Illus.). 32p. 1989. 12.95x (ISBN 0-8160-2042-6). Facts on File.

NEWSPAPERS–FICTION

Kroll, Steven. Newsman Ned & the Broken Rules. Brunkus, Denise, illus. (ps-2). 1989. pap. 2.95 (ISBN 0-318-41673-5). Scholastic Inc.

Norby, Lisa. Star Reporter. LC 89-31869. 112p. (Orig.). (gr. 3-7). 1989. pap. 2.95 (ISBN 0-679-80065-4, Bullseye Bks). Knopf.

Roos, Stephen. Twelve-Year-Old Vows Revenge after Being Dumped by Extraterrestrial on First Date. 1990. 13.95 (ISBN 0-385-30042-5). Doubleday.

NEWTON, SIR ISAAC, 1642-1727

Ipsen, David C. Isaac Newton: Reluctant Genius. LC 84-1581. (Illus.). 96p. (gr. 5-9). 1985. 16.95 (ISBN 0-89490-090-0). Enslow Pubs.

Tiner, John H. Isaac Newton: The True Story of His Life. Biel, Bill & Biel, Bill, illus. LC 75-32562. (gr. 3-6). 1976. pap. 6.95 (ISBN 0-915134-95-0). Mott Media.

NIAGARA, FORT, N. Y.–FICTION

Orton, Helen F. The Gold-Laced Coat. rev. ed. Ball, Robert, illus. 226p. (gr. 4-8). pap. 5.95 (ISBN 0-941967-07-7). Old Fort Niagara Assn.

NIAGARA FALLS–HISTORY

Granfield, Linda. All about Niagara Falls: Fascinating Facts, Dramatic Discoveries. Hemsworth, Sandi & Cupples, Pat, illus. LC 88-13408. 80p. (gr. 3-7). 1989. PLB 11.88 (ISBN 0-688-08456-7); pap. 7.95 (ISBN 0-688-08810-4, Pub. by Beech Tree Bks). Morrow Jr Bks.

NICARAGUA

Adams, Faith. Nicaragua: Struggling with Change. LC 86-11608. (Illus.). 152p. (gr. 5 up). 1987. PLB 14.95 (ISBN 0-87518-340-9, Dillon). Macmillan Child Grp.

Gelman, Rita G. Inside Nicaragua. (Illus.). 192p. (gr. 10-12). 1990. 14.95 (ISBN 0-531-15085-2). Watts.

Simons, John & Ward, Kay. Noah & His Great Ark. Ward, Kay, ed. (Illus.). 16p. (Orig.). (gr. 3-7). 1987. pap. text ed. 2.50 (ISBN 0-937039-00-4). Sun Pr FL.

Singleton, Kathy. Noah's Big Boat. Baker, Arthur, illus. 32p. (gr. k-3). 1990. saddle-stitched 1.25 (ISBN 0-8028-5051-0). Eerdmans.

Smith, Roger. How the Animals Saved the Ark & Put Two & Two Together. (Illus.). (ps-3). 1989. pap. 11.95 (ISBN 0-671-66560-X). S&S Trade.

Smithson, Colin & Smithson, Sheila. Noah's Great Big Boat. Smithson, Colin & Smithson, Sheila, illus. 32p. (ps-3). 1991. 4.95 (ISBN 0-310-56180-9, Youth Bks). Zondervan.

Spier & Jones. Noah's Ark. 1989. 17.95 (ISBN 0-525-44525-0, DCB). Dutton Child Bks.

Spier, Peter. Noah's Ark. 48p. (ps). 1981. pap. 6.95 (ISBN 0-385-17302-4, Zephyr BFYR). Doubleday.

Stirrup Associates, Inc. Staff. My Jesus Pocketbook of Noah & the Floating Zoo. Harvey, Bonnie C. & Phillips, Cheryl M., eds. Fulton, Ginger A., illus. LC 83-51680. 32p. (ps-3). 1984. pap. 0.69 (ISBN 0-937420-10-7). Stirrup Assoc.

Thompson, Don. Captain Noah. Meyer, Rita, illus. 32p. (gr. 3-5). pap. 1.19 (ISBN 0-87123-696-6). Bethany Hse.

Thorne, Jenny. Noah's Ark. Thorne, Jenny, illus. 12p. (ps-k). 1989. 3.50 (ISBN 0-689-71306-1, Aladdin). Macmillan Child Grp.

Vos Wezeman, Phyllis & Wiessner, Colleen A. Noah's Noises. 33p. (Orig.). (gr. 1-6). 1988. pap. 5.95 (ISBN 0-940754-58-4). Ed Ministries.

Yeatman, Linda. Noah's Ark. Gault, Bob, illus. 12p. (ps-3). 1984. 6.95 (ISBN 0-698-20598-7, Coward). Putnam Pub Group.

NOBEL PRIZES
Magill, Frank N., ed. Nobel Prize Winners, 3 vols. 1364p. (gr. 9-12). 1989. Set. PLB 210.00x (ISBN 0-89356-557-1, Magill Bks). Salem Pr.

NOISE
Bailey, Donna. What We Can Do about Noise & Fumes. (Illus.). 32p. (gr. k-4). 1991. PLB 11.40 (ISBN 0-531-11018-4). Watts.

Petty, Kate. What's That Noise? Kopper, Lisa, illus. 32p. (gr. k-3). 1986. lib. bdg. 7.79 (ISBN 0-531-10175-4). Watts.

Ross, Katharine. The Little Noisy Book. Hirashima, Jean, illus. LC 88-62100. 28p. (ps). 1989. bds. 2.95 (ISBN 0-394-82907-7, Random Juv). Random.

NOISE–FICTION
Hughes, Shirley. Noisy. LC 84-12632. (Illus.). 24p. (gr. k-1). 1985. 4.95 (ISBN 0-688-04203-1). Lothrop.

McGovern, Ann. Too Much Noise. (gr. k-3). 1967. 14.95 (ISBN 0-395-18110-0). HM.

Wells, Rosemary. Noisy Nora. Wells, Rosemary, illus. LC 72-6068. 40p. (ps-2). 1973. 10.95 (ISBN 0-8037-6638-6); PLB 9.89 (ISBN 0-8037-6639-4). Dial Bks Young.

Wheedle on the Needle. (gr. 1-6). 1975. pap. 2.95 (ISBN 0-8431-0564-X). Price Stern.

Ziefert, Harriet. Andy Toots His Horn. Hoffmann, Sanford, illus. (Orig.). (ps-3). 1988. pap. 3.50 (ISBN 0-14-050813-9, Puffin). Puffin Bks.

NOMADS
Sussman, Susan. Casey the Nomad. Tucker, Kathleen, ed. Shefts, Joelle, illus. (gr. 3-6). 1985. 9.95 (ISBN 0-8075-1068-8). A Whitman.

NONCONFORMITY
see Dissent

NONSENSE VERSES
see also Limericks

Base, Graeme, illus. Jabberwocky: From Lewis Carroll's Through the Looking Glass. 32p. 1989. 12.95 (ISBN 0-8109-1150-7). Abrams.

Brett, Jan & Lear, Edward. Owl & the Pussycat. (Illus.). 32p. (ps-3). 1991. 14.95 (ISBN 0-399-21925-0, Putnam). Putnam Pub Group.

Brewton, Sara & Brewton, John E. Laughable Limericks. Fetz, Ingrid, illus. LC 65-16179. 160p. (gr. 3-6). 1990. PLB 12.89 (ISBN 0-690-04887-4, Crowell Jr Bks). HarpC Child Bks.

Brown, Marc. Pickle Things. Brown, Marc, illus. LC 80-10540. 48p. (ps-3). 1980. 5.95 (ISBN 0-8193-1027-1). Parents.

Calmenson, Stephanie. Ten Furry Monsters. Chambliss, Maxie, illus. LC 84-4998. 48p. (ps-3). 1984. 5.95 (ISBN 0-8193-1128-6). Parents.

Carroll, Lewis. Humorous Verse of Lewis Carroll. (Illus.). 446p. (gr. 1 up). 1933. pap. 9.95 (ISBN 0-486-20654-8). Dover.

—Jabberwocky. Zalben, Jane B., illus. LC 77-75040. (gr. 1 up). 1977. 11.95 (ISBN 0-7232-6145-8). Warne.

Chmielewski, Gary. Tongue Twisters. Clark, Ron G., illus. LC 86-17701. (gr. 2-3). 1986. 12.66 (ISBN 0-86592-685-9). Rourke Corp.

Ciardi, John. I Met a Man. Osborne, Robert. (Illus.). 80p. (gr. k-3). 1973. pap. 6.95 (ISBN 0-395-17447-3, Sandpiper). HM.

—Man Who Sang the Sillies. Gorey, Edward, illus. LC 61-11734. (gr. 4-6). 1961. 8.95 (ISBN 0-397-30568-0, Lipp Jr Bks); PLB 11.89i (ISBN 0-397-30569-9, Lipp Jr Bks). HarpC Child Bks.

Clark, Emma C. Never Saw a Purple Cow. (ps-3). 1991. 18.95 (ISBN 0-316-14500-9). Little.

Cole, Joanna & Calmenson, Stephanie. Miss Mary Mack: And Other Children's Street Rhymes. Tiegreen, Alan, illus. LC 89-37266. 64p. (gr. 2 up). 1990. PLB 11.88 (ISBN 0-688-08330-7); pap. 6.95 (ISBN 0-688-09749-9, Pub. by Beech Tree Bks). Morrow Jr Bks.

Cole, William, ed. Oh, Such Foolishness! De Paola, Tomie, illus. LC 78-1622. 96p. (gr. 3-6). 1978. 11.95 (ISBN 0-397-31807-3, Lipp Jr Bks). HarpC Child Bks.

De Regniers, Beatrice S. May I Bring a Friend? Montresor, Beni, illus. LC 64-19562. 48p. (ps-2). 1971. 13.95 (ISBN 0-689-20615-1, Atheneum Child Bk). Macmillan Child Grp.

Dr. Seuss. The Butter Battle Book. Dr. Seuss, illus. LC 83-21286. 48p. (gr. 5 up). 1984. (Random Juv); 9.95 (ISBN 0-394-86580-4); lib. bdg. 12.99 (ISBN 0-394-96580-9). Random.

—Cat in the Hat. Dr. Seuss, illus. LC 56-5470. 72p. (gr. 1-2). 1957. 6.95 (ISBN 0-394-80001-X); lib. bdg. 7.99 (ISBN 0-394-90001-4). Beginner.

—Did I Ever Tell You How Lucky You Are? Dr. Seuss, illus. (ps-4). 1973. 9.95 (ISBN 0-394-82719-8, Random Juv); PLB 11.99 (ISBN 0-394-92719-2). Random.

—Dr. Seuss's ABC. Dr. Seuss, illus. LC 63-9810. 72p. (gr. k-3). 1960. 6.95 (ISBN 0-394-80030-3); lib. bdg. 7.99 (ISBN 0-394-90030-8). Beginner.

—Fox in Socks. Dr. Seuss, illus. LC 65-10484. 72p. (gr. k-3). 1965. 6.95 (ISBN 0-394-80038-9); lib. bdg. 7.99 (ISBN 0-394-90038-3). Beginner.

—Green Eggs & Ham. Dr. Seuss, illus. LC 60-13493. 72p. (gr. 1-2). 1960. 6.95 (ISBN 0-394-80016-8); lib. bdg. 7.99 (ISBN 0-394-90016-2). Beginner.

—Hop on Pop. Dr. Seuss, illus. LC 63-9810. 72p. (gr. 1-2). 1963. 6.95 (ISBN 0-394-80029-X); lib. bdg. 7.99 (ISBN 0-394-90029-4). Beginner.

—Horton Hatches the Egg. Dr. Seuss, illus. (gr. k-3). 1940. 10.95 (ISBN 0-394-80077-X, Random Juv); lib. bdg. 10.99 (ISBN 0-394-90077-4). Random.

—Horton Hears a Who. Dr. Seuss, illus. (gr. k-3). 1954. 11.95 (ISBN 0-394-80078-8, Random Juv); PLB 12.99 (ISBN 0-394-90078-2). Random.

—How the Grinch Stole Christmas. Dr. Seuss, illus. (gr. k-3). 1957. 8.95 (ISBN 0-394-80079-6, Random Juv); PLB 7.99 (ISBN 0-394-90079-0). Random.

—I Can Lick Thirty Tigers Today & Other Stories. Dr. Seuss, illus. (gr. k-3). 1969. 9.95 (ISBN 0-394-80094-X, Random Juv); lib. bdg. 7.99 (ISBN 0-394-90094-4). Random.

—I Had Trouble in Getting to Solla Sollew. Dr. Seuss, illus. (ps-3). 1965. (Random Juv); lib. bdg. 12.99 (ISBN 0-394-90092-8). Random.

—If I Ran the Zoo. Dr. Seuss, illus. (gr. k-3). 1966. 9.95 (ISBN 0-394-80081-8, Random Juv); lib. bdg. 11.99 (ISBN 0-394-90081-2). Random.

—Lorax. Dr. Seuss, illus. (gr. 2-3). 1971. 11.95 (ISBN 0-394-82337-0, Random Juv); lib. bdg. 12.99 (ISBN 0-394-92337-5). Random.

—McElligot's Pool. Dr. Seuss, illus. (gr. k-3). 1947. 9.95 (ISBN 0-394-80083-4, Random Juv); lib. bdg. 11.99 (ISBN 0-394-90083-9). Random.

—Oh, Say Can You Say? Dr. Seuss, illus. LC 78-20716. (gr. 1-4). 1979. 6.95 (ISBN 0-394-84255-3, BYR); lib. bdg. 7.99 (ISBN 0-394-94255-8). Beginner.

—On Beyond Zebra. Dr. Seuss, illus. (ps-3). 1955. 10.95 (ISBN 0-394-80084-2, Random Juv); lib. bdg. 9.99 (ISBN 0-394-90084-7). Random.

—One Fish Two Fish Red Fish Blue Fish. Dr. Seuss, illus. LC 60-7180. 72p. (gr. 1-2). 1966. 6.95 (ISBN 0-394-80013-3); PLB 7.99 (ISBN 0-394-90013-8). Beginner.

—Scrambled Eggs Super! Dr. Seuss, illus. (gr. k-3). 1953. lib. bdg. 12.99 (ISBN 0-394-90085-5). Random.

—Sneetches & Other Stories. Dr. Seuss, illus. (gr. k-4). 1961. 9.95 (ISBN 0-394-80089-3, Random Juv); lib. bdg. 10.99 (ISBN 0-394-90089-8). Random.

—There's a Wocket in My Pocket! Dr. Seuss, illus. LC 74-5516. 36p. (ps-1). 1974. 6.95 (ISBN 0-394-82920-4, Random Juv); lib. bdg. 7.99 (ISBN 0-394-92920-9). Random.

Hamoy, Carol. What's Wrong? What's Wrong? Hamoy, Carol, illus. (gr. k-3). 1965. 8.95 (ISBN 0-685-00564-X). Astor-Honor.

Heilbroner, Joan. This Is the House Where Jack Lives. Aliki, illus. LC 62-7311. 64p. (gr. k-3). 1962. PLB 11.89 (ISBN 0-06-022286-7). HarpC Child Bks.

Hunter, Julius. Absurd Alphabedtime Stories. Gomez, Ronald, illus. LC 76-22534. (gr. k-4). 1976. 2.95 (ISBN 0-8272-0012-9). CBP.

Lear, Edward. The Complete Nonsense of Edward Lear. Lear, Edward, illus. Jackson, H., intro. by. (Illus.). xxix, 287p. (gr. 4-6). pap. 5.95 (ISBN 0-486-20167-8). Dover.

—An Edward Lear Alphabet. Newsom, Carol, illus. LC 82-10037. 32p. (gr. k-3). 1983. PLB 11.88 (ISBN 0-688-00965-4). Lothrop.

—Lear's Nonsense ABCs. LC 90-53464. (Illus.). 120p. (ps-8). 1991. 4.95 (ISBN 0-89471-985-8). Running Pr.

—The Owl & the Pussy-Cat. Voce, Louise, illus. LC 90-39673. 32p. (ps up). 1991. 13.95 (ISBN 0-688-09536-4); PLB 13.88 (ISBN 0-688-09537-2). Lothrop.

—The Owl & the Pussycat. rev. ed. Stevens, Janet, illus. LC 82-12092. 32p. (ps-3). 1983. reinforced bdg. 14.95 (ISBN 0-8234-0474-9). Holiday.

Lear, Edward & Nash, Ogden. Scroobious Pip. Burkert, Nancy E., illus. LC 68-10373. (gr. 3 up). 1968. 14.95 (ISBN 0-06-023764-3); PLB 14.89 (ISBN 0-06-023765-1). HarpC Child Bks.

Le Sieg, Theodore. Maybe You Should Fly a Jet! Maybe You Should Be a Vet. Smollin, Michael J., illus. LC 80-5084. 48p. (ps-3). 1980. lib. bdg. 7.99 (ISBN 0-394-94448-8); pap. 6.95 (ISBN 0-394-84448-3). Beginner.

Lopshire, Robert. Put Me in the Zoo. LC 60-13494. (Illus.). 72p. (gr. 1-2). 1960. 6.95 (ISBN 0-394-80017-6); lib. bdg. 7.99 (ISBN 0-394-90017-0). Beginner.

Lord, John V. & Burroway, Janet. The Giant Jam Sandwich. Lord, John V., illus. LC 72-13578. 32p. (gr. k-3). 1987. 15.95 (ISBN 0-395-16033-2); pap. 3.95 (ISBN 0-395-44237-0). HM.

McClintock, Mike. Stop That Ball! LC 59-9741. (Illus.). (gr. 1-2). 1959. 6.95 (ISBN 0-394-80010-9); lib. bdg. 7.99 (ISBN 0-394-90010-3). Beginner.

Morrison, Bill. Squeeze a Sneeze. Morrison, Bill, illus. LC 76-62503. (gr. k-3). 1977. 13.95 (ISBN 0-395-25151-6). HM.

Nash, Ogden. Custard the Dragon. Nash, Linell, illus. (gr. k-3). 1973. lib. bdg. 14.95 (ISBN 0-316-59841-0). Little.

Palmer, Michele, ed. Rainy Day Rhymes: A Collection of Chants, Forecasts & Tales. Guerin, Penny, illus. LC 84-60412. 24p. (Orig.). (gr. k up). 1984. pap. 2.95 (ISBN 0-932306-02-0). Rocking Horse.

Pape, D. L. King Robert, the Resting Ruler. LC 68-56823. (Illus.). 48p. (gr. 2-5). 1968. PLB 10.95 (ISBN 0-87783-021-5). Oddo.

—Scientist Sam. LC 68-56826. (Illus.). 48p. (gr. 2-5). 1968. PLB 10.95 (ISBN 0-87783-034-7). Oddo.

Patz, Nancy. Moses Supposes His Toeses Are Roses: And Seven Other Silly Old Rhymes. Patz, Nancy, illus. LC 82-3099. 32p. (ps-3). 1983. 13.95 (ISBN 0-15-255690-7, HJ). HarBraceJ.

Raskin, Ellen. Twenty-Two, Twenty-Three. LC 76-5475. (Illus.). 32p. (gr. k-3). 1976. 7.95 (ISBN 0-689-30529-X, Atheneum Childrens Bks). Macmillan Child Grp.

Stiles, Barbara J. Trinkets & Toads & Other Treasures. LC 91-60705. 48p. 1991. 12.95 (ISBN 0-9622057-3-7); pap. 8.95 (ISBN 0-9622057-2-9). Manzanita Canyon.

Inspire children to enjoy books! Give them a reason to want to learn to read! Provide the means for them to have fun with words! Children love silly, rhythmic nonsensical verse. Do you make learning fun for young children by using handclapping rhymes & funny poems? Preschool & early grades will identify with, want to share & have read to them the alliterative verse found in this book. Do you provide books for preschool children? This book offers the lapreading set the chance to cuddle & comprehend, basic ingredients for success & security. Offer them a firm literary beginning. Do you give children a place of their own, to study, to share? Furnish them the seeds for their future, time, caring, knowledge, your gifts to young minds. Find these inspirations in TRINKETS & TOADS. The author & artist have successfully integrated verse & vision to bring together an attractive, eye catching book for the young of all ages. Imaginative illustrations in classic sepia tones are on each of the 48 pages. TRINKETS & TOADS is a delightful discovery & a continuation of the appeal found in the author's first book, Cheeky Rubs. Both books are available with fast response from Baker & Taylor & Ingram Book Company. *Publisher Provided Annotation.*

Westcott, Nadine B. The Lady with the Alligator Purse. (ps-3). 1990. pap. 4.95 (ISBN 0-316-93136-5). Little.

Westcott, Nadine B., adapted by. & illus. The Lady with the Alligator Purse. LC 87-21368. (ps-3). 1988. 12.95 (ISBN 0-316-93135-7, Joy St Bks). Little.

Wittels, Harriet & Greisman, Joan. Things I Hate! LC 73-11053. (Illus.). 32p. (ps-3). 1973. 16.95 (ISBN 0-87705-096-1). Human Sci Pr.

Ziegler, Sandra K. Knock-Knocks, Limericks, & Other Silly Sayings. Magnuson, Diana, illus. LC 82-19764. 48p. (gr. 1-5). 1983. PLB 13.27 (ISBN 0-516-01872-8); pap. 3.95 (ISBN 0-516-41872-6). Childrens.

NONVIOLENCE
Lucas, Eileen. Peace on the Playground: Nonviolent Ways of Problem-Solving. (Illus.). 64p. (gr. 5-8). 1991. PLB 11.90 (ISBN 0-531-20047-7). Watts.

NORMANDY, ATTACK ON, 1944

Bliven, Bruce, Jr. Story of D-Day: June 6, 1944. (Illus.). (gr. 6-8). 1963. (Random Juv); lib. bdg. 8.99 (ISBN 0-394-90362-5). Random.

Miller, Marilyn. D-Day. LC 84-40380. (Illus.). 64p. (gr. 5 up). 1986. 16.98 (ISBN 0-382-06825-4); pap. 7.95 (ISBN 0-382-06972-2). Silver Burdett Pr.

Stein, R. Conrad. The Story of D-Day. Dunnington, Tom, illus. LC 77-5089. 32p. (gr. 3-5). 1977. PLB 13.27 (ISBN 0-516-04609-8); pap. 3.95 (ISBN 0-516-44609-6). Childrens.

NORMANS

see also Northmen

NORSEMEN

see Northmen

NORTH AMERICA

Georges, D. V. North America. LC 86-9638. (Illus.). 48p. (gr. k-4). 1986. PLB 14.60 (ISBN 0-516-01294-0); pap. 4.95 (ISBN 0-516-41294-9). Childrens.

Newhouse, Elizabeth L., ed. The Story of America. LC 84-2018. (Illus.). (gr. 4-8). 1984. lib. bdg. 21.95 (ISBN 0-87044-535-9, 00535); 19.95 (ISBN 0-87044-508-1). Natl Geog.

Sabin, Louis. North America. Eitzen, Allan, illus. LC 84-8625. 32p. (gr. 3-6). 1985. PLB 9.49 (ISBN 0-8167-0240-3); pap. text ed. 2.95 (ISBN 0-8167-0241-1). Troll Assocs.

NORTH AMERICA–DISCOVERY AND EXPLORATION

see America–Discovery and Exploration

NORTH AMERICA–HISTORY

Andrews, C. L. Story of Sitka. 142p. (gr. 9 up). pap. 9.95 (ISBN 0-8466-0094-3, S94). Shorey.

Shaw, George C. Vancouver's Discovery of Puget Sound. 28p. (gr. 9 up). pap. 1.95 (ISBN 0-8466-0102-8, S102). Shorey.

NORTH AMERICAN INDIANS

see Indians of North America

NORTH ATLANTIC TREATY ORGANIZATION

Ferrara, Peter L. NATO: An Entangled Alliance. 128p. (gr. 7-12). 1984. PLB 12.90 (ISBN 0-531-04759-8). Watts.

NORTH CAROLINA

Aylesworth, Thomas G. & Aylesworth, Virginia L. Lower Atlantic (North Carolina, South Carolina) (Illus.). 64p. (gr. 4-6). 1991. PLB 16.95 (ISBN 0-7910-1042-2). Chelsea Hse.

Campbell, William A. Casting Your Vote in North Carolina. 2nd ed. 25p. (gr. 10-12). 1990. pap. text ed. 5.00 (ISBN 1-56011-171-2). Institute Government.

Carole Marsh North Carolina Books, 31 bks. Set. 638.45 (ISBN 0-7933-1308-2). Gallopade Pub Group.

Carpenter, Allan. North Carolina. new ed. LC 79-682. (Illus.). 96p. (gr. 4 up). 1979. PLB 19.93 (ISBN 0-516-04133-9). Childrens.

Charlet, James D., et al. North Carolina: Our People, Places, & Past Student Workbook. Charlet, James D., illus. 300p. 1988. wkbk. 49.95 (ISBN 0-935911-13-8). Cornucop Pub.

Fradin, Dennis. North Carolina: In Words & Pictures. LC 79-25291. (Illus.). 48p. (gr. 2-5). 1980. PLB 15.93 (ISBN 0-516-03933-4); pap. 4.95 (ISBN 0-516-43933-2). Childrens.

Gasque, Pratt. Rum Gully Tales from Tuck'em Inn. (Illus.). 148p. 1990. 15.95 (ISBN 0-87844-094-1); pap. 8.95 (ISBN 0-87844-095-X). Sandlapper Pub Co.

Marsh, Carole. Avast, Ye Slobs! North Carolina Pirate Trivia. (Illus.). 1990. PLB 19.95 (ISBN 0-7933-0859-3); pap. 14.95 (ISBN 0-7933-0858-5); computer disk 29.95 (ISBN 0-7933-0860-7). Gallopade Pub Group.

—The Beast of the North Carolina Bed & Breakfast. (Illus.). 1990. PLB 19.95 (ISBN 0-7933-1830-0); pap. 14.95 (ISBN 0-7933-1831-9); computer disk 29.95 (ISBN 0-7933-1832-7). Gallopade Pub Group.

—The Hard-to-Believe-But-True! Book of North Carolina History, Mystery, Trivia, Legend, Lore, Humor & More. (Illus.). 1990. PLB 19.95 (ISBN 0-7933-0856-9); pap. 14.95 (ISBN 0-7933-0855-0); computer disk 29.95 (ISBN 0-7933-0857-7). Gallopade Pub Group.

—Hot Shot: Photography for Kids. (Illus., Orig.). (gr. 3-12). 1986. 19.95 (ISBN 1-55609-171-0); pap. 14.95 (ISBN 0-935326-79-0). Gallopade Pub Group.

—If My North Carolina Mama Ran the World! (Illus.). 1990. lib. bdg. 19.95 (ISBN 0-7933-1833-5); pap. 14.95 (ISBN 0-7933-1834-3); computer disk 29.95 (ISBN 0-7933-1835-1). Gallopade Pub Group.

—Let's Quilt North Carolina & Stuff It Topographically! (Illus.). 1990. PLB 19.95 (ISBN 1-55609-925-8); pap. 14.95 (ISBN 1-55609-050-1); computer disk 29.95 (ISBN 1-55609-926-6). Gallopade Pub Group.

—North Carolina & Other State Greats (Biographies) (Illus.). 1990. PLB 19.95 (ISBN 1-55609-937-1); pap. 14.95 (ISBN 1-55609-938-X); computer disk 29.95 (ISBN 1-55609-939-8). Gallopade Pub Group.

—North Carolina Bandits, Bushwackers, Outlaws, Crooks, Devils, Ghosts, Desperadoes & Other Assorted & Sundry Characters! (Illus.). 1990. PLB 19.95 (ISBN 0-7933-0841-0); pap. 14.95 (ISBN 0-7933-0840-2); computer disk 29.95 (ISBN 0-7933-0842-9). Gallopade Pub Group.

—North Carolina Classic Christmas Trivia: Stories, Recipes, Activities, Legends, Lore & More. (Illus.). 1990. PLB 19.95 (ISBN 0-7933-0844-5); pap. 14.95 (ISBN 0-7933-0843-7); computer disk 29.95 (ISBN 0-7933-0845-3). Gallopade Pub Group.

—The North Carolina Hot Air Balloon Mystery. (Illus.). (gr. 2-9). 1990. 19.95 (ISBN 0-7933-2615-X); pap. 14.95 (ISBN 0-7933-2616-8); computer disk 29.95 (ISBN 0-7933-2617-6). Gallopade Pub Group.

—North Carolina Jography: A Fun Run Through the Tarheel State. (Illus.). 50p. (Orig.). (gr. 4-8). 1986. pap. 14.95 (ISBN 0-935326-81-2). Gallopade Pub Group.

—North Carolina Kid's Cookbook: Recipes, How-to, History, Lore & More. (Illus.). 1990. PLB 19.95 (ISBN 0-7933-0853-4); pap. 14.95 (ISBN 0-7933-0852-6); computer disk 29.95 (ISBN 0-7933-0854-2). Gallopade Pub Group.

—North Carolina Quiz Bowl Crash Course! (Illus.). 1990. PLB 19.95 (ISBN 1-55609-934-7); pap. 14.95 (ISBN 1-55609-935-5); computer disk 29.95 (ISBN 1-55609-936-3). Gallopade Pub Group.

—North Carolina School Trivia: An Amazing & Fascinating Look at Our State's Teachers, Schools & Students! (Illus.). 1990. PLB 19.95 (ISBN 0-7933-0850-X); pap. 14.95 (ISBN 0-7933-0849-6); computer disk 29.95 (ISBN 0-7933-0851-8). Gallopade Pub Group.

—North Carolina Silly Basketball Sportsmysteries, Vol. 1. (Illus.). 1990. PLB 19.95 (ISBN 0-7933-0847-X); pap. 14.95 (ISBN 0-7933-0846-1); computer disk 29.95 (ISBN 0-7933-0848-8). Gallopade Pub Group.

—North Carolina Silly Basketball Sportsmysteries, Vol. 2. (Illus.). 1990. PLB 19.95 (ISBN 0-7933-1836-X); pap. 14.95 (ISBN 0-7933-1837-8); computer disk 29.95 (ISBN 0-7933-1838-6). Gallopade Pub Group.

—North Carolina Silly Football Sportmysteries, Vol. 2. (Illus.). 1990. PLB 19.95 (ISBN 1-55609-930-4); pap. 14.95 (ISBN 1-55609-931-2); computer disk 29.95 (ISBN 1-55609-932-0). Gallopade Pub Group.

—North Carolina Silly Football Sportsmysteries, Vol. 1. (Illus.). 1990. PLB 19.95 (ISBN 1-55609-927-4); pap. 14.95 (ISBN 1-55609-928-2); computer disk 29.95 (ISBN 1-55609-929-0). Gallopade Pub Group.

—North Carolina Silly Trivia! (Illus.). 1990. PLB 19.95 (ISBN 1-55609-921-5); pap. 14.95; computer disk 29.95 (ISBN 1-55609-922-3). Gallopade Pub Group.

—North Carolina's (Most Devastating!) Disasters & (Most Calamitous!) Catastrophies! (Illus.). 1990. PLB 19.95 (ISBN 0-7933-0838-0); pap. 14.95 (ISBN 0-7933-0837-2); computer disk 29.95 (ISBN 0-7933-0839-9). Gallopade Pub Group.

—North Carolina's Scariest Swamp: The Great Dismal. (Illus.). (gr. 3 up). 1990. lib. bdg. 19.95 (ISBN 0-7933-1270-1); pap. 14.95 (ISBN 0-7933-1271-X); computer disk 29.95 (ISBN 0-7933-1272-8). Gallopade Pub Group.

Stein, R. Conrad. North Carolina. LC 89-17298. 144p. (gr. 4 up). 1989. PLB 25.27 (ISBN 0-516-00479-4). Childrens.

Turner Educational Services, Inc. Staff & Clark, James I. North Carolina. 48p. (gr. 3 up). 1986. PLB 17.32 (ISBN 0-86514-454-0); pap. text ed. 9.27 (ISBN 0-86514-529-6); cancelled Beta video (ISBN 0-86514-079-0); cancelled VHS video (ISBN 0-86514-154-1); cancelled 3/4" video (ISBN 0-86514-229-7); cancelled tchr's. study guide; cancelled student activity bk. (ISBN 0-86514-379-X); cancelled index. Raintree Pubs.

NORTH CAROLINA–FICTION

Taylor, Theodore. Teetoncey & Ben O'Neal. Cuffari, Richard, illus. 192p. (gr. 5-7). 1991. pap. 3.50 (ISBN 0-380-71025-0, Camelot). Avon.

Wolfe, Thomas. Look Homeward, Angel. 1920. pap. 12.95 (ISBN 0-684-71941-X, Scribner). Macmillan.

NORTH CAROLINA–HISTORY

Carriker, S. David. North Carolina Railroads: The Common Carrier Railroads of North Carolina. 66p. 1989. pap. 15.00 (ISBN 0-936013-08-7). Herit Pub NC.

Tate, Suzanne. Memories of Manteo & Roanoke Island, N. C. Melvin, James, illus. Basnight, Cora M., as told by. LC 88-60590. (Illus.). 52p. (Orig.). (gr. 7-12). 1988. pap. 5.95 (ISBN 0-9616344-2-1). Nags Head Art.

NORTH CENTRAL STATES

see Middle West

NORTH DAKOTA

Carole Marsh North Dakota Books, 31 bks. Set. 638.45 (ISBN 0-7933-1309-0). Gallopade Pub Group.

Carpenter, Allan. North Dakota. new ed. LC 79-11470. (Illus.). 96p. (gr. 4 up). 1979. PLB 19.93 (ISBN 0-516-04134-7). Childrens.

Fradin, Dennis. North Dakota: In Words & Pictures. Wahl, Richard, illus. LC 80-26480. 48p. (gr. 2-5). 1981. PLB 15.93 (ISBN 0-516-03934-2). Childrens.

Marsh, Carole. Avast, Ye Slobs! North Dakota Pirate Trivia. (Illus.). 1990. PLB 19.95 (ISBN 0-7933-0883-6); pap. 14.95 (ISBN 0-7933-0882-8); computer disk 29.95 (ISBN 0-7933-0884-4). Gallopade Pub Group.

—The Beast of the North Dakota Bed & Breakfast. (Illus.). 1990. PLB 19.95 (ISBN 0-7933-1839-4); pap. 14.95 (ISBN 0-7933-1840-8); computer disk 29.95 (ISBN 0-7933-1841-6). Gallopade Pub Group.

—The Hard-to-Believe-But-True! Book of North Dakota History, Mystery, Trivia, Legend, Lore, Humor & More. (Illus.). 1990. PLB 19.95 (ISBN 0-7933-0880-1); pap. 14.95 (ISBN 0-7933-0879-8); computer disk 29.95 (ISBN 0-7933-0881-X). Gallopade Pub Group.

—If My North Dakota Mama Ran the World! (Illus.). 1990. lib. bdg. 19.95 (ISBN 0-7933-1842-4); pap. 14.95 (ISBN 0-7933-1843-2); computer disk 29.95 (ISBN 0-7933-1844-0). Gallopade Pub Group.

—Let's Quilt North Dakota & Stuff It Topographically! (Illus.). 1990. PLB 19.95 (ISBN 1-55609-946-0); pap. 14.95 (ISBN 1-55609-135-4); computer disk 29.95 (ISBN 1-55609-947-9). Gallopade Pub Group.

—The North Dakota Air Balloon Mystery. (Illus.). (gr. 2-9). 1990. 19.95 (ISBN 0-7933-2624-9); pap. 14.95 (ISBN 0-7933-2625-7); computer disk 29.95 (ISBN 0-7933-2626-5). Gallopade Pub Group.

—North Dakota & Other State Greats (Biographies) (Illus.). 1990. PLB 19.95 (ISBN 1-55609-976-2); pap. 14.95 (ISBN 1-55609-977-0); computer disk 29.95. Gallopade Pub Group.

—North Dakota Bandits, Bushwackers, Outlaws, Crooks, Devils, Ghosts, Desperadoes & Other Assorted & Sundry Characters! (Illus.). 1990. PLB 19.95 (ISBN 0-7933-0865-8); pap. 14.95 (ISBN 0-7933-0864-X); computer disk 29.95 (ISBN 0-7933-0866-6). Gallopade Pub Group.

—North Dakota Classic Christmas Trivia: Stories, Recipes, Activities, Legends, Lore & More! (Illus.). 1990. PLB 19.95 (ISBN 0-7933-0868-2); pap. 14.95 (ISBN 0-7933-0867-4); computer disk 29.95 (ISBN 0-7933-0869-0). Gallopade Pub Group.

—North Dakota Coastales. (Illus.). 1990. PLB 19.95; pap. 14.95 (ISBN 1-55609-971-1); computer disk 29.95 (ISBN 1-55609-972-X). Gallopade Pub Group.

—North Dakota "Jography" A Fun Run Thru Our State! (Illus.). 1990. PLB 19.95 (ISBN 1-55609-943-6); pap. 14.95 (ISBN 1-55609-944-4); computer disk 29.95 (ISBN 1-55609-945-2). Gallopade Pub Group.

—North Dakota Kid's Cookbook: Recipes, How-to, History, Lore & More! (Illus.). 1990. PLB 19.95 (ISBN 0-7933-0877-1); pap. 14.95 (ISBN 0-7933-0876-3); computer disk 29.95 (ISBN 0-7933-0878-X). Gallopade Pub Group.

—North Dakota Quiz Bowl Crash Course! (Illus.). 1990. PLB 19.95 (ISBN 1-55609-973-8); pap. 14.95 (ISBN 1-55609-974-6); computer disk 29.95 (ISBN 1-55609-975-4). Gallopade Pub Group.

—North Dakota School Trivia: An Amazing & Fascinating Look at Our State's Teachers, Schools & Students! (Illus.). 1990. PLB 19.95 (ISBN 0-7933-0874-7); pap. 14.95 (ISBN 0-7933-0873-9); computer disk 29.95 (ISBN 0-7933-0875-5). Gallopade Pub Group.

—North Dakota Silly Basketball Sportsmysteries, Vol. 1. (Illus.). 1990. PLB 19.95 (ISBN 0-7933-0871-2); pap. 14.95 (ISBN 0-7933-0870-4); computer disk 29.95 (ISBN 0-7933-0872-0). Gallopade Pub Group.

—North Dakota Silly Basketball Sportsmysteries, Vol. 2. (Illus.). 1990. PLB 19.95; pap. 14.95 (ISBN 0-7933-1846-7); computer disk 29.95 (ISBN 0-7933-1847-5). Gallopade Pub Group.

—North Dakota Silly Football Sportsmysteries, Vol. 1. (Illus.). 1990. PLB 19.95 (ISBN 1-55609-948-7); pap. 14.95 (ISBN 1-55609-949-5); computer disk 29.95. Gallopade Pub Group.

—North Dakota Silly Football Sportsmysteries, Vol. 2. (Illus.). 1990. PLB 19.95 (ISBN 1-55609-967-3); pap. 14.95 (ISBN 1-55609-968-1); computer disk 29.95 (ISBN 1-55609-969-X). Gallopade Pub Group.

—North Dakota Silly Trivia! (Illus.). 1990. PLB 19.95 (ISBN 1-55609-940-1); pap. 14.95 (ISBN 1-55609-941-X); computer disk 29.95 (ISBN 1-55609-942-8). Gallopade Pub Group.

—North Dakota's (Most Devastating!) Disasters & (Most Calamitous!) Catastrophies! (Illus.). 1990. PLB 19.95 (ISBN 0-7933-0862-3); pap. 14.95 (ISBN 0-7933-0861-5); computer disk 29.95 (ISBN 0-7933-0863-1). Gallopade Pub Group.

Turner Program Services, Inc. Staff & Clark, James I. North Dakota. LC 85-9974. 48p. (gr. 3 up). 1985. PLB 17.32 (ISBN 0-86514-440-0); pap. text ed. 9.27 (ISBN 0-86514-515-6); cancelled Beta video (ISBN 0-86514-065-0); cancelled VHS video (ISBN 0-86514-140-1); cancelled 3/4" video (ISBN 0-86514-215-7); cancelled tchr's. guide (ISBN 0-86514-290-4); cancelled student activity bk. (ISBN 0-86514-365-X); cancelled index. Raintree Pubs.

Tweton, D. Jerome & Jelliff, Theodore B. North Dakota: The Heritage of a People. LC 76-27123. (Illus.). (gr. 7 up). 1976. 12.85 (ISBN 0-911042-19-9). N Dak Inst.

NORTH DAKOTA–FICTION

Sypher, Lucy J. Cousins & Circuses. Abel, Ray, illus. 250p. (gr. 3-7). 1991. pap. 3.95 (ISBN 0-14-034551-5, Puffin). Puffin Bks.

Wilder, Laura I. By the Shores of Silver Lake. rev. ed. Williams, Garth, illus. LC 52-7529. 292p. (gr. 4-7). 1961. 14.95 (ISBN 0-06-026416-0); PLB 14.89 (ISBN 0-06-026417-9). HarpC Child Bks.

NORTH POLE

see also Arctic Regions

NORTHMEN

Atkinson, I. The Viking Ships. LC 77-17510. (Illus.). 48p. (gr. 7 up). 1979. pap. 5.95 (ISBN 0-521-21951-5). Cambridge U Pr.

Birkett, Alaric. Vikings. (gr. 5-8). 1985. pap. 10.95 (ISBN 0-7175-1321-1). Dufour.

Costumes of the Saxons & Vikings. 72p. (gr. 7-11). 1991. 19.95 (ISBN 0-7134-5750-3, Pub. by Batsford UK). Trafalgar Sq.

Humble, Richard. The Age of Leif Eriksson. Hook, Richard, illus. LC 89-8867. 32p. (gr. 5-8). 1989. PLB 11.90 (ISBN 0-531-10741-8). Watts.

Italia, Bob. The Vikings. Walner, Rosemary, ed. (Illus.). 32p. (gr. 4). 1990. PLB 11.95 (ISBN 0-939179-93-8). Abdo & Dghtrs.
Matthews, Rupert. Viking Explorers. (Illus.). 24p. (gr. k-4). 1990. PLB 10.40 (ISBN 0-531-18346-7). Watts.
Mulvihill, Margaret. Viking Longboats. Smith, Tony, illus. LC 89-31565. 32p. (gr. 3-6). 1989. PLB 11.90 (ISBN 0-531-17168-X). Watts.
Odijk, Pamela. The Vikings. Easton, Emily, ed. (Illus.). 48p. (gr. 5-8). 1990. lib. bdg. 16.98 (ISBN 0-382-09893-5). Silver Burdett Pr.
Schiller, Barbara. Eric the Red & Leif the Lucky. LC 78-18055. (Illus.). 48p. (gr. 4-7). 1979. PLB 9.89 (ISBN 0-89375-174-X); pap. 2.95 (ISBN 0-89375-166-9). Troll Assocs.
Triggs, Tony P. Viking Warriors. LC 90-858. (Illus.). 24p. (gr. 2-5). 1991. PLB 10.40 (ISBN 0-531-18356-4, Pub. by Bookwright Pr). Watts.
Viking Sailor. (Illus.). (gr. 3-8). lib. bdg. 14.00 (ISBN 0-86592-141-5). Rourke Corp.
The Vikings. (Illus.). (gr. 5 up). 3.50 (ISBN 0-7214-0945-8). Ladybird Bks.

NORTHMEN–FICTION

Abraham, Norma J. Erik of the Dragon Ships. Steiner, Pat, illus. LC 83-50987. 163p. (Orig.). (gr. 8-11). 1983. pap. 3.95 (ISBN 0-912661-00-3). Woodsong Graph.
Benchley, Nathaniel. Beyond the Mists. LC 75-9389. 160p. (gr. 7 up). 1975. PLB 10.89 (ISBN 0-06-020460-5). HarpC Child Bks.
Campbell, Civardi. Viking Raiders. (gr. 4-9). 1977. 7.95 (ISBN 0-86020-086-8, Usborne-Hayes); PLB 13.96 (ISBN 0-88110-102-8); pap. 6.95 (ISBN 0-86020-085-X). EDC.
De Goscinny, Rene. Le Bouclier Arverne. (FRE.). (gr. 7-9). 19.95 (ISBN 0-685-23433-9, FC883). French & Eur.
—Le Combat des Chefs. (FRE.). (gr. 7-9). 19.95 (ISBN 0-685-23429-0, FC879). French & Eur.
De Goscinny, Rene & Uderzo, M. Domaine des Dieux. (FRE., Illus.). (gr. 7-9). 19.95 (ISBN 0-685-28430-1, FC886). French & Eur.
Goscinny, R. & Uderzo, M. The Great Crossing. (Illus.). 15.95 (ISBN 0-686-56214-3). French & Eur.
Goscinny, Rene. Le Tour de Gaulle. (FRE., Also avail. in Span.). (gr. 3-8). 15.95 (ISBN 0-685-23428-2). French & Eur.
Goscinny, Rene de & Uderzo, M. Asterix & the Goths. (Illus.). (gr. 7-10). 15.95 (ISBN 0-686-56209-7). French & Eur.
—Asterix Gladiator. (LAT., Illus.). 15.95 (ISBN 0-686-56274-7). French & Eur.
—Asterix in Britain. (Illus.). 15.95 (ISBN 0-686-56202-X). French & Eur.
Janeway, Elizabeth. The Vikings. LC 81-867. (Illus.). 160p. (gr. 5-9). 1981. pap. 3.95 (ISBN 0-394-84885-3). Random.
Jones, Terry. The Saga of Eric the Viking. large type ed. 248p. (gr. 3 up). 1990. lib. bdg. 16.95x (ISBN 0-7451-1152-1, Lythway Large Print). G K Hall.
Molan, Chris, as told by. The Viking Saga. (Illus.). 32p. (gr. k-5). 1985. PLB 16.67 (ISBN 0-8172-2503-X); pap. 9.27 (ISBN 0-8172-2511-0). Raintree Pubs.
Treece, Henry. Road to Miklagard. Price, Christine, illus. LC 57-12280. (gr. 6-10). 1957. 18.95 (ISBN 0-87599-118-1). S G Phillips.
—Viking's Dawn. Price, C., illus. LC 56-9962. (gr. 7-9). 1956. 18.95 (ISBN 0-87599-117-3). S G Phillips.
—Westward to Vinland. Stobbs, William, illus. (gr. 8 up). 1967. 18.95 (ISBN 0-87599-136-X). S G Phillips.

NORTHWEST, OLD

see also Middle West

NORTHWEST, OLD–FICTION

Silver, Jeffrey H. The Rainier Ice Caves & Other Northwest Stories. Topolski, Diane F., illus. 32p. (gr. 5 up). 1983. pap. 4.00 (ISBN 0-910867-01-1). Silver Seal Bks.

NORTHWEST PASSAGE

Brown, Warren. The Search for the Northwest Passage. Goetzmann, William H., ed. Collins, Michael, intro. by. (Illus.). 112p. (gr. 5 up). 1991. PLB 18.95 (ISBN 0-7910-1297-2). Chelsea Hse.

NORTHWESTERN STATES

Herda, D. J. Environmental America: The Northwestern States. (Illus.). 64p. (gr. 5-8). 1991. PLB 13.90 (ISBN 1-878841-10-6). Millbrook Pr.

NORWAY

Gilseth, Margaret C. Fjord Magic: Getting Acquainted with Norway. Edwards, Helen, illus. 125p. (gr. 4 up). 1989. pap. text ed. 7.95 (ISBN 0-9619327-2-4). Askeladd Pr.
Hintz, Martin. Norway. LC 82-9400. (Illus.). (gr. 5-9). 1982. PLB 25.27 (ISBN 0-516-02780-8). Childrens.
Lerner Publications, Department of Geography Staff, ed. Norway in Pictures. (Illus.). 64p. (gr. 5 up). 1990. PLB 12.95 (ISBN 0-8225-1871-6). Lerner Pubns.
Lye, Keith. Take a Trip to Norway. (Illus.). (gr. k-3). 1985. PLB 7.99 (ISBN 0-531-04885-3). Watts.
St. John, Jetty. A Family in Norway. (Illus.). 32p. (gr. 2-5). 1988. lib. bdg. 9.95 (ISBN 0-8225-1681-0). Lerner Pubns.
Zickgraf, Ralph. Norway. (Illus.). (gr. 5 up). 1990. 14.95 (ISBN 0-7910-1100-3). Chelsea Hse.

NORWAY–FICTION

Aamundsen, Nina R. Two Short & One Long. 112p. (gr. 4-8). 1990. 13.95 (ISBN 0-395-52434-2). HM.
Egner, Thorbjorn. Karius & Baktus. Sevig, Mike, tr. from NOR. LC 86-62750. (gr. 1-4). 1986. write for info. (ISBN 0-9615394-1-0). Skandisk.
Ibsen, Henrik. Peer Gynt. Canon, R. R., intro. by. (gr. 10 up). pap. 1.50 (ISBN 0-8049-0133-3, CL-133). Airmont.
McSwigan, Marie. Snow Treasure. (Illus.). (gr. 6-9). pap. 2.50 (ISBN 0-590-41148-9). Scholastic Inc.
—Snow Treasure. LaBlanc, Andre, illus. 156p. (gr. 4-6). 1986. pap. 2.25 (ISBN 0-590-33992-3, Apple Paperbacks). Scholastic Inc.
Marron, Carol A. Last Look from the Mountain. Ray, Deborah K., illus. LC 83-6450. 32p. (gr. 3-6). 1983. PLB 14.65g (ISBN 0-940742-17-9). Raintree Pubs.

NORWEGIANS IN THE U. S.

Cornelius, James. The Norwegian Americans. Moynihan, Daniel P., intro. by. (Illus.). 112p. (gr. 5 up). 1989. lib. bdg. 17.95 (ISBN 0-87754-892-7). Chelsea Hse.
Hillbrand, Percie V. The Norwegians in America. rev. ed. LC 67-15683. (Illus.). 80p. (gr. 5 up). PLB 11.95 (ISBN 0-8225-0243-7); pap. 3.95 (ISBN 0-8225-1041-3). Lerner Pubns.

NOTATION, MUSICAL

see Musical Notation

NOVA SCOTIA–FICTION

James, Janet C. Jeremy Gates & the Magic Key. 101p. (gr. 9-12). 1986. 7.95 (ISBN 0-920806-32-5, Pub. by Penumbra Pr CN). U of Toronto Pr.

NOVELISTS

Blair, Gwenda. Laura Ingalls Wilder. Allen, Thomas B., illus. 64p. (gr. 1-4). 1981. lib. bdg. 6.99 (ISBN 0-399-61139-8, Putnam); pap. 5.95 (ISBN 0-399-20953-0). Putnam Pub Group.

NUCLEAR ENERGY

Ardley, Neil. Atoms & Energy. LC 76-13597. (Illus.). 48p. (gr. 5 up). 1976. 3.95 (ISBN 0-531-02442-3); PLB 11.40 (ISBN 0-531-01200-X). Watts.
Boy Scouts of America. Atomic Energy. (Illus.). 80p. (gr. 6-12). 1983. pap. 1.85 (ISBN 0-8395-3275-X, 3275). BSA.
Fradin, Dennis. Nuclear Energy. (Illus.). (gr. k-4). 1987. PLB 14.60 (ISBN 0-516-01237-1). Childrens.
Halacy, Dan. Nuclear Energy. rev. ed. Schreiber, Norman, rev. by. LC 84-7361. (Illus.). 88p. (gr. 4-6). 1984. PLB 10.40 (ISBN 0-531-04829-2). Watts.

NUCLEAR ENGINEERING

Harwell, Christine C. & Harwell, Mark A. Nuclear Famine. LC 87-70224. (Illus.). 16p. (Orig.). (gr. 10 up). 1990. pap. text ed. 2.15 (ISBN 0-89278-185-8, 45-9785). Carolina Biological.
Ligou, Jacques P. Elements of Nuclear Engineering. 508p. (gr. 6 up). 1986. text ed. 180.00 (ISBN 3-7186-0363-2, Pub. by Harwood Acad Pubs). Gordon & Breach.

NUCLEAR PHYSICS

see also Chemistry, Physical and Theoretical; Nuclear Engineering; Radioactivity

Ardley, Neil. Atoms & Energy. LC 76-13597. (Illus.). 48p. (gr. 5 up). 1976. 3.95 (ISBN 0-531-02442-3); PLB 11.40 (ISBN 0-531-01200-X). Watts.

NUCLEAR POWER

see also Atomic Bomb; Nuclear Engineering

Arnold, Guy. Facts on Nuclear Energy. (Illus.). 32p. (gr. 5-8). 1990. PLB 11.90 (ISBN 0-531-11088-5). Watts.
—Facts on Nuclear Energy. 1990. 11.90 (ISBN 0-531-14069-5). Watts.
Asimov, Isaac. How Did We Find Out about Nuclear Power? LC 76-12067. (Illus.). (gr. 4 up). 1976. PLB 12.85 (ISBN 0-8027-6266-2). Walker & Co.
Bernards, Neal. Nuclear Power: Examining Cause & Effect Relationships. (Illus.). 32p. (gr. 3-6). 1990. PLB 8.95 (ISBN 0-89908-607-1). Greenhaven.
Dineen, Jacqueline. Nuclear Power. 32p. (gr. 4-8). 1988. lib. bdg. 12.95 (ISBN 0-89490-220-2). Enslow Pubs.
Kruschke, Earl R. & Jackson, Byron M. Nuclear Energy Policy: A Reference Handbook. 250p. 1990. lib. bdg. 39.50 (ISBN 0-87436-238-5). ABC-CLIO.
Pringle, Laurence. Nuclear Energy: Troubled Past, Uncertain Future. LC 88-28664. (Illus.). 128p. (gr. 7 up). 1989. 13.95 (ISBN 0-02-775391-3, Mcmillan Child Bk). Macmillan Child Grp.
Story of Nuclear Power. (ARA., Illus.). (gr. 5-12). 3.50x (ISBN 0-86685-228-X). Intl Bk Ctr.

NUCLEAR POWER–FICTION

Krogman, Dane & Holelson, Doug. Skeleton Boy: The Nuclear Hero. (Illus.). 80p. (gr. 6-12). 1982. 8.95 (ISBN 0-910519-00-5). Daneco Pubns.
Moeri, Louise. Downwind. (gr. k-12). 1987. pap. 2.75 (ISBN 0-440-92132-5, LFL). Dell.
Thompson, Julian. A Band of Angels. 304p. (gr. 7 up). 1987. pap. 2.95 (ISBN 0-590-43124-2). Scholastic Inc.

NUCLEAR POWER PLANTS

Hawkes, Nigel. Nuclear Power. (Illus.). 48p. (gr. 5 up). 1990. lib. bdg. 18.00 (ISBN 0-86592-098-2); lib. bdg. 13.50s.p. (ISBN 0-685-36380-5). Rourke Corp.
—Nuclear Safety. (Illus.). 32p. (gr. 4-8). 1987. lib. bdg. 8.90 (ISBN 0-531-17040-3, Gloucester Pr). Watts.
Helgerson, Joel. Nuclear Accidents. Solomon, Maury, ed. (Illus.). 128p. (gr. 7 up). 1988. PLB 12.90 (ISBN 0-531-10330-7). Watts.
Moeri, Louise. Downwind. 144p. (gr. 4-7). 1984. 13.95 (ISBN 0-525-44096-8, DCB). Dutton Child Bks.

NUCLEAR SUBMARINES

Graham, Ian. Attack Submarine. (Illus.). 32p. (gr. 5-9). 1989. PLB 8.90 (ISBN 0-531-17156-6). Watts.

NUCLEAR TEST BAN

see Disarmament

NUCLEAR WARFARE

Bender, David L. & Leone, Bruno, eds. Nuclear Arms Annual, 1989. 144p. (gr. 10 up). 1989. pap. text ed. 5.45 (ISBN 0-89908-545-8). Greenhaven.
Brown, Adam. Nuclear Weapons. (Illus.). 48p. (gr. 5 up). 1987. PLB 14.60 (ISBN 0-86592-278-0). Rourke Corp.
Feldbaum, Carl B. & Bee, Ronald J. Looking the Tiger in the Eye: Confronting the Nuclear Threat. LC 85-48253. (Illus.). 320p. (gr. 7 up). 1988. 14.95 (ISBN 0-06-020414-1); PLB 14.89 (ISBN 0-06-020415-X). HarpC Child Bks.
Fleisher, Paul. Understanding the Vocabulary of the Nuclear Arms Race. LC 87-15430. (Illus.). 192p. (gr. 5 up). 1988. PLB 14.95 (ISBN 0-87518-352-2, Dillon). Macmillan Child Grp.
Martin, Laurence W. Nuclear Warfare. Gibbons, Tony, et al, illus. 48p. (gr. 5 up). 1989. 9.95 (ISBN 0-8225-1384-6). Lerner Pubns.
Sanford, James, Jr. Nuclear War Diary. Alexander, Frank, ed. Sanford, James, Jr. & Bates, Dawn, illus. 186p. (gr. 7-12). 1989. pap. 5.95 (ISBN 0-915256-28-2, 130). Front Row.
Smoke, Richard. Nuclear Weapons: A Changing Arms Race. 160p. (gr. 7 up). 1991. PLB 15.85 (ISBN 0-8027-8117-9); pap. 8.95 (ISBN 0-8027-7369-9). Walker & Co.
—Think about Nuclear Arms Control: Understanding the Arms Race. (Illus.). 178p. 1988. PLB 14.85 (ISBN 0-8027-6761-3); pap. 5.95 (ISBN 0-8027-6762-1). Walker & Co.
Williams, Gene B. Nuclear War, Nuclear Winter. (Illus.). 128p. (gr. 7-12). 1987. PLB 12.90 (ISBN 0-531-10416-8). Watts.

NUCLEAR WARFARE–FICTION

Godfrey, Martyn. The Last War. LC 88-11459. (Illus.). 96p. (Orig.). (gr. 5 up). 1989. pap. 2.95 (ISBN 0-02-041791-8, Collier Young Ad). Macmillan Child Grp.
Miklowitz, Gloria D. After the Bomb. 160p. (Orig.). (gr. 7 up). 1985. pap. 2.25 (ISBN 0-590-33287-2, Point). Scholastic Inc.
Swindells, Robert. Brother in the Land. LC 84-22362. 160p. (gr. 6 up). 1985. 10.95 (ISBN 0-8234-0556-7). Holiday.

NUCLEAR WEAPONS AND DISARMAMENT

see Disarmament

NUMBER CONCEPT

Adler, David A. Roman Numerals. Barton, Byron, illus. LC 77-2270. 40p. (gr. 1-4). 1977. PLB 14.89 (ISBN 0-690-01302-7, Crowell Jr Bks). HarpC Child Bks.
Alexander, Lloyd. The Book of Three. 192p. (gr. 5-9). 1980. pap. 3.50 (ISBN 0-440-90702-0, LFL). Dell.
Allen, Robert. One-Two-Three: First Counting Book. Weissman, Mottke, photos by. (Illus.). 72p. (ps-1). 1981. 3.95 (ISBN 0-448-41055-9, G&D). Putnam Pub Group.
Argon, Hilda. Counting Book. (Illus.). 20p. (Orig.). (ps-7). 1981. pap. 3.75 (ISBN 0-915347-15-6). Pueblo Acoma Pr.
Bathtime Numbers. (ps up). 1990. PLB 3.98 (ISBN 0-7924-5361-1, Mallard Pr). BDD Promo Bk.
Berenstain, Stan & Berenstain, Janice. Bears on Wheels. LC 72-77840. (Illus.). (ps-1). 1969. 6.95 (ISBN 0-394-80967-X, Random Juv); lib. bdg. 7.99 (ISBN 0-394-90967-4). Random.
Bernstein, Bob. Numbers Count. 96p. (gr. 2-7). 1990. 8.95 (ISBN 0-86653-542-X, GA1151). Good Apple.
Boyle, Sallie, et al. Blends, Digraphs & Counting by Twos, Fives, Tens. (Illus.). 32p. (ps-3). 1984. pap. 1.98 (ISBN 0-88724-162-X, CD-0920). Carson-Dellos.
Brown, Mik. Mik Brown's 123. (Illus.). 32p. (ps-k). 1989. pap. 2.95 (ISBN 0-8249-8374-2). Ideals.
Carle, Eric. My Very First Book of Numbers. reissued ed. Carle, Eric, illus. LC 72-83777. 10p. (ps-1). 1991. bds. 4.95 (ISBN 0-694-00012-4, Crowell Jr Bks). HarpC Child Bks.
Carona, Philip. Numbers. LC 82-4455. (gr. k-4). 1982. 14.60 (ISBN 0-516-01634-2). Childrens.
Carroll, Jeri A. Let's Learn about Numbers. Skiles, Janet, illus. 64p. (ps-2). 1986. wkbk. 6.95 (ISBN 0-86653-354-0, GA 792). Good Apple.
Carson, Patti & Dellosa, Janet. Beginning Numbers: One Through Ten. (Illus.). 20p. (ps-2). 1984. pap. 5.95 (ISBN 0-88724-136-0, CD-0570). Carson Dellos.
—Fun with Numbers. Carson, Patti & Dellosa, Janet, illus. 32p. (gr. k-1). 1984. pap. 1.98 (ISBN 0-88724-075-5, CD-7018). Carson-Dellos.
Childs, Phyllis, et al. First Book of Numbers. 55p. (ps-k). 1985. wkbk. 4.95 (ISBN 0-931749-02-6). PJC Lrng Mtrls.
Colors, Shapes, Words, & Numbers. Date not set. 5.98 (ISBN 0-517-68231-1). Outlet Bk Co.
Counting. (Illus.). (ps). 1992. 3.50 (ISBN 0-7214-5207-8). Ladybird Bks.
Counting Rhymes Board Book. (ps). 1959. bds. 3.95 (ISBN 0-448-03078-0, G&D). Putnam Pub Group.
Dellosa, Janet, et al. Colors & Counting Zero Through Nine. (Illus.). 32p. (ps-1). 1984. pap. 1.98 (ISBN 0-88724-158-1, CD-0922). Carson-Dellos.
—Consonants & Counting Zero Through Twenty. (Illus.). 32p. (ps-2). 1984. pap. 1.98 (ISBN 0-88724-161-1, CD-0921). Carson-Dellos.
Disney, Walt, Productions Staff. Adventures with Letters & Numbers. LC 85-43076. 80p. (Orig.). 1985. pap. 5.95 (ISBN 0-553-05533-X). Bantam.
Dreaming Numbers. 1990. text ed. 3.95 cased (ISBN 0-7214-5272-8). Ladybird Bks.
Feelings, Muriel. Moja Means One: A Swahili Counting Book. Feelings, Tom, illus. LC 76-134856. (ps-3). 1987. 13.95 (ISBN 0-8037-5776-X); PLB 13.89 (ISBN 0-8037-5777-8). Dial Bks Young.

Friskey, Margaret. Chicken Little Count-To-Ten. Evans, K., illus. 32p. (gr. k-3). 1946. PLB 14.60 (ISBN 0-516-03431-6). Childrens.
Fujikawa, Gyo. One, Two, Three, A Counting Book. Fujikawa, Gyo, illus. 14p. (ps). 1981. 2.25 (ISBN 0-448-15085-9, G&D). Putnam Pub Group.
Garcia, Yolanda. Celebremos con Numeros. (SPA., Illus.). 60p. (gr. k-2). 1986. pap. text ed. 7.95 (ISBN 0-935303-01-4). Victory Pub.
Gillen, Patricia B. My Signing Book of Numbers. LC 87-28758. (Illus.). 56p. (ps up). 1987. 10.95 (ISBN 0-930323-37-8, Kendall Green Pubns). Gallaudet Univ Pr.
Gregorich, Barbara. Contando del 1 al 10: Counting 1 to 10. Hoffman, Joan, ed. Shepherd-Bartram, tr. from ENG. Pape, Richard, illus. (SPA.). 32p. (Orig.). 1987. wkbk. 1.99 (ISBN 0-938256-79-3). Sch Zone Pub Co.
Henry Hound's One-Two-Three. (ps-k). 1990. bds. 3.95 (ISBN 0-7214-9124-3). Ladybird Bks.
Hindley. Counting Book. (gr. k-2). 1979. 6.95 (ISBN 0-86020-361-1, Usborne-Hayes); PLB 11.96 (ISBN 0-88110-066-8). EDC.
Hornnes, Esther & Magos, Eunice. Sew & Know: Puppet Projects to Teach Numbers, 1-12. Sussman, Ellen, ed. Rundell, Wendi S., illus. 28p. (Orig.). (gr. k-1). 1982. pap. text ed. 4.95 (ISBN 0-933606-17-6, MS-615). Monkey Sisters.
Hyman, Jane. Gumby Book of Numbers. LC 86-6193. (Illus.). 32p. (ps-3). 1986. 5.95 (ISBN 0-385-23455-4); PLB 5.95 (ISBN 0-385-23847-9). Doubleday.
Katz, Bobbi. Ten Little Care Bears Counting Book. Barto, Bobbi, illus. LC 83-60084. 14p. (ps-k). 1983. 4.95 (ISBN 0-394-86088-8). Random.
Kehl, Richard. How to Make a Zero Backwards. 1989. pap. 2.95 (ISBN 0-590-42547-1). Scholastic Inc.
Krampe, Leesa. My Number Book. Curlee, Jane, illus. 126p. (ps-1). 1986. pap. text ed. 3.95 (ISBN 0-932957-99-4). Natl School.
—My Number Word Book. Ehrlich, Doris, ed. O'Rourke, Dawn, illus. 100p. (Orig.). (ps-1). 1987. pap. text ed. 3.95 (ISBN 0-932957-94-3). Natl School.
Krulik, Nancy E. I Am Curious about Numbers. Wildman, George, illus. 48p. (Orig.). (ps-2). 1987. pap. 1.95 (ISBN 0-590-41046-6). Scholastic Inc.
LeGros, Lucy C. Instant Centers - Numbers 10-20. LeGros, Ivor L., illus. 33p. (gr. k-2). 1988. tchr's ed. 5.95 (ISBN 0-937306-07-X). Creat Res NC.
—Instant Centers: Numbers. (Illus.). 48p. (Orig.). (gr. k-2). 1984. pap. 5.95 (ISBN 0-937306-05-3). Creat Res NC.
Le Sieg, Theodore. Ten Apples up on Top. LC 61-7068. (Illus.). 72p. (gr. 1-2). 1961. 6.95 (ISBN 0-394-80019-2); lib. bdg. 7.99 (ISBN 0-394-90019-7). Beginner.
Lottridge, Celia B. One Watermelon Seed. Patkau, Karen, illus. 24p. (ps up). 1990. pap. 6.95 (ISBN 0-19-540735-0). Oxford U Pr.
Maestro, Betsy. Harriet Goes to the Circus: A Number Concept Book. Maestro, Giulio, illus. LC 76-40204. (ps-1). 1989. Crown.
Moncure, Jane B. My Eight Book. Hohag, Linda, illus. LC 85-30962. 32p. (ps-2). 1986. lib. bdg. 11.97 (ISBN 0-89565-319-2). Childs World.
—My Five Book. Hohag, Linda, illus. LC 85-9699. 32p. (ps-2). 1985. PLB 11.97 (ISBN 0-89565-316-8). Childs World.
—My Four Book. Hohag, Linda, illus. LC 85-9700. 32p. (ps-2). 1985. PLB 11.97 (ISBN 0-89565-315-X). Childs World.
—My Nine Book. Hohag, Linda, illus. LC 85-30959. 32p. (ps-2). 1986. lib. bdg. 11.97 (ISBN 0-89565-320-6). Childs World.
—My One Book. Peltier, Pam, illus. LC 85-5897. 32p. (ps-2). 1985. PLB 11.97 (ISBN 0-89565-312-5). Childs World.
—My Seven Book. Hohag, Linda, illus. LC 86-2594. 32p. (ps-2). 1986. PLB 11.97 (ISBN 0-89565-318-4). Childs World.
—My Six Book. Hohag, Linda, illus. LC 85-30961. 32p. (ps-2). 1986. lib. bdg. 11.97 (ISBN 0-89565-317-6). Childs World.
—My Ten Book. Hohag, Linda, illus. LC 86-2293. 32p. (ps-2). 1986. lib. bdg. 11.97 (ISBN 0-89565-321-4). Childs World.
—My Three Book. Hohag, Linda, illus. LC 85-5898. 32p. (ps-2). 1985. PLB 11.97 (ISBN 0-89565-314-1). Childs World.
—My Two Book. Peltier, Pam, illus. LC 85-7885. 32p. (ps-2). 1985. PLB 11.97 (ISBN 0-89565-313-3). Childs World.
Moss, David. Numbers. 1989. 4.99 (ISBN 0-517-69423-9). Outlet Bk Co.
My First Book of Numbers. (ps-2). bds. 2.50 (ISBN 0-448-02679-1, G&D). Putnam Pub Group.
Nedobeck, Don. Nedobeck's Numbers Book. 26p. (gr. 1-8). 1988. 9.95 (ISBN 0-944314-01-5). New Wrinkle.
Neff, Carolyn & Verett, Dotty. Digit Days. Draze, Dianne, ed. Franklin, Jean, illus. 32p. (gr. 4-6). 1983. 5.00 (ISBN 0-931724-24-4). Dandy Lion.
Numbers. (Illus.). (ps-k). 3.50 (ISBN 0-7214-1115-0). Ladybird Bks.
Numbers. (Illus.). (ps-k). 3.50 (ISBN 0-7214-8101-9). Ladybird Bks.
Numbers Dot-to-Dot. (Illus.). 24p. (ps-k). 1986. 3.98 (ISBN 0-86734-063-0, FS-3055). Schaffer Pubns.
Numbers Ten to One Hundred. (Illus.). 32p. (gr. k-1). 1985. pap. write for info. (ISBN 0-307-03586-7, Pub. by Golden Bks). Western Pub.
OcKenga, Starr & Doolittle, Eileen. World of Wonders: A Trip Though Numbers. (Illus.). 48p. 1988. 16.95 (ISBN 0-395-48726-9). HM.
O'Halloran, Tim. Know Your Numbers. O'Halloran, Tim, illus. 38p. (ps-1). 1983. 10.95 (ISBN 0-88625-045-5). Durkin Hayes Pub.
Oliver, Stephen, photos by. My First Look at Numbers. LC 89-63088. (Illus.). 24p. (ps-k). 1990. 6.95 (ISBN 0-679-80533-8). McKay.
Oxenbury, Helen. Helen Oxebury's Numbers of Things. Oxenbury, Helen, illus. LC 83-5263. 32p. (ps-3). 1983. pap. 9.95 (ISBN 0-385-29288-0); pap. 9.95 (ISBN 0-385-29289-9). Delacorte.
Pagnucci, Susan. Number Chomp. (Illus.). 48p. (Orig.). (gr. 1-2). 1984. Incl. reproducible math sheets with numbers 0-9 addition & subtraction. 4.50 (ISBN 0-929326-04-0). Bur Oak Pr Inc.
Peppe, Rodney. Circus Numbers. Peppe, Rodney, illus. LC 75-86381. (ps-3). 1969. 5.95 (ISBN 0-440-01288-0); pap. 3.69 (ISBN 0-440-01289-9). Delacorte.
Peter Rabbit's 1 2 3 Frieze. 1988. 5.00 (ISBN 0-7232-5630-6). Warne.
Quality Time Workbooks: I Know Numbers. 1991. 1.98 (ISBN 0-8317-7295-6). Smithmark.
Robinson, Shari. A First Number Book. Murdocca, Sal, illus. LC 80-83587. 96p. (gr. k-4). 1981. PLB 11.85 (ISBN 0-448-13922-7, G&D); pap. 3.95 (ISBN 0-448-47335-6). Putnam Pub Group.
Ross, Shirley & McCord, Cindy. Number Monsters. 64p. (ps-2). 1987. 6.95 (ISBN 0-912107-65-0). Monday Morning Bks.
Schaffer, Frank, Publications Staff. Beginning Activities with Numbers. (Illus.). 24p. (ps-k). 1980. 3.98 (ISBN 0-86734-014-2, FS 3027). Schaffer Pubns.
—Getting Ready for Math. (Illus.). 24p. (ps-k). 1980. 3.98 (ISBN 0-86734-020-7, FS 3033). Schaffer Pubns.
—Numbers. (Illus.). 24p. (ps-2). 1978. wkbk. 3.98 (ISBN 0-86734-002-9, FS 3003). Schaffer Pubns.
Schwartz, David M. How Much Is a Million? Kellogg, Steven, illus. LC 84-5736. 40p. (gr. k-5). 1985. PLB 14.88 (ISBN 0-688-04050-0); 15.00 (ISBN 0-688-04049-7). Lothrop.
Shearer, Marilyn J. The Lonely Ten: A Book of Counting for Preschool & Above. Bostic, Alex, illus. 16p. (Orig.). (ps-6). 1992. pap. 19.95 (ISBN 0-685-30094-3). L Ashley & Joshua.
—The Lonely Ten: A Book of Simple Addition for Preschool & Above. Bostic, Alex, illus. 16p. (Orig.). (ps-6). 1991. 19.95 (ISBN 0-685-30093-5). L Ashley & Joshua.
Sitomer, Mindel & Sitomer, Harry. How Did Numbers Begin? LC 75-11756. (Illus.). 40p. (gr. k-3). 1976. PLB 12.89 (ISBN 0-690-00794-9, Crowell Jr Bks). HarpC Child Bks.
Smalley, Guy, illus. My Very Own Book of Numbers. 28p. (ps-2). 1989. 9.95 (ISBN 0-929793-00-5). Camex Bks Inc.
Srivastava, Jane J. Number Families. Ehlert, Lois, illus. LC 78-19511. (gr. 2-5). 1979. PLB 12.89 (ISBN 0-690-03924-7, Crowell Jr Bks). HarpC Child Bks.
Stuart, Daryl. Quality Time Little Readers: I Know My Numbers. 1991. 1.49 (ISBN 0-8317-7268-9). Smithmark.
Tarrant, Margaret. My First Book of Numbers. (ps-3). 1989. 6.95 (ISBN 0-8249-8383-1). Ideals.
Taulbee, Annette. Numbers. (Illus.). 24p. (ps-k). 1986. 3.98 (ISBN 0-86734-061-4, FS-3053). Schaffer Pubns.
Tudor, Tasha. One Is One. Tudor, Tasha, illus. LC 56-11381. (ps-1). 1988. pap. 4.95 (ISBN 0-02-688535-2, Aladdin). Macmillan Child Grp.
Tyler, J. & Round, G. Counting up to Ten. (Illus.). 24p. (ps up). 1987. pap. 3.50 (ISBN 0-7460-0217-3). EDC.
Van der Meer, Ron & Van der Meer, Atie. Fun with Numbers. (Illus.). 10p. (ps-1). 1990. 5.95 (ISBN 0-399-21788-6, Putnam). Putnam Pub Group.
Verkouteren, J. Adrian. A Study of Numbers. 355p. (gr. 5-8). 1981. pap. text ed. 12.95 (ISBN 0-685-32862-7). Longman.
Warren, Jean. One - Two - Three Books. Bittinger, Gayle, ed. Walker, Cora, illus. LC 89-50120. 80p. (Orig.). 1989. pap. text ed. 6.95 (ISBN 0-911019-23-5). Warren Pub Hse.
Wilkes & Zeff. First Book of Numbers. (gr. k-3). 1982. 10.95 (ISBN 0-86020-665-3, Usborne-Hayes). EDC.
Zaslavsky, Claudia. Count on Your Fingers African Style. Pinkney, Jerry, illus. LC 77-26586. 32p. (gr. k-3). 1980. (Crowell Jr Bks); PLB 12.89 (ISBN 0-690-03865-8, Crowell Jr Bks). HarpC Child Bks.
—Zero! Is It Something? Is It Nothing? Bassett, Jeni, illus. 32p. (gr. k-4). 1989. PLB 12.90 (ISBN 0-531-10693-4). Watts.
Ziefert, Harriet. Bears One, Two, Three. Baruffi, Andrea, illus. LC 89-32650. 24p. (Orig.). (ps-2). 1989. pap. 2.25 (ISBN 0-394-84877-2). Random.
Zimmermann, H. Werner. Alphonse Knows...Zero Is Not Enough. (Illus.). 24p. (ps-2). 1990. bds. 9.95 laminated (ISBN 0-19-540797-0). Oxford U Pr.

NUMBERS THEORY

Dilson, Jesse. Abacus. Pozzi, Angela, illus. (gr. 5-8). 1975. pap. 6.95 (ISBN 0-312-00140-1). St Martin.
Fisher, Leonard E. Number Art: Thirteen 1 2 3s from Around the World. Fisher, Leonard E., illus. LC 82-5050. 64p. (gr. 3-7). 1984. 14.95 (ISBN 0-02-735240-4, Four Winds). Macmillan Child Grp.
Hershey, Robert L. How to Think with Numbers. 142p. (gr. 7 up). 1987. pap. 7.95 (ISBN 0-939765-14-4, GK108). Janson Pubns.
Hoffman, Joan. Numbers One to Twelve. rev. ed. Cook, Chris, illus. 32p. (ps-1). 1987. wkbk. 1.99 (ISBN 0-938256-26-2). Sch Zone Pub Co.
Richards, Elspeth & Fernyhough, Frances. Fun with Numbers. Kerr, Angela, illus. 24p. (gr. k-3). 1987. pap. 2.95 (ISBN 0-385-23844-4, Zephyr-BFYR). Doubleday.
Tallarico, Tony. Numbers. (Illus.). 12p. (gr. 3-8). 1982. pap. 3.95 (ISBN 0-89828-303-5). Tuffy Bks.
Wheeler, Sharon, ed. Number Skills. Richesson, Robin, illus. (ps). 1984. wkbk 1.95 (ISBN 0-916119-04-1). Creat Teach Pr.

NUMISMATICS

see also Coins

Counting One, Two, Three. (Illus.). (ps). 1985. bds. 2.98 (ISBN 0-517-47338-0). Outlet Bk Co.
Davis, Nancy M., et al. Numbers. Davis, Nancy M., illus. 26p. (Orig.). (ps-2). 1986. pap. 4.95 (ISBN 0-937103-14-4). DaNa Pubns.
Hoban, Tana. Twenty-Six Letters & Ninety-Nine Cents. LC 86-11993. (Illus.). 32p. (ps-3). 1987. 14.95 (ISBN 0-688-06361-6); PLB 14.88 (ISBN 0-688-06362-4). Greenwillow.
Hobson, Burton H. Coin Collecting As a Hobby. rev. ed. Obojski, Robert, ed. LC 67-27759. (Illus.). 192p. (gr. 4-10). 1986. 9.95 (ISBN 0-8069-4748-9); PLB 13.29 (ISBN 0-8069-4749-7). Sterling.
Patton, Sally. Numismatics: A Coin Word. 1980. 12.95 (ISBN 0-685-30593-7, ZS07-V). Zephyr Pr AZ.

NUNS

see Monasticism and Religious Orders for Women

NURSERY RHYMES

Adams, Pam, illus. There Was an Old Lady. 16p. (ps-2). 1975. 8.00 (ISBN 0-85953-021-3, Pub. by Child's Play England). Childs Play.
—This Is the House That Jack Built. 16p. (Orig.). (ps-2). 1977. pap. 5.00 (ISBN 0-85953-075-2, Pub. by Child's Play England). Childs Play.
—This Old Man. 16p. (Orig.). (ps-2). 8.00 (ISBN 0-85953-027-2, Pub. by Child's Play England); pap. 5.00 (ISBN 0-85953-026-4, Pub. by Child's Play England). Childs Play.
Ahlberg, Janet & Ahlberg, Allan. Peek-a-Boo! LC 81-1925. (Illus.). (ps-1). 1981. pap. 11.95 (ISBN 0-670-54598-8). Viking Child Bks.
Alchemy II, Inc. Staff, illus. The Little Red Hen. 26p. (ps). 1988. incl. cassette 9.95 (ISBN 1-55578-905-6). Worlds Wonder.
Ali-El, Yusuf. Once upon a Ryme Tyme for Growing Minds. Pride, Alexis, et al, illus. LC 83-90101. 90p. (gr. k-5). 1983. pap. 9.95 (ISBN 0-912475-09-9). Natl Res Unltd.
Amoss, Berthe. Mother Goose Rhymes. Amoss, Berthe, illus. 10p. (ps-7). 1989. pap. 2.95 (ISBN 0-922589-02-X). More Than Card.
Anglund, Joan W. In a Pumpkin Shell. Anglund, Joan W., illus. LC 60-10243. (ps-2). 1977. pap. 3.95 (ISBN 0-15-644425-9, VoyB). HarBraceJ.
—In a Pumpkin Shell: A Mother Goose ABC. Anglund, Joan W., illus. LC 60-10243. (gr. k-3). 1960. 10.95 (ISBN 0-15-238269-0, HJ). HarBraceJ.
Animal Rhymes. (Illus.). (ps). pap. 1.25 (ISBN 0-7214-9549-4). Ladybird Bks.
Aragon, Hilda, illus. My First Nursery Rhyme Book. 28p. (Orig.). (ps-7). 1981. pap. 3.75 (ISBN 0-915347-07-5). Pueblo Acoma Pr.
Arnsteen, Katy K. Mother Goose Rhymes: Hide 'n' Seek. 1990. 3.99 (ISBN 0-517-02630-9). Crown.
Atkinson, Allen, illus. The Cat & the Fiddle & Other Favorites. 64p. (Orig.). (gr. k). 1985. pap. 2.50 (ISBN 0-553-15321-8). Bantam.
—Humpty Dumpty & Other Favorites. 64p. (Orig.). (gr. k). 1985. pap. 2.50 (ISBN 0-553-15340-4). Bantam.
—Jack & Jill & Other Favorites. 64p. (Orig.). 1986. pap. 2.50 (ISBN 0-553-15354-4). Bantam.
—Little Bo-Peep & Other Favorites. 64p. (Orig.). 1986. pap. 2.50 (ISBN 0-553-15353-6). Bantam.
—Little Boy Blue & Other Favorites. 64p. (Orig.). (gr. k). 1985. pap. 2.50 (ISBN 0-553-15320-X). Bantam.
—Mary Had a Little Lamb & Other Favorites. (Orig.). (gr. k). 1985. pap. 2.50 (ISBN 0-553-15319-6). Bantam.
—Simple Simon & Other Favorites (Mother Goose) 64p. (Orig.). 1986. pap. 2.50 (ISBN 0-553-15322-6). Bantam.
Bailey, Emma. Quality Time Little Readers: Mother Goose Nursery Rhymes. 1991. 1.49 (ISBN 0-8317-7272-7). Smithmark.
Baring-Gould, S. A Book of Nursery Songs & Rhymes. (ps-4). 59.95 (ISBN 0-87968-768-1). Gordon Pr.
Baron, Michelle. A Hector Nursery Rhyme: Hey Diddle Diddle. Mazurek, Theresa, et al, illus. 26p. (ps). 1987. Packaged with pre-programmed audio cass. tape. 9.95 (ISBN 0-934323-48-8). Alchemy Comms.
—A Hector Nursery Rhyme: Hickory, Dickory, Dock. Mazurek, Theresa, et al, illus. 26p. (ps). 1987. Packaged with pre-programmed audio cass. tape. 9.95 (ISBN 0-934323-50-X). Alchemy Comms.
—A Hector Nursery Rhyme: Little Bo Beep. Mazurek, Theresa, et al, illus. 26p. (ps). 1987. Packaged with pre-programmed audio cass. tape. 9.95 (ISBN 0-934323-54-2). Alchemy Comms.
—Hey Diddle Diddle. Alchemy II, Inc. Staff, illus. 26p. (ps). 1988. incl. cassette 9.95 (ISBN 1-55578-919-6). Worlds Wonder.
—Hickory Dickory Dock. Alchemy II, Inc. Staff, illus. 26p. (ps). 1988. incl. cassette 9.95 (ISBN 1-55578-923-4). Worlds Wonder.

—Little Boy Blue. Alchemy II, Inc. Staff, illus. 26p. (ps). 1988. incl. cassette 9.95 (ISBN 1-55578-918-8). Worlds Wonder.
Barr, Marilynn G. Mother Goose Caboose. 256p. (ps-2). 1991. write for info. (ISBN 0-86653-618-3, GA1337). Good Apple.
Baum, L. Frank. Mother Goose in Prose. (gr. k up). 1986. 4.98 (ISBN 0-685-16878-6, 519046). Outlet Bk Co.
Bayley, Nicola. Hush-a-Bye Baby & Other Bedtime Rhymes. Bayley, Nicola, illus. 32p. (ps-k). 1986. 10.95 (ISBN 0-02-708610-0, Mcmillan Child Bk). Macmillan Child Grp.
—Nicola Bayley's Book of Nursery Rhymes. Bayley, Nicola, illus. LC 76-57923. 32p. (ps-2). 1990. pap. 3.95 (ISBN 0-679-80204-5, Dragonfly Bks). Knopf.
Beall, Pamela C. & Nipp, Susan H. Wee Color Wee Sing Nursery Rhymes & Lullabies. Klein, Nancy, illus. 48p. (ps-7). 1987. pap. 1.95 (ISBN 0-8431-1900-4); bk, cass. & markers 9.95 (ISBN 0-8431-1925-X). Price Stern.
—Wee Sing Nursery Rhymes & Lullabies. (Illus.). 64p. (Orig.). (ps-2). 1985. pap. 9.95 incl. cass. (ISBN 0-8431-1422-3); pap. 2.95 (ISBN 0-8431-1438-X). Price Stern.
Becker, Lois & Stratton, Mark. A Hector Nursery Rhyme: Little Miss Muffet. Mazurek, Theresa, et al, illus. 26p. (ps). 1987. Packaged with pre-programmed audio cass. tape. 9.95 (ISBN 0-934323-52-6). Alchemy Comms.
—A Hector Nursery Rhyme: Mistress Mary. Mazurek, Theresa, et al, illus. 26p. (ps). 1987. Packaged with pre-programmed audio cass. tape. 9.95 (ISBN 0-934323-49-6). Alchemy Comms.
—Little Miss Muffet. Alchemy II, Inc. Staff, illus. 26p. (ps). 1988. incl. cassette 9.95 (ISBN 1-55578-922-6). Worlds Wonder.
Bedtime Rhymes. (Illus.). (ps). pap. 1.25 (ISBN 0-7214-9551-6). Ladybird Bks.
Bernal, Richard. Night, Mother Goose. Bernal, Richard, illus. 24p. 1990. 11.95 (ISBN 0-8092-4305-9, Calico Bks). Contemp Bks.
Big & Little. (Illus.). (ps-k). 3.50 (ISBN 0-7214-1178-9). Ladybird Bks.
The Blue Match the Rhyme Book. (gr. 2-6). Date not set. 4.95 (ISBN 1-879332-01-9). XYZ Group.
Bodecker, N. M. It's Raining Said John Twaining: Danish Nursery Rhymes. Bodecker, N. M., illus. LC 72-85912. 32p. (ps-3). 1973. 6.95 (ISBN 0-689-30316-5, M K McElderry); (Aladdin). Macmillan Child Grp.
Book of Rhymes. (Illus.). (ps-5). 8.95 (ISBN 0-7214-7513-2). Ladybird Bks.
Bracken, Carolyn, illus. Humpty Dumpty & Other Rhymes. (ps-k). 3.95 (ISBN 0-7214-5194-2). Ladybird Bks.
—Jack & Jill & Other Rhymes. (ps-k). 3.95 (ISBN 0-7214-5193-4). Ladybird Bks.
—Little Bo-Peep & Other Rhymes. (ps-k). 3.95 (ISBN 0-7214-5195-0). Ladybird Bks.
—Old Mother Hubbard & Other Rhymes. (ps-k). 3.95 (ISBN 0-7214-5196-9). Ladybird Bks.
Brown, Marc. Play Rhymes. 1987. 12.95 (ISBN 0-525-44336-3, DCB). Dutton Child Bks.
Brown, Marc, ed. Hand Rhymes. Brown, Marc, illus. LC 84-25918. 32p. (ps-1). 1985. 13.95 (ISBN 0-525-44201-4, DCB). Dutton Child Bks.
Bunny's First Birthday. (Illus.). (ps-k). 3.50 (ISBN 0-7214-0301-8). Ladybird Bks.
Butterworth, Nick. Nick Butterworth's Book of Nursery Rhymes. (ps-3). 1991. 14.95 (ISBN 0-670-83551-X). Viking Child Bks.
Caldecott, Randolph, illus. Sing a Song of Sixpence. (ps up). 1988. Repr. of 1888 ed. 8.95 (ISBN 0-8120-5900-X). Barron.
Cauley, Lorinda B. The Three Little Kittens. (Illus.). 32p. (ps-1). 1982. 7.95 (ISBN 0-399-20855-0, Putnam); pap. 3.95 (ISBN 0-399-20856-9). Putnam Pub Group.
Causley, Charles. Early in the Morning. Foreman, Michael, illus. LC 86-50709. (ps-3). 1987. pap. 14.95 (ISBN 0-670-80810-5). Viking Child Bks.
Chandler, Jean, illus. The Humpty Dumpty Book. 24p. (ps-k). 1987. pap. write for info. (ISBN 0-307-10052-9, Pub. by Golden Bks). Western Pub.
Children's Treasury: Mother Goose Nursery Rhymes. 1990. 7.98 (ISBN 0-8317-1361-5). Smithmark.
Chorao, Kay. The Baby's Bedtime Book. Chorao, Kay, illus. LC 84-6067. (ps). 1989. 13.95 (ISBN 0-525-44149-2, DCB); bk & cassette 18.95 (ISBN 0-525-44506-4). Dutton Child Bks.
—The Baby's Lap Book. (Illus.). (ps-k). 1977. 12.95 (ISBN 0-525-26100-1, DCB). Dutton Child Bks.
—Baby's Lap Book. Rashad, Phylicia, read by. 64p. (ps). 1991. 13.95 (ISBN 0-525-44604-4, DCB); incl. audiocassette 18.95 (ISBN 0-525-44628-1). Dutton Child Bks.
Chusid, Nancy. Favorite Nursery Songs. Chusid, Nancy, illus. 32p. (Orig.). (gr. 2-6). 1990. pap. 6.95 incl. cassette (ISBN 1-878624-05-9). McClanahan Bk.
The Classic Mother Goose. LC 88-70839. (Illus.). 56p. (gr. k up). 1988. 9.98 (ISBN 0-89471-654-9, Pub. by Courage Books). Running Pr.
Cocca-Leffler, Maryann, illus. Hey Diddle Diddle: My First Book of Nursery Rhymes. 18p. (ps). 1991. 3.95 (ISBN 0-448-40107-X, G&D). Putnam Pub Group.
Cole, Joanna & Calmenson, Stephanie, eds. The Read-Aloud Treasury: Favorite Nursery Rhymes, Poems, Stories & More for the Very Young. Schweninger, Ann, illus. 256p. 1988. pap. 18.95 (ISBN 0-385-18560-X). Doubleday.
Conover, Chris. Mother Goose & the Sly Fox. (ps up). 1989. 13.95 (ISBN 0-374-35072-8). FS&G.
Cooney, et al. Tortillitas Para Mama: And Other Nursery Rhymes, Spanish & English. Cooney, Barbara, illus. LC 81-4823. 32p. (gr. k-3). 1981. 14.95 (ISBN 0-8050-0285-5); pap. 5.95 (ISBN 0-8050-0317-7). H Holt & Co.
Counting Rhymes. (ps). 1982. 2.95 (ISBN 0-86112-085-X). Borden.
Courson, Diana. Let's Learn about Fairy Tales & Nursery Rhymes. 64p. (ps-2). 1988. wkbk. 6.95 (ISBN 0-86653-437-7, GA1040). Good Apple.
Cutts, David, retold by. House That Jack Built. Silverstein, Don, illus. LC 78-18951. 32p. (gr. k-2). 1979. PLB 9.79 (ISBN 0-89375-127-8); pap. 1.95 (ISBN 0-89375-105-7). Troll Assocs.
De Angeli, Marguerite. Book of Nursery & Mother Goose Rhymes. De Angeli, Marguerite, illus. (gr. k-5). 1954. pap. 19.95 (ISBN 0-385-07232-5). Doubleday.
—Marguerite De Angeli's Book of Nursery & Mother Goose Rhymes. De Angeli, Marguerite, illus. LC 54-9838. (gr. k-5). 1979. pap. 18.95 (ISBN 0-685-01499-1, Zephyr BFYR); pap. 7.95 (ISBN 0-385-15291-4). Doubleday.
Decker, Marjorie A. Rock-a-Bye Prayers: Christian Mother Goose. 1990. 6.95 (ISBN 0-529-06843-5). World Bible.
Delacre, Lulu. Arroz Con Leche. Delacre, Lulu, illus. 1992. pap. 3.95 (ISBN 0-590-41886-6, Blue Ribbon Bks). Scholastic Inc.
De la Mare, Walter. Rhymes & Verses: Collected Poems for Young People. Blaisdell, Elinore, illus. 368p. (gr. 2-4). 1988. 15.95 (ISBN 0-8050-0847-0); pap. 7.95 (ISBN 0-8050-0848-9). H Holt & Co.
Demi. Dragon Kites & Dragonflies: A Collection of Chinese Nursery Rhymes. LC 86-7637. (Illus.). 32p. (ps-3). 1986. 14.95 (ISBN 0-15-224199-X, HJ). HarBraceJ.
Dennis the Dragon. (Illus.). (ps-k). 3.50 (ISBN 0-7214-0611-4). Ladybird Bks.
Dennis the Dragon Finds a New Job. (Illus.). (ps-k). 3.50 (ISBN 0-7214-0753-6). Ladybird Bks.
De Paola, Tomie, selected by. & illus. Tomie De Paola's Favorite Nursery Tales. 128p. (gr. 1 up). 1986. 17.95 (ISBN 0-399-21319-8, Putnam). Putnam Pub Group.
De Regniers, Beatrice S. Jack & the Beanstalk. Wilsdorf, Anne, illus. LC 85-7946. 48p. (ps-2). 1985. 12.95 (ISBN 0-689-31174-5, Atheneum Child Bk). Macmillan Child Grp.
Dodson, Fitzhugh. I Wish I Had a Computer That Makes Waffles: Teaching Your Child with Modern Nursery Rhymes. LC 78-13178. (Illus.). 80p. (ps-3). 1978. pap. 9.95 (ISBN 0-86679-006-3). Oak Tree Pubns.
Domain, Public. The "Match the Rhyme" Value Pack: The Blue Match the Rhyme Book; the Red Match the Rhyme Book; the Green Match the Rhyme Book. (gr. 2-6). 1991. 4.95 (ISBN 1-879332-04-3). XYZ Group.
—The Red Match the Rhyme Book. (gr. 2-6). 1991. 4.95 (ISBN 1-879332-02-7). XYZ Group.
Domanska, Janina. A Was an Angler. LC 88-35589. (Illus.). 32p. (ps up). 1991. 13.95 (ISBN 0-688-06990-8); PLB 13.88 (ISBN 0-688-06991-6). Greenwillow.

Dowell, Ruth I. Move Over, Mother Goose Series. Doolittle, et al, illus. (Orig.). (ps-5). Date not set. pap. write for info (ISBN 0-945842-24-4). Pollyanna Prodns.
Move Over Mother Goose!, ISBN 0-945842-00-7 $6.00; Jiggle on the Doorknob, ISBN 0-945842-01-5 $4.00; Watch Out, Pollyanna!, ISBN 0-945842-02-3 $4.00; Let's Talk!, ISBN 0-945842-03-1 $6.00; Think About It, ISBN 0-945842-04-X $3.00; Alphabet-ter Letter Rhymes, ISBN 0-945842-05-8 $6.00; Busy Being Me, ISBN 0-945842-07-4 $6.00; Pollyanna Herself, ISBN 0-945842-08-2 $6.00; I Say...You Say!, ISBN 0-945842-12-0 $9.95; Mother Ruth's Rhymes, ISBN 0-945842-13-9 $12.00; Alphabet-ter Letter Rhymes Activity Book, ISBN 0-945842-14-7 $6.00. Fingerplays, action verses & a wide subject range of rhymes to grow by. Indexed for concepts & the curriculum: story rhymes that "grab children & hold on!" *Publisher Provided Annotation.*

Downy Duckling. (Illus.). (ps-k). 3.50 (ISBN 0-7214-0210-0). Ladybird Bks.
Dr. Seuss. Mister Brown Can Moo, Can You. Dr. Seuss, illus. (ps-1). 1970. 6.95 (ISBN 0-394-80622-0, Random Juv); lib. bdg. 7.99 (ISBN 0-394-90622-5). Random.
Engen, Rodney, intro. by. Kate Greenaway's Mother Goose: The Complete Facsimile Sketchbooks. McTigue, Bernard, frwd. by. (Illus.). 96p. (gr. 2 up). 1988. 19.95 (ISBN 0-8109-1031-4). Abrams.
Eulalie, illus. Mother Goose Rhymes. 48p. (ps-3). 1978. 4.95 (ISBN 0-448-40114-2, G&D). Putnam Pub Group.
Falconer, Elizabeth. The House That Jack Built. Falconer, Elizabeth, illus. 32p. 1990. 13.95 (ISBN 0-8249-8459-5). Ideals.
Father Gander, pseud. Father Gander Nursery Rhymes. Blattel, Carolyn & Blair, Janice, illus. LC 85-72785. 47p. (ps up). 1985. 14.95 (ISBN 0-911655-12-3, Dist. by Ingram Bookpeople). Advocacy Pr.
Favorite Counting Rhymes. (Illus.). 32p. (gr. k-2). 1988. 4.95 (ISBN 0-87449-412-5). Modern Pub NYC.
Favorite Mother Goose & Animal Tales. (Illus.). 72p. (ps-1). 1989. write for info. (ISBN 0-307-15822-5, Pub. by Golden Bks). Western Pub.
Favorite Nursery Classics. LC 62-15043. (ps-2). 1978. write for info. (ISBN 0-528-82216-0). Checkerboard Pr.
Favorite Nursery Rhymes. 1989. 2.98 (ISBN 0-517-69216-3). Outlet Bk Co.
Fletcher, Cynthia H. My Jesus Pocketbook of Nursery Rhymes. Sherman, Erin, illus. LC 80-52041. 32p. (Orig.). (ps-3). 1980. pap. 0.69 (ISBN 0-937420-00-X). Stirrup Assoc.
Fujikawa, Gyo, illus. Baby Mother Goose. LC 88-60965. 24p. (ps-1). 1989. pap. 4.95 (ISBN 0-394-89032-9). Random.
—Mother Goose. (ps-2). 1968. 7.95 (ISBN 0-448-01810-1, G&D). Putnam Pub Group.
Galdone, Paul. Cat Goes Fiddle-i-Fee. Galdone, Paul, illus. LC 85-2686. 32p. (ps-3). 1985. 12.95 (ISBN 0-89919-336-6, Clarion). Ticknor & Fields.
—Three Little Kittens. Galdone, Paul, illus. LC 86-2655. 32p. (ps-2). 1988. 13.95 (ISBN 0-89919-426-5, Pub. by Clarion); pap. 4.95 (ISBN 0-89919-796-5, Pub. by Clarion). Ticknor & Fields.
Galdone, Paul, retold by. & illus. The Gingerbread Boy. LC 74-11461. 40p. (ps-3). 1983. 13.95 (ISBN 0-395-28799-5, Clarion); pap. 4.95 (ISBN 0-89919-163-0, Clarion). HM.
Gleiter, Jan. Color Rhymes. (Illus.). 32p. (ps-3). 1986. PLB 13.31 (ISBN 0-8172-2441-6); pap. 9.27 (ISBN 0-8172-2446-7). Raintree Pubs.
—Picture Rhymes. (Illus.). 32p. (ps-3). 1986. PLB 13.31 (ISBN 0-8172-2443-2); pap. 9.27 (ISBN 0-8172-2448-3). Raintree Pubs.
—Shape Rhymes. (Illus.). 32p. (ps-3). 1986. PLB 13.31 (ISBN 0-8172-2444-0); pap. 9.27 (ISBN 0-8172-2449-1). Raintree Pubs.
Gorsline, Douglas, illus. Nursery Rhymes. LC 76-24168. (ps-2). 1977. pap. 1.95 (ISBN 0-394-83550-6, Random Juv). Random.
Graham, Terry. Let Loose on Mother Goose. LC 81-80248. (Illus.). 96p. (gr. k-1). 1982. pap. text ed. 7.95 (ISBN 0-86530-030-5, IP 30-5). Incentive Pubns.
The Green Match the Rhyme Book. (gr. 2-6). Date not set. 4.95 (ISBN 1-879332-03-5). XYZ Group.
Gregory Griggs: And Other Nursery Rhyme People. (ps-3). 1987. pap. 3.95 (ISBN 0-688-07042-6, Mulberry Bks). Macmillan.
Gutmann, Bessie P. Nursery Poems & Prayers. (Illus.). 32p. 1990. 9.95 (ISBN 0-448-23458-0, G&D). Putnam Pub Group.
Hale, Sarah J. Mary Had a Little Lamb. DePaola, Tomie, illus. 32p. (ps-3). 1984. reinforced bdg 14.95 (ISBN 0-8234-0509-5); pap. 5.95 (ISBN 0-8234-0519-2). Holiday.
—Mary Had a Little Lamb. 32p. (ps-1). 1990. 12.95 (ISBN 0-590-43773-9). Scholastic Inc.
Hall, Douglas. Douglas Hall's Nursery Rhymes. 1989. 4.98 (ISBN 0-671-07573-X). S&S Trade.
Hannant, Judith S. Doorknob Collection of Nursery Rhymes. (ps). 1991. 12.95 (ISBN 0-316-34343-9). Little.
Harrison, Michael & Stuart-Clark, Christopher, eds. The Oxford Treasury of Children's Poems. (Illus.). 174p. (gr. k up). 1988. 17.95 (ISBN 0-19-276055-6). Oxford U Pr.
Harte, Cheryl, illus. Sing a Song of Mother Goose: Yellow Ladder Books for Toddlers Through 4 Years. 16p. (ps). 1988. pap. 5.95 bk. & cassette pkg. (ISBN 0-394-89404-9, Random Juv). Random.
Hastings, Scott E., Jr. Miss Mary Mac All Dressed in Black: Tongue Twisters, Jump-Rope Rhymes, & Other Children's Lore from New England. 128p. (Orig.). 1990. pap. 8.95 (ISBN 0-87483-156-3). August Hse.
Hawkins, Colin & Hawkins, Jacqui. Old Mother Hubbard. LC 84-18333. 22p. (gr. k-2). 1985. 10.95 (ISBN 0-399-21162-4, Putnam). Putnam Pub Group.
Hayes, Sarah. Clap Your Hands: Finger Rhymes. Goffe, Toni, illus. LC 87-16958. (ps-1). 1988. 13.00 (ISBN 0-688-07692-0); lib. bdg. 12.88 (ISBN 0-688-07693-9). Lothrop.
Heller, Ruth. The Reason for a Flower. Heller, Ruth, illus. (ps-2). 1983. 8.95 (ISBN 0-448-14495-6, G&D). Putnam Pub Group.
Here We Go Round the Mulberry Bush. (Illus.). (ps-1). 3.50 (ISBN 0-7214-5137-3). Ladybird Bks.
Hoberman, Mary Ann. The Cozy Book. Chen, Tony, illus. LC 80-10916. 48p. (gr. k-3). 1982. pap. 12.95 (ISBN 0-670-24447-3). Viking Child Bks.
Hoguet, Susan R. Solomon Grundy. Hoguet, Susan R., illus. LC 85-20453. 32p. (ps-3). 1986. 13.95 (ISBN 0-525-44239-1, DCB). Dutton Child Bks.

Holmes, Martha. Time to Rhyme. (Illus.). 52p. (gr. k-1). 1990. lib. bdg. 17.95 (ISBN 0-89796-042-4). New Dimens Educ.

Hooker, Yvonne. Round in a Circle. Michelini, Carlo A., illus. (ps-1). 1983. 5.95 (ISBN 0-448-01455-6, G&D). Putnam Pub Group.

Hopkins, Lee B. Animals from Mother Goose. 1989. 6.95 (ISBN 0-15-200406-8). HarbraceJ.

—People from Mother Goose. 1989. 6.95 (ISBN 0-15-200558-7). HarbraceJ.

The House That Jack Built. (Illus.). (ps-1). 3.50 (ISBN 0-7214-0963-6). Ladybird Bks.

Howard, Nina. Barber, Barber, Shave a Pig. Rayl, Eleanor, illus. 16p. (ps-k). 1981. tchr's ed. 4.95 (ISBN 0-917206-13-4). Children Learn Ctr.

Hudak, I., ed. Sing a Song of Sixpence: English Nursery Rhymes. Degryse, L., illus. 50p. (ps-8). 1988. 13.95 (ISBN 963-13-2641-1, Pub. by Corvina Budapest). Intl Spec Bk.

Hunter, Emily. My Bedtime Nursery Rhyme Book. (Illus.). (ps-1). 1991. 11.99 (ISBN 0-89081-890-8). Harvest Hse.

Ideals Staff. Christian Bedtime Rhymes. Hook, Frances, illus. 32p. (gr. k-6). 1985. 3.95 (ISBN 0-8249-8070-0). Ideals.

Irani, Meheru. Nursery Rhymes in Meher's Time. White, Susan, illus. (gr. 3 up). 1977. pap. text ed. 5.95 (ISBN 0-913078-29-8). Sheriar Pr.

Ireson, Barbara, ed. The Faber Book of Nursery Verse. Adamson, George, illus. LC 83-1522. 286p. (ps-3). 1983. pap. 9.95 (ISBN 0-571-13079-8). Faber & Faber.

Ivimey, John W. The Complete Story of the Three Blind Mice. LC 87-689. (gr. k-3). 1987. 13.95 (ISBN 0-89919-481-8, Pub. by Clarion). Ticknor & Fields.

Izawa, Tadasu & Hijikata, Shigemi, illus. A Puppet Treasure Book of Nursery Rhymes. 96p. (ps-1). 1981. 5.95 (ISBN 0-448-12288-X, G&D). Putnam Pub Group.

Jeffers, Susan. If Wishes Were Horses: Mother Goose Rhymes. Jeffers, Susan, illus. LC 79-9986. (ps-3). 1979. 13.95 (ISBN 0-525-32531-X, DCB). Dutton Child Bks.

Johnson, Jane. A Book of Nursery Riddles. Johnson, Jane, illus. LC 84-15677. 32p. (gr. k-3). 1985. 9.95 (ISBN 0-395-37766-8). HM.

Jones, Carol, illus. Old MacDonald Had a Farm. (ps-3). 1989. 10.95 (ISBN 0-395-49212-2). HM.

Kemp, Moira, illus. Baa, Baa, Black Sheep. 10p. (ps). 1991. bds. 4.95 (ISBN 0-525-67331-8, Lodestar Bks). Dutton Child Bks.

—Hey Diddle Diddle. 10p. (ps). 1991. bds. 4.95 (ISBN 0-525-67329-6, Lodestar Bks). Dutton Child Bks.

—Hickory, Dickory, Dock. 10p. (ps). 1991. bds. 4.95 (ISBN 0-525-67328-8, Lodestar Bks). Dutton Child Bks.

—This Little Piggy. 10p. (ps). 1991. bds. 4.95 (ISBN 0-525-67326-1, Lodestar Bks). Dutton Child Bks.

Kennedy, Pamela, compiled by. Nursery Songs & Lap Games. Covell, Joan, illus. 32p. 1990. 13.95 (ISBN 0-8249-8486-2); incl. 50-min. cassette 17.95 (ISBN 0-8249-7399-2). Ideals.

Kent, Jack. Jack Kent's Book of Nursery Tales. (Illus.). (ps-1). 1970. Random.

Knapp, John, II. My Book of Bible Rhymes. Deckert, Dianne T., illus. (ps-2). 1982. 12.95 (ISBN 1-55513-161-1, 51615). Cook.

Lamont, Priscilla. Ring-a-Round-a Rosy, Nursery Rhymes, Action Rhymes & Lullabies. (ps). 1990. 15.95 (ISBN 0-316-51292-3, Joy St Bks). Little.

Landgren, Le. Old Mother Bear's Book of Hug Rhymes. Cannon, Christy, illus. LC 88-38973. 40p. (Orig.). (ps-9). 1989. pap. 6.95 (ISBN 0-943367-02-6). Princess Pub.

Launchberry, Jane. In Nursery Rhyme Land. 1988. 2.98 (ISBN 0-671-09597-8). S&S Trade.

Lehman, Patricia J. & Padzik, Alicja, eds. At Babci's Knee. Zurawiecka, Aska, tr. Knowlton, Barbara W., illus. LC 85-51371. (ENG & POL.). 165p. (Orig.). (ps). 1985. pap. 25.00 (ISBN 0-935003-01-0); cassette incl. (ISBN 0-935003-00-2). Talent Ed.

Leib, Mani. Yingl Tsingl Khvat. Lissitzky, El, illus. 32p. (ps-5). 11.95 (ISBN 0-918825-52-0); lib. bdg. 11.75x (ISBN 0-918825-54-7). Moyer Bell Limited.
The delightful nursery rhymes tell of an adventurous soul who dreams of riding off on a magic horse to find a better life, & does. A dual language book, the Yiddish facsimile of the 1991 Russian edition features startling fresh black-&-white drawings by the pre-eminent Constructivist artist, El Lisssitzky. The English version reproduces the illustrations, & is the first translation of this beloved story by the poet who sucessfully revived the Yiddish ballad. ***Publisher Provided Annotation.***

LeMair, Henriette W., illus. Little Songs of Long Ago. 64p. 1988. 13.95 (ISBN 0-399-21643-X, Philomel Bks). Putnam Pub Group.

Levy, Sara G. Mother Goose Rhymes for Jewish Children. Robinson, Jessie B., illus. (ps-2). 1979. pap. 8.95 (ISBN 0-8197-0254-4). Bloch.

Lines, Kathleen. Lavender's Blue. Jones, Harold, illus. 180p. (ps-7). 1990. pap. 10.95 (ISBN 0-19-272208-5). Oxford U Pr.

Lines, Kathleen, ed. Lavender's Blue: A Book of Nursery Rhymes. Jones, Harold, illus. 180p. 1987. 19.95 (ISBN 0-19-279537-6). Oxford U Pr.

Little Boy Blue. (Illus.). pap. 0.59 (ISBN 0-685-74083-8). Guild Bks.

Little Jack Horner. (Illus.). pap. 0.59 (ISBN 0-685-74086-2). Guild Bks.

Lobel, Arnold, selected by. & illus. The Random House Book of Mother Goose: A Treasury of 306 Timeless Nursery Rhymes. LC 86-47532. 176p. (gr. 2-6). 1986. 14.95 (ISBN 0-394-86799-8, Random Juv); lib. bdg. 14.99 (ISBN 0-394-96799-2, Random Juv). Random.

Lobel, Arnold, illus. Arnold Lobel's Little Library of Nursery Rhymes, 3 bks. (ps-1). 1990. Set, 24p. ea. slipcased 7.95 (ISBN 0-679-80660-1). Random.

Loomans, Diane, et al. Positively Mother Goose. Kramer, Linda, ed. Henrichson, Ronda, illus. LC 90-52634. 32p. 1991. 14.95 (ISBN 0-915811-24-3). H J Kramer Inc.

McCord, David. All Day Long. Kane, Henry B., illus. (gr. 5 up). 1966. 12.95 (ISBN 0-316-55508-8). Little.

Mcrae, Rodney. Who Killed Cock Robin? 1990. 13.95 (ISBN 0-385-30085-9). Doubleday.

Magos, Eunice & Hornnes, Esther. Nursery Rhymes & Numbers. Sussman, Ellen, ed. Burris, Priscilla, illus. 36p. (Orig.). (gr. k-2). 1984. pap. text ed. 4.95 (ISBN 0-933606-26-5, MS-624). Monkey Sisters.

Marcus, Leonard S. & Schwartz, Amy, eds. Mother Goose's Little Misfortunes. Schwartz, Amy, illus. LC 89-77425. 32p. 1990. 15.95 (ISBN 0-02-781431-9, Bradbury Pr). Macmillan Child Grp.

Marshall, James. James Marshall's Mother Goose. Marshall, James, illus. LC 79-2574. 40p. (ps-6). 1986. pap. 3.95 (ISBN 0-374-43723-8). FS&G.

—Old Mother Hubbard & Her Wonderful Dog. (ps-3). 1991. 13.95 (ISBN 0-374-35621-1). FS&G.

Mary Had a Little Lamb. (Illus.). pap. 0.59 (ISBN 0-685-74085-4). Guild Bks.

Mary-Mary Quite Contrary. (Illus.). pap. 0.59 (ISBN 0-685-74084-6). Guild Bks.

Mervyn Mouse. (Illus.). (ps-k). 3.50 (ISBN 0-7214-0614-9). Ladybird Bks.

Morninghouse, Sundaira. Nightfeathers: Black Goose Rhymes. Kim, Jody, illus. LC 89-63264. 32p. (gr. 1-4). 1989. 9.95 (ISBN 0-940880-27-X); pap. text ed. 4.95 (ISBN 0-940880-28-8). Open Hand.

Mother Goose Rhymes. rev. ed. 14p. (ps). 1990. write for info. (ISBN 0-307-12253-0, Golden Bks.). Western Pub.

Muldrow, Diane, selected by. My Little Book of Mother Goose Rhymes. (Illus.). 24p. (ps-k). 1989. pap. write for info. (ISBN 0-307-11756-1, Pub. by Golden Bks). Western Pub.

Mulherin, Jennifer, ed. Popular Nursery Rhymes. (Illus.). (ps-1). 1983. 8.95 (ISBN 0-448-01346-0, G&D). Putnam Pub Group.

Muppet Babies Classic Nursery Rhymes. 32p. (ps-8). 1991. 14.95 (ISBN 0-88363-691-3). H L Levin.

My Big Book of Nursery Rhymes. 1990. 7.99 (ISBN 0-517-69683-5). Outlet Bk Co.

My First Nursery Rhymes. (Illus.). 32p. (ps). 1985. 3.95 (ISBN 0-394-87687-3). Random.

Neilson, Gena. Favorite Rhymes. (Illus.). (ps-1). 1986. pap. 9.95 (ISBN 0-937763-02-0). Lauri Inc.

Nic Leodhas, Sorche. Always Room for One More. Hogrogian, Nonny, illus. LC 65-12881. 32p. (gr. k-2). 1965. reinforced bdg. 13.95 (ISBN 0-8050-0331-2); pap. 4.95 (Owlet Bk.) (ISBN 0-8050-0330-4). H Holt & Co.

Nudelman, Edward D., frwd. by. The Jessie Willcox Smith Mother Goose. enhanced ed. (Illus.). 192p. 1991. 24.95 (ISBN 0-88289-844-2); deluxe ed. 75.00 (ISBN 0-88289-830-2). Pelican.

Nursery Rhymes. (ps-k). 3.95 (ISBN 0-7214-5056-3). Ladybird Bks.

Nursery Rhymes. (Illus.). 24p. (gr. k-2). 1988. 3.95 (ISBN 0-87449-499-0). Modern Pub NYC.

Nursery Rhymes: Kiddy Big Book. (ps up). 1990. PLB 4.98 (ISBN 0-7924-5194-5, Mallard Pr). BDD Promo Bk.

Offen, Hilda, illus. My Favorite Nursery Rhymes. (ps-5). 1987. pap. 9.95 (ISBN 0-671-64705-9, Little Simon). S&S Trade.

—A Treasury of Mother Goose. (gr. 1 up). 1984. pap. 9.95 (ISBN 0-671-50118-6, Little Simon). S&S Trade.

Old King Cole. (Illus.). pap. 0.59 (ISBN 0-685-74103-6). Guild Bks.

Old MacDonald's Farm. (Illus.). (ps-1). 3.50 (ISBN 0-7214-5085-7). Ladybird Bks.

The Old Woman Who Lived in a Shoe. (Illus.). pap. 0.59 (ISBN 0-685-74082-X). Guild Bks.

One, Two, Buckle My Shoe. (Illus.). (ps-1). 1990. 3.50 (ISBN 0-7214-1265-3). Ladybird Bks.

Opie, Iona & Opie, Peter, eds. Oxford Nursery Rhyme Book. Hassall, Joan, illus. (ps-3). 1955. 29.95x (ISBN 0-19-869112-2). Oxford U Pr.

Opie, Peter & Opie, Iona, eds. Tail Feathers from Mother Goose: The Opie Rhyme Book. (Illus.). (ps up). 1988. 15.95 (ISBN 0-316-65081-1). Little.

Oxenbury, Helen, illus. Tiny Tim. Bennett, Jill, selected by. LC 81-68916. (Illus.). 32p. (ps-3). 1982. PLB 10.95 (ISBN 0-685-01402-9); pap. 10.95 (ISBN 0-385-29055-1). Delacorte.

Palmer, Michele, ed. A Mother Goose Feast: Rhymes & Recipes. LC 79-65819. (Illus.). (ps-12). 1979. pap. 1.95 (ISBN 0-932306-01-2). Rocking Horse.

Patience, J. The Land of Nursery Rhymes. (Illus.). (ps-1). 1985. 1.98 (ISBN 0-517-43878-X). Outlet Bk Co.

Pearson, Tracey C. Old MacDonald Had a Farm. Pearson, Tracey C., illus. LC 83-18815. 32p. (ps-2). 1986. pap. 4.95 (ISBN 0-8037-0274-4). Dial Bks Young.

Peppe, Rodney. First Nursery Rhymes. (Illus.). 32p. (ps up). 1988. bds. 10.95 (ISBN 0-19-520711-4). Oxford U Pr.

—The House That Jack Built. Peppe, Rodney, illus. 32p. (ps-3). 1985. pap. 4.95 (ISBN 0-385-28430-6). Delacorte.

Petersham, Maud & Petersham, Miska. The Rooster Crows. Petersham, Maud & Petersham, Miska, illus. LC 46-446. 64p. (ps-2). 1969. 13.95 (ISBN 0-02-773100-6, Mcmillan Child Bk). Macmillan Child Grp.

—The Rooster Crows: A Book of American Rhymes & Jingles. Petersham, Maud & Petersham, Miska, illus. LC 87-1138. 64p. (ps-3). 1987. pap. 4.95 (ISBN 0-689-71153-0, Aladdin). Macmillan Child Grp.

Playtime Rhymes. (Illus.). (ps). pap. 1.25 (ISBN 0-7214-9552-4). Ladybird Bks.

Pooley, Sarah. A Day of Rhymes. LC 87-3020. (Illus.). 80p. (ps-3). 1988. Knopf.

Potter, Beatrix. Appley Dapply's Nursery Rhymes. 1987. 5.95 (ISBN 0-7232-3481-7); pap. 2.25 (ISBN 0-7232-3506-6). Warne.

—Beatrix Potter's Nursery Rhyme Book. 56p. (ps-4). 1984. 10.95 (ISBN 0-7232-3254-7). Warne.

—Cecily Parsley's Nursery Rhymes. Atkinson, Allen, illus. 1983. pap. 2.25 (ISBN 0-553-15229-7). Bantam.

—Cecily Parsley's Nursery Rhymes. 1987. 5.95 (ISBN 0-7232-3482-5); pap. 2.25 (ISBN 0-7232-3507-4). Warne.

Prelutsky, Jack. The Mean Old Mean Hyena. Lobel, Arnold, illus. LC 78-2300. 32p. (gr. k-3). 1978. PLB 11.88 (ISBN 0-688-84163-5). Greenwillow.

Prelutsky, Jack, ed. Read-Aloud Rhymes for the Very Young. Brown, Marc, illus. Trelease, Jim, intro. by. LC 86-7147. (Illus.). 112p. (ps-3). 1988. bk. & cassette pkg. 19.95 (ISBN 0-394-89833-8). Knopf.

Price, S. Treasury of Nursery Stories. 1991. 9.98 (ISBN 0-7924-5493-6). BDD Promo Bk.

Provensen, Alice & Provensen, Martin, illus. Old Mother Hubbard. LC 76-24176. 32p. (ps-2). 1982. lib. bdg. 5.99 (ISBN 0-394-93460-1); pap. 1.95 saddle stitched (ISBN 0-394-83460-7). Random.

Punnett, Dick & Dunnington, Tom. Peek-a-Boo Sue. LC 84-23003. (Illus.). 32p. (gr. k-3). 1985. lib. bdg. 10.95 (ISBN 0-89565-305-2). Childs World.

Purnell. Rhyme Time Books: Humpty Dumpty. 1989. 1.98 (ISBN 0-671-09369-X). S&S Trade.

Ra, Carol F. Trot, Trot to Boston. Stock, Catherine, illus. LC 86-7354. 32p. (ps). 1987. 12.95 (ISBN 0-688-06190-7); PLB 12.88 (ISBN 0-688-06191-5). Lothrop.

Rackham, Arthur. Mother Goose, the Old Nursery Rhymes. (Illus.). (ps-6). 1978. Repr. of 1912 ed. lib. bdg. 12.00 luxury ed. (ISBN 0-932106-02-1, Pub by Marathon Pr). S J Durst.

Rao, Anthony, illus. The Highlights Book of Nursery Rhymes. LC 73-10279. 32p. (Orig.). (ps-4). 1974. text ed. 3.95 (ISBN 0-87534-771-1). Highlights.

Real Mother Goose Husky Books, 4 vols. 24p. (gr. 2-6). write for info. Vol. 1 Blue (ISBN 0-528-82424-4). Vol. 2 Yellow (ISBN 0-528-82425-2). Vol. 3 Green (ISBN 0-528-82435-X). Vol. 4 Red (ISBN 0-528-82436-8). Checkerboard Pr.

Reid, Barbara, illus. Sing a Song of Mother Goose. (ps-1). 1989. pap. 8.95 (ISBN 0-590-41698-7). Scholastic Inc.

Rhyming Rabbit. 1989. text ed. 3.95 cased (ISBN 0-7214-5232-9). Ladybird Bks.

Rojankovsky, Feodor. Tall Book of Mother Goose. Rojankovsky, Feodor, illus. (ps-1). 1942. 7.95i (ISBN 0-06-025055-0). HarpC Child Bks.

Rosenberg, Amye & Chamberlain, Margaret, illus. My Book of Bedtime Rhymes. (ps-2). 3.95 (ISBN 0-7214-5108-X). Ladybird Bks.

—My Book of Nursery Rhymes. (ps-2). 3.95 (ISBN 0-7214-5105-5). Ladybird Bks.

—My Book of Playtime Rhymes. (ps-2). 3.95 (ISBN 0-7214-5107-1). Ladybird Bks.

Rossetti, Christina G. Sing Song: A Nursery Rhyme Book. Hughes, Arthur, illus. LC 68-55822. x, 130p. (gr. 3-7). 1969. pap. 4.50 (ISBN 0-486-22107-5). Dover.

Scarry, Richard. Richard Scarry's Mother Goose Scratch & Sniff Book. (Illus.). 32p. (ps-2). 1989. write for info. (ISBN 0-307-13543-8, Pub. by Golden Bks). Western Pub.

Schenk de Regniers, Beatrice. It Does Not Say Meow & Other Animal Riddle Rhymes. LC 72-75704. 40p. (gr. k-3). 1983. pap. 4.95 (ISBN 0-89919-043-X, Clarion). HM.

Schwartz, Alvin. I Saw You in the Bathtub: And Other Folk Rhymes. Hoff, Syd, illus. LC 88-16111. 64p. (ps-2). 1991. pap. 3.50 (ISBN 0-06-444151-2, Trophy). HarpC Child Bks.

Scott, Louise B. Rhymes for Learning Times. LC 82-73392. 145p. (Orig.). (ps). 1984. pap. 15.95 (ISBN 0-513-01763-1). Denison.

Sendak, Maurice. Hector Protector & As I Went over the Water: Two Nursery Rhymes. Sendak, Maurice, illus. LC 65-21388. 64p. (ps-1). 1990. pap. 5.95 (ISBN 0-06-443237-8, Trophy). HarpC Child Bks.

Seven Little Hippos. 1991. pap. 13.95 (ISBN 0-671-72964-0). S&S Trade.

Sharon, et al. Sharon, Lois & Bram's Mother Goose Songs, Finger Rhymes, Tickling Verses, Games & More. Kovalski, Mary A., illus. 92p. (ps-2). 1986. 16.95i (ISBN 0-316-78281-5, 782815); pap. 9.95i (ISBN 0-316-78282-3). Little.

Sharon, Lois & Bram Staff. Sharon, Lois & Bram's Mother Goose: Songs, Finger Rhymes, Tickling Verses, Games & More. Kovalski, Mary A., illus. LC 85-48024. 92p. (ps-2). 1986. 16.95 (ISBN 0-685-11909-2); pap. 8.70 (ISBN 0-685-11910-6). Atlantic Monthly.

Sharpe, Caroline, et al, illus. Rhyme Readers One to Eight, 8 bks. (ps-1). 1986. Set. pap. text ed. 18.80 (ISBN 1-55624-001-5). Wright Group.

Sieveking, Anthea. Mary Had a Little Lamb & Other Animal Rhymes. (ps-3). 1991. bds. 5.95 (ISBN 0-8120-6217-5). Barron.

Sieveking, Anthea, illus. Polly Put the Kettle on & Other Play Rhymes. 12p. (ps-3). 1991. bds. 5.95 (ISBN 0-8120-6218-3). Barron.

—Rub a Dub Dub & Other Water Rhymes. 12p. (ps-3). 1991. bds. 5.95 (ISBN 0-8120-6219-1). Barron.

—Twinkle, Twinkle, Little Star & Other Bedtime Rhymes. 12p. (ps-3). 1991. bds. 5.95 (ISBN 0-8120-6220-5). Barron.

Sing or Say Best Loved Nursery Rhymes. 1990. 5.98 (ISBN 0-8317-7810-5). Smithmark.

Smith, Beverly J. Long & Short of Mother Goose Set. Kempster, Teddy, ed. Holtman, Noelle M., illus. (Orig.). (gr. 2-4). 1989. pap. text ed. 4.95 (ISBN 0-88336-983-4). New Readers.

Smoke & Fluff. (Illus.). (ps-k). 3.50 (ISBN 0-7214-0208-9). Ladybird Bks.

Smollin, Michael J., illus. The Sesame Street Players Present Mother Goose. LC 81-52979. 32p. (ps-1). 1982. Random.

Spier, Peter. To Market, to Market. Spier, Peter, illus. LC 67-18664. 52p. (gr. 1-3). 1967. 8.95a (ISBN 0-385-08755-1); pap. 5.95 (ISBN 0-385-09081-1). Doubleday.

Stevens, Janet, illus. The House That Jack Built: A Mother Goose Nursery Rhyme. LC 84-15832. 32p. (ps-2). 1985. PLB 14.95 (ISBN 0-8234-0548-6). Holiday.

Stories & Rhymes for under Fives. 1990. 7.99 (ISBN 0-517-69420-4). Outlet Bk Co.

Stryker & Bingham. Mother Nature Nursery Rhymes. Paine, ed. Itoko Maeno, illus. 32p. (ps-6). 1990. PLB 14.95 (ISBN 0-911655-01-8). Advocacy Pr.

Swan, Frances M. Once upon a Rhyme. Criscuolo, Edna, illus. 48p. 1984. pap. 2.00 (ISBN 0-9602126-2-0). F M Swan.

Szekeres, Cyndy, selected by. & illus. Cyndy Szekeres' Mother Goose Rhymes. LC 86-81596. 48p. (ps-3). 1987. write for info. (ISBN 0-307-15560-9, Pub. by Golden Bks). Western Pub.

Tarrant. Nursery Rhymes & Fairy Tales. 1984. 5.98 (ISBN 0-671-06535-1). S&S Trade.

Tate, Carole. Rhymes & Ballads of London. LC 72-90691. (Illus.). 32p. (gr. k-4). 1973. 6.95 (ISBN 0-87592-042-X). Scroll Pr.

There Was an Old Woman Who Swallowed a Fly. (Illus.). (ps-1). 1990. 3.50 (ISBN 0-7214-1266-1). Ladybird Bks.

Thumbelina. 1989. 2.98 (ISBN 0-517-69214-7). Outlet Bk Co.

Underhill, Liz. One, Two, Tie Up My Shoe: A New Look at an Old Nursery Rhyme. Underhill, Liz, illus. LC 89-28587. 32p. 1990. PLB 12.95 (ISBN 1-55670-142-X). Stewart Tabori & Chang.

Uttley, Alison. Ten Candelight Tales. Hawkins, Irene, illus. 112p. (gr. k-2). 1991. pap. 3.95 (ISBN 0-571-14289-3). Faber & Faber.

Warlow, Aidan, ed. Start with Rhymes, Nos. 1-6: The Grand Old Duke of York; Humpty Dumpty; Bed Time; Fishing; Three Blind Mice & Jack & Jill, 6 bks. Smith, Lesley, et al, illus. 48p. (gr. k-1). 1988. Set. pap. text ed. 29.60 (ISBN 1-55624-517-3). Wright Group.

—Start with Rhymes, Nos. 7-12: Little Miss Muffett; Baa Baa Black Sheep; 1, 2 Buckle My Shoe; Rain; In a Dark Dark Wood & Round the Moon, 6 bks. Smith, Lesley, et al, illus. 48p. (Orig.). (gr. k-1). 1988. Set. pap. text ed. 29.60 (ISBN 1-55624-518-1). Wright Group.

Wasmuth, Eleanor, illus. Jack & Jill. (ps). 1986. 2.95 (ISBN 0-671-61729-X, Little Simon). S&S Trade.

—The Old Woman in a Shoe. (ps). 1986. 2.95 (ISBN 0-671-61728-1, Little Simon). S&S Trade.

Watson, Clyde. Catch Me & Kiss Me & Say It Again. Watson, Wendy, illus. LC 78-17644. 64p. (gr. 1-12). 1983. 10.95 (ISBN 0-399-20948-4, Philomel); pap. 5.95 (ISBN 0-399-20954-9). Putnam Pub Group.

—Father Fox's Pennyrhymes. reissued ed. Watson, Wendy, illus. LC 71-146291. 64p. (gr. k-3). 1971. 13.95 (ISBN 0-690-29213-9, Crowell Jr Bks); PLB 13.89 (ISBN 0-690-29214-7, Crowell Jr Bks). HarpC Child Bks.

Weinburg, Larry. Guess a Rhyme: Poems to Complete! Riddles to Solve! McKie, Roy, illus. LC 81-15689. 32p. (gr. 1-4). 1982. pap. 2.25 (ISBN 0-394-85062-9). Random.

Westcott, Nadine B. House That Jack Built: Pop-up, Pull-tab, Playtime Book. (ps-3). 1991. 14.95 (ISBN 0-316-93138-1). Little.

Westcott, Nadine B., illus. Peanut Butter & Jelly: A Play Rhyme. LC 86-32889. (gr. 4-7). 1987. 11.95 (ISBN 0-525-44317-7, DCB). Dutton Child Bks.

Wiggin, Kate D., et al, eds. Pinafore Palace: A Book of Rhymes for the Nursery. LC 72-8290. (ps-1). Repr. of 1907 ed. 21.00 (ISBN 0-8369-6399-7). Ayer Co Pubs.

Wildsmith, Brian. Cat on the Mat. (Illus.). 16p. 1987. pap. 2.95 (ISBN 0-19-272123-2). Oxford U Pr.

—Mother Goose: Nursery Rhymes. (Illus.). 80p. (ps up). 1987. 14.95 (ISBN 0-19-279611-9); pap. 8.95 (ISBN 0-19-272180-1). Oxford U Pr.

Wilkin, Eloise, illus. Nursery Rhymes. LC 78-64606. (ps). 1979. bds. 3.95 (ISBN 0-394-84129-8, Random Juv). Random.

—Rock-a-Bye Baby. LC 84-60029. (ps up). 1984. 5.95 (ISBN 0-394-86798-X, Pub. by BYR). Random.

Williams, Barbara L. Barbara Lee's Nursery Rhymes & Poems for Young Children. 1990. 6.95 (ISBN 0-533-08985-9). Vantage.

Williams, Jenny, illus. Ride a Cockhorse: Animal Rhymes. LC 86-19844. (ps-1). 1987. 3.95 (ISBN 0-8037-0389-9). Dial Bks Young.

Withers, Carl. Eenie-Meenie-Minie-Mo & Other Counting-Out Rhymes. Ripley, Elizabeth, illus. 44p. (ps up). 1970. pap. 2.50 (ISBN 0-486-22414-7). Dover.

Wood, Jenny. First Songs & Action Rhymes. McEwan, Chris, illus. LC 90-44773. 64p. (ps-k). 1991. bds. 6.95 POB (ISBN 0-689-71472-6, Aladdin). Macmillan Child Grp.

Wright, Blanche F., illus. The Real Mother Goose, 4 bks. 96p. (ps-2). Set Incl. cassettes. pap. 14.98 (ISBN 1-55886-018-5). Smarty Pants.

—The Real Mother Goose, Vol. I. 24p. (ps-2). Incl. cassettes. pap. 4.98 (ISBN 1-55886-012-6). Smarty Pants.

—The Real Mother Goose, Vol. II. 24p. (ps-2). Incl. cassettes. pap. 4.98 (ISBN 1-55886-013-4). Smarty Pants.

—The Real Mother Goose, Vol. III. 24p. (ps-2). Incl. cassettes. pap. 4.98 (ISBN 1-55886-014-2). Smarty Pants.

—The Real Mother Goose, Vol. IV. 24p. (ps-2). Incl. cassettes. pap. 4.98 (ISBN 1-55886-015-0). Smarty Pants.

Wyndham, Robert. Chinese Mother Goose Rhymes. Young, Ed, illus. 48p. (ps-k). 1989. pap. 5.95 (ISBN 0-399-21718-5, Pub. by Sandcastle Bks). Putnam Pub Group.

Wyndham, Robert, selected by. Chinese Mother Goose Rhymes. Young, Ed, illus. (ps-k). 1989. 14.95 (ISBN 0-685-36240-X, Philomel Bks). Putnam Pub Group.

Zaslow, David B. & Inada, Lawson F. Hey Diddle Rock. Bullock, Kathleen, illus. 32p. (Orig.). (ps-8). 1986. pap. 7.95 (ISBN 0-89411-006-3). Kids Matter.

—Humpty Dumpty Rock. Bullock, Kathleen, illus. 32p. (Orig.). (ps-8). 1986. pap. 7.95 (ISBN 0-89411-007-1). Kids Matter.

—Rock-a-Doodle-Doo. Bullock, Kathleen, illus. 32p. (Orig.). (ps-8). 1986. pap. 7.95 (ISBN 0-89411-005-5). Kids Matter.

Zokeisha. Mother Goose House. Klimo, Kate, ed. Zokeisha, illus. 16p. (ps-k). 1983. 2.95 (ISBN 0-671-46127-3, Little Simon). S&S Trade.

NURSERY RHYMES–DICTIONARIES

Magos, Eunice & Hornnes, Esther. Nursery Rhymes & Numbers. Sussman, Ellen, ed. Burris, Priscilla, illus. 36p. (Orig.). (gr. k-2). 1984. pap. text ed. 4.95 (ISBN 0-933606-26-5, MS-624). Monkey Sisters.

Opie, Iona & Opie, Peter, eds. Oxford Dictionary of Nursery Rhymes. (Illus.). (ps-3). 1951. 47.50x (ISBN 0-19-869111-4). Oxford U Pr.

NURSERY SCHOOLS

see also Kindergarten

Brown, Jerome C. Mother Goose PaperCrafts. (gr. k-5). 1989. pap. 7.95 (ISBN 0-8224-3154-8). Fearon Teach Aids.

Isaak, Betty. Sequencing Seal. Armstrong, Bev, illus. 24p. (ps). 1982. wkbk. 2.95 (ISBN 0-88160-090-3, LW 124). Learning Wks.

Lamarche, Beth A. Classification: Preschool - Kindergarten. Rittenour, Gary, illus. 64p. (Orig.). (ps-k). 1987. pap. text ed. 4.95 (ISBN 0-88724-242-1, CO-0938). Carson-Dellos.

Rogers, Fred. Going to Day Care. LC 84-24940. (Illus.). 32p. (gr. k-2). 1985. 12.95 (ISBN 0-399-21235-3, Putnam); pap. 5.95 (ISBN 0-399-21237-X, Putnam). Putnam Pub Group.

Twinn, Michael, illus. I Go to Nursery School. 8p. (ps-2). 1977. 2.00 (ISBN 0-85953-070-1, Pub. by Child's Play England). Childs Play.

Tyler, Sydney B. Young Think Program Two. 90p. (Orig.). (gr. k-1). 1988. pap. text ed. 25.00 report cover (ISBN 0-912781-13-0). Thomas Geale.

NURSERY SCHOOLS–FICTION

Breinburg, Petronella. Shawn Goes to School. Lloyd, Errol, illus. LC 73-8003. 32p. (ps-2). 1974. PLB 14.89 (ISBN 0-690-00277-7, Crowell Jr Bks). HarpC Child Bks.

Lewis, Shari. Baby Lamb Chop Loves Nursery School. Beylon, Cathy, illus. 12p. (ps-k). 1991. bds. 3.95 (ISBN 0-679-81725-5). Random.

Radlauer, Ruth S. Molly. McCully, Emily A., illus. (ps-2). 1987. 10.95 (ISBN 0-13-599762-3). P-H.

Rockwell, Harlow. My Nursery School. 32p. (ps). 1984. pap. 3.95 (ISBN 0-14-050478-8, Puffin). Puffin Bks.

Wolde, Gunilla. Betsy's First Day at Nursery School. LC 76-9322. (Illus.). (ps-k). 1982. 1.95 (ISBN 0-394-85381-4, Random Juv); lib. bdg. 4.99 (ISBN 0-394-95381-9). Random.

NURSES AND NURSING

see also Children–Care and Hygiene; First Aid; Hospitals

Bauer, Judith. What's It Like to Be a Nurse. Pellaton, Karen E., illus. LC 89-34387. 32p. (gr. k-3). 1989. lib. bdg. 10.89 (ISBN 0-8167-1809-1); pap. text ed. 2.50 (ISBN 0-8167-1810-5). Troll Assocs.

Behrens, June. I Can Be a Nurse. LC 85-29086. (Illus.). 32p. (gr. k-3). 1986. PLB 13.93 (ISBN 0-516-01893-0); pap. 3.95 (ISBN 0-516-41893-9). Childrens.

Collins, David. Florence Nightingale. (gr. 3-6). 1985. pap. 6.95 (ISBN 0-88062-126-5). Mott Media.

Cosner, Shaaron. War Nurses. (gr. 7 up). 1988. 16.95 (ISBN 0-8027-6826-1); 17.85 (ISBN 0-8027-6828-8). Walker & Co.

Everygirls Nurse Stories. (gr. 6-10). PLB 6.70 (ISBN 0-8313-0054-X). Lantern.

Heron, Jackie. Exploring Careers in Nursing. rev. ed. 144p. (gr. 7-12). 1990. 12.95 (ISBN 0-8239-1136-5). Rosen Group.

Seide, Diane. Nurse Power: New Vistas in Nursing. LC 85-15851. 128p. (gr. 7 up). 1986. 12.95 (ISBN 0-525-67173-0, Lodestar Bks). Dutton Child Bks.

Witty, Margot. A Day in the Life of an Emergency Room Nurse. Lewis, Sarah, photos by. LC 78-68842. (Illus.). 32p. (gr. 4-8). 1980. PLB 11.79 (ISBN 0-89375-226-6); pap. 2.95 (ISBN 0-89375-230-4); cassettes avail. Troll Assocs.

NURSES AND NURSING–FICTION

Barrett, Marsha. Servant with a Smile. Swain, John & Stevens, Bill, photos by. (Illus.). 40p. (Orig.). (gr. 1-3). 1985. pap. 2.00 (ISBN 0-317-18029-0). Home Mission.

Belloc, Hilaire. Jim, Who Ran Away from His Nurse, & Was Eaten by a Lion. Chess, Victoria, illus. (gr. 2 up). 1987. 12.95 (ISBN 0-316-13815-0); pap. 4.95 (ISBN 0-316-13816-9). Little.

Ellis, Joyce. Tiffany. LC 86-70910. 160p. (Orig.). (gr. 9-12). 1986. pap. 3.95 (ISBN 0-87123-893-4). Bethany Hse.

Newell, Hope. Cap for Mary Ellis. LC 53-8547. (gr. 7 up). 1953. PLB 12.89 (ISBN 0-06-024526-3). HarpC Child Bks.

NURSING

see Nurses and Nursing

NUTRITION

see also Diet; Digestion; Food; Metabolism; Vitamins

Adams, Marylou. Brighten up at Breakfast: Helpful Tips for Heavenly Bodies. Adams, Marylou, illus. LC 81-51601. 120p. (gr. 2-7). 1981. plastic comb 7.95 (ISBN 0-9606248-0-5). Starbright.

American Health Foundation Staff. Great Meals, Great Snacks, Great Kids. 1990. pap. 4.95 (ISBN 0-590-43382-2). Scholastic Inc.

Austin, Trina K. All Aboard the S. S. Nutrient. (Illus.). 26p. (Orig.). (gr. k-4). 1986. pap. 6.50 (ISBN 0-9615840-0-9). Trinas Pr.

Bailey, Donna. Energy for Our Bodies. LC 90-39295. (Illus.). 48p. (gr. 2-5). 1990. PLB 15.96 (ISBN 0-8114-2521-5). Steck-V.

Berry, Joy. Every Kid's Guide to Nutrition & Health Care. Batholomew, illus. 48p. (gr. 3-7). 1987. 4.95 (ISBN 0-516-21413-6); PLB 14.60 (ISBN 0-516-01413-7). Childrens.

Carratello, Patricia. Food & Nutrition. Carratello, Patricia, illus. 38p. (gr. 1-4). 1980. wkbk. 5.95 (ISBN 1-55734-212-1). Tchr Create Mat.

Carratello, Patty. Nutrition & Me. Wright, Theresa, illus. 48p. (gr. 1-5). 1987. wkbk. 5.95 (ISBN 1-55734-222-9). Tchr Create Mat.

Epstein, Rachel. Eating Habits & Disorders. (Illus.). (gr. 6-12). 1990. 18.95 (ISBN 0-7910-0048-6). Chelsea Hse.

Food & Digestion. 48p. (gr. 5-8). 1988. PLB 12.98 (ISBN 0-382-09704-1); 9.74s.p. (ISBN 0-685-24612-4). Silver Burdett Pr.

Galperin, Anne. Nutrition. (Illus.). (gr. 5 up). 1991. 18.95 (ISBN 0-7910-0024-9). Chelsea Hse.

Greenbaum, David & Wasser, Edward. My First Health & Nutrition Coloring Book: Mr. Carrots Coloring Book. Puglisi, Lou, illus. 40p. (Orig.). (gr. 2). 1988. pap. 0.99 (ISBN 0-9621833-0-X). D Greenbaum.

Hamm, Anita M. Lisa in Sugarland, a Child's Book on Nutrition to Be Digested Before Eating. (gr. 1-4). 1978. 3.50x (ISBN 0-935513-02-7). Samara Pubns.

Isphording, Julie. Food Fun For Kids: A Recipe Coloring Book. Wolterman, Jan, ed. (Illus.). 48p. (gr. 1-6). 1991. pap. 6.95 spiral bdg. (ISBN 0-9629589-0-5). Kids Kitchen.
An entertaining & educational cookbook for children filled with nourishing adventures. Authored by Julie Isphording, one of America's favorite women marathoners, FOOD FUN FOR KIDS portrays fruit, vegetable, & whole grains as they grow using food caricatures & features

delicious recipes high in fiber, low in fat & all sugar-free. Designed for children ages 5 to 10, FOOD FUN FOR KIDS' 48 pages are filled with funny food friend recipes, Foodles, jokes, funny food-facts & puzzles. Blank placemats, with a food alphabet border, are included for children to draw or paint. These placemats can be laminated & used at dinnertime with the family or given as gifts to grandparents & teachers. FOOD FUN FOR KIDS is the answer to that age old question every parent asks, "How can we get our children to eat what's good for them?" FOOD FUN FOR KIDS measures 8 1/2" by 11" with red spiral binding.
Publisher Provided Annotation.

Jacobson, Michael & Hill, Laura. Kitchen Fun for Kids: Healthy Recipes & Nutrition Facts for 7-12 Year Old Cooks. 128p. (gr. 2-7). 1991. 12.95 (ISBN 0-8050-1609-0). H Holt & Co.

Jacobson, Michael F., et al. Safe Food: Eating Wisely in a Risky World. (Illus.). 252p. (Orig.). 1991. pap. 9.95 (ISBN 1-879326-01-9). Living Planet Pr.

Jennings, Terry. Food. LC 88-22866. (Illus.). 32p. (gr. 3-6). 1989. PLB 14.60 (ISBN 0-516-08402-X); pap. 4.95 (ISBN 0-516-48402-8). Childrens.

Lee, Sally. New Theories on Diet & Nutrition. 1990. PLB 13.40 (ISBN 0-531-10930-5). Watts.

LeMaster, Leslie J. Nutrition. LC 85-7728. (Illus.). 45p. (gr. k-3). 1985. PLB 14.60 (ISBN 0-516-01271-1); pap. 4.95 (ISBN 0-516-41271-X). Childrens.

Marbach, Ellen S., et al. Nutrition in a Changing World: A Curriculum for Primary Level. LC 79-11776. (Illus., Orig.). (gr. 1-3). 1979. pap. 8.95 (ISBN 0-8425-1660-3). Brigham.

Moncure, Jane B. The Healthkin Food Train. Endres, Helen, illus. LC 82-14710. 32p. (ps-2). 1982. lib. bdg. 10.95 (ISBN 0-89565-240-4). Childs World.

Montgomery, Paul J. Nutritional Analysis of Ready-to-Eat Cereal. rev. ed. 274p. (gr. 7 up). 1989. pap. text ed. 19.95 (ISBN 0-9621865-0-3). Prod Info Analysis.

—Nutritional Cereal Counter. (Illus.). 92p. (Orig.). (gr. 9 up). 1989. pap. 2.95 (ISBN 0-9621865-1-1). Prod Info Analysis.

Neff, Fred. Keeping Fit Handbook for Physical Conditioning & Better Health. Reid, James, illus. LC 75-38478. 56p. (gr. 5 up). 1977. PLB 8.95 (ISBN 0-8225-1157-6). Lerner Pubns.

O'Connell, Lily H., et al. Nutrition in a Changing World: Grade Five. (Illus.). 152p. (Orig.). (gr. 5). 1981. pap. text ed. 11.95 (ISBN 0-8425-1916-5). Brigham.

Orlandi, Mario, et al. Nutrition. (Illus.). 128p. 1988. 18.95x (ISBN 0-8160-1670-4). Facts on File.

Parker, Steve. Eating a Meal: How You Eat, Drink & Digest. (Illus.). 32p. (gr. k-4). 1991. PLB 11.40 (ISBN 0-531-14086-5). Watts.

Peavy, Linda & Smith, Ursula. Food, Nutrition, & You. LC 82-5694. (Illus.). 192p. (gr. 6 up). 1982. 13.95 (ISBN 0-684-17461-8, Scribners Young Read). Macmillan Child Grp.

Rhodes, Janis. Nutrition Mission. 48p. (ps-2). 1982. 5.95 (ISBN 0-86653-092-4, GA 443). Good Apple.

Rosenthal, Etta. Nutrition Expedition. 48p. (gr. 4-6). 1980. 5.95 (ISBN 0-88160-036-9, LW 221). Learning Wks.

Roth, Geneen. Breaking Free from Compulsive Eating. 256p. (gr. 9-12). Date not set. pap. 4.50 (ISBN 0-451-15439-8, Sig). NAL-Dutton.

—Feeding the Hungry Heart: The Experience of Compulsive Eating. 224p. (gr. 9-12). Date not set. pap. 4.50 (ISBN 0-451-15825-3, Sig). NAL-Dutton.

Salter, Charles A. Looking Good, Eating Right: A Sensible Guide to Proper Nutrition & Weight Loss for Teens. (Illus.). 144p. (gr. 7 up). 1991. PLB 13.90 (ISBN 1-56294-047-3). Millbrook Pr.

—The Vegetarian Teen. (Illus.). 112p. (gr. 7 up). 1991. PLB 13.90 (ISBN 1-56294-048-1). Millbrook Pr.

Sanders, Pete. Food & Hygiene. (Illus.). 32p. (gr. 2-5). 1990. PLB 10.40 (ISBN 0-531-17243-0). Watts.

Seixas, Judith S. Junk Food--What It Is, What It Does. Huffman, Tom, illus. LC 83-14135. 48p. (gr. 1-3). 1984. 12.95 (ISBN 0-688-02559-5); PLB 12.88 (ISBN 0-688-02560-9). Greenwillow.

Singer, Marcia. Eating for a Fresh Start: A P.L.A.Y. Book. Rendal, Camille, illus. LC 90-91969. 64p. (Orig.). (gr. 1-7). 1990. pap. write for info. (ISBN 0-9622543-1-2). PLAY House.
A family guide to beginning vegetarianism & ecologically sound eating habits. Easy to follow help with sprouting, food combining, good digestion practices & yummy recipes.

Features scientific definitions, charming illustrations, activities, "rap" style verse. Promotes physical, mental & emotional health. "Sorely needed as an educational tool."-- Malibu Action For Safe Food. "Helpful introduction to healthful, planet-healing cuisine."-- Michael Klaper, M.D., EarthSave. "Balances sound nutritional principles with games & activities.--Marilyn Diamond, Fit For Life. "Helps children be more aware & healthy."--John Robbins, Diet For A New America. "I particularly like the drawings & simple recipes."--Kim Fella, Pres. Peace Child Foundation. "Pictures, recipes, poetry, hard facts for kids who like food."-- Carolyn Rueben, LA Weekly "Excellent intro to healthy eating habits for any kid or parent."--Garbage Magazine. "On our reference list for school health coordinators."--Susan Lordi, LA County Office of Education. "Also creates awareness about animal rights, environmental concerns."-- Vegetarian Society of So. CA. "Nice beginner's guide."--Gabriel Cousens, M.D., Spiritual Nutrition. "Promotes dieting practices uniquely."--Sandra French, LB Unified School District. "Magically creative teaching tool."-- Kathy Arnos, Mother-to-Mother newsletter.
Publisher Provided Annotation.

Tatchell, J. & Fraser, K. Food Fitness & Health. (Illus.). 96p. (gr. 6-10). 1987. 10.95 (ISBN 0-7460-0079-0). EDC.

Tatchell, J. & Wells, D. You & Your Food: Understanding Nutrition, Calories, Vitamins & the Things You Eat. (Illus.). 48p. (gr. 6-10). 1986. PLB 13.96 (ISBN 0-88110-222-9); pap. 6.95 (ISBN 0-86020-939-3). EDC.

Thompson, Paul. Nutrition. 72p. (gr. 4-8). 1981. lib. bdg. 10.40 (ISBN 0-531-04328-2). Watts.

Thornton, Claire & Cambruzzi, Doris. Learning with ABC's: Fruits & Vegetables to Grow On. Arthur, Lorraine, illus. 32p. (gr. 2-7). 1986. casebound 4.95 (ISBN 0-87403-127-3, 3607). Standard Pub.

—Learning with Colors: Meat to Grow On. Arthur, Lorraine, illus. 32p. (gr. 2-7). 1986. casebound 4.95 (ISBN 0-87403-128-1, 3608). Standard Pub.

—Learning with Numbers: Bread & Cereal to Grow On. Arthur, Lorraine, illus. 32p. (gr. 2-7). 1986. casebound 4.95 (ISBN 0-87403-129-X, 3609). Standard Pub.

—Learning with Shapes: Milk to Grow On. Arthur, Lorraine, illus. 32p. (gr. 2-7). 1986. casebound 4.95 (ISBN 0-87403-130-3, 3610). Standard Pub.

Ward, Brian. Diet: And Health. LC 90-31200. (Illus.). 32p. 1991. PLB 11.40 (ISBN 0-531-14095-4). Watts.

Ward, Brian R. Diet & Nutrition. (Illus.). 48p. (gr. 4-12). 1987. PLB 12.40 (ISBN 0-531-10259-9). Watts.

O

OAK
Hogan, Paula Z. The Oak Tree. LC 78-21183. (Illus.). 32p. (gr. 1-4). 1979. PLB 16.67 (ISBN 0-8172-1251-5). Raintree Pubs.

—The Oak Tree. LC 78-21183. (Illus.). 32p. (gr. 1-4). 1984. PLB 27.99 incl. cassette (ISBN 0-8172-2230-8); cassette 14.00 (ISBN 0-685-09510-X). Raintree Pubs.

OAKLEY, ANNIE, 1860-1926
Annie Oakley. (Illus.). (gr. 2-5). 1989. 27.99 (ISBN 0-8172-2955-8). Raintree Pubs.

Gleiter, Jan & Thompson, Kathleen. Annie Oakley. Miyake, Yoshi, illus. 32p. (gr. 2-5). 1986. PLB 16.67 (ISBN 0-8172-2641-9). Raintree Pubs.

Levine, Ellen. Ready, Aim, Fire! The Real Adventures of Annie Oakley. (gr. 5-7). 1989. pap. 2.75 (ISBN 0-590-41877-7). Scholastic Inc.

Wilson, Ellen. Annie Oakley. (Illus.). 192p. (gr. 2-6). 1989. pap. 3.95 (ISBN 0-689-71346-0, Aladdin). Macmillan Child Grp.

OBESITY
see Weight Control
OBSCENITY (LAW)--FICTION
Martin, Katherine. Night Riding. LC 89-2711. 208p. 1989. 12.95 (ISBN 0-679-80064-6); PLB 13.99 (ISBN 0-679-90064-0). Knopf.

OBSERVATORIES, ASTRONOMICAL
see Astronomical Observatories

OBSTETRICS
see Childbirth
OCCULT SCIENCES
see also Astrology; Divination; Fortune Telling; Magic; Superstition; Witchcraft
Berger, Melvin. The Supernatural: From ESP to UFO's. LC 77-2829. (gr. 6 up). 1977. 12.95 (ISBN 0-354-17625-0, Crowell Jr Bks). HarpC Child Bks.

Duncan, David. Strange but True: Twenty-Two Amazing Stories. (gr. 4-6). 1974. pap. 2.25 (ISBN 0-590-03528-2, Schol Pap). Scholastic Inc.

Herbst, Judith. Bio Amazing: A Casebook of Unsolved Human Mysteries. LC 85-7446. 156p. (gr. 5 up). 1985. 12.95 (ISBN 0-689-31151-6, Atheneum Child Bk). Macmillan Child Grp.

Hunt, Roderick. Ghosts, Witches & Things Like That. 144p. 1990. pap. 10.95 (ISBN 0-19-278130-8). Oxford U Pr.

Matthews, Rupert. The Supernatural. Dennis, Peter, illus. LC 89-886. 48p. (gr. 4-6). 1989. PLB 12.40 (ISBN 0-531-18289-4). Watts.

Singer, Marcia. Crystal Kids: PLAYBook. Rendal, Camille, illus. LC 89-90988. 64p. (Orig.). 1989. pap. 9.95 (ISBN 0-9622543-0-4). PLAY House.
Metaphysics, meditations, creative healing arts & crystal fun for beginners of all ages. Softcover feast of enchanting, colorable illustrations, storyline, songs & "eduP.L.A.Y.tional" activities. Stimulates creativity, self-esteem & imagination skills. Enhances parent-child communications too. Experts recommend it as a year round gift for children & parents to share: "We need more books like this."--Terry Cole-Whittaker. "Wonderful fun tool introducing the world of crystals... topics covered in loving detail."-- newsletter Psychic Research Institute (Marcel Vogel). "Every page is a multifacted lesson/game...creative experience, delightfully endearing artwork."--Lee Perry, Whole Life Times. "My son enjoyed it."--Katrina Raphaell, Crystal Healing. "A light, joyful experience."--Frank Alper, D.D., Pres. AZ Metaphysical Society. "Fills hole in contemporary literature for children."--Wabun Wind, Lightseeds. "Healthful, helpful, positive, loving tool."--United Sensitive of America. "Inspiring, refreshing for all ages."-- Kenny Kingston, Psychic to the Stars. "Delightful drawings, charming & informative text."--Laiura Wilson, (Louise) Hay House "Wondrous journey for the child in us all."-- Richard Hatch, "ALL MY CHILDREN" (TV). "Expansive, not violent or condescending...I was tempted to get out my crayons & do a little doodling myself!"--Terry Sweeney, ex "Saturday Night Live" (TV). "Great pictures, songs, pretend games with crystals."--Lezli Censullo, Alternatives Newsletter.
Publisher Provided Annotation.

Wilcox, Tamara. Mysterious Detectives: Psychics. LC 77-14315. (Illus.). 48p. (gr. 4 up). 1983. PLB 17.32 (ISBN 0-8172-1061-X); pap. 9.27 (ISBN 0-8172-2162-X). Raintree Pubs.

OCCULT SCIENCES--FICTION
Ames, Mildred. Conjuring Summer In. LC 85-45821. 224p. (gr. 7 up). 1986. 12.95 (ISBN 0-06-020053-7); PLB 12.89 (ISBN 0-06-020054-5). HarpC Child Bks.

Bellairs, John. The Figure in the Shadows. Mayer, Mercer, illus. LC 74-2885. 168p. (gr. 4-7). 1975. PLB 13.89 (ISBN 0-8037-4917-1). Dial Bks Young.

—The House with a Clock in Its Walls. LC 72-7600. (Illus.). 192p. (gr. 4-7). 1984. 13.95 (ISBN 0-8037-3821-8); PLB 13.89 (ISBN 0-8037-3823-4). Dial Bks Young.

DeFelice, Cynthia C. The Strange Night Writing of Jessamine Colter. LC 88-4325. 56p. (gr. 5 up). 1988. 11.95 (ISBN 0-02-726451-3, Mcmillan Child Bk). Macmillan Child Grp.

Gifaldi, David. Yours Till Forever. LC 88-35725. 96p. (gr. 7 up). 1989. 11.95 (ISBN 0-397-32355-7, Lipp Jr Bks); PLB 11.89 (ISBN 0-397-32356-5, Lipp Jr Bks). HarpC Child Bks.

Lunn, Janet. Shadow in Hawthorn Bay. LC 87-4297. 192p. (gr. 7 up). 1987. 13.95 (ISBN 0-684-18843-0, Scribners Young Read). Macmillan Child Grp.

Shute, Linda. Clever Tom & the Leprechaun. Shute, Linda, illus. LC 87-29671. 32p. (gr. k-3). 1988. 12.95 (ISBN 0-688-07488-X); PLB 12.88 (ISBN 0-688-07489-8). Lothrop.

Stratton, Robin L. Raising the Pentagon: Three Ancient Sorcerers Caught in a Time Warp Find Themselves in 20th Century Boston. 240p. (Orig.). 1990. pap. 9.95 (ISBN 0-9626541-1-6). Mockngbrd Square.

OCCUPATION, CHOICE OF

see Vocational Guidance

OCCUPATIONAL THERAPY–VOCATIONAL GUIDANCE

Brown, Margaret F. Careers in Occupational Therapy. Rosen, Ruth, ed. (gr. 7-12). 1989. PLB 12.95 (ISBN 0-8239-0981-6). Rosen Group.

OCCUPATIONS

see also Professions; Vocational Guidance; also names of countries, cities, etc. with the subdivision Occupations (e.g. U. S.–Occupations); also such headings as Law–Vocational Guidance

Bell, Rivian & Koenig, Teresa. Careers with a Record Company. LC 82-20840. (Illus.). 36p. (gr. 2-5). 1983. PLB 7.95 (ISBN 0-8225-0348-4). Lerner Pubns.

Brill, M. I Can Be a Lawyer. LC 87-13227. (Illus.). 32p. (gr. k-3). 1987. PLB 13.93 (ISBN 0-516-01911-2); pap. 3.95 (ISBN 0-516-41911-0). Childrens.

Civardi, Anne. Things People Do. Cartwright, Stephen, illus. 38p. (ps-4). 1986. 10.95 (ISBN 0-86020-864-8, Pub. by Usborne); PLB 12.96 (ISBN 0-88110-236-9). EDC.

Downes, Paul, ed. Career Profile Guide. 250p. (gr. 7-10). 1986. pap. text ed. 48.50 (ISBN 0-912578-90-4). Chron Guide.

Eubank, Mary G. & Hollingsworth, Mary. King's Workers. 1990. write for info. (ISBN 0-8499-0827-2). Word Bks.

Farr, J. Michael & Amore, JoAnn. Exploring Careers: The World of Work & You. Reader, Spring D., photos by. (Illus.). 33p. (gr. 6-12). 1989. wkbk. 1.95 (ISBN 0-942784-28-6, JW EXPAB). Jist Works.

Fitz-Gerald, C. I Can Be a Textile Worker. LC 87-10716. (Illus.). 32p. (gr. k-3). 1987. PLB 13.93 (ISBN 0-516-01912-0). Childrens.

Florian, Douglas. People Working. Florian, Doug, illus. LC 82-45188. 32p. (ps-3). 1983. PLB 12.89 (ISBN 0-690-04264-7, Crowell Jr Bks). HarpC Child Bks.

Fricke, Pam. Careers with an Electric Company. Blumenfeld, Milton J., illus. LC 83-26807. 36p. (gr. 2-5). 1984. lib. bdg. 7.95 (ISBN 0-8225-0375-1). Lerner Pubns.

Giblin, James C. Chimney Sweeps: Yesterday & Today. Tomes, Margot, illus. LC 81-43878. 64p. (gr. 4-7). 1987. pap. 5.95 (ISBN 0-06-446061-4, Trophy). HarpC Child Bks.

Greene, Carol. I Can Be a Salesperson. LC 89-15848. 32p. (gr. k-3). 1989. PLB 13.93 (ISBN 0-516-01959-7); pap. 3.95 (ISBN 0-516-41959-5). Childrens.

Hefter, Richard. Bears at Work. Hefter, Richard, illus. LC 83-2192. 32p. (ps-1). 1983. 5.95 (ISBN 0-911787-00-3). Optimum Res Inc.

—Jobs for Bears. Hefter, Richard, illus. LC 83-2197. 32p. (ps-1). 1983. 5.95 (ISBN 0-911787-02-X). Optimum Res Inc.

Hepworth, R. Stunt People. (Illus.). 32p. (gr. 4 up). Date not set. PLB 14.00 (ISBN 0-86592-415-5). Rourke Corp.

I Want to Be... (Illus.). 32p. (gr. 2-5). 1985. 3.95 (ISBN 0-394-87691-1). Random.

Imershein, Betsy. The Work People Do, 3 bks. (Illus.). 1990. Set, 32p. ea. lib. bdg. 29.94 (ISBN 0-671-94097-X); Set, 32p. ea. pap. 14.85 (ISBN 0-671-94098-8). Messner.

Keran, Shirley. Underwater Specialists. LC 88-14890. (Illus.). 48p. (gr. 5-6). 1988. PLB 10.95 (ISBN 0-89686-400-6, Crestwood Hse). Macmillan Child Grp.

LaValla, P. Land, Search, Rescue Unit. (Illus.). 32p. (gr. 4 up). Date not set. PLB 14.00 (ISBN 0-86592-416-3). Rourke Corp.

Lillegard, Dee. I Can Be a Beautician. LC 87-13835. (Illus.). 32p. (gr. k-3). 1987. PLB 13.93 (ISBN 0-516-01910-4). Childrens.

McCombs, Barbara L. & Brannan, Linda. Do. (Illus.). 32p. (Orig.). (gr. 7-12). 1990. Set. 10 wkbks. & tchr's. guide 44.95 (ISBN 1-56119-061-6); tchr's. guide 1.95 (ISBN 1-56119-006-3); software 39.95 (ISBN 1-56119-103-5). Educ Pr MD.

—Done on Time. (Illus.). 32p. (Orig.). (gr. 7-12). 1990. Set. 10 wkbks. & tchr's. guide 44.95 (ISBN 1-56119-082-9); tchr's. guide 1.95 (ISBN 1-56119-048-9); software 39.95 (ISBN 1-56119-124-8). Educ Pr MD.

—Making the Best Use of Time. (Illus.). 32p. (Orig.). (gr. 7-12). 1990. Set. 10 wkbks. & tchr's. guide 44.95 (ISBN 1-56119-073-X); tchr's. guide 1.95 (ISBN 1-56119-030-6); software 39.95 (ISBN 1-56119-115-9). Educ Pr MD.

McGee, William & Kabes, Todd. The Basic Guide to Resume Writing & Job Interviews. 75p. (Orig.). 1989. pap. 6.50 (ISBN 0-9622594-0-3). Advantage Video.

Matthias, Catherine. Puedo Ser un Policia. LC 84-12106. (SPA., Illus.). 32p. (gr. k-3). 1987. PLB 13.93 (ISBN 0-516-31840-3); pap. 3.95 (ISBN 0-516-51840-2). Childrens.

Mendelsohn, A. Pocket Guide to Job Interviewing. rev. ed. Chavez, Joseph, ed. 45p. (gr. 8 up). 1981. text ed. 1.50 (ISBN 0-918443-00-8, AJDBI101). Job Data.

Merriam, Eve. Daddies at Work. Fernandez, Eugenie, illus. (ps-2). 1989. pap. 5.95 (ISBN 0-671-64873-X). S&S Trade.

—Mommies at Work. Fernandex, Eugenie, illus. (ps-2). 1989. pap. 5.95 (ISBN 0-671-64386-X). S&S Trade.

Moncure, Jane B. What Can We Play Today? Hohag, Linda, illus. LC 87-32565. 32p. (ps-2). 1987. PLB 11.97 (ISBN 0-89565-412-1); pap. 6.96 (ISBN 0-89565-441-5). Childs World.

—Word Bird's Hats. Gohman, Vera, illus. LC 81-18065. (ps-2). 1982. lib. bdg. 11.97 (ISBN 0-89565-221-8). Childs World.

Otfinoski, Steven. Tony the Night Custodian. (Illus.). 40p. (gr. 7-12). 1977. pap. text ed. 2.65 (ISBN 0-915510-21-9). Janus Bks.

Pickering, R. I Can Be an Archaeologist. LC 87-14683. (Illus.). 32p. (gr. k-3). 1987. PLB 13.93 (ISBN 0-516-01909-0); pap. 3.95 (ISBN 0-516-41909-9). Childrens.

Piltch, Benjamin. Real Jobs for Real People. (Illus.). 64p. (gr. 3). 1988. pap. text ed. 3.75 (ISBN 0-88323-246-4, 208); tchr's. key 1.25 (ISBN 0-318-33408-9, 263). Pendergrass Pub.

Rice, Melanie. All about Things People Do. 1990. 11.95 (ISBN 0-385-26756-8). Doubleday.

Rockwell, Anne. When We Grow Up. Rockwell, Anne, illus. LC 80-21768. (ps-1). 1981. 10.95 (ISBN 0-525-42575-6, Dutton). NAL-Dutton.

Rosen, Mike. People at Work. LC 89-11328. (Illus.). 64p. (gr. 2-3). 1990. PLB 12.95 (ISBN 0-8368-0034-6). Gareth Stevens Inc.

San Diego Zoo Doctor. 1991. pap. 14.95 (ISBN 0-671-73921-2). S&S Trade.

Scarry, Richard. Mein Allerschonstes Buch Vom Backen Bauen und Flugzeugfliegen. (GER., Illus.). 1970. 12.95x (ISBN 3-7735-4927-X). Intl Learn Syst.

—Richard Scarry's What Do People Do All Day? (Illus.). (ps-3). 1968. 9.95 (ISBN 0-394-81823-7). Random.

Stewart, David. Fathering & Career: Keeping a Healthy Balance. 2nd ed. LC 87-63156. 16p. (gr. 7 up). 1987. pap. 1.95 (ISBN 0-934426-16-3). NAPSAC Reprods.

Stewart, Gail. Off-Shore Oil Rig Workers. LC 88-12006. (Illus.). 48p. (gr. 5-6). 1988. PLB 10.95 (ISBN 0-89686-397-2, Crestwood Hse). Macmillan Child Grp.

—Smokejumpers & Forest Firefighters. LC 88-12008. (Illus.). 48p. (gr. 5-6). 1988. PLB 10.95 (ISBN 0-89686-398-0, Crestwood Hse). Macmillan Child Grp.

—Stuntpeople. LC 88-14946. (Illus.). 48p. (gr. 5-6). 1988. PLB 10.95 (ISBN 0-89686-396-4, Crestwood Hse). Macmillan Child Grp.

What People Do. (Illus.). 80p. (gr. k-6). 1986. pap. 13.27 (ISBN 0-8172-2588-9). Raintree Pubs.

White, Dana. High-Rise Workers. LC 88-11991. (Illus.). 48p. (gr. 5-6). 1988. PLB 10.95 (ISBN 0-89686-402-2, Crestwood Hse). Macmillan Child Grp.

Wurmfeld, Hope H. Trucker. Wurmfeld, Hope H., illus. LC 89-3296. 64p. (gr. 3 up). 1990. 14.95 (ISBN 0-02-793581-7, Mcmillan Child Bk). Macmillan Child Grp.

Zink, Richard M. Jobs: How to Get the Job You Want. 4th, rev. ed. (Illus.). 32p. (gr. 9-12). 1991. pap. 14.95 (ISBN 0-939469-22-7). Zinks Career Guide.

OCCUPATIONS–FICTION

Allen, Jeffrey. Mary Alice, Operator Number Nine. Marshall, James, illus. 32p. (gr. 1-3). 1975. lib. bdg. 14.95i (ISBN 0-316-03425-8). Little.

Bourque, Nina. The Best Trade of All. Urbanovic, Jackie, illus. LC 83-7352. 32p. (gr. 3-6). 1983. PLB 14.65 (ISBN 0-940742-33-0). Raintree Pubs.

Conford, Ellen. A Job for Jenny Archer. Palmisciano, Diane, illus. LC 87-24424. 76p. (gr. 3-5). 1988. 9.95 (ISBN 0-316-15262-5). Little.

—A Job for Jenny Archer. (gr. 2-4). 1990. pap. 2.95 (ISBN 0-316-15349-4). Little.

Grossman, Patricia. The Night Ones. D'Andrade, Diane, ed. Dabcovich, Lydia, illus. 32p. (ps-3). 1991. 13.95 (ISBN 0-15-257438-7). HarBraceJ.

Harwood, Pearl A. Mr. Bumba's New Job. Folger, Joseph, illus. LC 64-19774. 32p. (gr. k-3). 1964. PLB 4.95 (ISBN 0-8225-0105-8). Lerner Pubns.

Hill, Eric. Who Does What? 20p. (ps-k). 1982. 4.95 (ISBN 0-8431-0909-2). Price Stern.

Joslin, Sesyle. What Do You Do, Dear? Sendak, Maurice, illus. LC 84-43139. 48p. 1958. 13.95 (ISBN 0-201-09387-1); PLB 13.89 (ISBN 0-06-023075-4). HarpC Child Bks.

Pearson, Gayle. The Coming Home Cafe. LC 88-3448. 208p. (gr. 6 up). 1988. 14.95 (ISBN 0-689-31338-1, Atheneum Child Bk). Macmillan Child Grp.

Scarry, Richard. Richard Scarry's Busiest People Ever. LC 76-8123. (Illus.). (ps-2). 1976. lib. bdg. 9.99 (ISBN 0-394-93293-5, Random Juv); PLB 9.95 (ISBN 0-394-83293-0). Random.

—Richard Scarry's Postman Pig & His Busy Neighbors. LC 77-91646. (Illus.). (ps-2). 1978. lib. bdg. 5.99 (ISBN 0-394-93898-4, Random Juv). Random.

Trella, Phyllis. A Peek at Occupations. Trella, Phyllis, illus. LC 82-73692. 48p. (gr. 2-6). write for info. (ISBN 0-914201-03-4). Cheeruppet.

Wood, Phyllis A. A Five-Color Buick & a Blue-Eyed Cat. LC 74-19156. 126p. (gr. 7 up). 1975. 7.95 (ISBN 0-664-32562-9, Westminster). Westminster John Knox.

OCEAN

see also Icebergs; Oceanography; Seashore; Storms; Tides

Adams, Pam. The Ocean. 32p. (ps). 1984. 8.00 (ISBN 0-85953-193-7, Child's Play England). Childs Play.

Adler, David. Our Amazing Ocean. Veno, Joseph, illus. LC 82-17373. 32p. (gr. 3-6). 1983. PLB 10.59 (ISBN 0-89375-882-5); pap. text ed. 2.95 (ISBN 0-89375-883-3). Troll Assocs.

Althea. Signposts of the Sea. (Illus.). 32p. (gr. 5-7). 1983. pap. 2.95 (ISBN 0-521-27171-1). Cambridge U Pr.

Amery. At the Seaside. Cartwright, illus. 20p. (ps). 1985. 2.95 (ISBN 0-86020-855-9, Pub. by Usborne). EDC.

Bright, Michael. The Dying Sea. FS-Aladdin Staff, ed. Hayward, Ron, illus. LC 88-50523. 32p. (gr. 4-9). 1988. PLB 8.99 (ISBN 0-531-17126-4, Gloucester Pr). Watts.

Carter, Katharine J. Oceans. LC 81-17093. (Illus.). 48p. (gr. k-4). 1982. PLB 14.60 (ISBN 0-516-01639-3); pap. 4.95 (ISBN 0-516-41639-1). Childrens.

Cook, Jan L. The Mysterious Undersea World. LC 79-1791. (Illus.). 104p. (gr. 3-8). 1980. 6.95 (ISBN 0-87044-317-8); PLB 8.50 (ISBN 0-87044-322-4). Natl Geog.

De Beauregard, Diane C. The Blue Planet: Seas & Oceans. Bogard, Vicki, tr. from FRE. Lepagnol, Cyril, illus. LC 89-8912. 38p. (gr. k-5). 1989. 4.95 (ISBN 0-944589-22-7, 022). Young Discovery Lib.

Gibbs, B. Ocean Facts. (Illus.). 48p. (gr. 3-7). 1991. lib. bdg. 12.96 (ISBN 0-88110-531-7, Usborne); pap. 5.95 (ISBN 0-7460-0621-7, Usborne). EDC.

Gould, G. The Seas, Reading Level 5. (Illus.). 32p. (gr. 3-6). Date not set. PLB 13.26 ea. Rourke Corp.

Heinrichs, Susan. The Atlantic Ocean. LC 86-9578. (Illus.). 48p. (gr. k-4). 1986. PLB 14.60 (ISBN 0-516-01289-4). Childrens.

—The Indian Ocean. LC 86-9579. (Illus.). 48p. (gr. k-4). 1986. PLB 14.60 (ISBN 0-516-01293-2). Childrens.

Hopkins, Lee B. The Sea Is Calling Me. Gaffney-Kessell, W., illus. LC 85-16412. (gr. 4-6). 1986. 14.95 (ISBN 0-15-271155-4, HJ). Harbracej.

Illustrated World Oceans. 1991. pap. 12.95 (ISBN 0-671-74128-4). S&S Trade.

Lambert, David & McConnell, Anita. Seas & Oceans. LC 84-1654. (Illus.). 64p. (gr. 7 up). 1985. 15.95 (ISBN 0-8160-1064-1). Facts on File.

Little People Big Book about the Sea. 64p. (ps-1). 1989. write for info. (ISBN 0-8094-7475-1); PLB write for info. (ISBN 0-8094-7476-X). Time-Life.

A Look at the Earth Around Us: Oceans. (gr. 3-6). 1981. incl. cass. & tchr's. guide 28.95 (ISBN 0-686-73885-3, 04916). Natl Geog.

Matthews, Rupert. Record Breakers of the Sea. LC 89-35503. (Illus.). 32p. (gr. 2-6). 1989. PLB 9.59 (ISBN 0-8167-1925-X); pap. text ed. 2.50 (ISBN 0-8167-1926-8). Troll Assocs.

Mitgutsch, Ali. From Sea to Salt. Mitgutsch, Ali, illus. LC 84-17466. 24p. (ps-3). 1985. PLB 6.95 (ISBN 0-87614-232-3). Carolrhoda Bks.

Myerson, A. Lee. Seawater: A Delicate Balance. 64p. (gr. 6-12). 1988. lib. bdg. 15.95 (ISBN 0-89490-157-5). Enslow Pubs.

Noel, Spike. Fish & the Sea. (Illus.). 64p. (gr. 7 up). 1972. 14.95 (ISBN 0-7136-1239-8). Dufour.

Polking, Kirk. Oceans of the World: Our Essential Resource. (Illus.). 136p. (gr. 6-9). 1983. pap. 14.95 (ISBN 0-399-20919-0, Philomel). Putnam Pub Group.

Pomeroy, Johanna P. Content Area Reading Skills Oceans: Main Idea. (Illus.). (gr. 4). 1987. pap. text ed. 3.25 (ISBN 0-89525-857-9). Ed Activities.

Robinson, W. Wright. Incredible Facts about the Ocean: The Restless Blue Salt Water, Vol. 1. LC 85-25430. (Illus.). 96p. (gr. 4 up). 1986. lib. bdg. 11.95 (ISBN 0-87518-317-4, Dillon). Macmillan Child Grp.

—Incredible Facts about the Ocean, Vol. 3: How We Use It, How We Abuse It. (Illus.). 128p. (gr. 4 up). 1990. PLB 11.95 (ISBN 0-87518-435-9, Dillon). Macmillan Child Grp.

Sabin, Francene. Oceans. Goldsborough, June, illus. LC 84-8590. 32p. (gr. 3-6). 1985. PLB 9.49 (ISBN 0-8167-0216-0); pap. text ed. 2.95 (ISBN 0-8167-0217-9). Troll Assocs.

Sabin, Louis. Wonders of the Sea. Dodson, Bert, illus. LC 81-3334. 32p. (gr. 2-4). 1982. PLB 10.89 (ISBN 0-89375-578-8); pap. text ed. 2.95 (ISBN 0-89375-579-6); cassette 9.95 (ISBN 0-685-04957-4). Troll Assocs.

The Sea. (Illus.). 80p. (gr. k-6). 1986. pap. 13.27 (ISBN 0-8172-2586-2). Raintree Pubs.

Seymour, Peter. What's in the Deep Blue Sea? Carter, David A., illus. LC 90-80884. 18p. (ps-2). 1990. 10.95 (ISBN 0-8050-1449-7). H Holt & Co.

Tesar, Jenny. Threatened Oceans. Cayne, Bernard S., ed. (Illus.). 128p. (gr. 7-12). 1992. lib. bdg. 18.95x (ISBN 0-8160-2494-4). Facts on File.

Thompson, Brenda & Overbeck, Cynthia. Under the Sea. Beisner, Monica, illus. LC 76-22470. 24p. (gr. k-3). 1977. PLB 5.95 (ISBN 0-8225-1363-3). Lerner Pubns.

Tyler. The Seas. (gr. 3-6). 1976. pap. 6.95 (ISBN 0-86020-064-7, Usborne-Hayes). EDC.

Williams, Brian. The Sea. (Illus.). 48p. (gr. 5-8). 1991. PLB 13.90 (ISBN 0-531-19146-X, Warwick). Watts.

OCEAN–ECONOMIC ASPECTS

see Marine Resources

OCEAN–FICTION

Barklem, Jill. Sea Story. (Illus.). 32p. (ps-3). 1991. 9.95 (ISBN 0-399-21844-0, Philomel Bks). Putnam Pub Group.

Bozanich, Tony L. Captain Flounder, His Sole Brothers & Friends. Isaksen, Lisa A., ed. Isaksen, Patricia, illus. 16p. (ps-4). 1984. pap. 4.95 (ISBN 0-930655-00-1). Antarctic Pr.
Who is Captain Flounder? Skipper Tony L. Bozanich has created this famous flatfish fisherman who finds his life's reward on the bottom of the sea. This enchanting fish story, a series of rhymes which capture the true spirit of the sea, is a delightful children's book entitled "Captain Flounder, His Sole Brothers & Friends". With salty characters colorfully illustrated by Lisa A. Isaksen, Captain Flounder comes alive in an underwater wonderland for kids to explore! Bozanich, owner & skipper of the purse seiner "Antarctic", has been on the water for over 50 years. He has fished the Pacific Coastal waters from Alaska to California but calls the Puget Sound his home. He has a wealth of information, stories, & anecdotes about the high times & the disastrous times of fishing. His experience of the sea enables him to create this salty story now being read & enjoyed by all ages. ***Publisher Provided Annotation.***

Burchard, Peter. Sea Change. LC 84-47524. (Illus.). 116p. (gr. 7 up). 1984. 9.95 (ISBN 0-374-36460-5). FS&G.
Coles, Allison. Michael & the Sea. Charlton, Michael, illus. 28p. (ps up). 1985. 3.95 (ISBN 0-88110-268-7). EDC.
Disney, Walt, Productions Staff. Donald at Sea. Disney, Walt, Productions Staff, illus. 10p. (ps). 1984. vinyl bdg 2.95 (ISBN 0-394-86751-3, Pub. by BYR). Random.
Levinson, Riki. Our Home Is the Sea. Luzak, Dennis, illus. LC 87-36419. 32p. (gr. k-3). 1988. pap. 13.95 (ISBN 0-525-44406-8, DCB). Dutton Child Bks.
Paterson, Diane. The Bathtub Ocean. Patterson, Diane, illus. LC 78-72517. (ps-2). 1985. 6.95 (ISBN 0-8037-0460-7). Dial Bks Young.
Tomkins, Jasper. The Hole in the Ocean. Tomkins, Jasper, illus. LC 83-82782. 60p. (gr. k-6). 1984. pap. 7.95 (ISBN 0-914676-73-3). Green Tiger Pr.

OCEAN BOTTOM
Booth, Eugene. Under the Ocean. LC 77-7983. (Illus.). (gr. k-3). 1977. PLB 13.32 (ISBN 0-8393-0108-1). Raintree Pubs.

OCEAN CABLES
see Cables, Submarine

OCEAN LIFE
see Marine Biology

OCEAN ROUTES
see Trade Routes

OCEAN TRAVEL–FICTION
Huff, Barbara. Welcome Aboard: Traveling on an Ocean Liner. Maxtone-Graham, John, frwd. by. LC 86-34315. 128p. (gr. 4 up). 1987. 13.95 (ISBN 0-89919-503-2, Pub. by Clarion). Ticknor & Fields.
Kurth, Heinz. Sam at the Sea. (Illus.). 32p. (gr. k-2). 1986. 12.95 (ISBN 0-437-53623-8, Pub. by W Heinemann Ltd). Trafalgar Sq.

OCEAN WAVES
Rogers, Daniel. Waves, Tides & Currents. LC 90-551. (Illus.). 32p. (gr. 4-7). 1991. PLB 11.90 (ISBN 0-531-18370-X). Watts.

OCEANIA
see Islands of the Pacific

OCEANOGRAPHY
see also Marine Biology; Marine Resources; Navigation; Ocean Waves; Submarine Geology
Asimov, Isaac. How Did We Find Out about Life in the Deep Sea? Wool, David, illus. (gr. 4-7). 1981. lib. bdg. 10.85 (ISBN 0-8027-6428-2). Walker & Co.
Baker, Lucy. Life in the Oceans. (Illus.). 32p. (gr. 5-8). 1990. PLB 11.40 (ISBN 0-531-10981-X). Watts.
Blair, Carvel. Exploring the Sea: Oceanography Today. Rimson, Ole & Luke, Melinda, eds. McNaught, Harry, illus. LC 85-43336. 96p. (gr. 5 up). 1986. lib. bdg. 9.99 (ISBN 0-394-95927-2); pap. 8.95 (ISBN 0-394-85927-8). Random.
Boyer, Robert E. Oceanography. 2nd ed. LC 74-1649. (Illus.). 48p. (gr. 7-12). 1987. pap. 5.95 (ISBN 0-8331-6611-5, 6611). Hubbard Sci.
Bramwell, Martyn. Oceanography. (Illus.). 48p. (gr. 7-9). 1990. 12.90 (ISBN 0-531-19510-4). Watts.
Center for Environmental Education Staff. The Ocean: Consider the Connections. Maraniss, Linda & Bierce, Rose, eds. Perry, Jill, illus. Asimov, Isaac, frwd. by. (Illus.). 104p. (Orig.). (gr. 2-6). 1985. pap. 8.95 wkbk. (ISBN 0-9615294-0-7). Ctr Env Educ.
Conway, Lorraine. Oceanography. 64p. (gr. 5 up). 1982. 6.95 (ISBN 0-86653-066-5, GA401). Good Apple.
Daegling, Mary. Monster Seaweeds: The Story of the Giant Kelps. LC 86-13591. (Illus.). 120p. (gr. 4 up). 1986. PLB 11.95 (ISBN 0-87518-350-6, Dillon). Macmillan Child Grp.
Embry, Lynn. Scientific Encounters of the Mysterious Sea. McClure, Nancee, illus. 64p. (gr. 4-7). 1987. pap. 6.95 (ISBN 0-86653-407-5, GA1013). Good Apple.
Fine, John C. Oceans in Peril. Fine, John C., illus. LC 86-26546. 128p. (gr. 5 up). 1987. 15.95 (ISBN 0-689-31328-4, Atheneum Child Bk). Macmillan Child Grp.
Goldin, Augusta. Bottom of the Sea. Emberley, Ed E., illus. LC 66-10194. 40p. (gr. k-3). 1967. PLB 13.89 (ISBN 0-690-15864-5, Crowell Jr Bks). HarpC Child Bks.
Life in the Water. (Illus.). 88p. (ps-3). 1989. 15.93 (ISBN 0-8094-4853-X); lib. bdg. 21.27 (ISBN 0-8094-4854-8). Time-Life.
Lye, Keith. The Ocean Floor. LC 90-549. (Illus.). 32p. (gr. 4-7). 1991. PLB 11.90 (ISBN 0-531-18369-6). Watts.
Moore, Chris. Oceans. 1988. pap. 5.95 (ISBN 0-14-032472-0, Puffin). Puffin Bks.
Morris, R. Ocean Life. Jackson, Ian, et al, illus. 32p. (gr. 3-6). 1983. 7.95 (ISBN 0-86020-754-4, Usborne-Haynes); PLB 13.96 (ISBN 0-88110-149-4, Usborne-Haynes); pap. 5.95 (ISBN 0-86020-753-6, Usborne-Haynes). EDC.
Oceanography. (Illus.). 72p. (gr. 6-12). 1983. pap. 1.85 (ISBN 0-8395-3306-3, 3306). BSA.
Pearce, Q. L. Tidal Waves & Other Ocean Wonders. Steltenpohl, Jane, ed. Fraser, Mary A., illus. 64p. (gr. 4-6). 1989. PLB 12.98 (ISBN 0-671-68532-5); pap. 5.95 (ISBN 0-671-68647-X). Messner.
Robinson, W. Wright. Incredible Facts about the Ocean: The Land Below, the Life Within, Vol. 2. LC 85-25430. (Illus.). 120p. (gr. 4 up). 1987. PLB 11.95 (ISBN 0-87518-358-1, Dillon). Macmillan Child Grp.
Sibbald, Jean. Homes In the Sea: From the Shore to the Deep. LC 85-6865. (Illus.). 96p. (gr. 4 up). 1986. PLB 11.95 (ISBN 0-87518-304-2, Dillon). Macmillan Child Grp.
—Sea Babies: New Life In the Ocean. LC 85-7039. (Illus.). 88p. (gr. 4 up). 1986. PLB 11.95 (ISBN 0-87518-305-0, Dillon). Macmillan Child Grp.
—Strange Eating Habits of Sea Creatures. LC 85-11621. (Illus.). 112p. (gr. 4 up). 1986. PLB 11.95 (ISBN 0-87518-349-2, Dillon). Macmillan Child Grp.
Simon, Seymour. How to Be an Ocean Scientist in Your Own Home. Carter, David A., illus. LC 87-45988. 144p. (gr. 5-9). 1988. 12.95 (ISBN 0-397-32291-7, Lipp Jr Bks); PLB 12.89 (ISBN 0-397-32292-5, Lipp Jr Bks). HarpC Child Bks.
Whipple, A. B. Restless Oceans. (Illus.). 176p. (gr. 7 up). 1983. 18.60 (ISBN 0-8094-4340-6); lib. bdg. 24.60 (ISBN 0-8094-4341-4). Time-Life.

OCEANOGRAPHY–FICTION
Olsen, E. A. Mystery at Salvage Rock. LC 68-16401. (Illus.). 48p. (gr. 3 up). 1970. PLB 10.95 (ISBN 0-87783-027-4); pap. 3.94 deluxe ed. (ISBN 0-87783-101-7); cassette 10.60x (ISBN 0-87783-195-5). Oddo.
Reese, Bob. Coral Reef. LC 82-23610. (Illus.). 24p. (ps-2). 1983. PLB 11.27 (ISBN 0-516-02312-8); pap. 2.95 (ISBN 0-516-42312-6). Childrens.

OCEANOGRAPHY–RESEARCH
see also Skin Diving; Underwater Exploration

OCEANOLOGY
see Oceanography

OCELOTS–FICTION
Bunny. Tigger: Story of a Mayan Ocelot. LC 66-12746. (Illus.). (gr. k-2). 1974. 6.95 (ISBN 0-87208-009-9). Island Pr Pubs.
Wicker, Ireene. How the Ocelots Got Their Spots. Perrot, Catherine, illus. 32p. (gr. 2-4). 1976. 6.95 (ISBN 0-8184-0231-8). Carol Pub Group.

OCTOPUS
Carrick, Carol. Octopus. Carrick, Donald, illus. LC 77-12769. 32p. (gr. 1-4). 1979. 14.95 (ISBN 0-395-28777-4, Clarion). HM.
Green, Carl R. & Sanford, William R. The Octopus. LC 88-5435. (Illus.). 48p. (gr. 5-6). 1988. PLB 10.95 (ISBN 0-89686-386-7, Crestwood Hse). Macmillan Child Grp.
Lauber, Patricia. An Octopus Is Amazing. Keller, Holly, illus. LC 89-29300. 32p. (ps-1). 1990. 12.95 (ISBN 0-690-04801-7, Crowell Jr Bks); PLB 13.89 (ISBN 0-690-04803-3, Crowell Jr Bks). HarpC Child Bks.
Schultz, Ellen. I Can Read About the Octopus. LC 78-73715. (gr. 2-4). 1979. pap. 1.95 (ISBN 0-89375-213-4). Troll Assocs.

OCTOPUS–FICTION
Barrett, John. Oscar, the Selfish Octopus. Servello, Joseph, illus. LC 78-18760. 32p. (ps-3). 1978. 16.95 (ISBN 0-87705-335-9). Human Sci Pr.
Brandenberg, Franz. Otto Is Different. Stevenson, James, illus. LC 84-13654. 24p. (gr. k-3). 1985. 11.75 (ISBN 0-688-04253-8); PLB 11.88 (ISBN 0-688-04254-6). Greenwillow.
Kraus, Robert, et al. Herman the Helper Cleans Up. Dewey, Ariane, illus. 10p. (ps). 1981. pap. 2.95 vinyl (ISBN 0-671-42555-2, Little Simon). S&S Trade.
Most, Bernard. My Very Own Octopus. D'Andrade, Diane, ed. (Illus.). 32p. (Orig.). 1991. pap. 4.95 (ISBN 0-15-256345-8, HJ). HarBraceJ.
Terris, Susan. Octopus Pie. LC 83-11517. 166p. (gr. 5 up). 1983. 11.95 (ISBN 0-374-35571-1). FS&G.
Waber, Bernard. I Was All Thumbs. Waber, Bernard, illus. LC 75-11689. 48p. (gr. k-3). 1990. 13.95 (ISBN 0-395-21404-1); pap. 4.95 (ISBN 0-395-53969-2). HM.

OFFICE WORK–TRAINING
see Business Education

OFFICIALS
see names of countries, cities, etc. and organizations with subdivision Officials and Employees, e.g. U. S.–Officials and Employees

OGLETHORPE, JAMES EDWARD, 1696-1785
Blackburn, Joyce. James Edward Oglethorpe. (gr. 7-11). 1983. 9.95 (ISBN 0-396-08158-4, Putnam). Putnam Pub Group.

OHIO
Burke, James L. & Davison, Kenneth E. Ohio's Heritage. LC 83-20091. (Illus.). 340p. (gr. 7). 1984. text ed. 19.50x (ISBN 0-87905-109-4, Peregrine Smith). Gibbs Smith Pub.
Carole Marsh Ohio Books, 31 bks. Set. 638.45 (ISBN 0-7933-1310-4). Gallopade Pub Group.
Carpenter, Allan. Ohio. new ed. LC 78-16162. (Illus.). 96p. (gr. 4 up). 1979. PLB 19.93 (ISBN 0-516-04135-5). Childrens.
Cockley, David H. Over the Falls: A Child's Guide to Chagrin Falls. Ascherman, Herbert, Jr., photos by. (Illus.). 24p. (Orig.). (gr. 1-6). 1981. pap. 2.25 (ISBN 0-940900-00-9). Aschley Pr.
Fox, Mary V. Ohio. (Illus.). 72p. (gr. 4-9). 1987. PLB 10.40 (ISBN 0-531-10392-7). Watts.
Fradin, Dennis. Ohio: In Words & Pictures. Ulm, Robert, illus. LC 76-46941. 48p. (gr. 2-5). 1977. PLB 15.93 (ISBN 0-516-03935-0). Childrens.
Hall, Betty L. Ohio Survival. rev. ed. 160p. (gr. 10-12). 1986. pap. text ed. 5.84 (ISBN 0-936159-00-6). Westwood Pr.
Kent, Deborah. Ohio. LC 88-38401. (Illus.). 144p. (gr. 4 up). 1989. PLB 25.27 (ISBN 0-516-00481-6). Childrens.
Lewis, Lois F. Carlin School, A History Book: The Story of a School in Ravenna, Ohio, U. S. A. Lewis, William B., illus. 28p. (Orig.). (gr. 5). 1989. pap. text ed. write for info. (ISBN 0-9620136-3-3). L F Lewis.
—Tappan School, a History Book: The Story of a School in Ravenna, Ohio, U. S. A. Lewis, William B., illus. 28p. (Orig.). (gr. 5). 1989. pap. text ed. write for info. (ISBN 0-9620136-1-7). L F Lewis.
Marsh, Carole. Avast, Ye Slobs! Ohio Pirate Trivia. (Illus.). 1990. PLB 19.95 (ISBN 0-7933-0908-5); pap. 14.95 (ISBN 0-7933-0907-7); computer disk 29.95 (ISBN 0-7933-0909-3). Gallopade Pub Group.
—The Beast of the Ohio Bed & Breakfast. (Illus.). 1990. PLB 19.95 (ISBN 0-7933-0905-0); pap. 14.95 (ISBN 0-7933-1848-3); computer disk 29.95 (ISBN 0-7933-1849-1). Gallopade Pub Group.
—The Hard-to-Believe-But-True! Book of Ohio History, Mystery, Trivia, Legend, Lore, Humor & More. (Illus.). 1990. PLB 19.95 (ISBN 0-7933-0904-2); pap. 14.95 (ISBN 0-7933-0903-4); computer disk 29.95 (ISBN 0-7933-0906-9). Gallopade Pub Group.
—If My Ohio Mama Ran the World! (Illus.). 1990. lib. bdg. 19.95 (ISBN 0-7933-1850-5); pap. 14.95 (ISBN 0-7933-1851-3); computer disk 29.95 (ISBN 0-7933-1852-1). Gallopade Pub Group.
—Let's Quilt Ohio & Stuff It Topographically! (Illus.). 1990. PLB 19.95; pap. 14.95 (ISBN 1-55609-095-1); computer disk 29.95 (ISBN 1-55609-985-1). Gallopade Pub Group.
—Ohio & Other State Greats (Biographies) (Illus.). 1990. PLB 19.95 (ISBN 1-55609-998-3); pap. 14.95 (ISBN 1-55609-999-1); computer disk 29.95 (ISBN 1-55609-854-5). Gallopade Pub Group.
—Ohio Bandits, Bushwackers, Outlaws, Crooks, Devils, Ghosts, Desperadoes & Other Assorted & Sundry Characters! (Illus.). 1990. PLB 19.95 (ISBN 0-7933-0889-5); pap. 14.95 (ISBN 0-7933-0888-7); computer disk 29.95 (ISBN 0-7933-0890-9). Gallopade Pub Group.
—Ohio Classic Christmas Trivia: Stories, Recipes, Activities, Legends, Lore & More! (Illus.). 1990. PLB 19.95 (ISBN 0-7933-0892-5); pap. 14.95 (ISBN 0-7933-0891-7); computer disk 29.95 (ISBN 0-7933-0893-3). Gallopade Pub Group.
—Ohio Coastales. (Illus.). 1990. PLB 19.95 (ISBN 1-55609-992-4); pap. 14.95 (ISBN 1-55609-993-2); computer disk 29.95 (ISBN 1-55609-994-0). Gallopade Pub Group.
—The Ohio Hot Air Balloon Mystery. (Illus.). (gr. 2-9). 1990. 19.95 (ISBN 0-7933-2633-8); pap. 14.95 (ISBN 0-7933-2634-6); computer disk 29.95 (ISBN 0-7933-2635-4). Gallopade Pub Group.
—Ohio "Jography" A Fun Run Thru Our State! (Illus.). 1990. PLB 19.95 (ISBN 1-55609-981-9); pap. 14.95 (ISBN 1-55609-982-7); computer disk 29.95 (ISBN 1-55609-983-5). Gallopade Pub Group.
—Ohio Kid's Cookbook: Recipes, How-to, History, Lore & More! (Illus.). 1990. PLB 19.95 (ISBN 0-7933-0901-8); pap. 14.95 (ISBN 0-7933-0900-X); computer disk 29.95 (ISBN 0-7933-0902-6). Gallopade Pub Group.
—Ohio Quiz Crash Course! (Illus.). 1990. PLB 19.95 (ISBN 1-55609-995-9); pap. 14.95 (ISBN 1-55609-996-7); computer disk 29.95 (ISBN 1-55609-997-5). Gallopade Pub Group.

—Ohio School Trivia: An Amazing & Fascinating Look at Our State's Teachers, Schools & Students! (Illus.). 1990. PLB 19.95 (ISBN 0-7933-0898-4); pap. 14.95 (ISBN 0-7933-0897-6); computer disk 29.95 (ISBN 0-7933-0899-2). Gallopade Pub Group.

—Ohio Silly Basketball Sportsmysteries, Vol. 1. (Illus.). 1990. PLB 19.95 (ISBN 0-7933-0895-X); pap. 14.95 (ISBN 0-7933-0894-1); computer disk 29.95 (ISBN 0-7933-0896-8). Gallopade Pub Group.

—Ohio Silly Basketball Sportsmysteries, Vol. 2. (Illus.). 1990. PLB 19.95; pap. 14.95 (ISBN 0-7933-1854-8); computer disk 29.95 (ISBN 0-7933-1855-6). Gallopade Pub Group.

—Ohio Silly Football Sportsmysteries, Vol. 1. (Illus.). 1990. PLB 19.95 (ISBN 1-55609-986-X); pap. 14.95 (ISBN 1-55609-987-8); computer disk 29.95 (ISBN 1-55609-988-6). Gallopade Pub Group.

—Ohio Silly Football Sportsmysteries, Vol. 2. (Illus.). 1990. PLB 19.95 (ISBN 1-55609-989-4); pap. 14.95 (ISBN 1-55609-990-8); computer disk 29.95 (ISBN 1-55609-991-6). Gallopade Pub Group.

—Ohio Silly Trivia1. (Illus.). 1990. PLB 19.95 (ISBN 1-55609-979-7); pap. 14.95 (ISBN 1-55609-112-5); computer disk 29.95 (ISBN 1-55609-980-0). Gallopade Pub Group.

—Ohio's (Most Devastating!) Disasters & (Most Calamitous!) Catastrophies! (Illus.). 1990. PLB 19.95 (ISBN 0-7933-0886-0); pap. 14.95 (ISBN 0-7933-0885-2); computer disk 29.95 (ISBN 0-7933-0887-9). Gallopade Pub Group.

Regina, Karen & Rhodes, Gregory L., eds. Cincinnati: An Urban History Sourcebook, Bk. 1. LC 87-72186. (Illus.). 88p. (Orig.). (gr. 4-6). 1988. pap. text ed. 6.95 (ISBN 0-911497-01-3). Cinc Hist Soc.

—Cincinnati: An Urban History Sourcebook, Bk. II. LC 87-72186. (Illus.). 88p. (Orig.). (gr. 7-8). 1988. pap. text ed. 6.95 (ISBN 0-911497-02-1). Cinc Hist Soc.

Stith, Bari O. Lake County, Ohio: One Hundred Fifty Years of Tradition: An Illustrated History. (Illus.). 128p. (gr. 7 up). 1988. 25.95 (ISBN 0-89781-249-2). Windsor Pubns Inc.

Thompson, Kathleen. Ohio. LC 87-26482. 48p. (gr. 3 up). 1988. 17.32 (ISBN 0-86514-455-9); cancelled tchr's. study guide (ISBN 0-317-67106-5); cancelled Beta video (ISBN 0-317-67107-3); cancelled VHS video (ISBN 0-86514-155-X); cancelled 3/4" video (ISBN 0-86514-230-0). Raintree Pubs.

OHIO–FICTION

Hamilton, Virginia. The House of Dies Drear. Keith, Eros, illus. LC 68-23059. 256p. (gr. 6-9). 1984. 14.95 (ISBN 0-02-742500-2, Mcmillan Child Bk); pap. 3.95 (ISBN 0-02-043520-7, Collier). Macmillan Child Grp.

McCloskey, Robert. Lentil. (ps-3). 1978. pap. 3.95 (ISBN 0-14-050287-4, Puffin). Puffin Bks.

OHIO–HISTORY–FICTION

Fradin, Dennis. Ohio: In Words & Pictures. Ulm, Robert, illus. LC 76-46941. 48p. (gr. 2-5). 1977. PLB 15.93 (ISBN 0-516-03935-0). Childrens.

OIL

see Petroleum

OIL ENGINES

see Gas and Oil Engines

OIL WELLS

see Petroleum

OKLAHOMA

Aylesworth, Thomas G. & Aylesworth, Virginia L. South Central (Louisiana, Arkansas, Missouri, Kansas, Oklahoma) (Illus.). 64p. (gr. 3 up). 1992. PLB 16.95 (ISBN 0-7910-1047-3). Chelsea Hse.

Carole Marsh Oklahoma Books, 31 bks. Set. 638.45 (ISBN 0-7933-1311-2). Gallopade Pub Group.

Carpenter, Allan. Oklahoma. new ed. LC 79-10592. (Illus.). 96p. (gr. 4 up). 1979. PLB 19.93 (ISBN 0-516-04136-3). Childrens.

Ferguson, Elva S. They Carried the Torch: The Story of Oklahoma's Pioneer Newspapers. Griffis, Molly L., ed. Ferguson, Benton, illus. Johnson, Edith, intro. by. LC 89-80349. (Illus.). 84p. (gr. 8 up). 1989. pap. 5.00 (ISBN 0-9618634-8-X). Levite Apache.

Fradin, Dennis. Oklahoma: In Words & Pictures. Wahl, Richard, illus. LC 80-26961. 48p. (gr. 2-5). 1981. PLB 15.93 (ISBN 0-516-03936-9). Childrens.

Heinrichs, Ann. Oklahoma. LC 88-11743. (Illus.). 144p. (gr. 4 up). 1988. PLB 25.27 (ISBN 0-516-00482-4). Childrens.

Kirschstein, Carolyn V. Hooray for Oklahoma (1889) Merrell, David, illus. 48p. (gr. k-4). 1989. write for info. B C Pub Inc.

Marsh, Carole. Avast, Ye Slobs! Oklahoma Pirate Trivia. (Illus.). 1990. PLB 19.95 (ISBN 0-7933-0932-8); pap. 14.95 (ISBN 0-7933-0931-X); computer disk 29.95 (ISBN 0-7933-0933-6). Gallopade Pub Group.

—The Beast of the Oklahoma Bed & Breakfast. (Illus.). 1990. PLB 19.95 (ISBN 0-7933-1869-6); pap. 14.95 (ISBN 0-7933-1870-X); computer disk 29.95 (ISBN 0-7933-1871-8). Gallopade Pub Group.

—The Hard-to-Believe-But-True! Book of Oklahoma History, Mystery, Trivia, Legend, Lore, Humor & More. (Illus.). 1990. PLB 19.95 (ISBN 0-7933-0929-8); pap. 14.95 (ISBN 0-7933-0928-X); computer disk 29.95 (ISBN 0-7933-0930-1). Gallopade Pub Group.

—If My Oklahoma Mama Ran the World! (Illus.). 1990. lib. bdg. 19.95 (ISBN 0-7933-1875-0); pap. 14.95 (ISBN 0-7933-1876-9); computer disk 29.95 (ISBN 0-7933-1877-7). Gallopade Pub Group.

—Let's Quilt Oklahoma & Stuff It Topographically! (Illus.). 1990. PLB 19.95 (ISBN 0-7933-1860-2); pap. 14.95 (ISBN 0-7933-1861-0); computer disk 29.95 (ISBN 0-7933-1862-9). Gallopade Pub Group.

—Oklahoma & Other State Greats (Biographies) (Illus.). 1990. PLB 19.95 (ISBN 0-7933-1878-5); pap. 14.95 (ISBN 0-7933-1879-3); computer disk 29.95 (ISBN 0-7933-1880-7). Gallopade Pub Group.

—Oklahoma Bandits, Bushwackers, Outlaws, Crooks, Devils, Ghosts, Desperadoes & Other Assorted & Sundry Characters! (Illus.). 1990. PLB 19.95 (ISBN 0-7933-0914-X); pap. 14.95 (ISBN 0-7933-0913-1); computer disk 29.95 (ISBN 0-7933-0915-8). Gallopade Pub Group.

—Oklahoma Classic Christmas Trivia: Stories, Recipes, Activities, Legends, Lore & More! (Illus.). 1990. PLB 19.95 (ISBN 0-7933-0917-4); pap. 14.95 (ISBN 0-7933-0916-6); computer disk 29.95 (ISBN 0-7933-0918-2). Gallopade Pub Group.

—Oklahoma Coastales. (Illus.). 1990. PLB 19.95 (ISBN 0-7933-1872-6); pap. 14.95 (ISBN 0-7933-1873-4); computer disk 29.95 (ISBN 0-7933-1874-2). Gallopade Pub Group.

—The Oklahoma Hot Air Balloon Mystery. (Illus.). (gr. 2-9). 1990. 19.95 (ISBN 0-7933-2642-7); pap. 14.95 (ISBN 0-7933-2643-5); computer disk 29.95 (ISBN 0-7933-2644-3). Gallopade Pub Group.

—Oklahoma "Jography" A Fun Run Thru Our State! (Illus.). 1990. PLB 19.95 (ISBN 0-7933-1858-0); pap. 14.95 (ISBN 1-55609-086-2); computer disk 29.95 (ISBN 0-7933-1859-9). Gallopade Pub Group.

—Oklahoma Kid's Cookbook: Recipes, How-to, History, Lore & More! (Illus.). 1990. PLB 19.95 (ISBN 0-7933-0926-3); pap. 14.95 (ISBN 0-7933-0925-5); computer disk 29.95 (ISBN 0-7933-0927-1). Gallopade Pub Group.

—Oklahoma Quiz Bowl Crash Course! (Illus.). 1990. PLB 19.95 (ISBN 0-7933-1881-5); pap. 14.95 (ISBN 0-7933-1882-3); computer disk 29.95 (ISBN 0-7933-1883-1). Gallopade Pub Group.

—Oklahoma School Trivia: An Amazing & Fascinating Look at Our State's Teachers, Schools & Students! (Illus.). 1990. PLB 19.95 (ISBN 0-7933-0923-9); pap. 14.95 (ISBN 0-7933-0922-0); computer disk 29.95 (ISBN 0-7933-0924-7). Gallopade Pub Group.

—Oklahoma Silly Basketball Sportsmysteries, Vol. 1. (Illus.). 1990. PLB 19.95 (ISBN 0-7933-0920-4); pap. 14.95 (ISBN 0-7933-0919-0); computer disk 29.95 (ISBN 0-7933-0921-2). Gallopade Pub Group.

—Oklahoma Silly Basketball Sportsmysteries: Oklahoma Bks, Vol. 2. (Illus.). 1990. PLB 19.95 (ISBN 0-7933-1884-X); pap. 14.95 (ISBN 0-7933-1885-8); computer disk 29.95 (ISBN 0-7933-1886-6). Gallopade Pub Group.

—Oklahoma Silly Football Sportsmysteries, Vol. 1. (Illus.). 1990. PLB 19.95 (ISBN 0-7933-1863-7); pap. 14.95 (ISBN 0-7933-1864-5); computer disk 29.95 (ISBN 0-7933-1865-3). Gallopade Pub Group.

—Oklahoma Silly Football Sportsmysteries, Vol. 2. (Illus.). 1990. PLB 19.95 (ISBN 0-7933-1866-1); pap. 14.95 (ISBN 0-7933-1867-X); computer disk 29.95 (ISBN 0-7933-1868-8). Gallopade Pub Group.

—Oklahoma Silly Trivia! (Illus.). 1990. PLB 19.95; pap. 14.95 (ISBN 1-55609-082-X); computer disk 29.95 (ISBN 0-7933-1857-2). Gallopade Pub Group.

—Oklahoma's (Most Devastating!) Disasters & (Most Calamitous!) Catastrophies! (Illus.). 1990. PLB 19.95 (ISBN 0-7933-0911-5); pap. 14.95 (ISBN 0-7933-0910-7); computer disk 29.95 (ISBN 0-7933-0912-3). Gallopade Pub Group.

Turner Educational Services Inc. Staff & Clark, James I. Oklahoma. 48p. (gr. 3 up). 1986. text ed. 17.32 (ISBN 0-86514-456-7); pap. text ed. 9.27 (ISBN 0-86514-531-8); cancelled Beta video (ISBN 0-86514-081-2); cancelled VHS video (ISBN 0-86514-156-8); cancelled 3/4" video (ISBN 0-86514-231-9); cancelled tchr's. study guide (ISBN 0-86514-306-4); cancelled student activity bk. (ISBN 0-86514-381-1); cancelled index. Raintree Pubs.

OKLAHOMA–FICTION

Hinton, Susie E. Outsiders. (gr. 7 up). 1967. pap. 12.95 (ISBN 0-670-53257-6). Viking Child Bks.

Thomas, Joyce C. Marked by Fire. 160p. (gr. 7 up). 1982. pap. 2.95 (ISBN 0-380-79327-X, Flare). Avon.

OKLAHOMA–HISTORY

Meinders, LaDonna K. Leaves in the Wind. Loftin, Beth, illus. Wheeler, J. Clyde, intro. by. LC 89-81374. (Illus.). 152p. 1989. 15.95 (ISBN 0-934188-31-9). Evans Pubns.

Newsom, D. Earl. The Birth of Oklahoma. (Illus.). 178p. (gr. 5-12). 1983. 14.95 (ISBN 0-934188-08-4). Evans Pubns.

Wagoner, Jay J. Oklahoma! Boutas, Nora, illus. LC 89-90110. 229p. 1989. lib. bdg. 20.00 (ISBN 0-9622361-0-1). Thunderbird Bks.

Wise, Lu C. Oklahoma's First Ladies. LC 83-82947. (Illus.). 88p. (gr. 5-12). 1984. 14.95 (ISBN 0-934188-10-6). Evans Pubns.

OKLAHOMA–HISTORY–FICTION

Kirschstein, Carolyn. Hooray for Oklahoma Eighteen Eighty-Nine. (Illus.). 72p. (gr. k-4). 1989. 9.95 (ISBN 0-926521-00-4). B C Pub Inc.

OLD AGE

see also Aged

Darling, David. Could You Ever Live Forever? (Illus.). 60p. (gr. 5 up). 1991. 14.95 (ISBN 0-87518-457-X, Dillon). Macmillan Child Grp.

Farber, Norma. How Does It Feel to Be Old? Hyman, Trina S., illus. LC 79-11516. (ps-3). 1988. 12.95 (ISBN 0-525-32414-3, DCB); pap. 3.95 (ISBN 0-525-44367-3, DCB). Dutton Child Bks.

Worth, Richard. You'll Be Old Someday, Too. LC 85-29419. 128p. (gr. 7-12). 1986. lib. bdg. 12.90 (ISBN 0-531-10158-4). Watts.

OLD AGE–FICTION

Bedard, Michael. Redwork. LC 89-27983. 272p. (gr. 7 up). 1990. 15.95 (ISBN 0-689-31622-4, Atheneum Child Bk). Macmillan Child Grp.

Coutant, Helen. The Gift. Mai, Vo-Dinh, illus. LC 82-7810. 48p. (gr. 2-5). 1983. 9.95 (ISBN 0-394-85499-3). Knopf.

Ethridge, Kenneth E. Viola, Furgy, Bobbi & Me. LC 88-28429. 168p. 1989. 13.95 (ISBN 0-8234-0746-2). Holiday.

Fair, Sylvia. The Bedspread. Fair, Sylvia, illus. LC 81-11152. 32p. (gr. k-3). 1982. 14.95 (ISBN 0-688-00877-1). Morrow Jr Bks.

Fox, Mem. Night Noises. 1989. 13.95 (ISBN 0-15-200543-9). HarbraceJ.

Gondosch, Linda. Who's Afraid of Haggerty House? LC 86-24265. (gr. 4-6). 1987. 11.95 (ISBN 0-525-67198-6, Lodestar Bks). Dutton Child Bks.

—Who's Afraid of Haggerty House. 1989. pap. 2.75 (ISBN 0-671-67237-1, Minstrel Bks). PB.

Holl, Kristi D. Just Like a Real Family. LC 82-16239. 132p. (gr. 4-6). 1983. 12.95 (ISBN 0-689-30970-8, Atheneum Child Bk). Macmillan Child Grp.

Howe, James. Pinky & Rex & the Mean Old Witch. Sweet, Melissa, illus. LC 89-78204. 48p. (gr. k-3). 1991. SBE 11.95 (ISBN 0-689-31617-8, Atheneum Child Bk). Macmillan Child Grp.

Jones, Janice. Secrets of a Summer Spy. LC 89-38156. 192p. (gr. 5-9). 1990. 13.95 (ISBN 0-02-747861-0, Bradbury Pr). Macmillan Child Grp.

Kantrowitz, Mildred. Maxie. McCully, Emily A., illus. LC 80-15289. 36p. (ps-3). 1984. Repr. of 1970 ed. 12.95 (ISBN 0-02-749390-3, Four Winds). Macmillan Child Grp.

Martin, C. L. The Dragon Nanny. Rayevsky, Robert, illus. LC 90-39985. 32p. (gr. k-3). 1991. pap. 3.95 (ISBN 0-689-71451-3, Aladdin). Macmillan Child Grp.

Myers, Walter D. Won't Know Till I Get There. LC 81-71128. 192p. (gr. 7 up). 1982. pap. 11.95 (ISBN 0-670-77862-1). Viking Child Bks.

Rawlins, Donna. Digging to China. LC 89-42536. (Illus.). 32p. (ps-2). 1989. 12.95 (ISBN 0-531-05814-X); PLB 12.99 (ISBN 0-531-08414-0). Orchard Bks Watts.

Ruckman, Ivy. This Is Your Captain Speaking. (gr. 5 up). 1987. 14.95 (ISBN 0-8027-6734-6). Walker & Co.

Ryan, Mary C. The Voice from the Mendelsohns Maple. Roman, Irena, illus. LC 89-31569. 132p. (gr. 5-7). 1990. 13.95 (ISBN 0-316-76360-8). Little.

Rylant, Cynthia. Miss Maggie. DiGrazia, Thomas, illus. LC 82-18206. 32p. (gr. k-3). 1983. 11.95 (ISBN 0-525-44048-8, DCB). Dutton Child Bks.

Sakai, Kimiko. Sachiko Means Happiness. Arai, Tomie, illus. 32p. (gr. k-5). 1990. 12.95 (ISBN 0-89239-065-4). Childrens Book Pr.

Towne, Mary. Their House. LC 89-34969. 208p. (gr. 5 up). 1990. 13.95 (ISBN 0-689-31562-7, Atheneum Child Bk). Macmillan Child Grp.

Zolotow, Charlotte. I Know a Lady. Stevenson, James, illus. LC 83-25361. 24p. (gr. k-3). 1984. 14.95 (ISBN 0-688-03837-9); PLB 14.88 (ISBN 0-688-03838-7). Greenwillow.

Zolotow, Charlotte & Stevenson, James. I Know a Lady. (Illus.). 32p. (ps-3). 1986. pap. 3.95 (ISBN 0-14-050550-4, Puffin). Puffin Bks.

OLD TESTAMENT

see Bible. Old Testament

OLYMPIC GAMES

Arnold, Caroline. The Olympic Summer Games. (Illus.). 64p. (gr. 5-8). 1991. PLB 11.90 (ISBN 0-531-20052-3). Watts.

—The Olympic Winter Games. (Illus.). 64p. (gr. 5-8). 1991. PLB 11.90 (ISBN 0-531-20053-1). Watts.

Fradin, Dennis B. Olympics. LC 83-7214. (Illus.). 48p. (gr. k-4). 1983. PLB 14.60 (ISBN 0-516-01703-9); pap. 4.95 (ISBN 0-516-41703-7). Childrens.

Glubok, Shirley & Tamarin, Alfred. Olympic Games in Ancient Greece. LC 75-25408. (Illus.). 128p. (gr. 5-9). 1976. PLB 13.89 (ISBN 0-06-022048-1). HarpC Child Bks.

Jarrett, William. Timetables of Sports History: The Olympic Games. (Illus.). 96p. 1990. 17.95x (ISBN 0-8160-1921-5). Facts on File.

Lambert, David. Seas & Oceans. (Illus.). 48p. (gr. 5-8). 1987. PLB 14.98 (ISBN 0-382-09503-0). Silver Burdett Pr.

Milton, Joyce. Greg Louganis: Diving for Gold. LC 88-43496. (Illus.). 72p. (gr. 2-4). 1989. PLB 6.99 (ISBN 0-394-94586-7); pap. 2.95 (ISBN 0-394-84586-2). Random.

The Summer Olympics. 32p. (gr. 4). 1990. 12.95s.p. (ISBN 0-88682-318-8); 18.50 (ISBN 0-685-28233-3). Creative Ed.

Trella, Phyllis. Les Duit at the Olympics...& Be a Strong. Trella, Phyllis, illus. 48p. (gr. 2-6). write for info. (ISBN 0-914201-01-8). Cheeruppet.

Trenary, Jill. Day I Skated for the Gold. 1991. pap. 5.95 (ISBN 0-671-73348-6). S&S Trade.

OLYMPIC GAMES–FICTION

Baglio, Ben. The First Olympics, No. 77. 176p. (Orig.). (gr. 7 up). 1988. pap. 2.50 (ISBN 0-553-27063-X). Bantam.

Birenbaum, Barbara. The Olympic Glow. (Illus.). 48p. (gr. 3-5). 1990. pap. 5.95 (ISBN 0-935343-41-5) (ISBN 0-317-89492-7). Peartree.

Drake, Ann. Quigby & the Junior Olympic Games. Caroland, Mary, ed. LC 90-71142. 79p. (gr. 4-8). 1991. 6.95 (ISBN 1-55523-368-6). Winston-Derek.

Goscinny, Rene de & Uderzo, Albert. Asterix at the Olympic Games. 2nd ed. (Illus.). 48p. (gr. 10). 1984. pap. 4.95 (ISBN 2-205-06911-X). Dargaud Pub.

OMAN

Tilley, P. F. Oman. (Illus.). (gr. 5 up). 1988. 14.95 (ISBN 1-55546-172-7). Chelsea Hse.

ONE-ACT PLAYS

Jones, Michael P. Land of the Animal Spirits: A One Act Play. Willis, Kathy & Boldt, Jeaninefrwd. by. (Illus.). 132p. (Orig.). 1985. text ed. 15.00 (ISBN 0-89904-113-2); pap. text ed. 9.99 (ISBN 0-89904-114-0). Crumb Elbow Pub.

OPERA

see also Ballet

Biscardi, Cyrus H. The Storybook of Opera, Vol. II. Blythe, Anne, frwd. by. LC 86-81155. (Illus.). 224p. (gr. 7 up). 1987. lib. bdg. 23.95 (ISBN 0-918452-99-6); pap. 23.95 (ISBN 1-55691-006-1). Learning Pubns.

Brubaker, David. Court & Commedia. (Illus.). (gr. 7-12). 1975. PLB 14.95 (ISBN 0-8239-0317-6). Rosen Group.

Englander, Roger. Opera! What's All the Screaming About? LC 82-23742. (Illus.). 192p. (gr. 6 up). 1983. 12.95 (ISBN 0-8027-6491-6). Walker & Co.

John, Nicholas. Opera. 48p. (gr. 4-7). 1986. pap. 9.95 (ISBN 0-19-321335-4). Oxford U Pr.

Kerby, Mona. Beverly Sills: America's Own Opera Star. Hamanaka, Sheila, illus. 64p. (gr. 2-5). 1989. 10.95 (ISBN 0-670-82251-5). Viking Child Bks.

Neidorf, Mary. Operantics with Wolfgang Amadeus Mozart. LC 86-14435. 32p. (Orig.). (gr. 3-6). 1987. pap. 4.95 (ISBN 0-86534-092-7). Sunstone Pr.

Williams, Sylvia. Leontyne Price: Opera Superstar. LC 84-7617. (Illus.). 32p. (gr. 2-5). 1984. lib. bdg. 13.27 (ISBN 0-516-03531-2). Childrens.

OPERA–FICTION

Sparks, Richard W. A Candle Opera. Acheson, Robert B., illus. 54p. (gr. 1-10). 1983. pap. 5.95 (ISBN 0-9614185-0-8). S J F Co.

OPERETTA

see also Musical Revues, Comedies, etc.

OPIATES

see Narcotics

OPINION, PUBLIC

see Public Opinion

OPOSSUMS

Crofford, Emily. Opossum. LC 89-28269. (Illus.). 48p. (gr. 5 up). 1990. 10.95 (ISBN 0-89686-518-5, Crestwood Hse). Macmillan Child Grp.

Mizumura, Kazue. Opossum. Mizumura, Kazue, illus. LC 73-13514. 40p. 1974. PLB 12.89 (Crowell Jr Bks). HarpC Child Bks.

Rue, Leonard L., III & Owen, William. Meet the Opossum. (Illus.). 64p. (gr. 3-7). 1983. 8.95 (ISBN 0-396-08221-1, Putnam). Putnam Pub Group.

OPOSSUMS–FICTION

Fox, Mem. Possum Magic. Vivas, Julie, illus. 32p. (ps-2). 1990. 13.95 (ISBN 0-15-200572-2, Gulliver Bks). HarBraceJ.

Higgins, Kitty. Perry P. Plum the Possum. James, Robin, illus. 24p. 1990. pap. 5.95 (ISBN 0-8431-2743-0). Price Stern.

Jensen, Kiersten. Possum in the House. Sherwood, Rhoda, ed. Olliver, Tony, illus. LC 88-42910. 32p. (gr. 1-2). 1988. PLB 12.95 (ISBN 1-55532-933-0). Gareth Stevens Inc.

Pellowski, Michael J. Professor Possum's Great Adventure. Durrell, Julie, illus. LC 88-1281. 48p. (Orig.). (gr. 1-3). 1988. PLB 9.89 (ISBN 0-8167-1341-3); pap. text ed. 2.95 (ISBN 0-8167-1342-1). Troll Assocs.

Swartzentruber, Mrs. James. God Made the Opossum. 1976. 2.45 (ISBN 0-686-18187-5). Rod & Staff.

OPPENHEIMER, J. ROBERT, 1904-1967

Driemen, J. E. Atomic Dawn: A Biography of Robert Oppenheimer. LC 88-18968. (Illus.). 160p. (gr. 5 up). 1989. PLB 12.95 (ISBN 0-87518-397-2, Dillon). Macmillan Child Grp.

OPTICAL ILLUSIONS

Baum, Arline & Baum, Joseph. Opt: An Illusionary Tale. (Illus.). 32p. (ps-3). 1989. pap. 3.95 (ISBN 0-14-050573-3, Puffin). Puffin Bks.

Beeler, Nelson F. & Branley, Franklyn M. Experiments in Optical Illusion. Lyon, Fred H., illus. LC 51-5642. 114p. (gr. 5-9). 1951. PLB 12.89 (ISBN 0-690-27507-2, Crowell Jr Bks). HarpC Child Bks.

Brandes, Louis G. Can You Believe What You See? Illusions. Laycock, Mary, ed. Brandes, Louis G., illus. 96p. (Orig.). (gr. 4-10). pap. 12.50 (ISBN 0-918932-92-0). Activity Resources.

Brandreth, Gyles. The Great Book of Optical Illusions. Murphy, Rowan B. & Murphy, Albert, illus. LC 85-9898. 96p. (Orig.). (gr. 2 up). 1985. pap. 3.95 (ISBN 0-8069-6258-5). Sterling.

Carini, E. Take Another Look. (ps-3). 1969. pap. 1.50 (ISBN 0-685-03910-2). P-H.

Churchill, E. Richard. How to Make Optical Illusion Tricks & Toys. LC 89-26169. (Illus.). 128p. (Orig.). 1990. pap. 4.95 (ISBN 0-8069-6869-9). Sterling.

Gardner, Robert. Experimenting with Illusions. (gr. 4-7). 1990. PLB 12.40 (ISBN 0-531-10909-7). Watts.

Koziakin, Vladimir. Optical Illusions to Color. 1989. pap. 1.95 (ISBN 0-590-42199-9). Scholastic Inc.

Paraquin, Charles H. Eye Teasers: Optical Illusion Puzzles. Kuttner, Paul, tr. LC 76-21844. (Illus.). (gr. 3 up). 1976. 7.95 (ISBN 0-8069-4538-9); PLB 9.99 (ISBN 0-8069-4539-7). Sterling.

—World's Best Optical Illusions. Kuttner, Paul, tr. LC 87-13885. (Illus.). 96p. (Orig.). (gr. 4-12). 1987. pap. 4.95 (ISBN 0-8069-6644-0). Sterling.

Powers, Tom. Special Effects in the Movies. LC 89-12703. (Illus.). 96p. (gr. 5-8). 1989. PLB 11.95 (ISBN 1-56006-102-2). Lucent Bks.

Simon, Seymour. The Optical Illusion Book. LC 83-43222. (Illus.). 80p. (gr. 3-7). 1984. 12.88 (ISBN 0-688-03255-9); pap. 6.95 (ISBN 0-688-03254-0, Pub. by Beech Tree Bks). Morrow Jr Bks.

Supraner, Robyn. Stop & Look! Illusions. Barto, Renzo, illus. LC 80-23799. 48p. (gr. 1-5). 1981. PLB 11.89 (ISBN 0-89375-434-X); pap. 2.95 (ISBN 0-89375-435-8). Troll Assocs.

White, Lawrence B. & Brockel, Ray. Optical Illusions. Green, Anne C., illus. LC 86-510986. (gr. 4-9). 1986. PLB 10.40 (ISBN 0-531-10220-3). Watts.

OPTICAL MASERS

see Lasers

OPTICS

see also Color; Light; Radiation; Vision

Billings, Charlene W. Fiber Optics. (Illus.). 64p. (gr. 2-5). 1986. 12.99 (ISBN 0-399-61233-5, Putnam). Putnam Pub Group.

Hecht, Jeff. Optics: Light for a New Age. LC 87-23398. (Illus.). 44p. (gr. 5-9). 1988. 14.95 (ISBN 0-684-18879-1, Scribners Young Read). Macmillan Child Grp.

Wood, Robert W. Physics For Kids: 49 Easy Experiments with Optics. (Illus.). 176p. 1990. 16.95 (ISBN 0-8306-8402-6, 3402); pap. 9.95 (ISBN 0-8306-3402-9). TAB Bks.

OPTICS–EXPERIMENTS

Ardley, Neil. Science Book of Light. (gr. 4-7). 1991. 9.95 (ISBN 0-15-200577-3). HarBraceJ.

Beeler, Nelson F. & Branley, Franklyn M. Experiments in Optical Illusion. Lyon, Fred H., illus. LC 51-5642. 114p. (gr. 5-9). 1951. PLB 12.89 (ISBN 0-690-27507-2, Crowell Jr Bks). HarpC Child Bks.

OPTIONS

see Stock Exchange

OPTOMETRY

see also Eye

Silverstein, Alvin & Silverstein, Virginia B. Glasses & Contact Lenses: Your Guide to Eyes, Eyewear, & Eye Care. LC 88-13026. (Illus.). 144p. (gr. 7 up). 1989. 12.95 (ISBN 0-397-32184-8, Lipp Jr Bks); PLB 12.89 (ISBN 0-397-32185-6, Lipp Jr Bks). HarpC Child Bks.

ORANGE

Cleaver, Vera & Cleaver, Bill. Hazel Rye. LC 81-48603. 160p. (gr. 5-8). 1983. 12.95 (ISBN 0-397-31951-7, Lipp Jr Bks); PLB 12.89 (ISBN 0-397-31952-5, Lipp Jr Bks). HarpC Child Bks.

Moncure, Jane B. What Was It Before It Was Orange Juice? Lexa, Susan, illus. LC 85-11396. 32p. (ps-2). 1985. PLB 11.97 (ISBN 0-89565-322-2). Childs World.

ORATORY

see Public Speaking

ORBITING VEHICLES

see Artificial Satellites

ORCHARDS

see Fruit Culture

ORCHESTRA

see also Bands (Music)

Elliott, Donald. Alligators & Music. Arrowood, Clinton, illus. LC 84-13862. (gr. 8). 1984. (Pub. by Gambit); pap. 8.95 (ISBN 0-87645-118-0, Pub. by Gambit). Harvard Common Pr.

Elliott, Donald & Arrowood, Clinton L. Alligators & Music. LC 76-1569. (Illus.). (gr. 1 up). 1976. 12.95 (ISBN 0-685-01824-5, H C Press Gambit); pap. 8.95 (ISBN 0-685-01825-3, H C Press Gambit). S&S Trade.

Glass, Marvin. Animal Band. Glass, Marvin, illus. 12p. (gr. 2-4). 1990. bds. 3.95 (ISBN 1-878624-02-4). McClanahan Bk.

Hayes, Ann. Meet the Orchestra. D'Andrade, Diane, ed. Thompson, Karmen, illus. 32p. (ps-3). 1991. 13.95 (ISBN 0-15-200526-9, Gulliver Bks). HarBraceJ.

Posell, Elsa Z. This Is an Orchestra. rev. ed. (Illus.). 96p. (gr. 2-5). 1973. 13.95 (ISBN 0-395-17712-X). HM.

Storms, Laura. Careers with an Orchestra. Blumenfeld, Milton J., illus. LC 82-17284. 36p. (gr. 2-5). 1983. PLB 7.95 (ISBN 0-8225-0344-1). Lerner Pubns.

ORDNANCE

see also names of general and specific military ordnance, e.g. Atomic Weapons; also names of armies with the subdivision Ordnance and Ordnance Stores, e.g. U. S. Army–Ordnance and Ordnance Stores

OREGON

Bratvold, Gretchen. Oregon. (Illus.). 72p. (gr. 3-6). 1991. PLB 12.95 (ISBN 0-8225-2704-9). Lerner Pubns.

Carole Marsh Oregon Books, 31 bks. Set. 638.45 (ISBN 0-7933-1312-0). Gallopade Pub Group.

Carpenter, Allan. Oregon. new ed. LC 78-13955. (Illus.). 96p. (gr. 4 up). 1979. PLB 19.93 (ISBN 0-516-04137-1). Childrens.

Cloutier, James. This Day in Oregon. Cloutier, James, illus. LC 80-83719. 128p. 1981. pap. 6.95 (ISBN 0-918966-06-X). Image West.

Dodson, Benjamin C. The Promise of Oregon. Dodson, O. Ray, intro. by. 118p. (Orig.). (gr. 7-12). 1989. pap. 6.75 (ISBN 0-9620550-3-4). Dodson Assocs.

Fradin, Dennis. Oregon: In Words & Pictures. Wahl, Richard, illus. LC 80-15183. 48p. (gr. 3-8). 1980. PLB 15.93 (ISBN 0-516-03937-7). Childrens.

Jones, Michael P., ed. Oregon River Watch: A Contemporary History of Oregon's Waterways, Vol. 1. Bachmann, Mark, et al, illus. 48p. (Orig.). 1985. text ed. 9.95 (ISBN 0-89904-143-4); pap. text ed. 5.00 (ISBN 0-89904-144-2); composition 8.00 (ISBN 0-89904-145-0). Crumb Elbow Pub.

—Oregon River Watch: A Contemporary History of Oregon's Waterways, Vol. 2. Bachmann, Mark, et al, illus. 50p. (Orig.). 1985. text ed. 9.95 (ISBN 0-89904-146-9); pap. text ed. 5.00 (ISBN 0-89904-147-7); composition 8.00 (ISBN 0-89904-148-5). Crumb Elbow Pub.

Marsh, Carole. Avast, Ye Slobs! Oregon Pirate Trivia. (Illus.). 1990. PLB 19.95 (ISBN 0-7933-0956-5); pap. 14.95 (ISBN 0-7933-0955-7); computer disk 29.95. Gallopade Pub Group.

—The Beast of the Oregon Bed & Breakfast. (Illus.). 1990. PLB 19.95 (ISBN 0-7933-1901-3); pap. 14.95 (ISBN 0-7933-1902-1); computer disk 29.95 (ISBN 0-7933-1903-X). Gallopade Pub Group.

—The Hard-to-Believe-But-True! Book of Oregon History, Mystery, Trivia, Legend, Lore, Humor & More. (Illus.). 1990. PLB 19.95 (ISBN 0-7933-0953-0); pap. 14.95 (ISBN 0-7933-0952-2); computer disk 29.95 (ISBN 0-7933-0954-9). Gallopade Pub Group.

—If My Oregon Mama Ran the World! (Illus.). 1990. lib. bdg. 19.95 (ISBN 0-7933-1910-2); pap. 14.95 (ISBN 0-7933-1911-0); computer disk 29.95 (ISBN 0-7933-1912-9). Gallopade Pub Group.

—Let's Quilt Oregon & Stuff It Topographically! (Illus.). 1990. PLB 19.95 (ISBN 0-7933-1893-9); pap. 14.95 (ISBN 1-55609-132-X); computer disk 29.95 (ISBN 0-7933-1894-7). Gallopade Pub Group.

—Oregon & Other State Greats (Biographies) (Illus.). 1990. PLB 19.95 (ISBN 0-7933-1913-7); pap. 14.95 (ISBN 0-7933-1914-5); computer disk 29.95 (ISBN 0-7933-1915-3). Gallopade Pub Group.

—Oregon Bandits, Bushwackers, Outlaws, Crooks, Devils, Ghosts, Desperadoes & Other Assorted & Sundry Characters! (Illus.). 1990. PLB 19.95 (ISBN 0-7933-0938-7); pap. 14.95 (ISBN 0-7933-0937-9); computer disk 29.95 (ISBN 0-7933-0939-5). Gallopade Pub Group.

—Oregon Classic Christimas Trivia: Stories, Recipes, Activities, Legends, Lore & More! (Illus.). 1990. PLB 19.95 (ISBN 0-7933-0941-7); pap. 14.95 (ISBN 0-7933-0940-9); computer disk 29.95 (ISBN 0-7933-0942-5). Gallopade Pub Group.

—Oregon Coastales. (Illus.). 1990. PLB 19.95 (ISBN 0-7933-1907-2); pap. 14.95. Gallopade Pub Group.

—The Oregon Hot Air Balloon Mystery. (Illus.). (gr. 2-9). 1990. 19.95 (ISBN 0-7933-2651-6); pap. 14.95 (ISBN 0-7933-2652-4); computer disk 29.95 (ISBN 0-7933-2653-2). Gallopade Pub Group.

—Oregon "Jography" A Fun Run Thru Our State. (Illus.). 1990. PLB 19.95 (ISBN 0-7933-1890-4); pap. 14.95 (ISBN 0-7933-1891-2); computer disk 29.95 (ISBN 0-7933-1892-0). Gallopade Pub Group.

—Oregon Kid's Cookbook: Recipes, How-to, History, Lore & More! (Illus.). 1990. PLB 19.95 (ISBN 0-7933-0950-6); pap. 14.95 (ISBN 0-7933-0949-2); computer disk 29.95 (ISBN 0-7933-0951-4). Gallopade Pub Group.

—Oregon Quiz Bowl Crash Course! (Illus.). 1990. PLB 19.95 (ISBN 0-7933-1904-8); pap. 14.95 (ISBN 0-7933-1905-6); computer disk 29.95 (ISBN 0-7933-1906-4). Gallopade Pub Group.

—Oregon School Trivia: An Amazing & Fascinating Look at Our State's Teachers, Schools & Students. (Illus.). 1990. PLB 19.95 (ISBN 0-7933-0947-6); pap. 14.95 (ISBN 0-7933-0946-8); computer disk 29.95 (ISBN 0-7933-0948-4). Gallopade Pub Group.

—Oregon Silly Basketball Sportsmysteries, Vol. 1. (Illus.). 1990. PLB 19.95 (ISBN 0-7933-0944-1); pap. 14.95 (ISBN 0-7933-0943-3); computer disk 29.95 (ISBN 0-7933-0945-X). Gallopade Pub Group.

—Oregon Silly Basketball Sportsmysteries, Vol. 2. (Illus.). 1990. PLB 19.95 (ISBN 0-7933-1916-1); pap. 14.95 (ISBN 0-7933-1917-X); computer disk 29.95 (ISBN 0-7933-1918-8). Gallopade Pub Group.

—Oregon Silly Football Sportsmysteries, Vol. 1. (Illus.). 1990. PLB 19.95 (ISBN 0-7933-1895-5); pap. 14.95 (ISBN 0-7933-1896-3); computer disk 29.95 (ISBN 0-7933-1897-1). Gallopade Pub Group.

—Oregon Silly Football Sportsmysteries, Vol. 2. (Illus.). 1990. PLB 19.95 (ISBN 0-7933-1898-X); pap. 14.95 (ISBN 0-7933-1899-8); computer disk 29.95 (ISBN 0-7933-1900-5). Gallopade Pub Group.

—Oregon Silly Trivia! (Illus.). 1990. PLB 19.95 (ISBN 0-7933-1887-4); pap. 14.95 (ISBN 0-7933-1888-2); computer disk 29.95 (ISBN 0-7933-1889-0). Gallopade Pub Group.

—Oregon's (Most Deastating!) Disasters & (Most Calamitous!) Catastrophies! (Illus.). 1990. PLB 19.95 (ISBN 0-7933-0935-2); pap. 14.95 (ISBN 0-7933-0934-4); computer disk 29.95 (ISBN 0-7933-0936-0). Gallopade Pub Group.

Riegel, Martin P. Ghost Ports of the Pacific, Vol. II: Oregon. LC 89-90772. (Illus.). 52p. (Orig.). 1989. 11.00 (ISBN 0-944871-20-8); pap. 4.95 (ISBN 0-944871-21-6). Riegel Pub.
Stein, R. Conrad. Oregon. LC 88-38528. (Illus.). (gr. 4 up). 1989. PLB 25.27 (ISBN 0-516-00483-2). Childrens.
Stewart, Judi & Weit, Kathryn. Around Portland with Kids. rev. ed. (Illus.). 205p. (ps-7). 1987. pap. 9.95 (ISBN 0-9614261-2-8). Discovery Pr.
Turner Program Services, Inc. Staff & Clark, James I. Oregon. LC 85-9973. 48p. (gr. 3 up). 1985. PLB 17.32 (ISBN 0-86514-441-9); pap. text ed. 9.27 (ISBN 0-86514-516-4); cancelled Beta video (ISBN 0-86514-066-9); cancelled VHS video (ISBN 0-86514-141-X); cancelled 3/4" video (ISBN 0-86514-216-5); cancelled tchr's. guide (ISBN 0-86514-291-2); cancelled student activity bk. (ISBN 0-86514-366-8); cancelled index. Raintree Pubs.
Williams, William J., Jr. Where the Trails Are - Ashland-Medford & Beyond. rev. ed. Sisson, Bob, illus. 184p. 1990. pap. 7.95 (ISBN 0-9622114-1-9). B Williams.
Wood, Sharon. The Portland Bridge Book. Alley, Joy D., illus. (Orig.). (ps-7). 1989. pap. 12.95 (ISBN 0-87595-211-9). Oregon Hist.

OREGON–FICTION

Cleary, Beverly. Emily's Runaway Imagination. Krush, Joe & Krush, Beth, illus. LC 61-10939. 224p. (gr. 3-7). 1961. 12.95 (ISBN 0-688-21267-0); PLB 12.88 (ISBN 0-688-31267-5, Morrow Jr Bks). Morrow Jr Bks.
Killingsworth, Monte. Eli's Songs. LC 91-6452. 144p. (gr. 5 up). 1991. 12.95 (ISBN 0-689-50527-2, M K McElderry). Macmillan Child Grp.
Wood, Elizabeth L. Many Horses. Pollock, Dean, illus. (gr. 5-11). 1953. 7.95 (ISBN 0-8323-0175-2). Binford Mort.

OREGON–HISTORY

Barklow, Irene. From Trails to Rails: The Post Offices, Stage Stops, & Wagon Roads of Union County, Oregon. Evans, Jack, ed. (Illus.). 306p. (Orig.). (gr. 8up). 1987. 24.95 (ISBN 0-9618185-2-2); pap. 18.95 (ISBN 0-9618185-0-6). Enchant Pub Oregon.
Braly, David. Cattle Barons of Early Oregon. LC 78-105220. (Illus.). 44p. (gr. 7-12). 1982. pap. 4.50 (ISBN 0-942206-00-2). Mediaor Co.

OREGON TRAIL

Catrow, David J., III, illus. The Story of the Oregon Trail. LC 83-23997. 31p. (gr. 3-5). 1984. 13.27 (ISBN 0-516-04668-3); pap. 3.25 (ISBN 0-516-44668-1). Childrens.
Fisher, Leonard E. The Oregon Trail. LC 90-55103. (Illus.). 64p. (gr. 3-7). 1990. reinforced 14.95 (ISBN 0-8234-0833-7). Holiday.
Gildemeister, Jerry. A Letter Home. Gildemeister, Jerry & Gray, Don, illus. LC 87-1151. 120p. (gr. 4-12). 1987. 24.50 (ISBN 0-936376-04-X). Bear Wallow Pub.
Parkman, Francis. Oregon Trail. (gr. 6 up). 1964. pap. 1.50 (ISBN 0-8049-0037-X, CL-37). Airmont.
Santrey, Laurence. Oregon Trail. Livingston, Francis, illus. LC 84-2643. 32p. (gr. 3-6). 1985. PLB 9.49 (ISBN 0-8167-0196-2); pap. text ed. 2.95 (ISBN 0-8167-0197-0). Troll Assocs.

OREGON TRAIL–FICTION

Arntson, Herbert E. Caravan to Oregon. LC 57-13207. (Illus.). (gr. 7-11). 1957. 8.95 (ISBN 0-8323-0164-7). Binford Mort.
Stevens, Carla. Trouble for Lucy. Himler, Ronald, illus. LC 79-10445. (gr. 2-6). 1979. 13.95 (ISBN 0-395-28971-8, Clarion). HM.

ORELLANA, FRANCISCO DE, 1500?-1549?

Bernhard, Brendan. Pizarro, Orellana, & the Exploration of the Amazon. Goetzmann, William H., ed. Collins, Michael, intro. by. (Illus.). 112p. (gr. 5 up). 1991. PLB 18.95 (ISBN 0-7910-1305-7). Chelsea Hse.

ORGANIZED CRIME
see Racketeering
ORGANIZED LABOR
see Labor Unions
ORIENT
see East (Far East)
ORIENTATION

Lieberman, Lillian. Following Directions. 64p. (gr. 2-5). 1989. 6.95 (ISBN 0-912107-87-1, MM1904). Monday Morning Bks.
Orienteering. (Illus.). 32p. (gr. 6-12). 1974. pap. 1.85 (ISBN 0-8395-3385-3, 3385). BSA.

ORIGAMI
see also Paper Crafts

Araki, Chiyo. Origami in the Classroom, 2 vols. LC 65-13412. (Illus.). (gr. 1 up). 1965-68. bds. 13.95 ea. Vol. 1 (ISBN 0-8048-0452-4). Vol. 2 (ISBN 0-8048-0453-2). C E Tuttle.
Huber, Joanna & Claudius, Christel. Easy & Fun Paper Folding. LC 90-9829. (Illus.). 128p. (gr. 2-8). 1990. 12.95 (ISBN 0-8069-7444-3). Sterling.
Kasahara, Kunihiko. Creative Origami. LC 67-87040. (Illus.). 1977. pap. 15.95 (ISBN 0-87040-411-3). Japan Pubns USA.

Kitamura, Keiji. Origami Treasure Chest. (Illus.). 80p. (Orig.). pap. 16.95 (ISBN 0-87040-868-2). Japan Pubns USA. This origami source book contains a delightful array of figures & objects to make something that will appeal to every taste & whim! Easy-to-follow directions will help children of all ages create everything from exotic animals & flowers to useful boxes & envelopes. The cross-cultural holiday section contains unique decorations for both Western & Japanese celebrations. With full-color illustrations & step-by-step instructions, the book is sure to inspire origami enthusiasts of all levels of ability. The 86 projects make this book truly a "treasure chest" of ideas. *Publisher Provided Annotation.*

Medvene, Mark. Foilrigami. (Illus.). (gr. 4-7). 1968. 10.95 (ISBN 0-685-06619-3). Astor-Honor.
Montroll, John. Origami American Style. 32p. (gr. 2 up). 1990. pap. 6.00 (ISBN 0-9627254-0-4). Zenagraf.
—Origami Sculptures. 2nd ed. Montroll, Andrew, ed. Montroll, John, illus. 144p. 1990. pap. text ed. 9.95 (ISBN 1-877656-02-X). Antroll Pub.
Murray, William D. & Rigney, Francis J. Paper Folding for Beginners. (Illus.). (gr. 1 up). pap. 2.95 (ISBN 0-486-20713-7). Dover.
My First Origami, No. 1: Airplanes, Penguin, Ivy & Pinwheel. (gr. 1-3). 1989. bds. 2.95 incl. origami paper (ISBN 0-89346-317-5). Heian Intl.
My First Origami, No. 2: Waterbird, Hat, Bat & Turtle. (gr. 1-3). 1989. bds. 2.95 incl. origami paper (ISBN 0-89346-318-3). Heian Intl.
My First Origami, No. 3: Cap, Piano, Pigeon & Snake. (gr. 1-3). 1989. bds. 2.95 incl. origami paper (ISBN 0-685-27025-4). Heian Intl.
My First Origami, No. 4: Grasshopper, Cat, Fish & Boat. (gr. 1-3). 1989. bds. 2.95 incl. origami paper (ISBN 0-685-27026-2). Heian Intl.
My First Origami, No. 5: Crow, Flower, Cicada & Boots. (gr. 1-3). 1989. bds. 2.95 incl. origami paper (ISBN 0-685-27027-0). Heian Intl.
My First Origami, No. 6: Box, Sailboat, Table & Chair, & Angelfish. (gr. 1-3). 1989. bds. 2.95 incl. origami paper (ISBN 0-685-27028-9). Heian Intl.
Nakano, Dokuihtei. Easy Origami. Kenneway, Eric, tr. Nakano, Dokuihtei, illus. LC 85-40644. 64p. (gr. k-12). 1986. pap. 10.95 (ISBN 0-670-80382-0). Viking Child Bks.
Sakade, Florence. Origami, Japanese Paper Folding, 3 Vols. LC 57-10685. (Illus., Orig.). (gr. 2 up). Vol. 1. pap. 5.95 ea. (ISBN 0-8048-0454-0). Vol. 2 (ISBN 0-8048-0455-9). Vol. 3 (ISBN 0-8048-0456-7). C E Tuttle.
Sarasas, Claude. ABC's of Origami. Sarasas, Claude, illus. LC 64-17160. (gr. 3-8). 1964. bds. 11.95 (ISBN 0-8048-0000-6). C E Tuttle.
Saunders, Richard & Mackness, Brian. Horrorgami! (Illus.). 64p. (gr. 1-7). 1991. 14.95 (ISBN 0-8069-8480-5). Sterling.
Takahama, Toshie. Happy Origami. (Illus.). 60p. (Orig.). 1989. pap. 17.95 boxed set incl. 96 sheets origami paper (ISBN 0-87040-830-5). Japan Pubns USA.
—Joy of Origami: Ten Basic Folds Which Create Many Forms. (Illus.). 128p. (Orig.). 1984. pap. 10.95 (ISBN 0-87040-603-5). Japan Pubns USA.

Trodglen, James E., Jr. Super Origami: Book One. (Illus.). 44p. 1991. pap. 9.95 (ISBN 1-879610-01-9). Origami Intl. Like many simple ideas, SUPER ORIGAMI (tm), is a very beautiful thing. Imagine a colorful geometric square design printed on the best high gloss white paper. Now imagine that you can fold up that printed paper design into a bird, do that & the head, body, wings, tail, eyes, beak, feet, etc., all come out in the right places, & the right color! This is a very old idea with colorful detail added. The History of Origami, & folding instructions plus diagrams are included in the book. This book will teach a person how to fold three each of five large detailed Super Origami models, for a total of 15 models in each book. The Green Parrot, Sea Bird, Seal, Rooster, & Tropical Fish were carefully chosen to introduce BOOK ONE. The first four will stand on their feet, & three Tropical Fish make a delightful mobile to hang in your room. Twenty four more SUPER ORIGAMI (tm), books are in the planning stage. Representing 125 different & exciting Origami models. Order today, your satisfaction is guaranteed! *Publisher Provided Annotation.*

ORIGIN OF MAN
see Man–Origin and Antiquity
ORIGIN OF SPECIES
see Evolution
ORNAMENT
see Decoration and Ornament
ORNAMENTAL ALPHABETS
see Lettering
ORNAMENTAL DESIGN
see Design, Decorative
ORNITHOLOGY
see Birds
ORPHANS AND ORPHANS' HOMES–FICTION

Anderson, Margaret J. The Journey of the Shadow Bairns. Lincoln, Patricia H., illus. 196p. (gr. 5-9). 1980. Knopf.
Bethancourt, T. Ernesto. The Me Inside of Me. LC 85-10292. 156p. (gr. 5 up). 1985. 11.95 (ISBN 0-8225-0728-5). Lerner Pubns.
Bronte, Charlotte. Jane Eyre. Mitchell, Kathy, illus. (gr. 4 up). 1983. deluxe ed. 13.95 (ISBN 0-448-06031-0, G&D). Putnam Pub Group.
Burch, Robert. Skinny. LC 89-28225. 128p. (gr. 4-6). 1990. Repr. 14.95g (ISBN 0-8203-1223-1). U of Ga Pr.
Burnett, Frances. The Secret Garden. 1989. pap. 2.50 (ISBN 0-451-52080-7). NAL-Dutton.
Burnett, Frances H. The Secret Garden. 302p. 1981. Repr. PLB 19.95x (ISBN 0-89966-326-5). Buccaneer Bks.
—Secret Garden. (gr. k-6). 1989. pap. 3.50 (ISBN 0-440-47709-3, Pub. by Yearling Classics); pap. 2.75 (ISBN 0-440-97709-6, Dell Trade Pbks). Dell.
—The Secret Garden. (gr. 4-6). 1987. pap. 2.25 (ISBN 0-14-035004-7, Puffin). Puffin Bks.
—The Secret Garden. Mitchell, Kathy, illus. 320p. (gr. 4 up). 1987. 12.95 (ISBN 0-448-06029-9, G&D). Putnam Pub Group.
—The Secret Garden. Tudor, Tasha, illus. LC 62-17457. 256p. (gr. 4-8). 1987. pap. 3.50 (ISBN 0-06-440188-X, Trophy). HarpC Child Bks.
—The Secret Garden. McNulty, Faith, afterword by. 1987. pap. 2.95 (ISBN 0-451-52417-9, Sig Classics). NAL-Dutton.
—The Secret Garden. Allen, Thomas B., illus. Howe, James, adapted by. LC 86-17788. (Illus.). 72p. (gr. k-5). 1987. 13.95 (ISBN 0-394-86467-0, Random Juv); lib. bdg. 12.99 (ISBN 0-394-96467-5). Random.
—The Secret Garden. (gr. k-6). 8.98 (ISBN 0-517-63225-X). Outlet Bk Co.
—The Secret Garden. Hague, Michael, illus. LC 86-22780. 240p. (gr. 4-6). 1987. 18.95 (ISBN 0-8050-0277-4). H Holt & Co.
—The Secret Garden. 304p. (Orig.). (gr. 4-6). 1987. pap. 2.95 (ISBN 0-590-40720-1, Pub. by Apple Classics). Scholastic Inc.
—The Secret Garden. Lowry, Lois, intro. by. 256p. 1987. pap. 2.95 (ISBN 0-553-21201-X, Bantam Classics). Bantam.
—The Secret Garden. Betts, Louise, adapted by. LC 87-15490. (Illus.). (gr. 3-6). 1987. PLB 12.89 (ISBN 0-8167-1203-4); pap. 3.95 (ISBN 0-8167-1204-2). Troll Assocs.
—The Secret Garden. 360p. 1987. pap. 4.95 (ISBN 0-19-281772-8). Oxford U Pr.
—The Secret Garden. Sanderson, Ruth, illus. LC 86-46002. 240p. 1988. 18.95 (ISBN 0-394-55431-0). Knopf.
—The Secret Garden. 304p. (gr. 4-7). 1987. pap. 2.95 (ISBN 0-590-43346-6). Scholastic Inc.
—Secret Garden. 1987. pap. 3.50 (ISBN 0-440-40055-4). Dell.
—Secret Garden. 288p. 1990. pap. 2.50 (ISBN 0-8125-0501-8). Tor Bks.
—Secret Garden. Howell, Troy, illus. 272p. (gr. 4 up). 1987. 10.95 (ISBN 0-681-40056-0). Longmeadow Pr.
—Secret Garden. 1991. pap. 3.99 (ISBN 0-8125-1910-8). Tor Bks.
Burnett, Francis H. The Secret Garden: A Young Reader's Edition of the Classic Story. Abr. ed. Crawford, Dale, illus. LC 90-80198. 56p. (gr. 1 up). 1990. 9.98 (ISBN 0-89471-860-6, Courage Bks). Running Pr.
Byrum, Isabel. How John Became a Man. 64p. (gr. 7 up). pap. 0.75 (ISBN 0-686-29118-2). Faith Pub Hse.
Carlson, Natalie S. Happy Orpheline. Williams, Garth, illus. LC 57-9260. 112p. (gr. 3-6). 1957. PLB 13.89 (ISBN 0-06-021007-9). HarpC Child Bks.
Cassedy, Sylvia. Lucie Babbidge's House. LC 89-1296. 256p. (gr. 4-7). 1989. 12.95 (ISBN 0-690-04796-7, Crowell Jr Bks); PLB 12.89 (ISBN 0-690-04798-3, Crowell Jr Bks). HarpC Child Bks.
Cleaver, Vera & Cleaver, Bill. Where the Lilies Bloom. LC 75-82402. (Illus.). 176p. (gr. 4-9). 1969. 14.95 (ISBN 0-397-31111-7, Lipp Jr Bks). HarpC Child Bks.
Cohen, Barbara. The Orphan Game. (gr. 3-7). 1989. pap. 2.75 (ISBN 0-553-15706-X, Skylark). Bantam.
Cunningham, Julia. Dorp Dead. Spanfeller, J., illus. (gr. 5-9). 1965. lib. bdg. 6.99 (ISBN 0-394-91089-3). Pantheon.
Dickens, Charles. Oliver Twist. (gr. 9 up). 1964. pap. 3.50 (ISBN 0-8049-0009-4, CL-9). Airmont.
—Oliver Twist. (gr. 4 up). 1989. pap. 4.87 (ISBN 0-582-52279-X, 73808). Longman.

—Oliver Twist. 496p. (gr. 9-12). Date not set. pap. 2.50 (ISBN 0-451-51685-0, Sig Classics). NAL-Dutton.
—Oliver Twist. abridged ed. Martin, Les, adapted by. Zallinger, Jean, illus. LC 89-24279. 96p. (Orig.). (gr. 2-6). 1990. PLB 5.99 (ISBN 0-679-90391-7); pap. 2.95 (ISBN 0-679-80391-2). Random.
Dupasquier, Philippe. Jack at Sea. (Illus.). 32p. (gr. 2-6). 1987. 12.95 (ISBN 0-13-509209-4). P-H.
Eckles, Melita Z. The Horse That Blew Up. LC 89-52188. (Illus.). 35p. (gr. 2-5). 1990. pap. 4.95 (ISBN 1-55523-319-8). Winston-Derek.
Edwards, Julie. Mandy. Brown, Judith G., illus. LC 76-157901. 224p. (gr. 3-6). 1989. pap. 3.95 (ISBN 0-06-440296-7, Trophy). HarpC Child Bks.
Ehrlich, Amy. Annie: The Storybook Based on the Movie. LC 81-15416. (Illus.). 64p. (gr. 5 up). 1982. Random.
Eliot, George. Silas Marner. (gr. 9 up). 1964. pap. 2.50 (ISBN 0-8049-0014-0, CL-14). Airmont.

Gabel, Susan L. Where the Sun Kisses the Sea. Bowring, Joanne, illus. LC 89-16296. 32p. (ps-5). 1989. 15.95 (ISBN 0-944934-00-5). Perspect Indiana. Gorgeous full color water color illustrations illuminate the poetry-tinged language of this story for all ages of a young boy's journey home. Though his caregivers in the orphanage in a far away land have been kind & his life secure & comfortable, the boy dreams of a smaller house, with only a few children, where everyone shares the same family name. As he flies across the sea, we share his fears & apprehensions as well as his ultimate joy in a forever family. Appropriate for children adopted at an older age either in the U.S. or internationally. Well reviewed by every adoption-related periodical & School Library Journal. Other adoption related children's books from Perspectives Press include Jane Schnitter's WILLIAM IS MY BROTHER (family built by birth & adoption), Janice Koch's OUR BABY: A BIRTH & ADOPTION STORY (sex education), Anne Brodzinsky's THE MULBERRY BIRD (a birthmother's viewpoint), Ann Angel's REAL FOR SURE SISTER (transracial adoption); & Susan Gabel's FILLING IN THE BLANKS: A GUIDED LOOK AT GROWING UP ADOPTED (adolescence). Distributed by Ingram, Baker & Taylor or contact the publisher at (317) 872-3055. *Publisher Provided Annotation.*

Godden, Rumer. The Story of Holly & Ivy. Cooney, Barbara, illus. LC 84-25799. 32p. (ps-5). 1985. pap. 13.95 (ISBN 0-670-80622-6). Viking Child Bks.
Goffstein, M. B. Goldie the Dollmaker. Goffstein, M. B., illus. LC 79-85369. 64p. (ps up). 1980. 8.95 (ISBN 0-374-32739-4); pap. 3.45 (ISBN 0-374-42740-2). FS&G.
Great Expectations. (Illus.). 48p. (gr. 4 up). 1988. PLB 17.32 (ISBN 0-8172-2762-8); pap. 9.27 (ISBN 0-8172-2766-0). Raintree Pubs.
Gruelle, Johnny. Orphan Annie Story Book. 2nd ed. 100p. (gr. k-5). 1989. Repr. of 1921 ed. 14.95 (ISBN 0-9617367-9-8). Guild Pr IN.
Hardy, Thomas. Tess of the D'Urbervilles. Hogan, A. H., intro. by. (gr. 11 up). pap. 3.50 (ISBN 0-8049-0082-5, CL-82). Airmont.
Heidi. (Illus.). (gr. 1). 3.50 (ISBN 0-7214-5169-1). Ladybird Bks.
Heidi. (Illus.). (gr. 3-5). 1990. 3.50 (ISBN 0-7214-1210-6). Ladybird Bks.
Henry, Marguerite. Sea Star: Orphan of Chincoteague. (Illus.). (gr. k-9). 1989. pap. 2.25 (ISBN 0-590-41537-9). Scholastic Inc.
Holland, Isabelle. God, Mrs. Muskrat & Aunt Dot. Krush, Beth & Krush, Joe, illus. LC 82-23794. 78p. (gr. 4-8). 1983. 10.00 (ISBN 0-664-32703-6, Westminster). Westminster John Knox.
Levin, Betty. Brother Moose. LC 89-34437. (gr. 5 up). 1990. 12.95 (ISBN 0-688-09266-7). Greenwillow.
Lindbergh, Anne M. Nobody's Orphan. (gr. 3-7). 1987. pap. 2.95 (ISBN 0-380-70395-5, Camelot). Avon.
Major, Kevin. Hold Fast. 176p. (gr. 7 up). 1981. pap. 3.25 (ISBN 0-440-93756-6, LE). Dell.
Montgomery, Lucy M. Anne of Green Gables, Vol. 1. (gr. 4-7). 1984. pap. 2.95 (ISBN 0-553-15327-7). Bantam.
Newton, Suzanne. M. V. Sexton Speaking. LC 91-2397. 192p. (gr. 7 up). 1981. pap. 9.95 (ISBN 0-670-44505-3). Viking Child Bks.
—M. V. Sexton Speaking. 198p. (ps up). 1990. pap. 3.95 (ISBN 0-14-032356-2, Puffin). Puffin Bks.
Nixon, Joan L. In the Face of Danger. (gr. 7 up). 1989. pap. 3.50 (ISBN 0-553-28196-8, Starfire). Bantam.
—In the Face of Danger: The Orphan Train Quartet, No. 3. 160p. (gr. 7 up). 1988. 14.95 (ISBN 0-553-05490-2, Starfire). Bantam.
—The Specter. LC 82-70322. 160p. (gr. 7 up). 1982. pap. 12.95 (ISBN 0-385-28948-0). Delacorte.
Oliver Twist. (Illus.). (gr. 3-5). 3.50 (ISBN 0-7214-0823-0). Ladybird Bks.
Reeder, Carolyn. Shades of Gray. 176p. (gr. 3-7). 1989. 12.95 (ISBN 0-02-775810-9, Mcmillan Child Bk). Macmillan Child Grp.
Roberts, Willo D. Eddie & the Fairy Godpuppy. Morrill, Leslie, illus. LC 83-15678. 136p. (gr. 3-5). 1984. 12.95 (ISBN 0-689-31021-8, Atheneum Child Bk). Macmillan Child Grp.
The Secret Garden. (Illus.). (gr. 3-5). 3.50 (ISBN 0-7214-0632-7). Ladybird Bks.
Snyder, Vern W. For the Lov'va Winkie. 135p. 1988. write for info.; pap. write for info. V W Snyder.
—For the Lov'va Winkie. 90p. (gr. 3 up). 1989. pap. 8.95 (ISBN 0-926366-00-9). V W Snyder.
Spyri, Johanna. Heidi. (gr. k-1). 1986. 8.98 (ISBN 0-685-16841-7, 618141). Outlet Bk Co.
Stahl, Hilda. Sadie Rose & the Cottonwood Creek Orphan. LC 88-71808. 128p. (gr. 4-7). 1989. pap. 4.95 (ISBN 0-89107-513-5, Crossway Bks). Good News.
Talbot, Charlene J. An Orphan for Nebraska. Brown, Judith G., illus. LC 78-12179. 216p. (gr. 3-7). 1979. 14.95 (ISBN 0-689-30698-9, Atheneum Childrens Bks). Macmillan Child Grp.
Van Vorst, M. L. A Norse Lullaby. Tomes, Margot, illus. LC 87-31058. 32p. (ps-1). 1988. 12.95 (ISBN 0-688-05812-4); PLB 12.88 (ISBN 0-688-05813-2). Lothrop.
Wallace, Barbara B. Peppermints in the Parlor. LC 80-12326. 216p. (gr. 4-6). 1980. 14.95 (ISBN 0-689-30790-X, Atheneum Child Bk). Macmillan Child Grp.
Warner, Gertrude C. Boxcar Children. LC 42-1418. (gr. 3-8). 1989. PLB 9.95 (ISBN 0-8075-0851-9); pap. 3.50 (ISBN 0-8075-0852-7). A Whitman.
Webster, Jean. Daddy-Long-Legs. Hearn, Michael P., afterword by. 1988. pap. 2.50 (ISBN 0-451-52187-0, Sig Classics). NAL-Dutton.
Wickstrom, Lois. Oliver. (Illus.). 32p. 1991. 14.95 (ISBN 0-9611872-5-5). Our Child Pr.
Zistel, Era. Orphan. Coombs, Christine, illus. 64p. (Orig.). (gr. 4 up). 1990. pap. 11.95 (ISBN 0-9617426-5-8). J N Townsend.

ORWELL, GEORGE, 1903-1950

Flynn, Nigel. Orwell. (Illus.). 112p. (gr. 7 up). 1990. lib. bdg. 18.60 (ISBN 0-86593-018-X); lib. bdg. 13.95s.p. Rourke Corp.
Manovrier, Lynne. Animal Farm: A Study Guide. (gr. 6-10). 1983. tchr's. ed. & wkbk. 14.95 (ISBN 0-88122-021-3). LRN Links.

OSCEOLA, SEMINOLE CHIEF, 1800?-1838

Clark, Electa. Osceola: Young Seminole Indian. (Illus.). (gr. 3-7). 5.95 (ISBN 0-672-50144-9, Bobbs). Macmillan.
Oppenheim, Joanne. Osceola, Seminole Warrior. LC 78-60116. (Illus.). 48p. (gr. 4-6). 1979. PLB 9.89 (ISBN 0-89375-158-8); pap. 2.95 (ISBN 0-89375-148-0). Troll Assocs.
Zadra, Dan. Indians of America: Osceola. rev. ed. (gr. 2-4). 1987. PLB 11.50s.p. (ISBN 0-88682-162-2); 16.45 (ISBN 0-318-32941-7). Creative Ed.

OSTEOLOGY

see Bones

OSTRICHES

Arnold, Caroline. Ostriches & Other Flightless Birds. Hewett, Richard R., illus. 48p. (gr. 2-5). 1990. PLB 12.95 (ISBN 0-87614-377-X). Carolrhoda Bks.
Green, Carl R. & Sanford, William R. The Ostrich. LC 87-20175. (Illus.). 48p. (gr. 5-6). 1987. PLB 10.95 (ISBN 0-89686-336-0, Crestwood Hse). Macmillan Child Grp.
Saunier, Nadine. The Ostrich. Leduc, Anne, illus. 20p. (ps). 1989. 5.95 (ISBN 0-8120-5983-2). Barron.
Stone, L. Ostriches. (Illus.). 24p. (gr. k-5). 1989. lib. bdg. 11.93 (ISBN 0-86592-323-X). Rourke Corp.

OSTRICHES–FICTION

Brown, Kent. Why Can't I Fly? 1990. 13.95 (ISBN 0-385-41208-8). Doubleday.
Herman, Erwin & Herman, Agnes. The Yanov Torah. Kahn, Katherine J., illus. LC 85-5269. 48p. (gr. 5 up). 1985. 10.95 (ISBN 0-930494-45-8); pap. 5.95 (ISBN 0-930494-46-6). Kar Ben.

OTTERS

Ashby, Ruth. Jane Goodall's Animal World: Sea Otters. Goodall, Jane, intro. by. LC 89-38552. (Illus.). 32p. (gr. 3-7). 1990. 11.95 (ISBN 0-689-31472-8, Atheneum Child Bk). Macmillan Child Grp.
Banks, Martin. Discovering Otters. Caulkins, Janet, ed. (Illus.). 48p. (gr. 1-6). 1988. PLB 11.90 (ISBN 0-531-18227-4, Pub. by Bookwright Pr). Watts.
Goodall, Jane. Jane Goodall's Animal World: Sea Otters. 32p. (gr. 3-7). 1990. pap. 3.95 (ISBN 0-689-71394-0, Aladdin). Macmillan Child Grp.
Graves, Jack A. What Is a California Sea Otter? Cooke, Ralph W., illus. (gr. 3 up). 1977. pap. 3.95 (ISBN 0-910286-61-2). Boxwood.
Hurd, Edith T. Song of the Sea Otter. Dewey, Jennifer, illus. LC 83-4675. 48p. (gr. 2-7). 1983. (Pant Bks Young); PLB 9.95 (ISBN 0-394-86191-4). Pantheon.
Leon, Vicki. A Raft of Sea Otters. (Illus.). 40p. (Orig.). (ps-12). 1987. pap. 5.95 (ISBN 0-918303-13-3). Blake Pub.
Otter. 1990. 2.95 (ISBN 0-8378-2056-1). Gibson.
Royston, Angela. The Otter. Allen, Graham, illus. 24p. (Orig.). (ps-2). 1988. pap. 2.95 (ISBN 0-8249-8245-2). Ideals.
Schneider, Jeff. My Friend the Sea Otter: An Ocean Magic Book. Spoon, Wilfred, illus. LC 90-61578. 12p. (ps). 1991. 4.95g (ISBN 1-877779-10-5). Schneider Educational.
Shaw, Evelyn. Sea Otters. Pape, Cheryl, illus. LC 79-2017. 64p. (gr. k-3). 1980. 7.64i (ISBN 0-06-025613-3). HarpC Child Bks.

OTTERS–FICTION

Allen, Laura J. Ottie & the Star. Allen, Laura J., illus. LC 78-22485. 32p. (ps-3). 1979. HarpC Child Bks.
Benchley, Nathaniel. Oscar Otter. Lobel, Arnold, illus. LC 66-11499. 64p. (gr. k-3). 1966. PLB 11.89 (ISBN 0-06-020472-9). HarpC Child Bks.
—Oscar Otter. Lobel, Arnold, illus. LC 66-11499. 64p. (gr. k-3). 1980. pap. 3.50 (ISBN 0-06-444025-7, Trophy). HarpC Child Bks.
Burdick, Margaret. Bobby Otter & the Blue Boat. Burdick, Margaret, illus. 32p. (ps-3). 1987. 11.95 (ISBN 0-316-11616-5). Little.
Burgess, Thornton. Little Joe Otter. 103p. 1981. Repr. PLB 17.95x (ISBN 0-89966-353-2). Buccaneer Bks.
—Little Joe Otter. 169p. 1981. Repr. PLB 17.95 (ISBN 0-89967-027-X). Harmony Raine.
Chandrasekhar, Aruna. Oliver & the Oil Spill. Thatch, Nancy R., ed. Chandrasekhar, Aruna, illus. Melton, David, intro. by. (Illus.). 26p. (gr. k-4). 1991. PLB 12.95 (ISBN 0-933849-33-8). Landmark Edns.
Craft, Mary L. Little Orphan Otter. Craft, Mary L., illus. 20p. (Orig.). (gr. k-12). 1989. pap. text ed. 5.25 (ISBN 0-9624842-0-2). M Craft.
Higgins, Kitty. Tippy Potter the Otter. James, Robin, illus. 24p. 1990. pap. 5.95 (ISBN 0-8431-2499-7). Price Stern.
Hunt, Robert. Buffy: The Sea Otter. Teason, James, illus. LC 74-735892. (gr. 2-5). 1978. 6 bks. & 1 cass. 29.95 (ISBN 0-89290-033-4); 1 bk. & 1 cass. 10.95 (ISBN 0-685-04633-8). Soc for Visual.
Savage, Deborah. A Rumor of Otters. (gr. 6 up). 1986. 12.95 (ISBN 0-395-41186-6). HM.
Williamson, Henry. Tarka the Otter: The Joyful Water-Life & Death in the Two Rivers. Finch, Robert, intro. by. LC 90-55169. (Illus.). 276p. 1990. pap. 9.95 (ISBN 0-8070-8507-3). Beacon Pr.

OUTBOARD MOTORS

see Motorboats

OUTDOOR COOKERY

Boy Scouts of America. Cooking. LC 19-600. (Illus.). 80p. (gr. 6-12). 1986. pap. 1.85 (ISBN 0-8395-3257-1, 3257). BSA.

OUTDOOR LIFE

see also Camping; Country Life; Hiking; Mountaineering; Nature Study; Sports; Wilderness Survival

Allison, Linda. The Wild Inside: Sierra Club's Guide to Great Outdoors. Allison, Linda, illus. 144p. (gr. 3-7). 1988. pap. 7.95 (ISBN 0-316-03434-7). Little.
Beame, Rona. Backyard Explorer Kit. LC 88-51582. (Illus.). 64p. (gr. k-5). 1989. pap. 9.95 (ISBN 0-89480-343-3, 1343). Workman Pub.
Brimner, Larry D. Footbagging. Rakos, Jennie, ed. (Illus.). 72p. (gr. 7-9). 1988. 10.40 (ISBN 0-531-10477-X). Watts.
Disney, Walt, Productions Staff. The Outdoor Adventure Book. LC 77-74468. (Illus.). (gr. 2-6). 1977. (Random Juv); lib. bdg. 4.99 (ISBN 0-394-93601-9). Random.
Humberstone, Eliot. Things Outdoors. (gr. 2-5). 1981. (Usborne-Hayes); PLB 11.96 (ISBN 0-88110-019-6); pap. 3.95 (ISBN 0-86020-464-2). EDC.
Kaplan, Andrew. Careers for Outdoor Types. (Illus.). 64p. (gr. 7 up). 1991. PLB 12.90 (ISBN 1-56294-022-8). Millbrook Pr.
Klingel, Fitterer. Outdoor Safety. (Illus.). 32p. (ps up). 1986. PLB 10.95s.p. (ISBN 0-88682-082-0); 15.65 (ISBN 0-685-09469-3). Creative Ed.
Oakland, Don. Wildwoods Dad. Schley, Cynthia, illus. 220p. (Orig.). (gr. 5 up). 1987. pap. 6.95 (ISBN 0-9615242-1-9). Oak Pr.
Olsen, Larry D. Outdoor Survival Skills. rev. ed. (Illus.). (gr. 6 up). 1988. pap. 9.95 (ISBN 0-9620429-0-0). Salmon Falls Pub.
Outdoor Fun. (gr. 4-7). 1990. 12.95 (ISBN 0-316-67738-8, Joy St Bks). Little.
Paulsen, Gary. Woodsong. Paulsen, Ruth W., illus. LC 89-70835. 144p. (gr. 7 up). 1990. 12.95 (ISBN 0-02-770221-9, Bradbury Pr). Macmillan Child Grp.
Sanders, Pete. Outdoors. (Illus.). 32p. (gr. k-6). 1989. PLB 11.90 (ISBN 0-531-17182-5). Watts.
Sobol, Donald J. Encyclopedia Brown's Book of the Wacky Outdoors. Enik, Ted, illus. LC 87-7851. 112p. (gr. 3-7). 1987. 12.95 (ISBN 0-688-06635-6). Morrow Jr Bks.
Sun Bear. At Home in the Wilderness. Rev. ed. (Illus.). 90p. (gr. 4 up). 1973. pap. 5.95 (ISBN 0-87961-004-2). Naturegraph.

OUTDOOR LIFE–FICTION

Christopher, John. The White Mountains. LC 67-10362. 192p. (gr. 5-9). 1970. 13.95 (ISBN 0-02-718360-2, Mcmillan Child Bk); pap. 3.95 (ISBN 0-02-042710-7, Collier Young Ad). Macmillan Child Grp.

Disney, Walt, Productions Staff. The Outdoor Adventure Book. LC 77-74468. (Illus.). (gr. 2-6). 1977. (Random Juv); lib. bdg. 4.99 (ISBN 0-394-93601-9). Random.

Henckel, Mark. It's Tough to Be Small in the Big Outdoors. 1990. pap. 4.95 (ISBN 0-945960-04-2). Outlaw MT.

—Sis' Revenge: Oh Brother, This Is Fishing. Walton, Jeri D., ed. Potter, John, illus. 32p. (ps-2). 1989. pap. 4.95 (ISBN 0-945960-03-4). Outlaw MT.

Kjelgaard, Jim. Big Red. Kuhn, Bob, illus. 254p. (gr. 6 up). 1956. 14.95 (ISBN 0-8234-0007-7). Holiday.

Montgomery, Rutherford G. Pekan the Shadow. Nenninger, Jerome D., illus. LC 78-84779. (gr. 8-12). 1970. 3.95 (ISBN 0-87004-132-0). Caxton.

Rajkumar, Rosy. Lark in Central Park. (gr. 2-5). 1989. 6.95 (ISBN 0-533-08042-8). Vantage.

Seton, Ernest T. Two Little Savages. (Illus.). 286p. (gr. 4-8). 1903. pap. 6.95 (ISBN 0-486-20985-7). Dover.

Wallerstein, James S. The Trail of Danger. Giordano, Richard, illus. 248p. (gr. 4-12). 1972. 5.95 (ISBN 0-912388-03-X). Aurelon.

OUTDOOR SURVIVAL

see Wilderness Survival

OUTER BANKS–NORTH CAROLINA–HISTORY–ANECDOTES, FACETIAE, SATIRE, ETC.

Preston, Judy J. The Outer Banks Story. Preston, Judy J., illus. 117p. (Orig.). (gr. 5 up). 1985. pap. 3.49 (ISBN 0-9613824-0-6). Seabright.

OUTER SPACE

Alter, Anna. Destination Outer Space. (gr. 6 up). 1988. 4.95 (ISBN 0-8120-3839-8). Barron.

Asimov, Isaac. Colonizing the Planets & Stars. LC 89-4644. 32p. (gr. 3-4). 1989. PLB 11.95 (ISBN 1-55532-372-3). Gareth Stevens Inc.

—Exploding Suns: The Secrets of the Supernovas. 288p. (gr. 9-12). Date not set. pap. 4.50 (ISBN 0-317-02724-7, Ment). NAL-Dutton.

—How Did We Find Out about Outer Space? 64p. (gr. 5 up). 1977. PLB 11.85 (ISBN 0-8027-6284-0). Walker & Co.

Attalides, Stephanos. Journey into Space: Adventure Box IV. Attalides, Stephanos, illus. 12p. (ps up). 1988. 4.95 (ISBN 0-694-00266-6). HarpC Child Bks.

Bailey, Donna. Far Out in Space. LC 90-40083. (Illus.). 48p. (gr. 2-5). 1990. PLB 15.96 (ISBN 0-8114-2525-8). Steck-V.

Baker, D. Stepping into Space, 6 bks, Reading Level 3. (Illus.). 144p. (gr. 2-6). Date not set. PLB write for info. (ISBN 0-86592-968-8). Rourke Corp.

—Today's World in Space, 6 bks, Set I, Reading Level 5. (Illus.). 288p. (gr. 3-8). Date not set. Set. PLB 111.60 (ISBN 0-86592-403-1). Rourke Corp.

—Voices in the Sky, Reading Level 3. (Illus.). 32p. (gr. 2-6). Date not set. PLB 13.20 (ISBN 0-86592-972-6). Rourke Corp.

Baker, David. Believe It Or Not Space Facts, Reading Level 5. (Illus.). 48p. (gr. 3-8). Date not set. 18.60 (ISBN 0-86592-407-4). Rourke Corp.

—Living in Space. (Illus.). 48p. (gr. 3-8). 1989. lib. bdg. 18.60 (ISBN 0-86592-401-5). Rourke Corp.

—Today's World in Space, 6 bks, Set II, Reading Level 5. (Illus.). 288p. (gr. 3-8). Date not set. Set. PLB 111.60 (ISBN 0-86592-370-1). Rourke Corp.

Baxter, Leon. Baxter's Book of Space. (Illus.). 24p. (gr. 2-5). 1990. pap. 3.95 (ISBN 0-8249-8377-7). Ideals.

Bernards, Neal. Living in Space: Opposing Viewpoints. LC 90-3727. (Illus.). 112p. (gr. 3-8). 1990. PLB 13.95 (ISBN 0-89908-075-8). Greenhaven.

Boney, Lesley, illus. Space. 48p. (gr. k-5). 1988. pap. 2.95 (ISBN 0-8431-2247-1). Price Stern.

Branley, Franklyn M. Mysteries of Outer Space. Bensusen, Sally J., illus. LC 84-13683. 96p. (gr. 5-9). 1985. 11.95 (ISBN 0-525-67149-8, Lodestar Bks). Dutton Child Bks.

Carrie, Christopher. Mission to the Space Station. (Illus.). 40p. (gr. k up). 1990. 1.59 (ISBN 0-86696-247-6). Binney & Smith.

Cleeve, Roger. Outer Space. Steltenpohl, Jane, ed. (Illus.). 32p. (gr. 3-5). 1990. PLB 10.98 (ISBN 0-671-68628-3); pap. 4.95 (ISBN 0-671-68631-3). Messner.

Cooper, Heather & Henbest, Nigel. Galaxies & Quasars. LC 86-50351. (Illus.). 32p. (gr. 4-12). 1987. PLB 8.99 (ISBN 0-531-10265-3). Watts.

Daniels, Patricia, ed. Let's Discover Outer Space. (Illus.). 80p. (gr. k-6). 1986. pap. 13.27 (ISBN 0-8172-2595-1). Raintree Pubs.

DeBruin, Jerry. Young Scientists Explore: Inner & Outer Space. Czernick, Charlene, illus. 32p. (gr. 4 up). 1983. wkbk. 4.95 (ISBN 0-86653-152-1, GA 457). Good Apple.

Donnelly, Judy & Kramer, Sydelle. Space Junk: Pollution Beyond the Earth. (Illus.). 112p. (gr. 4-7). 1990. 12.95 (ISBN 0-688-08678-0); PLB 12.88 (ISBN 0-688-08679-9, Morrow Jr Bks). Morrow Jr Bks.

Furniss, Tim. Exploitation of Space. (Illus.). 48p. (gr. 5 up). 1990. lib. bdg. 18.00 (ISBN 0-86592-097-4); lib. bdg. 13.50s.p. (ISBN 0-685-36377-5). Rourke Corp.

—Space. Farmer, Andrew, illus. LC 85-51185. 32p. (gr. 4-9). 1985. PLB 11.90 (ISBN 0-531-10087-1). Watts.

Greenberg, Judith E. & Carey, Helen H. Space. Karpinski, Rick, illus. 32p. (gr. 2-4). 1990. 16.67 (ISBN 0-8172-3754-2); PLB 11.99. Raintree Pubs.

Holland, Margaret & Cooper, David. A Look Around Space. 24p. (gr. k-3). 1986. 1.95 (ISBN 0-87406-037-0). Willowisp Pr.

Isaaman. Computer Spacegames. 48p. (gr. 5-9). 1983. pap. 3.95 (ISBN 0-86020-683-1, 24062); lib. bdg. 10.96 (ISBN 0-88110-133-8). EDC.

Jones, Brian. Space: A Three-Dimensional Journey. Clifton-Dey, Richard, illus. 14p. (gr. k-4). 1991. 15.95 (ISBN 0-8037-0759-2). Dial Bks Young.

—Space Exploration. LC 89-11359. (Illus.). 64p. (gr. 4-6). 1989. PLB 12.95 (ISBN 0-8368-0004-4). Gareth Stevens Inc.

Kay, Jerry. Living in Space. Allison, Linda & Wells, William S., illus. 22p. (Orig.). (gr. 3-7). 1988. 9.95 (ISBN 0-929201-06-X). Kay Productions.

Kerrod, Robin. Big Book of Space. 1988. 5.98 (ISBN 0-8317-0860-3). Smithmark.

Knight, Brian. Space Mobiles. (Illus.). 28p. (Orig.). (gr. 4 up). pap. 4.95 (ISBN 0-906212-38-3). Parkwest Pubns.

Kohler, Pierre. Earth & the Conquest of Space. (gr. 6 up). 1988. 4.95 (ISBN 0-8120-3831-2). Barron.

Little People Big Book about Space. 64p. (ps-1). 1990. write for info. (ISBN 0-8094-7500-6); lib. bdg. write for info. (ISBN 0-8094-7501-4). Time-Life.

Mackie, Dan. Space Tour. Hughes, Mark, illus. 32p. (gr. 5-9). 1986. PLB 10.99 (ISBN 0-87617-007-6, Pub. by C Hayes Pr). Penworthy Pub.

Marsh, Carole. Kids & Space: Look Forward, Plan, Prepare, Go! (Illus.). (gr. 3-8). 1990. PLB 19.95 (ISBN 0-7933-0003-7); pap. 14.95 (ISBN 0-7933-0004-5); computer disk 29.95 (ISBN 0-7933-0005-3). Gallopade Pub Group.

Mayes, S. What's Out in Space? (Illus.). 24p. (gr. 1-4). 1990. lib. bdg. 11.96 (ISBN 0-88110-443-4, Usborne); pap. 3.95 (ISBN 0-7460-0430-3, Usborne). EDC.

Moche, Dinah. My First Book About Space. Alley, Robert, illus. 24p. (ps-3). 1982. pap. write for info. (ISBN 0-307-11870-3, Golden Bks.). Western Pub.

Moncure, Jane B. Magic Monsters Learn about Space. Sommers, Linda, illus. LC 79-25765. (ps-3). 1980. PLB 11.97 (ISBN 0-89565-119-X). Childs World.

Montgomery, Raymond A. Space & Beyond. large type ed. Granger, Paul, illus. 117p. (gr. 3-7). 1987. Repr. of 1979 ed. 8.95 (ISBN 0-942545-11-7); PLB 9.95 (ISBN 0-942545-16-8, Dist. by Grolier). Grey Castle.

Podendorf, Illa. Space. LC 82-4507. (gr. k-4). 1982. 14.60 (ISBN 0-516-01650-4); pap. 4.95 (ISBN 0-516-41650-2). Childrens.

Quinn, Kaye. Mission: Space. Quinn, Kaye, illus. 40p. (gr. 2-6). 1986. pap. 2.50 (ISBN 0-8431-1894-6). Price Stern.

Reid, S. Space Facts: Records-Lists-Facts-Comparisons. (Illus.). 48p. (gr. 3-7). 1987. PLB 12.96 (ISBN 0-88110-240-7); pap. 5.95 (ISBN 0-7460-0024-3). EDC.

Rickard, Graham. Homes in Space. (Illus.). 32p. (gr. 2-5). 1989. 9.95 (ISBN 0-8225-2125-3). Lerner Pubns.

Ridpath, Ian. Space. (Illus.). 48p. (gr. 5-8). 1991. PLB 13.90 (ISBN 0-531-19144-3, Warwick). Watts.

Seevers, James. Space. rev. ed. LC 87-20801. (Illus.). 48p. (gr. 2-6). 1987. PLB 17.32 (ISBN 0-8172-3260-5); pap. 9.27 (ISBN 0-8172-3285-0). Raintree Pubs.

Space. (Illus.). 32p. (Orig.). (gr. 3-6). 1989. pap. 2.95 (ISBN 0-8431-2374-5). Price Stern.

Space. (Illus.). (gr. 5 up). 3.50 (ISBN 0-7214-0832-X). Ladybird Bks.

Spangenberg, Ray & Moser, Diane. Living & Working in Space. (Illus.). 136p. 1989. 22.95x (ISBN 0-8160-1849-9). Facts on File.

Spizzirri Publishing Co. Staff. Space Explorers: An Educational Coloring Book. Spizzirri, Linda, ed. Spizzirri, Peter M., illus. 32p. (gr. 1-8). 1981. pap. 1.95 (ISBN 0-86545-037-4). Spizzirri.

Tong, Gary. Gary Tong's Crazy Cut-Outs from Outer Space. (Illus.). (ps-3). pap. 2.25 (ISBN 0-686-91619-0). Scholastic Inc.

Weissman, Paul & Harris, Alan. The Great Voyager Adventure. (Illus.). 64p. (gr. 5-9). 1990. 10.95 (ISBN 0-671-72539-4); lib. bdg. 12.98 (ISBN 0-671-72538-6). Messner.

OUTER SPACE–COMMUNICATION

see Interstellar Communication

OUTER SPACE–EXPLORATION

Arno, Roger. The Story of Space & Rockets. (Illus.). (gr. 5). 1978. pap. 3.95 (ISBN 0-88388-063-6). Bellerophon Bks.

Baker, David. Factories in Space. LC 87-16689. (Illus.). 48p. (gr. 3-8). 1987. PLB 18.60 (ISBN 0-86592-409-0). Rourke Corp.

—I Want to Fly the Shuttle. LC 87-20467. (Illus.). 48p. (gr. 3-8). 1987. PLB 18.60 (ISBN 0-86592-406-6). Rourke Corp.

—Journey to the Outer Planets. LC 87-19888. (Illus.). 48p. 1987. PLB 18.60 (ISBN 0-86592-405-8). Rourke Corp.

—Pease in Space. LC 87-19885. (Illus.). 48p. (gr. 3-8). 1987. PLB 18.60 (ISBN 0-86592-408-2). Rourke Corp.

Barrett, Norman. The Picture World of Space Voyages. (Illus.). 32p. (gr. k-4). 1990. PLB 11.40 (ISBN 0-531-14057-1). Watts.

Berger, Melvin. Space Shots, Shuttles & Satellites. LC 83-19279. (Illus.). 80p. (gr. 4-6). 1984. 7.99 (ISBN 0-399-61210-6, Putnam). Putnam Pub Group.

Billings, Charlene W. Space Station: Bold New Step Beyond Earth. (gr. 2-5). 1986. 9.95 (ISBN 0-396-08730-2, Putnam). Putnam Pub Group.

Branley, Franklyn M. Journey into a Black Hole. Simont, Marc, illus. LC 85-48249. 32p. (ps-3). 1986. PLB 13.89 (ISBN 0-690-04544-1, Crowell Jr Bks). HarpC Child Bks.

Cohen, Lynn. Air & Space. 64p. (ps-2). 1988. 6.95 (ISBN 0-912107-80-4, MM984). Monday Morning Bks.

Cole, Joanna. The Magic School Bus Lost in the Solar System. Degen, Bruce, illus. (ps-3). 1990. 13.95 (ISBN 0-590-41428-3). Scholastic Inc.

Cromie, William. Skylab: The Story of Man's First Station in Space. LC 74-25983. (Illus.). 192p. (gr. 7 up). 1976. pap. 10.95 (ISBN 0-679-20300-1). McKay.

Davidson, Jeff. Voyage to the Planets. (Illus.). 32p. (gr. 3-8). 1990. 3.95 (ISBN 0-87406-491-0, 51-20543-8). Willowisp Pr.

Donnelly, Judy. Moonwalk: The First Trip to the Moon. Davidson, Dennis, illus. LC 88-23668. 48p. (Orig.). (gr. 2-4). 1989. PLB 6.99 (ISBN 0-394-92457-6); pap. 2.95 (ISBN 0-394-82457-1). Random.

Fradin, Dennis B. Space Colonies. LC 85-7722. (Illus.). 48p. (gr. k-4). 1985. PLB 14.60 (ISBN 0-516-01273-8); pap. 4.95 (ISBN 0-516-41273-6). Childrens.

Kennedy, Gregory P. The First Men in Space. Goetzmann, William H., ed. Collins, Michael, intro. by. (Illus.). 112p. (gr. 5 up). 1991. PLB 18.95 (ISBN 0-7910-1324-3). Chelsea Hse.

Kerrod, Robin. The Challenge of Space. LC 79-64385. (Illus.). 36p. (gr. 3-6). 1980. PLB 9.95 (ISBN 0-8225-1177-0). Lerner Pubns.

—Mission Outer Space. LC 79-64388. (Illus.). 36p. (gr. 3-6). 1980. PLB 9.95 (ISBN 0-8225-1180-0). Lerner Pubns.

Lord, Suzanne. A Day in Space. (Illus.). 32p. (Orig.). (gr. k-3). 1986. pap. 1.95 (ISBN 0-590-40152-1). Scholastic Inc.

McGowen, Tom. Album of Space Flight. Ruth, Rod, illus. 64p. (gr. 3-7). 1987. pap. 4.95 (ISBN 0-02-688502-6). Checkerboard Pr.

Magill, Frank N., intro. by. Magill's Survey of Science, 5 vols. 2328p. (gr. 9-12). 1989. Set. 425.00 (ISBN 0-89356-600-4). Salem Pr.

Mammana, Dennis. Start Exploring Space: A Fact-Filled Coloring Book. Driggs, Helen, illus. 128p. (Orig.). (ps-8). 1991. pap. 7.95 (ISBN 0-89471-864-9). Running Pr.

Maurer, Richard. The Nova Space Explorer's Guide: Where to Go & What to See. LC 84-24905. (Illus.). 118p. (gr. 5 up). 1988. 15.95 (ISBN 0-517-55752-5, C N Potter Bks); (C N Potter Bks). Crown.

Moche, Dinah. The Golden Book of Space Exploration. LaPadula, Tom, illus. (ps-7). 1990. write for info. (ISBN 0-307-15855-1, Pub. by Golden Bks). Western Pub.

Newton, David E. U. S. & Soviet Space Programs: A Comparison. Rasof, Henry, ed. (Illus.). 144p. (gr. 7-12). 1988. PLB 12.90 (ISBN 0-531-10515-6). Watts.

Ride, Sally & Okie, Susan. To Space & Back. LC 85-23757. (Illus.). 96p. (gr. 1 up). 1989. Repr. of 1985 ed. 16.95 (ISBN 0-688-06159-1). Lothrop.

Ridpath, Ian. Space. (Illus.). 48p. (gr. 5-8). 1991. PLB 13.90 (ISBN 0-531-19144-3, Warwick). Watts.

Sabin, Louis. Space Exploration & Travel. Moylan, Holly, illus. LC 84-2698. 32p. (gr. 3-6). 1985. PLB 9.49 (ISBN 0-8167-0258-6); pap. text ed. 2.95 (ISBN 0-8167-0259-4). Troll Assocs.

Solomon, Maury. An Album of Voyager. (Illus.). 64p. (gr. 5-8). 1990. PLB 13.90 (ISBN 0-531-10876-7). Watts.

Spangenberg, Ray & Moser, Diane. Living & Working in Space. (Illus.). 136p. 1989. 22.95x (ISBN 0-8160-1849-9). Facts on File.

—Opening the Space Frontier. (Illus.). 136p. 1989. 22.95x (ISBN 0-8160-1848-0). Facts on File.

Sullivan, George. Day We Walked On the Moon. 1990. 14.95 (ISBN 0-590-43632-5, Scholastic Hardcover). Scholastic Inc.

Vogt, Gregory. Apollo & the Moon Landing. (Illus.). 112p. (gr. 4-6). 1991. PLB 19.00 (ISBN 1-878841-31-9); pap. 4.95 (ISBN 1-878841-37-8). Millbrook Pr.

—Space Explorers. Sloan, Frank, ed. (Illus.). 32p. (gr. 7-9). 1990. PLB 11.90 (ISBN 0-531-10461-3). Watts.

—Voyager. (Illus.). 112p. (gr. 4-6). 1991. PLB 19.25 (ISBN 1-56294-050-3). Millbrook Pr.

Von Brook, Patricia, et al, eds. Space Exploration: The Dream & the Reality. rev. ed. (Illus.). 84p. (gr. 7-12). 1990. pap. text ed. 18.95 (ISBN 1-878623-08-7). Info Plus TX.

Wright, Pearce. The Space Race. (Illus.). 32p. (gr. 4-8). 1987. PLB 8.90 (ISBN 0-531-17041-1, Gloucester Pr). Watts.

OUTER SPACE–FICTION

Bell, Lucille H. Glow in the Dark Trip to the Planets. (ps-3). 1990. write for info. (ISBN 0-307-06250-3). Western Pub.

Clark, Margaret G. Barney in Space. (Illus.). 160p. (gr. 3-7). 1981. 8.95 (ISBN 0-396-08001-4, Putnam). Putnam Pub Group.

Davis, Natalie L. The Space Twin. Taylor, Neil, illus. 112p. (gr. 4-8). 1987. 7.95 (ISBN 1-55523-037-7). Winston-Derek.

De Weese, Gene. Black Suits from Outer Space. (gr. k-6). 1989. pap. 2.95 (ISBN 0-440-40196-8). Dell.

Disney, Walt, Productions Staff. Walt Disney Productions Presents "The Black Hole" LC 79-10622. (Illus.). (ps-3). 1979. 4.95 (ISBN 0-394-84279-0, Random Juv); lib. bdg. 4.99 (ISBN 0-394-94279-5). Random.

Etra, Jon & Spinner, Stephanie. Aliens for Lunch. Bjorkman, Steve, illus. LC 90-39417. 64p. (Orig.). (gr. 2-4). 1991. PLB 6.99 (ISBN 0-679-91056-5); pap. 2.50 (ISBN 0-679-81056-0). Random.

Etra, Jonathan & Spinner, Stephanie. Aliens for Breakfast. Bjorkman, Steve, illus. LC 88-6653. 64p. (Orig.). (gr. 2-4). 1988. lib. bdg. 6.99 (ISBN 0-394-92093-7, Random Juv); pap. 2.50 (ISBN 0-394-82093-2, Random Juv). Random.

Freeman, Mae B. & Freeman, Ira M. The Sun, the Moon, & the Stars. rev. ed. Martin, Rene, illus. LC 78-64604. (gr. 2-4). 1979. 8.95 (ISBN 0-394-80110-5, Random Juv); lib. bdg. 5.99 (ISBN 0-394-90110-X). Random.

Greer, Gery & Ruddick, Bob. Let Me off This Spaceship! Sims, Blanche C., illus. LC 90-32045. 64p. (gr. 2-5). 1991. 12.95 (ISBN 0-06-021605-0); PLB 12.89 (ISBN 0-06-021606-9). HarpC Child Bks.

Heinlein, Robert A. Tunnel in the Sky. reissued ed. LC 55-10142. 288p. (gr. 7 up). 1988. 14.95 (ISBN 0-684-18916-X, Scribners Young Read). Macmillan Child Grp.

Johnson, Crockett. Harold's Trip to the Sky. Johnson, Crockett, illus. LC 57-9262. (gr. k-3). 1957. PLB 11. 89 (ISBN 0-06-022986-1). HarpC Child Bks.

L'Engle, Madeleine. A Swiftly Tilting Planet. (gr. 7 up). 1979. pap. 3.50 (ISBN 0-440-90158-8, LFL). Dell.

Marshall, Edward. Space Case. Marshall, James, illus. LC 80-13369. 32p. (ps-3). 1980. 13.95 (ISBN 0-8037-8005-2); PLB 12.89 (ISBN 0-8037-8007-9). Dial Bks Young.

Marzollo, Jean & Marzollo, Claudio. Jed's Junior Space Patrol. Rose, David, illus. LC 81-12483. 56p. (ps-3). 1982. PLB 7.89 (ISBN 0-8037-4287-8). Dial Bks Young.

Noakes, Polly. Sally Sky Diver. (Illus.). 32p. (ps-3). 1990. 10.95 (ISBN 0-8249-8468-4). Ideals.

O'Neill, Mary. Power Failure. Bindon, John, illus. LC 90-11148. 32p. (gr. 3-6). 1991. PLB 12.89 (ISBN 0-8167-2288-9); pap. text ed. 3.95 (ISBN 0-8167-2289-7). Troll Assocs.

Paton Walsh, Jill. The Green Book. Bloom, Lloyd, illus. LC 81-12620. 80p. (gr. 5 up). 1982. 11.95 (ISBN 0-374-32778-5); pap. 2.95 (ISBN 0-374-42802-6, Sunburst). FS&G.

Peterson, Melvin N. David's Star Studded Adventures. (Illus.). 58p. (gr. 1-4). 1988. spiral binding 48.00 (ISBN 0-938880-07-1). MNP Star.

Pinkwater, Daniel M. Fat Men from Space. (Illus.). 64p. (gr. 3-7). 1977. 9.95 (ISBN 0-396-07461-8, Putnam). Putnam Pub Group.

Quinn, Kaye. Trip to the Lost Planet. (Illus.). 48p. (Orig.). (gr. k-3). 1989. pap. 2.95 (ISBN 0-8431-2708-2). Price Stern.

Rays First Spaceship Ride. 60p. (gr. 3-4). pap. write for info. Rapcom Enter.

Riding, Julia. Space Traders Unlimited. LC 87-24165. 160p. (gr. 6 up). 1988. 13.95 (ISBN 0-689-31409-4, Atheneum Child Bk). Macmillan Child Grp.

Rotsler, William. The Star Trek II Gift Set, 3 vols. Boxed Set. pap. 9.50 (ISBN 0-317-12429-3, Little Simon). S&S Trade.

—Star Trek III: Plot-It-Yourself Adventure Stories, the Vulcan Treasure. Barish, Wendy, ed. 128p. (Orig.). (gr. 3 up). 1984. pap. 3.85 (ISBN 0-671-50138-0, Little Simon). S&S Trade.

—Star Trek III Short Stories. Barish, Wendy, ed. 160p. (Orig.). (gr. 3 up). 1984. pap. 3.85 (ISBN 0-671-50139-9, Little Simon). S&S Trade.

Sadler, Marilyn. Alistair in Outer Space. LC 84-4896. 1989. 13.95 (ISBN 0-671-66678-9); pap. 5.95 (ISBN 0-671-67938-4). S&S Trade.

Schade, Susan, ed. Space Rock. Buller, Jon, illus. LC 87-12762. 48p. (Orig.). (gr. 2-3). 1989. lib. bdg. 6.99 (ISBN 0-394-99384-5, Random Juv); pap. 2.95 (ISBN 0-394-89384-0, Random Juv). Random.

Spinelli, Jerry. Space Station Seventh Grade. LC 82-47915. 192p. (gr. 7 up). 1982. 14.95 (ISBN 0-316-80709-5). Little.

—Space Station Seventh Grade. (gr. 7-12). 1984. pap. 2.95 (ISBN 0-440-96165-3, LFL). Dell.

Stern, Leonard & Price, Roger. Mad Libs from Outer Space. (Illus.). 48p. (Orig.). (gr. 3 up). 1989. pap. 2.95 (ISBN 0-8431-2443-1). Price Stern.

Williams, Geoff. Aliens Next Door: Book & Cassette in 3-D Sound. (Illus.). 32p. (gr. 2-5). 1989. bk. & cass. 8.95 (ISBN 0-8431-2746-5); pap. 2.95 (ISBN 0-8431-2376-1). Price Stern.

Williams, Jay & Abrashkin, Raymond. Danny Dunn & the Voice from Space. Summers, Leo, illus. LC 67-22974. (gr. 4-6). 1982. pap. 1.95 (ISBN 0-671-42684-2, Archway). PB.

Yolen, Jane. Commander Toad & the Big Black Hole. Degen, Bruce, illus. LC 82-23524. (gr. 1-4). 1983. PLB 9.99 (ISBN 0-698-30741-0, Coward); pap. 5.95 (ISBN 0-698-20594-4). Putnam Pub Group.

OUTLAWS

see Robbers and Outlaws

OVERLAND JOURNEYS TO THE PACIFIC

Parkman, Francis. Oregon Trail. (gr. 6 up). 1964. pap. 1.50 (ISBN 0-8049-0037-X, CL-37). Airmont.

OVERLAND JOURNEYS TO THE PACIFIC–FICTION

Coerr, Eleanor. The Josefina Story Quilt. Degen, Bruce, illus. LC 85-45260. 64p. (gr. k-3). 1986. 11.95 (ISBN 0-06-021348-5); PLB 11.89 (ISBN 0-06-021349-3). HarpC Child Bks.

Fleischman, Sid. Mr. Mysterious & Company. Von Schmidt, Eric, illus. (gr. 4-6). 1962. 14.95 (ISBN 0-316-28578-1, Joy St Bks). Little.

Mason, Miriam E. Young Mister Meeker & His Exciting Journey to Oregon. (gr. 3-6). 1952. 4.95 (ISBN 0-672-50599-1, Bobbs). Macmillan.

OVERWEIGHT

see Weight Control

OWENS, JESSE, 1913-

Gentry, Tony. Jesse Owens. King, Coretta Scott, intro. by. (Illus.). (gr. 5 up). 1990. 17.95 (ISBN 1-55546-603-6); pap. 9.95 (ISBN 0-7910-0247-0). Chelsea Hse.

Jesse Owens. 48p. (gr. 5-6). 1989. PLB 10.95 (ISBN 0-685-26352-5). Capstone Pr.

Sabin, Francene. Jesse Owens, Olympic Hero. Frenck, Hal, illus. LC 85-1101. 48p. (gr. 4-6). 1986. lib. bdg. 10.79 (ISBN 0-8167-0551-8); pap. text ed. 2.95 (ISBN 0-8167-0552-6). Troll Assocs.

OWLS

Bailey, Jill. Life Cycle of an Owl. (ps-3). 1990. PLB 8.99 (ISBN 0-531-18315-7). Watts.

Brown, Fern G. Owls. Perrotta, Mary, ed. (Illus.). 64p. (gr. 3-5). 1991. PLB 11.90 (ISBN 0-531-20008-6). Watts.

Burton, Jane. Buffy the Barn Owl. LC 89-11410. (Illus.). 32p. (gr. 2-3). 1989. PLB 10.95 (ISBN 0-8368-0202-0). Gareth Stevens Inc.

—Snowy the Barn Owl. Burton, Jane, photos by. LC 89-42694. (Illus.). 24p. (Orig.). (ps-3). 1989. PLB 5.99 (ISBN 0-394-92268-9); pap. 1.95 (ISBN 0-394-82268-4). Random.

Butterworth, Christine & Bailey, Donna. Owls. LC 90-37529. (Illus.). 32p. (gr. 1-4). 1990. PLB 14.64 (ISBN 0-8114-2643-2). Steck-V.

Coldrey, Jennifer. The Owl in the Tree. Oxford Scientific Film Staff, illus. LC 87-9915. 32p. (gr. 4-6). 1987. PLB 10.95 (ISBN 1-55532-272-7). Gareth Stevens Inc.

Heinrich, Bernd. Owl in the House. Heinrich, Bernd, illus. Calaprice, Alice, adapted by. (gr. 5-9). 1990. 14. 95 (ISBN 0-316-35456-2, Joy St Bks). Little.

Hunt, Patricia. Snowy Owls. (gr. 2-5). 1982. 8.95 (ISBN 0-396-08073-1, Putnam). Putnam Pub Group.

Kalman, Bobbie. Owls. Loates, Glen, illus. 56p. (gr. 3-4). 1987. 15.95 (ISBN 0-86505-164-X); pap. 7.95 (ISBN 0-86505-184-4). Crabtree Pub Co.

Kappeler, Markus. Owls. (Illus.). 32p. (gr. 4-6). 1991. PLB 11.95 (ISBN 0-8368-0687-5). Gareth Stevens Inc.

Nero, Robert. Owls in North America. Karstad, Aleta, illus. 40p. (Orig.). (gr. 2-6). 1990. pap. 4.95 (ISBN 0-920534-42-2, Pub. by Hyperion Pr Ltd CN). Sterling.

Saintsing, David. The World of Owls. Oxford Scientific Films Staff, illus. LC 87-6537. 32p. (gr. 2-3). 1987. PLB 10.95 (ISBN 1-55532-301-4). Gareth Stevens Inc.

Selsam, Millicent E. & Hunt, Joyce. A First Look at Owls, Eagles, & Other Hunters of the Sky. Springer, Harriet, illus. 32p. (gr. 6-9). 1986. 10.95 (ISBN 0-8027-6625-0); PLB 10.85 (ISBN 0-8027-6642-0). Walker & Co.

Stone, Lynn M. The Great Horned Owl. (Illus.). 48p. (gr. 5-6). 1987. PLB 10.95 (ISBN 0-89686-325-5, Crestwood Hse). Macmillan Child Grp.

Wexo, John B. Owls. 24p. (gr. 4). 1989. 11.95s.p. (ISBN 0-88682-268-8); 17.10 (ISBN 0-685-28184-1). Creative Ed.

Wildlife Education, Ltd. Staff. Owls. Boyer, Trevor, et al, illus. 20p. (Orig.). (gr. 5 up). 1985. pap. 2.25 (ISBN 0-937934-32-1). Wildlife Educ.

OWLS–FICTION

Bunting, Eve. The Man Who Could Call Down Owls. Mikolaycak, Charles, illus. LC 83-17568. 32p. (gr. k-3). 1984. 13.95 (ISBN 0-02-715380-0, Mcmillan Child Bk). Macmillan Child Grp.

Dragonwagon, Crescent. Your Owl Friend. Bornstein, Ruth, illus. LC 76-58725. (gr. k-3). 1977. HarpC Child Bks.

Gullander, Elizabeth. Oswald Hoot: The Owl Who Was Scared of the Dark. Youra, Dan, illus. 64p. (ps-6). 1982. PLB 7.95 (ISBN 0-940828-06-5); pap. 4.95 (ISBN 0-940828-05-7). Olympic Pub.

Hale, Janet C. The Owl's Song. (gr. 5 up). 1991. pap. 2.95 (ISBN 0-553-28829-6, Starfire). Bantam.

Harris, Nicholas. Owlbert. Horvat, Karl J., illus. LC 89-4445. 32p. (gr. 2-3). 1989. PLB 12.95 (ISBN 0-8368-0110-5). Gareth Stevens Inc.

Hooker, Yvonne. I Am an Owl. (Illus.). 24p. (gr. k-2). 1982. 5.95 (ISBN 0-448-01451-3, G&D). Putnam Pub Group.

Hoopes, Lyn L. My Own Home. Richardson, Ruth, illus. LC 90-4386. 32p. (gr. k-3). 1991. 13.95 (ISBN 0-06-022570-X); PLB 13.89 (ISBN 0-06-022571-8). HarpC Child Bks.

Hutchins, Pat. Good-Night, Owl. Hutchins, Pat, illus. LC 72-186355. 32p. (ps-2). 1972. 12.95 (ISBN 0-02-745900-4, Mcmillan Child Bk). Macmillan Child Grp.

—Good Night, Owl. LC 89-17708. 32p. (ps-3). 1990. pap. 3.95 (ISBN 0-689-71371-1, Aladdin). Macmillan Child Grp.

Jones, Donna J. Oolik: The Owl Who Couldn't Whoo. Grove, Jason, illus. 29p. (Orig.). (gr. k-5). 1987. pap. 3.50 (ISBN 0-9617382-0-0). Glacier Pub.

Kennedy, X. J. The Owlstone Crown. Chessare, Michele, illus. LC 81-3513. 224p. (gr. 3-6). 1983. 11.95 (ISBN 0-689-50207-9, M K McElderry). Macmillan Child Grp.

Kraus, Robert. Owliver. Aruego, Jose & Dewey, Ariane, illus. LC 80-13664. (ps). 1987. pap. 12.95 (ISBN 0-671-66523-5). S&S Trade.

Lear, Edward. The Owl & the Pussycat. (ps-1). 1989. 13. 95 (ISBN 0-89919-505-9, Pub. by Clarion); pap. 4.95 (ISBN 0-89919-854-6, Pub. by Clarion). Ticknor & Fields.

Leonard, Marcia. Little Owl Leaves the Nest. Newson, Carol, illus. 32p. 1984. pap. 2.75 (ISBN 0-553-15460-5). Bantam.

Lobel, Arnold. Owl at Home. Lobel, Arnold, illus. LC 74-2630. 64p. (gr. k-3). 1975. 11.95 (ISBN 0-06-023948-4); PLB 11.89 (ISBN 0-06-023949-2). HarpC Child Bks.

—Owl at Home. Lobel, Arnold, illus. LC 74-2630. 64p. (gr. k-3). 1987. incl. cassette 5.98 (ISBN 0-694-00176-7, Trophy); pap. 3.50 (ISBN 0-06-444034-6, Trophy). HarpC Child Bks.

McGuire, Leslie. Baby Night Owl: Just Right for 3's & 4's. Szilagyi, Mary, illus. LC 88-43033. 32p. (ps). 1989. (Random Juv); lib. bdg. 5.99 (ISBN 0-394-99986-X). Random.

Matthews, Morgan. Whoo's Too Tired? Kolding, Richard M., illus. LC 88-1285. 48p. (Orig.). (gr. 1-3). 1988. PLB 9.89 (ISBN 0-8167-1331-6); pap. text ed. 2.95 (ISBN 0-8167-1332-4). Troll Assocs.

Maurice, Dominique. The Tale about the Owl. (Illus.). 8p. (Orig.). (gr. 7-9). 1982. pap. 2.50 (ISBN 0-914676-59-8). Green Tiger Pr.

Mowat, Farley. Owls in the Family. Frankenberg, Robert, illus. (ps up). 1962. 14.95 (ISBN 0-316-58641-2, Pub. by Atlantic-Little, Brown). Little.

—Owls in the Family. (gr. 4-7). 1985. pap. 2.95 (ISBN 0-553-15585-7). Bantam.

Nicoll, Helen & Pienkowski, Jan. Owl at School. (Illus.). 32p. (ps). 1984. 15.95 (ISBN 0-317-00752-1, Pub. by W Heinemann Ltd). Trafalgar Sq.

Ollie the Owl. (Illus.). (ps-1). 2.98 (ISBN 0-517-46984-7). Outlet Bk Co.

Shles, Larry. The Adventure of the Squib Owl: Squib Ser. Shles, Larry, illus. Date not set. pap. 7.95 each (ISBN 0-915190-85-0). Jalmar Pr.

Squib the Owl series, written & whimsically illustrated by Larry Shles, teaches self-esteem & personal & social responsibility as it entertains. The author uses the name Squib to personify the small vunerable part of us all that struggles & at times feels helpless in an enormous world filled with emotions. This Series, five volumes, traces the adventures of this tiny owl as he struggles with his feelings searching at least for understanding. Each of the five titles explores a different vulnerability. MOTHS & MOTHERS, FEATHERS & FATHERS (explores feelings); HOOTS & TOOTS & HAIRY BRUTES (explores disabilities); ALIENS IN MY NEST (explores adolescent behavior); HUGS & SHRUGS (explores inner peace). The latest volume DO I HAVE TO GO TO SCHOOL TODAY? is great for the young reader who needs encouragement from teachers who accept him "just as he is". Brilliantly simple, yet realistically complex, Squib personifies each & every one of us. He is a reflection of what we are, & what we can become. Every reader who has struggled with life's limitations will recognize his own struggles & triumphs in the microcosm of Squib's forest world - in Squib we find a parable for all ages from 8-80.

Publisher Provided Annotation.

—Hoots & Toots & Hairy Brutes, Vol. 2: The Continuing Adventures of Squib. 2nd ed. Shles, Larry, illus. LC 89-83466. 80p. (gr. k-8). 1989. pap. 7.95 (ISBN 0-915190-56-7, JP9056-7). Jalmar Pr.

—Moths & Mothers, Feathers & Fathers, Vol. 1: A Story about a Tiny Owl Named Squib. 2nd ed. Winch, Bradley, ed. Shles, Larry, illus. LC 89-83467. 56p. (gr. k-8). 1989. pap. 7.95 (ISBN 0-915190-57-5, JP9057-5). Jalmar Pr.

Shles, Lawrence. Hoots & Toots & Hairy Brutes: Squib the Owl Saves the Day. Shles, Lawrence, illus. 70p. (gr. k-3). 1984. 10.95; pap. 4.95. HM.

Thaler, Mike. Owly. Wiesner, David, illus. LC 81-47727. 32p. (ps-3). 1982. 12.95 (ISBN 0-06-026151-X). HarpC Child Bks.

OWLS–POETRY

Livingston, Myra C. If the Owl Calls Again: A Collection of Owl Poems. Frasconi, Antonio, illus. LC 89-27659. 128p. (gr. 5 up). 1990. 13.95 (ISBN 0-689-50501-9, M K McElderry). Macmillan Child Grp.

P

PACIFIC CABLE
see Cables, Submarine
PACIFIC ISLANDS
see Islands of the Pacific
PACIFIC OCEAN
Heinrichs, Susan. The Pacific Ocean. LC 86-9653. (Illus.). 48p. (gr. k-4). 1986. PLB 14.60 (ISBN 0-516-01295-9); pap. 4.95 (ISBN 0-516-41295-7). Childrens.
PACIFIC STATES
Lawson, Don. The Pacific States. 96p. (gr. 4 up). 1984. lib. bdg. 10.40 (ISBN 0-531-04733-4). Watts.
Riegel, Martin P. Ghost Ports of the Pacific, Vol. III: Washington. LC 89-90772. (Illus.). 52p. (Orig.). 1989. 11.00 (ISBN 0-944871-22-4); pap. 4.95 (ISBN 0-944871-23-2). Riegel Pub.
Yocom, Charles & Dasmann, Raymond. Pacific Coastal Wildlife Region. rev. ed. (Illus.). 120p. (gr. 4 up). 1965. 13.95 (ISBN 0-911010-05-X); pap. 6.95 (ISBN 0-911010-04-1). Naturegraph.
PAGEANTS
see also Mysteries and Miracle Plays
Randolph, Sallie G. Putting on Perfect Proms, Programs, & Pageants. (Illus.). 144p. (gr. 9-12). 1991. PLB 12.90 (ISBN 0-531-11061-3). Watts.
PAINE, THOMAS, 1737-1809
Vail, John. Thomas Paine. Schlesinger, Arthur M., Jr., intro. by. (Illus.). 112p. (gr. 5 up). 1990. 17.95 (ISBN 1-55546-819-5). Chelsea Hse.
PAINTED GLASS
see Glass Painting and Staining
PAINTERS
see also Artists;
also names of individual painters
Ventura, Piero. Great Painters. Ventura, Piero, illus. LC 84-3423. 160p. (gr. 5 up). 1984. 20.95 (ISBN 0-399-21115-2, Putnam). Putnam Pub Group.
PAINTERS, AMERICAN
Goldstein, Ernest. Grant Wood: American Gothic. (Illus.). 52p. (gr. 9-12). 1984. pap. 9.95 (ISBN 0-317-02721-2). NAL-Dutton.
Meyer, Susan E. Mary Cassatt. (Illus.). 80p. (gr. 7 up). 1990. 18.95 (ISBN 0-8109-3154-0). Abrams.
O'Kelley, Mattie L. From the Hills of Georgia: An Autobiography in Paintings. LC 83-9414. (Illus.). 32p. (ps-3). 1986. 14.95 (ISBN 0-316-63800-5, Joy St Bks); pap. 6.95 (ISBN 0-316-63799-8, Joy St Bks). Little.
Reef, Pat D. William Thon, Painter. (Illus.). 56p. (gr. 4-7). 1991. pap. 12.95 (ISBN 0-933858-28-0). Kennebec River.
PAINTERS' MATERIALS
see Artists' Materials
PAINTING
see also Animal Painting and Illustration; Color; Flower Painting and Illustration; Impressionism (Art); Landscape Painting; Paintings
Beaton, Clare. Make & Play: Face Painting. 1990. pap. 2.95 (ISBN 0-531-15161-1). Watts.
—Make & Play: T-Shirt Painting. 1990. pap. 2.95 (ISBN 0-531-15164-6). Watts.
Canady, Robert & Annis, Scott. Color in Iowa Coloring Album. (Illus.). 32p. (Orig.). (gr. 1-5). 1984. pap. 3.95 (ISBN 0-9615584-0-7). Little Gnome.
Foster, P. Guide to Painting. (Illus.). 32p. (gr. 5-10). 1981. PLB 13.96 (ISBN 0-88110-026-9); pap. 6.95 (ISBN 0-86020-546-0). EDC.
Haldane, Suzanne. Painting Faces. LC 88-3706. (Illus.). 32p. (gr. 3 up). 1988. 13.95 (ISBN 0-525-44408-4, DCB). Dutton Child Bks.
Hodge, Anthony. Painting. Hodge, Anthony, illus. Kline, M., ed. 32p. (gr. 5-9). 1991. PLB 11.90 (ISBN 0-531-17299-6, Gloucester Pr). Watts.
Looking at Painting. 48p. (gr. 4-8). 1990. 13.95 (ISBN 1-85435-102-8). Marshall Cavendish.
The Paint Book. (gr. 1 up). 1990. pap. 4.95 (ISBN 0-671-70365-X). S&S Trade.
Pluckrose, Henry. Paints. Fairclough, Chris, photos by. Franklin Watts Ltd., ed. LC 87-50906. (Illus.). 32p. (gr. 1-9). 1988. PLB 11.90 (ISBN 0-531-10471-0). Watts.
Triado, Juan-Ramon. The Key to Painting. (Illus.). 80p. (gr. 8 up). 1990. PLB 15.95 (ISBN 0-8225-2050-8). Lerner Pubns.
PAINTING–FICTION
Agge, Jon. Incredible Painting of Felix. (gr. 4-8). 1990. pap. 4.95 (ISBN 0-374-43582-0, Sunburst). FS&G.
Alcorn, Johnny. Rembrandt's Beret. Alcorn, Stephen, illus. LC 90-42330. 32p. (gr. k up). 1991. 13.95 (ISBN 0-688-10206-9, Tambourine Bks); PLB 13.88 (ISBN 0-688-10207-7, Tambourine Bks). Morrow.
Asch, Frank. Bread & Honey. Asch, Frank, illus. LC 81-16893. 48p. (ps-3). 1982. 5.95 (ISBN 0-8193-1077-8); PLB 5.95 (ISBN 0-8193-1078-6). Parents.
Berman, Linda. The Goodbye Painting. Hannon, Mark, illus. LC 81-20217. 32p. (ps-3). 1982. 16.95 (ISBN 0-89885-074-6). Human Sci Pr.
Clement, Claude. The Painter & the Wild Swans. Clement, Frederic, illus. LC 86-2154. 32p. (gr. k up). 1986. 13.95 (ISBN 0-8037-0268-X). Dial Bks Young.
Demi. Liang & the Magic Paintbrush. Demi, illus. LC 80-11351. 32p. (gr. k-3). 1988. pap. 3.95 (ISBN 0-8050-0801-2). H Holt & Co.
Harwood, Pearl A. Mr. Bumba's Tuesday Club. Folger, Joseph, illus. LC 65-27998. 32p. (gr. k-3). 1966. PLB 4.95 (ISBN 0-8225-0110-4). Lerner Pubns.
Liang & the Magic Paintbrush. LC 80-11351. (Illus.). 32p. (gr. k-2). 1980. 14.95 (ISBN 0-8050-0220-0). H Holt & Co.
Schwartz, Amy. Begin at the Beginning. Schwartz, Amy, illus. LC 82-48257. 32p. (ps-3). 1983. PLB 12.89 (ISBN 0-06-025228-6). HarpC Child Bks.
Spier, Peter. Oh, Were They Ever Happy. Spier, Peter, illus. LC 77-78144. 48p. (gr. k-3). 1978. 12.95 (ISBN 0-385-13175-5); pap. 10.95 (ISBN 0-385-13176-3). Doubleday.
Ventura, Piero & Ventura, Marisa. The Painter's Trick. Ventura, Piero & Ventura, Marisa, illus. LC 76-54411. (gr. k-2). 1977. (Random Juv); lib. bdg. 6.99 (ISBN 0-394-93320-6). Random.
PAINTING–HISTORY
Peppin. Story of Painting. (Illus.). 32p. 1980. PLB 13.96 (ISBN 0-88110-030-7); pap. 6.95 (ISBN 0-86020-441-3). EDC.
PAINTING, RELIGIOUS
see Christian Art and Symbolism
PAINTING–TECHNIQUE
Brown, Charlene & Davis, Carolyn. Craft Painting Fun: How to Paint on Objects. Sprague, Sydney, ed. Davis, Carolyn, illus. 64p. (Orig.). 1991. pap. text ed. 5.95 (ISBN 1-56010-071-0, BA12). W Foster Pub.
Lerner, Sharon. Self-Portrait in Art. LC 64-8202. (Illus.). (gr. 5 up). 1965. PLB 5.95 (ISBN 0-8225-0154-6). Lerner Pubns.
Momiyama, Nanae. Sumi-E: An Introduction to Ink Painting. LC 67-15320. (Illus.). (gr. 7-9). 1967. pap. 5.95 (ISBN 0-8048-0554-7). C E Tuttle.
Muller, Brunhild. Painting with Children. 1988. pap. 8.50 (ISBN 0-86315-052-7, 20240). Gryphon Hse.
Testa, Fulvio. If You Take a Paintbrush: A Book of Colors. Testa, Fulvio, illus. LC 82-45512. 32p. (ps-2). 1983. 10.95 (ISBN 0-8037-3829-3). Dial Bks Young.
Tofts, Hannah. Paint Book. (ps-3). 1990. pap. 11.95 (ISBN 0-671-70364-1). S&S Trade.
PAINTINGS
see also Portraits
Levine, Bobbie, et al. A Child's Walk Through Twentieth Century American Painting & Sculpture. (Illus.). 29p. (gr. 2-6). 1986. spiral bdg. 1.50 (ISBN 0-912303-37-9). Michigan Mus.
Martin, Mary & Zorn, Steven. Start Exploring Masterpieces: A Fact-Filled Coloring Book. rev. ed. (Illus.). 178p. (gr. 2 up). 1990. pap. 7.95 (ISBN 0-89471-801-0). Running Pr.
Nigg, Joe. Strength of Lions & the Flight of Eagles: Gryphons. (Illus.). 12p. (Orig.). (gr. 7-9). 1982. pap. 2.50 (ISBN 0-88138-004-0). Green Tiger Pr.
Yenawine, Philip. Stories. (Illus.). (gr. 2-5). 1991. 14.00 (ISBN 0-385-30256-8); PLB 14.99 (ISBN 0-385-30316-5). Delacorte.
PAINTINGS–FICTION
King, Clive. Me & My Million. LC 78-22501. (gr. 5 up). 1979. 8.79 (ISBN 0-690-03971-9, Crowell Jr Bks). HarpC Child Bks.
Wilde, Oscar. Picture of Dorian Gray. (gr. 9 up). 1964. pap. 2.50 (ISBN 0-8049-0039-6, CL-39). Airmont.
PAIR SYSTEM
see Binary System (Mathematics)
PAKISTAN
Caldwell, John C. Pakistan. (Illus.). (gr. 5 up). 1988. 14.95 (ISBN 0-222-00907-1). Chelsea Hse.
Cumming, David. Pakistan. Bull, Peter, illus. Holmes, Jimmy, photos by. LC 88-27553. (Illus.). 48p. (gr. 3-6). 1989. PLB 12.40 (ISBN 0-531-18268-1). Watts.
Doherty, Katherine M. & Doherty, Craig A. Benazir Bhutto. (Illus.). 144p. (gr. 9-12). 1990. PLB 13.90 (ISBN 0-531-10936-4). Watts.
Hughes, Libby. From Prison to Prime Minister: A Biography of Benazir Bhutto. (Illus.). 128p. (gr. 5 up). 1990. PLB 12.95 (ISBN 0-87518-438-3, Dillon). Macmillan Child Grp.
Lye, Keith. Take a Trip to Pakistan. (Illus.). 32p. (gr. k-3). 1985. PLB 7.99 (ISBN 0-531-04886-1). Watts.
Mohamed, Amin. We Live in Pakistan. (Illus.). 64p. (gr. k up). 1984. PLB 9.49 (ISBN 0-531-03817-3). Watts.
Scarsbrook, Ailsa & Scarsbrook, Alan. A Family in Pakistan. LC 85-6886. (Illus.). 32p. (gr. 2-5). 1985. PLB 9.95 (ISBN 0-8225-1662-4). Lerner Pubns.
Shaw, Denis. Pakistani Twins. Spence, Geraldine, illus. (gr. 6-9). 1965. 9.95 (ISBN 0-8023-1094-X). Dufour.
Yusufali, Jabeen. Pakistan: An Islamic Treasure. (Illus.). 128p. (gr. 5 up). 1990. 12.95 (ISBN 0-685-33008-7, Dillon); PLB 12.95 (ISBN 0-685-33009-5). Macmillan Child Grp.
PAKISTANIS IN THE U. S.
Bagai, Leona B. The East Indians & Pakistanis in America. rev. ed. LC 67-15680. (Illus.). 64p. (gr. 5 up). 1972. PLB 9.95 (ISBN 0-8225-0210-0). Lerner Pubns.
PALACES
Odor, Ruth S. Learning about Castles & Palaces. Halverson, Lynn, illus. LC 82-9567. 48p. (gr. 2-6). 1982. 17.27 (ISBN 0-516-06537-8). Childrens.
PALEOLITHIC PERIOD
see Stone Age
PALEONTOLOGY
see Fossils
PALESTINE
Gilmour, David. The Palestinians. (Illus.). 32p. (gr. 4-9). 1986. PLB 8.90 (ISBN 0-531-17031-4, Pub. by Gloucester). Watts.
Reische, Diana. Arafat & the Palestine Liberation Organization. (Illus.). 160p. (gr. 9-12). 1991. PLB 13.90 (ISBN 0-531-11000-1). Watts.
PALESTINE–FICTION
Speare, Elizabeth G. Bronze Bow. 256p. (gr. 6 up). 1961. 13.95 (ISBN 0-395-07113-5). HM.
—The Bronze Bow. LC 61-10640. (Illus.). 272p. (gr. 6 up). 1973. pap. 7.95 (ISBN 0-395-13719-5, Sandpiper). HM.
Thoene, Bodie. The Key to Zion. LC 88-7439. 352p. (Orig.). (gr. 11 up). 1988. pap. 7.95 (ISBN 1-55661-034-3). Bethany Hse.
PALESTINE–HISTORY
Britton, Colleen. Palestine Thirty A. D. You Are There. Britton, Colleen, illus. 73p. (Orig.). (ps-6). 1987. pap. 12.95 (ISBN 0-940754-38-X). Ed Ministries.
PALSY, CEREBRAL
see Cerebral Palsy
PANAMA
Griffiths, John. Take a Trip to Panama. LC 89-8929. (Illus.). 32p. (gr. 3-5). 1989. PLB 10.90 (ISBN 0-531-10736-1). Watts.
Haynes, Tricia. Panama. (Illus.). (gr. 5 up). 1988. 14.95 (ISBN 0-222-00961-6). Chelsea Hse.
Lerner Publications, Department of Geography Staff. Panama in Pictures. (Illus.). 64p. (gr. 5 up). 1987. PLB 12.95 (ISBN 0-8225-1818-X). Lerner Pubns.
Stewart, Gail B. Panama. LC 90-36249. (Illus.). 48p. (gr. 5-6). 1990. RSBE 10.95 (ISBN 0-89686-536-3, Crestwood Hse). Macmillan Child Grp.
PANAMA CANAL
Oliver, Carl R. Panama's Canal. (Illus.). 128p. (gr. 9-12). 1990. PLB 13.90 (ISBN 0-531-10958-5). Watts.
St. George, Judith. The Panama Canal: Gateway to the World. 144p. (gr. 5 up). 1989. 14.95 (ISBN 0-399-21637-5, Putnam). Putnam Pub Group.
Stein, R. Conrad. The Story of the Panama Canal. LC 82-4565. (Illus.). (gr. 3-6). 1982. PLB 13.27 (ISBN 0-516-04640-3). Childrens.
PANCRAS, SAINT, d. 304
Ongaro, A. St. Pancratius. (gr. 4-8). 2.00 (ISBN 0-8198-0220-4); pap. 1.25 (ISBN 0-8198-0221-2). Dghtrs St Paul.
PANDAS
Bailey, Jill. Project Panda. LC 90-9802. (Illus.). 48p. (gr. 3-7). 1990. PLB 17.28 (ISBN 0-8114-2704-8). Steck-V.
Barrett, N. S. Pandas. FS Staff, ed. (Illus.). 32p. (gr. 4-9). 1988. PLB 11.40 (ISBN 0-531-10530-X). Watts.
Barrett, Norman. Pandas. (SPA., Illus.). 32p. (gr. k-4). 1990. PLB 11.40 (ISBN 0-531-07908-2). Watts.
—Picture Library: Pandas. 1990. pap. 3.95 (ISBN 0-531-15206-5). Watts.
Bracken, Carolyn, illus. Panda. 6p. (ps-k). 1981. 2.50 (ISBN 0-671-42530-7, Little Simon). S&S Trade.
Bright, Michael. Giant Panda. (Illus.). 32p. (gr. 5-6). 1989. PLB 11.90 (ISBN 0-531-17140-X). Watts.
Crump, Donald J., ed. Playful Pandas, Bk. 1 of 2. (Illus.). (ps-3). 1991. Set. 19.95 (ISBN 0-317-99618-5). Natl Geog.
Goodall, Jane, ed. Jane Goodall's Animal World: Pandas. (Illus.). 32p. (gr. 3-7). 1989. pap. 3.95 (ISBN 0-689-71319-3, Aladdin). Macmillan Child Grp.
Green, Carl R. & Sanford, William R. The Giant Panda. LC 87-14002. (Illus.). 48p. (gr. 5-6). 1987. PLB 10.95 (ISBN 0-89686-331-X, Crestwood Hse). Macmillan Child Grp.
Gross, Ruth B. Book about Pandas. (Illus.). (gr. k-3). 1974. pap. 1.95 (ISBN 0-590-31865-9). Scholastic Inc.
—A Book about Pandas. (Illus.). 32p. (gr. k-3). 1991. pap. 2.50 (ISBN 0-590-43492-6). Scholastic Inc.
Hoffman, Mary. Panda. LC 84-15882. (Illus.). 24p. (gr. k-5). 1985. PLB 13.32 (ISBN 0-8172-2407-6). Raintree Pubs.
MacClintock, Dorcas. Red Pandas: A Natural History. Young, Ellan, illus. LC 88-3528. 112p. (gr. 7 up). 1988. 13.95 (ISBN 0-684-18677-2, Scribners Young Read). Macmillan Child Grp.
Martin, L. Panda. (Illus.). 24p. (gr. k-5). Date not set. PLB 11.93 (ISBN 0-86592-996-3). Rourke Corp.
Masui, Mitsuko. Pandas of the World. Ooka, Diane, tr. (Illus.). 32p. (gr. k-2). 1989. 11.95 (ISBN 0-89346-314-0). Heian Intl.
The Panda. (Illus.). (gr. 2-5). 1988. pap. 2.50 (ISBN 0-8167-1573-4). Troll Assocs.
Pandas. (Illus.). 32p. (gr. 2-6). 1989. pap. 4.95 (ISBN 0-14-034174-9, Puffin). Puffin Bks.
Petty, Kate. Pandas. (Illus.). 24p. (gr. k-3). 1991. PLB 10.40 (ISBN 0-531-17287-2, Gloucester Pr). Watts.
Propper. Panda, Reading Level 3-4. (Illus.). 28p. (gr. 2-5). Date not set. PLB 14.60 (ISBN 0-86592-851-7). Rourke Corp.
Rothaus, Jim. Giant Pandas. 24p. (gr. 3). 1988. 17.10 (ISBN 0-88682-228-9); PLB 11.95s.p. (ISBN 0-318-37911-2). Creative Ed.
San Diego Panda. 1991. pap. 14.95 (ISBN 0-671-73922-0). S&S Trade.
Schlein, Miriam. Jane Goodall's Animal World: Pandas. Goodall, Jane, intro. by. (Illus.). 32p. (gr. 3-7). 1989. 11.95 (ISBN 0-689-31471-X, Atheneum Child Bk). Macmillan Child Grp.
Schmidt, Annemarie & Schmidt, Christian R. Bears. (Illus.). 32p. (gr. 4-6). 1991. PLB 11.95 (ISBN 0-8368-0684-0). Gareth Stevens Inc.
Standring, Gillian. Pandas. (Illus.). 32p. (gr. k-4). 1991. RLB 11.90 (ISBN 0-531-18397-1, Pub. by Boatwright Pr). Watts.
Wong, O. Giant Pandas. LC 87-10717. (Illus.). 48p. (gr. k-4). 1987. PLB 14.60 (ISBN 0-516-01241-X); pap. 4.95 (ISBN 0-516-41241-8). Childrens.

PANDAS–FICTION

Bonners, Susan. Panda. (gr. k-6). 1988. pap. 3.95 (ISBN 0-440-40110-0, YB). Dell.

Calmenson, Stephanie. Dinner at the Panda Palace. Westcott, Nadine B., illus. LC 90-33720. 32p. (ps-3). 1991. 14.95 (ISBN 0-06-021010-9); PLB 14.89 (ISBN 0-06-021011-7). HarpC Child Bks.

Cosgrove, Stephen. Ming Ling. James, Robin, illus. 32p. (Orig.). (gr. k-4). 1978. pap. 2.95 (ISBN 0-8431-0592-5). Price Stern.

Day, David. The Emperor's Panda. Beddows, Eric, illus. LC 86-32818. 112p. (gr. 3-5). 1987. 12.95 (ISBN 0-396-09036-2, Putnam). Putnam Pub Group.

Dowell, Olivia S. The First Adventure of Peter Nelson Panda. West, Linnea F., illus. 16p. (gr. 2-4). 1986. pap. 5.95 (ISBN 0-9617624-0-3). Bear Tracks Pub.

Eisemann, Henry. Su-Su, the Fremont School Panda. Steinberg, Chris, illus. 22p. (Orig.). (gr. k-6). 1987. pap. 6.95 (ISBN 0-938129-03-1). Emprise Pubns.

Foreman, Michael. Panda & the Bunyips. Foreman, Michael, illus. LC 87-9842. 32p. (ps-6). 1988. 10.95 (ISBN 0-8052-4041-1). Schocken.

Frazer, Benjamin. Copper the Cat & the Adventure of the Stranded Panda. Faulkner, Matt, illus. 32p. 1990. 9.95 (ISBN 0-8092-4270-2, Calico Bks). Contemp Bks.

Gackenbach, Dick. Poppy the Panda. Gackenbach, Dick, illus. LC 84-4952. 32p. (ps-3). 1984. 13.95 (ISBN 0-89919-276-9, Clarion). HM.

Gross, Ruth B. Book about Pandas. (Illus.). (gr. k-3). 1974. pap. 1.95 (ISBN 0-590-31865-9). Scholastic Inc.

Hoban, Tana. Panda, Panda. Hoban, Tana, illus. LC 86-3088. 12p. (ps). 1986. pap. 3.95 (ISBN 0-688-06564-3). Greenwillow.

Hunt, Robert. Beishung: The Giant Panda. Dunnington, Tom, illus. LC 74-735891. (gr. 2-5). 1978. 6 bks. & 1 cass. 29.95 (ISBN 0-89290-032-6); 1 bk. & 1 cass. 10. 95 (ISBN 0-685-04628-1). Soc for Visual.

Kim, Joy. You Look Funny! Boyd, Patti, illus. LC 86-30839. 32p. (gr. k-2). 1987. PLB 7.06 (ISBN 0-8167-0976-9); pap. text ed. 1.95 (ISBN 0-8167-0977-7). Troll Assocs.

Krauss, Robert. Milton the Early Riser. Aruego, Jose & Dewey, Ariane, illus. LC 81-9460. (ps). 1987. pap. 13. 95 (ISBN 0-671-66272-4); pap. 5.95 (ISBN 0-671-66911-7). S&S Trade.

Leonard, Marcia & Schmidt, Karen. Little Panda Gets Lost. 32p. (Orig.). (gr. 1). 1985. pap. 2.50 (ISBN 0-553-15302-1). Bantam.

Liu Qian. Panda Bear Goes Visiting. (Illus.). 22p. (gr. 3-4). 1982. 3.95 (ISBN 0-8351-1108-3); pap. 2.95 (ISBN 0-8351-1139-3). China Bks.

McClung, Robert M. Lili: A Giant Panda of Sichuan. Brady, Irene, illus. LC 87-28271. 96p. (gr. 3-7). 1988. 12.95 (ISBN 0-688-06942-8); PLB 12.88 (ISBN 0-688-06943-6, Morrow Jr Bks). Morrow Jr Bks.

Ono, Koichi. Little Panda Bear. McClain, Mary, illus. 12p. (ps-2). 1982. 4.95 (ISBN 0-671-42549-8, Little Simon). S&S Trade.

Temko, Florence. Paper Pandas & Jumping Frogs. Jackson, Paul, illus. Petersen, Richard, et al, photos by. LC 86-70960. (Illus.). 135p. (gr. 3-6). 1986. pap. 11.95 (ISBN 0-8351-1770-7). China Bks.

Willard, Nancy. Papa's Panda. Hoban, Lillian, illus. LC 78-31787. (ps-2). 1979. 5.95 (ISBN 0-15-259462-0, HJ). HarBraceJ.

PANICS

see Depressions

PANTHERS

Kappeler, Markus. Big Cats. (Illus.). 32p. (gr. 4-6). 1991. PLB 11.95 (ISBN 0-8368-0685-9). Gareth Stevens Inc.

Sateren, Shelley S. Black Panther. LC 89-28267. (Illus.). 48p. (gr. 5 up). 1990. 10.95 (ISBN 0-89686-519-3, Crestwood Hse). Macmillan Child Grp.

PANTHERS–FICTION

Sampson, Fay. Josh's Panther. (Illus.). 96p. (gr. 3-5). 1988. 13.95 (ISBN 0-575-03914-0, Pub. by Gollancz England). Trafalgar Sq.

PANTOMIMES

see also Shadow Pantomimes and Plays

PAPER

Limousin, Odile. The Story of Paper. Matthews, Sarah, tr. from FRE. Brusch, Beat, illus. LC 87-31752. 38p. (gr. k-5). 1988. 4.95 (ISBN 0-944589-16-2, 162). Young Discovery Lib.

Paper. (ARA., Illus.). (gr. 5-8). 3.50x (ISBN 0-86685-213-1). Intl Bk Ctr.

Sneider, Cary I. & Barber, Jacqueline. Paper Towel Testing. Bergman, Lincoln & Fairwell, Kay, eds. Bevilacqua, Carol, illus. Hoyt, Richard, photos by. (Illus.). 29p. (Orig.). (gr. 5-9). 1987. pap. 6.50 (ISBN 0-912511-65-6). Lawrence Science.

Witcombmsia, Gerald, illus. Paper. 32p. (gr. 3-5). 1985. 5. 95x (ISBN 0-86685-450-9). Intl Bk Ctr.

PAPER–HISTORY

Cosner, Shaaron. Paper Through the Ages. Kiedrowski, Priscilla, illus. LC 84-7760. 48p. (gr. k-4). 1984. PLB 9.95 (ISBN 0-87614-270-6). Carolrhoda Bks.

Smith, Elizabeth S. Paper. LC 84-7271. (Illus.). 64p. (gr. 4 up). 1984. PLB 10.85 (ISBN 0-8027-6569-6). Walker & Co.

PAPER CRAFTS

see also names of paper crafts, e.g. Origami

Araki, Chiyo. Origami in the Classroom, 2 vols. LC 65-13412. (Illus.). (gr. 1 up). 1965-68. bds. 13.95 ea. Vol. 1 (ISBN 0-8048-0452-4). Vol. 2 (ISBN 0-8048-0453-2). C E Tuttle.

Barr, Marilyn G. Paper Bags: Patterns for Cut-&-Play Fun. (Illus.). 64p. (ps-k). 1989. 6.95 (ISBN 0-685-31233-X, MM1915). Monday Morning Bks.

Barr, Marilynn G. Paper Plates. (Illus.). 64p. (ps-k). 1989. 6.95 (ISBN 0-912107-98-7, MM1916). Monday Morning Bks.

—Paper Rolls. (Illus.). 64p. (ps-k). 1989. 6.95 (ISBN 1-878279-00-9, MM1917). Monday Morning Bks.

Boden, Arthur & Woodside, John. Boden's Beasts. Boden, Art, illus. (gr. 1-5). 1964. 8.95 (ISBN 0-8392-3045-1). Astor-Honor.

Borja, Corinne & Borja, Robert. Making Chinese Paper Cuts. Tucker, Kathleen, ed. Borja, Corinne & Borja, Robert, illus. LC 79-18358. (gr. 3-8). 1980. PLB 12.95 (ISBN 0-8075-4948-7). A Whitman.

Bottomley, Jim. Paper Projects for Creative Kids of All Ages. 160p. (gr. 5 up). 1983. pap. 12.95 (ISBN 0-316-10349-7). Little.

Brown, Charlene & Davis, Carolyn. Paper Art Fun. Davis, Carolyn, illus. 64p. (Orig.). 1988. pap. text ed. 5.95 (ISBN 0-929261-31-3, BA06). W Foster Pub.

Brown, James C. Papercrafts for All Seasons. (Illus.). (gr. 3-12). 1984. pap. 4.95 (ISBN 0-8224-5189-1). Fearon Teach Aids.

Brown, Jerome C. Fables & Tales PaperCrafts. (gr. k-5). 1989. pap. 7.95 (ISBN 0-8224-3155-6). Fearon Teach Aids.

—Holiday Crafts & Greeting Cards. (gr. 3-6). 1982. pap. 5.95 (ISBN 0-8224-5194-8). Fearon Teach Aids.

—Paper Designs. (gr. 1-6). 1982. pap. 5.95 (ISBN 0-8224-5193-X). Fearon Teach Aids.

—Puppets & Mobiles. (gr. 1-6). 1982. pap. 5.95 (ISBN 0-8224-5195-6). Fearon Teach Aids.

Burt, Erica. Paper. (Illus.). 32p. (gr. 2-6). 1990. lib. bdg. 13.26 (ISBN 0-86592-488-0); lib. bdg. 9.95s.p. Rourke Corp.

Chernoff, Goldie T. Easy Costumes You Don't Have to Sew. LC 76-46428. (Illus.). 48p. (gr. 1-3). 1984. 12.95 (ISBN 0-02-718230-4, Four Winds). Macmillan Child Grp.

Churchill, E. Richard. Building with Paper. LC 89-26220. (Illus.). 128p. 1990. 14.95 (ISBN 0-8069-5772-7). Sterling.

—Fantastic Flying Paper Toys. LC 90-39007. (Illus.). 96p. (Orig.). (gr. 4-10). 1990. pap. 3.95 (ISBN 0-8069-7460-5). Sterling.

Corwin, Judith H. Papercrafts. Corwin, Judith H., illus. IRosoff, ed. (Illus.). 72p. (gr. 2-4). 1988. PLB 11.90 (ISBN 0-531-10465-6). Watts.

Curtis, A. & Hindley, J. The KnowHow Book of Paper Fun: Lots of Things to Make from Paper & Card. (Illus.). 32p. (gr. 3-6). 1977. pap. 5.95 (ISBN 0-86020-001-9). EDC.

D'Amato, Janet & D'Amato, Alex. Cardboard Carpentry. D'Amato, Jane & D'Amato, Alex, illus. Thompson, Morton, intro. by. (gr. 2-5). PLB 11.95 (ISBN 0-87460-085-5). Lion Bks.

DeRosemond, Peggy. A Royal Romance Paper Dolls. (gr. 8-12). 1984. pap. 4.00 (ISBN 0-914510-14-2). Evergreen.

Devonshire, Hilary. Moving Art. (Illus.). 48p. (gr. 5-8). 1990. PLB 11.90 (ISBN 0-531-14076-8). Watts.

Forte, Imogene. Paper Capers. LC 84-62932. (Illus.). 80p. (gr. k-6). 1985. 3.95 (ISBN 0-86530-097-6, IP 91-1). Incentive Pubns.

Gibson, R. Paperplay. (Illus.). 32p. (ps-3). 1989. lib. bdg. 13.96 (ISBN 0-88110-422-1, Usborne); pap. 5.95 (ISBN 0-7460-0466-4). EDC.

Grater, Michael. Make It in Paper: Creative Three-Dimensional Paper Projects. (Illus.). 96p. (gr. 5 up). 1983. pap. 4.95 (ISBN 0-486-24468-7). Dover.

Irvine, Joan. How to Make Pop-Ups. Reid, Barbara, illus. LC 87-28306. 96p. (gr. 3-7). 1988. PLB 12.88 (ISBN 0-688-07903-2); pap. 6.95 (ISBN 0-688-07902-4, Pub. by Beech Tree Bks). Morrow Jr Bks.

Johnston, Mary G. Paper Sculpture. rev. & enl. ed. LC 64-24721. (Illus.). (gr. 4-12). 1965. 9.95 (ISBN 0-87192-019-0). Davis Mass.

Leonard, Kay. Paper Kaleidoscopes. (Illus.). 40p. (gr. k-12). 1989. pap. 5.95 (ISBN 0-685-26430-0). Pelona Pr.

Lohf, Sabine. Things I Can Make with Paper. (Illus.). 32p. (ps-3). 1989. 6.95 (ISBN 0-87701-671-2). Chronicle Bks.

McGraw, Shelia. Papier Mache for Kids. (Illus.). 72p. 1991. 17.95 (ISBN 0-920668-92-5); pap. 9.95 (ISBN 0-920668-93-3). Firefly Bks Ltd.
Papier Mache expert Sheila McGraw published PAPIER MACHE TODAY in 1990 to great reviews & strong sales. Now she has created a how-to-book for kids that explores this versatile & absorbing craft on levels that are comfortable for children. By experimenting & simplifying, she has created a variety of projects that fit the level of skill, the hand size, & the attention span of kids. All of the projects are bright, engaging & fun. They include monsters, masks, animals, jewellery, & more. While papier mache is the original "recycled" art form, this book takes it a step further, using paper towel & toilet paper tubes, newspaper, bleach bottles, twigs, plastic bags & many other "found" items that are usually doomed to the garbage bag. Each how-to step is matched with a clear full-color photograph. Directions are straightforward, concise, & simple. The introduction to each project features photos of many variations to stimulate the imagination. Each features a sidebar as well, reminding readers of basic techniques & paste recipe. This alleviates the need to go hunting throughout the book with pasty hands. A chapter on finishing includes collage, decoupage, sponge painting & other painting techniques. Clear symbols denote where an adult's help or supervision may be required.
Publisher Provided Annotation.

Magos, Eunice & Hornnes, Esther. Alphabet Paper Dolls & Number Paper Dolls. Sussman, Ellen, intro. by. Burris, Priscilla, illus. (ps). 1988. Alpha, 56 p. pap. 4.95 (ISBN 0-933606-59-1, MS-659); Number, 52 p. pap. 4.95 (ISBN 0-933606-60-5, MS-660). Monkey Sisters.

Mah, Ronald. Predator Prey Puppets & Toys: Eight Paper Animal Projects to Make. Mah, Ronald, illus. 32p. (ps-3). 1986. pap. 3.95 (ISBN 0-9615903-1-9). Symbiosis Bks.

Medvene, Mark. Foilrigami. (Illus.). (gr. 4-7). 1968. 10.95 (ISBN 0-685-06619-3). Astor-Honor.

Murray, William D. & Rigney, Francis J. Paper Folding for Beginners. (Illus.). (gr. 1 up). pap. 2.95 (ISBN 0-486-20713-7). Dover.

Oldfield, Margaret J. Tell & Draw Paper Cut-Outs. Oldfield, Margaret J., illus. (Orig.). (gr. k-2). 1988. pap. 3.50 (ISBN 0-934876-23-1, 23). Creative Storytime.

Olson, Margaret J. Tell & Draw Animal Cut-outs. 3rd ed. (gr. k-2). 1963. pap. 3.00 (ISBN 0-934876-15-0). Creative Storytime.

Sakade, Florence. Origami, Japanese Paper Folding, 3 Vols. LC 57-10685. (Illus., Orig.). (gr. 2 up). Vol. 1. pap. 5.95 ea. (ISBN 0-8048-0454-0). Vol. 2 (ISBN 0-8048-0455-9). Vol. 3 (ISBN 0-8048-0456-7). C E Tuttle.

Sarasas, Claude. ABC's of Origami. Sarasas, Claude, illus. LC 64-17160. (gr. 3-8). 1964. bds. 11.95 (ISBN 0-8048-0000-6). C E Tuttle.

Simon, Seymour. The Paper Airplane Book. (gr. 4-6). 1976. pap. 3.95 (ISBN 0-14-030925-X, Puffin). Puffin Bks.

Supraner, Robyn. Fun with Paper. Barto, Renzo, illus. LC 80-19859. 48p. (gr. 1-5). 1981. PLB 11.89 (ISBN 0-89375-430-7); pap. 2.95 (ISBN 0-89375-431-5). Troll Assocs.

Temko, Florence. Paper Tricks. Winchester, Linda, illus. 48p. (gr. 3 up). 1988. pap. 1.95 (ISBN 0-590-41129-2). Scholastic Inc.

Thieme, Jeanne. American Girls PaperDolls: Kirsten, Samantha & Molly Paperdolls with All of Their Lovely Old-Fashioned Clothes. (Illus.). 32p. (Orig.). (gr. 2-5). 1989. pap. 6.95 (ISBN 0-937295-60-4). Pleasant CO.

Tofts, Hannah. Paper Book. 1990. 11.95 (ISBN 0-671-70366-8); pap. 4.95 (ISBN 0-671-70367-6). S&S Trade.

—Three-D. (ps-3). 1990. pap. 11.95 (ISBN 0-671-70370-6, SSJ); pap. 4.95 (ISBN 0-685-34801-6). S&S Trade.

Valentine, Malcolm. How to Make Your Own Recycled Paper. (Illus.). 32p. (Orig.). 1990. pap. 4.50 (ISBN 0-85532-670-0, Pub. by Search Pr UK). A Schwartz & Co.

Westphal, Arnold C. Paper & Scissors Truth Talks, No. 5. 1971. perfect bdg. 4.95 (ISBN 0-915398-08-4). Visual Evangels.

Zubrowski, Bernie. Messing Around with Drinking Straw Construction: A Children's Museum Activity Book. Fleischer, Stephanie, illus. 64p. (gr. 3-7). 1981. pap. 7.95 (ISBN 0-316-98875-8). Little.

PAPER FOLDING

see Paper Crafts

PAPER MAKING AND TRADE

see also Book Industries and Trade

Bourgeois, Paulette. Amazing Paper Book. (gr. 4-8). 1990. pap. 6.68 (ISBN 0-201-52377-9). Addison-Wesley.

Boy Scouts of America. Pulp & Paper. (Illus.). 40p. (gr. 6-12). 1974. pap. 1.85 (ISBN 0-8395-3343-8, 3343). BSA.

Gibbons, Gail. Paper, Paper Everywhere. Gibbons, Gail, illus. LC 82-3109. 32p. (ps-3). 1983. 10.95 (ISBN 0-15-259488-4, HJ). HarBraceJ.

Grummer, Arnold E. Paper by Kids. rev. ed. LC 79-22904. (Illus.). 116p. (gr. 5 up). 1980. PLB 12.95 (ISBN 0-87518-191-0, Dillon). Macmillan Child Grp.

The Manufacturing of Pulp & Paper: Science & Engineering Concepts. 113p. 1988. pap. 12.00 (ISBN 0-89852-448-2, 0101R148). TAPPI.

Mitgutsch, Ali. From Wood to Paper. Lerner, Mark, tr. from GER. Mitgutsch, Ali, illus. 24p. (ps-3). 1986. lib. bdg. 6.95 (ISBN 0-87614-296-X). Carolrhoda Bks.

PAPER SCULPTURE

see Paper Crafts

PAPER WORK

see Paper Crafts

PAPIER-MACHE

see Paper Crafts

PARABLES

see also Allegories; Fables; Jesus Christ–Parables

Butterworth, Nick. Parables, 4 vols. Inkpen, Mick, illus. LC 85-21816. (ps-3). 1986. 3.95 ea. Vol. 1: The House on the Rock (ISBN 0-88070-146-3). Vol. 2: The Lost Sheep (ISBN 0-88070-147-1) (ISBN 0-88070-145-5). Vol. 4: The Two Sons (ISBN 0-88070-148-X). Multnomah.

Castagnola, Lawrence. Parables for Little People. Muren, Nancy LaBerge, illus. Quinn, Francis A. LC 86-62628. (Illus.). 101p. (Orig.). (gr. 4 up). 1982. pap. text ed. 7.95 (ISBN 0-685-06197-3). Resource Pubns.

Jackson, Neta. The Hamster Who Got Himself Stuck. Babbitt, Anne, illus. 25p. (ps-3). 1991. 3.99 (ISBN 0-88070-416-0). Multnomah.

—The Parrot Who Talked Too Much. Babbitt, Anne, illus. 25p. (ps-3). 1991. 3.99 (ISBN 0-88070-415-2). Multnomah.

LeFevre, G. L. Parables & Miracles of Jesus. 16p. (Orig.). (gr. 3-6). 1982. pap. 0.98 (ISBN 0-87239-580-4, 2807). Standard Pub.

Lippman, Peter. From Here to There. Lippman, Peter, illus. LC 75-19947. 48p. (gr. 1 up). 1975. pap. 5.00 (ISBN 0-912846-11-9). Bookstore Pr.

Reid, John C. Bird Life in Wington: Practical Parables for Young People. Weidenaar, Reynold H., illus. 142p. (gr. 1-4). 1990. pap. 8.95 (ISBN 0-8028-4062-0). Eerdmans.

PARACHUTING

see Skydiving

PARADES–FICTION

Baker, Eugene. Shadowing the Suspect. Axeman, Lois, illus. LC 80-13982. 32p. (gr. 2-5). 1980. PLB 9.48 (ISBN 0-89565-152-1). Childs World.

—Spotting the Fakes-Counterfeits & Forgeries. Axeman, Lois, illus. LC 80-15998. 32p. (gr. 2-5). 1980. PLB 9.48 (ISBN 0-89565-153-X). Childs World.

Bunting, Eve. St. Patrick's Day in the Morning. Brett, Jan, illus. LC 79-15934. 32p. (ps-3). 1983. 13.95 (ISBN 0-395-29098-8, Clarion); pap. 4.95 (ISBN 0-89919-162-2). HM.

Crews, Donald. Parade. LC 82-20927. (Illus.). (ps-3). 1986. 3.95 (ISBN 0-688-06520-1, Mulberry). Morrow.

Haynes, Mary. The Great Pretenders. LC 90-32162. 144p. (gr. 4-7). 1990. 12.95 (ISBN 0-02-743452-4, Bradbury Pr). Macmillan Child Grp.

How I Saw the Parade (EV, Unit 4. (gr. 1). 1991. 5-pack 21.25 (ISBN 0-88106-732-6). Charlesbridge Pub.

Mockrin, Ida. The Big Parade. Brodsky, Harry, illus. 16p. (ps-1). 1983. pap. 2.00 (ISBN 0-9612244-0-1). Honeycomb Pr.

Shachtman, Tom. Parade! Saaf, Chuck, illus. LC 85-42795. 64p. (gr. 4-6). 1985. 14.95 (ISBN 0-02-782540-X, Mcmillan Child Bk). Macmillan Child Grp.

Ziefert, Harriet. Parade. 1990. 9.95 (ISBN 0-553-05862-2, Little Rooster). Bantam.

PARAGUAY

Haverstock, Nathan A. Paraguay in Pictures. (Illus.). 64p. (gr. 5 up). 1987. PLB 12.95 (ISBN 0-8225-1819-8). Lerner Pubns.

Moms, Marion. Paraguay. (Illus.). (gr. 5 up). 1988. 14.95 (ISBN 1-55546-184-0). Chelsea Hse.

PARASITES

see also Bacteriology; Insects, Injurious and Beneficial

PARCEL POST

see Postal Service

PAREJA, JUAN DE, 1606-1670–FICTION

De Trevino, Elizabeth B. I, Juan De Pareja. LC 65-19330. 192p. (gr. 7 up). 1987. (Sunburst); pap. 3.50 (ISBN 0-374-43525-1, Sunburst). FS&G.

PARENT AND CHILD

see also Children–Management; Fathers; Mothers

Adoff, Arnold. Black Is Brown Is Tan. McCully, Emily A., illus. LC 73-9855. 32p. (ps-3). 1973. 14.95i (ISBN 0-06-020083-9); PLB 14.89 (ISBN 0-06-020084-7). HarpC Child Bks.

Bailey, Marilyn. Single-Parent Families. LC 89-1415. (Illus.). 48p. (gr. 4 up). 1989. 10.95 (ISBN 0-89686-437-5, Crestwood Hse). Macmillan Child Grp.

Berry, Joy. Every Kid's Guide to Laws That Relate to Parents & Children. Bartholomew, illus. 48p. (gr. 3-7). 1987. 4.95 (ISBN 0-516-21411-X); PLB 14.60 (ISBN 0-516-01411-0). Childrens.

—Every Kid's Guide to Understanding Parents. Bartholomew, illus. 48p. (gr. 3-7). 1987. 4.95 (ISBN 0-516-21416-0); PLB 14.60 (ISBN 0-516-01416-1). Childrens.

Berry, Joy W. Teach Me About Mommies & Daddies. Dickey, Kate, ed. LC 85-45078. (Illus.). 36p. (ps). 1986. 4.98 (ISBN 0-685-10717-5). Grolier Inc.

—What to Do When Your Mom or Dad Says..."Be Prepared!" LC 81-83790. (Illus.). 48p. (gr. 3 up). 1982. lib. bdg. 14.60 (ISBN 0-516-02566-X). Childrens.

—What to Do When Your Mom or Dad Says..."Earn Your Allowance!" LC 81-83791. (Illus.). 48p. (gr. 3 up). 1982. lib. bdg. 14.60 (ISBN 0-516-02568-6). Childrens.

Bratman, Fred. Everything You Need to Know When a Parent Dies. (gr. 7-12). 1991. PLB 12.95 (ISBN 0-8239-1324-4). Rosen Group.

Brown, Fern G. Teen Guide to Caring for Your Unborn Baby. LC 88-51487. (Illus.). 62p. (gr. 7-12). 1989. PLB 12.40 (ISBN 0-531-10668-3). Watts.

Cain, V. M. Steps of Love: Single Adoptive Parenting. 133p. (Orig.). 1988. text ed. write for info.; pap. write for info. V M H Cain.

Chapian, Marie. Mothers & Daughters. LC 88-4199. 176p. (Orig.). (gr. 8 up). 1988. pap. 6.95 (ISBN 1-55661-007-6). Bethany Hse.

Clinton, Patrick. I Can Be a Father. LC 88-11749. (Illus.). 32p. (gr. k-3). 1988. PLB 13.93 (ISBN 0-516-01904-X); pap. 3.95 (ISBN 0-516-41904-8). Childrens.

Coleman, William L. The Great Date Wait & Other Hazards. LC 82-1233. 138p. (Orig.). (gr. 7 up). 1982. pap. 5.95 (ISBN 0-87123-348-7). Bethany Hse.

Corey, Dorothy. You Go Away. Rubin, Caroline & Axeman, Lois, illus. LC 75-33015. 32p. (ps). 1975. PLB 9.75 (ISBN 0-8075-9441-5). A Whitman.

Craven, Linda. Stepfamilies: New Patterns of Harmony. LC 82-60652. (Illus.). 192p. (gr. 7 up). 1983. lib. bdg. 13.98 (ISBN 0-671-44080-2); pap. 4.95 (ISBN 0-671-49486-4). Messner.

Davis, Ken. How to Live with Your Parents Without Losing Your Mind. (gr. 7 up). 1988. pap. 6.95 (ISBN 0-310-32331-2, 11791P, Pub. by Youth Spec). Zondervan.

Dinkmeyer, Don, Sr., et al. PREP for Effective Family Living. (gr. 7 up). 1985. 99.50 (ISBN 0-88671-225-4). Am Guidance.

Dragonwagon, Crescent. Will It Be Okay? Shecter, Ben, illus. LC 76-48859. (ps-3). 1977. PLB 12.89 (ISBN 0-06-021738-3). HarpC Child Bks.

Duggan, Maureen H. Mommy Doesn't Live Here Anymore. Liberman, Jane, illus. 48p. (Orig.). (ps-7). 1987. pap. 8.95 (ISBN 0-944453-01-5). B Brae. "Mommy Doesn't Live Here Anymore" - a sensitive chronicle of a mother's alcoholism & how it affected her children. It has successfully captured the essence of life within an alcoholic family: the stresses, tensions, pressures & pains. Most importantly, it has done so from the vantage point of the child, as the child reflects upon the total experience. No other work has presented such a realistic portrayal of the magnitude of suffering, emotional pain & psychic turmoil of young children within alcoholic families. It reveals the thoughts, reasoning, feelings & behaviors of children in alcoholic homes, & yet, accomplishes such spirit of understanding & sympathy within an overall message of hope & help for our children. "Mommy Doesn't Live Here Anymore" is an inspirational work, revealing that the tragedies of familial alcoholism & tragic consequences for our youth need to be dealt with in a personal & delicate manner." Maureen Duggan has always been regarded highly for her thoughtful & gentle manner, compassionate understanding, & her acute sensitivity towards alcoholics & family needs. Her own serenity & spirituality are guides for many seeking their own honesty & fulfillment."--Nelson C. Acquilano, Executive Director, Council on Alcoholism of The Finger Lakes, N.Y. *Publisher Provided Annotation.*

Evans, Marla D. This Is Me & My Single Parent: A Discovery Workbook for Children & Single Parents to Work on Together. (Illus.). 80p. (Orig.). (gr. 2-6). 1989. pap. 12.95 (ISBN 0-945354-17-7, 4177). Magination Pr.

Fitz-Gerald, Christine M. I Can Be a Mother. LC 87-35189. (Illus.). 32p. (gr. k-3). 1988. PLB 13.93 (ISBN 0-516-01914-7); pap. 3.95 (ISBN 0-516-41914-5). Childrens.

Gardner, Richard A. The Boys & Girls Book about One-Parent Families. LC 78-18388. (Illus.). 122p. (gr. k-8). 1983. pap. 3.95 (ISBN 0-933812-16-7). Creative Therapeutics.

Gibson, R. Odds & Ends. (Illus.). 32p. (ps-2). 1991. lib. bdg. 13.96 (ISBN 0-88110-488-4, Usborne); pap. 5.95 (ISBN 0-7460-0633-0, Usborne). EDC.

Gilbert, Sara. How to Live with a Single Parent. LC 81-12413. 128p. (gr. 7 up). 1982. PLB 12.88 (ISBN 0-688-00633-7). Lothrop.

Havens, Ami. Now You're Talking. Richey, Donald, illus. LC 90-10764. 128p. (gr. 5-9). 1990. lib. bdg. 10.89 (ISBN 0-8167-2142-4); pap. text ed. 2.95 (ISBN 0-8167-2143-2). Troll Assocs.

Klein, David & Klein, Marymae E. Your Parents & Your Self: Alike-Unlike, Agreeing-Disagreeing. LC 86-20390. 176p. (gr. 6 up). 1986. 13.95 (ISBN 0-684-18684-5, Scribners Young Read). Macmillan Child Grp.

Lash, Michele, et al. My Kind of Family: A Book for Kids in Single-Parent Homes. LC 90-31471. (Illus.). 208p. (ps-6). 1990. plastic comb spiral bdg. 16.95 (ISBN 0-914525-13-1); pap. 16.95 plastic comb spiral (ISBN 0-914525-12-3). Waterfront Bks.

LeShan, Eda. When a Parent Is Very Sick. (Illus.). 112p. (gr. 3-7). 1986. 14.95 (ISBN 0-316-52162-0, Joy St Bks). Little.

—When Grownups Drive You Crazy. LC 87-22005. 128p. (gr. 3-7). 1988. 12.95 (ISBN 0-02-756340-5, Mcmillan Child Bk). Macmillan Child Grp.

Lindsay, Jeanne W. Do I Have a Daddy? A Story about a Single-Parent Child. 2nd ed. Boeller, Cheryl, illus. 48p. 1991. 12.95 (ISBN 0-930934-45-8); pap. 5.95 (ISBN 0-930934-44-X). Morning Glory.

Making Parents Proud. 48p. (gr. 6-8). 1990. pap. 6.95 (ISBN 1-55945-107-6). Group Pub.

Marsh, Carole. Meet in the Middle: The Parents Test - The Kids Test. (Illus.). (gr. 4 up). 1983. 14.95 (ISBN 0-935326-24-3). Gallopade Pub Group.

Mayle, Peter. Why Are We Getting a Divorce? Robins, Arthur, illus. LC 87-12105. 32p. (gr. k-3). 1988. PLB 11.95 (ISBN 0-517-56527-7, Harmony). Crown.

Newquist, Larry W., Jr. How to Take Advantage of Your Parents. LC 88-70059. 80p. (Orig.). (gr. 12). 1988. 8.95 (ISBN 0-945474-13-X); pap. 4.95 (ISBN 0-945474-12-1). Atomic Bks.

Parramon, J. M., et al. Parents. 32p. (gr. 3-5). Eng. ed. pap. 3.95 (ISBN 0-8120-3852-5); Span. ed.: Los Padres. pap. 4.95 (ISBN 0-8120-3856-8). Barron.

Rashkis, Harold A. & Tashjian, Levon D. Understanding Your Parents. LC 78-60444. (Illus.). 154p. (gr. 9-12). 1978. 6.95 (ISBN 0-89313-009-5). Lippincott.

Reich, Hanns, ed. Children & Their Mothers. (Illus.). 64p. (ps up). 1983. 4.95 (ISBN 0-8090-1513-7, Terra Magica). Hill & Wang.

Roop, Peter & Roop, Connie. Keep the Lights Burning, Abbie. Hanson, Peter E., illus. LC 84-27446. 40p. (gr. k-4). 1985. lib. bdg. 9.95 (ISBN 0-87614-275-7); pap. 5.95 (ISBN 0-87614-454-7). Carolrhoda Bks.

Ryan, Elizabeth A. Straight Talk about Parents. 144p. 1989. 15.95x (ISBN 0-8160-1526-0). Facts on File.

Siegel, Eli. Children's Guide to Parents & Other Matters: Little Essays for Children & Others. LC 78-171393. (Illus.). (gr. 1-6). 1971. text ed. 6.50 (ISBN 0-910492-16-6). Definition.

Silverstein, Herma. Teen Guide to Single Parenting. LC 88-51486. (Illus.). 62p. (gr. 7-12). 1989. PLB 12.40 (ISBN 0-531-10669-1). Watts.

Webb, Margot. Coping with Overprotective Parents. Rosen, Ruth, ed. (gr. 7-12). 1990. lib. bdg. 12.95 (ISBN 0-8239-1088-1). Rosen Group.

PARENT AND CHILD–FICTION

Alexander, Martha. When the New Baby Comes, I'm Moving Out. Alexander, Martha, illus. LC 79-4275. (ps-2). 1979. 9.95 (ISBN 0-8037-9557-2); PLB 9.89 (ISBN 0-8037-9558-0). Dial Bks Young.

Asch, Frank. Bread & Honey. Asch, Frank, illus. LC 81-16893. 48p. (ps-3). 1982. 5.95 (ISBN 0-8193-1077-8); PLB 5.95 (ISBN 0-8193-1078-6). Parents.

Barrett, John. Daniel Discovers Daniel. Servello, Joe, illus. LC 79-17897. 32p. (gr. k-5). 1980. 16.95 (ISBN 0-87705-423-1). Human Sci Pr.

Black, Claudia. My Dad Loves Me, My Dad Has a Disease. LC 59-776. (Illus.). 84p. (Orig.). (gr. k-9). 1982. pap. 8.95 (ISBN 0-9607940-2-6). MAC Pub.

Blue, Rose. Wishful Lying. Hartman, Laura, illus. LC 79-21806. 32p. (ps-3). 1980. 16.95 (ISBN 0-87705-473-8). Human Sci Pr.

Bunn, Scott. Just Hold On. LC 82-70316. 160p. (gr. 7 up). 1982. pap. 9.95 (ISBN 0-385-28490-X). Delacorte.

Bunting, Eve. Sharing Susan. LC 90-27097. 128p. (gr. 4-7). 1991. 13.95 (ISBN 0-06-021693-X); PLB 13.89 (ISBN 0-06-021694-8). HarpC Child Bks.

Burningham, John. Come Away from the Water, Shirley. Burningham, John, illus. LC 77-483. 32p. (gr. 1-2). 1977. 12.95 (ISBN 0-690-01360-4, Crowell Jr Bks); PLB 12.89 (ISBN 0-690-01361-2). HarpC Child Bks.

Bussard, Paula. The Glad I Gotcha Day. Goodridge, Larry, illus. 28p. (gr. k-3). 1985. 1.39 (ISBN 0-87239-963-X, 3383). Standard Pub.

Caines, Jeannette. Abby. Kellogg, Steven, illus. LC 73-5480. 32p. (ps-3). 1973. PLB 12.89 (ISBN 0-06-020922-4). HarpC Child Bks.

Cannon, Bettie. Begin the World Again. LC 90-46596. 192p. (gr. 7 up). 1991. SBE 13.95 (ISBN 0-684-19292-6, Scribners Young Read). Macmillan Child Grp.

Christopher, John. The Guardians. LC 78-99118. 192p. (gr. 5-9). 1972. pap. 4.95 (ISBN 0-02-042680-1, Collier Young Ad). Macmillan Child Grp.

Cleary, Beverly. Dear Mr. Henshaw. large type ed. Zelinsky, Paul O., illus. 141p. (gr. 2-6). 1987. Repr. of 1983 ed. lib. bdg. 14.95 (ISBN 1-55736-001-4). ABC-CLIO.
—Ramona & Her Father. Tiegreen, Alan, illus. LC 77-1614. 192p. (gr. 3-7). 1977. 13.95 (ISBN 0-688-22114-9); PLB 13.88 (ISBN 0-688-32114-3). Morrow.
Colman, Hila. Weekend Sisters. LC 85-5665. 176p. (gr. 7 up). 1985. 11.95 (ISBN 0-688-05785-3). Morrow Jr Bks.
Dahl, Roald. Danny: The Champion of the World. Bennett, Jill, illus. 208p. (gr. 3 up). 1975. lib. bdg. 13.99 (ISBN 0-394-93103-3). Knopf.
Danziger, Paula. The Divorce Express. 160p. (gr. 7 up). 1983. pap. 3.25 (ISBN 0-440-92062-0, LFL). Dell.
—Everyone Else's Parents Said Yes. (gr. k-6). 1990. pap. 3.50 (ISBN 0-440-40333-2, YB). Dell.
De Balzac, Honore. Pere Goriot. Canon, R. R., intro. by. (gr. 10 up). pap. 1.50 (ISBN 0-8049-0084-1, CL-84). Airmont.
Dumond, Michael. Dad Is Leaving Home. 196p. (gr. 7-12). 1987. PLB 12.95 (ISBN 0-8239-0699-X). Rosen Group.
Eyles, Heather. Well, I Never! Ross, Tony, illus. 32p. (ps-3). 1990. 11.95 (ISBN 0-87951-383-7). Overlook Pr.
Fenner, Carol. A Summer of Horses. LC 88-45878. 144p. (Orig.). (gr. 3-6). 1989. lib. bdg. 7.99 (ISBN 0-394-90480-X); pap. 2.95 (ISBN 0-394-80480-5). Knopf.
Fitzhugh, Louise. Nobody's Family Is Going to Change. LC 74-19152. 222p. (gr. 3 up). 1974. 13.95 (ISBN 0-374-35539-8). FS&G.
Ford, Barbara. The Eagles' Child. LC 90-5633. 160p. (gr. 3-7). 1990. 12.95 (ISBN 0-02-735405-9, Mcmillan Child Bk). Macmillan Child Grp.
Graeber, Charlotte T. The Thing in Kat's Attic. McCully, Emily A., illus. LC 84-8117. 80p. (gr. 1-4). 1984. 9.95 (ISBN 0-525-44146-8, DCB). Dutton Child Bks.
Grant, Cynthia D. Kumquat May, I'll Always Love You. LC 85-23037. 216p. (gr. 8 up). 1986. 14.95 (ISBN 0-689-31198-2, Atheneum Child Bk). Macmillan Child Grp.
Green, Phyllis. A New Mother for Martha. Luks, Margaret. LC 78-16731. (Illus.). 32p. (gr. k-3). 1978. 16.95 (ISBN 0-87705-330-8). Human Sci Pr.
Haynes, Betsy. Fabulous Five Parent Game. (ps-1). 1989. pap. 2.75 (ISBN 0-553-15670-5, #06). Bantam.
Hoban, Julia. Amy Loves the Rain. Hoban, Lillian, illus. LC 88-45851. 32p. (ps). 1989. 9.95 (ISBN 0-06-022357-X); PLB 9.89 (ISBN 0-06-022358-8). HarpC Child Bks.
—Amy Loves the Snow. Hoban, Lillian, illus. LC 76-45852. 24p. (ps). 1989. 9.95 (ISBN 0-06-022361-8); PLB 9.89 (ISBN 0-06-022395-2). HarpC Child Bks.
Johnson, Angela. Tell Me a Story, Mama. Soman, David, illus. LC 88-17917. 32p. (ps-1). 1989. 13.95 (ISBN 0-531-05794-1); PLB 13.99 (ISBN 0-531-08394-2). Orchard Bks Watts.
Kaye, Marilyn. Camp Sunnyside Friends, No. 11: The Problem with Parents. 128p. 1991. pap. 2.95 (ISBN 0-380-76183-1, Camelot). Avon.
Lee, Joanna. I Want to Keep My Baby! 176p. (Orig.). (gr. 9-12). 1977. pap. 3.50 (ISBN 0-451-15733-8, Sig). NAL-Dutton.
Macaulay, David. Black & White. Macaulay, David, illus. 32p. 1990. 14.95 (ISBN 0-395-52151-3). HM.
McGrath, Bob. I'm a Good Mommy. (Illus.). 48p. (ps-2). 1989. pap. 7.95 incl. audiocassette (ISBN 0-8431-2769-4). Price Stern.
—You're a Good Daddy. (Illus.). 48p. (ps-2). 1989. pap. 7.95 incl. audiocassette (ISBN 0-8431-2771-6). Price Stern.
Mahy, Margaret. The Catalogue of the Universe. LC 85-72262. 192p. (gr. 9 up). 1986. 15.95 (ISBN 0-689-50391-1, M K McElderry). Macmillan Child Grp.
Martin, Katherine. Night Riding. LC 89-2711. 208p. 1989. 12.95 (ISBN 0-679-80064-6); PLB 13.99 (ISBN 0-679-90064-0). Knopf.
Mazer, Harry. The Dollar Man. 190p. (Orig.). (gr. k-12). 1975. pap. 2.95 (ISBN 0-440-94484-8, LFL). Dell.
Mazer, Norma F. Up in Seth's Room. LC 79-2102. 208p. (gr. 7 up). 1979. pap. 7.95 (ISBN 0-385-29058-6). Delacorte.
Mills, Claudia. Boardwalk with Hotel. 144p. (gr. 7-12). 1986. pap. 2.50 (ISBN 0-553-15397-8, Skylark). Bantam.
Morris-Vann, Artie M. My Mom Keeps Hitting Me...But. Orlowski, Dennis, illus. 32p. (Orig.). (ps-5). 1981. pap. 6.50x (ISBN 0-940370-02-6); counseling activity guide-abused children 6.50 (ISBN 0-940370-06-9). Aid-U Pub.
Roberts, Willo D. Don't Hurt Laurie! Sanderson, Ruth, illus. LC 76-46569. 176p. (gr. 4-6). 1977. 13.95 (ISBN 0-689-30571-0, Atheneum Child Bk). Macmillan Child Grp.
Rockwell, Anne & Rockwell, Harlow. Can I Help? LC 82-15375. (Illus.). 24p. (ps-k). 1982. 8.95 (ISBN 0-02-777720-0, Mcmillan Child Bk). Macmillan Child Grp.
Rodgers, Mary. Freaky Friday. LC 74-183158. 156p. (gr. 5 up). 1973. pap. 3.50 (ISBN 0-06-440046-8, Trophy). HarpC Child Bks.
Rylant, Cynthia. Birthday Presents. Stevenson, Sucie, illus. LC 87-5485. 32p. (ps-1). 1987. 13.95 (ISBN 0-531-05705-4); PLB 13.99 (ISBN 0-531-08305-5). Orchard Bks Watts.
Schlein, Miriam. Big Talk. rev. ed. Auclair, Joan, illus. LC 89-35343. 32p. (ps-1). 1990. 12.95 (ISBN 0-02-781231-6, Bradbury Pr). Macmillan Child Grp.
Steiner, Barbara. Tessa. LC 87-31524. 224p. (gr. 7 up). 1988. 12.95 (ISBN 0-688-07232-1, Morrow Junior Books). Morrow.
Stock, Catherine. Christmas Time. Stock, Catherine, illus. LC 89-71249. 32p. (ps-1). 1990. 11.95 (ISBN 0-02-788403-1, Bradbury Pr). Macmillan Child Grp.
Teibl, Margaret. Davey Come Home. Smith, Jacqueline B., illus. LC 78-22477. 64p. (gr. 1-5). 1979. 7.95i (ISBN 0-06-026135-8). HarpC Child Bks.
Valens, Amy. Jesse's Day Care. Brown, Richard, illus. 32p. (ps-2). 1990. 13.95 (ISBN 0-395-53357-0). HM.
Willey, Margaret. Finding David Dolores. LC 85-45252. 192p. (gr. 7 up). 1986. PLB 10.89 (ISBN 0-06-026484-5). HarpC Child Bks.
Winthrop, Elizabeth. Sloppy Kisses. Burgess, Anne, illus. (ps-3). 1983. pap. 3.95 (ISBN 0-14-050433-8, Puffin). Puffin Bks.
Wood, Audrey. Weird Parents. Fogelman, Phyllis J., ed. Wood, Audrey, illus. LC 88-25742. 32p. (ps-3). 1990. 11.95 (ISBN 0-8037-0648-0); PLB 11.89 (ISBN 0-8037-0649-9). Dial Bks Young.
Wright, Betty R. My New Mom & Me. Day, Betsy, illus. Silverman, Manuel S. LC 80-25529. (Illus.). (gr. k-6). 1981. PLB 16.67 (ISBN 0-8172-1368-6). Raintree Pubs Ltd.
You're Not My Parents! (Illus.). (gr. 5 up). 1991. pap. 3.50. Ladybird Bks.
Zemach, Margot. To Hilda for Helping. LC 77-87584. (Illus.). 32p. (ps-3). 1977. 11.95 (ISBN 0-374-37663-8). FS&G.
Ziefert, Harriet. Before I Was Born. Coes, Rufus, illus. LC 88-37255. 40p. (ps-1). 1989. 11.95 (ISBN 0-394-85128-5); lib. bdg. 12.99 (ISBN 0-394-95128-X). Knopf.
Zolotow, Charlotte. The Quiet Mother & the Noisy Little Boy. Simont, Marc, illus. LC 88-936. 32p. (ps-3). 1989. 12.95 (ISBN 0-06-026978-2); PLB 12.89 (ISBN 0-06-026979-0). HarpC Child Bks.

PARIS

Clay, Rebecca. Kidding Around Paris: A Young Person's Guide to the City. Lambert, Mary, illus. 64p. (Orig.). (gr. 3 up). 1991. pap. 9.95 (ISBN 0-945465-82-3). John Muir.
Hovey, Tamara. Paris Underground. LC 90-7980. (Illus.). 96p. (gr. 5 up). 1991. 14.95 (ISBN 0-531-05931-6); PLB 14.99 (ISBN 0-531-08531-7). Orchard Bks Watts.

PARIS–FICTION

Bemelmans, Ludwig. Madeline's Rescue. Bemelmans, Ludwig, illus. 64p. (gr. k-3). 1977. pap. 3.95 (ISBN 0-14-050207-6, Puffin). Puffin Bks.
Carlson, Natalie S. Family under the Bridge. Williams, Garth, illus. LC 58-5292. 112p. (gr. 3-7). 1958. PLB 13.89 (ISBN 0-06-020991-7). HarpC Child Bks.
Cunningham, Julia. Flight of the Sparrow. LC 80-12788. 144p. (gr. 5-9). 1980. Pantheon.
Donovan, Donna. Countdown on the Metro. (Illus.). 14p. (gr. 3-7). 1988. incl. puzzle 9.95 (ISBN 0-922242-07-0). Lombard Mktg.
Dragonwagon, Crescent. Winter Holding Spring. Himler, Ronald, illus. LC 88-13747. 32p. (gr. 2-5). 1990. 11.95 (ISBN 0-02-733122-9, Mcmillan Child Bk). Macmillan Child Grp.
Fattah, Michel. Lacey in Paris. Voight, Linda, illus. LC 90-52812. 40p. (gr. k-4). 1991. 12.95 (ISBN 0-915677-49-0). Roundtable Pub.
Fender, Kay. Odette: A Springtime in Paris. Dumas, Philippe, illus. 32p. (ps-3). 1991. 10.95 (ISBN 0-916291-33-2). Kane-Miller Bk.
Hugo, Victor. Hunchback of Notre Dame. Canon, R. R., intro. by. (gr. 11 up). pap. 2.25 (ISBN 0-8049-0162-7, CL-162). Airmont.
Lamerisse, Albert. The Red Balloon. 32p. (gr. 6). 1990. 10.95s.p. (ISBN 0-88682-304-8); 15.65 (ISBN 0-685-28219-8). Creative Ed.
Lamorisse, Albert. Red Balloon. Lamorisse, Albert, photos by. LC 57-9229. (Illus.). 45p. (gr. 3-7). 1967. 13.95 (ISBN 0-685-01494-0). Doubleday.
Poulet, Virginia. Blue Bug Goes to Paris. Anderson, Peggy P., illus. LC 85-31390. 32p. (ps-3). 1986. PLB 14.60 (ISBN 0-516-03480-4). Childrens.

PARIS–POETRY

Bemelmans, Ludwig. Madeline. Bemelmans, Ludwig, illus. LC 39-21791. (gr. k-3). 1977. pap. 3.95 incl. cassette (ISBN 0-14-050198-3, Puffin). Puffin Bks.
—Madeline & the Bad Hat. Bemelmans, Ludwig, illus. LC 57-62. (gr. k-3). 1977. pap. 3.95 (ISBN 0-14-050206-8, Puffin). Puffin Bks.
—Madeline & the Gypsies. Bemelmans, Ludwig, illus. (gr. k-3). 1959. pap. 13.95 (ISBN 0-670-44682-3). Viking Child Bks.
—Madeline's Rescue. Bemelmans, Ludwig, illus. LC 53-8709. 56p. (gr. k-3). 1953. pap. 13.95 (ISBN 0-670-44716-1). Viking Child Bks.
Bemmelmans, Ludwig. Madeline. Bemelmans, Ludwig, illus. LC 68-666. (gr. k-3). 1958. pap. 13.95 (ISBN 0-670-44580-0). Viking Child Bks.
—Madeline & the Bad Hat. Bemelmans, Ludwig, illus. (gr. k-3). 1957. pap. 13.95 (ISBN 0-670-44614-9). Viking Child Bks.

PARKS, GORDON ALEXANDER BUCHANON, 1912-

Berry, Skip. Gordon Parks. King, Coretta Scott, intro. by. (Illus.). 112p. (gr. 5 up). 1991. lib. bdg. 17.95 (ISBN 1-55546-604-4). Chelsea Hse.

PARKS, ROSA, 1903-

Celsi, Teresa. Rosa Parks & the Montgomery Bus Boycott. (Illus.). 32p. (gr. 2-4). 1991. PLB 11.50 (ISBN 1-878841-14-9); pap. 3.95 (ISBN 1-878841-34-3). Millbrook Pr.
Friese, Kai J. Rosa Parks: The Movement Organizes. Gallin, Richard, ed. Young, Andrew, intro. by. (Illus.). 128p. (gr. 5 up). 1990. lib. bdg. 16.98 (ISBN 0-382-09927-3); pap. 7.95 (ISBN 0-382-24065-0). Silver Burdett Pr.
Greenfield, Eloise. Rosa Parks. Marlow, Eric, illus. LC 72-83782. 40p. (gr. 1-5). 1973. PLB 14.89 (ISBN 0-690-71211-1, Crowell Jr Bks). HarpC Child Bks.

PARKS–FICTION

Booth, Eugene. In the Park. LC 77-7622. (Illus.). 24p. (gr. k-3). 1977. PLB 13.32 (ISBN 0-8393-0106-5). Raintree Pubs.
Hamilton, Dorothy. Busboys at Big Bend. Ponter, James, illus. LC 74-8689. 112p. (gr. 8-12). 1974. o. p. 4.95 (ISBN 0-8361-1744-1); pap. 3.95 (ISBN 0-8361-1745-X). Herald Pr.
Hughes, Shirley. When We Went to the Park. LC 84-12624. (Illus.). 24p. (gr. k-1). 1985. 4.95 (ISBN 0-688-04204-X). Lothrop.
Lamb, Wendy. Sparks in the Park. (Orig.). (gr. k up). 1989. pap. 3.50 (ISBN 0-440-20415-1, LFL). Dell.
Lowry, Lois. Taking Care of Terrific. LC 82-23331. 160p. (gr. 5 up). 1983. 13.95 (ISBN 0-395-34070-5). HM.
Matthias, Catherine. Over-Under. Sharp, Gene, illus. LC 83-21005. 32p. (ps-2). 1984. lib. bdg. 11.93 (ISBN 0-516-02048-X); pap. 2.95 (ISBN 0-516-42048-8). Childrens.
Rockwell, Anne. Hugo at the Park. Rockwell, Anne, illus. LC 89-2417. 32p. (ps-k). 1990. 13.95 (ISBN 0-02-777301-9, Mcmillan Child Bk). Macmillan Child Grp.
Takeshita, Fumiko. The Park Bench. Kanagy, Ruth A., tr. from JPN. Suzuki, Mamoru, illus. 40p. (ps-3). 1988. 11.95 (ISBN 0-916291-15-4). Kane-Miller Bk.
Zolotow, Charlotte. Park Book. Rey, H. A., illus. LC 44-9471. 32p. (ps-1). 1986. PLB 12.89 (ISBN 0-06-026973-1). HarpC Child Bks.

PARKS–VOCATIONAL GUIDANCE

Aska, Warabe. Who Hides in the Park. (Illus.). 36p. (ps up). 1986. text ed. 17.95 (ISBN 0-88776-182-8, Dist. by U of Toronto Pr). Tundra Bks.

PARLIAMENTARY PRACTICE

Jones, O. Garfield. Parliamentary Procedure at a Glance. (gr. 9 up). 1971. pap. 4.95 (ISBN 0-8015-5766-6, 0481-140, Dutton). NAL-Dutton.
Powers, David G. & Harmon, Mary K. How to Run a Meeting. rev. ed. Green, Anne C., illus. LC 84-23441. 72p. (gr. 4-6). 1985. lib. bdg. 10.40 (ISBN 0-531-04641-9). Watts.
Russell, Kenneth L., ed. How in Parliamentary Procedure. 5th ed. (Illus.). 74p. (gr. 9-12). 1990. pap. text ed. 2.00 (ISBN 0-8134-2871-8, 2171); pap. text ed. 1.80 ea. 10-49 copies; pap. text ed. 1.60 ea. 50-99 copies; pap. text ed. 1.40 ea. 100 or more. Inter Print Pubs.

PARROTS

Braithwaite, Althea & Rubin, Carolyn. Parrots. McGirr, Barbara & Gill, Peter, illus. 24p. (gr. k-3). 1989. pap. 3.95 (ISBN 0-88462-175-8); PLB 8.95 (ISBN 0-88462-174-X). Dearborn Finan.
Dunnahoo, Terry. The Lost Parrots of America. LC 89-7846. (Illus.). 48p. (gr. 4-5). 1989. 10.95 (ISBN 0-89686-461-8, Crestwood Hse). Macmillan Child Grp.
Gabin, Martin. Your First Parrot. (Illus.). 36p. (Orig.). 1991. pap. 1.95 (ISBN 0-86622-070-4, YF-113). TFH Pubns.
Serventy, Vincent. Parrot. (Illus.). 24p. (gr. k-5). 1986. PLB 13.32 (ISBN 0-8172-2705-9). Raintree Pubs.
Wildlife Education, Ltd. Staff. Parrots. Boyer, Trevor, illus. 20p. (gr. 5 up). 1984. pap. text ed. 2.25 (ISBN 0-937934-27-5). Wildlife Educ.
Wolter, Annette. African Gray Parrots. (Illus.). 64p. (gr. 4 up). 1987. pap. 4.95 (ISBN 0-8120-3773-1). Barron.
—Parakeets. (Illus.). (gr. k-12). 1982. pap. 4.95 (ISBN 0-8120-2423-0). Barron.

PARROTS–FICTION

Allen, Linda. When Granfather's Parrot Inherits. (gr. 3-7). 1990. 12.95 (ISBN 0-316-03413-4, Joy St Bks). Little.
Anders, Rebecca. Lorito the Parrot. Hammarberg, Dyan, tr. from FRE. LC 76-1208. (Illus.). 24p. (gr. k-4). 1976. PLB 6.95 (ISBN 0-87614-068-1). Carolrhoda Bks.
Benitez, Mirna. Super Parrot. (Illus.). 32p. (gr. 1-4). 1989. PLB 13.32 (ISBN 0-8172-3503-5). Raintree Pubs.
Clifford, Eth. Harvey's Wacky Parrot Adventure. 112p. (gr. 3-7). 1990. 13.95 (ISBN 0-395-53352-X). HM.
Demuth. Max, the Bad Talking Parrot. (gr. 5-8). 1986. 12.95 (ISBN 0-396-08767-1, Putnam). Putnam Pub Group.
Demuth, Patricia B. Max, the Bad-Talking Parrot. Zaunders, Bo, illus. 1990. 12.95 (ISBN 0-525-44613-3, DCB); pap. 3.95 (ISBN 0-525-44595-1, DCB). Dutton Child Bks.
Jackson, Neta. The Parrot Who Talked Too Much. Babbitt, Anne, illus. 25p. (ps-3). 1991. 3.99 (ISBN 0-88070-415-2). Multnomah.
King-Smith, Dick. Harry's Mad. (gr. 3-6). 1988. 11.95 (ISBN 0-517-56254-5). Crown.
Phillips, Todd-Michael. Somewhere: As Told by Garret the Parrot. Walsh, Lori, illus. LC 90-90193. 40p. (Orig.). (ps-3). Date not set. pap. 6.50 (ISBN 0-9626557-0-8). Word Blossoms.

Remkiewicz, Frank. The Last Time I Saw Harris. LC 90-40263. (Illus.). 32p. (gr. k up). 1991. 13.95 (ISBN 0-688-10291-3); PLB 13.88 (ISBN 0-688-10292-1). Lothrop.

Robinson, Ronald W. Stanley, the Talking Parrot. Todd, Thomas, illus. LC 89-60801. 22p. (Orig.). (gr. 3-4). 1989. Incl. cassette & filmstrip pkg. 12.95 (ISBN 0-9622692-2-0); Incl. cassette pkg. 8.95 (ISBN 0-9622692-1-2); pap. 4.95 (ISBN 0-9622692-0-4). R W Robinson.

Slaughter, Hope. Plato's Fine Feathers. Shearer, Hope, illus. LC 84-4830. 32p. (ps-3). 1984. PLB 8.95 (ISBN 0-931093-00-7); pap. 3.95 (ISBN 0-685-15364-9). Red Hen Pr.

Solomon, Helen. Polly Jumped over the Moon. Rosato, Amelia & Inwood, Gary, illus. LC 88-45475. 32p. (ps-2). 1989. 9.95 (ISBN 0-397-32328-X, Lipp Jr Bks); PLB 9.89 (ISBN 0-397-32329-8). HarpC Child Bks.

Swan, Walter. Stick 'em up! I've Got You Covered! Swan, Deloris, ed. Asch, Connie, illus. 16p. (Orig.). (ps-8). 1989. pap. 1.50 (ISBN 0-927176-03-3). Swan Enterp.

Vail, Virginia. Animal Inn: Parrot Fever, No. 10. (gr. 4-7). 1990. pap. 2.75 (ISBN 0-590-42801-2). Scholastic Inc.

Weber, Kathryn. Molly Moonshine & Timothy. Downey, Jane, illus. 44p. (gr. 2-4). 1990. pap. 2.95 (ISBN 1-878438-01-8). Ranch House Pr.

Woolf, Virginia. The Widow & the Parrot. Bell, Julian, illus. Bell, Quentin, afterword by. (Illus.). 32p. (gr. 2-7). 1988. 12.95 (ISBN 0-15-296783-4). HarBraceJ.

Zacharias, Thomas. Where Is the Green Parrot? 1990. 12.95 (ISBN 0-385-30091-3). Doubleday.

PASCAL (COMPUTER PROGRAM LANGUAGE)

Nance, Douglas W. Pascal: Introduction to Programming & Problem Solving. (Illus.). 630p. (gr. 9-12). 1986. text ed. 34.25 (ISBN 0-314-93206-2). West Pub.

PASSIONS

see Emotions

PASSIVE RESISTANCE

see also Nonviolence

PASSOVER

Adler, David A. Passover Fun Book: Puzzles, Riddles, Magic & More. (Illus.). (gr. k-5). 1978. saddlewire bdg. 3.95 (ISBN 0-88482-759-3, Bonim Bks). Hebrew Pub.

—A Picture Book of Passover. Heller, Linda, illus. LC 81-6983. 32p. (gr. k-3). 1982. reinforced bdg. 13.95 (ISBN 0-8234-0439-0); pap. 5.95 (ISBN 0-8234-0609-1). Holiday.

Atlas, Susan. Passover Passage. 5.95 (ISBN 0-933873-46-8). Torah Aura. Rebecca Able learns about Jewish history & culture while spending a Passover holiday on-board her grandparents sailboat in the Caribbean. This adolescent novel explores the meaning of family, traditional Jewish values & growing up. Through Becca's eyes, the reader sees, feels, hears & smells what it's like to be an adolescent a-sail for the first time.

Publisher Provided Annotation.

Auerbach, Julie J. Everything's Changing It's Pesach. Radin, Chari, intro. by. LC 86-2717. (Illus.). 24p. (ps-3). 1986. pap. 3.95 (ISBN 0-930494-53-9). Kar Ben.

Bin-Nun, Judy & Cooper, Nancy. Pesach: A Holiday Funtext. Steinberger, Heidi, illus. 32p. (Orig.). (gr. 1-3). 1983. pap. text ed. 5.00 (ISBN 0-8074-0161-7, 101310). UAHC.

Chaikin, Miriam. Ask Another Question: The Story & Meaning of Passover. Friedman, Marvin, illus. LC 84-12744. 96p. (gr. 3-6). 1986. 13.95 (ISBN 0-89919-281-5, Pub. by Clarion). Ticknor & Fields.

Chanover, Hyman & Chanover, Alice. Pesah Is Coming. Kessler, Leonard, illus. (gr. k-2). 1956. 5.95 (ISBN 0-8381-0713-3, 10-713). United Syn Bk.

—Pesah Is Here. Kessler, Leonard, illus. (gr. k-2). 1956. 5.95 (ISBN 0-8381-0714-1). United Syn Bk.

DePaola, Tomie. My First Passover. (Illus.). 12p. 1991. 5.95 (ISBN 0-399-21784-3, Putnam). Putnam Pub Group.

Groner, Judye & Wikler, Madeline. Where is the Afikomen. Schanzer, Roz, illus. LC 89-63254. 12p. (ps). 1989. bds. 4.95 (ISBN 0-929371-06-2). Kar Ben.

Halper, Roe. Passover Haggadah. Halper, Roe, illus. 40p. (Orig.). 1986. pap. 5.00 (ISBN 0-916326-03-9). Bayberry Pr.

Miller, Deborah U. Only Nine Chairs-A Tall Tale for Passover. LC 82-80035. (Illus.). 40p. (ps-3). 1982. pap. 4.95 (ISBN 0-930494-13-X). Kar Ben.

Nerlove, Miriam. Passover. Levine, Abby, ed. Nerlove, Miriam, illus. 24p. (ps-1). 1989. 10.95 (ISBN 0-8075-6360-9). A Whitman.

Oren, Rony. The Animated Haggadah (1990 Edition) (Illus.). 54p. 1990. 14.95 (ISBN 0-944007-43-0). Shapolsky Pubs.

Pliskin, Jacqueline. My Animated Haggadah & Story of Passover. (Illus.). 48p. (gr. 5-8). 1989. pap. 5.95 (ISBN 0-933503-28-8). Shapolsky Pubs.

Rosen, Anne, et al. Family Passover. Salzmann, Laurence, photos by. LC 79-89298. 64p. (gr. 2 up). 1980. 8.95 (ISBN 0-8276-0169-7). JPS Phila.

Rudin, Jacob. Haggadah for Children. (gr. 3 up). 1973. 2.25x (ISBN 0-8197-0032-0). Bloch.

Schwartz, Lynne S. The Four Questions. Sherman, Ori, illus. LC 88-18881. 40p. (ps up). 1989. 15.95 (ISBN 0-8037-0600-6); PLB 15.89 (ISBN 0-8037-0601-4). Dial Bks Young.

Silberg, Francis B. The Story of Passover for Children. Britt, Stephanie, illus. 24p. (ps-1). 1989. pap. 3.95 (ISBN 0-8249-8309-2). Ideals.

Silverman, Maida. Festival of Freedom: The Story of Passover. Ewing, Carolyn, illus. (gr. 1-5). 1988. pap. 7.95 (ISBN 0-671-64567-6, Little Simon); pap. 2.95 (ISBN 0-671-66340-2). S&S Trade.

Simon, Norma. My Family Seder. Weiss, Harvey, illus. (ps-k). 1961. plastic cover 4.50 (ISBN 0-8381-0710-9, 10-710). United Syn Bk.

—Passover. Shimin, Symeon, illus. LC 65-11644. (gr. k-3). 1965. PLB 12.89 (ISBN 0-690-61094-7, Crowell Jr Bks). HarpC Child Bks.

Wark, Mary A. We Tell It to Our Children: The Story of Passover: A Haggadah for Seders with Young Children. 2nd ed. Oskow, Craig, illus. Lerner, Leigh D., frwd. by. LC 88-92282. (Illus.). 126p. (Orig.). (ps-6). 1988. pap. 5.95 wire bdg. (ISBN 0-9619880-8-8). Mensch Makers Pr.

Wark, MaryAnn B. We Tell It to Our Children: The Story of Passover (Leader Edition with Puppets) A Haggadah for Seders with Young Children. Oskow, Cragi, illus. Lerner, Leigh D., frwd. by. LC 87-63604. (Illus.). 150p. (Orig.). (ps-6). 1988. pap. 11.95 wire-o (ISBN 0-9619880-9-6). Mensch Makers Pr.

Children's active participatory Haggadah makes Passover story into an engaging drama of the Exodus story. A complete guide, including multi-national recipes, for putting on the traditional Seder meal for passover. Text is a musical puppet show with Judaically-meaningful lyrics set to simple American folk tunes. Everyone participates in singing throughout the service. This Leader edition has 9 cut out puppets who are the "guests" from the past, who in a "you-are-there" style tell the story of the Exodus. Parts for non-readers & early readers. Guest edition - no puppets with full text also available. Endorsed by rabbis, religious educators (Jewish & Christian), children's book store owners, preschool teachers, parents & grandparents nationwide. For home or model seders. Authentically Jewish; easy for non-Jews. Developmentally appropriate for children. Downright fun for adults. Other unique features include the Passover food sysmbols, like matzah, explained at the appropriate time in the story; special sections to personalize & teach about world Jewry. Difficult concepts like slavery are taught through action, songs, & pictures. Lyrics respond to children's thinking while tackling complicated issues surrounding freedom. Plentiful, detailed drawings emphasize immediacy of ideas & illustrate every idea & ceremonial symbol.

Publisher Provided Annotation.

Wengrov, Charles. The Story of Passover. (Illus.). (gr. k-7). 1965. pap. 2.50 (ISBN 0-914080-54-7). Shulsinger Sales.

Wikler, Madeline & Groner, Judye. I Have Four Questions. Radin, Chari M., illus. LC 88-83570. 12p. (ps). 1989. bds. 4.95 (ISBN 0-930494-90-3). Kar Ben.

Zwebner, Janet. The Animated Haggadah Activity Book. 48p. (ps-8). 1990. pap. 5.95 (ISBN 0-944007-46-5). Shapolsky Pubs.

PASTEUR, LOUIS, 1822-1895

Bains, Rae. Louis Pasteur. Smolinski, Dick, illus. LC 84-2748. 32p. (gr. 3-6). 1985. PLB 9.49 (ISBN 0-8167-0148-2); pap. text ed. 2.95 (ISBN 0-8167-0149-0). Troll Assocs.

Greene, Carol. Louis Pasteur: Enemy of Disease. Dobson, Steven, illus. LC 90-2197. 48p. (gr. k-3). 1990. PLB 15.27 (ISBN 0-516-04216-5); pap. 4.95 (ISBN 0-516-44216-3). Childrens.

Johnson, Spencer. The Value of Believing in Yourself: The Story of Louis Pasteur. 2nd ed. Pileggi, Steven, illus. LC 76-55225. (gr. k-6). 1976. 9.95 (ISBN 0-916392-06-6, Pub. by Value Communications). Oak Tree Pubns.

Rich, Beverly. Louis Pasteur: The Scientist Who Found the Cause of Infectious Disease & Invented Pasteurization. LC 88-24867. (Illus.). 64p. (gr. 5-6). 1989. PLB 12.95 (ISBN 1-55532-839-3). Gareth Stevens Inc.

Sabin, Francene. Louis Pasteur: Young Scientist. Swan, Susan, illus. LC 82-15924. 48p. (gr. 4-6). 1983. PLB 10.79 (ISBN 0-89375-853-1); pap. text ed. 2.95 (ISBN 0-89375-854-X). Troll Assocs.

Tames, Richard. Louis Pasteur. (Illus.). 32p. (gr. 5-8). 1990. PLB 11.90 (ISBN 0-531-14025-3). Watts.

PASTIMES

see Amusements; Games; Recreation; Sports

PASTORS

see Clergy

PATHOLOGICAL PSYCHOLOGY

see Psychology, Pathological

PATHOLOGY

see also Bacteriology; Immunity; Medicine

Guthrie, Donna W. Grandpa Doesn't Know It's Me: A Family Adjusts to Alzheimer's Disease. Arnsteen, Katy, illus. Aronson, Miriam, intro. by. (Illus.). (ps-5). 1986. 16.95 (ISBN 0-89885-302-8); pap. 9.95 (ISBN 0-89885-308-7). Human Sci Pr.

PATRICK, SAINT, 373?-463?

Turcotte, Mary C. The Wind at My Back: The Life of St. Patrick. Bliss, Bob, illus. 115p. (gr. 3 up). 1991. 4.95 (ISBN 0-8198-8236-4). Dghtrs St Paul.

PATRIOTIC SONGS

see National Songs

PATRIOTISM

Brady, Janeen. Take Your Hat Off When the Flag Goes By. Perry, Scott & Hulet, Grant, illus. 22p. (Orig.). (gr. k-6). 1987. activity bk. 2.25 (ISBN 0-944803-31-8); Set of 20. wkbk. 12.00 (ISBN 0-944803-34-2); cassette & bk. 9.95 (ISBN 0-944803-32-6); dialogue bk. 1.25 (ISBN 0-944803-33-4); songbk. 7.95 (ISBN 0-944803-29-6). Brite Intl.

Davis, Nancy M., et al. Patriotism. Davis, Nancy M., illus. 34p. (Orig.). (ps-5). 1986. pap. 4.95 (ISBN 0-937103-19-5). DaNa Pubns.

Johnson, Linda C. Patriotism. (Illus.). 64p. (gr. 7-12,RL 4-6). 1990. PLB 12.95 (ISBN 0-8239-1114-4). Rosen Group.

Szumski, Bonnie. Patriotism: Recognizing Stereotypes. (Illus.). 32p. (gr. 3-6). 1990. PLB 8.95 (ISBN 0-89908-640-3). Greenhaven.

PATTERNS FOR DRESSMAKING

see Dressmaking

PATTON, GEORGE SMITH, 1885-1945

Carpenter. George Smith Patton, Jr, Reading Level 6. (Illus.). 112p. (gr. 4 up). Date not set. PLB 18.60 (ISBN 0-685-37266-9). Rourke Corp.

Carpenter, Allen. George Patton...The Lost Romantic. (Illus.). 112p. (gr. 4-8). 1987. PLB 18.60 (ISBN 0-86625-329-7). Rourke Corp.

Finke, Blythe F. General Patton: Fearless Military Leader. Rahmas, D. Steve, ed. LC 76-190251. 32p. (gr. 7-12). 1972. lib. bdg. 4.20 incl. catalog cards (ISBN 0-87157-534-5). SamHar Pr.

Peifer, Charles, Jr. Soldier of Destiny: A Biography of George Patton. LC 88-20265. (Illus.). 128p. (gr. 5 up). 1988. PLB 12.95 (ISBN 0-87518-395-6, Dillon). Macmillan Child Grp.

PAUL, SAINT, APOSTLE

Dean, Bessie. Paul, God's Special Missionary. 72p. (Orig.). (gr. k-5). 1980. pap. 5.95 (ISBN 0-88290-152-4). Horizon Utah.

De Graaf, Anne. Paul: A Change of Heart. Montero, Jose P., illus. 32p. (gr. 1-3). 1990. 7.95 (ISBN 0-8028-5034-0). Eerdmans.

Ham, Wayne. Paul's First Missionary Journey. (Illus.). 24p. 1989. pap. 3.75 (ISBN 0-8309-0538-3). Herald Hse.

Parry, Alan & Parry, Linda. Paul Meets Jesus. Parry, Alan, illus. 24p. (ps). 1990. pap. 0.99 (ISBN 0-8066-2480-9, 9-2480). Augsburg Fortress.

Storr, Catherine. St. Peter & St. Paul. Peppe, Mark, illus. LC 84-18078. 32p. (gr. k-4). 1985. PLB 14.65 (ISBN 0-8172-1998-6). Raintree Pubs.

Vos Wezeman, Phyllis & Wiessner, Colleen A. Saul to Paul: Enlightened to Serve. 32p. (Orig.). (gr. 1-6). 1989. pap. 5.95 (ISBN 0-940754-74-6). Ed Ministries.

PEACE

see also Disarmament; War

Aaseng, Nathan. The Peace Seekers: The Nobel Peace Prize. (Illus.). 80p. (gr. 5 up). 1987. PLB 11.95 (ISBN 0-8225-0654-8). Lerner Pubns.

Careme, Maurice. The Peace. Neumeyer, Helen, tr. Felix, Monique, illus. 8p. (Orig.). (gr. 7-9). 1982. pap. 2.50 (ISBN 0-914676-68-7). Green Tiger Pr.

Durell, Ann & Sachs, Marilyn, eds. The Big Book for Peace. (Illus.). (gr. 2-7). 1990. 16.95 (ISBN 0-525-44605-2, DCB). Dutton Child Bks.

Obold, Ruth. Prepare for Peace, Pt. I. (Illus.). 40p. (gr. 1-3). 1986. 6.25 (ISBN 0-87303-116-4). Faith & Life.

—Prepare for Peace, Pt. II. (Illus.). 48p. (gr. 4-6). 1986. 6.25 (ISBN 0-87303-117-2). Faith & Life.

—Prepare for Peace, Pt. III. (Illus.). 55p. (gr. 7-8). 1986. 6.25 (ISBN 0-87303-118-0). Faith & Life.
Scholes, Katherine. Peace Begins with You. (Illus.). (gr. 1-5). 1990. 11.95 (ISBN 0-316-77436-7). Little.
Webster-Doyle, Terrence. Fighting the Invisible Enemy: Understanding the Effects of Conditioning. (Illus.). 164p. (gr. 5-12). 1990. 15.95 (ISBN 0-942941-19-5); pap. 10.95 (ISBN 0-942941-18-7). Atrium Pubns.
—Peace, the Enemy of Freedom: The Myth of Non-Violence. (Illus.). 157p. (gr. 5-12). 1991. pap. 9.95 (ISBN 0-942941-12-8). Atrium Pubns.
—Tug of War: Peace Through Understanding Conflict. (Illus.). 106p. (gr. 5-12). 1990. 14.95 (ISBN 0-942941-21-7); pap. 9.95 (ISBN 0-942941-20-9). Atrium Pubns.
Whitman, Edmund S. Little Pax. Ely, Gladys, illus. LC 74-182528. 120p. (gr. 5-9). 1972. 3.75 (ISBN 0-8356-0428-4, Quest). Theos Pub Hse.

PEACE–FICTION

Douglis, Marjie. Peace Porridge. Peterson, Pete, ed. French, Ed, illus. 122p. (gr. 3-6). 1986. pap. 3.95 (ISBN 0-934998-22-1). Bethel Pub.
Roberson, Maxine M. Peace Is... Unada, illus. 32p. (gr. 1-4). 1987. casebound 4.95 (ISBN 0-87403-323-3, 3668). Standard Pub.

PEAFOWL–FICTION

Peet, Bill. The Spooky Tail of Prewitt Peacock. (Illus.). (gr. k-3). 1979. pap. 3.95 (ISBN 0-395-28159-8). HM.
—The Spooky Tail of Prewitt Peacock. Peet, Bill, illus. LC 72-7930. 32p. (gr. k-3). 1973. 13.95 (ISBN 0-395-15494-4). HM.

PEANUTS–FICTION

Asher, Sandy. Teddy Teaberry's Peanutty Problem. (gr. k-6). 1989. pap. 2.95 (ISBN 0-440-40229-8, YB). Dell.

PEARL FISHERIES–FICTION

O'Dell, Scott. Black Pearl. Johnson, Milton, illus. LC 67-23311. 160p. (gr. 7 up). 1967. 13.95 (ISBN 0-395-06961-0). HM.

PEARL HARBOR, ATTACK ON, 1941

Bachrach, Deborah. Pearl Harbor: Opposing Viewpoints. LC 88-24288. (Illus.). 112p. (gr. 3-8). 1988. PLB 13.95 (ISBN 0-89908-059-6). Greenhaven.
Black, Wallace B. & Blashfield, Jean F. Pearl Harbor. LC 90-45621. (Illus.). 48p. (gr. 5-6). 1991. RSBE 11.95 (ISBN 0-89686-555-X, Crestwood Hse). Macmillan Child Grp.
Dunnahoo, Terry. Pearl Harbor: America Enters the War. (Illus.). 144p. (gr. 7-12). 1991. PLB 12.90 (ISBN 0-531-11010-9). Watts.
Harris, Nathan. Pearl Harbor. (Illus.). 64p. (gr. 6-8). 1987. 19.95 (ISBN 0-85219-669-5, Pub. by Batsford England). Trafalgar Sq.
Lord, Walter. Day of Infamy. (gr. 8 up). 1983. pap. 4.95 (ISBN 0-553-26777-9, Falcon). Bantam.
Shapiro, William E. Pearl Harbor. LC 84-7324. (Illus.). 103p. (gr. 7-12). 1984. PLB 12.90 (ISBN 0-531-04865-9). Watts.
Stein, R. Conrad. The Story of the U. S. S. Arizona. Dunnington, Tom, illus. LC 76-26572. 32p. (gr. 3-5). 1977. PLB 13.27 (ISBN 0-516-04642-X); pap. 3.95 (ISBN 0-516-44642-8). Childrens.

PEARLS–FICTION

Heine, Helme. The Pearl. Heine, Helme, illus. LC 84-72404. 32p. (gr. k-4). 1985. 13.95 (ISBN 0-689-50321-0, M K McElderry). Macmillan Child Grp.
Torre, Betty L., retold by. The Luminous Pearl: A Chinese Folktale. Inouye, Carol, illus. LC 89-70999. 32p. (ps-3). 1990. 14.95 (ISBN 0-531-05890-5); PLB 14.99 (ISBN 0-531-08490-6). Orchard Bks Watts.

PEASANT ART

see Art Industries and Trade; Folk Art

PEBBLES

see Rocks

PECOS BILL

Anderson, J. I. I Can Read About Pecos Bill. Killgrew, John, illus. LC 76-54575. (gr. 2-5). 1977. pap. 1.95 (ISBN 0-89375-042-5). Troll Assocs.

PEDAGOGY

see Education; Teaching

PEDDLERS AND PEDDLING–FICTION

Davis, Edward E. Bruno the Pretzel Man. Simont, Marc, illus. LC 84-47630. 64p. (gr. 2-5). 1984. HarpC Child Bks.
McDonald, Megan. The Potato Man. Lewin, Ted, illus. LC 90-7758. 32p. (ps-2). 1991. 14.95 (ISBN 0-531-05914-6); PLB 14.99 (ISBN 0-531-08514-7). Orchard Bks Watts.
Shannon, George. The Piney Woods Peddler. Tafuri, Nancy, illus. LC 81-2219. 32p. (gr. k-3). 1981. PLB 14.88 (ISBN 0-688-84304-2). Greenwillow.
Shelby, Anne. We Keep a Store. Ward, John, illus. LC 89-35105. 32p. (ps-2). 1990. 14.95 (ISBN 0-531-05856-5); PLB 14.99 (ISBN 0-531-08456-6). Orchard Bks Watts.

PEDIATRICS

see Children–Care and Hygiene; Children–Diseases

PEDIGREES

see Heraldry

PELICANS

Green, Carl R. & Sanford, William R. The Pelicans. LC 87-22251. (Illus.). 48p. (gr. 5-6). 1987. PLB 10.95 (ISBN 0-89686-337-9, Crestwood Hse). Macmillan Child Grp.
Stone, Lynn. The Pelican. LC 89-26049. (Illus.). 60p. (gr. 3 up). 1990. 12.95 (ISBN 0-87518-430-8, Dillon); PLB 10.95 (ISBN 0-685-31385-9). Macmillan Child Grp.
Stone, Lynn M. Pelicans. LC 88-26428. (Illus.). (gr. 2-4). 1989. PLB 11.93 (ISBN 0-86592-322-1). Rourke Corp.

PELICANS–FICTION

O'Reilly, Edward. Brown Pelican at the Pond. Strange, Florence, illus. LC 78-58689. (gr. k-4). 1979. 7.95 (ISBN 0-931644-01-1). Manzanita Pr.
Reese, Bob. Wellington Pelican. LC 82-23587. (Illus.). 24p. (ps-2). 1983. PLB 11.27 (ISBN 0-516-02316-0); pap. 2.95 (ISBN 0-516-42316-9). Childrens.
Roa, Annia. Peter Pelican-Pedro Pelicano. Henry, William, illus. LC 64-22715. (SPA & ENG.). (gr. k-4). 1974. 8.95 (ISBN 0-87208-006-4). Island Pr Pubs.
Thiele, Colin. Storm Boy. Schoenherr, John, illus. LC 77-25675. 64p. (gr. 2-5). 1978. PLB 12.89 (ISBN 0-06-026134-X). HarpC Child Bks.
Wildsmith, Brian. Pelican. Wildsmith, Brian, illus. LC 82-12431. 64p. (ps-2). 1983. lib. bdg. 10.99 (ISBN 0-394-95668-0). Pantheon.

PEN DRAWING–STUDY AND TEACHING

Evans, Lee. Basic Pen & Ink Sketching for Pathfinders III: A Y. E. S. Book. Gattis, L. S., ed. (Illus.). 20p. (Orig.). (gr. 5-6). 1987. tchrs. ed 5.00 (ISBN 0-936241-34-9). Cheetah Pub.

PENAL CODES

see Criminal Law

PENAL INSTITUTIONS

see Prisons

PENAL LAW

see Criminal Law

PENCIL DRAWING–STUDY AND TEACHING

Hobbis, Charles I. Pencil Drawing for the Architect. (gr. 10-12). 1954. 9.95 (ISBN 0-85458-100-6); pap. 7.95 (ISBN 0-85458-101-4). Transatl Arts.
Mitgutsch, Ali. From Graphite to Pencil. Mitgutsch, Ali, illus. LC 84-17469. 24p. (ps-3). 1985. PLB 6.95 (ISBN 0-87614-231-5). Carolrhoda Bks.

PENGUINS

Allen, Douglas. The Penguin in the Snow. Oxford Scientific Film Staff, illus. LC 87-9968. 32p. (gr. 4-6). 1987. PLB 10.95 (ISBN 1-55532-270-0). Gareth Stevens Inc.
Arnold, Caroline. Penguin. Hewett, Richard, photos by. LC 87-31458. (Illus.). 48p. (gr. 2-5). 1988. 12.95 (ISBN 0-688-07706-4); PLB 12.88 (ISBN 0-688-07707-2). Morrow.
Barrett, Norman. Penguins. LC 90-32151. (Illus.). 32p. (gr. k-4). 1991. PLB 11.40 (ISBN 0-531-14114-4). Watts.
Bonners, Susan. A Penguin Year. Bonners, Susan, illus. LC 79-53595. 48p. (ps-3). 1981. 11.95 (ISBN 0-685-01398-7); PLB 12.95 (ISBN 0-385-28022-X). Delacorte.
Coldrey, Jenny. Penguins. Oxford Scientific Films, et al, photos by. (Illus.). 32p. (gr. 2-5). 1984. 10.95 (ISBN 0-233-97524-1). Andre Deutsch.
Cowcher, Helen. Antarctica. Cowcher, Helen, illus. 32p. (ps-3). 1990. incl. audiocassette 17.95 (ISBN 0-924483-24-5). Soundprints.
Dalmais. Penguin, Reading Level 3-4. (Illus.). 28p. (gr. 2-5). Date not set. PLB 14.60 (ISBN 0-86592-854-1). Rourke Corp.
Dewey, Jennifer O. The Adelie Penguin. Dewey, Jennifer O., illus. LC 88-13010. 48p. (gr. 3-6). 1989. 15.95 (ISBN 0-316-18207-9). Little.
Frank, Sid & Melick, Arden. The Presidents: Tidbits & Trivia. rev. ed. Dobbins, Dwight, illus. LC 79-47990. 160p. (gr. 5-8). 1982. pap. 10.95 (ISBN 0-8437-3351-9). Hammond Inc.
Hoffman, Mary. Penguin. LC 84-18045. (Illus.). 24p. (gr. k-5). 1985. PLB 13.32 (ISBN 0-8172-2415-7). Raintree Pubs.
Hogan, Paula Z. The Penguin. Strigenz, Geri K., illus. LC 78-21225. 32p. (gr. 1-4). 1979. PLB 16.67 (ISBN 0-8172-1257-4). Raintree Pubs.
—The Penguin. LC 78-21225. (Illus.). 32p. (gr. 1-4). 1984. PLB 27.99 incl. cassette (ISBN 0-8172-2231-6); cassette 14.00 (ISBN 0-685-09515-0). Raintree Pubs.
Johnson, Sylvia A. Penguins. LC 80-28180. (Illus.). 48p. (gr. 4 up). 1981. PLB 14.95 (ISBN 0-8225-1453-2). Lerner Pubns.
Lepthien, Emilie U. Penguins. LC 82-17911. (Illus.). 48p. (gr. k-4). 1983. PLB 14.60 (ISBN 0-516-01683-0); pap. 4.95 (ISBN 0-516-41683-9). Childrens.
Paladino, Catherine. Pomona: The Birth of a Penguin. (Illus.). (gr. 2-4). 1991. 11.95 (ISBN 0-531-15212-X); PLB 12.90 (ISBN 0-531-10988-7). Watts.
The Penguin. (gr. 2-5). 1988. pap. 2.50 (ISBN 0-8167-1572-6). Troll Assocs.
Royston, Angela. The Penguin. Allen, Graham, illus. 24p. (Orig.). (ps-2). 1988. pap. 2.95 (ISBN 0-8249-8246-0). Ideals.
Saintsing, David. The World of Penguins. Oxford Scientific Films Staff, illus. LC 87-6536. 32p. (gr. 2-3). 1987. PLB 10.95 (ISBN 1-55532-274-3). Gareth Stevens Inc.
Schneider, Jeff. My Friend the Penguin: An Ocean Magic Book. Spoon, Wilfred, illus. LC 90-61577. 12p. (ps). 1991. 4.95g (ISBN 1-877779-09-1). Schneider Educational.
Stone, Lynn M. The Penguins. (Illus.). 48p. (gr. 5-6). 1987. PLB 10.95 (ISBN 0-89686-326-3, Crestwood Hse). Macmillan Child Grp.
—Penguins. LC 88-31606. (Illus.). (gr. 2-4). 1989. PLB 11.93 (ISBN 0-86592-325-6). Rourke Corp.
Strange, Ian J. Penguin World. (gr. 7-11). 1981. 8.95 (ISBN 0-396-08000-6, Putnam). Putnam Pub Group.
Todd, Frank S. Sea World Book of Penguins. LC 86-25588. (Illus.). 96p. (gr. 4-6). 1981. 12.95 (ISBN 0-15-271949-0, HJ). HarBraceJ.
—The Sea World Book of Penguins. Todd, Frank S., photos by. LC 80-25588. (Illus.). 96p. (gr. 4-7). 1984. pap. 9.95 (ISBN 0-15-271951-2, VoyB). HarBraceJ.
Wexo, John B. Penguins. 24p. (gr. 4). 1989. 11.95s.p. (ISBN 0-88682-263-7); 17.10 (ISBN 0-685-28179-5). Creative Ed.
Wildlife Education, Ltd. Staff. Penguins. Stuart, Walter & Boyer, Trevor, illus. 20p. (gr. 5 up). 1983. pap. 2.25 (ISBN 0-937934-17-8). Wildlife Educ.

PENGUINS–FICTION

Atwater, Richard & Atwater, Florence. Mr. Popper's Penguins. (Illus.). 144p. (gr. 3-6). 1978. 3.50 (ISBN 0-440-45934-6, YB). Dell.
—Mr. Popper's Penguins. Lawson, Robert, illus. (gr. 3 up). 1938. 14.95 (ISBN 0-316-05842-4). Little.
Benson, Patrick. Little Penguin. (Illus.). 32p. (ps-2). 1991. 14.95 (ISBN 0-399-21757-6, Philomel Bks). Putnam Pub Group.
Brenner, Barbara. Walt Disney's The Penguin That Hated the Cold. (Illus.). (ps-3). 1973. (Random Juv). Random.
Gay, Michel. Bibi Takes Flight. Gay, Michel, illus. LC 87-28262. 40p. (ps-1). 1988. 12.95 (ISBN 0-688-06828-6); PLB 12.88 (ISBN 0-688-06829-4, Morrow Jr Bks). Morrow Jr Bks.
Glimmerveen, Ulco. A Tale of Antarctica. Glimmerveen, Ulco, illus. 32p. (gr. 1-4). 1990. 12.95 (ISBN 0-590-43360-1). Scholastic Inc.
Hammond, Jane. Pete the Penguin. (ps-k). 1984. pap. 1.50 (ISBN 0-87162-394-3, D5607). Warner Pr.
Howe, Caroline W. Counting Penguins Zero to Nine. LC 82-48860. (Illus.). 32p. (ps-1). 1983. 7.64i (ISBN 0-06-022618-8). HarpC Child Bks.
Hunt, Robert. Glu the Emperor Penguin. Producciones Ancora, illus. LC 77-736442. 16p. (gr. 2-5). 1978. pap. 29.95 6 bks. & 1 cass. (ISBN 0-89290-027-X); pap. 10. 95 1 bk. & 1 cass. (ISBN 0-685-04644-3). Soc for Visual.
Jenkin-Pearce, Susie. Peppi & Poppy Search for Santa. (Illus.). 32p. (gr. k-3). 1988. 8.95 (ISBN 0-8120-4129-1). Barron.
Lester, Helen. Tacky the Penguin. Munsinger, Lynn, illus. LC 87-30684. 32p. (ps-3). 1988. 13.95 (ISBN 0-395-45536-7). HM.
—Tacky the Penguin. Munsinger, Lynn, illus. 32p. (gr. k-3). 1990. pap. 3.95 (ISBN 0-395-56233-3). HM.
Little, Karen E. Penguin Partners. (Illus.). (ps-1). 1981. 4.50 (ISBN 0-913545-05-8). Moonlight FL.
The Littlest Penguin, Unit 3. (gr. 1). 1991. 5-pack 21.25 (ISBN 0-88106-725-3). Charlesbridge Pub.
Mitra, Annie. Penguin Moon. Mitra, Annie, illus. LC 88-32797. 32p. (ps-1). 1989. reinforced bdg. 13.95 (ISBN 0-8234-0749-7). Holiday.
Monsell, Mary E. The Mysterious Cases of Mr. Pin. Christelow, Eileen, illus. LC 88-8102. 64p. (gr. 1-4). 1989. 11.95 (ISBN 0-689-31435-3, Atheneum Child Bk). Macmillan Child Grp.
Obedin, Harry. Peter Penguin & the Polar Sea. Strecker, Rebekah J., illus. LC 88-63171. 32p. (Orig.). (ps-4). 1989. lib. bdg. 15.95 (ISBN 0-943990-55-6); pap. 8.95 (ISBN 0-943990-54-8). Parenting Pr.
A Penguin Year. 48p. (Orig.). (gr. k-6). 1989. pap. 3.95 (ISBN 0-440-40151-8, YB). Dell.
Peter Penguin. (Illus.). (ps). 1.79 (ISBN 0-517-46419-5). Outlet Bk Co.
Pfister, Marcus. Penguin Pete. Pfister, Marcus, illus. LC 87-1627. 32p. (gr. k-3). 1987. 13.95 (ISBN 1-55858-018-2). North-South Bks NYC.
—Penguin Pete & Pat. Pfister, Marcus, illus. Bell, Anthea, tr. from GER. LC 88-25296. (Illus.). 32p. (gr. k-3). 1989. 13.95 (ISBN 1-55858-003-4). North-South Bks NYC.
—Penguin Pete's New Friends. Pfister, Marcus, illus. LC 87-72037. 32p. (gr. k-3). 1988. 13.95 (ISBN 1-55858-025-5). North-South Bks NYC.
Playful Penguins, EV Unit 3. (gr. 1). 1991. 5-pack 21.25 (ISBN 0-88106-723-7). Charlesbridge Pub.
Strodder, Chris. A Sky for Henry. Kennedy, Emilie, illus. 32p. (ps-3). 1985. pap. 4.95 (ISBN 0-931093-03-1). Red Hen Pr.
Tripp, Valerie. Los Pinguinos Se Ponen a Pintar (The Penguins Paint) Martin, Sandra K., illus. LC 87-14081. (SPA.). 24p. (ps-2). 1990. PLB 12.33 (ISBN 0-516-31567-6); pap. 3.95 (ISBN 0-516-51567-5). Childrens.
Wilhelm, Hans. Don't Give Up, Josephine! Wilhelm, Hans, illus. LC 84-24849. 40p. (ps-3). 1985. (Random Juv); lib. bdg. 7.99 (ISBN 0-394-97244-9). Random.
Wood, Audrey. Little Penguin's Tale. 1989. 13.95 (ISBN 0-15-246475-1). HarbraceJ.

PENICILLIN

Jacobs, Francine. Breakthrough: The True Story of Penicillin. (Illus.). 128p. (gr. 7-11). 1985. 10.95 (ISBN 0-396-08579-2, Putnam). Putnam Pub Group.

PENITENTIARIES

see Prisons

PENNSYLVANIA

Carole Marsh Pennsylvania Books, 31 bks. Set. 638.45 (ISBN 0-7933-1313-9). Gallopade Pub Group.
Carpenter, Allan. Pennsylvania. new ed. LC 78-5089. (Illus.). 96p. (gr. 4 up). 1978. PLB 19.93 (ISBN 0-516-04138-X). Childrens.
Cooper, Richard & Crary, Ryland. The Politics of Progress. (gr. 7-12). 1982. 9.95 (ISBN 0-931992-42-7). Penns Valley.

Fradin, Dennis. Pennsylvania: In Words & Pictures. LC 79-24942. (Illus.). 48p. (gr. 2-5). 1980. PLB 15.93 (ISBN 0-516-03938-5); pap. 4.95 (ISBN 0-516-43938-3). Childrens.

McGough, Michael R. Pennsylvania from Wilderness Colony to National Leader. (Illus.). 44p. (gr. 4-6). 1989. pap. text ed. 5.95 (ISBN 0-939631-15-6). Thomas Publications.

Marsh, Carole. Avast, Ye Slobs! Pennsylvania Pirate Trivia. (Illus.). 1990. PLB 19.95 (ISBN 0-7933-0980-8); pap. 14.95 (ISBN 0-7933-0979-4); computer disk 29.95 (ISBN 0-7933-0981-6). Gallopade Pub Group.

—The Beast of the Pennsylvania Bed & Breakfast. (Illus.). 1990. PLB 19.95 (ISBN 0-7933-1933-1); pap. 14.95 (ISBN 0-7933-1934-X); computer disk 29.95 (ISBN 0-7933-1935-8). Gallopade Pub Group.

—The Hard-to-Believe-But-True! Book of Pennsylvania History, Mystery, Trivia, Legend, Lore. Humor & More. (Illus.). 1990. PLB 19.95 (ISBN 0-7933-0977-8); pap. 14.95 (ISBN 0-7933-0976-X); computer disk 29.95 (ISBN 0-7933-0978-6). Gallopade Pub Group.

—If My Pennsylvania Mama Ran the World! (Illus.). 1990. lib. bdg. 19.95 (ISBN 0-7933-1939-0); pap. 14.95 (ISBN 0-7933-1940-4); computer disk 29.95 (ISBN 0-7933-1941-2). Gallopade Pub Group.

—Let's Quilt Pennsylvania & Stuff It Topographically! (Illus.). 1990. PLB 19.95 (ISBN 0-7933-1925-0); pap. 14.95 (ISBN 1-55609-059-5); computer disk 29.95 (ISBN 0-7933-1926-9). Gallopade Pub Group.

—Pennsylvania & Other State Greats (Biographies) (Illus.). 1990. PLB 19.95 (ISBN 0-7933-1942-0); pap. 14.95 (ISBN 0-7933-1943-9); computer disk 29.95 (ISBN 0-7933-1944-7). Gallopade Pub Group.

—Pennsylvania Bandits, Bushwackers, Outlaws, Crooks, Devils, Ghosts, Desperadoes & Other Assorted & Sundry Characters! (Illus.). 1990. PLB 19.95 (ISBN 0-7933-0962-X); pap. 14.95 (ISBN 0-7933-0961-1); computer disk 29.95 (ISBN 0-7933-0963-8). Gallopade Pub Group.

—Pennsylvania Classic Christmas Trivia: Stories, Recipes, Activities, Legends, Lore & More! (Illus.). 1990. PLB 19.95 (ISBN 0-7933-0965-4); pap. 14.95 (ISBN 0-7933-0964-6); computer disk 29.95 (ISBN 0-7933-0966-2). Gallopade Pub Group.

—Pennsylvania Coastales. (Illus.). 1990. PLB 19.95 (ISBN 0-7933-1936-6); pap. 14.95 (ISBN 0-7933-1937-4); computer disk 29.95 (ISBN 0-7933-1938-2). Gallopade Pub Group.

—The Pennsylvania Hot Air Balloon Mystery. (Illus.). (gr. 2-9). 1990. 19.95 (ISBN 0-7933-2660-5); pap. 14.95 (ISBN 0-7933-2661-3); computer disk 29.95 (ISBN 0-7933-2662-1). Gallopade Pub Group.

—Pennsylvania "Jography" A Fun Run Thru Our State! (Illus.). 1990. PLB 19.95 (ISBN 0-7933-1922-6); pap. 14.95 (ISBN 0-7933-1923-4); computer disk 29.95 (ISBN 0-7933-1924-2). Gallopade Pub Group.

—Pennsylvania Kid's Cookbook: Recipes, How-to, History, Lore & More! (Illus.). 1990. PLB 19.95 (ISBN 0-7933-0974-3); pap. 14.95 (ISBN 0-7933-0973-5); computer disk 29.95 (ISBN 0-7933-0975-1). Gallopade Pub Group.

—Pennsylvania Quiz Bowl Crash Course! (Illus.). 1990. PLB 19.95 (ISBN 0-7933-1945-5); pap. 14.95 (ISBN 0-7933-1946-3); computer disk 29.95 (ISBN 0-7933-1947-1). Gallopade Pub Group.

—Pennsylvania School Trivia: An Amazing & Fascinating Look at Ou State's Teachers, Schools & Students! (Illus.). 1990. PLB 19.95 (ISBN 0-7933-0971-9); pap. 14.95 (ISBN 0-7933-0970-0); computer disk 29.95 (ISBN 0-7933-0972-7). Gallopade Pub Group.

—Pennsylvania Silly Basketball Sportsmysteries, Vol. 1. (Illus.). 1990. PLB 19.95 (ISBN 0-7933-0968-9); pap. 14.95 (ISBN 0-7933-0967-0); computer disk 29.95 (ISBN 0-7933-0969-7). Gallopade Pub Group.

—Pennsylvania Silly Basketball Sportsmysteries, Vol. 2. (Illus.). 1990. PLB 19.95 (ISBN 0-7933-1948-X); pap. 14.95 (ISBN 0-7933-1949-8); computer disk 29.95 (ISBN 0-7933-1950-1). Gallopade Pub Group.

—Pennsylvania Silly Football Sportsmysteries, Vol. 1. (Illus.). 1990. PLB 19.95 (ISBN 0-7933-1927-7); pap. 14.95 (ISBN 0-7933-1928-5); computer disk 29.95 (ISBN 0-7933-1929-3). Gallopade Pub Group.

—Pennsylvania Silly Football Sportsmysteries, Vol. 2. (Illus.). 1990. PLB 19.95 (ISBN 0-7933-1930-7); pap. 14.95 (ISBN 0-7933-1931-5); computer disk 29.95 (ISBN 0-7933-1932-3). Gallopade Pub Group.

—Pennsylvania Silly Trivia! (Illus.). 1990. PLB 19.95 (ISBN 0-7933-1919-6); pap. 14.95 (ISBN 0-7933-1920-X); computer disk 29.95 (ISBN 0-7933-1921-8). Gallopade Pub Group.

—Pennsylvania's (Most Devastating!) Disasters & (Most Calamitous!) Catastrophies! (Illus.). 1990. PLB 19.95 (ISBN 0-7933-0959-X); pap. 14.95 (ISBN 0-7933-0958-1); computer disk 29.95 (ISBN 0-7933-0960-3). Gallopade Pub Group.

Shebar, Sharon S. & Shebar, Susan E. Pennsylvania. (Illus.). 72p. (gr. 4-9). 1987. pap. 10.40 (ISBN 0-531-10393-5). Watts.

Shires, H. Bess & March, Rita N. Adventures in Pennsylvania. (gr. 5-6). 1984. pap. 4.95 (ISBN 0-931992-12-5). Penns Valley.

Turner Program Services, Inc. Staff & Clark, James I. Pennsylvania. LC 85-9972. 48p. (gr. 3 up). 1985. PLB 17.32 (ISBN 0-86514-442-7); pap. text ed. 9.27 (ISBN 0-86514-517-2); cancelled Beta video (ISBN 0-86514-067-7); cancelled VHS video (ISBN 0-86514-142-8); cancelled 3/4" video (ISBN 0-86514-217-3); cancelled tchr's. guide (ISBN 0-86514-292-0); cancelled student activity bk. (ISBN 0-86514-367-6); cancelled index. Raintree Pubs.

Wallower, Lucille. All about Pennsylvania. Wholey, Ellen J., ed. Wallower, Lucille, illus. (gr. 3-4). 1984. pap. 4.55 (ISBN 0-931992-05-2). Penns Valley.

—Your Pennsylvania. Brebner, Daphne B. & Stevens, S. K., eds. (gr. 4-6). 1959. 6.35 (ISBN 0-931992-07-9). Penns Valley.

—Your State: Pennsylvania. Gump, Patricia L., ed. (gr. 3-4). 1984. pap. 4.90 (ISBN 0-931992-09-5). Penns Valley.

Wallower, Lucille & Wier, Bernice. The New Pennsylvania Primer. (gr. 3-4). 1984. 9.45 (ISBN 0-931992-04-4). Penns Valley.

PENNSYLVANIA–FICTION

Fritz, Jean. The Cabin Faced West. Rojankovsky, Feodor, illus. (gr. 4-7). 1958. 8.95 (ISBN 0-698-20016-0, Coward). Putnam Pub Group.

—The Cabin Faced West. Rojanovsky, Feodor, illus. (gr. 1-7). 1987. pap. 3.95 (ISBN 0-14-032256-6, Puffin). Puffin Bks.

Knight, James E. The Farm, Life in Colonial Pennsylvania. Milone, Karen, illus. LC 81-23083. 32p. (gr. 5-9). 1982. PLB 10.79 (ISBN 0-89375-730-6); pap. text ed. 2.95 (ISBN 0-89375-731-4). Troll Assocs.

PENNSYLVANIA–HISTORY

Cooper, Richard & Crary, Ryland. The Politics of Progress. (gr. 7-12). 1982. 9.95 (ISBN 0-931992-42-7). Penns Valley.

Cornell, William A. & Altland, Millard. Our Pennsylvania Heritage. LC 78-50430. (gr. 7-12). 1983. 15.95 (ISBN 0-931992-21-4). Penns Valley.

Fradin, Dennis B. The Pennsylvania Colony. LC 88-11975. 160p. (gr. 4 up). 1988. PLB 22.60 (ISBN 0-516-00390-9). Childrens.

McElroy, Janice H., ed. Our Hidden Heritage: Pennsylvania Women in History. LC 83-71272. (Illus.). 440p. (gr. 7-8). 1983. pap. 12.00 (ISBN 0-9611476-0-1). Am Assn U.

Wallower, Lucille. Indians of Pennsylvania Workshop. LC 76-12651. (gr. 3-4). 1985. pap. 4.90 (ISBN 0-931992-53-2). Penns Valley.

PENNSYLVANIA DUTCH

Ammon, Richard. Growing up Amish. LC 88-27493. (Illus.). 80p. (gr. 3 up). 1989. 12.95 (ISBN 0-689-31387-X, Atheneum Child Bk). Macmillan Child Grp.

Faber, Doris. Amish. (gr. 4-7). 1991. pap. 12.95 (ISBN 0-385-26130-6). Doubleday.

Smucker, Barbara. Amish Adventure. Price, Caroline, illus. LC 83-80892. 144p. (Orig.). (gr. 6-9). 1983. pap. 6.50 (ISBN 0-8361-3339-0). Herald Pr.

Troyer, Terry L. Amish Life Style Illustrated. Smith, Tilman R., intro. by. LC 82-90105. (Illus.). 96p. (gr. 6-12). 1982. 19.95 (ISBN 0-943314-00-3). TLT.

Wallower, Lucille. The Pennsylvania Dutch. Gump, Patricia L., ed. (gr. 3-4). 1971. pap. 3.75 (ISBN 0-931992-31-1). Penns Valley.

PENNSYLVANIA DUTCH–FICTION

Milhous, Katherine. The Egg Tree. Milhous, Katherine, illus. LC 50-6817. 32p. (gr. 1-4). 1971. 12.95 (ISBN 0-684-12716-4, Scribners Young Read). Macmillan Child Grp.

PENNSYLVANIA GERMANS

see Pennsylvania Dutch

PENOLOGY

see Prisons

PEOPLE'S DEMOCRACIES

see Communist Countries

PEOPLE'S REPUBLIC OF CHINA

see China (People'S Republic of China)

PERCEPTION

Adler, David A. Three-D, Two-D, One-D. LC 74-5156. (Illus.). 40p. (gr. k-3). 1974. (Crowell Jr Bks); PLB 12.89 (ISBN 0-690-00543-1). HarpC Child Bks.

Allington, Richard L. Opposites. Conner, Eulala, illus. LC 79-20525. 32p. (gr. k-3). 1985. PLB 15.33 (ISBN 0-8172-1279-5); pap. 9.27 (ISBN 0-8172-2484-X). Raintree Pubs.

Church, Ellin B. What Now? 64p. (gr. k-3). 1983. 6.95 (ISBN 0-912107-07-3). Monday Morning Bks.

—What Works? 64p. (gr. k-3). 1984. 6.95 (ISBN 0-912107-15-4). Monday Morning Bks.

—What's This? 64p. (gr. k-3). 1984. 6.95 (ISBN 0-912107-14-6). Monday Morning Bks.

—What's Up? 64p. (gr. k-3). 1983. 6.95 (ISBN 0-912107-09-X). Monday Morning Bks.

—What's Wrong? 64p. (gr. k-3). 1983. 6.95 (ISBN 0-912107-08-1). Monday Morning Bks.

Cohen, Lynn. Exploring My World. 64p. (ps-k). 1986. 6.95 (ISBN 0-912107-47-2). Monday Morning Bks.

Cosgrove, Stephen. T.J. Flopp: From the Land of Barely There. Edelson, Wendy, illus. LC 89-9329. 32p. 1989. 9.95 (ISBN 0-88070-281-8). Multnomah.

Gillham, Bill. What's the Difference? Horne, Fiona, illus. LC 85-28138. (gr. 3-6). 1986. 5.95 (ISBN 0-399-21321-X, Putnam). Putnam Pub Group.

Hayes, Dympna & Lehman, Melanie. Fun with Opposites. Davis, Annelies, illus. 32p. (ps). 1987. PLB 13.85 (ISBN 0-88625-142-7); pap. 2.50 (ISBN 0-685-30765-4). Durkin Hayes Pub.

Hoban, Tana. Is It Rough? Is It Smooth? Is It Shiny? Hoban, Tana, illus. LC 83-25460. 32p. (ps-1). 1984. 13.95 (ISBN 0-688-03823-9); PLB 13.88 (ISBN 0-688-03824-7). Greenwillow.

McMillan, Dana. Sorting & Sequencing. 64p. (gr. k-2). 1985. 8.95 (ISBN 0-912107-34-0). Monday Morning Bks.

Pesiri, Evelyn. Learn to See. Pesiri, Evelyn, illus. 64p. (gr. k-3). 1985. wkbk. 6.95 (ISBN 0-86653-286-2, GA 674). Good Apple.

Thomson, Ruth. All about Opposites. Sleight, Katy, illus. LC 87-42586. 32p. (gr. 1-2). 1987. PLB 10.95 (ISBN 1-55532-315-4). Gareth Stevens Inc.

Tyler, J. & Round, G. Opposites. (Illus.). 24p. (ps up). 1987. pap. 3.50 (ISBN 0-7460-0219-X). EDC.

Wassermann, Selma & Wassermann, Jack. The Book of Comparing. Smith, Dennis, illus. 32p. (gr. k-3). 1990. lib. bdg. 12.85 (ISBN 0-8027-6944-6); pap. 4.95 (ISBN 0-8027-9451-3). Walker & Co.

Watson, C. Opposites. (Illus.). 24p. (ps-2). 1983. 2.95 (ISBN 0-86020-758-7). EDC.

Wheeler, Sharon. Opposites. Richesson, Robin, illus. (ps). 1984. wkbk 1.95 (ISBN 0-916119-05-X). Creat Teach Pr.

—Sequencing. Richesson, Robin, illus. (ps). 1984. wkbk 1.95 (ISBN 0-916119-10-6). Creat Teach Pr.

Wheeler, Sharon, ed. Same-Different. Koeller, Nina C., illus. (ps). 1984. wkbk 1.95 (ISBN 0-916119-07-6). Creat Teach Pr.

—Visual Skills. Richesson, Robin, illus. (ps). 1984. wkbk. 1.95 (ISBN 0-916119-08-4). Creat Teach Pr.

PERCUSSION INSTRUMENTS

see also names of percussion instruments, e.g. Drums

Navarro, Frank. Hot Riffs. LC 88-60168. 32p. (Orig.). (gr. 10-12). 1989. pap. 4.95 (ISBN 0-9620045-0-2). Hot Riffs.

PERFORMING ARTS

see also Theater;

also art forms performed on stage or screen, e.g. Ballet

Exploring the Arts Series, 4 vols. (gr. 4-8). 1990. Set. 55.00 (ISBN 1-85435-101-X). Marshall Cavendish.

Let's Discover Sport & Entertainment. (Illus.). 80p. (gr. k-6). 1981. pap. text ed. 13.27 (ISBN 0-8172-1768-1). Raintree Pubs.

Reisfield, Randi. So You Want to Be a Star: A Teenager's Guide to Breaking into Showbusiness. Clancy, Lisa, ed. (Illus.). 224p. (Orig.). (gr. 6 up). 1990. pap. 2.95 (ISBN 0-671-70192-4, Archway). PB.

Straub, Cindie & Straub, Matthew. Mime: Basic for Beginners. (Illus., Orig.). (gr. 7-12). 1984. pap. 12.95 (ISBN 0-8238-0263-9). Plays.

PERIODICALS

see also Newspapers

Merrison, Tim. Comics & Magazines. Stefoff, Rebecca, ed. LC 90-13985. (Illus.). 32p. (gr. 4-8). 1991. PLB 17.26 (ISBN 0-944483-97-6). Garrett Ed Corp.

Walden, Kim. Magazines. LC 88-29289. (Illus.). 48p. (gr. 6-12). 1989. PLB 12.95 (ISBN 0-86307-979-2). Marshall Cavendish.

PERRY, MATTHEW CALBRAITH, 1794-1858

Kuhn, Ferdinand. Commodore Perry & the Opening of Japan. (Illus.). (gr. 4-6). 1955. 2.95 (ISBN 0-394-80356-6). Random.

PERSONAL APPEARANCE

see Beauty, Personal

PERSONAL DEVELOPMENT

see Personality; Success

PERSONAL FINANCE

see Finance, Personal

PERSONAL GROOMING

see Beauty, Personal

PERSONAL LIBERTY

see Liberty

PERSONALITY

see also Individuality

Ask about Who I Am. 64p. (gr. 4-5). 1987. PLB 18.25 (ISBN 0-8172-2883-7); pap. 13.27 (ISBN 0-8172-2895-0). Raintree Pubs.

Beckman, Jean E. Why? There Is More to You Than Meets the Eye. (Illus.). 50p. (Orig.). (gr. 9-12). 1981. pap. 4.25 (ISBN 0-941992-00-4). Los Arboles Pub.

Brown, Tricia. Someone Special, Just Like You. Ortiz, Fran, photos by. (Illus.). 64p. (gr. k-2). 1984. 15.95 (ISBN 0-8050-0481-5). H Holt & Co.

Carroll, Jeri. Let's Learn about Magnificent Me. Foster, Tom, illus. 64p. (ps-2). 1987. pap. 7.95 (ISBN 0-86653-384-2, GA1010). Good Apple.

Ets, Marie H. Just Me. Ets, Marie H., illus. (gr. k-3). 1985. bk. & cassette 19.95 (ISBN 0-941078-75-2); pap. 12.95 bk. & cassette (ISBN 0-941078-73-6); cassette, 4 paperbacks & guide 27.95 (ISBN 0-941078-74-4). Live Oak Media.

Fass, Bernie & Caggiano, Rosemary. The Power Is You. 48p. (gr. 2-12). 1979. pap. 10.95 (ISBN 0-86704-005-X). Clarus Music.

Freed, Alvyn M. TA for Tots, Vol. II. Dick, JoAnn, illus. LC 76-19650. (Orig.). (ps-3). 1980. pap. 12.95 (ISBN 0-915190-25-7, JP9025-7). Jalmar Pr.

Hallinan, P. K. I'm Glad to Be Me. LC 77-6327. (Illus.). 32p. (ps-3). 1977. PLB 13.27 (ISBN 0-516-03509-6). Childrens.

Markert, Christopher. This Person Is You. LC 68-28486. (Illus., Orig.). (gr. 10 up). 1968. pap. 2.95 (ISBN 0-8283-1016-5). Branden Pub Co.

Peebles, Catherine & Edge, Denzil. A Natural Curiosity: Taffy's Search for Self. LC 87-36882. (Illus., Orig.). 1988. pap. 6.95 (ISBN 0-939991-01-2). Learning KY.

Schwartz, Linda. The Month-To-Month Me. 48p. (gr. 4-6). 1976. 5.95 (ISBN 0-88160-021-0, LW 205). Learning Wks.

Spier, Peter. People. Spier, Peter, illus. LC 78-19832. 48p. (gr. 1-3). 1980. PLB 13.95 (ISBN 0-385-13181-X); pap. 14.99 (ISBN 0-385-13182-8). Doubleday.

Ward, Hiley H. Feeling Good about Myself. Novello, Joseph, intro. by. LC 82-25613. 166p. (gr. 6 up) 1983. 11.95 (ISBN 0-664-32704-4, Westminster). Westminster John Knox.

PERSONALITY-FICTION

American Etiquette Institute Staff. Eddycat & Buddy Entertain a Guest, Bk. 5. (Illus.). 32p. (gr. k-3). 1991. 13.95 (ISBN 1-879322-14-5). Amer Etiquette Inst.

—Eddycat & Gabby Gorilla Babysit, Bk. 9. (Illus.). 32p. (gr. k-3). 1991. 13.95 (ISBN 1-879322-18-8). Amer Etiquette Inst.

—Eddycat Attends Sunshine's Birthday Party, Bk. 3. (Illus.). 32p. (gr. k-3). 1991. 13.95 (ISBN 1-879322-12-9). Amer Etiquette Inst.

—Eddycat Brings Soccer to Mannersville, Bk. 8. (Illus.). 32p. (gr. k-3). 1991. 13.95 (ISBN 1-879322-17-X). Amer Etiquette Inst.

—Eddycat Goes on Vacation with the Ducks, Bk. 11. (Illus.). 32p. (gr. k-3). 1991. 13.95 (ISBN 1-879322-20-X). Amer Etiquette Inst.

—Eddycat Goes Shopping with Becky, Bk. 6. (Illus.). 32p. (gr. k-3). 1991. 13.95 (ISBN 1-879322-15-3). Amer Etiquette Inst.

—Eddycat Helps Sunshine Plan Her Party, Bk. 2. (Illus.). 32p. (gr. k-3). 1991. 13.95 (ISBN 1-879322-11-0). Amer Etiquette Inst.

—Eddycat Introduces Leonardo Lion, Bk. 12. (Illus.). 32p. (gr. k-3). 1991. 13.95 (ISBN 1-879322-21-8). Amer Etiquette Inst.

—Eddycat Introduces Mannersville, USA, Bk. 1. (Illus.). 32p. (gr. k-3). 1991. 13.95 (ISBN 1-879322-10-2). Amer Etiquette Inst.

—Eddycat Serves Grandma's Birthday Brunch, Bk. 10. (Illus.). 32p. (gr. k-3). 1991. 13.95 (ISBN 1-879322-19-6). Amer Etiquette Inst.

—Eddycat Teaches Telephone Skills, Bk. 4. (Illus.). 32p. (gr. k-3). 1991. 13.95 (ISBN 1-879322-13-7). Amer Etiquette Inst.

—Eddycat Visits Wright Street School, Bk. 7. (Illus.). 32p. (gr. k-3). 1991. 13.95 (ISBN 1-879322-16-1). Amer Etiquette Inst.

Angell, Judie. Secret Selves. 192p. (gr. 7 up). 1981. pap. 2.25 (ISBN 0-440-97716-9, LE). Dell.

Breitmeyer, Lois & Leithauser, Gladys. Who Should I Be? 1991. pap. 2.95 (ISBN 0-8091-6599-6). Paulist Pr.

Bunting, Eve. The Cloverdale Switch. LC 79-2404. (gr. 7 up). 1979. (Lipp Jr Bks). HarpC Child Bks.

Charaleone. All I See Is Part of Me. Aldrich, Cynthia, illus. 56p. (gr. 2-8). 1989. 14.95 (ISBN 0-935699-03-1). Illum Arts.

A rhythmic tale of one child's journey to self-discovery, this richly illustrated story has received an exceptional response across the country. In addition to parents & children, enthusiasts include teachers, librarians, pediatricians & other health professionals. Dr. Michael E. Ogle, Ph.D., Clinical Psychologist, states "All I See Is Part of Me should be required reading by prospective mothers & fathers, educators, mental health practitioners & their patients... This book is a prescription for child-rearing & the goal of psychotherapy." Now in its 1st reprint, All I See Is Part of Me communicates simple & enduring truths enhanced by brilliant, full-color illustrations. "Sister star, How can it be That I am you & you are me?" She glowed, "You're larger than you know, You are everyplace there is to go. You have a body, this is true... But look at what's inside of you!" According to Gerald G. Jampolsky, M.D., Founder of the Center for Attitudinal Healing, "This warm, gentle, tender, trusting book is just what the world needs." All I See Is Part of Me is a delight for children of all ages - a book whose message is never forgotten!

Publisher Provided Annotation.

Conford, Ellen. Why Me? 156p. (gr. 5 up). 1985. 14.95 (ISBN 0-316-15326-5). Little.

Evans, Mari. I Look at Me. (ps-2). 1974. pap. 2.50 (ISBN 0-88378-038-0). Third World.

Grant, Eva. I Hate My Name. Mayo, Gretchen, illus. Hollingsworth, Charles, intro. by. LC 80-14428. (Illus.). 32p. (gr. k-6). 1980. PLB 16.67 (ISBN 0-8172-1362-7). Raintree Pubs.

Hargreaves, Roger. Mr. Dizzy. Hargreaves, Roger, illus. 32p. (ps-k). 1982. pap. 1.25 (ISBN 0-8431-1132-1). Price Stern.

—Mr. Impossible. Hargreaves, Roger, illus. 32p. 1981. pap. 1.25 (ISBN 0-8431-0819-3). Price Stern.

—Mr. Nonsense. Hargreaves, Roger, illus. 32p. (ps-k). 1981. pap. 1.25 (ISBN 0-8431-0821-5). Price Stern.

—Mr. Nonsense. 32p. (ps up). 1978. PLB 8.70s.p. (ISBN 0-87191-820-X); PLB 12.45 (ISBN 0-685-09339-5). Creative Ed.

—Mr. Small. Hargreaves, Roger, illus. 32p. (ps-k). 1981. pap. 1.25 (ISBN 0-8431-0823-1). Price Stern.

—Mr. Sneeze. Hargreaves, Roger, illus. 32p. (ps-k). 1982. pap. 1.25 (ISBN 0-8431-1125-9). Price Stern.

—Mr. Snow. Hargreaves, Roger, illus. 32p. (ps-k). 1982. pap. 1.25 (ISBN 0-8431-1133-X). Price Stern.

—Mr. Stingy. Hargreaves, Roger, illus. 32p. (ps-k). 1982. pap. 1.25 (ISBN 0-8431-1130-5). Price Stern.

—Mr. Tall. Hargreaves, Roger, illus. 32p. (ps-k). 1982. pap. 1.25 (ISBN 0-8431-1126-7). Price Stern.

Hazen, Barbara S. To Be Me. Hook, Frances, illus. LC 75-12960. (ps-2). 1975. 12.96 (ISBN 0-913778-09-5). Childs World.

Krauss, Ruth. I'll Be You-You Be Me. Sendak, Maurice, illus. (gr. k-5). 1973. pap. 8.00 (ISBN 0-912846-14-3). Bookstore Pr.

Lester, Alison. Clive Eats Alligators. LC 85-17213. (ps-3). 1986. 12.95 (ISBN 0-395-40775-3). HM.

Lovelace, Maud H. Betsy in Spite of Herself. Neville, Vera, illus. LC 46-11995. 272p. (gr. 4-7). 1980. pap. 3.50 (ISBN 0-06-440111-1, Trophy). HarpC Child Bks.

McDonnell, Janet & Ziegler, Sandra. What's So Special about Me? I'm One of a Kind. Friedman, Joy, illus. LC 88-2872. 32p. (ps-2). 1988. PLB 11.97 (ISBN 0-89565-419-9). Childs World.

McPhail, David. Something Special. McPhail, David, illus. 32p. (ps-3). 1988. 12.95 (ISBN 0-316-56324-2). Little.

Miles, Betty. Looking On. LC 77-15946. (gr. 4-8). 1978. lib. bdg. 10.99 (ISBN 0-394-93582-9); PLB 6.95 (ISBN 0-394-83582-4). Knopf.

Mr. Skinny. Hargreaves, Roger. 32p. (ps-k). 1981. pap. 1.25 (ISBN 0-8431-0822-3). Price Stern.

Nordlicht, Lillian. I Love to Laugh. Davis, Allen, illus. Silverman, Manuel, intro. by. LC 80-14399. (Illus.). 32p. 1980. 39.95 (ISBN 0-8172-1364-3). Raintree Pubs.

O'Leary, Daniel J. & Dalton, Kathleen. Where Is God? Sabatte, Frank, illus. 1991. pap. 2.95 (ISBN 0-8091-6598-8). Paulist Pr.

Roe, Eileen. All I Am. LC 88-30510. (Illus.). 32p. (ps-1). 1990. 12.95 (ISBN 0-02-777372-8, Bradbury Pr). Macmillan Child Grp.

Rosen, Lillian. Just Like Everybody Else. LC 81-47534. 155p. (gr. 7-12). 1981. 12.95 (ISBN 0-15-241652-8, HJ). HarBraceJ.

Saunders, Susan. Twin Trouble. 107p. (gr. 3-5). 1989. PLB 5.99 (ISBN 0-394-99606-2); pap. 2.95 (ISBN 0-394-89606-8). Knopf.

Sutton, Jane. Definitely Not Sexy. LC 88-18127. 160p. (gr. 7 up). 1988. 12.95 (ISBN 0-316-82325-2). Little.

PERSONNEL SERVICE IN EDUCATION
see also Counseling; Dropouts; Vocational Guidance

PERSPECTIVE
see also Drawing

PERSUASION (RHETORIC)
see Public Speaking; Rhetoric

PERU

Lerner Publications, Department of Geography Staff. Peru in Pictures. (Illus.). 64p. (gr. 5 up). 1987. PLB 12.95 (ISBN 0-8225-1820-1). Lerner Pubns.

Peru. (Illus.). (gr. 5 up). 1988. 14.95 (ISBN 0-222-00952-7). Chelsea Hse.

St. John, Jetty. A Family in Peru. (Illus.). 32p. (gr. 2-5). 1987. PLB 9.95 (ISBN 0-8225-1669-1). Lerner Pubns.

PERU-ANTIQUITIES
McMullen, David. Mystery in Peru: The Lines of Nazca. LC 77-10456. (Illus.). 48p. (gr. 4 up). 1983. PLB 17.32 (ISBN 0-8172-1058-X); pap. 9.27 (ISBN 0-8172-2163-8). Raintree Pubs.

PERU-FICTION
Clark, Ann N. Secret of the Andes. Charlot, Jean, illus. (gr. 4-8). 1952. pap. 14.95 (ISBN 0-670-62975-8). Viking Child Bks.

PESTS
see Fungi; Insects, Injurious and Beneficial

PESTICIDE POLLUTION
see Pesticides and the Environment

PESTICIDES AND THE ENVIRONMENT
Lee, Sally. Pesticides. (Illus.). 144p. (gr. 9-12). 1991. PLB 12.90 (ISBN 0-531-13017-7). Watts.

PET (COMPUTER)
Kressen, David P. Teach Your Computer to Think in BASIC. Jacobs, Russell, ed. (Illus.). 88p. (gr. 5 up). 1983. pap. text ed. 7.50 (ISBN 0-918272-10-6). Jacobs.

PETER, SAINT, APOSTLE
Barrett, Ethel. Peter. LC 81-52942. 128p. (Orig.). (gr. 3 up). 1982. pap. text ed. 3.95 (ISBN 0-8307-0768-9, 5810809). Regal.

Daughters of St. Paul. The Fisher Prince. (gr. 3-7). 3.00 (ISBN 0-8198-0233-6); pap. 2.00 (ISBN 0-685-01442-8). Dghtrs St Paul.

De Graaf, Anne. Peter: The Fisher of Men. Montero, Jose P., illus. 32p. (gr. 1-3). 1990. 7.95 (ISBN 0-8028-5033-2). Eerdmans.

Storr, Catherine. St. Peter & St. Paul. Peppe, Mark, illus. LC 84-18078. 32p. (gr. k-4). 1985. PLB 14.65 (ISBN 0-8172-1998-6). Raintree Pubs.

The Story of Peter the Fisherman. (Illus.). (gr. 4). 3.50 (ISBN 0-7214-0274-7). Ladybird Bks.

PETER 1ST, EMPEROR AND TSAR OF RUSSIA, 1672-1725
Stanley, Diane. Peter the Great. Stanley, Diane, illus. LC 85-13060. 32p. (gr. k-3). 1986. 13.95 (ISBN 0-02-786790-0, Four Winds). Macmillan Child Grp.

PETROLEUM
Ardley, Neil. Oil Rigs. Stefoff, Rebecca, ed. LC 90-40246. (Illus.). 48p. (gr. 4-7). 1990. PLB 17.26 (ISBN 0-944483-76-3). Garrett Ed Corp.

Asimov, Isaac. How Did We Find Out about Oil? Wool, David, illus. 64p. (gr. 5-8). 1980. PLB 10.85 (ISBN 0-8027-6381-2). Walker & Co.

Bailey, Donna. Energy from Oil & Gas. LC 90-39300. (Illus.). 48p. (gr. 2-5). 1990. PLB 15.96 (ISBN 0-8114-2518-5). Steck-V.

Mitgutsch, Ali. From Oil to Gasoline. Mitgutsch, Ali, illus. LC 80-29562. 24p. (ps-3). 1981. PLB 6.95 (ISBN 0-87614-160-2). Carolrhoda Bks.

Oil. (Illus.). (gr. 5 up). lib. bdg. 15.93 (ISBN 0-86592-262-4). Rourke Corp.

Robson, Pat, illus. Oil. 32p. (gr. 3-5). 1985. 5.95x (ISBN 0-86685-449-5). Intl Bk Ctr.

PETROLEUM-FICTION
Hawthorne, Dorothy. Chocolate Wildcat. Washington, Bill, illus. LC 87-72602. (gr. 4-6). 1988. PLB 11.95 (ISBN 0-931722-64-0); pap. 5.95 (ISBN 0-931722-65-9). Corona Pub.

Rice, James. Gaston Drills an Offshore Oil Well. Rice, James, illus. LC 82-11240. 48p. (gr. 4 up). 1982. 11.95 (ISBN 0-88289-289-4). Pelican.

PETROLEUM ENGINES
see Gas and Oil Engines

PETROLEUM INDUSTRY AND TRADE
Lynch, Michael. How Oil Rigs Are Made. (Illus.). 32p. (gr. 7 up). 1986. 12.95 (ISBN 0-8160-0041-7). Facts on File.

Mitgutsch, Ali. From Oil to Gasoline. Mitgutsch, Ali, illus. LC 80-29562. 24p. (ps-3). 1981. PLB 6.95 (ISBN 0-87614-160-2). Carolrhoda Bks.

Scott, Elaine. Oil! Getting It, Shipping It, Selling It. LC 83-19653. 96p. (gr. 4-7). 1985. 13.95 (ISBN 0-7232-6260-8). Warne.

PETROLEUM INDUSTRY AND TRADE-FICTION
Thiele, Colin. Fight Against Albatross Two. LC 75-37104. 254p. (gr. 7 up). 1976. PLB 12.89 (ISBN 0-06-026099-8). HarpC Child Bks.

PETROLEUM PRODUCTS
Brice, Raphaelle. From Oil to Plastic. Matthews, Sarah, tr. from FRE. Kniffke, Sophie, illus. LC 87-31753. 38p. (gr. k-5). 1988. 4.95 (ISBN 0-944589-17-0, 170). Young Discovery Lib.

PETS
see also Domestic Animals;
also names of animals, e.g. Cats; Dogs

Animal Answers: Small Pets. (ps up) 1989. PLB 3.98 (ISBN 0-7924-5120-1, Mallard Pr). BDD Promo Bk.

Animal Friends. (Illus.). 88p. (ps-3). 1989. 15.93 (ISBN 0-8094-4849-1); lib. bdg. 21.27 (ISBN 0-8094-4850-5). Time-Life.

Arnold, Caroline. Pets Without Homes. Hewett, Richard, illus. LC 83-2106. 48p. (gr. k-3). 1983. 14.95 (ISBN 0-89919-191-6, Clarion). HM.

Baby Pet Animals. (Illus.). (ps). pap. 1.25 (ISBN 0-7214-9547-8). Ladybird Bks.

Bare, Colleen S. To Love a Cat. (gr. 5-8). 1986. 10.95 (ISBN 0-396-08834-1, Putnam). Putnam Pub Group.

—To Love a Dog. (gr. k-3). 1987. 12.95 (ISBN 0-396-09057-5, Putnam). Putnam Pub Group.

Berry, Joy W. Teach Me about Pets. Dickey, Kate, ed. LC 85-45081. (Illus.). 36p. (ps). 1986. 4.98 (ISBN 0-685-10720-5). Grolier Inc.

Blumberg, Leda. Pets. (Illus.). 72p. (gr. 4up). PLB 10.40 (ISBN 0-531-04649-4). Watts.

Broekel, Ray. Gerbil Pets & Other Small Rodents. LC 82-23501. (Illus.). 48p. (gr. k-4). 1983. PLB 14.60 (ISBN 0-516-01679-2). Childrens.

Chrystie, Frances N. Pets. rev. 3rd ed. Griffin, Gillett, illus. (gr. 4 up). 1974. 16.95 (ISBN 0-316-14051-1). Little.

Cousins, Lucy. Pet Animals. Cousins, Lucy, illus. LC 90-36260. (ps). 1991. bds. 3.95 (ISBN 0-688-10073-2, Tambourine Bks). Morrow.

Cowing, Renee. The Complete Book of Pet Names. LC 90-81851. 112p. 1990. 9.95 (ISBN 0-9626950-2-5). Fireplug CA.

"A charming book about naming your pet (the author) has a light touch to go with her massive research into the arcane world of naming cats & dogs. She notes wisely that the first burst of joy in naming a pet has got to

withstand a long period of time...the book also contains a complete section on celebrity pets & the 50 most popular cat & dog names in the country. The alphabet section is illustrated with clever drawings."--Jack Russell, San Mateo Times. "I highly reccommend Ms. Cowing's compilation of canine monikers."--Jay Stuller, Author & Journalist. To order: From Fireplug Press, P.O. Box 283, San Mateo, CA 94401. ($9.95 plus $1.00 postage & handling) or from Baker & Taylor.
Publisher Provided Annotation.

Davis, A. This Is My Pet. (Illus.). 12p. (ps-1). 1987. 2.50 (ISBN 0-88625-139-7). Durkin Hayes Pub.
Felder, Deborah G. The Kids' World Almanac of Animals & Pets. Lane, John, illus. 1990. 14.95 (ISBN 0-88687-556-0); pap. 6.95 (ISBN 0-88687-555-2). Pharos Bks NY.
Friends & Pets. (ps). 1982. 3.95 (ISBN 0-86112-084-1). Borden.
Fujikawa, Gyo. Puppies, Pussycats & Other Friends. (ps-k). 1975. 4.50 (ISBN 0-448-11920-X, G&D). Putnam Pub Group.
Hill. Small Pets. Cork, Barbara, ed. Jackson, Ian & Shields, Chris, illus. (gr. 3-6). 6.95 (ISBN 0-86020-649-1, 15121); pap. 4.50 (ISBN 0-86020-648-3, 15122); lib. bdg. 11.96 (ISBN 0-88110-087-0). EDC.
Hill, R. Pets & Pet Care. 24p. (gr. 1-4). 1983. 10.95 (ISBN 0-86020-650-5). EDC.
Holmes, Jean E. Norah's Ark. Woolsey, Raymond H., ed. 128p. 1989. pap. 4.95 (ISBN 0-8280-0417-X). Review & Herald.
Jameson, Pam & Hearne, Tina. Responsible Pet Care, 6 bks, Reading Level 3. (Illus.). 192p. (gr. 2-5). Date not set. Set. PLB 84.00 (ISBN 0-86625-188-X). Rourke Corp.
McPherson, Mark. Choosing Your Pet. Bernstein, Dianne, illus. LC 84-226. 48p. (gr. 3-7). 1985. PLB 9.89 (ISBN 0-8167-0111-3); pap. text ed. 2.95 (ISBN 0-8167-0112-1). Troll Assocs.
Mitchell, Victor. Pets. Mitchell, Victor, illus. 16p. (gr. k up). 1988. pap. 1.95 (ISBN 0-7459-1469-1). Lion USA.
My Book of Baby Pet Animals. (ps-2). 3.95 (ISBN 0-7214-5151-9). Ladybird Bks.
Pets. (Illus.). 64p. (gr. 6-12). 1984. pap. 1.85 (ISBN 0-8395-3281-4, 3281). BSA.
Pets. (Illus.). 32p. (ps-1). 1986. pap. 1.25 (ISBN 0-8431-1519-X). Price Stern.
Pets. LC 90-49259. 24p. (ps-k). 1991. pap. 6.95 (ISBN 0-689-71404-1, Aladdin). Macmillan Child Grp.
Podendorf, Illa. Pets. LC 81-7679. (Illus.). 48p. (gr. k-4). 1981. PLB 14.60 (ISBN 0-516-01641-5). Childrens.
Polikoff, Barbara G. My Parrot Eats Baked Beans: Kids Talk about Their Pets. Levine, Abby, ed. (Illus.). 56p. (gr. 1-7). 1988. PLB 10.95 (ISBN 0-8075-5349-2). A Whitman.
Pope, Joyce. Taking Care of Your Gerbil. 1990. pap. 3.95 (ISBN 0-531-15168-9). Watts.
—Taking Care of Your Guinea Pig. (Illus.). 32p. (gr. 4-9). 1990. PLB 10.90 (ISBN 0-685-13496-2); pap. 3.95 (ISBN 0-531-15169-7). Watts.
Roy, Ron. What Has Ten Legs & Eats Cornflakes? Cherry, Lynne, illus. 48p. (ps-3). 1982. 13.95 (ISBN 0-89919-119-3, Clarion). HM.
Seltzer, Meyer. Petcetera: The Pet Riddle Book. Fay, Ann, ed. (Illus.). 32p. (gr. 1-5). 1988. PLB 8.95 (ISBN 0-8075-6515-6). A Whitman.
Simon, Seymour. Pets in a Jar: Collecting & Caring for Small Animals. Fraser, Betty, illus. (gr. 4-8). 1979. pap. 5.95 (ISBN 0-14-049186-4, Puffin). Puffin Bks.
Smith, Lane. The Big Pets. Smith, Lane, illus. 32p. (ps-3). 1991. 14.95 (ISBN 0-670-83378-9). Viking Child Bks.
Tallarico, Tony, illus. Pets. 12p. (ps-1). 1990. bds. 3.95 (ISBN 0-89828-400-7). Tuffy Bks.
Vail, Virginia. Adopt-A-Pet. 128p. (Orig.). (gr. 4-6). 1987. pap. 2.50 (ISBN 0-590-40185-8). Scholastic Inc.
—Animal Inn, No. 5: Adopt a Pet. 1987. pap. 2.75 (ISBN 0-590-43431-4). Scholastic Inc.
Vrbova, Zuza. Junior Pet Care Koi for Ponds. McAulay, Robert, illus. 48p. (gr. 1-6). 1990. PLB 9.95 (J-008). TFH Pubns.
Weber, William J. Care of Uncommon Pets. LC 78-14093. (Illus.). 224p. (gr. 5 up). 1979. 10.95 (ISBN 0-8050-0294-4); pap. 5.95 (ISBN 0-8050-0320-7). H Holt & Co.
Wexler, Jerome. Pet Mice. Tucker, Kathleen, ed. (Illus.). 48p. (gr. 2-8). 1989. PLB 13.95 (ISBN 0-8075-6524-5). A Whitman.

PETS–FICTION

Alexander, Martha. No Ducks in Our Bathtub. Alexander, Martha, illus. LC 72-7598. 32p. (ps-2). 1985. 8.95 (ISBN 0-8037-6239-9); PLB 8.89 (ISBN 0-8037-6217-8). Dial Bks Young.
Angell, Judie. A Home Is to Share... & Share... & Share. LC 83-21356. 112p. (gr. 4-6). 1984. 12.95 (ISBN 0-02-705830-1, Bradbury Pr). Macmillan Child Grp.
Armstrong, Jennifer. Too Many Pets. (gr. 4-7). 1990. pap. 2.75 (ISBN 0-553-15804-X). Bantam.
Bragg, Ruth. Mrs. Muggle's Sparkle. Bragg, Ruth, illus. LC 89-31371. 28p. (ps up). 1990. 14.95 (ISBN 0-88708-106-1). Picture Bk Studio.
Carlson, Natalie S. A Pet for the Orphelines. (gr. k-6). 1988. pap. 2.75 (ISBN 0-440-46838-8, YB). Dell.
—A Pet for the Orphelines. (gr. 1-4). 1988. 2.75 (ISBN 0-440-40014-7, Pub. by Yearling Classics). Dell.
—A Pet for the Orphelines. (gr. 3-6). 14.50 (ISBN 0-8446-6373-5). Peter Smith.
Carris, Joan D. Pets, Vets, & Marty Howard. (gr. k-6). 1987. pap. 2.95 (ISBN 0-440-46855-8, Yearling). Dell.
Chalmers, Mary. Six Dogs, Twenty-Three Cats, Forty-Five Mice, & One Hundred Sixteen Spiders. Chalmers, Mary, illus. LC 83-49482. 40p. (gr. k-3). 1986. 11.95 (ISBN 0-06-021188-1); PLB 11.89 (ISBN 0-06-021189-X). HarpC Child Bks.
Corrin, Sara & Corrin, Stephen. Pet Stories for Children. Bennett, Jill, illus. 160p. (gr. 2-7). 1985. 11.95 (ISBN 0-571-13642-7). Faber & Faber.
Davies, Andrew & Davies, Diana. Poonam's Pets. Dowling, Paul, illus. 32p. (ps-2). 1990. pap. 12.95 (ISBN 0-670-83321-5). Viking Child Bks.
De Hamel, Joan. Hemi's Pet. LC 86-26905. (ps-2). 1987. 12.95 (ISBN 0-395-43665-6). HM.
DePaola, Tomie. Little Grunt & the Big Egg: A Prehistoric Fairy Tale. DePaola, Tomie, illus. LC 88-17009. 32p. 1990. PLB 14.95 (ISBN 0-8234-0730-6). Holiday.
Ernst, Lisa C. Nattie Parsons' Good-Luck Lamb. (Illus.). 32p. (ps-3). 1990. pap. 3.95 (ISBN 0-14-050772-8, Puffin). Puffin Bks.
Freeman, Lydia & Freeman, Don. Pet of the Met. (Illus.). 64p. (ps-3). 1953. pap. 13.95 (ISBN 0-670-54875-8). Viking Child Bks.
Gackenbach, Dick. Do You Love Me? Gackenbach, Dick, illus. LC 74-34104. 48p. (ps-4). 1979. 14.95 (ISBN 0-395-28794-4, Clarion). HM.
Galvani, Maureen. Me & My Cat. Galvani, Maureen, illus. LC 88-33310. 24p. 1989. 10.95 (ISBN 0-87226-410-6, Bedrick Blackie). P Bedrick Bks.
Graham, Amanda. Who Wants Arthur? Gynell, Donna, illus. LC 86-42812. 32p. (gr. 2-3). 1987. PLB 12.95 (ISBN 1-55532-868-7). Gareth Stevens Inc.
Graham, Bob. Pete & Roland. Smith, Peter & Graham, Bob, illus. LC 83-23402. 32p. (ps-2). 1984. pap. 5.95 (ISBN 0-670-54912-6). Viking Child Bks.
Greeley, Valerie, illus. Pets. LC 83-22509. 12p. (ps). 1984. bds. 3.95 (ISBN 0-911745-21-1, Bedrick Blackie). P Bedrick Bks.
Gregorich, Barbara. I Want a Pet. Hoffman, Joan, ed. Schneider, Rex, illus. 16p. (Orig.). (gr. k-2). 1984. pap. 1.95 (ISBN 0-88743-003-1, 06003). Sch Zone Pub Co.
Greydanus, Rose. Let's Get a Pet. Sweat, Lynn, illus. LC 87-10938. 32p. (gr. k-2). 1988. PLB 7.06 (ISBN 0-8167-0986-6); pap. text ed. 1.95 (ISBN 0-8167-0987-4). Troll Assocs.
Haywood, Carolyn. Eddie's Menagerie. Fetz, Ingrid, illus. LC 78-6519. (gr. 4-6). 1978. PLB 12.88 (ISBN 0-688-32158-5). Morrow Jr Bks.
Himmel, Roger J. Kindness to Animals. Manoni, Mary H., ed. Peters, Luther J. & Ross, Connie, illus. (gr. k-3). 1978. pap. text ed. 29.95 6 bks. & 1 cass. (ISBN 0-89290-048-2); pap. text ed. 10.95 1 bk. & 1 cass. (ISBN 0-685-04653-2). Soc for Visual.
Howard, Jean G. Half a Cage. Howard, Jean G., illus. LC 78-62962. (gr. 4-12). 1978. 3.50 (ISBN 0-930954-07-6). Tidal Pr.
Keats, Ezra J. Pet Show! Keats, Ezra J., illus. LC 86-17225. 40p. (gr. k-3). 1987. pap. 4.50 (ISBN 0-689-71159-X, Aladdin). Macmillan Child Grp.
Kellogg, Steven. Can I Keep Him? Kellogg, Steven, illus. LC 72-142453. (ps-3). 1985. 12.95 (ISBN 0-8037-0988-9); PLB 12.89 (ISBN 0-8037-0989-7). Dial Bks Young.
—The Mysterious Tadpole. LC 77-71517. (Illus.). (ps-3). 1977. 14.95 (ISBN 0-8037-6245-3); PLB 14.89 (ISBN 0-8037-6246-1). Dial Bks Young.
Kimmel, Eric. I Took My Frog to the Library. Sims, Blanche, illus. 32p. (ps-3). 1990. pap. 12.95 (ISBN 0-670-82418-6). Viking Child Bks.
Kline, Suzy. Herbie Jones & Hamburger Head. Williams, Richard, illus. 112p. (gr. 2-6). 1989. 12.95 (ISBN 0-399-21748-7, Putnam). Putnam Pub Group.
McBrier, Michael. Oliver & the Runaway Alligator. Sims, Blanche, illus. LC 86-7120. 96p. (Orig.). (gr. 3-6). 1987. PLB 9.89 (ISBN 0-8167-0818-5); pap. text ed. 2.95 (ISBN 0-8167-0819-3). Troll Assocs.
—Oliver's Back-Yard Circus. Sims, Blanche, illus. LC 86-40378. 96p. (Orig.). (gr. 3-6). 1987. PLB 9.89 (ISBN 0-8167-0822-3); pap. text ed. 2.95 (ISBN 0-8167-0823-1). Troll Assocs.
—Oliver's High-Flying Adventure. Sims, Blanche, illus. LC 86-16038. 96p. (Orig.). (gr. 3-6). 1987. PLB 9.89 (ISBN 0-8167-0820-7); pap. text ed. 2.95 (ISBN 0-8167-0821-5). Troll Assocs.
McBrier, Page. Oliver's Lucky Day. Sims, Blanche, illus. LC 85-8437. 96p. (gr. 3-6). 1986. lib. bdg. 9.89 (ISBN 0-8167-0537-2); pap. text ed. 2.95 (ISBN 0-8167-0538-0). Troll Assocs.
—Secret of the Missing Camel. Sims, Blanche, illus. LC 86-887. 96p. (Orig.). (gr. 3-6). 1986. PLB 9.89 (ISBN 0-8167-0816-9); pap. text ed. 2.95 (ISBN 0-8167-0817-7). Troll Assocs.
McPhail, David. Emma's Pet. McPhail, David, illus. LC 85-4414. 24p. (ps-k). 1985. 9.95 (ISBN 0-525-44210-3, DCB). Dutton Child Bks.
—Emma's Pet. McPhail, David, illus. LC 85-4414. 24p. (ps-k). 1988. pap. 3.95 (ISBN 0-525-44430-0, DCB). Dutton Child Bks.
Manes, Stephen. The Great Gerbil Roundup. McKinley, John, illus. LC 88-2266. 112p. (gr. 3-7). 1991. pap. 3.50 (ISBN 0-06-440375-0, Trophy). HarpC Child Bks.
Martin. Jessi Ramsey Pet Sitter. (ps-1). 1989. PLB 2.75 (ISBN 0-590-42006-2, BSC #22). Scholastic Inc.
Morgan, Michaela. Edward Gets a Pet. Porter, Sue, illus. (ps-1). 1988. 8.95 (ISBN 0-525-44349-5, 0869-260, DCB). Dutton Child Bks.
Oke, Janette. A Cote of Many Colors. Mann, Brenda, illus. 128p. (Orig.). (gr. 3 up). 1987. pap. 4.95 (ISBN 0-934998-27-2). Bethel Pub.
Oram, Hiawyn. A Boy Wants a Dinosaur. (ps-3). 1991. bds. 13.95 jacketed (ISBN 0-374-30939-6). FS&G.
Orgel, Doris. Whiskers Once & Always. Newsom, Carol, illus. LC 86-5468. 80p. (gr. 2-5). 1986. pap. 10.95 (ISBN 0-670-80959-4). Viking Child Bks.
Parish, Peggy. No More Monsters for Me. Simont, Marc, illus. LC 81-47111. 64p. (gr. k-3). 1981. 11.95 (ISBN 0-06-024657-X); PLB 11.89 (ISBN 0-06-024658-8). HarpC Child Bks.
Pershall, Mary K. Hello, Barney! Wilson, Mark, illus. 32p. (ps-3). 1989. pap. 11.95 (ISBN 0-670-82406-2). Viking Child Bks.
Phillips, Joan. Mickey Mouse & the Pet Show. (Illus.). 40p. (gr. k-2). 1989. write for info. (ISBN 0-307-11684-0, Pub. by Golden Bks). Western Pub.
Plummer, Louise. A Walk to Grow On. Cook, Tom, illus. 40p. (ps-3). 1985. 5.95 (ISBN 0-910313-85-7). Parker Bros.
Rockwell, Anne & Rockwell, Harlow. I Love My Pets. LC 82-15188. (Illus.). 24p. (ps-k). 1982. 8.95 (ISBN 0-02-777710-3, Mcmillan Child Bk). Macmillan Child Grp.
Schlein, Miriam. That's Not Goldie! Magurn, Susan G., illus. LC 90-31560. 40p. (ps-1). 1990. PLB 13.95 (ISBN 0-671-70005-7). S&S Trade.
Schmeltz, Susan A. Pets I Wouldn't Pick. Appleby, Ellen, illus. LC 81-11071. 48p. (ps-3). 1982. 5.95 (ISBN 0-8193-1073-5); PLB 5.95 (ISBN 0-8193-1074-3). Parents.
Scruton, Clive. Mary's Pets. Scruton, Clive, illus. LC 88-12895. 32p. (ps-k). 1989. 10.95 (ISBN 0-688-08520-2). Lothrop.
Selden, George. Harry Cat's Pet Puppy. 176p. (gr. 2-6). 1975. pap. 3.25 (ISBN 0-440-45647-9, YB). Dell.
—Harry Cat's Pet Puppy. Williams, Garth, illus. LC 74-12436. 160p. (gr. 3 up). 1974. 13.95 (ISBN 0-374-32856-0). FS&G.
Sendak, Maurice & Margolis, Matthew. Some Swell Pup: Or Are You Sure You Want a Dog? Sendak, Maurice, illus. LC 75-42870. 32p. (ps up). 1985. 10.95 (ISBN 0-374-37134-2). FS&G.
Squire, Ann. One Hundred & One Questions & Answers about Pets & People. Karas, Brian, illus. LC 87-36457. 96p. (gr. 3-7). 1988. 13.95 (ISBN 0-02-786580-0, Mcmillan Child Bk). Macmillan Child Grp.
Swanson, Harry. Pets & Pathos. rev. ed. Swanson, Harry, illus. 52p. (gr. 9-12). 1989. pap. 5.00 (ISBN 1-878200-03-8). SwanMark Bks.
Taylor, Mark. The Great Rescue. Brett, Jan, illus. LC 83-25113. 40p. (gr. 1-5). 1984. 6.95 (ISBN 0-910313-28-8); incl. cassette 7.95 (ISBN 0-910313-61-X). Parker Bros.
Vail, Virginia. Pets Are For Keeps. 128p. (Orig.). (gr. 3-6). 1986. pap. 2.50 (ISBN 0-590-40181-5, Apple Paperbacks). Scholastic Inc.

White, James E. The Triumphs of Trisha & Tripod: Tripod Finds a Home. Senf, Richard L., illus. 22p. 1991. pap. 7.95 (ISBN 0-9629102-0-1). Pyramid TX. About a little handicapped girl named Trisha who dreams of finding a pet to share her love with. The story centers around a three-legged dog named Tripod, who is headed for the humane shelter's version of death row when he is rescued & adopted by Trisha. Trisha always wanted a "big fluffy dog with a fat waggily tail." But, Tripod hardly fitted that description. He's a brown mongrel but to Trisha he was the most wonderful thing that had ever happened in her life. When Trisha sees the doomed Tripod, she understands that just because Tripod lacks a leg, he doesn't lack in an abundance of puppy love. The triumphs of Trisha & Tripod teaches children to love people & animals just for what they are. The world is not perfect & neither are people. As cruel as children may seem at times to other children & other children's pets, they should be taught to

be giving. We must learn to love without compromise. That's what the triumphs of Trisha & Tripod is all about.
Publisher Provided Annotation.

Wood, Phyllis A. A Five-Color Buick & a Blue-Eyed Cat. LC 74-19156. 126p. (gr. 7 up). 1975. 7.95 (ISBN 0-664-32562-9, Westminster). Westminster John Knox.

Yashima, Mitsu & Yashima, Taro. Momo's Kitten. Yashima, Taro, illus. (gr. k-2). 1977. pap. 3.95 (ISBN 0-14-050200-9, Puffin). Puffin Bks.

Ziefert, Harriet. Pet Day. Brown, Richard, illus. (gr. 2-4). 1987. 7.95 (ISBN 0-316-98766-2). Little.

—Pet Day (Mr. Rose's Class) Brown, Richard, illus. 64p. 1988. pap. 2.50 (ISBN 0-553-15620-9, Skylark). Bantam.

PHANTOMS
see Apparitions; Ghosts

PHARMACY
see also Drugs

Monroe, Judy. Prescription Drugs. LC 88-22911. (Illus.). 48p. (gr. 5-6). 1988. PLB 10.95 (ISBN 0-89686-414-6, Crestwood Hse). Macmillan Child Grp.

PHEASANTS
Endo, Kimio. The Pheasant. Pohl, Kathy, ed. LC 85-28207. (Illus.). 32p. (gr. 3-7). 1986. PLB 16.67 (ISBN 0-8172-2549-8); pap. text ed. 9.27 (ISBN 0-8172-2574-9). Raintree Pubs.

Holmgren, Virginia. The Pheasant. LC 82-23672. (Illus.). 48p. (gr. 4 up). 1983. lib. bdg. 10.95 (ISBN 0-89686-222-4, Crestwood Hse). Macmillan Child Grp.

PHILADELPHIA
Balcer, Bernadette & O'Byrne-Pelham, Fran. Philadelphia. LC 88-20198. (Illus.). 60p. (gr. 3 up). 1989. PLB 12.95 (ISBN 0-87518-388-3, Dillon). Macmillan Child Grp.

Clay, Rebecca. Kidding Around Philadelphia: A Young Person's Guide to the City. (Illus.). 64p. (gr. 3 up). 1990. pap. 9.95 (ISBN 0-945465-71-8). John Muir.

Loewen, N. Philadelphia. (Illus.). (gr. 5 up). 1989. lib. bdg. 14.60 (ISBN 0-86592-542-9). Rourke Corp.

PHILADELPHIA–HISTORY–FICTION
Knight, James E. Seventh & Walnut, Life in Colonial Philadelphia. Guzzi, George, illus. LC 81-24036. 32p. (gr. 5-9). 1982. PLB 10.79 (ISBN 0-89375-740-3); pap. text ed. 2.95 (ISBN 0-89375-741-1). Troll Assocs.

Ratner-Gantshar, Barbara. Philadelphia: The City & the Bell. Miller, Wynne, ed. LC 76-43573. (Illus.). (gr. 4-8). 1976. 3.98 (ISBN 0-686-16319-2); tchr's. & research guide 3.48 (ISBN 0-686-16320-6). Artistic Endeavors.

PHILADELPHIA PHILLIES (BASEBALL TEAM)
Ashburn, Richie & Lewis, Allen. Richie Ashburn's Phillies Trivia. LC 83-3335. (Illus.). 128p. (Orig.). (gr. 5 up). 1983. lib. bdg. 15.90 (ISBN 0-89471-220-9); pap. 7.95 (ISBN 0-89471-219-5). Running Pr.

PHILANTHROPY
see Gifts; Social Work

PHILIP, KING (METACOMET) SACHEM OF THE WAMPANOAGS, d. 1676
Fradin, Dennis B. King Philip: Indian Leader. LC 88-31344. (Illus.). 48p. (gr. 3-6). 1990. PLB 14.95 (ISBN 0-89490-231-8). Enslow Pubs.

PHILIPPINE ISLANDS
Bailey, Donna & Sproule, Anna. Philippines. LC 90-9547. (Illus.). 32p. (gr. 2-5). 1990. PLB 14.64 (ISBN 0-8114-2564-9). Steck-V.

Harper, Peter & Peplow, Evelyn. Philippines Handbook. (Illus.). 96p. (Orig.). 1991. pap. 12.95 (ISBN 0-918373-62-X). Moon Pubns CA.

Haskins, James. Corazon Aquino: Leader of the Philippines. LC 87-24440. (Illus.). 128p. (gr. 6-12). 1988. lib. bdg. 17.95 (ISBN 0-89490-152-4). Enslow Pubs.

Lawson, Don. The New Philippines. rev. ed. (Illus.). 128p. (gr. 7-12). 1986. PLB 12.90 (ISBN 0-531-10269-6). Watts.

Lepthien, Emilie U. Corazon Aquino: President of the Philippines. LC 87-14030. (Illus.). 32p. (gr. 2-5). 1987. PLB 13.27 (ISBN 0-516-04170-3); pap. 2.95 (ISBN 0-516-44170-1). Childrens.

—The Philippines. LC 83-23152. (Illus.). 128p. (gr. 5-9). 1984. lib. bdg. 25.27 (ISBN 0-516-02782-4). Childrens.

Lerner Publications, Department of Geography Staff, ed. Phillipines in Pictures. (Illus.). 64p. (gr. 5 up). 1989. PLB 12.95 (ISBN 0-8225-1863-5). Lerner Pubns.

Lye, Keith. Take a Trip to the Philippines. LC 85-50164. (Illus.). 32p. (gr. 1-6). 1985. PLB 7.99 (ISBN 0-531-10013-8). Watts.

Nadel, Laurie. Corazon Aquino: Journey to Power. LC 86-33266. 93p. (gr. 6 up). 1987. lib. bdg. 13.98 (ISBN 0-671-63950-1). Messner.

Nance, John. Lobo of the Tasaday: A Stone Age Boy Meets the Modern World. Nance, John, illus. LC 81-14113. 56p. (gr. 3-7). 1982. 9.95 (ISBN 0-394-85077-7). Pantheon.

Sonneborn, Liz. The Philippines. (Illus.). (gr. 5 up). 1988. 14.95 (ISBN 0-7910-0105-9). Chelsea Hse.

Willis, Doris. Teacher's Guide to Pearl Makers. Lansdale, Paul, illus. 64p. (Orig.). 1989. pap. 5.95 (ISBN 0-377-00194-5). Friendship Pr.

PHILIPPINE ISLANDS–FICTION
Fuentes, Vilma M. Pearl Makers: Six Stories about the Children in the Philippines. (Illus., Orig.). (gr. 1-6). 1989. 4.95 (ISBN 0-377-00191-0). Friendship Pr.

Richardson, Arleta. Andrew's Secret. Payne, Peggy & Yoder, Tamra, eds. Secaur, Emiline, illus. 30p. (Orig.). (gr. 1-3). 1989. pap. 3.00 (ISBN 0-89367-143-6). Light & Life.

PHILOLOGY
see Language and Languages

PHILOLOGY, COMPARATIVE
Here are entered comparative studies of languages. General works on the history, philosophy, origin, etc. of languages are entered under Language and Languages.
see also Language and Languages

PHILOSOPHERS
Falcone, Vincent J. Great Thinkers, Great Ideas: An Introduction to Western Thought. LC 88-1639. 274p. (Orig.). (gr. 11-12). 1988. pap. text ed. 17.50 (ISBN 0-88427-075-0). North River.

Ozmon, H. Twelve Great Western Philosophers. Steinbauer, S., illus. LC 68-16403. 48p. (gr. 4 up). 1967. PLB 9.95 (ISBN 0-87783-046-0); pap. 3.94 deluxe ed (ISBN 0-87783-115-7). Oddo.

Russell, Bertrand. Bertrand Russell. Redpath, Ann, ed. Delessert, Etienne, illus. 32p. (gr. 9 up). 1986. PLB 10.45s.p. (ISBN 0-88682-012-X); 14.95 (ISBN 0-685-10393-5). Creative Ed.

PHILOSOPHY
see also Belief and Doubt; Ethics; God; Knowledge, Theory of; Logic; Mind and Body; Psychology; Universe also general subjects with the subdivision Philosophy, e.g. History–Philosophy, etc.

Falcone, Vincent J. Great Thinkers, Great Ideas: An Introduction to Western Thought. LC 88-1639. 274p. (Orig.). (gr. 11-12). 1988. pap. text ed. 17.50 (ISBN 0-88427-075-0). North River.

Franco, Eloise. The Young Look. (Illus.). (gr. 3-7). 1979. pap. 4.95 (ISBN 0-87516-294-0). DeVorss.

Lipman, Matthew. Kio & Gus. LC 79-9315. 77p. (gr. 3-4). 1982. pap. 9.00 (ISBN 0-916834-19-0, TX942-173). Inst Advncmnt Philos Child.

—Pixie. LC 81-67706. 98p. (Orig.). (gr. 3-4). 1981. pap. 9.00 (ISBN 0-916834-17-4, TX782-682). Inst Advncmnt Philos Child.

Roets, Lois. Philosophy & Philosophers. 48p. (gr. 5-12). 1987. pap. 8.00 tchr's. manual & text in one volume (ISBN 0-911943-12-9). Leadership Pub.

PHILOSOPHY–DICTIONARIES
Goodman, Florence G. A Young Person's Philosophical Dictionary. (gr. 5-12). 1978. pap. 7.95x (ISBN 0-917232-06-2). Gee Tee Bee.

PHILOSOPHY, MODERN
see also Evolution; Existentialism

PHILOSOPHY, MORAL
see Ethics

PHILOSOPHY AND RELIGION
see also Religion–Philosophy

PHILOSOPHY OF RELIGION
Van Dam, Eva. The Magic Life of Milarepa: Tibet's Great Yogi. LC 90-43321. (Illus.). 80p. (Orig.). (gr. 6 up). 1991. pap. 16.00 (ISBN 0-87773-473-9). Shambhala Pubns.

PHONETICS
see also Speech; Voice

Auld, Janice L. Cut & Paste Phonics: Extra Help for Troublesome Letter Combinations. (gr. 1-3). 1985. pap. 6.95 (ISBN 0-8224-5540-4). Fearon Teach Aids.

Bachman, Barbara. Frisky Phonics Fun I. Bachman, Barbara, illus. 152p. (gr. 1-3). 1984. wkbk. 10.95 (ISBN 0-86653-195-5, GA 548). Good Apple.

—Frisky Phonics Fun II. Bachman, Barbara, illus. 152p. (gr. 1-3). 1984. wkbk. 10.95 (ISBN 0-86653-212-9, GA 549). Good Apple.

Fields, Harriette. Phonics for the New Reader: Step-by-Step. Cox, Anne, illus. LC 90-70334. 128p. (ps-2). 1991. 17.95x (ISBN 0-9625802-0-1). Words Pub CO. "The author provides a ready-to-use blueprint for helping young children understand phonics & provides the necessary tools for that understanding," says former President of the National Association of State Boards of Education, Roseann Bentley. "This book provides clear, well-organized directions", & "I think this would be an excellent book for people striving to learn English as a second language." TABLE OF CONTENTS: Lesson 1- Letter Names, Shapes & Sounds; Lesson 2- Short Vowels; Lesson 3- Long Vowels; Lesson 4- Special Words & Letters; Lesson 5- Reading Consonant Combinations; Lesson 6- Reading Vowel Combinations; Lesson 7- Special Vowel Combinations; Lesson 8- Reading Vowel-Consonant Combinations.
Publisher Provided Annotation.

Foltzer, Monica. Professor Phonics Gives Sound Advice. 12th ed. Hoffmann, Jo-

Ann, illus. 1990. pap. text ed. 6.80 (ISBN 0-9607918-0-9, A 505419). St Ursula.
PROFESSOR PHONICS GIVES SOUND ADVICE, the primary book, is unique in that it has the only totally organized phonics system. All of the consonant sounds are taught around four categories of vowels. It is so streamlined that all 42 basic sounds are taught on 23 pages interspersed with practice pages. Sounds arranged in more difficult spelling patterns follow. A SOUND TRACK TO READING has exactly the same format but starts with two-syllable words. All the basic sounds are taught on 14 pages. This advanced book is not geared for intermediate grades & up. Phonics is NOT reading. It is reading's only sure foundation for unlocking unknown words. The system also contains 38 PICTURE KEY WORD CARDS, MANUALS & a SPELLING WORD LIST. At the end of the year, first graders can spell 1500 words without memorizing. Taking regular spelling first helps greatly. The ten percent of non-phonetic words then fall into place. Systematic, intensive phonics should be taught first & fast before sight words are introduced because all one does is slide sounds together. Anyone can teach another to read in this manner if one has an organized system. As Mary Pride says in her New Big Book Of Home Learning, "The program author really knows her stuff."
Publisher Provided Annotation.

—Spelling Phonics Gives Sound Advice. 5th ed. 16p. 1984. pap. text ed. 1.20x (ISBN 0-9607918-2-5, 801878). St Ursula.

Kirsten, Suzanne. Begin with Phonics. Kahn, Betsey, ed. LC 81-85695. (Illus.). 80p. (Orig.). (gr. 1-4). 1982. pap. 4.95 (ISBN 0-89709-033-0). Liberty Pub.

Lockhart, Charlotte F. Discover Intensive Phonics for Yourself. rev. ed. Griffin, Glen C., frwd. by. LC 83-71502. 452p. 1983. tchrs. ed. 49.95 (ISBN 0-9605654-1-8). Char-L.

Magos, Eunice & Hornnes, Esther. Fairy Tales & Phonics. Sussman, Ellen, ed. Burris, Priscilla, illus. 36p. (Orig.). (gr. k-2). 1984. pap. text ed. 4.95 (ISBN 0-933606-25-7, MS-625). Monkey Sisters.

Moncure, Jane B. Word Bird Makes Words with Pig. LC 83-23945. (Illus.). 32p. (gr. k-2). 1984. PLB 11.97 (ISBN 0-89565-262-5). Childs World.

Mylet, Trish & Sheffield, Antoinette. The Bed. Burton, Barry W., ed. (Illus.). 16p. (ps-2). 1988. pap. text ed. 5.00 (ISBN 0-945590-04-0). Sizzy Bks.

—The Box. Burton, Barry W., ed. (Illus.). 16p. (ps-2). 1988. pap. text ed. 5.00 (ISBN 0-945590-08-3). Sizzy Bks.

—Dod & Bob. Burton, Barry W., ed. (Illus.). 16p. (ps-2). 1988. pap. text ed. 5.00 (ISBN 0-945590-07-5). Sizzy Bks.

—Hun & Sum. Burton, Barry W., ed. (Illus.). 16p. (ps-2). 1988. pap. text ed. 5.00 (ISBN 0-945590-09-1). Sizzy Bks.

—The Hut. Burton, Barry W., ed. (Illus.). 16p. (ps-2). 1988. pap. text ed. 5.00 (ISBN 0-945590-10-5). Sizzy Bks.

—Jan & Pam. Burton, Barry W., ed. (Illus.). 16p. (ps-2). 1988. pap. text ed. 5.00 (ISBN 0-945590-01-6). Sizzy Bks.

—Pals. Burton, Barry W., ed. (Illus.). 20p. (ps-2). 1988. pap. text ed. 5.00 (ISBN 0-945590-11-3). Sizzy Bks.

—The Pit. Burton, Barry W., ed. (Illus.). 16p. (ps-2). 1988. pap. text ed. 5.00 (ISBN 0-945590-06-7). Sizzy Bks.

—Rex & Tex. Burton, Barry W., ed. (Illus.). 16p. (ps-2). 1988. pap. text ed. 5.00 (ISBN 0-945590-03-2). Sizzy Bks.

—Siz & Liz. Burton, Barry W., ed. (Illus.). 16p. (ps-2). 1988. pap. text ed. 5.00 (ISBN 0-945590-05-9). Sizzy Bks.

—The Van. Burton, Barry W., ed. (Illus.). 16p. (ps-2). 1988. pap. text ed. 5.00 (ISBN 0-945590-02-4). Sizzy Bks.

Palker, Kathy. Vowel Puzzles. Fowler, Christopher & Clapsdale, Mark, illus. 32p. (gr. 1-2). 1984. pap. 1.98 (ISBN 0-88724-095-X, CD-7034). Carson-Dellos.

Schaffer, Frank, Publications Staff. Getting Ready for Phonics. (Illus.). 24p. (ps-k). 1980. wkbk. 3.98 (ISBN 0-86734-018-5, FS 3031). Schaffer Pubns.
—Phonics: Consonants. (Illus.). 24p. (ps-2). 1978. wkbk. 3.98 (ISBN 0-86734-003-7, FS 3004). Schaffer Pubns.
—Phonics: Vowels. (Illus.). 24p. (gr. 1-3). 1978. wkbk. 3.98 (ISBN 0-86734-004-5, FS 3005). Schaffer Pubns.
Stringham, Alene. Get Set to Learn Phonics. Sussman, Ellen, intro. by. Burris, Priscilla, illus. 64p. (Orig.). (ps-2). 1989. pap. 6.95 (ISBN 0-933606-69-9). Monkey Sisters.
Taulbee, Annette. Phonics. (Illus.). 24p. (ps-k). 1986. 3.98 (ISBN 0-86734-066-5, FS-3058). Schaffer Pubns.

PHONICS
see Phonetics
PHONOGRAPH
see also Sound–Recording and Reproducing
PHONOLOGY
see Phonetics
PHOTOGRAPHERS
Gherman, Beverly. Georgia O'Keefe: The "Wideness & Wonder" of Her World. LC 85-26860. (Illus.). 144p. (gr. 4 up). 1986. 13.95 (ISBN 0-689-31164-8, Atheneum Child Bk). Macmillan Child Grp.
Jann, Gayle. A Day in the Life of a Photographer. Jann, Gayle, illus. LC 87-13751. 32p. (gr. 4-8). 1988. PLB 11.79 (ISBN 0-8167-1123-2); pap. text ed. 2.95 (ISBN 0-8167-1124-0). Troll Assocs.

PHOTOGRAPHY
see also Cameras; Nature Study
Czaja, Paul C. Writing with Light: A Simple Workshop in Basic Photography. LC 72-93261. 96p. (gr. 6 up). 1973. 12.95 (ISBN 0-85699-068-X). Chatham Pr.
Fischer, Robert. Trick Photography: Crazy Things You Can Do with Cameras. LC 80-22333. (Illus.). 160p. (gr. 8 up). 1980. 9.95 (ISBN 0-87131-332-4); pap. 5.95 (ISBN 0-87131-335-9). M Evans.
Freeman, Tony. Photography. LC 83-7359. (Illus.). 48p. (gr. k-4). 1983. PLB 14.60 (ISBN 0-516-01704-7). Childrens.
Hasanati, J. A. Sell Your Photos Overseas. Williams, Curtis, ed. 100p. Date not set. 10.00 (ISBN 0-317-94052-X). Creative Enterprise.
Kohn, Eugene. Photography: A Manual for Shutterbugs. Plasencia, Peter P., illus. Noa, Pedro A., photos by. (Illus.). (gr. 3-7). 1965. pap. 1.25 (ISBN 0-685-03891-2). P-H.
Mitchell, Barbara. Click! A Story about George Eastman. Hosking-Smith, Jan, illus. 64p. (gr. 3-6). 1986. PLB 9.95 (ISBN 0-87614-289-7); pap. 4.95 (ISBN 0-87614-472-5). Carolrhoda Bks.
Moss, Miriam. Fashion Photographer. LC 90-15059. (Illus.). 32p. (gr. 5-6). 1991. RSBE 11.95 (ISBN 0-89686-608-4, Crestwood Hse). Macmillan Child Grp.
Owens-Knudsen, Vic. Photography Basics: An Introduction for Young People. Petronella, Michael, illus. LC 83-9775. 48p. (gr. 5-9). 1983. 9.95 (ISBN 0-13-664995-5). P-H.
Peach, S. & Butterfield, M. Photography from Beginner to Expert. (Illus.). 48p. (gr. 6 up). 1987. PLB 13.96 (ISBN 0-88110-292-X); pap. 6.95 (ISBN 0-7460-0107-X). EDC.
Photography. (Illus.). 64p. (gr. 6-12). 1983. pap. 1.85 (ISBN 0-8395-3334-9, 3334). BSA.
PHOTOGRAPHY, ARTISTIC
Hoban, Tana. Shadows & Reflections. LC 89-30461. (Illus.). 32p. (ps up). 1990. 12.95 (ISBN 0-688-07089-2); lib. bdg. 12.88 (ISBN 0-688-07090-6). Greenwillow.
Lynch, Marietta & Perry, Patricia. No More Monkeys: A Photographic Version of the Children's Finger Game. (Orig.). (ps-3). pap. 2.95 (ISBN 0-9610962-0-9). M Lynch.
PHOTOGRAPHY–ESTHETICS
see Photography, Artistic
PHOTOGRAPHY–FICTION
Calvert, Patricia. Yesterday's Daughter. LC 86-13753. 144p. (gr. 7 up). 1986. 12.95 (ISBN 0-684-18746-9, Scribners Young Read). Macmillan Child Grp.
Levoy, Myron. Pictures of Adam. LC 85-45268. 224p. (gr. 6-9). 1986. PLB 12.89 (ISBN 0-06-023829-1). HarpC Child Bks.
Willard, Nancy. Simple Pictures Are Best. DePaola, Tomie, illus. LC 78-6424. (ps-3). 1978. pap. 3.95 (ISBN 0-15-682625-9, VoyB). HarBraceJ.
Yates, Madeleine. It's School Picture Day. Sims, Blanche, illus. 32p. (gr. k-3). 1987. pap. 1.00 (ISBN 0-687-19730-9). Abingdon.
PHOTOGRAPHY–VOCATIONAL GUIDANCE
Blumenfeld, Milton J. Careers in Photography. Blumenfeld, Milton J., photos by. LC 79-16299. (Illus.). 36p. (gr. 2-5). 1979. PLB 7.95 (ISBN 0-8225-0338-7). Lerner Pubns.
Henderson, Kathy. Market Guide for Young Artists & Photographers. LC 90-39084. (Illus.). 176p. (Orig.). (gr. 3 up). 1990. pap. 10.95 (ISBN 1-55870-176-1, Shoe Tree Pr). Betterway Pubns.
Osinki, Christine. I Can Be a Photographer. LC 85-30854. (Illus.). 32p. (gr. k-3). 1986. PLB 13.93 (ISBN 0-516-01894-9). Childrens.
PHOTOGRAPHY OF ANIMALS
see also Animal Painting and Illustration

Arrabito, James. Cameras at the Zoo. Glaser, Mary J., illus. 16p. (Orig.). (gr. 3-10). 1991. pap. 4.95 (ISBN 0-9622596-0-8). Arraster Pub.

CAMERAS AT THE ZOO, is an elementary instruction book providing quick & easy tips to create special pictures. Photography basics, as well as artistic insights are covered. Written & photographed by Northwest award winning commercial photographer James Arrabito, CAMERAS AT THE ZOO, is printed on recycled paper combined with a durable waterproof coating, the size is perfect to fit in the amateur's camera bag or parent's knap sack. The book is recommended for ages 10 to adult. The suggested retail price of $4.95 meets the need for a how-to photography book under five dollars. Available at the WOODLAND PARK ZOO BOOK STORE, several Northwest book stores, & a few selected camera stores, or purchase publisher direct (prices include shipping & handling) SORRY NO C.O.D. "CAMERAS AT THE ZOO, fills the need for a simple field guide to a hobby families can do all their lives. Kids love to take pictures to "show & tell, to Grandma's", Arrabito says. "And it's fun & surprisingly cheap to blow a picture up to poster size & put it on your wall. It's a real confidence-builder. Published by ARRASTAR PUBLISHING'S, HAPPY KIDS, c/o P.O. BOX 916, EVERETT, WASHINGTON 98201.
Publisher Provided Annotation.

Campbell, John C. Two Dogs Plus. Cunningham, Imogen & Richardson, David, illus. 95p. (Orig.). (gr. 8 up). 1984. pap. text ed. 9.95 (ISBN 0-9613596-0-9); pap. 7.95 (ISBN 0-685-09160-0). Deer Creek Pr.
PHOTOSYNTHESIS
Asimov, Isaac. How Did We Find out about Photosynthesis. Kors, Erika, illus. 32p. (gr. 1-4). 1989. 11.95 (ISBN 0-8027-6899-7); PLB 12.85 (ISBN 0-8027-6886-5). Walker & Co.
Nakatani, Herbert Y. Photosynthesis. Head, J. J., ed. Steffen, Ann T., illus. LC 84-45838. 16p. (Orig.). (gr. 10 up). 1988. pap. text ed. 2.15 (ISBN 0-89278-109-2, 45-9793). Carolina Biological.
PHYSICAL CHEMISTRY
see Chemistry, Physical and Theoretical
PHYSICAL CULTURE
see Physical Education and Training
PHYSICAL EDUCATION AND TRAINING
see also Athletics; Coaching (Athletics); Exercise; Games; Gymnastics; Health Education; Physical Fitness; Sports; also names of kinds of exercises, e.g. Fencing; Judo
Bershad, Carol & Bernick, Deborah. Bodyworks: The Kids' Guide to Food & Physical Fitness. Selig, Heidi J., illus. 240p. (gr. 5-9). 1981. Random.
Black, John & Evans, Patrick. John Black Presents Power Build. (Illus.). 92p. 1990. pap. 9.95 (ISBN 0-929994-05-1). Crains Muscle.
Heron, Jackie. Careers in Health & Fitness. rev. ed. Rosen, Ruth, ed. (Illus.). 160p. (gr. 7 up). 1990. 12.95 (ISBN 0-8239-1162-4). Rosen Group.
Isberg, Emily. Peak Performance. (gr. 3 up). 1989. pap. 14.95 (ISBN 0-671-67750-0); pap. 5.95 (ISBN 0-671-67745-4). S&S Trade.
Jarrell, Steve. Working Out with Weights. LC 77-1919. (gr. 8 up). 1978. pap. 7.95 (ISBN 0-668-04221-4). Prentice Hall Pr.
McNichols, Joan & McNichols, Larry. Sports. Meyers, Barbara, illus. (Orig.). (gr. 1-9). 1974. pap. 6.95 (ISBN 0-918932-41-6). Activity Resources.
Ponce, Omar. Educate para una Mejor Condicion Fisica: Guia Basica para el Desarrollo de un Programa de Eficiencia Fisica. Figueroa, Ivelisse, illus. (SPA.). 75p. (Orig.). 1986. write for info. B Ponce.
Stillwell, Jim. The Perceptual-Motor Activities Book. Gimlin, Rick & Kamiya, Artie, illus. 96p. (Orig.). (gr. k-6). 1990. pap. 10.00 (ISBN 0-945872-05-4). Great Activities Pub Co.
Thomas, Art. Merry-Go-Rounds. Overlie, George, illus. LC 81-3825. 48p. (gr. k-4). 1981. PLB 9.95 (ISBN 0-87614-168-8). Carolrhoda Bks.
PHYSICAL FITNESS
Diet & Exercise. (Illus.). (gr. 5 up). lib. bdg. 14.00 (ISBN 0-86625-280-0). Rourke Corp.
Fraser, K. & Tatchell, J. You & Your Fitness & Health. (Illus.). 48p. (gr. 6-10). 1987. PLB 13.96 (ISBN 0-88110-234-2); pap. 6.95 (ISBN 0-7460-0004-9). EDC.
Hammer, Arnold. The Rosen Photo Guide to a Career in Health & Fitness. (Illus.). (gr. 7-12). 1988. lib. bdg. 12.95 (ISBN 0-8239-0820-8). Rosen Group.

Hyman, Jane & Millen-Posner, Barbara. The Fitness Book: The Diet & Exercise Book. Barish, Wendy, ed. (Illus.). 192p. (gr. 5 up). 1984. pap. 3.95 (ISBN 0-671-46433-7, Little Simon); PLB 9.49 (ISBN 0-685-09179-1). S&S Trade.

Maitland, William J. Weight Training for Gifted Athletes. Mollen, Art, intro. by. LC 89-90833. (Illus.). 147p. (Orig.). (gr. 8 up). 1990. pap. 17.95 (ISBN 0-936759-01-1). Maitland Enter.
Co-educational training & nutrition information for recreational through professional athletes ages 14 through adult. Endorsed by Dr. Art Mollen. Has easy-to-read large print with explicit photos for each exercise. Text is block paragraphs & non-technical language allowing quick sight reading. In-season - off-season schedules are discussed using psycho-physiological & plyometric disciplines. Warm-ups - warm-downs with proper & improper stretching are discussed fully. Development of the human body from childhood to maturation with muscle-skeletal diagrams. Charts for record of progress & alternate advanced exercises. Table of contents-bibliography. Author has trained & coached athletes in all sports for thirty years including recreational training activities for fitness. "Makes good sense for improving skills"--Dr. Art Mollen. "...I found your book. Used it - our game has improved immensely"--John Barclay, Hockey Coach, Phoenix, Arizona. "Taught me a great deal about training young athletes"--Michael Johnson, YMCA Coach, N.J. "Finally the answers I've been seeking in language I can understand"--Cara Schappat, Bangor, Maine. Also see BEGINNING WEIGHT TRAINING FOR YOUNG ATHLETES - AGES 12 THROUGH ADULT by same author.
Publisher Provided Annotation.

Martinez, Alicia. Feeling Fit. Richey, Donald, illus. LC 90-10864. 128p. (gr. 5-9). 1990. PLB 10.89 (ISBN 0-8167-2140-8); pap. text ed. 2.95 (ISBN 0-8167-2141-6). Troll Assocs.
Personal Fitness. (Illus.). 56p. (gr. 6-12). 1990. pap. 1.85 (ISBN 0-8395-3286-5, 3286A). BSA.
Physical Fitness Skill Book. (Illus.). 32p. (gr. 3-4). 1975. pap. 1.50x (ISBN 0-8395-6590-9, 6590); tchr's. guide , 12 pgs. 0.50x (ISBN 0-8395-8230-7); troop leader's can-do kit , 24 pgs. 0.50 (ISBN 0-8395-8210-2). BSA.
Roberts, Alison J. Fun with Fitness. Hayes, Dympna, ed. Mansfield, Renee & Pawczuk, Eugene, illus. 32p. (gr. 2). 1987. PLB 13.85 (ISBN 0-88625-167-2); pap. 2.50 (ISBN 0-88625-157-5). Durkin Hayes Pub.

Schade, Charlene. Move with Me One Two Three. Ziebarth, Pat, ed. Pileggi, Steve, illus. Senter, Sheri, intro. by. (Illus.). 58p. (Orig.). (ps-1). 1988. Includes audio cassette. 16.90 (ISBN 0-924860-00-6). Exer Fun Pub.
"Move With Me 1, 2, 3" blends the concepts of movement, numbers & animals with music. Providing learning through play, the book gives children the numerals 1 to 20, the names of 20 animals & 20 basic fitness moves. Each left-hand page presents one sentence which tells of the animal, number & movement. The numeral is under the sentence to reinforce the counting concept. On the opposite page, Steve Pileggi provides black-line, whimsical illustrations of the animals & their movements. The learning process continues with music & lyrics on the accompanying audio cassette by gold

record song writers Jim & Dee Patton. The 20 activity songs plus a title song will make feet tap, bodies sway & faces smile. Author Charlene Schade also wrote the companion book "Move With Me From A to Z" which has an accompanying audio cassette by Don Dunn. Schade, a UCLA graduate in physical education/dance, gives workshops & presentations for local, state, national & international organizations. Charlene Schade, Steve Pileggi & the Pattons have combined efforts to provide kids with a fun way to be active, involved learners. "Move With Me 1, 2, 3" is a terrific investment for anyone interested in providing excellent learning materials & having fun with kids ages 2-7. *Publisher Provided Annotation.*

Simon, Nissa. Good Sports: Plain Talk about Health & Fitness for Teens. Tobin, Patricia, illus. LC 89-78556. 128p. (gr. 7 up). 1990. 13.95 (ISBN 0-690-04902-1, Crowell Jr Bks); PLB 13.89 (ISBN 0-690-04904-8, Crowell Jr Bks). HarpC Child Bks.

Sullivan, George. Better Weight Training for Boys. (Illus.). 64p. (gr. 8-12). Date not set. pap. 3.95 (ISBN 0-396-08293-9, Putnam). Putnam Pub Group.

Time-Life Books Editors. Super Firm: Tough Workouts. (Illus.). 144p. 1989. 17.27 (ISBN 0-8094-6134-X); lib. bdg. 23.27 (ISBN 0-8094-6135-8). Time-Life.

—Walking & Running. (Illus.). 144p. 1989. 17.27 (ISBN 0-8094-6130-7); lib. bdg. 23.27 (ISBN 0-8094-6131-5). Time-Life.

Von Yon, Anthony. How to Slam Dunk: The Human Dynamics of Bodies in Motion & the Theory of Dunk Radiation. (Illus.). 70p. (Orig.). (gr. 9-12). 1988. pap. text ed. 6.95 (ISBN 0-942385-00-4). Nutshell Pub.

Ward, Brian R. Exercise & Fitness. FS Staff, ed. (Illus.). 48p. (gr. 4-9). 1988. PLB 12.40 (ISBN 0-531-10562-8). Watts.

Zeldis, Yona. Coping with Beauty, Fitness & Fashion. Rosen, Ruth, ed. Daven, Douglas, illus. LC 86-24850. 128p. (gr. 7 up). 1987. PLB 12.95 (ISBN 0-8239-0731-7). Rosen Group.

PHYSICAL GEOGRAPHY

see also Climate; Earth; Earthquakes; Glaciers; Ice; Icebergs; Lakes; Meteorology; Mountains; Ocean; Rivers; Tides; Volcanoes; Winds

Seddon, Tony & Bailey, Jill. Physical World. LC 87-6855. (Illus.). 160p. (gr. 3 up). 1987. 12.95 (ISBN 0-385-24179-8). Doubleday.

PHYSICAL STAMINA

see Physical Fitness

PHYSICAL THERAPY–VOCATIONAL GUIDANCE

Paige, David. A Day in the Life of a Sports Therapist. Ruhlin, Roger, illus. LC 84-2433. 32p. (gr. 4-8). 1985. PLB 11.79 (ISBN 0-8167-0099-0); pap. text ed. 2.95 (ISBN 0-8167-0100-8). Troll Assocs.

PHYSICAL TRAINING

see Physical Education and Training

PHYSICALLY HANDICAPPED

see also Blind; Deaf

Alexander, Sally. Mom Can't See Me. Ancona, George, illus. LC 89-13241. 48p. (gr. 1-5). 1990. 14.95 (ISBN 0-02-700401-5, Mcmillan Child Bk). Macmillan Child Grp.

Bergman, Thomas. On Our Own Terms: Children Living with Physical Handicaps. LC 88-42973. (Illus.). 48p. (gr. 4-5). 1989. PLB 10.95 (ISBN 1-55532-942-X). Gareth Stevens Inc.

Bernstein, Joanne E. & Fireside, Bryna. Special Parents, Special Children. Mathews, Judith, ed. Bernstein, Michael, photos by. (Illus.). 48p. (gr. 3-7). 1991. 11.50 (ISBN 0-8075-7559-3). A Whitman.

Berry, Joy. About Physical Disabilities. Bartholomew, illus. 48p. (gr. 3 up). 1990. PLB 14.60 (ISBN 0-516-02954-1); 6.95 (ISBN 0-516-22954-0). Childrens.

Boy Scouts of America. Handicap Awareness. (Illus.). 48p. (gr. 6-12). 1981. pap. 1.85 (ISBN 0-8395-3370-5, 3370). BSA.

Cattoche, Robert J. Computers for the Disabled. LC 86-9184. (Illus.). 96p. (gr. 5-8). 1986. PLB 10.40 (ISBN 0-531-10212-2). Watts.

Chaney, Sky & Fisher, Pam, eds. The Discovery Book: A Helpful Guide for the World Written by Children with Disabilities. rev. ed. (Illus.). 100p. (gr. 3-10). 1989. pap. 7.95 (ISBN 0-9616891-1-0). UCPANB.

Exley, Helen. What It's Like to Be Me. 2nd ed. (Illus.). 127p. (gr. 4-11). 1984. pap. 10.95 (ISBN 0-377-00144-9). Friendship Pr.

Greenfield, Eloise & Revis, Alesia. Alesia. Ford, George, illus. Bond, Sandra T., photos by. (Illus.). 80p. (gr. 5 up). 1981. 9.95 (ISBN 0-399-20831-3, Philomel). Putnam Pub Group.

Johnson, Ann D. The Value of Facing a Challenge: The Story of Terry Fox. Pileggi, Steve, illus. LC 83-8542. 64p. (gr. k-6). 1985. 9.95 (ISBN 0-7172-8134-5, Pub. by Value Communications). Oak Tree Pubns.

Peterson, Jeanne W. I Have a Sister, My Sister Is Deaf. Ray, Deborah, illus. LC 76-24306. (gr. k-3). 1977. 13.95 (ISBN 0-06-024701-0); PLB 13.89 (ISBN 0-06-024702-9). HarpC Child Bks.

Physical Handicaps. (Illus.). (gr. 6-12). 1993. 18.95 (ISBN 0-7910-0073-7). Chelsea Hse.

Powers, Mary E. Our Teacher's in a Wheelchair. Tucker, Kathleen, ed. Powers, Mary E., illus. LC 86-1623. 32p. (ps-3). 1986. 10.95 (ISBN 0-8075-6240-8). A Whitman.

Prall, Jo. My Sister's Special. Gray, Linda, photos by. LC 85-13209. 32p. (gr. k-3). 1985. PLB 14.60 (ISBN 0-516-03862-1). Childrens.

Richmond, Sandra. Wheels for Walking. Kroupa, Melanie, ed. LC 85-70855. 196p. (gr. 6 up). 1985. 13.95 (ISBN 0-316-74439-5, Joy St Bks). Little.

Stein, Sara B. About Handicaps. LC 73-15270. (Illus.). 48p. (ps-8). 1984. 8.95 (ISBN 0-8027-7225-0); pap. write for info. (ISBN 0-685-07283-5). Walker & Co.

—About Handicaps. LC 73-15270. (Illus.). 48p. (gr. 1 up). 1974. 12.95 (ISBN 0-8027-6174-7). Walker & Co.

PHYSICALLY HANDICAPPED–BIOGRAPHY

Gibson, William. The Miracle Worker. (gr. 6-9). 1984. pap. 3.50 (ISBN 0-553-24778-6). Bantam.

Greenfield, Eloise & Revis, Alesia. Alesia. Ford, George, illus. Bond, Sandra T., photos by. (Illus.). 80p. (gr. 5 up). 1981. 9.95 (ISBN 0-399-20831-3, Philomel). Putnam Pub Group.

Hafford, Jeannette N. Tiny Goes to the Doctor. 48p. (Orig.). (gr. 3-8). 1990. pap. write for info. Tinys Self Help Bks.

Killilea, Marie. Karen. 286p. (gr. 5 up). 1980. pap. 3.50 (ISBN 0-440-94376-0, LFL). Dell.

Martin, Patricia S. Ted Kennedy Jr. He Faced His Challenge. (Illus.). 24p. (gr. 1-4). 1987. PLB 12.33 (ISBN 0-86592-174-1). Rourke Corp.

Miller, Robyn. Robyn's Book: A True Diary. 179p. (Orig.). (gr. 7 up). 1986. pap. 2.25 (ISBN 0-590-41331-7, Point). Scholastic Inc.

Rosenberg, Maxine B. My Friend Leslie: The Story of a Handicapped Child. Ancona, George, photos by. LC 82-12734. (Illus.). (gr. 1-3). 1983. 13.95 (ISBN 0-688-01690-1); PLB 13.88 (ISBN 0-688-01691-X). Lothrop.

PHYSICALLY HANDICAPPED–EDUCATION

Miller, Mary Beth & Ancona, George. Handtalk School. LC 90-24030. (Illus.). 32p. (ps-6). 1991. 14.95 (ISBN 0-02-700912-2, Four Winds). Macmillan Child Grp.

PHYSICALLY HANDICAPPED–FICTION

Andrews, Jean F. Hasta Luego, San Diego. LC 90-27125. 104p. (Orig.). (gr. 3-6). 1991. pap. 4.95 (ISBN 0-930323-83-1, Pub. by K Green Pubns). Gallaudet Univ Pr.

Burnett, Frances. The Secret Garden. 1989. pap. 2.50 (ISBN 0-451-52080-7). NAL-Dutton.

Burnett, Frances H. The Secret Garden. 302p. 1981. Repr. PLB 19.95x (ISBN 0-89966-326-5). Buccaneer Bks.

—Secret Garden. (gr. k-6). 1989. pap. 3.50 (ISBN 0-440-47709-3, Pub. by Yearling Classics); pap. 2.75 (ISBN 0-440-97709-6, Dell Trade Pbks). Dell.

—The Secret Garden. (gr. 4-6). 1987. pap. 2.25 (ISBN 0-14-035004-7, Puffin). Puffin Bks.

—The Secret Garden. Mitchell, Kathy, illus. 320p. (gr. 4 up). 1987. 12.95 (ISBN 0-448-06029-9, G&D). Putnam Pub Group.

—The Secret Garden. Tudor, Tasha, illus. LC 62-17457. 256p. (gr. 4-8). 1987. pap. 3.50 (ISBN 0-06-440188-X, Trophy). HarpC Child Bks.

—The Secret Garden. McNulty, Faith, afterword by. 1987. pap. 2.95 (ISBN 0-451-52417-9, Sig Classics). NAL-Dutton.

—The Secret Garden. Allen, Thomas B., illus. Howe, James, adapted by. LC 86-17788. (Illus.). 72p. (gr. k-5). 1987. 13.95 (ISBN 0-394-86467-0, Random Juv); lib. bdg. 12.99 (ISBN 0-394-96467-5). Random.

—The Secret Garden. (gr. k-6). 8.98 (ISBN 0-517-63225-X). Outlet Bk Co.

—The Secret Garden. Hague, Michael, illus. LC 86-22780. 240p. (gr. 4-6). 1987. 18.95 (ISBN 0-8050-0277-4). H Holt & Co.

—The Secret Garden. 304p. (Orig.). (gr. 4-6). 1987. pap. 2.95 (ISBN 0-590-40720-1, Pub. by Apple Classics). Scholastic Inc.

—The Secret Garden. Lowry, Lois, intro. by. 256p. 1987. pap. 2.95 (ISBN 0-553-21201-X, Bantam Classics). Bantam.

—The Secret Garden. Betts, Louise, adapted by. LC 87-15490. (Illus.). (gr. 3-6). 1987. PLB 12.89 (ISBN 0-8167-1203-4); pap. 3.95 (ISBN 0-8167-1204-2). Troll Assocs.

—The Secret Garden. 360p. 1987. pap. 4.95 (ISBN 0-19-281772-8). Oxford U Pr.

—The Secret Garden. Sanderson, Ruth, illus. LC 86-46002. 240p. 1988. 18.95 (ISBN 0-394-55431-0). Knopf.

—The Secret Garden. Hughes, Shirley, illus. 240p. (gr. 5 up). 1989. pap. 18.95 (ISBN 0-670-82571-9). Viking Child Bks.

—The Secret Garden. 304p. (gr. 4-7). 1987. pap. 2.95 (ISBN 0-590-43346-6). Scholastic Inc.

—Secret Garden. 1987. pap. 3.50 (ISBN 0-440-40055-4). Dell.

—Secret Garden. 288p. 1990. pap. 2.50 (ISBN 0-8125-0501-8). Tor Bks.

—Secret Garden. Howell, Troy, illus. 272p. (gr. 4 up). 1987. 10.95 (ISBN 0-681-40056-0). Longmeadow Pr.

—Secret Garden. 1991. pap. 3.99 (ISBN 0-8125-1910-8). Tor Bks.

Burnett, Francis H. The Secret Garden: A Young Reader's Edition of the Classic Story. Abr. ed. Crawford, Dale, illus. LC 90-80198. 56p. (gr. 1 up). 1990. 9.98 (ISBN 0-89471-860-6, Courage Bks). Running Pr.

Carlson, Judy. Here Comes Kate! (Illus.). 32p. (gr. 1-4). 1989. PLB 13.32 (ISBN 0-8172-3515-9). Raintree Pubs.

Carlson, Nancy. Arnie & the New Kid. (Illus.). 32p. (ps-2). 1990. pap. 11.95 (ISBN 0-670-82499-2). Viking Child Bks.

Gerson, Corrine. Passing Through. 208p. (gr. 8 up). 1980. pap. 1.50 (ISBN 0-440-96958-1, LFL). Dell.

Gould, Marilyn. Golden Daffodils. LC 84-40758. 1985. PLB 12.89 (ISBN 0-397-32164-3, Lipp Jr Bks). HarpC Child Bks.

Halvorson, Marilyn. Hold on, Geronimo. LC 87-25656. 240p. (gr. 7 up). 1988. pap. 14.95 (ISBN 0-385-29665-7). Delacorte.

Henriod, Lorraine. Grandma's Wheelchair. Tucker, Kathy, ed. LC 81-12918. (Illus.). 32p. (ps-1). 1982. PLB 12.95 (ISBN 0-8075-3035-2). A Whitman.

Holcomb, Nan. A Smile from Andy. Yoder, Dot, illus. 32p. (ps-2). 1989. pap. 5.95 (ISBN 0-944727-04-2). Jason & Nordic Pubs.

Holland, Isabelle. The Unfrightened Dark. LC 89-31570. 128p. (gr. 6-8). 1990. 13.95 (ISBN 0-316-37173-4). Little.

Howard, Ellen. Circle of Giving. LC 83-15631. 112p. (gr. 4-6). 1984. 12.95 (ISBN 0-689-31027-7, Atheneum Child Bk). Macmillan Child Grp.

Howe, James. A Night Without Stars. LC 82-16278. 192p. (gr. 4-7). 1983. 13.95 (ISBN 0-689-30957-0, Atheneum Child Bk). Macmillan Child Grp.

Klusmeyer, Joann. Shelly from Rockytop Farm. Taylor, Neil, illus. 65p. (gr. 3-6). 1986. 5.95 (ISBN 1-55523-014-8). Winston-Derek.

Kneeland, Linda C. Cookie. Fargo, Todd, illus. 32p. (ps-2). 1989. pap. 5.95 (ISBN 0-944727-05-0). Jason & Nordic Pubs.

Knowles, Anne. Under the Shadow. LC 82-48857. 128p. (gr. 5 up). 1983. PLB 11.89 (ISBN 0-06-023222-6). HarpC Child Bks.

Lasker, Joe. Nick Joins In. Tucker, Kathleen, ed. Lasker, Joe, illus. LC 79-29637. 32p. (gr. 1-3). 1980. PLB 12.95 (ISBN 0-8075-5612-2). A Whitman.

Little, Jean. Listen for the Singing. LC 90-40019. 272p. (gr. 4-7). 1991. PLB 14.89 (ISBN 0-06-023910-7). HarpC Child Bks.

Madsen, Jane M., et al. Please Don't Tease Me. 32p. (gr. 3-4). 1980. pap. 2.95 (ISBN 0-8170-0876-4). Judson.

Perske, Robert. Don't Stop the Music. (gr. 12 up). 1986. pap. 9.95 (ISBN 0-687-11060-2). Abingdon.

—Show Me No Mercy: A Compelling Story of Remarkable Courage. 144p. (Orig.). (gr. 12 up). 1984. pap. 9.95 (ISBN 0-687-38435-4). Abingdon.

Rabe, Berniece. The Balancing Girl. Hoban, Lillian, illus. LC 80-22100. (ps-2). 1981. 12.95 (ISBN 0-525-26160-5, 0995-300, DCB). Dutton Child Bks.

—Margaret's Moves. LC 86-11592. (Illus.). 96p. (gr. 3-6). 1987. 10.95 (ISBN 0-525-44271-5, DCB). Dutton Child Bks.

Reuter, Margaret. My Mother Is Blind. Lanier, Philip, illus. LC 78-12645. 32p. (ps-3). 1979. PLB 13.27 (ISBN 0-516-02021-8). Childrens.

Richmond, Sandra. Wheels for Walking. (Illus.). 176p. (gr. 9-12). 1988. pap. 2.50 (ISBN 0-451-15235-2, Sig). NAL-Dutton.

Rogers, Fred. Josephine, the Short-Neck Giraffe. Dastolfo, Frank & Howard, John, illus. 32p. (ps-4). pap. 4.95 (ISBN 0-685-05751-8). Pro Ed.

Rosofsky, Iris. My Aunt Ruth. LC 90-4940. 224p. (gr. 7 up). 1991. 13.95 (ISBN 0-06-025087-9); PLB 13.89 (ISBN 0-06-025088-7). HarpC Child Bks.

Sanford, Agnes. Melissa & the Little Red Book. Heinen, Sandy, illus. (gr. 1-6). pap. 2.25 (ISBN 0-910924-81-3). Macalester.

The Secret Garden. (Illus.). (gr. 3-5). 3.50 (ISBN 0-7214-0632-7). Ladybird Bks.

Smith, Elizabeth S. A Service Dog Goes to School: The Story of a Dog Trained to Help the Disabled. Petruccio, Steven, illus. LC 88-17598. 64p. (gr. 1-4). 1988. 12.95 (ISBN 0-688-07648-3); PLB 12.88 (ISBN 0-688-07649-1, Morrow Jr Bks). Morrow Jr Bks.

Springer, Nancy. Colt. (gr. 4-7). 1991. 13.95 (ISBN 0-8037-1022-4). Dial Bks Young.

Strachan, Ian. Flawed Glass. (gr. 9-12). 1990. 14.95 (ISBN 0-316-81813-5). Little.

Taylor, Theodore. Tuck Triumphant. (gr. 5-7). 1991. 14.95 (ISBN 0-385-41480-3). Doubleday.

Van Raven, Pieter. The Great Man's Secret. (Illus.). 176p. (gr. 5-9). 1991. pap. 3.95 (ISBN 0-14-034390-3, Puffin). Puffin Bks.

Voigt, Cynthia. Izzy, Willy-Nilly. 1987. pap. 3.50 (ISBN 0-449-70214-6, Juniper). Fawcett.

White, James E. The Triumphs of Trisha & Tripod: Tripod Finds a Home. Senf, Richard L., illus. 22p. 1991. pap. 7.95 (ISBN 0-9629102-0-1). Pyramid TX. About a little handicapped girl named Trisha who dreams of finding a pet to share her love with. The story centers around a three-legged dog named Tripod, who is headed for the humane

shelter's version of death row when he is rescued & adopted by Trisha. Trisha always wanted a "big fluffy dog with a fat waggily tail." But, Tripod hardly fitted that description. He's a brown mongrel but to Trisha he was the most wonderful thing that had ever happened in her life. When Trisha sees the doomed Tripod, she understands that just because Tripod lacks a leg, he doesn't lack in an abundance of puppy love. The triumphs of Trisha & Tripod teaches children to love people & animals just for what they are. The world is not perfect & neither are people. As cruel as children may seem at times to other children & other children's pets, they should be taught to be giving. We must learn to love without compromise. That's what the triumphs of Trisha & Tripod is all about.
Publisher Provided Annotation.

Winthrop, Elizabeth. Marathon Miranda. (gr. 4 up). 1990. pap. 3.95 (ISBN 0-14-034391-1, Puffin). Puffin Bks.

Zelonky, Joy. I Can't Always Hear You. Bejna, Barbara & Jensen, Shirlee, illus. Geist, Chris, intro. by. LC 79-23891. 32p. (gr. k-6). 1980. PLB 16.67 (ISBN 0-8172-1355-4). Raintree Pubs.

PHYSICIANS

see also Women As Physicians;
also names of specialists, e.g. Surgeons

Bauer, Judith. What's It Like to Be a Doctor. Burns, Raymond, illus. LC 89-34398. 32p. (gr. k-3). 1989. lib. bdg. 10.89 (ISBN 0-8167-1801-6); pap. text ed. 2.50 (ISBN 0-8167-1802-4). Troll Assocs.

Berger, et al. A Visit to the Doctor. (Illus.). (ps-1). pap. 2.95 (ISBN 0-448-14001-2, G&D). Putnam Pub Group.

Berry, Joy W. Teach Me about the Doctor. Dickey, Kate, ed. (Illus.). 36p. (ps). 1986. 4.98 (ISBN 0-685-10723-X). Grolier Inc.

DeSantis, Kenny. A Doctor's Tools. Agre, Patricia A., photos by. (Illus.). 48p. (gr. k-3). 1985. 9.95 (ISBN 0-396-08516-4, Putnam); pap. 3.95 (ISBN 0-396-08739-6, Putnam). Putnam Pub Group.

Drescher, Joan. Your Doctor, My Doctor. 32p. (gr. 1-3). 1987. 10.95 (ISBN 0-8027-6668-4); PLB 11.85 (ISBN 0-8027-6669-2). Walker & Co.

Ferris, Jeri. Native American Doctor: The Story of Susan LaFlesche Picotte. (Illus.). 80p. (gr. 3-6). 1991. PLB 11.95 (ISBN 0-87614-443-1). Carolrhoda Bks.

Gaffney, Timothy. Jerrold Petrofsky: Biomedical Pioneer. LC 83-25268. (Illus.). 128p. (gr. 4 up). 1984. lib. bdg. 15.93 (ISBN 0-516-03201-1). Childrens.

Hankin, Rebecca. I Can Be a Doctor. LC 84-23304. (Illus.). 32p. (gr. k-3). 1985. lib. bdg. 13.93 (ISBN 0-516-01846-9); pap. 3.95 (ISBN 0-516-41846-7). Childrens.

—Puedo Ser Medico: I Can Be a Doctor. LC 84-23304. (SPA., Illus.). 32p. (gr. k-3). 1990. PLB 13.93 (ISBN 0-516-31846-2). Childrens.

Lappin, Myra & Feinglass, Sanford. Need a Doctor? (Illus.). 64p. (gr. 7-12). 1981. pap. text ed. 3.95 (ISBN 0-915510-58-8). Janus Bks.

Rockwell, Harlow. My Doctor. Rockwell, Harlow, illus. LC 72-92442. 24p. (ps-1). 1973. 12.95 (ISBN 0-02-777480-5, Mcmillan Child Bk). Macmillan Child Grp.

Rogers, Fred. Going to the Doctor. Judkis, Jim, illus. 32p. (ps-2). 1986. 12.95 (ISBN 0-399-21298-1, Putnam); pap. 5.95 (ISBN 0-399-21299-X, Putnam). Putnam Pub Group.

Watson, Jane W., et al. My Friend the Doctor: A Read-Together Book for Parents & Children. rev. & updated ed. Smith, Catherine B., illus. 32p. (ps up). 1987. pap. 3.50 (ISBN 0-517-56485-8). Crown.

PHYSICIANS–FICTION

Cole, Joanna. Doctor Change. Carrick, Donald, illus. LC 86-881. 32p. (ps-3). 1986. 12.95 (ISBN 0-688-06135-4); lib. bdg. 12.88 (ISBN 0-688-06136-2, Morrow Jr Bks). Morrow Jr Bks.

Cronin, A. J. The Citadel. (gr. 7 up). 1983. 16.45 (ISBN 0-316-16158-6); pap. 8.95i (ISBN 0-316-16183-7). Little.

De Brunhoff, Laurent. Babar Chez le Docteur. (FRE.). (gr. 2-3). 4.95 (ISBN 0-685-28425-5). French & Eur.

Freeman, Don. Corduroy's Busy Street & Corduroy Goes to the Doctor, 2 bks. McCue, Lisa, illus. (ps-k). 1989. Repr. of 1987 ed. bds. 12.95 incl. cass. (ISBN 0-87499-133-1). Live Oak Media.

Kuklin, Susan. When I See My Doctor. LC 87-25621. (Illus.). 32p. (ps-1). 1988. 13.95 (ISBN 0-02-751232-0, Bradbury Pr). Macmillan Child Grp.

Lowry, Lois. Anastasia, Ask Your Analyst. (Orig.). (gr. 4-6). 1985. pap. 2.95 (ISBN 0-440-40289-1, YB). Dell.

McCue, Lisa. Corduroy Goes to the Doctor. (Illus.). (ps). 1987. pap. 2.95 (ISBN 0-670-81495-4). Viking Child Bks.

Medearis, Mary. Big Doc's Girl. LC 84-45641. 142p. (gr. 7-12). 1985. pap. 7.95 (ISBN 0-87483-105-9). August Hse.

Revich, S. J. Ezra the Physician. Hinlicky, Gregg, illus. 126p. (gr. 5-7). 1988. 9.95 (ISBN 0-935063-63-3); pap. 7.95 (ISBN 0-935063-64-1). CIS Comm.

Schwartz, Joel L. Shrink. (Orig.). (gr. 3-6). 1986. pap. 2.75 (ISBN 0-440-47687-9, YB). Dell.

Sommers, Tish. Big Bird Goes to the Doctor. Cooke, Tom, illus. LC 85-81562. 32p. (ps-k). 1986. write for info. (ISBN 0-307-12019-8, Pub. by Golden Bks). Western Pub.

Tannenbaum, D. Leb. A Visit to the Doctor. Leder, Dora, illus. 64p. (ps-2). 1981. pap. 3.95 (ISBN 0-671-43205-2, Little Simon). S&S Trade.

Twinn, Michael, illus. A Visit to the Doctor. (Orig.). (ps-2). 1977. 2.00 (ISBN 0-85953-067-1, Pub. by Child's Play England). Childs Play.

PHYSICISTS

Ferguson, Kitty. Stephen Hawking: Quest for a Theory of the Universe. (Illus.). 240p. (gr. 9-12). 1991. PLB 14.90 (ISBN 0-531-11067-2). Watts.

Magill, Frank N., ed. Nobel Prize Winners, 3 vols. 1364p. (gr. 9-12). 1989. Set. PLB 210.00x (ISBN 0-89356-557-1, Magill Bks). Salem Pr.

Simon, Sheridan. Unlocking the Universe: A Biography of Stephen Hawking. (Illus.). 112p. (gr. 5 up). 1991. 12.95 (ISBN 0-87518-455-3, Dillon). Macmillan Child Grp.

PHYSICS

see also Chemistry, Physical and Theoretical; Electricity; Electronics; Gravitation; Light; Liquids; Magnetism; Matter; Mechanics; Music–Acoustics and Physics; Nuclear Physics; Optics; Radiation; Radioactivity; Relativity (Physics); Sound; Thermodynamics

Apfel, Necia H. It's All Elementary: From Atoms to the Quantum World of Quarks, Leptons, & Gluons. LC 84-9718. (Illus.). 160p. (gr. 4 up). 1985. PLB 12.88 (ISBN 0-688-04093-4). Lothrop.

Barr, George. Sports Science for Young People. 1990. pap. 3.95 (ISBN 0-486-26527-7). Dover.

Crump, Donald J., ed. Fun with Physics. LC 86-8501. (Illus.). 104p. (gr. 5 up). 1986. 6.95 (ISBN 0-87044-576-6); lib. bdg. 8.50 (ISBN 0-87044-581-2). Natl Geog.

—How Things Work. LC 81-47894. (Illus.). 104p. (gr. 7 up). 1983. 6.95 (ISBN 0-87044-425-5); PLB 8.50 (ISBN 0-87044-430-1). Natl Geog.

Fitzpatrick, Julie. Balancing. (Illus.). 32p. (gr. 3-5). 1988. PLB 9.96 (ISBN 0-382-09535-9). Silver Burdett Pr.

—Bounce, Stretch & Spring. (Illus.). (gr. 3-5). 1988. PLB 9.96 (ISBN 0-382-09537-5). Silver Burdett Pr.

Hoyt, Marie A. Kitchen Chemistry & Front Porch Physics. Finkler, C. Etana, illus. 60p. (Orig.). (gr. 3-8). 1983. pap. 5.00 (ISBN 0-914911-00-7). Educ Serv Pr.
KITCHEN CHEMISTRY & FRONT PORCH PHYSICS for children ages 7-14 has instructions on how to make a SHOEBOX CHEMISTRY SET to be used in performing the 32 science experiments which demystify physics & chemistry. Its use of common materials & everyday household chemicals make the teaching of science fun, safe & in-depth. The simple understandable reading level enables students to discover science concepts by "Hands On" experience. Additionally, the glossary teacher-parent guide along with the Future Scientists of America awards make this book a science treasure to teachers, children, science group leaders & parents of both mainstream & minorities alike.
Publisher Provided Annotation.

—Workbook Game Sheets for Kitchen Chemistry & Front Porch Physics. Green, Victor D. & Loor, Robin, illus. 44p. (Orig.). (gr. 3-8). 1983. pap. text ed. 4.00 (ISBN 0-914911-02-3). Educ Serv Pr.

Kraul, Walter. Earth, Water, Fire & Air: Playful Explorations in the Four Elements. (Illus.). 120p. (gr. 4-8). pap. 12.95 (ISBN 0-86315-090-X, Pub. by Floris Bks UK). Gryphon Hse.

Lampton, Christopher. Sailboats, Flag Poles, Cranes: Using Pulleys as Simple Machines. (Illus.). 32p. (gr. 2-4). 1991. PLB 15.25 (ISBN 1-56294-026-0). Millbrook Pr.

—Superconductors. LC 88-31562. (Illus.). 96p. (gr. 6 up). 1989. PLB 16.95 (ISBN 0-89490-203-2). Enslow Pubs.

Marsh, Carole. Phyzzics for Kids. (gr. 4-9). 1989. 19.95 (ISBN 1-55609-258-X); pap. 14.95 (ISBN 1-55609-245-8); computer disk 29.95 (ISBN 1-55609-340-3). Gallopade Pub Group.

Stacy, Tom. Earth, Sea & Sky. Vestal, J., ed. Forsey, Chris, illus. 40p. (gr. 4-5). 1991. PLB 11.40 (ISBN 0-531-19106-0). Watts.

Stockley, C. Dictionary of Physics: The Facts You Need to Know - At a Glance. (Illus.). 128p. (gr. 6 up). 1988. PLB 15.96 (ISBN 0-88110-308-X); pap. 9.95 (ISBN 0-86020-987-3). EDC.

Stwertka, Albert & Srwertka, Eve. Physics: From Newton to the Big Bang. LC 86-5669. (Illus.). 96p. (gr. 4-9). 1986. PLB 10.40 (ISBN 0-531-10224-6). Watts.

Wingate, P. Essential Physics. (Illus.). 64p. 1991. lib. bdg. 12.96 (ISBN 0-685-38859-X, Usborne); pap. 5.95 (ISBN 0-7460-0703-5). EDC.

Wood, Robert W. Physics for Kids: Forty-Nine Easy Experiments with Electricity & Magnetism. (Illus.). 192p. 1990. 16.95 (ISBN 0-685-32939-9, 3412); pap. 9.95 (ISBN 0-8306-3412-6). TAB Bks.

PHYSICS–EXPERIMENTS

Challand, Helen J. Activities in the Physical Sciences. LC 83-26224. (Illus.). 96p. (gr. 5 up). 1984. lib. bdg. 17.27 (ISBN 0-516-00504-9). Childrens.

Gardner, Robert. Famous Experiments You Can Do. (Illus.). 144p. (gr. 9-12). 1990. PLB 12.90 (ISBN 0-531-10883-X). Watts.

Mandell, Muriel. Physics Experiments for Children. Matsuda, S., illus. LC 68-9308. (gr. 3-10). 1968. pap. 2.95 (ISBN 0-486-22033-8). Dover.

Vancleave, Janice. Physics for Every Kid: One Hundred One Easy Experiments That Really Work. 1991. pap. text ed. 10.95 (ISBN 0-471-52505-7). Wiley.

Ward, Alan. Experimenting with Surface Tension & Bubbles. Flax, Zena, illus. 48p. (gr. 2-7). 1991. PLB 12.95 (ISBN 0-7910-1513-0). Chelsea Hse.

PHYSIOGRAPHY

see Physical Geography

PHYSIOLOGICAL CHEMISTRY

see also Cells; Digestion; Metabolism; Poisons; Vitamins

PHYSIOLOGY

see also Anatomy; Blood; Bones; Cells; Digestion; Growth; Nervous System; Nutrition; Old Age; Reproduction; Respiration; Senses and Sensation
also names of organs, e.g. Heart

Elting, Mary. Macmillan Book of the Human Body. LC 85-24204. (Illus.). 80p. (gr. 3-7). 1986. 15.95 (ISBN 0-02-733440-6, Mcmillan Child Bk). Macmillan Child Grp.

Gabb, Michael. The Human Body. (Illus.). 48p. (gr. 5-8). 1991. PLB 13.90 (ISBN 0-531-19145-1, Warwick). Watts.

How Our Bodies Work Series, 8 vols. (Illus.). 384p. (gr. 5-8). 1988. Set. 103.84g (ISBN 0-382-09733-5); Set. 77.88s.p. (ISBN 0-685-37315-0). Silver Burdett Pr.

Kolkmeyer, Alexandra. The Clear Red Stone: A Myth & the Meaning of Menstruation. Goldstein, Lynn, ed. Kirby, Thomas, illus. LC 82-2956. 64p. (gr. 3-12). 1982. text ed. 9.50 (ISBN 0-942524-01-2). In Sight Pr NM.

Lauber, Patricia. Your Body & How It Works. (Illus.). (gr. 3-5). 1966. (Random Juv); PLB 10.99 (ISBN 0-394-90125-8). Random.

Little, Marjorie. The Endocrine System. (Illus.). (gr. 5-12). 1990. 18.95 (ISBN 0-7910-0016-8). Chelsea Hse.

Settel, Joanne & Baggett, Nancy. Why Does My Nose Run? & Other Questions Kids Ask About Their Bodies. Tunney, Linda, illus. LC 84-21549. 80p. (gr. 4-6). 1985. 11.95 (ISBN 0-689-31078-1, Atheneum Child Bk). Macmillan Child Grp.

Skin, Hair, Teeth. 48p. (gr. 5-8). 1988. PLB 11.96 (ISBN 0-382-09706-8); 9.98s.p. (ISBN 0-685-24613-2). Silver Burdett Pr.

Ward, Brian R. Birth & Growth. LC 82-50055. (Illus.). 48p. (gr. 4 up). 1983. PLB 12.40 (ISBN 0-531-04459-9). Watts.

—Body Maintenance. (Illus.). 48p. (gr. 4 up). 1983. PLB 12.40 (ISBN 0-531-04457-2). Watts.

What's Inside My Body? (Illus.). 24p. (ps-3). 1991. 8.95 (ISBN 1-879431-07-6); PLB 9.99 (ISBN 1-879431-22-X). Dorling Kindersley.
Designed to satisfy a child's natural curiosity, the WHAT'S INSIDE? series gives a fascinating behind-the-scenes look at an array of subjects. Each book features bright, full color photography & overlay illustrations that show the inner workings of an object, from a shell to a teddy bear to a goldfish. Short, easy-to-read labels & leader lines make this a terrific series for beginning readers, & are great for reading aloud, too. The perfect answer to one of the questions children ask most often: WHAT'S INSIDE? Taken together, Dorling Kindersley's WHAT'S INSIDE? series serves as a valuable reference tool for home, school, & library.
Publisher Provided Annotation.

You & Your Body. (Illus.). 80p. (gr. k-6). 1986. pap. 13. 27 (ISBN 0-8172-2589-7). Raintree Pubs.

PIANISTS

Guerry, Jack. Silvio Scionti: Remembering a Master Pianist & Teacher. Dolch, Jessie, ed. (Illus.). 240p. (gr. 10 up). 1991. 25.00 (ISBN 0-929398-27-0). UNTX Pr.

PIANISTS–FICTION

Goffstein, M. B. Two Piano Tuners. LC 71-106399. (Illus.). 72p. (ps-3). 1977. 9.95 (ISBN 0-374-38019-8). FS&G.

PIANO

Beirne, Barbara. A Pianist's Debut: Preparing for the Concert Stage. Beirne, Barbara, photos by. (Illus.). 56p. (gr. 2-5). 1990. PLB 12.95 (ISBN 0-87614-432-6). Carolrhoda Bks.

Blocksma, Mary. The Marvelous Music Machine: A Story of the Piano. Richter, Mischa, illus. LC 84-4892. 64p. (gr. 3-7). 1984. 10.95 (ISBN 0-13-559410-3). P-H.

Brimhall, John. Children's Piano Method. (Illus.). 64p. (Orig.). (gr. 1-6). 1984. pap. text ed. 5.95 (ISBN 0-8494-2887-4, T430). Hansen Ed Mus.

Czerny, Carl. School of Velocity for Piano, Op. 299, Complete Edition. 101p. 1903. pap. 6.00 (ISBN 0-8258-0108-7, L 338). Fischer Inc NY.

Kochevitsky, George. Art of Piano Playing: A Scientific Approach. (Illus.). 80p. (gr. 9 up). 1967. pap. text ed. 10.95 (ISBN 0-87487-068-2). Summy-Birchard.

Lubin, Ernest. A Start at the Piano. LC 78-110975. (Orig.). (gr. 5-8). 1977. pap. 8.95 (ISBN 0-8256-2636-6, Amsco Music). Music Sales.

Patrick, Ann. Let's Make Piano Music with Marvin, Bk. 3. 40p. (Orig.). (gr. k-7). 1987. pap. 6.95 (ISBN 0-685-17364-X). Centerstream Pub.

Philipp, Lillie H. Piano Technique: Tone, Touch, Phrasing & Dynamics. (Illus.). 90p. (gr. 7 up). 1982. pap. 5.95 (ISBN 0-486-24272-2). Dover.

Poffenberger, Nancy. Instant Piano Fun: Book One. 34p. (gr. 4). 1985. pap. 8.95 (ISBN 0-938293-25-7). Fun Pub OH.

—Now! Instant Keyboard Fun I. 32p. (gr. 4 up). 1985. pap. 4.95 (ISBN 0-938293-39-7). Fun Pub OH.

Storr, Catherine. The Nutcracker. Tchaikovsky, contrib. by. (Illus.). 32p. (ps up). 1988. pap. 9.95 (ISBN 0-571-10080-5). Faber & Faber.

Thomas, A. First Book of the Piano. (Illus.). 64p. (gr. 2-6). 1988. PLB 13.96 (ISBN 0-88110-332-2); pap. 7.95 (ISBN 0-7460-0197-5). EDC.

PIANO MUSIC

Amaldev, Jerry. India: Raga for the Piano. 32p. (Orig.). (gr. k-12). 1981. pap. text ed. 5.95 (ISBN 0-87487-104-2). Summy-Birchard.

Brimhall, John. My Favorite Easy Classics, Bk. 5. 128p. (Orig.). (gr. 1-3). 1984. pap. text ed. 10.95 (ISBN 0-8494-2182-9, 0116). Hansen Ed Mus.

Bryansky, Faina. The Key to Music Making, Pt. I: Piano Method for Beginners. Squillace, Albert & Kuznetsov, Eugene, illus. LC 88-50726. 48p. (gr. 1-5). 1988. pap. 8.00 (ISBN 0-929571-00-2). White Lilac Pr.

Chopin, Frederic. Waltzes for Piano. 80p. 1902. pap. 7.50 (ISBN 0-8258-0103-6, L 309). Fischer Inc NY.

Clark, Frances. Look & Listen, Pt. A. Goss, Louise & Kraehenbuehl, Davidcontrib. by. 48p. (Orig.). (gr. k-6). 1962. pap. text ed. 2.95 (ISBN 0-87487-176-X). Summy-Birchard.

—Look & Listen, Pt. B. Goss, Louise & Kraehenbuehl, Davidcontrib. by. 48p. (Orig.). (gr. k-12). 1962. pap. text ed. 2.95 (ISBN 0-87487-177-8). Summy-Birchard.

—Look & Listen, Pt. C. Goss, Louise & Kraehenbuehl, Davidcontrib. by. 48p. (Orig.). (gr. k-12). 1962. pap. text ed. 2.95 (ISBN 0-87487-178-6). Summy-Birchard.

—Look & Listen, Pt. D. Goss, Louise & Kraehenbuehl, Davidcontrib. by. 48p. (Orig.). (gr. k-12). 1962. pap. text ed. 2.95 (ISBN 0-87487-179-4). Summy-Birchard.

Clark, Frances & Goss, Louise. Write & Play Time, Pt. A. 64p. (Orig.). (gr. k-6). 1974. pap. text ed. 9.95 (ISBN 0-87487-196-4). Summy-Birchard.

Collins, Ann & Clary, Linda. Sing & Play--Preschool Piano Book One. (Illus.). 60p. (ps). 1987. spiral bdg. 5.00 (ISBN 0-87563-307-2). Stipes.

Cramer, J. B. Fifty Selected Studies for Piano. Von Bulow, Hans, ed. 116p. 1946. pap. 12.00 (ISBN 0-8258-0138-9, L 525). Fischer Inc NY.

Czerny, Carl. One Hundred Practical Exercises for Piano, Op. 139. 76p. 1905. pap. 6.95 (ISBN 0-8258-0134-6). Fischer Inc NY.

—Thirty New Studies in Technic for Piano, Op. 849. 56p. 1907. pap. 6.75 (ISBN 0-8258-0127-3, L 487). Fischer Inc NY.

Dittenhaver, Sarah L., et al. Tune Time, 2 pts. rev. ed. Goss, Louise, ed. 48p. (gr. k-6). 1973. pap. text ed. 6.95 pt. A (ISBN 0-87487-194-8); pap. text ed. 6.95 pt. B (ISBN 0-87487-195-6). Summy-Birchard.

Eckstein, Maxwell, ed. Let Us Have Music for Piano: Seventy-Four Famous Melodies, Vol. 2. 111p. pap. 8.95 (ISBN 0-8258-0048-X, 03127). Fischer Inc NY.

—Let Us Have Music for Piano: Seventy-Four Melodies, Vol. 1. 112p. pap. 8.95 (ISBN 0-8258-0047-1, 02942). Fischer Inc NY.

Faber, Nancy & Faber, Randall. ChordTime Piano Hymns: Level 2 - I, IV, V7 Chords in Keys of C,G & F. McLean, Edwin, ed. Terpstra, Gwen, illus. 24p. (gr. 2-4). 1988. pap. 4.95 (ISBN 0-929666-03-8). FJH Music Co Inc.

—PlayTime Piano Christmas: Level 1 - Five Finger Melodies. McLean, Edwin, ed. Terpstra, Gwen, illus. 24p. (gr. 1-3). 1988. pap. 4.95 (ISBN 0-929666-02-X). FJH Music Co Inc.

—PlayTime Piano Hymns: Level One - Five Finger Melodies. McLean, Edwin, ed. Terpstra, Gwen, illus. 24p. (gr. 1-3). 1988. pap. 4.95 (ISBN 0-929666-00-3). FJH Music Co Inc.

—PlayTime Piano Popular: Level One - Five Finger Melodies. McLean, Edwin, ed. Terpstra, Gwen, illus. 24p. (gr. 1-3). 1988. pap. 4.95 (ISBN 0-929666-01-1). FJH Music Co Inc.

Goss, Louise & McArtot, Marion. Technic Time, Pt. A. 48p. (Orig.). (gr. k-6). 1974. pap. text ed. 6.95 (ISBN 0-87487-189-1). Summy-Birchard.

Goss, Louise, ed. Themes from Masterworks, 3 bks. 16p. (Orig.). (gr. k-12). 1970. pap. text ed. 5.95 Bk. 1 (ISBN 0-87487-191-3); pap. text ed. 5.95 Bk. 2 (ISBN 0-87487-192-1); pap. text ed. 5.95 Bk. 3 (ISBN 0-87487-193-X). Summy-Birchard.

Grove, Roger. Riches of Rag. 16p. (Orig.). (gr. k-12). 1976. pap. text ed. 5.95 (ISBN 0-87487-188-3). Summy-Birchard.

Hammond, Vicky L. & Dalby, Judy N. Primary Passages Plus: Favorite Songs & Hymns Arranged for Newcomers to the Piano. Waller, Nancy G., illus. 32p. (Orig.). 1989. pap. 5.95 (ISBN 0-9624262-3-7). Hammond Dalby Music.

Hammond, Vicky L. & Smith, Jerry. Accent on Youth: Piano Solos of Favorite Songs & Hymns. 24p. (Orig.). 1989. pap. 6.95 (ISBN 0-9624262-7-X). Hammond Dalby Music.

Hanon & Lindquist, A. Technical Variants. 32p. (Orig.). (gr. k-12). 1929. pap. text ed. 5.95 (ISBN 0-87487-657-5). Summy-Birchard.

Hawthorn, P. Easy Piano Classics. (Illus.). 64p. (gr. 2-6). 1991. lib. bdg. 13.96 (ISBN 0-88110-424-8, Usborne); pap. 7.95 (ISBN 0-7460-0643-8, Usborne). EDC.

Hawthorn, P. & Armstrong, S. The Usborne Book of Easy Piano Tunes. (Illus.). 64p. (gr. 2-6). 1989. lib. bdg. 13.96 (ISBN 0-88110-410-8, Usborne); pap. 7.95 (ISBN 0-7460-0459-1, Usborne). EDC.

Kraehenbuehl, David, et al. Supplementary Solos: Level 1. Clark, Frances & Goss, Louise, eds. 32p. (gr. k-12). 1979. pap. text ed. 5.95 (ISBN 0-87487-105-0). Summy-Birchard.

—Supplementary Solos: Level 2. Clark, Frances & Goss, Louise, eds. 32p. (gr. k-12). 1980. pap. text ed. 5.95 (ISBN 0-87487-106-9). Summy-Birchard.

Lemoine, H. Etudes Enfantines for Piano, Op. 37. 52p. 1904. pap. 7.00 (ISBN 0-8258-0106-0, L 323). Fischer Inc NY.

Singing Keys Omnibus. 64p. (Orig.). (gr. 6-12). 1946. pap. text ed. 9.95 (ISBN 0-87487-651-6). Summy-Birchard.

Storr, Catherine. Hansel & Gretel. Humperdinck, Engelbert, contrib. by. (Illus.). 32p. (ps up). 1988. 15. 00 (ISBN 0-571-10082-1); pap. 9.95 (ISBN 0-571-10083-X). Faber & Faber.

—The Nutcracker. Tchaikovsky, contrib. by. (Illus.). 32p. (ps up). 1988. pap. 9.95 (ISBN 0-571-10080-5). Faber & Faber.

Summy Piano Solo Package: Advanced, No. 501. (Illus.). 32p. (gr. 10-12). 1976. pap. text ed. 5.95 (ISBN 0-87487-656-7). Summy-Birchard.

Summy Piano Solo Package: Elementary, No. 101. (Illus.). 32p. (Orig.). (gr. k-2). 1976. pap. text ed. 5.95 (ISBN 0-87487-652-4). Summy-Birchard.

Summy Piano Solo Package: Intermediate, No.301. 32p. (Orig.). (gr. 5-8). 1976. pap. text ed. 5.95 (ISBN 0-87487-654-0). Summy-Birchard.

Summy Piano Solo Package: Late Elementary, No.201. 32p. (Orig.). (gr. 2-6). 1976. pap. text ed. 5.95 (ISBN 0-87487-653-2). Summy-Birchard.

Summy Piano Solo Package: Late Intermediate, No.401. 32p. (Orig.). (gr. 8-10). 1976. pap. text ed. 5.95 (ISBN 0-87487-655-9). Summy-Birchard.

Wolff, B. The Little Pischna: Forty-Eight Preparatory Exercises for Piano. (ENG & GER.). 1907. pap. 4.00 (ISBN 0-8258-0122-2, L 475). Fischer Inc NY.

PICASSO, PABLO, 1881-1972

Giraudy, Daniele, text by. Pablo Picasso: The Minotaur, An Art Play Book. (Illus.). 32p. (gr. 2 up). 1988. 17.95 (ISBN 0-8109-1471-9). Abrams.

Lyttle, Richard B. Pablo Picasso: The Man & the Image. (Illus.). 192p. (gr. 7 up). 1989. 15.95 (ISBN 0-689-31393-4, Atheneum Child Bk). Macmillan Child Grp.

Raboff, Ernest. Pablo Picasso. Picasso, Pablo, illus. LC 87-45156. 32p. (gr. 1 up). 1987. 11.95 (ISBN 0-397-32224-0, Lipp Jr Bks). HarpC Child Bks.

—Pablo Picasso. Picasso, Pablo, illus. LC 87-45147. 32p. (gr. 1 up). 1987. pap. 7.95 (ISBN 0-06-446068-1, Trophy). HarpC Child Bks.

—Pablo Picasso. 1987. pap. 7.95 (ISBN 0-06-446067-3). HarpC Child Bks.

Sommer, Robin L. & MacDonald, Patricia. Pablo Picasso. (Illus.). 128p. (gr. 7-9). 1990. 14.95 (ISBN 0-382-24031-6); lib. bdg. 17.98 (ISBN 0-382-09903-6). Silver Burdett Pr.

Venezia, Mike. Picasso. Venezia, Mike, illus. LC 87-33023. 32p. (gr. 1-3). 1988. PLB 14.60 (ISBN 0-516-02271-7); pap. 4.95 (ISBN 0-516-42271-5). Childrens.

PICKLING

see Canning and Preserving

PICKNICKING

Brown, Marc. Pickle Things. (Illus.). 48p. (ps-2). 1991. pap. 2.95 (ISBN 0-448-40105-3, G&D). Putnam Pub Group.

PICTOGRAPHS

see Picture Writing

PICTORIAL WORKS

see Pictures

PICTURE BOOKS

Here are entered actual picture books (including Big Books, board books, etc.).

Aardema, Verna. Oh, Kojo! How Could You? Brown, Marc, illus. LC 84-1710. 32p. (ps-3). 1984. 12.95 (ISBN 0-8037-0006-7); PLB 12.89 (ISBN 0-8037-0007-5). Dial Bks Young.

ABC. (ps-1). 1985. 2.95 (ISBN 0-671-51083-5, Little Simon). S&S Trade.

ABC: Kiddy Big Book. (ps up). 1990. PLB 4.98 (ISBN 0-7924-5191-0, Mallard Pr). BDD Promo Bk.

ABC Rhymes. 1984. 2.95 (ISBN 0-671-49685-9, Little Simon). S&S Trade.

Aber, Linda. You're A Star, Snoopy! (Illus.). 24p. (ps-3). 1990. pap. write for info. (ISBN 0-307-11728-6, Pub. by Golden Bks). Western Pub.

Aber, Linda W. & Aber, Hal. More Stuck on Stickers. (Illus.). 48p. (Orig.). (gr. 4-6). 1984. pap. 5.95 (ISBN 0-590-33360-7). Scholastic Inc.

—Rainbow Sticker Riot. Aber, Linda W. & Aber, Hal, illus. 24p. (Orig.). (gr. 2-6). 1985. pap. 2.95 (ISBN 0-590-33388-7). Scholastic Inc.

Abramson, Lillian & Robinson, Jessie. Alef Bet Fun. (Illus.). (gr. 2-4). 1957. pap. 4.95x (ISBN 0-8197-0028-2). Bloch.

Ackerman, Angela, illus. My Pillow Book: Blue Ladder Books for Babies Through 16 Months. 10p. (ps). 1988. 5.95 (ISBN 0-394-89402-2, Random Juv). Random.

Adams, Pam. The Fairground. (Illus.). 32p. (ps). 1984. 8.00 (ISBN 0-85953-194-5, Child's Play England). Childs Play.

—Oh, Soldier! Soldier! (ps-3). 1990. pap. 5.95 (ISBN 0-85953-092-2, Pub. by Child's Play England). Childs Play.

Adams, Pam, illus. Angels. 24p. (Orig.). (ps-2). 1974. 4.50 (ISBN 0-85953-034-5, Pub. by Child's Play England). Childs Play.

—The Best Things. 24p. (ps-2). 1974. 4.50 (ISBN 0-85953-031-0, Pub. by Child's England). Childs Play.

—How Many? 16p. (Orig.). (ps-2). 1975. pap. 2.00 (ISBN 0-85953-045-0, Pub. by Child's Play England). Childs Play.

—Same & Different. 16p. (Orig.). (ps-2). 1975. pap. 2.00 (ISBN 0-85953-043-4, Pub. by Child's Play England). Childs Play.

—Shopping Day. 24p. (ps-2). 1974. 4.50 (ISBN 0-85953-033-7, Pub. by Child's Play England). Childs Play.

Addison-Wesley Staff. The Farmer & the Beet. (Illus.). (gr. k-2). 1988. text ed. 31.75 (ISBN 0-201-19318-3); pap. text ed. 12.95 (ISBN 0-201-19059-1). Addison-Wesley.

—The Gingerbread Man. (Illus.). 16p. (gr. k-2). 1989. text ed. 31.75 (ISBN 0-201-19320-5); pap. text ed. 12. 95 (ISBN 0-201-19064-8). Addison-Wesley.

—Goldilocks & the Three Bears. (Illus.). (gr. k-2). 1988. pap. text ed. 31.75 (ISBN 0-201-19319-1). Addison-Wesley.

—Goldilocks & the Three Bears Little Book. (Illus.). 16p. (gr. k-3). 1989. text ed. 12.95 (ISBN 0-201-19065-6); pap. text ed. 4.50 (ISBN 0-201-19055-9). Addison-Wesley.

—The Hare & the Tortoise. (Illus.). 16p. (gr. k-2). 1989. 31.75 (ISBN 0-201-19324-8); pap. text ed. 12.95 (ISBN 0-201-19369-8). Addison-Wesley.

—How the Moon Got in the Sky. (Illus.). (gr. k-2). 1989. 31.75 (ISBN 0-201-19325-6); pap. text ed. 12.95 (ISBN 0-201-19366-3). Addison-Wesley.

—The Little Red Hen. (Illus.). 16p. (gr. k-2). 1989. text ed. 31.75 (ISBN 0-201-19323-X); pap. text ed. 12.95 (ISBN 0-201-19368-X). Addison-Wesley.

—The Three Little Pigs. 16p. (gr. k-2). 1988. text ed. 31. 75 (ISBN 0-201-19322-1); pap. 12.95 (ISBN 0-201-19066-4). Addison-Wesley.

Addy, Sharon H. A Visit with Great-Grandma. Fay, Ann, ed. (Illus.). 32p. (gr. 1-3). 1989. 12.95g (ISBN 0-8075-8497-5). A Whitman.

Adler, David A. I Know I'm a Witch. Stevenson, Sucie, illus. LC 86-33508. 32p. (gr. k-3). 1988. 13.95 (ISBN 0-8050-0427-0). H Holt & Co.

—A Picture Book of George Washington. Wallner, John & Wallner, Alexandra, illus. LC 88-16384. 32p. (gr. k-3). 1989. reinforced bdg. 13.95 (ISBN 0-8234-0732-2); pap. 5.95 (ISBN 0-8234-0800-0). Holiday.

—A Picture Book of Jewish Holidays. Heller, Linda, illus. LC 81-2765. 32p. (gr. k-3). 1981. reinforced bdg. 13. 95 (ISBN 0-8234-0396-3); pap. 5.95 (ISBN 0-8234-0756-X). Holiday.

Adoff, Arnold. Hard to Be Six. Hanna, Cheryl, illus. LC 89-45903. 32p. (gr. k-3). 1990. 12.95 (ISBN 0-688-09013-3); lib. bdg. 12.88 (ISBN 0-688-09579-8). Lothrop.

Adshead, Paul. Peacock on the Roof. (ps-3). 1990. pap. 5.95 (ISBN 0-85953-307-7). Childs Play.

Adventures of the Pea Pod Kids. (ps-5). 1988. incl. 3 dolls & 5 playsettings 19.95 (ISBN 0-698-12011-6, Coward). Putnam Pub Group.

Ahlberg, Janet. Peek-A-Boo. (ps). 1990. 4.95 (ISBN 0-670-83283-9). Viking Child Bks.

Ahlberg, Janet & Ahlberg, Allan. The Baby's Catalogue. Ahlberg, Janet & Ahlberg, Allan, illus. 32p. (gr. k up). 1986. pap. 5.95 (ISBN 0-316-02038-9). Little.

—Each Peach Pear Plum. Ahlberg, Janet & Ahlberg, Allan, illus. 32p. (ps-1). 1986. pap. 3.95 (ISBN 0-14-050639-X, Puffin). Puffin Bks.

—Each Peach Pear Plum: An I-Spy Story. LC 79-16726. (Illus.). 32p. (gr. k-3). 1979. pap. 12.95 (ISBN 0-670-28705-9). Viking Child Bks.

—Peek-a-Boo. (Illus.). 32p. (ps-k). 1984. pap. 3.95 (ISBN 0-14-050107-X, Puffin). Puffin Bks.

Aitken, Amy. Ruby, The Red Knight. Aitken, Amy, illus. LC 82-9590. 32p. (gr. k-2). 1983. 12.95 (ISBN 0-02-700340-X, Bradbury Pr). Macmillan Child Grp.

Albertsen, June. Two Are Twins. Anton, Karen, illus. LC 86-70195. 31p. (ps-3). 1987. pap. 5.95 (ISBN 0-9615839-0-8). Double Talk.

Alcott, Louisa May. Little Men. 240p. (gr. 4-6). 1984. pap. 2.25 (ISBN 0-14-035018-7, Puffin). Puffin Bks.

Alexander, Liza. Big Bird the Artist: A Story about Addition & Subtraction. (Illus.). 32p. (ps-k). 1989. pap. write for info. (ISBN 0-307-13110-6, Pub. by Golden Bks). Western Pub.

—A Day in the Country: An Alphabet Story. Wetzel, Rick, illus. LC 87-81932. 32p. (ps-k). 1988. write for info. (ISBN 0-307-13106-8, Pub. by Golden Bks). Western Pub.

—Grover's Amazing Dream: A Storybook Introducing New Words. Cooke, Tom, illus. LC 87-83490. 32p. (ps-1). 1988. write for info. (ISBN 0-307-13108-4). Western Pub.

—Nothing to Do. Cooke, Tom, illus. LC 87-81761. 32p. (ps-k). 1988. write for info. (ISBN 0-307-12024-4, Pub. by Golden Bks). Western Pub.

—Sesame Street: Ernie & Twiddlebug Town Fair. 1990. pap. write for info. (ISBN 0-307-10030-8, Golden Pr). Western Pub.

—Sesame Street: Splish Splashy Day. (Illus.). 24p. (ps-k). 1989. pap. write for info. (ISBN 0-307-10064-2, Pub. by Golden Bks). Western Pub.

—A Visit to the Sesame Street Museum. Mathiew, Joe, illus. LC 87-1685. 32p. (gr. 3-6). 1987. lib. bdg. 5.99 (ISBN 0-394-98715-2); pap. 2.25 (ISBN 0-394-88715-8). Random.

Alexander, Lloyd. The Kestrel. 256p. (gr. 7 up). 1983. pap. 3.50 (ISBN 0-440-94393-0, LFL). Dell.

Alexander, Martha. Blackboard Bear. Alexander, Martha, illus. (gr. k-3). 1988. PLB 9.89 (ISBN 0-8037-0652-9). Dial Bks Young.

—I'll Protect You from the Jungle Beasts. Alexander, Martha, illus. LC 73-6015. 32p. (ps-2). 1983. 8.95 (ISBN 0-8037-4308-4); PLB 8.89 (ISBN 0-8037-4309-2). Dial Bks Young.

—Maybe a Monster. Alexander, Martha, illus. LC 68-28732. 32p. (ps-2). 1985. 8.95 (ISBN 0-8037-5508-2); PLB 8.89 (ISBN 0-8037-5513-9). Dial Bks Young.

—Out, Out, Out. Alexander, Martha, illus. LC 68-15251. (gr. k-3). 1968. 6.95 (ISBN 0-8037-6663-7); PLB 6.95 (ISBN 0-685-01457-6). Dial Bks Young.

Alexander, Sue. Small Plays for Special Days. Huffman, Tom, illus. LC 76-28424. 64p. (ps-1). 1988. pap. 4.95 (ISBN 0-89919-798-1, Pub. by Clarion). Ticknor & Fields.

—There's More...Much More. Brewster, Patience, illus. (ps-3). 12.95 (ISBN 0-317-62359-1, Gulliver Bks). HarBraceJ.

Aliki. The Two of Them. LC 79-10161. (ps-3). 1987. pap. 4.95 (ISBN 0-688-07337-9, Mulberry). Morrow.

Allard, Harry. Miss Nelson Has a Field Day. Marshall, James, illus. 32p. (gr. k-3). 1988. pap. 3.95 (ISBN 0-395-48654-8, Sandpiper). HM.

—Miss Nelson Is Back. Marshall, James, illus. 1988. pap. 7.95 incl. cass. (ISBN 0-395-48872-9). HM.

Allard, Harry & Marshall, James. The Stupids Take Off. Allard, Harry & Marshall, James, illus. 32p. (gr. k-3). 1989. 13.95 (ISBN 0-395-50068-0). HM.

Allbright, Viv. Ten Go Hopping. Allbright, Viv, illus. LC 85-13010. 29p. (ps-k). 1985. 6.95 (ISBN 0-571-13473-4). Faber & Faber.

Allen, Constance. Grover's Book of Cute Things to Touch. (ps). 1990. write for info. (ISBN 0-307-12320-0, Golden Pr). Western Pub.

—Sesame Street: Sleep Tight! Prebenna, David, illus. (ps-k). 1991. pap. write for info. (ISBN 0-307-10026-X, Golden Pr). Western Pub.

Allen, Jonathan. My Cat. LC 85-24614. (Illus.). 32p. (ps-2). 1986. 9.95 (ISBN 0-8037-0292-2). Dial Bks Young.

Allen, Laura J. Where Is Freddy? Allen, Laura J., illus. LC 85-45275. 64p. (gr. k-3). 1986. 11.95 (ISBN 0-06-020098-7). HarpC Child Bks.

Allert, Kathy. Kate Greenaway Paper Dolls in Full Color. 1981. pap. 3.50 (ISBN 0-486-24153-X). Dover.

Alley, R. W. The Clever Carpenter: (Just Right for 4's & 5's) Alley, R. W., illus. LC 87-43195. 32p. (ps-k). 1988. 4.95 (ISBN 0-394-89934-2, Random Juv); lib. bdg. 5.99 (ISBN 0-394-99934-7, Random Juv). Random.

—Watch Out, Cyrus! A Wacky Adventure on Land, on Sea & in the Air. (Illus.). 24p. (ps-2). 1990. 4.95 (ISBN 0-448-44001-6, G&D). Putnam Pub Group.

—Wee Wheels. (Illus.). 24p. (ps). 1990. bds. 2.50 (ISBN 0-448-02260-5, G&D). Putnam Pub Group.

Alley, R. W., illus. Busy Farm Trucks. 12p. (ps up). 1986. pap. 5.95 (ISBN 0-448-09883-0, G&D). Putnam Pub Group.

Almaraz, Humberto. Santa Will Love My Tree (Play Format) Almaraz, Humberto, illus. & intro. by. 12p. (Orig.). (ps-3). 1982. pap. 5.00 incl. 45 rpm record (ISBN 0-9616528-1-0). Alpha-Beto Music.

—Santa Will Love My Tree (Story Format) Almaraz, Humberto, illus. & intro. by. 12p. (Orig.). (ps-2). 1982. pap. 5.00 incl. 45 rpm record (ISBN 0-9616528-0-2). Alpha-Beto Music.

Alphabet. (Illus.). 12p. (gr. k-2). 1982. bds. 3.95 (ISBN 0-87449-175-4). Modern Pub NYC.

Alvarez, Juan. Jose Rabbit's Southwest Adventures: An ABC Coloring Book with Spanish Words. Alvarez, Juan, illus. 32p. (Orig.). (gr. 2-3). 1990. pap. 3.95 (ISBN 1-878610-00-7). Red Crane Bks.

Alverson, Charles. The Princess & the Mirror. Southgate, Mark, illus. 32p. (gr. k-3). 1989. 13.95 (ISBN 0-86264-174-8, Pub. by Anderson Pr UK). Trafalgar Sq.

Amadeo, Diana. There's a Little Bit of Me in Jamey. Fay, Ann, ed. Friedman, Judith, illus. (gr. 1-4). 1989. 10.95g (ISBN 0-8075-7854-1). A Whitman.

Amazing Dinosaurs: The Fastest, the Smallest, the Fiercest, & the Tallest. (ps-1). 1991. write for info. (ISBN 0-307-15747-4, Golden Pr). Western Pub.

American Colortype Co., Staff. Cut & Assemble Paper Dollhouse Furniture. 1981. pap. 4.95 (ISBN 0-486-24150-5). Dover.

Amerikaner, Susan. My Silly Book of ABC's. Brook, Bonnie, ed. Ziegler, Judy, illus. 32p. (ps-1). 1989. 4.95 (ISBN 0-671-68119-2); PLB 8.98 (ISBN 0-671-68363-2). Silver Pr.

—My Silly Book of Colors. Brook, Bonnie, ed. Ziegler, Judy, illus. 32p. (ps-1). 1989. 4.95 (ISBN 0-671-68120-6); PLB 8.98 (ISBN 0-671-68364-0). Silver Pr.

—My Silly Book of Counting. Brook, Bonnie, ed. Ziegler, Judy, illus. 32p. (ps-1). 1989. 4.95 (ISBN 0-671-68121-4); PLB 8.98 (ISBN 0-671-68365-9). Silver Pr.

—My Silly Book of Opposites. Brook, Bonnie, ed. Ziegler, Judy, illus. 32p. (ps-1). 1989. 4.95 (ISBN 0-671-68122-2); PLB 8.98 (ISBN 0-671-68366-7). Silver Pr.

—Silly Me! Books, 4 bks. Ziegler, Judy, illus. (ps-1). 1990. Set, 24p. ea. 19.80 (ISBN 0-671-93116-4); Set, 24p. ea. lib. bdg. 35.92 (ISBN 0-671-93137-7). Messner.

Amery. On the Farm. Cartwright, Stephen, illus. 20p. (ps). 1984. 2.95 (ISBN 0-86020-853-2, Pub. by Usborne). EDC.

Amery, H. The Farm Picture Book. 12p. (ps up). 1988. 2.95 (ISBN 0-7460-0128-2). EDC.

—The Seaside Picture Book. 12p. (ps up). 1988. 2.95 (ISBN 0-7460-0137-1). EDC.

—The Zoo Picture Book. 12p. (ps up). 1988. 2.95 (ISBN 0-7460-0127-4). EDC.

Amstutz, Beverly. Touch Me Not! (Illus.). 20p. (ps-7). 1983. pap. 2.50x (ISBN 0-937836-09-5). Precious Res.

Anastasio, Dina & Hohman, William. Letters & Sounds: Get Set Learning Skills Workbook. Fitzgerald, Theresa, illus. 32p. (ps-3). 1988. pap. 1.95 (ISBN 0-590-40549-7). Scholastic Inc.

Ancona, George & Miller, Mary B. Handtalk Zoo. Ancona, George, illus. LC 88-36861. 32p. 1989. 14.95 (ISBN 0-02-700801-0, Four Winds). Macmillan Child Grp.

Andersen, Hans Christian. The Emperor & the Nightingale. Van Nutt, Robert, illus. Tuber, Joel, adapted by. LC 88-11541. (Illus.). 44p. (ps up). 1988. 14.95 (ISBN 0-88708-082-0, Rabbit Ears); bk. & cass. pkg. 19.95 (ISBN 0-88708-087-1). Picture Bk Studio.

—The Emperor's New Clothes. LC 81-43313. (Illus.). 32p. (ps-3). 1987. pap. 3.95 (ISBN 0-06-443142-8, Trophy). HarpC Child Bks.

—The Little Mermaid. Iwasaki, Chihiro, illus. LC 84-9490. 32p. (gr. 2 up). 1984. 15.95 (ISBN 0-907234-59-3). Picture Bk Studio.

—The Nightingale. Le Gallienne, Eva, tr. from DAN. Burkert, Nancy E., illus. LC 64-18574. 48p. (gr. 2-6). 1985. pap. 6.95 (ISBN 0-06-443070-7, Trophy). HarpC Child Bks.

—The Snow Queen. Lewis, Naomi, tr. Barrett, Angela, illus. Lewis, Naomi, intro. by. LC 87-28789. (Illus.). 48p. (ps up). 1988. 15.95 (ISBN 0-8050-0830-6). H Holt & Co.

—Thumbelina. Roberts, Tom, adapted by. Johnson, David, illus. LC 89-8484. 32p. (gr. 1 up). 1989. 14.95 (ISBN 0-88708-113-4, Rabbit Ears); incl. cassette 19.95 (ISBN 0-88708-114-2). Picture Bk Studio.

—Thumbeline. Zwerger, Lisbeth, illus. LC 85-12062. 28p. (gr. 1 up). 1985. 14.95 (ISBN 0-88708-006-5). Picture Bk Studio.

—The Ugly Duckling. Van Nutt, Robert, illus. LC 86-185. 48p. (gr. k up). 1986. 12.95 (ISBN 0-394-88403-5); incl. cassette 15.95 (ISBN 0-394-88298-9). Knopf.

—The Ugly Duckling. Bell, Anthea, tr. Marks, Alan, illus. LC 89-3975. 42p. (gr. k up). 1990. 14.95 (ISBN 0-88708-116-9). Picture Bk Studio.

Anderson, Carol J. Alphabet Soup. Harding, Trish T., illus. 60p. (gr. k-4). 1989. 12.95 (ISBN 0-935317-26-0). Blue Heron WA.

Anderson, Debby. Christmas Joy. (Illus.). 32p. (ps-2). 1988. bds. 3.95 (ISBN 1-55513-862-4, Chariot Bks). Cook.

—Here & There, Everywhere! (Illus.). 18p. (ps). 1988. bds. 4.95 (ISBN 1-55513-643-5, Chariot Bks). Cook.

—Jesus Loves Me. (Illus.). 18p. (ps). 1988. bds. 4.95 (ISBN 1-55513-647-8, Chariot Bks). Cook.

—My Friend Noah. (Illus.). 18p. (ps). 1988. bds. 4.95 (ISBN 1-55513-665-6, Chariot Bks). Cook.

Anderson, Marcie. The Clumsy Kitty. (Illus.). 24p. (ps-3). 1988. pap. 0.99 (ISBN 0-87406-333-7). Willowisp Pr.

Anderson, Paul S. Storytelling with the Flannel Board, 3 Bks, Bk. 1. Francis, Irene, illus. LC 21-650. 270p. (ps). 1963. 15.95 (ISBN 0-513-00105-0). Denison.

—Storytelling with the Flannel Board, 3 Bks, Bk. 2. Arms, William, illus. LC 21-650. 260p. (ps). 1970. 15.95 (ISBN 0-513-00137-9). Denison.

Anderson, Peggy P. Time for Bed, the Babysitter Said. LC 86-27388. (ps). 1987. 12.95 (ISBN 0-395-41851-8). HM.

Anderson, Sara. Colors. Anderson, Sara, illus. 16p. (ps). 1988. comb bdg. 7.95 (ISBN 0-525-44401-7, DCB). Dutton Child Bks.

—Numbers. Anderson, Sara, illus. 22p. (ps). 1988. comb bdg. 7.95 (ISBN 0-525-44404-1, DCB). Dutton Child Bks.

Andrews, Jan. Very Last First Time. Wallace, Ian, illus. LC 85-71606. 32p. (gr. k-4). 1986. 14.95 (ISBN 0-689-50388-1, M K McElderry). Macmillan Child Grp.

Andrews, Margaret A. The Cooldles. 1989. 6.95 (ISBN 0-533-08231-5). Vantage.

Anglund, Joan W. Baby's First Book. Anglund, Joan W., illus. 12p. (ps). 1985. 3.99 (ISBN 0-394-87470-6, Random Juv). Random.

—How Many Days Has Baby To Play? Anglund, Joan W., illus. LC 87-19665. 24p. (ps-3). 1988. 7.95 (ISBN 0-15-200460-2, Gulliver Bks). HarBraceJ.

—The Joan Walsh Anglund I Love You Book & Doll Set. Anglund, Joan W., illus. LC 88-60060. 24p. (ps-1). 1988. book & doll pkg. 5.95 (ISBN 0-394-89338-7, Random Juv). Random.

—Morning Is a Little Child. Anglund, Joan W., illus. LC 69-11592. (gr. 4-6). 1969. 7.95 (ISBN 0-15-255652-4, HJ). HarBraceJ.

Animal Alphabet. (ps-1). 1987. 6.95 (ISBN 0-448-01466-1, G&D). Putnam Pub Group.

Animal Babies at the Zoo. (ps-1). 1985. 4.95 (ISBN 0-671-54736-4, Little Simon). S&S Trade.

Animal Fun. 1986. 1.98 (ISBN 0-685-16868-9, 614979). Outlet Bk Co.

Animal Shape Board Book: The Circus Clown. 1988. 1.98 (ISBN 0-671-09437-8). S&S Trade.

Animal Shape Board Book: The Hungry Caterpillar. 1988. 1.98 (ISBN 0-671-09436-X). S&S Trade.

Animal Shape Board Book: The Playful Puppy. 1988. 1.98 (ISBN 0-671-09435-1). S&S Trade.

Animals. (ps-k). 0.75 (ISBN 0-8091-6542-2). Paulist Pr.

Animals' ABC's. (Illus.). (ps-3). 1988. 8.95 (ISBN 0-8167-1443-6). Troll Assocs.

Anno, Mitsumasa. Anno's Alphabet: An Adventure in Imagination. Anno, Mitsumasa, illus. LC 73-21652. 64p. (ps up). 1988. pap. 6.95 (ISBN 0-06-443190-8, Trophy). HarpC Child Bks.

—Anno's Counting Book. LC 76-28977. (Illus.). 32p. (ps-3). 1986. pap. 5.95 (ISBN 0-06-443123-1, Trophy). HarpC Child Bks.

—Anno's Faces. Anno, Mitsumasa, illus. 32p. (ps). 1989. 11.95 (ISBN 0-399-21711-8, Philomel Bks). Putnam Pub Group.

—Anno's Mask. (Illus.). 24p. (ps-k). 1990. 10.95 (ISBN 0-399-21860-2, Philomel Bks). Putnam Pub Group.

—Anno's Peekaboo. (Illus.). 32p. (ps-k). 1988. 9.95 (ISBN 0-399-21520-4, Philomel Bks). Putnam Pub Group.

Anno, Mitsumasa & Anno, Mitsumasa. Topsy Turvies. (Illus.). 32p. (gr. k up). 1989. 13.95 (ISBN 0-399-21557-3, Philomel Bks). Putnam Pub Group.

Anno, Mitsumasa, illus. Anno's U. S. A. LC 83-13107. (gr. 3 up). 1983. 11.95 (ISBN 0-399-20974-3, Philomel Bks); signed limited ed. 35.00 (ISBN 0-399-21053-9, Philomel Bks). Putnam Pub Group.

Anno, Mitsumasa, et al. All in a Day. (Illus.). 32p. (ps-k). 1990. 14.99g (ISBN 0-399-61292-0, Philomel Bks). Putnam Pub Group.

Another Adventure Staff. Color My World. Hicks, Russell, et al, illus. 22p. (ps). 1988. write for info. incl. pre-programmed audiotape (ISBN 0-934323-72-0). Alchemy Comms.

—Counting Is Fun. Armstrong, Julie, et al, illus. 22p. (ps). 1988. write for info. incl. audio tape (ISBN 0-934323-71-2). Alchemy Comms.

—Easy As ABC. Hicks, Russell, et al, illus. 22p. (ps). 1988. write for info. incl. pre-programmed audiotape (ISBN 0-934323-76-3). Alchemy Comms.

—Just about the Size of It! Armstrong, Julie, et al, illus. 22p. (ps). 1988. write for info. incl. pre-programmed audiotape (ISBN 0-934323-78-X). Alchemy Comms.

—Shapes Are Everywhere. Armstrong, Julie, et al, illus. 22p. (ps). 1988. write for info. incl. pre-programmed audiotape (ISBN 0-934323-73-9). Alchemy Comms.

—Up, down & All Around. Mazurek, Theresa, et al, illus. 22p. (ps). 1988. write for info. incl. pre-programmed audiotape (ISBN 0-934323-77-1). Alchemy Comms.

Appelbaum, Neil. Is There a Hole in Your Head? Appelbaum, Neil, illus. (gr. k-3). 1963. 8.95 (ISBN 0-8392-3012-5). Astor-Honor.

Appiah, Sonia. Amoko & Efua Bear. Easmon, Carol, illus. LC 88-8343. 32p. (ps-1). 1989. 13.95 (ISBN 0-02-705591-4, Mcmillan Child Bk). Macmillan Child Grp.

Appleby, Ellen, illus. Peek-A-Boo. 16p. (ps-k). 1990. bds. 3.95 casebound (ISBN 0-671-70722-1). S&S Trade.

Apy, Deborah, retold by. Beauty & the Beast. Hague, Michael, illus. LC 83-5495. 72p. (ps up). 1988. pap. 6.95 (ISBN 0-8050-0948-5). H Holt & Co.

Archambault, John. Counting Sheep. Rombola, John, illus. 32p. (ps-2). 1989. 14.95 (ISBN 0-8050-1135-8). H Holt & Co.

Ardizzone, Edward. Tim All Alone. (Illus.). 48p. (ps-7). 1990. pap. 6.95 (ISBN 0-19-272125-9). Oxford U Pr.

Are You My Friend. 12p. (ps). 1988. 4.95 (ISBN 0-8120-5943-3). Barron.

Argent, Kerry & Trinca, Rod. One Woolly Wombat. LC 84-21854. (Illus.). 32p. (ps-1). 1985. 12.95 (ISBN 0-916291-00-6). Kane Miller Bk.

Arnold, Arnold. Antique Paper Dolls, 1915-1920. 1976. pap. 3.95 (ISBN 0-486-23176-3). Dover.
Aronin, Ben. The Secret of the Sabbath Fish. Rieger, Shay, illus. LC 78-63437. (gr. k-4). 1979. 8.95 (ISBN 0-8276-0110-7). JPS Phila.
The Artist, the Book & the Child: An Exhibition of Original Art for Children's Books. (Illus.). 60p. 1989. pap. 17.00 (ISBN 0-89792-120-8). Ill St Museum.
Aruego, Jose. Look What I Can Do! Aruego, Jose, illus. LC 87-21743. 32p. (ps-1). 1988. pap. 3.95 (ISBN 0-689-71205-7, Aladdin). Macmillan Child Grp.
Aruego, Jose & Dewey, Ariane. We Hide, You Seek. LC 78-13638. (Illus.). 32p. (ps-3). 1988. pap. 4.95 (ISBN 0-688-07815-X, Mulberry). Morrow.
Arvetis, Chris & Palmer, Carole. Why Does It Float? Buckley, James, illus. 32p. (ps-3). 1984. Repr. 3.95 (ISBN 0-528-82399-X). Checkerboard Pr.
—Why Does It Fly? Buckley, James, illus. 32p. (ps-3). 1984. Repr. 3.95 (ISBN 0-528-82074-5). Checkerboard Pr.
—Why Does It Rain? Buckley, James, illus. 32p. (ps-3). 1984. Repr. 3.95 (ISBN 0-528-82073-7, Checkerbord Pr). Macmillan.
—Why Does It Snow? Buckley, James, illus. 32p. (ps-3). 1984. 3.95 (ISBN 0-528-82823-1). Checkerboard Pr.
—Why Is It Dark? Buckley, James, illus. 32p. (ps-3). 1984. 3.95 (ISBN 0-528-82075-3). Checkerboard Pr.
Asch, Frank. I Can Roar. Asch, Frank, illus. 14p. (ps-1). 1988. pap. 3.95 (ISBN 0-517-56120-4). Crown.
—Moongame. (Illus.). 32p. (gr. k-4). 1987. PLB 11.95 (ISBN 0-671-66452-2); pap. 4.95 (ISBN 0-671-66453-0). S&S Trade.
Aseltine, Lorraine. First Grade Can Wait. Tucker, Kathleen, ed. (Illus.). 32p. (ps-2). 1988. PLB 10.95 (ISBN 0-8075-2451-4). A Whitman.
Aseltine, Lorraine, et al. I'm Deaf, & It's Okay. (Illus.). 40p. (gr. 1-4). 1986. 10.95 (ISBN 0-8075-3472-2). A Whitman.
Ashton, Elizabeth A. An Old-Fashioned ABC Book. Smith, Jessie W., illus. 32p. (ps-3). 1990. pap. 14.95 (ISBN 0-670-83048-8). Viking Child Bks.
At Home. (Illus.). (ps-k). 3.95 (ISBN 0-7214-5041-5). Ladybird Bks.
Atlas, Ron. Looking for Zebra. Arnold, Tedd, illus. Elck, Peter. 28p. (ps). 1986. pap. 4.95 (ISBN 0-671-62923-9, Little Simon). S&S Trade.
Attalides, Stephanos. Jungle Explorers: Adventure Box II. LC 85-45421. (Illus.). 28p. (ps up). 1986. 3.95 (ISBN 0-694-00083-3). HarpC Child Bks.
—Treasures of the Deep: Adventure Box I. LC 85-45420. (Illus.). 28p. (ps up). 1986. 3.95 (ISBN 0-694-00082-5). HarpC Child Bks.
Autumn Rose Diaries Garfield. 1987. 9.98 (ISBN 0-89954-727-3). Antioch Pub Co.
Autumn Rose Diaries Kittens & Hearts. 1987. 9.98 (ISBN 0-89954-722-2). Antioch Pub Co.
Averill, Esther. Jenny's Birthday Book. Averill, Esther, illus. LC 54-6589. 32p. (gr. k-3). 1954. PLB 14.89 (ISBN 0-06-020251-3). HarpC Child Bks.
Away in a Manger. 10p. (ps-2). 1989. pap. 4.95 (ISBN 0-448-04186-3, G&D). Putnam Pub Group.
Awdry, W. Catch Me, Catch Me! A Thomas the Tank Engine Story. Bell, Owain, illus. LC 89-37547. 24p. (Orig.). (ps-2). 1990. pap. 2.25 (ISBN 0-679-80485-4). McKay.
—Thomas the Tank Engine ABC: (Just Right for 2's & 3's) McArthur, Kenny, photos by. LC 89-10605. (Illus.). 24p. (ps). 1990. 4.95 (ISBN 0-679-80362-9). McKay.
—Thomas the Tank Engine Starter Library, 4 bks. Dalby, C. Reginald, illus. (ps-3). 1990. Repr. of 1945 ed. boxed set 19.95 (ISBN 0-679-80792-6). Random.
Aylesworth, Jim. Mr. McGill Goes to Town. Graham, Thomas, illus. 32p. (ps-1). 1989. 13.95 (ISBN 0-8050-0772-5). H Holt & Co.
—Mother Halverson's New Cat. Goffe, Toni, illus. LC 88-29279. 32p. (gr. k-3). 1989. 13.95 (ISBN 0-689-31465-5, Atheneum Child Bk). Macmillan Child Grp.
—One Crow: A Counting Rhyme. Young, Ruth, illus. LC 85-45856. 32p. (ps-1). 1988. 12.95 (ISBN 0-397-32174-0, Lipp Jr Bks); PLB 12.89 (ISBN 0-397-32175-9). HarpC Child Bks.
—Two Terrible Frights. Christelow, Eileen, illus. LC 86-25859. 32p. (ps-2). 1987. 13.95 (ISBN 0-689-31327-6, Atheneum Child Bk). Macmillan Child Grp.
Ayres, Pam. Guess What? Lacome, Julie, illus. LC 87-2718. 32p. (ps-k). 1988. 7.95 (ISBN 0-394-89287-9). Knopf.
—Guess Who? Lacome, Julie, illus. LC 87-2716. 32p. (ps-k). 1988. 7.95 (ISBN 0-394-89288-7). Knopf.
—When Dad Cuts Down the Chestnut Tree. Percy, Graham, illus. LC 87-35299. 32p. (ps-3). 1988. Knopf.
—When Dad Fills in the Garden Pond. Percy, Graham, illus. LC 87-35356. 32p. (ps-3). 1988. 3.82 (ISBN 0-394-80441-4). Knopf.
Babbitt, Natalie. The Something. (Illus.). (ps-3). 1987. pap. 2.95 (ISBN 0-374-46464-2). FS&G.
Baby. (Illus.). (ps-k). 3.95 (ISBN 0-7214-5159-4). Ladybird Bks.
Baby. (Illus.). (ps). 3.50 (ISBN 0-7214-1121-5). Ladybird Bks.
Baby Animals. (Illus.). 12p. (gr. k-2). 1983. bds. 3.95 (ISBN 0-87449-176-2). Modern Pub NYC.
Baby Animals. (Illus.). 24p. (gr. k-2). 1988. 3.95 (ISBN 0-87449-500-8). Modern Pub NYC.
Baby Bear Learns Numbers. 1988. 3.99 (ISBN 0-517-65510-1). Crown.
Baby Bear Learns Opposites. 1988. 2.99 (ISBN 0-517-65511-X). Crown.
Baby Bears At Snacktime. 1988. bds. 1.99 (ISBN 0-517-66704-5). Crown.
Baby Bear's Best Friends. (Illus.). (ps-k). 6.95 (ISBN 0-7214-9104-9). Ladybird Bks.
Baby Bears Get Dressed. 1988. bds. 1.99 (ISBN 0-517-66703-7). Crown.
Baby Bear's Hide & Seek. (Illus.). (ps-k). 6.95 (ISBN 0-7214-9103-0). Ladybird Bks.
Baby Bear's Noisy Farm. (Illus.). (ps-k). 6.95 (ISBN 0-7214-9101-4). Ladybird Bks.
Baby Bear's Shopping Day. (Illus.). (ps-k). 6.95 (ISBN 0-7214-9102-2). Ladybird Bks.
The Baby Born in a Stable: The Christmas Story. Bd. with The Secret Journey: Mary & Joseph. (ps-3). bk. & cassette 6.95 (ISBN 0-570-08054-1, 59-2105). Concordia.
Baby Care Bears' Animal Friends. LC 84-61936. 14p. (ps). 1985. bds. 2.95 (ISBN 0-394-87044-1, Random Juv). Random.
Baby Daisy's Walk. (Illus.). 10p. (ps). 1986. write for info (ISBN 0-307-06095-0, Pub. by Golden Bks). Western Pub.
Baby Dinosaur's Busy Day. 24p. (ps-1). 1988. 5.95 (ISBN 0-8431-4730-X). Price Stern.
Baby Donald at the Playground. (Illus.). 10p. (ps). 1986. write for info (ISBN 0-307-06096-9, Pub. by Golden Bks.). Western Pub.
Baby Jesus. 12p. (ps). 1986. 3.25 (ISBN 0-8378-5089-4). Gibson.
Baby Mickey Plays Hide & Seek. (Illus.). 10p. (ps). 1986. write for info (ISBN 0-307-06097-7, Pub. by Golden Bks). Western Pub.
Baby Mickey's Toys. (Illus.). 10p. (ps). 1986. write for info (ISBN 0-307-06098-5, Pub. by Golden Bks.). Western Pub.
Baby Mini Memory Album. 1988. pap. 3.95 (ISBN 0-89954-894-6). Antioch Pub Co.
Baby's Animal Sounds. (Illus.). 8p. 1989. 3.95 (ISBN 0-448-02786-0, G&D). Putnam Pub Group.
Baby's Blue Picture Book. (Illus.). (ps). 3.50 (ISBN 0-7214-1089-8). Ladybird Bks.
Baby's First Book. (Illus.). (ps). 3.50 (ISBN 0-7214-1082-0). Ladybird Bks.
Baby's First Rattle. (ps). 1990. bds. 2.95 (ISBN 0-671-47668-8, Little Simom). S&S Trade.
Baby's First Things. (Illus.). 8p. 1989. 3.95 (ISBN 0-448-02788-7, G&D). Putnam Pub Group.
Baby's First Things. (Illus.). (ps). 2.50 (ISBN 0-7214-9092-1). Ladybird Bks.
Baby's Green Picture Book. (Illus.). (ps). 3.50 (ISBN 0-7214-1101-0). Ladybird Bks.
Baby's Little Engine That Could. (Illus.). 8p. 1989. 3.95 (ISBN 0-448-02785-2, G&D). Putnam Pub Group.
Baby's Mother Goose. (Illus.). (ps). 1978. 2.50 (ISBN 0-448-46804-2, G&D). Putnam Pub Group.
Baby's Mother Goose. (Illus.). 8p. 1989. 3.95 (ISBN 0-448-02790-9, G&D). Putnam Pub Group.
Baby's Peek-a-Boo. (Illus.). 8p. 1989. 3.95 (ISBN 0-448-02789-5, G&D). Putnam Pub Group.
Baby's Red Picture Book. (Illus.). (ps). 3.50 (ISBN 0-7214-1088-X). Ladybird Bks.
Baby's Sweet Dreams. (Illus.). 8p. 1989. 3.95 (ISBN 0-448-02787-9, G&D). Putnam Pub Group.
Baby's Things. (ps). 1954. 2.50 (ISBN 0-448-03048-9, G&D). Putnam Pub Group.
Baby's Yellow Picture Book. (Illus.). (ps). 3.50 (ISBN 0-7214-1100-2). Ladybird Bks.
Baehr, Patricia. School Isn't Fair. Alley, R. W., illus. LC 88-21461. 32p. (ps-k). 1989. 13.95 (ISBN 0-02-708130-3, Four Winds). Macmillan Child Grp.
Baker, Arthur. Cut & Assemble Paper Airplanes That Fly. 1982. pap. 3.95 (ISBN 0-486-24302-8). Dover.
Baker, Barbara. Digby & Kate. Winborn, Marsha, illus. LC 87-24455. 48p. (ps-2). 1988. 9.95 (ISBN 0-525-44370-3, 0966-290, DCB). Dutton Child Bks.
Baker, Betty. The Turkey Girl. Berson, Harold, illus. LC 82-17285. 64p. (gr. 1-4). 1983. 9.95 (ISBN 0-02-708260-1, Mcmillan Child Bk). Macmillan Child Grp.
Baker, Darrell, illus. Baby Donald's Busy Play Group. LC 87-81947. 14p. (ps-1). 1988. write for info. (ISBN 0-307-12316-2). Western Pub.
—Disney Babies Nursery Rhymes. LC 87-83006. 12p. (ps). 1988. write for info. (ISBN 0-307-06082-9). Western Pub.
—Disney Babies on the Go. LC 87-83008. 12p. (ps). 1988. write for info. (ISBN 0-307-06099-3). Western Pub.
—Disney Babies Rock-a-Bye. LC 87-83007. 12p. (ps). 1988. write for info. (ISBN 0-307-06084-5). Western Pub.
—Disney Babies What's up High? LC 87-83009. 12p. (ps). 1988. write for info. (ISBN 0-307-06100-0). Western Pub.
Baker, Leslie. The Third-Story Cat. Baker, Leslie, illus. 32p. (ps-3). 1987. 12.95 (ISBN 0-316-07832-8). Little.
Baker, Pamela J. My First Book of Sign. Gillen, Patricia B, illus. LC 86-14937. iv, 76p. (ps-3). 1986. 12.95 (ISBN 0-930323-20-3, Kendall Green Pubns). Gallaudet Univ Pr.
Baker, Rosemary. What Am I? A Bible Animal Activity Book. 32p. (gr. k-4). 1988. pap. 1.99 (ISBN 0-8163-0716-4). Pacific Pr Pub Assn.
Balestrino, Philip. The Skeleton Inside You. Bolognese, Don, illus. LC 85-42982. 40p. (ps-3). 1986. pap. 4.95 (ISBN 0-06-445039-2, Trophy). HarpC Child Bks.
Balian, Lorna. The Sweet Touch. 48p. (Orig.). (gr. 1-2). pap. 5.95 (ISBN 0-687-40774-5). Abingdon.
Ball, Jacqueline. Riddles about Baby Animals. Brook, Bonnie, ed. (Illus.). 32p. (ps-3). 1989. 5.95 (ISBN 0-671-68577-5); PLB 10.98 (ISBN 0-671-68576-7). Silver Pr.
—Riddles about Our Bodies. Brook, Bonnie, ed. (Illus.). 32p. (ps-3). 1989. 5.95 (ISBN 0-671-68579-1); PLB 10.98 (ISBN 0-671-68578-3). Silver Pr.
—Riddles about the Seasons. Brook, Bonnie, ed. (Illus.). 32p. (ps-3). 1989. 5.95 (ISBN 0-671-68583-X); PLB 10.98 (ISBN 0-671-68582-1). Silver Pr.
—Riddles about the Senses. Brook, Bonnie, ed. (Illus.). 32p. (ps-3). 1989. 5.95 (ISBN 0-671-68581-3); PLB 10.98 (ISBN 0-671-68580-5). Silver Pr.
Ball, Jacqueline A. What Can It Be, 8 bks. (Illus.). (gr. k-3). 1990. Set, 32p. ea. 47.60 (ISBN 0-671-94104-6); Set, 32p. ea. lib. bdg. 109.80 (ISBN 0-671-94103-8). Messner.
Balzola, Asun. Munia & the Day Things Went Wrong. (Illus.). 24p. (gr. k-2). 1988. 11.95 (ISBN 0-521-35643-1). Cambridge U Pr.
—Munia & the Orange Crocodile. (Illus.). 24p. (gr. k-2). 1988. 11.95 (ISBN 0-521-35642-3). Cambridge U Pr.
Bang, Molly. The Paper Crane. LC 84-13546. (gr. k-3). 1987. pap. 4.95 (ISBN 0-688-07333-6, Mulberry). Morrow.
Bang, Molly G. The Grey Lady & the Strawberry Snatcher. LC 85-29224. (Illus.). 48p. (ps-3). 1984. 14. 95 (ISBN 0-02-708140-0, Four Winds). Macmillan Child Grp.
Bank Street College of Education Editors. ABC Come Play with Me. (Illus.). 64p. (ps-k). 1985. 3.95 (ISBN 0-8120-3617-4). Barron.
—All Around the House. (Illus.). 64p. (ps-k). 1985. 2.95 (ISBN 0-8120-3613-1). Barron.
—All Around the Neighborhood. (Illus.). 64p. (ps-k). 1985. 2.95 (ISBN 0-8120-3612-3). Barron.
—Get Ready to Read. (Illus.). 64p. (ps-k). 1985. 3.95 (ISBN 0-8120-3616-6). Barron.
—Let's Take a Ride. (gr. 1-2). 1986. pap. 2.95 (ISBN 0-8120-3623-9). Barron.
Banks, Kate. Alphabet Soup. Sis, Peter, illus. LC 87-3191. 32p. (ps-2). 1988. 12.95 (ISBN 0-394-89151-1); lib. bdg. 11.99 (ISBN 0-394-99151-6). Knopf.
Banner, Angela. Ant & Bee: Alphabetical Story for Tiny Tots. Ward, Bryan, illus. 96p. (ps-1). 5.95 (ISBN 0-434-92966-2, Pub. by W Heinemann Ltd). Trafalgar Sq.
—Ant & Bee & the ABC. (Illus.). 96p. (ps-1). 1989. 5.95 (ISBN 0-434-92967-0, Pub. by W Heinemann Ltd). Trafalgar Sq.
—Ant & Bee & the Doctor. Ward, Bryan, illus. 96p. (ps-1). 5.95 (ISBN 0-434-92968-9, Pub. by W. Heinemann Ltd). Trafalgar Sq.
—Ant & Bee & the Rainbow. Ward, Bryan, illus. 96p. (ps-1). 5.95 (ISBN 0-434-92972-7, Pub. by W. Heinemann Ltd). Trafalgar Sq.
—Ant & Bee & the Secret. (Illus.). 96p. (ps-1). 1989. 5.95 (ISBN 0-434-92959-X, Pub. by W Heinemann Ltd). Trafalgar Sq.
—Ant & Bee Go Shopping. Ward, Bryan, illus. 96p. (ps-1). 5.95 (ISBN 0-434-92970-0, Pub. by W Heinemann Ltd). Trafalgar Sq.
—Ant & Bee Time. (Illus.). 94p. (ps-3). 1988. 5.95 (ISBN 0-434-92961-1, Pub. by W Heinemann Ltd). Trafalgar Sq.
—Around the World with Ant & Bee. (Illus.). 96p. (ps-1). 1989. 5.95 (ISBN 0-434-92958-1, Pub. by W Heinemann Ltd). Trafalgar Sq.
—Happy Birthday with Ant & Bee. (Illus.). 96p. (ps-1). 1989. 5.95 (ISBN 0-434-92963-8, Pub. by W Heinemann Ltd). Trafalgar Sq.
—More & More Ant & Bee. (Illus.). 96p. (ps-1). 1989. 5.95 (ISBN 0-434-92962-X, Pub. by W Heinemann Ltd). Trafalgar Sq.
—More Ant & Bee. (Illus.). 96p. (ps-1). 1989. 5.95 (ISBN 0-434-92965-4, Pub. by W Heinemann Ltd). Trafalgar Sq.
—One, Two, Three with Ant & Bee. (Illus.). 96p. (ps-1). 1989. 5.95 (ISBN 0-434-92964-6, Pub. by W Heinemann Ltd). Trafalgar Sq.
Bantock, Nick, retold by. & illus. There Was an Old Lady. (gr. 4 up). 1990. pap. 7.95 (ISBN 0-670-83194-8). Viking Penguin.
Barbaresi, Nina. Firemouse. 40p. (ps-3). 1987. PLB 10.95 (ISBN 0-517-56337-1). Crown.
Barbaresi, Nina, illus. Baby's First Book of Colors. LC 85-62638. 12p. (ps). 1986. 3.95 (ISBN 0-448-10827-5, Platt & Munk). Putnam Pub Group.
—Tough Trucks. 12p. (ps up). 1986. pap. 5.95 (ISBN 0-448-09884-9, G&D). Putnam Pub Group.
Barborak, Gary & Kveton, Lisa. Gentle Giants: A Child's Adventure with the Five Senses. Kveton, Lisa, illus. 40p. (ps-k). 1989. write for info. Blue Norther.
Barkan, Joanne. Whiskerville Bake Shop. Schmidt, Karen L., illus. 12p. (ps-k). 1990. bds. 3.50 (ISBN 0-448-19467-8, G&D). Putnam Pub Group.
—Whiskerville Firehouse. Schmidt, Karen L., illus. 12p. (ps-k). 1990. bds. 3.50 (ISBN 0-448-19468-6, G&D). Putnam Pub Group.
—Whiskerville Post Office. Schmidt, Karen L., illus. 12p. (ps-k). 1990. bds. 3.50 (ISBN 0-685-32321-8, G&D). Putnam Pub Group.
Barklem, Jill. Autumn Story. (ps-3). 1989. 8.95 (ISBN 0-399-21754-1, Philomel Bks). Putnam Pub Group.
—Spring Story. (ps-3). 1989. 8.95 (ISBN 0-399-21751-7, Philomel Bks). Putnam Pub Group.

—Summer Story. (ps-3). 1989. 8.95 (ISBN 0-399-21753-3, Philomel Bks). Putnam Pub Group.
—Winter Story. (ps-3). 1989. incl. cass. 8.95 (ISBN 0-399-21752-5, Philomel Bks). Putnam Pub Group.
Barks, Carl. Walt Disney's Donald & Daisy Comic Album. Barks, Carl, illus. Blum, Geoffrey, intro. by. (Illus.). 48p. (Orig.). (ps up). 1988. pap. 5.95 (ISBN 0-944599-11-7). Gladstone Pub.
—Walt Disney's Donald Duck Adventures Album. Barks, Carl, illus. Blum, Geoffrey, intro. by. (Illus.). 48p. (Orig.). (ps up). 1988. pap. 5.95 (ISBN 0-944599-13-3). Gladstone Pub.
—Walt Disney's Donald Duck Adventures Album. Barks, Carl, illus. Blum, Geoffrey, intro. by. (Illus.). 48p. (Orig.). (ps up). 1989. pap. 5.95 (ISBN 0-944599-15-X). Gladstone Pub.
—Walt Disney's Uncle Scrooge Album. Barks, Carl, illus. Blum, Geoffrey, intro. by. (Illus.). 48p. (Orig.). (ps up). 1988. pap. 5.95 (ISBN 0-944599-14-1). Gladstone Pub.
—Walt Disney's Uncle Scrooge Comic Album. Barks, Carl, illus. Blum, Geoffrey, intro. by. (Illus.). 48p. (Orig.). (ps up). 1988. pap. 5.95 (ISBN 0-944599-10-9). Gladstone Pub.
Barlass, Gail. Dinosquares: A Modern Dinosaur Book for Imaginative Children. Hansen, Ron, ed. & illus. LC 87-62124. 24p. (ps-3). 1988. pap. 3.95 (ISBN 0-943925-07-X). Purple Turtle Bks.
Barnes-Murphy, Rowan, illus. One, Two, Buckle My Shoe: A Book of Counting Rhymes. (ps-3). 1988. pap. 10.95 (ISBN 0-671-63791-6, Little Simon). S&S Trade.
Baron, Michelle. One More Spot. Forsse, Ken, ed. High, David, et al, illus. 26p. (ps). 1985. incl. pre-programmed audio-cassette 9.95. Alchemy Comms.
—Safe at Home with Teddy Ruxpin. Armstrong, Julie, et al, illus. 34p. (ps). 1988. write for info. incl. audio tape (ISBN 0-934323-70-4). Alchemy Comms.
—Water Safety with Teddy Ruxpin. Armstrong, Julie, et al, illus. 34p. (ps). 1988. incl. audio tape 9.95 (ISBN 0-934323-74-7). Alchemy Comms.
Baron, Michelle, adapted by. The Golden Touch: A Greek Myth (King Midas) Hicks, Russell, et al, illus. 26p. (ps). 1987. Packaged with pre-programmed audio cass. tape. 9.95 (ISBN 0-934323-63-1). Alchemy Comms.
Baron, Phil. Anything in the Soup. Levitt, Lenny, contrib. by. Hicks, Russell, et al, illus. 34p. (ps). 1987. incl. cass. 9.95 (ISBN 0-934323-44-5). Alchemy Comms.
—The Autumn Adventure. Forsse, Ken, ed. High, David, et al, illus. 26p. (ps). 1986. 9.95 (ISBN 0-934323-18-6); audio cassette tape incl. Alchemy Comms.
—Fire Safety with Teddy Ruxpin. Armstrong, Julie, et al, illus. 22p. (ps). 1988. write for info. incl. pre-programmed audiotape (ISBN 0-934323-75-5). Alchemy Comms.
—Gizmos & Gadgets. (Illus.). 34p. (ps). 1987. packaged with pre-programmed audio cass. tape 9.95 (ISBN 0-934323-45-3). Alchemy Comms.
—Let's Learn about Opposites. Hicks, Russell, et al, illus. 22p. (ps). 1988. write for info. incl. audio tape (ISBN 0-934323-69-0). Alchemy Comms.
—Medicine Wagon. Forsse, Ken, ed. High, David, et al, illus. 26p. (ps). 1985. incl. pre-programmed audio-cassette 9.95 (ISBN 0-934323-17-8). Alchemy Comms.
—Quiet Please. Hicks, Russell, et al, illus. 34p. (ps). 1987. incl. pre-programmed audio cass. 9.95 (ISBN 0-934323-40-2). Alchemy Comms.
—Wooly & the Giant Snowzos. Hicks, Russell, et al, illus. 34p. (ps). 1987. incl. pre-programmed audio cass. 9.95 (ISBN 0-934323-42-9). Alchemy Comms.
Barone, Shirley A. Bugs - Bugs - Bugs, Vol. 10. Coleman, Debbie, illus. 44p. (Orig.). (ps-2). Date not set. pap. write for info. Toad Hse Bks.
—Easter Parade, Vol. 6. Coleman, Debbie, illus. 44p. (Orig.). (ps-2). 1990. pap. write for info. Toad Hse Bks.
—Funny Dinosaurs, Vol. 4. Coleman, Debbie, illus. 44p. (Orig.). (ps-2). 1989. pap. write for info. Toad Hse Bks.
—Halloween Fun for Everyone, Vol. 1. Coleman, Debbie, illus. 44p. (Orig.). (ps-2). 1989. pap. 1.69 (ISBN 0-685-30447-7). Toad Hse Bks.
—Happy Valentines, Vol. 5. Coleman, Debbie, illus. 44p. (Orig.). (ps-2). 1990. pap. text ed. write for info. Toad Hse Bks.
—I Know My ABC's, Vol. 13. Coleman, Debbie, illus. 44p. (Orig.). (ps-2). Date not set. pap. write for info. Toad Hse Bks.
—I Know My Numbers, Vol. 14. Coleman, Debbie, illus. 44p. (Orig.). (ps-2). Date not set. pap. write for info. Toad Hse Bks.
—I Like Monsters, Vol. 9. Coleman, Debbie, illus. 44p. (Orig.). (ps-2). Date not set. pap. write for info. Toad Hse Bks.
—In My Toy Box, Vol. 8. Coleman, Debbie, illus. 44p. (Orig.). (ps-2). Date not set. pap. write for info. Toad Hse Bks.
—Kittens & Puppies, Vol. 11. Coleman, Debbie, illus. 44p. (Orig.). (ps-2). Date not set. pap. write for info. Toad Hse Bks.
—Let's Give Thanks, Vol. 2. Coleman, Debbie, illus. 44p. (Orig.). (ps-2). 1989. pap. 1.75 (ISBN 0-685-30448-5). Toad Hse Bks.
—Meet My Friends: Children of the World, Vol. 15. Coleman, Debbie, illus. 44p. (Orig.). (ps-2). Date not set. pap. write for info. Toad Hse Bks.
—My Teddy Bears, Vol. 12. Coleman, Debbie, illus. 44p. (Orig.). (ps-2). Date not set. pap. write for info. Toad Hse Bks.
—A Shoe for You, Vol. 7. Coleman, Debbie, illus. 44p. (Orig.). (ps-2). Date not set. pap. write for info. Toad Hse Bks.
—A Time for Joy (Christmas, Vol. 3. Coleman, Debbie, illus. 44p. (Orig.). (ps-2). 1989. pap. write for info. Toad Hse Bks.
Barrett, John E., photos by. Big Bird Is Yellow: A Sesame Street Book of Colors. LC 89-63996. (Illus.). 14p. (ps). 1990. bds. 3.95 (ISBN 0-679-80752-7). Random.
Barrett, Judi. Animals Should Definitely Not Act Like People. Barrett, Ron, illus. 32p. (ps-1). 1988. pap. 3.95 (ISBN 0-689-71287-1, Aladdin). Macmillan Child Grp.
—Animals Should Definitely Not Wear Clothing. Barrett, Ron, illus. 32p. (ps-1). 1988. pap. 3.95 (ISBN 0-689-70807-6, Aladdin). Macmillan Child Grp.
Barrett, Judith. Pickles Have Pimples: And Other Silly Statements. Johnson, Lonnie S., illus. LC 85-20073. 32p. (ps-2). 1986. 12.95 (ISBN 0-689-31187-7, Atheneum Child Bk). Macmillan Child Grp.
—A Snake Is Totally Tail. Johnson, Lonni S., illus. LC 87-1123. 32p. (ps-1). 1987. pap. 3.95 (ISBN 0-689-71148-4, Aladdin). Macmillan Child Grp.
Barry, Robert. Mr. Willoby's Christmas Tree. Galdone, Paul, illus. (gr. k-3). 1963. text ed. 12.95 (ISBN 0-07-003877-5). McGraw.

Bartlett, Jaye. Caterpillar Had a Dream: A Poetic Story about Dreams Coming True. (Illus.). 1991. 8.95 (ISBN 1-878064-02-9). TLC Bks.
"Caterpillar" isn't about pots of gold at the end of the rainbow. "Caterpillar" is about a dream, & the courage to try. Parents & children alike will be thrilled & inspired by Caterpillar's heartening adventure as he finds the courage & determination to make his dream come true.
Publisher Provided Annotation.

—Caterpillar Had a Dream: A Story about Dreams Coming True. Dubina, Alan, illus. 38p. (Orig.). (ps up). 1990. PLB 11.95 incl. cassette (ISBN 1-878064-00-2). New Age CT.
CATERPILLAR HAD A DREAM is a heartening story, written to encourage children to follow their dreams. The poetic book contains 38 pages of magical poetry & endearing color illustrations. CATERPILLAR HAD A DREAM is the first release in a series of twelve planned children's books. The series is being released under the Logo "Tender Loving Caretaker of Planet Earth." A portion of profits from the 'Caretaking Series' is donated to the World Children's Day Foundation, Washington, D.C., to help facilitate & encourage children to become active participant of "Caretaking Projects" in their communities. "CATERPILLAR HAD A DREAM is inspiring & enchanting! It's our two daughters' favorite story book & audio cassette. I feel it's one of the best stories for children I've ever read."--Lee Rector, Publisher, I.S.I. Publications, Tampa, Florida.
Publisher Provided Annotation.

—Freddy the Elephant: The Story of a Sensitive Leader. Dubina, Alan, illus. 45p. (Orig.). (ps up). 1991. pap. 11.95 incl. cassette (ISBN 1-878064-01-0). New Age CT.
Freddy doesn't like himself. He is chubby & can't move very fast. His mentor, Gran-Fada, King of all the Elephants, recognizes Freddy's potential, & encourages Freddy with his majestic understanding. As Freddy grows & learns to accept himself, hope triumphs over low self-esteem. Every child & adult will identify with Freddy's many trials & tribulations, & will cherish the memory of their own "sensitive leader."
Publisher Provided Annotation.

Barton, Byron. Where's Al? LC 78-171866. (Illus.). 32p. (ps). 1989. pap. 4.95 (ISBN 0-395-51582-3, Clarion Bks). HM.
Bassett, Lisa. Beany Wakes up for Christmas. Bassett, Jeni, illus. 32p. (ps-3). 1988. 12.95 (ISBN 0-399-21668-5, Putnam). Putnam Pub Group.
Bastin, Marjolein. Vera the Mouse. (ps-k). 1986. Four-bk. boxed set. 11.95 (ISBN 0-8120-7391-6); 2.95 ea. Barron.
Bathtime. (Illus.). (ps). 3.50 (ISBN 0-7214-9085-9). Ladybird Bks.
Battistella, B. The Legend of Little White Hood. (gr. 1 up). 1988. pap. 1.75 (ISBN 0-8198-4405-5). Dghtrs St Paul.
Bauer, Caroline F. Midnight Snowman. Stock, Catherine, illus. LC 86-26540. 32p. (ps-2). 1987. 13.95 (ISBN 0-689-31294-6, Atheneum Child Bk). Macmillan Child Grp.
Baum, L. Frank. Wonderful Wizard of Oz Pop Ups. 1991. slipcased 12.99 (ISBN 0-517-06094-9). Crown.
Baum, Louis. I Want to See the Moon. Daly, Niki, illus. LC 88-33061. 32p. (ps-3). 1989. cloth 11.95 (ISBN 0-87951-367-5). Overlook Pr.
Baum, Susan. Busy Farm. (Illus.). 24p. (ps). 1988. 5.95 (ISBN 0-448-19064-8, G&D). Putnam Pub Group.
—Busy Town. (Illus.). 24p. (ps-1). 1988. 5.95 (ISBN 0-448-19065-6, G&D). Putnam Pub Group.
—Gear Bear's Good Morning. (Illus.). 14p. (ps). 1988. bds. 3.50 (ISBN 0-448-19061-3, G&D). Putnam Pub Group.
—Goodnight, Gear Bear. (Illus.). 14p. (ps). 1988. bds. 3.50 (ISBN 0-448-19060-5, G&D). Putnam Pub Group.
Baum, Susan, illus. & created by. Busy Birthday. 24p. (ps-k). 1988. 5.95 (ISBN 0-448-09280-8, G&D). Putnam Pub Group.
—Busy School. 24p. (ps-k). 1988. 5.95 (ISBN 0-448-09279-4, G&D). Putnam Pub Group.
—Gear Bear Loves Color! A Gear Bear Lift-the-Flap Book. 24p. (ps-k). 1988. 10.95 (ISBN 0-448-09282-4, G&D). Putnam Pub Group.
Bauman, A. F. Guess Where You're Going, Guess What You'll Do. Kelley, True, illus. 32p. (ps-k). 1989. 13.95 (ISBN 0-395-50211-X). HM.
Bayley, Nicola. As I Was Going Up & Down & Other Nonsense Rhymes. (Illus.). 32p. (ps-k). 1986. 10.95 (ISBN 0-02-708590-2, Mcmillan Child Bk). Macmillan Child Grp.
Baynes, Pauline, illus. Noah & the Ark. LC 87-46412. 32p. (ps up). 1988. 14.95 (ISBN 0-8050-0886-1). H Holt & Co.
Baynton, Martin. Fifty & the Great Race. Baynton, Martin, illus. (gr. k-3). 1986. 5.95 (ISBN 0-517-56354-1). Crown.
—Fifty Gets the Picture. Baynton, Martin, illus. (gr. k-3). 1986. 5.95 (ISBN 0-517-56355-X). Crown.
Beall, Pamela C. Wee Color Wee Sing & Play. 1986. pap. 1.95 (ISBN 0-8431-1240-9). Price Stern.
Beall, Pamela C. & Nipp, Susan. Wee Color Wee Sing Australia. 48p. (ps-2). 1988. pap. 1.95 (ISBN 0-8431-4725-3); audio pkg. 9.95 (ISBN 0-8431-2320-6). Price Stern.
—Wee Color Wee Sing Dinosaurs. 48p. (ps-2). 1988. pap. 1.95 (ISBN 0-8431-4726-1); audio pkg. 9.95 (ISBN 0-8431-2321-4). Price Stern.
—Wee Color Wee Sing King Cole's Party. 48p. (ps-2). 1988. pap. 1.95 (ISBN 0-8431-4728-8); audio pkg. 9.95 (ISBN 0-8431-2323-0). Price Stern.
Beall, Pamela C. & Nipp, Susan H. King Cole's Party. Klein, Nancy, illus. (ps-2). 1987. 19.95 (ISBN 0-8431-4714-8); incl. audiocassette soundtrack 23.95 (ISBN 0-8431-4715-6). Price Stern.
—Wee Color Wee Sing. Klein, Nancy, illus. 48p. (Orig.). (ps-2). 1988. incl. cassettes & pens 9.95 (ISBN 0-8431-1237-9). Price Stern.
—Wee Color Wee Sing & Play. Klein, Nancy, illus. 48p. (Orig.). (ps-2). 1988. incl. cass. & pens 9.95 (ISBN 0-8431-1224-7). Price Stern.
—Wee Color Wee Sing Around the Campfire. Klein, Nancy, illus. 48p. (Orig.). (ps-2). 1988. incl. cassettes & pens 9.95 (ISBN 0-8431-1760-5). Price Stern.
—Wee Color Wee Sing Silly Songs. Klein, Nancy, illus. 48p. (Orig.). (ps-2). 1988. incl. cassettes & pens 9.95 (ISBN 0-8431-1776-1). Price Stern.
Beasley, Roberta, illus. Baby's Cradle Songs. 12p. (ps). 1986. 3.95 (ISBN 0-394-88242-3, Random Juv). Random.
Beatrix Potter's Address Book. 160p. 1982. 6.95 (ISBN 0-7232-2900-7). Warne.
Beckett, Sheilah, illus. Lullaby & Good Night. 32p. (ps-2). 1987. pap. 1.95 (ISBN 0-448-19082-6, Platt & Munk); write for info. bk & cass. (Platt & Munk). Putnam Pub Group.
Beckmann, Beverly. Numbers in God's World. (ps). 1983. 6.95 (ISBN 0-570-04083-3, 56-1438). Concordia.
Bedtime. (Illus.). (ps). 3.50 (ISBN 0-7214-1087-1). Ladybird Bks.
Beisner, Monika. Secret Spells & Curious Charms. (Illus.). 32p. 1988. pap. 3.95 (ISBN 0-374-46600-9). FS&G.

—Topsy Turvy. LC 87-45751. (Illus.). 32p. (ps up). 1988. 12.95 (ISBN 0-374-37679-4). FS&G.

Bell, Anthea. Swan Lake. Iwasaki, Chihiro, illus. LC 86-9509. 28p. (gr. 1 up). 1986. 15.95 (ISBN 0-88708-028-6). Picture Bk Studio.

Bell, Owain. Thomas the Tank Engine Books. Bell, Owain, illus. (ps-2). 1990. 5.95 (Random Juv); pap. 2.95. Random.

Bell, Owain, illus. Thomas the Tank Engine Says Goodnight. 12p. (ps-k). 1990. sponge filled 3.95 (ISBN 0-679-80791-8). Random.

Bell, Richard. Deep in the Wood. (Illus.). 28p. (ps-2). 1988. pap. 6.95 (ISBN 0-434-92849-6, Pub. by W Heinemann Ltd). Trafalgar Sq.

Bell, Robert. Amazing Dinosaur Facts. (Illus.). 24p. (ps-3). 1990. pap. write for info. (ISBN 0-307-12575-0, Pub. by Golden Bks). Western Pub.

—My First Book of Space Coloring & Activity Book. Epstein, Len, et al, illus. 160p. (gr. 1 up). 1986. pap. 6.95 (ISBN 0-671-62407-5, Little Simon). S&S Trade.

Bell, Sally. Gingerbread Man. (ps-3). 1990. write for info. (ISBN 0-307-11592-5). Western Pub.

Bellamy, David. Our Changing World: The Roadside. Dow, Jill, illus. 32p. (gr. 1-5). 1988. 9.95 (ISBN 0-517-56976-0, C N Potter Bks). Crown.

—Our Changing World: The Rock Pool. Dow, Jill, illus. 32p. (gr. 1-5). 1988. 9.95 (ISBN 0-517-56977-9, C N Potter Bks). Crown.

Bellows, Cathy. Four Fat Rats. Bellows, Cathy, illus. LC 85-31836. 32p. (ps-3). 1987. 12.95 (ISBN 0-02-708830-8, Mcmillan Child Bk). Macmillan Child Grp.

—The Royal Raccoon. Bellows, Cathy, illus. LC 88-8282. 32p. (ps-3). 1989. 13.95 (ISBN 0-02-709031-0, Mcmillan Child Bk). Macmillan Child Grp.

Bellville, Cheryl W. Round-Up. (Illus.). 32p. (gr. k-4). 1982. PLB 9.95 (ISBN 0-87614-187-4). Carolrhoda Bks.

Bellville, Rod & Bellville, Cheryl W. Stockyards. LC 83-18839. (Illus.). 32p. (gr. k-4). 1984. PLB 9.95 (ISBN 0-87614-224-2). Carolrhoda Bks.

Bemelmans, Ludwig. Madeline. Bemelmans, Ludwig, illus. LC 39-21791. (gr. k-3). 1977. pap. 3.95 incl. cassette (ISBN 0-14-050198-3, Puffin). Puffin Bks.

—Madeline & the Bad Hat. Bemelmans, Ludwig, illus. LC 57-62. (gr. k-3). 1977. pap. 3.95 (ISBN 0-14-050206-8, Puffin). Puffin Bks.

—Madeline & the Gypsies. Bemelmans, Ludwig, illus. (gr. k-3). 1959. pap. 13.95 (ISBN 0-670-44682-3). Viking Child Bks.

—Madeline's Christmas. (ps-3). 1988. pap. 3.95 (ISBN 0-14-050666-7, Puffin). Puffin Bks.

—Madeline's Rescue. Bemelmans, Ludwig, illus. LC 53-8709. 56p. (gr. k-3). 1953. pap. 13.95 (ISBN 0-670-44716-1). Viking Child Bks.

Bemmelmans, Ludwig. Madeline. Bemelmans, Ludwig, illus. LC 68-666. (gr. k-3). 1958. pap. 13.95 (ISBN 0-670-44580-0). Viking Child Bks.

—Madeline & the Bad Hat. Bemelmans, Ludwig, illus. (gr. k-3). 1957. pap. 13.95 (ISBN 0-670-44614-9). Viking Child Bks.

—Madeline in London. Bemelmans, Ludwig, illus. (gr. k-3). 1961. pap. 14.95 (ISBN 0-670-44648-3). Viking Child Bks.

Benchley, Nathaniel. Oscar Otter. Lobel, Arnold, illus. LC 66-11499. 64p. (gr. k-3). 1966. PLB 11.89 (ISBN 0-06-020472-9). HarpC Child Bks.

—Red Fox & His Canoe. Lobel, Arnold, illus. LC 64-16650. 64p. (gr. k-3). 1985. pap. 3.50 (ISBN 0-06-444075-3, Trophy). HarpC Child Bks.

—Sam the Minuteman. Lobel, Arnold, illus. LC 68-10211. 64p. (gr. k-3). 1987. pap. 3.50 (ISBN 0-06-444107-5, Trophy). HarpC Child Bks.

Benjamin, Alan. Busy Bunnies. Santoro, Christopher, illus. 16p. (ps). 1988. 3.95 (ISBN 0-671-64807-1, Little Simon). S&S Trade.

—Dear Santa. Woodward, Theresa, illus. & (ps). 1986. pap. 2.95 (ISBN 0-671-62919-0, Little Simon). S&S Trade.

—Ducky's Easter Surprise. Santoro, Christopher, illus. 16p. 1988. 3.95 (ISBN 0-671-64808-X, Little Simon). S&S Trade.

—Happy Days. Woodward, Theresa, illus. & (ps). 1986. pap. 2.95 (ISBN 0-671-62920-4, Little Simon). S&S Trade.

—Rat-a-Tat, Pitter Pat. Miller, Margaret, illus. LC 87-568. 40p. (ps-k). 1987. (Crowell Jr Bks); PLB 11.89 (ISBN 0-690-04611-1). HarpC Child Bks.

Benjamin, Alan & Woodward, Theresa. I Went Shopping. (Illus.). (ps). 1986. pap. 2.95 (ISBN 0-671-62921-2, Little Simon). S&S Trade.

—We Took a Ride. (Illus.). (ps). 1986. pap. 2.95 (ISBN 0-671-62922-0, Little Simon). S&S Trade.

Bennett, David. Fire. Kightley, Rosalinda, illus. 1989. 3.95 (ISBN 0-553-05813-4). Bantam.

Bennett, Marian, ed. My Family & Friends. Hand, Judy, illus. 10p. (ps). 1985. 3.95 (ISBN 0-87239-912-5, 2752). Standard Pub.

Bennett, Nancy & Bennett, Pearl. My ABC Book. Bennett, Pearl, illus. 54p. (ps-1). 1988. wkbk. 12.00 (ISBN 0-9622242-0-0). Red Baron Pub Co.

The Berenstain Bears Meet Santa Claus. incl. cassette 5.95 (ISBN 0-685-29550-8). Random.

Berenstain, Janice. Berenstain Bears & the Trouble with Friends. 1987. pap. 2.25 (ISBN 0-394-87339-4). Random.

Berenstain, Michael. The Biggest Dinosaurs. (Illus.). 24p. (ps-k). 1989. pap. write for info. (ISBN 0-307-11977-7, Pub. by Golden Bks). Western Pub.

—The Horned Dinosaur: Triceratops. (Illus.). 24p. (ps-k). 1989. pap. write for info. (ISBN 0-307-11979-3, Pub. by Golden Bks). Western Pub.

—King of the Dinosaurs: Tyrannosaurus Rex. (Illus.). 24p. (ps-k). 1989. pap. write for info. (ISBN 0-307-11976-9, Pub. by Golden Bks). Western Pub.

Berenstain, Stan. Berenstain Bear's Around the Clock-Coloring Book. 1987. pap. 0.49 (ISBN 0-394-88263-6). Random.

—Berenstain Bear's Bear Scout-Coloring Book. 1987. pap. 0.49 (ISBN 0-394-88260-1). Random.

—Berenstain Bear's Count on Numbers Coloring Book. 1987. pap. 0.49 (ISBN 0-394-88264-4). Random.

—Berenstain Bear's Safety First-Coloring Book. 1987. pap. 0.49 (ISBN 0-394-88259-8). Random.

—Berenstain Bears Storytime Color Book. 1989. pap. 0.66 (ISBN 0-394-82368-0, Random Juv). Random.

Berenstain, Stan & Berenstain, Jan. El Bebe de los Osos Berenstain: (The Berenstain Bears' New Baby) De Cuenca, Pilar & Alvarez, Ines, trs. from ENG. Berenstain, Stan & Berenstain, Jan, illus. LC 81-12193. (SPA.). 32p. (Orig.). (ps-3). 1982. lib. bdg. 5.99 (ISBN 0-394-95144-1); pap. 2.25 (ISBN 0-394-85144-7). Random.

—The Berenstain Bears & the Week at Grandma's. Berenstain, Stan & Berenstain, Jan, illus. LC 85-25743. 32p. (ps-1). 1990. pap. 3.50 incl. puppet (ISBN 0-394-82714-7). Random.

—The Berenstain Bears' Trouble at School. Berenstain, Stan & Berenstain, Jan, illus. LC 86-4999. 32p. (ps-1). 1990. pap. 3.50 incl. puppet (ISBN 0-394-82715-5). Random.

Berenstain, Stan & Berenstain, Janice. Bears' Picnic. LC 66-10156. (Illus.). 72p. (gr. k-3). 1966. 6.95 (ISBN 0-394-80041-9); lib. bdg. 7.99 (ISBN 0-394-90041-3). Beginner.

—The Berenstain Bears & the In-Crowd. LC 88-32095. (Illus.). 32p. (Orig.). (ps-1). 1989. lib. bdg. 5.99 (ISBN 0-394-93013-4); pap. 2.25 (ISBN 0-394-83013-X). Random.

—The Berenstain Bears & Too Much Vacation. LC 88-32094. (Illus.). 32p. (Orig.). (ps-1). 1989. PLB 5.99 (ISBN 0-394-93014-2); pap. 2.25 (ISBN 0-394-83014-8). Random.

—The Berenstain Bears Go Out for the Team. LC 85-30164. (Illus.). 32p. (ps-1). 1987. lib. bdg. 5.99 (ISBN 0-394-97338-0, Random Juv); pap. 2.25 (ISBN 0-394-87338-6). Random.

—The Berenstain Bears' Make & Do Book. Berenstain, Stan & Berenstain, Janice, illus. 64p. (ps-3). 1984. pap. 3.95 (ISBN 0-394-86895-1, Random Juv). Random.

—The Berenstain Bears Meet Santa Bear. Berenstain, Stan & Berenstain, Jan, illus. LC 84-4829. 32p. (ps-1). 1984. lib. bdg. 5.99 (ISBN 0-394-96880-8, Random Juv); pap. 2.25 (ISBN 0-394-86880-3). Random.

—The Bike Lesson. Berenstain, Stan, illus. 64p. (ps-1). 1987. pap. 1.75 incl. cassette (ISBN 0-394-88846-4, Random Juv). Random.

—The Day of the Dinosaur. Berenstain, Michael, illus. LC 87-9828. 32p. (gr. k-3). 1987. lib. bdg. 5.99 (ISBN 0-394-99130-3, Random Juv); pap. 2.25 (ISBN 0-394-89130-9, Random Juv). Random.

—He Bear She Bear & Bears on Wheels. Berenstain, Stan & Berenstain, Janice, illus. (ps-1). 1989. bk. & cassette 7.95 (ISBN 0-394-82952-2). Random.

—Old Hat, New Hat. (Illus.). (ps-1). 1970. 6.95 (ISBN 0-394-80669-7, Random Juv); lib. bdg. 6.99 (ISBN 0-394-90669-1). Random.

Berenzy, Alix. A Frog Prince. Berenzy, Alix, illus. 32p. 1989. 13.95 (ISBN 0-8050-0426-2). H Holt & Co.

Berger, Melvin. Early Humans: A Pop-Up Book. (Illus.). 18p. (ps up). 1988. 13.95 (ISBN 0-399-21476-3, Putnam). Putnam Pub Group.

—Prehistoric Mammals: A New World Pop-Up Book. Cremins, Robert, illus. Moseley, Keith, contrib. by. (Illus.). 18p. (gr. 3-6). 1986. 12.95 (ISBN 0-399-21312-0, G&D). Putnam Pub Group.

Bergey, Alyce. Beggar's Greatest Wish. (gr. 4-6). 1969. pap. 1.39 (ISBN 0-570-06040-0, 59-1155). Concordia.

Bergstrom, Gunilla. Who's Scaring Alfie Atkins? Sandin, Joan, tr. from SWE. Bergstrom, Gunilla, illus. 32p. (ps up). 1987. 6.95 (ISBN 9-12-958318-7, Pub. by R & S Bks). FS&G.

Bernstein, Sharon C. A Family That Fights. Levine, Abby, ed. Ritz, Karen, illus. 32p. (gr. 1-5). 1991. 10.95 (ISBN 0-8075-2248-1). A Whitman.

Berridge, Celia. At My House. Berridge, Celia, illus. LC 86-31590. 24p. (ps). 1987. 3.95 (ISBN 0-394-89166-X, Random Juv); lib. bdg. 7.99 (ISBN 0-394-99166-4, Random Juv). Random.

—At the Playground. Berridge, Celia, illus. LC 86-31588. 24p. (ps). 1987. 3.95 (ISBN 0-394-89164-3, Random Juv); lib. bdg. 7.99 (ISBN 0-394-99164-8, Random Juv). Random.

Berry, Joy W. Teach Me about Looking. Dickey, Kate, ed. LC 85-45086. (Illus.). 36p. (ps). 1986. 4.98 (ISBN 0-685-10725-6). Grolier Inc.

Beskow, Elsa. Around the Year. (Illus.). (ps-2). 1988. 14.95 (ISBN 0-86315-075-6, 20245). Gryphon Hse.

—Pelle's New Suit. Beskow, Elsa, illus. 16p. (ps-1). 1929. PLB 13.89 (ISBN 0-06-020496-6). HarpC Child Bks.

—Peter in Blueberry Land. (ps-2). 1988. 14.95 (ISBN 0-86315-050-0, 20237). Gryphon Hse.

—The Tale of the Little, Little Old Woman. Beskow, Elsa, illus. (ps). 1989. 10.95 (ISBN 0-86315-079-9, 20246). Gryphon Hse.

Best Friends. 32p. (gr. 1-8). 1988. poster bk. 1.95 (ISBN 0-87406-340-X). Willowisp Pr.

Better Homes & Gardens Editors. Dandy Dinosaurs. (Illus.). 32p. 1989. 4.95 (ISBN 0-696-01881-0). Meredith Bks.

—Day & Night. (Illus.). 32p. 1989. 4.95 (ISBN 0-696-01882-9). Meredith Bks.

—Water Wonders. (Illus.). 32p. 1989. pap. 3.95 (ISBN 0-696-01883-7). Meredith Bks.

Betty Bird. 12p. (ps-1). 1989. bds. 14.95 (ISBN 0-87449-644-6). Modern Pub NYC.

Beyl, Judith. Sunshine, Rainbows & Friends. Sydlik, Danilea & Campbell, Elisa L., illus. LC 80-50828. 83p. (Orig.). (ps-k). 1980. pap. 5.95 (ISBN 0-933308-01-9). Harper SF.

Beylon, Cathy, illus. The Glo Friends Glo-Year-Round Book. LC 85-63344. 14p. (ps-1). 1986. 4.95 (ISBN 0-394-88246-6, Random Juv). Random.

Bible Promises. 32p. (ps-2). 1988. pap. 0.69 (ISBN 1-55513-337-1, Chariot Bks). Cook.

Big & Little. (Illus.). (ps-k). 1990. bds. 3.50 (ISBN 0-7214-9120-0). Ladybird Bks.

Big & Little. (Illus.). (ps-2). 3.50 (ISBN 0-7214-0612-2). Ladybird Bks.

Big & Little Pack, No. 466. (Illus.). (ps-k). incl. chart & activity bk. 6.95 (ISBN 0-7214-5163-2). Ladybird Bks.

Big Animal ABC Pop-Up. 1989. 4.98 (ISBN 0-8317-0868-9). Smithmark.

Big Dinosaur Pop-Up. 1989. 4.98 (ISBN 0-8317-0866-2). Smithmark.

Big Fish Story Share-a-Story Unit. (Illus.). 32p. (ps-2). 1987. 64.87 (ISBN 0-516-49541-0). Childrens.

A Big Year on Sesame Street. 1989. write for info. (ISBN 0-307-15550-1, Golden Bks). Western Pub.

Billout, Guy. By Camel or by Car: A Look at Transportation. Billout, Guy, illus. 32p. 1983. 8.95 (ISBN 0-13-109603-6, Pub. by Treehouse); pap. 5.95 (ISBN 0-13-109595-1). P-H.

The Bionic Six Super Picture Book. (ps-5). 1987. pap. 5.95 (ISBN 0-448-19057-5, G&D). Putnam Pub Group.

Birch, David. The King's Chessboard. Grebu, Devis, illus. LC 87-20164. 32p. (gr. k up). 1988. 10.95 (ISBN 0-8037-0365-1); PLB 10.89 (ISBN 0-8037-0367-8). Dial Bks Young.

Bird, E. J. Chuck Wagon Stew. (Illus.). 72p. (gr. 2-6). 1988. 9.95 (ISBN 0-87614-313-3); pap. 4.95 (ISBN 0-87614-498-9). Carolrhoda Bks.

—How Do Bears Sleep? (Illus.). 32p. (ps-3). 1989. PLB 12.95 (ISBN 0-87614-384-2); pap. 5.95 (ISBN 0-685-26814-4). Carolrhoda Bks.

Bishop, Claire H. The Five Chinese Brothers. (Illus.). (gr. k-3). 1938. 7.95 (ISBN 0-698-20044-6, Coward). Putnam Pub Group.

Black, Irma S. Little Old Man Who Could Not Read. Fleishman, Seymour, illus. LC 68-9115. (gr. k-2). 1968. PLB 11.50 (ISBN 0-8075-4621-6). A Whitman.

Blacker, Terence. If I Could Work. Winn, Chris, illus. LC 87-3972. 32p. (ps-2). 1988. 12.95 (ISBN 0-397-32245-3, Lipp Jr Bks); PLB 12.89 (ISBN 0-397-32255-0). HarpC Child Bks.

Blades, Ann. Spring. Blades, Ann, illus. LC 89-2424. 10p. (ps). 1990. board 4.95 (ISBN 0-688-09230-6). Lothrop.

Blathwayt, Benedict. Bear's Adventure. Blathwayt, Benedict, illus. LC 88-2696. 32p. (ps-1). 1988. lib. bdg. 10.99 (ISBN 0-394-90568-7). Knopf.

Blegvad, Lenore. Anna Banana & Me. Blegvad, Erik, illus. (gr. 1-3). 1988. bk. & cassette 19.95 (ISBN 0-87499-104-8); bk. & cassette 12.95 (ISBN 0-87499-103-X); 4 cassettes & guide 27.95 (ISBN 0-87499-105-6). Live Oak Media.

Blocksma, Mary. All My Toys Are on the Floor. Kalthoff, Sandra C., illus. LC 85-27000. 24p. (ps-2). 1986. PLB 12.33 (ISBN 0-516-01579-6); pap. 3.95 (ISBN 0-516-41579-4). Childrens.

—Rub-aDub-Dub - What's in the Tub? Kalthoff, Sandra C., illus. LC 84-12139. 24p. (ps-2). 1984. lib. bdg. 12.33 (ISBN 0-516-01586-9); pap. 3.95 (ISBN 0-516-41586-7). Childrens.

Blonder. Wee Wonders of Nature. (gr. 2 up). 1988. 2.50 (ISBN 0-448-09254-9, G&D). Putnam Pub Group.

Blonder, Ellen, illus. My Very First Things. (ps). 1988. bds. 2.50 (ISBN 0-448-09253-0, G&D). Putnam Pub Group.

Bloss, Janet A. Ballet Bunny. (Illus.). 24p. (ps-3). 1989. pap. 1.95 (ISBN 0-87406-374-4). Willowisp Pr.

Blume, Judy. Freckle Juice. Lisker, Sonia O., illus. LC 85-280. 40p. (gr. 1-3). 1984. Repr. of 1971 ed. 12.95 (ISBN 0-02-711690-5, Four Winds). Macmillan Child Grp.

—The One in the Middle Is the Green Kangaroo. Aitken, Amy, illus. LC 80-29664. 40p. (gr. k-3). 1982. 12.95 (ISBN 0-02-711060-5, Bradbury Pr). Macmillan Child Grp.

Blumenthal, Nancy. Count-a-Saurus. Kaufman, Robert, illus. LC 88-21320. 24p. (ps-3). 1989. 12.95 (ISBN 0-02-749391-1, Four Winds). Macmillan Child Grp.

Boase, Wendy. Hide & Seek Books. (Illus.). (ps-1). pap. 1.95 ea. Random.

Bober, Natalie S., compiled by. Let's Pretend: Poems of Flight & Fancy. Bell, Bill, illus. Boler, Natalie S., intro. by. (Illus.). 64p. (ps-3). 1986. pap. 13.95 (ISBN 0-670-81176-9). Viking Child Bks.

Boccaccio, Giovanni. Chichibo & the Crane. Luzatti, Lele, illus. (gr. 1-6). 1961. 8.95 (ISBN 0-8392-3004-4). Astor-Honor.

Boegehold, Betty D. Horse Called Starfire. 1990. 9.99 (ISBN 0-553-05861-4). Bantam.

Bohatta, Ida. All of the Birds. (Illus.). Date not set. 2.00 (ISBN 0-317-93762-6). W J Fantasy.
—Barlithe Ice Bear. (Illus.). Date not set. 2.00 (ISBN 0-317-93758-8). W J Fantasy.
—Bow Wow. (Illus.). Date not set. 2.00 (ISBN 0-317-93754-5). W J Fantasy.
—The Brown Family. (Illus.). Date not set. 2.00 (ISBN 0-317-93761-8). W J Fantasy.
—The Busy Savers. (Illus.). Date not set. 2.00 (ISBN 0-317-93765-0). W J Fantasy.
—The Cloud Kitchen. (Illus.). Date not set. 2.00 (ISBN 0-317-93759-6). W J Fantasy.
—The Hardworking Bee. (Illus.). Date not set. 2.00 (ISBN 0-317-93764-2). W J Fantasy.
—The Little Advent Book. (Illus.). Date not set. 2.00 (ISBN 0-317-93766-9). W J Fantasy.
—The Merry Hoppers. (Illus.). Date not set. 2.00 (ISBN 0-317-93756-1). W J Fantasy.
—Raindrops. (Illus.). Date not set. 2.00 (ISBN 0-317-93763-4). W J Fantasy.
—St. Nicholas. (Illus.). Date not set. 2.00 (ISBN 0-317-93767-7). W J Fantasy.
—Shooting Stars. (Illus.). Date not set. 2.00 (ISBN 0-317-93757-X). W J Fantasy.
—Sleepy Time Illustrated Book Collection, 30 Bks. (Illus.). Date not set. write for info. W J Fantasy.
—Velvet Paws. (Illus.). Date not set. 2.00 (ISBN 0-317-93760-X). W J Fantasy.
—Wixi the Easter Rabbit. (Illus.). Date not set. 2.00 (ISBN 0-317-93755-3). W J Fantasy.
Boholm-Olsson, Eva. Tuan. Van Don, Pham, illus. Jonasson, Dianne, tr. (Illus.). 32p. (ps up). 1988. 11.95 (ISBN 9-12-958766-2, R & S Bks). FS&G.
Bond, Felicia. Four Valentines in a Rainstorm. Bond, Felicia, illus. LC 82-45586. 32p. (gr. k-3). 1990. pap. 3.95 (ISBN 0-06-443216-5, Trophy). HarpC Child Bks.
—The Halloween Performance. Bond, Felicia, illus. LC 82-45920. 32p. (ps-3). 1987. pap. 3.95 (ISBN 0-06-443155-X, Trophy). HarpC Child Bks.
—Poinsettia & the Firefighters. Bond, Felicia, illus. LC 83-46169. 32p. (ps-3). 1988. pap. 4.95 (ISBN 0-06-443160-6, Trophy). HarpC Child Bks.
Bonhomme, Isabelle, illus. Cinderella. 24p. (ps-2). 1988. bk. & audiocassette 6.95 (ISBN 0-8120-4043-0). Barron.
Bonsall, Crosby. The Day I Had to Play with My Sister. Bonsall, Crosby, illus. LC 72-76507. 32p. (ps-2). 1988. pap. 2.95 (ISBN 0-06-444117-2, Trophy). HarpC Child Bks.
—Who's Afraid of the Dark? Bonsall, Crosby, illus. LC 79-2700. 32p. (ps-2). 1985. pap. 2.95 (ISBN 0-06-444071-0, Trophy). HarpC Child Bks.
Bonsall, Crosby N. It's Mine: A Greedy Book. Bonsall, Crosby N., illus. LC 64-11839. 32p. (gr. k-3). 1964. PLB 10.89 (ISBN 0-06-020586-5). HarpC Child Bks.
Boola's Secrets. (Illus.). 26p. (ps-1). 1988. pap. 2.95 incl. sticker pgs. (ISBN 0-671-66867-6). S&S Trade.
Boon, Emilie. Belinda's Balloon. Boon, Emilie, illus. LC 84-21771. 32p. (ps-1). 1985. 8.95 (ISBN 0-394-87342-4). Knopf.
—It's Spring, Peterkin. Boon, Emilie, illus. LC 85-62015. 14p. (ps). 1986. bds. 3.95 (ISBN 0-394-87997-X). Random.
Boone, Debby. Bedtime Hugs for Little Ones. Ferrer, Gabri, illus. LC 87-81035. 64p. (ps-1). 1988. 10.99 (ISBN 0-89081-616-6). Harvest Hse.
Bottner, Barbara. Zoo Song. Munsinger, Lynn, illus. (gr. k-3). 1989. pap. 2.50 (ISBN 0-590-33773-4). Scholastic Inc.
Bougon, Claude. The Cross-Eyed Rabbit. Bougon, Claude, illus. LC 87-22847. 32p. (gr. k-3). 1988. Repr. of 1984 ed. 12.95 (ISBN 0-689-50443-8, M K McElderry). Macmillan Child Grp.
A Boy for Flops. (Illus.). 32p. (gr. k-2). 1989. 4.95 (ISBN 0-87449-583-0). Modern Pub NYC.
Boyd, Lizi. Half Wild & Half Child. (ps-3). 1989. pap. 11.95 (ISBN 0-670-82072-5). Viking Child Bks.
Boyd, Paxxy. Baby Animals. (ps-1). 1985. 2.95 (ISBN 0-671-51085-1, Little Simon). S&S Trade.
Boyle, Sallie. Basic Sight Words. Carson, Patti & Dellosa, Janet, illus. 32p. (ps-1). 1984. pap. 1.98 (ISBN 0-88724-092-5, CD-7031). Carson-Dellos.
Boynton, Sandra. But Not the Hippopotamus. Klimo, Kate, ed. Boynton, Sandra, illus. 14p. (ps-k). 1982. 3.95 (ISBN 0-671-44904-4, Little Simon). S&S Trade.
—Opposites. Klimo, Kate, ed. Boynton, Sandra, illus. (ps-k). 1982. 3.95 (ISBN 0-671-44903-6, Little Simon). S&S Trade.
Bracken, Carolyn. Peter Rabbit's Pockets. Bracken, Carolyn, illus. 8p. (ps). 1982. pap. 3.95 (ISBN 0-671-44528-6, Little Simon). S&S Trade.
Bracken, Carolyn, illus. The Busy School Bus. 12p. (ps up). 1986. pap. 5.95 (ISBN 0-448-09880-6, G&D). Putnam Pub Group.
Bracken, Carolyn & Barbaresi, Nina, illus. Baby Seal. (ps). 1984. pap. 2.95 (ISBN 0-671-50031-7, Little Simon). S&S Trade.
—Duckling. (ps). 1991. pap. 2.95 (ISBN 0-671-50030-9, Little Simon). S&S Trade.
Bradman, Tony. The Bad Babies' Counting Book. Van der Beek, Debbie, illus. LC 86-71. 32p. (ps-2). 1986. Set. 4.95 (ISBN 0-394-88352-7); lib. bdg. 5.99 (ISBN 0-394-98352-1). Knopf.
—Look Out, He's Behind You! Chamberlain, Margaret, illus. 32p. (ps-3). 1988. 11.95 (ISBN 0-399-21485-2, Putnam). Putnam Pub Group.
Brady, Esther W. Toliver's Secret. Cuffari, Richard, illus. 176p. (gr. 3-7). 1988. pap. 3.95 (ISBN 0-517-56910-8). Crown.
Brady, Susan. Find My Blanket. Brady, Susan, illus. LC 87-45310. 32p. (ps-1). 1988. 11.95 (ISBN 0-397-32247-X, Lipp Jr Bks); PLB 11.89 (ISBN 0-397-32248-8). HarpC Child Bks.
Bragg, Michael, illus. Monday's Child. 32p. (ps-1). 1989. 15.95 (ISBN 0-575-04097-1, Pub. by Gollancz England). Trafalgar Sq.
Brandenburg, Franz. Nice New Neighbours. Aliki, illus. 32p. (gr. k-3). pap. 2.25 (ISBN 0-317-69660-2). Scholastic Inc.
Branley, Franklyn M. Flash, Crash, Rumble & Roll. Emberley, Barbara & Emberley, Ed E., illus. LC 84-48532. 32p. (ps-3). 1987. incl. cassette 7.95 (ISBN 0-694-00200-3, Trophy); pap. 4.50 (ISBN 0-06-445012-0, Trophy). HarpC Child Bks.
—Journey into a Black Hole. Simont, Marc, illus. LC 85-48249. 32p. (gr. k-3). 1988. pap. 4.50 (ISBN 0-06-445075-9, Trophy). HarpC Child Bks.
—Snow Is Falling. rev. ed. Keller, Holly, illus. LC 85-48256. 32p. (ps-3). 1986. pap. 4.50 (ISBN 0-06-445058-9, Trophy). HarpC Child Bks.
Braumiller, Tanya. Visiting Gig Harbor. Hamer, Bonnie, illus. (Orig.). (gr. 1-4). 1983. pap. 2.75 (ISBN 0-933992-28-9). Coffee Break.
Brenner, Barbara. Lion & Lamb Step Out. 1990. 9.99 (ISBN 0-553-05860-6). Bantam.
—Moon Boy. 1990. 9.99 (ISBN 0-553-05858-4). Bantam.
—Wagon Wheels. Bologneze, Don, illus. LC 76-21391. 64p. (ps-3). 1984. pap. 3.50 (ISBN 0-06-444052-4, Trophy). HarpC Child Bks.
Bridle, Martin. Hey Presto! Eaton, Sue, illus. LC 87-33375. 32p. (ps-3). 1988. 12.95 (ISBN 0-87226-182-4, Bedrick Blackie). P Bedrick Bks.
Bridwell, Norman. Clifford, the Small Red Puppy. Bridwell, Norman, illus. 32p. (gr. k-3). 1985. pap. 1.95 (ISBN 0-590-33583-9). Scholastic Inc.
—Clifford's Christmas. Bridwell, Norman, illus. (gr. k-3). 1984. pap. 1.95 (ISBN 0-590-40221-8). Scholastic Inc.
—Where Is Clifford: A Lift-a-Flap Book. 1989. pap. 10.95 (ISBN 0-590-42925-6). Scholastic Inc.
Brierley, Louise, illus. The Twelve Days of Christmas. LC 86-45290. 32p. (gr. 1-5). 1986. 12.95 (ISBN 0-8050-0035-6). H Holt & Co.
Briggs, Raymond. The Snowman. Briggs, Raymond, illus. LC 78-55904. 32p. (Orig.). (ps-2). 1986. pap. 4.95 book & doll pkg. (ISBN 0-394-88466-3, Random Juv). Random.
Bright, Robert. Georgie. Bright, Robert, illus. 44p. (gr. k-1). 1944. pap. 7.95 (ISBN 0-385-07307-0). Doubleday.
—Georgie & the Robbers. Bright, Robert, illus. LC 63-11384. 28p. (ps-1). 1963. pap. 5.95 (ISBN 0-385-04483-6); pap. 2.50 (ISBN 0-385-13341-3). Doubleday.
—My Red Umbrella. LC 59-7928. (Illus.). 32p. (ps-1). 1985. 8.95 (ISBN 0-688-05249-5, Morrow Junior Books); pap. 3.95 (ISBN 0-688-05250-9, Morrow Junior Books). Morrow.
Brinckloe, Julie. A Stitch in Time for the Brothers Rhyme. Brinckloe, Julia, illus. LC 84-17721. 32p. (gr. 3-6). 1985. PLB 27.99 (ISBN 0-8172-2284-7); PLB 14.65 (ISBN 0-940742-44-6). Raintree Pubs.
Brooke, Leslie. Johnny Crow's Garden. Brooke, Leslie, illus. 64p. (ps-3). 1986. 4.95 (ISBN 0-7232-3429-9). Warne.
—Johnny Crow's Party. Brooke, Leslie, illus. 64p. (ps-3). 1986. 4.95 (ISBN 0-7232-3428-0). Warne.
Brooks, Andreas, illus. The Pudgy Book of Make-Believe. 16p. (gr. k). 1984. 2.95 (ISBN 0-448-10209-9, G&D). Putnam Pub Group.
Brown, Jeff. Flat Stanley. Ungerer, Tomi, illus. LC 63-17525. 64p. (gr. 1-5). 1964. PLB 13.89 (ISBN 0-06-020681-0). HarpC Child Bks.
Brown, Jerome C. Dinosaur Color & Pattern Book. (gr. k-3). 1989. pap. 7.95 (ISBN 0-8224-2322-7). Fearon Teach Aids.
Brown, Judith G. The Mask of the Dancing Princess. Brown, Judith G., illus. LC 88-27151. 48p. (gr. k-3). 1989. 14.95 (ISBN 0-689-31427-2, Atheneum Child Bk). Macmillan Child Grp.
Brown, Laurence K. & Brown, Mark. Visiting the Art Museum. (ps-4). 1990. 12.95 (ISBN 0-525-44233-2, DCB); pap. 4.95 (ISBN 0-525-44568-4, DCB). Dutton Child Bks.
Brown, Marc. Arthur's Eyes. Brown, Marc, illus. 32p. (ps-3). 1986. pap. 4.95 (ISBN 0-316-11069-8, Joy St Bks). Little.
—Arthur's Valentine. Brown, Marc, illus. 32p. (ps-3). 1988. pap. 4.95 (ISBN 0-316-11187-2, Joy St Bks). Little.
—D. W. All Wet. (ps-3). 1991. pap. 4.95 (ISBN 0-316-11268-2). Little.
—D. W. Flips. Brown, Marc, illus. (ps-2). 1987. 10.95 (ISBN 0-316-11239-9, Joy St Bks). Little.
—D. W. Flips. (ps-3). 1991. pap. 4.95 (ISBN 0-316-11269-0). Little.
—The Silly Tail Book. Brown, Marc, illus. LC 83-2250. 48p. (ps-3). 1983. 5.95 (ISBN 0-8193-1109-X). Parents.
—Silly Tail Book: Gold Banner Bks. (ps-2). 1990. pap. 2.95 (ISBN 0-448-04342-4, G&D). Putnam Pub Group.
Brown, Marc, illus. One, Two Buckle My Shoe. 8p. (ps-k). 1989. 5.95 (ISBN 0-525-44462-9, DCB). Dutton Child Bks.
Brown, Marcia. Dick Whittington & His Cat. Brown, Marcia, illus. LC 50-9157. 32p. (gr. k-3). 1988. Repr. of 1950 ed. PLB 13.95 (ISBN 0-684-18998-4, Scribners Young Read). Macmillan Child Grp.
—Once a Mouse. Brown, Marcia, illus. 32p. (gr. k-4). 1989. pap. 3.95 (ISBN 0-689-71343-6, Aladdin). Macmillan Child Grp.
—Stone Soup. Brown, Marcia, illus. (gr. 1-4). 1987. incl. cassette 19.95 (ISBN 0-87499-053-X); pap. 12.95 incl. cassette (ISBN 0-87499-052-1); 4 paperbacks, cassette & guide 27.95 (ISBN 0-87499-054-8). Live Oak Media.
Brown, Margaret W. A Child's Good Night Book. Charlot, Jean, illus. LC 84-43123. 32p. (ps-2). 1986. pap. 4.95 (ISBN 0-06-443114-2, Trophy). HarpC Child Bks.
—Christmas in the Barn. Cooney, Barbara, illus. LC 85-42738. 32p. (ps-3). 1985. pap. 3.95 (ISBN 0-06-443082-0, Trophy). HarpC Child Bks.
—Goodnight Moon. Hurd, Clement, illus. LC 47-30762. 36p. (ps-1). 1947. 10.95 (ISBN 0-06-020705-1); PLB 10.89 (ISBN 0-06-020706-X). HarpC Child Bks.
—Goodnight Moon. (gr. k-3). 1984. incl. cassette 19.95 (ISBN 0-941078-30-2); pap. 12.95 incl. cassette (ISBN 0-941078-28-0); incl. 4 bks., cassette, & guide 27.95 (ISBN 0-317-07120-3). Live Oak Media.
—The Goodnight Moon Room: A Pop-Up Book. Hurd, Clement, illus. LC 83-48169. 10p. (ps-1). 1985. 10.95 (ISBN 0-694-00003-5). HarpC Child Bks.
—Important Book. Weisgard, Leonard, illus. LC 49-9133. 22p. (ps-1). 1949. 12.95 (ISBN 0-06-020720-5); PLB 12.89 (ISBN 0-06-020721-3). HarpC Child Bks.
—The Important Book. Weisgard, Leonard, illus. LC 49-9133. 24p. (gr. k-3). 1990. pap. 4.95 (ISBN 0-06-443227-0, Trophy). HarpC Child Bks.
—Indoor Noisy Book. Weisgard, Leonard, illus. LC 42-23589. 42p. (ps-3). 1942. PLB 12.89 (ISBN 0-06-020821-X). HarpC Child Bks.
—The Little Fir Tree. Cooney, Barbara, illus. LC 85-42743. 40p. (ps-3). 1985. pap. 3.50 (ISBN 0-06-443083-9, Trophy). HarpC Child Bks.
—The Runaway Bunny. Hurd, Clement, illus. LC 71-183168. 32p. (ps). 1991. bds. 6.95 (ISBN 0-06-107429-2). HarpC Child Bks.
—Sleepy Little Lion. Ylla, photos by. LC 47-11482. (Illus.). 24p. (gr. k-3). 1947. PLB 12.89 (ISBN 0-06-020771-X). HarpC Child Bks.
—Wait Till the Moon Is Full. Williams, Garth, illus. LC 48-9278. 32p. (ps-1). 1948. 14.95 (ISBN 0-06-020800-7); PLB 12.89 (ISBN 0-06-020801-5). HarpC Child Bks.
—Where Have You Been? 32p. (gr. k-3). pap. 1.95 (ISBN 0-590-00348-8). Scholastic Inc.
Brown, Michael. Baby's Santa Mouse. (Illus.). (ps). 1983. 3.95 (ISBN 0-448-03091-8, G&D). Putnam Pub Group.
Brown, Richard. Cookie Monster's Good Time to Eat! (Illus.). 14p. (ps-k). 1989. write for info. (ISBN 0-307-12259-X, Pub. by Golden Bks). Western Pub.
—One Hundred Words about Animals. Brown, Richard, illus. LC 86-22774. 32p. (ps). 1987. 5.95 (ISBN 0-15-200550-1, Gulliver Bks). HarBraceJ.
—One Hundred Words about My House. LC 87-7574. (Illus.). 32p. (gr. 3-5). 1988. 6.95 (ISBN 0-15-200552-8, Gulliver Bks). HarBraceJ.
Brown, Richard, illus. Sesame Street, Cookie Monster's Book of Cookie Shapes. 24p. (ps-k). 1979. pap. write for info (ISBN 0-307-10074-X, Pub. by Golden Bks). Western Pub.
Brown, Ruth. Our Cat Flossie. Monfried, Lucia, ed. Brown, Ruth, illus. 32p. (ps-1). 1986. 10.95 (ISBN 0-525-44256-1, DCB). Dutton Child Bks.
Browne, Anthony. Look What I've Got! LC 87-26066. (Illus.). 32p. (ps-3). 1988. lib. bdg. 11.99 (ISBN 0-394-99860-X); pap. text ed. 3.95 (ISBN 0-394-89860-5). Knopf.
—Piggybook. Browne, Anthony, illus. LC 86-3008. 32p. (ps-3). 1986. 14.95 (ISBN 0-394-88416-7); lib. bdg. 12.99 (ISBN 0-394-98416-1). Knopf.
Browne, Gerard. The Car & Truck Lift-the-Flap Book. Browne, Gerard, illus. LC 88-29994. 18p. (gr. 2-5). 1989. 12.95 (ISBN 0-525-67273-7, Lodestar Bks). Dutton Child Bks.
Bruce, Linda. Al Phillip Bettle. Bruce, Linda, illus. (gr. k-3). 1965. 8.95 (ISBN 0-8392-3050-8). Astor-Honor.
Bryan, Ashley. Turtle Knows Your Name. Bryan, Ashley, illus. LC 89-2. 32p. (ps-2). 1989. 13.95 (ISBN 0-689-31578-3, Atheneum Child Bk). Macmillan Child Grp.
Buckingham, John. The Middle of the Pond. Terry, Angeline & Blackburn, Sylvia, eds. Woodson, Mini, illus. 32p. (gr. k-2). 1988. 8.50 (ISBN 0-943153-01-8); pap. 4.25 (ISBN 0-943153-02-6). Stafford Lowery.
Buckley, Paul. Amy Belligera & the Fireflies. Tucker, Kathleen, ed. Buckley, Kate, illus. 32p. (ps-3). 1987. PLB 12.95 (ISBN 0-8075-0324-X). A Whitman.
Buckley, Richard & Williams, Alex. The Bird Who Couldn't Fly. (Illus.). 32p. (ps-1). 1989. 15.95 (ISBN 0-340-41990-3, Pub. by Hodder & Stoughton UK). Trafalgar Sq.
Bucknall, Caroline. One Bear in the Picture. Bucknall, Caroline, illus. LC 87-6891. 32p. (ps-2). 1988. 11.95 (ISBN 0-8037-0463-1). Dial Bks Young.
Buell, Ellen L., ed. Treasury of Little Golden Books. 120p. (ps-2). 1989. write for info. (ISBN 0-307-86540-1, Golden Bks). Western Pub.

Bulla, Clyde R. Singing Sam. Magurn, Susan, illus. LC 88-19758. 48p. (Orig.). (gr. 1-3). 1989. PLB 6.99 (ISBN 0-394-91977-7); pap. 2.95 (ISBN 0-394-81977-2). Random.

Bullock, Gloria S. & Crocitto, Jane B. Shopping at the Ani-Mall. Weinberger, Jane, ed. DeVito, Pam, illus. LC 90-70475. 44p. (ps-3). 1991. pap. 9.95 (ISBN 0-932433-72-3). Windswept Hse.

Bunsen, Rick, ed. Golden Christmas Treasury. rev. & enl. ed. LC 84-72934. (Illus.). 96p. (gr. k-12). 1989. write for info. (ISBN 0-307-95585-0, Pub. by Golden Bks). Western Pub.

Bunting, Eve. Demetrius & the Golden Goblet. Hague, Michael, illus. LC 79-14865. 48p. (gr. 1-5). 1980. 8.95 (ISBN 0-15-223186-2, HJ). HarBraceJ.

—Ghost's Hour, Spook's Hour. Carrick, Donald, illus. LC 86-31674. 32p. (ps). 1989. pap. 4.95 (ISBN 0-395-51583-1, Clarion Bks). HM.

—No Nap. Meddaugh, Susan, illus. LC 88-35256. 32p. (ps-k). 1989. 13.95 (ISBN 0-89919-813-9, Clarion Bks). HM.

Burditt, Faraday & Holley, Cynthia. Every Day in Every Way. (ps). 1989. pap. 11.95 (ISBN 0-8224-2507-6). Fearon Teach Aids.

Burgess, Thornton W. The Adventures of Jimmy Skunk. Cady, Harrison, illus. 128p. (ps-3). 1987. pap. 2.95 (ISBN 0-316-11662-9). Little.

Burn, Doris. Andrew-Henry's Meadow. Burn, Doris, illus. (gr. k-3). 1965. PLB 4.99 (ISBN 0-698-30011-4, Coward). Putnam Pub Group.

Burningham, John. The Blanket. Burningham, John, illus. LC 76-17630. (ps-1). 1962. PLB 11.89 (ISBN 0-690-01270-5, Crowell Jr Bks). HarpC Child Bks.

—The Cupboard. Burningham, John, illus. LC 76-17797. (ps-1). 1966. 7.95 (ISBN 0-690-01300-0, Crowell Jr Bks). HarpC Child Bks.

—The Dog. Burningham, John, illus. LC 76-17626. (ps-1). 1985. (Crowell Jr Bks). HarpC Child Bks.

—The Friend. Burningham, John, illus. LC 76-16436. (ps-1). 1966. PLB 11.89 (ISBN 0-690-01274-8, Crowell Jr Bks). HarpC Child Bks.

—Mr. Gumpy's Motor Car. (Illus.). (gr. 1-3). 1983. pap. 3.50 (ISBN 0-14-050300-5, Puffin). Puffin Bks.

—Trubloff: The Mouse Who Wanted to Play the Balalaika. (ps). 1965. lib. bdg. write for info. (ISBN 0-394-97316-X, Random Juv). Random.

Burnnett, Carroll. Kikko's Tracks. Burnnett, Carroll, illus. 28p. (Orig.). (ps up). 1988. pap. 6.95 (ISBN 0-9619414-1-3). Foto Fantasi Pr.

Burton, Jane. Caper the Kid. Burton, Jane, photos by. LC 88-6485. (Illus.). 24p. (ps-3). 1988. lib. bdg. 5.99 (ISBN 0-394-99962-2, Random Juv); (Random Juv). Random.

—Chester the Chick. LC 87-20677. (Illus.). 24p. (ps-3). 1988. (Random Juv); pap. 2.25 (ISBN 0-394-89640-8). Random.

—Dabble the Duckling. Burton, Jane, photos by. LC 88-2730. (Illus.). 24p. (Orig.). (ps-3). 1988. lib. bdg. 5.99 (ISBN 0-394-99960-6, Random Juv); pap. 1.95 (ISBN 0-394-89960-1, Random Juv). Random.

—Freckles the Rabbit. Burton, Jane, photos by. LC 87-20812. (Illus.). 24p. (ps-3). 1988. (Random Juv). Random.

—Ginger the Kitten. Burton, Jane, photos by. LC 87-16660. (Illus.). 24p. (ps-3). 1988. (Random Juv). Random.

—Jack the Puppy. Burton, Jane, photos by. LC 87-16432. (Illus.). 24p. (ps-3). 1988. lib. bdg. 5.99 (ISBN 0-394-99641-0, Random Juv). Random.

Burton, Virginia L. Choo Choo. (Illus.). 48p. (gr. k-3). 1973. 14.95 (ISBN 0-395-17684-0). HM.

—Little House. (Illus.). (gr. k-3). 1978. 13.95 (ISBN 0-395-18156-9); pap. 4.95 (ISBN 0-395-25938-X). HM.

—Mike Mulligan & His Steam Shovel. (Illus.). (gr. k-3). 1939. PLB 11.95 (ISBN 0-395-06681-6). HM.

Bussard, Paula. The Glad I Gotcha Day. Goodridge, Larry, illus. 28p. (gr. k-3). 1985. 1.39 (ISBN 0-87239-963-X, 3383). Standard Pub.

Busy Days. (Illus.). 6p. (ps-2). 1987. bds. 3.95 (ISBN 0-87449-569-5). Modern Pub NYC.

Butler, Joyce. The Duchess Who Lived in the Mansion. Troise-Heidel, Theresa, illus. LC 86-50877. 66p. (ps-6). 1986. pap. 3.95 (ISBN 0-932433-24-3). Windswept Hse.

Butler, M. Christina. Too Many Eggs. LC 83-49007. (Illus.). (gr. k-12). 1988. 12.95 (ISBN 0-87923-741-4). Godine.

A Butterfly Doesn't Waddle, A Goldfish Doesn't Bark, A Frog Doesn't Gallop & A Gopher Doesn't Build a Nest. (Illus.). (ps-k). 1989. pap. 3.95 ea., 12pgs. ea. A Butterfly Doesn't Waddle (ISBN 0-87449-766-3). A Goldfish Doesn't Bark (ISBN 0-87449-767-1). A Frog Doesn't Gallop (ISBN 0-87449-768-X). A Gopher Doesn't Build a Nest (ISBN 0-87449-769-8). Modern Pub NYC.

Butterworth, Nick. The Good Stranger. Inkpen, Mick, illus. (ps-3). 1989. 4.95 (ISBN 0-310-55940-5). Zondervan.

—The Little Gate. Inkpen, Mick, illus. (ps-3). 1989. 4.95 (ISBN 0-310-55970-7). Zondervan.

—The Rich Farmer. Inkpen, Mick, illus. (ps-3). 1989. 4.95 (ISBN 0-310-55960-X). Zondervan.

—The Ten Silver Coins. Inkpen, Mick, illus. (ps-3). 1989. 4.95 (ISBN 0-310-55950-2). Zondervan.

Butterworth, Oliver. The Enormous Egg. Darling, Louis, illus. (gr. 4-6). 1956. 14.95 (ISBN 0-316-11904-0, Pub. by Atlantic Monthly Pr). Little.

Button, Beth. Yes-No, Stop-Go. Sussman, Ellen, ed. Burris, Priscilla, illus. 56p. (Orig.). (ps-3). 1990. pap. text ed. 6.95 (ISBN 0-933606-82-6, MS-686). Monkey Sisters.

Buxbaum, Susan K. & Gelman, Rita G. Splash! All about Baths. Cocca-Leffler, Maryann, illus. 32p. (ps-3). 1987. 14.95 (ISBN 0-316-30726-2). Little.

Cahill, Chris. Bear Magic. Young, Ruth & Rose, Mitchell, illus. LC 89-61636. 12p. (ps-1). 1990. bds. 5.95 incl. finger puppet (ISBN 1-877779-00-8). Schneider Educational.

—Bunny Magic. Young, Ruth & Rose, Mitchell, illus. LC 89-61633. 12p. (ps-1). 1990. bds. 5.95 incl. finger puppet (ISBN 1-877779-02-4). Schneider Educational.

Caines, Jeannette. Abby. Kellogg, Steven, illus. LC 73-5480. 32p. (ps-3). 1984. pap. 4.95 (ISBN 0-06-443049-9, Trophy). HarpC Child Bks.

—Just Us Women. Cummings, Pat, illus. LC 81-48655. 32p. (gr. k-3). 1984. pap. 4.95 (ISBN 0-06-443056-1, Trophy). HarpC Child Bks.

Caldecott, Randolph. A Second Collection: Sing a Song for Sixpence, the Three Jovial Hunters. Caldecott, Randolph, illus. 64p. 1986. 4.95 (ISBN 0-7232-3433-7). Warne.

—A Third Caldecott Collection: The Queen of Hearts, The Farmer's Boy. Caldecott, Randolph, illus. 64p. 1986. 4.95 (ISBN 0-7232-3434-5). Warne.

Calder, Lyn. Blue-Ribbon Friends. LC 90-85433. (Illus.). 32p. (gr. k-3). 1991. 5.95 (ISBN 1-56282-034-6, Disney Pr). W Disney Pub.

—Gold-Star Homework. LC 90-85434. (Illus.). 32p. (gr. k-3). 1991. 5.95 (ISBN 1-56282-035-4, Disney Pr). W Disney Pub.

—Minnie 'n Me: The Perfect Bow. Shakespeare, Sue, illus. (ps-k). 1991. pap. write for info. (ISBN 0-307-10025-1, Golden Pr). Western Pub.

Calder, Lyn, retold by. Little Red Hen. Severn, Jeffrey, illus. LC 87-91771. 24p. (ps-k). 1988. pap. write for info. (ISBN 0-307-10097-9, Pub. by Golden Bks). Western Pub.

—Little Red Riding Hood. Super, Terri, illus. LC 87-81772. 24p. (ps-k). 1988. pap. write for info. (ISBN 0-307-10098-7, Pub. by Golden Bks). Western Pub.

Calder, S. J. If You Were a Bird. Brook, Bonnie, ed. Van Wright, Cornelius, illus. 32p. (ps-1). 1989. 4.95 (ISBN 0-671-68599-6); PLB 9.98 (ISBN 0-671-68595-3). Silver Pr.

—If You Were a Cat. Brook, Bonnie, ed. Van Wright, Cornelius, illus. 32p. (ps-1). 1989. 4.95 (ISBN 0-671-68604-6); PLB 9.98 (ISBN 0-671-68598-8). Silver Pr.

—If You Were a Fish. Brook, Bonnie, ed. (Illus.). 32p. (ps-1). 1989. 4.95 (ISBN 0-671-68602-X); PLB 9.98 (ISBN 0-671-68596-1). Silver Pr.

—If You Were an Ant. Brook, Bonnie, ed. Van Wright, Cornelius, illus. 32p. (ps-1). 1989. 4.95 (ISBN 0-671-68603-8); PLB 9.98 (ISBN 0-671-68597-X). Silver Pr.

Calders, Pere. Brush. Feitlowitz, Marguerite, tr. from SPA. Vendrell, Carme S., illus. LC 85-23873. 32p. (ps-3). 1986. 10.95 (ISBN 0-916291-05-7). Kane-Miller Bk.

Calhoun, Mary. Cross-Country Cat. Ingraham, Erick, illus. LC 78-31718. (gr. k-3). 1979. 12.95 (ISBN 0-688-22186-6); PLB 12.88 (ISBN 0-688-32186-0, Morrow Jr Bks); pap. 4.95 (ISBN 0-685-03414-3, Mulberry Bks). Morrow Jr Bks.

—Hungry Leprechaun. Duvoisin, Roger, illus. LC 62-7214. 32p. (gr. k-3). 1962. PLB 12.88 (ISBN 0-688-31713-8). Morrow Jr Bks.

Calmenson, Stephanie. Babies. Wilburn, Kathy, illus. LC 86-81490. 22p. (ps). 1987. write for info. (ISBN 0-307-12118-6, Golden Bks). Western Pub.

—The Birthday Hat. Gantner, Susan, illus. 32p. (gr. 1-3). 1983. pap. 3.50 (ISBN 0-448-21705-8, G&D). Putnam Pub Group.

—Eureeka's Castle: Magellan's Hats. Prebenna, David, illus. (ps-k). 1991. bds. 1.95 (ISBN 0-307-06112-4, Golden Pr). Western Pub.

—Where Is Grandma Potamus. Gantner, Susan, illus. 32p. (gr. 1-3). 1983. pap. 3.50 (ISBN 0-448-21706-6, G&D). Putnam Pub Group.

Calmunson, Stephanie. Little Bunny. (ps-1). 1985. 2.95 (ISBN 0-671-53110-7, Little Simon). S&S Trade.

—The Little Bunny. Chambliss, Maxie, illus. (gr. 2-6). 1986. 4.95 (ISBN 0-671-62079-7, Little Simon). S&S Trade.

—Little Chick. (ps-1). 1985. 2.95 (ISBN 0-671-53111-5, Little Simon). S&S Trade.

—The Little Chick. Chambliss, Maxie, illus. (gr. 2-6). 1986. 4.95 (ISBN 0-671-62080-0, Little Simon). S&S Trade.

—The Shaggy Little Monster. Chambliss, Maxie, illus. (ps-1). 1986. 4.95 (ISBN 0-671-62738-4, Little Simon). S&S Trade.

Calrenson, Stephanie. Tiger's Bedtime. Cooke, Tom, illus. (ps-k). 1991. pap. write for info. (ISBN 0-307-11510-0, Golden Pr). Western Pub.

Campbell, Louise A. & Bowers, Grace A. Muffin, The Maine Puffin. Mason, MacAdam L., illus. 40p. (Orig.). (gr. k-3). 1988. pap. 9.95 (ISBN 0-9621949-0-5). Muffin Enter.
There's a lovable, colorful bird that lives off the coast of Maine. He learns to swim, learns to take a bath & learns to eat by himself. He catches a cold & meets a new friend. He's Muffin, an Atlantic Puffin growing up on the islands off the Maine coast. With his mother & father, his friends & the wide open ocean he learns everything a young person would...well, almost everything. Muffin learns to fly, too. MUFFIN, THE MAINE PUFFIN is a children's book written by first-time authors Louise Campbell & Grace Bowers. The colorful illustrations by MacAdam Lee Mason are perfectly matched to these seven stories of the triumphs & obstacles of growing & learning. MUFFIN, THE MAINE PUFFIN is a wonderful idea for children (or grandchildren) 4 to 8 years old.
Publisher Provided Annotation.

Campbell, Peter. Harry's Bee. LC 74-156105. (gr. 1-3). 1971. 5.95 (ISBN 0-672-51587-3, Bobbs). Macmillan.

Campbell, Rod. Buster Gets Dressed. (gr. 1-3). 1988. 4.95 (ISBN 0-8120-5922-0). Barron.

—Buster Keeps Warm. (gr. 1-3). 1988. 4.95 (ISBN 0-8120-5923-9). Barron.

—Dear Zoo. Campbell, Rod, illus. LC 82-83224. 22p. (ps-1). 1986. 9.95 (ISBN 0-02-716440-3, Four Winds). Macmillan Child Grp.

—Dear Zoo. (ps-k). 1987. pap. 4.95 (ISBN 0-317-62180-7, Puffin). Puffin Bks.

—I'm a Mechanic. 12p. (ps-2). 1986. bds. 6.95 (ISBN 0-8120-5768-6). Barron.

—I'm a Nurse. 12p. (ps-2). 1986. bds. 6.95 (ISBN 0-8120-5769-4). Barron.

—It's Mine. (Illus.). 24p. (ps). 1988. 8.95 (ISBN 0-8120-5921-2). Barron.

—Oh Dear! Campbell, Rod, illus. LC 84-3993. 20p. (ps-1). 1986. 8.95 (ISBN 0-02-716430-6, Four Winds). Macmillan Child Grp.

Cannon, Frances A. A Picture Book. Petz, Rita K., ed. Carr, Linda, illus. (gr. 4-6). write for info. Rapcom Enter.

Caple, Kathy. Harry's Smile. Caple, Kathy, illus. LC 87-5094. 32p. (gr. k-3). 1987. 12.95 (ISBN 0-395-43417-3). HM.

Carey, Karla. Julie & Jackie at Christmas-Time: The Play & Musical Play (with Music Book, Story-&-Song Cassette & Piano Cassette) Nolan, Dennis, illus. LC 88-12909. 39p. 1990. pap. 35.00 complete pkg. (ISBN 1-55768-151-1); pap. 25.00 book only (ISBN 1-55768-026-4); story-&-song or piano cass. 8.00 (ISBN 0-685-19710-7). LC Pub.

—Julie & Jackie Go a'Journeying: The Play & Musical Play (with Music Book, Story-&-Song Cassette & Piano Cassette) Nolan, Dennis, illus. LC 88-9171. 73p. 1990. pap. 35.00 complete pkg. (ISBN 1-55768-153-8); pap. 25.00 book only (ISBN 1-55768-028-0); story-&-song or piano cass. 8.00 (ISBN 0-685-19711-5). LC Pub.

—Julie & Jackie on the Ranch: The Play & Musical Play (with Music Book, Story-&-Song Cassette & Piano Cassette) Nolan, Dennis, illus. LC 88-12911. 46p. 1990. pap. 35.00 complete pkg. (ISBN 1-55768-154-6); pap. 25.00 book only (ISBN 1-55768-029-9); story-&-song or piano cass. 8.00 (ISBN 0-685-19712-3). LC Pub.

Carey, Mary. Donald Duck, TV Star! LC 87-83491. (Illus.). 40p. (gr. k-2). 1988. write for info. (ISBN 0-307-11695-6). Western Pub.

Carle, Eric. All Around Us. Carle, Eric, illus. LC 86-9354. (ps up). 1986. pap. 11.95 (ISBN 0-88708-016-2). Picture Bk Studio.

—Do You Want to Be My Friend? Carle, Eric, illus. LC 70-140643. 32p. (ps-2). 1971. 13.95 (ISBN 0-690-24276-X, Crowell Jr Bks); PLB 13.89 (ISBN 0-690-01137-7, Crowell Jr Bks). HarpC Child Bks.

—Do You Want to Be My Friend? Carle, Eric, illus. LC 70-140643. 32p. (ps-2). 1987. pap. 5.95 (ISBN 0-06-443127-4, Trophy). HarpC Child Bks.

—The Grouchy Ladybug. LC 77-3170. (Illus.). 48p. (ps-2). 1986. pap. 4.95 (ISBN 0-06-443116-9, Trophy). HarpC Child Bks.

—A House for Hermit Crab. LC 87-29261. (Illus.). 32p. 1987. 15.95 (ISBN 0-88708-056-1). Picture Bk Studio.

—The Mixed-Up Chameleon. rev. ed. LC 83-45950. (Illus.). 32p. (ps-3). 1988. pap. 5.95 (ISBN 0-06-443162-2, Trophy). HarpC Child Bks.

—My Very First Book of Food. Carle, Eric, illus. LC 85-45259. 10p. (ps-k). 1986. 2.95 (ISBN 0-694-00130-9, Crowell Jr Bks). HarpC Child Bks.

—My Very First Book of Growth. Carle, Eric, illus. LC 85-47893. 10p. (ps-k). 1986. 2.95 (ISBN 0-694-00092-2, Crowell Jr Bks). HarpC Child Bks.

—My Very First Book of Heads & Tails. Carle, Eric, illus. LC 85-45260. 10p. (ps-k). 1986. 2.95 (ISBN 0-694-00128-7, Crowell Jr Bks). HarpC Child Bks.

—My Very First Book of Homes. Carle, Eric, illus. LC 85-47891. 10p. (ps-k). 1986. 2.95 (ISBN 0-694-00094-9, Crowell Jr Bks). HarpC Child Bks.

—My Very First Book of Motion. Carle, Eric, illus. LC 85-47892. 10p. (ps-k). 1986. 2.95 (ISBN 0-694-00093-0, Crowell Jr Bks). HarpC Child Bks.
—My Very First Book of Sounds. Carle, Eric, illus. LC 85-45261. 10p. (ps-k). 1986. 2.95 (ISBN 0-694-00131-7, Crowell Jr Bks). HarpC Child Bks.
—My Very First Book of Tools. Carle, Eric, illus. LC 85-45258. 10p. (ps-k). 1986. 2.95 (ISBN 0-694-00129-5, Crowell Jr Bks). HarpC Child Bks.
—My Very First Book of Touch. Carle, Eric, illus. LC 84-47894. 10p. (ps-k). 1986. 2.95 (ISBN 0-694-00095-7, Crowell Jr Bks). HarpC Child Bks.
—One, Two, Three to the Zoo. (Illus.). 34p. (ps-2). 1990. pap. 5.95 (ISBN 0-399-21970-6, Sandcastle Bks). Putnam Pub Group.
—Rooster's off to See the World. LC 86-25509. (Illus.). 28p. (ps up). 1987. 15.95 (ISBN 0-88708-042-1). Picture Bk Studio.
—Secret Birthday Message. Carle, Eric, illus. LC 75-168726. 26p. (ps-3). 1972. 13.95 (ISBN 0-690-72347-4, Crowell Jr Bks); PLB 14.89 (ISBN 0-690-72348-2). HarpC Child Bks.
—Secret Birthday Message. Carle, Eric, illus. LC 85-45403. 26p. (ps-3). 1986. pap. 5.95 (ISBN 0-06-443099-5, Trophy). HarpC Child Bks.
—The Tiny Seed. Carle, Eric, illus. LC 86-2534. 32p. (gr. k up). 1987. 15.95 (ISBN 0-88708-015-4). Picture Bk Studio.
—The Very Busy Spider. Carle, Eric, illus. 32p. (ps-2). 1989. 16.95 (ISBN 0-399-21166-7, Philomel Bks); pap. 4.95 (ISBN 0-399-21592-1). Putnam Pub Group.
—The Very Hungry Caterpillar: La Oruga Muy Hambrienta. Carle, Eric, illus. (SPA.). (ps up). 1990. 15.95 (ISBN 0-399-21933-1, Philomel Bks). Putnam Pub Group.
Carlson, Nancy. Louanne Pig in Making the Team. Carlson, Nancy, illus. (gr. k-3). 1987. 19.95 (ISBN 0-685-18332-7); pap. 12.95 (ISBN 0-87499-038-6); 4 paperbacks, cassette & guide 27.95 (ISBN 0-87499-036-X). Live Oak Media.
—Louanne Pig in the Mysterious Valentine. Carlson, Nancy, illus. (gr. 1-3). 1988. bk. & cassette 19.95 (ISBN 0-87499-087-4); bk. & cassette 12.95 (ISBN 0-87499-086-6); 4 cassettes & guide 27.95 (ISBN 0-87499-088-2). Live Oak Media.
—Louanne Pig in The Perfect Family. Carlson, Nancy, illus. (gr. k-3). 1987. incl. cassette 19.95 (ISBN 0-87499-037-8); pap. 12.95 incl. cassette (ISBN 0-87499-035-1); 4 paperbacks, cassette & guide 27.95 (ISBN 0-685-18333-5). Live Oak Media.
—Loudmouth George & The Big Race. Carlson, Nancy, illus. (gr. k-3). 1986. incl. cassette 19.95 (ISBN 0-317-59227-0); pap. 12.95 incl. cassette (ISBN 0-87499-029-7); 4 paperbacks, cassette & guide 27.95 (ISBN 0-87499-031-9). Live Oak Media.
Carlstrom, Nancy W. Graham Cracker Animals 1-2-3. Sandford, John, illus. LC 88-13434. 32p. (ps-1). 1989. 13.95 (ISBN 0-02-717270-8, Mcmillan Child Bk). Macmillan Child Grp.
—Jesse Bear, What Will You Wear? Degen, Bruce, illus. LC 85-10610. 32p. (ps-k). 1986. 13.95 (ISBN 0-02-717350-X, Mcmillan Child Bk). Macmillan Child Grp.
—Wild Wild Sunflower Child Anna. Pinkney, Jerry, illus. LC 86-18226. 32p. (ps-1). 1987. 13.95 (ISBN 0-02-717360-7, Mcmillan Child Bk). Macmillan Child Grp.
Carmichael, Hoagy. Raffles & Other Singing Stories. Stearns, Helen M., ed. Urbahn, Clara, illus. 44p. (ps up). 1989. incl. cass. 25.00 (ISBN 0-9614281-5-5). Cricketfield Pr.
Carr, Jo. Trouble with Tikki. Petie, Haris, illus. LC 71-115459. (gr. k-2). 1970. 6.70 (ISBN 0-8313-0013-2). Lantern.
Carratello, Patricia. My Body. Carratello, Patricia, illus. 37p. (gr. 1-4). 1980. wkbk. 5.95 (ISBN 1-55734-211-3). Tchr Create Mat.
Carratello, Patty. Brett, My Pet. Spivak, Darlene, ed. Spence, Paula, illus. 16p. (gr. k-2). 1988. wkbk. 1.95 (ISBN 1-55734-387-X). Tchr Create Mat.
—My Cap. Spivak, Darlene, ed. Smythe, Linda, illus. 16p. (gr. k-2). 1988. wkbk. 1.95 (ISBN 1-55734-386-1). Tchr Create Mat.
Carrick, Carol. Ben & the Porcupine. Carrick, Donald, illus. LC 80-214020. 32p. (ps-3). 1985. pap. 4.95 (ISBN 0-89919-348-X, Clarion). HM.
—Left Behind. Carrick, Donald, illus. LC 88-1040. 32p. (gr. k-3). 1988. 13.95 (ISBN 0-89919-535-0, Pub. by Clarion). Ticknor & Fields.
—Old Mother Witch. Carrick, Donald, illus. LC 75-4609. 32p. (ps). 1989. pap. 4.95 (ISBN 0-395-51584-X, Clarion Bks). HM.
—Patrick's Dinosaurs. Carrick, Donald, illus. LC 83-2049. (gr. k-3). 1985. pap. 4.95 (ISBN 0-89919-402-8, Pub. by Clarion). Ticknor & Fields.
—What Happened to Patrick's Dinosaurs? Carrick, Doral, illus. 1988. pap. 7.95 incl. cass. (ISBN 0-89919-838-4, Clarion Bks). HM.
Carrick, Donald. Patrick's Dinosaurs. (ps-3). 1987. incl. cass. 6.95 (ISBN 0-317-64570-6). HM.
Carrie, Christopher. Astronauts to Diving Ducks. (Illus.). 40p. (Orig.). (gr. k up). 1989. pap. 1.49 (ISBN 0-86696-219-0). Binney & Smith.
—Elephants to Haunted Houses. (Illus.). 40p. (Orig.). (gr. k up). 1989. pap. 1.49 (ISBN 0-86696-225-5). Binney & Smith.
—Everything Has a Shape. (Illus.). 40p. (Orig.). (ps up). 1989. pap. 1.99 (ISBN 0-86696-222-0). Binney & Smith.
—Going Places. (Illus.). 40p. (Orig.). (ps up). 1989. pap. 1.99 (ISBN 0-86696-221-2). Binney & Smith.
—Growing Up. (Illus.). 40p. (Orig.). (ps up). 1989. pap. 1.99 (ISBN 0-86696-220-4). Binney & Smith.
—Icebergs to Lazy Lizards. (Illus.). 40p. (Orig.). (gr. k up). 1989. pap. 1.49 (ISBN 0-86696-226-3). Binney & Smith.
—Measurement. (Illus.). 12p. (Orig.). (gr. 3-6). 1987. pap. 4.70 (ISBN 0-86696-206-9). Binney & Smith.
—Monsters to Playful Penquins. (Illus.). 40p. (Orig.). (gr. k up). 1989. pap. 1.49 (ISBN 0-86696-227-1). Binney & Smith.
—My Perfect Pet. (Illus.). 40p. (Orig.). (ps up). 1989. pap. 1.99 (ISBN 0-86696-218-2). Binney & Smith.
—Quilts to Unusual Unicorns. (Illus.). 40p. (Orig.). (gr. k up). 1989. pap. 1.49 (ISBN 0-86696-229-8). Binney & Smith.
—Smiles, Giggles & Frowns. (Illus.). 40p. (Orig.). (ps up). 1989. pap. 1.99 (ISBN 0-86696-223-9). Binney & Smith.
—So Big. (Illus.). 32p. Date not set. 2.70 (ISBN 0-86696-205-0). Binney & Smith.
—Time. (Illus.). 12p. (Orig.). (gr. 3-6). 1987. pap. 4.70 (ISBN 0-86696-207-7). Binney & Smith.
—Volcanoes to Zany Zebras. (Illus.). 40p. (Orig.). (gr. k up). 1989. pap. 1.49 (ISBN 0-86696-230-1). Binney & Smith.
Carrier, Lark. Do Not Touch. LC 87-32730. (Illus.). (ps-12). 1988. 15.95 (ISBN 0-88708-061-8). Picture Bk Studio.
—A Perfect Spring. Carrier, Lark, illus. LC 89-49262. 32p. (ps up). 1989. 14.95 (ISBN 0-88708-131-2). Picture Bk Studio.
—Scout & Cody. Carrier, Lark, illus. LC 86-883. 28p. (ps up). 1987. 14.95 (ISBN 0-88708-013-8). Picture Bk Studio.
—Snowy Path: A Christmas Journey. Carrier, Lark, illus. LC 89-8449. 28p. (ps up). 1989. 15.95 (ISBN 0-88708-121-5). Picture Bk Studio.
—There Was a Hill... Carrier, Lark, illus. LC 84-25536. 40p. (ps up). 1985. 15.95 (ISBN 0-907234-70-4). Picture Bk Studio.
Carrier, Roch. The Hockey Sweater. Fischman, Sheila, tr. from FRE. Cohen, Sheldon, illus. 24p. (gr. 1 up). 1984. text ed. 14.95 (ISBN 0-88776-169-0, Dist. by U of Toronto Pr); pap. 6.95 (ISBN 0-88776-174-7). Tundra Bks.
Carroll, Lewis. Jabberwocky. Tucker, Kathleen, ed. Buckley, Kate, illus. LC 84-17339. 32p. (gr. k up). 1985. PLB 10.95 (ISBN 0-8075-3747-0). A Whitman.
Cars & Trucks. (Illus.). 24p. (gr. k-2). 1988. 3.95 (ISBN 0-87449-501-6). Modern Pub NYC.
Carter, Anne. Molly in Danger. Butler, John, illus. (ps-2). 1987. PLB 5.95 (ISBN 0-517-56534-X). Crown.
—Scurry's Treasure. Butler, John, illus. (gr. k-3). 1987. PLB 5.95 (ISBN 0-517-56535-8). Crown.
Carter, David A. How Many Bugs in a Box? (ps-1). 1988. pap. 11.95 (ISBN 0-671-64965-5, Little Simon). S&S Trade.
—Surprise Party: A Lift-up Pop-up Book. (Illus.). 16p. 1990. 14.95 (ISBN 0-448-40062-6, G&D). Putnam Pub Group.
—What's in My Pocket? A Pop-up & Peek-in Book. Carter, David A., illus. 10p. (ps-k). 1989. 8.95 (ISBN 0-399-21685-5, Putnam). Putnam Pub Group.
Carter, Margaret. Go Away, William. Wright, Carol, illus. LC 88-8314. 32p. (ps-1). 1989. 11.95 (ISBN 0-02-717791-2, Mcmillan Child Bk). Macmillan Child Grp.
Cartlidge, Michelle. Bear in the Forest. Cartlidge, Michelle, illus. 12p. (ps). 1991. bds. 3.50 (ISBN 0-525-44674-5, DCB). Dutton Child Bks.
—Dressing Teddy. Cartlidge, Michelle, illus. (Orig.). (ps up). 1986. pap. 3.95 (ISBN 0-14-032067-9, Puffin). Puffin Bks.
—Duck in the Pond. Cartlidge, Michelle, illus. 12p. (ps). 1991. bds. 3.50 (ISBN 0-525-44675-3, DCB). Dutton Child Bks.
—Elephant in the Jungle. Cartlidge, Michelle, illus. 12p. (ps). 1991. bds. 3.50 (ISBN 0-525-44676-1, DCB). Dutton Child Bks.
—Mouse in the House. Cartlidge, Michelle, illus. 12p. (ps). 1991. bds. 3.50 (ISBN 0-525-44678-8, DCB). Dutton Child Bks.
—Mouse's Christmas Tree. Cartlidge, Michelle, illus. 8p. (Orig.). (ps up). 1986. pap. 3.95 (ISBN 0-14-032066-0, Puffin). Puffin Bks.
—Teddy's Birthday Party. Cartlidge, Michelle, illus. 8p. (Orig.). (ps up). 1986. pap. 3.95 (ISBN 0-14-032068-7, Puffin). Puffin Bks.
—Teddy's Christmas. Cartlidge, Michelle, illus. 32p. (ps). 1986. pap. 9.95 (ISBN 0-671-62912-3, Little Simon). S&S Trade.
—Teddy's Dinner. Cartlidge, Michelle, illus. (ps). 1986. 2.95 (ISBN 0-671-61347-2, Little Simon). S&S Trade.
—Teddy's Garden. Cartlidge, Michelle, illus. (ps). 1986. 2.95 (ISBN 0-671-61346-4, Little Simon). S&S Trade.
—Teddy's House. Cartlidge, Michelle, illus. (ps). 1986. 2.95 (ISBN 0-671-61345-6, Little Simon). S&S Trade.
—Teddy's Toys. Cartlidge, Michelle, illus. (ps). 1986. 2.95 (ISBN 0-671-61348-0, Little Simon). S&S Trade.
Cartwright, Stephen. Find the Bird. Cartwright, Stephen, illus. Zeff, C. (Illus.). 12p. (ps). 1984. bds. 2.95 (ISBN 0-86020-719-6, Pub. by Usborne). EDC.
—Find the Duck. Cartwright, Stephen, illus. Zeff, C. (Illus.). 12p. (ps). 1984. bds. 2.95 (ISBN 0-86020-714-5, Pub. by Usborne). EDC.
—Find the Kitten. Cartwright, Stephen, illus. Zeff, C. (Illus.). 12p. (ps). 1984. bds. 2.95 (ISBN 0-86020-718-8, Pub. by Usborne). EDC.
—Find the Piglet. Cartwright, Stephen, illus. Zeff, C. (Illus.). 12p. (ps). 1984. bds. 2.95 (ISBN 0-86020-716-1, Pub. by Usborne). EDC.
—Find the Puppy. Cartwright, Stephen, illus. Zeff, C. (Illus.). 12p. (ps). 1984. bds. 2.95 (ISBN 0-86020-717-X, Pub. by Usborne). EDC.
—Find the Teddy. Cartwright, Stephen, illus. Zeff, C. (Illus.). 12p. (ps). 1984. bds. 2.95 (ISBN 0-86020-715-3, Pub. by Usborne). EDC.
Case, Elinor. Humphrey, Wimsey & Doo. Taylor, Marie, illus. 48p. (Orig.). (ps-6). 1984. pap. 5.95 (ISBN 0-910781-02-8). G Whittell Mem.
A Case of the Giggles, Now That's Funny!, Cutchie-Cutchie Coo! & No Laughing Matter. (Illus.). (gr. k-2). Date not set. pap. 3.95 ea., 24pgs. ea. A Case of the Giggles (ISBN 0-87449-787-6). Now That's Funny (ISBN 0-87449-788-4). Cutchie-Cutchie Coo (ISBN 0-87449-789-2). No Laughing Matter (ISBN 0-87449-790-6). Modern Pub NYC.
The Case of the Missing Lettuce. (Illus.). 64p. (gr. k-2). 1989. 6.95 (ISBN 0-87449-508-3). Modern Pub NYC.
The Case of the Vanishing House. (Illus.). 64p. (gr. k-2). 1989. 6.95 (ISBN 0-87449-510-5). Modern Pub NYC.
Caseley, Judith. Silly Baby. LC 87-4097. (Illus.). 24p. (ps-3). 1988. 11.95 (ISBN 0-688-07355-7); lib. bdg. 11.88 (ISBN 0-688-07356-5). Greenwillow.
The Caterpillar Who Turned into a Butterfly. 16p. (ps-k). 1980. 2.95 (ISBN 0-671-41347-3, Little Simon). S&S Trade.
Cat's Book of Opposites: Animal Board Book. 1989. bds. 1.98 (ISBN 0-8317-0346-6). Smithmark.
Cauley, Lorinda B. The Ugly Duckling. Canley, Lorinda B., illus. LC 79-12340. 48p. (gr. k-3). 1979. pap. 4.95 (ISBN 0-15-692528-1, VoyB). HarBraceJ.
Causley, Charles. Quack! Said the Billy-Goat. Firth, Barbara, illus. LC 85-27167. 24p. (ps-2). 1986. pap. 2.50 (ISBN 0-06-443104-5, Trophy). HarpC Child Bks.
Cazet, Denys. December Twenty-Fourth. Cazet, Denys, illus. LC 86-8247. 32p. (ps-2). 1986. 12.95 (ISBN 0-02-717950-8, Bradbury Pr). Macmillan Child Grp.
—Frosted Glass. Cazet, Denys, illus. LC 86-26822. 32p. (ps-2). 1987. 12.95 (ISBN 0-02-717960-5, Bradbury Pr). Macmillan Child Grp.
—Good Morning, Maxine! Cazet, Denys, illus. LC 88-2889. 32p. (ps-2). 1989. 13.95 (ISBN 0-02-717940-0, Bradbury Pr). Macmillan Child Grp.
Ceccarelli, Serge, illus. The Three Little Pigs. 24p. (ps-2). 1988. bk. & audiocassette 6.95 (ISBN 0-8120-4041-4). Barron.
Cecil, Laura. Listen to This. Clark, Emma C., illus. LC 87-8556. 96p. (ps-3). 1988. 15.00 (ISBN 0-688-07617-3). Greenwillow.
Cecotti, Loralie. Seattle Center. Hamer, Bonnie, illus. 24p. (Orig.). (gr. 1-4). 1983. pap. 2.75 (ISBN 0-933992-30-0). Coffee Break.
Chadwick, Kenneth E. A Hear Do'n Sing Book: Little Bitty You Little Bitty Me. Boss, Jackie, illus. (ps). 1979. 4.25 (ISBN 0-9603698-0-5). Bet-Ken Prods.
Chalmers, Mary. A Christmas Story. rev. ed. Chalmers, Mary, illus. LC 56-8143. 24p. (ps-1). 1987. pap. 2.95 (ISBN 0-06-443156-8, Trophy). HarpC Child Bks.
—Easter Parade. Chalmers, Mary, illus. LC 87-45277. 32p. (ps-1). 1990. pap. 4.95 (ISBN 0-06-443219-X, Trophy). HarpC Child Bks.
Chambliss, Maxie, illus. I Know an Old Lady. 1987. pap. 5.95 incl. audiocassette (ISBN 0-553-45901-5). Bantam.
Chandler, Jean, illus. The Humpty Dumpty Book. 24p. (ps-k). 1987. pap. write for info. (ISBN 0-307-10052-9, Pub. by Golden Bks). Western Pub.
Chandoha, Walter, photos by. Puppies & Kittens. (Illus.). (ps). 1983. 3.95 (ISBN 0-448-40874-0, G&D). Putnam Pub Group.
Chaplin, Susan. I Can Sign My ABCs. McCaul, Laura, illus. LC 86-22890. 56p. (ps-1). 1986. 8.95 (ISBN 0-930323-19-X, Kendall Green Pubns). Gallaudet Univ Pr.
Chapman, Carol. Barney Bipple's Magic Dandelions. Kellogg, Steven, illus. LC 77-5747. 32p. (gr. k-3). 1988. 13.95 (ISBN 0-525-44449-1, DCB). Dutton Child Bks.

Charaleone. All I See Is Part of Me. Aldrich, Cynthia, illus. 56p. (gr. 2-8). 1989. 14.95 (ISBN 0-935699-03-1). Illum Arts.
A rhythmic tale of one child's journey to self-discovery, this richly illustrated story has received an exceptional response across the country. In addition to parents & children, enthusiasts include teachers, librarians, pediatricians & other health professionals. Dr. Michael E. Ogle, Ph.D., Clinical Psychologist, states "All I See Is Part of Me should be required reading by prospective mothers & fathers, educators, mental

health practitioners & their patients... This book is a prescription for child-rearing & the goal of psychotherapy." Now in its 1st reprint, All I See Is Part of Me communicates simple & enduring truths enhanced by brilliant, full-color illustrations. "Sister star, How can it be That I am you & you are me?" She glowed, "You're larger than you know, You are everyplace there is to go. You have a body, this is true... But look at what's inside of you!" According to Gerald G. Jampolsky, M.D., Founder of the Center for Attitudinal Healing, "This warm, gentle, tender, trusting book is just what the world needs." All I See Is Part of Me is a delight for children of all ages - a book whose message is never forgotten!
Publisher Provided Annotation.

Charles, Donald. Gordito, Gordon Gato Galano: (Fat, Fat Calico Cat) Charles, Donald, illus. LC 77-7154. (SPA.). 32p. (ps-2). 1988. PLB 14.60 (ISBN 0-516-33456-5); pap. 3.95 (ISBN 0-516-53456-4). Childrens.

Charles, Oz. How Is a Crayon Made? (Illus.). (gr. 1-5). 1990. 9.95 (ISBN 0-671-63756-8); pap. 3.95 (ISBN 0-671-69437-5). S&S Trade.

Charlie Cricket. 12p. (ps-1). 1989. bds. 14.95 (ISBN 0-87449-643-8). Modern Pub NYC.

Charlie the Noisy Caterpillar. (Illus.). (ps-2). 3.95 (ISBN 0-7214-9597-4). Ladybird Bks.

Charlip, Remy. Fortunately. Charlip, Remy, illus. LC 80-36956. 48p. (ps-3). 1984. Repr. of 1964 ed. 13.95 (ISBN 0-02-718100-6, Four Winds). Macmillan Child Grp.

Charlip, Remy & Joyner, Jerry. Thirteen. LC 75-8875. (Illus.). 40p. (gr. 1-3). 1984. Repr. of 1975 ed. 13.95 (ISBN 0-02-718120-0, Four Winds). Macmillan Child Grp.

Charlot, Martin. Sunnyside Up. LC 73-173473. (Illus.). (gr. 1-7). 1972. 5.95 (ISBN 0-685-02677-9). Island Heritage.

Charlton, Michael. Wheezy. (ps-2). 1988. 10.95 (ISBN 0-318-37402-1). Random.

Chartier, Normand. Jingle Bells: Chubby Board Book. 1989. 3.95 (ISBN 0-671-68269-5). S&S Trade.

Chase, Edith N. The New Baby Calf. Reid, Barbara, illus. 32p. (gr. k-3). pap. 2.50 (ISBN 0-590-00349-6). Scholastic Inc.

Cherry, Lynne. Orangutan. LC 86-24025. (Illus.). 16p. (ps-k). 1987. 3.50 (ISBN 0-525-44301-0, DCB). Dutton Child Bks.

Chetwin, Grace. Mr. Meredith & the Truly Remarkable Stone. Stock, Catherine, illus. LC 87-37435. 32p. (gr. k-3). 1989. 13.95 (ISBN 0-02-718313-0, Bradbury Pr). Macmillan Child Grp.

Chevalier, Christa. Spence & the Mean Old Bear. Levine, Abby, ed. LC 86-1570. (Illus.). 32p. (ps-1). 1986. 10. 95 (ISBN 0-8075-7572-0). A Whitman.

—Spence Is Small. Levine, Abby, ed. Chevalier, Christa, illus. LC 87-2054. (ps-3). 1987. PLB 10.95 (ISBN 0-8075-7567-4). A Whitman.

Chiefari. Kids Are Baby Goats. (gr. 5-8). 1984. 9.95 (ISBN 0-396-08316-1, Putnam). Putnam Pub Group.

Children's Television Workshop Staff. Who's Hiding? Cooke, Tom, illus. LC 84-81602. 14p. (ps-k). 1986. write for info. (ISBN 0-307-12157-7, Pub. by Golden Bks). Western Pub.

Chochola, Frantisek. The Forest. (Illus.). (ps). 1988. bds. 5.50 (ISBN 0-86315-073-X, 20234). Gryphon Hse.

—On the Farm. (ps). 1988. bds. 5.50 (ISBN 0-86315-051-9, 20235). Gryphon Hse.

Chorao, Kay, illus. Baby's Good Morning Book. Collins, Judy, contrib. by. LC 86-6415. (Illus.). 64p. (ps). 1990. 13.95 (ISBN 0-525-44257-X, DCB); incl. audio cass. 17.95 (ISBN 0-525-44627-3, DCB). Dutton Child Bks.

Christiansen, C. B. My Mother's House, My Father's House. Trivas, Irene, illus. LC 88-16802. 32p. (gr. k-3). 1989. 13.95 (ISBN 0-689-31394-2, Atheneum Child Bk). Macmillan Child Grp.

Chubby Bear. 1984. 2.95 (ISBN 0-671-50949-7, Little Simon). S&S Trade.

Chubby Bear Goes to the Moon. 1984. 2.95 (ISBN 0-671-50953-5, Little Simon). S&S Trade.

Chubby Chums: Chick, 3 bks. (Illus.). 36p. (ps). 1991. Set. bds. 7.95 incl. doll (ISBN 0-671-70802-3, Little Simon). S&S Trade.

Chubby Chums: Panda, 3 bks. (Illus.). 36p. (ps). 1991. Set. bds. 7.95 incl. doll (ISBN 0-671-70803-1, Little Simon). S&S Trade.

Chubby Snowman. 1984. 2.95 (ISBN 0-671-50948-9, Little Simon). S&S Trade.

Chubby Train. 1984. 2.95 (ISBN 0-671-50951-9, Little Simon). S&S Trade.

Chubby Tugboat. 1984. 2.95 (ISBN 0-671-50950-0, Little Simon). S&S Trade.

Circle Circus. 6p. (Orig.). (ps-2). 1989. pap. 5.95 (ISBN 0-8431-2326-5). Price Stern.

Circle Zoo. (Illus.). 6p. (Orig.). (ps-2). 1989. pap. 5.95 (ISBN 0-8431-2327-3). Price Stern.

The Circus. (Illus.). 12p. (gr. k-2). 1983. bds. 3.95 (ISBN 0-87449-178-9). Modern Pub NYC.

Civardi, Anne. Potty Time. Langley, Jonathan, illus. 24p. (ps). 1988. pap. 6.95 (ISBN 0-671-65896-4, Little Simon). S&S Trade.

Cleary, Beverly. The Real Hole. rev. ed. Stevens, Mary, illus. LC 85-18815. 32p. (ps-1). 1986. 11.95 (ISBN 0-688-05850-7); PLB 11.88 (ISBN 0-688-05851-5). Morrow.

—Ribsy. Darling, Louis, illus. 192p. (gr. 3-7). 1982. pap. 3.25 (ISBN 0-440-47456-6, YB). Dell.

Clements, Andrew. Big Al. Yoshi, illus. LC 88-15129. 28p. (ps up). 1988. 14.95 (ISBN 0-88708-075-8). Picture Bk Studio.

—Noah & the Ark & the Animals. Gantschev, Ivan, illus. LC 84-9438. 28p. (gr. 1 up). 1984. 14.95 (ISBN 0-907234-58-5). Picture Bk Studio.

Clements, Jehan. Alfred the Ant: The First Storytelling "Flip Over" Picture Book. Clements, Jehan, illus. LC 89-61138. 48p. (gr. k-3). 1991. 20.00 (ISBN 0-9622500-0-7). Strytllr Co. The Storyteller Company presents a new concept in storytelling & story reading in the classroom. The unique format of the First Storytelling "Flip Over" Picture Book, is especially designed for elementary school teachers to use in the classroom. The children will just flip over The Very First Storytelling "Flip Over" Picture Book. ALFRED THE ANT, an ant who lives in Central Park, will be The First Storytelling "Flip Over" Picture Book. This Pre-Bound Teacher's Edition contains 48 9" X 12" "Flip Over" pages, including a Teacher's Guide for grades K-3. Part I: The Storytelling version of ALFRED THE ANT, as told by Jehan Clements, also has suggested follow up activities for the children. Part II: The Illustrated Version of ALFRED THE ANT has 13 full color, full sized illustrations for the children. There are 13 full color reduced size illustrations, with large text type, for the teachers. There are also two master copies of the classroom activity pages & authors notes.
Publisher Provided Annotation.

Clemons, Martha & Hartley, Barb. Buncho. Kratzer, Erica, illus. 28p. (Orig.). (gr. k-3). Date not set. pap. write for info. Clemons Hartley.

Climo, Shirley. The Cobweb Christmas. Lasker, Joe, illus. LC 81-43879. 32p. (ps-3). 1986. pap. 4.50 (ISBN 0-06-443110-X, Trophy). HarpC Child Bks.

Clothes. (Illus.). (ps). 3.50 (ISBN 0-7214-9086-7). Ladybird Bks.

Coats, Laura J. Goodyear the City Cat. Coats, Laura J., illus. LC 86-23782. 32p. (gr. k-3). 1987. 12.95 (ISBN 0-02-719051-X, Mcmillan Child Bk). Macmillan Child Grp.

—Mr. Jordan in the Park. Coats, Laura J., illus. LC 88-13295. 32p. (gr. k-3). 1989. 13.95 (ISBN 0-02-719053-6, Mcmillan Child Bk). Macmillan Child Grp.

Cobb, Vicki. Skyscraper Going Up! Strajan, John, illus. LC 86-47795. 18p. (gr. 1-5). 1987. 14.95 (ISBN 0-690-04525-5, Crowell Jr Bks). HarpC Child Bks.

Cocca-Leffler, Maryann, illus. These Are Baby's Things. 14p. (ps). 1990. bds. 3.95 (ISBN 0-679-80167-7). Random.

Coerr, Eleanor. Big Balloon Race. Croll, Carolyn, illus. LC 80-8368. 64p. (gr. k-3). 1984. incl. cassette 5.98 (ISBN 0-694-00162-7, Trophy); pap. 3.50 (ISBN 0-06-444053-2, Trophy). HarpC Child Bks.

Cohen, Barbara. Molly's Pilgrim. Deraney, Michael J., illus. LC 83-797. 32p. (gr. 2-5). 1983. 12.95 (ISBN 0-688-02103-4); PLB 12.88 (ISBN 0-688-02104-2). Lothrop.

Cohen, Hennig & Coffin, Tristram P., eds. Folklore of American Holidays. 431p. (gr. 3-12). 1986. 80.00x (ISBN 0-8103-2126-2). Gale.

Cohen, Marsha, illus. Baby's Favorite Things. 12p. (ps). 1986. 3.95 (ISBN 0-394-88243-1, Random Juv). Random.

Cohen, Miriam. Best Friends. Hoban, Lillian, illus. 32p. (ps-1). 1989. pap. 3.95 (ISBN 0-689-71334-7, Aladdin). Macmillan Child Grp.

—It's George! Hoban, Lillian, illus. LC 86-19384. 24p. (ps-2). 11.95 (ISBN 0-688-06812-X); lib. bdg. 11.88 (ISBN 0-688-06813-8). Greenwillow.

—The New Teacher. Hoban, Lillian, illus. 32p. (ps-1). 1989. pap. 3.95 (ISBN 0-689-71332-0, Aladdin). Macmillan Child Grp.

—Will I Have a Friend? Hoban, Lillian, illus. LC 67-10127. 32p. (gr. k-1). 1967. 12.95 (ISBN 0-02-722790-1, Mcmillan Child Bk). Macmillan Child Grp.

—Will I Have a Friend? Hoban, Lillian, illus. 32p. (ps-1). 1989. pap. 3.95 (ISBN 0-689-71333-9, Aladdin). Macmillan Child Grp.

Cole, Babette. The Smelly Book. Cole, Babette, illus. 40p. (gr. k-5). 1988. pap. 10.95 (ISBN 0-671-65670-8, Little Simon). S&S Trade.

Cole, Betsy. Green Creatures Ten to One. Happe, Cary, illus. LC 88-71429. 32p. (Orig.). (gr. k-3). 1988. pap. 4.95 (ISBN 0-9620606-0-7). Adventure VA.

Cole, Brock. The Giant's Toe. (Illus.). 32p. (ps up). 1988. pap. 3.95 (ISBN 0-374-42557-4). FS&G.

Cole, Joann. Norma Jean, Jumping Bean. Munsinger, Lynn, illus. LC 86-15588. 48p. (gr. 1-3). 1987. lib. bdg. 6.99 (ISBN 0-394-98668-7, Random Juv); pap. 2.95 (ISBN 0-394-88668-2). Random.

Cole, Joanna. Anna Banana: One Hundred One Jump-Rope Rhymes. Tiegreen, Alan, illus. LC 88-29108. 64p. (gr. 3-7). 1989. 13.95 (ISBN 0-688-07788-9); pap. 6.95 (ISBN 0-688-08809-0, Pub. by Beech Tree Bks). Morrow Jr Bks.

—The Clown-Arounds. Smath, Jerry, illus. LC 81-4662. 48p. (ps-3). 1981. 5.95 (ISBN 0-8193-1059-X); PLB 5.95 (ISBN 0-8193-1060-3). Parents.

Colladi, Carlo. The Adventures of Pinocchio: The Ultimate Illustrated Edition. (Illus.). 160p. (ps up). write for info. Bantam.

Collier, Jaunell & Hill, Marie. I Love You. Collier, Jaunell, illus. 27p. (Orig.). 1983. write for info. (ISBN 0-918464-58-7). Irresistible.

Collins, Crystal. Teddy Bear Paper Dolls. 1983. pap. 3.50 (ISBN 0-486-24550-0). Dover.

Collins, Doris. Fun Times Growing Up. Walsh, Janice, illus. 24p. (Orig.). (gr. k-3). 1988. pap. 7.95 (ISBN 0-9621650-0-X). Periwinkle MA.

Collins, Grace. Willy, Zilly & the Little Bantams. LC 88-51662. (Illus.). 32p. (gr. 1-3). 1988. 10.25x (ISBN 0-943864-54-2). Davenport.

Collins, Pat L. Waiting for Baby Joe. Tucker, Kathy, ed. Dunn, Joan W., illus. 40p. (ps-2). 1990. PLB 10.95 (ISBN 0-8075-8625-0). A Whitman.

Collins, Sterling C. Doll-Victorian Mouse Paper Dolls in Full Color. 1986. pap. 3.95 (ISBN 0-486-25045-8). Dover.

Collins-sterling, Crystal. Panda-Paper Dolls. 1989. pap. 2.95 (ISBN 0-486-25929-3). Dover.

Collis, Len. My Little Vacation Book. Reeves, Eira, illus. 24p. (ps-3). 1988. 3.50 (ISBN 0-8120-5918-2). Barron.

Color Match Ups. (Illus.). 12p. (ps-1). 1988. 5.95 (ISBN 0-8431-2660-4). Price Stern.

Colors. (ps-1). 1985. 2.95 (ISBN 0-671-54749-6, Little Simon). S&S Trade.

Colors. (Illus.). (ps-k). bds. 3.50 (ISBN 0-7214-9600-8). Ladybird Bks.

Colors. (Illus.). 12p. (gr. k-2). 1982. bds. 3.95 (ISBN 0-87449-174-6). Modern Pub NYC.

Colors & Shapes. 32p. (ps-k). 1986. write for info. wkbk. (ISBN 0-307-05165-X, Pub. by Golden Bks). Western Pub.

Colossal Book of Dinosaurs. 240p. (gr. k-2). 1989. 19.95 (ISBN 0-87449-649-7). Modern Pub NYC.

Come to the Circus. 16p. (ps-k). 1980. pap. 2.95 (ISBN 0-671-41479-8, Little Simon). S&S Trade.

Cook, Scott, illus. The Gingerbread Boy. LC 86-31278. 32p. (ps-1). 1987. 7.95 (ISBN 0-394-88698-4); lib. bdg. 7.99 (ISBN 0-394-98698-9). Knopf.

Cooke, Tom, illus. Grover's Adventure under the Sea. LC 88-61629. 14p. (ps). 1989. bds. 2.95 (ISBN 0-394-81951-9). Random.

—Hide-&-Seek Camping Trip. (ps). bds. 2.95 (ISBN 0-317-99898-6). Random.

—The Hide & Seek Camping Trip: A Sesame Street Book. LC 89-61021. 14p. (ps). 1990. 2.95 (ISBN 0-685-31775-7). Random.

—Sesame Street Hide-&-Seek Safari. LC 87-61638. 14p. (ps). 1988. bds. 2.95 (ISBN 0-394-89474-X, Random Juv). Random.

Cooney, Nancy E. Umbrella Day. Mathis, Melissa B., illus. 32p. (ps-2). 1989. 14.95 (ISBN 0-399-21523-9, Philomel Bks). Putnam Pub Group.

Cooper, Susan. The Selkie Girl. Hutton, Warwick, illus. LC 86-70147. 32p. (gr. k-4). 1986. 13.95 (ISBN 0-689-50390-3, M K McElderry). Macmillan Child Grp.

Cope, Wendy. Twiddling Your Thumbs. (Illus.). 32p. (ps-3). 1988. 10.95 (ISBN 0-571-14791-7). Faber & Faber.

Corey, Dorothy. Everybody Takes Turns. Ann, Fay, ed. Axeman, Lois, illus. LC 79-18652. (ps-1). 1980. PLB 9.75 (ISBN 0-8075-2166-3). A Whitman.

—New Shoes! Fay, Ann, ed. Leder, Dora, illus. LC 84-17381. 32p. (ps-2). 1985. 12.95 (ISBN 0-8075-5583-5). A Whitman.

—A Shot for Baby Bear. Fay, Ann, ed. Cushman, Doug, illus. 24p. (ps-1). 1989. 10.95g (ISBN 0-8075-7348-5). A Whitman.

—Will It Ever Be My Birthday? Fay, Ann, ed. LC 86-1565. (Illus.). 32p. (ps-1). 1986. PLB 12.95 (ISBN 0-8075-9106-8). A Whitman.

Cornell, Donald. Ice Told Tales. Rosoff, Barbara, tr. Cornell, Donald, illus. (ENG & FRE.). 58p. (Orig.). (ps-2). 1991. pap. 4.00 (ISBN 0-9620738-1-4). D Cornell.

Corrigan, Dorothy D. Watch Out for the Golly Whompers. McBride, Michael, illus. LC 88-50754. 35p. (gr. k-3). 1988. 6.95 (ISBN 1-55523-149-7). Winston-Derek.

Corrin, Sara & Corrin, Stephen, eds. Stories for Eight-Year-Olds & Other Young Readers. Hughes, Shirley, illus. 192p. (gr. 2-4). 1984. 12.95 (ISBN 0-571-09332-9); pap. 9.95 (ISBN 0-571-12969-2). Faber & Faber.

—Stories for Six-Year Olds & Other Young Readers. Hughes, Shirley, illus. 198p. (gr. k-2). 1984. 12.95 (ISBN 0-571-08114-2); pap. 9.95 (ISBN 0-571-12959-5). Faber & Faber.

Corwin, Judith H. Patriotic Fun. Corwin, Judith H., illus. LC 85-18730. 64p. (gr. 3 up). 1986. PLB 10.29 (ISBN 0-671-50799-0); PLB 7.71s.p.; pap. 4.95 (ISBN 0-671-55378-X); pap. 3.71s.p. Messner.

Cosgrove, Shaerie. On Grandma's Lap. McGlinn, Merry A., illus. 32p. (ps-3). 1989. pap. 4.95 incl. cassette (ISBN 0-8249-7321-6). Ideals.

—A Sunny Song. McGlinn, Merry A., illus. 32p. (ps-3). 1989. pap. 4.95 incl. cassette (ISBN 0-8249-7320-8). Ideals.

Cosgrove, Stephen. Balderdash. Gedrose, Ed, illus. 32p. (ps up). 1991. 14.95 (ISBN 1-55868-045-4). Gr Arts Ctr Pub.
There was a place called Bugaboo where elfin creatures called Woodsprites lived. But also there, in the darkened shadows of Bugaboo, lived Balderdash, the king of twisty snakes & skittering things. He was the leader of any puffery shaded black & grey that whisked about the night scaring wit & wisdom from those not wise. So frightened were the Woodsprites of Balderdash & all that they commanded that they wouldn't work in the garden for fear of the daytime shadows. No one would gather nuts or berries for fear of being away from the protective wrap of the nighttime fires. With no one to work the garden & no one to gather berries, there was no food, & without food, the Woodsprites were very hungry indeed. Thus begins Stephen Cosgrove's classic tale of BALDERDASH as illustrated by Ed Gedrose, one of the Northwest's premier fantasy artists. BALDERDASH is added with great pride as the fourth book in the DreamMaker Classic series. Children of all ages learn not to fear the dark, the shadows, & those things that imagination can make.
Publisher Provided Annotation.

—**The Dream Stealer. Heyer, Carol, illus. LC 89-83843. 48p. (gr. 1-4). 1990. 16.95 (ISBN 1-55868-009-8); pap. 5.95 (ISBN 1-55868-021-7); pap. 12.95 incl. audio (ISBN 1-55868-042-X). Gr Arts Ctr Pub.**
THE DREAM STEALER is the first of the Dream Maker Classics by Stephen Cosgrove. A twisted, masked gnome, the Dream Stealer, has been taking good dreams from the children of Chimera. The tale is woven around Michael & Gabby's efforts to capture the gnome & release the dreams. Illustrated by Carol Heyer, THE DREAM STEALER is certain to enchant one & all.
Publisher Provided Annotation.

—The Fanny. James, Robin, illus. LC 86-15589. (gr. k-2). 1986. 12.66 (ISBN 0-317-58037-X). Rourke Corp.

—**Harmony. Casad, Michael, illus. LC 89-83842. 72p. (gr. 7 up). 1991. 24.95 (ISBN 1-55868-008-X). Gr Arts Ctr Pub.**
For the past several years, the national
news media has reflected man's fascination with one of the most spiritual of all creatures - the whale. More & more people have followed the news stories with a sense of awe & wonder. The story, as sung by the whales, is narrated by Harmony & accented by characters such as Rhapsody, his mother; Symphony, the leader of the pod; & Cacophony, the mad bull. Through the eyes of Harmony, we view a panoramic picture relating the history of a pod of whales from the beginning of time to their ultimate beached destruction. Interwoven is the story of man & his senseless obsession with traditions, which could lead ultimately to his own destruction. Meant for the entire family, this novel is one of the first of its kind to include original color illustrations. HARMONY, the first in the trilogy, "Song of the Sea," concerns itself with man's relationship to nature. Michael Casad's 25 years of experience encompass everything from commissions by various foreign countries & portraits of famous personalities, to a 70' x 23' mural.
Publisher Provided Annotation.

—Heidi's Rose. Edelson, Wendy, illus. LC 90-71079. 32p. 1991. 14.95 (ISBN 1-55868-033-0). Gr Arts Ctr Pub.
Set high in the mountains at Timberline Lodge, the story begins as a Saint Bernard arrives at the lodge. Wearing a beautiful locket, the huge dog arouses the curiosity of Rose, the innkeeper's daughter. But no one can get close to the animal to see what is in the locket. Accustomed to getting her own way, Rose schemes to get the locket so she can look inside. But adventure overtakes both girl & dog. Stephen Cosgrove is the author of more than 150 children's books. Wendy Edelson's illustrations have won numerous awards.
Publisher Provided Annotation.

—Leo the Lop: Tail Two. James, Robin, illus. 32p. (Orig.). (gr. k-6). 1978. pap. 2.95 (ISBN 0-8431-0572-0). Price Stern.
—Maui-Maui. James, Robin, illus. 32p. (gr. k-6). 1979. pap. 2.95 (ISBN 0-8431-0573-9). Price Stern.

—Prancer. Heyer, Carol, illus. LC 89-83843. 32p. (gr. k-7). 1990. 14.95 (ISBN 0-685-27179-X); pap. 5.95 (ISBN 1-55868-020-9); pap. 12.95 incl. audio (ISBN 1-55868-041-1). Gr Arts Ctr Pub.
Stephen Cosgrove, master lecturer & storyteller, narrates the audio cassette which accompanies the softcover edition of PRANCER. The original music score enriches this twenty-two minute spellbinding audio tape that brings the magic of PRANCER to life.
Publisher Provided Annotation.

—Read Aloud Topsy-Turvy Library, 26 vols. Reasoner, Charles, illus. (ps-3). 1988. Set. 155.48 (ISBN 0-87475-600-6). Stuttman.

Cosgrove, Stephen E. Gigglesnitcher. James, Robin, illus. 48p. (gr. k-9). 1991. 16.95 (ISBN 1-55868-034-9). Gr Arts Ctr Pub.
The GIGGLESNITCHER has stolen all of Levity Tree's giggle blossoms & laughing leaves, & now nothing is as it
should be on the island of Serendipity. The birds have stopped singing, the animals are grumpy, & the Muffin Muncher is so upset his tears are creating a flood in the village! Leo the Lop & magical Flutterby, the winged horse, come to the rescue & try to persuade the thief to change his ways. This is a Serendipity adventure by Stephen Cosgrove to warm the hearts of readers young & old. The illustrations by Robin James are the perfect accompaniment to this enchanting tale.
Publisher Provided Annotation.

—Terrybrook Dragon. McNatt, Richard, illus. 32p. (gr. k-7). 1990. 14.95 (ISBN 1-55868-036-5). Gr Arts Ctr Pub.
TERRYBROOK DRAGON is a tale about the banished prince who must protect his mother, the queen, & his princess sister from the terrible Terrybrook Dragon. The prince's father left the three alone to go out into the world & secure a new castle for his family - much like fathers now, who are forced to leave home to find better jobs to support their families. This is a timeless story of families separated by circumstances beyond their control. It is a metaphor relating to family problems, values, & personal worth. The combination of Cosgrove & McNatt is not new. Together they created the 6-book series, "The Snuffin Chronicles." McNatt also did extensive work for Disney Studios where he illustrated many of the "Winnie the Pooh" books.
Publisher Provided Annotation.

Costa, Nicoletta. My Poke & Look Busy Book. (Illus.). 44p. (ps-2). 1990. bds. 13.95 (ISBN 0-448-21034-7, G&D). Putnam Pub Group.

Count Ten Baby Animals. (Illus.). 6p. (gr. k-2). 1988. bds. 6.95 (ISBN 0-87449-452-4). Modern Pub NYC.

Count Ten Circus Friends. (Illus.). 6p. (gr. k-2). 1988. bds. 6.95 (ISBN 0-87449-455-9). Modern Pub NYC.

Count Ten Fun & Games. (Illus.). 6p. (gr. k-2). 1988. bds. 6.95 (ISBN 0-87449-454-0). Modern Pub NYC.

Count Ten Playtime Toys. (Illus.). 6p. (gr. k-2). 1988. bds. 6.95 (ISBN 0-87449-453-2). Modern Pub NYC.

Counting One, Two, Three. (Illus.). (ps). 1985. bds. 2.98 (ISBN 0-517-47338-0). Outlet Bk Co.

Counting Rhymes. 1984. 2.95 (ISBN 0-671-49684-0, Little Simon). S&S Trade.

Courtney, Richard, illus. Dinosaurs: Giants of the Earth. Moseley, Keith, designed by. (Illus.). 12p. (ps-3). 1988. 5.95 (ISBN 0-448-19302-7, G&D). Putnam Pub Group.

—Prehistoric Mammals: After the Dinosaurs. Moseley, Keith, designed by. (Illus.). 12p. (ps-3). 1988. 5.95 (ISBN 0-448-19303-5, G&D). Putnam Pub Group.

—Pterosaurs: The Flying Reptiles. Moseley, Keith, designed by. (Illus.). 12p. (ps-3). 1988. 5.95 (ISBN 0-448-19301-9, G&D). Putnam Pub Group.

Cousins, Lucy. Maisy Goes to Bed. (ps). 1990. 10.95 (ISBN 0-316-15832-1). Little.

Coville, Bruce. The Foolish Giant. Coville, Katherine, illus. LC 77-18522. 48p. (ps-2). 1990. pap. 3.95 (ISBN 0-06-443229-7, Trophy). HarpC Child Bks.

Coville, Bruce & Coville, Katherine. Sarah's Unicorn. Coville, Bruce & Coville, Katherine, illus. LC 85-42749. 48p. (gr. 1-4). 1985. pap. 3.50 (ISBN 0-06-443084-7, Trophy). HarpC Child Bks.

Cowell, Phyllis F. The Baby Hugs Bear & Baby Tugs Bear Alphabet Book. (Illus.). 40p. (ps). 1984. 5.95 (ISBN 0-910313-72-5). Parker Bros.

Cox, David. Bossyboots. Cox, David, illus. (ps-3). 1988. PLB 10.95 (ISBN 0-517-56491-2). Crown.

Coxe, Molly. Louella & the Yellow Balloon. Coxe, Molly, illus. LC 87-30379. 32p. (ps-2). 1988. 12.95 (ISBN 0-690-04746-0, Crowell Jr Bks); PLB 12.89 (ISBN 0-690-04748-7). HarpC Child Bks.

Craft, Ruth. The Winter Bear. Blegvad, Erik, illus. 32p. (ps-3). 1989. pap. 3.95 (ISBN 0-689-71342-8, Aladdin). Macmillan Child Grp.

Cresswell, Helen. Trouble. Chamberlain, Margaret, illus. 32p. (ps-2). 1988. 10.95 (ISBN 0-525-44396-7, DCB). Dutton Child Bks.

Crews, Donald. Harbor. LC 81-6607. (ps-1). 1987. pap. 3.95 (ISBN 0-688-07332-8, Mulberry). Morrow.

—Parade. Crews, Donald, illus. LC 82-20927. 32p. (gr. k-3). 1983. 13.95 (ISBN 0-688-01995-1); PLB 13.88 (ISBN 0-688-01996-X). Greenwillow.

—Truck. LC 79-19031. (Illus.). 32p. (ps-2). 1980. 13.95 (ISBN 0-688-80244-3); PLB 13.88 (ISBN 0-688-84244-5). Greenwillow.

Cristini, Ermanno & Puricelli, Luigi. In My Garden. Cristini, Ermanno & Puricelli, Luigi, illus. LC 85-9402. 28p. (ps up). 1985. 12.95 (ISBN 0-907234-05-4). Picture Bk Studio.

—In the Pond. Cristini, Ermanno & Puricelli, Luigi, illus. LC 84-972. 28p. (ps up). 1985. 12.95 (ISBN 0-907234-43-7). Picture Bk Studio.

—In the Woods. Cristini, Ermanno & Puricelli, Luigi, illus. LC 83-8153. 28p. (ps up). 1985. 12.95 (ISBN 0-907234-31-3). Picture Bk Studio.

Critter Sitters Board Books. Incl. The Seasons; Rainy Day Play; Nursery Rhymes; Our Friends; A Busy Day; Toys. (ps-4). 1984. Checkerboard Pr.

Critter Sitters Cloth Books. Incl. Playtime (ISBN 0-528-87080-7); Mother Goose (ISBN 0-528-87081-5); On the Farm (ISBN 0-528-87083-1). (ps-4). 1983. write for info. Checkerboard Pr.

Cross, Molly. Wait for Me! Mathieu, Joe, illus. LC 87-12926. 40p. (ps-3). 1987. 4.95 (ISBN 0-394-89135-X, Random Juv). Random.

Cross, Verda. Great-Grandma Tells of Threshing Day. Tucker, Kathleen, ed. Owens, Gail, illus. 40p. (gr. 1-6). 1991. 14.95 (ISBN 0-8075-3042-5). A Whitman.

Crowe, Robert L. Clyde Monster. Chorao, Kay, illus. (ps-3). 1987. 12.95 (ISBN 0-525-28025-1, DCB); pap. 3.95 (ISBN 0-525-44289-8, DCB). Dutton Child Bks.

—Tyler Toad & the Thunder. Chorao, Kay, illus. LC 80-347. 32p. (ps-1). 1986. pap. 4.95 (ISBN 0-525-44243-X, DCB). Dutton Child Bks.

Crowther, Robert. Most Amazing Hide & Seek Opposites Book. Crowther, Robert, illus. LC 85-42757. 12p. (ps-3). 1985. pap. 12.95 pop-up (ISBN 0-670-80121-6). Viking Child Bks.

—Pop Goes the Weasel! Twenty-Five Pop-Up Nursery Rhymes. (Illus.). (ps-3). 1987. Pop-Up ed. pap. 14.95 (ISBN 0-670-81815-1). Viking Child Bks.

—Robert Crowther's Most Amazing Pop-Up Book of Machines. (ps-3). 1988. pap. 14.95 (ISBN 0-670-82339-2). Viking Child Bks.

Crozat, Francois. I Am a Little Bear. (Illus.). 24p. (ps). 1989. 8.95 (ISBN 0-8120-5903-4). Barron.

—I Am a Little Rabbit. (Illus.). 24p. (ps). 1989. 7.95 (ISBN 0-8120-5905-0). Barron.

Cruickshank, Kathy. The Baby Book. Cruickshank, Kathy, illus. (ps-k). 1991. pap. 1.50 (ISBN 0-307-10029-4, Golden Pr). Western Pub.

Crump, Fred, Jr. A Rose for Zemira. Crump, Fred, illus. LC 88-50758. 45p. (gr. k-3). 1988. pap. 4.95 (ISBN 1-55523-151-9). Winston-Derek.

Cuddle's Bathtime. (ps). 3.50 (ISBN 0-86112-275-5, Pub. by Brimax Bks). Borden.

Cuddle's Bedtime. (ps). 3.50 (ISBN 0-86112-278-X, Pub. by Brimax Bks). Borden.

Cuddle's Mealtime. (ps). 3.50 (ISBN 0-86112-276-3, Pub. by Brimax Bks). Borden.

Cuddle's Playtime. (ps). 3.50 (ISBN 0-86112-277-1, Pub. by Brimax Bks). Borden.

Cuddly Casey. 12p. (ps-1). 1989. bds. 5.95 (ISBN 0-87449-710-8). Modern Pub NYC.

Un Cuento Gracioso de Peces (A Funny Fish Story) LC 83-24058. (ENG & SPA.). (ps-2). 1989. PLB 14.60 (ISBN 0-516-32986-3); pap. 3.95 (ISBN 0-516-52986-2). Childrens.

Cummings, e. e. Little Tree. Ray, Deborah K., illus. LC 86-30940. 32p. (gr. k-4). 1988. PLB 10.95 (ISBN 0-517-56598-6). Crown.

Cunliffe, John. Riddles & Rhymes & Rigmaroles. Pendle, Alexy, illus. 80p. (gr. 1-5). 1982. 10.95 (ISBN 0-233-96306-5). Andre Deutsch.

Curran, Eileen. Hello, Farm Animals. Goldsborough, June, illus. LC 84-8657. 32p. (gr. k-2). 1985. PLB 10.89 (ISBN 0-8167-0345-0); pap. text ed. 2.95 (ISBN 0-8167-0346-9). Troll Assocs.

—Life in the Meadow. Watling, James, illus. LC 84-12384. 32p. (gr. k-2). 1985. PLB 10.89 (ISBN 0-8167-0343-4); pap. 2.95 (ISBN 0-8167-0344-2). Troll Assocs.

—Little Christmas Elf. Page, Don, illus. LC 84-8628. 32p. (gr. k-2). 1985. PLB 10.89 (ISBN 0-8167-0352-3); pap. text ed. 2.95 (ISBN 0-8167-0432-5). Troll Assocs.

—Look at a Tree. Goldsborough, June, illus. LC 84-8843. 32p. (gr. k-2). 1985. PLB 10.89 (ISBN 0-8167-0349-3); pap. text ed. 2.95 (ISBN 0-8167-0350-7). Troll Assocs.

Cushman, Doug. Nasty Kyle the Crocodile. Cushman, Doug, illus. (ps-1). 1983. 5.95 (ISBN 0-448-16592-9, G&D). Putnam Pub Group.

Cushman, Doug, illus. The Pudgy Fingers Counting Book. 16p. (ps-3). 1983. pap. 2.95 (ISBN 0-448-10202-1, G&D). Putnam Pub Group.

Cutchins, Judy & Johnston, Ginny. Scoots, the Bog Turtle. Smith, Frances, illus. 32p. (gr. 1-4). 1989. 12.95 (ISBN 0-689-31440-X, Atheneum Child Bk). Macmillan Child Grp.

Cutting, Brian & Cutting, Jillian. A Small World. Webb, David, illus. 16p. (Orig.). (gr. k-2). 1988. pap. text ed. 23.00 (ISBN 1-55911-039-2). Wright Group.

—Whose Eggs Are These? Hyndman, Rosanne, illus. 16p. (Orig.). (gr. k-2). 1988. pap. text ed. 23.00 (ISBN 1-55911-037-6). Wright Group.

—Whose Eggs Are These, 6 bks. Hyndman, Rosanne, illus. 16p. (Orig.). (gr. k-2). 1988. Set. pap. text ed. 19.80 (ISBN 1-55911-038-4). Wright Group.

Cuyler, Margery. Freckles & Jane. Morrill, Leslie H., illus. LC 88-32068. 32p. (ps-2). 1989. 14.95 (ISBN 0-8050-0643-5). H Holt & Co.

—Shadow's Baby. Weiss, Ellen, illus. LC 88-35257. 32p. (ps-1). 1989. 13.95 (ISBN 0-89919-831-7, Clarion Bks). HM.

Dabcovich, Lydia. Busy Beavers. Dabcovich, Lydia, illus. LC 87-27190. 32p. (ps). 1988. 11.95 (ISBN 0-525-44384-3, 01160-350, DCB). Dutton Child Bks.

Dabney, Joy, illus. A Book about Me. 32p. (gr. k-3). 1987. wkbk. 2.50 (ISBN 0-939985-00-4). Creative Dimensions.

Dalgliesh, Alice. The Little Wooden Farmer. Lobel, Anita, illus. LC 87-1125. 32p. (ps-1). 1988. pap. 4.95 (ISBN 0-689-71180-8, Aladdin). Macmillan Child Grp.

Daly, Kathleen N. Baby Jesus. Cummins, Jim, illus. 14p. (ps-2). bds. 2.95 (ISBN 0-528-82491-0). Checkerboard Pr.

—Jesus Our Friend. Cummins, Jim, illus. 14p. (ps-2). 1987. bds. 2.95 (ISBN 0-528-82494-5). Checkerboard Pr.

—Joseph & His Brothers. Cummins, Jim, illus. 14p. (ps-2). 1984. bds. 2.95 (ISBN 0-528-82493-7). Checkerboard Pr.

—Noah & the Ark. Cummins, Jim, illus. 14p. (gr. 3-7). bds. 2.95 (ISBN 0-528-82490-2). Checkerboard Pr.

—The Shyest 'Kid in the 'Patch. Lace, Lynn, illus. 40p. (gr. 1-5). 1984. 5.95 (ISBN 0-910313-30-X). Parker Bros.

—Strawberry Shortcake & Pets on Parade. Sustendal, Pat, illus. 40p. (ps-3). 1983. cancelled 5.95 (ISBN 0-910313-06-7). Parker Bros.

Daly, Niki. Not So Fast, Songololo. Daly, Niki, illus. LC 85-70134. 32p. (gr. k-3). 1986. 13.95 (ISBN 0-689-50367-9, M K McElderry). Macmillan Child Grp.

—Not So Fast, Songololo. (ps-3). 1987. pap. 3.50 (ISBN 0-14-050715-9, Puffin). Puffin Bks.

D'Andrea, Deborah B. If I Were a Bunny, Or a Panda, or a Monkey, or... Ayers, Michael B., illus. 8p. (ps-1). 1989. bds. 6.95 (ISBN 1-878338-00-5). Picture Me Bks.

—If I Were a Fairy, Or a Ballerina, or a Witch, or... Ayers, Michael B., illus. 8p. (ps-1). 1989. bds. 6.95 (ISBN 1-878338-01-3). Picture Me Bks.

—If I Were a Pirate, Or a Cowboy, or a Knight, or... Ayers, Michael B., illus. 8p. (ps-1). 1989. bds. 6.95 (ISBN 1-878338-02-1). Picture Me Bks.

Daniel, Becky & Daniel, Charlie. I Wonder. 48p. (gr. k-3). 1980. 5.95 (ISBN 0-916456-82-X, GA 192). Good Apple.

Daniels, Joan. Listen & Do Stories. Rittenour, Gary, illus. 64p. (gr. k-3). 1986. pap. write for info. (ISBN 0-88724-170-0, CD-0923). Carson-Dellos.

Dantzer-Rosenthal, Marya. Some Things Are Different, Some Things Are the Same. Tucker, Kathleen, ed. (Illus.). 32p. (ps-2). 1986. 12.95 (ISBN 0-8075-7535-6). A Whitman.

Daugherty, James. Andy & the Lion. Daugherty, James, illus. LC 38-27390. 80p. (gr. 1-4). 1938. pap. 13.95 (ISBN 0-670-12433-8). Viking Child Bks.

Davis, A. This Is My Playworld. (Illus.). 12p. (ps-1). 1987. 2.50 (ISBN 0-88625-141-9). Durkin Hayes Pub.

—This Is My Workout. (Illus.). 12p. (ps-1). 1987. 2.50 (ISBN 0-88625-140-0). Durkin Hayes Pub.

Davis, Jim. Garfield Goes to the Farm. Fentz, Mike & Fentz, Larry, illus. 64p. (ps-3). 1985. pap. 2.95 (ISBN 0-394-87614-8, Random Juv). Random.

—Garfield the Fussy Cat. Simone, Norma, text by. (Illus.). 24p. (Orig.). (ps-3). 1988. pap. write for info. (ISBN 0-307-13958-1). Western Pub.

—Garfield Touch-&-Go-Seek: Things to Touch, See, & Smell. Klimo, Kate, ed. Davis, Jim, illus. LC 85-61210. 14p. (ps). 1986. bds. 5.95 (ISBN 0-394-87799-3). Random.

—Garfield Water Fun. Davis, Jim, illus. 10p. (gr. 1-4). 1985. vinyl 2.95 (ISBN 0-394-87360-2, Random Juv). Random.

—Garfield's Furry Tales. Davis, Jim, illus. 48p. (gr. k up). 1989. 9.95 (ISBN 0-448-09286-7, G&D). Putnam Pub Group.

—Garfield's Picnic Adventure. Harris, Jack C., text by. (Illus.). 24p. (Orig.). (ps-3). 1988. pap. write for info. (ISBN 0-307-13959-X). Western Pub.

—Garfield's Picnic Adventure. Harris, Jack C., text by. LC 87-83011. (Illus.). 24p. (Orig.). (ps-3). 1988. pap. write for info. (ISBN 0-307-11738-3). Western Pub.

Davis, Robert C. The E-waa, Vol. 1. Tremblay, Martin, illus. LC 91-61838. 28p. (Orig.). 1991. pap. 5.50g (ISBN 0-9629949-0-1). Across the Road.
"The E-Waa" is for children & for those who enjoy reading to them. It is a wonderful bedtime story. There's a freshness about the style & story that makes for delightful reading. The use of poetry to tell such a story adds to the charm of the book. Worthy to mention: the illustrations are graphic & heighten interest. An added dimension is that they are colorbook quality. The E-waa is a friendly beast that tells Baby-waas stories at night with hopes of keeping them in bed. He tells his stories much the same way as humans do when trying to keep their children in bed at bedtime. He is a friendly fellow who loves to eat car parts. He loves his Baby-waas, & human children everywhere. Much to the dismay of the E-waa & She-waa, the Baby-waas sometimes sneak junk food at bedtime. The Baby-waas sorrowfully admit giving in to the temptation & eating their nightlight. The E-waa tells the Baby-waas a bedtime story about how human children look, play after bedtime, & sometimes eat junk food like Baby-waas do. The story teaches that viewpoint can make a difference in how much alike all are despite the differences.
Publisher Provided Annotation.

Davoll, Barbara. A Sunday Surprise. Hockerman, Dennis, illus. 24p. 1988. 5.99 (ISBN 0-89693-405-5); cassette 8.99 (ISBN 0-89693-616-3). Victor Bks.

Day, O. M. ABC's of Bugs & Beasts. Day, O. M., illus. 31p. (Orig.). (gr. 3-12). 1991. pap. 11.95 (ISBN 0-9629795-1-1). Klar-Iden Pub.
ABC's of Bugs & Beasts is primarily a picture book with colorful & comical illustrations of insects & animals. Critics have called O. M. Day's book a work of art with depth & value above mere "read-to-me" entertainment. The book is meant to instill in children the concern for an interest in all living creatures, & to stimulate a desire for reading. O. M. Day specifically chose the insect to show that even they have a design in nature's plan, be it for good or for bad. Although focused to the younger child, older children also should have an interest. Various zoos find this publication appealing as well & are ordering. With the combination of the amusing illustrations & alphabet limericks, ABC's of Bugs & Beasts informs & entertains children. Klar-Iden, the publisher of ABC's of Bugs & Beasts is committed to publish only a small number of books each year, because it is their desire to produce quality rather than quantity. O. M. Day's book met their criteria. To order please contact Klar-Iden Publishing, 6963 Douglas Boulevard, Box #115, Granite Bay, CA 95661 or call (415) 856-1059.
Publisher Provided Annotation.

De Beaumont, Madame. Beauty & the Beast. Shumate, Mark, adapted by. Hicks, Russell, illus. 26p. (ps). 1987. Packaged with pre-programmed audio cass. tape. 9.95 (ISBN 0-934323-66-6). Alchemy Comms.

De Brunhoff, Jean. Babar & His Children. Haas, Merle, tr. (Illus.). (ps). 1969. 8.95 (ISBN 0-394-80577-1, Random Juv); lib. bdg. 8.99 (ISBN 0-394-90577-6). Random.

—Babar & Zephir. Haas, Merle, tr. (Illus.). (ps). 1969. 9.95 (ISBN 0-394-80579-8, Random Juv); lib. bdg. 5.99 (ISBN 0-394-90579-2). Random.

—The Story of Babar. (Illus.). (ps). 1937. 9.95 (ISBN 0-394-80575-5, Random Juv); PLB 10.99 (ISBN 0-394-90575-X). Random.

—Travels of Babar. (Illus.). (ps). 1967. 9.95 (ISBN 0-394-80576-3, Random Juv); lib. bdg. 7.99 (ISBN 0-394-90576-8). Random.

De Brunhoff, Laurent. Babar's Counting Book. De Brunhoff, Laurent, illus. LC 85-19652. 36p. (ps). 1986. 10.00 (ISBN 0-394-87517-6); PLB 10.99 (ISBN 0-394-97517-0). Random.

—Babar's French Lessons. (Illus.). (ps). 1963. 11.00 (ISBN 0-394-80587-9, Random Juv); lib. bdg. 5.99 (ISBN 0-394-90587-3). Random.

—Babar's Trunk, 4 bks. Incl. Babar at the Seashore; Babar the Gardener; Babar Goes Skiing; Babar on a Picnic. (ps-2). 1969. Set. slipcased 9.95 (ISBN 0-394-80585-2). Random.

De Brunhoff, Laurent, illus. Babar's Busy Week. LC 89-64400. 22p. (ps). 1990. bds. 2.95 (ISBN 0-679-80664-4). Random.

Deck the Halls. 10p. (ps-2). 1989. pap. 4.95 (ISBN 0-448-04185-5, G&D). Putnam Pub Group.

Decker, Marjorie. Animal Friends. (ps). 1989. 6.95 (ISBN 0-529-06689-0). World Bible.

De Cuenca, Pilar. Cinco Ciente Palabras Nuevas Para Ti. Alvarez, Ines, tr. McNaught, Harry, illus. LC 81-13766. 32p. (ps-3). 1982. lib. bdg. 5.99 (ISBN 0-394-95145-X); pap. 2.25 (ISBN 0-394-85145-5). Random.

DeFelice, Cynthia C. The Dancing Skeleton. Parker, Robert Andrew, illus. LC 88-30245. 32p. (gr. k-3). 1989. 13.95 (ISBN 0-02-726452-1, Mcmillan Child Bk). Macmillan Child Grp.

Degen, Bruce. Jamberry. Degen, Bruce, illus. (gr. k-3). 1986. incl. cassette 19.95 (ISBN 0-87499-028-9); pap. 12.95 incl. cassette (ISBN 0-87499-026-2); 4 paperbacks, cassette & guide 27.95 (ISBN 0-87499-027-0). Live Oak Media.

De Goscinny, Rene. Le Devin. (gr. 7-9). 19.95 (ISBN 0-685-33972-6, FC890). French & Eur.

De'Ham, Claude, illus. Playtime. 20p. (Orig.). (ps-2). 1975. pap. 2.00 (ISBN 0-85953-038-8, Pub. by Child's Play England). Childs Play.

De Hieronymis, Elve F. At the Seashore. (Illus.). 16p. (gr. 1 up). 1989. 8.95 (ISBN 0-8120-5996-4). Barron.

—A Night at the Circus. (Illus.). 16p. 1989. 8.95 (ISBN 0-8120-5995-6). Barron.

Delacre, Lulu. Lullabies. (ps-5). 1984. 2.95 (ISBN 0-671-49686-7, Little Simon). S&S Trade.

Delaney, Molly. My Sister. Delaney, Molly, illus. LC 88-29278. 32p. (gr. k-3). 1989. 12.95 (ISBN 0-689-31460-4, Atheneum Child Bk). Macmillan Child Grp.

Delarce, Lulu. Kitten Rhymes. 1984. 2.95 (ISBN 0-671-49687-5, Little Simon). S&S Trade.

Delessert, Etienne. A Long Long Song. LC 87-73491. (Illus.). 32p. (ps up). 1988. 13.95 (ISBN 0-374-34638-0). FS&G.

Delton, Judy. I'll Never Love Anything Ever Again: Concept Bks. Fay, Ann, ed. Daniel, Alan, illus. 32p. (ps-3). 1985. PLB 10.95 (ISBN 0-8075-3521-4). A Whitman.

—I'm Telling You Now. Hoban, Lillian, illus. LC 82-17714. 32p. (ps-k). 1985. pap. 3.95 (ISBN 0-525-44221-9, DCB). Dutton Child Bks.

—It Happened on Thursday. Pacini, Kathy, ed. Goldsborough, June, illus. LC 77-19086. (gr. 1-3). 1978. PLB 10.95 (ISBN 0-8075-3669-5). A Whitman.

—My Mother Lost Her Job Today. Fay, Ann, ed. Trivas, Irene, illus. LC 80-19067. 32p. (gr. k-3). 1980. PLB 10.95 (ISBN 0-8075-5359-X). A Whitman.

Delton, Judy & Tucker, Dorothy. My Grandma's in a Nursing Home. Tucker, Kathleen, ed. Robinson, Charles, illus. LC 86-1640. 32p. (gr. 1-5). 1986. PLB 10.95 (ISBN 0-8075-5333-6). A Whitman.

Demi. Cuddly Chick. Demi, illus. 12p. (ps). 1987. bds. 6.95 (ISBN 0-448-19154-7, G&D). Putnam Pub Group.

—Demi's Basket of Books, 4 bks. Demi, illus. 40p. (ps-k). 1989. Set. bds. 4.95 slipcase (ISBN 0-448-14975-3, G&D). Putnam Pub Group.

—Demi's Count the Animals One-Two-Three. Demi, illus. LC 85-81653. 48p. (ps-2). 1986. PLB 9.95 (ISBN 0-448-18980-1, G&D). Putnam Pub Group.

—Demi's Count the Animals 1 2 3. (Illus.). 48p. 1990. pap. 5.95 (ISBN 0-448-19166-0, G&D). Putnam Pub Group.

—Demi's Find the Animal A B C. (Illus.). 48p. 1990. pap. 5.95 (ISBN 0-448-19165-2, G&D). Putnam Pub Group.

—Downy Duckling. Demi, illus. 12p. (ps). 1987. bds. 6.95 (ISBN 0-448-19153-9, G&D). Putnam Pub Group.

—Fleecy Lamb. Demi, illus. 12p. (gr. 4 up). 1987. 6.95 (ISBN 0-448-19152-0, G&D). Putnam Pub Group.

—Fuzzy Wuzzy Puppy. (Illus.). 12p. (ps). 1986. pap. 5.95 (ISBN 0-448-18985-2, G&D). Putnam Pub Group.

—Jolly Koala Bear. Demi, illus. 12p. (ps). 1989. 6.95 (ISBN 0-448-19156-3, G&D). Putnam Pub Group.

—Roly-Poly Panda. Demi, illus. 12p. (ps). 1989. 6.95 (ISBN 0-448-19155-5, G&D). Putnam Pub Group.

—So Soft Kitty. Demi, illus. 12p. (ps). 1986. pap. 5.95 (ISBN 0-448-18986-0, G&D). Putnam Pub Group.

Demi, retold by. & illus. Demi's Reflective Fables. LC 87-83261. 32p. 1988. 15.95 (ISBN 0-448-09281-6, G&D). Putnam Pub Group.

Deming, A. G. Who Is Tapping at My Window? Wellington, Monica, illus. 24p. (ps-k). 1988. 10.95 (ISBN 0-525-44383-5, 01063-320, DCB). Dutton Child Bks.

Denton, Kady M. The Picnic. Denton, Kady M., illus. LC 87-71868. 32p. (ps-1). 1988. 11.95 (ISBN 0-525-44376-2, 01160-350, DCB). Dutton Child Bks.

Denton, Terry. Felix & Alexander. Denton, Terry, illus. 32p. (gr. k-3). 1988. 13.95 (ISBN 0-395-48661-0). HM.

—Home Is the Sailor. Denton, Terry, illus. 32p. (gr. k-3). 1989. 13.95 (ISBN 0-395-51525-4). HM.

DePaola, Tomie. Baby's First Christmas. (Illus.). 12p. (ps). 1988. bds. 4.95 (ISBN 0-399-21591-3, Putnam). Putnam Pub Group.

De Paola, Tomie. Big Anthony & the Magic Ring. De Paola, Tomie, illus. LC 78-23631. 32p. (ps-3). 1979. 13.95 (ISBN 0-15-207124-5); pap. 3.95 (ISBN 0-15-611907-2). HarBraceJ.

—The Comic Adventures of Old Mother Hubbard & Her Dog. LC 80-19270. (Illus.). 32p. (ps-3). 1981. 13.95 (ISBN 0-15-219541-6, HJ); pap. 3.95 (ISBN 0-15-219542-4, PL). HarBraceJ.

—Giorgio's Village. De Paola, Tomie, illus. 6p. (gr. 1 up). 1982. 12.95 (ISBN 0-399-20854-2, Putnam). Putnam Pub Group.

DePaola, Tomie. Haircuts for the Woolseys. DePaola, Tomie, illus. 24p. (ps-1). 1989. 5.95 (ISBN 0-399-21662-6, Putnam). Putnam Pub Group.

—Nana Upstairs & Nana Downstairs. (Illus.). (gr. 1-3). 1978. pap. 3.95 (ISBN 0-14-050290-4, Puffin). Puffin Bks.

De Paola, Tomie. Oliver Button Is a Sissy. De Paola, Tomie, illus. LC 78-12624. 48p. (ps-3). 1979. 11.95 (ISBN 0-15-257852-8, HJ). HarBraceJ.

DePaola, Tomie. Sing, Pierrot, Sing. LC 83-8403. (Illus.). 32p. (Orig.). (ps-3). 1987. pap. 3.95 (ISBN 0-15-274989-6, VoyB). HarBraceJ.

De Paola, Tomie. Sing, Pierrot, Sing: A Picture Book in Mime. De Paola, Tomie, illus. LC 83-8403. 32p. (ps-3). 1983. 12.95 (ISBN 0-15-274988-8, HJ). HarBraceJ.

DePaola, Tomie, illus. Hey Diddle Diddle: And Other Mother Goose Rhymes. (gr. 1 up). 1988. pap. 4.95 (ISBN 0-399-21589-1, Putnam). Putnam Pub Group.

De Poix, Carol. Jo, Flo & Yolanda. (Illus.). 35p. (Orig.). (ps-1). 1973. pap. 4.95 (ISBN 0-914996-04-5). Lollipop Power.

De Regniers, Beatrice S. May I Bring a Friend? Montresor, Beni, illus. LC 64-19562. 48p. (ps-2). 1971. 13.95 (ISBN 0-689-20615-1, Atheneum Child Bk). Macmillan Child Grp.

—May I Bring a Friend? Montresor, Beni, illus. 48p. (gr. k-3). 1989. pap. 3.95 (ISBN 0-689-71353-3, Aladdin). Macmillan Child Grp.

—May I Bring a Friend? (ps-3). 1974. pap. 4.95 (ISBN 0-689-70405-4, Aladdin). Macmillan Child Grp.

—The Snow Party. Myers, Bernice, illus. LC 88-13332. 32p. (ps-3). 1989. 12.95 (ISBN 0-688-08570-9); PLB 12.88 (ISBN 0-688-08571-7). Lothrop.

De Regniers, Beatrice S. & Haas, Irene. Little House of Your Own. Haas, Irene, illus. LC 86-27013. (gr. k-3). 1955. 9.95 (ISBN 0-15-245787-9, HJ). HarBraceJ.

Deverell, Catherine. Grandpa Told Me So. Petach, Heidi, illus. LC 87-62600. 20p. (ps). 1988. pap. 1.59 (ISBN 0-87403-387-X, 24-02017). Standard Pub.

DeVito, Pam. Lydia & the Purple Paint. Weinberger, Jane, ed. DeVito, Pam, illus. LC 89-50681. 52p. (ps-4). 1989. pap. 5.95 (ISBN 0-932433-59-6). Windswept Hse.

Dewey, Ariane. The Tea Squall. LC 87-14868. (Illus.). 40p. (gr. 1-4). 1988. 11.95 (ISBN 0-688-07492-8); lib. bdg. 11.88 (ISBN 0-688-07493-6). Greenwillow.

Dickens, Charles. A Christmas Carol. Zwerger, Lisbeth, illus. LC 88-15161. 60p. (gr. 5 up). 1988. 19.95 (ISBN 0-88708-069-3). Picture Bk Studio.

—A Christmas Carol: A Changing Picture & Lift-the-Flap Book. Taylerson, Kareen, illus. 32p. (ps-3). 1989. pap. 14.95 (ISBN 0-670-82694-4). Viking Child Bks.

Dickson, Anna H. Oh, I Am So Embarrassed! Cooke, Tom, illus. LC 87-81782. 32p. (ps-1). 1988. write for info. (ISBN 0-307-12027-9). Western Pub.

—Where's My Blankie? Nicklalus, Carol, illus. LC 83-83278. 32p. (ps). 1984. write for info. (ISBN 0-307-12013-9, 12013, Golden Bks). Western Pub.

DiFiori, Lawrence. The Truck Book. DiFiori, Lawrence, illus. LC 83-83106. (ps). 1984. write for info. (ISBN 0-307-12299-9, Golden Bks). Western Pub.

Dijs, Carla. Are You My Daddy? Dijs, Carla, illus. 12p. (ps). 1990. casebound 5.95 (ISBN 0-671-70227-0). S&S Trade.

—Are You My Mommy? Dijs, Carla, illus. 12p. (ps). 1990. casebound 5.95 (ISBN 0-671-70226-2). S&S Trade.

—Big & Small. Dijs, Carla, illus. 10p. (ps-k). 1989. 7.95 (ISBN 0-448-09075-9, G&D). Putnam Pub Group.

—How Many? Dijs, Carla, illus. 10p. (ps-k). 1989. 7.95 (ISBN 0-448-09076-7, G&D). Putnam Pub Group.

—Who Sees You? at the Ocean. (ps-2). 1987. 3.95 (ISBN 0-448-34350-9, G&D). Putnam Pub Group.

—Who Sees You? at the Zoo. (ps-2). 1987. 3.95 (ISBN 0-448-34353-3, G&D). Putnam Pub Group.

—Who Sees You? in the Forest. (ps-2). 1987. 3.95 (ISBN 0-448-34351-7, G&D). Putnam Pub Group.

—Who Sees You? on the Farm. (ps-3). 1987. 3.95 (ISBN 0-448-34352-5, G&D). Putnam Pub Group.

Dijs, Carla, illus. Let's Go Out. 12p. (ps-k). 1988. 5.95 (ISBN 0-448-19182-2, G&D). Putnam Pub Group.

—Little Helpers. 12p. (ps-k). 1988. 5.95 (ISBN 0-448-19180-6, G&D). Putnam Pub Group.

—My Busy Day. 12p. (ps-k). 1988. 5.95 (ISBN 0-448-19181-4, G&D). Putnam Pub Group.

Dils, Tracey E. Words! Words! Words! Robison, Don, illus. 24p. (Orig.). (ps-2). 1988. pap. 1.00 (ISBN 0-87406-242-X). Willowisp Pr.

Dinosaurs & Other Monsters from the Past. 1987. pap. 2.25 (ISBN 0-89954-742-7). Antioch Pub Co.

Dinosaurs & Prehistoric Creatures. (Illus.). 240p. (gr. k-2). 1989. 19.95 (ISBN 0-87449-513-X). Modern Pub NYC.

Dinosaurs of the Land, Sea & Air. (Illus.). 240p. (gr. k-2). 1989. 19.95 (ISBN 0-87449-512-1). Modern Pub NYC.

Disney. Disney Babies Word Book: At Home. 1990. 5.98 (ISBN 0-8317-2302-5). Smithmark.

—Disney Babies Word Book: In the City. 1990. 5.98 (ISBN 0-8317-2301-7). Smithmark.

—Disney Babies Word Book: In the Country. 1990. 5.98 (ISBN 0-8317-2304-1). Smithmark.

—Disney Babies Word Book: On Vacation. 1990. 5.98 (ISBN 0-8317-2303-3). Smithmark.

—Peter Pan. 1990. 5.98 (ISBN 0-8317-2473-0). Smithmark.

—Prince & the Pauper. 1990. 5.98 (ISBN 0-8317-2433-1). Smithmark.

Disney Babies, Baby Mickey's Word Book. (Illus.). 24p. (ps-k). 1987. pap. write for info. (ISBN 0-307-10088-X, Pub. by Golden Bks). Western Pub.

Disney Babies Company & Disney, Walt. Disney Babies Bathtime. (Illus.). (ps). 1990. pap. 2.95 (ISBN 0-671-62930-1, Little Simon). S&S Trade.

Disney Babies First Words. LC 86-72424. 12p. (ps). 1988. pap. write for info. (ISBN 0-307-06058-6, Pub. by Golden Bks). Western Pub.

Disney Babies Good Night. LC 87-81754. (Illus.). 12p. (ps). 1988. write for info. (ISBN 0-307-06067-5, Pub. by Golden Bks). Western Pub.

Disney Classics: A Treasury of Best-loved Tales. (ps-3). 1990. write for info. (ISBN 0-307-15536-6). Western Pub.

Disney, Walt. Baby Talk. (ps). 1986. pap. 2.95 (ISBN 0-671-62934-4, Little Simon). S&S Trade.

—Baby Time. (ps). 1986. pap. 2.95 (ISBN 0-671-62935-2, Little Simon). S&S Trade.

—Walt Disney's Giant ABC Book. 1990. 19.98 (ISBN 0-7924-5186-4). BDD Promo Bk.

Disney, Walt, Productions Staff. Colors, Shapes, & Sizes. LC 85-43077. 80p. (Orig.). 1985. pap. 5.95 (ISBN 0-553-05534-8). Bantam.

—How It Works in the City. (gr. 4-6). write for info. (ISBN 0-89434-046-8). Ferguson.

—How It Works in the Country. (gr. 4-6). write for info. (ISBN 0-89434-047-6). Ferguson.

—How It Works in the Home. (gr. 4-6). write for info. (ISBN 0-89434-048-4). Ferguson.

—Mickey & the Haunted House: A Book of Hidden Surprises. Disney, Walt, Productions Staff, illus. LC 84-60291. 14p. (ps). 1984. bds. 4.95 (ISBN 0-394-86772-6, Pub. by BYR). Random.

—Mickey at Home. Walt Disney Productions, illus. LC 84-60185. 28p. (ps). 1984. bds. 2.95 (ISBN 0-394-86768-8, Pub. by BYR). Random.

—Mickey's Pop-Up Book of Opposites. (Illus.). 14p. (ps-1). 1985. 6.95 (ISBN 0-394-87347-5, Random Juv). Random.

—Mickey's Toy Shop. Disney, Walt, Productions Staff, illus. 10p. (ps). 1984. vinyl bdg 2.95 (ISBN 0-394-86750-5, Pub. by BYR). Random.

Disney's Duck Tales: The Great Lost Treasure Hunt. (ps). 1989. pap. write for info. (ISBN 0-307-12565-3, Pub. by Golden Bks). Western Pub.

Disney's Pop-up Book of Colors. LC 90-85431. (Illus.). 12p. (ps-1). 1991. 6.95 (ISBN 1-56282-020-6, Disney Pr). W Disney Pub.

Disney's Pop-up Book of Numbers. LC 90-85432. (Illus.). 12p. (ps-1). 1991. 6.95 (ISBN 1-56282-021-4, Disney Pr). W Disney Pub.

Disney's Pop-up Book of Opposites. LC 90-85429. (Illus.). 12p. (ps-1). 1991. 6.95 (ISBN 1-56282-018-4, Disney Pr). W Disney Pub.

Disney's Pop-up Book of Shapes. LC 90-85430. (Illus.). 12p. (ps-1). 1991. 6.95 (ISBN 1-56282-019-2, Disney Pr). W Disney Pub.

Disney's Read-It-Yourself Storybook. (gr. k-2). 1991. 10.50 (ISBN 0-307-16556-6, Golden Pr). Western Pub.

Disney's The Little Mermaid: Pop-up Book. LC 90-85428. (Illus.). 12p. (gr. 1-5). 1991. 9.95 (ISBN 1-56282-017-6, Disney Pr). W Disney Pub.

Disney's Two-Minute Stories: Mickey Mouse & Friends. (ps-1). 1991. 4.25 (ISBN 0-307-12193-3, Golden Pr). Western Pub.

Do I Belong Here? 12p. (ps). 1988. 4.95 (ISBN 0-8120-5946-8). Barron.

Dr. Seuss. I Am Not Going to Get up Today! Stevenson, James, illus. 32p. (ps-1). 1990. pap. 6.95 (ISBN 0-679-80307-6); cass. incl. McKay.

Dodd, Lynley. Dragon in a Wagon. Sherwood, Rhoda, ed. Dodd, Lynley, illus. LC 88-42925. 32p. (gr. 1-2). 1988. PLB 10.95 (ISBN 1-55532-911-X). Gareth Stevens Inc.

—Hairy Maclary-Scattercat. Dodd, Lynley, illus. LC 86-42797. 32p. (gr. 1-2). 1988. PLB 10.95 (ISBN 1-55532-123-2). Gareth Stevens Inc.

—Hairy Maclasy's Caterwaul Caper. Dodd, Lynley, illus. LC 88-42926. 32p. (ps-2). 1989. PLB 10.95 (ISBN 1-55532-910-1). Gareth Stevens Inc.

Dodson, Peter. Baby Dinosaurs. (gr. 4-7). 1990. pap. 2.50 (ISBN 0-590-40276-5). Scholastic Inc.

Dollhouse. 8p. (ps). 1990. bds. 2.95 (ISBN 0-671-49718-9, Little Simon). S&S Trade.

Dolson, Gina, ed. Lisa & the Magic Doll: Russian & Ukrainian Fairy Tales. Mandeville, Jerry & Brodsky, Anna, trs. from RUS & UKR. Mawolski, Stanley M., illus. 56p. (Orig.). (gr. 4-10). 1986. pap. 4.50x (ISBN 0-914265-07-5). New Eng Pub MA.

Domanska, Janina, illus. If All the Seas Were One Sea. reissued ed. LC 73-146621. 32p. (ps-2). 1987. 13.95 (ISBN 0-02-732540-7, Mcmillan Child Bk). Macmillan Child Grp.
Donahue, Marilyn. A Place to Belong. LC 88-14808. (gr. 3-7). 1988. pap. 4.49 (ISBN 1-55513-757-1, Chariot Bks). Cook.
Donovan, Melanie, selected by. The Mother Goose Word Book. Schweninger, Ann, illus. LC 86-81489. 22p. (ps). 1987. write for info. (ISBN 0-307-12119-4, Pub. by Golden Bks). Western Pub.
Dorros, Arthur. Por Fin Es Carnaval. Dorros, Sandra M., tr. Club De Madres Virgen Del Carmen Staff, illus. LC 90-36222. (SPA.). 32p. (ps-3). 1991. 13.95 (ISBN 0-525-44690-7, DCB). Dutton Child Bks.
Douglas-Hamilton, Oria. The Elephant Family Book. Douglas-Hamilton, Iain, photos by. LC 89-77319. (Illus.). 56p. (ps up). 1990. 15.95 (ISBN 0-88708-126-6). Picture Bk Studio.
Dowdell, D. Secrets of the ABCs. LC 65-22301. (Illus.). 64p. (gr. 2 up). 1968. PLB 10.95 (ISBN 0-87783-035-5). Oddo.
Down by the Station. 24p. 1987. pap. 2.95 (ISBN 0-553-15575-X). Bantam.
Doyle, Elizabeth. Strawberry Shortcake & the Birthday Surprise. Sustendal, Pat, illus. 40p. (ps-3). 1983. cancelled 5.95 (ISBN 0-910313-11-3). Parker Bros.
Dragon's Wagon. 12p. (ps-1). 1989. bds. 3.95 (ISBN 0-87449-635-7). Modern Pub NYC.
Dragonwagon, Crescent. Alligator Arrived with Apples: A Potluck Alphabet Feast. Aruego, Jose & Dewey, Ariane, illus. LC 86-37. 40p. (gr. k-3). 1987. 15.95 (ISBN 0-02-733090-7, Mcmillan Child Bk). Macmillan Child Grp.
—Half a Moon & One Whole Star. Pinkney, Jerry, illus. LC 85-13818. 32p. (gr. k-3). 1986. 13.95 (ISBN 0-02-733120-2, Mcmillan Child Bk). Macmillan Child Grp.
—I Hate My Sister Maggie. Morrill, Leslie, illus. LC 88-8197. 32p. (gr. k-3). 1989. 11.95 (ISBN 0-02-733150-4, Mcmillan Child Bk). Macmillan Child Grp.
—This Is the Bread I Baked for Ned. Seltzer, Isadore, illus. LC 88-22619. 32p. (gr. k-3). 1989. 13.95 (ISBN 0-02-733220-9, Mcmillan Child Bk). Macmillan Child Grp.
Drayton, Grace G. Adventures of Dolly Dingle Paper Dolls. 1985. pap. 3.95 (ISBN 0-486-24809-7). Dover.
Drescher, Henrik. Simon's Book. LC 82-24931. (Illus.). 32p. (gr. k-3). 1983. 14.95 (ISBN 0-688-02085-2); lib. bdg. 14.88 (ISBN 0-688-02086-0). Lothrop.
—Simon's Book. 40p. (gr. k-3). 1987. 3.95 (ISBN 0-590-41934-X). Scholastic Inc.
—Whose Furry Nose? Drescher, Henrik, illus. LC 87-45151. 32p. (gr. k-3). 1987. 11.95 (ISBN 0-397-32236-4, Lipp Jr Bks); PLB 11.89 (ISBN 0-397-32243-7). HarpC Child Bks.
—Whose Scaly Tail? Drescher, Henrik, illus. LC 87-45152. 32p. (gr. k-3). 1987. 11.95 (ISBN 0-397-32237-2, Lipp Jr Bks); PLB 11.89 (ISBN 0-397-32244-5). HarpC Child Bks.
Drescher, Joan. My Mother's Getting Married. Drescher, Joan, illus. LC 84-18642. 32p. (ps-3). 1986. PLB 10.89 (ISBN 0-8037-0176-4). Dial Bks Young.
—Your Family, My Family. Drescher, Joan, illus. 32p. (gr. 2-5). 1980. PLB 13.85 (ISBN 0-8027-6383-9). Walker & Co.
Dr. Seuss. Dr. Seuss's ABC. (Illus.). 64p. (ps-1). 1988. pap. 6.95 bk. & cassette pkg. (ISBN 0-394-89784-6, Random Juv). Random.
—Dr. Seuss's Sleep Book. Dr. Seuss, illus. (gr. 3-7). 1962. 13.00 (ISBN 0-394-80091-5, Random Juv); lib. bdg. 13.99 (ISBN 0-394-90091-X). Random.
—Fox in Socks. Dr. Seuss, illus. LC 65-10484. 72p. (gr. k-3). 1965. 6.95 (ISBN 0-394-80038-9); lib. bdg. 7.99 (ISBN 0-394-90038-3). Beginner.
—Hop on Pop. Dr. Seuss, illus. 64p. (ps-1). 1987. pap. 6.95 incl. cassette (ISBN 0-394-89222-4, Random Juv). Random.
—Horton Hears a Who. Dr. Seuss, illus. (gr. k-3). 1954. 11.95 (ISBN 0-394-80078-8, Random Juv); PLB 12.99 (ISBN 0-394-90078-2). Random.
—Horton Hears a Who! Hoffman, Dustin, narrated by. LC 54-7012. (Illus.). 72p. (ps-1). 1990. pap. 10.95 incl. cassette (ISBN 0-679-80003-4). Random.
—I Am Not Going to Get up Today! Stevenson, James, illus. LC 87-11466. 48p. (gr. k-3). 1987. 6.95 (ISBN 0-394-89217-8, Random Juv); lib. bdg. 7.99 (ISBN 0-394-99217-2). Random.
—I Can Lick Thirty Tigers Today & Other Stories. Dr. Seuss, illus. (gr. k-3). 1969. 9.95 (ISBN 0-394-80094-X, Random Juv); lib. bdg. 7.99 (ISBN 0-394-90094-4). Random.
—I Can Read with My Eyes Shut! Dr. Seuss, illus. 40p. (ps-1). 1987. Incl. cassette. pap. 6.95 (ISBN 0-394-88767-0, Random Juv). Random.
—I Had Trouble in Getting to Solla Sollew. Dr. Seuss, illus. (ps-3). 1965. (Random Juv); lib. bdg. 12.99 (ISBN 0-394-90092-8). Random.
—If I Ran the Zoo. Dr. Seuss, illus. (gr. k-3). 1966. 9.95 (ISBN 0-394-80081-8, Random Juv); lib. bdg. 11.99 (ISBN 0-394-90081-2). Random.
—King's Stilts. Dr. Seuss, illus. (gr. k-3). 1939. 9.95 (ISBN 0-394-80082-6, Random Juv); lib. bdg. 8.99 (ISBN 0-394-90082-0). Random.
—McElligot's Pool. Dr. Seuss, illus. (gr. k-3). 1947. 9.95 (ISBN 0-394-80083-4, Random Juv); lib. bdg. 11.99 (ISBN 0-394-90083-9). Random.
—Marvin K. Mooney, Will You Please Go Now. Dr. Seuss, illus. (ps-2). 1972. 6.95 (ISBN 0-394-82490-3, Random Juv); lib. bdg. 7.99 (ISBN 0-394-92490-8). Random.
—Oh Say Can You Say? Dr. Seuss, illus. 40p. (ps-1). 1987. Incl. cassette. pap. 6.95 (ISBN 0-394-88769-7, Random Juv). Random.
—There's a Wocket in My Pocket & Marvin K. Mooney Will You Please Go Now! Dr. Seuss, illus. (ps-1). 1989. bk. & cassette 7.95 (ISBN 0-394-82954-9). Random.
Dryden, Emma. Good Morning - Good Night. Kolding, Richard M., illus. 9p. (ps). 1990. bds. 4.95 (ISBN 0-679-80066-2). Random.
Dubanevich, Arlene. Pigs at Christmas. Dubanevich, Arlene, illus. LC 86-6891. 32p. (ps-2). 1986. 13.95 (ISBN 0-02-733160-1, Bradbury Pr). Macmillan Child Grp.
—Pigs at Christmas. Dubanevich, Arlene, illus. 32p. (ps-3). 1989. pap. 3.95 (ISBN 0-689-71344-4, Aladdin). Macmillan Child Grp.
Du Bois, William P. Bear Party. (ps-1). 1987. pap. 3.95 (ISBN 0-14-050793-0, Puffin). Puffin Bks.
Duchess of York. Budgie at Bendick's Point. Richardson, John, illus. (ps-1). 1989. pap. 11.95 (ISBN 0-671-67684-9). S&S Trade.
—Budgie the Little Helicopter. Richardson, John, illus. (ps-1). 1989. pap. 11.95 (ISBN 0-671-67683-0). S&S Trade.
Dudley, Dick. One Big Bear. Paris, Pat, illus. 12p. (ps-k). 1988. 8.95 (ISBN 0-8120-5951-4). Barron.
Duke, Kate. Bedtime. Duke, Kate, illus. LC 84-73140. (ps). 1986. bds. 2.95 (ISBN 0-525-44207-3, DCB). Dutton Child Bks.
—Clean-Up Day. Duke, Kate, illus. LC 84-73139. (ps). 1986. bds. 2.95 (ISBN 0-525-44208-1, DCB). Dutton Child Bks.
—Guinea Pigs Far & Near. Duke, Kate, illus. LC 84-1580. 24p. (ps-1). 1989. pap. 3.95 (ISBN 0-525-44480-7, DCB). Dutton Child Bks.
—The Playground. Duke, Kate, illus. LC 84-73141. 12p. (ps). 1986. bds. 2.95 (ISBN 0-525-44206-5, DCB). Dutton Child Bks.
—What Bounces? Duke, Kate, illus. LC 84-73138. 12p. (ps). 1986. 2.95 (ISBN 0-525-44209-X, DCB). Dutton Child Bks.
Dumond, Val. Visiting Olympia. Ballman, Jean, illus. 24p. (Orig.). (gr. 1-4). 1983. pap. 2.75 (ISBN 0-933992-39-4). Coffee Break.
Dunbar, Fiona. You'll Never Guess! Dunbar, Fiona, illus. LC 90-2795. 40p. (ps-3). 1991. 11.95 (ISBN 0-8037-0871-8). Dial Bks Young.
Duncan, Riana. If You Were a... LC 86-17368. 30p. (ps-1). 1987. 8.95 (ISBN 0-8120-5801-1). Barron.
—When Emily Woke up Angry. Duncan, Riana, illus. 32p. (ps-1). 1989. incl. dust jacket 9.95 (ISBN 0-8120-5985-9). Barron.
Dunn, Joyce E. Riding on a School Bus. rev. ed. Dunn, Joyce E., illus. Doyle, James M., intro. by. (Illus.). 56p. (gr. k-1). 1989. pap. 4.95 (ISBN 0-9624280-0-0). SPI Pub.
Dunn, Judy. The Little Duck. Dunn, Phoebe, photos by. LC 75-36467. (Illus.). 32p. (ps-1). 1976. lib. bdg. 5.99 (ISBN 0-394-93247-1); pap. 2.25 (ISBN 0-394-83247-7). Random.
Dunn, Phoebe. Baby's Busy Year. LC 89-51127. (Illus.). 28p. (ps). 1990. 2.95 (ISBN 0-679-80260-6). McKay.
—Busy Busy Toddlers. LC 86-62247. (Illus.). 14p. (ps). 1987. 1.95 (ISBN 0-394-88604-6, Random Juv). Random.
Dunn, Phoebe, photos by. Baby's Animal Friends. LC 87-61462. (Illus.). 28p. (ps). 1988. bds. 2.95 (ISBN 0-394-89583-5, Random Juv). Random.
—I'm a Baby. LC 86-61904. (Illus.). 14p. 1987. pap. 1.95 (ISBN 0-394-88605-4, Random Juv). Random.
Dunrea, Olivier. Deep Down Underground. Dunrea, Olivier, illus. LC 88-13534. 32p. (ps-2). 1989. 13.95 (ISBN 0-02-732861-9, Mcmillan Child Bk). Macmillan Child Grp.
Durrell, Julie. It's My Birthday! An Animal Guessing Game. (Illus.). 24p. (ps-2). 1990. 4.95 (ISBN 0-448-44000-8, G&D). Putnam Pub Group.
—Peek-a-Boo. Bahr, Amy C. & Klimo, Kate, eds. Durrell, Julie, illus. 8p. (ps). 1982. pap. 3.95 (ISBN 0-671-45546-X, Little Simon). S&S Trade.
Durrell, Julie, illus. The Pudgy Book of Toys. 16p. (ps-3). 1983. pap. 2.95 (ISBN 0-448-10201-3, G&D). Putnam Pub Group.
Duvoisin, Roger. Our Veronica Goes to Petunia's Farm. Duvoisin, Roger, illus. (gr. k-3). 1962. lib. bdg. 6.99 (ISBN 0-394-91469-4). Knopf.
—Petunia. Duvoisin, Roger, illus. (gr. k-3). 1962. lib. bdg. 8.99 (ISBN 0-394-90865-1). Knopf.
—Petunia, Beware! Duvoisin, Roger, illus. (gr. 1-3). 1964. lib. bdg. 12.99 (ISBN 0-394-90867-8). Knopf.
—Petunia, I Love You. Duvoisin, Roger, illus. (gr. k-3). 1965. lib. bdg. 12.99 (ISBN 0-394-90870-8). Knopf.
—Petunia the Silly Goose Stories: Five Read-Aloud Classics. Duvoisin, Roger, illus. LC 86-2783. 160p. (ps-3). 1987. 15.95 (ISBN 0-394-88292-X); lib. bdg. 15.99 (ISBN 0-394-98292-4). Knopf.
—Veronica. Duvoisin, Roger, illus. (gr. k-3). 1961. lib. bdg. 13.99 (ISBN 0-394-91792-8). Knopf.
Dyer, Jane. Moo, Moo Peekaboo. Dyer, Jane, illus. LC 85-61530. (ps). 1986. 2.95 (ISBN 0-394-87883-3, Random Juv). Random.
Eastman, Kevin & Laird, Peter, eds. The Teenage Mutant Ninja Turtles Pop-Up Book. (Illus.). 12p. (ps-5). 1990. pap. 9.95 (ISBN 0-679-81313-6). Random.
Eastman, Philip D. Sam & the Firefly. LC 58-11966. (Illus.). 72p. (gr. 1-2). 1958. 6.95 (ISBN 0-394-80006-0); lib. bdg. 7.99 (ISBN 0-394-90006-5). Beginner.
Eberle, Irmengarde. Picture Stories for Children. (gr. k-6). 1988. pap. 2.95 (ISBN 0-440-40031-7, YB). Dell.
Eberts, Marjorie & Gisler, Margaret. Pancakes, Crackers & Pizza: A Book of Shapes. Hayes, Steven, illus. LC 84-7699. 32p. (ps-2). 1984. lib. bdg. 11.93 (ISBN 0-516-02063-3); pap. 2.95 (ISBN 0-516-42063-1). Childrens.
Eccles, Anne M. New Mexico Activity & Coloring Book. (Illus.). 32p. (ps-8). 1987. activity & coloring book 2.95 (ISBN 0-9618555-1-7). Anne M Eccles.
Edens, Cooper. Caretakers of Wonder. 2nd ed. 40p. (ps up). 1987. 4.95 (ISBN 0-317-57053-6). Green Tiger Pr.
—Helping the Animals. Day, Alexandra, illus. (ps up). 1987. 3.95 (ISBN 0-317-57051-X). Green Tiger Pr.
—Helping the Flowers. Day, Alexandra, illus. (ps up). 1987. 3.95 (ISBN 0-317-57052-8). Green Tiger Pr.
—Helping the Night. Day, Alexandra, illus. (ps up). 1987. 3.95 (ISBN 0-317-57050-1). Green Tiger Pr.
—Helping the Sun. Day, Alexandra, illus. (ps up). 1987. 3.95 (ISBN 0-317-57049-8). Green Tiger Pr.
Edens, Cooper & Day, Alexandra. Children of Wonder. 14p. (Orig.). (ps-2). 1987. 3.95 ea. Vol. 1 "Helping the Sun (ISBN 0-88138-083-0). Vol. 2 "Helping the Animals (ISBN 0-88138-085-7). Vol. 3 "Helping the Flowers (ISBN 0-88138-086-5). Vol. 4 "Helping the Night (ISBN 0-88138-084-9). Green Tiger Pr.
Edge, Terry. The Fluppets Storybook. King, Ian, illus. 32p. (ps-2). 1988. 13.95 (ISBN 0-09-172729-4, Pub. by Hutchinson UK). Trafalgar Sq.
Edwards, Patricia. Chester & Uncle Willoughby. Allison, Diane W., illus. 48p. (gr. 1-3). 1987. 14.95 (ISBN 0-316-21173-7). Little.
Ehrlich, Amy. Bunnies & Their Grandma. Henry, Marie H., illus. LC 84-20030. 32p. (ps-2). 1985. 7.95 (ISBN 0-8037-0186-1). Dial Bks Young.
—Bunnies on Their Own. Henry, Marie H., illus. LC 85-20467. 32p. (ps-2). 1986. 7.95 (ISBN 0-8037-0256-6). Dial Bks Young.
—Emma's New Pony. Brown, Richard, photos by. (Illus.). 32p. (ps-3). 1988. (Random Juv); pap. 1.95 (ISBN 0-394-89210-0, Random Juv). Random.
—Leo, Zack & Emmie. Kellogg, Steven, illus. 64p. (ps-3). 1981. pap. 4.95 (ISBN 0-8037-4760-8, Dial Easy to Read). Puffin Bks.
Ehrlich, Doris. Animal Alphabet. 2nd ed. O'Rourke, Dawn M., illus. 36p. (ps-k). 1988. pap. text ed. 80.00 classroom pack (ISBN 0-932957-90-0); tchr's. ed. 4.50 (ISBN 0-932957-91-9); wkbk. 3.90 (ISBN 0-932957-89-7); wall posters 17.50 (ISBN 0-932957-96-X). Natl School.
Eisenberg, Ann. I Can Celebrate. Schanzer, Roz, illus. LC 88-83567. 12p. (ps). 1989. bds. 4.95 (ISBN 0-930494-93-8). Kar Ben.
Elliott, Dan. The Adventures of Ernie & Bert at the South Pole. Cooke, Tom, illus. LC 84-60187. 32p. (ps-3). 1984. pap. 1.25 (ISBN 0-394-86299-6, Pub. by BYR). Random.
Elsie. (Illus.). (ps-2). 3.95 (ISBN 0-7214-9595-8). Ladybird Bks.
Elsie's Clean Day. 24p. (ps). 1988. pap. 1.29 (ISBN 0-02-898134-0). Checkerboard Pr.
Elzbieta. Dikou & the Baby Star. Elzbieta, illus. LC 88-302. 32p. (ps-3). 1988. 11.95i (ISBN 0-690-04719-3, Crowell Jr Bks); PLB 11.89 (ISBN 0-690-04721-5). HarpC Child Bks.
Emberley, Barbara. Drummer Hoff. Emberley, Ed E., illus. LC 74-8201. 32p. (gr. k-4). 1985. PLB 12.95 (ISBN 0-671-66682-7); pap. 5.95 (ISBN 0-671-66745-9). S&S Trade.
Emberley, Ed E. Ed Emberley's ABC. Emberley, Ed E., illus. (ps-1). 1987. pap. 8.95 (ISBN 0-316-23427-3). Little.
—Green Says Go. LC 68-21165. (Illus.). (ps-3). 1972. lib. bdg. 14.95 (ISBN 0-316-23599-7). Little.
—Klippity Klop. Emberley, Ed E., illus. 32p. (gr. k-3). 1974. lib. bdg. 10.95 (ISBN 0-316-23607-1). Little.
Emberley, Ed E. & Emberley, Rebecca. Ed Emberley's Big Red Drawing Book, Vol. 1. Emberley, Ed E. & Emberley, Rebecca, illus. 96p. (gr. 1-5). 1987. 14.95 (ISBN 0-316-23434-6); pap. 7.95 (ISBN 0-316-23435-4). Little.
Emberley, Ed E., illus. First Words: Animals. (ps). 1987. pap. 3.50 (ISBN 0-316-23428-1). Little.
—First Words: Cars, Boats, & Planes. (ps). 1987. pap. 3.50 (ISBN 0-316-23430-3). Little.
—First Words: Home. (ps). 1987. pap. 3.50 (ISBN 0-316-23433-8). Little.
—First Words: Sounds. (ps). 1987. pap. 3.50 (ISBN 0-316-23431-1). Little.
Emerson, Sally, compiled by. The Nursery Treasury: A Collection of Rhymes, Poems, Lullabies & Games. Maclean, Moira & Maclean, Colin, illus. 128p. 1988. pap. 17.95 (ISBN 0-385-24650-1). Doubleday.
Emmert, Michelle. I'm the Big Sister Now. Levine, Abby, ed. Owens, Gail, illus. 32p. (gr. 2-6). 1989. PLB 12.95 (ISBN 0-8075-3458-7). A Whitman.
Enchanting Fairy Tales. 192p. (gr. k-2). 1989. 14.95 (ISBN 0-87449-695-0). Modern Pub NYC.

Endersby, Frank. Jasmine & the Cat. (Illus.). 12p. (ps). 1984. 3.50 (ISBN 0-85953-183-X, Child's Play England). Childs Play.
—Jasmine & the Flowers. 12p. (ps). 1984. 3.50 (ISBN 0-85953-184-8, Child's Play England). Childs Play.
—Jasmine's Bath Time. 12p. (ps). 1984. 3.50 (ISBN 0-85953-185-6, Child's Play England). Childs Play.
—Jasmine's Bed Time. 12p. (ps). 1984. 3.50 (ISBN 0-85953-186-4, Child's Play England). Childs Play.
—The Pet Shop. (ps). 1984. 3.50 (ISBN 0-317-07210-2, Child's Play England). Childs Play.
—Pocket Money. (ps). 1984. 3.50 (ISBN 0-85953-190-2, Child's Play England). Childs Play.
Endersby, Frank, ed. Wall Paper. 12p. (ps). 1984. 3.50 (ISBN 0-85953-188-0, Child's Play England). Childs Play.
Erickson, Mary. Six Busy Days. LC 88-11803. (Illus.). 32p. (ps-2). 1988. 9.95 (ISBN 1-55513-699-0, Chariot Bks). Cook.
Erickson, Phoebe. Who's in the Mirror? (gr. 1-3). Repr. of 1965 ed. PLB 4.95 (ISBN 0-317-13837-5). P Erickson.
Ernie Gets Lost. (Illus.). 24p. (ps-3). 1987. pap. write for info incl. cassette (ISBN 0-307-13947-6, Pub. by Golden Bks). Western Pub.
Ernst, Kathryn F. Danny & His Thumb. De Paola, Tomie, illus. (ps-3). 1975. (Pub. by Treehouse); pap. 4.95 (ISBN 0-13-196808-4). P-H.
Ernst, Lisa C. Sam Johnson & the Blue Ribbon Quilt. LC 82-9980. (Illus.). 32p. (gr. k-3). 1983. lib. bdg. 12.88 (ISBN 0-688-01517-4). Lothrop.
—When Bluebell Sang. Ernst, Lisa C., illus. LC 88-22262. 32p. (ps-2). 1989. 12.95 (ISBN 0-02-733561-5, Bradbury Pr). Macmillan Child Grp.
Espelt, J. M. & Ginesta, M. The Blue Hat. (Illus.). 48p. (ps-2). pap. 2.95 (ISBN 0-8431-2202-1). Price Stern.
Estes, Eleanor. Hundred Dresses. Slobodkin, Louis, illus. LC 44-8963. (gr. k-3). 1944. 14.95 (ISBN 0-15-237374-8, HJ). HarBraceJ.
Ets, Marie H. Gilberto & the Wind. Ets, Marie H., illus. (ps-1). 1963. pap. 12.95 (ISBN 0-670-34025-1). Viking Child Bks.
—Just Me. Ets, Marie H., illus. (ps-2). 1965. pap. 14.95 (ISBN 0-670-41109-4). Viking Child Bks.
Evans, Larry. Invisibles Two. (Illus.). 40p. (Orig.). 1981. pap. 3.50 (ISBN 0-8431-1711-7). Price Stern.
Evans, Phillip. City. (ps). 1990. 14.60 (ISBN 0-8172-3668-6). Raintree Pubs.
—Doing. (ps). 1990. 14.60 (ISBN 0-8172-3651-1). Raintree Pubs.
—Farm. (ps). 1990. 14.60 (ISBN 0-8172-3671-6). Raintree Pubs.
F. J. Strauss Co., Inc. Staff. Dino. 10p. (ps). Date not set. write for info. vinyl. F J Strauss.
—In Air. 10p. (ps). Date not set. write for info. vinyl (ISBN 0-945987-14-5). F J Strauss.
—My First Read 'n Play Alphabet Book. 10p. (ps). Date not set. write for info. vinyl (ISBN 0-945987-15-3). F J Strauss.
—On Land. 10p. (ps). Date not set. write for info. vinyl (ISBN 0-945987-12-9). F J Strauss.
—On Sea. 10p. (ps). Date not set. write for info. vinyl (ISBN 0-945987-13-7). F J Strauss.
Faces in Places, Famous Faces, Funny Faces & Happy Faces. (Illus.). (gr. k-2). 1989. bds. 4.95 ea., 12pgs. ea. Faces in Places (ISBN 0-87449-727-2). Famous Faces (ISBN 0-87449-728-0). Funny Faces (ISBN 0-87449-729-9). Happy Faces (ISBN 0-87449-730-2). Modern Pub NYC.
Facklam, Margery. But Not Like Mine. Bassett, Jeni, illus. LC 86-33588. 20p. (gr. 3-5). 1988. 6.95 (ISBN 0-15-200585-4, Gulliver Bks). HarBraceJ.
—So Can I. Bassett, Jeni, illus. LC 86-33720. 28p. (gr. 3-5). 1988. 6.95 (ISBN 0-15-200419-X, Gulliver Bks). HarBraceJ.
Factor, June. Micky the Mighty Magpie. Webb, Melissa, illus. 32p. (ps-3). 1986. pap. 9.95 (ISBN 0-670-80788-5). Viking Child Bks.
Farbanish, Lori, illus. The Owl & the Pussycat. 18p. (ps). 1988. bds. 3.95 (ISBN 0-448-10229-3, G&D). Putnam Pub Group.
Farley, Walter. The Black Stallion Picture Book. LC 78-20653. (Illus.). (gr. 1-6). 1979. (Random Juv); lib. bdg. 6.99 (ISBN 0-394-94174-8). Random.
Farm Sounds: A Cozy Cloth Book. (Illus.). 6p. (ps-1). 1987. pap. 2.95 (ISBN 0-553-18349-4). Bantam.
Farris, Stella. The Magic Teddy Bear. Farris, Stella, illus. LC 79-2394. 30p. (ps-2). 1987. 4.95 (ISBN 0-694-00172-4). HarpC Child Bks.
Fassler, Joan. Howie Helps Himself. Lasker, Joe, illus. LC 74-12284. 32p. (gr. k-2). 1975. PLB 12.95 (ISBN 0-8075-3422-6). A Whitman.
Fast Jets & Planes. 1988. pap. 2.25 (ISBN 0-89954-871-7). Antioch Pub Co.
Favorite Things. (Illus.). 12p. (ps). 1989. 5.95 (ISBN 0-02-689193-X). Checkerboard Pr.
Feczko, Kathy. Three Little Chicks. Harvey, Paul, illus. LC 84-8629. 32p. (gr. k-2). 1985. PLB 10.89 (ISBN 0-8167-0355-8); pap. text ed. 2.95 (ISBN 0-8167-0435-X). Troll Assocs.
—Umbrella Parade. Borgo, Deborah C., illus. LC 84-8650. 32p. (gr. k-2). 1985. PLB 10.89 (ISBN 0-8167-0356-6); pap. text ed. 2.95 (ISBN 0-8167-0436-8). Troll Assocs.
Feeling Afraid. (ps-k). 0.75 (ISBN 0-8091-6544-9). Paulist Pr.
Feeling Happy. (ps-k). 0.75 (ISBN 0-8091-6543-0). Paulist Pr.
Feelings, Mariel & Feelings, Tom. Jambo Means Hello: Swahili Alphabet Book. (Illus.). 56p. (gr. k-3). 1985. pap. 4.95 (ISBN 0-8037-4428-5, Dial Pied Piper). Puffin Bks.
Fehlner, Paul. The Story of Christmas. (Illus.). 24p. (ps-3). 1989. pap. write for info. (ISBN 0-307-11710-3, Pub. by Golden Bks). Western Pub.
Feldman, Thea. Giant Work Machines. LaPadula, Tom, illus. LC 87-81783. 48p. (ps-3). 1988. write for info. (ISBN 0-307-15566-8). Western Pub.
Felix, Monique, illus. If I Were a Sheep. 12p. (Orig.). (gr. 7-9). 1982. pap. 2.50 (ISBN 0-914676-67-9). Green Tiger Pr.
Fentz, Mike. Garfield Looks for Pooky: Help Garfield Find His Teddy Bear. Fentz, Mike, illus. LC 85-61209. 14p. (ps). 1986. 4.95 (ISBN 0-394-87800-0, Random Juv). Random.
Fern, Eugene. Pepito's Story. Fern, Eugene, illus. LC 90-23639. 52p. (ps-3). 1991. Repr. of 1960 ed. smythe sewn 14.95 (ISBN 1-878274-04-X). Yarrow Pr.
Fernandes, Eugenie. My Birthday Book. (ps-1). 1988. bds. 3.50 (ISBN 0-7214-5097-0). Ladybird Bks.
—My Busy Day Book. (ps-1). 1988. bds. 2.95 (ISBN 0-7214-5096-2). Ladybird Bks.
—My Rainy Day Book. (ps-1). 1988. bds. 3.50 (ISBN 0-7214-5095-4). Ladybird Bks.
—My Sunny Day Book. (ps-1). 1988. bds. 3.50 (ISBN 0-7214-5094-6). Ladybird Bks.
Fernandes, Eugenie, illus. My Bathtime Book. (ps-k). bds. 3.50 (ISBN 0-7214-5072-5). Ladybird Bks.
—My Bedtime Book. (ps-k). bds. 3.50 (ISBN 0-7214-5073-3). Ladybird Bks.
—My Going Out Book. (ps-k). bds. 3.50 (ISBN 0-7214-5074-1). Ladybird Bks.
—My Playtime Book. (ps-k). bds. 3.50 (ISBN 0-7214-5071-7). Ladybird Bks.
—One Light, One Sun. 32p. (ps-2). 1988. PLB 9.95 (ISBN 0-517-56785-7). Crown.
Fetch, Flops! Fetch! (Illus.). 32p. (gr. k-2). 1989. 4.95 (ISBN 0-87449-581-4). Modern Pub NYC.
Field, Rachel. General Store. Parker, Nancy W., illus. LC 87-21641. 24p. (ps-1). 1988. 11.95 (ISBN 0-688-07353-0); lib. bdg. 11.88 (ISBN 0-688-07354-9). Greenwillow.
Fire Engines. (ps-2). 1971. 2.95 (ISBN 0-448-02683-X, G&D). Putnam Pub Group.
Firmin, Peter. Boastful Mr. Bear. Firmin, Peter, illus. (ps-1). 1989. 8.95 (ISBN 0-440-50083-4). Delacorte.
—Foolish Miss Crow. Firmin, Peter, illus. (ps-1). 1989. 8.95 (ISBN 0-440-50082-6). Delacorte.
—Happy Miss Rat. Firmin, Peter, illus. (ps-1). 1989. 8.95 (ISBN 0-440-50081-8). Delacorte.
—Hungry Mr. Fox. Firmin, Peter, illus. (ps-1). 1989. 8.95 (ISBN 0-440-50034-6). Delacorte.
First Big Talkabout. (Illus.). (ps-5). 8.95 (ISBN 0-7214-7504-3). Ladybird Bks.
A First Book for Bedtime. (Illus.). 32p. (gr. k-2). 1986. 4.95 (ISBN 0-87449-193-2). Modern Pub NYC.
A First Book of Colors. (Illus.). 32p. (gr. k-2). 1986. 4.95 (ISBN 0-87449-191-6). Modern Pub NYC.
A First Book of Counting. (Illus.). 32p. (gr. k-2). 1986. 4.95 (ISBN 0-87449-190-8). Modern Pub NYC.
A First Book of Do's & Don'ts. (Illus.). 32p. (gr. k-2). 1986. 4.95 (ISBN 0-87449-192-4). Modern Pub NYC.
A First Book of Fairy Tales. (Illus.). 32p. (gr. k-2). 1988. 4.95 (ISBN 0-87449-379-X). Modern Pub NYC.
A First Book of Opposites. (Illus.). 32p. (gr. k-2). 1988. 4.95 (ISBN 0-87449-377-3). Modern Pub NYC.
A First Book of Shapes. (Illus.). 32p. (gr. k-2). 1988. 4.95 (ISBN 0-87449-380-3). Modern Pub NYC.
A First Book of Words. (Illus.). 32p. (gr. k-2). 1988. 4.95 (ISBN 0-87449-378-1). Modern Pub NYC.
First Graders of A. R. Shepherd Washington, D. C. A Caterpillar's Wish. (Illus.). 24p. (Orig.). (ps-2). 1988. pap. 2.95 (ISBN 0-87406-307-8). Willowisp Pr.
Fisher, Barbara. Linkups. (Illus., Orig.). (ps-3). 1977. pap. 2.00 slipcased (ISBN 0-934830-05-3). Ten Penny.
Fisher, Leonard E. Look Around! A Book about Shapes. (Illus.). 32p. (ps-1). 1989. pap. 3.95 (ISBN 0-14-050572-5, Puffin). Puffin Bks.
Fitzhugh, Louise. I Am Five. Fitzhugh, Louise, illus. LC 78-50404. (ps-2). 1978. PLB 5.47 (ISBN 0-440-03953-3); pap. 5.95 (ISBN 0-440-03952-5). Delacorte.
Flack, Marjorie. Ask Mr. Bear. LC 58-24158. (Illus.). 32p. 1968. 11.95 (ISBN 0-02-735390-7, Mcmillan Child Bk). Macmillan Child Grp.
Fleming, Denise, illus. It Feels Like Christmas! A Book of Surprises to Touch, See & Sniff. LC 84-60622. (ps). 1984. bds. 5.95 (ISBN 0-394-86862-5, Pub. by BYR). Random.
Flops in Space. (Illus.). 32p. (gr. k-2). 1989. 4.95 (ISBN 0-87449-582-2). Modern Pub NYC.
Flops Pretends. (Illus.). 32p. (gr. k-2). 1989. 4.95 (ISBN 0-87449-580-6). Modern Pub NYC.
Florian, Douglas. A Winter Day. LC 86-33524. (Illus.). 24p. (ps-1). 1987. 11.75 (ISBN 0-688-07351-4); lib. bdg. 11.88 (ISBN 0-688-07352-2). Greenwillow.
Flournoy, Valerie. The Best Time of Day. Ford, George, illus. LC 77-91641. (ps-2). 1979. lib. bdg. 4.99 (ISBN 0-394-93799-6, Random Juv); pap. 1.25 (ISBN 0-394-83799-1). Random.
—The Patchwork Quilt. Pinkey, Jerry, illus. LC 84-1711. (gr. 4-8). 1985. 13.95 (ISBN 0-8037-0097-0); PLB 13.89 (ISBN 0-8037-0098-9). Dial Bks Young.
Floyd, James C. Some Gentle Moving Thing. 2nd ed. McBride, Michael, illus. LC 82-60198. 70p. (gr. 7-9). 1982. 6.95 (ISBN 0-938232-11-8). Winston-Derek.
Fluffy Bunny. 12p. (ps up). 1987. 6.95 (ISBN 0-448-19151-2, G&D). Putnam Pub Group.
Flying Colors. 24p. (gr. k-2). 1989. 3.95 (ISBN 0-87449-671-3). Modern Pub NYC.
Fontane, Theodor. Nick Ribbeck of Ribbeck of Havelland. Bell, Anthea, tr. from GER. Koci, Marta, illus. LC 90-7164. 32p. (gr. k up). 1990. 15.95 (ISBN 0-88708-149-5). Picture Bk Studio.
Footprint's of a Chickie. 24p. (gr. k-2). 1990. 3.95 (ISBN 0-87449-667-5). Modern Pub NYC.
Ford, Barbara. Black Bear: The Spirit of the Wilderness. 192p. (gr. 7 up). 1981. 8.95 (ISBN 0-395-30444-X). HM.
Ford, George. Baby's First Picture Book. Ford, George, illus. LC 79-62941. (ps). 1979. 3.50 (ISBN 0-394-84245-6, Random Juv). Random.
Foreman, Mark. Scraps. (Illus.). 32p. (ps-2). 1991. 15.95 (ISBN 0-86264-306-6, Pub. by Andersen Pr UK). Trafalgar Sq.
Foreman, Michael. The Angel & the Wild Animal. Foreman, Michael, illus. LC 88-16822. 32p. (ps-2). 1989. 13.95 (ISBN 0-689-31492-2, Atheneum Child Bk). Macmillan Child Grp.
—Ben's Baby. Foreman, Michael, illus. LC 87-25943. 32p. (ps-1). 1988. 14.95 (ISBN 0-06-021843-6); PLB 14.89 (ISBN 0-06-021844-4). HarpC Child Bks.
—War & Peas. LC 74-10368. (Illus.). 32p. (ps-3). 1974. PLB 13.89 (ISBN 0-690-00629-2, Crowell Jr Bks). HarpC Child Bks.
Foreman, Michael & Gray, Nigel. I'll Take You to Mrs. Cole. (Illus.). 32p. (gr. k-3). 1986. 11.95 (ISBN 0-930267-21-4). Bergh Pub.
Forrester, John. The Forbidden Beast. LC 88-2643. (Illus.). 144p. (gr. 7 up). 1990. pap. 3.50 (ISBN 0-06-447012-1, Trophy). HarpC Child Bks.
Forsse, Ken. The Day Teddy Met Grubby. High, David, et al, illus. 26p. (ps). 1985. 9.95 (ISBN 0-934323-19-4); pre-programmed audio-cassette tape incl. Alchemy Comms.
—Teddy Ruxpin Lullabies II. Hicks, Russell, et al, illus. 26p. (ps). 1988. 21.00 (ISBN 0-934323-68-2); pre-programmed audiocassette incl. Alchemy Comms.
Forsse, Ken & Angelos, Bill. The Third Crystal. Hicks, Russell, et al, illus. 34p. (ps). 1987. incl. cass. 9.95 (ISBN 0-934323-43-7). Alchemy Comms.
Forsse, Ken & Baron, Michelle. Tweeg Gets the Tweezles. Hicks, Russell, et al, illus. 34p. (ps). 1987. incl. cass. 9.95 (ISBN 0-934323-41-0). Alchemy Comms.
Forte, Imogene. Dinosaur Learning Fun. (Illus.). 48p. (ps-3). 1987. pap. 2.95 (ISBN 0-86530-145-X, IP 100-6). Incentive Pubns.
—Fairy Tale Learning Fun. (Illus.). 48p. (ps-3). 1987. pap. 2.95 (ISBN 0-86530-146-8, IP 100-7). Incentive Pubns.
—Monster Learning Fun. (Illus.). 48p. (ps-3). 1987. pap. 2.95 (ISBN 0-86530-147-6, IP 100-8). Incentive Pubns.
—Mother Goose Learning Fun. (Illus.). 48p. (ps-3). 1987. pap. 2.95 (ISBN 0-86530-148-4, IP 100-5). Incentive Pubns.
Fowler, Richard. Let's Make It Go from Side to Side. Fowler, Richard, illus. 8p. (ps). 1990. Repr. of 1985 ed. bds. 4.95 (ISBN 0-88335-898-0, AT03). Milliken Pub Co.
—Let's Make It Go In & Out. Fowler, Richard, illus. 8p. (ps). 1990. Repr. of 1984 ed. bds. 4.95 (ISBN 0-88335-737-2, AT01). Milliken Pub Co.
—Let's Make It Go Round. Fowler, Richard, illus. 8p. (ps). 1990. Repr. of 1984 ed. bds. 4.95 (ISBN 0-88335-738-0, AT02). Milliken Pub Co.
—Little's Noisy Boat. Fowler, Richard, illus. LC 85-80927. 20p. (ps-1). 1986. pap. 9.95 (ISBN 0-448-18979-8, G&D). Putnam Pub Group.
—Mr. Little's Noisy Plane: A Lift-the-Flap Book. Fowler, Richard, illus. 20p. (ps-1). 1988. 11.95 (ISBN 0-448-19007-9, G&D). Putnam Pub Group.
—Mr. Little's Noisy Truck: A Life-the-Flap Book. Fowler, Richard, illus. 20p. (ps-1). 1989. 11.95 (ISBN 0-448-19021-4, G&D). Putnam Pub Group.
Fox, Mem. Hattie & the Fox. Mullins, Patricia, illus. LC 88-5058. 32p. (ps-2). 1988. text ed. 12.95 (ISBN 0-02-735470-9, Bradbury Pr); pap. 16.95 big book (ISBN 0-02-735471-7). Macmillan Child Grp.
—Shoes from Grandpa. Mullins, Patricia, illus. LC 89-35401. 32p. (ps-1). 1990. 13.95 (ISBN 0-531-05848-4); PLB 13.99 (ISBN 0-531-08448-5). Orchard Bks Watts.
Fraidy Cat's Halloween Pop-Up Storybook. (ps-3). 1990. pap. 2.95 (ISBN 0-8167-2194-7). Troll Assocs.
Frankel, Alona. Mi Bacinica y Yo (Once upon a Potty) (SPA.). 36p. (ps). 1986. Hers. 4.95 (ISBN 0-8120-5751-1); His. (ISBN 0-8120-5750-3). Barron.
Frascino, Edward. Nanny Noony & the Magic Spell. Frascino, Edward, illus. 32p. (gr. k-3). 1988. 14.95 (ISBN 0-945912-00-5). Pippin Pr.
Freddie Frog. 12p. (ps-1). 1989. bds. 14.95 (ISBN 0-87449-642-X). Modern Pub NYC.
Freedman, Sally. Devin's New Bed. Levine, Abby, ed. LC 86-15823. (Illus.). 32p. (ps). 1986. PLB 12.95 (ISBN 0-8075-1565-5). A Whitman.
Freeman, Don. Beady Bear. Freeman, Don, illus. LC 54-12295. 48p. (ps-1). 1954. 13.95 (ISBN 0-670-15056-8). Viking Child Bks.
—The Chalk Box Story. Freeman, Don, illus. LC 76-10169. 40p. (gr. 1-3). 1976. 13.95 (ISBN 0-397-31699-2). HarpC Child Bks.

—Corduroy. Freeman, Don, illus. LC 68-16068. 32p. 1968. pap. 11.95 (ISBN 0-670-24133-4). Viking Child Bks.
—Corduroy, Edicion Espanola. Freeman, Don, illus. (SPA.). 32p. (ps-3). 1988. pap. 11.95 (ISBN 0-670-82265-5). Viking Child Bks.
—Dandelion. Freeman, Don, illus. LC 64-21472. 48p. (ps-2). 1964. pap. 12.95 (ISBN 0-670-25532-7). Viking Child Bks.
—Mop Top. Freeman, Don, illus. (ps-1). 1955. pap. 13.95 (ISBN 0-670-48882-8). Viking Child Bks.
—Norman the Doorman. Freeman, Don, illus. (ps-3). 1989. pap. 4.95 (ISBN 0-14-050288-2, Puffin). Puffin Bks.
—A Pocket for Corduroy. LC 77-16123. (Illus.). (gr. 3-5). 1978. pap. 11.95 (ISBN 0-670-56172-X). Viking Child Bks.
—A Rainbow of My Own. 32p. (ps-2). 1978. pap. 3.95 (ISBN 0-14-050328-5, Puffin). Puffin Bks.
—Rainbow of My Own. (Illus.). (gr. k-3). 1966. pap. 13. 95 (ISBN 0-670-58928-4). Viking Child Bks.
Friendly Pets. 14p. (ps). 1979. bds. 2.25 (ISBN 0-448-16279-2, G&D). Putnam Pub Group.
Friends at School. (Illus.). 12p. (ps-5). 1989. pap. text ed. 1.95 (ISBN 0-02-689210-3). Checkerboard Pr.
Friskey, Margaret. Chicken Little Count-To-Ten. Evans, K., illus. 32p. (gr. k-3). 1946. PLB 14.60 (ISBN 0-516-03431-6). Childrens.
—Seven Diving Ducks. Morey, Jean, illus. LC 65-20889. 32p. (gr. k-3). 1965. PLB 14.60 (ISBN 0-516-03605-X). Childrens.
Frog. (ps-k). 1986. 4.95 (ISBN 1-55513-175-1, Chariot Bks). Cook.
Front, Sheila. Scary Book. Front, Charles, illus. 32p. (gr. k-3). 1986. 10.95 (ISBN 0-233-97751-1). Andre Deutsch.
Front, Sheila & Front, Charles. One Rich Rajah. Front, Sheila & Front, Charles, illus. 24p. (ps-2). 1988. 10.95 (ISBN 0-233-98101-2). Andre Deutsch.
Frost, Marie. Grandma's Secret. Ham, John, illus. LC 87-91988. 32p. (gr. k-2). 1988. 1.99 (ISBN 0-87403-393-4, 24-03803). Standard Pub.
Fuchshuber, Annegert. The Cuckoo-Clock Cuckoo. 32p. (gr. k-4). 1988. lib. bdg. 12.95 (ISBN 0-87614-320-6); pap. 5.95 (ISBN 0-87614-499-7). Carolrhoda Bks.
—The Cuckoo-Clock Cuckoo. (Illus.). 32p. (gr. k-4). 1989. pap. 5.95 (ISBN 0-685-24889-5, First Ave Edns). Lerner Pubns.
—Giant Story - Mouse Tale: A Half Picture Book. (Illus.). 32p. (ps-3). 1988. lib. bdg. 12.95 (ISBN 0-87614-319-2); pap. 5.95 (ISBN 0-87614-500-4). Carolrhoda Bks.
Fujikawa, Gyo. Babes of the Wild. Fujikawa, Gyo, illus. 16p. (ps). 1989. Repr. bds. 6.95 (ISBN 1-55987-008-7, Sunny Bks). J B Comns.
—Betty Bear's Birthday. Fujikawa, Gyo, illus. 16p. (ps). 1989. Repr. bds. 6.95 (ISBN 1-55987-011-7, Sunny Bks). J B Comns.
—Can You Count? Fujikawa, Gyo, illus. 16p. (ps). 1989. Repr. of 1977 ed. bds. 6.95 (ISBN 1-55987-003-6, Sunny Bks). J B Comns.
—Good Morning! Fujikawa, Gyo, illus. 14p. (ps). 1981. 2.25 (ISBN 0-448-15084-0, G&D). Putnam Pub Group.
—Gyo Fujikawa's Come Follow Me. Fujikawa, Gyo, illus. 80p. 1989. 13.95 (ISBN 0-448-04303-3, G&D). Putnam Pub Group.
—Gyo Fujikawa's Oh, What a Busy Day! Fujikawa, Gyo, illus. 80p. 1989. 13.95 (ISBN 0-448-04304-1, G&D). Putnam Pub Group.
—Let's Eat. Fujikawa, Gyo, illus. 16p. (ps). 1989. Repr. of 1975 ed. bds. 6.95 (ISBN 1-55987-005-2, Sunny Bks). J B Comns.
—Let's Grow a Garden. Fujikawa, Gyo, illus. 16p. (ps). 1989. Repr. bds. 6.95 (ISBN 1-55987-010-9, Sunny Bks). J B Comns.
—Let's Play. Fujikawa, Gyo, illus. 16p. (ps). 1989. Repr. of 1975 ed. bds. 6.95 (ISBN 0-317-93045-1, Sunny Bks). J B Comns.
—Millie's Secret. Fujikawa, Gyo, illus. 16p. (ps). 1989. bds. 6.95 (ISBN 1-55987-006-0, Sunny Bks). J B Comns.
—Mother Goose. Fujikawa, Gyo, illus. 14p. (ps-k). 1981. 2.25 (ISBN 0-448-15091-3, G&D). Putnam Pub Group.
—My Favorite Thing. Duenewald, Doris, ed. (Illus.). (ps-1). 1978. 3.50 (ISBN 0-448-14727-0, G&D). Putnam Pub Group.
—My Favorite Thing. Fujikawa, Gyo, illus. 16p. (ps). 1989. Repr. of 1978 ed. bds. 6.95 (ISBN 1-55987-004-4, Sunny Bks). J B Comns.
—Our Best Friends. Fujikawa, Gyo, illus. 16p. (ps). 1989. Repr. bds. 6.95 (ISBN 1-55987-009-5, Sunny Bks). J B Comns.
—Puppies, Pussycats & Other Friends. Fujikawa, Gyo, illus. 16p. (ps). 1989. Repr. of 1977 ed. bds. 6.95 (ISBN 1-55987-000-1, Sunny Bks). J B Comns.
—See What I Can Be! (Illus.). 24p. (gr. 1-3). 1990. bds. 2.50 (ISBN 0-448-09257-3, G&D). Putnam Pub Group.
—Sleepy Time. Fujikawa, Gyo, illus. 16p. (ps). 1989. Repr. of 1975 ed. bds. 6.95 (ISBN 1-55987-001-X, Sunny Bks). J B Comns.
—Sunny Books - Four-Favorite Tales, 4 bks, No. 1. Fujikawa, Gyo, illus. (ps). 1989. Repr. of 1975 ed. Boxed set, 4 books, 16 pgs. ea. bds. write for info. (ISBN 1-55987-040-0, Sunny Bks). J B Comns.
—Sunny Books - Four-Favorite Tales, 4 bks, No. 2. Fujikawa, Gyo, illus. (ps). 1989. Repr. Boxed set, four bks., 16 pgs. ea. bds. write for info. (ISBN 1-55987-041-9, Sunny Bks). J B Comns.
—Sunny Books - Four-Favorite Tales, 4 bks, No. 3. Fujikawa, Gyo, illus. (ps). Repr. Boxed set, four bks., 16 pgs. ea. bds. write for info. (ISBN 1-55987-042-7, Sunny Bks). J B Comns.
—Surprise! Surprise! Fujikawa, Gyo, illus. (gr. k-3). 1978. 3.50 (ISBN 0-448-14557-X, G&D). Putnam Pub Group.
—Surprise! Surprise! Fujikawa, Gyo, illus. 16p. (ps). 1989. Repr. bds. 6.95 (ISBN 1-55987-007-9, Sunny Bks). J B Comns.
Fujikawa, Gyo, illus. Babies. (ps). 1963. bds. 3.95 (ISBN 0-448-03084-5, G&D). Putnam Pub Group.
—Good Night, Sleep Tight, Shh... 22p. (ps). 1990. bds. 2.95 (ISBN 0-679-80845-0). Random.
Fun & Games Sticker Book: Haunted House. (ps up). 1990. 2.98 (ISBN 0-8317-3650-X). Smithmark.
Fun & Games Sticker Book: Nutcracker. (ps up). 1990. pap. 2.98 (ISBN 0-8317-3653-4). Smithmark.
Fun & Games Sticker Book: Pirates. (ps up). 1990. pap. 2.98 (ISBN 0-8317-3651-8). Smithmark.
Funakoshi, Canna. One Morning. LC 86-91538. (Illus.). 34p. (ps-3). 1986. 11.95 (ISBN 0-88708-033-2). Picture Bk Studio.
Funtime ABC & 123. (Illus.). 24p. (gr. k-2). 1988. 3.95 (ISBN 0-87449-498-2). Modern Pub NYC.
Fusako Ishinabe. Hiro's Pillow. Young, Richard G., ed. Kaisei - Sha, tr. LC 89-11768. (Illus.). 32p. (gr. 1-3). 1989. PLB 13.26 (ISBN 0-944483-44-5). Garrett Ed Corp.
Fyleman, Rose. Fairy Went A-Marketing. Henterly, Jamichael, illus. (ps-1). 1986. 11.95 (ISBN 0-525-44258-8, DCB). Dutton Child Bks.
G. A. T. abouts Alphabet Contest. 24p. (gr. k-2). 1990. 3.95 (ISBN 0-87449-702-7). Modern Pub NYC.
G. A. T. abouts Build with Shapes. 24p. (gr. k-2). 1990. 3.95 (ISBN 0-87449-699-3). Modern Pub NYC.
G. A. T. abouts Colorful Card. 24p. (gr. k-2). 1990. 3.95 (ISBN 0-87449-701-9). Modern Pub NYC.
G. A. T. abouts Count at the Zoo. 24p. (gr. k-2). 1990. 3.95 (ISBN 0-87449-700-0). Modern Pub NYC.
Gackenbach, Dick. Hurray for Hattie Rabbit! Gackenbach, Dick, illus. LC 85-45828. 32p. (gr. k-3). 1986. 10.95 (ISBN 0-06-021960-2); PLB 10.89 (ISBN 0-06-021983-1). HarpC Child Bks.
—Timid Timothy's Tongue Twisters. Gackenbach, Dick, illus. (gr. k-3). 1989. bk. & cassette 19.95 (ISBN 0-87499-128-5); bk. & cassette 12.95 (ISBN 0-87499-127-7); 4 cassettes & guide 27.95 (ISBN 0-87499-129-3). Live Oak Media.
—With Love from Gran. Gackenbach, Dick, illus. LC 88-35248. 32p. (ps). 1989. 13.95 (ISBN 0-89919-842-2, Clarion Bks). HM.
Gag, Wanda. The Funny Thing. Gag, Wanda, illus. (gr. 1-3). 1960. PLB 6.99 (ISBN 0-698-30097-1, Coward). Putnam Pub Group.
—Millions of Cats. Gag, Wanda, illus. 112p. (gr. k-3). 1977. 7.95 (ISBN 0-698-20091-8, Coward); pap. 3.95 (ISBN 0-698-20434-4). Putnam Pub Group.
—Millions of Cats. (Illus.). 32p. (ps-k). 1928. 9.95 (ISBN 0-317-99864-1, Coward). Putnam Pub Group.
—Nothing at All. Gag, Wanda, illus. (gr. 1-3). 1941. PLB 6.99 (ISBN 0-698-30264-8, Coward). Putnam Pub Group.
Gaines, M. C., ed. Picture Stories from the Bible: The New Testament in Full-Color Comic-Strip Form. Cameron, Don, illus. LC 80-51593. 144p. (gr. 3-10). 1980. Repr. of 1946 ed. 12.95 (ISBN 0-934386-02-1). Scarf Pr.
Galbraith, Richard. Reuben Runs Away. LC 88-11741. (Illus.). 32p. (ps-2). 1989. 12.95 (ISBN 0-531-05790-9); PLB 12.99 (ISBN 0-531-08390-X). Orchard Bks Watts.
Galdone, Paul. Cat Goes Fiddle-I-Fee. LC 85-2686. (Illus.). (ps-1). 1988. pap. 4.95 (ISBN 0-89919-705-1, Pub. by Clarion). Ticknor & Fields.
—Henny Penny. Galdone, Paul, illus. LC 68-24735. 32p. (ps-3). 1984. pap. 4.95 (ISBN 0-89919-225-4, Pub. by Clarion). Ticknor & Fields.
—The Little Red Hen. LC 84-4311. (Illus.). 48p. (ps-3). 1985. pap. 4.95 (ISBN 0-89919-349-8, Pub. by Clarion). Ticknor & Fields.
Galdone, Paul, retold by. & illus. The Monster & the Tailor. LC 82-1246. 32p. (ps-1). 1988. pap. 4.95 (ISBN 0-89919-796-7, Pub. by Clarion). Ticknor & Fields.
Galvin, Matthew R. Clouds & Clocks: A Story for Children Who Soil. Ferraro, Sandra, illus. LC 89-12278. 48p. 1989. 15.95 (ISBN 0-945354-18-5); pap. 5.95 (ISBN 0-945354-15-0). Magination Pr.
Gambill, Henrietta D. Thank You, God, for Christmas. Hutton, Kathryn, illus. LC 87-91997. 32p. (gr. k-2). 1988. 1.99 (ISBN 0-87403-402-7, 24-03812). Standard Pub.
Ganly, Helen. Jyoti's Journey. Ganly, Helen, illus. 32p. (ps-3). 1986. 11.95 (ISBN 0-233-97899-2). Andre Deutsch.
Gantos, Jack. Rotten Ralph. Rubel, Nicole, illus. 1988. Incl. cass. pap. 7.95 (ISBN 0-395-48873-7). HM.
—Rotten Ralph's Trick or Treat. Rubel, Nicole, illus. 32p. (gr. k-3). 1988. pap. 4.95 (ISBN 0-395-48655-6, Sandpiper). HM.
Gantschev, Ivan. Where Is Mr. Mole? Clements, Andrew, tr. Gantschev, Ivan, illus. LC 89-8778. 28p. (ps up). 1989. 15.95 (ISBN 0-88708-109-6). Picture Bk Studio.
Garcia, Gloria. Be My Friend. (ps). 1990. 7.95 (ISBN 0-85953-421-9). Childs Play.
—Flying High. 1990. 7.95 (ISBN 0-85953-424-3). Childs Play.
—I Can't Stop Now. (ps). 1990. 7.95 (ISBN 0-85953-423-5). Childs Play.
—Life on the Ocean Wave. (ps). 1990. 7.95 (ISBN 0-85953-422-7). Childs Play.
Garcia, Richard. My Aunt Otilia's Spirits: Los Espiritus de Mi Tia Otilia. Rea, Jesus G., tr. Cherin, Robin & Reyes, Roger I., illus. (ENG & SPA.). 24p. (gr. 2-9). 1987. 12.95 (ISBN 0-89239-029-8). Childrens Book Pr.
Garcia de Lynam, Alicia. It's Mine. Garcia de Lynam, Alicia, illus. LC 87-24649. 32p. (ps-k). 1988. 8.95 (ISBN 0-8037-0509-3). Dial Bks Young.
Gardener, Beau. The Look Again...& Again, & Again, & Again Book. LC 84-748. (Illus.). 32p. (ps-3). 1983. 11. 00 (ISBN 0-688-03805-0); lib. bdg. 10.08 (ISBN 0-688-03806-9). Lothrop.
Gardner, Beau. Can You Imagine? A Counting Book. (Illus.). 32p. 1987. 12.95 (ISBN 0-399-22027-5, Putnam). Putnam Pub Group.
—Have You Ever Seen...? An ABC Book. (Illus.). 32p. (gr. k-3). 1986. 10.95 (ISBN 0-396-08825-2, Putnam). Putnam Pub Group.
—What Is It? A Spin-About Book. Gardner, Beau, illus. 16p. (ps-3). 1989. 10.95 (ISBN 0-399-21664-2, Putnam). Putnam Pub Group.
Gardner, Karen A. My Life As a Hand. rev. ed. (Illus.). 37p. (ps-2). 1984. Set of 1-4. PLB 1.70 (ISBN 0-931421-03-9). Hlth Pub SF.
—My Life As a Nose. rev. ed. (Illus.). 37p. (ps-2). 1984. Set of 1-4. PLB 1.70 (ISBN 0-931421-04-7). Hlth Pub SF.
—My Life As A Tongue. rev. ed. (Illus.). 37p. (ps-2). 1984. Set of 1-4. PLB 1.70 (ISBN 0-931421-05-5). Hlth Pub SF.
—My Life As an Eye. rev. ed. (Illus.). 37p. (ps-2). 1984. Set of 1-4. PLB 1.70 (ISBN 0-931421-02-0). Hlth Pub SF.
Garfield-Beach Key Lock Diary. 1988. 9.98 (ISBN 0-89954-900-4). Antioch Pub Co.
Garfield-Beach Photo Album. 1988. 8.98 (ISBN 0-89954-901-2). Antioch Pub Co.
Garis, Howard R. Uncle Wiggily to the Rescue. Chambless-Rigie, Jane, illus. 32p. (ps-2). 1987. pap. 1.95 (ISBN 0-448-34305-3, G&D). Putnam Pub Group.
—Uncle Wiggily's Picture Book. Campbell, Lansing & San Souci, Daniel, illus. (gr. k-4). 1989. 11.95 (ISBN 0-448-09079-1, G&D). Putnam Pub Group.
Garland, Sarah. Oh, No! (Illus.). 32p. (ps-1). 1990. pap. 8.95 (ISBN 0-670-83075-5). Viking Child Bks.
Gas Station. 8p. (ps). 1990. bds. 2.95 (ISBN 0-671-49715-4, Little Simon). S&S Trade.
Gathrid, Erin, created by. A Zoo for You. Tilley, Debbie, illus. LC 84-52555. 28p. (ps). 1985. bds. 6.95 (ISBN 0-915391-04-X, Pub. by Mad Hatter Bks). Slawson Comm.
Gay, Marie-Louise. Rainy Day Magic. Tucker, Kathy, ed. Gay, Marie-Louise, illus. 32p. (ps-2). 1989. PLB 12.95 (ISBN 0-8075-6767-1). A Whitman.
Gee, John. Hidden Pictures: Favorites by John Gee. (Illus.). 32p. (Orig.). (gr. 1-6). 1981. pap. 2.95 (ISBN 0-87534-230-2). Highlights.
Geisert, Arthur. The Ark. Geisert, Arthur, illus. LC 88-15889. 48p. (ps up). 1988. 15.95 (ISBN 0-395-43078-X). HM.
Geiss, Tony. Honk If You Like Honkers: A Sesame Street Book with a Honker That Really Honks. Cooke, Tom, illus. LC 85-63546. 16p. (gr. k-1). 1986. 1.29 (ISBN 0-394-87989-9, Random Juv). Random.
Gelbard, Jane & Polivy, Betsy B. My Bye-Bye Bottle Book. Klonsky, Arthur, photos by. (Illus.). 14p. (ps). 1989. bds. 3.95 (ISBN 0-448-21526-8, G&D). Putnam Pub Group.
—My Dressing Book. Klonsky, Arthur, photos by. (Illus.). 14p. (ps). 1989. bds. 3.95 (ISBN 0-448-21527-6, G&D). Putnam Pub Group.
—My Eating Book. Klonsky, Arthur, photos by. (Illus.). 14p. (ps). 1989. bds. 3.95 (ISBN 0-448-21528-4, G&D). Putnam Pub Group.
—My Sharing Book. Klonsky, Arthur, photos by. (Illus.). 14p. (ps). 1989. bds. 3.95 (ISBN 0-448-21529-2, G&D). Putnam Pub Group.
Gellman, Ellie. Tamar's Sukkah. Kahn, Katherine J., illus. LC 88-23388. 32p. (ps-2). 1988. pap. 4.95 (ISBN 0-930494-79-2). Kar Ben.
Gelman, Rita G. Cats & Mice. Gurney, Eric, illus. 48p. (gr. k-3). Big Book. 19.50 (ISBN 0-590-71592-5); pap. 1.95 (ISBN 0-590-71593-3). Scholastic Inc.
—Stop Those Painters! Gerberg, Mort, illus. 32p. (ps-2). 1989. pap. 2.50 (ISBN 0-590-40959-X, Hello Reader). Scholastic Inc.
Genet, Barbara. Ta-Poo-Ach Means Apple. Genet, Barbara, illus. LC 85-60009. 46p. (ps-3). 1985. 8.00 (ISBN 0-86705-015-2). AIRE.
Genia, illus. The Little Red Hen. 24p. (ps-2). 1988. Incl. cass. bk & audiocassette 6.95 (ISBN 0-8120-4042-2). Barron.
Gentle Friends. 12p. (ps-1). 1988. bds. 5.95 (ISBN 0-87449-628-4). Modern Pub NYC.
Georgiady, Nicholas P. & Romano, Louis G. Trudi La Cane. Thorne, Patrice, tr. Wilson, Dagmar, illus. 32p. (gr. 1-4). 1982. pap. write for info. Argee Pubs.

Geras, Adele. Nursery School Rabbit. Julian-Ottie, Vanessa, illus. LC 86-20283. 32p. (ps-3). 1987. lib. bdg. 5.99 (ISBN 0-394-98712-8, Random Juv). Random.
Gere, Bill. The Truck Book. LaPadula, Tom, illus. 24p. (ps-k). 1987. pap. write for info. (ISBN 0-307-10051-0, Pub. by Golden Bks). Western Pub.
Gerez, Toni de, retold by. Louhi, Witch of North Farm: A Finnish Tale. Cooney, Barbara, illus. (ps-3). 1988. pap. 4.95 (ISBN 0-14-050529-6, Puffin). Puffin Bks.
Geringer, Laura. A Three Hat Day. Lobel, Arnold, illus. LC 85-42640. 32p. (ps-3). 1987. pap. 4.95 (ISBN 0-06-443157-6, Trophy). HarpC Child Bks.
Gerrard, Roy. The Favershams. (Illus.). 32p. (gr. 2 up). 1987. pap. 3.95 (ISBN 0-374-42293-1). FS&G.
Gerstein, Mordicai. The Seal Mother. Gerstein, Mordicai, illus. LC 82-29295. 32p. (ps-3). 1986. 10.95 (ISBN 0-8037-0302-3); PLB 10.89 (ISBN 0-8037-0303-1). Dial Bks Young.
—William, Where Are You? Gerstein, Mordicai, illus. LC 84-21479. 32p. (ps-1). 1986. 7.95 (ISBN 0-517-55644-8). Crown.
Gerver, Jane, ed. My First Book of Telling Time. McCarthy, Kathleen, et al, illus. 32p. (gr. k-2). 1986. wkbk. 3.95 (ISBN 0-394-88167-2). Random.
Gerver, Jane E. Happy Bear, Christmas Star. Barto, Bobbi, illus. LC 90-60174. 32p. (Orig.). (ps-3). 1990. pap. 2.25 (ISBN 0-679-80858-2). Random.
Gibbons, Gail. The Milk Makers. Gibbons, Gail, illus. LC 86-22148. 32p. (gr. k-3). 1987. pap. 3.95 (ISBN 0-689-71116-6, Aladdin). Macmillan Child Grp.
—The Pottery Place. Gibbons, Gail, illus. LC 86-32790. 32p. (ps-3). 1987. 12.95 (ISBN 0-15-263265-4, HJ). HarBraceJ.
—Sun up, Sun Down. LC 82-23420. (Illus.). 32p. (Orig.). (ps-3). 1987. pap. 4.95 (ISBN 0-15-282782-X, VoyB). HarBraceJ.
—Trucks. Gibbons, Gail, illus. LC 81-43039. 32p. (ps-1). 1985. pap. 3.95 (ISBN 0-06-443069-3, Trophy). HarpC Child Bks.
Giff, Patricia R. The Almost Awful Play. Natti, Susanna, illus. (gr. 2-4). 1989. bk. & cassette 19.95 (ISBN 0-87499-116-1); bk. & cassette 12.95 (ISBN 0-87499-115-3); pap. 27.95 4 cassettes & guide (ISBN 0-87499-117-X). Live Oak Media.
—Happy Birthday, Ronald Morgan! Natti, Susanna, illus. LC 85-32303. 32p. (ps-4). 1986. pap. 10.95 (ISBN 0-670-80741-9). Viking Child Bks.
—Happy Birthday, Ronald Morgan. Natti, Susanna, illus. (gr. 2-4). 1989. bk. & cassette 19.95 (ISBN 0-87499-122-6); bk. & cassette 12.95 (ISBN 0-87499-121-8); 4 cassettes & guide 27.95 (ISBN 0-87499-123-4). Live Oak Media.
—Have You Seen Hyacinth Macaw? 128p. (gr. k-6). 1982. pap. 2.95 (ISBN 0-440-43450-5, YB). Dell.
—Today Was a Terrible Day. Natti, Susanna, illus. 32p. 1984. pap. 3.95 (ISBN 0-14-050453-2, Puffin). Puffin Bks.
—Today Was a Terrible Day. Natti, Susanna, illus. 32p. (ps-k). 1984. pap. 3.95 incl. cassette (Penguin Bks). Viking Penguin.
Gikow, Louise. The Muppet Babies at the Circus. Spaar, Kathy, illus. LC 84-61436. 24p. (ps-k). 1985. bds. 4.95 (ISBN 0-394-87105-7, Random Juv). Random.
—Muppet Kids in Good-Bye, Horace Hamster. Brannon, Tom, illus. (ps-3). 1991. pap. 1.25 (ISBN 0-307-12655-2, Golden Pr). Western Pub.
—Muppet Kids in Mom's Having a Baby. Cooke, Tom, illus. (ps-3). 1991. pap. write for info. (ISBN 0-307-12661-7, Golden Pr). Western Pub.
—Muppet Kids in Scooter Can't Read. Leigh, Tom, illus. (ps-3). 1991. pap. write for info. (ISBN 0-307-12656-0, Golden Pr). Western Pub.
—The Tale of the Bunny Picnic: A Jim Henson Picture Book. Hearn, Diane D., illus. 40p. (ps-4). 1988. pap. 3.95 (ISBN 0-590-40837-2). Scholastic Inc.
Gilchrist, Guy. Tiny Dinos Fun at the Beach: A Book of Actions. Gilchrist, Guy, illus. LC 87-40337. (ps-1). 1988. 4.95 (ISBN -155782-013-9). Warner Bks.
Giles, Lucille. Color Me Brown. rev. ed. Holmes, Louis F., illus. 47p. (gr. k-6). 1974. pap. 5.00 (ISBN 0-87485-017-7). Johnson Chi.
Gill, Bob. What Color Is Your World. Gill, Bob, illus. (gr. k-3). 1963. 10.95 (ISBN 0-8392-3042-7). Astor-Honor.
Gilleo, Alma, ed. Donkey Lettuce. LC 74-734826. (Illus.). (gr. 1-3). 1976. 6 bks. & 1 cass. 29.95 (ISBN 0-685-25745-2, BC002-4); 1 bk. & 1 cass. 10.95 (ISBN 0-89290-007-5). Soc for Visual.
—It's Perfectly True. LC 76-730153. (Illus.). (gr. 1-3). 1976. 6 bks. & 1 cass. 29.95 (ISBN 0-89290-001-6, BC001-2); 1 bk. & 1 cass. 10.95 (ISBN 0-318-42847-4). Soc for Visual.
Gillham, Bill. And So Can I! Gillham, Bill, photos by. (Illus.). 32p. (ps-k). 1987. 8.95 (ISBN 0-399-21448-8, Putnam). Putnam Pub Group.
—The Early Words Picture Book. Grainger, Sam, illus. 32p. (ps-k). 1985. 7.95 (ISBN 0-698-20583-9, Coward); pap. 4.95 (ISBN 0-698-20621-5, Coward). Putnam Pub Group.
—The First Words Picture Book. Grainger, Sam, photos by. LC 81-12452. (Illus.). 32p. (gr. 1-5). 1982. 7.95 (ISBN 0-698-20560-X, Coward); pap. 3.95 (ISBN 0-698-20605-3). Putnam Pub Group.
—Where Does It Go? Horne, Fiona, illus. LC 85-28139. 24p. (ps-1). 1986. 5.95 (ISBN 0-399-21322-8, Putnam). Putnam Pub Group.
Gillon, Edmund. Cut & Assemble a Western Frontier Town. 1950. pap. 5.95 (ISBN 0-486-23736-2). Dover.
—Cut & Assemble an Early New England Village. 1950. pap. 5.95 (ISBN 0-486-23536-X). Dover.
Gillon, Edmund V. Cut & Assemble-Victorian Houses. 1980. pap. 5.95 (ISBN 0-486-23849-0). Dover.
—Cut & Assemble Victorian Seaside Resort. 1986. pap. 5.95 (ISBN 0-486-25097-0). Dover.
Gilson, Jamie. Can't Catch Me, I'm the Gingerbread Man. 128p. (gr. 4-7). 1989. pap. 2.75 (ISBN 0-671-69160-0, Minstrel Bks). PB.
Ginsburg, Mirra. The Chick & the Duckling. Aruego, Jose & Dewey, Ariane, illus. 32p. (ps-1). 1988. pap. 4.95 (ISBN 0-689-71226-X, Aladdin). Macmillan Child Grp.
Giovanni, Nikki. Spin a Soft Black Song. rev. ed. Martins, George, illus. LC 84-19287. 64p. (gr. 2 up). 1985. 11.95 (ISBN 0-8090-8796-0). Hill & Wang.
—Spin a Soft Black Song. rev. ed. Martins, George, illus. (gr. k up). 1987. pap. 3.50 (ISBN 0-374-46469-3). FS&G.

Girard, Linda W. Adoption Is for Always. Levine, Abby, ed. LC 86-15843. (Illus.). 32p. (gr. 2-5). 1986. 10.95 (ISBN 0-8075-0185-9). A Whitman. STARRED, SCHOOL LIBRARY JOURNAL. "Celia (who appears to be five or six years old) has always known that she was adopted, but she is just beginning to understand the significance of the word. Although her parents deal with her questions with honesty & love, Celia experiences a confused mixture of fear & anger.... This well-written book succeeds as a story as well as bibliotherapy. Information a young child can understand about adoption is skillfully integrated into the text. Expressive pencil drawings within colored borders enhance the story. One of the best titles about adoption available for young children. "This is attractive & absorbing-- a very good source for adults looking for ways to deal with children's feelings about adoption."-- BOOKLIST.
Publisher Provided Annotation.

—At Daddy's on Saturdays. Levine, Abby, ed. (Illus.). 32p. (gr. k-3). 1987. PLB 12.95 (ISBN 0-8075-0475-0). A Whitman.
—Jeremy's First Haircut. Fay, Ann, ed. Begin, Mary J., illus. 32p. (ps-k). 1986. 11.50 (ISBN 0-8075-3805-1). A Whitman.
—We Adopted You, Benjamin Koo. Levine, Abby, ed. (Illus.). 32p. (gr. 2-6). 1989. 12.95 (ISBN 0-8075-8694-3). A Whitman.
Glass, Marvin. What Happened Today, Freddy Groundhog? (Illus.). 32p. (ps-2). 1988. PLB 12.95 (ISBN 0-517-57140-4). Crown.
Glazier, Nancy H. My Very Own Telephone Book. Hirtenstein, Ginna, illus. 28p. (ps-2). 1986. bds. 5.95 (ISBN 0-448-18978-X, G&D). Putnam Pub Group.
Gleeson, Brian, as told by. Pecos Bill. Raglin, Tim, illus. LC 88-11581. 36p. (ps up). 1988. 14.95 (ISBN 0-88708-081-2, Rabbit Ears); bk. & cass. pkg. 19.95 (ISBN 0-88708-086-3). Picture Bk Studio.
Glover, Susanne, et al. A Bulletin Board Book for All Seasons. 64p. (gr. k-6). 1980. 6.95 (ISBN 0-916456-79-X, GA 160). Good Apple.
Go to Sleep Baby Donald. (Illus.). (ps). 1986. pap. 3.95 (ISBN 0-671-62932-8, Little Simon). S&S Trade.
Goble, Paul. Beyond the Ridge. Goble, Paul, illus. LC 87-33113. 32p. 1989. 13.95 (ISBN 0-02-736581-6, Bradbury Pr). Macmillan Child Grp.
—The Dream Wolf. rev. ed. Goble, Paul, illus. LC 89-687. 32p. (ps-3). 1990. 14.95 (ISBN 0-02-736585-9, Bradbury Pr). Macmillan Child Grp.
—The Great Race. LC 85-4202. (Illus.). 32p. (ps-2). 1985. 13.95 (ISBN 0-02-736950-1, Bradbury Pr). Macmillan Child Grp.
—Star Boy. Goble, Paul, illus. LC 82-20599. 32p. (gr. k up). 1983. 14.95 (ISBN 0-02-722660-3, Bradbury Pr). Macmillan Child Grp.
God Made Apples. (ps). 1990. pap. 0.99 (ISBN 0-8007-7103-6). Revell.
God Made Friends. 8p. (ps). 1985. bds. 2.95 (ISBN 0-85648-865-8). Lion USA.
God Made My Family. 8p. (ps). 1985. bds. 2.95 (ISBN 0-85648-864-X). Lion USA.
God Made Oranges. (ps). 1990. pap. 0.99 (ISBN 0-8007-7104-4). Revell.
God Made Pears. (ps). 1990. pap. 0.99 (ISBN 0-8007-7105-2). Revell.
God Made Strawberries. (ps). 1990. pap. 0.99 (ISBN 0-8007-7106-0). Revell.
Goennel, Heidi. My Day. Goennel, Heidi, illus. (ps-1). 1988. 12.95 (ISBN 0-316-31839-6). Little.
Goffstein, Brooke. Our Prairie Home: A Picture Album. Goffstein, Brooke, illus. LC 87-30795. 32p. (ps up). 1988. 12.95 (ISBN 0-06-022290-5); PLB 12.89 (ISBN 0-06-022291-3). HarpC Child Bks.
Golden, Silvia. The King's Forest. Eichenauer, Gabriele G., illus. 1988. 14.95 (ISBN 0-86315-085-3, 20247). Gryphon Hse.
Goldilocks & the Three Bears & The Three Little Pigs, 2 bks. 40p. (ps-k). 1989. Set. incl. audio cassette 4.95 (ISBN 0-448-10231-5, G&D). Putnam Pub Group.
Goldman, Ronald & Lynch, Martha E. High Hat Story Bk. 2. (ps-1). 1986. 20.00 (ISBN 0-88671-245-9); lesson guide 6.50 (ISBN 0-88671-248-3); wkbk. 6.00 (ISBN 0-88671-249-1). Am Guidance.
Gomboli, Mario. Many Silly Animals. (Illus.). 8p. (ps-1). 1989. spiral bdg. 12.95 (ISBN 0-8120-5992-1). Barron.
—Many Silly Machines. (Illus.). 8p. (ps-1). 1989. spiral bdg. 12.95 (ISBN 0-8120-5991-3). Barron.
Good, Elaine W. That's What Happens When It's Spring. Shenks, Susie, illus. LC 87-14964. 32p. (ps-1). 1987. 12.95 (ISBN 0-934672-53-9). Good Bks PA.
Good Morning, Sunshine. (ps-1). 1985. 4.95 (ISBN 0-671-54733-X, Little Simon). S&S Trade.
Good Night Stars. (ps-1). 1985. 4.95 (ISBN 0-671-54734-8, Little Simon). S&S Trade.
Goodall, John S. Creepy Castle. LC 74-16836. (Illus.). 60p. 1975. 12.95 (ISBN 0-689-50027-0, M K McElderry). Macmillan Child Grp.
—Lavinia's Cottage: A Pop-Up Story. LC 82-71160. (Illus.). 16p. (gr. 1-4). 1983. text ed. 13.95 (ISBN 0-689-50257-5, M K McElderry). Macmillan Child Grp.
—Paddy to the Rescue. LC 85-70231. (Illus.). 32p. 1986. 12.95 (ISBN 0-689-50330-X, M K McElderry). Macmillan Child Grp.
—Shrewbettina's Birthday. Goodall, John S., illus. LC 73-24238. 60p. (ps-3). 1983. pap. 3.95 (ISBN 0-685-07278-9, VoyB). HarBraceJ.
—The Surprise Picnic. LC 76-28455. (Illus.). 64p. 1977. 12.95 (ISBN 0-689-50074-2, M K McElderry). Macmillan Child Grp.
Goode, Diane. I Hear a Noise. Goode, Diane, illus. 32p. (ps-1). 1988. 12.95 (ISBN 0-525-44353-3, DCB). Dutton Child Bks.
Goodman, Beth. Big Top Pee-wee's Pals: A Color & Fun Book. (Illus.). 32p. (gr. k-3). 1988. pap. 1.95 (ISBN 0-590-42204-9, 050). Scholastic Inc.
Goodman, Michael E. Baseball's Best. (ps). 1989. pap. write for info. (ISBN 0-307-11730-8, Pub. by Golden Bks). Western Pub.
—Cars & Trucks. (Illus.). 24p. (ps-k). 1989. pap. write for info. (ISBN 0-307-11753-7, Pub. by Golden Bks). Western Pub.
Goodspeed, Peter. A Rhinoceros Wakes Me up in the Morning. Panek, Dennis, illus. 32p. (ps-k). 1984. pap. 3.95 (ISBN 0-14-050455-9, Puffin). Puffin Bks.
Gorbaty, Norman. Little Dinosaur. Gorbaty, Norman, illus. LC 87-61420. 24p. (ps-1). 1988. bk. & doll pkg. 4.95 (ISBN 0-394-89575-4, Random Juv). Random.
—Little Ernie's Animal Friends. 1987. 0.90 (ISBN 0-394-88508-2). Random.
—Sesame Street. 1987. 0.90 (ISBN 0-394-88504-X). Random.
—Sesame Street: At the Playground. 1987. 0.90 (ISBN 0-394-88503-1). Random.
—Sesame Street: Goodnight Little Grover. 1987. 0.90 (ISBN 0-394-88506-6). Random.
—Sesame Street: Playtime with Bigbird. 1987. 0.90 (ISBN 0-394-88507-4). Random.
—Sesame Street: Tubbie Time with Little Ernie. 1987. 0.90 (ISBN 0-394-88505-8). Random.
Gorbaty, Norman, tr. Baby in the Park. (Illus.). 12p. (ps). 1988. 2.95 (ISBN 0-394-81925-X, Random Juv). Random.
Gorbaty, Norman, illus. Baby Animals Say Hello. 12p. (ps). 1986. 3.95 (ISBN 0-394-88241-5, Random Juv). Random.
—Baby at Home. 12p. (ps). 1988. 2.95 (ISBN 0-394-81924-1, Random Juv). Random.
—Get up & Go, Little Dinosaur! LC 89-64282. 22p. (ps). 1990. bds. 2.95 (ISBN 0-679-80693-8). Random.
—What Do You See on Sesame Street? 12p. (ps). 1988. 3.95 (ISBN 0-394-80594-1, Random Juv). Random.
Gordon, Margaret. The Frogs' Holiday. (ps-2). 1987. pap. 9.95 (ISBN 0-670-80854-7). Viking Child Bks.
—Wilberforce Goes Shopping. LC 84-40846. (Illus.). 32p. (ps-1). 1985. pap. 8.95 (ISBN 0-670-80701-X). Viking Child Bks.
—Wilberforce Goes Shopping. (ps-1). 1987. pap. 3.50 (ISBN 0-14-050391-9, Puffin). Puffin Bks.
—Wilberforce Goes to a Party. (ps-1). 1987. pap. 3.50 (ISBN 0-14-050472-9, Puffin). Puffin Bks.
—Wilberforce Goes to Playgroup. (ps-1). 1988. 9.95 (ISBN 0-317-69204-6). Viking Penguin.
Gorey, Edward. Cat E Gory. LC 86-10938. (ps up). 1986. 8.95 (ISBN 0-915361-55-8). Adama Pubs Inc.
—The Wuggly Ump. Gorey, Edward, illus. LC 86-11273. (ps up). 1986. 6.95 (ISBN 0-915361-56-6, Dist. by Watts). Adama Pubs Inc.
Gottlieb, Dale. Big Dog. Gottlieb, Dale, illus. LC 88-5295. 32p. (ps-1). 1989. 11.95 (ISBN 0-688-07381-6); PLB 11.88 (ISBN 0-688-07382-4, Morrow Jr Bks). Morrow Jr Bks.
Gould, Deborah. Aaron's Shirt. Harness, Cheryl, illus. LC 88-10414. 32p. (ps-2). 1989. 12.95 (ISBN 0-02-736351-1, Bradbury Pr). Macmillan Child Grp.

Gould, Toni. Fun with the Fumble Families. LC 83-5928. (Illus.). (gr. 1-3). 1984. PLB 12.85 (ISBN 0-8027-9190-5); pap. 9.50 (ISBN 0-8027-9191-3). Walker & Co.
—Fun with Water & Ice. LC 83-5938. (Illus.). (gr. 1-3). 1984. PLB 12.85 (ISBN 0-8027-9192-1); pap. text ed. 9.50 (ISBN 0-8027-9194-8). Walker & Co.
Grades K-One Early Learner Workbook. 192p. (ps-1). 1990. pap. 4.95 wkbk. (ISBN 0-87449-999-2). Modern Pub NYC.
Grafton, Carol B. Cut & Use Stencil Alphabet. 1984. pap. 4.95 (ISBN 0-486-24623-X). Dover.
Graham, Bill. Can You See It? Horne, Fiona, illus. LC 85-28131. 24p. (ps-1). 1986. 5.95 (ISBN 0-399-21323-6, Putnam). Putnam Pub Group.
Gramatky, Hardie. Little Toot. Gramatky, Hardie, illus. LC 78-4801. (gr. k-3). 1978. 8.95 (ISBN 0-399-20144-0, Putnam); 9.99 (ISBN 0-399-60422-7, Putnam); pap. 5.95 (ISBN 0-399-20649-3, Putnam). Putnam Pub Group.
Grambling, Lois G. Hundred Million Reasons for Owning an Elephant: Or at Least a Dozen That I Can Think of Right Now. Learner, Vickie M., illus. 32p. (ps). 1990. 6.95 (ISBN 0-8120-6189-6). Barron.
Grand et Petit. (FRE., Illus.). 3.50 (ISBN 0-7214-0800-1). Ladybird Bks.
Grater, Michael. Cut & Fold Extraterrestrial Invaders That Fly. 1983. pap. 2.95 (ISBN 0-486-24478-4). Dover.
—Cut & Fold Paper Spaceships. 1981. pap. 2.95 (ISBN 0-486-23978-0). Dover.
—Cut & Make Monster Masks in Full Color. 1978. pap. 4.95 (ISBN 0-486-23576-9). Dover.
Gray, Catherine. One, Two, Three & Four: No More? Moss, Marissa, illus. 32p. (gr. k-3). 1988. 13.95 (ISBN 0-395-48293-3). HM.
Gray, Nigel. The One & Only Robin Hood. Craig, Helen, illus. LC 87-2680. 32p. (ps-3). 1987. 12.95 (ISBN 0-316-32578-3, Joy St Bks). Little.
Greaves, Margaret. The Lucky Coin. Underhill, Liz, illus. LC 89-19718. 12p. 1990. 14.95 (ISBN 1-55670-129-2). Stewart Tabori & Chang.
Greaves, Margaret, retold by. The Magic Flute: The Story of Mozart's Opera. Crespi, Francesca, illus. 32p. (ps-3). 1989. 13.95 (ISBN 0-8050-0887-X). H Holt & Co.
Green, Cecile. Tale of Theodore Bear. LC 68-56812. (Illus.). 32p. (gr. 1-2). 1968. PLB 9.95 (ISBN 0-87783-038-X). Oddo.
Green, Ivah. Splash & Trickle. LC 68-56818. (Illus.). 32p. (gr. 2-3). 1968. PLB 9.95 (ISBN 0-87783-037-1); pap. 3.94 deluxe ed. (ISBN 0-87783-109-2); cassette o.s.i. 7.94x (ISBN 0-87783-226-9). Oddo.
Greenaway, Kate. Kate Greenaway's Mother Goose. LC 87-9214. (Illus.). 12p. (ps up). 1988. 10.95 (ISBN 0-8037-0479-8). Dial Bks Young.
Greene, Carol. Ice Is...Whee! Sharp, Paul, illus. LC 82-19855. 32p. (ps-2). 1983. PLB 11.93 (ISBN 0-516-02037-4); pap. 2.95 (ISBN 0-516-42037-2). Childrens.
—The Pilgrims Are Marching. Dunnington, Tom, illus. LC 88-20219. 32p. (ps-2). 1988. PLB 14.60 (ISBN 0-516-08234-5); pap. 3.95 (ISBN 0-516-48234-3). Childrens.
Greenfield, Eloise. Me & Neesie. Barnett, Moneta, illus. LC 74-23078. 40p. (gr. k-3). 1984. pap. 4.95 (ISBN 0-06-443057-X, Trophy). HarpC Child Bks.
—She Come Bringing Me That Little Baby Girl. Steptoe, John, illus. LC 74-8104. 32p. (gr. k-3). 1990. 13.95 (ISBN 0-397-31586-4, Lipp Jr Bks); PLB 13.89 (ISBN 0-397-32478-2). HarpC Child Bks.
—Under the Sunday Tree. Ferguson, Amos, illus. LC 87-29373. 48p. (gr. 1 up). 1991. pap. 5.50 (ISBN 0-06-443257-2, Trophy). HarpC Child Bks.
Greenleaf, E. Who Wants to Nap? LC 68-56820. (Illus.). 32p. (gr. 2-3). PLB 9.95 (ISBN 0-87783-050-9). Oddo.
Greeson, Janet. The Stingy Baker. LaRochelle, David, illus. 32p. (ps-3). 1989. PLB 12.95 (ISBN 0-87614-378-8). Carolrhoda Bks.
Gregorich, Barbara. Hidden Pictures. Hoffman, Joan, ed. Pape, Richard, illus. 32p. (Orig.). (ps). 1983. wkbk. 1.99 (ISBN 0-938256-50-5). Sch Zone Pub Co.
—Jace, Mace, & the Big Race. Hoffman, Joan, ed. (Illus.). 16p. (Orig.). (gr. k-2). 1985. pap. 1.95 (ISBN 0-88743-018-X, 06018). Sch Zone Pub Co.
—Rhyming Pictures. Hoffman, Joan, ed. Pape, Richard, illus. 32p. (ps). 1983. wkbk. 1.99 (ISBN 0-938256-53-X). Sch Zone Pub Co.
Greta's Grand Prize, Petey's Penpalmanship, Friend's Forever & Patsy's Play. (Illus.). (gr. k-2). 1989. pap. 3.95 ea., 24pgs. ea. Greta's Grand Prize (ISBN 0-87449-731-0). Petey's Penpalmanship (ISBN 0-87449-732-9). Friend's Forever (ISBN 0-87449-733-7). Patsy's Play (ISBN 0-87449-734-5). Modern Pub NYC.
Gretz, Susanna. It's Your Turn, Roger! Gretz, Susanna, illus. LC 84-23879. 32p. (ps-2). 1985. 10.95 (ISBN 0-8037-0198-5). Dial Bks Young.
—Teddy Bears Go Shopping. Gretz, Susanna, illus. LC 85-4494. 32p. (gr. k-3). 1984. 13.95 (ISBN 0-02-737310-X, Four Winds). Macmillan Child Grp.
—Too Dark! Gretz, Susanna, illus. LC 85-12999. 10p. (ps-k). 1986. PLB 2.95 (ISBN 0-02-737410-6, Four Winds). Macmillan Child Grp.
Gretz, Susanna & Sage, Alison. Teddy Bears at the Seaside. Gretz, Susanna, illus. LC 88-11280. 32p. (gr. k-3). 1989. 12.95 (ISBN 0-02-738141-2, Four Winds). Macmillan Child Grp.
Grey, J. The Turtle Who Wanted to Run. LC 68-56813. (Illus.). 32p. (gr. 1-3). 1968. PLB 9.95 (ISBN 0-87783-045-2). Oddo.
Griffith, Linda, illus. Tommy's Toys. 12p. (ps). 1990. pap. 4.95 (ISBN 0-670-82941-2). Viking Child Bks.
—When Jenny Grows Up. 12p. (ps). 1990. pap. 4.95 (ISBN 0-670-82944-7). Viking Child Bks.
—When Ricky Reads. 12p. (ps). 1990. pap. 4.95 (ISBN 0-670-82942-0). Viking Child Bks.
—When Sue Pretends. 12p. (ps). 1990. pap. 4.95 (ISBN 0-670-82943-9). Viking Child Bks.
Grillis, Carla. Animals. (Illus.). (ps). 1988. bds. 5.50 (ISBN 0-86315-072-1, 20232). Gryphon Hse.
Grimes, Nikki. Something on My Mind. Feelings, Tom, illus. LC 77-86266. 32p. (gr. k up). 1986. pap. 4.95 (ISBN 0-8037-0273-6). Dial Bks Young.
Grimm, Jacob & Grimm, Wilhelm K. The Brave Little Tailor. Bell, Anthea, tr. Tharlet, Eve, illus. LC 88-33367. 28p. (ps up). 1989. 14.95 (ISBN 0-88708-091-X). Picture Bk Studio.
—Bremen Town Musicians. Bell, Anthea, tr. Palecek, Josef, illus. LC 88-15179. 32p. (ps up). 1988. 13.95 (ISBN 0-88708-071-5). Picture Bk Studio.
—The Fisherman & His Wife. Bell, Anthea, tr. Marks, Alan, illus. LC 88-15165. 28p. (ps up). 1989. 14.95 (ISBN 0-88708-072-3). Picture Bk Studio.
—The Fisherman & His Wife. Metaxas, Eric, tr. from GER. Bryan, Diana, illus. LC 89-28445. 32p. (ps up). 1990. 14.95 (ISBN 0-88708-122-3, Rabbit Ears). Picture Bk Studio.
—The Goose Girl. Bell, Anthea, tr. Bruntjen, Sabine, illus. LC 87-32109. 32p. (gr. k-3). 1988. 12.95 (ISBN 1-55858-056-5). North-South Bks NYC.
—Hansel & Gretel. Becker, Lois & Stratton, Mark, eds. (Illus.). 26p. (ps). 1987. Packaged with pre-programmed audio cass. tape. 9.95 (ISBN 0-934323-64-X). Alchemy Comms.
—Hansel & Gretel. LC 87-32833. 1988. 14.95 (ISBN 0-88708-068-5). Picture Bk Studio.
—Mother Holly. Watts, Bernadette, illus. & retold by. LC 77-185753. 32p. (gr. k-3). 1988. pap. 3.95 (ISBN 1-55858-057-3). North-South Bks NYC.
—Rapunzel. McKay, Sindy, adapted by. Hicks, Russell, et al, illus. 26p. (ps). 1987. Packaged with pre-programmed audio cass. tape. 9.95 (ISBN 0-934323-67-4). Alchemy Comms.
—The Seven Ravens. Zwerger, Lisbeth, illus. LC 83-61777. 28p. (gr. k up). 1989. 14.95 (ISBN 0-685-24950-6); pap. 5.95 (ISBN 0-685-24951-4). Picture Bk Studio.
—Snow White & the Seven Dwarfs. Iwasaki, Chihiro, illus. LC 85-12158. 40p. (gr. 1 up). 1985. 15.95 (ISBN 0-88708-012-X). Picture Bk Studio.
Grimm, Jacob, adapted by. The Complete Story of Snow White & the Seven Dwarfs: Based on the Walt Disney Motion Picture. Grimm, Wilhelm K. (Illus.). 80p. 1987. 19.95 (ISBN 0-8109-1515-4). Abrams.
Grindley, Sally. Knock, Knock! Who's There? Browne, Anthony, illus. LC 86-112. 32p. (ps-2). 1986. lib. bdg. 8.99 (ISBN 0-394-98400-5); PLB 7.95 (ISBN 0-394-88400-0). Knopf.
Groner, Judye & Wikler, Madeline. Shabbat Shalom. Yaffa, illus. LC 88-83568. 12p. (ps). 1989. bds. 4.95 (ISBN 0-930494-91-1). Kar Ben.
Gullette, Margaret M. The Lost Bellybutton. Udry, Leslie, illus. LC 76-26377. 32p. (Orig.). (ps-2). 1976. pap. 4.95 (ISBN 0-914996-11-8). Lollipop Power.
Gundersheimer, Karen. Happy Winter. Gundersheimer, Karen, illus. LC 81-48650. 40p. (ps-3). 1987. pap. 3.95 (ISBN 0-06-443151-7, Trophy). HarpC Child Bks.
Gunn, Robin J. When I Celebrate His Birthday. Acquistapace, David & Gary, N. C., illus. (ps). 1988. bds. 4.95 (ISBN 1-55513-567-6, Chariot Bks). Cook.
—When I Go to the Park. Acquistapace, David & Gary, N. C., illus. (ps). 1988. bds. 4.95 (ISBN 1-55513-589-7, Chariot Bks). Cook.
—When I Have a Babysitter. Acquistapace, David & Gary, N. C., illus. (ps). 1988. bds. 4.95 (ISBN 1-55513-573-0, Chariot Bks). Cook.
—When I Help My Mommy. Acquistapace, David & Gary, N. C., illus. (ps). 1988. bds. 4.95 (ISBN 1-55513-566-8, Chariot Bks). Cook.
Gurney, Nancy & Gurney, Eric. King, the Mice & the Cheese. Vallier, Jean, illus. LC 89-8463. 72p. (gr. k-3). 1965. 6.95 (ISBN 0-394-80039-7); lib. bdg. 7.99 (ISBN 0-394-90039-1). Random.
Gutelle, Andrew. Ernie & Bert's Different Day: A Story about Opposites & Other Relational Concepts. Ewers, Joseph, illus. LC 87-81930. 32p. (ps-k). 1988. write for info. (ISBN 0-307-13104-1, Pub. by Golden Bks). Western Pub.
—What's a Gonzo? Hunt, Judith, illus. 32p. (ps-2). 1986. pap. 1.95 (ISBN 0-517-56192-1). Crown.
Haas, Dorothy. The Baby Hugs Bear & Baby Tugs Bear Counting Book. Cooke, Tom, illus. 40p. (ps). 1984. 5.95 (ISBN 0-910313-71-7). Parker Bros.
Haas, Irene. The Maggie B. Haas, Irene, illus. LC 74-18183. 32p. (ps-2). 1975. 14.95 (ISBN 0-689-50021-1, M K McElderry). Macmillan Child Grp.
Haddock, Peter. Fairy Tale Shape Board Book: Cinderella. 1988. 2.49 (ISBN 0-671-09409-2). S&S Trade.
—Hansel & Gretel. 1988. 2.49 (ISBN 0-671-09408-4). S&S Trade.
Haddon, Mark. Gilbert's Gobstopper. Haddon, Mark, illus. LC 87-19961. 32p. (ps-3). 1988. 9.95 (ISBN 0-8037-0506-9). Dial Bks Young.
Hader, Bertha. Wee Willie Winkie. 1990. 3.98 (ISBN 0-8317-4270-4). Smithmark.
Hadithi, Mwenye. Crafty Chameleon. Kennaway, Adrienne, illus. 32p. (ps-3). 1987. 12.95 (ISBN 0-316-33723-4). Little.
Hague, Michael. Michael Hague's World of Unicorns. Hague, Michael, illus. LC 86-80453. 12p. (gr. k-3). 1986. 16.95 (ISBN 0-8050-0070-4). H Holt & Co.
Hague, Michael, illus. Magic Moments: A Book of Days. 96p. 1990. 14.95 (ISBN 1-55970-069-6). Arcade Pub Inc.
Haidle, Elizabeth. Elmer the Grump. Thatch, Nancy R., ed. Haidle, Elizabeth, illus. Melton, David, intro. by. LC 89-31872. (Illus.). 26p. (gr. k-5). 1989. lib. bdg. 12.95 (ISBN 0-933849-20-6). Landmark Edns.
Hale, Janet. Fall Think & Do Shape Books. Hale, Janet, illus. 48p. (gr. k-2). 1989. wkbk. 5.95 (ISBN 1-55734-127-3). Tchr Create Mat.
—Spring & Summer Think & Do Shape Books. Hale, Janet, illus. 48p. (gr. k-2). 1989. wkbk. 5.95 (ISBN 1-55734-129-X). Tchr Create Mat.
—Winter Think & Do Shape Books. Hale, Janet, illus. 48p. (gr. k-2). 1989. wkbk. 5.95 (ISBN 1-55734-128-1). Tchr Create Mat.
Hale, Sarah J. Mary Had a Little Lamb. DePaola, Tomie, illus. (ps-2). 1989. bk. & cassette 19.95 (ISBN 0-87499-125-0); pap. 12.95 bk. & cassette (ISBN 0-87499-124-2); pap. 27.95 4 cassettes & guide (ISBN 0-87499-126-9). Live Oak Media.
Haley, Gail E. A Story, a Story. Haley, Gail E., illus. LC 87-17412. 36p. (ps-3). 1988. pap. 4.95 (ISBN 0-689-71201-4, Aladdin). Macmillan Child Grp.
Hall, Katy & Eisenberg, Lisa. Buggy Riddles. Taback, Simms, illus. (gr. 2-5). 1989. bk. & cassette 19.95 (ISBN 0-87499-118-8); bk. & cassette 12.95 (ISBN 0-87499-119-6); 4 cassettes & guide 27.95 (ISBN 0-87499-120-X). Live Oak Media.
Hall, Susan T. Noah's Ark. Hall, Susan T., illus. 12p. (ps). Date not set. pap. text ed. 5.95 (ISBN 0-927106-03-5). Prod Concept.
—Perfect Pals. Hall, Susan T., illus. 12p. (ps). Date not set. pap. text ed. 5.95 (ISBN 0-927106-00-0). Prod Concept.
—So Sleepy. Hall, Susan T., illus. 12p. (ps). Date not set. pap. text ed. 5.95 (ISBN 0-927106-01-9). Prod Concept.
—So Sleepy Fuzzy Book. 10p. (ps). 1989. pap. 6.95 (ISBN 1-55513-280-4, Chariot Bks). Cook.
Haller, Danita R. Not Just Any Ring. Ray, Deborah K., illus. LC 81-14242. 48p. (gr. 1-5). 1982. Knopf.
Hallinan, P. K. We're Very Good Friends, My Aunt & I. Hallinan, P. K., illus. LC 89-35767. 32p. (ps-3). 1989. PLB 13.27 (ISBN 0-516-03655-6). Childrens.
—We're Very Good Friends, My Sister & I. Hallinan, P. K., illus. LC 89-35766. 32p. (ps-3). 1989. PLB 13.27 (ISBN 0-516-03656-4). Childrens.
Hallinan, Patrick. We're Very Good Friends, My Grandma & I. Hallinan, Patrick, illus. 24p. (ps-k). 1989. pap. 3.95 (ISBN 0-8249-8344-0). Ideals.
—We're Very Good Friends, My Grandpa & I. Hallinan, Patrick, illus. 24p. (ps-k). 1989. pap. 3.95 (ISBN 0-8249-8345-9). Ideals.
Halloween Night. 1989. pap. 5.95 (ISBN 0-553-45909-0). Bantam.
Halverson, Sandy. Book of Mormon Activity Book: Creative Scripture Learning Experiences for Children 4-12. Halverson, Sandy, illus. 80p. (gr. 3-8). 1982. pap. 9.95 (ISBN 0-88290-188-5, 4521). Horizon Utah.
Hamilton, Virginia. Dustland. LC 79-19003. 192p. (gr. 7 up). 1980. 13.00 (ISBN 0-688-80228-1); PLB 12.88 (ISBN 0-688-84228-3). Greenwillow.
Hamilton-Merritt, Jane. Our New Baby. Hamilton-Merritt, Jane, illus. 32p. (ps-k). 1982. 4.80 (ISBN 0-671-44416-6, Little Simon). S&S Trade.
Hamsa, Bobbie. Lucio el Sucio: (Dirty Larry) Sharp, Paul, illus. LC 83-10079. (SPA.). 32p. (ps-2). 1989. PLB 11.93 (ISBN 0-516-32040-8); pap. 2.95 (ISBN 0-516-52040-7). Childrens.
—Polly Wants a Cracker. Warshaw, Jerry, illus. LC 85-30000. 32p. (ps-2). 1986. PLB 11.93 (ISBN 0-516-02071-4); pap. 2.95 (ISBN 0-516-42071-2). Childrens.
Handford, Martin. The Great Waldo Search. Handford, Martin, illus. (ps up). 1989. 12.95 (ISBN 0-316-34282-3). Little.
—Where's Waldo? (ps up). 1987. 12.95 (ISBN 0-316-34293-9). Little.
Handy, Libby. Boss for a Week. 32p. (gr. k-3). Big Book. 19.50 (ISBN 0-590-36772-2); pap. 1.95 (ISBN 0-590-00351-8). Scholastic Inc.
Hansen, Kathleen. A New Sibling. 2nd ed. Silverthorn, Tina, illus. 16p. (ps). 1989. color book 1.95x (ISBN 0-685-29408-0). Time Grow Co.
Hansen, Rosanna. Horses & Ponies. Barrett, Peter, illus. LC 87-81777. 24p. (Orig.). (ps-3). 1988. pap. write for info. (ISBN 0-307-11741-3). Western Pub.
Hanson, Joan. More Similes. LC 78-70461. (Illus.). 32p. (ps-3). 1979. PLB 4.95 (ISBN 0-8225-1112-6). Lerner Pubns.
—More Sound Words. LC 78-70462. (Illus.). 32p. (ps-3). 1979. PLB 4.95 (ISBN 0-8225-1113-4). Lerner Pubns.
—Possessives: Monkey's Banana...Monkeys' Bananas, Thief's Mask...Thieves' Masks, & Other Words That Show Ownership. Hanson, Joan, photos by. LC 79-83842. (Illus.). 32p. (ps-3). 1979. PLB 4.95 (ISBN 0-8225-1115-0). Lerner Pubns.
Happy Bear Storytime. 1989. pap. 0.66 (ISBN 0-394-82362-1). Random.

Happy Bears ABC. 1989. pap. 0.66 (ISBN 0-394-82298-6). Random.
Happy Bears Number. 1989. pap. 0.66 (ISBN 0-394-82294-3). Random.
Happy Days. (Illus.). 6p. (ps-2). 1987. bds. 3.95 (ISBN 0-87449-570-9). Modern Pub NYC.
Happy Snowman. 12p. (ps-3). 1988. bds. 2.95 (ISBN 0-02-688791-6). Checkerboard Pr.
Harada, Joyce. It's the 0-1-2-3 Book. Harada, Joyce, illus. 32p. (ps-3). 1985. pap. 7.95 (ISBN 0-89346-252-7). Heian Intl.
Hargreaves, Roger. Mr. Muddle. Hargreaves, Roger, illus. 32p. (ps-k). 1981. pap. 1.25 (ISBN 0-8431-0820-7). Price Stern.
—Mr. Rush. (Illus.). 32p. (ps-3). 1982. pap. 1.25 (ISBN 0-8431-0880-0). Price Stern.
—Mr. Rush. 32p. (ps up). 1978. PLB 8.70s.p. (ISBN 0-87191-912-5); PLB 12.45 (ISBN 0-685-09343-3). Creative Ed.
—Mr. Silly. 32p. (ps up). 1972. PLB 8.70s.p. (ISBN 0-87191-767-X); PLB 12.45 (ISBN 0-685-09344-1). Creative Ed.
—Mr. Skinny. 32p. (ps up). 1978. PLB 8.70s.p. (ISBN 0-87191-823-4); PLB 12.45 (ISBN 0-685-09345-X). Creative Ed.
—Mr. Slow. 32p. (ps up). 1978. PLB 8.70s.p. (ISBN 0-87191-913-3); PLB 12.45 (ISBN 0-685-09347-6). Creative Ed.
—Mr. Small. 32p. (ps up). 1972. PLB 8.70s.p. (ISBN 0-87191-824-2); PLB 12.45 (ISBN 0-685-09348-4). Creative Ed.
—Mr. Sneeze. 32p. (ps up). 1971. PLB 8.70s.p. (ISBN 0-87191-914-1); PLB 12.45 (ISBN 0-685-09350-6). Creative Ed.
—Mr. Snow. 32p. (ps up). 1971. PLB 8.70s.p. (ISBN 0-87191-915-X); PLB 12.45 (ISBN 0-685-09351-4). Creative Ed.
Harness, Cheryl, illus. The Night-Light Mother Goose: Blue Ladder Books for Babies Through 16 Months. 24p. (ps). 1988. 5.95 (ISBN 0-394-89400-6, Random Juv). Random.
Harriman, Marinell & Harriman, Robert. A Myriad of Minstrels. Harriman, Marinell & Harriman, Robert, illus. 32p. (Orig.). (gr. 5-7). pap. 3.50 (ISBN 0-940920-00-X). Drollery Pr.
Harris, Audrey. Why Did He Die? Dalke, Susan, illus. LC 65-22217. (gr. k-5). 1965. PLB 5.95 (ISBN 0-8225-0256-9). Lerner Pubns.
Harris, Jack C. Big Boats, Little Boats. (Illus.). 24p. (ps). 1990. pap. write for info. (ISBN 0-307-11667-0, Pub. by Golden Bks). Western Pub.
—My First Book of Fire Trucks. (Illus.). 24p. (ps). 1990. pap. write for info. (ISBN 0-307-11666-2, Pub. by Golden Bks). Western Pub.
Harris, Jack C. & Kraft, Jim. Garfield's Longest Catnap. Davis, Jim, created by. (ps). 1989. pap. write for info. (ISBN 0-307-11727-8, Pub. by Golden Bks). Western Pub.
Harrison, David L. Little Boy Soup. Goffe, Toni, illus. (ps-2). 1990. 3.95 (ISBN 0-7214-5267-1). Ladybird Bks.
Harshman, Terry W. Porcupine's Pajama Party. Cushman, Doug, illus. LC 87-45681. 64p. (gr. k-3). 1988. 11.95 (ISBN 0-06-022248-4); PLB 11.89 (ISBN 0-06-022249-2). HarpC Child Bks.
Hart, Marj. Fold-&-Cut Stories & Fingerplays. (ps-3). 1987. pap. 8.95 (ISBN 0-8224-3150-5). Fearon Teach Aids.
Harte, Cheryl, illus. Bunny Rattle. 12p. (ps). 1989. sponge-filled cloth 4.95 (ISBN 0-394-89956-3). Random.
—Ducky Squeak. 12p. (ps). 1989. sponge-filled cloth 4.95 (ISBN 0-394-89955-5). Random.
—My Chalkboard Book: Green Ladder Books for Kids Through 6 Years. 14p. (ps-1). 1988. bds. 6.95 (ISBN 0-394-89401-4, Random Juv). Random.
Hartelius, Margaret A., illus. Over in the Meadow. 1987. pap. 5.95 incl. audiocassette (ISBN 0-553-45900-7). Bantam.
—The Twelve Days of Christmas. 1988. pap. 5.95 incl. audiocassette (ISBN 0-553-45906-6). Bantam.
Hartley, Al. Family Fun. Hartley, Al, illus. (gr. 1). 1988. pap. text ed. 0.99 (ISBN 1-55748-004-4). Barbour & Co.
—Flying Colors. Hartley, Al, illus. 32p. (gr. 1). 1988. pap. text ed. 0.99 (ISBN 1-55748-000-1). Barbour & Co.
—Fun in the Car. Hartley, Al, illus. 32p. (gr. 1). 1988. pap. text ed. 0.99 (ISBN 1-55748-001-X). Barbour & Co.
—Happy Home. Hartley, Al, illus. (gr. 1). 1988. pap. text ed. 0.99 (ISBN 1-55748-005-2). Barbour & Co.
—School Fun. Hartley, Al, illus. (gr. 1). 1988. pap. text ed. 0.99 (ISBN 1-55748-003-6). Barbour & Co.
Hartley, David. Wacky Fill-Ins, No. 1. 1989. pap. 1.95 (ISBN 0-590-42564-1). Scholastic Inc.
Hartley, David, ed. Freaky Fillins, No. 3. 48p. (Orig.). (gr. 3-5). 1980. pap. 1.50 (ISBN 0-937518-02-6). Hartley Hse.
Hartley, Deborah. Up North in Winter. Dabcovich, Lydia, illus. 32p. (ps-3). 1986. 11.95 (ISBN 0-525-44268-5, DCB). Dutton Child Bks.
Hartley, Melissa, ed. Freaky Fillins, No. 4. 48p. (Orig.). (gr. 3-5). 1980. pap. 1.50 (ISBN 0-937518-03-4). Hartley Hse.
Hartman, Gail. For Strawberry Jam or Fireflies. Weiss, Ellen, illus. LC 88-30509. 32p. (ps). 1989. 12.95 (ISBN 0-02-742990-3, Bradbury Pr). Macmillan Child Grp.
Hartsell, Lynn. Pitch in & Play Fair. Ewers, Joe & Sustendal, Pat, illus. 40p. (ps-3). write for info (ISBN 0-910313-75-X). Parker Bros.
Harwood, Pearl A. Mr. Bumba Has a Party. Folger, Joseph, illus. LC 64-19775. 32p. (gr. k-3). 1964. PLB 4.95 (ISBN 0-8225-0106-6). Lerner Pubns.
—Mr. Bumba Keeps House. Folger, Joseph, illus. LC 64-19772. 32p. (gr. k-3). 1964. PLB 4.95 (ISBN 0-8225-0103-1). Lerner Pubns.
—Mr. Bumba Plants a Garden. Folger, Joseph, illus. LC 64-19771. 32p. (gr. k-3). 1964. PLB 4.95 (ISBN 0-8225-0102-3). Lerner Pubns.
—Mr. Bumba Rides a Bicycle. Folger, Joseph, illus. LC 65-27997. 32p. (gr. k-3). 1966. PLB 4.95 (ISBN 0-8225-0109-0). Lerner Pubns.
—Mr. Bumba's Four-Legged Company. Folger, Joseph, illus. LC 65-27996. 32p. (gr. k-3). 1966. PLB 4.95 (ISBN 0-8225-0108-2). Lerner Pubns.
—Mr. Bumba's New Home. Folger, Joseph, illus. LC 64-19775. 32p. (gr. k-3). 1964. PLB 4.95 (ISBN 0-8225-0101-5). Lerner Pubns.
—Mr. Bumba's New Job. Folger, Joseph, illus. LC 64-19774. 32p. (gr. k-3). 1964. PLB 4.95 (ISBN 0-8225-0105-8). Lerner Pubns.
—Mr. Bumba's Tuesday Club. Folger, Joseph, illus. LC 65-27998. 32p. (gr. k-3). 1966. PLB 4.95 (ISBN 0-8225-0110-4). Lerner Pubns.
Haskins, Jim. Count Your Way Through China. Skoro, Martin, illus. 24p. (gr. 1-4). 1988. pap. 4.95 (ISBN 0-87614-486-5, First Ave Edns). Lerner Pubns.
—Count Your Way Through Japan. (Illus.). 24p. (gr. 1-4). 1987. lib. bdg. 11.95 (ISBN 0-87614-301-X); pap. 4.95 (ISBN 0-87614-485-7). Carolrhoda Bks.
—Count Your Way Through Russia. (Illus.). 24p. (gr. 1-4). 1987. lib. bdg. 11.95 (ISBN 0-87614-303-6); pap. 4.95 (ISBN 0-87614-488-1). Carolrhoda Bks.
Haus, Felice. Big Bird Flies Alone. Fritz, Ron, illus. LC 88-62523. 32p. (Orig.). (ps-3). 1989. pap. 1.25 (ISBN 0-394-83932-3). Random.
—Happy Birthday, Cookie Monster! A Step One Book. Nicklaus, Carol, illus. LC 85-25639. 32p. (ps-1). 1986. lib. bdg. 6.99 (ISBN 0-394-98182-0); pap. 2.95 (ISBN 0-394-88182-6). Random.
Hautzig, Deborah. Big Bird at the Beach. Nicklaus, Carol, illus. LC 89-61613. 32p. (Orig.). (ps-3). 1990. pap. 1.25 (ISBN 0-679-80159-6). McKay.
—Get Well, Granny Bird. Mathieu, Joe, illus. LC 88-18446. 40p. (ps-3). 1989. 4.95 (ISBN 0-394-82247-1); PLB 6.99 (ISBN 0-394-92247-6). Random.
—Happy Mother's Day. Chartier, Normand, illus. LC 88-14002. 32p. (Orig.). (ps-1). 1989. PLB 6.99 (ISBN 0-394-92204-2); pap. 2.95 (ISBN 0-394-82204-8). Random.
—It's a Secret! Leigh, Tom, illus. LC 87-20542. 40p. (ps-3). 1988. 4.95 (ISBN 0-394-89672-6, Random Juv); lib. bdg. 6.99 (ISBN 0-394-99672-0). Random.
—It's Easy! Mathieu, Joe, illus. LC 88-6441. 40p. (ps-3). 1988. 4.95 (ISBN 0-394-81376-6, Random Juv); (Random Juv). Random.
—Little Witch Book & Doll Package. Brown, Marc, illus. LC 87-63196. 24p. (ps-1). 1988. Book & doll pkg. 4.95 (ISBN 0-394-89813-3, Random Juv). Random.
—A Visit to the Sesame Street Library. Mathieu, Joe, illus. LC 85-18312. 32p. (ps-1). 1986. 2.25 (ISBN 0-394-87744-6); lib. bdg. 5.99 (ISBN 0-394-97744-0). Random.
Hautzig, Esther. Make It Special: Cards, Decorations, & Party Favors for Holiday & Other Celebrations. Weston, Martha, illus. LC 86-8616. 96p. (gr. 3-7). 1986. 12.95 (ISBN 0-02-743370-6, Mcmillan Child Bk). Macmillan Child Grp.
Havel, Jennifer. The Wacky Rulebook. Ewers, Joe, illus. 40p. (ps-3). write for info (ISBN 0-910313-77-6). Parker Bros.
Hawk, Steve. Skateboard Action. 1988. pap. 2.25 (ISBN 0-89954-859-8). Antioch Pub Co.
Hawkins, Colin. Mr. Wolf's Birthday Surprise. (Illus.). 32p. (ps-1). 1989. 13.95 (ISBN 0-434-94247-2, Pub. by W Heinemann Ltd). Trafalgar Sq.
Hawkins, Colin & Hawkins, Jacqui. The Elephant. Hawkins, Colin & Hawkins, Jacqui, illus. LC 85-40639. 12p. (ps-1). 1986. pap. 2.95 (ISBN 0-670-80314-6). Viking Child Bks.
—The House That Jack Built. (Illus.). 24p. (ps-1). 1990. 12.95 (ISBN 0-399-21941-2, Putnam). Putnam Pub Group.
—Max & the Magic Word. Hawkins, Colin & Hawkins, Jacqui, illus. 24p. (ps-k). 1986. pap. 8.95 (ISBN 0-670-80853-9). Viking Child Bks.
—Noah Built an Ark One Day. Hawkins, Colin, illus. 24p. (ps-1). 1989. 12.95 (ISBN 0-399-21626-X, Putnam). Putnam Pub Group.
—One Finger, One Thumb. LC 85-48299. (Illus.). (ps). 1986. pap. 2.95 (ISBN 0-316-35101-6, Joy St Bks). Little.
—Oops-a-Daisy. LC 85-48302. (Illus.). 14p. (ps). 1986. pap. 2.95 (ISBN 0-316-35102-4, Joy St Bks). Little.
—Where's Bear? LC 85-48301. (Illus.). 14p. (ps). 1986. pap. 2.95 (ISBN 0-316-35103-2, Joy St Bks). Little.
—Zug the Bug: A Flip-the-Page Rhyming Book. Hawkins, Colin, illus. 22p. (ps-3). 1988. 9.95 (ISBN 0-399-21556-5, Putnam). Putnam Pub Group.
Hawkins, Colin & Hawkins, Jacqui, eds. I Know an Old Lady Who Swallowed a Fly. Hawkins, Colin & Hawkins, Jacqui, illus. 24p. (ps-1). 1987. 11.95 (ISBN 0-399-21484-4, Putnam). Putnam Pub Group.
Hawthorne, Nathaniel & Andersen, Hans Christian. King Midas & The Emperor's New Clothes. (Illus.). 48p. (ps-3). 1985. 5.95 (ISBN 0-88110-253-9). EDC.
Hayden, Lea. Outside - Inside. Ewers, Joe, illus. 9p. 1990. bds. 4.95 (ISBN 0-679-80069-7). Random.
—Sunny Day - Rainy Day. Ewers, Joe, illus. 9p. (ps). 1990. bds. 4.95 (ISBN 0-679-80068-9). Random.
Hayes, Geoffrey. Patrick & His Grandpa. Hayes, Geoffrey, illus. LC 85-62403. 14p. (ps). 1986. bds. 3.95 (ISBN 0-394-87287-8). Random.
—Patrick & Ted at the Beach. Hayes, Geoffrey, illus. LC 86-43069. 32p. (ps-1). 1987. lib. bdg. 5.99 (ISBN 0-394-97289-9, Random Juv); pap. 1.95 (ISBN 0-394-87289-4). Random.
—Patrick & Ted Ride the Train: (Just Right for 4's & 5's) Hayes, Geoffrey, illus. LC 88-3084. 32p. (Orig.). (ps-k). 1988. (Random Juv); (Random Juv). Random.
—Patrick Buys a Coat. Hayes, Geoffrey, illus. LC 84-1659. 40p. (ps-1). 1985. Knopf.
—Patrick Buys a Coat. Hayes, Geoffrey, illus. LC 84-1659. 32p. (ps-1). 1989. pap. 2.95 (ISBN 0-685-32905-4). McKay.
—Patrick Eats His Dinner. Hayes, Geoffrey, illus. LC 84-5924. 40p. (ps-1). 1985. Knopf.
—Patrick Eats His Dinner. Hayes, Geoffrey, illus. LC 84-5924. 32p. (ps-1). 1989. pap. 2.95 (ISBN 0-685-32907-0). McKay.
—Patrick Goes to Bed. Hayes, Geoffrey, illus. LC 84-6099. 40p. (ps-1). 1985. 4.95 (ISBN 0-394-87264-9); lib. bdg. 5.99 (ISBN 0-394-97264-3). Knopf.
—Patrick Goes to Bed. Hayes, Geoffrey, illus. LC 84-6099. 32p. (ps-1). 1989. pap. 2.95 (ISBN 0-685-32906-2). McKay.
—Patrick Takes a Bath. Hayes, Geoffrey, illus. LC 84-1658. 32p. (ps-1). 1989. pap. 2.95 (ISBN 0-685-32908-9). McKay.
Hayes, Sarah. Bad Egg: The True Story of Humpty Dumpty. Voake, Charlotte, illus. 32p. (ps-3). 1987. 12.95 (ISBN 0-316-35184-9, Joy St Bks). Little.
—This Is the Bear. Craig, Helen, illus. LC 85-45752. 32p. (ps-2). 1986. PLB 11.89 (ISBN 0-397-32171-6, Lipp Jr Bks). HarpC Child Bks.
Hayward, Linda. Baby Moses. LC 88-25917. (Illus.). 32p. (Orig.). (ps-1). 1989. PLB 6.99 (ISBN 0-394-99410-8); pap. 2.95 (ISBN 0-394-89410-3). Random.
—Elmo Goes to Day Camp. Nicklaus, Carol, illus. LC 89-61614. 32p. (Orig.). 1990. pap. 1.25 (ISBN 0-679-80158-8). McKay.
—Gingham Collection: Goldilocks & the Three Little Bears, Little Red Riding Hood & The Three Little Pigs, 3 mini-bks. Linden, Madelaine G., illus. (Orig.). (ps-1). 1988. Set. 5.95 (ISBN 0-394-89637-8, Random Juv). Random.
—Grover's Summer Vacation. Fritz, Ron, illus. LC 88-62524. 32p. (Orig.). (ps-3). 1989. pap. 1.25 (ISBN 0-394-83969-2). Random.
—Hello, House! Munsinger, Lynn, illus. LC 86-22080. 32p. (Orig.). (ps-1). 1988. lib. bdg. 6.99 (ISBN 0-394-98864-7, Random Juv); pap. 2.95 (ISBN 0-394-88864-2). Random.
—Mine! A Sesame Street Book about Sharing: (Just Right for 2's & 3's) Gorbaty, Norman, illus. LC 87-42810. 24p. (ps). 1988. 4.95 (ISBN 0-394-89599-1, Random Juv). Random.
—Noah's Ark. Wright, Freire, illus. LC 86-17790. 32p. (ps-1). 1987. lib. bdg. 6.99 (ISBN 0-394-98716-0, Random Juv); pap. 2.95 (ISBN 0-394-88716-6). Random.
—Sounds & Letters. Nicklaus, Carol, illus. 96p. (ps-2). 1986. pap. 5.95 (ISBN 0-448-18991-7, G&D). Putnam Pub Group.
Hayward, Linda & Leigh, Tom. Early Bird on Sesame Street. 24p. (ps-3). 1988. pap. write for info. (ISBN 0-307-13815-1, 13815, Pub. by Golden Bks). Western Pub.
Haywood, Carolyn. B Is for Betsy. 144p. (gr. 1 up). 1987. 12.95 (ISBN 0-318-37339-4, HJ); pap. 4.95 (ISBN 0-318-37340-8, HJ). HarBraceJ.
—Primrose Day. Haywood, Carolyn, illus. LC 86-4620. 216p. (gr. k-3). 1986. pap. 4.95 (ISBN 0-15-263510-6, VoyB). HarBraceJ.
—Two & Two Are Four. Haywood, Carolyn, illus. LC 86-4619. 180p. (gr. k-3). 1986. pap. 4.95 (ISBN 0-15-291771-3, VoyB). HarBraceJ.
Hazen, Barbara S. Fang. Morrill, Leslie, illus. LC 86-28697. 32p. (ps-2). 1987. 12.95 (ISBN 0-689-31307-1, Atheneum Child Bk). Macmillan Child Grp.
—The Gorilla Did It. LC 87-23589. (Illus.). 32p. (ps-1). 1988. pap. 3.95 (ISBN 0-689-71214-6, Aladdin). Macmillan Child Grp.
Hearn, Michael P. The Porcelain Cat. Dillon, Leo & Dillon, Diane, illus. 32p. (gr. 1-3). 1987. 12.95 (ISBN 0-316-35330-2). Little.
Heesakkers, Wim. My Little Rooster Woodbook. (ps). 1985. 9.95 (ISBN 0-8120-5628-0). Barron.
Hefter, Richard. Yes & No: A Book of Opposites. 1980. text ed. 4.50 (ISBN 0-07-027809-1). McGraw.
Heine, Helme. The Most Wonderful Egg in the World. Heine, Helme, illus. LC 82-22251. 32p. (gr. k-3). 1987. pap. 3.95 (ISBN 0-689-71117-4, Aladdin). Macmillan Child Grp.
—Prince Bear. Heine, Helme, illus. LC 88-32576. 32p. (ps-3). 1989. 13.95 (ISBN 0-689-50484-5, M K McElderry). Macmillan Child Grp.
Hellard, Susan. Billy Goats Gruff: A Lift-the-Flap Book. Hellard, Susan, illus. 22p. (ps). 1986. 10.95 (ISBN 0-399-21291-4, Putnam). Putnam Pub Group.

—This Little Piggy. Hellard, Suzy, illus. 24p. (ps-3). 1989. 11.95 (ISBN 0-399-21625-1, Putnam). Putnam Pub Group.
—Time to Get Up. (Illus.). 24p. (ps-k). 1990. 12.95 (ISBN 0-399-21948-X, Putnam). Putnam Pub Group.
Hellard, Susan, adapted by. & illus. Froggie Goes A-Courting. 24p. (ps-3). 1988. 11.95 (ISBN 0-399-21508-5, Putnam). Putnam Pub Group.
Hellard, Susan, retold by. & illus. The Ugly Duckling. (gr. k-3). 1987. 10.95 (ISBN 0-399-21410-0, Putnam). Putnam Pub Group.
Helldorfer, M. C. Daniel's Gift. Downing, Julie, illus. LC 87-5160. 32p. (ps-3). 1987. 13.95 (ISBN 0-02-743511-3, Bradbury Pr). Macmillan Child Grp.
Hellen, Nancy. Old MacDonald Had a Farm. LC 89-25587. (Illus.). 18p. (ps-1). 1990. 13.95 (ISBN 0-531-05872-7). Orchard Bks Watts.
Heller, Ruth. How to Hide a Crocodile. Heller, Ruth, illus. 32p. (ps-2). 1986. 4.95 (ISBN 0-448-19028-1, G&D). Putnam Pub Group.
—How to Hide a Gray Tree Frog. Heller, Ruth, illus. 32p. (ps-2). 1986. 4.95 (ISBN 0-448-19026-5, G&D). Putnam Pub Group.
—How to Hide a Whippoorwill. Heller, Ruth, illus. 32p. (ps-2). 1986. 4.95 (ISBN 0-448-19027-3, G&D). Putnam Pub Group.
Hello God. 8p. (ps). 1985. bds. 2.95 (ISBN 0-85648-863-1). Lion USA.
Hellsing, Lennart. Cantankerous Crow. Stroyer, Paul, illus. (gr. k-3). 1962. 9.95 (ISBN 0-8392-3002-8). Astor-Honor.
Helstrom, David C. My Tacoma Dome. Hamer, Bonnie, illus. 24p. (Orig.). (gr. 1-4). 1983. pap. 2.75 (ISBN 0-933992-29-7). Coffee Break.
—Visiting Mt. Rainier. Harder, Arvid & Hamer, Bonnie, illus. 28p. (Orig.). (gr. 1-4). 1984. pap. 2.75 (ISBN 0-933992-37-8). Coffee Break.
Henderson, Kathy. Don't Interrupt. Hellard, Sue, illus. (gr. 1-3). 1988. 8.95 (ISBN 0-8120-5785-6). Barron.
—Sam & the Big Machines. (Illus.). (ps-1). 1987. 10.95 (ISBN 0-233-97802-X). Andre Deutsch.
Henkes, Kevin. Bailey Goes Camping. (Illus.). 24p. (ps-1). 1989. pap. 3.95 (ISBN 0-14-050979-8, Puffin). Puffin Bks.
—Sheila Rae, the Brave. LC 87-62370. (ps-3). 1988. pap. 3.95 (ISBN 0-14-050897-X, Puffin). Puffin Bks.
—A Weekend with Wendell. (ps-3). 1987. pap. 3.95 (ISBN 0-14-050728-0, Puffin). Puffin Bks.
Hennessy, B. G. The Dinosaur Who Lived in My Backyard. Davis, Susan, illus. LC 87-19867. 32p. (ps-1). 1988. pap. 12.95 (ISBN 0-670-81685-X). Viking Child Bks.
Henny Penny. (Illus.). 24p. (ps-k). 1988. 1.29 (ISBN 0-02-898133-2). Checkerboard Pr.
Henry, Gilson. Animal Squares: An Animal Picture & Rhyme Book for Imaginative Children. Hansen, Ronnie, ed. & illus. LC 87-62123. 24p. (ps-4). 1987. pap. 3.95 (ISBN 0-943925-01-0). Purple Turtle Bks.
—How the Tooth Fairy Got Her Job. Eide, Joyce, illus. LC 87-62126. 24p. (ps-5). pap. 3.95 (ISBN 0-943925-03-7). Purple Turtle Bks.
Here Comes Tootle. 1990. pap. write for info. (ISBN 0-307-06110-8, Golden Pr). Western Pub.
Herman, Gail. The Haunted House: Book & Puzzle Set. Nicklaus, Carol, illus. 24p. (ps-1). 1989. 5.95 (ISBN 0-394-82717-1). Random.
Hersom, Kathleen & Hersom, Donald. The Copycat. Stock, Catherine, illus. LC 88-34166. 32p. (ps-2). 1989. 12.95 (ISBN 0-689-31448-5, Atheneum Child Bk). Macmillan Child Grp.
Hest, Amy. The Crack of Dawn Walkers. Schwartz, Amy, illus. LC 83-19597. 32p. (ps-2). 1984. 11.95 (ISBN 0-02-743710-8, Mcmillan Child Bk). Macmillan Child Grp.
—The Midnight Eaters. Gundersheimer, Karen, illus. LC 88-24381. 32p. (gr. k-3). 1989. 12.95 (ISBN 0-02-743630-6, Four Winds). Macmillan Child Grp.
Heuck, Sigrid. Who Stole the Apples? Heuck, Sigrid, illus. LC 86-2977. 32p. (ps-1). 1986. 8.95 (ISBN 0-394-88371-3). Knopf.
Heuninck, Ronald. A New Day. (Illus.). (ps). 1988. bds. 5.50 (ISBN 0-685-25277-9, 20233). Gryphon Hse.
Hickman, Martha W. Lost & Found. Boddy, Joe, illus. 32p. (ps-3). 1987. 1.00 (ISBN 0-687-22777-1). Abingdon.
—Lost & Found. Boddy, Joe, illus. 32p. (ps-3). 1987. 1.00 (ISBN 0-687-22777-1). Abingdon.
Hide-&-Seek Duck. (ps-k). Date not set. write for info. (ISBN 0-307-12235-2, Golden Pr). Western Pub.
Highlights Editors. Hidden Pictures & Other Challengers. (Illus.). 32p. (Orig.). (gr. 1-6). 1981. pap. 2.95 (ISBN 0-87534-227-2). Highlights.
—Hidden Pictures & Other Fun. (Illus.). 32p. (Orig.). (gr. 1-6). 1981. pap. 2.95 (ISBN 0-87534-178-0). Highlights.
—Hidden Pictures & Other Puzzlers. (Illus.). 32p. (Orig.). (gr. 1-6). 1981. pap. 2.95 (ISBN 0-87534-180-2). Highlights.
—Hidden Pictures with Picture Clues & Other Games. (Illus.). 32p. (Orig.). (gr. 1-6). 1981. pap. 2.95 (ISBN 0-87534-226-4). Highlights.
Hilary Hippo, Movie Star. 24p. (ps-1). 1988. 5.95 (ISBN 0-8431-4729-6). Price Stern.
Hill, Eric. Here's Spot! Hill, Eric, illus. (ps-2). 1984. 19.95 (ISBN 0-399-21167-5, Putnam). Putnam Pub Group.
—Spot Counts from One to Ten. Hill, Eric, illus. 14p. (ps-k). 1989. bds. 3.95 (ISBN 0-399-21672-3, Putnam). Putnam Pub Group.
—Spot Goes to the Circus. Hill, Eric, illus. LC 85-24471. 22p. (ps). 1986. 10.95 (ISBN 0-399-21317-1, Putnam). Putnam Pub Group.
—Spot Learns to Count. Hill, Eric, illus. (ps-2). 1983. pap. 1.95 (ISBN 0-399-20985-9, Putnam). Putnam Pub Group.
—Spot Looks at Colors. Hill, Eric, illus. 14p. (ps-k). 1986. 3.75 (ISBN 0-399-21349-X, Putnam). Putnam Pub Group.
—Spot Looks at Opposites. Hill, Eric, illus. 14p. (ps-k). 1989. bds. 3.75 (ISBN 0-399-21681-2, Putnam). Putnam Pub Group.
—Spot Looks at Shapes. Hill, Eric, illus. 14p. (ps-1). 1986. 3.50 (ISBN 0-399-21350-3, Putnam). Putnam Pub Group.
—Spot Looks at the Weather. Hill, Eric, illus. 14p. (ps-k). 1989. bds. 3.75 (ISBN 0-399-21673-1, Putnam). Putnam Pub Group.
—Spot Tells the Time. Hill, Eric, illus. (ps-2). 1983. pap. 1.95 (ISBN 0-399-20986-7, Putnam). Putnam Pub Group.
—Spot Va a la Granja. (SPA., Illus.). 22p. (ps-1). 1987. 11.95 (ISBN 0-399-21463-1, Putnam). Putnam Pub Group.
—Spot Va al Circo (Spot Goes to the Circus) Hill, Eric, illus. (SPA.). 22p. (ps). 1986. 11.95 (ISBN 0-399-21318-X, Putnam). Putnam Pub Group.
—Spot's Alphabet. Hill, Eric, illus. (ps-2). 1983. pap. 1.95 (ISBN 0-399-20984-0, Putnam). Putnam Pub Group.
—Spot's Big Book of Words - El Libro Grande de las Palabras de Spot. Hill, Eric, illus. (SPA & ENG.). 32p. (ps-1). 1989. 10.95 (ISBN 0-399-21689-8, Putnam). Putnam Pub Group.
—Spot's Busy Year. Hill, Eric, illus. (ps-2). 1983. pap. 1.95 (ISBN 0-399-20987-5, Putnam). Putnam Pub Group.
—Spot's Doghouse. Hill, Eric, illus. (ps-1). 1986. pap. 15.95 (ISBN 0-399-21366-X, Putnam). Putnam Pub Group.
—Spot's First Christmas. Hill, Eric, illus. LC 82-23073. (ps-2). 1983. 10.95 (ISBN 0-399-20963-8, Putnam). Putnam Pub Group.
—Spot's First Words. Hill, Eric, illus. 14p. 1986. 3.75 (ISBN 0-399-21348-1, Putnam). Putnam Pub Group.
—Where's Spot? (Illus.). 22p. (ps-1). 1980. 10.95 (ISBN 0-399-20758-9, Putnam). Putnam Pub Group.
—Where's Spot? A Lift-the-Flap Book Miniature Edition. Hill, Eric, illus. 22p. (ps-k). 1990. pap. 4.95 (ISBN 0-399-21822-X, Putnam). Putnam Pub Group.
Hill, Eric, ed. Ayna Boby. (ARA., Illus.). 24p. (ps-2). 1988. 10.95 (ISBN 0-940793-01-6, Pub. by Crocodile Bks.). Interlink Pub.
—Boby Yath'hab Ilal Madrasa. (ARA., Illus.). 24p. (ps-2). 1988. 10.95 (ISBN 0-940793-03-2, Pub. by Crocodile Bks). Interlink Pub.
—Khatawat Boby Al- Oula. (ARA., Illus.). 22p. (ps-2). 1988. 10.95 (ISBN 0-940793-02-4, Pub. by Crocodile Bks.). Interlink Pub.
—Spot Goes to School. (ARA & ENG., Illus.). 24p. (ps-2). 1988. 10.95 (ISBN 0-940793-06-7, Pub. by Crocodile Bks.). Interlink Pub.
—Spot's First Walk. (ARA & ENG., Illus.). 24p. (ps-2). 1988. 10.95 (ISBN 0-940793-05-9, Pub. by Crocodile Bks). Interlink Pub.
—Where's Spot. (ENG & ARA., Illus.). 24p. (ps-2). 1988. 10.95 (ISBN 0-940793-04-0, Pub. by Crocodile Bks). Interlink Pub.
Hilleary, Jane K. Fletcher & the Great Big Dog. Brown, Richard, illus. 32p. (gr. k-3). 1988. 13.95 (ISBN 0-395-46761-6). HM.
Hillert, Margaret. Guess, Guess. O'Connell, Ruth, illus. 24p. (gr. k-1). 1988. 4.99 (ISBN 0-87403-456-6, 24-03695). Standard Pub.
—Jesus Grows Up. Endres, Helen, illus. 24p. (gr. k-1). 1988. 3.95 (ISBN 0-87403-459-0, 24-03698). Standard Pub.
—Lightning Bugs & Lullabies. Hand, Judy, illus. LC 87-91992. 32p. (gr. k-2). 1988. 1.99 (ISBN 0-87403-397-7, 24-03807). Standard Pub.
Hilton, Lisa & Kirkpatrick, Sandra L. If Dinosaurs Were Alive Today. Chewning, Randy, illus. 32p. (ps-3). 1988. 8.95 (ISBN 0-8431-2309-5). Price Stern.
Himmel, Roger J. Columbus & the Explorers of Tumtum. (Illus.). (gr. k-3). 1981. 1 bk. & 1 cass. 10.95 (ISBN 0-318-42856-3, BC18-2); 6 bks. & 1 cass. 29.95 (ISBN 0-89290-156-X). Soc for Visual.
—Happy New Year in Tumtum. (Illus.). (gr. k-3). 1981. 6 bks. & 1 cass. 29.95 (ISBN 0-89290-157-8, BC18-3); 1 bk. & 1 cass. 10.95 (ISBN 0-318-42857-1). Soc for Visual.
—Lollipop's Thanksgiving in Canada. (Illus.). (gr. k-3). 1981. 6 bks. & 1 cass. 29.95 (ISBN 0-89290-155-1, BC18-1); 1 bk. & 1 cass. 10.95 (ISBN 0-318-42855-5). Soc for Visual.
—Thanksgiving in TumTum. Manoni, Mary H., ed. LC 79-739481. (Illus.). (gr. k-3). 1978. 6 bks. & 1 cass. 29.95 (ISBN 0-89290-038-5, BC008-2); 1 bk. & 1 cass. 10.95 (ISBN 0-685-25746-0). Soc for Visual.
—Tumtum Celebrates Lincoln's Birthday. (Illus.). (gr. k-3). 1981. 6 bks. & 1 cass. 29.95 (ISBN 0-89290-158-6, BC18-4); 1 bk. & 1 cass. 10.95 (ISBN 0-318-42858-X). Soc for Visual.
Himmelman, John. Amanda & the Witch Switch. (ps-3). 1987. pap. 3.95 (ISBN 0-14-050635-7, Puffin). Puffin Bks.
—Fix-It Family Series, 4 vols. Himmelman, John, illus. 192p. (ps-3). 1990. Set. PLB 35.92 (ISBN 0-671-31232-4); Set. PLB 26.94s.p.; Set. pap. 14.00 (ISBN 0-671-31233-2); Set. pap. 10.50s.p. Silver Pr.
Hindley, Judy. Once There Was a House: And You Can Make It. Bartelt, Robert, illus. LC 86-42927. 32p. (ps-2). 1987. lib. bdg. 5.99 (ISBN 0-394-98772-1, Random Juv); pap. 1.95 (ISBN 0-394-88772-7). Random.
Hindley, Judy & Reyes, Gregg. Once There Was a Knight & You Can Be One too! Bartelt, Robert, illus. LC 87-20485. 32p. (ps-2). 1988. lib. bdg. 5.99 (ISBN 0-394-99007-2, Random Juv). Random.
Hines, Anna G. All by Myself. LC 84-19882. (Illus.). 32p. (ps). 1985. 13.95 (ISBN 0-89919-293-9, Clarion). HM.
—All By Myself. (ps-k). 10.95 (ISBN 0-317-38428-7, Clarion). Ticknor & Fields.
—Daddy Makes the Best Spaghetti. Hines, Anna G., illus. LC 85-13993. 32p. (ps-1). 1988. pap. 4.95 (ISBN 0-89919-794-9, Pub. by Clarion). Ticknor & Fields.
—I'll Tell You What They Say. Hines, Anna G., illus. LC 86-4743. 24p. (ps-1). 1987. 11.75 (ISBN 0-688-06486-8); PLB 11.88 (ISBN 0-688-06487-6). Greenwillow.
—Maybe a Band-Aid Will Help. (Illus.). (ps-1). 1990. pap. 3.95 (ISBN 0-525-44561-7, DCB). Dutton Child Bks.
Hirschi & Burrell. Who Lives in the Mountains? (gr. 5-8). 1989. 9.95 (ISBN 0-399-21900-5, Putnam). Putnam Pub Group.
—Who Lives on the Prairie? (gr. 5-8). 1989. 9.95 (ISBN 0-399-21901-3, Putnam). Putnam Pub Group.
Hirschi, Ron. Who Lives in the Alligator Swamp? Burrell, Galen, photos by. (Illus.). (ps-2). 1987. 9.95 (ISBN 0-396-09123-7, Putnam); pap. 3.95 (ISBN 0-396-09124-5, Putnam). Putnam Pub Group.
—Who Lives in the Forest? Burrell, Galen, photos by. (Illus.). (ps-2). 1987. 9.95 (ISBN 0-396-09121-0, Putnam); pap. 3.95 (ISBN 0-396-09122-9, Putnam). Putnam Pub Group.
Hirsh, Marilyn. Joseph Who Loved the Sabbath. Grebu, Devis, illus. LC 86-1335. 32p. (ps-3). 1986. pap. 11.95 (ISBN 0-670-81194-7). Viking Child Bks.
—Joseph Who Loved the Sabbath. Grebu, Devis, illus. 32p. (ps-3). 1988. pap. 3.95 (ISBN 0-14-050670-5, Puffin). Puffin Bks.
Hissey, Jane. The Jane Hissey Collection, 3 bks. (Illus.). 96p. 1991. Set. slipcase 14.95 (ISBN 0-399-21758-4, Philomel Bks). Putnam Pub Group.
—Little Bear Lost. Hissey, Jane, illus. 32p. (ps-1). 1989. 14.95 (ISBN 0-399-21743-6, Philomel Bks). Putnam Pub Group.
—Little Bear's Storytime, 3 bks. (Illus.). 96p. 1991. Plush Box Set. 21.95 (ISBN 0-399-21762-2, Philomel Bks). Putnam Pub Group.
—Old Bear Birthday Book. 128p. (gr. 1 up). 1990. 6.95 (ISBN 0-8120-6154-3). Barron.
Hoban, Julia. Amy Loves the Sun. Hoban, Lillian, illus. LC 87-45987. 24p. (ps). 1988. 9.95 (ISBN 0-06-022396-0); PLB 9.89 (ISBN 0-06-022397-9). HarpC Child Bks.
—Amy Loves the Wind. Hoban, Lillian, illus. LC 87-45986. 24p. (ps). 1988. 9.95 (ISBN 0-06-022402-9); PLB 9.89 (ISBN 0-06-022403-7). HarpC Child Bks.
Hoban, Lillian. Arthur's Christmas Cookies. Hoban, Lillian, illus. LC 72-76596. 64p. (gr. k-3). 1984. incl. cassette 5.98 (ISBN 0-694-00160-0, Trophy); pap. 3.50 (ISBN 0-06-444055-9, Trophy). HarpC Child Bks.
—Arthur's Funny Money. Hoban, Lillian, illus. LC 80-7903. 64p. (gr. k-3). 1984. incl. cassette 5.98 (ISBN 0-694-00173-2, Trophy); pap. 3.50 (ISBN 0-06-444048-6, Trophy). HarpC Child Bks.
—Arthur's Honey Bear. Hoban, Lillian, illus. LC 73-14324. 64p. (gr. k-3). 1982. incl. cassette 5.98 (ISBN 0-694-00116-3, Trophy); pap. 3.50 (ISBN 0-06-444033-8, Trophy). HarpC Child Bks.
—The Sugar Snow Spring. Hoban, Lillian, illus. LC 72-9866. 48p. (ps-3). 1973. PLB 11.89 (ISBN 0-06-022334-0). HarpC Child Bks.
Hoban, Russell. Baby Sister for Frances. Hoban, Lillian, illus. LC 64-15154. 32p. (gr. k-3). 1964. 12.95 (ISBN 0-06-022335-9); PLB 12.89 (ISBN 0-06-022336-7). HarpC Child Bks.
—Bargain for Frances. Hoban, Lillian, illus. LC 70-85033. 64p. (gr. k-3). 1970. 11.95 (ISBN 0-06-022329-4); PLB 11.89 (ISBN 0-06-022330-8). HarpC Child Bks.
—Bedtime for Frances. Williams, Garth, illus. LC 60-8347. 32p. (gr. k-3). 1960. 12.95 (ISBN 0-06-022350-2); PLB 12.89 (ISBN 0-06-022351-0). HarpC Child Bks.
—Best Friends for Frances. Hoban, Lillian, illus. LC 71-77935. 32p. (ps-3). 1969. 12.95 (ISBN 0-06-022327-8); PLB 13.89 (ISBN 0-06-022328-6). HarpC Child Bks.
—Birthday for Frances. Hoban, Lillian, illus. LC 68-24321. 32p. (gr. k-3). 1968. 13.95 (ISBN 0-06-022338-3); PLB 13.89 (ISBN 0-06-022339-1). HarpC Child Bks.
—Bread & Jam for Frances. Hoban, Lillian, illus. LC 64-19605. 32p. (gr. k-3). 1965. 13.95 (ISBN 0-06-022359-6); PLB 13.89 (ISBN 0-06-022360-X). HarpC Child Bks.
Hoban, Tana. A Children's Zoo. Hoban, Tana, illus. LC 84-25318. 24p. (ps-1). 1985. 13.95 (ISBN 0-688-05202-9); lib. bdg. 13.88 (ISBN 0-688-05204-5). Greenwillow.

—Dots, Spots, Speckles, & Stripes. (ps-3). 1987. 11.75 (ISBN 0-688-06862-6); PLB 11.88 (ISBN 0-688-06863-4). Greenwillow.
—I Read Signs. LC 83-1482. (ps-1). 1987. pap. 4.95 (ISBN 0-688-07331-X, Mulberry). Morrow.
—Look Again! LC 72-127469. (Illus.). 40p. (ps-2). 1971. 12.95 (ISBN 0-02-744050-8, Mcmillan Child Bk). Macmillan Child Grp.
—Look! Look! Look! Hoban, Tina, illus. LC 87-25655. 40p. (ps-1). 1988. 12.95 (ISBN 0-688-07239-9); lib. bdg. 12.88 (ISBN 0-688-07240-2). Greenwillow.
—Take Another Look. LC 80-21342. (Illus.). 32p. (ps-3). 1981. PLB 14.88 (ISBN 0-688-84298-4). Greenwillow.
—What Is It? Hoban, Tana, illus. LC 84-13483. 12p. (ps). 1985. bds. 4.95 (ISBN 0-688-02577-3). Greenwillow.
Hoban, Tana, illus. Shapes & Things. LC 70-102965. 32p. (ps-2). 1970. 13.95 (ISBN 0-02-744060-5, Mcmillan Child Bk). Macmillan Child Grp.
Hoberman, Mary Ann. A House Is a House for Me. Fraser, Betty, illus. LC 77-15518. (gr. k-3). 1978. pap. 13.95 (ISBN 0-670-38016-4). Viking Child Bks.
—A House Is a House for Me. Fraser, Betty, illus. 48p. Big Book. 19.50 (ISBN 0-590-71695-6); pap. 2.50 (ISBN 0-590-71696-4). Scholastic Inc.
Hofer, Angelika. The Lion Family Book. Ziesler, Gunter, illus. LC 88-15139. 52p. (gr. k up). 1988. 15.95 (ISBN 0-88708-070-7). Picture Bk Studio.
Hoff, Syd. Grizzwold. LC 63-14366. (Illus.). 64p. (gr. k-3). 1984. pap. 3.50 (ISBN 0-06-444057-5, Trophy). HarpC Child Bks.
—Julius. Hoff, Syd, illus. LC 59-7981. 64p. (gr. k-3). 1988. pap. 3.50 (ISBN 0-06-444119-9, Trophy). HarpC Child Bks.
—Little Chief. Hoff, Syd, illus. LC 61-12098. 64p. (gr. k-3). 1990. pap. 3.50 (ISBN 0-06-444135-0, Trophy). HarpC Child Bks.
—Who Will Be My Friends? Hoff, Syd, illus. LC 60-14096. 32p. (ps-2). 1985. pap. 2.95 (ISBN 0-06-444072-9, Trophy). HarpC Child Bks.
Hoffman, E. T. & Richardson, Jean. The Nutcracker. Crespi, Francesca, illus. 32p. (ps-2). 1990. lib. bdg. 14.95 (ISBN 1-55970-105-6). Arcade Pub Inc.
Hoffman, G., illus. The Adventures of the Little Mouse. 24p. (gr. 4-7). 1988. bk. & audiocassette 6.95 (ISBN 0-8120-4039-2). Barron.
Hoffman, Phyllis. Baby's First Year. Wilson, Sarah, illus. LC 86-45768. 32p. (ps). 1988. 12.95 (ISBN 0-06-022551-3); PLB 12.89 (ISBN 0-06-022552-1). HarpC Child Bks.
—We Play. Wilson, Sarah, illus. LC 89-36381. 32p. (ps). 1990. 12.95 (ISBN 0-06-022557-2); PLB 12.89 (ISBN 0-06-022558-0). HarpC Child Bks.
Hoffmann, E. T. The Strange Child. Zweger, Lisbeth, illus. LC 84-8404. 28p. (gr. 3 up). 1984. 16.95 (ISBN 0-907234-60-7). Picture Bk Studio.
Hofman, Ginnie. The Runaway Teddy Bear. Hofman, Ginnie, illus. LC 84-23740. 32p. (ps-3). 1986. lib. bdg. 5.99 (ISBN 0-394-96286-9, Random Juv); pap. 1.95 (ISBN 0-394-86286-4). Random.
Hofstrand, Mary. By the Sea. Hofstrand, Mary, illus. LC 88-16756. 32p. (ps-3). 1989. 11.95 (ISBN 0-689-31421-3, Atheneum Child Bk). Macmillan Child Grp.
Hogrogian, Nonny. Noah's Ark. Hogrogian, Nonny, illus. LC 86-97. 40p. (ps-3). 1986. 12.95 (ISBN 0-394-88191-5); lib. bdg. 12.99 (ISBN 0-394-98191-X). Knopf.
—One Fine Day. Hogrogian, Nonny, illus. LC 75-119834. 32p. (gr. k-3). 1974. pap. 3.95x (ISBN 0-02-043620-3, Aladdin). Macmillan Child Grp.
—One Fine Day. 1971. 13.95 (ISBN 0-02-744000-1, Mcmillan Child Bk). Macmillan Child Grp.
Hokey Pokey Did It. (Illus.). (ps-2). 1990. 3.95 (ISBN 0-7214-9608-3). Ladybird Bks.
Holcomb, Nan. Andy Finds a Turtle. Yoder, Dot, illus. 32p. (Orig.). (ps-2). 1988. pap. 5.95 (ISBN 0-944727-02-6). Jason & Nordic Pubs.
—Danny & the Merry-Go-Round. Lucia, Virginia, illus. 32p. (Orig.). 1988. pap. 5.95 (ISBN 0-944727-00-X). Jason & Nordic Pubs.
—How About A Hug. Taggart, Tricia, illus. 32p. (Orig.). (ps). 1988. pap. 5.95 (ISBN 0-944727-01-8). Jason & Nordic Pubs.
Holden, L. Dwight. Gran-Gran's Best Trick: A Story for Children Who Have Lost Someone They Love. Chesworth, Michael, illus. LC 89-8336. 48p. 1989. 15.95 (ISBN 0-945354-19-3); pap. 5.95 (ISBN 0-945354-16-9). Magination Pr.
Holden, Queen. Best Friends-Paper Dolls in Full Color. 1985. pap. 3.50 (ISBN 0-486-24973-5). Dover.
Holder, Bill & Farquhar, John. Jets & Bombers. 32p. (gr. 1-8). 1989. 3.95 (ISBN 0-87406-385-X). Willowisp Pr.
—Monster Trucks. 32p. (gr. 1-8). 1988. 3.95 (ISBN 0-87406-241-1). Willowisp Pr.
Holder, Heidi, illus. Crows: An Old Rhyme. LC 87-45364. 32p. (ps up). 1987. 14.95 (ISBN 0-374-31660-0). FS&G.
Holl, Adelaide. My Weekly Reader Picture Word Book. Perry, Alfred, illus. 128p. (ps-k). 1981. pap. 5.95 (ISBN 0-671-42542-0, Little Simon). S&S Trade.
—Rain Puddle. Duvoisin, Roger, illus. LC 65-22026. 32p. (gr. k-3). 1965. PLB 14.88 (ISBN 0-688-51096-5). Lothrop.
Hollow, Fern. All in a Day. (Illus.). (ps-1). 1985. 2.98 (ISBN 0-517-48288-6). Outlet Bk Co.
Holt, Ginny. Me & My Spoon. (Illus.). 24p. (ps-4). 1989. bds. 5.95 (ISBN 0-394-82156-4). Random.
Holt, Virginia. Nine Little Popples. Gray, J. M., illus. LC 85-63347. 14p. (ps). 1986. 1.95 (ISBN 0-394-88254-7, Random Juv). Random.
Home. (Illus.). (ps-k). 3.95 (ISBN 0-7214-5157-8). Ladybird Bks.
Home. (Illus.). (ps). 3.50 (ISBN 0-7214-1097-9). Ladybird Bks.
Hooker, Ruth. Sara Loves Her Big Brother. Tucker, Kathleen, ed. Apple, Margot, illus. 32p. (ps-1). 1987. PLB 12.95 (ISBN 0-8075-7244-6). A Whitman.
Hooker, Yvonne. The Little Red Ant. Vanetti, Giorgio, illus. LC 84-80289. (ps-1). 1984. 6.95 (ISBN 0-448-01456-4, G&D). Putnam Pub Group.
—Splish, Splash! Pazzaglia, Nadia, illus. (ps-1). 1983. 6.95 (ISBN 0-448-01454-8, G&D). Putnam Pub Group.
Hooks, William A., et al. Let's Get Dressed! Bank Street College Media Group, ed. Schick, Joel, illus. 32p. (Orig.). (ps). 1986. write for info. (ISBN 0-9617460-0-9). Levi Strauss.
Hooks, William H. The Three Little Pigs & the Fox. Schindler, S. D., illus. LC 88-29296. 32p. (gr. k-3). 1989. 13.95 (ISBN 0-02-744431-7, Mcmillan Child Bk). Macmillan Child Grp.
Hooper, Meredith. Seven Eggs. McKenna, Terry, illus. LC 84-43159. 20p. (ps-3). 1986. 3.95 (ISBN 0-694-00144-9). HarpC Child Bks.
Hoopes, Lyn L. Mommy, Daddy, Me. Bornstein, Ruth L., illus. LC 87-45286. 32p. (ps-2). 1988. 12.95 (ISBN 0-06-022549-1); PLB 12.89 (ISBN 0-06-022550-5). HarpC Child Bks.
Hop Like a Bunny! Waddle Like a Duck! 24p. (ps-3). 1987. pap. write for info incl. cassette (ISBN 0-307-13993-X, Pub. by Golden Bks). Western Pub.
Hopkins, Lee B. Surprises. Lloyd, Megan, illus. LC 83-47712. 64p. (gr. k-3). 1986. pap. 3.50 (ISBN 0-06-444105-9, Trophy). HarpC Child Bks.
Horlin, Jean-Pierre. At Our House. De Boeck, Francine, illus. 32p. (ps-1). 1988. 6.95 (ISBN 0-671-66134-5, Little Simon). S&S Trade.
—Out & About. De Boeck, Francine, illus. 32p. (ps-1). 1988. 6.95 (ISBN 0-671-66139-6, Little Simon). S&S Trade.
Horsey's Carriage. 12p. (ps-1). 1989. bds. 3.95 (ISBN 0-87449-633-0). Modern Pub NYC.
Hot! 40p. (gr. 3-6). 1988. 2.95 (ISBN 0-87406-356-6). Willowisp Pr.
Hotshots, illus. Cabbage Patch Kids Adventure. 24p. (gr. 1-5). 1984. 5.95 (ISBN 0-910313-31-8). Parker Bros.
Howard, Elizabeth F. Chita's Christmas Tree. Cooper, Floyd, illus. LC 88-26250. 32p. (ps-2). 1989. 13.95 (ISBN 0-02-744621-2, Bradbury Pr). Macmillan Child Grp.
Howl-Oween Party Pop-up Storybook. 10p. (ps-3). 1990. 3.95 (ISBN 0-8167-2186-6). Troll Assocs.
Hoy, Joanne H. Have Fun, Balloons. 32p. (ps-1). 1985. pap. 2.95 (ISBN 0-931093-02-3). Red Hen Pr.
Hoye, Jessie & Taylor, Stephanie. The Frogs Party. McEntee, Steve, illus. 20p. (Orig.). (gr. 1). 1989. pap. 2.95 plastic paper (ISBN 0-317-94121-6). Kidzco Pub.
Huang, Benrei, illus. Boo! Guess Who? LC 89-61374. 14p. (ps). 1990. bds. 2.95 (ISBN 0-679-80278-9). Random.
Huberman, Caryn & Wetzel, JoAnne. Onstage Backstage. Huberman, Caryn & Wetzel, JoAnne, photos by. (Illus.). 56p. (gr. 2-5). 1987. PLB 12.95 (ISBN 0-87614-307-9). Carolrhoda Bks.
Hudson, Cheryl W. Afro-Bets A B C Book. Hudson, Cheryl W., illus. LC 87-81580. 24p. (ps-3). 1987. pap. 3.95 (ISBN 0-940975-00-9). Just Us Bks.
—Afro-Bets 1 2 3 Book. Hudson, Cheryl W., illus. LC 87-82952. 24p. (ps-3). 1988. pap. 3.95 (ISBN 0-940975-01-7). Just Us Bks.
Hugh Pine. 96p. (ps-1). 1983. pap. 2.50 (ISBN 0-553-15558-X, Skylark). Bantam.
Hughes, Alice. Mickey Mouse & His Boat. Waltz, Dick, illus. LC 87-83494. 40p. (gr. k-2). 1988. write for info. (ISBN 0-307-11692-1). Western Pub.
Hughes, Barbara & Dwiggins, Gwen. God Loves Children. Dow, Bonnie, illus. (ps-3). 0.99 (ISBN 0-8091-6562-7). Paulist Pr.
—God Loves Colors. Dow, Bonnie, illus. (ps-3). 0.99 (ISBN 0-8091-6566-X). Paulist Pr.
—God Loves Fun. Dow, Bonnie, illus. (ps-3). 0.99 (ISBN 0-8091-6564-3). Paulist Pr.
—God Loves Love. Dow, Bonnie, illus. (ps-3). 0.99 (ISBN 0-8091-6565-1). Paulist Pr.
—God Loves Seasons. Dow, Bonnie, illus. (ps-3). 0.99 (ISBN 0-8091-6563-5). Paulist Pr.
Hughes, Margaret A. A Birthday Surprise. Hicks, Russell, et al, illus. 26p. (ps). 1987. Packaged with pre-programmed audio cass. tape. 15.00 (ISBN 0-934323-61-5). Alchemy Comms.
Hughes, Shirley. Alfie Gives a Hand. Hughes, Shirley, illus. LC 83-14883. 32p. (ps-1). 1984. 12.95 (ISBN 0-688-02386-X); PLB 14.88 (ISBN 0-688-02387-8). Lothrop.
—Alfie's Feet. LC 82-13012. (Illus.). 32p. (ps-3). 1988. pap. 3.95 (ISBN 0-688-07812-5, Mulberry). Morrow.
—All Shapes & Sizes. LC 86-2734. (Illus.). 24p. (ps). 1986. 4.95 (ISBN 0-688-04205-8). Lothrop.
—Angel Mae: A Tale of Trotter Street. Hughes, Shirley, illus. LC 89-45288. 32p. (ps-1). 1989. 12.95 (ISBN 0-688-08538-5); PLB 12.88 (ISBN 0-688-08539-3). Lothrop.
—Colors. LC 86-2732. (Illus.). 24p. (ps). 1986. 4.95 (ISBN 0-688-04206-6). Lothrop.
—Lucy & Tom's A. B. C. 's. Hughes, Shirley, illus. LC 86-40022. 32p. (ps-1). 1986. pap. 11.95 (ISBN 0-670-81256-0). Viking Child Bks.
—Lucy & Tom's A. B. C.'s. (ps-1). 1987. pap. 4.95 (ISBN 0-14-050697-7, Puffin). Puffin Bks.
—Lucy & Tom's Christmas. Hughes, Shirley, illus. LC 86-40023. 32p. (ps-1). 1986. pap. 11.95 (ISBN 0-670-81255-2). Viking Child Bks.
—Lucy & Tom's Christmas. (ps-1). 1987. pap. 4.95 (ISBN 0-14-050698-5, Puffin). Puffin Bks.
—Two Shoes, New Shoes. LC 86-2733. (Illus.). 24p. (ps). 1986. 4.95 (ISBN 0-688-04207-4). Lothrop.
Hulbert, Jay. The Bedtime Beast. (Illus.). 32p. (gr. 1-4). 1989. PLB 13.32 (ISBN 0-8172-3516-7). Raintree Pubs.
Hurd, Edith T. Day the Sun Danced. Hurd, Clement, illus. LC 64-16641. 32p. (gr. k-3). 1966. PLB 13.89 (ISBN 0-06-022692-7). HarpC Child Bks.
—Johnny Lion's Book. Hurd, Clement, illus. LC 65-14490. 64p. (gr. k-3). 1965. PLB 11.89 (ISBN 0-06-022706-0). HarpC Child Bks.
Hurd, Thacher. Axle the Freeway Cat. Hurd, Thacher, illus. LC 80-8432. 32p. (ps-3). 1988. pap. 3.95 (ISBN 0-06-443173-8, Trophy). HarpC Child Bks.
—Mama Don't Allow. Hurd, Thacher, illus. LC 83-47703. 40p. (ps-3). 1985. pap. 4.95 (ISBN 0-06-443078-2, Trophy). HarpC Child Bks.
—Mystery on the Docks. Hurd, Thacher, illus. LC 82-48261. 32p. (gr. k-3). 1984. pap. 4.95 (ISBN 0-06-443058-8, Trophy). HarpC Child Bks.
—A Night in the Swamp: A Moveable Book. Hurd, Thacher, illus. LC 86-45616. 12p. (ps-k). 1987. 7.95 (ISBN 0-694-00177-5). HarpC Child Bks.
Hutchins, Pat. Changes, Changes. Hutchins, Pat, illus. LC 86-22331. 32p. (ps-1). 1987. pap. 4.95 (ISBN 0-689-71137-9, Aladdin). Macmillan Child Grp.
—Good-Night, Owl. Hutchins, Pat, illus. LC 72-186355. 32p. (ps-2). 1972. 12.95 (ISBN 0-02-745900-4, Mcmillan Child Bk). Macmillan Child Grp.
—Rosie's Walk. Hutchins, Pat, illus. LC 68-12090. 32p. (ps-1). 1968. SBE 13.95 (ISBN 0-02-745850-4, Mcmillan Child Bk). Macmillan Child Grp.
—The Surprise Party. reissued ed. LC 86-7255. (Illus.). 32p. (ps-3). 1986. 12.95 (ISBN 0-02-745930-6, Mcmillan Child Bk). Macmillan Child Grp.
—The Very Worst Monster. LC 84-5928. (Illus.). 32p. (ps-3). 1988. pap. 3.95 (ISBN 0-688-07816-8, Mulberry). Morrow.
Hutton, Warwick. Theseus & the Minotaur. Hutton, Warwick, illus. LC 88-26875. 32p. (gr. 1-5). 1989. 13.95 (ISBN 0-689-50473-X, M K McElderry). Macmillan Child Grp.
Hyman, Jane. Gumby Book of Colors. LC 86-6222. (Illus.). 32p. (ps-3). 1986. 5.95 (ISBN 0-385-23454-6); PLB 5.95 (ISBN 0-385-23845-2). Doubleday.
—Gumby Book of Letters. LC 86-6216. (Illus.). 32p. (ps-3). 1986. 5.95 (ISBN 0-685-38408-X); PLB 5.97 (ISBN 0-685-38409-8). Doubleday.
—Gumby Book of Shapes. LC 86-6194. (Illus.). 32p. (ps-3). 1986. 5.95 (ISBN 0-385-23453-8); PLB 5.95 (ISBN 0-385-23848-7). Doubleday.
I Am an Owl. (Illus.). 24p. (ps-k). 1989. 7.95 (ISBN 0-448-21027-4, G&D). Putnam Pub Group.
I Can, Can You? 1984. 3.95 (ISBN 0-671-49316-7, Little Simon). S&S Trade.
I Can See, Hear, Smell, Taste & Touch. (Illus.). (ps). 1985. bds. 3.98 (ISBN 0-517-47340-2). Outlet Bk Co.
I Know Colors. 1990. 2.98 (ISBN 0-8317-7253-0). Smithmark.
I Learn Letters: A Jumbo Board Book. (Illus.). 16p. (ps-1). 1987. pap. 5.95 (ISBN 0-553-18351-6). Bantam.
I Learn Numbers: A Jumbo Board Book. (Illus.). 16p. (ps-1). 1987. 5.95 (ISBN 0-553-18350-8). Bantam.
I Love Cats Share-a-Story Unit. (Illus.). 32p. (ps-2). 1987. 58.20 (ISBN 0-516-49543-7). Childrens.
Ichikawa, Satomi, illus. Happy Birthday! A Book of Birthday Celebrations. 64p. (ps up). 1988. 13.95 (ISBN 0-399-21421-6, Philomel Bks). Putnam Pub Group.
If I Could Be a Circus Clown. (Illus.). 24p. (gr. k-2). 1988. 4.95 (ISBN 0-87449-463-X). Modern Pub NYC.
If I Knew How to Fly a Rocket. (Illus.). 24p. (gr. k-2). 1988. 4.95 (ISBN 0-87449-461-3). Modern Pub NYC.
If I Went Sailing Out to Sea. (Illus.). 24p. (gr. k-2). 1988. 4.95 (ISBN 0-87449-462-1). Modern Pub NYC.
I'm a Little Baby. (ps). 1990. bds. 2.95 (ISBN 0-671-44567-7, Little Simon). S&S Trade.
I'm a Little Choo-Choo. (ps). 1990. bds. 2.95 (ISBN 0-671-44568-5, Little Simon). S&S Trade.
Immel, Mary B. No Longer Sings the Brown Thrush. 208p. (Orig.). (gr. 4-8). 1988. pap. 7.95 (ISBN 0-8272-2509-1). CBP.
Imoto, Yoko. Skipper at the Beach. Imoto, Yoko, illus. 32p. (ps-1). 1989. 5.95 (ISBN 0-448-09293-X, G&D). Putnam Pub Group.
—Skipper is the Daddy. Imoto, Yoko, illus. 32p. (ps-1). 1989. 5.95 (ISBN 0-448-09294-8, G&D). Putnam Pub Group.
—Skipper Plants a Tulip. Imoto, Yoko, illus. 32p. (ps-1). 1989. 5.95 (ISBN 0-448-09292-1, G&D). Putnam Pub Group.
—Skipper's New Red Pants. Imoto, Yoko, illus. 32p. (ps-1). 1989. 5.95 (ISBN 0-448-09291-3, G&D). Putnam Pub Group.

Imoto, Yoko, illus. The Picture Book of Cats. Dayton, Linnea & Weller-Watson, Karen, eds. (Illus.). 36p. (ps up). 1985. 7.95 (ISBN 0-915391-14-7, Pub. by Mad Hatter Bks). Slawson Comm.
Impey, Rose. Joe's Cafe. (ps-3). 1991. 14.95 (ISBN 0-316-41777-7). Little.
Indoor Things. (Illus.). (ps-k). 3.95 (ISBN 0-7214-5141-1). Ladybird Bks.
Ingoglia, Gina. Those Mysterious Dinosaurs. (Illus.). 24p. (ps-k). 1989. pap. write for info. (ISBN 0-307-11747-2, Pub. by Golden Bks). Western Pub.
Intervisional Communications Staff. Viking Circus Block Books: Circus Parade Zoo-A Book in-a-Box with a Performing Picture, 3 vols. LC 83-80225. (Illus.). (gr. 1-5). 1983. Set. 10.95. Viking Child Bks.
Is This My Spaceship? 12p. (ps). 1988. 4.95 (ISBN 0-8120-5945-X). Barron.
Isaak, Betty. Perception Panda. Armstrong, Bev, illus. 24p. (ps). 1982. wkbk. 2.95 (ISBN 0-88160-088-1, LW 122). Learning Wks.
Isadora, Rachel. Ben's Trumpet. Isadora, Rachel, illus. LC 78-12885. 32p. (gr. k-3). 1979. 13.00 (ISBN 0-688-80194-3). Greenwillow.
—I Touch. Isadora, Rachel, illus. LC 84-13673. 32p. (ps). 1985. 11.75 (ISBN 0-688-04255-4); lib. bdg. 11.88 (ISBN 0-688-04256-2). Greenwillow.
Isami, Ikuyo. The Fox's Egg. Isami, Ikuyo, illus. 40p. (ps-2). 1989. 12.95 (ISBN 0-87614-339-7). Carolrhoda Bks.
Issacsen-Bright, Margaret H. Monster Don't Scare Me. Hickman, Estella, illus. 32p. (Orig.). (gr. k-2). 1988. pap. 1.95 (ISBN 0-87406-344-2). Willowisp Pr.
Ivanovsky, Elisabeth. Things in My House. (Illus.). (ps). 1985. bds. 3.98 (ISBN 0-517-47341-0). Outlet Bk Co.
—What Color Is It. (Illus.). (ps). 1985. bds. 3.98 (ISBN 0-517-47342-9). Outlet Bk Co.
—What Time Is It? (Illus.). (ps). 1985. bds. 3.98 (ISBN 0-517-47343-7). Outlet Bk Co.
Ivimey, John W. The Complete Story of the Three Blind Mice. Galdone, Paul, illus. 32p. (ps). 1989. pap. 4.95 (ISBN 0-395-51585-8, Clarion Bks). HM.
Izawa, Tadasu & Hijikata, Shigemi, illus. My First Book. (ps-1). 1983. 5.95 (ISBN 0-448-12287-1, G&D). Putnam Pub Group.
Izawa, Tadasu & Hijkata, Shigemi, illus. What Time Is It? 18p. (gr. k-2). 1981. (G&D); PLB 2.99 (ISBN 0-448-03701-7, G&D). Putnam Pub Group.
Jabar, Cynthia. Party Day! Jabar, Cynthia, illus. (ps-1). 1987. 11.95 (ISBN 0-316-43456-6, Joy St Bks). Little.
Jack & the Beanstalk. 24p. (Orig.). 1988. pap. write for info. (ISBN 0-307-13969-7). Western Pub.
Jaffrey, Madhur. Seasons of Splendor. Foreman, Michael, illus. (ps up). pap. 7.95 (ISBN 0-317-62172-6, Puffin). Puffin Bks.
James, Betsy. The Dream Stair. Watson, Richard J., illus. LC 89-36420. 32p. (gr. k-2). 1990. 13.95 (ISBN 0-06-022787-7); PLB 13.89 (ISBN 0-06-022788-5). HarpC Child Bks.
—What's That Room For? James, Betsy, illus. LC 87-24462. 32p. (ps-1). 1988. 11.95 (ISBN 0-525-44382-7, 01160-350, DCB). Dutton Child Bks.
James, Emily. Willow & the Brownies. Segrelles, Vicente, illus. LC 87-62953. 24p. (ps-3). 1988. pap. 1.25 (ISBN 0-394-89801-X, Random Juv). Random.
Janosch. The Cricket & the Mole. Janosch, illus. Bell, Anthea, tr. (Illus.). 70p. (ps-1). 8.95 (ISBN 0-86264-043-1, Pub. by Anderson Pr UK). Trafalgar Sq.
Jarrell, Mary. The Knee-Baby. Shimin, Symeon, illus. LC 73-75295. 32p. (ps up). 1973. 10.95 (ISBN 0-374-34246-6). FS&G.
Jean, Priscilla. Pattie Round & Wally Square. Jean, Priscilla, illus. (gr. k-3). 1965. 8.95 (ISBN 0-8392-3048-6). Astor-Honor.
Jeffers, Susan. The Three Jovial Huntsmen. Jeffers, Susan, illus. 32p. (ps-2). 1989. pap. 3.95 (ISBN 0-689-71309-6, Aladdin). Macmillan Child Grp.
—Wild Robin. Jeffers, Susan, illus. LC 76-21343. 40p. (ps-3). 1986. pap. 4.95 (ISBN 0-525-44244-8, DCB). Dutton Child Bks.
Jemima Puddle-Duck. (Illus.). (ps-2). 1.95 (ISBN 0-7214-5218-3). Ladybird Bks.
Jenkin-Pearce, Susie. Bad Boris Goes to School. Jenkin-Pearce, Susie, illus. 32p. (ps-1). 1989. 12.95 (ISBN 0-02-747621-9, Mcmillan Child Bk). Macmillan Child Grp.
Jensen, Kent W. Slippers & Wraparound Wraps. Traba, Henry & Faigin, Cecilia, illus. 41p. (ps-2). Date not set. pap. 7.95 (ISBN 0-9621024-0-7). K Jensen.
Jensen, Virginia A. Catching. LC 83-13152. (Illus.). (ps-4). 1984. pap. 12.95 (ISBN 0-399-20997-2, Philomel). Putnam Pub Group.
Jeram, Anita. It Was Jake. (ps-3). 1991. 14.95 (ISBN 0-316-46120-2). Little.
Jeremy Mouse & Mr. Puffle. (Illus.). (ps-2). 3.50 (ISBN 0-7214-0921-0). Ladybird Bks.
Jeschke, Susan. Perfect the Pig. Jeschke, Susan, illus. LC 80-39998. 40p. (gr. k-3). 1981. 13.95 (ISBN 0-8050-0704-0). H Holt & Co.
Jessie Willcox Smith Mother Goose. (ps up). 1986. 7.98 (ISBN 0-685-16881-6, 603578). Outlet Bk Co.
Jingle Bells. 10p. (ps-2). 1989. pap. 4.95 (ISBN 0-448-04184-7, G&D). Putnam Pub Group.
Johnson, Crockett. Harold & the Purple Crayon. Johnson, Crockett, illus. LC 55-7683. (gr. k-3). 1958. 10.95 (ISBN 0-06-022935-7); PLB 10.89 (ISBN 0-06-022936-5). HarpC Child Bks.
—Harold's Trip to the Sky. Johnson, Crockett, illus. LC 57-9262. (gr. k-3). 1957. PLB 11.89 (ISBN 0-06-022986-1). HarpC Child Bks.
—Will Spring Be Early or Will Spring Be Late? Johnson, Crockett, illus. LC 59-9424. 48p. (gr. k-3). 1961. PLB 12.89 (ISBN 0-690-89423-6, Crowell Jr Bks). HarpC Child Bks.
Johnson, George C., illus. Baby's First Words. 20p. (ps-1). 1986. bds. 3.95 (ISBN 0-448-03093-4, G&D). Putnam Pub Group.
Johnson, Neil. Born to Run: A Racehorse Grows Up. (Illus.). 32p. (gr. k-3). 1988. pap. 13.95 (ISBN 0-590-41237-X, Scholastic Hardcover). Scholastic Inc.
Johnson, Ryerson. Why Is Baby Crying? Tucker, Kathy, ed. DiSalvo-Ryan, DyAnne, illus. 32p. (ps-2). 1989. PLB 12.95 (ISBN 0-8075-9084-3). A Whitman.
Johnson, Sue. Popsicles Are Cold: Storybook for Young Children in Sign Languages. Herigstad, Joni, illus. 30p. (Orig.). (ps-3). pap. 4.50 (ISBN 0-916708-12-8). Modern Signs.
Johnson, Susan. Erte Fashion Paper Dolls of the Twenties. 1979. pap. 3.95 (ISBN 0-486-23627-7). Dover.
Johnson, William R. Color Monkeys. Johnson, Pauline, ed. (Illus.). 48p. (ps-2). 1989. write for info. (ISBN 0-936917-05-9, B608). Blip Prods.
—Dinosaurs & Other Prehistorics. Johnson, Pauline D., ed. Johnson, William R., illus. 48p. (gr. 3-6). 1986. pap. 4.95 (ISBN 0-936917-02-4, B606). Blip Prods.
—Kids of the World: Cursive. Johnson, Pauline D., ed. Johnson, William R., illus. 48p. (gr. 3-6). 1986. pap. 4.95 (ISBN 0-936917-01-6, B604). Blip Prods.
—Kids of the World: Manuscript. Johnson, Pauline D., ed. Johnson, William R., illus. 48p. (Orig.). (ps-2). 1986. pap. 4.95 (ISBN 0-936917-00-8, B603). Blip Prods.
—Monthly Calendars. Johnson, Pauline, ed. (Illus.). 48p. (gr. k-4). 1989. write for info. (ISBN 0-936917-04-0, B607). Blip Prods.
—Numbers One to Twenty: The Circus & the Bees. Johnson, Pauline D., ed. Johnson, William R., illus. 48p. (ps-2). 1986. pap. 4.95 (ISBN 0-936917-03-2, B605). Blip Prods.
Johnston, Norma. The Delphic Choice. LC 88-24570. 208p. (gr. 7 up). 1989. 13.95 (ISBN 0-02-747711-8, Four Winds). Macmillan Child Grp.
Johnston, S. Paper Doll-Godey Fashion. 1979. pap. 3.95 (ISBN 0-486-23511-4). Dover.
Johnston, Tony. Five Little Foxes & the Snow. Szekeres, Cyndy, illus. LC 87-45144. 32p. (ps-3). 1987. pap. 4.95 (ISBN 0-06-443149-5, Trophy). HarpC Child Bks.
Jonas, Ann. Reflections. LC 86-33545. (Illus.). 24p. (gr. k-3). 1987. 13.95 (ISBN 0-688-06140-0); lib. bdg. 13.88 (ISBN 0-688-06141-9). Greenwillow.
—Round Trip. (Illus.). 32p. (gr. k-3). 1984. pap. 3.95 (ISBN 0-590-40956-5). Scholastic Inc.
Jones, Carolyn E. Lottie Moon Storybook. Ellis, Debbie, illus. 20p. (gr. k-4). 1984. pap. 2.50 (ISBN 0-9616996-0-4). Honor Pub.
Jones, Kathleen I. I Am This & More, Bk. 1. Jones, Kert, illus. 12p. (ps-5). 1989. write for info. (ISBN 0-9624790-0-4). Kindle Bks.
Jones, Rebecca. The Biggest (& Best) Flag That Ever Flew. Geer, Charles, illus. LC 87-40609. 32p. (ps). 1988. 6.95 (ISBN 0-87033-381-X). Tidewater.
Jones, Rebecca C. Down at the Bottom of the Deep Dark Sea. Wright-Frierson, Virginia, illus. LC 90-33981. 40p. (ps-k). 1991. RSBE 13.95 (ISBN 0-02-747901-3, Bradbury Pr). Macmillan Child Grp.
Joos, Francoise & Joos, Frederic. Sarah & the Stone Man. (Illus.). 32p. (gr. k-2). 1989. 13.95 (ISBN 0-86264-202-7, Pub. by Anderson Pr UK). Trafalgar Sq.
Jordan, MaryKate. Losing Uncle Tim. Levine, Abby, ed. Wennekes, Ron, illus. 32p. (gr. 2-6). 1989. PLB 12.95 (ISBN 0-8075-4756-5). A Whitman.
Jorgensen, Gail. Crocodile Beat. Mullins, Patricia, illus. LC 89-578. 32p. (ps-1). 1989. 13.95 (ISBN 0-02-748010-0, Bradbury Pr). Macmillan Child Grp.
Joseph, Lorraine F. My Island: A Picture Storybook. Washington, Helen, illus. 23p. (Orig.). (gr. k-3). 1985. pap. 2.95 (ISBN 0-935357-00-9). Cric Prod.
Joshua James Likes Trucks Share-a-Story Unit. (Illus.). 32p. (ps-2). 1987. 58.20 (ISBN 0-516-49545-3). Childrens.
Josiah, the Boy King. (ps-2). 1988. pap. 0.79 (ISBN 1-55513-918-3, Chariot Bks). Cook.
Joslin, Sesyle. What Do You Do, Dear? Sendak, Maurice, illus. LC 84-43139. 48p. (ps-3). 1986. pap. 3.50 (ISBN 0-06-443113-4, Trophy). HarpC Child Bks.
—What Do You Say, Dear? Sendak, Maurice, illus. LC 84-43140. 48p. (ps-3). 1986. pap. 4.50 (ISBN 0-06-443112-6, Trophy). HarpC Child Bks.
Joyce, William. George Shrinks. Joyce, William, illus. LC 83-47697. 32p. (ps-2). 1985. 13.95 (ISBN 0-06-023070-3); PLB 13.89 (ISBN 0-06-023071-1). HarpC Child Bks.
Juster, Norton. As: A Surfeit of Similes. Small, David, illus. LC 88-8449. 80p. 1989. 9.95 (ISBN 0-688-08139-8); PLB 9.88 (ISBN 0-688-08140-1, Morrow Jr Bks). Morrow Jr Bks.
Kachenmeister, Cherryl. On Monday When It Rained. Berthiaume, Tom, photos by. (Illus.). 40p. (gr. k-3). 1989. 10.95 (ISBN 0-395-51940-3). HM.
Kahalewai, Marilyn. Whose Slippers Are Those? Kahalewai, Marilyn, illus. LC 87-92272. 16p. (ps-6). 1988. 9.95 (ISBN 0-935848-58-4). Bess Pr.
Kahn, Peggy. Popple Opposites. Ewers, Joe, illus. LC 85-63459. 28p. (ps). 1986. 2.95 (ISBN 0-394-88266-0, Random Juv). Random.
Kahn, Peggy & Beylon, Cathy. When Do You Snuzzle a Wuzzle? LC 84-62808. (Illus.). 14p. (gr. 2-5). 1985. 1.95 (ISBN 0-394-87433-1, Random Juv). Random.
Kalin, Robert. Jump, Frog, Jump! Barton, Byron, illus. 32p. (gr. k-3). Big Book. 19.50 (ISBN 0-590-71722-7); pap. 2.95 (ISBN 0-590-71723-5). Scholastic Inc.
Kalmenoff, Matthew. Dinosaur Dioramas to Cut & Assemble. 1983. pap. 4.95 (ISBN 0-486-24541-1). Dover.
Kamen, Gloria. Paddle, Said the Swan. Kamen, Gloria, illus. LC 88-16749. 32p. (ps-1). 1989. 12.95 (ISBN 0-689-31330-6, Atheneum Child Bk). Macmillan Child Grp.
Kanao, Keiko. Kitten up a Tree. Spinner, Stephanie, ed. Greenstein, Mina, designed by. LC 86-21075. (Illus.). 24p. (ps-1). 1987. 7.95 (ISBN 0-394-88817-0). Knopf.
Kantrowitz, Mildred. Willy Bear. Parker, Nancy W., illus. 32p. (ps-1). 1989. pap. 3.95 (ISBN 0-689-71345-2, Aladdin). Macmillan Child Grp.
Kaplan, Carol B. The Brown Bear Who Wasn't. Bolinske, Janet L., ed. Quenell, Midge, illus. LC 87-63000. (ps-k). 1988. 17.95 (ISBN 0-88335-753-4); pap. 4.95 (ISBN 0-88335-076-9). Milliken Pub Co.
—The Underground Tea Party. Bolinske, Janet L., ed. Quenell, Midge, illus. LC 87-62996. 24p. (Orig.). (ps-k). 1988. spiral-bound Big Book 17.95 (ISBN 0-88335-758-5); pap. 4.95 (ISBN 0-88335-080-7). Milliken Pub Co.
Karlin, Nurit. The Dream Factory. Karlin, Nurit, illus. LC 87-45311. 32p. (ps-1). 1988. 12.95 (ISBN 0-397-32211-9, Lipp Jr Bks); PLB 12.89 (ISBN 0-397-32212-7). HarpC Child Bks.
—The Tooth Witch. Karlin, Nurit, illus. LC 84-62553. 32p. (ps-2). 1985. pap. 4.95 (ISBN 0-06-443079-0, Trophy). HarpC Child Bks.
Kassirer, Norma. Magic Elizabeth. Krush, Joe, illus. LC 66-11910. 176p. (gr. 2-6). 1990. pap. 3.50 (ISBN 0-679-80261-4, Bullseye Bks). Knopf.
Kates, Louise. Make Believe with the Muppet Babies: A Storybook. Cooke, Tom, illus. LC 86-42543. 32p. (gr. 3-7). 1986. 4.95 (ISBN 0-394-88184-2, Random Juv). Random.
Katz, Bobbi. The Creepy Crawly Book: With Reusable Stickers. Schindler, S. D., illus. 24p. (ps-1). 1989. 5.95 (ISBN 0-394-82709-0). Random.
—Play with the Care Bears. Katz, Bobbi, illus. LC 84-61375. 14p. (ps). 1985. pap. 4.95 (ISBN 0-394-87098-0, Random Juv). Random.
—The Runaway Ball. Brackman, Bob, illus. 14p. (ps-3). 1986. 5.95 (ISBN 0-394-87429-3). Random.
—Tick Tock, Let's Read the Clock: Green Ladder Books for Kids Through 6 Years. Nicklaus, Carol, illus. 16p. (ps-1). 1988. incl. clock 6.95 (ISBN 0-394-89399-9, Random Juv). Random.
Katz, Bobbi & Moseley, Keith. The Fox in the Farmyard. Wilson, Ann, illus. 14p. (ps-3). 1986. 5.95 (ISBN 0-394-87428-5). Random.
Kaufman, Curt & Kaufman, Gita. Hotel Boy. Curt, Kaufman, illus. LC 86-25925. 40p. (gr. k-3). 1987. 11.95 (ISBN 0-689-31287-3, Atheneum Child Bk). Macmillan Child Grp.
Kawami, David. Cut & Assemble Paper Dragons That Fly. 1989. pap. 3.50 (ISBN 0-486-25325-2). Dover.
Keathley, Jean. Pennies, Nickels, & Dreams. Graves, Helen, ed. LC 88-50117. 44p. (gr. k-3). 1988. 7.95 (ISBN 1-55523-137-3). Winston-Derek.
Keats, Ezra J. Jennie's Hat. Keats, Ezra J., illus. LC 66-15683. 32p. (gr. k-3). 1966. 13.95i (ISBN 0-06-023113-0); PLB 13.89 (ISBN 0-06-023114-9). HarpC Child Bks.
—Jennie's Hat. Keats, Ezra J., illus. LC 66-15683. 32p. (ps-3). 1985. pap. 4.95 (ISBN 0-06-443072-3, Trophy). HarpC Child Bks.
—Letter to Amy. Keats, Ezra J., illus. LC 68-24329. (gr. k-3). 1968. 14.95 (ISBN 0-06-023108-4); PLB 14.89 (ISBN 0-06-023109-2). HarpC Child Bks.
—Regards to the Man in the Moon. Keats, Ezra J., illus. 32p. (gr. k-3). 1987. pap. 3.95 (ISBN 0-689-71160-3, Aladdin Bks). Macmillan Child Grp.
—The Snowy Day. Keats, Ezra J., illus. LC 62-15441. 40p. (ps-1). 1962. pap. 11.95 (ISBN 0-670-65400-0). Viking Child Bks.
—The Trip. LC 77-24907. (ps-3). 1987. pap. 4.95 (ISBN 0-688-07328-X, Mulberry). Morrow.
—Whistle for Willie. Keats, Ezra J., illus. LC 64-13595. (ps-1). 1977. pap. 3.95 (ISBN 0-14-050202-5, Puffin). Puffin Bks.
—Whistle for Willie. Keats, Ezra J., illus. (ps-1). 1964. pap. 12.95 (ISBN 0-670-76240-7). Viking Child Bks.
Keller, Holly. Geraldine's Blanket. LC 83-14062. (Illus.). 32p. (ps-3). 1988. pap. 3.95 (ISBN 0-688-07810-9, Mulberry). Morrow.
Keller, Irene. The Thingumajig Book of Manners. Keller, Dick, illus. 32p. (ps-3). 1989. pap. 3.95 (ISBN 0-8249-8346-7). Ideals.
Kelley, True. Look Baby! Listen Baby! Do Baby! Kelley, True, illus. LC 87-6800. (ps). 1987. 9.95 (ISBN 0-525-44320-7, DCB). Dutton Child Bks.
Kellogg, Steven. Aster Aardvark's Alphabet Adventures. Kellogg, Steven, illus. LC 87-5715. 40p. (gr. k up). 1987. 13.95 (ISBN 0-688-07256-9); lib. bdg. 13.88 (ISBN 0-688-07257-7, Morrow Jr Bks). Morrow Jr Bks.

Kent, Jack. Ice Cream Soup. Herman, Gail, retold by. Alley, R. W., illus. LC 89-43680. 24p. (Orig.). (ps-2). 1990. pap. 2.25 (ISBN 0-679-80790-X). Random.
—Little Peep. Kent, Jack, illus. 32p. (ps up). 1989. pap. 12.95 (ISBN 0-671-67051-4); pap. 5.95 (ISBN 0-671-67052-2). S&S Trade.
—The Wizard. rev. ed. Kent, Jack, illus. 32p. (gr. k-3). pap. 5.95 (ISBN 0-317-93485-6). WW Pr.
Kent, Lorna, et al, illus. More & More: The Shopping List; Just Out for a Walk; Up in the Big Tree; All Dressed Up; In My Pocket & Off on Holiday, 6 bks. 96p. (gr. k-1). Set. pap. text ed. 28.90 (ISBN 1-55624-257-3). Wright Group.
Kent, Richard. Play On! 2nd ed. LC 85-50588. 124p. (gr. 9-12). 1989. 5.95 (ISBN 0-932433-04-9). Windswept Hse.
Kepes, Juliet. Cock-A-Doodle-Doo. Kepes, Juliet, illus. LC 76-44433. (ps-2). 1978. 6.95 (ISBN 0-394-83867-X). Pantheon.
—Frogs Merry. Kepes, Juliet, illus. (ps-2). 1963. lib. bdg. 6.99 (ISBN 0-394-91176-8). Pantheon.
Ker, John. BMX in Action. 1988. pap. 2.25 (ISBN 0-89954-780-X). Antioch Pub Co.
Kesselman, Wendy. Emma. Cooney, Barbara, illus. LC 84-48783. 32p. (ps-3). 1985. pap. 4.95 (ISBN 0-06-443077-4, Trophy). HarpC Child Bks.
Kessler, Ethel & Kessler, Leonard. Are There Seals in the Sandbox? Kessler, Leonard, illus. 22p. (ps). 1990. casebound with padded cover 4.95 (ISBN 0-671-70539-3, Little Simon). S&S Trade.
—Is There a Horse in Your House? Kessler, Leonard, illus. 22p. (ps). 1990. casebound with padded cover 4.95 (ISBN 0-671-70540-7). S&S Trade.
Khalsa, Dayal K. Baabee Books, Series II, 4 Bks, Bks. 5-8. (Illus.). 48p. (ps). 1983. Set. text ed. 12.95 (ISBN 0-88776-150-X). Tundra Bks.
—Bon Voyage Baabee. (Illus.). 12p. (ps). 1984. text ed. 2.95 (ISBN 0-88776-146-1). Tundra Bks.
—Happy Birthday Baabee. (Illus.). 12p. (ps). 1984. text ed. 2.95 (ISBN 0-88776-144-5, Dist. by U of Toronto Pr). Tundra Bks.
—Merry Christmas Baabee. (Illus.). 12p. (ps). 1984. text ed. 2.95 (ISBN 0-88776-145-3). Tundra Bks.
—Sleepers. (Illus.). 24p. (ps-1). 1988. PLB 7.95 (ISBN 0-517-56917-5, C N Potter Bks). Crown.
—Welcome Twins. (Illus.). 12p. (ps). 1984. text ed. 2.95 (ISBN 0-88776-147-X). Tundra Bks.
Kidner, Maria C. ABC Come See Wyoming. Campbell, Loreen, illus. 56p. (Orig.). (gr. k-3). 1990. pap. 4.95 (ISBN 0-9625920-0-5). Rainbow Rhapsody.
Kightley, Rosalinda. The Farmer. Kightley, Rosalinda, illus. LC 87-15261. 32p. (ps-2). 1988. 12.95 (ISBN 0-02-750290-2, Mcmillan Child Bk). Macmillan Child Grp.
—The Farmer. Kightley, Rosalinda, illus. LC 88-19431. 32p. (ps-2). 1989. pap. 3.95 (ISBN 0-689-71222-7, Aladdin). Macmillan Child Grp.
—The Postman. LC 87-14160. (Illus.). 32p. (ps-2). 1988. 12.95 (ISBN 0-02-750270-8, Mcmillan Child Bk). Macmillan Child Grp.
—The Postman. Kightley, Rosalinda, illus. LC 88-19431. 32p. (ps-2). 1989. pap. 3.95 (ISBN 0-689-71223-5, Aladdin). Macmillan Child Grp.
Kilroy, Sally. Market Day. Kilroy, Sally, illus. 16p. (gr. 1-3). 1986. pap. 2.95 (ISBN 0-670-80339-1). Viking Child Bks.
Kindergarten Skills. (ps). 1985. 3.95 (ISBN 0-394-87707-1, Random Juv). Random.
Kindergarteners of Paul Mort Elementary. Looking for a Rainbow. (Illus.). 24p. (gr. k-3). 1987. 2.95 (ISBN 0-87406-227-6). Willowisp Pr.
King, Celia. Seven Ancient Wonders: A Pop-up Book. (Illus.). 7p. 1990. text ed. 8.95 (ISBN 0-87701-707-7). Chronicle Bks.
King, P. E. Down on the Funny Farm: A Step Two Book. Graham, Alastair, illus. LC 85-11893. 48p. (gr. 1-3). 1986. PLB 6.99 (ISBN 0-394-97460-3); pap. 2.95 (ISBN 0-394-87460-9). Random.
King, Tony. The Moving Animal Book. King, Tony, illus. (ps up). 1983. 9.95 (ISBN 0-399-20964-6, Putnam). Putnam Pub Group.
Kingshead Corporation Staff. Cut-Color & Create: Make Your Own: Dinosaur Playmates. (Illus.). 24p. (ps-8). Date not set. pap. write for info. (ISBN 1-55941-041-8). Kingshead Corp.
—Cut-Color & Create: Make Your Own: Fashions of the Ages. (Illus.). 24p. (ps-8). Date not set. pap. write for info. (ISBN 1-55941-028-0). Kingshead Corp.
—Cut-Color & Create: Make Your Own: Land of the Dinosaurs. (Illus.). 24p. (ps-8). Date not set. pap. write for info. (ISBN 1-55941-040-X). Kingshead Corp.
—Cut-Color & Create: Make Your Own: Space Settlers. (Illus.). 24p. (ps-8). Date not set. pap. write for info. (ISBN 1-55941-042-6). Kingshead Corp.
Kingsley, Emily P. A Baby Sister for Herry. Walz, Richard, illus. LC 83-83280. 24p. (ps). 1984. write for info. (ISBN 0-307-12011-2, 12011, Golden Bks). Western Pub.
—Sesame Street Big Bird & Little Bird's Book of Big & Little. Delaney, A., illus. 24p. (ps-k). 1977. pap. write for info (ISBN 0-307-10073-1, Pub. by Golden Bks). Western Pub.
—The Sesame Street Pet Show. Chartier, Normand, illus. 24p. (ps-3). 1988. pap. write for info. (ISBN 0-307-13819-4, 13819, Pub. by Golden Bks). Western Pub.
Kingsley, Pearl. Sesame Street: One Two Three Storybook. 1986. pap. 4.95 (ISBN 0-394-88302-0). Random.
King-Smith, Dick. Farmer Bungle Forgets. LC 87-1163. (Illus.). 32p. (ps-1). 1987. 12.95 (ISBN 0-689-31370-5, Atheneum Child Bk). Macmillan Child Grp.
Kipling, Rudyard. The Elephant's Child. Raglin, Tim, illus. LC 86-377. 48p. (gr. k up). 1986. incl. cassette 14.95 (ISBN 0-394-88300-4); 12.95 (ISBN 0-394-88401-9). Knopf.
—How the Camel Got His Hump. Raglin, Tim, illus. LC 88-33366. 32p. (ps up). 1989. 14.95 (ISBN 0-88708-096-0, Rabbit Ears); incl. cassette 19.95 (ISBN 0-88708-097-9). Picture Bk Studio.
—How the Rhinoceros Got His Skin. Raglin, Tim, illus. LC 88-11439. 28p. (ps up). 1988. 14.95 (ISBN 0-88708-078-2, Rabbit Ears); bk. & cass. pkg. 19.95 (ISBN 0-88708-083-9). Picture Bk Studio.
Kirkwood, Ken & Marshall, Ray. Search for the Rare Plumidor. Kirkwood, Ken, illus. (gr. 1-7). 1983. 9.95 (ISBN 0-399-20967-0, Philomel). Putnam Pub Group.
Kitamura, Satoshi. Captain Toby. Kitamura, Satoshi, illus. LC 88-15029. 24p. (ps-1). 1988. 10.95 (ISBN 0-525-44414-9, DCB). Dutton Child Bks.
—Lily Takes a Walk. Kitamura, Satoshi, illus. LC 87-8894. (ps-1). 1987. 9.95 (ISBN 0-525-44333-9, DCB). Dutton Child Bks.
—What's Inside? Kitamura, Satoshi, illus. 32p. (ps up). 1987. pap. 3.95 (ISBN 0-374-48324-8). FS&G.
—When Sheep Cannot Sleep. (Illus.). 32p. (ps up). 1988. pap. 3.95 (ISBN 0-374-48359-0). FS&G.
Kitties' Purr-fect Caper. 24p. (gr. k-2). 1990. 3.95 (ISBN 0-87449-668-3). Modern Pub NYC.
Kitty's Book of Shapes. 1988. 2.99 (ISBN 0-517-66173-X). Crown.
Kline, Suzy. The Hole Book. Newton, Laurie, illus. 24p. (ps-k). 1989. 9.95 (ISBN 0-399-21719-3, Putnam). Putnam Pub Group.
—Ooops! Fay, Ann, ed. Leder, Dora, illus. 32p. (ps-2). 1988. PLB 12.95 (ISBN 0-8075-6122-3). A Whitman.
—Ooops! Leder, Dora, illus. 32p. (ps). 1989. pap. 3.95 (ISBN 0-14-050986-0, Puffin). Puffin Bks.
Klinting, Lars. Regal: The Golden Eagle. Bernstein, Alan, tr. (Illus.). 32p. (ps up). 1988. 6.95 (ISBN 9-12-958774-3, R & S Bks). FS&G.
Knight, Hilary. Hilary Knight's the Owl & the Pussycat. (Illus.). 32p. (ps-3). 1989. pap. 3.95 (ISBN 0-689-71331-2, Aladdin). Macmillan Child Grp.
—Where's Wallace? LC 64-19717. (ps-3). 1964. 14.95 (ISBN 0-06-023170-X); PLB 14.89 (ISBN 0-06-023171-8). HarpC Child Bks.
—Where's Wallace? Knight, Hilary, illus. LC 64-19717. 48p. (ps-3). 1986. pap. 4.95 (ISBN 0-06-443094-4, Trophy). HarpC Child Bks.
Knight, Joan. The Baby Who Would Not Come Down. Santini, Debrah, illus. LC 89-3987. 28p. (ps up). 1989. 14.95 (ISBN 0-88708-107-X). Picture Bk Studio.
—Tickle-Toe Rhymes. Wallner, John, illus. LC 88-60088. 32p. (ps-2). 1989. 13.95 (ISBN 0-531-05773-9); PLB 13.99 (ISBN 0-531-08373-X). Orchard Bks Watts.
Know an Old Lady. 24p. 1987. pap. 2.95 (ISBN 0-553-15574-1). Bantam.
Kobayashi, Yuji. Miss Josephine's Secret Walk. (Illus.). 32p. (ps-2). 1987. 11.95 (ISBN 0-88138-096-2). Green Tiger Pr.
Koller, Jackie F. Impy for Always. (ps-3). 1991. pap. 2.95 (ISBN 0-316-50149-2). Little.
Komaiko, Leah. Earl's Too Cool for Me. Cornell, Laura, illus. LC 87-30803. 40p. (gr. k-3). 1990. pap. 4.95 (ISBN 0-06-443245-9, Trophy). HarpC Child Bks.
—My Perfect Neighborhood. Westman, Barbara, illus. LC 89-37871. 32p. (ps-3). 1990. 13.95 (ISBN 0-06-023287-0); PLB 13.89 (ISBN 0-06-023288-9). HarpC Child Bks.
Komori, Atsushi. Animal Mothers. Yabuuchi, Masayuki, illus. LC 82-22411. (ps-1). 1983. 8.95 (ISBN 0-399-20980-8, Philomel). Putnam Pub Group.
Koontz, Robin M. Dinosaur Dream. Koontz, Robin M., illus. 32p. (ps-1). 1988. 12.95 (ISBN 0-399-21669-3, Putnam). Putnam Pub Group.
Koontz, Robin M., illus. This Old Man: The Counting Song. 32p. (ps-1). 1988. 12.95 (ISBN 0-396-09120-2, Putnam). Putnam Pub Group.
Koralek, Jenny. The Cobweb Curtain: A Christmas Story. Baynes, Pauline, illus. LC 88-27035. 32p. 1989. 13.95 (ISBN 0-8050-1051-3). H Holt & Co.
Korman, Justine. Daffy Duck in Duck Troop to the Rescue. (Illus.). 24p. (ps). 1990. pap. write for info. (ISBN 0-307-11658-1, Pub. by Golden Books). Western Pub.
Korschunow, Irina. Small Fur. Skofield, James, tr. from GER. Michl, Reinhard, illus. LC 87-45289. 80p. (gr. 1-4). 1988. 12.95 (ISBN 0-06-023247-1); PLB 12.89 (ISBN 0-06-023248-X). HarpC Child Bks.
Kovacs, Deborah. A Day in Space. 160p. (gr. k-3). 1986. pap. 2.50 (ISBN 0-590-41099-7). Scholastic Inc.
—Woody's First Dictionary. Rose, Eve, illus. 24p. (ps-2). 1988. 3.95 (ISBN 0-448-09287-5, G&D). Putnam Pub Group.
Kovalski, Maryann. Wheels on the Bus. (ps-4). 1990. pap. 4.95 (ISBN 0-316-50259-6, Joy St Bks). Little.
Kowalczyk, Carolyn. El Morado Es Parte del Arco Iris (Purple Is Part of a Rainbow) Sharp, Gene, illus. LC 85-11693. (SPA.). 32p. (ps-2). 1988. PLB 11.27 (ISBN 0-516-32068-8); pap. 2.95 (ISBN 0-516-52068-7). Childrens.
Kraft, Jim. Garfield & the Haunted Diner: A Lift-the-Flap Book. Fentz, Mike, illus. Davis, Jim, created by. (Illus.). 24p. 1989. 10.95 (ISBN 0-448-00398-8, G&D). Putnam Pub Group.
Krahn, Fernando. Amanda & the Mysterious Carpet. Krahn, Fernando, illus. LC 84-14201. 32p. (ps-3). 1985. 13.95 (ISBN 0-89919-258-0, Clarion). HM.
Kraul, Edward G. & Beatty, Judith. Little Herman Meets la Llorona at the Santa Fe Fiestas: A Story-Color Book in English & Spanish. Gomez, Jose, illus. (ENG & SPA.). 24p. (gr. 3-6). 1989. story-color book 2.95 (ISBN 0-945937-03-2). Word Process.
Kraus, Robert. Buggy Bear Cleans Up. Brook, Bonnie, ed. Kraus, Robert, illus. 48p. (ps-3). 1989. PLB 8.98 (ISBN 0-671-68608-9); pap. 3.50 (ISBN 0-671-68612-7). Silver Pr.
—Bunny's Nutshell Library, 4 bks. Kraus, Robert, illus. Incl. The First Robin (ISBN 0-06-023285-4); Juniper (ISBN 0-06-023295-1); The Silver Dandelion (ISBN 0-06-023300-1); Springfellow's Parade. LC 65-11450. (gr. 1 up). 1965. Set. 10.95 (ISBN 0-06-023225-0). HarpC Child Bks.
—Ella the Bad Speller. Brook, Bonnie, ed. Kraus, Robert, illus. 48p. (ps-3). 1989. PLB 8.98 (ISBN 0-671-68606-2); pap. 3.50 (ISBN 0-671-68610-0). Silver Pr.
—Good Morning, Miss Gator. Brook, Bonnie, ed. Kraus, Robert, illus. 48p. (ps-3). 1989. PLB 8.98 (ISBN 0-671-68605-4); pap. 3.50 (ISBN 0-671-68609-7). Silver Pr.
—Happy City. Kraus, Robert, illus. (ps). 1987. pap. 2.95 (ISBN 0-671-62933-6, Little Simon). S&S Trade.
—Happy Farm. Kraus, Robert, illus. (ps). 1987. pap. 2.95 (ISBN 0-671-62936-0, Little Simon). S&S Trade.
—Here Comes Tardy Toad. Brook, Bonnie, ed. Kraus, Robert, illus. 48p. (ps-3). 1989. PLB 8.98 (ISBN 0-671-68607-0); pap. 3.50 (ISBN 0-671-68611-9). Silver Pr.
—How Spider Saved Halloween. 40p. (gr. k-3). pap. 2.50 (ISBN 0-590-41395-3). Scholastic Inc.
—Squeaky. (Illus.). 10p. (ps). 1982. vinyl cover 3.50 (ISBN 0-671-44861-7, Little Simon). S&S Trade.
Krauss, Ruth. Big & Little. Szilagyi, Mary, illus. 32p. (ps-3). 1988. pap. 12.95 (ISBN 0-590-41707-X). Scholastic Inc.
—Big & Little. Szilagyi, Mary, illus. 32p. (ps-1). 1991. pap. 3.95 (ISBN 0-590-40699-X). Scholastic Inc.
—Birthday Party. Sendak, Maurice, illus. (gr. k-3). 1957. PLB 11.89 (ISBN 0-06-023330-3). HarpC Child Bks.
—Carrot Seed. Johnson, Crockett, illus. LC 45-4530. 24p. (gr. k-3). 1945. 10.95 (ISBN 0-06-023350-8); PLB 10.89 (ISBN 0-06-023351-6). HarpC Child Bks.
—The Carrot Seed. Johnson, Crockett, illus. (ps-3). 1990. incl. cass. 19.95 (ISBN 0-87499-177-3); pap. 12.95 incl. cass. (ISBN 0-87499-176-5); Set; incl. 4 bks., guide, & cass. pap. 27.95 (ISBN 0-685-38538-8). Live Oak Media.
—Growing Story. Rowand, Phyllis, illus. LC 47-30688. (gr. k-3). 1947. 11.95i (ISBN 0-06-023380-X). HarpC Child Bks.
—The Happy Day. Simont, Marc, illus. LC 49-10568. 36p. (gr. k-3). 1989. pap. 3.95 (ISBN 0-06-443191-6, Trophy). HarpC Child Bks.
—A Hole Is to Dig. Sendak, Maurice, illus. 48p. (gr. k-3). pap. 2.25 (ISBN 0-590-40788-0). Scholastic Inc.
—A Hole Is to Dig: A First Book of Definitions. Sendak, Maurice, illus. LC 52-7731. 48p. (ps up). 1989. pap. 3.95 (ISBN 0-06-443205-X, Trophy). HarpC Child Bks.
—Hole Is to Dig: A First Book of First Definitions. Sendak, Maurice, illus. LC 52-7731. (ps-1). 1952. 12.95 (ISBN 0-06-023405-9); PLB 13.89 (ISBN 0-06-023406-7). HarpC Child Bks.
—I'll Be You & You Be Me. Sendak, Maurice, illus. LC 54-9214. (gr. k-3). 1954. PLB 12.89 (ISBN 0-06-023431-8). HarpC Child Bks.
—Very Special House. Sendak, Maurice, illus. LC 53-7115. (ps-1). 1953. 12.89 (ISBN 0-685-02070-3). HarpC Child Bks.
Krementz, Jill. Jack Goes to the Beach. Krementz, Jill, photos by. LC 85-62038. (Illus.). 14p. (ps). 1986. bds. 3.95 (ISBN 0-394-88001-3). Random.
Krensky, Stephen. Lionel at Large. Natti, Susanna, illus. LC 85-1450. 56p. (ps-3). 1986. 9.95 (ISBN 0-8037-0240-X); PLB 8.89 (ISBN 0-8037-0241-8). Dial Bks Young.
Kroeber, Theodora. Green Christmas. Larrecq, John M., illus. LC 67-26304. (gr. k-2). 1967. 6.95 (ISBN 0-87466-047-5, Pub. by Parnassus). HM.
Kroll, Steven. Don't Get Me in Trouble. Glass, Marvin, illus. 32p. (gr. k-2). 1987. PLB 11.95 (ISBN 0-517-56724-5). Crown.
—The Hokey-Pokey Man. Ray, Deborah K., illus. LC 88-17012. 32p. (gr. k-3). 1989. reinforced bdg. 14.95 (ISBN 0-8234-0728-4). Holiday.
—Pigs in the House. Kirk, Tim, illus. LC 83-13310. 48p. (ps-3). 1983. 5.95 (ISBN 0-8193-1111-1). Parents.
Krueger, Ron, et al. Bearly There at All. French, Marty, illus. 26p. (ps up). 1986. Incl. cass. 7.95 (ISBN 1-55578-106-3). Worlds Wonder.
Krulik, Nancy E. Big Top Pee-wee: A Color & Fun Book. (Illus.). 32p. (gr. k-3). 1988. pap. 1.95 (ISBN 0-590-42203-0, 049). Scholastic Inc.
Kudrna, C. Imbior. To Bathe a Boa. Kudrna, C. Imbiore., illus. 32p. (ps-4). 1986. PLB 12.95 (ISBN 0-87614-306-0); pap. 5.95 (ISBN 0-87614-490-3). Carolrhoda Bks.
Kuklin, Susan. Going to My Ballet Class. Kuklin, Susan, illus. LC 88-37556. 32p. (ps-2). 1989. 12.95 (ISBN 0-02-751235-5, Bradbury Pr). Macmillan Child Grp.
—Taking My Cat to the Vet. Kuklin, Susan, illus. LC 88-5052. 32p. (ps-1). 1988. 12.95 (ISBN 0-02-751233-9, Bradbury Pr). Macmillan Child Grp.

—Taking My Dog to the Vet. Kuklin, Susan, illus. LC 88-5047. 32p. (ps-1). 1988. 12.95 (ISBN 0-02-751234-7, Bradbury Pr). Macmillan Child Grp.

Kunhardt, Dorothy. Pat the Bunny. Kunhardt, Dorothy, illus. (ps). 1988. Includes Touch & Feel Book with Plush Doll. pap. write for info. (ISBN 0-307-14000-8, Pub. by Golden Bks). Western Pub.

Kunhardt, Edith. The Airplane Book. Bracken, Carolyn, illus. 24p. (ps-k). 1987. pap. write for info. (ISBN 0-307-10083-9, Pub. by Golden Bks). Western Pub.

—How Speedy Is a Cheetah? Roe, Richard, illus. 32p. (ps-2). 1987. pap. 1.95 (ISBN 0-448-19081-8, Platt & Munk). Putnam Pub Group.

—I Want to Be a Farmer. Kunhardt, Edith, photos by. (Illus.). 32p. (ps-2). 1989. 6.95 (ISBN 0-448-09068-6, G&D). Putnam Pub Group.

—I Want to Be a Fire Fighter. Kunhardt, Edith, photos by. (Illus.). 32p. (ps-2). 1989. 6.95 (ISBN 0-448-09069-4, G&D). Putnam Pub Group.

—Pat the Cat. Kunhardt, Edith, illus. LC 83-83106. (ps-3). 1984. write for info. comb. bdg. (ISBN 0-307-12001-5, 12001, Golden Bks). Western Pub.

Kurz, Ann. Cranberries from A to Z: An Educational Picture Book. Kurz, Ann, illus. LC 89-61059. 32p. (gr. k-8). 1989. PLB 13.95 (ISBN 0-9622784-0-8). Cranberry Origs.

Kuskin, Karla. The Dallas Titans Get Ready for Bed. Simont, Marc, illus. LC 83-49470. 48p. (ps-3). 1988. pap. 3.95 (ISBN 0-06-443180-0, Trophy). HarpC Child Bks.

—Jerusalem, Shining Still. Frampton, David, illus. LC 86-25841. 32p. (gr. 1 up). 1990. pap. 5.50 (ISBN 0-06-443243-2, Trophy). HarpC Child Bks.

—The Philharmonic Gets Dressed. Simont, Marc, illus. LC 81-48658. 48p. (ps-3). 1986. pap. 3.95 (ISBN 0-06-443124-X, Trophy). HarpC Child Bks.

—Roar & More. rev. ed. Kuskin, Karla, illus. LC 89-15650. 48p. (ps-1). 1990. pap. 3.95 (ISBN 0-06-443244-0, Trophy). HarpC Child Bks.

LaBelle, Susan. Flopsy, Mopsy & Cottontail: A Little Book of Paper Dolls in Full Color. (Illus.). 48p. (gr. 1 up). 1983. pap. 2.95 (ISBN 0-486-24376-1). Dover.

Lacome, Julie, illus. Words. 32p. (ps-k). 1986. pap. 3.95 (ISBN 0-448-10831-3, G&D). Putnam Pub Group.

Ladybird Words & Pictures. (Illus.). (ps-k). 8.95 (ISBN 0-7214-7542-6). Ladybird Bks.

Lamont, Priscilla. Our Mammoth Goes to School. Lamont, Pricilla, illus. LC 86-26939. 32p. (gr. 4-8). 1988. 11.95 (ISBN 0-15-258837-X, HJ). HarBraceJ.

Langstaff, John & Rojankovsky, Feodor. Over in the Meadow. Rojankovsky, Feodor, illus. LC 57-8587. 32p. (ps-3). 1973. pap. 3.95 (ISBN 0-15-670500-1, VoyB). HarBraceJ.

Lansky, Vicki. Koko Bear's Big Earache: Preparing for Ear Tube Surgery. (Orig.). (ps). 1990. pap. 4.95 (ISBN 0-916773-26-4). Book Peddlers.

—Koko Bear's New Babysitter. (Orig.). (ps). 1989. pap. 3.95 (ISBN 0-916773-24-8). Book Peddlers.

—Koko Bear's New Potty, No. 1. Prince, Jane L., illus. 32p. 1986. pap. 3.50 (ISBN 0-553-34243-6). Bantam.

Laporte, Michel. Investigate with Prune & Prosper at the Beach. Poulot, Alexandra, illus. 24p. (ps-3). 1989. 6.95 (ISBN 0-8120-6101-2). Barron.

—Investigate with Prune & Prosper at the Zoo. Poulot, Alexandra, illus. 24p. (ps-3). 1989. 6.95 (ISBN 0-8120-6102-0). Barron.

—Investigate with Prune & Prosper on the Farm. Poulot, Alexandra, illus. 24p. (ps-3). 1989. 6.95 (ISBN 0-8120-6103-9). Barron.

La Rochelle, David. A Christmas Guest. Skoro, Martin, illus. 32p. (ps-3). 1988. PLB 12.95 (ISBN 0-87614-325-7); pap. 5.95 (ISBN 0-87614-506-3). Carolrhoda Bks.

LaRochelle, David. A Christmas Guest. Skoro, Martin, illus. 32p. (ps-3). 1989. pap. 5.95 (ISBN 0-685-25636-7, First Ave Edns). Lerner Pubns.

Lasker, Joe. He's My Brother. Lasker, Joe, illus. LC 73-7318. 40p. (ps-2). 1974. PLB 12.95 (ISBN 0-8075-3218-5). A Whitman.

—A Tournament of Knights. Lasker, Joe, illus. LC 85-48075. 32p. (gr. 3 up). 1989. pap. 4.95 (ISBN 0-06-443192-4, Trophy). HarpC Child Bks.

Latta, Rich. Mother Goose Puzzles, No. 1. (Illus.). 48p. (ps). 1988. pap. 2.95 (ISBN 0-8431-2229-3). Price Stern.

Lattimore, Eleanor F. Little Pear. Lattimore, Eleanor F., illus. LC 31-22069. (gr. k-3). 1968. pap. 3.95 (ISBN 0-15-652799-5, VoyB). HarBraceJ.

Lauber, Patricia. Journey to the Planets. rev. ed. (Illus.). (gr. 5 up). 1987. PLB 14.95 (ISBN 0-517-56548-X). Crown.

—The News about Dinosaurs. Gurche, John, et al, illus. LC 88-24140. 48p. (gr. 1-5). 1989. 15.95 (ISBN 0-02-754520-2, Bradbury Pr). Macmillan Child Grp.

Laurin, Anne. Perfect Crane. Mikolaycak, Charles, illus. LC 80-7912. 32p. (gr. 1-4). 1987. pap. 4.95 (ISBN 0-06-443154-1, Trophy). HarpC Child Bks.

Lavie, Arlette. Half a World Away. (ps-3). 1990. pap. 3.95 (ISBN 0-85953-334-4). Childs Play.

Lavut, Karen. Jacques' Jungle Ballet. Rigg, Nicola, illus. LC 89-1985. 32p. (ps-2). 1989. 13.95 (ISBN 0-8050-1123-4). H Holt & Co.

Lawrence, Jim. Shy Little Kitten's Secret Place. (Illus.). 24p. (ps up). 1990. write for info. (ISBN 0-307-12089-9, Pub. by Golden Bks). Western Pub.

Leaf, Munro. Safety Can Be Fun. 2nd rev. ed. Leaf, Munro, illus. LC 86-45499. 48p. (ps-2). 1988. pap. 3.95 (ISBN 0-06-443111-8, Trophy). HarpC Child Bks.

—The Story of Ferdinand. Lawson, Robert, illus. (ps-3). 1988. pap. 9.95 (ISBN 0-14-095075-3, Puffin); bk. & t-shirt 9.95 (ISBN 0-318-37105-7, Puffin); bk. & cassette 6.95 (ISBN 0-318-37106-5, Puffin). Puffin Bks.

Lear, Edward. The Owl & the Pussycat. Berg, Ron, illus. 24p. (gr. k-3). pap. 2.50 (ISBN 0-590-00350-X). Scholastic Inc.

—The Scroobious Pip. Burkett, Nancy E., illus. LC 68-10373. 32p. (gr. 1-3). 1987. pap. 5.95 (ISBN 0-06-443132-0, Trophy). HarpC Child Bks.

LeCain, Errol. Thorn Rose. (Illus.). (ps-3). 1978. pap. 3.95 (ISBN 0-14-050222-X, Puffin). Puffin Bks.

Leder, Dora, illus. Let's Peek in Santa's Pack. LC 89-61375. 14p. (ps). 1990. bds. 2.95 (ISBN 0-679-80277-0). Random.

Lee, Jeanne M., retold by. & illus. Toad Is the Uncle of Heaven: A Vietnamese Folk Tale. LC 85-5639. 32p. (gr. 4-7). 1989. pap. 4.95 (ISBN 0-8050-1147-1). H Holt & Co.

Leedy, Loreen. Big, Small, Short, Tall. Leedy, Loreen, illus. LC 86-46203. 32p. (ps-1). 1987. reinforced bdg. 12.95 (ISBN 0-8234-0645-8). Holiday.

—Pingo the Plaid Panda. Leedy, Loreen, illus. LC 88-17005. 32p. (ps-3). 1989. reinforced bdg. 13.95 (ISBN 0-8234-0727-6). Holiday.

Leffler, Maryann C. My A B C's at Home. (Illus.). 24p. (ps). 1990. bds. 2.50 (ISBN 0-448-02257-5, G&D). Putnam Pub Group.

Le Guin, Ursula K. Fire & Stone. LC 88-16799. (Illus.). 32p. (gr. 1-3). 1989. 13.95 (ISBN 0-689-31408-6, Atheneum Child Bk). Macmillan Child Grp.

Lehman, James H. The Saga of Shakespeare Pintlewood & the Great Silver Fountain Pen. Raschka, Christopher, illus. LC 90-82303. 32p. (gr. k-3). 1990. PLB 13.95 (ISBN 1-878925-00-8). Brotherstone Pubs. Shakespeare Pintlewood is an ant. Because he is small, he sees things as children do. After a heroic struggle to write with his large silver pen, he becomes a great literary ant. But he still doesn't know any children. So he shoulders his pen & sets out to find them. Lehman's wry, gentle story & Raschka's warm, delicately humorous illustrations, full of inviting detail, give an ant's eye (Child's eye) view of the hard work & pleasure of writing, of the deep satisfaction stories produce when they bring people together. Readers of all ages are charmed by Shakey & his quest to know & love children. "This is a good book. I liked it when Shakey slid across the spilled ink & when he rode on the little chair. Other kids would like Shakey."--Jennifer, age 5. "All the kids liked it. They wanted to know what happened to the pen. They really listened intently. It really grabbed their interest."--elementary special education teacher. "My daughter loves it. She took it to school & had her teacher read it in class."--mother of 7-year-old. "This book has good values--creativity, persistence, love & loyalty. Raschka's illustrations are inventive, bright, & detailed."--Ann Arbor News.
Publisher Provided Annotation.

Lehmann, Terry & Nobisso, Joi. How to Fill an Empty Lap. Greenberg, Melanie, illus. 32p. (Orig.). (ps). 1980. pap. text ed. 3.00 (ISBN 0-940112-00-0). Little Feat.

Leigh, Tom, illus. The Sesame Street Word Book. 72p. (ps). 1983. write for info. (ISBN 0-307-15549-8, 15818, Golden Bks). Western Pub.

LeMair, Henriette W., illus. Baby's Diary. 112p. (ps up). 1987. 11.95 (ISBN 0-399-21454-2, Philomel Bks). Putnam Pub Group.

Lemke, Horst, illus. Places & Faces. LC 78-160446. 32p. (ps-k). 8.95 (ISBN 0-87592-041-1). Scroll Pr.

The Lemonade Mystery. (Illus.). 64p. (gr. k-2). 1989. 6.95 (ISBN 0-87449-509-1). Modern Pub NYC.

L'Engle, Madeleine. A Wrinkle in Time. 224p. (gr. 4up). 1988. limited edition 50.00 (ISBN 0-374-38614-5). FS&G.

Lenski, Lois. Cowboy Small. LC 60-12094. (Illus.). (gr. k-3). 1980. 5.25 (ISBN 0-8098-1021-2). McKay.

—Little Airplane. Lenski, Lois, illus. LC 59-12487. (gr. k-3). 1980. 5.25 (ISBN 0-8098-1004-2). McKay.

—Little Auto. Lenski, Lois, illus. LC 58-14239. (gr. k-3). 1980. 5.25 (ISBN 0-8098-1001-8). McKay.

—Little Farm. Lenski, Lois, illus. LC 58-12902. (gr. k-3). 1980. 5.25 (ISBN 0-8098-1009-3). McKay.

—Lois Lenski's Big Big Book of Mr. Small. (Illus.). 300p. (ps-1). 1985. 5.98 (ISBN 0-517-46307-5). Outlet Bk Co.

—More Mr. Small. (ps-3). 1980. 9.95 (ISBN 0-8098-6300-6, Walk). McKay.

Leo the Lop Plush Gift Set. (Illus., Orig.). 1989. incl. plush toy, 2 bks, audiocass, 2 bkmarks 24.95 (ISBN 0-8431-5819-0). Price Stern.

Leonard, Marcia. Birthday in a Bathtub. Brook, Bonnie, ed. Wallner, John, illus. 24p. (ps-1). 1989. 4.95 (ISBN 0-671-68592-9); PLB 9.98 (ISBN 0-671-68588-0). Silver Pr.

—Counting Kangaroos, A Book about Numbers. Palmisciano, Diane, illus. LC 89-4960. 24p. (gr. k-2). 1990. PLB 8.79 (ISBN 0-8167-1722-2); pap. text ed. 1.95 (ISBN 0-8167-1723-0). Troll Assocs.

—The Kitten Twins: A Book about Opposites. Cocca-Leffler, Maryann, illus. LC 89-4945. 24p. (gr. k-2). 1990. PLB 7.89 (ISBN 0-8167-1724-9); pap. text ed. 1.95 (ISBN 0-8167-1725-7). Troll Assocs.

—Noisy Neighbors: A Book about Animal Sounds. Weissman, Bari, illus. LC 89-4959. 24p. (gr. k-2). 1990. PLB 8.79 (ISBN 0-8167-1726-5); pap. text ed. 1.95 (ISBN 0-8167-1727-3). Troll Assocs.

—Paintbox Penguins, A Book about Colors. Palmisciano, Diane, illus. LC 89-4979. 24p. (gr. k-2). 1990. lib. bdg. 8.79 (ISBN 0-8167-1716-8); pap. text ed. 1.95 (ISBN 0-8167-1717-6). Troll Assocs.

—Rainboots for Breakfast. Brook, Bonnie, ed. Himmelman, John, illus. 24p. (ps-1). 1989. 4.95 (ISBN 0-671-68591-0); PLB 9.98 (ISBN 0-671-68587-2). Silver Pr.

—Shopping for Snowflakes. Brook, Bonnie, ed. Himmelman, John, illus. 24p. (ps-1). 1989. 4.95 (ISBN 0-671-68594-5); PLB 9.98 (ISBN 0-671-68590-2). Silver Pr.

—Swimming in the Sand. Brook, Bonnie, ed. Wallner, John, illus. 24p. (ps-1). 1989. 4.95 (ISBN 0-671-68593-7); PLB 9.98 (ISBN 0-671-68589-9). Silver Pr.

—What Next, 4 bks. Himmelman, John & Wallner, John, illus. (ps-1). 1990. Set, 24p. ea. 19.80 (ISBN 0-671-94102-X); Set, 24p. ea. lib. bdg. 39.92 (ISBN 0-671-94101-1). Messner.

—What's Missing? Ser, 4 vols. Cushman, Doug & Banek, Yvette, illus. 96p. (ps-1). 1990. Set. 19.80 (ISBN 0-671-94433-9); Set. 14.85s.p.; Set. PLB 39.92 (ISBN 0-671-94432-0); Set. PLB 29.94s.p. Silver Pr.

LeSieg, Theo. The Pop-up Mice of Mr. Brice. McKie, Roy, illus. LC 89-60507. 20p. (ps-3). 1989. 9.95 (ISBN 0-679-80132-4, Random Juv). Random.

Le Sieg, Theodore. Ten Apples up on Top. LC 61-7068. (Illus.). 72p. (gr. 1-2). 1961. 6.95 (ISBN 0-394-80019-2); lib. bdg. 7.99 (ISBN 0-394-90019-7). Beginner.

—Wacky Wednesday. Booth, George, illus. LC 74-5520. 48p. (gr. k-4). 1974. 6.95 (ISBN 0-394-82912-3, Bergin & Garvey); lib. bdg. 7.99 (ISBN 0-394-92912-8, Bergin & Garvey). Beginner.

Lessac, Frane. My Little Island. Lessac, Frane, illus. LC 84-48355. 48p. (ps-3). 1987. pap. 4.95 (ISBN 0-06-443146-0, Trophy). HarpC Child Bks.

Lester, Alison. Rosie Sips Spiders. Lester, Alison, illus. 32p. (ps-k). 1989. 13.95 (ISBN 0-395-51526-2). HM.

Lester, Helen. Pookins Gets Her Way. Munsinger, Lynn, illus. (ps-3). 1990. 12.95 (ISBN 0-395-42636-7); pap. 4.95 (ISBN 0-395-53965-X). HM.

Le Tord, Bijou. Joseph & Nellie. LC 85-26662. (Illus.). 32p. (ps-2). 1986. 11.95 (ISBN 0-02-756450-9, Bradbury Pr). Macmillan Child Grp.

—The Little Hills of Nazareth. LeTord, Bijou, illus. LC 86-32657. 32p. (ps up). 1988. 12.95 (ISBN 0-02-756480-0, Bradbury Pr). Macmillan Child Grp.

Let's Eat! - Colors. (ps-k). 1989. pap. write for info. (ISBN 0-307-04728-8). Western Pub.

Let's Feed the Animals: A Lift-the-Flap Book. (Illus.). 24p. (ps-1). 1987. pap. 5.95 (ISBN 0-553-18352-4). Bantam.

Let's Get Dressed! - Numbers. (ps-k). 1989. pap. write for info. (ISBN 0-307-04727-X). Western Pub.

Let's Go, Feet! (Illus.). 16p. (ps). 1988. 3.95 (ISBN 0-8431-2233-1). Price Stern.

Let's Sing & Play. (Illus.). (ps-3). pap. write for info. (ISBN 0-307-13976-X, Golden Bks). Western Pub.

LeValley, Norma. A Tree for Me. Darcy, Tom, illus. LC 87-70974. 50p. (ps-2). 1987. pap. 5.95 (ISBN 0-9618740-0-7). Caring Tree.

Levine, Abby. What Did Mommy Do Before You? Fay, Ann, ed. (Illus.). 32p. (ps-3). 1988. PLB 12.95 (ISBN 0-8075-8819-9). A Whitman.

—You Push, I Ride. Tucker, Kathleen, ed. Apple, Margot, illus. 32p. (ps). 1989. PLB 12.95 (ISBN 0-8075-9444-X). A Whitman.

Levine, Abby & Levine, Sarah. Sometimes I Wish I Were Mindy. Sims, Blanche, illus. LC 85-15549. 32p. (gr. 2-5). 1986. 10.95 (ISBN 0-8075-7542-9). A Whitman.

Levine, Abby & Tucker, Kathy, eds. Too Much Mush! Parkinson, Kathy, illus. 32p. (ps-2). 1989. PLB 12.95 (ISBN 0-8075-8025-2). A Whitman.

Levinson, Nancy S. Clara & the Bookwagon. Croll, Carolyn, illus. LC 86-45773. 64p. (gr. k-3). 1988. 11. 95 (ISBN 0-06-023837-2); PLB 11.89 (ISBN 0-06-023838-0). HarpC Child Bks.

Levinson, Riki. DinnieAbbieSister-r-r! Cagancherry, Helen, illus. LC 86-10663. 96p. (gr. 1-3). 1987. 11.95 (ISBN 0-02-757380-X, Bradbury Pr). Macmillan Child Grp.

—I Go with My Family to Grandma's. Goode, Diane, illus. 32p. (ps-1). 1990. 11.95 (ISBN 0-525-44261-8, DCB); pap. 3.95 (ISBN 0-525-44557-9, DCB). Dutton Child Bks.

—Touch! Touch! Kelley, True, illus. LC 86-29056. 24p. (ps). 1987. 7.95 (ISBN 0-525-44309-6, Dutton). NAL-Dutton.

Levy, Nathan & Levy, Janet. There Are Those. Edwards, Joan, illus. LC 82-81111. 32p. (ps up). 1990. 21.95 (ISBN 0-9608240-0-6). NL Assoc Inc.
If you have gifted children in your life, this book "There Are Those," will put their special qualities into poetic words for you. The joy, excitement, challenge & frustration that the very bright children bring to themselves & to those around them are brought alive in this highly acclaimed poem. This hardcover book is illustrated with brilliant designs in vivid color. Destined to become a classic, this book will be loved by children from 8-88!
Publisher Provided Annotation.

Lewin, Betsy. Hip Hippo Hooray! (Illus.). 32p. (gr. 5-8). 1982. 9.95 (ISBN 0-396-08032-4, Putnam). Putnam Pub Group.

Lewis, Naomi, ed. The Twelve Dancing Princesses & Other Tales from Grimm. Postma, Lidia, illus. LC 85-6964. 100p. (ps up). 1986. 14.95 (ISBN 0-8037-0237-X). Dial Bks Young.

Lewis, Paul O. Davy's Dream. (Illus.). 64p. (ps-6). 1988. 14.95 (ISBN 0-941831-32-9); pap. 9.95 (ISBN 0-941831-28-0). Beyond Words Pub.

—P. Bear's New Years Party - A Counting Book. (Illus.). 24p. (ps-1). 1989. 12.95 (ISBN 0-941831-21-3); pap. 8.95 (ISBN 0-941831-29-9). Beyond Words Pub.

—The Starlight Bride. (Illus.). 40p. (ps-6). 1988. cloth 14. 95 (ISBN 0-941831-33-7); pap. 9.95 (ISBN 0-941831-25-6). Beyond Words Pub.

Lewis, Shari. One-Minute Greek Myths. Ewing, C. S., illus. 48p. (ps-3). 1987. 6.95 (ISBN 0-385-23849-5); pap. 9.95 (ISBN 0-385-23423-6). Doubleday.

Lewison, Wendy C. Where Is Sammy's Smile: A Lift-the-Flap Book. Bratun, Katy, illus. 24p. (ps-k). 1989. 10.95 (ISBN 0-448-40150-9, G&D). Putnam Pub Group.

Lexau, Joan M. Don't Be My Valentine. Hoff, Syd, illus. LC 85-42621. 64p. (gr. k-3). 1988. pap. 3.50 (ISBN 0-06-444115-6, Trophy). HarpC Child Bks.

—Strawberry Shortcake & Sad Mister Sun. Sustendal, Pat, illus. 40p. (ps-3). 1983. cancelled 5.95 (ISBN 0-910313-10-5). Parker Bros.

Lightbody, Nancy K. & Malley, Sarah H. Observa-Story: Portland to Cut & Color. Malley, Sarah H., illus. LC 76-54460. (gr. 1-4). 1976. pap. 1.25 (ISBN 0-9600612-5-8). Greater Portland.

Lights Off. (Illus.). 24p. (gr. k-2). 1989. bds. 3.95 (ISBN 0-87449-591-1). Modern Pub NYC.

Lillegard, Dee. Where Is It? Sharp, Gene, illus. LC 84-7005. 32p. (ps-2). lib. bdg. 11.93 (ISBN 0-516-02065-X); pap. 2.95 (ISBN 0-516-42065-8). Childrens.

Lillington, Kenneth, text by. A Christmas Carol. Dickens, Charles, contrib. by. (Illus.). 32p. (gr. k up). 1988. pap. 9.95 (ISBN 0-571-10093-7). Faber & Faber.

—The Mikado: Easy Piano Picture Book. Sullivan, Arthur, contrib. by. (Illus.). 32p. (gr. k up). 1988. pap. 9.95 (ISBN 0-571-10085-6). Faber & Faber.

Lindberg, Becky T. Speak up, Chelsea Martin! Tucker, Kathleen, ed. Poydar, Nancy, illus. 128p. (gr. 2-4). 1991. 10.50 (ISBN 0-8075-7552-6). A Whitman.

Linden, Madelaine G. Under the Blanket. Linden, Madelaine G., illus. (ps-3). 1987. 12.95 (ISBN 0-316-52626-6). Little.

Lindgren, Astrid. Christmas in the Stable. LC 62-14449. (Illus.). (gr. 1-3). 1979. PLB 6.99 (ISBN 0-698-30042-4, Coward); pap. text ed. 4.95 (ISBN 0-698-20489-1, Coward). Putnam Pub Group.

—I Don't Want to Go to Bed. Lucas, Barbara, tr. from SWE. Wikland, Ilon, illus. 32p. (ps up). 1988. 12.95 (ISBN 9-12-959066-3, R & S Bks). FS&G.

—I Want a Brother or Sister. Wikland, Ilon, illus. Bibb, Eric, tr. (Illus.). 32p. (ps up). 1988. 10.95 (ISBN 9-12-958778-6, R & S Bks). FS&G.

—The Tomten. Wiberg, Harald, illus. LC 61-10658. (gr. 1-3). 1979. 8.95 (ISBN 0-698-20147-7, Coward); (Coward); pap. 6.95 (ISBN 0-698-20487-5, Coward). Putnam Pub Group.

—The Tomten & the Fox. Wiberg, Harald, illus. LC 65-25501. (ps-2). 1979. pap. 4.95 (ISBN 0-698-20488-3, Coward). Putnam Pub Group.

Lindsey, Marilyn L. The Little Lost Sheep. O'Connell, Ruth, illus. LC 87-91993. (gr. k-2). 1988. 1.99 (ISBN 0-87403-398-5, 24-03808). Standard Pub.

Linehan, Patricia. See What I Can Do! Rader, Laura, illus. 24p. (ps). 1990. bds. 2.50 (ISBN 0-448-02259-1, G&D). Putnam Pub Group.

Linn, Margot. A Trip to the Dentist. Siracusa, Catherine, illus. LC 87-14884. 20p. (ps-k). 1988. 9.95i (ISBN 0-06-025829-2). HarpC Child Bks.

—A Trip to the Doctor. Siracusa, Catherine, illus. LC 87-15004. 20p. (ps-k). 1988. 9.95i (ISBN 0-06-025839-X); PLB 10.89 (ISBN 0-06-025843-8). HarpC Child Bks.

Lionni, Leo. Alexander & the Wind-up Mouse. reissue ed. Lionni, Leo, illus. LC 76-77423. 32p. (ps-2). 1991. 15. 00 (ISBN 0-394-80914-9); lib. bdg. 15.99 (ISBN 0-394-90914-3). Knopf.

—Frederick. Lionni, Leo, illus. (gr. k-3). 1973. pap. 2.95 (ISBN 0-394-82614-0). Pantheon.

—Inch by Inch. (Illus.). (gr. k-1). 1962. 10.95 (ISBN 0-8392-3010-9). Astor-Honor.

—Little Blue & Little Yellow. (Illus.). (gr. k-1). 1959. 10. 95 (ISBN 0-8392-3018-4). Astor-Honor.

—On My Beach There Are Many Pebbles. (Illus.). (gr. k-1). 1961. 10.95 (ISBN 0-8392-3024-9). Astor-Honor.

—Pouce par Pouce. (FRE., Illus.). (gr. k-1). 1961. 10.95 (ISBN 0-8392-3028-1). Astor-Honor.

Lion's Chair. 12p. (ps-1). 1989. bds. 3.95 (ISBN 0-87449-634-9). Modern Pub NYC.

Lippman, Peter. Peter Lippman's Numbers. (gr. 2 up). 1988. 8.95 (ISBN 0-448-19105-9, G&D). Putnam Pub Group.

—Peter Lippman's Opposites. (gr. 2 up). 1988. 8.95 (ISBN 0-448-19106-7, G&D). Putnam Pub Group.

Little Bear Counts His Favorite Things. (ps-k). Date not set. write for info. (ISBN 0-307-12289-1, Golden Pr). Western Pub.

Little Bear Paints a Picture. 1988. 1.98 (ISBN 0-671-09562-5). S&S Trade.

Little Bears Go Visiting the Hawaiian Islands, Bk. 23. (ps-1). write for info. (ISBN 0-931363-23-3). Celia Totus Enter.

Little Bears Visit the Ocean Beach, Bk. 22. (ps-1). write for info. (ISBN 0-931363-21-7). Celia Totus Enter.

A Little Book of Numbers. 16p. (ps-k). 1980. pap. 2.95 (ISBN 0-671-41346-5, Little). S&S Trade.

The Little Engine That Could. (ps-5). 1988. incl. 3 dolls 19.95 (ISBN 0-698-12013-2, Playland Bks). Putnam Pub Group.

The Little Engine That Could & the Big Chase. (ps-2). 1988. incl. cassette 5.95 (ISBN 0-448-19108-3, G&D). Putnam Pub Group.

The Little Green Caterpillar. (Illus.). 24p. (ps-k). 1989. 7.95 (ISBN 0-448-21029-0, G&D). Putnam Pub Group.

Little Kids at Home. (Illus.). 48p. (gr. k-2). 1989. pap. 5.95 (ISBN 0-87449-680-2). Modern Pub NYC.

Little Kids at Play. (Illus.). 48p. (gr. k-2). 1989. pap. 5.95 (ISBN 0-87449-679-9). Modern Pub NYC.

Little Kids at School. (Illus.). 48p. (gr. k-2). 1989. pap. 5.95 (ISBN 0-87449-677-2). Modern Pub NYC.

Little Kids in the Neighborhood. (Illus.). 48p. (gr. k-2). 1989. pap. 5.95 (ISBN 0-87449-678-0). Modern Pub NYC.

Little Mouse Around the House. 24p. (ps-1). 1988. 5.95 (ISBN 0-8431-4731-8). Price Stern.

Little Pioneer Bears, Bk. 21. (ps-1). write for info. (ISBN 0-931363-20-9). Celia Totus Enter.

Little Rabbit's Garden. 12p. (ps). 1985. 3.95 (ISBN 0-394-87112-X, Random Juv). Random.

Little Red Riding Hood. (Illus.). (ps-5). 1989. incl. dolls & play settings 13.95 (ISBN 0-698-12046-9, Playland Bks). Putnam Pub Group.

Little Red Riding Hood. (Illus.). 20p. (ps-2). 1990. 5.95 (ISBN 0-8120-6163-2). Barron.

Little Red Riding Hood Pop-Up. 10p. 1990. 9.95 (ISBN 0-8431-2851-8). Price Stern.

Little Treasury of Walt Disney. 1986. 5.98 (ISBN 0-685-16883-2, 616300). Outlet Bk Co.

Littledale, Freya. Peter & the North Wind. Howell, Troy, illus. 32p. (gr. k-3). 1989. pap. 2.50 (ISBN 0-590-40629-9). Scholastic Inc.

Littlejohn, Claire, illus. Aesop's Fables: A Pull-the-Tab-Pop-Up-Book. LC 87-24478. 14p. (ps up). 1988. 13.95 (ISBN 0-8037-0487-9). Dial Bks Young.

Littler, Angela. What Can You Series, 4 bks. Galvani, Maureen, illus. 20p. (gr. 2-5). 1988. Set. 15.80 (ISBN 0-671-93015-X). Messner.

Livermore, Elaine. Looking for Henry. Livermore, Elaine, illus. 48p. (gr. k-3). 1988. 12.95 (ISBN 0-395-44240-0). HM.

Lloyd, David. Duck. Voake, Charlotte, illus. LC 87-26200. 32p. (ps-k). 1988. (Lipp Jr Bks); PLB 12.89 (ISBN 0-397-32275-5). HarpC Child Bks.

—The Stopwatch. Dale, Penny, illus. LC 85-27146. 32p. (ps-2). 1986. pap. 2.50 (ISBN 0-06-443107-X, Trophy). HarpC Child Bks.

Lloyd, Errol. Nine at Carnival. Lloyd, Errol, illus. LC 78-4776. (ps-2). 1979. (Crowell Jr Bks); PLB 9.89 (ISBN 0-690-03892-5). HarpC Child Bks.

Lobato, Arcadio. Just One Wish. Clements, Andrew, tr. from GER. Lobato, Arcadio, illus. LC 89-49263. 32p. (ps up). 1990. 14.95 (ISBN 0-88708-134-7). Picture Bk Studio.

Lobel, Anita. Potatoes, Potatoes. Lobel, Anita, illus. LC 67-16231. 48p. (gr. k-3). 1984. PLB 11.89 (ISBN 0-685-02068-1). HarpC Child Bks.

Lobel, Arnold. The Book of Pigericks (Pig Limericks) Lobel, Arnold, illus. LC 82-47730. 48p. (ps up). 1988. pap. 4.95 (ISBN 0-06-443163-0, Trophy). HarpC Child Bks.

—Days with Frog & Toad. Lobel, Arnold, illus. LC 78-21786. 64p. (ps-3). 1985. (Trophy); pap. 3.50 (ISBN 0-06-444058-3, Trophy). HarpC Child Bks.

—Frog & Toad All Year. Lobel, Arnold, illus. LC 76-2343. 64p. (ps-3). 1985. (Trophy); pap. 3.50 (ISBN 0-06-444059-1, Trophy). HarpC Child Bks.

—Frog & Toad Are Friends. Lobel, Arnold, illus. LC 73-105492. 64p. (ps-3). 1985. (Trophy); pap. 3.50 (ISBN 0-06-444020-6, Trophy). HarpC Child Bks.

—Frog & Toad Together. Lobel, Arnold, illus. LC 73-183163. 64p. (ps-3). 1985. (Trophy); pap. 3.50 (ISBN 0-06-444021-4, Trophy). HarpC Child Bks.

—Giant John. Lobel, Arnold, illus. LC 64-16639. 32p. (gr. k-3). 1964. PLB 13.89 (ISBN 0-06-022946-2). HarpC Child Bks.

—Grasshopper on the Road. Lobel, Arnold, illus. LC 77-25653. 64p. (gr. k-3). 1986. pap. 3.50 (ISBN 0-06-444094-X, Trophy). HarpC Child Bks.

—Holiday for Mister Muster. Lobel, Arnold, illus. LC 63-15323. 32p. (gr. k-3). 1963. PLB 12.89 (ISBN 0-06-023956-5). HarpC Child Bks.

—Humpty Dumpty Book & Doll Set. Lobel, Arnold, illus. 24p. (ps-k). 1988. book & doll pkg. 4.95 (ISBN 0-394-89936-9, Random Juv). Random.

—Martha the Movie Mouse. Lobel, Arnold, illus. 32p. (gr. k-3). 1966. PLB 12.89 (ISBN 0-06-023970-0). HarpC Child Bks.

—Mouse Soup. Lobel, Arnold, illus. LC 76-41517. 64p. (gr. k-3). 1986. (Trophy); pap. 3.50 (ISBN 0-06-444041-9, Trophy). HarpC Child Bks.

—On the Day Peter Stuyvesant Sailed into Town. Lobel, Arnold, illus. LC 75-148420. 48p. (ps-3). 1987. pap. 4.95 (ISBN 0-06-443144-4, Trophy). HarpC Child Bks.

—Prince Bertram the Bad. Lobel, Arnold, illus. LC 63-8741. 32p. (gr. k-3). 1963. PLB 12.89 (ISBN 0-06-023976-X). HarpC Child Bks.

—Small Pig. Lobel, Arnold, illus. LC 69-10213. 64p. (gr. k-3). 1988. pap. 3.50 (ISBN 0-06-444120-2, Trophy). HarpC Child Bks.

—The Turnaround Wind. Lobel, Arnold, illus. LC 87-45293. 32p. (ps-3). 1988. 12.95 (ISBN 0-06-023987-5); PLB 12.89 (ISBN 0-06-023988-3). HarpC Child Bks.

Locker, Thomas. Family Farm. Locker, Thomas, illus. LC 87-19645. 32p. (ps up). 1988. 15.00 (ISBN 0-8037-0489-5); PLB 14.89 (ISBN 0-8037-0490-9). Dial Bks Young.

Loelling, Carol. Whose House Is This? (Illus.). 22p. (ps-4). 1978. 5.95 (ISBN 0-8431-0444-9). Price Stern.

Logan, Les. The Game. 160p. (Orig.). (gr. 7-12). 1986. pap. 2.25 (ISBN 0-553-25211-9). Bantam.

Look at Me. (Illus.). (ps). 3.50 (ISBN 0-7214-0853-2). Ladybird Bks.

Look at This. (Illus.). (ps-5). 3.50 (ISBN 0-7214-0013-2); No. 1. wkbk. 1.95; Series S05, Set 1. flash cards 4.75; Series S05, Set 2. flash cards 4.75. Ladybird Bks.

Lorenz, Lee. A Weekend in the Country. (Illus.). 32p. (ps-3). 1988. pap. 4.95 (ISBN 0-13-948191-5, Little Simon). S&S Trade.

Lorenzen, Anna L. Tiger. Craft, Mary, illus. 22p. (Orig.). (gr. 1-2). 1989. pap. text ed. 2.95 (ISBN 0-9626133-0-4). ALL Ventura Pub.

Love, Marsha L. The Vitamin Parade. LC 89-51346. (Illus.). 44p. (gr. k-3). 1989. 5.95 (ISBN 1-55523-264-7). Winston-Derek.

Lowry, Lois. All about Sam. (Illus.). 144p. (gr. 1-5). 1988. 12.95 (ISBN 0-395-48662-9). HM.

Ludwig, Lyndell. The Little White Dragon. Ludwig, Lyndell, illus. 23p. (gr. 5 up). 1989. pap. 4.95 (ISBN 0-9621782-0-9). Star Dust Bks.
"THE LITTLE WHITE DRAGON" This timeless, well loved tale from ancient China takes you into the world of a wonderful little dragon intent on exploring everything both inside & outside of his realm. At one point he even changes himself into a little fish so he can dive into the waters of the deep sea. However, after numerous adventures, including a miraculous escape, he decides that, after all, it is much better just to be the dragon he really is, with untold worlds yet to discover. The third in a series of authentic Chinese tales in picture book form, delightfully told & illustrated by the author who is well qualified both as an illustrator & in her knowledge of the Chinese language. ("Like the tales of Rudyard Kipling 'these stories' transport children to another time & a different, fascinating world."--Creative

Arts). Children are important! As the world changes cultures are blending. And stories from distant lands such as China are enormously valuable in broadening the scope for growth & understanding. They are also fun to read. TS'AO CHUNG WEIGHS AN ELEPHANT ("...splendid, vibrantly colored paintings..."--Publishers Weekly) & THE SHOEMAKER'S GIFT are also available from Star Dust Books at $4.95 each.
Publisher Provided Annotation.

Lundell, Margaretta. The Land of Colors. Pazzaglia, Nadia, illus. LC 84-81410. 24p. (ps-k). 1989. 7.95 (ISBN 0-448-21028-2, G&D). Putnam Pub Group.
Lundell, Margo. What Does Baby See? Pagnoni, Roberta, illus. 24p. (ps-k). 1990. bds. 8.95 (ISBN 0-448-19098-2, G&D). Putnam Pub Group.
—Woody, Be Good! A First Book of Manners. Rose, Eve, illus. 24p. (ps-2). 1988. 3.95 (ISBN 0-448-09288-3, G&D). Putnam Pub Group.
Lunn, Carolyn. Spiders & Webs. Dunnington, Tom, illus. LC 89-34665. 32p. (ps-2). 1989. PLB 11.93 (ISBN 0-516-02093-5); pap. 2.95 (ISBN 0-516-42093-3). Childrens.
Lurie, Morris. The Story of Imelda, Who Was Small. Denton, Terry, illus. 32p. (gr. k-3). 1988. 13.95 (ISBN 0-395-48663-7). HM.
Lustig, Loretta, illus. The Pop-Up Book of Trucks. LC 73-19318. (ps-2). 1974. 7.95 (ISBN 0-394-82826-7, Random Juv). Random.
Luton, Mildred. Little Chicks' Mothers & All the Others. Rae, Mary M., illus. 32p. (ps-3). 1983. pap. 12.50 (ISBN 0-670-43113-3). Viking Child Bks.
Luttrell, Ida. Mattie & the Chicken Thief. Hurd, Thacher, illus. LC 87-24451. (ps-3). 1988. 12.95 (ISBN 0-396-09126-1, Perigee Bks). Putnam Pub Group.
Lydon, Kerry R. A Birthday for Blue. Levine, Abby, ed. Hays, Michael, illus. 32p. (gr. k-3). 1989. 12.95g (ISBN 0-8075-0774-1). A Whitman.
Lynn, Sara. Clothes. Lynn, Sara, illus. 14p. (ps). 1986. bds. 2.95 (ISBN 0-689-71095-X, Aladdin Bks). Macmillan Child Grp.
—Farm Animals. Lynn, Sara, illus. 14p. (ps). 1987. bds. 2.95 (ISBN 0-689-71100-X, Aladdin Bks). Macmillan Child Grp.
—Garden Animals. Lynn, Sara, illus. 14p. (ps). 1987. bds. 2.95 (ISBN 0-689-71101-8, Aladdin Bks). Macmillan Child Grp.
Lynn, Sara & Kightley, Rosalinda. ABC. (Illus.). 32p. (ps-1). 1986. pap. 6.95 (ISBN 0-316-49930-7). Little.
—Colors. Lynn, Sara, illus. 32p. (ps-1). 1986. pap. 6.95 (ISBN 0-316-54002-1). Little.
—One Two Three. (Illus.). 32p. (ps-1). 1986. pap. 6.95 (ISBN 0-316-54004-8). Little.
—Shapes. Lynn, Sara & Knightley, Rosalind, illus. 32p. (ps-1). 1986. pap. 6.95 (ISBN 0-316-54005-6). Little.
Lyon, David. The Runaway Duck. LC 84-5677. (ps-1). 1987. pap. 3.95 (ISBN 0-688-07334-4, Mulberry). Morrow.
McAllister, Angela. The King Who Sneezed. Henwood, Simon, illus. LC 88-6858. 32p. (gr. k-3). 1988. 12.95 (ISBN 0-688-08327-7); PLB 12.88 (ISBN 0-688-08328-5, Morrow Jr Bks). Morrow Jr Bks.
McArthur, Nancy. Pickled Peppers. Brunkus, Denise, illus. (gr. 1-4). 1988. pap. 2.50 (ISBN 0-590-40997-2). Scholastic Inc.
Mccaughrean, Geraldine. My First Space Pop-up Book. 1990. 7.95 (ISBN 0-671-67571-0). S&S Trade.
McCay, Winsor. Complete Little Nemo in Slumberland, Vol. II. Marschall, Richard, ed. & intro. by. (Illus.). 96p. (gr. 6 up). 1989. 29.95 (ISBN 0-924359-02-1). Remco Wrldserv Bks.
McClain, Mary. Baby's Pockets. McClain, Mary, illus. 8p. (ps). 1981. pap. 3.95 (ISBN 0-671-43204-4, Little Simon). S&S Trade.
McCloskey, Robert. Blueberries for Sal. McCloskey, Robert, illus. LC 48-4955. (ps-1). 1976. pap. 3.95 (ISBN 0-14-050169-X, Puffin). Puffin Bks.
—Blueberries for Sal. McCloskey, Robert, illus. LC 48-4955. 56p. (ps-1). 1948. pap. 13.95 (ISBN 0-670-17591-9). Viking Child Bks.
—Lentil. McCloskey, Robert, illus. (gr. k-3). 1940. pap. 14.95 (ISBN 0-670-42357-2). Viking Child Bks.
—Make Way for Ducklings. McCloskey, Robert, illus. (gr. k-3). 1941. pap. 12.95 (ISBN 0-670-45149-5). Viking Child Bks.
—Time of Wonder. McCloskey, Robert, illus. 64p. (gr. k-3). 1989. pap. 4.95 (ISBN 0-14-050201-7, Puffin). Puffin Bks.
McConnell, Nancy P. Different & Alike. Duell, Nancy, illus. LC 87-73309. 40p. (gr. 1-6). pap. text ed. 3.20 (ISBN 0-944943-00-4). Current Inc.
McCue, Dick. Baby Elephant's Bedtime. McCue, Lisa, illus. 12p. (ps). 1990. bds. 2.95 (ISBN 0-671-55853-6, Little Simon). S&S Trade.
—Bunny's Numbers. McCue, Lisa, illus. 12p. (ps). 1990. bds. 2.95 (ISBN 0-671-50944-6, Little Simon). S&S Trade.
—Panda's Playtime. McCue, Lisa, illus. 12p. (ps). 1990. bds. 2.95 (ISBN 0-671-55850-1, Little Simon). S&S Trade.
—Raccoon's Hide & Seek. McCue, Lisa, illus. 12p. (ps). 1990. bds. 2.95 (ISBN 0-671-55854-4, Little Simon). S&S Trade.
McCue, Dick & McCue, Lisa. Puppy's Day. (ps). 1984. 2.95 (ISBN 0-671-50945-4, Little Simon). S&S Trade.
McCue, Lisa. Kittens Love. McCue, Lisa, illus. LC 89-61137. 24p. (ps-1). 1990. 4.95 (ISBN 0-394-82876-3). Random.
—Nighty-Night, Little One. McCue, Lisa, illus. LC 87-42786. 28p. (ps). 1988. bds. 2.95 (ISBN 0-394-89476-6, Random Juv). Random.
—Puppies Love. McCue, Lisa, illus. LC 89-61140. 24p. (ps-1). 1990. 4.95 (ISBN 0-394-82875-5). Random.
McCue, Lisa, illus. Kitten's Christmas. 1985. 2.95 (ISBN 0-671-55851-X, Little Simon). S&S Trade.
—Puppy Peek-a-Boo. LC 88-60759. 14p. (ps). 1989. bds. 2.95 (ISBN 0-394-81950-0). Random.
—Whose Little Baby Says...? 14p. (ps). 1990. bds. 3.95 (ISBN 0-679-80168-5). Random.
McCully. Tiny Tickle Book. (gr. 2 up). 1988. 2.50 (ISBN 0-448-09255-7, G&D). Putnam Pub Group.
McCully, Emily A. First Snow. McCully, Emily A., illus. LC 84-43244. 32p. (ps-1). 1985. PLB 12.89 (ISBN 0-06-024129-2). HarpC Child Bks.
—First Snow. McCully, Emily A., illus. LC 84-43244. 32p. (ps-1). 1988. pap. 3.95 (ISBN 0-06-443181-9, Trophy). HarpC Child Bks.
—New Baby. McCully, Emily A., illus. LC 87-45294. 32p. (ps-1). 1988. 12.95 (ISBN 0-06-024130-6); PLB 12.89 (ISBN 0-06-024131-4). HarpC Child Bks.
—Picnic. McCully, Emily A., illus. LC 83-47913. 32p. (ps-1). 1989. pap. 3.95 (ISBN 0-06-443199-1, Trophy). HarpC Child Bks.
—School. McCully, Emily A., illus. LC 87-156. 32p. (ps-2). 1987. PLB 12.89 (ISBN 0-06-024133-0). HarpC Child Bks.
—School. McCully, Emily A., illus. LC 87-156. 32p. (ps-1). 1990. pap. 3.95 (ISBN 0-06-443233-5, Trophy). HarpC Child Bks.
McCully, Emily A., illus. The Baby Bubble Book. 24p. (ps). 1988. bds. 2.50 (ISBN 0-448-09256-5, G&D). Putnam Pub Group.
McCurdy, Michael. The Devils Who Learned to Be Good. McCurdy, Michael, illus. 32p. (gr. 2-5). 1987. 13.95 (ISBN 0-316-55527-4, Joy St Bks). Little.
McDaniel, Becky B. Katie Can. Axeman, Lois, illus. LC 87-5190. 32p. (ps-2). 1987. PLB 11.93 (ISBN 0-516-02082-X); pap. 2.95 (ISBN 0-516-42082-8). Childrens.
McDermott, Gerald. Daniel O'Rourke. McDermott, Gerald, illus. LC 85-20188. 32p. (ps-3). 1986. pap. 12. 95 (ISBN 0-670-80924-1). Viking Child Bks.
—The Stonecutter. (Illus.). (gr. 1-3). 1978. pap. 4.95 (ISBN 0-14-050289-0, Puffin). Puffin Bks.
MacDonald, George. The Christmas Stories of George MacDonald. LC 81-68187. (gr. 1 up). 1981. 12.95 (ISBN 0-89191-491-9, 54916). Cook.
MacDonald, Sharon. We Learn All about Community Helpers. (ps-1). 1988. pap. 6.95 (ISBN 0-8224-4599-9). Fearon Teach Aids.
—We Learn All about Dinosaurs. (ps-1). 1988. pap. 6.95 (ISBN 0-8224-4595-6). Fearon Teach Aids.
—We Learn All about Fall. (ps-1). 1988. pap. 6.95 (ISBN 0-8224-4596-4). Fearon Teach Aids.
—We Learn All about Farms. (ps-1). 1988. pap. 6.95 (ISBN 0-8224-4594-8). Fearon Teach Aids.
—We Learn all about the Circus. (ps-1). 1988. pap. 6.95 (ISBN 0-8224-4598-0). Fearon Teach Aids.
—We Learn All about Winter. (ps-1). 1988. pap. 6.95 (ISBN 0-8224-4597-2). Fearon Teach Aids.
Macdonald, Suse. Alphabatics. LC 85-31429. (Illus.). 64p. (ps up). 1986. 15.95 (ISBN 0-02-761520-0, Bradbury Pr). Macmillan Child Grp.
MacDonald, Suse & Oakes, Bill. Numblers. MacDonald, Suse & Oakes, Bill, illus. LC 87-32736. 32p. (ps-1). 1988. 13.95 (ISBN 0-8037-0547-6); PLB 13.89 (ISBN 0-8037-0548-4). Dial Bks Young.
McDonell, Marcella A. Barney the Magical Snail. Steyn, Anette, illus. 40p. (ps). 1989. 8.95 (ISBN 0-317-93668-9). Charming World.
McDonnell, Christine. Lucky Charms & Birthday Wishes. De Groat, Diane, illus. LC 83-19861. 96p. (gr. 2-5). 1984. pap. 11.95 (ISBN 0-670-44430-8). Viking Child Bks.
McDonnell, Janet. Polka-Dot Puppy's New House: A Book about Counting. Hohag, Linda, illus. LC 88-11941. 32p. (ps-2). 1988. PLB 11.97 (ISBN 0-89565-380-X); pap. 6.96 (ISBN 0-89565-500-4). Childs World.
McDowell, Josh & McDowell, Dottie. Katie's Adventure at Blueberry Pond. (Illus.). 32p. (ps-2). 1988. 8.95 (ISBN 1-55513-598-6, Chariot Bks). Cook.
—Pizza for Everyone. LC 88-14041. (Illus.). 32p. (ps-2). 1988. 8.95 (ISBN 1-55513-596-X, Chariot Bks). Cook.
McFarland, Kathleen & Larkin, Judy. Colleen Marie. (Illus.). 56p. (Orig.). (ps). 1985. pap. write for info. (ISBN 0-9621691-1-0, TX 1-705-162). B Bumpers Inc.
MacFarlane, Kee & Cunningham, Carolyn. Steps to Healthy Touching. Mortenson, Bob, illus. 144p. (Orig.). (gr. k-7). 1988. wkbk. 19.95 (ISBN 0-685-20041-8, 1400). Kidsrights.
McGee, Shelagh. Dressing up. (Illus.). 20p. (ps). 1988. 4.95 (ISBN 0-8120-5881-X). Barron.
McGinley, Phyllis. Year Without a Santa Claus. Werth, Kurt, illus. (gr. k-3). 1981. 12.95 (ISBN 0-397-30399-8, Lipp Jr Bks); PLB 14.89 (ISBN 0-397-31969-X). HarpC Child Bks.
McGovern, Ann. Too Much Noise. Taback, Simms, illus. 48p. (gr. k-3). pap. 2.25 (ISBN 0-317-69684-X). Scholastic Inc.
MacHaffie, Ingeborg. Henry: The Heron. Blumenstein, Amy, illus. Mouck, Mike, frwd. by. (Illus.). 55p. (Orig.). (ps). 1988. lib. bdg. 7.95 (ISBN 0-9609374-3-9). Skribent.
Mack, Gail. Yesterday's Snowman. Blegvad, Erik, illus. LC 78-6090. (ps-2). 1979. Pantheon.
McKee, David. Elmer. McKee, David, illus. LC 89-2285. 32p. (ps-2). 1989. Repr. of 1968 ed. 12.95 (ISBN 0-688-09171-7); PLB 12.88 (ISBN 0-688-09172-5). Lothrop.
—King Rollo's Letter: And Other Stories. (Illus.). 28p. (gr. k-3). 1989. 13.95 (ISBN 0-86264-076-8, Pub. by Anderson Pr UK). Trafalgar Sq.
Mackenzie, Jill W. The Golden Fairy. LC 90-70311. (Illus.). 44p. (gr. 1-6). 1990. 5.95 (ISBN 1-55523-336-8). Winston-Derek.
MacKenzie, Joy. Bible Read-to-Me. LC 87-18337. 48p. (ps-2). 1988. 9.95 (ISBN 1-55513-861-6, Chariot Bks). Cook.
—Bible Read-to-Me. LC 87-18334. 48p. (ps-2). 1988. 9.95 (ISBN 1-55513-480-7, Chariot Bks). Cook.
McKernan, Llewellyn T. Bird Alphabet, Happy Day Book. Petach, Heidi, illus. LC 87-91986. (gr. k-2). 1988. 1.99 (ISBN 0-87403-391-8, 24-03801). Standard Pub.
McKie, Roy & Eastman, Philip D. Snow. LC 62-15114. (Illus.). 72p. (gr. 1-2). 1962. 6.95 (ISBN 0-394-80027-3); lib. bdg. 7.99 (ISBN 0-394-90027-8). Beginner.
McKissack, Patricia. Quien Viene? (Who Is Coming?) Martin, Clovis, illus. LC 86-11805. (SPA & ENG.). 32p. (ps-2). 1989. PLB 11.93 (ISBN 0-516-32073-4); pap. 2.95 (ISBN 0-516-52073-3). Childrens.
McKissack, Patricia & McKissack, Fredrick. Constance Stumbles. Dunnington, Tom, illus. 32p. (ps-2). 1988. PLB 11.93 (ISBN 0-516-02086-2); pap. 2.95 (ISBN 0-317-69612-2). Childrens.
—The King's New Clothes. Connelly, Gwen, illus. LC 86-33422. 32p. (gr. k-3). 1987. PLB 11.93 (ISBN 0-516-02365-9); pap. 3.95 (ISBN 0-516-42365-7). Childrens.
—Messy Bessey. LC 87-15079. (Illus.). (ps-3). 1987. PLB 11.93 (ISBN 0-516-02083-8); pap. 2.95 (ISBN 0-516-42083-6). Childrens.
—Three Billy Goats Gruff. Dunnington, Tom, illus. LC 86-33450. 32p. (ps-2). 1987. PLB 11.93 (ISBN 0-516-02366-7); pap. 3.95 (ISBN 0-516-42366-5). Childrens.
McKissack, Patricia C. Quien Es Quien? (Who Is Who?) Allen, Elizabeth M., illus. LC 83-7361. (SPA.). 32p. (ps-2). 1989. PLB 11.93 (ISBN 0-516-32042-4); pap. 2.95 (ISBN 0-516-52042-3). Childrens.
McKissack, Patricia C. & McKissack, Frederick. Messy Bessey's Closet. Hackney, Rick, illus. LC 89-34667. 32p. (ps-2). 1989. PLB 11.93 (ISBN 0-516-02091-9); pap. 2.95 (ISBN 0-516-42091-7). Childrens.
McLeod, Emilie W. The Bear's Bicycle. McPhail, David, illus. (gr. 1-3). 1986. incl. cassette 19.95 (ISBN 0-87499-025-4); pap. 12.95 incl. cassette (ISBN 0-87499-023-8); 4 paperbacks, cassette & guide 27.95 (ISBN 0-87499-024-6). Live Oak Media.
McLerran, Alice. The Mountain That Loved a Bird. Carle, Eric, illus. LC 85-9391. 32p. (ps up). 1985. 15. 95 (ISBN 0-88708-000-6). Picture Bk Studio.
McMillan, Bruce. The Alphabet Symphony. (Illus.). 32p. (gr. k-2). 1989. 15.00 (ISBN 0-317-93064-8). Apple Isl Bks.
—Becca Backward, Becca Frontward: A Book of Concept Pairs. LC 86-7221. (Illus.). 32p. (ps-1). 1986. 12.95 (ISBN 0-688-06282-2); PLB 12.88 (ISBN 0-688-06283-0). Lothrop.
—Step by Step. (Illus.). 28p. (ps-2). 1990. PLB 15.00 (ISBN 0-685-35118-1). Apple Isl Bks.
—Time to... McMillan, Bruce, photos by. LC 89-2325. (Illus.). 32p. (ps-2). 1989. 13.95 (ISBN 0-688-08855-4); PLB 13.88 (ISBN 0-688-08856-2). Lothrop.
McMillan, Naomi. Wish You Were Here. LC 90-85435. (Illus.). 32p. (gr. k-3). 1991. 5.95 (ISBN 1-56282-036-2, Disney Pr). W Disney Pub.
McNaught, Harry, illus. Words to Grow On. LC 84-6880. 24p. (ps-1). 1984. 3.95 (ISBN 0-394-86103-5, Pub. by BYR); lib. bdg. 4.99 (ISBN 0-394-96103-X). Random.
McNulty, Faith. How to Dig a Hole to the Other Side of the World. Simont, Marc, illus. LC 78-22479. 32p. (gr. k-3). 1990. pap. 4.95 (ISBN 0-06-443218-1, Trophy). HarpC Child Bks.
—The Lady & the Spider. Marstall, Bob, illus. LC 85-5427. 48p. (gr. 1-4). 1987. pap. 4.95 (ISBN 0-06-443152-5, Trophy). HarpC Child Bks.
McPhail, David. The Bear's Toothache. McPhail, David, illus. (gr. k-2). 1986. incl. cassette 19.95 (ISBN 0-87499-081-5); pap. 12.95 incl. cassette (ISBN 0-87499-080-7); 4 paperbacks, cassette & guide 27.95 (ISBN 0-87499-082-3). Live Oak Media.
—Emma's Pet. McPhail, David, illus. (ps-2). 1988. bk. & cassette 19.95 (ISBN 0-87499-107-2); bk. & cassette 12.95 (ISBN 0-87499-106-4); 4 cassettes & guide 27. 95 (ISBN 0-87499-108-0). Live Oak Media.
—First Flight. (Illus.). (ps-3). 1991. Repr. 4.95 (ISBN 0-316-56332-3, Joy St Bks). Little.

—Fix-It. McPhail, David, illus. (gr. k-3). 1988. bk. & cassette 19.95 (ISBN 0-87499-084-X); bk. & cassette 12.95 (ISBN 0-87499-083-1); 4 cassettes & guide 27. 95 (ISBN 0-87499-085-8). Live Oak Media.
—Fix-It. McPhail, David, illus. 112p. (ps-k). 1987. pap. 3.95 (ISBN 0-525-44323-1, 0383-120, DCB). Dutton Child Bks.
—Great Cat. (Illus.). 32p. (gr. k up). 1986. pap. 4.95 (ISBN 0-525-44273-1, DCB). Dutton Child Bks.
—Pig Pig & the Magic Photo Album. McPhail, David, illus. LC 85-20459. 24p. (ps-3). 1986. 10.95 (ISBN 0-525-44238-3, DCB). Dutton Child Bks.
—Pig Pig Rides. McPhail, David, illus. (gr. 1-3). 1988. bk. & cassette 19.95 (ISBN 0-87499-090-4); bk. & cassette 12.95 (ISBN 0-87499-089-0); 4 cassettes & guide 27. 95 (ISBN 0-87499-091-2). Live Oak Media.
—The Train. (Illus.). (ps-k). 1979. pap. 4.95 (ISBN 0-14-050302-1, Puffin). Puffin Bks.
McPherson, Betty. A Mayflower Adventure. Stefano, Nancy Di, illus. 32p. (ps-1). 1985. 6.00 (ISBN 0-918823-00-5). Boyce-Pubns.
—The Small Patriot. (Illus.). 32p. (ps-1). 1987. 6.00 (ISBN 0-918823-01-3). Boyce-Pubns.
McQueen. Baby Farm Love. (gr. 2 up). 1988. 2.50 (ISBN 0-448-09251-4, G&D). Putnam Pub Group.
—What Does Sunny Bunny Love? (gr. 2 up). 1988. 2.50 (ISBN 0-448-09252-2, G&D). Putnam Pub Group.
McQueen, John T. A World Full of Monsters. Brown, Marc, illus. LC 85-48257. 32p. (gr. k-3). 1989. pap. 3.95 (ISBN 0-06-443206-8, Trophy). HarpC Child Bks.
McQueen, Lucinda. Counting Bears. (Illus.). 24p. (gr. 1-3). 1990. bds. 2.50 (ISBN 0-448-02263-X, G&D). Putnam Pub Group.
McQueen, Lucinda & Guitar, Jeremy. Tidy Pig: Just Right for 4's & 5's. LC 87-43347. (Illus.). 32p. (ps-k). 1989. Random.
McQueen, Lucinda, illus. Pudgy Zoo Babies. 16p. 1989. bds. 2.95 (ISBN 0-448-02256-7, G&D). Putnam Pub Group.
McQueen, Lucinda & Guitar, Jeremy, illus. Otis Lee. 12p. (gr. 1-5). 1984. 4.00 (ISBN 0-910313-33-4). Parker Bros.
Maddern, Eric. Earth Story. Duff, Leo, illus. 32p. (gr. 1 up). 1988. 11.95 (ISBN 0-8120-5909-3). Barron.
—Life Story. Duff, Leo, illus. LC 87-73253. 32p. (gr. 1 up). 1988. 11.95 (ISBN 0-8120-5941-7). Barron.
Madsen, Ross M. Perrywinkle & the Book of Magic Spells. Zimmer, Dirk, illus. LC 85-15932. 48p. (ps-3). 1986. 8.95 (ISBN 0-8037-0242-6); PLB 8.89 (ISBN 0-8037-0243-4). Dial Bks Young.
Maestro, Betsy & Maestro, Giulio. Harriet the Elephant, 4 bks. Maestro, Betsy & Maestro, Giulio, illus. Incl. Harriet at School. LC 83-27225. 1984; Harriet at Play. LC 83-27226. 1984; Harriet at Work. LC 83-26364. 1989; Harriet at Home. LC 83-26365. 1984. (Illus.). (ps-1). 1984. Crown.
Maestro, Giulio & Maestro, Betsy. The Guessing Game. (Illus.). 32p. (gr. 1-3). 1983. pap. 3.50 (ISBN 0-448-21701-5, G&D). Putnam Pub Group.
Magni, Laura. Come to the Park. Cluet, Jaume, illus. 16p. (ps up). 1989. 8.95 (ISBN 0-8120-5994-8). Barron.
Magnus, Erica. The Boy & the Devil. Magnus, Erica, illus. 32p. (ps-3). 1986. PLB 12.95 (ISBN 0-87614-305-2). Carolrhoda Bks.
Magorian, James. Fimperings & Torples. LC 81-69872. 44p. (gr. 4-6). 1981. pap. 3.00 (ISBN 0-930674-06-5). Black Oak.
—Imaginary Radishes. LC 79-53857. 32p. (gr. 3-5). 1980. 5.00 (ISBN 0-930674-03-0). Black Oak.
Maguire, Arlene. Life's Changes. Holtman, Noel, illus. LC 91-9353. 32p. (Orig.). (ps-5). 1991. 6.95 (ISBN 0-941992-26-8). Los Arboles Pub.
Mahy, Margaret. Boy Who Was Followed Home. Kellogg, Steven, illus. LC 75-2866. 32p. (ps-3). 1986. 13.95 (ISBN 0-8037-0286-8). Dial Bks Young.
—Seventeen Kings & Forty-Two Elephants. MacCarthy, Patricia, illus. LC 87-5311. 32p. (ps-3). 1987. 11.95 (ISBN 0-8037-0458-5). Dial Bks Young.
Majewski, Joe. A Friend for Oscar Mouse. Majewska, Maria, illus. LC 86-32879. 32p. (ps-2). 1988. 11.95 (ISBN 0-8037-0348-1). Dial Bks Young.
Major, Beverly. Playing Sardines. Glass, Andrew, illus. LC 87-9621. 32p. (ps-2). 1988. pap. 12.95 (ISBN 0-590-41153-5, Scholastic Hardcover). Scholastic Inc.
Make-Believe Moon. 12p. (ps-1). 1988. bds. 5.95 (ISBN 0-87449-627-6). Modern Pub NYC.
Mallett, Jerry J. & Bartch, Marian R. Stories to Draw. 52p. (Orig.). (ps-3). 1982. pap. 6.95x (ISBN 0-913853-00-3). Freline.
Mammoth Book of Dinosaurs. 240p. (gr. k-2). 1989. 19. 95 (ISBN 0-87449-650-0). Modern Pub NYC.
Mandel, Peter. Ballerina Bunny Loves to Dance. 1987. pap. 2.25 (ISBN 0-89954-674-9). Antioch Pub Co.
Manning, Paul. Boy. Bayley, Nicola, illus. LC 87-14202. 24p. (ps-1). 1988. RSBE 8.95 (ISBN 0-02-762251-7, Mcmillan Child Bk). Macmillan Child Grp.
—Clown. Bayley, Nicola, illus. LC 87-14148. 24p. (ps-1). 1988. 8.95 (ISBN 0-02-762254-1, Mcmillan Child Bk). Macmillan Child Grp.
—Cook. Bayley, Nicola, illus. LC 87-14147. 24p. (ps-1). 1988. 8.95 (ISBN 0-02-762252-5, Mcmillan Child Bk). Macmillan Child Grp.
—Fisherman. Bayley, Nicola, illus. LC 87-14168. 24p. (ps-1). 1988. 8.95 (ISBN 0-02-762253-3, Mcmillan Child Bk). Macmillan Child Grp.
Manushkin, Fran. Baby, Come Out! Himler, Ronald, illus. LC 78-183159. 32p. (ps-3). 1984. pap. 2.95 (ISBN 0-06-443050-2, Trophy). HarpC Child Bks.
—Glow in the Dark Mother Goose. (ps-3). 1990. write for info. (ISBN 0-307-06251-1). Western Pub.
—Puppies & Kittens. (Illus.). 24p. (ps-k). 1989. pap. write for info. (ISBN 0-307-11806-1, Pub. by Golden Bks). Western Pub.
—Sweetie in "What's for Lunch?" (Illus.). (ps-k). 1991. bds. 1.95 (ISBN 0-307-06117-5, Golden Pr). Western Pub.
Mariotti, Mario. Hanimations. (Illus.). 40p. (ps-4). 1989. 10.95 (ISBN 0-916291-22-7). Kane-Miller Bk.
—Humages. Marchiori, Roberto, illus. LC 85-70420. (Orig.). 1985. pap. 7.95 (ISBN 0-88138-058-X). Green Tiger Pr.
Maris, Ron. Are You There, Bear? Maris, Ron, illus. 32p. (ps-1). 1986. pap. 3.50 (ISBN 0-14-050524-5, Puffin). Puffin Bks.
—Hold Tight, Bear! (ps-1). 1989. 12.95 (ISBN 0-440-50152-0). Delacorte.
—I Wish I Could Fly. Maris, Ron, illus. LC 86-9797. 32p. (ps-1). 1987. 13.95 (ISBN 0-688-06654-2); PLB 13.88 (ISBN 0-688-06655-0). Greenwillow.
Mark, Jan. Fur. Voake, Charlotte, illus. LC 85-45681. 24p. (ps-2). 1986. pap. 2.50 (ISBN 0-06-443100-2, Trophy). HarpC Child Bks.
—Fur. Voake, Charlotte, illus. LC 85-45539. 24p. (ps-2). 1986. PLB 11.89 (ISBN 0-397-32170-8, Pub. by Lipp Jr Bks). HarpC Child Bks.
Marks, Alan. Nowhere to be Found. Marks, Alan, illus. LC 87-32729. 28p. (ps up). 1988. 14.95 (ISBN 0-88708-062-6). Picture Bk Studio.
Marksbury, Tina, illus. Nighty-Night, Teddy Beddy Bear. 12p. (ps). 1986. 3.95 (ISBN 0-394-88244-X, Random Juv). Random.
Marsh, Carole. Snowshoe & Earmuff Go West. (Illus.). (ps-3). 1989. 19.95 (ISBN 1-55609-304-7); pap. 14.95 (ISBN 1-55609-303-9). Gallopade Pub Group.
Marshall, James. Fox on the Job. Marshall, James, illus. LC 87-15589. 48p. (gr. k-3). 1988. 9.95 (ISBN 0-8037-0350-3); PLB 9.89 (ISBN 0-8037-0351-1). Dial Bks Young.
—George & Martha Round & Round. Marshall, James, illus. LC 88-14739. 48p. (gr. k-3). 1988. 13.95 (ISBN 0-395-46763-2). HM.
—Goldilocks & the Three Bears. Marshall, James, illus. LC 87-32983. 32p. (ps-3). 1988. 12.95 (ISBN 0-8037-0542-5); PLB 12.89 (ISBN 0-8037-0543-3). Dial Bks Young.
—The Guest. Marshall, James, illus. 40p. (gr. k-3). 1981. pap. 4.95 (ISBN 0-395-31127-6). HM.
—Red Riding Hood. LC 86-16722. (Illus.). 32p. (ps-3). 1987. 10.95 (ISBN 0-8037-0344-9); PLB 10.89 (ISBN 0-8037-0345-7). Dial Bks Young.
—What's the Matter with Carruthers? Marshall, James, illus. LC 72-75607. 32p. (gr. k-3). 1987. pap. 3.95 (ISBN 0-395-45358-5). HM.
—Willis. Marshall, James, illus. LC 74-5259. (gr. k-3). 1974. 13.95 (ISBN 0-395-19494-6). HM.
—Yummers! Marshall, James, illus. LC 72-5400. 32p. (gr. k-3). 1973. 12.95 (ISBN 0-395-14757-3). HM.
—Yummers Too. Marshall, James, illus. LC 86-10667. 32p. (gr. k-3). 1986. 12.95 (ISBN 0-395-38990-9). HM.
Martin, Bill, Jr. & Archambault, John. Chicka Chicka Boom Boom. Ehlert, Lois, illus. (gr. 2-6). 1989. pap. 13.95 (ISBN 0-671-67949-X). S&S Trade.
—Here Are My Hands. Rand, Ted, illus. LC 86-25842. 32p. (ps-2). 1987. 14.95 (ISBN 0-8050-0328-2). H Holt & Co.
—Here Are My Hands. Rand, Ted, illus. LC 86-25842. 32p. (ps-1). 1989. pap. 4.95 (ISBN 0-8050-1168-4). H Holt & Co.
—Listen to the Rain. Endicott, James, illus. LC 88-6502. 32p. (gr. k-3). 1988. 13.95 (ISBN 0-8050-0682-6). H Holt & Co.
—Up & down on the Merry-Go-Round. Rand, Ted, illus. LC 87-28836. 32p. (gr. k-3). 1988. 12.95 (ISBN 0-8050-0681-8). H Holt & Co.
Martin, C. L. The Dragon Nanny. Rayevsky, Robert, illus. LC 87-7674. 32p. (gr. k-3). 1988. 14.95 (ISBN 0-02-762440-4, Mcmillan Child Bk). Macmillan Child Grp.
Martin, Charles E. Sam Saves the Day. Martin, Charles E., illus. LC 86-19594. 32p. (gr. k-3). 1990. pap. 4.95 (ISBN 0-06-443230-0, Trophy). HarpC Child Bks.
—Summer Business. Martin, Charles E., illus. 32p. (gr. k-3). 1990. pap. 4.95 (ISBN 0-06-443231-9, Trophy). HarpC Child Bks.
Martin, Dick. Cut & Assemble the Emerald City. 1980. pap. 5.95 (ISBN 0-486-24053-3). Dover.
—Cut & Assemble Wizard of Oz Theatre. 1985. pap. 4.95 (ISBN 0-486-24799-6). Dover.
Martin, Jacqueline B. Bizzy Bones & the Lost Quilt. Qrmai, Stella, illus. LC 87-13577. (ps-3). 1988. 12.95 (ISBN 0-688-07407-3); PLB 12.88 (ISBN 0-688-07408-1). Lothrop.
Martin, Janet. Ten Little Babies Counts. Watson, Michael, photos by. (Illus.). (ps). 1986. bds. 3.95 (ISBN 0-312-79112-7). St Martin.
—Ten Little Babies Dress. Watson, Michael, photos by. (Illus.). 14p. 1986. bds. 3.95 (ISBN 0-312-79113-5). St Martin.
—Ten Little Babies Eat. Watson, Michael, photos by. (Illus.). 14p. (ps). 1986. bds. 3.95 (ISBN 0-312-79114-3). St Martin.
—Ten Little Babies Play: A Book of Colors. Watson, Michael, photos by. (Illus.). 14p. (ps). 1986. bds. 3.95 (ISBN 0-312-79115-1). St Martin.
Martin, Phyllis. A New Blanket for Josh. Connelly, Gwen, illus. LC 87-91995. 32p. (gr. k-2). 1988. 2.50 (ISBN 0-87403-400-0, 24-03810). Standard Pub.
Martin, Rodney. The Making of a Picture Book. Siow, John, illus. LC 88-42911. 32p. (gr. 3-4). 1989. PLB 12. 95 (ISBN 1-55532-958-6). Gareth Stevens Inc.
Marzollo, Jean. The Rebus Treasury. Carson, Carol D., illus. LC 85-16133. 64p. (ps up). 1986. 14.95 (ISBN 0-8037-0254-X); PLB 14.89 (ISBN 0-8037-0255-8). Dial Bks Young.
—The Three Little Kittens. Thornton, Shelley, illus. 32p. (Orig.). (ps-1). 1986. pap. 1.95 (ISBN 0-590-33370-4, SeeSaw Books). Scholastic Inc.
Maslen, Bobby L. Bob Books for Beginning Readers, Set I. (Illus.). 144p. (ps). 1983. Set of 12 bks. pap. 13.95 (ISBN 0-9612104-0-0). Bob Bks.
Mason, Evelyn. The Baby Hugs Bear & Baby Tugs Bear Look & Find Book. Cooke, Tom, illus. 40p. (ps). 1984. 5.95 (ISBN 0-910313-73-3). Parker Bros.
Mason, Lura. A Book of Boxes. (ps-1). 1989. pap. 11.95 (ISBN 0-671-67801-9). S&S Trade.
Mason, Margo. Go Away, Crows! Prebenna, David, illus. 32p. (ps-1). 1989. 3.50 (ISBN 0-553-34725-X). Bantam.
—Rover. Hoffman, Sandy, illus. 32p. (ps-1). write for info. Bantam.
—Winter Coats. (ps-k). 1989. 8.95 (ISBN 0-553-05818-5). Bantam.
—Winter Coats. 1989. pap. 3.50 (ISBN 0-553-34726-8). Bantam.
Massi, Jeri. Crown & Jewel. (Illus.). 160p. (Orig.). (gr. 5). 1987. pap. 4.95 (ISBN 0-89084-390-2). Bob Jones Univ Pr.
Mastrangelo, Judy. What Do Bunnies Do All Day? Mastrangelo, Judy, illus. 32p. (ps-1). 1989. 11.95 (ISBN 0-8249-8311-4). Ideals.
Matarasso, Janet. Why Can't You Grow Up? Chambers, Margaret, illus. LC 85-25539. 24p. (ps-2). 1986. 11.95 (ISBN 0-521-32125-5). Cambridge U Pr.
Mathers, Petra. Theodor & Mr. Balbini. Mathers, Petra, illus. LC 87-45860. 32p. (gr. k-3). 1988. 11.95 (ISBN 0-06-024122-5); PLB 11.89 (ISBN 0-06-024144-6). HarpC Child Bks.
Mathiesen, Egon. Jungle in the Wheat Field. (Illus.). (gr. k-3). 1960. 9.95 (ISBN 0-8392-3014-1). Astor-Honor.
—Oswald the Monkey. (Illus.). (gr. k-3). 1959. 9.95 (ISBN 0-8392-3025-7). Astor-Honor.
Mathieu, Joe. Big Bird's Big Book. Mathieu, Joe, illus. 12p. (ps-1). 1987. 29.95 (ISBN 0-394-89128-7, Random Juv). Random.
—Sesame Street Wheel Books. Mathieu, Joe, illus. (ps-2). 1989. 2.95 (ISBN 0-318-41489-9). Random.
Mathieu, Joe, illus. Sesame Street Fire Trucks. 14p. (ps-k). 1988. bds. 2.95 (ISBN 0-394-89952-0, Random Juv). Random.
—Trucks in Your Neighborhood. 14p. (ps-k). 1988. bds. 2.95 (ISBN 0-394-89951-2, Random Juv). Random.
Matthews, Rupert. The Great Dinosaur Pop-up Book. Johnson, Karen, illus. LC 88-361. 24p. (gr. 2-6). 1989. 13.95 (ISBN 0-8037-0549-2). Dial Bks Young.
Matthias, Catherine. Arriba y Abajo: (Over-Under) Sharp, Gene, illus. LC 83-21005. (SPA.). 32p. (ps-2). 1989. PLB 11.93 (ISBN 0-516-32048-3); pap. 2.95 (ISBN 0-516-52048-2). Childrens.
—Sal y Entra: (Out the Door) Neill, Eileen M., illus. LC 81-17060. (SPA.). 32p. (ps-2). 1989. PLB 11.93 (ISBN 0-516-33560-X); pap. 2.95 (ISBN 0-516-53560-9). Childrens.
Matura, Mustapha. Moon Jump. Gifford, Jane, illus. LC 88-6788. 32p. (ps-1). 1988. lib. bdg. 11.99 (ISBN 0-685-20042-6). Knopf.
Matus, Jean L. Pip of Weeville. Gemmill, Courtenay, ed. Toler, Sand, illus. LC 88-70820. 24p. (gr. k-2). 1988. 11.95 (ISBN 0-945938-00-4). Clark-Davis.
Mayer, Marianna. The Little Jewel Box. (Illus.). (ps-3). 1986. 10.95 (ISBN 0-8037-0148-9). Dial Bks Young.
Mayer, Mercer. Astronaut Critter. Mayer, Mercer, illus. (ps-1). 1986. 3.95 (ISBN 0-671-61142-9, Little Simon). S&S Trade.
—Baby Sister Says No. Mayer, Mercer, illus. LC 86-82368. 24p. (gr. 4-8). 1987. pap. write for info. (ISBN 0-307-11949-1, Pub. by Golden Bks). Western Pub.
—A Boy, a Dog, a Frog & a Friend. LC 70-134857. (ps-2). 1985. 8.95 (ISBN 0-8037-0754-1); PLB 8.89 (ISBN 0-8037-0755-X); pap. 2.95 (ISBN 0-8037-0804-1). Dial Bks Young.
—Cowboy Critter. Mayer, Mercer, illus. (ps-1). 1986. 3.95 (ISBN 0-671-61141-0, Little Simon). S&S Trade.
—Fireman Critter. Mayer, Mercer, illus. (ps-1). 1986. 3.95 (ISBN 0-671-61143-7, Little Simon). S&S Trade.
—Hiccup. LC 76-2284. (Illus.). (ps-2). 1978. pap. 3.95 (ISBN 0-8037-3590-1, 0383-120). Dial Bks Young.
—I Just Forgot. Mayer, Mercer, illus. LC 87-81779. 24p. (Orig.). (ps-3). 1988. pap. write for info. (ISBN 0-307-11975-0). Western Pub.
—Just a Daydream. (Illus.). 24p. (ps-3). 1989. pap. write for info. (ISBN 0-307-11973-4, Pub. by Golden Bks). Western Pub.
—Just a Mess. Mayer, Mercer, illus. LC 86-82369. 24p. (gr. 4-8). 1987. pap. write for info. (ISBN 0-307-11948-3, Pub. by Golden Bks). Western Pub.
—Just a Nap. (Illus.). 24p. (ps-k). 1989. pap. write for info. (ISBN 0-307-11713-8, Pub. by Golden Bks). Western Pub.

—Just a Snowy Day. (Illus.). 20p. (gr. k). 1983. write for info. comb. bdg. (ISBN 0-307-12156-9, 12156, Golden Bks). Western Pub.
—Just Camping Out. (Illus.). 24p. (ps-k). 1989. pap. write for info. (ISBN 0-307-11714-6, Pub. by Golden Bks). Western Pub.
—Just for You. Mayer, Mercer, illus. 24p. (ps-3). 1975. pap. write for info. (ISBN 0-307-11838-X, Golden Bks.). Western Pub.
—Just Go to Bed. rev. ed. Mayer, Mercer, illus. 24p. (ps-3). 1985. pap. write for info. (ISBN 0-307-11940-8, 11940, Pub. by Golden Bks). Western Pub.
—Just Grandma & Me. (Illus.). 24p. (ps-3). 1985. pap. write for info. (ISBN 0-307-11893-2, Golden Bks). Western Pub.
—Just Grandpa & Me. Mayer, Mercer, illus. 24p. (ps-3). 1985. pap. write for info. (ISBN 0-307-11936-X, Pub. by Golden Bks). Western Pub.
—Just Me & My Babysitter. Mayer, Mercer, illus. 24p. (Orig.). (ps-3). 1986. pap. write for info. (ISBN 0-307-11945-9, Pub. by Golden Bks). Western Pub.
—Just Me & My Little Sister. Mayer, Mercer, illus. 24p. (Orig.). (ps-3). 1986. pap. write for info. (ISBN 0-307-11946-7, Pub. by Golden Bks). Western Pub.
—Just Me & My Puppy. Mayer, Mercer, illus. 24p. (ps-3). 1985. pap. write for info. (ISBN 0-307-11937-8, Pub. by Golden Bks). Western Pub.
—Just My Friend & Me. Mayer, Mercer, illus. 1988. write for info. (ISBN 0-307-11947-5, 11947, Pub. by Golden Bks). Western Pub.
—Just Shopping with Mom. (Illus.). 24p. (ps-3). 1989. pap. write for info. (ISBN 0-307-11972-6, Pub. by Golden Bks). Western Pub.
—Little Critter's Christmas Book. (ps-1). 1989. write for info. (ISBN 0-307-15849-7, Golden Bks). Western Pub.
—Little Critter's Holiday Fun. Mayer, Mercer, illus. 24p. (Orig.). (ps-3). 1984. pap. 3.95 (ISBN 0-590-33658-4). Scholastic Inc.
—Little Critter's the Fussy Princess. (Illus.). 24p. (ps-2). 1989. write for info. (ISBN 0-307-12090-2, Pub. by Golden Bks). Western Pub.
—Little Sister's Birthday. Mayer, Mercer, illus. LC 87-83017. 40p. (gr. k-2). 1988. write for info. (ISBN 0-307-11665-4). Western Pub.
—Me Too! Mayer, Mercer, illus. 24p. (ps-3). 1985. pap. write for info. (ISBN 0-307-11941-6, Pub. by Golden Bks). Western Pub.
—Mercer Mayer's Little Critter's Day. (Illus.). 12p. (ps). 1989. bds. write for info. (ISBN 0-307-06107-8, Pub. by Golden Bks). Western Pub.
—The New Baby. Mayer, Mercer, illus. 24p. (ps-3). 1985. pap. write for info. (ISBN 0-307-11942-4, Pub. by Golden Bks). Western Pub.
—The Picnic. Mayer, Mercer, illus. LC 87-83015. 40p. (gr. k-2). 1988. write for info. (ISBN 0-307-11663-8). Western Pub.
—Policeman Critter. Mayer, Mercer, illus. (ps-1). 1986. 3.95 (ISBN 0-671-61140-2, Little Simon). S&S Trade.
—Staying Overnight. Mayer, Mercer, illus. LC 87-83014. 40p. (gr. k-2). 1988. write for info. (ISBN 0-307-11662-X). Western Pub.
—Terrible Troll. Mayer, Mercer, illus. LC 68-28730. (gr. k-3). 1968. PLB 11.89 (ISBN 0-8037-8621-2). Dial Bks Young.
—There's a Nightmare in My Closet. Mayer, Mercer, illus. LC 68-15250. (ps-3). 1990. 12.95 (ISBN 0-8037-8682-4); PLB 12.89 (ISBN 0-8037-8683-2); pap. 3.95 (ISBN 0-8037-8574-7); guide 16.95 (ISBN 0-8037-0843-2). Dial Bks Young.
—There's Something in My Attic. Mayer, Mercer, illus. LC 86-32875. 32p. (ps-3). 1988. 11.95 (ISBN 0-8037-0414-3); PLB 11.89 (ISBN 0-8037-0415-1). Dial Bks Young.
—These Are My Pets. Mayer, Mercer, illus. LC 87-83016. 40p. (gr. k-2). 1988. write for info. (ISBN 0-307-11664-6). Western Pub.
—This Is My House. Mayer, Mercer, illus. LC 87-116603. 40p. (gr. k-2). 1988. write for info. (ISBN 0-307-11660-3). Western Pub.
—The Trip. Mayer, Mercer, illus. LC 87-83013. 40p. (gr. k-2). 1988. write for info. (ISBN 0-307-11661-1). Western Pub.
—When I Get Bigger. Mayer, Mercer, illus. 24p. (ps-3). 1985. pap. write for info. (ISBN 0-307-11943-2, Pub. by Golden Bks). Western Pub.
Mayer, Mercer & Mayer, Marianna. One Frog Too Many. Mayer, Mercer, illus. LC 75-6325. 32p. (ps-2). 1985. 9.95 (ISBN 0-8037-4838-8); PLB 9.89 (ISBN 0-8037-4858-2). Dial Bks Young.
Mayer-Skumanz, Lene. Caroline Moves In. Sklenitzka, Franz S., illus. 96p. (gr. 1-3). 1988. pap. 2.95 (ISBN 0-8120-3938-6). Barron.
Mazer, Anne. Watch Me. Schuett, Stacey, illus. LC 89-34920. 40p. (ps-k). 1990. 12.95 (ISBN 0-394-82946-8); lib. bdg. 13.99 (ISBN 0-394-92946-2). McKay.
Meddaugh, Susan. Maude & Claude Go Abroad. Meddaugh, Susan, illus. (gr. k-3). 1980. 7.95 (ISBN 0-395-29162-3). HM.
Meggendorfer, Lothar. The Doll's House: A Reproduction of the Antique Pop-up Book. Meggendorfer, Lothar, illus. Shiller, Justin G., notes by. LC 79-5072. (Illus.). (gr. k-3). 1989. pap. 8.95 (ISBN 0-670-27761-4). Viking Child Bks.
Mendoza, George. Hunter I Might Have Been. (Illus.). (gr. 3-5). 1968. 10.95 (ISBN 0-8392-3064-8). Astor-Honor.
Menten, Ted. Cut & Use Stencil Bunny Rabbit. 1985. pap. 4.95 (ISBN 0-486-24909-3). Dover.
—Folk Art Cut & Use Stencils. 1985. pap. 4.95 (ISBN 0-486-24838-0). Dover.
—Ships & Boats Punch Out Stencils. 1986. pap. 3.50 (ISBN 0-486-25049-0). Dover.
—Teddy Bear-Cut & Use Stencils. 1983. pap. 4.95 (ISBN 0-486-24595-0). Dover.
—Teddy Bear Punch Out Stencils. 1985. pap. 3.50 (ISBN 0-486-24832-1). Dover.
Menten, Theodore. Art Deco Cut & Use Stencils. 1977. pap. 4.95 (ISBN 0-486-23551-3). Dover.
—Victorian Fashion Paper Dolls from Harper's Bazar, 1867-1898. 1979. pap. 3.95 (ISBN 0-486-23453-3). Dover.
Merriam, Eve. Halloween A B C. Smith, Lane, illus. LC 86-23772. 52p. (gr. k up). 1987. 14.95 (ISBN 0-02-766870-3, Mcmillan Child Bk). Macmillan Child Grp.
Meryl, Debra. Baby's Peek-a-Boo Album. Kelley, True, illus. 24p. (ps). 1989. 10.95 (ISBN 0-448-15375-0, G&D). Putnam Pub Group.
Messenger, Jannat. Lullaby & Goodnight: A Bedtime Book with Music. Messenger, Jannat, illus. 12p. (ps-1). 1988. bds. 10.95 (ISBN 0-689-71268-5, Aladdin). Macmillan Child Grp.
—Twinkle Twinkle Little Star: A Lullaby Book with Lights & Music. Messenger, Jannat, illus. 12p. (ps-1). 1987. bds. 10.95 (ISBN 0-689-71136-0, Aladdin). Macmillan Child Grp.
Meyrick, Kathryn. Hazel's Healthy Halloween. (ps-3). 1990. pap. 5.95 (ISBN 0-85953-308-5). Childs Play.
—Musical Life of Gustav Mole. (ps-3). 1990. pap. 5.95 (ISBN 0-85953-347-6). Childs Play.
Michaela, Muntean. Muppet Babies Through The Year. McNally, Bruce, illus. LC 83-16041. 32p. (ps-1). 1984. 3.95 (ISBN 0-394-86544-8, Random Juv). Random.
Michels, Tilde. Sophie the Rag Picker. Michels, Tilde, illus. (gr. k-1). 1962. 10.95 (ISBN 0-8392-3036-2). Astor-Honor.
—Who's That Knocking at My Door? Michl, Reinhard, illus. 28p. (ps-3). 1986. 7.95 (ISBN 0-8120-5732-5). Barron.
Mike, Jan & Lowmiller, Cathie. Bizagolaa; Apache Cut & Color Book. Lowmiller, Cathie, illus. 32p. (Orig.). (gr. k-6). 1989. pap. 3.95 (ISBN 0-918080-46-0). Treasure Chest.
Mike, Jan M. Desert Seasons. Mike, Samuel A., illus. 32p. (gr. k-8). 1991. pap. 7.95 (ISBN 0-918080-49-5). Treasure Chest.
Miles, Sally. Alfi & the Dark. Le Cain, Errol, illus. LC 88-1043. 32p. (ps-1). 1988. 13.95 (ISBN 0-87701-527-9). Chronicle Bks.
Milios, Rita. Bears, Bears Everywhere. (ps-2). 1988. PLB 11.93 (ISBN 0-516-02085-4); pap. 2.95 (ISBN 0-516-42085-2). Childrens.
—Osos, osos, aqui y alli: (Bears, Bears, Everywhere) Dunnington, Tom, illus. LC 87-33780. (ENG & SPA.). 32p. (ps-2). 1989. PLB 11.93 (ISBN 0-516-32085-8); pap. 2.95 (ISBN 0-516-52085-7). Childrens.
—Yo Soy (I Am) Martin, Clovis, illus. LC 87-5163. (SPA.). 32p. (ps-2). 1990. PLB 11.93 (ISBN 0-516-32081-5); pap. 2.95 (ISBN 0-516-52081-4). Childrens.
Miller, Albert G. Sesame Street Storybook. 1986. pap. 6.95 (ISBN 0-394-88301-2). Random.
Miller, Edna. Mousekin Finds a Friend. Miller, Edna, illus. (ps-3). 1971. (Pub. by Treehouse). P-H.
Miller, J. P., illus. What Did Santa Bring? LC 83-63317. 12p. (ps). 1984. bds. 1.95 (ISBN 0-394-86749-1, Random Juv). Random.
Miller, M. L. Dizzy from Fools. Tharlet, Eve, illus. LC 85-9390. 32p. (gr. 1 up). 1985. 13.95 (ISBN 0-88708-004-9). Picture Bk Studio USA.
Miller, Margaret. More First Words: Every Day. Miller, Margaret, illus. LC 89-82634. 14p. (ps). 1991. 3.95 (ISBN 0-694-00304-2). HarpC Child Bks.
—More First Words: My Birthday. Miller, Margaret, illus. LC 89-82635. 14p. (ps). 1991. 3.95 (ISBN 0-694-00302-6). HarpC Child Bks.
—More First Words: On My Street. Miller, Margaret, illus. LC 89-82633. 14p. (ps). 1991. 3.95 (ISBN 0-694-00303-4). HarpC Child Bks.
—More First Words: Playtime. Miller, Margaret, illus. LC 89-82632. 14p. (ps). 1991. 3.95 (ISBN 0-694-00301-8). HarpC Child Bks.
Miller, Nell. Strawberry Shortcake & the Crazy Baking Contest. Sustendal, Pat, illus. 40p. (ps-3). 1983. 5. 95cancelled (ISBN 0-910313-09-1). Parker Bros.
Millios, Rita. I Am. Martin, Clovis, illus. LC 87-5163. 32p. (ps-2). 1987. PLB 11.93 (ISBN 0-516-02081-1); pap. 2.95 (ISBN 0-516-42081-X). Childrens.
Milne, A. A. House at Pooh Corner: A Pop-Up Book. (Illus.). 12p. (ps up). 1986. 10.95 (ISBN 0-525-44245-6, DCB). Dutton Child Bks.
—Now We Are Six. Shepard, Ernest H., illus. 112p. (ps up). 1988. 9.95 (ISBN 0-525-44446-7, DCB). Dutton Child Bks.
—Pooh's Adventures with Christopher Robin. (Illus.). 18p. (ps-4). 1986. 2.98 (ISBN 0-525-44262-6, DCB). Dutton Child Bks.
—Pooh's Adventures with Eeyore & Tigger. (ps-4). 1986. 2.98 (ISBN 0-525-44263-4, DCB). Dutton Child Bks.
—Pooh's Adventures with Piglet. 18p. (ps-4). 1986. 2.98 (ISBN 0-525-44264-2, DCB). Dutton Child Bks.
—When We Were Very Young. Shepard, Ernest H., illus. 112p. (ps up). 1988. 9.95 (ISBN 0-525-44445-9, DCB). Dutton Child Bks.
—Winnie-the-Pooh Goes Exploring. (ps-4). 1986. 2.98 (ISBN 0-525-44269-3, DCB). Dutton Child Bks.
—Winnie-the-Pooh's Calendar Book 1987. Shepard, Ernest H., illus. (ps up). 1986. 4.95 (ISBN 0-525-44235-9, Dutton). NAL-Dutton.
—Winnie-the-Pooh's Revolving Picture Book. 1990. 12.95 (ISBN 0-525-44645-1, DCB). Dutton Child Bks.
Minarik, Else H. Kiss for Little Bear. Sendak, Maurice, illus. LC 57-9263. 32p. (gr. k-3). 1968. 10.95 (ISBN 0-06-024298-1); PLB 10.89 (ISBN 0-06-024299-X). HarpC Child Bks.
—Little Bear. LC 57-9263. (Illus.). 64p. (gr. k-3). 1978. incl. cassette 5.98 (ISBN 0-694-00113-9, Trophy); pap. 3.50 (ISBN 0-06-444004-4, Trophy). HarpC Child Bks.
Miranda, Anne. Baby-Sit, Vol. 1. (ps). 1990. 9.95 (ISBN 0-316-57454-6, Joy St Bks). Little.
—Baby Talk. Stott, Dorothy, illus. 16p. (ps). 1987. 9.95 (ISBN 0-525-44319-3, 0772-230, DCB). Dutton Child Bks.
—Baby Walk. Stott, Dorothy, illus. 14p. (ps). 1988. 8.95 (ISBN 0-525-44421-1, DCB). Dutton Child Bks.
Miranda the Magnificent. (Illus.). (ps-2). 1990. 3.95 (ISBN 0-7214-9609-1). Ladybird Bks.
Miss Lori. Shapeless & the Magic Box, Bk. 1. White, Lori G., ed. Miss Lori, illus. 18p. (Orig.). (ps-1). 1990. pap. 11.99 (ISBN 0-9623368-3-1). Shapeless Enterprises.
—Shapeless & the Magic Box, Bk. 2. White, Lori G., ed. Miss Lori, illus. 18p. (Orig.). (ps-1). 1991. pap. 11.99 (ISBN 0-9623368-8-2). Shapeless Enterprises.
Mitchell, Cindy. Happy Hands & Feet. LC 88-82903. (Illus.). 80p. (ps-3). 1989. pap. text ed. 7.95 (ISBN 0-86530-062-3, IP 166-0). Incentive Pubns.
Mitchell, Evelyn. My Dog Sam. 1989. 4.95 (ISBN 0-533-07763-X). Vantage.
Mitchell, Kathy. Silent Night: A Christmas Book with Lights & Music. Mitchell, Kathy, illus. 12p. (ps-3). 1989. bds. 10.95 (ISBN 0-689-71330-4, Aladdin). Macmillan Child Grp.
Modan, Shula. Why Jonathan Doesn't Cry. Leon, Yael, illus. (ps-2). 1988. 7.95 (ISBN 1-55774-022-4, Dist. by Watts). Adama Pubs Inc.
Modell, Frank. One Zillion Valentines. LC 81-2215. (ps-3). 1987. pap. 3.95 (ISBN 0-688-07329-8, Mulberry). Morrow.
Moerbeek, Kees. New at the Zoo: A Mix-&-Match Pop-up Book. Moerbeek, Kees, illus. LC 89-60077. 10p. (ps-1). 1989. bds. 7.95 (ISBN 0-679-80076-X, Random Juv). Random.
—Who's Peeking at Me: A Pop-Up Book. (Illus.). 12p. (ps-3). 1989. 8.95 (ISBN 0-8431-2410-5). Price Stern.
Mogensen, Jan. The Forty-Six Little Men. LC 90-36470. (Illus.). 28p. (ps up). 1991. 13.95 (ISBN 0-688-09283-7); PLB 13.88 (ISBN 0-688-09284-5). Greenwillow.
Mohr, Joseph. Silent Night. Jeffers, Susan, illus. LC 84-8113. 32p. (ps up). 1984. 14.95 (ISBN 0-525-44144-1, DCB); pap. 4.95 (ISBN 0-8037-4443-9, DCB). Dutton Child Bks.
Molly's Monsters. (ps-2). 1988. incl. cassette 5.95 (ISBN 0-448-19100-8, G&D). Putnam Pub Group.
Molnar, Dorothy E. & Fenton, Stephen H. Who Will Pick Me up When I Fall? Mathews, Judith, ed. Trivas, Irene, illus. 32p. (ps-2). 1991. 12.95 (ISBN 0-8075-9072-X). A Whitman.
Moncure, Jane B. Apes Find Shapes. Freidman, Joy, illus. LC 87-11747. 32p. (ps-2). 1987. PLB 11.97 (ISBN 0-89565-364-8); pap. 6.96 (ISBN 0-89565-437-7). Childs World.
—Away Went the Farmer's Hat. Hohag, Linda, illus. LC 87-11742. 32p. (ps-2). 1987. PLB 11.97 (ISBN 0-89565-367-2); pap. 6.96 (ISBN 0-89565-430-X). Childs World.
—The Bears Upstairs. Knipper, Sue, illus. LC 87-11715. 32p. (ps-2). 1987. PLB 11.97 (ISBN 0-89565-373-7); pap. 6.96 (ISBN 0-89565-446-6). Childs World.
—A Color Clown Comes to Town. Hohag, Lindq, illus. LC 87-11605. 32p. (ps-2). 1987. lib. bdg. 11.97 (ISBN 0-89565-369-9); pap. 6.96 (ISBN 0-89565-444-X). Childs World.
—A Dragon in a Wagon. Hohag, Linda, illus. LC 87-11755. 32p. (ps-2). 1987. PLB 11.97 (ISBN 0-89565-400-8); pap. 6.96 (ISBN 0-89565-428-8). Childs World.
—Hop-skip-jump-a-roo Zoo. Hohag, Linda, illus. LC 87-11743. 32p. (ps-2). 1987. PLB 11.97 (ISBN 0-89565-371-0); pap. 6.96 (ISBN 0-89565-447-4). Childs World.
—Let's Take a Walk in the Zoo. Axeman, Lois, illus. LC 86-20744. 32p. (ps-2). 1986. lib. bdg. 11.97 (ISBN 0-89565-356-7). Childs World.
—Little Too-Tall. Hohag, Linda, illus. LC 87-11632. 32p. (ps-2). 1987. PLB 11.97 (ISBN 0-89565-374-5); pap. 6.96 (ISBN 0-89565-448-2). Childs World.
—Magic Monsters Learn about Manners. Sommers, Linda, illus. LC 79-24528. (ps-3). 1980. PLB 11.97 (ISBN 0-89565-118-1). Childs World.
—Mousekin's Special Day. Williams, Jenny, illus. LC 87-11750. 32p. (ps-2). 1987. PLB 11.97 (ISBN 0-89565-366-4); pap. 6.96 (ISBN 0-89565-442-3). Childs World.
—My First Book. Hutton, Kathryn, illus. LC 84-17455. 32p. (ps-2). 1984. PLB 11.97 (ISBN 0-89565-271-4); pap. 6.96 (ISBN 0-89565-334-6). Childs World.
—One Tricky Monkey Up on Top. Freidman, Joy, illus. LC 87-11612. 32p. (ps-2). 1987. PLB 11.97 (ISBN 0-89565-365-6); pap. 6.96 (ISBN 0-89565-436-9). Childs World.

—A Pocketful of Pets. Hohag, Linda, illus. LC 87-11748. 32p. (ps-2). 1987. PLB 11.97 (ISBN 0-89565-370-2); pap. 6.96 (ISBN 0-89565-432-6). Childs World.
—What Do You Do with a Grumpy Kangaroo? Hohag, Linda, illus. LC 87-11731. 32p. (ps). 1987. PLB 11.97 (ISBN 0-89565-372-9); pap. 6.96 (ISBN 0-89565-440-7). Childs World.
—What Do You Say When a Monkey Acts This Way? Super, Terri, illus. LC 87-11736. 32p. (ps-2). 1987. PLB 11.97 (ISBN 0-89565-368-0); pap. 6.96 (ISBN 0-89565-443-1). Childs world.
—Where? Axeman, Lois, illus. LC 83-7307. 32p. (gr. k-2). 1983. 12.60 (ISBN 0-516-06593-9); pap. 3.95 (ISBN 0-516-46593-7). Childrens.
—Word Bird's Christmas Words. Gohman, Vera, illus. LC 86-31666. 32p. (gr. k-2). 1987. PLB 11.97 (ISBN 0-89565-361-3); pap. 6.96 (ISBN 0-89565-394-X). Childs World.
—Word Bird's Circus Surprise. Hohag, Linda, illus. LC 80-29528. 32p. (ps-1). 1983. pap. 3.95 (ISBN 0-516-46554-6). Childrens.
—Word Bird's Easter Words. Axeman, Lois, illus. 32p. (gr. k-2). 1987. PLB 11.97 (ISBN 0-89565-363-X); pap. 6.96 (ISBN 0-89565-395-8). Childs World.
—Word Bird's Halloween Words. Gohman, Vera, illus. LC 86-31024. 32p. (gr. k-2). 1987. PLB 11.97 (ISBN 0-89565-359-1); pap. 6.96 (ISBN 0-89565-396-6). Childs World.
—Word Bird's Thanksgiving Words. Hohag, Linda, illus. LC 86-32639. 32p. (gr. k-2). 1987. PLB 11.97 (ISBN 0-89565-360-5); pap. 6.96 (ISBN 0-89565-397-4). Childs World.
—Word Bird's Valentine Day Words. Fullam, Sue M., illus. 32p. (gr. k-2). 1987. PLB 11.97 (ISBN 0-89565-362-1); pap. 6.96 (ISBN 0-89565-398-2). Childs World.
Monsell, Mary. Underwear! Levine, Abby, ed. Munsinger, Lynn, illus. 24p. (ps-2). 1988. PLB 10.95 (ISBN 0-8075-8308-1). A Whitman.
The Monster Mystery. (Illus.). 64p. (gr. k-2). 1989. 6.95 (ISBN 0-87449-511-3). Modern Pub NYC.
Monster Pop-Up. (ps-3). 1988. 8.95 (ISBN 0-8167-1445-2). Troll Assocs.
Montgomery, H. Mongoose Magoo. LC 68-56822. (Illus.). 64p. (gr. 2-5). 1968. PLB 10.95 (ISBN 0-87783-026-6); pap. 3.94 deluxe ed. (ISBN 0-87783-100-9). Oddo.
Moore, Clement C. Night Before Christmas. Fujikawa, Gyo, illus. 5.95 (ISBN 0-448-02935-9, G&D). Putnam Pub Group.
—The Night Before Christmas. Rogers, Jacqueline, illus. 32p. (ps-2). 1987. pap. 1.95 (ISBN 0-448-34300-2, Platt & Munk). Putnam Pub Group.
—The Night Before Christmas: A Revolving Picture & Lift-the-Flap Book. Ives, Penny, illus. 14p. 1988. 14.95 (ISBN 0-399-21544-1, Putnam). Putnam Pub Group.
Moore, Frank J. The Incredible Moving Picture Book. 32p. (gr. 1 up). 1987. pap. 3.95 (ISBN 0-486-25374-0). Dover.
Moore, Inga. Rose & the Nightingale. (Illus.). 32p. (gr. k-2). 1991. 13.95 (ISBN 0-86264-223-X, Pub. by Andersen Pr UK). Trafalgar Sq.
—The Sorcerer's Apprentice. Moore, Inga, illus. LC 88-27195. 32p. (gr. k-3). 1989. 13.95 (ISBN 0-02-767645-5, Mcmillan Child Bk). Macmillan Child Grp.
Moore, Lilian. Junk Day on Easy Street & Other Easy-To-Read Stories. Lobel, Arnold, illus. (gr. 1-4). 1991. pap. 2.75 (ISBN 0-553-15627-6, Skylark). Bantam.
Mooser, Stephen & Oliver, Lin. The Fat Cat. Day, Susan, illus. LC 87-40339. (ps-2). 1990. 4.95 (ISBN 1-55782-022-8). Warner Bks.
—Tad & Dad. Day, Susan, illus. LC 87-40340. (ps-2). 1990. 4.95 (ISBN 1-55782-023-6). Warner Bks.
More ABCs - N-Z. 24p. (Orig.). (ps). pap. 3.95 (ISBN 0-8431-3139-X); Little Q Electronic Wand pkg. 7.00 (ISBN 0-318-39959-8). Price Stern.
More Shapes & Colors. (Illus.). 32p. (ps). 1986. write for info. wkbk. (ISBN 0-307-03592-1, Pub. by Golden Bks). Western Pub.
Morehead, Ruth J. The Christmas Story with Holly Babes. Morehead, Ruth J., illus. LC 85-32305. 32p. (ps-1). 1986. pap. 2.25 (ISBN 0-394-88051-X, Random Juv); cassette pkg. 5.95 (ISBN 0-394-89058-2). Random.
Morgan, Mary. Wee Seasons. (Illus.). 24p. (ps). 1990. bds. 2.50 (ISBN 0-448-02261-3, G&D). Putnam Pub Group.
Morgan, Mary, illus. The Pudgy Merry Christmas Book. 16p. 1989. bds. 2.95 (ISBN 0-448-02262-1, G&D). Putnam Pub Group.
—Sleepy Time. LC 89-63997. 14p. (ps). 1990. bds. 3.95 (ISBN 0-679-80753-5). Random.
Morgan, Michaela. The Monster Is Coming. Porter, Sue, illus. LC 87-45568. 24p. (ps-1). 1988. flap bk. 8.95 (ISBN 0-694-00238-0). HarpC Child Bks.
Morris, Ann. Bundle Up! Falconer, Elizabeth, illus. (ps-k). 1987. 3.95 (ISBN 0-671-63368-6, Little Simon). S&S Trade.
—The Cinderella Rebus Book. Rylands, Ljiljana, illus. LC 88-1451. 32p. (ps-3). 1989. 13.95 (ISBN 0-531-05761-5); PLB 13.99 (ISBN 0-531-08361-6). Orchard Bks Watts.
—Clothes. Roffey, Maureen, illus. 24p. (ps). 1989. 2.95 (ISBN 0-8249-8290-8). Ideals.
—Cuddle Up. Roffey, Maureen, illus. LC 85-45335. 16p. (ps). 1986. 3.50 (ISBN 0-694-00072-8). HarpC Child Bks.
—Happy Birthday! Falconer, Elizabeth, illus. 32p. (ps-k). 1987. 3.95 (ISBN 0-671-63365-1, Little Simon). S&S Trade.
—Home. Roffey, Maureen, illus. 24p. (ps). 1989. 2.95 (ISBN 0-8249-8291-6). Ideals.
—My Cat Peter. Falconer, Elizabeth, illus. 32p. (ps-k). 1987. 3.95 (ISBN 0-671-63366-X, Little Simon). S&S Trade.
—Toys. Roffey, Maureen, illus. 24p. (ps). 1989. 2.95 (ISBN 0-8249-8289-4). Ideals.
Morris, Dean. Cats. (ps). 1990. pap. 11.99 (ISBN 0-8172-3230-3). Raintree Pubs.
Morris, Neil & Morris, Ting. Where's My Hat? Clarke, Anna, illus. 24p. (gr. k-3). 1983. 6.95 (ISBN 0-316-58378-2). Little.
Morris, Winifred. Just Listen. Clark, Patricia C., illus. LC 89-15084. 32p. (ps-2). 1990. 11.95 (ISBN 0-689-31588-0, Atheneum Child Bk). Macmillan Child Grp.
—The Magic Leaf. Chen, Ju-Hong, illus. LC 86-28898. 32p. (ps-3). 1987. 13.95 (ISBN 0-689-31358-6, Atheneum Child Bk). Macmillan Child Grp.
Morrison, Blake. The Yellow House. Craig, Helen, illus. 32p. (ps-3). 1987. 12.95 (ISBN 0-15-299820-9, HJ). HarBraceJ.
Mosel, Arlene. Tikki Tikki Tembo. Lent, Blair, illus. LC 68-11839. 48p. (gr. k-2). 1968. 14.95 (ISBN 0-8050-0662-1). H Holt & Co.
Mosel, Arlene, retold by. Tikki Tikki Tembo. Lent, Blair, illus. LC 68-11839. 48p. (ps-2). 1989. pap. 5.95 (ISBN 0-8050-1166-8). H Holt & Co.
Moseley, Keith. The Ghosts of Creepy Castle. (gr. 2 up). 1988. 7.95 (ISBN 0-448-09290-5, G&D). Putnam Pub Group.
—Things in Mouldy Manor. (gr. 2 up). 1988. 7.95 (ISBN 0-448-09289-1, G&D). Putnam Pub Group.
Moseley, Keith & Everitt-Stewart, Andy. The Door under the Stairs. (Illus.). 12p. 1990. 8.95 (ISBN 0-448-40044-8, G&D). Putnam Pub Group.
—Some Bodies in the Attic. (Illus.). 12p. 1990. 8.95 (ISBN 0-448-40043-X, G&D). Putnam Pub Group.
Mosley, Francis. The Dinosaur Eggs. (Illus.). 32p. (ps-2). 1988. 9.95 (ISBN 0-8120-5910-7). Barron.
Moss, Jeffrey. Sesame Street: ABC Storybook. 1986. pap. 5.95 (ISBN 0-394-88303-9). Random.
Moss, Marissa. Who Was It? Moss, Marissa, illus. (gr. k-3). 1989. 13.95 (ISBN 0-395-49699-3). HM.
Most, Bernard. My Very Own Octopus. Most, Bernard, illus. LC 80-12786. 32p. (ps-3). 1980. 14.95 (ISBN 0-15-256641-4, HJ). HarBraceJ.
Mother Goose. 1984. 3.95 (ISBN 0-671-49315-9, Little Simon). S&S Trade.
Motyka, Sally M. An Ordinary Day. Ayers, Donna, illus. (ps-1). 1989. pap. 13.95 (ISBN 0-671-67118-9). S&S Trade.
The Mouse. LC 88-16778. 16p. (Orig.). 1988. pap. 3.95 (ISBN 0-8092-4464-0, Calico Bks). Contemp Bks.
Mouse's Book of Months. (ps-1). 1987. 6.95 (ISBN 0-448-01465-3, G&D). Putnam Pub Group.
Move over Roger. 24p. (ps-k). 1988. 1.29 (ISBN 0-02-898130-8). Checkerboard Pr.
Mueller, Virginia. A Halloween Mask for Monster. Fay, Ann, ed. Munsinger, Lynn, illus. LC 86-1569. 24p. (ps-k). 1986. 10.95 (ISBN 0-8075-3134-0). A Whitman.
—A Halloween Mask for Monster. Munsinger, Lynn, illus. (ps-1). 1988. pap. 3.95 (ISBN 0-14-050879-1, Puffin). Puffin Bks.
—Monster & the Baby. Munsinger, Lynn, illus. (ps-1). 1988. pap. 3.95 (ISBN 0-14-050880-5, Puffin). Puffin Bks.
—Monster Can't Sleep. Fay, Ann, ed. Munsinger, Lynn, illus. LC 86-1568. 24p. (ps-k). 1986. PLB 10.95 (ISBN 0-8075-5261-5). A Whitman.
—Monster Goes to School. Levine, Abby, ed. Munsinger, Lynn, illus. 24p. (ps-1). 1991. 10.95 (ISBN 0-8075-5264-X). A Whitman.
—Monster's Birthday Hiccups. Levine, Abby, ed. Munsinger, Lynn, illus. 24p. (ps-1). 1991. 10.95 (ISBN 0-8075-5267-4). A Whitman.
Muldoon, Kathleen M. Princess Pooh. Mathews, Judith, ed. Shute, Linda, illus. 32p. (gr. 2-5). 1989. PLB 12.95 (ISBN 0-8075-6627-6). A Whitman.
Muldron, Diane. Walt Disney's Bambi: Count to Five. Langley, Bill & Wakeraw, Diana, illus. (ps-k). 1991. bds. write for info. (ISBN 0-307-06114-0, Golden Pr). Western Pub.
Munger, Carol V. Billy Groat. Decker, Tim, illus. LC 87-71679. 23p. (Orig.). 1990. pap. 4.00 (ISBN 0-916383-45-8). Aegina Pr.
Muntean, Michaela. Ernie's Window: A Neighborhood Story. (Illus.). 32p. (ps). 1990. pap. write for info. (ISBN 0-307-13112-2, Pub. by Golden Bks). Western Pub.
—We're Counting on You, Grover! Ewers, Joe, illus. (ps-k). 1991. write for info. (ISBN 0-307-12050-3, Golden Pr). Western Pub.
Murphy, Elspeth C. Barney Wigglesworth & the Birthday Surprise. Yakovetic, illus. LC 88-4346. 32p. (ps-2). 1988. 6.49 (ISBN 1-55513-696-6, Chariot Bks). Cook.
—Barney Wigglesworth & the Church Flood. Yakovetic, illus. LC 88-5008. 32p. (ps-2). 1988. 6.49 (ISBN 1-55513-685-0, Chariot Bks). Cook.
—Barney Wigglesworth & the Party That Almost Wasn't. Yakovetic, illus. LC 88-4342. 32p. (ps-2). 1988. 6.49 (ISBN 1-55513-684-2, Chariot Bks). Cook.
—Barney Wigglesworth & the Smallest Christmas Pageant. Yakovetic, illus. LC 88-5009. 32p. (ps-2). 1988. 6.49 (ISBN 1-55513-686-9, Chariot Bks). Cook.
—Kids Can Be Wise Too. LC 87-35539. 24p. (ps-2). 1988. pap. 3.49 (ISBN 1-55513-893-4, Chariot Bks). Cook.
—Sometimes I Get Scared. Nelson, Jane E., illus. (gr. k-2). 1980. pap. 2.95 (ISBN 0-89191-275-4, 52753). Cook.
—What Can I Say to You, God? Nelson, Jane E., illus. (gr. k-2). 1980. pap. 2.95 (ISBN 0-89191-276-2). Cook.
—Where Are You, God? Nelson, Jane E., illus. (gr. k-2). 1980. pap. 2.95 (ISBN 0-89191-274-6). Cook.
Murphy, Jill. Five Minutes' Peace. Murphy, Jill, illus. 32p. (ps-k). 1986. 9.95 (ISBN 0-399-21354-6, Putnam). Putnam Pub Group.
Murphy, Jim. The Last Dinosaur. Weatherby, Mark A., illus. LC 87-3008. 32p. (gr. 1-3). 1988. pap. 13.95 (ISBN 0-590-41097-0, Scholastic Hardcover). Scholastic Inc.
Murrow, Liza K. Good-Bye, Sammy. Owens, Gail, illus. LC 88-17011. 32p. (ps-3). 1989. reinforced bdg. 13.95 (ISBN 0-8234-0726-8). Holiday.
Musetti, Bernadette & Brennan, Pat. I Wrote This Book: My Picture & Storybook, Vols. 1-6. (Illus.). 300p. (ps-3). Date not set. Set. write for info. Lil Push Pub.
My Animal Friends on the Farm. 12p. (ps). 1986. 3.25 (ISBN 0-8378-5090-8). Gibson.
My Bible Friends. (Illus.). 1989. pap. 0.99 ea. David (ISBN 0-8024-3248-4). James (ISBN 0-8024-3247-6). Joseph (ISBN 0-8024-3249-2). Mary (ISBN 0-8024-3245-X). Noah (ISBN 0-8024-3244-1). Paul (ISBN 0-8024-3246-8). Set of 6 (ISBN 0-8024-3243-3). Moody.
My Big Book of Fairy Tales: A Treasury of Favorite Stories for Children. 1987. 8.98 (ISBN 0-671-08503-4). S&S Trade.
My Big Picture Book ABC. (ps-1). 1987. 1.75 (ISBN 0-448-46535-3, Platt & Munk). Putnam Pub Group.
My Biggest Playtime Book Ever. 1987. 8.98 (ISBN 0-671-07933-6). S&S Trade.
My Book of Favorite Fairy Tales. 1985. 5.98 (ISBN 0-671-06930-6). S&S Trade.
My Book of One Minute Stories & Verses. 1987. 3.98 (ISBN 0-671-08500-X). S&S Trade.
My Busy Day. (Illus.). 12p. (ps). 1989. 5.95 (ISBN 0-02-689194-8). Checkerboard Pr.
My Cricket Book of Mother Goose. (ps-1). 1987. 3.50 (ISBN 0-448-46536-1, Platt & Munk). Putnam Pub Group.
My Day. 16p. (ps-k). 1980. bds. 2.95 (ISBN 0-671-41344-9, Little). S&S Trade.
My Day. (Illus.). (ps). 3.50 (ISBN 0-7214-0784-6). Ladybird Bks.
My Favorite Friends. (Illus.). 24p. (gr. k-2). 1989. 6.95 (ISBN 0-87449-584-9). Modern Pub NYC.
My Favorite Games & Toys. (Illus.). 24p. (gr. k-2). 1989. 6.95 (ISBN 0-87449-585-7). Modern Pub NYC.
My Favorite Places. (Illus.). 24p. (gr. k-2). 1989. 6.95 (ISBN 0-87449-586-5). Modern Pub NYC.
My Favorite Things to Do. (Illus.). 24p. (gr. k-2). 1989. 6.95 (ISBN 0-87449-587-3). Modern Pub NYC.
My First ABC Book. 32p. (Orig.). (ps). wkbk. 4.95 (ISBN 0-8431-3101-2). Price Stern.
My First Book of Dinosaurs. 24p. (Orig.). (ps). 1988. pap. 3.95 (ISBN 0-8431-3143-8); Little Q Answer Wand 7.00 (ISBN 0-318-39955-5). Price Stern.
My First Book: Telling Time. 1991. 2.98 (ISBN 0-8317-3255-5). Smithmark.
My First Counting Book. 32p. (Orig.). (ps). wkbk. 4.95 (ISBN 0-8431-3104-7). Price Stern.
My First Numbers. 32p. (Orig.). (ps.). 1988. wkbk. 4.95 (ISBN 0-8431-3102-0). Price Stern.
My First Picture Dictionary. (ps-1). 1985. 5.98 (ISBN 0-517-44379-1). Outlet Bk Co.
My First Picture Word Book. (Illus.). (ps-1). 1985. 3.98 (ISBN 0-517-46373-3). Outlet Bk Co.
My First Reading Book. 32p. (Orig.). (ps-1). wkbk. 4.95 (ISBN 0-8431-3107-1). Price Stern.
My First Vocabulary. 32p. (Orig.). (ps). wkbk. 4.95 (ISBN 0-8431-3108-X). Price Stern.
My First Words. 32p. (Orig.). (ps). wkbk. 4.95 (ISBN 0-8431-3100-4). Price Stern.
My House. (Illus.). 12p. (gr. k-2). 1983. bds. 3.95 (ISBN 0-87449-177-0). Modern Pub NYC.
My Little Bible Picture Book. LC 88-4575. (Illus.). 80p. (ps). 1988. 5.95 (ISBN 1-55513-513-7, Chariot Bks). Cook.
My Little Duck Woodbook. 8p. (ps). 1986. bds. 15.95 (ISBN 0-8120-5694-9). Barron.
My Little Sheep Woodbook. 8p. (ps). 1986. bds. 13.95 (ISBN 0-8120-5695-7). Barron.
My Mini Rooster Woodbook. 8p. (ps). 1986. bds. 5.95 (ISBN 0-8120-5702-3). Barron.
My Plane Bath Book. (Illus.). (ps). 1989. vinyl 4.95 (ISBN 0-8167-1604-8). Troll Assocs.
My Rocket Bath Book. (Illus.). (ps). 1989. vinyl 4.95 (ISBN 0-8167-1606-4). Troll Assocs.
My Submarine Bath Book. (Illus.). (ps). 1989. 4.95 (ISBN 0-318-41873-8). Troll Assocs.
My Toys. (Illus.). 12p. (gr. k-2). 1983. bds. 3.95 (ISBN 0-87449-022-7). Modern Pub NYC.
My Train Bath Book. (ps). 1989. vinyl 4.95 (ISBN 0-8167-1605-6). Troll Assocs.
My Very First Words. 24p. (Orig.). (ps). 1988. pap. 3.95 (ISBN 0-8431-3136-5); Little Q Electronic Answer Wand 7.00 (ISBN 0-318-39950-4). Price Stern.
Myller, Rolf. How Big Is a Foot? (Illus.). 36p. (gr. 1-3). 1972. (Atheneum Child Bk); pap. 0.95 (ISBN 0-689-70306-6). Macmillan Child Grp.

Napoli, Donna J. The Hero of Barletta. Gustafson, Dana, illus. 48p. (gr. k-4). 1988. lib. bdg. 9.95 (ISBN 0-87614-277-3). Carolrhoda Bks.
Nash, Corey. I'm Growing Up! Things I Can Do by Myself. Wells, Chrissie, illus. (ps-k). 1990. 4.95 (ISBN 1-55782-028-7). Warner Bks.
Nash, Ogden. Custard the Dragon. Nash, Linell, illus. (gr. k-3). 1973. lib. bdg. 14.95 (ISBN 0-316-59841-0). Little.
La Navidad de Azulin. LC 87-15793. (SPA., Illus.). 32p. (gr. k-3). 1987. PLB 14.60 (ISBN 0-516-33483-2); pap. 3.95 (ISBN 0-516-53480-7). Childrens.
Naylor, Phyllis R. Keeping a Christmas Secret. Shiffman, Lena, illus. LC 88-29277. 32p. (ps-2). 1989. 13.95 (ISBN 0-689-31447-7, Atheneum Child Bk). Macmillan Child Grp.
Neasi, Barbara. Sweet Dreams. Martin, Clovis, illus. LC 87-15083. 32p. (ps-2). 1987. PLB 11.93 (ISBN 0-516-02084-6); pap. 2.95 (ISBN 0-516-42084-4). Childrens.
Nerlove, Miriam. Halloween. Levine, Abby, ed. Nerlove, Miriam, illus. 24p. (ps-1). 1989. PLB 10.95 (ISBN 0-8075-3131-6). A Whitman.
—Hanukkah. Levine, Abby, ed. Nerlove, Miriam, illus. 24p. (ps-1). 1989. PLB 10.95 (ISBN 0-8075-3143-X). A Whitman.
—I Made a Mistake. Nerlove, Miriam, illus. LC 85-6018. 32p. (ps-2). 1985. 12.95 (ISBN 0-689-50327-X, M K McElderry). Macmillan Child Grp.
Nesbit, Edith. The Deliverers of Their Country. Zwerger, Lisbeth, illus. LC 85-9389. 32p. (gr. 3-5). 1985. 15.95 (ISBN 0-88708-005-7). Picture Bk Studio.
Ness, Evaline. Sam, Bangs & Moonshine. Ness, Evaline, illus. LC 66-10113. 48p. (ps-2). 1966. 14.95 (ISBN 0-8050-0314-2); pap. 4.95 (ISBN 0-8050-0315-0). H Holt & Co.
Nessi, Barbara J. A Minute Is a Minute. Martin, Clovis, illus. 32p. (ps-3). 1988. PLB 13.93 (ISBN 0-516-03491-X); pap. 3.95 (ISBN 0-516-43491-8). Childrens.
Nevins, Kathy. Dot-to-Dot Dinos. (Illus.). 48p. (Orig.). (gr. k-3). 1989. pap. 2.95 (ISBN 0-8431-2338-9). Price Stern.
New Walt Disney Treasury. rev. ed. 96p. (ps-3). 1989. write for info. (ISBN 0-307-15546-3, Golden Bks). Western Pub.
Newberry, Clare T. April's Kittens. Newberry, Clare T., illus. LC 40-32442. (gr. k-3). 1940. PLB 10.89 (ISBN 0-06-024401-1). HarpC Child Bks.
Newell, Peter. The Hole Book. LC 84-52396. (Illus.). 50p. (gr. k-4). 1985. Repr. of 1902 ed. 12.95 (ISBN 0-8048-1498-8). C E Tuttle.
Newell, Peter S. Topsys & Turvys. LC 87-51208. (gr. k-4). 1988. 12.95 (ISBN 0-8048-1551-8). C E Tuttle.
—Topsys & Turvys, No. 2. LC 87-51208. (gr. k-4). 1988. 12.95 (ISBN 0-8048-1552-6). C E Tuttle.
Newman, Al. Fraid E. Cat. Doody, Jim, illus. LC 88-60439. 32p. (ps-1). 1989. book & toy set 4.95 (ISBN 0-394-81969-1). Random.
—Giggle E. Goose. Doody, Jim, illus. LC 88-60440. 32p. (ps-1). 1989. book & toy set 4.95 (ISBN 0-394-81971-3). Random.
—Grub E. Dog. Doody, Jim, illus. LC 88-60438. 32p. (ps-1). 1989. book & toy sets 4.95 (ISBN 0-394-81970-5). Random.
—Gruff E. Bear. Doody, Jim, illus. LC 88-60437. 32p. (ps-1). 1989. book & toy set 4.95 (ISBN 0-394-81972-1). Random.
Newton, Laura. Me & My Aunts. Fay, Ann, ed. Oz, Robin, illus. LC 86-15950. 32p. (ps-2). 1986. PLB 12.95 (ISBN 0-8075-5029-9). A Whitman.
Newton, Laura P. William the Vehicle King. Rogers, Jackie, illus. LC 86-33412. 32p. (ps-2). 1987. 12.95 (ISBN 0-02-768230-7, Bradbury Pr). Macmillan Child Grp.
Nichol, B. P. Once: A Lullaby. Lobel, Anita, illus. LC 85-9942. 24p. (ps-1). 1986. 11.95 (ISBN 0-688-04284-8); PLB 11.88 (ISBN 0-688-04285-6). Greenwillow.
Nic Leodhas, Sorche. Always Room for One More. Hogrogian, Nonny, illus. LC 65-12881. 32p. (gr. k-2). 1965. reinforced bdg. 13.95 (ISBN 0-8050-0331-2); pap. 4.95 (Owlet Bk.) (ISBN 0-8050-0330-4). H Holt & Co.
Nicoll, Helen & Pienkowski, Jan. Meg & Mog. (Illus.). (ps-2). 1976. pap. 3.50 (ISBN 0-14-050117-7, Puffin). Puffin Bks.
—Meg & Mog Birthday Book. 32p. (ps-k). 1984. pap. 3.50 (ISBN 0-14-050345-5, Puffin). Puffin Bks.
—Mog's Box. (Illus.). 32p. (ps-k). 1987. 15.95 (ISBN 0-434-95658-9, Pub. by W Heinemann Ltd). Trafalgar Sq.
Nikola-Lisa, W. One, Two, Three Thanksgiving! Levine, Abby, ed. Kramer, Robin, illus. 32p. (ps-1). 1991. 12.95 (ISBN 0-8075-6109-6). A Whitman.
Nims, Bonnie L. Where Is the Bear? Fay, Ann, ed. Wallner, John, illus. LC 87-25321. 24p. (ps-2). 1988. PLB 10.95 (ISBN 0-8075-8933-0). A Whitman.
Nister, Ernest. The Children's Picture Book. Nister, Ernest, illus. LC 80-7613. 18p. (ps-3). 1980. pop-up bk. 9.95 (ISBN 0-385-28173-0). Delacorte.
—Christmas Surprises: An Antique Revolving Picture Book. (Illus.). 20p. 1990. 16.95 (ISBN 0-399-22160-3, Philomel Bks). Putnam Pub Group.
—Good Friends. (Illus.). 1989. pap. 4.95 (ISBN 0-399-21729-0, Philomel Bks). Putnam Pub Group.
—The Great Panorama Picture Book. Nister, Ernest, illus. LC 82-70305. 18p. (ps-3). 1982. pop-up bk. 8.95 (ISBN 0-385-28327-X). Delacorte.
—Land of Sweet Surprises: An Antique Revolving Picture Books. Nister, Ernest, illus. (gr. k up). 1983. 10.95 (ISBN 0-399-20993-X, Philomel). Putnam Pub Group.
—Magic Windows: An Antique Revolving Picture Book. (Illus.). 14p. (ps up). 1981. 10.95 (ISBN 0-399-20773-2, Philomel). Putnam Pub Group.
—My Picture Puzzle Book: Reproductions of Antique Pictures. (Illus.). 10p. 1991. incl. 40 puzzle pieces 12.95 (ISBN 0-399-21855-6, Philomel Bks). Putnam Pub Group.
—Our Baby. (Illus.). 32p. 1991. 15.95 (ISBN 0-399-21856-4, Philomel Bks). Putnam Pub Group.
—Our Farmyard: A Pop-up Book with Punch-out Play Figures. Nister, Ernest, illus. 12p. (ps-3). 1991. 13.95 (ISBN 0-525-44689-3, DCB). Dutton Child Bks.
—Pop up Mother Goose Favorites. 1989. 12.95 (ISBN 0-525-44504-8, DCB). Dutton Child Bks.
—Surprising Pictures for Little Folk. (Illus.). (ps up). 1987. 10.95 (ISBN 0-399-21423-2, Philomel Bks). Putnam Pub Group.
—We Visit the Farm. Nister, Ernest, illus. (gr. k up). 1989. 13.95 (ISBN 0-399-21724-X, Philomel Bks). Putnam Pub Group.
—We Visit the Seashore: An Antique Book. (Illus.). 24p. (ps-5). 1990. 14.95 (ISBN 0-399-21956-0, Philomel Bks). Putnam Pub Group.
Nister, Ernest, illus. Moving Pictures: An Antique Picture Book. 12p. (ps up). 1985. 10.95 (ISBN 0-399-21272-8, Philomel). Putnam Pub Group.
Nixon, Joan L. Beats Me, Claude. Pearson, Tracey C., illus. (ps-3). 1988. pap. 3.95 (ISBN 0-14-050847-3, Puffin). Puffin Bks.
Nodset, Joan L. Go Away, Dog. Bonsall, Crosby, illus. LC 63-11162. (gr. k-3). 1963. PLB 11.89 (ISBN 0-06-024556-5). HarpC Child Bks.
—Who Took the Farmer's Hat? Siebel, Fritz, illus. LC 62-17964. 32p. (gr. k-3). 1963. PLB 12.89 (ISBN 0-06-024566-2). HarpC Child Bks.
—Who Took the Farmer's Hat? Siebel, Fritz, illus. LC 62-17964. 32p. (ps-2). 1988. pap. 3.95 (ISBN 0-06-443174-6, Trophy). HarpC Child Bks.
Noll, Sally. Jiggle Wiggle Prance. Noll, Sally, illus. LC 86-18322. 24p. (ps-1). 1987. 11.75 (ISBN 0-688-06760-3); PLB 11.88 (ISBN 0-688-06761-1). Greenwillow.
Nordtvedt, Matilda. Ladybugs Bees & Butterfly Trees. LC 84-24343. 160p. (Orig.). (ps). 1985. pap. 5.95 (ISBN 0-87123-820-9). Bethany Hse.
North, Carol, retold by. The Gingerbread Man. Nez, John, illus. LC 87-81770. 24p. (ps-k). 1988. pap. write for info. (ISBN 0-307-10096-0, Pub. by Golden Bks). Western Pub.
Norton, Mary. Borrowers. Krush, Beth & Krush, Joe, illus. LC 53-7870. (gr. 3 up). 1953. 13.95 (ISBN 0-15-209987-5, HJ). HarBraceJ.
—Borrowers Afield. Krush, Beth & Krush, Joe, illus. LC 55-11011. (gr. 3 up). 1955. 12.95 (ISBN 0-15-210166-7, HJ). HarBraceJ.
—Borrowers Aloft. Krush, Beth & Krush, Joe, illus. LC 61-11751. (gr. 3 up). 1961. 12.95 (ISBN 0-15-210524-7, HJ). HarBraceJ.
Nothing-to-Do Puppy. (ps-k). Date not set. write for info. (ISBN 0-307-12237-9, Golden Pr). Western Pub.
Now I'm Sleepy: A Cozy Cloth Book. (Illus.). 6p. (ps). 1987. pap. 2.95 (ISBN 0-553-18331-1). Bantam.
Numbers. (Illus.). 12p. (gr. k-2). 1982. bds. 3.95 (ISBN 0-87449-021-9). Modern Pub NYC.
Numbers: Kiddy Big Book. (ps up). 1990. PLB 4.98 (ISBN 0-7924-5195-3, Mallard Pr). BDD Promo Bk.
Numbers Up! 24p. (gr. k-2). 1990. 3.95 (ISBN 0-87449-669-1). Modern Pub NYC.
Nunes, Susan. Tiddalick the Frog. Chen, Ju-Hong, illus. 32p. (gr. k-3). 1989. 13.95 (ISBN 0-689-31502-3, Atheneum Child Bk). Macmillan Child Grp.
Nygren, Tord. The Red Thread. (Illus.). 32p. (ps up). 1988. 12.95 (ISBN 9-12-959005-1, R & S Bks). FS&G.
Oakley, Graham. Graham Oakley's Magical Changes. Oakley, Graham, illus. LC 79-2784. 32p. (gr. 1 up). 1987. 5.95 (ISBN 0-689-71179-4, Aladdin). Macmillan Child Grp.
Oakley, John. Would You Be Scared? (Illus.). 32p. (ps-1). 1987. 10.95 (ISBN 0-233-97922-0). Andre Deutsch.
Obligado, Lilian. Guess the Animal! 1990. pap. write for info. (ISBN 0-307-12165-8, Golden Pr). Western Pub.
O'Brien, Anne S. I'm Not Tired. LC 85-5645. (Illus.). 14p. (gr. k). 1985. 3.95 (ISBN 0-03-005009-X, O'Brien Board Bks.). H Holt & Co.
O'Brien, John & Cusack, Margaret, illus. The Calico Mother Goose. LC 88-22196. 80p. 1988. 14.95 (ISBN 0-8092-4491-8, Calico Bks). Contemp Bks.
O'Brien, Theresa. Little Fish in a Big Pond. (ps-3). 1990. pap. 3.95 (ISBN 0-85953-391-3). Childs Play.
O'Connor, Jane. The Care Bears' Party Cookbook. Sustendal, Pat, illus. LC 84-18252. 48p. (gr. k-3). 1985. lib. bdg. 6.99 (ISBN 0-394-97305-4, Random Juv); pap. 2.95 (ISBN 0-394-87305-X). Random.
Octopus's Walker. 12p. (ps-1). 1989. bds. 3.95 (ISBN 0-87449-636-5). Modern Pub NYC.
Oda, Stephanie C. My Nighttime Book. 12p. (ps). 1986. 3.25 (ISBN 0-8378-5091-6). Gibson.
—One-Two-Three God Is Good to Me. 12p. (ps). 1986. 2.95 (ISBN 0-8378-5092-4). Gibson.
Oechsle, Robert. Ducky, Ucky & Mucky. (Illus.). 40p. (ps). 1985. pap. 7.95 (ISBN 0-9603376-0-1). Flourtown Pub.
Ogle, Lucille & Thoburn, Tina. The Golden Picture Dictionary. Knight, Hilary, illus. (ps-3). 1989. write for info. (ISBN 0-307-17861-7, Pub. by Golden Bks). Western Pub.
O'Halloran, Tim. Words Around Us. O'Halloran, Tim, illus. 48p. (ps-k). 1985. 10.95 (ISBN 0-88625-124-9). Durkin Hayes Pub.
Oivardi, Anne & Philpot, Graham. My First Picture Dictionary. (Illus.). 64p. (gr. 1-3). 1989. incl. dust jacket 7.95 (ISBN 0-8120-5961-1). Barron.
Oliver, Stephen, photos by. Home. LC 89-63092. (Illus.). 24p. (ps-k). 1990. Repr. of 1990 ed. 6.95 (ISBN 0-679-80622-9). Random.
—Seasons. LC 89-63094. (Illus.). 24p. (ps-k). 1990. Repr. of 1990 ed. 6.95 (ISBN 0-679-80621-0). Random.
—Touch. LC 89-63095. (Illus.). (ps-k). 1990. Repr. of 1990 ed. 6.95 (ISBN 0-679-80623-7). Random.
Olson, Arielle N. The Lighthouse Keeper's Daughter. Wentworth, Elaine, illus. 32p. (ps-3). 1987. 14.95 (ISBN 0-316-65057-9). Little.
On the Beach. (Illus.). (ps-5). 3.50 (ISBN 0-7214-8001-2); wkbk. A 1.95. Ladybird Bks.
On the Farm. (Illus.). (ps). 3.50 (ISBN 0-7214-0786-2). Ladybird Bks.
On the Move. (Illus.). (ps). 3.50 (ISBN 0-7214-0752-8). Ladybird Bks.
One Green Frog. (Illus.). 24p. (ps-k). 1989. 7.95 (ISBN 0-448-21031-2, G&D). Putnam Pub Group.
One-Two-Three. 1984. 3.95 (ISBN 0-671-49314-0, Little Simon). S&S Trade.
One-Two-Three. (Illus.). (ps-k). bds. 3.50 (ISBN 0-7214-9583-4). Ladybird Bks.
One Two Three Board Book. (ps). 1958. bds. 3.95 (ISBN 0-448-03076-4, G&D). Putnam Pub Group.
One, Two, Three Board Shape Book. (Illus.). (ps). 1985. bds. 1.69 (ISBN 0-517-46320-2). Outlet Bk Co.
O'Neal, Zibby. Maude & Walter. Chambliss, Maxie, illus. LC 84-48357. 32p. (ps-2). 1985. 11.95 (ISBN 0-397-32150-3, Lipp Jr Bks). HarpC Child Bks.
O'Neill, Catharine. Mrs. Dunphy's Dog. (Illus.). 32p. (ps-3). 1989. pap. 3.95 (ISBN 0-14-050622-5, Puffin). Puffin Bks.
O'Neill, Catherine. Mrs. Dunphy's Dog. (ps-3). 1987. pap. 12.95 (ISBN 0-670-81135-1). Viking Child Bks.
Oppenheim, Joanne. Have You Seen Birds? Reid, Barbara, illus. (ps-2). 1988. Big book. 19.50 (ISBN 0-590-71576-3); pap. 2.95 (ISBN 0-590-40890-9). Scholastic Inc.
—Wake Up, Baby-Bank Street. (ps-3). 1990. PLB 9.99 (Little Rooster); pap. 3.50. Bantam.
Oppenheim, Joanne F. You Can't Catch Me! Shachat, Andrew, illus. LC 86-7211. 32p. (gr. k). 1986. 12.95 (ISBN 0-395-41452-0). HM.
Opposites. (Illus.). (ps-k). bds. 3.50 (ISBN 0-7214-9601-6). Ladybird Bks.
Opposites. (Illus.). (ps-2). 1.95 (ISBN 0-7214-5185-3). Ladybird Bks.
Oram, Hiawyn & Ross, Tony. Anyone Seen Harry Lately? (Illus.). 32p. (gr. 1-4). 1989. 13.95 (ISBN 0-86264-198-5, Pub. by Anderson Pr UK). Trafalgar Sq.
Ormerod, Jan. Kitten Day. Ormerod, Jan, illus. LC 88-26687. 22p. (ps-1). 1989. 13.95 (ISBN 0-688-08536-9); PLB 13.88 (ISBN 0-688-08537-7). Lothrop.
—Moonlight. (Illus.). 32p. (ps-k). 1984. pap. 3.50 (ISBN 0-14-050372-2, Puffin). Puffin Bks.
—One Hundred One Things to Do with a Baby. Ormerod, Jan, illus. 32p. (ps-3). 1986. pap. 3.50 (ISBN 0-14-050447-8, Puffin). Puffin Bks.
—Sunshine. (Illus.). 32p. (ps-k). 1984. pap. 3.50 (ISBN 0-14-050362-5, Puffin). Puffin Bks.
Ormondroyd, Edward. Broderick. Larrecq, John M., illus. LC 77-83752. (gr. k-3). 1969. (Pub. by Parnassus); PLB 4.77 (ISBN 0-686-86580-4). HM.
—Theodore's Rival. Larrecq, John M., illus. LC 76-156876. 40p. (ps-3). 1971. (Pub. by Parnassus); PLB 4.59 (ISBN 0-87466-001-7). HM.
Ostheeven, Ingrid. Jonathan Mouse at the Circus. Lanning, Rosemary, tr. Mathieu, Agnes, illus. LC 87-42980. 32p. (gr. k-3). 1988. 12.95 (ISBN 1-55858-055-7). North-South Bks NYC.
Otter Swims. LC 83-22004. (Illus.). 20p. (ps-1). 4.95; PLB 6.99. Sierra.
Our Motor Car. 8p. (ps-2). 1977. 2.00 (ISBN 0-85953-069-8, Pub. by Child's Play England). Childs Play.
Outdoor Things. (Illus.). (ps-k). 3.95 (ISBN 0-7214-5142-X). Ladybird Bks.
Oxenbury, Helen. All Fall Down. Oxenbury, Helen, illus. 10p. (ps-k). 1987. bds. 4.95 (ISBN 0-02-769040-7, Aladdin). Macmillan Child Grp.
—Baby's First Book & Doll. (Illus.). 1986. bds. 9.95 (ISBN 0-671-93991-2, Little Simon). S&S Trade.
—Clap Hands. Oxenbury, Helen, illus. 10p. (ps). 1987. bds. 4.95 (ISBN 0-02-769030-X, Aladdin). Macmillan Child Grp.
—Good Night, Good Morning. LC 81-69272. 14p. (ps-k). 1982. bds. 3.50 (ISBN 0-8037-2980-4). Dial Bks Young.
—I Hear. Oxenbury, Helen, illus. LC 85-61367. 14p. (ps). 1986. 3.95 (ISBN 0-394-87481-1). Random.
—I See. Oxenbury, Helen, illus. LC 85-61365. 14p. (ps). 1986. Repr. of 1986 ed. bds. 3.95 (ISBN 0-394-87479-X). Random.
—Pippo Gets Lost. Oxenbury, Helen, illus. 14p. (ps-k). 1989. bds. 5.95 (ISBN 0-689-71336-3, Aladdin). Macmillan Child Grp.
—Say Goodnight. Oxenbury, Helen, illus. 10p. (ps). 1987. bds. 4.95 (ISBN 0-02-769010-5, Aladdin). Macmillan Child Grp.

—Tickle, Tickle. Oxenbury, Helen, illus. 10p. (ps). 1987. bds. 4.95 (ISBN 0-02-769020-2, Aladdin). Macmillan Child Grp.
—Tom & Pippo & the Dog. Oxenbury, Helen, illus. 14p. (ps-k). 1989. Repr. bds. 5.95 (ISBN 0-689-71338-X, Aladdin). Macmillan Child Grp.
—Tom & Pippo Go Shopping. Oxenbury, Helen, illus. 14p. (ps-1). 1989. pap. 5.95 (ISBN 0-689-71278-2, Aladdin). Macmillan Child Grp.
—Tom & Pippo in the Garden. Oxenbury, Helen, illus. 14p. (ps-1). 1989. pap. 5.95 (ISBN 0-689-71275-8, Aladdin). Macmillan Child Grp.
—Tom & Pippo in the Snow. Oxenbury, Helen, illus. 14p. (ps-k). 1989. Repr. bds. 5.95 (ISBN 0-689-71337-1, Aladdin). Macmillan Child Grp.
—Tom & Pippo Make a Friend. Oxenbury, Helen, illus. 14p. (ps-k). 1989. Repr. bds. 5.95 (ISBN 0-689-71339-8, Aladdin). Macmillan Child Grp.
—Tom & Pippo See the Moon. Oxenbury, Helen, illus. 14p. (ps-1). 1989. pap. 5.95 (ISBN 0-689-71277-4, Aladdin). Macmillan Child Grp.
—Tom & Pippo's Day. Oxenbury, Helen, illus. 14p. (ps-1). 1989. pap. 5.95 (ISBN 0-689-71276-6, Aladdin). Macmillan Child Grp.
—Working. Oxenbury, Helen, illus. 7p. (ps). 1990. bds. 3.50 (ISBN 0-671-42112-3, Little Simon). S&S Trade.
Oxford Scientific Films Staff. Matchmaking. (Illus.). 32p. (gr. k up). 1987. 12.95 (ISBN 0-399-21451-8, Putnam). Putnam Pub Group.
Pace, Betty. Chris Gets Ear Tubes. Hutton, Katherine, illus. LC 87-26759. 48p. (ps-2). 1987. 4.95 (ISBN 0-930323-36-X, Kendall Green Pubns). Gallaudet Univ Pr.
Packard, Mary. Disney's Two-Minute Good Night Stories. Langley, Bill, et al, illus. LC 87-83200. 36p. (ps-1). 1988. write for info. (ISBN 0-307-12181-X). Western Pub.
—Two-Minute Bedtime Stories. Wilburn, Kathy, illus. LC 87-83202. 36p. (ps-1). 1988. write for info. (ISBN 0-307-12183-6). Western Pub.
Packard, Mary, adapted by. Disney's Two-Minute Classics. LC 87-83199. (Illus.). 36p. (ps-1). 1988. write for info. (ISBN 0-307-12180-1). Western Pub.
Paige, Rae. Sesame Street: The Whole Wide World. 1990. pap. write for info. (ISBN 0-307-15826-8, Pub. by Golden Bks). Western Pub.
Palazzo, Tony. The Biggest & the Littlest Animals. Palazzo, Tony, illus. LC 77-112374. 40p. (gr. k-3). 1973. PLB 11.95 (ISBN 0-87460-225-4). Lion Bks.
Palmer, Bernard & Palmer, Marjorie. Who Helps. Webb, Gary A., illus. 32p. (Orig.). (ps-k). 1982. pap. 3.95 (ISBN 0-934998-08-6). Bethel Pub.
Palmer, Mary R. Clean As a Whistle. LC 90-70148. 48p. (gr. 1-4). 1990. pap. 7.95 (ISBN 0-932433-66-9). Windswept Hse.
Palmisciano, Diane. Garden Partners. Palmisciano, Diane, illus. LC 88-16741. 32p. (gr. k-3). 1989. 12.95 (ISBN 0-689-31415-9, Atheneum Child Bk). Macmillan Child Grp.
Panda Climbs. LC 83-17462. (Illus.). 20p. (ps-1). 4.95 (ISBN 0-685-11108-3); PLB 6.99 (ISBN 0-685-11109-1). Sierra.
Pape, D. L. Liz Dearly's Silly Glasses. LC 68-56824. (Illus.). 48p. (gr. 2-5). 1968. PLB 10.95 (ISBN 0-87783-023-1). Oddo.
—Professor Fred & the Fid Fuddlephone. LC 68-56825. (Illus.). 48p. (gr. 2-5). 1968. PLB 10.95 (ISBN 0-87783-032-0). Oddo.
—Scientist Sam. LC 68-56826. (Illus.). 48p. (gr. 2-5). 1968. PLB 10.95 (ISBN 0-87783-034-7). Oddo.
—Shoemaker Fooze. Frank, Lola E., illus. LC 68-56827. 48p. (gr. 2-5). 1969. PLB 10.95 (ISBN 0-87783-036-3). Oddo.
—Three Thinkers of Thay-Lee. LC 68-56828. (Illus.). 48p. (gr. 2-5). 1968. PLB 10.95 (ISBN 0-87783-040-1). Oddo.
Parachute Press Staff. The Twelve Days of Christmas. 24p. 1988. pap. 2.50 (ISBN 0-553-15638-1, Bantam Aud Pub). Bantam.
Paris, Pat, illus. Bear Cubs. 10p. (ps). 1989. 4.95 (ISBN 0-8120-5987-5). Barron.
—Bunnies. 10p. (ps). 1989. 4.95 (ISBN 0-8120-5990-5). Barron.
—Kittens. 10p. (ps). 1989. 4.95 (ISBN 0-8120-5989-1). Barron.
—Puppies. 10p. (ps). 1989. 4.95 (ISBN 0-8120-5988-3). Barron.
Parish, Peggy. Amelia Bedelia. Siebel, Fritz, illus. LC 63-14367. 32p. (gr. k-3). 1983. pap. 3.50 (ISBN 0-06-443036-7, Trophy). HarpC Child Bks.
—Amelia Bedelia & the Surprise Shower. Siebel, Fritz, illus. LC 66-18655. 64p. (gr. k-3). 1966. 11.95 (ISBN 0-06-024642-1); PLB 11.89 (ISBN 0-06-024643-X). HarpC Child Bks.
—Amelia Bedelia & the Surprise Shower. Siebel, Fritz, illus. LC 66-18655. 64p. (gr. k-3). 1986. pap. 5.98 incl. cassette (ISBN 0-694-00161-9, Trophy). HarpC Child Bks.
—Come Back, Amelia Bedelia. Tripp, Wallace, illus. LC 73-121799. 64p. (gr. k-3). 1986. incl. cassette 5.98 (ISBN 0-694-00112-0, Trophy); pap. 3.50 (ISBN 0-06-444016-8, Trophy). HarpC Child Bks.
—Ootah's Lucky Day. Funai, Mamoru, illus. LC 70-105467. 64p. (gr. k-3). 1970. PLB 11.89 (ISBN 0-06-024645-6). HarpC Child Bks.
—Play Ball, Amelia Bedelia. Tripp, Wallace, illus. 64p. (gr. k-3). pap. 1.95 (ISBN 0-590-06203-4). Scholastic Inc.
—Scruffy. Oechsli, Kelly, illus. LC 87-45564. 64p. (gr. k-3). 1988. 11.95 (ISBN 0-06-024659-6); PLB 11.89 (ISBN 0-06-024660-X). HarpC Child Bks.
—Scruffy. Oechsli, Kelly, illus. LC 87-45564. 64p. (gr. k-3). 1990. pap. 3.50 (ISBN 0-06-444137-7, Trophy). HarpC Child Bks.
—Willy Is My Brother. Rogers, Jacqueline, illus. (ps up). 1989. 12.95 (ISBN 0-385-29723-8). Delacorte.
Park, Ruth. Playing Beatie Bow. 200p. (gr. 5-9). 1984. pap. 3.95 (ISBN 0-14-031460-1, Puffin). Puffin Bks.
Parke, Sara. No Fair Peeking. LC 90-85436. (Illus.). 32p. (gr. k-3). 1991. 5.95 (ISBN 1-56282-037-0, Disney Pr). W Disney Pub.
Parker, Joy. Henry: The Story of a Mole. (Illus.). 48p. (gr. 1-4). 1989. 13.95 (ISBN 0-09-173447-9, Pub. by Hutchinson UK). Trafalgar Sq.
Parker, Robert A. An Autumn Tale. Parker, Robert A., illus. 40p. (gr. 2 up). 1988. 14.95 (ISBN 0-945912-02-1). Pippin Pr.
—A Spring Story. Parker, Robert A., illus. 40p. (gr. 2 up). 1989. PLB 14.95 (ISBN 0-945912-06-4). Pippin Pr.
Parkhurst, Carole. Visiting Tacoma. Hamer, Bonnie, illus. 24p. (Orig.). (gr. 1-4). 1983. pap. 2.75 (ISBN 0-933992-38-6). Coffee Break.
Parkinson, Kathy, illus. The Enormous Turnip. 32p. (gr. k-3). 1986. 12.95 (ISBN 0-8075-2062-4). A Whitman.
Parkinson, Kathy & Parkinson, Kathy, illus. The Farmer in the Dell. 32p. (ps-2). 1988. PLB 12.95 (ISBN 0-8075-2271-6). A Whitman.
Parnall, Peter. Cats from Away. Parnall, Peter, illus. LC 88-30532. 32p. (gr. 1 up). 1989. 13.95 (ISBN 0-02-770150-6, Mcmillan Child Bk). Macmillan Child Grp.
Partin, Charlotte C. Daydreams & Sunbeams: An Album of Framable Word Pictures. Partin, Robin C., illus. 18p. (Orig.). (gr. 7 up). 1987. pap. 4.00 (ISBN 0-9619816-0-1). C C Partin.
The Party Animals Colorful Picnic. 24p. (gr. k-2). 1989. 4.95 (ISBN 0-87449-692-6). Modern Pub NYC.
The Party Animals Come Celebrate. 24p. (gr. k-2). 1989. 4.95 (ISBN 0-87449-690-X). Modern Pub NYC.
The Party Animals Countdown to Fun. 24p. (gr. k-2). 1989. 4.95 (ISBN 0-87449-691-8). Modern Pub NYC.
The Party Animals Fun Shapes. 24p. (gr. k-2). 1989. 4.95 (ISBN 0-87449-693-4). Modern Pub NYC.
Pashuk, Lauren. Fun with Colors. Pashuk, Lauren, illus. 32p. (ps-k). 1985. pap. 2.50 (ISBN 0-88625-106-0). Durkin Hayes Pub.
Paterson, Cynthia & Paterson, Brian. The Foxwood Smugglers. (Illus.). 32p. (ps-3). 1989. incl. dust jacket 6.95 (ISBN 0-8120-5984-0). Barron.
Patrick, Denice. Look Inside a House. (Illus.). 16p. (ps-1). 1989. 9.95 (ISBN 0-448-19351-5, G&D). Putnam Pub Group.
—Look Inside a Ship. (Illus.). 16p. (ps-1). 1989. 9.95 (ISBN 0-448-19352-3, G&D). Putnam Pub Group.
—Look Inside Your Body. (Illus.). 16p. (ps-1). 1989. bds. 9.95 (ISBN 0-448-21033-9, G&D). Putnam Pub Group.
Patrick, Denice & Ingoglia, Gina. Look Inside a Tree. Gomboli, Mary, illus. LC 88-82991. 16p. (ps-1). 1989. bds. 9.95 (ISBN 0-685-29301-7, G&D). Putnam Pub Group.
Patrick, Gloria. This Is. Hanson, Joan, illus. LC 70-84092. 96p. (ps-3). 1970. PLB 4.95 (ISBN 0-87614-003-7). Carolrhoda Bks.
Patterson, Francine. Koko's Story. Cohn, Ronald H., photos by. (Illus.). 40p. 1988. pap. 4.95 (ISBN 0-590-41364-3). Scholastic Inc.
Patterson, Geoffrey. The Goose That Laid the Golden Egg: Re-Told from Aesop. Patterson, Geoffrey, illus. 32p. (ps-2). 1986. 10.95 (ISBN 0-233-97878-X). Andre Deutsch.
—Working Horse. Patterson, Geoffrey, illus. 32p. (gr. 2-5). 1986. 10.95 (ISBN 0-233-97786-4). Andre Deutsch.
Patty Cake. 12p. (ps-1). 1989. bds. 5.95 (ISBN 0-87449-713-2). Modern Pub NYC.
Patz, Nancy. No Thumpin' No Bumpin' No Rumpus Tonight! Patz, Nancy, illus. LC 88-7717. 32p. (gr. k-3). 1990. 13.95 (ISBN 0-689-31510-4, Atheneum Child Bk). Macmillan Child Grp.
—Sarah Bear & Sweet Sidney. Patz, Nancy, illus. LC 88-21300. 32p. (ps-2). 1989. 13.95 (ISBN 0-02-770270-7, Four Winds). Macmillan Child Grp.
Paulsen, Gary. Hatchet. (gr. 5-9). 1988. pap. 3.95 (ISBN 0-14-032724-X, Puffin). Puffin Bks.
—Hatchet Rack Trim. (gr. 4-7). 1989. pap. 3.95 (ISBN 0-14-034371-7, Puffin). Puffin Bks.
Payne, Emmy. Katy No-Pocket. (gr. 1-3). 1973. reinforced bdg. 13.95 (ISBN 0-395-17104-0). HM.
A Pea Pod Christmas. (ps-5). 1988. incl. 3 dolls 19.95 (ISBN 0-698-12012-4, Playland Bks). Putnam Pub Group.
Pea Pod Doll House. 1988. 19.95 (ISBN 0-698-12002-7, Playland Bks). Putnam Pub Group.
Pea Pod Pop-Ups. (Illus.). (ps up). 1988. 19.95 (ISBN 0-698-12000-0, Playland Bks); 3 dolls incl. Putnam Pub Group.
Pea Pod Tree Fort. 1988. 19.95 (ISBN 0-698-12003-5, Playland Bks). Putnam Pub Group.
Pearce, Colin. The Monkey & the Crocodile. (Illus.). (ps-2). 1990. 12.95 (ISBN 0-8423-4537-X). Tyndale.
Pearl, Lizzy. What Have I Lost? Langley, Jonathan, illus. LC 87-9087. 10p. (ps-k). 1988. 4.95 (ISBN 0-8037-0482-8). Dial Bks Young.
—What Time Is It? Langley, Jonathan, illus. LC 87-9093. 10p. (ps-k). 1988. 4.95 (ISBN 0-8037-0480-1). Dial Bks Young.
Pearse, Patricia. See How You Grow. Riddell, Edwina, illus. LC 87-33268. 32p. (gr. 1-4). 1988. 11.95 (ISBN 0-8120-5936-0). Barron.
Pearson, Kit. The Sky Is Falling. 256p. (gr. 3-7). 1990. pap. 12.95 (ISBN 0-670-82849-1). Viking Child Bks.
Pearson, Susan. The Baby & the Bear. Carlson, Nancy, illus. (ps-k). 1987. pap. 3.95 (ISBN 0-670-81299-4). Viking Child Bks.
—The Day Porkchop Climbed the Christmas Tree. Brown, Rick, illus. (gr. k-3). 9.95 (ISBN 0-317-62031-2). P-H.
—My Favorite Time of Year. Wallner, John, illus. LC 87-45296. 32p. (ps-3). 1988. 12.95 (ISBN 0-06-024681-2); PLB 12.89 (ISBN 0-06-024682-0). HarpC Child Bks.
—When the Baby Went to Bed. Carlson, Nancy, illus. (ps-k). 1987. pap. 3.95 (ISBN 0-670-81300-1). Viking Child Bks.
Pearson, Tracey C. Sing a Song of Sixpence. Pearson, Tracey C., illus. LC 84-14206. 32p. (ps-2). 1988. 10.95 (ISBN 0-8037-0151-9, 0383-120); PLB 10.89 (ISBN 0-8037-0152-7, 0383-120); pap. 3.95 (ISBN 0-8037-0492-5, 0383-120). Dial Bks Young.
Peaslee, Ann & De Witt, Sorena. Guess What Day It Is? Clayson, David N., illus. 210p. (gr. 3-6). 1988. pap. 14.50 (ISBN 0-89346-305-1). Heian Intl.
Peckham, Pamela. Stories of Tommy's Toy Animal Collection. 1988. 6.95 (ISBN 0-533-07906-3). Vantage.
Peeples, H. I. The Itty-Bitty Kiddies Wake Up. Montgomery, Michael, illus. 24p. 1990. 7.95 (ISBN 0-8092-4345-8, Calico Bks). Contemp Bks.
Peet, Bill. Big Bad Bruce. (gr. 3 up). 1987. Incl. cass. pap. 7.95 (ISBN 0-395-45741-6). HM.
—Chester the Worldly Pig. (Illus.). 48p. (gr. k-3). 1980. 13.95 (ISBN 0-395-18470-3). HM.
—Eli. Peet, Bill, illus. LC 77-17500. 48p. (gr. k-3). 1984. pap. 3.95 (ISBN 0-395-36611-9). HM.
—Farewell to Shady Glade. (Illus.). 48p. (gr. k-3). 1966. 13.95 (ISBN 0-395-18975-6); pap. 4.95 (ISBN 0-395-31128-4). HM.
—Hubert's Hair-Raising Adventure. (Illus.). 36p. (gr. k-3). 1959. 13.95 (ISBN 0-395-15083-3). HM.
—Kermit the Hermit. (Illus.). (gr. k-3). 1980. 13.95 (ISBN 0-395-15084-1); pap. 4.95 (ISBN 0-395-29607-2). HM.
—The Kweeks of Kookatumdee. Peet, Bill, illus. 32p. (gr. k-3). 1988. pap. 4.95 (ISBN 0-395-48656-4, Sandpiper). HM.
—Smokey. (Illus.). (gr. k-3). 1962. 12.95 (ISBN 0-395-15992-X). HM.
—Zella, Zack, & Zodiac. (Illus.). 32p. (gr. k-3). 1989. pap. 4.95 (ISBN 0-395-52207-2). HM.
Peifer, Jane & Nolt, Marilyn. Good Thoughts about Me. (Illus.). 24p. (Orig.). (ps-2). 1985. pap. 2.95 (ISBN 0-8361-3389-7). Herald Pr.
—Good Thoughts at Bedtime. (Illus.). 24p. (Orig.). (ps-2). 1985. pap. 2.95 (ISBN 0-8361-3388-9). Herald Pr.
Pellegrino, Virginia. Listen to the City. (Illus.). 16p. (ps). 1988. 3.95 (ISBN 0-8431-2311-7); bk. & cassette 6.95 (ISBN 0-8431-2315-X). Price Stern.
—Listen to the Country. (Illus.). 16p. (ps). 1988. 3.95 (ISBN 0-8431-2310-9); bk. & cassette 6.95 (ISBN 0-8431-2314-1). Price Stern.
Pellowski, Michael J. Little Lost Unicorn. (Illus.). 24p. (ps-3). 1989. pap. 1.95 (ISBN 0-317-93832-0). Willowisp Pr.
—The Puppy Nobody Wanted. (Illus.). 24p. (ps-3). 1988. pap. 0.99 (ISBN 0-317-93827-4). Willowisp Pr.
Peppe, Rodney. Circus Numbers. Peppe, Rodney, illus. LC 75-86381. (ps-3). 1969. 5.95 (ISBN 0-440-01288-0); pap. 3.69 (ISBN 0-440-01289-9). Delacorte.
—Circus Numbers: A Counting Book. (Illus.). 32p. (ps-2). 1985. 11.95 (ISBN 0-385-29424-7). Delacorte.
—Little Dolls. LC 83-40274. (Illus.). 14p. (gr. k-1). 1984. pap. 2.95 (ISBN 0-670-43182-6). Viking Child Bks.
—Little Numbers. LC 83-40275. (Illus.). 14p. (gr. k-1). 1984. pap. 2.95 (ISBN 0-670-43248-2). Viking Child Bks.
—Thumbprint Circus. Peppe, Rodney, illus. (ps-1). 1989. 12.95 (ISBN 0-440-50154-7). Delacorte.
Perez, Carla & Robison, Deborah. Your Turn, Doctor. Robison, Deborah, illus. LC 81-68778. 32p. (ps-2). 1984. pap. 3.95 (ISBN 0-8037-0061-X). Dial Bks Young.
Perkins, Al. Nose Book. McKie, Roy, illus. LC 71-117540. (ps-1). 1970. 6.95 (ISBN 0-394-80623-9, Random Juv); lib. bdg. 7.99 (ISBN 0-394-90623-3). Random.
Perkins, Myrna. What Does A Spider Do? Perkins, William C. & Perkins, Lori L., illus. 20p. (Orig.). (ps-3). 1985. pap. 3.95 (ISBN 0-937729-00-0). Markins Enter.
—What Is This? Perkins, William C. & Perkins, Lori L., illus. 36p. (Orig.). (ps-3). 1986. pap. 4.95 (ISBN 0-937729-01-9). Markins Enter.
—What Makes Honey? Perkins, William C. & Perkins, Lori L., illus. 32p. (Orig.). (ps-3). pap. 3.95 (ISBN 0-937729-03-5). Markins Enter.
Perrault, Charles. The Pancake That Ran Away & Toads & Diamonds. (Illus.). 48p. (ps-3). 1985. 5.95 (ISBN 0-88110-254-7). EDC.
Perrine, Mary. Nannabah's Friend. Weisgard, Leonard, illus. 32p. (gr. k-3). 1989. pap. 4.95 (ISBN 0-395-52020-7). HM.
Perugini, Donna. Don't Hug a Grudge. (Orig.). (gr. k-3). 1987. 3.98 (ISBN 0-89274-433-2). Harrison Hse.

Pesiri, Evelyn. Learn to Hear. Pesiri, Evelyn, illus. 64p. (gr. k-3). 1986. wkbk. 6.95 (ISBN 0-86653-337-0, GA 675). Good Apple.
—Learn to Think. Pesiri, Evelyn, illus. 64p. (gr. k-3). 1986. wkbk. 6.95 (ISBN 0-86653-343-5, GA 676). Good Apple.
Pesiri, Evelyn, ed. & illus. Learn to Write. 64p. (gr. k-3). 1986. wkbk. 6.95 (ISBN 0-86653-342-7, GA 791). Good Apple.
Peters, Lisa W. The Sun, the Wind & the Rain. Rand, Ted, illus. LC 87-23808. 32p. (ps-2). 1988. 13.95 (ISBN 0-8050-0699-0). H Holt & Co.
Peters, Sharon. Pussycat Kite. Hall, Susan T., illus. LC 84-8632. 32p. (gr. k-2). 1985. PLB 10.89 (ISBN 0-8167-0358-2); pap. text ed. 2.95 (ISBN 0-8167-0438-4). Troll Assocs.
Petersham, Maud & Petersham, Miska. The Box with Red Wheels. reissued ed. Petersham, Maud & Petersham, Miska, illus. LC 49-11325. 32p. (ps-1). 1986. 12.95 (ISBN 0-02-771350-4, Mcmillan Child Bk). Macmillan Child Grp.
—Circus Baby. Petersham, Maud & Petersham, Miska, illus. LC 50-9295. 32p. (ps-1). 1968. 13.95 (ISBN 0-02-771670-8, Mcmillan Child Bk). Macmillan Child Grp.
—The Circus Baby. Petersham, Maud & Petersham, Miska, illus. LC 88-7369. 32p. (ps-1). 1989. pap. 3.95 (ISBN 0-689-71295-2, Aladdin). Macmillan Child Grp.
Peterson, Elizabeth J. Christina & the Little Red Bird. Mcknight, C. D., illus. 23p. (Orig.). (ps-1). pap. 5.95 (ISBN 0-938911-02-3). Indiv Educ Syst.
Peterson, Jeanne W. I Have a Sister, My Sister Is Deaf. Ray, Deborah, illus. LC 76-24306. 32p. (ps-3). 1984. pap. 4.95 (ISBN 0-06-443059-6, Trophy). HarpC Child Bks.
Peterson, John. The Littles Go to School. 80p. (gr. k-3). 1985. pap. 2.50 (ISBN 0-590-42129-8). Scholastic Inc.
Petty, Kate. Staying Overnight. FS-Aladdin Staff, ed. Kopper, Lisa, illus. 24p. 1988. PLB 5.29 (ISBN 0-531-17106-X, Gloucester Pr). Watts.
Pevsner, Stella. How Could You Do It, Diane? LC 88-35923. 192p. (gr. 5-9). 1989. 13.95 (ISBN 0-395-51041-4, Clarion Bks). HM.
Pfeffer, Susan B. What Do You Do When Your Mouth Won't Open? 128p. (gr. 4-8). 1982. pap. 2.75 (ISBN 0-440-49320-X, YB). Dell.
Pfloog, Jan. The Farm Book. (Illus.). 24p. (ps-k). 1989. pap. write for info. (ISBN 0-307-58117-9, Pub. by Golden Bks). Western Pub.
—The Kitten Book. (Illus.). 24p. (ps-k). 1968. pap. write for info. (ISBN 0-307-10079-0, Pub. by Golden Bks). Western Pub.
—The Puppy Book. (Illus.). 24p. (ps-k). 1968. pap. write for info (ISBN 0-307-10078-2, Pub. by Golden Bks). Western Pub.
—The Zoo Book. (Illus.). 24p. (ps-k). 1989. pap. write for info. (ISBN 0-307-58118-7, Pub. by Golden Bks). Western Pub.
Phillips, Joan. Donald Duck & the Garden. Mateu, Franc, illus. LC 87-83492. 40p. (gr. k-2). 1988. write for info. (ISBN 0-307-11694-8). Western Pub.
—Donald Duck at the Toy Store. Ito, Willy & Wilson, Roy, illus. LC 87-83493. 40p. (gr. k-2). 1988. write for info. (ISBN 0-307-11693-X). Western Pub.
—Peek-a-Boo! I See You! Wilburn, Kathy, illus. (ps). 1983. 3.95 (ISBN 0-448-03092-6, G&D). Putnam Pub Group.
—Tiger Is a Scaredy Cat: A Step One Book. Gorbaty, Norman, illus. LC 85-19673. 32p. (ps-1). 1986. lib. bdg. 6.99 (ISBN 0-394-98056-5); pap. 2.95 (ISBN 0-394-88056-0). Random.
Phillips, Tamara. Day Care ABC. Levine, Abby, ed. Leder, Dora, illus. (ps-2). 1989. PLB 12.95 (ISBN 0-8075-1483-7). A Whitman.
Pickart, Joan Elliott. Mixed Signals. 1990. pap. 2.50 (ISBN 0-553-44018-7, Loveswept). Bantam.
Picture Book for Baby. (Illus.). (ps). 3.50 (ISBN 0-7214-0749-8). Ladybird Bks.
Picture Book One in Arabic. (ARA., Illus.). (gr. 1-3). 3.50x (ISBN 0-86685-214-X). Intl Bk Ctr.
Picture Book Two in Arabic. (ARA., Illus.). (gr. 1-3). 3.50x (ISBN 0-686-53062-4). Intl Bk Ctr.
Picture Reading. (Illus.). (ps-2). 3.50 (ISBN 0-7214-0854-0). Ladybird Bks.
Picture Reading Rhymes. (Illus.). (ps-2). 3.50 (ISBN 0-7214-1182-7). Ladybird Bks.
Picture Reading Stories. (Illus.). (ps-2). 1990. 3.50 (ISBN 0-7214-1204-1). Ladybird Bks.
Picture Word Book. (Illus.). (ps-k). 8.95 (ISBN 0-7214-7510-8). Ladybird Bks.
Piemontes, Grayce. Classic Shirley Temple-Paperdolls. 1989. pap. 3.95 (ISBN 0-486-25193-4). Dover.
Pienkowski, Jan. Faces. Pienkowski, Jan, illus. 24p. (ps-k). 1991. bds. 2.95 (ISBN 0-671-72846-6, Little Simon). S&S Trade.
—Farm-Nursery Board Book. 1990. 2.95 (ISBN 0-671-70476-1). S&S Trade.
—Food. Pienkowski, Jan, illus. 24p. (ps-k). 1991. bds. 2.95 (ISBN 0-671-72845-8, Little Simon). S&S Trade.
—Homes-Nursery Board Book. (ps). 1990. 2.95 (ISBN 0-671-70478-8). S&S Trade.
—Nursery Board Books. (ps-2). 1990. pap. 2.95 (ISBN 0-685-31424-3). S&S Trade.
—Oh My, a Fly! Pienkowski, Jan, illus. 10p. (ps up). 1989. pop-up book 8.95 (ISBN 0-8431-2765-1). Price Stern.
—Sizes. Pienkowski, Jan, illus. 24p. (ps-k). 1991. bds. 2.95 (ISBN 0-671-72844-X, Little Simon). S&S Trade.
—Time. Pienkowski, Jan, illus. 24p. (ps-k). 1991. bds. 2.95 (ISBN 0-671-72847-4, Little Simon). S&S Trade.
—Weather - Nursery Board Book. (ps). 1990. 2.95 (ISBN 0-671-70479-6). S&S Trade.
—Zoo - Nursery Board Book. (ps). 1990. 2.95 (ISBN 0-671-70477-X). S&S Trade.
Piers, Helen. Peekaboo, 4 bks. Incl. Bk. No. 1. Peekaboo Kitten. LC 85-80827. 1986; Bk. No. 2. Peekaboo Mouse. LC 85-80824. 1986; Bk. No. 3. Peekaboo Puppy. LC 85-80826. 1986; Bk. No. 4. Peekaboo Rabbit. LC 85-80825. 1986. (Illus.). 12p. (ps-k). 1986. 2.95 ea. (HJ). HarbraceJ.
Pillinger, Ian. Animal Shape Board Book: The Little Kitten. 1988. 1.98 (ISBN 0-671-09434-3). S&S Trade.
Pincus, Harriet. Minna & Pippin. Pincus, Harriet, illus. LC 70-188253. 32p. (ps up). 1972. 7.95 (ISBN 0-374-34991-6). FS&G.
Pinkerton, Susan. Concoctions. 64p. (ps-3). 1987. 6.95 (ISBN 0-912107-58-8). Monday Morning Bks.
Pinkwater, Daniel. The Frankenbagel Monster. Pinkwater, Daniel, illus. (gr. k-3). 1986. 9.95 (ISBN 0-525-44260-X, DCB). Dutton Child Bks.
—Guys from Space. Pinkwater, Daniel, illus. LC 88-13485. 32p. (gr. k-3). 1989. 13.95 (ISBN 0-02-774672-0, Mcmillan Child Bk). Macmillan Child Grp.
—Uncle Melvin. Pinkwater, Daniel, illus. LC 88-27178. 32p. (gr. k-3). 1989. 13.95 (ISBN 0-02-774675-5, Mcmillan Child Bk). Macmillan Child Grp.
Piper, Watty. The Little Engine That Could. Walz, Richard, illus. LC 99-44044. 12p. (ps-2). 1984. 7.95 (ISBN 0-448-18963-1, Platt & Munk). Putnam Pub Group.
Pittman, Helena C. The Gift of the Willows. Pittman, Helena C., illus. 32p. (gr. k-4). 1988. 12.95 (ISBN 0-87614-354-0). Carolrhoda Bks.
—Miss Hindy's Cats. Pittman, Helena C., illus. LC 89-22214. 32p. (ps-3). 1990. pap. 12.95 (ISBN 0-87614-368-0). Carolrhoda Bks.
A Place at the Table. (Illus.). 24p. (gr. k-2). 1989. bds. 3.95 (ISBN 0-685-39485-9). Modern Pub NYC.
Places to Go. (Illus.). (ps-k). 3.95 (ISBN 0-7214-5039-3). Ladybird Bks.
Playskool Preschool Staff. Storyland Fun. 1989. pap. write for info. (ISBN 0-307-02391-5, Pub. by Golden Bks). Western Pub.
—Who Says Moo? 1989. pap. write for info. (ISBN 0-307-02393-1, Pub. by Golden Bks). Western Pub.
—Zoo for You. 1989. pap. write for info. (ISBN 0-307-01423-1, Pub. by Golden Bks). Western Pub.
Playtime. (Illus.). (ps). 2.50 (ISBN 0-7214-9089-1). Ladybird Bks.
Plume, Ilse. The Bremen-Town Musicians. Plume, Ilse, illus. LC 86-42990. 32p. (ps-3). 1987. pap. 5.95 (ISBN 0-06-443141-X, Trophy). HarpC Child Bks.
Plumme, Don E. The Wuzzles & the Creepasaurs: A Story in Rhyme. Stuhmer, Bob, illus. LC 85-18289. 32p. (ps-3). 1986. 4.95 (ISBN 0-394-87877-9). Random.
Poelker, Kathy. At the Firehouse. Judge, Matt, ed. Hedran, Susan, illus. 8p. (Orig.). (ps-3). 1988. pap. text ed. 15.00 (ISBN 0-929842-00-6). Hawthorne Pubs.
—One Little Drop of Sunshine. Judge, Matt, ed. Hedran, Susan, illus. 8p. (Orig.). (ps-3). 1988. pap. text ed. 15.00 (ISBN 0-929842-01-4). Hawthorne Pubs.
Poky Little Puppy's Day at the Fair. 1990. pap. write for info. (ISBN 0-307-12162-3, Pub. by Golden Bks). Western Pub.
Polette, Nancy. E Is for Everybody: A Manual for Bringing Fine Picture Books into the Hands & Hearts of Children. 2nd ed. LC 82-10508. 194p. (gr. 1-7). 1982. 20.00 (ISBN 0-8108-1579-6). Scarecrow.
Polka Dot Pony. 12p. (ps-1). 1988. bds. 5.95 (ISBN 0-87449-626-8). Modern Pub NYC.
Pollock, Penny. The Spit Bug Who Couldn't Spit. Cauley, Lorinda B., illus. 48p. 1982. PLB 6.99 (ISBN 0-399-61152-5, Putnam). Putnam Pub Group.
Polter, David. Say Hello to the Care Bear Cousins. Neher, Julie & Redding, Jane, illus. 64p. (ps-3). 1985. pap. 2.95 (ISBN 0-394-87114-6, Random Juv). Random.
Polushkin, Maria. Here's That Kitten. Lewin, Betsy, illus. LC 89-829. 32p. (ps-k). 1990. 12.95 (ISBN 0-02-774741-7, Bradbury Pr). Macmillan Child Grp.
—Who Said Meow? Weiss, Ellen, illus. LC 87-28073. 32p. (ps). 1988. 12.95 (ISBN 0-02-774770-0, Bradbury Pr). Macmillan Child Grp.
Pomaska, Anna. Cut & Assemble a Peter Rabbit. 1984. pap. 4.95 (ISBN 0-486-24713-9). Dover.
—Easy Mazes Activity Book. (Illus.). (ps up). 1988. pap. 1.00 (ISBN 0-486-25531-X). Dover.
—The Little Alphabet Follow-the-Dots Book. (ps up). 1988. pap. 1.00 (ISBN 0-486-25623-5). Dover.
—The Little Dinosaur Activity Book. (ps up). 1987. pap. 1.00 (ISBN 0-486-25344-9). Dover.
—The Little Follow the Dots Book. 1986. pap. 1.00 (ISBN 0-486-25157-8). Dover.
—The Little Seashore Activity Book. (ps up). 1988. pap. 1.00 (ISBN 0-486-25608-1). Dover.
Pomerantz, Charlotte. All Asleep. Tafuri, Nancy, illus. 32p. (ps-1). 1986. pap. 3.95 (ISBN 0-14-050548-2, Puffin). Puffin Bks.
—How Many Trucks Can a Tow Truck Tow. Alley, R. W., illus. LC 89-3657. 24p. (ps-k). 1987. PLB 5.99 (ISBN 0-394-98775-6); pap. 4.95 (ISBN 0-394-88775-1). Random.
—The Piggy in the Puddle. Marshall, James, illus. 32p. (ps-1). 1989. pap. 3.95 (ISBN 0-689-71293-6, Aladdin). Macmillan Child Grp.
Pop - Up Goldilocks & the Three Bears. 1989. 13.95 (ISBN 0-698-12050-7, Playland Bks); doll incl. Putnam Pub Group.
Porter, Sue. One Potato. Porter, Sue, illus. LC 88-35361. 32p. (ps-1). 1989. 12.95 (ISBN 0-02-774910-X, Bradbury Pr). Macmillan Child Grp.
Potter, Beatrix. Babys Book. rev. ed. 1988. 7.99 (ISBN 0-517-67576-5). Crown.
—The Beatrix Potter Story Chest. Potter, Beatrix, illus. (ps-3). 1986. Set. pap. 7.95 (ISBN 0-7232-5161-4). Warne.
—Beatrix Potter's Birthday Book. Linder, Enid, ed. Potter, Beatrix, illus. LC 73-89833. 156p. (gr. 1 up). 1974. 6.95 (ISBN 0-7232-1758-0); leather bdg. 11.95 (ISBN 0-7232-1815-3). Warne.
—Jemima Puddle-Duck Bath Book. (Illus.). 8p. (ps). 1988. pap. 2.95 waterproof (ISBN 0-7232-3512-0). Warne.
—Jeremy Fisher Bath Book. (Illus.). 8p. (ps). 1989. 2.95 (ISBN 0-7232-3513-9). Warne.
—Letters to Children. (Illus.). 48p. (gr. 2 up). 1986. pap. 5.95 (ISBN 0-8027-7293-5). Walker & Co.
—Meet Hunca Munca. Potter, Beatrix, illus. 12p. (ps). 1986. bds. 2.95 (ISBN 0-7232-3421-3). Warne.
—Meet Jemima Puddle-Duck. Potter, Beatrix, illus. 12p. (ps). 1986. bds. 2.95 (ISBN 0-7232-3420-5). Warne.
—Meet Peter Rabbit. Potter, Beatrix, illus. 12p. (ps). 1986. bds. 2.95 (ISBN 0-7232-3418-3). Warne.
—Meet Tom Kitten. Potter, Beatrix, illus. 12p. (ps). 1986. bds. 2.95 (ISBN 0-7232-3419-1). Warne.
—My Peter Rabbit Learning Box: Peter Rabbit's 123 & Peter Rabbit's ABC. (ps-3). 1988. Boxed Set. 13.95 (ISBN 0-7232-5168-1). Warne.
—The Original Peter Rabbit Miniature Collection, No. I. Potter, Beatrix, illus. (ps-3). 1986. pap. 4.95 (ISBN 0-7232-5022-7). Warne.
—The Original Peter Rabbit Miniature Collection II. (ps-3). 1988. pap. 4.95 (ISBN 0-7232-5023-5). Warne.
—The Peter Rabbit Cut-Out Book. Potter, Beatrix, illus. (ps-3). 1986. pap. 3.95 (ISBN 0-7232-3331-4). Warne.
—The Tailor of Gloucester. Jorgensen, David, illus. LC 88-11510. 44p. (ps up). 1988. 14.95 (ISBN 0-88708-080-4, Rabbit Ears); bk. & cass. pkg. 19.95 (ISBN 0-88708-085-5). Picture Bk Studio.
—The Tale of Benjamin Bunny. Leach, Rosemary, read by. Davis, Carl, contrib. by. (Illus.). (ps-3). 1989. pap. 6.95 incl. tape (ISBN 0-7232-3628-3). Warne.
—Tale of Benjamin Bunny Pop Up. 1988. 3.99 (ISBN 0-517-67096-8). Crown.
—The Tale of Jemima Puddle-Duck. West, Timothy, read by. Davis, Carl, contrib. by. (Illus.). (ps-3). 1989. pap. 6.95 incl. tape (ISBN 0-7232-3630-5). Warne.
—Tale of Jemima Puddle Duck Pop-Up. 1988. 3.99 (ISBN 0-517-67097-6). Crown.
—The Tale of Mr. Jeremy Fisher. LC 74-75269. (Illus.). 59p. (gr. 2-4). 1974. pap. 1.75 (ISBN 0-486-23066-X). Dover.
—The Tale of Mr. Jeremy Fisher. Jorgensen, David, illus. LC 88-34668. 32p. (ps up). 1989. 14.95 (ISBN 0-88708-094-4, Rabbit Ears); incl. cassette 19.95 (ISBN 0-88708-095-2). Picture Bk Studio.
—The Tale of Mrs. Tiggy-Winkle. Routledge, Patricia, read by. Davis, Carl, contrib. by. (Illus.). (ps-3). 1989. pap. 6.95 incl. tape (ISBN 0-7232-3629-1). Warne.
—The Tale of Peter Rabbit. Jorgensen, David, illus. LC 88-11509. 36p. (ps up). 1988. 14.95 (ISBN 0-317-89758-6, Rabbit Ears); bk. & cass. pkg. 19.95 (ISBN 0-88708-084-7). Picture Bk Studio.
—Tale of Peter Rabbit Pop Up. 1988. 3.99 (ISBN 0-517-67098-4). Crown.
—Tale of Tom Kitten Pop-Up. 1988. 3.99 (ISBN 0-517-67099-2). Crown.
—The Two Bad Mice Pop-Up Book. Potter, Beatrix, illus. (ps-3). 1986. 11.95 (ISBN 0-7232-3360-8). Warne.
—Where's Tom Kitten? 24p. (ps-3). 1990. 6.95 (ISBN 0-7232-3597-X). Warne.
—The World of Peter Rabbit Postcard Book. (Illus.). 1990. pap. 6.95 (ISBN 0-7232-3647-X). Warne.
—The World of Peter Rabbit Sticker Book. Twinn, Colin, illus. 32p. (ps-3). 1990. pap. 5.95 (ISBN 0-7232-3645-3). Warne.
Poulet, Virginia. Blue Bug's Christmas. LC 87-15793. (Illus.). 32p. (ps-3). 1987. PLB 14.60 (ISBN 0-516-03483-9); pap. 3.95 (ISBN 0-516-43483-7). Childrens.
—El Tesoro de Azulin: Blue Bug's Treasure. Maloney, M. & Fleming, S., illus. LC 75-40352. (SPA.). 32p. (ps-2). 1988. PLB 14.60 (ISBN 0-516-33424-7); pap. 3.95 (ISBN 0-516-53424-6). Childrens.
Powell, Patricia. Diddle Diddle Red Hot Fiddle. Metrejean, Nikki N., illus. 32p. (gr. 1-8). 1990. pap. text ed. 6.95 (ISBN 0-944512-01-1). Radiant LA.
Pragoff, Fiona. Fiona Pragoff Board Books. (Illus.). (ps). 1988. pap. 4.95 (ISBN 0-318-32999-9). Doubleday.
—Growing. LC 87-5239. (Illus.). 20p. (gr. k-3). 1987. 6.95 (ISBN 0-385-24174-7). Doubleday.
—How Many? From Zero to Twenty. LC 87-5053. (Illus.). 28p. (gr. k-3). 1987. pap. 6.95 (ISBN 0-385-24172-0). Doubleday.
Prater, John. Gilbert. (ps-1). 1988. 10.95 (ISBN 0-318-37400-5). Random.
Precek, Katharine W. Penny in the Road. Cullen-Clark, Patricia, illus. LC 88-13331. 32p. (gr. k-3). 1989. 14.95 (ISBN 0-02-774970-3, Mcmillan Child Bk). Macmillan Child Grp.

Prelutsky, Jack. Circus! Lobel, Arnold, illus. 32p. (ps-2). 1989. pap. 3.95 (ISBN 0-689-70806-8, Aladdin). Macmillan Child Grp.
—The Terrible Tiger. Lobel, Arnold, illus. 32p. (ps-2). 1989. pap. text ed. 3.95 (ISBN 0-689-71300-2, Aladdin). Macmillan Child Grp.
Preschool Early Learner Workbook. 192p. (ps-1). 1990. pap. 4.95 wkbk. (ISBN 0-87449-989-5). Modern Pub NYC.
Price, Donna. Greenberg's German LGB Coloring Book. (Illus.). 32p. (Orig.). (gr. k-5). 1988. text ed. 3.50 (ISBN 0-317-64973-6, 10-7020G). Greenberg Pub Co.
—Greenberg's LGB Coloring Book. (Illus.). 32p. (Orig.). (gr. k-5). 1987. pap. 3.50 (ISBN 0-89778-093-0, 10-7020). Greenberg Pub Co.
Price, El-Louise. Counting Katie's Gifts. Boddy, Joe, illus. LC 87-91987. 32p. (gr. k-2). 1988. 1.99 (ISBN 0-87403-392-6, 24-03802). Standard Pub.
Price, Mathew & Claverie, Jean. Peekaboo. Claverie, Jean, illus. LC 84-40451. 20p. (ps-k). 1985. 9.95 (ISBN 0-394-87142-1). Knopf.
La Primera Pascua de Spot (Spot's First Easter) (SPA.). 22p. (ps-1). 11.95 (ISBN 0-399-21551-4, Putnam). Putnam Pub Group.
Prince, Pamela. Once upon a Time. Smith, Jesse W., illus. LC 87-33359. 48p. (ps up). 1988. 12.95 (ISBN 0-517-56832-2, Harmony). Crown.
Pringle, Laurence. Jesse Builds a Road. Morrill, Leslie H., illus. LC 88-29297. 32p. (ps-1). 1989. 13.95 (ISBN 0-02-775311-5, Mcmillan Child Bk). Macmillan Child Grp.
Provensen, Alice & Provensen, Martin. The Glorious Flight Across the Channel with Louis Bleriot. LC 82-7034. (Illus.). 40p. (gr. 5-8). 1983. pap. 14.95 (ISBN 0-670-34259-9). Viking Child Bks.
—El Libro de las Estaciones. Cuenca, Pilar de & Alvarez, Ines, trs. LC 81-13821. (SPA., Illus.). 32p. (ps-3). 1982. lib. bdg. 5.99 (ISBN 0-394-95143-3); pap. 2.25 (ISBN 0-394-85143-9). Random.
Provensen, Alice & Provensen, Martin, illus. A Peaceable Kingdom: The Shaker Abecedarius. Barsam, Richard M., afterword by. (gr. k-3). 1981. pap. 4.95 (ISBN 0-14-050370-6, Puffin). Puffin Bks.
Proysen, Alf. Mrs. Pepperpot in the Magic Wood. Berg, Bjorn, illus. 128p. (gr. 1-4). 1988. pap. 3.95 (ISBN 0-14-030538-6, Puffin). Puffin Bks.
Pryor, Ainslie. The Baby Blue Cat & the Dirty Dog Brothers. (Illus.). 32p. (ps-3). 1989. pap. 3.95 (ISBN 0-14-050769-8, Puffin). Puffin Bks.
—The Baby Blue Cat Who Said No. Pryor, Ainslie, illus. LC 87-21026. 32p. (ps-k). 1988. 11.95 (ISBN 0-670-81780-5). Viking Child Bks.
Pryor, Bonnie & Baird, Anne. Happy Birthday, Mama! Bracken, Carolyn & Fernandes, Eugenie, illus. (ps). 1987. 3.95 (ISBN 0-671-63757-6, Little Simon). S&S Trade.
—Ride Away! Bracken, Carolyn & Fernandes, Eugenie, illus. (ps). 1987. 3.95 (ISBN 0-671-64307-X, Little Simon). S&S Trade.
Puppy, Teddy, Kitty & Bunny. (Illus.). (ps-k). 1990. pap. 5.95 ea., 8pgs. ea. Puppy (ISBN 0-87449-819-8). Teddy (ISBN 0-87449-820-1). Kitty (ISBN 0-87449-821-X). Bunny (ISBN 0-87449-822-8). Modern Pub NYC.
Purviance, Susan & O'Shell, Marcia. Alphabet Annie Announces an All-American Book. Brunner-Strosser, Ruth, photos by. (Illus.). 56p. (ps up). 1988. 15.95 (ISBN 0-395-48070-1). HM.
Quackenbush, Robert. Henry Babysits. Quackenbush, Robert, illus. LC 83-2247. 48p. (ps-3). 1983. 5.95 (ISBN 0-8193-1107-3); lib. bdg. 5.95 (ISBN 0-8193-1108-1). Parents.
—Mouse Feathers. Quackenbush, Robert, illus. LC 87-15690. 40p. (gr. k-3). 1988. 12.95 (ISBN 0-89919-527-X, Pub. by Clarion). Ticknor & Fields.
Questron Staff. ABC Dinosaurs in the Woods. (ps-3). 1987. pap. 3.95 (ISBN 0-394-89053-1). Random.
Quinn, Kaye. Under the Big Top. (Illus.). 48p. (Orig.). (ps-2). 1989. pap. 2.95 (ISBN 0-8431-2729-5). Price Stern.
Rabe, Berniece. A Smooth Move. Tucker, Kathleen, ed. Sims, Blanche, illus. LC 87-2099. (gr. 1-4). 1987. PLB 11.50 (ISBN 0-8075-7486-4). A Whitman.
Rabe, Tish. My Name Is Ernie. Swanson, Maggie, illus. (ps-k). 1991. pap. write for info. (ISBN 0-307-11513-5, Golden Pr). Western Pub.
Rackham, Arthur, illus. Sixty Fairy Tales of the Brothers Grimm. (gr. 2-7). 8.98 (ISBN 0-517-28525-8). Outlet Bk Co.
Rader, Laura, illus. The Pudgy Where Is Your Nose? Book. 16p. 1989. bds. 2.95 (ISBN 0-448-02258-3, G&D). Putnam Pub Group.
Radin, Ruth Y. High in the Mountains. Young, Ed, illus. LC 88-13395. 32p. (gr. k-4). 1989. 13.95 (ISBN 0-02-775650-5, Mcmillan Child Bk). Macmillan Child Grp.
Radke, Lee. The Birthday Surprise. 32p. (ps-1). 1990. 6.95 (ISBN 0-8062-3617-5). Carlton.
Rae, Mary M. The Farmer in the Dell: A Singing Game. 32p. (ps-1). 1988. pap. 12.95 (ISBN 0-670-81853-4). Viking Child Bks.
Raffi. Baby Beluga. Wolff, Ashley, illus. LC 89-49367. 32p. (ps-2). 1990. 10.00 (ISBN 0-517-57839-5); PLB 10.99 (ISBN 0-517-57840-9). Crown.
—Down by the Bay. Westcott, Nadine B., illus. 32p. (ps-2). 1988. PLB 10.95 (ISBN 0-517-56644-3). Crown.
—Down by the Bay. Westcott, Nadine B., illus. LC 87-750291. 32p. (ps-2). 1988. pap. 3.95 (ISBN 0-517-56645-1). McKay.
—One Light, One Sun. Fernandes, Eugenie, illus. LC 87-22256. 32p. (ps-2). 1990. pap. 3.95 (ISBN 0-517-57644-9). McKay.
—Shake My Sillies Out. Allender, David, illus. LC 87-750478. 32p. (ps-2). 1988. pap. 3.95 (ISBN 0-517-56647-8). McKay.
—Wheels on the Bus. Wickstrom, Sylvie K., illus. LC 87-30126. 32p. (ps-2). 1990. pap. 3.95 (ISBN 0-517-57645-7). McKay.

Raichert, Lane. D.C. Hopper, the First Starbunny. Raichert, Lane, illus. LC 91-23055. 32p. (gr. 2-6). 1991. 15.95 (ISBN 1-880009-81-1, DC-P1). Blue Zero Pub.
Why is D.C. Hopper, a respected doctor of applied carrotology, building a rocket in his garage? Why has he left his job just when everybody needs him the most? Why is he walking around his apartment in a color coordinated space suit? Has the poor rabbit gone harebrained? No one is sure. All they know is that D.C. is obsessed with the dream of visiting space. Hurled from the safety of his home planet, D.C. Hopper discovers that the rewards from following your dreams are far more than can be imagined. In warm color pencil illustrations, rich with detail & humor, Lane Raichert's first picture book shows that there is truly hope for the future. D.C. Hopper, The First Starbunny, is printed on 100 pound acid free paper with illustrations printed at a line resolution of 225 - a level usually reserved for limited art prints. Don't miss the stunning achievement of this important new author. Blue Zero Publishing Company, PO Box 10699, Burbank, CA, 91510. Call (818) 840-0918 or fax (818) 840-8503.
Publisher Provided Annotation.

Rand, Ted & Lear, Edward. The Jumblies. (Illus.). 32p. (ps-3). 1989. 14.95 (ISBN 0-399-21632-4, Putnam). Putnam Pub Group.
Rao, Anthony. Cut & Make Animal Masks. 1989. pap. 4.95 (ISBN 0-486-25199-3). Dover.
—Dinosaurs! LC 79-63241. (Illus.). (ps-3). 1979. 2.50 (ISBN 0-448-46532-9, G&D); PLB 7.95 (ISBN 0-448-13079-3, G&D). Putnam Pub Group.
Rappaport, Doreen. The Boston Coffee Party. McCully, Emily A., illus. LC 87-45301. 64p. (gr. k-3). 1988. 11.95 (ISBN 0-06-024824-6); PLB 11.89 (ISBN 0-06-024825-4). HarpC Child Bks.
Rasbach, Hubert H. The Dinkywinkies & Snickity Snackety Snort. Ingram, Fred & Jennings, Elkay, illus. LC 79-89378. (ps-4). 1982. 6.95 (ISBN 0-934822-05-0). Plus One Pub.
Raskin, Ellen. Nothing Ever Happens on My Block. Raskin, Ellen, illus. 32p. (gr. k-4). 1989. pap. 3.95 (ISBN 0-689-71335-5, Aladdin). Macmillan Child Grp.
Ray, Margret & Shalleck, Alan J. Curious George Goes to an Ice Cream Shop. (Illus.). 32p. (ps-2). 1989. 9.95 (ISBN 0-395-51943-8); pap. 2.95 (ISBN 0-395-51937-3). HM.
Rayner, Shoo. My First Picture Joke Book. (Illus.). 32p. (ps-1). 1990. pap. 11.95 (ISBN 0-670-82450-X). Viking Child Bks.
Raynor, Mary, illus. Thank You for the Tadpole. LC 87-474. (gr. k-2). 1988. pap. 2.50 (ISBN 0-317-69488-X). Delacorte.
Razzi, Jim. Big Wheel Super Car. Lapinski, Joe, illus. 32p. (gr. 1-7). 1988. pap. 4.95 (ISBN 0-590-41470-4). Scholastic Inc.
—The Very Best Christmas Present. Fernandes, Henry, illus. LC 87-83045. 24p. (Orig.). (ps-3). 1988. pap. write for info. (ISBN 0-307-11711-1). Western Pub.
Razzi, Jim, adapted by. Friends in Need. (Illus.). 24p. (ps-3). 1988. pap. 2.25 (ISBN 0-448-09358-8, G&D); pap. 5.95 incl. audio cassette (ISBN 0-448-09352-9, G&D). Putnam Pub Group.
—The Search for the Great Valley. (Illus.). 24p. (ps-3). 1988. pap. 2.25 (ISBN 0-448-09357-X, G&D); pap. 5.95 incl. audio cassette (ISBN 0-448-09353-7, G&D). Putnam Pub Group.
Read a Picture: Colors & Numbers. 1991. 4.98 (ISBN 0-8317-7353-7). Smithmark.
Read a Picture: Let's Go. 1991. 4.98 (ISBN 0-8317-7354-5). Smithmark.
Read a Picture: Rhymes & Stories. 1991. 4.98 (ISBN 0-8317-7352-9). Smithmark.
Real Mother Goose Clock Book. Wright, Blanche F., illus. 22p. (ps-2). 6.95 (ISBN 1-56288-095-0). Checkerboard Pr.
Reed, Louise D. DG & You. (Illus.). 21p. (ps-1). 1989. 6.95 (ISBN 0-533-08029-0). Vantage.
Reese, Bob. Who's a Silly Egg? Jordan, Alton, ed. (Illus.). (gr. k-3). 1981. PLB 7.95 (ISBN 0-89868-092-1, Read Res); pap. text ed. 2.95 (ISBN 0-89868-103-0). ARO Pub.
Reese, Bob, et al. Buppet Character Book Set, 10 bks. Jordan, Alton, ed. (Illus.). (gr. k-3). 1981. Set. PLB 79.50 (ISBN 0-89868-088-3, Read Res); pap. 29.50 (ISBN 0-89868-099-9). ARO Pub.
Reese, Ron. Toy Bear. Jordan, Alton, ed. Reese, Bob, illus. (gr. k-3). 1975. PLB 5.95 (ISBN 0-89868-016-6, Read Res); pap. text ed. 2.50 (ISBN 0-89868-049-2). ARO Pub.
Reeves, Mona R. I Had a Cat. Downing, Julie, illus. LC 87-37608. 32p. (ps-2). 1989. 13.95 (ISBN 0-02-775731-5, Bradbury Pr). Macmillan Child Grp.
—The Spooky Eerie Night Noise. Yalowitz, Paul, illus. LC 89-447. 32p. (ps-2). 1989. 12.95 (ISBN 0-02-775732-3, Bradbury Pr). Macmillan Child Grp.
Reichmeier, Betty, illus. Potty Time! Yellow Ladder Books for Toddlers Through 4 Years. 10p. 1988. vinyl 7.00 (ISBN 0-394-89403-0, Random Juv). Random.
Reid, John C. Parables from the Animal Kingdom. Hayes, Theresa, ed. Stone, Bryan, illus. LC 87-32922. 96p. (ps-3). 1988. 5.95 (ISBN 0-87403-500-7, 14-02872). Standard Pub.
Reid, Saralou L. Mommakitty's Surprise: "Skyler" LC 88-60613. (Illus.). (gr. k-3). write for info. (ISBN 0-9620420-0-5); lib. bdg. write for info. (ISBN 0-9620420-1-3); pap. write for info. (ISBN 0-9620420-3-X). Surge Pub.
Reif, Patricia. Big Work Machines. LaPadula, Tom, illus. 24p. (ps-3). 1984. pap. write for info. (ISBN 0-307-11897-5, Golden Bks). Western Pub.
Reisberg. Baby Rattlesnake. 32p. (gr. 3-4). 1990. 13.95 (ISBN 0-8172-3660-0). Raintree Pubs.
Reiss, John J. Colors. Reiss, John J., illus. LC 86-22189. 32p. (ps-2). 1987. pap. 3.95 (ISBN 0-689-71119-0, Aladdin). Macmillan Child Grp.
—Numbers. Reiss, John J., illus. LC 86-22243. 32p. (ps-2). 1987. pap. 3.95 (ISBN 0-689-71120-4, Aladdin). Macmillan Child Grp.
—Shapes. LC 73-76545. (Illus.). 32p. (ps-2). 1982. 13.95 (ISBN 0-02-776190-8, Bradbury Pr). Macmillan Child Grp.
—Shapes. Reiss, John J., illus. LC 86-22164. 32p. (ps-2). 1987. pap. 3.95 (ISBN 0-689-71121-2, Aladdin). Macmillan Child Grp.
Reit, Seymour. Flying School Bus. 1990. pap. write for info. (ISBN 0-307-10032-4, Golden Pr). Western Pub.
—Things That Go: A Traveling Alphabet. 1990. 9.99 (ISBN 0-553-05856-8). Bantam.
Reptiles & Amphibians Color & Story Album. pap. 3.95 (ISBN 0-8431-1765-6). Price Stern.
Rey, H. A. Cecily G. & the Nine Monkeys. Rey, H. A., illus. 32p. (gr. 1-3). 1974. 12.95 (ISBN 0-395-18430-4). HM.
—Curious George. (Illus.). 56p. (gr. k-3). 1973. 12.95 (ISBN 0-395-15993-8). HM.
—Curious George Gets a Medal. (Illus.). 48p. (gr. k-3). 1957. 12.95 (ISBN 0-395-16973-9). HM.
—Curious George Paper Doll. 1982. pap. 3.95 (ISBN 0-486-24386-9). Dover.
—Curious George Rides a Bike. (Illus.). 48p. (gr. k-3). 1952. 12.95 (ISBN 0-395-16964-X). HM.
—Curious George Takes a Job. (Illus.). 48p. (gr. k-3). 1973. 12.95 (ISBN 0-395-15086-8). HM.
Rey, H. A. & Rey, Margaret. Curious George Goes to the Hospital. (Illus.). 48p. (gr. 1-5). 1973. 12.95 (ISBN 0-395-18158-5); pap. 3.95 (ISBN 0-395-07062-7). HM.
Rey, Margaret & Rey, H. A. Curious George Flies a Kite. (Illus.). 80p. (gr. k-3). 1973. 12.95 (ISBN 0-395-16965-8). HM.
—Pretzel. Rey, H. A., illus. LC 44-9584. 32p. (ps-1). 1944. PLB 13.89 (ISBN 0-06-024911-0). HarpC Child Bks.
Rey, Margaret & Shalleck, Alan J. Curious George & the Dinosaur. (Illus.). 32p. (ps-2). 1989. 9.95 (ISBN 0-395-51941-1); pap. 2.95 (ISBN 0-395-51936-5). HM.
—Curious George at the Beach. (Illus.). 32p. (ps-2). 1988. 9.95 (ISBN 0-395-48666-1); pap. 2.95 (ISBN 0-395-48660-2). HM.
—Curious George at the Railroad Station. (Illus.). 32p. (ps-2). 1988. 9.95 (ISBN 0-395-48667-X); pap. 2.95 (ISBN 0-395-48657-2). HM.
—Curious George Goes to a Restaurant. (Illus.). 32p. (ps-2). 1988. 9.95 (ISBN 0-395-48664-5); pap. 2.95 (ISBN 0-395-48658-0). HM.
—Curious George Goes to School. (Illus.). 32p. (ps-2). 1989. 9.95 (ISBN 0-395-51944-6); pap. 2.95 (ISBN 0-395-51939-X). HM.
—Curious George Goes to the Dentist. (Illus.). 32p. (ps-2). 1989. 9.95 (ISBN 0-685-26499-8); pap. 2.95 (ISBN 0-395-51938-1). HM.
—Curious George Visits an Amusement Park. (Illus.). 32p. (ps-2). 1988. 9.95 (ISBN 0-395-48665-3); pap. 2.95 (ISBN 0-395-48659-9). HM.
Rey, Margaret & Shalleck, Allan J. Curious George & the Pizza. 1988. pap. 6.95 incl. cass. (ISBN 0-395-48874-5). HM.
—Curious George at the Fire Station. 1988. pap. 6.95 incl. cass. (ISBN 0-395-48875-3). HM.

Reynolds, Annette. The Christmas Baby. (Illus.). 12p. (ps-1). 1987. bds. 6.95 (ISBN 0-7459-1368-7). Lion USA.
—The First Christmas Presents. (Illus.). 12p. (ps-1). 1987. bds. 6.95 (ISBN 0-7459-1369-5). Lion USA.
Rice, Eve. Aren't You Coming Too? Parker, Nancy W., illus. LC 86-33506. 32p. (ps-3). 1988. 11.95 (ISBN 0-688-06446-9); lib. bdg. 11.88 (ISBN 0-688-06447-7). Greenwillow.
—Benny Bakes a Cake. LC 80-17313. (Illus.). 32p. (ps-3). 1999. pap. 3.95 (ISBN 0-688-07814-1, Mulberry). Morrow.
—City Night. Sis, Peter, illus. 24p. (ps-1). 1987. PLB 11.88 (ISBN 0-688-06857-X); pap. 11.75 (ISBN 0-688-06856-1). Greenwillow.
—Goodnight, Goodnight. LC 79-17253. (Illus.). (ps-1). 1980. 13.95 (ISBN 0-688-80254-0); PLB 13.88 (ISBN 0-688-84254-2). Greenwillow.
—Oh, Lewis! Rice, Eve, illus. LC 73-19057. 32p. (ps-k). 1987. PLB 12.95 (ISBN 0-02-775990-3). Macmillan.
—Sam Who Never Forgets. LC 76-30370. (ps-3). 1987. pap. 3.95 (ISBN 0-688-07335-2, Mulberry). Morrow.
Rice, Melanie & Rice, Chris. All About Me. Smith, Lesley, illus. LC 87-15498. 48p. (ps-3). 1988. PLB 11.99 (ISBN 0-385-24282-4); pap. 10.95 (ISBN 0-385-24281-6). Doubleday.
Richard Scarry's Splish-Splash Sounds. (Illus.). (gr. k-9). 1988. pap. 1.50 (ISBN 0-318-36478-6). Scholastic Inc.
Richardson, Gale T. Serenity, Courage & Wisdom. 2p. (ps). 1989. 3.50 (ISBN 0-9614337-2-8). Poetry Unltd.
Richardson, Jean. Thomas's Sitter. Holmes, Dawn, illus. LC 90-13799. 32p. (ps-1). 1991. SBE 13.95 (ISBN 0-02-776146-0, Four Winds). Macmillan Child Grp.
Richardson, Judith B. The Way Home. Mavor, Salley, illus. LC 88-35951. 32p. (ps-1). 1991. RSBE 13.95 (ISBN 0-02-776145-2, Mcmillan Child Bk). Macmillan Child Grp.
Richardson, Lee. Sophie's Surprise. 2nd ed. Holt, Shirley, illus. 28p. (gr. 3-8). 1984. 16.95 (ISBN 0-9613476-0-0). Shirlee.
Richmond, Gary. Howard the Horrible Gets Even. 32p. 1990. write for info. (ISBN 0-8499-0744-6). Word Bks.
Ricklen, Neil. Baby's ABC. 1990. 4.95 (ISBN 0-671-69540-1). S&S Trade.
—Babys Big & Little. 1990. 4.95 (ISBN 0-671-69542-8). S&S Trade.
—Baby's Colors. 1990. 4.95 (ISBN 0-671-69539-8). S&S Trade.
—Baby's 1-2-3. 1990. 4.95 (ISBN 0-671-69541-X). S&S Trade.
Ricklin, Neil. Baby's Friends. 1986. 4.95 (ISBN 0-671-62076-2). S&S Trade.
—Baby's Toys. 1986. 4.95 (ISBN 0-671-62078-9). S&S Trade.
Ricklin, Neil, photos by. Daddy & Me. (Illus.). 28p. (ps). 1988. 4.95 (ISBN 0-671-64537-4). S&S Trade.
—Grandma & Me. (Illus.). 28p. (ps-k). 1988. 4.95 (ISBN 0-671-64540-4). S&S Trade.
—Grandpa & Me. (Illus.). 28p. (ps-k). 1988. 4.95 (ISBN 0-671-64539-0). S&S Trade.
—Mommy & Me. (Illus.). 28p. (ps-k). 1988. 4.95 (ISBN 0-671-64538-2). S&S Trade.
Riddell, Chris. The Trouble with Elephants. Riddell, Chris, illus. LC 87-24963. 32p. (ps-2). 1990. pap. 4.95 (ISBN 0-06-443170-3, Trophy). HarpC Child Bks.
Riddell, Edwina. My First Animal Word Book. (Illus.). 32p. (ps). 1989. 9.95 (ISBN 0-8120-6127-6). Barron.
—One Hundred First Words. (Illus.). 32p. (ps). 1988. 8.95 (ISBN 0-8120-5786-4). Barron.
Ridgeway, Frank. Bugs Bunny in the Little Surprise. (Illus.). 24p. (ps). 1990. pap. write for info. (ISBN 0-307-11668-9, Pub. by Golden Bks). Western Pub.
Riehecky, Janet. Polka-Dot Puppy's Visitor: A Book about Opposites. Hohag, Linda, illus. LC 88-10935. 32p. (ps-2). 1988. PLB 11.97 (ISBN 0-89565-378-8); pap. 6.96 (ISBN 0-89565-502-0). Childs World.
—Polka-Dot Puppy's Walk: A Book about Sequences. Hohag, Linda, illus. LC 88-10934. 32p. (ps-2). 1988. PLB 11.97 (ISBN 0-89565-379-6); pap. 6.96 (ISBN 0-89565-501-2). Childs World.
Riggio, Anita. Wake Up, William! LC 86-25866. (Illus.). 32p. (ps-1). 1987. 12.95 (ISBN 0-689-31344-6, Atheneum Child Bk). Macmillan Child Grp.
Ringstad, Muriel. Eye of the Changer. Croly, Donald, illus. LC 83-7121. 64p. (Orig.). (gr. 4 up). 1984. pap. 9.95 (ISBN 0-88240-251-X). Alaska Northwest.
Riorden, James, retold by. Babes in the Woods. Cladecott, Randolph, illus. 32p. (ps up). 1989. incl. dust jacket 10.95 (ISBN 0-8120-5964-6). Barron.
Rippon, Penelope. My Day. LC 89-52175. (ps). 1990. 12.95 (ISBN 0-670-83459-9). Viking Child Bks.
Robbins, Ken. City-Country: A Car Trip in Photographs. LC 85-40165. (Illus.). 32p. (gr. k-12). 1985. pap. 12.95 (ISBN 0-670-80743-5). Viking Child Bks.
Roberts, Sarah. The Adventures of Grover in Outer Space. McPheeters, Neal, illus. LC 84-60188. 32p. (ps-3). 1984. pap. 1.25 (ISBN 0-394-86300-3, Pub. by BYR). Random.
Roberts, Tom. The Three Billy Goats Gruff. Jorgensen, David, illus. LC 89-32138. 32p. (gr. 1 up). 1989. 14.95 (ISBN 0-88708-117-7, Rabbit Ears); incl. cassette 19.95 (ISBN 0-88708-118-5). Picture Bk Studio.
—The Three Little Pigs. Jorgensen, David, illus. LC 89-70097. 32p. (ps up). 1989. 14.95 (ISBN 0-88708-132-0, Rabbit Ears); incl. cass. 19.95 (ISBN 0-88708-133-9). Picture Bk Studio.
Roberts, Willo D. Don't Hurt Laurie! Sanderson, Ruth, illus. LC 87-21742. 176p. (gr. 3-7). 1988. pap. 3.95 (ISBN 0-689-71206-5, Aladdin). Macmillan Child Grp.
Robins, Joan. Addie Meets Max. Truesdell, Sue, illus. LC 84-48329. 32p. (ps-2). 1988. pap. 2.95 (ISBN 0-06-444116-4, Trophy). HarpC Child Bks.
Robinson, Colin. Bye-Bye Fly. (ps-k). 1988. 9.95 (ISBN 0-318-37401-3). Random.
Robinson, Joan G. About Teddy Robinson. Robinson, Joan G., illus. 122p. (gr. 1-4). 1975. pap. 3.50 (ISBN 0-14-030752-4, Penguin Bks). Viking Penguin.
Robinson, Marlene M. Who Knows This Nose? (gr. 5-8). 1983. 10.95 (ISBN 0-396-08205-X, Putnam). Putnam Pub Group.
Robison, Caroline B. The Mouse Factory, Pt. III: Clara. (Illus.). 23p. 1988. 4.95 (ISBN 0-533-07738-9). Vantage.
Roche, P. K. Jump All the Morning. (ps-k). 1987. pap. 3.95 (ISBN 0-14-050681-0, Puffin). Puffin Bks.
Rockwell, Anne. Albert B. Cub & Zebra: An Alphabet Storybook. Rockwell, Anne, illus. LC 76-54224. 32p. (ps-1). 1987. pap. 4.95 (ISBN 0-06-443140-1, Trophy). HarpC Child Bks.
—Apples & Pumpkins. Rockwell, Lizzy, illus. LC 88-22628. 24p. (ps-1). 1989. 12.95 (ISBN 0-02-777270-5, Mcmillan Child Bk). Macmillan Child Grp.
—At Night. Rockwell, Anne, illus. LC 85-47740. 15p. (ps). 1986. 2.50 (ISBN 0-694-00076-0, Crowell Jr Bks). HarpC Child Bks.
—Bear Child's Book of Hours. Rockwell, Anne, illus. LC 86-24245. 32p. (ps-2). 1987. 7.95 (ISBN 0-694-00196-1, Crowell Jr Bks); PLB 12.89 (ISBN 0-690-04551-4). HarpC Child Bks.
—Big Wheels. Rockwell, Anne, illus. LC 85-16248. (ps-1). 1986. 12.95 (ISBN 0-525-44226-X, DCB). Dutton Child Bks.
—Bikes. Rockwell, Ann, illus. LC 86-19923. (ps-1). 1987. 11.95 (ISBN 0-525-44287-1, DCB). Dutton Child Bks.
—Handy Hank Will Fix It. Rockwell, Anne, illus. LC 87-22865. 32p. (ps-2). 1988. 13.95 (ISBN 0-8050-0697-4). H Holt & Co.
—Hugo at the Window. Rockwell, Anne, illus. LC 87-11058. 32p. (ps-k). 1988. 13.95 (ISBN 0-02-777330-2, Mcmillan Child Bk). Macmillan Child Grp.
—In Our House. Rockwell, Anne, illus. LC 85-47535. 32p. (ps-1). 1985. 7.95 (ISBN 0-694-00038-8, Crowell Jr Bks); PLB 12.89 (ISBN 0-690-04488-7). HarpC Child Bks.
—In the Morning. Rockwell, Anne, illus. LC 85-47742. 15p. (ps). 1986. 2.50 (ISBN 0-694-00078-7, Crowell Jr Bks). HarpC Child Bks.
—In the Rain. Rockwell, Anne, illus. LC 85-47743. 15p. (ps). 1986. 2.50 (ISBN 0-694-00079-5, Crowell Jr Bks). HarpC Child Bks.
—My Baby-Sitter. Rockwell, Harlow, illus. LC 85-5000. 24p. (ps-k). 1985. 8.95 (ISBN 0-02-777780-4, Mcmillan Child Bk). Macmillan Child Grp.
—My Spring Robin. Rockwell, Harlow & Rockwell, Lizzy, illus. LC 88-13333. 24p. (ps-1). 1989. 12.95 (ISBN 0-02-777611-5, Mcmillan Child Bk). Macmillan Child Grp.
—Things That Go. Rockwell, Anne, illus. LC 86-6199. (ps-1). 1986. 10.95 (ISBN 0-525-44266-9, DCB). Dutton Child Bks.
—Things That Go. (ps-3). 1991. pap. 3.95 (ISBN 0-525-44703-2, Dutton Unicorn). Puffin Bks.
—Things to Play With. Rockwell, Anne, illus. LC 87-33399. 24p. (ps-1). 1988. 11.95 (ISBN 0-525-44409-2, DCB). Dutton Child Bks.
—Trains. Rockwell, Anne, illus. LC 87-22180. 24p. (ps-1). 1988. 12.95 (ISBN 0-525-44377-0, 01063-320, DCB). Dutton Child Bks.
Rockwell, Anne & Rockwell, Harlow. Happy Birthday to Me. Rockwell, Anne & Rockwell, Harlow, illus. LC 81-3738. 24p. (ps-k). 1981. 8.95 (ISBN 0-02-777680-8, Mcmillan Child Bk). Macmillan Child Grp.
—I Play in My Room. Rockwell, Anne & Rockwell, Harlow, illus. LC 81-2634. 24p. (ps-k). 1981. 8.95 (ISBN 0-02-777670-0, Mcmillan Child Bk). Macmillan Child Grp.
Roe, Eileen. Staying with Grandma. Rogers, Jacqueline, illus. LC 87-37611. 32p. (ps-1). 1989. 12.95 (ISBN 0-02-777371-X, Bradbury Pr). Macmillan Child Grp.
Roffey, Maureen. Bathtime. Roffey, Maureen, illus. LC 88-21372. 32p. (ps). 1989. 12.95 (ISBN 0-02-777161-X, Four Winds). Macmillan Child Grp.
—Home Sweet Home. Roffey, Maureen, illus. (ps-1). 1983. 7.95 (ISBN 0-698-20595-2, Coward). Putnam Pub Group.
—I Spy at the Zoo. Roffey, Maureen, illus. LC 87-12116. 32p. (ps-2). 1988. 12.95 (ISBN 0-02-777150-4, Four Winds). Macmillan Child Grp.
—I Spy at the Zoo. Roffey, Maureen, illus. LC 88-19360. 32p. (ps-2). 1989. pap. 3.95 (ISBN 0-689-71227-8, Aladdin). Macmillan Child Grp.
—I Spy on Vacation. Roffey, Maureen, illus. LC 87-12115. 32p. (ps-2). 1988. 12.95 (ISBN 0-02-777160-1, Four Winds). Macmillan Child Grp.
—I Spy on Vacation. LC 88-19438. (Illus.). 32p. (ps-2). 1989. pap. 3.95 (ISBN 0-689-71228-6, Aladdin). Macmillan Child Grp.
—Look, There's My Hat! Roffey, Maureen, illus. LC 84-60908. 32p. (ps-2). 1985. 8.95 (ISBN 0-399-21192-6, Putnam). Putnam Pub Group.
—The Make-Your-Own Pop-up Circus. Roffey, Maureen, illus. 26p. (Orig.). (gr. k-4). 1984. pap. 7.95 (ISBN 0-698-20596-0, Coward). Putnam Pub Group.
—Mealtime. Roffey, Maureen, illus. LC 88-21347. 32p. (ps). 1989. 12.95 (ISBN 0-02-777151-2, Four Winds). Macmillan Child Grp.
Rogers, Fred. No One Can Ever Take Your Place. Sustendal, Pat, illus. LC 87-43242. 32p. (Orig.). (ps-1). 1988. lib. bdg. 5.99 (ISBN 0-394-98779-9, Random Juv). Random.
—Wishes Don't Make Things Come True. Sustendal, Pat, illus. LC 87-4447. 32p. (ps-1). 1987. (Random Juv); (Random Juv). Random.
Rogers, Jean. Runaway Mittens. Munoz, Rie, illus. LC 87-12024. 24p. (ps-3). 1988. 13.95 (ISBN 0-688-07053-1); lib. bdg. 13.88 (ISBN 0-688-07054-X). Greenwillow.
Rogers, Marion. Caribbean ABC. Roger, Marion, illus. 26p. (Orig.). (ps-1). pap. 3.50 (ISBN 0-935357-02-5). CRIC Prod.
Rogers, Paul. Somebody's Awake. Corfield, Robin B., illus. 24p. (ps-k). 1989. 10.95 (ISBN 0-689-31490-6, Atheneum Child Bk). Macmillan Child Grp.
—Somebody's Sleepy. Corfield, Robin B., illus. 24p. (ps-k). 1989. 10.95 (ISBN 0-689-31491-4, Atheneum Child Bk). Macmillan Child Grp.
Rojankovsky, Feodor. Animals on the Farm. Rojankovsky, Feodor, illus. LC 67-18586. (gr. k-3). 1967. lib. bdg. 14.99 (ISBN 0-394-91875-4). Knopf.
A Rooster Reminds Peter. (ps-2). 1988. pap. 0.79 (ISBN 1-55513-920-5, Chariot Bks). Cook.
Rose, Dorothy. I Wish That I Could Have a Pet. Oechsli, Kelly, illus. 24p. (ps-2). 1987. 2.25 (ISBN 0-671-63654-5, Little Simon). S&S Trade.
Rosen, Michael. Down at the Doctor's: The Sick Book. Blake, Quentin, illus. 24p. (gr. k-4). 1988. 10.95 (ISBN 0-13-218942-9, Little Simon). S&S Trade.
—Hard-Boiled Legs: The Breakfast Book. Blake, Quentin, illus. (gr. k-4). 1986. 10.95 (ISBN 0-13-383746-7). P-H.
—Quick, Let's Get out of Here. Blake, Quentin, illus. 96p. (gr. k-5). 1984. 10.95 (ISBN 0-233-97559-4). Andre Deutsch.
—We're Going on a Bear Hunt. Oxenbury, Helen, illus. LC 88-13338. 40p. (ps-4). 1989. 14.95 (ISBN 0-689-50476-4, M K McElderry). Macmillan Child Grp.
Rosenberg, Amye, illus. The Pudgy Peek-a-Boo Book. 16p. (ps). 1983. pap. 2.95 (ISBN 0-448-10205-6, G&D). Putnam Pub Group.
Rosenblatt, Arthur S. The Care Bears Battle the Freeze Machine. Ewers, Joe, illus. 40p. (ps-3). 1984. 5.95 (ISBN 0-910313-15-6). Parker Bros.
—Runners to the Rescue. Ewers, Joe, illus. 40p. (ps-3). write for info (ISBN 0-910313-76-8). Parker Bros.
—Strawberry Shortcake & the Deep, Dark Woods. Sustendal, Pat, illus. 40p. (ps-3). 1983. cancelled 5.95 (ISBN 0-910313-07-5). Parker Bros.
Rosenkrans, B. Things I Love the Most. Costa, Nicoletta, illus. 24p. (gr. k-1). 1985. 6.95 (ISBN 0-448-01458-0, G&D). Putnam Pub Group.
Rosner, Ruth. Arabba, Gah, Zee, Marissa & Me! Fay, Ann, ed. Rosner, Ruth, illus. 32p. (ps-3). 1987. PLB 12.95 (ISBN 0-8075-0442-4). A Whitman.
Ross, Andrea. Oscar Crab & Rallo Car. LC 86-72872. 64p. (Orig.). (ps-2). 1987. pap. 5.00 (ISBN 0-916383-18-0). Aegina Pr.
Ross, Dave. Baby Hugs. Ross, Dave, illus. LC 87-498. 32p. (ps up). 1987. 6.95 (ISBN 0-694-00221-6, Crowell Jr Bks); PLB 12.89 (ISBN 0-690-04639-1). HarpC Child Bks.
Ross, K. K. Cozy in the Woods. Dyer, Jane, illus. LC 88-63931. 28p. (ps). 1990. 2.95 (ISBN 0-394-85400-4). Random.
Ross, Katharine. Can You Say Dinosaur: Book & Puzzle Set. Santoro, Christopher, illus. 24p. (ps-4). 1989. bds. 5.95 book & puzzle (ISBN 0-394-89957-1). Random.
—My Favorite Things Book & Puzzle Set: Blue Ladder Books for Babies Through 16 Months. Harte, Cheryl, illus. 14p. (ps). 1988. bds. 5.95 book & puzzle set (ISBN 0-394-89190-2, Random Juv). Random.
—Sweetie & Petie: (Just Right for 3's & 4's) McCue, Lisa, illus. LC 87-35434. 32p. (ps). 1988. (Random Juv); lib. bdg. 5.99 (ISBN 0-394-99864-2, Random Juv). Random.
—When You Were a Baby: Yellow Ladder Books for Toddlers Through 4 Years. Dunn, Phoebe, photos by. LC 87-37464. (Illus.). 32p. (ps). 1988. (Random Juv); (Random Juv). Random.
Ross, Katherine. The Baby's Animal Party. McCue, Lisa, illus. LC 84-43117. 32p. (ps-2). 1986. 5.95 (ISBN 0-394-87355-6); lib. bdg. 6.99 (ISBN 0-394-97355-0). Random.
—The Fuzzytail Friends' Great Egg Hunt. McCue, Lisa, illus. LC 87-50812. 14p. (ps). 1988. bds. 2.95 (ISBN 0-394-89475-8, Random Juv). Random.
Ross, Marie. An Opossum Story. (Illus.). 29p. 1988. 6.95 (ISBN 0-533-07793-1). Vantage.
Ross, Tony. Lazy Jack. Ross, Tony, illus. LC 85-16180. 32p. (ps-3). 1986. 11.95 (ISBN 0-8037-0275-2). Dial Bks Young.
—Oscar Got the Blame. Ross, Tony, illus. LC 87-15543. 32p. (ps-3). 1988. 11.95 (ISBN 0-8037-0497-6); PLB 11.89 (ISBN 0-8037-0499-2). Dial Bks Young.
—This Old Man. 12p. (ps-1). 1990. pap. 9.95 (ISBN 0-689-71386-X, Aladdin). Macmillan Child Grp.
—Towser & the Funny Face. Ross, Tony, illus. 32p. (ps-1). 1987. 5.95 (ISBN 0-86264-077-6, Pub. by Anderson Pr UK). Trafalgar Sq.
—Towser & the Haunted House. Ross, Tony, illus. 32p. (ps-1). 1987. 5.95 (ISBN 0-86264-079-2, Pub. by Anderson Pr UK). Trafalgar Sq.

—Towser & the Magic Apple. Ross, Tony, illus. 32p. (ps-1). 1987. 5.95 (ISBN 0-86264-078-4, Pub. by Anderson Pr UK). Trafalgar Sq.

Roth, Harold. Babies Love a Checkup. Roth, Harold, illus. LC 85-82141. 14p. (ps). 1986. pap. 2.50 (ISBN 0-448-10683-3, G&D). Putnam Pub Group.

—Babies Love a Goodnight Hug. (Illus.). 14p. (ps-2). 1986. pap. 2.50 (ISBN 0-448-10677-9, G&D). Putnam Pub Group.

—Babies Love Autumn Days. Roth, Harold, illus. LC 85-82138. 14p. (ps). 1986. pap. 2.50 (ISBN 0-448-10680-9, G&D). Putnam Pub Group.

—Babies Love Nursery School. Roth, Harold, illus. LC 85-82140. (ps). 1986. pap. 2.50 (ISBN 0-448-10682-5, G&D). Putnam Pub Group.

—Babies Love Spring Days. (Illus.). 14p. (ps-2). 1986. pap. 2.50 (ISBN 0-448-10679-5, G&D). Putnam Pub Group.

—Babies Love Summer Days. (Illus.). 14p. (ps-2). 1986. pap. 2.50 (ISBN 0-448-10678-7, G&D). Putnam Pub Group.

—Babies Love the Playground. (Illus.). 14p. (ps-2). 1986. pap. 2.50 (ISBN 0-448-10676-0, G&D). Putnam Pub Group.

—Babies Love Winter Days. Roth, Harold, illus. LC 85-82139. 14p. (ps). 1986. pap. 2.50 (ISBN 0-448-10681-7, G&D). Putnam Pub Group.

—Let's Look All Around the Farm. Roth, Harold, photos by. (Illus.). 24p. (ps). 1988. 7.95 (ISBN 0-448-10687-6, G&D). Putnam Pub Group.

—Let's Look All Around the House. Roth, Harold, illus. 24p. (ps). 1988. 7.95 (ISBN 0-448-10685-X, G&D). Putnam Pub Group.

—Let's Look All Around the Town. Roth, Harold, illus. 24p. (ps). 1988. 7.95 (ISBN 0-448-10684-1, G&D). Putnam Pub Group.

—Let's Look for Surprises All Around. Roth, Harold, photos by. (Illus.). 24p. (ps). 1988. 7.95 (ISBN 0-448-10686-8, G&D). Putnam Pub Group.

Rottinghuis, W. Trompy, No. 3. (Illus.). 20p. (ps-1). 1989. 3.95 (ISBN 0-88625-251-2). Durkin Hayes Pub.

Rowan, Peter. Can You Get Warts from Touching Toads? Ask Dr. Pete. Blake, Quentin, illus. 112p. (gr. 3-7). 1987. lib. bdg. 9.79 (ISBN 0-671-63469-0); pap. 5.95 (ISBN 0-671-64263-4). Silver Burdett Pr.

Roy, Cal. Time Is Day. (Illus.). (gr. k-3). 1968. 9.95 (ISBN 0-8392-3065-6). Astor-Honor.

Roy, Ron. Big & Small, Short & Tall. Cherry, Lynne, illus. LC 85-19544. (gr. 1-4). 1986. 12.95 (ISBN 0-89919-355-2, Pub. by Clarion). Ticknor & Fields.

—Whose Hat Is That? Hausherr, Rosmarie, illus. LC 86-17553. 40p. (ps-2). 1987. 12.95 (ISBN 0-89919-446-X, Pub. by Clarion). Ticknor & Fields.

—Whose Shoes Are These? Hausherr, Rosmarie, photos by. LC 87-24279. (Illus.). 40p. (ps-2). 1988. 12.95 (ISBN 0-318-35963-4, Pub. by Clarion). Ticknor & Fields.

Rub-a-Dub-Dub - What's in the Tub? Share-a-Story Unit. (Illus.). 32p. (ps-2). 1987. 64.87 (ISBN 0-516-49547-X). Childrens.

Rudner, Barry. The Bumblebee & the Ram. Fahsbender, Thomas, illus. LC 89-81585. 32p. (Orig.). 1989. pap. 4.95 (ISBN 0-925928-03-8). Tiny Thought.

—The Handstand. Fahsbender, Thomas, illus. 32p. 1991. pap. 4.95 (ISBN 0-925928-05-4). Tiny Thought.

—Nonsense. Fahsbender, Thomas, illus. (gr. k-6). 1990. write for info. (ISBN 0-925928-04-6). Tiny Thought.

—Will I Still Have to Make My Bed In The Morning? (Illus.). 32p. 1991. pap. 4.95 (ISBN 0-925928-10-0). Tiny Thought.

Rumney, Donna. My Picture Book about Me. (Illus.). 20p. (ps). 1988. write for info. My Picture Bks.

Running Press Staff. The Dinosaurs Postcard Book. (Illus.). 64p. (Orig.). (gr. k up). 1987. pap. 6.95 (ISBN 0-89471-553-4). Running Pr.

Running Press Staff, ed. KIDZ Mother Goose Car Rhyme Book & Audiocassette. (Illus.). 128p. (Orig.). (gr. 1 up). 1991. incl. 60-min. audiocass. 9.95 (ISBN 1-56138-019-9). Running Pr.

Rupprecht, Maureen, illus. Cabbage Patch Kids Jumbo Activity & Coloring Book. 128p. 1984. pap. 2.50 (ISBN 0-910313-34-2). Parker Bros.

Ruschak, Lynette. Snack Attack: A Tasty Pop Up Book. Carter, David A., illus. 12p. (ps-3). 1990. pap. 8.95 (ISBN 0-671-70448-6). S&S Trade.

Russo, Marisabina. The Line-up Book. Russo, Marisabina, illus. LC 85-24907. 24p. (ps-1). 1986. 11.75 (ISBN 0-688-06204-0); PLB 11.88 (ISBN 0-688-06205-9). Greenwillow.

—Only Six More Days. LC 86-19586. (Illus.). 32p. (ps-3). 1988. 11.95 (ISBN 0-688-07071-X); lib. bdg. 11.88 (ISBN 0-688-07072-8). Greenwillow.

Rutland, Jonathan. UFOs. Full, Roger, illus. LC 87-4793. 24p. (gr. 2-5). 1987. lib. bdg. 5.99 (ISBN 0-394-99211-3, Random Juv); (BYR). Random.

Ryan, Cheli D. Hildilid's Night. Lobel, Arnold, illus. LC 86-5294. 32p. (ps-2). 1986. 12.95 (ISBN 0-02-777260-8, Mcmillan Child Bk). Macmillan Child Grp.

Ryan, Will. Double Grubby. Forsse, Ken, ed. High, David, et al, illus. 26p. (ps). 1985. incl. pre-programmed audio-cassette 9.95 (ISBN 0-934323-15-1). Alchemy Comms.

—Grundo Springtime Singtime. Forsse, Ken, ed. High, David, et al, illus. 26p. (ps). 1985. 9.95 (ISBN 0-934323-14-3); pre-programmed audio-cassette tape incl. Alchemy Comms.

—Uncle Grubby. Forsse, Ken, ed. High, David, et al, illus. 26p. (ps). 1985. 9.95 (ISBN 0-934323-20-8); audio cassette incl. Alchemy Comms.

Ryan, Will, adapted by. The Grasshopper & the Ant: An Aesop Fable. Hicks, Russell, et al, illus. 26p. (ps). 1987. Packaged with pre-programmed audio cass. tape. 9.95 (ISBN 0-934323-62-3). Alchemy Comms.

Ryder, Joanne. Under the Moon: Just Right for 3's & 4's. Harness, Cheryl, illus. LC 88-11512. 32p. (ps). 1989. 4.95 (ISBN 0-394-81960-8); PLB 5.99 (ISBN 0-394-91960-2). Random.

Rylant, Cynthia. Henry & Mudge Get the Cold Shivers: The Seventh Book of Their Adventures. Stevenson, Sucie, illus. LC 88-18854. 48p. (gr. 1-3). 1989. 11.95 (ISBN 0-02-778011-2, Bradbury Pr). Macmillan Child Grp.

—Henry & Mudge in Puddle Trouble: The Second Book of Their Adventures. Stevenson, Sucie, illus. LC 86-13616. 48p. (gr. 1-3). 1987. 11.95 (ISBN 0-02-778002-3, Bradbury Pr). Macmillan Child Grp.

—Henry & Mudge in the Green Time: The Third Book of Their Adventures. Stevenson, Sucie, illus. LC 86-26386. 48p. (gr. 1-3). 1987. 11.95 (ISBN 0-02-778003-1, Bradbury Pr). Macmillan Child Grp.

—Henry & Mudge under the Yellow Moon: The Fourth Book of Their Adventures. Stevenson, Sucie, illus. LC 86-26390. 48p. (gr. 1-3). 1987. 11.95 (ISBN 0-02-778004-X, Bradbury Pr). Macmillan Child Grp.

—Mr. Griggs' Work. Downing, Julie, illus. LC 88-1484. 32p. (ps-2). 1989. 12.95 (ISBN 0-531-05769-0); PLB 12.99 (ISBN 0-531-08369-1). Orchard Bks Watts.

Sadler, Marilyn. The Copykitty. (Illus.). 24p. (ps). 1990. pap. write for info. (ISBN 0-307-11657-3, Pub. by Golden Bks). Western Pub.

Safari Adventure. (ps-3). 1988. 8.95 (ISBN 0-8167-1444-4). Troll Assocs.

Sage, Chris. That's Mine, That's Yours. (ps). 1991. 12.95 (ISBN 0-670-83746-6). Viking Child Bks.

—The Trouble with Babies. Sage, Angie, illus. 32p. (ps-1). 1990. pap. 11.95 (ISBN 0-670-82392-9). Viking Child Bks.

St. John, Patricia. Star of Light. (gr. 5-8). 1953. pap. 4.50 (ISBN 0-8024-0004-3). Moody.

Salazar, Yolanda L. The Beestys' Journey, 20 Vols, Vol. 1. Kelley, Midorie, illus. 36p. (gr. 3 up). 1989. write for info. ADAPT Pub Co.

—The Beestys' What Color Is... Kelley, Midorie, illus. 10p. (ps). 1989. 7.95 (ISBN 0-317-94002-3). ADAPT Pub Co.

—The Beesty's What Shape Is... Kelley, Midorie, illus. 10p. (ps). 1989. 7.95 (ISBN 0-317-94001-5). ADAPT Pub Co.

—The Beestys' What Time Is... Kelley, Midorie, illus. 10p. (ps). 1989. 7.95 (ISBN 0-317-94003-1). ADAPT Pub Co.

Salter-Mathieson, Nigel. Little Chief Mischief. Gruen, Chuck, illus. (gr. 2-7). 1962. 10.95 (ISBN 0-8392-3020-6). Astor-Honor.

Saltzberg, Barney. Hi Bird, Bye Bird. (Illus.). 10p. (ps). 1989. 5.95 (ISBN 0-8120-6161-6). Barron.

—What Would You Do with a Bone? (Illus.). 10p. (ps). 1989. 5.95 (ISBN 0-8120-6162-4). Barron.

Salzman, Yuri, retold by. & illus. The Three Little Pigs. LC 87-81773. 24p. (ps-k). 1988. pap. write for info. (ISBN 0-307-10099-5, Pub. by Golden Bks). Western Pub.

Sammy Siren. 12p. (ps-1). 1989. bds. 14.95 (ISBN 0-87449-641-1). Modern Pub NYC.

Samuels, Vyanne. Carry Go Bring Come. Northway, Jennifer, illus. LC 89-1528. 32p. (ps-2). 1989. 13.95 (ISBN 0-02-778121-6, Four Winds). Macmillan Child Grp.

Sandberg, Inger. Dusty Wants to Borrow Everything. Sandberg, Lasse, illus. Maurer, Judy A., tr. (Illus.). 32p. (ps up). 1988. 6.95 (ISBN 9-12-958782-4, R & S Bks). FS&G.

Sanders, Scott R. Aurora Means Dawn. Kastner, Jill, illus. LC 88-24127. 32p. (gr. 1-5). 1989. 12.95 (ISBN 0-02-778270-0, Bradbury Pr). Macmillan Child Grp.

Sanford, Doris. Once I Was a Thief. (ps-3). 1990. 6.99 (ISBN 0-88070-347-4). Multnomah.

San Souci, Daniel, illus. The Bedtime Book. LC 85-12898. 48p. (gr. k-3). 1985. PLB 11.79. Messner.

Sara & the Shy Elephant, Freddie & the Farsighted Frog, Troy & the Tiny Mouse & Bonnie & the Floppy-Eared Bunny. (Illus.). (gr. k-2). Date not set. pap. 3.95 ea., 24pgs. ea. Sara & the Shy Elephant (ISBN 0-87449-762-0). Freddie & the Farsighted Frog (ISBN 0-87449-763-9). Troy & the Tiny Mouse (ISBN 0-87449-764-7). Bonnie & the Floppy-Eared Bunny (ISBN 0-87449-765-5). Modern Pub NYC.

Sasaki, Isao. Snow. LC 82-2659. (Illus.). 32p. (gr. 4-8). 1982. pap. 9.95 (ISBN 0-670-65364-0). Viking Child Bks.

Saunier, Nadine. The Cat. Wirth, Pascale, illus. 20p. (ps). 1988. 5.95 (ISBN 0-8120-5933-6). Barron.

—The Elephant. Raison, Isabelle, illus. 20p. (ps). 1988. 5.95 (ISBN 0-8120-5935-2). Barron.

—The Giraffe. Leduc, Anne, illus. 20p. (ps). 1988. 5.95 (ISBN 0-8120-5930-1). Barron.

—The Lion. Raison, Isabelle, illus. 20p. (ps). 1988. 5.95 (ISBN 0-8120-5934-4). Barron.

—The Panda. Geneste, Marcelle, illus. 20p. (ps). 1988. 5.95 (ISBN 0-8120-5931-X). Barron.

—The Rabbit. Geneste, Marcelle, illus. 20p. (ps). 1988. 5.95 (ISBN 0-8120-5932-8). Barron.

Sawyer, Ruth. Roller Skates. Angelo, Valenti, illus. 192p. (gr. 4-7). 1969. pap. 1.50 (ISBN 0-440-47499-X, YB). Dell.

Say, Allen. A River Dream. Say, Allen, illus. 32p. (gr. k-3). 1988. 14.95 (ISBN 0-395-48294-1). HM.

Scarry, Huck, illus. My First Picture Dictionary. LC 76-24174. (ps-2). 1978. lib. bdg. 5.99 (ISBN 0-394-93486-5, Random Juv); pap. 2.25 (ISBN 0-394-83486-0). Random.

Scarry, Patsy. Patsy Scarry's Big Bedtime Storybook. Saekeres, Cyndy, illus. LC 79-5450. 72p. (ps-1). 1990. pap. 9.95 (ISBN 0-679-80756-X). Random.

Scarry, Richard. The Best Mistake Ever! A Step Two Book. Scarry, Richard, illus. LC 84-2029. 48p. (ps-2). 1984. lib. bdg. 6.99 (ISBN 0-394-96816-6, Pub. by BYR); pap. 2.95 (ISBN 0-394-86816-1). Random.

—The Bunny Book. (Illus.). 24p. (ps-k). 1987. pap. write for info (ISBN 0-307-10048-0, Pub. by Golden Bks). Western Pub.

—I Am a Bunny. Scarry, Richard, illus. 22p. (gr. k-2). 1967. write for info. (ISBN 0-307-12125-9, Golden Bks.). Western Pub.

—Pig Will - Pig Won't. Scarry, Richard, illus. 9p. (ps). 1990. bds. 4.95 (ISBN 0-679-80067-0). Random.

—Richard Scarry's ABC's. Scarry, Richard, illus. (ps-k). 1991. pap. 1.25 (ISBN 0-307-11515-1, Golden Pr). Western Pub.

—Richard Scarry's All about Cars. (Illus.). 12p. (ps). 1989. bds. write for info. (ISBN 0-307-06103-5, Pub. by Golden Bks). Western Pub.

—Richard Scarry's Bedtime Stories. reissue ed. LC 86-484. (Illus.). 32p. (ps-1). 1989. pap. 1.95 (ISBN 0-394-88269-5). Random.

—Richard Scarry's Best Busy Year Ever. Scarry, Richard, illus. (ps-1). 1991. 5.25 (ISBN 0-307-15748-2, Golden Pr). Western Pub.

—Richard Scarry's Best Friend Ever. (Illus.). 24p. (ps-k). 1989. pap. write for info. (ISBN 0-307-11715-4, Pub. by Golden Bks). Western Pub.

—Richard Scarry's Best Word Book Ever. Scarry, Richard, illus. (ps-3). 1963. write for info. (ISBN 0-307-15510-2, Golden Bks). Western Pub.

—Richard Scarry's Busy Busy World. Scarry, Richard, illus. (gr. k-5). write for info. (ISBN 0-307-15511-0, Golden Bks). Western Pub.

—Richard Scarry's Counting Book. (Illus.). 24p. (ps). 1990. pap. write for info. (ISBN 0-307-11659-X, Pub. by Golden Bks). Western Pub.

—Richard Scarry's Great Big Air Book. Scarry, Richard, illus. LC 79-146649. (gr. k-3). 1971. 8.95 (ISBN 0-394-82167-X, Random Juv). Random.

—Richard Scarry's Great Big Schoolhouse. Scarry, Richard, illus. (ps-2). 1969. 8.95 (ISBN 0-394-80874-6, Random Juv). Random.

—Richard Scarry's Just Right Word Book: (Just Right for 2's & 3's) Scarry, Richard, illus. LC 89-42839. 24p. (ps). 1990. 4.95 (ISBN 0-679-80073-5). McKay.

—Richard Scarry's Lowly Worm's Schoolbag, 4 bks. Scarry, Richard, illus. 18p. (ps-k). 1987. (Random Juv); Lowly Learns about Colors. write for info. (ISBN 0-394-87873-6); Lowly Learns His ABC's. write for info. (ISBN 0-394-87874-4); Lowly Learns to Count. write for info. (ISBN 0-394-87875-2); Lowly Learns Words. write for info. (ISBN 0-394-87872-8). Random.

—Richard Scarry's Splish-Splash Sounds. Scarry, Richard, illus. 24p. (Orig.). (ps-3). 1988. pap. write for info. (ISBN 0-307-13964-6). Western Pub.

—Richard Scarry's Things That Go. Scarry, Richard, illus. 24p. (ps-3). 1987. write for info. (ISBN 0-307-11817-7, Pub. by Golden Bks). Western Pub.

Scarry, Richard, illus. Richard Scarry's Little Miss Muffet & Other Rhymes. LC 88-80232. 12p. (ps). 1988. write for info. (ISBN 0-307-06101-9). Western Pub.

—Richard Scarry's Simple Simon & Other Rhymes. LC 88-80233. 12p. (ps). 1988. write for info. (ISBN 0-307-06102-7). Western Pub.

Scary! Spooky! 32p. 1989. pap. 1.95 (ISBN 0-317-91022-1). Tor Bks.

Schatell, Brian. The McGoonys Have a Party. Schatell, Brian, illus. LC 85-40095. 32p. (gr. k-3). 1985. PLB 12.89 (ISBN 0-685-10299-8, Lipp Jr Bks); PLB 12.89 (ISBN 0-397-32124-4). HarpC Child Bks.

Scheer, Julian. Rain Makes Applesauce. Bileck, Marvin, illus. 36p. (gr. k-3). 1964. 14.95 (ISBN 0-8234-0091-3). Holiday.

Scheffler, Ursel. Stop Your Crowing, Kasimir! Brix-Henker, Silke, illus. 32p. (gr. k-3). 1988. lib. bdg. 12.95 (ISBN 0-87614-323-0). Carolrhoda Bks.

Scheidl, Gerda M. Flowers for the Snowman. Lanning, Rosemary, tr. Wilkon, Jozef, illus. LC 88-42532. 32p. (gr. k-3). 1988. 12.95 (ISBN 1-55858-068-9). North-South Bks NYC.

Schmidt, Karen L., illus. My First Book of Baby Animals. LC 85-62639. 12p. (ps). 1986. 3.95 (ISBN 0-448-10826-7, Platt & Munk). Putnam Pub Group.

Schneider, Erika, illus. The Twelve Days of Christmas. LC 84-9489. 12p. (gr. 1 up). 1984. 4.95 (ISBN 0-907234-62-3). Picture Bk Studio.

Schneider, Howie & Seligson, Susan. Amos: The Story of an Old Dog & His Couch. Schneider, Howie, illus. LC 87-2813. 32p. (ps-3). 1987. 13.95 (ISBN 0-316-77404-9). Little.

Schneidewind, Barbara F. Mali Lelani & Bo: Of Treedle-dee-dees & Rocks Called Joe. 1989. 6.95 (ISBN 0-533-08309-5). Vantage.

Schoepfer, G. R. River of Miracles. Schoepfer, Virginia B., ed. Brenes, Irma M., illus. (gr. 1-11). 1978. pap. text ed. 2.75x (ISBN 0-931436-01-X, Children's Books). G R Schoepfer.
Schongut, Emanuel. Catch Kitten. Klimo, Kate, ed. Schongut, Emanuel, illus. 14p. (ps-k). 1983. 3.95 (ISBN 0-671-46382-9, Little Simon). S&S Trade.
—Hush Kitten. Klimo, Kate, ed. Schongut, Emanuel, illus. 14p. 1983. 3.95 (ISBN 0-671-46386-1, Little Simon). S&S Trade.
School. (Illus.). (ps-k). 3.95 (ISBN 0-7214-5160-8). Ladybird Bks.
Schoolhouse. 8p. (ps). 1990. bds. 2.95 (ISBN 0-671-49717-0, Little Simon). S&S Trade.
Schoop, Janice. Boys Don't Knit. Beingessner, Laura, illus. 30p. (ps-3). 1988. pap. 4.95 (ISBN 0-86543-077-2). Africa World.
Schroeder, Ruth. The Adventure of Fifi's Honey Bee Bears & the Big Bee Hive. Dixon, David, illus. 28p. (gr. k-5). 1987. PLB 8.95 (ISBN 0-935087-24-9). R & D Bks.
Schubert, Dieter. Where's My Monkey. LC 86-16578. (Illus.). 32p. (ps-2). 1987. 10.95 (ISBN 0-8037-0069-5). Dial Bks Young.
Schulthess, Daniele, illus. Hello, Words! 48p. (ps-3). 1989. 9.95 (ISBN 0-8120-5788-0). Barron.
Schulz, Charles M. Happy Halloween, Snoopy! (Illus.). 24p. (ps-3). 1989. pap. write for info. (ISBN 0-307-11974-2, Pub. by Golden Bks). Western Pub.
Schumacher, Claire. Tommy the Winner. Schumacher, Claire, illus. LC 90-38437. 40p. (ps-1). 1991. 13.95 (ISBN 0-06-026904-9); PLB 13.89 (ISBN 0-06-026905-7). HarpC Child Bks.
Schwartz, Alvin. In a Dark, Dark Room. LC 83-47699. (Illus.). 64p. (gr. k-3). 1986. incl. cassette 5.98 (ISBN 0-694-00163-5, Trophy); pap. 3.50 (ISBN 0-06-444090-7, Trophy). HarpC Child Bks.
—Ten Copycats in a Boat & Other Riddles. Simont, Marc, illus. LC 79-2811. 64p. (gr. k-3). 1985. pap. 3.50 (ISBN 0-06-444076-1, Trophy). HarpC Child Bks.
Schwartz, Amy. Bea & Mr. Jones. Schwartz, Amy, illus. LC 81-18041. 32p. (ps-2). 1982. 11.95 (ISBN 0-02-781430-0, Bradbury Pr). Macmillan Child Grp.
—Begin at the Beginning. Scwartz, Amy, illus. LC 82-48257. 32p. (gr. k-3). 1984. pap. 3.50 (ISBN 0-06-443060-X, Trophy). HarpC Child Bks.
Schwartz, David M. How Much Is a Million? Kellogg, Stephen, illus. 40p. (gr. k-3). 1987. Big Book. 19.50 (ISBN 0-590-71767-7). Scholastic Inc.
—How Much Is a Million? Kellogg, Stephen, illus. 40p. (gr. 1-4). 1986. pap. 3.95 (ISBN 0-590-43614-7). Scholastic Inc.
Schwartz, Henry. How I Captured a Dinosaur. Schwartz, Amy, illus. LC 88-1482. 32p. (ps-2). 1989. 12.95 (ISBN 0-531-05770-4); PLB 12.99 (ISBN 0-531-08370-5). Orchard Bks Watts.
Schweninger, Ann. Off to School! (Illus.). 32p. (ps-3). 1989. pap. 3.95 (ISBN 0-14-050661-6, Puffin). Puffin Bks.
—Valentine Friends. LC 87-22326. 32p. (ps-1). 1988. pap. 10.95 (ISBN 0-670-81448-2). Viking Child Bks.
Sclavi, Tiziano. The Planet Putipoo. Lagana, Giuseppe, illus. 16p. 1989. 8.95 (ISBN 0-8120-5997-2). Barron.
Scott, Ann H. Sam. Shimin, Symeon, illus. (ps-3). 1967. text ed. 14.95 (ISBN 0-07-055803-5). McGraw.
—Someday Rider. Himler, Ronald, illus. LC 88-35255. 32p. (ps-1). 1989. 13.95 (ISBN 0-89919-792-2, Clarion Bks). HM.
Scribner, Toni, illus. The Glo Friends' Good Night Book. LC 85-60757. 28p. (ps). 1986. 2.95 (ISBN 0-394-87797-7). Random.
—Where's Baby? LC 86-43148. 14p. (ps). 1987. bds. 2.95 (ISBN 0-394-89071-X, Random Juv). Random.
Seablom, Seth H. Seattle Coloring Guide. Seablom, Seth H., illus. (gr. 4-6). 1977. pap. 2.50 (ISBN 0-918800-01-3). Seablom.
Seaman, Rosie. Discovering Plants & Animals. (ps-k). 1987. pap. 5.95 (ISBN 0-8224-1928-9). Fearon Teach Aids.
Segal, Lore. All the Way Home. Marshall, James, illus. LC 73-82699. 32p. (ps-3). 1973. 8.95 (ISBN 0-374-30215-4). FS&G.
—All the Way Home. Marshall, James, illus. 32p. (ps up). 1988. pap. 3.95 (ISBN 0-374-40355-4). FS&G.
Seiden, Art, illus. Trucks. (ps). 1983. 3.95 (ISBN 0-448-40873-2, G&D). Putnam Pub Group.
Selman, LaRue. Boots, Two. Jordan, Alton, ed. (Illus.). (gr. k-3). 1981. PLB 7.95 (ISBN 0-89868-094-8, Read Res); pap. text ed. 2.95 (ISBN 0-89868-105-7). ARO Pub.
Selsam, Millicent E. & Hunt, Joyce. Keep Looking! Chartier, Normand, illus. LC 88-1416. 32p. (gr. k-3). 1989. 14.95 (ISBN 0-02-781840-3, Mcmillan Child Bk). Macmillan Child Grp.
Sendak, Maurice. Alligators All Around: An Alphabet. Sendak, Maurice, illus. LC 62-13315. 32p. (ps-3). 1991. pap. 2.95 (ISBN 0-06-443254-8, Trophy). HarpC Child Bks.
—Chicken Soup with Rice. Sendak, Maurice, illus. 32p. (gr. k-3). 1986. Big book. 19.50 (ISBN 0-685-11908-4); pap. 2.50 (ISBN 0-590-41033-4). Scholastic Inc.
—Chicken Soup with Rice: A Book of Months. Sendak, Maurice, illus. LC 62-13315. 32p. (ps-3). 1991. pap. 2.95 (ISBN 0-06-443253-X, Trophy). HarpC Child Bks.
—Hector Protector & As I Went over the Water: Two Nursery Rhymes. Sendak, Maurice, illus. LC 65-21388. 64p. (ps-1). 1990. pap. 5.95 (ISBN 0-06-443237-8, Trophy). HarpC Child Bks.
—Higglety Pigglety Pop! Or There Must be More to Life. LC 67-18553. (Illus.). 80p. (gr. k-4). 1979. pap. 5.95 (ISBN 0-06-443021-9, Trophy). HarpC Child Bks.
—In the Night Kitchen. Sendak, Maurice, illus. LC 70-105483. 48p. (ps-3). 1970. 14.95 (ISBN 0-06-025489-0); PLB 14.89 (ISBN 0-06-025490-4). HarpC Child Bks.
—In the Night Kitchen. Sendak, Maurice, illus. LC 70-105483. 48p. (ps-3). 1985. pap. 4.95 (ISBN 0-06-443086-3, Trophy). HarpC Child Bks.
—Kenny's Window. LC 56-5148. (Illus.). 64p. (gr. k-3). 1956. 12.95 (ISBN 0-06-025494-7); PLB 11.89 (ISBN 0-06-025495-5). HarpC Child Bks.
—Maurice Sendak's Really Rosie. (Illus.). 48p. (gr. k-4). 1986. pap. 8.95 (ISBN 0-06-443138-X, Trophy). HarpC Child Bks.
—Outside over There. Sendak, Maurice, illus. LC 79-2682. 40p. (ps up). 1989. pap. 7.95 (ISBN 0-06-443185-1, Trophy). HarpC Child Bks.
—Pierre: A Cautionary Tale. Sendak, Maurice, illus. LC 62-13315. 48p. (ps-3). 1991. pap. 2.95 (ISBN 0-06-443252-1, Trophy). HarpC Child Bks.
—Pierre: A Cautionary Tale in Five Chapters & a Prologue. Sendak, Maurice, illus. 48p. (ps-3). 1962. PLB 12.89 (ISBN 0-06-025965-5). HarpC Child Bks.
—Sign on Rosie's Door. Sendak, Maurice, illus. LC 60-9451. 48p. (gr. k-3). 1960. 12.95 (ISBN 0-06-025505-6); PLB 12.89 (ISBN 0-06-025506-4). HarpC Child Bks.
—Very Far Away. Sendak, Maurice, illus. LC 57-5356. (gr. k-3). 1962. 11.95 (ISBN 0-06-025514-5); PLB 11.89 (ISBN 0-06-025515-3). HarpC Child Bks.
—Where the Wild Things Are. new ed. Sendak, Maurice, illus. LC 63-21253. 48p. (ps up). 1988. pap. 4.95 (ISBN 0-06-443178-9, Trophy). HarpC Child Bks.
Serfozo, Mary. Who Said Red? Narahashi, Keiko, illus. LC 88-9345. 32p. (ps-1). 1988. PLB 12.95 (ISBN 0-689-50455-1, M K McElderry). Macmillan Child Grp.
—Who Wants One? Narahashi, Keiko, illus. LC 88-26614. 32p. (ps-1). 1989. 12.95 (ISBN 0-689-50474-8, M K McElderry). Macmillan Child Grp.
Sesame Street A-Z. 32p. (Orig.). (ps). wkbk. 4.95 (ISBN 0-8431-3113-6). Price Stern.
Sesame Street Book 'n' Tape Gift Pack. (ps-3). 1989. write for info. incl. 3 cassettes (ISBN 0-307-13939-5, 13939, Pub. by Golden Bks). Western Pub.
Sesame Street Editors. The Sesame Street ABC Book of Words. McNaught, Harry, illus. LC 86-62405. 48p. (ps-k). 1988. (Random Juv); pap. 10.95 (ISBN 0-394-88880-4). Random.
Sesame Street Favorites. (ps-3). 1990. write for info. (ISBN 0-307-15537-4). Western Pub.
Sesame Street Little Golden Books, 6 bks. (ps-1). 1978. Set. write for info (ISBN 0-307-15518-8, Golden Bks). Western Pub.
Sesame Street Staff. Ernie & Bert Can...Can You. Smollin, Michael J., illus. LC 81-83696. 28p. (ps). 1982. 2.95 (ISBN 0-394-85150-1). Random.
—Sesame Street Mix or Match Storybook. Mathieu, Joe, illus. LC 77-70853. (ps-1). 1977. bds. 3.50 (ISBN 0-394-83547-6, Random Juv). Random.
Sesame Street 1-10. 32p. (Orig.). (ps). wkbk. 4.95 (ISBN 0-8431-3106-3). Price Stern.
Sewall, Marcia. Animal Song. Sewall, Marcia, illus. LC 87-4092. (ps-1). 1988. 14.95 (ISBN 0-316-78191-6, Joy Street Bks). Little.
Seymour, Peter. Baby Animals at Play. (ps-3). 1983. 5.95 (ISBN 0-531-02192-0). Watts.
—If Pigs Could Fly: A Pop-Up Book. (Illus.). 12p. 1989. 7.95 (ISBN 0-8431-2411-3). Price Stern.
—What's in the Jungle. Carter, David A., illus. LC 87-81818. 18p. (ps-k). 1988. 10.95 (ISBN 0-8050-0688-5). H Holt & Co.
Shannon, George. Dancing the Breeze. Rogers, Jacqueline, illus. LC 88-37598. 32p. (ps-1). 1991. RSBE 13.95 (ISBN 0-02-782190-0, Bradbury Pr). Macmillan Child Grp.
Shapes. (Illus.). 12p. (gr. k-2). 1982. bds. 3.95 (ISBN 0-87449-179-7). Modern Pub NYC.
Shapes: Kiddy Big Book. (ps up). 1990. PLB 4.98 (ISBN 0-7924-5196-1, Mallard Pr). BDD Promo Bk.
Shapiro, Arnold. Could I Keep Him? Paris, Pat, illus. 14p. (ps-k). 1990. 12.95 (ISBN 0-8120-4492-4). Barron.
—Pop up House on Main Street. 1989. 4.95 (ISBN 0-671-67553-2). S&S Trade.
Shapiro, Mary S. My Playbook, One, Bk. 4. 01/1986 ed. Hinchberger, William D., illus. 12p. (ps-k). wkbk 3.50x (ISBN 0-934361-04-5). Kinder Read.
—Play. Wisniewski, Dennis, photos by. (Illus.). 14p. (ps-k). 1985. 3.50 (ISBN 0-934361-02-9); Set. write for info. Kinder Read.
—Red, Green, Yellow. Hron, Debi, illus. 12p. (ps-k). 1985. 3.50 (ISBN 0-934361-01-0); Set. write for info. Kinder Read.
—Stop, Start. Hron, Debi, illus. 14p. (ps-k). 1985. 3.50 (ISBN 0-934361-03-7); Set. write for info. (ISBN 0-934361-00-2). Kinder Read.
Sharks-Sticker Book. 1989. pap. 2.25 (ISBN 0-89954-129-1). Antioch Pub Co.
Sharmat, Andrew. Smedge. Demarest, Chris L., illus. LC 88-13733. 32p. (ps-3). 1989. 13.95 (ISBN 0-02-782261-3, Mcmillan Child Bk). Macmillan Child Grp.
Sharmat, Marjorie. My Mother Never Listens to Me. Tucker, Kathleen, ed. Munsinger, Lynn, illus. LC 84-17201. 32p. (ps-3). 1984. 10.95 (ISBN 0-8075-5347-6). A Whitman.
Sharmat, Marjorie W. Goodnight, Andrew, Goodnight, Craig. Chalmers, Mary, illus. LC 69-10205. 32p. (ps-3). 1969. PLB 11.89 (ISBN 0-06-025548-X). HarpC Child Bks.
—A Hot Thirsty Day. Wells, Rosemary, illus. LC 86-3478. 32p. (gr. 1-4). 1986. pap. 3.95 (ISBN 0-689-71079-8, Aladdin). Macmillan Child Grp.
—Nate the Great Goes Down. (ps-3). 1991. pap. 2.95 (ISBN 0-440-40438-X). Dell.
Shaw, Charles G. It Looked Like Spilt Milk. Shaw, Charles G., illus. LC 47-30767. 30p. (ps-2). 1947. 11.95 (ISBN 0-06-025566-8); PLB 12.89 (ISBN 0-06-025565-X). HarpC Child Bks.
—It Looked Like Spilt Milk. Shaw, Charles G., illus. LC 47-30767. 32p. (ps-2). 1988. pap. 3.95 (ISBN 0-06-443159-2, Trophy). HarpC Child Bks.
—It Looked Like Spilt Milk. Shaw, Charles G., illus. (ps-2). 1988. pap. 19.95 incl. cassette (ISBN 0-87499-110-2); bk. & cassette 12.95 (ISBN 0-87499-109-9); 4 cassettes & guide 27.95 (ISBN 0-87499-111-0). Live Oak Media.
Shaw, Nancy. Sheep in a Jeep. Apple, Margot, illus. 32p. (ps-k). 1988. pap. 3.95 (ISBN 0-395-47030-7, Sandpiper). HM.
Shearer, Marilyn J. The Adventures of Curious Eric: Learning Concepts. Roberts, Tom, illus. LC 90-60397. 16p. (ps-6). 1990. 19.95 (ISBN 0-685-33064-8); pap. 10.95 (ISBN 1-878389-01-7). L Ashley & Joshua.
Sheldon, Dyan. I Forgot. Rogan, John, illus. LC 87-14850. 32p. (ps-2). 1988. 12.95 (ISBN 0-02-782471-3, Four Winds). Macmillan Child Grp.
—I Forgot. Rogan, John, illus. LC 88-19440. 32p. (ps-2). 1989. pap. 3.95 (ISBN 0-689-71211-1, Aladdin). Macmillan Child Grp.
Shepperson, Bob. The Sandman. Shepperson, Bob, illus. 32p. (ps-3). 1990. 12.95 (ISBN 0-374-36405-2); pap. 4.95 (ISBN 0-374-46450-2). FS&G.
Shine, Deborah. The Little Engine That Could Pudgy Word Book. Ong, Christina, illus. 18p. (ps). 1988. bds. 2.95 (ISBN 0-448-19054-0, G&D). Putnam Pub Group.
—The Pudgy I Love You Book. Coville, Katherine D., illus. 18p. (ps). 1988. bds. 2.95 (ISBN 0-448-19056-7, G&D). Putnam Pub Group.
—The Pudgy Noisy Book. McCord, Kathleen G., illus. 18p. (ps). 1988. bds. 2.95 (ISBN 0-448-19055-9, G&D). Putnam Pub Group.
Shorto, Russell & Cwiklik, Robert. A Baseball Bat. LC 88-19356. (Illus.). 24p. (Orig.). 1988. pap. 6.95 (ISBN 0-8092-4468-3, Calico Bks). Contemp Bks.
—A Crayon. LC 88-19325. (Illus.). 24p. (Orig.). 1988. pap. 6.95 (ISBN 0-8092-4467-5, Calico Bks). Contemp Bks.
—Ice Cream. LC 88-17761. (Illus.). 24p. (Orig.). 1988. pap. 6.95 (ISBN 0-8092-4466-7, Calico Bks). Contemp Bks.
—A Penny. LC 88-19320. (Illus.). 24p. (Orig.). 1988. pap 6.95 (ISBN 0-8092-4469-1, Calico Bks). Contemp Bks.
Showers, Paul. A Baby Starts to Grow. Fry, Rosalind, illus. LC 85-43024. 40p. (ps-3). 1986. pap. 4.50 (ISBN 0-06-445044-9, Trophy). HarpC Child Bks.
—A Drop of Blood. rev. ed. Madden, Paul, illus. LC 85-43021. 32p. (gr. k-4). 1989. pap. 4.50 (ISBN 0-06-445090-2, Trophy). HarpC Child Bks.
—What Happens to a Hamburger. rev. ed. Rockwell, Anne, illus. LC 84-48784. 32p. (gr. k-3). 1985. pap. 4.50 (ISBN 0-06-445013-9, Trophy). HarpC Child Bks.
—Your Skin & Mine. Galdone, Paul, illus. LC 85-43022. 40p. (ps-3). 1985. pap. 4.50 (ISBN 0-06-445045-7, Trophy). HarpC Child Bks.
Shulevitz, Uri. Dawn. Shulevitz, Uri, illus. 32p. (ps up). 1988. 4.95 (ISBN 0-374-41689-3). FS&G.
—One Monday Morning. Shulevitz, Uri, illus. LC 66-24483. (gr. k-3). 1974. 14.95 (ISBN 0-684-13195-1, Scribners Young Read). Macmillan Child Grp.
—Rain Rain Rivers. (Illus.). 32p. 1988. pap. 3.95 (ISBN 0-374-46195-3). FS&G.
Sibbett, Ed. American Indian Cut & Use Stencils. pap. 4.95 (ISBN 0-486-24183-1). Dover.
—Cut & Make Christmas Decorations. 1985. pap. 3.95 (ISBN 0-486-24912-3). Dover.
—Decorative Americana Cut & Use Stencils. 1985. pap. 4.95 (ISBN 0-486-24970-0). Dover.
—Decorative Cut & Use Stencils. 1988. pap. 4.95 (ISBN 0-486-23880-6). Dover.
—Holidays & Special Occasions, Cut & Use Stencils. 1986. pap. 4.95 (ISBN 0-486-25052-0). Dover.
—Messages & Greetings Cut & Use Stencils. 1985. pap. 4.95 (ISBN 0-486-24965-4). Dover.
Sibbick, John, illus. Creatures of Long Ago: Dinosaurs, No. 1. (gr. k-3). 1989. 19.95 (ISBN 0-87044-723-8). Natl Geog.
Sibley, Brian. Pooh Sketchbook. (Illus.). 96p. (gr. 5up). 1984. 11.95 (ISBN 0-525-44084-4, Dutton). NAL-Dutton.
Siebert, Diane. Mojave. Minor, Wendell, illus. LC 86-24329. 32p. (ps up). 1988. 14.95 (ISBN 0-690-04567-0, Crowell Jr Bks); PLB 14.89 (ISBN 0-690-04569-7, Crowell Jr Bks). HarpC Child Bks.
—Truck Song. LC 83-46173. (Illus.). 32p. (ps-3). 1987. pap. 4.95 (ISBN 0-06-443134-7, Trophy). HarpC Child Bks.

—Truck Song. Barton, Byron, illus. (gr. k-3). 1988. bk. & cassette 19.95 (ISBN 0-87499-093-9); bk. & cassette 12.95 (ISBN 0-87499-092-0); 4 cassettes & guide 27. 95 (ISBN 0-87499-094-7). Live Oak Media.
Silbert, Linda P. & Silbert, Alvin J. My Own Book of Wishes. (Illus.). (gr. k-6). 1976. wkbk. 4.98 (ISBN 0-89544-016-4). Silbert Bress.
Silverman, Erica. Warm in Winter. Deraney, Michael J., illus. LC 88-22691. 32p. (gr. k-3). 1989. 13.95 (ISBN 0-02-782661-9, Mcmillan Child Bk). Macmillan Child Grp.
Silverman, Maida. Baby's First Body Book. Kramer, Robin, illus. (ps-1). 1987. 3.95 (ISBN 0-448-10554-3, G&D). Putnam Pub Group.
—Baby's First Finger Rhymes. Miller, Susan, illus. (ps-1). 1987. 3.95 (ISBN 0-448-10556-X, G&D). Putnam Pub Group.
—Big Bear's Balloon, a Counting Book. Mahan, Benton, illus. 24p. (ps-1). 1986. pap. 3.95 (ISBN 0-448-01462-9, G&D). Putnam Pub Group.
—Bunny's ABC Box. Blonder, Ellen, illus. 24p. (ps-1). 1986. pap. 3.95 (ISBN 0-448-01464-5, G&D). Putnam Pub Group.
—Ladybug's Color Book. Duell, Nancy, illus. 24p. (ps-1). 1986. pap. 3.95 (ISBN 0-448-01461-0, G&D). Putnam Pub Group.
—Mouse's Shape Book. Marvin, Frederic, illus. 24p. (ps-1). 1986. pap. 3.95 (ISBN 0-448-01463-7, G&D). Putnam Pub Group.
—Piggy's Good Food: A Mealtime Word Book. Blonder, Ellen, illus. (ps-1). 1987. 3.95 (ISBN 0-448-10557-8, G&D). Putnam Pub Group.
Silverstein, Shel. Lafcadio, the Lion Who Shot Back. Silverstein, Shel, illus. LC 62-13320. 112p. (gr. 3-6). 1963. 13.95 (ISBN 0-06-025675-3); PLB 13.89 (ISBN 0-06-025676-1). HarpC Child Bks.
—A Light in the Attic. Silverstein, Shel, illus. LC 80-8453. 176p. 1981. 14.95 (ISBN 0-06-025673-7); PLB 14.89 (ISBN 0-06-025674-5). HarpC Child Bks.
—Where the Sidewalk Ends: Poems & Drawings. Silverstein, Shel, illus. LC 70-105486. 176p. (gr. 4 up). 1974. 14.95 (ISBN 0-06-025667-2); PLB 14.89 (ISBN 0-06-025668-0). HarpC Child Bks.
Simmonds, Posy. Fred. Simmonds, Posy, illus. LC 86-21395. 32p. (gr. k up). 1988. 9.95 (ISBN 0-394-88627-5). Knopf.
Simon, Norma. Cats Do, Dogs Don't. Levine, Abby, ed. (Illus.). 32p. (ps-4). 1986. 12.95 (ISBN 0-8075-1102-1). A Whitman.
—Children Do, Grownups Don't. Tucker, Kathleen, ed. Cogancherry, Helen, illus. LC 87-2205. (ps-3). 1987. PLB 12.95 (ISBN 0-8075-1144-7). A Whitman.
—I Am Not a Crybaby! Tucker, Kathleen, ed. Cogancherry, Helen, illus. 40p. (gr. 1-4). 1989. 12.95g (ISBN 0-8075-3447-1). A Whitman.
—I Was So Mad! Leder, Dora, illus. LC 73-22425. 40p. (gr. k-2). 1974. PLB 10.95 (ISBN 0-8075-3520-6). A Whitman.
—I'm Busy, Too. Tucker, Kathleen, ed. Leder, Dora, illus. LC 79-18374. (ps-1). 1980. PLB 10.95 (ISBN 0-8075-3464-1). A Whitman.
—Nobody's Perfect, Not Even My Mother. Tucker, Kathleen, ed. Leder, Dora, illus. LC 81-520. 32p. (gr. k-3). 1981. PLB 10.95 (ISBN 0-8075-5707-2). A Whitman.
—The Saddest Time. (Illus.). 40p. (gr. 1-4). 1986. 10.95 (ISBN 0-8075-7203-9). A Whitman.
—Wedding Days. Tucker, Kathleen, ed. (Illus.). 32p. (ps-4). 1988. PLB 12.95 (ISBN 0-8075-8703-6). A Whitman.
—What Do I Do: English - Spanish Edition. Lasker, Joe, illus. LC 74-79544. 40p. (ps-2). 1969. PLB 12.95 (ISBN 0-8075-8823-7). A Whitman.
—What Do I Say. Lasker, Joe, illus. LC 67-17420. (ENG & SPA.). (ps-2). 1967. 12.95 (ISBN 0-8075-8828-8); PLB 12.95 (ISBN 0-8075-8826-1). A Whitman.
Simpson, Bert & Simpson, Bonnie. Shake My Sillies Out. Allender, David, illus. 32p. (ps-2). 1988. PLB 9.95 (ISBN 0-517-56646-X). Crown.
Sing-Along Favorites. (Illus.). (ps-3). pap. write for info. (ISBN 0-307-13977-8, Golden Bks). Western Pub.
Singer, Marilyn. Turtle in July. Pinkney, Jerry, illus. LC 89-2745. 32p. (gr. k-3). 1989. 13.95 (ISBN 0-02-782881-6, Mcmillan Child Bk). Macmillan Child Grp.
Sipherd, Ray. When Is My Birthday? Cooke, Tom, illus. LC 88-80284. 32p. (ps-1). 1988. write for info. (ISBN 0-307-12028-7). Western Pub.
Sis, Peter. Waving. LC 86-25762. (Illus.). 24p. (ps-1). 1988. 11.95 (ISBN 0-688-07159-7); lib. bdg. 11.88 (ISBN 0-688-07160-0). Greenwillow.
Sizes: Kiddy Big Book. (ps up). 1990. PLB 4.98 (ISBN 0-7924-5197-X, Mallard Pr). BDD Promo Bk.
Sklenitzka, Franz S. The Red Sports Car. (Illus.). 96p. (gr. 1-3). 1988. pap. 2.95 (ISBN 0-8120-3937-8). Barron.
Skurzynski, Gloria. The Minstrel in the Tower. Heller, Julek, illus. LC 87-26614. 64p. (Orig.). (gr. 2-4). 1988. lib. bdg. 6.99 (ISBN 0-394-99598-8, Random Juv); pap. 1.95 (ISBN 0-394-89598-3). Random.
Slater, Teddy. The Big Book of Real Fire Trucks. Mones, illus. 48p. (gr. 1-4). 1987. 7.95 (ISBN 0-448-19176-8, G&D). Putnam Pub Group.
Slater, Teddy, adapted by. Walt Disney's Dumbo. Dias, Ron, illus. LC 88-80740. 24p. (ps-1). 1988. write for info. (ISBN 0-307-11994-7). Western Pub.
Sleator, William. The Duplicate. LC 87-30562. 160p. (gr. 5-11). 1988. 13.95 (ISBN 0-525-44390-8, 01258-370, DCB). Dutton Child Bks.
Slegers, Guusje. Toys. (ps). 1987. 1.95 (ISBN 0-8120-5802-X). Barron.
Slier, Debby. Baby's Places. 1989. 2.95 (ISBN 0-02-689330-4). Checkerboard Pr.
Slier, Deborah, ed. Baby's Words. 12p. (ps). 1988. bds. 2.95 (ISBN 1-56288-085-3). Checkerboard Pr.
—Busy Baby. 12p. (ps). 1988. bds. 2.95 (ISBN 1-56288-086-1). Checkerboard Pr.
—Farm Animals. (Illus.). 12p. (ps). 1988. 2.95 (ISBN 1-56288-084-5). Checkerboard Pr.
—Hello Baby. (Illus.). 12p. (ps). 1988. bds. 2.95 (ISBN 1-56288-087-X). Checkerboard Pr.
Slobodkina, Esphyr. Caps for Sale. Slobodkina, Esphyr, illus. LC 84-43122. 48p. (ps-2). 1987. pap. 3.95 (ISBN 0-06-443143-6, Trophy). HarpC Child Bks.
—Caps for Sale. Slobodkina, Esphyr, illus. (gr. k-3). 1987. incl. cassette 19.95 (ISBN 0-87499-059-9); pap. 12.95 incl. cassette (ISBN 0-87499-058-0); 4 paperbacks, cassette & guide 27.95 (ISBN 0-87499-060-2). Live Oak Media.
Small, Ernest & Lent, Blair. Baba Yaga. (Illus.). 48p. (gr. k-3). 1966. 13.95 (ISBN 0-395-16975-5). HM.
Small, Terry. Tails, Claws, Fangs & Paws: An Alpha Beast Caper. Small, Terry, illus. 32p. (ps-3). 1990. 13. 95 (ISBN 0-553-05852-5). Bantam.
Smallman, Clare & Riddell, Edwina. Outside In. (Illus.). 32p. (ps-2). 1986. 12.95 (ISBN 0-8120-5760-0). Barron.
Smath, Jerry, illus. Peek-a-Bug. LC 89-61381. 14p. (ps). 1990. 2.95 (ISBN 0-685-31774-9). Random.
Smiling Sandy. 12p. (ps-1). 1989. bds. 5.95 (ISBN 0-87449-712-4). Modern Pub NYC.
Smith, A. G. Civil War Paper Soldiers in Full Color. 1985. pap. 4.95 (ISBN 0-486-24987-5). Dover.
—Cut & Assemble a Medieval Castle. 1984. pap. 5.95 (ISBN 0-486-24663-9). Dover.
—Cut & Assemble an Early American Seaport. 1984. pap. 5.95 (ISBN 0-486-24754-6). Dover.
—Cut & Assemble an Old Fashioned Carousel in Full Color. 1985. pap. 5.95 (ISBN 0-486-24992-1). Dover.
—Cut & Assemble an Old-Fashioned Train. 1989. pap. 5.95 (ISBN 0-486-25324-4). Dover.
—Cut & Assemble Circus Parade. 1985. pap. 5.95 (ISBN 0-486-24861-5). Dover.
—Cut & Assemble New York Harbor. 1986. pap. 4.95 (ISBN 0-486-25026-1). Dover.
—Cut & Assemble 3-D Geometric Shapes. 1986. pap. 5.95 (ISBN 0-486-25093-8). Dover.
—Dinosaur Punch out Stencils. 1989. pap. 3.50 (ISBN 0-486-25305-8). Dover.
—Easy-to-Make Playtime Castle. 1989. pap. 2.95 (ISBN 0-486-25469-0). Dover.
—Easy-to-Make Playtime Farm. 1989. pap. 2.95 (ISBN 0-486-25585-9). Dover.
—Easy-to-Make Playtime Village. 1989. pap. 2.95 (ISBN 0-486-25478-X). Dover.
—Fun with Dinosaur Stencils. 1989. pap. 1.00 (ISBN 0-486-25450-X). Dover.
—Fun with Favorite Pets Stencils. 1989. pap. 1.00 (ISBN 0-486-25451-8). Dover.
Smith, Barry. Cumberland Road. Smith, Barry, illus. 32p. (gr. k-3). 1989. 9.95 (ISBN 0-395-51739-7). HM.
—Tom & Annie Go Shopping. Smith, Barry, illus. 32p. 1989. 9.95 (ISBN 0-395-51738-9). HM.
Smith, Bobby J. Mama Catfis H. 35p. 1988. 4.95 (ISBN 0-533-06530-5). Vantage.
Smith, Bron. The Great Thistledown Flood. Smith, Bron, illus. LC 89-31540. 32p. (Orig.). (ps-3). 1989. 4.99 (ISBN 0-89081-751-0). Harvest Hse.
Smith, Debbie. The Peter Rabbit Craft Book. (gr. k-5). 1988. 7.95 (ISBN 0-7232-3440-X). Warne.
Smith, Donald. Who's Wearing My Baseball Cap? LC 86-23957. (Illus.). 12p. (ps-k). 1987. 2.95 (ISBN 0-8037-0396-1). Dial Bks Young.
Smith, Jacqueline B., illus. The Three Billy Goats Gruff. 18p. (ps). 1988. bds. 3.95 (ISBN 0-448-10230-7, G&D). Putnam Pub Group.
Smith, Jennifer. Grover & the New Kid. Cooke, Tom, illus. LC 86-42965. 40p. (ps-3). 1987. 4.95 (ISBN 0-394-88519-8, Random Juv); lib. bdg. 6.99 (ISBN 0-394-98519-2). Random.
Smith, Jessie. Grover's Day at the Beach: A Counting Story. Cooke, Tom, illus. 32p. (ps-k). 1988. write for info. (ISBN 0-307-13105-X, Pub. by Golden Bks). Western Pub.
—Sesame Street: Going Places. Ewers, Joseph, illus. LC 87-81768. 24p. (ps-k). 1988. pap. write for info. (ISBN 0-307-10057-X, Pub. by Golden Bks). Western Pub.
Smith, Robert K. Jelly Belly. 160p. (gr. 4-9). 1982. pap. 3.25 (ISBN 0-440-44207-9, YB). Dell.
Smith, Wendy. Think Hippo! (Illus.). 28p. (ps-2). 1989. PLB 12.95 (ISBN 0-87614-372-9). Carolrhoda Bks.
—Twice Mice. (Illus.). 28p. (ps-2). 1989. PLB 12.95 (ISBN 0-87614-371-0). Carolrhoda Bks.
Smithson, Colin & Smithson, Sheila. Jonah's Fish Story. Smithson, Colin & Smithson, Sheila, illus. 32p. (ps-3). 1990. 4.95 (ISBN 0-310-56200-7, Youth Bks). Zondervan.
—Samson's Haircut. 32p. (ps-3). 1989. 4.95 (ISBN 0-310-56190-6, Youth Bks). Zondervan.
Smollin, Michael J., illus. Santa's Workshop. LC 83-63315. 12p. (ps). 1984. bds. 1.95 (ISBN 0-394-86747-5, Random Juv). Random.
Snakes-Sticker Book. 1989. pap. 2.25 (ISBN 0-89954-127-5). Antioch Pub Co.
Snow, Pegeen. Come los Guisantes, Cuanto Antes: (Eat Your Peas, Louise!) Venezia, Mike, illus. LC 84-27445. (ENG & SPA.). 32p. (ps-2). 1989. PLB 11.93 (ISBN 0-516-32067-X); pap. 2.95 (ISBN 0-516-52067-9). Childrens.
So Many Buttons. (Illus.). 24p. (gr. k-2). 1989. bds. 3.95 (ISBN 0-87449-589-X). Modern Pub NYC.
Solomon, Chuck. Our Little League. (Illus.). 40p. (ps-2). 1988. PLB 10.95 (ISBN 0-517-56798-9). Crown.
Somme, Lauritz & Kalas, Sybille. The Penguin Family Book. LC 87-32830. (Illus.). (ps-12). 1988. 15.95 (ISBN 0-88708-057-X). Picture Bk Studio.
Sommer, Ann. Youngest Shepherd. (ps-2). 1989. 11.95 (ISBN 1-55513-602-8). Cook.
Sommers, Tish. A Bird's Best Friend. Swanson, Maggie, illus. 24p. (ps-3). 1987. pap. write for info incl. cassette (ISBN 0-307-13945-X, Pub. by Golden Bks). Western Pub.
Song Book 'n' Tape Gift Pack. (Illus.). 24p. (Orig.). (ps-3). 1988. pap. write for info. (ISBN 0-307-13806-2). Western Pub.
Sorenson, Jane B. Quiet Moments with Young Children. Wigginton, Shirley, ed. Johnson, Diane, tr. 128p. (Orig.). (gr. 1-3). 1988. pap. 3.95 (ISBN 0-87403-472-8, 2804). Standard Pub.
Southgate, Mark. The Fisherman & His Wife. (Illus.). 32p. (gr. k-3). 1988. 13.95 (ISBN 0-86264-160-8, Pub. by Anderson Pr UK). Trafalgar Sq.
Sowden, Henry. The Grand Old Duke of York. (Illus.). 20p. (ps). 1989. 8.95 (ISBN 0-575-04081-5, Pub. by Gollancz England). Trafalgar Sq.
Spar, J. Willy, a Story of Water. LC 68-56819. (Illus.). 32p. (gr. 2-3). 1968. PLB 9.95 (ISBN 0-87783-051-7); pap. 3.94 deluxe ed (ISBN 0-87783-117-3). Oddo.
Special Days. (Illus.). 6p. (ps-2). 1987. bds. 3.95 (ISBN 0-87449-571-7). Modern Pub NYC.
Spier, Peter. Dreams. Spier, Peter, illus. LC 85-13130. 32p. (ps-3). 1986. PLB 12.99 (ISBN 0-385-19337-8). Doubleday.
—Fast-Slow High-Low: A Book of Opposites. Spier, Peter, illus. LC 72-76207. 48p. (gr. k-3). 1972. pap. 10.95 (ISBN 0-385-06781-X); pap. 10.95 (ISBN 0-385-02876-8); pap. 2.95 (ISBN 0-685-01490-8). Doubleday.
—Fox Went Out on a Chilly Night. Spier, Peter, illus. LC 60-7139. 42p. (gr. k-3). 1961. pap. 11.95 (ISBN 0-385-07990-7). Doubleday.
—Oh, Were They Ever Happy! LC 77-78144. (Illus.). 48p. (ps-3). 1988. pap. 6.95 (ISBN 0-385-24477-0, Zephyr-BFYR). Doubleday.
—Peter Spier's Rain. Spier, Peter, illus. LC 81-43506. 40p. (ps-3). 1982. PLB 12.95 (ISBN 0-385-15485-2, Zephyr-BFYR). Doubleday.
—Star-Spangled Banner. Spier, Peter, illus. LC 73-79112. 48p. (gr. 1 up). 1986. pap. 8.00 (ISBN 0-385-23401-5, Pub. by Zephyr-BFYR). Doubleday.
Spires, Elizabeth. The Falling Star. Michelini, Carlo A., illus. LC 84-80288. 24p. (ps-k). 1989. 7.95 (ISBN 0-448-21026-6, G&D). Putnam Pub Group.
Spirit, Bonnie. It's Fun to Read Coloring, Vol. 1. Lightfoot, Patricia, illus. 10p. (Orig.). (ps up). 1988. pap. text ed. 3.95 (ISBN 0-9614089-1-X). Avitar Bks.
—Pink Rose Bush. Lightfoot, Patricia, illus. 64p. (ps up). 1985. text ed. 9.95 (ISBN 0-9614089-0-1). Avitar Bks.
Spivak, Darlene. My Favorite Things. Olsen, Shirley, illus. 48p. (gr. k-2). 1988. wkbk. 5.95 (ISBN 1-55734-375-6). Tchr Create Mat.
Spizzirri Publishing Co. Staff. Animal Alphabet: An Educational Coloring Book. Spizzirri, Linda, ed. (Illus.). 32p. (gr. 1-8). 1982. pap. 1.95 (ISBN 0-86545-042-0). Spizzirri.
—Cats of the Wild: An Educational Coloring Book. Spizzirri, Linda, ed. (Illus.). 32p. (gr. 1-8). 1982. pap. 1.95 (ISBN 0-86545-045-5). Spizzirri.
—Counting & Coloring Dinosaurs: An Educational Coloring Book. Spizzirri, Linda, ed. (Illus.). 32p. (gr. 1-8). 1982. pap. 1.95 (ISBN 0-86545-044-7). Spizzirri.
—Endangered Species: An Educational Coloring Book. Spizzirri, Linda, ed. (Illus.). 32p. (gr. 1-8). 1982. pap. 1.95 (ISBN 0-86545-041-2). Spizzirri.
—Kachina Dolls: An Educational Coloring Book. Spizzirri, Linda, ed. (Illus.). 32p. (gr. 1-8). 1982. pap. 1.95 (ISBN 0-86545-046-3). Spizzirri.
—Picture Dictionary: An Educational Coloring Book. Spizzirri, Linda, ed. (Illus.). 32p. (gr. 1-8). 1982. pap. 1.95 (ISBN 0-86545-049-8). Spizzirri.
—Planets: An Educational Coloring Book. Spizzirri, Linda, ed. (Illus.). 32p. (gr. 1-8). 1982. pap. 1.95 (ISBN 0-86545-043-9). Spizzirri.
—Whales: An Educational Coloring Book. Spizzirri, Linda, ed. (Illus.). 32p. (gr. 1-8). 1982. pap. 1.95 (ISBN 0-86545-039-0). Spizzirri.
Spizzirri Publishing Inc Staff. Atlantic Fish: An Educational Coloring Book. Spizzirri, Linda, ed. (Illus.). 32p. (gr. 1-8). 1989. pap. 1.95 (ISBN 0-86545-135-4). Spizzirri.
—Butterfly Mazes: An Educational-Activity Coloring Book. Spizzirri, Linda, ed. (Illus.). 32p. (gr. 1-8). 1989. pap. 0.99 (ISBN 0-86545-146-X). Spizzirri.
—Eskimos: An Educational Coloring Book. Spizzirri, Linda, ed. (Illus.). 32p. (gr. 1-8). 1989. pap. 1.95 (ISBN 0-86545-140-0). Spizzirri.
—Farm Animals: An Educational Coloring Book. Spizzirri, Linda, ed. (Illus.). 32p. (gr. 1-8). 1989. pap. 1.95 (ISBN 0-86545-141-9). Spizzirri.
—Mammal Mazes: An Educational-Activity Coloring Book. Spizzirri, Linda, ed. (Illus.). 32p. (gr. 1-8). 1989. pap. 0.99 (ISBN 0-86545-144-3). Spizzirri.

—Pacific Fish: An Educational Coloring Book. Spizzirri, Linda, ed. (Illus.). 32p. (gr. 1-8). 1989. pap. 1.95 (ISBN 0-86545-136-2). Spizzirri.
—Penguins: An Educational Coloring Book. Spizzirri, Linda, ed. (Illus.). 32p. (gr. 1-8). 1989. pap. 1.95 (ISBN 0-86545-134-6). Spizzirri.
—Pioneers: An Educational Coloring Book. Spizzirri, Linda, ed. (Illus.). 32p. (gr. 1-8). 1989. pap. 1.95 (ISBN 0-86545-138-9). Spizzirri.
—Shell Mazes: An Educational-Activity Coloring Book. Spizzirri, Linda, ed. (Illus.). 32p. (gr. 1-8). 1989. pap. 0.99 (ISBN 0-86545-145-1). Spizzirri.
—State Flowers: An Educational Coloring Book. Spizzirri, Linda, ed. (Illus.). 32p. (gr. 1-8). 1989. pap. 1.95 (ISBN 0-86545-142-7). Spizzirri.
—Tree Mazes: An Educational-Activity Coloring Book. Spizzirri, Linda, ed. (Illus.). 32p. (gr. 1-8). 1989. pap. 0.99 (ISBN 0-86545-143-5). Spizzirri.
Spot Va a la Escuela (Spot Goes to School) (SPA., Illus.). 22p. (gr. 3-7). 1985. 11.95 (ISBN 0-399-21223-X, Putnam). Putnam Pub Group.
Springate, Kay W. Let's Learn about Letters. Skiles, Janet, illus. 64p. (ps-2). 1986. wkbk. 6.95 (ISBN 0-86653-362-1, GA 794). Good Apple.
A Square Deal. 24p. (gr. k-2). 1989. 3.95 (ISBN 0-87449-670-5). Modern Pub NYC.
Squirrel Nutkin. (Illus.). (ps-2). 1.95 (ISBN 0-7214-5139-X). Ladybird Bks.
Stadler, John. Cat at Bat. Stadler, John, illus. LC 87-36400. 32p. (ps-2). 1988. 9.95 (ISBN 0-525-44416-5, DCB). Dutton Child Bks.
—Snail Saves the Day. Stadler, John, illus. LC 85-47539. 32p. (ps-3). 1988. pap. 3.95 (ISBN 0-06-443161-4, Trophy). HarpC Child Bks.
Standiford, Natalie. The Best Little Monkeys in the World. Knight, Hilary, illus. LC 86-15425. 48p. (gr. 1-3). 1987. lib. bdg. 6.99 (ISBN 0-394-98616-4, Random Juv); pap. 2.95 (ISBN 0-394-88616-X, Random Juv). Random.
Stanek, Muriel. All Alone after School. Fay, Ann, ed. Owens, Gay, illus. LC 84-17243. 32p. (gr. 1-4). 1985. PLB 10.95 (ISBN 0-8075-0278-2). A Whitman.
—My Mom Can't Read. Levine, Abby, ed. Rogers, Jacqueline, illus. LC 86-1637. 32p. (gr. 1-4). 1986. 10.95 (ISBN 0-8075-5343-3). A Whitman.
—Starting School. Fay, Ann, ed. De Luna, Tony & De Luna, Betty, illus. LC 81-297. 32p. (ps-1). 1981. PLB 9.75 (ISBN 0-8075-7617-4). A Whitman.
Stanton, Elizabeth & Stanton, Henry. Sometimes I Like to Cry. Rubin, Caroline, ed. Leyden, Richard, illus. LC 77-19131. 32p. (ps-2). 1978. PLB 12.95 (ISBN 0-8075-7537-2). A Whitman.
—The Very Messy Room. Rubin, Caroline, ed. Leyden, Richard, illus. LC 78-1031. 32p. (gr. 1-3). 1978. PLB 12.95 (ISBN 0-8075-5077-9). A Whitman.
Stanton, P. The Yellow Star Sticker. Moser, Jeanie W., illus. (gr. k-3). Bk. & cassette 4.95 (ISBN 0-932715-08-7). Evans FL.
Starting School. (Illus.). (ps). 3.50 (ISBN 0-7214-1086-3). Ladybird Bks.
Stearns, Helen M. The Space Cadet & the Marionette. Urbahn, Clara, illus. 36p. 1986. 8.95 (ISBN 0-9614281-2-0); cassette 4.95. Cricketfield Pr.
Stehr, Frederic. Quack-Quack. Stehr, Frederic, illus. LC 86-46349. 32p. (ps up). 1987. 9.95 (ISBN 0-374-36161-4). FS&G.
Steig, William. Brave Irene. (Illus.). 32p. (ps up). 1988. pap. 4.95 (ISBN 0-374-40927-7). FS&G.
—Roland the Minstrel Pig. (Illus.). (gr. k-3). 1968. 12.95 (ISBN 0-06-025761-X). HarpC Child Bks.
—Solomon the Rusty Nail. Steig, William, illus. 32p. (ps up). 1985. 13.95 (ISBN 0-374-37131-8). FS&G.
—Solomon the Rusty Nail. (Illus.). 32p. (ps up). 1987. pap. 3.95 (ISBN 0-374-46903-2). FS&G.
—Yellow & Pink. LC 84-80503. 32p. (ps up). 1988. pap. 3.95 (ISBN 0-374-48735-9). FS&G.
Stelson, Caren B. Safari. Stelson, Kim A., illus. 40p. (gr. k-4). 1988. PLB 12.95 (ISBN 0-87614-324-9); pap. 5.95 (ISBN 0-87614-512-8). Carolrhoda Bks.
Steptoe, John. Stevie. Steptoe, John L., illus. LC 69-16700. 32p. (ps-3). 1969. PLB 12.89 (ISBN 0-06-025764-4). HarpC Child Bks.
—Stevie. LC 69-16700. (Illus.). 32p. (ps-3). 1986. pap. 4.95 (ISBN 0-06-443122-3, Trophy). HarpC Child Bks.
—Stevie. Steptoe, John, illus. (gr. 1-4). 1987. incl. cassette 19.95 (ISBN 0-87499-050-5); pap. 12.95 incl. cassette (ISBN 0-87499-049-1); 4 paperbacks, cassette & guide 27.95 (ISBN 0-87499-051-3). Live Oak Media.
Sterbenz, Carol E. The Dog Album: A Pet Owner's Memory Book. Sterbenz, Carol E., et al, illus. 32p. (ps up). 12.95 (ISBN 0-399-21460-7, Putnam). Putnam Pub Group.
Stevens, Kathleen. The Beast in the Bathtub. Bowler, Ray, illus. LC 86-45074. 32p. (ps-3). 1987. pap. 5.95 (ISBN 0-06-443121-5, Trophy). HarpC Child Bks.
Stevenson, James. Emma. LC 84-4141. (gr. k-3). 1987. pap. 3.95 (ISBN 0-688-07336-0, Mulberry). Morrow.
—Grandpa's Great City Tour: An Alphabet Book. Stevenson, James, illus. LC 83-1459. 48p. (gr. k-3). 1983. PLB 12.95 (ISBN 0-688-02324-X); 12.88 (ISBN 0-688-02323-1). Greenwillow.
—We Hate Rain! LC 87-21204. (Illus.). 32p. (gr. k-3). 1988. 11.95 (ISBN 0-688-07786-2); lib. bdg. 11.88 (ISBN 0-688-07787-0). Greenwillow.
—The Wish Card Ran Out! Stevenson, James, illus. LC 80-22139. 32p. (gr. k-4). 1981. 11.75 (ISBN 0-688-80305-9). Greenwillow.
Stevenson, Jocelyn. Anybody Can Play. Phillips, Beverly, illus. 24p. (ps-3). pap. write for info. (ISBN 0-307-13814-3, 13814, Pub. by Golden Bks). Western Pub.
—When Grover Moved to Sesame Street. Cooke, Tom, illus. 24p. (ps-3). 1987. pap. write for info incl. cassette (ISBN 0-307-13949-2, Pub. by Golden Bks). Western Pub.
Stevenson, Sucie. Christmas Eve. Stevenson, Sucie, illus. LC 88-18172. 32p. (ps-3). 1988. 12.95 (ISBN 0-399-21667-7, Putnam). Putnam Pub Group.
—Jessica the Blue Streak. LC 88-17920. (Illus.). 32p. (ps-1). 1989. 12.95 (ISBN 0-531-05798-4); PLB 12.99 (ISBN 0-531-08398-5). Orchard Bks Watts.
Stewart, Frances T. & Stewart, Charles P. Noah & the Rainbow Promise. (Illus.). (ps up). 1986. pap. 6.95 (ISBN 0-8054-4187-5). Broadman.
Sticker Book Animals. 1989. pap. 2.98 (ISBN 0-8317-0327-X). Smithmark.
Stickland, Paul. Diggers. Stickland, Paul, illus. 16p. (ps-1). 1988. 3.95 (ISBN 0-8249-8256-8). Ideals.
—Machines As Big As Monsters. LC 88-26511. (Illus.). 32p. (gr. k-3). 1989. lib. bdg. 10.99 (ISBN 0-394-93913-1). Random.
—Trucks. Stickland, Paul, illus. 16p. (ps-1). 1988. 3.95 (ISBN 0-8249-8259-2). Ideals.
Stiles, Norman. Sesame Street, the Ernie & Bert Book. Mathieu, Joe, illus. 24p. (ps-k). 1977. pap. write for info. (ISBN 0-307-10072-3, Pub. by Golden Bks). Western Pub.
Stiles, Norman & Wilcox, Daniel. Grover & the Everything in the Whole Wide World Museum. Mathieo, Joe, illus. LC 73-18736. 32p. (ps-k). 1974. pap. 2.25 (ISBN 0-394-82707-4, Random Juv). Random.
Stinson, Kathy. Big Or Little. Baird Lewis, Robin, illus. 32p. (gr. k-2). 1983. 12.95 (ISBN 0-920236-30-8); pap. 4.95 (ISBN 0-920236-32-4). Firefly Bks Ltd.
—Red Is Best. Baird, Robin L., illus. 32p. (gr. k-3). 1982. 12.95 (ISBN 0-920236-24-3); pap. 4.95 (ISBN 0-920236-26-X). Firefly Bks Ltd.
Stock, Catherine. Alexander's Midnight Snack: A Little Elephant's ABC. Stock, Catherine, illus. LC 88-2608. 40p. (ps-1). 1988. 13.95 (ISBN 0-89919-512-1, Pub. by Clarion). Ticknor & Fields.
—The Birthday Present. Stock, Catherine, illus. LC 90-1914. 32p. (ps-1). 1991. SBE 11.95 (ISBN 0-02-788401-5, Bradbury Pr). Macmillan Child Grp.
—Sophie's Knapsack. LC 87-3103. (Illus.). (ps-2). 1988. 12.95 (ISBN 0-688-06457-4); 12.88 (ISBN 0-688-06458-2). Lothrop.
Stockton, Frank R. The Griffin & the Minor Canon. Sendak, Maurice, illus. LC 85-45827. 56p. (gr. 2 up). 1987. pap. 4.95 (ISBN 0-06-443126-6, Trophy). HarpC Child Bks.
Stoddard, Darrell. The Hero. Jordan, Alton, ed. Reese, Bob, illus. (gr. k-3). 1974. PLB 5.95 (ISBN 0-89868-001-8); pap. 2.50 (ISBN 0-89868-034-4). ARO Pub.
Stolz, Mary. Storm in the Night. Cummings, Pat, illus. LC 85-45838. 32p. (gr. k-3). 1990. pap. 4.95 (ISBN 0-06-443256-4, Trophy). HarpC Child Bks.
Stone, Jon. Big Bird in China. (Illus.). (gr. 4-8). 1983. lib. bdg. 7.99 (ISBN 0-394-95645-1). Random.
Stoneback, Jean C. Pup Pup & Murray Find a New Home. Weisbecker, Gene, illus. 45p. (Orig.). (ps). 1984. pap. 4.00 (ISBN 0-931440-09-2). Stoneback Pub.
Stortz, Diane M. Daytime & Nighttime. Huffman, Deborah, illus. LC 87-62598. 20p. (ps). 1988. 1.59 (ISBN 0-87403-385-3, 24-02015). Standard Pub.
—Where Does the Puppy Live? Hackney, richard, illus. LC 87-62602. (ps). 1988. 1.59 (ISBN 0-87403-389-6, 24-02019). Standard Pub.
—Who Tells the Wind? Rigo, Christian, tr. LC 87-62603. 20p. (ps). 1988. 1.59 (ISBN 0-87403-390-X, 24-02020). Standard Pub.
Stott, Dot, illus. The Three Little Kittens. 16p. (ps-1). 1984. 3.95 (ISBN 0-448-10216-1, G&D). Putnam Pub Group.
Stouffer, Marty. Wild Animal Babies. (Illus.). 24p. (ps-3). 1990. pap. write for info. (ISBN 0-307-12576-9, Pub. by Golden Bks). Western Pub.
Stowell, Gordon. Ark & Animals Sticker. (Orig.). (ps-3). 1987. pap. 6.95 (ISBN 0-8024-8475-1). Moody.
—Little Fish Surprise Picture Books. Roe, Earl O., ed. Incl. Noah's Big Boat. pap. 0.79 (ISBN 0-8307-1129-5, 5608701); Joseph & His Dreams (ISBN 0-8307-1130-9, 5608702); David the Shepherd Boy (ISBN 0-8307-1131-7, 5608703); Christmas in Bethlehem. pap. 0.79 (ISBN 0-8307-1132-5, 5608704); The Wise Men Find Jesus. pap. 0.79 (ISBN 0-8307-1133-3, 5608705); The Little Man's Happy Day. pap. 0.79 (ISBN 0-8307-1134-1, 5608706); The Great Big Picnic (ISBN 0-8307-1136-8, 5608707); The First Easter (ISBN 0-8307-1137-6, 5608708). (Illus.). 16p. (Orig.). (gr. 1 up). 1986. Set. 4.74 (ISBN 0-685-14585-9); 0.79 ea. Regal.
Strand, Mark. Rembrandt Takes a Walk. Grooms, Red, illus. (gr. 3 up). 1987. 14.95 (ISBN 0-517-56293-6). Crown.
Strauss, F. J., Co., Inc. Staff. Monkey & Friends. Strauss, F. J., Co., Inc. Staff, illus. 10p. (ps). write for info. vinyl (ISBN 0-945987-07-2). F J Strauss.
—Muffy & Billy Car Book. Strauss, F. J., Co., Inc. Staff, illus. 8p. (ps). write for info. vinyl (ISBN 0-945987-03-X). F J Strauss.
—Muffy & Billy Dress-up Book. Strauss, F. J., Co., Inc. Staff, illus. 10p. (ps). write for info. vinyl (ISBN 0-945987-01-3). F J Strauss.
—Muffy & Billy Read 'n Play Book. Strauss, F. J., Co., Inc. Staff, illus. 10p. (ps). write for info. vinyl (ISBN 0-945987-00-5). F J Strauss.
—Muffy & Billy Town Book. Strauss, F. J., Co., Inc. Staff, illus. 8p. (ps). write for info. vinyl (ISBN 0-945987-02-1). F J Strauss.
—My Rubber Ducky. Strauss, F. J., Co., Inc. Staff, illus. 10p. (ps). write for info. vinyl (ISBN 0-945987-05-6). F J Strauss.
—My Rubber Ducky Bath Book. Strauss, F. J., Co., Inc. Staff, illus. 8p. (ps). write for info. vinyl (ISBN 0-945987-04-8). F J Strauss.
—On the Farm. Strauss, F. J., Co., Inc. Staff, illus. 10p. (ps). write for info. vinyl (ISBN 0-945987-06-4). F J Strauss.
Struble, Steve. To See or Not to See. Pohl, Kathy, ed. Garcia, Tom, illus. LC 85-15487. 32p. (gr. 2-4). 1986. PLB 16.67 (ISBN 0-8172-2700-8). Raintree Pubs.
Stuart, Alexander & Vendrell, Carme S. Joe, Jo-Jo & the Monkey Masks. (Illus.). 32p. (gr. 1-4). 1989. 13.95 (ISBN 0-86264-199-3, Pub. by Anderson Pr UK). Trafalgar Sq.
Suire, Diane D. Polka-Dot Puppy's Birthday: A Book about Colors. Hohag, Linda, illus. LC 88-10937. 32p. (ps-2). 1988. PLB 11.97 (ISBN 0-89565-381-8); pap. 6.96 (ISBN 0-89565-499-7). Childs World.
Sullivan, Dianna. Make Your Own Adventure Books. Ecker, Beverly, illus. 48p. (gr. 1-4). 1988. wkbk. 5.95 (ISBN 1-55734-395-0). Tchr Create Mat.
—Make Your Own Fable & Fairy Tale Books. Ecker, Beverly, illus. 48p. (gr. 1-4). 1988. wkbk. 5.95 (ISBN 1-55734-392-6). Tchr Create Mat.
—Make Your Own Happy Times Books. Ecker, Beverly, illus. 48p. (gr. 1-4). 1988. wkbk. 5.95 (ISBN 1-55734-394-2). Tchr Create Mat.
—Make Your Own Holiday Books. Ecker, Beverly, illus. 48p. (gr. 1-4). 1988. wkbk. 5.95 (ISBN 1-55734-393-4). Tchr Create Mat.
Sun, Ming-Ju. Japanese Kimono-Paper Dolls. 1986. pap. 3.95 (ISBN 0-486-25094-6). Dover.
Sunny Days. (Illus.). 6p. (ps-2). 1987. bds. 3.95 (ISBN 0-87449-572-5). Modern Pub NYC.
Super, Terri, illus. Animal Babies. LC 86-72426. 12p. (ps). 1988. pap. write for info. (ISBN 0-307-06056-X, Pub. by Golden Bks). Western Pub.
—The Pudgy Pat-a-Cake. 16p. (ps). 1983. pap. 2.95 (ISBN 0-448-10204-8, G&D). Putnam Pub Group.
—The Three Little Pigs. 16p. (ps-1). 1984. 3.95 (ISBN 0-448-10214-5, G&D). Putnam Pub Group.
Suppertime for Frieda Fuzzypaws. (ps-k). Date not set. write for info. (ISBN 0-307-12234-4, Golden Pr). Western Pub.
Surowiecki, Sandra L. Joshua's Day. 2nd ed. LC 77-20479. (Illus.). 27p. (ps-1). 1977. pap. 5.95 (ISBN 0-914996-18-5). Lollipop Power.
Surprise Dinosaur! (ps-1). 1988. 3.95 (ISBN 0-671-66712-2, Little Simon). S&S Trade.
Surprise Fire Engine! (ps-1). 1987. bds. 3.95 (ISBN 0-317-66512-X, Little Simon). S&S Trade.
Sussman, Ellen. Teaching Train. Burris, Priscilla, illus. 44p. (Orig.). (ps-k). 1988. pap. 4.95 (ISBN 0-933606-65-6). Monkey Sisters.
Sustendal, Pat, illus. The Trim-the-Tree Counting Book. LC 83-63314. 12p. (ps). 1984. bds. 1.95 (ISBN 0-394-86748-3, Random Juv). Random.
Sutcliff, Rosemary. Flame-Colored Taffeta. 120p. (gr. 5 up). 1986. 11.95 (ISBN 0-374-32344-5). FS&G.
Sutherland, Harry A. Dad's Car Wash. Chambliss, Maxie, illus. LC 87-15183. 32p. (ps-1). 1988. 12.95 (ISBN 0-689-31335-7, Atheneum Child Bk). Macmillan Child Grp.
Sutton, Scott E. Oh No, More Wizard Lessons! Sutton, Scott E., illus. 35p. (gr. 2-4). 1986. 12.95 (ISBN 0-9617199-2-3). Sutton Pubns.
Sutton, Valerie J. & Beekman, Betty. Goldilocks & the Three Bears: Written in Sutton Sign Writing. (gr. 1 up). 1981. pap. text ed. 3.00x (ISBN 0-914336-34-7). Ctr Sutton Movement.
Svensson, Borje, illus. Let's Take a Trip Around the Airport. 12p. (ps). 1988. 9.95 (ISBN 0-8431-2294-3). Price Stern.
—Let's Take a Trip Around the Harbor. 12p. (ps). 1988. 9.95 (ISBN 0-8431-2295-1). Price Stern.
Swanson, Harry. Oscar Otter Meets the Mayor. Swanson, Harry, illus. 48p. (Orig.). (ps-6). 1989. pap. 5.00 (ISBN 1-878200-02-X). SwanMark Bks.
Sweet Dreams. 12p. (ps-1). 1988. bds. 5.95 (ISBN 0-87449-625-X). Modern Pub NYC.
Szekeres, Cyndy. Cyndy Szekeres' Counting Book One to Ten. (Illus.). 22p. (gr. k). 1984. write for info. (ISBN 0-307-12141-0, 12140, Golden Bks). Western Pub.
—Cyndy Szekeres' Nice Animals. 1990. pap. write for info. (ISBN 0-307-06109-4, Golden Pr). Western Pub.
—Good Night, Sweet Mouse. Szekeres, Cyndy, illus. LC 87-81789. 20p. (ps). 1988. write for info. (ISBN 0-307-12159-3). Western Pub.
—Thumpity Thump Gets Dressed. Szekeres, Cyndy, illus. LC 83-83284. 16p. (ps-k). 4.95 (ISBN 0-307-12203-4, 12233, Golden Bks). Western Pub.
Tabby Max. (Illus.). (ps-2). 3.95 (ISBN 0-7214-9594-X). Ladybird Bks.
Tabler, Judith. The New Puppy. Sustendal, Pat, illus. LC 85-62016. 14p. (ps). 1986. 3.95 (ISBN 0-394-88038-2, Random Juv). Random.

Tafuri, Nancy. Early Morning in the Barn. Tafuri, Nancy, illus. 24p. (ps). 1990. pap. 3.95 (ISBN 0-14-050511-3, Puffin). Puffin Bks.
—In a Red House. Tafuri, Nancy, illus. LC 86-27114. (ps). 1987. Board book. pap. 3.95 (ISBN 0-688-07185-6). Greenwillow.
—One Wet Jacket. LC 87-8439. (Illus.). 12p. (ps). 1988. Board Book. pap. 3.95 (ISBN 0-688-07465-0). Greenwillow.
—Spots, Feathers, & Curly Tails. LC 87-15638. (Illus.). 32p. (ps-1). 1988. 11.95 (ISBN 0-688-07536-3); lib. bdg. 11.88 (ISBN 0-688-07537-1). Greenwillow.
Tagel, Peggy. Pop-up Baby Bunny. (Illus.). 14p. (ps-1). 1991. 3.95 (ISBN 0-448-40054-5, G&D). Putnam Pub Group.
—Pop-up Little Duck. (Illus.). 14p. 1991. 3.95 (ISBN 0-448-40056-1, G&D). Putnam Pub Group.
—Pop-up Tiny Chick. (Illus.). 14p. 1991. 3.95 (ISBN 0-448-40055-3, G&D). Putnam Pub Group.
Taggart, George. Bible Promises for Tiny Tots, II. Coffen, Richard W., ed. 32p. (Orig.). (ps). 1985. pap. 4.50 (ISBN 0-8280-0246-0). Review & Herald.
Takihara, Koji. Rolli. LC 87-29262. (Illus.). (ps-12). 1988. 14.95 (ISBN 0-88708-058-8). Picture BK Studio.
Talbot, John. The Raries. (Illus.). 32p. (gr. k-3). 1989. 13.95 (ISBN 0-86264-144-6, Pub. by Anderson Pr UK). Trafalgar Sq.
Talbott, Hudson. We're Back: A Dinosaur's Story. 32p. (ps-2). 1988. PLB 12.95 (ISBN 0-517-56599-4). Crown.
The Tale of Peter Rabbit & Chicken Little, 2 bks. 40p. (ps-k). 1989. Set. pap. 4.95 incl. audio cassette (ISBN 0-448-10232-3, G&D). Putnam Pub Group.
Tallarico, Tony, illus. All Through the Year. 14p. (ps). 1980. 2.25 (ISBN 0-448-16278-4, G&D). Putnam Pub Group.
—At Home. 28p. (ps-1). 1984. bds. 2.95 (ISBN 0-89828-055-9). Tuffy Bks.
—Colors. 28p. (ps). 1988. bds. 3.50 (ISBN 0-89828-060-5, 80605). Tuffy Bks.
—Fire Engines. 12p. (ps-1). 1990. bds. 3.95 (ISBN 0-89828-401-5). Tuffy Bks.
—Happy Birthday. 12p. (ps-1). 1985. bds. 3.95 (ISBN 0-89828-313-2, 83132). Tuffy Bks.
—Haunted House. 48p. (ps-1). 1990. 1.39 (ISBN 0-89828-403-1). Tuffy Bks.
—Here We Go. 28p. (ps). 1988. 2.95 (ISBN 0-89828-061-3). Tuffy Bks.
—How Many? 28p. (ps-1). 1984. bds. 2.95 (ISBN 0-89828-052-4). Tuffy Bks.
—I Love My Family. 12p. (ps-1). 1985. bds. 3.95 (ISBN 0-89828-314-0, 83140). Tuffy Bks.
—Nursery Rhymes. 12p. (ps). 1988. bds. 3.95 (ISBN 0-89828-320-5, 04013). Tuffy Bks.
—Opposites. 12p. (ps). 1988. 3.95 (ISBN 0-89828-319-1). Tuffy Bks.
—Peter Rabbit's Family. 12p. (ps). 1988. 3.95 (ISBN 0-89828-312-4). Tuffy Bks.
—Shapes. 12p. (ps-1). 1985. bds. 3.95 (ISBN 0-89828-315-9). Tuffy Bks.
—Skitter Bugs. 14p. (ps). 1980. 2.25 (ISBN 0-448-16277-6, G&D). Putnam Pub Group.
—Time To... 28p. (ps-1). 1984. bds. 2.95 (ISBN 0-89828-050-8). Tuffy Bks.
—Trucks & Cars. 14p. (ps). 1980. 2.50 (ISBN 0-448-16275-X, G&D). Putnam Pub Group.
—What's Opposite? 28p. (ps-1). 1984. bds. 2.95 (ISBN 0-89828-054-0). Tuffy Bks.
—Who Am I? 28p. (ps-1). 1984. bds. 2.95 (ISBN 0-89828-053-2). Tuffy Bks.
Tangvald, Christine. Mom & Dad Don't Live Together Anymore. LC 87-34211. 24p. (ps-2). 1988. 7.95 (ISBN 1-55513-502-1, Chariot Bks). Cook.
Tangvald, Christine H. The Bible Is for Me. Nelson, Donna, illus. 24p. (ps-2). 1988. pap. 2.95 (ISBN 1-55513-706-7, Chariot Bks). Cook.
—Christmas Is for Me. Nelson, Donna, illus. 24p. (ps-2). 1988. pap. 2.95 (ISBN 1-55513-705-9, Chariot Bks). Cook.
Tarrant, Margaret, illus. My First Book of Nursery Rhymes. 64p. (ps-k). 1988. 6.95 (ISBN 0-8249-8267-3). Ideals.
Tax, Meredith. Families. Hafner, Marilyn, illus. 32p. (ps-3). 1981. 14.95 (ISBN 0-316-83240-5, Pub. by Atlantic). Little.
Taylor, Anelise. Lights Off, Lights On. (Illus.). 32p. (ps-k). 1989. pap. 4.95 (ISBN 0-19-272193-3). Oxford U Pr.
Taylor, E. J. Goose Eggs. Taylor, E. J., illus. LC 84-905. 32p. (ps-3). 1985. Knopf.
Taylor, Judy. My Cat. Cartwright, Reg, illus. LC 88-22127. 32p. (ps-2). 1989. pap. 3.95 (ISBN 0-689-71209-X, Aladdin). Macmillan Child Grp.
—My Dog. Cartwright, Reg, illus. LC 88-19441. 32p. (ps-2). 1989. pap. 3.95 (ISBN 0-689-71210-3, Aladdin). Macmillan Child Grp.
Taylor, Kenneth. New Testament in Pictures for Little Eyes. (Illus.). 155p. (Orig.). 1989. pap. 5.95 (ISBN 0-8024-0682-3). Moody.
Taylor, Kenneth N. Giant Steps for Little People. 64p. (ps-1). 1985. 10.95 (ISBN 0-8423-1023-1). Tyndale.
Taylor, Mark A. I See Christmas Coming! Hand, Judy, illus. LC 87-62601. 20p. (ps). 1988. 1.59 (ISBN 0-87403-388-8, 24-02018). Standard Pub.
Teach Me Now 1. 80p. (ps). 4.95 (ISBN 1-55976-401-5); 6.99 (ISBN 0-685-17899-4). CEF Press.
Teach Me Now 3. 80p. (ps). 4.95 (ISBN 1-55976-403-1); 6.99 (ISBN 0-685-17902-8). CEF Press.
Teach Me Now 4. 80p. (ps). 4.95 (ISBN 1-55976-404-X); 6.99 (ISBN 0-685-17903-6). CEF Press.
The Teddy Bears' Picnic: Mini-Sticker Book. 24p. (ps-k). 1988. pap. 1.95 (ISBN 0-8249-8229-0). Ideals.
Teddy Ruxpin Sings Love Songs. 26p. (Orig.). (ps). 1987. incl. pre-programmed audio cass. tape 14.50 (ISBN 0-934323-53-4). Alchemy Comms.
Teddy's Best Toys. 12p. (ps). 1985. 3.95 (ISBN 0-394-87111-1, Random Juv). Random.
Teen Creed Key Lock Diary. 1988. 9.98 (ISBN 0-89954-700-1). Antioch Pub Co.
Teitelbaum, Michael. Disney's Duck Tales: Journey to Magic Island. (Illus.). 24p. (ps-k). 1989. pap. write for info. (ISBN 0-307-11754-5, Pub. by Golden Bks). Western Pub.
Tenaille, Marie. The Day the Dragon Came to School. Charney, Didi, tr. from FRE. Hulne, Violayne, illus. 36p. (Orig.). (gr. 1-3). 1988. pap. 2.95 (ISBN 0-689-71192-1, Aladdin Bks). Macmillan Child Grp.
Testa, Fulvio. If You Look Around You. LC 83-5310. (Illus.). 32p. (ps-2). 1987. pap. 3.95 (ISBN 0-8037-0432-1). Dial Bks Young.
—Wolf's Favor. Testa, Fulvio, illus. LC 85-15934. 32p. (ps-3). 1986. 11.95 (ISBN 0-8037-0244-2). Dial Bks Young.
Thackray, Patricia. Sesame Street: Big Bird Gets Lost. (Illus.). 32p. (ps-2). 1989. write for info. (ISBN 0-307-13524-1, Pub. by Golden Bks). Western Pub.
Thaler, Mike. In the Middle of the Puddle. Degen, Bruce, illus. LC 85-45830. 32p. (ps-1). 1988. 11.95 (ISBN 0-06-026053-X); PLB 11.89 (ISBN 0-06-026054-8). HarpC Child Bks.
—Pack 109. Chartier, Normand, illus. 48p. (ps-2). 1988. 9.95 (ISBN 0-525-44393-2, 0966-290, DCB). Dutton Child Bks.
Thayer, Jane. Quiet on Account of Dinosaur. Fleishman, Seymour, illus. LC 64-10028. 32p. (ps-3). 1964. PLB 12.88 (ISBN 0-688-31632-8); pap. 3.95 (ISBN 0-688-08292-0, Mulberry Bks). Morrow Jr Bks.
Theobalds, Prue, illus. The Teddy Bear's Picnic. 8p. (gr. k-5). 1986. pap. 5.95 (ISBN 0-87226-098-4, Bedrick Blackie). P Bedrick Bks.
Thigpen, Paul. Angels in the Air - ABC's. (ps-3). 1986. 1.95 (ISBN 6-125-52134-6, 52134, Chariot Bks). Cook.
—Guest of the Animals - One, Two, Threes. (Illus.). (ps-3). 1986. pap. 1.95 (ISBN 6-125-52126-5, Chariot Bks). Cook.
Things I Like to Do. (ps-1). 1985. 4.95 (ISBN 0-671-54735-6, Little Simon). S&S Trade.
Things That Go. (Illus.). (ps-k). 3.95 (ISBN 0-7214-5140-3). Ladybird Bks.
Things That Go Board Shape Book. (Illus.). (ps). 1985. bds. 1.69 (ISBN 0-517-46322-9). Outlet Bk Co.
Things That Move. (Illus.). (ps-k). 3.95 (ISBN 0-7214-5040-7). Ladybird Bks.
Things to Play With. (Illus.). (ps-k). 3.95 (ISBN 0-7214-5144-6). Ladybird Bks.
Things to Wear. (Illus.). (ps-k). 3.95 (ISBN 0-7214-5143-8). Ladybird Bks.
This Is Me. Blegvad, Lenore. LC 85-61671. 28p. (ps-k). 1986. bds. 2.95 (ISBN 0-394-87816-7). Random.
Thoburn, Tina, compiled by. My First Golden Dictionary. Chandler, Jean, illus. LC 87-81750. 24p. 1988. write for info. (ISBN 0-307-11992-0, Pub. by Golden Bks). Western Pub.
Thomas Gets Tricked. (ps-3). 1990. pap. 1.95 (Random Juv). Random.
Thomas, Iolette. Janine & the New Baby. Northway, Jennifer, illus. (ps-2). 1987. 10.95 (ISBN 0-233-97916-6). Andre Deutsch.

Thomasson, Merry. Hey Look at Me! Baby Days. 20p. (ps-2). 1990. 9.95 (ISBN 0-9615407-5-3). Thomasson-Grant.
One of nine in a personalized book series featuring your child with Look at ME Windows. Simply tape your child's photo inside the back cover & watch their delight as they become the star of the book. Record special moments when your baby learns to crawl, talk & feed him or herself. A delightful gift for parents & grandparents. Other "Hey Look at Me!" Books include: Here We Go; I Can Be; I Like To Dream; I Can Draw; I Like To Play (a book for boys); I Like To Play (a book for girls); I Can Help; Wee Babies.
Publisher Provided Annotation.

—Hey Look at Me! I Like to Play Book for Girls. (ps-2). 1990. 9.95 (ISBN 0-9615407-4-5). Merrybooks VA.
Thompson, Brian. Puffin First Picture Dictionary. Berridge, Celia, illus. 38p. (ps-3). 1989. pap. 3.95 (ISBN 0-14-050777-9, Puffin). Puffin Bks.
Thompson, Carol. The Funnybone Book of Jokes & Riddles. Andriani, Vincent, illus. 32p. (ps-2). 1987. pap. 1.95 (ISBN 0-448-19080-X, Platt & Munk). Putnam Pub Group.
—My Big Farm Book. Battaglia, Aurelius, illus. (ps-1). 1987. 1.75 (ISBN 0-448-46534-5, Platt & Munk). Putnam Pub Group.
Thompson, Emily. Just Like Ernie. Cooke, Tom, illus. LC 87-81762. 32p. (ps-k). 1988. write for info. (ISBN 0-307-12025-2, Pub. by Golden Bks). Western Pub.
Thompson, Frances M. Miss Circo Comes Apart at the Seams. Holt, Cather C., illus. 18p. (Orig.). (gr. k-3). 1986. pap. 3.95 (ISBN 0-9616207-0-6). Bks By Brooks.
Thompson, Susan L. One More Thing, Dad. Tucker, Kathleen, ed. Leder, Dora, illus. LC 79-27887. (ps-1). 1980. PLB 9.75 (ISBN 0-8075-6095-2). A Whitman.
Thomson, Pat. Best Thing of All. Chamberlain, Margaret, illus. 32p. (gr. 1-4). 1990. 13.95 (ISBN 0-575-04578-7, Pub. by Gollancz UK). Trafalgar Sq.
Thomson, Ruth. All about One, Two, Three. Ursell, Martin, illus. LC 87-42593. 32p. (gr. 1-2). 1987. PLB 10.95 (ISBN 1-55532-316-2). Gareth Stevens Inc.
—My First Easy & Fun, 6 vols. (Illus.). (gr. 1-2). 1987. Set. lib. bdg. 65.70 (ISBN 1-55532-418-5). Gareth Stevens Inc.
—Playtime. Galletly, Mike, photos by. (Illus.). 20p. (ps up). 1989. incl. dust jacket 6.95 (ISBN 0-8120-5963-8). Barron.
Thorne, Jenny. Baby's Bible Stories: Adam & Eve. Thorne, Jenny, illus. 12p. (ps-k). 1989. Repr. bds. 3.50 (ISBN 0-689-71305-3, Aladdin). Macmillan Child Grp.
—Baby's Bible Stories: Jonah & the Whale. Thorne, Jenny, illus. 12p. (ps-k). 1989. Repr. bds. 3.50 (ISBN 0-689-71307-X, Aladdin). Macmillan Child Grp.
—Baby's Bible Stories: The Walls of Jericho. Thorne, Jenny, illus. 12p. (ps-k). 1989. Repr. bds. 3.50 (ISBN 0-689-71308-8, Aladdin). Macmillan Child Grp.
Three Billy Goats Gruff. (Illus.). 24p. (Orig.). (gr. k-3). 1988. pap. write for info. (ISBN 0-307-13968-9). Western Pub.
Tierney, Tom. Abraham Lincoln & His Family - Paper Dolls. 1989. pap. 3.95 (ISBN 0-486-26024-0). Dover.
—American Family of the Civil War Era Paper Dolls in Full Color. 1985. pap. 3.95 (ISBN 0-486-24833-X). Dover.
—American Family of the Colonial Era Paper Dolls in Full Color. 1982. pap. 3.95 (ISBN 0-486-24394-X). Dover.
—Carmen Miranda Paper Dolls in Full Color. 1982. pap. 3.95 (ISBN 0-486-24285-4). Dover.
—Chanel Fashions: Review Paper Dolls in Full Color. 1986. pap. 3.95 (ISBN 0-486-25105-5). Dover.
—Diana & Prince Charles Fashion Paper Dolls in Full Color. 1985. pap. 3.95 (ISBN 0-486-24961-1). Dover.
—Great Black Entertainers Paper Dolls. 1984. pap. 3.95 (ISBN 0-486-24748-1). Dover.
—Great Empresses & Queen Paper Dolls. 1982. pap. 3.95 (ISBN 0-486-24268-4). Dover.
—Great Fashion Design of the Fifties, Paper Dolls in Full Color. 1985. pap. 3.95 (ISBN 0-486-24960-3). Dover.
—Great Fashion Designs of the Belle Epoque, Paper Dolls in Full Color. 1983. pap. 3.95 (ISBN 0-486-24425-3). Dover.
—Great Fashion Designs of the 30s Paper Dolls. 1989. pap. 3.95 (ISBN 0-486-24724-4). Dover.
—Greta Garbo Paper Dolls in Full Color. 1985. pap. 3.95 (ISBN 0-486-24802-X). Dover.
—Joan Crawford Paper Dolls in Full Color. 1983. pap. 3.95 (ISBN 0-486-24569-1). Dover.
—Legendary Baseball Stars Paper Dolls. 1985. pap. 3.95 (ISBN 0-486-24846-1). Dover.
—Little Cupid Dolls-Paper Dolls. 1986. pap. 2.50 (ISBN 0-486-25028-8). Dover.
—Marilyn Monroe-Paper Dolls. 1980. pap. 3.95 (ISBN 0-486-23769-9). Dover.
—More Erte Fashion Paper Dolls in Full Color. 1984. pap. 3.95 (ISBN 0-486-24630-2). Dover.
—Paper Doll-Gibson Girl. 1985. pap. 3.95 (ISBN 0-486-24980-8). Dover.
—Paper Doll-Judy Garland. 1982. pap. 3.95 (ISBN 0-486-24404-0). Dover.
—Poiret Fashion Design Paper Dolls in Full Color. 1985. pap. 3.95 (ISBN 0-486-24952-2). Dover.
—Ronald Reagan-Paper Dolls in Full Color. 1984. pap. 3.95 (ISBN 0-486-24628-0). Dover.
—Santa Claus-Paper Dolls in Full Color. 1983. pap. 3.95 (ISBN 0-486-24546-2). Dover.
—Three Little Kittens Paper Dolls in Full Color. 1986. pap. 3.50 (ISBN 0-486-25065-2). Dover.
—Vivien Leigh Paper Dolls in Full Color. pap. 3.95 (ISBN 0-486-24207-2). Dover.
Time for Play. (Illus.). 12p. (ps). 1989. text ed. 5.95 (ISBN 0-02-689191-3). Checkerboard Pr.
Time-Life Books Editors. The Great ABC Treasure Hunt: A Hidden Picture Alphabet Book. (Illus.). 56p. (ps-2). 1991. write for info. (ISBN 0-8094-9254-7); lib. bdg. write for info. (ISBN 0-8094-9255-5). Time-Life.
—Guess Who? A Lift-the-Flap Animal Book. (Illus.). 20p. (ps-2). 1990. write for info. (ISBN 0-8094-9250-4); lib. bdg. write for info. (ISBN 0-8094-9251-2). Time-Life.
Time to Clean. 12p. (ps-1). 1989. bds. 5.95 (ISBN 0-87449-620-9). Modern Pub NYC.
Time to Eat. 12p. (ps-1). 1989. bds. 5.95 (ISBN 0-87449-618-7). Modern Pub NYC.
Time to Go. 12p. (ps-1). 1989. bds. 5.95 (ISBN 0-87449-619-5). Modern Pub NYC.

Titherington, Jeanne. Big World, Small World. Titherington, Jeanne, illus. LC 84-4140. 24p. (ps-1). 1985. 11.75 (ISBN 0-688-04022-5); PLB 11.88 (ISBN 0-688-04023-3). GreenWillow.

Todd, H. E. & Biro, Val. The Sleeping Policeman. (Illus.). 32p. (ps-1). 1989. 13.95 (ISBN 0-340-41299-2, Pub. by Hodder & Stoughton UK). Trafalgar Sq.

Toddling Terry. 12p. (ps-1). 1989. bds. 5.95 (ISBN 0-87449-711-6). Modern Pub NYC.

Tolkien, J. R. R. Oliphaunt. Hinton, Hank, illus. 16p. 1989. 3.95 (ISBN 0-8092-4353-9, Calico Bks). Contemp Bks.

Tomkins, Jasper. When Bear Bakes a Cake. 60p. (Orig.). (ps-2). 1987. 8.95 (ISBN 0-88138-082-2). Green Tiger Pr.

Tompert, Ann. Will You Come Back for Me? Tucker, Kathleen, ed. (Illus.). 32p. (ps-k). 1988. PLB 12.95 (ISBN 0-8075-9112-2). A Whitman.

Tong, Gary. Gary Tong's Crazy Cut-Outs. (ps-3). pap. 2.25 (ISBN 0-590-32264-8). Scholastic Inc.

Tons-of-Fun from A-Z. 24p. (gr. k-2). 1989. 3.95 (ISBN 0-87449-672-1). Modern Pub NYC.

Topek, Susan R. Israel Is... Kahn, Katherine J., illus. LC 88-83569. 12p. (ps). 1989. bds. 4.95 (ISBN 0-930494-92-X). Kar Ben.

Trabucco, Anita. Tony's Shapes Come Back. 1988. 5.95 (ISBN 0-533-07889-X). Vantage.

El Traje Nuevo del Emperador: (The King's New Clothes) LC 86-33422. (ENG & SPA.). (ps-2). 1989. PLB 11.93 (ISBN 0-516-32365-2); pap. 3.95 (ISBN 0-516-52365-1). Childrens.

Tran-Khan-Tuyet. The Little Weaver of Thai-Yen Village. rev. ed. Hom, Nancy, illus. (ENG & VIE.). 24p. (gr. 2-9). 1987. 12.95 (ISBN 0-89239-030-1). Childrens Book Pr.

A Treasury of Disney Little Golden Books: 22 Best-Loved Disney Stories. (ps-1). 1991. write for info. (ISBN 0-307-15509-9, Golden Pr). Western Pub.

Tresselt, Alvin. Hide & Seek Fog. Duvoisin, Roger, illus. LC 65-14087. 32p. (ps-3). 1988. pap. 3.95 (ISBN 0-688-07813-3, Mulberry). Morrow.

—The Rabbit Story. Ewing, Carolyn, illus. LC 88-32594. 32p. (ps-2). 1989. 12.95 (ISBN 0-688-08650-0); PLB 12.88 (ISBN 0-688-08651-9). Lothrop.

—White Snow Bright Snow. Duvoisin, Roger, illus. LC 88-10018. (ps-3). 1988. pap. 3.95 (ISBN 0-688-08294-7, Mulberry). Morrow.

Tresselt, Alvin R. Autumn Harvest. Duvoisin, Roger, illus. LC 51-8824. 32p. (gr. k-3). 1951. PLB 15.88 (ISBN 0-688-51155-4). Lothrop.

Trip, Valerie. The Singing Dog. Kalthoff, Sandra C., illus. LC 86-14797. 24p. (ps-2). 1986. PLB 12.33 (ISBN 0-516-01578-8); pap. 3.95 (ISBN 0-516-41578-6). Childrens.

Tripp, Valerie. Baby Koala Finds a Home. Kalthoff, Sandra C., illus. LC 87-6325. 24p. (ps-2). 1987. PLB 12.33 (ISBN 0-516-01577-X); pap. 3.95 (ISBN 0-516-41577-8). Childrens.

—The Penguins Paint. LC 87-14081. (Illus.). 24p. (ps-2). 1987. PLB 12.33 (ISBN 0-516-01567-2); pap. 3.95 (ISBN 0-516-41567-0). Childrens.

—Pequeno Coala busca casa: (Baby Koala Finds a Home) Kalthoff, Sandra C., illus. LC 87-6325. (SPA & ENG.). 24p. (ps-2). 1989. PLB 12.33 (ISBN 0-516-31577-3); pap. 3.95 (ISBN 0-516-51577-2). Childrens.

Troll. Kites That Really Fly. 14p. (gr. 5-9). 1991. pap. 5.95 (ISBN 0-8167-2357-5). Troll Assocs.

—Photo Fun Book Baby Animals. 12p. (ps-3). 1991. pap. 5.95 (ISBN 0-8167-2085-1). Troll Assocs.

Tsuchiya, Yukio. Faithful Elephants. Dykes, Tomoko T., tr. from JPN. Lewin, Ted, illus. 32p. (ps up). 1988. 13.95 (ISBN 0-395-46555-9). HM.

Tsutsui, Yoriko. Anna's Secret Friend. Hayashi, Akiko, illus. 32p. (ps-1). 1989. pap. 3.95 (ISBN 0-14-050731-0, Puffin). Puffin Bks.

Tudor, Tasha. Dolls' Christmas. Tudor, Tasha, illus. LC 59-12744. (gr. k-3). 1979. 6.95 (ISBN 0-8098-1026-3); pap. 4.95 (ISBN 0-8098-2912-6). McKay.

—First Delights: A Book About the Five Senses. Tudor, Tasha, illus. 32p. (ps-1). 1988. 8.95 (ISBN 0-448-09327-8, G&D). Putnam Pub Group.

—Tale for Easter. Tudor, Tasha, illus. LC 62-8626. (gr. k-3). 1985. 6.95 (ISBN 0-8098-1008-5); pap. 4.95 (ISBN 0-8098-1807-8). McKay.

—A Tale for Easter. LC 88-30675. (Illus.). 36p. (ps-2). 1989. Repr. of 1941 ed. 5.95 (ISBN 0-394-84404-1). Random.

Tufts, Mary L. The Wee Kitten Who Sucked Her Thumb. McQueen, Lucinda, illus. 32p. (ps-2). 1986. pap. 1.95 (ISBN 0-448-19076-1, G&D). Putnam Pub Group.

Tunis, John R. The Kid Comes Back. LC 46-25250. 256p. (gr. 5 up). 1990. 11.95 (ISBN 0-688-09289-6); pap. 4.95 (ISBN 0-688-09290-X, Pub. by Beech Tree Bks). Morrow Jr Bks.

Turkle, Brinton. Do Not Open. Turkle, Brinton, illus. LC 80-10289. 32p. (ps-2). 1985. pap. 3.95 (ISBN 0-525-44224-3, DCB). Dutton Child Bks.

—Obadiah the Bold. Turkle, Brinton, illus. LC 65-13350. (gr. k-3). 1977. pap. 3.95 (ISBN 0-14-050233-5, Puffin). Puffin Bks.

—Obadiah the Bold. Turkle, Brinton, illus. (gr. k-3). 1965. pap. 13.95 (ISBN 0-670-52001-2). Viking Child Bks.

Turnbull, Ann. The Sand Horse. Foreman, Michael, illus. LC 89-9. 32p. (gr. k-3). 1989. 13.95 (ISBN 0-689-31581-3, Atheneum Child Bk). Macmillan Child Grp.

Turner, Ann. Hedgehog for Breakfast. McCue, Lisa, illus. LC 88-8228. 32p. (ps-2). 1989. 13.95 (ISBN 0-02-789241-7, Mcmillan Child Bk). Macmillan Child Grp.

Turner, Gwenda. Playbook. (ps-1). 1987. pap. 3.50 (ISBN 0-14-050695-0, Puffin). Puffin Bks.

Tusa, Tricia. Sherman & Pearl. Tusa, Tricia, illus. LC 88-1630. 32p. (gr. k-3). 1989. 13.95 (ISBN 0-02-789542-4, Mcmillan Child Bk). Macmillan Child Grp.

Twinn, Colin, illus. Bunnykins Counting Book. 32p. (ps-1). 1988. 4.95 (ISBN 0-7232-3564-3). Warne.

—Bunnykins Nursery Rhymes. 32p. (ps-1). 1988. 4.95 (ISBN 0-7232-3563-5). Warne.

Tyler, J. Dot to Dot Animals: On the Farm. (Illus.). 24p. (ps-2). 1990. pap. 3.50 (ISBN 0-7460-0595-4, Usborne). EDC.

Tyler, J. & Stitt, S. Bedtime Words. (Illus.). 16p. (ps up). 1988. 2.95 (ISBN 0-7460-0222-X); PLB 6.96 (ISBN 0-88110-329-2). EDC.

—Toy Words. (Illus.). 16p. (ps up). 1988. 2.95 (ISBN 0-7460-0220-3). EDC.

Tyler, Jan. Holly Lolly. Mattingly, Jennie, ed. LC 87-50981. (Illus.). 44p. (gr. k-3). 1987. 7.95 (ISBN 1-55523-084-9). Winston-Derek.

Tyler, Linda. The Sick-in-Bed Birthday Book. Davis, Susan, illus. 32p. (ps-1). 1988. pap. 12.95 (ISBN 0-670-81823-2). Viking Child Bks.

Tyler, Linda W. Waiting for Mom. Davis, Susan, illus. 32p. (ps-2). 1989. pap. 3.95 (ISBN 0-14-050652-7, Puffin). Puffin Bks.

—When Daddy Comes Home. Davis, Susan, illus. LC 85-31459. 32p. (ps-1). 1986. pap. 9.95 (ISBN 0-670-80301-4). Viking Child Bks.

Udry, Janice M. Let's Be Enemies. Sendak, Maurice, illus. LC 61-5777. 32p. (ps-1). 1961. 12.95 (ISBN 0-06-026130-7); PLB 12.89 (ISBN 0-06-026131-5). HarpC Child Bks.

—Let's Be Enemies. Sendak, Maurice, illus. LC 61-5777. 32p. (ps-2). 1988. pap. 4.50 (ISBN 0-06-443188-6, Trophy). HarpC Child Bks.

—Moon Jumpers. Sendak, Maurice, illus. 32p. (gr. k-2). 1959. 13.95 (ISBN 0-06-026145-5). HarpC Child Bks.

—Tree Is Nice. Simont, Marc, illus. LC 56-5153. 32p. (ps-1). 1957. 11.95 (ISBN 0-06-026155-2); PLB 12.89 (ISBN 0-06-026156-0). HarpC Child Bks.

—A Tree Is Nice. Simont, Marc, illus. LC 56-5153. 32p. (ps-3). 1987. pap. 4.95 (ISBN 0-06-443147-9, Trophy). HarpC Child Bks.

—What Mary Jo Shared. Mill, Eleanor, illus. LC 66-16082. 40p. (gr. k-2). 1966. PLB 12.95 (ISBN 0-8075-8842-3). A Whitman.

—What Mary Jo Shared. Mill, Eleanor, illus. (gr. k-3). 1970. pap. 2.25 (ISBN 0-590-40731-7). Scholastic Inc.

Ueno, Noriko. Elephant Buttons. Ueno, Noriko, illus. LC 72-10264. 32p. (ps up). 1973. PLB 11.89 (ISBN 0-06-026161-7). HarpC Child Bks.

Uncle Peasley & the Pea Pod Kids. (Illus.). (ps up). 1988. 19.95 (ISBN 0-698-12001-9, Playland Bks); 3 dolls incl. Putnam Pub Group.

Ungerer, Tomi. The Beast of Monsieur Racine. Ungerer, Tomi, illus. LC 74-149216. 32p. (ps-3). 1971. 11.95 (ISBN 0-374-30640-0). FS&G.

—Crictor. LC 58-5288. (Illus.). 32p. (ps-3). 1983. pap. 4.95 (ISBN 0-06-443044-8, Trophy). HarpC Child Bks.

—The Three Robbers. Ungerer, Tomi, illus. LC 87-11549. 32p. (ps-3). 1987. Repr. of 1962 ed. 14.95 (ISBN 0-689-31391-8, Atheneum Child Bk). Macmillan Child Grp.

Unwin, Charlotte. Let's Pretend. Dann, Penny & Kindberg, Sally, illus. LC 87-19963. 24p. (ps-3). 1989. 4.95 (ISBN 0-8037-0507-7). Dial Bks Young.

Upton, Bertha. Vegemen's Revenge. Upton, Florence, illus. 64p. (Orig.). (gr. 7-9). 1987. Repr. of 1897 ed. 9.95 (ISBN 0-88138-081-4). Green Tiger Pr.

Vaes, Alain. The Porcelain Pepper Pot. (ps-3). 1987. pap. 4.95 (ISBN 0-14-050727-2, Puffin). Puffin Bks.

Van, Kampen Vlasta. Orchestranimals. 1990. pap. 12.95 (ISBN 0-590-43149-8). Scholastic Inc.

Van Allsburg, Chris. Two Bad Ants. Van Allsburg, Chris, illus. 32p. (ps up). 1988. 16.95 (ISBN 0-395-48668-8). HM.

Van Der Meer, Ron. What Is the Time. (ps-1). 1990. pap. 4.95 (ISBN 0-8167-2176-9). Troll Assocs.

Van der Meer, Ron & Van der Meer, Atie. Fun with Shapes. (Illus.). 10p. (ps-1). 1990. 7.99 (ISBN 0-399-21787-8, Putnam). Putnam Pub Group.

Van Leeuwen, Jean. Oliver, Amanda & Grandmother Pig. Schweninger, Ann, illus. LC 86-243326. 56p. (ps-3). 1987. 9.95 (ISBN 0-8037-0361-9); PLB 9.89 (ISBN 0-8037-0362-7). Dial Bks Young.

Van Loon, Joan & Van Loon, John. Jelly, Chips & Caramel Whips. (gr. 1-3). 1988. 13.95 (ISBN 0-09-148830-3, Pub. by Hutchinson UK). Trafalgar Sq.

Varley, Susan. Badger's Parting Gifts. Varley, Susan, illus. LC 83-17500. 32p. (gr. k-3). 1984. 13.95 (ISBN 0-688-02699-0); lib. bdg. 13.88 (ISBN 0-688-02703-2). Lothrop.

Vaughn, Salle W. A Little One's Draw a Story Drawing Book. Vaughn, Jimmy, illus. 120p. (ps-5). 1990. wkbk, incl. protective envelope & rainbow drawing pencil 35.00 (ISBN 0-9625832-0-0). Crystal TX.

Velthuijs, Max. A Birthday Cake for Little Bear. Lanning, Rosemary, tr. Velthuijs, Max, illus. LC 87-73270. 32p. (gr. k-3). 1988. 9.95 (ISBN 1-55858-046-8). North-South Bks NYC.

Velveteen Rabbit's Pockets. (ps). 1985. pap. 3.95 (ISBN 0-671-52404-6, Little Simon). S&S Trade.

Vesey, A. Merry Christmas, Thomas! (ps-3). 1988. pap. 3.95 (ISBN 0-14-050803-1, Puffin). Puffin Bks.

Vigna, Judith. Boot Weather. Fay, Ann, ed. Vigna, Judith, illus. 32p. (ps-2). 1989. 12.95g (ISBN 0-8075-0837-3). A Whitman.

—Mommy & Me by Ourselves Again. Fay, Ann, ed. Vigna, Judith, illus. LC 87-2059. 32p. (ps-3). 1987. PLB 12.95 (ISBN 0-8075-5232-1). A Whitman.

—Nobody Wants a Nuclear War. Tucker, Kathleen, ed. Vigna, Judith, illus. 40p. (gr. 1-4). 1986. 12.95 (ISBN 0-8075-5739-0). A Whitman.

—She's Not My Real Mother. Fay, Ann, ed. Vigna, Judith, illus. LC 80-19073. 32p. (gr. k-3). 1980. PLB 12.95 (ISBN 0-8075-7340-X). A Whitman.

Vincent, Gabrielle. Ernest & Celestine's Patchwork Quilt. Vincent, Gabrielle, illus. LC 84-25891. 16p. (ps-1). 1985. 5.25 (ISBN 0-688-04557-X). Greenwillow.

—Ernest & Celestine's Picnic. LC 82-2909. (Illus.). 24p. (ps-3). 1988. pap. 3.95 (ISBN 0-688-07809-5, Mulberry). Morrow.

—Merry Christmas, Ernest & Celestine. LC 83-14155. (ps-3). 1987. pap. 3.95 (ISBN 0-688-07330-1, Mulberry). Morrow.

Viney, Marie-Laure, illus. Tom Thumb. 24p. (ps-2). 1988. bk & audiocassette 6.95 (ISBN 0-8120-4038-4). Barron.

Viorst, Judith. Alexander & the Terrible, Horrible, No Good, Very Bad Day. Ada, Alma F., tr. Cruz, Ray, illus. (SPA.). 32p. (gr. k-4). 1989. pap. 3.95 (ISBN 0-689-71350-9, Aladdin). Macmillan Child Grp.

—Alexander, Que Era Rico el Domingo Pasado. Ada, Alma F., tr. Cruz, Ray, illus. LC 89-6503. (SPA.). 32p. (gr. k-4). 1989. 12.95 (ISBN 0-689-31590-2, Atheneum Child Bk). Macmillan Child Grp.

—Alexander, Who Used to Be Rich Last Sunday. Ada, Alma F., tr. Cruz, Ray, illus. (SPA.). 32p. (gr. k-4). 1989. pap. 3.95 (ISBN 0-689-71351-7, Aladdin). Macmillan Child Grp.

—Alexander y el Dia Terrible, Horrible, Espantoso, Horroroso. Ada, Alma F., tr. Cruz, Ray, illus. (SPA.). 32p. (gr. k-4). 1989. 12.95 (ISBN 0-689-31591-0, Atheneum Child Bk). Macmillan Child Grp.

—The Good-Bye Book. Chorao, Kay, illus. LC 87-1778. 32p. (ps-1). 1988. 12.95 (ISBN 0-689-31308-X, Atheneum Child Bk). Macmillan Child Grp.

—I'll Fix Anthony. Lobel, Arnold, illus. LC 87-18725. 32p. (gr. k-4). 1988. pap. 3.95 (ISBN 0-689-71202-2, Aladdin). Macmillan Child Grp.

—My Mama Says There Aren't Any: Zombies, Ghosts, Vampires, Creatures, Demons, Monsters, Friends, Goblins, or Things. Chorao, Kay, illus. LC 87-18733. 48p. (gr. k-4). 1987. pap. 3.95 (ISBN 0-689-71204-9, Aladdin). Macmillan Child Grp.

—The Tenth Good Thing about Barney. Blegvad, Erik, illus. 32p. (gr. k-4). 1987. pap. 3.95 (ISBN 0-689-71203-0, Aladdin). Macmillan Child Grp.

Vipont, Elfrida. The Elephant & the Bad Baby. Briggs, Raymond, illus. 32p. (ps-3). 1986. 12.95 (ISBN 0-698-20039-X, Coward); pap. 4.95 (ISBN 0-698-20625-8). Putnam Pub Group.

Vita-finzi, Claudio. Pop up Planet Earth. 1989. pap. 13.95 (ISBN 0-671-67573-7). S&S Trade.

Voake, Charlotte. First Things First. Voake, Charlotte, illus. 48p. (ps-k). 1988. 12.95 (ISBN 0-316-90510-0, Joy St Bks). Little.

Vonk, Idalee. Storytelling with the Flannel Board, Bk. 3. LC 21-650. 313p. (ps). 1983. 15.95 (ISBN 0-513-01762-3). Denison.

Wabbes, Marie. Happy Birthday, Little Rabbit. Wabbes, Marie, illus. 24p. (ps-k). 1987. pap. 4.95 (ISBN 0-87113-129-3, Joy St Bks). Little.

—It's Snowing, Little Rabbit. Wabbes, Marie, illus. 24p. (ps-k). 1987. pap. 4.95 (ISBN 0-87113-128-5, Joy St Bks). Little.

Waber, Bernard. Anteater Named Arthur. Waber, Bernard, illus. LC 67-20374. 48p. (gr. k-3). 1977. 13.95 (ISBN 0-395-20336-8); pap. 4.95 (ISBN 0-395-25936-3). HM.

—House on East Eighty-Eighth Street. (Illus.). 48p. (gr. k-3). 1973. 13.95 (ISBN 0-395-18157-7). HM.

—The House on East Eighty-Eighth Street. Waber, Bernard, illus. (ps up). Date not set. pap. 6.95 incl. cass. (ISBN 0-395-48878-8). HM.

—Lovable Lyle. LC 69-14728. (Illus.). (gr. k-3). 1977. 13.95 (ISBN 0-395-19858-5); pap. 4.95 (ISBN 0-395-25378-0). HM.

—Lyle & the Birthday Party. (Illus.). (gr. k-3). 1966. 13.95 (ISBN 0-395-15080-9). HM.

—Lyle, Lyle, Crocodile. (Illus.). (gr. k-3). 1965. 13.95 (ISBN 0-395-16995-X). HM.

—You Look Ridiculous Said the Rhinoceros to the Hippopotamus. (Illus.). (gr. k-3). 1973. reinforced bdg. 13.95 (ISBN 0-395-07156-9). HM.

Wadsworth, Olive A. Over in the Meadow. Keats, Ezra J., illus. (Orig.). (ps-2). 1985. (Blue Ribbon Bks); pap. 3.95 (ISBN 0-590-40981-6). Scholastic Inc.

Wagner, E. Vernel. Dinosaurs & Prehistoric Animals Coloring Book. Wagner, E. Vernel, illus. 64p. (gr. 3-5). 1988. pap. 3.00 (ISBN 0-941875-05-9, WB02). Wolverine Gallery.

Wagner, Karen. Silly Fred. Chartier, Normand, illus. LC 88-22620. 32p. (gr. k-3). 1989. 13.95 (ISBN 0-02-792280-4, Mcmillan Child Bk). Macmillan Child Grp.

Wahl, Jan. The Golden Christmas Tree. Weisgard, Leonard, illus. LC 87-82738. 32p. (gr. 1 up). 1988. write for info. (ISBN 0-307-10420-6). Western Pub.

—Humphrey's Bear. Joyce, William, illus. LC 85-5541. 32p. (ps-2). 1989. pap. 4.95 (ISBN 0-8050-1169-2). H Holt & Co.

Waite, Michael. Casey, the Greedy Young Cowboy. LC 37-35512. (Illus.). 32p. (ps-2). 1988. 7.95 (ISBN 1-55513-615-X, Chariot Bks). Cook.

—Sir Maggie, the Mighty. LC 87-35527. (Illus.). 32p. (ps-2). 1988. 7.95 (ISBN 1-55513-616-8, Chariot Bks). Cook.

Waite, Michael P. Boggin, Blizzy, & Sleeter the Cheater. LC 87-35510. (Illus.). 32p. (ps-2). 1988. 7.95 (ISBN 1-55513-618-4, Chariot Bks). Cook.

—Max & the Big Fat Lie. LC 87-35511. (Illus.). 32p. (ps-2). 1988. 7.95 (ISBN 1-55513-617-6, Chariot Bks). Cook.

Walking in Two Worlds: Paper Doll Book for Girls, Bk. 50. (ps-3). write for info. (ISBN 0-931363-50-0). Celia Totus Enter.

Walking in Two Worlds: Paper Doll Book for Boys, Bk. 51. (ps-3). write for info. (ISBN 0-931363-51-9). Celia Totus Enter.

Wallner, John, illus. Look & Find. 12p. (ps-2). 1988. 7.95 (ISBN 0-448-19068-0, G&D). Putnam Pub Group.

—What's Wrong Here? 12p. (ps-2). 1988. 7.95 (ISBN 0-448-19067-2, G&D). Putnam Pub Group.

Wallner, S. J. Hans & the Golden Stirrup. LC 68-56815. (Illus.). 48p. (gr. 2-3). PLB 10.95 (ISBN 0-87783-016-9); pap. 3.94 deluxe ed. (ISBN 0-87783-093-2). Oddo.

Walt Disney Company Staff. Disney's Ducktales: Down the Drain. (Illus.). 24p. (ps-3). 1990. pap. write for info. (ISBN 0-307-11726-X, Pub. by Golden Bks). Western Pub.

—Walt Disney's Peter Pan. (Illus.). 24p. (ps-2). 1989. write for info. (ISBN 0-307-12081-3, Pub. by Golden Bks). Western Pub.

Walt Disney Staff. Little Mermaid: Disney Bath Book. 1990. 5.98 (ISBN 0-8317-2305-X). Smithmark.

Walt Disney's Bambi's Fragrant Forest. LC 74-33127. 32p. (ps-2). 1988. write for info. (ISBN 0-307-13530-6). Western Pub.

Walt Disney's Dumbo. 24p. (ps-k). 1977. pap. write for info (ISBN 0-307-10076-6, Pub. by Golden Bks). Western Pub.

Walt Disney's Peter Pan to the Rescue. (Illus.). 24p. (ps-3). 1989. pap. write for info. (ISBN 0-307-12566-1, Pub. by Golden Bks). Western Pub.

Walt Disney's Pinocchio. (Illus.). 24p. (ps-k). 1988. pap. write for info. (ISBN 0-307-10093-6, Pub. by Golden Bks). Western Pub.

Walt Disney's the Mickey Mouse Book. (Illus.). 24p. (ps-k). 1965. pap. write for info (ISBN 0-307-10077-4, Pub. by Golden Bks). Western Pub.

Walt Disney's Winnie the Pooh Scratch & Sniff Book. (Illus.). 32p. (ps-2). 1989. write for info. (ISBN 0-307-13528-4, Pub. by Golden Bks). Western Pub.

Walter, Marion. Look at Annette. Haber-Schaim, Navah, illus. LC 77-186592. 32p. (ps-3). 1977. 5.95 (ISBN 0-87131-071-6). M Evans.

—Make a Bigger Puddle, Make a Smaller Worm. Walter, Marion, illus. LC 70-186593. 32p. (ps-3). 1970. 5.95 (ISBN 0-87131-073-2). M Evans.

Walter, Mildred P. Ty's One-Man Band. Tomes, Margot, illus. LC 80-11224. 40p. (gr. k-3). 1987. Repr. of 1980 ed. 13.95 (ISBN 0-02-792300-2, Pub. by Four Winds Pr). Macmillan Child Grp.

Wang, Mary L. The Ant & the Dove. Walters, Mary C., illus. LC 89-34414. 32p. (ps-2). 1989. PLB 11.93 (ISBN 0-516-02367-5); pap. 3.95 (ISBN 0-516-42367-3). Childrens.

—The Frog Prince. Connelly, Gwen, illus. LC 86-11796. 32p. (ps-2). 1986. PLB 11.93 (ISBN 0-516-03983-0); pap. 3.95 (ISBN 0-516-43983-9). Childrens.

—El Leon y el Raton: The Lion & the Mouse. Dunnington, Tom, illus. LC 85-31441. (SPA.). 32p. (ps-2). 1988. PLB 11.93 (ISBN 0-516-33981-8); pap. 3.95 (ISBN 0-516-53981-7). Childrens.

Ward, Helen. Animal Homes. (Illus.). 24p. (ps-1). 1989. 6.95 (ISBN 0-8431-2342-7). Price Stern.

Ward, Lynd. Biggest Bear. (Illus.). 88p. (gr. k-3). 1952. 13.95 (ISBN 0-395-14806-5). HM.

—The Silver Pony: A Story in Pictures. Ward, Lynd, illus. LC 72-5402. 192p. (gr. k-3). 1973. 14.95 (ISBN 0-395-14753-0). HM.

Warner, Jerry S. Charlie McTwiddle & the Wobbly-Wheeled Sputter Putter Popper. Telfer, Judy, ed. Conlin, Jim, illus. LC 90-70308. 128p. (gr. 3-7). 1990. PLB 12.95 (ISBN 0-9626293-0-8). Windsor Medallion.

Warren, Jean. Animal Rhymes: Reproducible Pre-Reading Books for Young Children. Bittinger, Gayle, ed. Buskirk, Judith P., illus. 160p. 1990. pap. text ed. 12.95 (ISBN 0-911019-34-0). Warren Pub Hse.

—Everyday Patterns: Multi-Sized Patterns for Making Cut-Outs, Puppets, & Learning Games. Bittinger, Gayle, ed. Mohrmann, Gary, illus. 240p. (Orig.). 1990. pap. text ed. 12.95 (ISBN 0-911019-35-9). Warren Pub Hse.

—Nature Patterns: Multi-Sized Patterns for Making Cut-Outs, Puppets & Learning Games. Bittinger, Gayle, ed. Mohrmann, Gary, illus. 240p. (Orig.). 1990. pap. text ed. 12.95 (ISBN 0-911019-36-7). Warren Pub Hse.

—Object Rhymes: Reproducible Pre-Reading Books for Young Children. Bittinger, Gayle, ed. Tourtillotte, Barb, illus. 160p. (Orig.). 1990. pap. text ed. 12.95 (ISBN 0-911019-33-2). Warren Pub Hse.

Washington, Ned. When You Wish Upon a Star. Day, Alexandra, illus. 36p. (ps-1). 1987. 15.95 (ISBN 0-88138-087-3). Green Tiger Pr.

Wasmuth, Eleanor. An Alligator Day. (Illus.). 32p. (gr. 1-3). 1983. pap. 3.50 (ISBN 0-448-21703-1, G&D). Putnam Pub Group.

—The Picnic Basket. (Illus.). 32p. (gr. 1-3). 1983. pap. 3.50 (ISBN 0-448-21704-X, G&D). Putnam Pub Group.

Wasmuth, Eleanor, illus. Hey Diddle Diddle. 1986. 2.95 (ISBN 0-671-61726-5, Little Simon). S&S Trade.

—Jack & Jill. (ps). 1986. 2.95 (ISBN 0-671-61729-X, Little Simon). S&S Trade.

—The Old Woman in a Shoe. (ps). 1986. 2.95 (ISBN 0-671-61728-1, Little Simon). S&S Trade.

—This Little Pig. (ps). 1986. 2.95 (ISBN 0-671-61727-3, Little Simon). S&S Trade.

Watanabe, Shigeo. How Do I Put It On? Ohtomo, Yasuo, illus. 32p. 1991. 10.99 (ISBN 0-399-21850-5, Philomel Bks); pap. 4.95 (ISBN 0-399-21849-1, Philomel Bks). Putnam Pub Group.

—I Can Build a House! Ohtomo, Yasuo, illus. 32p. (ps-2). 1985. 8.95 (ISBN 0-399-20950-6, Philomel); pap. 3.95 (ISBN 0-399-21041-5, Philomel). Putnam Pub Group.

—I Can Take a Walk! Ohtomo, Yasuo, illus. 32p. 1991. 10.99 (ISBN 0-399-21848-3, Philomel Bks); pap. 4.95 (ISBN 0-399-21847-5, Philomel Bks). Putnam Pub Group.

—Let's Go Swimming. Ohtomo, Yasuo, illus. 32p. (ps-2). 1990. 10.95 (ISBN 0-399-21896-3, Philomel Bks). Putnam Pub Group.

—What a Good Lunch! (Illus.). 32p. (ps-2). 1991. 10.99 (ISBN 0-399-21846-7, Philomel Bks); pap. 4.95 (ISBN 0-399-21845-9, Philomel Bks). Putnam Pub Group.

—Where's My Daddy? (Illus.). 32p. 1991. 10.99 (ISBN 0-399-21852-1, Philomel Bks); pap. 4.95 (ISBN 0-399-21851-3, Philomel Bks). Putnam Pub Group.

Waters, Kate. Lion Dancer: Ernie Wan's Chinese New Year. (ps-3). 1991. pap. 3.95 (ISBN 0-590-43047-5). Scholastic Inc.

Watson. The Shop. (gr. k-2). 1980. 6.95 (ISBN 0-86020-393-X, Usborne-Hayes); PLB 11.96 (ISBN 0-88110-069-2); pap. 2.95 (ISBN 0-86020-390-5). EDC.

Watson, Claire. Big Creatures from the Past: A Pop-up Book. Cremins, Robert, illus. 14p. (gr. k-4). 1990. 14.95 (ISBN 0-399-22159-X, Putnam). Putnam Pub Group.

Watson, Clyde. Father Fox's Pennyrhymes. Watson, Wendy, illus. LC 71-146291. 56p. (ps-3). 1987. pap. 4.95 (ISBN 0-06-443137-1, Trophy). HarpC Child Bks.

Watson, E. Elaine. My Feet Are for Walking. Pride, Barbara, illus. 20p. (ps). 1986. casebound 1.59 (ISBN 0-87403-136-2, 2006). Standard Pub.

Watson, Jane W., et al. Sometimes a Family Has to Move. (Illus.). 32p. (ps-1). 1988. pap. 3.95 (ISBN 0-517-56593-5). Crown.

—Sometimes a Family Has to Split Up. (Illus.). 32p. (ps-1). 1988. pap. 4.99 (ISBN 0-517-56811-X). Crown.

Watson, Wendy. Wendy Watson's Mother Goose. Watson, Wendy, illus. LC 88-37913. (ps-2). 1989. 19.95 (ISBN 0-688-05708-X). Lothrop.

Wattenberg, Jane. Mrs. Mustard's Baby Faces. (Illus.). 6p. (ps). 1989. 4.95 (ISBN 0-87701-659-3). Chronicle Bks.

—Mrs. Mustard's Beastly Babies. (Illus.). 7p. (ps). 1990. board book 4.95 (ISBN 0-87701-683-6). Chronicle Bks.

Webb, David, illus. A Small World, 6 bks. 16p. (Orig.). (gr. k-2). 1988. Set. pap. text ed. 19.80 (ISBN 1-55911-040-6). Wright Group.

Webber, Helen. Good Night, Night. Webber, Helen, illus. (gr. k-6). 1968. 8.95 (ISBN 0-8392-3054-0). Astor-Honor.

—My Kite Is the Magic Me. Webber, Helen, illus. (gr. k-6). 1968. 8.95 (ISBN 0-8392-3055-9). Astor-Honor.

—Sea Is My Blanket. (Illus.). (gr. k-6). 1968. 8.95 (ISBN 0-8392-3057-5). Astor-Honor.

—Summer Sun. Webber, Helen, illus. (gr. k-6). 1968. 8.95 (ISBN 0-8392-3056-7). Astor-Honor.

—Webber Quartet, 4 Vols. (gr. k-6). Set. deluxe slipcase 35.00 (ISBN 0-8392-3070-2). Astor-Honor.

Weber, Bernard. Ira Says Goodbye. Weber, Bernard, illus. 40p. (ps-3). 1988. 13.95 (ISBN 0-395-48315-8). HM.

Weimann, Elaine & Friedman, Rita. The Cotton Candy Caper. (Illus.). 30p. (ps-1). 1985. PLB 10.50 (ISBN 0-89796-988-X). New Dimens Educ.

—A Dozen Delicious Doughnuts. (Illus.). 30p. (ps-1). 1988. PLB 10.50 (ISBN 0-89796-803-4). New Dimens Educ.

—Gooey Gum Is Not for Chewing. (Illus.). 30p. (ps-1). 1985. PLB 10.50 (ISBN 0-89796-989-8). New Dimens Educ.

—The Incredible Inventor. (Illus.). 30p. (ps-1). 1985. PLB 10.50 (ISBN 0-89796-985-5). New Dimens Educ.

—The Inimitable Mr. X. (Illus.). 30p. (ps-1). 1986. PLB 10.50 (ISBN 0-89796-992-8). New Dimens Educ.

—Jingling, Jangling Joggers. (Illus.). 30p. (ps-1). 1986. PLB 10.50 (ISBN 0-89796-994-4). New Dimens Educ.

—The Longest Kick. (Illus.). 30p. (ps-1). 1986. PLB 10.50 (ISBN 0-89796-990-1). New Dimens Educ.

—Lovely Lemon Lollies. (Illus.). 30p. (ps-1). 1978. PLB 10.50 (ISBN 0-89796-802-6). New Dimens Educ.

—Meet Me at the Market. (Illus.). 30p. (ps-1). 1978. PLB 10.50 (ISBN 0-89796-801-8). New Dimens Educ.

—A Most Unusual Umbrella. (Illus.). 30p. (ps-1). 1986. PLB 10.50 (ISBN 0-89796-999-5). New Dimens Educ.

—The Noisy Nose Nanny. (Illus.). 30p. (ps-1). 1985. PLB 10.50 (ISBN 0-89796-986-3). New Dimens Educ.

—The Optimistic Optimist. (Illus.). 30p. (ps-1). 1986. PLB 10.50 (ISBN 0-89796-996-0). New Dimens Educ.

—Popping Pointy Patches. (Illus.). 30p. (ps-1). 1985. PLB 10.50 (ISBN 0-89796-984-7). New Dimens Educ.

—The Rubberbit Roundup. (Illus.). 30p. (ps-1). 1986. PLB 10.50 (ISBN 0-89796-998-7). New Dimens Educ.

—The Super Sock Sensation. (Illus.). 30p. (ps-1). 1985. PLB 10.50 (ISBN 0-89796-987-1). New Dimens Educ.

—To Be or Not to Be...Quiet. (Illus.). 30p. (ps-1). 1986. PLB 10.50 (ISBN 0-89796-997-9). New Dimens Educ.

—Vanishing Vests. (Illus.). 30p. (ps-1). 1978. PLB 10.50 (ISBN 0-89796-804-2). New Dimens Educ.

—Wonderful Winks & Weather Wishes. (Illus.). 30p. (ps-1). 1986. PLB 10.50 (ISBN 0-89796-995-2). New Dimens Educ.

—The Yawn Maker. (Illus.). 30p. (ps-1). 1986. PLB 10.50 (ISBN 0-89796-993-6). New Dimens Educ.

—Zipping Zippers Save the Zoo. (Illus.). 30p. (ps-1). 1986. PLB 10.50 (ISBN 0-89796-991-X). New Dimens Educ.

Weimann, Elayne & Friedman, Rita. The A-Choo Confusion. Callen, Elizabeth, illus. 30p. (ps-1). 1988. PLB 10.50 (ISBN 0-89796-000-9). New Dimens Educ.

—The Best Quiet Meter. Callen, Elizabeth, illus. 30p. (ps-1). 1989. PLB 10.50 (ISBN 0-89796-016-5). New Dimens Educ.

—Buttonyms for Safety. Callen, Elizabeth, illus. 30p. (ps-1). 1989. PLB 10.50 (ISBN 0-89796-001-7). New Dimens Educ.

—The Cotton Candy Creature. Callen, Elizabeth, illus. 30p. (ps-1). 1989. PLB 10.50 (ISBN 0-89796-002-5). New Dimens Educ.

—The Dictionary Doughnut Shop. Callen, Elizabeth, illus. 30p. (ps-1). 1989. PLB 10.50 (ISBN 0-89796-003-3). New Dimens Educ.

—Exercise Excitement. Callen, Elizabeth, illus. 30p. (ps-1). 1988. PLB 10.50 (ISBN 0-89796-004-1). New Dimens Educ.

—Fantastic Friendship. Callen, Elizabeth, illus. 30p. (ps-1). 1988. PLB 10.50 (ISBN 0-89796-005-X). New Dimens Educ.

—Gooey Gumball Game. Callen, Elizabeth, illus. 30p. (ps-1). 1989. PLB 10.50 (ISBN 0-89796-006-8). New Dimens Educ.

—The Hat House Hotel. Callen, Elizabeth, illus. 30p. (ps-1). 1988. PLB 10.50 (ISBN 0-89796-007-6). New Dimens Educ.

—Inchy the Incredible Invention. Callen, Elizabeth, illus. 30p. (ps-1). 1988. PLB 10.50 (ISBN 0-89796-008-4). New Dimens Educ.

—The Kazoo Kicker. Callen, Elizabeth, illus. 30p. (ps-1). 1989. PLB 10.50 (ISBN 0-89796-010-6). New Dimens Educ.

—Lemonberry Lollipops. Callen, Elizabeth, illus. 30p. (ps-1). 1989. PLB 10.50 (ISBN 0-89796-011-4). New Dimens Educ.

—Mr. J's Junkyard. Callen, Elizabeth, illus. 30p. (ps-1). 1989. PLB 10.50 (ISBN 0-89796-009-2). New Dimens Educ.

—Mr. X's Mix-ups. Callen, Elizabeth, illus. 30p. (ps-1). 1989. PLB 10.50 (ISBN 0-89796-023-8). New Dimens Educ.

—Munching Magic. Callen, Elizabeth, illus. 30p. (ps-1). 1988. PLB 10.50 (ISBN 0-89796-012-2). New Dimens Educ.

—Ostrich Express. Callen, Elizabeth, illus. 30p. (ps-1). 1988. PLB 10.50 (ISBN 0-89796-014-9). New Dimens Educ.

—Parking Pandemonium. Callen, Elizabeth, illus. 30p. (ps-1). 1989. PLB 10.50 (ISBN 0-89796-015-7). New Dimens Educ.

—The Rubber Band Runner Champion. Callen, Elizabeth, illus. 30p. (ps-1). 1989. PLB 10.50 (ISBN 0-89796-017-3). New Dimens Educ.

—Say No & Fly Away! Callen, Elizabeth, illus. 30p. (ps-1). 1988. PLB 10.50 (ISBN 0-89796-013-0). New Dimens Educ.

—Super Socks for Courage. Callen, Elizabeth, illus. 30p. (ps-1). 1989. PLB 10.50 (ISBN 0-89796-018-1). New Dimens Educ.

—Tall Toothbrush Retires. Callen, Elizabeth, illus. 30p. (ps-1). 1988. PLB 10.50 (ISBN 0-89796-019-X). New Dimens Educ.

—Valuable Volunteers. Callen, Elizabeth, illus. 30p. (ps-1). 1989. PLB 10.50 (ISBN 0-89796-021-1). New Dimens Educ.

—The Worry Machine. Callen, Elizabeth, illus. 30p. (ps-1). 1989. PLB 10.50 (ISBN 0-89796-022-X). New Dimens Educ.

—Yawn-Maker Wanted. Callen, Elizabeth, illus. 30p. (ps-1). 1989. PLB 10.50 (ISBN 0-89796-024-6). New Dimens Educ.

—You Forget Too. Callen, Elizabeth, illus. 30p. (ps-1). 1989. PLB 10.50 (ISBN 0-89796-020-3). New Dimens Educ.

—Zip Codes. Callen, Elizabeth, illus. 30p. (ps-1). 1989. PLB 10.50 (ISBN 0-89796-025-4). New Dimens Educ.

Weingarten, Elaine. The Dog Who Didn't Know about Snow. Sweeney, Phyllis, illus. 58p. (ps-3). 1988. text ed. 13.50 (ISBN 0-89777-703-4, 97005). Soc Issues.

—Kenny the Caterpillar. Sweeney, Phyllis, illus. 30p. (ps-3). 1988. text ed. 13.50 (ISBN 0-89777-702-6, 97003). Soc Issues.

—One Duck. Sweeney, Phyllis, illus. 56p. (ps-3). 1988. text ed. 13.50 (ISBN 0-89777-700-X, 97001). Soc Issues.

—The Robin Who Was Afraid to Fly. Sweeney, Phyllis, illus. 50p. (ps-3). 1988. text ed. 13.50 (ISBN 0-89777-701-8, 97002). Soc Issues.

Weiss, Ellen. Muppet Kids in Kermit's Bad Dreams. Brannon, Tom, illus. (ps-3). 1991. pap. write for info. (ISBN 0-307-12662-5, Golden Pr). Western Pub.

—Muppet Kids in Piggy Takes a Dare. Brannon, Tom, illus. (ps-3). 1991. pap. write for info. (ISBN 0-307-12658-7, Golden Pr). Western Pub.

—Muppet Kids in Too Many Promises. Brannon, Tom, illus. (ps-3). 1991. pap. write for info. (ISBN 0-307-12654-4, Golden Pr). Western Pub.

—Muppet Kids in Worried about Divorce. Cooke, Tom, illus. (ps-3). 1991. pap. 1.25 (ISBN 0-307-12657-9, Golden Pr). Western Pub.

—Oh Beans! Starring Wax Bean. Hall, Susan, illus. LC 88-4902. 32p. (gr. k-3). 1989. PLB 8.79 (ISBN 0-8167-1408-8); pap. text ed. 1.95 (ISBN 0-8167-1409-6). Troll Assocs.

—A Visit to the Sesame Street Zoo. Leigh, Tom, illus. LC 88-3201. 32p. (Orig.). (ps-1). 1988. lib. bdg. 5.99 (ISBN 0-394-90447-8, Random Juv); pap. 2.25 (ISBN 0-394-80447-3, Random Juv). Random.

Weiss, Nicki. Barney Is Big. LC 87-8546. (Illus.). 24p. (ps-1). 1988. 11.95 (ISBN 0-688-07586-X); lib. bdg. 11.88 (ISBN 0-688-07587-8). Greenwillow.

—Barney Is Big. 1989. pap. 3.95 (ISBN 0-14-054059-8, Puffin). Puffin Bks.

—If You're Happy & You Know It. LC 86-753170. (Illus.). 40p. (gr. k-3). 1987. 14.95 (ISBN 0-688-06444-2). Greenwillow.

—Princess Pearl. (ps-3). 1987. pap. 3.95 (ISBN 0-14-050759-0, Puffin). Puffin Bks.

Welber, Robert. The Winter Picnic. Ray, Deborah, illus. (ps-3). 1973. pap. 0.95 (ISBN 0-394-82621-3). Pantheon.

Well, Rosemary. Max's Bedtime. Wells, Rosemary, illus. LC 84-14968. 12p. (ps-k). 1985. bds. 3.95 (ISBN 0-8037-0160-8). Dial Bks Young.

Wells, Rosemary. Abdul. Wells, Rosemary, illus. LC 74-18595. 40p. (ps-3). 1986. pap. 3.50 (ISBN 0-8037-0281-7). Dial Bks Young.

—Benjamin & Tulip. Wells, Rosemary, illus. LC 73-6018. 32p. (ps-2). 1973. 8.95 (ISBN 0-8037-1808-X); PLB 9.89 (ISBN 0-8037-2057-2); pap. 3.50 (ISBN 0-8037-0545-X). Dial Bks Young.

—Hooray for Max. Wells, Rosemary, illus. (ps). 1986. bds. 15.95 2 bks. & doll (ISBN 0-8037-0202-7); Max doll 8.95 (ISBN 0-8037-0203-5). Dial Bks Young.

—Max's Bath. Wells, Rosemary, illus. LC 84-14969. 12p. (ps-k). 1985. bds. 3.95 (ISBN 0-8037-0162-4). Dial Bks Young.

—Max's Birthday. Wells, Rosemary, illus. LC 84-14970. 12p. (ps-k). 1985. bds. 3.50 (ISBN 0-8037-0163-2). Dial Bks Young.

—Noisy Nora. 40p. (gr. k-3). pap. 1.95 (ISBN 0-590-00352-6). Scholastic Inc.

Wells, Tony. All Sorts. Wells, Tony, illus. 32p. (Orig.). (ps-1). 1988. pap. 4.95 (ISBN 0-689-71185-9, Aladdin). Macmillan.

—What You Can See by the Sea? (ps up). 1990. PLB 4.98 (ISBN 0-7924-5177-5, Mallard Pr). BDD Promo Bk.

—What You Can See in the Forest? (ps up). 1990. PLB 4.98 (ISBN 0-7924-5176-7, Mallard Pr). BDD Promo Bk.

—What You Can See in the Town? (ps up). 1990. PLB 4.98 (ISBN 0-7924-5178-3, Mallard Pr). BDD Promo Bk.

—What You Can See on the Farm? (ps up). 1990. PLB 4.98 (ISBN 0-7924-5179-1, Mallard Pr). BDD Promo Bk.

Werner, Jane. The Tall Book of Make-Believe. Williams, Garth, illus. 92p. (gr. k-3). 1950. 7.95i (ISBN 0-06-026505-1). HarpC Child Bks.

West, Cindy. Mickey Mouse & the Peanuts. Biggs, Gene & Wilson, Roy, illus. LC 87-83495. 40p. (gr. k-2). 1988. write for info. (ISBN 0-307-11691-3). Western Pub.

—Minnie 'n' Me: the Surprise Friend. (ps-3). 1990. write for info. (ISBN 0-307-11588-7). Western Pub.

—Welcome to Little Golden Book Land. (Illus.). (ps-2). 1989. write for info. (ISBN 0-307-12084-8, Golden Bks). Western Pub.

West, Colin. Have You Seen the Crocodile? West, Colin, illus. LC 85-45748. 24p. (ps-2). 1986. pap. 3.95 (ISBN 0-06-443101-0, Trophy). HarpC Child Bks.

—Have You Seen the Crocodile? West, Colin, illus. LC 85-45751. 24p. (ps-2). 1986. PLB 11.89 (ISBN 0-397-32172-4, Lipp Jr Bks). HarpC Child Bks.

—Hello, Great Big Bullfrog. West, Colin, illus. LC 87-3729. 24p. (ps-2). 1988. 10.95 (ISBN 0-397-32249-6, Lipp Jr Bks). HarpC Child Bks.

—The "Hello, Great Big Bullfrog" LC 87-8452. (Illus.). 24p. (ps-2). 1989. pap. 3.95 (ISBN 0-06-443165-7, Trophy). HarpC Child Bks.

—The King's Toothache. Dalton, Anne, illus. LC 87-3713. 32p. (ps-2). 1988. 12.95 (ISBN 0-397-32251-8, Lipp Jr Bks); PLB 12.89 (ISBN 0-397-32252-6). HarpC Child Bks.

—Not Me, Said the Monkey. West, Colin, illus. LC 87-3712. 24p. (ps-2). 1988. 10.95 (ISBN 0-397-32253-4, Lipp Jr Bks); PLB 12.89 (ISBN 0-397-32254-2). HarpC Child Bks.

—Pardon?" Said the Giraffe. West, Colin, illus. LC 85-45747. 24p. (ps-2). 1986. pap. 3.95 (ISBN 0-06-443102-9, Trophy). HarpC Child Bks.

—Pardon?" Said the Giraffe. West, Colin, illus. LC 85-45750. 24p. (ps-2). 1986. PLB 11.89 (ISBN 0-397-32173-2, Lipp Jr Bks). HarpC Child Bks.

West, Cyndy. I Am Mickey Mouse. DiCicco, Sue, illus. (ps-k). 1991. 3.50 (ISBN 0-307-12166-6, Golden Pr). Western Pub.

Westcott, Nadine B. Getting Up. Westcott, Nadine B., illus. LC 86-28721. (ps). 1987. pap. 4.95 (ISBN 0-316-93131-4, Joy St Bks). Little.

—Going to Bed. Westcott, Nadine B., illus. LC 86-28767. (ps). 1987. pap. 4.95 (ISBN 0-316-93132-2, Joy St Bks). Little.

Wetzel, Rick & Swanson, Maggie. Big Bird's Bedtime Story. Wetzel, Rick & Swanson, Maggie, illus. LC 87-4764. 32p. (ps-1). 1987. lib. bdg. 5.99 (ISBN 0-394-99126-5, Random Juv); pap. 2.25 (ISBN 0-394-89126-0, Random Juv). Random.

Weyn, Suzanne. Chip'n'Dale's Rescue Rangers: The Missing Eggs Caper. Edwards, Paul, illus. (ps). 1989. pap. write for info. (ISBN 0-307-11718-9, Pub. by Golden Bks). Western Pub.

What Belongs? (Illus.). 12p. (ps-1). 1988. 5.95 (ISBN 0-8431-2662-0). Price Stern.

What Do Babies Do. LC 84-61897. 14p. (ps). 1985. bds. 1.95 (ISBN 0-394-87279-7, Random Juv). Random.

What Do Toddlers Do? LC 84-61895. (Illus.). 14p. (ps). 1985. pap. 1.95 (ISBN 0-394-87280-0, Random Juv). Random.

What Should I Choose? (Illus.). 24p. (gr. k-2). 1989. bds. 3.95 (ISBN 0-87449-590-3). Modern Pub NYC.

Whatever Happened to the Dinosaurs? LC 84-37795. 32p. (Orig.). (ps-3). 1987. pap. 4.95 (ISBN 0-15-295296-9, VoyB). HarBraceJ.

What's So Funny, Puppies? 24p. (gr. k-2). 1990. 3.95 (ISBN 0-87449-666-7). Modern Pub NYC.

Wheeler, Cindy. Marmalade's Christmas Present. Wheeler, Cindy, illus. LC 83-24406. 32p. (ps-1). 1984. Knopf.

—Rose. Wheeler, Cindy, illus. LC 83-19985. 32p. (ps-1). 1985. lib. bdg. 10.99 (ISBN 0-394-96233-8). Knopf.

—Sally Wants to Help: (Just Right for 2's & 3's) Wheeler, Cindy, illus. LC 88-3152. 24p. (ps). 1988. 4.95 (ISBN 0-394-89339-5, Random Juv). Random.

Wheels. (Illus.). (ps). 3.50 (ISBN 0-7214-9088-3). Ladybird Bks.

Wheels Go Round. (Illus.). 24p. (ps-k). 1989. 7.95 (ISBN 0-448-21030-4, G&D). Putnam Pub Group.

Wheels That Work. 16p. (ps-k). 1988. 2.95 (ISBN 0-671-64872-1, Little Simon). S&S Trade.

Whelan, Gloria. A Week of Raccoons. Munsinger, Lynn, illus. LC 87-16800. 40p. (ps-1). 1988. 11.95 (ISBN 0-394-88396-9); lib. bdg. 12.99 (ISBN 0-394-98396-3). Knopf.

Whelchel, Sandy. A Day in Blue: Follow Freddy Falcon on a Child's Tour of the U. S. Air Force Academy. Brandt, Bill, illus. 28p. (gr. k-4). 1986. pap. 2.95 (ISBN 1-878406-00-0). Parker Dstb.

Where Do We Live? (ps-k). 1986. 4.95 (ISBN 1-55513-176-X, Chariot Bks). Cook.

Where's Baby Mickey. (Illus.). (ps). 1986. pap. 3.95 (ISBN 0-671-62931-X, Little Simon). S&S Trade.

Whitehead, Patricia. Arnold Plays Baseball. Karas, Brian, illus. LC 84-8827. 32p. (gr. k-2). 1985. PLB 10.89 (ISBN 0-8167-0367-1); pap. text ed. 2.95 (ISBN 0-8167-0368-X). Troll Assocs.

—Best Halloween Book. Britt, Stephanie, illus. LC 84-8828. 32p. (gr. k-2). 1985. PLB 10.89 (ISBN 0-8167-0373-6); pap. text ed. 2.95 (ISBN 0-8167-0374-4). Troll Assocs.

—Best Thanksgiving Book. Hall, Susan T., illus. LC 84-8831. 32p. (gr. k-2). 1985. PLB 10.89 (ISBN 0-8167-0371-X); pap. text ed. 2.95 (ISBN 0-8167-0372-8). Troll Assocs.

—Best Valentine Book. Harvy, Paul, illus. LC 84-8829. 32p. (gr. k-2). 1985. PLB 10.89 (ISBN 0-8167-0369-8); pap. text ed. 2.95 (ISBN 0-8167-0370-1). Troll Assocs.

—Christmas Alphabet Book. Borgo, Deborah C., illus. LC 84-8830. 32p. (gr. k-2). 1985. PLB 10.89 (ISBN 0-8167-0365-5); pap. text ed. 2.95 (ISBN 0-8167-0366-3). Troll Assocs.

—Here Comes Hungry Albert. Karas, G. Brian, illus. LC 84-8835. 32p. (gr. k-2). 1985. PLB 10.89 (ISBN 0-8167-0379-5); pap. text ed. 2.95 (ISBN 0-8167-0380-9). Troll Assocs.

—Let's Go to the Farm. Gold, Ethel, illus. LC 84-8834. 32p. (gr. k-2). 1985. lib. bdg. 10.89 (ISBN 0-8167-0377-9); pap. 2.95 (ISBN 0-8167-0378-7). Troll Assocs.

—Let's Go to the Zoo. Boyd, Patti, illus. LC 84-8832. 32p. (gr. k-2). 1985. PLB 10.89 (ISBN 0-8167-0375-2); pap. text ed. 2.95 (ISBN 0-8167-0376-0). Troll Assocs.

—What a Funny Bunny. Page, Don, illus. LC 84-8833. 32p. (gr. k-2). 1985. PLB 10.89 (ISBN 0-8167-0361-2); pap. text ed. 2.95 (ISBN 0-8167-0362-0). Troll Assocs.

Whitelaw, Nancy. A Beautiful Pearl. Tucker, Kathleen, ed. Friedman, Judith, illus. 32p. (gr. 2-5). 1991. 12.95 (ISBN 0-8075-0599-4). A Whitman.

Who Belongs? (Illus.). 12p. (ps-1). 1988. 5.95 (ISBN 0-8431-2661-2). Price Stern.

Who Changes into What? (Illus.). 10p. (gr. k-3). 1986. 4.95 (ISBN 0-8431-1558-0). Price Stern.

Who Eats What? (Illus.). 10p. (gr. k-3). 1986. 4.95 (ISBN 0-8431-1559-9). Price Stern.

Who Is in the Water? (Illus.). 10p. (gr. k-3). 1986. 4.95 (ISBN 0-8431-1560-2). Price Stern.

Who Lives Here? (Illus.). 10p. 1986. 4.95 (ISBN 0-8431-1557-2). Price Stern.

Whose Baby Are You. Dunn, Phoebe, et al, photos by. LC 86-62382. (Illus.). 18p. (ps). 1987. 4.95 (ISBN 0-394-88629-1, Random Juv). Random.

Whyte, Malcolm. Huggs & Cuddles Teddy Bear Funbook. (gr. 2 up). pap. 3.50 (ISBN 0-8431-1757-5). Troubador Pr.

Wickstrom, Sylvie K., illus. Wheels on the Bus. 32p. (ps-2). 1988. PLB 9.95 (ISBN 0-517-56784-9). Crown.

Wiggs, Susan. The Canary Who Sailed with Columbus. Roberts, Melissa, ed. Anderson, Sharon, illus. 48p. (ps-2). 1989. 12.95 (ISBN 0-89015-719-7, Pub. by Panda Bks). Eakin Pr.

Wik, Lars, photos by. Baby's First Words. LC 84-60700. (Illus.). 28p. (ps). 1985. pap. 2.95 (ISBN 0-394-86945-1, Random Juv). Random.

Wikler, Madeline & Groner, Judye. I Have Four Questions. Radin, Chari M., illus. LC 88-83570. 12p. (ps). 1989. bds. 4.95 (ISBN 0-930494-90-3). Kar Ben.

Wilburn, Kathy, illus. Pudgy Pals. 16p. (ps). 1983. pap. 2.95 (ISBN 0-448-10203-X, G&D). Putnam Pub Group.

—The Pudgy Rock-a-Bye Book. 16p. (ps). 1983. pap. 2.95 (ISBN 0-448-10206-4, G&D). Putnam Pub Group.

Wild, Anne. The Egyptians Pop-Up. (Illus.). 32p. (gr. 5-9). 1986. pap. 6.95 (ISBN 0-906212-44-8, Tarquin). Parkwest Pubns.

Wild West Bears, Bk. 24. (ps-1). write for info. (ISBN 0-931363-22-5). Celia Totus Enter.

Wilde, Irma, illus. Baby's Farm Animals. 20p. (ps-1). 1986. bds. 3.95 (ISBN 0-448-03094-2, G&D). Putnam Pub Group.

Wilde, Oscar. The Canterville Ghost. Zwerger, Lisbeth, illus. LC 86-8179. (gr. 4 up). 1986. 15.95 (ISBN 0-88708-027-8). Picture Bk Studio.

Wildsmith, Brian. The Circus. (Illus.). (ps-3). 1970. pap. 6.95x (ISBN 0-19-272102-X). Oxford U Pr.

—Goat's Trail. Wildsmith, Brian, illus. LC 86-2731. 40p. (gr. k-3). 1986. 10.95 (ISBN 0-394-88276-8); lib. bdg. 12.99 (ISBN 0-394-98276-2). Knopf.

—Python's Party. (Illus.). 32p. (ps up). 1991. pap. 6.95 (ISBN 0-19-272229-8, 12355). Oxford U Pr.

Wilhelm, Hans. Oh, What a Mess. (Illus.). 32p. (gr. k-3). 1988. PLB 12.95 (ISBN 0-517-56909-4). Crown.

Wilkin, Eloise. Baby's Bedtime. Wilkin, Eloise, illus. 12p. (ps). 1985. 2.95 (ISBN 0-448-10429-6, G&D). Putnam Pub Group.

—Baby's House. Wilkin, Eloise, illus. 12p. (ps). 1985. 2.95 (ISBN 0-448-10426-1, G&D). Putnam Pub Group.

—Baby's Toys. Wilkin, Eloise, illus. 12p. (ps). 1985. 2.95 (ISBN 0-448-10427-X, G&D). Putnam Pub Group.

Wilkin, Eloise, illus. Baby Looks. LC 86-80140. 12p. (ps). 1988. pap. write for info. (ISBN 0-307-06049-7). Western Pub.

—Play with Me. LC 86-80141. 12p. (ps). 1988. pap. write for info. (ISBN 0-307-06048-9, Pub. by Golden Bks). Western Pub.

Willard, Nancy. The Marzipan Moon. Sewall, Marcia, illus. LC 80-24221. 48p. (ps-3). 1981. pap. 3.95 (ISBN 0-15-252963-2, VoyB). HarBraceJ.

—The Mountains of Quilt. DePaola, Tomie, illus. LC 86-19577. 40p. (ps-3). 1987. 12.95 (ISBN 0-15-256010-6, HJ). HarBraceJ.

—The Nightgown of the Sullen Moon. McPhail, David, illus. LC 83-8472. 32p. (Orig.). (ps-3). 1987. pap. 3.95 (ISBN 0-15-257430-1, VoyB). HarBraceJ.

Williams, Barbara. Donna Jean's Disaster. Levine, Abby, ed. Apple, Margot, illus. 32p. (gr. 1-5). 1986. PLB 10.95 (ISBN 0-8075-1682-1). A Whitman.

Williams, Garth. Rabbits' Wedding. Williams, Garth, illus. LC 58-5285. 30p. (ps-1). 1958. 13.95 (ISBN 0-06-026495-0); PLB 14.89 (ISBN 0-06-026496-9). HarpC Child Bks.

Williams, Helen, illus. & compiled by. The Language of Flowers. 32p. (ps up). 1988. 10.95 (ISBN 0-525-44391-6, 01063-320, DCB). Dutton Child Bks.

Williams, Jay. Everyone Knows What a Dragon Looks Like. 32p. (gr. k-3). 1984. pap. 5.95 (ISBN 0-02-045600-X, Aladdin). Macmillan Child Grp.

Williams, Linda. The Little Old Lady Who Was Not Afraid of Anything. Lloyd, Megan, illus. LC 85-48250. 32p. (ps-2). 1986. 13.95 (ISBN 0-690-04584-0, Crowell Jr Bks); PLB 13.89 (ISBN 0-690-04586-7). HarpC Child Bks.

—The Little Old Lady Who Was Not Afraid of Anything. Lloyd, Megan, illus. LC 85-48250. 32p. (ps-2). 1988. pap. 3.95 (ISBN 0-06-443183-5, Trophy). HarpC Child Bks.

Williams, Marcia. The First Christmas. Williams, Marcia, illus. LC 88-1961. 32p. (Orig.). (ps-1). 1988. 4.95 (ISBN 0-394-80434-1, Random Juv). Random.

Williams, Margery. The Velveteen Rabbit. Graham, Florence, illus. 32p. (ps-2). 1987. pap. 1.95 (ISBN 0-448-19083-4, Platt & Munk); incl. cassette 5.95 (ISBN 0-448-19086-9, Platt & Munk). Putnam Pub Group.

Williams, Susan. Poppy's First Year. Williams, Susan, illus. LC 88-21345. 32p. (ps-2). 1989. 13.95 (ISBN 0-02-793031-9, Four Winds). Macmillan Child Grp.

Williams, Vera B. Music, Music for Everyone. LC 83-14196. (Illus.). 32p. (ps-3). 1988. pap. 3.95 (ISBN 0-688-07811-7, Mulberry). Morrow.

Willis, Jeanne. The Long Blue Blazer. Varley, Susan, illus. LC 87-24453. 32p. (ps-2). 1988. 11.95 (ISBN 0-525-44381-9, 01160-350, DCB). Dutton Child Bks.

Willis, Val. The Secret in the Matchbox. Shelley, John, photos by. LC 87-46000. (Illus.). 32p. (gr. 3 up). 1988. 12.95 (ISBN 0-374-36603-9). FS&G.

Wilson, Sarah. Beware the Dragons! Wilson, Sarah, illus. LC 85-42164. 32p. (ps-3). 1988. pap. 4.95 (ISBN 0-06-443186-X, Trophy). HarpC Child Bks.

—Three in a Ballon. 1990. pap. 12.95 (ISBN 0-590-42631-1). Scholastic Inc.

Winborn, Marsha, illus. Inside Sesame Street. 22p. (ps). 1986. write for info. (ISBN 0-307-12142-9, Pub. by Golden Bks.). Western Pub.

Windham, Sophie, retold by. & illus. Noah's Ark: A Peek-Through-the-Window Book. 32p. (ps-1). 1989. 14.95 (ISBN 0-399-21564-6, Putnam). Putnam Pub Group.

Windham, Sophie, illus. Twelve Days of Christmas. 32p. (ps-1). 1986. pap. 13.95 (ISBN 0-399-21327-9, Putnam). Putnam Pub Group.

Windsor, Patricia. The Sandman's Eyes. (gr. k-12). 1987. pap. 2.95 (ISBN 0-440-97585-9, LFL). Dell.

Winik, J. T. Fun with Numbers. Winik, J. T., illus. 32p. (ps-k). 1985. pap. 2.50 (ISBN 0-88625-104-4). Durkin Hayes Pub.

Winik, J. T. & Pashuk, Lauren. Fun from A-Z. Winik, J. T. & Pashuk, Lauren, illus. 32p. (ps-k). 1985. pap. 2.50 (ISBN 0-88625-105-2). Durkin Hayes Pub.

Winter, Ginny L. What's in My Tree. Winter, Ginny L., illus. (gr. k-1). 1962. 8.95 (ISBN 0-8392-3044-3). Astor-Honor.

Winter, Jeanette, illus. Hush Little Baby. LC 83-12182. 36p. (ps-1). 1984. (Pant Bks Young). Pantheon.

Winthrop, Elizabeth. Grover Sleeps Over. Swanson, Maggie, illus. LC 83-83279. 32p. (ps). 1984. write for info. (ISBN 0-307-12010-4, 12010, Golden Bks). Western Pub.

—Shoes. Joyce, William, illus. LC 85-45841. 32p. (ps-2). 1986. 12.95 (ISBN 0-06-026591-4); PLB 13.89 (ISBN 0-06-026592-2). HarpC Child Bks.

—Shoes. Joyce, William, illus. LC 85-45841. 32p. (ps-3). 1988. pap. 3.95 (ISBN 0-06-443171-1, Trophy). HarpC Child Bks.

—Shoes. Joyce, William, illus. (ps-1). 1988. bk. & cassette 19.95 (ISBN 0-87499-113-7); bk. & cassette 12.95 (ISBN 0-87499-112-9); 4 cassettes & guide 27.95 (ISBN 0-87499-114-5). Live Oak Media.

—Strawberry Shortcake & the Big Balloon Race. Sustendal, Pat, illus. 40p. (ps-3). 1983. cancelled 5.95 (ISBN 0-910313-08-3). Parker Bros.

Wiskur, Darrell. Mary's Merry Chase. Silver Dollar City, Inc. Staff, ed. Wiskur, Darrell, illus. (ps-1). 1977. 1.99g (ISBN 0-686-19126-9). Silver Dollar.

Witch Who Changed Her Ways Pop-Up. 10p. (ps-3). 1990. 3.95 (ISBN 0-8167-2184-X). Troll Assocs.

Witkowski, George. The Cloudbumpers. (Illus.). 54p. (gr. k-4). 1987. pap. 4.95 (ISBN 0-941889-00-9). Kiddyhawk Pub.

Witte, Eve & Witte, Pat. Touch Me Book. Rockwell, Harlow, illus. (ps). 1961. write for info (ISBN 0-307-12146-1, Golden Bks). Western Pub.

Wittman, Sally. A Special Trade. Gundersheimer, Karen, illus. LC 77-25673. 32p. (ps-2). 1985. pap. 4.95 (ISBN 0-06-443071-5, Trophy). HarpC Child Bks.

Wolde, Gunilla. Betsy & the Doctor. Wolde, Gunilla, illus. LC 78-50057. 24p. (ps). 1978. 4.95 (ISBN 0-394-83782-7). Random.

—Betsy's Baby Brother. Wolde, Gunilla, illus. LC 75-7568. 24p. (ps). 1990. 4.95 (ISBN 0-394-83162-4). Random.

—Betsy's First Day at Day Care. Wolde, Gunilla, illus. LC 76-9322. 24p. (ps). 1976. 4.95 (ISBN 0-394-83327-9). Random.

—This Is Betsy. Wolde, Gunilla, illus. LC 75-7566. 24p. (ps). 1990. 4.95 (ISBN 0-394-83161-6). Random.

Wolf, Aline D. A Book about Anna: For Children & Their Parents. Rajpar, Shamin & Wolf, Gerald, illus. LC 80-84874. 56p. (Orig.). (ps-k). 1981. 9.95x (ISBN 0-685-03953-6); pap. 5.95x (ISBN 0-9601016-4-0). Parent-Child Pr.

Wolf, Bernard. In the Year of the Tiger. Wolf, Bernard, photos by. LC 87-22007. (Illus.). 128p. (gr. 5 up). 1988. 14.95 (ISBN 0-02-793390-3, Mcmillan Child Bk). Macmillan Child Grp.

Wolf, Janet. Adelaide to Zeke. Wolf, Janet, illus. LC 86-45770. 32p. (ps-2). 1987. 11.95 (ISBN 0-06-026597-3); PLB 11.89 (ISBN 0-06-026598-1). HarpC Child Bks.

Wolf, Jill. Bartleby's One-Bad-Day-After-Another. Wasmuth, Eleanor, illus. 24p. (ps-3). 1984. pap. 1.95. Antioch Pub Co.

—Bears in Toyland. 1988. pap. 2.25 (ISBN 0-89954-785-0). Antioch Pub Co.

—Teddy Bear's Easter Picnic. Nelson, Linda K., illus. 24p. (gr. 3-7). 1985. pap. 2.25 (ISBN 0-89954-424-X). Antioch Pub Co.

—Troll's Christmas. Till, Tom, illus. 24p. (gr. 3-7). 1981. pap. 2.25 (ISBN 0-89954-460-6). Antioch Pub Co.

Wolf, Jim. Wise Quacks. 1988. pap. 2.25 (ISBN 0-89954-950-0). Antioch Pub Co.

Wolff, Ashley. Only the Cat Saw. (Illus.). (ps-3). 1988. pap. 3.95 (ISBN 0-14-050853-8, Puffin). Puffin Bks.

—A Year of Beasts. Wolff, Ashley, illus. LC 85-27419. 32p. (ps-1). 1986. 11.95 (ISBN 0-525-44240-5, DCB). Dutton Child Bks.

—A Year of Birds. (ps-3). 1988. pap. 3.95 (ISBN 0-14-050854-6, Puffin). Puffin Bks.

Wood, Audrey. Heckedy Peg. Wood, Don, illus. LC 86-33639. 32p. (ps-3). 1987. 14.95 (ISBN 0-15-233678-8, HJ). HarBraceJ.

—Presto Change-O. (Illus.). 32p. (ps-2). 1983. 5.50 (ISBN 0-85953-181-3, Child's Play England). Childs Play.

—Three Sisters. Hoffman, Rosekrans, illus. LC 85-29392. 48p. (ps-3). 1986. 9.95 (ISBN 0-8037-0279-5); PLB 9.89 (ISBN 0-8037-0280-9). Dial Bks Young.

Wood, Don. Little Mouse, the Red Ripe Strawberry & the Big Hungry Bear. (ps-3). 1990. pap. 5.95 (ISBN 0-85953-012-4). Childs Play.

—Quick As a Cricket. (ps-3). 1990. pap. 5.95 (ISBN 0-85953-306-9). Childs Play.

Wood, Don & Wood, Audrey. Piggies. Perlman, Willa, ed. Wood, Don, illus. 32p. (ps-1). 1991. 13.95 (ISBN 0-15-256342-3). HarBraceJ.

Wood, Leslie. Bump, Bump, Bump. (Illus.). 16p. 1987. pap. 2.95 (ISBN 0-19-272162-3). Oxford U Pr.

Woody, Marilyn. God Made My World. John, Joyce, illus. 14p. (ps). 1988. bds. 6.95 (ISBN 1-55513-320-7, Chariot Bks). Cook.

Woody, Marilyn J. God Cares for Me. John, Joyce, illus. 14p. (ps). 1988. bds. 6.95 (ISBN 1-55513-319-3, Chariot Bks). Cook.

Wooly Has Two Dozen Sisters. 24p. (gr. k-2). 1990. 3.95 (ISBN 0-87449-665-9). Modern Pub NYC.

World Around Us. (Illus.). (ps-7). 1987. 5.95 (ISBN 0-553-05411-2). Bantam.

Worley, Daryl. Billy & the Big Truck. Daab, John, illus. 32p. (ps). Date not set. 9.95 (ISBN 0-924067-06-3). Tyke Corp.

—Billy & the Bright Red Ball. Daab, John, illus. 32p. (ps). Date not set. 9.95 (ISBN 0-924067-05-5). Tyke Corp.

—Billy & the Chocolate Chip Cookies. Daab, John, illus. 32p. (ps). 1989. 9.95 (ISBN 0-924067-02-0). Tyke Corp.

—Billy & the Department Store. Daab, John, illus. 32p. (ps). Date not set. 9.95 (ISBN 0-924067-04-7). Tyke Corp.

—Billy & the Scary Things. Daab, John, illus. (ps). Date not set. 9.95 (ISBN 0-924067-03-9). Tyke Corp.

Wormell, Christopher. Alphabet of Animals. LC 90-2774. 64p. 1990. 17.95 (ISBN 0-8037-0876-9). Dial Bks Young.

Worth, Bonnie. Baby Kermit's Opposites. 1988. write for info. (ISBN 0-02-689109-3). Checkerboard Pr.

Worthington, Joan & Worthington, Phoebe. Teddy Bear Farmer. (ps-1). pap. 2.95 (ISBN 0-317-62188-2, Puffin). Puffin Bks.

Worthington, P., et al. Teddy Bear Postman. 1987. pap. 7.95 (ISBN 0-670-80798-2). Viking Child Bks.

Worthington, Phoebe. Teddy Bear Postman. (ps-1). 1987. pap. 2.95 (ISBN 0-14-050500-8, Puffin). Puffin Bks.

Wright, Friere & Foreman, Michael. Seven in One Blow. Wright, Friere & Foreman, Michael, illus. 32p. (ps-3). 1981. lib. bdg. 4.99 (ISBN 0-394-93805-4). Random.

Wylie, Joanne. Un Cuento de Peces y Sus Formas. Kratky, Lada, tr. Wylie, David, illus. LC 85-23264. (SPA.). 32p. (ps-2). 1986. PLB 14.60 (ISBN 0-516-32985-5); pap. 3.95 (ISBN 0-516-52985-4). Childrens.

Wyllie, Stephen & Axworthy, Anni. The Great Race. Wyllie, Stephen & Axworthy, Anni, illus. LC 86-45498. 16p. (ps-3). 1987. 8.95 (ISBN 0-694-00126-0). HarpC Child Bks.

Yashima, Taro. Umbrella. Yashima, Taro, illus. (ps-1). 1977. pap. 3.95 (ISBN 0-14-050240-8, Puffin). Puffin Bks.

—Umbrella. Yashima, T., illus. (ps-1). 1958. pap. 13.95 (ISBN 0-670-73858-1). Viking Child Bks.

Yeatman, Linda. Pickles. Littlewood, Valerie, illus. (Illus.). 64p. (gr. 2-5). 1988. pap. 2.95 (ISBN 0-8120-3955-6). Barron.

Yektai, Niki. Bears in Pairs. De Groat, Diane, illus. LC 86-18828. 32p. (ps-k). 1987. 13.95 (ISBN 0-02-793691-0, Bradbury Pr). Macmillan Child Grp.

—Crazy Clothes. Stevenson, Sucie, illus. LC 87-15312. 32p. (ps-2). 1988. 12.95 (ISBN 0-02-793692-9, Bradbury Pr). Macmillan Child Grp.

—What's Missing. Ryan, Susannah, illus. LC 87-784. 32p. (ps-1). 1989. 12.95 (ISBN 0-89919-510-5, Pub. by Clarion). Ticknor & Fields.

Yezback, Steven A. Pumpkinseeds. Thompson, Mozelle, illus. LC 76-77825. (gr. k-3). 1969. 5.95 (ISBN 0-672-50437-5, Bobbs). Macmillan.

Yogesvara dosa-Jyotirmayi. Gopal the Invincible. Bhaktivedanta Swami Prabhupado, A. C., tr. Sunita-devi dosa, illus. 15p. (gr. 3 up). 1983. 7.95 (ISBN 0-89647-017-2). Bala Bks.

Yolen, Jane. All in the Woodland Early: An ABC Book. Zalben, Jane B., illus. (ps-3). 1983. pap. 5.95 (ISBN 0-399-20969-7, Philomel). Putnam Pub Group.

—The Emperor & the Kite. Young, Ed, illus. 32p. (ps-2). 1988. 13.95 (ISBN 0-399-21499-2, Philomel Bks). Putnam Pub Group.

—The Girl Who Loved the Wind. Young, Ed, illus. LC 85-43037. 32p. (gr. k-3). 1987. pap. 4.50 (ISBN 0-06-443088-X, Trophy). HarpC Child Bks.

—An Invitation to the Butterfly Ball: A Counting Rhyme. Zalben, Jane B., illus. (ps-3). 1983. pap. 5.95 (ISBN 0-399-20972-7, Philomel). Putnam Pub Group.

—No Bath Tonight. Parker, Nancy W., illus. LC 77-26605. 32p. (gr. k-3). 1989. pap. 3.95 (ISBN 0-06-443179-7, Trophy). HarpC Child Bks.

—The Three Bears Rhyme Book. Dyer, Jane, illus. LC 86-19514. 32p. (ps-3). 1987. 14.95 (ISBN 0-15-286386-9, HJ). HarBraceJ.

Yolen, Jane, et al, eds. Dragons & Dreams. LC 85-45384. 192p. (gr. 5-9). 1986. 12.95 (ISBN 0-06-026792-5); PLB 12.89 (ISBN 0-06-026793-3). HarpC Child Bks.

Youldon, Gillian. Sizes. Youldon, Gillian, illus. 32p. (gr. 1-3). 1987. PLB 9.40 (ISBN 0-531-00442-2). Watts.

Young, James. Alligator Cookies. (Illus.). 32p. (ps-3). 1988. 6.95 (ISBN 0-8431-2297-8). Price Stern.

Young, Ruth & Rose, Mitchell, illus. Spider Magic. LC 89-61632. 12p. (ps-1). 1990. bds. 5.95 incl. finger puppet (ISBN 1-877779-03-2). Schneider Educational.

—Turtle Magic. LC 89-61634. 12p. (ps-1). 1990. bds. 5.95 incl. finger puppet (ISBN 1-877779-01-6). Schneider Educational.

Young, Sheila. Betty Bonnet Paper Dolls in Full Color. 1982. pap. 3.95 (ISBN 0-486-24415-6). Dover.

—Lettie Lane Paper Doll. 1981. pap. 3.95 (ISBN 0-486-24089-4). Dover.

Younger, Jesse. The Fire Engine Book. Battaglia, Aurelius, illus. 24p. (ps-k). 1987. pap. write for info (ISBN 0-307-10082-0, Pub. by Golden Bks). Western Pub.

Zabar, Abbie. Alphabet Soup. Zabar, Abbie, illus. 32p. 1990. 14.95 (ISBN 1-55670-154-3). Stewart Tabori & Chang.

Zakhoder, Boris. Rosachok: A Russian Story. Mills, Yaroslava, illus. LC 72-10148. (gr. k-3). 1970. PLB 12.88 (ISBN 0-688-51113-9). Lothrop.

Zalben, Jane B. Beni's First Chanukah. Zalben, Jane B., illus. LC 86-33634. 32p. (gr. k-3). 1988. 12.95 (ISBN 0-8050-0479-3). H Holt & Co.

Zeifert, Harriet. Good Night' Lewis! Nicklaus, Carol, illus. 32p. (gr. 2-6). 1986. pap. 4.95 incl. night light (ISBN 0-394-88139-7). Random.

Zelinsky, Paul O. & Zhitov, Boris. How I Hunted the Little Fellows. Zelinsky, Paul O., illus. 64p. (gr. k-3). 1979. 8.95 (ISBN 0-396-07692-0, Putnam). Putnam Pub Group.

Zemach, M. The Judge: An Untrue Tale. Zemach, Margot, illus. 48p. (ps up). 1988. pap. 4.95 (ISBN 0-374-43962-1). FS&G.

Zemach, Margot. Jake & Honeybunch Go to Heaven. Zemach, Margot, illus. 40p. (ps up). 1987. pap. 4.95 (ISBN 0-374-43714-9). FS&G.

—The Little Red Hen. (ps-3). 1987. pap. 3.95 (ISBN 0-14-050567-9, Puffin). Puffin Bks.

—The Three Wishes: An Old Story. Zemach, Margot, illus. LC 86-80956. 32p. (ps up). 1986. 13.95 (ISBN 0-374-37529-1). FS&G.

Zemach, Margot, illus. Hush, Little Baby. 32p. (Orig.). (ps-1). 1987. 11.95 (ISBN 0-525-44296-0, 01160-350, DCB); pap. 3.95 (ISBN 0-525-44297-9, 0383-120, DCB). Dutton Child Bks.

Zemke, Deborah. The Way It Happened. Zemke, Deborah, illus. 32p. (gr. k-3). 1988. 13.95 (ISBN 0-395-47984-3). HM.

Zerner, Jesse, illus. Astro-Dots: Find the Constellations. 64p. (Orig.). (ps-7). 1985. pap. 3.95 (ISBN 0-913319-01-5). Sunstone Pubns.

Ziefert, Harriet. All Clean! Drescher, Henrik, illus. LC 85-45331. 26p. (ps). 1986. 3.95 (ISBN 0-694-00100-7). HarpC Child Bks.

—All Gone! Drescher, Henrik, illus. LC 85-45329. 26p. (ps). 1986. 3.95 (ISBN 0-694-00098-1). HarpC Child Bks.

—Andy Toots His Horn. Hoffman, Sanford, illus. LC 87-25339. 32p. (ps-3). 1988. pap. 8.95 (ISBN 0-670-82035-0). Viking Child Bks.

—Animal Count. Baum, Susan, illus. 20p. (ps-1). 1989. pap. 4.95 (ISBN 0-14-054174-8, Puffin). Puffin Bks.

—Baby Ben's Bow-Wow Book. Gorbaty, Norman, illus. LC 83-63539. (ps). 1984. bds. 2.95 (ISBN 0-394-86821-8, Pub. by BYR). Random.

—Baby Ben's Busy Book. Gorbaty, Norman, illus. LC 83-63538. (ps). 1984. bds. 2.95 (ISBN 0-394-86819-6, Pub. by BYR). Random.

—Baby Ben's Noisy Book. Gorbaty, Norman, illus. LC 83-63541. (ps). 1984. bds. 2.95 (ISBN 0-394-86822-6, Pub. by BYR). Random.

—Bear Gets Dressed. Lobel, Arnold, illus. LC 85-45338. 16p. (ps). 1986. 4.95 (ISBN 0-694-00086-8). HarpC Child Bks.

—Bear Goes Shopping. Lobel, Arnold, illus. LC 85-45336. 16p. (ps). 1986. 4.95 (ISBN 0-694-00085-X). HarpC Child Bks.

—The Best Castle Ever. Nicklaus, Carol, illus. LC 88-26317. 24p. (Orig.). (ps-2). 1989. pap. 2.25 (ISBN 0-394-81997-7). Random.

—Birthday Card, Where Are You? Brown, Richard, illus. (ps-1). 1985. pap. 4.95 (ISBN 0-14-050536-9, Puffin). Puffin Bks.

—Boats. Baum, Susan, illus. 20p. (ps-1). 1989. pap. 4.95 (ISBN 0-14-054175-6, Puffin). Puffin Bks.

—Breakfast Time! Ernst, Lisa C., illus. (ps). 1988. pap. 3.95 (ISBN 0-670-81579-9). Viking Child Bks.

—Bye, Bye, Daddy! Ernst, Lisa C., illus. (ps). 1988. pap. 3.95 (ISBN 0-670-81581-0). Viking Child Bks.

—Can You Play. Smith, Mavis, illus. LC 88-24025. 24p. (Orig.). (ps-2). 1989. pap. 2.25 (ISBN 0-394-82001-0). Random.

—Cat Games. Schumacher, Claire, illus. LC 87-25428. 32p. (ps-3). 1988. pap. 8.95 (ISBN 0-670-82031-8). Viking Child Bks.

—A Clean House for Mole & Mouse. Prebenna, David, illus. LC 87-25420. 32p. (ps-3). 1988. pap. 8.95 (ISBN 0-670-82032-6). Viking Child Bks.

—Cock-a-Doodle-Doo! Drescher, Henrik, illus. LC 85-45330. 26p. (ps). 1986. 3.95 (ISBN 0-694-00099-X). HarpC Child Bks.

—Count with Little Bunny. Ernst, Lisa C., illus. (ps-1). 1988. pap. 5.95 (ISBN 0-670-82308-2). Viking Child Bks.

—Daddy, Can You Play with Me? Boon, Emilie, illus. (ps-k). 1988. pap. 4.95 (ISBN 0-14-050895-3, Puffin). Puffin Bks.

—Dark Night, Sleepy Night. Baruffi, Andrea, illus. LC 87-25405. 32p. (ps-3). 1988. pap. 8.95 (ISBN 0-670-82034-2). Viking Child Bks.

—Don't Cry, Baby Sam. Brown, Richard, illus. 20p. (gr. 2-6). 1988. pap. 4.95 (ISBN 0-14-050858-9, Puffin). Puffin Bks.

—Feed Little Bunny. Ernst, Lisa C., illus. (ps-1). 1988. pap. 5.95 (ISBN 0-670-82309-0). Viking Child Bks.

—Flip the Switch. Gorbaty, Norman, illus. 24p. (ps). 1984. 4.95 (ISBN 0-448-19102-4, G&D). Putnam Pub Group.

—Follow Me! (Illus.). 32p. (ps-2). 1990. pap. 8.95 (ISBN 0-670-83197-2). Viking Child Bks.

—Going on a Lion Hunt. Smith, Mavis, illus. 20p. (ps). 1989. pap. 4.95 (ISBN 0-14-054083-0, Puffin). Puffin Bks.

—Here Comes a Bus. 20p. (gr. 2-6). 1988. pap. 4.95 (ISBN 0-14-050857-0, Puffin). Puffin Bks.

—How Big Is Big? Baruffi, Andrea, illus. LC 88-612151. 32p. (ps-3). 1989. pap. 3.50 (ISBN 0-14-050983-6, Puffin). Puffin Bks.

—In a Scary Old House. Smith, Mavis, illus. 20p. (ps). 1989. pap. 5.95 (ISBN 0-14-054082-2, Puffin). Puffin Bks.

—Let's Get Dressed. Ernst, Lisa C., illus. (ps). 1988. pap. 3.95 (ISBN 0-670-81580-2). Viking Child Bks.

—Let's Trade. Morgan, Mary, illus. LC 88-62150. 32p. (ps-3). 1989. pap. 3.50 (ISBN 0-14-050982-8, Puffin). Puffin Bks.

—Let's Watch Nicky. Brown, Richard, illus. 26p. (ps-3). 1986. pap. 2.95 (ISBN 0-670-81296-X). Viking Child Bks.

—Little Bunny's Melon Patch. Ernst, Lisa C., illus. 20p. (ps-3). 1990. pap. 4.95 (ISBN 0-14-054262-0, Puffin). Puffin Bks.

—Little Bunny's Noisy Friends. Ernst, Lisa C., illus. 20p. (ps-3). 1990. pap. 4.95 (ISBN 0-14-054263-9, Puffin). Puffin Bks.

—Mommy, Where Are You? Boon, Emilie, illus. (ps-k). 1988. pap. 5.95 (ISBN 0-14-050894-5, Puffin). Puffin Bks.

—A New Coat for Anna. Lobel, Anita, illus. LC 86-2722. 40p. (ps-3). 1986. PLB 11.99 (ISBN 0-394-97426-3). Knopf.

—Nicky's Friends. (Illus.). 14p. (ps). 1986. pap. 2.95 (ISBN 0-670-81298-6). Viking Child Bks.

—Nicky's Picnic. Brown, Richard, illus. 20p. (Orig.). (ps-k). 1986. pap. 4.95 (ISBN 0-14-050584-9, Puffin). Puffin Bks.

—No More TV, Sleepy Dog. Gorbaty, Norman, illus. LC 88-26316. 24p. (Orig.). (ps-2). 1989. pap. 2.25 (ISBN 0-394-81996-9). Random.

—No, No, Nicky! Brown, Richard, illus. 14p. (ps). 1986. pap. 2.95 (ISBN 0-670-81297-8). Viking Child Bks.

—Piggety Pig Books, 6 of ea. title. Prebenna, David, illus. 96p. (ps-k). 1988. 2.95 (ISBN 0-316-98758-1). Little.

—Play with Little Bunny. Ernst, Lisa C., illus. (ps-1). 1986. pap. 5.95 (ISBN 0-670-80359-6). Viking Child Bks.

—Please Let It Snow. Brown, Rick, illus. LC 88-62145. 32p. (ps-3). 1989. pap. 3.50 (ISBN 0-14-050981-X, Puffin). Puffin Bks.

—The Prince Has a Boo-Boo. Alley, R. W., illus. LC 88-26322. 24p. (Orig.). (ps-2). 1989. PLB 2.25 (ISBN 0-394-81999-3). Random.

—Push the Button. Gorbaty, Norman, illus. 24p. (ps). 1984. 4.95 (ISBN 0-448-19101-6, G&D). Putnam Pub Group.

—Run! Run! Drescher, Henrik, illus. LC 85-45328. 26p. (ps). 1986. 3.95 (ISBN 0-694-00097-3). HarpC Child Bks.

—So Big! Smith, Mavis, illus. LC 86-61785. 14p. (ps). 1987. 2.95 (ISBN 0-394-88555-4, Random Juv). Random.

—So Busy! Smith, Mavis, illus. LC 86-61787. 14p. (ps). 1987. 2.95 (ISBN 0-394-88557-0, Random Juv). Random.

—So Clean! Smith, Mavis, illus. LC 86-61786. 14p. (ps). 1987. 2.95 (ISBN 0-394-88556-2, Random Juv). Random.

—So Hungry! Nicklaus, Carol, illus. LC 87-4763. 32p. (ps-1). 1987. lib. bdg. 6.99 (ISBN 0-394-99127-3, Random Juv); pap. 2.95 (ISBN 0-394-89127-9, Random Juv). Random.

—Stitches. (Illus.). 32p. (ps-2). 1990. pap. 8.95 (ISBN 0-670-83202-2). Viking Child Bks.

—Strike Four! Smith, Mavis, illus. LC 87-25412. 32p. (ps-3). 1988. pap. 8.95 (ISBN 0-670-82033-4). Viking Child Bks.

—Surprise! Morgan, Mary, illus. LC 87-26217. 32p. (ps-3). 1988. pap. 8.95 (ISBN 0-670-82036-9). Viking Child Bks.

—Turn the Dial. Gorbaty, Norman, illus. 24p. (ps). 1984. 4.95 (ISBN 0-448-19103-2, G&D). Putnam Pub Group.

—Turn the Key. Gorbaty, Norman, illus. 24p. (ps). 1984. 4.95 (ISBN 0-448-19104-0, G&D). Putnam Pub Group.

—The Wheels on the Bus. Baruffi, Andrea, illus. LC 89-38100. 24p. (Orig.). (ps-2). 1990. pap. 2.25 (ISBN 0-394-84870-5). Random.

—When the TV Broke. Smith, Mavis, illus. LC 88-62153. 32p. (ps-3). 1989. pap. 3.50 (ISBN 0-14-050984-4, Puffin). Puffin Bks.

—Where Is My Dinner? Taback, Simms, illus. 24p. (ps). 1985. 3.95 (ISBN 0-448-19129-6, G&D). Putnam Pub Group.

—Where Is My Family? Taback, Simms, illus. 24p. (ps). 1985. 3.95 (ISBN 0-448-19128-8, G&D). Putnam Pub Group.

—Where Is My Friend? Zaback, Simms, illus. 24p. (ps). 1985. 3.95 (ISBN 0-448-19127-X, G&D). Putnam Pub Group.

Ziefert, Harriet & Smith, Mavis. So Little! LC 86-61788. (Illus.). 14p. (ps). 1987. 2.95 (ISBN 0-394-88558-9, Random Juv). Random.

Zinnemann-Hope, Pam. Find Your Coat, Ned. Denton, Kady M., illus. LC 86-33729. 32p. (ps-2). 1988. Repr. of 1986 ed. 6.95 (ISBN 0-689-50426-8, M K McElderry). Macmillan Child Grp.

—Let's Play Ball, Ned. Denton, Kady M., illus. LC 86-33808. 32p. (ps-2). 1988. Repr. of 1987 ed. 6.95 (ISBN 0-689-50427-6, M K McElderry). Macmillan Child Grp.

Zion, Gene. Dear Garbage Man. Graham, Margaret B., illus. LC 57-5355. (gr. k-3). 1957. PLB 12.89 (ISBN 0-06-026841-7). HarpC Child Bks.

—Dear Garbage Man. Graham, Margaret B., illus. LC 57-5355. 32p. (ps-3). 1988. pap. 4.95 (ISBN 0-06-443177-0, Trophy). HarpC Child Bks.

—Harry by the Sea. Graham, Margaret B., illus. LC 65-21302. 32p. (gr. k-3). 1965. 13.95 (ISBN 0-06-026855-7); PLB 13.89 (ISBN 0-06-026856-5). HarpC Child Bks.

—Harry the Dirty Dog. Graham, Margaret B., illus. LC 56-8137. 32p. (gr. k-3). 1956. 13.95 (ISBN 0-06-026865-4); PLB 13.89 (ISBN 0-06-026866-2). HarpC Child Bks.

—No Roses for Harry. Graham, Margaret B., illus. LC 58-7752. (gr. k-3). 1958. 13.95 (ISBN 0-06-026890-5); PLB 13.89 (ISBN 0-06-026891-3). HarpC Child Bks.

Zokeisha. A Little Book of Colors. Klimo, Kate, ed. Zokeisha, illus. 16p. 1982. 2.95 (ISBN 0-671-45570-2, Little Simon). S&S Trade.

—Mouse House. Klimo, Kate, ed. Zokeisha, illus. 16p. 1983. 2.95 (ISBN 0-671-46129-X, Little Simon). S&S Trade.

—Things I Like to Look At. Zokeisha, illus. 16p. (ps-k). 1981. 2.95 (ISBN 0-671-44451-4, Little Simon). S&S Trade.

Zolotow, Charlotte. Big Brother. Chalmers, Mary, illus. LC 60-5794. 32p. (ps-1). 1960. PLB 12.89 (ISBN 0-06-026921-9, C Zolotow Bks). HarpC Child Bks.

—Big Sister & Little Sister. Alexander, Martha, illus. 24p. (gr. k-3). 1966. 13.95 (ISBN 0-06-026925-1); PLB 13.89 (ISBN 0-06-026926-X). HarpC Child Bks.

—Do You Know What I'll Do? Williams, Garth, illus. LC 58-7755. 32p. (ps-1). 1958. 12.95 (ISBN 0-06-026930-8); PLB 12.89 (ISBN 0-06-026940-5). HarpC Child Bks.

—The Hating Book. Shecter, Ben, illus. LC 69-14444. 32p. (ps-3). 1969. 11.95 (ISBN 0-06-026923-5); PLB 11.89 (ISBN 0-06-026924-3). HarpC Child Bks.

—I Like to Be Little. Blegvad, Eric, illus. LC 83-45056. 32p. (gr. k-4). 1990. pap. 3.95 (ISBN 0-06-443248-3, Trophy). HarpC Child Bks.

—If It Weren't for You. Reissue. ed. Shecter, Ben, illus. LC 66-15682. 32p. (gr. k-3). 1966. 12.95 (ISBN 0-06-026942-1); PLB 12.89 (ISBN 0-06-026943-X). HarpC Child Bks.

—Mister Rabbit & the Lovely Present. Sendak, Maurice, illus. LC 62-7590. (gr. k-3). 1962. 13.95 (ISBN 0-06-026945-6); PLB 12.89 (ISBN 0-06-026946-4). HarpC Child Bks.

—Mr. Rabbit & the Lovely Present. Sendak, Maurice, illus. (gr. k-3). 1987. incl. cassette 19.95 (ISBN 0-87499-047-5); pap. 12.95 incl. cassette (ISBN 0-87499-046-7); 4 paperbacks, cassette & guide 27.95 (ISBN 0-87499-048-3). Live Oak Media.

—My Friend John. Shecter, Ben, illus. LC 68-10209. (gr. k-3). 1968. 12.95 (ISBN 0-06-026947-2, C Zolotow Bks); PLB 13.89 (ISBN 0-06-026948-0, C Zolotow Bks). HarpC Child Bks.

—Over & Over. Williams, Garth, illus. LC 56-8149. (gr. k-2). 1957. 11.95i (ISBN 0-06-026955-3). HarpC Child Bks.

—Park Book. Rey, H. A., illus. LC 44-9471. 32p. (ps-1). 1986. PLB 12.89 (ISBN 0-06-026973-1). HarpC Child Bks.

—The Park Book. Rey, H. A., illus. LC 44-9471. 32p. (ps-3). 1986. pap. 4.95 (ISBN 0-06-443092-8, Trophy). HarpC Child Bks.

—The Quarreling Book. Lobel, Arnold, illus. LC 63-14445. 32p. (gr. k-3). 1963. 12.95 (ISBN 0-06-026975-8); PLB 11.89 (ISBN 0-06-026976-6). HarpC Child Bks.

—The Quarreling Book. Lobel, Arnold, illus. LC 63-14445. 32p. (gr. k-3). 1982. pap. 3.95 (ISBN 0-06-443034-0, Trophy). HarpC Child Bks.

—The Sky Was Blue. Williams, Garth, illus. LC 62-13328. (gr. k-3). 1963. PLB 13.89 (ISBN 0-06-027001-2). HarpC Child Bks.

—Sleepy Book. Plume, Ilse, illus. LC 87-45861. 32p. (ps-1). 1988. 12.95 (ISBN 0-06-026967-7); PLB 13.89 (ISBN 0-06-026968-5). HarpC Child Bks.

—Sleepy Book. Plume, Ilse, illus. LC 87-45861. 32p. (ps-1). 1990. pap. 4.95 (ISBN 0-06-443239-4, Trophy). HarpC Child Bks.

—Some Things Go Together. Gundersheimer, Karen, illus. LC 82-48694. 24p. (ps-2). 1987. pap. 3.95 (ISBN 0-06-443133-9, Trophy). HarpC Child Bks.

—Someday. Lobel, Arnold, illus. LC 64-16654. 32p. (gr. k-3). 1965. PLB 12.89 (ISBN 0-06-027016-0). HarpC Child Bks.

—Storm Book. Graham, Margaret B., illus. LC 52-7880. (gr. k-3). 1952. PLB 13.89 (ISBN 0-06-027026-8). HarpC Child Bks.

—The Storm Book. Graham, Margaret B., illus. LC 52-7880. 32p. (ps-3). 1989. pap. 4.50 (ISBN 0-06-443194-0, Trophy). HarpC Child Bks.

—Three Funny Friends. Chalmers, Mary, illus. LC 61-5779. 32p. (ps-1). 1961. PLB 12.89 (ISBN 0-06-027040-3). HarpC Child Bks.

—When I Have a Little Boy. Knight, Hilary, illus. LC 67-14072. 32p. (ps-3). 1988. pap. 2.95 (ISBN 0-06-443176-2, Trophy). HarpC Child Bks.

—When I Have a Little Girl. Knight, Hilary, illus. LC 65-24656. 32p. (gr. k-3). 1965. 12.95 (ISBN 0-06-027045-4); PLB 12.89 (ISBN 0-06-027046-2). HarpC Child Bks.

—When I Have a Little Girl. Knight, Hilary, illus. LC 65-24656. 32p. (ps-3). 1988. pap. 2.95 (ISBN 0-06-443175-4, Trophy). HarpC Child Bks.

—William's Doll. Pene du Boid, William, illus. LC 70-183173. 32p. (ps-3). 1985. pap. 4.95 (ISBN 0-06-443067-7, Trophy). HarpC Child Bks.

Zoo. 8p. (ps). bds. 2.95 (ISBN 0-671-49716-2, Little Simon). S&S Trade.

PICTURE GALLERIES

see Art–Galleries and Museums

PICTURE POSTERS

see Posters

PICTURE WRITING

see also Hieroglyphics

Hofsinde, Robert. Indian Sign Language. Hofsinde, Robert, illus. LC 56-5178. (gr. 5 up). 1956. PLB 12.88 (ISBN 0-688-31610-7, Morrow Junior Books). Morrow.

PICTURES

see also Cartoons and Caricatures; Paintings; Portraits also names of countries, states, etc. with the subdivision Description and Travel, e.g. U. S.–Description and Travel, etc.; and names of cities with the subdivision Description, e.g. New York (City)–Description

Gregorich, Barbara. Alike-Not Alike & Go-Togethers: Kindergarten. Hoffman, Joan, ed. Koontz, Robin M., illus. 32p. (gr. k). 1990. wkbk. 3.49 (ISBN 0-88743-176-3). Sch Zone Pub Co.

PICTURES, HUMOROUS

see Cartoons and Caricatures

Edens, Cooper. With Secret Friends. LC 84-149490. (Illus.). 48p. (gr. 7-12). 1981. pap. 8.95 (ISBN 0-914676-57-1). Green Tiger Pr.

PIERCE, FRANKLIN, PRES. U. S., 1804-1869

Brown, Fern G. Franklin Pierce: Fourteenth President of the United States. Young, Richard G., ed. LC 88-30050. (Illus.). (gr. 5-9). 1989. PLB 17.26 (ISBN 0-944483-25-9). Garrett Ed Corp.

Simon, Charnan. Franklin Pierce: Fourteenth President of the United States. LC 88-10883. (Illus.). 100p. (gr. 3 up). 1988. PLB 17.27 (ISBN 0-516-01357-2). Childrens.

PIGEONS

Morrison, Susan D. The Passenger Pigeon. LC 89-31839. (Illus.). 48p. (gr. k-4). 1990. 10.95 (ISBN 0-89686-457-X, Crestwood Hse). Macmillan Child Grp.

Schlein, Miriam. Pigeons. Miller, Margaret, photos by. LC 88-35286. (Illus.). 48p. (gr. 2-6). 1989. 12.95 (ISBN 0-690-04808-4, Crowell Jr Bks); PLB 12.89 (ISBN 0-690-04810-6, Crowell Jr Bks). HarpC Child Bks.

PIGEONS–FICTION

Alexander, Martha. Out, Out, Out. Alexander, Martha, illus. LC 68-15251. (gr. k-3). 1968. 6.95 (ISBN 0-8037-6663-7); PLB 6.95 (ISBN 0-685-01457-6). Dial Bks Young.

Baker, Jeannie. Home in the Sky. Baker, Jeannie, illus. LC 83-25379. 32p. (gr. k-3). 1984. 13.00 (ISBN 0-688-03841-7); PLB 11.96 (ISBN 0-688-03842-5). Greenwillow.

Benchley, Nathaniel. Walter, the Homing Pigeon. Darrow, Whitney, Jr., illus. LC 79-2696. 32p. (gr. 1-4). 1981. HarpC Child Bks.

Graeber, Charlotte T. Grey Cloud. Bloom, Lloyd, illus. LC 79-14673. 128p. (gr. 3-7). 1984. 12.95 (ISBN 0-02-736910-2, Four Winds). Macmillan Child Grp.

Mukerji, Dhan G. Gay-Neck: The Story of a Pigeon. Artzybasheff, Boris, illus. (gr. 4 up). 1968. 14.95 (ISBN 0-525-30400-2, DCB). Dutton Child Bks.

Overbeck, Cynthia. Tanya the Turtledove. Hammarberg, Dyan, tr. from FRE. LC 76-29464. (Illus.). 24p. (gr. k-4). 1977. PLB 6.95 (ISBN 0-87614-084-3). Carolrhoda Bks.

Renton, Alice. Victoria: The Biography of a Pigeon. (gr. 7 up). 1988. pap. 3.50 (ISBN 0-8041-0395-X). Ivy Books.

PIGMENTATION

see Color of Animals; Color of Man

PIGMIES

see Pygmies

PIGS

Ahlstrom, Mark & Schroeder, Howard. The Wild Pigs. LC 86-2282. (Illus.). 48p. (gr. 5-6). 1986. PLB 10.95 (ISBN 0-89686-272-0, Crestwood Hse). Macmillan Child Grp.

Munsch, Robert. Pigs. Martchenko, Michael, illus. 24p. (gr. k-2). 1989. 12.95 (ISBN 1-550370-39-1); pap. 4.95 (ISBN 1-550370-38-3). Firefly Bks Ltd.

Royston, Angela. Pig. 1990. PLB 10.40 (ISBN 0-531-19080-3). Watts.

Stone, Lynn. Pigs. (Illus.). 24p. (gr. k-5). 1990. lib. bdg. 11.93 (ISBN 0-86593-037-6); lib. bdg. 8.95s.p. (ISBN 0-685-36312-0). Rourke Corp.

PIGS–FICTION

Addison-Wesley Staff. The Three Little Pigs Little Book. (Illus.). 16p. (gr. k-3). 1989. pap. text ed. 4.50 (ISBN 0-201-19058-3). Addison-Wesley.

—Los Tres Cerditos - Little Book. (SPA., Illus.). 16p. (gr. k-3). 1989. pap. text ed. 4.50 (ISBN 0-201-19710-3). Addison-Wesley.

—Los Tres Cerditos Big Book. (SPA., Illus.). 16p. (gr. k-3). 1989. pap. text ed. 31.75 (ISBN 0-201-19938-6). Addison-Wesley.

Adler, C. S. Good-Bye Pink Pig. 176p. (gr. 3-7). 1986. pap. 2.75 (ISBN 0-380-70175-8, Camelot). Avon.

—Help, Pink Pig! 160p. (gr. 3-7). 1990. 14.95 (ISBN 0-399-22183-2, Putnam). Putnam Pub Group.

Alexander, Martha. Pigs Say Oink. Alexander, Martha, illus. 32p. (ps-3). 1981. Random.

Amery, H. Pig Gets Stuck. (Illus.). 16p. (ps). 1989. 2.95 (ISBN 0-7460-0259-9, Usborne); lib. bdg. 7.96 (ISBN 0-88110-374-8, Usborne). EDC.

—Three Little Pigs. Cartwright, Stephen, illus. 16p. (ps-2). 1987. 2.95 (ISBN 0-7460-0189-4); PLB 6.96 (ISBN 0-88110-293-8). EDC.

Ashwill, Beverly. Jeffrey, the Littlest Pig. Ashwill, Betty J., illus. LC 90-83312. 24p. (ps-3). 1990. pap. 3.98 (ISBN 0-941381-06-4). BJO Enterprises.

Battaglia, Aurelius, illus. Three Little Pigs. LC 76-24170. 32p. (ps-2). 1982. lib. bdg. 5.99 (ISBN 0-394-93459-8); pap. 2.25 saddle stitched (ISBN 0-394-83459-3). Random.

Bawden, Nina. The Peppermint Pig. 160p. (gr. 5 up). 1988. pap. 4.95 (ISBN 0-440-40122-4, Pub. by Yearling Classics). Dell.

Bell, Sally, retold by. The Three Little Pigs. Dolce, J. Ellen, illus. (ps-1). 1991. write for info. (ISBN 0-307-11598-4, Golden Pr). Western Pub.

Bianchi, J. The Swine Snafu. (Illus.). 24p. (ps-8). 1988. 12.95 (ISBN 0-921285-14-0); pap. 4.95 (ISBN 0-921285-12-4). Firefly Bks Ltd.

Bishop, Gavin. Three Little Pigs. Bishop, Gavin, illus. LC 89-10871. 32p. (ps-3). 1990. 12.95 (ISBN 0-590-43358-X). Scholastic Inc.

Bloom, Suzanne. We Keep a Pig in the Parlor. Bloom, Suzanne, illus. 32p. (ps-1). 1988. 13.95 (ISBN 0-517-56829-2, C N Potter Bks). Crown.

Bond, Felicia. Mary Betty Lizzie McNutt's Birthday. Bond, Felicia, illus. (ps-3). 1983. PLB 11.89 (ISBN 0-690-04256-6, Crowell Jr Bks). HarpC Child Bks.

Bond, Michael. The Tales of Olga Da Polga. Helweg, Hans, illus. LC 88-31444. 128p. (gr. 3-7). 1989. Repr. of 1973 ed. 11.95 (ISBN 0-02-711731-6, Mcmillan Child Bk). Macmillan Child Grp.

Bonsall, Crosby N. Piggle. Bonsall, Crosby, illus. LC 73-5478. 64p. (gr. k-3). 1973. PLB 11.89 (ISBN 0-06-020580-6). HarpC Child Bks.

Boynton, Sandra. Hester in the Wild. LC 78-67026. (Illus.). 32p. (ps-3). 1979. HarpC Child Bks.

Brenner, Barbara. Walt Disney's The Three Little Pigs. (Illus.). (ps-3). 1973. 6.95 (ISBN 0-394-82522-5, Random Juv); lib. bdg. 4.99 (ISBN 0-394-92522-X). Random.

Brooks, Walter R. Freddy & the Perilous Adventure. Morrill, Leslie & Wiese, Kurt, illus. LC 85-14653. 256p. (gr. 3-7). 1986. lib. bdg. 9.99 (ISBN 0-394-97601-0). Knopf.

—Freddy Goes Camping. Morrill, Leslie & Wiese, Kurt, illus. LC 48-8629. 264p. (gr. 3-7). 1986. lib. bdg. 9.99 (ISBN 0-394-97602-9); pap. 4.95 (ISBN 0-394-87602-4). Knopf.

—Freddy the Politician. Morrill, Leslie, illus. LC 85-14713. 264p. (gr. 3-7). 1986. pap. 3.95 (ISBN 0-394-87600-8). Knopf.

Browne, Anthony. Piggybook. Browne, Anthony, illus. LC 86-3008. 32p. (ps-3). 1990. pap. 4.95 (ISBN 0-679-80837-X, Dragonfly Bks). Knopf.

Bucknall, Caroline. The Three Little Pigs. Bucknall, Caroline, illus. LC 86-16716. 32p. (ps-2). 1987. 10.95 (ISBN 0-8037-0100-4). Dial Bks Young.

Carlson, Nancy. I Like Me! (Illus.). 32p. (ps-1). 1990. pap. 3.95 (ISBN 0-14-050819-8, Puffin). Puffin Bks.

—Louanne Pig in the Mysterious Valentine. (ps-3). 1987. pap. 3.95 (ISBN 0-14-050604-7, Puffin). Puffin Bks.

—Louanne Pig in the Talent Show. Carlson, Nancy, illus. 32p. (ps-3). 1986. pap. 3.95 (ISBN 0-14-050603-9, Puffin). Puffin Bks.

—Louanne Pig in The Talent Show. Carlson, Nacy, illus. (gr. k-3). 1987. incl. cassette 19.95 (ISBN 0-87499-065-3); pap. 12.95 incl. cassette (ISBN 0-87499-064-5); 4 paperbacks, cassette & guide 27.95 (ISBN 0-87499-066-1). Live Oak Media.

—Louanne Pig in the Witch Lady. Carlson, Nancy, illus. 32p. (ps-3). 1986. pap. 3.95 (ISBN 0-14-050602-0, Puffin). Puffin Bks.

—Louanne Pig in Witch Lady. Carlson, Nancy, illus. (gr. k-3). 1987. incl. cassette 19.95 (ISBN 0-87499-068-8); pap. 12.95 incl. cassette (ISBN 0-87499-067-X); 4 paperbacks, guide & cassette 27.95 (ISBN 0-87499-069-6). Live Oak Media.

Celsi, Teresa. The Fourth Little Pig. Cushman, Doug, illus. 24p. (ps-3). 1990. PLB 12.33 (ISBN 0-8172-3577-9); PLB 9.25 (ISBN 0-685-33574-7). Raintree Pubs.

Charles, Donald. Paddy Pigs Poems. 1989. pap. 13.95 (ISBN 0-671-67081-6). S&S Trade.

Chorao, Kay. Ups & Downs with Oink & Pearl. Chorao, Kay, illus. LC 85-45264. 64p. (gr. k-3). 1986. PLB 11.89 (ISBN 0-06-021275-6). HarpC Child Bks.

Christian, Mary B. Goody Sherman's Pig. Zimmer, Dirk, illus. LC 90-35181. 48p. (gr. 2-6). 1991. RSBE 12.95 (ISBN 0-02-718251-7, Mcmillan Child Bk). Macmillan Child Grp.

Claverie, Jean. The Three Little Pigs. Claverie, Jean, illus. Crawford, Elizabeth, tr. from GER. LC 88-25327. (Illus.). 32p. (gr. k-3). 1989. 13.95 (ISBN 1-55858-004-2). North-South Bks NYC.

Copeland, Colene. Priscilla. Harrison, Edith, illus. LC 81-80663. 212p. (Orig.). (gr. 3 up). 1981. 8.95 (ISBN 0-939810-01-8); pap. 3.95 (ISBN 0-939810-02-6). Jordan Valley.

Corbalis, Judy. Porcellus the Flying Pig. Craig, Helen, illus. LC 88-3976. 32p. (gr. 1-5). 1988. 12.95 (ISBN 0-8037-0486-0). Dial Bks Young.

Crawford, Thomas. Pig Who Saved the Day. (Illus.). (gr. 3-4). 1972. pap. 1.95 (ISBN 0-89375-049-2). Troll Assocs.

Crozat, Francois. I Am a Little Pig. (Illus.). (ps-3). 1991. large 7.95 (ISBN 0-8120-6201-9); miniature 2.95 (ISBN 0-8120-6222-1). Barron.

De Brunhoff, Laurent. The One Pig with Horns. Howard, Richard, tr. from FRE. De Brunhoff, Laurent, illus. LC 78-4917. (gr. k-3). 1979. Pantheon.

Dubanevich, Arlene. Pig William. 32p. (gr. k-3). 1990. pap. 3.95 (ISBN 0-689-71372-X, Aladdin). Macmillan Child Grp.

—The Piggest Show on Earth. LC 88-11742. (Illus.). 32p. (ps-1). 1989. 13.95 (ISBN 0-531-05789-5); PLB 13.99 (ISBN 0-531-08389-6). Orchard Bks Watts.

—Pigs in Hiding. Dubanevich, Arlene, illus. LC 83-1409. 32p. (ps-1). 1984. 13.95 (ISBN 0-02-732140-1, Four Winds). Macmillan Child Grp.

Dunn, Judy. The Little Pig. Dunn, Phoebe, photos by. LC 86-42956. (Illus.). 32p. (ps-3). 1987. (Random Juv); pap. 1.95 (ISBN 0-394-88774-3). Random.

Edwards, Pat. Nelda. LC 86-27219. (gr. 3-7). 1987. 12.95 (ISBN 0-395-43021-6). HM.

Fleming, Susan. The Pig at Thirty-Seven Pinecrest Drive. LC 80-22391. (Illus.). 130p. (gr. 3-5). 1981. 9.95 (ISBN 0-664-32676-5, Westminster). Westminster John Knox.

Frost, Erica. The Littlest Pig. Paterson, Diane, illus. LC 85-14121. 48p. (Orig.). (gr. 1-3). 1986. PLB 9.89 (ISBN 0-8167-0654-9); pap. text ed. 2.95 (ISBN 0-8167-0655-7). Troll Assocs.

Gackenbach, Dick. Harvey the Foolish Pig. Gackenbach, Dick, illus. LC 87-15691. 32p. (gr. k-3). 1988. 13.95 (ISBN 0-89919-540-7, Pub. by Clarion). Ticknor & Fields.

Galdone, Paul. The Amazing Pig. LC 80-16990. (Illus.). 32p. (ps-3). 1981. 13.95 (ISBN 0-395-29101-1, Clarion). HM.

—Three Little Pigs. Galdone, Paul, illus. LC 75-123456. (ps-3). 1979. 13.95 (ISBN 0-395-28813-4, Clarion). HM.

—The Three Little Pigs. Galdone, Paul, illus. LC 75-123456. 40p. (Orig.). (ps-3). 1984. pap. 4.95 (ISBN 0-89919-275-0, Pub. by Clarion). Ticknor & Fields.

—Three Little Pigs. (gr. 1 up). 1987. incl. cass. 6.95 (ISBN 0-317-64579-X). HM.

Geisert, Arthur. Pa's Balloon & Other Pig Tales. Geisert, Arthur, illus. LC 83-18552. 96p. (gr. k-3). 1984. 12.95 (ISBN 0-395-35381-5, 5-86480). HM.

—Pigs from A to Z. Geisert, Arthur, illus. LC 86-18542. 64p. (gr. 2 up). 1986. 15.95 (ISBN 0-395-38509-1). HM.

Gikow, Louise. Baby Piggy at the Bat. Chauhan, Manhar, illus. LC 86-62182. 32p. (ps-3). 1987. pap. 1.25 (ISBN 0-394-88783-2, Random Juv). Random.

Gilman, Phoebe. Wonderful Pigs of Jillian Jiggs. 1989. pap. 2.50 (ISBN 0-590-41341-4). Scholastic Inc.

Grace, Eileen, illus. Three Little Pigs. LC 80-27483. 32p. (gr. k-2). 1981. PLB 9.79 (ISBN 0-89375-462-5); pap. text ed. 1.95 (ISBN 0-89375-463-3). Troll Assocs.

Gray, Nigel. Little Pig's Tale. Rees, Mary, illus. LC 90-30642. 32p. (ps-2). 1990. 12.95 (ISBN 0-02-736942-0, Mcmillan Child Bk). Macmillan Child Grp.

—Pigs Can't Fly. Vendrell, Carme S., illus. 32p. (ps-1). 1991. 15.95 (ISBN 0-86264-272-8, Pub. by Andersen Pr UK). Trafalgar Sq.

Gustafson, Anita. The Case of the Purloined Pork. Gordon, Melinda, illus. 32p. (gr. 2-3). 1985. 7.95 (ISBN 0-88700-004-5). Natl Live Stock.

Haswell, Peter. Pog. LC 88-34466. (Illus.). 32p. (ps-1). 1989. 13.95 (ISBN 0-531-05843-3); PLB 13.99 (ISBN 0-531-08443-4). Orchard Bks Watts.

Hawkins, Colin & Hawkins, Jacqui. Mig the Pig. Hawkins, Colin, illus. 22p. (gr. k-1). 1984. 9.95 (ISBN 0-399-21061-X, Putnam). Putnam Pub Group.

Heine, Helme. The Pigs' Wedding. Heine, Helme, illus. LC 78-57691. 32p. (ps-3). 1986. 13.95 (ISBN 0-689-50409-8, M K McElderry). Macmillan Child Grp.

—The Pigs' Wedding. Heine, Helme, illus. 32p. (gr. k-3). 1991. pap. 4.95 (ISBN 0-689-71478-5, Aladdin). Macmillan Child Grp.

—Seven Wild Pigs. LC 87-3448. (Illus.). 120p. (gr. k up). 1988. Repr. of 1986 ed. 18.95 (ISBN 0-689-50439-X, M K McElderry). Macmillan Child Grp.

Hoban, Lillian. Mr. Pig & Family. Hoban, Lillian, illus. LC 80-7771. 64p. (gr. k-3). 1980. PLB 9.89 (ISBN 0-06-022384-7). HarpC Child Bks.

—Mr. Pig & Sonny Too. LC 76-58731. (Illus.). 64p. (gr. k-3). 1977. PLB 11.89 (ISBN 0-06-022341-3). HarpC Child Bks.

—Mr. Pig & Sonny Too. LC 76-58731. (Illus.). 64p. (gr. k-3). 1977. PLB 11.89 (ISBN 0-06-022341-3). HarpC Child Bks.

Hoban, Russell. The Marzipan Pig. Blake, Quentin, illus. LC 86-24253. 40p. (gr. 1-4). 1987. 10.95 (ISBN 0-374-34859-6). FS&G.

—The Marzipan Pig. Blake, Quentin, illus. 40p. (gr. 1 up). 1989. pap. 3.95 (ISBN 0-374-44750-0). FS&G.

Hofstrand, Mary. Albion Pig. Hofstrand, Mary, illus. LC 83-17496. 40p. (ps-k). 1984. lib. bdg. 10.99 (ISBN 0-394-96255-9). Knopf.

—By the Sea. (Illus.). 32p. (ps-3). 1990. pap. 3.95 (ISBN 0-14-054208-6, Puffin). Puffin Bks.

Horejs, Vit. Pig & Bear. Henstra, Friso, illus. LC 88-21304. 48p. (gr. 2-4). 1989. 11.95 (ISBN 0-02-744421-X, Four Winds). Macmillan Child Grp.

Hulbert, Jay. Pete Pig Cleans Up. (Illus.). 32p. (gr. 1-4). 1989. PLB 12.33 (ISBN 0-8172-3504-3). Raintree Pubs.

Hunt, Rod. Piglet Goes to the Rescue. Gordon, Mike, illus. 32p. (ps). 1987. 5.95 (ISBN 0-09-167240-6, Pub. by Hutchinson UK). Trafalgar Sq.

Hynard, Julia. Percival's Party: A Story about Numbers. Thatcher, Francis, illus. LC 82-22114. 32p. (ps-3). 1983. PLB 15.93 (ISBN 0-516-08941-2). Childrens.

Inkpen, Mick. Gumboot's Chocolatey Day. 1991. 12.99 (ISBN 0-385-41490-0); pap. 11.95 (ISBN 0-385-41489-7). Doubleday.

—If I Had a Pig. Inkpen, Mick, illus. (ps). 1988. 7.95 (ISBN 0-316-41887-0). Little.

Jeschke, Susan. Perfect the Pig. Jeschke, Susan, illus. 48p. (ps-3). 1985. pap. 2.50 (ISBN 0-590-33741-6). Scholastic Inc.

—Perfect the Pig. Jeschke, Susan, illus. 40p. (gr. k-3). 1985. pap. 2.95 (ISBN 0-590-43710-0). Scholastic Inc.

Jewell, Nancy. Cheer up, Pig. Shecter, Ben, illus. LC 74-20385. 32p. (ps-3). 1975. PLB 11.89 (ISBN 0-06-022838-5). HarpC Child Bks.

Johnston, Tony. Farmer Mack Measures His Pig. Lloyd, Megan, illus. LC 85-45254. 32p. (gr. k-3). 1986. PLB 11.89 (ISBN 0-06-023018-5). HarpC Child Bks.

Jose, Eduard, adapted by. The Three Little Pigs: A Classic Tale. McDonnell, Janet, tr. from SPA. Asensio, Augusti, illus. LC 88-35314. 32p. (gr. 1-4). 1988. PLB 10.95 (ISBN 0-89565-459-8). Childs World.

Kaplan, Carol & Becker, Sandi. Three Piggy Opera. Mitter, Kathy, illus. 25p. (ps). 1989. tchr's. ed. 16.95 (ISBN 0-88734-407-0). Players Pr.

Kaplan, Carol B. The Picky Pig. Bolinske, Janet L., ed. Quenell, Midge, illus. LC 87-62998. 24p. (Orig.). (ps-k). 1988. spiral bdg. 17.95 (ISBN 0-88335-756-9); pap. 4.95 (ISBN 0-88335-078-5). Milliken Pub Co.

Kasza, Keiko. The Pigs' Picnic. Kasza, Keiko, illus. 32p. (ps-1). 1988. PLB 13.95 (ISBN 0-399-21543-3, Putnam). Putnam Pub Group.

Kemp, Gene. Tamworth Pig Stories. Dinan, Carolyn, illus. 224p. (ps-4). 1987. laminated boards 9.95 (ISBN 0-571-14931-6). Faber & Faber.

King-Smith, Dick. Ace: The Very Important Pig. Hemmant, Lynette, illus. LC 90-1447. 144p. (gr. 2-7). 1990. 13.00 (ISBN 0-517-57832-8); PLB 13.99 (ISBN 0-517-57833-6). Crown.

—Babe: The Gallant Pig. Rayner, Mary, illus. LC 84-11429. 176p. 1988. 11.95 (ISBN 0-517-55556-5). Crown.

—Babe the Gallant Pig: The Gallant Pig. (gr. k-6). 1987. pap. 2.95 (ISBN 0-440-40420-7, YB). Dell.

—Pigs Might Fly. Rayner, Mary, illus. LC 81-11525. 156p. (gr. 3-7). 1982. pap. 12.95 (ISBN 0-670-55506-1). Viking Child Bks.

—Pigs Might Fly. Rayner, Mary, illus. 168p. (gr. 4-6). 1984. pap. 2.50 (ISBN 0-590-40839-9, Apple Paperbacks). Scholastic Inc.

—Pigs Might Fly. (gr. 4 up). 1990. pap. 3.95 (ISBN 0-14-034537-X, Puffin). Puffin Bks.

—Pigs Might Fly. 168p. (gr. 3-7). 1984. pap. 2.75 (ISBN 0-590-43341-5). Scholastic Inc.

Koscielniak, Bruce. Hector & Prudence. Koscielniak, Bruce, illus. LC 88-31359. 40p. (ps-2). 1990. 12.95 (ISBN 0-394-84514-5); lib. bdg. 14.99 (ISBN 0-394-94514-X). McKay.

—Hector & Prudence - All Aboard! Koscielniak, Bruce, illus. LC 89-2008. 40p. (ps-2). 1990. 12.95 (ISBN 0-679-80486-2); PLB 13.99 (ISBN 0-679-90486-7). Knopf.

Krause, Ute. Pig Surprise. Krause, Ute, illus. LC 88-31108. 32p. (ps-3). 1989. 11.95 (ISBN 0-8037-0714-2). Dial Bks Young.

Kujoko. Pig Tales: The Adventures of Arnold the Chinese Potbelly Miniature Pig. Clifford, Sandy, illus. 21p. (Orig.). (ps-8). 1988. pap. 4.95 (ISBN 0-9623210-0-1). Kiyoko & Co.

Laird, Donivee. The Three Little Hawaiian Pigs & the Magic Shark. Jossem, Carol, illus. LC 81-67047. 40p. (ps-3). 1981. 7.95x (ISBN 0-940350-19-X). Barnaby Bks.

Laird, Elizabeth. The Day Sidney Ran Off. Reeder, Colin, illus. LC 90-11154. 32p. (gr. k up). 1991. 10.95 (ISBN 0-688-10241-7, Tambourine Bks); PLB 10.88 (ISBN 0-688-10242-5, Tambourine Bks). Morrow.

Latta, Richard. This Little Pig Had a Riddle. Fay, Anne, ed. Munsinger, Lynn, illus. LC 83-26112. 32p. (gr. 1-5). 1984. PLB 8.95 (ISBN 0-8075-7893-2). A Whitman.

Lawson, John. If Pigs Could Fly. 144p. (gr. 5-9). 1989. 13.95 (ISBN 0-395-50928-9). HM.

Leonard, Marcia. Little Pig's Birthday. Hockerman, Dennis, illus. 32p. 1984. pap. 2.50 (ISBN 0-553-15267-X). Bantam.
Levine, Abby. You Push, I Ride. (ps). 1990. pap. 3.95 (ISBN 0-14-054180-2, Puffin). Puffin Bks.
Lobel, Arnold. Small Pig. Lobel, Arnold, illus. LC 69-10213. 64p. (gr. k-3). 1969. PLB 11.89 (ISBN 0-06-023932-8). HarpC Child Bks.
—A Treeful of Pigs. Lobel, Anita, illus. 32p. (gr. k-3). 1988. pap. 3.95 (ISBN 0-590-41280-9, Blue Ribbon Bks). Scholastic Inc.
Lorenz, Lee. A Weekend in the Country. Lorenz, Lee, illus. 32p. (gr. k-3). 1985. 11.95 (ISBN 0-13-947961-9). P-H.
Lowry, Lois. Anastasia, Ask Your Analyst. LC 83-26687. 128p. (gr. 3-6). 1984. 13.95 (ISBN 0-395-36011-0, 5-90388). HM.
McPhail, David. Pig Pig & the Magic Photo Album. (Illus.). (ps-3). 1989. pap. 3.95 (ISBN 0-525-44539-0, DCB). Dutton Child Bks.
—Pig Pig Gets a Job. (ps-3). 1990. 12.95 (ISBN 0-525-44619-2, DCB). Dutton Child Bks.
—Pig Pig Goes to Camp. LC 83-1412. (Illus.). 24p. (ps-3). 1983. 12.95 (ISBN 0-525-44064-X, 0966-290, DCB). Dutton Child Bks.
—Pig Pig Goes to Camp. McPhail, David, illus. 24p. (ps-3). 1987. pap. 3.95 (ISBN 0-525-44302-9, DCB). Dutton Child Bks.
—Pig Pig Grows Up. LC 80-377. (Illus.). 32p. (ps-2). 1985. 11.95 (ISBN 0-525-37027-7, DCB); pap. 3.95 (ISBN 0-525-44195-6, DCB). Dutton Child Bks.
—Pig Pig Grows Up. McPhail, David, illus. (ps-2). 1985. pap. 12.95 incl. cassette (ISBN 0-941078-94-9); incl. cassette 19.95 (ISBN 0-941078-96-5); incl. cassette 4 paperbacks guide 27.95 (ISBN 0-941078-95-7). Live Oak Media.
—Pig Pig Rides. McPhail, David, illus. 32p. (ps-3). 1982. 13.95 (ISBN 0-525-44024-0, DCB). Dutton Child Bks.
—Pig Pig Rides. McPhail, David, illus. LC 82-9777. 24p. (ps-3). 1985. pap. 3.95 (ISBN 0-525-44222-7, DCB). Dutton Child Bks.
Magorian, James. The Three Diminutive Pigs. LC 88-71605. 20p. (gr. 1-4). 1988. pap. 3.00 (ISBN 0-930674-30-8). Black Oak.
Marshall, James, retold by. & illus. The Three Little Pigs. LC 88-33411. (ps-3). 1989. 12.95 (ISBN 0-8037-0591-3); PLB 12.89 (ISBN 0-8037-0594-8). Dial Bks Young.
Moore, Inga. The Truffle Hunter. (Illus.). 32p. (ps-3). 1987. 10.95 (ISBN 0-916291-09-X). Kane-Miller Bk.
Mori, Tuyosi. Socrates & the Three Little Pigs. Anno, Mitsumasa, illus. LC 85-21564. 44p. (gr. 2 up). 1986. 13.95 (ISBN 0-399-21310-4, Putnam). Putnam Pub Group.
Orbach, Ruth. Apple Pigs. Orbach, Ruth, illus. (gr. 1-4). 1981. 6.95 (ISBN 0-529-05332-2, Philomel Bks); pap. 3.95 (ISBN 0-399-20797-X, Philomel). Putnam Pub Group.
Overbeck, Cynthia. Curly the Piglet. Hammarberg, Dyan, tr. LC 76-3431. (ENG., Illus.). 24p. (gr. k-4). 1976. PLB 6.95 (ISBN 0-87614-069-X). Carolrhoda Bks.
Patterson, Geoffrey. A Pig's Tale. Patterson, Geoffrey, illus. LC 82-72113. 32p. (gr. k-3). 1984. 9.95 (ISBN 0-233-97477-6). Andre Deutsch.
Peck, Robert N. A Day No Pigs Would Die. 144p. (gr. 7 up). 1979. pap. 3.50 (ISBN 0-440-92083-3, LFL). Dell.
Peet, Bill. Chester the Worldly Pig. (Illus.). 48p. (gr. k-3). 1980. 13.95 (ISBN 0-395-18470-3). HM.
—Chester the Worldly Pig. Peet, Bill, illus. (gr. k-3). 1978. pap. 4.95 (ISBN 0-395-27271-8). HM.
Pennington, Eunice. Perry, the Pet Pig. Pennington, Eunice, illus. (gr. 4-7). 1966. 3.00 (ISBN 0-685-19374-8, 911120-06-8); pap. 1.00 (ISBN 0-685-19375-6). Pennington.
Peppe, Rodney. Huxley Pig the Clown. 1990. 8.95 (ISBN 0-385-29819-6). Doubleday.
—Huxley Pig's Airplane. Peppe, Rodney, illus. (ps-2). 1990. 8.95 (ISBN 0-385-30038-7). Doubleday.
—Huxley Pig's Model Car. 1991. pap. 8.95 (ISBN 0-385-30238-X). Doubleday.
Peters, Sharon. Rub-a-Dub Suds. Carter, Penny, illus. LC 86-30856. 32p. (gr. k-2). 1987. PLB 7.06 (ISBN 0-8167-0984-X); pap. text ed. 1.95 (ISBN 0-8167-0985-8). Troll Assocs.
Pizer, Abigail. Penelope Pig. (Illus.). 32p. (ps-2). 1989. PLB 8.95 (ISBN 0-87614-366-4). Carolrhoda Bks.
Pomerantz, Charlotte. The Piggy in the Puddle. Marshall, James, illus. LC 73-6047. 32p. (ps-1). 1974. 13.95 (ISBN 0-02-774900-2, Mcmillan Child Bk). Macmillan Child Grp.
Porte, Barbara A. Ruthann & Her Pig. LC 88-31452. (Illus.). 96p. (gr. 2-5). 1989. 14.95 (ISBN 0-531-05825-5); PLB 14.99 (ISBN 0-531-08425-6). Orchard Bks Watts.
Potter, Beatrix. The Tale of Little Pig Robinson. 1987. 5.95 (ISBN 0-7232-3478-7); pap. 2.25 (ISBN 0-7232-3503-1). Warne.
Radford, Derek. Piggy at the Wheel. Radford, Derek, illus. 16p. (ps-2). 1988. pap. 6.95 (ISBN 0-671-65265-6, Little Simon). S&S Trade.
Rayner, Mary. Garth Pig & the Ice Cream Lady. LC 77-1647. (Illus.). 32p. (ps-3). 1978. 13.95 (ISBN 0-689-30598-2, Atheneum Child Bk). Macmillan Child Grp.
—Mr. & Mrs. Pig's Evening Out. Rayner, Mary, illus. LC 76-4476. 32p. (ps-2). 1976. 13.95 (ISBN 0-689-30530-3, Atheneum Child Bk). Macmillan Child Grp.
—Mrs. Pig Gets Cross & Other Stories. Rayner, Mary, illus. LC 86-13433. (ps-3). 1987. 11.95 (ISBN 0-525-44280-4, DCB). Dutton Child Bks.
—Mrs. Pig Gets Cross & Other Stories. (ps-3). 1991. pap. 5.95 (ISBN 0-525-44705-9, Unicorn Pbks). Dutton Child Bks.
—Mrs. Pig's Bulk Buy. Rayner, Mary, illus. LC 80-19875. 32p. (ps-2). 1981. 13.95 (ISBN 0-689-30831-0, Atheneum Child Bk). Macmillan Child Grp.
Rockwell, Anne. The Old Woman & Her Pig & Ten Other Stories. Rockwell, Anne, illus. LC 78-13901. (gr. 1 up). 1979. (Crowell Jr Bks); PLB 13.89 (ISBN 0-690-03928-X, Crowell Jr Bks). HarpC Child Bks.
Rodda, Emily. The Pigs Are Flying! Young, Noela, illus. LC 88-2449. 160p. (gr. 4-6). 1988. Repr. of 1986 ed. 12.95 (ISBN 0-688-08130-4). Greenwillow.
—The Pigs Are Flying! (Illus.). 144p. (gr. 2 up). 1989. pap. 2.95 (ISBN 0-380-70555-9, Camelot). Avon.
Romanova, Natalia. Once There Was a Tree. 1985. 13.95 (ISBN 0-8037-0235-3). Dial Bks Young.
Root, Phyllis & Marron, Carol A. No Place for a Pig. Jarvis, Nathan Y., illus. LC 84-17729. 32p. (gr. 3-6). 1985. PLB 14.65 (ISBN 0-940742-46-2); cassette 14.00 (ISBN 0-685-09934-2); incl. cassette 27.99 (ISBN 0-8172-2286-3). Raintree Pubs.
Sanford, Monard G. The Free Pigs. Bookless, George, ed. Skivington, Janice, illus. LC 86-63205. 21p. (ps-5). 1987. PLB 13.00 (ISBN 0-940273-00-4). Mill Creek Ent.
Saunders, Susan. The Daring Rescue of Marlon the Swimming Pig. Owens, Gail, illus. LC 87-4633. 64p. (gr. 2-4). 1987. lib. bdg. 6.99 (ISBN 0-394-98293-2, Random Juv); pap. 1.95 (ISBN 0-394-88293-8, Random Juv). Random.
Scally, Kevin. Save the Three Pigs. Scally, Kevin, illus. 32p. (ps-3). 1984. 3.95 (ISBN 0-448-11127-6, G&D). Putnam Pub Group.
Schwartz, Mary A. Spiffen: A Tale of a Tidy Pig. Levine, Abby, ed. Munsinger, Lynn, illus. 32p. (ps-3). 1988. PLB 12.95 (ISBN 0-8075-7580-1). A Whitman.
Scieszka, Jon. The True Story of the Three Little Pigs. Smith, Lane, illus. 32p. (ps up). 1989. pap. 14.95 (ISBN 0-670-82759-2). Viking Child Bks.
Sleator, William. Interstellar Pig. LC 84-4132. 192p. (gr. 7 up). 1984. 12.95 (ISBN 0-525-44098-4, DCB). Dutton Child Bks.
Steig, William. The Amazing Bone. Steig, William, illus. LC 76-26479. 32p. (ps-3). 1983. 16.95 (ISBN 0-374-30248-0). FS&G.
—Roland the Minstrel Pig. (Illus.). (gr. k-3). 1968. 12.95 (ISBN 0-06-025761-X). HarpC Child Bks.
—Roland the Minstrel Pig. Steig, William, illus. 32p. (ps-3). 1988. pap. 5.95 (ISBN 0-671-66841-2). S&S Trade.
Stepto, Michele. Snuggle Piggy & the Magic Blanket. Monfried, Lucia, ed. Himmelman, John, illus. LC 86-23943. (ps-k). 1987. 9.95 (ISBN 0-525-44308-8, DCB). Dutton Child Bks.
—Snuggle Piggy & the Magic Blanket. Monfried, Lucia, ed. Himmelman, John, illus. LC 86-23943. 24p. (ps). 1990. pap. 3.95 (ISBN 0-525-44609-5, DCB). Dutton Child Bks.
Stine, Bob. The Pigs' Book of World Records. Lippman, Peter, illus. LC 79-5239. 96p. (gr. 3 up). 1980. (Random Juv); pap. 4.99 (ISBN 0-394-94402-X). Random.
Stolz, Mary. Emmett's Pig. Williams, Garth, illus. LC 58-7763. 64p. (gr. k-3). 1959. PLB 11.89 (ISBN 0-06-025856-X). HarpC Child Bks.
Tharlet, Eve. Little Pig, Big Trouble. Clements, Andrew, tr. Tharlet, Eve, illus. LC 89-31369. (ps up). 1989. 14.95 (ISBN 0-88708-073-1). Picture Bk Studio.
Thompson, Carol. In My Bathroom. LC 89-31720. 1990. 8.95 (ISBN 0-385-29856-0). Doubleday.
—In My Bedroom. 1990. 8.95 (ISBN 0-385-29857-9). Doubleday.
Three Little Pigs. (FRE.). (gr. k-3). 4.25 (ISBN 0-685-28448-4). French & Eur.
Three Little Pigs. Facsimile ed. LC 86-33407. (Illus.). 56p. (gr. k-5). 1987. Repr. of 1924 ed. 11.95 (ISBN 0-916410-38-2). A D Bragdon.
Three Little Pigs. 1989. 2.98 (ISBN 0-671-06785-0). S&S Trade.
Three Little Pigs. 1988. 2.98 (ISBN 0-671-10041-6). S&S Trade.
Three Little Pigs. (Illus.). (ps-2). 3.95 (ISBN 0-7214-5059-8). Ladybird Bks.
Three Little Pigs. (Illus.). (gr. k). 3.50 (ISBN 0-7214-5134-9). Ladybird Bks.
The Three Little Pigs. (Illus.). (ps-4). 3.50 (ISBN 0-7214-1174-6). Ladybird Bks.
Tyler, Linda. The Sick-in-Bed Birthday. Davis, Susan, illus. 32p. (ps-3). 1990. pap. 3.95 (ISBN 0-14-050783-3, Puffin). Puffin Bks.
Uttley, Alison. Magic Water. Percy, Graham, illus. 32p. (ps-2). 1989. bds. 4.95 laminated (ISBN 0-571-15163-9). Faber & Faber.
—Sam Pig & His Fiddle. Percy, Graham, illus. (ps-2). 1989. bds. 4.95 laminated (ISBN 0-571-15162-0). Faber & Faber.
—Sam Pig & the Cuckoo Clock. Percy, Graham, illus. 32p. (ps-2). 1990. bds. 4.95 laminated (ISBN 0-571-15468-9). Faber & Faber.
—Sam Pig & the Dragon. (Illus.). 32p. (ps-2). 1989. bds. 4.95 laminated (ISBN 0-571-15294-5). Faber & Faber.
—Sam Pig & the Hurdy-Gurdy Man. (Illus.). 32p. (ps-2). 1989. bds. 4.95 laminated (ISBN 0-571-15076-4). Faber & Faber.
—Sam Pig & the Wind. (Illus.). 32p. (ps-2). 1989. laminated 4.95 (ISBN 0-571-15295-3). Faber & Faber.
—Sam Pig at the Theatre. Percy, Graham, illus. 32p. (ps-2). 1990. bds. 4.95 laminated (ISBN 0-571-15471-9). Faber & Faber.
—Sam Pig's Trousers. Percy, Graham, illus. 32p. (ps-2). 1989. laminated 4.95 (ISBN 0-571-15293-7). Faber & Faber.
Van, Leeuwan J. Oliver Pig at School. LC 89-25607. (ps-3). 1990. 9.89 (ISBN 0-8037-0812-2); PLB 9.89 (ISBN 0-8037-0813-0). Dial Bks Young.
Van Leeuwen, Jean. Amanda Pig & Her Big Brother Oliver. Schweninger, Ann, illus. LC 82-70188. 56p. (ps-3). 1982. PLB 9.89 (ISBN 0-8037-0017-2); pap. 4.95 (ISBN 0-8037-0016-4). Dial Bks Young.
—Cuentos de la Cerdita Amanda. (SPA.). 5.95 (ISBN 0-685-31018-3). Santillana.
—More Tales of Amanda Pig. Schweninger, Ann, illus. LC 84-28775. 56p. (ps-3). 1985. 8.95 (ISBN 0-8037-0223-X); PLB 9.89 (ISBN 0-8037-0224-8). Dial Bks Young.
—More Tales of Amanda Pig. Schweninger, Ann, illus. LC 84-28775. 56p. (ps-3). 1988. pap. 4.95 (ISBN 0-8037-0502-6). Dial Bks Young.
—Oliver, Amanda, & Grandmother Pig. 1990. pap. 4.95 (ISBN 0-8037-0745-2, Dial Easy to Read). Puffin Bks.
—Tales of Amanda Pig. Schweninger, Ann, illus. LC 82-23545. 56p. (ps-3). 1983. PLB 9.89 (ISBN 0-8037-8450-3); pap. 4.95 (ISBN 0-8037-8443-0). Dial Bks Young.
—Tales of Oliver Pig. Lobel, Arnold, illus. LC 79-4276. 64p. (ps-3). 1979. PLB 9.89 (ISBN 0-8037-8736-7); pap. 4.95 (ISBN 0-8037-8737-5). Dial Bks Young.
Wallner, John. The Three Little Pigs. (ps-k). 1987. pap. 7.95 (ISBN 0-670-81707-4). Viking Child Bks.
West, Keith. Little Pig's Special Day. (Illus.). (ps-3). 1991. 13.95 (ISBN 0-399-22209-X, Putnam). Putnam Pub Group.
White, E. B. Charlotte's Web. Williams, Garth, illus. LC 52-9760. (gr. 2-6). 1952. 10.95 (ISBN 0-06-026385-7); PLB 11.89 (ISBN 0-06-026386-5). HarpC Child Bks.
Winthrop, Elizabeth. Sloppy Kisses. Burgess, Anne, illus. (ps-3). 1983. pap. 3.95 (ISBN 0-14-050433-8, Puffin). Puffin Bks.
Wood, Don. Piggies. (ps). 1991. 13.95 (ISBN 0-15-256341-5). HarBraceJ.
Yolen, Jane. Picnic with Piggins. Dyer, Jane, illus. 32p. (gr. 4-8). 1988. 14.95 (ISBN 0-15-261534-2). HarBraceJ.
Zemach, Margot. The Three Little Pigs. (Illus.). 32p. (ps up). 1991. pap. 3.95 (ISBN 0-374-47717-5, Di Capua Bks). FS&G.
Zindel, Paul. The Pigman. LC 68-10784. 192p. (gr. 7 up). 1968. 13.95 (ISBN 0-06-026827-1); PLB 13.89 (ISBN 0-06-026828-X). HarpC Child Bks.

PIGS–POETRY

Lobel, Arnold. The Book of Pigericks. Lobel, Arnold, illus. LC 82-47730. 48p. (gr. k-3). 1983. 14.95 (ISBN 0-06-023982-4); PLB 14.89 (ISBN 0-06-023983-2). HarpC Child Bks.
MacDonald, Elizabeth. Miss Poppy & the Honey Cake. Smith, Claire, illus. LC 88-3851. 32p. (ps-2). 1989. 8.95 (ISBN 0-8037-0578-6). Dial Bks Young.

PIKE, ZEBULLON MONTGOMERY, 1779-1813

Stallones, Jared. Zebulon Pike & the Explorers of the American West. Goetzmann, William H., ed. Collins, Michael, intro. by. (Illus.). 112p. (gr. 5 up). 1991. PLB 18.95 (ISBN 0-7910-1317-0). Chelsea Hse.

PILGRIM FATHERS

Bains, Rae. Pilgrims & Thanksgiving. Wenzel, David, illus. LC 84-2686. 32p. (gr. 3-6). 1985. PLB 9.49 (ISBN 0-8167-0222-5); pap. text ed. 2.95 (ISBN 0-8167-0223-3). Troll Assocs.
Boynton, Alice B. Priscilla Alden & the Story of the First Thanksgiving. Brook, Bonnie, ed. Kiefer, Christa, illus. 32p. (gr. k-2). 1990. 5.95 (ISBN 0-671-69111-2); PLB 10.98 (ISBN 0-671-69105-8). Silver Pr.
Brown, Margaret W., ed. Homes in the Wilderness: A Pilgrim's Journal of Plymouth Plantation in 1620, by William Bradford & Others of the Mayflower Company. LC 87-27321. (Illus.). 76p. (gr. 5-12). 1988. PLB 16.00 (ISBN 0-208-02197-3, Linnet); pap. 8.95 (ISBN 0-208-02269-4, Linnet). Shoe String.
Caselli, Giovanni. An Irish Pilgrim. Caselli, Giovanni, illus. LC 86-71706. 29p. (gr. 3-9). 1987. 12.95 (ISBN 0-87226-108-5). P Bedrick Bks.
Dalgliesh, Alice. Thanksgiving Story. Sewell, Helen, illus. (gr. k-3). 1950. 9.95 (ISBN 0-684-12330-4, Scribners Young Read). Macmillan Child Grp.
Greene, Carol. The Pilgrims Are Marching. Dunnington, Tom, illus. LC 88-20219. 32p. (ps-2). 1988. PLB 14.60 (ISBN 0-516-08234-5); pap. 3.95 (ISBN 0-516-48234-3). Childrens.
Licht, Fred. Shelter the Pilgrim. 48p. (gr. 6). 1990. 10.95s.p. (ISBN 0-88682-307-2); 15.65 (ISBN 0-685-28222-8). Creative Ed.
McGovern, Ann. The Pilgrim's First Thanksgiving. Lasker, Je, illus. 48p. (gr. k-5). 1984. pap. 2.50 (ISBN 0-590-40617-5). Scholastic Inc.
Payne, Elizabeth. Meet the Pilgrim Fathers. Vestal, H. B., illus. (gr. 4 up). 1966. lib. bdg. 8.99 (ISBN 0-394-90063-4, Random Juv). Random.
Richards, Norman. The Story of the Mayflower Compact. Wiskur, Darrell, illus. LC 67-22901. 32p. (gr. 2-5). 1967. PLB 13.27 (ISBN 0-516-04625-X); pap. 3.95 (ISBN 0-516-44625-8). Childrens.

Sewall, Marcia. The Pilgrims of Plimoth. Sewall, Marcia, illus. LC 86-3362. 48p. (gr. 2 up). 1986. 14.95 (ISBN 0-689-31250-4, Atheneum Child Bk). Macmillan Child Grp.
Siegel, Beatrice. Fur Trappers & Traders: The Indians, the Pilgrims, & the Beaver. Bock, William S., illus. LC 80-7671. 64p. (gr. 3-7). 1987. PLB 11.85 (ISBN 0-8027-6397-9). Walker & Co.
—A New Look at the Pilgrims: Why They Came to America. Morris, Douglas, illus. LC 76-57060. 82p. (gr. 3-7). 1987. Repr. of 1977 ed. 13.85 (ISBN 0-8027-6292-1). Walker & Co.
Wisler, G. Clifton. This New Land. LC 87-17749. (gr. 5 up). 1987. 13.95 (ISBN 0-8027-6726-5); PLB 14.85 (ISBN 0-8027-6727-3). Walker & Co.

PILGRIM FATHERS–FICTION

Daugherty, James. The Landing of the Pilgrims. LC 80-21430. (Illus.). 160p. (gr. 5-9). 1981. PLB 7.99 (ISBN 0-685-04232-4, Random Juv); pap. 3.95 (ISBN 0-394-84697-4). Random.

Gay, David. Voyage to Freedom: Story of the Pilgrim Fathers. 149p. 1984. pap. 7.95 (ISBN 0-85151-384-0). Banner of Truth.
"You are standing on a narrow quay-side waiting to board a small sailing ship. You are about to make an exciting but dangerous & uncomfortable voyage..." So begins the racy & imaginative account of the voyage of the Mayflower which David Gay has written specially for young people. His exciting historical narrative follows the nine week passage of the Pilgrims through the eyes of an imaginary family, Matthew & Martha Lovelace, with their typical children, Justice & Prudence. They encounter such fascinating characters as Master Reynolds, John Howland & William Butten - all of whom really took The Mayflower's historic voyage. Here are three thousand miles of adventure, written with a sensitive appreciation of God's care for his people, & young people's love for adventure.
Publisher Provided Annotation.

The Seekers. 1987. pap. 3.95 (ISBN 0-14-032320-1, Puffin). Puffin Bks.
Taylor, Helen L. Little Pilgrim's Progress. (gr. 2-6). pap. 4.95 (ISBN 0-8024-0003-5). Moody.

PILOTING (AERONAUTICS)

see Airplanes–Piloting

PILOTS, AIRPLANE

see Air Pilots

PILOTS AND PILOTAGE

see also Navigation

Thompson, Jonathon. Air Raiders. (Illus.). 75p. (gr. 6-12). 4.50 (ISBN 0-933479-02-6). Thompson.
—Superflyer: Captain John Champion Flyer. 40p. (gr. 3-6). 3.95 (ISBN 0-933479-08-5). Thompson.
Thompson, Jonathon, Jr. Air Raiders Two. (Illus.). 70p. (gr. 7-12). 1987. 4.60 (ISBN 0-933479-10-7). Thompson.

PIONEER LIFE

see Frontier and Pioneer Life

PIRATES

see also Privateering

Drechsler, Lawrence. The Pirates. LC 85-52401. (Illus., Orig.). (gr. 6 up). pap. write for info. (ISBN 0-935143-01-7). Treadle Pr.
McCall, Edith. Pirates & Privateers. Palm, Felix, illus. LC 63-15637. 128p. (gr. 3-10). 1980. PLB 14.60 (ISBN 0-516-03360-3). Childrens.
McWilliams, Karen. Pirates. 64p. (gr. 3-5). 1989. PLB 11.90 (ISBN 0-531-10464-8). Watts.
Marrin, Albert. The Sea Rovers: Pirates, Privateers & Buccaneers. LC 83-15886. (Illus.). 224p. (gr. 6 up). 1984. 14.95 (ISBN 0-689-31029-3, Atheneum Child Bk). Macmillan Child Grp.
Marsh, Carole. Avast, Ye Slobs! The Book of Silly Pirate Trivia. (Illus., Orig.). (gr. 1-12). 1986. PLB 19.95 (ISBN 1-55609-281-4); pap. 14.95 (ISBN 0-935326-82-0). Gallopade Pub Group.
Stein, R. Conrad. The Story of the Barbary Pirates. LC 82-4436. (Illus.). (gr. 3-6). 1982. PLB 13.27 (ISBN 0-516-04632-2). Childrens.
Wright, Rachel. Pirates. (Illus.). 32p. (gr. k-4). 1991. PLB 11.40 (ISBN 0-531-14156-X). Watts.

PIRATES–FICTION

Ambrus, Victor G. Blackbeard the Pirate. (Illus.). 32p. (gr. 2 up). 1990. pap. 5.95 (ISBN 0-19-272220-4). Oxford U Pr.
Arden, William. The Mystery of the Purple Pirate. LC 82-372. (Illus.). 192p. (gr. 4-7). 1982. lib. bdg. 6.99 (ISBN 0-394-94951-X); pap. 2.95 (ISBN 0-394-84951-5). Random.
Asch, Frank. Pearl's Pirates. Asch, Frank, illus. LC 86-19621. 160p. (gr. k-3). 1987. pap. 13.95 (ISBN 0-385-29546-4). Delacorte.
—Pearl's Pirates. (gr. k-6). 1989. pap. 3.25 (ISBN 0-440-40245-X, YB). Dell.
Avi. Captain Grey. Mikolaycak, Charles, illus. LC 76-41182. (gr. 5 up). 1977. Pantheon.
Bashful Bard. Pirates. Bashful Bard, illus. LC 89-84960. 24p. (Orig.). (ps-1). 1989. pap. 2.99 (ISBN 1-877906-00-X). Kenney Pubns.
Burningham, John. Come Away from the Water, Shirley. LC 77-483. (Illus.). 32p. (ps-3). 1983. pap. 5.95 (ISBN 0-06-443039-1, Trophy). HarpC Child Bks.
Coerr, Eleanor. The Bell Ringer & the Pirates. Sandin, Joan, illus. LC 82-47700. 64p. (gr. k-3). 1983. PLB 10.89 (ISBN 0-06-021355-8). HarpC Child Bks.
Giff, Patricia R. The Gift of the Pirate Queen. Rutherford, Jenny, illus. 160p. (gr. 4-8). 1983. pap. 3.25 (ISBN 0-440-43046-1, Pub. by Yearling Classics). Dell.
Gilbert & Sullivan. The Pirates of Penzance. Botsford, Ward, adapted by. Sorel, Edward, illus. LC 81-5173. 48p. (gr. 5 up). 1981. Random.
Haseley, Dennis. The Pirate Who Tried to Capture the Moon. Truesdell, Susan, illus. LC 82-47734. 48p. (gr. k-4). 1983. PLB 11.89 (ISBN 0-06-022227-1). HarpC Child Bks.
Homer, Larona. Blackbeard the Pirate & Other Stories of the Pine Barrens. Bock, William S., illus. 96p. (gr. 3-5). 1987. pap. 8.95 (ISBN 0-912608-04-8). Mid Atlantic.
Isadora, Rachel. The Pirates of Bedford Street. LC 84-25904. (Illus.). 32p. (ps-3). 1988. 11.95 (ISBN 0-688-05206-1); lib. bdg. 11.88 (ISBN 0-688-05208-8). Greenwillow.
Kennedy, Richard. Amy's Eyes. Egielski, Richard, illus. LC 82-48841. 448p. (ps up). 1985.. 14.95 (ISBN 0-06-023219-6). HarpC Child Bks.
Kingsley, Emily P. Garfield the Pirate. Davis, Jim, illus. 32p. (ps). 1982. pap. 1.25 (ISBN 0-394-85445-4). Random.
Marc & John. Swashbucklers: The Raid; The Cook; The Rock; The Cannon; The Storm & The Map, 6 bks. Marc & John, illus. 96p. (gr. k-1). Set. pap. text ed. 28.90 (ISBN 1-55624-255-7). Wright Group.
Nelson, Ginger K. The Pirate's Revenge. Kratoville, Betty L., ed. Lucey, Jack, illus. 64p. (gr. 3-9). 1989. lib. bdg. 4.95 (ISBN 0-87879-654-1, High Noon Books). Acad Therapy.
Oleksy, Walter. The Pirates of Deadman's Cay. LC 82-8488. (Illus.). 112p. (gr. 7-9). 1982. 9.95 (ISBN 0-664-32693-5, Westminster). Westminster John Knox.
Poskitt, Kjartan. The Mystery of the Pirate's Treasure. Higham, David, illus. 24p. (gr. k-3). 1991. pap. 4.95 (ISBN 0-8249-8417-X). Ideals.
Ryan, John. Pugwash & the Ghost Ship. Ryan, John, illus. LC 68-23218. (gr. k-3). 1968. 18.95 (ISBN 0-87599-146-7). S G Phillips.
Scieszka, Jon. The Not-So-Jolly-Roger. Smith, Lane, illus. 64p. (gr. 3-7). 1991. 10.95 (ISBN 0-670-83754-7). Viking Child Bks.
Shub, Elizabeth. Cutlass in the Snow. Isadora, Rachel, illus. LC 85-5442. 48p. (gr. 1-4). 1986. 11.95 (ISBN 0-688-05927-9); PLB 11.88 (ISBN 0-688-05928-7). Greenwillow.
Sohl, Marcia & Dackerman, Gerald. Treasure Island. 16p. (gr. 4-10). 1976. pap. 2.95 (ISBN 0-88301-106-9); pap. 1.25 student activity bk. (ISBN 0-88301-185-9). Pendulum Pr.
Stevenson, Robert Louis. Reader's Digest Best Loved Books for Young Readers: Treasure Island. Ogburn, Jackie, ed. Glanzman, Louis S., illus. 144p. (gr. 4-12). 1989. 3.99 (ISBN 0-945260-23-7). Choice Pub NY.
—Treasure Island. (gr. 7 up). pap. 2.75 (ISBN 0-8049-0002-7, CL-2). Airmont.
—Treasure Island. (Illus.). (gr. 1-9). 1947. deluxe ed. 10.95 (ISBN 0-448-06025-6, G&D). Putnam Pub Group.
—Treasure Island. (Illus.). (gr. 6-9). 1978. 2.95 (ISBN 0-448-14920-6, G&D). Putnam Pub Group.
—Treasure Island. 224p. (gr. 2-5). 1984. pap. 2.25 (ISBN 0-14-035016-0, Puffin). Puffin Bks.
—Treasure Island. (gr. 7-12). 1972. pap. 2.25 (ISBN 0-590-40105-X, Schol Pap). Scholastic Inc.
—Treasure Island. Letley, Emma, ed. (gr. 7-12). 1985. pap. 2.25 (ISBN 0-19-281681-0). Oxford U Pr.
—Treasure Island. (gr. k-6). 1986. 7.98 (ISBN 0-685-16845-X, 618168). Outlet Bk Co.
—Treasure Island. Iljinski, Igor, illus. 192p. (gr. 4 up). 1989. 14.95 (ISBN 0-8120-5942-5). Barron.
—Treasure Island. Wyeth, N. C., illus. LC 89-43034. 274p. 1989. Repr. 12.98 (ISBN 0-89471-778-2, Courage Books). Running Pr.
—Treasure Island. abridged ed. Norby, Lisa, adapted by. Fernandez, Fernando, illus. LC 89-70039. 96p. (Orig.). (gr. 2-6). 1990. PLB 5.99 (ISBN 0-679-90402-6); pap. 2.95 (ISBN 0-679-80402-1). Random.
—Treasure Island. 1991. pap. 3.75 (ISBN 0-425-12335-9). Berkley Pub.
Townsend, Tom. Powderhorn Passage: Sequel to Where the Pirates Are, Vol. 3. Roberts, Melissa, ed. (gr. 4-7). 1988. 8.95 (ISBN 0-89015-642-5, Pub. by Panda Bks). Eakin Pr.
Treasure Island. (Illus.). (gr. 3-5). 3.50 (ISBN 0-7214-0597-5). Ladybird Bks.
Vinton, Iris. Look Out for Pirates. LC 61-7790. (Illus.). 72p. (gr. 1-2). 1961. lib. bdg. 7.99 (ISBN 0-394-90022-7). Beginner.
Ward, Helen. The Moonrat & the White Turtle. Ward, Helen, illus. (ps-4). 1990. 13.95 (ISBN 0-8249-8467-6). Ideals.
Wilhelm, Hans. Pirates Ahoy! Wilhelm, Hans, illus. LC 87-30197. 40p. (ps-3). 1987. 5.95 (ISBN 0-8193-1162-6). Parents.
—Pirates Ahoy. Wilhelm, Hans, illus. 48p. (ps-2). 1990. pap. 2.95 (ISBN 0-448-04340-8, G&D). Putnam Pub Group.

PIUS 5TH, SAINT, POPE, 1566-1572

Daughters of St. Paul. No Place for Defeat. (gr. 3-9). 3.00 (ISBN 0-8198-0241-7). Dghtrs St Paul.

PIUS 10TH, SAINT, POPE, 1835-1914

Windeatt, Mary F. St. Pius X. Harmon, Gedge, illus. 32p. (gr. 1-5). 1989. Repr. of 1954 ed. wkbk. 3.00 (ISBN 0-89555-371-6). TAN Bks Pubs.

PIZARRO, FRANCISCO, 1470?-1541

Bernhard, Brendan. Pizarro, Orellana, & the Exploration of the Amazon. Goetzmann, William H., ed. Collins, Michael, intro. by. (Illus.). 112p. (gr. 5 up). 1991. PLB 18.95 (ISBN 0-7910-1305-7). Chelsea Hse.

PLACE NAMES

see Names, Geographical

PLAGUE–FICTION

Swindells, Robert. A Serpent's Tooth. LC 88-24635. 144p. (gr. 4-7). 1989. 13.95 (ISBN 0-8234-0743-8). Holiday.

PLANE GEOMETRY

see Geometry

PLAGUE

Biel, Timothy L. The Black Death. LC 89-112269. (Illus.). 64p. (gr. 5-8). 1989. PLB 11.95 (ISBN 1-56006-001-8). Lucent Bks.
Tolan, Stephanie S. Plague Year. LC 89-13605. (Illus.). 208p. (gr. 7 up). 1990. 12.95 (ISBN 0-688-08801-5). Morrow Jr Bks.
Turner, Derek. The Black Death. Reeves, Marjorie, ed. (Illus.). 96p. (gr. 7-12). 1978. pap. text ed. 8.60 (ISBN 0-582-31097-0, 78068). Longman.

PLANETS

see also Life on Other Planets; Solar System; Stars; also names of planets, e.g. Venus (Planet)

Asimov, Isaac. How Did We Find Out about Neptune? Kors, Erika, illus. 64p. (gr. 5 up). 1990. 12.95 (ISBN 0-8027-6981-0); lib. bdg. 13.85 (ISBN 0-8027-6982-9). Walker & Co.
—Jupiter: The Spotted Giant. LC 88-42893. (Illus.). 32p. (gr. 3-4). 1989. PLB 11.95 (ISBN 1-55532-363-4). Gareth Stevens Inc.
—Neptune: The Farthest Giant. LC 89-43136. (Illus.). 32p. (gr. 3-4). 1990. PLB 12.95 (ISBN 1-55532-369-3). Gareth Stevens Inc.
—Saturn: The Ringed Beauty. LC 88-17563. (Illus.). 32p. (gr. 3-4). 1988. PLB 11.95 (ISBN 1-55532-364-2). Gareth Stevens Inc.
—Uranus: The Sideways Planet. LC 87-42594. (Illus.). 32p. (gr. 3-4). 1988. PLB 11.95 (ISBN 1-55532-324-3). Gareth Stevens Inc.
Bailey, Donna. The Far Planets. LC 90-40081. (Illus.). 48p. (gr. 2-5). 1990. PLB 15.96 (ISBN 0-8114-2524-X). Steck-V.
—The Near Planets. LC 90-40078. (Illus.). 48p. (gr. 2-5). 1990. PLB 15.96 (ISBN 0-8114-2523-1). Steck-V.
Barrett, Norman. The Picture World of Planets. (Illus.). 32p. (gr. k-4). 1990. PLB 11.40 (ISBN 0-531-14054-7). Watts.
—Planets. Marffy, Janos & Willard, Stuart, illus. LC 85-50159. 32p. (gr. 3-5). 1985. PLB 11.40 (ISBN 0-531-10005-7). Watts.
Bendick, Jeanne. Moons & Rings: Companions to the Planets. (Illus.). 32p. (gr. k-2). 1991. PLB 11.90 (ISBN 1-56294-000-7); pap. 3.95 (ISBN 1-878841-54-8). Millbrook Pr.
Branley, Franklyn M. Mysteries of the Planets. Bensusen, Sally J., illus. LC 87-20086. 80p. (gr. 5-9). 1988. 13.95 (ISBN 0-525-67240-0, Lodestar Bks). Dutton Child Bks.
—The Planets in Our Solar System. rev. ed. Madden, Don, illus. LC 86-47530. 32p. (ps-3). 1987. 13.95 (ISBN 0-690-04579-4, Crowell Jr Bks); PLB 13.89 (ISBN 0-690-04581-6). HarpC Child Bks.
—Saturn: The Spectacular Planet. Kessler, Leonard, illus. LC 81-43890. 64p. (gr. 3-6). 1987. pap. 4.95 (ISBN 0-06-446056-8, Trophy). HarpC Child Bks.
—Uranus: The Seventh Planet. Buchanan, Yvonne, illus. LC 87-35046. 64p. (gr. 3-6). 1988. 11.95 (ISBN 0-690-04685-5, Crowell Jr Bks); PLB 11.89 (ISBN 0-690-04687-1, Crowell Jr Bks). HarpC Child Bks.
Fradin, Dennis B. Jupiter. LC 89-9983. 48p. (gr. k-4). 1989. PLB 14.60 (ISBN 0-516-01173-1); pap. 4.95 (ISBN 0-516-41173-X). Childrens.
—Pluto. LC 89-9925. 48p. (gr. k-4). 1989. PLB 14.60 (ISBN 0-516-01175-8); pap. 4.95 (ISBN 0-516-41175-6). Childrens.
—Saturn. LC 88-39117. (Illus.). 48p. (gr. k-4). 1989. PLB 14.60 (ISBN 0-516-01166-9); pap. 4.95 (ISBN 0-516-41166-7). Childrens.
—Uranus. LC 89-9984. 48p. (gr. k-4). 1989. PLB 14.60 (ISBN 0-516-01177-4); pap. 4.95 (ISBN 0-516-41177-2). Childrens.
Gallant, Roy. The Planets: Exploring the Solar System. rev. ed. LC 84-29725. (Illus.). 192p. (gr. 7 up). 1990. Repr. of 1982 ed. 15.95 (ISBN 0-02-735773-2, Four Winds). Macmillan Child Grp.
Gallant, Roy A. The Planets: Exploring the Solar System. LC 84-29725. (Illus.). 192p. (gr. 7 up). 1984. Repr. of 1982 ed. 15.95 (ISBN 0-02-736930-7, Four Winds). Macmillan Child Grp.

Greenberg, Judith E. & Carey, Helen H. Space. Karpinski, Rick, illus. 32p. (gr. 2-4). 1990. 16.67 (ISBN 0-8172-3754-2); PLB 11.99. Raintree Pubs.

Herbst, Judith. The Golden Book of Stars & Planets. LaPadula, Tom, illus. 48p. (gr. 3-7). 1988. write for info. (ISBN 0-307-15572-2). Western Pub.

Jackson, Kim. The Planets. Watling, James, illus. LC 84-16451. 32p. (gr. k-2). 1985. lib. bdg. 10.89 (ISBN 0-8167-0450-3); pap. text ed. 2.95 (ISBN 0-8167-0451-1). Troll Assocs.

Jay, Michael. Planets. (Illus.). 32p. (gr. k-3). 1987. PLB 7.99 (ISBN 0-531-10278-5). Watts.

Kerrod, Robin. Big Book of Stars & Planets. 1990. 5.98 (ISBN 0-8317-0861-1). Smithmark.

Lampton, Christopher. Stars & Planets: A Useful & Entertaining Tool to Guide Youngsters into the Twenty-First Century. Miller, Ron, illus. LC 87-13628. 48p. (gr. 1-7). 1988. PLB 11.99 (ISBN 0-385-23786-3); pap. 10.95 (ISBN 0-385-23785-5). Doubleday.

Landau, Elaine. Jupiter. (Illus.). 64p. (gr. 3-5). 1991. PLB 11.90 (ISBN 0-531-20015-9). Watts.

—Neptune. (Illus.). 64p. (gr. 3-5). 1991. PLB 11.90 (ISBN 0-531-20014-0). Watts.

—Saturn. (Illus.). 64p. (gr. 3-5). 1991. PLB 11.90 (ISBN 0-531-20013-2). Watts.

Lauber, Patricia. Journey to the Planets. LC 82-1426. (Illus.). 90p. (gr. 5 up). 1984. 13.95 (ISBN 0-517-54477-6). Crown.

—Journey to the Planets. 2nd, rev. ed. NASA Staff, illus. LC 90-33102. 1990. 15.95 (ISBN 0-517-58121-3); PLB 16.99 (ISBN 0-517-58125-6). Crown.

Maynard. Stars & Planets: Discovering the Secrets of the Sky at Night. (Illus.). 32p. (gr. 4-8). 1976. PLB 13.96 (ISBN 0-88110-313-6); pap. 6.95 (ISBN 0-86020-094-9). EDC.

Nourse, Alan E. The Giant Planets. rev. ed. (Illus.). 72p. (gr. 4 up). 1982. PLB 10.40 (ISBN 0-531-00816-9). Watts.

Petty, Kate. The Planets. Saunders, Mike, illus. 32p. (gr. k-3). 1984. lib. bdg. 10.90 (ISBN 0-531-04734-2). Watts.

Radlauer, Ruth & Stembridge, Charles. Planets. LC 83-21043. (Illus.). 48p. (gr. 3 up). 1984. lib. bdg. 15.93 (ISBN 0-516-07838-0); pap. 4.95 (ISBN 0-516-47838-9). Childrens.

Reigot, Betty P. A Book about Planets. Hanke, Ted, illus. 39p. (Orig.). (gr. k-3). 1981. pap. 2.95 (ISBN 0-590-40313-3, Schol Pap). Scholastic Inc.

Robson, Denny. The Planets. (Illus.). 32p. (gr. k-4). 1991. PLB 11.90 (ISBN 0-531-17335-6, Gloucester Pr). Watts.

Rutland, Jonathan. The Planets. Jobson, Ron, illus. LC 86-26219. 24p. (gr. 2-5). 1987. lib. bdg. 6.99 (ISBN 0-394-98972-4, Random Juv); pap. 2.95 (ISBN 0-394-88972-X). Random.

Schecter, Darrow. I Can Read About Planets. new ed. LC 78-66272. (Illus.). (gr. 3-6). 1979. pap. 1.95 (ISBN 0-89375-215-0). Troll Assocs.

Simon, Seymour. Jupiter. LC 85-2922. (Illus.). 32p. (ps-3). 1988. 14.95 (ISBN 0-688-05796-9); PLB 14.88 (ISBN 0-688-05797-7, Morrow Jr Bks); pap. 4.95 (ISBN 0-688-08403-6, Mulberry Bks). Morrow Jr Bks.

—Saturn. LC 85-2995. (Illus.). 32p. (ps-3). 1988. 14.95 (ISBN 0-688-05798-5); lib. bdg. 14.88 (ISBN 0-688-05799-3, Morrow Jr Bks); pap. 4.95 (ISBN 0-688-08404-4, Mulberry Bks). Morrow Jr Bks.

—Uranus. LC 86-31223. (Illus.). 32p. (ps-3). 1987. 13.00 (ISBN 0-688-06582-1); lib. bdg. 12.88 (ISBN 0-688-06583-X, Morrow Jr Bks). Morrow Jr Bks.

Vogt, Gregory. Mars & the Inner Planets. (Illus.). 72p. (gr. 4 up). 1982. PLB 10.40 (ISBN 0-531-04384-3). Watts.

PLANETS, LIFE ON OTHER
see Life on Other Planets

PLANNED PARENTHOOD
see Birth Control

PLANNING, ECONOMIC
see Economic Policy
see names of countries, states, etc. with the subdivision Economic Policy, e.g. U. S.–Economic Policy

PLANNING, NATIONAL
see Economic Policy
see names of countries with the subdivision Economic Policy, Social Policy; e.g. U. S.–Economic Policy; U. S.–Social policy

PLANS
see Geometrical Drawing; Map Drawing; Maps; Mechanical Drawing

PLANT BREEDING
see also Plant Propagation

PLANT FORMS IN DESIGN
see Design, Decorative

PLANT PHYSIOLOGY
see also Growth (Plants)

PLANT PROPAGATION
see also Seeds

Jordan, Helene J. Seeds by Wind & Water. Hogner, Nils, illus. LC 62-12820. (gr. k-3). 1962. write for info. (ISBN 0-690-72452-7, Crowell Jr Bks). HarpC Child Bks.

Lauber, Patricia. From Flower to Flower: Animals & Pollination. Wexler, Jerome, photos by. (gr. 3-6). 1987. 13.95 (ISBN 0-517-55539-5). Crown.

PLANTING
see Agriculture; Gardening

PLANTS
see also Desert Plants; Flowers; Gardening; House Plants; Marine Plants; Shrubs; Weeds
also names of plants (e.g. Mosses, etc.)

Animals, Birds, Bees, & Flowers. Date not set. 5.98 (ISBN 0-517-68230-3). Outlet Bk Co.

Baker, Margaret. Discovering the Folklore of Plants. (Illus.). 72p. (gr. 6 up). 1975. pap. 3.00 (ISBN 0-913714-04-6). Legacy Bks.

Bates, Jeffrey. Seeds to Plants: Projects with Botany. (Illus.). 32p. (gr. 5-9). 1991. PLB 11.90 (ISBN 0-531-17292-9, Gloucester Pr). Watts.

Bender, Lionel. Plants. Franklin Watts Ltd., ed. Khan, Aziz, illus. 40p. (gr. 7-9). 1988. PLB 12.40 (ISBN 0-531-17094-2, Gloucester Pr). Watts.

Borland, Hal. Plants of Christmas. Dowden, Anne O., illus. LC 87-552. 32p. (gr. 3 up). 1987. Repr. of 1969 ed. 13.95 (ISBN 0-690-04649-9, Crowell Jr Bks); PLB 14.89 (ISBN 0-690-04650-2, Crowell Jr Bks). HarpC Child Bks.

Burnie, David. Plant. King, Dave, et al, illus. LC 88-27172. 64p. (gr. 5 up). 1989. 13.95 (ISBN 0-394-82252-8); PLB 14.99 (ISBN 0-394-92252-2). Knopf.

Carle, Eric. The Tiny Seed. 2nd ed. Carle, Eric, illus. LC 86-2534. 36p. (gr. k up). 1990. Repr. of 1987 ed. 4.95 (ISBN 0-88708-155-X). Picture Bk Studio.

Carratello, John & Carratello, Patty. Hands on Science: Plants. Wright, Terry, illus. 32p. (gr. 2-5). 1988. wkbk. 4.95 (ISBN 1-55734-224-5). Tchr Create Mat.

Challand, Helen. Plants Without Seeds. LC 85-30935. (Illus.). 48p. (gr. k-4). 1986. PLB 14.60 (ISBN 0-516-01286-X). Childrens.

Conway, Lorraine. Plants. 64p. (gr. 5 up). 1980. 6.95 (ISBN 0-916456-69-2, GA 176). Good Apple.

—Plants & Animals in Nature. Akins, Linda, illus. 64p. (gr. 5 up). 1986. wkbk. 6.95 (ISBN 0-86653-356-7, GA 797). Good Apple.

Cork, Barbara. Plant Life. Jackson, Ian, illus. 32p. (gr. 6up). 1984. PLB 13.96 (ISBN 0-88110-169-9); pap. 5.95 (ISBN 0-86020-755-2). EDC.

Crowell, Robert L. The Lore & Legends of Flowers. Dowden, Anne O., illus. LC 79-7829. 88p. (gr. 7 up). 1982. 14.95 (ISBN 0-690-03991-3, Crowell Jr Bks); PLB 14.89 (ISBN 0-690-04035-0, Crowell Jr Bks). HarpC Child Bks.

Facklam, Howard & Facklam, Margery. Plants: Extinction or Survival? 96p. (gr. 6 up). 1990. 16.95 (ISBN 0-89490-248-2). Enslow Pubs.

Gale, Frank C. & Gale, Clarice W. Experiences with Plants for Young Children. Solis-Navarro, Kelly, illus. Durett, Mary E., frwd. by. LC 78-88376. (Illus.). (ps-3). 1975. 10.95x (ISBN 0-87015-211-4). Pacific Bks.

Gibbons, Gail. From Seed to Plant. Gibbons, Gail, illus. LC 90-47037. 32p. (ps-3). 1991. PLB 14.95 (ISBN 0-8234-0872-8). Holiday.

Goldish, Meish. How Do Plants Get Food? (Illus.). 32p. (gr. 1-4). 1989. PLB 13.32 (ISBN 0-8172-3507-8). Raintree Pubs.

Holly, Brian. Plants & Flowers. McGee, Martin, illus. 32p. (gr. 3-7). 1985. pap. 3.50 (ISBN 0-88625-114-1). Durkin Hayes Pub.

Janulewicz, Mike. Plants. 40p. (gr. 4-8). 1984. lib. bdg. 12.40 (ISBN 0-531-03477-1). Watts.

Jordan, Helene J. How a Seed Grows. Low, Joseph, illus. LC 60-11541. 33p. (gr. k-3). 1972. pap. 4.95 (ISBN 0-690-40646-0, Crowell Jr Bks). HarpC Child Bks.

Kirkpatrick, Rena K. Look at Seeds & Weeds. rev. ed. King, Debbie, illus. LC 84-26226. 32p. (gr. 2-4). 1985. PLB 15.99 (ISBN 0-8172-2357-6); pap. text ed. 9.27 (ISBN 0-8172-2382-7). Raintree Pubs.

Kuchalla, Susan. All about Seeds. McBee, Jane, illus. LC 81-11480. 32p. (gr. k-2). 1982. lib. bdg. 10.89 (ISBN 0-89375-658-X); pap. 2.95 (ISBN 0-89375-659-8). Troll Assocs.

Lauber, Patricia. Seeds: Pop Stick Glide. Wexler, Jerome, photos by. LC 80-14553. (Illus.). 64p. (gr. 2-4). 1988. 12.95 (ISBN 0-517-54165-3). Crown.

Lerner, Carol. Plant Families. Lerner, Carol, illus. LC 88-26653. 32p. (gr. 4 up). 1989. 12.95 (ISBN 0-688-07881-8); PLB 12.88 (ISBN 0-688-07882-6, Morrow Jr Bks). Morrow Jr Bks.

Madgwick, Wendy. Flowering Plants. LC 90-9572. (Illus.). 48p. (gr. 5-9). 1990. PLB 18.60 (ISBN 0-8114-2730-7). Steck-V.

Marcus, Elizabeth. Amazing World of Plants. Boyd, Patti, illus. LC 83-4836. 32p. (gr. 3-6). 1984. lib. bdg. 10.59 (ISBN 0-89375-967-8); pap. text ed. 2.95 (ISBN 0-89375-968-6). Troll Assocs.

Miner, O. Irene. Plants We Know. LC 81-9929. 48p. (gr. k-4). 1981. PLB 14.60 (ISBN 0-516-01642-3); pap. 4.95 (ISBN 0-516-41642-1). Childrens.

Moncure, Jane B. What Plants Need: The Rabbit Who Knew. Dunnington, Tom, illus. LC 89-24001. 32p. (ps-2). 1990. lib. bdg. 11.97 (ISBN 0-89565-559-4). Childs World.

Nussbaum, Hedda. Plants Do Amazing Things. Mathieu, Joe, illus. LC 75-36471. 72p. (gr. 2-3). 1977. 7.95 (ISBN 0-394-83232-9, Random Juv); lib. bdg. 8.99 (ISBN 0-394-93232-3). Random.

Overbeck, Cynthia. Carnivorous Plants. LC 81-17234. (Illus.). 48p. (gr. 4 up). 1982. PLB 14.95 (ISBN 0-8225-1470-2, First Ave Edns); pap. 5.95 (ISBN 0-8225-9535-4, First Ave Edns). Lerner Pubns.

Penn, Linda. Wild Plants & Animals. Weiser, Liz, illus. 32p. (gr. k-3). 1986. wkbk. 4.95 (ISBN 0-86653-351-6, GA 687). Good Apple.

—Young Scientist Explore: The Kingdom of Plants. Scott, Elaine, illus. 32p. (gr. k-3). 1985. wkbk. 4.95 (ISBN 0-86653-315-X, GA 651). Good Apple.

Plant Science. (Illus.). 48p. (gr. 6-12). 1983. pap. 1.85 (ISBN 0-8395-3396-9, 3396). BSA.

Plants. LC 87-16543. (Illus.). 96p. (gr. 3 up). 1987. PLB 240.00 set (ISBN 0-317-64438-6); pap. 13.27 (ISBN 0-8172-3054-8). Raintree Pubs.

Plants. (Illus.). (gr. k-3). 3.95 (ISBN 0-7214-5214-0). Ladybird Bks.

Plants. 1991. pap. 3.95 (ISBN 0-7214-5327-9). Ladybird Bks.

Plants & People. (gr. 3-6). 1981. incl. cass. & tchr's. guide 28.95 (ISBN 0-686-73889-6, 04915). Natl Geog.

Pringle, Laurence. Being a Plant. Brickman, Robin, illus. LC 82-45915. 96p. (gr. 7 up). 1983. (Crowell Jr Bks); PLB 12.89 (ISBN 0-690-04347-3). HarpC Child Bks.

Quinn, Kaye. The World's Wierdest Plants. (Illus.). 80p. (Orig.). (gr. 2-4). 1989. pap. 2.50 (ISBN 0-8431-2379-6). Price Stern.

Rahn, Joan E. Plants Up Close. (Illus.). (gr. 2-5). 1981. 13.95 (ISBN 0-395-31677-4). HM.

Reading, Susan. Plant Partnerships. 64p. 1990. 15.95x. Facts on File.

Ricciuti, Edward R. Plants in Danger. Zwinger, Ann, illus. LC 77-25669. (gr. 7-9). 1979. 10.10i (ISBN 0-06-024978-1). HarpC Child Bks.

Riehecky, Janet. What Plants Give Us: The Gift of Life. Collette, Rondi, illus. LC 90-30374. 32p. (ps-2). 1990. lib. bdg. 11.97 (ISBN 0-89565-570-5). Childs World.

Ring, Elizabeth. Tiger Lilies & Other Beastly Plants. Bash, Barbara, illus. LC 84-7499. 32p. (gr. 3 up). 1985. 9.95 (ISBN 0-8027-6540-8). Walker & Co.

Sabin, Louis. Plants, Seeds & Flowers. Moylan, Holly, illus. LC 84-2720. 32p. (gr. 3-6). 1985. PLB 9.49 (ISBN 0-8167-0226-8); pap. text ed. 2.95 (ISBN 0-8167-0227-6). Troll Assocs.

Selsam, Millicent E. & Hunt, Joyce. A First Look at the World of Plants. Springer, Harriett, illus. LC 77-78088. (gr. 1-4). 1978. PLB 9.85 (ISBN 0-8027-6299-9). Walker & Co.

Taylor, Barbara. Growing Plants. (Illus.). 40p. (gr. k-4). 1991. PLB 11.90 (ISBN 0-531-19128-1, Warwick). Watts.

Warren, Elizabeth. I Can Read About Trees & Plants. LC 74-24991. (Illus.). (gr. 2-4). 1975. pap. 1.95 (ISBN 0-89375-069-7). Troll Assocs.

Webster, Vera. Plant Experiments. LC 82-9448. (Illus.). (gr. k-4). 1982. PLB 14.60 (ISBN 0-516-01638-5); pap. 4.95 (ISBN 0-516-41638-3). Childrens.

PLANTS, CULTIVATED
see also House Plants; Plants, Edible

Rahn, Joan E. More Plants That Changed History. LC 84-21563. 136p. (gr. 5 up). 1985. 12.95 (ISBN 0-689-31099-4, Atheneum Child Bk). Macmillan Child Grp.

PLANTS–ECOLOGY
see Botany–Ecology

PLANTS, EDIBLE

Sweet, Muriel. Common Edible & Useful Plants of the West. rev. ed. LC 76-58. (Illus.). 64p. (gr. 4 up). 1976. 10.95 (ISBN 0-87961-047-6); pap. 3.95 (ISBN 0-87961-046-8). Naturegraph.

PLANTS–FICTION

Cates, Joe W. Carl the Cactus. Cates, Joe W., illus. 64p. (Orig.). (gr. k-6). 1986. PLB 9.95 (ISBN 0-942403-03-7); pap. 7.00 (ISBN 0-942403-01-0). J Barnaby Dist.

Flora, James. The Great Green Turkey Creek Monster. Flora, James, illus. LC 75-43894. 32p. (gr. k-4). 1976. 14.95 (ISBN 0-689-50060-2, M K McElderry). Macmillan Child Grp.

Kerven, Rosalind. The Tree in the Moon & Other Legends of Plants & Trees. (Illus.). 1989. 13.95 (ISBN 0-521-34269-4). Cambridge U Pr.

Krauss, Ruth. The Carrot Seed. Johnson, Crockett, illus. LC 45-4530. 32p. (ps-1). 1989. pap. 3.95 (ISBN 0-06-443210-6, Trophy). HarpC Child Bks.

McArthur, Nancy. The Return of the Plant That Ate Dirty Socks. 128p. (Orig.). (gr. 5-6). 1990. pap. 2.95 (ISBN 0-380-75873-3, Camelot). Avon.

Marbach, Ethel. The Cabbage Moth & the Shamrock. Hague, Michael, illus. 32p. (ps-2). 1991. jacketed, reinforced bdg. 9.00 (ISBN 0-671-74864-5, Green Tiger). S&S Trade.

Reese, Bob. Lactus Cactus. LC 81-3866. (Illus.). 24p. (ps-2). 1981. PLB 11.27 (ISBN 0-516-02304-7); pap. 2.95 (ISBN 0-516-42304-5). Childrens.

Rey, H. A. Elizabite: Adventures of a Carnivorous Plant. Rey, H. A., illus. 32p. (ps-3). 1990. Repr. of 1942 ed. lib. bdg. 17.00 (ISBN 0-208-02288-0, Linnet). Shoe String.

PLANTS–GROWTH
see Growth (Plants)

PLANTS–PROPAGATION
see Plant Propagation

PLANTS, USEFUL
see Botany, Economic; Plants, Edible

PLASTIC MATERIALS
see Plastics

PLASTICS

Cash, Terry. Plastics. Stefoff, Rebecca, ed. Barber, Ed, photos by. LC 90-40368. (Illus.). 26p. (gr. 3-5). 1990. PLB 15.93 (ISBN 0-944483-70-4). Garrett Ed Corp.

Dineen, Jacqueline. Plastics. 32p. (gr. 4-8). 1988. lib. bdg. 12.95 (ISBN 0-89490-221-0). Enslow Pubs.

Lambert, M. Plastics. (Illus.). 48p. (gr. 5 up). Date not set. PLB 15.93 (ISBN 0-86592-269-1). Rourke Corp.

PLATYPUS

Spanjian, Beth. Baby Duckbill. (ps-1). 1990. write for info. (ISBN 0-307-12600-5). Western Pub.

PLAY

see also Amusements; Games; Recreation; Sports

Appelbaum, Samuel, et al. The Way They Play, Bk. 13. (Illus.). 288p. (gr. 9-12). 14.95 (ISBN 0-86622-009-7, Z-76). Paganiniana Pubns.

Bauer, Lois M. & Reed, Barbara A. Dance & Play Activities for the Elementary Grades, 2 Vols. (Illus.). (gr. 1-6). 1967. Vol. 1. 4.50 (ISBN 0-910354-02-2); Vol. 2. 4.98 (ISBN 0-910354-07-3). Chartwell.

Boyd, L. M. Clancy's Treasure Book for Children. Boyd, L. M., illus. 166p. (Orig.). (gr. k-5). 1981. pap. 7.95 (ISBN 0-941620-34-4). Carson Ent.

Chlad, Dorothy. Jugando en el Patio de Recreo: Playing on the Playground. Halverson, Lydia, illus. LC 87-5197. (SPA.). 32p. (ps-2). 1988. PLB 14.60 (ISBN 0-516-31989-2); pap. 3.95 (ISBN 0-516-51989-1). Childrens.

Johnson, Eleanor. Whistle Him In. (gr. 2-5). 1985. pap. 6.95 (ISBN 0-930096-70-3). G Gannett.

Lamb, Sandra & Bellows, Dena. Parties for Home & School: A Piece of Cake. Hyndman, Kathryn, illus. 144p. (ps-4). 1985. wkbk. 10.95 (ISBN 0-86653-328-1, GA 647). Good Apple.

Let's Play. (Illus.). 12p. (ps). 1978. 3.95 (ISBN 0-448-40872-4, G&D). Putnam Pub Group.

Oxenbury, Helen. Playing. Oxenbury, Helen, illus. 14p. (ps-k). 1981. 3.95 (ISBN 0-671-42109-3, Little Simon). S&S Trade.

Pragoff, Fiona. Odd One Out. (Illus.). 16p. (ps-k). 1989. 5.95 (ISBN 0-385-26410-0, Zephyr-BFYR). Doubleday.

Trencher, Barbara R. Child's Play: An Activities & Materials Handbook. Fritts, Susan, illus. LC 76-46501. 160p. (gr. 3 up). 1976. pap. text ed. 14.95 (ISBN 0-89334-003-0). Humanics Ltd.

PLAY-FICTION

Adorjan, Carol. I Can! Can You? rev. ed. Levine, Abby, ed. Nerlove, Miriam, illus. 24p. (ps). 1990. 10.95 (ISBN 0-8075-3491-9). A Whitman.

Alexander, Martha. Blackboard Bear. Alexander, Martha, illus. (gr. k-3). 1988. PLB 9.89 (ISBN 0-8037-0652-9). Dial Bks Young.

Alexander, Sue. Lila on the Landing. Eagle, Ellen, illus. LC 87-301. 64p. (gr. 2-5). 1987. 13.95 (ISBN 0-89919-340-4, Pub. by Clarion). Ticknor & Fields.

Allen, Pamela. I Wish I Had a Pirate Suit. (ps). 1990. 12.95 (ISBN 0-670-82475-5). Viking Child Bks.

Baillie, Allan. Drac & the Gremlin. Tanner, Jane, illus. LC 88-20275. 32p. (ps-3). 1989. 11.95 (ISBN 0-8037-0628-6). Dial Bks Young.

Beylon, Cathy, illus. Billy & Belly Button, It's Playtime. 14p. (ps-3). 1985. 4.95 (ISBN 0-448-41202-0, G&D). Putnam Pub Group.

Brandenberg, Franz. Leo & Emily's Big Ideas. Aliki, illus. LC 81-6424. 56p. (gr. 1-3). 1982. 9.00 (ISBN 0-688-00754-6); PLB 10.88 (ISBN 0-688-00755-4). Greenwillow.

Carlson, Nancy. Harriet & the Roller Coaster. LC 81-18138. (Illus.). 32p. (ps-3). 1982. lib. bdg. 9.95 (ISBN 0-87614-183-1). Carolrhoda Bks.

Cartwright, Stephen. Who Can Hop? (ps up). 1989. PLB 5.98 (ISBN 0-7924-5043-4, Mallard Pr). BDD Promo Bk.

Chevalier, Christa. Spence Isn't Spence Anymore. Levine, Abby, ed. Chevalier, Christa, illus. 32p. (ps-1). 1985. 10.95 (ISBN 0-8075-7565-8). A Whitman.

Ets, Marie H. Play with Me. (ps-k). 1976. pap. 3.95 (ISBN 0-14-050178-9, Puffin). Puffin Bks.

Gaban, Jesus. Harry's Sandbox Surprise. Colorado, Nani, illus. 16p. (ps-1). 1991. PLB 10.95 (ISBN 0-8368-0716-2). Gareth Stevens Inc.

Hartman, Gail. For Sand Castles or Seashells. Weiss, Ellen, illus. LC 89-35994. 32p. (ps). 1990. 12.95 (ISBN 0-02-743091-X, Bradbury Pr). Macmillan Child Grp.

Hines, Anna G. It's Just Me, Emily. Hines, Anna G., illus. (ps-1). 1987. 12.95 (ISBN 0-89919-487-7, Pub. by Clarion). Ticknor & Fields.

I Can Jump. 24p. (ps-2). 1989. pap. 1.29 (ISBN 0-02-898253-3). Checkerboard Pr.

Katz, Kitty. Play with Me. Rosenberg, Amye, illus. 8p. (ps). 1982. 4.95 (ISBN 0-448-46830-1, G&D). Putnam Pub Group.

Kellogg, Steven. Won't Somebody Play with Me? LC 72-708. (Illus.). (gr. k-3). 1976. pap. 4.95 (ISBN 0-8037-9612-9). Dial Bks Young.

Kent, Jack. Joey. LC 84-4694. (Illus.). 32p. (gr. k-4). 1987. PLB 11.95 (ISBN 0-671-66459-X); pap. 5.95 (ISBN 0-671-66460-3). S&S Trade.

Kingman, Lee. Catch the Baby! (ps). 1990. 12.95 (ISBN 0-670-81751-1). Viking Child Bks.

Lomasney, Eileen. What Do You Do with the Rest of the Day, Mary Ann? 1991. pap. 3.95 (ISBN 0-8091-6601-1). Paulist Pr.

Mayer, Mercer. Construction Critter. 1987. 3.95 (ISBN 0-671-61145-3). S&S Trade.

—Doctor Critter. 1987. 3.95 (ISBN 0-671-61147-X). S&S Trade.

Michaels, Ski. Something New to Do. Palmer, Jan, illus. LC 85-14021. 48p. (Orig.). (gr. 1-3). 1986. PLB 9.89 (ISBN 0-8167-0634-4); pap. text ed. 2.95 (ISBN 0-8167-0635-2). Troll Assocs.

Moss, Marissa. Want to Play? Moss, Marissa, illus. 32p. (ps-3). 1990. 12.95 (ISBN 0-395-52022-3). HM.

O'Brien, Anne S. Come Play with Us. LC 85-5644. (Illus.). 14p. (ps-k). 1985. pap. 3.95 (ISBN 0-03-005008-1). H Holt & Co.

—I Want That! LC 85-5640. (Illus.). 14p. (ps). 1985. 3.95 (ISBN 0-03-005012-X, O'Brien Board Bks.). H Holt & Co.

Orgel, Doris. Sarah's Room. LC 63-13675. (Illus.). (gr. k-3). 1963. 11.95 (ISBN 0-06-024605-7). HarpC Child Bks.

Peppe, Rodney. Huxley Pig's Model Car. 1991. pap. 8.95 (ISBN 0-385-30238-X). Doubleday.

Pocock, Rita. Annabelle & the Big Slide. (ps-k). 1989. 10.95 (ISBN 0-15-200407-6, Gulliver Bks). HarBraceJ.

Ross, Pat. M & M & Haunted House Game. (gr. 4 up). 1990. pap. 2.95 (ISBN 0-14-034577-9, Puffin). Puffin Bks.

Shearer, Marilyn J. I Like to Play. Roberts, Tom, illus. 16p. (Orig.). (ps-6). 1992. 19.95 (ISBN 0-685-30097-8); pap. 10.95 (ISBN 0-685-30098-6). L Ashley & Joshua.

Sinnett, Kate. My Five Disguises. Lewis, Anthony, illus. LC 90-44374. 28p. (gr. 4-8). 1991. 12.95 (ISBN 0-87226-444-0). P Bedrick Bks.

Townson, Hazel. What on Earth...? (ps-3). 1991. 13.95 (ISBN 0-316-85138-8). Little.

Van Allsburg, Chris. Jumanji. Van Allsburg, Chris, illus. (gr. 3 up). 1981. 15.95 (ISBN 0-395-30448-2). HM.

Van Der Beek, Deborah. Alice's Blue Cloth. (Illus.). 32p. (ps-k). 1989. 11.95 (ISBN 0-399-21622-7, Putnam). Putnam Pub Group.

Watanabe, Shigeo. Daddy, Play with Me! Ohtomo, Yasuo, illus. (ps). 1986. 3.95 (ISBN 0-399-21334-1, Philomel). Putnam Pub Group.

Wildsmith, Brian. Carousel. Wildsmith, Brian, illus. LC 88-846. 32p. (ps-2). 1989. 12.95 (ISBN 0-394-81937-3); lib. bdg. 12.99 (ISBN 0-394-91937-8). Knopf.

Ziefert, Harriet. Come out, Jessie! Smith, Mavis, illus. LC 90-41880. 32p. (ps-1). 1991. 4.95 (ISBN 0-06-107414-4). HarpC Child Bks.

Zokeisha. Things I Like to Play With. Zokeisha, illus. 16p. (ps-k). 1981. 2.95 (ISBN 0-671-44450-6, Little Simon). S&S Trade.

PLAY CENTERS

see Playgrounds

PLAY DIRECTION (THEATER)

see Theater–Production and Direction

PLAY PRODUCTION

see Amateur Theatricals; Theater–Production and Direction

PLAY WRITING

see Drama–Technique

PLAYGROUNDS

Gibbons, Gail. Playgrounds. Gibbons, Gail, illus. LC 84-19285. 32p. (ps-3). 1985. reinforced bdg. 14.95 (ISBN 0-8234-0553-2). Holiday.

Penn, Linda. Parks & Playgrounds. Scott, Elaine, illus. 32p. (gr. k-3). 1986. wkbk. 4.95 (ISBN 0-86653-350-8, GA 685). Good Apple.

PLAYGROUNDS-FICTION

Barnes, Jill & Kanabe, Junkichi. Road Roller Saves the Day. Rubin, Caroline, ed. Japan Foreign Rights Centre Staff, tr. from JPN. Emu, Namae, illus. LC 90-3841. 40p. (gr. k-3). 1990. PLB 14.60 (ISBN 0-944483-81-X). Garrett Ed Corp.

Gordon, Sharon. Playground Fun. Karas, G. Brian, illus. LC 86-30854. 32p. (gr. k-2). 1987. lib. bdg. 7.06 (ISBN 0-8167-0990-4); pap. text ed. 1.95 (ISBN 0-8167-0991-2). Troll Assocs.

Wilmer, Diane. The Playground. rev. ed. Chamberlain, Margaret, illus. 32p. (gr. k-2). 1990. Repr. of 1986 ed. PLB 9.45 (ISBN 1-878363-10-7). Forest Hse.

PLAYING CARDS

see Cards

PLAYS

Alexander, Sue. Small Plays for Special Days. Huffman, Tom, illus. LC 76-28424. 64p. (gr. 2-4). 1979. 13.95 (ISBN 0-395-28761-8, Clarion). HM.

Andersen, Hans Christian. The Red Shoes. Schmidt, Hans J., retold by. (gr. k-12). 1969. pap. 2.50x (ISBN 0-88020-048-0). Dramatic Pub.

Ashby, Sylvia. Once upon a Broomstick: A Halloween Happening in One Act. (Illus.). 28p. (Orig.). (gr. 1-8). 1990. pap. 2.25 (ISBN 0-88680-329-2). I E Clark.

Avery, Helen P. The Ghost of Canterville Hall. 1977. 4.50 (ISBN 0-87602-112-7). Anchorage.

Ayckbourn, Alan. Mr. A's Amazing Maze Plays. 96p. 1990. pap. 7.95 (ISBN 0-571-14160-9). Faber & Faber.

Battle of San Pascual: Mini-Play. (gr. 5 up). 1978. 5.00 (ISBN 0-89550-308-5). Stevens & Shea.

Beiner, Stan J. Sedra Scenes: Skits for Every Torah Portion. LC 82-71282. 225p. (Orig.). (gr. 6-12). 1982. pap. text ed. 9.50 (ISBN 0-86705-007-1). AIRE.

Bellville, Cheryl W. Theater Magic: Behind the Scenes at a Children's Theater. Bellville, Cheryl W., illus. LC 86-9757. 48p. (gr. k-4). 1986. PLB 12.95 (ISBN 0-87614-278-1). Carolrhoda Bks.

Bennett, Rowena. Creative Plays & Programs for Holidays. (gr. 2-6). pap. 13.95 (ISBN 0-8238-0005-9). Plays.

Birch, Beverly, retold by. Shakespeare's Stories: Comedies. Tarrant, Carol, illus. LC 88-16947. 128p. (gr. 3-7). 1988. 12.95x (ISBN 0-87226-191-3). P Bedrick Bks.

—Shakespeare's Stories: Histories. Green, Robina, illus. LC 88-15693. 128p. (gr. 3-7). 1988. 12.95x (ISBN 0-87226-192-1). P Bedrick Bks.

Bland, Joellen. Stage Plays from the Classics. LC 87-14669. (Orig.). (gr. 7-12). 1987. pap. 13.95 (ISBN 0-8238-0281-7). Plays.

Boiko, Claire. Children's Plays for Creative Actors. 384p. (gr. 3-7). 1985. pap. 13.95 (ISBN 0-8238-0267-1). Plays.

Bradley, Alfred & Bond, Michael. Paddington on Stage. Fortnum, Peggy, illus. LC 76-62497. (gr. 2-5). 1977. 13.95 (ISBN 0-395-25155-9). HM.

Brill, Michael E. The Masque of Beauty & the Beast. 1979. 4.50 (ISBN 0-87602-156-9). Anchorage.

Broadhurst, Alan. The Great Cross-Country Race. 1965. 5.50 (ISBN 0-87602-133-X). Anchorage.

—Young Dick Whittington. 1964. 4.50 (ISBN 0-87602-224-7). Anchorage.

Brooks, Courtaney. The Case of the Stolen Dinosaur: A Play in Two Versions: Stage & Radio. Way, Merrilee, illus. 26p. (Orig.). (gr. 4 up). 1983. pap. text ed. 4.00x (ISBN 0-941274-02-0). Belnice Bks.

—Eight Steps to Choral Reading. Way, Marrilee, illus. (Orig.). (gr. 1 up). 1983. pap. text ed. 3.00x (ISBN 0-941274-01-2). Belnice Bks.

—Little Red & the Wolf: A Puppet Play. Way, Merrilee, illus. (gr. k up). 1983. pap. text ed. 2.50x (ISBN 0-941274-04-7). Belnice Bks.

—Pardner & Freddie: A Puppet Play. Way, Merrilee, illus. (gr. k up). 1983. pap. text ed. 2.50x (ISBN 0-941274-03-9). Belnice Bks.

Brown, Regina. Play at Your House. Brown, Regina, illus. (gr. 3-7). 1962. 8.95 (ISBN 0-8392-3027-3). Astor-Honor.

Bruestle, Beaumont. The Wonderful Tang. 1952. 4.50 (ISBN 0-87602-222-0). Anchorage.

Burchard, Rachael C. Hallelujah Hopscotch. 1986. pap. 3.00x (ISBN 0-88020-128-2). Dramatic Pub.

Bush, Max. The Voyage of the Dragonfly. 1989. Playscript. 4.50 (ISBN 0-87602-287-5). Anchorage.

Campbell, Ken. Skungpoomery. 47p. 1988. pap. 5.95 (ISBN 0-413-33910-6, A0263). Heinemann Ed.

Carey, Karla. Julie & Jackie at Christmas-Time: The Play & Musical Play (with Music Book, Story-&-Song Cassette & Piano Cassette) Nolan, Dennis, illus. LC 88-12909. 39p. 1990. pap. 35.00 complete pkg. (ISBN 1-55768-151-1); pap. 25.00 book only (ISBN 1-55768-026-4); story-&-song or piano cass. 8.00 (ISBN 0-685-19710-7). LC Pub.

—Julie & Jackie at the Circus: The Play & Musical Play (with Music Book, Story-&-Song Cassette & Piano Cassette) Nolan, Dennis, illus. LC 88-12910. 44p. 1990. pap. 35.00 complete pkg. (ISBN 1-55768-152-X); pap. 25.00 book only (ISBN 1-55768-177-5); story-&-song or piano cass. 8.00 (ISBN 1-55768-027-2). LC Pub.

The talent behind the Julie & Jackie Children's Series: Karla Carey, well-known California author-composer. "Outstanding composer," said Frederick Jagel (former Metropolitan Opera & teacher in San Francisco). "Up-&-coming San Francisco composer's brilliant music brings inspiration in song" (Army of Stars coast-to-coast broadcast, USA & Canada). In speaking of another work, R. Frederick Henry (prominent artist & teacher in Berkeley, California) said, "These etudes, Poems for Piano, are a treasure belonging in the active repertoire of every pianist." Karla Carey now brings remarkable descriptive music & fascinating stories to each of these five children's books. Dennis Nolan, now-renowned award-winning illustrator, at an early age on his first professional assignment, provided the 71 charming colorful pictures in the five Julie & Jackie books - which will bring encouragement to all budding artists. The Series (" Christmastime," "Calendar," "Circus," "Journeying," "Ranch") brings fun while teaching. A child reads & listens to cassette, while watching colorful pictures & learning from storytellers & songs that bring the many characters to life. Each production includes: Children's Book, Music Book & Musical Play (complete instructions, explicit detail, laymen's terms, dialogue

hints, directions, gestures, song-presentation, costuming, choreography, stage-settings, property, lighting) each book with cassette.
Publisher Provided Annotation.

—Julie & Jackie Go a'Journeying: The Play & Musical Play (with Music Book, Story-&-Song Cassette & Piano Cassette) Nolan, Dennis, illus. LC 88-9171. 73p. 1990. pap. 35.00 complete pkg. (ISBN 1-55768-153-8); pap. 25.00 book only (ISBN 1-55768-028-0); story-&-song or piano cass. 8.00 (ISBN 0-685-19711-5). LC Pub.
—Julie & Jackie on the Ranch: The Play & Musical Play (with Music Book, Story-&-Song Cassette & Piano Cassette) Nolan, Dennis, illus. LC 88-12911. 46p. 1990. pap. 35.00 complete pkg. (ISBN 1-55768-154-6); pap. 25.00 book only (ISBN 1-55768-029-9); story-&-song or piano cass. 8.00 (ISBN 0-685-19712-3). LC Pub.
Charpentier, Aristide-Christian. The Violin of Passing Time. 1972. 4.50 (ISBN 0-87602-217-4). Anchorage.
Chinese in America: Mini-Play. (gr. 5up). 1975. 6.50 (ISBN 0-89550-350-6). Stevens & Shea.
Chokai, M. Sherlock Holmes & the Jewel & Other Short Plays. Biswas, Dolly, illus. 169p. (gr. 6). 1983. pap. 3. 95x (ISBN 0-86131-330-5). Apt Bks.
Chorpenning, Charlotte B. The Adventures of Tom Sawyer. (gr. k-12). 1956. pap. 2.25x (ISBN 0-88020-008-1). Dramatic Pub.
—Alice in Wonderland. rev. ed. (gr. k-12). 1959. pap. 2. 25x (ISBN 0-88020-018-9). Dramatic Pub.
—Cinderella. 1940. 4.50 (ISBN 0-87602-116-X). Anchorage.
—Hansel & Gretel. (gr. k-12). 1956. pap. 2.25x (ISBN 0-88020-029-4). Dramatic Pub.
—Jack & the Beanstalk. 1935. 4.50 (ISBN 0-87602-143-7). Anchorage.
—Rip Van Winkle. (gr. k-12). 1954. pap. 2.25x (ISBN 0-88020-050-2). Dramatic Pub.
—Robinson Crusoe. 1952. 4.50 (ISBN 0-87602-192-5). Anchorage.
—Rumpelstiltskin. 1944. 4.50 (ISBN 0-87602-195-X). Anchorage.
—The Sleeping Beauty. 1947. 4.50 (ISBN 0-87602-203-4). Anchorage.
Conradson, Shari. Just Junior High. 52p. (Orig.). (gr. 6-9). 1989. pap. 5.00 (ISBN 0-9620445-1-2). J Muckle.
Cullen, Alan. The Beeple. 1968. 4.50 (ISBN 0-87602-108-9). Anchorage.
—The Man in the Moon. 1964. 4.50 (ISBN 0-87602-153-4). Anchorage.
—Trudi & the Minstrel. 1957. 4.50 (ISBN 0-87602-214-X). Anchorage.
Cullen, Allan. Niccolo & Nicolette. 1957. 4.50 (ISBN 0-87602-162-3). Anchorage.
Dahl, Roald. Charlie & the Chocolate Factory. Schindelman, Joseph, illus. (gr. 5 up). 1991. 15.00 (ISBN 0-394-81011-2); PLB 13.99 (ISBN 0-394-91011-7). Knopf.
Davenport, May. Two Plays. LC 75-55603. (gr. 5-12). 1977. 2.50x (ISBN 0-9603118-0-7). Davenport.
Davis, Ossie. Langston: A Play. LC 82-70314. 144p. (gr. 7 up). 1982. pap. 11.95 (ISBN 0-385-28543-4). Delacorte.
Dean, Lois. Fox in a Fix. 1959. 4.00 (ISBN 0-87602-128-3). Anchorage.
Dinges, Susan & Thomas, Sue. Curtain II: Creative Drama for Children 9-12. (ps-7). 1986. 15.00 (ISBN 0-89824-168-5). Trillium Pr.
Doyle, Sharon E. In Other Words. 1976. 4.00 (ISBN 0-87602-141-0). Anchorage.
Dunster, Mark. Chimney. 14p. (Orig.). 1990. pap. 4.00 (ISBN 0-89642-180-5). Linden Pubs.
Engelhardt, James F. & Weiss, Carol. Fir Tree. 1986. score 35.00x (ISBN 0-88020-124-X); pap. 2.50x libretto (ISBN 0-88020-123-1). Dramatic Pub.
Falls, Gregory A. & Beattie, Kurt. The Odyssey. 1978. 5.00 (ISBN 0-87602-238-7). Anchorage.
Farnagle, A. E. The Not So Goody Gum Drop Shop: A Play in One Act. 32p. (Orig.). (gr. 3-8). 1984. pap. 3.50 (ISBN 0-916565-06-8). Whitehall Pr.
Fauquez, Arthur. Don Quixote of La Mancha. 1967. 4.50 (ISBN 0-87602-121-6). Anchorage.
—The Man Who Killed Time. 1964. 4.50 (ISBN 0-87602-154-2). Anchorage.
—Reynard the Fox. 5.50 (ISBN 0-87602-187-9). Anchorage.
Fisher, Aileen. Year-Round Programs for Young Players. LC 85-8153. 334p. (Orig.). (gr. 3-7). 1985. 14.95 (ISBN 0-8238-0266-3). Plays.
Fisher, Aileen, ed. Holiday Programs for Boys & Girls. 393p. (gr. 2-6). 1986. pap. 12.95 (ISBN 0-8238-0277-9). Plays.
Fox, Phyllis W. & Coleman, David. Cinderella. (gr. k-12). 1978. pap. 2.50x (ISBN 0-88020-002-2); vocal & instrumental score 9.00x (ISBN 0-88020-003-0). Dramatic Pub.
Gallo, Donald R., ed. Center Stage: One-Act Plays for Teenage Readers & Actors. LC 90-4050. 384p. (gr. 7 up). 1990. 16.95 (ISBN 0-06-022170-4); PLB 16.89 (ISBN 0-06-022171-2). HarpC Child Bks.
Glennon, William. The Adventures of Harlequin. (gr. k-12). 1968. pap. 2.25x (ISBN 0-88020-007-3). Dramatic Pub.
—Aladdin. (gr. k-12). 1956. pap. 2.25x (ISBN 0-88020-009-X). Dramatic Pub.
—Ali Baba & the Magic Cave. (gr. k-12). 1969. pap. 2. 25x (ISBN 0-88020-010-3). Dramatic Pub.
—Alice in Wonderland. (gr. k-12). 1967. pap. 2.25x (ISBN 0-88020-011-1). Dramatic Pub.
—Beauty & the Beast. (gr. k-12). 1966. pap. 2.25x (ISBN 0-88020-012-X). Dramatic Pub.
—Cinderella. (gr. k-12). 1969. pap. 2.25x (ISBN 0-88020-013-8). Dramatic Pub.
—Hansel & Gretel. (gr. k-12). 1966. pap. 2.25x (ISBN 0-88020-014-6). Dramatic Pub.
—Jack & the Beanstalk. (gr. k-12). 1969. pap. 2.25x (ISBN 0-88020-015-4). Dramatic Pub.
—My Friend, the Fox. (gr. k-12). 1968. pap. 2.25x (ISBN 0-88020-016-2). Dramatic Pub.
—The Pied Piper. (gr. k-12). 1968. pap. 2.25x (ISBN 0-88020-017-0). Dramatic Pub.
Goldberg, Moses. Aladdin: A Participation Play. 1977. 4.50 (ISBN 0-87602-101-1). Anchorage.
—The Analysis of Mineral Number Four. (Orig.). (gr. 4 up). 1982. playscript 4.50 (ISBN 0-87602-234-4). Anchorage.
—The Men's Cottage. (Orig.). (gr. 4 up). 1980. playscript 4.50 (ISBN 0-87602-229-8). Anchorage.
—The Outlaw Robin Hood. 1967. 4.50 (ISBN 0-87602-168-2). Anchorage.
—The Wind in the Willows. 1974. 4.50 (ISBN 0-87602-220-4). Anchorage.
Golden, Joseph. Johnny Moonbeam & the Silver Arrow. 1962. 4.50 (ISBN 0-87602-144-5). Anchorage.
Graczyk, Ed. Appleseed. 1971. 4.50 (ISBN 0-87602-106-2). Anchorage.
—Livin' de Life. 1970. 4.50 (ISBN 0-87602-151-8). Anchorage.
—The Rude Mechanicals. 1970. 4.50 (ISBN 0-87602-194-1). Anchorage.
Grecian, Phil. Dragon of Nitt. 1986. pap. 2.50x (ISBN 0-88020-122-3). Dramatic Pub.
Greidanus, Aad. Two Pails of Water. 1965. 4.50 (ISBN 0-87602-215-8). Anchorage.
Grenzeback, Joe & Bergh, Haakon. Sing Ho for a Prince (Sleeping Beauty) (gr. k-12). 1957. pap. 2.50x (ISBN 0-88020-054-5); 15.00x (ISBN 0-88020-055-3). Dramatic Pub.
Hall, Robin. Three Tales from Japan. 1973. 4.50 (ISBN 0-87602-209-3). Anchorage.
Hamlett, Christina. Humorous Plays for Teenagers. LC 86-16916. (Orig.). (gr. 7-12). 1987. pap. 12.00 (ISBN 0-8238-0276-0). Plays.
Harder, Eleanor & Harder, Ray. The Near-Sighted Knight & the Far-Sighted Dragon: Musical. 1977. 4.50 (ISBN 0-87602-161-5). Anchorage.
—Sacramento Fifty Miles: Musical. 1969. 4.50 (ISBN 0-87602-198-4). Anchorage.
Harris, Aurand. Androcles & the Lion: Musical. 1964. 4.50 (ISBN 0-87602-105-4). Anchorage.
—The Arkansaw Bear. (Orig.). (gr. 5 up). 1980. playscript 4.50 (ISBN 0-87602-226-3). Anchorage.
—The Brave Little Tailor. 1961. 4.50 (ISBN 0-87602-109-7). Anchorage.
—A Doctor in Spite of Himself. 1968. 4.50 (ISBN 0-87602-120-8). Anchorage.
—Huck Finn's Story. 42p. 1988. Playscript. 4.50 (ISBN 0-87602-280-8). Anchorage.
—Peck's Bad Boy. 1974. playscript 4.50 (ISBN 0-87602-170-4). Anchorage.
—Pocahontas. 1961. 4.50 (ISBN 0-87602-177-1). Anchorage.
—Rags to Riches: Musical. 1966. 4.50 (ISBN 0-87602-185-2). Anchorage.
—Star Spangled Salute. 1974. 4.50 (ISBN 0-87602-205-0). Anchorage.
Harris, Aurand & Shakespeare, William. Robin Goodfellow. 1977. 4.50 (ISBN 0-87602-190-9). Anchorage.
Havilan, Amorie & Smith, Lyn. Easy Plays for Preschoolers to Third Graders. LC 85-6521. (Illus.). 160p. (ps-3). 1985. pap. 14.95 (ISBN 0-937552-15-1). Quail Ridge.
Haycock, Kate. Plays. Stefoff, Rebecca, ed. LC 90-13937. (Illus.). 32p. (gr. 4-8). 1991. PLB 17.26 (ISBN 0-944483-98-4). Garrett Ed Corp.
Herbert, Victor. Babes in Toyland: Musical. Holamon, Ken, adapted by. (Orig.). (ps up). 1987. playscript 5.50 (ISBN 0-87602-275-1). Anchorage.
Herlihy, Dirlie. Ludie's Song. 224p. (gr. 4 up). 1990. pap. 3.95 (ISBN 0-14-034245-1, Puffin). Puffin Bks.
Hume, Pat. Dick Whittington & His Amazing Cat. (Orig.). (gr. k up). 1980. 4.50 (ISBN 0-87602-230-1). Anchorage.
Jackson, R. Eugene. Babes in Toyland: Stage Magic Plays for Children's Theatre. Alette, Carl, adapted by. (Illus.). 48p. (Orig.). 1987. pap. 4.00 (ISBN 0-88680-267-9); piano-vocal score 15.00 (ISBN 0-88680-268-7). I E Clark.
—Christmas with the Three Bears. Alette, Carl, contrib. by. (Illus.). 48p. (Orig.). (gr. 1-10). 1990. pap. 4.00 (ISBN 0-88680-326-8); musical score 10.00 (ISBN 0-88680-327-6). I E Clark.
Jetsmark, Torben. Peter the Postman. 37p. 1988. Playscript. 4.50 (ISBN 0-87602-279-4). Anchorage.
Jonson, Marian. The Beauty of the Dreaming Wood. (gr. k-12). 1973. 2.25x (ISBN 0-85343-510-3). Dramatic Pub.
—The Cricket on the Hearth. (gr. k-12). 1957. pap. 2.25x (ISBN 0-88020-023-5). Dramatic Pub.
—Greensleeves' Magic. (gr. k-12). 1954. pap. 2.50x (ISBN 0-88020-000-6). Dramatic Pub.
—Snow White & the Seven Dwarfs. (gr. k-12). 1957. pap. 2.25x (ISBN 0-88020-057-X). Dramatic Pub.
Julian, Faye. A Magic Christmas: A Play for Children in One Act. (Illus.). 28p. (gr. k-12). 1983. pap. 1.50 (ISBN 0-88680-121-4). I E Clark.
Kamerman, Sylvia E., ed. Plays from Favorite Folk Tales. LC 87-12960. (Orig.). (gr. 2 up). 1987. pap. 12.95 (ISBN 0-8238-0280-9). Plays.
Kaplan, Carol B. Holiday Plays. Mitter, Kathy, illus. 37p. (ps). 1989. tchr's. ed. 16.95 (ISBN 0-88734-410-0). Players Pr.
Kesselman, Wendy. Becca: (Musical) 61p. 1988. playscript 5.50 (ISBN 0-87602-277-8). Anchorage.
King, Martha B. Riddle Me Ree. 1977. 4.50 (ISBN 0-87602-188-7). Anchorage.
—The Snow Queen & the Goblin. (gr. k-12). 1956. pap. 2.00x (ISBN 0-88020-056-1). Dramatic Pub.
—The Witch's Lullaby. (gr. k-12). 1955. pap. 2.25x (ISBN 0-88020-073-1). Dramatic Pub.
Kipling, Rudyard. Just So Stories: Adapted from the Book by Rudyard Kipling. Dubay, Brenda J., contrib. by. (Illus.). 36p. (Orig.). (ps-7). 1990. pap. 3.00 (ISBN 0-88680-333-0). I E Clark.
Koste, Glasgow V. Scraps: The Ragtime Girl of Oz. 1986. write for info. (ISBN 0-88020-127-4). Dramatic Pub.
Koste, Virginia G. The Medicine Show. 1975. 4.50 (ISBN 0-87602-258-1). Anchorage.
Kral, Brian. Apologies. 42p. (Orig.). (gr. 9-12). 1988. playscript 5.00 (ISBN 0-87602-278-6). Anchorage.
—East of the Sun, West of the Moon. 56p. (Orig.). (ps up). 1987. playscript 5.50 (ISBN 0-87602-273-5). Anchorage.
—Ransom of Red Chief. (Orig.). (gr. 3 up). 1980. playscript 4.50 (ISBN 0-87602-227-1). Anchorage.
Kraus, Joanna. The Dragon Hammer & the Tale of Oniroku. LC 77-83857. (Illus.). 64p. (gr. 3-5). 1977. pap. 4.95 (ISBN 0-932720-17-X); 7.95 (ISBN 0-932720-18-8). New Plays Inc.
Kraus, Joanna H. The Shaggy Dog Murder Trial. (Orig.). (gr. 4-7). 1988. playscript 3.50 (ISBN 0-87602-274-3). Anchorage.
Laing, John. One Cool Cat. 56p. 1988. pap. 5.95 (ISBN 0-413-54220-3, A0197). Heinemann Ed.
Landes, William-Alan. Aladdin n' His Magic Lamp. rev. ed. LC 89-43679. 52p. (gr. 3-12). 1985. pap. text ed. 6.00 (ISBN 0-88734-102-0); tchr's. ed. 30.00 (ISBN 0-88734-003-2). Players Pr.
—Jack 'n the Beanstalk. rev. ed. LC 89-43681. (gr. 3-12). 1985. pap. text ed. 6.00 (ISBN 0-88734-101-2); tchr's. ed. 30.00 (ISBN 0-88734-001-6). Players Pr.
—Jack 'n the Beanstalk: Music & Lyrics. rev. ed. (gr. 3-12). 1985. pap. text ed. 15.00 (ISBN 0-88734-000-8). Players Pr.
—Peter N' the Wolf. rev. ed. LC 89-69871. (gr. 3-12). 1988. pap. text ed. 6.00 (ISBN 0-88734-106-3); tchr's. ed. 30.00 (ISBN 0-88734-013-X). Players Pr.
—Rapunzel 'N the Witch. rev. ed. LC 89-43682. (gr. 3-12). 1985. pap. text ed. 6.00 (ISBN 0-88734-107-1); tchr's. ed. 30.00 (ISBN 0-88734-007-5). Players Pr.
—Rhyme Tyme. rev. ed. LC 89-63869. (gr. 3-12). 1985. pap. text ed. 6.00 (ISBN 0-88734-108-X). Players Pr.
Landes, William-Alan & Rizzo, Jeff. Rhyme Tyme: Music & Lyrics. rev. ed. (gr. 3-12). 1985. pap. text ed. 15.00 (ISBN 0-88734-008-3). Players Pr.
Levitt, Saul. Jim Thorpe, All American. (Orig.). (gr. 4 up). 1980. playscript 5.00 (ISBN 0-87602-237-9). Anchorage.
Longmeyer, Carole M. An American Mystery: Script. (Orig.). (gr. 3-12). 1983. pap. 20.00 play (ISBN 0-935326-50-2). Gallopade Pub Group.
McAlvay, Nora & Chorpenning, Charlotte B. Flibbertygibbet. 1952. 4.50 (ISBN 0-87602-127-5). Anchorage.
McAlvay, Nora & Chropenning, Charlotte B. The Elves & the Shoemaker. 1946. 4.50 (ISBN 0-87602-124-0). Anchorage.
McCaslin, Nellie. Little Snow Girl. (gr. k-12). 1963. pap. 2.00x (ISBN 0-88020-037-5). Dramatic Pub.
—The Rabbit Who Wanted Red Wings. (gr. k-12). 1963. pap. 2.00x (ISBN 0-88020-045-6). Dramatic Pub.
Maccoby, Annie & Church, Jeff. Alien Equation. 1986. pap. 2.50x (ISBN 0-88020-129-0). Dramatic Pub.
McDonough, Jerome. Limbo. 28p. (Orig.). (gr. 7 up). 1984. pap. 2.00 (ISBN 0-88680-219-9). I E Clark.
—Not Even A. Mouse: A Chris-Mouse Tale. (Illus.). 20p. (Orig.). (gr. k-9). 1984. pap. 1.50 (ISBN 0-88680-220-2). I E Clark.
McDonough, Jerome, adapted by. Alice: A One-Act Play. (Illus.). 36p. (Orig.). (gr. 4-12). 1990. pap. 2.75 (ISBN 0-88680-336-5). I E Clark.
McKenna, Helen. Young Hickory. 1940. 4.50 (ISBN 0-87602-225-5). Anchorage.
Mahlmann, Lewis & Jones, David C. Puppet Plays for Young Players. 194p. (gr. 3-7). 1985. pap. 12.00 (ISBN 0-8238-0269-8). Plays.
Martin, Judith & Ashwander, Donald. Christmas All over the Place. 22p. (Orig.). (ps-12). 1977. playscript 3.50 (ISBN 0-87602-113-5). Anchorage.
—The Lost & Found Christmas. 14p. (Orig.). (ps up). 1977. playscript 3.50 (ISBN 0-87602-152-6). Anchorage.
—The Runaway Presents. 16p. (Orig.). (ps up). 1977. playscript 3.50 (ISBN 0-87602-197-6). Anchorage.
—Wiggle Worm's Surprise. 16p. (Orig.). (ps up). 1977. playscript 3.50 (ISBN 0-87602-218-2). Anchorage.

Melanos, Jack. Rapunzel & the Witch. 4.50 (ISBN 0-87602-186-0). Anchorage.
Miller, Helen L. First Plays for Children. 295p. (gr. 1-3). 1985. pap. 10.95 (ISBN 0-8238-0268-X). Plays.
—Special Plays for Holidays. LC 86-9332. (Orig.). (gr. 1-6). 1986. pap. 12.00 (ISBN 0-8238-0275-2). Plays.
Miller, Kathryn S. Blue Horses. 30p. (gr. 5-7). 1982. saddle-stitched 2.50x (ISBN 0-88020-107-X). Dramatic Pub.
—Haunted Houses. 1986. pap. 2.50x (ISBN 0-88020-121-5). Dramatic Pub.
—The Shining Moment: (Musical) 1989. Playscript. 4.50 (ISBN 0-87602-286-7). Anchorage.
Miller, Lucille. Heidi. 1936. 4.50 (ISBN 0-87602-136-4). Anchorage.
Miller, Madge. Alice in Wonderland. 1953. 4.50 (ISBN 0-87602-104-6). Anchorage.
—Hansel & Gretel. 4.50 (ISBN 0-87602-135-6). Anchorage.
—The Land of the Dragon. 1946. 4.50 (ISBN 0-87602-148-8). Anchorage.
—The Pied Piper of Hamelin. 1951. 4.50 (ISBN 0-87602-174-7). Anchorage.
—Pinocchio. 1954. 4.00 (ISBN 0-87602-175-5). Anchorage.
—The Princess & the Swineherd. 1946. 4.50 (ISBN 0-87602-181-X). Anchorage.
—Robinson Crusoe. 1954. 4.00 (ISBN 0-87602-193-3). Anchorage.
—The Unwicked Witch. 1964. 4.50 (ISBN 0-87602-216-6). Anchorage.
Miller, Sarah W. Bible Dramas for Older Boys & Girls. LC 75-95409. (gr. 3-6). 1970. pap. 4.95 (ISBN 0-8054-7506-0). Broadman.
Miller, Schultz K. You Don't See Me. 1985. pap. 2.50x (ISBN 0-88020-120-7). Dramatic Pub.
Mofid, Bijan. The Butterfly. 1974. 4.50 (ISBN 0-87602-111-9). Anchorage.
Molyneux, Lynn & Gordner, Brad. Act It Out: Original Plays Plus Crafts for Costumes & Scenery. Marasco, Pam, illus. 192p. (gr. 2-6). 1986. spiral bdg. 12.95 (ISBN 0-685-29139-1). Trellis Bks Inc.
Mother Jones: Mini-Play. (gr. 5up). 1975. 6.50 (ISBN 0-89550-367-0). Stevens & Shea.
Murray, John. Fifteen Plays for Today's Teenagers. new rev. ed. 353p. (gr. 7-12). 1985. pap. 13.95 (ISBN 0-8238-0271-X). Plays.
—Mystery Plays for Young Actors. (Orig.). (gr. 5-12). 1984. pap. 12.95 (ISBN 0-8238-0265-5). Plays.
Musil, Rosemary G. The Ghost of Mr. Penny. 1940. 4.50 (ISBN 0-87602-129-1). Anchorage.
Norris, James. Aladdin & the Wonderful Lamp. 1940. 4.50 (ISBN 0-87602-102-X). Anchorage.
—Robin Hood. 1952. 4.50 (ISBN 0-87602-191-7). Anchorage.
Nursey-Bray, Rosemary. Through the Looking Glass & What Alice Found There. (Orig.). (ps up). 1987. playscript 5.00 (ISBN 0-87602-276-X). Anchorage.
Pearson, Carol L. Don't Count Your Chickens until They Cry Wolf: Musical. 1979. 4.50 (ISBN 0-87602-122-4). Anchorage.
Peter N' the Wolf: Music & Lyrics. rev. ed. (gr. 3-12). 1985. pap. text ed. 15.00 (ISBN 0-88734-012-1). Players Pr.
Porter, Steven. The Prairie Man. LC 89-92532. 62p. 1990. pap. text ed. 6.00 (ISBN 0-9625372-0-9). Phantom Pubns.
Pugh, Shirley. In One Basket. 1972. 4.50 (ISBN 0-87602-140-2). Anchorage.
Rapunzel 'N the Witch: Music & Lyrics. rev. ed. (gr. 3-12). 1985. pap. text ed. 15.00 (ISBN 0-88734-006-7). Players Pr.
Reed, Roland. The Miser. 1973. 4.50 (ISBN 0-87602-158-5). Anchorage.
Robinette, Joseph. ABC (America Before Columbus) 40p. (gr. k-8). 1984. pap. 2.50 (ISBN 0-88680-212-1). I E Clark.
Rockwell, Thomas. How to Eat Fried Worms: And Other Plays. Schick, Joel, illus. LC 78-72854. (gr. 4-7). 1980. 9.95 (ISBN 0-440-03498-1); PLB 9.89 (ISBN 0-440-03499-X). Delacorte.
Ross, Monica L. Montana Molly & the Peppermint Kid: (Musical) 1989. Playscript. 4.50 (ISBN 0-87602-285-9). Anchorage.
—Wilma's Revenge. 1989. Playscript. 4.50 (ISBN 0-87602-288-3). Anchorage.
Rumble, Patricia B. The Archer & the Princess: A Comedy Based on a Russian Folk Tale. (Illus.). 48p. (Orig.). (gr. 4-10). 1990. pap. 3.00 (ISBN 0-88680-334-9). I E Clark.
Russell, Willey. Our Day Out. 56p. 1988. pap. 7.95x (ISBN 0-413-54870-8, A0201). Heinemann Ed.
Saunders, Dudley. Dracula's Treasure. 1975. 4.50 (ISBN 0-87602-123-2). Anchorage.
Schuyler, Royce. Boomerang: A One-Act Play for Grades 7-9. Kester, Ellen S., ed. Omoto, Larry, illus. 50p. (Orig.). Date not set. pap. text ed. 6.95 (ISBN 0-685-26284-7). Pickwick Pubs.
—Boomerang: Drama for Study & Performance. Kester, Ellen S., ed. Omoto, Larry, illus. 100p. (Orig.). Date not set. pap. text ed. 35.00 (ISBN 0-685-26285-5). Pickwick Pubs.
Seale, Jan E. Texas History Classroom Plays, Vol. 1. (Illus.). 56p. (gr. 4-8). 1986. PLB 4.25 (ISBN 0-317-89748-9). Knowing Pr.
—Texas History Plays Series. (Illus.). (ps-8). 1986. PLB 89.95 (ISBN 0-317-89749-7). Knowing Pr.
Seale, Nancy. The Little Princess, Sara Crewe. (Orig.). 1982. playscript 5.00 (ISBN 0-87602-231-X). Anchorage.
Sexton, Nancy N., et al. My Days As a Youngling, John Jacob Niles. (Orig.). (gr. 4 up). 1982. playscript 5.50 (ISBN 0-87602-239-5). Anchorage.
Shakespeare, William. King Henry IV, Pt. II. Girling, Zoe. (gr. 10 up). pap. 0.60. Airmont.
—King Henry V. Thomas, Clara. (gr. 10 up). pap. 0.60 (ISBN 0-8049-1017-0). Airmont.
—Macbeth. Stewart, Diana, adapted by. LC 81-19273. (Illus.). 48p. (gr. 4 up). 1983. PLB 17.32 (ISBN 0-8172-1681-2); pap. 9.27 (ISBN 0-8172-2014-3). Raintree Pubs.
—A Midsummer Night's Dream. Stewart, Diana, adapted by. LC 81-19272. (Illus.). 48p. (gr. 4 up). 1983. PLB 17.32 (ISBN 0-8172-1680-4); pap. 9.27 (ISBN 0-8172-2015-1). Raintree Pubs.
—A Midsummer Night's Dream. Pickett, Cecil, adapted by. (Illus.). 32p. (gr. 7 up). 1984. pap. 1.50 (ISBN 0-88680-214-8). I E Clark.
—Twelfth Night. abr. ed. Pickett, Cecil, adapted by. (Illus.). 36p. (gr. 7 up). 1984. pap. 1.50 (ISBN 0-88680-213-X). I E Clark.
Siks, Geraldine B. The Sandalwood Box. 1954. 4.50 (ISBN 0-87602-199-2). Anchorage.
Spencer, Sara. Little Women. 1940. 4.50 (ISBN 0-87602-150-X). Anchorage.
—Tom Sawyer. 1935. 4.50 (ISBN 0-87602-211-5). Anchorage.
Steins, Richar. Berlin. (gr. 7-12). 1991. PLB 14.95 (ISBN 0-8239-1216-7). Rosen Group.
Sternberg, Pat & Beechman, Dolly. Sojourner. 46p. 1989. Playscript. 4.50 (ISBN 0-87602-283-2). Anchorage.
Still, James, adapted by. The Velveteen Rabbit. 33p. (Orig.). 1989. playscript 4.50 (ISBN 0-87602-289-1). Anchorage.
Sunanda. Stories & Plays for Children. 91p. (gr. 3-8). 1984. pap. 2.50 (ISBN 0-89071-329-4, Pub. by Sri Aurobindo Ashram India). Aurobindo Assn.
Surface, Mary H. Prodigy: Wolfgang Amadeus Mozart: (Musical) 50p. 1988. Playscript. 4.50 (ISBN 0-87602-281-6). Anchorage.
Thane, Adele. Plays from Famous Stories & Fairy Tales. (gr. 4-7). pap. 15.00 (ISBN 0-8238-0060-1). Plays.
—The Wizard of Oz. 1957. 4.50 (ISBN 0-87602-221-2). Anchorage.
Thurston, Cheryl M. A Frog King's Daughter Is Nothing to Sneeze At. LC 88-93068. (Orig.). (gr. k-12). 1990. pap. 10.00 (ISBN 0-88734-513-1). Players Pr.
Triangle Shirtwaist Fire: Mini-Play. (gr. 5 up). 1975. 6.50 (ISBN 0-89550-369-7). Stevens & Shea.
Urquhart, John, et al. Nightingale (A Participation Play) (Orig.). (gr. k up). 1983. pap. 4.00 (ISBN 0-87602-245-X). Anchorage.
Vos, Eric. Professor Filarsky's Miraculous Invention. 1980. 4.50. Anchorage.
Vos, Erik. The Dancing Donkey: Musical. 1965. 4.50 (ISBN 0-87602-117-8). Anchorage.
Water for the Angels: Mini-Play. (gr. 5 up). 1978. 6.50 (ISBN 0-89550-332-8). Stevens & Shea.
Whiting, Frank. Huckleberry Finn. 1948. 4.50 (ISBN 0-87602-138-0). Anchorage.
Wilde, Oscar & Payne, Darwin R. The Canterville Ghost. (gr. k-12). 1963. pap. 2.25x (ISBN 0-88020-021-9). Dramatic Pub.
Williams, Guy. David & Goliath. LC 90-53572. (Orig.). (gr. 3 up). 1991. pap. 5.00 (ISBN 0-88734-411-9). Players Pr.
Wilson, Alice, et al. Flashback! (Orig.). (gr. k up). 1980. pap. 4.50 (ISBN 0-87602-259-X). Anchorage.
Wise, Arthur & Wise, Sarah. Six Christian One-Act Plays for Young Adults. 52p. (gr. 7-12). pap. 5.00 (ISBN 0-88680-178-8). I E Clark.
Young, Ruth. Starring Francine & Dave: Three One-Act Plays. LC 88-60093. (Illus.). 32p. (ps-2). 1988. 13.95 (ISBN 0-531-05781-X); PLB 13.99 (ISBN 0-531-08381-0). Orchard Bks Watts.
Zarambouka, Sofia. Irene. Zarambouka, Sofia & Loftin, Tee, trs. (Illus.). 42p. (gr. k-3). 1979. 8.95 (ISBN 0-934812-00-4). Tee Loftin.
Zeder, Susan. Ozma of Oz: A Tale of Time. (Orig.). (gr. 4 up). 1981. playscript 5.00 (ISBN 0-87602-233-6). Anchorage.
Zeder, Suzan. The Play Called Noah's Flood. (Orig.). (gr. 4 up). 1985. pap. 5.00 (ISBN 0-87602-247-6). Anchorage.
—Step on a Crack. 1976. 4.50 (ISBN 0-87602-207-7). Anchorage.
Zeder, Suzan L. An Evening at Versailles. Moliere, J. B., contrib. by. 1989. Playscript. 5.00 (ISBN 0-87602-284-0). Anchorage.
—In a Room Somewhere: (Musical) 60p. 1988. Playscript. 5.00 (ISBN 0-87602-282-4). Anchorage.

PLAYS, CHRISTMAS
see Christmas Plays

PLAYS FOR CHILDREN
see Plays

PLAYWRIGHTS
see Dramatists

PLAYWRITING
see Drama–Technique

PLUMBING
Plumbing. (Illus.). 40p. (gr. 6-12). 1965. pap. 1.85 (ISBN 0-8395-3386-1, 3386). BSA.

PLUMBING–VOCATIONAL GUIDANCE
Lillegard, Dee & Stoker, Wayne. I Can Be a Plumber. LC 86-30950. (Illus.). 32p. (gr. k-3). 1987. PLB 13.93 (ISBN 0-516-01906-6). Childrens.

PLUTO (PLANET)
Asimov, Isaac. Pluto: A Double Planet? LC 89-11290. (Illus.). 32p. (gr. 3-4). 1989. PLB 11.95 (ISBN 1-55532-373-1). Gareth Stevens Inc.

PLYMOUTH, MASSACHUSETTS–HISTORY
Fritz, Jean. Who's That Stepping on Plymouth Rock? Handelsman, J. B., illus. LC 74-30593. 32p. (gr. 2-6). 1975. 8.95 (ISBN 0-698-20325-9, Coward). Putnam Pub Group.

POCAHONTAS, 1595?-1617
D'Aulaire, Ingri. Pocahontas. 1989. pap. 7.95 (ISBN 0-385-26607-3). Doubleday.
D'Aulaire, Ingri & D'Aulaire, Edgar P. Pocahontas. D'Aulaire, Ingri & D'Aulaire, Edgar P., illus. 48p. (gr. 1-4). 1985. pap. 13.95 (ISBN 0-385-07454-9). Doubleday.
Fritz, Jean. The Double Life of Pocahontas. Young, Ed, illus. LC 83-9662. 96p. (gr. 4-8). 1983. 12.95 (ISBN 0-399-21016-4, Putnam). Putnam Pub Group.
—The Double Life of Pocahontas. large type ed. (Illus.). 128p. (gr. 4-8). 1991. Repr. of 1983 ed. PLB 17.95 (ISBN 1-55905-092-6). Grey Castle.
Greene, Carol. Pocahontas: Daughter of a Chief. Dobson, Steven, illus. LC 88-11978. 48p. (gr. k-3). 1988. PLB 15.27 (ISBN 0-516-04203-3); pap. 4.95 (ISBN 0-516-44203-1). Childrens.
Jassem, Kate. Pocahontas, Girl of Jamestown. LC 78-18045. (Illus.). 48p. (gr. 4-6). 1979. PLB 9.89 (ISBN 0-89375-152-9); pap. 2.95 (ISBN 0-89375-142-1). Troll Assocs.
Richards, Dorothy F. Pocahontas, Child-Princess. Nelson, John, illus. LC 78-7719. (gr. k-4). 1978. PLB 10.95 (ISBN 0-89565-035-5). Childs World.
Santrey, Laurence. Pocahontas. Wenzel, David, illus. LC 84-8443. 32p. (gr. 3-6). 1985. PLB 9.49 (ISBN 0-8167-0276-4); pap. text ed. 2.95 (ISBN 0-8167-0277-2). Troll Assocs.

POCAHONTAS, 1595?-1617–FICTION
Bulla, Clyde R. Pocahontas & the Strangers. Burchard, Peter, illus. 176p. (gr. 2-6). 1988. pap. 2.50 (ISBN 0-590-41711-8). Scholastic Inc.
Gleiter, Jan & Thompson, Kathleen. Pocahontas. LC 84-9819. (Illus.). 32p. (gr. 2-5). 1984. PLB 16.67 (ISBN 0-8172-2118-2); PLB 27.99 incl. cassette (ISBN 0-8172-2240-5); pap. 9.27 (ISBN 0-8172-2261-8); pap. 23.95 (ISBN 0-8172-2271-5); cassette 14.00 (ISBN 0-685-09501-0). Raintree Pubs.
O'Dell, Scott. The Serpent Never Sleeps: A Novel of Jamestown & Pocahontas. (gr. 8 up). 1988. pap. 3.50 (ISBN 0-449-70328-2, Juniper). Fawcett.

POE, EDGAR ALLAN, 1809-1849–FICTION
Avi. The Man Who Was Poe. LC 89-42537. 224p. (gr. 6-8). 1989. 13.95 (ISBN 0-531-05833-6); PLB 13.99 (ISBN 0-531-08433-7). Orchard Bks Watts.

POETICS
Here are entered works on the art and technique of poetry. Works on the appreciation and philosophy of poetry are entered under Poetry.
see also Rhythm; Versification
Hardt, Elaine. Writing Poetry. Kruck, Gerry, illus. 32p. (Orig.). (gr. 1-9). 1983. pap. 1.95 (ISBN 0-940406-09-8). Perception Pubns.
Hayes, Dympna. Fun with Rhymes. Davis, Annelies, illus. 32p. (gr. 1). 1987. PLB 13.85 (ISBN 0-88625-165-6); pap. 2.50 (ISBN 0-88625-144-3). Durkin Hayes Pub.
Kuskin, Karla. Near the Window Tree: Poems & Notes. Kuskin, Karla, illus. LC 74-20394. 64p. (gr. 2-6). 1975. PLB 12.89 (ISBN 0-06-023540-3). HarpC Child Bks.
Livingston, Myra C. Poem-Making: Ways to Begin Writing Poetry. LC 90-5012. 176p. (gr. 4-8). 1991. 15.95 (ISBN 0-06-024019-9); PLB 15.89 (ISBN 0-06-024020-2). HarpC Child Bks.
Raffel, Burton. How to Read a Poem: Metrics. 260p. (gr. 9-12). 1989. pap. 8.95 (ISBN 0-452-00917-0, Mer). NAL-Dutton.
Ryan, Margaret. How to Read & Write Poems. (Illus.). 64p. (gr. 5-8). 1991. PLB 11.90 (ISBN 0-531-20043-4). Watts.
Spellman, Linda. Poetry Party. 48p. (gr. 4-6). 1981. 5.95 (ISBN 0-88160-038-5, LW 223). Learning Wks.
Wainwright, James. Poetivities - Intermediate. 64p. (gr. 4-6). 1989. 6.95 (ISBN 0-86653-488-1, GA1090). Good Apple.
—Poetivities - Primary. 64p. (gr. 1-3). 1989. 6.95 (ISBN 0-86653-484-9, GA1089). Good Apple.

POETRY
see also Ballads; Hymns; Love Poetry; Nature in Poetry also American Poetry; English Poetry, etc.; and general subjects, names of historical events, places and famous persons with the subdivision Poetry, e.g. Animals–poetry
Adoff, Arnold. Birds. Howell, Troy, illus. LC 81-47753. 64p. (gr. k-5). 1982. PLB 11.89 (ISBN 0-685-02079-7, Lipp Jr Bks); PLB 11.89 (ISBN 0-397-31950-9). HarpC Child Bks.
—Chocolate Dreams. MacCombie, Turi, illus. LC 88-27208. 64p. (gr. 3 up). 1989. 13.95 (ISBN 0-688-06822-7); PLB 13.88 (ISBN 0-688-06823-5). Lothrop.
—In for Winter, Out for Spring. Ingber, Bonnie, ed. Pinkney, Jerry, illus. 48p. (ps-3). 1991. 14.95 (ISBN 0-15-238637-8). HarBraceJ.
Agard, John. Life Doesn't Frighten Me at All. (Illus.). 96p. (gr. 6 up). 1990. 14.95 (ISBN 0-8050-1237-0). H Holt & Co.

Ain, Diantha. What Do You Know about Succotash? Poems & Drawings. Ain, Diantha, illus. 75p. (Orig.). (gr. 1-6). Date not set. pap. 7.95 (ISBN 0-925360-01-5). Geste Pub.

Allum, Faith T. Respite. Allum, Lois Saarinen, illus. 48p. (Orig.). (gr. 6 up). 1985. pap. 3.00 (ISBN 0-9613349-2-4). F T Allum.

Amos, Winsom. Youth Poems. Jones, Jean, illus. 24p. (Orig.). (gr. 6-12). 1983. pap. 1.75x (ISBN 0-932510-00-0). Soma Pr.

Anglund, Joan W. The Joan Walsh Anglund Book of Poetry. Anglund, Joan W., illus. LC 87-4429. 48p. (ps-3). 1987. 9.95 (ISBN 0-394-88465-5, Random Juv); lib. bdg. 9.99 (ISBN 0-394-98465-X). Random.

Ashley, Jill. Riddles about Christmas. Brook, Bonnie, ed. Gray, Rob, illus. 32p. (ps-3). 1990. 5.95 (ISBN 0-671-70554-7); PLB 10.98 (ISBN 0-671-70552-0). Silver Pr.

Astley, Neil, ed. Bossy Parrot. LC 87-73294. (Illus.). 64p. (Orig.). (gr. 1 up). 1988. pap. 10.95 (ISBN 1-85224-040-7, Pub. by Bloodaxe Bks). Dufour.

Axeman, Lois, illus. Holidays. LC 84-9429. 32p. (gr. k-3). 1984. PLB 11.97 (ISBN 0-89565-266-8). Childs World.

Barker, Cicely M. Flower Fairies of the Garden. Barker, Cicely M., illus. (ps up). 1991. 5.95 (ISBN 0-7232-3758-1). Viking Child Bks.

Bauer, Caroline F., ed. Windy Day: Stories & Poems. Zimmer, Dirk, illus. LC 86-42994. 96p. (gr. 2-5). 1988. 11.95 (ISBN 0-397-32207-0, Lipp Jr Bks); PLB 12.89 (ISBN 0-397-32208-9). HarpC Child Bks.

Behn, Robin. Paper Bird. LC 87-51682. 88p. 1988. 15.95 (ISBN 0-89672-164-7); pap. 9.95 (ISBN 0-89672-163-9). Tex Tech Univ Pr.

Bennett, Jill. People Poems. Sharratt, Nick, illus. 32p. (gr. k up). 1990. bds. 9.95 laminated (ISBN 0-19-276086-6). Oxford U Pr.

Bernal, Richard. Night, Zoo. Bernal, Richard, illus. 24p. (gr. 2-5). 1989. 11.95 (ISBN 0-8092-4396-2, Calico Bks). Contemp Bks.

Berry, James. When I Dance. Ingber, Bonnie, ed. Barbour, Karen, illus. 128p. (gr. 7 up). 1991. 15.95 (ISBN 0-15-295568-2). HarBraceJ.

Blankenship, Judy, illus. Teddy Beddy Bear's Bedtime Songs & Poems. LC 84-4837. 32p. (ps). 1984. pap. 2.25 saddle-stitched (ISBN 0-394-86826-9, Pub. by BYR). Random.

Blishen, Edward, ed. The Oxford Book of Poetry for Children. Wildsmith, Brian, illus. LC 83-21500. 168p. (Orig.). (gr. k up). 1984. pap. 12.95 (ISBN 0-911745-34-3). P Bedrick Bks.

—Oxford Book of Poetry for Children. Wildsmith, Brian, illus. 168p. (gr. k-5). 1987. 16.95 (ISBN 0-19-276031-9). Oxford U Pr.

Bober, Natalie S., compiled by. Let's Pretend: Poems of Flight & Fancy. Bell, Bill, illus. Boler, Natalie S., intro. by. (Illus.). 64p. (ps-3). 1986. pap. 13.95 (ISBN 0-670-81176-9). Viking Child Bks.

Bogan, Louise & Smith, William J. The Golden Journey: Two Hundred Twenty-Five Poems for Young People. 320p. 1989. leatherette 9.95 (ISBN 0-8092-4249-4). Contemp Bks.

Bonner, Ann & Bonner, Roger. Earlybirds...Earlywords. LC 72-89449. (Illus.). 32p. (ps-2). 1973. 7.95 (ISBN 0-87592-013-6). Scroll Pr.

Brewton, John E., et al. In the Witch's Kitchen: Poems for Halloween. Barton, Harriett, illus. LC 79-7822. 96p. (gr. 2-5). 1980. PLB 13.89 (ISBN 0-690-04062-8, Crowell Jr Bks). HarpC Child Bks.

Brewton, Sara, et al. Quarks, Quasars & Other Quirks: Quizzical Poems for the Supersonic Age. Blake, Quentin, illus. LC 76-54747. 128p. (gr. 4 up). 1977. 12.95 (ISBN 0-690-01286-1, Crowell Jr Bks). HarpC Child Bks.

Brewton, Sara, et al, eds. Of Quarks, Quasars, & Other Quirks: Quizzical Poems for the Supersonic Age. Blake, Quentin, illus. LC 76-54747. 128p. (gr. 5 up). 1990. PLB 13.89 (ISBN 0-690-04885-8, Crowell Jr Bks). HarpC Child Bks.

Brooke, L. Leslie. Rhymes from Ring O'Rose. (ps-3). 1987. 4.95 (ISBN 0-7232-3529-5). Warne.

Brown, Marcia. Shadow. Brown, Marcia, illus. LC 86-3432. 38p. (ps-12). 1986. pap. 3.95 (ISBN 0-689-71084-4, Aladdin). Macmillan Child Grp.

Brown, Margaret W. Nibble Nibble: Poems for Children. Weisgard, Leonard, illus. LC 84-43128. 64p. 1959. PLB 12.89 (ISBN 0-201-09291-3). HarpC Child Bks.

Burton, Michael H. In the Light of a Child: Fifty-two Verses for Children & the Child in Every Human Being. McHenry, Kitsy & Geard, David, illus. Burton, Michael, intro. by. 62p. (Orig.). (gr. 4). 1989. pap. text ed. 12.95 (ISBN 0-932776-17-5). Adonis Pr.

Carroll, Lewis. The Walrus & the Carpenter. Zalben, Jane B., illus. LC 85-7591. 32p. (gr. 2-4). 1990. pap. 4.95 (ISBN 0-8050-1482-9). H Holt & Co.

Carson, Jo. Stories I Ain't Told Nobody Yet: Selections from the People Pieces. LC 88-19821. 96p. (gr. 7 up). 1989. 13.95 (ISBN 0-531-05808-5); PLB 13.99 (ISBN 0-531-08408-6). Orchard Bks Watts.

Cassedy, Sylvia. Roomrimes. Chessare, Michele, illus. LC 86-4583. 80p. (gr. k-3). 1987. 12.95 (ISBN 0-690-04466-6, Crowell Jr Bks); PLB 12.89 (ISBN 0-690-04467-4, Crowell Jr Bks). HarpC Child Bks.

The Caterpillar. LC 88-18899. 16p. (Orig.). 1988. pap. 3.95 (ISBN 0-8092-4465-9, Calico Bks). Contemp Bks.

Cendrars, Blaise. Shadow. Marcia, Brown, tr. from FRE. & illus. LC 81-9424. 40p. (gr. 2 up). 1982. 14.95 (ISBN 0-684-17226-7, Scribners Young Read). Macmillan Child Grp.

Chapman, Jean. Cat Will Rhyme with Hat. LC 86-17817. (Illus.). 96p. (gr. 4 up). 1986. 12.95 (ISBN 0-684-18747-7, Scribners Young Read). Macmillan Child Grp.

Charles, Donald. Paddy Pigs Poems. 1989. pap. 13.95 (ISBN 0-671-67081-6). S&S Trade.

Christison, Mary Ann. English Through Poetry. Peterson, Kathleen, illus. 130p. (gr. 3-6). 1982. pap. text ed. 8.95 (ISBN 0-88084-002-1). Alemany Pr.

Church, Elmer T. Walk with Me in White. LC 86-81184. 154p. 1986. perfect bdg. 5.98 (ISBN 0-318-21723-6). E T Church.

Ciardi, John. Doodle Soup. Nacht, Merle, illus. LC 85-814. 64p. (gr. 2-5). 1985. 12.95 (ISBN 0-395-38395-1). HM.

—Fast & Slow: Poems for Advanced Children of Beginning Parents. Gaver, Becky, intro. by. LC 74-22405. (Illus.). 68p. (gr. k-3). 1978. 12.95 (ISBN 0-395-20282-5). HM.

—Mummy Took Cooking Lessons & Other Poems. Nacht, Merle, illus. 64p. (gr. 2-8). 1990. 13.95 (ISBN 0-395-53351-1). HM.

—The Reason for the Pelican. Corcoran, Mark, illus. 16p. (ps). 1989. 3.95 (ISBN 0-8092-4398-9, Calico Bks). Contemp Bks.

—You Read to Me, I'll Read to You. Gorey, Edward, illus. LC 62-16296. 64p. (gr. k-6). 1961. PLB 11.89 (ISBN 0-685-02089-4, Lipp Jr Bks); PLB 11.89 (ISBN 0-397-30646-6). HarpC Child Bks.

—You Read to Me, I'll Read to You. Gorey, Edward, illus. LC 62-16296. 64p. (gr. k-4). 1987. pap. 5.95 (ISBN 0-06-446060-6, Trophy). HarpC Child Bks.

Cirillo, Louise G. Fun Verse for the Young & the Young in Heart. (Illus.). (gr. 1-3). 5.95 (ISBN 0-533-06369-8). Vantage.

Clark, Ann N. In My Mother's House. Herrara, Velino, illus. 64p. (ps up). 1991. 15.95 (ISBN 0-670-83917-5). Viking Child Bks.

Clifford, Eth. The Remembering Box. Diamond, Donna, illus. 64p. (gr. 2-5). 1985. 12.95 (ISBN 0-395-38476-1). HM.

Cohen, Shari. Prime Time Rhyme. (gr. k-6). 1990. 10.95 (ISBN 0-9620467-4-4). Forward March.
Grandmas, babysitters, strange people, neighbors, teachers, roller coasters, frogs, clothes, dogs, toothfairies, chickenpox, food, treehouses, romance (romance?), & a guy named "Stu" are all taken on in this light-hearted look at growing up. Share these & many more secret thoughts & feelings about school, friends, family, & life in general with "Prime Time Rhyme's seventy-three humorous poems about the joys & struggles of childhood. HIDE ME: My grandmother dressed me today/She sent me to school/In loud checkered shorts/And a Mickey Mouse belt/And a wide striped shirt/With a collar of felt/A polka dot vest/With buttons that shine/Gray flannel socks/That are one of a kind/High leather boots/With buckles up the side/Even grandmothers should know/That a kid has his pride!
Publisher Provided Annotation.

Cole, Joanna. New Treasury of Children's Poetry. Brown, Judith G., illus. LC 83-20821. 224p. (ps-8). 1984. pap. 17.95 (ISBN 0-385-18539-1). Doubleday.

Cole, William. Beastly Boys & Ghastly Girls. (gr. 4 up). 1977. pap. 1.25 (ISBN 0-440-40467-3, YB). Dell.

—Oh, How Silly! Ungerer, Tomi, illus. 80p. (gr. 2 up). 1990. pap. 3.95 (ISBN 0-14-034441-1, Puffin). Puffin Bks.

—Oh, What Nonsense. Ungerer, Tomi, illus. 80p. (gr. 2 up). 1990. pap. 3.95 (ISBN 0-14-034442-X, Puffin). Puffin Bks.

Cole, William, ed. Poem Stew. Weinhaus, Karen, illus. LC 81-47106. 96p. (gr. 3-6). 1981. PLB 11.89 (ISBN 0-685-02084-3, Lipp Jr Bks); PLB 11.89 (ISBN 0-397-31964-9). HarpC Child Bks.

Coleridge, Sara. January Brings the Snow: A Seasonal Hide-&-Seek Book. LC 88-28609. (Illus.). 28p. (ps-3). 1989. 14.95 (ISBN 0-531-05824-7). Orchard Bks Watts.

Connelly, Gwen, illus. Adventures. LC 83-25212. 32p. (gr. k-3). 1984. PLB 11.97 (ISBN 0-89565-265-X). Childs World.

Creedon, Sharon. A Look over the Edge. Waterline, Wendy, illus. 16p. (gr. k-4). 1987. pap. 5.95 (ISBN 0-9620446-0-1). Sunset Mktg.

The Crocodile. LC 88-18878. (Illus.). 16p. (Orig.). 1988. pap. 3.95 (ISBN 0-8092-4462-4, Calico Bks). Contemp Bks.

Crosby, Alexander L., photos by. Crazy to Be Alive in Such a Strange World: Poems about People. Larrick, Nancy, selected by. LC 76-49667. (Illus.). 192p. (gr. 5 up). 1989. pap. 6.95 (ISBN 0-87131-566-1). M Evans.

Crossley-Holland, Kevin. Under the Sun & over the Moon. Penney, Ian, illus. 32p. 1989. 15.95 (ISBN 0-399-21946-3, Putnam). Putnam Pub Group.

Cummings, e. e. In Just-Spring. Goennel, Heidi, illus. LC 87-14342. 32p. (ps-3). 1988. 14.95 (ISBN 0-316-16390-2). Little.

Cummings, e. e., et al. Spooky Poems. Bennett, Jill, compiled by. Rees, Mary, illus. (ps-3). 1989. 13.95 (ISBN 0-316-08987-7, Joy St Bks). Little.

Dahl, Roald. Dirty Beasts. Blake, Quentin, illus. LC 85-594. 32p. (gr. 1 up). 1986. pap. 4.95 (ISBN 0-14-050435-4, Puffin). Puffin Bks.

—Rhyme Stew. Blake, Quentin, illus. 80p. (gr. 4 up). 1990. pap. 14.95 (ISBN 0-670-82916-1). Viking Penguin.

—Roald Dahl's Revolting Rhymes. Blake, Quentin, illus. LC 82-15263. 48p. (gr. 3-6). 1983. 14.00 (ISBN 0-394-85422-5); lib. bdg. 14.99 (ISBN 0-394-95422-X). Knopf.

Dakos, Kalli. If You're Not Here, Please Raise Your Hand: Poems about School. Karas, G. Brian, illus. LC 89-71530. 64p. (gr. 2-6). 1990. 12.95 (ISBN 0-02-725581-6, Four Winds). Macmillan Child Grp.

Daniel, Mark. Child's Treasury of Animal Verse. (ps up). 1989. 16.95 (ISBN 0-8037-0606-5). Dial Bks Young.

Daniel, Mark, ed. A Child's Treasury of Poems. LC 86-2194. (Illus.). 160p. (ps up). 1986. 15.95 (ISBN 0-8037-0330-9). Dial Bks Young.

Davenport, May, ed. Watch Out, the Tide. LC 86-91602. 84p. (Orig.). (gr. 7-12). 1987. pap. 3.95x (ISBN 0-943864-48-8). Pogosticks by Andrea Ross. Ginger: Poof! Bam! Growl! by Andrea Ross. Poems by Kay Garrard. Davenport.

Davis, Hubert J. What Will the Weather Be?, No. 1: A Folk Weather Calendar. Turner, Erin, illus. LC 88-17869. 40p. (Orig.). (gr. k-12). 1988. pap. 4.95 (ISBN 0-936015-11-X). Pocahontas Pr.

—What Will the Weather Be?, No. 2: Animal Signs. Turner, Erin, illus. LC 90-22327. 56p. (Orig.). (gr. k-12). 1991. pap. 5.95 (ISBN 0-936015-12-8). Pocahontas Pr.

Decker, Marjorie A. Christian Mother Goose - Rock-a-Bye-Bible. (Illus.). 96p. (ps-k). 1987. text ed. 6.95 (ISBN 0-529-06481-2). World Bible.

DeWitt, Jim. Fingernail Souffle. Cole, Bradley, illus. 136p. (Orig.). (gr. 4-12). 1987. pap. 6.00 (ISBN 0-915199-03-3). Pen Dec.

—Jammy Donuts a Season After. LC 83-90481. (Illus.). 64p. (Orig.). (gr. 4-12). 1984. pap. text ed. 5.95 (ISBN 0-915199-04-1). Pen-Dec.

—Quiet-Time Thoughts. LC 83-90474. (Illus.). 64p. (Orig.). (gr. 3-10). 1984. pap. text ed. 5.95 (ISBN 0-915199-00-9). Pen Dec.

—Sharpshooting at Kinkajous. Cole, Bradley, illus. 136p. (gr. 4-12). 1987. pap. 6.00 (ISBN 0-915199-06-8). Pen Dec.

Dickinson, Emily. A Brighter Garden. Ackerman, Karen, compiled by. Tudor, Tasha, illus. 63p. 1990. 17.95 (ISBN 0-399-21490-9, Philomel Bks). Putnam Pub Group.

—Poems for Youth. Hampson, Alfred L., ed. Hauman, George & Hauman, Doris, illus. (gr. 7-10). 1934. 12.95 (ISBN 0-316-18418-7). Little.

Disney. Disney Minnie N' Me Book of Poems. 1990. 5.98 (ISBN 0-8317-2349-1). Smithmark.

Dituro, William J. Who Would I Be If My Father Were Me? (gr. 3-5). 1989. 6.95 (ISBN 0-533-08118-1). Vantage.

Dolce, J. Ellen, illus. Baby's Mother Goose. LC 87-81921. 12p. (ps). 1988. write for info. (ISBN 0-307-06066-7, Pub. by Golden Bks). Western Pub.

Duncan, Lois. From Spring to Spring: Poems & Photographs. LC 82-11100. (Illus.). 96p. (gr. 3-7). 1982. 10.95 (ISBN 0-664-32695-1, Westminster). Westminster John Knox.

—Songs from Dreamland. Chorao, Kay, illus. LC 88-21742. 48p. (ps-1). 1989. 11.95 (ISBN 0-394-89904-0). Knopf.

Dunlop, Emma E. & Paris, Pat. Have You Snuzzled a Wuzzle Today? LC 85-2141. (Illus.). 32p. (gr. 4-8). 1985. 4.95 (ISBN 0-394-87495-1, Random Juv). Random.

Dunnington, Tom, illus. Animals. LC 83-25213. 32p. (gr. k-3). 1984. PLB 9.95 (ISBN 0-89565-264-1). Childs World.

Eakins, Margaret, et al, illus. A Patter of Poems: The Chickens; Little Piggy-Wig; Cats; Pitter Patter; One, Two & The Bird Table, 6 bks. 96p. (gr. k-1). Set. pap. text ed. 28.90 (ISBN 1-55624-253-0). Wright Group.

Eastwick, Ivy O. In & Out the Windows: Happy Poems for Children. Barth, Gillian, illus. Swinger, Marlys. LC 73-90841. (Illus.). 80p. (ps-3). 1969. 7.50 (ISBN 0-87486-007-5). Plough.

Eavey, Louise. Happiness Rhymes for Children. Murphy, Emmy L., illus. (ps-1). 1969. pap. 1.95 (ISBN 0-915374-09-9, 09-0). Rapids Christian.

Edey, Marion & Grider, Dorothy. The Jolly Woodchuck. Carmi, Giora, illus. 16p. (ps). 1989. 3.95 (ISBN 0-8092-4399-7, Calico Bks). Contemp Bks.

Edwards, Richard. A Mouse in My Roof. 1990. 13.95 (ISBN 0-385-30035-2). Doubleday.

Eggleton, Jill. I Dream. Biro, Val, illus. 24p. (Orig.). (gr. k-2). 1988. pap. text ed. 28.00 (ISBN 1-55624-957-8). Wright Group.

—I Dream, 6 bks. Biro, Val, illus. 24p. (Orig.). (gr. k-2). 1988. Set. pap. text ed. 26.60 (ISBN 1-55624-962-4). Wright Group.

—Now I Am Five. Moxley, Susan, illus. 24p. (Orig.). (gr. k-2). 1988. pap. text ed. 28.00 (ISBN 1-55624-958-6). Wright Group.

—Now I Are, 6 bks. Moxley, Susan, illus. 24p. (Orig.). (gr. k-2). 1988. Set. pap. text ed. 26.60 (ISBN 1-55624-963-2). Wright Group.

Eliot, T. S. Growltiger's Last Stand & Other Poems. Le Cain, Errol, illus. 32p. (ps up). 1987. 13.95 (ISBN 0-374-32809-9, Co-pub. by HarBraceJ). FS&G.

Esbensen, Barbara J. Cold Stars & Fireflies: Poems of the Four Seasons. Bonners, Susan, illus. LC 83-45051. 80p. (gr. 3-7). 1991. PLB 14.89 (ISBN 0-690-04363-5, Crowell Jr Bks). HarpC Child Bks.

—Words with Wrinkled Knees. Stadler, John, illus. LC 85-47886. 48p. (gr. 2-7). 1987. 11.95 (ISBN 0-690-04504-2, Crowell Jr Bks); PLB 13.89 (ISBN 0-690-04505-0, Crowell Jr Bks). HarpC Child Bks.

Farjeon, Eleanor. Eleanor Farjeon's Poems for Children. LC 51-11164. 256p. (gr. 4 up). 1984. PLB 12.89 (ISBN 0-685-17657-6, Lipp Jr Bks); PLB 12.89 (ISBN 0-397-32091-4). HarpC Child Bks.

Farjeon, Eleanor, et al. A First Album of Poems: Waves; Here Is the Ostrich; What Is Pink?; Birthdays; Months of the Year & Hurt No Living Thing, 6 bks. (Illus.). 96p. (gr. k-2). Set. pap. text ed. 28.90 (ISBN 1-55624-254-9). Wright Group.

Fast, Suellen M. Celebrations of Daughterhood. Serman, Gina L., ed. LC 85-72281. 68p. (Orig.). (gr. 1 up). 1985. pap. 8.00 (ISBN 0-935281-06-1). Daughter Cult.

Feldman, Jacqueline. The Lavender Box. Hoffman, Nannette, illus. LC 89-85206. 41p. (gr. k-6). 1990. 10.95 (ISBN 0-9623903-0-5). Ellicott Pr.
A small boy disappears into a very large hat; a child silently shares poignant feelings with a chipmunk; a little girl preaches the rules of etiquette to a bee. Poems dealing with nature & the pleasures of domestic life transform childhood experiences into rhythmic images. And in the final offering, a lavender box becomes a metaphor for the entire book. Although these poems were written for children aged 3 to 11, Ms. Feldman's awareness of & wonder at the workings of a child's mind give readers of all ages an exhilarating & joyous experience. The poems are beautifully complemented by Nannette Hoffman's whimsical black & white drawings. "A resonant voice is gently in tune with the imagination of children in this poetry collection...the imagery reverberates on every page." SCHOOL LIBRARY JOURNAL. "In rhythmical, memorable verse, she recreates-- for children & adult readers alike-- a child's sense of wonder." -- Anne Whitehouse, reviewer for THE NEW YORK TIMES. "Quite a treasure box of a book." --THE BOOK READER.
Publisher Provided Annotation.

Ferris, Helen, ed. Favorite Poems Old & New. Weisgard, Leonard, illus. LC 57-11418. 598p. (gr. 3-7). 1957. pap. 18.95 (ISBN 0-385-07696-7). Doubleday.

Field, Eugene. The Gingham Dog & the Calico Cat. Street, Janet, illus. 32p. 1990. 14.95 (ISBN 0-399-22151-4, Philomel Bks). Putnam Pub Group.

—Poems of Childhood. (Illus.). (gr. 4 up). 1969. pap. 1.95 (ISBN 0-8049-0211-9, CL-211). Airmont.

Fields, Richard L. Haiku Animal World. Lam, Fahn, illus. 80p. (Orig.). (gr. 6-12). 1989. pap. 7.95 (ISBN 0-927256-00-2). ELF Assocs.

—Haiku Fin & Fathom World. (Illus.). 86p. (Orig.). (gr. 6-12). 1989. pap. 7.95 (ISBN 0-317-93460-0). ELF Assocs.

—Haiku Wing & Feather World. (Illus.). 108p. (Orig.). (gr. 6-12). 1989. pap. 7.95 (ISBN 0-317-93461-9). ELF Assocs.

—Haiku Zing & Sting World. (Illus.). 70p. (Orig.). (gr. 6-12). 1989. pap. 7.95 (ISBN 0-317-93459-7). ELF Assocs.

First Poems. (Illus.). 24p. (ps-3). 1979. pap. 1.25 (ISBN 0-448-49611-9, G&D). Putnam Pub Group.

Fisher, Aileen. Always Wondering: Some Favorite Poems of Aileen Fisher. Sandin, Joan, illus. LC 90-23069. 96p. (gr. 2-6). 1991. 13.95 (ISBN 0-06-022851-2); PLB 13.89 (ISBN 0-06-022858-X). HarpC Child Bks.

Fisher, Barbara. Dan. Fisher, Barbara, illus. 20p. (Orig.). (gr. k-5). 1981. pap. 2.00 (ISBN 0-934830-19-3). Ten Penny.

Fisher, Barbara & Spiegel, Richard, eds. In Search of a Song: PS-114, Vol. 1. (Illus.). 90p. (Orig.). (gr. k-6). 1981. pap. 2.00 (ISBN 0-934830-25-8). Ten Penny.

—In Search of a Song: PS-276, Vol. 2. (Illus.). 90p. (Orig.). (gr. k-6). 1981. pap. 2.00 (ISBN 0-934830-26-6). Ten Penny.

—More Poetry Hunter. (Illus.). 92p. (Orig.). (gr. 3 up). 1981. pap. 2.00 (ISBN 0-934830-23-1). Ten Penny.

—Poetry Hunter, No. 1. (Illus.). 92p. (Orig.). (gr. k-6). 1981. pap. 2.00 (ISBN 0-934830-21-5). Ten Penny.

—Still More Poetry Hunter. (Illus.). 36p. (Orig.). (gr. k-6). 1981. pap. 2.00 (ISBN 0-934830-24-X). Ten Penny.

Fisher, Robert. Funny Folk: Poems about People. (Illus.). 80p. (gr. 3-6). 1986. 13.95 (ISBN 0-571-13793-8). Faber & Faber.

Fisher, Robert, ed. Amazing Monsters: Verses to Thrill & Chill. Allen, Rowena, illus. 96p. (gr. k-5). 1982. pap. 5.95 (ISBN 0-571-13925-6). Faber & Faber.

—Witch Words: Poems of Magic & Mystery. Felts, Shirley, illus. 80p. (gr. 3-6). 1987. laminated boards 9.95 (ISBN 0-571-14559-0). Faber & Faber.

Fitch, Marguerite. Samuel Francis Smith: My Country 'tis of Thee. (Illus.). (gr. 3-6). 1987. pap. 6.95 (ISBN 0-88062-049-8). Mott Media.

Flashinski, Linda. Just As We Are. Flashinski, Todd, illus. 120p. (gr. k-8). 1987. spiral bdg. 11.95 (ISBN 0-9619625-0-X); lib. bdg. 14.95 (ISBN 0-9619625-1-8). Lavinia Pub.

Fleischman, Paul. I Am Phoenix: Poems for Two Voices. Nutt, Ken, illus. LC 85-42615. 64p. (gr. 3-8). 1985. 11.95 (ISBN 0-06-021881-9); PLB 11.89 (ISBN 0-06-021882-7). HarpC Child Bks.

—Joyful Noise: Poems for Two Voices. Beddows, Eric, illus. LC 87-45280. 64p. (gr. 3-8). 1988. 13.95 (ISBN 0-06-021852-5); PLB 12.89 (ISBN 0-06-021853-3). HarpC Child Bks.

Forelle, Helen. Mortimer Meets Melody. Leih, Janet, ed. Stevens, Barbara, illus. 20p. (gr. 1-3). 1981. pap. 3.00 (ISBN 1-877649-02-3). Tesseract SD.

Fort, Chloe F. A Variety of Verse for the Very Young. Malone, David, illus. 32p. (ps). 1990. 8.95 (ISBN 0-9626343-0-1). C F Fort.
Sam was the model for the English teacher portrayed in the movie "The Dead Poet Society". Sam is the author of several books, some scholarly, some a collection of charming essays, such as "The Right Distance," "May Day," "Still Life," & "Let it Ride." "It is really good. It has a wonderful lyric sense & the poems are full of color. Like 'Secret Place', the poems are green & quiet. They make one imagine the world & change sight. One looks out & then turns inward to dream, carried along in part by the music of the verse. In truth, the poems are not just for the young; they are for me & thee, all of us who have a furrow across our brows."--Sam Pickering, Jr. "It was with growing delight that I read the little book A VARIETY OF VERSE FOR THE VERY YOUNG, by Chloe Frierson Fort. The poems in this gentle book seemed to take me back to my childhood when my mother would read to me from Robert Louis Stevenson's A CHILD'S GARDEN OF VERSES & other special books. I feel that this beautiful book would appeal to the children of today & to their sense of wonder at the magic & beauty of the world around them, & I warmly recommend it."--Carroll Miller, Branch Librarian.
Publisher Provided Annotation.

Foster, John, compiled by. A First Poetry Book. Orr, Chris, et al, illus. 128p. (gr. 1-3). 1980. 11.95 (ISBN 0-19-918113-6); pap. 5.95 (ISBN 0-19-918112-8). Oxford U Pr.

Fowke, Edith. Ring Around the Moon: Two Hundred Songs, Tongue Twisters, Riddles & Rhymes for Children. Brown, Judith G., illus. 160p. (gr. k-5). 1987. pap. 12.95 (ISBN 1-55021-006-8, Pub. by NC Press Ltd). U of Toronto Pr.

Frank, Josette, selected by. Snow Toward Evening, a Year in a River Valley. Locker, Thomas, illus. LC 89-48307. 32p. 1990. 15.95 (ISBN 0-8037-0810-6); PLB 15.89 (ISBN 0-8037-0811-4). Dial Bks Young.

Frasier, Elizabeth. Wow! What a Wonderful World. Black, Robert, illus. 32p. (Orig.). (gr. k-4). 1990. pap. 4.50 (ISBN 1-879253-00-3). Apex Creat.
The Author's desire to make children feel "upbeat" & positive about themselves & their world has been a driving force throughout her career as an early childhood specialist, & in the writing of her first book. Wow! What A Wonderful World is a cleverly convincing, entertaining, instructive & timely book for children, ages 5 through 9. It tells in fanciful verse about technological advancements made in the modern world. It touches on topics such as housing, household conveniences, space travel, computers, music, medicine & modern games. The book begins with a humorous personal letter to children, highlighting some changes that have occured over the past few decades, which tend to make the world a more wonderful place in which to live. Frasier writes: Dear children, Why have I written this book? I have written it because you may not know how much the world has changed for the better. Being young, you have no basis for comparisons. You see I remember when there were mainly two kinds of cars--Ford & Chevrolet, & tennis shoes were just tennis shoes, except for some high tops, some low. Now there are so many wonderful choices for almost everything. You can purchase bathtubs & telephones in any color you like & ice cream in at least 31 flavors. There are hundreds of different kinds of cars & trucks, a brand explosion in tennis shoes, & much more. WOW! What A Wonderful World.
Publisher Provided Annotation.

Fratti, Mario, et al. Thank You, Gorbachev! 70p. (Orig.). 1990. pap. write for info. (ISBN 0-9626427-0-3). Wall to Wall.

Froman, Robert. Seeing Things: A Book of Poems. Barber, Ray, illus. LC 73-18494. 64p. (gr. 4-8). 1974. PLB 13.89 (ISBN 0-685-02103-3, Crowell Jr Bks, Crowell Jr Bks). HarpC Child Bks.

Frost, Robert. Birches. Young, Ed, illus. LC 87-46359. 32p. (gr. 1-5). 1988. 13.95 (ISBN 0-8050-0570-6). H Holt & Co.

—Christmas Trees. Rand, Ted, illus. LC 89-48899. (gr. 3 up). 1990. 14.95 (ISBN 0-8050-1208-7). H Holt & Co.

—A Swinger of Birches: Poems of Robert Frost for Young People. Koeppen, Peter, illus. Fadiman, Clifton, intro. by. LC 82-5517. (Illus.). 80p. (gr. 4 up). 1982. 21.95 (ISBN 0-916144-92-5); pap. 14.95 (ISBN 0-916144-93-3); cass. & bk. 23.90 (ISBN 0-685-05629-5, 102-5); cassette only 8.95 (ISBN 0-88045-099-1). Stemmer Hse.

Fujikawa, Gyo, illus. Child's Book of Poems. LC 75-86696. (gr. k-4). 1969. 7.95 (ISBN 0-448-01876-4, G&D). Putnam Pub Group.

Fukijawa, Gyo, illus. Gyo Fujikawa's a Child's Book of Poems. 80p. (gr. k up). 1989. 13.95 (ISBN 0-448-04302-5, G&D). Putnam Pub Group.

Gaber, Susan. Favorite Poems for Children Coloring Book. (Illus.). 48p. (Orig.). (ps-3). 1980. pap. 2.95 (ISBN 0-486-23923-3). Dover.

Gaige, Amity. We Are a Thunderstorm. Thatch, Nancy R., ed. Melton, David, intro. by. LC 90-5922. (Illus.). 26p. 1990. lib. bdg. 12.95 (ISBN 0-933849-27-3). Landmark Edns.

Galdone, Paul. Little Bo-Peep. Galdone, Paul, illus. LC 85-14914. 32p. (ps-3). 1986. 12.95 (ISBN 0-89919-395-1, Pub. by Clarion). Ticknor & Fields.

Garcia, Conrad. Thinking in Poetry. 65p. (Orig.). (gr. 10-12). Date not set. pap. 7.50 (ISBN 0-9621124-0-2). C Garcia.

Giovanni, Nikki. Ego Tripping & Other Poems for Young People. Ford, George, illus. LC 73-81745. 37p. (gr. 2-7). 1974. pap. 7.95 (ISBN 1-55652-062-X). L Hill Bks.

—Vacation Time: Poems for Children. Russo, Marisabina, illus. LC 79-91643. 32p. (gr. 7 up). 1981. pap. 5.95 (ISBN 0-688-00507-1). Morrow.

Gleiter, Jan. Counting Rhymes. (Illus.). 32p. (ps-3). 1986. PLB 13.31 (ISBN 0-8172-2442-4); pap. 9.98 (ISBN 0-8172-2447-5). Raintree Pubs.

Glenn, Mel. Back to Class: Poems by Mel Glenn. Bernstein, Michael J., photos by. LC 88-2835. (Illus.). 112p. (gr. 7 up). 1988. 13.95 (ISBN 0-89919-656-X, Pub. by Clarion). Ticknor & Fields.

—Class Dismissed! High School Poems. Berstein, Michael J., photos by. LC 81-38441. (gr. 9 up). 1982. 13.95 (ISBN 0-89919-075-8, Pub. by Clarion). Ticknor & Fields.

—Class Dismissed: More High School Poems, No. II. Bernstein, Michael J., photos by. LC 86-2671. (Illus.). 96p. (gr. 8 up). 1986. 12.95 (ISBN 0-89919-443-5, Pub. by Clarion). Ticknor & Fields.

Goldblatt, Eli. Leo Loves Round. Osterweil, Wendy, illus. LC 89-35277. 32p. (Orig.). (ps-1). 1990. pap. 6.95 (ISBN 0-943173-49-3). Harbinger AZ.

Goodrich, Patricia. Barefeet & Bellybuttons: Poems & Activities to Tickle a Child. Boytin, Michael, illus. 46p. (gr. k-4). 1989. pap. 5.00 (ISBN 0-9625348-1-1). P Goodrich.

Goulet, Rosalina M. Poems of Childhood: Mga Tula ng Kabataan. (TAG & ENG., Illus.). 106p. (Orig.). (gr. k-2). 1989. pap. 7.50x (ISBN 971-10-0349-X, Pub. by New Day Pub Philippines). Cellar.

Granville, Katherine H. Let's Go See. (gr. 4 up). 1981. 6.50 (ISBN 0-9623897-1-4). Catalyst Pr.

Gravel, Fern, pseud. Oh Millersville! Andrews, Clarence A., tr. LC 41-3646. (Illus.). 128p. (gr. 3 up). 1981. PLB 8.95 (ISBN 0-934582-01-7); pap. 5.95. Midwest Heritage.

Greenfield, Eloise. Honey, I Love & Other Love Poems. Dillon, Diane & Dillon, Leo, illus. LC 85-45398. 48p. (gr. 1-4). 1986. pap. 3.50 (ISBN 0-06-443097-9, Trophy). HarpC Child Bks.

—Nathaniel Talking. Gilchrist, Jan S., illus. 32p. (gr. k-5). 1988. 11.95 (ISBN 0-86316-200-2). Writers & Readers.

Hall, Steven. Down Came the Sun. Steffan, Leonard, illus. Hall, Mary A. LC 72-176097. (Illus.). 64p. (gr. 3 up). 1972. 8.95 (ISBN 0-87929-010-2). Barlenmir.

Halloran, Phyllis. I'd Like to Hear a Flower Grow. Reynolds, Carol, illus. LC 89-60979. 56p. (gr. k-8). 1989. 12.95 (ISBN 0-943867-02-9). Reading Inc.

Hammond, Doreen. Freda the Frog & Other Poems. 48p. (gr. 7-10). 1986. pap. 20.00X (ISBN 0-317-52593-X, Pub. by A H Stockwell England). State Mutual Bk.

Harper, Jo. The Harper's Voices: Caves & Cowboys: Family Song Book. George, R. Jefferson, photos by. Boustany, Robert, illus. (ENG & SPA.). 20p. (Orig.). (gr. 1-5). 1988. pap. 10.95 incl. cassette (ISBN 0-929932-00-5). Harpers Voice.

—The Harper's Voices: Pals, Potions, & Pixies: Family Songbook. George, R. Jefferson, photos by. Boustany, Robert, illus. (SPA & ENG.). 20p. (Orig.). (gr. 1-5). 1988. pap. 10.95 incl. cassette (ISBN 0-929932-01-3). Harpers Voice.

Harrison, Michael & Stuart-Clark, Christopher. The Oxford Book of Story Poems. (Illus.). 176p. (gr. 3 up). 1990. jacketed 17.95 (ISBN 0-19-276087-4). Oxford U Pr.

Harrison, Ted. Children of the Yukon. LC 77-79543. (Illus.). (gr. 1-4). 1977. pap. 6.95 (ISBN 0-88776-163-1). Tundra Bks.

Hazard, James. Look Both Ways. 55p. (Orig.). (gr. 4-6). 1987. pap. 4.25 (ISBN 0-935399-03-8). Main St Pub.

Hazeltine, Alice I., compiled by. The Year Around: Poems for Children. Hazeltine, Smith, compiled by. LC 72-11921. (gr. 7 up). 1973. Repr. of 1956 ed. 15.00 (ISBN 0-8369-6403-9). Ayer Co Pubs.

Hearne, Betsy. Love Lines: Poetry in Person. LC 87-1737. 72p. (gr. 9 up). 1987. 10.95 (ISBN 0-689-50437-3, M K McElderry). Macmillan Child Grp.

Hedge-Cheney, Jacquelyn & Cheney, Roland J. The Little Daisy Girl & Other Poems. Hedge-Cheney, Jacquelyn & Cheny, Roland J., illus. 48p. (Orig.). (gr. 6 up). 1989. pap. write for info (ISBN 0-9621283-0-9). Lil Daisy Bks.

Hegler, Michele & Hegler, Jodi. Faces of the World. Cuthbert, Peter, illus. 79p. (gr. 9-12). 1989. pap. 7.95 (ISBN 0-945362-02-1). Best Sllrs TX.

Heylen, Jill & Jellett, Celia, eds. Someone Is Flying Balloons. Argent, Kerry, illus. LC 85-23136. 136p. (gr. 5-7). 1986. 14.95 (ISBN 0-932238-33-5, Pub. by Mad Hatter Bks). Slawson Comm.

Higman, Anita. Willing to Grow. Cuthbert, Peter, illus. 45p. (gr. 9-12). 1988. pap. 4.95 (ISBN 0-945362-01-3). Best Sllrs TX.

Hill, Charlotte M. Poetry for Wee Folks. Hill, Fred D., ed. Young, Elaine, et al, illus. LC 88-70281. 31p. (gr. k-3). 1988. 11.95 (ISBN 0-9620182-0-1); pap. 6.95 (ISBN 0-9620182-2-8). Charill Pubs. Poetry For Wee Folks is a collection of contemporary poems for young children, particularly, African/American Children. The author, Charlotte M. Hill, a retired teacher, has written the book from a child's perspective. She has attempted to help children gain an appreciation of their heritage & to cultivate positive self-images in them. The poems reflect her 26 years experience with children whom she has observed at work & at play. The poetry & colorful illustrations highlight such topics as: a. self-pride b. self-discipline c. truthfulness d. learning e. love of family f. responsibility g. fun & fantasy. Reviews & endorsement from administrators, teachers, parents, librarians, newspapers & magazines have been excellent. Says Ebony Magazine's August 1988 Special Edition- "Poetry for Wee Folks explores a variety of emotions, events & situations- from Christmas to the use of correct English. Mrs. Hill displays a keen sense of the rhythms of children's speech, but Poetry For Wee Folks is enjoyable reading for the entire family." Charill Publishers has published a 5 volume collection of 'Wee Folks Readers' written by Hill & a modern day fairy tale by Fred Hill. ***Publisher Provided Annotation.***

Hill, H, compiled by. New Coasts & Strange Harbors: Discovering Poems. Perkins, A, compiled by. LC 74-12343. (Illus.). 224p. (gr. 7 up). 1974. 12.95 (ISBN 0-690-00271-8, Crowell Jr Bks). HarpC Child Bks.

Hill, Helen, et al. Dusk to Dawn: Poems of Night. Burgess, Anne, illus. LC 80-770. 64p. (gr. 5 up). 1981. 11.95i (ISBN 0-690-04065-2, Crowell Jr Bks). HarpC Child Bks.

Hillman, Priscilla. Merry Mouse Christmas ABC. Hillman, Priscilla, illus. LC 79-6586. 32p. (ps-1). 1980. pap. 4.95 (ISBN 0-385-15596-4). Doubleday.

The Hippopotamus. LC 88-16777. (Illus.). 16p. (Orig.). 1988. pap. 3.95 (ISBN 0-8092-4463-2, Calico Bks). Contemp Bks.

Hodgson, Harriet W. My First Fourth of July Book. Hohag, Linda, illus. LC 86-30987. 32p. (ps-2). 1987. PLB 14.60 (ISBN 0-516-02907-X); pap. 3.95 (ISBN 0-516-42907-8). Childrens.

Homer. The Iliad. Shaw, Charlie, illus. Stewart, Diana, adapted By. LC 80-15669. (Illus.). 48p. (gr. 4 up). 1983. PLB 17.32 (ISBN 0-8172-1663-4); pap. 9.27 (ISBN 0-8172-2011-9). Raintree Pubs.

—The Odyssey. Hack, Konrad, illus. Stewart, Diana, adapted by. LC 79-24480. (Illus.). 48p. (gr. 4 up). 1983. PLB 17.32 (ISBN 0-8172-1654-5); pap. 9.27 (ISBN 0-8172-2017-8). Raintree Pubs.

Hopkins, Lee B. Elves, Fairies & Gnomes. Hoffman, Rosekrans, illus. LC 79-19753. (ps-2). 1980. Knopf.

—The Sky Is Full of Song. Zimmer, Dirk, illus. LC 82-48263. 48p. (gr. k-3). 1987. pap. 4.95 (ISBN 0-06-446064-9, Trophy). HarpC Child Bks.

Hopkins, Lee B., compiled by. By Myself. Coalson, Glo, illus. LC 79-7830. 40p. (gr. 1-3). 1980. 11.95 (ISBN 0-690-04070-9, Crowell Jr Bks). HarpC Child Bks.

Hopkins, Lee B., ed. Morning, Noon & Nightime, Too. Hannans, Nancy, illus. LC 78-22484. 64p. (gr. 2-5). 1980. PLB 11.89 (ISBN 0-06-022577-7). HarpC Child Bks.

—Rainbows Are Made: Poems by Carl Sandburg. Eichenberg, Fritz, illus. LC 82-47934. (gr. k up). 1982. 17.95 (ISBN 0-15-265480-1, HJ). HarBraceJ.

—Side by Side: Poems to Read Together. Knight, Hilary, illus. 96p. (gr. 1 up). 1988. pap. 14.95 (ISBN 0-671-63579-4). S&S Trade.

Huff, Barbara A. Once Inside the Library, Vol. 1. (ps-4). 1990. 14.95 (ISBN 0-316-37967-0). Little.

Huffaker, Alice. That First Christmas Day. Neeley, Keith, illus. (Orig.). 1989. pap. 3.25 (ISBN 0-8024-2637-9). Moody.

Hughes, Roger. The Hippopotamus's Birthday: And Other Poems about Animals & Birds. (Illus.). 28p. (ps-2). 1988. 15.95 (ISBN 0-340-38681-9, Pub. by Hodder & Stoughton UK). Trafalgar Sq.

Hughes, Ted. Meet My Folks! Adamson, George, illus. 64p. (gr. 3 up). 1987. pap. 6.95 (ISBN 0-571-13644-3). Faber & Faber.

Hummel, Berta. The Hummel. Hummel, Berta, illus. 1972. 15.75 (ISBN 0-88431-129-5). IBD Ltd.

Jabar, Cynthia. Bored Blue? Think What You Can Do. (ps-3). 1991. 14.95 (ISBN 0-316-43458-2). Little.

Jackson, Bobby. Pops, Chops & Crops. LC 89-51297. 44p. (gr. k-3). 1990. 5.95 (ISBN 1-55523-259-0). Winston-Derek.

Janeczko, Paul, ed. Poetspeak. 256p. (gr. 7 up). 1991. pap. 8.95 (ISBN 0-02-043850-8, Collier Young Ad). Macmillan Child Grp.

Janeczko, Paul B. Brickyard Summer. Rush, Ken, illus. LC 89-42542. 64p. (gr. 7 up). 1989. 13.95 (ISBN 0-531-05846-8); PLB 13.99 (ISBN 0-531-08446-9). Orchard Bks Watts.

—The Place My Words Are Looking For: What Poets Say about & Through Their Work. LC 89-39331. 160p. (gr. 4-8). 1990. 13.95 (ISBN 0-02-747671-5, Bradbury Pr). Macmillan Child Grp.

Janeczko, Paul B., selected by. The Music of What Happens: Poems That Tell Stories. LC 87-30791. 208p. (gr. 7 up). 1988. 14.95 (ISBN 0-531-05757-7); PLB 14.99 (ISBN 0-531-08357-8). Orchard Bks Watts.

Janeczko, Paul B., compiled by. This Delicious Day: Sixty-Five Poems. LC 87-7717. 96p. (gr. 4-6). 1987. 11.95 (ISBN 0-531-05724-0); PLB 11.99 (ISBN 0-531-08324-1). Orchard Bks Watts.

Janger, Kathie, ed. Rainbow Collection, 1987: Stories & Poetry by Young People. Ishikawa, Yoko, illus. Johnson, Rafer, intro. by. (Illus.). 160p. (gr. 1-8). 1987. pap. text ed. 6.00 (ISBN 0-929889-02-9). Young Writers Contest Found.

—Rainbow Collection, 1988: Stories & Poetry by Young People. Turtiainen, Tuomas, illus. Valenti, Jack, intro. by. (Illus.). 160p. (gr. 1-8). 1988. pap. 6.00 (ISBN 0-929889-03-7). Young Writers Contest Found.

Janger, Kathie & Korenblit, Joan, eds. Rainbow Collection, 1985: Stories & Poetry by Young People. Allen, Steve, frwd. by. 160p. (gr. 1-8). 1985. pap. 6.00 (ISBN 0-929889-00-2). Young Writers Contest Found.

—Rainbow Collection, 1986: Stories & Poetry by Young People. Scott, Willard, frwd. by. 160p. (gr. 1-8). 1986. pap. 6.00 (ISBN 0-929889-01-0). Young Writers Contest Found.

Johnson, George F. Poems & Things, Vol. 1. 98p. (Orig.). (gr. 9-12). 1989. write for info. G F Johnson.

Johnson, Kristopher K. A Day Without Cartoons: Poetry for Gifted Students. Kester, Ellen S., ed. (Illus.). 50p. (Orig.). (gr. 3-8). Date not set. pap. 6.95 (ISBN 0-685-26282-0). Pickwick Pubs.

Johnston, Tony. I'm Gonna Tell Mama I Want an Iguana. Hoban, Lillian, illus. 32p. (ps-3). 1990. 14.95 (ISBN 0-399-21934-X, Putnam). Putnam Pub Group.

Jones, Charla. Poetry Patterns. (Illus.). 32p. (gr. 3-6). 1985. pap. 4.95 (ISBN 0-913839-31-0). Bk Lures.

Joseph, Lynn. Coconut Kind of Day. 32p. 1990. 13.95 (ISBN 0-688-09119-9); PLB 13.88 (ISBN 0-688-09120-2). Lothrop.

Katz, Bobbi. Month by Month: A Care Bear Book of Poems. Barto, Bobbi, illus. LC 84-3283. 40p. (ps-3). 1984. 3.95 (ISBN 0-394-86719-X, Random Juv); lib. bdg. 4.99 (ISBN 0-394-96719-4). Random.

—Poems for Small Friends. Fujikawa, Ayo, illus. LC 88-27444. 32p. (ps-1). 1989. Random.

Katz, Bobbi, ed. A Popple in Your Pocket & Other Funny Poems. Ewers, Joe, illus. LC 85-43342. 32p. (gr. k-5). 1986. 4.95 (ISBN 0-394-88042-0). Random.

Keel-Williams, Mildred. Legacies of a Shopping Bag Lady: Poems of Life. Holmes, Darryl, ed. George, Anthony & Washington, Ruby, photos by. Harewood, Lasana K., frwd. by. LC 84-62520. (Illus.). 72p. (Orig.). (gr. 7 up). 1984. pap. 6.00 (ISBN 0-9614084-1-3). Mus Fed Ink.

Kellogg, Mary G. Doing Things & Happenings. Rytter, Peggy, illus. LC 80-80271. 90p. (gr. 1-6). 1979. 6.95 (ISBN 0-9603972-0-5); pap. 4.95 (ISBN 0-9603972-1-3). Bks by Kellogg.

Kenneally, Christy. Miracles & Me: Poems for Children. Ortiz, Gloria C., illus. 64p. (gr. 2-3). 1986. pap. 3.95 (ISBN 0-8091-6558-9). Paulist Pr.

Kennedy, X. J. Brats. Watts, James, illus. LC 85-20018. 48p. (gr. 3 up). 1986. 11.95 (ISBN 0-689-50392-X, M K McElderry). Macmillan Child Grp.

—The Forgetful Wishing Well: Poems for Young People. Incisa, Monica, illus. LC 84-45977. 96p. (gr. 4 up). 1985. 11.95 (ISBN 0-689-50317-2, M K McElderry). Macmillan Child Grp.

—Fresh Brats. Watts, James, illus. LC 89-38031. 48p. (gr. 3-5). 1990. 12.95 (ISBN 0-689-50499-3, M K McElderry). Macmillan Child Grp.

—Ghastlies, Goops & Pincushions: Nonsense Verse. Barrett, Ron, illus. (gr. 3 up). 1989. 12.95 (ISBN 0-689-50477-2, M K McElderry). Macmillan Child Grp.

—The Kite That Braved Old Orchard Beach: Year-Round Poems for Young People. LC 90-20100. (Illus.). 96p. (gr. 4 up). 1991. SBE 12.95 (ISBN 0-689-50507-8, M K McElderry). Macmillan Child Grp.

Kennedy, X. J. & Kennedy, Dorothy M. Knock at a Star: A Child's Introduction to Poetry. Weinhaus, Karen A., illus. 160p. (gr. 2-6). 1985. 14.95 (ISBN 0-316-48853-4); pap. 7.95 (ISBN 0-316-48854-2). Little.

Khayyam, Omar. Rubaiyat of Omar Khayyam. Fitzgerald, Edward, tr. (Illus.). (gr. 9 up). 1969. pap. 1.95 (ISBN 0-8049-0204-6, CL-204). Airmont.

Kimball, Richard S. A Funny Feeling. Reid, William K., Jr., illus. LC 87-32155. 64p. (Orig.). (gr. 3 up). 1988. pap. 7.95 (ISBN 0-944443-00-1). Green Timber.
This collection of 41 cleverly illustrated poems explores common feelings & sayings about them for entertainment & enlightenment of youngsters aged eight & above. Eight-

year olds will identify with Reginald Botts who was "tied up in knots & couldn't get his thoughts undone." Ten-year olds will enjoy the image of Louise being made small by the weight of the grudge she carries. Twelve-year olds will sympathize with Annie who has reached the age "when staying in means being left out" & "going out means being in." Everybody will be delighted by "tongue tied" Sid & by the many other characters & poems. With humor, this book allows readers & listeners to think about their own funny feelings & can open the way for discussion with parents, teachers, counselors, church groups, & friends. Paperback, $7.95.
Publisher Provided Annotation.

Klawitter, P. Poetry Parade. (gr. 4-6). 1987. 5.95 (ISBN 0-88160-156-X, LW 274). Learning Wks.

Knudson, R. R. & Swenson, May, eds. American Sports Poems. LC 87-24384. 240p. (gr. 6 up). 1988. 15.95 (ISBN 0-531-05753-4); PLB 15.99 (ISBN 0-531-08353-5). Orchard Bks Watts.

Koch, Kenneth & Farrell, Kate. Talking to the Sun: An Illustrated Anthology of Poems for Young People. LC 85-15428. 112p. (gr. 7 up). 1985. 19.95 (ISBN 0-8050-0144-1). H Holt & Co.

Krauss, Ruth. Monkey Day. Rowand, Phyllis, illus. 23p. (gr. k-5). 1973. pap. 8.00 (ISBN 0-912846-05-4). Bookstore Pr.

Kruss, James & Lewis, Naomi. Johnny Longnose. Eidrigevicius, Stasys, illus. LC 89-42612. 32p. (gr. k-3). 1990. 13.95 (ISBN 1-55858-023-9). North-South Bks NYC.

Kuskin, Karla. Dogs & Dragons, Trees & Dreams: A Collection of Poems. Kuskin, Karla, illus. LC 79-2814. 96p. (gr. 1-6). 1980. PLB 13.89 (ISBN 0-06-023544-6). HarpC Child Bks.

Langill, Ellen. Pompey Poems... Celebrating a Cat. Davenport, May, illus. LC 86-91603. 64p. (Orig.). (gr. 7-12). 1986. 10.25x (ISBN 0-943864-28-3); pap. 3.50x (ISBN 0-943864-26-7). Davenport.

Larrick, Nancy. Merry-Go-round Poetry Book. (ps-3). 1989. 14.95 (ISBN 0-385-30115-4). Doubleday.

—To the Moon & Back: A Collection of Poems. (ps-3). 1991. pap. 14.95 (ISBN 0-385-30159-6). Doubleday.

—When the Dark Comes Dancing: A Bedtime Poetry Book. Wallner, John, illus. LC 81-428. (ps-2). 1983. 17.95 (ISBN 0-399-20807-0, Philomel). Putnam Pub Group.

Lash, Jamie S. Righteous Rhymes, Vol. 1. Jackson, Jeff, illus. 24p. (gr. 2-7). 1983. pap. 2.95 (ISBN 0-915775-00-X, Dist. by Stardust). Love Song Mess Assn.

Lash, Jamie S., ed. Righteous Rhymes, Vol. 2. Jackson, Jeff, illus. 24p. (Orig.). 1987. pap. 2.95 (ISBN 0-915775-01-8). Love Song Mess Assn.

Lawrence, D. H. Birds, Beasts & the Third Thing: Poems. Provensen, Martin & Provensen, Alice, illus. LC 81-70405. 40p. 1982. 13.95 (ISBN 0-670-16779-7). Viking Child Bks.

Lear, Edward. The Owl & the Pussycat. Littlejohn, Clare, illus. LC 86-46115. 14p. (ps-3). 1987. 6.95 (ISBN 0-694-00193-7). HarpC Child Bks.

Le Mair, Henriette W., ed. & illus. Our Old Nursery Rhymes. 64p. (gr. k up). 1989. 13.95 (ISBN 0-399-21722-3, Philomel Bks). Putnam Pub Group.

Leo, Kathleen R., et al, eds. Waiting for the Apples. LC 82-62746. (Illus.). 100p. (Orig.). (gr. k up). 1983. pap. 6.50 (ISBN 0-9606678-2-2). Sylvan Pubns.

Lester, Julius. Who I Am. Gahr, David, illus. LC 73-15447. 64p. (gr. 7 up). 1974. 5.95 (ISBN 0-8037-8758-8). Dial Bks Young.

Levy, Nathan & Levy, Janet. There Are Those. Edwards, Joan, illus. LC 82-81111. 32p. (ps up). 1990. 21.95 (ISBN 0-9608240-0-6). NL Assoc Inc.
If you have gifted children in your life, this book "There Are Those," will put their special qualities into poetic words for you. The joy, excitement, challenge & frustration that the very bright children bring to themselves & to those around them are brought alive in this highly acclaimed poem. This hardcover book is illustrated with brilliant designs in vivid color. Destined to become a classic, this book will be loved by children from 8-88!
Publisher Provided Annotation.

Lewis, Claudia L. Long Ago in Oregon. Fontaine, Joel, illus. LC 86-45781. 64p. (gr. 3-7). 1987. 11.95 (ISBN 0-06-023839-9); PLB 11.89 (ISBN 0-06-023840-2). HarpC Child Bks.

Lewis, T., illus. The Calico Mother Goose Book of Earth, Moon & Sky. 32p. (gr. 2-5). 1989. 8.95 (ISBN 0-8092-4394-6, Calico Bks). Contemp Bks.

Lindbloom, James A. Make the Morning. Lindbloom, Nancy, illus. (gr. 3-8). 1977. pap. 3.00 (ISBN 0-89409-007-0). Childrens Art.

Lindsay, Vachel. Johnny Appleseed & Other Poems. 129p. 1981. Repr. PLB 11.95x (ISBN 0-89966-365-6). Buccaneer Bks.

—Johnny Appleseed & Other Poems. 138p. 1981. PLB 11.95x (ISBN 0-89967-039-3). Harmony Raine.

Little, Lessie J. Children of Long Ago: Poems. Gilchrist, Jan S., illus. 32p. (gr. 2-5). 1988. 13.95 (ISBN 0-399-21473-9, Philomel Bks). Putnam Pub Group.

Livingston, Myra C. Dilly Dilly Piccalilli: Poems for the Very Young. Christelow, Eileen, illus. (gr. 1 up). 1989. 12.95 (ISBN 0-689-50466-7, M K McElderry). Macmillan Child Grp.

—I Like You, If You Like Me: Poems of Friendship. LC 86-21108. 160p. (gr. 5 up). 1987. 12.95 (ISBN 0-689-50408-X, M K McElderry). Macmillan Child Grp.

—Monkey Puzzle & Other Poems. Frasconi, Antonio, illus. LC 84-3050. 64p. (gr. 6 up). 1984. 11.95 (ISBN 0-689-50310-5, M K McElderry). Macmillan Child Grp.

—Poems for Mothers. Ray, Deborah K., illus. LC 87-19629. 32p. (gr. k-3). 1988. reinforced bdg. 13.95 (ISBN 0-8234-0678-4). Holiday.

—Remembering & Other Poems. LC 89-2654. 64p. (gr. 3-7). 1989. 12.95 (ISBN 0-689-50489-6, M K McElderry). Macmillan Child Grp.

—A Song I Sang to You: A Selection of Poems. Tomes, Margot, illus. LC 84-4585. 96p. (ps-3). 1984. 12.95 (ISBN 0-15-277105-0, HJ). HarBraceJ.

—There Was a Place: And Other Poems. LC 88-12832. 40p. (gr. 3-7). 1988. 11.95 (ISBN 0-689-50464-0, M K McElderry). Macmillan Child Grp.

—Up in the Air. Fisher, Leonard E., illus. LC 88-23293. 32p. (gr. k-3). 1989. reinforced bdg. 14.95 (ISBN 0-8234-0736-5). Holiday.

—Valentine Poems. Livingston, Myra C., selected by. LC 85-31723. (Illus.). 32p. (gr. k-3). 1987. reinforced bdg. 13.95 (ISBN 0-8234-0587-7). Holiday.

—Worlds I Know & Other Poems. Arnold, Tim, illus. LC 85-7344. 64p. (gr. 4-7). 1985. text ed. 12.95 (ISBN 0-689-50332-6, Pub. by M K McElderry). Macmillan Child Grp.

Livingston, Myra C., selected by. Halloween Poems. Gammell, Stephen, illus. LC 89-1741. 32p. (gr. k-3). 1989. PLB 13.95 (ISBN 0-8234-0762-4). Holiday.

Livingston, Myra C., ed. Lots of Limericks. Perry, Rebecca, illus. LC 91-329. 128p. (gr. 3 up). 1991. 13.95 (ISBN 0-689-50531-0, M K McElderry). Macmillan Child Grp.

Livingston, Myra C., selected by. New Year's Poems. Tomes, Margot, illus. LC 86-22885. 32p. (gr. k-3). 1987. reinforced bdg. 12.95 (ISBN 0-8234-0641-5). Holiday.

—Poems for Grandmothers. Cullen-Clark, Patricia, illus. LC 90-55102. 32p. (gr. k-3). 1990. reinforced 12.95 (ISBN 0-8234-0830-2). Holiday.

—Poems for Jewish Holidays. Bloom, Lloyd, illus. LC 85-27179. 32p. (gr. 1-4). 1986. reinforced bdg. 13.95 (ISBN 0-8234-0606-7). Holiday.

Livingston, Myra C., ed. Thanksgiving Poems. Gammell, Stephen, illus. LC 85-762. 32p. (gr. 1-4). 1985. reinforced bdg. 13.95 (ISBN 0-8234-0570-2). Holiday.

Longfellow, Henry Wadsworth. Paul Revere's Ride. Parker, Nancy W., illus. LC 84-4139. 48p. (gr. 1 up). 1985. 14.95 (ISBN 0-688-04014-4); PLB 14.88 (ISBN 0-688-04015-2). Greenwillow.

Lyon, George-Ella. Together. LC 89-2892. (Illus.). 32p. (ps-1). 1989. 14.95 (ISBN 0-531-05831-X); PLB 14.99 (ISBN 0-531-08431-0). Orchard Bks Watts.

McCord, Catherine G. Of Butterflies & Buttercups. Scudder, Barbara J., illus. LC 85-61275. 64p. (gr. 5-12). 1985. 12.50 (ISBN 0-9614997-0-2). Buttercup Bks.

McCord, David. One at a Time. Kane, Henry B., illus. (gr. 4 up). 1986. 18.95 (ISBN 0-316-55516-9). Little.

—Speak Up: More Rhymes of the Never Was & Always Is. Simont, Marc, illus. 80p. (gr. 5 up). 1980. 13.95 (ISBN 0-316-55517-7). Little.

—Take Sky. Kane, Henry B., illus. (gr. 4 up). 1962. 12.95 (ISBN 0-316-55509-6). Little.

McCracken, Lisa. The Lilies' Edge. Taylor, Neil, illus. LC 86-40282. 48p. (gr. 1-3). 1987. 5.95 (ISBN 1-55523-036-9). Winston-Derek.

McCullough, Frances, ed. Love Is Like the Lion's Tooth. LC 77-25659. 96p. (gr. 7 up). 1984. 12.95 (ISBN 0-06-024138-1); PLB 12.89 (ISBN 0-06-024139-X). HarpC Child Bks.

McMahon, Sean, ed. Poolbeg Book of Children's Verse. 240p. 1987. pap. 9.95 (ISBN 0-905169-88-3, Pub. by Poolbeg Press Ltd Eire). Dufour.

Mcmillan, Bruce. One Sun: A Book of Terse Verse. Mcmillan, Bruce, illus. LC 89-24625. 32p. (ps-3). 1990. PLB 14.95 (ISBN 0-8234-0810-8). Holiday.

McNaughton, Colin. Who's Been Sleeping in My Porridge? McNaughton, Colin, illus. 96p. (gr. k-4). 1990. 15.95 (ISBN 0-8249-8455-2). Ideals.

MacPherson, Jennifer B. To Attempt a Tower. LC 85-90339. 84p. (gr. 9-12). 1985. 16.95 (ISBN 0-9614849-0-X); pap. 8.95 (ISBN 0-9614849-1-8). MacPherson Pub.

Magorian, James. The Witches' Olympics. LC 83-71262. 44p. (gr. 4-7). 1983. pap. 5.00 (ISBN 0-930674-10-3). Black Oak.

Maguire, Arlene. Life's Changes. Holtman, Noel, illus. LC 91-9353. 32p. (Orig.). (ps-5). 1991. 6.95 (ISBN 0-941992-26-8). Los Arboles Pub.

Manes, Stephen. Some of the Adventures of Rhode Island Red. Joyce, William, illus. LC 89-35397. 128p. (gr. 3-7). 1990. 10.95 (ISBN 0-397-32347-6, Lipp Jr Bks); PLB 10.89 (ISBN 0-397-32348-4, Lipp Jr Bks). HarpC Child Bks.

Marrs, Carol R. Pet Cobwebs. Marrs, Greg, illus. 112p. (gr. 1 up). 1988. 12.95 (ISBN 0-9621234-0-4). Funny Farm Pr.

Marsh, James. Bizarre Birds & Beasts: Animal Verses. 1991. 12.95 (ISBN 0-8037-1046-1). Dial Bks Young.

Matanah. Love Bones. Ridge, Delores F., ed. 75p. (Orig.). (gr. 9). 1974. pap. text ed. 4.95 (ISBN 0-9600978-1-3). Knees Pbk.

Mazer, Norma F. & Lewis, Margorie. Waltzing on Water: Poetry by Women. (Orig.). (gr. k-12). 1989. pap. 3.50 (ISBN 0-440-20257-4, LFL). Dell.

Mendoza, George & Wilson, Gahan. Hairticklers. (Illus.). 128p. (gr. 5 up). 1989. cloth 13.95 (ISBN 0-89815-332-8); pap. 8.95 (ISBN 0-89815-330-1). Ten Speed Pr.

Mennella, Roxanna. Roxanna Mennella, in Search of a Song: Inner Clockwork, Vol. 8. Fisher, Barbara, ed. (Illus.). 10p. (Orig.). (gr. 5-9). 1985. pap. 2.00 (ISBN 0-934830-36-3). Ten Penny.

Merriam, Eve. Chortles: New & Selected Wordplay Poems. Hamanaka, Sheila, illus. LC 88-29129. 64p. (gr. 3-7). 1989. 11.95 (ISBN 0-688-08152-5); PLB 11.88 (ISBN 0-688-08153-3, Morrow Jr Bks). Morrow Jr Bks.

—Fresh Paint: New Poems. Frampton, David, illus. LC 85-23742. 48p. (gr. 5 up). 1986. 12.95 (ISBN 0-02-766860-6, Mcmillan Child Bk). Macmillan Child Grp.

—A Poem for a Pickle: Funnybone Verses. Hamanaka, Sheila, illus. LC 88-22047. 40p. (gr. k up). 1989. 12.95 (ISBN 0-688-08137-1); PLB 12.88 (ISBN 0-688-08138-X, Morrow Jr Bks). Morrow Jr Bks.

—A Sky Full of Poems. Gaffney-Kessell, Walter, illus. (Orig.). (gr. k-6). 1986. pap. 3.25 (ISBN 0-440-47986-X, YB). Dell.

—You Be Good & I'll Be Night: Jump-on-the-Bed-Poems. Schmidt, Karen L., illus. LC 87-24859. 40p. (ps-2). 1988. 13.95 (ISBN 0-688-06742-5); PLB 13.88 (ISBN 0-688-06743-3, Morrow Jr Bks). Morrow Jr Bks.

Millay, Edna St. Vincent. Edna St. Vincent Millay's Poems Selected for Young People. Keller, Ronald, illus. LC 77-25671. 120p. (gr. 7 up). 1979. 13.95 (ISBN 0-06-024218-3). HarpC Child Bks.

Miller, May. Halfway to the Sun. Pauker, John, intro. by. LC 81-50427. (Illus.). 50p. (Orig.). (gr. 6). 1981. pap. text ed. 7.00 (ISBN 0-931846-17-X). Wash Writers Pub.

Miller, Vousette T. Poems by Shining Star: The Voice of Shining Star. 16p. (Orig.). (ps-6). 1990. pap. write for info. wkbk. (ISBN 0-9619641-1-1). Vous Etes Tres Belle.

Milne, A. A. Now We Are Six. Shepard, Ernest H., illus. 112p. (ps up). 1988. 9.95 (ISBN 0-525-44446-7, DCB). Dutton Child Bks.

—When We Were Very Young. Shepard, Ernest H., illus. 112p. (ps up). 1988. 9.95 (ISBN 0-525-44445-9, DCB). Dutton Child Bks.

Milnes, Gerald. Granny Will Your Dog Bite? And Other Mountain Rhymes. Root, Kimberly, illus. LC 88-27350. 48p. 1990. 14.95 (ISBN 0-394-84749-0); PLB 15.99 (ISBN 0-394-94749-5). Knopf.

Mitchell, Adrian. Nothingmas Day & Other Poems for Kids & Their Allies. Lawrence, John, illus. 96p. (gr. 2-8). 1987. pap. 8.95 (ISBN 0-8052-8168-1, Pub. by Allison & Busby England). Schocken.

Molner, Gwen. I Said to Sam. Freire, Carlos, illus. 48p. (gr. k-3). Big Book. pap. 22.00 (ISBN 0-590-71360-4); pap. 2.50 (ISBN 0-590-71367-1). Scholastic Inc.

Moncure, Jane B. My First Thanksgiving Book. Connelly, Gwen, illus. LC 84-9433. 32p. (ps-2). 1984. PLB 14.60 (ISBN 0-516-02903-7); pap. 3.95 (ISBN 0-516-42903-5). Childrens.

—Wishes, Whispers & Secrets. Hook, Frances, illus. LC 78-31295. (ps-3). 1979. PLB 12.96 (ISBN 0-89565-024-X). Childs World.

Montgomery, Michael. Night, America. (Illus.). 24p. (ps). 1989. 11.95 (ISBN 0-8092-4397-0, Calico Bks). Contemp Bks.

Moore, Clement C. The Night Before Christmas. Gorsline, Douglas, illus. LC 75-7511. 32p. (gr. 2-6). 1975. pap. 2.25 (ISBN 0-394-83019-9, Random Juv). Random.

—The Night Before Christmas. Wilburn, Kathy, illus. 24p. (ps-1). 1985. write for info. (ISBN 0-307-10202-5, Pub. by Golden Bks). Western Pub.

—The Night Before Christmas: An Antique Reproduction of a Christmas Classic. (Illus.). 32p. 1989. 15.95 (ISBN 0-399-21614-6, Philomel Bks). Putnam Pub Group.

Morrison, Lillian. Best Wishes, Amen: A New Collection of Autograph Verses. Lustig, Loretta, illus. LC 74-2456. 208p. (gr. 4-6). 1989. pap. 4.50 (ISBN 0-06-446089-4, Trophy). HarpC Child Bks.

Morton, Miriam. The Moon Is Like a Silver Sickle: A Celebration of Poetry by Russian Children. LC 72-77768. (Illus.). (gr. 5 up). 1972. 4.95 (ISBN 0-671-65198-6, Little Simon). S&S Trade.

Moss, Graveyard. Graveyard Moss Is Still Alive. 48p. (Orig.). (gr. 9). 1988. pap. 5.00 (ISBN 0-945237-00-6). Morgan Virginia Pub.

Moss, Jeffrey. The Butterfly Jar. Demarest, Chris, illus. (ps up). 1989. 14.95 (ISBN 0-553-05704-9). Bantam.

Most, Bernard. Four & Twenty Dinosaurs. Most, Bernard, illus. LC 89-34472. 40p. (ps-2). 1990. 8.95 (ISBN 0-06-024376-7); PLB 13.89 (ISBN 0-06-024377-5). HarpC Child Bks.

Mother Goof, pseud. The Sheep That Was Allergic to Wool. Mother Goof, illus. LC 89-61740. 17p. (Orig.). (gr. 1-2). 1989. text ed. 3.00 (ISBN 0-685-26114-X). Sunflower Hill.

Myers, Garry C. Christmas Wishes. 32p. (gr. 2-6). 3.95 (ISBN 0-87534-602-2). Highlights.

—Wishes. 32p. (gr. 4-6). Repr. of 1969 ed. 3.95 (ISBN 0-87534-601-4). Highlights.

Nash, Ogden. The Cruise of the Aardvark. Watson, Wendy, illus. 48p. (ps up). 1989. pap. 5.95 (ISBN 0-87131-570-X). M Evans.

—Custard & Company. Blake, Quentin, illus. 128p. (gr. 2-6). 1985. 12.95 (ISBN 0-316-59834-8); pap. 6.95 (ISBN 0-316-59855-0). Little.

Neville, Mary, ed. If a Poem Bothers You. (Illus.). 64p. (Orig.). (gr. 2-6). 1991. pap. 3.75x (ISBN 0-913678-14-7). New Day Pr.

Newell, Peter. The Slant Book. Newell, Peter, illus. LC 67-12304. 50p. (gr. k-4). 1967. Repr. of 1910 ed. 12.95 (ISBN 0-8048-0532-6). C E Tuttle.

Nichols, Grace. Come on into My Tropical Garden: Poems for Children. Binch, Caroline, illus. LC 89-36335. 48p. (gr. 2-6). 1990. 10.95 (ISBN 0-397-32350-6, Lipp Jr Bks); PLB 10.89 (ISBN 0-397-32349-2, Lipp Jr Bks). HarpC Child Bks.

Nielsen-Barsuhn, Rochelle. In Fall. Claude, Marie, illus. LC 85-12817. 32p. (ps-2). 1985. PLB 11.95 (ISBN 0-89565-329-X). Childs World.

Nister, Ernest. Christmas Surprises: An Antique Revolving Picture Book. (Illus.). 20p. 1990. 16.95 (ISBN 0-399-22160-3, Philomel Bks). Putnam Pub Group.

—A Day in the Country. (Illus.). 10p. 1990. 5.95 (ISBN 0-399-21959-5, Philomel Bks). Putnam Pub Group.

—Favorite Animals. (Illus.). 10p. 1989. pap. 4.95 (ISBN 0-399-21728-2, Philomel Bks). Putnam Pub Group.

—My Best Friend. (Illus.). 10p. 1990. 5.95 (ISBN 0-399-21960-9, Philomel Bks). Putnam Pub Group.

Nister, Ernest & Bingham, Clifton. Revolving Pictures. LC 79-12438. (Illus.). (ps-4). 1981. 10.95 (ISBN 0-399-20802-X, Philomel). Putnam Pub Group.

Norman, Charles. The Hornbean Tree & Other Poems. Rand, Ted, illus. LC 87-12033. 32p. (gr. k-4). 1988. 12.95 (ISBN 0-8050-0417-3). H Holt & Co.

Norskog, Howard L. High Country Ballads: Cowboy Poetry. 80p. (Orig.). (gr. 8 up). 1988. pap. 6.99 (ISBN 0-685-30409-4). H L Norskog.

—Yesterdays Trails: Cowboy Poetry. 49p. (gr. 8 up). 1989. pap. 6.99 (ISBN 0-685-30410-8). H L Norskog.

Noyes, Alfred. The Highwayman. Mikolaycak, Charles, illus. LC 83-725. 40p. (gr. 5 up). 1983. 11.95 (ISBN 0-688-02117-4). Lothrop.

Nye, Robert. Beowulf. 96p. (gr. 5 up). 1982. pap. 2.95 (ISBN 0-440-90560-5, LFL). Dell.

NYS Waterways Project Child Poet Supplement. (Illus.). 7p. (Orig.). (gr. 1-5). 1979. pap. 0.50 (ISBN 0-934830-17-7). Ten Penny.

O'Brien, John, illus. The Calico Mother Goose Book of Games, Riddles, & Tongue Twisters. 48p. (gr. 2-5). 1989. 9.95 (ISBN 0-8092-4395-4, Calico Bks). Contemp Bks.

Pagliaro, Penny, ed. I Like Poems & Poems Like Me. Kim Chee, Wendy, illus. LC 76-50343. (gr. 1-6). 1977. PLB 7.95 (ISBN 0-916630-03-X). Pr Pacifica.

Pagnucci, Gianfranco, ed. Face the Poem. (Illus.). 32p. (Orig.). (gr. 2-8). 1979. Incl. animal poems with animal face masks for choral readings. 3.95 (ISBN 0-929326-02-4). Bur Oak Pr Inc.

Paul, Ted. The Christmas Collie. Kummer, Mary, illus. 42p. (ps-7). 1989. 12.95 (ISBN 0-89802-548-6). Beautiful Am.

Peck, Richard. Sound & Silences. (gr. k-12). 1990. pap. 3.95 (ISBN 0-440-98171-9, LFL). Dell.

Perry, Marion. Dishes. Walsh, Joy, ed. Michael, Linda, illus. 25p. Date not set. pap. 5.00 (ISBN 0-938838-29-6). Textile Bridge.

Petersham, Maud & Petersham, Miska. The Rooster Crows: A Book of American Rhymes & Jingles. Petersham, Maud & Petersham, Miska, illus. LC 87-1138. 64p. (ps-3). 1987. pap. 4.95 (ISBN 0-689-71153-0, Aladdin). Macmillan Child Grp.

Peterson, Gayle & Kelley, Ying, eds. A Chance to Live: Children's Poems & Songs for Peace in a Nuclear Age. (Illus.). 102p. (gr. 4-9). 1985. Incl. cassette. 12.95 (ISBN 0-939508-03-6). Resc World Hlth.

Philipps, Myra. Smooth As Silk. 2nd ed. Ramon, Estelle, illus. (gr. 3 up). 1979. 1.95 (ISBN 0-686-10960-0). Basin Pub.

Plath, Sylvia. The Bed Book. McCully, Emily A., illus. LC 76-3825. 40p. (ps-3). 1976. 12.95 (ISBN 0-06-024746-0). HarpC Child Bks.

—The Bed Book. McCully, Emily A., illus. LC 76-3825. 40p. (ps-3). 1989. pap. 5.95 (ISBN 0-06-443184-3, Trophy). HarpC Child Bks.

Plotz, Helen. Imagination's Other Place: Poems of Science & Mathematics. Reissue. ed. Leighton, Clare, illus. LC 55-9216. 200p. (gr. 7 up). 1987. PLB 12.89 (ISBN 0-690-04700-2, Crowell Jr Bks). HarpC Child Bks.

Pomerantz, Charlotte. All Asleep. Tafuri, Nancy, illus. 32p. (ps-1). 1986. pap. 3.95 (ISBN 0-14-050548-2, Puffin). Puffin Bks.

Poskanzer, Susan. Riddles about Hannukah. Brook, Bonnie, ed. Gray, Rob, illus. 32p. (ps-3). 1990. 5.95 (ISBN 0-671-70555-5); PLB 10.98 (ISBN 0-671-70553-9). Silver Pr.

Poulin, Stephane. Pourrais-Tu Arreter Josephine? (FRE., Illus.). 24p. (ps-3). 1989. 12.95 (ISBN 0-88776-217-4); pap. 6.95 (ISBN 0-88776-228-X). Tundra Bks.

Prelutsky, Jack. The Baby Uggs Are Hatching! Stevenson, James, illus. LC 81-7266. 32p. (gr. k-3). 1982. 13.95 (ISBN 0-688-00922-0); PLB 13.88 (ISBN 0-688-00923-9). Greenwillow.

—The Headless Horseman Rides Tonight. Lobel, Arnold, illus. LC 80-10372. 40p. (gr. 1-4). 1980. 13.95 (ISBN 0-688-80273-7); PLB 13.88 (ISBN 0-688-84273-9). Greenwillow.

—It's Thanksgiving. Hafner, Marylin, illus. LC 81-1929. 48p. (gr. 1-3). 1982. 12.95 (ISBN 0-688-00441-5); lib. bdg. 12.88 (ISBN 0-688-00442-3). Greenwillow.

—My Parents Think I'm Sleeping. Abolafia, Yossi, illus. LC 84-13640. 48p. (gr. 2-4). 1985. 13.95 (ISBN 0-688-04018-7); lib. bdg. 13.88 (ISBN 0-688-04019-5). Greenwillow.

—The New Kid on the Block. Stevenson, James, illus. LC 83-20621. 160p. (gr. 1 up). 1984. 14.95 (ISBN 0-688-02271-5); PLB 14.88 (ISBN 0-688-02272-3). Greenwillow.

—Nightmares: Poems to Trouble Your Sleep. Lobel, Arnold, illus. LC 76-4820. 40p. (gr. 3 up). 1976. 13.95 (ISBN 0-688-80053-X); PLB 13.88 (ISBN 0-688-84053-1). Greenwillow.

—The Queen of Eene. Chess, Victoria, illus. LC 77-17311. 32p. (gr. k-3). 1978. PLB 14.88 (ISBN 0-688-84144-9). Greenwillow.

—Rainy, Rainy Saturday. Hafner, Marilyn, illus. LC 79-22217. 48p. (gr. 1-3). 1980. 13.95 (ISBN 0-688-80252-4); PLB 13.88 (ISBN 0-688-84252-6). Greenwillow.

—Ride a Purple Pelican. Williams, Garth, illus. LC 84-6024. 64p. (ps up). 1986. 15.95 (ISBN 0-688-04031-4). Greenwillow.

—Rolling Harvey Down the Hill. Chess, Victoria, illus. LC 79-18236. 32p. (gr. k-3). 1980. 12.95 (ISBN 0-688-80258-3); PLB 12.88 (ISBN 0-688-84258-5). Greenwillow.

—The Sheriff of Rottenshot. Chess, Victoria, illus. LC 81-6420. 32p. (gr. k-3). 1982. 12.95 (ISBN 0-688-00205-6); PLB 13.88 (ISBN 0-688-00198-X). Greenwillow.

—The Snopp on the Sidewalk & Other Poems. Barton, Byron, illus. LC 76-46323. 32p. (gr. 3 up). 1977. PLB 11.88 (ISBN 0-688-84084-1). Greenwillow.

—Tyrannosaurus Was a Beast. LC 87-25131. (Illus.). 32p. (ps-6). 1988. 13.95 (ISBN 0-688-06442-6); lib. bdg. 13.88 (ISBN 0-688-06443-4). Greenwillow.

Prelutsky, Jack, intro. by. Poems of A. Nonny Mouse. Drescher, Henrik, illus. LC 89-31672. 48p. (gr. 1-7). 1989. 12.95 (ISBN 0-394-88711-5); lib. bdg. 14.99 (ISBN 0-394-98711-X). Knopf.

Provensen, Alice & Provensen, Martin, illus. A Peaceable Kingdom: The Shaker Abecedarius. Barsam, Richard M., afterword by. LC 78-125. 42p. (gr. k-2). 1978. pap. 13.95 (ISBN 0-670-54500-7). Viking Child Bks.

Pyle, Howard. The Wonder Clock or, Four & Twenty Marvelous Tales, Being One for Each Hour of the Day. (Illus.). xiv, 319p. (gr. 3-6). pap. 7.95 (ISBN 0-486-21446-X). Dover.

Rabbitts, Muriel J. Thought of Childhood. 1991. 10.95 (ISBN 0-533-09371-6). Vantage.

Reece, Colleen L. My First Christmas Book. Hohag, Linda, illus. LC 84-9431. 32p. (ps-2). 1984. lib. bdg. 14.60 (ISBN 0-516-02901-0); pap. 3.95 (ISBN 0-516-42901-9). Childrens.

—My First Halloween Book. Peltier, Pam, illus. LC 84-9431. 32p. (ps-2). 1984. PLB 14.60 (ISBN 0-516-02902-9); pap. 3.95 (ISBN 0-516-42902-7). Childrens.

Reeves, James. Ragged Robin, Poems from A to Z. (ps-4). 1990. 16.95 (ISBN 0-316-73829-8). Little.

Rice, James. Texas Night Before Christmas. Rice, James, illus. 32p. (gr. 1-6). 1986. 11.95 (ISBN 0-88289-603-2). Pelican.

Ricken, Robert. Love Me When I'm Most Unlovable, Vol. II. 32p. (gr. 6-9). 1987. pap. 3.00 (ISBN 0-88210-198-6). Natl Assn Principals.

Riley, James W. Joyful Poems for Children. LC 60-14663. (gr. 2-6). 1960. 5.95 (ISBN 0-672-50342-5, Bobbs). Macmillan.

Rivlin, Asher E. & Gimmestad, Nancy, eds. Poetry Unfolding Basic Kit. 450p. (gr. 4-12). 1983. pap. 200.00 (ISBN 0-915291-05-3). Know Unltd.

Roche, P. K. At Christmas Be Merry: Poems for Christmas Week. Roche, P. K., illus. LC 84-21917. 32p. (ps-3). 1986. pap. 11.95 (ISBN 0-670-80421-5). Viking Child Bks.

Rockwell, Harlow. My Kitchen. LC 79-15929. (Illus.). 24p. (ps-2). 1980. 13.95 (ISBN 0-688-80236-2); PLB 12.88 (ISBN 0-688-84236-4). Greenwillow.

Rodriguez, Alejo. Simple Poems for Children: Hey What Kind of World Is This? LC 90-71368. 126p. (gr. 3-9). 1991. pap. 5.95 (ISBN 1-55523-393-7). Winston-Derek.

Rosen, Michael. Don't Put the Mustard in the Custard. Blake, Quentin, illus. 32p. (gr. 2-5). 1986. 10.95 (ISBN 0-233-97784-8). Andre Deutsch.

—Mind Your Own Business. Blake, Quentin, illus. LC 74-9969. 96p. (gr. 3 up). 1974. 18.95 (ISBN 0-87599-209-9). S G Phillips.

Ross, Gwendolyn. A Child's Treasure for a Lifetime. 24p. (gr. 2-6). 1988. pap. 2.95 (ISBN 0-88144-134-1). Christian Pub.

Rossen, Estelle R. Poems & Short Stories for Children's Delight, Illustrated. (Illus.). 112p. (Orig.). (gr. 3-6). 1991. pap. 6.95 (ISBN 0-8059-3159-7). Dorrance.

Royds, Caroline. Poems for Young Children. Moore, Inga, illus. LC 86-1290. 64p. (ps-3). 1986. 9.95 (ISBN 0-385-23524-0). Doubleday.

Rutherford, Erica. The Owl & the Pussycat. (Illus.). 24p. (gr. 1 up). 1986. text ed. 12.95 (ISBN 0-88776-181-X, Dist. by Univ. of Toronto Pr). Tundra Bks.

Ryder, Joanne. Inside Turtle's Shell & Other Poems of the Field. Bonners, Susan, illus. LC 84-833. 64p. (gr. 2-5). 1985. 10.95 (ISBN 0-02-778010-4, Mcmillan Child Bk). Macmillan Child Grp.

Rylant, Cynthia. Soda Jerk. Catalanotto, Peter, illus. LC 89-35654. 48p. (gr. 7 up). 1990. 14.95 (ISBN 0-531-05864-6); PLB 14.99 (ISBN 0-531-08464-7). Orchard Bks Watts.

—This Year's Garden. Szilagyi, Mary, illus. LC 84-10974. 32p. (gr. k-3). 1984. 13.95 (ISBN 0-02-777970-X, Bradbury Pr). Macmillan Child Grp.

Saltoon, Diana. Four Hands: Green Gulch Poems. 25p. (Orig.). (gr. 7 up). 1988. pap. 2.95 (ISBN 0-931191-08-4). Rob Briggs.

Samuels, Frederick, ed. Intense Experience: Social Psychology Through Poetry. 160p. (Orig.). 1990. pap. 12.95 (ISBN 0-9617481-6-8). Oyster River Pr.
Poems selected for illustrative & poetic value, with discussions, an exemplary student paper with poems, an essay comparing methods & goals of science & poetry & an index of concepts such as alienation, basic human needs, communication, conflict, death, dreams, ethnic loyalty, empathy, labeling, loneliness, perception affected by attitudes, projection. Excellent resource book for high school American Lit., Writing & Psychology courses. "Samuels' innovative teaching, combining social science with humanistic concerns of writers, inspires students to express their heartfelt experience...a beautiful collection by students & more seasoned poets."--Arnold Linsky, WEVO, NH Public Radio interview.
Publisher Provided Annotation.

Sanchez, Sonia. It's a New Day: Poems for Young Brothas & Sistuhs. Olugebefola, Ademola & Sherman, Ed, illus. LC 72-155311. (gr. 5 up). 1971. 3.00 (ISBN 0-685-00867-3); pap. 3.00 (ISBN 0-910296-60-X). Broadside Pr.

Sandburg, Carl. Early Moon. Daugherty, James, illus. LC 77-16488. (gr. 5 up). 1978. pap. 1.95 (ISBN 0-15-627326-8, VoyB). HarBraceJ.

—Sandburg Treasury: Prose & Poetry for Young People. Bacon, Paul, illus. LC 79-120818. (gr. 7 up). 1970. 24.95 (ISBN 0-15-270180-X, HJ). HarBraceJ.

Sandcastles & Cucumber Ships Last Forever. LC 78-74555. 48p. (Orig.). (gr. 3-8). 2.95 (ISBN 0-916872-06-8). Delafield Pr.

Scherer, Catharine D. Ladybug. Legman, Linda C., illus. LC 83-70738. 10p. (gr. 6-11). 1983. 2.95 (ISBN 0-9611024-0-3). Drum Assocs.

Schwartz, Alvin, ed. I Saw You in the Bathtub & Other Folk Rhymes. Hoff, Syd, illus. LC 88-16111. 64p. (gr. k-3). 1989. 11.95 (ISBN 0-06-025298-7); PLB 11.89 (ISBN 0-06-025299-5). HarpC Child Bks.

Scott, Bob. The Backcountry. Arcade, Greg, illus. 24p. (gr. 4-12). 1989. cardstock cover 5.00 (ISBN 0-9621201-0-3). B Scott Bks.

Seabrooke, Brenda. Judy Scuppernong. (gr. 4-7). 1990. 12.95 (ISBN 0-525-65038-5, Cobblehill Bks). Dutton Child Bks.

Seeley, Laura L. The Book of Shadowboxes: A Story of the ABC's. Seeley, Laura L., illus. 64p. (ps-3). 1990. 15.95 (ISBN 0-934601-65-8). Peachtree Pubs.

Sendak, Maurice. Seven Little Monsters. Sendak, Maurice, illus. LC 76-18400. (gr. 1 up). 1977. PLB 12.89 (ISBN 0-06-025478-5). HarpC Child Bks.

Service, Robert. The Cremation of Sam McGee. Harrison, Ted, illus. LC 86-14971. 32p. (ps up). 1987. 15.95 (ISBN 0-688-06903-7). Greenwillow.

Sesame Street Staff. Big Bird's Rhyming Book. Chartier, Norm, illus. LC 78-68790. (ps-3). 1979. 7.95 (ISBN 0-394-84140-9, Random Juv). Random.

Seven Little Hippos. 1991. pap. 13.95 (ISBN 0-671-72964-0). S&S Trade.
Shapes & Colors. (Illus.). (ps-k). 3.50 (ISBN 0-7214-1177-0). Ladybird Bks.
Sherry, Helen J. Splashes. Sherry, Helen J., illus. 36p. (Orig.). 1989. pap. 2.75 (ISBN 0-922273-00-6). Chocho Bks.
Silverstein, Shel. Where the Sidewalk Ends: Poems & Drawings. Silverstein, Shel, illus. LC 70-105486. 176p. (gr. 4 up). 1974. 14.95 (ISBN 0-06-025667-2); PLB 14.89 (ISBN 0-06-025668-0). HarpC Child Bks.
Simmie, Lois. Auntie's Knitting a Baby. LC 88-42546. (Illus.). 80p. (gr. 3-5). 1988. 11.95 (ISBN 0-531-05762-3); 11.99 (ISBN 0-531-08362-4). Orchard Bks Watts.
Skofield, James. Crow Moon, Worm Moon. Powzyk, Joyce, illus. LC 89-1370. 32p. (gr. k-3). 1990. 13.95 (ISBN 0-02-782915-4, Four Winds). Macmillan Child Grp.
Smith, Janet A., ed. The Faber Book of Children's Verse. 412p. (gr. 4 up). 1953. pap. 8.95 (ISBN 0-571-05457-9). Faber & Faber.
Spier, Peter. London Bridge Is Falling Down. LC 67-17695. (Illus.). (gr. k-3). 1972. pap. 6.95 (ISBN 0-385-08025-5, Zephyr). Doubleday.
Starbird, Kaye. The Covered Bridge House & Other Poems. Arnosky, Jim, illus. LC 79-11418. 64p. (gr. 3-7). 1985. 12.95 (ISBN 0-02-786850-8, Four Winds). Macmillan Child Grp.
Steele, Susanna. Mother Gave a Shout: Poems by Women & Girls. Styles, Morag, ed. Ray, Jane, illus. 128p. (gr. 3-8). 1991. 14.95 (ISBN 0-912078-90-1). Volcano Pr.
Stevenson, Robert Louis. A Child's Garden of Verses. Fujikawa, Gyo, illus. LC 85-12766. (gr. k-3). 1957. 6.95 (ISBN 0-448-02878-6, G&D). Putnam Pub Group.
—A Child's Garden of Verses. LC 85-12766. (Illus.). (gr. 3-5). 1950. pap. 2.95 (ISBN 0-14-030022-8, Puffin). Puffin Bks.
—A Child's Garden of Verses. Tudor, Tasha, illus. LC 85-12766. 72p. (ps up). 1988. 12.95 (ISBN 0-02-689093-3). Macmillan Child Grp.
—A Child's Garden of Verses. Robinson, Charles, illus. (gr. 1 up). 1976. pap. 4.95 (ISBN 0-85967-313-8, Pub. by Scolar Pr UK). Gower Pub Co.
—A Child's Garden of Verses. Wildsmith, Brian, illus. 96p. (gr. 1-4). 14.95 (ISBN 0-19-276032-7); pap. 10.95 (ISBN 0-19-276065-3). Oxford U Pr.
—A Child's Garden of Verses. LC 85-12766. (gr. 5-6). 12.95 (ISBN 0-89190-739-4, Pub. by Am Repr). Amereon Ltd.
—A Child's Garden of Verses. Foreman, Michael, illus. LC 85-12766. 128p. (ps-3). 1985. 14.95 (ISBN 0-385-29430-1). Delacorte.
—A Child's Garden of Verses. LC 88-43564. 160p. 1989. 4.95 (ISBN 0-89471-715-4). Running Pr.
—A Child's Garden of Verses. Lewis, T., illus. 64p. 1989. 14.95 (ISBN 0-8092-4356-3, Calico Bks). Contemp Bks.
—A Child's Garden of Verses. (Illus.). 128p. 1989. 15.95 (ISBN 0-87701-608-9). Chronicle Bks.
—Child's Garden of Verses. 1984. 4.98 (ISBN 0-671-06537-8). S&S Trade.
—Child's Garden of Verses. (Illus.). 112p. (gr. k up). 1991. 13.95 (ISBN 0-399-21818-1, Philomel Bks). Putnam Pub Group.
—Gyo Fujikawa's Original a Child's Garden of Verses. Fujikawa, Gyo, illus. 112p. 1988. 13.95 (ISBN 0-448-09278-6, G&D). Putnam Pub Group.
—The Land of Nod & Other Poems for Children. Hague, Michael, illus. LC 87-26533. 64p. (gr. k-2). 1988. 16.95 (ISBN 0-8050-0746-6). H Holt & Co.
—The Moon. Saldutti, Denise, illus. LC 83-47704. 32p. (ps-3). 1986. pap. 4.95 (ISBN 0-06-443098-7, Trophy). HarpC Child Bks.
—My Shadow. Rand, Ted, illus. 32p. 1990. 14.95 (ISBN 0-399-22216-2, Putnam). Putnam Pub Group.
—Poems from a Child's Garden of Verses. Littlejohn, Clare, illus. LC 86-46114. 14p. (ps-3). 1987. 6.95 (ISBN 0-694-00192-9). HarpC Child Bks.
—Poems from a Child's Garden of Verses. (ps-2). 1988. 4.95 (ISBN 0-7232-3525-2). Warne.
Stiles, Barbara J. Cheeky Rubs. Arthur, John, illus. LC 89-164732. 20p. (ps-5). 1989. text ed. 12.95 (ISBN 0-9622057-1-0); pap. text ed. 7.95 (ISBN 0-9622057-0-2). Manzanita Canyon.
Stopple, Libby. A Box of Peppermints. Dromgoole, Dick, ed. Bell, Martha, illus. LC 75-20957. 96p. (gr. 2-10). 1975. 12.95 (ISBN 0-913632-08-2); pap. 7.95 (ISBN 0-913632-07-4). Am Univ Artforms.
Stortz, Diane M. Little Poems for Little People. Rigo, Christina, illus. 24p. (ps). 1986. pap. 0.49 (ISBN 0-87403-157-5, 2117). Standard Pub.
Strauss, Gwen. Trail of Stones. Browne, Anthony, illus. LC 89-38358. 40p. 1990. 6.95 (ISBN 0-679-80582-6); PLB 9.99 (ISBN 0-679-90582-0). McKay.
Stuart, Monica & Soper, Gill. Ten Little Fingers: Craft Ideas for Young Children. 96p. (gr. 4-7). 1975. pap. 9.95 (ISBN 0-571-10828-8). Faber & Faber.
Suire, Diane D. Seasons. Connelly, Gwen, illus. LC 89-773. 32p. (gr. k-3). 1989. lib. bdg. 11.97 (ISBN 0-89565-503-9). Childs World.
Sullivan, Charles, ed. Imaginary Gardens: American Poetry & Art for Young People. (Illus.). 112p. 1989. 19.95 (ISBN 0-8109-1130-2). Abrams.
Swann, Brian. A Basket Full of White Eggs: Riddle-Poems. Goembel, Ponder, illus. LC 87-11220. 32p. (gr. k-3). 1988. 14.95 (ISBN 0-531-05734-8); PLB 14.99 (ISBN 0-531-08334-9). Orchard Bks Watts.
Tarrant, Margaret. My First Book of Poems. (ps-3). 1989. 6.95 (ISBN 0-8249-8384-X). Ideals.
Thomas, Marlo. Free to Be...You & Me. Hart, Carole, ed. 1987. pap. 9.95 (ISBN 0-317-62189-0). McGraw.
Tolkien, J. R. R. Bilbo's Last Song. Baynes, Pauline, illus. 32p. 1990. 14.95 (ISBN 0-395-53810-6). HM.
A Treasury of Playtime Poems. 80p. 1990. 15.95 (ISBN 0-8249-8485-4). Ideals.
Tripp, Wallace. A Great Big Ugly Man Came Up & Tied His Horse to Me: A Book of Nonsense Verse. (Illus.). 48p. (gr. k-12). 1974. lib. bdg. 14.95 (ISBN 0-316-85280-5); pap. 6.95 (ISBN 0-316-85281-3). Little.
Tripp, Wallace & Belloc, Hilaire. The Bad Child's Pop-up Book of Beasts. (Illus.). 12p. (gr. 1-5). 1987. 13.95 (ISBN 0-399-21431-3, Putnam). Putnam Pub Group.
Tucker, Kerry & Morgan, Hal, eds. The Kids' Bathtub Rhyme Book. Marsh, Susan, illus. 12p. (Orig.). (ps-1). 1988. pap. 4.95 (ISBN 0-942820-25-8). Steam Pr MA.
Turner, Ann. Street Talk. (gr. 4-7). 1986. 11.95 (ISBN 0-395-39971-8). HM.
Velez, Jennicel. Poemas. Mendoza, Ester F., pref. by. LC 83-3526. (SPA.). xvii, 56p. (gr. 3-7). 1983. pap. 2.00 (ISBN 0-8477-0063-1). U of PR Pr.
Viorst, Judith. If I Were in Charge of the World & Other Worries. Cherry, Lynn, illus. LC 81-2342. 64p. (gr. 3 up). 1981. 13.95 (ISBN 0-689-30863-9, Atheneum Child Bk). Macmillan Child Grp.
Wahl, John & Wahl, Stacey. I Can Count the Petals of a Flower. 2nd, rev. ed. LC 85-13670. (Illus.). 36p. (ps-1). 1985. 8.00 (ISBN 0-87353-224-4). NCTM.
Wallace, Daisy, ed. Fairy Poems. Hyman, Trina S., illus. LC 79-18763. 32p. (gr. 1-4). 1980. reinforced bdg. 12.95 (ISBN 0-8234-0371-8). Holiday.
—Ghost Poems. LC 78-11028. (Illus.). 32p. (gr. k-3). 1990. reinforced 12.95 (ISBN 0-8234-0344-0); pap. 4.95 (ISBN 0-8234-0849-3). Holiday.
—Witch Poems. Hyman, Trina S., illus. LC 76-9036. 32p. (gr. k-3). 1990. reinforced bdg. 12.95 (ISBN 0-8234-0281-9); pap. 4.95 (ISBN 0-8234-0850-7). Holiday.
Walter, Dean S. Pages of My Mind. Teasley, Jamie, ed. 45p. 1990. pap. 4.95 (ISBN 1-55523-280-9). Winston-Derek.
Walters, J. Donald. Ring, Bluebell, Ring! Potapovskaya, Bella, illus. 130p. (ps-12). 1989. pap. 7.95 (ISBN 0-916124-33-9, CCP4). Crystal Clarity.
Waters, Fiona, ed. Whiskers & Paws. Julian-Ottie, Vanessa, illus. LC 89-77349. 32p. 1990. 9.95 (ISBN 0-940793-51-2, Pub. by Crocodile Bks). Interlink Pub.
Wells, Carolyn. A Christmas Alphabet. (Illus.). 32p. 1989. 15.95 (ISBN 0-399-21683-9, Putnam). Putnam Pub Group.
West, Colin. A Moment in Rhyme. LC 86-24287. (Illus.). 32p. (ps-3). 1987. 11.95 (ISBN 0-8037-0259-0). Dial Bks Young.
Wheeler, Kim. Loves of the Cat: An Illustrated Anthology of Old & Modern Cat Poems. Wheeler, Kim, ed. LC 85-63189. (Illus.). 101p. (Orig.). (gr. 5 up). 1985. pap. 5.75 (ISBN 0-9615937-0-9). Star City Pubns.
Whipple, Laura, ed. Animals Animals. Carle, Eric, illus. LC 88-31646. 96p. (ps-3). 1989. 18.95 (ISBN 0-399-21744-4, Philomel Bks). Putnam Pub Group.
Whitman, Walt. Poems of Walt Whitman: Leaves of Grass. Powell, Lawrence C., ed. LC 64-20689. (Illus.). 169p. (gr. 7 up). 1966. PLB 12.89 (ISBN 0-690-64431-0, Crowell Jr Bks). HarpC Child Bks.
Wiands, Catherine. Positive Strokes for Little Folks, Vols. 1-7. 2nd ed. Ziebarth, Pat, ed. 32p. (Orig.). (gr. 1-6). 1983. pap. 2.50 (ISBN 0-943262-00-3); Set of 7. pap. write for info. Transitions.
Wilkins, Sarah. Sarah Wilkins, in Search of a Song, Vol. 7. Fisher, Barbara, ed. 22p. (Orig.). (gr. 5-8). 1984. pap. 2.00 (ISBN 0-934830-35-5). Ten Penny.
Willard, Nancy. A Visit to William Blake's Inn: Poems for Innocent & Experienced Travelers. Provensen, Alice & Provensen, Martin, illus. LC 80-27403. 44p. (ps-3). 1981. 13.95 (ISBN 0-15-293822-2, HJ). HarBraceJ.
Wilner, Isabel. The Poetry Troupe: Poems to Read Aloud. LC 77-9439. (Illus.). 224p. (gr. 3-7). 1977. 14.95 (ISBN 0-684-15198-7, Scribner). Macmillan.

Wilson, Jean A. Come Follow Me. Massmann, Jane H., illus. 26p. (ps-3). 1989. 12.95 (ISBN 0-911586-01-6). Wahr.
Jean Wilson's second book of verses for children 3-7, follows the children through the seasons for discovery, learning & questioning. The children go to a supermarket, slide down a hill, ride a bike, go to a band concert, feel a live rabbit, a horse, see their shadows, wonder about frost, leaves, snowmen, play jacks, go to a birthday party, wonder about raindrops, & go to bed (but, according to the last verse, not without washing their feet). Reality based, vivid illustrations, accurate animal drawings & musical instruments. Again, Wilson adds another dimension to her whimsical verses through thoughtful questions posed by the child narrator.
Publisher Provided Annotation.

—The Garden Zoo. 20p. 1985. pap. 3.95 (ISBN 0-911586-00-8). Wahr.
Discover in the back yard. Pussy willows have faces; a rabbit is larger than life. Jean Wilson, grandmother, political activist, former college administrator, tucked in "suitcase notes" when her husband & children traveled. These suitcase notes form the core of her first book of children's verses. Twenty-two pages of Jean Wilson's warm, witty & wise verses will surprise & delight readers - & listeners - of all ages as they did her own children. Art teacher Joan Otis's over size illustrations augment the agelessness, fun, wonder & lovingness expressed in the verses.
Publisher Provided Annotation.

Withers, Carl. A Rocket in My Pocket: The Rhymes & Chants of Young Americans. Suba, Sussanne, illus. 224p. (gr. 1-6). 1988. 14.95 (ISBN 0-8050-0821-7); pap. 7.50 (ISBN 0-8050-0804-7). H Holt & Co.
Wood, Robert W. How to Tell the Birds from the Flowers. (Illus.). 64p. (gr. 4 up). 1959. pap. 1.95 (ISBN 0-486-20523-1). Dover.
Worth, Valerie. Small Poems. Babbitt, Natalie, illus. LC 72-81488. 48p. (gr. 3 up). 1972. 8.95 (ISBN 0-374-37072-9). FS&G.
—Small Poems Again. Babbitt, Natalie, illus. LC 85-47513. 48p. (gr. 3 up). 1986. 8.95 (ISBN 0-374-37074-5). FS&G.
—Still More Small Poems. Babbitt, Natalie, illus. LC 78-11739. 48p. (gr. 3 up). 1978. 8.95 (ISBN 0-374-37258-6). FS&G.
Yeoman, John. Our Village. Blake, Quentin, illus. LC 88-895. 48p. (gr. 1-3). 1988. 13.95 (ISBN 0-689-31451-5, Atheneum Child Bk). Macmillan Child Grp.
Yolen, Jane. Best Witches. Primavera, Elise, illus. 48p. (gr. k-4). 1989. 14.95 (ISBN 0-399-21539-5, Putnam). Putnam Pub Group.
—Bird Watch. Lewin, Ted, illus. 48p. 1990. 15.95 (ISBN 0-399-21612-X, Philomel Bks). Putnam Pub Group.
—Dinosaur Dances. Degen, Bruce, illus. 40p. 1990. 14.95 (ISBN 0-399-21629-4, Putnam). Putnam Pub Group.
Zaslow, David. A Rose by Any Other Name. (Illus.). 96p. (Orig.). 1980. pap. 4.95 (ISBN 0-89411-002-0). Kids Matter.
—Somedays It Feels Like It Wants to Rain. Fink, Grace, illus. LC 76-46244. (gr. 2-6). 1976. pap. 3.95 (ISBN 0-89411-001-2). Kids Matter.
Zito, Penny. Through My Eyes - A Teenage Look at Life. York, Sherri, ed. LC 87-50257. (Illus.). 152p. (gr. 7 up). 1987. 7.95 (ISBN 1-55523-075-X). Winston-Derek.
Zolotow, Charlotte. Flocks of Birds. rev. ed. Bornstein, Ruth L., illus. LC 81-43029. 32p. (ps-3). 1981. 11.95 (ISBN 0-690-04112-8, Crowell Jr Bks). HarpC Child Bks.

POETRY–COLLECTIONS

see also American Poetry–Collections; English Poetry–Collections

Adoff, Arnold. All the Colors of the Race. Steptoe, John, illus. LC 81-11777. 64p. (gr. 5 up). 1982. 13.95 (ISBN 0-688-00879-8); PLB 13.88 (ISBN 0-688-00880-1). Lothrop.
Adoff, Arnold, ed. I Am the Darker Brother: An Anthology of Modern Poems by Negro Americans. LC 68-12077. (Illus.). 128p. (gr. 7 up). 1970. pap. 4.95 (ISBN 0-02-041120-0, Collier Young Ad). Macmillan Child Grp.
—The Poetry of Black America: Anthology of the Twentieth Century. Brooks, Gwendolyn, intro. by. LC 72-76518. 576p. (gr. 7 up). 1973. 24.95 (ISBN 0-06-020089-8); PLB 24.89 (ISBN 0-06-020090-1). HarpC Child Bks.
Ainsworth, Catherine H. Jump Rope Verses Around the United States. LC 75-4827. 24p. (ps-12). 1976. 4.00 (ISBN 0-933190-01-8). Clyde Pr.
Alexander, Martha. Poems & Prayers for the Very Young. (Illus.). (ps-1). 1973. pap. 2.25 (ISBN 0-394-82705-8, Random Juv). Random.
Amery, H., compiled by. The Usborne Book of Creepy Poems. (Illus.). 32p. (gr. 2-6). 1990. lib. bdg. 13.96 (ISBN 0-88110-444-2, Usborne); pap. 5.95 (ISBN 0-7460-0440-0, Usborne). EDC.
Antologia de Poesia-Primavera: Anthology of Poetry-Spring. (SPA.). (gr. k-6). 1990. 6.95 (ISBN 0-935303-02-2). Victory Pub.

Bassett, Harmon. Children's Daily Verses for Growing up the Easy Way with Fun & Play. LC 88-47545. (Illus.). 150p. (gr. 2-7). 1988. 19.95 (ISBN 0-88164-712-8); pap. 15.95 (ISBN 0-88164-713-6). ABBE Pubs Assn.

Bayer, Jane. A, My Name Is Alice. Kellogg, Steven, illus. LC 84-7059. (gr. k-3). 1984. 14.95 (ISBN 0-8037-0123-3); PLB 14.89 (ISBN 0-8037-0124-1). Dial Bks Young.

Bedtime Bear's Book of Bedtime Poems. Leder, Dora, illus. 40p. (ps-3). 1983. lib. bdg. 4.99 (ISBN 0-394-95956-6). Random.

Bell, Bill, illus. Let's Pretend: Poems Collected by Natalie Bober. 72p. (ps-3). 1990. pap. 4.95 (ISBN 0-14-032132-2, Puffin). Puffin Bks.

The Best Stories & Poems from Lollipops Magazine. 64p. (ps-2). 1990. 6.95 (ISBN 0-86653-564-0, GA1161). Good Apple.

The Big Little Golden Book of Funny Poems. (Illus.). (gr. k-9). 1988. pap. 1.39 (ISBN 0-318-36462-X). Scholastic Inc.

Bradford, Gigi & Moos, Michael, eds. Sixteen Toes: Anthology. (Illus.). (gr. 2-7). 1978. pap. 2.50 (ISBN 0-930970-00-4). O'Neill Pr.

Brewton, Sara & Brewton, John E, eds. America Forever New: A Book of Poems. Grifalconi, Ann, illus. LC 67-23663. 278p. (gr. 5 up). 1989. PLB 13.89 (ISBN 0-690-04764-9, Crowell Jr Bks). HarpC Child Bks.

Brewton, Sara & Brewton, John E., eds. Shrieks at Midnight: Macabre Poems, Eerie & Humorous. Raskin, Ellen, illus. LC 69-11824. 177p. (gr. 4 up). 1969. 13.95 (ISBN 0-690-73518-9, Crowell Jr Bks). HarpC Child Bks.

Caddy, John, ed. A Box of Night Mirrors. Schanilec, Gaylord, illus. 120p. (Orig.). 1980. pap. 5.00 (ISBN 0-927663-11-2). COMPAS.

Chisholm, Louey, ed. The Golden Staircase: Poems & Verses for Children. LC 79-51973. (Illus.). (gr. 3-8). 1980. Repr. of 1906 ed. 23.50x (ISBN 0-89609-182-1). Roth Pub Inc.

Chorao, Kay. The Baby's Bedtime Book. Chorao, Kay, illus. LC 84-6067. (ps). 1989. 13.95 (ISBN 0-525-44149-2, DCB); bk & cassette 18.95 (ISBN 0-525-44506-4). Dutton Child Bks.

Cole, Joanna & Calmenson, Stephanie, eds. The Read-Aloud Treasury: Favorite Nursery Rhymes, Poems, Stories & More for the Very Young. Schweninger, Ann, illus. 256p. 1988. pap. 18.95 (ISBN 0-385-18560-X). Doubleday.

Collen, Arne. Friends & Fiends. (Illus.). 72p. (Orig.). (gr. 7 up). 1989. pap. write for info. Eagleye Bks Intl.

Cook, Roy J., ed. One Hundred & One Famous Poems. (Illus.). 186p. (gr. 9-12). 1990. Repr. lib. bdg. 19.95x (ISBN 0-89966-667-1). Buccaneer Bks.

Corrin, Sara & Corrin, Stephen, eds. Once upon a Rhyme: One Hundred One Poems for Young Children. Bennett, Jill, illus. 160p. (gr. 1-4). 1982. 13.95 (ISBN 0-571-11913-1). Faber & Faber.

Corrin, Sara, et al. Stories for Five Year-Olds & Other Young Readers. Corrin, Stephen, ed. Hughes, Shirley, illus. 168p. (ps-5). 1973. 12.95 (ISBN 0-571-10162-3); pap. 9.95 (ISBN 0-685-03338-4). Faber & Faber.

Corrin, Sara, et al, eds. Stories for Under-Fives. Hughes, Shirley, illus. 158p. (ps-5). 1974. 12.95 (ISBN 0-571-10371-5); pap. 9.95 (ISBN 0-571-12920-X). Faber & Faber.

Cummings, e. e. Hist Whist & Other Poems for Children. Firmage, George J., ed. (Illus.). (gr. 3 up). 1983. 12.95 (ISBN 0-87140-640-3). Liveright.

De la Mare, Walter. Peacock Pie: A Book of Rhymes. Ardizzone, Edward, illus. 128p. (gr. 3-7). 1988. pap. 7.95 (ISBN 0-571-14963-4). Faber & Faber.

De Regniers, Beatrice, et al, eds. Sing a Song of Popcorn: Every Child's Book of Poems. (Illus.). 160p. (gr. k up). 1988. pap. 16.95 (ISBN 0-590-40645-0, Scholastic Hardcovers). Scholastic Inc.

De Regniers, Beatrice S., et al, eds. Sing a Song of Popcorn: Every Child's Book of Poems. 160p. (ps-8). 1991. write for info. tchr's. guide (ISBN 0-590-43035-1). Scholastic Inc.

Dittberner-Jax, Norita, ed. The Ragged Heart. Wood, Marce, illus. 164p. (Orig.). 1989. pap. 8.00 (ISBN 0-927663-14-7). COMPAS.

Doan, Eleanor. A Child's Treasury of Verse. Munger, Nancy, illus. 208p. (gr. 1-6). 1987. pap. 10.95 (ISBN 0-310-23801-3, 9545P). Zondervan.

Dunning, Stephen, et al, eds. Reflections on a Gift of Watermelon Pickle & Other Modern Verse. LC 66-8763. (Illus.). 144p. (gr. 7 up). 1966. 14.95 (ISBN 0-688-41231-9); PLB 13.88 (ISBN 0-688-51231-3). Lothrop.

Egan, Louise B., ed. The Classic Treasury of Children's Poetry. LC 89-83327. (Illus.). 56p. (gr. 1 up). 1990. 9.98 (ISBN 0-89471-802-9, Pub. by Courage Bks). Running Pr.

Elementary School Children of California. The Poetry Express, Nineteen Eighty-Eight: A Collection of Poetry by the Children of California. Reed, John M. & Gillman, Lillian E., eds. Hayden, Jaime, contrib. by. 192p. (ps-6). 1988. 8.95 (ISBN 0-317-93373-6). Other Eye.

Elementary School Children of Oregon. Rhyme Time, Nineteen Eighty-Eight: A Collection of Poetry by the Children of Oregon. Reed, John M. & Gillman, Lillian E., eds. Hayden, Jaime, contrib. by. 104p. (Orig.). (ps-6). 1988. 6.95 (ISBN 0-317-93374-4). Other Eye.

Elementary School Children of Washington State. A Child's Eye View: A Collection of Poetry by the Children of Washington State, Vol. 1. Reed, John M. & Gillman, Lillian E., eds. Hayden, Jaime, contrib. by. 143p. (ps-6). 1987. 7.95 (ISBN 0-317-93371-X). Other Eye.

—A Child's Eye View: A Collection of Poetry by the Children of Washington State, Vol. 2. Reed, John M. & Gillman, Lillian E., eds. Hayden, Jaime, contrib. by. 200p. (ps-6). 1988. 7.95 (ISBN 0-317-93372-8). Other Eye.

Elliot, J. W. Mother Goose: Or National Nursery Rhymes & Nursery Songs. Dalziel, illus. 111p. (gr. 4 up). 1981. Repr. of 1873 ed. lib. bdg. 40.00 (ISBN 0-940070-14-6). Doll Works.

Ernest, P. Edward, ed. Family Album of Favorite Poems. Vosburgh, Leonard, illus. LC 83-16028. (gr. 7-9). 1959. 15.95 (ISBN 0-399-12932-4, G&D). Putnam Pub Group.

Farber, Norma & Livingston, Myra C., eds. These Small Stones. Livingston, Myra C., intro. by. LC 87-264. 128p. (gr. 3-7). 1987. 12.95 (ISBN 0-06-024013-X); PLB 12.89 (ISBN 0-06-024014-8). HarpC Child Bks.

Ferris, Helen, ed. Favorite Poems Old & New. Weisgard, Leonard, illus. LC 57-11418. 598p. (gr. 3-7). 1957. pap. 18.95 (ISBN 0-385-07696-7). Doubleday.

Field, Eugene. Wynken, Blynken & Nod. Jeffers, Susan, illus. (ps-1). 1985. pap. 4.95 (ISBN 0-525-44199-9, 0383-120, DCB). Dutton Child Bks.

Fifty-Two Stories & Poems for Children. (Illus.). 160p. (gr. 2-5). 1987. casebd. 7.95 (ISBN 0-570-04158-9, 56-1616). Concordia.

Fisher, Barbara & Spiegel, Richard, eds. Streams. (Illus.). 138p. (Orig.). (gr. 9-12). 1987. pap. 5.00 (ISBN 0-934830-39-8). Ten Penny.

—Streams, No. 2. (Illus.). 142p. (gr. 9-12). 1988. pap. 5.00 (ISBN 0-934830-42-8). Ten Penny.

—Streams, No. 3. (Illus.). (gr. 9-12). 1989. pap. 5.00 (ISBN 0-934830-43-6). Ten Penny.

—Subway Slams. (Illus.). 48p. (Orig.). (gr. k-8). 1981. pap. 2.00 (ISBN 0-934830-22-3). Ten Penny.

Fisher, Robert, ed. Ghosts Galore: Haunting Verse. Allen, Rowena, illus. 96p. (gr. 4-6). 1986. pap. 5.95 (ISBN 0-571-13926-4). Faber & Faber.

Foster, John. Let's Celebrate: Festival Poems. (Illus.). 112p. (gr. 3 up). 1990. 13.95 (ISBN 0-19-276083-1). Oxford U Pr.

Foster, John & Curless, Alan. A Second Poetry Book. White, Martin & Wright, Joseph, illus. 128p. (gr. 4-6). 1987. 11.95 (ISBN 0-19-918137-3); pap. 5.95 (ISBN 0-19-918136-5). Oxford U Pr.

Foster, John, compiled by. Another Fifth Poetry Book. (Illus.). 128p. (gr. 5-7). 1989. bds. 11.95 laminated (ISBN 0-19-917128-9); pap. 5.95 (ISBN 0-19-917127-0). Oxford U Pr.

—Another First Poetry Book. (Illus.). 128p. (ps-6). 1988. bds. 11.95 (ISBN 0-19-917120-3); pap. 5.95 (ISBN 0-19-917119-X). Oxford U Pr.

—Another Second Poetry Book. (Illus.). 128p. (ps-6). 1988. bds. 11.95 (ISBN 0-19-917122-X); pap. 5.95 (ISBN 0-19-917121-1). Oxford U Pr.

—Another Third Poetry Book. (Illus.). 128p. (ps-6). 1988. bds. 11.95 (ISBN 0-19-917124-6); pap. 5.95 (ISBN 0-19-917123-8). Oxford U Pr.

—A Fifth Poetry Book. (Illus.). 128p. 1987. 11.95 (ISBN 0-19-916054-6); pap. 5.95 (ISBN 0-19-916053-8). Oxford U Pr.

—A Fourth Poetry Book. Benton, Peter, et al, illus. 128p. 1987. 11.95 (ISBN 0-19-918152-7); pap. 5.95 (ISBN 0-19-918151-9). Oxford U Pr.

Frank, Josette, ed. Poems to Read to the Very Young. Wilkin, Eloise, illus. LC 82-518. 48p. (ps-3). 1982. pap. 7.95 (ISBN 0-394-85188-9). Random.

—Poems to Read to the Very Young. Wilson, Dagmar, illus. LC 87-23234. 32p. (ps-1). 1988. lib. bdg. 5.99 (ISBN 0-394-99768-9, Random Juv); pap. 2.25 (ISBN 0-394-89768-4). Random.

Froman, Robert. Seeing Things: A Book of Poems. Barber, Ray, illus. LC 73-18494. 64p. (gr. 4-8). 1974. PLB 13.89 (ISBN 0-685-02103-3, Crowell Jr Bks, Crowell Jr Bks). HarpC Child Bks.

Gaige, Grace, ed. Recitations for Younger Children. LC 78-74816. (gr. 3-8). 1979. Repr. of 1927 ed. 19.50x (ISBN 0-89609-134-1). Roth Pub Inc.

Galdone, Paul, adapted by. & illus. Over in the Meadow. (ps-1). 1989. 13.95 (ISBN 0-671-66449-2); pap. 5.95 (ISBN 0-671-67837-X). S&S Trade.

Gordon, Ruth, ed. Time Is the Longest Distance. LC 90-4947. 96p. (gr. 7 up). 1991. 13.95 (ISBN 0-06-022297-2); PLB 13.89 (ISBN 0-06-022424-X). HarpC Child Bks.

—Under All Silences: The Many Shades of Love (An Anthology of Poems Selected by Ruth Gordon) LC 85-45845. 128p. (gr. 7 up). 1987. 12.95 (ISBN 0-06-022154-2); PLB 12.89 (ISBN 0-06-022155-0). HarpC Child Bks.

Harrison, Michael, compiled by. Splinters: A Book of Very Short Poems. Heap, Sue, illus. 128p. (gr. 5 up). 1989. jacketed 10.95 (ISBN 0-19-276072-6). Oxford U Pr.

Hopkins, Lee B., ed. Click, Rumble, Roar: Poems about Machines. Audette, Anna H., illus. LC 86-47746. 48p. (gr. 2-6). 1987. (Crowell Jr Bks); PLB 11.89 (ISBN 0-690-04589-1, Crowell Jr Bks). HarpC Child Bks.

—Hey-How for Halloween! McGaffrey, Janet, illus. LC 74-5601. 32p. (gr. 1-5). 1974. 12.95 (ISBN 0-15-233900-0, HJ). HarBraceJ.

—More Surprises. Lloyd, Megan, illus. LC 86-45335. 64p. (gr. k-3). 1987. 11.95i (ISBN 0-06-022604-8); PLB 11.89 (ISBN 0-06-022605-6). HarpC Child Bks.

—A Song in Stone. Audette, Anna H., photos by. LC 82-45589. (Illus.). 48p. (gr. 2-6). 1983. (Crowell Jr Bks); PLB 11.89 (ISBN 0-690-04270-1). HarpC Child Bks.

—Surprises. LC 83-47712. (Illus.). 64p. (gr. k-3). 1984. 11.95 (ISBN 0-06-022584-X); PLB 11.89 (ISBN 0-06-022585-8). HarpC Child Bks.

Huber, Miriam B., et al, eds. The Poetry Book: Vol. 4. Hartwell, Marjorie, illus. LC 79-51968. (gr. 4). 1980. Repr. of 1926 ed. 18.00x (ISBN 0-89609-183-X). Roth Pub Inc.

Huigin, S. O. Scary Poems for Rotten Kids. (Illus.). 32p. (ps-8). 1988. pap. 4.95 (ISBN 0-88753-177-6). Firefly Bks Ltd.

Janeczko, Paul B., ed. Going over to Your Place: Poems for Each Other. LC 86-26439. 176p. (gr. 7 up). 1987. 13.95 (ISBN 0-02-747670-7, Bradbury Pr). Macmillan Child Grp.

—Pocket Poems: Selected for a Journey. LC 84-21537. 160p. (gr. 7 up). 1985. 12.95 (ISBN 0-02-747820-3, Bradbury Pr). Macmillan Child Grp.

Janeczko, Paul B., selected by. Preposterous: Poems of Youth. LC 90-39644. 144p. (gr. 7 up). 1991. 13.95 (ISBN 0-531-05901-4); PLB 13.99 (ISBN 0-531-08501-5). Orchard Bks Watts.

Janeczko, Paul B., ed. Strings: A Gathering of Family Poems. LC 83-19033. 144p. (gr. 7 up). 1984. 12.95 (ISBN 0-02-747790-8, Bradbury Pr). Macmillan Child Grp.

Janger, Kathie, ed. Rainbow Collection, 1989: Stories & Poetry by Young People. Viorst, Judith, frwd. by. Sarecky, Melody, illus. 176p. (gr. 1-8). 1989. pap. 6.00 (ISBN 0-929889-04-5). Young Writers Contest Found.

—Rainbow Collection, 1990: Stories & Poetry by Young People. Sarecky, Melody, illus. Bush, Barbara, frwd. by. (Illus.). 176p. 1990. pap. 6.00 (ISBN 0-929889-06-1). Young Writers Contest Found.

Josefowitz, Natasha. A Hundred Scoops of Ice Cream. 1989. pap. 3.95 (ISBN 0-671-67744-6, Touchstone Bks). S&S Trade.

Kroll, Steven. It's April Fools' Day! Bassett, Jeni, illus. LC 88-28434. 32p. (ps-3). 1990. PLB 14.95 (ISBN 0-8234-0747-0). Holiday.

Kuskin, Karla. Any Me I Want to Be. Kuskin, Karla, illus. LC 77-105485. 64p. (gr. 1-4). 1972. PLB 11.89 (ISBN 0-06-023616-7). HarpC Child Bks.

Larke, Joe. Can't Reach the Itch. Larke, Karol, illus. 72p. (gr. 1-6). 1988. 10.00x (ISBN 0-9620112-1-5). Grin A Bit.

Larrick, Nancy. Bring Me All Your Dreams. LC 79-26892. 128p. (gr. 10 up). 1988. pap. 6.95 (ISBN 0-87131-550-5). M Evans.

Larrick, Nancy, compiled by. The Merry-Go-Round Poetry Book. Gundersheimer, Karen, illus. 1989. 14.95 (ISBN 0-385-29814-5). Delacorte.

Leary, Lory B. An Alaskan Child's Garden of Verse. Leary, Lory B., illus. 40p. (Orig.). (gr. 6 up). 1989. pap. 6.95x (ISBN 0-924663-02-2). Alaskan Viewpoint.

Lewis, C. S. The Magician's Nephew. 192p. (gr. 4 up). 1970. pap. 3.50 (ISBN 0-02-044230-0, Collier Young Ad). Macmillan Child Grp.

Lewis, Naomi, ed. Messages: A Book of Poems. LC 85-10326. 255p. (gr. 7 up). 1985. pap. 5.95 (ISBN 0-571-13647-8). Faber & Faber.

Livingston, Myra C. Birthday Poems. Tomes, Margot, illus. LC 89-2114. 32p. (gr. k-3). 1989. reinforced 13.95 (ISBN 0-8234-0783-7). Holiday.

—Sky Songs. Fisher, Leonard E., illus. LC 83-12955. 32p. (gr. 1-4). 1984. reinforced bdg 14.95 (ISBN 0-8234-0502-8). Holiday.

Livingston, Myra C., compiled by. Cat Poems. Hyman, Trina S., illus. LC 86-14810. 32p. (gr. k-3). 1987. PLB 13.95 (ISBN 0-8234-0631-8). Holiday.

Livingston, Myra C., ed. Easter Poems. Wallner, John, illus. LC 84-15866. 32p. (gr. k-3). 1985. reinforced bdg. 13.95 (ISBN 0-8234-0546-X). Holiday.

—Poems for Fathers. Casilla, Robert, illus. LC 88-17010. 32p. (gr. k-3). 1989. reinforced bdg. 13.95 (ISBN 0-8234-0729-2). Holiday.

MacKenthum, Carole. Poems, Prayers & Projects. Valentino, Carla & McClure, Nancee, illus. 48p. (gr. 3-7). 1984. wkbk. 6.95 (ISBN 0-86653-177-7, SS 812). Good Apple.

Malley, Barbara & Allen, Frances. Poetry with a Purpose. Lawrence, Grace, illus. 128p. (gr. 4-7). 1987. pap. 9.95 (ISBN 0-86653-415-6, GA 1018). Good Apple.

Mastrangelo, Judy & Mastrangelo, Judy, illus. The Sandman: And Other Sleepy-Time Rhymes. LC 90-34513. 48p. (ps-2). 1990. 4.95 (ISBN 0-88101-105-3). Unicorn Pub.

Mitchell, Adrian. Strawberry Drums. 1991. PLB 14.99 (ISBN 0-385-30287-8); pap. 13.95. Delacorte.

Moore, Clement C. The Night Before Christmas. Gustafson, Scott, illus. LC 85-40334. 32p. (ps-3). 1985. 12.95 (ISBN 0-394-54809-4). Knopf.

Moore, Peggy S. My Very First book of Poetry & Other Things. Moore, Peggy S., illus. 16p. (gr. 3-5). 1982. pap. 1.98 (ISBN 0-9613078-0-3). Detroit Black.

Morrison, Lillian, ed. Yours Till Niagara Falls: A Book of Autograph Verses. Wickstrom, Sylvie, illus. LC 89-82520. 192p. (gr. 3-7). 1990. PLB 11.89 (ISBN 0-690-04876-9, Crowell Jr Bks). HarpC Child Bks.

—Yours Till Niagara Falls: A Book of Autograph Verses. Wickstrom, Sylvie, illus. LC 89-82520. 192p. (gr. 3-7). 1990. pap. 4.95 (ISBN 0-06-446104-1, Trophy). HarpC Child Bks.

Nunez, Ana R. Antologia de Poesia Infantil. LC 85-81795. (SPA.). 180p. (Orig.). (gr. 3-12). 1985. pap. 9.95 (ISBN 0-89729-369-X). Ediciones.

Palmer, Mary R. Mother Moose Rhymes. (gr. 2-5). 1986. pap. 7.95 (ISBN 0-930096-75-4). G Gannett.

Poet's Workshop Staff. Black American History: Rap & Rhyme. 8p. (gr. 6-12). 1989. pap. text ed. 2.50 (ISBN 0-913597-53-8, Pub. by Alpha Pyramis). Prosperity & Profits.

Prelutsky, Jack. Kermit's Garden of Verses. McNally, Bruce, illus. LC 82-480. 64p. (gr. 4-6). 1982. lib. bdg. 5.99 (ISBN 0-394-95410-6). Random.

—The Random House Book of Poetry for Children. Lobel, Arnold, illus. LC 81-85940. 248p. (gr. 1-5). 1983. 16.95 (ISBN 0-394-85010-6); lib. bdg. 16.99 (ISBN 0-394-95010-0). Random.

Prelutsky, Jack, ed. Read Aloud Rhymes for the Very Young. Brown, Marc, illus. Trelease, Jim, intro. by. LC 86-7147. (Illus.). 112p. (ps-3). 1986. 15.95 (ISBN 0-394-87218-5); lib. bdg. 15.99 (ISBN 0-394-97218-X). Knopf.

Reynolds, James J., ed. Modern Poetry for Children, Bk. 8. LC 30-10164. (gr. 4). 1979. Repr. of 1928 ed. 15.00x (ISBN 0-89609-167-8). Roth Pub Inc.

Rhyming: Cut & Paste & More. 32p. (gr. 1). 1983. pap. 1.98 (ISBN 0-88724-011-9, CD-7012). Carson-Dellos.

Rhys, Grace L., ed. The Children's Garland of Verse. Robinson, Charles, illus. LC 79-51958. (gr. 2-6). 1980. 25.00x (ISBN 0-89609-200-3). Roth Pub Inc.

Roche, P. K., selected by. & illus. At Christmas Be Merry. 32p. (ps-1). 1989. pap. 3.95 (ISBN 0-14-050680-2, Puffin). Puffin Bks.

Roes, Mimi. Poems for Young Children. Fuhrman, James, illus. (ps-6). 1979. pap. 1.95x (ISBN 0-89780-003-6). NAR Prodns.

Rosenbloom, Joseph. World's Best Funny Rhymes. Behr, Joyce, illus. LC 88-13937. (Orig.). (gr. 2-6). 1989. pap. 4.95 (ISBN 0-8069-6968-7). Sterling.

Ross, Tony, illus. The Pop-up Book of Nonsense Verse. LC 89-60365. 12p. (ps-5). 1989. 12.95 (ISBN 0-394-84964-7, Random Juv). Random.

Scott, Louise. Quiet Times. 66p. (ps). 1986. saddle stitched 9.95 (ISBN 0-513-01785-2). Denison.

Sneve, Virginia H., ed. Dancing Teepees: Poems of American Indian Youth. Gammell, Stephen, illus. LC 88-11075. 32p. (gr. 1-4). 1989. reinforced bdg. 14.95 (ISBN 0-8234-0724-1). Holiday.

Sproxton, Mildred. Children's Treasure House of Poetry. (gr. 7-10). 1986. 22.00x (ISBN 0-7223-2073-6, Pub. by A H Stockwell England). State Mutual Bk.

Suire, Diane D., ed. Family. Hohag, Linda, illus. LC 89-772. 32p. (gr. k-3). 1989. PLB 11.97 (ISBN 0-89565-504-7). Childs World.

Szekeres, Cyndy, selected by. & illus. Cyndy Szekeres' Book of Poems. LC 86-23418. 48p. (gr. 2-5). 1987. Repr. of 1981 ed. write for info. (ISBN 0-307-15596-X, Pub. by Golden Bks). Western Pub.

Taylor, Phoebe, ed. Thoughts for the Free Life: Lao Tsu to the Present. 2nd ed. Buckley, Cicely, illus. 110p. (Orig.). (gr. 8 up). 1989. pap. 10.00 (ISBN 0-9617481-5-X). Oyster River Pr. With foreward & indices of 77 authors & 27 languages of origin. Illustrated with beautiful suggestive drawings by Cicely. Ideas from the cultures of 5 continents, 25 centuries, on the art of living. Free thought, the Natural Way, Life in Time...In exquisite book-making, with English translations often along side the originals. It is a joy to come upon its varied treasure. Among the jewels: Sophocles, Tagore, Cervantes, Isaiah, Job, the Palestinian poets, Neruda, Schweitzer, May Sarton, American Indian Wisdom. This is a book of inspiration & a peacemaking book. The preface tells how it was begun by a philospher & psychologist, while working on his dissertation at Harvard in the 1920's, on Belief & Behavior. "Truly a peacemaking book."--M. Grierson, Smith College Archivist Emeritus. "The native vision, the gift of seeing truly, with wonder & delightful insight into the natural world, is informed by a certain attitude of reverence & respect....In addition to the eye, it involves intelligence, the instinct & the imagination. It is the perception not only of objects & forms but also of essence & ideals."--J. Scott Momaday;

1934 Kiowa Indian.
Publisher Provided Annotation.

Tudor, Tasha, illus. First Poems of Childhood. 32p. (ps-1). 1990. 8.95 (ISBN 0-448-09326-X, G&D). Putnam Pub Group.

Untermeyer, Louis, ed. Rainbow in the Sky: Golden Anniversary Edition. Birch, Reginald, illus. LC 84-19306. 528p. (gr. 3-6). 1985. 19.95 (ISBN 0-15-265479-8, HJ). HarBraceJ.

Wade, Theodore E., Jr., ed. With Joy, Poems for Children. rev. ed. LC 88-72233. (Illus.). 48p. (gr. k-7). 1988. pap. 2.95 (ISBN 0-930192-20-6). Gazelle Pubns.

Wallace, Daisy, ed. Monster Poems. Chorao, Kay, illus. LC 75-17680. 32p. (gr. k-3). 1990. reinforced 12.95 (ISBN 0-8234-0268-1); pap. 4.95 (ISBN 0-8234-0848-5). Holiday.

Webber, Helen. How Long Is Long Ago & Other Poems. Webber, Helen, illus. (gr. k-6). 1968. 8.95 (ISBN 0-8392-3068-0). Astor-Honor.

Wilhelm, Hans. Mother Goose on the Loose. Wilhelm, Hans, illus. LC 88-37925. 24p. (gr. k-5). 1989. 4.95 (ISBN 0-8069-6990-3). Sterling.

Worth, Valerie. More Small Poems. Babbitt, Natalie, illus. LC 76-28323. 48p. (gr. 3 up). 1976. 8.95 (ISBN 0-374-35022-1). FS&G.

Young Folks' Book of Mirth: A Collection of the Best Fun in Prose & Verse. LC 79-51961. (gr. 2-6). 1980. Repr. of 1924 ed. 19.75x (ISBN 0-89609-197-X). Roth Pub Inc.

POETRY–INDEXES
Damon, Valerie H. Grindle Lamfoon & the Procurnious Fleekers. Damon, Dave, ed. Damon, Valerie H., illus. LC 78-64526. (gr. 1-12). 1979. 12.95 (ISBN 0-932356-05-2); fleeker ed. 14.95 (ISBN 0-932356-06-0). Star Pubns MO.

POETS
see also Dramatists
Bernotas, Bob. Amiri Baraka (Le Roi Jones) King, Coretta Scott, intro. by. (Illus.). 112p. (gr. 5 up). 1991. PLB 17.95 (ISBN 0-7910-1117-8). Chelsea Hse.

Bhatt, H. D. Kalidas. (Illus.). (gr. 3-8). 1979. pap. 3.95 (ISBN 0-89744-144-3). Auromere.

Bodie, Idella. A Hunt for Life's Extras: The Story of Archibald Rutledge. (Illus.). 176p. (gr. 5-12). 1986. pap. 6.95 (ISBN 0-87844-073-9). Sandlapper Pub Co.

Levinson, Nancy S. I Lift My Lamp: Emma Lazarus & the Statue of Liberty. LC 86-4394. (Illus.). 128p. (gr. 5-9). 1986. 13.95 (ISBN 0-525-67180-3, Lodestar Bks). Dutton Child Bks.

Longo, Lucas. Robert Frost: Twentieth Century Modern American Poet Laureate. Rahmas, D. Steve, ed. LC 70-190239. 32p. (gr. 7-12). 1972. lib. bdg. 4.20 incl. catalog cards (ISBN 0-87157-521-3). SamHar Pr.

POETS–FICTION
Cole, William, ed. Poem Stew. Weinhaus, Karen, illus. LC 81-47106. 96p. (gr. 2-6). 1983. pap. 4.95 (ISBN 0-06-440136-7, Trophy). HarpC Child Bks.

Siebert, Diane. Heartland. Minor, Wendell, illus. LC 87-29380. 32p. (ps-3). 1989. 13.95 (ISBN 0-690-04730-4, Crowell Jr Bks); PLB 13.89 (ISBN 0-690-04732-0). HarpC Child Bks.

Yolen, Jane. The Stone Silences. 128p. (gr. 7 up). 1984. 10.95 (ISBN 0-399-20971-9, Philomel). Putnam Pub Group.

POETRY–PHILOSOPHY
see Poetry
POETRY–SELECTIONS
see Poetry–Collections
POETRY–TECHNIQUE
see Poetics
POETRY FOR CHILDREN
see Nursery Rhymes; Poetry
POETRY OF LOVE
see Love Poetry
POETRY OF NATURE
see Nature in Poetry
POISONOUS PLANTS
Coil, Suzanne M. Poisonous Plants. (Illus.). 64p. (gr. 3-5). 1991. PLB 11.90 (ISBN 0-531-20017-5). Watts.

Lerner, Carol. Dumb Cane & Daffodils: Poisonous Plants in the House & Garden. Lerner, Carol, illus. LC 89-33622. 32p. 1990. 13.95 (ISBN 0-688-08791-4); PLB 13.88 (ISBN 0-688-08796-5, Morrow Jr Bks). Morrow Jr Bks.

—Moonseed & Mistletoe: A Book of Poisonous Wild Plants. LC 87-13989. (Illus.). 32p. (ps up). 1988. 12.95 (ISBN 0-688-07307-7); PLB 12.88 (ISBN 0-688-07308-5, Morrow Jr Bks). Morrow Jr Bks.

POISONS
Chlad, Dorothy. Poisons Make You Sick. Halverson, Lydia, illus. LC 83-24029. 32p. (ps-2). 1984. lib. bdg. 14.60 (ISBN 0-516-01976-7); pap. 3.95 (ISBN 0-516-41976-5). Childrens.

Gay, Kathlyn. Silent Killers: Radon & Other Hazards. Kline, M., ed. (Illus.). (gr. 6-12). 1988. PLB 12.90 (ISBN 0-531-10598-9). Watts.

Kronenwetter, Michael. Managing Toxic Wastes. Steltenpohl, Jane, ed. (Illus.). 126p. (gr. 7-10). 1989. lib. bdg. 12.98 (ISBN 0-671-69051-5). Messner.

Kusinitz, Marc. Poisons & Toxins. (Illus.). (gr. 6-12). 1992. 18.95 (ISBN 0-7910-0074-5). Chelsea Hse.

Zipko, Stephen J. Toxic Threat: How Hazardous Substances Poison Our Lives. rev. ed. Steltenpohl, Jane, ed. (Illus.). 208p. (gr. 7 up). 1990. PLB 12.98 (ISBN 0-671-69330-1); pap. 5.95 (ISBN 0-671-69331-X). Messner.

POLAND
Craig, Mary. Lech Walesa: The Leader of Solidarity & Campaigner for Freedom & Human Rights in Poland. LC 88-17732. (Illus.). 68p. (gr. 5-6). 1990. PLB 12.95 (ISBN 1-55532-821-0). Gareth Stevens Inc.

Donica, Ewa & Sharman, Tim. We Live in Poland. LC 84-73583. (Illus.). 64p. (gr. 7-9). 1985. 9.49 (ISBN 0-531-03819-X, Pub. by Bookwright Pr). Watts.

Greene, Carol. Poland. LC 82-19737. (Illus.). 128p. (gr. 5-9). 1983. PLB 25.27 (ISBN 0-516-02783-2). Childrens.

Holland, Gini. Poland. LC 89-43181. (Illus.). 64p. (gr. 5-6). 1991. PLB 12.95 (ISBN 0-8368-0233-0). Gareth Stevens Inc.

Lye, Keith. Take a Trip to Poland. (Illus.). (gr. k-3). 1985. PLB 7.99 (ISBN 0-531-04887-X). Watts.

Pfeiffer, Christine. Poland: Land of Freedom Fighters. (Illus.). 144p. (gr. 5 up). 1991. PLB 14.95 (ISBN 0-87518-464-2, Dillon). Macmillan Child Grp.

Popescu, Julian. Poland. (Illus.). (gr. 5 up). 1988. 14.95 (ISBN 0-222-01036-3). Chelsea Hse.

Sandak, Cass R. Poland. LC 85-26596. (Illus.). 72p. (gr. 4-9). 1986. lib. bdg. 10.40 (ISBN 0-531-10126-6). Watts.

Stewart, Gail B. Poland. LC 90-35498. (Illus.). 48p. (gr. 5-6). 1990. RSBE 10.95 (ISBN 0-89686-549-5, Crestwood Hse). Macmillan Child Grp.

Zyskind, Sara. Stolen Years. LC 81-1953. 288p. (gr. 6 up). 1981. 11.95 (ISBN 0-8225-0766-8). Lerner Pubns.

POLAND–FICTION
Seidler, Babara. The Legend of King Piast. Kedron, Jane, tr. Rosinski, Grzegorz, illus. (gr. 2-8). 1977. pap. 1.00 (ISBN 0-917004-08-6). Kosciuszko.

Singer, Isaac Bashevis. The Fools of Chelm & Their History. Shub, Elizabeth, tr. from YID. Shulevitz, Uri, illus. LC 73-81500. 64p. (gr. 3 up). 1973. 11.95 (ISBN 0-374-32444-1). FS&G.

POLAR EXPEDITIONS
see Antarctic Regions; Arctic Regions; Polar Regions; South Pole
POLAR REGIONS
see also Antarctic Regions; Arctic Regions; South Pole
Byles, Monica. Life in the Polar Lands. (Illus.). 32p. (gr. 5-8). 1990. PLB 11.40 (ISBN 0-531-10982-8). Watts.

James, Barbara. Conserving the Polar Regions. LC 90-46064. (Illus.). 48p. (gr. 4-9). 1990. PLB 18.60 (ISBN 0-8114-2393-X). Steck-V.

Lambert, David. Polar Regions. (Illus.). 48p. (gr. 5-8). 1987. PLB 14.98 (ISBN 0-382-09502-2). Silver Burdett Pr.

Stewart, G. In the Polar Regions. (Illus.). 32p. (gr. 3-8). 1989. lib. bdg. 13.26 (ISBN 0-86592-108-3). Rourke Corp.

Stone, L. Arctic Tundra. (Illus.). 48p. (gr. 4-8). 1989. lib. bdg. 14.00 (ISBN 0-86592-436-8). Rourke Corp.

POLES IN THE U. S.
Toor, Rachel. The Polish Americans. Moynihan, Daniel P., intro. by. 112p. (Orig.). (gr. 5 up). 1988. 17.95 (ISBN 0-87754-895-1); pap. 9.95 (ISBN 0-7910-0274-8). Chelsea Hse.

Wytrwal, Joseph. The Poles in America. LC 68-31506. (Illus.). 88p. (gr. 5 up). 1969. PLB 11.95 (ISBN 0-8225-0218-6); pap. 3.95 (ISBN 0-8225-1019-7). Lerner Pubns.

POLICE
see also Crime and Criminals; Criminal Investigation; Detectives; Secret Service;
also names of cities with the subdivision Police, e.g. N. Y. (city)–Police, etc.
Barrett, Norman. Picture World of Police Vehicles. LC 90-31020. (Illus.). 32p. (gr. k-4). 1991. PLB 11.40 (ISBN 0-531-14092-X). Watts.

Broekel, Ray. Police. LC 81-7693. (Illus.). 48p. (gr. k-4). 1981. PLB 13.27 (ISBN 0-516-01643-1). Childrens.

—La Policia. Kratky, Lada, tr. from ENG. LC 81-7693. (SPA., Illus.). 48p. (gr. k-4). 1984. lib. bdg. 14.60 (ISBN 0-516-31643-5); pap. 4.95 (ISBN 0-516-51643-4). Childrens.

Campling, Elizabeth. Timeline: The Police. (Illus.). 64p. (gr. 7-10). 1989. 19.95 (ISBN 0-85219-789-6, Pub. by Batsford England). Trafalgar Sq.

Dick, Jean. Bomb Squads & Swat Teams. LC 88-15907. (Illus.). 48p. (gr. 5-6). 1988. PLB 10.95 (ISBN 0-89686-401-4, Crestwood Hse). Macmillan Child Grp.

Dolan, Edward F. The Police in American Society. Rasof, Henry, ed. LC 88-14265. (Illus.). 160p. (gr. 7-12). 1988. PLB 13.90 (ISBN 0-531-10608-X). Watts.

Dumpleton, John. Law & Order: The Story of the Police. (Illus.). (gr. 3-7). 1983. Repr. of 1963 ed. 14.95 (ISBN 0-7136-1079-4). Dufour.

Hannum, Dotti. A Visit to the Police Station. Flanagen, Romie, photos by. LC 84-12700. (Illus.). 32p. (gr. k-3). 1985. PLB 14.60 (ISBN 0-516-01493-5); pap. 3.95 (ISBN 0-516-41493-3). Childrens.

Hewett, Joan. Motorcycle on Patrol: The Story of a Highway Officer. Hewett, Richard, illus. LC 86-2689. 48p. (gr. 3 up). 1986. 12.95 (ISBN 0-89919-372-2, Pub. by Clarion). Ticknor & Fields.

Hunter, David. Black Friday Coming Down. LC 89-70361. 240p. 1990. 14.95 (ISBN 1-558-53061-4). Rutledge Hill Pr.

Johnson, Jean. Police Officers: A to Z. (Illus.). 48p. (gr. k-3). 1986. 11.95 (ISBN 0-8027-6614-5); lib. bdg. 12.85 (ISBN 0-8027-6615-3). Walker & Co.

Nau, Patrick. State Patrol. Nau, Pat, photos by. LC 83-2716. (Illus.). 32p. (gr. k-4). 1984. PLB 9.95 (ISBN 0-87614-264-1). Carolrhoda Bks.

POLICE–FICTION
Baum, L. Frank. Policeman Bluejay. LC 81-9044. (gr. 1-6). 1981. Repr. of 1907 ed. 35.00x (ISBN 0-8201-1367-0). Schol Facsimiles.
Corbett, Scott. Cop's Kid. (Illus.). (gr. 4-6). 1968. 13.95 (ISBN 0-316-15660-4, Joy St Bks). Little.
Morey, Walt. The Lemon Meringue Dog. LC 80-171. 176p. (gr. 4-7). 1980. 13.95 (ISBN 0-525-33455-6, DCB). Dutton Child Bks.
Thomson, Andy. Sheriff at Waterstop. (Illus.). 133p. (Orig.). (gr. 4-6). 1987. pap. 4.95 (ISBN 0-89084-371-6). Bob Jones Univ Pr.
Whitman, Ken & Wilkey, Chris. Mutazoids. Sumner, Robert, ed. Radford, Stephan, illus. 98p. (Orig.). (gr. 10-12). 1989. pap. text ed. 12.95 (ISBN 0-685-29088-3). Whit Prodns.
POLICE–VOCATIONAL GUIDANCE
Martin, John H. A Day in the Life of a Police Cadet. Jann, Gayle, illus. LC 84-2578. 32p. (gr. 4-8). 1985. PLB 11.79 (ISBN 0-8167-0103-2); pap. text ed. 2.95 (ISBN 0-8167-0104-0). Troll Assocs.
Matthias, Catherine. I Can Be a Police Officer. LC 84-12106. (Illus.). 32p. (gr. k-3). 1984. lib. bdg. 13.93 (ISBN 0-516-01840-X); pap. 3.95 (ISBN 0-516-41840-8). Childrens.
Pellowski, Michael J. What's It Like to Be a Police Officer. Dolobowsky, Mena, illus. LC 89-34395. 32p. (gr. k-3). 1989. lib. bdg. 10.89 (ISBN 0-8167-1811-3); pap. text ed. 2.50 (ISBN 0-8167-1812-1). Troll Assocs.
Smith, Carter. A Day in the Life of an FBI Agent-in-Training. Jantzen, Franz, illus. LC 90-11150. 32p. (gr. 4-8). 1991. PLB 11.79 (ISBN 0-8167-2210-2); pap. text ed. 2.95 (ISBN 0-8167-2211-0). Troll Assocs.
POLICE DOGS
Curtis, Patricia. Dogs on the Case: Search Dogs Who Help Save Lives & Enforce the Law. Cupp, David, photos by. LC 88-37990. (Illus.). 128p. (gr. 5-9). 1989. 15.95 (ISBN 0-525-67274-5, Lodestar Bks). Dutton Child Bks.
Emert, Phyllis R. Law Enforcement Dogs. LC 85-21351. (Illus.). 48p. (gr. 5-6). 1985. 10.95 (ISBN 0-89686-284-4, Crestwood Hse). Macmillan Child Grp.
McPherson, Jan. The Dog School. LC 90-10085. (Illus.). 24p. (gr. 1-4). 1990. PLB 15.96 (ISBN 0-8114-2697-1). Steck-V.
POLITENESS
see Courtesy; Etiquette
POLITICAL CRIMES AND OFFENSES
Raynor, Thomas P. Terrorism. 160p. (gr. 7 up). 1982. PLB 11.90 (ISBN 0-531-04499-8). Watts.
POLITICAL CRIMES AND OFFENSES–FICTION
Cormier, Robert. After the First Death. LC 78-11770. (Illus.). (gr. 7-12). 1979. 7.95 (ISBN 0-394-84122-0); lib. bdg. 12.99 (ISBN 0-394-94122-5). Pantheon.
Hale, Edward E. Man Without a Country & Other Stories. (gr. 5 up). 1968. pap. 1.95 (ISBN 0-8049-0185-6, CL-185). Airmont.
POLITICAL ECONOMY
see Economics
POLITICAL PARTIES
see also Politics, Practical
also names of parties, e.g. Democratic Party
POLITICAL SCIENCE
see also Church and State; Citizenship; Civil Rights; Communism; Democracy; Government, Resistance to; Kings and Rulers; Law; Liberty; Local Government; Revolutions; State Governments; World Politics
Arab-Israeli Issue. LC 86-20259. (Illus.). (gr. 7 up). 1987. 17.26 (ISBN 0-86592-029-X). Rourke Corp.
Coffey, William E., et al. West Virginia Government. Buckalew, Marshall & Thoenen, Eugenia G., eds. (Illus.). 112p. (Orig.). (gr. 8). 1984. pap. 10.00 (ISBN 0-914498-05-3). WV Hist Ed Found.
Cook, J. Introduction to Politics & Governments. 48p. (gr. 6 up). 1981. pap. 6.95 (ISBN 0-7460-0047-2). EDC.
DeBiase, Louis A. How to Break into Politics on a Shoestring. Lyon, Lucinda, illus. 61p. (Orig.). (gr. 9-12). 1981. pap. 4.95 (ISBN 0-686-31571-5). Louvin Pub.
Hyde, Margaret O. & Forsyth, Elizabeth H. Terrorism. 160p. (gr. 9-12). 1987. 11.95 (ISBN 0-399-61240-8, Putnam). Putnam Pub Group.
Kronenwetter, Michael. Are You a Liberal? Are You A Conservative? (Illus.). 96p. (gr. 7-12). 1984. lib. bdg. 12.90 (ISBN 0-531-04751-2). Watts.
Lee, Richard S. & Lee, Mary P. Careers for Women in Politics. Rosen, Ruth, ed. (gr. 7-12). 1989. PLB 12.95 (ISBN 0-8239-0966-2). Rosen Group.
Lewis, Barbara A. A Kid's Guide to Social Action: How to Solve the Social Problems You Choose - & Turn Creative Thinking Into Positive Action. Espeland, Pamela, ed. (Illus.). 160p. (Orig.). (gr. 5 up). 1991. pap. 14.95 (ISBN 0-915793-29-6). Free Spirit Pub.
Machiavelli, Niccolo. Prince. Detmold, C. E., intro. by. (gr. 11 up). pap. 2.50 (ISBN 0-8049-0056-6, CL-56). Airmont.
Plato. Plato's Republic. Jowett, Benjamin, tr. Gemme, F., intro. by. (gr. 11 up). 1968. pap. 2.75 (ISBN 0-8049-0172-4, CL-172). Airmont.
Raynor, Thomas P. Politics, Power & People: Four Governments in Action. 128p. (gr. 7 up). lib. bdg. 12.90 (ISBN 0-531-04662-1). Watts.
Samuels, Cynthia K. It's a Free Country! A Young Person's Guide to Politics & Elections. LC 87-30857. (Illus.). 144p. (gr. 5 up). 1988. 13.95 (ISBN 0-689-31416-7, Atheneum Child Bk). Macmillan Child Grp.
Sharman, Tim. Rise of Solidarity. LC 86-20276. (Illus.). 78p. (gr. 7 up). 1987. 17.26 (ISBN 0-86592-030-3). Rourke Corp.
Suez Crisis. (Illus.). (gr. 7 up). lib. bdg. 17.26 (ISBN 0-86592-026-5). Rourke Corp.
POLITICS, PRACTICAL
see also Elections
Buhay, Debra. Black & White of Politics. 30p. (gr. 12). Date not set. pap. 2.00 (ISBN 1-878056-03-4). D Hockenberry.
POLITICS, PRACTICAL–FICTION
Eyerly, Jeannette. Radigan Cares. LC 71-11722. (gr. 7-9). 1970. 6.50 (ISBN 0-397-31151-6, Lipp Jr Bks). HarpC Child Bks.
Fritz, Jean. Shh! We're Writing the Constitution. De Paola, Tomie, illus. 64p. (gr. 3-7). 1987. 13.95 (ISBN 0-399-21403-8, Putnam); pap. 5.95 (ISBN 0-399-21404-6, Putnam). Putnam Pub Group.
Kemp, Gene. The Turbulent Term of Tyke Tiler. (Illus.). 118p. (gr. 5-8). 1980. 10.95 (ISBN 0-571-10966-7). Faber & Faber.
Nixon, Joan L. Candidate for Murder. 1991. 14.95 (ISBN 0-385-30257-6). Delacorte.
POLLS, ELECTION
see Elections
POLLUTION OF AIR
see Air–Pollution
POLLUTION OF WATER
see Water–Pollution
POLO, MARCO, 1254?-1324?
Ceserani, Gian P. Marco Polo. Ventura, Piero, illus. 40p. (gr. 3-7). 1982. 9.95 (ISBN 0-399-20843-7, Philomel). Putnam Pub Group.
Greene, Carol. Marco Polo: Voyager to the Orient. LC 86-29977. (Illus.). 112p. (gr. 4 up). 1987. PLB 17.27 (ISBN 0-516-03229-1). Childrens.
Humble, Richard. Travels of Marco Polo. 1990. PLB 11.90 (ISBN 0-531-14022-9). Watts.
Italia, Bob. Marco Polo. Walner, Rosemary, ed. (Illus.). 32p. (gr. 4). 1990. PLB 11.95 (ISBN 0-939179-92-X). Abdo & Dghtrs.
Marco Polo. (ARA., Illus.). (gr. 5-12). 3.50x (ISBN 0-86685-207-7). Intl Bk Ctr.
Reynolds, Kathy, ed. Marco Polo. Woods, Dan, illus. LC 86-6678. 32p. (gr. 2-5). 1986. PLB 16.67 (ISBN 0-8172-2627-3); pap. text ed. 9.27 (ISBN 0-8172-2635-4). Raintree Pubs.
Rosen, Mike. The Travels of Marco Polo. Bull, Peter, illus. LC 88-23375. 32p. (gr. 4-6). 1989. PLB 11.40 (ISBN 0-531-18241-X). Watts.
Roth, Susan L. Marco Polo. (ps-3). 1991. 14.95 (ISBN 0-385-26495-X); PLB 15.99 (ISBN 0-385-26555-7). Doubleday.
Stefoff, Rebecca. Marco Polo. (Illus.). 112p. (gr. 5 up). 1992. PLB 18.95 (ISBN 0-7910-1294-8). Chelsea Hse.
POLTERGEISTS
see Ghosts
POLYMERS AND POLYMERIZATION
see also Plastics
POMPEII
Andrews, Ian. Pompeii. (Illus.). 48p. (gr. 7 up). 1978. pap. 5.95 (ISBN 0-521-20973-0). Cambridge U Pr.
Biel, Timothy L. Pompeii. LC 89-9395. (Illus.). 64p. (gr. 5-8). 1989. PLB 11.95 (ISBN 1-56006-000-X). Lucent Bks.
Connolly, Peter. Pompeii. (Illus.). 80p. (gr. 6 up). 1990. bds. 16.95 laminated (ISBN 0-19-917159-9). Oxford U Pr.
Goor, Ron & Goor, Nancy. Pompeii: Exploring a Roman Ghost Town. Goor, Ron & Goor, Nancy, illus. LC 85-47895. 128p. (gr. 5-9). 1986. 13.95 (ISBN 0-690-04515-8, Crowell Jr Bks); PLB 13.89 (ISBN 0-690-04516-6, Crowell Jr Bks). HarpC Child Bks.
Rosen, Mike. The Destruction of Pompeii. Caulkins, Janet, ed. (Illus.). 32p. (gr. k-6). 1988. PLB 10.90 (ISBN 0-531-18159-6, Pub. by Bookwright Pr). Watts.
POND ECOLOGY
see Fresh-Water Biology
Michels, Tilde. At the Frog Pond. Ignatowicz, Nina, tr. from GER. Michl, Reinhard, illus. LC 88-37835. 32p. (ps-4). 1989. 11.95 (ISBN 0-397-32314-X, Lipp Jr Bks); PLB 11.89 (ISBN 0-397-32315-8). HarpC Child Bks.
PONIES
see also Horses
Brady, Irene. America's Horses & Ponies. Brady, Irene, illus. 202p. (gr. 4 up). 1976. pap. 9.95 (ISBN 0-395-24050-6, Sandpiper). HM.
British Horse Society & Pony Club Staff. The Pony Club Book, No. 2. (Illus.). 60p. (gr. 1-6). 1988. 14.95 (ISBN 0-901366-17-X, Pub. by Threshold Bks). Half Halt Pr.
Burton, Jane. Dizzie the Pony. LC 89-11395. (Illus.). 32p. (gr. 2-3). 1989. PLB 10.95 (ISBN 0-8368-0207-1). Gareth Stevens Inc.
—Pacer the Pony. Burton, Jane, photos by. LC 89-42693. (Illus.). 24p. (Orig.). (ps-3). 1989. PLB 5.99 (ISBN 0-394-92271-9). Random.
Dennis, Wesley. Flip. Dennis, Wesley, illus. (ps-1). 1977. pap. 3.95 (ISBN 0-14-050203-3, Puffin). Puffin Bks.
—Flip & the Morning. Dennis, Wesley, illus. LC 51-13521. (ps-1). 1977. pap. 3.95 (ISBN 0-14-050204-1, Puffin). Puffin Bks.
Folsom, Franklin. Sand Dune Pony. (Illus.). 250p. (gr. 3-6). 1991. pap. 8.95 (ISBN 0-911797-99-8). R Rinehart Inc.
McGowan, E. M. Horses & Ponies, A Photo-Fact Book. (Illus., Orig.). 1988. pap. 1.95 (ISBN 0-942025-26-1). Kidsbks.
The Pony. Date not set. write for info. W J Fantasy.
Rawson, C. & Spector, J. Riding & Pony Care. 32p. (gr. 2 up). 1987. PLB 13.96 (ISBN 0-88110-297-0); pap. 7.95 (ISBN 0-7460-0111-8). EDC.
Robison, Nancy. The Ponies. LC 83-7833. (Illus.). 48p. (gr. 4 up). 1983. PLB 9.95 (ISBN 0-89686-229-1, Crestwood Hse). Macmillan Child Grp.
Royston, Angela. Pony. 1990. PLB 10.40 (ISBN 0-531-19081-1). Watts.
PONIES–FICTION
Bangs, Edward. Yankee Doodle. Kellogg, Steven, illus. 40p. (ps-3). 1984. 13.95 (ISBN 0-02-749800-X, Four Winds). Macmillan Child Grp.
Brady, Irene. Doodlebug. Brady, Irene, illus. LC 77-4168. 40p. (gr. 1-5). 1977. 13.95 (ISBN 0-395-25782-4). HM.
Campbell, John N. Gator: The Cowpony Goes to School. (Illus.). 72p. (gr. 4-7). 1990. 8.95 (ISBN 0-89015-699-9, Pub. by Panda Bks). Eakin Pr.

Cooley, Regina F. The Magic Christmas Pony. Hansen, Han H., illus. 36p. (gr. 1-5). 1991. 19.95 (ISBN 1-880450-04-6). Capstone Pub.
A carousel pony mysteriously disappears in the night, magically reappearing on Christmas Eve in the doorway of Frederick & Valentina's bedroom. With grandparents sleeping unaware in the next room, the Magic Christmas Pony whisks the mystified children to the Forbidden City in China. There they meet the Dragon of Fantasy, a close friend of the Magic Christmas Pony, & enjoy a Dragon banquet. After dining with the many Dragons, their adventure continues. They meet the Emperor & Empress of China & are further entranced by traditional Chinese dances & entertainment. Frederick & Valentina's exposure to the culture & traditions of the Chinese royalty becomes educational as well as entertaining. The Forbidden City comes to life with the rich detail provided by Regina Francoise Cooley, the author, whose thorough research lends a realistic backdrop to this enchanting tale. Hans Henrik Hansen, a well known illustrator from Denmark, has established his reputation in the plate collecting world with collectors plates from both Bing & Grondahl & Royal Copenhagen. His unique use of brilliant saturated color & superb detail has created a book worthy of being called a collectors item. Capstone Publishing Inc. is proud to present this mesmerizing & timeless story.
Publisher Provided Annotation.

Cosgrove, Stephen. Mumkin. James, Robin, illus. LC 86-15635. (gr. k-2). 1986. 12.66 (ISBN 0-86592-242-X). Rourke Corp.
Crompton, Anne E. The Snow Pony. 128p. (gr. 4-7). Date not set. 14.95 (ISBN 0-8050-1573-6). H Holt & Co.
Davis, Jim. My Little Pony Through the Seasons. Allert, Kathy, illus. 64p. (ps-3). 1985. pap. 2.95 (ISBN 0-394-87387-4, Random Juv). Random.
Fidler, Kathleen. Haki the Shetland Pony. 142p. (gr. 5-8). 1989. pap. 5.95 (ISBN 0-86241-075-4, Pub. by Cnngt Pub Ltd). Trafalgar Sq.
Hall, Lynn. Mrs. Portree's Pony. LC 85-43353. 96p. (gr. 4-7). 1986. 12.95 (ISBN 0-684-18576-8, Scribners Young Read). Macmillan Child Grp.
Hamilton, Dorothy. Cricket. Van Demark, Paul, illus. LC 74-30421. 80p. (gr. 3-7). 1975. pap. 3.95 (ISBN 0-8361-1761-1). Herald Pr.
Henry, Marguerite. Sea Star, Orphan of Chincoteague. 2nd ed. Dennis, Wesley, illus. 176p. (gr. 3-7). 1991. pap. 3.95 (ISBN 0-689-71530-7, Aladdin). Macmillan Child Grp.
Kirkwood, James. There Must Be a Pony. 1989. pap. 4.50 (ISBN 0-440-20238-8). Dell.
Kuchn, Nora A. Thunder, the Maverick Mustang. 96p. 1991. pap. 6.95 (ISBN 0-8163-0932-9). Pacific Pr Pub Assn.
Matthews, Maria. My Little Pony: Baby Firefly's Adventure & Other My Little Pony Stories. Beylon, Cathy, illus. LC 85-42537. 32p. (gr. 1-5). 1985. 4.95 (ISBN 0-394-87386-6, Random Juv). Random.

My Little Pony Sea Ponies Water Fun. Woods, Mia, illus. 10p. (ps). 1985. vinyl 2.95 (ISBN 0-394-86996-6, Random Juv). Random.
My Little Pony Story. 1989. pap. 0.66 (ISBN 0-394-82361-3). Random.
Penner, Fred & Oberman, Sheldon. Julie Gerond & the Polka Dot Pony. Pakarnyk, Alan, illus. 32p. (gr. 2-6). 1990. pap. 5.95 (ISBN 0-920534-70-8, Pub. by Hyperion Pr Ltd CN). Sterling.
Primavera, Elise. Basil & Maggie. Primavera, Elise, illus. LC 82-48455. 32p. (gr. 1-3). 1983. (Lipp Jr Bks). HarpC Child Bks.
Steinbeck, John. The Red Pony. reissue ed. Dennis, Wesley, illus. (gr. 7 up). 1986. pap. 15.95 (ISBN 0-670-59184-X). Viking Child Bks.
Thompson, Polly. My Little Pony: Where Is Cuddles? A Book of Hidden Surprises. Dyer, Jane, illus. LC 85-60496. 14p. (gr. 2-4). 1985. 4.95 (ISBN 0-394-87425-0, Random Juv). Random.
Timm, Carey. My Little Pony Learns to Count. Stott, Dot, illus. LC 85-60498. 14p. (gr. 2-6). 1985. 3.95 (ISBN 0-394-87388-2, Random Juv). Random.
Ward, Lynd. The Silver Pony: A Story in Pictures. Ward, Lynd, illus. LC 72-5402. 192p. (gr. k-3). 1973. 14.95 (ISBN 0-395-14753-0). HM.
Weber, Kathryn. Midnite & Mark. Hamilton, Sandi, illus. LC 83-8622. 64p. (Orig.). (gr. 4-6). 1983. pap. 3.95 (ISBN 0-88100-021-3). Ranch House Pr.

PONTIAC, OTTAWA CHIEF, d. 1769

Fleischer, Jane. Pontiac, Chief of the Ottawas. LC 78-18050. (Illus.). 48p. (gr. 4-6). 1979. PLB 9.89 (ISBN 0-89375-156-1); pap. 2.95 (ISBN 0-89375-146-4); cassette avail. Troll Assocs.
Wheeler, Jill. The Story of Pontiac. Deegan, Paul, ed. Dodson, Liz, illus. 32p. (gr. 4). 1989. PLB 11.95 (ISBN 0-939179-69-5). Abdo & Dghtrs.
Zadra, Dan. Indians of America: Pontiac. rev. ed. (gr. 2-4). 1987. PLB 11.50s.p. (ISBN 0-88682-160-6); 16.45 (ISBN 0-685-19790-5). Creative Ed.

PONY EXPRESS

DiCerto, Joseph J. The Pony Express: Hoofbeats in the Wilderness. (Illus.). 64p. (gr. 3-5). 1989. PLB 11.90 (ISBN 0-531-10751-5). Watts.
Lake, A. L. Pony Express. (Illus.). 32p. (gr. 3-8). 1990. PLB 17.26 (ISBN 0-86625-368-8). Rourke Corp.
McCall, Edith. Mail Riders. Eckart, Frances, illus. LC 61-10103. 128p. (gr. 3-10). 1980. PLB 14.60 (ISBN 0-516-03347-6). Childrens.
Stein, R. Conrad. The Story of the Pony Express. LC 81-4558. (Illus.). 32p. (gr. 3-6). 1981. PLB 13.27 (ISBN 0-516-04631-4). Childrens.

POODLES

Moncure, Jane B. Mr. Doodle Had a Poodle. Hohag, Linda, illus. LC 87-15808. 32p. (ps-2). 1987. PLB 11.97 (ISBN 0-89565-409-1); pap. 6.96 (ISBN 0-89565-429-6). Childs World.

POPES

Daughters of St. Paul. Karol from Poland. (gr. 4-9). write for info. Dghtrs St Paul.
—No Place for Defeat. (gr. 3-9). 3.00 (ISBN 0-8198-0241-7). Dghtrs St Paul.
Sullivan, George. Pope John Paul II: The People's Pope. LC 83-40395. (Illus.). 120p. (gr. 7 up). 1984. 11.95 (ISBN 0-8027-6523-8). Walker & Co.
Walch, Timothy. John Paul Second. (Illus.). (gr. 5 up). 1990. 17.95 (ISBN 1-55546-839-X). Chelsea Hse.
Wolfe, Rinna. The Singing Pope: The Story of Pope John Paul II. (Illus.). 128p. (gr. 6-8). 1984. 8.95 (ISBN 0-8164-0472-0). Harper SF.

POPULAR GOVERNMENT

see Democracy

POPULAR MUSIC

see Music, Popular (Songs, etc.)

POPULATION

see also Birth Control
also names of countries, cities, etc. with the subdivision Population, e.g. U. S.–Population

Aaseng, Nathan. Overpopulation: Crisis or Challenge? (Illus.). 160p. (gr. 9-12). 1991. PLB 12.90 (ISBN 0-531-11006-0). Watts.
Becklake, John. Population Explosion. 1990. PLB 11.90 (ISBN 0-531-17198-1). Watts.
Fairfield, Shelia. Peoples & Nations, 5 vols. (Illus.). 320p. (gr. 5-6). 1988. Set. PLB 69.75 (ISBN 1-55532-936-5). Gareth Stevens Inc.
Gallant, Roy A. The Peopling of Planet Earth: Human Population Growth Through the Ages. LC 89-34575. (Illus.). 176p. (gr. 3-7). 1990. 15.95 (ISBN 0-02-735772-4, Mcmillan Child Bk). Macmillan Child Grp.
Hoff, Mary & Rodgers, Mary M. Our Endangered Planet: Population Growth. (Illus.). 64p. 1991. PLB 15.95 (ISBN 0-8225-2502-X). Lerner Pubns.
McGraw, Eric. Population Growth. (Illus.). 48p. (gr. 5 up). 1987. Set. PLB 72.00 (ISBN 0-317-60380-9); PLB 18.00 (ISBN 0-86592-276-4). Rourke Corp.
Maifair, Linda. People & Places. Burris, Priscilla, illus. Sussman, Ellen, intro. by. (Illus.). 64p. (gr. 3-6). 1989. pap. 6.95 (ISBN 0-933606-72-9). Monkey Sisters.
The World's Children, 5 vols. LC 88-21723. (Illus.). 240p. (gr. 4-9). 1988. Set. 69.95 (ISBN 0-86307-987-3). Marshall Cavendish.

POPULATION, FOREIGN

see Immigration and Emigration

PORCELAIN ENAMELS

see Enamel and Enameling

PORCUPINES

Blassingame, Wyatt. Porcupines. (gr. 2-5). 1982. 8.95 (ISBN 0-396-08074-X, Putnam). Putnam Pub Group.
Dalmais. Porcupine, Reading Level 3-4. (Illus.). 28p. (gr. 2-5). Date not set. PLB 14.60 (ISBN 0-86592-852-5). Rourke Corp.
Schneider, Jeff. My Friend the Porpoise: An Ocean Magic Book. Spoon, Wilfred, illus. LC 90-61572. 12p. (ps). 1991. 4.95g (ISBN 1-877779-07-5). Schneider Educational.
Sherrow, Victoria. The Porcupine. (Illus.). 60p. (gr. 3 up). 1991. PLB 12.95 (ISBN 0-87518-442-1, Dillon). Macmillan Child Grp.

PORCUPINES–FICTION

Ben & the Porcupine. 32p. (ps-3). 1981. 13.95 (ISBN 0-395-30171-8, Clarion). HM.
Christian, Mary B. Penrod's Pants. Dyer, Jane, illus. LC 85-11545. 56p. (gr. 1-4). 1986. 9.95 (ISBN 0-02-718520-6, Mcmillan Child Bk). Macmillan Child Grp.
—Penrod's Pants. 56p. (gr. 1-4). 1989. pap. 3.95 (ISBN 0-689-71340-1, Aladdin). Macmillan Child Grp.
—Penrod's Party. Schindler, S. D., illus. LC 89-37203. 48p. (gr. 1-4). 1990. 11.95 (ISBN 0-02-718525-7, Mcmillan Child Bk). Macmillan Child Grp.
Greenleaf, E. Pricky, a Pet Porcupine. LC 65-22311. (Illus.). 48p. (gr. 2-5). 1968. PLB 10.95 (ISBN 0-87783-031-2); pap. 3.94 deluxe ed. (ISBN 0-87783-158-0). Oddo.
Harshman, Terry W. Porcupine's Pajama Party. Cushman, Doug, illus. LC 87-45681. 64p. (gr. k-3). 1990. pap. 3.50 (ISBN 0-06-444140-7, Trophy). HarpC Child Bks.
Lester, Helen. A Porcupine Named Fluffy. LC 85-24820. 32p. (ps-3). 1989. 13.95 (ISBN 0-395-36895-2); pap. 4.95 (ISBN 0-395-52018-5). HM.
Littke, Lael. The Day Porcupine Put on the Dog at Peanut Butter Pond. Britt, Stephanie M., illus. 36p. (ps-1). 1990. pap. 15.95 incl. audiocassette (ISBN 1-55999-123-2). LinguiSystems.
Stren, Patti. Hug Me. LC 76-58694. (Illus.). (gr. k-3). 1977. PLB 11.89 (ISBN 0-06-026081-5). HarpC Child Bks.
Thomas, Patricia. One & Only Super-Duper, Golly-Whopper, Jim-Dandy, Really-Handy Clock-Tock Stopper. 32p. 1990. 13.95 (ISBN 0-688-09340-X); PLB 13.88 (ISBN 0-688-09341-8). Lothrop.
Van De Wetering, Janwillem. Hugh Pine & the Good Place. Munsinger, Lynn, illus. LC 86-3108. 80p. (gr. 3 up). 1986. 12.95 (ISBN 0-395-40147-X). HM.
Zalben, Jane B. Porcupine's Christmas Blues. Zalben, Jane B., illus. 32p. 1982. 9.95 (ISBN 0-399-20893-3, Philomel). Putnam Pub Group.

PORPOISES

Gordon, Sharon. Dolphins & Porpoises. Goldsborough, June, illus. LC 84-8594. 32p. (gr. k-2). 1985. PLB 10.89 (ISBN 0-8167-0340-X); pap. text ed. 2.95 (ISBN 0-8167-0443-0). Troll Assocs.
Hatherly, Janelle & Nicholls, Delia. Dolphins & Porpoises. 72p. 1990. 17.95x (ISBN 0-8160-2272-0). Facts on File.
McGowen, Tom. Album of Whales. Ruth, Rod, illus. 64p. (gr. 4-7). 1980. write for info. (ISBN 0-528-82287-X). Checkerboard Pr.
Patent, Dorothy H. Dolphins & Porpoises. LC 87-45332. (Illus.). 96p. (gr. 4 up). 1987. reinforced bdg. 14.95 (ISBN 0-8234-0663-6). Holiday.
—Looking at Dolphins & Porpoises. LC 88-39985. (Illus.). 48p. (gr. 1-4). 1989. reinforced bdg. 12.95 (ISBN 0-8234-0748-9). Holiday.

PORPOISES–FICTION

Dominick, Bayard. Joe, a Porpoise. (Illus.). (gr. 3-5). 1968. 10.95 (ISBN 0-8392-3067-2). Astor-Honor.
Geaghan Alessi, Louise. Poindexter the Porpoise. (ps-7). 1989. 5.95 (ISBN 0-533-07978-0). Vantage.

POST OFFICE

see Postal Service

PORTRAIT PAINTING

see also Crayon Drawing

PORTRAITS

see also Cartoons and Caricatures

Coen, Rena N. Kings & Queens in Art. LC 64-8042. (Illus.). (gr. 5 up). 1965. PLB 5.95 (ISBN 0-8225-0155-4). Lerner Pubns.
Lerner, Sharon. Self-Portrait in Art. LC 64-8202. (Illus.). (gr. 5 up). 1965. PLB 5.95 (ISBN 0-8225-0154-6). Lerner Pubns.

PORTS

see Harbors

PORTUGAL

Cross, Esther & Cross, Wilbur. Portugal. LC 85-26991. (Illus.). 127p. (gr. 5-6). 1986. PLB 25.27 (ISBN 0-516-02778-6). Childrens.
Lye, Keith. Take a Trip to Portugal. LC 86-50019. (Illus.). 32p. (gr. 1-6). 1986. PLB 7.99 (ISBN 0-531-10196-7). Watts.
Selfridge, John. Portugal. (Illus.). (gr. 5 up). 1990. 14.95 (ISBN 0-7910-1366-9). Chelsea Hse.

PORTUGAL–FICTION

Hope, Laura L. Bobbsey Twins' Search for the Green Rooster. (gr. 1-4). 1965. 4.50 (ISBN 0-448-08058-3, G&D). Putnam Pub Group.
L'Engle, Madeleine. The Arm of the Starfish. LC 65-10919. 256p. (gr. 7 up). 1965. 16.95 (ISBN 0-374-30396-7). FS&G.

POSSUM

see Opossums

POSTAGE STAMPS

Boy Scouts of America. Stamp Collecting. (Illus.). 48p. (gr. 6-12). 1974. pap. 1.85 (ISBN 0-8395-3359-4, 3359). BSA.
Hobson, Burton. Stamp Collecting As a Hobby. rev. & enl. ed. Obojski, Robert, ed. LC 86-6015. (Illus.). 192p. (gr. 4-10). 1986. flexiband 9.95 (ISBN 0-8069-4794-2). Sterling.
Jacobsen, Karen. Stamps. LC 83-7591. (Illus.). 48p. (gr. k-4). 1983. PLB 14.60 (ISBN 0-516-01709-8). Childrens.
Lewis, Brenda R. Stamps! A Young Collector's Guide. (Illus.). 96p. (gr. 5-9). 1991. 14.95 (ISBN 0-525-67341-5, Lodestar Bks). Dutton Child Bks.
Macdonald, David S., ed. U. S. Liberty Album. (Illus.). 416p. (gr. 6 up). 1984. text ed. 18.95 (ISBN 0-937458-29-5). Harris & Co.
Schwarz, Ted. The Beginner's Guide to Stamp Collecting. 192p. (gr. 12 up). 1983. pap. 10.95 (ISBN 0-668-05551-0). Prentice Hall Pr.

POSTAL SERVICE

see also Pony Express

Barklow, Irene. The Old & the New: History of the Post Offices of Wallowa County. (Illus.). 184p. (Orig.). (gr. 8 up). 1987. pap. 11.95 (ISBN 0-9618185-1-4). Enchant Pub Oregon.
Bolger, William F., intro. by. All about Letters. Rev. ed. LC 82-600601. (Illus.). 64p. (gr. 9-12). 1982. pap. 2.50x (ISBN 0-685-06202-3, 01135). USPS.
—P. S. Write Soon! All about Letters. LC 82-600641. (Illus.). 64p. (Orig.). (gr. 4-8). 1982. pap. 2.50x (ISBN 0-8141-3796-2, 37962). USPS.
Gibbons, Gail. The Post Office Book: Mail & How It Moves. Gibbons, Gail, illus. LC 85-45397. 32p. (gr. k-4). 1986. pap. 4.95 (ISBN 0-06-446029-0, Trophy). HarpC Child Bks.
Johnson, Jean. Postal Workers: A to Z. (Illus.). 48p. (gr. 1-3). 1987. 11.95 (ISBN 0-8027-6663-3); PLB 12.85 (ISBN 0-8027-6664-1). Walker & Co.
Matthews, Morgan. What's It Like to Be a Postal Worker. Hicks, Mark A., illus. LC 89-34385. 32p. (gr. k-3). 1989. lib. bdg. 10.89 (ISBN 0-8167-1813-X); pap. text ed. 2.50 (ISBN 0-8167-1814-8). Troll Assocs.
Roth, Harold. First Class! The Postal System in Action. LC 82-14520. (Illus.). 56p. (gr. 3-7). 1983. Pantheon.
Ziegler, Sandra. A Visit to the Post Office. Holmes, Dave, photos by. LC 89-35061. 32p. (ps-3). 1989. lib. bdg. 14.60 (ISBN 0-516-01487-0); pap. 3.95 (ISBN 0-516-41487-9). Childrens.

POSTAL SERVICE–FICTION

Ahlberg, Janet & Ahlberg, Allan. The Jolly Postman. Ahlberg, Janet & Ahlberg, Allan, illus. 32p. (gr. k-3). 1986. 15.95 (ISBN 0-316-02036-2). Little.
Craven, Carolyn. What the Mailman Brought. De Paola, Tomie, illus. LC 85-19076. 40p. (gr. k-2). 1987. 13.95 (ISBN 0-399-21290-6, Putnam). Putnam Pub Group.
Gibbons, Gail. The Post Office Book. Gibbons, Gail, illus. LC 81-43888. 32p. (gr. k-3). 1982. 13.95 (ISBN 0-690-04198-5, Crowell Jr Bks); PLB 12.89 (ISBN 0-690-04199-3). HarpC Child Bks.
Gormley, Beatrice. Mail-Order Wings. McCully, Emily A., illus. 164p. (gr. 3-7). 1984. pap. 2.95 (ISBN 0-380-67421-1, Camelot). Avon.
Hedderwick, Mairi. Katie Morag Delivers the Mail. (ps-3). 1988. 13.95 (ISBN 0-316-35405-8). Little.
Henri, Adrian. The Postman's Palace. Henwood, Simon, illus. LC 90-30568. 32p. (ps-2). 1990. 13.95 (ISBN 0-689-31667-4, Atheneum Child Bk). Macmillan Child Grp.
La Bianca, Cory. Legend of Snowshoe Thompson. (Illus.). 32p. (Orig.). 1989. pap. 6.95 (ISBN 0-929796-01-2). Dry Canyon Pr.
Maury, Inez. My Mother the Mail Carrier - Mi Mama la Cartera. Alemany, Norah, tr. McCrady, Lady, illus. LC 76-14275. (ENG & SPA.). 32p. (Orig.). (gr. k-4). 1976. 7.95 (ISBN 0-935312-23-4). Feminist Pr.
Pollak, Felix. The Castle & the Flaw. 1963. pap. 4.00 (ISBN 0-685-01010-4). Elizabeth Pr.

POSTERS

see also Signs and Signboards

Beatrix Potter Posters, No. I. 1990. 9.95 (ISBN 0-7232-5641-1). Warne.
Brown, Charlene & Davis, Carolyn. Poster Fun. (Illus.). 64p. (Orig.). 1988. pap. 5.95 (ISBN 0-929261-30-5, BA05). W Foster Pub.
Droscher, Elke. The Victorian Sticker Postcard Book. (Illus.). 64p. (Orig.). pap. 6.95 (ISBN 0-89471-384-1). Running Pr.

POTTER, BEATRIX, 1866-1943

Aldis, Dorothy. Nothing Is Impossible - The Story of Beatrix Potter. Cuffari, Richard, illus. (gr. 4-6). 1988. 18.75 (ISBN 0-8446-6359-X). Peter Smith.
Collins, David R. The Country Artist: A Story about Beatrix Potter. Wilken, Mark, illus. 56p. (gr. 3-6). 1989. 9.95 (ISBN 0-87614-344-3); pap. 4.95 (ISBN 0-87614-509-8). Carolrhoda Bks.
Taylor, Judith, et al. Beatrix Potter, 1866-1943: The Artist & Her World. 244p. (gr. 9 up). 1988. pap. 19.95 (ISBN 0-7232-3561-9). Warne.
Taylor, Judy. Beatrix Potter: Artist, Storyteller & Countrywoman. (Illus.). 224p. (gr. 9 up). 1987. 24.95 (ISBN 0-7232-3314-4). Warne.

POTTERS–FICTION

Johnston, Norma. The Potter's Wheel. LC 87-24697. 256p. (gr. 7 up). 1988. 12.95 (ISBN 0-688-06463-9). Morrow Jr Bks.

POTTERY

Dixon, Annabelle. Clay. Stefoff, Rebecca, ed. Barber, Ed, photos by. LC 90-40369. (Illus.). 26p. (gr. 3-5). 1990. PLB 15.93 (ISBN 0-944483-69-0). Garrett Ed Corp.

Florian, Douglas. A Potter. LC 90-33940. (Illus.). 24p. (ps up). 1991. 13.95 (ISBN 0-688-10100-3); PLB 13.88 (ISBN 0-688-10101-1). Greenwillow.
Leach, Bernard. Potter's Book. (gr. 9-12). 1946. pap. 10.00 (ISBN 0-693-01157-2). Transatl Arts.
Potter, T. Pottery. (Illus.). 48p. (gr. 6 up). 1986. PLB 13.96 (ISBN 0-88110-319-5); pap. 5.95 (ISBN 0-86020-944-X). EDC.
Pottery. (Illus.). 64p. (gr. 6-12). 1969. pap. 1.85 (ISBN 0-8395-3314-4, 3314). BSA.
Roussel, Mike. Clay. (Illus.). 32p. (gr. 2-6). 1990. lib. bdg. 13.26 (ISBN 0-86592-485-6); lib. bdg. 9.95s.p. (ISBN 0-685-36301-5). Rourke Corp.

POTTERY–FICTION

Fowler, Virginie. Clayworks: Colorful Crafts from Around the World. Fowler, Virginie, illus. (gr. 5 up). 1986. 11.95 (ISBN 0-13-136417-0). P-H.
French, Fiona. The Magic Vase. (Illus.). 32p. (gr. 2 up). 1991. bds. 13.95 laminated (ISBN 0-19-279875-8). Oxford U Pr.

POULTRY

see also names of domesticated birds, e.g. Ducks; Geese; Turkeys, etc.

Back, Christine. Chicken & Egg. LC 86-10019. 1989. 6.95 (ISBN 0-382-09292-9); PLB 9.98 (ISBN 0-382-09284-8); pap. 3.95 (ISBN 0-382-09959-1). Silver Burdett.
Burton, Jane. Chester the Chick. LC 89-11421. (Illus.). 32p. (gr. 2-3). 1989. PLB 10.95 (ISBN 0-8368-0204-7). Gareth Stevens Inc.
Coldrey, Jennifer. Chicken on the Farm. LC 86-5716. (Illus.). 32p. (gr. 4-6). 1986. 10.95 (ISBN 1-55532-067-8). Gareth Stevens Inc.
Royston, Angela. Hen. (ps-3). 1990. PLB 10.40 (ISBN 0-531-19079-X). Watts.
Selsam, Millicent E. Egg to Chick. rev. ed. Wolff, Barbara, illus. LC 74-85034. 64p. (ps-3). 1970. PLB 11.89 (ISBN 0-06-025290-1). HarpC Child Bks.
—Egg to Chick. Wolff, Barbara, illus. LC 74-85034. 64p. (gr. k-3). 1987. pap. 3.50 (ISBN 0-06-444113-X, Trophy). HarpC Child Bks.
Stone, Lynn. Chickens. (Illus.). 24p. (gr. k-5). 1990. lib. bdg. 11.93 (ISBN 0-86593-034-1); lib. bdg. 8.95s.p. (ISBN 0-685-36308-2). Rourke Corp.

POULTRY–FICTION

Alexander, Linda. Job Well Done. Petie, Haris, illus. (gr. 1-4). PLB 6.70 (ISBN 0-8313-0002-7). Lantern.
Benchley, Nathaniel. Strange Disappearance of Arthur Cluck. Lobel, Arnold, illus. LC 67-4151. 64p. (gr. k-3). 1967. PLB 11.89 (ISBN 0-06-020478-8). HarpC Child Bks.

POVERTY

see also names of countries with the subdivision Economic Conditions and Social Conditions e.g. U. S. –Economic Conditions; U. S.–Social Conditions

Barrett, John M. It's Hard Not to Worry: Stories for Children about Poverty. (Illus., Orig.). (gr. 1-6). 1988. pap. 4.75 (ISBN 0-377-00178-3). Friendship Pr.
Coil, Suzanne. The Poor in America. Steltenpohl, Jane, ed. (Illus.). 136p. (gr. 7-10). 1989. lib. bdg. 12.98 (ISBN 0-671-69052-3). Messner.
Dando, William A. & Dando, Caroline Z. A Reference Guide to World Hunger. 128p. (gr. 6 up). 1991. PLB 17.95 (ISBN 0-89490-326-8). Enslow Pubs.
Davis, Bertha. Poverty in America: What We Do About It. (Illus.). 144p. (gr. 9-12). 1991. PLB 12.90 (ISBN 0-531-13016-9). Watts.
Dudley, William, ed. Poverty: Opposing Viewpoints. LC 87-36794. (Illus.). (gr. 10 up). 1988. lib. bdg. 15.95 (ISBN 0-89908-432-X); pap. text ed. 8.95 (ISBN 0-89908-407-9). Greenhaven.
Kosof, Anna. Homeless in America. Kline, M., ed. (Illus.). 96p. (gr. 7-12). 1988. PLB 11.90 (ISBN 0-531-10519-9). Watts.
O'Neill, Terry. The Homeless: Distinguishing Between Fact & Opinion. (Illus.). 32p. (gr. 3-6). 1990. PLB 8.95 (ISBN 0-89908-605-5). Greenhaven.
Orr, Lisa, ed. The Homeless: Opposing Viewpoints. LC 89-25734. (Illus.). 216p. (gr. 10 up). 1990. lib. bdg. 15.95 (ISBN 0-89908-476-1); pap. text ed. 8.95 (ISBN 0-89908-451-6). Greenhaven.
O'Sullivan, Carol. Poverty: Locating the Authors Main Idea. (Illus.). 32p. (gr. 3-6). 1990. PLB 8.95 (ISBN 0-89908-641-1). Greenhaven.

POVERTY–FICTION

Kallstrom, Theresa. Lyndy. York, Sherri, ed. Iarsen, Barbara, illus. LC 87-50259. 44p. (Orig.). (gr. 3 up). 1987. pap. 3.95 (ISBN 1-55523-081-4). Winston-Derek.
Meltzer, Milton. Poverty in America. LC 85-31963. 128p. (gr. 7 up). 1986. 12.95 (ISBN 0-688-05911-2). Morrow Jr Bks.

POWER (MECHANICS)

see also Electric Power; Force and Energy; Machinery; Water Power

Branley, Franklyn M. Energy for the Twenty First Century. Roth, Henry, illus. LC 74-31144. 96p. (gr. 5 up). 1975. 12.95 (ISBN 0-690-00756-6, Crowell Jr Bks). HarpC Child Bks.
Neal, Philip. Energy, Power Sources & Electricity. (Illus.). 48p. (gr. 6-9). 1989. 19.95 (ISBN 0-85219-776-4, Pub. by Batsford England). Trafalgar Sq.
Pluckrose, Henry. Move It! 1990. PLB 10.40 (ISBN 0-531-14020-2). Watts.

POWER BOATS

see Motorboats

POWER RESOURCES

see also Electric Power; Fuel; Solar Energy; Water Power

Arnold, Guy. Facts on Water, Wind & Solar Power. (Illus.). 32p. (gr. 5-8). 1990. PLB 11.90 (ISBN 0-531-11089-3). Watts.
Asimov, Isaac. How Did We Find Out about Solar Power? Wool, David, illus. 64p. (gr. 4-7). 1983. PLB 12.85 (ISBN 0-8027-6423-1). Walker & Co.
Bailey, Donna. Energy All Around Us. LC 90-39294. (Illus.). 48p. (gr. 2-5). 1990. PLB 15.96 (ISBN 0-8114-2520-7). Steck-V.
Baker, Susan. First Look at Using Energy. LC 91-2372. (Illus.). 32p. (gr. 1-2). 1991. PLB 10.95 (ISBN 0-8368-0680-8). Gareth Stevens Inc.
Branley, Franklyn M. Energy for the Twenty First Century. Roth, Henry, illus. LC 74-31144. 96p. (gr. 5 up). 1975. 12.95 (ISBN 0-690-00756-6, Crowell Jr Bks). HarpC Child Bks.
—Feast or Famine? The Energy Future. Roth, Henry, illus. LC 79-7817. 128p. (gr. 5 up). 1980. 12.95 (ISBN 0-690-04040-7, Crowell Jr Bks); (TYC-J). HarpC Child Bks.
Brown, Julie & Brown, Robert. Earth's Energy & Fuel. LC 91-2803. (Illus.). 64p. (gr. 2-3). 1991. PLB 12.95 (ISBN 0-8368-0077-X). Gareth Stevens Inc.
Catherall, Ed. Exploring Energy Sources. LC 90-21764. (Illus.). 48p. (gr. 3-7). 1991. PLB 18.60 (ISBN 0-8114-2597-5). Steck-V.
Davis, Bertha & Whitfield, Susan. The Coal Question. LC 82-4716. (Illus.). 96p. (gr. 7 up). 1982. PLB 12.90 (ISBN 0-531-04484-X). Watts.
Diener, Carolyn S., et al. Energy: A Curriculum Unit for Three, Four & Five Year Olds. LC 81-83050. (Illus.). 112p. (ps-k). 1982. pap. 9.95 (ISBN 0-89334-069-3). Humanics Ltd.
Dineen, Jacqueline. Energy from Sun, Wind, & Tide. 32p. (gr. 4-8). 1988. lib. bdg. 12.95 (ISBN 0-89490-214-8). Enslow Pubs.
Fogel, Barbara. Energy: Choices for the Future. LC 85-10516. (Illus.). 103p. (gr. 8 up). 1985. PLB 12.90 (ISBN 0-531-10060-X). Watts.
Gardner, Robert. Energy Projects for Young Scientists. 1989. pap. 5.95 (ISBN 0-531-15129-8). Watts.
Gibson, Michael. The Energy Crisis. (Illus.). 48p. (gr. 5 up). 1987. PLB 18.00 (ISBN 0-86592-277-2). Rourke Corp.
Herda, D. J. & Madden, Margaret L. Energy Resources: Towards a Renewable Future. (Illus.). 144p. (gr. 9-12). 1991. PLB 12.90 (ISBN 0-531-11005-2). Watts.
Jennings, Terry. Energy. LC 88-36214. (Illus.). 32p. (gr. 3-6). 1989. PLB 14.60 (ISBN 0-516-08438-0); pap. 4.95 (ISBN 0-516-48438-9). Childrens.
Johnstone, Hugh. Facts on Future Energy Possibilities. (Illus.). 32p. (gr. 5-8). 1990. PLB 11.90 (ISBN 0-531-11087-7). Watts.
Knowledge Unlimited Staff. Energy: Conserving a Vital Resource. (Illus.). 19p. (Orig.). (gr. 4-12). 1984. tchr's guide 13.00 (ISBN 0-915291-22-3). Know Unltd.
Lambert, Mark. Energy Technology. (Illus.). 48p. (gr. 5-8). 1991. RLB 12.40 (ISBN 0-531-18457-9, Pub. by Boatwright Pr). Watts.
Lyttle, Richard B. Shale Oil & Tar Sands: The Promises & Pitfalls. LC 82-6913. (Illus.). 96p. (gr. 7 up). 1982. PLB 12.90 (ISBN 0-531-04489-0). Watts.
McKie, Robin. Energy. (Illus.). 48p. (gr. 7-9). 1990. 12.90 (ISBN 0-531-19509-0). Watts.
Mason, John. Power Station Sun: The Story of Energy. (Illus.). 48p. (gr. 1-4). 1987. 12.95x (ISBN 0-8160-1778-6). Facts on File.
Podendorf, Illa. Energy. LC 81-12309. (Illus.). 48p. (gr. k-4). 1982. PLB 14.60 (ISBN 0-516-01625-3). Childrens.
Pringle, Laurence. Chains, Webs, & Pyramids: The Flow of Energy in Nature. LC 75-1084. (Illus.). (gr. 4-7). 1975. 12.95 (ISBN 0-690-00562-8, Crowell Jr Bks); (Crowell Jr Bks). HarpC Child Bks.
Radford, Don. Looking at Energy. (Illus.). 72p. (gr. 7-12). 1984. 18.95 (ISBN 0-7134-3486-4, Pub. by Batsford England). Trafalgar Sq.
Saving Energy. (gr. 3-6). 1981. incl. cass. & tchr's. guide 28.95 (ISBN 0-686-73893-4, 04917). Natl Geog.
Schulz, Charles M. Charlie Brown's Encyclopedia of Energy. Schulz, Charles M., illus. LC 82-3767. 128p. (gr. 2-5). 1982. lib. bdg. 9.99 (ISBN 0-394-94682-0). Random.
Seidenberg, Steven. Fuel & Energy. LC 90-23743. (Illus.). 64p. (gr. 4-6). 1991. PLB 12.95 (ISBN 0-8368-0052-4). Gareth Stevens Inc.
Snyder, Thomas F. Energy Searchbook. Cullinan, Dorothy K., illus. Snyder, Thomas F., intro. by. 56p. (gr. 4-12). 1982. pap. text ed. 8.08 (ISBN 0-07-059472-4). McGraw.
Strachan, James. Future Sources. LC 85-70597. (Illus.). 31p. (gr. 4-8). 1985. PLB 11.90 (ISBN 0-531-17004-7, Gloucester Pr). Watts.
Taylor, Barbara. Energy & Power. (Illus.). 32p. (gr. 5-8). 1990. PLB 11.40 (ISBN 0-531-14080-6). Watts.
Yanda, Bill. Rads, Ergs, & Cheeseburgers: The Kid's Guide to Energy & the Environment. (Illus.). 108p. (Orig.). (gr. 3 up). 1991. pap. 12.95 (ISBN 0-945465-75-0). John Muir.

POWER SUPPLY

see Power Resources

PRACTICAL POLITICS

see Politics, Practical

PRAIRIE DOGS

Beers, Dorothy S. The Prairie Dog. (Illus.). 60p. (gr. 3 up). 1990. PLB 12.95 (ISBN 0-87518-444-8, Dillon). Macmillan Child Grp.

PRAIRIE-DOGS–FICTION

Latham, Launa. Grandma Prairie Dog's Unwelcome Visitor. Lathem, Launa, illus. 32p. (Orig.). (gr. k-4). 1987. pap. 2.95 (ISBN 0-937573-00-0, 2811). T Sawyer Bks.
Oetting, R. Prairie Dog Town. LC 68-56829. (Illus.). 48p. (gr. 2-5). 1968. PLB 10.95 (ISBN 0-87783-030-4); pap. 3.94 deluxe ed. (ISBN 0-87783-157-2). Oddo.
Oke, Janette. Prairie Dog Town. Mann, Brenda, illus. 140p. (gr. 3 up). 1988. pap. 4.95 (ISBN 0-934998-31-0). Bethel Pub.

PRAIRIES

Kurelek, William. A Prairie Boy's Winter. Kurelek, William, illus. LC 73-8913. 48p. (gr. k-3). 1984. 13.95 (ISBN 0-395-17708-1); pap. 4.95 (ISBN 0-395-36609-7). HM.
Lawlor, Laurie. Addie Across the Prairie. LC 85-15548. (Illus.). 128p. (gr. 2-5). 1986. 10.50 (ISBN 0-8075-0165-4). A Whitman.
Rowan, James P. Prairies & Grasslands. LC 83-7310. (Illus.). 48p. (gr. k-4). 1983. PLB 14.60 (ISBN 0-516-01706-3); pap. 4.95 (ISBN 0-516-41706-1). Childrens.

PRAYER

see also Prayers

Alleman, Herman C. Prayers for Girls. (gr. 4-8). 6.95 (ISBN 0-8407-5242-3). Nelson.
Bogot, Howard & Syme, Daniel. Prayer Is Reaching. Ruthen, Marlene L., illus. 32p. (ps). 1982. text ed. 4.00 (ISBN 0-8074-0172-2, 101230). UAHC.
Branson, Mary. Adventures in Prayer: A Prayer Guide for Children. (Illus.). 127p. (Orig.). (gr. 4-6). 1988. pap. 4.95 (ISBN 0-936625-14-7, New Hope AL). Womans Mission Union.
Catholic Children's Prayer Book. 1986. 5.95 (ISBN 0-88271-127-X). Regina Pr.
Center for Learning Network. Praying with Children, Bk. 1. (Illus.). 112p. (gr. 1-3). 1991. pap. text ed. 12.95 (ISBN 1-56077-028-7). Ctr Learning.
—Praying with Children, Bk. 2. (Illus.). 112p. (gr. 4-6). 1991. pap. text ed. 12.95 (ISBN 1-56077-029-5). Ctr Learning.
Chandler, Linda S. When I Talk to God. LC 84-4967. (Illus.). (gr. k-3). 1984. 6.95 (ISBN 0-8054-4291-X, 4242-91). Broadman.
Chapian, Marie. Am I the Only One Here with Faded Genes? LC 87-11611. (Illus.). 192p. 1987. pap. 6.95 (ISBN 0-87123-945-0). Bethany Hse.
Chapman, Kathryn. God & I Can Talk: A Prayer Guide for Children. (Illus.). 104p. (Orig.). (gr. 1-3). 1988. pap. 4.95 (ISBN 0-936625-15-5, New Hope AL). Womans Mission Union.
Coleman, William. Friends Forever. LC 87-700. 160p. (Orig.). 1987. pap. 5.95 (ISBN 0-87123-959-0). Bethany Hse.
Cosby, Clair G. Junior High's a Jungle. LC 87-27040. 88p. (Orig.). (gr. 7-9). 1988. pap. 4.95 (ISBN 0-8361-3455-9). Herald Pr.
Gibbons, Ted. Amen! An Interrupted Prayer. 6p. Date not set. pap. text ed. 1.95 (ISBN 0-929985-00-1). Sonos.
Groth, J. L. Prayer: Learning How to Talk to God. LC 56-1395. (gr. 1 up). 1983. pap. 3.95 (ISBN 0-570-07799-0). Concordia.
Hague, Michael. A Child's Book of Prayers. LC 85-8380. (Illus.). 32p. (gr. k-2). 1985. 13.95 (ISBN 0-8050-0211-1). H Holt & Co.
Heerey, Frances. My First Prayer Book. 1986. pap. 3.95 (ISBN 0-88271-131-8). Regina Pr.
Hugh, Mitchell. Always Take Time to Pray. (Illus.). (gr. k-6). 1973. visualized song 4.99 (ISBN 3-90117-014-6). CEF Press.
Kelling, Furn F. Prayer Is... (Illus.). (gr. k-3). 1979. 6.95 (ISBN 0-8054-4256-1, 4242-56). Broadman.
Merrell, Karen D. Prayer. 23p. (ps-2). 1975. pap. 4.95 (ISBN 0-87747-562-8). Deseret Bk.
Nystrom, Carolyn. What Is Prayer? 32p. (ps-2). 1980. pap. 3.95 (ISBN 0-8024-6156-5). Moody.
O'Connor, Francine M. The ABC's of Prayer...for Children. Boswell, Kathryn, illus. 32p. (gr. 1-5). 1989. pap. 2.95 (ISBN 0-89243-317-5). Liguori Pubns.
Prayer: How to Talk to God. (Illus.). (gr. 1-8). 1970. pap. text ed. 3.95 (ISBN 0-86508-153-0). BCM Pubn.
Prayers for a Small Child. LC 83-16050. 24p. (ps-1). 1984. 6.95 (ISBN 0-394-86281-3, Random Juv). Random.
Sattgast, L. J. & Elkins, Jan. Teach Me about Prayer. Davis, Deena, ed. Flint, Russ, illus. 32p. (gr. 1-4). 1990. 4.99 (ISBN 0-88070-382-2). Multnomah.
Silverman, Morris & Silverman, Hillel. Prayer Book for Summer Camps. (gr. 3-12). 8.95x (ISBN 0-87677-060-X); pap. 6.95x (ISBN 0-87677-061-8). Prayer Bk.
Smith, Judy G. Teaching Children about Prayer. 25p. (Orig.). (gr. 4-6). 1988. pap. 6.95 (ISBN 0-940754-56-8). Ed Ministries.
Titherington, Jeanne. Child's Prayer. Titherington, Jeanne, illus. LC 88-16566. 24p. (ps up). 1989. 13.95 (ISBN 0-688-08317-X); PLB 13.88 (ISBN 0-688-08318-8). Greenwillow.
Touching Incidents & Remarkable Answers to Prayer. 135p. (gr. k up). pap. 1.00 (ISBN 0-686-29172-7). Faith Pub Hse.

PRAYERS

see also Prayer

Alexander, Martha. Poems & Prayers for the Very Young. (Illus.). (ps-1). 1973. pap. 2.25 (ISBN 0-394-82705-8, Random Juv). Random.
Alleman, Herman C. Prayers for Boys. LC 81-142145. (gr. 4-9). pap. 6.95 (ISBN 0-8407-5241-5). Nelson.

Armstrong, William. Health, Happiness, Humor & Holiness: As Seen Through Children's Eyes. Graves, Helen, ed. LC 86-51342. (Illus.). 86p. (gr. 3-8). 1987. pap. text ed. 5.95 (ISBN 1-55523-065-2). Winston-Derek.
Batchelor, Mary. The Lion Book of Bible Stories & Prayers. (Illus.). 96p. (gr. 1-5). 1989. 11.95 (ISBN 0-85648-239-0). Lion USA.
—Lion Book of Children's Prayers. (Illus.). 96p. 1984. 11.95 (ISBN 0-85648-070-3). Lion USA.
Baynes, Pauline, compiled by. & illus. Thanks Be to God: Prayers from Around the World. LC 89-28622. 32p. (gr. k-8). 1990. 11.95 (ISBN 0-02-708541-4, Mcmillan Child Bk). Macmillan Child Grp.
Bishop, Roma, compiled by. & illus. A Little Book of Prayers. 32p. (ps-3). 1987. 7.95 (ISBN 0-316-09660-1). Little.
Bly, Stephen & Bly, Janet. Devotions with a Difference. LC 82-8304. 128p. (gr. 3 up). 1982. pap. 5.95 (ISBN 0-8024-1789-2). Moody.
Book of Prayers. (Illus.). (gr. 2-4). 3.50 (ISBN 0-7214-0521-5). Ladybird Bks.
Brown, Angela. Prayers That Avail Much for Children. (Illus.). 32p. (Orig.). (gr. 1-3). 1983. pap. 3.98 (ISBN 0-89274-296-8). Harrison Hse.
Butcher, Sam. Precious Moments Prayers for Boys & Girls. 1989. 9.95 (ISBN 0-8407-7230-0). Nelson.
Carr & Paquet. God, I've Got to Talk to You Again! LC 59-1315. 24p. (Orig.). (gr. k-4). 1985. pap. 1.39 (ISBN 0-570-06197-0, 59-1315). Concordia.
Champlin, Joseph M. & Haggerty, Brian A. Together in Peace for Children. LC 76-26348. (Illus.). 72p. (gr. 2-7). 1976. 1.50 (ISBN 0-87793-119-4). Ave Maria.
Coleman, William L. The Sleep Tight Book. LC 82-12953. 125p. (Orig.). (ps up). 1982. pap. 5.95 (ISBN 0-87123-577-3). Bethany Hse.
Costello, Gwen. Prayer Services for Religious Educators: Services for Catechists, Teachers, Parents, Children, Teenagers, & Parish Ministers. LC 88-51811. (Illus.). 80p. 1989. tchr's. ed. 9.95 (ISBN 0-89622-390-6). Twenty-Third.
—Praying With Children: Twenty-Eight Services for Various Occasions. LC 90-70560. 96p. (Orig.). (gr. 2-6). 1990. pap. 9.95 (ISBN 0-89622-439-2). Twenty-Third.
Daughters of St Paul. My Prayer Book. (gr. 3 up). 1978. plastic bdg. 2.00 (ISBN 0-8198-0359-6); pap. 1.25 (ISBN 0-8198-0360-X). Dghtrs St Paul.
Dear God. (ps). 2.95 (ISBN 0-86112-218-6, Pub. by Brimax Bks). Borden.
De Gasztold, Carmen B. Prayers from the Ark. (FRE.). (gr. 3-8). 29.95 (ISBN 0-685-11511-9). French & Eur.
Dellinger, A. & Fletcher, S. Bedtime Prayers. (ps-3). pap. 0.59 (ISBN 0-570-08314-1, 56HH1446). Concordia.
Dinter, B. Tell Me about Jesus. (Illus.). 80p. (ps). 1991. 3.95 (ISBN 0-8146-1881-2). Liturgical Pr.
Dixon, Dorothy. Teaching Young Children to Care: Thirty-Seven Activities for Developing Self-Esteem. LC 90-70418. 88p. (Orig.). (gr. k-3). 1990. pap. 9.95 (ISBN 0-89622-436-8). Twenty-Third.
—Teaching Young Children to Care: Thirty-Seven Activities for Developing Concern for Others. LC 90-70417. (Illus.). 88p. (Orig.). (gr. k-3). 1990. pap. 9.95 (ISBN 0-89622-437-6). Twenty-Third.
Donze, Mary T. In My Heart Room, Bk. 2: More Love Prayers for Children. LC 90-70810. (Illus.). 80p. (Orig.). (gr. 1-5). 1990. pap. 2.95 (ISBN 0-89243-329-9). Liguori Pubns.
Field, Rachel. Prayer for a Child. Jones, Elizabeth O., illus. LC 44-47191. 32p. (ps-1). 1968. 11.95 (ISBN 0-02-735190-4, Mcmillan Child Bk). Macmillan Child Grp.
Fletcher, Sarah. Prayers for Little People. Kueker, Don, illus. 32p. (gr. 3-7). 1974. pap. 2.29 (ISBN 0-570-03429-9, 56-1184). Concordia.
Foss, Allen J. Walking in God's Truth: Ten Commandments-Lord's Prayer. rev. ed. Rinden, David, intro. by. Heiman, Lori, illus. 276p. (gr. 6-8). 1989. pap. text ed. 4.95 (ISBN 0-943167-04-3). Faith & Fellowship Pr.
Fox, Robert J. A Prayer Book for Young Catholics. LC 82-81318. 168p. (gr. 4-8). 1982. pap. 4.95 leatherette (ISBN 0-87973-370-5, 370). Our Sunday Visitor.
Gates of Wonder: Prayerbook for Young Children. (Illus.). 48p. (ps-8). 1990. 12.95 (ISBN 0-88123-009-X). Central Conf.
Gockel, Herman W. & Saleska, Edward J., eds. Child's Garden of Prayer. (Illus.). (gr. k-2). 1981. pap. 2.29 (ISBN 0-570-03412-4, 56-1016). Concordia.
God Bless. (ps). 2.95 (ISBN 0-86112-195-3, Pub. by Brimax Bks). Borden.
God Made. (ps). 2.95 (ISBN 0-86112-219-4, Pub. by Brimax Bks). Borden.
Gompertz, Helen. First Prayers. (Illus.). 32p. (ps-3). 1983. 6.95 (ISBN 0-8170-1013-0). Judson.
Good Night, God. 8p. (ps). 1985. bds. 2.95 (ISBN 0-85648-862-3). Lion USA.
Gooding, Margaret K. A Growing-up Year. 70p. (gr. 6-7). 1988. write for info. (ISBN 0-933840-34-9). Unitarian Univ.
Groth, Lynn. Reaching Tender Hearts, 3 vols. Grunze, R., ed. May, Lawrence & Steele, Lawrence, illus. (Orig.). (ps-k). 1988. Set. pap. text ed. write for info. (ISBN 0-938272-45-4). WELS Board.
—Reaching Tender Hearts, Vol. 3. Grunze, R., ed. May, Lawrence & Steele, Lawrence, trs. (Illus.). 163p. (Orig.). (gr. k). 1988. pap. text ed. 8.95 (ISBN 0-938272-44-6). WELS Board.
Harmer, Juliet. Prayers for Children. (ps-3). 1990. 12.95 (ISBN 0-670-83348-7). Viking Child Bks.
Have You Got a Minute, GOD? Prayers by Teens. (Illus.). 32p. (Orig.). (gr. 7-12). pap. write for info. (ISBN 0-937997-15-3). Hi-Time Pub.
Hayes, Edward J., et al. Catholicism & Reason. 256p. (gr. 8-12). 1981. pap. 5.95 (ISBN 0-913382-23-X, 103-14); tchr's manual 3.00 (ISBN 0-913382-25-6, 103-15). Prow Bks-Franciscan.
Hein, Lucille E. I Can Make My Own Prayers. LC 72-154026. (Illus.). (gr. k-4). 1971. pap. 3.95 (ISBN 0-8170-0851-9). Judson.
Heinrich, Annette. Not a Hollywood Family: Realistic Devotions for Teens. 110p. (Orig.). (gr. 7 up). 1989. pap. 5.95 (ISBN 0-87788-584-2). Shaw Pubs.
—One in a Zillion: Realistic Devotions for Teens. 112p. (Orig.). (gr. 9-12). 1990. pap. 5.95 (ISBN 0-87788-621-0). Shaw Pubs.
Henderson, Felicity. My Little Box of Prayers, 4 bks. Goffe, Toni, illus. 32p. (ps). 1988. Set. casebound 9.95 (ISBN 0-7459-1250-8). Lion USA.
Hodgson, Joan. Our Father. Ripper, Peter, illus. (ps-3). 1977. pap. 2.95 (ISBN 0-85487-040-7). DeVorss.
Hopkins, Lee B. And God Bless Me: Prayers, Lullabies, & Dream-Poems. Lincoln, Patricia H., illus. LC 81-8376. 32p. (ps-2). 1982. Knopf.
Jahsmann, Allan H. & Simon, Martin P. Little Visits with God. (gr. k-3). 1957. 9.95 (ISBN 0-570-03016-1, 6-1055); pap. 7.95 (ISBN 0-570-03032-3, 6-1158). Concordia.
Johnson, Ruth I. Devotions for Early Teens. (gr. 7-12). 1960-74. Vol. 1. pap. 2.95 (ISBN 0-8024-2181-4); Vol. 3. pap. 2.95—o.p. (ISBN 0-8024-2183-0). Moody.
Jones, Chris. Lord, I Want to Tell You Something: Prayers for Boys. LC 73-78266. (Illus.). 96p. (Orig.). (gr. 5-8). 1973. pap. 4.95 (ISBN 0-8066-1330-0, 10-4100, Augsburg). Augsburg Fortress.
Keleman, Julie. Lent Is for Children: Stories, Activities, Prayers. 64p. (Orig.). (gr. 4-8). 1988. pap. 1.95 (ISBN 0-89243-280-2). Liguori Pubns.
Kennedy, Pamela. A Child's Book of Prayers. Wilson, Kathy, tr. (Illus.). 32p. (ps-3). 1989. 5.95 (ISBN 0-8249-8343-2). Ideals.
—Little Treasury of Prayers, 6 bks. Wilson, Katherine, illus. (ps-3). 1989. Set. bds. 7.95 (ISBN 0-8249-8394-7). Ideals.
—Prayers at Eastertime. Britt, Stephanie, illus. 24p. (ps-k). 1990. pap. 3.95 (ISBN 0-8249-8422-6). Ideals.
Klug, Ron. You Promised, Lord: Prayers for Boys. LC 83-70502. 80p. (Orig.). (gr. 3-7). 1983. pap. 4.95 (ISBN 0-8066-2008-0, 10-7417, Augsburg). Augsburg Fortress.
Kramer, William A. Teenagers Pray. LC 55-12193. (gr. 8-12). 1956. 5.95 (ISBN 0-570-03018-8, 6-1054). Concordia.
Larrick, Nancy. Tambourines! Tambourines to Glory! Prayers & Poems. LC 81-23158. (Illus.). 122p. (gr. 3-7). 1982. 8.95 (ISBN 0-664-32689-7, Westminster). Westminster John Knox.
Little Folded Hands. rev. ed. LC 59-12074. (gr. 1-5). 1959. 4.95 (ISBN 0-570-03417-5, 56-1038); pap. 1.99 laminated (ISBN 0-570-03416-7, 56-1037). Concordia.
Littleton, Mark R. Beefin' Up: Daily Feed for Amazing Grazing. Heaney, Liz, ed. LC 89-29297. 140p. (Orig.). (gr. 7-12). 1990. pap. 7.95 (ISBN 0-88070-317-2). Multnomah.
The Lord's Prayer & Other Prayers. (Illus.). (gr. 2-4). 3.50 (ISBN 0-7214-0809-5). Ladybird Bks.
McEntee, Sean & Breen, Michael. Lectionary for Masses with Children: Cycle A. vi, 216p. (Orig.). (gr. 1-6). 1989. pap. 19.95 (ISBN 0-89622-411-2). Twenty-Third.
McKissack, Patricia & McKissack, Fredrick. When Do You Talk to God? Prayers for Small Children. Gumble, Gary, illus. LC 86-71903. 32p. (Orig.). (gr. 3-8). 1986. pap. 4.95 (ISBN 0-8066-2239-3, 10-7078, Augsburg). Augsburg Fortress.
Moskowitz, Nachama S. Bridge to Prayer: The Jewish Worship Workbook, Vol. II. (Illus.). 144p. (gr. 6-7). 1989. pap. text ed. 6.00 (ISBN 0-8074-0432-2, 123596). UAHC.
My First Box of Prayers, 4 bks. (Illus.). (gr. 2 up). 1988. adhesive board 7.95 (ISBN 0-687-27539-3). Abingdon.
My First Prayer Book. (Illus.). 32p. (ps-2). 1985. 1.95 (ISBN 0-225-66387-2). Harper SF.
Newman, Marjorie, ed. My Book of Favorite Prayers. Pasifull, Linda, illus. LC 89-82555. 28p. (ps-2). 1990. pap. 8.95 (ISBN 0-8066-2469-8, 9-2469). Augsburg Fortress.
Noble, Trudy V. God Answers Children's Prayers Too. Carmen, Dave, illus. LC 85-217377. 30p. (ps-4). 1990. write for info. (ISBN 0-9620133-0-7). Joy Deliverance.
Odor, Ruth. Prayers for Boys. (gr. 3-6). 1985. pap. 0.69 pocket size (ISBN 0-87239-825-0, 2815). Standard Pub.
—Prayers for Girls. (gr. 3-6). 1985. pap. 0.69 pocket size (ISBN 0-87239-826-9, 2816). Standard Pub.
Pappas, Michael G. Sweet Dreams for Little Ones. Wenz-Vietor, Ilse, illus. 64p. (Orig.). 1985. pap. 7.95 (ISBN 0-86683-641-1, AY8156). Harper SF.
Prayers for Children. 32p. (gr. k-5). 1985. 3.95 (ISBN 0-8249-8023-9). Ideals.
Reeves, Eira. Thank You God for Our Day in the Country. 24p. (Orig.). (ps). 1988. pap. 1.95 (ISBN 0-8170-1135-8). Judson.
—Thank You God for Our Day in the Town. (Illus.). 24p. (Orig.). (ps). 1988. pap. 1.95 (ISBN 0-8170-1136-6). Judson.
—Thank You God for Our Day Indoors. (Illus.). 24p. (Orig.). (ps). 1988. pap. 1.95 (ISBN 0-8170-1137-4). Judson.
—Thank You God for Our Day on the Beach. (Illus.). 24p. (Orig.). (ps). 1988. pap. 1.95 (ISBN 0-8170-1134-X). Judson.
Riley, Anne. Help Me. LC 90-82929. (Illus.). 10p. 1990. text ed. 3.95 (ISBN 0-8066-2495-7, 9-2495). Augsburg Fortress.
—I'm Sorry. LC 90-82927. (Illus.). 10p. 1990. text ed. 3.95 (ISBN 0-8066-2494-9, 9-2494). Augsburg Fortress.
—Please God. LC 90-82930. (Illus.). 10p. 1990. text ed. 3.95 (ISBN 0-8066-2496-5, 9-2496). Augsburg Fortress.
—Thank You. LC 90-82928. (Illus.). 10p. 1990. text ed. 3.95 (ISBN 0-8066-2493-0, 9-2493). Augsburg Fortress.
Schaap, James C. Intermission: Breaking Away with God. Treman, Terry, illus. LC 85-4156. 224p. (Orig.). (gr. 7 up). 1985. pap. 10.95 (ISBN 0-930265-06-8). CRC Pubns.
Schmidt, J. David. Graffiti: Devotions for Girls. new ed. (Illus.). 128p. (Orig.). (gr. 8-12). 1983. pap. 6.95 (ISBN 0-8007-5115-9, Power Bks). Revell.
—Graffiti: Devotions for Guys. new ed. (Illus.). 128p. (Orig.). (gr. 8-12). 1983. pap. 6.95 (ISBN 0-8007-5114-0, Power Bks). Revell.
Schreivogel, Paul A. Small Prayers for Small Children. Holmgren, George E., illus. LC 76-135226. 32p. (gr. k-4). 1980. pap. 4.95 (ISBN 0-8066-1804-3, 10-5836, Augsburg). Augsburg Fortress.
Sorensen, David A. It's a Mystery to Me, Lord: Bible Devotions for Boys. LC 85-22993. 112p. (Orig.). (gr. 3-7). 1985. pap. 4.95 (ISBN 0-8066-2183-4, 10-3445, Augsburg). Augsburg Fortress.
Sorenson, Stephen W. Lord, I Want to Know You Better: Story Devotions for Boys. LC 81-52280. 112p. (Orig.). (gr. 3-7). 1982. pap. 4.95 (ISBN 0-8066-1912-0, 10-4103, Augsburg). Augsburg Fortress.
Tarrant, Margaret, illus. My First Book of Prayers. 64p. (ps-2). 1988. 6.95 (ISBN 0-8249-8268-1). Ideals.
Thank You God. (ps). 2.95 (ISBN 0-86112-196-1, Pub. by Brimax Bks). Borden.
Tucker, Jeff & Tucker, Ramona. Life Oughta Come with Directions! Realistic Devotions for Teens. 112p. (Orig.). (gr. 9-12). 1990. pap. 5.95 (ISBN 0-87788-496-X). Shaw Pubs.
Tudor, Tasha. First Graces. Tudor, Tasha, illus. LC 59-12017. (gr. k-3). 1978. pap. 6.95 (ISBN 0-8098-1953-8). McKay.
—First Prayers. Tudor, Tasha, illus. LC 59-9631. (gr. k-3). 1978. protestant ed. 6.95 (ISBN 0-8098-1952-X). McKay.
—Tasha Tudor's Treasure, 3 vols. 144p. (gr. k-4). 1981. 13.95 (ISBN 0-679-20983-2). McKay.
Tudor, Tasha, tr. First Graces. LC 88-30673. (Illus.). 48p. (ps-2). 1989. Repr. of 1955 ed. 6.95 (ISBN 0-394-84409-2). Random.
Tullis, Dawn. Teach Us to Pray. 2.25 (ISBN 0-686-13717-5). Crusade Pubs.
Wangerin, W., Jr. & Jennings, A. God, I've Gotta Talk to You. (Illus.). 32p. (gr. k-4). 1974. pap. 1.39 (ISBN 0-570-06086-9, 59-1301). Concordia.
Watson, Carol, compiled by. Three Hundred Sixty-Five Children's Prayers. (Illus.). 160p. 1989. text ed. 12.95 (ISBN 0-7459-1454-3); white ed. 24.95 (ISBN 0-7459-1721-6). Lion USA.
Webb, Barbara O. Now What, Lord? Bible Devotions for Girls. LC 85-22884. 112p. (Orig.). (gr. 3-7). 1985. pap. 4.95 (ISBN 0-8066-2182-6, 10-4680, Augsburg). Augsburg Fortress.
Westberg, Barbara. Rhymes, Riddles & Reasons, Vol. I: Genesis, A Devotional Book for Children. Bernard, David, ed. Agnew, Tim, illus. LC 90-38218. 224p. (Orig.). (gr. 3-7). 1991. pap. 6.95 (ISBN 0-932581-75-7). Word Aflame.

PRAYING MANTIS

Lavies, Bianca. Backyard Hunter: The Praying Mantis. 1990. 13.95 (ISBN 0-525-44547-1, DCB). Dutton Child Bks.
Pohl, Kathleen. The Praying Mantis. (Illus.). 32p. (gr. 3-7). 1986. PLB 16.67 (ISBN 0-8172-2715-6); pap. text ed. 9.27 (ISBN 0-8172-2733-4). Raintree Pubs.

PREACHERS

see Clergy

PRECIOUS METALS

see also Gold; Silver

PRECIOUS STONES

see also Gems;
also names of precious stones, e.g. Diamonds

Jackson, Julia. Gemstones: Treasures from the Earth's Crust. LC 88-1380. (Illus.). 104p. (gr. 6-12). 1989. PLB 17.95 (ISBN 0-89490-201-6). Enslow Pubs.
Symes, R. F. & Harding, Roger. Crystal & Gem. Keates, Colin, photos by. LC 90-4930. (Illus.). 64p. (gr. 5 up). 1991. 15.00 (ISBN 0-679-80781-0); PLB 15.99 (ISBN 0-679-90781-5). Knopf.

PREGNANCY

see also Childbirth

Arnold, Lisa E. You Know You're Really Pregnant When... (Illus.). 64p. 1987. 9.95 (ISBN 0-8431-1916-0). Price Stern.

Arthur, Shirley M. Surviving Teen Pregnancy: Your Choices, Dreams & Decisions. Lindsay, Jeanne, ed. (Illus.). 192p. (Orig.). (gr. 1-8). 1991. 15.95 (ISBN 0-930934-46-6); pap. 9.95 (ISBN 0-930934-47-4). Morning Glory.

Beyer, Kay. Coping with Teen Parenting. Rosen, Ruth, ed. (gr. 7-12). 1990. lib. bdg. 12.95 (ISBN 0-8239-1155-1). Rosen Group.

Bowe-Gutman, Sonia. Teen Pregnancy. 72p. (gr. 6 up). 1987. PLB 11.95 (ISBN 0-8225-0039-6). Lerner Pubns.

Brinkley, Ginny & Sampson, Sherry. Young & Pregnant: A Book for You. Cooper, Gail S., illus. Mahan, Charles, intro. by. (Illus.). 80p. (Orig.). (gr. 7-12). 1989. pap. text ed. 4.95x (ISBN 0-317-93681-6). Pink Inc.

Glore, John. Teenage Parents. (Illus.). 64p. (gr. 7 up). 1990. lib. bdg. 15.93 (ISBN 0-86593-080-5); lib. bdg. 11.95s.p. (ISBN 0-685-36299-X). Rourke Corp.

Guernsey, JoAnn B. Teen Pregnancy. LC 89-1384. (Illus.). 48p. (gr. 4 up). 1989. 10.95 (ISBN 0-89686-435-9, Crestwood Hse). Macmillan Child Grp.

Hales, Dianne. Pregnancy & Birth. (Illus.). (gr. 6-12). 1989. 18.95 (ISBN 0-7910-0040-0). Chelsea Hse.

Hughes, Tracy. Everything You Need to Know about Teen Pregnancy. Rosen, Roger, ed. Glassman, Richard, photos by. (Illus.). 64p. (gr. 7 up). 1988. lib. bdg. 12.95 (ISBN 0-8239-0810-0). Rosen Group.

Jakobson, Cathryn. Teenage Pregnancy. rev. ed. 160p. (gr. 7 up). 1991. PLB 15.85 (ISBN 0-8027-8128-4); pap. 8.95 (ISBN 0-8027-7372-9). Walker & Co.

Kuklin, Susan. What Do I Do Now? (Illus.). 1991. 15.95 (ISBN 0-399-21843-2, Putnam); pap. 7.95 (ISBN 0-399-22043-7, Putnam). Putnam Pub Group.

Kurland, Adrienne. Coping with Being Pregnant. Rosen, Ruth, ed. LC 88-18433. (gr. 7 up). 1988. lib. bdg. 12.95 (ISBN 0-8239-0791-0). Rosen Group.

Lindsay, Jeanne W. & Brunelli, Jean. Teens Parenting - Your Pregnancy & Newborn Journey: How to Take Care of Yourself & Your Newborn When You're a Pregnant Teen. (Illus.). 192p. (Orig.). (gr. 6 up). 1991. text ed. 15.95 (ISBN 0-930934-51-2); pap. text ed. 9.95 (ISBN 0-930934-50-4); wkbk. 2.50 (ISBN 0-930934-60-1). Morning Glory.

McGuire, Paula. It Won't Happen to Me: Teenagers Talk about Pregnancy. LC 82-72754. 224p. (gr. 7 up). 1983. 14.95 (ISBN 0-385-29244-9); pap. 6.95 (ISBN 0-685-06445-X). Delacorte.

—It Won't Happen to Me: Teenagers Talk about Pregnancy. Ryan, George M., frwd. by. 1923. pap. 6.95 (ISBN 0-385-29201-5, Delta). Dell.

Minor, Nancy & Bradley, Patricia. Coping with School-Age Motherhood. (gr. 7-12). 1979. PLB 12.95 (ISBN 0-8239-0923-9). Rosen Group.

Newton, David E. Particle Accelerations. (Illus.). 128p. (gr. 10-12). 1990. 12.40 (ISBN 0-531-10671-3). Watts.

Nixon, Joan L. Before You Were Born. McIlrath, James, illus. LC 79-91741. 32p. (ps up). 1980. pap. 5.95 (ISBN 0-87973-343-8). Our Sunday Visitor.

Roggow, Linda & Owens, Carolyn. Handbook for Pregnant Teenagers. (Orig.). (gr. 9-12). 1990. pap. 7.95 (ISBN 0-310-45821-8, 12734P). Zondervan.

Silverstein, Herma. Teenage & Pregnant: What You Can Do. (Illus.). (gr. 7 up). 1989. lib. bdg. 13.98 (ISBN 0-671-65221-4); pap. 5.95 (ISBN 0-671-65222-2). Messner.

Simpson, Carolyn. Coping with An Unplanned Pregnancy. Rosen, Ruth, ed. (gr. 7-12). 1990. lib. bdg. 12.95 (ISBN 0-8239-1145-4). Rosen Group.

Truss, Jan. Bird at the Window. LC 79-1999. 224p. (gr. 7 up). 1980. 8.95 (ISBN 0-06-026137-4). HarpC Child Bks.

Vondra, Mary & Vondra, Lisa. Pregnant, This Time It's Me: For Teens Who Have Just Found Out They're Pregnant. Borum, Shari, illus. 24p. (Orig.). 1985. pap. 2.50 (ISBN 0-685-30731-X). Centering Corp.

PREHISTORY

see Stone Age

PREJUDICES AND ANTIPATHIES

Berry, Joy. Every Kid's Guide to Overcoming Prejudice & Discrimination. Bartholomew, illus. 48p. (gr. 3-7). 1987. 4.95 (ISBN 0-516-21414-4); PLB 14.60 (ISBN 0-516-01414-5). Childrens.

Guggenheim, Hans. World of Wonderful Difference. (gr. 5-8). 5.00x (ISBN 0-87068-371-3, Pub. by Friendly Hse). Ktav.

Lang, Susan S. Extremist Groups in America. 1990. PLB 13.90 (ISBN 0-531-10901-1). Watts.

Pascoe, Elaine. Racial Prejudice. LC 85-8816. (Illus.). 128p. (gr. 7 up). 1985. PLB 12.90 (ISBN 0-531-10057-X). Watts.

PREJUDICES AND ANTIPATHIES–FICTION

Betancourt, Jeanne. More Than Meets the Eye. 1990. 14.95 (ISBN 0-553-05871-1). Bantam.

Bush, Lawrence. Rooftop Secrets & Other Stories of Anti-Semitism. Vorspan, Albert, commentary by. LC 86-1362. (Illus.). 144p. (Orig.). (gr. 7 up). 1986. pap. text ed. 7.95 (ISBN 0-8074-0314-8, 121720). UAHC.

Campbell, Will. Chester & Chun Ling. Hsieh, Jim, illus. (gr. 2 up). 1989. 12.95 (ISBN 0-687-06481-3). Abingdon.

Doleski, Teddi. Silvester & the Oogaloo Boogalo. 1990. 2.95 (ISBN 0-8091-6596-1). Paulist Pr.

Levitin, Sonia. The Return. LC 86-25891. 224p. (gr. 5 up). 1987. 13.95 (ISBN 0-689-31309-8, Atheneum Child Bk). Macmillan Child Grp.

McClaskey, Marilyn H. What Kind of Name Is Juan? Rosen, Roger, ed. (gr. 7 up). 1989. lib. bdg. 12.95 (ISBN 0-8239-0830-5). Rosen Group.

Neville, Emily C. Berries Goodman. LC 65-19485. (gr. 5-9). 1975. pap. 3.50 (ISBN 0-06-440072-7, Trophy). HarpC Child Bks.

Oram, Hiawyn. Just Like Us. Baird, Daniel, illus. 32p. (gr. 2-4). 1988. Repr. of 1987 ed. 11.95 (ISBN 0-8192-1472-8). Morehouse Pub.

Shaw, Diana. What You Don't Know Can Hurt You, Vol. 1. 1990. 13.95 (ISBN 0-316-78344-7, Joy St Bks). Little.

Smith, Rukshana. Sumitra's Story. LC 82-19794. 168p. (gr. 6). 1983. 9.95 (ISBN 0-698-20579-0, Coward). Putnam Pub Group.

Sorenson, Jane. Another Jennifer. Endres, Helen, illus. 144p. (gr. 5-8). 1986. 3.95 (ISBN 0-87403-088-9, 3741). Standard Pub.

Swope, Sam. The Araboolies of Liberty Street. Root, Barry, illus. LC 88-12687. 32p. (ps-3). 1989. 14.95 (ISBN 0-517-56960-4, C N Potter Bks); PLB 14.99 (ISBN 0-517-57411-X). Crown.

Tunis, John R. All-American. 1989. pap. 3.95 (ISBN 0-15-202292-9). HarbraceJ.

Wainwright, Richard M. Montanas Escalar. Crompton, Jack, illus. (SPA.). 64p. 1991. 15.00 (ISBN 0-9619566-5-8). Family Life.

—Mountains to Climb. Crompton, Jack, illus. 64p. 1990. 13.95 (ISBN 0-9619566-3-1). Family Life.

PRESCHOOL EDUCATION

see Nursery Schools

PRESENTS

see Gifts

PRESERVATION OF FOOD

see Food–Preservation

PRESERVATION OF FORESTS

see Forests and Forestry

PRESERVATION OF NATURAL RESOURCES

see Conservation of Natural Resources

PRESERVATION OF WILDLIFE

see Wildlife–Conservation

PRESERVATION OF ZOOLOGICAL SPECIMENS

see Zoological Specimens–Collection and Preservation

PRESERVING

see Canning and Preserving

PRESIDENTS–FRANCE

Our Forty-First President: George Bush. 96p. (gr. 2-6). 1989. pap. 2.50 (ISBN 0-590-42644-3). Scholastic Inc.

Sabin, Francene. Young Thomas Jefferson. Baxter, Robert, illus. LC 85-1093. 48p. (gr. 4-6). 1985. lib. bdg. 10.79 (ISBN 0-8167-0561-5); pap. text ed. 2.95 (ISBN 0-8167-0562-3). Troll Assocs.

PRESIDENTS–U. S.

Aten, Jerry. Presidential Leaders. Hierstein, Judy, illus. 64p. (gr. k-4). 1986. wkbk. 6.95 (ISBN 0-86653-347-8, GA 697). Good Apple.

—Presidents. Hyndman, Kathryn, illus. 176p. (gr. 4 up). 1985. wkbk. 12.95 (ISBN 0-86653-281-1, GA 627). Good Apple.

Barrett, Marvin. Meet Thomas Jefferson. Torres, Angelo, illus. (gr. 2-6). 1967. (Random Juv); lib. bdg. 8.99 (ISBN 0-394-90067-7). Random.

Beckman, Beatrice. I Can Be President. LC 84-12653. (Illus.). 32p. (gr. k-3). 1984. lib. bdg. 13.93 (ISBN 0-516-01841-8); pap. 3.95 (ISBN 0-516-41841-6). Childrens.

Behrens, June. George Bush: Forty-First President of the United States. LC 89-693. (Illus.). 32p. (gr. 2-5). 1989. PLB 13.27 (ISBN 0-516-04172-X); pap. 3.95 (ISBN 0-516-44172-8). Childrens.

Blassingame, Wyatt. The Look-It-up Book of Presidents. rev. ed. LC 84-2114. (Illus.). 160p. 1988. pap. 4.95 (ISBN 0-394-81973-X, Random Juv). Random.

—The Look-It-Up Book of Presidents. rev. ed. LC 89-10519. (Illus.). (gr. 5-9). 1990. 10.95 (ISBN 0-679-80353-X); PLB 11.99 (ISBN 0-679-90353-4); pap. 5.95 (ISBN 0-679-80358-0). McKay.

—The Look-It-Up Book of Presidents: Updated, Revised & Newly Illustrated with Photographs & Old Prints. LC 84-2114. (Illus.). 160p. (gr. 5-9). 1984. 9.95 (ISBN 0-394-86839-0, Random Juv); lib. bdg. 9.99 (ISBN 0-394-96839-5). Random.

Brandt, Keith. President. Dole, Bob, illus. LC 84-2652. 32p. (gr. 3-6). 1985. PLB 9.49 (ISBN 0-8167-0268-3); pap. text ed. 2.95 (ISBN 0-8167-0269-1). Troll Assocs.

Bumann, Joan & Patterson, John. Our American Presidents. (Illus.). 176p. (gr. 3-8). 1989. 2.95 (ISBN 0-87406-072-9, 57-19148-6). Willowisp Pr.

Cary, Barbara. Meet Abraham Lincoln. Davis, J., illus. (gr. 2-6). 1965. 5.95 (ISBN 0-394-80057-5, Random Juv); lib. bdg. 8.99 (ISBN 0-394-90057-X). Random.

Clinton, Susan. Benjamin Harrison. LC 89-33751. 100p. (ps up). 1989. PLB 17.27 (ISBN 0-516-01370-X). Childrens.

Coy, Harold. Presidents. (Illus.). (gr. 4-6). 1977. PLB 10.40 s&l (ISBN 0-531-02906-9). Watts.

D'Aulaire, Ingri & D'Aulaire, Edgar P. Abraham Lincoln. rev. ed. (gr. k-4). 1957. pap. 10.95 (ISBN 0-385-07669-X). Doubleday.

—George Washington. D'Aulaire, Ingri & D'Aulaire, Edgar P., illus. LC 36-27417. 64p. (gr. 1-4). 1936. pap. 13.95 (ISBN 0-385-07306-2). Doubleday.

Falkof, Lucille. Ulysses S. Grant: 18th President of the United States. Young, Richard G., ed. LC 87-32817. (Illus.). (gr. 5-9). 1988. PLB 17.26 (ISBN 0-944483-02-X). Garrett Ed Corp.

Fisher, Leonard E. The White House. LC 89-1990. (Illus.). 96p. (gr. 3-7). 1989. reinforced 14.95 (ISBN 0-8234-0774-8). Holiday.

Fox, Mary V. Mister President: The Story of Ronald Reagan. rev. ed. LC 86-4420. (Illus.). 160p. (gr. 5-12). 1986. PLB 18.95 (ISBN 0-89490-130-3). Enslow Pubs.

Gamiello, Elvira. America's Presidents Activity & Fun Book. (Illus., Orig.). (gr. 4-6). 1989. pap. 1.95 (ISBN 0-942025-51-2). Kidsbks.

George Bush: The Story of Our Forty-First President. (gr. 2-6). 1989. pap. 2.95 (ISBN 0-440-40174-7, YB). Dell.

Goldman, Phyllis B., ed. Monkeyshines on the United States Presidents: Games, Puzzles, & Trivia. (Illus.). 97p. (gr. 4 up). 1990. pap. 12.95x (ISBN 0-9620900-1-8). NC Learn Inst Fitness.

Graves, Charles P. John F. Kennedy. Frame, Paul, illus. 80p. (gr. 1-7). 1981. pap. 2.95 (ISBN 0-440-44242-7, YB). Dell.

Green, Carl & Sanford, William. Presidency. (Illus.). 96p. (gr. 7 up). 1990. lib. bdg. 18.60 (ISBN 0-86593-084-8); lib. bdg. 13.95s.p. (ISBN 0-685-36360-0). Rourke Corp.

Greenblatt, Miriam. James K. Polk: 11th President of the United States. Young, Richard G., ed. LC 87-35981. (Illus.). (gr. 5-9). 1988. PLB 17.26 (ISBN 0-944483-04-6). Garrett Ed Corp.

Greene, Carol. Los Presidentes. Kratky, Lada, tr. LC 85-31848. (SPA., Illus.). 48p. (gr. k-4). 1986. PLB 14.60 (ISBN 0-516-31928-0); pap. 4.95 (ISBN 0-516-51928-X). Childrens.

—Presidents. LC 84-7719. (Illus.). 48p. (gr. k-4). 1984. lib. bdg. 14.60 (ISBN 0-516-01928-7); pap. 4.95 (ISBN 0-516-41928-5). Childrens.

Heilbroner, Joan. Meet George Washington. Mays, Victor, illus. (gr. 2-6). 1967. 4.95 (ISBN 0-394-80058-3, Random Juv); lib. bdg. 8.99 (ISBN 0-394-90058-8). Random.

Honey, Michael. Milestone Documents in the National Archives: Records of Impeachment. LC 86-16307. (Illus.). 23p. (Orig.). 1987. pap. text ed. 2.50x (ISBN 0-911333-49-5). Natl Archives & Records.

Kent, Zachary. George Bush. LC 89-33744. 100p. (gr. 3 up). 1989. PLB 17.27 (ISBN 0-516-01374-2); pap. 6.95 (ISBN 0-516-41374-0). Childrens.

Krulik, Nancy E. Meet the Presidents: A Book to Color. Roper, Robert, illus. 48p. (gr. 1-4). 1988. pap. 1.95 (ISBN 0-590-41977-3). Scholastic Inc.

Law, Kevin J. Millard Fillmore: Thirteenth President of the United States. Young, Richard G., ed. LC 89-25651. (Illus.). 128p. (gr. 5-9). 1990. PLB 17.26 (ISBN 0-944483-61-5). Garrett Ed Corp.

Lindop, Edmund. Presidents by Accident. (Illus.). 208p. (gr. 9-12). 1991. PLB 14.90 (ISBN 0-531-11059-1). Watts.

Moncure, Jane B. My First Presidents' Day Book. Halverson, Lydia, illus. LC 87-10309. 32p. (ps-2). 1987. PLB 14.60 (ISBN 0-516-02910-X); pap. 3.95 (ISBN 0-516-42910-8). Childrens.

North, Sterling. Abe Lincoln: Log Cabin to White House. LC 87-4654. (Illus.). 160p. (gr. 5-9). 1987. lib. bdg. 8.99 (ISBN 0-394-90361-7, Random Juv); pap. 3.95 (ISBN 0-394-89179-1). Random.

Parker, Nancy W. The President's Car. Parker, Nancy W., illus. LC 79-7898. 64p. (gr. 3-5). 1981. 11.95i (ISBN 0-690-03963-8, Crowell Jr Bks). HarpC Child Bks.

Plischke, Elmer. Presidential Diplomacy: A Chronology of Summit Visits, Trips & Meetings. LC 85-13833. 270p. (gr. 10-12). 1986. lib. bdg. 18.00 (ISBN 0-379-12088-7). Oceana.

Saunders, Susan. A Book of U. S. Presidents. 1989. pap. 2.50 (ISBN 0-590-42662-1). Scholastic Inc.

Simon, Charnan. Chester A. Arthur. LC 89-35386. 100p. (gr. 3 up). 1989. PLB 17.27 (ISBN 0-516-01369-6). Childrens.

Smith, Kathie B. Abraham Lincoln. Seward, James, illus. LC 86-28060. 24p. (gr. 4-6). 1987. PLB 7.98 (ISBN 0-671-64148-4); PLB 5.99s.p. (ISBN 0-685-18829-9). Messner.

Stevens, Rita. Chester A. Arthur: 21st President of the United States. Young, Richard G., ed. LC 87-36120. (Illus.). (gr. 5-9). 1989. PLB 17.26 (ISBN 0-944483-05-4). Garrett Ed Corp.

Sufrin, Mark. George Bush: The Story of the Forty-First President of the United States. (gr. 5 up). 1989. 12.95 (ISBN 0-440-50158-X). Delacorte.

Sullivan, George. Facts & Fun about the Presidents. 96p. (Orig.). (gr. 3-7). 1987. pap. 2.25 (ISBN 0-590-40204-8). Scholastic Inc.

—George Bush. Steltenpohl, Jane, ed. (Illus.). 128p. (gr. 6-10). 1989. lib. bdg. 11.98 (ISBN 0-671-64599-4); pap. 5.95 (ISBN 0-671-67814-0). Messner.

—Mr. President. 1989. pap. 2.75 (ISBN 0-590-42659-1). Scholastic Inc.

—Mr. President: A Book of U. S. Presidents. 144p. (gr. 3-7). pap. 2.95 (ISBN 0-590-40955-7). Scholastic Inc.

—Mr. President: A Book on U. S. Presidents. (Illus.). 160p. (gr. 3-7). 1985. 8.95 (ISBN 0-396-08737-X, Putnam). Putnam Pub Group.

Swerdlick, Harriet & Reiter, Edith. President Games: Puzzles, Quizzes, & Mind Teasers for Every George, Abe, & Lyndon! 48p. (Orig.). (gr. 3 up). 1988. pap. 2.95 incl. chipboard (ISBN 0-8431-2240-4). Price Stern.

White, Nancy B. Meet John F. Kennedy. (Illus.). (gr. 2-5). 1965. 6.95 (ISBN 0-394-80059-1, Random Juv); lib. bdg. 8.99 (ISBN 0-394-90059-6). Random.

PRESIDENTS–U. S.–ELECTION

Hargrove, Jim. The Story of Presidential Elections. LC 88-1021. (Illus.). 31p. (gr. 3-6). 1988. PLB 13.27 (ISBN 0-516-04737-X); pap. 3.95 (ISBN 0-516-44737-8). Childrens.

Hewett, Joan. Getting Elected: The Diary of a Campaign. Hewett, Richard, illus. LC 88-11109. 48p. (gr. 4-7). 1989. 13.95 (ISBN 0-525-67259-1, Lodestar Bks). Dutton Child Bks.

Raber, Thomas R. Presidential Campaign. (Illus.). 88p. (gr. 4 up). 1988. lib. bdg. 10.95 (ISBN 0-8225-1750-7). Lerner Pubns.

PRESIDENTS–U. S.–FICTION

Adams, Laurie & Coudert, Allison. Who Wants a Turnip for President, Anyway? 96p. (Orig.). 1990. pap. 2.75 (ISBN 0-553-15432-X). Bantam.

Brown, Marc. Arthur Meets the President. (ps-3). 1991. 14.95 (ISBN 0-316-11265-8). Little.

Service, Pamela F. A Question of Destiny. LC 85-21466. 168p. (gr. 5-9). 1986. 13.95 (ISBN 0-689-31181-8, Atheneum Child Bk). Macmillan Child Grp.

PRESIDENTS–U. S.–POWER

see Executive Power–U. S.

PRESIDENTS–U. S.–STAFF

Bruce, Preston & Johnson, Katharine. From the Door of the White House. LC 81-23672. (Illus.). 160p. (gr. 6 up). 1984. 12.95 (ISBN 0-688-00883-6). Lothrop.

Sullivan, George. How the White House Really Works. LC 88-16409. (Illus.). 128p. (gr. 5-9). 1989. 15.95 (ISBN 0-525-67266-4, Lodestar Bks). Dutton Child Bks.

PRESIDENTS–U. S.–WIVES

Behrens, June. Barbara Bush: First Lady of Literacy. LC 90-2201. (Illus.). 32p. (gr. 2-5). 1990. PLB 13.27 (ISBN 0-516-04275-0); pap. 3.95 (ISBN 0-516-44275-9). Childrens.

Shelley, Mary V. & Munro, Sandra H. Harriet Lane, First Lady of the White House. LC 80-20151. (Illus.). 48p. (gr. 4-6). 1980. 6.95 (ISBN 0-915010-29-1). Sutter House.

Winner, David. Eleanor Roosevelt: Defender of Human Rights & Democracy. LC 91-291. (Illus.). 68p. (gr. 5-6). 1991. PLB 13.95 (ISBN 0-8368-0218-7). Gareth Stevens Inc.

PRESIDENTS' WIVES

see Presidents–U. S.–Wives

PRESLEY, ELVIS ARON, 1935-1977

Alico, Stella H. Elvis Presley - The Beatles. Cruz, E. R. & Guanlao, Ernie, illus. (gr. 4-12). 1979. pap. text ed. 2.95 (ISBN 0-88301-352-5); wkbk 1.25 (ISBN 0-88301-376-2). Pendulum Pr.

Elvis Presley. 48p. (gr. 5-6). 1989. PLB 10.95 (ISBN 0-685-26353-3). Capstone Pr.

Loewen, L. Elvis. (Illus.). 112p. (gr. 5 up). 1989. lib. bdg. 17.26 (ISBN 0-86592-606-9). Rourke Corp.

Love, Robert. Elvis Presley. LC 86-5656. (Illus.). 128p. (gr. 7-12). 1986. PLB 13.90 (ISBN 0-531-10239-4). Watts.

Rubel, David. Elvis Presley: The Rise of Rock & Roll. (Illus.). 96p. (gr. 7 up). 1991. PLB 19.95 (ISBN 1-878841-18-1). Millbrook Pr.

Wootton, Richard. Elvis. LC 84-17970. (Illus.). 128p. (gr. 5 up). 1985. lib. bdg. 6.99 (ISBN 0-394-97046-2, Random Juv). Random.

PRESS

see Journalism; Newspapers; Periodicals

PREVENTION OF ACCIDENTS

see Accidents–Prevention

PREVENTION OF CRUELTY TO ANIMALS

see Animals–Treatment

PREVENTION OF FIRE

see Fire Prevention

PREVENTIVE MEDICINE

see Bacteriology; Hygiene; Immunity; Public Health

PRIMARY EDUCATION

see Education, Elementary

PRIMATES

see also Man; Monkeys

Barrett, N. S. Monkeys & Apes. FS Staff, ed. (Illus.). 32p. (gr. 1-6). 1988. PLB 11.40 (ISBN 0-531-10529-6). Watts.

Bogard, Vicki, tr. from FRE. Monkeys, Apes & Other Primates. Wallis, Diz, illus. LC 89-5378. 38p. (gr. k-5). 1989. 4.95 (ISBN 0-944589-26-X, 026). Young Discovery Lib.

Chivers, David. Gorillas & Chimps. (Illus.). 32p. (gr. 1-6). 1987. PLB 11.90 (ISBN 0-531-17051-9, Gloucester Pr). Watts.

Green, Carl R. & Sanford, William R. The Orangutan. LC 87-19811. (Illus.). 48p. (gr. 5-6). 1987. PLB 10.95 (ISBN 0-89686-335-2, Crestwood Hse). Macmillan Child Grp.

Harrison, Virginia. How Mountain Gorillas Live. Nichols, Michael, illus. LC 91-2022. 32p. (gr. 2-3). 1991. PLB 11.95 (ISBN 0-8368-0446-5). Gareth Stevens Inc.

—Mountain Gorillas & Their Young. Nichols, Michael, illus. LC 91-7600. 32p. (gr. 2-3). 1991. PLB 11.95 (ISBN 0-8368-0445-7). Gareth Stevens Inc.

Hogan, Paula Z. The Gorilla. LC 79-13602. (Illus.). 32p. (gr. 1-4). 1981. PLB 27.99 incl. cassette (ISBN 0-8172-1845-9) (ISBN 0-685-09541-X). Raintree Pubs.

Ritchie, Rita. Mountain Gorillas in Danger. Nichols, Michael, photos by. LC 91-10831. (Illus.). 32p. (gr. 2-3). 1991. PLB 11.95 (ISBN 0-8368-0447-3). Gareth Stevens Inc.

Selsam, Millicent E. & Hunt, Joyce. A First Look at Monkeys & Apes. Springer, Harriett, illus. LC 78-74164. (gr. 1-4). 1979. lib. bdg. 9.85 (ISBN 0-8027-6359-6). Walker & Co.

Spizzirri Publishing Co. Staff. Primates: An Educational Coloring Book. Spizzirri, Linda, ed. Fuller, Glenn, et al, illus. 32p. (gr. 1-8). 1981. pap. 1.95 (ISBN 0-86545-030-7). Spizzirri.

PRIME MINISTERS–GREAT BRITAIN

Faber, Doris. Margaret Thatcher: Britain's Iron Lady. Masheris, Robert, illus. 64p. (gr. 2-6). 1986. pap. 3.95 (ISBN 0-14-032160-8, Puffin). Puffin Bks.

PRIMERS

see also Alphabet Books

Bank Street College of Education Editors. It's about Time: Play Time - Work Time - Learning Time. (Illus.). 64p. (ps-k). 1985. 2.95 (ISBN 0-8120-3611-5). Barron.

—One to Ten More Counting Fun. (Illus.). 64p. (ps-k). 1985. 3.95 (ISBN 0-8120-3614-X). Barron.

—One, Two, Three Come Count with Me. (Illus.). 64p. (ps-k). 1985. 3.95 (ISBN 0-8120-3615-8). Barron.

Berenstain, Stan & Berenstain, Janice. The Bear Detectives. Berenstain, Stan & Berenstain, Janice, illus. LC 75-1603. 48p. (gr. k-3). 1975. 6.95 (ISBN 0-394-83127-6); lib. bdg. 7.99 (ISBN 0-394-93127-0). Beginner.

—Bears' Christmas. LC 79-117542. (Illus.). 72p. (gr. k-3). 1970. 5.95 (ISBN 0-394-80090-7); lib. bdg. 6.99 (ISBN 0-394-90090-1). Beginner.

Forman-Hitt, Kathy & Young, Janet. Beginning Reading Five. Wheeler, Sharon, ed. Richesson, Robin, illus. (ps). 1986. wkbk. 1.95 (ISBN 0-916119-22-X). Creat Teach Pr.

Gackenbach, Dick. Claude & Pepper. Gackenbach, Dick, illus. LC 75-25507. 32p. (ps-2). 1979. 13.95 (ISBN 0-395-28793-6, Clarion). HM.

—Hattie Rabbit. LC 75-37018. (Illus.). 32p. (ps-3). 1976. PLB 10.89 (ISBN 0-06-021940-8). HarpC Child Bks.

Hill, Charlotte M. Wee Folks Learn to Read, Bk. One: A Phonetic Approach to Beginning Reading. Young, Elaine & Hill, Fred D., eds. LC 90-83256. (Illus., Orig.). (gr. k-3). 1990. pap. text ed. 7.95 (ISBN 0-9620182-3-6). Charill Pubs.

Hoff, Syd. Albert the Albatross. Hoff, Syd, illus. LC 61-5767. 32p. (gr. k-3). 1961. PLB 10.89 (ISBN 0-06-022446-0). HarpC Child Bks.

—Barkley. Hoff, Syd, illus. LC 75-6290. 32p. (gr. k-3). 1975. PLB 10.89 (ISBN 0-06-022448-7). HarpC Child Bks.

Hurd, Edith T. Come & Have Fun. Hurd, Clement, illus. LC 62-13324. 32p. (gr. k-3). 1962. PLB 10.89 (ISBN 0-06-022681-1). HarpC Child Bks.

Kalb, Jonah. The Easy Baseball Book. Kossin, Sandy, illus. LC 75-44085. 64p. (gr. 2-5). 1976. 14.95 (ISBN 0-395-24385-8). HM.

Learn with E.T.: Colors. (Illus.). 24p. 1983. pap. 1.95 (ISBN 0-671-47727-7, Little Simon). S&S Trade.

Learn with E.T.: Words. (Illus.). 24p. 1983. pap. 1.95 (ISBN 0-671-46438-8, Little Simon). S&S Trade.

Lorian, Nicole. Popple Peeking. Beylon, Cathy, illus. 24p. (ps-1). 1986. 5.95 (ISBN 0-394-88040-4). Random.

McClintock, Mike. What Have I Got? Kessler, Leonard, illus. LC 60-11197. (gr. k-2). 1961. PLB 9.89 (ISBN 0-06-024141-1). HarpC Child Bks.

Marshall, James. Speedboat. Marshall, James, illus. LC 75-40349. 48p. (gr. 1-4). 1976. 13.95 (ISBN 0-395-24384-X). HM.

Minarik, Else H. Cat & Dog. Siebel, Fritz, illus. LC 60-14998. 32p. (gr. k-2). 1960. PLB 10.89 (ISBN 0-06-024221-3). HarpC Child Bks.

Moncure, Jane B. My "a" Sound Box. Peltier, Pam, illus. LC 84-17024. 32p. (ps-2). 1984. PLB 11.97 (ISBN 0-89565-296-X); pap. 6.96 (ISBN 0-89565-335-4). Childs World.

—Watch Out! Word Bird. Hohag, Linda S., illus. (ps-2). 1982. lib. bdg. 11.97 (ISBN 0-89565-219-6). Childs World.

Morris, Robert A. Dolphin. Funai, Mamoru, illus. LC 75-6292. 64p. (gr. k-3). 1975. PLB 11.89 (ISBN 0-06-024342-2). HarpC Child Bks.

Parish, Peggy. Good Work, Amelia Bedelia. Sweat, Lynn, illus. LC 75-20360. 56p. (gr. 1-4). 1976. 12.95 (ISBN 0-688-80022-X); PLB 12.88 (ISBN 0-688-84022-1). Greenwillow.

Prather, Gloria A. & Prather, Alfred G. My First Reader & Skills Book: One Hundred Words Plus. Prather, Arden C., ed. Hafer, Dick, illus. 36p. (Orig.). (gr. 1-3). 1988. pap. write for info. (ISBN 0-9619655-2-5). Academic Packs Co.

Prather, Gloria M. & Prather, Alfred G. Especially for Special Children: The A-B-C's of Super Stars. Prather, Arden C., ed. Hafer, Dick, illus. 30p. (Orig.). 1988. Picture bk. PLB write for info. (ISBN 0-9619655-3-3). Academic Packs Co.

Punnett, Dick. Talk-along-Help Dress Priscilla. Dunnington, Tom, illus. LC 84-23030. 32p. (ps). 1985. lib. bdg. 11.97 (ISBN 0-89565-217-X). Childs World.

Punnett, Richard D. Help Jumbo Escape. Dunnington, Tom, illus. LC 81-21667. 32p. (ps-2). 1982. lib. bdg. 11.97 (ISBN 0-89565-214-5). Childs World.

—Name Lizzy's Colors. Dunnington, Tom, illus. LC 82-1172. 32p. (ps-2). 1982. lib. bdg. 11.97 (ISBN 0-89565-216-1). Childs World.

—Name Patty's Pets. Dunnington, Tom, illus. LC 81-18056. 32p. (ps-2). 1982. lib. bdg. 11.97 (ISBN 0-89565-213-7). Childs World.

Schreckhise, Roseva. What Was It Before It Was My Chair? McLean, Mina G., illus. LC 85-13238. 32p. (ps-2). 1985. PLB 11.97 (ISBN 0-89565-326-5). Childs World.

—What Was It Before It Was My Sweater? Endres, Helen, illus. LC 85-11401. 32p. (ps-2). 1985. PLB 11.97 (ISBN 0-89565-324-9). Childs World.

Schulman, Janet. The Big Hello. Hoban, Lillian, illus. LC 75-33672. (gr. 1-4). 1976. 13.95 (ISBN 0-688-80036-X). Greenwillow.

Spizman, Robyn. Bulletin Boards: For Reading, Spelling & Language Skills. Pesiri, Evelyn, illus. 64p. (gr. k-6). 1984. wkbk. 6.95 (ISBN 0-86653-210-2, GA 574). Good Apple.

Tuhy, Arleen A. A Silly Book. Tuhy, Arleen A., illus. 18p. (Orig.). (ps-3). 1990. pap. 3.00 (ISBN 0-9625059-1-9). Fountain Light Pr.

—This Is My First Book. (Illus.). 15p. (ps-3). 1990. pap. 2.00 (ISBN 0-9625059-3-5). Fountain Light Pr.

Tyler, J. & Stitt, S. Outdoor Words. (Illus.). 16p. (ps). 1989. 2.95 (ISBN 0-7460-0435-4, Usborne); lib. bdg. 6.96 (ISBN 0-88110-393-4, Usborne). EDC.

—Shopping Words. (Illus.). 16p. (ps). 1989. 2.95 (ISBN 0-7460-0436-2, Usborne); lib. bdg. 6.96 (ISBN 0-88110-394-2, Usborne). EDC.

White, Curlie. Children's First Action Words. rev. ed. (gr. k-2). 1992. 7.95 (ISBN 0-8062-4125-X). Carlton.

Wise, Francis H. & Wise, Joyce M. Fun in the Sun. Wise, Joyce M., illus. 21p. (ps-1). 1975. pap. 1.50 (ISBN 0-915766-30-2). Wise Pub.

—Jay's Fat Cat. Wise, Joyce M., illus. 20p. (ps-1). 1974. pap. text ed. 1.50 (ISBN 0-915766-29-9). Wise Pub.

PRINCE EDWARD ISLAND–FICTION

Montgomery, L. M. Anne of Green Gables. 320p. (gr. 7-12). 1976. pap. 2.95 (ISBN 0-553-24295-4). Bantam.

Montgomery, Lucy M. Anne of Green Gables, Vol. 1. (gr. 4-7). 1984. pap. 2.95 (ISBN 0-553-15327-7). Bantam.

PRINCES AND PRINCESSES–FICTION

Andersen, Hans Christian. The Princess & the Pea. Bell, Anthea, tr. Tharlet, Eve, illus. LC 87-13913. (ps up). 1987. 13.95 (ISBN 0-88708-052-9). Picture Bk Studio.

Armstrong, Alice C. Princess McGuffy & the Little Rebel. 1988. 8.95 (ISBN 0-533-07708-7). Vantage.

Ashby, Sylvia. Shining Princess of the Slender Bamboo. (Illus.). 44p. (Orig.). (gr. 6 up). 1987. pap. 3.50 (ISBN 0-88680-266-0). I E Clark.

Bawden, Nina. Princess Alice. Gili, Phillida, illus. 32p. (ps-3). 1986. 10.95 (ISBN 0-233-97746-5). Andre Deutsch.

Bianchi, J. Princess Frownsalot. (Illus.). 24p. (ps-8). 1987. 12.95 (ISBN 0-921285-06-X); pap. 4.95 (ISBN 0-921285-04-3). Firefly Bks Ltd.

Birrer, Cynthia & Birrer, William. The Lady & the Unicorn. Birrer, Cynthia & Birrer, William, illus. LC 86-20872. 32p. (ps-3). 1987. 12.95 (ISBN 0-688-04037-3). Lothrop.

Bos, Burny. Prince Valentino. De Beer, Hans, illus. LC 89-43247. 32p. (gr. k-3). 1990. 13.95 (ISBN 1-55858-089-1). North-South Bks NYC.

Brentano, Clemens. The Legend of Rosepetal. Zwerger, Lisbeth, illus. LC 84-27386. 32p. (gr. 2-6). 1985. 16.95 (ISBN 0-907234-71-2). Picture Bk Studio.

Burnett, Frances H. A Little Princess. 232p. 1981. Repr. PLB 15.95 (ISBN 0-89966-327-3). Buccaneer Bks.

—A Little Princess. 300p. 1977. PLB 15.95x (ISBN 0-89967-005-9). Harmony Raine.

—A Little Princess. 256p. (Orig.). (gr. 4-6). 1987. pap. 2.95 (ISBN 0-590-40719-8, Pub. by Apple Classics). Scholastic Inc.

—A Little Princess. Adorjan, Carol M., adapted by. Marvin, Frederic, illus. LC 87-15485. 48p. (gr. 3-6). 1988. PLB 12.89 (ISBN 0-8167-1201-8); pap. text ed. 3.95 (ISBN 0-8167-1202-6). Troll Assocs.

—A Little Princess. Henterly, Jamichael, illus. 288p. (gr. 4 up). 1989. 12.95 (ISBN 0-448-09299-9, G&D). Putnam Pub Group.

—The Lost Prince. (gr. 4-6). 1986. pap. 2.25 (ISBN 0-14-035071-3, Puffin). Puffin Bks.

Cartwright & Rawson. Princes & Princesses. (gr. k-4). 1980. 6.95 (ISBN 0-86020-383-2, Usborne-Hayes); pap. 3.95 (ISBN 0-86020-382-4). EDC.

Christopher, John. The Prince in Waiting. LC 70-119838. 192p. (gr. 5-9). 1974. pap. 4.95 (ISBN 0-02-042400-0, Collier Young Ad). Macmillan Child Grp.

Conford, Ellen. A Royal Pain. 176p. (gr. 7 up). 1986. pap. 11.95 (ISBN 0-590-33269-4, Scholastic Hardcover). Scholastic Inc.

—A Royal Pain. 176p. (Orig.). (gr. 7 up). 1987. pap. 2.50 (ISBN 0-590-40548-9, Point). Scholastic Inc.

—Royal Pain. 1987. pap. 2.75 (ISBN 0-590-43437-3). Scholastic Inc.

Cosgrove, Stephen E. Terrybrook Dragon. McNatt, Richard, illus. 32p. (gr. k-7). 1990. 14.95 (ISBN 1-55868-036-5). Gr Arts Ctr Pub. TERRYBROOK DRAGON is a tale about the banished prince who must protect his mother, the queen, & his princess sister from the terrible Terrybrook Dragon. The prince's father left the three alone to go out into the world & secure a new castle for his

family - much like fathers now, who are forced to leave home to find better jobs to support their families. This is a timeless story of families separated by circumstances beyond their control. It is a metaphor relating to family problems, values, & personal worth. The combination of Cosgrove & McNatt is not new. Together they created the 6-book series, "The Snuffin Chronicles." McNatt also did extensive work for Disney Studios where he illustrated many of the "Winnie the Pooh" books.
Publisher Provided Annotation.

Curtis, Dorris. Skammy: Prince of Troy. Curtis, Dorris, illus. 231p. (gr. 5-9). 1988. lib. bdg. 18.50 (ISBN 0-944436-04-8). Univ Central AR Pr.
Skammy: Prince of Troy
Recommended reading group: 10-15 years. It captures the imagination, & connects young readers to the origins of western values. Skammy: Prince of Troy is an exciting story of adventure & mighty deeds which will appeal to both the imagination & the intellect of young readers. But this book offers more than mere entertainment. It does what the deepest thinkers about literature have always said good books should do. It teaches as it entertains. It clarifies & enhances life. It struggles with great questions of life, death, & immortality. It offers models of human thought, behavior, & morality ranging from heroism, courage, integrity, & endurance to cowardice & treachery. Prince Skamandrios (Skammy to his family & friends) is initiated into the adult world of violence & intrigue early in life because the Greek armies are threatening the walls of his hometown of Troy & because he is the son of Hector, the heroic champion of the city....all of this against the backdrop of the war that defined patriotism & heroism, as well as waste & inhumanity, in the art & literature of western civilization.
Publisher Provided Annotation.

Dalton, Anne. Prince Star. (Illus.). 32p. (gr. k-3). 1985. 14.95 (ISBN 0-7182-2101-X, Pub. by W Heinemann Ltd). Trafalgar Sq.

Dasent, George W., tr. East o' the Sun, West o' the Moon. Barlow, Gillian, illus. LC 87-32679. 32p. (ps-3). 1988. PLB 13.95 (ISBN 0-399-21570-0, Philomel Bks). Putnam Pub Group.

Davis, Jim. Garfield the Knight in Shining Armor. Davis, Jim, illus. 32p. (ps). 1982. pap. 1.25 (ISBN 0-394-85446-2). Random.

Davis, Michael. The Flower Princess. Luongo, Aldo, illus. 32p. (gr. k-12). 1989. write for info.; PLB write for info. R Bane Ltd.

De Camp, L. Sprague. Undesired Princess & the Enchanted Bunny. 1990. pap. 3.95 (ISBN 0-671-69875-3). S&S Trade.

De Paola, Tomie. The Prince of the Dolomites. De Paola, Tomie, illus. LC 79-18524. 48p. (ps-3). 1980. pap. 4.50 (ISBN 0-15-674432-5, VoyB). HarBraceJ.

De Saint-Exupery, Antoine. Petit Prince. (FRE.). (gr. 3-8). write for info. French & Eur.

Galoete, Mario, Jr. The Hermit Prince. 60p. 1988. 6.95 (ISBN 0-533-07705-2). Vantage.

Gold, Auner. The Marrano Prince. Hinlicky, Gregg, illus. 286p. (gr. 9-12). 1988. 13.95 (ISBN 0-935063-39-0); text ed. 10.95 (ISBN 0-935063-40-4). CIS Comm.

Goodman, Robert B. & Spicer, Robert A. Kaguya Hime: The Shimmering Princess. Johnson, Victor, ed. Suyeoka, George, illus. LC 75-18791. (gr. 1-7). 1974. 5.95 (ISBN 0-89610-005-7). Island Heritage.

Gouffe, Marie A. Treasures Beyond the Snows. Sellon, Michael B., illus. LC 77-95392. (gr. 3-9). 1970. 3.75 (ISBN 0-8356-0026-2, Quest). Theos Pub Hse.

Harris, Aurand. The Flying Prince. (Orig.). (gr. k up). 1985. 4.50 (ISBN 0-87602-262-X). Anchorage.

Haugaard, Erik C. Princess Horrid. Hearne, Diane D., illus. LC 89-8227. 48p. (gr. k-4). 1990. 14.95 (ISBN 0-02-743445-1, Mcmillan Child Bk). Macmillan Child Grp.

Helprin, Mark, as told by. Swan Lake. Van Allsburg, Chris, illus. (gr. 1-8). 1989. 19.95 (ISBN 0-395-49858-9). HM.

Honey, Elizabeth. Princess Beatrice & the Rotten Robber. (Illus.). 32p. (ps-3). 1989. pap. 10.95 (ISBN 0-670-82272-8). Viking Child Bks.

Hope, Anthony. The Heart of Princess Osra. 250p. Repr. of 1896 ed. PLB 17.95x (ISBN 0-89966-477-6). Buccaneer Bks.

Johnson, Crockett. Frowning Prince. Johnson, Crockett, illus. (gr. 1-4). 1974. Repr. 15.00 (ISBN 0-912846-09-7). Bookstore Pr.

Karpin, Florence. The Prince in the Golden Tower. Palladini, David, illus. 32p. (ps-3). 1989. pap. 14.95 (ISBN 0-670-82218-3). Viking Child Bks.

Krulik, Nancy E. Prince & the Pauper. 1990. pap. 2.75 (ISBN 0-590-44364-X). Scholastic Inc.

Latella, Lisa. A Song for the Prince. Latella, Lisa, illus. 36p. (Orig.). (gr. k up). 1984. pap. write for info. (ISBN 0-9608592-1-7). Gallery Arts.

LeCain, Errol. Twelve Dancing Princesses. 32p. (ps-k). 1981. pap. 3.95 (ISBN 0-14-050322-6, Puffin). Puffin Bks.

Lee, Nancy. Amber's Rainbow. 23p. (gr. 3 up). 1988. 5.95 (ISBN 0-533-07999-3). Vantage.

Lewis, C. S. The Horse & His Boy. Baynes, Pauline, illus. LC 54-12817. 202p. (gr. 4 up). 1988. 12.95 (ISBN 0-02-757650-7, Mcmillan Child Bk); pap. 3.50 (ISBN 0-02-044200-9, Collier). Macmillan Child Grp.

—Prince Caspian. Baynes, Pauline, illus. LC 85-18999. 192p. (gr. 4 up). 1986. pap. 5.95 (ISBN 0-02-044430-3, Collier Young Ad). Macmillan Child Grp.

Lewis, Paul O. The Starlight Bride. (Illus.). 40p. (ps-6). 1988. cloth 14.95 (ISBN 0-941831-33-7); pap. 9.95 (ISBN 0-941831-25-6). Beyond Words Pub.

Littke, Lael. Prom Dress. 176p. (Orig.). (gr. 6-10). 1989. pap. 2.95 (ISBN 0-590-44237-6). Scholastic Inc.

A Little Princess. (Illus.). (gr. 3-5). 3.50 (ISBN 0-7214-0863-X). Ladybird Bks.

Lowry, Lois. Anastasia. write for info. HM.

Luth, Sophie A. The Special Princess. McColgan, Susie, illus. 36p. 1990. glossy cover 5.95 (ISBN 0-9626153-0-7). Luth & Assocs.

Lynch, Patricia. Brogeen & the Princess of Sheen. (gr. 1 up). 1986. pap. 11.95 (ISBN 0-85105-905-8, Pub. by Colin Smythe Ltd Britain). Dufour.

MacDonald, George. The Light Princess & Other Tales. (Illus.). 288p. (gr. 5-8). 1989. pap. 6.95 (ISBN 0-86241-164-5, Pub. by Cnngt Pub Ltd). Trafalgar Sq.

—Little Daylight. Ingraham, Erick, adapted by. & illus. LC 85-29769. 40p. (gr. 2 up). 1988. 12.95 (ISBN 0-688-06300-4); PLB 12.88 (ISBN 0-688-06301-2, Morrow Jr Bks). Morrow Jr Bks.

—The Princess & Curdie. 306p. 1989. Repr. lib. bdg. 26.95x (ISBN 0-89966-591-8). Buccaneer Bks.

—The Princess & The Goblin. 1986. pap. 4.95 (ISBN 0-440-47189-3, Yearling Classics). Dell.

—The Princess & the Goblin. Smith, Jesse W., illus. Glassman, Peter, afterword by. LC 86-2532. (Illus.). 208p. (ps up). 1986. 17.95 (ISBN 0-688-06604-6). Morrow Jr Bks.

—The Princess & the Goblin. 1989. Repr. lib. bdg. 26.95x (ISBN 0-89966-598-5). Buccaneer Bks.

—The Princess & the Goblin, The Princess & Curdie. McGillis, Roderick, ed. 480p. 1990. pap. 5.95 (ISBN 0-19-282579-8). Oxford U Pr.

Manson, Frank A. The Adventures of Prince Albert & the Royal Dinosaurs. Henley, Joan, illus. 144p. (gr. 2-7). 1990. 11.95 (ISBN 0-918339-17-0). Vandamere.

Mayer, Marianna. Twelve Dancing Princess. Craft, Kinuko Y., illus. LC 83-1034. 40p. (ps up). 1989. 14.95 (ISBN 0-688-08051-0); PLB 14.88 (ISBN 0-688-02026-7, Morrow Jr Bks). Morrow Jr Bks.

Moodie, Fiona. The Sugar Prince. (Illus.). (ps-3). 1987. 12.95 (ISBN 1-55774-005-4, Dist. by Watts). Adama Pubs Inc.

Murphy, Shirley R. Nightpool. LC 85-42626. 256p. (gr. 7 up). 1985. PLB 11.89 (ISBN 0-685-10298-X). HarpC Child Bks.

Peck, Richard. Princess Ashley. (gr. k-12). 1988. pap. 3.25 (ISBN 0-440-20206-X, LFL). Dell.

Philip, Neil, ed. Guleesh & the King of France's Daughter. Underhill, Henry, illus. 32p. (ps-5). 1986. 11.95 (ISBN 0-399-21391-0, Philomel). Putnam Pub Group.

Pilny, Marie. The Three Princes of Serendip. 160p. (gr. 4-10). 1987. write for info. (ISBN 0-932806-03-1). Synergy Pubns.

Poole, Josephine, retold by. The Sleeping Beauty. Morin, Edmund, illus. 24p. (ps up). 1989. incl. dust jacket 10.95 (ISBN 0-8120-5965-4). Barron.

Ross, Tony. I Want My Potty. (Illus.). 24p. (ps-k). 1988. pap. 6.95 (ISBN 0-916291-14-6). Kane-Miller Bk.

Saint-Exupery, Antoine de. The Little Prince. Woods, Katherine, tr. LC 67-1144. (Illus.). 113p. (gr. 4-6). 1968. pap. 3.95 (ISBN 0-15-652820-7, Harv). HarBraceJ.

Sampson, Fay. Pangur Ban. (Illus.). 128p. (Orig.). (gr. 4-8). 1989. pap. 3.95 (ISBN 0-85648-580-2). Lion USA.

Shearer, Marilyn J. The Nubian Princess. Walker, Larry, illus. 16p. (Orig.). (ps-6). Date not set. 19.95 (ISBN 0-685-30091-9); pap. 10.95 (ISBN 0-685-30092-7). L Ashley & Joshua.

Simpson, Juwairiah J. L. The Princess Who Wanted to Be Poor. American Trust Publications, ed. (Illus.). 52p. 1987. pap. 4.75 (ISBN 0-89259-104-8). Am Trust Pubns.

Swiderska, Barbara. The Fisherman's Bride. Swiderska, Barbara, illus. LC 78-148051. 32p. (ps-3). 8.95 (ISBN 0-87592-018-7). Scroll Pr.

Thomas, Jane R. The Princess in the Pigpen. LC 89-856. 128p. (gr. 3-7). 1989. 13.95 (ISBN 0-395-51587-4, Clarion Bks). HM.

Thurber, James. Many Moons. Simont, Marac, illus. LC 89-36465. 48p. (ps-3). 1990. 14.95 (ISBN 0-15-251872-X). HarBraceJ.

Trout, John M. Princess Fanisha: The Whispering Waters, Bk. 2. Trout, John M., illus. 180p. (Orig.). (gr. 4 up). 1984. pap. 5.95x (ISBN 0-914970-49-6). Conch Mag.

Twain, Mark. The Prince & the Pauper. 256p. (gr. 3-7). 1983. pap. 2.25 (ISBN 0-14-035017-9, Puffin). Puffin Bks.

—The Prince & the Pauper. (gr. k-6). 1985. pap. 4.95 (ISBN 0-440-47186-9, Pub. by Yearling Classics). Dell.

Vesey, A. The Princess & the Frog. Vesey, A., illus. 32p. (ps-3). 1985. 14.95 (ISBN 0-316-90036-2, 900362, Joy St Bks). Little.

—The Princess & the Frog. (Illus.). 32p. (Orig.). (ps-3). 1988. pap. 3.95 (ISBN 0-14-050802-3, Puffin). Puffin Bks.

White, John. The Sword Bearer. LC 86-2860. (Illus.). 320p. (Orig.). (gr. 4 up). 1986. pap. 10.95 (ISBN 0-87784-590-5). InterVarsity.

Wilde, Oscar & Riswold, G. Happy Prince. (gr. 1-4). 1971. pap. 1.95 (ISBN 0-13-384057-3). P-H.

Wood, Audrey. Princess & the Dragon. Wood, Audrey, illus. 32p. (ps-2). 1981. 5.50 (ISBN 0-85953-150-3, Pub. by Child's Play England). Childs Play.

—Princess & the Dragon. 1989. pap. 2.50 (ISBN 0-85953-013-2). Childs Play.

Ziefert, Harriet. The Prince's Tooth Is Loose. Alley, R. W., illus. LC 89-36433. 24p. (Orig.). (ps-2). 1990. pap. 2.25 (ISBN 0-394-84840-3). Random.

PRINTING
see also Books

Althea. Making a Book. (Illus.). 26p. (gr. 2-5). 1983. pap. 3.95 (ISBN 0-521-27159-2). Cambridge U Pr.

Brommer, Gerald F. Relief Printmaking. LC 77-113860. (Illus.). (gr. 7-12). 14.95 (ISBN 0-87192-034-4). Davis Mass.

Caselli, Giovanni. German Printer. Caselli, Giovanni, illus. LC 86-71707. 29p. (gr. 3-7). 1987. 12.95 (ISBN 0-87226-109-3). P Bedrick Bks.

Cross, Jeanne. Simple Printing Methods. Cross, Jeanne, illus. LC 72-39812. 48p. (gr. 6 up). 1972. 18.95 (ISBN 0-87599-192-0). S G Phillips.

Devonshire, Hilary. Printing. FS-Ltd Staff, ed. (Illus.). 32p. (gr. 1-6). 1988. PLB 11.90 (ISBN 0-531-10555-5). Watts.

Graphic Arts. (Illus.). 64p. (gr. 6-12). 1988. pap. 1.85 (ISBN 0-8395-3374-8, 3374). BSA.

Hart, Tony. Printing & Patterns. (Illus.). 32p. (gr. 1-4). 1984. 5.95 (ISBN 0-7182-2953-3, Pub. by w Heinemann Ltd). Trafalgar Sq.

O'Neill, Catherine. Let's Visit a Printing Plant. Parker, James W., illus. LC 87-3484. 32p. (gr. 2-4). 1988. PLB 10.79 (ISBN 0-8167-1163-1); pap. text ed. 2.95 (ISBN 0-8167-1164-X). Troll Assocs.

Tofts, Hannah. Print Book. (ps-3). 1990. pap. 11.95 (ISBN 0-671-70368-4); pap. 4.95 (ISBN 0-671-70369-2). S&S Trade.

PRISON ESCAPES
see Escapes

PRISONS
see also Crime and Criminals; Criminal Law; Escapes

Bernards, Neal & Szumski, Bonnie. Prisons: Detecting Bias. (Illus.). 32p. (gr. 3-6). 1990. PLB 8.95 (ISBN 0-89908-604-7). Greenhaven.

Gordon, Vivian V. & Smith-Owens, Lois. Prisons & the Criminal Justice System. 160p. (gr. 7 up). 1991. PLB 15.85 (ISBN 0-8027-8121-7); pap. 8.95 (ISBN 0-8027-7370-2). Walker & Co.

Johnson, Spencer. The Value of Kindness: The Story of Elizabeth Fry. 2nd ed. Pileggi, Steve, illus. LC 76-55339. (gr. k-6). 1976. 9.95 (ISBN 0-916392-09-0, Pub. by Value Communications). Oak Tree Pubns.

Mitford, Jessica. Kind & Unusual Punishment: The Prison Business. LC 74-3262. (gr. 9 up). 1974. pap. 8.76 (ISBN 0-394-71093-2, Vin). Random.

O'Neill, Judith. Transported to Van Diemen's Land. (Illus.). 48p. (gr. 7 up). 1977. pap. 5.95 (ISBN 0-521-21231-6). Cambridge U Pr.

Weiss, Ann E. Prisons: A System in Trouble. 160p. (gr. 6 up). 1988. lib. bdg. 18.95 (ISBN 0-89490-165-6). Enslow Pubs.

PRISONS–FICTION

Bosse, Malcolm J. The Seventy-Nine Squares. LC 79-7591. (gr. 7 up). 1979. 9.57i (ISBN 0-690-03999-9, Crowell Jr Bks). HarpC Child Bks.

De Jenkins, Lyll B. The Honorable Prison. 208p. (gr. 7 up). 1989. pap. 3.95 (ISBN 0-14-032952-8, Puffin). Puffin Bks.

Sebestyen, Ouida. The Girl in the Box: The Diary of Anne Frank. 160p. (gr. 7 up). 1988. 12.95 (ISBN 0-316-77935-0, Joy St Bks). Little.

Takashima, Shizuye. A Child in Prison Camp. (Illus.). 100p. (gr. 4 up). 1991. pap. 7.95 (ISBN 0-88776-241-7). Tundra Bks.

PRIVACY, RIGHT OF
Taylor, L. B., Jr. Electronic Surveillance. (Illus.). 128p. (gr. 7-12). 1987. lib. bdg. 12.90 (ISBN 0-531-10328-5). Watts.
PRIVATE THEATRICALS
see Amateur Theatricals
PRIVATEERING
Cook, Fred J. Privateers of Seventy Six. LC 75-30808. (Illus.). 192p. (gr. 10 up). 1976. 7.95 (ISBN 0-672-52127-X, Bobbs). Macmillan.
PRIZE FIGHTING
see Boxing
PROBES, SPACE
see Space Probes
PROBLEM CHILDREN
see also Juvenile Delinquency
Champ, Laurna J. Resolving Behavior Problems: The Learning Styles Approach. (Illus.). 36p. (Orig.). (ps-6). 1988. 3.95 (ISBN 0-944697-05-4). Beeby Champ.
PROBLEM CHILDREN–FICTION
Fassler, Joan. The Boy with a Problem: Johnny Learns to Share His Troubles. LC 78-147125. (Illus.). 32p. (ps-3). 1971. 16.95 (ISBN 0-87705-054-6). Human Sci Pr.
—Don't Worry Dear. Kranz, Stewart, illus. LC 74-147124. 32p. (ps-3). 1971. 16.95 (ISBN 0-87705-055-4). Human Sci Pr.
McCoy, Diana L. A Special Place: A Child's Story about Entering Counseling for Children Ages 4 Through 6. Brown, Wynne, illus. 24p. (Orig.). (ps-1). 1988. pap. 5.50 (ISBN 0-9619250-2-7). Magic Lantrn.
—A Special Place: A Child's Story about Entering Counseling for Children Ages 7 Through 10. Brown, Wynne, illus. 32p. (gr. 2-5). 1988. pap. text ed. 5.50 (ISBN 0-9619250-3-5). Magic Lantrn.
Weber, Lenora M. Come Back, Wherever You Are. LC 69-13643. (gr. 7 up). 1969. 14.95 (ISBN 0-690-20123-0, Crowell Jr Bks). HarpC Child Bks.
PROBLEM SOLVING–DATA PROCESSING
Youngs, Bettie B. Problem Solving Skills for Children. 69p. (gr. k-6). 1989. pap. text ed. 9.95 (ISBN 0-940221-01-2); tchr's. ed. 10.00 (ISBN 0-685-25381-3); wkbk. 10.00 (ISBN 0-685-25382-1); lab manual 10.00 (ISBN 0-685-25383-X). Lrng Tools-Bilicki Pubns.
PRODUCTION
see Economics; Industry
PRODUCTS, COMMERCIAL
see Commercial Products
PRODUCTS, WASTE
see Waste Products
PROFESSION, CHOICE OF
see Vocational Guidance
PROFESSIONS
see also Occupations; Vocational Guidance; also names of professions (e.g. Law; Medicine); also Law–Vocational Guidance; music–Vocational guidance
Southworth, Scott. Exploring High-Tech Careers. rev. ed. Rosen, Roger, ed. 118p. (gr. 7-12). 1988. 12.95 (ISBN 0-8239-0796-1). Rosen Group.
Stern, Benjamin J. Opportunities in Machines Shop Trades. (gr. 8 up). 1986. 12.95 (ISBN 0-8442-6147-5, VGM Career Horzns); pap. 9.95 (ISBN 0-8442-6148-3, VGM Career Horzns). Natl Textbk.
PROFESSORS
see Teachers
PROGRAMMING (ELECTRONIC COMPUTERS)
Ault, Rosalie S. Basic. (gr. 7 up). 1983. 13.95 (ISBN 0-395-34927-3). HM.
Bailey, Harold J., et al. Apple LOGO: Activities for Exploring Turtle Graphics. (Illus.). 256p. (gr. 5 up). 1984. pap. 14.95 (ISBN 0-89303-312-X). Brady Bks.
Carlson, Edward H. Compute's Kids & the Commodore 128. (gr. k up). 1986. pap. 14.95 (ISBN 0-87455-032-7). Compute Pubns.
Dewhirst, John. A Child's Guide to the Apple Micro. LC 85-47805. (Illus.). 96p. (gr. 2 up). 1985. pap. 8.50 (ISBN 0-521-31300-7). Cambridge U Pr.
Downes, Paul, ed. C-LECT Jr. (Orig.). (gr. 7-10). 1986. write for info. instr's. guide, 6p. (ISBN 0-912578-92-0); wkbk., 12p. 1.25 (ISBN 0-912578-91-2). Chron Guide.
Feeman, Jeff & Feeman, Maryellen. Discovery Learning with LOGO III. Rittenour, Gary & Fowler, Christopher, illus. 32p. (gr. 3 up). 1984. pap. 1.98 (ISBN 0-88724-111-5, CD-9054). Carson-Dellos.
—Problem Solving with BASIC. Fowler, Christopher & Rittenour, Gary, illus. 32p. (gr. 5 up). 1984. pap. 1.98 (ISBN 0-88724-105-0, CD-9048). Carson-Dellos.
Feeman, Maryellen & Feeman, Jeff. BASIC Programming I. Fowler, Christopher & Rittenour, Gary, illus. 32p. (gr. 2 up). 1984. pap. 1.98 (ISBN 0-88724-106-9, CD-9049). Carson Dellos.
—BASIC Programming II. Fowler, Christopher & Rittenour, Gary, illus. 32p. (gr. 2 up). 1984. pap. 1.98 (ISBN 0-88724-107-7, CD-9050). Carson-Dellos.
—BASIC Programming III. Rittenour, Gary, illus. 32p. (gr. 3 up). 1984. pap. 1.98 (ISBN 0-88724-108-5, CD-9051). Carson-Dellos.
—Discovery Learning with LOGO I. Rittenour, Gary & Fowler, Christopher, illus. 32p. (gr. 2 up). 1984. pap. 1.98 (ISBN 0-88724-109-3, CD-9052). Carson-Dellos.
—Discovery Learning with LOGO II. Rittenour, Gary & Fowler, Jeff, illus. 32p. (gr. 3 up). 1984. pap. 1.98 (ISBN 0-88724-110-7, CD-9053). Carson-Dellos.
Galanter, Eugene. Advanced Programming Handbook. LC 83-26697. (Illus.). 192p. (gr. 7 up). 1984. 14.95 (ISBN 0-399-50975-5, G&D); pap. 8.95 (ISBN 0-399-50976-3). Putnam Pub Group.
Hoglund, Barry A. LOGO Aide. (Illus.). 142p. (gr. k-12). 1984. 34.99 (ISBN 0-9613902-0-4, 15135). August Pubns.
Jones, Roblyn K. Programming Professor. Armstrong, Bev, illus. 56p. (gr. 4-8). 1983. pap. 6.95 (ISBN 0-88160-102-0, LW 242). Learning Wks.
—Programming Puzzlers. 48p. (gr. 4-8). 1984. 5.95 (ISBN 0-88160-111-X, LW 249). Learning Wks.
Lampton, Christopher. How to Create Adventure Games. LC 85-26511. 72p. (gr. 4-9). PLB 10.40 (ISBN 0-531-10119-3). Watts.
Leonard. Learning BASIC, Bk. 1. 48p. (gr. 4-8). 1988. pap. text ed. 2.30 (ISBN 0-913684-10-4). Key Curr Pr.
—Learning BASIC, Bk. 2. 48p. (gr. 4-8). 1988. pap. text ed. 2.30 (ISBN 0-913684-11-2). Key Curr Pr.
—Learning BASIC, Bk. 3. 48p. (gr. 4-8). 1988. pap. text ed. 2.30 (ISBN 0-913684-12-0). Key Curr Pr.
—Learning BASIC: Answers & Notes. 32p. (gr. 4-8). 1988. pap. text ed. 2.95 (ISBN 0-913684-14-7). Key Curr Pr.
Luehrmann, Arthur & Peckham, Herbert. Hands-on Appleworks Reproduction Masters. (Illus.). 128p. (Orig.). (gr. 7-12). 1987. pap. 29.95 (ISBN 0-941681-09-2). Computer Lit Pr.
Muller, Jim. One-Two-Three My Computer & Me: A LOGO Funbook for Kids. (gr. 3 up). 1984. (Reston); Commodore 64. pap. 15.95 (ISBN 0-8359-5244-4). P-H.
Nance, Douglas W. Pascal: Introduction to Programming & Problem Solving. (Illus.). 630p. (gr. 9-12). 1986. text ed. 34.25 (ISBN 0-314-93206-2). West Pub.
Simon, Seymour. Turtle Talk: A Beginner's Book of Logo. Emberley, Barbara & Emberley, Ed E., illus. LC 85-47890. 32p. (gr. 1-4). 1986. 13.95i (ISBN 0-690-04521-2, Crowell Jr Bks); PLB 13.89 (ISBN 0-690-04522-0, Crowell Jr Bks). HarpC Child Bks.
Stevens, Lawrence. Computer Programming Basics: An Introduction for Young People. Seiden, Art, illus. 48p. 1984. 9.95 (ISBN 0-13-164260-X). P-H.
Taft, David. Computer Programming. Art, Hayward, illus. 40p. (gr. 4-8). 1986. lib. bdg. 11.90 (ISBN 0-531-19007-2, Warwick). Watts.
Wagner, Roger. Assembly Lines the Book. rev., 2nd ed. (Illus.). 273p. (Orig.). pap. 19.95 (ISBN 0-927796-99-6); Apple format disk 15.95 (ISBN 0-927796-24-4). R Wagner Pub.
Watson, Nancy R. Taking off with BASIC on the Commodore 64. (Illus.). 208p. (gr. 5 up). 1984. pap. 12.95 (ISBN 0-89303-868-7). Brady Bks.
PROGRAMMING (ELECTRONIC COMPUTERS) –VOCATIONAL GUIDANCE
Kaplan, Andrew. Careers for Computer Buffs. (Illus.). 64p. (gr. 7 up). 1991. PLB 12.90 (ISBN 1-56294-021-X). Millbrook Pr.
PROGRESS
see also Civilization; Social Change
PROHIBITION–FICTION
Peck, Robert N. Justice Lion. 264p. (gr. 7 up). 1981. 13.95 (ISBN 0-316-69658-7). Little.
PROJECT APOLLO
see Apollo Project
PROPAGANDA
see also Advertising
PROPAGATION OF PLANTS
see Plant Propagation
PROPHETS
Hardy, Linda C. Boys Who Became Prophets. Grover, Nina, illus. LC 82-2373. 72p. (gr. k-12). 1982. 6.95 (ISBN 0-87747-900-3). Deseret Bk.
Hashim, A. S. Stories of Some of the Prophets, Vol. I. pap. 5.95 (ISBN 0-686-18402-5); pap. 49.50 entire series (ISBN 0-686-18403-3). Kazi Pubns.
—Stories of Some of the Prophets, Vol II. pap. 5.95 (ISBN 0-686-18400-9); pap. 49.50 entire series (ISBN 0-686-18401-7). Kazi Pubns.
McMinn, Tom. Prophets: Preachers for God. Fields, Don, illus. (gr. 1-6). 1979. 5.95 (ISBN 0-8054-4250-2, 4242-50). Broadman.
Overholtzer, Ruth. Elisha. Biel, Bill, illus. 33p. (gr. k-6). 1967. pap. text ed. 9.45 (ISBN 1-55976-010-9). CEF Press.
PROSODY
see Versification
PROSPECTING
Rynerson, Fred. Exploring & Mining for Gems & Gold in the West. (Illus.). 204p. (gr. 4 up). 1970. 14.95 (ISBN 0-911010-61-0); pap. 7.95 (ISBN 0-911010-60-2). Naturegraph.
PROSPECTING–FICTION
Coombs, Charles. Young Atom Detective. (Illus.). (gr. 4-7). PLB 6.70 (ISBN 0-8313-0021-3). Lantern.
PROTECTION OF ANIMALS
see Animals–Treatment
PROTECTION OF CHILDREN
see Child Welfare
PROTECTION OF ENVIRONMENT
see Environmental Protection
PROTECTION OF WILDLIFE
see Wildlife–Conservation
PROTEST
see Dissent
PROTESTANT REFORMATION
see Reformation
PROTESTANTISM
see also Reformation
Pelley, Ronn T. In Word & Deed: A Student's Beginning Guide to Understanding the Luthern Worship Service. (Illus.). 32p. (gr. 4-6). 1986. pap. 2.95 (ISBN 0-933350-49-X). Morse Pr.
PROVERBS
see also Epigrams
Burgest, David R. Proverbs for the Young...& the Not So Young. Burgest, David R., II, illus. 75p. (Orig.). (gr. 7-12). 1989. pap. write for info. Self-Taught Pubs.
Davidson, Alice J. Alice in Bibleland Storybooks: Psalms & Proverbs. Marshall, Victoria, illus. 32p. (gr. 3 up). 1984. 4.95 (ISBN 0-8378-5069-X). Gibson.
Fraser, Betty. First Things First: An Illustrated Collection of Sayings Useful & Familiar for Children. Fraser, Betty, illus. LC 86-42993. 32p. (gr. k-3). 1990. 12.95 (ISBN 0-06-021854-1); PLB 12.89 (ISBN 0-06-021855-X). HarpC Child Bks.
Fulton, Ginger A. When I'm a Mommy: A Little Girl's Paraphrase of Proverbs 31. (Illus.). (gr. 1-4). 1984. pap. 3.25 (ISBN 0-8024-0367-0). Moody.

Taylor, Phoebe, ed. Thoughts for the Free Life: Lao Tsu to the Present. 2nd ed. Buckley, Cicely, illus. 110p. (Orig.). (gr. 8 up). 1989. pap. 10.00 (ISBN 0-9617481-5-X). Oyster River Pr. With foreward & indices of 77 authors & 27 languages of origin. Illustrated with beautiful suggestive drawings by Cicely. Ideas from the cultures of 5 continents, 25 centuries, on the art of living. Free thought, the Natural Way, Life in Time...In exquisite book-making, with English translations often along side the originals. It is a joy to come upon its varied treasure. Among the jewels: Sophocles, Tagore, Cervantes, Isaiah, Job, the Palestinian poets, Neruda, Schweitzer, May Sarton, American Indian Wisdom. This is a book of inspiration & a peacemaking book. The preface tells how it was begun by a philospher & psychologist, while working on his dissertation at Harvard in the 1920's on Belief & Behavior. "Truly a peacemaking book."--M. Grierson, Smith College Archivist Emeritus. "The native vision, the gift of seeing truly, with wonder & delightful insight into the natural world, is informed by a certain attitude of reverence & respect....In addition to the eye, it involves intelligence, the instinct & the imagination. It is the perception not only of objects & forms but also of essence & ideals."--J. Scott Momaday; 1934 Kiowa Indian.
Publisher Provided Annotation.

PSALMODY
see Church Music; Hymns
PSYCHIATRISTS–FICTION
Galvin, Matthew R. Ignatius Finds Help: A Story About Psychotherapy for Children. Ferraro, Sandra, illus. LC 87-34899. 48p. (ps-6). 1988. 14.95 (ISBN 0-945354-01-0); pap. 5.95 (ISBN 0-945354-00-2). Magination Pr.
Lowry, Lois. Anastasia Ask Your Analyst. large type ed. 176p. 1989. Repr. of 1984 ed. PLB 15.95 (ISBN 1-55736-133-9, Crnrstn Bks). ABC-CLIO.
Zindel, Bonnie. Dr. Adriana Earthlight, Student Shrink. 144p. (gr. 7 up). 1988. pap. 11.95 (ISBN 0-670-81647-7). Viking Child Bks.
PSYCHIATRY
see also Psychotherapy
Sanders, Corine & Turner, Cynthia. Coping. Villalpando, Eleanor, illus. 64p. (gr. 2-8). 1983. wkbk. 7.95 (ISBN 0-9607366-2-X, GA 494). Good Apple.
PSYCHICAL RESEARCH
see also Apparitions; Dreams; Extrasensory Perception; Ghosts; Hypnotism; Mind and Body; Thought Transference
Psychics & ESP. 48p. (gr. 4-5). 1989. PLB 10.95 (ISBN 0-685-26399-1). Capstone Pr.
Seeing the Future. 48p. (gr. 4-5). 1989. PLB 10.95 (ISBN 0-685-26400-9). Capstone Pr.
Tuhy, Arleen A. From the Universe to You. (Illus.). 23p. (Orig.). (gr. k-6). 1990. pap. 4.25 (ISBN 0-9625059-5-1). Fountain Light Pr.
Whitney, Joy. Starlink: The Book of Knowledge of Anton--Communique from the Pleiades. 166p. (Orig.). 1989. pap. 12.95 (ISBN 0-317-93870-3). Starset Pub.

PSYCHICAL RESEARCH-FICTION

Conford, Ellen. And This Is Laura. (gr. 5-7). 1988. pap. 2.75 (ISBN 0-671-67879-5, Archway). PB.

Kassem, Lou. A Summer for Secrets. 112p. 1989. pap. 2.95 (ISBN 0-380-75759-1, Camelot). Avon.

PSYCHOANALYSIS

see also Dreams; Hypnotism; Mind and Body; Psychology; Psychology, Pathological

Stwertka, Eve. Psychoanalysis: From Freud to the Age of Therapy. Kline, M., ed. (Illus.). 96p. (gr. 7-9). 1988. PLB 10.40 (ISBN 0-531-10481-8). Watts.

PSYCHOLOGY

see also Attitude (Psychology); Emotions; Imagination; Individuality; Intellect; Perception; Personality; Psychical Research; Psychoanalysis; Reasoning; Senses and Sensation; Social Psychology; Thought and Thinking

Anderson, Jill. Thinking, Changing, Rearranging: Improving Self Esteem in Young People. LC 88-2289. (Illus.). 80p. (gr. 2). 1990. Repr. of 1981 ed. wkbk. 7.50 (ISBN 0-943920-30-2). Metamorphous Pr.

Barden, Renardo. Fears & Phobias. LC 89-1340. (Illus.). 48p. (gr. 4 up). 1989. 10.95 (ISBN 0-89686-441-3, Crestwood Hse). Macmillan Child Grp.

Buckalew, M. W., Jr. Learning to Control Stress. rev. ed. Gahan, Nancy L., illus. (gr. 7-12). 1982. PLB 12.95 (ISBN 0-8239-0496-2). Rosen Group.

Cohen, Daniel & Cohen, Susan. Teenage Stress: Understanding the Tensions You Feel at Home, at School & among Your Friends. LC 83-16477. 160p. (gr. 5 up). 1983. 13.95 (ISBN 0-87131-423-1). M Evans.

Diebert, Linda. Motivational Magic. (Illus.). 128p. (ps-2). 1990. 9.95 (ISBN 0-86653-535-7, GA1137). Good Apple.

Dinkmeyer, Don, Sr. & Dinkmeyer, Don, Jr. Developing Understanding of Self & Others (DUSO) Storybook, No. 1. (gr. k-4). 1982. pap. text ed. 34.50 (ISBN 0-88671-278-5, 5505). Am Guidance.

First Experiences. 96p. (ps up) 1987. 8.95 (ISBN 0-7460-0049-9). EDC.

Freed, Alvyn M. Transactional Analysis: Transactional Analysis for Everybody Ser. (Illus.). (gr. 1-3). Date not set. write for info (ISBN 0-915190-84-2). Jalmar Pr.
Stress, realization of self worth & anxiety are universal problems, bound by neither age nor ethnic background. Tots, teenagers & children of all ages experience these problems. Now there is a way to help them realize their self esteem through Transactional Analysis. The TA books have established "I'M OK YOU'RE OK" as a household concept. TA FOR TOTS (& Other Prinzes) newly revised, deals with a full range of feelings that help tots, from four years old, realize their intrinsic worth as human beings & build & strengthen their self-esteem. TA FOR KIDS has already proven to be an ideal book to help youngsters, from nine to thirteen years old, develop self-esteem, esteem of others, social & personal responsibility, critical thinking & independent judgement. TA FOR TEENS is aimed at telling teens, from thirteen to eighteen years old, & their (people in charge) that they are OK. Teens is designed to bring teenagers into closer & more satisfying relationships. Dr. Freed offers new choices & options to teenagers dealing with the dilemmas of growing up, in a positive way. Transactional Analysis is a simple-to-use way to understand & respect one's own feelings & those of others. THE ORIGINAL WARM FUZZY TALE originated the concept of Warm Fuzzies & Cold Pricklies, (a fairy tale in every sense, with a moral). A beautifully illustrated book for kids from five to one hundred & five. Great for parents & care-givers.
Publisher Provided Annotation.

Freed, Alvyn M. & Freed, Margaret. TA for Kids (& Grownups Too) 3rd rev ed. Hackney, Rick, illus. LC 77-81761. (gr. 4-7). 1977. pap. 9.95 (ISBN 0-915190-09-5, JP9009-5). Jalmar Pr.

Gibbons, Julie. My Secret Place. Gibbons, Julie, illus. 20p. (Orig.). (gr. 1-4). 1975. pap. 4.95 (ISBN 0-911336-61-3). Sci of Mind.

—There Is Only One Me. 20p. (gr. 1-4). 1974. pap. 4.95 (ISBN 0-911336-56-7). Sci of Mind.

Goley, Elaine. Believing in Yourself, Reading Level 2. (Illus.). 32p. (gr. 1-4). Date not set. PLB 13.26 (ISBN 0-86592-398-1). Rourke Corp.

Gordon, James. Stress Management. (Illus.). (gr. 6-12). 1990. 18.95 (ISBN 0-7910-0042-7). Chelsea Hse.

Grewe, Georgeanne & Glover, Susanne. Motivational Units for Spring. (Illus.). 144p. (gr. 2-6). 1990. 10.95 (ISBN 0-86653-524-1, GA1145). Good Apple.

Ignoffo, Matthew. Coping with Your Inner Critic. Rosen, Ruth, ed. (gr. 7-12). 1989. PLB 12.95 (ISBN 0-8239-1001-6). Rosen Group.

Jones, Bill. What's on Your Mind? Thinking the Right Stuff. LC 89-83737. 64p. (Orig.). (gr. 7-12). 1989. pap. 4.50 (ISBN 0-89840-256-5). Heres Life.

Kerr, M. E. Me Me Me Me Me: Not a Novel. LC 82-48521. 224p. (gr. 7 up). 1983. 12.95 (ISBN 0-06-023192-0); PLB 12.89 (ISBN 0-06-023193-9). HarpC Child Bks.

Kincher, Jonni. Psychology for Kids: Forty Fun Tests That Help You Learn about Yourself. Bach, Julie, ed. Maclean & Tuminell, illus. Elliott, Thomas, frwd. by. 160p. (Orig.). (gr. 4 up). 1990. pap. 11.95 (ISBN 0-915793-23-7). Free Spirit Pub.

Knox, Jean. Learning Disabilities. (Illus.). (gr. 6-12). 1989. 18.95 (ISBN 0-7910-0049-4); pap. 9.95 (ISBN 0-7910-0529-1). Chelsea Hse.

Lawless, Joann A. Mysteries of the Mind. LC 77-10726. (Illus.). 48p. (gr. 4 up). 1983. PLB 17.32 (ISBN 0-8172-1066-0); pap. 9.27 (ISBN 0-8172-2161-1). Raintree Pubs.

Mahoney, Bateman & Mahoney, Bill. Macho: Is This What I Really Want? 1986. pap. 6.00 (ISBN 0-87738-024-4). Youth Ed.

Sylvester, Sandra. Living with Stress - Middle School. 64p. (gr. 5-9). 1991. 6.95 (ISBN 0-86653-594-2). Good Apple.

—Living with Stress - Primary. 64p. (gr. 1-4). 1991. 6.95 (ISBN 0-86653-593-4). Good Apple.

Wayman, Joe. Let's Talk about It! Wayman, Joe, illus. 96p. (gr. 1-8). 1986. wkbk. 8.95 (ISBN 0-86653-372-9, GA 799). Good Apple.

Wilson, Marie M. Nellie's Girl Two. (Illus.). 156p. (ps up). 1988. PLB 11.00 (ISBN 0-9615259-1-6). Wilson Oregon.

PSYCHOLOGY, ABNORMAL

see Psychology, Pathological

PSYCHOLOGY, APPLIED

see also Counseling; Human Relations

Elchoness, Monte. Why Can't Anyone Hear Me? A Guide for Surviving Adolescence. 2nd, rev. ed. Elchoness, Monte, illus. LC 86-737. 200p. (gr. 6-12). 1989. pap. 10.95 (ISBN 0-936781-06-8, Dist. by Publishers Group West). Monroe Pr.

Kalb, Jonah & Viscott, David. What Every Kid Should Know. LC 75-45123. (Illus.). 128p. (gr. 5-9). 1976. 13.95 (ISBN 0-395-24386-6). HM.

LeShan, Eda. What Makes Me Feel This Way? Growing up with Human Emotions. Weil, Lisl, illus. LC 71-165573. 128p. (gr. 3-6). 1974. 13.95 (ISBN 0-02-757320-6, Mcmillan Child Bk); pap. 3.95 (ISBN 0-02-044340-4, Aladdin). Macmillan Child Grp.

Silbert, Linda P. & Silbert, Alvin. My Own Book of Feelings. (Illus.). (gr. k-8). 1977. 4.98 (ISBN 0-89544-017-2, 017). Silbert Bress.

PSYCHOLOGY, CHILD

see Child Study

PSYCHOLOGY-DICTIONARIES

Berger, Gilda. Psychology Words. LC 85-8889. (Illus.). 96p. (gr. 7 up). 1986. lib. bdg. 9.59 (ISBN 0-671-54291-5). Messner.

PSYCHOLOGY, INDUSTRIAL

see Psychology, Applied

PSYCHOLOGY, MEDICAL

see Psychology, Pathological

PSYCHOLOGY, PATHOLOGICAL

see also Mental Illness; Psychiatry; Psychoanalysis

Friedland, Bruce. Personality Disorders. (Illus.). (gr. 6-12). 1991. 18.95 (ISBN 0-7910-0051-6). Chelsea Hse.

PSYCHOLOGY, PRACTICAL

see Psychology, Applied

Herzfeld, Gerald & Powell, Robin. Coping for Kids: A Complete Stress-Control Program for Students Ages 8-18. 202p. (gr. 3-12). 1985. pap. 47.95x (ISBN 0-87628-234-6); wkbk. 5.95x (ISBN 0-317-43482-9). Ctr Appl Res.

PSYCHOLOGY, SOCIAL

see Social Psychology

PSYCHOPATHOLOGY

see Psychology, Pathological

PSYCHOPATHY

see Psychology, Pathological

PSYCHOSES

see Mental Illness

PSYCHOTHERAPY

Freed, Alvyn M. TA for Tots Coloring Book. (ps-3). 1976. pap. 1.95 (ISBN 0-915190-33-8, JP9033-8). Jalmar Pr.

Nemiroff, Marc A. & Annunziata, Jane. A Child's First Book about Play Therapy. Scott, Margaret, illus. LC 90-49954. 60p. (Orig.). (ps-2). 1990. 19.95

(ISBN 1-55798-112-4, 460-0180); pap. text ed. write for info. (ISBN 1-55798-089-6, 460-0170). Am Psychol. What is play therapy? Who goes to play therapy, & why? What happens in a session? This book answers these questions for children when psychotherapy is being considered -- in words & images that 4-7 year olds can understand. The following issues are addressed in simple language with many colorful illustrations: Things a child does that indicate a possible problem; How a child enters treatment; The therapist's office & equipment; The activity of play therapy; Confidentiality; How a child improves over time; & How treatment will end. The book is written in a way that a child can understand but says things that adults need to know, too. Beginning therapy for a child & parent is a time of curiosity, questions, & worry. Help make this task easier by purchasing A CHILD'S FIRST BOOK ABOUT PLAY THERAPY now!
Publisher Provided Annotation.

PTOMAINE POISONING

see Food Poisoning

PUBLIC FINANCE

see Finance

PUBLIC HEALTH

see also Cemeteries; Communicable Diseases; Hospitals; Noise; Refuse and Refuse Disposal; Sanitation; Sewage Disposal; Water–Pollution; Water Supply

Hampton, J. World Health. (Illus.). 48p. (gr. 5 up). Date not set. PLB 18.00 (ISBN 0-86592-281-0). Rourke Corp.

Public Health. (Illus.). 56p. (gr. 6-12). 1985. pap. 1.85 (ISBN 0-8395-3251-2, 3251). BSA.

Sully, Nina. Health. (Illus.). 72p. (gr. 7-12). 1983. 19.95 (ISBN 0-7134-4447-9, Pub. by Batsford England). Trafalgar Sq.

PUBLIC OPINION

see also Attitude (Psychology)

also names of countries with the subdivision Foreign Opinion, u. s.–Foreign Opinion

Roets, Lois F. Survey & Public Opinion Research. 2nd ed. 120p. (gr. 3 up). 1988. 14.00 (ISBN 0-911943-14-5). Leadership Pub.

PUBLIC PLAYGROUNDS

see Playgrounds

PUBLIC SPEAKING

see also Acting; Debates and Debating

Berry, Marilyn. Help Is on the Way for Group Reports. Bartholomew, illus. 48p. (gr. 4-6). 1987. PLB 14.60 (ISBN 0-516-03281-X). Childrens.

Carratello, Patricia. I Can Give a Speech. Chacon, Rick, illus. 32p. (gr. 3-6). 1981. 4.95 (ISBN 1-55734-327-6). Tchr Create Mat.

Colligan, Louise. The A-Plus Guide to Giving a Speech. 1989. pap. 2.50 (ISBN 0-590-42147-6). Scholastic Inc.

Detz, Joan. You Mean I Have to Stand Up & Say Something? Marshall, David, illus. LC 86-3611. 86p. (gr. 5-9). 1986. 12.95 (ISBN 0-689-31221-0, Atheneum Child Bk). Macmillan Child Grp.

Dunbar, Robert E. Making Your Point. 1990. PLB 12.90 (ISBN 0-531-10905-4). Watts.

Public Speaking. (Illus.). 44p. (gr. 6-12). 1969. pap. 1.85 (ISBN 0-8395-3373-X, 3373). BSA.

Ryan, Margaret. So You Have to Give a Speech. LC 86-23354. (Illus.). 127p. (gr. 7-12). 1987. lib. bdg. 12.90 (ISBN 0-531-10337-4). Watts.

PUBLIC UTILITIES

see also Railroads; Telephone; Water Supply

PUBLISHERS AND PUBLISHING

see also Book Industries and Trade; Books; Printing

Bold, Mary. Publish Your Own Book: A Resource Book for Young Authors. Small, Carol B., illus. LC 86-91615. 36p. (Orig.). (gr. 5 up). 1986. pap. 6.95 (ISBN 0-938267-02-7). Bold Prodns.

Publish-A-Book Complete Clipper Set, 15 titles. (gr. 1-6). Date not set. Set. 299.11 (ISBN 0-8172-2522-6). Raintree Pubs.

Publish-A-Book Complete Set, 16 titles. (gr. 1-6). Date not set. Set. pap. text ed. 190.00 (ISBN 0-8172-2517-X). Raintree Pubs.

Publish-A-Book Fall 1990 Winners, 5 titles. (gr. 1-6). Date not set. Set. 62.50 (ISBN 0-8172-2516-1). Raintree Pubs.

Publish-A-Book Fall 1990 Winners, 4 titles. (gr. 1-6). Date not set. Set. 83.96 (ISBN 0-8172-2790-3). Raintree Pubs.

Publish-A-Book Previous Winners, 11 titles. (gr. 1-6). Date not set. Set. 137.50 (ISBN 0-8172-2520-X). Raintree Pubs.

PUBLISHING
see Publishers and Publishing
PUERTO RICANS IN THE U. S.
Larsen, Ronald J. The Puerto Ricans in America. (Illus.). 80p. (gr. 5 up). 1989. PLB 9.95 (ISBN 0-8225-0238-0). Lerner Pubns.
PUERTO RICANS IN THE U. S.–FICTION
Mohr, Nicholasa. Going Home. LC 85-20621. 176p. (gr. 5-8). 1986. 13.95 (ISBN 0-8037-0269-8); PLB 13.89 (ISBN 0-8037-0338-4). Dial Bks Young.
Simon, Norma. What Do I Do: English - Spanish Edition. Lasker, Joe, illus. LC 74-79544. 40p. (ps-2). 1969. PLB 12.95 (ISBN 0-8075-8823-7). A Whitman.
PUERTO RICO
Griffiths, John. Take a Trip to Puerto Rico. LC 89-8930. (Illus.). 32p. (gr. 3-5). 1989. PLB 10.90 (ISBN 0-531-10737-X). Watts.
Lerner Publications, Department of Geography Staff. Puerto Rico in Pictures. (Illus.). 64p. (gr. 5 up). 1987. PLB 12.95 (ISBN 0-8225-1821-X). Lerner Pubns.
Turner Program Services, Inc. Staff & Clark, James I. Puerto Rico. 48p. (gr. 3 up). 1985. PLB 17.32 (ISBN 0-86514-443-5); pap. text ed. 9.27 (ISBN 0-86514-518-0); cancelled tchr's. guide (ISBN 0-86514-293-9); cancelled student activity bk. (ISBN 0-86514-368-4); cancelled 3/4" video (ISBN 0-86514-218-1); cancelled Beta video (ISBN 0-86514-068-5); cancelled VHS video (ISBN 0-86514-143-6); cancelled index. Raintree Pubs.
PUERTO RICO–BIOGRAPHY
Luis Monz Marin. (gr. 2-6). 1989. 15.33 (ISBN 0-318-41744-8); pap. 9.27 (ISBN 0-318-41745-6). Raintree Pubs.
Luis Munoz Marin. (Illus.). 32p. (gr. 3-6). 1988. PLB 16.67 (ISBN 0-8172-2907-8). Raintree Pubs.
PUERTO RICO–FICTION
Barsy, Kalman. Del Nacimiento de la Isla de Boriken. Quintero, Nora, illus. LC 82-83288. (SPA.). 76p. (gr. 6). 1982. pap. 7.50 (ISBN 0-940238-01-2). Ediciones Huracan.
Misla, Victor M. Little Anabo from Boriken. Misla, Victor M., illus. 28p. (Orig.). (gr. 6-7). 1987. pap. 5.00 (ISBN 0-9626870-0-6). NW Monarch Pr.
PUERTO RICO–HISTORY
Luis Munoz Marin. (Illus.). 32p. (gr. 3-6). 1988. PLB 16.67 (ISBN 0-8172-2907-8). Raintree Pubs.
Pico, Isabel, et al, eds. Mujeres de Puerto Rico. 2nd ed. Marichal, Carmen & Delano, Jack, illus. (SPA.). 41p. (gr. 1-6). 1984. pap. text ed. 2.50 (ISBN 0-8477-2474-3). U of PR Pr.
PUFFINS
Gibbons, Gail. The Puffins Are Back! Gibbons, Gail, illus. LC 90-30525. 32p. (gr. 3-5). 1991. 13.95 (ISBN 0-06-021603-4); PLB 13.89 (ISBN 0-06-021604-2). HarpC Child Bks.
Gove, Doris. Miracle at Egg Rock: A Puffin's Story. Bishop, Bonnie, illus. LC 85-7050. 48p. (Orig.). (gr. 1-4). 1985. pap. 6.95 (ISBN 0-89272-205-3). Down East.
Martin, Lynne. Puffin, Bird of the Open Seas. Lewin, Ted, illus. LC 76-3486. (gr. 3-7). 1976. PLB 12.88 (ISBN 0-688-32074-0). Morrow.
PUGILISM
see Boxing
PUMAS
Robinson, Sandra C. Mountain Lion: Puma, Panther, Painter Cougar. (Illus.). 64p. (gr. 4-6). 1991. pap. 6.95 (ISBN 1-879373-00-9). R Rinehart Inc.
Stone, L. Cougars. (Illus.). 24p. (gr. k-5). 1989. lib. bdg. 11.94 (ISBN 0-86592-505-4). Rourke Corp.
—Jaguars. (Illus.). 24p. (gr. k-5). 1989. lib. bdg. 11.93 (ISBN 0-86592-506-2). Rourke Corp.
PUMPKIN–FICTION
Chevalier, Christa. Little Green Pumpkins. Tucker, Cathy, ed. LC 81-12999. (Illus.). 32p. (ps-1). 1982. PLB 11.50 (ISBN 0-8075-4593-7). A Whitman.
Cole, Bruce. The Pumpkinville Mystery. Warhola, James, illus. (gr. 1-4). 1987. 10.95 (ISBN 0-13-741620-2). P-H.
Friskey, Margaret. The Perky Little Pumpkin. Dunnington, Tom, illus. LC 90-38376. 32p. (ps-3). 1990. PLB 14.60 (ISBN 0-516-03564-9); pap. 4.95 (ISBN 0-516-43564-7). Childrens.
Johnston, Tony. The Vanishing Pumpkin. DePaola, Tomie, illus. 32p. (ps-2). 1990. 13.99g (ISBN 0-399-61303-X, Putnam); pap. 4.95 (ISBN 0-399-20992-1, Putnam). Putnam Pub Group.
Kaslow, Florence R. The Puzzled Pumpkin. Phillips, Jennifer, illus. LC 91-60798. 24p. (Orig.). (gr. k-4). 1991. pap. 4.95 (ISBN 0-9628321-0-3). Pumpkin Patch Pubs.
Kellogg, Steven. The Mystery of the Flying Orange Pumpkin. Kellogg, Steven, illus. LC 80-11748. 32p. (ps-2). 1980. 8.95 (ISBN 0-8037-6115-5); PLB 8.89 (ISBN 0-8037-6116-3). Dial Bks Young.
King, Elizabeth. Pumpkin Patch. (ps-3). 1990. 13.95 (ISBN 0-525-44640-0, DCB). Dutton Child Bks.
Kroll, Steven. The Biggest Pumpkin Ever. Bassett, Jeni, illus. 32p. (gr. k-3). 1985. pap. 2.50 (ISBN 0-590-41113-6). Scholastic Inc.
Titherington, Jeanne. Pumpkin, Pumpkin. Titherington, Jeanne, illus. LC 84-25334. 24p. (ps-1). 1986. 13.95 (ISBN 0-688-05695-4); PLB 13.88 (ISBN 0-688-05696-2). Greenwillow.
PUNCH AND JUDY
see Puppets and Puppet Plays
PUNCHED CARD SYSTEMS
see Information Storage and Retrieval Systems
PUNCTUATION
Alward, Edgar C. & Dale, E. Up Your Punctuation! An Almost Non-Grammatical Approach to Punctuation. 112p. (Orig.). (gr. 9-12). 1988. pap. 12.95 (ISBN 0-9620092-0-2). Pine Isl Pr.
Armstrong, Beverly. Punctuation Passport. 38p. (gr. 4-7). 1979. 6.95 (ISBN 0-88160-029-6, LW 214). Learning Wks.
Berry, Marilyn. Help Is on the Way for Punctuation. (Illus.). 48p. (gr. 4-6). 1987. pap. 4.95 (ISBN 0-516-43287-7). Childrens.
Carratello, Patricia. I Can Capitalize. Chacon, Rick, illus. 32p. (gr. 3-6). 1983. wkbk. 4.95 (ISBN 1-55734-331-4). Tchr Create Mat.
—I Can Punctuate. Chacon, Rick, illus. 32p. (gr. 3-6). 1983. wkbk. 4.95 (ISBN 1-55734-332-2). Tchr Create Mat.
Carratello, Patty. It's Easy to Capitalize. Wright, Theresa, illus. 32p. (gr. 1-4). 1988. 4.95 (ISBN 1-55734-322-5). Tchr Create Mat.
—It's Easy to Punctuate. Spence, Paula & Wright, Theresa, illus. 32p. (gr. 1-4). 1988. wkbk. 4.95 (ISBN 1-55734-321-7). Tchr Create Mat.
Cushman, Jack L. Punctuation & Capitalization Flipper. (Illus.). 49p. (gr. 5 up). 1989. Repr. of 1974 ed. trade edition 5.95 (ISBN 1-878383-00-0). C Lee Pubns.
Gregorich, Barbara. Apostrophe, Colon, Hyphen. Pape, Richard, illus. 24p. (gr. 3-4). 1980. wkbk. 2.95 (ISBN 0-89403-593-2). EDC.
—Comma. Pape, Richard, illus. 24p. (gr. 3-4). 1980. wkbk. 2.95 (ISBN 0-89403-595-9). EDC.
—Period, Question Mark, Exclamation Mark. Pape, Richard, illus. 24p. (gr. 3-4). 1980. wkbk. 2.95 (ISBN 0-89403-592-4). EDC.
Sebranek, Patrick & Meyer, Verne. Punctuation Pockets: A Student Folder. (Illus.). (gr. 7-12). 1984. pap. text ed. 0.95x (ISBN 0-9605312-8-9). Write Source.
Spellman, Linda. More Creative Investigations. 48p. (gr. 4-8). 1984. 5.95 (ISBN 0-88160-114-4, LW 246). Learning Wks.
Sweeney, Kathy, et al. Punctuation. 64p. (gr. 2-4). 1985. 6.95 (ISBN 0-912107-37-5). Monday Morning Bks.
Tilkin, Sheldon. Quotation Marks & Underlining. Pape, Richard, illus. 24p. (gr. 3-4). 1980. 2.95 (ISBN 0-89403-594-0). EDC.
PUPPETS AND PUPPET PLAYS
Aaseng, Nathan. Jim Henson: Muppet Master. (Illus.). 40p. (gr. 4-9). 1988. 9.95 (ISBN 0-8225-1615-2). Lerner Pubns.
Abelson, Danny. The Muppets Take Manhattan: The Storybook Based on the Movie. LC 83-19153. (Illus.). 64p. (ps-4). 1984. 6.95 (ISBN 0-394-86386-0, Random Juv); lib. bdg. 7.99 (ISBN 0-394-96386-5, BYR). Random.
Bailey, Vanessa. Puppets: Games & Projects. (Illus.). 32p. (gr. 2-4). 1991. PLB 11.40 (ISBN 0-531-17269-4, Gloucester Pr). Watts.
Baird, Bil. Art of the Puppet. (Illus.). (gr. 9 up). 1966. 35.00 (ISBN 0-8238-0067-9). Plays.
Bivens, Ruth. Aunt Ruth's Puppet Scripts, Bk. I. (Orig.). (gr. 1-8). 1986. Incl. cassette narration. pap. 19.95 (ISBN 0-89265-096-6). Randall Hse.
—Aunt Ruth's Puppet Scripts, Bk. III. 55p. (gr. 1-6). 1987. 19.95 (ISBN 0-89265-119-9); cassette incl. Randall Hse.

Brooks, Courtaney. Plays & Puppets &cetera. 7th ed. Runyan, Merrilee, illus. LC 81-68933. 100p. (Orig.). (gr. k up). 1981. pap. text ed. 14.95 (ISBN 0-941274-00-4). Belnice Bks.
"Drama celebrates our differences & uses them. Plays draw out our individuality (which) is never wrong; it is ours--unique. We can all learn, for we're not like little cups waiting to be filled, but like lamps ready to be turned on." These excerpts sum up the philosophy that makes PLAYS & PUPPETS &CETERA much more powerful than the average how-to text. Brooks mixes a complete outlining of puppet & drama basics with a wonderfully positive attitude of respect & joy for life & its possibilities. Her explanations offer sufficient know-how to allow any teacher to carry a group through a show from start to curtain. As a first time student teacher, I used the book to coordinate a play-project with six fourth-graders. One parent wrote a thank-you note telling us it was the first time she had heard her daughter speak above a whisper in public. I used the book again to help an adult troupe of Spanish-speaking novice players stage a Christmas story."--

BREAKTHROUGH Winter/Summer 1990. (Illustrated puppet directions; 7 sample plays for puppets or people actors with casts of 4 to 6, simple costuming, such as ears for a dog or cat, & props).
Publisher Provided Annotation.

Buchwald, Claire. The Puppet Book: How to Make & Operate Puppets & Stage a Puppet-Play. Jakubiszyn, Audrey, illus. LC 90-38080. 134p. (Orig.). 1990. pap. 12.95 (ISBN 0-8238-0293-0). Plays.
Collodi, Carlo. Pinocchio. (gr. 4-6). 1985. pap. 2.95 (ISBN 0-14-035037-3, Puffin). Puffin Bks.
Ferguson, Helen S. Bring on the Puppets. LC 75-5217. (Illus.). 40p. (Orig.). (gr. k-6). 1975. pap. 4.95 (ISBN 0-8192-1195-8). Morehouse Pub.
Forte, Imogene. Puppets. LC 84-62934. (Illus.). 80p. (gr. k-6). 1985. pap. text ed. 3.95 (ISBN 0-86530-101-8, IP 91-5). Incentive Pubns.
Galdston, Olive. Play with Puppets. rev. ed. Galdston, Olive, illus. 52p. (Orig.). (ps up). 1971. pap. 1.50x (ISBN 0-686-01100-7); pap. text ed. 1.50x (ISBN 0-936426-07-1). Play Schs.
Hart, Marj & Shelly, Walt. Pom-Pom Puppets, Stories, & Stages. (gr. 5-8). 1989. pap. 12.95 (ISBN 0-8224-5596-X). Fearon Teach Aids.
Joyce, Joy. Me & More Shadows. Treadway, Jerry, ed. Ross, Ray, intro. by. (Illus.). 62p. (gr. 1-6). 1981. pap. text ed. 10.95 (ISBN 0-9605984-1-3). Joy-Co.
—Me & My Shadows. Treadway, Jerry, ed. Ross, Ray, intro. by. (Illus.). 58p. (gr. 1-6). 1981. pap. text ed. 10.95 (ISBN 0-9605984-0-5). Joy-Co.
Keefe, Betty. Fingerpuppets, Fingerplays & Holidays. (Illus.). 136p. (ps-3). 1984. spiral bdg. 17.95 (ISBN 0-938594-05-2). Spec Lit Pr.
Kingshead Corporation Staff. Cut, Color & Create: Make Your Own: Paperplate Puppets. Kingshead Corporation Staff, illus. 24p. (ps-3). 1987. pap. 2.97 (ISBN 1-55941-002-7). Kingshead Corp.
Ludwig, Nancy. Easter Puppets & Plays. Fowler, Christopher, illus. 31p. (ps-4). 1984. pap. 1.98 (ISBN 0-88724-154-9, CD-8056). Carson-Dellos.
—February Puppets & Plays. Carson, Patti & Dellosa, Janet, illus. 31p. (ps-4). 1984. pap. 1.98 (ISBN 0-88724-156-5, CD-8058). Carson-Dellos.
McKay, Sindy. Something's Fishy. Alchemy II, Inc., illus. 26p. (ps up). 1986. 12.95 (ISBN 1-55578-610-3). Worlds Wonder.
Marks, Burton & Marks, Rita. Puppet Plays & Puppet-Making. 64p. (gr. 3-7). 1985. pap. 6.95 (ISBN 0-8238-0272-8). Plays.
Martin, Sidney & McMillan, Dana. Puppet Costumes. 64p. (gr. 1-6). 1986. 6.95 (ISBN 0-912107-45-6). Monday Morning Bks.
Mehrens, Gloria & Wick, Karen. Bagging It with Puppets. (gr. k-2). 1988. pap. 15.95 (ISBN 0-8224-0677-2). Fearon Teach Aids.
Mister Tom. Six Silly Puppet Plays, Vol. I. Neely, David, ed. Neely, Heather, illus. LC 89-50784. 44p. (Orig.). (gr. 4-6). 1989. spiral bdg. 6.95 (ISBN 0-925237-05-1). Ten Pubns.
—Six Silly Puppet Plays, Vol. 2. Neely, David, ed. Neely, Heather, illus. 32p. (Orig.). (gr. k-3). 1989. pap. 6.95 spiral bdg. (ISBN 0-925237-06-X). Ten Pubns.
More Puppet Plays & Patter. (gr. 3-8). 1980. pap. 3.00 (ISBN 0-914318-06-3). V S Morris.
Oldfield, Margaret J. Finger Puppets & Finger Plays. (Illus.). (ps-3). 1982. pap. 3.00 (ISBN 0-934876-18-5). Creative Storytime.
—Tell & Draw Paper Bag Puppet Book. 2nd ed. Oldfield, Margaret J., illus. (gr. k-2). 1981. pap. 5.95 (ISBN 0-934876-16-9). Creative Storytime.
Olson, Margaret J. Tell & Draw Animal Cut-outs. 3rd ed. (gr. k-2). 1963. pap. 3.00 (ISBN 0-934876-15-0). Creative Storytime.
Philpott, V. & McNeil, M. J. The KnowHow Book of Puppets: A Simple Guide to Making & Working Puppets. (Illus.). 32p. (gr. 3-6). 1977. pap. 5.95 (ISBN 0-86020-003-5). EDC.
Poskanzer, Susan C. Puppeteer. Paterson, Diane, illus. LC 88-10042. 32p. (gr. k-2). 1988. PLB 10.89 (ISBN 0-8167-1432-0); pap. text ed. 2.50 (ISBN 0-8167-1433-9). Troll Assocs.
Renfro, Nancy. Puppet Shows Made Easy! Cromack, Celeste, ed. Renfro, Nancy, illus. 96p. (Orig.). (gr. 2-12). 18.95 (ISBN 0-685-07862-0); pap. 12.95 (ISBN 0-931044-13-8). Renfro Studios.
Renfro, Nancy & Armstrong, Beverly. Make Amazing Puppets. 32p. (gr. 1-6). 1979. 3.95 (ISBN 0-88160-007-5, LW 109). Learning Wks.
River, Chatham. Make a Pinocchio String Puppet. 1990. 4.99 (ISBN 0-517-69513-8). Outlet Bk Co.
Sierra, Judy. Fantastic Theater: Puppets & Plays for Young Performers & Young Audiences. 280p. 1991. 35.00 (ISBN 0-8242-0809-9). Wilson.
Sims, J. Puppets for Dreaming & Scheming. (gr. 1-6). 1988. 15.95 (ISBN 0-88160-167-5, LW 277). Learning Wks.
Spence, Rodney. Seventy-Six Short Scripts for Puppet Plays. Baldman, Craig, illus. LC 87-32921. (gr. 2-5). 1988. 9.95 (ISBN 0-87403-481-7, 14-03327). Standard Pub.

Suib, Leonard & Broadman, Muriel. Marionettes: How to Make & Perform with Them. (gr. 5 up). 17.75 (ISBN 0-318-42069-4). Peter Smith.

Supraner, Robyn & Supraner, Lauren. Plenty of Puppets to Make. Barto, Renzo, illus. LC 80-23785. 48p. (gr. 2-5). 1981. PLB 11.89 (ISBN 0-89375-432-3); pap. 2.95 (ISBN 0-89375-433-1). Troll Assocs.

Walker, Lois. Instant Puppets for Kids. Goddard, Lori & Porter, Debbie, illus. 63p. 1989. pap. text ed. 9.95 (ISBN 0-921217-30-7, 00658, Pub. by Pembroke Canada). Heinemann Ed.

Warshawsky, Gale. Creative Puppetry for Jewish Kids. 192p. (Orig.). (gr. 4-7). 1985. pap. text ed. 13.50 (ISBN 0-86705-017-9). AIRE.

Woods, Geraldine. Jim Henson: From Puppets to Muppets. LC 86-11624. (Illus.). 64p. (gr. 3 up). 1987. PLB 10.95 (ISBN 0-87518-348-4, Dillon). Macmillan Child Grp.

Wright, Lyndie. Puppets. Fairclough, Chris, photos by. (Illus.). 48p. (gr. 3-6). 1989. PLB 11.90 (ISBN 0-531-10635-7). Watts.

Zokeisha. Mother Goose. Zokeisha, illus. 12p. (ps-2). 1981. 2.95 (ISBN 0-671-42643-5, Little Simon). S&S Trade.

PUPPETS AND PUPPET PLAYS-FICTION

Barkan, Joanne. Boober's Colorful Soup. 1988. write for info. (ISBN 0-02-689135-2). Checkerboard Pr.

Barken, Joanne. Kermit's Mixed-up Message. Attinello, Lauren, illus. 32p. (Orig.). (gr. k-3). 1987. pap. 2.50 (ISBN 0-590-40704-X, Hello Reader). Scholastic Inc.

Baron, Michelle. Nanny Piggy. Alchemy II, Inc, illus. 26p. (ps up). 1987. 12.95 (ISBN 1-55578-602-2). Worlds Wonder.

Becker, Lois & Stratton, Mark. Muppet Babies on Twinkledink. Alchemy II, Inc., illus. 26p. (ps up). 1987. 12.95 (ISBN 1-55578-606-5). Worlds Wonder.

Big Bird Beep Books Starter Pack. (ps-k). 1989. pap. write for info. (ISBN 0-307-04725-3). Western Pub.

Borkan, Joanne. Doozer's Big & Little. 1988. write for info. (ISBN 0-02-689138-7). Checkerboard Pr.

Bove, Linda. Sesame Street Sign Language ABC with Linda Bove. Cooke, Tom, illus. Shevett, Anita & Shevett, Anita, photos by. LC 85-1845. (Illus.). 32p. (gr. 3-8). 1985. lib. bdg. 5.99 (ISBN 0-394-97516-2, Random Juv); pap. 2.25 (ISBN 0-394-87516-8). Random.

Brandenberg, Franz. Aunt Nina's Visit. Aliki, illus. LC 83-16531. 32p. (gr. k-3). 1984. 12.95 (ISBN 0-688-01764-9); PLB 14.88 (ISBN 0-688-01766-5). Greenwillow.

Campbell, Louisa. Ernie Gets Lost. Cooke, Tom, illus. 32p. (gr. k-3). 1985. write for info. (ISBN 0-307-12015-5, Pub. by Golden Bks). Western Pub.

Chaney, Steve. The Puppet in the Big Black Box. Katz, Richard, illus. 32p. (gr. k-3). 1989. write for info. Stiff Lip.

Collodi, C. The Adventures of Pinocchio. Chiesa, Carol D., tr. from ITA. Mussino, Attilio, illus. LC 88-26684. 320p. (gr. 3 up). 1989. 24.95 (ISBN 0-02-722821-5, Mcmillan Child Bk). Macmillan Child Grp.

Collodi, Carlo. Adventures of Pinocchio. (Illus.). (gr. 4 up). pap. 1.75 (ISBN 0-8049-0101-5, CL-101). Airmont.

—Pinocchio: A Classic Tale. Jose, Eduard, adapted by. Moncure, Jane B., tr. from SPA. Asensio, Augusti, illus. LC 88-35308. 32p. 1988. PLB 10.95 (ISBN 0-89565-458-X). Childs World.

—Pinocchio & the Great Whale. Cutts, David E., adapted by. Paterson, Diane, illus. LC 81-16026. 32p. (gr. 2-5). 1982. PLB 10.79 (ISBN 0-89375-720-9); pap. text ed. 2.95 (ISBN 0-89375-721-7). Troll Assocs.

—Pinocchio & the Puppet Show. Cutts, David E., adapted by. Paterson, Diane, illus. LC 81-16001. 32p. (gr. 2-5). 1982. PLB 10.79 (ISBN 0-89375-714-4); pap. text ed. 2.95 (ISBN 0-89375-715-2); avail. cassettes. Troll Assocs.

—Pinocchio Goes to School. Cutts, David E., adapted by. Paterson, Diane, illus. LC 81-15312. 32p. (gr. 2-5). 1982. PLB 10.79 (ISBN 0-89375-718-7); pap. text ed. 2.95 (ISBN 0-89375-719-5). Troll Assocs.

—Pinocchio Meets the Cat & Fox. Cutts, David E., adapted by. Paterson, Diane, illus. LC 81-16427. 32p. (gr. 2-5). 1982. PLB 10.79 (ISBN 0-89375-716-0); pap. text ed. 2.95 (ISBN 0-89375-717-9). Troll Assocs.

Cooke, Tom, illus. Bert & Ernie on the Go. LC 80-54574. 16p. (ps-2). 1981. 6.95 (ISBN 0-394-84869-1). Random.

Disney, Walt, Productions Staff. Walt Disney's Pinocchio. (Illus.). (ps-3). 1973. 5.95 (ISBN 0-394-82626-4, Random Juv); lib. bdg. 4.99 (ISBN 0-394-92626-9). Random.

Elliott, Dan. Grover Learns to Read. Chartier, Normand, illus. LC 84-27692. 40p. (ps-3). 1985. 4.95 (ISBN 0-394-87498-6, Random Juv); lib. bdg. 6.99 (ISBN 0-394-97498-0). Random.

—Two Wheels for Grover. Mathieu, Joe, illus. LC 84-4732. 40p. (ps-3). 1984. 4.95 (ISBN 0-394-86586-3, Pub. by BYR); lib. bdg. 6.99 (ISBN 0-394-96586-8). Random.

Fleischman, Paul. Shadow Play. Beddows, Eric, illus. LC 89-26874. 48p. (gr. 2 up). 1990. 14.95 (ISBN 0-06-021858-4); PLB 14.89 (ISBN 0-06-021865-7). HarpC Child Bks.

Forte, Imogene. The Puppet Factory. LC 83-82048. (Illus.). 96p. (gr. 2-6). 1984. pap. text ed. 7.95 (ISBN 0-86530-036-4, IP 36-4). Incentive Pubns.

Gikow, Louise. Baby Fozzie's Magic Show. 1989. write for info. (ISBN 0-02-689156-5). Macmillan.

—Baby Gonzo's Amusement Park. 1989. write for info. (ISBN 0-02-689157-3). Checkerboard Pr.

—Baby Kermit & the Magic Trunk. Spahr, Kathy, illus. 26p. (ps up). 1987. 12.95 (ISBN 1-55578-601-4). Worlds Wonder.

—Baby Rowlf & the Boomtown Bandits. Cooke, Tom, illus. 26p. (ps up). 1987. 12.95 (ISBN 1-55578-600-6). Worlds Wonder.

—Muppet Babies & the Magic Garden. Attinello, Lauren, illus. 26p. (ps up). 1987. 12.95 (ISBN 1-55578-608-1). Worlds Wonder.

—Muppet Babies at Playground. 1989. write for info. (ISBN 0-02-689163-8). Checkerboard Pr.

—Sleeptime Baby Animals. 1989. write for info. (ISBN 0-02-689164-6). Checkerboard Pr.

Gilchrist, Brad & Gilchrist, Guy. Muppets, No. 4: Chickens Are People Too. 128p. (Orig.). 1985. pap. 1.95 (ISBN 0-8125-7369-2, Dist. by Warner Pub Services & St. Martin's Press). Tor Bks.

—Muppets, No. 5: On the Town. 128p. (Orig.). 1986. pap. 1.95 (ISBN 0-8125-7371-4, Dist. by Warner Pub Services & St. Martin's Press). Tor Bks.

Gilchrist, Guy & Gilchrist, Brad. Muppets No. Three: Froggy Mountain Breakdown. 128p. (Orig.). 1985. pap. 1.95 (ISBN 0-8125-7367-6, Dist. by Warner Pub Services & St. Martin's Press). Tor Bks.

Gilcow, Louise. Baby Kermit's Christmas. 1988. write for info. (ISBN 0-02-689160-3). Checkerboard Pr.

Gondosch, Linda. The Monsters of Marble Avenue. (Illus.). (gr. 2-4). 1988. 10.95 (ISBN 0-316-31991-0). Little.

Hautzig, Deborah. It's Not Fair. Leigh, Tom, illus. LC 85-30154. 40p. (ps-3). 1986. 4.95 (ISBN 0-394-88151-6, Random Juv). Random.

Hayward, Linda. A Day in the Life of Oscar the Grouch. 24p. (ps-3). 1989. pap. write for info. (ISBN 0-307-14030-X). Western Pub.

Kirk, Tim, illus. The Muppet Babies' Busy Day. 12p. (ps). 1985. 2.95 (ISBN 0-394-87448-X, Random Juv). Random.

McKay, Sindy. Color Crazy. Alchemy II, Inc., illus. 26p. (ps up). 1987. 12.95 (ISBN 1-55578-609-X). Worlds Wonder.

McKay, Sindy & Swerdlove, Larry. Radio Station K-E-R-M. Alchemy II, Inc., illus. 26p. (ps up). 1987. 12.95 (ISBN 1-55578-607-3). Worlds Wonder.

McNaught, Harry. Muppets in My Neighborhood. McNaught, Harry, illus. LC 77-74472. (ps-k). 1977. bds. 3.95 (ISBN 0-394-83593-X, Random Juv). Random.

Muntean, Michaela. Baby Fozzie Goes Camping. Wilson, Ann, illus. 26p. (ps up). 1987. 12.95 (ISBN 1-55578-604-9). Worlds Wonder.

Muppets, Muppets, Muppets. (ps-2). 1986. 6.98 (ISBN 0-685-16866-2, 618109). Outlet Bk Co.

Paterson, Katherine. The Master Puppeteer. Wells, Haru, illus. 180p. (gr. 5 up). 1981. pap. 2.95 (ISBN 0-380-53322-7, 60065-X, Camelot). Avon.

—The Master Puppeteer. Wells, Haru, illus. LC 75-8614. 192p. (gr. 6 up). 1976. 14.95 (ISBN 0-690-00913-5, Crowell Jr Bks). HarpC Child Bks.

—The Master Puppeteer. Wells, Haru, illus. LC 75-8614. 192p. (gr. 4 up). 1989. pap. 3.50 (ISBN 0-06-440281-9, Trophy). HarpC Child Bks.

Paul, Emily. Count with Baby Kermit. 1988. write for info. (ISBN 0-02-689136-0). Checkerboard Pr.

—Muppet Babies on the Move. 1988. write for info. (ISBN 0-02-689108-5). Checkerboard Pr.

Pauli, Emily. Mokey Fraggles New Colors. 1988. write for info. (ISBN 0-02-689114-X). Checkerboard Pr.

Peters, Sharon. Una Funcion De Titeres. Lee, Alana, illus. (SPA.). 32p. (gr. k-2). 1981. PLB 7.06 (ISBN 0-89375-551-6). Troll Assocs.

Pinocchio. (FRE.). 6.25 (ISBN 0-685-33974-2). French & Eur.

Pinocchio. (Illus.). 18p. (ps-1). 1979. 3.95 (ISBN 0-448-09752-4, G&D). Putnam Pub Group.

Pinocchio. (Illus.). (ps-3). 1985. 2.98 (ISBN 0-517-28809-5). Outlet Bk Co.

Pinocchio. (Illus.). (ps-4). 3.50 (ISBN 0-7214-0589-4). Ladybird Bks.

Pinocchio. (FRE., Illus.). (gr. 2). 3.50 (ISBN 0-7214-1281-5). Ladybird Bks.

Pinocho. (SPA.). (gr. 2). 1990. casebound 3.50 (ISBN 0-7214-1412-5). Ladybird Bks.

Prady, Bill. Muppet Babies & the Time Machine. Brannon, Tom, illus. 26p. (ps up). 1987. 12.95 (ISBN 1-55578-605-7). Worlds Wonder.

Riordan, James. Pinocchio. Ambrus, Victor G., illus. 96p. (gr. 3 up). 1988. 18.95 (ISBN 0-19-279855-3). Oxford U Pr.

Roberts, Sarah. Ernie's Big Mess. Mathieu, Joe, illus. LC 81-2464. 40p. (gr. k-2). 1981. 4.95 (ISBN 0-394-84847-0); lib. bdg. 6.99 (ISBN 0-394-94847-5). Random.

—I Want to Go Home. Mathieu, Joe, illus. LC 84-11725. 40p. (ps-3). 1985. 4.95 (ISBN 0-394-87027-1, Random Juv); PLB 6.99 (ISBN 0-394-97027-6). Random.

Ross, Anna. I Did It! Gorbaty, Norman, illus. LC 89-34543. 24p. (ps). 1990. 3.95 (ISBN 0-394-86019-5). Random.

—I Have to Go. Gorbaty, Norman, illus. LC 89-34542. 24p. (ps). 1990. 3.95 (ISBN 0-394-86051-9). Random.

—Naptime. Gorbaty, Norman, illus. LC 89-34545. 24p. (ps). 1990. 3.95 (ISBN 0-394-85828-X). Random.

—Quiet Time. Gorbaty, Norman, illus. LC 89-24354. 24p. (ps). 1991. 3.95 (ISBN 0-394-85495-0). Random.

—Say the Magic Word, Please. Gorbaty, Norman, illus. LC 89-34544. 24p. (ps). 1990. 3.95 (ISBN 0-394-85857-3). Random.

Ross, Harry. Fraggles Alphabet Pie. 1988. write for info. (ISBN 0-02-689115-8). Checkerboard Pr.

—Wembley Fraggles Big Bigger Biggest. 1988. write for info. (ISBN 0-02-689113-1). Checkerboard Pr.

Ross, Harvey. Fraggles Counting Book. 1988. write for info. (ISBN 0-02-689112-3). Checkerboard Pr.

Sesame Street Staff. Cookie Monster, Where Are You? Jones, Randy, illus. LC 75-39342. (ps-3). 1976. 7.95 (ISBN 0-394-83257-4, Random Juv). Random.

—Your Friends from Sesame Street. Smollin, Michael J., illus. (ps). 1979. 3.50 (ISBN 0-394-84137-9, Random Juv). Random.

Spahr, Kathy, illus. The Muppet Babies Night Light Book. LC 84-62047. 14p. (gr. 3-6). 1985. bds. 4.95 (ISBN 0-394-87274-6, Random Juv). Random.

Stevenson, Jocelyn. The Great Muppet Caper. LC 81-4583. (Illus.). 64p. (gr. 4-7). 1981. lib. bdg. 6.99 (ISBN 0-394-94874-2). Random.

Stone, Jon. Would You Like to Play Hide & Seek in This Book with Lovable, Furry Old Grover? Smollin, Michael J., illus. LC 76-8120. (ps-1). 1976. pap. 2.25 (ISBN 0-394-83292-2). Random.

Sustendal, Pat, illus. Sesame Street Farm Friends. 12p. (ps). 1985. 3.95 (ISBN 0-394-87466-8, Random Juv). Random.

Szekeres, Cyndy. A Fine Mouse Band. 24p. (ps-k). 1989. pap. write for info. (ISBN 0-307-11999-8, Pub. by Golden Bks). Western Pub.

Weiss, Ellen. Baby Gonzo in Backwardsland. DiCicco, Sue, illus. 26p. (ps up). 1987. 12.95 (ISBN 1-55578-603-0). Worlds Wonder.

Worth, Bonnie. Baby Kermit's Opposites. 1988. write for info. (ISBN 0-02-689109-3). Checkerboard Pr.

—Fraggles Adding Fraggles. 1989. write for info. (ISBN 0-02-689262-6). Checkerboard Pr.

—Fraggles Book of Cooperation. 1989. write for info. (ISBN 0-02-689263-4). Checkerboard Pr.

—Muppet Babies Head to Toe. 1989. write for info. (ISBN 0-02-689260-X). Checkerboard Pr.

—Muppet Babies Seasons. 1989. write for info. (ISBN 0-02-689261-8). Checkerboard Pr.

—Muppet Babies Shape Machine. 1988. write for info. (ISBN 0-02-689107-7). Checkerboard Pr.

—Muppet Babies Word Book. 1988. write for info. (ISBN 0-02-689106-9). Checkerboard Pr.

PURCHASING
see Shopping

PURIM (FEAST OF ESTHER)

Chaikin, Miriam. Make Noise, Make Merry: The Story & Meaning of Purim. Demi, illus. LC 82-12926. 96p. (gr. 3-6). 1986. pap. 4.95 (ISBN 0-89919-424-9, Pub. by Clarion); pap. 4.95 (ISBN 0-685-06203-1). Ticknor & Fields.

Silverman, Maida. Festival of Esther: The Story of Purim. Ewing, Carolyn S., illus. (gr. 1-5). 1989. pap. 8.95 (ISBN 0-671-67200-2); pap. 2.95 (ISBN 0-671-67663-6). S&S Trade.

Simon, Norma. Happy Purim Night. Gordon, Ayala, illus. (ps-k). plastic cover 4.50 (ISBN 0-8381-0706-0, 10-706). United Syn Bk.

—Purim Party. Gordon, Ayala, illus. (ps-k). 1959. plastic cover 4.50 (ISBN 0-8381-0707-9). United Syn Bk.

Stuhlman, Daniel D. My Own Pesah Story. Klugman, Micha, illus. (Orig.). (gr. 1-6). 1981. Personalized Version. pap. 3.95x (ISBN 0-934402-09-4); Trade Version. pap. 3.00 (ISBN 0-934402-10-8); Seder cards 1.50 (ISBN 0-934402-11-6). BYLS Pr.

Wengrov, Charles. The Story of Purim. (Illus.). (gr. k-7). 1965. pap. 2.50 (ISBN 0-914080-53-9). Shulsinger Sales.

Zwerm, Raymond A. & Marcus, Audrey F. Purim Album. (Illus.). 32p. (gr. k-3). 1981. 10.95 (ISBN 0-8074-0154-4, 101250). UAHC.

PURITANS-FICTION

Hawthorne, Nathaniel. Scarlet Letter. Levin, Harry, ed. LC 60-2662. (gr. 9 up). 1960. pap. 7.56 (ISBN 0-395-05142-8, RivEd). HM.

Speare, Elizabeth G. Witch of Blackbird Pond. (Illus.). 256p. (gr. 7 up). 1958. 13.95 (ISBN 0-395-07114-3). HM.

PUZZLES

Adler, David A. Bible Fun Book: Puzzles, Riddles, Magic, & More. (Illus., Orig.). (gr. 1-5). 1979. pap. 3.95 (ISBN 0-88482-769-0). Hebrew Pub.

Arboleda, Alba, et al. Outer Space Adventures. (Illus.). 32p. (gr. 3 up). 1986. incl. hand held Decoder 5.95 (ISBN 0-88679-462-5). Educ Insights.

Armstrong, Beverly. All Occasion Pages. 32p. (gr. 1-6). 1982. 3.95 (ISBN 0-88160-014-8, LW 117). Learning Wks.

Baker & Boyington. Down East Puzzles & Word Games. Hassett, John, illus. 80p. (Orig.). 1989. pap. 3.95 (ISBN 0-89272-272-X). Down East.

Ball, Jacqueline A. A Puzzle for Apatosaurus. (gr. 4-7). 1990. pap. 2.95 (ISBN 0-06-106002-X, PL). HarperCollins.

Barr, Marilyn. ABC Puzzles. (Illus.). 64p. (ps-1). 1989. 6.95 (ISBN 0-912107-96-0, MM1913). Monday Morning Bks.

Barr, Stephen. Puzzlequiz: Wit Twisters, Brain Teasers, Riddles, Puzzles & Tough Questions. LC 89-46070. (Illus.). 144p. 1990. pap. 5.95 (ISBN 0-06-091974-4, PL). HarperCollins.

Beisner, Monika. Catch That Cat! A Picture Book of Rhymes & Puzzles. (Illus.). 32p. 1990. 13.95 (ISBN 0-374-31226-5). FS&G.

Brain-Bending Mazes. (gr. 2-5). 1987. pap. 1.49 (ISBN 0-671-64357-6, Little Simon). S&S Trade.

Bright, Leonard D. The Gifted Kids Guide to Puzzles & Mind Games. (Illus.). 143p. pap. 7.95 (ISBN 0-936750-15-4). Paradon Pub Co.

Bureloff, Morris. Brain-Busting Decode Puzzles. Laycock, Mary, ed. Bureloff, Morris, illus. 64p. (gr. 7-10). 1985. pap. 6.95 (ISBN 0-918932-86-6). Activity Resources.

Cool, Jeannie. Word Picture Puzzles. (gr. 3-6). 1985. pap. 0.69 pocket size (ISBN 0-87239-822-6, 2812). Standard Pub.

Cron, Mary. Magic Penny Puzzlers, No. 1. (Illus.). 48p. 1990. pap. 2.95 (ISBN 0-8431-2751-1). Price Stern.

—Magic Penny Puzzlers, No. 2. (Illus.). 48p. 1990. pap. 2.95 (ISBN 0-8431-2752-X). Price Stern.

—Magic Penny Puzzlers, No. 3. (Illus.). 48p. 1990. pap. 2.95 (ISBN 0-8431-2753-8). Price Stern.

—Magic Penny Puzzlers, No. 4. (Illus.). 48p. 1990. pap. 2.95 (ISBN 0-8431-2754-6). Price Stern.

Crossword Puzzle Adventures. (gr. 2-5). 1987. pap. 1.79 (ISBN 0-671-64356-8, Little Simon). S&S Trade.

Crowther, Jean D. Book of Mormon Puzzles & Pictures for Young Latter-Day Saints. LC 77-74495. (Illus.). 56p. (gr. 3 up). 1977. pap. 5.50 (ISBN 0-88290-080-3). Horizon Utah.

The Dell Book of Cryptograms. 1989. pap. 6.95 (ISBN 0-440-50091-5). Dell.

Dolby, K., et al. Second Usborne Book of Puzzle Adventures. (Illus.). 144p. (gr. 3-8). 1990. pap. 9.95 (ISBN 0-7460-0310-2, Usborne). EDC.

Doolittle, Eileen. The Ark in the Attic: An Alphabet Adventure. Ockenga, Starr, photos by. LC 86-45534. (ps up). 1987. 19.95 (ISBN 0-87923-684-1). Godine.

Ecklund, Larry & Silvani, Harold. Interesting Facts Number Puzzles. 74p. (gr. 3-8). 1978. 6.95 (ISBN 1-878669-05-2, 4462); wkbk., incl. tchr's. ed. 6.95 ea. Bk. 1: Addition (4462). Bk. 2: Subtraction, 1977 (ISBN 1-878669-06-0, 4463). Bk. 3: Multiplication (4464). Bk. 4: Division (4465). Crea Tea Assocs.

Evans, Larry. Three-D Mazes, Vol. 1. (Illus.). 40p. 1976. pap. 3.50 (ISBN 0-8431-1744-3). Price Stern.

Fisher, John. John Fisher's Magic Book. De Paola, Tomie, illus. (gr. 5-8). 1975. pap. 1.95 (ISBN 0-13-510222-7, Pub. by Treehouse). P-H.

Gamiello, Elvira. Hidden Messages You Can Solve. (Illus., Orig.). (gr. 4-6). 1989. pap. 1.95 (ISBN 0-942025-41-5). Kidsbks.

—Search-A-Picture Puzzles. (Illus., Orig.). (gr. 4-6). 1987. pap. 1.95 (ISBN 0-942025-07-5). Kidsbks.

—Secret Codes & Other Word Games. (Illus., Orig.). (gr. 4-6). 1988. pap. 1.95 (ISBN 0-942025-45-8). Kidsbks.

—Secret Jokes & Hidden Riddles Activity & Fun Book. (Illus., Orig.). (gr. 4-6). 1989. pap. 1.95 (ISBN 0-942025-25-3). Kidsbks.

—Sharks Activity & Game Book. (Illus., Orig.). (gr. 4-6). 1988. pap. 1.95 (ISBN 0-942025-46-6). Kidsbks.

—Snowy Days Activity & Game Book. (Illus., Orig.). (gr. 4-6). 1989. pap. 1.95 (ISBN 0-942025-36-9). Kidsbks.

—Spooky Haunted House Puzzles. (Illus.). 64p. (Orig.). (gr. 4-6). 1987. pap. 1.95 (ISBN 0-942025-06-7). Kidsbks.

—Summertime Puzzle & Fun Book. (Illus., Orig.). (gr. 4-6). 1989. pap. 1.95 (ISBN 0-942025-62-8). Kidsbks.

—Sunny Days Word Games & Mazes. (Illus., Orig.). (gr. 4-6). 1988. pap. 1.95 (ISBN 0-942025-40-7). Kidsbks.

—Super Secret Codes & Jokes. (Illus., Orig.). (gr. 4-6). 1990. pap. 1.95 (ISBN 0-942025-44-X). Kidsbks.

—What's Wrong Here. (Illus., Orig.). (gr. 4-6). 1989. pap. 1.95 (ISBN 0-942025-91-1). Kidsbks.

Gardner, Martin. The Snark Puzzle Book. Holiday, Henry & Tenniel, John, illus. 124p. (gr. 3 up). 1990. Repr. of 1973 ed. PLB 13.95 (ISBN 0-87975-583-0). Prometheus Bks.

Goldberg, Steve. Pholdit. (gr. 3 up). 1972. 4.95 (ISBN 0-918932-67-X). Activity Resources.

Gomi, Taro. Who Ate It? (Illus.). 24p. (ps). 1991. PLB 7.90 (ISBN 1-56294-010-4). Millbrook Pr.

—Who Hid It? (Illus.). 24p. (ps). 1991. PLB 7.90 (ISBN 1-56294-011-2). Millbrook Pr.

Graham, Dennis, et al. Culture Trek. (Illus.). 32p. (gr. 3 up). 1989. incl. hand held Decoder 5.95 (ISBN 0-88679-572-9). Educ Insights.

—Exploring America. (Illus.). 32p. (gr. 3 up). 1989. incl. hand held Decoder 5.95 (ISBN 0-88679-573-7). Educ Insights.

—Prehistoric Life. (Illus.). 32p. (gr. 3 up). 1989. incl. hand held Decoder 5.95 (ISBN 0-88679-571-0). Educ Insights.

—Undersea Adventures. (Illus.). 32p. (gr. 3 up). 1989. incl. hand held Decoder 5.95 (ISBN 0-88679-574-5). Educ Insights.

Graham, Harriet. The Chinese Puzzle. LC 88-6771. 192p. (gr. 5-9). 1988. 13.95 (ISBN 0-395-47689-5). HM.

Hall, John. Maze Craze Three. (Illus.). 40p. (gr. 1-12). 1974. pap. 3.50 (ISBN 0-8431-1734-6). Price Stern.

—Maze Craze Two. (Illus.). 40p. (gr. 1-12). 1973. pap. 3.50 (ISBN 0-8431-1733-8). Price Stern.

Hallett, Bill & Hallett, Jane. National Park Service: Activities & Adventures for Kids. Paltrow, Robert, illus. 32p. (Orig.). (gr. 3-8). 1991. activity bk. 3.95 (ISBN 1-877827-07-X). Look & See.

Harris, Tina, et al. Worldwide Wonders. (Illus.). 32p. (gr. 3 up). 1986. incl. hand held Decoder 5.95 (ISBN 0-88679-461-7). Educ Insights.

—Inventions & Discoveries. (Illus.). 32p. (gr. 3 up). 1989. incl. hand held Decoder 5.95 (ISBN 0-88679-458-7). Educ Insights.

Haunted House Detect-a-Word. (Illus.). (gr. k-9). 1988. pap. 1.95 (ISBN 0-318-36487-5). Scholastic Inc.

Hayes. Picture Puzzles. (Illus.). 32p. (gr. 2-6). 1988. pap. 2.95 (ISBN 0-88625-147-8). Durkin Hayes Pub.

Heimann, Rolf. Amazing Mazes. (gr. 4-7). 1990. pap. 3.95 (ISBN 0-8167-2201-3). Troll Assocs.

Heller, Ruth. Maze Craze. (Illus.). 40p. (gr. 1-12). 1971. pap. 3.50 (ISBN 0-8431-1732-X). Price Stern.

Highlights Editors. Hidden Pictures & Other Puzzlers. (Illus.). 32p. (Orig.). (gr. 1-6). 1981. pap. 2.95 (ISBN 0-87534-180-2). Highlights.

Highlights for Children Staff. Puzzlemania. Highlights for Children Staff, illus. (gr. 3-7). 1989. pap. 2.98 48p. (ISBN 0-87534-701-0); pap. 2.98 32p. (ISBN 0-87534-801-7). Highlights.

—Puzzlemania. Highlights for Children Staff, illus. (gr. 3-7). 1989. pap. 2.98 48p. (ISBN 0-87534-702-9); pap. 2.98 32p. (ISBN 0-87534-802-5). Highlights.

—Puzzlemania. Highlights for Children Staff, illus. (gr. 3-7). 1989. pap. 2.98 48p. (ISBN 0-87534-703-7); pap. 2.98 32p. (ISBN 0-87534-803-3). Highlights.

—Puzzlemania. Highlights for Children Staff, illus. (gr. 3-7). 1989. pap. 2.98 48p. (ISBN 0-87534-704-5); pap. 2.98 32p. (ISBN 0-87534-804-1). Highlights.

—Puzzlemania. Highlights for Children Staff, illus. (gr. 3-7). 1989. pap. 2.98 48p. (ISBN 0-87534-705-3); pap. 2.98 32p. (ISBN 0-87534-805-X). Highlights.

—Puzzlemania. Highlights for Children Staff, illus. (gr. 3-7). 1989. pap. 2.98 48p. (ISBN 0-87534-706-1); pap. 2.98 32p. (ISBN 0-87534-806-8). Highlights.

—Puzzlemania. Highlights for Children Staff, illus. (gr. 3-7). 1989. pap. 2.98 48p. (ISBN 0-87534-707-X); pap. 2.98 32p. (ISBN 0-87534-807-6). Highlights.

—Puzzlemania. Highlights for Children Staff, illus. (gr. 3-7). 1989. pap. 2.98 48p. (ISBN 0-87534-708-8); pap. 2.98 32p. (ISBN 0-87534-808-4). Highlights.

—Puzzlemania. Highlights for Children Staff, illus. (gr. 3-7). 1989. pap. 2.98 48p. (ISBN 0-87534-709-6); pap. 2.98 32p. (ISBN 0-87534-809-2). Highlights.

—Puzzlemania. Highlights for Children Staff, illus. (gr. 3-7). 1989. pap. 2.98 48p. (ISBN 0-87534-710-X); pap. 2.98 32p. (ISBN 0-87534-810-6). Highlights.

Hite, Nancy. A Pocket Book of Puzzles. 200p. (ps up). 1979. 6.95 (ISBN 0-916456-47-1, GA98). Good Apple.

Holland, Penny & Kubota, Carole. Puzzles & Thinking Games. (Illus.). 32p. (gr. 3 up). 1986. incl. hand held Decoder 5.95 (ISBN 0-88679-459-5). Educ Insights.

Hovanex, Helene. Riddled with Puzzles. 64p. (gr. 3-7). 1986. pap. 1.95 (ISBN 0-590-33823-4). Scholastic Inc.

Interesting Facts Number Puzzles: Addition, Subtraction, Multiplication & Division, 4 bks. Set. write for info (ISBN 1-878669-04-4). Crea Tea Assocs.

Jenkins, Lee. Time & Time Again. Laycock, Mary, ed. Gittings, Elisa, illus. 72p. (Orig.). (gr. 1-6). 1985. pap. text ed. 6.95 (ISBN 0-918932-85-8). Activity Resources.

Johnson, William. Dinosaur Fun Book. (Illus.). 48p. (gr. k-12). 1979. pap. 3.50 (ISBN 0-8431-1704-4). Price Stern.

King, Colin. Amazing Book of Puzzles & Tricks. 1990. 3.50 (ISBN 0-517-69194-9). Outlet Bk Co.

Lasley, Mary. A Day at the Beach. 4p. (ps-2). 1990. incl. 24 puzzle pieces 10.95 (ISBN 0-88679-843-4). Educ Insights.

—A Day at the Park. 4p. (ps-2). 1990. incl. 24 puzzle pieces 10.95 (ISBN 0-685-38496-9). Educ Insights.

—Do-It-Yourself Story Puzzle Book. Brown, Amy L., illus. 2p. (ps). 1988. 9.95 (ISBN 0-9622406-0-5). MOL Bks.

Lattimore, Deborah. Digging into the Past. (Illus.). 32p. (gr. 3 up). 1986. incl. hand held Decoder 5.95 (ISBN 0-88679-460-9). Educ Insights.

Leigh, S. The Haunted Tower. (Illus.). 48p. 1989. lib. bdg. 10.96 (ISBN 0-88110-367-5); pap. 4.50 (ISBN 0-685-36292-2). EDC.

—Puzzle Island. (Illus.). 32p. (ps up). 1991. lib. bdg. 13.96 (ISBN 0-88110-558-9, Usborne); pap. 5.95 (ISBN 0-7460-0596-2, Usborne). EDC.

Levy, Nathan. Stories with Holes, Vols. 1-8. 20p. 1990. pap. 5.00 ea. (ISBN 1-878347-11-X). NL Assocs.
"Stories With Holes" is the result of several years' accumulation, by the author & others, of puzzling stories that lend themselves to what I call thinking games. The games have become the means for hundreds of teachers to carry on a totally enjoyable process of training students in critical & imaginative thinking.
Publisher Provided Annotation.

Macdonald, Suse. Puzzlers. LC 88-33392. 1989. 13.89 (ISBN 0-8037-0690-1); PLB 13.95 (ISBN 0-8037-0689-8). Dial Bks Young.

Maleska, Eugene T., ed. Children's Word Games & Crossword Puzzles, Vol. 1. LC 86-888. 80p. (gr. 1-3). 1986. pap. 5.95 (ISBN 0-8129-1243-8, Times Bks). Random.

—Children's Word Games & Puzzles. 2nd ed. LC 86-886. 80p. (gr. 3 up). 1986. pap. 5.95 (ISBN 0-8129-1308-6, Times Bks). Random.

Mallett, Jerry J. Library Skills Activity Puzzles Series, 5 bks. Incl. Book Bafflers. 1982. pap. text ed. 9.95 (ISBN 0-87628-188-9); Dictionary Puzzlers. 1982. pap. text ed. 9.95 (ISBN 0-87628-273-7); Lively Locators. 1982. pap. text ed. 9.95 (ISBN 0-87628-539-6); Reading Incentives. 1982. pap. text ed. 9.95 (ISBN 0-87628-719-4); Resource Rousers. 1982. pap. text ed. 9.95 (ISBN 0-87628-741-0). (gr. 2-6). 1988. pap. text ed. 32.95x ea., 64 pgs. ea. (ISBN 0-87628-537-X). Ctr Appl Res.

Martin, Sidney & McMillan, Dana. Brain Boosters. 64p. (gr. 1-6). 1986. 6.95 (ISBN 0-912107-43-X). Monday Morning Bks.

Maschke, Ruby A. Bible Puzzles for Children. 64p. (gr. 4-6). 1986. pap. 6.95 (ISBN 0-8170-1095-5). Judson.

Mind Teasers. 48p. (Orig.). 1982. pap. 2.95 (ISBN 0-8431-0293-4). Price Stern.

Nister, Ernest. My Picture Puzzle Book: Reproductions of Antique Pictures. (Illus.). 10p. 1991. incl. 40 puzzle pieces 12.95 (ISBN 0-399-21855-6, Philomel Bks). Putnam Pub Group.

Oliver, M. Agent Arthur's Jungle Journey. (Illus.). 48p. 1989. lib. bdg. 10.96 (ISBN 0-88110-334-9); pap. 4.50 (ISBN 0-7460-0141-X). EDC.

Orleans, Jacob S. Great Big Book of Pencil Puzzles. pap. 5.95 (ISBN 0-399-50942-9, Perigee Bks). Putnam Pub Group.

Packard, Mary. Puzzle Party. Barish, Wendy, ed. 64p. (gr. 7 up). 1984. pap. 2.95 (ISBN 0-671-47730-7, Little Simon). S&S Trade.

Pape, Donna L. The Children's Arkansas Puzzle Book. Mueller, Virginia & Karle, Carol, illus. 28p. (gr. k up). 1984. pap. 2.95 (ISBN 0-914546-55-4). Rose Pub.

Pape, Donna L., et al. The Vermont Puzzle Book. 96p. (Orig.). 1987. pap. 4.95 (ISBN 0-88150-092-5). Countryman.

Paraquin, Charles. Optical Illusion Puzzles. Kuttner, Paul, tr. LC 83-18198. (Illus.). 96p. (Orig.). (gr. 7 up). 1984. 12.95 (ISBN 0-8069-6868-0). Sterling.

Pelham, David. Dimensional Mazes. LC 88-40373. 12p. 1989. pap. 14.95 (ISBN 0-670-82709-6). Viking Penguin.

Peter Rabbit's Puzzle Book. 1987. pap. 3.95 (ISBN 0-7232-3441-8). Warne.

Phillips, Dave, illus. Hidden Treasure Maze Book. 48p. (Orig.). (gr. 2 up). 1984. pap. 2.95 (ISBN 0-486-24566-7). Dover.

Play-by-Play. (gr. 3-7). 1990. pap. 3.95 (ISBN 0-316-94670-2). Little.

Pragoff, Fiona. Odd One Out. (Illus.). 16p. (ps-k). 1989. 5.95 (ISBN 0-385-26410-0, Zephyr-BFYR). Doubleday.

Puzzles & Puzzlers. (Illus.). 96p. (gr. 2-5). 1988. pap. 2.95 (ISBN 0-8431-2273-0). Price Stern.

Ranucci, Ernest R. & Rollins, Wilma E. Brain Drain, 2 bks. Klassen, Grace & Nachtigall, Kelly, illus. 70p. (gr. 6-12). Bks. A & B. write for info. incl. tchr's. ed. (ISBN 1-878669-09-5, 4301); wkbk., tchr's. ed. 6.95 ea. Bk. A, 1975 (ISBN 1-878669-10-9, 4301). Bk. B, 1978 (4420). Crea Tea Assocs.

Razzi, Jim & Looney, Jack. The Ghostbusters Two Joke, Puzzle, & Game Book. Ahar, Jackie, illus. 96p. (Orig.). (gr. 2-8). 1989. pap. 4.95 (ISBN 1-55704-048-6). Newmarket.

Revealing Hidden Pictures. (Illus.). 64p. (gr. 2-5). 1990. pap. 1.79 (ISBN 0-671-72336-7). S&S Trade.

RGA Staff. Math Mixers. 32p. 1989. pap. 1.95 (ISBN 0-317-91014-0). Tor Bks.

Selsam, Millicent E. Is This a Baby Dinosaur? & Other Science Picture Puzzles. LC 72-76508. (Illus.). 32p. (gr. k-3). 1984. pap. 4.95 (ISBN 0-06-443054-5, Trophy). HarpC Child Bks.

Sensational Search-a-Words. (Illus.). 64p. (gr. 2-5). 1990. pap. 1.79 (ISBN 0-671-72334-0). S&S Trade.

Silvani, Harold. Animal Number Puzzles. 50p. (gr. 2-4). 1971. wkbk. 6.95 (ISBN 1-878669-25-7, 4015). Crea Tea Assocs.

—Famous Athletes Number Puzzles. Sharpsteen, Linda, illus. 28p. (gr. 4-6). 1975. wkbk. 6.95 (ISBN 1-878669-23-0, 4161). Crea Tea Assocs.

—Presidents Number Puzzles, 2 bks. 46p. Bks. A & B. write for info. set (ISBN 1-878669-15-X, 4158); wkbk. 6.95 ea. Bk. A, Grades 3-5, 1977 (4158). Bk. B, Grades 4-7, 1973 (4159). Crea Tea Assocs.

Simon & Schuster Staff. Amazing Mazes. (Illus.). 64p. (gr. 2-5). 1990. pap. 1.79 (ISBN 0-671-72333-2). S&S Trade.

Smart, Margaret A. & Laycock, Mary. Create a Cube. Kyzer, Walter & Kyzer, Martha, illus. 64p. (Orig.). (gr. 4-12). 1985. pap. text ed. 6.95 (ISBN 0-918932-84-X). Activity Resources.

Sorensen, Mathew D. Mat's Mazes. Sorensen, Mathew, illus. 32p. (Orig.). (gr. 3-6). 1988. pap. 1.98 (ISBN 0-9621376-1-8). SH Ltd Pubs.

Spivak, Darlene E. Scrambled Word Puzzles. Spivak, Darlene E., illus. 48p. (gr. 2-5). 1987. wkbk. 5.95 (ISBN 1-55734-066-8). Tchr Create Mat.

Studio D Staff. Fantastic Book of Picture Puzzles. LC 88-38022. (Illus.). 128p. (gr. 3-10). 1989. pap. 4.95 (ISBN 0-8069-6961-X). Sterling.

Tailor, Z. Little Red Riding Hood "Puzzle 'n Book" Belli, Fred, illus. 8p. (gr. k up). Date not set. PLB write for info. ABC Child Bks.
Tallarico, Anthony. Find Freddie. (Illus.). 24p. (Orig.). 1988. pap. 2.95 (ISBN 0-942025-65-2). Kidsbks.
—Hunt for Hector. (Illus.). 24p. (Orig.). 1988. pap. 2.95 (ISBN 0-942025-68-7). Kidsbks.
—Look for Lisa. (Illus.). 24p. (Orig.). 1988. pap. 2.95 (ISBN 0-942025-66-0). Kidsbks.
—Search for Sam. (Illus.). 24p. (Orig.). 1988. pap. 2.95 (ISBN 0-942025-67-9). Kidsbks.
Tallarico, Tony. Mr. Merlin's Puzzle & Game Book. Klimo, Kate, ed. Tallarico, Tony, illus. 64p. (Orig.). (gr. 3-6). 1981. pap. 2.95 (ISBN 0-671-44492-1, Little Simon). S&S Trade.
Townsend, Charles B. World's Most Baffling Puzzles. (Illus.). 128p. (gr. 4-11). 1991. 12.95 (ISBN 0-8069-5832-4). Sterling.
—The World's Most Challenging Puzzles. LC 88-19729. (Illus.). 128p. (gr. 10-12). 1988. 12.95 (ISBN 0-8069-6730-7). Sterling.
—The World's Most Challenging Puzzles. LC 88-19729. (Illus.). 128p. (gr. 3-9). 1989. pap. 4.95 (ISBN 0-8069-6731-5). Sterling.
—World's Toughest Puzzles. LC 89-49131. (Illus.). 96p. 1990. 12.95 (ISBN 0-8069-6962-8). Sterling.
Treat, Lawrence. You're the Detective! Twenty-Four Solve-Them-Yourself Picture Mysteries. Borowik, Kathleen, illus. LC 82-49346. 80p. (Orig.). (gr. 3-6). 1983. pap. 7.95 (ISBN 0-87923-478-4). Godine.
Troll. Brain Teasers & Puzzles for Kids. 32p. (ps-3). 1991. pap. 1.95 (ISBN 0-8167-2247-1). Troll Assocs.
Tyler. Number Puzzles. (gr. 2-5). 1980. PLB 12.96 (ISBN 0-88110-050-1, Usborne-Hayes); pap. 3.95 (ISBN 0-86020-435-9). EDC.
—Picture Puzzles. (gr. 2-5). 1980. (Usborne-Hayes); PLB 12.96 (ISBN 0-88110-049-8); pap. 3.95 (ISBN 0-86020-433-2). EDC.
Walter, Marion. The Mirror Puzzle Book. (Illus.). 32p. (gr. 2 up). 1985. pap. 5.95 (ISBN 0-906212-39-1). Parkwest Pubns.
Waters, G. Time Train to Ancient Rome. (Illus.). 48p. (gr. 3-5). 1988. PLB 10.96 (ISBN 0-88110-302-0); pap. 4.50 (ISBN 0-7460-0153-3). EDC.
Waters, G., et al. Puzzle Adventures: Dinosaur Expedition, Bus Trip, Time Train. (Illus.). 144p. (gr. 3-5). 1988. pap. 9.95 (ISBN 0-7460-0155-X). EDC.
Weyn, Suzanne. HBO Encyclopedia Puzzle Book. 1989. pap. 2.50 (ISBN 0-590-42651-6). Scholastic Inc.
Wheeler, Joan & Carter, Sharon. Brain Benders. 48p. (gr. 4-6). 1982. 5.95 (ISBN 0-88160-048-2, LW 234). Learning Wks.

PYGMIES

Jones. Pygmies of Central Africa, Reading Level 5. (Illus.). 48p. (gr. 4-8). Date not set. PLB 15.33 (ISBN 0-86625-268-1). Rourke Corp.

PYRAMIDS

Abels, Harriette S. The Pyramids. LC 87-15455. (Illus.). 48p. (gr. 5-6). 1987. PLB 10.95 (ISBN 0-89686-345-X, Crestwood Hse). Macmillan Child Grp.
The Great Pyramid of Cheops. 48p. (gr. 4-5). 1989. PLB 10.95 (ISBN 0-685-26410-6). Capstone Pr.
Millard, Anne. Pyramids. LC 88-83093. (Illus.). 32p. (gr. 5-7). 1989. PLB 11.90 (ISBN 0-531-17154-X, Gloucester Pr). Watts.
Mitchell, Barbara. The Pyramids: Opposing Viewpoints. LC 87-8392. (Illus.). 96p. (gr. 3-10). 1987. lib. bdg. 13. 95 (ISBN 0-89908-051-0). Greenhaven.
Steel, Anne. Egyptian Pyramids. (gr. 4-7). 1990. PLB 10. 40 (ISBN 0-531-18325-4). Watts.

Q

QUAKERS

see Friends, Society of

QUANTUM THEORY

see also Chemistry; Force and Energy; Radiation; Relativity (Physics); Thermodynamics

QUARANTINE

see Communicable Diseases

QUASARS

Berger, Melvin. Quasars, Pulsars & Black Holes in Space. new ed. LC 76-50057. (Illus.). (gr. 3-6). 1977. PLB 6.99 (ISBN 0-399-61051-0). Putnam Pub Group.
Jespersen, James & Fitz-Randolph, Jane. From Quarks to Quasars: A Tour of the Universe. Hiscock, Bruce, illus. LC 86-17276. 224p. (gr. 7 up). 1987. 16.95 (ISBN 0-689-31270-9, Atheneum Child Bk). Macmillan Child Grp.

QUASI-STELLAR RADIO SOURCES

see Quasars

QUEBEC, BATTLE OF, 1759

Ochoa, George. The Fall of Quebec & the French & Indian War. (Illus.). 64p. 1990. lib. bdg. 16.98 (ISBN 0-382-09954-0); pap. 7.95 (ISBN 0-382-09950-8). Silver Burdett Pr.

QUEBEC (PROVINCE)

LeVert, Suzanne. Quebec. Berton, Pierre, intro. by. (Illus.). 64p. (gr. 3 up). 1991. PLB 16.95 (ISBN 0-7910-1030-9). Chelsea Hse.

QUEBEC (PROVINCE)–FICTION

Mangin, Marie-France. Suzette & Nicholas & the Seasons Clock. Ichikawa, Satomi, illus. 32p. (ps-k). 1982. 8.95 (ISBN 0-399-20832-1, Philomel). Putnam Pub Group.

QUEENS

see also Kings and Rulers;
also names of countries with the subdivision Kings and Rulers (e.g. Great Britain–Kings and Rulers;); and names of queens, e.g. Elizabeth 2nd, Queen of Great Britain

QUERIES

see Questions and Answers

QUESTIONS AND ANSWERS

Adler, David. All about the Moon. Burns, Raymond, illus. LC 82-17422. 32p. (gr. 3-6). 1983. PLB 10.59 (ISBN 0-89375-886-8); pap. text ed. 2.95 (ISBN 0-89375-887-6). Troll Assocs.
—Amazing Magnets. Lawler, Dan, illus. LC 82-17377. 32p. (gr. 3-6). 1983. PLB 10.59 (ISBN 0-89375-894-9); pap. text ed. 2.95 (ISBN 0-89375-895-7). Troll Assocs.
Alden, Laura. When. Axeman, Lois, illus. LC 83-7305. 32p. (gr. k-2). 1983. 12.60 (ISBN 0-516-06592-0); pap. 3.95 (ISBN 0-516-46592-9). Childrens.
Amazing Book of Quizzes. 1990. 3.99 (ISBN 0-517-69193-0). Outlet Bk Co.
Ardley, Bridget & Ardley, Neil. The Random House Book of 1001 Questions & Answers. LC 88-23200. (Illus.). 176p. (Orig.). (gr. 3-7). 1989. PLB 12.99 (ISBN 0-394-99992-4); pap. 12.95 (ISBN 0-394-89992-X). Random.
Arvetis, Chris & Palmer, Carole. Why Is the Grass Green? LC 85-60558. 32p. (ps-3). 1985. write for info. (ISBN 0-528-82670-0). Checkerboard Pr.
Barish, Wendy, ed. The Simon & Schuster Color Illustrated Question & Answer Book: What Is It? (Illus.). 128p. (gr. 8-12). 1984. Repr. of 1984 ed. text ed. 8.95 (ISBN 0-685-09144-9, Little Simon). S&S Trade.
Branley, Franklyn M. Gravity Is a Mystery. rev. ed. Madden, Don, illus. LC 85-48247. 32p. (ps-3). 1986. pap. 4.50 (ISBN 0-06-445057-0, Trophy). HarpC Child Bks.
Campbell, John P. Campbell's Middle School Quiz Book No. 1. 326p. (Orig.). (gr. 5-8). 1985. pap. 13.95x (ISBN 0-9609412-4-X). Patricks Pr.
—Campbell's Potpourri III of Quiz Bowl Questions. 288p. (Orig.). (gr. 7-12). 1985. pap. 13.95x (ISBN 0-9609412-5-8). Patricks Pr.
Clark, Roberta. Why? Axeman, Lois, illus. LC 83-7306. 32p. (gr. k-2). 1983. 12.60 (ISBN 0-516-06594-7); pap. 3.95 (ISBN 0-516-46594-5). Childrens.
Cohen, Daniel. The Simon & Schuster Question & Answer Book: Computers. (gr. 9-12). 1983. lib. bdg. 9.29 (ISBN 0-671-49750-2). S&S Trade.
Dickinson, Jane. All about Trees. D'Adamo, Anthony, illus. LC 82-17382. 32p. (gr. 3-6). 1983. PLB 10.59 (ISBN 0-89375-892-2); pap. text ed. 2.95 (ISBN 0-89375-893-0). Troll Assocs.
Duffy, Robert. Children's Quiz Book. 132p. 1988. pap. 5.95 (ISBN 1-85371-020-2, Pub. by Poolbeg Pr UK). Dufour.
Eichel, C. & Sanders, E. Question Collection. (gr. 4 up). 1988. 7.95 (ISBN 0-88160-153-5, LW 271). Learning Wks.
Elting, Mary & Wyler, Rose. The Answer Book about You. Tallarico, Tony, illus. 1980. 6.95 (ISBN 0-448-16566-X, G&D). Putnam Pub Group.
Firth, Lesley, ed. When Did It Happen. (Illus.). 128p. (gr. 3-7). 1986. pap. 8.95 (ISBN 0-671-60426-0, Little Simon); pap. 7.95 (ISBN 0-671-72497-5). S&S Trade.
Ganeri, Anita. Animal Babies. Taylor, Kate, illus. 32p. (ps-1). Date not set. 6.95 (ISBN 0-8120-6241-8). Barron.
—Animal Movements. Taylor, Kate, illus. 32p. (ps-1). Date not set. 6.95 (ISBN 0-8120-6238-8). Barron.
—Animal Talk. Taylor, Kate, illus. 32p. (ps-1). Date not set. 6.95 (ISBN 0-8120-6239-6). Barron.
Giddis, Diane. Name the Seven Dwarfs: And Other Numerical Diversions. Ladenheim-Gil, Randy, ed. LC 90-6083. 224p. 1990. 15.95 (ISBN 0-688-09388-4). Morrow.
Graham, Lawrence & Graham, Betty J. The Teenager's Ask & Answer Book. LC 86-702. 160p. (gr. 7 up). 1986. lib. bdg. 11.29 (ISBN 0-671-60167-9). Messner.
Greeley, Valerie. Where's My Share? Greeley, Valerie, illus. LC 89-13299. 32p. (ps-1). 1990. 11.95 (ISBN 0-02-736761-4, Mcmillan Child Bk). Macmillan Child Grp.
Greene, Constance C. Ask Anybody. 160p. (gr. k-6). 1984. pap. 2.75 (ISBN 0-440-40330-8, YB). Dell.
Guess What? (ps up). 1990. PLB 5.98 (ISBN 0-7924-5162-7, Mallard Pr). BDD Promo Bk.
Guess What. (Illus.). (ps-5). 3.50 (ISBN 0-7214-8005-5); wkbk. C 1.95. Ladybird Bks.
Guess Where? (ps up). 1990. PLB 5.98 (ISBN 0-7924-5163-5, Mallard Pr). BDD Promo Bk.
Guess Who? (ps up). 1990. PLB 5.98 (ISBN 0-7924-5164-3, Mallard Pr). BDD Promo Bk.
Guess Who? (ps up). 1990. PLB 5.98 (ISBN 0-7924-5165-1, Mallard Pr). BDD Promo Bk.
Hayes. Brain Twisters. (Illus.). 32p. (gr. 2-6). 1988. pap. 2.95 (ISBN 0-88625-149-4). Durkin Hayes Pub.
—Number Mysteries. (Illus.). 32p. (gr. 2-6). 1988. pap. 2.95 (ISBN 0-88625-145-1). Durkin Hayes Pub.
—Word Teasers. (Illus.). 32p. (gr. 2-6). 1988. pap. 2.95 (ISBN 0-88625-148-6). Durkin Hayes Pub.
How, Why, Where & When. (Illus.). 32p. (gr. k-4). 1985. 3.95 (ISBN 0-394-87695-4). Random.
Jefferies, Lawrence. Air, Air, Air. Johnson, Lewis, illus. LC 82-15808. 32p. (gr. 3-6). 1983. PLB 10.59 (ISBN 0-89375-880-9); pap. text ed. 2.95 (ISBN 0-89375-881-7). Troll Assocs.
—All about Stars. Veno, Joseph, illus. LC 82-20027. 32p. (gr. 3-6). PLB 10.59 (ISBN 0-89375-888-4); pap. text ed. 2.95 (ISBN 0-89375-889-2). Troll Assocs.
—Amazing World of Animals. D'Adamo, Anthony, illus. LC 82-20061. 32p. (gr. 3-6). 1983. PLB 10.59 (ISBN 0-89375-898-1); pap. text ed. 2.95 (ISBN 0-89375-899-X). Troll Assocs.
The Julian Messner Color Illustrated Question & Answer Book: What Is It? 1984. pap. 8.95 (ISBN 0-685-09674-2, Little Simon). S&S Trade.
Knight, David C. All about Sound. Johnson, Lewis, illus. LC 82-17387. 32p. (gr. 3-6). 1983. PLB 10.59 (ISBN 0-89375-878-7); pap. text ed. 2.95 (ISBN 0-89375-879-5). Troll Assocs.
Lahey, Richard. Quiz Bowl I. Sellers, Marci, illus. 56p. (Orig.). (gr. 4-12). 1982. tchr's. manual 6.95 (ISBN 0-88047-012-7, 8216). DOK Pubs.
—Quiz Bowl II. Sellers, Marci, illus. 56p. (Orig.). (gr. 4-12). 1984. 6.95 (ISBN 0-88047-037-2, 8408). DOK Pubs.
Leokum, Arkady. Still More Tell Me Why. Koehler, Cynthia & Koehler, Alvin, illus. (gr. k-6). 1968. 9.95 (ISBN 0-448-04458-7, G&D). Putnam Pub Group.
—Tell Me Why. rev. ed. (Illus.). 208p. (gr. 2-9). 1986. No. 1. 9.95 ea. (ISBN 0-448-22501-8, G&D). No. 2 (ISBN 0-448-22502-6). No. 3 (ISBN 0-448-22503-4). No. 4 (ISBN 0-448-22504-2). Putnam Pub Group.
—Tell Me Why, No. 5. (Illus.). 176p. (gr. 2-9). 1988. 9.95 (ISBN 0-448-19069-9, G&D). Putnam Pub Group.
Marsh, Carole. Autumn: Silly Trivia. Marsh, Carole, illus. (Orig.). (gr. 2-9). 1986. 19.95 (ISBN 1-55609-274-1); pap. 14.95 (ISBN 0-685-14606-5). Gallopade Pub Group.
—The Crazy Comet Silly Trivia Book. (Illus.). 60p. (Orig.). (gr. 2-12). 1985. pap. 14.95 (ISBN 0-935326-64-2). Gallopade Pub Group.
—Dinosaur Trivia for Kids: I'm Saury! (Illus., Orig.). (gr. 2 up). 1986. PLB 19.95 (ISBN 1-55609-162-1); pap. 14.95 (ISBN 0-935326-54-5). Gallopade Pub Group.
—Quiz Bowl Crash Course. (gr. 5 up). 1989. 19.95 (ISBN 1-55609-288-1); pap. 14.95 (ISBN 1-55609-195-8); computer disk 29.95 (ISBN 1-55609-289-X). Gallopade Pub Group.
—The Secret of Somerset Place S. P. A. R. K. Kit. (Illus., Orig.). (gr. 3-9). 1986. pap. 24.95 (ISBN 0-935326-20-0). Gallopade Pub Group.
—Tyrannosaurus & Other Wrecks: Fossil Trivia for Kids. (Illus., Orig.). (gr. 2 up). 1986. 19.95 (ISBN 1-55609-166-4); pap. 14.95 (ISBN 0-935326-56-1). Gallopade Pub Group.
Maynard, Christopher. War Vehicles. LC 79-5063. (Illus.). 36p. (gr. 3-6). 1980. PLB 9.95 (ISBN 0-8225-1185-1). Lerner Pubns.
Minn, Loretta B. Trek for Trivia. Jurgens, Steve, illus. 48p. (gr. 3-8). 1985. wkbk. 6.95 (ISBN 0-86653-291-9, GA 646). Good Apple.
Moncure, Jane B. How? LC 83-18974. (Illus.). 32p. (gr. k-2). 1984. PLB 12.60 (ISBN 0-516-06595-5); pap. 3.95 (ISBN 0-516-46595-3). Childrens.
—Who? Axeman, Lois, illus. LC 83-19025. 32p. (gr. k-2). 1984. pap. 3.95 (ISBN 0-516-46596-1). Childrens.
OWL Magazine Editors. The Kids' Question & Answer Book. (Illus.). 80p. (gr. 3-7). 1988. 9.95 (ISBN 0-448-19221-7, G&D). Putnam Pub Group.
OWL Magazine Editors Staff. The Kids' Question & Answer Book Two. (Illus.). 80p. (gr. 3-7). 1988. 9.95 (ISBN 0-448-09276-X, G&D). Putnam Pub Group.
Packard, Mary. My First Answer Book. Allert, Kathy, illus. (ps-5). 1984. pap. 7.95 (ISBN 0-671-49312-4, Little Simon). S&S Trade.
Pansini, Anna, ed. Great Answer Book. Kinnealy, Janice, illus. LC 90-44452. 48p. (gr. 3-6). 1991. PLB 10.89 (ISBN 0-8167-2308-7); pap. text ed. 2.95 (ISBN 0-8167-2309-5). Troll Assocs.
—I Wonder Why. Barto, Renzo, illus. LC 90-44455. 48p. (gr. k-2). 1990. PLB 10.89 (ISBN 0-8167-2304-4); pap. text ed. 2.95 (ISBN 0-8167-2305-2). Troll Assocs.
—Kids' Question & Answer Book. Barto, Renzo, illus. LC 90-43969. 48p. (gr. 2-4). 1990. PLB 10.89 (ISBN 0-8167-2306-0); pap. text ed. 2.95 (ISBN 0-8167-2307-9). Troll Assocs.
Phillips, Louis. Celebrity Quiz. Schwartz, Betty, ed. 64p. (gr. 3-7). 1984. pap. 2.95 (ISBN 0-671-44921-4, Little Simon). S&S Trade.
—How Do You Get a Horse Out of the Bathtub? Profound Answers to Preposterous Questions. Stevenson, James, illus. 80p. (gr. 1 up). 1983. pap. 10. 95 (ISBN 0-670-38119-5). Viking Child Bks.
—Two Hundred Sixty-Three Brain Busters: Just How Smart Are You, Anyway? Stevenson, James, illus. LC 85-40444. 87p. (gr. 4-7). 1985. pap. 10.95 (ISBN 0-670-80412-6). Viking Child Bks.
Quinsey, Mary Beth. Why Does That Man Have Such a Big Nose? Chan, Wilson, illus. LC 85-63760. 32p. (Orig.). (ps-1). 1986. lib. bdg. 14.95 (ISBN 0-943990-25-4); pap. 4.95 (ISBN 0-943990-24-6). Parenting Pr.
Reece, Colleen L. What? Axeman, Lois, illus. LC 83-7308. 32p. (gr. k-2). 1983. 12.60 (ISBN 0-516-06591-2); pap. 3.95 (ISBN 0-516-46591-0). Childrens.
Richardson, Joy. What Happens When..., 12 vols. (Illus.). (gr. 2-3). 1986. Set. PLB 131.40 (ISBN 1-55532-122-4). Gareth Stevens Inc.
Rolde, Neil. So You Think You Know Maine. LC 84-47758. (Illus.). 216p. (Orig.). (gr. 6-12). 1984. pap. 13. 95 (ISBN 0-88448-025-9). Tilbury Hse.
Ruben, Patrica. True or False? LC 77-25285. (Illus.). 32p. (gr. k-3). 1978. (Lipp Jr Bks); pap. 3.50 (ISBN 0-397-31802-2). HarpC Child Bks.

Schulz, Charles M. Charlie Brown's Fifth Super Book of Questions & Answers: About All Kinds of Things & How They Work! Schulz, Charles M., illus. LC 79-28441. 160p. (gr. 3-6). 1981. Random.
Schwartz, L. Junior Question Collection. (gr. 1-6). 1988. 7.95 (ISBN 0-88160-169-1, LW 279). Learning Wks.
—Trivia Trackdown - Animals & Science. (gr. 4-6). 1985. 3.95 (ISBN 0-88160-119-5, LW 252). Learning Wks.
—Trivia Trackdown - Social Studies & Famous People. (gr. 4-6). 1985. 3.95 (ISBN 0-88160-120-9, LW 253). Learning Wks.
Simon, Seymour. The Dinosaur Is the Biggest Animal That Ever Lived & Other Wrong Ideas You Thought Were True. Maestro, Giulio, illus. LC 83-48960. 64p. (gr. 2-5). 1984. 12.95 (ISBN 0-397-32075-2, Lipp Jr Bks); PLB 12.89 (ISBN 0-397-32076-0, Lipp Jr Bks). HarpC Child Bks.
—The Dinosaur Is the Biggest Animal That Ever Lived, & Other Wrong Ideas You Thought Were True. Maestro, Giulio, illus. LC 83-48960. 64p. (gr. 2-5). 1986. pap. 3.95 (ISBN 0-06-446053-3, Trophy). HarpC Child Bks.
Souter, John C. Trivia. 96p. (gr. 8-12). 1984. 4.95 (ISBN 0-8423-7338-1). Tyndale.
Stanish, Bob. Mindglow. Stanish, Jon, illus. 96p. (gr. 3-12). 1986. wkbk. 9.95 (ISBN 0-86653-346-X, GA 693). Good Apple.
Trivia Fun & Games. (Illus.). 32p. (gr. 4 up). 1985. 3.95 (ISBN 0-394-87694-6). Random.
Tunney, Christopher. Aircraft. LC 79-64384. (Illus.). 36p. (gr. 3-6). 1980. PLB 9.95 (ISBN 0-8225-1176-2). Lerner Pubns.
What Is It? (gr. 1 up). 1984. pap. 11.95 (ISBN 0-671-53129-8, Little Simon). S&S Trade.
Willis, William M. The Children's Question Book: A Parent Teacher Guide. LC 81-83727. 115p. (Orig.). (gr. 1 up). 1981. pap. text ed. 7.95 (ISBN 0-9607028-1-4). Ocean East.
Woolger, David. Who Do You Think You Are? (Illus.). 128p. (gr. 6 up). 1990. jacketed 16.95 (ISBN 0-19-276074-2). Oxford U Pr.

QUILTS
see Coverlets

QUIZ BOOKS
see Questions and Answers

QUOTATIONS
see also Proverbs

Alvarez del Real, Maria E., ed. Frases Celebres De Todos los Tiempos. (SPA., Illus.). 336p. (Orig.). 1988. pap. 4.00x (ISBN 0-944499-40-6). Editorial Amer.
Lawson, Robert. Watchwords of Liberty: A Pageant of American Quotations. Lawson, Robert, illus. 117p. (gr. 4 up). 1986. pap. 7.95 (ISBN 0-316-51754-2). Little.

R

RABBIS

Elkins, Dov P. God's Warriors: Dramatic Adventures of Rabbis in Uniform. LC 74-226. (Illus.). 92p. (gr. 5 up). 1974. 7.95 (ISBN 0-8246-0168-8). Jonathan David.
Goldman, Alex J. The Greatest Rabbis Hall of Fame. (gr. 7 up). 1987. 14.95 (ISBN 0-933503-11-3); pap. 7.95 (ISBN 0-933503-14-8). Shapolsky Pubs.
Karlenstein, Tzira. Reb Aryeh: A Portrait of the Jerusalem Tzaddik Reb Aryeh Levin. (Illus.). (gr. 4-7). 1989. 11.95 (ISBN 0-87306-490-9). Feldheim.
Piontac, Nechemiah. The Arizal: The Life & Times of Rabbi Yitzchak Luria. Weinbach, Shaindel, tr. from HEB. Bardugo, Miriam, illus. 288p. (gr. 5-12). 1988. 12.95 (ISBN 0-89906-835-9); pap. 9.95 (ISBN 0-89906-836-7). Mesorah Pubns.
Rabbi Mindy Avra Portnoy. Ima on the Bima: My Mommy Is a Rabbi. Rubin, Steffi, illus. LC 86-3023. 32p. (ps-4). 1986. 10.95 (ISBN 0-930494-55-5); pap. 4.95 (ISBN 0-930494-54-7). Kar Ben.

RABBIS–VOCATIONAL GUIDANCE

Gottschalk, Alfred. To Learn & to Teach Your Life as a Rabbi. (Illus.). (gr. 7-12). 1988. lib. bdg. 12.95 (ISBN 0-8239-0700-7). Rosen Group.

RABBITS

Animal Answers: Rabbits. (ps up). 1989. PLB 3.98 (ISBN 0-7924-5121-X, Mallard Pr). BDD Promo Bk.
Barrett, Norman. Rabbits. (Illus.). 32p. (gr. k-4). 1990. PLB 11.40 (ISBN 0-531-14033-4). Watts.
Brown, Margaret W. The Runaway Bunny. Hurd, Clement, illus. LC 71-183168. 40p. (ps-2). 1942. 11.95 (ISBN 0-06-020765-5); PLB 10.89 (ISBN 0-06-020766-3). HarpC Child Bks.
Bunnies. (Illus.). 7p. (ps-1). 1975. 2.50 (ISBN 0-448-09737-0, G&D). Putnam Pub Group.
Bunnies & Rabbits. (Illus.). 32p. (ps-1). 1986. pap. 1.25 (ISBN 0-8431-1520-3). Price Stern.
Burton, Jane. Freckles the Rabbit. Taylor, Kim, illus. LC 89-11396. 32p. (gr. k-3). 1989. PLB 10.95 (ISBN 0-8368-0208-X). Gareth Stevens Inc.
Coldrey, Jennifer. The Rabbit in the Fields. LC 85-30298. (Illus.). 32p. (gr. 4-6). 1987. 10.95 (ISBN 1-55532-061-9). Gareth Stevens Inc.
—The World of Rabbits. LC 85-28988. (Illus.). 32p. (gr. 2-3). 1986. 10.95 (ISBN 1-55532-064-3). Gareth Stevens Inc.
Drenchko, John D. A True Story about Button. 1989. 6.95 (ISBN 0-533-07972-1). Vantage.
Dunn, Judy. The Little Rabbit. Dunn, Phoebe, illus. LC 79-5241. 32p. (ps). 1980. lib. bdg. 5.99 (ISBN 0-394-94377-5, Random Juv); pap. 2.25 (ISBN 0-394-84377-0). Random.
Green, Carl R. & Sanford, William R. The Rabbit. LC 88-9601. (Illus.). 48p. (gr. 5-6). 1988. PLB 10.95 (ISBN 0-89686-387-5, Crestwood Hse). Macmillan Child Grp.
Hearne, T. Rabbits. (Illus.). 32p. (gr. 2-5). 1989. lib. bdg. 14.00 (ISBN 0-86625-187-1). Rourke Corp.
Henrie, Fiona. Rabbits. (gr. 2-5). 1980. PLB 10.90 (ISBN 0-531-04122-0, G10). Watts.
Hoban, Tana. Where Is It? LC 73-8573. (Illus.). 32p. (ps-1). 1974. 12.95 (ISBN 0-02-744070-2, Mcmillan Child Bk). Macmillan Child Grp.
Jewell, Nancy. The Snuggle Bunny. Chalmers, Mary, illus. LC 73-183171. 32p. (ps-3). 1972. 11.95 (ISBN 0-06-022833-4). HarpC Child Bks.
Komoda, Beverly. The Too Hot Day. Komoda, Beverly, illus. LC 90-1620. 32p. (ps-1). 1991. 14.95 (ISBN 0-06-021611-5); PLB 14.89 (ISBN 0-06-021612-3). HarpC Child Bks.
McCue, Lisa, illus. Bunnies Love. LC 90-61307. 24p. (ps-1). 1991. 4.95 (ISBN 0-679-80385-8). Random.
Mangas, Brian. A Nice Surprise for Father Rabbit. Levitt, Sidney, illus. 32p. (ps-1). 1991. pap. 2.25 (ISBN 0-671-73277-3, Little Simon). S&S Trade.
Mathews, Louise. Bunches & Bunches of Bunnies. Bassett, Jeni, illus. 32p. (gr. k-3). 1978. 10.95 (ISBN 0-396-07601-7, Putnam). Putnam Pub Group.
Moncure, Jane B. Rabbits' Habits. Peltier, Pam, illus. LC 87-12841. 32p. (ps-2). 1987. PLB 11.97 (ISBN 0-89565-406-7); pap. 6.96 (ISBN 0-89565-450-4). Childs World.
Peet, Bill. Huge Harold. (Illus.). 48p. (gr. k-3). 1974. 13.95 (ISBN 0-395-18449-5). HM.
Petty, Kate. Rabbits. Thompson, George, illus. LC 89-50456. 32p. (gr. k-2). 1989. PLB 10.40 (ISBN 0-531-17160-4, Gloucester Pr). Watts.
Pope, Joyce. Taking Care of Your Rabbit. (Illus.). 32p. (gr. 4-6). 1990. PLB 10.90 (ISBN 0-531-10189-4); pap. 3.95 (ISBN 0-531-15171-9). Watts.
Porter, Keith. Discovering Rabbits & Hares. (Illus.). (gr. 4-9). 1986. PLB 11.90 (ISBN 0-531-18054-9, Pub. by Bookwright). Watts.
Potter, Beatrix. The Tale of Peter Rabbit. Potter, Beatrix, illus. 24p. (ps-2). Date not set. incl. cassette 5.98 (ISBN 1-55886-055-X). Smarty Pants.
Pouyanne. Hare, Reading Level 3-4. (Illus.). 28p. (gr. 2-5). Date not set. PLB 14.60 (ISBN 0-86592-853-3). Rourke Corp.
Rabbit. 1990. 2.95 (ISBN 0-8378-2052-9). Gibson.
Rabbit Raising. (Illus.). 32p. (gr. 6-12). 1974. pap. 1.85 (ISBN 0-8395-3375-6, 3375). BSA.
Riehecky, Janet. Saving the Forests: A Rabbit's Story. Hohag, Linda, illus. LC 89-28122. 32p. (ps-2). 1990. lib. bdg. 11.97 (ISBN 0-89565-561-6). Childs World.
Snell, Nigel. Sam's Rabbit. Snell, Nigel, illus. 32p. 1989. 4.95 (ISBN 0-8120-6123-3). Barron.
Sproule, Anna & Sproule, Michael. Rabbits. Caulkins, Janet, ed. (Illus.). 48p. (gr. 1-6). 1988. PLB 11.90 (ISBN 0-531-18217-7, Pub. by Bookwright Pr). Watts.
Steinberg, Phil. You & Your Pet: Rodents & Rabbits. Cummings, Christine, illus. LC 78-54365. 64p. (gr. 4 up). 1979. PLB 6.95 (ISBN 0-8225-1256-4). Lerner Pubns.
Vernier, Louise. Your First Rabbit. (Illus.). 36p. (Orig.). 1991. pap. 1.95 (ISBN 0-86622-071-2, YF-114). TFH Pubns.
Vrbova, Zuza. Rabbits. McAulay, Robert, illus. 48p. 1990. PLB 9.95 (ISBN 0-86622-550-1, J-001). TFH Pubns.
Watson, Carol. If You Were a Rabbit. Cony, Frances, illus. 24p. (ps-2). 1990. 1.95 (ISBN 1-878624-24-5, 1553800024). McClanahan Bk.
Williams, Margery. The Velveteen Rabbit: Or, How Toys Become Real. Hague, Michael, illus. LC 82-15606. 48p. (gr. k-2). 1983. 11.95 (ISBN 0-8050-0209-X). H Holt & Co.
York, Carol B. Rabbit Magic. 128p. (gr. 2-5). 1991. pap. 2.50 (ISBN 0-590-43894-8). Scholastic Inc.
Zolotow, Charlotte. The Bunny Who Found Easter. Peterson, Betty F., illus. 32p. (gr. k-3). 1983. 13.95 (ISBN 0-395-27677-2); pap. 4.95 (ISBN 0-395-34068-3). HM.

RABBITS–FICTION

Aardema, Verna. Rabbit Makes a Monkey of Lion. Pinkney, Jerry, illus. LC 86-11523. 32p. (ps-3). 1989. 11.95 (ISBN 0-8037-0297-3); PLB 11.89 (ISBN 0-8037-0298-1). Dial Bks Young.
Aardema, Verna, retold by. Who's in Rabbit's House? Dillon, Leo & Dillon, Diane, illus. LC 77-71514. 32p. (gr. k-3). 1977. 14.95 (ISBN 0-8037-9550-5); PLB 14.89 (ISBN 0-8037-9551-3). Dial Bks Young.
—Who's in Rabbit's House? Dillon, Leo & Dillon, Diane, illus. LC 77-71514. 32p. (ps-3). 1979. pap. 4.95 (ISBN 0-8037-9549-1). Dial Bks Young.
Adams, Adrienne. The Easter Egg Artists. Adams, Adrienne, illus. LC 90-1097. 32p. (gr. k-3). 1991. pap. 4.95 (ISBN 0-689-71481-5, Aladdin). Macmillan Child Grp.
—The Great Valentine's Day Balloon Race. Adams, Adrienne, illus. LC 86-3382. 32p. (gr. k-3). 1986. pap. 4.95 (ISBN 0-689-71085-2, Aladdin). Macmillan Child Grp.
Addison-Wesley Staff. El Conejo la Tortuga - Big Book. (SPA., Illus.). 16p. (gr. k-3). 1989. pap. text ed. 31.75 (ISBN 0-201-19937-8). Addison-Wesley.
—El Conejo la Tortuga - Little Book. (SPA., Illus.). 16p. (gr. k-3). 1989. pap. text ed. 4.50 (ISBN 0-201-19709-X). Addison-Wesley.
—The Hare & the Tortoise Little Book. (Illus.). 16p. (gr. k-3). 1989. pap. text ed. 4.50 (ISBN 0-201-19365-5). Addison-Wesley.
Adler, David A. Bunny Rabbit Rebus. Linden, Madelaine G., illus. LC 82-45574. 40p. (gr. 1-4). 1983. (Crowell Jr Bks); PLB 10.89 (ISBN 0-690-04197-7, Crowell Jr Bks). HarpC Child Bks.
—Bunny Rabbit Rebus. Linden, Madelaine G., illus. (ps-3). 1987. pap. 3.95 (ISBN 0-14-050775-2, Puffin). Puffin Bks.
The Adventures of Jason Jackrabbit. LC 89-2164. 48p. (gr. k-4). 1990. 9.95 (ISBN 0-937460-60-5). Hendrick-Long.
Anderson, Lena. Bunny Bath. Anderson, Lena, illus. LC 89-63049. (ps-k). 1991. bds. 3.95 (ISBN 91-29-59652-1). R & S Books.
—Bunny Box. (Illus.). 20p. (ps). 1991. bds. 3.95 (ISBN 91-29-59858-3, Pub. by R&S Bks). FS&G.
—Bunny Fun. (Illus.). 20p. (ps). 1991. bds. 3.95 (ISBN 91-29-59860-5, Pub. by R&S Bks). FS&G.
—Bunny Surprise. Anderson, Lena, illus. LC 89-63050. (ps-k). 1991. bds. 3.95 (ISBN 91-29-59654-8). R & S Books.
Anderson, Lena, illus. Bunny Party. (ps). 1989. bds. 3.95 (ISBN 9-12-959134-1, Pub. by R & S Bks). FS&G.
—Bunny Story. (ps). 1989. bds. 3.95 (ISBN 9-12-959132-5, Pub. by R & S Bks). FS&G.
Baber, Frank, illus. The Adventures of Brer Rabbit. Spriggs, Ruth, retold By. (Illus.). 96p. (ps-5). 1980. write for info. (ISBN 0-528-82300-0). Checkerboard Pr.
Bailey, Carolyn S. The Little Rabbit Who Wanted Red Wings. Santoro, Chris, illus. 32p. (ps-1). 1988. pap. 1.95 (ISBN 0-448-19089-3, Platt & Munk); write for info. bk. & case (ISBN 0-448-19093-1, Platt & Munk). Putnam Pub Group.
Ballman, Wanda. Jack the Jack Rabbit. (Illus.). 16p. (gr. k-4). 1991. 2.95 (ISBN 0-8059-3178-3). Dorrance.
Bate, Lucy. Little Rabbit's Loose Tooth. De Groat, Diane, illus. LC 75-6833. 32p. (gr. k-3). 1988. PLB 13.95 (ISBN 0-517-52240-3); pap. 3.95 (ISBN 0-517-55122-5). Crown.
Becker, John. Seven Little Rabbits. Cooney, Barbarba, illus. 32p. (ps-2). 1985. pap. 3.95 (ISBN 0-590-41197-7, Blue Ribbon Bks.); incl. cassette 6.95 (ISBN 0-590-63196-9). Scholastic Inc.
Bergstrom, Gunilla. Is That a Monster, Alfie Atkins? Swindells, Robert, tr. (Illus.). 28p. (ps up). 1989. 6.95 (ISBN 9-12-959136-8, Pub. by R & S Bks). FS&G.
Berry, Gail. Barry Bundy & the Honest Pie. Gartner, Kate, illus. 1989. 5.95 (ISBN 0-533-07735-4). Vantage.
Billam, Rosemary. Fuzzy Rabbit. Julian-Ottie, Vanessa, illus. LC 83-17637. 32p. (ps-3). 1984. (Random Juv); pap. 2.25 (ISBN 0-394-86346-1). Random.
—Fuzzy Rabbit in the Park. Julian-Ottie, Vanessa, illus. LC 85-10794. 32p. (ps-3). 1986. pap. 1.95 (ISBN 0-394-87863-9). Random.
Billy the Brave Bunny. 1988. 2.99 (ISBN 0-517-66780-0). Crown.
Binford, Dale. Rabbits Can't Dance! Binford, Dale, illus. LC 89-42640. 24p. (gr. 1-2). 1989. PLB 12.95 (ISBN 0-8368-0106-7). Gareth Stevens Inc.
Blau, Judith. Bunny Mitten's Book. Blau, Judith, illus. 7p. (ps). 1991. incl. puppet 5.95 (ISBN 0-679-81315-2). Random.
Boujon, Claude. Bon Appetit, Mr. Rabbit. Boujon, Claude, illus. LC 87-4199. 32p. (gr. k-3). 1987. 12.95 (ISBN 0-689-50425-X, M K McElderry). Macmillan Child Grp.
Bracken, Carolyn, illus. Bunny. 6p. (ps-k). 1981. cloth ed. 2.50 (ISBN 0-671-42531-5, Little Simon). S&S Trade.
Brambledown: Blackberry Bunny. 1990. 3.98 (ISBN 0-8317-0971-5). Smithmark.
Br'er Rabbit & the Briar Patch. 1989. 5.98 (ISBN 0-685-28324-0, Mallard Pr). BDD Promo Bk.
Brickey, Louise. Pouche: The Assistant to the Easter Bunny. rev. ed. (Illus.). 36p. (gr. k-3). 1989. Repr. of 1987 ed. write for info. Cottontail Creations.
Brown, Cathy J. & Paterson, Debi. Bouncy Bunny's Birthday: A Family Story about Bravery. Adams, Kathy R., illus. LC 86-61065. 32p. (Orig.). (gr. 1-3). 1985. pap. 8.75 (ISBN 0-9614796-0-4). C J Brown.
—Bouncy Bunny's Birthday: A Family Story about Bravery. Adams, Kathy R., illus. 32p. (Orig.). (gr. 1-3). 1985. pap. 8.75 (ISBN 0-318-19386-8). Offset Hse.
Brown, Marc. The Bionic Bunny Show. Brown, Laurene K., illus. 32p. (ps-3). 1985. 14.95 (ISBN 0-316-11120-1, Joy St Bks); pap. 5.95 (ISBN 0-316-10992-4, Joy St Bks). Little.
—What Do You Call a Dumb Bunny? & Other Rabbit Riddles, Games, Jokes & Cartoons. Brown, Marc, illus. LC 82-21650. 32p. (ps-3). 1983. 12.95 (ISBN 0-316-11117-1, Joy St Bks); pap. 4.95 (ISBN 0-316-11119-8, Joy St Bks). Little.
Brown, Margaret W. Goodnight Moon. Hurd, Clement, illus. LC 47-30762. 36p. (ps-1). 1947. 10.95 (ISBN 0-06-020705-1); PLB 10.89 (ISBN 0-06-020706-X). HarpC Child Bks.
—Goodnight Moon. Hurd, Clement, illus. LC 47-30762. (ps-2). 1977. pap. 3.95 (ISBN 0-06-443017-0, Trophy). HarpC Child Bks.

—The Runaway Bunny. Hurd, Clement, illus. LC 71-183168. 40p. (ps-2). 1977. pap. 3.95 (ISBN 0-06-443018-9, Trophy). HarpC Child Bks.

—The Runaway Bunny. Hurd, Clement, illus. (gr. k-3). 1985. incl. cassette 19.95 (ISBN 0-941078-78-7); pap. 12.95 incl. cassette (ISBN 0-941078-76-0); cassette, 4 paperbacks & guide 27.95 (ISBN 0-941078-77-9). Live Oak Media.

Bugs Bunny & Friends. 1990. Boxed set. write for info. (ISBN 0-307-15538-2). Western Pub.

Bugs Bunny Stories. 1990. pap. write for info. (ISBN 0-307-15827-6, Golden Pr). Western Pub.

Burgess, Thornton. The Adventures of Peter Cottontail. (Illus.). (ps-8). 1990. Repr. lib. bdg. 18.95x (ISBN 0-89966-664-7). Buccaneer Bks.

Burningham, John. The Rabbit. LC 75-4566. (Illus.). (ps-1). 1975. PLB 11.89 (ISBN 0-690-00907-0, Crowell Jr Bks). HarpC Child Bks.

Caitlin, Stephen. Busy Bunnies. Mahan, Ben, illus. LC 87-10912. 32p. (gr. k-2). 1988. PLB 10.89 (ISBN 0-8167-1083-X); pap. text ed. 2.95 (ISBN 0-8167-1084-8). Troll Assocs.

Caldwell, Mary. Morning, Rabbit, Morning. Schweninger, Ann, illus. LC 81-47724. 32p. (ps-1). 1982. 10.95i (ISBN 0-06-020939-9). HarpC Child Bks.

Calmenson, Stephanie. Wanted: Warm, Furry Friend. Schwartz, Amy, illus. LC 88-13405. 32p. (gr. k-3). 1990. 13.95 (ISBN 0-02-716390-3, Mcmillan Child Bk). Macmillan Child Grp.

Carlson, Nancy. Bunnies & Their Hobbies. Carlson, Nancy, illus. LC 83-23161. 32p. (ps-3). 1984. PLB 9.95 (ISBN 0-87614-257-9). Carolrhoda Bks.

—Bunnies & Their Hobbies. LC 84-26458. (Illus.). 32p. (ps-3). 1985. pap. 3.95 (ISBN 0-14-050538-5, Puffin). Puffin Bks.

—Bunnies & Their Sports. LC 86-1337. (ps-3). 1987. pap. 11.95 (ISBN 0-670-81109-2). Viking Child Bks.

—Bunnies & Their Sports. (Illus.). 32p. (ps-3). 1989. pap. 3.95 (ISBN 0-14-050617-9, Puffin). Puffin Bks.

—Loudmouth George & the Big Race. Carlson, Nancy, illus. 32p. (ps-3). 1986. pap. 3.95 (ISBN 0-14-050516-4, Puffin). Puffin Bks.

Cartlidge, Michelle. Little Bunny's Picnic. 1990. 9.95 (ISBN 0-525-44560-9, DCB). Dutton Child Bks.

Castle, Caroline, retold by. Hare & the Tortoise. Weevers, Peter, illus. LC 84-9569. 32p. (ps-3). 1987. pap. 4.95 (ISBN 0-8037-0147-0). Dial Bks Young.

Christelow, Eileen. Henry & the Dragon. Christelow, Eileen, illus. LC 83-14405. 32p. (ps-2). 1984. 13.95 (ISBN 0-89919-220-3, Clarion). HM.

Cleveland, David. The April Rabbits. Karlin, Nurit, illus. 32p. (gr. k-3). 1988. pap. 2.25 (ISBN 0-590-41288-4). Scholastic Inc.

—The April Rabbits. Karlin, Nurit, illus. 32p. (gr. k-3). 1986. pap. 2.50 (ISBN 0-590-42369-X). Scholastic Inc.

Cloke, Rene. Br'er Rabbit Stories. 1988. 2.98 (ISBN 0-671-06187-9). S&S Trade.

Colmenson, Stephenie. Hopscotch, the Tiny Bunny. Lanza, Barbara, illus. (ps-3). 1991. pap. 1.75 (ISBN 0-307-12617-X, Golden Pr). Western Pub.

Cook, Elizabeth, adapted by. Rabbit Who Overcame Fear: A Jataka Tale. Meller, Eric, illus. Tulku, Tarthang, intro. by. (Illus.). 32p. (Orig.). (gr. k-4). 1991. 12. 95 (ISBN 0-89800-212-5); pap. 5.95 (ISBN 0-89800-211-7). Dharma Pub. The latest in a series of children's stories drawn from the rich storytelling tradition of ancient India, China & Tibet, presented for the first time in large picture-book format. Stories in the Jataka Tales promote the values of compassion, peace, friendship, & kindness, opening the door for parent & child to discuss the importance of these issues. In this story, a young rabbit, startled from sleep by a loud noise & shaking, springs into flight in fear of an earthquake. His panic spreads, endangering other animals who follow his blind rush toward a cliff. They are saved by a compassionate lion who teaches them how to investigate the source of fear before jumping to unwise conclusions. An instructive tale told with warmth & humor. Vibrant color. Ages 3-8. Available in English, Portuguese, German, Dutch. Valuable for multicultural education, English as second language classes. Call Dharma Publishing, (800) 873-4276 for a free brochure of other books in this series. *Publisher Provided Annotation.*

Cooper, Helen. Ella & the Rabbit. Cooper, Helen, illus. LC 90-34499. 32p. (ps-3). 1990. 12.95 (ISBN 0-940793-62-8, Crocodile Bks). Interlink Pub.

Cornell, S. A. Flying Carrots. Jones, John, illus. LC 85-14093. 48p. (Orig.). (gr. 1-3). 1986. PLB 9.89 (ISBN 0-8167-0640-9); pap. text ed. 2.95 (ISBN 0-8167-0641-7). Troll Assocs.

Cosgrove, Stephen. Buttermilk. James, Robin, illus. 32p. (gr. 5-9). 1986. pap. 2.95 (ISBN 0-8431-1565-3). Price Stern.

—T.J. Flopp: From the Land of Barely There. Edelson, Wendy, illus. LC 89-9329. 32p. 1989. 9.95 (ISBN 0-88070-281-8). Multnomah.

Cosgrove, Stephen E. Derby Downs. Edelson, Wendy, illus. 32p. (ps-3). 1990. lib. bdg. 12.96 (ISBN 0-89565-659-0). Childs World.

Cousins, Lucy. What Can Rabbit Hear? LC 90-21212. (Illus.). 12p. 1991. 12.95 (ISBN 0-688-10455-X, Tambourine Bks). Morrow.

Crooks, Linda H., et al. Kindergang Kindergarten Skills Booklets, Featuring Ready Rabbit, Booklet 4. 2nd ed. Crooks, Linda H., illus. (gr. k). 1988. Repr. of 1985 ed. tchr's. ed. 9.19 (ISBN 1-877594-04-0); wkbk. 1.59 (ISBN 0-317-93577-1). I Can.

Crozat, Francois. I Am a Little Rabbit-Mini. 24p. (ps). 1990. 2.95 (ISBN 0-8120-6194-2). Barron.

Cry Bunny. 1989. text ed. 3.95 cased (ISBN 0-7214-5234-5). Ladybird Bks.

Dalmais, Anne-Marie. The Busy Day of Jack Rabbit. Percy, Graham, illus. 32p. (ps-3). 1990. 5.95 (ISBN 0-374-31004-1). FS&G.

Daniel, Kira. Habits of Rabbits. Croll, Carolyn, illus. LC 85-14122. 48p. (Orig.). (gr. 1-3). 1986. PLB 9.89 (ISBN 0-8167-0632-8); pap. text ed. 2.95 (ISBN 0-8167-0633-6). Troll Assocs.

DeJong, Meindert. Shadrach. Sendak, Maurice, illus. LC 53-5250. 192p. (gr. 3-6). 1953. PLB 14.89 (ISBN 0-06-021546-1). HarpC Child Bks.

—Shadrach. Sendak, Maurice, illus. LC 53-5250. 192p. (gr. 3-6). 1980. pap. 3.50 (ISBN 0-06-440115-4, Trophy). HarpC Child Bks.

Delton, Judy. Hired Help for Rabbit. McCue, Lisa, illus. LC 87-15254. 32p. (gr. k-3). 1988. 12.95 (ISBN 0-02-728470-0, Mcmillan Child Bk). Macmillan Child Grp.

—Rabbit Finds a Way. Lasker, Joe, illus. 32p. (ps-3). 1988. pap. 3.95 (ISBN 0-517-55948-X). Crown.

—Rabbit's New Rug. Brown, Marc, illus. LC 79-16639. 40p. (ps-3). 1980. 5.95 (ISBN 0-8193-1009-3); PLB 5.95 (ISBN 0-8193-1010-7). Parents.

Dickinson, Susan. Brer Rabbit & the Peanut Patch. rev. ed. Frankland, David, illus. 32p. (gr. k-2). 1990. Repr. of 1985 ed. PLB 9.45 (ISBN 1-878363-18-2). Forest Hse.

Disney. Br'er Rabbit & the Rabbit Patch. (ps up). 1990. PLB 5.98 (ISBN 0-7924-5055-8, Mallard Pr). BDD Promo Bk.

Dodge, Nancy C. Thumpy's Story: A Story of Love & Grief Shared. Veara, Kevin, illus. LC 84-61293. 24p. (gr. k-12). 1985. pap. 5.95 (ISBN 0-918533-00-7). Prairie Lark.

Eagle, Mike. The Marathon Rabbit. Eagle, Mike, illus. LC 84-27944. 48p. (gr. k-3). 1986. 12.95 (ISBN 0-03-004058-2). H Holt & Co.

The Easter Bunny's Helper. 1989. text ed. 3.95 cased (ISBN 0-7214-5233-7). Ladybird Bks.

Ehrlich, Amy. Bunnies All Day Long. Henry, Marie H., illus. LC 84-20031. 32p. (ps-2). 1989. 7.95 (ISBN 0-8037-0226-4); pap. 3.95 (ISBN 0-8037-0641-3). Dial Bks Young.

—Bunnies at Christmastime. Henry, Marie, illus. LC 86-2202. 32p. (ps-2). 1989. 11.95 (ISBN 0-8037-0321-X); pap. 3.95 (ISBN 0-8037-0702-9). Dial Bks Young.

Erlich, Amy. Bunnies & Their Grandma. Henry, Marie H., illus. LC 84-20030. 32p. (ps-2). 1989. pap. 3.95 (ISBN 0-8037-0640-5). Dial Bks Young.

Ernst, Lisa C. Miss Penny & Mr. Grubbs. Ernst, Lisa C., illus. LC 90-43175. 40p. (ps-2). 1991. RSBE 14.95 (ISBN 0-02-733563-1, Bradbury Pr). Macmillan Child Grp.

Everett, Louise. Bubble Gum in the Sky. Harvey, Paul, illus. LC 86-30859. 32p. (gr. k-2). 1988. PLB 7.06 (ISBN 0-8167-0998-X); pap. text ed. 1.95 (ISBN 0-8167-0999-8). Troll Assocs.

Feczko, Kathy. The Great Bunny Race. Jones, John, illus. LC 84-8634. 32p. (gr. k-2). 1985. PLB 10.89 (ISBN 0-8167-0357-4); pap. text ed. 2.95 (ISBN 0-8167-0437-6). Troll Assocs.

Fisher, Aileen. Listen, Rabbit. Shimin, Symeon, illus. LC 64-10860. 44p. (gr. k-3). 1964. PLB 12.89 (ISBN 0-690-49592-7, Crowell Jr Bks). HarpC Child Bks.

—Rabbits, Rabbits. Niemann, Gail, illus. LC 82-48849. 32p. (gr. k-3). 1983. 12.95i (ISBN 0-06-021896-7). HarpC Child Bks.

Frieze, A. & Potter, Beatrix. The Rabbit's Christmas Party. (Illus.). 1989. pap. 4.95 (ISBN 0-7232-3566-X). Warne.

Gackenbach, Dick. Hattie Be Quiet, Hattie Be Good. LC 76-58697. (Illus.). 32p. (ps-3). 1977. PLB 10.89 (ISBN 0-06-021952-1). HarpC Child Bks.

—Hattie Rabbit. LC 75-37018. (Illus.). 32p. (ps-3). 1976. PLB 10.89 (ISBN 0-06-021940-8). HarpC Child Bks.

—Hattie Rabbit. Gackenbach, Dick, illus. LC 75-37018. 32p. (ps-2). 1990. pap. 2.95 (ISBN 0-06-444133-4, Trophy). HarpC Child Bks.

—Mother Rabbit's Son Tom. LC 76-18399. (Illus.). 32p. (gr. k-3). 1977. PLB 9.89 (ISBN 0-06-021948-3). HarpC Child Bks.

Gag, Wanda. ABC Bunny. Gag, Wanda, illus. LC 33-27359. (gr. k-2). 1978. 8.95 (ISBN 0-698-20000-4, Coward); 6.99g (ISBN 0-698-30000-9, Coward); pap. 4.95 (ISBN 0-698-20465-4, Coward). Putnam Pub Group.

Giant Treasury of Peter Rabbit. (gr. k-6). 1985. 5.95 (ISBN 0-517-31687-0). Outlet Bk Co.

Giff, Patricia R. Monster Rabbit Runs. (gr. 4-7). 1991. pap. 2.95 (ISBN 0-440-40424-X). Dell.

Gikow, Louise. The Tale of the Bunny Picnic: A Jim Henson Picture Book. Hearn, Diane D., illus. (gr. k-3). 1987. pap. 12.95 (ISBN 0-590-40443-1, Scholastic Hardcover). Scholastic Inc.

Hall, Susan T. Bunny Tail. Hall, Susan T., illus. (ps-k). 1991. 4.95 (ISBN 0-307-12901-2, Golden Pr). Western Pub.

Hamley, Dennis. Hare's Choice. Rutherford, Meg, illus. (gr. 3-7). 1990. 13.95 (ISBN 0-385-30050-6). Doubleday.

Hardgrove, Nelle. Hurrah for Funny Bunny. Goodman, Joe, ed. (Illus.). 48p. 1987. pap. write for info. (ISBN 0-9619227-1-0). N A Hardegrove.

Harris, Joel C. Jump Again! More Adventures of Brer Rabbit. Moser, Barry, illus. & adapted by. 48p. (ps-3). 1987. 16.95 (ISBN 0-15-241352-9, HJ). HarBraceJ.

—Jump: The Adventures of Brer Rabbit. Parks, Van D. & Jones, Malcolm, eds. Goldberg, Whoopi, read by. LC 86-7654. (Illus.). 48p. (ps-3). 1986. incl. musical cassette 15.95 (ISBN 0-15-241350-2, HJ). HarBraceJ.

Hayward, Linda. Sunny Day Bunny. McQueen, Lucinda, illus. 12p. (ps-1). 1986. 5.95 (ISBN 0-448-10452-0, G&D). Putnam Pub Group.

Heyward, Du Bose. The Country Bunny & the Little Gold Shoes. Flack, Marjorie, illus. 48p. (gr. k-3). 1974. reinforced bdg. 13.95 (ISBN 0-395-15990-3); pap. 4.95 (ISBN 0-395-18557-2, Sandpiper). HM.

Heyward, DuBose. The Country Bunny & the Little Gold Shoes. Flack, Marjorie, illus. (ps-3). 1989. pap. 6.95 incl. cassette (ISBN 0-395-52140-8). HM.

Hopkins, Margo. Honey Rabbit. Szekeres, Cyndy, illus. 14p. (ps). 1982. write for info. (ISBN 0-307-12268-9, Golden Bks). Western Pub.

Houston, Julie. Too Many Bunnies. (Illus.). 24p. (gr. k-2). 1986. 1.95 (ISBN 0-87406-179-2, 23-14391-1). Willowisp Pr.

Howard, Katherine. Little Bunny Follows His Nose. Miller, J. P., illus. 32p. (ps-2). 1971. write for info. (ISBN 0-307-13536-5, Golden Bks.). Western Pub.

Howe, Deborah & Howe, James. Bunnicula: A Rabbit Tale of Mystery. Daniel, Alan, illus. LC 78-11472. 112p. (gr. 4-6). 1979. 12.95 (ISBN 0-689-30700-4, Atheneum Child Bk). Macmillan Child Grp.

—Bunnicula: A Rabbit-Tale of Mystery. Daniel, Alan, illus. 100p. (gr. 3-7). 1980. pap. 3.50 (ISBN 0-380-51094-4, Camelot). Avon.

Howe, James. The Celery Stalks at Midnight. Morrill, Leslie, illus. LC 83-2665. 128p. (gr. 4-6). 1983. 12.95 (ISBN 0-689-30987-2, Atheneum Child Bk). Macmillan Child Grp.

—The Celery Stalks at Midnight. Morrill, Leslie H., illus. 128p. (gr. 3-7). 1984. pap. 3.50 (ISBN 0-380-69054-3, 69054-3, Camelot). Avon.

Hunds, Hargrave, illus. Bunny Sees. 10p. (gr. k). 1985. 2.95 (ISBN 0-448-10577-2, G&D). Putnam Pub Group.

Huriet, Genevieve. Beechwood Bunny Tales Series. Jouannigot, Loic, illus. (gr. k-2). 1991. Set. lib. bdg. 51.80 (ISBN 0-8368-0359-0). Gareth Stevens Inc.

—Dandelion's Vanishing Vegetable Garden. Jouannigot, Loic, illus. LC 90-4857. 32p. (gr. k-2). 1991. lib. bdg. 12.95 (ISBN 0-8368-0526-7). Gareth Stevens Inc.

—Mistletoe & the Baobab Tree. Jouannigot, Loic, illus. LC 90-4856. 32p. (gr. k-2). 1991. lib. bdg. 12.95 (ISBN 0-8368-0527-5). Gareth Stevens Inc.

—Perriwinkle at the Full Moon Ball. Jouannigot, Loic, illus. LC 90-4859. 32p. (gr. k-2). 1991. lib. bdg. 12.95 (ISBN 0-8368-0525-9). Gareth Stevens Inc.

—Poppy's Dance. Jouannigot, Loic, illus. LC 90-4858. 32p. (gr. k-2). 1991. lib. bdg. 12.95 (ISBN 0-8368-0528-3). Gareth Stevens Inc.

Hynard, Stephen. Snowy the Rabbit: A Story about Colors. Thatcher, Francis, illus. LC 82-22108. 32p. (gr. k-3). 1983. PLB 15.93 (ISBN 0-516-08942-0). Childrens.

Jarrell, Randall. The Gingerbread Rabbit. Williams, Garth, illus. LC 63-16364. 56p. (gr. k-3). 1972. pap. 2.95 (ISBN 0-02-043900-8, Aladdin). Macmillan Child Grp.

Kaplan, Carol B. The Not-So-Fast Rabbit. Bolinske, Janet L., ed. Quenell, Midge, illus. LC 87-62997. 24p. (Orig.). (ps-k). 1988. 17.95 (ISBN 0-88335-755-0); pap. 4.95 (ISBN 0-88335-079-3). Milliken Pub Co.

Keller, Irene. Benjamin Rabbit & the Fire Chief. Keller, Dick, illus. 32p. (ps-k). 1990. pap. 3.95 (ISBN 0-8249-8447-1). Ideals.

—Benjamin Rabbit & the Stranger Danger. (Illus.). 32p. (gr. k-3). 1985. 8.95 (ISBN 0-396-08655-1, Putnam). Putnam Pub Group.

Kennedy, Pamela. A, B, C, Bunny. Kobobel, Janet, ed. Chartier, Normand, illus. 12p. (ps-k). 1990. bds. 3.99 (ISBN 0-929608-69-0). Focus Family.

—All Mine, Bunny. Kobobel, Janet, ed. Chartier, Normand, illus. 12p. (ps-k). 1990. bds. 3.99 (ISBN 0-929608-65-8). Focus Family.

—Night, Night, Bunny. Kobobel, Janet, ed. Chartier, Normand, illus. 12p. (ps-k). 1990. bds. 3.99 (ISBN 0-929608-70-4). Focus Family.

—Oh, Oh, Bunny. Kobobel, Janet, ed. Chartier, Normand, illus. 12p. (ps-k). 1990. bds. 3.99 (ISBN 0-929608-67-4). Focus Family.

—One, Two, Three, Bunny. Kobobel, Janet, ed. Chartier, Normand, illus. 12p. (ps-k). 1990. bds. 3.99 (ISBN 0-929608-68-2). Focus Family.

—Red, Yellow, Blue, Bunny. Kobobel, Janet, ed. Chartier, Normand, illus. 12p. (ps-k). 1990. bds. 3.99 (ISBN 0-929608-66-6). Focus Family.

Komoda, Beverly. The Winter Day. Komoda, Beverly, illus. LC 91-104. 32p. (ps-1). 1991. 13.95 (ISBN 0-06-023301-X); PLB 13.89 (ISBN 0-06-023302-8). HarpC Child Bks.

Koscielniak, Bruce. Euclid Bunny Delivers the Mail. Koscielniak, Bruce, illus. LC 90-4696. 40p. (ps-2). 1991. 13.95 (ISBN 0-679-81069-2); lib. bdg. 14.99 (ISBN 0-679-91069-7). Knopf.

Kraus, Robert. Daddy Long Ears. Kraus, Robert, illus. (ps-1). 1989. 4.95 (ISBN 0-671-67415-3). S&S Trade.

—Daddy Long Ears Christmas Surprise. 1989. pap. 4.95 (ISBN 0-671-68150-8). S&S Trade.

Kroll, Steven. The Big Bunny & the Magic Show. Stevens, Janet, illus. LC 85-14147. 32p. (ps-3). 1986. reinforced bdg. 14.95 (ISBN 0-8234-0589-3). Holiday.

—The Big Bunny & the Magic Show. Stevens, Janet, illus. 32p. (ps-2). 1987. pap. 3.95 (ISBN 0-590-44633-9). Scholastic Inc.

Kunhardt, Dorothy. Pat the Bunny. Kunhardt, Dorothy, illus. (ps). 1942. write for info. (ISBN 0-307-12000-7, Golden Bks). Western Pub.

Laird, Rebecca. Robinson Rabbit, What Do You Hear? Boddy, Joe, illus. LC 89-82550. 32p. (ps-k). 1990. pap. 4.95 (ISBN 0-8066-2463-9, 9-2463). Augsburg Fortress.

Lawhead, Stephen R. Brown Ears: The Adventures of a Lost & Found Rabbit. Heaney, Liz, ed. Fuller, Bob, illus. LC 88-33039. 90p. (ps-6). 1989. 9.95 (ISBN 0-88070-270-2). Multnomah.

Lawson, Robert. Rabbit Hill. (Illus.). (gr. 1-3). 1977. pap. 3.95 (ISBN 0-14-031010-X, Puffin). Puffin Bks.

—Robbut: A Tale of Tails. Lawson, Robert, illus. LC 89-32367. 94p. (gr. 2-6). 1989. Repr. of 1948 ed. lib. bdg. 14.50 (ISBN 0-208-02236-8, Linnet). Shoe String.

Leedy, Loreen. The Bunny Play. Leedy, Loreen, illus. LC 87-17793. 32p. (ps-2). 1988. reinforced bdg. 12.95 (ISBN 0-8234-0679-2). Holiday.

Lester, Julius. The Tales of Uncle Remus: The Adventures of Brer Rabbit, Vol. I. Pinckney, Jerry, illus. LC 85-20449. (ps up). 1987. 16.95 (ISBN 0-8037-0271-X); PLB 16.89 (ISBN 0-8037-0272-8). Dial Bks Young.

Le Tord, Bijou. Rabbit Seeds. Le Tord, Bijou, illus. LC 84-28736. (ps-2). 1984. 10.95 (ISBN 0-02-756420-7, Four Winds). Macmillan Child Grp.

Lewis, Naomi. Hare & Badger Go to Town. Ross, Tony, illus. 32p. (ps-1). 1987. 9.95 (ISBN 0-905478-94-0, Pub. by Century UK). Trafalgar Sq.

Lian, Ann & Lian, Leslie. The Fourteen Carat Caper. LC 88-51031. (Illus.). 44p. 1988. 5.95 (ISBN 1-55523-171-3). Winston-Derek.

Liberati, Bruce D. Bunnylove & the Three Ways to Love. Liberati, Zona, ed. (Illus.). (gr. 1-6). 1989. write for info. Word Dist Intl.

Little Bunnies All Through the Year. 1990. text ed. 3.95 cased (ISBN 0-7214-5289-2). Ladybird Bks.

Little Bunnies Around Town. 1990. text ed. 3.95 cased (ISBN 0-7214-5290-6). Ladybird Bks.

Little Bunnies at Home. 1990. text ed. 3.95 cased (ISBN 0-7214-5288-4). Ladybird Bks.

Little Bunnies on the Move. 1990. text ed. 3.95 cased (ISBN 0-7214-5291-4). Ladybird Bks.

Little Bunnies on Vacation. 1990. text ed. 3.95 cased (ISBN 0-7214-5292-2). Ladybird Bks.

Little Rabbit Who Wanted Red Wings. (Illus.). 24p. (ps-3). 1978. pap. 2.50 (ISBN 0-448-46525-6, G&D). Putnam Pub Group.

Macdonald, Maryann. Rosie Runs Away. Sweet, Melissa, illus. LC 89-27575. 32p. (ps-2). 1990. 12.95 (ISBN 0-689-31625-9, Atheneum Child Bk). Macmillan Child Grp.

Malinowski, Stanley B. & Melodia, Thomas V. The Easter Bunny Comes to Forgottenville. 48p. (ps-3). 1988. 11.95 (ISBN 0-941316-02-5). TSM Books.

Mangas, Brian. Carrot Delight. 1990. pap. 5.95 (ISBN 0-671-67886-8). S&S Trade.

—A Nice Surprise for Father Rabbit. Levitt, Sidney, illus. (ps). 1989. pap. 5.95 (ISBN 0-671-67194-4). S&S Trade.

—You Don't Get a Carrot Unless You're a Bunny. Levitt, Sidney, illus. 1989. pap. 5.95 (ISBN 0-671-67201-0). S&S Trade.

Manushkin, Fran. Be Brave, Baby Rabbit. (ps-3). 1990. 14.99 (ISBN 0-517-57574-4, CRNP). Crown.

—Little Rabbit's Baby Brother. De Groat, Diane, illus. Bate, Lucy, created by. (Illus.). (ps-3). 1988. 12.95 (ISBN 0-517-56251-0). Crown.

Martin, Rafe. Foolish Rabbit's Big Mistake. (Illus.). 32p. (ps-3). 1991. pap. 6.95 (ISBN 0-399-21778-9, Putnam). Putnam Pub Group.

Martin, Rafe, rev. by. Foolish Rabbit's Big Mistake. Young, Ed, illus. LC 84-11665. 32p. (gr. k-3). 1985. 13.95 (ISBN 0-399-21178-0, Putnam). Putnam Pub Group.

Matthews, Morgan. Houdini, the Vanishing Hare. Gustafson, Dana, illus. LC 88-1286. 48p. (Orig.). (gr. 1-4). 1989. PLB 9.89 (ISBN 0-8167-1343-X); pap. text ed. 2.95 (ISBN 0-8167-1344-8). Troll Assocs.

May, Robert E. How Billy Joe Bobtail Met Texas Slim. McQueen, Don, illus. 32p. (gr. k-7). 1987. lib. bdg. 11.89 (ISBN 0-87397-303-8); pap. 5.95 (ISBN 0-87397-300-3). Strode.

Meroux, Felix. The Prince of the Rabbits. Edens, Copper, illus. LC 84-81640. 40p. (Orig.). (ps-3). 1984. pap. 8.95 (ISBN 0-88138-030-X, Star & Elephant Bks.). Green Tiger Pr.

Michaels, Tilde. Rabbit Spring. James, J. Alison & Bhend, Kathi, illus. LC 87-18107. 96p. (gr. 7-11). 1989. 11.95 (ISBN 0-15-200568-4, Gulliver Bks). HarBraceJ.

Michels, Tilde. Rabbit Spring. Bhend, Kathi, illus. LC 87-18107. 96p. (gr. 1-4). 1990. pap. 2.95 (ISBN 0-679-80153-7). McKay.

Miller, J. P. Learn to Count with Little Rabbit. Miller, J. P., illus. LC 83-21100. 24p. (ps-1). 1984. 3.95 (ISBN 0-394-86149-3, Random Juv). Random.

—Little Rabbit. (ps-k). 1987. write for info incl. doll. Random.

—Little Rabbit Goes to the Doctor. (ps-k). 1987. pap. 3.95 (ISBN 0-394-87991-0, Random Juv). Random.

—Little Rabbit Takes a Walk. Miller, J. P., illus. LC 86-61525. 24p. (ps-1). 1987. pap. 4.95 bk. & doll pkg. (ISBN 0-394-88667-4). Random.

—What Time Is It, Little Rabbit? Miller, J. P., illus. LC 85-2225. 24p. (ps-1). 1985. 3.95 (ISBN 0-394-87533-8, Random Juv). Random.

—Yoo-Hoo Little Rabbit. Miller, J. P., illus. LC 85-61529. (ps). 1986. 2.95 (ISBN 0-394-87884-1, Random Juv). Random.

Miller, Minnie T. Why the March Hare Went Mad & Other Stories. 55p. (gr. k-4). 1972. 5.00 (ISBN 0-87881-002-1). Mojave Bks.

Miller, Sherry. The Day Happy E. Bunny Lost His Cotton Tail. Martinez, Jesse, illus. 16p. (Orig.). (gr. k-5). 1983. pap. 0.49 saddle-stitched. Double M Pub.

Modesitt, Jeanne. Vegetable Soup. Spowart, Robin, illus. LC 87-11169. 32p. (ps-1). 1988. 13.95 (ISBN 0-02-767630-7, Mcmillan Child Bk). Macmillan Child Grp.

Nakano, Mei T. Riko Rabbit. LC 82-81737. (gr. 2-5). 1982. pap. 5.95 (ISBN 0-942610-00-8). Mina Pr.

Nash, Corey, retold by. Little Treasury of Peter Rabbit. Potter, Beatrix, illus. (ps). 1983. 6.95 (ISBN 0-517-41069-9, Chatham River Pr). Outlet Bk Co.

New Boots for Rabbit. 1989. text ed. 3.95 cased (ISBN 0-7214-5230-2). Ladybird Bks.

Olson, Jim. The Reindeer & the Easter Bunny. Van Vleck, Jane & Olson, Sally, eds. (Illus.). 18p. (Orig.). (gr. 1-4). 1981. pap. 4.95 (ISBN 0-943806-00-3). Neahtawanta Pr.

Orstadius, Brita. The Dolphin Journey. Didoff, Lennart, illus. Bibb, Eric, tr. (Illus.). 28p. (ps up). 1989. 12.95 (ISBN 9-12-959138-4, Pub. by R & S Bks). FS&G.

Paxton, Tom. Jennifer's Rabbit. Ayers, Donna, illus. LC 87-14113. 32p. (ps-1). 1988. 12.95 (ISBN 0-688-07431-6); lib. bdg. 12.88 (ISBN 0-688-07432-4, Morrow Jr Bks). Morrow Jr Bks.

Peppe, Rodney. Run Rabbit, Run! A Pop-Up Book. Peppe, Rodney, illus. LC 82-70307. 12p. (ps-3). 1982. pap. 8.95 (ISBN 0-385-28851-4). Delacorte.

Peter Rabbit. (Illus.). (ps-2). 1.95 (ISBN 0-7214-5138-1). Ladybird Bks.

Peter Rabbit: A Beatrix Potter Bath Book. 8p. (ps). 1989. 2.95 (ISBN 0-7232-3584-8). Warne.

Peter Rabbit & His Friends. 1985. 2.95 (ISBN 0-671-52698-7, Little Simon). S&S Trade.

Peter Rabbit & His Friends Word Book. 1989. 4.99 (ISBN 0-517-64156-9). Crown.

Peter Rabbit's 1 2 3 Frieze. 1988. 5.00 (ISBN 0-7232-5630-6). Warne.

Pitcher, Diana. The Mischief Maker. Dove, Sally, illus. 64p. 1990. pap. 5.95 (ISBN 0-86486-106-0, Pub. by D Philip South Africa). Interlink Pub.

Pizer, Abigail. Loppylugs. (Illus.). 32p. (ps-2). 1990. pap. 11.95 (ISBN 0-670-83209-X). Viking Child Bks.

Potter, Beatrix. Beatrix Potter & Peter Rabbit Classic Treasury. 1988. 9.99 (ISBN 0-517-67150-6). Crown.

—Beatrix Potter Tale of Baby Da. (gr. k up). 1979. 17.00 (ISBN 0-8378-8011-4). Gibson.

—The Big Peter Rabbit Book. 64p. (gr. 1-3). 1987. 8.95 (ISBN 0-7232-3409-4). Warne.

—Birthday Book of Peter Rabbit. (Illus.). 256p. (ps up). 1983. 4.98 (ISBN 0-517-40303-X, Greenwich Hse). Outlet Bk Co.

—The Complete Adventures of Peter Rabbit. 80p. (ps-3). 1984. pap. 6.95 (ISBN 0-14-050444-3, Puffin). Puffin Bks.

—The Complete Adventures of Peter Rabbit. Potter, Beatrix, illus. 96p. (ps-3). 1987. 12.95 (ISBN 0-7232-2951-1). Warne.

—Complete Tales of Peter Rabbit: And Other Favorite Stories. Santore, Charles, illus. LC 86-10116. 54p. (gr. k up). 1986. 9.98 (ISBN 0-89471-460-0, Pub. by Courage Bks). Running Pr.

—El Cuento de Perico, el Conejo Travieso. (SPA., Illus.). 64p. 1988. 5.95 (ISBN 0-7232-3556-2). Warne.

—El Cuento del Conejito Benjamin. (SPA., Illus.). 64p. 1988. 5.95 (ISBN 0-7232-3558-9). Warne.

—Meet Benjamin Bunny. (Illus.). 12p. (ps). 1987. bds. 2.95 (ISBN 0-7232-3451-5). Warne.

—Meet Peter Rabbit. Potter, Beatrix, illus. 12p. (ps). 1986. bds. 2.95 (ISBN 0-7232-3418-3). Warne.

—My Peter Rabbit Play Box. 1991. bds. 14.95 incl. tape & toy (ISBN 0-7232-3794-8). Warne.

—Original Peter Rabbit Mini Collection. (Illus.). 1989. Twelve-copy drawer. pap. 14.95 (ISBN 0-7232-5173-8). Warne.

—Original Peter Rabbit Mini Collection IV. (ps-3). 1990. pap. 4.95 (ISBN 0-7232-5076-6). Warne.

—The Original Peter Rabbit Miniature Collection, No. III. (Illus.). (ps-3). 1989. pap. 4.95 set of 4 in slipcase (ISBN 0-7232-5070-7). Warne.

—Original Peter Rabbit Miniature Collection V. (ps-3). 1990. pap. 4.95 (ISBN 0-7232-5078-2). Warne.

—Original Peter Rabbit Miniature Collection VI. 1991. pap. 5.95 (ISBN 0-7232-3764-6). Warne.

—The Original Peter Rabbit Miniature Collection VI. (Illus.). (ps-3). 1991. pap. 4.95 (ISBN 0-7232-5079-0). Warne.

—Peter Rabbit. LC 87-24226. (Illus.). 64p. (gr. k-5). 1989. 11.95 (ISBN 0-916410-24-2). A D Bragdon.

—Peter Rabbit & Benjamin Bunny Coloring Book. (Illus.). (gr. 1 up). 1987. pap. 1.49 (ISBN 0-671-62987-5, Little Simon). S&S Trade.

—Peter Rabbit & Friends: Three Complete Tales, 3 vols. (Illus.). 178p. (gr. 2 up). 1985. Set. pap. 5.25 (ISBN 0-486-24772-4). Dover.

—The Peter Rabbit & His Friends Sticker Book. 1988. pap. 5.95 (ISBN 0-7232-3537-6). Warne.

—Peter Rabbit Comes Home. 1988. 2.99 (ISBN 0-517-60596-1). Crown.

—Peter Rabbit in Mr. McGregor's Garden. 1988. 2.99 (ISBN 0-517-60597-X). Crown.

—The Peter Rabbit Make-a-Mobile Book. (ps-3). 1987. pap. 3.95 (ISBN 0-7232-3426-4). Warne.

—The Peter Rabbit Nursery Frieze. (Illus.). (ps-k). 1989. shrink-wrapped 5.00 (ISBN 0-7232-3583-X). Warne.

—The Peter Rabbit Pop-Up Book. 12p. 1983. 12.95 (ISBN 0-7232-2950-3). Warne.

—Peter Rabbit Sticker Book. Potter, Beatrix, illus. 32p. (ps-3). 1985. pap. 4.95 (ISBN 0-7232-3345-4). Warne.

—Peter Rabbit with Many Other Beloved Beatrix Potter Characters Coloring Book. (Illus.). (gr. 1 up). 1987. pap. 1.49 (ISBN 0-671-62984-0, Little Simon). S&S Trade.

—Peter Rabbit's Christmas Book. (ps-3). 1990. pap. 5.95 (ISBN 0-7232-3778-6). Warne.

—Peter Rabbit's Colors. 48p. (ps-k). 1988. 6.95 (ISBN 0-7232-3612-7); frieze 5.00 (ISBN 0-7232-3613-5). Warne.

—Peter Rabbit's One Two Three. (ps-k). 1988. 6.95 (ISBN 0-7232-3424-8). Warne.

—Pierre Lapin: Peter Rabbit. (FRE., Illus.). (gr. 3-7). 1973. 5.00 (ISBN 0-7232-0650-3). Warne.

—Scenes from the Tale of Peter Rabbit. (Illus.). 1989. 6.95 (ISBN 0-7232-3547-3). Warne.

—The Story of a Fierce Bad Rabbit. 1987. 5.95 (ISBN 0-7232-3479-5); pap. 2.25 (ISBN 0-7232-3504-X). Warne.

—The Story of Miss Moppet. 1987. 5.95 (ISBN 0-7232-3480-9); pap. 2.25 (ISBN 0-7232-3505-8). Warne.

—The Tailor of Gloucester. 1987. 5.95 (ISBN 0-7232-3462-0); pap. 2.25 (ISBN 0-7232-3487-6). Warne.

—The Tale of Benjamin Bunny. Stewart, Pat, illus. LC 74-78812. 59p. (gr. 2 up). 1974. pap. 1.75 (ISBN 0-486-21102-9). Dover.

—The Tale of Benjamin Bunny. Kirk, Tim, illus. LC 80-27468. 32p. (gr. k-3). 1981. PLB 9.79 (ISBN 0-89375-484-6); pap. text ed. 1.95 (ISBN 0-89375-485-4). Troll Assocs.

—The Tale of Benjamin Bunny. Atkinson, Allen, illus. 64p. 1984. pap. 2.25 (ISBN 0-553-15203-3). Bantam.

—The Tale of Benjamin Bunny. (Illus.). 64p. (ps-3). 1986. 3.95 (ISBN 0-671-62925-5, Little Simon). S&S Trade.

—The Tale of Benjamin Bunny. LC 87-40283. (Illus.). (ps up). 1990. incl. audio cassettes 6.95 (ISBN 1-55782-016-3). Warner Bks.

—The Tale of Benjamin Bunny. 1987. 5.95 (ISBN 0-7232-3463-9); pap. 2.25 (ISBN 0-7232-3488-4). Warne.

—Tale of Benjamin Bunny. 1988. 2.50 (ISBN 0-517-65277-3). Crown.

—Tale of Benjamin Bunny. (Illus.). (ps). 1991. pap. 1.99 (ISBN 0-7232-3768-9). Warne.

—The Tale of Benjamin Bunny Paint with Water Book. (Illus.). (gr. 1 up). 1987. pap. 1.49 (ISBN 0-671-62986-7, Little Simon). S&S Trade.

—Tale of Benjamin Bunny-Sticker. 1990. pap. 2.95 (ISBN 0-671-69254-2). S&S Trade.

—The Tale of Benjamin Bunny with Peter Rabbit Sticker Book. (Illus.). (gr. 1 up). 1986. pap. 1.49 (ISBN 0-671-62580-2, Little Simon). S&S Trade.

—The Tale of Ginger & Pickles. 1987. 5.95 (ISBN 0-7232-3477-9); pap. 2.25 (ISBN 0-7232-3502-3). Warne.

—The Tale of Jemima Puddle-Duck. 1987. pap. 2.25 (ISBN 0-7232-3493-0). Warne.

—The Tale of Johnny Town-Mouse. (ps-3). 1987. 5.95 (ISBN 0-7232-3472-8); pap. 2.25 (ISBN 0-7232-3497-3). Warne.

—The Tale of Little Pig Robinson. 1987. 5.95 (ISBN 0-7232-3478-7); pap. 2.25 (ISBN 0-7232-3503-1). Warne.

—The Tale of Mr. Jeremy Fisher. 1987. 5.95 (ISBN 0-7232-3466-3); pap. 2.25 (ISBN 0-7232-3491-4). Warne.

—The Tale of Mr. Tod. 1987. 5.95 (ISBN 0-7232-3473-6); pap. 2.25 (ISBN 0-7232-3498-1). Warne.

—The Tale of Mrs. Tiggy-Winkle. 1987. 5.95 (ISBN 0-7232-3465-5); pap. 2.25 (ISBN 0-7232-3490-6). Warne.

—The Tale of Mrs. Tittlemouse. 1987. 5.95 (ISBN 0-7232-3470-1); pap. 2.25 (ISBN 0-7232-3495-7). Warne.

—The Tale of Peter Rabbit. (Illus.). 60p. (gr. 1-5). 1972. pap. 1.75 (ISBN 0-486-22827-4). Dover.

—The Tale of Peter Rabbit. Bloom, Claire, narrated by. 1984. pap. 5.95 incl. cassette (ISBN 0-89845-500-6, TBC5006, Caedmon). HarperAudio.

—The Tale of Peter Rabbit. Graham, Florence, illus. LC 85-70809. 13p. (ps). 1986. 3.95 (ISBN 0-448-10224-2, G&D). Putnam Pub Group.

—The Tale of Peter Rabbit. McPhail, David, illus. 32p. (Orig.). (gr. k-3). 1986. pap. 2.50 (ISBN 0-590-41101-2); incl. cassette 5.95 (ISBN 0-590-63091-1). Scholastic Inc.

—Tale of Peter Rabbit. (ps). 1991. pap. 1.99 (ISBN 0-7232-3765-4). Warne.

—The Tale of Peter Rabbit. (Illus.). 64p. (ps-3). 1986. 3.95 (ISBN 0-671-62924-7, Little Simon). S&S Trade.

—The Tale of Peter Rabbit. LC 87-40282. (Illus.). (ps up). 1990. incl. audio cassettes 6.95 (ISBN 1-55782-015-5). Warner Bks.

—The Tale of Peter Rabbit. Leach, Rosemary, read by. Davis, Carl, contrib. by. (Illus.). (ps-3). 1989. pap. 6.95 incl. tape (ISBN 0-7232-3627-5). Warne.

—The Tale of Peter Rabbit. (ps-3). 1987. 5.95 (ISBN 0-7232-3460-4); pap. 2.25 (ISBN 0-7232-3485-X). Warne.

—Tale of Peter Rabbit. McPhail, David, illus. (ps-1). 1989. 11.95 (ISBN 0-590-42268-5, Scholastic Hardcover). Scholastic Inc.

—Tale of Peter Rabbit. 1988. 2.50 (ISBN 0-517-65276-5). Crown.

—The Tale of Peter Rabbit. Graham, Florence, illus. 32p. 1991. pap. 1.95 (ISBN 0-448-40061-8, Platt & Munk Pubs). Putnam Pub Group.

—The Tale of Peter Rabbit: A Coloring Book in Signed English. Miller, Ralph R., illus. Roy, Howard L., et al. (Illus.). 64p. (ps-2). 1986. pap. 4.95 (ISBN 0-930323-29-7, Pub. by K Green Pubns). Gallaudet Univ Pr.

—The Tale of Peter Rabbit & Other Stories. Delacre, Lulu, illus. 1985. pap. 6.95 (ISBN 0-671-52403-8, Little Simon). S&S Trade.

—Tale of Peter Rabbit & Other Stories. 1983. pap. 2.25 (ISBN 0-553-15202-5). Bantam.

—The Tale of Peter Rabbit Paint with Water Book. (Illus.). (gr. 1 up). 1987. pap. 1.49 (ISBN 0-671-62983-2, Little Simon). S&S Trade.

—The Tale of Peter Rabbit Sticker Book. (Illus.). (gr. 1 up). 1986. pap. 1.49 (ISBN 0-671-62579-9, Little Simon). S&S Trade.

—Tale of Peter Rabbit Sticker Book. 1990. pap. 2.95 (ISBN 0-671-69255-0). S&S Trade.

—The Tale of Pigling Bland. 1987. 5.95 (ISBN 0-7232-3474-4); pap. 2.25 (ISBN 0-7232-3499-X). Warne.

—The Tale of Samuel Whiskers. 1987. 5.95 (ISBN 0-7232-3475-2); pap. 2.25 (ISBN 0-7232-3500-7). Warne.

—The Tale of Squirrel Nutkin. 1987. 5.95 (ISBN 0-7232-3461-2); pap. 2.25 (ISBN 0-7232-3486-8). Warne.

—The Tale of the Flopsy Bunnies. 64p. (gr. 1 up). 1985. pap. 1.75 (ISBN 0-486-24806-2). Dover.

—The Tale of the Flopsy Bunnies. (Illus.). 64p. (ps-3). 1987. 3.95 (ISBN 0-671-63237-X, Little Simon). S&S Trade.

—The Tale of the Flopsy Bunnies. 1987. 5.95 (ISBN 0-7232-3469-8); pap. 2.25 (ISBN 0-7232-3494-9). Warne.

—The Tale of the Pie & the Patty-Pan. 1987. 5.95 (ISBN 0-7232-3476-0); pap. 2.25 (ISBN 0-7232-3501-5). Warne.

—The Tale of Timmy Tiptoes. 1987. 5.95 (ISBN 0-7232-3471-X); pap. 2.25 (ISBN 0-7232-3496-5). Warne.

—The Tale of Tom Kitten. 1987. pap. 2.25 (ISBN 0-7232-3492-2). Warne.

—The Tale of Two Bad Mice. 1987. pap. 2.25 (ISBN 0-7232-3489-2). Warne.

—Tales of Peter Rabbit & His Friends, 2 vols. in 1. 1988. 6.99 (ISBN 0-517-44901-3). Crown.

—A Tiny Tale of Peter Rabbit. Carlson, David, illus. 14p. (ps-k). 1982. bd 3.50 (ISBN 0-671-44518-9, Little Simon). S&S Trade.

—What Time Is It, Peter Rabbit? (Illus.). (ps-k). 1989. 6.95 (ISBN 0-7232-3586-4). Warne.

—Where's Peter Rabbit? Twinn, Colin, illus. (ps-3). 1988. 6.95 (ISBN 0-7232-3519-8). Warne.

—Yours Affectionately, Peter Rabbit. Potter, Beatrix, illus. 96p. 1983. 6.95 (ISBN 0-7232-3178-8). Warne.

Potter, Beatrix, illus. My Peter Rabbit Birthday - Address Book Gift Set. 160p. 1990. Set. 13.95 (ISBN 0-7232-5156-8). Warne.

—The Peter Rabbit Sticker Book. rev. ed. 20p. (ps-3). 1991. pap. 5.95 (ISBN 0-7232-3979-7). Warne.

—The Peter Rabbit Theatre. (gr. k-5). 1983. 5.00 (ISBN 0-7232-3180-X). Warne.

Quackenbush, Robert. Funny Bunnies. LC 84-4314. (Illus.). 48p. (ps-2). 1984. 12.95 (ISBN 0-89919-267-X, Clarion). HM.

Quakenbush, Robert. Funny Bunnies on the Run. Quakenbush, Robert, illus. (gr. k-3). 1989. 13.95 (ISBN 0-318-41694-8, Pub. by Clarion). Ticknor & Fields.

Raichert, Lane. D.C. Hopper, the First Starbunny. Raichert, Lane, illus. LC 91-23055. 32p. (gr. 2-6). 1991. 15.95 (ISBN 1-880009-81-1, DC-P1). Blue Zero Pub.

Why is D.C. Hopper, a respected doctor of applied carrotology, building a rocket in his garage? Why has he left his job just when everybody needs him the most? Why is he walking around his apartment in a color coordinated space suit? Has the poor rabbit gone harebrained? No one is sure. All they know is that D.C. is obsessed with the dream of visiting space. Hurled from the safety of his home planet, D.C. Hopper discovers that the rewards from following your dreams are far more than can be imagined. In warm color pencil illustrations, rich with detail & humor, Lane Raichert's first picture book shows that there is truly hope for the future. D.C. Hopper, The First Starbunny, is printed on 100 pound acid free paper with illustrations printed at a line resolution of 225 - a level usually reserved for limited art prints. Don't miss the stunning achievement of this important new author. Blue Zero Publishing Company, PO Box 10699, Burbank, CA, 91510. Call (818) 840-0918 or fax (818) 840-8503.

Publisher Provided Annotation.

Rees, Ennis. Brer Rabbit & His Tricks. (ps-3). 1990. pap. 5.95 (ISBN 0-929077-10-5). WaterMark Inc.

—More Brer Rabbit & His Tricks. 1990. pap. 5.95 (ISBN 0-929077-11-3). WaterMark Inc.

Reinheimer, Joel. The Adventure of Squeek the Rabbit. 1990. 6.95 (ISBN 0-533-08900-X). Vantage.

Richardson, Jean. Tag-along Timothy Tours Alaska. Eakin, Edwin M., ed. Edington, Jo A., illus. 48p. (gr. 2-3). 1989. 12.95 (ISBN 0-89015-706-5, Pub. by Panda Bks). Eakin Pr.

Roberts, Bethany. Waiting-for-Spring Stories. Joyce, William, illus. LC 83-49486. 32p. (ps-3). 1984. PLB 14.89 (ISBN 0-06-025062-3). HarpC Child Bks.

Ronnie the Rabbit. (Illus.). (ps-1). 2.98 (ISBN 0-517-46986-3). Outlet Bk Co.

Rosen, Michael. Little Rabbit Foo Foo. LC 90-9598. (Illus.). 32p. (ps-1). 1990. pap. 12.95 (ISBN 0-671-70968-2). S&S Trade.

Rosenberg, Amye. Rabbit's Rainy Day. (Illus.). 40p. (gr. k-2). 1989. write for info. (ISBN 0-307-11689-1, Pub. by Golden Bks). Western Pub.

Sadler, Marilyn. The Very Bad Bunny. LC 84-3319. (Illus.). 48p. (ps-3). 1984. 6.95 (ISBN 0-394-86861-7, Pub. by BYR); lib. bdg. 7.99 (ISBN 0-394-96861-1). Beginner.

Sanderson, Ruth, illus. The Pudgy Bunny Book. 16p. (gr. k). 1984. 2.95 (ISBN 0-448-10210-2, G&D). Putnam Pub Group.

Saunders, Susan. Back to Nature. (Illus., Orig.). (gr. 3-5). 1987. pap. 2.50 (ISBN 0-671-62714-7, Minstrel Bks). PB.

—Narrow Escape. Ross, Larry, illus. (Orig.). (gr. 3-5). 1987. pap. 2.50 (ISBN 0-671-62718-X, Minstrel Bks). PB.

—Stop the Presses. (Illus., Orig.). (gr. 3-5). 1987. pap. 2.50 (ISBN 0-671-62715-5, Minstrel Bks). PB.

Scarry, Patsy. Patsy Scarry's Big Bedtime Storybook. Szekeres, Cyndy, illus. LC 79-5450. 72p. (ps-2). 1980. bds. 8.95 (ISBN 0-394-83268-X). Random.

Scarry, Richard. I Am a Bunny. Scarry, Richard, illus. 22p. (gr. k-2). 1967. write for info. (ISBN 0-307-12125-9, Golden Bks.). Western Pub.

—Richard Scarry's Naughty Bunny. (Illus.). 24p. (ps-2). 1989. write for info. (ISBN 0-307-12092-9, Pub. by Golden Bks). Western Pub.

—Watch Your Step, Mr. Rabbit! Scarry, Richard, illus. LC 90-34336. 24p. (Orig.). (ps-2). 1991. pap. 2.25 (ISBN 0-679-81072-2). Random.

Scherer, Bonnie. Benjy's New Home. McCracken, Bill, illus. LC 89-60806. 7p. 1989. pap. 1.50 (ISBN 0-9622421-0-1). B Scherer.

Written & published in Billings, MT, BENJY'S NEW HOME is a story about a Cottontail rabbit who discovered that moving can be an exciting new experience. Children of all ages will delight in following Benjy's adventures. About the Author, Benjy's New Home is the first published effort of author Bonnie Scherer, stemming from her own close encounter of a personal kind with a rabbit who took up residence in her front yard. A registered nurse & multi-talented mother of two sons, Bonnie & her husband Jered are residents of Billings, Montana. She has inspired & encouraged many people across the nation with her unpublished (as yet) writings on the trials, tribulations & victories of a cancer patient, also stemming from personal experience. A sequel to Benjy's New Home is already in first draft. About the Illustrator, Bill McCracken has "strewn" his work across America in the form of portraits, illustrations & advertising art. A native of South Dakota & a resident of Florida for many years, Bill & his wife Mony now live in Mobile, Alabama where he is employed as a media minister with Alabama's largest church. Look for The Rescue of Rusty Rabbit by B. Scherer (Easter 1992) dealing with children obeying their parents.

Publisher Provided Annotation.

Scherer, Bonnie L. The Rescue of Rusty Rabbit. Roberts, Mary & Hendricks, Janie, eds. Thayer, Carolyn, illus. LC 90-63373. 12p. (Orig.). (gr. 1-6). 1991. pap. text ed. write for info. (ISBN 0-9622421-1-X). B Scherer.

Schlachter, Rita. Winter Fun. Swan, Susan, illus. LC 85-14008. 48p. (Orig.). (gr. 1-3). 1986. PLB 9.89 (ISBN 0-8167-0584-4); pap. text ed. 2.95 (ISBN 0-8167-0585-2). Troll Assocs.

Schoder, Judy. Funny Bunny. Wasserman, Dan, ed. Reese, Bob, illus. (gr. k-1). 1979. PLB 7.95 (ISBN 0-89868-069-7); pap. 2.95 (ISBN 0-89868-080-8). ARO Pub.

Schweninger, Ann. Birthday Wishes. Schweninger, Ann, illus. LC 85-20178. 32p. (ps-1). 1986. 10.95 (ISBN 0-670-80742-7). Viking Child Bks.

—Birthday Wishes. (Illus.). (ps-1). 1987. pap. 3.95 (ISBN 0-14-050682-9, Puffin). Puffin Bks.

—Christmas Secrets. Schweninger, Ann, illus. 32p. (ps-1). 1986. pap. 3.95 (ISBN 0-14-050577-6, Puffin). Puffin Bks.

—Halloween Surprises. Schweninger, Ann, illus. 32p. (ps-1). 1986. pap. 3.95 (ISBN 0-14-050634-9, Puffin). Puffin Bks.

Smith, Cara L. Twenty-Six Rabbits Run Riot. (ps-4). 1990. 12.95 (ISBN 0-316-80185-2). Little.

Smith, Doris S. The Travels of J. B. Rabbit. LC 82-80876. (Illus.). 48p. (gr. k-2). 1982. 5.95 (ISBN 0-448-16585-6, G&D). Putnam Pub Group.

Smith, Maggie. Noly Poly Rabbit Tail & Me. 1990. 13.95 (ISBN 0-688-09570-4); PLB 13.88 (ISBN 0-688-09571-2). Lothrop.

Solotaroff, Gregoire. Don't Call Me Little Bunny. LC 88-45430. (Illus.). 32p. (ps up). 1988. 13.95 (ISBN 0-374-35012-4). FS&G.

Steiner, Jorg. Rabbit Island. Lammers, Ann C., tr. Muller, Jorg, illus. 30p. (ps-3). 9.95 (ISBN 0-930267-00-1). Bergh Pub.

Stevenson, James. The Great Big Especially Beautiful Easter Egg. LC 82-11731. (ps-3). 1990. 4.95 (ISBN 0-688-09355-8, Mulberry). Morrow.

Stinson, Kathy. Teddy Rabbit. Poulin, Stephane, illus. 32p. (gr. k-3). 1988. 12.95 (ISBN 1-550370-17-0); pap. 4.95 (ISBN 1-550370-16-2). Firefly Bks Ltd.

The Story of Peter Rabbit. (Illus.). 24p. (ps-k). 1988. 1.29 (ISBN 0-02-898131-6). Checkerboard Pr.

Strangelo, Judy M. What Do Bunnies Do All Day? (Illus.). 32p. (ps-k). 1991. pap. 4.95 (ISBN 0-8249-8509-5). Ideals.

Sundeen, Poppy. Rosie, the Rosedown Rabbit: A Storybook to Color. West, Joanne, ed. & illus. 26p. (Orig.). 1988. pap. text ed. 5.95 (ISBN 0-929317-00-9). Rosedown Plantation.

Supraner, Robyn. Mrs. Wigglesworth's Secret. Harvey, Paul, illus. LC 78-18041. 48p. (gr. 2-4). 1979. 10.89 (ISBN 0-89375-097-2); pap. 2.95 (ISBN 0-89375-085-9). Troll Assocs.

Szekeres, Cyndy. Things Bunny Sees. (ps-3). 1990. write for info. (ISBN 0-307-11591-7). Western Pub.

—What Bunny Loves. (ps-3). 1990. write for info. (ISBN 0-307-11590-9). Western Pub.

Tafuri, Nancy. Rabbit's Morning. Tafuri, Nancy, illus. LC 84-10229. 24p. (ps-1). 1985. 13.95 (ISBN 0-688-04063-2); PLB 13.88 (ISBN 0-688-04064-0). Greenwillow.

Tallarico, Tony, illus. Meet Peter Rabbit. 12p. (ps). 1988. 3.95 (ISBN 0-89828-321-3, 04014). Tuffy Bks.

—Peter Rabbit's Big Adventure. 12p. (ps). 1988. 3.95 (ISBN 0-89828-324-8). Tuffy Bks.

—A Tale of Peter Rabbit. 12p. (ps). 1988. 3.95 (ISBN 0-89828-322-1). Tuffy Bks.

Taylor, Judy. That Naughty Rabbit. 96p. (ps up). 1987. 15.95 (ISBN 0-7232-3442-6). Warne.

Teitelbaum, Michael, retold by. Little Bunny's Magic Nose. Macombi, Turi, illus. (ps-2). 1991. 5.25 (ISBN 0-307-15701-6, Golden Pr). Western Pub.
Tejima, Keizaburo. Ho-Limlim: A Rabbit Tale from Japan. (Illus.). 40p. (ps-3). 1990. 14.95 (ISBN 0-399-22156-5, Philomel Bks). Putnam Pub Group.
Thomas, Patricia. Stand Back, Said the Elephant, I'm Going to Sneeze! Tripp, Wallace, illus. LC 89-43215. 32p. (ps-2). 1990. 13.95 (ISBN 0-688-09338-8); lib. bdg. 13.88 (ISBN 0-688-09339-6). Lothrop.
A Tiny Tale of Peter Rabbit. 1985. 2.95 (ISBN 0-671-52695-2, Little Simon). S&S Trade.
Tom Kitten Mittens & Moppet: A Beatrix Potter Bath Book. 1989. 2.95 (ISBN 0-7232-3585-6). Warne.
Tummy Trouble. 64p. (gr. 6-12). 1989. pap. 7.95 (ISBN 0-685-30117-6, Disney Movie Books). WD Pub.
Twinn, Colin. Bunnykins Colors. 24p. 1991. 5.95 (ISBN 0-7232-3793-X). Warne.
—Bunnykins Rhyming Games. (Illus.). 23p. (ps-1). 1989. 4.95 (ISBN 0-7232-3603-8). Warne.
Unruh, John. Bright Eyes: The Life of a Baby Jack Rabbit. LC 80-18667. (Illus.). 112p. (Orig.). (gr. 4 up). 1980. pap. 4.95 (ISBN 0-914598-02-3). Padre Prods.
Uttley, Alison. Fuzzypeg Goes to School. 1990. 4.98 (ISBN 0-8317-5629-2). Smithmark.
—Little Grey Rabbit's House. Jaques, Faith, illus. 32p. (ps-2). 1983. pap. 8.95 (ISBN 0-399-20943-3, Philomel). Putnam Pub Group.
—Little Grey Rabbit's Party. 1990. 4.98 (ISBN 0-8317-5628-4). Smithmark.
Uttley, Allison. Hare & the Easter Eggs. 1990. 4.98 (ISBN 0-8317-5625-X). Smithmark.
Valloglise, P. Luc. The Search for the Rabbit. 138p. (gr. 7 up). 1988. pap. 8.00 (ISBN 0-934852-55-3). Lorien Hse.
Vanemst, Charlotte. Little Rabbit's Big Day, Vol. 1. (ps-3). 1990. 12.95 (ISBN 0-316-89623-3, Joy St Bks). Little.
Velveteen Rabbit. 1990. 2.98 (ISBN 0-8317-7259-X). Smithmark.
Wahl, Jan. Doctor Rabbit's Foundling. 1990. pap. 3.95 (ISBN 0-671-69008-6). S&S Trade.
—Doctor Rabbit's Lost Scout. 1990. pap. 3.95 (ISBN 0-671-69007-8). S&S Trade.
—Rabbits on Roller Skates! Allender, David, illus. 32p. (ps-2). 1988. PLB 6.95 (ISBN 0-517-56997-3). Crown.
Waldrop, Ruth. Bunny Rabbits in Mother Gooseland. Hendrix, Hurston H., illus. LC 86-61389. (Orig.). (ps-3). 1987. pap. 4.95 (ISBN 0-317-59032-4); cassette 4.95 (ISBN 0-317-59033-2). RuSk Inc.
Walt Disney Productions Presents Brer Rabbit & His Friends. (Illus.). (ps-3). 1974. 5.95 (ISBN 0-394-82774-0, Random Juv); lib. bdg. 4.99 (ISBN 0-394-92774-5). Random.
Warrener. Bunnykins in the Kitchen. 1987. 4.95 (ISBN 0-670-80569-6). Viking Penguin.
—Bunnykins in the Snow. Hayward, Walter, illus. 24p. (ps-1). 1986. pap. 4.95 (ISBN 0-670-80568-8). Viking Child Bks.
—Picnic for Bunnykins. Hayward, Walter, illus. LC 83-23532. 24p. (ps-3). 1985. pap. 4.95 (ISBN 0-670-80052-X). Viking Child Bks.
Wayland, April H. To Rabbittown. Spowart, Robin, illus. (gr. 2-5). 1989. pap. 12.95 (ISBN 0-590-40852-6). Scholastic Inc.
Weedn, Flavia. Flavia & the Velveteen Rabbit. (Illus.). 52p. 1990. 16.00 (ISBN 0-929632-10-9). Applause Inc.
Weiss, Jaqueline S. Young Brer Rabbit & Other Trickster Tales from the Americas. Arrowood, Clinton, illus. Pellowski, Anne, intro. by. (Illus.). 80p. (gr. 3-7). 1985. 14.95 (ISBN 0-88045-037-1). Stemmer Hse.
Where Is Grandma Rabbit? 1989. text ed. 3.95 cased (ISBN 0-7214-5231-0). Ladybird Bks.
Wilhelm, Hans. Bunny Trouble. (Illus.). 40p. (Orig.). (ps-3). 1987. pap. 3.95 (ISBN 0-590-44632-0); Book & cassette. 6.95 (ISBN 0-590-63153-5). Scholastic Inc.
Williams, Garth. Rabbits' Wedding. Williams, Garth, illus. LC 58-5285. 30p. (ps-1). 1958. 13.95 (ISBN 0-06-026495-0); PLB 14.89 (ISBN 0-06-026496-9). HarpC Child Bks.
Williams, Margery. Margery Williams "The Velveteen Rabbit" Eastman, David, ed. Schindler, S. D., illus. LC 87-11269. 32p. (gr. k-4). 1987. PLB 9.79 (ISBN 0-8167-1061-9); pap. text ed. 1.95 (ISBN 0-8167-1062-7). Troll Assocs.
—Miniature Velveteen Rabbit Gift Set. Green, Michael, illus. 88p. (ps-8). 1991. incl. plush bunny 9.95 (ISBN 0-89471-978-5). Running Pr.
—The Velveteen Rabbit. (Illus.). 40p. (gr. 1-9). 1982. pap. 2.95 (ISBN 0-380-58156-6, Flare). Avon.
—Velveteen Rabbit. Nicholson, William, illus. 47p. (gr. 3-5). 1991. PLB (ISBN 0-385-07748-3); pap. 9.95 (ISBN 0-385-07725-4); pap. 15.95 slipcased (ISBN 0-385-00913-5). Doubleday.
—Velveteen Rabbit. Klimo, Kate, ed. Ho, Tien, illus. 48p. 1983. pap. 8.95 (ISBN 0-671-44498-0, Little Simon). S&S Trade.
—The Velveteen Rabbit. Nicholson, William, illus. 44p. (gr. k up). 1979. pap. 2.95 (ISBN 0-380-00255-8, Camelot). Avon.
—The Velveteen Rabbit. LC 81-1454. (Illus.). (ps up). deluxe ed. 7.95 (ISBN 0-89471-153-9); lib. bdg. 12.90 (ISBN 0-89471-127-X); pap. 3.95 (ISBN 0-89471-128-8). Running Pr.
—The Velveteen Rabbit. Jorgensen, David, illus. 48p. (ps up). 1985. with cassette 13.95 (ISBN 0-394-87712-8); 11.95 (ISBN 0-394-87711-X). Knopf.
—The Velveteen Rabbit. Green, Michael, illus. LC 89-42996. 96p. (gr. 1-8). 1989. 4.95 (ISBN 0-89471-755-3). Running Pr.
—The Velveteen Rabbit. Jorgensen, David, illus. LC 85-4257. 48p. (ps-2). 1990. pap. 3.95 (ISBN 0-679-80333-5). McKay.
—The Velveteen Rabbit: A Board Book. Jorgensen, David, illus. LC 89-63161. 10p. (ps). 1990. bds. 3.95 (ISBN 0-679-80644-X). McKay.
—The Velveteen Rabbit: Or How Toys Become Real. Green, Michael, illus. LC 81-1454. 48p. (Orig.). (gr. k-12). 1984. 9.98 (ISBN 0-89471-266-7, Pub. by Courage Bks); Book & plush toy gift set. 11.49 (ISBN 0-89471-885-1). Running Pr.
Williams, Margery & Le Mesurier, John. The Velveteen Rabbit. (Illus.). 24p. (ps-2). Date not set. incl. cassette 5.98 (ISBN 1-55886-065-7). Smarty Pants.
Wise, Francis H. & Wise, Joyce M. Jack, the Rabbit. (Illus.). 21p. (gr. 1). 1976. pap. 1.50. Wise Pub.

Woods, Becky. A Rocky Mountain Rabbit. LC 90-70093. (Illus.). 86p. (gr. 4-8). 1990. 12.95 (ISBN 0-932433-65-0). Windswept Hse.

Worth, Bonnie. Peter Cottontail's Surprise. Hildebrandt, Greg, illus. LC 84-28031. 48p. (ps-2). 1985. 4.95 (ISBN 0-88101-015-4). Unicorn Pub.
Yazaki, Setsuo. Little Bunny's Christmas Present. Ooka, D. T., tr. from JPN. Kuroi, Ken, illus. 32p. (ps-8). 1983. 11.95 (ISBN 0-89346-225-X). Heian Intl.
Yost, Carolyn K. Mother Rabbit Knew. Gardner, Katherine L., tr. (Illus.). 32p. (gr. k-2). 1989. pasted 1.99 (ISBN 0-87403-595-3, 3855). Standard Pub.
Zolotow, Charlotte. Mister Rabbit & the Lovely Present. Sendak, Maurice, illus. LC 62-7590. (gr. k-3). 1962. 13.95 (ISBN 0-06-026945-6); PLB 12.89 (ISBN 0-06-026946-4). HarpC Child Bks.
—Mr. Rabbit & the Lovely Present. Sendak, Maurice, illus. LC 62-7590. 32p. (ps-3). 1977. pap. 4.50 (ISBN 0-06-443020-0, Trophy). HarpC Child Bks.

RACCOONS

Holmgren, Virginia C. Raccoons: In Folklore, History & Today's Backyards. (Illus.). 208p. (Orig.). 1990. pap. 10.95 (ISBN 0-88496-312-8). Capra Pr.
Kostyal, Karen. Raccoons. Crump, Donald J., ed. (Illus.). 32p. (ps-3). 1987. Set. 10.95 (ISBN 0-87044-677-0); Set. lib. bdg. 12.95 (ISBN 0-87044-682-7). Natl Geog.
Nentl, Jerolyn. Raccoon. LC 83-21072. (Illus.). 48p. (gr. 5-6). 1984. PLB 10.95 (ISBN 0-89686-246-1, Crestwood Hse). Macmillan Child Grp.
North, Sterling. Rascal: A Memoir of a Better Era. Shoenherr, John, illus. LC 63-13882. (gr. 4 up). 1984. 13.95 (ISBN 0-525-18839-8, DCB). Dutton Child Bks.
Raccoon. 1990. 2.95 (ISBN 0-8378-2051-0). Gibson.
Stone, Lynn. Raccoons. (Illus.). 24p. (gr. k-5). 1990. lib. bdg. 11.93 (ISBN 0-86593-045-7); lib. bdg. 8.95s.p. Rourke Corp.

RACCOONS–FICTION

Arnosky, Jim. Raccoons & Ripe Corn. Arnosky, Jim, illus. LC 87-4243. 32p. (ps-3). 1987. 13.95 (ISBN 0-688-05455-2); PLB 13.88 (ISBN 0-688-05456-0). Lothrop.
Barrett, John. Zeke Hatfield & a Ghost Named Rocky. Ruth, Red, illus. (gr. k-10). 1978. 1.99 (ISBN 0-686-22892-8). Silver Dollar.
Brown, Margaret W. Wait Till the Moon Is Full. Williams, Garth, illus. LC 48-9278. 32p. (ps-1). 1948. 14.95 (ISBN 0-06-020800-7); PLB 12.89 (ISBN 0-06-020801-5). HarpC Child Bks.
Bussard, Paula. Rascal's Close Call. Goodridge, Larry, illus. 28p. (gr. k-3). 1985. 1.39 (ISBN 0-87239-962-1, 3382). Standard Pub.
Deitz, Lawrence. Jimmy Coon Story Book, No. 1. McCoy, Beverly, illus. 34p. (Orig.). 1985. pap. 2.95 (ISBN 0-934750-79-3). Mntn Memories Bks.
—Jimmy Coon Story Book, No. 2. McCoy, Beverly, illus. 37p. 1985. pap. 2.95 (ISBN 0-934750-42-4). Mntn Memories Bks.
—Jimmy Coon Story Book, No. 5. (Illus.). 40p. (Orig.). (ps up). 1986. pap. 2.95 (ISBN 0-938985-02-7). Mntn Memories Bks.
Keane, Glen. Adam Raccoon & the Circusmaster. LC 86-26889. 1989. 6.95 (ISBN 1-55513-090-9). Cook.
—Adam Raccoon & the Flying Machine. LC 88-17006. (Illus.). 48p. (ps-2). 1989. 6.95 (ISBN 1-55513-287-1). Cook.
—Adam Raccoon at Forever Falls. LC 86-24318. (ps-3). 6.95 (ISBN 1-55513-087-9). Cook.
—Adam Raccoon in Lost Woods. LC 86-30951. (ps-3). 6.95 (ISBN 1-55513-088-7). Cook.
Langstaff, Dorothea. Raccoons in Trouble. 32p. (ps-1). 1990. 6.95 (ISBN 0-8062-3653-1). Carlton.
Leonard, Marcia & DeRosa. Little Raccoon Goes to the Beach. (ps-7). 1987. pap. 2.50 (ISBN 0-553-15326-9). Bantam.
Leslie. Ringo, the Robber Raccoon. 1984. 10.95 (ISBN 0-396-08323-4, Putnam). Putnam Pub Group.
Poskanzer, Susan C. Little Raccoon Who Could. Hall, Susan, illus. LC 85-14020. 48p. (Orig.). (gr. 1-3). 1986. PLB 9.89 (ISBN 0-8167-0624-7); pap. text ed. 2.95 (ISBN 0-8167-0625-5). Troll Assocs.
Renner, Beverly H. The Hideaway Summer. Sanderson, Ruth, illus. LC 77-11848. (gr. 4-6). 1978. 8.95i (ISBN 0-06-024862-9). HarpC Child Bks.
Ricky the Raccoon. (Illus.). (ps-1). 2.98 (ISBN 0-517-46985-5). Outlet Bk Co.
Roddy, Lee. D J Dillon & the Legend of the White Raccoon. 144p. (gr. 3-7). 1986. pap. 4.99 (ISBN 0-89693-500-0). Victor Bks.
Stamper, Jamie. Kitty the Raccoon. 2nd ed. Heinonen, Susan, illus. 50p. (gr. k-10). 1989. pap. 7.95 (ISBN 0-9623072-0-3). S Ink WA.

RACE

Gay, Kathlyn. The Rainbow Effect: Interracial Families. LC 86-26689. (Illus.). 144p. (gr. 7-12). 1987. PLB 12.90 (ISBN 0-531-10343-9). Watts.

RACE DISCRIMINATION

see Race Problems

RACE PROBLEMS

see also Discrimination; Immigration and Emigration; Intercultural Education;
also names of countries, cities, etc. with the subdivision Race Relations, e.g. U. S.–Race Relations

Cohen, Susan & Cohen, Daniel. Racism. 192p. (gr. 8 up). 1991. 14.95 (ISBN 0-87131-626-9). M Evans.
Mckissack, Patricia. Taking a Stand Against Racism & Racial Discrimination. 1990. PLB 13.40 (ISBN 0-531-10924-0). Watts.
Mizell, Linda. Racism. 160p. (gr. 7 up). 1991. PLB 15.85 (ISBN 0-8027-8113-6); pap. 8.95 (ISBN 0-8027-7365-6). Walker & Co.

RACE PROBLEMS–FICTION

Armstrong, William H. Sour Land. LC 70-135783. 128p. (gr. 7 up). 1991. PLB 13.89 (ISBN 0-06-020142-8). HarpC Child Bks.
—Sour Land. LC 70-135783. 128p. (gr. 7 up). 1976. pap. 3.50 (ISBN 0-06-440074-3, Trophy). HarpC Child Bks.
Blume, Judy. Iggie's House. LC 70-104340. 128p. (gr. 4-6). 1982. 12.95 (ISBN 0-02-711040-0, Bradbury Pr). Macmillan Child Grp.
Carlson, Natalie S. Empty Schoolhouse. Kaufmann, John, illus. LC 65-11452. 128p. (gr. 2-6). 1965. PLB 14.89 (ISBN 0-06-020981-X). HarpC Child Bks.
Gordon, Sheila. Waiting for the Rain. LC 87-7638. 224p. (gr. 7 up). 1987. 12.95 (ISBN 0-531-05726-7); PLB 12.99 (ISBN 0-531-08326-8). Orchard Bks Watts.
Jackson, Jesse. Call Me Charley. Spiegel, Doris, illus. LC 45-9807. 156p. (gr. 5 up). 1945. PLB 13.89 (ISBN 0-06-022786-9). HarpC Child Bks.
Komai, Felicia, ed. Cry, the Beloved Country. (gr. 9 up). 1954. pap. 1.35 (ISBN 0-377-80501-7). Friendship Pr.
Miles, Betty. All It Takes Is Practice. LC 76-13057. 128p. (gr. 3-7). 1989. pap. 2.95 (ISBN 0-394-82053-3). Knopf.
Paton, Alan. Cry, the Beloved Country. 1977. 35.00x (ISBN 0-684-15559-1, Scribner); pap. 9.95 (ISBN 0-684-71863-4, Scribner); pap. text ed. 11.25 (ISBN 0-684-51544-X, Scribner). Macmillan.
Sebestyen, Ouida. Words by Heart. 144p. (gr. 4-8). 1983. pap. 3.50 (ISBN 0-553-27179-2, Starfire). Bantam.
Viglucci, Pat C. Cassandra Robbins, Esq. 176p. (Orig.). (gr. 8-12). 1987. pap. 4.95 (ISBN 0-938961-01-2, Stamp Out Sheep Pr). Sq One Pubs.

RACES OF MAN

see Ethnology

RACKETEERING

Randall, Denise. Drugs & Organized Crime. (ps-3). 1990. PLB 11.90 (ISBN 0-531-10933-X). Watts.

RADAR

see also Radar; Sound–Recording and Reproducing

Hitzeroth, Deborah. Radar: The Silent Detector. LC 90-35500. (Illus.). 96p. (gr. 5-8). 1990. PLB 15.95 (ISBN 1-56006-201-0). Lucent Bks.

RADIATION

see also Light; Radioactivity; Sound

Fradin, Dennis. Radiation. (Illus.). (gr. k-4). 1987. 14.60 (ISBN 0-516-01238-X). Childrens.
Price, Stern & Sloan Staff. Radiation. (Illus.). 32p. (gr. 7-12). 1987. pap. 2.95 (ISBN 0-8431-4291-X). Price Stern.

RADICALS AND RADICALISM

see Revolutions

RADIO

Aero Products Research, Inc., Industries Division Staff. Official CB Crossword Puzzles for Big Dummy's. (Illus.). (gr. 8 up). 1977. pap. 1.98 (ISBN 0-912682-18-3). Aero Products.
Balcziak, B. Radio. (Illus.). 48p. (gr. 4-8). 1989. lib. bdg. 14.00 (ISBN 0-86592-057-5). Rourke Corp.
Carter, Alden R. Radio: From Marconi to the Space Age. (Illus.). 96p. (gr. 4-9). 1987. PLB 10.40 (ISBN 0-531-10310-2). Watts.
Ferrell, Nancy W. The New World of Amateur Radio. LC 86-10991. (Illus.). 72p. (gr. 4-9). 1986. PLB 10.40 (ISBN 0-531-10219-X). Watts.
Hawkins. Audio & Radio. 32p. (gr. 5-9). 1982. 7.95 (ISBN 0-86020-642-4, Usborne-Hayes); PLB 13.96 (ISBN 0-88110-001-3); pap. 5.95 (ISBN 0-86020-641-6). EDC.
Piersel. Photophonics I. (Illus.). (gr. 1-5). 1968. pap. 1.99x (ISBN 0-87783-073-8); tchr's guide 0.29x (ISBN 0-685-03702-9). Oddo.
—Photophonics II. (Illus.). (gr. 1-5). 1968. pap. 2.39x (ISBN 0-87783-074-6); tchr's guide 0.29x (ISBN 0-685-03703-7). Oddo.
Radio. (Illus.). 72p. (gr. 6-12). 1989. pap. 1.85 (ISBN 0-8395-3333-0, 3333). BSA.
Sabin, Louis. Television & Radio. Veno, Joseph, illus. LC 84-8446. 32p. (gr. 3-6). 1985. PLB 9.49 (ISBN 0-8167-0310-8); pap. text ed. 2.95 (ISBN 0-8167-0311-6). Troll Assocs.

RADIO–BROADCASTING

see Radio Broadcasting

RADIO–VOCATIONAL GUIDANCE

Lerner, Mark. Careers with a Radio Station. Blumenfeld, Milton J., illus. LC 82-20349. 36p. (gr. 2-5). 1983. PLB 7.95 (ISBN 0-8225-0312-3). Lerner Pubns.

RADIO ASTRONOMY

see also names of celestial radio sources, e.g. Quasars

RADIO BROADCASTING

see also Television Broadcasting

Conford, Ellen. Strictly for Laughs. LC 85-9450. 155p. (gr. 7-10). 1985. 12.95 (ISBN 0-448-47754-8, Putnam). Putnam Pub Group.

Coyle, Rebecca. Radio. LC 88-29290. (Illus.). 48p. (gr. 6-12). 1989. PLB 12.95 (ISBN 0-86307-977-6). Marshall Cavendish.

Kuslan, Louis I. & Kuslan, Richard D. Ham Radio. (gr. 7 up). 1981. 10.95 (ISBN 0-13-372334-8). P-H.

Wong, Michael A. A Day in the Life of a Disc Jockey. Jann, Gayle, illus. LC 87-10943. 32p. (gr. 4-8). 1988. PLB 11.79 (ISBN 0-8167-1125-9); pap. text ed. 2.95 (ISBN 0-8167-1126-7). Troll Assocs.

RADIO JOURNALISM

see Journalism; Radio Broadcasting

RADIO SCRIPTS

Adorjan, Carol & Rasovsky, Yuri. WKID: Easy Radio Plays. (Illus.). 80p. (gr. 3-8). 1988. pap. 9.95 (ISBN 0-8075-9155-6). A Whitman.

RADIO SHACK COMPUTERS

see Trs-80 Computers

RADIOACTIVE SUBSTANCE

see Radioactivity

RADIOACTIVE WASTES

Johnstone, Hugh. Facts on Nuclear Waste & Radioactivity. (ps-3). 1990. PLB 11.90 (ISBN 0-531-10913-5). Watts.

RADIOACTIVITY

see also Nuclear Physics

Johnstone, Hugh. Facts on Nuclear Waste & Radioactivity. (ps-3). 1990. PLB 11.90 (ISBN 0-531-10913-5). Watts.

Milne, Lorus & Milne, Margery. Understanding Radioactivity. Hiscock, Bruce, illus. LC 88-7382. 80p. (gr. 3-7). 1989. 12.95 (ISBN 0-689-31362-4, Atheneum Child Bk). Macmillan Child Grp.

Murray, Raymond L. & Powell, Judith A. Understanding Radioactive Waste. 3rd, rev. ed. LC 88-22134. (Illus.). 184p. (gr. 6-12). 1989. pap. 12.50 (ISBN 0-935470-42-5). Battelle.

RADIUM

see also Radioactivity

RAILROADS

see also Subways

Barton, Byron. Trains. Barton, Byron, illus. LC 85-47898. 32p. (ps-k). 1986. 4.95 (ISBN 0-694-00061-2, Crowell Jr Bks); PLB 11.89 (ISBN 0-690-04534-4). HarpC Child Bks.

Broekel, Ray. Trains. (Illus.). 48p. (gr. k-4). 1981. PLB 14.60 (ISBN 0-516-01652-0); pap. 4.95 (ISBN 0-516-41652-9). Childrens.

Brown, David. Guide to Model Railways. (gr. 4-9). 1980. 7.95 (ISBN 0-86020-504-5, Usborne); PLB 13.96 (ISBN 0-88110-023-4); pap. 4.95 (ISBN 0-86020-503-7). EDC.

Chlad, Dorothy. Stop, Look, & Listen for Trains. LC 83-7213. (Illus.). 32p. (ps-2). 1983. lib. bdg. 14.60 (ISBN 0-516-01988-0); pap. 3.95 (ISBN 0-516-41988-9). Childrens.

Crews, Donald. Freight Train. LC 78-2303. (Illus.). 32p. (gr. k-3). 1978. 13.95 (ISBN 0-688-80165-X); PLB 13.88 (ISBN 0-688-84165-1). Greenwillow.

Dreher, Jean. Iron Horses-Iron Men. (Illus.). 130p. (gr. 10 up). 1984. 12.95 (ISBN 0-912113-20-0); pap. 5.95 (ISBN 0-912113-21-9). Railhead Pubns.

Gibbons, Gail. Trains. LC 86-19595. (Illus.). 32p. (ps-3). 1988. 14.95g (ISBN 0-8234-0640-7); pap. 5.95 (ISBN 0-8234-0699-7). Holiday.

Harvey, T. Railroads. LC 79-5062. (Illus.). 36p. (gr. 3-6). 1980. PLB 8.95 (ISBN 0-8225-1184-3, First Ave Edns); pap. 4.95 (ISBN 0-8225-9539-7, First Ave Edns). Lerner Pubns.

Kanetzke, Howard W. Trains & Railroads. rev. ed. LC 87-20813. (Illus.). 48p. (gr. 2-6). 1987. PLB 17.32 (ISBN 0-8172-3263-X); pap. 9.27 (ISBN 0-8172-3288-5). Raintree Pubs.

Matthews, L. Railroaders. (Illus.). 32p. (gr. 3-8). Date not set. PLB 17.26 (ISBN 0-86625-366-1). Rourke Corp.

Miller, Marilyn. The Transcontinental Railroad. rev. ed. (Illus.). 64p. (gr. 5 up). 1989. pap. 7.95 (ISBN 0-382-09912-5). Silver Burdett Pr.

Railroading. (Illus.). 48p. (gr. 6-12). 1978. pap. 1.85 (ISBN 0-8395-3292-X, 3292). BSA.

Rutland. Supertrains. rev. ed. (gr. 4-6). 1984. (Usborne-Hayes); PLB 12.96 (ISBN 0-88110-125-7); pap. 5.95 (ISBN 0-86020-180-5). EDC.

RAILROADS–FICTION

Awdry, W. Breakfast-Time for Thomas: Based on the Railway Series. Bell, Owain, illus. LC 89-62527. 32p. (Orig.). (ps-3). 1990. pap. 1.25 (ISBN 0-679-80409-9). McKay.

—James & the Foolish Freight Cars. LC 91-8035. (Illus.). 32p. (ps-2). 1991. 3.50 (ISBN 0-679-82086-8, Random Juv). Random.

—Meet Thomas the Tank Engine & His Friends. McArthur, Kenny, et al, illus. LC 89-32299. 32p. (ps-1). 1989. 6.95 (ISBN 0-679-80102-2, Random Juv); PLB 8.99 (ISBN 0-679-90102-7). Random.

—Percy Runs Away. LC 91-8707. (Illus.). 32p. (ps-2). 1991. 3.50 (ISBN 0-679-82087-6, Random Juv). Random.

—Thomas Breaks the Rules. LC 91-2428. (Illus.). 32p. (ps-2). 1991. 3.50 (ISBN 0-679-82088-4, Random Juv). Random.

—Thomas Gets Tricked & Other Stories: Based on the Railway Series. McArthur, Kenny, photos by. LC 89-8502. (Illus.). 32p. (ps-3). 1989. PLB 5.99 (ISBN 0-679-90100-0); pap. 2.25 (ISBN 0-679-80100-6). Random.

—Thomas the Tank Engine ABC: (Just Right for 2's & 3's) McArthur, Kenny, photos by. LC 89-10605. (Illus.). 24p. (ps). 1990. 4.95 (ISBN 0-679-80362-9). McKay.

—Thomas the Tank Engine & the Great Race. Bell, Owain, illus. 7p. (ps-k). 1989. bds. 6.95 with plastic wheels (ISBN 0-679-80000-X, Random Juv). Random.

—Thomas the Tank Engine's Noisy Trip. Bell, Owain, illus. LC 89-60089. 28p. 1989. bds. 2.95 (ISBN 0-679-80083-2, Random Juv). Random.

—Toby the Tram Engine. LC 91-7770. (Illus.). 32p. (ps-2). 1991. 3.50 (ISBN 0-679-82095-7, Random Juv). Random.

—Trouble for Thomas & Other Stories: Based on the Railway Series. McArthur, Kenny, photos by. LC 89-8503. (Illus.). 32p. (ps-3). 1989. PLB 5.99 (ISBN 0-679-90101-9); pap. 2.25 (ISBN 0-679-80101-4). Random.

Aylesworth, Jim. Country Crossing. Rand, Ted, illus. LC 89-78184. 32p. (ps-2). 1991. SBE 13.95 (ISBN 0-689-31580-5, Atheneum Child Bk). Macmillan Child Grp.

Barkan, Joanne. Whiskerville Train Station. (Illus.). 12p. (ps-k). 1991. bds. 3.95 (ISBN 0-448-40088-X, G&D). Putnam Pub Group.

Bibliotheca Press Staff. Posie the Positive Train: Story Edition. (gr. 4-9). 1990. 12.95 (ISBN 0-939476-27-4, Pub. by Biblio Pr GA); pap. 9.95 (ISBN 0-939476-28-2, Pub. by Biblio Pr GA). Prosperity & Profits.

Brewer, Raphael. The Adventures of Little Puff. 1989. 6.95 (ISBN 0-533-08084-3). Vantage.

Brown, Margaret W. Two Little Trains. LC 84-43138. 40p. 1986. PLB 12.89 (ISBN 0-06-020768-X). HarpC Child Bks.

Burningham, John. Hey! Get off Our Train. Burningham, John, illus. LC 89-15802. 48p. (ps-4). 1990. 15.00 (ISBN 0-517-57638-4); PLB 14.99 (ISBN 0-517-57643-0). Crown.

Burton, Virginia L. Choo Choo: The Story of a Little Engine Who Ran Away. Burton, Virginia L., illus. LC 37-19461. 56p. (Orig.). (gr. k-8). 1988. pap. 3.95 (ISBN 0-395-47942-8). HM.

Cox, Willis. Phillip's Train Ride to the Christmas Tree Farm. LC 88-110861. pap. 3.95 (ISBN 0-944119-20-4). Andover Junction.

Cross, Genevieve. The Engine That Lost Its Whistle. 10th ed. Cross, Genevieve, illus. 32p. (gr. 1-3). 1988. pap. 12.50 (ISBN 0-9621162-0-3). Van Buren Cty Hist Soc.

Fowler, Richard. Mr. Little's Noisy Train. (ps-1). 1987. 11.95 (ISBN 0-448-19212-8, G&D). Putnam Pub Group.

French, Susan M. The Magic Train. Lynn, Patty, illus. 24p. (Orig.). (gr. k-1). 1990. pap. 0.99 (ISBN 1-878624-33-4). McClanahan Bk.

Gauch, Patricia L. Christina Katerina & the Great Bear Train. Primavera, Elise, illus. 32p. 1990. 14.95 (ISBN 0-399-21623-5, Putnam). Putnam Pub Group.

Goble, Paul. Death of the Iron Horse. Goble, Paul, illus. LC 85-28011. 32p. (gr. k-3). 1987. 13.95 (ISBN 0-02-737830-6, Bradbury Pr). Macmillan Child Grp.

Green, Suzanne. The Little Choo-Choo: Sounds, Sights & Opposites. Fujita, Miho, illus. 14p. (ps-k). 1988. pap. 8.95 incl. pull toy (ISBN 0-385-24426-6). Doubleday.

Hamilton, Dorothy. The Blue Caboose. Needler, Jerry, illus. LC 72-5474. 135p. (gr. 3-6). 1973. pap. 3.95 (ISBN 0-8361-1696-8). Herald Pr.

Hines, Gary. A Ride in the Crummy. Hines, Anna G., illus. LC 90-30848. 24p. (ps up). 1991. 13.95 (ISBN 0-688-09691-3); PLB 13.88 (ISBN 0-688-09692-1). Greenwillow.

Howard, Elizabeth F. The Train to Lulu's. Casilla, Robert, illus. LC 86-33429. 32p. (ps-2). 1988. 13.95 (ISBN 0-02-744620-4, Bradbury Pr). Macmillan Child Grp.

Ingoglia, Gina. Tootle & Katy Caboose: A Special Treasure. (Illus.). 24p. (ps-2). 1989. write for info. (ISBN 0-307-12087-2, Pub. by Golden Bks). Western Pub.

Johnson, John E., illus. Here Comes the Train. 14p. (gr. 2-5). 1985. 2.95 (ISBN 0-394-87551-6, Random Juv). Random.

Keats, Ezra J. John Henry: An American Legend. Schwartz, Anne, ed. LC 65-11444. (Illus.). 32p. (ps-3). 1987. lib. bdg. 11.99 (ISBN 0-394-99052-8); pap. 5.00 (ISBN 0-394-89052-3). Knopf.

Lippman, Peter. Busy Trains. Lippman, Peter, illus. LC 77-86145. 32p. (ps-3). 1981. lib. bdg. 5.99 (ISBN 0-394-93748-1); pap. 2.25 (ISBN 0-394-83748-7). Random.

The Little Engine That Could. (Illus.). 48p. (gr. 1-7). anniv. ed. 7.95 (ISBN 0-448-47373-9, G&D). Putnam Pub Group.

The Little Engine That Could. (Illus.). (ps-12). 1988. 3.95 (ISBN 0-448-09827-X, G&D). Putnam Pub Group.

Lyon, George E. A Regular Rolling Noah. Gammell, Stephen, illus. 32p. (gr. k-3). 1991. pap. 4.95 (ISBN 0-689-71449-1, Aladdin). Macmillan Child Grp.

McPhail, David. The Train. (gr. 3-6). 1977. lib. bdg. 13.95 (ISBN 0-316-56316-1, Joy St Bks). Little.

Nesbit, Edith. The Railway Children. Butts, Dennis, ed. 224p. 1991. pap. 3.95 (ISBN 0-19-282659-X, 11912). Oxford U Pr.

Pano the Train. (ps-3). 1989. Incl. cass. write for info. (ISBN 0-307-13680-9, 13680, Pub. by Golden Bks). Western Pub.

Peet, Bill. Caboose Who Got Loose. Peet, Bill, illus. LC 79-155554. 48p. (gr. k-3). 1980. 13.95 (ISBN 0-395-14805-7); pap. 4.95 (ISBN 0-395-28715-4). HM.

—The Caboose Who Got Loose. (gr. 3 up). 1987. pap. 7.95 incl. cassette (ISBN 0-395-45740-8). HM.

Piper, Watty. The Easy-to-Read-Little Engine That Could. Retan, Walter, adapted by. Mateus, illus. 32p. (ps-2). 1986. pap. 1.95 (ISBN 0-448-19078-8, G&D); incl. cassette 5.95 (ISBN 0-448-19088-5). Putnam Pub Group.

—The Little Engine That Could. 40p. 1981. Repr. PLB 15.95x (ISBN 0-89966-366-4). Buccaneer Bks.

—The Little Engine That Could. 69p. 1981. Repr. PLB 10.95x (ISBN 0-89967-040-7). Harmony Raine.

—The Little Engine That Could Board Book. (Illus.). 12p. (ps). 1991. bds. 4.95 (ISBN 0-448-40101-0, G&D). Putnam Pub Group.

—The Little Engine That Could: Miniature Edition. Hauman, George & Hauman, Doris, illus. 48p. 1990. pap. 2.95 (ISBN 0-448-40071-5, Platt & Munk Pubs). Putnam Pub Group.

—The Little Engine That Could: Sixtieth Anniversary Edition. Hauman, George & Hauman, Doris, illus. 48p. 1990. 12.95 (ISBN 0-448-40041-3, Platt & Munk Pubs). Putnam Pub Group.

Piper, Watty, retold by. The Little Engine That Could. (Illus.). (ps). 1980. junior ed. 3.95 (ISBN 0-448-40035-9, G&D). Putnam Pub Group.

Reynolds, Malvina. Morningtown Ride. Leeman, Michael, illus. 20p. (ps-4). 1984. 10.95 (ISBN 0-931793-00-9). Turn The Page.

Siebert, Diane. Train Song. Wimmer, Mike, illus. LC 88-389. 32p. (ps-3). 1990. 14.95 (ISBN 0-690-04726-6, Crowell Jr Bks); PLB 14.89 (ISBN 0-690-04728-2, Crowell Jr Bks). HarpC Child Bks.

Tallarico, Tony, illus. Little Engine That Could. 12p. (ps-1). 1990. bds. 3.95 (ISBN 0-89828-402-3). Tuffy Bks.

Terhune, Albert P. Caleb Conover: Railroader. 111p. 1981. Repr. PLB 12.95x (ISBN 0-89966-349-4). Buccaneer Bks.

—Caleb Conover, Railroader. 189p. 1981. Repr. PLB 12.95x (ISBN 0-89967-023-7). Harmony Raine.

The Train. (gr. k). 1982. 3.95 (ISBN 0-448-12539-0, G&D). Putnam Pub Group.

Warner, Gertrude C. Caboose Mystery. LC 66-10791. (Illus.). 128p. (gr. 3-7). 1966. PLB 9.95 (ISBN 0-8075-1008-4). A Whitman.

RAILROADS–HISTORY

Bowler, Michael. The Official British Rail Book of Trains for Young People. (Illus.). 160p. (gr. 4-8). 1987. pap. 14.95 (ISBN 0-09-161510-0, Pub. by Hutchinson UK). Trafalgar Sq.

Carriker, S. David. North Carolina Railroads: The Common Carrier Railroads of North Carolina. 66p. 1989. pap. 15.00 (ISBN 0-936013-08-7). Herit Pub NC.

Edmisten, Donald D. Every Wheel That Turns: Spinning True Tales of California Rails. Rockefeller, Ruth, frwd. by. (Illus.). 53p. (Orig.). 1989. pap. write for info. (ISBN 0-9626263-0-9). DonSyl Pubns.

Forde, Hugo J., ed. A Compendia of Jargon Signals-Whistle Talk-Signs of the American Railroad. (Illus.). 86p. (Orig.). 1989. pap. 7.95 (ISBN 0-9620909-0-5). J Chesterfield Bks.

Jefferis, David. Trains: The History of Railroads. (Illus.). 32p. (gr. 5-8). 1991. PLB 11.90 (ISBN 0-531-14192-6). Watts.

MacDonald, Fiona. A Nineteenth Century Railway Station: Inside Story. James, John, illus. 48p. (gr. 5 up). 1990. 16.95 (ISBN 0-87226-341-X). P Bedrick Bks.

McKissack, Patricia & McKissack, Frederick. A Long Hard Journey. 144p. (gr. 7-9). 1990. 17.95 (ISBN 0-8027-6884-9); PLB 18.85 (ISBN 0-8027-6885-7). Walker & Co.

Miller, Marilyn. The Trans-Continental Railroad. LC 85-40167. (Illus.). 64p. (gr. 5 up). 1985. 16.98 (ISBN 0-382-06824-6). Silver Burdett Pr.

Nathan, Adele G. The Building of the First Transcontinental Railroad. (Illus.). (gr. 4-6). 1950. Random.

Nicholson, Loren. Rails Across the Ranchos: The Pacific Coastline of Southern Pacific Railroad. (Illus.). 197p. (gr. 10-12). 1980. text ed. 18.95 (ISBN 0-913548-72-3). CA HPA.

Serpico, Phil. Santa Fe Route to the Pacific. Serpico, Phil, illus. LC 87-46360. 150p. (gr. 6 up). 1988. 25.00 (ISBN 0-88418-000-X). Omni Hawthorne.

Stein, R. Conrad. The Story of the Golden Spike. Dunnington, Tom, illus. LC 78-4042. 32p. (gr. 3-6). 1978. PLB 13.27 (ISBN 0-516-04621-7). Childrens.

RAILROADS–MODELS

Ferguson, Jane & Ferguson, Gary. Narrow Gauge Fun. Kirkeeide, Deborah, illus. 24p. (ps-6). 1987. pap. 1.98 (ISBN 0-9624846-1-X). J & G Ferguson.

—Sawtooth Mountain Fun. Jenney, David, illus. 24p. (ps-6). 1982. pap. 1.98 (ISBN 0-9624846-0-1). J & G Ferguson.

Herda, D. J. Model Railroads. (Illus.). 72p. (gr. 4 up). 1982. PLB 10.40 (ISBN 0-531-04466-1). Watts.

LaVoie, Roland. Roland LaVoie's Model Railroading with Lionel Trains. 96p. (Orig.). (gr. 9-12). 1989. pap. 19.95 (ISBN 0-89778-054-X, 10-6745). Greenberg Pub Co.

National TCA Book Committee Staff, et al. Lionel Trains: Standard of the World, 1900-1943. 2nd ed. Witalis-Burke Agency Staff, illus. (Illus.). 256p. 1989. Repr. of 1976 ed. 34.95 (ISBN 0-917896-02-5); prepub. 24.95 (ISBN 0-317-93968-8). TCA PA.

Retan, Walter. The Big Book of Real Trains. Courtney, Richard, illus. 48p. (gr. 1-4). 1987. 7.95 (ISBN 0-448-19178-4, G&D). Putnam Pub Group.

Weiss, Harvey. How to Run a Railroad: Everything You Need to Know about Model Trains. Weiss, Harvey, illus. LC 76-18128. 96p. (gr. 4-7). 1983. pap. 4.95i (ISBN 0-690-04329-5, Crowell Jr Bks). HarpC Child Bks.

RAILROADS–ROLLING STOCK

see Locomotives

RAILROADS–STATIONS

Dupasquier, Philippe. The Train Station. Scally, Kevin, illus. 24p. (ps-1). 1984. 3.95 (ISBN 0-448-19051-6, G&D). Putnam Pub Group.

Slote, Alfred. Omega Station. Kramer, Anthony, illus. LC 82-48461. 160p. (gr. 2-5). 1983. 12.95 (ISBN 0-397-32035-3, Lipp Jr Bks); (Lipp Jr Bks). HarpC Child Bks.

RAILROADS–TRAINS

Better Homes & Gardens Books Editors. Trains & Railroads. (Illus.). 32p. (ps-8). 1991. 4.95 (ISBN 0-696-01937-X). Meredith Bks.

Cave, Ron & Cave, Joyce. What about-Trains? West, David, illus. LC 82-81169. 32p. (gr. k-3). 1982. lib. bdg. 10.90 (ISBN 0-531-03467-4). Watts.

Crews, Donald. Freight Train. (Illus.). 24p. (ps-k). 1985. pap. 3.95 (ISBN 0-14-050480-X, Puffin). Puffin Bks.

Kanetzke, Howard W. Trains & Railroads. rev. ed. LC 87-20813. (Illus.). 48p. (gr. 2-6). 1987. PLB 17.32 (ISBN 0-8172-3263-X); pap. 9.27 (ISBN 0-8172-3288-5). Raintree Pubs.

McPhail, David. Train. (ps-3). 1990. pap. 4.95 (ISBN 0-316-56331-5, Joy St Bks). Little.

Marshall, Ray & Bradley, John. The Train: Watch It Work. Marshall, Ray & Bradley, John, illus. 1986. pap. 13.95 (ISBN 0-670-81134-3). Viking Child Bks.

Piper, Watty. The Fast Rolling Little Engine That Could. Super, Terri, illus. LC 85-70661. 12p. (ps). 1985. 5.95 (ISBN 0-448-09878-4, G&D). Putnam Pub Group.

Rosenblatt, Arthur. The Magical Train. Yealdhall, Gary, illus. 32p. (ps-3). 1985. pap. 0.99 (ISBN 0-87372-008-3). Parker Bros.

Steele, Philip. Trains. LC 90-41179. (Illus.). 32p. (gr. 5-6). 1991. SBE 9.95 (ISBN 0-89686-523-1, Crestwood Hse). Macmillan Child Grp.

Yepsen, Roger. Train Talk: Guide to Lights, Hand Signals & Whistles. LC 83-4062. (Illus.). 96p. (gr. 4-7). 1983. (Pant Bks Young). Pantheon.

RAILROADS, UNDERGROUND

see Subways

RAILROADS–VOCATIONAL GUIDANCE

Matthews, Morgan. What's It Like to Be a Railroad Worker. Sweat, Lynn, illus. LC 89-34389. 32p. (gr. k-3). 1989. lib. bdg. 10.89 (ISBN 0-8167-1815-6); pap. text ed. 2.50 (ISBN 0-8167-1816-4). Troll Assocs.

RAILWAYS

see Railroads

RAIN AND RAINFALL

see also Floods; Meteorology; Snow; Storms

Brandt, Keith. What Makes It Rain? Miyake, Yoshi, illus. LC 81-7495. 32p. (gr. 2-4). 1982. PLB 10.89 (ISBN 0-89375-582-6); pap. text ed. 2.95 (ISBN 0-89375-583-4). Troll Assocs.

Bright, Michael. Tropical Rainforest. (Illus.). 32p. (gr. 2-4). 1991. PLB 11.90 (ISBN 0-531-17301-1, Gloucester Pr). Watts.

Green, Ivah. Splash & Trickle. Connor, Bil, illus. (gr. 2-3). 1978. pap. 1.25 (ISBN 0-89508-062-1). Rainbow Bks.

Greene, Carol. Rain! Rain! LC 82-9509. (Illus.). (ps-2). 1982. PLB 11.93 (ISBN 0-516-02034-X); pap. 2.95 (ISBN 0-516-42034-8). Childrens.

Kirkpatrick, Rena K. Look at Rainbow Colors. rev. ed. Barnard, Anna, illus. LC 84-26250. 32p. (gr. 2-4). 1985. PLB 15.99 (ISBN 0-8172-2356-8); pap. text ed. 9.27 (ISBN 0-8172-2381-9). Raintree Pubs.

Mayes, S. What Makes It Rain? (Illus.). 24p. (gr. 1-4). 1989. lib. bdg. 11.96 (ISBN 0-88110-379-9, Usborne); pap. 3.95 (ISBN 0-7460-0274-2, Usborne). EDC.

Moncure, Jane B. Rain: A Great Day for Ducks. Friedman, Joy, illus. LC 89-24010. 32p. (ps-2). 1990. lib. bdg. 11.97 (ISBN 0-89565-553-5). Childs World.

Robson, Pat, illus. Rain. 32p. (gr. 3-5). 1985. 5.95x (ISBN 0-86685-451-7). Intl Bk Ctr.

Shulevitz, Uri. Rain Rain Rivers. Shulevitz, Uri, illus. LC 73-85370. 32p. (ps-3). 1969. 13.95 (ISBN 0-374-36171-1). FS&G.

Stanish, Bob. Connecting Rainbows. 96p. (gr. 3-12). 1982. 9.95 (ISBN 0-86653-081-9, GA 426). Good Apple.

Steele, Philip. Rain: Causes & Effects. (Illus.). 32p. (gr. 5-8). 1991. PLB 11.90 (ISBN 0-531-10989-5). Watts.

Wyler, Rose. Raindrops & Rainbows. Steltenpohl, Jane, ed. Petruccio, Steven, illus. 32p. (gr. k-2). 1989. lib. bdg. 11.98 (ISBN 0-671-66346-1); pap. 4.95 (ISBN 0-671-66350-X). Messner.

RAIN AND RAINFALL–FICTION

Aardema, Verna. Bringing the Rain to Kapiti Plain. Vidal, Beatriz, illus. LC 80-25886. 32p. (ps). 1981. 14.95 (ISBN 0-8037-0809-2); PLB 13.89 (ISBN 0-8037-0807-6). Dial Bks Young.

Alexander, Martha. We Never Get to Do Anything. Alexander, Martha, illus. (ps-3). 1985. PLB 7.89 (ISBN 0-8037-9416-9). Dial Bks Young.

Bauer, Caroline F., ed. Rainy Day: Stories & Poems. Chessare, Michele, illus. LC 85-45170. 96p. (gr. 2-5). 1986. 13.95 (ISBN 0-397-32104-X, Lipp Jr Bks); PLB 13.89 (ISBN 0-397-32105-8, Lipp Jr Bks). HarpC Child Bks.

Bonnici, Peter. The First Rains. Kopper, Lisa, illus. LC 84-14979. 24p. (ps-3). 1985. PLB 9.95 (ISBN 0-87614-228-5). Carolrhoda Bks.

Boon, Emilie. Peterkin's Wet Walk. Boon, Emilie, illus. LC 83-8937. 32p. (gr. k-2). 1984. Random.

Branley, Franklyn M. Rain & Hail. Barton, Harriett, illus. LC 83-45058. 40p. (gr. k-3). 1983. PLB 13.89 (ISBN 0-690-04353-8, Crowell Jr Bks). HarpC Child Bks.

Brittain, Bill. Dr. Dredd's Wagon of Wonders. Glass, Andrew, illus. LC 86-45775. 208p. (gr. 3-7). 1987. 13.95 (ISBN 0-06-020713-2); PLB 13.89 (ISBN 0-06-020714-0). HarpC Child Bks.

Corrin, Ruth. It Always Rains for Jackie. Pye, Trevor, illus. 32p. (ps-2). 1990. bds. 8.95 (ISBN 0-19-558205-5). Oxford U Pr.

Ehlert, Lois. Planting a Rainbow. 32p. (ps-3). 1988. 14.95 (ISBN 0-15-262609-3). HarBraceJ.

Feagan, Mary. Questions to Ask a Cat When It Comes Home from a Trip. (Illus.). 24p. (gr. k-3). 1988. 3.95 (ISBN 0-929986-63-6). Rainbow Cat Pubs.

—The Rainbow Child. (Illus.). 20p. (gr. 1-4). 1988. 8.95 (ISBN 0-929986-06-7). Rainbow Cat Pubs.

Gordon, Sheila. Waiting for the Rain. (gr. 7 up). 1989. pap. 3.50 (ISBN 0-553-27911-4, Starfire). Bantam.

Hallinan, P. K. My Very Best Rainy Day. (Illus.). 24p. (Orig.). (ps-3). 1991. pap. 3.95 (ISBN 0-8249-8497-8). Ideals.

Hooks, William H. Rainbow Ribbon. 1991. 11.95 (ISBN 0-670-82866-1). Viking Child Bks.

Kalan, Robert. Rain. Crews, Donald, illus. LC 77-25312. 24p. (gr. k-3). 1978. PLB 13.88 (ISBN 0-688-84139-2). Greenwillow.

Maas, Virginia. Niddy Noddy the Noodlemaker. McIntosh, Carolyn, illus. 12p. (ps-2). 1981. pap. 2.75 (ISBN 0-933992-15-7). Coffee Break.

McCaughren, Tom. Rainbows of the Moon. 160p. (gr. 9-12). 1989. 13.95 (ISBN 0-947962-45-X, Pub. by Childrens Pr). Irish Bks Media.

McCoy, James C. Darby's Rainbow. Walker, Timothy, illus. Davenport, May, intro. by. LC 88-70551. (Illus.). 32p. (gr. k-3). 1990. pap. 3.50x (ISBN 0-943864-52-6). Davenport.

Munsch, Robert. Mud Puddle. Suomalaimen, Sami, illus. 32p. (gr. k-3). 1982. pap. 4.95 (ISBN 0-920236-28-6). Firefly Bks Ltd.

Ourth, John & Sawitz, Mike. Hooray, It's Raining. 48p. (gr. k-6). 1979. 5.95 (ISBN 0-916456-50-1, GA110). Good Apple.

Palazzo, Janet. Rainy Day Fun. Ulrich, George, illus. LC 87-10842. 32p. (gr. k-2). 1987. PLB 10.89 (ISBN 0-8167-1095-3); pap. text ed. 2.95 (ISBN 0-8167-1096-1). Troll Assocs.

Rupprecht, Siegfried P. The Tale of the Vanishing Rainbow. Wilkon, Jozef, illus. Lewis, Naomi, tr. from GER. LC 88-43120. (Illus.). 32p. (gr. k-3). 1989. 14.95 (ISBN 1-55858-001-8). North-South Bks NYC.

Ryder, Joanne. A Wet & Sandy Day. LC 76-18401. (Illus.). (gr. k-3). 1977. 6.95 (ISBN 0-06-025158-1). HarpC Child Bks.

Scheffler, Ursel. A Walk in the Rain. Wensell, Ulises, illus. 32p. (ps-2). 1986. 7.95 (ISBN 0-399-21267-1, Putnam). Putnam Pub Group.

Serfozo, Mary. Rain Talk. Narahashi, Keiko, illus. LC 89-12178. 32p. (ps-3). 1990. 12.95 (ISBN 0-689-50496-9, M K McElderry). Macmillan Child Grp.

Spier, Peter. Peter Spier's Rain. LC 81-43506. (Illus.). (gr. k-3). 1987. pap. 6.95 (ISBN 0-385-24105-4, Pub. by Zephyr-BFYR). Doubleday.

Sweeney, Joyce. Right Behind the Rain. LC 86-19953. 192p. (gr. 7 up). 1987. pap. 14.95 (ISBN 0-385-29551-0). Delacorte.

Taylor, Mark A. It's Raining! It's Raining! Rigo, Christina, illus. 20p. (ps). 1987. 1.59 (ISBN 0-87403-311-X, 2011). Standard Pub.

Taylor, Theodore. Walking up a Rainbow. (gr. k-12). 1988. pap. 2.95 (ISBN 0-440-99326-1, LFL); pap. 2.95 (ISBN 0-440-20039-3). Dell.

RAIN AND RAINFALL–POETRY

Palmer, Michele, ed. Rainy Day Rhymes: A Collection of Chants, Forecasts & Tales. Guerin, Penny, illus. LC 84-60412. 24p. (Orig.). (gr. k up). 1984. pap. 2.95 (ISBN 0-932306-02-0). Rocking Horse.

Sears, Peter. Gonna Bake Me a Rainbow Poem. 1990. pap. 2.95 (ISBN 0-590-43085-8). Scholastic Inc.

RAINFALL

see Rain and Rainfall

RANCH LIFE

see also Cowboys

Ashabranner, Brent. Born to the Land: An American Portrait. Conklin, Paul, photos by. (Illus.). 144p. (gr. 5 up). 1989. 14.95 (ISBN 0-399-21716-9, Putnam). Putnam Pub Group.

Braly, David. Cattle Barons of Early Oregon. LC 78-105220. (Illus.). 44p. (gr. 7-12). 1982. pap. 4.50 (ISBN 0-942206-00-2). Mediaor Co.

Henderson, Kathy. I Can Be a Rancher. LC 90-37678. (Illus.). 32p. (gr. k-3). 1990. PLB 13.93 (ISBN 0-516-01962-7); pap. 3.95 (ISBN 0-516-41962-5). Childrens.

Reeve, Agnesa, compiled by. & intro. by. My Dear Mollie: Love Letters of a Texas Sheep Rancher. (Illus.). 192p. 1990. 17.95 (ISBN 0-937460-62-1). Hendrick-Long.

RANCH LIFE–FICTION

Aaron, Chester. Duchess. LC 81-47755. 192p. (gr. 7 up). 1982. PLB 11.89 (ISBN 0-397-31948-7, Lipp Jr Bks). HarpC Child Bks.

Carey, Karla. Julie & Jackie on the Ranch: The Narration & Music Book. Nolan, Dennis, illus. 91p. 1990. pap. 18.95 complete pkg. (ISBN 0-685-35757-0); pap. 9.95 (ISBN 1-55768-204-6); cassette 9.95 (ISBN 0-685-35758-9). LC Pub.

Cleaver, Vera & Cleaver, Bill. The Kissimmee Kid. LC 80-29262. 160p. (gr. 5 up). 1981. PLB 12.88 (ISBN 0-688-51992-X). Lothrop.

Dominick, Bayard. Sam, a Goat. (Illus.). (gr. 3-5). 1968. 9.95 (ISBN 0-8392-3062-1). Astor-Honor.

Kehret, Peg. Nightmare Mountain. Mckeating, Eileen, illus. LC 89-1535. 176p. (gr. 5 up). 1989. 13.95 (ISBN 0-525-65008-3, Cobblehill Bks). Dutton Child Bks.

Kuchn, Nora A. Thunder, the Maverick Mustang. 96p. 1991. pap. 6.95 (ISBN 0-8163-0932-9). Pacific Pr Pub Assn.

Nelson, A. A Long Hard Day on the Ranch. (Illus.). 24p. (ps-8). 1989. pap. 4.95 (ISBN 0-88753-184-9). Firefly Bks Ltd.

Noble, Trinka H. Meanwhile Back at the Ranch. Ross, Tony, illus. LC 86-11651. 32p. (ps-3). 1987. 11.95 (ISBN 0-8037-0353-8); PLB 13.89 (ISBN 0-8037-0354-6). Dial Bks Young.

Pryor, Bonnie. Mr. Munday & the Rustlers. Manyum, Wallop, illus. LC 87-17539. 32p. (ps-3). 1987. PLB 12.95 (ISBN 0-13-604737-8). P-H.

Saban, Vera. Johnny Egan of the Paintrock. Saban, Sonja, illus. LC 85-30958. 130p. (Orig.). (gr. 4-8). 1986. pap. 7.95x (ISBN 0-914565-13-3). Capstan Pubns.

Ten-year-old Johnny lives on a cattle ranch in the Big Horn Basin of Wyoming, where he is joined by his 14-year-old cousin. They live the life of typical boys: with the same joys & sadness, hopes & fears that youngsters are familiar with today. There is adventure & some mystery. There are problems & there are some decisions to be made. Young people reading this book will readily identify with all the situations & be inspired & encouraged with the working out of the lives of these two boys. The family travels in a horse-drawn wagon, but there are such things as automobiles & telephones, too. It's an interesting era for the reader to become acquainted with, & particularly in this part of America, one of our newest frontiers. The illustrations by Sonja Bernard, from suggestions by fourth-grade readers of the manuscript, add even more interest to the book. To order this book & for additional information on other TimberTrails Books, call (307) 568-2604.

Publisher Provided Annotation.

Schaefer, Jack. Shane. McCormick, J., illus. (gr. 7 up). 1954. 13.95 (ISBN 0-395-07090-2). HM.

Steinbeck, John. Of Mice & Men. (gr. 9-12). 1970. pap. 2.75 (ISBN 0-553-26675-6). Bantam.

Weber, Lenora M. How Long Is Always? LC 75-1937. 226p. (gr. 7 up). 1970. 14.95 (ISBN 0-690-40680-0, Crowell Jr Bks). HarpC Child Bks.

RANDOLPH, ASA PHILIP, 1889-

Hanley, Sally. A. Philip Randolph. King, Coretta Scott, intro. by. (Illus.). 112p. (gr. 5 up). 1989. 17.95 (ISBN 1-55546-607-9); pap. 9.95 (ISBN 0-7910-0222-5). Chelsea Hse.

RAPE

Bode, Janet. The Voices of Rape. 144p. (gr. 9-12). 1990. 11.95 (ISBN 0-531-15184-0); PLB 12.90 (ISBN 0-531-10959-3). Watts.

Booher, Dianna D. Rape: What Would You Do If...? LC 81-914. 128p. (gr. 7 up). 1983. lib. bdg. 12.98 (ISBN 0-671-42201-4); pap. 4.95 (ISBN 0-671-49485-6). Messner.

Booher, Dianne D. Rape: What Would You Do If? rev. ed. 160p. (gr. 7 up). 1991. PLB 13.98 (ISBN 0-671-74538-7); pap. 6.95 (ISBN 0-671-74546-8). Messner.

Dizeno, Patricia. Why Me? The Story of Jenny. (gr. 7 up). 1976. pap. 2.95 (ISBN 0-380-00563-8, Flare). Avon.

Guernsey, JoAnn B. Rape. LC 90-33666. (Illus.). 48p. (gr. 5-6). 1990. RSBE 10.95 (ISBN 0-89686-533-9, Crestwood Hse). Macmillan Child Grp.

Shuker-Haines, Frances. Everything You Need to Know about Date Rape. Rosen, Ruth, ed. (gr. 7-12). 1989. PLB 12.95 (ISBN 0-8239-1013-X). Rosen Group.

Sloan, Irving J., ed. The Law of Rape. 150p. (gr. 9-12). 1991. lib. bdg. 17.50 (ISBN 0-379-11171-3). Oceana.

RAPE–FICTION

Abbey, Deirdre. Shadows after Closing. Fowles, Jeri, illus. (Orig.). (gr. 6-12). 1988. pap. 2.95 (ISBN 0-939400-04-9). RWS Bks.

Miklowitz, Gloria D. Did You Hear What Happened to Andrea? LC 78-72972. 1979. 7.95 (ISBN 0-440-01923-0). Delacorte.

—Did You Hear What Happened to Andrea? 176p. (gr. 7 up). 1986. pap. 1.75 (ISBN 0-440-91853-7, LE). Dell.

My Father Raped Me: Frances Ann Speaks Out. (Illus.). (gr. 5 up). 1977. 4.95 (ISBN 0-685-03566-2). New Seed.

Peck, Richard. Are You in the House Alone? (gr. 10 up). 1976. pap. 12.95 (ISBN 0-670-13241-1). Viking Child Bks.

RATS

Zinsser, Hans. Rats, Lice & History. (gr. 9 up). 1984. (Pub. by Atlantic Monthly Pr); pap. 8.95 (ISBN 0-316-98896-0). Little.

RATS–FICTION

Allen, Jeffery. Nosey Mrs. Rat. Marshall, James, illus. LC 84-19618. 32p. (ps-3). 1985. pap. 11.95 (ISBN 0-670-80880-6). Viking Child Bks.

Browning, Robert. The Pied Piper of Hamelin: A Classic Tale. Jose, Eduard, adapted by. Suire, Diane D., tr. from SPA. Rovira, Francesc, illus. LC 88-35313. 32p. (gr. 1-4). 1988. PLB 10.95 (ISBN 0-89565-471-7). Childs World.

The Cat & the Rat EV, Unit 6. (gr. 2). 1991. 5-pack 21.25 (ISBN 0-88106-750-4). Charlesbridge Pub.

Conly, Jane L. R-T, Margaret, & the Rats of NIMH. Lubin, Leonard, illus. LC 89-19968. 288p. (gr. 4-7). 1990. 12.95 (ISBN 0-06-021363-9); PLB 12.89 (ISBN 0-06-021364-7). HarpC Child Bks.

—R-T, Margaret, & the Rats of NIMH. 1990. 12.89 (ISBN 0-06-023647-7). HarpC Child Bks.

—Rasco & the Rats of NIMH. Lubin, Leonard, illus. LC 85-42634. 288p. (gr. 4-7). 1986. 12.95 (ISBN 0-06-021361-2); PLB 12.89 (ISBN 0-06-021362-0). HarpC Child Bks.

Firmin, Peter. Happy Miss Rat. 1990. pap. 2.95 (ISBN 0-440-40382-0, YB). Dell.

Giff, Patricia R. Rat Teeth. (gr. k-6). 1990. pap. 3.25 (ISBN 0-440-47457-4, YB). Dell.

Hamilton, Carol. The Dawn Seekers. Levine, Abby, ed. LC 86-15820. (Illus.). 144p. (gr. 3-7). 1987. PLB 10.50 (ISBN 0-8075-1480-2). A Whitman.

La Fontaine. The Lion & the Rat. Wildsmith, Brian, illus. 32p. 1987. 12.95 (ISBN 0-19-279607-0); pap. 5.95 (ISBN 0-19-272167-4). Oxford U Pr.

Levitin, Sonia. Rita, the Weekend Rat. Shortall, Leonard, illus. 144p. (Orig.). (gr. 3-7). 1980. pap. 1.95 (ISBN 0-590-30378-3, Schol Pap). Scholastic Inc.

—Rita, the Weekend Rat. 1989. pap. 2.50 (ISBN 0-590-42245-6). Scholastic Inc.

McCutcheon, Elsie. The Rat War. LC 85-4593. 111p. (gr. 4 up). 1986. 10.95 (ISBN 0-374-36182-7). FS&G.

O'Donovan, Dermot. Silas Rat & the Nuclear Tail. Booth, Tim, illus. 125p. 1988. pap. 7.95 (ISBN 0-947962-22-0, Pub. by Children's Pr). Irish Bks Media.

Porte, Barbara A. Harry in Trouble. 1990. pap. 2.95 (ISBN 0-440-40370-7, YB). Dell.

Sharmat, Marjorie W. Mooch the Messy. Shecter, Ben, illus. LC 76-3842. 64p. (gr. k-3). 1976. PLB 11.89 (ISBN 0-06-025532-3). HarpC Child Bks.

Spicer, Venetia. The Adventures of Chatrat. (Illus.). 48p. 1981. 9.95 (ISBN 0-7043-2269-2, Pub. by Quartet England). Charles River Bks.

Storr, Catherine, retold by. The Pied Piper of Hamelin. LC 84-26971. (Illus.). 32p. (gr. k-5). 1984. PLB 16.67 (ISBN 0-8172-2107-7); PLB 27.99 incl. cassette (ISBN 0-8172-2238-3); cassette 14.00 (ISBN 0-685-09502-9). Raintree Pubs.

Vlakos, Jon, illus. Ladle Rat Rotten Hut. 6th ed. 12p. 1988. pap. 2.00 (ISBN 0-934714-05-3). Swamp Pr.

Westcott, Alvin. Billy Lump's Adventure. LC 68-56817. (Illus.). 32p. (gr. 2-4). 1968. PLB 9.95 (ISBN 0-87783-002-9). Oddo.

RAVENS–FICTION

Aiken, Joan. Mortimer's Cross. Blake, Quentin, illus. LC 83-49475. 160p. (gr. 3-6). 1984. HarpC Child Bks.

Dewey, Jennifer O. Clem: The Story of a Raven. (Illus.). 128p. (gr. 7-11). 1986. 11.95 (ISBN 0-396-08728-0, Putnam). Putnam Pub Group.

Elijah & the Ravens. (ps). 1991. Set of 6. pap. 3.95 (ISBN 0-8007-7117-6). Revell.

Manley, Seon. A Present for Charles Dickens. LC 82-24862. (Illus.). 124p. (gr. 5 up). 1983. 12.95 (ISBN 0-664-32706-0, Westminster). Westminster John Knox.

READERS

Here are entered school readers in english. For readers in other languages, use the name of the language with the subdivision Readers, e.g. French Language–Readers.

see also Primers

Adventure at the Castle. (Illus.). (ps-5). 3.50 (ISBN 0-7214-0022-1). Ladybird Bks.

Adventure on the Island. (Illus.). (ps-5). 3.50 (ISBN 0-7214-0010-8); Series S05, Set 1. flash cards 4.75; Series S05, Set 2. flash cards 4.75. Ladybird Bks.

Amery, H. Black Knights Victory. (Illus.). 24p. (ps-2). 1987. 3.95 (ISBN 0-7460-0157-6); PLB 7.96 (ISBN 0-88110-299-7). EDC.

—Going Swimming. (Illus.). 24p. (ps-2). 1987. 3.95 (ISBN 0-7460-0065-0); PLB 7.96 (ISBN 0-88110-261-X). EDC.

—The Mammoth Hunt. (Illus.). 24p. 1987. 3.95 (ISBN 0-7460-0158-4); PLB 7.96 (ISBN 0-88110-291-1). EDC.

Ames, Gerald & Wyler, Rose. Prove It! Stubis, Talivaldis, illus. LC 62-21288. 64p. (gr. k-3). 1963. PLB 11.89 (ISBN 0-06-020051-0). HarpC Child Bks.

Averill, Esther. Fire Cat. Averill, Esther, illus. LC 60-10234. 64p. (gr. k-3). 1960. PLB 11.89 (ISBN 0-06-020196-7). HarpC Child Bks.

Baker, Betty. Little Runner of the Longhouse. Lobel, Arnold, illus. LC 62-8040. 64p. (gr. k-3). 1962. PLB 11.89 (ISBN 0-06-020341-2). HarpC Child Bks.

Balcomb, Philip E. The Clock Repair First Reader: Second Steps for the Beginner. Balcomb, Philip E., illus. 160p. (Orig.). (gr. 9 up). 1989. pap. 14.95 (ISBN 0-9620456-1-6). Tempus Pr.

Begin, S., et al. Suspicious Minds: A Radio Play Developing Listening Strategies & Lifeskills. 1990. pap. text ed. 10.12 (ISBN 0-8013-0287-0, 75937); cass. 26.21 (ISBN 0-8013-0288-9, 75938). Longman.

Beginning to Read, I. 32p. (gr. k-1). 1985. pap. write for info. (ISBN 0-307-03587-5, Pub. by Golden Bks). Western Pub.

Beginning to Read, II. (Illus.). 32p. (gr. k-1). 1985. pap. write for info. (ISBN 0-307-03588-3, Pub. by Golden Bks). Western Pub.

Benchley, Nathaniel. Red Fox & His Canoe. Lobel, Arnold, illus. LC 64-16650. 64p. (gr. k-3). 1964. PLB 11.89 (ISBN 0-06-020476-1). HarpC Child Bks.

The Big House. (Illus.). (ps-5). 3.50 (ISBN 0-7214-0544-4). Ladybird Bks.

The Big Secret. (Illus.). (ps-2). 1990. 3.50 (ISBN 0-7214-1324-2); parent/tchr's. guide 3.95 (ISBN 0-7214-4203-X). Ladybird Bks.

Bolinske, Janet L., ed. Big Bug Softcover Package. (Illus., Orig.). (gr. k-1). 1989. Set of 6 bks., 24 pgs. ea. bk. pap. 27.00 (ISBN 0-88335-539-6). Milliken Pub Co.

Bonsall, Crosby N. Case of the Cat's Meow. Bonsall, Crosby N., illus. LC 65-11451. 64p. (gr. k-3). 1965. PLB 11.89 (ISBN 0-06-020561-X). HarpC Child Bks.

—Case of the Dumb Bells. Bonsall, Crosby N., illus. LC 66-8267. 64p. (gr. k-3). 1966. PLB 11.89 (ISBN 0-06-020624-1). HarpC Child Bks.

—Case of the Hungry Stranger. Bonsall, Crosby N., illus. LC 63-17947. 64p. (gr. k-3). 1963. PLB 11.89 (ISBN 0-06-020571-7). HarpC Child Bks.

—Tell Me Some More. Siebel, Fritz, illus. LC 61-5773. 64p. (gr. k-3). 1961. PLB 11.89 (ISBN 0-06-020601-2). HarpC Child Bks.

—What Spot? Bonsall, Crosby N., illus. LC 63-8005. 64p. (gr. k-3). 1963. PLB 11.89 (ISBN 0-06-020611-X). HarpC Child Bks.

—Who's a Pest? Bonsall, Crosby N., illus. LC 62-13310. 64p. (gr. k-3). 1962. PLB 11.89 (ISBN 0-06-020621-7). HarpC Child Bks.

Books Are Exciting. (Illus.). (ps-5). 3.50 (ISBN 0-7214-0646-7). Ladybird Bks.

Booth, Eugene. At the Circus. Collard, Derek, illus. LC 77-7946. 24p. (gr. k-3). 1985. PLB 13.32 (ISBN 0-8393-0112-X); pap. text ed. 9.27 (ISBN 0-8393-0162-6). Raintree Pubs.

—At the Fair. Collard, Derek, illus. LC 77-7961. 24p. (gr. k-3). 1985. PLB 13.32 (ISBN 0-8393-0114-6); pap. text ed. 9.27 (ISBN 0-8393-0163-4). Raintree Pubs.

—On the Farm. LC 77-7965. (Illus.). 24p. (gr. k-3). 1985. PLB 13.32 (ISBN 0-8393-0113-8); pap. 9.27 (ISBN 0-8393-0170-7). Raintree Pubs.

Boyd, Frances & Quinn, David. Stories from Lake Wobegon: Advanced Listening & Conversation Skills. 1990. pap. text ed. 12.93 (ISBN 0-8013-0312-5, 78017); cass. 26.21 (ISBN 0-8013-0492-X, 78344). Longman.

Boys & Girls. (Illus.). (ps-5). 3.50 (ISBN 0-7214-0015-9); Series No. S705. wkbk. 1.95; Series S05, Set 1. flash cards 4.75; Series S05, Set 2. flash cards 4.75. Ladybird Bks.

Bradshaw, Georgene & Wrighton, Charlene. Zoo-Phonics Level B Reader: (a-b-c) (Illus.). 48p. (gr. 1). 1987. pap. text ed. 4.50 (ISBN 0-9617342-2-1). Zoo-phonics.

Bradshaw, Georgene E. & Wrighton, Charlene A. A Zoo-Phonics Reader: Level A. Clark, Irene, illus. 32p. (ps-1). 1986. pap. text ed. 3.50 (ISBN 0-9617342-1-3). Zoo-Phonics.

—Zoo-Phonics Reader: Level B (d-e-f) (Illus.). 48p. (gr. 1). 1987. pap. text ed. 4.50 (ISBN 0-9617342-3-X). Zoo-phonics.

—Zoo-Phonics Reader: Level C (g-h-i) (Illus.). 48p. (gr. 1). 1988. pap. text ed. 5.50 (ISBN 0-9617342-4-8). Zoo-phonics.

Brandenberg, Franz. It's Not My Fault. Aliki, illus. LC 79-24157. 64p. (gr. 1-3). 1980. 10.95 (ISBN 0-688-80235-4). Greenwillow.

Brannon, Tom & Cooke, Tom, illus. Open Sesame Multilevel Book. Baigelman, Simon, photos by. pap. 6.75 (ISBN 0-19-434261-1). Oxford U Pr.

Brooks, Robert F. Nwandu's Child of Life Reader. (Illus.). 20p. (Orig.). (gr. k-4). pap. 2.00 (ISBN 0-936868-00-7). Freeland Pubns.

Burke, Suzanne. Ollie Owl. Jordan, Alton, ed. Reese, Bob, illus. (gr. k-3). 1975. PLB 5.95 (ISBN 0-89868-015-8, Read Res); text ed. 2.50 soft bd. (ISBN 0-89868-048-4). ARO Pub.

—Our Parade. Jordan, Alton, ed. Thompson, Sherry, illus. (gr. k-3). 1975. PLB 5.95 (ISBN 0-89868-017-4, Read Res); pap. text ed. 2.50 (ISBN 0-89868-050-6). ARO Pub.

A Busy Night. (Illus.). (ps-2). 1990. 3.50 (ISBN 0-7214-1329-3); parent/tchr's. guide 3.95. Ladybird Bks.

Carlile, Candy. Book Report Big Top. 48p. (gr. 1-4). 1980. 5.95 (ISBN 0-88160-009-1, LW 111). Learning Wks.

Chapman, Mary W. Why? McKissack, Patricia & McKissack, Fredrick, eds. LC 88-60387. (Illus.). 32p. (Orig.). (gr. 1-3). 1988. text ed. 8.95 (ISBN 0-88335-781-X); pap. text ed. 4.95 (ISBN 0-88335-793-3). Milliken Pub Co.

Childs, Phyllis. The Language Ladder, Bk. I. Sterling, Suzanne, illus. 76p. (ps-k). 1985. wkbk. 6.50 (ISBN 0-931749-01-8). PJC Lrng Mtrls.

Chodkowski, Dick. Snakes Alive! It's Reptile Clive! McKissack, Patricia & McKissack, Fredrick, eds. Chodkowski, Dick, illus. LC 88-60391. 32p. (Orig.). (gr. 1-3). 1990. text ed. 8.95 (ISBN 0-88335-787-9); pap. text ed. 4.95 (ISBN 0-88335-799-2). Milliken Pub Co.

Civardi, A. The Big Match. (Illus.). 24p. (ps-2). 1987. 3.95 (ISBN 0-7460-0160-6); PLB 7.96 (ISBN 0-88110-298-9). EDC.

—The Builder. (Illus.). 24p. (ps-2). 1987. 3.95 (ISBN 0-7460-0053-7); PLB 7.96 (ISBN 0-88110-264-4). EDC.

—The Farmer. (Illus.). 24p. (gr. 1-3). 1987. 3.95 (ISBN 0-7460-0052-9); PLB 7.96 (ISBN 0-88110-263-6). EDC.

—The Great Race. (Illus.). 24p. 1988. 3.95 (ISBN 0-7460-0162-2); PLB 7.96 (ISBN 0-88110-309-8). EDC.

Collins, David R. Grandfather Woo Goes to School. McKissack, Patricia & McKissack, Fredrick, eds. Wilson, Deborah, illus. LC 88-60389. 32p. (Orig.). (gr. 1-3). 1990. text ed. 8.95 (ISBN 0-88335-784-4); pap. text ed. 4.95 (ISBN 0-88335-796-8). Milliken Pub Co.

Complete Softcover Library, 64 bks. (Illus., Orig.). (gr. k-3). 1989. Set. pap. 285.00 (ISBN 0-88335-716-X). Milliken Pub Co.

The Cooking Pot, 6 bks. 16p. (Orig.). (gr. k-2). 1987. Set. pap. text ed. 19.80 (ISBN 1-55624-735-4). Wright Group.

Cowley, Joy. Along Comes Jake. Paul, Korky, illus. 16p. (gr. k-2). 1989. pap. text ed. 23.00 (ISBN 1-55911-292-1). Wright Group.

—Along Comes Jake, 6 bks. Paul, Korky, illus. 16p. (gr. k-2). 1986. Set. pap. text ed. 19.80 (ISBN 1-55911-371-5). Wright Group.

—Baby Gets Dressed. Belton, Robyn, illus. 8p. (gr. k-2). 1989. pap. text ed. 15.00 (ISBN 1-55911-274-3). Wright Group.

—Baby Gets Dressed, 6 bks. Belton, Robyn, illus. 8p. (gr. k-2). 1986. Set. pap. text ed. 12.60 (ISBN 1-55911-335-9). Wright Group.

—Boggywooga, 6 bks. Gardiner, Deirdre, illus. 16p. (Orig.). (gr. k-2). 1987. Set. pap. text ed. 19.80 (ISBN 1-55624-746-X). Wright Group.

—Boggywooga. Gardiner, Deirdre, illus. 16p. (Orig.). (gr. k-2). 1987. pap. text ed. 23.00 (ISBN 1-55624-169-0). Wright Group.

—La Casa de Tio Totio. Paul, Korky, illus. (SPA.). 8p. (gr. k-2). 1989. pap. text ed. 15.00 (ISBN 1-55911-395-2). Wright Group.

—La Casa de Tio Totio, 6 bks. Korky, Paul, illus. (SPA.). 8p. (gr. k-2). 1989. Set. pap. text ed. 12.60 (ISBN 1-55911-396-0). Wright Group.

—The Cooking Pot. Breeze, Lynn, illus. 16p. (Orig.). (gr. k-2). 1987. pap. text ed. 23.00 (ISBN 1-55624-158-5). Wright Group.

—El Desayuno de Huggles. Fuller, Elizabeth, illus. (SPA.). 8p. (gr. k-2). 1989. pap. text ed. 15.00 (ISBN 1-55911-399-5). Wright Group.

—El Desayuno de Huggles. Fuller, Elizabeth, illus. (SPA.). 8p. (gr. k-2). 1989. pap. text ed. 12.60 (ISBN 1-55911-400-2). Wright Group.

—Good for You. Fuller, Elizabeth, illus. 16p. (gr. k-2). 1989. pap. text ed. 23.00 (ISBN 1-55911-287-5). Wright Group.

—Good for You, 6 bks. Fuller, Elizabeth, illus. 16p. (gr. k-2). 1986. Set. pap. text ed. 19.80 (ISBN 1-55911-363-4). Wright Group.

—The Ha-Ha Powder, 6 bks. Kincaid, Eric, illus. 16p. (Orig.). (gr. k-2). 1987. Set. pap. text ed. 19.80 (ISBN 1-55624-748-6). Wright Group.

—The Ha-Ha Powder. Kincaid, Eric, illus. 16p. (Orig.). (gr. k-2). 1987. pap. text ed. 23.00 (ISBN 1-55624-171-2). Wright Group.

—Huggles' Breakfast. Fuller, Elizabeth, illus. 8p. (gr. k-2). 1989. pap. text ed. 15.00 (ISBN 1-55911-276-X). Wright Group.

—Huggles' Breakfast, 6 bks. Fuller, Elizabeth, illus. 8p. (gr. k-2). 1986. Set. pap. text ed. 12.60 (ISBN 1-55911-337-5). Wright Group.

—A Hundred Hugs, 6 bks. Fuller, Elizabeth, illus. 16p. (Orig.). (gr. k-2). 1987. Set. pap. text ed. 19.80 (ISBN 1-55624-747-8). Wright Group.

—A Hundred Hugs. Fuller, Elizabeth, illus. 16p. (Orig.). (gr. k-2). 1987. pap. text ed. 23.00 (ISBN 1-55624-170-4). Wright Group.

—I Can Jump. Nightingale, Sandy, illus. 8p. (gr. k-2). 1989. pap. text ed. 15.00 (ISBN 1-55911-283-2). Wright Group.

—I Can Jump, 6 bks. Nightingale, Sandy, illus. 8p. (gr. k-2). 1986. Set. pap. text ed. 12.60 (ISBN 1-55911-357-X). Wright Group.

—Just This Once, 6 bks. Fuller, Elizabeth, illus. 16p. (Orig.). (gr. k-2). 1987. Set. pap. text ed. 19.80 (ISBN 1-55624-743-5). Wright Group.

—Just This Once. Fuller, Elizabeth, illus. 16p. (Orig.). (gr. k-2). 1987. pap. text ed. 23.00 (ISBN 1-55624-166-6). Wright Group.

—The Long, Long Tale. Beasley, Madeline, illus. 8p. (gr. k-2). 1989. pap. text ed. 15.00 (ISBN 1-55911-277-8). Wright Group.
—The Long, Long Tale, 6 bks. Beasley, Madeline, illus. 8p. (gr. k-2). 1986. Set. pap. text ed. 12.60 (ISBN 1-55911-341-3). Wright Group.
—Mr. Grump. Hodder, Wendy, illus. 16p. (gr. k-2). 1989. pap. text ed. 23.00 (ISBN 1-55911-288-3). Wright Group.
—Mr. Grump, 6 bks. Hodder, Wendy, illus. 16p. (gr. k-2). 1986. Set. pap. text ed. 19.80 (ISBN 1-55911-361-8). Wright Group.
—Mr. Whisper. Kincaid, Eric, illus. 16p. (Orig.). (gr. k-2). 1987. pap. text ed. 23.00 (ISBN 1-55624-163-1). Wright Group.
—Noise. Matijasevic, Astrid, illus. 16p. (Orig.). (gr. k-2). 1987. pap. text ed. 23.00 (ISBN 1-55624-159-3). Wright Group.
—El Pastel de Cumpleanos. Webb, Jenni, illus. (SPA.). 8p. (gr. k-2). 1989. pap. text ed. 15.00 (ISBN 1-55911-397-9). Wright Group.
—El Pastel de Cumpleanos. Webb, Jenni, illus. (SPA.). 8p. (gr. k-2). 1989. pap. text ed. 12.60 (ISBN 1-55911-398-7). Wright Group.
—The Poor, Sore Paw, 6 bks. Kincaid, Eric, illus. 16p. (Orig.). (gr. k-2). 1987. Set. pap. text ed. 19.80 (ISBN 1-55624-739-7). Wright Group.
—The Poor, Sore Paw. Kincaid, Eric, illus. 16p. (Orig.). (gr. k-2). 1987. pap. text ed. 23.00 (ISBN 1-55624-162-3). Wright Group.
—Quack, Quack, Quack, 6 bks. Fowler, Jeff, illus. 16p. (Orig.). (gr. k-2). 1987. Set. pap. text ed. 19.80 (ISBN 1-55624-745-1). Wright Group.
—Quack, Quack, Quack! Fowler, Jeff, illus. 16p. (Orig.). (gr. k-2). 1987. pap. text ed. 23.00 (ISBN 1-55624-168-2). Wright Group.
—Ratty-Tatty. Matijasevic, Astrid, illus. 16p. (Orig.). (gr. k-2). 1987. pap. text ed. 23.00 (ISBN 1-55624-164-X). Wright Group.
—The Secret of Spooky House. Paul, Korky, illus. 16p. (Orig.). (gr. k-2). 1987. pap. text ed. 23.00 (ISBN 1-55624-173-9). Wright Group.
—The Seed, 6 bks. Webb, Philip, illus. 16p. (gr. k-2). 1986. Set. pap. text ed. 19.80 (ISBN 1-55911-373-1). Wright Group.
—Shark in a Sack. Van der Voo, Jan, illus. 8p. (gr. k-2). 1989. pap. text ed. 15.00 (ISBN 1-55911-285-9). Wright Group.
—Shark in a Sack, 6 bks. Van der Voo, Jan, illus. 8p. (gr. k-2). 1986. Set. pap. text ed. 12.60 (ISBN 1-55911-353-7). Wright Group.
—Snap! Van der Voo, Jan, illus. (SPA.). 8p. (gr. k-2). 1989. pap. text ed. 15.00 (ISBN 1-55911-393-6). Wright Group.
—Snap! Van der Voo, Jan, illus. (SPA.). 8p. (gr. k-2). 1989. pap. text ed. 12.60 (ISBN 1-55911-394-4). Wright Group.
—Sopa Fuchi. McRae, Rodney, illus. (SPA.). 8p. (gr. k-2). 1989. pap. text ed. 15.00 (ISBN 1-55911-401-0). Wright Group.
—Sopa Fuchi. McRae, Rodney, illus. (SPA.). 8p. (gr. k-2). 1989. pap. text ed. 12.60 (ISBN 1-55911-402-9). Wright Group.
—Tiburon en un Saco. Van der Voo, Jan, illus. (SPA.). (gr. k-2). 1989. pap. text ed. 15.00 (ISBN 1-55911-392-8). Wright Group.
—Tiburon en un Saco: (Shark in a Sack Big Book) Van der Voo, Jan, illus. (SPA.). (gr. k-2). 1989. Set. pap. text ed. 12.60 (ISBN 1-55911-391-X). Wright Group.
—Uncle Buncle's House. Paul, Korky, illus. 8p. (gr. k-2). 1989. pap. text ed. 15.00 (ISBN 1-55911-282-4). Wright Group.
—Uncle Buncle's House, 6 bks. Paul, Korky, illus. 8p. (gr. k-2). 1986. Set. pap. text ed. 12.60 (ISBN 1-55911-347-2). Wright Group.
—Vete! (SPA., Illus.). 8p. (gr. k-2). 1989. pap. text ed. 12.00 (ISBN 1-55911-405-3). Wright Group.
—Vete! (SPA., Illus.). 8p. (gr. k-2). 1989. pap. text ed. 12.60 (ISBN 1-55911-406-1). Wright Group.
—What Is a Huggles? Fuller, Elizabeth, illus. 8p. (gr. k-2). 1989. pap. text ed. 15.00 (ISBN 1-55911-278-6). Wright Group.
—What Is a Huggles, 6 bks. Fuller, Elizabeth, illus. 8p. (gr. k-2). 1986. Set. pap. text ed. 12.60 (ISBN 1-55911-345-6). Wright Group.
—What Would You Like? Matijasevic, Astrid, illus. 16p. (gr. k-2). 1989. pap. text ed. 23.00 (ISBN 1-55911-286-7). Wright Group.
—What Would You Like, 6 bks. Matijasevic, Astrid, illus. 16p. (gr. k-2). 1986. Set. pap. text ed. 19.80 (ISBN 1-55911-365-0). Wright Group.
—When Itchy Witchy Sneezes. Hodder, Wendy, illus. 8p. (gr. k-2). 1989. pap. text ed. 15.00 (ISBN 1-55911-281-6). Wright Group.
—When Itchy Witchy Sneezes, 6 bks. Hodder, Wendy, illus. 8p. (gr. k-2). 1986. Set. pap. text ed. 12.60 (ISBN 1-55911-349-9). Wright Group.
—The Wind Blows Strong. Smillie-McHoull, Vicki, illus. 16p. (gr. k-2). 1989. pap. text ed. 23.00 (ISBN 1-55911-291-3). Wright Group.
—The Wind Blows Strong, 6 bks. Smillie-McHoull, Vicki, illus. 16p. (gr. k-2). 1986. Set. pap. text ed. 19.80 (ISBN 1-55911-369-3). Wright Group.
—Yo Puedo Brincar. Nightingale, Sandy, illus. (SPA.). 8p. (gr. k-2). 1989. pap. text ed. 15.00 (ISBN 1-55911-403-7). Wright Group.
—Yo Puedo Brincar. Nightingale, Sandy, illus. (SPA.). 8p. (gr. k-2). 1989. pap. text ed. 12.60 (ISBN 1-55911-404-5). Wright Group.
—Yuk Soup. McRae, Rodney, illus. 8p. (gr. k-2). 1989. pap. text ed. 15.00 (ISBN 1-55911-279-4). Wright Group.
—Yuk Soup, 6 bks. McRae, Rodney, illus. 8p. (gr. k-2). 1986. Set. pap. text ed. 12.60 (ISBN 1-55911-343-X). Wright Group.
Crane, Barbara J. The Baby Jay. (Illus.). (gr. k-2). 1977. pap. 4.50 (ISBN 0-89075-095-5). Crane Pub Co.
Crooks, Linda H., et al. Kindergang Kindergarten Skills Booklets, Featuring Busy Bear, Booklet 3. 2nd ed. Crooks, Linda H., illus. (gr. k). 1988. Repr. of 1985 ed. tchr's. ed. 9.19 (ISBN 1-877594-03-2); wkbk. 1.59 (ISBN 0-317-93575-5). I Can.
—Kindergang Kindergarten Skills Booklets, Featuring Lucky Lion, Booklet 1. 2nd ed. Crooks, Linda H., illus. (gr. k). 1988. Repr. of 1985 ed. tchr's. ed. 9.19 (ISBN 1-877594-01-6); wkbk. 1.59 (ISBN 0-317-93571-2). I Can.
Cutting, Brian & Cutting, Jill. Fact & Fantasy - Emergent Level: It Takes Time to Grow; What Am I?; A Small World; What Else?; Space; Alien at the Zoo; The Hermit Crab; Underwater Journey; Are You a Ladybug?; Dinosaurs; What Lives in These Eggs?; The Dandelion; I Wonder; Reading Is Everywhere; Together; Wheels; Clouds; The New Building; Dreams; Building; The Tree; Captain B's Ark; Math Is Everywhere & Sunshine Street, 24 bks. (Illus.). 384p. (gr. k-1). Set. pap. text ed. 65.90 (ISBN 1-55911-058-9). Wright Group.
Cutting, Brian & Cutting, Jillian. Fact & Fantasy Social Studies - Emergent Level: I Wonder; Reading Is Everywhere; Together; Wheels; Clouds; The New Building; Dreams; Building & The Tree, 9 bks. (Illus.). 144p. (gr. k-1). Set. pap. text ed. 24.60 (ISBN 1-55911-025-2). Wright Group.
—What Am I? Astin, David, illus. 16p. (Orig.). (gr. k-2). 1988. pap. text ed. 23.00 (ISBN 1-55911-027-9). Wright Group.
—What Am I, 6 bks. Astin, David, illus. 16p. (Orig.). (gr. k-2). 1988. Set. pap. text ed. 19.80 (ISBN 1-55911-028-7). Wright Group.
Cutting, Jillian. Look... Van der Voo, Jan, illus. 8p. (gr. k-2). 1989. pap. text ed. 15.00 (ISBN 1-55911-272-7). Wright Group.
—Look.., 6 bks. Van der Voo, Jan, illus. 8p. (gr. k-2). 1986. Set. pap. text ed. 12.60 (ISBN 1-55911-329-4). Wright Group.
—Shopping. Van der Voo, Jan, illus. 8p. (Orig.). (gr. k-2). 1989. pap. text ed. 15.00 (ISBN 1-55911-270-0). Wright Group.
—Shopping, 6 bks. Van der Voo, Jan, illus. 8p. (gr. k-2). 1986. Set. pap. text ed. 12.60 (ISBN 1-55911-325-1). Wright Group.
—The Space Ark. Van der Voo, Jan, illus. 8p. (gr. k-2). 1989. pap. text ed. 15.00 (ISBN 1-55911-273-5). Wright Group.
—The Space Ark, 6 bks. Van der Voo, Jan, illus. 8p. (gr. k-2). 1986. Set. pap. text ed. 12.60 (ISBN 1-55911-331-6). Wright Group.
The Day Trip. (Illus.). (ps-2). 1990. 3.50 (ISBN 0-7214-1320-X); parent/tchr's. guide 3.95. Ladybird Bks.
Deans, Virginia B. Kate's Scarf. Deans, Virgina B., illus. LC 82-70228. 136p. (Orig.). (gr. 5-12). 1985. pap. 4.50x (ISBN 0-943864-36-4). Davenport.
Delton, Judy. My Mom Hates Me in January. Faulkner, John, illus. LC 77-5749. (gr. 1-3). 1977. PLB 10.95 (ISBN 0-8075-5356-5). A Whitman.
Dodd, Lynley. Dragon in a Wagon. Sherwood, Rhoda, ed. Dodd, Lynley, illus. LC 88-42925. 32p. (gr. 1-2). 1988. PLB 10.95 (ISBN 1-55532-911-X). Gareth Stevens Inc.
Dodd, Lynley & Croser, Nigel. Gold Star First Readers, 10 vols. Aldridge, George, illus. 360p. (gr. 1-2). 1989. Set. PLB 109.50 (ISBN 0-8368-0260-8). Gareth Stevens Inc.
The Dog Who Came to Dinner. (Illus.). (ps-k). Date not set. lib. bdg. 6.95 (ISBN 0-685-38658-9, TK2294). Modern Curr.
The Dolphin Chase. (Illus.). (ps-2). 1990. 3.50 (ISBN 0-7214-1327-7); parent/tchr's. guide 3.95. Ladybird Bks.
Donatelli, Betty. A Good Book to Toot About. Donatelli, Betty, illus. 11p. (Orig.). (gr. 1-2). 1984. pap. 1.00 (ISBN 0-912981-10-5). Hse Bon Giovanni.
Doyle, Arthur Conan. The Hound of the Baskervilles. (Illus.). (gr. k-6). 1979. pap. text ed. 4.25x (ISBN 0-19-581211-5). Oxford U Pr.
The Dragon's Egg. (Illus.). (ps-2). 3.50 (ISBN 0-7214-0929-6); parent-teacher guide avail. Ladybird Bks.
The Dream. (Illus.). (ps-2). 1990. 3.50 (ISBN 0-7214-1319-6); parent/tchr's. guide 3.95 (ISBN 0-00-004198-X); Series 9011-6, No. 6. activity bk. 2.95 (ISBN 0-7214-3225-5). Ladybird Bks.
Duyff, Roberta L. Smiles for Smiles. McKissack, Patricia & McKissack, Fredrick, eds. Dorenkamp, Michelle, illus. LC 88-60386. 32p. (Orig.). (gr. 1-3). 1988. text ed. 8.95 (ISBN 0-88335-780-1); pap. text ed. 4.95 (ISBN 0-88335-792-5). Milliken Pub Co.
Easy to Sound. (Illus.). (ps-5). 3.50 (ISBN 0-7214-0031-0). Ladybird Bks.
Enjoying Reading. (Illus.). (ps-5). 3.50 (ISBN 0-7214-0552-5). Ladybird Bks.
Everyday Things. (Illus.). (ps-k). 3.95 (ISBN 0-7214-5042-3). Ladybird Bks.
The Fierce Giant. (Illus.). (ps-2). 1990. 3.50 (ISBN 0-7214-1325-0); parent/tchr's. guide 3.95. Ladybird Bks.
Fire in the Grass. (Illus.). (ps-2). 3.50 (ISBN 0-7214-0969-5); parent-teacher guide avail. Ladybird Bks.
First Word Book. (Illus.). (ps-k). 3.50 (ISBN 0-7214-8104-3). Ladybird Bks.
First Words. (Illus.). (ps-2). 1990. 3.50 (ISBN 0-7214-1338-2); parent/tchr's. guide 3.95 (ISBN 0-7214-3219-0). Ladybird Bks.
Forman-Hitt, Kathy & Young, Janet. Beginning Reading Five. Wheeler, Sharon, ed. Richesson, Robin, illus. (ps). 1986. wkbk. 1.95 (ISBN 0-916119-22-X). Creat Teach Pr.
Forte, Imogene. Read about It: Middle Grades. LC 82-80502. (Illus.). 80p. (gr. 4-6). 1982. pap. text ed. 7.95 (ISBN 0-86530-007-0, IP 070). Incentive Pubns.
Frankel, Julie. Hare & Bear Go Shopping. McKissack, Patricia & McKissack, Fredrick, eds. Smith, Ted, illus. LC 88-60394. 32p. (Orig.). (gr. 1-3). 1990. text ed. 8.95 (ISBN 0-88335-778-X); pap. text ed. 4.95 (ISBN 0-88335-790-9). Milliken Pub Co.
Friskey, Margaret. Pollito Pequenito Cuenta hasta Diez. Kratky, Lada, tr. from ENG. Evans, K., illus. (SPA.). 32p. (gr. k-3). 1984. lib. bdg. 14.60 (ISBN 0-516-33431-X); pap. 3.95 (ISBN 0-516-53431-9). Childrens.
Fun with Sounds. (Illus.). (ps-5). 3.50 (ISBN 0-7214-0551-7). Ladybird Bks.
Georgiady, Nicholas P. & Romano, Louis G. Gertie the Duck. Wilson, Dagmar, illus. (gr. 1-3). 1982. lib. ed. 2.97 (ISBN 0-695-43363-6); pap. 1.50 (ISBN 0-685-10942-9). Follett Pr.
Goldstein, Nettie & Warner, Norma. How Hip Are You, Bk 1. (Illus.). (gr. 5-12). 1977. wkbk. 4.95 (ISBN 0-87594-160-5); wkbk. 4.95 (ISBN 0-685-00790-1). Book-Lab.
Goley. Respect, Reading Level 2. (Illus.). 32p. (gr. 1-4). Date not set. PLB 13.26 (ISBN 0-86592-387-6). Rourke Corp.
Gordon, Sharon. Christmas Surprise. Magine, John, illus. 32p. (gr. k-2). 1980. PLB 7.06 (ISBN 0-89375-373-4); pap. 1.95 (ISBN 0-89375-273-8). Troll Assocs.
—Dinosaur in Trouble. Harvey, Paul, illus. 32p. (gr. k-2). 1980. PLB 7.06 (ISBN 0-89375-374-2); pap. 1.95 (ISBN 0-89375-274-6). Troll Assocs.
—Easter Bunny's Lost Egg. Magine, Sharon, illus. 32p. (gr. k-2). 1980. PLB 7.06 (ISBN 0-89375-375-0); pap. 1.95 (ISBN 0-89375-275-4). Troll Assocs.
—Friendly Snowman. Magine, John, illus. 32p. (gr. k-2). 1980. PLB 7.06 (ISBN 0-89375-377-7); pap. 1.95 (ISBN 0-89375-277-0). Troll Assocs.
—Pete the Parakeet. Harvey, Paul, illus. 32p. (gr. k-2). 1980. PLB 7.06 (ISBN 0-89375-384-X); pap. 1.95 (ISBN 0-89375-284-3). Troll Assocs.
—Sam the Scarecrow. Silverstein, Don, illus. 32p. (gr. k-2). 1980. PLB 7.06 (ISBN 0-89375-387-4); pap. 1.95 (ISBN 0-89375-287-8). Troll Assocs.
—Three Little Witches. Sims, Deborah, illus. 32p. (gr. k-2). 1980. PLB 7.06 (ISBN 0-89375-390-4); pap. 1.95 (ISBN 0-89375-290-8). Troll Assocs.
—What a Dog. Sims, Deborah, illus. 32p. (gr. k-2). 1980. PLB 7.06 (ISBN 0-89375-393-9); pap. 1.95 (ISBN 0-89375-293-2). Troll Assocs.
Graham, Carolyn. The Electric Elephant & Other Stories. (Illus., Orig.). (gr. 7-12). 1982. pap. text ed. 6.50x (ISBN 0-19-503229-2). Oxford U Pr.
Greene, Carol. Miss Apple's Hats. McKissack, Patricia & McKissack, Fredrick, eds. Martin, Clovis, illus. LC 88-60395. 32p. (Orig.). (gr. 1-3). 1988. text ed. 8.95 (ISBN 0-88335-779-8); pap. text ed. 4.95 (ISBN 0-88335-791-7). Milliken Pub Co.
Gregorich, Barbara. The Comprehension Adventure. 48p. (gr. 7-12). 1984. 5.95 (ISBN 0-88160-109-8, LW 1004). Learning Wks.
—The Fox, the Goose & the Corn: Reading Workbook. Hoffman, Joan, ed. Laurent, Richard & Pape, Richard, illus. 32p. (Orig.). (gr. k-2). 1988. 1.99 (ISBN 0-88743-107-0). Sch Zone Pub Co.
—It's Magic. Hoffman, Joan, ed. Pape, Richard, illus. 32p. (gr. k-2). 1987. 1.99 (ISBN 0-88743-104-6, 02604). Sch Zone Pub Co.
—Nicole Digs a Hole. Hoffman, Joan, ed. Brooks, Nan, illus. 32p. (gr. k-2). 1987. wkbk. 1.99 (ISBN 0-88743-101-1, 02601). Sch Zone Pub Co.
—Reading Railroad. Hofman, Joan, ed. Alexander, Barbara, et al, illus. 32p. (ps-1). 1986. wkbk. 1.99 (ISBN 0-88743-130-5, 02506). Sch Zone Pub Co.
—Trouble Again: Reading Workbook. Hoffman, Joan, ed. Murdocca, Sal & Pape, Richard, illus. 32p. (Orig.). (gr. k-2). 1988. 1.99 (ISBN 0-88743-110-0). Sch Zone Pub Co.
—What Order? Hoffman, Joan, ed. Pape, Richard, illus. 32p. (ps). 1983. wkbk. 1.99 (ISBN 0-938256-61-0). Sch Zone Pub Co.
Greydanus, Rose. Animals at the Zoo. Hall, Susan T., illus. 32p. (gr. k-2). 1980. PLB 7.06 (ISBN 0-89375-371-8); pap. 1.95 (ISBN 0-89375-271-1). Troll Assocs.
—Big Red Fire Engine. Harvey, Paul, illus. 32p. (gr. k-2). 1980. PLB 7.06 (ISBN 0-89375-372-6); pap. 1.95 (ISBN 0-89375-272-X). Troll Assocs.
—Climb Aboard. Ulrich, George, illus. LC 87-19150. 32p. (gr. k-2). 1988. PLB 10.89 (ISBN 0-8167-1099-6); pap. text ed. 2.95 (ISBN 0-8167-1100-3). Troll Assocs.
—Freddie the Frog. (Illus.). 32p. (gr. k-2). 1980. PLB 7.06 (ISBN 0-89375-376-9); pap. 1.95 (ISBN 0-89375-276-2). Troll Assocs.
—Mike's New Bike. Sims, Deborah, illus. 32p. (gr. k-2). 1980. PLB 7.06 (ISBN 0-89375-382-3); pap. 1.95 (ISBN 0-89375-282-7). Troll Assocs.

—My Secret Hiding Place. Harvey, Paul, illus. 32p. (gr. k-2). 1980. PLB 7.06 (ISBN 0-89375-383-1); pap. 1.95 (ISBN 0-89375-283-5). Troll Assocs.

—Susie Goes Shopping. Apple, Margot, illus. 32p. (gr. k-2). 1980. PLB 7.06 (ISBN 0-89375-389-0); pap. 1.95 (ISBN 0-89375-289-4). Troll Assocs.

—Tree House Fun. Demarest, Chris, illus. 32p. (gr. k-2). 1980. PLB 7.06 (ISBN 0-89375-391-2); pap. 1.95 (ISBN 0-89375-291-6). Troll Assocs.

—Willie the Slowpoke. Eberbach, Andrea, illus. 32p. (gr. k-2). 1980. PLB 7.06 (ISBN 0-89375-394-7); pap. 1.95 (ISBN 0-89375-294-0); cassette 8.95 (ISBN 0-685-04954-X). Troll Assocs.

The Griffle & Mr. Gotobed. (Illus.). (ps-2). 3.50 (ISBN 0-7214-0918-0); parent-teacher guide avail. Ladybird Bks.

The Gruffle. (Illus.). (ps-2). 3.50 (ISBN 0-7214-0928-8); parent-teacher guide avail. Ladybird Bks.

The Gruffle in Puddle Lane. (Illus.). (ps-2). 3.50 (ISBN 0-7214-0935-0); parent-teacher guide avail. Ladybird Bks.

Hal Finds a Home. (Illus.). (ps-k). Date not set. lib. bdg. 6.95 (ISBN 0-685-38660-0, TK38812). Modern Curr.

Halloran, Phyllis. Oh, Brother! Oh, Sister! McKissack, Patricia & McKissack, Fredrick, eds. Shoemaker, Katheryn, illus. LC 88-60392. 32p. (Orig.). (gr. 1-3). 1988. text ed. 8.95 (ISBN 0-88335-788-7); pap. text ed. 4.95 (ISBN 0-88335-767-4). Milliken Pub Co.

Harris, Raymond. Best Short Stories: Advanced Level. Burgoyne, Mari-Ann S., illus. 560p. (Orig.). (gr. 9 up). 1980. text ed. 16.00 (ISBN 0-89061-705-8, 620H); pap. text ed. 12.75 (ISBN 0-89061-701-5, 620). Jamestown Pubs.

Have a Go. (Illus.). (ps-5). 3.50 (ISBN 0-7214-0474-X); No. 2. wkbk. 1.95; Series S05, Set 1. flash cards 4.75; Series S05, Set 2. flash cards 4.75. Ladybird Bks.

Hayward, Linda. Sail Away! A Phonic Reader with Learning Cards: Blue Ladder Books for Kids Through 6 Years. Nicklaus, Carol, illus. 24p. (ps-1). 1988. pap. 5.95 incl. flash cards (ISBN 0-394-89480-4, Random Juv). Random.

Heilbroner, Joan. Happy Birthday Present. Chalmers, Mary, illus. LC 61-12094. 64p. (gr. k-3). 1961. PLB 11.89 (ISBN 0-06-022271-9). HarpC Child Bks.

—This Is the House Where Jack Lives. Aliki, illus. LC 62-7311. 64p. (gr. k-3). 1962. PLB 11.89 (ISBN 0-06-022286-7). HarpC Child Bks.

Herman, Gail. The Fire Engine: Green Ladder Books for Kids Through 6 Years. Burton, Jane, photos by. (Illus.). 24p. (ps-1). 1988. incl. puzzle 5.95 (ISBN 0-394-89673-4, Random Juv). Random.

Heyer, Sandra. More True Stories in the News: A Beginning Reader. (Illus.). 1989. pap. text ed. 8.21 (ISBN 0-8013-0223-4, 75881). Longman.

Hickory Mouse. (Illus.). (ps-2). 3.50 (ISBN 0-7214-0937-7); parent-teacher guide avail. Ladybird Bks.

Hiller, Margaret. Who Goes to School? (Illus.). (ps-k). Date not set. pap. 3.50 (ISBN 0-685-38662-7, TK2383). Modern Curr.

—The Witch Who Went... (Illus.). (ps-k). Date not set. lib. bdg. 6.95 (ISBN 0-8136-5105-0). Modern Curr.

Hillert, Margaret. Funny Baby. (Illus.). (ps-k). Date not set. pap. 3.50 (ISBN 0-685-38659-7, TK2301). Modern Curr.

—Purple Pussycat. (Illus.). (ps-k). Date not set. lib. bdg. 6.95 (ISBN 0-8136-5072-0, TK2357). Modern Curr.

—The Snow Baby. (Illus.). (ps-k). Date not set. lib. bdg. 6.95 (ISBN 0-8136-5055-0, TK2363). Modern Curr.

Hoban, Russell. Bargain for Frances. Hoban, Lillian, illus. LC 70-85033. 64p. (gr. k-3). 1970. 11.95 (ISBN 0-06-022329-4); PLB 11.89 (ISBN 0-06-022330-8). HarpC Child Bks.

—Tom & the Two Handles. Hoban, Lillian, illus. LC 65-11459. 64p. (gr. k-3). 1965. PLB 11.89 (ISBN 0-06-022431-2). HarpC Child Bks.

Hoff, Syd. Chester. Hoff, Syd, illus. LC 61-5768. 64p. (gr. k-3). 1961. PLB 11.89 (ISBN 0-06-022456-8). HarpC Child Bks.

—Danny & the Dinosaur. Hoff, Syd, illus. LC 58-7754. 64p. (gr. k-3). 1958. 11.95 (ISBN 0-06-022465-7); PLB 11.89 (ISBN 0-06-022466-5). HarpC Child Bks.

—Grizzwold. Hoff, Syd, illus. LC 64-14366. 64p. (gr. k-3). 1963. PLB 11.89 (ISBN 0-06-022481-9). HarpC Child Bks.

—Julius. Hoff, Syd, illus. LC 59-8971. 64p. (gr. k-3). 1959. PLB 11.89 (ISBN 0-06-022491-6). HarpC Child Bks.

—Little Chief. Hoff, Syd, illus. LC 61-12098. 64p. (gr. k-3). 1961. PLB 10.89 (ISBN 0-685-02062-2). HarpC Child Bks.

—Oliver. Hoff, Syd, illus. LC 60-5779. 64p. (gr. k-3). 1960. PLB 11.89 (ISBN 0-06-022516-5). HarpC Child Bks.

—Sammy the Seal. Hoff, Syd, illus. LC 59-5316. 64p. (gr. k-3). 1959. PLB 11.89 (ISBN 0-06-022526-2). HarpC Child Bks.

—Stanley. Hoff, Syd, illus. LC 62-8873. 64p. (gr. k-3). 1962. PLB 11.89 (ISBN 0-06-022536-X). HarpC Child Bks.

—Who Will Be My Friends? Hoff, Syd, illus. 32p. (gr. k-2). 1960. PLB 10.89 (ISBN 0-06-022556-4). HarpC Child Bks.

Hoffman, Joan. Mouse & Owl. Gregorich, Barbara, ed. Sanford, John, illus. 32p. (gr. k-2). 1987. wkbk. 1.99 (ISBN 0-88743-102-X, 02602). Sch Zone Pub Co.

How Can I, Dainty Dinosaur? (Illus.). (ps-k). Date not set. lib. bdg. 6.95 (ISBN 0-8136-5226-X, TK7291); pap. 3.50 (ISBN 0-685-38661-9, TK7294). Modern Curr.

Hsiung, S. I. Lady Precious Stream. Taylor, C. W., retold by. (Illus.). (gr. k-6). 1971. pap. text ed. 3.95x (ISBN 0-19-638235-1). Oxford U Pr.

Hurd, Edith T. Last One Home Is a Green Pig. Hurd, Clement, illus. LC 59-8972. 64p. (gr. k-3). 1959. PLB 11.89 (ISBN 0-06-022716-8). HarpC Child Bks.

I Like to Write. (Illus.). (ps-5). 3.50 (ISBN 0-7214-0479-0); No. 2. wkbk. 1.95. Ladybird Bks.

I Wish. (Illus.). (ps-5). 3.50 (ISBN 0-7214-8004-7); 1.95 (ISBN 0-7214-8009-8). Ladybird Bks.

I'm Reading...All By Myself! rev. ed. 34p. (gr. k-2). 1982. incl. cass. 12.95 (ISBN 0-88679-249-5). Educ Insights.

Irving, N. The Biggest. (Illus.). 24p. (ps-2). 1988. 3.95 (ISBN 0-7460-0159-2); PLB 7.96 (ISBN 0-88110-310-1). EDC.

—The Fastest. (Illus.). 24p. (gr. 1-3). 1988. 3.95 (ISBN 0-7460-0161-4); PLB 7.96 (ISBN 0-88110-311-X). EDC.

Isaak, Betty. Garbage Games. 112p. (gr. 1-4). 1980. 9.95 (ISBN 0-88160-012-1, LW 115). Learning Wks.

It Will Be Fun, Dainty Dinosaur. (Illus.). (ps-k). Date not set. pap. 3.50 (ISBN 0-8136-5715-6, TK7298). Modern Curr.

Jaspersohn, William. How the Forest Grew. Eckart, Chuck, illus. LC 79-16286. 56p. (gr. 1 up). 1989. Repr. of 1980 ed. 12.95 (ISBN 0-688-80232-X). Greenwillow.

Johnson, Crockett. Picture for Harold's Room. Johnson, Crockett, illus. LC 60-6372. (gr. k-3). 1960. PLB 11.89 (ISBN 0-06-023006-1). HarpC Child Bks.

Johnson, John E., illus. My First Book of Things. LC 78-64609. (ps). 1979. 3.95 (ISBN 0-394-84128-X, Random Juv). Random.

Jump from the Sky. (Illus.). (ps-5). 3.50 (ISBN 0-7214-0545-2). Ladybird Bks.

Kapelman, Helen H. Nini's Way, Bk. 1. Kapelman, Helen H., illus. (gr. k-2). 1988. 4.95 (ISBN 0-9621807-0-X). H H Kapelman.

Kate & the Crocodile. (Illus.). (ps-2). 1990. 3.50 (ISBN 0-7214-1318-8); parent/tchr's. guide 3.95; Series 9011-5, No. 5. activity bk. 1.95 (ISBN 0-7214-3224-7). Ladybird Bks.

Kessler, Leonard. Here Comes the Strikeout. Kessler, Leonard, illus. LC 65-10728. 64p. (gr. k-3). 1965. 11.95 (ISBN 0-06-023155-6); PLB 11.89 (ISBN 0-06-023156-4). HarpC Child Bks.

Learning Is Fun. (Illus.). (ps-5). 3.50 (ISBN 0-7214-0628-9). Ladybird Bks.

Lecourt, Nancy. Rainbow. 32p. (gr. 2). 1980. pap. 1.95 (ISBN 0-8127-0290-5). Review & Herald.

Let Me Write. (Illus.). (ps-5). 3.50 (ISBN 0-7214-0027-2); No. 3. wkbk. 1.95 (ISBN 0-00-004185-8). Ladybird Bks.

Let's Play. (Illus.). (ps-2). 1990. 3.50 (ISBN 0-7214-1314-5); parent/tchr's. guide 3.95; Series 9011-1, No. 1. activity bk. 1.95 (ISBN 0-7214-3220-4). Ladybird Bks.

Lewison, Wendy C., et al. But Why? Reading Workbook. Murdocca, Sal, illus. Pape, Richard, designed by. (Illus.). 32p. (Orig.). (gr. k-2). 1988. wkbk. 1.99 (ISBN 0-88743-109-7). Sch Zone Pub Co.

Lexau, Joan M. Rooftop Mystery. Hoff, Syd, illus. LC 68-16821. 64p. (gr. k-3). 1968. PLB 11.89 (ISBN 0-06-023865-8). HarpC Child Bks.

Litchfield, Ada B. A Cane in Her Hand. Rubin, Caroline, ed. Mill, Eleanor, illus. LC 77-14255. (gr. 1-3). 1977. PLB 12.95 (ISBN 0-8075-1056-4). A Whitman.

The Little Monster. (Illus.). (ps-2). 3.50 (ISBN 0-7214-0926-1). Ladybird Bks.

Look Out! It's Magic! (Illus.). (ps-2). 3.50 (ISBN 0-7214-0913-X). Ladybird Bks.

Lucky Dip. (Illus.). (ps-5). 3.50 (ISBN 0-7214-8000-4); wkbk. A 1.95 (ISBN 0-7214-8007-1). Ladybird Bks.

McFarland, Philip J., et al. Focus on People. (Illus.). (gr. 8). 1981. text ed. 32.60 (ISBN 0-395-29356-1); tchr's. guide 11.16 (ISBN 0-395-29357-X). HM.

McGuffey, William H. The Original McGuffey's Eclectic Series, 7 Vols. (gr. k-12). 1982. Repr. of 1837 ed. 89.95 (ISBN 0-88062-014-5). Mott Media.

McKissack, Patricia & McKissack, Fredrick. No Need for Alarm. Smith, Phil, illus. LC 88-60388. 32p. (Orig.). (gr. 1-3). 1990. text ed. 8.95 (ISBN 0-88335-783-6); pap. text ed. 4.95 (ISBN 0-88335-795-X). Milliken Pub Co.

McKissack, Patricia & McKissack, Fredrick. Reading Well Softcover Package, 24 bks. (Illus., Orig.). (gr. 1-3). 1989. Set, 32p. ea. pap. 107.00 (ISBN 0-88335-739-9). Milliken Pub Co.

McKissack, Patricia & McKissack, Fredrick. A Troll in a Hole. Bartholomew, illus. LC 88-60384. 32p. (Orig.). (gr. 1-3). 1988. text ed. 8.95 (ISBN 0-88335-782-8); pap. text ed. 4.95 (ISBN 0-88335-794-1). Milliken Pub Co.

McKissack, Patricia & McKissack, Frederick, eds. Reading Well Hardcover Package, 24 bks. (Illus.). (gr. 1-3). 1989. Set, 32p. ea. 190.00 (ISBN 0-88335-717-8). Milliken Pub Co.

The Magic Box. (Illus.). (ps-2). 3.50 (ISBN 0-7214-0941-5). Ladybird Bks.

Magic Music. (Illus.). (ps-2). 1990. 3.50 (ISBN 0-7214-1323-4); parent/tchr's. guide 3.95. Ladybird Bks.

The Magic Paintbrush. (Illus.). (gr. 1). 3.50 (ISBN 0-7214-5124-1). Ladybird Bks.

The Magic Stone. (Illus.). (gr. 1). 3.50 (ISBN 0-7214-5176-4). Ladybird Bks.

The Magician's Party. (Illus.). (ps-2). 3.50 (ISBN 0-7214-5025-3). Ladybird Bks.

The Magician's Raindrops. (Illus.). (ps-2). 3.50 (ISBN 0-7214-5089-X). Ladybird Bks.

Matijasevic, Astrid, illus. Ratty-Tatty, 6 bks. 16p. (Orig.). (gr. k-2). 1987. Set. pap. text ed. 19.80 (ISBN 1-55624-740-0). Wright Group.

Me & Other People. (Illus.). (ps-k). 3.95 (ISBN 0-7214-5038-5). Ladybird Bks.

Minarik, Else H. Father Bear Comes Home. Sendak, Maurice, illus. LC 59-5794. 64p. (gr. k-3). 1959. 11.95 (ISBN 0-06-024230-2); PLB 11.89 (ISBN 0-06-024231-0). HarpC Child Bks.

—Little Bear. Sendak, Maurice, illus. 64p. (gr. k-3). 1957. 11.95i (ISBN 0-06-024240-X); PLB 11.89 (ISBN 0-06-024241-8). HarpC Child Bks.

—Little Bear's Friend. Sendak, Maurice, illus. LC 60-6370. 64p. (gr. k-3). 1960. 11.95i (ISBN 0-06-024255-8); PLB 11.89 (ISBN 0-06-024256-6). HarpC Child Bks.

—Little Bear's Visit. Sendak, Maurice, illus. LC 61-11451. 64p. (ps-3). 1961. 11.95 (ISBN 0-06-024265-5); PLB 11.89 (ISBN 0-06-024266-3). HarpC Child Bks.

—No Fighting, No Biting! Sendak, Maurice, illus. LC 58-5293. 64p. (gr. k-3). 1958. 11.95 (ISBN 0-06-024290-6); PLB 11.89 (ISBN 0-06-024291-4). HarpC Child Bks.

Mr. Pitter-Patter & the Magician. (Illus.). (ps-2). 3.50 (ISBN 0-7214-0917-2). Ladybird Bks.

Mr. Whisper, 6 bks. 16p. (Orig.). (gr. k-2). 1987. Set. pap. text ed. 19.80 (ISBN 1-55624-742-7). Wright Group.

Moncure, Jane B. My "c" Sound Box. Sommers, Linda, illus. LC 78-23638. (ps-2). 1979. PLB 11.97 (ISBN 0-89565-052-5); pap. 6.96 (ISBN 0-89565-191-2). Child's World.

—My "g" Sound Box. Sommers, Linda, illus. LC 78-22037. (ps-2). 1979. PLB 11.97 (ISBN 0-89565-053-3); pap. 6.96 (ISBN 0-89565-193-9). Childs World.

—My "j" Sound Box. Sommers, Linda, illus. LC 78-23178. (ps-2). 1979. PLB 11.97 (ISBN 0-89565-049-5); pap. 6.96 (ISBN 0-89565-196-3). Childs World.

—My "k" Sound Box. Sommers, Linda, illus. LC 78-22034. (ps-2). 1979. PLB 11.97 (ISBN 0-89565-050-9); pap. 6.96 (ISBN 0-89565-192-0). Childs World.

—My "m" Sound Box. Sommers, Linda, illus. LC 78-24458. (ps-2). 1979. PLB 11.97 (ISBN 0-89565-051-7); pap. 6.96 (ISBN 0-89565-194-7). Childs World.

—My "n" Sound Box. Sommers, Linda, illus. LC 78-22053. (ps-2). 1979. PLB 11.97 (ISBN 0-89565-054-1); pap. 6.96 (ISBN 0-89565-195-5). Childs World.

—My "q" Sound Box. Sommers, Linda, illus. LC 79-13085. (ps-2). 1979. PLB 11.97 (ISBN 0-89565-100-9); pap. 6.96 (ISBN 0-89565-197-1). Childs World.

—My Sound Parade. Sommers, Linda, illus. LC 79-15930. (ps-2). 1979. PLB 11.97 (ISBN 0-89565-103-3); pap. 6.96 (ISBN 0-89565-200-5). Childs World.

—My "v" Sound Box. Sommers, Linda, illus. LC 79-13084. (ps-2). 1979. PLB 11.97 (ISBN 0-89565-101-7); pap. 6.96 (ISBN 0-89565-198-X). Childs World.

—My "x, y, z" Sound Box. Sommers, Linda, illus. LC 79-13086. (ps-2). 1979. PLB 11.97 (ISBN 0-89565-102-5); pap. 6.96 (ISBN 0-89565-199-8). Childs World.

—Play with A & T. McCallum, Jodi, illus. LC 89-774. 32p. (gr. k-2). 1989. PLB 11.97 (ISBN 0-89565-505-5). Childs World.

—Play with E & D. (Illus.). 32p. (gr. k-2). 1989. PLB 11.97 (ISBN 0-89565-508-X). Childs World.

—Play with I & G. (Illus.). 32p. (gr. k-2). 1989. PLB 11.95 (ISBN 0-89565-507-1). Childs World.

—Play with O & G. (Illus.). 32p. (gr. k-2). 1989. PLB 11.95 (ISBN 0-89565-506-3). Childs World.

—Play with U & G. (Illus.). 32p. (gr. k-2). 1989. PLB 11.95 (ISBN 0-89565-509-8). Childs World.

—Short A & Long A Play a Game. Endres, Helen, illus. LC 79-10300. (gr. k-2). 1979. PLB 11.97 (ISBN 0-89565-089-4). Childs World.

—Short E & Long E Play a Game. Endres, Helen, illus. LC 79-10305. (gr. k-2). 1979. PLB 11.97 (ISBN 0-89565-090-8). Childs World.

—Short I & Long I Play a Game. Endres, Helen, illus. LC 79-10303. (gr. k-2). 1979. PLB 11.97 (ISBN 0-89565-091-6). Childs World.

—Short O & Long O Play a Game. Endres, Helen, illus. LC 79-10304. (gr. k-2). 1979. PLB 11.97 (ISBN 0-89565-092-4). Childs World.

—Short U & Long U Play a Game. Endres, Helen, illus. LC 79-10306. (gr. k-2). 1979. PLB 11.97 (ISBN 0-89565-093-2). Childs World.

Moore, Elaine. Mixed-Up Sam. McKissack, Patricia & McKissack, Fredrick, eds. Boddy, Joe, illus. LC 88-60390. 32p. (Orig.). (gr. 1-3). 1988. text ed. 8.95 (ISBN 0-88335-786-0); pap. text ed. 4.95 (ISBN 0-88335-798-4). Milliken Pub Co.

More Sounds to Say. (Illus.). (ps-5). 3.50 (ISBN 0-7214-0029-9); No. 5. wkbk. 1.95. Ladybird Bks.

Morse, Joyce. Peter Sinks in the Water. 32p. (Orig.). (gr. 2). 1980. pap. 1.95 (ISBN 0-8127-0281-6). Review & Herald.

—Where Is Jesus? 32p. (gr. 2). 1980. pap. 1.95 (ISBN 0-8127-0280-8). Review & Herald.

Mylet, Trish & Sheffield, Antoinette. Children, Today's Joy & Tomorrow's Hope, 8 bks, Set 2. (Illus.). 224p. (gr. 1-3). 1991. Set. pap. text ed. 16.00 (ISBN 0-945590-62-8). Sizzy Bks. CHILDREN, SET 2 contains eight books of short stories & builds on the foundation of CHILDREN, SET 1. Each book consists of six stories. At least one story in each book has an O. Henry-type ending in which the child decides how the story ends. The child answers verbally, draws a picture or writes a note on a self expression page. Each story has a state reference page with a large dot-to-dot exercise in the shape of that state's outline. Featured in SET 2 are the District of Columbia & the 45 states not covered in SET 1. While continuing to incorporate geography, phonics (blends, digraphs, long & diverse vowels), number recognition, sentence completion & self-expression as in SET 1, SET 2 also explores the areas of zoology, botany, history & global unity. In the first five books each story is accompanied by a list of its vocabulary. Building on SET 1's themes of fun & fantasy, SET 2 expands & concludes with joy, fact & hope. These warmly written & illustrated books have been well received worldwide by Early Education, Special Education & English as a Second Language teachers, parents & most importantly, children.
Publisher Provided Annotation.

Myrick, Mildred. Secret Three. Lobel, Arnold, illus. LC 63-13323. 64p. (gr. k-3). 1963. PLB 11.89 (ISBN 0-06-024356-2). HarpC Child Bks.

Never Trust Dragons. (Illus.). (ps-2). 3.50 (ISBN 0-7214-0930-X). Ladybird Bks.

Noise, 6 bks. 16p. (Orig.). (gr. k-2). 1987. Set. pap. text ed. 19.80 (ISBN 1-55624-736-2). Wright Group.

Northrup, Melvin. Toby's Gift. 32p. (Orig.). (gr. 2). 1980. pap. 1.95 (ISBN 0-8127-0291-3). Review & Herald.

O. Henry, et al. The Gifts & Other Stories. (Illus.). (gr. 3up). 1974. pap. text ed. 4.25x (ISBN 0-19-580574-7). Oxford U Pr.

Old Mr. Gotobed. (Illus.). (ps-2). 3.50 (ISBN 0-7214-0934-2). Ladybird Bks.

On the Way to the Blue Mountains. (Illus.). (ps-2). 3.50 (ISBN 0-7214-0940-7). Ladybird Bks.

Open Door to Reading. (Illus.). (ps-5). 3.50 (ISBN 0-7214-0036-1). Ladybird Bks.

Our Friends. (Illus.). (ps-5). 3.50 (ISBN 0-7214-0508-8); No. 6. wkbk. 1.95 (ISBN 0-7214-3067-8); Series S05, Set 1. flash cards 4.75; Series S05, Set 2. flash cards 4.75. Ladybird Bks.

Out in the Sun. (Illus.). (ps-5). 3.50 (ISBN 0-7214-0541-X); No. 5. wkbk. 1.95; Series S05, Set 2. flash cards 4.75. Ladybird Bks.

Oxenbury, Helen. I Touch. Oxenbury, Helen, illus. LC 85-61366. 14p. (ps). 1986. Repr. of 1986 ed. bds. 3.95 (ISBN 0-394-87480-3). Random.

Paltrowitz, Stuart & Paltrowitz, Donna. Content Area Reading Skills-Competency Canada: Main Idea. (Illus.). (gr. 4). 1987. pap. text ed. 3.25 (ISBN 0-89525-853-6). Ed Activities.

—Content Area Reading Skills-Competency Mexico: Locating Details. (Illus.). (gr. 4). 1987. pap. text ed. 3.25 (ISBN 0-89525-854-4). Ed Activities.

—Content Area Reading Skills-Competency U. S. History: Detecting Sequence. (Illus.). (gr. 4). 1987. pap. text ed. 3.25 (ISBN 0-89525-856-0). Ed Activities.

—Content Area Reading Skills U. S. Geography: Cause & Effect. (Illus.). (gr. 4). 1987. pap. text ed. 3.25 (ISBN 0-89525-855-2). Ed Activities.

Pape, et al. Oddo Sound Series: 1968, 1974, 1978, 10 vols. (Illus.). (gr. 2-5). 1978. Set. PLB 109.50 (ISBN 0-87783-165-3). Oddo.

Parish, Peggy. Amelia Bedelia & the Surprise Shower. Siebel, Fritz, illus. LC 66-18655. 64p. (gr. k-3). 1966. 11.95 (ISBN 0-06-024642-1); PLB 11.89 (ISBN 0-06-024643-X). HarpC Child Bks.

—Come Back, Amelia Bedelia. Tripp, Wallace, illus. LC 73-121799. 64p. (ps-3). 1971. 11.95 (ISBN 0-06-024667-7); PLB 11.89 (ISBN 0-06-024668-5). HarpC Child Bks.

—Ootah's Lucky Day. Funai, Mamoru, illus. LC 70-105467. 64p. (gr. k-3). 1970. PLB 11.89 (ISBN 0-06-024645-6). HarpC Child Bks.

Peters, Sharon. Fun at Camp. Trivas, Irene, illus. 32p. (gr. k-2). 1980. PLB 7.06 (ISBN 0-89375-378-5); pap. 1.95 (ISBN 0-89375-278-9). Troll Assocs.

—Happy Birthday. Harvey, Paul, illus. 32p. (gr. k-2). 1980. PLB 7.06 (ISBN 0-89375-379-3); pap. 1.95 (ISBN 0-89375-279-7). Troll Assocs.

—Happy Jack. Harvey, Paul, illus. 32p. (gr. k-2). 1980. PLB 7.06 (ISBN 0-89375-380-7); pap. 1.95 (ISBN 0-89375-280-0). Troll Assocs.

—Messy Mark. Trivas, Irene, illus. 32p. (gr. k-2). 1980. PLB 7.06 (ISBN 0-89375-381-5); pap. 1.95 (ISBN 0-89375-281-9). Troll Assocs.

—Puppet Show. Lee, Alan, illus. 32p. (gr. k-2). 1980. PLB 6.11 (ISBN 0-89375-385-8); pap. 1.95 (ISBN 0-89375-286-X). Troll Assocs.

—Ready, Get Set, Go! Trivas, Irene, illus. 32p. (gr. k-2). 1980. PLB 7.06 (ISBN 0-89375-386-6); pap. 1.95 (ISBN 0-89375-285-1). Troll Assocs.

—Stop That Rabbit. Silverstein, Don, illus. 32p. (gr. k-2). 1980. PLB 7.06 (ISBN 0-89375-388-2); pap. 1.95 (ISBN 0-89375-288-6). Troll Assocs.

—Trick or Treat Halloween. Hall, Susan T., illus. 32p. (gr. k-2). 1980. PLB 7.06 (ISBN 0-89375-392-0); pap. 1.95 (ISBN 0-89375-292-4). Troll Assocs.

Phleger, Frederick B. Red Tag Comes Back. Lobel, Arnold, illus. LC 61-11452. 64p. (gr. k-3). 1961. PLB 11.89 (ISBN 0-06-024706-1). HarpC Child Bks.

Play with Us. (Illus.). (ps-5). 3.50 (ISBN 0-7214-0001-9); No. 1. wkbk. 1.95 (ISBN 0-7214-3062-7); Series S05, Set 1. flash cards 4.75. Ladybird Bks.

Poe, Edgar Allan. Tales of Mystery & Imagination, Retold by Henniker-Major. Owen, C., illus. (gr. 3 up). 1975. pap. text ed. 4.25x (ISBN 0-19-580511-9). Oxford U Pr.

Polette, Keith. The Winter Duckling. McKissack, Patricia & McKissack, Fredrick, eds. Martin, Clovis, illus. LC 88-60393. 32p. (Orig.). (gr. 1-3). 1990. text ed. 8.95 (ISBN 0-88335-777-1); pap. text ed. 4.95 (ISBN 0-88335-789-5). Milliken Pub Co.

Pollack, Cecelia. How Hip Are You, Bk. 2. (Illus.). (gr. 5-12). wkbk. 4.95 (ISBN 0-87594-161-3). Book Lab.

—How Hip Are You, Bk. 4. (Illus.). (gr. 5-12). wkbk. 4.95 (ISBN 0-87594-163-X). Book Lab.

Pomeroy, Johanna P. Content Area Reading Skills Electricity & Magnetism. (Illus.). (gr. 4). 1987. pap. text ed. 3.25 (ISBN 0-89525-859-5). Ed Activities.

—Content Area Reading Skills Geology: Detecting Sequence. (Illus.). (gr. 4). 1987. pap. text ed. 3.25 (ISBN 1-55737-085-0). Ed Activities.

—Content Area Reading Skills Light: Main Idea. (Illus.). (gr. 3). 1989. pap. text ed. 3.25 (ISBN 1-55737-687-5). Ed Activities.

—Content Area Reading Skills Machines: Detecting Sequence. (Illus.). (gr. 3). 1989. pap. text ed. 3.25 (ISBN 1-55737-690-5). Ed Activities.

—Content Area Reading Skills Matter: Locating Details. (Illus.). (gr. 4). 1988. pap. text ed. 3.25 (ISBN 1-55737-086-9). Ed Activities.

—Content Area Reading Skills Mechanics: Cause & Effect. (Illus.). (gr. 4). 1988. pap. text ed. 3.25 (ISBN 1-55737-088-5). Ed Activities.

—Content Area Reading Skills Oceans: Main Idea. (Illus.). (gr. 4). 1987. pap. text ed. 3.25 (ISBN 0-89525-857-9). Ed Activities.

—Content Area Reading Skills Our Earth: Locating Details. (Illus.). (gr. 3). 1989. pap. text ed. 3.25 (ISBN 1-55737-688-3). Ed Activities.

—Content Area Reading skills Reproduction & Heredity: Main Idea. (Illus.). (gr. 4). 1988. pap. text ed. 3.25 (ISBN 1-55737-087-7). Ed Activities.

—Content Area Reading Skills Solar System: Locating Details. (Illus.). (gr. 4). 1987. pap. text ed. 3.25 (ISBN 0-89525-858-7). Ed Activities.

—Content Area Reading Skills Sound & Hearing: Detecting Sequence. (Illus.). (gr. 4). 1987. pap. text ed. 3.25 (ISBN 0-89525-860-9). Ed Activities.

—Content Area Reading Skills Weather: Cause & Effect. (Illus.). (gr. 3). 1989. pap. text ed. 3.25 (ISBN 1-55737-689-1). Ed Activities.

Radlauer, Ed. Big Bears - Little Bears. Radlauer Productions Staff, illus. 32p. (ps-4). 1991. PLB 9.95 (ISBN 1-878363-34-4). Forest Hse. Forest House, a "sole source", no jobber/wholesaler sales, school & library publishing company, introduces our new for spring/fall 1991 series. All Forest House titles, in reinforced library bindings, are full, four color art which enhance & excite young & new readers. Our books encourage children & young adults, "to turn the page". Ed Radlauer introduces his first series for Forest House this spring. The RADLAUER BIG/LITTLE READERS, all done with actual photographs & easy text, show different examples of the concept, "Big & Little". Using full color photographs of bears, cats, & different vehicles with wheels, these delightful stories, done for pre K-4, are ideal for literature based reading. BIG BEARS/LITTLE BEARS, BIG CATS/LITTLE CATS, & BIG WHEELS/LITTLE WHEELS are 32 pages, $9.95 each. Each book has a glossary & word list. Series price: $29.85.
Publisher Provided Annotation.

Rayner, Mary. Rug. rev. ed. Rayner, Mary, illus. 32p. (gr. k-2). 1989. Repr. of 1989 ed. lib. bdg. 9.45 (ISBN 1-878363-03-4). Forest Hse.

Read & Write. (Illus.). (ps-5). 3.50 (ISBN 0-7214-0025-6); No. 1. wkbk. 1.95. Ladybird Bks.

Reading with Sounds. (Illus.). (ps-5). 3.50 (ISBN 0-7214-0549-5); No. 6. wkbk. 1.95. Ladybird Bks.

Ready Set Read Nonfiction Set, 6 titles. Date not set. Set. 55.50 (ISBN 0-8172-3589-2). Raintree Pubs.

Reese, Bob. Arbor Day. Jordan, Alton, ed. Reese, Bob, illus. (gr. k-3). 1977. PLB 5.95 (ISBN 0-89868-031-X, Read Res); pap. text ed. 2.50 (ISBN 0-89868-064-6). ARO Pub.

—Easter. Jordan, Alton, ed. Reese, Bob, illus. (gr. k-3). 1977. PLB 5.95 (ISBN 0-89868-032-8, Read Res); pap. text ed. 2.50 (ISBN 0-89868-065-4). ARO Pub.

—St. Patrick's Day. Jordan, Alton, ed. Reese, Bob, illus. (gr. k-3). 1977. PLB 5.95 (ISBN 0-89868-030-1, Read Res); pap. text ed. 2.50 (ISBN 0-89868-063-8). ARO Pub.

Reese, Bob, et al. Elephant Set, 10 bks. Jordon, Alton, ed. Reese, Bob, illus. (gr. k-6). 1977. Set. PLB 59.50 (ISBN 0-89868-011-5); Set. pap. 25.00 (ISBN 0-89868-044-1). ARO Pub.

—Holiday Series, 10 bks. Jordan, Alton, ed. Reese, Bob, illus. (gr. k-6). 1977. Set. PLB 59.50 (ISBN 0-89868-022-0); Set. pap. 25.00 (ISBN 0-89868-055-7). ARO Pub.

—I Can Read Underwater Series, 10 bks. Jordan, Alton, ed. Reese, Bob, illus. (gr. k-6). 1974. Set. PLB 59.50 (ISBN 0-89868-000-X); Set. pap. 25.00 (ISBN 0-89868-033-6). ARO Pub.

—Ten Word Books, 10 bks. Wasserman, Dan, ed. Reese, Bob, illus. (gr. k-6). Set. PLB 79.50 (ISBN 0-89868-066-2); Set. pap. 22.00 (ISBN 0-89868-077-8). ARO Pub.

Reese, Nancy. The Bee. Jordan, Alton, ed. Reese, Bob, illus. (gr. k-3). 1974. PLB 5.95 (ISBN 0-89868-005-0, Read Res); pap. text ed. 2.50 (ISBN 0-89868-038-7). ARO Pub.

—I Can Eat an Elephant. Jordan, Alton, ed. Reese, Bob, illus. (gr. k-3). 1975. PLB 5.95 (ISBN 0-89868-012-3, Read Res); pap. text ed. 2.50 (ISBN 0-89868-045-X). ARO Pub.

—New Year's. Jordan, Alton, ed. Reese, Bob, illus. (gr. k-3). 1977. PLB 5.95 (ISBN 0-89868-026-3, Read Res); text ed. 2.50 soft bd. (ISBN 0-89868-059-X). ARO Pub.

—Purple Bear. Jordan, Alton, ed. Reese, Bob, illus. (gr. k-3). 1975. PLB 5.95 (ISBN 0-89868-013-1, Read Res); pap. text ed. 2.50 (ISBN 0-89868-046-8). ARO Pub.

—Silly Egg. Jordan, Alton, ed. Reese, Bob, illus. (gr. k-3). 1974. PLB 5.95 (ISBN 0-89868-004-2, Read Res); pap. text ed. 2.50 (ISBN 0-89868-037-9). ARO Pub.

—Smiley Snake. Jordan, Alton, ed. Reese, Bob, illus. (gr. k-3). 1974. PLB 5.95 (ISBN 0-89868-010-7, Read Res); pap. text ed. 2.50 (ISBN 0-89868-043-3). ARO Pub.

—Valentine's Day. Jordan, Alton, ed. Reese, Bob, illus. (gr. k-3). 1977. PLB 5.95 (ISBN 0-89868-029-8, Read Res); pap. text ed. 2.50 (ISBN 0-89868-062-X). ARO Pub.

Reese, Ron. Crazy Cat. Jordan, Alton, ed. Reese, Bob, illus. (gr. k-3). 1974. PLB 5.95 (ISBN 0-89868-002-6, Read Res); pap. text ed. 2.50 (ISBN 0-89868-035-2). ARO Pub.

—Halloween. Jordan, Alton, ed. Reese, Robert, illus. (gr. k-3). 1977. PLB 5.95 (ISBN 0-89868-023-9, Read Res Ser.); pap. text ed. 2.50 (ISBN 0-89868-056-5). ARO Pub.

—Mosquito. Jordan, Alton, ed. Reese, Bob, illus. (gr. k-3). 1975. PLB 5.95 (ISBN 0-89868-014-X, Read Res); text ed. 2.50 soft bd. (ISBN 0-89868-047-6). ARO Pub.

—Sammy Skunk. Jordan, Alton, ed. Reese, Bob, illus. (gr. k-3). 1974. PLB 5.95 (ISBN 0-89868-009-3, Read Res); pap. text ed. 2.50 (ISBN 0-89868-042-5). ARO Pub.

Reiss, Elayne & Freidman, Rita. A-Choo. (Illus.). (gr. k-1). 1990. 10.50 (ISBN 0-89796-864-6). New Dimens Educ.

Reiss, Elayne & Friedman, Rita. A Buttonmat for Beautiful Buttons. (gr. k-1). 1978. 10.50 (ISBN 0-89796-865-4). New Dimens Educ.

Richard-Amato, Patricia A. Reading in the Content Areas: An Interactive Approach for Advanced Students. 1990. pap. text ed. 17.25 (ISBN 0-8013-0247-1, 75902). Longman.

Richecky, Janet. Excuse Me. Connelly, Gwen, illus. 32p. (ps-2). 1989. PLB 9.96 (ISBN 0-685-25651-0). Childs World.

Riehecky, Janet. After You. Connelly, Gwen, illus. 32p. (ps-2). 1989. PLB 9.96 (ISBN 0-89565-540-3). Childs World.

The Robbery. (Illus.). (ps-2). 1990. 3.50 (ISBN 0-7214-1328-5); parent/tchr's. guide 3.95. Ladybird Bks.

Roop, Peter & Roop, Connie. Snips the Tinker. McKissack, Patricia & McKissack, Fredrick, eds. Brown, Craig M., illus. LC 88-60385. 32p. (Orig.). (gr. 1-3). 1990. text ed. 8.95 (ISBN 0-88335-785-2); pap. text ed. 4.95 (ISBN 0-88335-797-6). Milliken Pub Co.

Salaz, Ruben D. Cosmic Reader of the Southwest for Young People. Aragon, Loretta, illus. (gr. 4 up). 1976. pap. 6.95 (ISBN 0-932492-00-2). Cosmic Hse NM.

—La Lectura Cosmica del Suroeste-para los Jovenes. Minkin, Rita, tr. from ENG. Aragon, Loretta, illus. (SPA.). (gr. 7 up). 1978. pap. 6.95 (ISBN 0-932492-01-0). Cosmic Hse NM.

The Sandalwood Girl. (Illus.). (ps-2). 3.50 (ISBN 0-7214-0939-3). Ladybird Bks.

Say the Sound. (Illus.). (ps-5). 3.50 (ISBN 0-7214-0028-0); No. 4. wkbk. 1.95. Ladybird Bks.

Scarry. Best Word Book. (FRE.). (gr. 3-8). 14.95 (ISBN 0-685-28441-7). French & Eur.

Seashell Magic. (Illus.). (ps-k). Date not set. pap. 3.50 (ISBN 0-8136-5691-5, TK7256). Modern Curr.

Selsam, Millicent E. Greg's Microscope. Lobel, Arnold, illus. LC 63-8002. 64p. (gr. k-3). 1963. PLB 11.89 (ISBN 0-06-025296-0). HarpC Child Bks.

Shebar, Sharon & Schoder, Judy. Groundhog Day. Jordan, Alton, ed. Reese, Bob, illus. (gr. k-3). 1977. PLB 5.95 (ISBN 0-89868-027-1, Read Res); pap. text ed. 2.50 (ISBN 0-89868-060-3). ARO Pub.

Sheffield, Antoinette & Mylet, Trish. Children, Today's Joy & Tomorrow's Hope, Set 1. (Illus.). 1991. write for info (ISBN 0-945590-74-1). Sizzy Bks. The CHILDREN, TODAY'S JOY & TOMORROW'S HOPE series consists of two sets of books. SET 1 contains 11 beginning reader & activity books. SET 2 contains eight books of short stories. The CHILDREN series consists of positive global readers incorporating geography (the fifty United States & the District of Columbia), phonics (short & long vowels, blends & digraphs), number recognition & self expression. SET 2 expands & explores the areas of zoology, botany, history & global unity. Each book in SET 1 & each story in SET 2 contains a state reference page with a large dot-to-dot exercise in the shape of that state's outline. The first sixteen books include sentence completion exercises & that story's word list. In SET 2 at least one story in each book has an O. Henry-type ending in which the child decides how the story ends. Each series includes a reference guide. Building on SET 1's themes of fun & fantasy, SET 2 expands & concludes with joy, fact & hope. This warmly written & illustrated series has been well received worldwide by Early Education, Special Education & English as a Second Language teachers, parents & most importantly children.
Publisher Provided Annotation.

Smee, Nicola. Down in the Woods. rev. ed. Smee, Nicola, illus. 32p. (gr. k-2). 1989. Repr. of 1985 ed. lib. bdg. 9.45 (ISBN 1-878363-00-X). Forest Hse.

Smith, Mary M. Orla's Upside Down Day. rev. ed. Lewis, Jan, illus. 32p. (gr. k-2). Repr. of 1989 ed. PLB 9.45 (ISBN 1-878363-05-0). Forest Hse.

Snow, Pegeen. Eat Your Peas, Louise! Venezia, Mike, illus. LC 84-27445. 32p. (ps-2). 1985. lib. bdg. 11.93 (ISBN 0-516-02067-6); pap. 2.95 (ISBN 0-516-42067-4). Childrens.

Speedsters Series. (Illus.). (gr. 1-3). write for info. (ISBN 0-525-44950-7). Dutton Child Bks. Speedsters are a unique series of fast & fun books for 7 to 10 year olds who are beginning to "really" read, but still need & enjoy pictures. Filling the gap between easy-to-read & "real" chapter books, Speedsters also appeals to

reluctant readers because of their unique open format & design. Snappy, upbeat & action-filled, they are sixty-four pages set in large type with lots of space between the lines, & line drawings & cartoon balloons on every page. Every Speedster is light, good-spirited, & child-oriented, on subjects ranging from sports to siblings to pets to magic. BCCB calls Speedsters "a truly audience aware series," & other reviews point out their direct appeal to kids, calling them "a sure pick for kids;" "a great choice for young readers just beyond the primer stage"-(Booklist); & "sure to appeal to newly independent readers"-(School Library Journal). As of Spring 1992, 12 Speedsters are available in hardcover & 4 as Puffin paperbacks, with more published every list. Contact publisher for individual titles.
Publisher Provided Annotation.

Spivak, Darlene. Special Times. Olsen, Shirley, illus. 48p. (gr. k-2). 1988. wkbk. 5.95 (ISBN 1-55734-376-4). Tchr Create Mat.

Stewart, Jeffrey E. Food! A Reading Program. (Illus.). 116p. (Orig.). 1987. pap. 32.50 (ISBN 1-877866-00-8). J E Stewart.

—More Food! A Reading Program. (Illus.). 116p. (Orig.). 1988. pap. 32.50 (ISBN 1-877866-01-6). J E Stewart.

Stolz, Mary. Emmett's Pig. Williams, Garth, illus. LC 58-7763. 64p. (gr. k-3). 1959. PLB 11.89 (ISBN 0-06-025856-X). HarpC Child Bks.

The Tale of a Tail. (Illus.). (ps-2). 3.50 (ISBN 0-7214-0916-4). Ladybird Bks.

Tessa & the Magician. (Illus.). (ps-2). 3.50 (ISBN 0-7214-0910-5). Ladybird Bks.

Tessa in Puddle Lane. (Illus.). (ps-2). 3.50 (ISBN 0-7214-0925-3). Ladybird Bks.

Things We Do. (Illus.). (ps-5). 3.50 (ISBN 0-7214-0540-1); No. 4. wkbk. 1.95 (ISBN 0-7214-3065-1); Series S05, Set 1. flash cards 4.75. Ladybird Bks.

Things We Like. (Illus.). (ps-5). 3.50 (ISBN 0-7214-0003-5); No. 3. wkbk. 1.95 (ISBN 0-7214-3064-3); Series S05, Set 1. flash cards 4.75. Ladybird Bks.

Thompson, Timothy J. Figs & Nuts. Thompson, Timothy J., illus. LC 80-83134. 15p. (Orig.). (ps-1). 1980. pap. text ed. 3.50 (ISBN 0-915676-03-6). Ed Sys Pub.

—Ten Red Rods. Thompson, Timothy J., illus. LC 80-83135. 16p. (Orig.). (ps-1). 1980. pap. text ed. 3.50 (ISBN 0-915676-02-8). Ed Sys Pub.

Tim Turns Green. (Illus.). (ps-2). 3.50 (ISBN 0-7214-0911-3). Ladybird Bks.

Tom's Storybook. (Illus.). (ps-2). 1990. 3.50 (ISBN 0-7214-1321-8); parent/tchr's. guide 3.95. Ladybird Bks.

Vickers, Kath. The Wizard & the Rainbow. Moxley, Susan, illus. 24p. (gr. 1-2). pap. text ed. 4.40 (ISBN 1-55624-151-8, WP1518). Wright Group.

—The Wizard & the Rainbow: Big Book. Moxley, Susan, illus. 24p. (gr. 1-2). pap. text ed. 26.00 (ISBN 1-55624-157-7, WP1577). Wright Group.

—A Wizard Came to Visit. Moxley, Susan, illus. 24p. (gr. 1-2). pap. text ed. 4.40 (ISBN 1-55624-150-X, WP150X). Wright Group.

—A Wizard Came to Visit: Big Book. Moxley, Susan, illus. 24p. (gr. 1-2). pap. text ed. 26.00 (ISBN 1-55624-156-9, WP1569). Wright Group.

Waugh, Charles & Greenberg, Martin, eds. The Newbery Award Reader. Hamilton, Virginia, intro. by. 320p. (gr. 7 up). 1984. 14.95 (ISBN 0-15-257034-9, HJ). HarBraceJ.

We Have Fun. (Illus.). (ps-5). 3.50 (ISBN 0-7214-0002-7); No. 2. wkbk. 1.95 (ISBN 0-7214-3063-5); Series S05, Set 1. flash cards 4.75. Ladybird Bks.

We Like to Help. (Illus.). (ps-5). 3.50 (ISBN 0-7214-0542-8); No. 6. wkbk. 1.95; Series S05, Set 2. flash cards 4.75. Ladybird Bks.

Weimann & Friedman. A-Choo. (Illus.). 30p. (gr. k-1). 1990. pap. 5.95 (ISBN 0-89796-200-1). New Dimens Educ.

—A Buttonmat for Beautiful Buttons. (Illus.). 30p. (gr. k-1). 1990. pap. 5.95 (ISBN 0-89796-201-X). New Dimens Educ.

—The Cotton Candy Caper. (Illus.). 30p. (gr. k-1). 1990. pap. 5.95 (ISBN 0-89796-202-8). New Dimens Educ.

—A Dozen Delicious Doughnuts. (Illus.). 30p. (gr. k-1). 1990. pap. 5.95 (ISBN 0-89796-203-6). New Dimens Educ.

—Fantastic Funny Feet. (Illus.). 30p. (gr. k-1). 1990. pap. 5.95 (ISBN 0-89796-205-2). New Dimens Educ.

—Gooey Gum Is Not for Chewing. (Illus.). 30p. (gr. k-1). 1990. pap. 5.95 (ISBN 0-89796-206-0). New Dimens Educ.

—Hat Helpers Hullabaloo. (Illus.). 30p. (gr. k-1). 1990. pap. 5.95 (ISBN 0-89796-207-9). New Dimens Educ.

—The Incredible Inventor. (Illus.). 30p. (gr. k-1). 1990. pap. 5.95 (ISBN 0-89796-208-7). New Dimens Educ.

—The Inimitable Mr. X. (Illus.). 30p. (gr. k-1). 1990. pap. 5.95 (ISBN 0-89796-223-0). New Dimens Educ.

—Jingling, Jangling Joggers. (Illus.). 30p. (gr. k-1). 1990. pap. 5.95 (ISBN 0-89796-209-5). New Dimens Educ.

—The Longest Kick. (Illus.). 30p. (gr. k-1). 1990. pap. 5.95 (ISBN 0-89796-210-9). New Dimens Educ.

—Lovely Lemon Lollies. (Illus.). 30p. (gr. k-1). 1990. pap. 5.95 (ISBN 0-89796-211-7). New Dimens Educ.

—Meet Me at the Market. (Illus.). 30p. (gr. k-1). 1990. pap. 5.95 (ISBN 0-89796-212-5). New Dimens Educ.

—A Most Unusual Umbrella. (Illus.). 30p. (gr. k-1). 1990. pap. 5.95 (ISBN 0-89796-220-6). New Dimens Educ.

—The Noisy Nose Nanny. (Illus.). 30p. (gr. k-1). 1990. pap. 5.95 (ISBN 0-89796-213-3). New Dimens Educ.

—The Optimistic Optimist. (Illus.). 30p. (gr. k-1). 1990. pap. 5.95 (ISBN 0-89796-214-1). New Dimens Educ.

—Popping Pointy Patches. (Illus.). 30p. (gr. k-1). 1990. pap. 5.95 (ISBN 0-89796-215-X). New Dimens Educ.

—The Rubberbit Roundup. (Illus.). 30p. (gr. k-1). 1990. pap. 5.95 (ISBN 0-89796-217-6). New Dimens Educ.

—Super Sock Sensation. (Illus.). 30p. (gr. k-1). 1990. pap. 5.95 (ISBN 0-89796-218-4). New Dimens Educ.

—The Tale of Tall Toothbrush. (Illus.). 30p. (gr. k-1). 1990. pap. 5.95 (ISBN 0-89796-219-2). New Dimens Educ.

—To Be or Not to Be...Quiet. (Illus.). 30p. (gr. k-1). 1990. pap. 5.95 (ISBN 0-89796-216-8). New Dimens Educ.

—Vanishing Vests. (Illus.). 30p. (gr. k-1). 1990. pap. 5.95 (ISBN 0-89796-221-4). New Dimens Educ.

—Wonderful Winks & Weather Wishes. (Illus.). 30p. (gr. k-1). 1990. pap. 5.95 (ISBN 0-89796-222-2). New Dimens Educ.

—The Yawn Maker. (Illus.). 30p. (gr. k-1). 1990. pap. 5.95 (ISBN 0-89796-224-9). New Dimens Educ.

—Zipping Zippers Save the Zoo. (Illus.). 30p. (gr. k-1). 1990. pap. 5.95 (ISBN 0-89796-225-7). New Dimens Educ.

Weimann & Friedman, Rita. The Exercise Expert. (Illus.). 30p. (gr. k-1). 1990. pap. 5.95 (ISBN 0-89796-204-4). New Dimens Educ.

Westcott, Alvin. Billy Lump's Adventure. LC 68-56817. (Illus.). 32p. (gr. 2-4). 1968. PLB 9.95 (ISBN 0-87783-002-9). Oddo.

What Time Is It Mr. Wolf? (Illus.). (ps-1). 3.50 (ISBN 0-7214-0871-0). Ladybird Bks.

When the Clock Struck Thirteen. (Illus.). (ps-2). 3.50 (ISBN 0-7214-0938-5). Ladybird Bks.

When the Magic Stopped. (Illus.). (ps-2). 3.50 (ISBN 0-7214-0924-5). Ladybird Bks.

Where We Go. (Illus.). (ps-5). 3.50 (ISBN 0-7214-0005-1); No. 5. wkbk. 1.95 (ISBN 0-7214-3066-X); Series S05, Set 1. flash cards 4.75 (ISBN 0-7214-3015-5); Series S05, Set 2. flash cards 4.75 (ISBN 0-7214-3016-3). Ladybird Bks.

Willoughby, Alana. Boots. Jordan, Alton, ed. Webster, Jeneanne, illus. (gr. k-3). 1974. PLB 5.95 (ISBN 0-89868-006-9, Read Res); pap. text ed. 2.50 (ISBN 0-89868-039-5, Read Res). ARO Pub.

—Christmas. Jordan, Alton, ed. Reese, Bob, illus. (gr. k-3). 1977. PLB 5.95 (ISBN 0-89868-025-5, Read Res); pap. text ed. 2.50 boxed (ISBN 0-89868-058-1, Read Res). ARO Pub.

—The Little Mouse. Jordan, Alton, ed. Reese, Bob, illus. (gr. k-3). 1974. PLB 5.95 (ISBN 0-89868-007-7, Read Res); text ed. 2.50 soft bd. (ISBN 0-89868-040-9). ARO Pub.

—Rain. Jordan, Alton, ed. Reese, Bob, illus. (gr. k-3). 1974. PLB 5.95 (ISBN 0-89868-003-4, Read Res); pap. text ed. 2.50 (ISBN 0-89868-036-0). ARO Pub.

—Spring. Jordan, Alton, ed. Thompson, Sherry, illus. (gr. k-3). 1975. PLB 5.95 (ISBN 0-89868-019-0, Read Res); pap. text ed. 2.50 (ISBN 0-89868-052-2). ARO Pub.

—Thanksgiving. Jordan, Alton, ed. Reese, Bob, illus. (gr. k-3). PLB 5.95 (ISBN 0-89868-024-7, Read Res); pap. text ed. 2.50 (ISBN 0-89868-057-3). ARO Pub.

—What Is Love. Jordan, Alton, ed. Thompson, Sherry, illus. (gr. k-3). 1975. PLB 5.95 (ISBN 0-89868-018-2, Read Res); pap. text ed. 2.50 (ISBN 0-89868-051-4). ARO Pub.

Wilmer, Diane. Gallop Off & Go! rev. ed. Petrone, Valeria, illus. 32p. (gr. k-2). 1989. Repr. of 1989 ed. lib. bdg. 9.45 (ISBN 1-878363-01-8). Forest Hse.

Wilmer, Diane & Currey, Anna. Mr. Pepino's Cabbage. rev. ed. Currey, Anna, illus. 32p. (gr. k-2). 1989. Repr. of 1989 ed. lib. bdg. 9.45 (ISBN 1-878363-02-6). Forest Hse.

Winder, Jack. Hands. Jordan, Alton, ed. Webster, Jeneanne, illus. (gr. k-3). 1975. PLB 5.95 (ISBN 0-89868-020-4, Read Res); pap. text ed. 2.50 (ISBN 0-89868-053-0). ARO Pub.

—Listening. Jordan, Alton, ed. Webster, Jeneanne, illus. (gr. k-3). 1975. PLB 5.95 (ISBN 0-89868-021-2, Read Res); text ed. 2.50 soft bd. (ISBN 0-89868-054-9). ARO Pub.

—Presidents Day. Jordan, Alton, ed. Reese, Bob, illus. (gr. k-3). 1977. PLB 5.95 (ISBN 0-89868-028-X, Read Res); pap. text ed. 2.50 (ISBN 0-89868-061-1). ARO Pub.

—Your Face. Jordan, Alton, ed. Reese, Bob, illus. (gr. k-3). 1974. PLB 5.95 (ISBN 0-89868-008-5, Read Res); pap. text ed. 2.50 (ISBN 0-89868-041-7). ARO Pub.

Wise, Francis H. Ann. Wise, Joyce M., ed. & illus. 21p. (ps-1). 1983. pap. 1.50 (ISBN 0-915766-60-4). Wise Pub.

—The Beach. Wise, Joyce M., ed. & illus. 21p. (ps-1). 1983. pap. 1.50 (ISBN 0-915766-63-9). Wise Pub.
—Ed, 20 bks. 3rd ed. Wise, Joyce M., ed. (Illus.). 21p. (ps-1). 1983. pap. 1.50 (ISBN 0-915766-59-0). Wise Pub.
Wise, Francis H. & Wise, Joyce M. Bernie, the Saint. new ed. (Illus.). 21p. (Orig.). (gr. 1). 1980. pap. 1.50 (ISBN 0-915766-41-8). Wise Pub.
—Park the Car. Wise, Joyce M., illus. (ps-1). 1975. pap. text ed. 1.50 (ISBN 0-915766-32-9). Wise Pub.
—Play Ball. Wise, Joyce M., illus. (ps-1). 1975. pap. text ed. 1.50 (ISBN 0-915766-31-0). Wise Pub.
—Sit By Me. Wise, Joyce M., illus. (ps-1). 1975. pap. text ed. 1.50 (ISBN 0-915766-33-7). Wise Pub.
Wiseman, Bernard. Morris Goes to School. Wiseman, Bernard, illus. LC 75-77944. 64p. (gr. k-3). 1970. PLB 11.89 (ISBN 0-06-026548-5). HarpC Child Bks.
Wittwer, Sylvan H. The Greenhouse Effect. Head, J. J., ed. Steffen, Ann T., illus. LC 84-45833. 16p. (Orig.). (gr. 10 up). 1988. pap. text ed. 2.15 (ISBN 0-89278-363-X, 45-9763). Carolina Biological.
Witty, Bruce. A Different Tune. Hoffman, Joan, ed. Laurent, Richard, illus. 32p. (gr. k-2). 1987. wkbk. 1.99 (ISBN 0-88743-103-8, 02603). Sch Zone Pub Co.
Witty, Bruce & Gregorich, Barbara. Noise in the Night: Reading Workbook. Hoffman, Joan, ed. Nerlove, Miriam & Pape, Richard, illus. 32p. (Orig.). (gr. k-2). 1988. 1.99 (ISBN 0-88743-106-2). Sch Zone Pub Co.
—The Raccoon on the Moon: Reading Workbook. Hoffman, Joan, ed. Sandford, John & Pape, Richard, illus. 32p. (Orig.). (gr. k-2). 1988. 1.99 (ISBN 0-88743-108-9). Sch Zone Pub Co.
Zion, Gene. Harry & the Lady Next Door. Graham, Margaret B., illus. LC 60-9452. 64p. (gr. k-3). 1978. pap. 3.50 (ISBN 0-06-444008-7, Trophy). HarpC Child Bks.

READING

Here are entered books on methods of teaching reading and general books on the art of reading. Works on teaching retarded readers are entered under Reading–Remedial Teaching. books on the cultural aspects of reading and general discussions of books to read are entered under Books and Reading.

see also Books and Reading

Aemmer, Gail. Read & Comprehend: Following Directions. Rittenour, Gary, illus. 20p. (gr. 3-4). pap. 5.95 (ISBN 0-88724-132-8, CD-0565). Carson-Dellos.
—Read & Comprehend: Following Directions. Black, Rebecca, illus. 20p. (gr. 2-3). pap. 5.95 (ISBN 0-88724-131-X, CD-0564). Carson-Dellos.
—Read & Comprehend: Following Directions. Zimmer, Ann, illus. 20p. (gr. 1-2). 1985. pap. 5.95 (ISBN 0-88724-130-1, CD-0563). Carson-Dellos.
—Read & Comprehend: Main Ideas. Inderhees, Joan, illus. 20p. (gr. 2-3). 1985. pap. 4.95 (ISBN 0-88724-126-3, CD-0559). Carson-Dellos.
—Read & Comprehend: Vocabulary Development. Rittenour, Gary, illus. 20p. (gr. 2-3). 1985. pap. 5.95 (ISBN 0-88724-121-2, CD-0549). Carson-Dellos.
Allington, Richard L. & Krull, Kathleen. Reading. Naprstek, Joel, illus. LC 80-16547. 32p. (ps-2). 1985. PLB 15.33 (ISBN 0-8172-1322-8); pap. 9.27 (ISBN 0-8172-2485-8). Raintree Pubs.
Appell, Clara & Appell, Morey. Glenn Learns to Read. 2nd ed. Szasz, Suzanne, photos by. Appell, Clara T., intro. by. LC 87-62285. (Illus.). 64p. (ps-2). 1987. pap. 6.25 (ISBN 0-943501-00-8). M L Appell.
Artman, John. Good Apple & Reading Fun. 144p. (gr. 3-7). 1981. 10.95 (ISBN 0-86653-046-0, GA 278). Good Apple.
Baggiani, J. M. & Tewell, V. M. Phonics; a Tool for Better Reading & Spelling, Bk. I. Birt, Jane L., illus. (gr. 1-2). 1982. pap. 9.50 student's copy (ISBN 0-934329-00-1); tchr's. manual 10.75 (ISBN 0-934329-01-X). Baggiani-Tewell.
—Phonics: A Tool for Better Reading & Spelling, Bk. II. Jacobson, Mary M., illus. (gr. 3-6). 1967. pap. 3.50 (ISBN 0-934329-02-8); wkbk. 2.00 (ISBN 0-934329-03-6). Baggiani-Tewell.
—Phonics: A Tool for Better Reading & Spelling, Bk. III. Jacobson, Mary M. & Davis, Mary I., illus. (gr. 5-12). 1984. pap. 5.75 (ISBN 0-934329-04-4); wkbk. 4.00 (ISBN 0-934329-05-2). Baggiani-Tewell.
Berkey, Geri A. Easy in Reading. Creative Teaching Assocs. Staff, illus. 66p. 1978. tchr's. handbk. 6.95 (ISBN 1-878669-27-3, 6073). Crea Tea Assocs.
Berry, Marilyn. Help Is on the Way for Reading Skills. (Illus.). 48p. (gr. 4-6). 1984. pap. 4.95 (ISBN 0-516-43232-X). Childrens.
Beyond Basics: A Developmental Reading Program. (Illus.). 216p. (Orig.). (gr. 4). 1986. pap. text ed. 9.75 (ISBN 0-89061-429-6); tchr's. ed. 15.00 (ISBN 0-89061-438-5). Jamestown Pubs.
Beyond Basics: A Developmental Reading Program. (Illus.). 216p. (gr. 5). pap. text ed. 9.75 (ISBN 0-89061-430-X); tchrs. ed. 15.00 (ISBN 0-89061-439-3). Jamestown Pubs.
Beyond Basics: A Developmental Reading Program. (Illus.). 216p. (gr. 6). pap. text ed. 9.75 (ISBN 0-89061-431-8); tchrs. ed. 15.00 (ISBN 0-89061-440-7). Jamestown Pubs.
Beyond Basics: A Developmental Reading Program. (Illus.). 216p. (gr. 7). pap. text ed. 9.75 (ISBN 0-89061-432-6); 15.00 (ISBN 0-89061-441-5). Jamestown Pubs.
Beyond Basics: A Developmental Reading Program. (Illus.). 216p. (gr. 8). 9.75 (ISBN 0-89061-433-4); tchr's. ed. 15.00 (ISBN 0-89061-442-3). Jamestown Pubs.
Beyond Basics: A Developmental Reading Program. (Illus.). 216p. (gr. 9). pap. text ed. 9.75 (ISBN 0-89061-434-2); tchrs. ed. 15.00 (ISBN 0-89061-443-1). Jamestown Pubs.
Beyond Basics: A Developmental Reading Program. (Illus.). 216p. (gr. 10). pap. text ed. 9.75 (ISBN 0-89061-435-0); tchrs. ed. 15.00 (ISBN 0-89061-444-X). Jamestown Pubs.
Beyond Basics: A Developmental Reading Program. (Illus.). 216p. (gr. 11). 9.75 (ISBN 0-89061-436-9); tchr's. ed. 15.00 (ISBN 0-89061-445-8). Jamestown Pubs.
Beyond Basics: A Developmental Reading Program. (Illus.). 216p. (gr. 12). pap. text ed. 9.75 (ISBN 0-89061-437-7); tchrs. ed. 15.00 (ISBN 0-89061-446-6). Jamestown Pubs.
Billings, Henry & Billings, Melissa. Heroes. (Illus.). 160p. (gr. 6 up). 1985. pap. text ed. 7.50x (ISBN 0-89061-450-4). Jamestown Pubs.
Blue, Rose. Me & Einstein: Breaking Through the Reading Barrier. Luks, Peggy, illus. (gr. 3 up). 1984. 16.95 (ISBN 0-87705-388-X); pap. 9.95 (ISBN 0-89885-185-8). Human Sci Pr.
Borba, Michele & Ungaro, Dan. Bookends. 128p. (gr. 1-4). 1982. 10.95 (ISBN 0-86653-065-7, GA 432). Good Apple.
Brooks, Bearl. Jumbo Reading Yearbook: Kindergarten. 96p. (gr. k). 1980. 18.00 (ISBN 0-8209-0011-7, JRY R). ESP.
Brown, Frances. My First Book of Words. LC 78-58344. 144p. (gr. k-6). 1979. Walker Educ.
Building Reading Skills, Level 1. (gr. 6). 1983. 19.98 (ISBN 0-88343-806-2); tchr's. manual 11.40 (ISBN 0-86609-040-1); vocabulary development skills level 4.14 (ISBN 0-88343-814-3); comprehension skills level 4.14 (ISBN 0-88343-815-1); study & research skills level 4.23 (ISBN 0-88343-817-8); literary appreciation skills level 4.23 (ISBN 0-88343-818-6). McDougal-Littell.
Butrick, Lyn M. If This... & That.. Then What, 3 vols. Cooper, William R., ed. Butrick, Lyn M., illus. LC 83-50783. 27p. (gr. 1-3). 1983. Set. pap. 15.80 (ISBN 0-914127-13-6); Vol. 1. 3.93 (ISBN 0-914127-04-7). Univ Class.
Carson, Patti & Dellosa, Janet. Christmas Reading & Activity Book. (Illus.). 32p. (gr. 1-3). 1983. pap. 1.98 (ISBN 0-88724-038-0, CD-8029). Carson-Dellos.
Carter, Mary. Reading for Comprehension Skills. (Illus.). (gr. 2-7). 1982. wkbk. 4.50 (ISBN 0-89525-177-9). Ed Activities.
Clay, Marie. Stones: Concepts About Print Test. (Orig.). (ps-2). 1980. pap. text ed. 3.00x (ISBN 0-685-02173-4, 00556). Heinemann Ed.
Cohen, Elaine R. Reading Comprehension Space Stories. King, Jerry, illus. 32p. (gr. 4-6). 1984. pap. 1.98 (ISBN 0-88724-088-7, CD-7027). Carson-Dellos.
Crane, Barbara J. BS Skillbooklet, No. I. (Illus.). (gr. k-2). 1982. pap. text ed. 2.14 ea. (ISBN 0-89075-031-9). Crane Pub Co.
Daniel, Becky. Reading Brainstorms. 80p. (gr. 1-4). 1990. 7.95 (ISBN 0-86653-560-8, GA1171). Good Apple.
—Reading Thinker Sheets. 64p. (gr. 4-8). 1989. 7.95 (ISBN 0-86653-501-2, GA1097). Good Apple.
Donatelli, Betty. Growing in Reading. Donatelli, Betty, illus. 11p. (Orig.). (gr. 1-2). 1984. pap. 1.00 (ISBN 0-912981-07-5). Hse Bon Giovanni.
—Merry Words for You. Donatelli, Betty, illus. 11p. (Orig.). (gr. 1-2). 1984. pap. 1.00 (ISBN 0-912981-09-1). Hse Bon Giovanni.
Dramer, Dan. Monsters. (Illus.). 160p. (gr. 6 up). 1985. pap. text ed. 7.50x (ISBN 0-89061-451-2). Jamestown Pubs.
Duncan, Leonard C. Learn to Read with Phonetic & Non-Phonetic Words. Incl. Bk. 1. 97p; Bk. 2. 85p (ISBN 0-941414-12-4); Bk. 3. 99p (ISBN 0-941414-13-2); Bk. 4. 110p (ISBN 0-941414-14-0); Bk. 5. Nursery Rhymes. 109p. (Illus., Orig.). (gr. 1-3). pap. 10.00 (ISBN 0-317-11632-0). LCD.
Evans, A. J. & Palmer, Marilyn. More Writing about Pictures: Using Pictures to Develop Language & Writing Skills. (gr. 1-3). 1982. Bk. 1: Familiar Places. pap. 3.95x (ISBN 0-8077-6037-4); Bk. 2: Action & Activity. pap. 3.95x (ISBN 0-8077-6038-2); Bk. 3: Supplement-Fables. pap. 3.95x (ISBN 0-8077-6039-0); tchr's. manual 2.95x (ISBN 0-8077-6040-4). Tchrs Coll.
Fearn, Leif. Reading in the Mind. 41p. (gr. 1-7). 1984. 25.00 (ISBN 0-940444-22-4). Kabyn.

Fields, Harriette. Phonics for the New Reader: Step-by-Step. Cox, Anne, illus. LC 90-70334. 128p. (ps-2). 1991. 17.95x (ISBN 0-9625802-0-1). Words Pub CO. "The author provides a ready-to-use blueprint for helping young children understand phonics & provides the necessary tools for that understanding," says former President of the National Association of State Boards of Education, Roseann Bentley. "This book provides clear, well-organized directions", & "I think this would be an excellent book for people striving to learn English as a second language." TABLE OF CONTENTS: Lesson 1- Letter Names, Shapes & Sounds; Lesson 2- Short Vowels; Lesson 3- Long Vowels; Lesson 4- Special Words & Letters; Lesson 5- Reading Consonant Combinations; Lesson 6- Reading Vowel Combinations; Lesson 7- Special Vowel Combinations; Lesson 8- Reading Vowel-Consonant Combinations.
Publisher Provided Annotation.

Finkelstein, Dave & London, Jack. Greater Nowheres. 1990. pap. 9.95 (ISBN 0-671-68485-X, Fireside). S&S Trade.
Forte, Imogene. Read about It: Beginning Readers. LC 82-81720. (Illus.). 80p. (gr. k-1). 1982. pap. text ed. 7.95 (ISBN 0-86530-005-4, IP 05-4). Incentive Pubns.
—Read about It: Primary. LC 82-80499. (Illus.). 80p. (gr. 2-4). 1982. pap. text ed. 7.95 (ISBN 0-86530-006-2, IP-062). Incentive Pubns.
—Skillstuff-Reading. LC 79-89158. (Illus.). 264p. (gr. 2-6). 1979. pap. text ed. 12.95 (ISBN 0-913916-79-X, IP-79X). Incentive Pubns.
Forte, Imogene, et al. Something Special. (Illus.). 200p. (ps-3). 1982. pap. text ed. 10.95 (ISBN 0-86530-001-1, IP-011). Incentive Pubns.
Foust, Sylvia J. Reading Comprehension. (Illus.). 48p. (gr. 2-6). 1986. wkbk. 5.95 (ISBN 1-55734-340-3). Tchr Create Mat.
Get Ready to Read. 32p. (ps-k). 1986. write for info. (ISBN 0-307-05162-5, Pub. by Golden Bks). Western Pub.
Getting Ready for Reading. 24p. (Orig.). (ps). 1988. pap. 3.95 (ISBN 0-8431-3135-7); Little Q Electronic Answer Wand 7.00 (ISBN 0-318-39960-1). Price Stern.
Gittings, Elisa. Shape Books. Gittings, Elisa, illus. (Orig.). (gr. k-3). 1974. pap. 4.50 (ISBN 0-918932-40-8). Activity Resources.
Gould, Toni S. & Warnke, Marie. Learn to Read Program. (gr. 1-3). 1985. 49.50 (ISBN 0-8027-9244-8). Walker & Co.
Gregorich, Barbara. Context Clues. Pape, Richard, illus. 24p. (gr. 3-4). 1980. wkbk. 2.95 (ISBN 0-89403-602-5). EDC.
—Reading. Hoffman, Joan, ed. Koontz, Robin M., illus. 32p. (gr. 1). 1988. wkbk. 1.49 (ISBN 0-88743-164-X). Sch Zone Pub Co.
—Reading. Hoffman, Joan, ed. Koontz, Robin M., illus. 32p. (gr. 2). 1988. wkbk. 1.49 (ISBN 0-88743-170-4). Sch Zone Pub Co.
—Reading: First Grade. Hoffman, Joan, ed. Koontz, Robin M., illus. 32p. (gr. 1). 1990. wkbk. 3.49 (ISBN 0-88743-183-6). Sch Zone Pub Co.
—Reading: Second Grade. Hoffman, Joan, ed. Koontz, Robin M., illus. 32p. (gr. 2). 1990. wkbk. 3.49 (ISBN 0-88743-189-5). Sch Zone Pub Co.
Gutkoska, Joseph P. Developing Comprehension Skills Through the Use of Analogies. (Orig.). (gr. 5-12). 1985. pap. 6.95 (ISBN 0-930723-00-7). Nutshell Enterprises.
Henry, Marcia K. Words. (gr. 3-9). 1990. write for info. (ISBN 1-878653-00-8). Lex Pr.
Herr, Selma E. Read for Understanding, Bk. I. new ed. Anyone Can Read Press Staff, ed. Herr, Selma E., illus. 225p. (Orig.). (gr. 6-12). 1987. pap. 6.95 (ISBN 0-914275-04-6). Anyone Can Read Bks.
Hodges, et al. Basic Studies: Reading & Word Skills. rev. ed. 271p. (gr. 4-8). 1988. pap. text ed. 17.00 (ISBN 0-913310-19-0). PAR Inc.
Hough, Belva L. Here's Help! For Primary Reading & Language Arts. (gr. 1-3). 1987. pap. 5.95 (ISBN 0-8224-3617-5). Fearon Teach Aids.
Howard, Mary C. Needing Reading. Sussman, Ellen, ed. Burris, Priscilla, illus. 72p. (gr. 3-6). 1984. pap. text ed. 7.95 (ISBN 0-933606-28-1, MS-626). Monkey Sisters.
Insel, Eunice & Edson, Ann. Ready-Go-Begin-To-Learn. (Illus.). (ps-1). 1980. wkbk. 4.25 (ISBN 0-89525-098-5). Ed Activities.
Johnson, Merideth. When I Learn to Read. 1990. 3.98 (ISBN 0-8317-9369-4). Smithmark.
King-Dickman, Kathy. Games That Teach: Dinosaurs: Children's Literature Through Whole Language - A Board Game. (Illus.). 20p. (gr. 1-6). 1990. pap. text ed. 10.00 incl. gameboard (ISBN 0-927867-06-0). SkippingStone Pr.
King-Dickman, Kathy & Kulp, Katherine. Games That Teach: Friendship: Children's Literature Through Whole Language - A Board Game. (Illus.). 20p. (gr. 1-6). 1990. pap. text ed. 10.00 incl. gameboard (ISBN 0-927867-08-7). SkippingStone Pr.
—Games That Teach: Humor: Children's Literature Through Whole Language - A Board Game. (Illus.). 20p. (gr. 1-6). 1990. pap. text ed. 10.00 incl. gameboard (ISBN 0-927867-07-9). SkippingStone Pr.

Kramkowski, Bernice C. Syllabic Reading. LC 83-90226. (Illus.). 118p. (Orig.). (gr. 1-5). 1983. comb bdg. 9.95 (ISBN 0-912145-00-5). MMI Pr.

LeGros, Lucy C. Reading Success for School & Home. rev. ed. (Illus.). 230p. (Orig.). 1989. pap. 10.95 (ISBN 0-318-41420-1). Creat Res NC.

Lieberman, Lillian. Reading Skills. 64p. (gr. k-3). 1985. 6.95 (ISBN 0-912107-36-7). Monday Morning Bks.

Lieberman, Lillian, et al. Ready to Read. 64p. (gr. k-2). 1986. 6.95 (ISBN 0-912107-52-9). Monday Morning Bks.

—Start to Read. 64p. (gr. k-2). 1986. 6.95 (ISBN 0-912107-53-7). Monday Morning Bks.

Littlefield, Kathy M. & Littlefield, Robert S. Read to Me! Stark, Steve, illus. 28p. (Orig.). (gr. 3-6). 1990. pap. text ed. 8.95 (ISBN 1-879340-04-6, K0105). Kidspeak.

Longanecker, Georgia. Howdy Out There! Phonics Fun. LC 76-62681. (Illus.). (ps-3). 1977. soft cover 6.95 (ISBN 0-9601126-1-8). Longanecker.

Maberly, Norman C. Mastering Speed Reading. 127p. (gr. 9-12). 1989. pap. 3.50 (ISBN 0-451-15511-4, Sig). NAL-Dutton.

—Mastering Speed Reading. 127p. (gr. 7 up). 1966. pap. 4.95 (ISBN 0-451-16644-2, Sig). NAL-Dutton.

Magos, Eunice & Hornnes, Esther. First Lessons in... Reading, Writing, Math, Science. Sussman, Ellen, intro. by. Burris, Priscilla, illus. 40p. (Orig.). (ps-1). 1987. Reading. pap. 4.95 (ISBN 0-933606-47-8, MS-647); Writing. pap. 4.95 (ISBN 0-933606-48-6, MS-648); Math. pap. 4.95 (ISBN 0-933606-49-4, MS-649); Science. pap. 4.95 (ISBN 0-933606-50-8, MS-650). Monkey Sisters.

Mauler, Cliff. Read Me: A Course of Study to Improve Your Reading Speed, Comprehension, Memory, & Concentration. Feild, Ann, illus. 191p. (gr. 9-12). 1979. spiral bdg. 14.95 (ISBN 0-9602842-0-6). Read Me Pub.

Mayer, Victoria I. Book Bridges One, No. 1: Extensions & Activities for "The Cay", "Island of the Blue Dolphins", "Call It Courage" Barchers, Suzanne I., ed. 100p. (Orig.). (gr. 5-6). 1990. pap. text ed. 15.00 (ISBN 0-927867-01-X). Skippingstone Pr.

Moon, Cliff & Moon, Bernice. Look at... Books, 6 Vols, Set 2. Lees, Beverly, et al, illus. 16p. (Orig.). (gr. 1-3). 1987. pap. text ed. 23.40 (ISBN 1-55624-121-6, WG1216). Wright Group.

More Letters & Sounds. (Illus.). 32p. (ps). 1986. write for info. wkbk. (ISBN 0-307-03593-X, Pub. by Golden Bks). Western Pub.

Murtha, Philly. Creative Reading: You Can Be a Free Reader. Redpath, Ann, ed. 32p. (gr. 6 up). 1984. PLB 9.95 (ISBN 0-87191-997-4); 14.25 (ISBN 0-685-10394-3). Creative Ed.

—Reading Fast: You Can Be a Reading Athlete. Redpath, Ann, ed. 32p. (gr. 4 up). 1984. PLB 9.95s.p. (ISBN 0-87191-996-6); PLB 14.25 (ISBN 0-685-10401-X). Creative Ed.

My First Reading Book. (Illus.). 32p. (ps-1). 1985. 3.95 (ISBN 0-394-87701-2). Random.

Mylet, Trish & Sheffield, Antoinette. Phonetic Readers for the Short Vowels: Jan & Pam, The Van, Rex & Tex, The Bed, Siz & Liz, The Pit, Dod & Bob, The Box, Hun & Sum, The Hut, & Pals, 11 bks. Burton, Barry W., ed. (Illus.). 180p. (ps-2). 1988. Set. pap. text ed. 16.00 (ISBN 0-945590-00-8). Sizzy Bks.

O'Connor, Katherine H. Read & Do: Learning to Follow Written Directions. rev. ed. (Illus.). 51p. (gr. 1-3). 1973. wkbk. 1.50 (ISBN 0-910812-09-8). Johnny Reads.

Peterson, Elizabeth J. Beginning Reading at Home. Dewagian, Jeanette, illus. 136p. (ps-1). Repr. of 1986 ed. 10 sets 19.95, (ISBN 0-938911-00-7). Indiv Educ Syst.

Piequet, Miriam. Fingertip Phonics. Anyone Can Read Staff, ed. Ritchie, Fern, illus. Piequet, M., intro. by. (Illus.). 290p. (Orig.). (gr. 1-12). 1985. 19.95 (ISBN 0-914275-05-4). Anyone Can Read Bks.

Price, Betty G. & Caujolle, Claude. See Me Read. Ferguson, Elizabeth T., illus. (ps-k). 1985. pap. 19.95 (ISBN 0-9614374-0-5). Prof Reading Serv.

Quality Time Workbooks: I'm Ready to Read. 1991. 1.98 (ISBN 0-8317-7296-4). Smithmark.

Read Today! Read Today, Unit 1. (gr. 1). 1991. 39.95 (ISBN 0-88106-700-8). Charlesbridge Pub.

Reading. (Illus.). 32p. (gr. 6-12). 1983. pap. 1.85 (ISBN 0-8395-3393-4, 3393). BSA.

Reading & Understanding Nonfiction: Level One. 372p. (gr. 9-10). 1989. 15.50 (ISBN 0-89061-690-6); pap. 12.50 (ISBN 0-89061-487-3); tchr's. ed. 2.95 (ISBN 0-89061-495-4). Jamestown Pubs.

Reading & Understanding Nonfiction: Level Two. 388p. (gr. 11-12). 1989. 16.50 (ISBN 0-89061-694-9); pap. 13.50 (ISBN 0-89061-491-1); tchr's. ed. 2.95 (ISBN 0-89061-499-7). Jamestown Pubs.

Reading & Understanding Plays: Level One. 404p. (gr. 9-10). 1989. 18.50 (ISBN 0-89061-691-4); pap. 15.50 (ISBN 0-89061-488-1); tchr's. ed. 2.95 (ISBN 0-89061-496-2). Jamestown Pubs.

Reading & Understanding Plays: Level Two. 356p. (gr. 11-12). 1989. 19.50 (ISBN 0-89061-695-7); pap. 16.50 (ISBN 0-89061-492-X); tchr's. ed. 2.95 (ISBN 0-89061-525-X). Jamestown Pubs.

Reading & Understanding Poems: Level One. 274p. (gr. 9-10). 1989. 12.50 (ISBN 0-89061-692-2); pap. 9.50 (ISBN 0-89061-489-X); tchr's. ed. 2.95 (ISBN 0-89061-497-0). Jamestown Pubs.

Reading & Understanding Poems: Level Two. 242p. (gr. 11-12). 1989. 13.50 (ISBN 0-89061-696-5); pap. 10.50 (ISBN 0-89061-493-8); tchr's. ed. 2.95 (ISBN 0-89061-526-8). Jamestown Pubs.

Reading & Understanding Short Stories: Level One. 356p. (gr. 9-10). 1989. 15.50 (ISBN 0-89061-689-2); pap. 12.50 (ISBN 0-89061-486-5); tchr's. ed. 2.95 (ISBN 0-89061-494-6). Jamestown Pubs.

Reading & Understanding Short Stories: Level Two. 340p. (gr. 11-12). 1989. 16.50 (ISBN 0-89061-693-0); pap. 13.50 (ISBN 0-89061-490-3); tchr's. ed. 2.95 (ISBN 0-89061-498-9). Jamestown Pubs.

Reading Help. 32p. (ps-1). 1984. 2.95 (ISBN 0-86653-244-7, GA 591). Good Apple.

Reading Help. 32p. (gr. k-2). 2.95 (ISBN 0-86653-245-5, GA 592). Good Apple.

Reading Help. 32p. (gr. 1-3). 2.95 (ISBN 0-86653-246-3, GA 594). Good Apple.

Reading Help. (gr. 2-4). 2.95 (ISBN 0-86653-247-1, GA 593, Dist. by Ingram). Good Apple.

Reading Readiness Staff. Reading Readiness. (Illus.). 32p. (ps). 1985. 3.95 (ISBN 0-394-87700-4). Random.

Reading, Writing & Arithmetic: Grade 2. 160p. 1973. pap. 1.95 (ISBN 0-448-02912-X, G&D). Putnam Pub Group.

Reed, Crafton C., III. Thiu Soo-Pr Pum-Kn: The Super Pumpkin. (Illus.). (gr. 2-5). 1980. pap. text ed. 3.50 (ISBN 0-87881-091-9). Mojave Bks.

Robinson, Jacqueline S. I'm Ready for Reading. (ps-k). 1990. 19.95 (ISBN 0-9624827-0-6). A Plus Lrn.

—More Ready for Reading. (gr. k-2). 1990. 19.95 (ISBN 0-9624827-1-4). A Plus Lrn.

Roderman, Winifred H. Reading & Following Directions. (Illus.). 64p. (gr. 7-12). 1978. pap. text ed. 3.95 (ISBN 0-915510-25-1). Janus Bks.

—Reading Schedules. (Illus.). 64p. (gr. 7-12). 1978. pap. text ed. 3.95 (ISBN 0-915510-23-5). Janus Bks.

Savage, John F. Dyslexia: Understanding Reading Problems. LC 85-8925. (Illus.). 96p. (gr. 4-8). 1985. lib. bdg. 10.98 (ISBN 0-671-54289-3). Messner.

—Dyslexia: Understanding Reading Problems. (Illus.). 96p. (gr. 4-8). 1985. lib. bdg. 10.98 (ISBN 0-685-28823-4). Silver Burdett Pr.

Schaffer, Frank, Publications Staff. Getting Ready for Reading. (Illus.). 24p. (ps-k). 1980. wkbk. 3.98 (ISBN 0-86734-019-3, FS 3032). Schaffer Pubns.

—Reading Comprehension. (Illus.). 24p. (gr. 3-5). 1978. wkbk. 3.98 (ISBN 0-86734-011-8, FS 3012). Schaffer Pubns.

Shangold, Helen. Cloze Stories for Reading Success. (gr. k-3). 1981. 13.95 (ISBN 0-8027-9124-7). Walker & Co.

Shapiro, Mary F. Learn-to-Read. Hinchberger, William D. & Hron, Debi, illus. 52p. (ps-k). 1986. 13.99 (ISBN 0-934361-11-8). Kinder Read.

Sharpe, Caroline, illus. Rhyme Readers, 6 vols, Vol. 9-14. 12p. (ps-1). 1987. Teacher's Notes incl. pap. 16.80 (ISBN 1-55624-125-9, WG1259). Wright Group.

Smith, Kathleen & Woods, Jennifer. Reading Skills Register. Sussman, Ellen, ed. (Illus.). 68p. (Orig.). (gr. 4-6). 1983. pap. text ed. 7.95 (ISBN 0-933606-24-9, MS-623). Monkey Sisters.

Spellman, Linda. Book Report Backpack. 48p. (gr. 4-6). 1980. 5.95 (ISBN 0-88160-035-0, LW 220). Learning Wks.

The Sport of Reading: Read Fast, Read Smart, Boost Your Grades. 24p. (gr. 4 up). write for info. (ISBN 0-930251-01-6). Bluechip Pubs.

Stauffer, Russell G. & Berg, Jean H. Super Reading Junior. 256p. 1981. pap. text ed. 49.95 (ISBN 1-55678-039-7); audiocassettes incl. Learn Inc.

Steffens, J. & Carr, J. Action & Adventure. (gr. 7-12). 1983. 9.95 (ISBN 0-88160-101-2, LW 1007). Learning Wks.

Sussman, Ellen. Smiling Sentences: Sight Word Activities to Cut & Paste. Bishara, Ann, illus. (gr. 2-3). 1978. pap. 4.95 (ISBN 0-933606-03-6, MS-601). Monkey Sisters.

—Sunny Sentences: Sight Word Activities to Cut & Paste. Bishara, Ann, illus. (gr. 1-2). 1978. pap. 4.95 (ISBN 0-933606-02-8, MS-600). Monkey Sisters.

Szabos, Janice. Reading - A Novel Approach. Filkins, Vanessa, illus. 112p. (gr. 4-8). 1984. wkbk. 9.95 (ISBN 0-86653-186-6, GA 529). Good Apple.

Tilkin, Sheldon L. Establishing Sequence. Conoway, Judith, illus. 24p. (gr. 3-4). 1980. wkbk. 2.95 (ISBN 0-89403-570-3). EDC.

—Finding the Main Idea. Conoway, Judith, illus. 24p. (gr. 3-4). 1980. wkbk. 2.95 (ISBN 0-89403-569-X). EDC.

—Following Directions. Conoway, Judith, illus. 24p. (gr. 3-4). 1980. wkbk. 2.95 (ISBN 0-89403-571-1). EDC.

—Recalling Details. Conoway, Judith, illus. 24p. (gr. 4-5). 1980. wkbk. 2.95 (ISBN 0-89403-568-1). EDC.

—Recognizing Cause & Effect. (Illus.). 24p. (gr. 3-4). 1980. 2.95 (ISBN 0-89403-574-6). EDC.

Tilkin, Sheldon L. & Conoway, Judith. Distinguishing Between Fact & Opinion. (Illus.). 24p. (gr. 4-5). 1980. wkbk. 2.95 (ISBN 0-89403-582-7). EDC.

—Drawing Conclusions. (Illus.). 24p. (gr. 3-4). 1980. wkbk. 2.95 (ISBN 0-89403-573-8). EDC.

—Drawing Conclusions. (Illus.). 24p. (gr. 4-5). 1980. wkbk. 2.95 (ISBN 0-89403-583-5). EDC.

—Establishing Sequence. (Illus.). 24p. (gr. 4-5). 1980. wkbk. 2.95 (ISBN 0-89403-580-0). EDC.

—Finding the Main Idea. (Illus.). 24p. (gr. 4-5). 1980. wkbk. 2.95 (ISBN 0-89403-579-7). EDC.

—Following Directions. (Illus.). 24p. (gr. 4-5). 1980. wkbk. 2.95 (ISBN 0-89403-581-9). EDC.

—Recalling Details. (Illus.). 24p. (gr. 4-5). 1980. wkbk. 2.95 (ISBN 0-89403-578-9). EDC.

—Recognizing Cause & Effect. (Illus.). 24p. (gr. 4-5). 1980. wkbk. 2.95 (ISBN 0-89403-584-3). EDC.

—Recognizing Mood, Character & Plot. (Illus.). 24p. (gr. 4-5). 1980. wkbk. 2.95 (ISBN 0-89403-586-X). EDC.

—Recognizing Mood, Character & Plot. (Illus.). 24p. (gr. 3-4). 1980. wkbk. 2.95 (ISBN 0-89403-576-2). EDC.

Tlkin, Sheldon L. & Conoway, Judith. Distinguishing Between Fact & Opinion. (Illus.). 24p. (gr. 3-4). 1980. wkbk. 2.95 (ISBN 0-89403-572-X). EDC.

Wayman, Joe. The Other Side of Reading. 144p. (gr. k-8). 1980. 11.95 (ISBN 0-916456-64-1, GA 183). Good Apple.

Zakalik, Leslie S. The Comprehension Carnival. 76p. (gr. 2-4). 1977. 7.95 (ISBN 0-88160-005-9, LW 106). Learning Wks.

Zimmer, Ann. Reading Readiness - Teaching. Carson, Patti, et al, illus. 32p. (ps-1). 1984. pap. 1.98 (ISBN 0-88724-097-6, CD-7036). Carson-Dellos.

READING–FICTION

Bloom, Daniel H. The Magic of Johnny Readingseed. Julien, Claudia, illus. 48p. (gr. 5-9). 1990. 9.95 (ISBN 0-944007-60-0). Shapolsky Pubs.

Booth, Eugene. In the Garden. LC 77-7628. (Illus.). 24p. (gr. k-3). 1977. PLB 13.32 (ISBN 0-8393-0115-4). Raintree Pubs.

Bowers, Ruth B. Little Thumb. LC 88-51387. (Illus.). 110p. (gr. k-3). 1989. pap. 5.95 (ISBN 1-55523-196-9). Winston-Derek.

Brown, Margaret W. Four Fur Feet. Charlip, Remy, illus. 48p. (gr. 1-3). 1989. Repr. of 1961 ed. 13.95 (ISBN 0-929077-03-2, Hopscotch Bks); PLB 12.95 (ISBN 0-317-92548-2, Hopscotch Bks). Watermark Inc.

Cohen, Miriam. When Will I Read? Hoban, Lillian, illus. LC 76-28320. 32p. (ps-3). 1977. 13.95 (ISBN 0-688-80073-4); PLB 13.88 (ISBN 0-688-84073-6). Greenwillow.

Cole, Joanna. Ready Set Read. 1990. 17.95 (ISBN 0-385-41416-1). Doubleday.

Cosgrove, Stephen. Ira Wordworthy. LC 89-13175. (Illus.). 1989. 6.95 (ISBN 0-88070-279-6). Multnomah.

Dr. Seuss. I Can Read with My Eyes Shut! Dr. Seuss, illus. LC 78-7193. (gr. 1-3). 1978. 6.95 (ISBN 0-394-83912-9); lib. bdg. 7.99 (ISBN 0-394-93912-3). Beginner.

Giff, Patricia R. The Girl Who Knew It All. 128p. (gr. k-6). 1989. pap. 2.95 (ISBN 0-440-42855-6, YB). Dell.

Gilson, Jamie. Do Bananas Chew Gum? LC 80-11414. 160p. (gr. 5-9). 1980. 12.95 (ISBN 0-688-41960-7); PLB 12.88 (ISBN 0-688-51960-1). Lothrop.

Greene, Constance C. Isabelle & Little Orphan Frannie. (gr. 4 up). 1990. pap. 3.95 (ISBN 0-14-032916-1, Puffin). Puffin Bks.

Hallinan, P. K. Just Open a Book. Hallinan, P. K., illus. LC 80-22099. 32p. (ps-3). 1981. PLB 13.27 (ISBN 0-516-03521-5); pap. 3.95 (ISBN 0-516-43521-3). Childrens.

Hoban, Lillian. Arthur's Prize Reader. Hoban, Lillian, illus. LC 77-25637. 64p. (ps-3). 1978. 11.95 (ISBN 0-06-022379-0); PLB 11.89 (ISBN 0-06-022380-4). HarpC Child Bks.

—Arthur's Prize Reader. LC 77-25637. (Illus.). 64p. (ps-3). 1985. incl. cassette 5.98 (ISBN 0-694-00016-7, Trophy); pap. 3.50 (ISBN 0-06-444049-4, Trophy). HarpC Child Bks.

Holland, Margaret. Guess Who Learned to Read. (Illus.). 24p. (ps-3). 1991. pap. 2.50 (ISBN 0-87406-535-6). Willowisp Pr.

Hubbard, Inez. Danny. Edgell, Kyle, illus. LC 84-62082. 48p. (Orig.). (gr. k-3). 1984. pap. 3.95 (ISBN 0-931571-00-6). Lifetime Pr.

Hutchins, Pat. The Tale of Thomas Mead. LC 79-6398. 1988. pap. 2.95 (ISBN 0-688-08422-2, Mulberry). Morrow.

Lester, Alison. Bibs & Boots. (Illus.). 16p. (ps-k). 1989. 3.50 (ISBN 0-670-81988-3). Viking Child Bks.

—Crashing & Splashing. (Illus.). 16p. (ps-k). 1989. pap. 3.50 (ISBN 0-670-81989-1). Viking Child Bks.

Olaf Reads, Unit 4. (gr. 1). 1991. 5-pack 21.25 (ISBN 0-88106-734-2). Charlesbridge Pub.

Paul, Sherry. Blossom Bird Falls in Love. Miller, Bob, illus. 32p. (Orig.). (ps-2). 1981. pap. 14.10 bks. only (ISBN 0-685-01192-5); pap. 16.20 bks & Skill Masters (ISBN 0-685-01193-3). CPI Pub.

—Blossom Bird Finds a Family. Miller, Bob, illus. 32p. (Orig.). (ps-2). 1981. pap. 14.10 set (ISBN 0-686-31343-7); Bks. & Skill Masters Set 16.20 (ISBN 0-685-01194-1). CPI Pub.

—Blossom Bird Goes South. Miller, Bob, illus. 32p. (Orig.). (ps-2). 1981. pap. 14.10 set (ISBN 0-675-01080-2); Bks. & Skillmasters set 16.20 (ISBN 0-685-01195-X). CPI Pub.

—Finn the Foolish Fish: Trouble with Bubbles. Miller, Bob, illus. 32p. (Orig.). (ps-2). pap. 14.10 set (ISBN 0-675-01084-5); Bks. & Skillmasters set 16.20 (ISBN 0-685-01196-8). CPI Pub.

—Two-B & the Rock 'n' Roll Band. Murphy, Bob, illus. 32p. (Orig.). (ps-2). pap. 14.10 set (ISBN 0-675-01082-9); Bks & Skillmasters set 16.20 (ISBN 0-685-01197-6). CPI Pub.

—Two-B & the Space Visitor. Murphy, Bob, illus. 32p. (Orig.). (ps-2). pap. 14.10 bks. only (ISBN 0-685-01198-4); pap. 16.20 Bks. & Skill Masters (ISBN 0-685-01199-2). CPI Pub.

Pelham, David. Worms Wiggle. Foreman, Michael, illus. (ps-1). 1989. pap. 8.95 (ISBN 0-671-67218-5). S&S Trade.

Roberts, Sarah. Bert & the Missing Mop Mix-Up. Mathieu, Joe, illus. LC 82-22971. 40p. (gr. k-2). 1983. lib. bdg. 6.99 (ISBN 0-394-95752-0); pap. 4.95 (ISBN 0-394-85752-6). Random.

Rowe, W. W. Small Tall Tales. LC 88-51388. 78p. 1989. 5.95 (ISBN 1-55523-200-0). Winston-Derek.

Shearer, Marilyn J. The Adventures of Curious Eric: Learning Concepts. Roberts, Tom, illus. LC 90-60397. 16p. (ps-6). 1990. 19.95 (ISBN 0-685-33064-8); pap. 10.95 (ISBN 1-878389-01-7). L Ashley & Joshua.

Sullivan Associates Staff. I Can Read, 8 bks. (gr. k-1). Set. pap. 27.00 (ISBN 0-8449-2998-0). Carroll CA.

Thomas, Claire & Thomas, Thornton. Naming Game: Storybook to Color. Jones, S. Max, illus. 22p. (Orig.). (gr. k-3). 1988. pap. 3.95 (ISBN 0-317-92517-2). Sparky Star Pr.

Ziefert, Harriet. Dr. Cat. LC 88-82403. (Illus.). 32p. (ps-3). 1989. pap. 8.95 (ISBN 0-670-82669-3). Viking Child Bks.

—How Big Is Big? LC 88-82402. (Illus.). 32p. (ps-3). 1989. pap. 8.95 (ISBN 0-670-82667-7). Viking Child Bks.

—Let's Trade. LC 88-82401. (Illus.). 32p. (ps-3). 1989. pap. 8.95 (ISBN 0-670-82666-9). Viking Child Bks.

—Please Let It Snow. LC 88-82399. (Illus.). 32p. (ps-3). 1989. pap. 8.95 (ISBN 0-670-82665-0). Viking Child Bks.

—When the TV Broke. LC 88-82404. (Illus.). 32p. (ps-3). 1989. pap. 8.95 (ISBN 0-670-82668-5). Viking Child Bks.

READING–REMEDIAL TEACHING

Dwyer, Kathleen M. What Do You Mean I Have a Learning Disability? (Illus.). 32p. (gr. 5-9). 1991. 14.95 (ISBN 0-8027-8102-0); pap. 15.85 (ISBN 0-8027-8103-9). Walker & Co.

Rue, Nancy N. Coping with An Illiterate Parent. Rosen, Roger, ed. 64p. (gr. 7-12). 1990. lib. bdg. 12.95 (ISBN 0-8239-1070-9). Rosen Group.

Williams, Patricia & Verner, Zenobia. Why Didn't I Think of That? Improving Reading Comprehension. (gr. 4-8). 1988. pap. 8.95 (ISBN 0-673-18247-9). Scott F.

READING–STUDY AND TEACHING
see Reading
READING CLINICS
see Reading–Remedial Teaching
READING INTERESTS
see Books and Reading
READING INTERESTS OF CHILDREN
see Children–Books and Reading
REAGAN, RONALD WILSON, PRESIDENT U.S., 1911-

Behrens, June. Ronald Reagan: An All-American. LC 81-9993. (Illus.). 32p. (gr. 2 up). 1981. PLB 13.27 (ISBN 0-516-03565-7). Childrens.

De La Mare, Walter. Peacock Pie: Power & Politics in the Reagan White House. LC 89-1828. (Illus.). (ps-6). 1989. 17.95 (ISBN 0-8050-1124-2). H Holt & Co.

Kent, Zachary. Ronald Reagan. LC 89-33746. 100p. (gr. 3 up). 1989. PLB 17.27 (ISBN 0-516-01373-4); pap. 6.95 (ISBN 0-516-41373-2). Childrens.

Lawson, Don. The Picture Life of Ronald Reagan. rev. ed. LC 84-673. (Illus.). 48p. (gr. k-3). 1985. lib. bdg. 7.99 (ISBN 0-531-04953-1). Watts.

—Ronald Reagan, the Picture Life. LC 80-29085. (gr. k-3). 1981. PLB 7.99 (ISBN 0-685-05324-5). Watts.

Robbins, Neal E. Ronald W. Reagan: Fortieth President of the United States. Young, Richard G., ed. LC 89-39955. (Illus.). 128p. (gr. 5-9). 1990. PLB 17.26 (ISBN 0-944483-66-6). Garrett Ed Corp.

Schwartzberg, Renee. Ronald Reagan. (Illus.). (gr. 5 up). 1991. 17.95 (ISBN 1-55546-849-7). Chelsea Hse.

Sullivan, George. Ronald Reagan. LC 85-13688. (Illus.). 128p. (gr. 5 up). 1985. lib. bdg. 10.98 (ISBN 0-671-60168-7). Messner.

REAL ESTATE
Here are entered general works on real property in the legal sense i.e., ownership of land and buildings (immovable property) as opposed to personal property. Works limited to the buying and selling of real property are entered under Real Estate business. general works on land without the ownership aspect are entered under Land.
see also Farms
REASONING
see also Intellect; Logic

Ceasar, Lisbeth D. Making Inferences. (gr. 1-3). 1986. pap. 6.95 (ISBN 0-8224-1477-5). Fearon Teach Aids.

Learning Works Staff. Solution Sleuth. (gr. 4-8). 1989. 7.95 (ISBN 0-88160-170-5, LW 278). Learning Wks.

Schwartz, L. Analogy Adventure. (gr. 4-8). 1989. 5.95 (ISBN 0-685-30890-1, LW 280). Learning Wks.

Schwatrz, L. Think on Your Feet. (gr. 4-8). 1989. 7.95 (ISBN 0-88160-172-1, LW 283). Learning Wks.

Tilkin, Sheldon L. & Conoway, Judith. Making Judgments. (Illus.). 24p. (gr. 3-4). 1980. wkbk. 2.95 (ISBN 0-89403-577-0). EDC.

—Making Judgments. (Illus.). 24p. (gr. 4-5). 1980. wkbk. 2.95 (ISBN 0-89403-587-8). EDC.

REBUSES
see Riddles
RECIPES
see Cookery

RECLAMATION OF LAND
Here are entered general works on reclamation, including drainage and irrigation.
see also Irrigation; Marshes; Sand
RECLAMATION OF LAND–FICTION
Sharpe, Susan. Waterman's Boy. LC 89-39332. 176p. (gr. 3-8). 1990. 12.95 (ISBN 0-02-782351-2, Bradbury Pr). Macmillan Child Grp.
RECONSTRUCTION
Here are entered works dealing with reconstruction in the u. s. following the Civil War.
see also Blacks; Ku Klux Klan
RECREATION
Here are entered works on the psychological and social aspects of recreation and works on organized recreational projects.
see also Amusements; Games; Hobbies; Play; Playgrounds; Sports

Cribbs, Dianna G. A Kid's Guide to Fishing & Fun Things to Do! Cribbs, Dianna G., illus. 113p. (gr. 1-5). 1990. pap. 6.95 (ISBN 0-943487-24-7). Sevgo Pr.

Feldscher, Sharla. The Kidfun Activity Book. LC 89-46088. 160p. (Orig.). (ps-3). 1990. pap. 6.95 (ISBN 0-06-096495-2, HarpT). HarperCollins.

The Griffle's Activity Book. (Illus.). (ps-2). 1.95 (ISBN 0-7214-3110-0). Ladybird Bks.

Kalman, Bobbie. People at Play. (Illus.). 32p. (gr. 2-3). 1986. 14.95 (ISBN 0-86505-069-4); pap. 6.95 (ISBN 0-86505-091-0). Crabtree Pub Co.

Penn, Linda. Parks & Playgrounds. Scott, Elaine, illus. 32p. (gr. k-3). 1986. wkbk. 4.95 (ISBN 0-86653-350-8, GA 685). Good Apple.

West, Rose. Go & Have a Good Time. (gr. 2-8). 1990. pap. 8.95 (ISBN 0-8224-3500-4). Fearon Teach Aids.

Winston, Lynn. Recreation & Sports: An Activity Guide. Garee, Betty, ed. LC 85-72420. 72p. (Orig.). (gr. 9-12). 1985. pap. 4.95 (ISBN 0-915708-18-3, #1770). Cheever Pub.

RECREATIONS, MATHEMATICAL
see Mathematical Recreations
RECREATIONS, SCIENTIFIC
see Scientific Recreations
RECTORS
see Clergy
RED CHINA
see China (People's Republic of China)
RED CROSS, U. S. AMERICAN NATIONAL RED CROSS
Barton, Clara. Story of the Red Cross. Gemme, Francis R., illus. (gr. 4 up). 1968. pap. 1.50 (ISBN 0-8049-0170-8, CL-170). Airmont.
REDUCING (BODY WEIGHT CONTROL)
see Weight Control
REDWOOD
Anderson, Tammy L., ed. California Redwoods Color Book. 26p. (ps-8). 1988. pap. 1.95 (ISBN 0-915687-03-8). FVN Corp.
REFERENCE BOOKS
see also Books and Reading–Best Books; Encyclopedias and Dictionaries

Anthony, Susan C. Facts Plus: An Almanac of Essential Information. LC 91-70863. (Illus.). 250p. (Orig.). (gr. 4-8). 1991. pap. 15.95 (ISBN 1-879478-00-5); 3 wire bound 16.95 (ISBN 1-879478-01-3). Instr Res Co. FACTS PLUS: AN ALMANAC OF ESSENTIAL INFORMATION is a concise, authoritative, user-friendly reference book compiled with students & classroom teachers in mind. Its clear, easy-to-read format, large type & 3,876 word index facilitate the learning of skills for information literacy. Included are sections on Time & Space; Science & Health; The Earth & Its People; The United States; Maps (a short atlas); Libraries & Books; The English Language; Writing; Music & Art; Math & Numbers; a Handbook of how-to information & a section of sources & notes with additional information. FACTS PLUS would be especially useful for educators emphasizing geography, integrating whole language across the curriculum, or utilizing real statistics to teach math problem solving. The Handbook includes guidelines for etiquette, interviewing, writing research reports, making speeches, & taking tests. This book is recommended for classrooms & libraries, for children in grades 4-8, for adults learning English or basic skills, or for anyone needing a source of

quick, up-to-date reference information. FACTS PLUS would be an excellent gift from parents or grandparents to their school-aged children. Quantity discounts are available to educational institutions for classroom sets. Reviewed in June 1, 1991 BOOKLIST/REFERENCE BOOKS BULLETIN. *Publisher Provided Annotation.*

Cook, Sybilla. Reference Flipper: A Guide to Reference Material. 49p. (gr. 1 up). 1988. Repr. of 1983 ed. trade edition 5.95 (ISBN 1-878383-09-4). C Lee Pubns.

Edwards, Candy. The Reference Point. LC 82-83712. (Illus.). 80p. (gr. 3-6). 1983. pap. text ed. 7.95 (ISBN 0-86530-042-9, IP 42-9). Incentive Pubns.

Finding Out about Everyday Things. 96p. (gr. 2-4). 1981. 11.95 (ISBN 0-86020-491-X). EDC.

Free Stuff Editors. Free Stuff for Kids. rev. ed. 1989. pap. 4.95 (ISBN 0-671-68988-6). S&S Trade.

Goldman, Phyllis B. Monkeyshines on Strange & Wonderful Facts. Grigni, John, illus. 116p. (Orig.). (ps-8). 1991. pap. 8.95 (ISBN 0-9620900-2-6). NC Learn Inst Fitness. Monkeyshines on Strange & Wonderful Facts, 98 page volume of fascinating facts & miscellany, interesting reference alternative, illus. 8.95 plus 1.00 p/h (ISBN 0-9620900-2-6). Also available, Monkeyshines on the United States Presidents (Games, Puzzles & Trivia) illus., 98p. Interesting, informative & enjoyable view of the lives & work of the first 40 U.S. Presidents 12.95 plus 1.00 p/h (ISBN 0-9620900-1-8). *Publisher Provided Annotation.*

Kid's Address & Writing Book. (Illus.). 112p. (Orig.). (ps-8). 1990. pap. 5.95 (ISBN 0-943400-45-7). Marlor Pr.

Martin, Claire & Martin, Steve. My Best Book: A Year-Long Record of "Personal Bests" Martin, Diane, illus. 40p. (Orig.). (gr. 3-5). 1988. pap. 7.95 (ISBN 0-929545-00-1). Black Birch Bks.

See & Explore Library, 4 vols. (Illus.). (gr. 3 up). 1991. 47.80 (ISBN 1-879431-67-X); lib. bdg. 51.96 (ISBN 1-879431-68-8). Dorling Kindersley. Dinosaurs & How They Lived. (SEE & EXPLORE LIBRARY) Steve Parker, author, 1991. (Illus.) 64 pp., gr. 3 up. Hardcover trade ed. 11.95 (ISBN 1-879431-13-0); lib. bdg. 12.99 (ISBN 1-879431-28-9). Dorling Kindersley, Inc. - Machines & How They Work. (SEE & EXPLORE LIBRARY) David Burnie, author. 1991. (Illus.) 64 pp., gr. 3 up. Hardcover trade ed. 11.95 (ISBN 1-879431-15-7); lib. bdg. 12.99 (ISBN 1-879431-30-0) Dorling Kindersley, Inc. - Sharks & Other Creatures of the Deep. (SEE & EXPLORE LIBRARY) Philip Steele, author. 1991. (Illus.) 64 pp., gr. 3 up. Hardcover trade ed. 11.95 (ISBN 1-879431-14-9); lib. bdg. 12.99 (ISBN 1-879431-31-9). Dorling Kindersley, Inc. - Space, Stars, Planets & Spacecraft. (SEE & EXPLORE LIBRARY) Sue Becklake, author. 1991. (Illus.) 64 pp, gr. 3 up Hardcover trade ed. 11.95 (ISBN 1-879431-14-9); lib. bdg. 12.99 (ISBN 1-879431-31-9). Dorling Kindersley, Inc.--The SEE & EXPLORE LIBRARY is a wide-ranging series of reference books, each of which is a treasure trove of information & detailed color illustrations. Every topic in the series has been carefully chosen not only to appeal to children's interests &

enthusiasms, but to stimulate them to find out more about the world they live in. Covering such areas as nature, history, earth sciences, anthropology & technology, the SEE & EXPLORE LIBRARY builds into a reference series of value to all young readers.
Publisher Provided Annotation.

Slater, Barbara & Slater, Ron. Tracking Down Trivia. 48p. (gr. 5-12). 1982. 5.95 (ISBN 0-86653-078-9, GA 423). Good Apple.

Webster's Beginning Book of Facts. (ps-2). 1978. 9.95 (ISBN 0-87779-074-4). Merriam-Webster Inc.

REFORM, SOCIAL
see Social Problems

REFORM OF CRIMINALS
see Crime and Criminals

REFORMATION
see also Protestantism

Fehlauer, Adolph. Life & Faith of Martin Luther. (gr. 6-9). 1981. pap. 6.95 (ISBN 0-8100-0125-X, 15N0376). Northwest Pub.

Schwiebert, Ernest G. Luther & His Times: The Reformation from a New Perspective. (Illus.). (gr. 9 up). 1950. 26.95 (ISBN 0-570-03246-6, 15-1164). Concordia.

REFUGEES

Hitchcox, Linda. Refugees. (Illus.). 32p. (gr. 5-8). 1990. PLB 8.90 (ISBN 0-531-17242-2). Watts.

Michener, James A. Bridge at Andau. (gr. 10 up). 1957. 19.95 (ISBN 0-394-41778-X). Random.

REFUGEES–FICTION

Crew, Linda. Children of the River. LC 88-20401. (gr. 7 up). 1989. 14.95 (ISBN 0-440-50122-9). Delacorte.

Holm, Anne. North to Freedom. 1990. pap. 3.95 (ISBN 0-15-257553-7). HarbraceJ.

REFUSE AND REFUSE DISPOSAL
see also Sewage Disposal; Waste Products; Water–Pollution

Bailey, Donna. What We Can Do about Litter. (Illus.). 32p. (gr. k-4). 1991. PLB 11.40 (ISBN 0-531-11016-8). Watts.

—What We Can Do about Recycling Garbage. (Illus.). 32p. (gr. k-4). 1991. PLB 11.40 (ISBN 0-531-11017-6). Watts.

Becklake, Sue. Waste Disposal & Recycling. (Illus.). 40p. (gr. 5-8). 1991. PLB 11.90 (ISBN 0-531-17305-4, Gloucester Pr). Watts.

Gay, Kathlyn. Garbage & Recycling. LC 91-7130. (Illus.). 128p. (gr. 6 up). 1991. PLB 17.95 (ISBN 0-89490-321-7). Enslow Pubs.

Hadingham, Evan & Hadingham, Janet. Garbage! Where It Comes from, Where It Goes. (Illus.). 48p. (gr. 5 up). 1990. PLB 14.95 (ISBN 0-671-69424-3); pap. 5.95 (ISBN 0-671-69426-X). S&S Trade.

Hawkes, Nigel. Facts on Domestic Waste & Industrial Pollutants. (ps-3). 1990. PLB 11.90 (ISBN 0-531-10912-7). Watts.

Miller, Christina G. & Berry, Louise A. Wastes. 72p. (gr. 4-9). 1986. lib. bdg. 10.40 (ISBN 0-531-10130-4). Watts.

O'Connor, Karen. Garbage: Our Endangered Planet. LC 89-9382. (Illus.). 96p. (gr. 5-8). 1989. PLB 11.95 (ISBN 1-56006-100-6). Lucent Bks.

Palmer, Joy. Recycling Metal. LC 90-32530. (Illus.). 32p. (gr. 9-12). 1991. PLB 11.40 (ISBN 0-531-14118-7). Watts.

—Recycling Plastic. LC 90-32527. (Illus.). 32p. (gr. 9-12). 1991. PLB 11.40 (ISBN 0-531-14119-5). Watts.

Pringle, Laurence. Throwing Things Away: From Middens to Resource Recovery. LC 83-46165. (Illus.). 128p. (gr. 7 up). 1986. 12.95 (ISBN 0-690-04420-8, Crowell Jr Bks); PLB 12.89 (ISBN 0-690-04421-6, Crowell Jr Bks). HarpC Child Bks.

Showers, Paul. Where Does the Garbage Go? Lustig, Loretta, illus. LC 73-14881. (ps-3). 1974. 7.95 (ISBN 0-690-00392-7, Crowell Jr Bks). HarpC Child Bks.

Stefoff, Rebecca. Recycling. (Illus.). 128p. (gr. 5 up). 1991. PLB 19.95 (ISBN 0-7910-1573-4). Chelsea Hse.

Weiss, Malcolm E. Toxic Waste: Cleanup or Coverup? (Illus.). (gr. 7 up). 1984. lib. bdg. 12.90 (ISBN 0-531-04755-5). Watts.

Wilcox, Charlotte. Trash! Bushey, Jerry, illus. 40p. (gr. k-4). 1988. PLB 12.95 (ISBN 0-87614-311-7); pap. 5.95 (ISBN 0-87614-511-X). Carolrhoda Bks.

REFUSE AND REFUSE DISPOSAL–FICTION

Himmel, Roger J. Avoiding Litter. Manoni, Mary H., ed. Peters, Luther J. & Ross, Connie, illus. (gr. k-3). 1978. pap. text ed. 29.95 6 bks. & 1 cass. (ISBN 0-89290-045-8); pap. text ed. 10.95 1 bk. & 1 cass. (ISBN 0-685-04625-7). Soc for Visual.

Madden, Don. The Wartville Wizard. Madden, Don, illus. LC 85-23159. 32p. (gr. k up). 1986. 12.95 (ISBN 0-02-762100-6, Mcmillan Child Bk). Macmillan Child Grp.

Wilcox, Charlotte. Trash! Bushey, Jerry, illus. 40p. (gr. k-4). 1989. pap. 5.95 (ISBN 0-685-25643-X, First Ave Edns). Lerner Pubns.

Zion, Gene. Dear Garbage Man. Graham, Margaret B., illus. LC 57-5355. (gr. k-3). 1957. PLB 12.89 (ISBN 0-06-026841-7). HarpC Child Bks.

REGATTAS
see Rowing

REGISTERS OF PERSONS
see names of countries, cities, etc. and names of colleges, universities, etc. with the subdivision Registers, e.g. U. S. –Registers

REHABILITATION
see classes of people with subdivision Rehabilitation, e.g. Physically Handicapped–Rehabilitation

REIGN OF TERROR
see France–History–Revolution, 1789-1799

REINDEER

Postell, Alice E. Where Did the Reindeer Come From? Alaska Experience the First Fifty Years. York, Susan P., ed. DeArmond, Robert N., frwd. by. LC 90-146. (Illus.). 144p. (gr. 9 up). 1990. write for info. (ISBN 0-9626090-0-5). Amaknak Pr.
The beginning of the domestic reindeer industry in Alaska reads like a story. The Reverend Sheldon Jackson, a Presbyterian Missionary, became the first Government Agent for Education in Alaska, & while on this assignment he learned of the near-starvation among Eskimos. White men had hunted, & driven off, their source of wildlife & seafood. The account of bringing reindeer from Siberia, & his efforts to prepare Alaska Natives to meet the influx of "outsiders" is filled with frustrations, excitement & intrigue. Cultural conflicts, tradition & superstitions were ever present. The endless Arctic nights & brief bug-infested summers added problems. Whaling ships frozen in Arctic ice demanded sacrifice of reindeer herds for relief. Reindeer Fairs were held to stimulate interest & competition among the herders. Epidemics of measles & smallpox decimated the Eskimo leadership that was developing. The Nome gold-rush added endless complications. The first 50 years of Reindeer Industry reached a milestone when the Reindeer Act of 1937 mandated that all reindeer be returned to Alaska Natives, for whom they were intended from the beginning. 15 boxed stories give details of leading characters as well as other interesting facts. 48 historic photos have informative captions. Map of Alaska, index & bibliography. This is exciting reading for all ages.
Publisher Provided Annotation.

REINDEER–FICTION

Daly, Eileeni. Rudolph the Red-Nosed Reindeer. Jancar, Milli, illus. 24p. (gr. 2-5). 1972. pap. write for info. (ISBN 0-307-10045-6, Pub. by Golden Bks). Western Pub.

Haywood, Carolyn. How the Reindeer Saved Santa. Ambrus, Victor G., illus. LC 85-28456. 32p. (ps-3). 1986. 12.95 (ISBN 0-688-05903-1, Morrow Junior Books); lib. bdg. 12.88 (ISBN 0-688-05904-X). Morrow.

LaGrange, Lynn M. Joey, the Little Reindeer & the Land of Forgotten Children. Hall, Kenneth L., illus. 40p. (ps-6). 1990. lib. bdg. 10.95 (ISBN 1-878790-02-1). Fables CO.

—Joey, the Little Reindeer & the Land of Forgotten Children. Hall, Kenneth L., illus. 40p. (ps-6). 1990. pap. 6.95 (ISBN 1-878790-05-6). Fables CO.

Marks, Johnny. Rudolph the Red-Nosed Reindeer. Shortall, Leonard, illus. LC 85-60077. 16p. (ps). 1985. bds. 6.95 (ISBN 0-394-87446-3, Random Juv). Random.

Olson, Jim. The Reindeer & the Easter Bunny. Van Vleck, Jane & Olson, Sally, eds. (Illus.). 18p. (Orig.). (gr. 1-4). 1981. pap. 4.95 (ISBN 0-943806-00-3). Neahtawanta Pr.

Pierce, Meredith A. The Woman Who Loved Reindeer. 242p. (gr. 5 up). 1985. 14.95 (ISBN 0-316-70742-2, 707422, Joy St Bks). Little.

RELATIVITY (PHYSICS)

Swisher, Clarice. Relativity: Opposing Viewpoints. LC 90-3910. (Illus.). 112p. (gr. 3-8). 1990. PLB 13.95 (ISBN 0-89908-076-6). Greenhaven.

Tauber, Gerald E. Relativity: From Einstein to Black Holes. Kline, M., ed. LC 87-25964. (Illus.). 128p. (gr. 6-12). 1988. PLB 12.40 (ISBN 0-531-10482-6). Watts.

RELAXATION
see Recreation

RELIGION
see also Belief and Doubt; Faith; God; Indians of North America–Religion and Mythology; Mythology; Religions; Spiritual Life; Superstition; Worship

Barker, Dan. Just Pretend: A Freethought Book for Children. Cuebas, Alma, illus. 72p. (Orig.). (ps-6). 1988. pap. 10.00 (ISBN 0-318-42495-9). Freedom Rel Found.

Berger, Gilda. Religion. 96p. (gr. 4 up). 1983. PLB 10.40 (ISBN 0-531-04538-2). Watts.

Cook, Bob. Speaking in Tongues: Is That All There Is? Van Someron, Terry, illus. 48p. (gr. 9-12). 1982. pap. text ed. 1.50 (ISBN 0-88243-932-4, 02-0932); leader's guide 3.95 (ISBN 0-88243-935-9, 02-0935). Gospel Pub.

Danjhal, Beryl. Sikhism. (Illus.). 72p. (gr. 7-12). 1987. 19.95 (ISBN 0-7134-5202-1, Pub. by Batsford England). Trafalgar Sq.

Daughters of St. Paul. God Loves Me. (gr. 1-6). 1982. pap. 1.95 (ISBN 0-8198-3032-1); tchr's. manual 3.95 (ISBN 0-8198-3031-3). Dghtrs St Paul.

Fahs, Sophia L. & Cobb, Alice. Old Tales for a New Day: Early Answers to Life's Eternal Questions. Stair, Gobin, illus. LC 80-84076. (gr. 3-9). 1980. 17.95 (ISBN 0-87975-138-X); tchr's manual o.p. 9.95 (ISBN 0-87975-131-2). Prometheus Bks.

Gardner, Hope C. & Gunnell, Sally. Teach Me in My Way: A Collection for L.D.S. Children. LC 80-84147. (ps-5). 1980. soft cover 5.95 (ISBN 0-913420-85-9). Olympus Pub Co.

Hartweg, Judy. Faithful Followers. Henson, Grace, illus. 48p. (gr. 1-3). 1984. wkbk. 6.95 (ISBN 0-86653-237-4, SS 822). Good Apple.

Johnson, Tom. What Religious Science Is. 18p. (gr. 7-12). 1989. Repr. of 1977 ed. 2.00 (ISBN 0-941992-19-5). Los Arboles Pub.

Makhlouf, Georgia. The Rise of Major Religions. Moeller, Walter O., tr. from FRE. Welply, Michael, illus. 77p. (gr. 7 up). 1988. 15.96 (ISBN 0-382-09482-4); 10.37s.p. (ISBN 0-685-18827-2). Silver Burdett Pr.

Martin, John D. Living Together on God's Earth. (gr. 3). 1974. 12.95x (ISBN 0-87813-915-X); tchr's. guide 19.65x (ISBN 0-87813-910-9). Christian Light.

Minchin-Comm, Dorothy. Gates of Promise. Wheeler, Gerald, ed. 96p. (gr. 7 up). 1989. pap. 6.95 (ISBN 0-8280-0470-6). Review & Herald.

The New Saint Joseph Baltimore Catechism, 2 bks. (gr. 3-8). No. 1, Gr. 3-5. 1.80 (ISBN 0-89942-241-1, 241/05); No. 2, Gr. 6-8. 1.95 (ISBN 0-89942-242-X, 242/05). Catholic Bk Pub.

Nystrom, Carolyn. Why Do I Do Things Wrong? 32p. (gr. 2). 1981. pap. 4.95 (ISBN 0-8024-5996-X). Moody.

Ruth, Eddie. I Didn't Eat the Apple. (Illus.). 28p. (Orig.). (gr. 1-4). 1981. pap. 3.00 saddle-stitched (ISBN 0-911826-23-8). Am Atheist.

—A Tale of Eternal Life. Fernandez, Oscar, illus. 38p. (Orig.). (gr. 1-4). 1981. pap. 2.00 saddle-stitched (ISBN 0-911826-32-7). Am Atheist.

St. Augustine. Confessions of Saint Augustine. (gr. 11 up). 1968. pap. 1.95 (ISBN 0-8049-0190-2, CL-190). Airmont.

VanderGriend, Donna. Faith Talk. 132p. (Orig.). (gr. 10-12). 1989. pap. text ed. 23.95 leader's guide (ISBN 0-930265-56-4). CRC Pubns.

RELIGION–PHILOSOPHY

Hamilton, Dorothy. Last One Chosen. Converse, James, illus. LC 82-3150. 112p. (Orig.). (gr. 5-10). 1982. pap. 3.95 (ISBN 0-8361-3306-4). Herald Pr.

Moore, Ruth N. The Sorrel Horse. LC 82-3136. 144p. (Orig.). (gr. 5-10). 1982. pap. 3.95 (ISBN 0-8361-3303-X). Herald Pr.

RELIGION–STUDY AND TEACHING
see Religious Education

RELIGION AND SCIENCE
see also Creation; Evolution; Man–Origin and Antiquity

Rohr, Janelle. Science & Religion: Opposing Viewpoints. LC 87-38066. (Illus.). (gr. 10 up). 1988. lib. bdg. 15.95 (ISBN 0-89908-431-1); pap. text ed. 8.95 (ISBN 0-89908-406-0). Greenhaven.

RELIGION AND STATE
see Church and State

RELIGIONS
see also Bahaism; Buddha and Buddhism; Christianity; Confucius and Confucianism; Hinduism; Judaism; Mythology; Religion; Sects

Cairns, Trevor, ed. Barbarians, Christians, & Muslims. LC 73-20213. (Illus.). 104p. (gr. 5 up). 1975. PLB 10.95 (ISBN 0-8225-0803-6). Lerner Pubns.

Faricy, Robert. A Pilgrim's Journal. LC 89-60634. 64p. (Orig.). 1989. pap. 5.95 (ISBN 1-55612-259-4). Sheed & Ward MO.

Singh, Bhagat. The Story of Krishna. (Illus.). 20p. (Orig.). (ps-5). 1976. pap. 2.50 (ISBN 0-89744-135-4, Pub. by Hemkunt India). Auromere.

Thomas, M. Angele & Ramey, Mary L. Many Children: Religions Around the World. Lucas, Patti L., illus. LC 87-91771. 70p. (Orig.). (gr. 2-6). 1987. pap. text ed. 6.95 (ISBN 0-9619293-0-8). M A Thomas.

Underwood, Lynn. Religion & Society. LC 90-20343. (Illus.). 64p. (gr. 4-6). 1991. PLB 12.95 (ISBN 0-8368-0022-2). Gareth Stevens Inc.

RELIGIONS–BIOGRAPHY
Here are entered collections of biographies of religious leaders not limited to the Christian religion.
see also Christian Biography
Clarke, Brenda. Fighting for Their Faith. LC 89-71372. (Illus.). 48p. (gr. 4-8). 1990. PLB 18.60 (ISBN 0-8114-2753-6). Steck-V.
David Livingstone. 1989. 3.50 (ISBN 0-7214-0168-6). Chr Lit.
Helen, Mary. Wait for Me: The Life of Junipero Serra. Thien, Denis, illus. 100p. (gr. 4-8). 1988. 3.00 (ISBN 0-8198-8232-1). Dghtrs St Paul.
Hofman, David. God & His Messengers. Rideout, Geoffrey & Zahra'i, Zohreh, illus. 1986. pap. write for info. (ISBN 0-85398-049-7). G Ronald Pub.
Lappin, Peter. Stories of Don Bosco. 2nd ed. LC 78-72525. (Illus.). 272p. (gr. 5-12). 1979. pap. 2.95 (ISBN 0-89944-036-3). Don Bosco Multimedia.
Majumdar, Lila. Jorasanko House. (Illus.). (gr. 1-9). 1979. pap. 2.50 (ISBN 0-89744-176-1). Auromere.
Treece, Patricia. Soldier of God. Chatton, Ray, illus. 32p. (gr. 1-8). 1982. pap. 1.00 (ISBN 0-913382-22-1, 111-1). Prow Bks-Franciscan.
Wylam, P. Guru Nanak. Biswas, Pulak, illus. (gr. 1-8). 1979. pap. 4.00 (ISBN 0-89744-154-0). Auromere.

RELIGIONS–FICTION
Baba Hari Dass. Mystic Monkey. Kelley, Elizabeth A., illus. LC 81-51051. 64p. (Orig.). (gr. 4-8). 1984. pap. 7.95 (ISBN 0-918100-05-4). Sri Rama.
Barrie, J. M. The Little Minister. 232p. 1981. Repr. PLB 18.95 (ISBN 0-89966-329-X). Buccaneer Bks.
—The Little Minister. 300p. 1980. Repr. PLB 18.95x (ISBN 0-89967-007-5). Harmony Raine.
Blume, Judy. Are You There, God? It's Me, Margaret. LC 79-122741. 160p. (gr. 4-6). 1982. 12.95 (ISBN 0-02-710990-9, Bradbury Pr). Macmillan Child Grp.
—Are You There God? It's Me, Margaret. LC 79-122741. 156p. (gr. 4-7). 1990. Repr. of 1970 ed. 12.95 (ISBN 0-02-710991-7, Bradbury Pr). Macmillan Child Grp.
Devi-Doolin, Daya. Dormck & the Temple of the Healing Light. LC 89-63461. (Illus.). 50p. (Orig.). (gr. 4-8). 1989. pap. text ed. 6.50 incl. cassette (ISBN 1-877945-05-6). Padaran Pubns.
Groner, Judyth & Wikler, Madeine. Let's Build a Sukkah. Kahn, Katherine J., illus. LC 86-81717. 12p. (ps). 1986. bds. 4.95 (ISBN 0-930494-58-X). Kar Ben.
Groner, Judyth & Wikler, Madeline. My First Seder. Kahn, Katherine J., illus. LC 86-81715. 12p. (ps). 1986. bds. 4.95 (ISBN 0-930494-61-X). Kar Ben.
Gruenbaum, Hannah. The Magic Carpet. Forst, Sigmund, illus. (ps-1). 1.50 (ISBN 0-685-86206-2). Feldheim.
Jones, Rebecca C. The Believers. 144p. (gr. 6 up). 1989. 13.95 (ISBN 1-55970-035-1). Arcade Pub Inc.
—The Believers. LC 89-84223. 192p. (gr. 3-7). 1991. pap. 3.95 (ISBN 0-679-80594-X, Bullseye Bks). Knopf.
Lee, Anthony A. The Proud Helper: A Story About 'Abdu'l-Baha in the Holy Land. Irvine, Rex J., illus. 24p. (gr. k-5). 1979. pap. 3.00 (ISBN 0-933770-03-0). Kalimat.
Le Guin, Ursula K. Solomon Leviathan's Nine Hundred Thirty-First Trip Around the World. Austin, Alicia, illus. 40p. (gr. 7 up). 1983. 70.00 (ISBN 0-941826-03-1). Cheap St.
Paterson, Katherine. Rebels of the Heavenly Kingdom. 240p. (gr. 7 up). 1984. pap. 2.95 (ISBN 0-380-68304-0, 68304, Flare). Avon.
Saypol, Judyth R. & Wikler, Madeline. The Purim Parade. Kahn, Katherine J., illus. LC 86-71816. 12p. (ps). 1986. bds. 4.95 (ISBN 0-930494-60-1). Kar Ben.

RELIGIOUS ART
see Christian Art and Symbolism

RELIGIOUS BELIEF
see Belief and Doubt; Faith
Bennett, Marian. God Made Me. (Illus.). (ps). 1988. 3.95 (ISBN 0-87403-381-0, 2748). Standard Pub.
—God's Gifts. (ps). 1988. 3.95 (ISBN 0-87403-382-9, 2750). Standard Pub.
Deverell, Catherine. Grandma Told Me So. (ps-k). 1988. 1.59 (ISBN 0-87403-386-1, 2016). Standard Pub.

RELIGIOUS BIOGRAPHY
see Christian Biography; Religions–Biography
Mohan, Claire J. A Red Rose for Frania: A Story of the Young Life of Francis Siedliska. Thomer, Susannah, illus. (gr. 4-7). 1989. PLB 5.95 (ISBN 0-9621500-8-8). Young Sparrow Pr.

RELIGIOUS CEREMONIES
see Rites and Ceremonies

RELIGIOUS DENOMINATIONS
see Sects

RELIGIOUS EDUCATION
see also Bible–Study; Character Education
Ahlers, Julia. Special Topics in Justice & Peace: Nine Articles for Student Handouts. Allaire, Barbara, ed. 48p. (Orig.). (gr. 11-12). 1990. pap. text ed. 8.95 stitched (ISBN 0-88489-244-1). St Mary's.
Beckman, Beverly. Shapes in God's World. LC 56-1462. (ps-k). 1984. 6.95 (ISBN 0-570-04094-9). Concordia.
—Sizes in God's World. (ps-k). 1984. 6.95 (ISBN 0-570-04095-7, 56-1463). Concordia.
Boden, Robert. Teen Talks with God. (gr. 7-12). 1980. pap. 3.95 (ISBN 0-570-03812-X, 12-2921). Concordia.
Case, Riley B., et al. We Believe--Sr. High. rev. ed. 64p. 1988. wkbk. 3.95 (ISBN 0-917851-26-9). Bristol Hse.
Caswell, Helen R. God's World Makes Me Feel So Little. Caswell, Helen R., illus. 32p. (gr. k-3). 1988. 4.95 (ISBN 0-687-15510-X). Abingdon.
Clark, Suzanne. Blackboard Blackmail. La Haye, Beverly. 220p. (Orig.). 1989. pap. 8.95 (ISBN 1-877818-02-X). Footstool Pubns.
Cone, Molly. About Belonging. Perl, Susan, illus. 64p. (Orig.). (gr. 1-2). 1972. pap. 5.00 (ISBN 0-8074-0234-6, 101083). UAHC.
Crowther, Jean D. Growing up in the Church: Gospel Principles & Practices for Children. rev. ed. Perry, Lucille R., illus. LC 67-25433. 84p. (gr. 2-6). 1973. Repr. of 1965 ed. 6.95 (ISBN 0-88290-024-2). Horizon Utah.
Cumming, James T. & Moll, Hans G. And, God, What About...? 1980. 5.95 (ISBN 0-570-03806-5, 12-2915). Concordia.
Fehlauer, Adolph. Catechism Lessons: Pupil's Book. Grunze, Richard, ed. May, Lawrence, illus. 336p. (gr. 5-6). 1981. 6.95 (ISBN 0-938272-09-8). WELS Board.
—Catechism Lessons-Teacher's Book. Grunze, R., ed. 392p. (gr. 5-6). 1978. 3-ring binder 9.95 (ISBN 0-938272-08-X). WELS Board.
Foling, Debra & Sherbondy, Sharon. Super Sketches for Youth Ministry: Thirty Creative Topical Dramas from Willow Creek Community Church. 192p. 1991. pap. 9.95 (ISBN 0-310-53411-9, Pub. by Youth Spec). Zondervan.
Fretz, Clarence Y. Story of God's People. (gr. 7). pap. 5.90x (ISBN 0-87813-900-1); tchrs. guide 6.95x (ISBN 0-87813-901-X). Christian Light.
Groomer, Vera. Quiet Because. (ps). 1979. pap. 2.15 (ISBN 0-8127-0253-0). Review & Herald.
—Talking to My Friend Jesus: Two - Four. 32p. (ps). 1980. pap. 2.15 (ISBN 0-8127-0273-5). Review & Herald.
Haas, Lois J. Tell Me about God: 12 Lessons, Vol. 1. (ps). 1966. complete kit 14.95 (ISBN 0-86508-011-9); text only 3.45 (ISBN 0-86508-012-7); color & action book 1.75 (ISBN 0-86508-013-5). BCM Pubn.
—Tell Me about Jesus: 16 Lessons, Vol. 2. (ps). 1967. complete kit 14.95 (ISBN 0-86508-014-3); text only 3.45 (ISBN 0-86508-015-1); color & action book 1.75 (ISBN 0-86508-016-X). BCM Pubn.
Hand, Phyllis. Celebrate God & Country. Nygaard, Elizabeth, illus. 144p. (gr. k-6). 1987. pap. 10.95 (ISBN 0-86653-390-7, SS 843). Good Apple.
Harrison House Staff. Confessions for Kids. Titolo, Nancy, illus. 29p. (Orig.). (gr. 1-3). 1984. pap. 0.98 (ISBN 0-89274-322-0). Harrison Hse.
Hillert, Margaret. God's Big Book. Hohag, Linda, illus. 24p. (gr. k-1). 1988. 4.99 (ISBN 0-87403-457-4, 24-03696). Standard Pub.
Hutchens, Paul. Sugar Creek Gang & the Chicago Adventure & One Stormy Day. (gr. 3-7). 1968. pap. 5.95 (ISBN 0-8024-1237-8). Moody.
—The Thousand Dollar Fish. (gr. 3-7). 1966. pap. 3.50 (ISBN 0-8024-4815-1). Moody.
—The Timber Wolf. (gr. 3-7). 1965. pap. 3.50 (ISBN 0-8024-4823-2). Moody.
Johnston, Dorothy G. & Abbas, Kathleen. Church Time for Children. LC 80-67855. 120p. (Orig.). (gr. 1-6). 1981. 10.95 (ISBN 0-89636-056-3). Accent Bks.
Lea, Thomas D. & Latham, Bill. Sigueme 3. Martinez, Mario, tr. from ENG. (SPA.). 128p. (Orig.). 1989. pap. 3.75 (ISBN 0-685-30878-2). Casa Bautista.
Lecciones y Actividades Misioneras para Ninos de 3 y 4 anos, No. 1. (SPA.). 96p. (ps). 1988. pap. 3.50 (ISBN 0-311-12039-3). Casa Bautista.
Lecciones y Actividades Misioneras Para Ninos de 3 y 4 Anos - Missionary Lessons & Activities for Children 3 & 4, No. 2. (SPA., Illus.). 96p. (Orig.). (ps). 1989. pap. 3.50 (ISBN 0-311-12044-X). Casa Bautista.
Lee, Sylvia, ed. The Holy Spirit in Christian Education. LC 88-80549. 144p. (Orig.). (gr. k up). 1988. pap. 2.95 tchr's. bk. (ISBN 0-88243-854-9, 02-0854). Gospel Pub.
Leichner, Jeannine T. Making Things Right: The Sacrament of Reconciliation. (Illus.). 62p. (Orig.). (gr. 2-4). 1980. pap. 3.50 (ISBN 0-87973-351-9, 351); Spanish Edition. 3.50 (ISBN 0-87973-349-7, 349). Our Sunday Visitor.
Leroy, Douglas. We Believe. Miller, Julius D., illus. 56p. (gr. 7-12). 1975. pap. 3.95 (ISBN 0-87148-906-6). Pathway Pr.
MacKenthun, Carole & Dwyer, Paulinus. Kindness. Filkins, Vanessa, illus. 48p. (gr. 2 up). 1987. pap. 6.95 (ISBN 0-86653-379-6, SS880). Good Apple.
Maughan, Joyce B. Talks for Tots. LC 85-70993. 171p. (ps-9). 1985. 8.95 (ISBN 0-87747-804-X). Deseret Bk.
Moffatt, M. Children's Word Liturgies, Vol. 2. 112p. (gr. k-6). 1987. pap. 9.95 (ISBN 0-8146-1538-4). Liturgical Pr.
Murphy, Elspeth C. Sometimes I Get Mad. (gr. k-2). 1981. pap. 2.95 (ISBN 0-89191-493-5, 54932). Cook.
—Sometimes I Have to Cry. Nelson, Jane, illus. (gr. k-2). 1981. pap. 2.95 (ISBN 0-89191-494-3, 54940). Cook.
—Sometimes I Need to Be Hugged. (Illus.). (gr. k-2). 1981. pap. 2.95 (ISBN 0-89191-492-7, 54924). Cook.
Neighbour, Ralph W., Jr. Sigueme, Edicion para Ninos. Geiger, Mary J. & Ditmore, Shirley, trs. from ENG. (SPA., Illus.). 64p. (Orig.). 1989. pap. 2.65 (ISBN 0-685-30879-0). Casa Bautista.
—Sigueme 2. Martinez, Mario, tr. from ENG. (SPA., Illus.). 128p. (Orig.). 1989. pap. 3.75 (ISBN 0-311-13843-8). Casa Bautista.
Nystrom, Carolyn. The Holy Spirit in Me. 32p. (ps-2). 1980. pap. 3.95 (ISBN 0-8024-6152-2). Moody.
Programas y Actividades para Muchachos y Jovencitos, No. 5. (SPA.). 96p. (gr. 4-10). 1988. pap. 3.50 (ISBN 0-311-12041-5). Casa Bautista.
Programas y Actividades para Muchachos y Jovencitos, No. 6. (SPA., Illus.). 96p. (Orig.). 1989. pap. 2.95 (ISBN 0-311-12046-6). Casa Bautista.
Programas y Actividades para Ninas y Jovencitas, No. 5. (SPA.). 96p. (gr. 4-10). 1988. pap. 3.50 (ISBN 0-311-12040-7). Casa Bautista.
Programas y Actividades para Ninas y Jovencitas, No. 6. (SPA., Illus.). 96p. (Orig.). 1989. pap. 2.95 (ISBN 0-311-12045-8). Casa Bautista.
Prose, Francine. Stories from Our Living Past. new ed. Harlow, Jules, ed. Weihs, Erika, illus. LC 74-8514. 128p. (gr. 3-4). 1974. 7.95 (ISBN 0-87441-081-9); wkbk. 1 2.95 (ISBN 0-87441-083-5); wkbk. 2 2.95 (ISBN 0-87441-084-3); tchr's guide 14.95 (ISBN 0-87441-082-7). Behrman.
St. John, Patricia M. Rainbow Garden. (gr. 2-5). pap. 4.50 (ISBN 0-8024-0028-0). Moody.
Schneck, Susan & Strohl, Mary. Vacation Bible School Ideas & Summertime Fun. (Illus.). 96p. (ps-2). 1989. 9.95 (ISBN 0-86653-477-6, SS1813). Good Apple.
Sherrill, Lou. Jovita Galan: Unselfish Teacher. LC 86-6110. (gr. 4-6). 1986. 5.95 (ISBN 0-8054-4326-6). Broadman.
Stadler, Bernice & Reese, Nancy. Celebrations of the Word for Children: Cycle C. LC 88-90102. 014p. (Orig.). (gr. 3-8). 1988. pap. text ed. 9.95 (ISBN 0-89622-362-0). Twenty-Third.
Vos Wezeman, Phyllis. Peacemaking Creatively Through the Arts: A Handbook for Educational Activities & Experiences for Children. Chase, Judith, illus. 238p. (Orig.). (gr. 1-8). 1990. pap. 15.95 (ISBN 1-877871-01-X). Ed Ministries.
Walsh, Chad. Knock & Enter. (Orig.). (gr. 6-9). 1953. pap. 4.95 (ISBN 0-8192-1076-5). Morehouse Pub.
Ward, Elaine. Using God's World in Christian Education. 12p. (Orig.). (gr. 1-8). 1987. pap. 5.75 (ISBN 0-940754-40-1). Ed Ministries.
Watkins, Dawn L. The Medallion. (Illus.). 223p. (Orig.). (gr. 4). 1985. pap. 6.94 (ISBN 0-89084-282-5). Bob Jones Univ Pr.
You Are an Acolyte: A Manual for Acolytes. (Illus.). (gr. 6-9). 1977. pap. 3.95 (ISBN 0-8066-1552-4, 10-7409, Augsburg). Augsburg Fortress.

RELIGIOUS FESTIVALS
see Fasts and Feasts

RELIGIOUS FREEDOM
see Religious Liberty

RELIGIOUS HISTORY
see Church History

RELIGIOUS LIBERTY
see also Church and State
Evans, J. Edward. Freedom of Religion. (Illus.). 88p. (gr. 4 up). 1990. PLB 10.95 (ISBN 0-8225-1754-X). Lerner Pubns.
Merlin, Lester. Courage for a Cross, Teacher's Guide To. (gr. 1-6). 1987. pap. 9.95 (ISBN 0-685-18066-2). Friendship Pr.
Walters, Jean. Freedom or Fear. 32p. (Orig.). 1984. pap. 3.50 (ISBN 0-941992-21-7). Los Arboles Pub.

RELIGIOUS LITERATURE
see also Catholic Literature
Angers, Joann. Meeting the Forgiving Jesus: A Child's First Penance Book. 32p. (gr. 1-3). 1984. pap. 2.50 (ISBN 0-89243-201-2). Liguori Pubns.
Barrett, Ethel. Cracker, the Horse Who Lost His Temper: Communicating Christian Values to Children. (ps-2). 1979. pap. 5.95 incl. cassette (ISBN 0-8307-0687-9, 5606403). Regal.
—Ice, Water & Snow. (gr. 2-6). 1980. pap. 5.95 incl. cass. (ISBN 0-8307-0690-9, 5606705). Regal.
—Sylvester the Three-Spined Stickleback. 24p. (gr. 2-6). 1980. pap. 5.95 incl. cass. (ISBN 0-8307-0688-7, 5606691). Regal.
Bhaktivedanta, Swami A. C. Prahlad, Picture & Story Book. LC 72-2032. (Illus.). (gr. 2-6). 1973. pap. 4.00 (ISBN 0-685-47513-1). Bhaktivedanta.
Burgess, Beverly C. The Little Red Hen. (Illus.). 32p. (gr. 1-3). 1984. pap. 3.98 (ISBN 0-89274-312-3). Harrison Hse.
—Little Red Riding Hood. (Illus.). 32p. (Orig.). (gr. 1-3). 1983. pap. 3.98 (ISBN 0-89274-289-5). Harrison Hse.
Coleman, William L. Listen to the Animals. LC 79-11312. 128p. (ps-6). 1979. pap. 5.95 (ISBN 0-87123-341-X). Bethany Hse.
—Singing Penguins & Puffed-up Toads. LC 81-1079. 125p. (ps-4). 1981. pap. 5.95 (ISBN 0-87123-554-4). Bethany Hse.
Dueland, Joy. God's Great Adventure. (Illus.). 111p. (ps up). 1980. 8.95 (ISBN 0-685-08285-7). Phunn Pubs.
Geller, Norman. Talk to God... I'll Get the Message: Catholic Version. Tomlinson, Albert, illus. 23p. (gr. 1-4). 1983. pap. 4.95 (ISBN 0-915753-03-0). N Geller Pub.
—Talk to God... I'll Get the Message: Jewish Version. Tomlinson, Albert J., illus. 23p. (gr. 1-4). 1983. pap. 4.95 (ISBN 0-915753-02-2). N Geller Pub.
—Talk to God... I'll Get the Message: Protestant Version. Tomlinson, Albert J., illus. 23p. (gr. 1-4). 1983. pap. 4.95 (ISBN 0-915753-04-9). N Geller Pub.
The Illustrated Pilgrim's Progress. (Illus.). 1989. 12.95 (ISBN 0-8423-1605-1). Tyndale.
Jones, Tim & Butterworth, Jim. Another Way of Putting It: Twenty Short Plays with a Point. 128p. (gr. 7-12). 1991. pap. 7.99 (ISBN 0-87403-854-5, 14-03354). Standard Pub.

L'Engle, Madeleine. Trailing Clouds of Glory: Spiritual Values in Children's Books. Brooke, Avery, contrib. by. LC 84-29081. 144p. (gr. 5-9). 1985. 12.95 (ISBN 0-664-32721-4, Westminster). Westminster John Knox.

Muhaiyaddeen, M. R. Bawa. Come to the Secret Garden: Sufi Tales of Wisdom. LC 83-49210. (Illus.). 450p. 1985. 20.00 (ISBN 0-914390-27-9). Fellowship Pr PA.

The Queen Who Saved Her People. 32p. (gr. 3-6). 1973. pap. 1.39 (ISBN 0-570-06075-3, 59-1194). Concordia.

Richardson, Arleta. In Grandma's Attic. LC 74-75541. 112p. (Orig.). (gr. 4-8). 1974. pap. 3.95 (ISBN 0-912692-32-4). Cook.

Richter, Betts & Jacobsen, Alice. Make It So! A Child's Book on Self-Direction Through Affirmations. 3rd ed. LC 79-84946. (Illus.). 55p. (gr. k-4). 1988. pap. 6.50 (ISBN 0-87516-599-0). DeVorss.

Rizzo, Kay D. Gospel in the Grocery Store. Wheeler, Penny E., ed. 96p. (gr. 7 up). 1989. pap. 4.95 (ISBN 0-8280-0446-3). Review & Herald.

Schlink, Basilea. What Made Them So Brave? (Illus.). (gr. 3 up). 1978. gift edition 2.25 (ISBN 3-87209-655-9). Evang Sisterhood Mary.

Tengbom, Mildred. Does Anybody Care How I Feel? LC 81-3808. 122p. (gr. 4 up). 1981. pap. 5.95 (ISBN 0-87123-142-5). Bethany Hse.

Wheeler, Penny E., ed. Morning Riser. 384p. (gr. 3-6). 1988. 9.50 (ISBN 0-8280-0457-9). Review & Herald.

Winn, Alison. Hello God. (gr. k-3). 1985. 3.95 (ISBN 0-87162-405-2, D4310). Warner Pr.

RELIGIOUS MUSIC

see Church Music

RELIGIOUS ORDERS

see Monasticism and Religious Orders

RELIGIOUS PAINTING

see Christian Art and Symbolism

RELIGIOUS POETRY

see also Carols; Hymns

Alexander, Martha. Poems & Prayers for the Very Young. (Illus.). (ps-1). 1973. pap. 2.25 (ISBN 0-394-82705-8, Random Juv). Random.

Fletcher, Cynthia H. My Jesus Pocketbook of Nursery Rhymes. Sherman, Erin, illus. LC 80-52041. 32p. (Orig.). (ps-3). 1980. pap. 0.69 (ISBN 0-937420-00-X). Stirrup Assoc.

Kenneally, Christy. Strings & Things: Poems & Other Messages for Children. (Orig.). (gr. 2-3). 1984. pap. 3.50 (ISBN 0-8091-6555-4). Paulist Pr.

Mitchell, Cynthia, ed. Here a Little Child I Stand: Poems of Prayer & Praise for Children. Ichikawa, Satomi, illus. LC 85-3450. 32p. (gr. k-3). 1985. 12.95 (ISBN 0-399-21244-2, Philomel). Putnam Pub Group.

RELIGIOUS SYMBOLISM

see Christian Art and Symbolism

REMBRANDT HERMANSZOON VAN RIJN, 1606-1669

Raboff, Ernest. Rembrandt. Rembrandt, illus. LC 87-45157. 32p. (gr. 1 up). 1987. 11.95 (ISBN 0-397-32228-3, Lipp Jr Bks). HarpC Child Bks.

—Rembrandt. Rembrandt, illus. LC 87-45148. 32p. (gr. 1 up). 1987. pap. 5.95 (ISBN 0-06-446072-X, Trophy). HarpC Child Bks.

Venezia, Mike. Rembrandt. Venezia, Mike, illus. LC 87-33014. 32p. (gr. 1-3). 1988. PLB 14.60 (ISBN 0-516-02272-5); pap. 4.95 (ISBN 0-516-42272-3). Childrens.

REMEDIAL READING

see Reading–Remedial Teaching

REMINGTON, FREDERIC, 1861-1909

Raboff, Ernest. Frederic Remington. Remington, Frederic, illus. LC 87-16865. 32p. (gr. 1 up). 1988. Repr. of 1973 ed. 11.95 (ISBN 0-397-32220-8, Lipp Jr Bks). HarpC Child Bks.

—Frederic Remington. Remington, Frederic, illus. LC 87-17698. 32p. (gr. 1 up). 1988. pap. 5.95 (ISBN 0-06-446079-7, Trophy). HarpC Child Bks.

RENAISSANCE

see also Art, Renaissance; Civilization, Medieval; Middle Ages

Sabin, Francene. Renaissance. Frenck, Hal, illus. LC 84-2695. 32p. (gr. 3-6). 1985. PLB 9.49 (ISBN 0-8167-0246-2); pap. text ed. 2.95 (ISBN 0-8167-0247-0). Troll Assocs.

RENAISSANCE–FICTION

Verges, Gloria & Verges, Oriol. The Renaissance. Rius, Maria & Peris, Carme, illus. 32p. (gr. 2-4). 1988. pap. 4.50 (ISBN 0-8120-3396-5); El Renacimiento. pap. 3.95 (ISBN 0-8120-3397-3). Barron.

RENOIR, PIERRE AUGUSTE, 1841-1919

Raboff, Ernest. Pierre-Auguste Renoir. Renoir, Pierre A., illus. LC 87-45154. 32p. (gr. 1 up). 1987. 11.95 (ISBN 0-397-32217-8, Lipp Jr Bks). HarpC Child Bks.

—Pierre-Auguste Renoir. Renoir, Pierre A., illus. LC 87-45145. 32p. (gr. 1 up). 1987. pap. 5.95 (ISBN 0-685-18215-0, Trophy). HarpC Child Bks.

REPAIRING

see also Building–Repair and Reconstruction

REPORTERS AND REPORTING

see also Journalism

Fitz-Gerald, Christine M. I Can Be a Reporter. LC 86-9614. (Illus.). 32p. (gr. k-3). 1986. PLB 13.93 (ISBN 0-516-01899-X); pap. 3.95 (ISBN 0-516-41899-8). Childrens.

Fleming, Thomas. Behind the Headlines. (gr. 5 up). 1989. 14.95 (ISBN 0-8027-6890-3); PLB 15.85 (ISBN 0-8027-6891-1). Walker & Co.

Trainer, David. A Day in the Life of a TV News Reporter. Sanacore, Stephen, photos by. LC 78-68810. (Illus.). 32p. (gr. 4-8). 1981. PLB 11.79 (ISBN 0-89375-228-2); pap. 2.95 (ISBN 0-89375-232-0); cassettes avail. Troll Assocs.

REPRODUCTION

see also Cells; Embryology; Pregnancy; Sex

Andry, Andrew C. & Schepp, Steven. How Babies Are Made. Hampton, Blake, illus. LC 99-944003. 88p. (ps up). 1984. pap. 8.95 (ISBN 0-316-04227-7). Little.

Avraham, Regina. The Reproductive System. (Illus.). (gr. 5-12). 1991. 18.95 (ISBN 0-7910-0025-7). Chelsea Hse.

Back, Christine. Chicken & Egg. LC 86-10019. 1989. 6.95 (ISBN 0-382-09292-9); PLB 9.98 (ISBN 0-382-09284-8); pap. 3.95 (ISBN 0-382-09959-1). Silver Burdett.

Knepp, Thomas H. Human Reproduction: Health & Hygiene. rev. ed. Lee, R. V., pref. by. LC 67-11701. (Illus.). 112p. (gr. 6 up). 1967. 4.95x (ISBN 0-8093-0263-2). S Ill U Pr.

McClung, Robert M. All about Animals & Their Young. (Illus.). (gr. 4-6). 1964. (Random Juv). Random.

Newman, Matt & Lemay, Nita K. Human Reproductive Systems. Green, James, et al, illus. (gr. 5-8). 1980. pap. text ed. 165.00 4 filmstrips, 4 cass., 24 skill sheets, Guide (ISBN 0-89290-101-2, A794-SATC). Soc for Visual.

Nilsson, Lennart. How Was I Born? Reproduction & Birth for Children. LC 75-24725. (Illus.). 32p. (ps-3). 1975. pap. 14.95 (ISBN 0-385-28624-4, Sey Lawr). Delacorte.

Pomeroy, Johanna P. Content Area Reading skills Reproduction & Heredity: Main Idea. (Illus.). (gr. 4). 1988. pap. text ed. 3.25 (ISBN 1-55737-087-7). Ed Activities.

Selsam, Millicent E. Egg to Chick. rev. ed. Wolff, Barbara, illus. LC 74-85034. 64p. (ps-3). 1970. PLB 11.89 (ISBN 0-06-025290-1). HarpC Child Bks.

Stein, Sara B. Making Babies. LC 73-15267. (Illus.). 48p. (gr. 1 up). 1974. 10.95 (ISBN 0-8027-6171-2). Walker & Co.

—Making Babies. LC 73-15267. (Illus.). 48p. (ps-8). 1984. pap. 7.95 (ISBN 0-8027-7221-8). Walker & Co.

Thiry, Joan. Discovering the Whole You. Titra, Stephen, illus. 64p. (Orig.). (gr. 5-6). 1991. pap. text ed. 5.25 (ISBN 0-935046-05-4); tchr's. edition 14.00. Chateau Thierry.

DISCOVERING THE WHOLE YOU presents a Family Life Unit in Human Reproduction as related to science units on human reproduction. It is created for use with middle-grade, preteen children. The facts of human reproduction are placed in context of animal reproduction from protozoa to mammals. Human reproduction is taught as part of a total person growth process. An important aspect of this approach is the emphasis on the emotional, mental, moral & social growth of the child entering puberty. The physical growth of the child is kept in the context of the development of all areas of personality growth. Rites of passage for those entering puberty are also presented as part of total personal growth. This total person development is based on the psychology of William Glasser, M.D. It is, therefore, an approach to positive emotional growth. The activities aim to strengthen the child's sense of self-worth, self-respect, self-responsibility. The projects & discussions are multicultural & intergenerational, especially in exploring rites of passage in various cultures. Parent involvement is an important aspect of this approach. There is an accompanying teacher/leader guide.

Publisher Provided Annotation.

Twist, Clint. Reproduction to Birth: Projects with Biology. (Illus.). 32p. (gr. 5-8). 1991. PLB 11.90 (ISBN 0-531-17294-5, Gloucester Pr). Watts.

REPTILES

see also Crocodiles; Lizards; Snakes; Turtles

Armstrong, B. Reptiles. 32p. (gr. 1-6). 1988. 3.95 (ISBN 0-88160-164-0, LW 269). Learning Wks.

Ballard, Lois. Reptiles. LC 81-38525. (Illus.). 48p. (gr. k-4). 1982. PLB 14.60 (ISBN 0-516-01644-X); pap. 4.95 (ISBN 0-516-41644-8). Childrens.

Bender, Lionel. Fish to Reptiles. Franklin Watts Ltd., ed. Khan, Aziz, illus. 40p. (gr. 7-9). 1988. PLB 12.40 (ISBN 0-531-17093-4, Gloucester Pr). Watts.

Berkowitz, Henry. Amphibians & Reptiles. Berkowitz, Henry, illus. 32p. (Orig.). (gr. 1-9). 1985. pap. 2.50 (ISBN 0-317-66182-5). Banyan Bks.

Caitlin, Stephen. Discovering Reptiles & Amphibians. Johnson, Pamela, illus. LC 89-4972. 32p. (gr. 2-4). 1990. PLB 10.89 (ISBN 0-8167-1753-2); pap. text ed. 2.95 (ISBN 0-8167-1754-0). Troll Assocs.

Cook, David. Small World of Reptiles. LC 80-85052. (gr. k-3). 1981. PLB 10.40 (ISBN 0-531-03455-0). Watts.

Cutts, David. I Can Read About Reptiles. LC 72-96954. (Illus.). (gr. 2-4). 1973. pap. 1.95 (ISBN 0-89375-058-1). Troll Assocs.

Find the Mistakes Science: Remarkable Reptiles. 48p. 1990. pap. 2.95 (ISBN 0-8431-2809-7). Price Stern.

Hornblow, Leonora & Hornblow, Arthur. Reptiles Do the Strangest Things. Frith, Michael K., illus. LC 70-106500. (gr. 2-4). 1970. 6.95 (ISBN 0-394-80074-5, Random Juv); lib. bdg. 8.99 (ISBN 0-394-90074-X, 90074). Random.

—Reptiles Do the Strangest Things. reissued ed. Graber, Jack, illus. LC 90-8598. 64p. (gr. 2-4). 1991. PLB 6.99 (ISBN 0-679-91158-8); pap. 3.95 (ISBN 0-679-81158-3). Random.

Johnston, Ginny & Cutchins, Judy. Scaly Babies: Reptiles Growing Up. LC 87-18599. 48p. (gr. 2-5). 1988. 13.95 (ISBN 0-688-07305-0); PLB 13.88 (ISBN 0-688-07306-9, Morrow Jr Bks). Morrow Jr Bks.

Kuchalla, Susan. What Is a Reptile? Harvey, Paul, illus. LC 81-11364. 32p. (gr. k-2). 1982. PLB 10.89 (ISBN 0-89375-672-5); pap. 2.95 (ISBN 0-89375-673-3). Troll Assocs.

Lindblom, Steven. Golden Book of Snakes & Other Reptiles. 1990. write for info. (ISBN 0-307-15852-7, Pub. by Golden Bks). Western Pub.

Ling, Mary. Amazing Crocodiles & Other Reptiles. Young, Jerry, photos by. LC 90-19239. (Illus.). 32p. (Orig.). (gr. 1-5). 1991. PLB 9.99 (ISBN 0-679-90689-4); pap. 6.95 (ISBN 0-679-80689-X). Knopf.

Losito, Linda, et al. Reptiles & Amphibians. (Illus.). 96p. 1989. 17.95x (ISBN 0-8160-1965-7). Facts on File.

McCarthy, Colin & Arnold, Nick. Reptile. Keates, Colin & Arnold, Nick, photos by. LC 90-4890. (Illus.). 64p. (gr. 5 up). 1991. 15.00 (ISBN 0-679-80783-7); PLB 15.99 (ISBN 0-679-90783-1). Knopf.

McConnell, Keith. The ReptAlphabet Encyclopedia. McConnell, Keith, illus. 48p. (Orig.). (gr. 4 up). 1984. pap. 5.95 (ISBN 0-88045-045-2). Stemmer Hse.

McGowen, Tom. Album of Snakes & Reptiles. Ruth, Rod, illus. 64p. (gr. 3-7). 1987. pap. 4.95 (ISBN 0-02-688503-4). Checkerboard Pr.

Martin, Louise. Reptile Discovery Library, 6 bks, Reading Level 2. (Illus.). 144p. (gr. k-5). Date not set. Set. PLB 71.60 (ISBN 0-86592-573-9). Rourke Corp.

Parker, Nancy W. Frogs, Toads, Lizards & Salamanders. Wright, Joan R., illus. (gr. 1 up). 1990. 13.95 (ISBN 0-688-08680-2); PLB 13.88 (ISBN 0-688-08681-0). Greenwillow.

Pope, Joyce. A Closer Look at Reptiles. rev. ed. 32p. (gr. 4-9). 1986. lib. bdg. 5.99 (ISBN 0-531-17014-4, Gloucester Pr). Watts.

Quinn, Kaye. Reptiles. Quinn, Kaye, illus. 40p. (gr. 2-6). 1987. pap. 2.50 (ISBN 0-8431-1892-X). Price Stern.

Reptile Study. (Illus.). 64p. (gr. 6-12). 1972. pap. 1.85 (ISBN 0-8395-3342-X, 3342A). BSA.

Reptiles. (gr. 4-6). pap. 2.95 (ISBN 0-8431-4273-1). Wonder.

Reptiles. 40p. (gr. 4 up). 1983. PLB 12.40 (ISBN 0-531-03475-5). Watts.

Reptiles. 32p. (Orig.). (gr. 1-3). 1988. pap. 2.95 (ISBN 0-8431-4298-7). Price Stern.

Reptiles. 20p. (gr. k up). 1990. laminated, wipe clean surface 3.95 (ISBN 0-88679-823-X). Educ Insights.

Sabin, Louis. Reptiles & Amphibians. Zink-White, Nancy, illus. LC 84-8445. 32p. (gr. 3-6). 1985. PLB 9.49 (ISBN 0-8167-0294-2); pap. text ed. 2.95 (ISBN 0-8167-0295-0). Troll Assocs.

Sattler, Helen R. Pterosaurs: The Flying Reptiles. Santoro, Christopher, illus. LC 84-4428. 48p. (gr. 1-4). 1985. PLB 12.88 (ISBN 0-688-03996-0). Lothrop.

Selsam, Millicent E. & Hunt, Joyce. A First Look at Snakes, Lizards & Other Reptiles. Springer, Harriet, illus. LC 74-26315. 32p. (gr. 1-4). 1975. PLB 12.85 (ISBN 0-8027-6211-5). Walker & Co.

Snakes & Reptiles. (Illus.). 32p. (gr. 2-6). 1989. pap. 3.50 (ISBN 0-88625-240-7). Durkin Hayes Pub.

Spellerberg, Ian & McKerchar, Marit. Reptile World. Quinn, David, illus. 32p. (gr. 4-7). 1985. PLB 13.96 (ISBN 0-88110-174-5, Pub. by Usborne); pap. 5.95 (ISBN 0-86020-845-1). EDC.

Spizzirri Publishing Co. Staff. Reptiles: An Educational Coloring Book. Spizzirri, Linda, ed. Fuller, Glenn, et al, illus. 32p. (gr. 1-8). 1981. pap. 1.95 (ISBN 0-86545-031-5). Spizzirri.

Steele, Philip. Reptiles. LC 90-42017. (Illus.). 32p. (gr. 5-6). 1991. SBE 9.95 (ISBN 0-89686-582-7, Crestwood Hse). Macmillan Child Grp.

Waldrop, Victor H., et al. The Unhuggables: The Truth about Snakes, Slugs, Skunks, Spiders, & Other Animals That Are Hard to Love. Pidgeon, Jean, illus. LC 88-19531. 96p. (gr. 2-7). 1988. 14.95 (ISBN 0-912186-91-7, 19419); PLB 17.95 (ISBN 0-912186-96-8, 19419). Natl Wildlife.

Wiessinger, John. Fish, Frogs & Snakes - Right Before Your Eyes. LC 89-1511. (Illus.). 64p. (gr. 4-10). 1989. PLB 15.95 (ISBN 0-89490-265-2). Enslow Pubs.
Wrigley, Robert E. Reptiles & Amphibians. Dahl, K. & Doran, J., illus. 40p. (Orig.). (gr. 2-6). 1990. pap. 4.95 (ISBN 0-920534-53-8, Pub. by Hyperion Pr Ltd CN). Sterling.

REPTILES, FOSSIL

see also Dinosaurs

Dixon, Dougal. A Closer Look at Prehistoric Reptiles. Orr, Richard, illus. 32p. (gr. 4 up). 1984. lib. bdg. 5.99 (ISBN 0-531-03480-1, Gloucester Pr). Watts.
Eldridge, David. Sea Monsters, Ancient Reptiles That Ruled the Sea. Nodel, Norman, illus. LC 79-87964. 32p. (gr. 3-6). 1980. PLB 10.79 (ISBN 0-89375-240-1); pap. 2.95 (ISBN 0-89375-244-4). Troll Assocs.
Gabriele, Joseph. Prehistoric Reptiles of the Sea & Air: Text Editions. Hurst, Maragaret, illus. 32p. (gr. 1-3). 1985. pap. 1.95 (ISBN 0-911211-58-6, Pub. by Know & Show Bks). Penny Lane Pubns.
Massare, Judy A. Prehistoric Marine Reptiles: Sea Monsters During the Age of Dinosaurs. (Illus.). 64p. (gr. 5-8). 1991. PLB 14.90 (ISBN 0-531-11022-2). Watts.
Steele, Philip. Extinct Reptiles: And Those in Danger of Extinction. (Illus.). 32p. (gr. 5-8). 1991. PLB 11.40 (ISBN 0-531-11030-3). Watts.

RESCUE WORK

see also First Aid

Barrett, Norman. Picture World of Air Rescue. LC 90-31222. (Illus.). 32p. (gr. k-4). 1991. PLB 11.40 (ISBN 0-531-14089-X). Watts.
—Picture World of Sea Rescue. LC 90-31019. (Illus.). 32p. (gr. k-4). 1991. PLB 11.40 (ISBN 0-531-14093-8). Watts.
Hull, Verne D. Pinky's Dog. (ps-1). 1989. 14.95 (ISBN 0-533-08194-7). Vantage.
Pike, D. Sea Rescue. (Illus.). 32p. (gr. 4 up). Date not set. PLB 14.00 (ISBN 0-86592-411-2). Rourke Corp.
Stewart, Janet & Pelowich, Nadia, eds. Amazing Rescues. (Illus.). 48p. (gr. 4). 1987. PLB 14.65 (ISBN 0-88625-172-9); pap. 5.95 (ISBN 0-88625-151-6). Durkin Hayes Pub.

RESCUE WORK–FICTION

Furman, Abraham L., ed. Teen-Age Great Rescue Stories. (gr. 6-10). PLB 6.70 (ISBN 0-8313-0050-7). Lantern.
Proysen, Alf. Mrs. Pepperpot to the Rescue. (gr. k-6). 1987. pap. 16.25 (ISBN 0-440-45597-9, YB). Dell.
Roddy, Lee. The Legend of Fire: A Ladd Family Adventure. rev. ed. Kobobel, Janet, ed. 148p. (gr. 3-6). 1988. pap. 4.99 (ISBN 0-929608-17-8). Focus Family.

RESEARCH

see also Learning and Scholarship; Psychical Research; also subjects with the subdivision Research, e.g. Agriculture–Research; Medicine–Research

Direct, R. F. Doing Basic Research for Pay. 130p. (gr. 10). 1988. pap. text ed. 39.95x (ISBN 0-945661-01-0). PASE Pubns.
Donovan, Melissa. Research Challanges. Schneider, Al, illus. 168p. (gr. 4-8). 1985. wkbk. 11.95 (ISBN 0-86653-271-4, GA 660). Good Apple.
Martin, Susan & Green, Harriet. Research Workout. Melton, Gerald, illus. 144p. (gr. 4-9). 1984. wkbk. 10.95 (ISBN 0-86653-194-7, GA 551). Good Apple.
Mealy, Virginia T. Tall Tale Research Book. (Illus.). 32p. (gr. 4-7). 1980. pap. 4.95 (ISBN 0-913839-11-6). Bk Lures.
Petreshene, Susan S. Advanced Research Pleasers. Sussman, Ellen, ed. Burris, Priscilla, illus. 48p. (gr. 6-8). 1985. pap. text ed. 5.95 (ISBN 0-933606-37-0, 636). Monkey Sisters.
—Research Pleasers. Sussman, Ellen, ed. Rundell, Wendi S., illus. (Orig.). (gr. 3-6). 1982. pap. text ed. 5.95 (ISBN 0-933606-19-2, MS-618). Monkey Sisters.
—Research Teasers. Sussman, Ellen, ed. Rundell, Wendi S., illus. (Orig.). (gr. 3-6). 1982. pap. text ed. 5.95 (ISBN 0-933606-18-4, MS-617). Monkey Sisters.
Polette, Nancy. Research Almanac. (Illus.). 172p. (gr. 4-9). 1986. pap. 14.95 (ISBN 0-913839-27-2). Bk Lures.
—The Research Project Book. (Illus.). 128p. (gr. 4-9). 1986. pap. 12.95 (ISBN 0-913839-51-5). Bk Lures.
—Research Without Copying. (Illus.). 32p. (gr. 4-9). 1988. pap. 4.95 (ISBN 0-913839-69-8). Bk Lures.
Schwartz, Linda. Search & Research. 48p. (gr. 4-6). 1984. 5.95 (ISBN 0-88160-116-0, LW 248). Learning Wks.
Suid, Murray. For the Love of Research. 64p. (gr. 4-6). 1986. 6.95 (ISBN 0-912107-50-2). Monday Morning Bks.
Weitzman, David. My Backyard History Book. Robertson, James, illus. 128p. (gr. 4 up). 1975. 14.95 (ISBN 0-316-92901-8); pap. 8.95 (ISBN 0-316-92902-6). Little.

RESIDENCES

see Architecture, Domestic; Houses

RESOURCES

see Marine Resources

RESPIRATION

Adler, David A. You Breathe In, You Breathe Out: All about Your Lungs. Roxas, Reni, ed. Paterson, Diane, illus. 32p. (gr. 1-4). 1991. PLB 12.90 (ISBN 0-531-10700-0). Watts.
Bailey, Donna. All about Your Lungs. LC 90-41009. (Illus.). 48p. (gr. 2-5). 1990. PLB 15.96 (ISBN 0-8114-2782-X). Steck-V.
Kittredge, Mary. The Respiratory System. Koop, C. Everett, intro. by. (Illus.). 112p. (gr. 5-12). 1989. 18.95 (ISBN 0-7910-0026-5). Chelsea Hse.
Kramer, Stephen P. Getting Oxygen. Bond, Felicia, illus. LC 85-47888. 64p. (gr. 3-7). 1986. PLB 11.89 (ISBN 0-690-04518-2, Crowell Jr Bks). HarpC Child Bks.
Lungs & Breathing. 48p. (gr. 5-8). 1988. PLB 11.96 (ISBN 0-382-09701-7); 9.74s.p. (ISBN 0-685-24609-4). Silver Burdett Pr.

Ostrow, William & Ostrow, Vivian. All about Asthma. Levine, Abby, ed. Sims, Blanche, illus. 32p. (gr. 3-7). 1989. PLB 10.95 (ISBN 0-8075-0276-6). A Whitman.
"Using his own experiences as illustrations, a young boy gives a clear & thorough picture of living with asthma. The text is well organized; chapters cover what asthma is & isn't, how its causes are determined, how it is treated, & most importantly, how to manage it. The emphasis is upbeat & positive; great care is taken to portray asthmatics as ordinary individuals who can lead normal lives...This is the best treatment of the subject currently available."--SCHOOL LIBRARY JOURNAL. "An excellent introduction for asthma sufferers & for the general public."--KIRKUS REVIEWS. Ages 8-12.
Publisher Provided Annotation.

Parker, Steve. The Lungs & Breathing. rev. ed. Mayron-Parker, Alan, contrib. by. (Illus.). 48p. (gr. 5-6). 1989. PLB 12.90 (ISBN 0-531-10710-8). Watts.
—The Lungs & Breathing. rev. ed. (Illus.). 48p. (gr. 5 up). 1991. pap. 4.95 (ISBN 0-531-24605-1). Watts.
Richardson, Joy. What Happens When You Breathe? LC 86-3728. (Illus.). 32p. (gr. 2-3). 1986. PLB 10.95 (ISBN 1-55532-103-8). Gareth Stevens Inc.
Savage, Eileen. Winning over Asthma. (Illus.). 40p. (Orig.). (ps-3). pap. write for info. (ISBN 0-9622868-0-X). Dolan Pr.
Silverstein, Alvin & Silverstein, Virginia B. Respiratory System: How Living Creatures Breathe. Bakacs, George, illus. (gr. 3-7). 1969. 10.95 (ISBN 0-13-774547-8). P-H.
Ward, Brian. Breathing: And Your Health. (Illus.). 32p. (gr. 5-8). 1991. PLB 11.40 (ISBN 0-531-14094-6). Watts.
—The Lungs & Breathing. (Illus.). 48p. (gr. 4 up). 1982. PLB 12.40 (ISBN 0-531-04358-4). Watts.

RESTAURANTS, BARS, ETC.

Gibbons, Gail. Marge's Diner. Gibbons, Gail, illus. LC 88-26789. 32p. (gr. 1-4). 1989. 12.95 (ISBN 0-690-04604-9, Crowell Jr Bks); PLB 12.89 (ISBN 0-690-04606-5, Crowell Jr Bks). HarpC Child Bks.
Lee, Mary P. & Lee, Richard. Careers in Restaurant Industry. rev. ed. Rosen, R., ed. (Illus.). 160p. (gr. 7-12). 1990. 12.95 (ISBN 0-8239-1142-X). Rosen Group.
Restaurateurs & Innkeepers. (Illus.). 176p. 1988. 17.95x (ISBN 0-8160-1451-5). Facts on File.

RESTAURANTS, BARS, ETC.–FICTION

Calmenson, Stephanie. Dinner at the Panda Palace. Westcott, Nadine B., illus. LC 90-33720. 32p. (ps-3). 1991. 14.95 (ISBN 0-06-021010-9); PLB 14.89 (ISBN 0-06-021011-7). HarpC Child Bks.
Cummings, Priscilla. Sid & Sal's Famous Channel Marker Diner. Cohen, A. R., illus. LC 9-65255. 30p. (gr. k-4). 1991. 8.95 (ISBN 0-87033-423-9). Tidewater.
Kovalski, Maryann. Pizza for Breakfast. Kovalski, Maryann, illus. LC 90-46078. 32p. (gr. k up). 1991. Repr. of 1990 ed. 13.95 (ISBN 0-688-10409-6); PLB 13.88 (ISBN 0-688-10410-X, Morrow Jr Bks). Morrow Jr Bks.
Peters, Sharon. Contento Juan. Harvey, Paul, illus. (SPA.). 32p. (gr. k-2). 1981. PLB 7.06 (ISBN 0-89375-552-4); pap. 1.95 (ISBN 0-685-04945-0). Troll Assocs.
Tchudi, Stephen. The Burg-O-Rama Man. LC 82-14075. 192p. (gr. 7 up). 1983. pap. 13.95 (ISBN 0-385-29239-2). Delacorte.

RETAIL TRADE

see also Advertising; Department Stores; Salesmen and Salesmanship

RETAIL TRADE–VOCATIONAL GUIDANCE

Koester, Pat. Careers in Fashion Retailing. Rosen, Ruth, ed. (gr. 7-12). 1990. PLB 12.95 (ISBN 0-8239-1007-5). Rosen Group.

REVERE, PAUL, 1735-1818

Brandt, Keith. Paul Revere: Son of Liberty. LC 81-23147. (Illus.). 48p. (gr. 4-6). 1982. PLB 10.79 (ISBN 0-89375-766-7); pap. text ed. 2.95 (ISBN 0-89375-767-5). Troll Assocs.
Forbes, Esther. America's Paul Revere. Ward, Lynd, illus. 48p. (gr. 3-5). 1990. pap. 4.95 (ISBN 0-395-24907-4). HM.
—America's Paul Revere. large type ed. (Illus.). 88p. (gr. 4-8). 1991. Repr. of 1946 ed. PLB 17.95 (ISBN 1-55905-093-4). Grey Castle.
—Paul Revere & the World He Lived In. (Illus.). 528p. (gr. 4-8). 1972. pap. 9.95 (ISBN 0-395-08370-2). HM.
Fritz, Jean. And Then What Happened, Paul Revere? Tomes, Margot, illus. 48p. (gr. 2-6). 1973. 9.95 (ISBN 0-698-20274-0, Coward); pap. 4.95 (ISBN 0-698-20541-3). Putnam Pub Group.
Gleiter, Jan & Thompson, Kathleen. Paul Revere. Balistreri, Francis, illus. 32p. (gr. 2-5). 1986. PLB 16.67 (ISBN 0-8172-2644-3); pap. text ed. 9.27 (ISBN 0-8172-2648-6). Raintree Pubs.
Grant, Matthew G. Paul Revere. LC 73-18076. 1988. PLB 11.50 (ISBN 0-87191-303-8); PLB 16.45 (ISBN 0-88682-186-X). Creative Ed.
—Paul Revere. LC 73-18076. 1988. PLB 11.50 (ISBN 0-87191-303-8); PLB 16.45 (ISBN 0-88682-186-X). Creative Ed.
Lee, Martin. Paul Revere. LC 86-23362. (Illus.). 96p. (gr. 4-8). 1987. PLB 10.40 (ISBN 0-531-10312-9). Watts.
Paul Revere. (Illus.). (gr. 2-5). 1989. 27.99 (ISBN 0-8172-2957-4); pap. 23.95 (ISBN 0-8172-2965-5). Raintree Pubs.
Stein, R. Conrad. The Story of Lexington & Concord. LC 82-23518. (Illus.). 32p. (gr. 3-6). 1983. PLB 13.27 (ISBN 0-516-04661-6); pap. 3.95 (ISBN 0-516-44661-4). Childrens.
Stevenson, Augusta. Paul Revere: Boston Patriot. Nicholas, Frank, illus. LC 86-10743. 192p. (gr. 2-6). 1986. pap. 3.95 (ISBN 0-02-042090-0, Aladdin). Macmillan Child Grp.
The Story of Paul Revere. (gr. k-6). 1990. pap. 2.95 (ISBN 0-440-40361-8, YB). Dell.

REVERE, PAUL, 1735-1818–FICTION

Lawson, Robert. Mr. Revere & I. (gr. 3-6). 1973. pap. 2.95 (ISBN 0-440-45897-8, YB). Dell.
—Mr. Revere & I. Lawson, Robert, illus. (gr. 7-10). 1953. 14.95 (ISBN 0-316-51739-9). Little.
—Mr. Revere & I. Lawson, Robert, illus. 152p. (gr. 3-6). 1988. pap. 5.95 (ISBN 0-316-51729-1). Little.

REVIEWS

see Book Reviews

REVIVAL OF LETTERS

see Renaissance

REVOLUTION, AMERICAN

see U. S.–History–Revolution

REVOLUTION, FRENCH

see France–History–Revolution, 1789-1799

REVOLUTIONS

see also France–History–Revolution, 1789-1799; Hungary–History–Revolution, 1956; Social Conflict; U. S. –History–Revolution

Millard. The Age of Revolution. (gr. 4-9). 1979. 7.95 (ISBN 0-86020-262-3, Usborne-Hayes); PLB 13.96 (ISBN 0-88110-112-5); pap. 6.95 (ISBN 0-86020-263-1). EDC.

REVOLUTIONS–FICTION

Townsend, John R. Kate & the Revolution. LC 81-48605. 219p. (gr. 7 up). 1983. PLB 12.89 (ISBN 0-397-32016-7, Lipp Jr Bks). HarpC Child Bks.

RHETORIC

see also Criticism; Debates and Debating; Letter Writing; Punctuation

Fearn, Leif. First I Think: Then I Write My Think. 160p. (gr. 3-12). 1981. 6.95 (ISBN 0-940444-13-5). Kabyn.
Fearn, Leif & Goldman, Elizabeth. Writing Kabyn: Assessment & Editing. 96p. (gr. 2-9). 1981. classroom kit 27.50 (ISBN 0-940444-11-9). Kabyn.
—Writing Kabyn: Products. 148p. (gr. 2-9). 1982. classroom kit 48.00 (ISBN 0-940444-09-7). Kabyn.
—Writing Kabyn: Sentences-Paragraphs. 125p. (gr. 2-9). 1982. classroom kit 69.00 (ISBN 0-940444-08-9). Kabyn.
—Writing Kabyn: Technology. 76p. (gr. 2-9). 1981. classroom Kit 49.00 (ISBN 0-940444-10-0). Kabyn.
Hunter, Mollie. Talent Is Not Enough: Mollie Hunter on Writing for Children. LC 76-3841. 144p. 1990. pap. 9.95 (ISBN 0-06-446105-X, Trophy). HarpC Child Bks.
Kane, Andrea L. & Martorana, Barbara. Writing Competency Practice. (gr. 7-12). 1980. wkbk. 5.75 (ISBN 0-89525-134-5). Ed Activities.
Littlefield, Kathy M. & Littlefield, Robert S. What's Your Point? Stark, Steve, illus. 32p. (Orig.). (gr. 3-6). 1990. pap. text ed. 8.95 (ISBN 1-879340-05-4, K0106). Kidspeak.
Newman, Gerald & Newman, Ebanor W. Writing Your College Admissions Essay. (Illus.). 128p. (gr. 7-12). 1987. PLB 12.90 (ISBN 0-531-10428-1). Watts.
Stevens, Jared & Michaels, Judy. How to Write for Everyday Living. (Illus.). (gr. 7 up). 1981. wkbk. 4.25 (ISBN 0-89525-132-9). Ed Activities.
Weisberg, Valerie H. Students' Discourse: Comprehensive Examples & Explanations of All Expository Modes & Argument, Precis, Narrative, Examination Writing & MLA Reccomendations for Research Paper Documentation Writing Exposition. 2nd ed. 126p. 1990. pap. 9.95. V H Pub.

RHINOCEROSES–FICTION

Alexander, Scott. Rhinoceros Success. 25th ed. Smallwood, Laurie, illus. LC 80-51648. 123p. (Orig.). (gr. 1 up). 1985. pap. 5.95 (ISBN 0-937382-00-0). Rhinos Pr.
Bailey, Jill. Mission Rhino. LC 90-32529. (Illus.). 48p. (gr. 3-7). 1990. PLB 17.28 (ISBN 0-8114-2702-1). Steck-V.

Bush, John. The Cross-with-Us Rhinoceros. Geraghty, Paul, illus. LC 88-3702. 32p. (ps-2). 1988. 13.95 (ISBN 0-525-44411-4, DCB). Dutton Child Bks.

De Brunhoff, Laurent. Isabelle's New Friend: A Babar Book. De Brunhoff, Laurent, illus. LC 89-3727. 32p. (ps-1). 1990. PLB 5.99 (ISBN 0-394-92880-6); pap. 2.25 (ISBN 0-394-82880-1). Random.

Green, Carl R. & Sanford, William R. The African Rhinos. (Illus.). 48p. (gr. 4-5). 1987. PLB 10.95 (ISBN 0-89686-327-1, Crestwood Hse). Macmillan Child Grp.

Kipling, Rudyard. How the Rhino Got His Skin: Just So Stories. Langley, Jonathan, illus. 24p. (ps-3). 1988. 5.95 (ISBN 0-399-21526-3, Philomel Bks). Putnam Pub Group.

Rogers, Alan. Red Rhino. Rogers, Alan, illus. LC 90-9830. 16p. (ps-1). 1990. PLB 9.95 (ISBN 0-8368-0403-1). Gareth Stevens Inc.

Rosner, Ruth. Rhinos Don't Climb! LC 83-47708. (Illus.). 32p. (ps-3). 1984. 12.95i (ISBN 0-06-025068-2). HarpC Child Bks.

Silverstein, Shel. Who Wants a Cheap Rhinoceros? rev. ed. LC 82-23945. (Illus.). 56p. (ps-3). 1983. 12.95 (ISBN 0-02-782690-2, Mcmillan Child Bk). Macmillan Child Grp.

Sis, Peter. Rainbow Rhino. Sis, Peter, illus. LC 87-2679. 40p. (ps-1). 1987. 11.95 (ISBN 0-394-89009-4); lib. bdg. 12.99 (ISBN 0-394-99009-9). Knopf.

RHODE ISLAND

Carole Marsh Rhode Island Books, 31 bks. Set. 638.45 (ISBN 0-7933-1314-7). Gallopade Pub Group.

Carpenter, Allan. Rhode Island. LC 78-16446. (Illus.). 96p. (gr. 4 up). 1979. PLB 19.93 (ISBN 0-516-04139-8). Childrens.

Fradin, Dennis. Rhode Island: In Words & Pictures. Wahl, Len, illus. LC 80-22497. 48p. (gr. 2-5). 1981. PLB 15.93 (ISBN 0-516-03939-3). Childrens.

Fradin, Dennis B. The Rhode Island Colony. LC 89-744. (Illus.). 160p. (gr. 4 up). 1989. PLB 22.60 (ISBN 0-516-00391-7). Childrens.

Gavan, Terrence. Complete Guide to Newport. (Illus.). 64p. (Orig.). 1988. pap. 5.95 (ISBN 0-929249-00-3). Pineapple Pubns.

Marsh, Carole. Avast, Ye Slobs! Rhode Island Pirate Trivia. (Illus.). 1990. PLB 19.95 (ISBN 0-7933-1004-0); pap. 14.95 (ISBN 0-7933-1003-2); computer disk 29.95 (ISBN 0-7933-1005-9). Gallopade Pub Group.

—The Beast of the Rhode Island Bed & Breakfast. (Illus.). 1990. PLB 19.95 (ISBN 0-7933-1965-X); pap. 14.95 (ISBN 0-7933-1966-8); computer disk 29.95 (ISBN 0-7933-1967-6). Gallopade Pub Group.

—The Hard-to-Believe-But-True! Book of Rhode Island History, Mystery, Trivia, Legend, Lore, Humor & More. (Illus.). 1990. PLB 19.95 (ISBN 0-7933-1001-6); pap. 14.95 (ISBN 0-7933-1000-8); computer disk 29.95 (ISBN 0-7933-1002-4). Gallopade Pub Group.

—If My Rhode Island Mama Ran the World! (Illus.). 1990. lib. bdg. 19.95 (ISBN 0-7933-1974-9); pap. 14. 95 (ISBN 0-7933-1975-7); computer disk 29.95 (ISBN 0-7933-1976-5). Gallopade Pub Group.

—Let's Quilt Rhode Island & Stuff it Topographically! (Illus.). 1990. PLB 19.95 (ISBN 0-7933-1957-9); pap. 14.95 (ISBN 1-55609-065-X); computer disk 29.95 (ISBN 0-7933-1958-7). Gallopade Pub Group.

—Rhode Island & Other State Greats (Biographies) (Illus.). 1990. PLB 19.95 (ISBN 0-7933-1977-3); pap. 14.95 (ISBN 0-7933-1978-1); computer disk 29.95 (ISBN 0-7933-1979-X). Gallopade Pub Group.

—Rhode Island Bandits, Bushwackers, Outlaws, Crooks, Devils, Ghosts, Desperadoes & Other Assorted & Sundry Characters! (Illus.). 1990. PLB 19.95 (ISBN 0-7933-0986-7); pap. 14.95; computer disk 29.95 (ISBN 0-7933-0987-5). Gallopade Pub Group.

—Rhode Island Classic Christmas Trivia: Stories, Recipes, Activities, Legends, Lore & More! (Illus.). 1990. PLB 19.95 (ISBN 0-7933-0989-1); pap. 14.95 (ISBN 0-7933-0988-3); computer disk 29.95 (ISBN 0-7933-0990-5). Gallopade Pub Group.

—Rhode Island Coastales. (Illus.). 1990. PLB 19.95 (ISBN 0-7933-1971-4); pap. 14.95 (ISBN 0-7933-1972-2); computer disk 29.95 (ISBN 0-7933-1973-0). Gallopade Pub Group.

—The Rhode Island Hot Air Balloon Mystery. (Illus.). (gr. 2-9). 1990. 19.95 (ISBN 0-7933-2669-9); pap. 14. 95 (ISBN 0-7933-2670-2); computer disk 29.95 (ISBN 0-7933-2671-0). Gallopade Pub Group.

—Rhode Island "Jography" A Fun Run Thru Our State! (Illus.). 1990. PLB 19.95 (ISBN 0-7933-1954-4); pap. 14.95 (ISBN 0-7933-1955-2); computer disk 29.95 (ISBN 0-7933-1956-0). Gallopade Pub Group.

—Rhode Island Kid's Cookbook: Recipes, How-to, History Lore & More! (Illus.). 1990. PLB 19.95 (ISBN 0-7933-0998-0); pap. 14.95 (ISBN 0-7933-0997-2); computer disk 29.95 (ISBN 0-7933-0999-9). Gallopade Pub Group.

—Rhode Island Quiz Bowl Crash Course! (Illus.). 1990. PLB 19.95 (ISBN 0-7933-1968-4); pap. 14.95 (ISBN 0-7933-1969-2); computer disk 29.95 (ISBN 0-7933-1970-6). Gallopade Pub Group.

—Rhode Island School Trivia: An Amazing & Fascinating Look at Our State's Teachers, Schools & Students! (Illus.). 1990. PLB 19.95 (ISBN 0-7933-0995-6); pap. 14.95 (ISBN 0-7933-0994-8); computer disk 29.95 (ISBN 0-7933-0996-4). Gallopade Pub Group.

—Rhode Island Silly Basketball Sportsmysteries, Vol. 1. (Illus.). 1990. PLB 19.95 (ISBN 0-7933-0992-1); pap. 14.95 (ISBN 0-7933-0991-3); computer disk 29.95. Gallopade Pub Group.

—Rhode Island Silly Basketball Sportsmysteries, Vol. 2. (Illus.). 1990. PLB 19.95 (ISBN 0-7933-1980-3); pap. 14.95 (ISBN 0-7933-1981-1); computer disk 29.95 (ISBN 0-7933-1982-X). Gallopade Pub Group.

—Rhode Island Silly Football Sportsmysteries, Vol. 1. (Illus.). 1990. PLB 19.95 (ISBN 0-7933-1959-5); pap. 14.95 (ISBN 0-7933-1960-9); computer disk 29.95 (ISBN 0-7933-1961-7). Gallopade Pub Group.

—Rhode Island Silly Football Sportsmysteries, Vol. 2. (Illus.). 1990. PLB 19.95 (ISBN 0-7933-1962-5); pap. 14.95 (ISBN 0-7933-1963-3); computer disk 29.95 (ISBN 0-7933-1964-1). Gallopade Pub Group.

—Rhode Island Silly Trivia! (Illus.). 1990. PLB 19.95 (ISBN 0-7933-1951-X); pap. 14.95 (ISBN 0-7933-1952-8); computer disk 29.95 (ISBN 0-7933-1953-6). Gallopade Pub Group.

—Rhode Island's (Most Devastating!) Disasters & (Most Calamitous!) Catastrophies! (Illus.). 1990. PLB 19.95 (ISBN 0-7933-0983-2); pap. 14.95 (ISBN 0-7933-0982-4); computer disk 29.95. Gallopade Pub Group.

Turner Programs Services, Inc. Staff, et al. Rhode Island. 48p. (gr. 3 up). 1986. PLB 17.32 (ISBN 0-86514-457-5); pap. text ed. 9.27 (ISBN 0-86514-532-6); cancelled Beta video (ISBN 0-86514-082-0); cancelled VHS video (ISBN 0-86514-157-6); cancelled 3/4" video (ISBN 0-86514-232-7); cancelled tchr's. study guide (ISBN 0-86514-307-2); cancelled student activity bk. (ISBN 0-86514-382-X); cancelled index. Raintree Pubs.

RHODE ISLAND–HISTORY

Gavan, Terrence. The Barons of Newport: A Guide to the Gilded Age. (Illus.). 88p. (Orig.). 1988. pap. 7.50 (ISBN 0-929249-01-1). Pineapple Pubns.

RHODESIA

Laure, Jason. Zimbabwe. LC 87-35426. (Illus.). 127p. (gr. 4-8). 1988. PLB 25.27 (ISBN 0-516-02704-2). Childrens.

RHYMES

see Limericks; Nonsense Verses; Nursery Rhymes; Poetry–Collections

Duncan, Lois. Birthday Moon. Davis, Susan, illus. 32p. (ps-3). 1989. 13.95 (ISBN 0-670-82238-8). Viking Child Bks.

RHYTHM

see also Versification

Hayes, Sarah. Stamp Your Feet. Ormerod, Jan, illus. LC 87-29779. 32p. (ps-1). 1988. 13.00 (ISBN 0-688-07694-7); PLB 12.88 (ISBN 0-688-07695-5). Lothrop.

Hello Rhythm: Rhythm Activities, Songs & Games to Develop Skills in Young Children. (ps-3). 1977. pap. 6.95 (ISBN 0-939514-01-X); album 9.95 (ISBN 0-685-03380-5); cassette 9.95 (ISBN 0-685-03381-3). Miss Jackie.

Lobel, Arnold. Whiskers & Rhymes. Lobel, Arnold, illus. LC 83-25424. 48p. (gr. k-3). 1985. 13.00 (ISBN 0-688-03835-2); lib. bdg. 12.88 (ISBN 0-688-03836-0). Greenwillow.

—Whiskers & Rhymes. LC 83-25424. 1988. pap. 3.95 (ISBN 0-688-08291-2, Mulberry). Morrow.

Morrison, Lillian. Rhythm Road: Poems to Move To. LC 87-4071. (gr. 4 up). 1988. PLB 13.95 (ISBN 0-688-07098-1). Lothrop.

RICE

Brice, Raphaelle. Rice: The Little Grain That Feeds the World. Bogard, Vicki, tr. from FRE. Riquier, Aline, illus. LC 90-50775. 38p. (gr. k-5). 1991. 4.95 (ISBN 0-944589-30-8, 308). Young Discovery Lib.

Johnson, Sylvia A. Rice. Moriya, Noboru, illus. 48p. (gr. 4 up). 1985. PLB 14.95 (ISBN 0-8225-1466-4). Lerner Pubns.

Thomson, Ruth. Rice. Stefoff, Rebecca, ed. Das, Prodeepta, photos by. LC 90-40367. (Illus.). 26p. (gr. 3-5). 1990. PLB 15.93 (ISBN 0-944483-71-2). Garrett Ed Corp.

RICE–FICTION

Pittman, Helena C. A Grain of Rice. LC 84-4670. (Illus.). (gr. k-4). 1986. 12.95 (ISBN 0-8038-2728-8); lib. bdg. 12.95 (ISBN 0-8038-9289-6). Hastings.

RICHARD 3RD, KING OF ENGLAND, 1452-1485–FICTION

Stevenson, Robert Louis. Black Arrow. (gr. 6 up). 1964. pap. 2.95 (ISBN 0-8049-0020-5, CL-20). Airmont.

RICHELIEU, ARMAND JEAN DU PLESSIS, CARDINAL, DUC DE, 1585-1642

Glossop, Pat. Cardinal Richelieu. (Illus.). (gr. 5 up). 1990. 17.95 (ISBN 1-55546-822-5). Chelsea Hse.

RIDDLES

see also Puzzles

Adler, David. The Dinosaur Princess & Other Prehistoric Riddles. (gr. k-3). 1990. pap. 2.75 (ISBN 0-553-15793-0, Skylark). Bantam.

Adler, David A. Bunny Rabbit Rebus. Linden, Madelaine G., illus. LC 82-45574. 40p. (gr. 1-4). 1983. (Crowell Jr Bks); PLB 10.89 (ISBN 0-690-04197-7, Crowell Jr Bks). HarpC Child Bks.

—The Carsick Zebra & Other Animal Riddles. De Paola, Tomie, illus. LC 82-48750. 64p. (gr. 1-4). 1983. reinforced bdg. 10.95 (ISBN 0-8234-0479-X). Holiday.

—The Carsick Zebra & Other Animal Riddles. De Paola, Tomie, illus. 64p. (Orig.). (gr. 1). 1985. pap. 2.25 (ISBN 0-553-15487-7). Bantam.

—The Dinosaur Princess & Other Prehistoric Riddles. Leedy, Loreen, illus. LC 87-25121. 64p. (gr. 1-4). 1988. reinforced bdg. 10.95 (ISBN 0-8234-0686-5). Holiday.

—The Purple Turkey & Other Thanksgiving Riddles. Hafner, Marylin, illus. LC 86-310. 64p. (gr. 1-4). 1986. reinforced bdg. 10.95 (ISBN 0-8234-0613-X). Holiday.

—Remember Betsy Floss & Other Colonial American Riddles. Wallner, John, illus. LC 87-45333. 64p. (gr. 1-4). 1987. reinforced bdg. 10.95 (ISBN 0-8234-0664-4). Holiday.

—A Teacher on Roller Skates & Other School Riddles. Wallner, John, illus. LC 89-1929. 64p. (gr. 1-4). 1989. reinforced 10.95 (ISBN 0-8234-0775-6). Holiday.

—The Twisted Witch & Other Spooky Riddles. Chess, Victoria, illus. LC 85-909. 64p. (gr. 1-4). 1985. reinforced bdg. 10.95 (ISBN 0-8234-0571-0). Holiday.

—The Twisted Witch & Other Spooky Riddles. 64p. 1986. pap. 2.25 (ISBN 0-553-15447-8). Bantam.

Adler, Larry. Help Wanted: Riddles about Jobs. Burke, Susan S., illus. 32p. (gr. 1-4). 1989. PLB 8.95 (ISBN 0-8225-2325-6). Lerner Pubns.

Ainsworth, Catherine H. Black & White & Said All over: Riddles. LC 72-5461. 36p. (ps-12). 1976. 4.00 (ISBN 0-933190-02-6). Clyde Pr.

Ask a Riddle, Unit 4. (gr. 1). 1991. 39.95 (ISBN 0-88106-727-X). Charlesbridge Pub.

Beisner, Monika. Monika Beisner's Book of Riddles. LC 83-81529. (Illus.). 32p. (ps up). 1983. 12.95 (ISBN 0-374-30866-7). FS&G.

Bernstein, Joanne & Cohen, Paul. Creepy, Crawly, Critter Riddles. Tucker, Kathleen, ed. Hoffman, Rosekrans, illus. 32p. (gr. 1-5). 1986. PLB 8.95 (ISBN 0-8075-1345-8). A Whitman.

—Riddles to Take on Vacation. Fay, Ann, ed. LC 87-2071. (Illus.). (gr. 1-5). 1987. PLB 8.95 (ISBN 0-8075-6999-2). A Whitman.

—Unidentified Flying Riddles. Fay, Ann, ed. Seltzer, Meyer, illus. LC 83-17097. 32p. (gr. 1-5). 1983. PLB 8.95 (ISBN 0-8075-8329-4). A Whitman.

Bernstein, Joanne E. & Cohen, Paul. Grand-Slam Riddles. Tucker, Kathleen, ed. (Illus.). 32p. (gr. 3-7). 1988. PLB 8.95 (ISBN 0-8075-3038-7). A Whitman.

—Happy Holiday Riddles to You. Fay, Ann, ed. Seltzer, Meyer, illus. 32p. (gr. 1-5). 1985. PLB 8.95 (ISBN 0-8075-3154-5). A Whitman.

—More Unidentified Flying Riddles. Seltzer, Meyer, illus. 32p. (gr. 1-5). 1985. 8.95 (ISBN 0-8075-5279-8). A Whitman.

—Sporty Riddles. Mathews, Judith, ed. Harvey, Paul, illus. 32p. (gr. 1-5). 1989. PLB 8.95 (ISBN 0-8075-7590-9). A Whitman.

—What Was the Wicked Witch's Real Name? & Other Character Riddles. Iosa, Ann, illus. 32p. (gr. 1-5). 1986. 8.95 (ISBN 0-8075-8854-7). A Whitman.

Bishop, Ann. Riddle Ages. Rubin, Caroline, ed. Warshaw, Jerry, illus. LC 77-12828. (gr. 1-4). 1977. PLB 8.95 (ISBN 0-8075-6965-8). A Whitman.

Brandreth, Gyles. The Big Book of Silly Riddles. Carter, John & Allen, Jonathan, illus. LC 86-29989. 128p. (gr. 2 up). 1987. 12.95 (ISBN 0-8069-6408-1); PLB 15.69 (ISBN 0-8069-6409-X). Sterling.

—The Big Book of Silly Riddles. Carter, John & Allen, Jonathan, illus. LC 86-29989. (gr. 2-8). 1988. pap. 3.95 (ISBN 0-8069-6782-X). Sterling.

Burns, Diane L. & Scholten, Dan. Here's to Ewe: Riddles about Sheep. Burke, Susan S., illus. 32p. (gr. 1-4). 1989. PLB 7.95 (ISBN 0-8225-2326-4). Lerner Pubns.

Burns, Marilyn. The One Dollar Word Riddle Book. Weston, Martha, illus. 48p. (Orig.). (gr. 3-8). 1990. pap. 6.95 (ISBN 0-685-31247-X). Cuisenaire.

Calmenson, Stephanie. What Am I? Very First Riddles. Gundersheimer, Karen, illus. LC 87-22959. 32p. (ps-2). 1989. 11.95 (ISBN 0-06-020997-6); PLB 11.89 (ISBN 0-06-020998-4). HarpC Child Bks.

Cerf, Bennett A. Bennett Cerf's Book of Animal Riddles. LC 64-11246. (gr. 2-3). 1964. lib. bdg. 7.99 (ISBN 0-394-90034-0). Beginner.

—Bennett Cerf's Book of Riddles. LC 60-13492. (Illus.). 72p. (gr. 1-2). 1966. 6.95 (ISBN 0-394-80015-X); lib. bdg. 7.99 (ISBN 0-394-90015-4). Beginner.

—More Riddles. LC 61-11727. (Illus.). 72p. (gr. k-3). 1961. 6.95 (ISBN 0-394-80024-9); lib. bdg. 7.99 (ISBN 0-394-90024-3). Beginner.

Chartier, Normand. Who Am I? 22p. (ps). 1978. write for info. (Golden Bks). Western Pub.

Chemielewski, Gary. Riddles. Clark, Ron G., illus. LC 86-17720. (gr. 2-3). 1986. PLB 12.66 (ISBN 0-86592-686-7). Rourke Corp.

Chmielewski, Gary. Teacher Jokes. Clark, Ron G., illus. LC 86-17773. (gr. 2-3). 1986. 12.66 (ISBN 0-86592-688-3). Rourke Corp.

De Regniers, Beatrice S. It Does Not Say Meow. Galdone, Paul, illus. LC 72-75704. 40p. (ps-3). 1979. 14.95 (ISBN 0-395-28822-3, Clarion). HM.

Electric Company Staff. Tickle Yourself Again with Riddles. Smollin, Michael J., illus. LC 78-19699. (gr. 1-5). 1988. pap. 2.95 (ISBN 0-394-84152-2, Random Juv). Random.

—Tickle Yourself with Riddles. Smollin, Mike, illus. LC 77-90197. 96p. (gr. 1-5). 1988. pap. 1.95 (ISBN 0-394-83783-5, Random Juv). Random.

Fox, Lori M. The Craziest Riddle Book in the World. Hoffman, Sanford, illus. LC 91-13209. 96p. (gr. 3-9). 1991. 12.95 (ISBN 0-8069-8406-6). Sterling.

—Oodles of Riddles. LC 89-4549. (Illus.). 96p. (gr. 2-8). 1989. 12.95 (ISBN 0-8069-6880-X); PLB 15.69 (ISBN 0-8069-6881-8). Sterling.

—Shake, Riddle & Roll. LC 89-26235. (Illus.). 96p. (gr. 2-8). 1990. 12.95 (ISBN 0-8069-7252-1); PLB 15.69 (ISBN 0-8069-7253-X). Sterling.

Gordon, Jeffie R. Hide & Shriek: Riddles about Ghosts & Goblins. (Illus.). 32p. (gr. 1-4). 1991. PLB 8.95 (ISBN 0-8225-2336-1). Lerner Pubns.

Hafner, Everett. Sports Riddles. Hafner, Marylin, illus. 48p. (gr. 1-4). 1991. pap. 3.95 (ISBN 0-14-032497-6, Puffin). Puffin Bks.

Hall, Katy. Garfield: Big Fat Book of Jokes & Riddles. Fentz, Mike, illus. LC 84-62725. 96p. (gr. 6-10). 1985. pap. 5.95 (ISBN 0-394-87414-5, Random Juv). Random.

Hall, Katy & Eisenberg, Lisa. Buggy Riddles. Taback, Simms, illus. LC 85-1450. 48p. (ps-3). 1986. 9.95 (ISBN 0-8037-0139-X); PLB 9.89 (ISBN 0-8037-0140-3). Dial Bks Young.

—Buggy Riddles. Taback, Simms, illus. LC 85-1450. 48p. (ps-3). 1988. pap. 4.95 (ISBN 0-8037-0554-9). Dial Bks Young.

—Fishy Riddles. LC 82-22135. (Illus.). 48p. (ps-3). 1983. PLB 9.89 (ISBN 0-8037-2431-4); pap. 4.95 (ISBN 0-8037-2419-5). Dial Bks Young.

—Fishy Riddles. Taback, Simms, illus. (gr. 3-5). 1985. bk. & cassette 19.95 (ISBN 0-941078-72-8); pap. 12.95 bk. & cassette (ISBN 0-941078-70-1); cassette, 4 paperbacks & guide 27.95 (ISBN 0-941078-71-X). Live Oak Media.

Heck, Joseph. Dinosaur Riddles. Barish, Wendy, ed. Hoffman, Sandy, illus. 128p. (gr. 3-7). 1982. pap. 3.80 (ISBN 0-671-45547-8, Little Simon); 9.29 (ISBN 0-685-05613-9). S&S Trade.

Hindman, Darwin A. Eighteen Hundred Riddles, Enigmas & Conundrums. 159p. (Orig.). (gr. 4 up). 1963. pap. 3.50 (ISBN 0-486-21059-6). Dover.

Jensen, Virginia A. & Edman, Polly. Red Thread Riddles. LC 79-28168. (Illus.). 24p. (Orig.). (ps). 1983. pap. 12.95 (ISBN 0-399-20955-7, Philomel). Putnam Pub Group.

Johnson, Harriet. Honolulu Zoo Riddles. Thompson, Judi, illus. (ps-5). 1974. pap. 1.25 (ISBN 0-914916-07-6). Topgallant.

Jokes & Riddles. 96p. (gr. 2-5). 1988. pap. 2.95 (ISBN 0-8431-2275-7). Price Stern.

Jones, Evelyn. World's Wackiest Riddle Book. Kendrick, Dennis, illus. LC 86-5960. 128p. (gr. 2 up). 1987. pap. 1.95 (ISBN 0-8069-6594-0). Sterling.

Keller, Charles. Count Draculations! Monster Riddles. Frascino, Edward, illus. 64p. (gr. 3-7). 1986. 10.95 (ISBN 0-13-183641-2). P-H.

—Take Me to Your Liter: Science & Math Jokes. Filling, Gregory, illus. 40p. (gr. 2-5). 1991. PLB 11.95 (ISBN 0-945912-13-7). Pippin Pr.

Keller, Charles & Baker, Richard, eds. Star-Spangled Banana: And Other Revolutionary Riddles. De Paola, Tomie. (Illus.). 62p. (gr. 2 up). 1974. 3.95 (ISBN 0-13-842971-5, Pub. by Treehouse). P-H.

Kessler, Leonard. Old Turtle's Ninety Knock-Knocks, Jokes, & Riddles. LC 89-77505. (Illus.). 48p. (gr. k up). 1991. 13.95 (ISBN 0-688-09585-2); PLB 13.88 (ISBN 0-688-09586-0). Greenwillow.

—Old Turtle's Riddle & Joke Book. Kessler, Leonard, illus. LC 85-12565. 48p. (gr. 1-4). 1986. 12.95 (ISBN 0-688-05953-8); PLB 12.88 (ISBN 0-688-05954-6). Greenwillow.

—Old Turtle's Riddle & Joke Book. (gr. k-6). 1990. pap. 2.95 (ISBN 0-440-40268-9, YB). Dell.

Lang, Margaret A. Gramma's Stories & Rhymes for Little Christians. Smith, Linda G., illus. 104p. (ps-5). 1982. 9.95. Lang Pubns.

Levine, Caroline. Silly School Riddles & Other Classroom Crack-Ups. Levine, Abby, ed. Munsinger, Lynn, illus. LC 84-17300. 32p. (gr. 1-5). 1984. 8.95 (ISBN 0-8075-7359-0). A Whitman.

Levine, Caroline A. The Silly Kid Joke Book. Maestro, Giulio, illus. LC 82-17727. 64p. (gr. 1-3). 1983. 10.95 (ISBN 0-525-44039-9, DCB). Dutton Child Bks.

Livingston, Myra C. My Head Is Red & Other Riddle Rhymes. LoPrete, Tere, illus. LC 89-24528. 32p. (gr. 6-9). 1990. PLB 12.95 (ISBN 0-8234-0806-X). Holiday.

McKie, Roy. The Riddle Book. LC 77-85237. (ps-2). 1978. lib. bdg. 5.99 (ISBN 0-394-93732-5, Random Juv); pap. 2.25 (ISBN 0-394-83732-0). Random.

Maestro, Giulio. A Raft of Riddles. Maestro, Giulio, illus. LC 82-2402. 64p. (gr. 3-7). 1982. 10.95 (ISBN 0-525-44017-8, 0869-260, DCB). Dutton Child Bks.

—Razzle-Dazzle Riddles. Maestro, Giulio, illus. LC 85-3785. 64p. (Orig.). (gr. 2-5). 1985. 11.95 (ISBN 0-89919-382-X, Clarion); pap. 4.95 (ISBN 0-89919-405-2). Ticknor & Fields.

—Riddle Romp. LC 83-2067. (Illus.). 64p. (gr. k-3). 1983. 13.95 (ISBN 0-89919-180-0, Pub. by Clarion); pap. 4.95 (ISBN 0-89919-207-6). Ticknor & Fields.

—Riddle Roundup: A Wild Bunch to Beef up Your Word Power. Maestro, Giulio, illus. LC 86-33404. 64p. (gr. 2-5). 1989. 13.95 (ISBN 0-89919-508-3, Clarion Bks); pap. 4.95 (ISBN 0-89919-537-7, Clarion Bks). HM.

—What's a Frank Frank? Tasty Homograph Riddles. Maestro, Giulio, illus. LC 84-5021. 64p. (gr. 2-5). 1984. 12.95 (ISBN 0-89919-297-1, Pub.by Clarion); pap. 4.95 (ISBN 0-89919-317-X). Ticknor & Fields.

—What's Mite Might? Homophone Riddles to Boost Your Word Power! Maestro, Giulio, illus. LC 86-2665. 64p. (gr. 2-5). 1986. 11.95 (ISBN 0-89919-434-6, Pub. by Clarion); pap. 4.95 (ISBN 0-89919-435-4). Ticknor & Fields.

Marzollo, Jean, compiled by. The Rebus Treasury. Carson, Carol D., illus. LC 85-16133. 64p. (ps up). 1989. pap. 5.95 (ISBN 0-8037-0644-8). Dial Bks Young.

Mase, Thomas. What's Gnu? Riddles from the Zoo. Burke, Susan S., illus. 32p. (gr. 1-4). 1989. PLB 8.95 (ISBN 0-8225-2330-2). Lerner Pubns.

Mickey Mouse Riddle Book. (Illus.). (ps-3). 1973. 6.95 (ISBN 0-394-82521-7, Random Juv); lib. bdg. 4.99 (ISBN 0-394-92521-1). Random.

Monteleone, Frank. Catchword: The Rebus Galore Book of Blackline Masters. Arena, John I., ed. Zwicky, Jill, illus. 96p. (Orig.). (gr. 4-12). 1989. wkbk. 8.50 (ISBN 0-87879-636-3, High Noon Books). Acad Therapy.

Morris, Ann. The Little Red Riding Hood Rebus Book. Rylands, Ljiljana, illus. LC 87-7696. 32p. (ps-3). 1987. 11.95 (ISBN 0-531-05730-5); PLB 11.99 (ISBN 0-531-08330-6). Orchard Bks Watts.

The Peek-a-Boo Riddle Book. 22p. 1985. 5.95 (ISBN 0-8431-1082-1). Price Stern.

Peterson, Scott K. Out on a Limb: Riddles about Trees & Plants. Burke, Susan S., illus. 32p. (gr. 1-4). 1989. PLB 8.95 (ISBN 0-8225-2328-0). Lerner Pubns.

—Wing It! Riddles about Birds. (Illus.). 32p. (gr. 1-4). 1991. PLB 8.95 (ISBN 0-8225-2333-7). Lerner Pubns.

Phillips, Louis. Going Ape: Jokes from the Jungle. Shein, Bob, illus. 64p. (gr. 2 up). 1990. pap. 3.95 (ISBN 0-14-032263-9, Puffin). Puffin Bks.

—Riddlegrams. (Illus.). 48p. (Orig.). (gr. 3-6). 1989. pap. 2.95 (ISBN 0-8431-2404-0). Price Stern.

—The Upside down Riddle Book. Gardner, Beau, illus. LC 82-73. 32p. (gr. k up). 1982. 14.95 (ISBN 0-688-00931-X); PLB 14.88 (ISBN 0-688-00932-8). Lothrop.

Pirotta, Saviour. Hey Riddle Riddle! Hellen, Nancy, illus. LC 88-34356. 32p. (gr. 2 up). 1989. 9.95 (ISBN 0-87226-408-4, Bedrick Blackie). P Bedrick Bks.

Reading Riddles. 32p. 1989. pap. 1.95 (ISBN 0-317-91020-5). Tor Bks.

Rosenbloom, Joseph. Biggest Riddle Book in the World. Behr, Joyce, illus. LC 76-1165. (gr. 5 up). 1979. 16.95 (ISBN 0-8069-4532-X); PLB 19.99 (ISBN 0-8069-4533-8); pap. 5.95 (ISBN 0-8069-8884-3). Sterling.

—The Funniest Riddle Book Ever! Wilhelm, Hans, illus. LC 84-16192. 24p. (ps up). 1985. 12.95 (ISBN 0-8069-4698-9); lib. bdg. 15.69 (ISBN 0-8069-4699-7). Sterling.

—Laughs, Hoots & Giggles: Riddles, Jokes, Knock-Knocks & Put-Downs. Behr, Joyce & Hoffman, Sanford, illus. 480p. (gr. 2 up). 1987. pap. 9.95 (ISBN 0-8069-6492-8). Sterling.

—Six Hundred Ninety-Six School Jokes & Riddles. Kendrick, Dennis, illus. 128p. (gr. 2 up). 1987. pap. 3.95 (ISBN 0-8069-6392-1). Sterling.

—Sports Riddles. Weissman, Sam Q., illus. LC 81-7232. 64p. (gr. 6 up). 1982. 8.95 (ISBN 0-15-277994-9, HJ). HarBraceJ.

—The Zaniest Riddle Book in the World. Hoffman, Sanford, illus. LC 83-18102. 128p. (gr. 3 up). 1985. 12.95 (ISBN 0-8069-4680-6); PLB 15.69 (ISBN 0-8069-4681-4); pap. 3.95 (ISBN 0-8069-6252-6). Sterling.

Rox, Lori M. Oodles of Riddles. Hoffman, Sanford, illus. LC 89-4549. 96p. (gr. 3-8). 1990. pap. 3.95 (ISBN 0-8069-7202-5). Sterling.

Salinas, Roger. Silly Ghost Riddles. Rodriguez, Carlos, illus. 32p. (Orig.). (gr. 3-5). 1987. pap. 2.95 (ISBN 0-942673-00-X). Salinas Salinas & Matthews.

Schaff, Joanne. What Am I? Schaff, Joanne, illus. 38p. (Orig.). (ps-3). 1987. pap. 1.99 (ISBN 0-9619365-0-9). Tree City Pr.

Schenk de Regniers, Beatrice. It Does Not Say Meow & Other Animal Riddle Rhymes. LC 72-75704. 40p. (gr. k-3). 1983. pap. 4.95 (ISBN 0-89919-043-X, Clarion). HM.

Schwartz, Alvin. Ten Copycats in a Boat & Other Riddles. Simont, Marc, illus. LC 79-2811. 64p. (gr. k-3). 1980. PLB 11.89 (ISBN 0-06-025238-3). HarpC Child Bks.

—Unriddling. Truesdell, Susan, illus. LC 82-48778. 128p. (gr. 4 up). 1983. PLB 12.89 (ISBN 0-397-32030-2, Lipp Jr Bks). HarpC Child Bks.

—Unriddling: All Sorts of Riddles to Puzzle Your Guessary. Truesdell, Sue, illus. LC 82-48778. 128p. (gr. 4 up). 1987. pap. 4.95 (ISBN 0-06-446057-6, Trophy). HarpC Child Bks.

Seltzer, Meyer. Petcetera: The Pet Riddle Book. Fay, Ann, ed. (Illus.). 32p. (gr. 1-5). 1988. PLB 8.95 (ISBN 0-8075-6515-6). A Whitman.

Sesame Street Staff. Sesame Street Pop-up Riddle Book. Sutherland, David, illus. LC 77-70852. (ps-3). 1977. bds. 8.95 (ISBN 0-394-83546-8, Random Juv). Random.

Shannon, J. Michael. Riddles & More Riddles. Magnuson, Diana, illus. LC 82-19765. 48p. (gr. 1-5). 1983. PLB 13.27 (ISBN 0-516-01873-6); pap. 3.95 (ISBN 0-516-41873-4). Childrens.

—Still More Riddles. Magnuson, Diana, illus. LC 85-29065. 48p. (gr. 3-6). 1986. lib. bdg. 13.27 (ISBN 0-516-01869-8); pap. 3.95 (ISBN 0-516-41869-6). Childrens.

Shofner, Myra. Second Ark Book of Riddles. Walles, Dwight, illus. (gr. 3-7). 1981. pap. 3.95 (ISBN 0-89191-531-1, 55319). Cook.

Sterne, Noelle. Tyrannosaurus Wrecks: A Book of Dinosaur Riddles. Chess, Victoria, illus. LC 78-22499. 32p. (gr. 1-4). 1979. PLB 12.89 (ISBN 0-690-03960-3, Crowell Jr Bks). HarpC Child Bks.

Swann, Brian. A Basket Full of White Eggs: Riddle-Poems. Goembel, Ponder, illus. LC 87-11220. 32p. (gr. k-3). 1988. 14.95 (ISBN 0-531-05734-8); PLB 14.99 (ISBN 0-531-08334-9). Orchard Bks Watts.

Swanson, June. That's for Shore: Riddles from the Beach. Burke, Susan S., illus. 32p. (gr. 1-4). 1991. PLB 8.95 (ISBN 0-8225-2332-9). Lerner Pubns.

Terban, Marvin. The Dove Dove: Funny Homograph Riddles. Huffman, Tom, illus. LC 88-2611. 64p. (gr. 4-7). 1988. 12.95 (ISBN 0-89919-723-X, Pub. by Clarion); pap. 4.95 (ISBN 0-89919-810-4, Pub. by Clarion). Ticknor & Fields.

—Eight Ate: A Feast of Homonym Riddles. Maestro, Giulio, illus. LC 81-12203. 64p. (gr. 1-3). 1982. 12.95 (ISBN 0-89919-067-7, Pub. by Clarion); pap. 4.95 (ISBN 0-89919-086-3). Ticknor & Fields.

—Too Hot to Hoot: Funny Palindrome Riddles. Maestro, Giulio, illus. LC 84-14942. 64p. (gr. 2-5). 1985. 12.95 (ISBN 0-89919-319-6, Pub. by Clarion); pap. 5.95 (ISBN 0-89919-320-X). Ticknor & Fields.

Thaler, Mike. The Riddle King's Camp Riddles. Harvey, Paul, illus. LC 88-63193. 32p. (gr. 1-5). 1989. pap. 1.25 (ISBN 0-394-83995-1, Random Juv). Random.

—The Riddle King's Food Riddles. Harvey, Paul, illus. LC 88-63190. 32p. (gr. 1-5). 1989. pap. 1.25 (ISBN 0-394-84041-0, Random Juv). Random.

—The Riddle King's Pet Riddles. Harvey, Paul, illus. LC 88-63191. 32p. (gr. 1-5). 1989. pap. 1.25 (ISBN 0-394-83977-3, Random Juv). Random.

—The Riddle King's School Riddles. Harvey, Paul, illus. LC 88-63192. 32p. (gr. 1-5). 1989. pap. 1.25 (ISBN 0-394-84004-6, Random Juv). Random.

Underwood, Ralph. Ask Me Another Riddle. Bonsall, Crosby, illus. LC 76-14690. (gr. k-7). 1976. pap. 4.95 (ISBN 0-448-12689-3, G&D). Putnam Pub Group.

Wallner, Alexandra. Ghoulish Giggles & Monster Riddles. Tucker, Kathy, ed. Wallner, Alexandra, illus. LC 82-10969. 32p. (gr. 1-5). 1982. PLB 8.95 (ISBN 0-8075-2863-3). A Whitman.

Walton, Rick & Walton, Ann. Ho Ho Ho! Riddles about Santa Claus. (Illus.). 32p. (gr. 1-4). 1991. PLB 8.95 (ISBN 0-8225-2337-X). Lerner Pubns.

—I Toad You So: Riddles about Frogs & Toads. Burke, Susan S., illus. 32p. (gr. 1-4). 1991. PLB 7.95 (ISBN 0-8225-2331-0). Lerner Pubns.

—On with the Show: Show Me Riddles. Burke, Susan S., illus. 32p. (gr. 1-4). 1989. PLB 8.95 (ISBN 0-8225-2327-2). Lerner Pubns.

—Weather or Not: Riddles for Rain & Shine. Burke, Susan S., illus. 32p. (gr. 1-4). 1989. PLB 8.95 (ISBN 0-8225-2329-9). Lerner Pubns.

Zimmerman, Andrea G. Riddle Zoo. 64p. (gr. 3-7). 1981. 9.25 (ISBN 0-525-38300-X, Dutton). NAL-Dutton.

RIDING

see Horsemanship

RIGHT OF PRIVACY

see Privacy, Right of

RIGHTS, CIVIL

see Civil Rights

RINGLING BROTHERS

Glendinning, Richard & Glendinning, Sally. The Ringling Brothers: Circus Family. Hutchinson, William, illus. 80p. (gr. 2-6). 1991. Repr. of 1972 ed. PLB 12.95 (ISBN 0-7910-1468-1). Chelsea Hse.

RIO GRANDE RIVER

Bragg, Bea. The Very First Thanksgiving: Pioneers on the Rio Grande. LC 89-15562. (Illus.). 64p. (Orig.). (gr. 3-5). 1989. pap. 7.95 (ISBN 0-943173-22-1). Harbinger AZ.

RITES AND CEREMONIES

see also Baptism; Fasts and Feasts; Funeral Rites and Ceremonies; Manners and Customs; Marriage Customs and Rites;

also classes of people and ethnic groups with the subdivision Rites and Ceremonies, e.g. Jews–Rites and Ceremonies

Guentert, Kenneth. The Young Server's Book of the Mass. LC 86-60894. 64p. (gr. 6-8). 1985. pap. 4.95 (ISBN 0-89390-078-8). Resource Pubns.

Kenny, Bernadette. Children's Liturgies: Seventy-Four Eucharistic Liturgies, Prayer Services & Penance Services Designed for Primary, Middle & Junior High Children. LC 77-74582. 176p. (gr. 1-8). 1977. pap. 10.95 (ISBN 0-8091-2030-5). Paulist Pr.

Lovasik, Lawrence G. The Seven Sacraments. (Illus.). (gr. 1-6). flexible bdg 0.95 (ISBN 0-89942-278-0, 278). Catholic Bk Pub.

RITUAL

see Rites and Ceremonies

RIVERA, DIEGO, 1886-1957

Cockcroft, James. Diego Rivera. (Illus.). 112p. (gr. 5 up). 1991. PLB 17.95 (ISBN 0-7910-1252-2). Chelsea Hse.

RIVERS

see also Dams; Floods; Water–Pollution; Water Power

also names of rivers

Bains, Rae. Wonders of Rivers. Miyake, Yoshi, illus. LC 81-7423. 32p. (gr. 2-4). 1982. PLB 10.89 (ISBN 0-89375-570-2); pap. text ed. 2.95 (ISBN 0-89375-571-0). Troll Assocs.

Baker, Susan. First Look at Rivers. LC 91-9419. (Illus.). 32p. (gr. 1-2). 1991. PLB 10.95 (ISBN 0-8368-0679-4). Gareth Stevens Inc.

Bellamy, David. Our Changing World: The River. Dow, Jill, illus. 24p. (gr. 1-4). 1988. bds. 9.95 (ISBN 0-517-56801-2, C N Potter Bks). Crown.

Bender, Lionel. River. FS-Watts Staff, ed. (Illus.). 32p. (gr. 1-6). 1988. PLB 11.90 (ISBN 0-531-10554-7). Watts.

Bentley, John & Charlton, Bill. Finding Out about Streams. (Illus.). 64p. (gr. 7-12). 1985. 19.95 (ISBN 0-7134-4425-8, Pub. by Batsford England). Trafalgar Sq.

Carlisle, Norman & Carlisle, Madelyn. Rivers. LC 81-38448. (Illus.). 48p. (gr. k-4). 1982. PLB 14.60 (ISBN 0-516-01645-8). Childrens.

Corke, Philip, illus. Rivers. 32p. (gr. 3-5). 1985. 5.95x (ISBN 0-86685-452-5). Intl Bk Ctr.

Crump, Donald J., ed. Let's Explore a River. (Illus.). (gr. k-4). 1988. Set. 10.95 (ISBN 0-685-31767-6); Set. PLB 12.95 (ISBN 0-685-31768-4). Natl Geog.

Emil, Jane. All about Rivers. LC 83-4868. (Illus.). 32p. (gr. 3-6). 1984. lib. bdg. 10.59 (ISBN 0-89375-979-1); pap. text ed. 2.95 (ISBN 0-89375-980-5). Troll Assocs.

Hester, Nigel. The Living River. (Illus.). 32p. (gr. 5-8). 1991. PLB 11.40 (ISBN 0-531-14121-7). Watts.

Morgan, Patricia G. A River Adventure. Plunkett, Micheal, illus. LC 87-3485. 32p. (gr. 3-6). 1987. PLB 10.79 (ISBN 0-8167-1171-2); pap. text ed. 2.95 (ISBN 0-8167-1172-0). Troll Assocs.

Mulherin, Jenny. Rivers & Lakes. LC 84-51228. (Illus.). 38p. (gr. 4-6). 1984. PLB 12.40 (ISBN 0-531-04836-5). Watts.

Parker, Steve. Pond & River. Dowell, Philip, photos by. LC 88-1575. (Illus.). 64p. (gr. 5 up). 1988. 15.00 (ISBN 0-394-89615-7); lib. bdg. 15.99 (ISBN 0-394-99615-1). Knopf.

Rowland-Entwistle, Theodore. Rivers & Lakes. (Illus.). 48p. (gr. 5-8). 1987. PLB 14.98 (ISBN 0-382-09499-9). Silver Burdett Pr.

Santrey, Laurence. Rivers. Sweat, Lynn, illus. LC 84-8818. 32p. (gr. 3-6). 1985. lib. bdg. 9.49 (ISBN 0-8167-0210-1); pap. text ed. 2.95 (ISBN 0-8167-0211-X). Troll Assocs.

Stewart, G. On the Water. (Illus.). 32p. (gr. 3-8). 1989. lib. bdg. 13.26 (ISBN 0-86592-109-1). Rourke Corp.

Swenson, Peter J. Secrets of Rivers & Streams. Jack, Susan, ed. Sabaka, Donna, illus. 90p. (gr. 4-10). 1982. pap. 3.95 (ISBN 0-930096-31-2). G Gannett.

Valiappa, Al. Story of Our Rivers: Book II. Chakravarty, Pranab, illus. (gr. 1-9). 1979. pap. 2.50 (ISBN 0-89744-184-2). Auromere.

RIVERS–FICTION

Baer, Judy. Silent Tears No More. LC 89-82689. 144p. (Orig.). (gr. 7-10). 1990. 3.95 (ISBN 1-55661-119-6). Bethany Hse.

Garden, Nancy. Peace, O River. 245p. (gr. 7 up). 1986. 12.95 (ISBN 0-374-35763-3). FS&G.

Grahame, Kenneth. The Wind in the Willows. Shepard, Ernest H., illus. 272p. (ps up). 1989. pap. 4.95 (ISBN 0-689-71310-X, Aladdin). Macmillan Child Grp.

Humphrey, Margo. River That Gave Gifts. (gr. 4-7). 1987. 12.95 (ISBN 0-89239-019-0). Childrens Book Pr.

Kherdian, David. Root River Run. Hogrogian, Nonny, illus. LC 84-14244. 160p. (gr. 7 up). 1984. 10.95 (ISBN 0-87614-274-9). Carolrhoda Bks.

Roddy, Lee. D. J. Dillon & the Hermit of Mad River. 132p. (gr. 3-7). 1988. pap. 4.99 (ISBN 0-89693-475-6). Victor Bks.

RIVERS–POLLUTION

see Water–Pollution

ROAD CONSTRUCTION

see Roads

ROAD RUNNER (BIRD)

Reese, Bob. Rapid Robert Roadrunner. LC 81-6090. (Illus.). 24p. (ps-2). 1981. PLB 11.27 (ISBN 0-516-02305-5); pap. 2.95 (ISBN 0-516-42305-3). Childrens.

ROAD SIGNS

see Signs and Signboards

ROADS

Gibbons, Gail. From Path to Highway: The Story of the Boston Post Road. Gibbons, Gail, illus. LC 85-47897. 32p. (gr. 1-4). 1986. (Crowell Jr Bks); PLB 13.89 (ISBN 0-690-04514-X). HarpC Child Bks.

—New Road! LC 82-45917. (Illus.). 32p. (gr. k-4). 1983. (Crowell Jr Bks); PLB 14.89 (ISBN 0-690-04343-0). HarpC Child Bks.

—New Road! Gibbons, Gail, illus. LC 82-45917. 32p. (gr. k-4). 1987. pap. 4.95 (ISBN 0-06-446059-2, Trophy). HarpC Child Bks.

Royston, Angela & Thompson, Graham. Monster Road Builders. (Illus.). 24p. (ps-2). 1989. 9.95 (ISBN 0-8120-6126-8). Barron.

Sandak, Cass R. Roads. (Illus.). 32p. (gr. k-4). 1984. lib. bdg. 10.90 (ISBN 0-531-04710-5). Watts.

Sauvain, Philip. Roads. Stefoff, Rebecca, ed. LC 90-40359. (Illus.). 48p. (gr. 4-7). 1990. PLB 17.26 (ISBN 0-944483-77-1). Garrett Ed Corp.

Unstead, R. J. Travel by Road Through the Ages. (Illus.). (gr. 7-10). 1967. 14.95 (ISBN 0-7136-1812-4). Dufour.

Williams, Owen. How Roads Are Made. (Illus.). 32p. 1989. 12.95x (ISBN 0-8160-2041-8). Facts on File.

ROADS–FICTION

Aiken, Joan. Tale of a One-Way Street. Pienkowski, Jan, illus. 128p. (gr. 3-7). 1986. pap. 3.95 (ISBN 0-14-031700-7, Puffin). Puffin Bks.

Bonham, Frank. Durango Street. (gr. 7 up). 1967. 15.95 (ISBN 0-525-28950-X, DCB). Dutton Child Bks.

Goodall, John S. The Story of a Main Street. Goodall, John S., illus. LC 87-60644. 60p. 1987. 14.95 (ISBN 0-689-50436-5, M K McElderry). Macmillan Child Grp.

Kehoe, Michael. Road Closed. LC 82-1312. (Illus.). 32p. (gr. k-4). 1982. lib. bdg. 9.95 (ISBN 0-87614-192-0). Carolrhoda Bks.

Lawrence, Louise. The Dram Road. LC 83-47601. 256p. (gr. 7 up). 1983. PLB 13.89 (ISBN 0-06-023748-1). HarpC Child Bks.

ROBBERS AND OUTLAWS

Lindgren, Astrid. Ronia, the Robber's Daughter. (Illus.). 176p. (gr. 4-7). 1985. pap. 3.95 (ISBN 0-14-031720-1, Puffin). Puffin Bks.

Yancey, Diane. Desperadoes & Dynamite: Train Robbery in the United States. (Illus.). 64p. (gr. 5-8). 1991. PLB 11.90 (ISBN 0-531-20038-8). Watts.

ROBBERS AND OUTLAWS–FICTION

Alexander, Martha. We're in Big Trouble, Blackboard Bear. Alexander, Martha, illus. LC 79-20631. (ps-2). 1980. 6.95 (ISBN 0-8037-9741-9); PLB 9.89 (ISBN 0-8037-9742-7). Dial Bks Young.

Avi. Man from the Sky. Wiesner, David, illus. LC 79-26909. 128p. (gr. 3-6). 1980. Knopf.

Bains, Rae. Case of the Great Train Robbery. Harvey, Paul, illus. LC 81-7525. 48p. (gr. 2-4). 1982. PLB 10.89 (ISBN 0-89375-588-5); pap. text ed. 2.95 (ISBN 0-89375-589-3). Troll Assocs.

Berry, James. A Thief in the Village & Other Stories. LC 87-24695. 160p. (gr. 6 up). 1988. PLB 12.95 (ISBN 0-531-05745-3); PLB 12.99 (ISBN 0-531-08345-4). Orchard Bks Watts.

Blackmore, R. D. Lorna Doone. 272p. (gr. 4-6). 1984. pap. 2.25 (ISBN 0-14-035021-7, Puffin). Puffin Bks.

Clifford, Eth. Just Tell Me When We're Dead! 144p. (gr. 4-6). 1985. pap. 2.50 (ISBN 0-590-33663-0, Apple Paperbacks). Scholastic Inc.

Dickens, Charles. Oliver Twist. 496p. (gr. 9-12). Date not set. pap. 2.50 (ISBN 0-451-51685-0, Sig Classics). NAL-Dutton.

—Oliver Twist. abridged ed. Martin, Les, adapted by. Zallinger, Jean, illus. LC 89-24279. 96p. (Orig.). (gr. 2-6). 1990. PLB 5.99 (ISBN 0-679-90391-7); pap. 2.95 (ISBN 0-679-80391-2). Random.

Duggan, Alice. Violet's Finest Hour. Stevenson, Harvey, illus. LC 91-52588. 64p. (gr. 1 up). 1991. text ed. 10.95 (ISBN 0-688-09456-2). Lothrop.

Ecke, Wolfgang. The Bank Holdup. Rettich, Rolf & Langenfass, Hansjorg, illus. 144p. (gr. 3-7). 1985. pap. 5.95 (ISBN 0-13-056474-5). P-H.

Fleischman, Sid. The Bloodhound Gang in the Case of the 264-Pound Burglar. Morrison, Bill, illus. LC 81-12066. 64p. (gr. 2-5). 1982. pap. 1.50 (ISBN 0-394-85108-0). Random.

—Humbug Mountain. Von Schmidt, Eric, illus. LC 78-9419. (gr. 4-6). 1978. 14.95i (ISBN 0-316-28569-2, Pub. by Atlantic Monthly Pr). Little.

—The Whipping Boy. Sis, Peter, illus. LC 85-17555. 96p. (gr. 2-6). 1986. PLB 13.95 (ISBN 0-688-06216-4). Greenwillow.

Galbraith, Kathryn O. Something Suspicious. 128p. (gr. 3 up). 1987. pap. 2.50 (ISBN 0-380-70253-3, Camelot). Avon.

Gezi, Kal & Bradford, Ann. The Mystery in the Secret Club House. McLean, Mina G., illus. LC 78-6418. (gr. k-3). 1978. PLB 9.96 (ISBN 0-89565-027-4). Childs World.

Harwood, Pearl A. Thief Visits Mr. & Mrs. Bumba. Overlie, George, illus. LC 70-156356. 32p. (gr. k-3). 1971. PLB 4.95 (ISBN 0-8225-0125-2). Lerner Pubns.

Haseley, Dennis. The Thieves' Market. Desimini, Lisa, illus. LC 90-38440. 32p. (gr. 1-5). 1991. 14.95 (ISBN 0-06-022492-4); PLB 14.89 (ISBN 0-06-022493-2). HarpC Child Bks.

Hogrogian, Nonny. The Contest. LC 75-40389. (Illus.). 32p. (gr. k-3). 1976. PLB 12.88 (ISBN 0-688-84042-6). Greenwillow.

Holland, Isabelle. Thief. (gr. 4 up). 1988. pap. 3.95 (ISBN 0-449-70269-3, Juniper). Fawcett.

McGovern, Ann. Robin Hood of Sherwood Forest. Sugarman, Tracy, illus. 128p. (gr. 4-6). 1987. pap. 2.50 (ISBN 0-590-40842-9, Pub. by Apple Classics). Scholastic Inc.

Mahy, Margaret. Great Piratical Rumbustification the Librarian & the Robbers. Blake, Quentin, illus. LC 85-45966. 64p. 1986. 11.95 (ISBN 0-87923-629-9). Godine.

Meltzer, Milton. The Terrorists. LC 82-48858. (Illus.). 192p. (gr. 7 up). 1983. PLB 12.89 (ISBN 0-06-024194-2). HarpC Child Bks.

Noyes, Alfred. The Highwayman. Keeping, Charles, illus. 32p. 1987. 14.95 (ISBN 0-19-279748-4); pap. 6.95 (ISBN 0-19-272133-X). Oxford U Pr.

Oana. Timmy Tiger & the Masked Bandit. LC 80-82955. (Illus.). 32p. (ps-4). 1981. PLB 9.95x (ISBN 0-87783-161-0). Oddo.

Oliver Twist. (Illus.). (gr. 3-5). 3.50 (ISBN 0-7214-0823-0). Ladybird Bks.

Palazzo-Craig, Janet. The Upside-Down Boy. Burns, Ray, illus. LC 85-14067. 48p. (Orig.). (gr. 1-3). 1986. PLB 9.89 (ISBN 0-8167-0604-2); pap. text ed. 2.95 (ISBN 0-8167-0605-0). Troll Assocs.

Parish, Peggy. The Cats' Burglar. Sweat, Lynn, illus. LC 82-11751. 64p. (gr. 1-3). 1983. 12.95 (ISBN 0-688-01825-4); PLB 12.88 (ISBN 0-688-01826-2). Greenwillow.

Rosenbloom, Joseph. Deputy Dan & the Bank Robbers. Raglin, Tim, illus. LC 84-159969. 48p. (gr. 2-3). 1985. lib. bdg. 6.99 (ISBN 0-394-97045-4, Random Juv); pap. 2.95 (ISBN 0-394-87045-X). Random.

Swan, Walter. Stick 'em up! I've Got You Covered! Swan, Deloris, ed. Asch, Connie, illus. 16p. (Orig.). (ps-8). 1989. pap. 1.50 (ISBN 0-927176-03-3). Swan Enterp.

Wettasinghe, Sybil. The Umbrella Thief. (Illus.). 32p. (ps-3). 1987. 11.95 (ISBN 0-916291-12-X). Kane-Miller Bk.

Wood, Audrey. Twenty-Four Robbers. 1989. pap. 2.50 (ISBN 0-85953-324-7). Childs Play.

Woods, Audrey. Twenty-Four Robbers. Woods, Audrey, illus. 32p. (ps-2). 1981. 5.50 (ISBN 0-85953-100-7, Pub. by Child's Play England). Childs Play.

ROBESON, PAUL

Greenfield, Eloise. Paul Robeson. Ford, George, illus. LC 74-13663. 40p. (gr. 1-5). 1975. PLB 14.89 (ISBN 0-690-00660-8, Crowell Jr Bks). HarpC Child Bks.

Hamilton, Virginia. Paul Robeson. LC 72-82892. (Illus.). 224p. 1974. 13.95 (ISBN 0-06-022188-7). HarpC Child Bks.

Paul Robeson: Mini Play. (gr. 5 up). 1977. 6.50 (ISBN 0-89550-371-9). Stevens & Shea.

Samuels, Steven. Paul Robeson. King, Coretta Scott, intro. by. (Illus.). 112p. (Orig.). (gr. 5 up). 1988. 17.95 (ISBN 1-55546-608-7); pap. 9.95 (ISBN 0-7910-0206-3). Chelsea Hse.

ROBIN HOOD

Green, Roger L. Adventures of Robin Hood. (Orig.). (gr. 2-5). 1984. pap. 2.25 (ISBN 0-14-035034-9, Puffin). Puffin Bks.

Haynes, Sarah, retold by. Robin Hood. Benson, Patrick, illus. 80p. (gr. 5-9). 1989. 12.95 (ISBN 0-8050-1206-0). H Holt & Co.

McGovern, Ann. Robin Hood of Sherwood Forest. Sugarman, Tracey, illus. 128p. (gr. 4-6). 1987. pap. 2.50 (ISBN 0-590-40842-9, Pub. by Apple Classics). Scholastic Inc.

Miles, Bernard. Robin Hood: His Life & Legend. Ambrus, Victor G., illus. LC 79-64615. 128p. (gr. 4 up). 12.95 (ISBN 0-02-689324-X). Checkerboard Pr.

Pyle, Howard. The Merry Adventures of Robin Hood. Pyle, Howard, illus. LC 68-55820. xxii, 296p. (gr. 3-6). 1968. pap. 6.95 (ISBN 0-486-22043-5). Dover.

Pyle, Howard, ed. Merry Adventures of Robin Hood. Smith, Lawrence B., illus. (gr. 4-6). Illus. Jr. Lib. o.p. 5.95 (ISBN 0-448-05820-0, G&D); Companion Lib. Ed. o.p. 2.95 (ISBN 0-448-05473-6); deluxe ed. 10.95 (ISBN 0-448-06020-5). Putnam Pub Group.

Robin Hood. 1988. 2.98 (ISBN 0-671-09223-5). S&S Trade.

Robin Hood. (Illus.). (gr. 3-7). 3.50 (ISBN 0-7214-0885-0). Ladybird Bks.

Storr, Catherine, retold by. Robin Hood. LC 83-24417. (Illus.). 32p. (gr. k-5). 1984. PLB 16.67 (ISBN 0-8172-2109-3); PLB 27.99 incl. cassette (ISBN 0-8172-2235-9); pap. 9.27g (ISBN 0-8172-2253-7); pap. text ed. 23.95 incl. cassette (ISBN 0-8172-2268-5); cassette 14.00 (ISBN 0-685-09498-7). Raintree Pubs.

Vivian, E. Charles. Adventures of Robin Hood. Vivian, E. Charles, illus. (gr. 5 up). pap. 1.75 (ISBN 0-8049-0067-1, CL-67). Airmont.

ROBINS–FICTION

Wheeler, Cindy. A Good Day, a Good Night. Wheeler, Cindy, illus. LC 79-3017. (ps-2). 1980. 8.61i (ISBN 0-397-31900-2, Lipp Jr Bks). HarpC Child Bks.

Wise Robin. (ARA., Illus.). (gr. 1-4). 3.50x (ISBN 0-86685-243-3). Intl Bk Ctr.

ROBINSON, BROOKS CALBERT, 1937-

Wolff, Rick. Brooks Robinson. Murray, Jim, intro. by. (Illus.). 64p. (gr. 3 up). 1991. PLB 14.95 (ISBN 0-7910-1186-0). Chelsea Hse.

ROBINSON, FRANK, 1935-

Macht, Norm. Frank Robinson. Murray, Jim, intro. by. (Illus.). 64p. (gr. 3 up). 1991. PLB 14.95 (ISBN 0-7910-1187-9). Chelsea Hse.

ROBINSON, JOHN ROOSEVELT, 1919-1972

Adler, David A. Jackie Robinson, He Was the First. (gr. 1-4). 1989. 12.95 (ISBN 0-8234-0734-9). Holiday.

—Jackie Robinson: He Was the First. Casilla, Robert, illus. LC 88-32394. (gr. 1-4). 1990. pap. 4.95 (ISBN 0-8234-0799-3). Holiday.

Cohen, Barbara. Thank You, Jackie Robinson. Cuffari, Richard, illus. LC 87-29341. (gr. 3-6). 1988. PLB 13.95 (ISBN 0-688-07909-1). Lothrop.

—Thank You, Jackie Robinson. 1989. pap. 2.75 (ISBN 0-590-42378-9). Scholastic Inc.

Davidson, Margaret. The Story of Jackie Robinson: Bravest Man in Baseball. (Orig.). (gr. k-6). 1988. pap. 2.95 (ISBN 0-440-40019-8, YB). Dell.

Farr, Naunerle C. Babe Ruth-Jackie Robinson. Caravana, Tony & Cruz, Nardo, illus. (gr. 4-12). 1979. pap. text ed. 2.95 (ISBN 0-88301-359-2); wkbk 1.25 (ISBN 0-88301-383-5). Pendulum Pr.

Golenbock, Peter. Teammates. Bacon, Paul, illus. (gr. 1-4). 1990. 15.95 (ISBN 0-15-200603-6). HarbraceJ.

Grabowski, John. Jackie Robinson. Murray, Jim, intro. by. (Illus.). 64p. (gr. 3 up). 1991. PLB 14.95 (ISBN 0-7910-1188-7). Chelsea Hse.

Johnson, Spencer. The Value of Courage: The Story of Jackie Robinson. LC 77-8865. 64p. (gr. k-6). 1977. 9.95 (ISBN 0-916392-12-0, Pub. by Value Communications); pap. 8.95 incl. cassette (ISBN 0-86679-063-2). Oak Tree Pubns.

O'Connor, Jim. Jackie Robinson & the Story of All-Black Baseball. Butcher, Jim, illus. LC 88-18466. 48p. (Orig.). (gr. 2-4). 1989. PLB 6.99 (ISBN 0-394-92456-8); pap. 2.95 (ISBN 0-394-82456-3). Random.

Robinson, Jackie & Duckett, Alfred. Breakthrough to the Big League: The Story of Jackie Robinson. large type ed. (Illus.). 160p. (gr. 4-8). 1991. Repr. of 1965 ed. PLB 17.95 (ISBN 1-55905-094-2). Grey Castle.

Sabin, Francene. Jackie Robinson. Sheean, Michael, illus. LC 84-2603. 32p. (gr. 3-6). 1985. PLB 9.49 (ISBN 0-8167-0164-4); pap. text ed. 2.95 (ISBN 0-8167-0165-2). Troll Assocs.

Scott, Richard. Jackie Robinson. King, Coretta Scott, intro. by. (Illus.). 112p. (Orig.). (gr. 5 up). 1987. 17.95 (ISBN 1-55546-609-5); pap. 9.95 (ISBN 0-7910-0200-4). Chelsea Hse.

Shorto, Russell. Jackie Robinson & the Breaking of the Color Barrier. (Illus.). 32p. (gr. 2-4). 1991. PLB 11.50 (ISBN 1-878841-15-7); pap. 3.95 (ISBN 1-878841-35-1). Millbrook Pr.

ROBOTS

Baldwin, Margaret & Peck, Gary. Robots & Robotics. 72p. (gr. 5 up). 1984. lib. bdg. 10.90 (ISBN 0-531-04705-9). Watts.

Barrett, N. S. Robots. (Illus.). 32p. (gr. 1-6). 1985. PLB 11.40 (ISBN 0-531-04947-7). Watts.

Cummings, Richard. Make Your Own Robots. 1985. 8.95 (ISBN 0-679-20686-8). McKay.

D'Ignazio, Fred. Working Robots. LC 81-17279. (Illus.). 160p. (gr. 7 up). 1981. 12.50 (ISBN 0-525-66740-7, Lodestar Bks). Dutton Child Bks.

Elting, Mary. The Answer Book about Robots & Other Inventions. Barnes-Murphy, Rowan, illus. 80p. (gr. 3-7). 1984. pap. 2.95 (ISBN 0-448-13802-6, G&D). Putnam Pub Group.

Gerver, Jane, ed. My Robot Book. McCarthy, Kathleen, et al, illus. 32p. (gr. 1-3). 1986. wkbk. 3.95 (ISBN 0-394-88170-2). Random.

Greene, Carol. Robots. LC 82-17872. (Illus.). 48p. (gr. k-4). 1983. PLB 14.60 (ISBN 0-516-01684-9). Childrens.

Harrar, George. Radical Robots: Can You Be Replaced? (Illus.). 48p. (gr. 5 up). 1990. PLB 14.95 (ISBN 0-671-69420-0); pap. 5.95 (ISBN 0-671-69421-9). S&S Trade.

Lauber, Patricia. Get Ready for Robots. Kelley, True, illus. LC 85-48255. 32p. (ps-3). 1987. PLB 13.89i (ISBN 0-690-04578-6, Crowell Jr Bks). HarpC Child Bks.

—Get Ready for Robots! Kelley, True, illus. LC 85-48255. 32p. (gr. k-3). 1988. pap. 4.50 (ISBN 0-06-445080-5, Trophy). HarpC Child Bks.

Lindblom, Steven. How to Build a Robot. Lindblom, Steven, illus. LC 84-45336. 96p. (gr. 4-7). 1985. 12.95 (ISBN 0-690-04441-0, Crowell Jr Bks); PLB 12.89 (ISBN 0-690-04442-9, Crowell Jr Bks). HarpC Child Bks.

Liptak, Karen. Robotics Basics. Petronella, Michael, illus. 48p. (gr. 3-7). 1984. 10.95 (ISBN 0-13-782087-9). P-H.

Price, Stern & Sloan Staff. Robots. (Illus.). 32p. (gr. 7-12). 1987. pap. 2.95 (ISBN 0-8431-4290-1). Price Stern.

Rex, Patricia. Robot Math. (ps-k). 1989. pap. 6.95 (ISBN 0-8224-5841-1). Fearon Teach Aids.

—Robot Readiness. (ps-k). 1989. pap. 6.95 (ISBN 0-8224-5842-X). Fearon Teach Aids.

—Robot Shapes. (ps-k). 1989. pap. 6.95 (ISBN 0-8224-5843-8). Fearon Teach Aids.

Richard, Graham. Robots. (Illus.). 32p. (gr. 1-6). 1986. PLB 8.99 (ISBN 0-531-18061-1, Pub. by Bookwright). Watts.

Riehecky, Janet. Robots: Here They Come! Hohag, Linda, illus. LC 90-30634. 32p. (ps-2). 1990. lib. bdg. 11.97 (ISBN 0-89565-577-2). Childs World.

Salant, Michael A. Our Industrious Robots: A Guide to What Robots Can Do & How They Work. LC 84-90027. (Illus.). 128p. (gr. 6 up). Date not set. 12.95 (ISBN 0-9609288-3-9); pap. 7.95 (ISBN 0-9609288-2-0). M A Salant.

Skurzynski, Gloria. Robots: Your High-Tech World. LC 89-70805. (Illus.). 64p. (gr. 4 up). 1990. 15.95 (ISBN 0-02-782917-0, Bradbury Pr). Macmillan Child Grp.

Sylvester, Diane. Inventions, Robots, Future. 112p. (gr. 4-6). 1984. 9.95 (ISBN 0-88160-108-X, LW 905). Learning Wks.

Vowles, Andrew. Robotics. Bastien, Charles, illus. 32p. (gr. 5-9). 1985. pap. 4.95 (ISBN 0-88625-113-3). Durkin Hayes Pub.

Winkles, Nels. If I Had a Robot... What to Expect from the Personal Robot. (gr. 8 up). 1984. pap. 9.95 (ISBN 0-88056-353-2). Weber Systems.

ROBOTS–FICTION

Altman, Adelaide. Professor Pishposh & the Robots. Altman, Adelaide, illus. 48p. (ps-2). 1988. 12.95 (ISBN 0-933905-05-X); pap. 9.95 (ISBN 0-933905-16-5). Claycomb Pr.

Asimov, Janet & Asimov, Isaac. Norby & the Court Jester. 128p. (gr. 3-7). 1991. 12.95 (ISBN 0-8027-8131-4); PLB 13.85 (ISBN 0-8027-8132-2). Walker & Co.

—Norby & the Queen's Necklace. LC 86-11120. 144p. (gr. 4-9). 1986. 11.95 (ISBN 0-8027-6659-5); PLB 12.85 (ISBN 0-8027-6660-9). Walker & Co.

—Norby & Yobo's Great Adventure. 224p. (gr. 4-9). 1989. 12.95 (ISBN 0-8027-6893-8); PLB 13.85 (ISBN 0-8027-6894-6). Walker & Co.

—Norby, the Mixed up Robot. LC 82-25173. 96p. (gr. 5-7). 1983. PLB 10.85 (ISBN 0-8027-6496-7). Walker & Co.

Black, Christopher. The Android Invasion. (Orig.). (gr. 4-8). 1984. pap. 2.50 (ISBN 0-440-40081-3, YB). Dell.

Bunting, Eve. The Robot Birthday. DeJohn, Marie, illus. LC 79-19185. 80p. (gr. 1-3). 1980. 7.95 (ISBN 0-525-38542-8, DCB). Dutton Child Bks.

Coombs, Patricia. Dorrie & the Witches' Camp. Coombs, Patricia, illus. LC 82-9986. 48p. (gr. 1-5). 1983. PLB 12.88 (ISBN 0-688-01508-5). Lothrop.

Corcoran, Mark, illus. The Mystery of the Rebellious Robot. LC 78-19701. (gr. 3-5). 1979. (Random Juv). Random.

Dupasquier, Philippe. Robot Named Chip. (ps-3). 1991. 12.95 (ISBN 0-670-83574-9). Viking Child Bks.

Fettig, Art. The Three Robots Find a Grandpa. Carpenter, Joe, illus. LC 84-80378. 96p. (Orig.). (gr. k-7). 1984. pap. 3.95 (ISBN 0-9601334-8-8); cassette incl. Growth Unltd.

Hoban, Lillian & Hoban, Phoebe. The Laziest Robot in Zone One. Hoban, Lillian, illus. LC 82-48613. 64p. (gr. k-3). 1983. 11.95 (ISBN 0-06-022349-9); PLB 11.89 (ISBN 0-06-022352-9). HarpC Child Bks.

Hoover, H. M. Orvis. 192p. (gr. 4 up). 1990. pap. 3.95 (ISBN 0-14-032113-6, Puffin). Puffin Bks.

Krahn, Fernando. Robot-Bot-Bot. LC 78-21959. (ps-1). 1979. 6.95 (ISBN 0-525-38545-2, DCB). Dutton Child Bks.

Kroll, Steven. Otto. Delaney, Ned, illus. LC 82-19024. 48p. (ps-3). 1983. 5.95 (ISBN 0-8193-1105-7); PLB 5.95 (ISBN 0-8193-1106-5). Parents.

Meddick, James. Robotman Takes Off, No. 1. 128p. (gr. 6 up). 1986. pap. 4.95 (ISBN 0-88687-250-2). Pharos Bks NY.

Pienkowski, Jan. Robot. Pienkowski, Jan, illus. 12p. (gr. 1 up). 1981. 9.95 (ISBN 0-440-07459-2). Delacorte.

Prince, Alison. The Type One Super Robot. Prince, Alison, illus. LC 87-14835. 128p. (gr. 3-6). 1988. PLB 12.95 (ISBN 0-02-775201-1, Pub. by Four Winds Pr). Macmillan Child Grp.

Robots in Space. 1989. pap. 0.66 (ISBN 0-394-82363-X). Random.

Slote, Alfred. My Robot Buddy. LC 75-9922. (Illus.). 96p. (gr. 3-5). 1975. 12.95 (ISBN 0-397-31641-0, Lipp Jr Bks). HarpC Child Bks.

Surprise Robot! (ps-1). 1987. bds. 3.95 (ISBN 0-317-66513-8, Little Simon). S&S Trade.

Taylor, Max. High Tech Howard: My Cousin the Droid. (Illus.). 128p. 1990. pap. 2.95 (ISBN 0-8431-2712-0). Price Stern.

—High-Tech Howard: The Halloween Hex. (Illus.). 128p. 1990. pap. 2.95 (ISBN 0-8431-2713-9). Price Stern.

Toomey, Mary R. Jamari. (Illus.). 1991. 6.95 (ISBN 0-533-09132-2). Vantage.

Traynor, Elizabeth. My Best Friend is a Robot: Light Fiction. (Illus.). 64p. (Orig.). (gr. 3-6). 1990. pap. 2.50 (ISBN 0-87406-529-1). Willowisp Pr.

Waddell, Martin. Harriet & the Robot. Burgess, Mark, illus. LC 86-17435. (gr. 3-7). 1987. 12.95 (ISBN 0-316-91624-2, Joy St Bks). Little.

—Harriet & the Robot. Burgess, Mark, illus. (gr. 3-5). 1988. pap. 2.50 (ISBN 0-671-66021-7, Minstrel Bks). PB.

Williams, Jeffery W. The Four Wheels of Justice Fighting Force: The Deadly Truckbots. Williams, Jeffery W., illus. 28p. (gr. 3 up). 1990. pap. 2.95 (ISBN 1-878392-02-6). R Kids Pub.

Wyatt, Pam. I Can Go! Buell-Bakke, Karen, illus. (ps-1). 1988. lib. bdg. 9.95 (ISBN 0-945286-00-7). Red Bus Pub.

Yolen, Jane. The Robot & Rebecca the Missing Owser. McCrady, Lady, illus. LC 81-4870. 96p. (gr. 3-6). 1981. lib. bdg. 4.99 (ISBN 0-394-94832-7). Knopf.

Zimmerman, R. D. Robot on the Rampage. (Illus.). 17p. (gr. 3-7). 1988. incl. puzzle 9.95 (ISBN 0-922242-09-7). Lombard Mktg.

ROCK CLIMBING

see Mountaineering

ROCK MUSIC

Adams, Barbara. Rock Video Strikes Again. (Orig.). (gr. 2-6). 1986. pap. 2.50 (ISBN 0-440-47170-2, YB). Dell.

Barnard, Stephen. Rock: An Illustrated History. (Illus.). 256p. (gr. 7 up). 1987. 60.00 (ISBN 0-02-870251-4). Schirmer Bks.

Berger, Gilda. U. S. A. for Africa, Rock Aid in the Eighties. LC 86-24718. (Illus.). 96p. (gr. 7-12). 1987. lib. bdg. 12.90 (ISBN 0-531-10299-8). Watts.

Blocher, Arlo. Rock. new ed. LC 75-39819. (Illus.). 32p. (gr. 5-10). 1976. PLB 10.79 (ISBN 0-89375-015-8); pap. 2.95 (ISBN 0-89375-031-X). Troll Assocs.

Busnar, Gene. The Picture Life of Whitney Houston. Rakos, Jennie, ed. (Illus.). 64p. (gr. k-6). 1988. PLB 10.90 (ISBN 0-531-10498-2). Watts.

Crocker, Chris. Cyndi Lauper. Arico, Diane, ed. (Illus.). 64p. (gr. 3-7). 1985. pap. 3.50 (ISBN 0-671-55475-1, Little Simon); 9.29 (ISBN 0-685-09958-X). S&S Trade.

—Wham! Arico, Diane, ed. (Illus.). 64p. (gr. 3-7). 1985. lib. bdg. 8.79 (ISBN 0-685-10386-2, Little Simon); pap. 3.50 (ISBN 0-685-10387-0). S&S Trade.

Fissinger. Hall & Oates. LC 83-71567. (Illus.). 32p. (ps up). 1983. PLB 9.75 (ISBN 0-89813-103-0); 13.95. Creative Ed.

—Pat Benatar. (Illus.). 32p. (gr. 4 up). 1983. PLB 9.75s.p. (ISBN 0-89813-101-4); PLB 13.95. Creative Ed.

Fornatale, Pete. The Story of Rock 'N' Roll. LC 86-28453. (Illus.). 224p. (gr. 5 up). 1987. 13.95 (ISBN 0-688-06276-8); pap. 7.95 (ISBN 0-688-06277-6, Pub. by Beech Tree Bks). Morrow Jr Bks.

Gray, Charlotte. Bob Geldof: The Rock Star Who Raised 140 Million Dollars for Famine Relief in Ethiopia. Sherwood, Rhoda, ed. LC 88-2231. (Illus.). 68p. (gr. 5-6). 1988. PLB 12.95 (ISBN 1-55532-814-8). Gareth Stevens Inc.

Green, Carl R. & Sanford, William R. Alabama. LC 86-13530. (Illus.). 32p. (gr. 4-5). PLB 9.95 (ISBN 0-89686-294-1, Crestwood Hse). Macmillan Child Grp.

Greenberg, Keith E. Bruce Springsteen. LC 85-18035. (Illus.). 40p. (gr. 4-9). 1986. lib. bdg. 9.95 (ISBN 0-8225-1608-X). Lerner Pubns.

—Cyndi Lauper. LC 85-10262. (Illus.). 32p. (gr. 4-9). 1985. PLB 9.95 (ISBN 0-8225-1605-5). Lerner Pubns.

—Rap. (Illus.). 40p. (gr. 4-9). 1988. 9.95 (ISBN 0-8225-1617-9). Lerner Pubns.

Kallen, Stuart. Renaissance of Rock: British Invasion - The Sixties. Italia, Bob, ed. (Illus.). 48p. (gr. 4). 1989. PLB 12.95 (ISBN 0-939179-75-X). Abdo & Dghtrs.

—Renaissance of Rock: Sounds of America - The Sixties. Italia, Bob, ed. (Illus.). 48p. (gr. 4). 1989. PLB 12.95 (ISBN 0-939179-74-1). Abdo & Dghtrs.

—Retrospect of Rock: The Eighties. Italia, Bob, ed. (Illus.). 48p. (gr. 4). 1989. PLB 12.95 (ISBN 0-939179-77-6). Abdo & Dghtrs.

—Revolution of Rock: The Seventies. Italia, Bob, ed. (Illus.). 48p. (gr. 4). 1989. PLB 12.95 (ISBN 0-939179-76-8). Abdo & Dghtrs.

—Roots of Rock, Vol. 1: Pre Fifties. Italia, Bob, ed. (Illus.). 48p. (gr. 4). 1989. lib. bdg. 12.95 (ISBN 0-939179-72-5). Abdo & Dghtrs.

—Roots of Rock, Vol. 2: The Fifties. Italia, Bob, ed. (Illus.). 48p. (gr. 4). 1989. PLB 12.95 (ISBN 0-939179-73-3). Abdo & Dghtrs.

Kaye, Annene. Van Halen. Arico, Diane, ed. (Illus.). 64p. (Orig.). (gr. 5 up). 1985. pap. 3.50 (ISBN 0-671-55031-4, Little Simon). S&S Trade.

Koenig, Terry. Bruce Springsteen. Schoeder, Howard, ed. LC 86-8961. (Illus.). 32p. (gr. 4-5). PLB 9.95 (ISBN 0-89686-303-4, Crestwood Hse). Macmillan Child Grp.

—Lionel Richie. LC 86-13588. (Illus.). 32p. (gr. 4-5). PLB 9.95 (ISBN 0-89686-302-6, Crestwood Hse). Macmillan Child Grp.

—Tina Turner. LC 86-8950. (Illus.). 32p. (gr. 4-5). PLB 9.95 (ISBN 0-89686-305-0, Crestwood Hse). Macmillan Child Grp.

Levy, A. Something Queer in Rock 'n' Roll. 48p. (gr. k-6). 1989. pap. 2.95 (ISBN 0-440-40159-3, YB). Dell.

Mabery, D. L. Julian Lennon. (Illus.). 40p. (gr. 4-9). 1986. lib. bdg. 9.95 (ISBN 0-8225-1607-1). Lerner Pubns.

—Tina Turner. (Illus.). 40p. (gr. 4-9). 1986. lib. bdg. 9.95 (ISBN 0-8225-1609-8). Lerner Pubns.

Manning, Steve. The Jacksons. LC 76-11634. (gr. 4 up). 1976. pap. 4.95 (ISBN 0-672-52275-6, Bobbs). Macmillan.

Martin, Susan. Duran Duran. 1984. pap. 3.50 (ISBN 0-671-53099-2, Little Simon); 8.29 (ISBN 0-685-09673-4). S&S Trade.

Matthews, Gordon. Madonna. Arico, Diane, ed. LC 85-10587. (Illus.). 64p. (gr. 8-12). 1985. lib. bdg. 8.79 (ISBN 0-671-60375-2, Little Simon); pap. 3.50 (ISBN 0-685-10385-4). S&S Trade.

—Prince. Arico, Diane, ed. (Illus.). 64p. (gr. 3 up). 1985. PLB 8.79 (ISBN 0-671-55477-8, Little Simon); pap. 3.50 (ISBN 0-685-09758-7). S&S Trade.

Paige, David. A Day in the Life of a Rock Musician. Ruhlin, Roger, photos by. LC 78-68808. (Illus.). 32p. (gr. 4-8). 1980. PLB 11.79 (ISBN 0-89375-225-8); pap. 2.95 (ISBN 0-89375-229-0). Troll Assocs.

Russell, Kate. Billy Idol. Arico, Diane, ed. LC 84-25807. (Illus.). 64p. (Orig.). (gr. 5 up). 1985. pap. 3.50 (ISBN 0-671-55474-3, Little Simon). S&S Trade.

Strasser, Todd. Rock It to the Top. 1987. write for info. Delacorte.

—Rock 'n Roll Nights. LC 81-12618. 224p. (gr. 7 up). 1982. pap. 10.95 (ISBN 0-385-28855-7). Delacorte.

Taylor, Paula. Elton John. (Illus.). (gr. 4 up). 1975. PLB 9.75 (ISBN 0-87191-457-3); 13.95 (ISBN 0-685-01254-9). Creative Ed.

Zadra, Dan. Bruce Springsteen. (Illus.). 32p. (gr. 4 up). 1983. PLB 9.75 (ISBN 0-88682-098-7). Creative Ed.

ROCKEFELLER, JOHN DAVISON, 1839-1937

Shuker, Nancy. John D. Rockefeller. Furstinger, Nancy, ed. (Illus.). 140p. (gr. 7-10). 1989. PLB 13.98 (ISBN 0-382-09583-9). Silver Burdett Pr.

ROCKET FLIGHT

see Space Flight

ROCKETRY

see also Guided Missiles; Rockets (Aeronautics); Space Vehicles

Branley, Franklyn M. Rockets & Satellites. rev. ed. Maestro, Giulio, illus. LC 86-47748. 32p. (ps-3). 1987. (Crowell Jr Bks); PLB 13.89 (ISBN 0-690-04593-X). HarpC Child Bks.

Lampton, Christopher. Rocketry: From Goddard to Space Travel. Kline, M., ed. (Illus.). 96p. (gr. 7-9). 1988. PLB 10.40 (ISBN 0-531-10483-4). Watts.

ROCKETS (AERONAUTICS)

see also Guided Missiles

Arno, Roger. The Story of Space & Rockets. (Illus.). (gr. 5). 1978. pap. 3.95 (ISBN 0-88388-063-6). Bellerophon Bks.

Asimov, Isaac. Rockets, Probes & Satellites. LC 87-42639. (Illus.). 32p. (gr. 3-4). 1988. PLB 11.95 (ISBN 1-55532-366-9). Gareth Stevens Inc.

—Rockets, Probes & Satellites. 1990. pap. 4.95 (ISBN 0-440-40351-0, YB). Dell.

Barrett, Norman. The Picture World of Rockets & Satellites. (Illus.). 32p. (gr. k-4). 1990. PLB 11.40 (ISBN 0-531-14055-5). Watts.

Furniss, Tim. Space Rocket. FS-Aladdin Staff, ed. Shone, Rob, illus. 32p. (gr. 4-9). 1988. PLB 11.90 (ISBN 0-531-17099-3, Gloucester Pr). Watts.

How It Works: The Motor Car. (ARA., Illus.). (gr. 5-12). 3.50x (ISBN 0-86685-256-5). Intl Bk Ctr.
Johnstone, Hugh. Aircraft & Rockets. (Illus.). 40p. (gr. 5-9). 1989. PLB 12.40 (ISBN 0-531-17185-X). Watts.
Myring. Rockets & Spaceflight. (gr. 2-5). 1982. (Usborne-Hayes); PLB 11.96 (ISBN 0-88110-017-X); pap. 3.95 (ISBN 0-86020-584-3). EDC.
Sabin, Francene. Rockets & Satellites. Maccabe, Richard, illus. LC 84-2738. 32p. (gr. 3-6). 1985. PLB 9.49 (ISBN 0-8167-0288-8); pap. text ed. 2.95 (ISBN 0-8167-0289-6). Troll Assocs.
Spizzirri Publishing Co. Staff. Rockets: An Educational Coloring Book. Spizzirri, Linda, ed. (Illus.). 32p. (gr. 1-8). 1986. pap. 1.95 (ISBN 0-86545-072-2). Spizzirri.

ROCKETS (AERONAUTICS)–FICTION

Newell, Peter. The Rocket Book. Newell, Peter, illus. LC 69-12080. 52p. (gr. k-4). 1969. Repr. of 1912 ed. 12.95 (ISBN 0-8048-0505-9). C E Tuttle.

ROCKETS (AERONAUTICS)–MODELS

Humphreys, B. J. A Hundred Ways to Save Money on Model Rocket Building. (Illus.). 1977. pap. text ed. 1.50 (ISBN 0-912468-19-X). CA Rocketry.

ROCKNE, KNUTE KENNETH, 1888-1931

Riper, Guernsey V., Jr. Knute Rockne: Young Athlete. Doremus, Robert, illus. LC 86-10791. 192p. (gr. 2-6). 1986. pap. 3.95 (ISBN 0-02-042110-9, Aladdin). Macmillan Child Grp.

ROCKS

see also Crystallography; Geology; Mineralogy

Arneson, D. J. Rocks & Minerals. Friedman, Howard, illus. 32p. (Orig.). 1990. pap. 2.50 (ISBN 0-942025-90-3). Kidsbks.
Bains, Rae. Rocks & Minerals. Maccabe, Richard, illus. LC 84-8644. 32p. (gr. 3-6). 1985. PLB 9.49 (ISBN 0-8167-0186-5); pap. text ed. 2.95 (ISBN 0-8167-0187-3). Troll Assocs.
Baylor, Byrd. Everybody Needs a Rock. Parnall, Peter, illus. LC 74-9163. 32p. (ps-3). 1974. 14.95 (ISBN 0-684-13899-9, Scribners Young Read). Macmillan Child Grp.
—Everybody Needs a Rock. Parnall, Peter, illus. LC 74-9163. 32p. (Orig.). (gr. k-3). 1985. pap. 4.95 (ISBN 0-689-71051-8, Aladdin). Macmillan Child Grp.
Brown, Vinson, et al. Rocks & Minerals of California. 3rd. rev. ed. LC 72-13423. (Illus.). 200p. (gr. 4 up). 1972. 15.95 (ISBN 0-911010-59-9); pap. 8.95 (ISBN 0-911010-58-0). Naturegraph.
Cork, B. & Bramwell, M. Rocks & Fossils. Jackson, I. & Suttie, A., illus. 32p. (gr. 5-8). 1983. PLB 13.96 (ISBN 0-88110-159-1); pap. 6.95 (ISBN 0-86020-765-X). EDC.
Gans, Roma. Rock Collecting. 2nd ed. Keller, Holly, illus. LC 83-46170. 32p. (gr. k-3). 1984. PLB 12.89 (ISBN 0-685-08451-5, Crowell Jr Bks). HarpC Child Bks.
—Rock Collecting. Keller, Holly, illus. LC 83-46170. 32p. (ps-3). 1987. pap. 4.50 (ISBN 0-06-445063-5, Trophy). HarpC Child Bks.
—Rock Collecting. (ps-3). 1984. PLB 13.89 (ISBN 0-690-04266-3, Crowell Jr Bks). HarperCollins.
Gattis, L. S., III. Rocks & Minerals for Pathfinders: A Basic Youth Enrichment Skill Honor Packet. (Illus.). 22p. (Orig.). (gr. 5 up). 1987. pap. 5.00 tchr's. ed. (ISBN 0-936241-29-2). Cheetah Pub.
Hyler, Nelson W. Rocks & Minerals. Shannon, Kenyon, illus. (gr. 4-6). pap. 2.95 (ISBN 0-8431-4274-X). Wonder.
Jennings, Terry. Rocks & Soil. LC 88-22889. (Illus.). 32p. (gr. 3-6). 1989. PLB 14.60 (ISBN 0-516-08407-0); pap. 4.95 (ISBN 0-516-48407-9). Childrens.
Kehoe, Michael. The Rock Quarry Book. Kehoe, Michael, illus. LC 80-28165. 32p. (gr. k-4). 1981. PLB 9.95 (ISBN 0-87614-142-4). Carolrhoda Bks.
Lampert, David. Rocks & Minerals. (Illus.). 32p. (gr. 4-9). 1986. PLB 7.99 (ISBN 0-531-10165-7). Watts.
McGowen, Tom. Album of Rocks & Minerals. Ruth, Rod, illus. 64p. (gr. 3 up). 1981. write for info. (ISBN 0-528-82400-7). Checkerboard Pr.
—Album of Rocks & Minerals. Ruth, Rod, illus. 64p. (gr. 3-7). 1987. pap. 4.95 (ISBN 0-02-688504-2). Checkerboard Pr.
Metcalf, Doris & Marson, Ron. Rocks & Minerals. Marson, Peg, illus. 88p. 1989. tchr's. ed. 15.70 (ISBN 0-941008-23-1). Tops Learning.
Podendorf, Illa. Rocks & Minerals. LC 81-38494. (Illus.). 48p. (gr. k-4). 1982. PLB 14.60 (ISBN 0-516-01648-2); pap. 4.95 (ISBN 0-516-41648-0). Childrens.
Rocks & Minerals. (Illus.). 32p. (gr. 1-4). 1987. pap. 2.95 (ISBN 0-8431-4296-0). Price Stern.
Selsam, Millicent E. & Hunt, Joyce. A First Look at Rocks. LC 83-40394. 32p. (gr. 1-4). 1984. PLB 12.85 (ISBN 0-8027-6531-9). Walker & Co.
Zim, Herbert S. & Shaffer, Paul R. Rocks & Minerals. Perlman, Raymond, illus. (gr. 6 up). 1957. pap. write for info. (ISBN 0-307-24499-7, Golden Pr). Western Pub.

ROCKS–AGE

see Geology, Stratigraphic

ROCKY MOUNTAINS–FICTION

MacDougall, Mary-Katherine. Black Jupiter. Gruver, Kate E., ed. Moyers, William, illus. 181p. (gr. 5 up). 8.95 (ISBN 0-940175-01-0). Now Comns.
"It was late for the horses to be so high in the mountains. By this time in other years they had already found winter quarters in a lower area. But this fall they were waiting for a colt." That colt was Black Jupiter. Snow came. The horses had to leave through the rock gateway the black mare could not yet get through. The stallion stayed with her. The next dawn the colt came but did not move or make a sound. The horses left the newborn colt alone in the snow. Jim Peters, a prospector, living alone in his cabin, was sensitive to wildlife. He felt something was wrong when he heard two horses leaving a day after the herd. He found Black Jupiter alive but not strong. He took him to his cabin. There are Gregg & Jenine Jordan, children of a mining engineer, a threat to Jim & his mining plans. In turn, Jim is suspected of stealing from the surveying crew. Black Jupiter, set in the Rocky Mountains with a factual copper mining background, is a mystery story of distrust & misunderstanding, healed by love & a colt. There is a happy Christmas chapter. Black & white illustrations.
Publisher Provided Annotation.

Woods, Becky. A Rocky Mountain Rabbit. LC 90-70093. (Illus.). 86p. (gr. 4-8). 1990. 12.95 (ISBN 0-932433-65-0). Windswept Hse.

RODENTIA

Pope, Joyce. Taking Care of Your Rats & Mice. Franklin Watts Ltd., ed. (Illus.). 32p. (gr. 7-9). 1990. PLB 10.90 (ISBN 0-531-10191-6); pap. 3.95 (ISBN 0-531-15172-7). Watts.
Steinberg, Phil. You & Your Pet: Rodents & Rabbits. Cummings, Christine, illus. LC 78-54365. 64p. (gr. 4 up). 1979. PLB 6.95 (ISBN 0-8225-1256-4). Lerner Pubns.

RODEOS

Bellville, Cheryl W. Rodeo. LC 84-14981. (Illus.). 32p. (gr. k-4). 1985. PLB 12.95 (ISBN 0-87614-272-2); pap. 4.95 (ISBN 0-87614-492-X). Carolrhoda Bks.
—Rodeo. (Illus.). 32p. (gr. k-4). 1985. pap. 4.95 (ISBN 0-685-25641-3, First Ave Edns). Lerner Pubns.
Berry, Barbara. Let'er Buck: The Rodeo. 5.95 (ISBN 0-672-51521-0, Bobbs). Macmillan.
Bryant, Thomas A. Rodeo, America's Number One Sport. 2nd ed. Wagner, E. Vernel, illus. (gr. 3-5). 1986. pap. 3.00 (ISBN 0-941875-00-8, WB1). Wolverine Gallery.
Coombs, Charles. Let's Rodeo! LC 85-8696. (Illus.). 128p. (gr. 4 up). 1986. 11.95 (ISBN 0-03-001207-4). H Holt & Co.
Fain, James W. Rodeos. LC 82-23460. (Illus.). 48p. (gr. k-4). 1983. PLB 14.60 (ISBN 0-516-01685-7). Childrens.
—Rodeos. LC 82-23460. (SPA.). 48p. (gr. k-4). 1987. PLB 14.60 (ISBN 0-516-31685-0); pap. 4.95 (ISBN 0-516-51685-X). Childrens.
Svendsen, Juanita B. & Strand, Julie. Goin' to the Rodeo. Lunsford, Heather, illus. 109p. (Orig.). (gr. k-8). 1986. pap. text ed. 10.00 (ISBN 0-685-18510-9). Collaborative Learn.

RODEOS–FICTION

Bly & Stephen. Crystals Rodeo Debut. LC 85-29063. 144p. (gr. 5-7). 1986. pap. 3.95 (ISBN 0-89191-605-9). Cook.
Bryant, Bonnie. Rodeo Rider. (gr. 4 up). 1990. pap. 2.95 (ISBN 0-553-15821-X). Bantam.

ROGERS, WILL, 1879-1935

Johnson, Spencer. The Value of Humor: The Story of Will Rogers. Pileggi, Steve, illus. LC 76-41782. (gr. k-6). 1976. 9.95 (ISBN 0-916392-05-8, Pub. by Value Communications). Oak Tree Pubns.

ROGUES AND VAGABONDS–FICTION

Fitzgerald, John D. The Great Brain Reforms. LC 72-7601. (Illus.). 176p. (gr. 4-7). 1973. 12.95 (ISBN 0-8037-3067-5); PLB 11.89 (ISBN 0-8037-3068-3). Dial Bks Young.

ROLLER-SKATING–FICTION

Diestel-Feddersen, Mary. Try Again, Sally Jane. Ashley, Yvonne, illus. LC 86-42810. 30p. (gr. 2-3). 1987. PLB 12.95 (ISBN 1-55532-150-X). Gareth Stevens Inc.
Fraser, Sheila. I Can Roller Skate. Kopper, Lisa, illus. 24p. (ps-3). 1991. 5.95 (ISBN 0-8120-6228-0). Barron.

ROLLING STOCK

see Locomotives

ROMAN CATHOLIC CHURCH

see Catholic Church

ROMAN LITERATURE

see Latin Literature

ROMAN MYTHOLOGY

see Mythology, Classical

ROME

Here are entered works about the Roman Empire. works only on the modern city of Rome are entered under Rome (City).

Amery & Vanage. Rome & Romans. (gr. 4-9). 1976. (Usborne-Hayes); PLB 13.96 (ISBN 0-88110-101-X); pap. 6.95 (ISBN 0-86020-070-1). EDC.
Bombarde, Odile & Moatti, Claude. Living in Ancient Rome. Matthews, Sarah, tr. from FRE. Place, Francois, illus. LC 87-37113. 38p. (gr. k-5). 1988. 4.95 (ISBN 0-944589-08-1, 081). Young Discovery Lib.
Church, Alfred J. Roman Life in the Days of Cicero. LC 61-24994. (gr. 7-11). 20.00 (ISBN 0-8196-0105-5). Biblo.
Davis, William S. Day in Old Rome. LC 61-24993. (Illus.). (gr. 7 up). 20.00 (ISBN 0-8196-0106-3). Biblo.
Hughes, Richard. There's No Place Like Rome. Wheeler, Jill, ed. Lowery, Carol, illus. 48p. (gr. 4). 1988. lib. bdg. 10.95 (ISBN 0-939179-45-8). Abdo & Dghtrs.
James, Simon. Rome. Shone, Rob, illus. 32p. (gr. 4-6). 1987. PLB 11.90 (ISBN 0-531-10399-4). Watts.
Kurtz, Irma & Unger-Hamilton, Clive. The Children's Guide to...Rome. Winn, Chris, illus. LC 85-22995. 96p. (gr. 3 up). 1986. 6.95 (ISBN 0-87226-054-2, Bedrick Blackie). P Bedrick Bks.
Lamprey, Louise. Children of Ancient Rome. LC 61-12876. (Illus.). (gr. 7-11). 18.00 (ISBN 0-8196-0114-4). Biblo.
Mulvihill, Margaret. Roman Forts. 1990. PLB 11.90 (ISBN 0-531-17201-5). Watts.
Rutland, Jonathan. See Inside a Roman Town. rev. ed. LC 85-52276. (Illus.). 32p. (gr. 4-9). 1986. PLB 11.90 (ISBN 0-531-19014-5, Pub. by Warwick). Watts.
Wilkes, John. The Roman Army. LC 76-22463. (Illus.). 52p. (gr. 5 up). 1977. PLB 9.95 (ISBN 0-8225-1210-6). Lerner Pubns.

ROME–BIOGRAPHY

Place, Robin. The Romans: Fact & Fiction. (Illus.). 32p. 1989. 10.50 (ISBN 0-521-33267-2); pap. 5.95 (ISBN 0-521-33787-9). Cambridge U Pr.

ROME–FICTION

Hawthorne, Nathaniel. Marble Faun. Fisher, N. H., intro. by. (gr. 11 up). pap. 1.95 (ISBN 0-8049-0104-X, CL-104). Airmont.

ROME–HISTORY

Abbott, Frank F. The Common People of Ancient Rome: Studies of Roman Life & Literature. LC 65-23487. (gr. 7 up). 1965. Repr. of 1911 ed. 20.00 (ISBN 0-8196-0157-8). Biblo.
—A History & Description of Roman Political Institutions. 3rd ed. LC 63-10766. 451p. (gr. 7 up). 1910. 20.00 (ISBN 0-8196-0117-9). Biblo.
—Society & Politics in Ancient Rome: Essays & Sketches. LC 63-10767. 267p. (gr. 7 up). 1909. 20.00 (ISBN 0-8196-0118-7). Biblo.
Artman, John. Ancient Rome. 64p. (gr. 4-8). 1991. 6.95 (ISBN 0-86653-638-8, GA1343). Good Apple.
Ballard, Robert D. Lost Wreck of the Isis. (gr. 4-7). 1990. 15.95 (ISBN 0-590-43852-2); pap. 6.95 (ISBN 0-590-43853-0). Scholastic Inc.
Brandt, Keith. Ancient Rome. Frenck, Hal, illus. LC 84-2684. 32p. (gr. 3-6). 1985. PLB 9.49 (ISBN 0-8167-0298-5); pap. text ed. 2.95 (ISBN 0-8167-0299-3). Troll Assocs.
Burland, Cottie A. Ancient Rome. (Illus.). (gr. 4-8). 1974. Repr. of 1958 ed. 8.95 (ISBN 0-7175-0015-2). Dufour.
Burrell, Roy. The Romans. Connolly, Peter, illus. 128p. (gr. 5-9). 1991. bds. 16.95 (ISBN 0-19-917162-9, 5084). Oxford U Pr.
Chisholm, Jan. Living in Roman Times. McCaig, Rob, illus. 24p. (gr. 3-6). 1982. pap. 4.50 (ISBN 0-86020-619-X); lib. bdg. 11.96 (ISBN 0-88110-105-2). EDC.
Hall, Andy & Hall, Maggie. The Romans Pop-Up. (Illus.). 32p. (Orig.). (gr. 3 up). 1985. pap. 6.95 (ISBN 0-906212-29-4). Parkwest Pubns.
Hodge, Peter. Roman House. (Illus.). 64p. (Orig.). (gr. 7-12). 1971. pap. text ed. 9.00 (ISBN 0-582-20300-7, 70709). Longman.
Lamprey, Louise. Children of Ancient Gaul. LC 60-16708. (Illus.). (gr. 7-11). 18.00 (ISBN 0-8196-0109-8). Biblo.
Moore, Frank G. The Roman's World. LC 65-23486. (Illus.). 502p. (gr. 7 up). 1936. 22.00 (ISBN 0-8196-0155-1). Biblo.
Odijk, Pamela. The Romans. (Illus.). 48p. (gr. 5-8). 1989. PLB 16.98 (ISBN 0-382-09885-4). Silver Burdett Pr.
The Roman World. 64p. (gr. 4-8). 1990. 13.95 (ISBN 0-86307-994-6). Marshall Cavendish.
The Romans. (Illus.). (gr. 5 up). 1990. pap. 3.50. Ladybird Bks.
Tingay, G. & Marks, A. The Romans. (Illus.). 96p. 1990. PLB 15.96 (ISBN 0-88110-439-6); pap. 9.95 (ISBN 0-7460-0340-4). EDC.
Whitehead, Albert C. The Standard Bearer: A Story of Army Life in the Time of Caesar. (Illus.). (gr. 7-11). 1943. 18.00 (ISBN 0-8196-0116-0). Biblo.

ROME–HISTORY–FICTION

Anderson, Paul L. Pugnax the Gladiator. LC 61-1111. (Illus.). (gr. 7-11). 1939. 15.00 (ISBN 0-8196-0104-7). Biblo.
—With the Eagles. LC 57-9447. (Illus.). (gr. 7-11). 1929. 18.00 (ISBN 0-8196-0100-4). Biblo.
Church, Alfred J. Lucius, Adventures of a Roman Boy. LC 60-16706. (gr. 7-11). 18.00 (ISBN 0-8196-0108-X). Biblo.

Wallace, Lewis. Ben Hur. 450p. 1981. Repr. lib. bdg. 24. 95x (ISBN 0-89966-289-7). Buccaneer Bks.
Wells, Reuben F. With Caesar's Legions. LC 60-16709. (Illus.). (gr. 7-11). 1951. 18.00 (ISBN 0-8196-0110-1). Biblo.
ROME-HISTORY-REPUBLIC, 510-30 B.C.
Judson, Harry P. Caesar's Army: A Study of the Military Art of the Romans in the Last Days of the Republic. LC 61-12877. (Illus.). 127p. (gr. 7 up). 1888. 22.00 (ISBN 0-8196-0113-6). Biblo.
ROME-HISTORY-EMPIRE, 30 B.C.-476 A.D.
Hughes, Jill. Imperial Rome. rev. ed. Lapper, Ivan, illus. LC 85-80644. 32p. (gr. 5-7). 1985. PLB 11.90 (ISBN 0-531-17003-9). Watts.
Roman Centurion. (Illus.). (gr. 3-8). lib. bdg. 14.00 (ISBN 0-86592-140-7). Rourke Corp.
ROOSEVELT, ELEANOR (ROOSEVELT) 1884-1962
Adler, David A. A Picture Book of Eleanor Roosevelt. Casilla, Robert, illus. LC 90-39212. 32p. (gr. k-3). 1991. PLB 14.95 (ISBN 0-8234-0856-6). Holiday.
Faber, Doris. Eleanor Roosevelt: First Lady of the World. Ruff, Donna, photos by. LC 84-20861. (Illus.). 64p. (gr. 2-6). 1985. pap. 10.95 (ISBN 0-670-80551-3). Viking Child Bks.
—Eleanor Roosevelt: First Lady of the World. Ruff, Doris, illus. 64p. (gr. 2-6). 1986. pap. 3.95 (ISBN 0-14-032103-9, Puffin). Puffin Bks.
Jacobs, William J. Eleanor Roosevelt: A Life of Happiness & Tears. (Illus.). (gr. 5-8). 1981. 10.95 (ISBN 0-698-20585-5, Coward). Putnam Pub Group.
Johnson, Ann D. The Value of Caring: The Story of Eleanor Roosevelt. LC 77-6656. (Illus.). (gr. k-6). 1977. 9.95 (ISBN 0-916392-11-2, Pub. by Value Communications). Oak Tree Pubns.
Sabin, Francene. Young Eleanor Roosevelt. Ramsey, Marcy D., illus. LC 89-33939. 48p. (gr. 4-6). 1989. PLB 10.79 (ISBN 0-8167-1779-6); pap. text ed. 2.95 (ISBN 0-8167-1780-X). Troll Assocs.
Toor, Rachel. Eleanor Roosevelt. Horner, Matina S., intro. by. (Illus.). 112p. (gr. 5 up). 1989. 17.95 (ISBN 1-55546-674-5). Chelsea Hse.
Weil, Ann. Eleanor Roosevelt. (Illus.). 192p. (gr. 2-6). 1989. pap. 3.95 (ISBN 0-689-71348-7, Aladdin). Macmillan Child Grp.
Winner, David. Eleanor Roosevelt: Defender of Human Rights & Democracy. LC 91-291. (Illus.). 68p. (gr. 5-6). 1991. PLB 13.95 (ISBN 0-8368-0218-7). Gareth Stevens Inc.
ROOSEVELT, FRANKLIN DELANO, PRESIDENT U. S. 1882-1945
Cross, Robin. Roosevelt: And the Americans at War. (Illus.). 64p. (gr. 5-8). 1990. PLB 11.90 (ISBN 0-531-17254-6). Watts.
Devaney, John. Franklin Delano Roosevelt, President. LC 86-46254. (Illus.). 76p. (gr. 5-9). 1987. 12.95 (ISBN 0-8027-6713-3); PLB 13.85 (ISBN 0-8027-6714-1). Walker & Co.
Farr, Naunerle C. Abraham Lincoln - Franklin D. Roosevelt. Redondo, Nestor & LoFamia, Jun, illus. (gr. 4-12). 1979. pap. text ed. 2.95 (ISBN 0-88301-354-1); wkbk. 1.25 (ISBN 0-88301-378-9). Pendulum Pr.
Freedman, Russell. Franklin Delano Roosevelt. (Illus.). 208p. (gr. 4 up). 1990. 16.95 (ISBN 0-89919-379-X, Clarion Bks). HM.
Greenblatt, Miriam. Franklin D. Roosevelt: Thirty-Second President of the United States. Young, Richard G., ed. LC 87-36121. (Illus.). (gr. 5-9). 1989. PLB 17.26 (ISBN 0-944483-06-2). Garrett Ed Corp.
Hacker, Jeffrey. Franklin D. Roosevelt. large type ed. (Illus.). 176p. (gr. 4-8). 1991. Repr. of 1983 ed. PLB 17.95 (ISBN 1-55905-096-9). Grey Castle.
Hacker, Jeffrey H. Franklin D. Roosevelt. (Illus.). 128p. (gr. 7 up). 1983. PLB 12.90 (ISBN 0-531-04592-7). Watts.
Israel, Fred L. Franklin D. Roosevelt. (Illus.). 112p. (gr. 5 up). 1985. lib. bdg. 17.95x (ISBN 0-87754-573-1); pap. 9.95 (ISBN 0-7910-0599-2). Chelsea Hse.
Italia, Bob. Franklin D. Roosevelt. Walner, Rosemary, ed. (Illus.). 32p. (gr. 4). 1990. PLB 11.95 (ISBN 0-939179-82-2). Abdo & Dghtrs.
Larsen, Rebecca. Franklin D. Roosevelt: Man of Destiny. (Illus.). 224p. (gr. 9-12). 1991. 14.95 (ISBN 0-531-15231-6); PLB 14.90 (ISBN 0-531-11068-0). Watts.
Osinski, Alice. Franklin D. Roosevelt. (Illus.). 100p. (gr. 3 up). 1989. PLB 17.27 (ISBN 0-516-01395-5); pap. 6.95 (ISBN 0-516-41395-3). Childrens.
Schlesinger, Arthur, Jr., intro. by. Franklin Roosevelt. (Illus.). 128p. (gr. 7-12). PLB 16.95 (ISBN 0-685-21876-7, 087250). Know Unltd.
Shebar, Sharon. Franklin D. Roosevelt & the New Deal. (Illus.). 144p. (gr. 3-6). 1987. pap. 4.95 (ISBN 0-8120-3916-5). Barron.
Sullivan, Wilson. Franklin Delano Roosevelt. LC 73-105906. 154p. (gr. 7 up). 1970. PLB 16.89 (ISBN 0-06-026087-4). HarpC Child Bks.
ROOSEVELT, FRANKLIN DELANO, PRESIDENT U. S. 1882-1945-DRAMA
Franklin D. Roosevelt Mini-Play: Mini-Play, 2 pts. (gr. 8 up). 1978. 6.50 ea.; Pt. 1. (ISBN 0-89550-314-X); Pt. 2. (ISBN 0-89550-319-0). Stevens & Shea.
ROOSEVELT, THEODORE, PRESIDENT U. S. 1858-1919
Kent, Zachary. Theodore Roosevelt. LC 87-35184. (Illus.). 100p. (gr. 3 up). 1988. PLB 17.27 (ISBN 0-516-01354-8); pap. 6.95 (ISBN 0-516-41354-6). Childrens.
McCafferty, Jim. Holt & the Teddy Bear. Davis, Florence S., illus. 40p. (gr. k-3). 1991. 12.95 (ISBN 0-88289-823-X). Pelican.
Markham, Lois. Theodore Roosevelt. large type ed. (Illus.). 96p. (gr. 4-8). 1991. Repr. of 1985 ed. PLB 17. 95 (ISBN 1-55905-098-5). Grey Castle.
Parks, Edd W. Teddy Roosevelt: All-Round Boy. Morrow, Gray, illus. 192p. (gr. 2-6). 1989. pap. 3.95 (ISBN 0-689-71349-5, Aladdin). Macmillan Child Grp.
Quackenbush, Robert. Don't You Dare Shoot That Bear. LC 84-4693. 1990. 11.95 (ISBN 0-671-66295-3, Wallaby); pap. 3.95 (ISBN 0-671-69440-5). S&S Trade.
Sabin, Lou. Teddy Roosevelt, Rough Rider. Baxter, Robert, illus. LC 85-1090. 48p. (gr. 4-6). 1985. lib. bdg. 10.79 (ISBN 0-8167-0555-0); pap. text ed. 2.95 (ISBN 0-8167-0556-9). Troll Assocs.
Stefoff, Rebecca. Theodore Roosevelt: 26th President of the United States. Young, Richard G., ed. LC 87-35953. (Illus.). (gr. 5-9). 1988. PLB 17.26 (ISBN 0-944483-09-7). Garrett Ed Corp.
Theodore Roosevelt: Mini-Play. (gr. 5 up). 1979. 6.50 (ISBN 0-89550-316-6). Stevens & Shea.
Whitelaw, Nancy. Theodore Roosevelt Takes Charge. Levine, Abby, ed. 176p. (gr. 4-8). 1991. 11.95 (ISBN 0-8075-7849-5). A Whitman.
ROOSEVELT, THEODORE, PRESIDENT U. S. 1858-1919-FICTION
Kay, Helen. The First Teddy Bear. Detwiler, Susan, illus. LC 85-2706. 40p. (gr. 1 up). 1985. 12.95 (ISBN 0-88045-042-8). Stemmer Hse.
Monjo, F. N. The One Bad Thing about Father. Negri, Rocco, illus. LC 71-85036. 64p. (gr. k-3). 1987. pap. 3.50 (ISBN 0-06-444110-5, Trophy). HarpC Child Bks.
ROOSTERS-FICTION
Berrill, Margaret. Chanticleer. Bottomley, Jane, illus. LC 86-6746. 32p. (gr. 2-5). PLB 16.67 (ISBN 0-8172-2626-5). Raintree Pubs.
Crawford, Thomas. Rooster Who Refused to Crow. (Illus.). (gr. 3-4). 1972. pap. 1.95 (ISBN 0-89375-050-6). Troll Assocs.
Fox, Robin. Poulet: A Rooster Who Laid Eggs. (FRE., Illus.). 3.50 (ISBN 0-685-11509-7). French & Eur.
Ginsburg, Mirra. The Magic Stove. Heller, Linda, illus. LC 82-12523. (gr. 2-4). 1983. 11.95 (ISBN 0-698-20566-9, Coward). Putnam Pub Group.
Peet, Bill. Cock-a-Doodle Dudley. Peet, Bill, illus. 48p. (gr. k-3). 1990. 14.95 (ISBN 0-395-55331-8). HM.
Peters, Sharon. The Rooster & the Weather Vane. Harvey, Paul, illus. LC 86-30838. 32p. (gr. k-2). 1987. PLB 7.06 (ISBN 0-8167-0980-7); pap. text ed. 1.95 (ISBN 0-8167-0981-5). Troll Assocs.
Soler, Dona K. For Love of Henry. (Illus.). 52p. (gr. 4-7). 1985. 5.95 (ISBN 0-8059-2974-6). Dorrance.
Toepperwein, Emilie & Toepperwein, Fritz. Chinto, The Chaparral Cock. (gr. 4-7). 2.95 (ISBN 0-910722-04-8). Highland Pr.
ROPE
Severn, Bill. Magic with Rope, Ribbon, & String. 224p. (gr. 6 up). 1981. 9.95 (ISBN 0-679-20813-5). McKay.
ROSH HASHONAH
Bin-Nun, Judy & Einhorn, Franne. Rosh Hashanah: A Holiday Funtext. Steinberger, Heidi, illus. (gr. 1-3). 1978. pap. 5.00 (ISBN 0-8074-0230-3, 101300). UAHC.
Chaikin, Miriam. Sound the Shofar: The Story & Meaning of Rosh HaShanah & Yom Kippur. Weihs, Erika, illus. LC 86-2651. 96p. (gr. 3-7). 1986. 13.95 (ISBN 0-89919-373-0, Pub. by Clarion); pap. 5.95 (ISBN 0-89919-427-3, Pub. by Clarion). Ticknor & Fields.
Eisenberg, Ann. I Can Celebrate. Schanzer, Roz, illus. LC 88-83567. 12p. (ps). 1989. bds. 4.95 (ISBN 0-930494-93-8). Kar Ben.
Friedman, Audrey M. & Zwerin, Raymond. High Holy Day Do It Yourself Dictionary. Ruten, Marlene L., illus. 32p. (gr. k-3). 1983. pap. 5.00 (ISBN 0-8074-0162-5, 101100). UAHC.
Gellman, Ellie. It's Rosh-Hashanah. Kahn, Katherine J., illus. LC 85-80783. 12p. (ps). 1985. bds. 4.95 (ISBN 0-930494-50-4). Kar Ben.
Goldin, Barbara D. World's Birthday. LC 89-29208. (ps-3). 1990. 13.95 (ISBN 0-15-299648-6). HarbraceJ.
Levin, Carol. A Rosh Hashanah Walk. Kahn, Katherine J., illus. LC 87-3106. (ps-3). 1987. 3.95 (ISBN 0-930494-70-9). Kar Ben.
Simon, Norma. Rosh Hashanah. Gordon, Ayala, illus. (ps-k). 1961. plastic cover 4.50 (ISBN 0-8381-0700-1). United Syn Bk.
ROSS, BETSY (GRISCOM) 1752-1836
Weil, Ann. Betsy Ross: Designer of Our Flag. LC 83-6375. 1983. pap. write for info. (ISBN 0-672-52785-5). Macmillan Child Grp.
—Betsy Ross: Designer of Our Flag. Fiorentino, Al, illus. LC 86-10775. 192p. (gr. 2 up). 1986. pap. 3.95 (ISBN 0-02-042120-6, Aladdin). Macmillan Child Grp.
ROUND TABLE
see Arthur, King
ROUTES OF TRADE
see Trade Routes
ROWING
Rowing. (Illus.). 48p. (gr. 6-12). 1981. pap. 1.85 (ISBN 0-8395-3392-6, 3392). BSA.
ROYALTY
see Kings and Rulers
RUBBER
Dineen, Jacqueline. Rubber. 32p. (gr. 4-8). 1988. lib. bdg. 12.95 (ISBN 0-89490-222-9). Enslow Pubs.
Graham, Ada & Graham, Frank. The Big Stretch: The Complete Book of the Amazing Rubber Band. Rosenblum, Richard, illus. LC 83-25615. 81p. (gr. 3-7). 1985. 9.95 (ISBN 0-394-85758-5). Knopf.
Mitgutsch, Ali. From Rubber Tree to Tire. Lerner, Mark, tr. from GER. Mitgutsch, Ali, illus. 24p. (ps-3). 1986. lib. bdg. 6.95 (ISBN 0-87614-297-8). Carolrhoda Bks.
RUINS
see Cities and Towns, Ruined, Extinct, Etc.
RULERS
see Kings and Rulers
RULES OF ORDER
see Parliamentary Practice
RUMANIA
Carran, Betty B. Romania. LC 87-35423. (Illus.). 124p. (gr. 4-8). 1988. PLB 25.27 (ISBN 0-516-02703-4). Childrens.
Lye, Keith. Take a Trip to Romania. Franklin Watts Ltd., ed. (Illus.). 32p. (ps-9). 1988. PLB 7.99 (ISBN 0-531-10468-0). Watts.
Stewart, Gail B. Romania. LC 90-24946. (Illus.). 48p. (gr. 5-6). 1991. RSBE 10.95 (ISBN 0-89686-600-9, Crestwood Hse). Macmillan Child Grp.
RUNAWAYS
Walsh, Joy & Fuda, Siri, eds. Life Junkies: On Our Own. (Illus.). 200p. (Orig.). (gr. 9-12). 1990. pap. 8.00 (ISBN 0-938838-51-2). Textile Bridge.
RUNAWAYS-FICTION
Alexander, Martha. And My Mean Old Mother Will Be Sorry, Blackboard Bear. Alexander, Martha, illus. LC 72-707. 32p. (ps-2). 1985. PLB 10.89 (ISBN 0-8037-0593-X). Dial Bks Young.
Bunting, Eve. The Hideout. D'Andrade, Diane, ed. 144p. (gr. 4-8). 1991. 14.95 (ISBN 0-15-233990-6). HarBraceJ.
Cleary, Beverly. Runaway Ralph. 176p. (gr. k-6). 1981. pap. 3.25 (ISBN 0-440-47519-8, YB). Dell.
Corcoran, Barbara. The Hideaway. LC 86-28849. 128p. (gr. 5-9). 1987. 12.95 (ISBN 0-689-31353-5, Atheneum Child Bk). Macmillan Child Grp.
Dragonwagon, Crescent & Zindel, Paul. To Take a Dare. LC 80-8441. 256p. (gr. 7 up). 1982. 12.95i (ISBN 0-06-026858-1); PLB 12.89 (ISBN 0-06-026859-X). HarpC Child Bks.
Garden, Nancy. Lark in the Morning. 288p. (gr. 9-12). 1991. 14.95 (ISBN 0-374-34338-1). FS&G.
Greenburg, Dan. The Bed Who Ran away from Home. Wallner, John, illus. LC 87-35144. 32p. (ps-3). 1991. 14.95 (ISBN 0-06-022279-4); PLB 14.89 (ISBN 0-06-022280-8). HarpC Child Bks.
Gregory, Kristiana. Legend of Jimmy Spoon. 1990. 15.95 (ISBN 0-15-200506-4). HarbraceJ.
Hamilton, Morse. Effie's House. LC 89-11918. 224p. (gr. 7 up). 1990. 13.95 (ISBN 0-688-09307-8). Greenwillow.
Jenkins, Jerry B. Good Sport, Bad Sport. (gr. 4-7). 1990. pap. 4.50 (ISBN 0-8024-0810-9). Moody.
—Two Runaways. (gr. 4-7). 1990. pap. 4.50 (ISBN 0-8024-0806-0). Moody.
—Yo Yo & Midnight. (gr. 4-7). 1990. pap. 4.50 (ISBN 0-8024-0809-5). Moody.
Jones, Adrienne. The Hawks of Chelney. Gammell, Stephen, illus. LC 77-11855. (gr. 7-9). 1978. 13.95 (ISBN 0-06-023057-6). HarpC Child Bks.
—Street Family. LC 85-45844. 288p. (gr. 7 up). 1987. PLB 13.89 (ISBN 0-06-023050-9). HarpC Child Bks.
Konigsburg, E. L. From the Mixed-Up Files of Mrs. Basil E. Frankweiler. 1987. pap. 3.95 (ISBN 0-689-71181-6, Aladdin). Macmillan Child Grp.
Lexau, Joan M. Emily & the Klunky Baby & the Next-Door Dog. Alexander, Martha, illus. LC 77-181789. 40p. (ps-3). 1972. 5.95 (ISBN 0-8037-2309-1); PLB 7.89 (ISBN 0-8037-2310-5). Dial Bks Young.
Major, Kevin. Hold Fast. 176p. (gr. 7 up). 1981. pap. 3.25 (ISBN 0-440-93756-6, LE). Dell.
O'Dell, Scott. Kathleen, Please Come Home. LC 78-3567. (gr. 7 up). 1978. 12.95 (ISBN 0-395-26453-7). HM.
Paulsen, Gary. Tiltawhirl John. 1990. pap. 3.95 (ISBN 0-14-034312-1, Puffin). Puffin Bks.
Pearson, Gayle. The Coming Home Cafe. LC 88-3448. 208p. (gr. 6 up). 1988. 14.95 (ISBN 0-689-31338-1, Atheneum Child Bk). Macmillan Child Grp.
Robins, Joan. Addie Runs Away. Truesdell, Sue, illus. LC 88-24350. 32p. (ps-2). 1991. pap. 3.50 (ISBN 0-06-444147-4, Trophy). HarpC Child Bks.
Shreve, Susan. The Revolution of Mary Leary. LC 82-185. 192p. (gr. 5-9). 1982. Knopf.
Silverstein, Alvin & Silverstein, Virginia B. Runaway Sugar: All about Diabetes. Barton, Harriett, illus. LC 80-8727. 48p. (gr. 3-5). 1981. PLB 12.89 (ISBN 0-397-31929-0, Lipp Jr Bks). HarpC Child Bks.
Thomas, Ruth. The Runaways. LC 88-8229. 304p. (gr. 3-7). 1989. 13.95 (ISBN 0-397-32344-1, Lipp Jr Bks); PLB 13.89 (ISBN 0-397-32345-X, Lipp Jr Bks). HarpC Child Bks.
Van Raven, Pieter. Pickle & Price. LC 89-10846. 224p. (gr. 7 up). 1990. 13.95 (ISBN 0-684-19162-8, Scribners Young Read). Macmillan Child Grp.
RUNNING
see Track Athletics
RURAL ARCHITECTURE
see Architecture, Domestic
RURAL LIFE
see Country Life; Outdoor Life

RURAL LIFE–FICTION

Casad, Mary B. Bluebonnet of the Hill Country. Binder, Pat, illus. (gr. k-4). 1983. 9.95 (ISBN 0-89015-395-7, Pub. by Panda Bks). Eakin Pr.

Kresel, Maryann. Thoughts of Yesterday. (Illus.). 106p. (Orig.). 1989. pap. 9.95 (ISBN 0-944958-37-0). Elfin Cove Pr.

RUSSELL, BILL, 1934-

Shapiro, Miles. Bill Russell. King, Coretta Scott, intro. by. (Illus.). 112p. (gr. 5 up). 1991. PLB 17.95 (ISBN 0-7910-1136-4). Chelsea Hse.

RUSSIAN LANGUAGE

Amery, Heather & Kirilenko, Katrina. The First Thousand Words in Russian. Cartwright, Stephen, illus. 64p. (gr. k-7). 1983. 11.95 (ISBN 0-86020-769-2). EDC.

Anpilogova, B. G., et al. Foundation Dictionary of Russian: Three Thousand High Semantic Frequency Words. (RUS & ENG.). 178p. (gr. 9-12). 1967. pap. 4.95 (ISBN 0-486-21860-0). Dover.

RUSSIAN LITERATURE–COLLECTIONS

Morton, Miriam, ed. A Harvest of Russian Children's Literature. Viguers, Ruth H., frwd. by. LC 67-21384. (Illus.). (ps up). 1967. 47.50x (ISBN 0-520-00886-3). U of Cal Pr.

RUSSIAN SATELLITE COUNTRIES
see Communist Countries

RUSSIANS IN THE U. S.

Eubank, Nancy. The Russians in America. LC 72-3598. (Illus.). 96p. (gr. 5 up). 1979. PLB 11.95 (ISBN 0-8225-0226-7); pap. 3.95 (ISBN 0-8225-1021-9). Lerner Pubns.

RUSSWURM, JOHN BROWN, 1799-1851

Borzendowski, Janice. John Russwurm. (Illus.). 112p. (gr. 5 up). 1989. 17.95 (ISBN 1-55546-610-9). Chelsea Hse.

RUTH (BIBLICAL CHARACTER)

Alexander, Matilda. Ruth. Butcher, Sam, illus. 48p. (gr. k-6). 1972. pap. text ed. 9.45 (ISBN 1-55976-017-6). CEF Press.

Barrett, Ethel. Ruth. LC 80-52961. 128p. (gr. 3-9). 1980. pap. 3.95 (ISBN 0-8307-0764-6, 5810418). Regal.

Parris, Paula. Ruth: Woman of Courage. Cassell, Robert, illus. (gr. 1-6). 1977. bds. 5.95 (ISBN 0-8054-4229-4, 4242-29). Broadman.

RUTH, GEORGE HERMAN, 1895-1948

Babe Ruth. 48p. (gr. 5-6). 1989. PLB 10.95 (ISBN 0-685-26354-1). Capstone Pr.

Bains, Rae. Babe Ruth. Smolinski, Dick, illus. LC 84-2595. 32p. (gr. 3-6). 1985. PLB 9.49 (ISBN 0-8167-0144-X); pap. text ed. 2.95 (ISBN 0-8167-0145-8). Troll Assocs.

Berke, Art. Babe Ruth: The Best There Ever Was. Rakos, Jennie, ed. (Illus.). 128p. (gr. 7-9). 1988. PLB 13.90 (ISBN 0-531-10472-9). Watts.

Brandt, Keith. Babe Ruth, Home Run Hero. Frenck, Hal, illus. LC 85-1091. 48p. (gr. 4-6). 1985. lib. bdg. 10.79 (ISBN 0-8167-0553-4); pap. text ed. 2.95 (ISBN 0-8167-0554-2). Troll Assocs.

Eisenberg, Lisa. The Story of Babe Ruth. (gr. k-6). 1990. pap. 2.95 (ISBN 0-440-40274-3, YB). Dell.

Farr, Naunerle C. Babe Ruth-Jackie Robinson. Caravana, Tony & Cruz, Nardo, illus. (gr. 4-12). 1979. pap. text ed. 2.95 (ISBN 0-88301-359-2); wkbk 1.25 (ISBN 0-88301-383-5). Pendulum Pr.

Macht, Norm. Babe Ruth. Murray, Jim, intro. by. (Illus.). 64p. (gr. 3 up). 1991. PLB 14.95 (ISBN 0-7910-1189-5). Chelsea Hse.

Van Riper, Guernsey, Jr. Babe Ruth: One of Baseball's Greatest. Fleishman, Seymour, illus. LC 86-10957. 192p. (gr. 2-6). 1986. pap. 3.95 (ISBN 0-02-042130-3, Aladdin). Macmillan Child Grp.

S

SABBATH

Groner, Judye & Wikler, Madeline. Shabbat Shalom. Yaffa, illus. LC 88-83568. 12p. (ps) 1989. bds. 4.95 (ISBN 0-930494-91-1). Kar Ben.

Kobre, Faige. A Sense of Shabbat. LC 89-40361. (Illus.). 32p. 1990. 11.95 (ISBN 0-933873-44-1). Torah Aura. In the sensuous photographs & simple text which make up this picture book, the taste, feel, sound, look & touch of Shabbat all make themselves manifest. The Shabbat presented here is at once holy & wonderous, & simultaneously, comfortable & familiar. It is a book the reader will go back to over & over. This book is a treasure.
Publisher Provided Annotation.

Robinson, Glen. Fifty-Two Things to Do on Sabbath. Wheeler, Gerald, ed. Kinzer, Kaaren, illus. (Orig.). 1983. pap. 2.95 (ISBN 0-8280-0199-5). Review & Herald.

Saypol, Judyth R. & Wikler, Madeline. Come Let Us Welcome Shabbat. LC 83-25638. (Illus.). 32p. (ps up) 1978. pap. 2.95 (ISBN 0-930494-04-0). Kar Ben.

Simon, Norma. Every Friday Night. Weiss, Harvey, illus. (ps-k). plastic cover 4.50 (ISBN 0-8381-0708-7). United Syn Bk.

SABBATH–FICTION

Ashton, Leila M. Today Is Friday. (Illus.). (ps-1). 1978. pap. 1.95 (ISBN 0-8127-0176-3). Review & Herald.

Blundell, Tony. Joe on Sunday. LC 86-30944. (Illus.). 32p. (ps-2). 1987. 10.95 (ISBN 0-8037-0446-1). Dial Bks Young.

SABIN, FLORENCE, 1871-1953

Kronstadt, Janet. Florence Sabin. Horner, Matina S., intro. by. (Illus.). 112p. (gr. 5 up). 1990. 17.95 (ISBN 1-55546-676-1). Chelsea Hse.

SACAJAWEA, 1786-1884

Bryant, Martha F. Sacajawea: A Native American Heroine. Gilliland, Hap, ed. Sargent, Heather & Gilliland, Hap, illus. 256p. (Orig.). 1989. 21.95 (ISBN 0-89992-420-4); pap. 15.95 (ISBN 0-89992-120-5). Coun India Ed.

Gleiter, Jan & Thompson, Kathleen. Sacagawea. Miyake, Yoshi, illus. 32p. (gr. 2-5). 1987. PLB 16.67 (ISBN 0-8172-2651-6); pap. 9.27 (ISBN 0-8172-2655-9). Raintree Pubs.

Jassem, Kate. Sacajawea, Wilderness Guide. new ed. LC 78-60118. (Illus.). 48p. (gr. 4-6). 1979. PLB 9.89 (ISBN 0-89375-160-X); pap. 2.95 (ISBN 0-89375-150-2). Troll Assocs.

Johnson, Ann D. The Value of Adventure: The Story of Sacajawea. LC 80-17623. (Illus.). 66p. (gr. k-6). 1980. 9.95 (ISBN 0-916392-59-7, Pub. by Value Communications). Oak Tree Pubns.

O'Dell, Scott. Streams to the River, River to the Sea: A Novel of Sacagawea. 1986. 14.95 (ISBN 0-395-40430-4). HM.

Seymour, Flora W. Sacagawea: American Pathfinder. Doremus, Robert, illus. 192p. (gr. 3-7). 1991. pap. 3.95 (ISBN 0-689-71482-3, Aladdin). Macmillan Child Grp.

SACRED ART
see Christian Art and Symbolism

SACRED MUSIC
see Church Music

SAFETY EDUCATION
see also Accidents–Prevention

Los Animales Pueden Ser Amigos Especiales. LC 84-23300. (SPA., Illus.). 32p. (ps-2). 1987. PLB 14.60 (ISBN 0-516-31978-7); pap. 3.95 (ISBN 0-516-51978-6). Childrens.

Bailie, Linda. Safe & Sound: Country & Backyard. (ps up). 1989. PLB 3.98 (ISBN 0-7924-5159-7, Mallard Pr). BDD Promo Bk.

—Safe & Sound: Town & Home. (ps up). 1989. PLB 3.98 (ISBN 0-7924-5158-9, Mallard Pr). BDD Promo Bk.

Bank Street College of Education Staff. Let's Stay Safe & Sound. (gr. 1-2). 1986. pap. 2.95 (ISBN 0-8120-3622-0). Barron.

Berry, Joy. Every Kid's Guide to Responding to Danger. Bartholomew, illus. 48p. (gr. 3-7). 1987. 4.95 (ISBN 0-516-21415-2); PLB 14.60 (ISBN 0-516-01415-3). Childrens.

Boyer. Let's Walk Safely. LC 80-82953. (Illus.). 32p. (gr. 1-6). 1981. PLB 9.95 (ISBN 0-87783-159-9). Oddo.

—Oddo Safety Series. (Illus.). (ps-6). Set of 4 vols. PLB 44.60 (ISBN 0-87783-170-X); three cassettes o.s.i. 23.82x (ISBN 0-87783-235-8). Oddo.

Brady, Janeen. Safety Kids Personal Safety, Vol. 1. Underwood, Oscar, tr. (SPA., Orig.). (gr. k-6). 1984. dialogue bk. 1.25 (ISBN 0-944803-18-0); Trans. by Oscar Underwood, in Spanish, 1984, 6pgs. pap. text ed. 1.25 dialogue bk. (ISBN 0-944803-19-9); songbk. 5.95 (ISBN 0-944803-15-6); act. bk. 2.25 (ISBN 0-944803-16-4); cassette & bk. 9.95 (ISBN 0-944803-17-2). Brite Intl.

—Safety Kids Personal Safety, Vol. 1. Twede, Evan, illus. 14p. (gr. k-6). 1983. Set of 20. wkbk. 12.00 (ISBN 0-944803-20-2). Brite Intl.

—Safety Kids Play it Smart: Stay Safe from Drugs, Vol. 2. Twede, Evan, illus. 14p. (gr. k-6). 1985. Set of 20. wkbk. 12.00 (ISBN 0-944803-25-3). Brite Intl.

Buschman, Janis & Hunley, Debbie. Strangers Don't Look Like the Big Bad Wolf! Lyons, Carole & Meyer, Linda D., eds. Megale, Marina, illus. McMorris, Sharon, intro. by. LC 85-80513. (Illus.). 38p. (Orig.). (gr. 2-4). 1985. lib. bdg. 9.00 (ISBN 0-932091-04-0); pap. 3.95 (ISBN 0-932091-05-9). Franklin Pr WA.

Carratello, Patricia. Let's Investigate Health & Safety. Carratello, Patricia, illus. 48p. (gr. 1-4). 1984. wkbk. 5.95 (ISBN 1-55734-214-8). Tchr Create Mat.

Chlad, Dorothy. Los Cerillos, los Encendedores y los Triquitraques No Son Juguetes. Halverson, Lydia, illus. LC 81-18125. (SPA.). 32p. (ps-2). 1987. PLB 14.60 (ISBN 0-516-31982-5); pap. 3.95 (ISBN 0-516-51982-4). Childrens.

—Cuando cruzo la calle. Kratky, Lada, tr. Halverson, Lydia, illus. LC 85-31397. (SPA.). 32p. (ps-2). 1986. PLB 14.60 (ISBN 0-516-31985-X); pap. 3.95 (ISBN 0-516-51985-9). Childrens.

—Cuando viajo en auto (When I Ride in a Car). Halverson, Lydia, illus. LC 83-7382. (ENG & SPA.). 32p. (ps-2). 1989. PLB 14.60 (ISBN 0-516-31987-6); pap. 3.95 (ISBN 0-516-51987-5). Childrens.

—Matches, Lighters, & Firecrackers Are not Toys. LC 81-18125. (Illus.). (gr. k-3). 1982. PLB 14.60 (ISBN 0-516-01982-1); pap. 3.95 (ISBN 0-516-41982-X). Childrens.

—Playing on the Playground. Halverson, Lydia, illus. LC 87-5197. 32p. (ps-2). 1987. PLB 14.60 (ISBN 0-516-01989-9); pap. 3.95 (ISBN 0-516-41989-7). Childrens.

—Strangers. LC 81-18109. (Illus.). (gr. k-3). 1982. PLB 14.60 (ISBN 0-516-01984-8); pap. 3.95 (ISBN 0-516-41984-6). Childrens.

—Viajando en Autobus (Riding on a Bus) Halverson, Lydia, illus. LC 85-12570. (SPA.). 32p. (ps-2). 1988. PLB 14.60 (ISBN 0-516-31979-5); pap. 3.95 (ISBN 0-516-51979-4). Childrens.

—When I Cross the Street. LC 81-18108. (Illus.). (gr. k-3). 1982. PLB 14.60 (ISBN 0-516-01985-6); pap. 3.95 (ISBN 0-516-41985-4). Childrens.

—When I Ride in a Car. LC 83-7382. (Illus.). 32p. (ps-2). 1983. lib. bdg. 14.60 (ISBN 0-516-01987-2); pap. 3.95 (ISBN 0-516-41987-0). Childrens.

Courson, Diana. Let's Learn about Safety. Foster, Tom, illus. 64p. (ps-2). 1987. pap. 6.95 (ISBN 0-86653-382-6, GA1011). Good Apple.

Crary, Elizabeth. I'm Lost. Megale, Marina, illus. LC 84-62128. 32p. (Orig.). (ps-2). 1985. PLB 14.95 (ISBN 0-943990-08-4); pap. 4.95 (ISBN 0-943990-09-2). Parenting Pr.

Darling, Kathy. Safe Kids, Healthy Kids. (Illus.). 64p. (ps-2). 1989. 6.95 (ISBN 0-912107-92-8, MM1909). Monday Morning Bks.

De Leeuw, Hendrik, et al. Fireproof Children Education Kit. (Illus.). 308p. (gr. k-6). 1990. 99.95 (ISBN 0-9626076-1-4). Natl Fire Serv Support Systs.

Educational Challenges Staff. Safe at Home, Safe Alone. (Illus.). 64p. (Orig.). (gr. 3-5). 1985. pap. 4.95 (ISBN 0-917917-01-4). Miles River. SAFE AT HOME, SAFE ALONE, Helps children ages 7 to 10 learn to manage responsibility for themselves. This multicultural activity book of exercises, games & puzzles is designed to provide a basis for adult & child discussions about aspects of spending time alone & unsupervised, including time management, self-reliance, safety & communications. This book is for all children, whether their parents are working or not. How to use time & how to plan food are two of the original kinds of things that are treated, in addition to standard subjects about fire prevention, taking care of house keys & giving accurate information to a helping person. A free Teacher's Guide is available.
Publisher Provided Annotation.

Elbek, Gail. What Every Child Must Know about Grownups. Jaworski, Jo, ed. Taylor, Neil, illus. LC 86-40333. 65p. (gr. k-4). 1987. 5.95 (ISBN 1-55523-015-6). Winston-Derek.

Forte, Imogene. I'm Ready to Learn about Safety. (Illus.). (gr. k-1). 1986. pap. text ed. 1.95 (ISBN 0-86530-120-4, IP 110-8). Incentive Pubns.

Gordon, Sol & Gordon, Judith. A Better Safe Than Sorry Book. Cohen, Viven, illus. (Orig.). (ps-4). 1984. pap. 7.95x (ISBN 0-934978-13-1). Ed U Pr.

Hubbard, Kate & Berlin, Evelyn. Help Yourself to Safety: A Guide to Avoiding Dangerous Situations with Strangers & Friends. Meyer, Linda D., ed. Megale, Marina, illus. Walsh, John & Walsh, Whiteintro. by. Lyons, Carole, ed. LC 84-82541. (Illus.). 48p. (Orig.). (gr. 4-6). 1985. lib. bdg. 9.00 (ISBN 0-932091-00-8); pap. 3.95 (ISBN 0-932091-01-6). Franklin Pr WA.

Jance, Judy. Dial Zero for Help: A Story of Parental Kidnapping. Meyer, Linda D. & Lyons, Carole, eds. Megale, Marina, illus. 30p. (Orig.). (gr. k-4). 1985. lib. bdg. 9.00 (ISBN 0-932091-06-7); pap. 3.95 (ISBN 0-932091-07-5). Franklin Pr WA.

—It's Not Your Fault. Meyer, Linda D. & Lyons, Carole R., eds. Megale, Mauna, illus. LC 85-70434. 32p. (gr. k-4). 1985. lib. bdg. 9.00 (ISBN 0-932091-03-2). Franklin Pr Wa.

—Welcome Home. Meyer, Linda D. & Lyons, Carole R., eds. Megale, Marina, illus. LC 86-80156. (Orig.). (gr. 3-6). 1986. pap. 3.95 (ISBN 0-932091-09-1). Franklin Pr WA.

Joyce, Irma. Never Talk to Strangers. Buckett, George, illus. (ps-3). Date not set. pap. write for info. (ISBN 0-307-12609-9, Golden Pr). Western Pub.

Klingel, Cynthia. Safety First: Fire. LC 86-72672. (ps up) 1986. PLB 10.95s.p. (ISBN 0-88682-080-4); PLB 15.65 (ISBN 0-685-18055-7). Creative Ed.

Klingel, Cynthia F. Safety First - School. LC 86-72593. (ps up). 1986. PLB 10.95 s.p. (ISBN 0-88682-084-7); PLB 15.65 (ISBN 0-685-17884-6). Creative Ed.

—Safety First - Water. LC 86-72673. (ps up). 1986. PLB 10.95s.p. (ISBN 0-88682-083-9); PLB 15.65 (ISBN 0-685-17886-2). Creative Ed.

Lewis, Cecilia H. Guardian Angel Health & Safety Series, Vol. I: Eleven Stories. 1989. 8.95 (ISBN 0-533-08326-5). Vantage.

McGee, Eddie. The Emergency Handbook. Arico, Diane, ed. Barnes-Murphy, Rowan, illus. 176p. (gr. 8-12). 1985. lib. bdg. 9.79 (ISBN 0-671-60484-8, Little Simon); pap. 4.95 (ISBN 0-671-60483-X). S&S Trade.

MacHovec, et al. The Aware Bears. Downey, John & Cohen, Lois, eds. (Illus., Orig.). (gr. k-2). 1988-91. Set. pap. 39.50 (ISBN 0-89976-236-0). Oceana Educ Comm.
Part of loving & caring for our children is making them aware. The AWARE BEARS teach our children to be street smart without being street scared. Ten full-color storybooks featuring two loveable pandas, Li & May-Ling Bear, present individual safety/awareness topics to children ages 4-7. This nationally acclaimed series teaches children to cope successfully with today's problems in non-threatening ways by using positive language designed to develop safety awareness skills as well as building thinking skills & self-confidence. The Reference Guide, available with purchase of the series, equips the adult with implementation tips. The objectives of each book are outlined along with awareness building activities (re-telling, role play, use of visuals, situations/solutions). Created under the supervision of a licensed clinical psychologist, & written by doctors & educators, these books speak to children in terms they can understand. Ten titles cover: latchkey issues, street safety, physical abuse, verbal abuse, multi-culturalism, drug abuse, fire safety, how diseases spread, strangers, identifying a "safe" adult when in need of help. $39.50 ten books plus guide. Ages 4-7.
Publisher Provided Annotation.

Molleson, Diane. I Am Curious About Safety: A Curious George Activity Book. 1989. pap. 1.95 (ISBN 0-590-42700-8). Scholastic Inc.

Poulet, Virginia. Blue Bug's Safety Book. Charles, Donald, illus. LC 72-8348. 32p. (gr. k-3). 1973. PLB 14.60 (ISBN 0-516-03419-7); pap. 3.95 (ISBN 0-516-43419-5). Childrens.

Reihecky, Janet. Carefulness. Hutton, Kathryn, illus. LC 89-71195. 32p. (gr. k-3). 1990. lib. bdg. 11.97 (ISBN 0-89565-564-0); pap. text ed. 6.96 (ISBN 0-89565-613-2). Childs World.

Safety. (Illus.). 48p. (gr. 6-12). 1986. pap. 1.85 (ISBN 0-8395-3347-0, 3347). BSA.

Santrey, Laurence. Safety. Gold, Ethel, illus. LC 84-2700. 32p. (gr. 3-6). 1985. PLB 9.49 (ISBN 0-8167-0230-6); pap. text ed. 2.95 (ISBN 0-8167-0231-4). Troll Assocs.

Scott, Kay & Shouse, Lucille. Help Me Bear Shows You How to Call 911. Semingson, Roberta, tr. Scott, Kay & Shouse, Lucille, illus. (ENG & SPA.). 16p. (Orig.). (gr. k-4). Date not set. write for info. tchr's. ed. (ISBN 0-9620819-1-4); write for info. color bk. (ISBN 0-9620819-0-6). L Shouse.

Thaxton, Kathi. Kids...Be on Guard. Rittenour, Gary, illus. 32p. 1985. pap. write for info. (ISBN 0-88724-169-7, CD-8061). Carson-Dellos.

—Safety Against Strangers. Rittenour, Gary, illus. 32p. 1985. pap. write for info. (ISBN 0-88724-168-9, CD-8060). Carson-Dellos.

Wathen, Judy & Sussman, Ellen. Teach Me Health & Safety. Burris, Priscilla, illus. 40p. (Orig.). (ps-k). 1989. pap. 4.95 (ISBN 0-933606-75-3); tchr's. guide avail. Monkey Sisters.

World Book, Inc. Staff, ed. Play It Safe! With the Alphabet Pals: Hide- & -Seek Safety. (Illus.). 20p. (ps). 1989. lib. bdg. write for info. (ISBN 0-7166-1901-6). World Bk.

SAFETY EDUCATION–FICTION

Berenstain, Stan & Berenstain, Janice. The Berenstain Bears Learn about Strangers. (Illus.). 32p. (ps-1). 1986. pap. 4.95 (ISBN 0-394-88346-2, Random Juv). Random.

Berry, Joy W. What to Do When Your Mom or Dad Says: "Be Careful!" Kelley, Orly, ed. Bartholomew, illus. LC 83-80837. 48p. (gr. k-6). 4.98 (ISBN 0-941510-12-3). Living Skills.

Boyer. Accident Kids. LC 73-93019. (Illus.). 32p. (gr. 2-5). 1974. PLB 9.95 (ISBN 0-87783-119-X); pap. 3.94 deluxe ed. (ISBN 0-87783-120-3). cassettes o.s.i. 7.94x (ISBN 0-87783-175-0). Oddo.

—Lucky Bus. LC 73-87801. (Illus.). 32p. (gr. k-2). 1974. PLB 12.35 prebound (ISBN 0-87783-131-9); cassette o.s.i. 7.94x (ISBN 0-87783-193-9). Oddo.

—Safety on Wheels. LC 73-87802. (Illus.). 32p. (gr. k-5). 1974. PLB 12.35 prebound (ISBN 0-87783-133-5); pap. 3.94 deluxe ed. (ISBN 0-87783-134-3); cassette 7. 94x (ISBN 0-87783-199-8). Oddo.

Chlad, Dorothy. Los Desconocidos. Kratky, Lada, tr. from ENG. Halverson, Lydia, illus. LC 81-18109. (SPA.). 32p. (ps-2). 1984. lib. bdg. 14.60 (ISBN 0-516-31984-1); pap. 3.95 (ISBN 0-516-51984-0). Childrens.

—Los Venenos te Hacen Dano. Kratky, Lada, tr. Halverson, Lydia, illus. LC 85-30738. (SPA.). 32p. (ps-2). 1986. PLB 14.60 (ISBN 0-516-31976-0); pap. 3.95 (ISBN 0-516-51976-X). Childrens.

Davidson, Alice J. Beware When Elephants Sneeze. (Illus.). 1986. 4.95 (ISBN 0-8378-5086-X). Gibson.

Franklin, Herb. Fireman Fred's, Fire Safety Coloring Book. Miller, Jackie, illus. 8p. (gr. 1-5). 1990. pap. 0.50 (ISBN 0-945145-02-0). Miller Family Pubns.

Gobbell, Phyllis & Laster, Jim. Safe Sally Seat Belt & the Magic Click. Britt, Stephanie, tr. (Illus.). 32p. (ps-k). 1990. pap. 3.95 (ISBN 0-8249-8446-3). Ideals.

Jagen, Edward J. A Good Knight Story: The Quest for the Missing Children. Gregory, G., et al, eds. Blank, Diane, et al, illus. McCarthy, Dennis, intro. by. 64p. (Orig.). (gr. k-7). 1990. pap. 14.95x (ISBN 0-9625641-0-9); wkbk. 4.95 (ISBN 0-9625641-2-5). White Feather & Co.

—The Quest of the Junior Blue Knights. Blank, Diane, illus. Jagen, E. J., intro. by. (Illus.). 32p. (gr. k-7). 1990. wkbk. 4.95 (ISBN 0-9625641-1-7). White Feather & Co.

Steel, Danielle. Martha & Hilary & the Stranger. (ps-3). 1991. 9.95 (ISBN 0-385-30212-6). Doubleday.

Tester, Sylvia R. Magic Monsters Learn about Safety. Magine, John, illus. LC 78-24365. (ps-3). 1979. PLB 11.97 (ISBN 0-89565-060-6). Childs World.

Wachter, Oralee. Close to Home. Aaron, Jane, illus. LC 86-6671. 48p. (Orig.). (ps-5). 1986. pap. 12.95 (ISBN 0-590-40330-3). Scholastic Inc.

SAFETY MEASURES

see Accidents–Prevention;
also subjects with the subdivision Safety Measures, e.g. Aeronautics–Safety Measures

SAHARA DESERT

Reynolds, Jan. Sahara. Peck, Tim & Ingber, Bonnie V., eds. Reynolds, Jan, illus. 32p. (gr. 2 up). 1990. 14.95. HarBraceJ.

—Sahara Vanishing Cultures. (gr. 4-7). 1991. write for info. (ISBN 0-15-269959-7). HarBraceJ.

SAHARA DESERT–FICTION

Kaufmann, Herbert. Adventure in the Desert. Karlin, Eugene, illus. (gr. 7 up). 1961. 10.95 (ISBN 0-8392-3000-1). Astor-Honor.

—Lost Sahara Trail. (gr. 7 up). 1962. 10.95 (ISBN 0-8392-3022-2). Astor-Honor.

Saint-Exupery, Antoine de. Little Prince. Woods, Katherine, tr. Saint-Exupery, Antoine de, illus. LC 67-1144. (gr. 3-7). 1943. 12.95 (ISBN 0-15-246503-0, HJ). HarBraceJ.

SAILING

see also Boats and Boating; Navigation

Bailey, Donna. Sailing. LC 90-36489. (Illus.). 32p. (gr. 1-4). 1990. PLB 14.64 (ISBN 0-8114-2853-2). Steck-V.

Barrett, Norman. Sailing. Franklin Watts Ltd., ed. (Illus.). 32p. (ps-6). 1988. 10.90 (ISBN 0-531-10351-X). Watts.

Burchard, Peter. Venturing: An Introduction to Sailing. (Illus.). 160p. (gr. 5 up). 1986. 17.95 (ISBN 0-316-11613-0). Little.

Clifford, Harold B. Clear Sailing. Alta, Ashley, illus. Ashley, Alta & Ashley, Altapref. by. LC 87-81501. (Illus.). 145p. (gr. 6-8). 1987. pap. 7.95 (ISBN 0-9614592-2-0). Grey Gull Pubns.

Jones, Claire. Sailboat Racing. LC 80-12846. (Illus.). 48p. (gr. 4-9). 1981. PLB 9.95 (ISBN 0-8225-0434-0). Lerner Pubns.

Rudder Editors. Good Sailing: An Illustrated Course on Sailing. (Illus.). (gr. 7 up). 1976. pap. 5.95 (ISBN 0-679-50630-6). McKay.

Slocombe, Lorna. Sailing Basics. Seiden, Art, illus. 48p. (gr. 3-7). 1982. 8.95 (ISBN 0-13-786053-6). P-H.

SAILING–FICTION

Haas, Irene. The Maggie B. Haas, Irene, illus. LC 74-18183. 32p. (ps-2). 1975. 14.95 (ISBN 0-689-50021-1, M K McElderry). Macmillan Child Grp.

Locke, Eleanor G., ed. Sail Away. Goodfellow, Robin, illus. 164p. (Orig.). 1987. pap. 15.95 (ISBN 0-913932-24-8). Boosey & Hawkes.

Locker, Thomas. Sailing with the Wind. Locker, Thomas, illus. LC 85-23381. 32p. (ps up). 1986. 15.00 (ISBN 0-8037-0311-2); PLB 14.89 (ISBN 0-8037-0312-0). Dial Bks Young.

Rand, Gloria. Salty Sails North. Rand, Ted, illus. LC 89-39063. 32p. 1990. 14.95g (ISBN 0-8050-1160-9). H Holt & Co.

Sinbad, the Sailor. (ARA., Illus.). (gr. 4-6). 3.95x (ISBN 0-86685-267-0). Intl Bk Ctr.

Smith, E. Boyd. The Seashore Book. Smith, E. Boyd, illus. LC 84-22483. 56p. (gr. k-12). 1985. Repr. of 1912 ed. 12.95 (ISBN 0-395-38015-4). HM.

Swolgaard, Carole. Sailboat Coloring Guide: A Great Five Star Super Deluxe Coloring Book. Seablom, Victoria, ed. Seablom, Seth H., illus. 32p. (Orig.). (gr. 1-6). 1979. pap. 2.50 saddle stitched (ISBN 0-918800-07-2). Seablom.

Weil, Ann. Red Sails to Capri. (gr. 5-9). 15.00 (ISBN 0-8446-6413-8). Peter Smith.

SAILORS

see Seamen

SAILORS' LIFE

see Seafaring Life

ST. LAWRENCE RIVER–FICTION

Holling, Holling C. Paddle-to-the-Sea. (Illus.). (gr. 4-6). 1980. 16.95 (ISBN 0-395-15082-5); pap. 7.95 (ISBN 0-395-29203-4). HM.

ST. LOUIS

Ford, Barbara. St. Louis. LC 88-35912. (Illus.). 60p. (gr. 3 up). 1989. lib. bdg. 12.95 (ISBN 0-87518-402-2, Dillon). Macmillan Child Grp.

ST. LOUIS–FICTION

Betancourt, Jeanne. Sweet Sixteen & Never... 144p. (Orig.). (gr. 7-12). 1987. pap. 2.95 (ISBN 0-553-25534-7, Starfire). Bantam.

ST. PATRICK'S DAY

Barth, Edna. Shamrocks, Harps, & Shillelaghs: The Story of the St. Patrick's Day Symbols. Arndt, Ursula, illus. LC 77-369. 96p. (gr. 3-6). 1982. 14.95 (ISBN 0-395-28845-2, Clarion); pap. 4.95 (ISBN 0-89919-038-3, Clarion). HM.

Davis, Nancy M., et al. St. Patrick's. Davis, Nancy M., illus. 29p. (Orig.). (ps-4). 1986. pap. 4.95 (ISBN 0-937103-08-X). DaNa Pubns.

Johnson, Pamela. Let's Celebrate St. Patricks's Day: A Book of Drawing Fun. LC 87-61374. (Illus.). (gr. 2-6). 1988. PLB 10.65 (ISBN 0-8167-1135-6); pap. 1.95 (ISBN 0-8167-1136-4). Troll Assocs.

Kessel, Joyce K. St. Patrick's Day. Gilchrist, Cathy, illus. LC 82-1254. 48p. (gr. k-4). 1982. lib. bdg. 9.95 (ISBN 0-87614-193-9); pap. 3.95 (ISBN 0-87614-482-2). Carolrhoda Bks.

Ziegler, Sandra. Our St. Patrick's Day Book. Connelly, Gwen, illus. LC 86-31726. 32p. (ps-3). 1987. PLB 11. 97 (ISBN 0-89565-344-3). Childs World.

ST. VALENTINE'S DAY

see Valentine's Day

SAINTS

see also Legends

Bisignano, Judith & Sanders, Corine. Saints Alive! Mirocha, Kay, illus. LC 86-63988. 64p. (gr. 5-7). 1987. wkbk. 6.95 (ISBN 1-55612-038-9). Sheed & Ward MO.

The Children's Book of Saints. (gr. 1-4). 1989. 5.95 (ISBN 0-88271-130-X). Regina Pr.

Daughters of St. Paul. Ahead of the Crowd. (gr. 3-7). 3.00 (ISBN 0-8198-0227-1); pap. 2.00 (ISBN 0-8198-0715-X). Dghtrs St Paul.

—Bells of Conquest. (gr. 3-7). 3.00 (ISBN 0-8198-0228-X); pap. 2.00 (ISBN 0-8198-1109-2). Dghtrs St Paul.

—The Country Road Home. (gr. 3-7). 3.00 (ISBN 0-8198-0232-8); pap. 2.00 (ISBN 0-8198-1412-1). Dghtrs St Paul.

—Fifty-Seven Saints for Boys & Girls. (Illus.). (gr. 5-8). 1963. 16.95 (ISBN 0-8198-0044-9); pap. 10.95 (ISBN 0-8198-0045-7). Dghtrs St Paul.

—Saints for Young People for Every Day, Vol. 1: January-June. (Illus.). 302p. (gr. 4-8). 6.00 (ISBN 0-8198-0143-7); pap. 4.50 (ISBN 0-8198-0144-5). Dghtrs St Paul.

—Wind & Shadows. (gr. 4-7). 3.00 (ISBN 0-8198-0174-7). Dghtrs St Paul.

Lappin, Peter. Dominic Savio Teenage Saint. rev. ed. LC 81-67928. 145p. (gr. 4-10). 1981. pap. 2.95 (ISBN 0-89944-055-X, Patron). Don Bosco Multimedia.

Lee, Frank. Bedtime Stories of the Saints, Bk. 1. rev ed. (Illus.). 96p. (ps-5). 1974. saddle stitch 3.95 (ISBN 0-89243-003-6, 27227). Liguori Pubns.

Panunzi, Paul. Love As Strong As Death. (gr. 3-7). 3.00 (ISBN 0-8198-0239-5). Dghtrs St Paul.

Patterson, Yvonne. Doubting Thomas. (gr. k-4). 1981. pap. 1.39 (ISBN 0-570-06144-X, 59-1261). Concordia.

Scotti, Juliet & Linksman, Ricki. Kirpal Singh: The Story of a Saint. 2nd ed. Tarrant, Valerie, illus. Zaffina, Bruno, intro. by. LC 77-79840. (Illus.). 96p. (gr. 1-7). 1982. pap. 12.95 (ISBN 0-918224-05-5). Sawan Kirpal Pubns.

Windeatt, Mary F. St. Christopher. Harmon, Gedge, illus. 32p. (gr. 1-5). 1989. Repr. of 1954 ed. wkbk. 3.00 (ISBN 0-89555-376-7). TAN Bks Pubs.

—St. Maria Goretti. Harmon, Gedge, illus. 32p. (gr. 1-5). 1989. Repr. of 1954 ed. wkbk. 3.00 (ISBN 0-89555-374-0). TAN Bks Pubs.

—St. Meinrad. Harmon, Gedge, illus. 32p. (gr. 1-5). 1989. Repr. of 1954 ed. wkbk. 3.00 (ISBN 0-89555-377-5). TAN Bks Pubs.

—St. Philomena. Harmon, Gedge, illus. 32p. (gr. 1-5). 1989. Repr. of 1954 ed. wkbk. 3.00 (ISBN 0-89555-373-2). TAN Bks Pubs.

Windham, Joan. Sixty Saints for Boys. 416p. (gr. 1-6). 1988. pap. 13.95 (ISBN 0-87061-149-6). Chr Classics.

—Sixty Saints for Girls. 384p. (gr. 1-6). 1988. pap. 13.95 (ISBN 0-87061-150-X). Chr Classics.

Young, John. Heroes of Faith: Stories of Saints for Young & Old. 1989. pap. 5.95 (ISBN 0-937032-61-1). Light&Life Pub Co MN.

SAINTS–DICTIONARIES

Daughters of St Paul. Saints for Young People for Every Day of the Year, Vol. 2: July to December. (Illus.). 338p. (gr. 4 up). 6.00 (ISBN 0-8198-0647-1); pap. 4.50 (ISBN 0-8198-0648-X). Dghtrs St Paul.

SAINTS–FICTION

De Paola, Tomie. Nuestra Senora de Guadalupe. De Paola, Tomie, illus. Belpre, Pura, tr. LC 79-19609. (SPA., Illus.). 48p. (gr. 1-4). 1980. reinforced bdg. 14.95 (ISBN 0-8234-0374-2); pap. 5.95 (ISBN 0-8234-0404-8). Holiday.

Hunger, Bill. When Two Saints Meet. Ripley, Jill, ed. Martin, Alice, et al, illus. 100p. (Orig.). (gr. 6-12). pap. 9.95 (ISBN 0-9625782-0-7). Two Saints Pub.

Talwalker, Gopinath. Some Indian Saints. Jomra, J., illus. 64p. (Orig.). (gr. 5 up). 1980. pap. 2.50 (ISBN 0-89744-208-3, Pub. by Natl Bk Trust India). Auromere.

Watts, Bernadette. St. Francis & the Proud Crow. LC 87-34942. (Illus.). 32p. (ps-2). 1988. 12.95 (ISBN 0-531-05758-5); PLB 12.99 (ISBN 0-531-08358-6). Orchard Bks Watts.

Windeatt, Mary F. St. Teresa of Avila. Harmon, Gedge, illus. 32p. (gr. 1-5). 1989. Repr. of 1954 ed. wkbk. 3.00 (ISBN 0-89555-372-4). TAN Bks Pubs.

SAINTS–LEGENDS

Egan, Patricia. Saint Patrick & the Snakes. (Illus.). 28p. (gr. 1-8). 1990. 9.95 (ISBN 1-85390-059-1, Pub. by Veritas Pubns Eire). Irish Bks Media.

Simms, George O. Brendan the Navigator: Exploring the Ancient World. LC 89-82004. (Illus.). 96p. (gr. 7-12). 1990. 13.95 (ISBN 0-86278-202-3, Pub. by O'Brien Pr IE). Dufour.

SALAMANDERS

Selsam, Millicent E. & Hunt, Joyce. A First Look at Frogs, Toads & Salamanders. Spunger, Harriett, illus. 32p. (gr. 2-4). 1976. PLB 12.85 (ISBN 0-8027-6244-1). Walker & Co.

SALEM, MASSACHUSETTS–HISTORY

Kent, Zachary. The Story of the Salem Witch Trials. Canaday, Ralph, illus. LC 86-9632. 32p. (gr. 3-6). 1986. PLB 13.27 (ISBN 0-516-04704-3); pap. 3.95 (ISBN 0-516-44704-1). Childrens.

SALESMEN AND SALESMANSHIP

see also Advertising; Business; Marketing

Boy Scouts of America. Salesmanship. LC 19-600. (Illus.). 40p. (gr. 6-12). 1987. pap. 1.85 (ISBN 0-8395-3351-9, 3351). BSA.

Estes, Sherrill Y. Sell Like a Pro! The Secrets of Consultative Selling. (Illus.). 192p. (gr. 7 up). 1988. 18.95 (ISBN 0-87491-917-7). Acropolis.

John, Hughes. Bob the Super Clerk. (Illus.). 40p. (gr. 7-12). 1975. pap. 2.65 (ISBN 0-915510-01-4). Janus Bks.

Mandino, Og. Greatest Salesman in the World. LC 68-10798. (gr. 9 up). 1987. 12.95 (ISBN 0-8119-0067-3). Lifetime.

SALESMEN AND SALESMANSHIP–FICTION

Field, Rachel. General Store. Laroche, Giles, illus. LC 87-37218. (ps-3). 1988. 15.95 (ISBN 0-316-28163-8). Little.

Merrill, Jean. The Pushcart War. Solbert, Ronni, illus. LC 84-43131. 224p. (gr. 5-8). 1964. 12.95 (ISBN 0-201-09313-8). HarpC Child Bks.

Schur, Maxine. Shnook the Peddler. Redpath, Dale, illus. LC 85-6807. 40p. (gr. 3-6). 1985. PLB 8.95 (ISBN 0-87518-298-4, Dillon). Macmillan Child Grp.

Williams-Garcia, Rita. Fast Talk on a Slow Track. 176p. (gr. 7 up). 1991. 14.95 (ISBN 0-525-67334-2, Lodestar Bks). Dutton Child Bks.

SALESMEN AND SALESMANSHIP–VOCATIONAL GUIDANCE

Epstein, Lawrence. Exploring Careers in Computer Sales. Rosen, Roger, ed. 64p. (gr. 7-12). 1990. lib. bdg. 12.95 (ISBN 0-8239-0667-1). Rosen Group.

SALK, JONAS, 1914-

Curson, Marjorie. Jonas Salk. Gallin, Richard, ed. (Illus.). 144p. (gr. 5-9). 1990. lib. bdg. 13.98 (ISBN 0-382-09966-4); pap. 7.95 (ISBN 0-382-09971-0). Silver Burdett Pr.

SALMON

Field, Nancy & Machlis, Sally. Discovering Salmon. Machlis, Sally, illus. 32p. (Orig.). (gr. k-6). 1984. pap. 3.50 (ISBN 0-941042-05-7). Dog Eared Pubns.

Hogan, Paula Z. The Salmon. Hockerman, Dennis, illus. LC 78-21178. 32p. (gr. 1-4). 1979. PLB 16.67 (ISBN 0-8172-1255-8). Raintree Pubs.

—The Salmon. LC 78-21178. (Illus.). 32p. (gr. 1-4). 1984. PLB 27.99 incl. cassette (ISBN 0-8172-2232-4); cassette 14.00 (ISBN 0-685-09509-6). Raintree Pubs.

Phleger, Frederick B. Red Tag Comes Back. Lobel, Arnold, illus. LC 61-11452. 64p. (gr. k-3). 1961. PLB 11.89 (ISBN 0-06-024706-1). HarpC Child Bks.

SALOMON, HAYM, 1740?-1785

Milgrim, Shirley. Haym Salomon: Liberty's Son. Fish, Richard, illus. LC 75-17349. 120p. (gr. 5-8). 1975. 5.95 (ISBN 0-8276-0073-9). JPS Phila.

SALOONS

see Restaurants, Bars, Etc.

SALT

Bracy, Norma M. Salt. (Illus.). 32p. (gr. k-12). 1986. pap. text ed. 2.00 (ISBN 0-915783-03-7). Book Binder.

Joly, Dominique. Grains of Salt. Perols, Sylvaine, illus. LC 87-34534. 38p. (gr. k-5). 1988. 4.95 (ISBN 0-944589-20-0, 200). Young Discovery Lib.

Mitgutsch, Ali. From Sea to Salt. Mitgutsch, Ali, illus. LC 84-17466. 24p. (ps-3). 1985. PLB 6.95 (ISBN 0-87614-232-3). Carolrhoda Bks.

SALUTATIONS

see Etiquette; Letter Writing

SALVADOR

Adams, Faith. El Salvador: Beauty among the Ashes. LC 85-6945. (Illus.). 136p. (gr. 5 up). 1986. lib. bdg. 14.95 (ISBN 0-87518-309-3, Dillon). Macmillan Child Grp.

Cheney, Glenn A. El Salvador: Country in Crisis. (Illus.). 96p. (gr. 7 up). 1982. PLB 12.90 (ISBN 0-531-04423-8). Watts.

—El Salvador: Country in Crisis. (gr. 4-7). 1990. PLB 12.90 (ISBN 0-531-10916-X). Watts.

Cummins, Ronnie & Welch, Rose. Children of the World: El Salvador. Welch, Rose, photos by. LC 89-43137. (Illus.). 64p. (gr. 5-6). 1990. PLB 12.95 (ISBN 0-8368-0220-9). Gareth Stevens Inc.

Haverstock, Nathan A. El Salavador in Pictures. (Illus.). 64p. (gr. 5 up). 1987. PLB 12.95 (ISBN 0-8225-1806-6). Lerner Pubns.

Sanders, Renfield. El Salvador. (Illus.). 96p. (gr. 5 up). 1988. lib. bdg. 14.95 (ISBN 1-55546-781-4). Chelsea Hse.

Stewart, Gail B. El Salvador. LC 90-47691. (Illus.). 48p. (gr. 5-6). 1991. RSBE 10.95 (ISBN 0-89686-602-5, Crestwood Hse). Macmillan Child Grp.

SALVAGE

see also Skin Diving; Shipwrecks

Graham, Ian. Salvage at Sea. (Illus.). 32p. (gr. 5-8). 1990. PLB 8.90 (ISBN 0-531-17177-9). Watts.

SALVATION ARMY

Exline, Barbara. Beyond the Battlefield. (Illus.). 78p. (Orig.). (gr. 7 up). 1986. pap. 3.25 (ISBN 0-89216-063-2). Salvation Army.

SAMSON, JUDGE OF ISRAEL–FICTION

Kolbrek, Loyal & Larsen, Chris. Samson's Secret. (Orig.). (ps-4). 1970. pap. 1.39 (ISBN 0-570-06052-4, 59-1168). Concordia.

SAN ANTONIO–FICTION

Bruni, Mary A. Rosita's Christmas Wish. Ricks, Thom, illus. LC 85-52040. 48p. (gr. k-8). 1985. 13.95 (ISBN 0-935857-00-1); ltd. ed. 125.00 (ISBN 0-935857-03-6); write for info. (ISBN 0-935857-09-5); pap. write for info. (ISBN 0-935857-01-X); pap. write for info. (ISBN 0-935857-10-9). Texart.

SAN FRANCISCO

Climo, Shirley. City! San Francisco. (Illus.). 64p. (gr. 3-7). 1990. 15.95 (ISBN 0-02-719030-7, Mcmillan Child Bk). Macmillan Child Grp.

Haddock, Patricia. San Francisco. LC 88-20200. (Illus.). 60p. (gr. 3 up). 1989. PLB 12.95 (ISBN 0-87518-383-2, Dillon). Macmillan Child Grp.

Wilder, Laura I. West from Home: Letters of Laura Ingalls Wilder, San Francisco 1915. MacBride, Roger L., ed. LC 73-14342. 176p. (gr. 7 up). 1974. 13.95 (ISBN 0-06-024110-1); PLB 13.89 (ISBN 0-06-024111-X). HarpC Child Bks.

Zibart, Rosemary. Kidding Around San Francisco: A Young Person's Guide to the City. St. Marie, Janice, illus. 64p. (Orig.). (gr. 3 up). 1989. pap. 9.95 (ISBN 0-945465-23-8). John Muir.

SAN FRANCISCO–BRIDGES

Kingston, Jeremy. How Bridges Are Made. (Illus.). 32p. (gr. 7 up). 12.95 (ISBN 0-8160-0040-9). Facts on File.

SAN FRANCISCO–EARTHQUAKE AND FIRE, 1906

Dudman, John. The San Francisco Earthquake. Caulkins, Janet, ed. (Illus.). 32p. (gr. 1-6). 1988. PLB 10.90 (ISBN 0-531-18163-4, Pub. by Bookwright Pr). Watts.

Hamilton, Sue. San Francisco Earthquake. Hamilton, John, ed. (Illus.). 32p. (gr. 4). 1989. PLB 11.95 (ISBN 0-939179-43-1). Abdo & Dghtrs.

House, James & Steffens, Bradley. The San Francisco Earthquake. LC 89-33558. (Illus.). 64p. (gr. 5 up). 1989. PLB 11.95 (ISBN 1-56006-003-4). Lucent Bks.

Levine, Ellen. If You Lived at the Time of the Great San Francisco Earthquake. Williams, Richard, illus. 64p. (Orig.). (gr. 2-5). 1987. pap. 2.95 (ISBN 0-590-43798-4). Scholastic Inc.

Stein, R. Conrad. The Story of the San Francisco Earthquake. LC 83-10135. (Illus.). 32p. (gr. 3-6). 1983. PLB 13.27 (ISBN 0-516-04664-0); pap. 3.95 (ISBN 0-516-44664-9). Childrens.

SAN FRANCISCO–FICTION

Caen, Herb. The Cable Car & the Dragon. Byfield, Barbara N., illus. LC 85-32004. 40p. 1986. 9.95 (ISBN 0-87701-390-X). Chronicle Bks.

Gordon, Jeffie R. Nora, No. 26. 224p. (Orig.). (gr. 7 up). 1987. pap. 2.75 (ISBN 0-590-41012-1, Sunfire). Scholastic Inc.

Levine, Ellen. If You Lived at the Time of the Great San Francisco Earthquake. Williams, Richard, illus. 64p. (gr. 2-5). 1987. pap. 2.50 (ISBN 0-590-40372-9). Scholastic Inc.

Yep, Laurence. Child of the Owl. LC 76-24314. 224p. (gr. 7 up). 1977. PLB 12.89 (ISBN 0-06-026743-7). HarpC Child Bks.

SAN FRANCISCO–HISTORY

Climo, Shirley. City! San Francisco. (Illus.). 64p. (gr. 3-7). 1990. 15.95 (ISBN 0-02-719030-7, Mcmillan Child Bk). Macmillan Child Grp.

Wilder, Laura I. West from Home: Letters of Laura Ingalls Wilder, San Francisco 1915. MacBride, Roger L., ed. LC 73-14342. (Illus.). 176p. (gr. 7 up). 1976. pap. 3.50 (ISBN 0-06-440081-6, Trophy). HarpC Child Bks.

SANATORIUMS

see Hospitals

SAND

De Paola, Tomie. The Quicksand Book. LC 76-28762. (Illus.). 32p. (gr. k-3). 1977. reinforced bdg. 14.95 (ISBN 0-8234-0291-6); pap. 5.95 (ISBN 0-8234-0532-X). Holiday.

Webb, Angela. Sand. (Illus.). 32p. (gr. k-3). 1987. PLB 10.90 (ISBN 0-531-10370-6). Watts.

SAND DUNES

Bannan, Jan G. Sand Dunes. (Illus.). 48p. (gr. 3-6). 1989. lib. bdg. 12.95 (ISBN 0-87614-321-4); pap. 6.95 (ISBN 0-87614-513-6). Carolrhoda Bks.

SAND DUNES–FICTION

Petrie, Catherine. Sandbox Betty. Elzaurdia, Sharon, illus. LC 81-15547. 32p. (ps-2). 1982. PLB 11.93 (ISBN 0-516-03578-9); pap. 2.95 (ISBN 0-516-43578-7). Childrens.

SANDBURG, CARL, 1878-1967

Hacker, Jeffrey H. Carl Sandburg. 128p. (gr. 7-12). 1984. lib. bdg. 12.90 (ISBN 0-531-04762-8). Watts.

Mitchell, Barbara. Good Morning Mr. President: A Story about Carl Sandburg. Collins, Dane, illus. LC 88-7265. 56p. (gr. 3-6). 1988. PLB 9.95 (ISBN 0-87614-329-X). Carolrhoda Bks.

Sandburg, Carl. Prairie-Town Boy. Hague, Michael & Krush, Joe, illus. 208p. (gr. 3-7). 1990. pap. 4.95 (ISBN 0-15-263332-4). HarBraceJ.

SANDWICHES

Gelman, Rita G. El Sandwich Mas Grande, Jamas. Gerberg, Mort, illus. Vasquez, Otto R., tr. (SPA., Illus.). 48p. (gr. k-3). 1987. pap. 2.95 (ISBN 0-590-40884-4). Scholastic Inc.

SANGER, MARGARET HIGGINS, 1883-1966

Topalian, Elyse. Margaret Sanger. 128p. (gr. 7 up). lib. bdg. 12.90 (ISBN 0-531-04763-6). Watts.

SANITARY AFFAIRS

see Sanitation

SANITATION

see also Cemeteries; Hygiene; Public Health; Refuse and Refuse Disposal; Water Supply; World War, 1939-1945–Medical and Sanitary Affairs

Poskanzer, Susan C. Sanitation Worker. Eitzen, Allan, illus. LC 88-10044. 32p. (gr. k-2). 1988. PLB 10.89 (ISBN 0-8167-1436-3); pap. text ed. 2.50 (ISBN 0-8167-1437-1). Troll Assocs.

SANTA CLAUS

Amoss, Berthe. What Did You Lose, Santa? Amoss, Berthe, illus. LC 86-33633. 24p. (ps-1). 1987. 3.95 (ISBN 0-694-00197-X). HarpC Child Bks.

Baum, L. Frank. The Life & Adventures of Santa Claus. (gr. 2-6). 1985. 4.98 (ISBN 0-517-42062-7). Outlet Bk Co.

—Life & Adventures of Santa Claus. 160p. 1986. pap. 2.25 (ISBN 0-451-52064-5, Sig Classics). NAL-Dutton.

—The Life & Adventures of Santa Claus. 13.95 (ISBN 0-8488-0428-7). Amereon Ltd.

Bonsall, Crosby N. Twelve Bells for Santa. Bonsall, Crosby N., illus. LC 76-58714. 64p. (ps-3). 1977. PLB 11.89 (ISBN 0-06-020582-2). HarpC Child Bks.

Briggs, Raymond. Father Christmas. Briggs, Raymond, illus. 32p. (gr. k-3). 1973. 9.95 (ISBN 0-698-20272-4, Coward). Putnam Pub Group.

—Father Christmas. (Illus.). 32p. (gr. k-3). 1977. pap. 3.95 (ISBN 0-14-050125-8, Puffin). Puffin Bks.

Brooke, Roger. Santa's Christmas Journey. LC 84-9796. (Illus.). 32p. (gr. k-5). 1984. PLB 16.67 (ISBN 0-8172-2116-6); PLB 27.99 incl. cassette (ISBN 0-8172-2244-8); pap. 9.27 (ISBN 0-8172-2259-6); pap. 23.95 incl. cassette (ISBN 0-8172-2269-3); cassette 14.00 (ISBN 0-685-08347-0). Raintree Pubs.

Brown, Marc. Arthur's Christmas. Brown, Marc, illus. LC 84-4373. (ps-3). 1985. 14.95 (ISBN 0-316-11180-5, Joy St Bks); pap. 4.95 (ISBN 0-316-10993-2). Little.

Civardi, Annie. The Secrets of Santa. Scruton, Clive, illus. LC 91-130. 32p. (ps-1). 1991. bds. 13.95 jacketed (ISBN 0-671-74270-1, S&S BYR). S&S Trade.

Clements, Andrew. Santa's Secret Helper. Santini, Debrah, illus. LC 90-8601. 32p. (gr. k up). 1990. 14.95 (ISBN 0-88708-136-3). Picture Bk Studio.

Cuyler, Margery. Fat Santa. LC 86-31962. 1989. pap. 4.95 (ISBN 0-8050-1167-6). H Holt & Co.

Ellison, Harold. Santa's Gone Away. LC 88-51034. 44p. (gr. k-3). 1988. 6.95 (ISBN 1-55523-180-2). Winston-Derek.

Fass, Bernie & Wolfson, Mack. United Santas of America. 48p. (gr. 3-12). 1987. pap. 15.95 (ISBN 0-86704-038-6); student bk. 2.95 (ISBN 0-86704-039-4). Clarus Music.

Giblin, James C. The Truth about Santa Claus. LC 85-47541. (Illus.). 96p. (gr. 3-7). 1985. 12.95 (ISBN 0-690-04483-6, Crowell Jr Bks); PLB 12.89 (ISBN 0-690-04484-4, Crowell Jr Bks). HarpC Child Bks.

Gimbel, Cheryl. Why Does Santa Celebrate Christmas? Lovelady, J., ed. Maners, Wendelin, illus. 36p. (gr. k up). 1990. 12.95 (ISBN 0-915190-67-2, JP9067-2). Jalmar Pr.

Hader, Bertha. Visit from Saint Nick. 1990. 3.98 (ISBN 0-8317-4274-7). Smithmark.

Hausman, Suzanne, illus. Yes, Virginia. 6.95 (ISBN 0-685-86235-6). Pubns Devl Co TX.

Haywood, Carolyn. Santa Claus Forever! Ambrus, Victor G., illus. LC 83-1017. 32p. (gr. k-3). 1983. 11.95 (ISBN 0-688-02344-4); lib. bdg. 11.88 (ISBN 0-688-02345-2). Morrow.

Hazen, Barbara S. The Story of Santa Claus. (Illus.). 32p. (ps up). 1989. write for info. (ISBN 0-307-12097-X, Pub. by Golden Bks). Western Pub.

Himmel, Roger J. Lollipop Dragon Helps Santa. Manoni, Mary H., ed. Peters, Luther J. & Ross, Connie, illus. LC 75-739480. (gr. k-3). 1978. pap. text ed. 29.95 6 bks. & 1 cass. (ISBN 0-89290-037-7); pap. text ed. 10.95 1 bk. & 1 cass. (ISBN 0-685-04659-1). Soc for Visual.

Hover, M. Here Comes Santa Claus. Santoro, Christopher, illus. 14p. (ps). 1982. write for info. (ISBN 0-307-12267-0, Golden Bks.). Western Pub.

Kahn, Peggy. The Care Bears Help Santa. Fleming, Denise, illus. LC 84-3385. 40p. (ps-3). 1984. 3.95 (ISBN 0-394-86807-2, Random Juv); lib. bdg. 4.99 (ISBN 0-394-96807-7, BYR). Random.

Kirk, Daniel. Santa Claus the Movie: Pop-up Panorama Book. Kirk, Daniel, illus. 12p. (ps-3). 1985. 7.95 (ISBN 0-448-10276-5, G&D). Putnam Pub Group.

Kroll, Steven. Santa's Crash-Bang Christmas. DePaola, Tomie, illus. LC 77-3025. 32p. (gr. k-3). 1977. reinforced bdg. 13.95 (ISBN 0-8234-0302-5); pap. 5.95 (ISBN 0-8234-0621-0). Holiday.

Kunnas, Mauri. Santa Claus & His Elves. Kunnas, Mauri, illus. Robbins, Maria R., tr. from FIN. LC 82-6043. (Illus.). 48p. (ps up). 1986. bds. 4.95 (ISBN 0-517-54781-3); pap. 4.95 (ISBN 0-517-55818-1). Crown.

Lane, Julie. The Life & Adventures of Santa Claus. (Illus.). 144p. 1987. 12.95 (ISBN 0-685-19459-0). Equity Pub NH.

—The Life & Legends of Santa Claus. Hokie, illus. Zinnott, Nicholas H., intro. by. LC 84-2741. (Illus.). 160p. (gr. 3-6). 1983. 10.95 (ISBN 0-917057-00-7). Tonnis.

M & M & the Santa Secrets. 1985. 9.95 (ISBN 0-670-80624-2). Viking Child Bks.

M & M & the Santa Secrets. (Illus.). 1987. pap. 3.95 (ISBN 0-14-032222-1, Puffin). Puffin Bks.

Mercurio, Helen C. The Miracle Santa's Beard. Mercurio, Mary M., ed. Adjoian, Eva M., illus. 29p. 1985. 12.00 (ISBN 0-9616079-0-4). Tiffany Pub.

Merriam, Robert L. Santa Claus' Snack. Roberts, William, illus. 14p. (ps-6). pap. 2.00x (ISBN 0-686-32491-9). R L Merriam.

Miller, Daisy. Santa's Reindeer: Santa Claus the Movie. Wilburn, Kathy, illus. 16p. (ps). 1985. 3.95 (ISBN 0-448-10222-6, G&D). Putnam Pub Group.

Miller, Sherry. Santa's Helper. Martinez, Jesse, illus. LC 83-72493. 32p. (Orig.). (gr. k-5). 1983. pap. 1.95 saddle-stitched (ISBN 0-913379-00-X). Double M Pub.

Mora, Emma. Mortimer Visits Santa Claus. Kennedy, illus. (ps-1). 1987. 3.95 (ISBN 0-8120-5808-9). Barron.

Oliver, Mary. Santa Claus the Movie: The Legend of Santa Claus. (Illus.). 24p. (ps-1). 1985. pap. 1.95 (ISBN 0-448-10280-3, G&D). Putnam Pub Group.

Peters, Sharon. Santa's New Sled. Dole, Bob, illus. LC 81-5028. 32p. (gr. k-2). 1981. PLB 10.89 (ISBN 0-89375-523-0); pap. text ed. 2.95 (ISBN 0-89375-524-9). Troll Assocs.

Pierce, Anne M. So Many Gifts. Campbell, Donna P., illus. 30p. (ps up). 1989. 14.95; 7.50x (ISBN 0-685-27188-9). Forword MN.

Richter, Konrad. Wipe Your Feet, Santa Claus. Wilkon, Jozef, illus. LC 85-7246. 24p. (gr. k-2). 1985. 13.95 (ISBN 1-55858-016-6). North-South Bks NYC.

Ross, Pat. M & M & the Santa Secrets. Hafner, Marylin, illus. (gr. 1-4). pap. 2.95 (ISBN 0-317-62234-X, Puffin). Puffin Bks.

Santa Claus Has a Busy Night. 3.95 (ISBN 0-7214-5077-6). Ladybird Bks.

Santa's New Suit Storybook. (ps-6). 1972. 3.00 (ISBN 0-686-00005-6). B A Scott.

Schmid, Eleonore. Wake up, Dormouse, Santa Claus Is Here. Schmid, Eleonore, illus. LC 89-42610. 32p. (gr. k-3). 1989. 14.95 (ISBN 1-55858-020-4). North-South Bks NYC.

Sharmat, Marjorie W. I'm Santa Claus & I'm Famous. Hafner, Marylin, illus. LC 90-55106. 32p. (ps-4). 1990. reinforced 14.95 (ISBN 0-8234-0826-4). Holiday.

Siegenthaler, Kathrin. Santa Claus & the Woodcutter. Crawford, Elizabeth, tr. from GER. Pfister, Marcus, illus. 32p. (gr. k-3). 1989. pap. 1.95 (ISBN 1-55858-032-8). North-South Bks NYC.

Stout, Robert T. Children's Favorite Story of Santa Claus. Stout, Robert T., illus. 32p. (ps-6). 1982. 5.95 (ISBN 0-911049-08-8); pap. 3.95 (ISBN 0-911049-04-5). Yuletide Intl.

—The Original Story of Santa Claus. Stout, Robert T., illus. 56p. (ps-8). 1981. 6.95 (ISBN 0-911049-00-2). Yuletide Intl.

Tulloch, Richard. Rain for Christmas. Harris, Wayne, illus. 32p. 1990. 9.95 (ISBN 0-521-37085-X). Cambridge U Pr.

Vinge, Joan D. The Santa Claus Storybook: Santa Claus the Movie. (Illus.). 64p. (gr. 3 up). 1985. 6.95 (ISBN 0-448-10281-1, G&D). Putnam Pub Group.

Waters, Meg. Santa Claus the Movie: The Elves at the Top of the World. (Illus.). 24p. (ps-1). 1985. pap. 1.95 (ISBN 0-448-10279-X, Pub. by G&D). Putnam Pub Group.

Weil, Lisl. Santa Claus Around the World. Weil, Lisl, illus. LC 87-45334. 32p. (gr. k-3). 1987. reinforced 13.95 (ISBN 0-8234-0665-2). Holiday.

Weinberg, Larry. Forgetful Bears Help Santa. 1989. pap. 2.50 (ISBN 0-590-40994-8). Scholastic Inc.

Winters, Faye H. The Year of Santa's Diet. Winters, Faye H., illus. 120p. (Orig.). (gr. 1-5). 1985. pap. 9.95 (ISBN 0-935011-00-5). Winters Pubns.

SANTA CLAUS–POETRY

Moore, Clement C. The Night Before Christmas. De Paola, Tomie, illus. LC 80-11758. 32p. (ps up). 1980. reinforced bdg. 14.95 (ISBN 0-8234-0414-5); pap. 5.95 (ISBN 0-8234-0417-X). Holiday.

—The Night Before Christmas. Amoss, Berthe, illus. 10p. (ps-7). 1989. pap. 3.95 (ISBN 0-922589-06-2). More Than Card.

SANTA FE, NEW MEXICO

Hillerman, Anne. Children's Guide to Santa Fe. LC 84-8782. (Illus.). 48p. (Orig.). (gr. 3 up). 1984. pap. 4.95 (ISBN 0-86534-030-7). Sunstone Pr.

York, Susan. Kidding Around Santa Fe: A Young Person's Guide to the City. Blakemore, Sally, illus. 64p. (Orig.). (gr. 3 up). 1991. pap. 9.95 (ISBN 0-945465-99-8). John Muir.

SANTA FE TRAIL

McCall, Edith. Wagons Over the Mountains. Rogers, Carol, illus. LC 61-10101. 128p. (gr. 3-10). 1980. PLB 14.60 (ISBN 0-516-03376-X). Childrens.

SANTA FE TRAIL–FICTION

Holling, Holling C. Tree in the Trail. (Illus.). (gr. 4-6). 16.95 (ISBN 0-395-18228-X). HM.

SARNOFF, DAVID, 1891-

Myers, Elisabeth P. David Sarnoff: Radio & TV Boy. (gr. 3-7). pap. 3.95 (ISBN 0-672-51754-X, Bobbs) (ISBN 0-672-71076-5). Macmillan.

SASQUATCH

Carmichael, Carrie. Big Foot: Man, Monster, or Myth? LC 77-21317. (Illus.). 48p. (gr. 4 up). 1977. PLB 17.32 (ISBN 0-8172-1052-0). Raintree Pubs.

Gaffron, Norma. Bigfoot: Opposing Viewpoints. (Illus.). 112p. (gr. 3-8). 1988. PLB 13.95 (ISBN 0-89908-058-8). Greenhaven.

Johnson, Mary E. & Johnson, Margie. Baby Bigfoot. (ps-3). 1977. pap. 1.25 (ISBN 0-686-21383-1). Animal Cracker.

Odor, Ruth S. Bigfoot. Magnuson, Diana, illus. LC 88-7882. 100p. (gr. 3-7). 1989. PLB 12.96 (ISBN 0-89565-455-5); pap. 7.95 (ISBN 0-89565-533-0). Childs World.

Place, Marion T. On the Track of Bigfoot. (Illus.). (gr. 5 up). 1980. pap. 1.95 (ISBN 0-671-41677-4). PB.

Sonberg, Lynn. The Bigfoot Mystery. (gr. 4-9). 1983. pap. 2.25 (ISBN 0-553-15436-2). Bantam.

SATAN

see Devil

SATELLITES, ARTIFICIAL

see Artificial Satellites

SAUDI ARABIA

Lerner Publications, Department of Geography Staff, ed. Saudi Arabia in Pictures. (Illus.). 64p. (gr. 5 up). 1989. 12.95 (ISBN 0-8225-1845-7). Lerner Pubns.

Lye, Keith. Take a Trip to Saudi Arabia. 32p. (gr. k-7). 1984. lib. bdg. 7.99 (ISBN 0-531-04872-1). Watts.

McCarthy, Kevin. Saudi Arabia: A Desert Kingdom. LC 85-6941. (Illus.). 128p. (gr. 5 up). 1986. PLB 14.95 (ISBN 0-87518-295-X, Dillon). Macmillan Child Grp.

Mulloy, Martin. Saudi Arabia. (Illus.). (gr. 5 up). 1988. 14.95 (ISBN 1-55546-179-4). Chelsea Hse.

SAUL, KING OF ISRAEL

Segal, Lore. The Story of King Saul & King David. LC 90-52544. (Illus.). 144p. 1991. 19.50 (ISBN 0-8052-4088-8). Pantheon.

Wengrov, Charles. Tales of King Saul. (Illus.). (gr. 5-10). 1969. 3.00 (ISBN 0-914080-21-0). Shulsinger Sales.

SAXONS

see Anglo-Saxons

SAYINGS

see Epigrams; Proverbs; Quotations

SCANDINAVIANS IN THE U. S.

Brownstone & Franck, eds. The Scandinavian-American Heritage. LC 88-45086. 128p. (gr. 5-9). 1988. 16.95 (ISBN 0-8160-1626-7). Facts On File.

SCARECROWS–FICTION

Fleischman, Sid. The Scarebird. Sis, Peter, illus. LC 87-4099. 32p. (gr. k-3). 1988. 13.95 (ISBN 0-688-07317-4); lib. bdg. 13.88 (ISBN 0-688-07318-2). Greenwillow.

Gordon, Sharon. Samuel el Espantapajaros. Silverstein, Don, illus. (SPA.). 32p. (gr. k-2). 1981. PLB 7.06 (ISBN 0-89375-556-7); pap. 1.95 (ISBN 0-685-04952-3). Troll Assocs.

Lewis, Rob. Hello Mr. Scarecrow. (Illus.). 28p. (ps up). 1988. pap. 3.95 (ISBN 0-374-42931-6). FS&G.

Lifton, Betty J. Joji & the Dragon. Mitsui, Eiichi, illus. LC 88-8434. 64p. (gr. 1-3). 1989. Repr. of 1957 ed. lib. bdg. 15.00 (ISBN 0-208-02245-7, Pub. by Linnet). Shoe String.

Oana, Katy D. Robbie & the Raggedy Scarecrow. LC 77-18349. (Illus.). 32p. (gr. 2-4). 1978. PLB 9.95 (ISBN 0-87783-154-8). Oddo.

—Robbie & the Raggedy Scarecrow. Stephens, Jacquelyn S., illus. LC 77-18349. (gr. k-2). 1978. PLB 5.95 (ISBN 0-89508-065-6). Rainbow Bks.

Stolz, Mary. The Scarecrows & Their Child. Schwartz, Amy, illus. LC 87-115. 80p. (gr. 3-6). 1987. 11.95 (ISBN 0-06-026007-6); PLB 11.89 (ISBN 0-06-026008-4). HarpC Child Bks.

SCENARIOS

see Television Plays

SCENERY

see Views

SCENERY (STAGE)

see Theaters–Stage Setting and Scenery

SCHOLARSHIP

see Learning and Scholarship

SCHOLARSHIPS, FELLOWSHIPS, ETC.

see also Student Loan Funds

Blum, Laurie. Free Money for Foreign Study: A Guide to More Than 1,000 Grants & Scholarships for Study Abroad. 256p. (gr. 11-12). 1991. lib. bdg. 24.95x (ISBN 0-8160-2450-2). Facts on File.

SCHOOL ADMINISTRATION AND ORGANIZATION

see also Teaching

Cobb, Vicki. The Secret Life of School Supplies. Morrison, Bill, illus. LC 81-47108. 96p. (gr. 5 up). 1981. PLB 13.89 (ISBN 0-397-31925-8, Lipp Jr Bks). HarpC Child Bks.

Rogers, Donald J. Banned! Censorship in the Schools. LC 87-7736. 128p. (gr. 5 up). 1987. lib. bdg. 12.98 (ISBN 0-671-63708-8). Messner.

Spizman, Robyn. Bulletin Boards: For Students to Make & Use. Pesiri, Evelyn, illus. 48p. (gr. k-6). 1984. wkbk. 5.95 (ISBN 0-86653-219-6, GA 571). Good Apple.

—Bulletin Boards: For the Whole School to Enjoy. Pesiri, Evelyn, illus. 48p. (gr. k-6). 1984. wkbk. 5.95 (ISBN 0-86653-260-9, GA 572). Good Apple.

—Bulletin Boards: Ideas to Reuse & Recycle. Pesiri, Evelyn, illus. 64p. (gr. k-6). 1984. wkbk. 6.95 (ISBN 0-86653-259-5, GA 565). Good Apple.

—Bulletin Boards: Letters, Borders & Background Materials. Pesiri, Evelyn, illus. 48p. (gr. k-6). 1984. wkbk. 5.95 (ISBN 0-86653-215-3, GA 566). Good Apple.

SCHOOL ATTENDANCE

see also Child Labor; Dropouts

Braithwaite, Althea. Starting School. Stubbs, Joanna, illus. 24p. (gr. k-2). 1990. pap. 1.95 (ISBN 1-878624-25-3). McClanahan Bk.

Gross, Alan. I Don't Want to Go to School. LC 81-17034. (Illus.). (ps-3). 1982. PLB 13.93 (ISBN 0-516-03496-0); pap. 3.95 (ISBN 0-516-43496-9). Childrens.

Paschos, Jacqueline & Destang, Francoise. Come to School. (ps). pap. 0.35 (ISBN 0-8091-6505-8). Paulist Pr.

Ready for School. (Illus.). 32p. (ps). 1985. pap. write for info. (ISBN 0-307-03585-9, Pub. by Golden Bks). Western Pub.

Shles, Larry. Do I have to Go to School Today? Squib Measures Up. Winch, Bradley L., ed. Shles, Larry, illus. 64p. (Orig.). (gr. k up). 1989. pap. 7.95 (ISBN 0-915190-62-1, JP9062-1). Jalmar Pr.

SCHOOL ATTENDANCE–FICTION

Cartwright, Stephen, illus. Going to School. 16p. (ps up). 1986. 2.95 (ISBN 0-86020-968-7). EDC.

Coles, Allison. Michael's First Day at School. Charlton, Michael, illus. 28p. (ps up). 1985. 3.95 (ISBN 0-88110-266-0). EDC.

Eyles, Heather. Well, I Never! Ross, Tony, illus. 32p. (ps-3). 1990. 11.95 (ISBN 0-87951-383-7). Overlook Pr.

Goodall, John S. Naughty Nancy Goes to School. Goodall, John S., illus. LC 85-70230. 32p. 1985. 12.95 (ISBN 0-689-50329-6, M K McElderry). Macmillan Child Grp.

Green, Wendy. Starting School. (ps-3). 1989. pap. 1.95 (ISBN 0-7459-1739-9). Lion USA.

Hogan, Paula Z. Sometimes I Don't Like School. Ford, Pam, illus. Smith, David L., intro. by. LC 79-24055. (Illus.). 32p. (gr. k-6). 1980. PLB 16.67 (ISBN 0-8172-1357-0). Raintree Pubs.

L'Engle, Madeleine. And Both Were Young. (Orig.). (gr. 7 up). 1983. pap. 3.50 (ISBN 0-440-90229-0, LFL). Dell.

Tester, Sylvia R. We Laughed a Lot, My First Day of School. Hook, Frances, illus. LC 78-10900. (ps-3). 1979. PLB 12.96 (ISBN 0-89565-020-7). Childs World.

SCHOOL LIBRARIES

see also Children's Literature; Libraries

Altman, David. Library Instruction for the High School Student. (Illus.). 56p. (gr. 9-12). 1988. wkbk. 39.00 (ISBN 0-936007-13-3, 3045); instr's. guide 15.95 (ISBN 0-936007-14-1). Meridian Educ.

Hart, Thomas L. Instruction in School Library Media Center Use, K-12. 2nd ed. LC 84-18405. 430p. (gr. k-12). 1985. pap. text ed. 15.00x (ISBN 0-8389-0418-1). ALA.

SCHOOL DROPOUTS

see Dropouts

SCHOOL LIFE

see Students

SCHOOL ENROLLMENT

see School Attendance

SCHOOL MANAGEMENT

see School Administration and Organization

SCHOOL INSPECTION

see School Administration and Organization

SCHOOL MUSIC

see Music–Study and Teaching

SCHOOL JOURNALISM

see College and School Journalism

SCHOOL NEWSPAPERS

see College and School Journalism

SCHOOL ORGANIZATION

see School Administration and Organization

SCHOOL PLAYGROUNDS

see Playgrounds

SCHOOL SPORTS

see also Coaching (Athletics)

Carlson, Nancy. Making the Team. Carlson, Nancy, illus. LC 85-3775. 32p. (ps-3). 1985. PLB 9.95 (ISBN 0-87614-281-1). Carolrhoda Bks.

Matovcik, Gerard. Academic Sportfolio: Excuse Notes Are No Excuse. Pranzo, Donard, ed. (Illus.). (gr. 9-12). 1989. portfolio ser. 50.00 (ISBN 0-924086-11-4). Acad Sportfolio.

Norberg, Jon. Academic Sportfolio. Gallup, Beth, ed. Norberg, Jon, illus. 1200p. (gr. 3-6). 1987. 495.00 (ISBN 0-685-24265-X). Acad Sportfolio.
—Academic Sportfolio: Excuse Notes Are No Excuse. Pranzo, Donard, ed. Norberg, Jon, illus. (gr. 3-6). 1987. portfolio ser. 50.00 (ISBN 0-924086-00-9). Acad Sportfolio.
Pranzo, Donard. Academic Sportfolio: Excuse Notes Are No Excuse. rev. ed. Gallup, Beth, ed. (Illus.). 1985. group of 40 lessons 249.00 (ISBN 0-924086-28-9); Group 1, 400 photo masters incl. write for info. (ISBN 0-924086-29-7); Group 2, 400 photo masters incl. write for info (ISBN 0-924086-30-0). Acad Sportfolio.

SCHOOL TEACHING
see Teaching

SCHOOL WITHDRAWALS
see Dropouts

SCHOOLS
see also Colleges and Universities; Education; Kindergarten

Althea. The School Fair. (Illus.). 26p. (gr. 2-5). 1983. pap. 3.95 (ISBN 0-521-27166-5). Cambridge U Pr.
Alvarez del Real, Maria E., ed. El Dato Escolar. 3rd ed. LC 81-72099. (SPA., Illus.). 352p. (gr. 2). 1985. pap. 6.00x (ISBN 0-944499-11-2). Editorial Amer.
—Diccionario Escolar. 2nd ed. LC 83-80787. (SPA., Illus.). 228p. (gr. 2). 1986. pap. 3.75x (ISBN 0-944499-13-9). Editorial Amer.
Arnold, Caroline. Where Do You Go to School? Bertol, Carole, illus. 32p. (gr. 1-3). 1982. lib. bdg. 10.90 (ISBN 0-531-04442-4). Watts.
Berry, Joy W. Teach Me about School. Dickey, Kate, ed. LC 85-45093. (Illus.). 36p. (ps). 1986. 4.98 (ISBN 0-685-10732-9). Grolier Inc.
—What to Do When Mom or Dad Says "Get Good Grades!" Bartholomew, illus. Berry, Joy W., intro. by. LC 81-83789. (Illus.). 48p. (gr. 3-7). 1982. 4.98 (ISBN 0-941510-01-8). Living Skills.
Blackburn, Lynn B. The Class in Room Forty-Four: When a Classmate Dies. Johnson, Joy, ed. Borum, Shari, illus. 24p. (Orig.). (gr. 1-6). 1990. pap. 3.50 (ISBN 1-56123-025-1). Centering Corp.
Collis, Len. My Little School Book. Reeves, Eira, illus. 24p. (ps-3). 1988. 3.50 (ISBN 0-8120-5916-6). Barron.
Gatch, Jean. School Makes Sense...Sometimes. Turnbull, Jean, illus. LC 80-10281. 32p. (gr. k-5). 1980. 16.95 (ISBN 0-87705-494-0). Human Sci Pr.
Kalman, Bobbie. Early Schools. (Illus.). 64p. (gr. 4-5). 1982. 14.95 (ISBN 0-86505-015-5); pap. 7.95 (ISBN 0-86505-014-7). Crabtree Pub Co.
Kuklin, Susan. Going to My Nursery School. Kuklin, Susan, illus. LC 89-37077. 40p. (ps-k). 1990. 12.95 (ISBN 0-02-751237-1, Bradbury Pr). Macmillan Child Grp.
Lewis, Lois F. Carlin School, A History Book: The Story of a School in Ravenna, Ohio, U. S. A. Lewis, William B., illus. 28p. (Orig.). (gr. 5). 1989. pap. text ed. write for info. (ISBN 0-9620136-3-3). L F Lewis.
—West Main School, a History Book: The Story of a School in Ravenna, Ohio, U. S. A. Lewis, William B., illus. (Orig.). (gr. 5). 1988. pap. text ed. 2.00 (ISBN 0-9620136-0-9). L F Lewis.
Loeper, John J. Going to School in 1876. LC 83-15669. (Illus.). 96p. (gr. 4-7). 1984. 12.95 (ISBN 0-689-31015-3, Atheneum). Macmillan Child Grp.
McCune, Dianne, et al. The Welcome Back to School Book. Hierstein, Judy, illus. 112p. (gr. k-4). 1987. pap. 9.95 (ISBN 0-86653-383-4, GA1001). Good Apple.
Osborne, Judy. My Teacher Said Goodbye Today: Planning for the End of the School Year. 2nd ed. Osborne, John, photos by. (Illus.). 39p. (ps-6). 1987. pap. text ed. 9.95 (ISBN 0-9618303-8-7). Emijo Pubns.
Petty, Kate. Starting School. Kopper, Lisa, illus. 24p. (gr. 1-3). 1987. PLB 5.29 (ISBN 0-531-17072-1, Gloucester Pr). Watts.
Scarry, Richard. Getting Ready for School. Scarry, Richard, illus. 32p. (ps-k). 1987. pap. 1.95 (ISBN 0-394-89040-X, Random Juv). Random.
Winitz, Harris. School: All about Language Ser. Baker, Syd, illus. 50p. (Orig.). (gr. 7 up). 1987. pap. text ed. 8.00 (ISBN 0-939990-49-0); incl. 2 cassettes 29.00 (ISBN 0-939990-66-0). Intl Linguistics.
Wirths, Claudine G. & Bowman-Kruhm, Mary. I Hate School! How to Hang In & When to Drop Out. Stren, Patti, illus. LC 85-48248. 128p. (gr. 7 up). 1986. pap. 7.95 (ISBN 0-06-446054-1, Trophy). HarpC Child Bks.

SCHOOLS–ADMINISTRATION
see School Administration and Organization

SCHOOLS–FICTION
see also Universities and Colleges–Fiction

Adams, Barbara. The Not-Quite-Ready-for-Prime-Time Bandits. (Orig.). (gr. 3-6). 1986. pap. 2.50 (ISBN 0-440-49551-2, YB). Dell.
Adler, C. S. The Once in a While Hero. 112p. 1982. 8.95 (ISBN 0-698-20553-7, Coward). Putnam Pub Group.
Adler, David A. Eaton Stanley & the Mind Control Experiment. Drescher, Joan, illus. LC 84-21135. 112p. (gr. 2-6). 1985. 11.95 (ISBN 0-525-44117-4, DCB). Dutton Child Bks.
Adler, Susan S. Samantha Learns a Lesson: A School Story. Thieme, Jeanne, ed. Niles, Nancy, illus. 72p. (gr. 2-5). 1990. PLB 12.95 (ISBN 0-937295-83-3). Pleasant Co.
Ahlberg, Allan. The Cinderella Show. Ahlberg, Janet, illus. (ps-3). 1987. pap. 4.95 (ISBN 0-670-81037-1). Viking Child Bks.
—Starting School. Ahlberg, Janet, illus. LC 88-50053. (ps-1). 1988. pap. 11.95 (ISBN 0-670-82175-6). Viking Child Bks.
Ahlberg, Janet. Starting School. 1990. pap. 3.95 (ISBN 0-14-050843-0, Puffin). Puffin Bks.
Albright, Molly. The Mascot Mess. Connor, Eulala, illus. LC 88-15879. 96p. (gr. 3-6). 1989. PLB 9.89 (ISBN 0-8167-1484-3); pap. text ed. 2.95 (ISBN 0-8167-1485-1). Troll Assocs.
Alexander, Liza. I Want to Go to School Too: A Story about Kindergarten. (Illus.). 1990. pap. write for info. (ISBN 0-307-13113-0, Pub. by Golden Bks). Western Pub.
Alexander, Martha. Move over, Twerp. Alexander, Martha, illus. 32p. (ps-2). 1989. pap. 3.95 (ISBN 0-8037-5814-6). Dial Bks Young.
Asher, Sandy. Missing Pieces. LC 83-14381. 144p. (gr. 7 up). 1984. 12.95 (ISBN 0-385-29318-6). Delacorte.
Avi. Nothing But the Truth: A Documentary Novel. LC 91-9200. (Illus.). 192p. (gr. 6 up). 1991. 14.95 (ISBN 0-531-05959-6); RLB 14.99 (ISBN 0-531-08559-7). Orchard Bks Watts.
Baker, Barbara. Third Grade Is Terrible. Shepherd, Roni, illus. LC 88-3631. 80p. (gr. 2-5). 1989. 11.95 (ISBN 0-525-44425-4, DCB). Dutton Child Bks.
Balducci, Carolyn. Is There a Life after Graduation, Henry Birnbaum? (Illus.). (gr. 7 up). 1971. 7.95 (ISBN 0-395-12749-1). HM.
Ball, Jacqueline A. Battle of the Class Clowns. 1990. pap. 2.95 (ISBN 0-06-106007-0, PL). HarperCollins.
Bates, A. Final Exam. 1990. pap. 2.95 (ISBN 0-590-43291-5, Point). Scholastic Inc.
Bates, Betty. Everybody Say Cheese. (gr. 3-6). 1986. pap. 2.50 (ISBN 0-440-42446-1, YB). Dell.
Bauer, Marion D. Like Mother, Like Daughter. LC 85-479. 156p. (gr. 5-9). 1985. 12.95 (ISBN 0-89919-356-0, Clarion). Ticknor & Fields.
Benteen, John. Traiganme Su Cabellera. new ed. Rios, Juan A., tr. from ENG. (SPA.). 160p. 1974. pap. 0.85 (ISBN 0-88473-533-8). Fiesta Pub.
Berenstain, Stan & Berenstain, Janice. The Berenstain Bears Go to School. LC 77-79853. (Illus.). (ps-2). 1978. lib. bdg. 5.99 (ISBN 0-394-93736-8, Random Juv); pap. 2.25 (ISBN 0-394-83736-3). Random.
Best of Friends: Sixth Grade Can Really Kill You; Sixth Grade Sleepover; Sixth Grade Secrets; & A Really Popular Girl. (gr. 2-6). 1989. pap. 11.00 boxed set (ISBN 0-590-63454-2). Scholastic Inc.
Birnbaum, Bette. My School, Your School. (Illus.). 24p. 1990. PLB 12.33 (ISBN 0-8172-3583-3). Raintree Pubs.
Bloom, Hanya. Vic the Vampire, No. 1: School Ghoul. (gr. 4-7). 1990. pap. 2.95 (ISBN 0-06-106004-6, Harp PBks). HarperCollins.
Blume, Judy. Tales of a Fourth Grade Nothing. (gr. k-6). 1976. pap. 3.50 (ISBN 0-440-48474-X, YB). Dell.
—Tales of a Fourth Grade Nothing. Doty, Roy, illus. LC 70-179050. 128p. (gr. 2-5). 1972. 10.95 (ISBN 0-525-40720-0, DCB). Dutton Child Bks.
Bottner, Barbara. Let Me Tell You Everything: Memoirs of a Lovesick Intellectual. LC 88-22066. 160p. (gr. 7 up). 1989. 12.95i (ISBN 0-06-020596-2); PLB 12.89 (ISBN 0-06-020597-0). HarpC Child Bks.
—The World's Greatest Expert on Absolutely Everything... Is Crying. Bottner, Barbara, illus. LC 83-49487. 128p. (gr. 3-6). 1984. PLB 12.89 (ISBN 0-06-020589-X). HarpC Child Bks.
Bourgeois, Paulette. Too Many Chicken! (ps-3). 1991. 12.95 (ISBN 0-316-10358-6). Little.
Bradford, Jan. Caroline Zucker Gets Her Wish. Ramsey, Marcy D., illus. LC 90-31549. 96p. (gr. 2-5). 1990. PLB 9.89 (ISBN 0-8167-2019-3); pap. text ed. 2.95 (ISBN 0-8167-2020-7). Troll Assocs.
Bradman, Tony. Michael. Ross, Tony, illus. LC 90-40523. 32p. (ps-2). 1991. 13.95 (ISBN 0-02-711850-9, Mcmillan Child Bk). Macmillan Child Grp.
Brittain, Bill. The Fantastic Freshman. LC 87-35051. 160p. (gr. 7 up). 1990. pap. 3.25 (ISBN 0-06-447016-4, Trophy). HarpC Child Bks.
Brown, Marc. Arthur's Teacher Trouble. Brown, Marc, illus. 32p. (ps-3). 1989. 13.95 (ISBN 0-316-11244-5, Joy St Bks); pap. 4.95 (ISBN 0-316-11186-4, Joy St Bks). Little.
—The True Francine. Brown, Marc, illus. 32p. (ps-3). 1981. 14.95 (ISBN 0-316-11212-7, Joy St Bks). Little.
Buchanan, Heather S. George & Matilda Mouse & the Floating School. LC 89-22036. (Illus.). 40p. (ps-3). 1990. PLB 13.95 (ISBN 0-671-70613-6). S&S Trade.
Bunting, Eve. Our Sixth-Grade Sugar Babies. LC 90-5487. 160p. (gr. 4-6). 1990. 12.95 (ISBN 0-397-32451-0, Lipp Jr Bks); PLB 12.89 (ISBN 0-397-32452-9, Lipp Jr Bks). HarpC Child Bks.
—Sixth-Grade Sleepover. (Illus.). 112p. (gr. 4-6). 1987. pap. 2.50 (ISBN 0-590-40554-3, Apple Paperbacks). Scholastic Inc.
Burch, Robert. Queenie Peavy. 160p. (gr. 3-7). 1987. pap. 3.95 (ISBN 0-14-032305-8, Puffin). Puffin Bks.
Burnett, Frances H. Little Princess. Tudor, Tasha, illus. LC 63-15435. (gr. 4-6). 1963. 12.95 (ISBN 0-397-30693-8, Lipp Jr Bks); PLB 12.89 (ISBN 0-397-31339-X, Lipp Jr Bks). HarpC Child Bks.
Burningham, John. The School. LC 75-4611. (Illus.). (ps-1). 1975. PLB 11.89 (ISBN 0-690-00903-8, Crowell Jr Bks). HarpC Child Bks.
Calmenson, Stephanie. The Principal's New Clothes. Brunkus, Denise, illus. (ps-3). 1989. pap. 12.95 (ISBN 0-590-41822-X). Scholastic Inc.
—The Principal's New Clothes. Brunkus, Denise, illus. 40p. (ps-2). 1991. pap. 3.95 (ISBN 0-590-44778-5, Blue Ribbon Bks). Scholastic Inc.
Carlson, Nancy. Loudmouth George & the Sixth Grade Bully. Carlson, Nancy, illus. (gr. k-3). 1986. pap. 12.95 incl. cassette (ISBN 0-87499-014-9); incl. cassette 19.95 (ISBN 0-87499-016-5); incl. cassette, 4 paperbacks guide 27.95 (ISBN 0-317-40166-1). Live Oak Media.
Carroll, Jeri, et al. Back to School in January. Smith, Bron, illus. 144p. (gr. k-5). 1989. wkbk. 10.95 (ISBN 0-86653-470-9, GA1067). Good Apple.

Case, Mary & Shaffer, Dianna. Katie Koala Bear in What Will Katie Wear to School? (Illus.). 20p. (Orig.). 1989. pap. 4.95 (ISBN 1-877995-06-1). Koala Pub Co.
Katie Koala in What Will Katie Wear To School? is the first of a series of story books for primary students. It is designed for whole language strategies in the classroom. Katie is a charming Koala bear. In this book, she gets ready for school & dresses for cold weather. What Katie wears to school each day is carefully recorded on the Koala's family calendar. A paper reproducible cutout is available with each book, so the add-on story can be told using the feltboard. A blank calendar & graphing strategies are included also.
Publisher Provided Annotation.

Caudill, Rebecca. Schoolhouse in the Woods. (gr. k-6). 1989. pap. 2.75 (ISBN 0-440-40170-4, YB). Dell.
—Schoolroom in the Parlor. (gr. k-6). 1989. pap. 2.75 (ISBN 0-440-40200-X, YB). Dell.
Cazet, Denys. Never Spit on Your Shoes. LC 89-35164. (Illus.). 32p. (ps-1). 1990. 14.95 (ISBN 0-531-05847-6); PLB 14.99 (ISBN 0-531-08447-7). Orchard Bks Watts.
Chapman, Carol. Herbie's Troubles. Oechsli, Kelley, illus. LC 80-21848. (ps-1). 1981. 11.95 (ISBN 0-525-31645-0, DCB). Dutton Child Bks.
Chardiet, Bernice. Best Teacher in the World. (ps-3). 1990. 11.95 (ISBN 0-590-44108-6, Scholastic Hardcover). Scholastic Inc.
Chardiet, Bernice & Maccarone, Grace. School Friends. Karas, G. Brian, illus. 32p. (ps-2). 1991. 2.50 (ISBN 0-590-43306-7). Scholastic Inc.
Christian, Mary B. But Everybody Does It: Peer Pressure. Brubaker, Lee W., illus. LC 85-17112. 72p. (Orig.). (gr. 4-7). 1986. pap. 3.95 (ISBN 0-570-03636-4, 39-1098). Concordia.
Clark, Catherine. What's So Funny about Ninth Grade? LC 91-2494. 128p. (gr. 7-9). 1991. lib. bdg. 9.89 (ISBN 0-8167-2396-6); pap. text ed. 2.95 (ISBN 0-8167-2397-4). Troll Assocs.
Clarke, John O. Teddy B. Zoot. (ps-3). 1990. 13.95 (ISBN 0-8050-1452-7). H Holt & Co.
Cleary, Beverly. Dear Mr. Henshaw. large type ed. Zelinsky, Paul O., illus. 141p. (gr. 2-6). 1987. Repr. of 1983 ed. lib. bdg. 14.95 (ISBN 1-55736-001-4). ABC-CLIO.
—Ellen Tebbits. Darling, Louis, illus. LC 51-11430. 160p. (gr. 3-7). 1951. 12.95 (ISBN 0-688-21264-6); PLB 12.88 (ISBN 0-688-31264-0, Morrow Jr Bks). Morrow Jr Bks.
—Jean & Johnny. Krush, Beth & Krush, Joe, illus. LC 59-7806. 288p. (gr. 6-9). 1959. 12.95 (ISBN 0-688-21740-0); PLB 12.88 (ISBN 0-688-31740-5, Morrow Jr Bks). Morrow Jr Bks.
—Muggie Maggie. Life, Kay, illus. LC 89-38959. 80p. (gr. 7 up). 1990. 11.95 (ISBN 0-688-08553-9); PLB 11.88 (ISBN 0-688-08554-7). Morrow.
—Otis Spofford. Darling, Louis, illus. LC 53-6660. (gr. 3-7). 1953. 12.95 (ISBN 0-688-21720-6); PLB 12.88 (ISBN 0-688-31720-0). Morrow Jr Bks.
—Ramona Quimby, Age 8. large type ed. Tiegreen, Alan, illus. 142p. (gr. 2-6). 1987. Repr. of 1981 ed. lib. bdg. 14.95 (ISBN 1-55736-000-6). ABC-CLIO.
—Ramona the Brave. Tiegreen, Alan, illus. LC 74-16494. 192p. (gr. 3-7). 1975. 13.95 (ISBN 0-688-22015-0); PLB 13.88 (ISBN 0-688-32015-5). Morrow.
—Ramona the Pest. Darling, Louis, illus. LC 68-12981. (gr. 3-7). 1968. 13.95 (ISBN 0-688-21721-4); PLB 13.88 (ISBN 0-688-31721-9). Morrow.
Cohen, Miriam. Best Friends. Hoban, Lillian, illus. LC 70-146620. 32p. (ps-1). 1971. 12.95 (ISBN 0-02-722800-2, Mcmillan Child Bk). Macmillan Child Grp.
—Don't Eat Too Much Turkey! Hoban, Lillian, illus. LC 86-25660. 32p. (gr. k-3). 1987. 13.95 (ISBN 0-688-07141-4); lib. bdg. 13.88 (ISBN 0-688-07142-2). Greenwillow.
—First Grade Takes a Test. Hoban, Lillian, illus. (gr. k-3). 1983. pap. 2.95 (ISBN 0-440-42500-X, YB). Dell.
—Jim's Dog Muffins. Hoban, Lillian, illus. LC 83-14090. 32p. (gr. k-3). 1984. 13.95 (ISBN 0-688-02564-1); PLB 13.88 (ISBN 0-688-02565-X). Greenwillow.

—Laura Leonora's First Amendment. (gr. 4-7). 1990. 14.95 (ISBN 0-525-67317-2, Lodestar Bks). Dutton Child Bks.
—No Good in Art. Hoban, Lillian, illus. LC 79-16566. 32p. (gr. k-3). 1980. PLB 13.88 (ISBN 0-688-84234-8). Greenwillow.
—See You in Second Grade! Hoban, Lillian, illus. LC 87-14869. 32p. (ps up). 1989. 13.95 (ISBN 0-688-07138-4); PLB 13.88 (ISBN 0-688-07139-2). Greenwillow.
—When Will I Read? Hoban, Lillian, illus. LC 76-28320. 32p. (ps-3). 1977. 13.95 (ISBN 0-688-80073-4); PLB 13.88 (ISBN 0-688-84073-6). Greenwillow.
—Will I Have a Friend? Hoban, Lillian, illus. LC 67-10127. 32p. (gr. k-1). 1967. 12.95 (ISBN 0-02-722790-1, Mcmillan Child Bk). Macmillan Child Grp.
Cole, Joanna. The Magic School Bus: At the Water Works. Degen, Bruce, illus. 40p. (gr. 1-4). 1986. pap. 12.95 (ISBN 0-590-40361-3, Scholastic Hardcover). Scholastic Inc.
—The Magic School Bus at the Waterworks. Degen, Bruce, illus. 40p. (gr. 1-4). 1988. pap. 3.95 (ISBN 0-590-40360-5). Scholastic Inc.
Conford, Ellen. The Alfred G. Graebner Memorial High School Handbook of Rules & Regulations. (gr. 7-9). 1988. pap. 2.50 (ISBN 0-671-67247-9, Archway). PB.
—The Alfred G. Graebner Memorial High School Handbook of Rules & Regulations. (gr. 7-12). 1976. 14.95 (ISBN 0-316-15293-5). Little.
—Dear Lovey Hart: I Am Desperate. 224p. (gr. 4-6). 1975. 14.95 (ISBN 0-316-15306-0). Little.
—Lenny Kandell, Smart Aleck. Gaffney-Kessell, Walter, illus. 128p. (gr. 4-6). 1983. 12.95 (ISBN 0-316-15313-3). Little.
—Lenny Kandell, Smart Aleck. Gaffney-Kessell, Walter, illus. 160p. (gr. 4-7). 1987. pap. 2.50 (ISBN 0-671-64190-5, Archway). PB.
—The Revenge of the Incredible Dr. Rancid & His Youthful Assistant, Jeffrey. 132p. (gr. 1-8). 1980. 14.95 (ISBN 0-316-15288-9). Little.
—Seven Days to a Brand-New Me. 96p. (gr. 5 up). 1981. 14.95 (ISBN 0-316-15311-7). Little.
Cooney, Linda A. Freshman. 240p. (Orig.). (gr. 7 up). 1987. pap. 2.50 (ISBN 0-317-55235-X). Scholastic Inc.
—Freshman Lies. 1991. pap. 3.50 (ISBN 0-06-106005-4, Harp PBks). HarperCollins.
—Junior. 240p. (Orig.). (gr. 7 up). 1988. pap. 2.50 (ISBN 0-590-41677-4). Scholastic Inc.
Cooper, Ilene. Choosing Sides. (Illus.). 218p. (gr. 3-7). 1991. pap. 3.95 (ISBN 0-14-034566-3, Puffin). Puffin Bks.
—Frances & Friends. Ortiz, Vilma, illus. LC 91-7504. 128p. (Orig.). (gr. 3-6). 1991. lib. bdg. 8.99 (ISBN 0-679-91113-8, Bullseye Bks); pap. 2.99 (ISBN 0-679-81113-3, Bullseye Bks). Knopf.
—Frances Four-eyes. Ortiz, Vilma, illus. LC 90-28270. 128p. (Orig.). (gr. 3-6). 1991. lib. bdg. 8.99 (ISBN 0-679-91112-X, Bullseye Bks); pap. 2.99 (ISBN 0-679-81112-5, Bullseye Bks). Knopf.
—Queen of the Sixth Grade. 160p. (gr. 3 up). 1990. pap. 3.95 (ISBN 0-14-034028-9, Puffin). Puffin Bks.
Corbett, Scott. Down with Wimps! Ross, Larry, illus. LC 84-1579. 96p. (gr. 3-6). 1984. 10.95 (ISBN 0-525-44108-5, DCB). Dutton Child Bks.
Coryell, Susan. Eaglebait. (gr. 7 up). 1989. 14.95 (ISBN 0-15-200442-4, Gulliver Bks). HarBraceJ.
Cossi, Olga. Gus the Bus. Schneider, Howie, illus. (ps-3). 1989. pap. 11.95 (ISBN 0-590-41616-2). Scholastic Inc.
Cowley, Joy. My Sloppy Tiger Goes to School, 6 bks. Stevenson, Peter, illus. 16p. (Orig.). (gr. k-2). 1987. Set. pap. text ed. 19.80 (ISBN 1-55624-749-4). Wright Group.
—My Sloppy Tiger Goes to School. Stevenson, Peter, illus. 16p. (Orig.). (gr. k-2). 1987. pap. text ed. 23.00 (ISBN 1-55624-172-0). Wright Group.
Crews, Donald. School Bus. LC 85-576. (Illus.). 32p. (ps-1). 1985. pap. 3.95 (ISBN 0-14-050549-0, Puffin). Puffin Bks.
Crutcher, Chris. Stotan! LC 85-12712. 192p. (gr. 7 up). 1986. reinforced trade ed. 10.25 (ISBN 0-688-05715-2). Greenwillow.
Cuyler, Margery. The Trouble with Soap. LC 81-12636. 144p. (gr. 5 up). 1982. 9.95 (ISBN 0-525-45111-0, DCB). Dutton Child Bks.
Danziger, Paula. The Cat Ate My Gymsuit. LC 74-5501. 128p. (gr. 7 up). 1974. 14.95 (ISBN 0-385-28183-8); PLB 14.95 (ISBN 0-385-28194-3). Delacorte.
—This Place Has No Atmosphere. (gr. k-6). 1989. pap. 3.25 (ISBN 0-440-40205-0, YB). Dell.
Davis, Melissa. Yearbook. 224p. (Orig.). (gr. 7 up). 1987. pap. 2.95 (ISBN 0-590-44118-3). Scholastic Inc.
DeClements, Barthe. How Do You Lose Those Ninth Grade Blues? LC 83-5750. 144p. (gr. 3-7). 1983. pap. 12.95 (ISBN 0-670-38122-5). Viking Child Bks.
—I Never Asked You to Understand Me. LC 85-40839. 144p. (gr. 7 up). 1986. pap. 12.95 (ISBN 0-670-80768-0). Viking Child Bks.
—Nothing's Fair in Fifth Grade. 144p. (gr. 3 up). 1990. pap. 2.95 (ISBN 0-14-034443-8, Puffin). Puffin Bks.
—Seventeen & In-Between. 180p. (gr. 7-9). 1984. pap. 13.95 (ISBN 0-670-63615-0). Viking Child Bks.
—Sixth Grade Can Really Kill You. LC 85-40382. 146p. (gr. 5-8). 1985. pap. 12.95 (ISBN 0-670-80656-0). Viking Child Bks.
Delton, Judy. The New Girl at School. Hoban, Lillian, illus. LC 79-11409. (gr. k-3). 1979. 12.95 (ISBN 0-525-35780-7, DCB). Dutton Child Bks.
Denton, Terry. The School for Laughter. Denton, Terry, illus. 32p. (gr. k-3). 1990. 13.95 (ISBN 0-395-53353-8). HM.
De Pressense, Domitille. Natalie: The Germ. (Illus.). 28p. (ps-1). 1990. pap. 3.95 (ISBN 0-8120-4509-2). Barron.
—Natalie: The Scribbles. (Illus.). 28p. (ps-1). 1990. pap. 3.95 (ISBN 0-8120-4508-4). Barron.
Dinan, Carolyn. Say Cheese! Dinan, Carolyn, illus. LC 85-40591. 32p. (ps-3). 1986. pap. 9.95 (ISBN 0-670-80954-3). Viking Child Bks.
Domke, Todd. Grounded. LC 81-14267. 192p. (gr. 4-7). 1982. pap. 9.95 (ISBN 0-394-85163-3). Knopf.
Du Jardin, Rosamond. Boy Trouble. Reissue. ed. LC 53-5423. 192p. (gr. 7 up). 1988. Repr. of 1953 ed. PLB 12.89 (ISBN 0-397-32263-1, Lipp Jr Bks). HarpC Child Bks.
Duncan, Lois. Wonder Kid Meets the Evil Lunch Snatcher. Sanfilippo, Margaret, illus. LC 87-26490. 76p. (gr. 7-10). 1988. 9.95 (ISBN 0-316-19558-8). Little.
Dunn, Ben. Ninja High School, Vol. 1: Graphic Album. 2nd ed. Castro, Carlos & Dunn, Ben, illus. 128p. (gr. 10). 1990. pap. 9.95 (ISBN 0-944735-13-4). Malibu Graphics.
Dygard, Thomas J. Forward Pass. LC 89-33427. (Illus.). 192p. (gr. 7 up). 1989. 11.95 (ISBN 0-688-07961-X). Morrow Jr Bks.
Elliott, Dan. Grover Goes to School. Chartier, Normand, illus. LC 81-15398. 40p. (gr. 1-3). 1982. lib. bdg. 6.99 (ISBN 0-394-95176-X); pap. 4.95 (ISBN 0-394-85176-5). Random.
Ellis, Jana. Better Than the Truth. LC 88-15881. 160p. (gr. 7 up). 1988. pap. text ed. 2.50 (ISBN 0-8167-1362-6). Troll Assocs.
—Never Stop Smiling. LC 88-12390. 160p. (gr. 7 up). 1988. pap. text ed. 2.50 (ISBN 0-8167-1360-X). Troll Assocs.
—Playing Games. LC 88-12389. 160p. (gr. 7 up). 1988. pap. text ed. 2.50 (ISBN 0-8167-1358-8). Troll Assocs.
Feder, Paula K. Where Does the Teacher Live? Hoban, Lillian, illus. LC 78-13157. (gr. k-3). 1979. 12.95 (ISBN 0-525-42586-1, DCB). Dutton Child Bks.
Fitzgerald, John D. The Great Brain at the Academy. 164p. (gr. k-6). 1982. pap. 2.95 (ISBN 0-440-43113-1, YB). Dell.
—The Great Brain at the Academy. Mayer, Mercer, illus. LC 72-712. 176p. (gr. 4-7). 1985. 12.95 (ISBN 0-8037-3039-X); PLB 11.89 (ISBN 0-8037-3040-3). Dial Bks Young.
Fitzhugh, Louise. Harriet the Spy. large type ed. Fitzhugh, Louise, illus. 282p. (gr. 2-6). 1987. Repr. of 1964 ed. lib. bdg. 13.95 (ISBN 1-55736-012-X). ABC-CLIO.
Frandsen, Karen G. I Started School Today. LC 83-23169. (Illus.). 32p. (ps-2). 1984. lib. bdg. 13.93 (ISBN 0-516-03495-2); pap. 3.95 (ISBN 0-516-43495-0). Childrens.
—Michael's New Haircut. Frandsen, Karen G., illus. LC 86-11696. 32p. (ps-3). 1986. PLB 13.93 (ISBN 0-516-03545-2); pap. 3.95 (ISBN 0-516-43545-0). Childrens.
Frederick, Ruth. Where's Tommy? O'Connell, Ruth A., illus. 32p. (gr. 1-2). 1991. pap. 3.99 saddle stitch (ISBN 0-87403-806-5, 24-03896). Standard Pub.
Geller, Mark. My Life in the Seventh Grade. LC 85-45265. 160p. (gr. 5-7). 1986. PLB 11.89 (ISBN 0-06-021982-3). HarpC Child Bks.
Giff, Patricia R. The Case of the Cool-Itch Kid. (gr. k-6). 1989. pap. 2.75 (ISBN 0-440-40199-2). Dell.
—The Fourth Grade Celebrity. 128p. (gr. k-6). 1989. pap. 2.95 (ISBN 0-440-42676-6, YB). Dell.
—Fourth Grade Celebrity. Morrill, Leslie, illus. 128p. (gr. 4-6). 1984. 8.95 (ISBN 0-385-28308-3). Delacorte.
—Garbage Juice for Breakfast. (gr. 1-4). 1989. pap. 2.75 (ISBN 0-440-40207-7, YB). Dell.
—New Kids of the Polk Street School, 6 vols. (gr. 4-7). 1990. pap. 16.50 boxed set (ISBN 0-440-36029-3). Dell.
—Pickle Puss. (Orig.). (gr. k-3). 1986. pap. 2.75 (ISBN 0-440-46844-2, YB). Dell.
—Pickle Puss. Sims, Blanche, illus. (ps-3). 1986. pap. 8.95 (ISBN 0-385-29477-8). Delacorte.
—Purple Climbing Days. Sims, Blanche, illus. (ps-3). 1986. pap. 8.95 (ISBN 0-385-29500-6). Delacorte.
—Say "Cheese" Sims, Blanche, illus. (ps-3). 1986. pap. 8.95 (ISBN 0-385-29501-4). Delacorte.
—Say "Cheese, No. 10. Sims, Blanche, illus. (gr. 6-9). 1985. pap. 2.75 (ISBN 0-440-47639-9, YB). Dell.
—Stacy Says Good-Bye. Sims, Blanche, illus. 80p. (gr. k-3). 1989. pap. 2.75 (ISBN 0-440-40135-6, YB). Dell.
—Sunny Side Up. (Orig.). (gr. k-3). 1986. pap. 2.75 (ISBN 0-440-48406-5, YB). Dell.
—Watch Out! Man-Eating Snake. 80p. (Orig.). (gr. k-6). 1988. pap. 2.75 (ISBN 0-440-40085-6, YB). Dell.
Gilden, Mel. Fifth Grade Monsters, No. 12: Werewolf Come Home. 1990. pap. 2.75 (ISBN 0-380-75908-X, Camelot). Avon.
—How to Be a Vampire in One Easy Lesson. 1990. pap. 2.75 (ISBN 0-380-75906-3, Camelot). Avon.
—Island of the Weird. 96p. 1990. pap. 2.75 (ISBN 0-380-75907-1, Camelot). Avon.
Gilson, Jamie. Hobie Hanson, Greatest Hero of the Mall. Riggio, Anita, illus. 160p. (gr. 3-6). 1990. pap. 2.95 (ISBN 0-671-70646-2, Minstrel Bks). PB.
Girion, Barbara. The Chicken Bone Wish. Cuffari, Richard, illus. 160p. (gr. 4-6). 1982. pap. 2.50 (ISBN 0-590-40870-4, Apple Paperbacks). Scholastic Inc.
Gordon, Sharon. Show & Tell. Kolding, Richard M., illus. LC 86-30855. 32p. (gr. k-2). 1987. PLB 7.06 (ISBN 0-8167-0994-7); pap. text ed. 1.95 (ISBN 0-8167-0995-5). Troll Assocs.
Gormley, Beatrice. Fifth Grade Magic. McCully, Emily A., illus. 128p. (gr. 3-7). 1984. pap. 2.95 (ISBN 0-380-67439-4, 60216-4, Camelot). Avon.
—More Fifth Grade Magic. 112p. 1990. pap. 2.95 (ISBN 0-380-70883-3, Camelot). Avon.
Goudge, Eileen. Winner All the Way. 160p. (Orig.). (gr. 7-12). 1984. pap. 2.25 (ISBN 0-440-99480-2, LFL). Dell.
Greene, Constance C. A Girl Called Al. 128p. (gr. 5-9). 1977. pap. 2.95 (ISBN 0-440-42810-6, YB). Dell.
Haas, Dorothy. Peanut Butter & Jelly: Trouble at Alcott School, No. 4. 1989. pap. 2.50 (ISBN 0-590-41509-3). Scholastic Inc.
Hackett, Christine. Little House in the Classroom. Filkins, Vanessa, illus. 112p. (gr. 3-5). 1989. wkbk. 9.95 (ISBN 0-86653-444-X, GA1052). Good Apple.
Hall, Lynn. The Giver. LC 84-27676. 128p. (gr. 7 up). 1985. 12.95 (ISBN 0-684-18312-9, Scribners Young Read). Macmillan Child Grp.
Hallinan, P. K. First Day of School. Hallinan, P. K., illus. 24p. (gr. k-6). 1987. 2.95 (ISBN 0-8249-8166-9). Ideals.
Hamilton, Dorothy. Rosalie. Unada, illus. LC 76-39961. 128p. (gr. 3-10). 1977. pap. text ed. 3.95 (ISBN 0-8361-1807-3). Herald Pr.
Hannan, Peter. School after Dark. Hannan, Peter, illus. LC 90-33407. 32p. (Orig.). (ps-2). 1991. PLB 8.99 (ISBN 0-679-90288-0); pap. 3.95 (ISBN 0-679-80288-6). Knopf.
Harrell, Janice. So Long, Senior Year. 155p. 1988. pap. 2.25 (ISBN 0-373-88038-3). Harlequin Bks.
Hart, Avery & Mantell, Paul. Ninth Grade Outcast. LC 91-2492. 128p. (gr. 7-9). 1991. lib. bdg. 9.89 (ISBN 0-8167-2392-3); pap. text ed. 2.95 (ISBN 0-8167-2393-1). Troll Assocs.
Haynes, Betsy. Grade Me. (gr. 7). 1989. pap. 2.75 (ISBN 0-685-33584-4). Bantam.
—Seventh-Grade Menace. (gr. 4 up). 1989. pap. 2.75 (ISBN 0-553-15763-9). Bantam.
Haywood, Carolyn. B Is for Betsy. Haywood, Carolyn, illus. LC 85-16381. (gr. 1-5). 1939. 12.95 (ISBN 0-15-204975-4, HJ). HarBraceJ.
—B Is for Betsy. Yakovetic, Joe, contrib. by. 168p. (gr. 2-5). 1990. pap. 3.95 (ISBN 0-15-204977-0). HarbraceJ.
—Back to School with Betsy. Haywood, Carolyn, illus. LC 85-16380. (gr. 1-5). 1943. 12.95 (ISBN 0-15-205512-6, HJ). HarBraceJ.
—Back to School with Betsy. Yakovetic, Joe, contrib. by. 192p. (gr. 2-5). 1990. pap. 3.95 (ISBN 0-15-205515-0). HarbraceJ.
—Betsy & Billy. Haywood, Carolyn, illus. LC 41-51926. (gr. 1-5). 1941. 12.95 (ISBN 0-15-206765-5, HJ). HarBraceJ.
—Betsy & Billy. Yakovetic, Joe, contrib. by. 156p. (gr. 2-5). 1990. pap. 3.95 (ISBN 0-15-206768-X). HarbraceJ.
—Betsy & the Boys. Yakovetic, Joe, contrib. by. 192p. (gr. 2-5). 1990. pap. 3.95 (ISBN 0-15-206947-X). HarbraceJ.
Henkes, Kevin. Chrysanthemum. LC 90-39803. (Illus.). 32p. (ps up). 1991. 13.95 (ISBN 0-688-09699-9); PLB 13.88 (ISBN 0-688-09700-6). Greenwillow.
Hentoff, Nat. Does This School Have Capital Punishment? 160p. (gr. 7-11). 1983. pap. 2.95 (ISBN 0-440-92070-1, LFL). Dell.
—This School Is Driving Me Crazy. 160p. (gr. 7 up). 1978. pap. 2.95 (ISBN 0-440-98702-4, LFL). Dell.
Herman, Charlotte. Millie Cooper, 3B. Cogancherry, Helen, illus. 80p. (gr. 3-7). 1986. pap. 3.95 (ISBN 0-14-032072-5, Puffin). Puffin Bks.
Herman, Gail. Time for School, Little Dinosaur. Gorbaty, Norman, illus. LC 89-70331. 24p. (Orig.). (ps-2). 1990. pap. 2.25 (ISBN 0-679-80789-6). Random.
Hermes, Patricia. Friends Are Like That. LC 83-18407. 128p. (gr. 4-6). 1984. 14.95 (ISBN 0-15-229722-7, HJ). HarBraceJ.
—I Hate Being Gifted. 144p. 1990. 14.95 (ISBN 0-399-21687-1, Putnam). Putnam Pub Group.
—A Place for Jeremy. LC 86-31793. (Illus.). 160p. (gr. 3-7). 1987. 13.95 (ISBN 0-15-262350-7). HarBraceJ.
Hiller, B. B. Rent a Third Grader. 192p. (gr. 2-4). 1988. pap. 2.75 (ISBN 0-590-40966-2). Scholastic Inc.
Hilton, James. Good-Bye, Mr. Chips. (Illus.). (gr. 7 up). 1962. 14.95 (ISBN 0-316-36420-7, Pub. by Atlantic Monthly Pr). Little.
—Goodbye, Mr. Chips. (gr. 7 up). 1969. pap. 2.95 (ISBN 0-553-25613-0). Bantam.
Hodgman, Ann. Rubberband Stew. (gr. 4 up). 1990. pap. 2.75 (ISBN 0-425-12267-0). Berkley Pub.
Hope, Laura L. Bobbsey Twins' Mystery at School. (gr. 1-4). 1930. 4.50 (ISBN 0-448-08004-4, G&D). Putnam Pub Group.
Hopkins, Lila. Talking Turkey. 1989. 12.95 (ISBN 0-531-15119-0). Watts.
Hopper, Nancy J. Hang on, Harvey! 96p. (gr. 5-9). 1984. pap. 2.25 (ISBN 0-440-43371-1, YB). Dell.
—The Interrupted Education of Huey B. 192p. (gr. 7 up). 1991. 14.95 (ISBN 0-525-67336-9, Lodestar Bks). Dutton Child Bks.
Hughes, Thomas. Tom Brown's School Days. Hearn, Michael P., intro. by. LC 52-8383. (gr. 7 up). 1986. pap. 2.95 (ISBN 0-451-52000-9, Sig Classics). NAL-Dutton.

—Tom Brown's School Days. 1987. Repr. lib. bdg. 21.95x (ISBN 0-89966-554-3). Buccaneer Bks.
Hughes, Thomas P. Tom Brown's Schooldays. Sanders, Andrew, ed. (Illus.). 456p. 1989. pap. 2.95 (ISBN 0-19-282198-9). Oxford U Pr.
Hurwitz, Johanna. Class Clown. Hamanaka, Sheila, illus. LC 86-23624. 112p. (gr. 1-4). 1987. 12.95 (ISBN 0-688-06723-9). Morrow Jr Bks.
—Class President. Hamanaka, Sheila, illus. LC 89-28600. 96p. (gr. 2 up). 1990. 12.95 (ISBN 0-688-09114-8). Morrow Jr Bks.
—Teacher's Pet. Hamamaka, Sheila, illus. LC 87-24003. 128p. (gr. 2-5). 1988. 12.95 (ISBN 0-688-07506-1). Morrow Jr Bks.
—Teacher's Pet. (gr. 2-5). 1989. pap. 2.75 (ISBN 0-590-42031-3, Apple Paperbacks). Scholastic Inc.
Jabar, Cynthia. Alice Ann Gets Ready for School, Vol. 1. 1989. 13.95 (ISBN 0-316-43457-4). Little.
Jackson, Kim. First Day of School. Goodman, John, illus. LC 84-8631. 32p. (gr. k-2). 1985. PLB 10.89 (ISBN 0-8167-0359-0); pap. text ed. 2.95 (ISBN 0-8167-0439-2). Troll Assocs.
Johnston, Annie F. The Little Colonel at Boarding School. (gr. 5 up). 13.95 (ISBN 0-89201-032-0). Zenger Pub.
Jones, William E. & Goldberg, Minerva J. Going to School. LC 68-56811. (Illus.). 32p. (ps-1). 1968. PLB 9.95 (ISBN 0-87783-015-0). Oddo.
Kahaner, Ellen. Fourth Grade Loser. Henderson, David F., illus. LC 90-26791. 96p. (gr. 3-5). 1991. lib. bdg. 9.89 (ISBN 0-8167-2384-2); pap. text ed. 2.95 (ISBN 0-8167-2385-0). Troll Assocs.
—What's So Great about Fourth Grade? Henry, Paul, illus. LC 89-20602. 96p. (gr. 3-5). 1989. PLB 9.89 (ISBN 0-8167-1702-8); pap. text ed. 2.95 (ISBN 0-8167-1703-6). Troll Assocs.
Kassem, Lou. Middle School Blues. 192p. (gr. 3-7). 1987. pap. 2.95 (ISBN 0-380-70363-7, Camelot). Avon.
—Middle School Blues. (gr. 4-7). 1986. 12.95 (ISBN 0-395-39499-6). HM.
Kaye, Marilyn. The Atonement of Mindy Wise. Van Doren, Liz, ed. 160p. (gr. 7 up). 1991. 15.95 (ISBN 0-15-200402-5, Gulliver Bks). HarBraceJ.
—A Friend Like Phoebe, No. 5. (gr. 3 up). 1989. 13.95 (ISBN 0-15-200450-5, Gulliver Bks). HarBraceJ.
Keller, Charles. School Daze. Weissman, Sam Q., illus. (gr. 2-5). 1981. pap. 3.95 (ISBN 0-13-793612-5, Pub. by Treehouse). P-H.
Keller, Holly. The New Boy. LC 90-41757. (Illus.). 24p. (ps up). 1991. 13.95 (ISBN 0-688-09827-4); PLB 13.88 (ISBN 0-688-09828-2). Greenwillow.
Kennedy, M. L. Junior High Jitters. 192p. (Orig.). (gr. 5-9). 1986. pap. 2.25 (ISBN 0-590-40342-7). Scholastic Inc.
Kenyon, Kate. Eight Grade Hero? 160p. (Orig.). (gr. 7 up). 1987. pap. 2.50 (ISBN 0-317-57585-6). Scholastic Inc.
—Eighth Grade to the Rescue. 160p. (Orig.). (gr. 7 up). 1987. pap. 2.50 (ISBN 0-590-40899-2). Scholastic Inc.
Kerby, Mona. Thirty-Eight Weeks Till Summer Vacation. Rosales, Melodye, illus. 128p. (gr. 3-7). 1989. pap. 11.95 (ISBN 0-670-82887-4). Viking Child Bks.
Kerr, M. E. Fell Back. LC 88-35762. 192p. (gr. 7 up). 1989. 11.95 (ISBN 0-06-023292-7); PLB 11.89 (ISBN 0-06-023293-5). HarpC Child Bks.
Kiesel, Stanley. The War Between the Pitiful Teachers & the Splendid Kids. 208p. (gr. 7 up). 1982. pap. 2.95 (ISBN 0-380-57802-6, 60179-6, Flare). Avon.
Kingman, Lee. Break a Leg, Betsy, Maybe. 192p. (gr. 7 up). 1979. pap. 1.50 (ISBN 0-440-90794-2, LFL). Dell.
Kirkland, Dianna C. Last Year I Failed...but. Orlowski, Dennis, illus. 32p. (Orig.). (ps-5). 1981. pap. 6.50 (ISBN 0-940370-04-2); counseling activity guide-failure 6.50 (ISBN 0-940370-07-7). Aid-U Pub.
Klein, Robin. Hating Alison Ashley. 186p. (gr. 5-9). 1985. pap. 3.95 (ISBN 0-14-031672-8, Puffin). Puffin Bks.
Kline, Suzy. Herbie Jones & the Class Gift. Williams, Richard, illus. 96p. (gr. 3-7). 1989. pap. 3.95 (ISBN 0-14-032723-1, Puffin). Puffin Bks.
—Horrible Harry in Room 2B. Remkiewicz, Frank, illus. 64p. (gr. 2-5). 1990. pap. 2.95 (ISBN 0-14-032825-4, Puffin). Puffin Bks.
Koosak, Tara. School Biz Is..., Bk. 1. rev. ed. LC 90-70016. (Illus.). 52p. (gr. 1-8). 1991. pap. 3.50 (ISBN 0-934426-33-3). NAPSAC Reprods.
Korman, Gordon. A Semester in the Life of a Garbage Bag. (gr. 7 up). 1989. pap. 2.75 (ISBN 0-590-40695-7, Point). Scholastic Inc.
—Son of Interflux. LC 86-6448. 288p. (gr. 7-10). 1986. pap. 12.95 (ISBN 0-590-40163-7). Scholastic Inc.
Korschunow, Irina. Adam Draws Himself a Dragon. Skofield, James, tr. from GER. Rahn, Mary, illus. LC 85-45256. 48p. (gr. k-3). 1986. PLB 11.89 (ISBN 0-06-023252-8). HarpC Child Bks.
Kraus, Robert. Miss Gator's School House, 6 bks. Kraus, Robert, illus. (gr. k-3). 1989. Set, 48p. ea. lib. bdg. 53.88 (ISBN 0-671-94105-4); Set, 48p. ea. pap. 21.00 (ISBN 0-671-94106-2). Messner.
—Spider's First Day at School. (Illus.). 32p. (Orig.). (ps-2). 1987. pap. 2.50 (ISBN 0-590-41091-1). Scholastic Inc.
Kroll, Steven. Otto. Delaney, Ned, illus. LC 82-19024. 48p. (ps-3). 1983. 5.95 (ISBN 0-8193-1105-7); PLB 5.95 (ISBN 0-8193-1106-5). Parents.
Landin, Les & Gardner, Mary. Homework Sweet Homework. 1990. pap. 4.95 (ISBN 0-8224-3603-5). Fearon Teach Aids.
Lasky, Kathryn. Pageant. LC 86-12087. 228p. (gr. 7 up). 1986. 14.95 (ISBN 0-02-751720-9, Four Winds). Macmillan Child Grp.
Lawlor, Laurie. How To Survive Third Grade. Levine, Abby, ed. (Illus.). 72p. (gr. 2-5). 1988. PLB 8.95 (ISBN 0-8075-3433-1). A Whitman.
L'Engle, Madeleine. And Both Were Young. (Orig.). (gr. 7 up). 1983. pap. 3.50 (ISBN 0-440-90229-0, LFL). Dell.
Lenski, Lois. Prairie School. LC 51-11169. (Illus.). 208p. (gr. 4-7). 1951. PLB 15.89 (ISBN 0-397-30194-4, Lipp Jr Bks). HarpC Child Bks.
Leonard, Marcia. Hannah the Hamster Hunter. Brook, Bonnie, ed. Chambliss, Maxie & Iosa, Ann, illus. 24p. (ps-1). 1990. 4.95 (ISBN 0-671-70404-4); lib. bdg. 9.98 (ISBN 0-671-70399-4). Silver Pr.
Leroe, Ellen. Meet Your Match, Cupid Delaney. (Illus.). 160p. (gr. 7 up). 1990. 13.95 (ISBN 0-525-67309-1, Lodestar Bks). Dutton Child Bks.
Leverich, Kathleen. Best Enemies. Lamb, Susan C., illus. LC 88-19150. (gr. 1 up). 1989. 10.95 (ISBN 0-688-08316-1). Greenwillow.
LeVert, John. The Flight of the Cassowary. 228p. (gr. 7 up). 1986. 14.95 (ISBN 0-316-52196-5, Pub. by Joy Street Bks). Little.
Levy, Elizabeth. Nice Little Girls. Gerstein, Mordicai, illus. LC 73-15394. (gr. k-3). 1978. pap. 2.75 (ISBN 0-440-06360-4). Delacorte.
—Something Queer at the Haunted School. Gerstein, Mordicai, illus. 48p. (gr. 1-4). 1983. pap. 2.75 (ISBN 0-440-48461-8, YB). Dell.
Lexau, Joan M. Olaf Reads. Weiss, Harvey, illus. (gr. k-3). 1965. PLB 6.46 (ISBN 0-8037-6559-2). Dial Bks Young.
Lindgren, Astrid. I Want to Go to School, Too! Lucas, Barbara, tr. from SWE. Wikland, Llon, illus. 32p. (ps up). 1987. 10.95 (ISBN 9-12-958328-4, Pub. by R & S Bks). FS&G.
Littke, Lael. Prom Dress. (gr. 6-10). 1989. pap. 2.75 (ISBN 0-590-41929-3). Scholastic Inc.
Little, Jean. Listen for the Singing. LC 90-40250. 272p. (gr. 4-7). 1991. pap. 3.95 (ISBN 0-06-440394-7, Trophy). HarpC Child Bks.
—Listen for the Singing. LC 90-40019. 272p. (gr. 4-7). 1991. PLB 14.89 (ISBN 0-06-023910-7). HarpC Child Bks.
Littledale, Freya. The Snow Child. Lavallee, Barbara & Shtainmets, Leon, illus. 32p. (gr. 2-5). 1989. pap. 2.50 (ISBN 0-590-42141-7). Scholastic Inc.
Lovelace, Maud H. Betsy & Joe. Neville, Vera, illus. LC 48-8096. 256p. (gr. 5 up). 1948. 14.95 (ISBN 0-690-13378-2, Crowell Jr Bks). HarpC Child Bks.
—Betsy Was a Junior. Neville, Vera, illus. LC 46-11995. 248p. (gr. 5 up). 1947. 14.95 (ISBN 0-690-13946-2, Crowell Jr Bks). HarpC Child Bks.
Maccarone, Grace. The Haunting of Grade Three. Oechsli, Ke-ly, illus. 96p. (Orig.). (gr. 4-6). 1987. pap. 2.50 (ISBN 0-590-40921-2, Lucky Star). Scholastic Inc.
McGuire, Leslie. Is There Life after Sixth Grade? Henry, Paul, illus. LC 89-20615. 96p. (gr. 4-6). 1990. PLB 9.89 (ISBN 0-8167-1706-0); pap. text ed. 2.95 (ISBN 0-8167-1707-9). Troll Assocs.
—The Terrible Truth about Third Grade. Henderson, David F., illus. LC 90-26788. 96p. (gr. 2-4). 1991. lib. bdg. 9.89 (ISBN 0-8167-2382-6); pap. text ed. 2.95 (ISBN 0-8167-2383-4). Troll Assocs.
McKenna, Colleen O. Fourth Grade Is a Jinx. LC 88-23897. 176p. (gr. 4-6). 1989. pap. 10.95 (ISBN 0-590-41735-5). Scholastic Inc.
—Fourth Grade Is a Jinx. (ps-3). 1990. pap. 2.75 (ISBN 0-590-41736-3). Scholastic Inc.
McKenzie, Ellen K. Stargone John. Low, William, illus. 80p. (gr. 2-4). 1990. 13.95 (ISBN 0-8050-1451-9). H Holt & Co.
McMullan, Kate. The Great Eggspectations of Lila Fenwick. De Groat, Diane, illus. 148p. (gr. 3-7). 1991. bds. 13.95 jacketed (ISBN 0-374-32774-2). FS&G.
Maguire, Jesse. Nowhere High No. 4: On the Edge. 192p. 1991. pap. 3.50 (ISBN 0-8041-0447-6). Ivy Books.
Major, Beverly. Playing Sardines. Glass, Andrew, illus. (ps-2). 1989. pap. 3.95 (ISBN 0-590-41154-3). Scholastic Inc.
Mallett, Jerry & Bartch, Marian. First-Last Gravelsburg Elementary School Spelling Bee. Smith, Mark D., illus. 55p. (gr. 2-5). 1986. PLB 7.05 (ISBN 0-8479-9928-9, 101440). Perma Bound.
Malmgren, Dallin. The Ninth Issue. LC 88-22881. (gr. 7 up). 1989. pap. 14.95 (ISBN 0-440-50124-5). Delacorte.
Martin, Ann M. Claudia & Middle School. (gr. 4-7). 1991. pap. 2.95 (ISBN 0-590-44082-9). Scholastic Inc.
—Stage Fright. Sims, Blanche, illus. 144p. (gr. 4-6). 1986. pap. 2.50 (ISBN 0-590-40874-7, Apple Paperbacks). Scholastic Inc.
Masters, Susan R. The Secret Life of Hubie Hartzel. Mayo, Gretchen W., illus. LC 89-36402. 144p. (gr. 3-7). 1990. 11.95 (ISBN 0-397-32399-9, Lipp Jr Bks); PLB 11.89 (ISBN 0-397-32400-6, Lipp Jr Bks). HarpC Child Bks.
Mazer, Harry. City Light. (gr. 7 up). 1989. pap. 2.75 (ISBN 0-590-40515-2, Point). Scholastic Inc.
Merry Christmas, What's Your Name. (ps-3). 1990. 11.95 (ISBN 0-590-44334-8, Scholastic Hardcover). Scholastic Inc.
Miklowitz, Gloria D. The Emerson High Vigilantes. LC 87-25657. 160p. (gr. 7 up). 1988. 14.95 (ISBN 0-385-29637-1). Delacorte.
Mitchell, Debbie. Diary of a First Class Jerk. LC 87-50267. 96p. (gr. 6-8). 1987. 8.95 (ISBN 1-55523-079-2). Winston-Derek.
Moncure, Jane B. What's So Special about Fall? I'm Going to School. Williams, Jenny, illus. LC 88-2868. 32p. (ps-2). 1988. PLB 9.95 (ISBN 0-89565-420-2). Childs World.
—Word Bird's New Friend. Hohag, Linda, illus. LC 90-37002. 32p. (ps-2). 1990. PLB 11.97 (ISBN 0-89565-616-7). Childs World.
Mooser, Stephen. It's a Weird, Weird School. 1989. 13.95 (ISBN 0-385-29812-9). Doubleday.
Morris, Judy K. The Kid Who Ran for Principal. LC 89-2729. 224p. (gr. 3-7). 1989. 12.95 (ISBN 0-397-32359-X, Lipp Jr Bks); PLB 12.89 (ISBN 0-397-32360-3, Lipp Jr Bks). HarpC Child Bks.
Moss, Marissa. Regina's Big Mistake. Moss, Marissa, illus. 32p. (gr. k-3). 1990. 13.95 (ISBN 0-395-55330-X). HM.
Mulford, Philippa G. The World Is My Eggshell. LC 85-16198. (gr. 7 up). 1986. pap. 14.95 (ISBN 0-385-29432-8). Delacorte.
Myers, Bernice. It Happens to Everyone. 1990. 12.95 (ISBN 0-688-09081-8); PLB 12.88 (ISBN 0-688-09082-6). Lothrop.
Naylor, Phyllis R. Reluctantly Alice. LC 90-37956. 192p. (gr. 3-7). 1991. SBE 13.95 (ISBN 0-689-31681-X, Atheneum Child Bk). Macmillan Child Grp.
Nesbit, Jeffrey A. The Great Nothing Strikes Back. 256p. (Orig.). (gr. 9-12). 1991. pap. 6.95 (ISBN 0-87788-323-8). Shaw Pubs.
Night School. (Illus.). (gr. 5 up). 1990. pap. 3.50. Ladybird Bks.
Nordstrom, Ursula. Secret Language. Chalmers, Mary, illus. LC 60-7701. 192p. (gr. 3-5). 1960. PLB 12.89 (ISBN 0-06-024576-X). HarpC Child Bks.
Norton, Nancy. Triple Trouble at Fairwood High, No. 3. (gr. 7-12). 1988. pap. 2.50 (ISBN 0-590-41975-7). Scholastic Inc.
Oppenheim, Joanne. Mrs. Peloki's Class Play. (Illus.). 32p. (ps-3). 1983. 10.95 (ISBN 0-396-08178-9, Putnam). Putnam Pub Group.
—Mrs. Peloki's Substitute. Zarins, Joyce A., illus. 32p. (ps-3). 1987. 12.95 (ISBN 0-396-08918-6, Putnam). Putnam Pub Group.
Palmer, Martha. Fractions. Hoffman, Joan, ed. Cook, Chris, illus. 32p. (gr. 5-6). 1981. wkbk. 1.99 (ISBN 0-938256-43-2). Sch Zone Pub Co.
Palumbo, Nancy. J.J. Goes to School: J.J. Va a L E'cole. Weaver, Judith, illus. 32p. (gr. k-6). 1989. wkbk. 5.95 (ISBN 0-927024-13-6). Crayons Pubns.
—J.J. Goes to School: J.J. Va a la Escuela. Weaver, Judith, illus. 32p. (gr. k-6). 1989. wkbk. 5.95 (ISBN 0-927024-12-8). Crayons Pubns.
Park, Barbara. Maxie, Rosie, & Earl...Partners in Grime. Strogart, Alexander, illus. LC 89-28027. 128p. (gr. 3-7). 1990. 12.95 (ISBN 0-679-80212-6); PLB 13.99 (ISBN 0-679-90212-0). McKay.
—Rosie Swanson: Fourth-Grade Geek for President. LC 91-8616. 114p. (gr. 3-6). 1991. 14.00 (ISBN 0-679-82094-9); lib. bdg. 14.99 (ISBN 0-679-92094-3). Knopf.
Pascal, Francine. Jealous Lies. 144p. (Orig.). (gr. 7-12). 1986. pap. 2.75 (ISBN 0-553-25816-8). Bantam.
—Lovestruck. 160p. (Orig.). (gr. 7-12). 1986. pap. 2.75 (ISBN 0-553-26750-7). Bantam.
—Spring Fever: Spring Super Edition, No. 2. 240p. (Orig.). (gr. 7-12). 1987. pap. 2.95 (ISBN 0-553-26420-6). Bantam.
—Sweet Valley Twins. 96p. (Orig.). (gr. 7-12). 1987. pap. 2.50 (ISBN 0-553-15474-5). Bantam.
—Winter Carnival. (Orig.). (gr. 7-12). 1986. pap. 2.95 (ISBN 0-553-26159-2). Bantam.
Pascal, Francine, created by. Against the Rules. 96p. (Orig.). (gr. 7-12). 1987. pap. 2.50 (ISBN 0-553-15518-0). Bantam.
—Alone in the Crowd. 160p. (Orig.). (gr. 7-12). 1986. pap. 2.75 (ISBN 0-553-26825-2). Bantam.
—Choosing Sides. 96p. (Orig.). (gr. 7-12). 1986. pap. 2.50 (ISBN 0-553-15459-1). Bantam.
—Leaving Home High. (Illus.). 144p. (gr. 7-12). 1987. pap. 2.95 (ISBN 0-553-27631-X). Bantam.
—The New Jessica. 160p. (Orig.). (gr. 7-12). 1986. pap. 2.75 (ISBN 0-553-26113-4). Bantam.
—Taking Sides. 160p. (Orig.). (gr. 7-12). 1986. pap. 2.75 (ISBN 0-553-25886-9). Bantam.
Paulsen, Gary. The Boy Who Owned the School. LC 89-23048. 112p. (gr. 6-8). 1990. 11.95 (ISBN 0-531-05865-4); PLB 11.99 (ISBN 0-531-08465-5). Orchard Bks Watts.
Peck, Robert N. Soup for President. (gr. 3-6). 1986. pap. 2.95 (ISBN 0-440-48188-0, YB). Dell.
—Soup on Wheels. Robinson, illus. LC 80-17661. 128p. (gr. 3 up). 1981. 6.95 (ISBN 0-394-84581-1); lib. bdg. 9.99 (ISBN 0-394-94581-6). Knopf.
Perkins, Thornton. Junior High Champs. Chappick, Joseph, illus. 49p. (Orig.). (gr. 6-9). 1989. pap. 3.00 (ISBN 0-9623407-0-7). NVEM.
Petersen, P. J. Going for the Big One. (gr. k-12). 1987. pap. 2.95 (ISBN 0-440-93158-4, LFL). Dell.
—Here's to the Sophomores. LC 83-14362. 192p. (gr. 7 up). 1984. pap. 13.95 (ISBN 0-385-29319-4). Delacorte.
—Here's to the Sophomores. 192p. (gr. 6 up). 1986. pap. 2.50 (ISBN 0-440-93394-3, LFL). Dell.
Pevsner, Stella. Cute Is a Four Letter Word. 190p. (gr. 3-6). 1980. 13.95 (ISBN 0-395-29106-2, Clarion). HM.

Poulet, Virginia. Blue Bug Goes to School. Anderson, Peggy P., illus. LC 84-23161. 32p. (ps-3). 1985. lib. bdg. 14.60 (ISBN 0-516-03416-2); pap. 3.95 (ISBN 0-516-43416-0). Childrens.

Pulver, Robin & R.W. Mrs. Toggle's Zipper. LC 88-37251. (Illus.). 32p. (ps-2). 1990. 12.95 (ISBN 0-02-775451-0, Four Winds Press). Macmillan Child Grp.

Quackenbush, Robert. First Grade Jitters. Quackenbush, Robert, illus. LC 81-47757. 32p. (gr. k-2). 1982. PLB 11.89 (ISBN 0-397-31981-9, Lipp Jr Bks). HarpC Child Bks.

Rabe, Berniece. The Balancing Girl. Hoban, Lillian, illus. LC 80-22100. (ps-2). 1981. 12.95 (ISBN 0-525-26160-5, 0995-300, DCB). Dutton Child Bks.

Ransom, Candice. Funniest Sixth Grade Video Ever. 144p. (Orig.). (gr. 4-8). 1991. pap. text ed. 2.50 (ISBN 0-87406-525-9). Willowisp Pr.

Ransom, Candice F. Ladies & Jellybeans. Steinhoff, Sharon, ed. 128p. (gr. 2-5). 1991. 12.95 (ISBN 0-02-775665-3, Bradbury Pr). Macmillan Child Grp.

Reuter, Bjarne. Buster, the Sheikh of Hope Street. Bell, Anthea, illus. 112p. (gr. 4 up). 1991. 13.95 (ISBN 0-525-44772-5, DCB). Dutton Child Bks.

Ritchie, Alan. Erin McEwan, Your Days Are Numbered. (gr. 4-7). 1990. 11.95 (ISBN 0-679-80321-1). Knopf.

—Erin McEwan, Your Days Are Numbered. (Illus.). 176p. (gr. 4-7). 1990. 11.95 (ISBN 0-685-31214-3); lib. bdg. 11.99 (ISBN 0-679-90321-6). McKay.

Robinson, Nancy K. Wendy & the Bullies. Fetz, Ingrid, illus. 128p. (gr. 2-5). 1987. 8.95 (ISBN 0-8038-8097-9). Hastings.

—Wendy & the Bullies. Fetz, Ingrid, illus. 128p. (Orig.). (gr. 3-5). 1983. pap. 2.50 (ISBN 0-590-32975-8, Apple Paperbacks). Scholastic Inc.

Roos, Stephen. My Horrible Secret. Newsom, Carol, illus. LC 82-14954. 128p. (gr. 4-6). 1983. pap. 10.95 (ISBN 0-385-29246-5). Delacorte.

—The Terrible Truth: Secrets of a Sixth-Grader. Newsom, Carol, illus. 128p. (gr. 4-7). 1991. pap. 3.25 (ISBN 0-440-48578-9, YB). Dell.

Ross, Pat. M & M & the Superchild Afternoon. Hafner, Marylin, illus. LC 86-28128. (gr. 1-4). 1987. pap. 9.95 (ISBN 0-670-81208-0). Viking Child Bks.

Roundabout Mulberry School. (ps-1). 1987. 5.95 (ISBN 0-448-11327-9, G&D). Putnam Pub Group.

Roy, Ron. Frankie Is Staying Back. Kessell, Walter, illus. 64p. (gr. 2-5). 1981. 8.95 (ISBN 0-395-31025-3, Clarion). HM.

Ruckman, Ivy. What's an Average Kid Like Me Doing Way up Here? LC 82-72820. 144p. (gr. 4-6). 1983. PLB 11.89 (ISBN 0-440-08893-3); pap. 11.95 (ISBN 0-385-29251-1). Delacorte.

Sachan, Louis. Wayside School Is Falling Down. Schick, Joel, illus. LC 88-674. 192p. (gr. 3-7). 1989. 12.95 (ISBN 0-688-07868-0). Lothrop.

Sachar, Louis. Sixth Grade Secrets. LC 86-4298. 208p. (gr. 4-6). 1987. pap. 12.95 (ISBN 0-590-40709-0, Scholastic Hardcover). Scholastic Inc.

—Sixth Grade Secrets. (gr. 3-7). 1989. pap. 2.75 (ISBN 0-590-40409-1, Apple Paperbacks). Scholastic Inc.

—Someday Angeline. Samuels, Barbara, illus. 160p. (Orig.). (gr. 3-7). 1991. pap. 3.50 (ISBN 0-380-83444-8, Camelot). Avon.

Sachs, Betsy. The Trouble with Santa. Apple, Margot, illus. LC 89-24257. 64p. (Orig.). (gr. 2-4). 1990. PLB 6.99 (ISBN 0-679-90410-7); pap. 2.50 (ISBN 0-679-80410-2). Random.

Sachs, Marilyn. Circles. LC 90-37516. 144p. (gr. 5-9). 1991. 14.95 (ISBN 0-525-44683-4, DCB). Dutton Child Bks.

Sansevere, Carol Q. The Real Scoop. 160p. (Orig.). (gr. 5-9). Date not set. pap. 2.95 (ISBN 1-55802-205-8). Lynx Bks.

Saunders, Susan. Starring Stephanie. (Illus.). 96p. (Orig.). (gr. 4-6). 1987. pap. 2.50 (ISBN 0-590-40642-6). Scholastic Inc.

Scarry, Richard. Richard Scarry's Great Big Schoolhouse. Scarry, Richard, illus. (ps-2). 1969. 8.95 (ISBN 0-394-80874-6, Random Juv). Random.

Schanback, Mindy. Does Third Grade Last Forever? Henry, Paul, illus. LC 89-20603. 96p. (gr. 2-4). 1990. PLB 9.89 (ISBN 0-8167-1700-1); pap. text ed. 2.95 (ISBN 0-8167-1701-X). Troll Assocs.

—What's New in Sixth Grade? LC 90-26792. 96p. (gr. 4-6). 1991. lib. bdg. 9.89 (ISBN 0-8167-2388-5); pap. text ed. 2.95 (ISBN 0-8167-2389-3). Troll Assocs.

Schulz, Charles M. It's Your First Kiss, Charlie Brown. LC 78-7460. (Illus.). (gr. 1 up). 1978. (Random Juv). Random.

Sells, Carole G. Rainbow Dragon: Lessons in Basic Values. Zellers, Toby, illus. Guese, Raymond F., intro. by. (Illus.). 34p. (Orig.). (ps-6). 1988. pap. 3.95 (ISBN 0-926739-00-X). Sells Pub.

Shalant, Phyllis. The Rock Star, the Rooster, & Me, the Reporter. Robinson, Charles, illus. 169p. (gr. 3-7). 1991. pap. 3.95 (ISBN 0-14-034596-5, Puffin). Puffin Bks.

Shannon, Jacqueline. Class Crush. 176p. (Orig.). (gr. 5-9). 1987. pap. 2.25 (ISBN 0-590-40407-5). Scholastic Inc.

Sharmat, Marjorie. Kids on the Bus, No. 3: Bully on the Bus. (gr. 4-7). 1991. pap. 2.95 (ISBN 0-06-106027-5, Harp PBks). HarperCollins.

—Kids on the Bus, No. 4: The Secret Notebook. (gr. 4-7). 1991. pap. 2.95 (ISBN 0-06-106028-3, Harp PBks). HarperCollins.

Sharmat, Marjorie & Sharmat, Mitchell. The Princess of the Fillmore Street School. Brunkus, Denise, illus. LC 89-1106. (gr. 2-4). 1989. 12.95 (ISBN 0-385-29811-0). Delacorte.

Sharmat, Marjorie W. Maggie Marmelstein for President. Shecter, Ben, illus. LC 75-6300. 128p. (gr. 4-6). 1975. PLB 13.89 (ISBN 0-06-025555-2). HarpC Child Bks.

—Maggie Marmelstein for President. LC 75-6300. (Illus.). 128p. (gr. 3-7). 1976. pap. 3.50 (ISBN 0-06-440079-4, Trophy). HarpC Child Bks.

Shaw, Janet. Kirsten Learns a Lesson: A School Story. Thieme, Jeanne, ed. Graef, Renee, illus. 72p. (gr. 2-5). 1990. PLB 12.95 (ISBN 0-937295-82-5). Pleasant Co.

Shles, Larry. Do I have to Go to School Today? Squib Measures Up. Winch, Bradley L., ed. Shles, Larry, illus. 64p. (Orig.). (gr. k up). 1989. pap. 7.95 (ISBN 0-915190-62-1, JP9062-1). Jalmar Pr.

Shreve, Susan. The Flunking of Joshua T. Bates. De Groat, Diane, illus. LC 83-19636. 96p. (gr. 2-6). 1984. 12.95 (ISBN 0-394-86380-1); lib. bdg. 12.99 (ISBN 0-394-96380-6). Knopf.

—The Flunking of Joshua T. Bates. De Groat, Diane, illus. 96p. (gr. 2-5). 1985. pap. 2.50 (ISBN 0-590-41189-6, Lucky Star). Scholastic Inc.

—The Flunking of Joshua T. Bates. 1985. pap. 2.50 (ISBN 0-590-42923-X). Scholastic Inc.

—The Gift of the Girl Who Couldn't Hear. LC 91-2247. 128p. (gr. 3-7). 1991. 12.95 (ISBN 0-688-10318-9, Tambourine Bks). Morrow.

Shusterman, Neal. The Shadow Club. LC 87-35369. 183p. (gr. 7-9). 1988. 12.95 (ISBN 0-316-77540-1). Little.

Sidney, Margaret. Five Little Peppers at School. 1987. Repr. lib. bdg. 21.95x (ISBN 0-89966-552-7). Buccaneer Bks.

—Five Little Peppers at School. (Orig.). (gr. k-6). 1988. pap. 4.95 (ISBN 0-440-40035-X, YB). Dell.

Singer, Marilyn. The Case of the Sabotaged School Play: A Sam & Dave Mystery. Glasser, Judy, illus. LC 83-48437. 64p. (gr. 3-7). 1987. pap. 3.50 (ISBN 0-06-440207-X, Trophy). HarpC Child Bks.

Skittles Make Believe School. (ps). 1976. 2.00 (ISBN 0-904494-25-X, Brimax Bks). Borden.

Smith, Janice L. It's Not Easy Being George: Stories about Adam Joshua (& His Dog) Gackenbach, Dick, illus. LC 88-33075. 128p. (gr. 1-4). 1989. 10.95 (ISBN 0-06-025852-7); PLB 10.89 (ISBN 0-06-025853-5). HarpC Child Bks.

Sommer, Karen. Satch & the Motormouth. (gr. 3-7). 1987. pap. 4.49 (ISBN 1-55513-063-1, Chariot Bks). Cook.

Sonnenmark, Laura A. Something's Rotten in the State of Maryland. 1990. pap. 12.95 (ISBN 0-590-42876-4). Scholastic Inc.

Spinelli, Jerry. Jason & Marceline. (gr. 6 up). 1986. 12.95 (ISBN 0-316-80719-2). Little.

Stahl, Hilda. Sendi Lee Mason & the Big Mistake. 128p. (Orig.). (gr. 1-4). 1991. pap. 4.95 (ISBN 0-89107-613-1). Good News.

Standish, Burt L. Frank Merriwell's Chums. Rudman, Jack, ed. (gr. 9 up). 9.95 (ISBN 0-8373-9302-7); pap. 3.95 (ISBN 0-8373-9002-8). F Merriwell.

Steel, Danielle. Martha's New School. Rogers, Jacqueline, illus. (ps-2). 1989. 8.95 (ISBN 0-385-29800-5). Delacorte.

Steffy, Jan. The School Picnic. Bond, Denny, illus. LC 87-14867. 32p. (ps-3). 1987. 12.95 (ISBN 0-934672-52-0). Good Bks PA.

Steiber, Ellen. Eighth Grade Changes Everything. LC 90-2495. 128p. (gr. 6-9). 1991. lib. bdg. 9.89 (ISBN 0-8167-2390-7); pap. text ed. 2.95 (ISBN 0-8167-2391-5). Troll Assocs.

Steiner, Barbara. Oliver Dibbs & the Dinosaur Cause. Christelow, Eileen, illus. LC 86-9941. 128p. (gr. 3-7). 1986. 12.95 (ISBN 0-02-787880-5, Four Winds). Macmillan Child Grp.

Stevenson, James. That Dreadful Day. Stevenson, James, illus. LC 84-4164. 32p. (gr. k-3). 1985. 11.75 (ISBN 0-688-04035-7); lib. bdg. 11.88 (ISBN 0-688-04036-5). Greenwillow.

Stine, Megan & Stine, H. William. How I Survived the Fifth Grade. LC 90-26790. 96p. (gr. 4-6). 1991. lib. bdg. 9.89 (ISBN 0-8167-2386-9); pap. text ed. 2.95 (ISBN 0-8167-2387-7). Troll Assocs.

Stolz, Mary. Bully of Barkham Street. Shortall, Leonard, illus. LC 68-2661. 224p. (gr. 3-6). 1963. PLB 14.89 (ISBN 0-06-025821-7). HarpC Child Bks.

Stretton, Barbara. The Truth of the Matter. LC 83-4305. 256p. (gr. 7-12). 1983. Knopf.

Surat, Michele. Angel Child, Dragon Child. Vo-Dinh Mai, illus. LC 83-8606. 32p. (gr. 3-6). 1983. PLB 14. 65 (ISBN 0-940742-12-8). Raintree Pubs.

Thompson, Julian F. Goofbang Value Daze. (gr. 7 up). 1989. pap. 12.95 (ISBN 0-590-41946-3). Scholastic Inc.

—Goofbang Value Daze. 1990. pap. 2.95 (ISBN 0-590-41945-5). Scholastic Inc.

Tolles, Martha. Who's Reading Darci's Diary? LC 84-10294. 128p. (gr. 4-6). 1984. 12.95 (ISBN 0-525-67153-6, Lodestar Bks). Dutton Child Bks.

Tomalin, Ruth. Another Day. 90p. (gr. 2-6). 1991. pap. 3.95 (ISBN 0-571-14393-8). Faber & Faber.

Tripp, Valerie. Molly Learns a Lesson: A School Story. Thieme, Jeanne, ed. Payne, C. F., illus. 72p. (gr. 2-5). 1990. PLB 12.95 (ISBN 0-937295-84-1). Pleasant Co.

—Samantha Saves the Day: A School Adventure. Thieme, Jeanne, ed. Grace, Robert & Niles, Nancy, illus. 72p. (gr. 2-5). 1990. PLB 12.95 (ISBN 0-937295-92-2). Pleasant Co.

Twohill, Maggie. Who Has the Lucky Duck in Class 4-B? LC 83-15719. 112p. (gr. 3-5). 1984. 10.95 (ISBN 0-02-789690-0, Bradbury Pr). Macmillan Child Grp.

Waddell, Martin. Harriet & the Haunted School. Burgess, Mark, illus. (gr. 2-6). 1986. pap. 2.50 (ISBN 0-671-62215-3, Minstrel Bks). PB.

Walsh, Jill P. Lost & Found. Rayner, Mary, illus. 32p. (gr. 1-3). 1985. 11.95 (ISBN 0-233-97672-8). Andre Deutsch.

Wardlaw, Lee. The Eye & I. Stouffer, Deborah, illus. 75p. (Orig.). (gr. 3-6). 1988. pap. 2.95 (ISBN 0-931093-10-4). Red Hen Pr.

Weiss, Leatie. My Teacher Sleeps in School. Weiss, Ellen, illus. LC 85-40449. 32p. (ps-3). 1985. pap. 3.95 (ISBN 0-14-050559-8, Puffin). Puffin Bks.

Weiss, Nicki. An Egg Is an Egg. (Illus.). 32p. (ps-1). 1990. 14.95 (ISBN 0-399-22182-4, Putnam). Putnam Pub Group.

Wells, Rosemary. Timothy Goes to School. Wells, Rosemary, illus. LC 80-20785. 32p. (ps-2). 1983. pap. 4.95 (ISBN 0-8037-0021-0). Dial Bks Young.

Weyn, Suzanne. All Alone in the Eighth Grade. LC 91-10162. 128p. (gr. 7-9). 1991. lib. bdg. 9.89 (ISBN 0-8167-2394-X); pap. text ed. 2.95 (ISBN 0-8167-2395-8). Troll Assocs.

Wilkinson, Brenda. Ludell & Willie. LC 76-18402. (gr. 7 up). 1977. PLB 13.89 (ISBN 0-06-026488-8). HarpC Child Bks.

Winthrop, Elizabeth. Luke's Bully. Porter, Pat G., illus. 64p. (gr. 2-5). 1990. pap. 11.95 (ISBN 0-670-83103-4). Viking Child Bks.

Wiseman, B. Morris Goes to School. LC 75-77944. (Illus.). 64p. (gr. k-3). 1983. pap. 3.50 (ISBN 0-06-444045-1, Trophy). HarpC Child Bks.

Wiseman, Bernard. Morris Goes to School. Wiseman, Bernard, illus. LC 75-77944. 64p. (gr. k-3). 1970. PLB 11.89 (ISBN 0-06-026548-5). HarpC Child Bks.

Wolfe, Elle. Palm Beach Prep, No. 3: The Girls Against the Boys, No. 3. (gr. 4-7). 1990. pap. 2.95 (ISBN 0-8125-1063-1). Tor Bks.

—Palm Beach Prep, No. 5: Troublemaker. (gr. 4-7). 1990. pap. 2.95 (ISBN 0-8125-1065-8). Tor Bks.

—Palm Beach Prep, No. 6: Upstaged, No. 6. (gr. 4-7). 1990. pap. 2.95 (ISBN 0-8125-1077-1). Tor Bks.

Wood, Phyllis A. Pass Me a Pine Cone. LC 82-1870. 160p. (gr. 7-9). 1982. 11.95 (ISBN 0-664-32692-7, Westminster). Westminster John Knox.

Woodruff, Elvira. Awfully Short for the Fourth Grade. 1990. pap. 2.95 (ISBN 0-440-40366-9, Pub. by Yearling Classics). Dell.

Yashima, Taro. Crow Boy. Yashima, T., illus. (gr. k-3). 1955. pap. 13.95 (ISBN 0-670-24931-9). Viking Child Bks.

Yolen, Jane & Greenberg, Martin H., eds. Things That Go Bump in the Night: A Collection of Original Stories. LC 88-39338. 288p. (gr. 5 up). 1989. 13.95 (ISBN 0-06-026802-6); PLB 13.89 (ISBN 0-06-026803-4). HarpC Child Bks.

Ziefert, Harriet. Egg-Drop Day. Brown, Richard, illus. LC 87-3125. 64p. (gr. 1-4). 1988. 8.95 (ISBN 0-316-98757-3). Little.

—Trip Day (Mr. Rose's Class) Brown, Richard, illus. 64p. 1988. pap. 2.50 (ISBN 0-553-15618-7, Skylark). Bantam.

—Worm Day (Mr. Rose's Class) Brown, Richard, illus. 64p. 1988. pap. 2.50 (ISBN 0-553-15619-5, Skylark). Bantam.

Zindel, Paul. Harry & Hortense at Hormone High. 160p. (gr. 7-12). 1985. pap. 2.95 (ISBN 0-553-25175-9, Starfire). Bantam.

SCHOOLS–MANAGEMENT AND ORGANIZATION

see School Administration and Organization

SCHOOLS, COMMERCIAL

see Business Education

SCHOOLS, MILITARY

see Military Education

SCHUBERT, FRANZ PETER, 1797-1828

Goffstein, M. B. Little Schubert. LC 72-79889. (Illus.). 48p. (gr. 2 up). 1985. 10.95 (ISBN 0-87923-540-3); pap. 6.95 (ISBN 0-87923-508-X). Godine.

Great Composers, Bk. 2: Handel, Hayden, Schubert. (Illus.). (gr. 5 up). 3.50 (ISBN 0-7214-0242-9). Ladybird Bks.

SCHWEITZER, ALBERT, 1875-1965

Bentley, James. Albert Schweitzer: The Doctor Who Devoted His Life to Africa's Sick. Lantier, Patricia, adapted by. LC 90-9974. (Illus.). 64p. (gr. 3-4). 1991. PLB 12.95 (ISBN 0-8368-0457-0). Gareth Stevens Inc.

—Albert Schweitzer: The Doctor Who Gave up a Brilliant Career to Serve the People of Africa. LC 88-17731. (Illus.). 68p. (gr. 5-6). 1989. PLB 12.95 (ISBN 1-55532-823-7). Gareth Stevens Inc.

Crawford, Gail & Renna, Giani. Albert Schweitzer. (Illus.). 104p. (gr. 5-8). 1990. 16.98 (ISBN 0-382-09976-1); pap. 8.95 (ISBN 0-382-24003-0). Silver Burdett Pr.

Johnson, Spencer. The Value of Dedication: The Story of Albert Schweitzer. Pileggi, Steve, illus. LC 79-21805. (gr. k-6). 1979. 9.95 (ISBN 0-916392-44-9, Pub. by Value Communications). Oak Tree Pubns.

Schweitzer, Albert. Albert Schweitzer. Repath, Ann, ed. Winston, Richard & Winston, Clara, trs. Delessert, Etienne, illus. 32p. (gr. 9 up). 1986. PLB 10.45 (ISBN 0-88682-013-8). Creative Ed.

SCIENCE

see also Astronomy; Bacteriology; Biology; Botany;
Chemistry; Crystallography; Ethnology; Fossils; Geology;
Mathematics; Meteorology; Mineralogy; Natural History;
Physics; Physiology; Space Sciences; Zoology;
also headings beginning with the word Scientific

Alberti, Delbert & Mason, George. Laboratory Laughter. Firmhand, Zelda, illus. (Orig.). (gr. 2-9). 1974. pap. 6.95 (ISBN 0-918932-25-4). Activity Resources.

Arvetis, Chris. What Is a Rainbow? (Illus.). 32p. (ps-3). 1988. pap. 1.95 (ISBN 0-02-688810-6). Checkerboard Pr.

—Why Does It Thunder & Lightning? (Illus.). 32p. (ps-3). 1988. pap. 1.95 (ISBN 0-02-688813-0). Checkerboard Pr.

—Why Is Grass Green? (Illus.). 32p. (ps-3). 1988. pap. 1.95 (ISBN 0-02-688812-2). Checkerboard Pr.

—Why Is the Sky Blue? (Illus.). 32p. (ps-3). 1988. pap. 1.95 (ISBN 0-02-688811-4). Checkerboard Pr.

Asimov, Isaac. How Was the Universe Born? LC 87-42602. (Illus.). 32p. (gr. 3-4). 1988. PLB 11.95 (ISBN 1-55532-358-8). Gareth Stevens Inc.

—Is There Life on Other Planets? LC 87-42603. (Illus.). 32p. (gr. 3-4). 1989. PLB 11.95 (ISBN 1-55532-359-6). Gareth Stevens Inc.

—Our Milky Way & Other Galaxies. LC 87-42597. (Illus.). (gr. 3-4). 1988. PLB 11.95 (ISBN 1-55532-352-9). Gareth Stevens Inc.

—Our Solar System. LC 87-42606. (Illus.). 32p. (gr. 3-4). 1988. PLB 11.95 (ISBN 1-55532-361-8). Gareth Stevens Inc.

—Quasars, Pulsars & Black Holes. LC 87-42596. (Illus.). 32p. (gr. 3-4). 1988. PLB 11.95 (ISBN 1-55532-351-0). Gareth Stevens Inc.

—Science Fiction, Science Fact. LC 87-42591. (Illus.). 32p. (gr. 3-4). 1989. PLB 11.95 (ISBN 1-55532-323-5). Gareth Stevens Inc.

—Space Spotter's Guide. LC 87-42600. (Illus.). 32p. (gr. 3-4). 1988. PLB 11.95 (ISBN 1-55532-356-1). Gareth Stevens Inc.

Barr, George. Science Projects for Young People. 153p. (gr. 5 up). 1986. pap. 3.50 (ISBN 0-486-25235-3). Dover.

—Sports Science for Young People. 1990. pap. 3.95 (ISBN 0-486-26527-7). Dover.

Beginning Science. (gr. 4-6). 1975. pap. 2.95 (ISBN 0-8431-4257-X). Price Stern.

Beginning Science. (Illus.). 32p. (ps up) 1986. 2.95 (ISBN 0-8431-4282-0). Price Stern.

Bender, David L. & Leone, Bruno, eds. Science & Technology Annual, 1989. 144p. (gr. 10 up). 1989. pap. text ed. 5.45 (ISBN 0-89908-552-0). Greenhaven.

Berenstain, Stan & Berenstain, Janice. The Berenstain Bears' Science Fair. Berenstain, Stan & Berenstain, Janice, illus. LC 76-8121. (gr. 1-4). 1977. PLB 11.99 (ISBN 0-394-93294-3, Random Juv). Random.

Berger, Melvin. Simple Science - Magnifying Glass. 1989. pap. 3.50 (ISBN 0-590-42385-1). Scholastic Inc.

—Simple Science Says: Take One Compass. 1990. pap. 3.50 (ISBN 0-590-42384-3). Scholastic Inc.

—Solids, Liquids & Gases: From Superconductors to the Ozone Layer. (Illus.). 80p. (gr. 5 up). 1989. 11.99 (ISBN 0-399-21731-2, Putnam). Putnam Pub Group.

—Wonders of Science. Karas, G. Brian, illus. 96p. (gr. 2-5). 1991. pap. 2.50 (ISBN 0-590-43472-1). Scholastic Inc.

Berry, Marilyn. Help Is on the Way for Science Skills. (Illus.). 48p. (gr. 4-6). 1987. PLB 14.60 (ISBN 0-516-03286-0); pap. 4.95 (ISBN 0-516-43286-9). Childrens.

Bochinski, Julianne B. The Complete Handbook of Science Fair Projects. 1991. text ed. 24.95 (ISBN 0-471-52729-7). Wiley.

Bombaugh, Ruth. Science Fair Success. (Illus.). 96p. (gr. 7-9). 1989. PLB 16.95 (ISBN 0-89490-197-4). Enslow Pubs.

Bramwell, Martyn. How Things Work. Mostyn, David, illus. 38p. (ps-3). 1985. PLB 10.95 (ISBN 0-86020-847-8, Pub. by Usborne). EDC.

Calder, Nigel & Newell, John. On the Frontiers of Science: How Scientists See Our Future. (Illus.). 256p. 1989. 35.00x (ISBN 0-8160-2205-4). Facts on File.

Carratello, John & Carratello, Patty. All about Science Fairs. Chellton, Anna, illus. 96p. (gr. 1-8). 1989. wkbk. 9.95 (ISBN 1-55734-228-8). Tchr Create Mat.

—Problem Solving Science Investigations. Chellton, Anna, illus. 96p. (gr. 1-8). 1989. wkbk. 9.95 (ISBN 1-55734-229-6). Tchr Create Mat.

Chisholm, J. Book of Science. Beeson, D., illus. 48p. (gr. 3-6). 1984. 14.95 (ISBN 0-86020-721-8). EDC.

Conaway, Judith. More Science Secrets. LC 86-16084. (Illus.). 48p. (gr. 1-5). 1987. PLB 11.89 (ISBN 0-8167-0866-5); pap. text ed. 2.95 (ISBN 0-8167-0867-3). Troll Assocs.

Cooper, Chris & Insley, Jane. How Does It Work. 64p. (gr. 4-7). 15.95 (ISBN 0-8160-1066-8). Facts on File.

Cooper, Chris & Osman, Tony. How Everyday Things Work. LC 84-1654. 64p. (gr. 7 up). 15.95 (ISBN 0-87196-988-2). Facts on File.

Crump, Donald J., ed. On the Brink of Tomorrow: Frontiers of Science. LC 81-48075. 200p. (gr. 7 up). 1982. 7.95 (ISBN 0-87044-414-X). Natl Geog.

—You Won't Believe Your Eyes. LC 86-7637. (Illus.). 104p. (gr. 3-8). 1987. 6.95 (ISBN 0-87044-611-8); PLB 8.50 (ISBN 0-87044-616-9). Natl Geog.

Daab, Marcia J. Science Fair Workshop. (gr. 4-8). 1990. pap. 6.95 (ISBN 0-8224-6374-1). Fearon Teach Aids.

DeBruin, Jerry. Creative Hands-on Science Cards & Activities. 336p. (gr. 3-9). 1990. 19.95 (ISBN 0-86653-538-1, GA1150). Good Apple.

—Rocks & Minerals. Swemba, Jeane, illus. 32p. (gr. 4 up). 1986. wkbk. 4.95 (ISBN 0-86653-341-9, GA 689). Good Apple.

—School Yard-Backyard, Cycles of Science. 160p. (gr. 3-9). 1989. 11.95 (ISBN 0-86653-489-X, GA1084). Good Apple.

—Young Scientists Explore: Animals, Bk. 2. 32p. (gr. 4 up). 1982. 4.95 (ISBN 0-86653-073-8, GA 406). Good Apple.

—Young Scientists Explore: The World Around Them, Bk. 1. 32p. (gr. 4 up). 1982. 4.95 (ISBN 0-86653-072-X, GA 405). Good Apple.

Diebert, Linda. Science for Me. 112p. (ps-2). 1991. 10.95 (ISBN 0-86653-597-7). Good Apple.

Dreher, Barbara S. Sounds of Science. LC 89-52116. (Illus.). 44p. (gr. k-3). 1990. 5.95 (ISBN 1-55523-310-4). Winston-Derek.

Durham, Quentin. Minigroup Science. (Illus.). 230p. (gr. 7-12). 1980. pap. 25.00 (ISBN 0-87879-244-9). Acad Therapy.

Embry, Lynn. Scientific Encounters of the Curious Kind. McClure, Nancee, illus. 64p. (gr. 4-7). 1984. wkbk 6.95 (ISBN 0-86653-176-9, GA 550). Good Apple.

—Scientific Encounters of the Endangered Kind. McClure, Nancee, illus. 64p. (gr. 4-7). 1986. 6. 95wkbk. (ISBN 0-86653-353-2, GA 694). Good Apple.

English, Timothy M. & English, Gayla I. Science Fun Centers. (Illus.). 48p. (Orig.). (gr. 3-5). 1990. pap. text ed. 4.69 (ISBN 1-878931-00-8, 3B90-001). English Enterprises.

Everix, Nancy. Windows to the World. Everix, Nancy, illus. 128p. (gr. 2-8). 1984. wkbk. 10.95 (ISBN 0-86653-173-4, GA 527). Good Apple.

Filson, Brent. Superconductors & Other New Breakthroughs in Science. (Illus.). 128p. (gr. 5-9). 1989. PLB 12.98 (ISBN 0-671-65857-3); PLB 9.74s.p. (ISBN 0-685-24680-9). Messner.

Fitzpatrick, Julia. Science Spirals, 7 bks. Bowles, Diana, illus. (gr. 2-5). 1988. Set, 32p. ea. lib. bdg. 69.72 (ISBN 0-382-09611-8). Silver Burdett Pr.

Fleisher, Paul. Secrets of the Universe: Discovering the Universal Laws of Science. Keeler, Patricia, illus. LC 86-14001. 224p. (gr. 5-9). 1987. 17.95 (ISBN 0-689-31266-0, Atheneum Child Bk). Macmillan Child Grp.

Ford, B. G. Do You Know? One Hundred Fascinating Facts. McNaught, Harry, illus. LC 78-62132. (ps-1). 1979. lib. bdg. 5.99 (ISBN 0-394-94070-9, Random Juv); pap. 1.95 (ISBN 0-394-84070-4). Random.

Forte, Imogene. Science Fun. LC 84-62935. (Illus.). 80p. (gr. k-6). 1985. pap. text ed. 3.95 (ISBN 0-86530-100-X, IP 91-4). Incentive Pubns.

Fox, Sally. Tasty Adventures in Science. Chemsley, Kim, illus. (gr. 3-6). 1962. PLB 6.70 (ISBN 0-8313-0037-X). Lantern.

Friedhoffer. Magic Tricks, Science Facts. 1990. pap. 5.95 (ISBN 0-531-15186-7). Watts.

Gabb, Michael. Everyday Science. LC 79-64387. (Illus.). 36p. (gr. 3-6). 1980. PLB 8.95 (ISBN 0-8225-1179-7, First Ave Edns); pap. 4.95 (ISBN 0-8225-9508-7, First Ave Edns). Lerner Pubns.

Gabet, Marcia. Fun with Science. Gabet, Marcia, illus. 48p. (gr. k-3). 1985. wkbk. 5.95 (ISBN 1-55734-036-6). Tchr Create Mat.

Gardner, Robert. Robert Gardner's Science Activity Books, 4 vols. (Illus.). 544p. (gr. 4-8). 1990. Set. PLB 47.92 (ISBN 0-671-94217-4); Set. PLB 35.94s.p.; Set. pap. 19.80 (ISBN 0-671-94218-2); Set. pap. 14.84s.p. Messner.

Godlewski, Lorraine, et al. Preparing for the Science RCT. (Illus., Orig.). 1987. wkbk. 3.45 (ISBN 0-937323-08-X). United Pub Co.

Goffstein, M. B. The School of Names. Goffstein, M. B., illus. LC 85-45419. 32p. (ps up) 1986. 12.95 (ISBN 0-06-021984-X). HarpC Child Bks.

Gottlieb, William P. Science Facts You Won't Believe. LC 82-20080. (Illus.). 128p. (gr. 6 up). 1983. PLB 11. 90 (ISBN 0-531-02875-5). Watts.

Grillone, Lisa & Gennaro, Joseph. Small Worlds Close Up. (Illus.). 64p. (gr. 3-6). 1987. 12.95 (ISBN 0-517-53289-1); pap. 4.95 (ISBN 0-685-17357-7). Crown.

Haines, Gail K. Micromysteries. (Illus.). 196p. (gr. 7-11). 1988. 14.95 (ISBN 0-396-09000-1, Putnam). Putnam Pub Group.

Hart-Davis, Adam. Scientific Eye: Exploring the Marvels of Science. LC 88-31333. (Illus.). 96p. (gr. 4 up) 1989. 14.95 (ISBN 0-8069-6920-2). Sterling.

Haught, James A. Science in a Nanosecond: Illustrated Answers to 100 Basic Science Questions. (Illus.). 110p. (Orig.). (gr. 4 up). 1991. pap. 12.95 (ISBN 0-87975-637-3). Prometheus Bks.

Henry, Lucia K. Science & Ourselves. (gr. 1-3). 1989. pap. 5.95 (ISBN 0-8224-6456-X). Fearon Teach Aids.

—Science in Special Places. (gr. 1-3). 1989. pap. 5.95 (ISBN 0-8224-6457-8). Fearon Teach Aids.

—Science Through the Seasons. (gr. 1-3). 1989. pap. 5.95 (ISBN 0-8224-6304-0). Fearon Teach Aids.

Hessler, Edward W. & Stubbs, Harriett. Acid Rain Science Projects. 20p. (Orig.). (gr. 5-12). 1987. pap. 9.95 (ISBN 0-935577-09-2). Acid Rain Found.

Hiscock, Bruce. The Big Rock. Hiscock, Bruce, illus. LC 87-31834. 32p. (gr. 1-5). 1988. 12.95 (ISBN 0-689-31402-7, Atheneum Child Bk). Macmillan Child Grp.

The How & Why Activity Wonder Book of Beginning Science. (Illus.). (gr. k-9). 1988. pap. 1.95 (ISBN 0-318-36492-1). Scholastic Inc.

Inquire Duplicating Master: Intermediate Science. (gr. 4-8). 1977. 8.95 (ISBN 0-89273-550-3). Educ Serv.

Iozzi, Louis A. & Bastardo, Peter J. Decisions for Today & Tomorrow. (gr. 9-12). 1990. tchr's. ed. 50.00 (ISBN 0-944584-22-5). Sopris.

Jennings, Terry. Balancing. Anstey, David, illus. 28p. (gr. k-4). 1989. PLB 10.40 (ISBN 0-531-17175-2). Watts.

—Structures. LC 88-22879. (Illus.). 32p. (gr. 3-6). 1989. PLB 14.60 (ISBN 0-516-08409-7); pap. 4.95 (ISBN 0-516-48409-5). Childrens.

Johnston, Tom. Light! Color! Action! Pooley, Sarah, illus. LC 87-42754. 32p. (gr. 4-6). 1988. PLB 10.95 (ISBN 1-55532-409-6). Gareth Stevens Inc.

—Science in Action, 6 vols. Pooley, Sarah, illus. 32p. (gr. 4-6). 1987. Set. PLB 65.70 (ISBN 1-55532-412-6). Gareth Stevens Inc.

Kanetzke, Howard W. Airplanes & Balloons. rev. ed. LC 87-23230. (Illus.). 48p. (gr. 2-6). 1987. PLB 17.32 (ISBN 0-8172-3251-6). Raintree Pubs.

Kerrod, Robin. Air in Action. (Illus.). 32p. (gr. 3-8). 1990. PLB 9.95 (ISBN 1-85435-152-4). Marshall Cavendish.

—All Around. (Illus.). 56p. (gr. 3-5). 1987. 14.95 (ISBN 0-382-09424-7). Silver Burdett Pr.

—Fire & Water. (Illus.). 32p. (gr. 3-8). 1990. PLB 9.95 (ISBN 1-85435-153-2). Marshall Cavendish.

—How Things Work. (Illus.). 32p. (gr. 3-8). 1990. PLB 9.95 (ISBN 1-85435-154-0). Marshall Cavendish.

—Is It Magic. (Illus.). 32p. (gr. 3-8). 1990. PLB 9.95 (ISBN 1-85435-155-9). Marshall Cavendish.

—Light Fantastic. (Illus.). 32p. (gr. 3-8). 1990. PLB 9.95 (ISBN 1-85435-156-7). Marshall Cavendish.

—Plants in Action. (Illus.). 32p. (gr. 3-8). 1990. PLB 9.95 (ISBN 1-85435-157-5). Marshall Cavendish.

—Science Alive Series, 4 bks. (Illus.). 224p. (gr. 3-5). 1989. Set. 59.80 (ISBN 0-382-09596-0). Silver Burdett Pr.

—Secrets of Science Series, 6 vols. (Illus.). (gr. 3-8). 1990. PLB 59.70 (ISBN 1-85435-151-6). Marshall Cavendish.

Kids' Smithsonian Experience. (Illus.). 32p. (ps-8). pap. 29.50 (ISBN 0-87474-585-3). Smithsonian.

Kuntz, Margy, et al. Big Fearon Book of Doing Science. (gr. 1-6). 1989. pap. 25.95 (ISBN 0-8224-2737-0). Fearon Teach Aids.

Lewis, James. Learn While You Scrub: Science in the Tub. 1989. pap. 6.95 (ISBN 0-671-68999-1). S&S Trade.

Library of Science, 7 vols. (Illus.). (gr. 4-9). Date not set. Set. 119.70x (ISBN 1-85435-069-2). Marshall Cavendish.

Light. (Illus.). (gr. 3-5). 3.50 (ISBN 0-7214-0657-2). Ladybird Bks.

Look at Science Series. (Illus.). (gr. 3 up). 1989. Set of 10 titles, 32 pp. ea. PLB 146.53 (ISBN 0-8172-2350-9); Set of 10 titles, 32 pp. ea. pap. 92.67 (ISBN 0-8172-2375-4). Raintree Pubs.

McAlpine, et al. What If? 80p. (gr. 4-6). 1985. pap. 9.00 (ISBN 0-685-30595-3, DP02-V). Zephyr Pr AZ.

McKelway, Margaret. A World of Things to Do. Crump, Donald J., ed. (Illus.). 104p. 1987. 6.95 (ISBN 0-87044-610-X); PLB 8.50 (ISBN 0-87044-615-0). Natl Geog.

McMillan, Dana & Martin, Shirley. Science Boosters. 64p. (gr. 2-6). 1988. 6.95 (ISBN 0-912107-82-0, MM998). Monday Morning Bks.

McNulty, Faith. Peeping in the Shell: A Whooping Crane Is Hatched. Brady, Irene, illus. LC 85-45837. 64p. (gr. 3-7). 1986. 11.95 (ISBN 0-06-024134-9); PLB 11.89 (ISBN 0-06-024135-7). HarpC Child Bks.

Markle, Sandra. Primary Science Sampler. 112p. (gr. 1-3). 1980. 9.95 (ISBN 0-88160-008-3, LW 110). Learning Wks.

—Science Mini-Mysteries. LC 87-17420. (Illus.). 72p. (gr. 3-7). 1988. 12.95 (ISBN 0-689-31291-1, Atheneum Child Bk). Macmillan Child Grp.

—Science Sampler. 112p. (gr. 4-8). 1980. 9.95 (ISBN 0-88160-031-8, LW 216). Learning Wks.

Marsh, Carole. Gee! Ology: Trivia for Kids. (Illus.). (gr. 3-12). 1989. PLB 19.95 (ISBN 1-55609-305-5); pap. 14.95 (ISBN 1-55609-306-3); computer disk 29.95 (ISBN 1-55609-307-1). Gallopade Pub Group.

Martin, Paul D. Science: It's Changing Your World. Crump, Donald J., ed. LC 85-2936. (Illus.). 104p. (gr. 3-8). 1985. 6.95 (ISBN 0-87044-516-2); PLB 8.50 (ISBN 0-87044-521-9). Natl Geog.

Mayes, S. Usborne Starting Point Science. (Illus.). 96p. (gr. 1-4). 1989. 11.95 (ISBN 0-7460-0481-8, Usborne). EDC.

Meyer, Jerome. Boiling Water in a Paper Cup & Other Unbelievables. (Illus.). (gr. 7-12). 1972. pap. 1.95 (ISBN 0-590-09146-8). Scholastic Inc.

Moutran, Julia S. Collecting Bugs & Things: A Science Activity Storybook. (Illus.). 48p. (gr. k up) 1988. pap. 2.95 (ISBN 0-8431-2226-9). Price Stern.

Nelson, Bonnie E. Science & Computer Activities for Children 3 to 9 Years Old. 2nd, rev. ed. (Illus.). 146p. (gr. k-3). 1988. 28.00x (ISBN 0-931642-21-3). Lintel.

Newton, David E. Science Ethics. (Illus.). 128p. (gr. 7-12). 1987. PLB 12.90 (ISBN 0-531-10419-2). Watts.

Norden, Carroll R. The Jungle. rev. ed. LC 87-20820. (Illus.). 48p. (gr. 2-6). 1987. PLB 17.32 (ISBN 0-8172-3256-7); pap. 9.27 (ISBN 0-8172-3281-8). Raintree Pubs.

Oxford Scientific Films Staff. Side by Side. (Illus.). 32p. (ps up). 1988. 13.95 (ISBN 0-399-21582-4, Putnam). Putnam Pub Group.

Pearce, Q. L. Amazing Science Series, 8 bks. (Illus.). 256p. (gr. 4-6). 1989. Set. PLB 103.84 (ISBN 0-671-94111-9); Set. pap. 47.60 (ISBN 0-671-94112-7). Messner.

Penn, Linda. Young Scientists Explore: Air, Land, & Water Life, Bk. 3. 32p. (gr. k-3). 1982. 4.95 (ISBN 0-86653-071-1, GA 404). Good Apple.

—Young Scientists Explore: The World of Nature, Bk. 1. 32p. (gr. k-3). 1982. 4.95 (ISBN 0-86653-069-X, GA 402). Good Apple.

Pollard, Michael. The House That Science Built. (Illus.). 48p. (gr. 1-4). 1987. 12.95x (ISBN 0-8160-1780-8). Facts on File.

Pringle, Laurence. Rain of Troubles: The Science & Politics of Acid Rain. LC 87-34950. (Illus.). 128p. (gr. 7 up). 1988. 13.95 (ISBN 0-02-775370-0, Mcmillan Child Bk). Macmillan Child Grp.

Pyke, Magnus. Weird & Wonderful Science Facts. Burton, Terry, illus. LC 83-24288. 128p. (gr. 5 up). 1985. pap. 3.95 (ISBN 0-8069-6254-2). Sterling.

Quinn, Kaye. Science Mysteries. (Illus.). 80p. (Orig.). (gr. 2-4). 1989. pap. 2.50 (ISBN 0-8431-2377-X). Price Stern.

Rahn, Joan E. Holes. Rahn, Joan E., illus. LC 83-16617. 32p. (gr. 2-5). 1984. 9.95 (ISBN 0-395-35389-0, 5-94126). HM.

Raintree Publishers Inc. The Poles. LC 87-28697. (Illus.). 64p. (Orig.). (gr. 5-9). 1988. PLB 19.99 (ISBN 0-8172-3078-5); pap. text ed. 11.93 (ISBN 0-8172-3095-5). Raintree Pubs.

Schaffer, Frank, Publications Staff. Getting Ready for Science. (Illus.). 24p. (ps-k). 1980. wkbk. 3.98 (ISBN 0-86734-021-5, FS 3034). Schaffer Pubns.

Schwartz, L. Trivia Trackdown - Animals & Science. (gr. 4-6). 1985. 3.95 (ISBN 0-88160-119-5, LW 252). Learning Wks.

Science Fun. 64p. (Orig.). (gr. k-1). 1984. pap. 1.25 (ISBN 0-448-16138-9, G&D, G&D). Putnam Pub Group.

Science Magic. 1987. write for info. P-H.

Science Starter. (Illus.). 88p. (ps-3). 1990. 15.93 (ISBN 0-8094-4881-5); lib. bdg. 21.27 (ISBN 0-8094-4882-3). Time-Life.

Science Surprises. (Illus.). 32p. (gr. 2-5). 1986. pap. 4.95 (ISBN 0-86020-914-8). EDC.

Science Tricks & Magic. (Illus.). 32p. (gr. 2-5). 1986. pap. 4.95 (ISBN 0-86020-916-4). EDC.

Science Yellow Pages for Students & Teachers. LC 87-82070. 64p. (gr. k-8). 1988. pap. text ed. 6.95 (ISBN 0-318-32626-4, IP 89-2). Incentive Pubns.

Selsam, Millicent E. Is This a Baby Dinosaur? & Other Science Picture Puzzles. LC 72-76508. (Illus.). 32p. (ps-3). 1972. PLB 13.89 (ISBN 0-06-025303-7). HarpC Child Bks.

Simon, Seymour. Einstein Anderson Sees Through the Invisible Man. Winkowski, Fred, illus. (gr. 3-7). 1987. pap. 3.95 (ISBN 0-14-032306-6, Puffin). Puffin Bks.

Stangl, Jean. The Tools of Science: Ideas & Activities for Guiding Young Scientists. rev. ed. (Illus.). 160p. 1989. 16.95 (ISBN 0-8306-9216-9); pap. 8.95 (ISBN 0-8306-3216-6). TAB Bks.

Stein, Sara. The Science Book. LC 79-64786. (Illus.). 288p. (gr. 4-7). 1980. pap. 9.95 (ISBN 0-89480-120-1, 291). Workman Pub.

Stetten, Mary. Let's Play Science. Stetten, Mary, illus. LC 78-24698. (ps-3). 1979. pap. 8.95 (ISBN 0-06-090711-8, CN-711, PL). HarperCollins.

Stine, Megan, et al. Smithsonian Science Activity Book. Solimini, Cheryl, ed. (Illus.). 100p. (gr. 2-6). 1987. pap. text ed. 8.95 (ISBN 0-939456-51-6). Galison.

Story of Science, Bk. 1. (ARA., Illus.). (gr. 5-12). 3.50x (ISBN 0-86685-229-8). Intl Bk Ctr.

Stwertka, Eve & Stwertka, Albert. Make It Graphic: Drawing Graphs for Science & Social Studies Projects. 64p. (gr. 4 up). 1985. lib. bdg. 9.29 (ISBN 0-671-54288-5). Messner.

Sullivan, Dianna J. Big & Easy Science. Adkins, Lynda, illus. 48p. (ps-2). 1988. wkbk. 5.95 (ISBN 1-55734-105-2). Tchr Create Mat.

Supraner, Robyn. Science Secrets. Barto, Renzo, illus. LC 80-23794. 48p. (gr. 1-5). 1981. PLB 11.89 (ISBN 0-89375-426-9); pap. 2.95 (ISBN 0-89375-427-7). Troll Assocs.

Things Around Us. (Illus.). 88p. (ps-3). 1989. 15.93 (ISBN 0-8094-4845-9); lib. bdg. 21.27 (ISBN 0-8094-4846-7). Time-Life.

Warren, Jean. Science Time. 80p. (gr. k-2). 1984. 7.95 (ISBN 0-912107-18-9). Monday Morning Bks.

Webster, David. How to Do a Science Project. LC 73-12214. (Illus.). 72p. (gr. 4 up). 1974. PLB 10.40 (ISBN 0-531-00817-7). Watts.

Weiss, Ann E. Seers & Scientists: Can the Future Be Predicted? (Illus.). 96p. (gr. 6 up). 1986. 13.95 (ISBN 0-15-272850-3, HJ). HarBraceJ.

White, Laurence B. Science Games & Puzzles. Brown, Marc T., illus. LC 84-40786. 1979. pap. 4.95 (ISBN 0-201-08606-9, Lipp Jr Bks). HarpC Child Bks.

—Science Toys & Tricks. Brown, Marc T., illus. LC 84-40787. 1980. pap. 4.95 (ISBN 0-201-08659-X, Lipp Jr Bks). HarpC Child Bks.

Why on Earth. LC 88-25486. 96p. (gr. 3-6). 1988. 7.95 (ISBN 0-87044-701-7); PLB 9.50 (ISBN 0-87044-706-8). Natl Geog.

Wicks, Keith. Science Can Be Fun. Kostal, Pavel, illus. 32p. (gr. 4-7). 1988. PLB 9.95 (ISBN 0-8225-0896-6, First Ave Edns); pap. 4.95 (ISBN 0-8225-9559-1, First Ave Edns). Lerner Pubns.

Wilkes. Simple Science. (Illus.). 38p. (gr. 2-5). 1983. 10.95 (ISBN 0-86020-761-7); PLB 12.96 (ISBN 0-88110-272-5). EDC.

Wilkins, Mary-Jane. Air, Light & Water. Forsey, Chris, illus. 40p. (gr. 4-5). 1991. PLB 11.40 (ISBN 0-531-19104-4). Watts.

Williams, Brenda & Williams, Brian. Earth, Sea & Sky. Forsey, Chris, illus. LC 90-42620. 40p. (Orig.). (gr. 2-5). 1991. pap. 3.95 (ISBN 0-679-80861-2). Random.

—The Random House Book of One Thousand-One Wonders of Science. Kerrod, Robin, et al, illus. LC 89-3954. 160p. 1990. PLB 11.99 (ISBN 0-679-90080-2); pap. 10.95 (ISBN 0-679-80080-8). McKay.

Wolfe, Constance. Search: A Research Guide for Science Fairs & Independent Study. 94p. (Orig.). (gr. 4-8). 1987. pap. text ed. 12.95 (ISBN 0-913705-30-6, ZB05-A). Zephyr Pr AZ.

Wood, Barbara S. Messages Without Words. rev. ed. LC 87-23315. (Illus.). 48p. (gr. 2-6). 1987. PLB 17.32 (ISBN 0-8172-3258-3); pap. 9.27 (ISBN 0-8172-3283-4). Raintree Pubs.

Woods, Geraldine. Science in Ancient Egypt. Rasof, Henry, ed. (Illus.). 96p. (gr. 5-8). 1988. PLB 10.40 (ISBN 0-531-10486-9). Watts.

Wyler, Rose. Science Fun Series, 6 vols. Stewart, Pat, illus. 288p. (gr. 2-4). 1987. Set. PLB 68.28 (ISBN 0-671-93016-8); Set. PLB 51.24s.p.; Set. pap. 29.70 (ISBN 0-671-93018-4); Set. pap. 22.26s.p. Messner.

SCIENCE–DATA PROCESSING

Adams, Richard C. Science with Computers. (Illus.). 128p. (gr. 7 up). 1987. PLB 12.90 (ISBN 0-531-10324-2). Watts.

SCIENCE–DICTIONARIES

Dempsey, Michael W. Children's First Science Encyclopedia. 1987. 6.98 (ISBN 0-671-07745-7). S&S Trade.

Engel, Leonard, ed. Junior Pictorial Encyclopedia of Science. Urey, Harold C., intro. by. (Illus.). (gr. 4-8). 11.25 (ISBN 0-8446-0089-X). Peter Smith.

Jugendhandbuch Naturwissen: Bausteine des Lebens, 6 vols, Vol. 1. (GER.). 144p. pap. 750.00 (ISBN 3-499-16203-2, M-7486, Pub. by Rowohlt). French & Eur.

Jugendhandbuch Naturwissen: Elektrizitaet und Elektronic, Vol. 6. (GER.). 144p. 1976. pap. 5.95 (ISBN 3-499-16208-3, M-7491, Pub. by Rowohlt). French & Eur.

Jugendhandbuch Naturwissen: Energie, Vol. 5. (GER.). 128p. 1976. pap. 5.95 (ISBN 3-499-16207-5, M-7490, Pub. by Rowohlt). French & Eur.

Jugendhandbuch Naturwissen: Erde und Weltall, Vol. 4. (GER.). 128p. 1976. pap. 5.95 (ISBN 3-499-16206-7, M-7489, Pub. by Rowohlt). French & Eur.

Jugendhandbuch Naturwissen: Saeugetiere, Vol. 3. (GER.). 144p. 1976. pap. 5.95 (ISBN 0-686-56619-X, M-7488, Pub. by Rowohlt). French & Eur.

Let's Discover, 16 vols. (Illus.). (gr. k-6). 1981. Set. PLB 330.67 (ISBN 0-8172-1782-7). Raintree Pubs.

New Encyclopedia of Science. (Illus.). 2300p. (gr. 7 up). 1985. Set of 16 vols. PLB 265.33 (ISBN 0-8172-5000-X). Raintree Pubs.

Pitt, Valeria. Enciclopedia Juvenil de la Ciencia. (SPA.). 260p. 1975. 95.00 (ISBN 84-272-5920-4, S-26475). French & Eur.

The Raintree Illustrated Science Encyclopedia, 18 vols. LC 78-12093. (Illus.). (gr. 3 up). 1991. Repr. of 1984 ed. PLB 398.67 (ISBN 0-8172-3800-X). Raintree Pubs.

Shaw, Jean M. & Dyches, Richard W. First Science Dictionary. Sornat, Czeslaw, illus. 104p. (gr. k-4). 1991. 14.95 (ISBN 0-531-15237-5); PLB 14.90 (ISBN 0-531-11110-5). Watts.

The Simon & Schuster Illustrated Dictionary of Science. (Illus.). (gr. 3 up). 1985. pap. 6.95 (ISBN 0-671-54547-7, Little Simon). S&S Trade.

Wertheim, J. & Oxlade, C. Dictionary of Science: Physics, Chemistry & Biology Facts. (Illus.). 128p. (gr. 6 up). 1988. pap. 21.95 (ISBN 0-86020-989-X). EDC.

World Book Editors Staff. Science Year, the World Book Science Annual, 1989. LC 65-21776. (Illus.). 400p. (gr. 7-12). 1988. lib. bdg. write for info. (ISBN 0-7166-0589-9). World Bk.

SCIENCE–EXPERIMENTS

see also particular branches of science with the subdivision Experiments, e.g. Chemistry–Experiments, etc.

Alexander, Alison. Science Magic: Scientific Experiments for Young Children. 1987. pap. 10.95 (ISBN 0-671-66368-2, PRHJ); pap. 5.95 (ISBN 0-671-66927-3). S&S Trade.

Allison, Linda & Katz, David. Gee Wiz! How to Mix Art & Science or the Art of Thinking Scientifically. Allison, Linda, illus. LC 83-9834. 128p. (gr. 4 up). 1983. 14.95 (ISBN 0-316-03444-4); pap. 8.95 (ISBN 0-316-03445-2). Little.

Amery. Experiments. (gr. 4-6). 1977. pap. 5.95 (ISBN 0-86020-135-X, Usborne-Hayes). EDC.

Ardley, Neil. Science Book of Color. (gr. 4-7). 1991. 9.95 (ISBN 0-15-200576-5). HarBraceJ.

—Science Book of Water. (gr. 4-7). 1991. 9.95 (ISBN 0-15-200575-7). HarBraceJ.

Barber, Jacqueline. Bubble-ology. Bergman, Lincoln & Fairwell, Kay, eds. Baker, Lisa H., et al, illus. Barber, Jacqueline & Sneider, Cary I., photos by. 53p. (gr. 5-9). 1987. pap. 7.50 (ISBN 0-912511-11-7). Lawrence Science.

Beller, Joel. So You Want to Do a Science Project! LC 81-7943. (Illus.). 160p. (gr. 5 up). 1982. PLB 9.95 (ISBN 0-668-04987-1, 4987). Prentice Hall Pr.

Bochinski, Julianne. Complete Handbook of Science Fair Projects. 1991. pap. text ed. 12.95 (ISBN 0-471-52728-9). Wiley.

Broekel, Ray. Experiments with Air. LC 87-34146. (Illus.). 48p. (gr. k-4). 1988. PLB 14.60 (ISBN 0-516-01213-4); pap. 4.95 (ISBN 0-516-41213-2). Childrens.

—Experiments with Straw & Paper. LC 90-2173. (Illus.). 48p. (gr. k-4). 1990. PLB 14.60 (ISBN 0-516-01104-9). Childrens.

—Experiments with Water. LC 87-34147. (Illus.). 48p. (gr. k-4). 1988. PLB 14.60 (ISBN 0-516-01215-0); pap. 4.95 (ISBN 0-516-41215-9). Childrens.

Brown, Bob. More Science for You: One Hundred Twelve Illustrated Experiments. (Illus.). 128p. (ps-8). 1988. 12.95 (ISBN 0-8306-9125-1, 3125); pap. 7.95 (ISBN 0-8306-3125-9, 3125). TAB Bks.

Brown, Sam E. Bubbles, Rainbows & Worms: Science Experiments for Pre-School Children. Stamper, Silas, illus. LC 80-84598. 105p. (ps-1). 1981. pap. 8.95 (ISBN 0-87659-100-4). Gryphon Hse.

Carson, Mary S. The Scientific Kid: Projects, Experiments, Adventures. LC 88-45551. 80p. (Orig.). 1989. pap. 11.95 (ISBN 0-06-096316-6, PL 6316, PL). HarperCollins.

Casn, Terry & Taylor, Barbara. One Hundred Seventy-Five More Science Experiments to Amuse & Amaze Your Friends. Kuo Kang Chen & Bull, Peter, illus. LC 90-39250. 176p. (Orig.). (gr. 4-7). 1991. pap. 10.95 (ISBN 0-679-80390-4). Random.

CES Industries, Inc. Staff. Ed-Lab Eight Hundred Experiment Manual: Thermal Probe Sensor. (Illus., Orig.). (gr. 9-12). 1983. pap. write for info. (ISBN 0-86711-073-2). CES Industries.

Challand, Helen. Activities in the Earth Sciences. LC 82-9444. (Illus.). (gr. 5 up). 1982. PLB 17.27 (ISBN 0-516-00506-5). Childrens.

—Activities in the Life Sciences. LC 82-9442. (Illus.). (gr. 5 up). 1982. PLB 17.27 (ISBN 0-516-00507-3). Childrens.

Challand, Helen J. Science Projects & Activities. Kimball, Linda H., illus. LC 84-23252. 93p. (gr. 5-8). 1985. lib. bdg. 17.27 (ISBN 0-516-00569-3). Childrens.

Clark, John G. Science Project Puzzlers: Starter Ideas for the Curious. Schwarz, Frank, illus. Stone, Harris. (Illus.). 61p. (gr. 7 up). 1981. pap. 4.95 (ISBN 0-13-795450-6, Pub. by Treehouse). P-H.

Cobb, Vicki. Bet You Can: Science Possibilities to Fool You. 112p. 1990. 12.95 (ISBN 0-688-09865-7). Lothrop.

—More Science Experiments You Can Eat. Maestro, Giulio, illus. LC 78-12732. (gr. 5 up). 1979. 12.95 (ISBN 0-397-31828-6, Lipp Jr Bks); PLB 12.89 (ISBN 0-397-31878-2, Lipp Jr Bks). HarpC Child Bks.

—More Science Experiments You Can Eat. LC 78-12732. (Illus.). 128p. (gr. 5-8). 1984. pap. 4.95 (ISBN 0-06-446003-7, Trophy). HarpC Child Bks.

—Science Experiments You Can Eat. Lippman, Peter, illus. LC 71-151474. 128p. (gr. 5-8). 1972. PLB 12.89 (ISBN 0-685-02086-X, Lipp Jr Bks). HarpC Child Bks.

—Science Experiments You Can Eat. Lippman, Peter, illus. LC 71-151474. 127p. (gr. 5-8). 1972. PLB 13.89 (ISBN 0-397-31487-6, Lipp Jr Bks). HarpC Child Bks.

—Science Experiments You Can Eat. LC 71-151474. (Illus.). 128p. (gr. 5-8). 1972. pap. 3.95 (ISBN 0-685-31398-0, Trophy). HarpC Child Bks.

Cobb, Vicki & Darling, Kathy. Bet You Can! Science Possibilities to Fool You. Ormai, Stella, illus. 112p. (gr. 3-7). 1983. pap. 2.95 (ISBN 0-380-82180-X, Camelot). Avon.

—Bet You Can't! Science Impossibilities to Fool You. Weston, Martha, illus. LC 79-9254. 128p. (gr. 5 up). 1980. 12.95 (ISBN 0-688-41905-4); PLB 12.88 (ISBN 0-688-51905-9). Lothrop.

—Bet You Can't: Science Impossibilities to Fool You. Weston, Martha, illus. 128p. (gr. 3-7). 1983. pap. 2.95 (ISBN 0-380-54502-0, Camelot). Avon.

Conaway, Judith. More Science Secrets. LC 86-16084. (Illus.). 48p. (gr. 1-5). 1987. PLB 11.89 (ISBN 0-8167-0866-5); pap. text ed. 2.95 (ISBN 0-8167-0867-3). Troll Assocs.

Davies, Kay. My Balloon. (ps-3). 1990. 6.95 (ISBN 0-385-41131-6); PLB 7.99 (ISBN 0-385-41199-5). Doubleday.

—My Mirror. 1990. 6.95 (ISBN 0-385-41128-6); PLB 7.99 (ISBN 0-385-41196-0). Doubleday.

DeBruin, Jerry. Creative, Hands-on Science Experiences. 256p. (gr. k-6). 1980. 15.95 (ISBN 0-916456-87-0, GA 165). Good Apple.

—Science Fairs with Style. 336p. (gr. 5-12). 1991. 19.95 (ISBN 0-86653-606-X, GA1325). Good Apple.

Echols, Jean C. Buzzing a Hive. Bergman, Lincoln & Fairwell, Kay, eds. Baker, Lisa H., illus. Curtis, Elizabeth, et al, photos by. (Illus.). 97p. (Orig.). (gr. 1-3). 1987. pap. 11.00 (ISBN 0-912511-12-5). Lawrence Science.

Filson, Brent. Famous Experiments & How to Repeat Them. Fuhrmann, Brigita, illus. LC 85-22259. 64p. (gr. 4 up). 1986. lib. bdg. 9.98 (ISBN 0-671-55687-8). Messner.

Flint, David. Weather & Climate: Projects with Geography. (Illus.). 32p. (gr. 5-8). 1991. PLB 11.90 (ISBN 0-531-17321-6, Gloucester Pr). Watts.

Gardner, Robert. Energy Projects. (Illus.). 128p. (gr. 7-12). 1987. PLB 12.90 (ISBN 0-531-10338-2). Watts.

—Experimenting with Sound. (Illus.). 128p. (gr. 9-12). 1991. PLB 12.40 (ISBN 0-531-12503-3). Watts.

—Ideas for Science Projects. (Illus.). 144p. (gr. 7-12). 1989. PLB 12.90 (ISBN 0-531-10246-7); pap. 5.95 (ISBN 0-531-15125-5). Watts.

—More Ideas for Science Projects. 1989. pap. 5.95 (ISBN 0-531-15126-3). Watts.

—Science Around the House. (Illus.). 136p. (gr. 4-8). 1989. PLB 11.98 (ISBN 0-671-54663-5); PLB 8.99s.p.; pap. 4.95 (ISBN 0-671-68139-7). Messner.

—Science Experiments. Rasof, Henry, ed. (Illus.). 72p. (gr. 5-7). 1988. PLB 10.40 (ISBN 0-531-10484-2). Watts.

Gardner, Robert & Webster, David. Science in Your Backyard. (Illus.). 136p. (gr. 4-8). 1989. PLB 11.98 (ISBN 0-671-55565-0); PLB 8.99s.p.; pap. 4.95 (ISBN 0-671-63835-1); pap. 3.71s.p. Messner.

Gore, Sheila. My Shadow. 1990. 6.95 (ISBN 0-385-41130-8); PLB 7.99 (ISBN 0-385-41198-7). Doubleday.

Gutnik, Martin J. Experiments That Explore the Greenhouse Effect. (Illus.). 72p. (gr. 5-8). 1991. PLB 13.90 (ISBN 1-56294-012-0). Millbrook Pr.

—How to Do a Science Project & Report. (gr. 7 up). 1980. PLB 10.90 (ISBN 0-531-04129-8). Watts.

Harlow, Rosie & Morgan, Gareth. Cycles & Seasons. Peperell, Liz, illus. 40p. (gr. 5-8). 1991. PLB 12.90 (ISBN 0-531-19123-0, Warwick). Watts.

—Energy & Growth. Kuo Kang Chen & Fitzsimmons, Cecilia, illus. 40p. (gr. 5-8). 1991. PLB 12.90 (ISBN 0-531-19124-9, Warwick). Watts.

—Observing Minibeasts. Kuo Kang Chen, illus. 40p. (gr. 5-8). 1991. PLB 12.90 (ISBN 0-531-19125-7, Warwick). Watts.

—Trees & Leaves. Peperell, Liz, illus. 40p. (gr. 5-8). 1991. PLB 12.90 (ISBN 0-531-19126-5, Warwick). Watts.

Herbert, Don. Mr. Wizard's Experiments for Young Scientists. Noonan, Dan, illus. LC 59-7907. 187p. (gr. 7 up). 1959. 16.95 (ISBN 0-385-07798-X). Doubleday.

—Mr. Wizard's Experiments for Young Scientists. 1990. pap. 7.95 (ISBN 0-385-26585-9). Doubleday.

—Mr. Wizard's Supermarket Science. McKie, Roy, illus. LC 79-27217. 96p. (gr. 4-7). 1980. lib. bdg. 9.99 (ISBN 0-394-93800-3); pap. 7.95 (ISBN 0-394-83800-9). Random.

Hessler, Edward W. & Stubbs, Harriett. Acid Rain Science Projects. 20p. (Orig.). (gr. 5-12). 1987. pap. 9.95 (ISBN 0-935577-09-2). Acid Rain Found.

Hoffman, Jane. Backyard Scientist: Series One. Ostroff, Lanny, illus. 52p. (Orig.). (gr. k-6). 1987. pap. text ed. 8.50 (ISBN 0-9618663-0-6). Backyard Scientist.

—Backyard Scientist: Series Two. (Illus.). (gr. 4-9). 1989. pap. 8.50 (ISBN 0-9618663-2-2). Backyard Scientist.

—Backyard Scientist, Series 3: Experiments in the Life Sciences. (Illus.). 52p. (gr. k-7). 1990. text ed. 8.50 (ISBN 0-9618663-3-0). Backyard Scientist.

—The Original Backyard Scientist. Ostroff, Lanny, illus. 58p. (Orig.). (gr. k-6). 1987. text ed. 8.50 (ISBN 0-9618663-1-4). Backyard Scientist.

Kelinson, Roberta M. & McGreevey, Carla. Blooming Experiments: Fun Science Activities for Language Enrichment Based on Benjamin Bloom's Taxonomy. 1988. pap. 13.95 (ISBN 1-55999-024-4). LinguiSystems.

Kelley, Colleen. Kids' Stuff: Simple Science & Nature Projects for Children. Kelley, Colleen, illus. 96p. (gr. k-6). 1989. pap. text ed. 4.95 (ISBN 0-9618052-2-6). Daily Hampshire.

Kramer, Alan. How to Make a Chemical Volcano & Other Mysterious Experiments. Harvey, Paul, illus. 112p. (gr. 5 up). 1991. pap. 6.95 (ISBN 0-531-15610-9). Watts.

Krieger, Melanie J. How to Excel in Science Competitions. (Illus.). 144p. (gr. 9-12). 1991. PLB 12.90 (ISBN 0-531-11004-4). Watts.

Lewis, James. Measure, Pour & Mix: Kitchen Science Tricks. 1990. write for info. (ISBN 0-88166-134-1, Dist. by S & S). Meadowbrook.

Lewis, Jim. Rub-a Dub-Dub, Science in the Tub. 1989. pap. 5.95 (ISBN 0-88166-161-9, Dist. by Simon & Schuster). Meadowbrook.

McCarthy, Donald W. Fun with Science-Magic. Cooper, William H., ed. LC 84-50893. (Illus.). 80p. (gr. 4-9). 1984. pap. 5.27 (ISBN 0-914127-15-2). Univ Class.

Mainwaring, Jane. My Feather. 1990. 6.95 (ISBN 0-385-41129-4); PLB 7.99 (ISBN 0-385-41197-9). Doubleday.

Mandell, Muriel. Simple Science Experiments with Everyday Materials. Zweifel, Frances W., illus. LC 88-31201. 128p. (gr. 4-10). 1989. 12.95 (ISBN 0-8069-6794-3). Sterling.

—Simple Weather Experiments with Everyday Materials. LC 90-37915. (Illus.). 128p. (gr. 4-10). 1990. 12.95 (ISBN 0-8069-7296-3). Sterling.

—Two Hundred & Twenty Easy-to-Do Science Experiments for Young People: Three Complete Books. 287p. (gr. 3 up). 1985. pap. 8.85 (ISBN 0-486-24874-7). Dover.

Markle, Sandra. Exploring Summer. Markle, Sandra, illus. LC 86-17322. 176p. (gr. 3-7). 1987. 14.95 (ISBN 0-689-31212-1, Atheneum Child Bk). Macmillan Child Grp.

—Power Up: Experiments, Puzzles & Games Exploring Electricity. LC 88-7772. (Illus.). 48p. (gr. 4-6). 1989. 13.95 (ISBN 0-689-31442-6, Atheneum Child Bk). Macmillan Child Grp.

—The Young Scientist's Guide to Successful Science Projects. Byrd, Bob, photos by. LC 89-45290. (Illus.). 128p. (gr. 3-7). lib. bdg. 12.88 (ISBN 0-688-07217-8). Lothrop.

Moche, Dinah. More Magic Science Tricks. (Orig.). (gr. 3-7). 1981. pap. 1.50 (ISBN 0-590-31847-0, Schol Pap). Scholastic Inc.

Munson, Howard R. Science Activities with Simple Things. (gr. 4-8). 1972. pap. 6.95 (ISBN 0-8224-6320-2). Fearon Teach Aids.

Nicholson, Shirley S. Nature's Merry - Go - Round. Sellon, Michael B., illus. LC 69-17716. (gr. 3-9). 1969. 3.75 (ISBN 0-8356-0003-3, Quest). Theos Pub Hse.

Ontario Science Center Staff. Scienceworks: Sixty-Five Experiments That Introduce the Fun & Wonder of Science. Holdcroft, Tina, illus. (gr. 2-7). 1986. pap. 8.61 (ISBN 0-201-16780-8). Addison-Wesley.

Orii, Eijo & Orii, Masako. Simple Science Experiments with Circles. Fujishima, Kaoru, et al, illus. Knopp, Jonathan, contrib. by. LC 88-23295. 32p. (gr. 2-3). 1989. PLB 10.95 (ISBN 1-55532-857-1). Gareth Stevens Inc.

—Simple Science Experiments with Light. Fujishima, Kaoru, et al, illus. Knopp, Jonathan, contrib. by. LC 88-23306. 32p. (gr. 2-3). 1989. PLB 10.95 (ISBN 1-55532-858-X). Gareth Stevens Inc.

—Simple Science Experiments with Marbles. Fujishima, Kaoru, et al, illus. Knopp, Jonathan, contrib. by. LC 88-23297. 32p. (gr. 2-3). 1989. PLB 10.95 (ISBN 1-55532-856-3). Gareth Stevens Inc.

—Simple Science Experiments with Optical Illusions. LC 88-24756. (Illus.). 32p. (gr. 2-3). 1989. PLB 10.95 (ISBN 1-55532-853-9). Gareth Stevens Inc.

—Simple Science Experiments with Ping-Pong Balls. Fujishima, Kaoru, et al, illus. Knopp, Jonathan, contrib. by. LC 88-22508. 32p. (gr. 2-3). 1989. PLB 10.95 (ISBN 1-55532-852-0). Gareth Stevens Inc.

—Simple Science Experiments with Starting & Stopping. Fujishima, Kaoru, et al, illus. Knopp, Jonathan, contrib. by. LC 88-20156. 32p. (gr. 2-3). 1989. PLB 10.95 (ISBN 1-55532-855-5). Gareth Stevens Inc.

—Simple Science Experiments with Straws. Fujishima, Kaoru, et al, illus. Knopp, Jonathan, contrib. by. LC 88-23298. 32p. (gr. 2-3). 1989. PLB 10.95 (ISBN 1-55532-854-7). Gareth Stevens Inc.

—Simple Science Experiments with Water. Fujishima, Kaoru, et al, illus. Knopp, Jonathan, contrib. by. LC 88-23304. 32p. (gr. 2-3). 1989. PLB 10.95 (ISBN 1-55532-859-8). Gareth Stevens Inc.

Parker, Steve. Nerves to Senses: Projects with Biology. (Illus.). 32p. (gr. 5-8). 1991. PLB 11.90 (ISBN 0-531-17295-3, Gloucester Pr). Watts.

Penrose, Gordon. Dr. Zeds Science Surprises. 1990. pap. 11.95 (ISBN 0-671-70542-3); pap. 5.95 (ISBN 0-671-70541-5). PB.

—Magic Mud & Other Great Experiments. (Illus.). 48p. (gr. 3-7). 1988. pap. 10.95 (ISBN 0-671-64969-8, Little Simon); pap. 6.95 (ISBN 0-671-65767-4, Little Simon). S&S Trade.

—Sensational Science Activities with Dr. Zed. (Illus.). 48p. (gr. 3-7). 1990. PLB 11.95 (ISBN 0-671-72552-1); pap. 5.95 (ISBN 0-671-72553-X). S&S Trade.

Reuben, Gabriel. Electricity Experiments for Children. (Illus.). 88p. (gr. 5-9). pap. 2.95 (ISBN 0-486-22030-3). Dover.

Simple Science Experiments, 8 vols. (Illus.). 256p. (gr. 2-3). 1988. Set. PLB 79.60 (ISBN 1-55532-937-3). Gareth Stevens Inc.

Smith, Norman F. How to Do Successful Science Projects. rev. ed. Steltenpohl, Jane, ed. (Illus.). 128p. (gr. 6-9). 1990. PLB 11.98 (ISBN 0-671-70685-3); pap. 5.95 (ISBN 0-671-70686-1). Messner.

Sneider, Cary I. Oobleck: What Do Scientists Do? rev. ed. Bergman, Lincoln & Fairwell, Kay, eds. Baker, Lisa H. & Peterson, Adria, illus. Sneider, Cary I., photos by. 28p. (gr. 4-8). 1988. pap. 6.50 (ISBN 0-912511-64-8). Lawrence Science.

Sneider, Cary I. & Gould, Alan. The Wizard's Lab. Bergman, Lincoln & Fairwell, Kay, eds. Bevilacqua, Carol & Klofkorn, Lisa, illus. Hoyt, Richard, photos by. 72p. 1989. pap. 49.50 (ISBN 0-912511-71-0). Lawrence Science.

Stacy, Dennis. Nifty (& Thrifty) Science Activities. (gr. 2-6). 1988. pap. 6.95 (ISBN 0-8224-4777-0). Fearon Teach Aids.

Stangl, Jean. The Tools of Science: Ideas & Activities for Guiding Young Scientists. rev. ed. (Illus.). 160p. 1989. 16.95 (ISBN 0-8306-9216-9); pap. 8.95 (ISBN 0-8306-3216-6). TAB Bks.

Stine, Megan, et al. More Science Activities. Solimini, Cheryl, ed. (Illus.). 100p. (gr. 2-6). 1988. pap. text ed. 8.95 (ISBN 0-939456-16-8). Galison.

—Still More Science Activities. 3rd ed. Taback, Simms, illus. Falk, John, intro. by. (Illus.). 100p. (gr. 2-6). 1989. pap. text ed. 8.95 (ISBN 0-929648-01-3). Galison.

Stone, George K. More Science Projects You Can Do. Hunter, Mel, illus. (gr. 5 up). 1981. pap. 3.95 (ISBN 0-13-600916-6, Pub. by Treehouse). P-H.

—Science Projects You Can Do. Peck, Stephen R., illus. 101p. (gr. 7-9). 1963. (Pub. by Treehouse); pap. 4.95 (ISBN 0-13-795328-3). P-H.

Sundquist, Nancy & Brin, Susannah. Fifty Science Experiments I Can Do. (Illus.). 48p. (gr. 1-5). 1988. pap. 2.95 (ISBN 0-8431-1867-9). Price Stern.

Taylor, Barbara. Air & Flight. (Illus.). 40p. (gr. k-4). 1991. PLB 11.90 (ISBN 0-531-19129-X, Warwick). Watts.

—Batteries & Magnets. (Illus.). 40p. (gr. k-4). 1991. PLB 11.90 (ISBN 0-531-19130-3, Warwick). Watts.

—Color & Light. (Illus.). 40p. (gr. k-4). 1991. PLB 11.90 (ISBN 0-531-19127-3, Warwick). Watts.

—Growing Plants. (Illus.). 40p. (gr. k-4). 1991. PLB 11.90 (ISBN 0-531-19128-1, Warwick). Watts.

—Sound & Music. (Illus.). 32p. (gr. 5-8). 1991. PLB 11.40 (ISBN 0-531-14185-3). Watts.

Taylor, Ron. Projects. (Illus.). 64p. (gr. 4-7). 1985. 15.95 (ISBN 0-8160-1076-5). Facts on File.

Thomas, David A. Math Projects for Young Scientists. Rasof, Henry, ed. (Illus.). 128p. (gr. 7-12). 1988. PLB 12.90 (ISBN 0-531-10523-7). Watts.

Tocci, Salvatore. How to Do a Science Fair Project. (Illus.). 128p. (gr. 7-12). 1989. PLB 12.90 (ISBN 0-531-10245-9); pap. 5.95 (ISBN 0-531-15123-9). Watts.

Twist, Clint. Reproduction to Birth: Projects with Biology. (Illus.). 32p. (gr. 5-8). 1991. PLB 11.90 (ISBN 0-531-17294-5, Gloucester Pr). Watts.

UNESCO Staff. Seven Hundred Science Experiments for Everyone. rev. ed. LC 64-10638. (Illus.). 252p. (gr. 5-9). 1964. pap. 13.95 (ISBN 0-385-05275-8). Doubleday.

Vancleave, Janice. Physics for Every Kid: One Hundred One Easy Experiments That Really Work. 1991. pap. text ed. 10.95 (ISBN 0-471-52505-7). Wiley.

Vessel, M. F. & Wong, H. H. Science Bulletin Boards. (gr. 1-8). 1962. pap. 5.95 (ISBN 0-8224-6290-7). Fearon Teach Aids.

Vowles, A. Amazing Experiments. (Illus.). 32p. (gr. 2-6). 1985. pap. 4.95 (ISBN 0-88625-073-0). Durkin Hayes Pub.

Walker, Diane A. & Hershey, Phillip. How to Master Science Labs. LC 86-24733. (Illus.). 128p. (gr. 7 up). 1989. PLB 12.90 (ISBN 0-531-10323-4); pap. 5.95 (ISBN 0-531-15124-7). Watts.

Walpole, Brenda. One Hundred Seventy-Five Science Experiments to Amuse & Amaze Your Friends. Kuo Kang Chen & Bull, Peter, illus. LC 88-4526. 176p. (Orig.). (gr. 4-7). 1988. pap. 10.95 (ISBN 0-394-89991-1, Random Juv). Random.

Webster, Vera. Experimentos Cientificos. Kratky, Lada, tr. LC 85-31403. (SPA., Illus.). 48p. (gr. k-4). 1986. PLB 14.60 (ISBN 0-516-31646-X); pap. 4.95 (ISBN 0-516-51646-9). Childrens.

—Science Experiments. LC 82-4429. (gr. k-4). 1982. PLB 14.60 (ISBN 0-516-01646-6); pap. 4.95 (ISBN 0-516-41646-4). Childrens.

Wellnitz, William R. Science Magic for Kids: Simple & Safe Experiments. (Illus.). 128p. 1990. 17.95 (ISBN 0-8306-8423-9, 3423); pap. 9.95 (ISBN 0-8306-3423-1). TAB Bks.

White, Laurence B., Jr. Science Games & Puzzles. Brown, Marc T., illus. LC 85-43035. 96p. (gr. 1-4). 1985. pap. 5.95 (ISBN 0-06-446013-4, Trophy). HarpC Child Bks.

—Science Toys & Tricks. Brown, Marc T., illus. LC 85-43036. 96p. (gr. 1-4). 1985. pap. 5.95 (ISBN 0-06-446014-2, Trophy). HarpC Child Bks.

White, Laurence B., Jr. & Broekel, Ray. Shazam! Simple Science Magic. Mathews, Judith, ed. Seltzer, Meyer, illus. 48p. (gr. 3-7). 1990. 11.95 (ISBN 0-8075-7332-9). A Whitman.

Wilkes, Angela. My First Science Book. (Illus.). 48p. (gr. 1-5). 1990. 11.95 (ISBN 0-679-80583-4); PLB 12.99 (ISBN 0-679-90583-9). Knopf.

Wong, Ovid. Experiments with Animal Behavior. LC 87-33779. (Illus.). 48p. (gr. k-4). 1988. PLB 14.60 (ISBN 0-516-01214-2); pap. 4.95 (ISBN 0-516-41214-0). Childrens.

Wong, Ovid K. Is Science Magic? LC 88-36961. (Illus.). 128p. (gr. 5 up). 1989. PLB 17.27 (ISBN 0-516-00570-7). Childrens.

Wyler, Rose. Science Fun with Drums, Bells, & Whistles. Stewart, Pat, illus. LC 87-7838. 48p. (gr. 2-4). 1987. PLB 11.38 (ISBN 0-671-63783-5); PLB 8.54s.p.; pap. 4.95 (ISBN 0-671-64760-1); pap. 3.71s.p. Messner.

—Science Fun With Mud & Dirt. Stewart, Pat, illus. 48p. (gr. 3). 1987. pap. 4.95 (ISBN 0-317-56794-2, Little Simon). S&S Trade.

—Science Fun with Mud & Dirt. Stewart, Pat, illus. LC 86-8388. 48p. (gr. 2-4). 1986. PLB 11.38 (ISBN 0-671-55569-3); PLB 8.54s.p.; pap. 4.95 (ISBN 0-671-62904-2); pap. 3.71s.p. Messner.

—Science Fun with Peanuts & Popcorn. Stewart, Pat, illus. 48p. (gr. 2-4). 1985. PLB 11.38 (ISBN 0-671-55572-3); PLB 8.54s.p.; pap. 4.95 (ISBN 0-671-62452-0); pap. 3.71s.p. Messner.

—Science Fun with Toy Boats & Planes. Stewart, Pat, illus. 48p. (gr. 3). 1987. pap. 4.95 (ISBN 0-317-56816-7, Little Simon). S&S Trade.

—Science Fun with Toy Cars & Trucks. Stewart, Pat, illus. LC 87-20326. 48p. (gr. 2-4). 1988. PLB 11.38 (ISBN 0-671-63784-3); PLB 8.54s.p.; pap. 4.95 (ISBN 0-671-65854-9); pap. 3.71s.p. Messner.

Zubrowski, Bernie. Balloons: Building & Experimenting with Inflatable Toys. Doty, Roy, illus. LC 89-37265. 80p. (gr. 3 up). 1990. PLB 12.88 (ISBN 0-688-08325-0); pap. 6.95 (ISBN 0-688-08324-2, Pub. by Beech Tree Bks). Morrow Jr Bks.

SCIENCE–FICTION

see Science Fiction

Asimov, Isaac, et al. Time Warps. Nass, Rikard & Nass, Rhonda, illus. LC 83-22888. 48p. (gr. 4-12). 1984. PLB 15.99 (ISBN 0-8172-1742-8). Raintree Pubs.

SCIENCE–HISTORY

Beshore, George. Science in Ancient China. LC 87-23748. (Illus.). 96p. (gr. 5-8). 1988. PLB 10.40 (ISBN 0-531-10485-0). Watts.

—Science in Early Islamic Culture. Rasof, Henry, ed. (Illus.). 72p. (gr. 5-8). 1988. PLB 10.40 (ISBN 0-531-10596-2). Watts.

Gay, Kathlyn. Science in Ancient Greece. Rasof, Henry, ed. (Illus.). 96p. (gr. 5-8). 1988. PLB 10.40 (ISBN 0-531-10487-7). Watts.

Harris, Jacqueline L. Science in Ancient Rome. Rasof, Henry, ed. (Illus.). 72p. (gr. 5-8). 1988. PLB 10.40 (ISBN 0-531-10595-4). Watts.

Moss, Carol. Science in Ancient Mesopotamia. Rasof, Henry, ed. (Illus.). 72p. (gr. 5-8). 1988. PLB 10.40 (ISBN 0-531-10594-6). Watts.

Ross, Frank. Oracles Bones, Stars & the Wheelbarrows: Ancient Chinese Science & Technology. 1990. pap. 4.95 (ISBN 0-395-54967-1). HM.

Ross, Frank, Jr. Oracle Bones, Stars, & Wheelbarrows: Ancient Chinese Science & Technology. Goodman, Michael, illus. (gr. 7 up). 1982. 8.95 (ISBN 0-395-32083-6). HM.

Tannenbaum, Beulah & Tannenbaum, Harold E. Science of the Early American Indians. Rasof, Henry, ed. (Illus.). 96p. (gr. 5-8). 1988. PLB 10.40 (ISBN 0-531-10488-5). Watts.

SCIENCE–METHODOLOGY

see also Logic

Kramer, Stephen P. How to Think Like a Scientist: Answering Questions by the Scientific Method. Bond, Felicia, illus. LC 85-43604. 48p. (gr. 3-7). 1987. 11.95 (ISBN 0-690-04563-8, Crowell Jr Bks); PLB 11.89 (ISBN 0-690-04565-4, Crowell Jr Bks). HarpC Child Bks.

Ruchlis, Hy. How Do You Know It's True? Discovering the Difference Between Science & Superstition. (Illus.). 100p. (Orig.). 1991. pap. 12.95 (ISBN 0-87975-657-8). Prometheus Bks.

SCIENCE–STUDY AND TEACHING

see also Nature Study

Geoffrion, Sondra. Power Study to up Your Grades in Science. LC 88-61275. 60p. (gr. 11 up). 1989. pap. text ed. 3.95 (ISBN 0-88247-785-4). R & E Pubs.

Ham, Karri & Uhlig, Janie. Science Stimulators. Sussman, Ellen, intro. by. Burris, Priscilla, illus. 64p. (Orig.). 1987. pap. text ed. 6.95 (ISBN 0-933606-55-9, MS-655). Monkey Sisters.

Katz, Phyllis. Exploring Science Through Art. (ps-3). 1990. PLB 11.90 (ISBN 0-531-10890-2). Watts.

Kumbaraci, Turkan & Gardenier, George H. Branching Trees: Statistical Methods: Games & Songs. Gardenier, Turhan K., illus. LC 89-90944. 27p. (gr. 1-8). 1989. 30.00x (ISBN 0-685-29039-5, 0003). Teka Trends. BRANCHING TREES provides a unique approach to teaching math without fear by combining poetry, music, & 3-D games. It simplifies complicated concepts used by scientists & industrial engineers & presents them using media familiar to children. It's sub-components are: a) FUN WITH NUMBERS presents an overview of terms such as "matrix", "run", & "factor". b) BRANCHES makes children use the "factorial" design & introduces them to Latin Square. c) COMPUTER MODELS designs a "metamodel" equation & plots it in 3-D form. d) TIME traces changes over time & relates it to quality control concepts with examples in environmental monitoring. e) TWO-by-TWO provides templates for "stem & leaf" charts, an innovation in statistical presentation, & presents methods to compare two sets of data. Provides a bridge between mathematics & science by illustrating how to design experiments with minimal cost. Methods for reducing sample size are illustrated & several such statistical plans, usually taught at college level (or post graduate level) are incorporated. Orientation is through use of poetry, music, & dexterity-oriented 3-D games. Music theory knowledge is not essential, because notes are presented in text form. Teamwork is emphasized by presenting dexterity tasks for groups of 4. Central theme of the examples is a planting exercise which can be tried out at school or home. The series have been pilot-tested at grades 2-3. Class exercise component (which can be duplicated by teacher) is incorporated. *Publisher Provided Annotation.*

Magos, Eunice & Hornnes, Esther. First Lessons in... Reading, Writing, Math, Science. Sussman, Ellen, intro. by. Burris, Priscilla, illus. 40p. (Orig.). (ps-1). 1987. Reading. pap. 4.95 (ISBN 0-933606-47-8, MS-647); Writing. pap. 4.95 (ISBN 0-933606-48-6, MS-648); Math. pap. 4.95 (ISBN 0-933606-49-4, MS-649); Science. pap. 4.95 (ISBN 0-933606-50-8, MS-650). Monkey Sisters.

Nicholson, Shirley S. Nature's Merry - Go - Round. Sellon, Michael B., illus. LC 69-17716. (gr. 3-9). 1969. 3.75 (ISBN 0-8356-0003-3, Quest). Theos Pub Hse.

Tchudi, Stephen. Probing the Unknown: From Myth to Science. LC 89-35938. (Illus.). 160p. 1990. 14.95 (ISBN 0-684-19086-9, Scribners Young Read). Macmillan Child Grp.

SCIENCE–VOCATIONAL GUIDANCE

Attonito, Joan K. A Science Lab. 72p. (gr. 4-6). 1982. 6.95 (ISBN 0-88047-009-7, 8212). DOK Pubs.

Shapiro, Stanley J. Exploring Careers in Science. rev. ed. Rosen, Ruth, ed. (gr. 7-12). 1989. PLB 12.95 (ISBN 0-8239-0969-7). Rosen Group.

SCIENCE–YEARBOOKS

Rand McNally Fact Books Staff. Rand McNally Fact Books. Incl. Aircraft. Maynard, Chris & Paton, John. write for info. (ISBN 0-528-87851-4); Space Flight. Cowley, Stewart. 96p. (gr. 4-7). pap. 3.50 (ISBN 0-528-87853-0); Dinosaur World. Lambert, David (ISBN 0-528-87854-9). (Illus.). 96p. (gr. 3-7). 1982. write for info. Checkerboard Pr.

World Book, Inc. Staff, ed. Science Year, 1990: The World Book Annual Science Supplement. LC 65-21776. (Illus.). 400p. (gr. 7-12). 1989. lib. bdg. write for info. (ISBN 0-7166-0590-2). World Bk.

SCIENCE AND RELIGION

see Religion and Science

SCIENCE AND SPACE

see Space Sciences

SCIENCE FICTION

Abels, Harriette S. A Forgotten World. Furan, Rodney & Furan, Barbara, illus. LC 79-4633. 48p. (gr. 3-5). 1979. PLB 9.95 (ISBN 0-89686-032-9, Crestwood Hse). Macmillan Child Grp.

—The Green Invasion. Furan, Rodney & Furan, Barbara, illus. LC 79-4639. 48p. (gr. 3-5). 1979. PLB 9.95 (ISBN 0-89686-030-2, Crestwood Hse). Macmillan Child Grp.

—Medical Emergency. Furan, Rodney & Furan, Barbara, illus. LC 79-9823. 48p. (gr. 3-5). 1979. PLB 9.95 (ISBN 0-89686-029-9, Crestwood Hse). Macmillan Child Grp.

—Meteor from the Moon. Furan, Rodney & Furan, Barbara, illus. LC 79-4650. 48p. (gr. 3-5). 1979. PLB 9.95 (ISBN 0-89686-025-6, Crestwood Hse). Macmillan Child Grp.

—Mystery on Mars. Furan, Rodney & Furan, Barbara, illus. LC 79-9923. 48p. (gr. 3-5). 1979. PLB 9.95 (ISBN 0-89686-024-8, Crestwood Hse). Macmillan Child Grp.

—Planet of Ice. Furan, Rodney & Furan, Barbara, illus. LC 79-9920. 48p. (gr. 3-5). 1979. PLB 9.95 (ISBN 0-89686-026-4, Crestwood Hse). Macmillan Child Grp.

—The Silent Invaders. Furan, Rodney & Furan, Barbara, illus. LC 79-4644. 48p. (gr. 3-5). 1979. PLB 9.95 (ISBN 0-89686-031-0, Crestwood Hse). Macmillan Child Grp.

—Strangers on NMA-6. Furan, Rodney & Furan, Barbara, illus. LC 79-4627. 48p. (gr. 3-5). 1979. PLB 7.95 (ISBN 0-89686-027-2, Crestwood Hse). Macmillan Child Grp.

—Unwanted Visitors. Furan, Rodney & Furan, Barbara, illus. LC 79-9922. 48p. (gr. 3-5). 1979. PLB 9.95 (ISBN 0-89686-028-0, Crestwood Hse). Macmillan Child Grp.

Alf: Mission to Mars. (Illus.). (gr. k-9). 1988. pap. 1.95 (ISBN 0-318-36458-1). Scholastic Inc.

Allington, Richard L. & Krull, Kathleen. Science. Teason, James, illus. LC 82-101711. 32p. (gr. k-3). 1985. PLB 15.33 (ISBN 0-8172-1387-2); pap. 9.27 (ISBN 0-8172-2486-6). Raintree Pubs.

Ames, Mildred. Anna to the Infinite Power. 208p. (gr. 7 up). 1985. pap. 2.50 (ISBN 0-590-41002-4, Point). Scholastic Inc.

Amthor, Terry K. Rivendell, the House of Elrond. McBride, Angus, illus. 36p. (Orig.). (gr. 10-12). 1987. pap. 7.00 (ISBN 0-915795-87-6, 8080). Iron Crown Ent Inc.

Anderson, Margaret J. In the Circle of Time. LC 78-10156. (gr. 5-9). 1979. lib. bdg. 6.99 (ISBN 0-394-94029-6). Knopf.

—The Mists of Time. LC 83-19555. 192p. (gr. 4 up). 1984. 10.95 (ISBN 0-394-86573-1). Knopf.

Angell, Judie. What's Best for You? 192p. (gr. 6-9). 1983. pap. 2.25 (ISBN 0-440-98959-0, LFL). Dell.

Anthony, Piers. Balook. Woodroffe, Patrick, illus. 200p. 1990. 24.95 (ISBN 0-88733-069-X). Underwood-Miller.

Armintrout, W. G. Death Game 2090. Barrett, Kevin, ed. Aulisio, Janet, et al, illus. 48p. (Orig.). (gr. 12). 1990. pap. 9.00 (ISBN 1-55806-132-0, 5106). Iron Crown Ent Inc.

Asch, Frank. Journey to Terezor. LC 88-45866. 176p. (gr. 3-7). 1989. 13.95 (ISBN 0-8234-0751-9). Holiday.

Asimov, Isaac. All the Troubles of World. 40p. (gr. 5). 1989. 10.95 (ISBN 0-88682-233-5). Creative Ed.

—Fantastic Voyage. 192p. (gr. 7 up). 1984. pap. 3.50 (ISBN 0-553-27151-2, Spectra). Bantam.

—Fantastic Voyage. 226p. (gr. 8 up). 1966. 16.95 (ISBN 0-395-07352-9). HM.

—Franchise. 40p. (gr. 5). 1989. 15.65 (ISBN 0-88682-232-7); PLB 10.95s.p. (ISBN 0-318-37908-2). Creative Ed.

—It's Such a Beautiful Day. Redpath, Ann, ed. Delessert, Etienne, illus. 64p. (gr. 4 up). 1985. 15.65s.p. (ISBN 0-88682-008-1); PLB 10.95s.p. (ISBN 0-685-10398-6). Creative Ed.

—Sally. 40p. (gr. 5). 1989. PLB 10.95s.p. (ISBN 0-88682-230-0); PLB 15.65 (ISBN 0-318-37912-0). Creative Ed.

Asimov, Isaac, et al, eds. Thinking Machines. Bond, Bruce, illus. LC 81-8662. 48p. (gr. 5-7). 1981. PLB 15.99 (ISBN 0-8172-1727-4). Raintree Pubs.

—Travels Through Time. Leonard, Thomas, illus. LC 81-8521. 48p. (gr. 5-7). 1981. PLB 15.99 (ISBN 0-8172-1726-6). Raintree Pubs.

—Wild Inventions. Ersland, William, illus. LC 81-8511. 48p. (gr. 5-7). 1981. PLB 15.99 (ISBN 0-8172-1728-2). Raintree Pubs.

—Young Mutants. LC 83-48444. 224p. (gr. 6-9). 1984. HarpC Child Bks.

—One Hundred Great Science Fiction Short Short Stories. 296p. (gr. 9 up). 1983. pap. 3.95 (ISBN 0-380-50733-1). Avon.

—Young Star Travelers. LC 85-45276. 240p. (gr. 7 up). 1986. PLB 12.89 (ISBN 0-06-020179-7). HarpC Child Bks.

Asimov, Janet. The Package in Hyperspace. Gampert, John, illus. (gr. 4-7). 1988. 13.95 (ISBN 0-8027-6822-9); PLB 14.85 (ISBN 0-8027-6823-7). Walker & Co.

Asimov, Janet & Asimov, Isaac. Norby Down to Earth. (Illus.). (gr. 4-9). 1989. 12.95 (ISBN 0-8027-6866-0); PLB 13.85 (ISBN 0-8027-6867-9). Walker & Co.

—Norby Finds a Villain. (gr. 4-9). 1987. 12.95 (ISBN 0-8027-6710-9); PLB 13.85 (ISBN 0-8027-6711-7). Walker & Co.

Baird, Thomas. Smart Rats. LC 90-4140. 224p. (gr. 7 up). 1990. 14.95 (ISBN 0-06-020364-1); PLB 14.89 (ISBN 0-06-020365-X). HarpC Child Bks.

—Smart Rats. LC 90-4140. 224p. (gr. 7 up). 1990. 14.95 (ISBN 0-06-020364-1); PLB 14.89 (ISBN 0-06-020365-X). HarpC Child Bks.

The Bank Street Book of Science Fiction. (Orig.). (gr. 4 up). 1989. pap. 3.95 (ISBN 0-671-63145-4, Minstrel Bks). PB.

Barrett, Kevin. Black Guard. Charlton, S. Coleman, ed. Jones, J. Wallace, et al, illus. 40p. (Orig.). (gr. 12). 1990. pap. 8.00 (ISBN 1-55806-115-0, 7012). Iron Crown Ent Inc.

Barron, Thomas A. Heartlight. 272p. (gr. 5-9). 1990. 15.95 (ISBN 0-399-22180-8, Philomel Bks). Putnam Pub Group.

Bellairs, John. The Eyes of the Killer Robot. LC 86-2148. 176p. (gr. 5 up). 1986. 11.95 (ISBN 0-8037-0324-4); PLB 11.89 (ISBN 0-8037-0325-2). Dial Bks Young.

Benet, Stephen Vincent. By the Waters of Babylon. 32p. (gr. 6). 1990. 10.45s.p. (ISBN 0-88682-294-7); 15.65 (ISBN 0-685-28209-0). Creative Ed.

Bennie, Scott. Day of the Destroyer. Bell, Rob, ed. Phillips, Joe & Dunn, Ben, illus. 32p. (Orig.). (gr. 12). 1990. pap. 7.00 (ISBN 1-55806-101-0, 408). Iron Crown Ent Inc.

Birkner, Malthias & Birkner, Karen. Denizens of the Dark Wood. Ney, Jessica, ed. McBride, Angus & Danforth, Liz, illus. 32p. (Orig.). (gr. 12). 1989. pap. 6.00 (ISBN 1-55806-081-2, 8111). Iron Crown Ent Inc.

Blackwood, Gary L. The Dying Sun. LC 88-27517. 208p. (gr. 6-9). 1989. 13.95 (ISBN 0-689-31482-5, Atheneum Child Bk). Macmillan Child Grp.

Bohl, Al. Zaanan: Fatal Limit. Bohl, Al, illus. 224p. (gr. 4-8). 1989. pap. text ed. 2.50 (ISBN 1-55748-101-6). Barbour & Co.

Bouton, Steve. Cyber Rogues. Barrett, Kevin, ed. Aulisio, Janet, illus. 32p. (Orig.). (gr. 12). 1990. pap. 10.00 (ISBN 1-55806-125-8, 5103). Iron Crown Ent Inc.

Bova, Ben. Millennium. (gr. 9 up). 1976. 8.95 (ISBN 0-394-49421-0). Random.

Bradbury, Ray. Dandelion Wine. (gr. 6 up). 1985. pap. 3.95 (ISBN 0-553-27753-7). Bantam.

—The Foghorn. Kelley, Gary, illus. 32p. 1987. PLB 10.95s.p. (ISBN 0-88682-107-X); 15.65 (ISBN 0-685-23213-1). Creative Ed.

—Illustrated Man. (gr. 6-12). 1969. pap. 3.50 (ISBN 0-553-25483-9). Bantam.

—Something Wicked This Way Comes. (gr. 6-12). 1983. pap. 3.50 (ISBN 0-553-25774-9). Bantam.

Bridges, Laurie. Magic Show. (ps-7). 1987. pap. 2.25 (ISBN 0-553-25096-5). Bantam.

Brinkley, Chad & Barrett, Kevin. The Body Bank. Aulisio, Janet, illus. 32p. (Orig.). (gr. 12). 1990. pap. 10.00 (ISBN 1-55806-128-2, 5104). Iron Crown Ent Inc.

Brown, Charles. Demons Rule. Bell, Rob, ed. Boonthanakit, Ted & Chacon, Joe, illus. 32p. (Orig.). (gr. 12). 1990. pap. 7.00 (ISBN 1-55806-110-X, 412). Iron Crown Ent Inc.

Bullock, Harold B. The Battle for the Worlds. Anderson, Jean, ed. Menefee, Paige & Smith, Patti, illus. Date not set. 14.95 (ISBN 0-9626219-4-3). Summit TX.

Cameron, Eleanor. Mr. Bass's Planetoid. Darling, Louis, illus. (gr. 3-7). 1958. 14.95 (ISBN 0-316-12525-3, Joy St Bks). Little.

Carlson, Dale. The Plant People. 96p. (gr. 5 up). 1979. pap. 1.25 (ISBN 0-440-96959-X, LFL). Dell.

Cartwright, Pauline. Escape from Zarcay. Campbell, Caroline, illus. LC 90-10075. 32p. (gr. 2-5). 1990. PLB 17.28 (ISBN 0-8114-2694-7). Steck-V.

Chew, Ruth. Earthstar Magic. Chew, Ruth, illus. LC 79-17927. (gr. 2-6). 1979. 8.95 (ISBN 0-8038-1955-2). Hastings.

Children of the Storm. 192p. (Orig.). (gr. 7-9). 1989. pap. 2.95 (ISBN 0-8041-0460-3). Ivy Books.

Christin, Pierre & Mezieres, Jean-Claude. Ambassador of the Shadows. (Illus.). 48p. pap. 4.95 (ISBN 2-205-06949-7). Dargaud Pub.

—Heroes of the Equinox. (Illus.). 48p. pap. 4.95 (ISBN 2-205-06575-0). Dargaud Pub.

—Welcome on Alfloflo. (Illus.). 48p. pap. 4.95 (ISBN 2-205-06951-9). Dargaud Pub.

—World Without Stars. (Illus.). 48p. pap. 4.95 (ISBN 2-205-06573-4). Dargaud Pub.

Christopher, John. The City of Gold & Lead. 2nd ed. LC 88-16118. (Illus.). 224p. (gr. 7 up). 1988. pap. 3.95 (ISBN 0-02-042701-8, Collier Young Ad). Macmillan Child Grp.

—Dragon Dance. LC 85-31149. 160p. (gr. 5-9). 1986. 12.95 (ISBN 0-525-44227-8, DCB). Dutton Child Bks.

—Empty World. (gr. 7-9). 1978. 13.95 (ISBN 0-525-29250-0, DCB). Dutton Child Bks.

—The Lotus Caves. LC 74-78074. 160p. (gr. 5-9). 1971. pap. 4.95 (ISBN 0-02-042690-9, Collier Young Ad). Macmillan Child Grp.

—Pool of Fire. LC 68-23062. 192p. (gr. 5-9). 1970. 12.95 (ISBN 0-02-718350-5, Mcmillan Child Bk); pap. 3.95 (ISBN 0-02-042720-4, Collier Young Ad). Macmillan Child Grp.

—The Pool of Fire. 2nd ed. LC 88-16117. 224p. (gr. 7 up). 1988. pap. 3.95 (ISBN 0-02-042721-2, Collier Young Ad). Macmillan Child Grp.

—The Prince in Waiting. (gr. 5-9). 1984. 15.25 (ISBN 0-8446-6157-0). Peter Smith.

—The Prince in Waiting. (Illus.). 224p. (gr. 7 up). 1989. pap. 3.95 (ISBN 0-02-042573-2, Collier Young Ad). Macmillan Child Grp.

—The Sword of the Spirits. 224p. (gr. 7 up). 1989. pap. 3.95 (ISBN 0-02-042574-0, Collier Young Ad). Macmillan Child Grp.

—The Tripods Trilogy. 2nd ed. 224p. (gr. 7 up). 1988. Boxed Set. pap. 11.95 (ISBN 0-02-042571-6, Collier Young Ad). Macmillan Child Grp.

—When the Tripods Came. 160p. (gr. 4-9). 1988. 12.95 (ISBN 0-525-44397-5, DCB). Dutton Child Bks.

—When the Tripods Came. LC 90-1436. 160p. (gr. 7 up). 1990. pap. 3.95 (ISBN 0-02-042575-9, Collier Young Ad). Macmillan Child Grp.

—The White Mountains. 2nd ed. LC 88-16119. (Illus.). 224p. (gr. 7 up). 1988. pap. 3.95 (ISBN 0-02-042711-5, Collier Young Ad). Macmillan Child Grp.

—Wild Jack. 2nd ed. 160p. (gr. 7 up). 1991. pap. 3.95 (ISBN 0-02-042576-7, Collier Young Ad). Macmillan Child Grp.

Cohen, Daniel. The Monsters of Star Trek. (Illus.). 128p. (gr. 4 up). 1989. pap. 2.75 (ISBN 0-671-68549-X, Archway). PB.

Cooke, Tim. Calenhad: A Beacon of Gondor. Ney, Jessica, ed. Martin, David, et al, illus. 48p. (Orig.). (gr. 12). 1990. pap. 9.00 (ISBN 1-55806-097-9, 8203). Iron Crown Ent Inc.

Cooper, Clare. Ashar of Qarius. 1990. 14.95 (ISBN 0-15-200409-2). HarbraceJ.

Corbett, Scott. The Deadly Hoax. LC 80-26552. (gr. 5 up). 1981. 9.25 (ISBN 0-525-28585-7, DCB). Dutton Child Bks.

Cover, Arthur B. The Rings of Saturn. 144p. (gr. 5 up). 1985. pap. 2.25 (ISBN 0-553-25797-8). Bantam.

Crist, Harold L. Twice a Hero. 112p. (Orig.). 1990. pap. 5.95 (ISBN 0-9621743-1-9). H L Crist.

Crowdis, John. Disaster on Adonis Three. LaDell, Leo, ed. Ridge, Jeff & Midgette, Darrell, illus. 32p. (Orig.). (gr. 12). 1989. pap. 6.00 (ISBN 1-55806-039-1, 9107). Iron Crown Ent Inc.

—Ghosts of the Southern Arduin. Ney, Jessica & Fenlon, Pete, eds. McBride, Angus & Midgette, Darrell, illus. 32p. (Orig.). (gr. 12). 1989. pap. 6.00 (ISBN 1-55806-030-8, 8109). Iron Crown Ent Inc.

—Hazards of the Harod Wood. Ney, Jessica, ed. McBride, Angus & Danforth, Liz, illus. 32p. (Orig.). (gr. 12). 1990. pap. 6.00 (ISBN 1-55806-096-0, 8112). Iron Crown Ent Inc.

—Rogues of the Borderlands. Ney, Jessica, ed. McBride, Angus & Jermy, Paul, illus. 40p. (Orig.). (gr. 12). 1990. pap. 7.00 (ISBN 1-55806-083-9, 8014). Iron Crown Ent Inc.

Crutchfield, Charles. Forest of Tears. Ney, Jessica, ed. McBride, Angus & Danforth, Liz, illus. 40p. (Orig.). (gr. 12). 1989. pap. 7.00 (ISBN 1-55806-084-7, 8015). Iron Crown Ent Inc.

—Warlords of the Desert. Ney, Jessica, ed. McBride, Angus & Robin, Jeremy, illus. 40p. (Orig.). (gr. 12). 1989. pap. 7.00 (ISBN 1-55806-058-8, 8012). Iron Crown Ent Inc.

Cunningham, Lowell. The Men in Black. Ulm, Chris, ed. Carruthers, Sandy, illus. 80p. 1990. pap. 7.95 (ISBN 0-944735-60-6). Malibu Graphics.

Curtis, Philip. Invasion from below the Earth. Ross, Tony, illus. LC 81-101. 128p. (gr. 3 up). 1981. Knopf.

Cutting, Jillian & Cutting, Brian. Fact & Fantasy Science - Emergent Level: It Takes Time to Grow; What Am I?; A Small World; What Else?; Space; Alien at the Zoo; The Hermit Crab; Underwater Journey; Are You a Ladybug?; Dinosaurs; What Lives in These Eggs? & The Dandelion, 12 bks. (Illus.). 192p. (gr. k-1). Set. pap. text ed. 33.10 (ISBN 1-55911-024-4). Wright Group.

Danziger, Paula. This Place Has No Atmosphere. (gr. k-12). 1987. pap. 3.25 (ISBN 0-440-98726-1, LFL). Dell.

—This Place Has No Atmosphere. large type ed. 190p. 1989. Repr. of 1986 ed. PLB 15.95 (ISBN 1-55736-130-4, Crnrstn Bks). ABC-CLIO.

Davis, Jim. Garfield in Space. LC 83-6061. (Illus.). 32p. (gr. k-5). 1983. pap. 1.25 (ISBN 0-394-86122-1). Random.

Defenders of the Earth: The Sun Stealers. (gr. k-9). 1988. pap. 1.95 (ISBN 0-318-36464-6). Scholastic Inc.

De Haven, Tom. Joe Gosh. Reese, Ralph, illus. (gr. 7 up). 1988. 15.95 (ISBN 0-8027-6824-5). Walker & Co.

Dereske, Jo. The Lone Sentinel. LC 88-36254. 176p. (gr. 4-8). 1989. 13.95 (ISBN 0-689-31552-X, Atheneum Child Bk). Macmillan Child Grp.

Dershem, Kurt. The Olympians. Bell, Rob, ed. Perez, George & Sutherland, Jackie, illus. 48p. (Orig.). (gr. 12). 1990. pap. 9.00 (ISBN 1-55806-114-2, 414). Iron Crown Ent Inc.

De Vos, Janifer C. The Purple Door. Davis, Deena, ed. Babbitt, Gwendolyn, illus. 140p. (Orig.). (gr. 3-6). 1990. pap. 5.95t (ISBN 0-88070-348-2). Multnomah.

DeWeese, Gene. Whatever Became of Aunt Margaret? 128p. (gr. 3-7). 1990. 13.95 (ISBN 0-399-21914-5, Putnam). Putnam Pub Group.

Dunn, Ben. Ninja High School, Vol. 2: Beware of Dog. Ulm, Chris, ed. Dunn, Ben, illus. 128p. 1990. pap. 9.95 (ISBN 0-944735-59-2). Malibu Graphics.

Eastman, Kevin & Laird, Peter. Teenage Mutant Ninja Turtles: Return of the Shredder. Mitchroney, Kevin, illus. 64p. 1990. pap. 5.95 (ISBN 0-679-80686-5); cass. incl. McKay.

Edwards, Roger. Max Science & the Glowing Firefly. Sanchez, Brenda L., ed. Beard, Derrick, illus. 26p. (gr. k-5). 1991. pap. 3.95 (ISBN 1-879350-01-7). Max Sci Pub.

Engdahl, Sylvia. Enchantress from the Stars. Shackell, Rodney, illus. 288p. (gr. 7 up). 1989. pap. 3.95 (ISBN 0-02-043031-0, Collier Young Ad). Macmillan Child Grp.

—The Far Side of Evil. Cufari, Richard, illus. 288p. (gr. 7 up). 1989. pap. 3.95 (ISBN 0-02-043041-8, Collier Young Ad). Macmillan Child Grp.

Eyes of the Tarot. (gr. 7-12). 1983. pap. 2.50 (ISBN 0-553-26685-3). Bantam.

Farrow, Peter & Lampert, Diane. Twyllyp. (Illus.). (gr. 3-7). 1963. 10.95 (ISBN 0-8392-3040-0). Astor-Honor.

Feild, William B., Jr. & Stassun, Peter G. Perils on the Sea of Rhun. Ney, Jessica, ed. Hook, Richard & Danforth, Liz, illus. 32p. (Orig.). (gr. 12). 1989. pap. 6.00 (ISBN 0-685-37962-0, 8110). Iron Crown Ent Inc.

Fenlon, Peter, ed. Lords of Middle-Earth, Vol. 2: The Mannish Races. McBride, Angus, illus. 112p. (Orig.). (gr. 10-12). 1987. pap. 12.00 (ISBN 0-915795-32-9, 8003). Iron Crown Ent Inc.

Ferrone, John M. Ghost Warriors. Ney, Jessica, ed. McBride, Angus & Danforth, Liz, illus. 48p. (Orig.). (gr. 12). 1990. pap. 10.00 (ISBN 1-55806-107-X, 8016). Iron Crown Ent Inc.

Foley, Tod. War on a Distant Moon. LaDell, Leo, ed. Velez, Waller & Waltrip, Jason, illus. 32p. (Orig.). (gr. 12). 1988. pap. 6.00 (ISBN 1-55806-020-0, 9104). Iron Crown Ent Inc.

Forrester, John. Bestiary Mountain. LC 86-45870. 160p. (gr. 7 up). 1987. pap. 2.75 (ISBN 0-06-447024-5, Trophy). HarpC Child Bks.

—The Secret of the Round Beast. LC 86-11800. 192p. (gr. 7 up). 1986. 13.95 (ISBN 0-02-735380-X, Bradbury Pr). Macmillan Child Grp.

French, Fiona. Future Story. LC 83-22317. (Illus.). 32p. (gr. 1-9). 11.95 (ISBN 0-911745-35-1). P Bedrick Bks.

Garfield, Leon. The Night of the Comet. (gr. k-6). 1988. pap. 3.25 (ISBN 0-440-40070-8, YB). Dell.

Gasperini, Jim. The Mystery of Atlantis. 144p. (Orig.). (gr. 5 up). 1985. pap. 2.25 (ISBN 0-553-25073-6). Bantam.

Gentle, Mary. Golden Witchbreed. (gr. 9-12). Date not set. pap. 3.95 (ISBN 0-451-13606-3, Sig). NAL-Dutton.

Gerrold, David. When Harlie Was One. 288p. 1988. pap. 3.95 (ISBN 0-553-26465-6, Spectra). Bantam.

—When Harlie Was Two. 240p. 1990. pap. 4.50 (ISBN 0-553-26466-4, Spectra). Bantam.

Gibson, Robert W. Captain Harlock Returns. Ulm, Chris, ed. Duke, Pat, et al, illus. 102p. 1991. pap. 9.95 (ISBN 0-944735-75-4). Malibu Graphics.

Gilden, Mel. Outer Space & All That Junk. LaVigne, Daniel, illus. LC 88-37110. 176p. (gr. 5-9). 1989. 12.95 (ISBN 0-397-32306-9, Lipp Jr Bks); PLB 12.89 (ISBN 0-397-32307-7, Lipp Jr Bks). HarpC Child Bks.

—The Planetoid of Amazement. LC 91-7261. 224p. (gr. 5-9). 1991. 14.95 (ISBN 0-06-021713-8); PLB 14.89 (ISBN 0-06-021714-6). HarpC Child Bks.

—The Return of Captain Conquer. (gr. 5-8). 1985. 12.95 (ISBN 0-685-11811-8). HM.

Goldin, Stephen & Mason, Mary. Jade Darcy & the Zen Pirates. (gr. 9-12). pap. 3.95 (ISBN 0-451-16157-2, Sig). NAL-Dutton.

Goscinny, Rene & Uderzo, Albert. Iter Gallicum. (Illus.). 48p. 7.95 (ISBN 0-685-09549-5). Dargaud Pub.

Greer, Gery & Ruddick, Bob. Max & Me & the Time Machine. LC 87-45284. 128p. (gr. 3-7). 1988. pap. 3.50 (ISBN 0-06-440222-3, Trophy). HarpC Child Bks.

Gross, Edward. The Alien Nation Companion. (Illus.). 112p. (gr. 9-12). 1991. pap. 12.95 (ISBN 0-9627508-1-6). Image NY.

Guymon, Maurine B. The Adventures of Micki Microbe. Zagone, Arlene T., illus. 88p. (gr. 2-5). 1987. 15.00 (ISBN 0-9618650-0-8). MoDel Pubs.
An imaginative & whimsical way of introducing children to various functions of the body while emphasizing good health. A lactic acid microbe, Micki, travels down Maggie's Throat Street when she takes a drink of milk. While visiting Tonsil Park & meeting the Pneumo Twins the microbes are detected by Watch Dog Cough & as he barks they are sent flying through the air landing on Jamie's ball. Now Jamie is the recipient & upon licking his fingers the microbes travel past his White Teeth Hills & find long chains of the streptococcus family in his Throat Street. In like manner Micki & other microbes travel from one child to another via apples, popsicles, pencils & spoons. Subsequent visits through the body introduces Lung House, Nose Cave, Tear Duct Waterfall, Windpipe Lane, etc. The White Corpuscle Policemen enter the story to destroy bad microbes & prevent infection in Blood River. Seventy three beautiful illustrations enhance the 88 page book. It has a sewn, hard bound laminated cover. Order from: MoDel Publishers, Box 645, Byron, CA 94514 or Baker Taylor; Select Books, Evanston, IL; Monroe Press, Sepulveda, CA.
Publisher Provided Annotation.

Hall, Barbara. Skeeball & the Secret of the Universe. LC 87-7730. 240p. (gr. 7 up). 1987. 12.95 (ISBN 0-531-05722-4); PLB 12.99 (ISBN 0-531-08322-5). Orchard Bks Watts.

Hamilton, Virginia. Planet of Junior Brown. large type, unabr. ed. 400p. (gr. 5 up). 1988. lib. bdg. 13.95 (ISBN 0-8161-4642-X). G K Hall.

Harris, Jack C. Photon-The Official Handbook. Bender, Howard, illus. (gr. k-5). 1987. pap. 4.95 (ISBN 0-448-48626-1, G&D). Putnam Pub Group.

Harris, Mark. The Doctor Who Technical Manual. Nathan-Turner, John, intro. by. LC 83-42868. (Illus.). 64p. (gr. 5 up). 1983. lib. bdg. 6.99 (ISBN 0-394-96214-1). Random.

Hayes, Bert. Nineteen Seventy-Eight: The Human Race Begins. Courington, D., as told to. (Illus.). 64p. (Orig.). Date not set. pap. 4.95 (ISBN 0-318-41429-5). M C Cook.

Heinlein, Robert. Time for the Stars. LC 90-33400. 256p. (gr. 7 up). 1990. 14.95 (ISBN 0-684-19211-X, Scribners Young Read). Macmillan Child Grp.

Heinlein, Robert A. Citizen of the Galaxy. (Illus.). (gr. 5-11). 1977. 15.00 (ISBN 0-684-15364-5, Scribner). Macmillan.

—Citizen of the Galaxy. LC 86-26172. 312p. (gr. 7 up). 1987. 14.95 (ISBN 0-684-18818-X, Scribners Young Read). Macmillan Child Grp.

Herbert, Frank. Dune Coloring Book, 12 bks. (Illus.). 48p. Set. pap. 23.40 (ISBN 0-448-81710-1, G&D). Putnam Pub Group.
Herman, Crystal D. Teenage Mutant Ninja Turtles: The First Battle. Mateu, Frank, illus. 32p. (Orig.). (ps-3). 1990. pap. 1.25 (ISBN 0-679-80668-7). McKay.
Hill, Douglas. The Caves of Klydor. LC 84-20481. 120p. (gr. 7up). 1985. 13.95 (ISBN 0-689-50320-2, M K McElderry). Macmillan Child Grp.
—The Caves of Klydor. 144p. 1986. pap. 2.75 (ISBN 0-553-25929-6, Spectra). Bantam.
Holm, Astrid. Teenage Mutant Ninja Turtles: The Final Lesson. Daste, Larry, illus. 32p. (Orig.). (ps-3). 1990. pap. 1.25 (ISBN 0-679-80669-5). McKay.
Hoover, H. M. The Delikon. 160p. (gr. 5-9). 1986. pap. 3.95 (ISBN 0-14-032167-5, Puffin). Puffin Bks.
—The Lost Star. 160p. (gr. 5-9). 1986. pap. 3.95 (ISBN 0-14-032166-7, Puffin). Puffin Bks.
—Orvis. 192p. (gr. 5 up). 1987. pap. 12.95 (ISBN 0-670-81117-3). Viking Child Bks.
—The Return to Earth. (gr. 5-9). 1988. pap. 3.95 (ISBN 0-14-032610-3, Puffin). Puffin Bks.
—The Shepherd Moon. LC 83-16784. 180p. (gr. 7 up). 1984. pap. 11.95 (ISBN 0-670-63977-X). Viking Child Bks.
Huddy, Delia. Time Piper. LC 78-24339. (gr. 7 up). 1979. 13.00 (ISBN 0-688-80212-5); PLB 12.88 (ISBN 0-688-84212-7). Morrow.
Hughes, Dean. Nutty Knows All. LC 90-40282. 160p. (gr. 3-7). 1991. pap. 3.95 (ISBN 0-689-71470-X, Aladdin). Macmillan Child Grp.
Hughes, Monica. Devil on My Back. LC 84-21657. 180p. (gr. 6-9). 1985. 13.95 (ISBN 0-689-31095-1, Atheneum Child Bk). Macmillan Child Grp.
—The Dream Catcher. LC 86-20584. 176p. (gr. 7 up). 1987. 13.95 (ISBN 0-689-31331-4, Atheneum Child Bk). Macmillan Child Grp.
Hunt, Dave. The Archon Conspiracy. LC 89-31535. 256p. (Orig.). (gr. 9 up). 1989. pap. 8.99 (ISBN 0-89081-766-9). Harvest Hse.
Hutchins, Hazel. Anastasia Morningstar. Tennent, Julie, illus. LC 89-38191. 96p. (gr. 2-5). 1990. 11.95 (ISBN 0-670-83140-9). Viking Child Bks.
Invaders of the Planet Earth. (Illus.). (gr. k-9). 1988. pap. 2.50 (ISBN 0-318-36500-6). Scholastic Inc.
Jackson, Steve & Livingstone, Ian. Rebel Planet. (Orig.). (gr. 5 up). 1986. pap. 2.50 (ISBN 0-440-97360-0, LFL). Dell.
Johnson, Annabel & Johnson, Edgar. The Danger Quotient. LC 83-48439. 224p. (gr. 7 up). 1987. pap. 2.95 (ISBN 0-06-447029-6, Trophy). HarpC Child Bks.
Johnson, Larry. Road Kill. Tabb, Doug, ed. (Illus.). 32p. (Orig.). (gr. 12). 1991. pap. 7.00 (ISBN 1-55806-117-7, 415). Iron Crown Ent Inc.
Johnston, Norma. The Dragon's Eye. LC 90-34388. 176p. (gr. 7 up). 1990. 13.95 (ISBN 0-02-747701-0, Four Winds). Macmillan Child Grp.
Journey to the Center of the Earth. (Illus.). (gr. 3-5). 3.50 (ISBN 0-7214-0596-7). Ladybird Bks.
Kane, Thomas. Tales of the Loremasters. Amthor, Terry K. & Ruemmler, John D., eds. Roberts, Tony & Jaquays, Paul, illus. 32p. (Orig.). (gr. 12). 1989. pap. 6.00 (ISBN 1-55806-073-1, 6004). Iron Crown Ent Inc.
Kane, Tom. Tales of the Loremasters, Book 2. Ruemmler, John D., ed. Martin, David & Jaquays, Paul, illus. 32p. (Orig.). (gr. 12). 1989. pap. 6.00 (ISBN 1-55806-034-0, 6008). Iron Crown Ent Inc.
Kidd, Ronald. The Glitch. LC 85-16040. (Illus.). 128p. (gr. 5-9). 1985. 11.95 (ISBN 0-525-67160-9, Lodestar Bks). Dutton Child Bks.
Klein, Robin. Halfway Across the Galaxy & Then Turn Left. 146p. (gr. 3-7). 1986. pap. 7.95 (ISBN 0-670-80636-6). Viking Child Bks.
—Halfway Across the Galaxy & Turn Left. 146p. (gr. 3-7). 1987. pap. 3.95 (ISBN 0-14-031843-7, Puffin). Puffin Bks.
Kochman, Charles. Photon-Double Trouble. Rosler, David, illus. (gr. k-5). 1987. pap. 2.25 (ISBN 0-448-48635-0, G&D). Putnam Pub Group.
Korman, Gordon. Son of Interflux. 288p. (gr. 7 up). 1988. pap. 2.50 (ISBN 0-590-41186-1, Point). Scholastic Inc.
Krensky, Stephen. Dragon Circle. 128p. (gr. 7 up). 1990. pap. 3.95 (ISBN 0-689-71365-7, Aladdin). Macmillan Child Grp.
LaDell, Leo. The Durandrium Find. Amthor, Terry K., ed. Velez, Waller & Martin, Ellisa, illus. 32p. (Orig.). (gr. 12). 1989. pap. 6.00 (ISBN 1-55806-021-9, 9105). Iron Crown Ent Inc.
—Legacy of the Ancients. Amthor, Terry K., ed. Ridge, Jeff & Waltrip, Jason, illus. 32p. (Orig.). (gr. 12). 1989. pap. 6.00 (ISBN 1-55806-035-9, 9106). Iron Crown Ent Inc.
Lapka, Fay S. Dark Is a Color. 264p. (Orig.). (gr. 9-12). 1990. pap. 6.95 (ISBN 0-87788-163-4). Shaw Pubs.
—Hoverlight. (Orig.). 1991. pap. 6.95 (ISBN 0-87788-352-1). Shaw Pubs.
Larson, Glen A. & Resnick, Michael. Battlestar Galactica No. 5: Galactica Discovers Earth. (Orig.). 1987. pap. 2.50 (ISBN 0-425-05249-4). Berkley Pub.
Lawhead, Stephen R. The Sword & the Flame. LC 83-73341. 348p. (gr. 7 up). 1984. pap. 9.95t (ISBN 0-89107-310-8, Crossway Bks). Good News.
Lawrence, Louise. Andra. LC 90-38595. 240p. (gr. 7 up). 1991. 14.95 (ISBN 0-06-023685-X); PLB 14.89 (ISBN 0-06-023705-8). HarpC Child Bks.
—Moonwind. LC 85-45507. 192p. (gr. 7 up). 1986. 12.95 (ISBN 0-06-023733-3); PLB 12.89 (ISBN 0-06-023734-1). HarpC Child Bks.
—Star Lord. LC 77-25674. (gr. 7 up). 1978. PLB 12.89 (ISBN 0-06-023777-5). HarpC Child Bks.
Lee, Robert C. Timequake. LC 82-13567. 152p. (gr. 5-9). 1982. 9.95 (ISBN 0-664-32698-6, Westminster). Westminster John Knox.
L'Engle, Madeleine. An Acceptable Time. (gr. 7 up). 1989. 13.95 (ISBN 0-374-30027-5). FS&G.
—Madeleine L'Engle's Time Quartet, 4 vols. (gr. 4 up). 1987. pap. 14.00 (ISBN 0-440-95208-5). Dell.
—Many Waters. LC 86-14911. 310p. (gr. 4 up). 1986. 15. 95 (ISBN 0-374-34796-4); limited ed. 50.00 (ISBN 0-374-34797-2). FS&G.
—A Swiftly Tilting Planet. LC 78-9648. 288p. (gr. 5 up). 1978. 15.95 (ISBN 0-374-37362-0). FS&G.
—Swiftly Tilting Planet. (gr. 4-7). 1981. pap. 3.50 (ISBN 0-440-40158-5). Dell.
—A Wind in the Door. 224p. (gr. 5-9). 1974. pap. 3.50 (ISBN 0-440-48761-7, YB). Dell.
—A Wrinkle in Time. 224p. (gr. 5-9). 1973. pap. 3.50 (ISBN 0-440-49805-8, YB). Dell.
—A Wrinkle in Time. LC 62-7203. 224p. (gr. 7 up). 1962. 15.95 (ISBN 0-374-38613-7). FS&G.
Leroe, Ellen. Robot Raiders. LC 86-45782. 192p. (gr. 6-9). 1987. 11.95 (ISBN 0-06-023835-6); PLB 11.89 (ISBN 0-06-023836-4). HarpC Child Bks.
Levy, Elizabeth, ed. Return of the Jedi Step-Up Movie Adventure. (Illus.). 72p. (gr. 1-3). 1983. lib. bdg. 8.99 (ISBN 0-394-96117-X). Random.
Lewis, C. S. The Chronicles of Narnia, 7 bks. Baynes, Pauline, illus. (gr. 4 up). 1983. Set. 79.95 (ISBN 0-02-757740-6). Macmillan Child Grp.
Loback, Tom. Halls of the Elven-King. Ruemmler, John D., ed. Martin, David, illus. 32p. (Orig.). (gr. 12). 1988. pap. 6.00 (ISBN 1-55806-015-4, 8204). Iron Crown Ent Inc.
Longyear, Barry B. The Homecoming. Clark, Alan M., illus. 224p. 1989. 15.95 (ISBN 0-8027-6863-6). Walker & Co.
The Lost World. (Illus.). (gr. 3-5). 3.50 (ISBN 0-7214-0711-0). Ladybird Bks.
Lynn, Haney. The Last Starfighter Storybook. (Illus.). 64p. 1984. pap. text ed. 6.95 (ISBN 0-399-21078-4, Putnam); pap. 83.40 sets of 12 (ISBN 0-399-21079-2). Putnam Pub Group.
McCaffrey, Anne. Dragondrums. Marcellino, Fred, illus. LC 78-11318. 256p. 1979. 15.95 (ISBN 0-689-30685-7, Atheneum Child Bk). Macmillan Child Grp.
—Dragonsong. Lydecker, Laura, illus. LC 75-30530. 224p. (gr. 5-9). 1976. 15.95 (ISBN 0-689-30507-9, Atheneum Childrens Bk). Macmillan Child Grp.
Macdonald, Caroline. The Lake at the End of the World. LC 88-25678. (Illus.). 208p. 1989. 12.95 (ISBN 0-8037-0650-2). Dial Bks Young.
McEvoy, Seth. Planet Hunters. 128p. (Orig.). (gr. 3 up). 1985. pap. 1.95 (ISBN 0-553-24532-5). Bantam.
—The Red Rocket. 120p. (Orig.). (gr. 4). 1985. pap. 2.25 (ISBN 0-553-26676-4). Bantam.
McKeage, Jeffrey. Dark Mage of Rhudaur. Ney, Jessica, ed. McBride, Angus & Danforth, Liz, illus. 40p. (Orig.). (gr. 12). 1989. pap. 7.00 (ISBN 1-55806-072-3, 8013). Iron Crown Ent Inc.
McKillip, Patricia A. The Changeling Sea. LC 88-3435. 160p. (gr. 5 up). 1988. 13.95 (ISBN 0-689-31436-1, Atheneum Child Bk). Macmillan Child Grp.
Maguire, Gregory. I Feel Like the Morning Star. LC 88-21544. 288p. (gr. 7 up). 1989. 14.95i (ISBN 0-06-024021-0); PLB 14.89 (ISBN 0-06-024022-9). HarpC Child Bks.
Manes, Stephen. That Game from Outer Space: The First Strange Thing That Happened to Oscar Noodleman. Auth, Tony, illus. 64p. (gr. 3-5). 1983. 11.95 (ISBN 0-525-44056-9, DCB). Dutton Child Bks.
Martin, George R. Aces High, No. 2. 288p. (Orig.). 1987. pap. 4.50 (ISBN 0-553-26464-8, Spectra). Bantam.
Marzollo, Jean & Marzollo, Claudio. Ruthie's Rude Friends. Meddaugh, Susan, illus. LC 84-1707. (ps-3). 1984. PLB 8.89 (ISBN 0-8037-0116-0). Dial Bks Young.
Mason, Anne. The Stolen Law. LC 85-45274. 224p. (gr. 7 up). 1986. PLB 11.89 (ISBN 0-06-024119-5). HarpC Child Bks.
Matsumoto, Leiji. Captain Harlock Television Scripts, Vol. 1. Villa, Mickie & Mason, Tom, eds. Dunn, Ben, illus. Gibson, Robert, intro. by. (Illus.). 152p. 1990. pap. 19.95 (ISBN 0-944735-63-0). Malibu Graphics.
Mayhar, Ardath. A Place of Silver Silence. Ortega, Pat, illus. (gr. 7 up). 1988. 15.95 (ISBN 0-8027-6825-3). Walker & Co.
Metos, Thomas H. Artificial Humans: Transplants & Bionics. Anderson, M. & Arico, D., eds. LC 85-29489. (Illus.). 96p. (gr. 5 up). 1985. lib. bdg. 10.98 (ISBN 0-671-44367-4). Messner.
Mixon, Laura J. Astropilots. (gr. 4-9). 1988. pap. 2.50 (ISBN 0-318-36513-8). Scholastic Inc.
Moore, Silas. Scarlet Arena 30303. Oddo, Genevieve, ed. Luering, Jacqueline M., illus. LC 74-190272. 196p. (gr. 8-12). 1972. PLB 3.95 (ISBN 0-87783-063-0). Oddo.
Morin, John B. Sea-Lords of Gondor. McBride, Angus, illus. Fenlon, Peter, ed. 64p. (Orig.). (gr. 10-12). 1987. pap. 12.00 (ISBN 0-915795-88-4, 3400). Iron Crown Ent Inc.
Mullin, Penn. A Message from Outer Space. Kratoville, Betty L., ed. Cincotta, Michael, illus. 64p. (gr. 3-9). 1989. lib. bdg. 4.95 (ISBN 0-87879-616-9, High Noon Books). Acad Therapy.
Murdock, M. S., et al. Arrival. LC 88-50404. 320p. (Orig.). 1988. pap. 3.95 (ISBN 0-88038-582-0). TSR Inc.
The Mysterious Island. (gr. 4 up). 1988. pap. 4.87 (ISBN 0-582-54143-3, 74253). Longman.
Nathan-Turner, John. Doctor Who: The Companions. Hughes, Stuart, illus. LC 86-6458. 48p. (gr. 5 up). 1986. (Random Juv); (Random Juv). Random.
Ney, Jessica, ed. The Necromancer's Lieutenant. Danforth, Liz & Martin, David, illus. 32p. (Orig.). (gr. 12). 1990. pap. 7.00 (ISBN 1-55806-113-4, 8113). Iron Crown Ent Inc.
Obergfoll, Michael. Super Santa of All Space & Beyond Assisted by His Galaxy Elves. Jew, Flora, illus. 38p. (gr. 2-12). 1988. 2.95 (ISBN 0-929052-00-5). Super Santa Prodns.
—Super Santa of All Space & Beyond Assisted by His Galaxy Elves: Coloring Activity Book. Obergfoll, Michael, illus. LC 72-847. 34p. (gr. 2-12). 1988. 10.95 (ISBN 0-929052-01-3). Super Santa Prodns.
O'Brien, Robert C. Z for Zachariah. LC 74-76736. 256p. (gr. 7 up). 1975. 14.95 (ISBN 0-689-30442-0, Atheneum Child Bk). Macmillan Child Grp.
Oxley, Dorothy. Quest. 144p. (Orig.). (gr. 7-10). 1990. pap. 3.95 (ISBN 0-7459-1846-8). Lion USA.
Packard, Edward. America: "Why Is There an Eye on a Pyramid on the One Dollar" LC 88-16912. 112p. 1989. pap. text ed. 3.95 (ISBN 0-07-047993-3). McGraw.
—Return to the Cave of Time. 128p. (Orig.). (gr. 4). 1985. pap. 2.25 (ISBN 0-553-25495-2). Bantam.
—The Third Planet from Altair. 128p. (Orig.). (gr. 5 up). 1989. pap. 2.50 (ISBN 0-553-23185-5). Bantam.
Pellowski, Michael J. Photon-Attack of the Tunnel-Dwellers. Rosler, David, illus. (gr. k-5). 1987. pap. 2.25 (ISBN 0-448-48636-9, G&D). Putnam Pub Group.
Pellowski, Michael J., adapted by. Silverhawks: The Menace of Mon Star. Fernandez, Fernando, illus. (gr. k-5). 1987. pap. 1.95 (ISBN 0-448-48634-2, G&D). Putnam Pub Group.
—Silverhawks: The Planet-Eater. Fernandez, Fernando, illus. (gr. k-5). 1987. pap. 1.95 (ISBN 0-448-48631-8, G&D). Putnam Pub Group.
—Silverhawks: The Sun Bandits. Fernandez, Fernando, illus. (gr. k-5). 1987. pap. 1.95 (ISBN 0-448-48632-6, G&D). Putnam Pub Group.
—Silverhawks: The Terror of the Time-Stopper. Fernandez, Fernando, illus. (gr. k-5). 1987. pap. 1.95 (ISBN 0-448-48633-4, G&D). Putnam Pub Group.
Petersen, P. J. Would You Settle for Improbable? 160p. (gr. 5-9). 1983. pap. 3.25 (ISBN 0-440-99733-X, LFL). Dell.
Pinkwater, Daniel. I Was a Second Grade Werewolf. Pinkwater, Daniel, illus. (gr. 1-3). 1986. incl. cassette 19.95 (ISBN 0-87499-010-6); pap. 12.95 incl. cassette (ISBN 0-87499-008-4); incl. cassette, 4 paperbacks guide 27.95 (ISBN 0-87499-009-2). Live Oak Media.
—I Was a Second Grade Werewolf. Pinkwater, Daniel, illus. (gr. k-2). 1985. pap. 3.95 (ISBN 0-525-44194-8, DCB). Dutton Child Bks.
—The Snarkout Boys & the Avocado of Death. LC 81-11737. 160p. (gr. 5 up). 1982. 12.95 (ISBN 0-688-00871-2). Lothrop.
Platt, Kin. Dracula, Go Home. Mayo, Frank, illus. 96p. (gr. 7 up). 1981. pap. 1.25 (ISBN 0-440-92022-1, LE). Dell.
Poppel, George. Planet of Trash. Moyer, Barry S., illus. 32p. (ps-3). 1987. 9.95 (ISBN 0-915765-42-X, Pub. by Panda Monium Bks.). Natl Pr Inc.
Pryor, Bonnie. Mr. Munday & the Space Creatures. Lorenz, Lee, illus. (ps-3). 1989. pap. 13.95 (ISBN 0-671-67114-6). S&S Trade.
Rattiner, Dan & Shepard, Richard. Attack of the Space Creatures. LC 79-67492. (Illus., Orig.). (gr. 1 up). 1980. pap. 4.95 (ISBN 0-932966-07-1). Permanent Pr.
Razzi, Jim. Tales from the Weird Zone, Bk. 1. Callahan, Kevin, illus. (Orig.). (gr. 4-7). 1986. pap. 2.50 (ISBN 0-671-63240-X, Minstrel Bks). PB.
Richelson, Geraldine, adapted by. The Star Wars Storybook. LC 77-90196. (gr. 4 up). 1978. (Random Juv). Random.
Roberts, Willo D. The Girl with the Silver Eyes. LC 80-12391. 192p. (gr. 4-7). 1980. 13.95 (ISBN 0-689-30786-1, Atheneum Child Bk). Macmillan Child Grp.
—The Girl with the Silver Eyes. 208p. (gr. 4-6). 1982. pap. 2.50 (ISBN 0-590-40950-6, Apple Paperbacks). Scholastic Inc.
Robot Changer: Master of Doom. (gr. k-9). 1988. pap. 1.95 (ISBN 0-318-36507-3). Scholastic Inc.
Robot Changer: Quest for Power. (gr. k-9). 1988. pap. 1.95 (ISBN 0-318-36506-5). Scholastic Inc.
Roth, Susan L. Fire Came to the Earth People. (Illus.). 32p. (gr. 1 up). 1988. 9.95 (ISBN 0-312-01723-5). St Martin.
Rubenstein, Gillian. Space Demons. (gr. 6-9). 1989. pap. 2.95 (ISBN 0-671-67912-0, Archway). PB.
Rubinstein, Gillian. Beyond the Labyrinth. LC 90-30627. 256p. (gr. 7 up). 1990. 14.95 (ISBN 0-531-05899-9); PLB 14.99 (ISBN 0-531-08499-X). Orchard Bks Watts.
—Skymaze. LC 90-43796. 192p. (gr. 6-9). 1991. 14.95 (ISBN 0-531-05929-4); PLB 14.99 (ISBN 0-531-08529-5). Orchard Bks Watts.

SCIENCE FICTION–HISTORY AND CRITICISM

SCIENTIFIC APPARATUS AND INSTRUMENTS

see also names of groups of instruments, e.g. Aeronautical Instruments; Astronomical Instruments; Chemical Apparatus; Electric Apparatus and Appliances; Meteorological Instruments

SCIENTIFIC EDUCATION

see Science–Study and Teaching

SCIENTIFIC EXPEDITIONS

see also names of regions explored, e.g. Antarctic Regions; Arctic Regions; and names of expeditions

SCIENTIFIC EXPERIMENTS

see Science–Experiments;
also particular branches of science with the subdivision Experiments, e.g. Chemistry–Experiments

SCIENTIFIC METHOD

see special subjects with the subdivision Methodology, e.g. Science–Methodology

SCIENTIFIC RECREATIONS

see also Mathematical Recreations

SCIENTISTS

see also Science–Vocational Guidance;
also classes of scientists, e.g. Astronomers; Chemists; Geologists; Mathematicians; Naturalists; Physicists, etc.; and names of scientists

Heckart, Barbara H. Edmond Halley: The Man & His Comet. LC 83-24000. (Illus.). 112p. (gr. 4 up). 1984. lib. bdg. 17.27 (ISBN 0-516-03202-X). Childrens.

McGovern, Ann. Shark Lady. Chew, Ruth, illus. 96p. (gr. k-3). 1987. pap. 2.25 (ISBN 0-590-41178-0). Scholastic Inc.

—Shark Lady: True Adventures of Eugenie Clark. Chew, Ruth, illus. LC 78-22126. 96p. (gr. 3-7). 1984. 12.95 (ISBN 0-02-767060-0, Four Winds). Macmillan Child Grp.

Metos, Thomas H. The New Eyes of the Scientist. Kline, M., ed. (Illus.). 128p. (gr. 6-12). 1988. 12.90 (ISBN 0-531-10609-8). Watts.

Polacco, Patricia. Meteor! Polacco, Patricia, illus. 32p. (gr. k-3). 1987. 13.95 (ISBN 0-399-21699-5, Putnam). Putnam Pub Group.

Rich, Beverly. Louis Pasteur: The Scientist Who Found the Cause of Infectious Disease & Invented Pasteurization. LC 88-24867. (Illus.). 64p. (gr. 5-6). 1989. PLB 12.95 (ISBN 1-55532-839-3). Gareth Stevens Inc.

Rosen, Sidney. Galileo & the Magic Numbers. Stein, Harve, illus. (gr. 7 up). 1958. 13.95 (ISBN 0-316-75704-7). Little.

Veglahn, Nancy. Women Scientists. (Illus.). 128p. (gr. 6-10). 1992. lib. bdg. 16.95x (ISBN 0-8160-2482-0). Facts on File.

Verheyden-Hilliard, Mary E. Mathematician & Computer Scientist, Caryn Navy. Rom, Holly M., illus. LC 87-82595. 32p. (Orig.). (gr. 1-4). 1988. pap. 4.50 (ISBN 0-932469-12-4). Equity Inst.

—Scientist & Activist, Phyllis Stearner. Rom, Holly M., illus. LC 87-82597. 32p. (Orig.). (gr. 1-4). 1988. pap. 4.50 (ISBN 0-932469-15-9). Equity Inst.

—Scientist & Physician, Judith Pachciarz. Stanier, Linda, illus. LC 87-82599. 32p. (Orig.). (gr. 1-4). 1988. pap. 4.50 (ISBN 0-932469-13-2). Equity Inst.

—Scientist & Strategist, June Rooks. Rom, Holly M., illus. LC 87-82596. 32p. (Orig.). (gr. 1-4). 1988. pap. 4.50 (ISBN 0-932469-14-0). Equity Inst.

—Scientist & Teacher, Anne Barrett Swanson. Rom, Holly M., illus. LC 87-82598. 32p. (Orig.). (gr. 1-4). 1988. pap. 4.50 (ISBN 0-932469-16-7). Equity Inst.

SCORPIONS

Mell, Jan. Scorpion. LC 89-28273. (Illus.). 48p. (gr. 4-5). 1990. 10.95 (ISBN 0-89686-520-7, Crestwood Hse). Macmillan Child Grp.

Myers, Walter D. Scorpions. LC 85-45815. 160p. (gr. 7 up). 1988. 12.95 (ISBN 0-06-024364-3); PLB 12.89 (ISBN 0-06-024365-1). HarpC Child Bks.

—Scorpions. LC 85-45815. 224p. (gr. 7 up). 1990. pap. 2.95 (ISBN 0-06-447066-0, Trophy). HarpC Child Bks.

SCOTCH IN THE U. S.

Aman, Catherine. The Scottish Americans. (Illus.). 112p. (gr. 5 up). 1991. lib. bdg. 17.95 (ISBN 1-55546-132-8). Chelsea Hse.

SCOTLAND

Lerner Publications, Department of Geography Staff, ed. Scotland in Pictures. (Illus.). 64p. (gr. 5 up). 1991. PLB 12.95 (ISBN 0-8225-1875-9). Lerner Pubns.

MacVicar, Angus. Scotland. (Illus.). (gr. 5 up). 1988. 14.95 (ISBN 0-222-01021-5). Chelsea Hse.

Meek, James. The Land & People of Scotland. LC 88-27215. (Illus.). 256p. (gr. 6 up). 1990. 17.95 (ISBN 0-397-32332-8, Lipp Jr Bks); PLB 14.89 (ISBN 0-397-32333-6, Lipp Jr Bks). HarpC Child Bks.

Oakley, C. A. The Second City: The Story of Glasgow. (Illus.). 304p. 1991. pap. 24.95 (ISBN 0-87226-439-4). P Bedrick Bks.

Scotland. (Illus.). (gr. 5 up). 3.50 (ISBN 0-7214-0946-6). Ladybird Bks.

Sutherland, Dorothy B. Scotland. LC 84-23227. (Illus.). 128p. (gr. 5-9). 1985. lib. bdg. 25.27 (ISBN 0-516-02787-5). Childrens.

Taylor, Doreen. Scotland. LC 90-10028. (Illus.). 96p. (gr. 6-11). 1990. PLB 18.60 (ISBN 0-8114-2431-6). Steck-V.

SCOTLAND–FICTION

Barrie, James. Little Minister. (gr. 10 up). 1968. pap. 0.75 (ISBN 0-8049-0187-2, CL-187). Airmont.

Cameron, Eleanor. Beyond Silence. LC 80-10350. (gr. 5-9). 1980. 9.95 (ISBN 0-525-26463-9, DCB). Dutton Child Bks.

Duncan, Jane. Janet Reachfar & the Kelpie. Hedderwick, Mairi, illus. LC 75-44166. 32p. (ps-3). 1976. 7.50 (ISBN 0-685-02316-8, Clarion). HM.

Hunter, Mollie. Cat, Herself. LC 85-45385. 288p. (gr. 6-9). 1986. PLB 12.89 (ISBN 0-06-022635-8). HarpC Child Bks.

—A Sound of Chariots. LC 72-76523. 256p. (gr. 7 up). 1972. PLB 12.89 (ISBN 0-06-022669-2). HarpC Child Bks.

—The Third Eye. LC 78-22159. (gr. 8 up). 1979. PLB 12.89 (ISBN 0-06-022677-3). HarpC Child Bks.

Kidnapped. (Illus.). (gr. 3-5). 3.50 (ISBN 0-7214-0862-1). Ladybird Bks.

MacDonald, George. Wee Sir Gibbie of the Highlands. Phillips, Michael R., ed. 240p. (gr. 2-7). 1990. 9.95 (ISBN 1-55661-139-0). Bethany Hse.

Ollivant, Alfred. Bob, Son of Battle. (Illus.). (gr. 5 up). pap. 2.50 (ISBN 0-8049-0141-4, CL-141). Airmont.

Smith, Alison. Come Away Home. Haeffele, Deborah, illus. LC 90-41534. 112p. (gr. 3-5). 1991. SBE 11.95 (ISBN 0-684-19283-7, Scribners Young Read). Macmillan Child Grp.

Stevenson, Robert Louis. Kidnapped. (gr. 8 up). 1964. pap. 1.95 (ISBN 0-8049-0010-8, CL-10). Airmont.

—Kidnapped. Ward, Lynd, illus. LC 99-933315. (gr. 4-6). companion lib. ed. o.p. 2.95 (ISBN 0-448-05474-4, G&D); il. jr. lib. o.p. 5.95 (ISBN 0-448-05815-4); deluxe ed. 11.95 (ISBN 0-448-06015-9). Putnam Pub Group.

Stewart, A. C. Ossian House. LC 76-9645. (gr. 6 up). 1976. PLB 18.95 (ISBN 0-87599-219-6). S G Phillips.

Wandelmaier, Roy. Mystery at Loch Ness. Mulkey, Kim, illus. LC 85-2532. 112p. (gr. 3-6). 1985. lib. bdg. 9.49 (ISBN 0-8167-0529-1); pap. text ed. 2.95 (ISBN 0-8167-0530-5). Troll Assocs.

SCOTLAND–HISTORY–FICTION

Forman, James D. Prince Charlie's Year. 144p. (gr. 7 up). 1991. 13.95 (ISBN 0-684-19242-X, Scribners Young Read). Macmillan Child Grp.

SCOTT, ROBERT FALCON, 1868-1912

Sipiera, Paul. Roald Amundsen & Robert Scott: Race for the South Pole. LC 90-2178. (Illus.). 128p. (gr. 3 up). 1990. PLB 25.27 (ISBN 0-516-03056-6). Childrens.

SCOUTS AND SCOUTING

see also Boy Scouts; Girl Scouts

Beard, Lina & Beard, Adelia. American Girls Handybook: How to Amuse Yourself & Others. LC 86-46262. 480p. 1987. 11.95 (ISBN 0-87923-666-3). Godine.

Toliusis, Juozas, ed. Ausra, Jubiliejine Stovykla. (LIT., Illus.). 72p. (gr. 1 up). 1983. pap. write for info. (ISBN 0-9611488-1-0). Lith Scouts.

SCOUTS AND SCOUTING–FICTION

Delton, Judy. Peanut Butter Pilgrims. 80p. (Orig.). (gr. k-6). 1988. pap. 2.50 (ISBN 0-440-40066-X, YB). Dell.

—The Pooped Troop. Tiegreen, Alan, illus. 80p. (ps-3). 1989. pap. 2.50 (ISBN 0-440-40184-4, YB). Dell.

Nye, Julie. Scout. 177p. (Orig.). 1987. pap. 4.95 (ISBN 0-89084-413-5). Bob Jones Univ Pr.

SCRIPTURES, HOLY

see Bible

SCUBA DIVING

see Skin Diving

SCULLING

see Rowing

SCULPTORS

Mercer, Charles. Statue of Liberty. LC 78-21305. (Illus.). 96p. (gr. 5 up). 1979. 17.95 (ISBN 0-399-20670-1, Putnam). Putnam Pub Group.

Reef, Pat. Bernard Langlais, Sculptor. LC 84-81337. (Illus.). 48p. (gr. 3-7). 1985. pap. 9.95 (ISBN 0-933858-06-X). Kennebec River.

Reichel, Cara. A Stone Promise. Thatch, Nancy R., ed. Reichel, Cara, illus. Melton, David, intro. by. (Illus.). 26p. (gr. 5 up). 1991. PLB 12.95 (ISBN 0-933849-35-4). Landmark Edns.

SCULPTURE

see also Mobiles (Sculpture); Modeling; Monuments

Brommer, Gerald F. Wire Sculpture & Other Three Dimensional Construction. LC 68-19999. (Illus.). (gr. 5-12). 1968. 14.95 (ISBN 0-87192-025-5). Davis Mass.

Johnson, Peter D., intro. by. Clay Modelling for Everyone: Sculpture, Pottery & Jewellery Without a Wheel. De la Bedoyere, C., tr. (Illus.). 112p. (Orig.). (gr. 7 up). 1988. pap. 14.95 (ISBN 0-85532-564-X, Pub. by Search Pr UK). Pathway Bk Serv.

Slade, Richard. Your Book of Modelling. (gr. 4 up). 1968. 7.95 (ISBN 0-571-08387-0). Transatl Arts.

SCULPTURE–FICTION

Fleischman, Paul. Graven Images. LC 81-48649. (Illus.). 96p. (gr. 6 up). 1982. 12.95 (ISBN 0-06-021906-8); PLB 12.89 (ISBN 0-06-021907-6). HarpC Child Bks.

SCULPTURE–HISTORY

Levine, Bobbie, et al. A Child's Walk Through Twentieth Century American Painting & Sculpture. (Illus.). 29p. (gr. 2-6). 1986. spiral bdg. 1.50 (ISBN 0-912303-37-9). Michigan Mus.

SCULPTURE, RELIGIOUS

see Christian Art and Symbolism

SCULPTURE–TECHNIQUE

see also Modeling

Sculpture. (Illus.). 24p. (gr. 6-12). 1969. pap. 1.85 (ISBN 0-8395-3322-5, 3322). BSA.

SEA

see Ocean

SEA ANIMALS

see Marine Animals

SEA FISHERIES

see Fisheries

SEA-HORSE

Clifford, Harold B. Sea Horse. Ashley, Alta, pref. by. & illus. Ashley, Alta, intro. by. LC 87-81502. 67p. (gr. 6-8). 1987. pap. 5.95 (ISBN 0-9614592-3-9). Grey Gull Pubns.

Morris, Robert A. Seahorse. Lobel, Arnold, illus. LC 70-146004. 64p. (gr. k-3). 1972. PLB 11.89 (ISBN 0-06-024339-2). HarpC Child Bks.

Schlein, Miriam. The Dangerous Life of the Sea Horse. Cole, Gwen, illus. LC 85-26857. 40p. (gr. 3-6). 1986. 12.95 (ISBN 0-689-31180-X, Atheneum Child Bk). Macmillan Child Grp.

SEA LIFE

see Seafaring Life; Seamen;

also names of countries with the subhead Navy, e.g., U. S. Navy

SEA LIONS

see Seals (Animals)

SEA MOSSES

see Algae

SEA POWER

see also Disarmament; Naval History; Warships; also names of countries with the subhead Navy or the subdivision History, Naval, e.g. U.S. Navy; U.S.–History, Naval, etc.

Walmer, Max & Rawlinson, Jon. Sea Power Library, 6 bks, Reading Level 5. (Illus.). 288p. (gr. 3-8). Date not set. Set. PLB 111.60 (ISBN 0-86625-087-5). Rourke Corp.

SEA ROUTES

see Trade Routes

SEA SHELLS

see Shells

SEA SHORE

see Seashore

SEA STORIES

Adams, Richard. Watership Down. LC 73-6044. 444p. (gr. 8 up). 1974. 35.00 (ISBN 0-02-700030-3). Macmillan.

Avi. The True Confessions of Charlotte Doyle. Murray, Ruth E., illus. LC 90-30624. 224p. (gr. 6-8). 1990. 14.95 (ISBN 0-531-05893-X); PLB 14.99 (ISBN 0-531-08493-0). Orchard Bks Watts.

Barber, Antonia. The Mousehole Cat. Bayley, Nicola, illus. LC 90-31533. 40p. (gr. k-3). 1990. 14.95 (ISBN 0-02-708331-4, Mcmillan Child Bk). Macmillan Child Grp.

Bligh, William. Mutiny on Board HMS Bounty. Teitel, N. R., intro. by. (gr. 8 up). pap. 1.95 (ISBN 0-8049-0088-4, CL-88). Airmont.

Carrie, Christopher. Search for the Sea Treasure. (Illus.). 40p. (gr. k up). 1990. 1.59 (ISBN 0-86696-246-8). Binney & Smith.

Chrisman, Arthur B. Shen of the Sea. Hasselriis, Else, illus. (gr. 4-7). 1968. 14.95 (ISBN 0-525-39244-0, DCB). Dutton Child Bks.

Conrad, Joseph. Lord Jim. Gemme, F. R., intro. by. (gr. 10 up). pap. 1.95 (ISBN 0-8049-0054-X, CL-54). Airmont.

Cooper, Susan. Seaward. LC 83-7055. 180p. (gr. 5 up). 1983. 12.95 (ISBN 0-689-50275-3, M K McElderry). Macmillan Child Grp.

Dana, Richard H. Two Years Before the Mast. Bennet, C. L., intro. by. (gr. 8 up). pap. 2.25 (ISBN 0-8049-0085-X, CL-85). Airmont.

Fenner, Phyllis R., ed. Stories of the Sea. Werth, Kurt, illus. (gr. 5-9). 1962. lib. bdg. 5.99 (ISBN 0-394-91678-6). Knopf.

Forester, C. S. Commodore Hornblower. (gr. 7 up). 1989. 17.95 (ISBN 0-316-28894-2); pap. 7.95 (ISBN 0-316-28938-8). Little.

—Lieutenant Hornblower. (gr. 7 up). 1984. 17.95 (ISBN 0-316-28907-8); pap. 8.95 (ISBN 0-316-28921-3). Little.

—Lord Hornblower, Vol. 1. (gr. 7 up). 1989. 17.95 (ISBN 0-316-28908-6); pap. 8.95 (ISBN 0-316-28943-4). Little.

—Mr. Midshipman Hornblower. (gr. 7 up). 1950. 17.95 (ISBN 0-316-28909-4). Little.

Holling, Holling C. Seabird. (Illus.). (gr. 4-6). 1973. 15.95 (ISBN 0-395-18230-1). HM.

Kipling, Rudyard. Captains Courageous. (gr. 6 up). 1964. pap. 1.75 (ISBN 0-8049-0027-2, CL-27). Airmont.

Lewis, Thomas P. Clipper Ship. Sandin, Joan, illus. LC 77-11858. 64p. (ps-3). 1978. 11.95 (ISBN 0-06-023808-9); PLB 11.89 (ISBN 0-06-023809-7). HarpC Child Bks.

Lightbourne, K. A. Grandfather Played the Trumpet: Sailors Fantasies. 375p. (Orig.). 1988. pap. 12.50 (ISBN 0-9621212-0-7). Sailors Fantasies Pub.

London, Jack. Martin Eden. (gr. 9 up). 1969. pap. 3.50 (ISBN 0-8049-0209-7, CL-209). Airmont.

—Sea Wolf. Gall, M., intro. by. (gr. 6 up). pap. 2.50 (ISBN 0-8049-0064-7, CL-64). Airmont.

Major, Kevin. Far from Shore. 224p. (gr. 7 up). 1983. pap. 2.95 (ISBN 0-440-92585-1, LFL). Dell.

Melville, Herman. Billy Budd. Fisher, N. H., intro. by. Bd. with The Encantadas. (gr. 9 up). pap. 1.75 (ISBN 0-8049-0116-3, CL-116). Airmont.

—Billy Budd. (gr. 9 up). 1982. pap. 2.50 (ISBN 0-685-03979-X, RE). PB.

—Billy Budd. (Illus.). 64p. (gr. 4-12). 1979. pap. text ed. 2.95 (ISBN 0-88301-385-1); student activity bk. 1.25 (ISBN 0-88301-409-2). Pendulum Pr.

—Moby Dick. (gr. 11 up). 1964. pap. 3.95 (ISBN 0-8049-0033-7, CL-33). Airmont.

—Moby Dick. new ed. Shapiro, Irwin, ed. Nino, Alex, illus. LC 73-75458. 64p. (Orig.). (gr. 5-10). 1973. pap. 2.95 (ISBN 0-88301-099-2). Pendulum Pr.

—Typee. Thomas, C., intro. by. (gr. 10 up). pap. 1.50 (ISBN 0-8049-0053-1, CL-53). Airmont.

O'Dell, Scott. Dark Canoe. LC 68-29334. (Illus.). 160p. (gr. 7 up). 1968. 13.95 (ISBN 0-395-06960-2). HM.

Paulsen, Gary. The Voyage of the Frog. LC 88-15261. (Illus.). 160p. (gr. 6-8). 1989. 12.95 (ISBN 0-531-05805-0); PLB 12.99 (ISBN 0-531-08405-1). Orchard Bks Watts.

Sobel, Barbara. The Jewels from the Sea. LC 87-81237. (gr. 3-6). 1987. 7.59 (ISBN 0-87386-043-8); bk. & cassette 16.99 (ISBN 0-317-55335-6); pap. 1.95 (ISBN 0-87386-042-X). Jan Prods.

Sohl, Marcia & Dackerman, Gerald. Moby Dick Student Activity Book. Nino, Alex, illus. (gr. 4-10). 1976. pap. 1.25 (ISBN 0-88301-181-6). Pendulum Pr.

Stevenson, Robert Louis. Master of Ballantrae. (gr. 8 up). 1964. pap. 1.95 (ISBN 0-8049-0047-7, CL-47). Airmont.

Swift, Hildegarde H. & Ward, Lynd. The Little Red Lighthouse & the Great Gray Bridge. LC 73-12861. (Illus.). 51p. (gr. k-3). 1974. pap. 4.95 (ISBN 0-15-652840-1, VoyB). HarBraceJ.
Verne, Jules. Twenty Thousand Leagues under the Sea. (gr. 8 up). 1964. pap. 1.95 (ISBN 0-8049-0012-4, CL-12). Airmont.
—Twenty Thousand Leagues under the Sea. new ed. Binder, Otto, ed. Gamboa, Romy & Patricio, Ernie, illus. LC 73-75466. 64p. (Orig.). (gr. 5-10). 1973. pap. 2.95 (ISBN 0-88301-104-2); student activity bk. 1.25 (ISBN 0-88301-180-8). Pendulum Pr.
—Twenty Thousand Leagues under the Sea. Butz, Steve, illus. Nordlicht, Lillian, adapted by. LC 79-23887. 48p. (gr. 4 up). 1983. PLB 17.32 (ISBN 0-8172-1652-9); pap. 9.27 (ISBN 0-8172-2028-3). Raintree Pubs.
Waters, Tony. Sailor's Bride. (ps-3). 1991. 14.99 (ISBN 0-385-41441-2); pap. 13.95 (ISBN 0-385-41440-4). Doubleday.
Williams, Jennifer. Stringbean's Trip to Shining Sea. 1990. pap. 3.95 (ISBN 0-590-42906-X). Scholastic Inc.
Williams, Vera B. Stringbean's Trip to The Shining Sea. Williams, Jennifer & Williams, Vera B., illus. LC 86-29502. 48p. (gr. k-3). 1988. 13.95 (ISBN 0-688-07161-9); lib. bdg. 13.88 (ISBN 0-688-07162-7). Greenwillow.

SEA WAVES
see Ocean Waves

SEAFARING LIFE
see also Seamen
Hoare, Robert. Travel by Sea. Unstead, R. J., ed. (gr. 7 up). 1965. 14.95 (ISBN 0-7136-0119-1). Dufour.
Life at the Seashore. (gr. 3-6). 1981. incl. cass. & tchr's. guide 28.95 (ISBN 0-686-74503-5, 04918). Natl Geog.

SEALS (ANIMALS)
Allan, Doug. The Seal on the Rocks. Oxford Scientific Film Staff, illus. LC 87-9950. 32p. (gr. 4-6). 1988. PLB 10.95 (ISBN 1-55532-271-9). Gareth Stevens Inc.
Baker, Lucy. Seals. (Illus.). 32p. (gr. 2-6). 1990. pap. 4.95 (ISBN 0-14-034436-5, Puffin). Puffin Bks.
Bare, Colleen S. Elephants on the Beach. Bare, Colleen S., photos by. LC 89-32267. (Illus.). 32p. (ps-3). 1990. 12.95 (ISBN 0-525-65018-0, Cobblehill Bks). Dutton Child Bks.
—Sea Lions. (gr. 2-5). Date not set. 9.95 (ISBN 0-396-08719-1, Putnam). Putnam Pub Group.
Barrett, Norman. Seals & Walruses. LC 90-32150. (Illus.). 32p. (gr. k-4). 1991. PLB 11.40 (ISBN 0-531-14115-2). Watts.
Burton, Jane. Surfer the Seal. Burton, Jane, photos by. LC 89-42695. (Illus.). 24p. (Orig.). (ps-3). 1989. PLB 5.99 (ISBN 0-394-92269-7). Random.
—Surfer the Seal. LC 89-11368. (Illus.). 32p. (gr. 2-3). 1989. PLB 10.95 (ISBN 0-8368-0210-1). Gareth Stevens Inc.
Cherry, Lynne, illus. Seal. LC 86-24030. (ps). 1987. bds. 3.50 (ISBN 0-525-44304-5, DCB); book & toy package 13.95 (ISBN 0-685-14572-7, DCB). Dutton Child Bks.
Cossi, Olga. Harp Seals. (Illus.). 48p. (gr. 2-5). 1991. PLB 12.95 (ISBN 0-87614-437-7). Carolrhoda Bks.
Cowcher, Helen. Antarctica. Cowcher, Helen, illus. 32p. (ps-3). 1990. incl. audiocassette 17.95 (ISBN 0-924483-24-5). Soundprints.
Dalmais. Seal, Reading Level 3-4. (Illus.). 28p. (gr. 2-5). Date not set. PLB 14.60 (ISBN 0-86592-867-3). Rourke Corp.
Duden, Jane. Harp Seal. LC 89-28274. (Illus.). 48p. (gr. 5 up). 1990. 10.95 (ISBN 0-89686-516-9, Crestwood Hse). Macmillan Child Grp.
Evans, Phyllis R. The Sea World Book of Seals & Sea Lions. LC 85-27100. (Illus.). (gr. 4-6). 1986. 15.95 (ISBN 0-15-271954-7, HJ); pap. 9.95 (ISBN 0-15-271955-5). HarBraceJ.
Green, Carl R. & Sanford, William R. The Elephant Seal. LC 87-22349. (Illus.). 48p. (gr. 5-6). 1987. PLB 10.95 (ISBN 0-89686-330-1, Crestwood Hse). Macmillan Child Grp.
Hoffman, Mary. Seal. LC 86-17806. (Illus.). 24p. (gr. k-5). 1987. PLB 13.32 (ISBN 0-8172-2702-4). Raintree Pubs.
Irving, Georgeanne. The True Story of Corky the Blind Seal. Kelly, Ken & Carrison, Ron, photos by. (Illus.). 32p. (Orig.). (gr. k-3). 1987. pap. 2.50 (ISBN 0-590-40718-X). Scholastic Inc.
Johnson, Sylvia A. Elephant Seals. Lanting, Frans, photos by. LC 88-12924. (Illus.). 48p. (gr. 4 up). 1989. PLB 14.95 (ISBN 0-8225-1487-7). Lerner Pubns.
Leon, Vicki. Seals & Sea Lions. (Illus.). 40p. (Orig.). (ps-12). 1988. pap. 5.95 (ISBN 0-918303-15-X, Little Simon). S&S Trade.
Martin, L. Seals. (Illus.). 24p. (gr. k-5). Date not set. PLB 11.93 (ISBN 0-86592-999-8). Rourke Corp.
Palmer, S. Sea Lions. (Illus.). 24p. (gr. k-5). 1989. lib. bdg. 11.93 (ISBN 0-86592-362-0). Rourke Corp.
—Sea Otters. (Illus.). 24p. (gr. k-5). 1989. lib. bdg. 11.93 (ISBN 0-86592-361-2). Rourke Corp.
Patent, Dorothy H. Seals, Sea Lions & Walruses. LC 90-55101. (Illus.). 96p. (gr. 3-7). 1990. reinforced 14.95 (ISBN 0-8234-0834-5). Holiday.
Petty, Kate. Seals. (Illus.). 24p. (gr. k-3). 1991. PLB 10.40 (ISBN 0-531-17285-6, Gloucester Pr). Watts.
Saintsing, David & Allan, Douglas. The World of Seals. LC 87-6524. (Illus.). 32p. (gr. 2-3). 1987. PLB 10.95 (ISBN 1-55532-300-6). Gareth Stevens Inc.
The Seal. (gr. 2-5). 1988. pap. 2.50 (ISBN 0-8167-1575-0). Troll Assocs.
Shaw, Evelyn. Elephant Seal Island. Pape, Cherryl, illus. LC 77-25649. 64p. (gr. k-3). 1978. PLB 11.89 (ISBN 0-06-025604-4). HarpC Child Bks.
Sherrow, Victoria. Seals, Sea Lions, & Walruses. (Illus.). 64p. (gr. 5-8). 1991. PLB 11.90 (ISBN 0-531-20028-0). Watts.
Wexo, John B. Seals, Sea Lions, Walruses. 24p. (gr. 4). 1989. 11.95s.p. (ISBN 0-88682-271-8); 17.10 (ISBN 0-685-28187-6). Creative Ed.
White, Sandra & Filisky, Michael. Sterling: The Rescue of a Baby Harbor Seal. (Illus.). 32p. (gr. 2-4). 1988. PLB 14.95 (ISBN 0-517-57112-9). Crown.
Wildlife Education, Ltd. Staff. Seals & Sea Lions. Stuart, Walter, illus. 20p. (Orig.). (gr. 5 up). 1985. pap. 2.25 (ISBN 0-937934-33-X). Wildlife Educ.

SEALS (ANIMALS)–FICTION
Aschenbrenner, Gerald. Jack, the Seal, & the Sea. Fink, Joanne, adapted by. Aschenbrenner, Gerald, illus. 30p. (gr. 2-5). 1988. PLB 14.98 (ISBN 0-382-09985-0); PLB 11.24s.p.; pap. 6.95 (ISBN 0-382-09986-9); pap. 5.21s.p. Silver Burdett Pr.
Davis, Deborah. The Secret of the Seal. Davis, Deborah, illus. (gr. 2 up). 1988. 13.95 (ISBN 0-517-56725-3). Crown.
Gerstein, Mordicai. The Seal Mother. (ps-3). 1990. pap. 3.95 (ISBN 0-8037-0743-6). Dial Bks Young.
Hertz, Ole. Tobias Goes Seal Hunting. Tobias, Tobi, tr. from DAN. Hertz, Ole, illus. LC 83-26357. 32p. (gr. k-3). 1984. PLB 7.95 (ISBN 0-87614-262-5). Carolrhoda Bks.
Hoff, Syd. Sammy the Seal. Hoff, Syd, illus. LC 59-5316. 64p. (gr. k-3). 1959. PLB 11.89 (ISBN 0-06-022526-2). HarpC Child Bks.
—Sammy the Seal. Hoff, Syd, illus. LC 59-5316. 64p. (gr. k-3). 1980. pap. 3.50 (ISBN 0-06-444028-1, Trophy). HarpC Child Bks.
Peck, Sylvia. Seal Child. (gr. 3-7). 1991. Repr. 3.50 (ISBN 0-553-15868-6, Skylark). Bantam.
Pope, Joyce. Seashores. (Illus.). 32p. (gr. 1-8). 1985. PLB 11.90 (ISBN 0-531-04951-5). Watts.
Sackett, Elisabeth. Danger on the Arctic Ice. (ps-3). 1991. 12.95 (ISBN 0-316-76598-8). Little.
Sammy Seal. (Illus.). (ps). 1.79 (ISBN 0-517-46416-0). Outlet Bk Co.
Shachtman, Tom. Driftwhistler: A Story of Daniel au Fond. (Illus.). 160p. (gr. 5 up). 1991. 14.95 (ISBN 0-8050-1285-0). H Holt & Co.
—Wavebender: A Story of Daniel au Fond. Henterly, Jamichael, illus. 160p. (gr. 5 up). 1989. 14.95 (ISBN 0-8050-0840-3). H Holt & Co.
Tafuri, Nancy. Follow Me! LC 89-23259. (Illus.). 24p. (ps up). 1990. 13.95 (ISBN 0-688-08773-6); lib. bdg. 13.88 (ISBN 0-688-08774-4). Greenwillow.
Watkins, Will. Sid Seal, Houseman. Goffe, Toni, illus. LC 88-60095. 96p. (gr. 2-5). 1989. 14.95 (ISBN 0-531-05784-4); PLB 14.99 (ISBN 0-531-08384-5). Orchard Bks Watts.

SEAMANSHIP
see also Navigation
Boy Scouts of America. Sea Exploring Manual. 272p. (gr. 6-12). 1987. pap. 8.75 (ISBN 0-8395-3229-6, 3239). BSA.

SEAMEN
see also Pilots and Pilotage; Seafaring Life
also names of countries with the subhead Navy, e.g. U.S. Navy, etc.
Strom, Kay M. John Newton: The Angry Sailor. (Orig.). (gr. 7-10). 1984. pap. 3.95 (ISBN 0-8024-0335-2). Moody.

SEAMEN–LEGENDS
Edwards, Roberta, retold by. Five Silly Fishermen: A Step One Book. Wickstrom, Sylvie, illus. LC 89-42508. 32p. (Orig.). (ps-1). 1989. PLB 6.99 (ISBN 0-679-90092-6, Random Juv); pap. 2.95 (ISBN 0-679-80092-1, Random Juv). Random.
Lobel, Arnold. Uncle Elephant. Lobel, Arnold, illus. LC 80-8944. 64p. (gr. k-3). 1981. 11.95 (ISBN 0-06-023979-4); PLB 11.89 (ISBN 0-06-023980-8). HarpC Child Bks.

SEARCH AND RESCUE OPERATIONS
see Rescue Work

SEASHORE
Booth, Eugene. At the Beach. LC 77-7659. (Illus.). (gr. k-3). 1985. PLB 13.32 (ISBN 0-8393-0111-1); pap. text ed. 9.27 (ISBN 0-8393-0161-8). Raintree Pubs.
Brown, Vinson. Exploring Pacific Coast Tide Pools. rev. & enl. ed. Rovetta, Ane, illus. 80p. (gr. 4 up). 1966. 14.95 (ISBN 0-87961-216-9); pap. 7.95 (ISBN 0-87961-217-7). Naturegraph.
Corbett, Julia. Sea Life at the Ocean's Edge. Warren, Hank & Moore, Shirley, eds. Kahler, Carole, illus. 24p. (gr. 4-6). 1984. pap. text ed. 3.95 (ISBN 0-685-34734-6). Pacif NW Natl Pks.
Crump, Donald J., ed. The World's Wild Shores. (Illus.). 1990. 7.95 (ISBN 0-87044-716-5); lib. bdg. 9.50 (ISBN 0-318-42775-3). Natl Geog.
Epstein, Samuel, et al. What's for Lunch? The Eating Habits of Seashore Creatures. Gaffney-Kessel, Walter, illus. LC 85-4964. 48p. (gr. 1-4). 1985. 11.95 (ISBN 0-02-733500-3, Mcmillan Child Bk). Macmillan Child Grp.
Farmer, Wesley M. Seashore Discoveries. Hamann, Jeff, illus. 124p. (Orig.). (gr. 9 up). 1986. pap. text ed. 7.95x (ISBN 0-937772-01-1). W M Farmer.
Fox, Paula. The Village by the Sea. LC 88-60099. 160p. (gr. 5-7). 1988. 13.95 (ISBN 0-531-05788-7); PLB 13.99 (ISBN 0-531-08388-8). Orchard Bks Watts.
Glaser, Michael. The Nature of the Seashore. Glaser, Michael, illus. 16p. (Orig.). (gr. 1-6). 1986. pap. 4.95 (ISBN 0-911635-02-5). Knickerbocker.
Goodall, John S. The Story of the Seashore. LC 89-8328. (Illus.). 54p. 1990. 14.95 (ISBN 0-689-50491-8, M K McElderry). Macmillan Child Grp.
Gregory, Elizabeth. Beach Colors & Beach Creatures. (Illus.). 1981. 6.95 (ISBN 0-933184-17-4); pap. 5.50 (ISBN 0-933184-18-2). Flame Intl.
Hecht, Jeff. Shifting Shores: Rising Seas, Retreating Coastlines. LC 89-37812. (Illus.). 160p. (gr. 7 up). 1990. 14.95 (ISBN 0-684-19087-7, Scribners Young Read). Macmillan Child Grp.
Hedgpeth, Joel. Common Seashore Life of Southern California. Hinton, Sam, illus. 64p. (gr. 4 up). 1961. 12.95 (ISBN 0-911010-63-7); pap. 5.95 (ISBN 0-911010-62-9). Naturegraph.
Hurd, Edith T. Starfish. Bloch, Lucienne, illus. LC 62-7742. 40p. (gr. k-2). 1962. PLB 13.89 (ISBN 0-690-77069-3, Crowell Jr Bks). HarpC Child Bks.
Jennings, Terry. Sea & Seashore. LC 89-454. (Illus.). 32p. (gr. 3-6). 1989. PLB 14.60 (ISBN 0-516-08441-0); pap. 4.95 (ISBN 0-516-48441-9). Childrens.
Kirkpatrick, Rena K. Look at Shore Life. rev. ed. Milne, Annabel & Stebbing, Peter, illus. LC 84-26249. 32p. (gr. 2-4). 1985. PLB 15.99 (ISBN 0-8172-2358-4); pap. text ed. 9.27 (ISBN 0-8172-2383-5). Raintree Pubs.
Lazier, Christine. Seashore Life. Bogard, Vicki, tr. from FRE. Underhill, Graham, illus. LC 90-50781. 38p. (gr. k-5). 1991. 4.95 (ISBN 0-944589-39-1, 391). Young Discovery Lib.
Lye, Keith. Coasts. Furstinger, Nancy, ed. (Illus.). 48p. (gr. 5-8). 1988. PLB 14.98 (ISBN 0-382-09790-4). Silver Burdett Pr.
Macht, Philip. Circles in the Sand. Rosenthal, Linda, illus. LC 84-90597. 64p. (gr. 7 up). 1985. 12.95 (ISBN 0-930339-00-2). Maxrom Pr.
Maidoff, Ilka. Let's Explore the Shore. (Illus.). (gr. 5 up). 1962. 9.95 (ISBN 0-8392-3017-6). Astor-Honor.
Malnig, Anita. Where the Waves Break: Life at the Edge of the Sea. LC 84-9614. (Illus.). 48p. (gr. 2-5). 1985. PLB 12.95 (ISBN 0-87614-226-9); pap. 6.95 (ISBN 0-87614-477-6). Carolrhoda Bks.
—Where the Waves Break: Life at the Edge of the Sea. (Illus.). 48p. (gr. 1-5). 1987. pap. 6.95 (ISBN 0-685-18836-1, First Ave Edns). Lerner Pubns.
Mason, Helen. Life at the Seashore. (Illus.). 32p. (gr. 2-5). 1990. PLB 14.25 (ISBN 0-88625-270-9); pap. 2.95 (ISBN 0-88625-269-5). Durkin Hayes Pub.
Miller, Christina G. & Berry, Louise A. Coastal Rescue: Preserving Our Seashores. LC 88-27250. (Illus.). 144p. (gr. 5-9). 1989. 12.95 (ISBN 0-689-31288-1, Atheneum Child Bk). Macmillan Child Grp.
O'Connor, Karen. Let's Take a Walk on the Beach. Axeman, Lois, illus. LC 86-9551. 32p. (ps-2). 1986. lib. bdg. 11.97 (ISBN 0-89565-354-0). Childs World.
Oda, Hidetomo. Animals of the Seashore. LC 85-28192. (Illus.). 32p. (gr. 3-7). 1986. PLB 16.67 (ISBN 0-8172-2543-9). Raintree Pubs.
Parker, Steve. Seashore. King, Dave, illus. LC 88-27173. 64p. (gr. 5 up). 1989. 15.00 (ISBN 0-394-82254-4); PLB 14.99 (ISBN 0-394-92254-9). Knopf.
Podendorf, Illa. Animals of Sea & Shore. LC 81-38453. (Illus.). 48p. (gr. k-4). 1982. PLB 14.60 (ISBN 0-516-01615-6); pap. 4.95 (ISBN 0-516-41615-4). Childrens.
Rius, Maria & Parramon, J. M. The Seaside. (ps). 1986. 6.95 (ISBN 0-8120-5747-3); pap. 3.95 (ISBN 0-8120-3699-9). Barron.
Rockwell, Anne. At the Beach. Rockwell, Harlow, illus. LC 86-2943. 24p. (ps-1). 1987. 12.95 (ISBN 0-02-777940-8, Mcmillan Child Bk). Macmillan Child Grp.
Salts, Bobbi. Beaches Are for Kids! An Activity Book for Kids. Parker, Steve, illus. 32p. (gr. 1-6). 1990. pap. 2.95 (ISBN 0-929526-09-0). Double B Pubns.
Schaper, Sue. The Seashore & Our Lighthouse. Mackler, Carole B., ed. Vanderwalten, Kate, illus. 24p. (gr. k-8). 1989. pap. 3.95 (ISBN 0-317-94103-8). SSGI Pr.
Silverstein, Alvin. Life in a Tidal Pool, Vol. 1. (gr. 4-7). 1990. 14.95 (ISBN 0-316-79120-2, Joy St Bks). Little.
Stevenson, James. July. Stevenson, James, illus. LC 88-37584. (gr. k up). 1990. 12.95 (ISBN 0-688-08822-8); PLB 12.88 (ISBN 0-688-08823-6). Greenwillow.
Stone, L. Seashores. (Illus.). 48p. (gr. 4-8). 1989. lib. bdg. 14.00 (ISBN 0-86592-435-X). Rourke Corp.
Swenson, Allan. Secrets of a Seashore. (Illus.). 80p. (gr. 4-10). 1981. pap. 3.95 (ISBN 0-930096-28-2). G Gannett.
Talkabout the Beach. (ARA., Illus.). (gr. 1-3). 3.50x (ISBN 0-86685-232-8). Intl Bk Ctr.
Taylor, Barbara. Ready Set Go: At the Seashore. 1991. 4.98 (ISBN 0-8317-7356-1). Smithmark.
Vasiliu, Mircea. A Day at the Beach. LC 76-24169. (ps-2). 1978. 2.25 (ISBN 0-394-83475-5, Random Juv). Random.
Wyler, Rose. Seashore Surprises. (Illus.). 32p. (gr. k-3). 1991. PLB 11.98 (ISBN 0-671-69165-1); pap. 4.95 (ISBN 0-671-69167-8). Messner.

SEASHORE–FICTION
Alexander, Sally. Sarah's Surprise. Kastner, Jill, illus. LC 89-36780. 32p. (gr. k-3). 1990. 13.95 (ISBN 0-02-700391-4, Mcmillan Child Bk). Macmillan Child Grp.
Avi. A Place Called Ugly. Adams, illus. LC 80-23326. 224p. (gr. 7-9). 1981. lib. bdg. 8.99 (ISBN 0-394-94755-X). Pantheon.

Cole, Sheila. When the Tide Is Low. Wright-Frierson, Virginia, illus. LC 84-10023. 32p. (ps-1). 1985. 12.95 (ISBN 0-688-04066-7); PLB 12.88 (ISBN 0-688-04067-5). Lothrop.
Craig, Janet. Homer the Beachcomber. Mahan, Ben, illus. LC 87-10913. 32p. (gr. k-2). 1988. PLB 10.89 (ISBN 0-8167-1085-6); pap. text ed. 2.95 (ISBN 0-8167-1086-4). Troll Assocs.
Dawe, Karen. The Beach Book & Beach Bucket. LC 87-40648. (Illus.). (gr. k-5). 1988. pap. 7.95 incl. bucket (ISBN 0-89480-590-8, 1590). Workman Pub.
Florian, Douglas. Beach Day. LC 89-1933. (Illus.). 32p. (ps up). 1990. 12.95 (ISBN 0-688-09104-0); lib. bdg. 12.88 (ISBN 0-688-09105-9). Greenwillow.
Gilbert, Jeanette. Seaside Stories. Barta, Beverly, ed. Feldmann, Susan, illus. 16p. (Orig.). (gr. 1-4). 1990. pap. write for info. (ISBN 0-9623503-0-3). Palm Pub.
Greenberg, Melanie H. At the Beach. Greenberg, Melanie H., illus. 24p. (ps-2). 1989. 11.95 (ISBN 0-525-44474-2, DCB). Dutton Child Bks.
Guild, Anne V. Mickey Mouse in Let's Go...on a Beach Picnic. Scholefield, Ron, et al, illus. 26p. (ps up). 1987. pap. 14.95 (ISBN 1-55578-800-9). Worlds Wonder.
Hope, Laura L. Bobbsey Twins' Secret at the Seashore. rev. ed. (gr. 1-4). 1936. 4.50 (ISBN 0-448-08003-6, G&D). Putnam Pub Group.
Hughes, Shirley. Here Comes Charlie Moon. Hughes, Shirley, illus. LC 85-24125. 128p. (gr. 2-5). 1986. Repr. of 1980 ed. 11.95 (ISBN 0-688-06401-9). Lothrop.
Jenkins, Jerry B. Big Trouble At the Beach. (gr. 4-7). 1990. pap. 4.50 (ISBN 0-8024-0812-5). Moody.
Kimball, Kathleen M. Big Foot, Little Foot. LoBue, Elisa M., illus. LC 78-68822. (ps). 1979. 6.95 (ISBN 0-933308-00-0). West Village.
Laird, Elizabeth & Madden, Olivia. The Inside Outing. Ward, Deborah, illus. 32p. (gr. k-2). 1988. 7.95 (ISBN 0-8120-5977-8). Barron.
Leopold, Nikia C. Sandcastle Seahorses. LC 87-35978. 45p. (Orig.). 1988. pap. 5.95 (ISBN 0-913123-17-X). Galileo.
Levy, Elizabeth. Something Queer on Vacation. Gerstein, Mordicai, illus. LC 78-72858. (gr. 1-3). 1980. 10.95 (ISBN 0-440-08346-X); pap. 6.95 (ISBN 0-385-28987-1). Delacorte.
Lewis, Shari. Baby Lamb Chop Loves the Beach. Beylon, Cathy, illus. 12p. (ps-k). 1991. bds. 3.95 (ISBN 0-679-81726-3). Random.
MacDonald, Maryann. Ben at the Beach. McTaggart, David, illus. 32p. (ps-3). 1991. 14.95 (ISBN 0-670-83920-5). Viking Child Bks.
Maestro, Betsy & Maestro, Giulio. Through the Year with Harriet. Maestro, Betsy & Maestro, Giulio, illus. LC 84-29339. 32p. (ps-1). 1986. PLB 12.95 (ISBN 0-517-55613-8). Crown.
Marshall, Edward. Three by the Sea. Marshall, James, illus. 48p. (ps-3). 1981. PLB 10.89 (ISBN 0-8037-8687-5); pap. 4.95 (ISBN 0-8037-8671-9). Dial Bks Young.
Nabb, Magdalen. Josie Smith at the Seashore. Vainio, Pirkko, illus. LC 89-8168. 96p. (gr. 1-5). 1990. 12.95 (ISBN 0-689-50492-6, M K McElderry). Macmillan Child Grp.
Oana. Bobby Bear Goes to the Beach. LC 80-82951. (Illus.). 32p. (ps-1). 1981. PLB 9.95 (ISBN 0-87783-153-X). Oddo.
Oxenbury, Helen. Beach Day. LC 81-69273. (Illus.). 14p. (ps-k). 1982. bds. 3.50 (ISBN 0-8037-0439-9). Dial Bks Young.
Pascal, Francine. Malibu Summer. 208p. (Orig.). (gr. 4). 1986. pap. 2.95 (ISBN 0-553-26050-2). Bantam.
Pirani, Felix. Abigail at the Beach. Roche, Christine, illus. LC 88-3824. 32p. (ps-2). 1989. 9.95 (ISBN 0-8037-0561-1). Dial Bks Young.
Rockwell, Anne. At the Beach. Rockwell, Harlow, illus. LC 90-45620. 24p. (ps-1). 1991. pap. 3.95 (ISBN 0-689-71494-7, Aladdin). Macmillan Child Grp.
Ryder, Joanne. A Wet & Sandy Day. LC 76-18401. (Illus.). (gr. k-3). 1977. 6.95 (ISBN 0-06-025158-1). HarpC Child Bks.
Rylant, Cynthia. Henry & Mudge & the Forever Sea: The Sixth Book of Their Adventures. Stevenson, Sucie, illus. LC 88-6130. 48p. (gr. 1-3). 1989. 11.95 (ISBN 0-02-778007-4, Bradbury Pr). Macmillan Child Grp.
Sargent, Susan & Wirt, Donna A. My Favorite Place. Eitzen, Allan, photos by. LC 83-2753. (Illus.). (gr. 1-3). 1983. pap. 0.20 (ISBN 0-687-27538-5). Abingdon.
Sharmat, Marjorie W. Nate the Great & the Boring Beach Bag. Simont, Marc, illus. 48p. (gr. 1-4). 1989. pap. 2.95 (ISBN 0-440-40168-2, YB). Dell.
Sis, Peter. Beach Ball. Sis, Peter, illus. LC 89-2076. 24p. (ps). 1990. 12.95 (ISBN 0-688-09181-4); PLB 12.88 (ISBN 0-688-09182-2). Greenwillow.
Smith, E. Boyd. The Seashore Book. Smith, E. Boyd, illus. LC 84-22483. 56p. (gr. k-12). 1985. Repr. of 1912 ed. 12.95 (ISBN 0-395-38015-4). HM.
Steele, David H. The Pebble Searcher. 16p. (gr. 7-10). 1986. 12.00X (ISBN 0-317-52595-6, Pub. by A H Stockwell England). State Mutual Bk.
Stevens, Kathleen. Bully for the Beast! Bowler, Ray, illus. LC 88-33090. 32p. (gr. 2-3). 1990. PLB 12.95 (ISBN 0-8368-0020-6). Gareth Stevens Inc.
Stevenson, James. Emma at the Beach. LC 88-3491. (Illus.). (gr. k up). 1990. 12.95 (ISBN 0-688-08806-6); lib. bdg. 12.88 (ISBN 0-688-08807-4). Greenwillow.
—The Worst Person in the World at Crab Beach. LC 86-31931. (Illus.). 32p. (gr. k-3). 1988. 13.95 (ISBN 0-688-07298-4); lib. bdg. 13.88 (ISBN 0-688-07299-2). Greenwillow.
Stevenson, Susie. Do I Have to Take Violet? (Illus.). 32p. (gr. k-3). 1987. 12.95 (ISBN 0-399-21700-2, Putnam). Putnam Pub Group.
Stine, R. L. Beach Party. 1990. pap. 2.95 (ISBN 0-590-43278-8). Scholastic Inc.
Streib, Sally. Treasures by the Sea. 159p. 1991. pap. 7.95 (ISBN 0-8163-0933-7). Pacific Pr Pub Assn.
Turkle, Brinton. Do Not Open. Turkle, Brinton, illus. LC 80-10289. 32p. (ps-2). 1981. pap. 13.95 (ISBN 0-525-28785-X, 01258-370, DCB). Dutton Child Bks.
Warner, Gertrude C. Mystery in the Sand. Cunningham, David, illus. LC 70-165823. 128p. (gr. 3-7). 1971. PLB 9.95 (ISBN 0-8075-5373-5). A Whitman.
Young, James. Og & Gargo at the Beach. (Illus.). 32p. (gr. 1-5). 1988. pap. 3.95 (ISBN 0-8431-2222-6). Price Stern.
Ziefert, Harriet. Max & Diana & the Beach Day. Johnson, Lonnie S., illus. LC 86-45339. 32p. (ps-2). 1987. 3.95 (ISBN 0-694-00091-4). HarpC Child Bks.
Zion, Gene. Harry by the Sea. Graham, Margaret B., illus. LC 65-21302. 32p. (ps-3). 1976. pap. 3.95 (ISBN 0-06-443010-3, JP 10, Trophy). HarpC Child Bks.

SEASONS

see also names of the seasons, e.g. Autumn, etc.

Alexander, Sue. There's More... Much More. Brewster, Patience, illus. LC 86-33632. 32p. (ps-3). 1987. 12.95 (ISBN 0-15-200605-2, Gulliver Bks). HarBraceJ.
Allison, Linda. The Reasons for Seasons: The Great Cosmic Megagalactic Trip Without Moving from Your Chair. Allison, Linda, illus. 128p. (gr. 4 up). 1975. 14.95 (ISBN 0-316-03439-8); pap. 8.95 (ISBN 0-316-03440-1). Little.
Asimov, Isaac. Why Are There Four Seasons? (Illus.). 24p. (gr. 2-3). 1991. PLB 11.95 (ISBN 0-8368-0439-2). Gareth Stevens Inc.
Baldwin, Barbara. Celebrate the Seasons. Sussman, Ellen, ed. Burris, Priscilla, illus. 68p. (gr. 1-6). 1983. pap. text ed. 7.95 (ISBN 0-933606-23-0, MS-621). Monkey Sisters.
Bank Street College of Education Editors. Let's Explore the Seasons. (gr. 1-2). 1986. pap. 2.95 (ISBN 0-8120-3625-5). Barron.
Bennett, David. Seasons. Kightley, Rosalinda, illus. 32p. (ps up). 1988. pap. 3.95 (ISBN 0-553-05480-5). Bantam.
Berenstain, Stan & Berenstain, Janice. The Bears Almanac. (gr. 1-4). 1973. (Random Juv); lib. bdg. 10.99 (ISBN 0-394-92693-5). Random.
Berger, Melvin. Seasons. (gr. 4-7). 1990. 11.95 (ISBN 0-385-24876-8); PLB 12.99 (ISBN 0-385-24877-6). Doubleday.
—Seasons. (gr. 4-7). 1990. 11.95 (ISBN 0-385-24876-8); PLB 12.99 (ISBN 0-385-24877-6). Doubleday.
Bilyeu, Linda M. Celebrate Spring. Grossmann, Dan, illus. 144p. (gr. k-3). 1984. wkbk. 10.95 (ISBN 0-86653-209-9, SS 836). Good Apple.
Borden, Louise. Caps, Hats, Socks, & Mittens: A Book about the Four Seasons. Hoban, Lillian, illus. 1992. pap. 3.95 (ISBN 0-590-44872-2). Scholastic Inc.
Borland, Hal. The Golden Circle: A Book of Months. Dowden, Anne O., illus. LC 77-23560. 64p. (gr. 5 up). 1977. 13.95 (ISBN 0-690-03803-8, Crowell Jr Bks). HarpC Child Bks.
Brandt, Keith. Wonders of the Seasons. Watling, James, illus. LC 81-7411. 32p. (gr. 2-4). 1982. PLB 10.89 (ISBN 0-89375-580-X); pap. text ed. 2.95 (ISBN 0-89375-581-8). Troll Assocs.
Branley, Franklyn M. Sunshine Makes the Seasons. rev. ed. Maestro, Giulio, illus. LC 85-47540. 32p. (ps-3). 1985. PLB 13.89 (ISBN 0-690-04482-8, Crowell Jr Bks). HarpC Child Bks.
Butler, Daphne. First Look at the Changing Seasons. LC 90-10246. (Illus.). 32p. (gr. 1-2). 1991. lib. bdg. 10.95 (ISBN 0-8368-0504-6). Gareth Stevens Inc.
Carr, Jan. I Am Curious about the Four Seasons. Campana, Manny, illus. 48p. (ps-2). 1988. pap. 1.95 (ISBN 0-590-41873-4). Scholastic Inc.
Carson, Patti, et al. Days, Months, Seasons. (Illus.). 20p. (gr. 2-4). 1984. pap. 5.95 (ISBN 0-88724-098-4, CD-0568). Carson-Dellos.
Cohen, Lynn. Weather & Seasons. 64p. (ps-2). 1988. 6.95 (ISBN 0-912107-79-0, MM983). Monday Morning Bks.
Coleridge, Sara. January Brings the Snow: A Seasonal Hide-&-Seek Book. LC 88-28609. (Illus.). 28p. (ps-3). 1989. 14.95 (ISBN 0-531-05824-7). Orchard Bks Watts.
Darling, Kathy. Kids & Seasons. (Illus.). 64p. (ps-2). 1989. 6.95 (ISBN 0-912107-93-6, MM1910). Monday Morning Bks.
Fass, Bernie & Caggiano, Rosemary. The Four Seasons. 48p. (gr. k-6). 1976. pap. 10.95 (ISBN 0-86704-001-7). Clarus Music.
Firmin, Peter, illus. Summer & Winter. 16p. (ps-1). 1986. 2.95 (ISBN 0-86020-964-4). EDC.
The Four Seasons. (Illus.). (ps). 1985. bds. 3.98 (ISBN 0-517-47339-9). Outlet Bk Co.
Goennel, Heidi. Seasons. Goennel, Heidi, illus. LC 85-31226. (gr. k-2). 1986. lib. bdg. 14.95 (ISBN 0-316-31836-1). Little.
Graube, Ireta S. Seasons - a Thematic Unit. Apodaca, Blanqui, illus. 80p. (ps-1). 1990. wkbk. 7.95 (ISBN 1-55734-251-2). Tchr Create Mat.
Greydanus, Rose. Changing Seasons. Hall, Susan, illus. LC 82-19959. 32p. (gr. k-2). 1983. PLB 10.89 (ISBN 0-89375-902-3); pap. 2.95 (ISBN 0-8167-1478-9). Troll Assocs.
Hand, Phyllis. Seasonal Bulletin Boards That Teach. Henson, Grace, illus. 48p. (gr. 1-5). 1984. wkbk. 6.95 (ISBN 0-86653-203-X, SS 820). Good Apple.
Harlow, Rosie & Morgan, Gareth. Cycles & Seasons. Peperell, Liz, illus. 40p. (gr. 5-8). 1991. PLB 12.90 (ISBN 0-531-19123-0, Warwick). Watts.
Kalman, Bobbie. Time & the Seasons. (Illus.). 32p. (gr. 2-3). 1986. 14.95 (ISBN 0-86505-072-4); pap. 6.95 (ISBN 0-86505-094-5). Crabtree Pub Co.
Lambert, David. The Seasons. (Illus.). 32p. (gr. k-3). 1983. PLB 7.99 (ISBN 0-531-04620-6). Watts.
Little People Big Book About Seasons. 64p. (ps-1). 1989. write for info. (ISBN 0-8094-7470-0); PLB write for info. (ISBN 0-8094-7471-9). Time-Life.
Magoldi, Mary. Daily Close-Ups for Spring. McClure, Nancee, illus. Russell, Bruce, ed. 96p. (gr. k-6). 1984. wkbk. 9.95 (ISBN 0-86653-255-2, GA 563). Good Apple.
—Daily Close-Ups for Winter. Hall, Robyn, illus. Russell, Bruce, ed. 96p. (gr. k-6). 1984. wkbk. 9.95 (ISBN 0-86653-256-0, GA 562). Good Apple.
Magoldi, Mary & Russell, Bruce. Daily Close-Ups for Fall. 96p. (gr. k-6). 1984. wkbk. 9.95 (ISBN 0-317-43006-8, GA 561). Good Apple.
Marcus, Elizabeth. Our Wonderful Seasons. Boyd, Patti, illus. LC 82-17372. 32p. (gr. 3-6). 1983. PLB 10.59 (ISBN 0-89375-896-5); pap. text ed. 2.95 (ISBN 0-89375-897-3). Troll Assocs.
Milburn, Constance. Let's Look at the Seasons. Caulkins, Janet, ed. (Illus.). 32p. (gr. k-6). 1988. PLB 10.90 (ISBN 0-531-18179-0, Pub. by Bookwright Pr). Watts.
Penn, Linda. Young Scientists Explore: Seasons. Scott, Elaine, illus. 32p. (gr. k-3). 1983. wkbk. 4.95 (ISBN 0-86653-123-8, GA 453). Good Apple.
Podendorf, Illa. Seasons. LC 81-7751. (Illus.). 48p. (gr. k-4). 1981. PLB 14.60 (ISBN 0-516-01647-4); pap. 4.95 (ISBN 0-516-41647-2). Childrens.
Provensen, Alice & Provensen, Martin. A Book of Seasons. Provensen, Alice & Provensen, Martin, illus. LC 75-36470. 32p. (ps-1). 1976. pap. 2.25 (ISBN 0-394-83242-6, Random Juv). Random.
Sabin, Francene. Seasons. Burns, Raymond, illus. LC 84-2713. 32p. (gr. 3-6). 1985. PLB 9.49 (ISBN 0-8167-0308-6); pap. text ed. 2.95 (ISBN 0-8167-0309-4). Troll Assocs.
Schulz, Charles M. Snoopy's Facts & Fun Book about Seasons. Schulz, Charles M., illus. LC 79-678. (ps-1). 1979. 2.95 (ISBN 0-394-84173-5, Random Juv); lib. bdg. 3.99 (ISBN 0-394-94173-X). Random.
Seasons. 48p. (gr. 1-5). 1985. pap. 1.29 (ISBN 0-317-28611-0). Crown.
Spizman, Robyn. Bulletin Boards: Seasonal Ideas & Activities. Pesiri, Evelyn, illus. 64p. (gr. k-6). 1984. wkbk. 6.95 (ISBN 0-86653-218-8, GA 568). Good Apple.
—Bulletin Boards to Promote Good Study Skills & Positive Self-Concept. Pesiri, Evelyn, illus. 48p. (gr. k-6). 1984. wkbk. 5.95 (ISBN 0-86653-261-7, GA 575). Good Apple.
Supraner, Robyn. I Can Read About Seasons. LC 74-24990. (Illus.). (gr. 2-4). 1975. pap. 1.95 (ISBN 0-89375-068-9). Troll Assocs.
Updike, John. A Child's Calendar. Burkert, Nancy E., illus. LC 61-21555. 32p. (gr. k-3). 1965. 11.95 (ISBN 0-394-81059-7); PLB 12.99 (ISBN 0-394-91059-1). Knopf.
Whitfield, Philip & Pope, Joyce. Why Do the Seasons Change? Questions on Nature's Rhythms & Cycles Answered by the Natural History Museum. LC 87-40133. 96p. (ps up). 1987. pap. 16.95 (ISBN 0-670-81860-7). Viking Child Bks.
Wildsmith, Brian. Seasons. (Illus.). 32p. (ps up). 1991. pap. 4.95 (ISBN 0-19-272175-5, 12409). Oxford U Pr.
Worth, Bonnie. Muppet Babies Seasons. 1989. write for info. (ISBN 0-02-689261-8). Checkerboard Pr.

SEASONS–FICTION

Beers, V. Gilbert, text by. Precious Moments Through-the-Year Stories. Butcher, Samuel J., illus. 288p. (gr. 2-6). 1989. 14.95 (ISBN 0-8010-0973-1). Baker Bk.
Blades, Ann. Fall. Blades, Ann, illus. (ps-k). 1990. bds. 4.95 (ISBN 0-688-09232-2). Lothrop.
Borden, Louise. Caps, Hats, Socks, & Mittens. Hoban, Lillian, illus. LC 87-28776. (ps-2). 1989. pap. 11.95 (ISBN 0-590-41257-4). Scholastic Inc.
Charles, Donald. Calico Cat's Year. LC 83-23160. (Illus.). 32p. (ps-3). 1984. lib. bdg. 14.60 (ISBN 0-516-03461-8). Childrens.
De Paola, Tomie. Four Stories for Four Seasons. De Paola, Tomie, illus. LC 76-8837. (ps-3). 1977. PLB 9.95 o. p. (ISBN 0-13-330175-3, Pub. by Treehouse); pap. 3.95 (ISBN 0-13-330100-1). P-H.
DePaola, Tomie. Four Stories for Four Seasons. LC 76-8837. (Illus.). 48p. (ps-2). 1987. PLB 12.95 (ISBN 0-671-66686-X). S&S Trade.
Dupasquier, Philippe. Our House on the Hill. (Illus.). 32p. (ps-3). 1990. pap. 3.95 (ISBN 0-14-054227-2, Puffin). Puffin Bks.
Gibbons, Gail. The Seasons of Arnold's Apple Tree. LC 84-4484. (Illus.). 32p. (ps-3). 1984. 13.95 (ISBN 0-15-271246-1, HJ). HarBraceJ.
Good, Elaine W. Fall Is Here! I Love It! Wenger, Susie S., illus. LC 90-71115. 32p. (ps-1). 1990. text ed. 12.95 (ISBN 1-56148-007-X). Good Bks PA.

Hopkins, Lee B., ed. The Sky Is Full of Song. Zimmer, Dirk, illus. LC 82-48263. 48p. (gr. 3-7). 1983. PLB 13.89 (ISBN 0-06-022583-1). HarpC Child Bks.

Maestro, Betsy & Maestro, Giulio. Through the Year with Harriet. Maestro, Betsy & Maestro, Giulio, illus. LC 84-29339. 32p. (ps-1). 1986. PLB 12.95 (ISBN 0-517-55613-8). Crown.

Meyer, Kathleen A. God Sends the Seasons. McIlrath, James, illus. LC 81-80712. 32p. (ps-2). 1981. 7.50 (ISBN 0-87973-668-2, 668). Our Sunday Visitor.

Patience, John. The Seasons in Fern Hollow. (Illus.). 64p. (ps-1). 2.98 (ISBN 0-517-45857-8). Outlet Bk Co.

Rylant, Cynthia. This Year's Garden. Szilagyi, Mary, illus. LC 86-22224. 32p. (ps-3). 1987. pap. 4.95 (ISBN 0-689-71122-0, Aladdin). Macmillan Child Grp.

Tafuri, Nancy. All Year Long. 32p. (ps-k). 1984. pap. 3.95 (ISBN 0-14-050479-6, Puffin). Puffin Bks.

Tallarico, Tony. Seasons. (Illus.). 12p. (ps). 1982. pap. 3.95 (ISBN 0-89828-301-9). Tuffy Bks.

Wildsmith, Brian. Seasons. Wildsmith, Brian, illus. (ps-3). 1980. 9.95 (ISBN 0-19-279730-1). Oxford U Pr.

Zolotow, Charlotte. Summer Is... Bornstein, Ruth L., illus. LC 82-45185. 32p. (gr. k-4). 1983. 13.95 (ISBN 0-690-04303-1, Crowell Jr Bks); PLB 13.89 (ISBN 0-690-04304-X, Crowell Jr Bks). HarpC Child Bks.

SEASONS–POETRY
Yolen, Jane. Ring of Earth: A Child's Book of Seasons. Wallner, John, illus. LC 86-4800. 32p. (ps-3). 1986. 14.95 (ISBN 0-15-267140-4, HJ). HarBraceJ.

SEATTLE
Bass, Sophie F. Pig-Tail Days in Old Seattle. Clark, Florenz, illus. LC 72-77591. 190p. (gr. 4-6). 1973. 12.50 (ISBN 0-8323-0206-6). Binford Mort.

Loewen, N. Seattle. (Illus.). (gr. 5 up). 1989. lib. bdg. 14.60 (ISBN 0-86592-545-3). Rourke Corp.

Steves, Rick. Kidding Around Seattle: A Young Person's Guide to the City. Meier, Melissa, illus. 64p. (Orig.). (gr. 3 up). 1991. pap. 9.95 (ISBN 0-945465-84-X). John Muir.

SEATTLE–FICTION
Wilbee, Brenda. Sweetbriar Spring. 224p. (Orig.). (gr. 11 up). 1989. pap. 5.99 (ISBN 0-89081-661-1). Harvest Hse.

SEAWEEDS
see Algae

SEX CRIMES
Benedict, Helen. Safe, Strong & Streetwise: The Teenager's Guide to Preventing Sexual Assault. (Illus.). 192p. (gr. 7 up). 1987. 14.95 (ISBN 0-316-08899-4); pap. 5.95 (ISBN 0-87113-100-5). Little.

Gorman, Carol. Pornography. Rosoff, Iris, ed. (Illus.). 144p. (gr. 7 up). 1988. PLB 12.90 (ISBN 0-531-10591-1). Watts.

SECONDARY EDUCATION
see Education, Secondary

SECONDARY SCHOOLS
see Education, Secondary; High Schools

SECRET SERVICE
see also Detectives; Spies;
also names of wars with the subdivision Secret Service, e.g. World War, 1939-1945–Secret Service, etc.
Campbell, Duncan. Secret Service. Franklin Watts Ltd., ed. (Illus.). 32p. (gr. 7-9). 1988. PLB 8.90 (ISBN 0-531-17079-9, Gloucester Pr). Watts.

SECRET WRITING
see Cryptography

SECTS
see also names of churches and sects, e.g. Methodist Church, etc.
Hamilton, Sue. The Death of a Cult Family: Jim Jones. Hamilton, John, ed. (Illus.). 32p. (gr. 4). 1989. PLB 10.95 (ISBN 0-939179-58-X). Abdo & Dghtrs.

Israel, Fred L. The Amish. Moynihan, Daniel P., intro. by. (Illus.). 112p. 1986. lib. bdg. 17.95 (ISBN 0-87754-853-6). Chelsea Hse.

Ross, Terry. Cults. (Illus.). 64p. (gr. 7 up). 1990. lib. bdg. 15.93 (ISBN 0-86593-070-8); lib. bdg. 11.95s.p. (ISBN 0-685-36323-6). Rourke Corp.

Tolan, Stephanie S. A Good Courage. LC 87-31306. 240p. (gr. 7 up). 1988. 12.95 (ISBN 0-688-07446-4). Morrow Jr Bks.

SECURITIES
see also Investments; Stocks

SECURITIES EXCHANGE
see Stock Exchange

SECURITY, INTERNATIONAL
see also Disarmament

SEDITION
see Political Crimes and Offenses; Revolutions

SEEDS
Jennings, Terry. Seeds. Franklin Watts Ltd., ed. Anstey, David, illus. 24p. (gr. k-3). 1988. PLB 10.40 (ISBN 0-531-17087-X, Gloucester Pr). Watts.

—Seeds & Seedlings. LC 88-22890. (Illus.). 32p. (gr. 3-6). 1989. PLB 14.60 (ISBN 0-516-08408-9); pap. 4.95 (ISBN 0-516-48408-7). Childrens.

Jordan, Helene J. Seeds by Wind & Water. Hogner, Nils, illus. LC 62-12820. (gr. k-3). 1962. write for info. (ISBN 0-690-72452-7, Crowell Jr Bks). HarpC Child Bks.

Kuchalla, Susan. All about Seeds. McBee, Jane, illus. LC 81-11480. 32p. (gr. k-2). 1982. lib. bdg. 10.89 (ISBN 0-89375-658-X); pap. 2.95 (ISBN 0-89375-659-8). Troll Assocs.

Lauber, Patricia & Wexler, Jerome. Seeds: Pop, Slick, Glide. (Illus.). 64p. (gr. 2-5). 1987. pap. 4.95 (ISBN 0-517-56348-7). Crown.

Merrill, Claire. A Seed Is a Promise. 1990. pap. 2.50 (ISBN 0-590-43454-3). Scholastic Inc.

Moncure, Jane B. How Seeds Travel: Popguns & Parachutes. Endres, Helen, illus. LC 89-71171. 32p. (ps-2). 1990. lib. bdg. 11.97 (ISBN 0-89565-569-1). Childs World.

Overbeck, Cynthia. How Seeds Travel. LC 81-17217. (Illus.). 48p. (gr. 4 up). 1982. PLB 14.95 (ISBN 0-8225-1474-5). Lerner Pubns.

—How Seeds Travel. Hani, Shabo, photos by. (Illus.). 48p. (gr. 4 up). Repr. of 1982 ed. 5.95g (ISBN 0-8225-9569-9). Lerner Pubns.

Sabin, Louis. Plants, Seeds & Flowers. Moylan, Holly, illus. LC 84-2720. 32p. (gr. 3-6). 1985. PLB 9.49 (ISBN 0-8167-0226-8); pap. text ed. 2.95 (ISBN 0-8167-0227-6). Troll Assocs.

Swartzentruber. God Makes Seeds That Grow. 1976. 2.45 (ISBN 0-686-18182-4). Rod & Staff.

Wexler, Jerome. Flowers Fruits Seeds. LC 86-30616. (Illus.). 32p. (ps-3). 1987. PLB 12.95 (ISBN 0-671-66372-0). S&S Trade.

SEEING EYE DOGS
see Guide Dogs

SEISMOGRAPHY
see Earthquakes

SEISMOLOGY
see Earthquakes

SELF-CONTROL
Conford, Ellen. Seven Days to a Brand-New Me. 120p. (gr. 7 up). 1982. pap. 2.50 (ISBN 0-590-40729-5, Point). Scholastic Inc.

Educational Assessment Publishing Company Staff. Parent - Child Learning Library: Self-Discipline. (Illus.). 32p. (ps). Date not set. text ed. 9.95 (ISBN 0-942277-60-0). Educ Assess Pub.

Erickson, Karen. I'm Brave! Roffey, Maureen, illus. 32p. (ps-k). 1989. pap. 5.95 (ISBN 0-670-82676-6). Viking Child Bks.

MacKenthun, Carole & Dwyer, Paulinus. Self-Control. Filkins, Vanessa, illus. 48p. (gr. 2 up). 1987. pap. 6.95 (ISBN 0-86653-396-6, SS878). Good Apple.

Moser, Adolph J. Don't Pop Your Cork on Mondays! The Children's Anti-Stress Book. Pilkey, Dav, illus. LC 88-13912. 48p. (gr. k up). 1988. lib. bdg. 12.95 (ISBN 0-933849-18-4). Landmark Edns.

Ward, Ruth M. Self Esteem: A Gift from God. (gr. 9 up). 1984. pap. 7.95 (ISBN 0-8010-9664-2). Baker Bk.

SELF-CULTURE
see also Books and Reading
Bold, Mary. How to Improve Your Mind over Summer Vacation. Small, Carol B., illus. 65p. (gr. 4-6). 1987. wkbk. 6.95 (ISBN 0-938267-05-1). Bold Prodns.

Christophersen, Susan & Farr, J. Michael. Knowing Yourself: Learning about Your Skills, Values & Planning Your Life. Croy, Greg, ed. Kreffel, Mike, illus. 64p. (gr. 9-12). 1990. pap. 6.95 (ISBN 0-942784-58-8, JWKM). Jist Works.

Duco, Joyce. Workbook for Self Image Is the Key. LC 89-92547. 26p. (Orig.). (gr. 7-12). 1990. Set. pap. 5.00 (ISBN 0-9612896-2-7). J Duco.

Hooker, Dennis. I Am (Already) Successful: Getting Motivated, Being Me. Holcomb, Ann, ed. Kreffel, Mike, illus. 156p. (gr. 7-12). 1990. pap. 6.95 (ISBN 0-942784-41-3, JWAM); instr's. manual. 32p. 12.95 (ISBN 0-942784-42-1, JAMIG). Jist Works.

Long, Lynellyn D. & Podnecky-Spiegel, Janet. In Print: Beginning Literacy Through Cultural Awareness. (Illus.). 192p. 1988. pap. text ed. 7.32 (ISBN 0-201-12023-2); tchrs., 128 p 7.95 (ISBN 0-201-12024-0). Addison-Wesley.

McGrath, Bob. Me Myself. (Illus.). 48p. (Orig.). 1989. pap. 7.95 incl. audiocassette (ISBN 0-8431-2770-8). Price Stern.

SELF-DEFENSE
see also Boxing; Judo; Karate
Harrington, Anthony P. Every Girl's Judo. (Illus.). (gr. 7 up). 11.95 (ISBN 0-87523-127-6). Emerson.

Mijares, David P. Modern Samurai Training. Mijares, David P., illus. 100p. (Orig.). 1989. pap. 9.95 (ISBN 0-9623400-0-6). Group M Probelications.

Neff, Fred. Basic Self-Defense Manual. Reid, James, illus. LC 75-38473. 56p. (gr. 5 up). 1976. PLB 8.95 (ISBN 0-8225-1152-5). Lerner Pubns.

—Foot-Fighting Manual for Self-Defense & Sport Karate. Reid, James, illus. LC 75-38474. 56p. (gr. 5 up). 1977. PLB 8.95 (ISBN 0-8225-1153-3). Lerner Pubns.

—Hand-Fighting Manual for Self-Defense & Sport Karate. Reid, James, illus. LC 75-38475. 56p. (gr. 5 up). 1977. PLB 8.95 (ISBN 0-8225-1154-1). Lerner Pubns.

—Lessons from the Art of Kempo: Subtle & Effective Self-Defense. Wolfe, Bob & Wolfe, Diane, photos by. (Illus.). 96p. (gr. 5 up). 1987. PLB 9.95 (ISBN 0-8225-1160-6, First Ave Edns); pap. 4.95 (ISBN 0-8225-9532-X, First Ave Edns). Lerner Pubns.

—Lessons from the Samurai: Ancient Self-Defense Strategies & Techniques. Wolfe, Bob & Wolfe, Diane, illus. 96p. (gr. 5 up). 1987. PLB 9.95 (ISBN 0-8225-1161-4, First Ave Edns); pap. 4.95 (ISBN 0-8225-9531-1, First Ave Edns). Lerner Pubns.

—Lessons from the Western Warriors: Dynamic Self-Defense Techniques. Wolfe, Bob & Wolfe, Diane, illus. 96p. (gr. 5 up). 1987. PLB 9.95 (ISBN 0-8225-1159-2, First Ave Edns); pap. 4.95 (ISBN 0-8225-9533-8, First Ave Edns). Lerner Pubns.

—Self-Protection Guide-Book for Girls & Women. Reid, James, illus. LC 75-38477. 56p. (gr. 5 up). 1977. PLB 8.95 (ISBN 0-8225-1156-8). Lerner Pubns.

Pacheco, Joseph B. Martial Arts for the Novice. Gilbert, Eric R., illus. (ENG & SPA.). 120p. (Orig.). (gr. 9-12). 1989. pap. 10.00 (ISBN 0-317-94016-3). Kyo-Sa Pub.

Pfluger, A. Karate: Basic Principles. Kuttner, Paul & Cunningham, Dale S., trs. LC 67-27760. (Illus.). (gr. 8 up). 1969. Repr. of 1967 ed. 6.95 (ISBN 0-8069-4432-3); PLB 7.49 (ISBN 0-8069-4433-1). Sterling.

Reisberg, Ken. Martial Arts. (Illus.). (gr. 4 up). 1979. s&l 10.40 (ISBN 0-531-04077-1). Watts.

SELF-GOVERNMENT
see Democracy

SELF-INSTRUCTION
see Self-Culture

Barker, Shane R. Finding a Friend in the Mirror. LC 88-21743. viii, 113p. (gr. 7-12). 1988. 8.95 (ISBN 0-87579-178-6). Deseret Bk.

SELF-RESPECT
Anderson, Lisa. Proud to Be Me, Peewee Platypus. Messer, Cathy, illus. 40p. (Orig.). (ps-4). 1990. pap. 12.95 (ISBN 0-9628323-0-8). Ridge Enter.

Dembrowsky, Constance H. Self Esteem. 371p. (Orig.). (gr. 6-9). 1983. pap. 7.95 wkbk. (ISBN 0-924609-01-X); tchr's. ed. 129.00 (ISBN 0-924609-00-1); parent's wkbk. 5.95 (ISBN 0-924609-03-6). Affect Skill.

Educational Assessment Publishing Company Staff. Parent - Child Learning Library: Self-Esteem. (Illus.). 40p. Date not set. text ed. 9.95 (ISBN 0-942277-53-8). Educ Assess Pub.

—Parent - Child Learning Library: Self-Esteem English Big Book. (Illus.). 40p. (gr. k-3). Date not set. text ed. 28.50 (ISBN 0-942277-46-5). Educ Assess Pub.

—Parent - Child Learning Library: Self-Esteem Spanish Big Book. (SPA., Illus.). 40p. (gr. k-3). Date not set. text ed. 28.50 (ISBN 0-942277-47-3). Educ Assess Pub.

—Parent - Child Learning Library: Self-Esteem Spanish Edition. (SPA.). 40p. (ps). Date not set. text ed. 9.95 (ISBN 0-942277-89-9). Educ Assess Pub.

—Parent - Child Learning Library: Your Uniqueness. (SPA., Illus.). 32p. (gr. k-3). Date not set. text ed. 28.50 (ISBN 0-942277-80-5). Educ Assess Pub.

—Parent - Child Learning Library: Your Uniqueness. (Illus.). 32p. (ps-k). Date not set. text ed. write for info. (ISBN 0-942277-63-5). Educ Assess Pub.

—Parent - Child Learning Library: Your Uniqueness English Big Book. (Illus.). 32p. (gr. k-3). Date not set. text ed. 28.50 (ISBN 0-942277-79-1). Educ Assess Pub.

—Parent - Child Learning Library: Your Uniqueness Spanish Edition. (SPA.). 32p. (ps). Date not set. text ed. 9.95 (ISBN 0-942277-95-3). Educ Assess Pub.

Espeland, Pamela & Wallner, Rosemary. Making the Most of Today: Daily Readings for Young People on Self-Awareness, Creativity & Self-Esteem. 380p. (Orig.). (gr. 6 up). 1991. pap. 8.95 (ISBN 0-915793-33-4). Free Spirit Pub.

Johnson, Julie T. Celebrate You: Building Your Self-Esteem. 72p. (gr. 5 up). 1990. PLB 11.95 (ISBN 0-8225-0046-9). Lerner Pubns.

Kramer, Patricia. Discovering Self-Confidence. (gr. 7-12). 1991. PLB 14.95 (ISBN 0-8239-1275-2). Rosen Group.

McAllister, Dawson. Self Esteem & Loneliness. Lamb, Jim, illus. (gr. 5-12). 1989. pap. 3.95 (ISBN 0-923417-02-8). Shepherd Minst.
—Student Conference Follow-Up Manual. Lamb, Jim, illus. (gr. 5-12). 1989. pap. 2.95 (ISBN 0-923417-10-9). Shepherd Minst.
McFarland, Rhoda. Coping Through Self-Esteem. Rosen, Ruth, ed. (gr. 7 up). 1988. lib. bdg. 12.95 (ISBN 0-8239-0790-2). Rosen Group.
—Coping with Stigma. Rosen, Ruth, ed. (gr. 7-12). 1989. PLB 12.95 (ISBN 0-8239-0998-0). Rosen Group.
Moser, Adolph. Don't Feed the Monster on Tuesdays! The Children's Self-Esteem Book. Thatch, Nancy R., ed. Melton, David, illus. Moser, Adolph, intro. by. (Illus.). 55p. (gr. k-12). 1991. PLB 12.95 (ISBN 0-933849-38-9). Landmark Edns.
Phillips, Ron & Brewer, Dan. Gem of the First Water: A Recovery Process for Troubled Teenagers. Stavrianoudakis, John, illus. LC 90-37990. 229p. (Orig.). (gr. 8-12). 1990. pap. 14.95 (ISBN 0-89390-181-4). Resource Pubns.
Rudner, Barry. The Bumblebee & the Ram. Fahsbender, Thomas, illus. LC 89-81585. 32p. (Orig.). 1989. pap. 4.95 (ISBN 0-925928-03-8). Tiny Thought.
Self-Esteem. (Illus.). 32p. (gr. 5 up). 1989. lib. bdg. 14.00 (ISBN 0-86625-288-6). Rourke Corp.
Trzcinski, Betty. All about Me, Myself & I: Blackline Masters Book. 80p. (Orig.). (gr. 3-6). 1989. tchr's. ed. 8.50 (ISBN 0-87879-863-3, High Noon Books). Acad Therapy.

SELLING

see Salesmen and Salesmanship

SEMANTICS

see also Words, New

Herman, Ethel & Everett, Karen H. Grammar-Semantics for Teens. (gr. 7-12). 1989. spiral wkbk. 49.90 (ISBN 1-55999-043-0). LinguiSystems.
—Semantics for Teens. (gr. 5-12). 1989. spiral wkbk. 24.95 (ISBN 1-55999-070-8). LinguiSystems.
Keffer, Christine & Long, Carolyn. Semantic Fitness. (gr. 8 up). 1986. spiral reproducible wkbk. 29.95 (ISBN 1-55999-069-4). LinguiSystems.
Tavzel, Carolyn. Blooming Holidays. (ps-5). 1989. pap. 13.95 (ISBN 1-55999-025-2). LinguiSystems.

SENATORS–U. S.

see U. S. Congress

SENEGAL

Department of Geography, Lerner Publications. Senegal in Pictures. (Illus.). 64p. (gr. 5 up). 1988. 12.95 (ISBN 0-8225-1827-9). Lerner Pubns.

SENSES AND SENSATION

see also Color Sense; Hearing; Smell; Touch; Vision

Aliki. My Five Senses. 228 ed. Aliki, illus. LC 88-853500. (gr. k-3). 1989. PLB 12.95 (ISBN 0-685-02100-9, Crowell Jr Bks); PLB 13.89 (ISBN 0-690-04794-0). HarpC Child Bks.
—My Five Senses. rev. ed. LC 88-35350. (Illus.). 32p. (gr. 1-3). 1989. pap. 4.50 (ISBN 0-06-445083-X, Trophy). HarpC Child Bks.
—My Five Senses. rev. ed. Aliki, illus. LC 88-35350. 32p. (ps-1). 1991. 19.95 (ISBN 0-06-020050-2). HarpC Child Bks.
Allington, Richard L. & Krull, Kathleen. Tasting. Spangler, Noel, illus. LC 79-29662. 32p. (gr. k-3). 1985. PLB 15.33 (ISBN 0-8172-1292-2); pap. 9.27 (ISBN 0-8172-2493-9). Raintree Pubs.
Bailey, Donna. All about Your Senses. LC 90-10051. (Illus.). 48p. (gr. 2-5). 1990. PLB 15.96 (ISBN 0-8114-2776-5). Steck-V.
Berry, Joy W. Teach Me about Tasting. Dickey, Kate, ed. LC 85-45088. (Illus.). 36p. (ps). 1986. 4.98 (ISBN 0-685-10727-2). Grolier Inc.
Brandt, Keith. Five Senses. Green, Gloria, illus. LC 84-2633. 32p. (gr. 3-6). 1985. PLB 9.49 (ISBN 0-8167-0168-7); pap. text ed. 2.95 (ISBN 0-8167-0169-5). Troll Assocs.
Broekel, Ray. Tus Cinco Sentidos. LC 84-7603. (SPA.). 48p. (gr. k-4). 1987. PLB 14.60 (ISBN 0-516-31932-9); pap. 4.95 (ISBN 0-516-51932-8). Childrens.
—Your Five Senses. LC 84-7603. (Illus.). 48p. (gr. k-4). 1984. lib. bdg. 14.60 (ISBN 0-516-01932-5); pap. 4.95 (ISBN 0-516-41932-3). Childrens.
Carratello, Patricia & Carratello, John. Let's Investigate the Senses. Chacon, Rick, illus. 48p. (gr. 1-4). 1984. wkbk. 5.95 (ISBN 1-55734-213-X). Tchr Create Mat.
Crowdy, Deborah. Let's Take a Walk in the Park. Axeman, Lois, illus. LC 86-17598. 32p. (ps-2). 1986. lib. bdg. 11.97 (ISBN 0-89565-357-5). Childs World.
DeBruin, Jerry. Young Scientists Explore: The Five Senses. Czerniak, Charlene, illus. 32p. (gr. 4 up). 1983. wkbk. 4.95 (ISBN 0-86653-114-9, GA 455). Good Apple.
The Five Senses. 48p. (gr. 5-8). 1988. PLB 12.98 (ISBN 0-382-09707-6); 9.74s.p. (ISBN 0-685-24614-0). Silver Burdett Pr.
Gardner, Karen A. My Life As an Ear. rev. ed. (Illus.). 37p. (ps-2). Set of 1-4. PLB 1.70 (ISBN 0-931421-01-2). Hlth Pub SF.
Gaskin, John. The Senses. LC 84-52328. (Illus.). 32p. (gr. 1-6). 1985. PLB 11.90 (ISBN 0-531-10051-0). Watts.
Holt, Pat. Gideon: God's Warrior. Brown, David S., illus. 32p. (gr. 1-6). 1986. 0.50 (ISBN 0-687-14220-2). Abingdon.
Hoover, Rosalie & Murphy, Barbara. Learning about Our Five Senses. 64p. (gr. k-3). 1981. 6.95 (ISBN 0-86653-013-4, GA 241). Good Apple.
Kahn, Peggy. Did You Ever Pet a Care Bear? Barto, Bobbi, illus. LC 83-60323. 14p. (ps-k). 1983. 6.95 (ISBN 0-394-86087-X). Random.
Kohl, Judith & Kohl, Herbert. The View from the Oak. Bayless, Roger, illus. 112p. (gr. 5 up). 1988. 13.95 (ISBN 0-316-50137-9). Little.
Littler, Angela. What Can You See. Galvani, Maureen & Littler, Angela, illus. 20p. (ps-1). 1988. 3.95 (ISBN 0-671-67228-2). Messner.
Martin, Paul D. Messengers to the Brain: Your Fantastic Five Senses. Crump, Donald J., ed. LC 82-45636. 104p. (gr. 3-8). 1984. 6.95 (ISBN 0-87044-499-9); PLB 8.50 (ISBN 0-87044-504-9). Natl Geog.
Micallef, Mary. Listening: The Basic Connection. Micallef, Mary, illus. 96p. (gr. 3-8). wkbk. 8.95 (ISBN 0-86653-188-2, GA 555). Good Apple.
Moncure, Jane B. The Five Senses: Treasures Outside. Axeman, Lois, illus. LC 90-30635. 32p. (ps-2). 1990. lib. bdg. 11.97 (ISBN 0-89565-575-6). Childs World.
—A Tasting Party. Axeman, Lois, illus. LC 82-4411. 32p. (ps-3). 1982. PLB 14.60 (ISBN 0-516-03253-4); pap. 3.95 (ISBN 0-516-43253-2). Childrens.
O'Connor, Karen. Let's Take a Walk on the Beach. Axeman, Lois, illus. LC 86-9551. 32p. (ps-2). 1986. lib. bdg. 11.97 (ISBN 0-89565-354-0). Childs World.
O'Connor, Karen & Crowdy, Deborah. Let's Take a Walk in the City. Axeman, Lois, illus. LC 86-20746. 32p. (ps-2). 1986. lib. bdg. 11.97 (ISBN 0-89565-355-9). Childs World.
Parker, Steve. Learning a Lesson: How You See, Think & Remember. (Illus.). 32p. (gr. k-4). 1991. PLB 11.40 (ISBN 0-531-14087-3). Watts.
—Nerves to Senses: Projects with Biology. (Illus.). 32p. (gr. 5-8). 1991. PLB 11.90 (ISBN 0-531-17295-3, Gloucester Pr). Watts.
—Touch, Taste & Smell. rev. ed. Mayron-Parker, Alan, contrib. by. (Illus.). 48p. (gr. 5-6). 1989. PLB 12.90 (ISBN 0-531-10655-1). Watts.
—Touch, Taste & Smell. rev. ed. (Illus.). 48p. (gr. 5 up). 1991. pap. 4.95 (ISBN 0-531-24607-8). Watts.
Parramon, J. M. & Puig, J. J. Taste. Rius, Maria, illus. 32p. (ps). 1985. pap. 4.95 (ISBN 0-8120-3566-6); Span. ed. pap. 4.95 (ISBN 0-8120-3608-5). Barron.
Parramon, J. M., et al. Five Senses, 5 bks. (ps). 1985. pap. 29.95 boxed set (ISBN 0-8120-7365-7). Barron.
Petty, Kate. What's That Taste? Kopper, Lisa, illus. 24p. (gr. 1-3). 1986. PLB 7.79 (ISBN 0-531-10258-0). Watts.
Pluckrose, Henry. Fingers & Feelers. (Illus.). 32p. (gr. k-4). 1990. PLB 10.40 (ISBN 0-531-14050-4). Watts.
—Tongues & Tasters. (Illus.). 32p. (gr. k-4). 1990. PLB 10.40 (ISBN 0-531-14049-0). Watts.
—Touching. Fairclough, Chris, photos by. 32p. (gr. k-3). 1986. lib. bdg. 7.99 (ISBN 0-531-10174-6). Watts.
Richardson, Joy. What Happens When You Touch & Feel? LC 86-3679. (Illus.). 32p. (gr. 2-3). 1986. PLB 10.95 (ISBN 1-55532-114-3). Gareth Stevens Inc.
Showers, Paul. In the Night. Keats, Ezra J., illus. LC 61-6138. 40p. (gr. k-3). 1961. PLB 13.89 (ISBN 0-690-44621-7, Crowell Jr Bks). HarpC Child Bks.
—Listening Walk. Aliki, illus. LC 61-10495. 40p. (gr. k-3). 1961. PLB 13.89 (ISBN 0-690-49663-X, Crowell Jr Bks). HarpC Child Bks.
Smith, Kathie B. & Crenson, Victoria. Tasting. LC 87-5884. (Illus.). 24p. (gr. k-3). 1987. PLB 9.59 (ISBN 0-8167-1014-7); pap. text ed. 1.95 (ISBN 0-8167-1015-5). Troll Assocs.
Smith, Kathie B. & Crenson, Victoria E. Rand McNally Question Books: The Senses. Storms, Robert S., illus. Incl. Seeing (ISBN 0-528-87152-8); Hearing (ISBN 0-528-87151-X); Thinking (ISBN 0-528-87154-4); Tasting (ISBN 0-528-87149-8); Smelling (ISBN 0-528-87153-6). (Illus.). 24p. (Orig.). (gr. k-3). 1986. pap. write for info. Macmillan.
Talbot, Mary. The Senses. (Illus.). (gr. 6-12). 1990. 18.95 (ISBN 0-7910-0027-3). Chelsea Hse.
Van Der Meer, Ron & Van Der Meer, Atie. Your Amazing Senses: Thirty-Six Games, Puzzles & Tricks to Show How Your Senses Work. Van Der Meer, Ron & Van Der Meer, Atie, illus. 12p. (gr. 4-7). 1987. pap. 9.95 (ISBN 0-689-71184-0, Aladdin). Macmillan Child Grp.
Ward, Brian. Touch, Taste & Smell. LC 82-50058. (Illus.). 48p. (gr. 4 up). 1982. PLB 12.40 (ISBN 0-531-04460-2). Watts.
Wood, Nicholas. Touch...What Do You Feel? Willey, Lynne, illus. LC 90-10925. 32p. (gr. k-3). 1990. PLB 10.89 (ISBN 0-8167-2126-2); pap. text ed. 2.95 (ISBN 0-8167-2127-0). Troll Assocs.
Ziefert, Harriet. What Do I Taste: The Five Senses. Smith, Mavis, illus. (ps-1). 1988. pap. 3.95 (ISBN 0-317-69282-8). Bantam.

SEPARATION (LAW)

see Divorce

SEQUOIA NATIONAL PARK

McCormick, Maxine. Sequoia & Kings Canyon. LC 88-20214. (Illus.). 48p. (gr. 4-5). 1988. 12.95 (ISBN 0-89686-409-X, Crestwood Hse). Macmillan Child Grp.

SEQUOYA, CHEROKEE INDIAN, 1700?-1843

Cwiklik, Robert. Sequoia. Furstinger, Nancy, ed. (Illus.). 142p. (gr. 5-7). 1989. PLB 12.98 (ISBN 0-382-09570-7); pap. 7.95 (ISBN 0-382-09759-9). Silver Burdett Pr.
Oppenheim, Joanne. Sequoyah, Cherokee Hero. new ed. LC 78-60117. (Illus.). 48p. (gr. 4-6). 1979. PLB 9.89 (ISBN 0-89375-159-6); pap. 2.95 (ISBN 0-89375-149-9). Troll Assocs.
Wheeler, Jill. The Story of Sequoyah. Deegan, Paul, ed. Dodson, Liz, illus. 32p. (gr. 4). 1989. PLB 11.95 (ISBN 0-939179-70-9). Abdo & Dghtrs.

SERIALS

see Periodicals

SERMON ON THE MOUNT

Coleman, Sheila S. Be Happy Attitudes for Children. Plunkett, Mark, ed. Ham, John & Willis, Diane, illus. 32p. (gr. 1 up). 1988. wkbk. 1.95 (ISBN 0-87403-509-0, 2819). Standard Pub.
Gonsalves, Carol. Sermon on the Mountain. (gr. k-4). 1981. pap. 1.39 (ISBN 0-570-06149-0, 59-1304). Concordia.

SERMONS

Benjamin, Don-Paul & Miner, Ron. Come Sit with Me Again: Sermons for Children. LC 86-30588. (Illus.). 128p. (Orig.). 1987. pap. 7.95 (ISBN 0-8298-0748-9). Pilgrim NY.
Cross, Luther. Object Lessons for Children. (Illus., Orig.). (gr. 2-5). 1967. pap. 4.95 (ISBN 0-8010-2315-7). Baker Bk.
Metcalf, Calvin S. Voices from the Bible: Dramatic Monologs in Worship. LC 90-53277. (Illus.). 144p. (Orig.). 1990. pap. 9.95 (ISBN 0-916260-70-4, B173). Meriwether Pub.
O'Connor, Francine M. The ABC's Lessons of Love: Sermon on the Mount for Children. Boswell, Kathryr, tr. (Illus.). 48p. (gr. 6-8). 1991. pap. text ed. 3.95 (ISBN 0-89243-345-0). Liguori Pubns.
Steindam, Harold. Growing Together: Sermons for Children. Heck, J. Parker, illus. LC 88-28718. 136p. (Orig.). 1989. pap. 8.95 (ISBN 0-8298-0800-0). Pilgrim NY.
Weisheit, E. Sixty-One Worship Talks for Children. rev. ed. LC 68-20728. (gr. 3-6). 1975. pap. 6.95 (ISBN 0-570-03714-X, 12-2616). Concordia.

SERPENTS

see Snakes

SERRA, JUNIPERO, 1713-1784

Duque, Sarah. Sally & Fr. Serra. (Illus.). 104p. (gr. 4-8). 1987. 9.95 (ISBN 0-89505-504-X). Tabor Pub.
Junipero Serra. (Illus.). 112p. (gr. 5 up). 1992. PLB 17.95 (ISBN 0-7910-1255-7). Chelsea Hse.

SERVICE STATIONS, AUTOMOBILE

see Automobiles–Service Stations

SET THEORY

see also Arithmetic; Numbers Theory

Oliver, Stephen, photos by. Sorting. LC 90-8575. (Illus.). 24p. (ps-k). 1991. 6.95 (ISBN 0-679-81162-1). Random.

SETS (MATHEMATICS)

see Set Theory

SEVEN WONDERS OF THE WORLD

McLeish, Kenneth. The Seven Wonders of the World. 32p. (gr. 4-7). 1986. 12.95 (ISBN 0-521-26538-X). Cambridge U Pr.

SEWAGE DISPOSAL

see also Refuse and Refuse Disposal; Water–Pollution

Miller, Christina G. & Berry, Louise A. Wastes. 72p. (gr. 4-9). 1986. lib. bdg. 10.40 (ISBN 0-531-10130-4). Watts.

SEWING

see also Dressmaking; Embroidery; Needlework

Arrants, Cheryl & Arrants, Dennis. Thimbelina & the Notion Parade. Arrants, Cheryl & Arrants, Dennis, illus. 32p. (Orig.). (gr. k-4). 1983. pap. text ed. 2.50 (ISBN 0-943704-03-0). Arrants & Assoc.
Bradley, Duane. Design It, Sew It, & Wear It: How to Make Yourself a Super Wardrobe Without Commercial Patterns. Corwin, Judith H., illus. LC 76-55732. (gr. 7 up). 1979. write for info. (ISBN 0-690-01297-7, Crowell Jr Bks); PLB 12.89 (ISBN 0-690-03839-9). HarpC Child Bks.
Cherry, Winky. My First Machine Sewing Book. Cherry, Winky, illus. 40p. (Orig.). (gr. 2 up). 1989. pap. 12.00 (ISBN 0-317-93839-8). ITS Pub.
—My First Sewing Book. Cherry, Winky, illus. 40p. (Orig.). (ps-6). 1984. pap. 10.00 (ISBN 0-317-93840-1). ITS Pub.
Coleman, Anne. Fabrics & Yarns. (Illus.). 32p. (gr. 2-6). 1990. lib. bdg. 13.26 (ISBN 0-86592-483-X); lib. bdg. 9.95s.p. Rourke Corp.
Gong, Linda & Echaore-Yoon, Susan. Basic Sewing. Kirk, Nancy, illus. 80p. (gr. 7-12). 1989. 19.95 (ISBN 0-88102-109-1); 3-ring binder 5.95 (ISBN 0-88102-110-5). Janus Bks.
Grogg, Evelyn. Kindergarten Pattern Book. Eberle, Sarah, rev. by. Greene, Tom, illus. 48p. (Orig.). (gr. k). 1981. pap. 5.95 (ISBN 0-87239-431-X, 2159). Standard Pub.
Hornnes, Esther & Magos, Eunice. Sew & Know: Puppet Projects to Teach Beginning Sounds. Sussman, Ellen, ed. Rundell, Wendi S., illus. 32p. (Orig.). (gr. k-1). 1982. pap. 4.95 (ISBN 0-933606-16-8, MS-614). Monkey Sisters.
Lawler, T. Sewing & Knitting. (Illus.). 64p. (gr. 5 up). Date not set. pap. 2.95 (ISBN 0-86020-311-5, Usborne). EDC.
Pyman, Kit, ed. Every Kind of Smocking. Messent, Jan, et al, illus. 126p. (Orig.). 1989. pap. 16.95 (ISBN 0-85532-632-8, Pub. by Search Pr UK). A Schwartz & Co.
Siegel, Beatrice. The Sewing Machine. LC 83-40397. 64p. (gr. 5 up). 1984. PLB 10.85 (ISBN 0-8027-6532-7). Walker & Co.
Wood, Marina. Crayon Creations. Wood, Marina, illus. 40p. (Orig.). (gr. 4-8). 1984. pap. 6.00 (ISBN 0-932946-12-7). Burdett CA.

SEX
see also Reproduction;
also headings beginning with the word Sexual

Bender, David L. & Leone, Bruno, eds. Human Sexuality Annual, 1989. 144p. (gr. 10 up). 1989. pap. text ed. 5.45 (ISBN 0-89908-549-0). Greenhaven.
—Male-Female Roles. 400p. (gr. 10 up). 1988. PLB 19.95 (ISBN 0-89908-534-2). Greenhaven.
Eager, George B. Love, Dating & Sex: What Teens Want to Know. Philbrook, Diana, illus. 208p. (Orig.). (gr. 6-12). 1989. pap. text ed. 9.95 (ISBN 0-9603752-8-7). Mailbox.
Fox, F. Earle. Biblical Sexuality & the Battle for Science. LC 88-80409. 208p. (Orig.). (gr. 9-12). 1988. pap. 5.45 (ISBN 0-945778-00-7). Emmaus Ministries.
Gittelsohn, Roland B. Love in Your Life: A Jewish View of Teenage Sexuality. (gr. 7-9). 1991. pap. 9.95 (ISBN 0-8074-0460-8, 142685). UAHC.
Hebert, Marie-Francine. The Stork Didn't Bring Me... Labrosse, Darcia, illus. (gr. k-7). 1988. Incl. one bk., one game, & one guide for parents. 12.95 (ISBN 0-88166-151-1, Dist. by Simon & Schuster). Meadowbrook.
Heron, Ann, ed. One Teenager in Ten: Writings by Gay & Lesbian Youth. 120p. (gr. 7-12). 1983. pap. 3.95 (ISBN 0-932870-26-0). Alyson Pubns.
Hunt, Morton. The Young Person's Guide to Love. LC 75-28371. 181p. (gr. 5 up). 1975. 12.95 (ISBN 0-374-38757-5). FS&G.
Hurst, Hugo. A Search for Meaning in Love, Sex, & Marriage. rev. ed. LC 75-9961. 234p. (gr. 11-12). 1975. pap. text ed. 6.50x (ISBN 0-88489-063-5); teaching manual 3.00x (ISBN 0-88489-119-4). St. Marys.
Hyde, Margaret O. Teen Sex. LC 88-101. 120p. (gr. 7-12). 1988. 9.95 (ISBN 0-664-32726-5, Westminster). Westminster John Knox.
Johnson, Kathryn T. & Balczon, Mary-Lynne J. The Sexual Dictionary: Terms & Expressions for Teens & Parents. Goodman, Frances B., ed. Johnson, Kathryn T., illus. 192p. 1991. pap. 12.95 (ISBN 0-89896-400-8). Larksdale.
Lawson, Michael & Skipp, David. Sexo y Mas: Guia Para la Juventud. (SPA., Illus.). 110p. (Orig.). (gr. 10-12). 1988. pap. 2.95 (ISBN 0-945792-02-6). Editorial Unilit.
Mast, Coleen K. Sex Respect: The Option of True Sexual Freedom: A Public Health Manual for Teachers. Evans, Wendy M. & Evans, Dolly B., illus. 61p. (Orig.). (gr. 7-9). 1986. pap. 12.95 (ISBN 0-945745-00-1). Respect Inc.
—Sex Respect: The Option of True Sexual Freedom: A Public Health Guide for Parents. Evans, Wendy M. & Evans, Dolly B., illus. 61p. (Orig.). (gr. 7-9). 1986. pap. text ed. 8.95 (ISBN 0-945745-01-X). Respect Inc.
—Sex Respect: The Option of True Sexual Freedom: A Public Health Workbook for Students. Evans, Wendy M. & Evans, Dolly B., illus. 61p. (Orig.). (gr. 7-9). 1986. pap. text ed. 7.95 (ISBN 0-945745-02-8). Respect Inc.
Melton, Tom. Sex from the Inside Out. Urschel, Judy, ed. Grounds, Vernon, frwd. by. (Orig.). (gr. 9-12). 1990. pap. text ed. 5.95 (ISBN 0-9625679-0-6). JTM Pr.
Nourse, Alan E. Teen Guide to Safe Sex. 1990. pap. 4.95 (ISBN 0-531-15211-1). Watts.
O'Neill, Terry & Bernards, Neal, eds. Male-Female Roles: Opposing Viewpoints. LC 89-23419. (Illus.). 261p. (gr. 10 up). 1989. lib. bdg. 15.95 (ISBN 0-89908-446-X); pap. 8.95 (ISBN 0-89908-421-4). Greenhaven.
Orr, Lisa, ed. Sexual Values: Opposing Viewpoints. LC 89-36527. (Illus.). 214p. (gr. 10 up). 1989. lib. bdg. 15.95 (ISBN 0-89908-445-1); pap. 8.95 (ISBN 0-89908-420-6). Greenhaven.
Polish, Daniel F., et al. Drug, Sex, & Integrity: What Does Judaism Say? Diaz, Jose, illus. (gr. 7-9). 1991. pap. 10.00 (ISBN 0-8074-0459-4, 168505). UAHC.
Sciacca, Fran & Sciacca, Jill. Sex: When to Say Yes. 1987. pap. 3.95 (ISBN 0-89066-099-9). World Wide Pubs.
Speck, Greg. Sex: It's Worth Waiting For. Hillam, Corbin A., illus. (Orig.). 1989. pap. 6.95 (ISBN 0-8024-7692-9). Moody.

SEX INSTRUCTION

Ameiss, Bill & Graver, Jane. Love, Sex & God. 128p. (gr. 9 up). pap. 7.95 (ISBN 0-570-08485-7, 14-1625). Concordia.
Bausch, William J. Becoming a Man: Basic Information, Guidance, & Attitudes on Sex for Boys. LC 87-51569. 324p. (Orig.). (gr. 5-12). 1988. pap. 9.95 (ISBN 0-89622-357-4). Twenty Third.
Bimler, Rich, illus. Sex & the New You. 64p. (gr. 6-9). pap. 7.95 (ISBN 0-570-08484-9, 14-1624). Concordia.
Blank, Joani. Playbook for Kids About Sex. Costanzo, Lana, illus. 56p. (gr. 2-6). 1980. pap. 5.00 (ISBN 0-9602324-6-X, Yes Pr). Down There Pr.
Bleich, Alan R. Coping with Health Risks & Risky Behavior. Rosen, Roger, ed. (gr. 7-12). 1990. lib. bdg. 12.95 (ISBN 0-8239-1072-5). Rosen Group.
Cole, Joanna. Asking about Sex & Growing Up: A Question-&-Answer Book for Boys & Girls. Tiegreen, Alan, illus. LC 87-26140. 96p. (gr. 3-7). 1988. 12.95 (ISBN 0-688-06927-4); pap. 4.95 (ISBN 0-688-06928-2, Pub. by Beech Tree Bks). Morrow Jr Bks.
—How You Were Born. LC 83-17314. (Illus.). 48p. (ps-3). 1984. 12.95 (ISBN 0-688-01710-X); lib. bdg. 12.88 (ISBN 0-688-01709-6, Morrow Jr Bks); pap. 4.95 (ISBN 0-685-08263-6, Mulberry Bks). Morrow Jr Bks.
Crawford, Kenneth & Simmons, Paul. Growing up with Sex. 80p. (gr. 7-9). 1973. pap. 6.95 (ISBN 0-8054-5312-1). Broadman.
Dawson, Barbara & Feibelman, Barbara. Sexuality Education: A Family Life Education Curriculum for Parents & Young Adolescents. LC 84-61333. 105p. (Orig.). (gr. 4-8). 1984. pap. 9.45 (ISBN 0-934586-14-4). Plan Parent.
Eager, George B. Love, Dating & Sex: What Teens Want to Know. Philbrook, Diana, illus. 208p. (gr. 6 up). 1989. PLB 12.95g (ISBN 0-9603752-9-5). Mailbox.
Edens, David. The Changing Me. 48p. (gr. 4-6). 1991. pap. 9.95 (ISBN 0-8054-4411-4). Broadman.
Elgin, Kathleen & Osterritter, John F. Twenty-Eight Days. LC 73-77779. (Illus.). 64p. (gr. 5 up). 1973. pap. 5.95 (ISBN 0-679-51382-5). McKay.
Family Life Education: Understanding Human Sexuality. (gr. 5-7). 1989. 29.00 (ISBN 1-877844-14-4, 2058). Meridian Educ.
Fiedler, Jean & Fiedler, Hal. Be Smart about Sex: Facts for Young People. LC 89-7919. (Illus.). 128p. (gr. 6 up). 1990. lib. bdg. 17.95 (ISBN 0-89490-168-0). Enslow Pubs.
Fox, Robert J. The Gift of Sexuality: A Guide for Young People. LC 88-63528. (Orig.). (gr. 9 up). 1989. pap. 7.95 (ISBN 0-87973-425-6, 425). Our Sunday Visitor.
Gitchel, Sam & Foster, Lorri. Let's Talk about...S-E-X: A Read & Discuss Guide for People 9 to 12 & Their Parents. Cooper, Andrea, illus. 59p. (gr. 4-8). 1983. pap. 4.95 (ISBN 0-9610122-0-X). Plan Par Ctrl CA.
Gordon, Sol. Protect Yourself from Becoming an Unwanted Parent. (Illus., Orig.). (gr. 9-12). 1983. pap. 1.95 (ISBN 0-934978-08-5). Ed U Pr.
Gordon, Sol & Cohen, Judith. Did the Sun Shine Before You Were Born: A Sex Education Primer. LC 74-82733. (ps-2). 1974. 6.95 (ISBN 0-89388-179-1). Okpaku Communications.
Gordon, Sol & Gordon, Judith. Did the Sun Shine Before You Were Born? A Sex Education Primer. (ps-3). 1982. pap. 7.95 (ISBN 0-934978-03-4). Ed-U Pr.
Graver, Jane. How You Are Changing. 64p. (gr. 3-6). 7.95 (ISBN 0-570-08483-0, 14-1623). Concordia.
Greene, Carol. Why Boys & Girls Are Different. 32p. (ps up). 6.95 (ISBN 0-570-08481-4, 14-1621). Concordia.
Griffin, Glen C. Not about Birds. Darley, Heidi, illus. LC 79-16653. 72p. (gr. 6-8). 1979. 5.95 (ISBN 0-87747-753-1). Deseret Bk.
—You Were Smaller Than a Dot. LC 72-90685. 31p. (gr. k-6). 1980. pap. 4.95 (ISBN 0-87747-817-1). Deseret Bk.
Hoch, Dean & Hoch, Nancy. The Sex Education Dictionary for Today's Teens & Preteens. Severe, Camille H., illus. LC 89-63577. 128p. (Orig.). (gr. 5-12). 1990. pap. 12.95 (ISBN 0-9624209-0-5). Landmark ID.
Hummel, Ruth. Where Do Babies Come From? 32p. (gr. 1-3). 6.95 (ISBN 0-570-08482-2, 14-1622). Concordia.
Jakobson, Cathryn. Teenage Pregnancy. rev. ed. 160p. (gr. 7 up). 1991. PLB 15.85 (ISBN 0-8027-8128-4); pap. 8.95 (ISBN 0-8027-7372-9). Walker & Co.
Jensen, Gordon D., et al. Human Sexuality. Head, J. J., ed. Botzis, Ka, et al, illus. LC 87-83058. 100p. (gr. 10 up). 1987. pap. text ed. 9.95 (ISBN 0-89278-091-6, 45-9591). Carolina Biological.
Johnson, Eric. Love & Sex in Plain Language. rev. ed. Mudd, Emily, intro. by. LC 84-48170. 160p. 1985. 15.95i (ISBN 0-06-015418-7, HarpT). HarperCollins.
Johnson, Eric W. People, Love, Sex & Families. Wool, David, illus. 144p. (gr. 4 up). 1985. PLB 14.85 (ISBN 0-8027-6605-6). Walker & Co.

Koch, Janice. Our Baby: A Birth & Adoption Story. Goldberg, Pat, illus. LC 85-6392. 27p. (ps-2). 1985. 10.95 (ISBN 0-9609504-3-5). Perspect Indiana.
A sex education book designed specifically for children who were adopted as babies into two parent families. Using correct anatomical terminology, the author, a science educator & adoptive parent, introduces the very young adoptee to the idea that there are two ways for grown ups to become parents: by birth & by adoption. In a format designed to be personalized with snapshots & words for an individual child it is explained that he was conceived by & born to birthparents & then adopted into a loving family who anticipated his arrival with excitement. Well reviewed in all adoption periodicals as well as by PARENT'S magazine & Planned Parenthood. Other adoption related children's books from Perspectives Press include Jane Schnitter's WILLIAM IS MY BROTHER (family built by birth & adoption), Anne Brodzinsky's THE MULBERRY BIRD (a birthmother's viewpoint), Ann Angel's REAL FOR SURE SISTER (transracial adoption); Susan Gabel's WHERE THE SUN KISSES THE SEA (international placement), & Susan Gabel's FILLING IN THE BLANKS: A GUIDED LOOK AT GROWING UP ADOPTED (adolescence). Distributed by Ingram, Baker & Taylor or contact the publisher at (317) 872-3055.
Publisher Provided Annotation.

Lena, Daniel S. & Howard, Marie. Hands off... I'm Special! How to Tell Your Boyfriend No. Bartimole, John, ed. (Illus.). 96p. (Orig.). (gr. 7 up). 1988. pap. 6.95 (ISBN 0-936320-30-3). Compact Bks.
Lester, Andrew D. Sex Is More Than a Word. 80p. (gr. 10-12). 1973. pap. 5.95 (ISBN 0-8054-5313-X). Broadman.
McIlhaney, Joe S., Jr. Sexuality & Sexually Transmitted Diseases: A Doctor Confronts the Myth of "Safe" Sex. 176p. (Orig.). 1990. pap. 8.95 (ISBN 0-8010-6274-8). Baker Bk.
Mahoney, Ellen V. Coping with Safer Sex. Rosen, Ruth, ed. (gr. 7-12). 1989. PLB 12.95 (ISBN 0-8239-0999-9). Rosen Group.
Mayle, Peter. What's Happening to Me? Walter, Paul & Robins, Arthur, illus. LC 75-14410. 56p. (gr. 3 up). 1975. 12.00 (ISBN 0-8184-0221-0); pap. 6.95 (ISBN 0-8184-0312-8). Carol Pub Group.
Miller, Deborah A. & Waigandt, Alex. Coping with Your Sexual Orientation. Rosen, Ruth, ed. (gr. 7-12). 1990. lib. bdg. 12.95 (ISBN 0-8239-1158-6). Rosen Group.
Morgan, Marcia K. My Feelings. 2nd ed. Hilty, Christi S., illus. (ps-5). 1984. pap. text ed. 3.95 (ISBN 0-930413-00-8, TX-1-361-947). Equal Just Con.
Nourse, Alan E. Safe Sex. Kline, M., ed. (Illus.). 64p. (gr. 6-12). 1988. PLB 12.40 (ISBN 0-531-10592-X). Watts.
Olson, Terrance D. & Wallace, Christopher M. Family Values & Sex Education. Haystead, Wes, ed. Day, Bruce, illus. 208p. (Orig.). (gr. 7-9). 1990. pap. text ed. 17.95 (ISBN 0-929608-86-0). Focus Family.
Orlandi, Mario, et al. Human Sexuality. (Illus.). 128p. 1989. 18.95x (ISBN 0-8160-1666-6). Facts on File.
Perl, Susan. So That's How I Was Born! Perl, Susan, illus. 48p. (ps-3). 1983. pap. 7.95 (ISBN 0-671-44501-4, Little Simon). S&S Trade.
Poe, Elizabeth. Focus on Sexuality. 225p. 1990. lib. bdg. 35.00 (ISBN 0-87436-116-8). ABC-Clio.
Pomeroy, Wardell B. Boys & Sex. rev. ed. 176p. (Orig.). (gr. 7 up). 1981. pap. 3.25 (ISBN 0-440-90753-5, LE). Dell.
—Boys & Sex. 3rd ed. 1991. pap. 15.95 (ISBN 0-385-30250-9). Doubleday.
—Boys & Sex. 3rd ed. 1991. pap. 3.95 (ISBN 0-440-20811-4). Dell.
—Girls & Sex. rev. ed. 176p. (Orig.). (gr. 7 up). 1981. pap. 3.25 (ISBN 0-440-92904-0, LE). Dell.
—Girls & Sex. 3rd ed. 1991. pap. 15.95 (ISBN 0-385-30251-7). Doubleday.
—Girls & Sex. 3rd ed. 1991. pap. 3.95 (ISBN 0-440-20812-2). Dell.
Rench, Janice E. Teen Sexuality: Decisions & Choices. (Illus.). 72p. (gr. 6 up). 1988. lib. bdg. 11.95 (ISBN 0-8225-0041-8). Lerner Pubns.
Tengbom, Mildred. Talking Together about Love & Sexuality. LC 85-22837. 160p. (gr. 4-8). 1985. pap. 5.95 (ISBN 0-87123-804-7). Bethany Hse.
Watkins, James N. Sex Is Not a Four-Letter Word. 1991. pap. 7.95 (ISBN 0-8423-7001-3). Tyndale.
Wingerd, William N. Understanding & Enjoying Adolescence. 1988. pap. text ed. 17.40 (ISBN 0-8013-0215-3, 75873). Longman.
Zimet, Susan & Goodman, Victor. The Great Cover-Up: A Condom Compendium. Silbur, Stephanie, illus. LC 88-92769. 136p. (Orig.). (gr. 10 up). 1989. pap. text ed. 5.95 (ISBN 0-9621700-0-3). Civan Inc.

SEX ROLE–FICTION

Davis, Jenny. Sex Education. LC 87-30441. 160p. (gr. 7 up). 1988. 13.95 (ISBN 0-531-05756-9); PLB 13.99 (ISBN 0-531-08356-X). Orchard Bks Watts.
—Sex Education. (gr. k-12). 1989. pap. 2.95 (ISBN 0-440-20483-6, LE). Dell.
Dygard, Thomas J. Forward Pass. LC 89-33427. (Illus.). 192p. (gr. 7 up). 1989. 11.95 (ISBN 0-688-07961-X). Morrow Jr Bks.
Green, Connie J. The War at Home. (gr. 7 up). 1989. 12.95 (ISBN 0-689-50470-5, M K McElderry). Macmillan Child Grp.
Hague, Kathleen & Hague, Michael. The Man Who Kept House. Hague, Michael, illus. LC 80-26258. 32p. (ps-3). 1981. 12.95 (ISBN 0-15-251698-0, HJ). HarBraceJ.
Knudson, R. R. Zanballer. 176p. (gr. 5-9). 1986. pap. 3.95 (ISBN 0-14-032168-3, Puffin). Puffin Bks.
—Zanbanger. LC 75-25416. 176p. (gr. 7 up). 1977. PLB 12.89 (ISBN 0-06-023214-5). HarpC Child Bks.
Meyer, Carolyn. Elliott & Win. LC 89-70868. 208p. (gr. 7 up). 1990. pap. 3.95 (ISBN 0-02-044702-7, Collier Young Ad). Macmillan Child Grp.

Miles, Betty. The Real Me. LC 74-160. 128p. (gr. 3-7). 1989. pap. 2.95 (ISBN 0-394-82588-8). Knopf.

Mulford, Philippa G. If It's Not Funny, Why Am I Laughing? LC 82-70321. 144p. (gr. 7 up). 1982. 9.95 (ISBN 0-440-03961-4). Delacorte.

Turin, Adela & Saccaro, Margherita. The Breadtime Story. (Illus.). 32p. (gr. 3-6). 1980. 6.95 (ISBN 0-904613-61-5). Writers & Readers.

Ure, Jean. What If They Saw Me Now? LC 83-14981. 160p. (gr. 7 up). 1984. 13.95 (ISBN 0-385-29317-8). Delacorte.

Waxman, Stephanie. What Is a Girl? What Is a Boy? Waxman, Stephanie, illus. LC 87-36528. 40p. (ps-2). 1989. Repr. 10.95 (ISBN 0-690-04709-6, Crowell Jr Bks); PLB 10.89 (ISBN 0-690-04711-8). HarpC Child Bks.

SEXUAL EDUCATION

see Sex Instruction

SEXUAL ETHICS

see also Birth Control

Black, Beryl. Coping with Sexual Harassment. Rosen, Ruth, ed. 149p. (gr. 7 up). 1987. PLB 12.95 (ISBN 0-8239-0732-5); pap. 7.95 (ISBN 0-8239-0764-3). Rosen Group.

Burns, Jim. Handling Your Hormones: The "Straight Scoop" on Love & Sexuality. rev. ed. LC 84-60033. 160p. (gr. 7-8). 1986. pap. 5.95 (ISBN 0-89081-532-1); leader's guide 5.95 (ISBN 0-89081-534-8); student growth guide 5.95 (ISBN 0-89081-535-6). Harvest Hse.

Fox, Robert J. The Gift of Sexuality: A Guide for Young People. LC 88-63528. (Orig.). (gr. 9 up). 1989. pap. 7.95 (ISBN 0-87973-425-6, 425). Our Sunday Visitor.

Mast, Coleen K. Sex Respect: The Option of True Sexual Freedom: A Public Health Workbook for Students. rev. ed. Forrestal, Julienne, ed. Greiner, William, illus. 118p. (gr. 7-9). 1990. pap. text ed. 8.95 (ISBN 0-945745-05-2). Respect Inc.

Nystrom, Carolyn & Floding, Matthew. Sexuality: God's Good Idea. (Illus.). 64p. (Orig.). (gr. 9-12). 1988. pap. 2.95 student ed. (ISBN 0-87788-764-0); tchr's. ed. 4.95 (ISBN 0-87788-765-9). Shaw Pubs.

Ozer, Elizabeth M. & Toure, Nkenge. Staying Safe: How to Protect Yourself Against Sexual Assault. Hamilton, Linda, illus. 23p. (Orig.). (gr. 2-6). pap. text ed. 3.00 (ISBN 0-318-04650-4). Rape Crisis Ctr.

Pomeroy, Wardell B. Girls & Sex. rev. ed. 176p. (Orig.). (gr. 7 up). 1981. pap. 3.25 (ISBN 0-440-92904-0, LE). Dell.

Sex: A Christian Perspective. 48p. (gr. 9-12). 1990. pap. 6.95 (ISBN 1-55945-206-4). Group Pub.

Stafford, Tim. Love, Sex & the Whole Person: Everything You Want to Know. 280p. 1991. pap. 9.95 (ISBN 0-310-71181-9, Campus Life). Zondervan.

SHADES AND SHADOWS

Cosgrove, Stephen E. Shadow Chaser. Edelson, Wendy, illus. 32p. (ps-3). 1990. lib. bdg. 12.96 (ISBN 0-89565-663-9). Childs World.

Dorros, Arthur. Me & My Shadow. (ps-3). 1990. pap. 12.95 (ISBN 0-590-42772-5). Scholastic Inc.

Gomi, Taro. Shadows. (Illus.). 22p. (ps-1). 1981. 3.50 (ISBN 0-89346-197-0). Heian Intl.

Goor, Ron & Goor, Nancy. Shadows: Here, There, & Everywhere. Goor, Ron, photos by. LC 81-43036. (Illus.). 48p. (gr. k-3). 1981. PLB 13.89 (ISBN 0-690-04133-0, Crowell Jr Bks). HarpC Child Bks.

Gore, Sheila. My Shadow. 1990. 6.95 (ISBN 0-385-41130-8); PLB 7.99 (ISBN 0-385-41198-7). Doubleday.

Hoban, Tana. Shadows & Reflections. LC 89-30461. (Illus.). 32p. (ps up). 1990. 12.95 (ISBN 0-688-07089-2); lib. bdg. 12.88 (ISBN 0-688-07090-6). Greenwillow.

Michaels, William. Clare & Her Shadow. Michaels, William, illus. 32p. (ps-k). 1991. lib. bdg. 15.00 (ISBN 0-208-02301-1, Linnet). Shoe String.

Montgomery, Rutherford G. Pekan the Shadow. Nenninger, Jerome D., illus. LC 78-84779. (gr. 8-12). 1970. 3.95 (ISBN 0-87004-132-0). Caxton.

Simon, Seymour. Shadow Magic. Ormai, Stella, illus. LC 84-4433. 48p. (ps-3). 1985. PLB 13.88 (ISBN 0-688-02682-6). Lothrop.

Webb, Phila H. & Corby, Jose. Shadowgraphs: Anyone Can Make. (Illus.). 32p. (gr. 1-4). 1991. Repr. of 1927 ed. 8.95 (ISBN 1-56138-014-8). Running Pr.

SHADOW PANTOMIMES AND PLAYS

Bursill, Henry. Hand Shadows to Be Thrown upon a Wall. 42p. (gr. 1-6). pap. 1.95 (ISBN 0-486-21779-5). Dover.

—More Hand Shadows to Be Thrown Upon a Wall. (Illus.). 39p. (gr. 1-6). 1971. pap. 1.95 (ISBN 0-486-21384-6). Dover.

Joyce, Joy. Me & More Shadows. Treadway, Jerry, ed. Ross, Ray, intro. by. (Illus.). 62p. (gr. 1-6). 1981. pap. text ed. 10.95 (ISBN 0-9605984-1-3). Joy-Co.

—Me & My Shadows. Treadway, Jerry, ed. Ross, Ray, intro. by. (Illus.). 58p. (gr. 1-6). 1981. pap. text ed. 10.95 (ISBN 0-9605984-0-5). Joy-Co.

SHAKERS

Campion, Nardi R. Mother Ann Lee, Morning Star of the Shakers. Sprigg, June, frwd. by. LC 90-50305. (Illus.). 205p. (gr. 9-10). 1990. pap. 10.95 (ISBN 0-87451-527-0). U Pr of New Eng.

Faber, Doris. The Perfect Life: The Shakers in America. LC 73-90968. (Illus.). 224p. (gr. 7 up). 1974. 12.95 (ISBN 0-374-35819-2). FS&G.

Ray, Mary L. Angel Baskets: A Little Story about the Shakers. Colquhoun, Jean, illus. LC 87-50789. 32p. (Orig.). 1987. pap. write for info. (ISBN 0-9609384-3-5). M Wetherbee.

Shaver, Elizabeth, ed. Fifteen Years a Shakeress. Shaker Almanac, 1886, NYS Library Staff & Lee, Elizabeth, illus. 105p. Date not set. Repr. of 1872 ed. perfect bdg. 5.95 (ISBN 0-318-49991-6). Shaker Her Soc.

Sherburne, Trudy R. As I Remember It: A Detailed Description of the North Family of the Watervliet, N. Y. Shaker Community. (Illus., Orig.). (gr. 5-10). 1987. pap. 4.95 (ISBN 0-944178-00-6). World Shaker.

SHAKESPEARE, WILLIAM, 1564-1616

Birch, Beverley. Shakespeare's Stories: Histories. Green, Robina, illus. LC 88-15693. 126p. 1990. pap. 6.95 (ISBN 0-87226-226-X). P Bedrick Bks.

—Shakespeare's Stories: Tragedies. Kerins, Tony, illus. LC 88-18112. 126p. 1990. pap. 6.95 (ISBN 0-87226-227-8). P Bedrick Bks.

Bloom, Harold, ed. Shylock. 224p. 1991. lib. bdg. 34.95 (ISBN 0-7910-0930-0). Chelsea Hse.

Chute, Marchette. An Introduction to Shakespeare. 128p. 1987. pap. 1.95 (ISBN 0-590-30263-9). Scholastic Inc.

Garfield, Leon. Shakespeare Stories. 1991. 24.95 (ISBN 0-395-56397-6). HM.

Harris Fair, Martha, et al. Shakespeare's Plays for Young People. Pigford, Barbara, illus. 37p. (Orig.). (gr. 2-9). 1982. pap. 10.00 (ISBN 0-911181-01-6). Harris Academy.

Marsh, Carole. Bill S: Shakespeare for Kids. (Illus.). (gr. 4-12). 1983. PLB 19.95 (ISBN 1-55609-156-7); pap. 14.95 (ISBN 0-935326-10-3). Gallopade Pub Group.

Martin, C. Shakespeare. (Illus.). 112p. (gr. 7 up). 1989. lib. bdg. 18.60 (ISBN 0-86592-296-9). Rourke Corp.

Marydass, C. A Compendium of Shakespeare. 180p. (gr. 7 up). 1988. text ed. 25.00x (ISBN 81-207-0713-3, Pub. by Sterling Pubs India). Apt Bks.

Mulherin, Jennifer. As You Like It: Shakespeare for Everyone. Thompson, George, illus. LC 90-478. 32p. (gr. 3-7). 1990. 10.95 (ISBN 0-87226-339-8). P Bedrick Bks.

Shakespeare, William. Shakespeare for Everyone, 6 vols. Mulherin, Jennifer, retold by. 192p. (gr. 5-12). 1988. Set, 6 vols. PLB 65.76 (ISBN 0-382-09811-0); Hamlet. pap. 11.90 (ISBN 0-382-09812-9). Macbeth. The Merchant of Venice. A Midsummer Night's Dream. Romeo & Juliet. Twelfth Night. Silver Burdett Pr.

Turner, Dorothy. William Shakespeare. (Illus.). 32p. (gr. 7-9). 1985. 11.90 (ISBN 0-531-00923-8, Pub. by Bookwright Pr). Watts.

SHAKESPEARE, WILLIAM, 1564-1616–ADAPTATIONS

Foster, Cass. Shakespeare for Children: The Story of Romeo & Juliet. Molyneux, Lisa, illus. LC 89-80371. 105p. (gr. 2 up). 1989. pap. 9.95 (ISBN 0-9619853-3-X). Five Star AZ.

—The Sixty-Minute Shakespeare: Romeo & Juliet. Hawkins, Mary E., ed. LC 89-82072. 136p. 1990. pap. 3.95 (ISBN 0-9619853-8-0); 5.00 (ISBN 1-877749-00-1). Five Star AZ.

Guida, Frank J. Shakespeare for Children, Vol. 1: Romeo & Juliet (with a Happy Ending) rev. ed. Guida, Frank J., illus. 20p. 1991. lib. bdg. write for info. (ISBN 1-878476-00-9). Rockmasters Intl.

Lamb, Charles & Lamb, Mary. Tales from Shakespeare. (gr. k-6). 1986. 8.98 (ISBN 0-685-16860-3, 621568). Outlet Bk Co.

Miles, Bernard. Favorite Tales from Shakespeare. Ambrus, Victor G., illus. LC 86-73174. 128p. (ps-8). 1987. write for info. (ISBN 0-02-689024-0). Macmillan.

Shakespeare, William. As You Like It. Gill, Roma, ed. (Illus.). 142p. 1987. pap. 6.95 (ISBN 0-19-831934-7). Oxford U Pr.

—Hamlet. Davidson, Diane, ed. LC 83-12310. (gr. 8-12). 1983. casebound 8.95 (ISBN 0-934048-13-4); pap. 4.95 (ISBN 0-934048-12-6). Swan Books.

—Macbeth: A Facing-Page Edition--The Original Text & a Translation into Modern English. Zuesse, Eric, tr. & intro. by. 192p. (Orig.). 1990. pap. 3.95 (ISBN 0-9628103-0-4). Shakespere VT. This represents a new alternative to the existing annotated editions of "Macbeth." On the facing page opposite the original text is no prose paraphrase, but a verse translation of it into modern English. Rather than employing modern-English word-by-word translations of isolated archaisms via footnotes such as are found in the annotated editions, this new edition avoids the disjointed word-by-word approach, by accompanying the original text with a running modern-English translation that's authentic in style to the original verse play, with the objective that a listener to the translation would think it to be the original--except that archaism-induced comprehension-problems, such as "kerns & gallowglasses," are gone. The translation doesn't aim to be a "Shakespeare-made-simple" text, but rather a literally high quality translation of one of the world's greatest dramas. This facing-page translation eliminates the need for annotations or footnotes in the original text. A preface, & "Note on Text & Translation," are included.

Publisher Provided Annotation.

—Merchant of Venice. Davidson, Diane, ed. LC 83-12308. (gr. 8-12). 1983. casebound 8.95 (ISBN 0-934048-09-6); pap. 4.95 (ISBN 0-934048-08-8). Swan Books.

—The Merchant of Venice. Gill, Roma, ed. (Illus.). 136p. 1987. pap. 6.95 (ISBN 0-19-831936-3). Oxford U Pr.

—Midsummer Night's Dream. Davidson, Diane, ed. LC 83-12311. (gr. 8-12). 1983. casebound 8.95 (ISBN 0-934048-11-8); pap. 4.95 (ISBN 0-934048-10-X). Swan Books.

—A Midsummer Night's Dream. Gill, Roma, ed. (Illus.). 118p. 1987. pap. 6.95 (ISBN 0-19-831938-X). Oxford U Pr.

—Othello. Gill, Roma, ed. (Illus.). 144p. (gr. 9 up). 1990. pap. 6.95 (ISBN 0-19-831953-3). Oxford U Pr.

—Romeo & Juliet. Davidson, Diane, ed. LC 83-12309. (gr. 8-12). 1983. pap. 4.95 (ISBN 0-934048-06-1). Swan Books.

—The Taming of the Shrew. Gill, Roma, ed. (Illus.). 144p. (gr. 6 up). 1990. pap. 6.95 (ISBN 0-19-831956-8). Oxford U Pr.

Stevenson, David, ed. Much Ado about Nothing. (gr. 9-12). Date not set. pap. 2.95 (ISBN 0-451-52159-5, Sig Classics). NAL-Dutton.

SHAKESPEARE, WILLIAM, 1564-1616–CONTEMPORARY ENGLAND

Shakespeare Country. (Illus.). (gr. 5 up). 3.50 (ISBN 0-7214-1003-0). Ladybird Bks.

SHAKESPEARE, WILLIAM, 1564-1616–CRITICISM, INTERPRETATION, ETC.

Eidenier, Betty. Warp Zone Shakespeare! Active Learning Lessons for the Gifted. (gr. 6-12). 1990. 12.00 (ISBN 0-910609-23-3). Gifted Educ Pr.

Kerr, Jessica. Shakespeare's Flowers. Dowden, Anne O., illus. LC 68-13585. 96p. (gr. 7 up). 1969. 14.95i (ISBN 0-690-73163-9, Crowell Jr Bks); (Crowell Jr Bks). HarpC Child Bks.

Kester, Ellen S. Word Magic: Shakespeare's Rhetoric for Gifted Students: Elementary & Secondary Shakespearian Excerpts. 2nd ed. Turner, Joseph R., III, illus. 194p. Date not set. pap. text ed. 35.00 (ISBN 0-685-26279-0). Pickwick Pubs.

Lipson, Greta & Solomon, Susan. Romeo & Juliet: Plainspoken. Kropa, Susan, illus. 256p. (gr. 7-12). 1985. 15.95 (ISBN 0-86653-283-8, GA 659). Good Apple.

Stockdale, Marina. William's Window: An Introduction to Shakespeare's Plays for Young People. 36p. (gr. 3-8). 1983. pap. 2.00 (ISBN 0-88680-209-1). I E Clark.

Walters, Michael E. Teaching Shakespeare to Gifted Students: An Examination of the Sensibility of Genius. (gr. 6-12). 1990. 12.00 (ISBN 0-910609-22-5). Gifted Educ Pr.

SHAKESPEARE, WILLIAM, 1564-1616–FICTION

Lepscky, Ibi. William Shakespeare. Cardoni, Paolo, illus. 28p. (gr. k-3). 1989. 7.95 (ISBN 0-8120-6106-3). Barron.

SHAKESPEARE, WILLIAM, 1564-1616, JULIUS CAESAR

Mulherin, Jennifer. Julius Caesar: Shakespeare for Everyone. Payne, Roger, illus. LC 90-476. 32p. (gr. 3-7). 1990. 12.95 (ISBN 0-87226-338-X). P Bedrick Bks.

Shakespeare, William. Julius Caesar. Davidson, Diane, ed. LC 83-12307. (gr. 8-12). 1983. 8.95 (ISBN 0-934048-05-3); pap. 4.95 (ISBN 0-934048-04-5). Swan Books.

—Julius Caesar. Gill, Roma, ed. (Illus.). 146p. 1987. pap. 6.95 (ISBN 0-19-831935-5). Oxford U Pr.

—Julius Caesar for Young People. Davidson, Diane, ed. LC 90-43038. (Illus.). 64p. (gr. 5-8). 1990. pap. text ed. 3.95 (ISBN 0-934048-22-3). Swan Books.

SHAKESPEARE, WILLIAM, 1564-1616, MACBETH

Shakespeare, William. Macbeth. Davidson, Diane, ed. LC 83-12312. (gr. 8-12). 1983. casebound 8.95 (ISBN 0-934048-03-7); pap. 4.95 (ISBN 0-934048-02-9). Swan Books.

—Macbeth. Gill, Roma, ed. (Illus.). 124p. 1987. pap. 6.95 (ISBN 0-19-831933-9). Oxford U Pr.

—Macbeth: A Facing-Page Edition--The Original Text & a Translation into Modern English. Zuesse, Eric, tr. & intro. by. 192p. (Orig.). 1990. pap. 3.95 (ISBN 0-9628103-0-4). Shakespere VT. This represents a new alternative to the existing annotated editions of "Macbeth." On the facing page

opposite the original text is no prose paraphrase, but a verse translation of it into modern English. Rather than employing modern-English word-by-word translations of isolated archaisms via footnotes such as are found in the annotated editions, this new edition avoids the disjointed word-by-word approach, by accompanying the original text with a running modern-English translation that's authentic in style to the original verse play, with the objective that a listener to the translation would think it to be the original--except that archaism-induced comprehension-problems, such as "kerns & gallowglasses," are gone. The translation doesn't aim to be a "Shakespeare-made-simple" text, but rather a literally high quality translation of one of the world's greatest dramas. This facing-page translation eliminates the need for annotations or footnotes in the original text. A preface, & "Note on Text & Translation," are included.
Publisher Provided Annotation.

SHAKESPEARE, WILLIAM, 1564-1616–STAGE HISTORY

Brown, John R. Shakespeare & His Theatre. Gentleman, David, illus. LC 81-8441. 64p. (gr. 6 up). 1982. 14.95 (ISBN 0-688-00850-X). Lothrop.

Hodges, C. Walter. Shakespeare's Theatre. (Illus.). 104p. (gr. 6-8). 1980. pap. 5.95 (ISBN 0-698-20511-1, Coward). Putnam Pub Group.

SHAPE

see Size and Shape

Pienkowski, Jan. Shapes. Pienkowski, Jan, illus. (ps). 1989. 2.95 (ISBN 0-671-68135-4). S&S Trade.

SHARES OF STOCK

see Stocks

SHARKS

Albert, Burton. Sharks & Whales. Ford, Pamela, illus. LC 78-66936. (gr. 1-6). 1979. 5.95 (ISBN 0-448-48990-2, G&D); PLB 5.29 (ISBN 0-448-13620-1). Putnam Pub Group.

—Sharks & Whales. Johnson, Pamela, illus. 48p. (gr. 2-5). 1989. 7.95 (ISBN 0-448-09077-5, G&D). Putnam Pub Group.

Barrett, Norman. Tiburones. (SPA., Illus.). 32p. (gr. k-4). 1990. PLB 11.40 (ISBN 0-531-07910-4). Watts.

Barrett, Norman S. Sharks. (Illus.). 32p. (gr. k-6). 1989. PLB 11.40 (ISBN 0-531-10704-3). Watts.

Berkowitz, Henry. Sharks: An Educational Coloring Book. (Illus.). 32p. (Orig.). (gr. 1-9). 1988. pap. 2.50 (ISBN 0-938059-01-7). Henart Bks.

Blassingame, Wyatt. Wonders of Sharks. 96p. 1984. 10.95 (ISBN 0-396-08463-X, Putnam). Putnam Pub Group.

Blumberg, Rhoda. Sharks. (Illus.). 72p. (gr. 4 up). 1976. PLB 10.40 (ISBN 0-531-00846-0). Watts.

Bunting, Eve. The Sea World Book of Sharks. Nicklin, Flip, photos by. LC 79-639201. (Illus.). 80p. (gr. 4-7). 1984. pap. 9.95 (ISBN 0-15-271952-0, VoyB). HarBraceJ.

Carrick, Carol. Sand Tiger Shark. Carrick, Donald, illus. LC 76-40206. (gr. 1-5). 1979. 13.95 (ISBN 0-395-28779-0, Clarion). HM.

Chinery, Michael. Shark. Doubilet, David, et al, illus. LC 90-33361. 32p. (gr. 4-6). 1990. lib. bdg. 10.89 (ISBN 0-8167-2104-1); pap. text ed. 2.95 (ISBN 0-8167-2105-X). Troll Assocs.

Coupe, Sheena & Coupe, Robert. Sharks. (gr. 3-10). 1990. 17.95 (ISBN 0-8160-2270-4). Facts on File.

Dingerkus, Guido. The Shark Watcher's Guide. Burkel, Dietrich, illus. 176p. (gr. 7 up). 1985. lib. bdg. 10.98 (ISBN 0-671-50234-4); pap. 5.95 (ISBN 0-671-68815-4). Messner.

Freedman, Russell. Sharks. Freedman, Russell, illus. LC 85-42881. 40p. (gr. 1-4). 1985. reinforced bdg. 12.95 (ISBN 0-8234-0582-6). Holiday.

Gay, Tanner O. Sharks in Action. Cassels, Jean, illus. 16p. (ps-3). 1990. pap. 6.95 (ISBN 0-689-71435-1, Aladdin). Macmillan Child Grp.

Green, Carl R. & Sanford, William R. The Great White Shark. LC 85-14936. (Illus.). 48p. (gr. 5-6). 1985. 10. 95 (ISBN 0-89686-281-X, Crestwood Hse). Macmillan Child Grp.

Hall, Howard. Sharks: The Perfect Predators. Leon, Vicki, ed. (Illus.). 40p. (Orig.). 1990. pap. 7.95 (ISBN 0-918303-24-9). Blake Pub.
Demon of the deep? Or an ancient & interesting animal with a key role in the checks & balances of the sea? Sharks, even the most ferocious species, are far from being mindless eating machines. With the help of lively, you-are-there text & 38 mind-boggling photographs, Sharks gives readers young & old a wealth of surprising facts & recent findings. Writer & photographer Howard Hall, long noted for his fine cinematography of sharks & other marine life, has put together a volume that brings action & humor to a favorite topic. Teachers will find this book especially useful because its non-grisly approach explodes myths & brings understanding. Sharks occupy a number of ecological niches within the sea; these are presented in a series of 11 by 17" color photos of uncanny detail. The saddle-stitched format of the Blake books lets pages open out flat, showing photographs to their best advantage. A succinct guide to where sharks can be seen in the wild & in captivity rounds out the book. This volume has especially easy-to-read text & captions. Its sturdy coated cover stands up well to heavy use.
Publisher Provided Annotation.

Herge. The Red Sea Sharks. (gr. k up). 1976. pap. 6.95 (ISBN 0-316-35848-7, Joy St Bks). Little.

McGovern, Ann. Sharks. Tinkelman, Murray, illus. (gr. k-3). 1977. pap. 1.75 (ISBN 0-590-10234-6). Scholastic Inc.

—Sharks. Tinkelman, Murray, illus. 48p. (gr. k-3). 1987. pap. 2.25 (ISBN 0-590-41360-0). Scholastic Inc.

McGowen, Tom. Album of Sharks. Ruth, Rod, illus. LC 77-5172. (gr. 5-7). 1987. write for info. (ISBN 0-528-82023-0); pap. write for info. (ISBN 0-02-688513-1). Checkerboard Pr.

—Album of Sharks. Ruth, Rod, illus. 64p. (gr. 3-7). 1987. pap. 4.95 (ISBN 0-318-32638-8). Checkerboard Pr.

Maestro, Betsy. Sea Full of Sharks. (ps-3). 1990. 12.95 (ISBN 0-590-43100-5). Scholastic Inc.

Naden, C. J. I Can Read About Sharks. LC 78-73736. (Illus.). (gr. 2-6). 1979. pap. 1.95 (ISBN 0-89375-218-5). Troll Assocs.

Palmer, S. Great White Sharks. (Illus.). 24p. (gr. k-5). Date not set. PLB 11.93 (ISBN 0-86592-462-7). Rourke Corp.

—Hammerhead Sharks. (Illus.). 24p. (gr. k-5). Date not set. PLB 11.93 (ISBN 0-86592-461-9). Rourke Corp.

—Mako Sharks. (Illus.). 24p. (gr. k-5). Date not set. PLB 11.93 (ISBN 0-86592-458-9). Rourke Corp.

—Nurse Sharks. (Illus.). 24p. (gr. k-5). Date not set. PLB 11.93 (ISBN 0-86592-459-7). Rourke Corp.

—Thresher Sharks. (Illus.). 24p. (gr. k-5). Date not set. PLB 11.93 (ISBN 0-86592-460-0). Rourke Corp.

—Whale Sharks. (Illus.). 24p. (gr. k-5). Date not set. PLB 11.93 (ISBN 0-86592-463-5). Rourke Corp.

Penny, Malcolm. Let's Look At Sharks. (ps-3). 1990. PLB 8.90 (ISBN 0-531-18308-4). Watts.

Penzler, Otto. Hunting the Killer Shark. LC 75-23409. (Illus.). 32p. (gr. 5-10). 1976. PLB 10.79 (ISBN 0-89375-009-3); pap. 2.95 (ISBN 0-89375-025-5). Troll Assocs.

Petty, Kate. Finding Out about Sharks. (Illus.). 32p. (gr. k-3). 1988. 2.50 (ISBN 0-87406-320-5). Willowisp Pr.

—Sharks. Johnson, Karen, illus. LC 85-80638. 32p. (gr. 2-4). 1990. PLB 10.90 (ISBN 0-531-10025-1); pap. 2.95 (ISBN 0-531-15155-7). Watts.

Radlauer, Edward. Shark Mania. LC 76-13500. (Illus.). (gr. 1-4). 1976. (Elk Grove Bks); pap. 3.95 (ISBN 0-516-47410-3). Childrens.

Reed, Don C. Sevengill Shark & Me. 1990. pap. 2.75 (ISBN 0-590-43497-7). Scholastic Inc.

—Sevengill: The Shark & Me. Johnson, Pamela F., illus. LC 86-2727. 144p. (gr. 5up). 1986. (Sierra Club Bk.); lib. bdg. 11.99 (ISBN 0-394-96926-X). Knopf.

Richards, Kay. Sharks. (Illus.). 32p. (gr. 3-8). 1990. 3.95 (ISBN 0-87406-449-X, 42-19344-4). Willowisp Pr.

Sattler, Helen R. Sharks, the Super Fish. Zallinger, Jean D., illus. LC 84-4381. 96p. (gr. 9 up). 1985. 15.95 (ISBN 0-688-03993-6). Lothrop.

Selsam, Millicent E., et al. A First Look at Sharks. Springer, Harriet, illus. (gr. k-3). 1979. PLB 12.85 (ISBN 0-8027-6373-1). Walker & Co.

Serventy, Vincent. Shark & Ray. LC 84-15097. (Illus.). 24p. (gr. k-5). 1984. PLB 13.32 (ISBN 0-8172-2402-5). Raintree Pubs.

Server, Lee. Sharks. 1989. 14.99 (ISBN 0-517-69091-8). Outlet Bk Co.

Sharks. 24p. (ps-2). 1989. pap. 1.29 (ISBN 0-02-898256-8). Checkerboard Pr.

Spizzirri Publishing Co. Staff. Sharks: An Educational Coloring Book. Spizzirri, Linda, ed. Fuller, Glenn, et al, illus. 32p. (gr. 1-8). 1981. pap. 1.95 (ISBN 0-86545-029-3). Spizzirri.

Stevens, John, ed. Sharks. LC 87-601. (Illus.). 240p. 1987. 35.00 (ISBN 0-8160-1800-6). Facts on File.

Waters, John F. Hungry Sharks. LC 72-7563. (Illus.). 40p. (ps-3). 1973. PLB 13.89 (ISBN 0-690-01121-0, Crowell Jr Bks). HarpC Child Bks.

Wheeler, Alwyne. Sharks. (Illus.). 32p. (gr. 1-6). 1987. PLB 11.90 (ISBN 0-531-17052-7, Gloucester Pr). Watts.

Wildlife Education, Ltd. Staff. Sharks. Hoopes, Barbara, illus. 20p. (gr. 5 up). 1983. pap. 2.25 (ISBN 0-937934-15-1). Wildlife Educ.

SHARKS–FICTION

Cowley, Joy. Shark in a Sack. Van der Voo, Jan, illus. 8p. (gr. k-2). 1989. pap. text ed. 15.00 (ISBN 1-55911-285-9). Wright Group.

—Shark in a Sack, 6 bks. Van der Voo, Jan, illus. 8p. (gr. k-2). 1986. Set. pap. text ed. 12.60 (ISBN 1-55911-353-7). Wright Group.

Crisfield, Deborah. Jaws. LC 90-47941. (Illus.). 48p. (gr. 5-6). 1991. RSBE 11.95 (ISBN 0-89686-578-9, Crestwood Hse). Macmillan Child Grp.

Keller, Charles. Smokey the Shark: And Other Fishy Stories. Lorenz, Lee, illus. (gr. 2-6). 1981. 8.95 (ISBN 0-13-814707-8). P-H.

Laird, Donivee M. Ula Li'i & the Magic Shark. LC 86-3390. (Illus.). 42p. (gr. k-3). 1985. 7.95x (ISBN 0-940350-12-2). Barnaby Bks.

McBarnet, Gill. The Shark Who Learned a Lesson. McBarnet, Gill, illus. 32p. (ps-2). Date not set. 7.95 (ISBN 0-9615102-5-0). Ruwanga Trad.

Mahy, Margaret. The Great White Man-Eating Shark: A Cautionary Tale. Allen, Jonathan, illus. (ps-3). 1990. 12.95 (ISBN 0-8037-0749-5). Dial Bks Young.

Thiele, Colin. Shadow Shark. LC 87-45566. 224p. (gr. 5-7). 1988. 13.95 (ISBN 0-06-026178-1); PLB 13.89 (ISBN 0-06-026179-X). HarpC Child Bks.

SHAVU'OTH (FEAST OF WEEKS)–FICTION

Wengrov, Charles. The Story of Shavuot. (Illus.). (gr. k-7). 1965. pap. 2.50 (ISBN 0-914080-55-5). Shulsinger Sales.

SHAYS' REBELLION, 1786-1787

Collier, James L. & Collier, Christopher. The Winter Hero. 208p. (gr. 7 up). 1985. pap. 2.25 (ISBN 0-590-33696-7, Point); tchr's. guide 1.25 (ISBN 0-590-40680-9). Scholastic Inc.

SHEEP

Ahlstrom, Mark. The Sheep. LC 83-25215. (Illus.). 48p. (gr. 5-6). 1984. PLB 10.95 (ISBN 0-89686-248-8, Crestwood Hse). Macmillan Child Grp.

Herriot, James. Smudge, the Little Lost Lamb. Brown, Ruth, illus. 32p. 1991. 13.00 (ISBN 0-312-06404-7). St Martin.

Hutchings, Tony. Little Woolly Lamb. Hutchings, Tony, illus. 12p. (ps-1). 1990. 4.95 (ISBN 1-878624-13-X, 1553800013). McClanahan Bk.

Keller, Holly. Ten Sleepy Sheep. Keller, Holly, illus. LC 83-1477. 32p. (gr. k-3). 1983. 10.25 (ISBN 0-688-02306-1); PLB 10.88 (ISBN 0-688-02307-X). Greenwillow.

Paladino, Catherine. Spring Fleece: A Day of Sheepshearing. (ps-3). 1990. 14.95 (ISBN 0-316-68890-8, Joy St Bks). Little.

Royston, Angela. Sheep. 1990. PLB 10.40 (ISBN 0-531-19082-X). Watts.

Stone, Lynn. Sheep. (Illus.). 24p. (gr. k-5). 1990. lib. bdg. 11.93 (ISBN 0-86593-038-4); lib. bdg. 8.95s.p. (ISBN 0-685-36313-9). Rourke Corp.

SHEEP–FICTION

Amery, H. The Naughty Sheep. (Illus.). 16p. (ps). 1989. 2.95 (ISBN 0-7460-0261-0, Usborne); lib. bdg. 7.96 (ISBN 0-88110-376-4, Usborne). EDC.

Barrett, Ethel. Blister Lamb-Gregory the Grub. (ps-2). 1978. pap. 5.95 incl. cass. (ISBN 0-8307-0420-5, 5602726). Regal.

Blanchard, Arlene. The Naughty Lamb. Wells, Tony, illus. LC 88-4098. 32p. (ps-1). 1989. 9.95 (ISBN 0-8037-0604-9); PLB 9.89 (ISBN 0-8037-0605-7). Dial Bks Young.

—The Naughty Lamb. Wells, Tony, illus. LC 88-4098. 32p. (ps-1). 1989. 9.95 (ISBN 0-8037-0577-8). Dial Bks Young.

Dudley, Dick. Ten Little Lambs. Paris, Pat, illus. 12p. (ps-k). 1988. 8.95 (ISBN 0-8120-5953-0). Barron.

Dunn, Judy. The Little Lamb. Dunn, Phoebe, illus. LC 76-24167. (ps-2). 1978. lib. bdg. 5.99 (ISBN 0-394-93455-5, Random Juv). Random.

—The Little Lamb. Dunn, Phoebe, illus. LC 76-24167. (ps-1). 1977. pap. 2.25 (ISBN 0-394-83455-0, Random Juv). Random.

Ernst, Lisa C. Nattie Parsons' Good-Luck Lamb. (Illus.). 32p. (ps-3). 1990. pap. 3.95 (ISBN 0-14-050772-8, Puffin). Puffin Bks.

Goffstein, M. B. Brookie & Her Lamb. rev. ed. Goffstein, M. B., illus. LC 67-26372. 32p. (ps-3). 1981. 6.95 (ISBN 0-374-30990-6). FS&G.

Grejniec, Michael. When I Open My Eyes. Grejniec, Michael, illus. 32p. (ps-1). 1990. 15.95 (ISBN 0-8050-1417-9). H Holt & Co.

Hammond, Jane. Larry the Lamb. (ps-k). 1983. pap. 1.50 (ISBN 0-87162-286-6, D5600). Warner Pr.

Hargreaves, Roger. Grandma Baa. Jolliffe, Gray, illus. LC 89-60417. 32p. (Orig.). (ps-3). 1989. pap. 1.95 (ISBN 0-679-80124-3). Random.

Hooks, William H. & Brenner, Barbara. Lion & Lamb, Level 3. Degen, Bruce, illus. (ps-3). 1989. pap. 3.50 (ISBN 0-553-34692-X). Bantam.

Hooks, William H. & Brenner, Barbara A. Lion & Lamb: Level 3. Degen, Bruce, illus. (ps-3). 1989. 9.99 (ISBN 0-553-05829-0). Bantam.

Inkpen, Mick. If I Had a Sheep. Inkpen, Mick, illus. (ps). 1988. 7.95 (ISBN 0-316-41888-9). Little.

Kitamura, Satoshi. When Sheep Cannot Sleep. LC 86-45000. (Illus.). 32p. (ps up). 1986. 9.95 (ISBN 0-374-38311-1). FS&G.

Krumgold, Joseph. And Now Miguel. Charlot, Jean, illus. LC 53-8415. 245p. (gr. 5 up). 1987. 12.95 (ISBN 0-690-09118-4, Crowell Jr Bks); PLB 12.89 (ISBN 0-690-04696-0, Crowell Jr Bks). HarpC Child Bks.

Lenski, Lois. Strawberry Girl. Lenski, Lois, illus. LC 45-7609. 192p. (gr. 4-6). 1945. 15.95 (ISBN 0-397-30109-X, Lipp Jr Bks); PLB 14.89 (ISBN 0-397-30110-3, Lipp Jr Bks). HarpC Child Bks.

Lewis, Kim. Emma's Lamb. Lewis, Kim, illus. LC 90-3863. 32p. (ps-1). 1991. SBE 13.95 (ISBN 0-02-758821-1, Four Winds). Macmillan Child Grp.

Lewis, Rob. Friska, the Sheep Who. LC 87-45756. (Illus.). 32p. (ps-k). 1988. 6.95 (ISBN 0-374-32461-1). FS&G.

Macaulay, David. BAAA. LC 85-2316. (Illus.). 64p. (gr. 6 up). 1985. 13.95 (ISBN 0-395-38948-8); pap. 4.95 (ISBN 0-395-39588-7). HM.

Maclean, Moira. Mary Had a Little Lamb. 1990. 9.95 (ISBN 0-385-41166-9). Doubleday.

Novak, Matt. While the Shepherd Slept. LC 90-7733. (Illus.). 32p. (ps-2). 1991. 13.95 (ISBN 0-531-05915-4); PLB 13.99 (ISBN 0-531-08515-5). Orchard Bks Watts.

O'Toole, Sharon S. Noodles: Sheep Security Guard. Morrill, Leslie, illus. 48p. (gr. 1-3). 1988. pap. 2.50 (ISBN 0-590-41208-6). Scholastic Inc.

Panek, Dennis. Ba Ba Sheep Wouldn't Go to Sleep. LC 88-60090. (Illus.). 32p. (ps-1). 1988. 13.95 (ISBN 0-531-05776-3); PLB 13.99 (ISBN 0-531-08376-4). Orchard Bks Watts.

Ray, Sandy. The Lamb. Sytsma, Cheryle, ed. (Illus.). 15p. (Orig.). Date not set. pap. write for info. (ISBN 1-879068-10-9). Ray-Ma Natsal.

Rogers, Paul T. Sheepchase. Berridge, Celia, illus. 32p. (Orig.). (ps-k). 1988. pap. 3.50 (ISBN 0-14-050561-X, Puffin). Puffin Bks.

Scheidl, Gerda M. Four Candles for Simon. Bell, Anthea, tr. Pfister, Marcus, illus. (GER.). 32p. (gr. k-3). 1989. pap. 1.95 (ISBN 1-55858-033-6). North-South Bks NYC.

Shaw, Elizabeth. Little Black Sheep. 1985. pap. 7.95 (ISBN 0-86278-102-7, Pub. by O'Brien Press Ltd Eire). Dufour.

Shaw, Nancy. Sheep in a Jeep. Apple, Margot, illus. LC 86-3101. 32p. (ps-k). 1986. 12.95 (ISBN 0-395-41105-X). HM.

Stubblefield, Fern. Tim & His Lamp. 52p. (gr. k-6). pap. 0.40 (ISBN 0-686-29170-0); pap. 1.00 3 copies (ISBN 0-686-29171-9). Faith Pub Hse.

Sundgaard, Arnold. The Lamb & the Butterfly. Carle, Eric, illus. LC 88-60092. 32p. (ps-2). 1988. 14.95 (ISBN 0-531-05779-8); PLB 14.99 (ISBN 0-531-08379-9). Orchard Bks Watts.

Wood, A. J. Sunny Stories: The Sheep that Liked to Sing. 1989. 1.98 (ISBN 0-671-09892-6). S&S Trade.

SHELLFISH

see Mollusks

SHELLS

see also Mollusks

Abbott, R. Tucker. Seashells of North America. Zim, Herbert S., ed. Sandstrom, George F., illus. (gr. 9 up). 1969. (Golden Pr); pap. write for info (ISBN 0-307-13657-4). Western Pub.

—Seashells of the World. Rev. ed. Zim, Herbert S., ed. Sandstrom, George F. & Sandstrom, Marita, illus. (gr. 9 up). 1985. pap. write for info. (ISBN 0-307-24410-5, Golden Pr). Western Pub.

Arthur, Alex. Shell. Einsiedel, Andreas, photos by. LC 88-13449. (Illus.). 64p. (gr. 5 up). 1989. 15.00 (ISBN 0-394-82256-0); lib. bdg. 14.99 (ISBN 0-394-92256-5). Knopf.

Cate, Jean M. & Raskin, Selma. It's Easy to Say Crepidula! A Phonetic Guide to Pronunciation of the Scientific Names of Sea Shells. Vasquez, Gina, illus. 158p. (Orig.). (gr. 5-7). 1986. pap. 19.95 (ISBN 0-938509-00-4). Pretty Penny Pr.

Florian, Douglas. Discovering Seashells. Florian, Douglas, illus. LC 86-11903. 32p. (ps-2). 1986. 12.95 (ISBN 0-684-18740-X, Scribners Young Read). Macmillan Child Grp.

Fredlee. Magic of Sea Shells. rev. ed. (Illus.). 36p. (gr. 1-3). 1985. pap. 3.25. Windward Pub.

Gattis, L. S., III. Shells for Pathfinders: A Basic Youth Enrichment Skill Honor Packet. (Illus.). 26p. (Orig.). (gr. 5 up). 1989. pap. 5.00 tchr's. ed. (ISBN 0-936241-47-0). Cheetah Pub.

Seashells. (gr. 4-6). 1984. 2.95 (ISBN 0-8431-4275-8). Price Stern.

Selsam, Millicent E. & Hunt, Joyce. A First Look at Seashells. Springer, Hariett, illus. LC 83-5876. 32p. (gr. 1-3). 1983. PLB 12.85 (ISBN 0-8027-6503-3). Walker & Co.

Victor, Joan B. Shells Are Skeletons. Victor, Joan B., illus. LC 75-23258. 40p. (gr. k-3). 1977. PLB 13.89 (ISBN 0-690-01038-9, Crowell Jr Bks). HarpC Child Bks.

SHEPHERDS–FICTION

Caudill, Rebecca. A Certain Small Shepherd. (gr. k-6). 1987. pap. 2.75 (ISBN 0-440-41194-7, YB). Dell.

Hackman, Martha. Komo the Shepherd Boy. Cesari, Aura, illus. 12p. (Orig.). (gr. 7-9). 1982. pap. 2.50 (ISBN 0-88138-002-4). Green Tiger Pr.

Haseley, Dennis. The Cave of Snores. Beddows, Eric, illus. LC 85-48845. 40p. (gr. k-4). 1987. 11.95 (ISBN 0-06-022214-X); PLB 11.89 (ISBN 0-06-022215-8). HarpC Child Bks.

LaGrange, Lynn M. Paul, the Shepherd Boy & the Birthday Sandals. Sanchez, Larry M., illus. 36p. (ps-6). 1990. lib. bdg. 10.95 (ISBN 1-878790-00-5). Fables CO.

—Paul, the Shepherd Boy & the Birthday Sandals. Sanchez, Larry M., illus. 36p. (ps-6). 1990. pap. 6.95 (ISBN 1-878790-03-X). Fables CO.

Lewis, Kim. The Shepherd Boy. Lewis, Kim, illus. LC 89-23679. 32p. (ps-1). 1990. 13.95 (ISBN 0-02-758581-6, Four Winds). Macmillan Child Grp.

Wright, Harold B. Shepherd of the Hills. rev. ed. Phillips, Michael R., ed. LC 88-10311. 256p. 1988. pap. 6.95 (ISBN 0-87123-916-7). Bethany Hse.

SHIP BUILDING

see Shipbuilding

SHIPBUILDING

see also Boatbuilding; Ships; Steamboats

Tunis, Edwin. Oars, Sails & Steam: A Picture Book of Ships. Tunis, Edwin, illus. LC 76-25453. (gr. 6 up). 1977. 24.95i (ISBN 0-690-01284-5, Crowell Jr Bks). HarpC Child Bks.

SHIPPING

Hartford, John. Steamboat in a Cornfield. LC 86-4154. (Illus.). (gr. 7 up). 1986. 10.95 (ISBN 0-517-56141-7). Crown.

SHIPS

see also Boats and Boating; Navigation; Sailing; Steamboats; Submarines; Warships

Ancona, George. Freighters: Cargo Ships & the People Who Work Them. LC 84-45059. (Illus.). 64p. (gr. 2-6). 1985. 12.95 (ISBN 0-690-04358-9, Crowell Jr Bks). HarpC Child Bks.

Atkinson, I. The Viking Ships. LC 77-17510. (Illus.). 48p. (gr. 7 up). 1979. pap. 5.95 (ISBN 0-521-21951-5). Cambridge U Pr.

Barrett, N. S. Ships. (Illus.). 32p. (gr. k-3). PLB 11.40 (ISBN 0-531-03722-3). Watts.

Barton, Byron. Boats. Barton, Byron, illus. LC 85-47900. 32p. (ps-k). 1986. 4.95 (ISBN 0-694-00059-0, Crowell Jr Bks); PLB 11.89 (ISBN 0-690-04536-0). HarpC Child Bks.

Buschini, Henny & Buschini, Luciano. The Ship in the Field. Buschini, Henny & Buschini, Luciano, illus. LC 77-174719. 32p. (gr. k-3). 1973. 6.95 (ISBN 0-87592-045-4). Scroll Pr.

Carter, Katherine. Ships & Seaports. LC 82-4463. (Illus.). (gr. k-4). 1982. PLB 14.60 (ISBN 0-516-01656-3); pap. 4.95 (ISBN 0-516-41656-1). Childrens.

Chant, Chris. Sailing Ships. Batchelor, John, illus. LC 88-28706. 63p. (gr. 3 up). 1990. PLB 16.95 (ISBN 1-85435-091-9). Marshall Cavendish.

Emert, Phyllis R. Mysteries of Ships & Planes. 1990. pap. 2.50 (ISBN 0-8125-9427-4). Tor Bks.

Gibbons, Gail. Boat Book. Gibbons, Gail, illus. LC 82-15851. 32p. (ps-3). 1983. reinforced bdg. 14.95 (ISBN 0-8234-0478-1); pap. 5.95 (ISBN 0-8234-0709-8). Holiday.

Hoare, Robert. Travel by Sea. Unstead, R. J., ed. (gr. 7 up). 1965. 14.95 (ISBN 0-7136-0119-1). Dufour.

Humble, Richard. Ships: Sailors & the Sea. (Illus.). 48p. (gr. 5-8). 1991. 13.95 (ISBN 0-531-15234-0); PLB 13.90 (ISBN 0-531-11092-3). Watts.

Johnstone, Hugh. Land & Sea Transport. (Illus.). 40p. (gr. 5-9). 1989. PLB 12.40 (ISBN 0-531-17186-8). Watts.

Let's Discover Ships & Boats. LC 80-22959. (Illus.). 80p. (gr. k-6). 1983. pap. text ed. 13.27 (ISBN 0-8172-1774-6). Raintree Pubs.

Mandell, Myles K. Micromodels: Make Your Own Six Little Ships. (gr. 2 up). 1983. 4.95 (ISBN 0-399-50853-8, Perigee Bks). Putnam Pub Group.

Matthews, Rupert. Let's Look At Ships & Boats. (ps-3). 1990. PLB 8.90 (ISBN 0-531-18322-X). Watts.

Price, Stern & Sloan Staff. Ships & Submarines. (Illus.). 32p. (gr. 7-12). 1987. pap. 2.95 (ISBN 0-8431-4289-8). Price Stern.

Relf, Patricia. The Big Book of Real Boats & Ships. LaPadula, Tom, illus. 48p. (gr. 1-4). 1990. 7.95 (ISBN 0-448-19189-X, G&D). Putnam Pub Group.

Riegel, Martin P. The Ships of the Orange Coast. Riegel, Martin P., illus. LC 88-92522. 40p. (Orig.). (gr. 9 up). 1988. PLB 11.00 (ISBN 0-944871-08-9); pap. 4.75 (ISBN 0-944871-09-7). Riegel Pub.

Rutland, Jonathan. Amazing Fact Book of Ships. (Illus.). 32p. (gr. 4-8). 1987. PLB 11.95 (ISBN 0-87191-849-8). Creative Ed.

Spizzirri Publishing Co. Staff. Ships: An Educational Coloring Book. Spizzirri, Linda, ed. Fuller, Glenn & Spizzirri, Peter M., illus. 32p. (gr. 1-8). 1981. pap. 1.95 (ISBN 0-86545-035-8). Spizzirri.

Thomas, David A. How Ships Are Made. LC 89-31328. (Illus.). 32p. (gr. 4-8). 1989. 12.95x (ISBN 0-8160-2040-X). Facts on File.

Tunis, Edwin. Oars, Sails & Steam: A Picture Book of Ships. Tunis, Edwin, illus. LC 76-25453. (gr. 6 up). 1977. 24.95i (ISBN 0-690-01284-5, Crowell Jr Bks). HarpC Child Bks.

Walmer, M. Frigates. (Illus.). 48p. (gr. 3-8). 1989. lib. bdg. 18.60 (ISBN 0-86625-082-4). Rourke Corp.

Williams, Brian. Ships & Other Seacraft. 96p. (gr. k-8). 1984. lib. bdg. 9.90 (ISBN 0-531-09229-1). Watts.

SHIPS–FICTION

Brett, Bernard. The Fighting Ship. Batchelor, John & Lapper, Ivan, illus. 96p. (gr. 7 up). 1988. 17.95 (ISBN 0-19-273155-6). Oxford U Pr.

Crawford, F. Marion. Nightmare Ship. Richardson, I. M., adapted by. Toulmin-Rothe, Ann, illus. LC 81-21805. 32p. (gr. 5-10). 1982. PLB 10.79 (ISBN 0-89375-632-6); pap. text ed. 2.95 (ISBN 0-89375-633-4). Troll Assocs.

Fredeking, Jean T. My Trip On a Ship. 16p. 1987. pap. 20.00x (ISBN 0-317-59267-X, Pub. by A H Stockwell England). State Mutual Bk.

Hawes, Charles B. The Dark Frigate. rev. ed. Chappell, Warren, illus. (gr. 7 up). 1971. 16.95 (ISBN 0-316-35096-6, Joy St Bks). Little.

The Mighty Ship. Date not set. write for info. Songbird & Seabird.

Ryan, John. Pugwash & the Ghost Ship. Ryan, John, illus. LC 68-23218. (gr. k-3). 1968. 18.95 (ISBN 0-87599-146-7). S G Phillips.

SHIPS–HISTORY

Berenstain, Michael. The Ship Book. (Illus.). (gr. k-3). 1978. 6.95 (ISBN 0-679-20449-0). McKay.

Burns, Phillys B. Iron Lady at Sea: From Shipyard to Voyage: A Story of the Great Iron-Hulled Sailing Ship, Star of India. (Illus.). 108p. (Orig.). 1988. pap. 6.95 (ISBN 0-685-20061-2). Cove Pr CA.

Lord, Walter. Night to Remember. (gr. 6-12). 1983. pap. 4.50 (ISBN 0-553-27827-4). Bantam.

Riegel, Martin P. Historic Ships of Hawaii. LC 88-92776. (Illus.). 44p. (Orig.). 1988. 11.00 (ISBN 0-944871-12-7); pap. 4.95 (ISBN 0-944871-13-5). Riegel Pub.

—Historic Ships of Oregon. LC 88-92771. (Illus.). 48p. (Orig.). 1988. 11.00 (ISBN 0-944871-14-3); pap. 4.95 (ISBN 0-944871-15-1). Riegel Pub.

—Historic Ships of Washington. LC 88-63929. (Illus.). 52p. (Orig.). 1988. 11.00 (ISBN 0-944871-16-X); pap. 4.95 (ISBN 0-944871-17-8). Riegel Pub.

—The Ships of the California Gold Rush. LC 88-92421. (Illus.). 48p. (Orig.). 1988. 11.00 (ISBN 0-944871-11-9); pap. 4.95 (ISBN 0-685-24979-4). Riegel Pub.

Ward, Ralph T. Ships Through History. LC 72-75895. (gr. 3-6). 1972. 8.95 (ISBN 0-672-51663-2, Bobbs). Macmillan.

SHIPS–MODELS

Herda, D. J. Model Boats & Ships. (Illus.). 72p. (gr. 4 up). 1982. PLB 10.40 (ISBN 0-531-04463-7). Watts.

SHIPWRECKS

see also Salvage; Survival (After Airplane Accidents, Shipwrecks, etc.);

also names of wrecked ships

Brown, Walter R. Sea Disasters. LC 84-40788. (Illus.). 112p. 1981. 11.95 (ISBN 0-201-09154-2, Lipp Jr Bks). HarpC Child Bks.

Fine, John C. Sunken Ships & Treasures. LC 86-3652. (Illus.). 128p. (gr. 3 up). 1986. 16.95 (ISBN 0-689-31280-6, Atheneum Child Bk). Macmillan Child Grp.

Humphrey, Kathryn L. Shipwrecks: Terror & Treasure. (Illus.). 64p. (gr. 5-8). 1991. PLB 11.90 (ISBN 0-531-20031-0). Watts.

SHIPWRECKS–FICTION

Defoe, Daniel. Robinson Crusoe. (gr. 6 up). 1964. pap. 2.25 (ISBN 0-8049-0022-1, CL-22). Airmont.

—Robinson Crusoe. (gr. 3-6). 1981. 6.95 (ISBN 0-86020-554-1, Usborne-Hayes); PLB 11.96 (ISBN 0-88110-062-5); pap. 3.95 (ISBN 0-86020-553-3). EDC.

Grimm, Jacob & Grimm, Wilhelm K. The Elves & the Shoemaker. Watts, Bernadette, illus. LC 85-63306. 32p. (gr. k-2). 1986. 14.95 (ISBN 1-55858-035-2). North-South Bks NYC.

Knox, Joann. Shipwrecked. 48p. (gr. 4-8). 1973. pap. 1.00 (ISBN 0-88243-773-9, 02-0773). Gospel Pub.

Robinson Crusoe. (gr. 4 up). 1988. pap. 4.87 (ISBN 0-582-54156-5, 74263). Longman.

Robinson Crusoe. (Illus.). (gr. 1). 3.50 (ISBN 0-7214-5123-3). Ladybird Bks.

Rowland, Della. A World of Shoes. Riccio, Frank, illus. 24p. 1989. 8.95 (ISBN 0-8092-4348-2, Calico Bks). Contemp Bks.

Swiss Family Robinson. 384p. (gr. 3-9). 1981. pap. 7.95 (ISBN 0-448-11022-9, G&D). Putnam Pub Group.

Treece, Henry. Further Adventures of Robinson Crusoe. Nickless, Will, illus. LC 58-9623. (gr. 7-11). 1958. 18.95 (ISBN 0-87599-116-5). S G Phillips.

Wandelmaier, Roy. Shipwrecked on Mystery Island. Pinkney, Brian J. LC 85-2531. (Illus.). 112p. (gr. 3-6). 1985. lib. bdg. 9.49 (ISBN 0-8167-0533-X); pap. text ed. 2.95 (ISBN 0-8167-0534-8). Troll Assocs.

Wulffson, Don. The Upside-Down Ship. Fay, Ann, ed. (Illus.). 128p. (gr. 4 up). 1986. 10.50 (ISBN 0-8075-8346-4). A Whitman.

SHOES AND SHOE INDUSTRY

Benjamin, Carol L. Cartooning for Kids. (Illus.). 80p. (gr. 3-8). 1987. pap. 4.95 (ISBN 0-06-446063-0, Trophy). HarpC Child Bks.

Cazet, Denys. Big Shoe, Little Shoe. Cazet, Denys, illus. LC 83-21362. 32p. (ps-2). 1984. 12.95 (ISBN 0-02-717820-X, Bradbury Pr). Macmillan Child Grp.

Cobb, Vicki. Sneakers Meet Your Feet. Cobb, Theo, illus. 48p. (gr. 4-6). 1985. 11.95 (ISBN 0-316-14896-2). Little.

Grainger, Sylvia. How to Make Your Own Moccasins. LC 77-4262. (gr. 5 up). 1977. (Lipp Jr Bks); pap. 3.95 (ISBN 0-397-31755-7). HarpC Child Bks.

—How to Make Your Own Moccasins. pap. 4.95 (ISBN 0-06-446036-3, Trophy). HarpC Child Bks.

Miller, Margaret. Whose Shoe? LC 90-38491. (Illus.). 40p. (ps up). 1991. 13.95 (ISBN 0-688-10008-2); PLB 13.88 (ISBN 0-688-10009-0). Greenwillow.

Mitgutsch, Ali. From Cow to Shoe. LC 80-29587. (Illus.). 24p. (ps-3). 1981. PLB 6.95 (ISBN 0-87614-151-3). Carolrhoda Bks.

Strauss, Lucy. The Story of Shoes. (Illus.). 32p. (gr. 1-4). 1989. PLB 13.32 (ISBN 0-8172-3534-5). Raintree Pubs.

Tafuri, Nancy. Two New Sneakers. LC 87-8418. (Illus.). 12p. (ps). 1988. bds. 3.95 (ISBN 0-688-07462-6). Greenwillow.

Young, Robert. Sneakers: The Shoes We Choose. (Illus.). 64p. (gr. 3 up). 1991. PLB 14.95 (ISBN 0-87518-460-X, Dillon). Macmillan Child Grp.

SHOOTING

see also Hunting

SHOOTING STARS

see Meteors

SHOPPER'S GUIDES

see Consumer Education; Shopping

SHOPPING

see also Consumer Education

Oliver, Stephen, photos by. Shopping. LC 90-23567. (Illus.). 24p. (ps-k). 1991. 7.00 (ISBN 0-679-81803-0, Random Juv). Random.

Sawyer, Jean. Our Village Shop. Jaques, Faith, illus. 32p. (Orig.). (gr. k-5). 1984. pap. 8.95 (ISBN 0-399-21023-7, Philomel). Putnam Pub Group.

Shopping. (Illus.). (ps). 3.50 (ISBN 0-7214-1120-7). Ladybird Bks.

Twinn, Michael, illus. Going Shopping. 8p. (ps-2). 1977. 2.00 (ISBN 0-85953-072-8, Pub. by Child's Play England). Childs Play.

Washington, Dolores E. Begin Basic Budget Saving Shopping Spending, Vol. I. 13p. (gr. 11 up). 1989. wkbk. 2.50x (ISBN 0-685-26101-8). Dew Educational.

SHOPPING–FICTION

Burningham, John. The Shopping Basket. LC 80-7987. (Illus.). 32p. (ps-2). 1980. 13.95 (ISBN 0-690-04082-2, Crowell Jr Bks). HarpC Child Bks.

Cutting, Jillian. Shopping. Van der Voo, Jan, illus. 8p. (Orig.). (gr. k-2). 1989. pap. text ed. 15.00 (ISBN 1-55911-270-0). Wright Group.

—Shopping, 6 bks. Van der Voo, Jan, illus. 8p. (gr. k-2). 1986. Set. pap. text ed. 12.60 (ISBN 1-55911-325-1). Wright Group.

Day, Alexandra. Carl Goes Shopping. (Illus.). (gr. 3 up). 1989. 9.95 (ISBN 0-374-31110-2). FS&G.

Edwards, Linda S. The Downtown Day. Edwards, Linda S., illus. LC 82-4645. 48p. (gr. k-3). 1983. 9.95 (ISBN 0-394-85407-1). Pantheon.

Fyleman, Rose. Fairy Went A-Marketing. (Illus.). (ps-1). 1990. pap. 3.95 (ISBN 0-525-44556-0, DCB). Dutton Child Bks.

Grossman, Bill. Tommy at the Grocery Store. Chess, Victoria, illus. LC 88-35756. 32p. (ps-2). 1989. 12.95 (ISBN 0-06-022408-8); PLB 12.89 (ISBN 0-06-022409-6). HarpC Child Bks.

Harwood, Pearl A. Mrs. Moon Goes Shopping. Overlie, George, illus. LC 67-15691. 32p. (gr. k-3). 1967. PLB 4.95 (ISBN 0-8225-0115-5). Lerner Pubns.

—Rummage Sale & Mr. & Mrs. Bumba. Overlie, George, illus. LC 70-156361. 32p. (gr. k-3). 1971. PLB 4.95 (ISBN 0-8225-0122-8). Lerner Pubns.

Haynes, Betsy. Mall Mania. (gr. 4-7). 1991. pap. 2.95 (ISBN 0-553-15852-X). Bantam.

Hutchins, Pat. Don't Forget the Bacon! LC 75-17935. (Illus.). 32p. (gr. k-3). 1976. 13.95 (ISBN 0-688-06787-5); PLB 13.88 (ISBN 0-688-06788-3). Greenwillow.

Lobel, Arnold. On Market Street. Lobel, Anita, illus. LC 80-21418. 40p. (gr. k-3). 1981. 13.95 (ISBN 0-688-80309-1); PLB 13.88 (ISBN 0-688-84309-3); Greenwillow.

Oxenbury, Helen. Shopping Trip. LC 81-69274. 14p. (ps-k). 1982. bds. 3.50 (ISBN 0-8037-7939-9). Dial Bks Young.

Peck, Richard. Secrets of the Shopping Mall. 192p. (gr. k-6). 1989. pap. 3.25 (ISBN 0-440-40270-0, LFL); pap. 3.50 (ISBN 0-440-98099-2). Dell.

Ross, Pat. M & M & the Big Bag. 48p. (ps-3). 1985. pap. 2.95 (ISBN 0-14-031852-6, Puffin). Puffin Bks.

—M & M & the Big Bag I Am Reading Book. Hafner, Marilyn, illus. LC 80-23299. 48p. (gr. 1-4). 1981. 6.95 (ISBN 0-394-84340-1). Pantheon.

Ziefert, Harriet. Max & Diana & the Shopping Trip. Johnson, Lonnie S., illus. LC 86-45340. 32p. (ps-2). 1987. 3.95 (ISBN 0-694-00088-4). HarpC Child Bks.

SHORT STORIES

Accorsi, William. Short Short Short Stories. LC 90-48179. (Illus.). 32p. (ps up). 1991. 13.95 (ISBN 0-688-10180-1); PLB 13.88 (ISBN 0-688-10181-X). Greenwillow.

Aiken, Joan. The Last Slice of Rainbow: And Other Stories. Berenzy, Alix, illus. LC 87-45271. 160p. (gr. 3-7). 1988. 12.95 (ISBN 0-06-020042-1); PLB 12.89 (ISBN 0-06-020043-X). HarpC Child Bks.

Alcott, Louisa May. Glimpses of Louisa: A Centennial Sampling of the Best Short Stories by Louisa May Alcott. (gr. 7 up). 1968. 19.95 (ISBN 0-316-03090-2). Little.

Aleichem, Sholom. Holiday Tales of Sholom Aleichem. Shevrin, Aliza, tr. DiGrazia, Thomas, illus. LC 79-753. 145p. (Orig.). (gr. 5 up). 1985. pap. 5.95 (ISBN 0-689-71034-8, Aladdin). Macmillan Child Grp.

Aleksin, Anatoly & Pettepiece, Thomas, eds. Face to Face: A Collection of Stories by Celebrated Soviet & American Writers. Downs, Hugh, intro. by. 256p. 1990. 14.95 (ISBN 0-399-21951-X, Philomel Bks). Putnam Pub Group.

Alexander, Liza. When Oscar Was a Little Grouch & Other Good-Night Stories. (Illus.). 24p. (ps-1). 1989. write for info. (Pub. by Golden Bks). Western Pub.

Allen, Steve & Meadows, Jayne. Shakin' Loose with Mother Goose. Bullock, Kathleen, illus. 128p. (ps-2). 1987. 4 bks. & 2 forty minute tapes in gift box ed. 19.95 (ISBN 0-89411-010-1). Kids Matter.

Allington, Richard L. & Krull, Kathleen. Stories. Cogancherry, Helen, illus. LC 82-10208. 32p. (gr. k-3). 1985. PLB 15.33 (ISBN 0-8172-1386-4); pap. 9.27 (ISBN 0-8172-2490-4). Raintree Pubs.

Alpha Pyramis Publishing Staff. Story Time Stories That Rhyme, Vol. 1: Fish Convention, Rainbow, Miss Divine Sunshine & Others. 35p. (gr. 4-12). 1990. pap. text ed. 15.95 (ISBN 0-913597-99-6, Pub. by Alpha Pyramis). Prosperity & Profits.

American Heritage Magazine Editorial Staff. The American Heritage Junior Library, 20 vols. (gr. 5-11). 1989. 14.95 ea. (ISBN 0-8167-1536-X). Troll Assocs.

Amery, H. First Stories. Cartwright, Stephen, illus. 48p. 1988. 7.95 (ISBN 0-7460-0191-6). EDC.

Andersen, Hans Christian. Eighty Fairy Tales. Keigwin, R. P., tr. LC 82-47882. 394p. (gr. k up). 1982. pap. 11.95 (ISBN 0-394-71055-X). Pantheon.

Anglund, Joan W. The Joan Walsh Anglund Storybook. LC 78-55913. (Illus.). (ps-2). 1978. (Random Juv); lib. bdg. 8.99 (ISBN 0-394-93803-8). Random.

Arnold, Arnold. Pictures & Stories from Forgotten Children's Books. (Illus.). 170p. (Orig.). (gr. k-6). 1970. pap. 7.50 (ISBN 0-486-22041-9). Dover.

Asch, Frank. George's Store. Wiseman, Bernard, illus. LC 82-22298. 48p. (ps-3). 1983. 5.95 (ISBN 0-8193-1101-4); PLB 5.95 (ISBN 0-8193-1102-2). Parents.

Asimov, Isaac, et al, eds. Young Witches & Warlocks. Asimov, Isaac, intro. by. LC 85-45849. 224p. (gr. 7 up). 1987. 12.95 (ISBN 0-06-020183-5); PLB 12.89 (ISBN 0-06-020184-3). HarpC Child Bks.

Babbitt, Natalie. The Devil's Other Storybook. LC 86-32760. (Illus.). 112p. (gr. 3 up). 1987. 10.95 (ISBN 0-374-31767-4). FS&G.

Bailey, Emma. Quality Time Little Readers: One Minute Bedtime Stories. 1991. 1.49 (ISBN 0-8317-7273-5). Smithmark.

Baisden, E. Bertram, et al. Anthology of Caribbean Short Stories. 125p. (Orig.). (gr. 7-12). 1989. pap. text ed. write for info. Caribbean Rsch Ctr.

Barrett, Peter. To Break the Silence: Thirteen Short Stories for Young Readers. (Orig.). (gr. k-12). 1986. pap. 3.25 (ISBN 0-440-98807-1, LFL). Dell.

Bauer, Caroline F., ed. Windy Day: Stories & Poems. Zimmer, Dirk, illus. LC 86-42994. 96p. (gr. 2-5). 1988. 11.95 (ISBN 0-397-32207-0, Lipp Jr Bks); PLB 12.89 (ISBN 0-397-32208-9). HarpC Child Bks.

Bernard, Robert, ed. All Problems Are Simple & Other Stories: Nineteen Views of the College Years. (gr. 12 up). 1988. 3.50 (ISBN 0-318-37398-X, LF). Dell.

The Best Stories & Poems from Lollipops Magazine. 64p. (ps-2). 1990. 6.95 (ISBN 0-86653-564-0, GA1161). Good Apple.

Bond, Michael. Paddington's Storybook. Fortnum, Peggy, illus. 160p. (gr. 1-5). 1984. 16.95 (ISBN 0-395-36667-4). HM.

Brana, Jorge A. The Brown Fox & Other Stories. (ps-8). 1990. 6.95 (ISBN 0-533-08669-8). Vantage.

Branfield, John. The Day I Shot My Dad: And Other Stories. 160p. (gr. 6-9). 1990. 18.95 (ISBN 0-575-04486-1, Pub. by Gollancz England). Trafalgar Sq.

Braun, P. C., ed. The Big Book of Favorite Horse Stories. Savitt, Sam, illus. 336p. (gr. 7 up). 1982. 9.95 (ISBN 0-448-42641-2, G&D). Putnam Pub Group.

Brooke, William J. A Telling of the Tales: Five Stories. Egielski, Richard, illus. LC 89-36588. 144p. (gr. 3-7). 1990. 12.95 (ISBN 0-06-020688-8); PLB 12.89 (ISBN 0-06-020689-6). HarpC Child Bks.

Brooks, Martha. Paradise Cafe & Other Stories. (gr. 7 up). 1990. 14.95 (ISBN 0-316-10978-9, Joy St Bks). Little.

Buck, Pearl S. The Enemy. LC 85-30005. 64p. (gr. 6 up). 1986. PLB 10.95s.p. (ISBN 0-88682-059-6); 15.65 (ISBN 0-685-12405-3). Creative Ed.

Bunyan, Paul. Pilgrims Progress in Modern English. 1984. pap. 0.50 (ISBN 0-87508-048-0). Chr Lit.

Cahill, Susan, ed. Women & Fiction: Short Stories by & About Women. (gr. 7 up). 1975. pap. 4.50 (ISBN 0-451-62411-4, ME2263, Ment). NAL-Dutton.

Calderon, Frank, ed. Washington Irving's Pilgrim of Love: From the Tales of the Alhambra. 2nd ed. Pontet, Daniel G., illus. 64p. (gr. 4 up). 1990. text ed. 19.95 (ISBN 0-939193-20-5). Edit Concepts.

Callen, Larry. Who Kidnapped the Sheriff? Gammill, Stephen L., illus. 176p. (gr. 4 up). 1985. 14.95 (ISBN 0-316-12499-0, Joy St Bks). Little.

Camille, Pamela, intro. by. Children of the Mountains: Short Stories by the Elementary School Children of Pagosa Springs, Colorado. LC 88-81602. (Illus.). 150p. (Orig.). (gr. 4-8). 1988. pap. 7.95 (ISBN 0-945985-01-0). Freedom Lights Pr.

Carlson, Anna L. Stories to Treasure. Wynne, Diana, illus. 24p. (Orig.). (ps-5). 1984. pap. 62.40 (ISBN 0-939938-06-5). Karwyn Ent.

Carlson, Natalie S. Talking Cat & Other Stories of French Canada. Duvoisin, Roger, illus. LC 52-5429. 92p. (gr. 3-6). 1952. PLB 12.89 (ISBN 0-06-021081-8). HarpC Child Bks.

Chadwick, Roxane. Once upon a Felt Board. Skiles, Janet, illus. 128p. (gr. k-4). wkbk. 10.95 (ISBN 0-86653-338-9, GA 798). Good Apple.

Chaikin, Miriam. Hinkle & Other Schlemiel Stories. (Illus.). 96p. (Orig.). (gr. 3-12). 1987. 10.95 (ISBN 0-933503-15-6). Shapolsky Pubs.

Chambers, Aidan, ed. Out of Time. LC 85-42631. 192p. (gr. 7 up). 1985. PLB 12.89 (ISBN 0-06-021202-0). HarpC Child Bks.

—Shades of Dark. LC 85-45840. 128p. (gr. 7 up). 1986. 11.95 (ISBN 0-06-021247-0). HarpC Child Bks.

Child Study Association of America. Read-to-Me Storybook Staff. Lenski, Lois L., illus. LC 47-31488. (ps-1). 1947. 12.95i (ISBN 0-690-68832-6, Crowell Jr Bks). HarpC Child Bks.

Chorao, Kay. The Baby's Story Book. Chorao, Kay, illus. LC 84-26005. (ps-1). 1989. 13.95 (ISBN 0-525-44200-6, DCB); bk. & cassette 17.95 (ISBN 0-525-44507-2). Dutton Child Bks.

—The Child's Story Book. Chorao, Kay, illus. LC 87-8899. 64p. (ps-3). 1987. 12.95 (ISBN 0-525-44328-2, 01258-370, DCB). Dutton Child Bks.

Christian, Peggy. The Old Coot. (Illus.). 64p. (gr. 3-5). 1991. SBE 11.95 (ISBN 0-689-31627-5, Atheneum Child Bk). Macmillan Child Grp.

Coates, Doreen, et al. Little Books, Nos. 1-6: Orange Level. Chesterman, Jo, et al, illus. 12p. (ps-1). 1986. Set. pap. text ed. 12.95 (ISBN 1-55624-062-7, WG0627). Wright Group.

Cole, Joanna & Calmenson, Stephanie, eds. The Read-Aloud Treasury: Favorite Nursery Rhymes, Poems, Stories & More for the Very Young. Schweninger, Ann, illus. 256p. 1988. pap. 18.95 (ISBN 0-385-18560-X). Doubleday.

Colum, Padraic. The Children of Odin: The Book of Northern Myths. reissued ed. Pogany, Willy, illus. LC 83-20368. 280p. (gr. 5up). 1984. 14.95 (ISBN 0-02-722890-8); pap. 7.95 (ISBN 0-02-042100-1, Collier Young Ad). Macmillan Child Grp.

Conford, Ellen. If This Is Love, I'll Take Spaghetti. 166p. (gr. 7 up). 1984. pap. 2.50 (ISBN 0-590-41210-8, Point). Scholastic Inc.

Corcoran, Clodagh. Baker's Dozen: An Anthology of New Fiction for Young People. 272p. 1990. pap. 6.95 (ISBN 1-85371-050-4, Pub. by Poolbeg Pr). Dufour.

Corrin, Sara & Corrin, Stephen, eds. Laugh out Loud: More Funny Stories for Children. Rose, Gerald, illus. 116p. (gr. k-2). 1991. pap. 2.95 (ISBN 0-571-14177-3). Faber & Faber.

—Stories for Nine-Year-Olds & Other Young Readers. Hughes, Shirley, illus. LC 79-670371. 160p. (gr. 2-5). 1979. 11.95 (ISBN 0-571-11409-1); pap. 9.95 (ISBN 0-571-12931-5). Faber & Faber.

Courageous Captain. 32p. (Orig.). (gr. 1-5). 1989. 12.95 (ISBN 0-89800-194-3); pap. 5.95 (ISBN 0-89800-195-1). Dharma Pub.

Crane, Stephen. Maggie & Other Stories. Gemme, F. R., intro. by. (gr. 11 up). pap. 2.75 (ISBN 0-8049-0166-X, CL-166). Airmont.

Crossley-Holland, Kevin, ed. The Dead Moon. Felts, Shirley, illus. 104p. (Orig.). (gr. 4 up). 1986. pap. 8.95 (ISBN 0-571-13879-9). Faber & Faber.

Crutcher, Chris. Athletic Shorts. LC 91-4418. (gr. 12 up). 1991. 13.95 (ISBN 0-688-10816-4). Greenwillow.

Dahl, Roald. Roald Dahl: Charlie & the Chocolate Factory, Charlie & the Great Glass Elevator & The BFG, 3 bks. 1989. Set. pap. 11.95 (ISBN 0-685-30573-2). Viking Penguin.

Davis, Richard H. Ranson's Folly & Other Stories. (gr. 9 up). 1968. pap. 1.95 (ISBN 0-8049-0192-9, CL-192). Airmont.

De Maupassant, Guy. Best Short Stories of Guy de Maupassant. Canon, R. R., intro. by. (gr. 9 up). pap. 2.75 (ISBN 0-8049-0161-9, CL-161). Airmont.

Demi, illus. A Chinese Zoo: Fables & Proverbs. LC 86-33562. 32p. (ps-3). 1987. 14.95 (ISBN 0-15-217510-5, HJ). HarBraceJ.

Dickens, Charles. The Bagman's Story. 48p. (gr. 4 up). 1983. PLB 10.95 (ISBN 0-87191-922-2). Creative Ed.

Disney Babies Bedtime Stories. (ps up). 1990. PLB 9.98 (ISBN 0-7924-5370-0, Mallard Pr). BDD Promo Bk.

Dittberner-Jax, Norita, ed. The Ragged Heart. Wood, Marce, illus. 164p. (Orig.). 1989. pap. 8.00 (ISBN 0-927663-14-7). COMPAS.

Donatelli, Betty. Sunny, Funny Stories. Donatelli, Betty, illus. 11p. (Orig.). (gr. 1-2). 1984. pap. 1.00 (ISBN 0-912981-08-3). Hse Bon Giovanni.

Doyle, Arthur Conan. Great Stories of Sherlock Holmes. 287p. (gr. 5 up). 1962. pap. 1.75 (ISBN 0-440-93190-8, LFL). Dell.

Dravich, Jay. Tales for a Child's Heart. Bernard, Lisa, illus. LC 80-50009. 136p. (Orig.). (gr. k-6). 1980. 12.00 (ISBN 0-686-27348-6); pap. 5.00 (ISBN 0-686-27349-4). Tari Bk Pubs.

Dr. Seuss. Yertle the Turtle & Other Stories. Dr. Seuss, illus. (gr. k-3). 1958. 12.95 (ISBN 0-394-80087-7, Random Juv); PLB 13.99 (ISBN 0-394-90087-1). Random.

Ellis, Joyce K., compiled by. Saved by a Broken Pole & Other Stories. 75p. (Orig.). (gr. 2-6). 1980. pap. 2.25 (ISBN 0-89323-007-3, 096). Bible Memory.

Erickson, John R. Alkali County Tales. Holmes, Gerald, illus. 100p. (Orig.). (gr. 3up). 1984. 9.95 (ISBN 0-916941-06-X); pap. 5.95 (ISBN 0-9608612-8-9). Maverick Bks.

Evans, Mary J. & Anderson, Deborah. Tales from Hans Christian Andersen. (gr. k up). 1983. pap. 4.50 (ISBN 0-87602-257-3). Anchorage.

Favorite Bedtime Stories. LC 64-17442. (ps-2). 1978. write for info. (ISBN 0-528-82217-9). Checkerboard Pr.

Favourite Stories from Vietnam. Cong-Huyen-Ton-Nu, retold by. 1978. pap. text ed. 2.50x (ISBN 0-686-60429-6, 00319). Heinemann Ed.

Fifty Stories for Eight-Year-Olds. (gr. 3). 1990. 7.98 (ISBN 0-8317-3278-4). Smithmark.

Fifty Stories for Seven-Year-Olds. (gr. 2). 1990. 7.98 (ISBN 0-8317-3277-6). Smithmark.

Fifty-Two Stories & Poems for Children. (Illus.). 160p. (gr. 2-5). 1987. casebd. 7.95 (ISBN 0-570-04158-9, 56-1616). Concordia.

First Bedtime Stories. 1991. 4.98 (ISBN 0-8317-3360-8). Smithmark.

Fisher, Barbara & Spiegel, Richard, eds. Streams. (Illus.). 138p. (Orig.). (gr. 9-12). 1987. pap. 5.00 (ISBN 0-934830-39-8). Ten Penny.

—Streams, No. 2. (Illus.). 142p. (gr. 9-12). 1988. pap. 5.00 (ISBN 0-934830-42-8). Ten Penny.

—Streams, No. 3. (Illus.). (gr. 9-12). 1989. pap. 5.00 (ISBN 0-934830-43-6). Ten Penny.

Fuentes, Vilma M. Kimod & the Swan Maiden. Inis, Ninabeth R., illus. 36p. (Orig.). (gr. k-3). 1984. pap. 3.50 (ISBN 0-318-04079-4, Pub. by New Day Philippines). Cellar.

Furman, Abraham L., ed. Everygirls Career Stories. (Illus.). (gr. 6-10). PLB 6.70 (ISBN 0-8313-0049-3). Lantern.

—Everygirls Companion. LC 68-11184. (gr. 5-9). 1968. PLB 6.70 (ISBN 0-685-13773-2). Lantern.

—Teen-Age Great Rescue Stories. (gr. 6-10). PLB 6.70 (ISBN 0-8313-0050-7). Lantern.

Gallo, Donald R. Connections: Short Stories by Outstanding Writers for Young Adults. 1989. 14.95 (ISBN 0-385-29815-3). Doubleday.

Gallo, Donald R., ed. Sixteen: Short Stories by Outstanding Writers for Young Adults. LC 84-3250. 208p. (gr. 7 up). 1984. 16.95 (ISBN 0-385-29346-1). Delacorte.

—Sixteen: Short Stories by Outstanding Young Adult Writers. 192p. (gr. 5-12). 1985. pap. 3.50 (ISBN 0-440-97757-6, LFL). Dell.

—Visions: Nineteen Short Stories by Outstanding Writers for Young Adults. (gr. k-12). 1988. pap. 3.50 (ISBN 0-440-20208-6, LFL). Dell.

—Visions: 19 Short Stories by Outstanding Writers for Young Adults. LC 87-6787. 240p. (gr. 7 up). 1987. pap. 16.95 (ISBN 0-385-29588-X). Delacorte.

Garner, Alan. A Bag of Moonshine. Lynch, Patrick J., illus. LC 86-13362. 160p. (gr. k-5). 1986. pap. 15.95 (ISBN 0-385-29517-0). Delacorte.

Goffstein, M. B. Family Scrapbook. Goffstein, M. B., illus. LC 78-51435. 48p. (ps up). 1978. 8.95 (ISBN 0-374-32269-4). FS&G.

Gold, Robert S. Stepping Stones: Seventeen Powerful Stories of Growing Up. 320p. (gr. 7 up). 1981. pap. 3.25 (ISBN 0-440-98269-3, LFL). Dell.

Goldsborough, June, illus. Stories to Grow On. LC 73-7200. 64p. (ps-3). write for info. (ISBN 0-528-82420-1). Checkerboard Pr.

Grender, Iris. Did I Ever Tell You...What the Children Told Me? Ross, Tony, illus. 86p. (gr. 1-3). 1987. 12.95 (ISBN 0-09-155280-X, Pub. by Hutchinson UK). Trafalgar Sq.

—The Second "Did I Ever Tell You...?" Ross, Tony, illus. 64p. (gr. 1-3). 1987. 12.95 (ISBN 0-09-133970-7, Pub. by Hutchinson UK). Trafalgar Sq.

—The Third "Did I Ever Tell You...?" Ross, Tony, illus. 64p. (gr. 1-3). 1987. 12.95 (ISBN 0-09-140370-7, Pub. by Hutchinson UK). Trafalgar Sq.

Hale, Edward E. Man Without a Country & Other Stories. (gr. 5 up). 1968. pap. 1.95 (ISBN 0-8049-0185-6, CL-185). Airmont.

Hall, Nancy C., ed. Platt & Munk Treasury of Stories for Children. LC 79-56868. (Illus.). 128p. (ps-3). 1981. 9.95 (ISBN 0-448-47722-X, G&D). Putnam Pub Group.

Hamel, Jean-Marie. Heart Tales: A Collection of Stories from a Child's Heart. Hamel, Jean-Marie, illus. 40p. (ps-3). 1990. 12.95g (ISBN 0-929684-50-8). Silver Forest Pub.

The Hands of Pablo Santos. 96p. (gr. 6-9). 1985. pap. 4.95 (ISBN 0-521-31706-1). Cambridge U Pr.

Hardegrove, Nelle A. Ten Stories for Children. Miller, Dennis, illus. 10p. (Orig.). (gr. 1-5). 1987. pap. text ed. 7.95 (ISBN 0-9619227-3-7). N A Hardegrove.

Harris, Raymond. Best Short Stories: Advanced Level. Burgoyne, Mari-Ann S., illus. 560p. (Orig.). (gr. 9 up). 1980. text ed. 16.00 (ISBN 0-89061-705-8, 620H); pap. text ed. 12.75 (ISBN 0-89061-701-5, 620). Jamestown Pubs.

—Best Short Stories, Middle Level. Lawrence, George, et al, illus. (gr. 6-10). 1983. text ed. 16.00 (ISBN 0-89061-322-2, 793H); pap. text ed. 12.75 (ISBN 0-89061-321-4, 793). Jamestown Pubs.

Harris, Rosemary. The Lotus & the Grail: Legends from East to East. Le Cain, Erro, illus. 272p. (gr. 7 up). 1985. pap. 7.95 (ISBN 0-571-13536-6). Faber & Faber.

Harun. Autumn Tales by Harun-of-UR. Date not set. write for info. Songbird & Seabird.

Harwood, Pearl A. Mrs. Moon's Story Hour. Overlie, George, illus. LC 67-15687. 32p. (gr. k-3). 1967. PLB 4.95 (ISBN 0-8225-0111-2). Lerner Pubns.

Heart of Gold. 32p. (Orig.). (gr. 1-5). 1989. 12.95 (ISBN 0-89800-192-7); pap. 5.95 (ISBN 0-89800-193-5). Dharma Pub.

Hitchcock, Alfred. Alfred Hitchcock's Spellbinders in Suspense. Isen, Harold, illus. (gr. 7-11). 1982. lib. bdg. 6.99 (ISBN 0-394-91665-4, Random Juv); pap. 3.95 (ISBN 0-394-84900-0). Random.

Holt, Virginia. Baby Kermit & the Dinosaur. Venning, Sue, illus. LC 86-62181. 32p. (ps-3). 1987. pap. 1.25 (ISBN 0-394-88782-4, Random Juv). Random.

Hwa-I Publishing Co., Staff. Chinese Children's Stories, Vol. 10: The Money Tree, The Coxcomb. Ching, Emily, et al, eds. Wonder Kids Publications Staff, tr. from CHI. Hwa-I Publishing Co., Staff, illus. LC 90-60792. 28p. (gr. 3-6). Repr. of 1988 ed. 7.95x (ISBN 1-56162-010-6). Wonder Kids.

—Chinese Children's Stories, Vol. 100: From Rice into Flowers, The Shy Rainbow. Ching, Emily, et al, eds. Wonder Kids Publications Staff, tr. from CHI. Hwa-I Publishing Co., Staff, illus. LC 90-60811. 28p. (gr. 3-6). Repr. of 1988 ed. 7.95x (ISBN 1-56162-100-5). Wonder Kids.

—Chinese Children's Stories, Vol. 12: The Snail & the Ox, Sparrows Can't Walk. Ching, Emily, et al, eds. Wonder Kids Publications Staff, tr. from CHI. Hwa-I Publishing Co., Staff, illus. LC 90-60793. 28p. (gr. 3-6). Repr. of 1988 ed. 7.95x (ISBN 1-56162-012-2). Wonder Kids.

—Chinese Children's Stories, Vol. 13: Rooster Summons the Sun, The White-Haired Bird. Ching, Emily, et al, eds. Wonder Kids Publications Staff, tr. from CHI. Hwa-I Publishing Co., Staff, illus. LC 90-60793. 28p. (gr. 3-6). Repr. of 1988 ed. 7.95x (ISBN 1-56162-013-0). Wonder Kids.

—Chinese Children's Stories, Vol. 14: Weasel Steals the Chickens, Why is the Crow Black? Ching, Emily, et al, eds. Wonder Kids Publications Staff, tr. from CHI. Hwa-I Publishing Co., Staff, illus. LC 90-60793. 28p. (gr. 3-6). Repr. of 1988 ed. 7.95x (ISBN 1-56162-014-9). Wonder Kids.

—Chinese Children's Stories, Vol. 15: Jiggle in the Wind, The Bat Can't See the Sun. Ching, Emily, et al, eds. Wonder Kids Publications Staff, tr. from CHI. Hwa-I Publishing Co., Staff, illus. LC 90-60793. 28p. (gr. 3-6). Repr. of 1988 ed. 7.95x (ISBN 1-56162-015-7). Wonder Kids.

—Chinese Children's Stories, Vol. 17: The Monkey & the Fire, Lazy Wife & the Bread Ring. Ching, Emily, et al, eds. Wonder Kids Publications Staff, tr. from CHI. Hwa-I Publishing Co., Staff, illus. LC 90-60794. 28p. (gr. 3-6). Repr. of 1988 ed. 7.95x (ISBN 1-56162-017-3). Wonder Kids.

—Chinese Children's Stories, Vol. 18: The Little Bamboo Pole, The Wise Old Man. Ching, Emily, et al, eds. Wonder Kids Publications Staff, tr. from CHI. Hwa-I Publishing Co., Staff, illus. LC 90-60794. 28p. (gr. 3-6). Repr. of 1988 ed. 7.95x (ISBN 1-56162-018-1). Wonder Kids.

—Chinese Children's Stories, Vol. 19: Crow Moves Away, Baby Lion & Baby Rhino. Ching, Emily, et al, eds. Wonder Kids Publications Staff, tr. from CHI. Hwa-I Publishing Co., Staff, illus. LC 90-60794. 28p. (gr. 3-6). Repr. of 1988 ed. 7.95x (ISBN 1-56162-019-X). Wonder Kids.

—Chinese Children's Stories, Vol. 20: Ah-Liu Picks Corn, Cuckoo's Winter. Ching, Emily, et al, eds. Wonder Kids Publications Staff, tr. from CHI. Hwa-I Publishing Co., Staff, illus. LC 90-60794. 28p. (gr. 3-6). Repr. of 1988 ed. 7.95x (ISBN 1-56162-020-3). Wonder Kids.

—Chinese Children's Stories, Vol. 22: The Steal a Bell, The Dropout. Ching, Emily, et al, eds. Wonder Kids Publications Staff, tr. from CHI. Hwa-I Publishing Co., Staff, illus. LC 90-60796. 28p. (gr. 3-6). Repr. of 1988 ed. 7.95x (ISBN 1-56162-022-X). Wonder Kids.

—Chinese Children's Stories, Vol. 23: Dummy Afa, The Fox in a Tiger's Suit. Ching, Emily, et al, eds. Wonder Kids Publications Staff, tr. from CHI. Hwa-I Publishing Co., Staff, illus. LC 90-60796. 28p. (gr. 3-6). Repr. of 1988 ed. 7.95x (ISBN 1-56162-023-8). Wonder Kids.

—Chinese Children's Stories, Vol. 24: Running Fifty vs. One-Hundred Strides, Atu Yanks the Rice Seedlings. Ching, Emily, et al, eds. Wonder Kids Publications Staff, tr. from CHI. Hwa-I Publishing Co., Staff, illus. LC 90-60796. 28p. (gr. 3-6). Repr. of 1988 ed. 7.95x (ISBN 1-56162-024-6). Wonder Kids.

—Chinese Children's Stories, Vol. 25: The Blindmen & the Elephant, Little Frog in the Well. Ching, Emily, et al, eds. Wonder Kids Publications Staff, tr. from CHI. Hwa-I Publishing Co., Staff, illus. LC 90-60796. 28p. (gr. 3-6). Repr. of 1988 ed. 7.95x (ISBN 1-56162-025-4). Wonder Kids.

—Chinese Children's Stories, Vol. 27: Sky-Mending Festival, Decorative Paper for Graves. Ching, Emily, et al, eds. Wonder Kids Publications Staff, tr. from CHI. Hwa-I Publishing Co., Staff, illus. LC 90-60797. 28p. (gr. 3-6). Repr. of 1988 ed. 7.95x (ISBN 1-56162-027-0). Wonder Kids.

—Chinese Children's Stories, Vol. 28: Mih-Ro River, The Herder & the Seamstress. Ching, Emily, et al, eds. Wonder Kids Publications Staff, tr. from CHI. Hwa-I Publishing Co., Staff, illus. LC 90-60797. 28p. (gr. 3-6). Repr. of 1988 ed. 7.95x (ISBN 1-56162-028-9). Wonder Kids.

—Chinese Children's Stories, Vol. 29: Moon Cake, Fei's Adventure. Ching, Emily, et al, eds. Wonder Kids Publications Staff, tr. from CHI. Hwa-I Publishing Co., Staff, illus. LC 90-60797. 28p. (gr. 3-6). Repr. of 1988 ed. 7.95x (ISBN 1-56162-029-7). Wonder Kids.

—Chinese Children's Stories, Vol. 30: La-Ba Porridge, The Stove God. Ching, Emily, et al, eds. Wonder Kids Publications Staff, tr. from CHI. Hwa-I Publishing Co., Staff, illus. LC 90-60797. 28p. (gr. 3-6). Repr. of 1988 ed. 7.95x (ISBN 1-56162-030-0). Wonder Kids.

—Chinese Children's Stories, Vol. 32: Dumplings, Ham. Ching, Emily, et al, eds. Wonder Kids Publications Staff, tr. from CHI. Hwa-I Publishing Co., Staff, illus. LC 90-60798. 28p. (gr. 3-6). Repr. of 1988 ed. 7.95x (ISBN 1-56162-032-7). Wonder Kids.

—Chinese Children's Stories, Vol. 34: The Stuffed Steamed Bao, Miss Freckle's Tofu. Ching, Emily, et al, eds. Wonder Kids Publications Staff, tr. from CHI. Hwa-I Publishing Co., Staff, illus. LC 90-60798. 28p. (gr. 3-6). Repr. of 1988 ed. 7.95x (ISBN 1-56162-034-3). Wonder Kids.

—Chinese Children's Stories, Vol. 35: Monks' Beef Stew, Yue's Tofu Store. Ching, Emily, et al, eds. Wonder Kids Publications Staff, tr. from CHI. Hwa-I Publishing Co., Staff, illus. LC 90-60798. 28p. (gr. 3-6). Repr. of 1988 ed. 7.95x (ISBN 1-56162-035-1). Wonder Kids.

—Chinese Children's Stories, Vol. 37: Confucius' Bookkeeping, The Scissors Shop. Ching, Emily, et al, eds. Wonder Kids Publications Staff, tr. from CHI. Hwa-I Publishing Co., Staff, illus. LC 90-60799. 28p. (gr. 3-6). Repr. of 1988 ed. 7.95x (ISBN 1-56162-037-8). Wonder Kids.

—Chinese Children's Stories, Vol. 38: The Peace Drum, Comb. Ching, Emily, et al, eds. Wonder Kids Publications Staff, tr. from CHI. Hwa-I Publishing Co., Staff, illus. LC 90-60799. 28p. (gr. 3-6). Repr. of 1988 ed. 7.95x (ISBN 1-56162-038-6). Wonder Kids.

—Chinese Children's Stories, Vol. 39: Brush Pen, Duan's Ink-Slab. Ching, Emily, et al, eds. Wonder Kids Publications Staff, tr. from CHI. Hwa-I Publishing Co., Staff, illus. LC 90-6079. 28p. (gr. 3-6). Repr. of 1988 ed. 7.95x (ISBN 1-56162-039-4). Wonder Kids.

—Chinese Children's Stories, Vol. 39: Noodles over the Bridge, Steamed Bread. Ching, Emily, et al, eds. Wonder Kids Publications Staff, tr. from CHI. Hwa-I Publishing Co., Staff, illus. LC 90-60798. 28p. (gr. 3-6). Repr. of 1988 ed. 7.95x (ISBN 1-56162-033-5). Wonder Kids.

—Chinese Children's Stories, Vol. 40: The Ink-Stick, Shiuan Paper. Ching, Emily, et al, eds. Wonder Kids Publications Staff, tr. from CHI. Hwa-I Publishing Co., Staff, illus. LC 90-60799. 28p. (gr. 3-6). Repr. of 1988 ed. 7.95x (ISBN 1-56162-040-8). Wonder Kids.

—Chinese Children's Stories, Vol. 42: Tiger Seeks a Master, Why Are Cats Afraid of Dogs? Ching, Emily, et al, eds. Wonder Kids Publications Staff, tr. from CHI. Hwa-I Publishing Co., Staff, illus. LC 90-60800. 28p. (gr. 3-6). Repr. of 1988 ed. 7.95x (ISBN 1-56162-042-4). Wonder Kids.

—Chinese Children's Stories, Vol. 43: The Bunny's Tail, Fox, Monkey, Rabbit & Horse. Ching, Emily, et al, eds. Wonder Kids Publications Staff, tr. from CHI. Hwa-I Publishing Co., Staff, illus. LC 90-60800. 28p. (gr. 3-6). Repr. of 1988 ed. 7.95x (ISBN 1-56162-043-2). Wonder Kids.

—Chinese Children's Stories, Vol. 44: Snake's Lost Drum, Ox & Buffalo Change Clothes. Ching, Emily, et al, eds. Wonder Kids Publications Staff, tr. from CHI. Hwa-I Publishing Co., Staff, illus. LC 90-60800. 28p. (gr. 3-6). Repr. of 1988 ed. 7.95x (ISBN 1-56162-044-0). Wonder Kids.

—Chinese Children's Stories, Vol. 45: The Goat & the Camel, The Wolf & the Pig. Ching, Emily, et al, eds. Wonder Kids Publications Staff, tr. from CHI. Hwa-I Publishing Co., Staff, illus. LC 90-60800. 28p. (gr. 3-6). Repr. of 1988 ed. 7.95x (ISBN 1-56162-045-9). Wonder Kids.

—Chinese Children's Stories, Vol. 47: The Crane-Riding Immortal, Lyu Dungbin & Guanyin. Ching, Emily, et al, eds. Wonder Kids Publications Staff, tr. from CHI. Hwa-I Publishing Co., Staff, illus. LC 90-60801. 28p. (gr. 3-6). Repr. of 1988 ed. 7.95x (ISBN 1-56162-047-5). Wonder Kids.

—Chinese Children's Stories, Vol. 48: Sir Thunder & Lady Lightning, The Door Guards. Ching, Emily, et al, eds. Wonder Kids Publications Staff, tr. from CHI. Hwa-I Publishing Co., Staff, illus. LC 90-60801. 28p. (gr. 3-6). Repr. of 1988 ed. 7.95x (ISBN 1-56162-048-3). Wonder Kids.

—Chinese Children's Stories, Vol. 49: The Slippery Nose Deity, Under the Moonlight. Ching, Emily, et al, eds. Wonder Kids Publications Staff, tr. from CHI. Hwa-I Publishing Co., Staff, illus. LC 90-60801. 28p. (gr. 3-6). Repr. of 1988 ed. 7.95x (ISBN 1-56162-049-1). Wonder Kids.

—Chinese Children's Stories, Vol. 50: Zung Kuei & the Little Ghost, Earth God & Earth Goddess. Ching, Emily, et al, eds. Wonder Kids Publications Staff, tr. from CHI. Hwa-I Publishing Co., Staff, illus. LC 90-60801. 28p. (gr. 3-6). Repr. of 1988 ed. 7.95x (ISBN 1-56162-050-5). Wonder Kids.

—Chinese Children's Stories, Vol. 52: Joining the Army, Beating up the Tiger. Ching, Emily, et al, eds. Wonder Kids Publications Staff, tr. from CHI. Hwa-I Publishing Co., Staff, illus. LC 90-60802. 28p. (gr. 3-6). Repr. of 1988 ed. 7.95x (ISBN 1-56162-052-1). Wonder Kids.

—Chinese Children's Stories, Vol. 53: Meeting an Angel, The Child in the Deer Skin. Ching, Emily, et al, eds. Wonder Kids Publications Staff, tr. from CHI. Hwa-I Publishing Co., Staff, illus. LC 90-60802. 28p. (gr. 3-6). Repr. of 1988 ed. 7.95x (ISBN 1-56162-053-X). Wonder Kids.

—Chinese Children's Stories, Vol. 54: The Story of Shun, Village of Filial Piety. Ching, Emily, et al, eds. Wonder Kids Publications Staff, tr. from CHI. Hwa-I Publishing Co., Staff, illus. LC 90-60802. 28p. (gr. 3-6). Repr. of 1988 ed. 7.95x (ISBN 1-56162-054-8). Wonder Kids.

—Chinese Children's Stories, Vol. 55: Two Baskets of Mulberries, Trun's Little Daughter. Ching, Emily, et al, eds. Wonder Kids Publications Staff, tr. from CHI. Hwa-I Publishing Co., Staff, illus. LC 90-60802. 28p. (gr. 3-6). Repr. of 1988 ed. 7.95x (ISBN 1-56162-055-6). Wonder Kids.

—Chinese Children's Stories, Vol. 57: The Little-Boy God, A Rooster's Egg. Ching, Emily, et al, eds. Wonder Kids Publications Staff, tr. from CHI. Hwa-I Publishing Co., Staff, illus. LC 90-60803. 28p. (gr. 3-6). Repr. of 1988 ed. 7.95x (ISBN 1-56162-057-2). Wonder Kids.

—Chinese Children's Stories, Vol. 58: Three Princes & the Firewood, Wang's Memory. Ching, Emily, et al, eds. Wonder Kids Publications Staff, tr. from CHI. Hwa-I Publishing Co., Staff, illus. LC 90-60803. 28p. (gr. 3-6). Repr. of 1988 ed. 7.95x (ISBN 1-56162-058-0). Wonder Kids.

—Chinese Children's Stories, Vol. 59: A Tankful of Water, The Little Hero. Ching, Emily, et al, eds. Wonder Kids Publications Staff, tr. from CHI. Hwa-I Publishing Co., Staff, illus. LC 90-60803. 28p. (gr. 3-6). Repr. of 1988 ed. 7.95x (ISBN 1-56162-059-9). Wonder Kids.

—Chinese Children's Stories, Vol. 60: Weighing an Elephant, The Distant Homeland. Ching, Emily, et al, eds. Wonder Kids Publications Staff, tr. from CHI. Hwa-I Publishing Co., Staff, illus. LC 90-60803. 28p. (gr. 3-6). Repr. of 1988 ed. 7.95x (ISBN 1-56162-060-2). Wonder Kids.

—Chinese Children's Stories, Vol. 61: To Catch the Suns, Two Quarrelsome Brothers. Ching, Emily, et al, eds. Wonder Kids Publications Staff, tr. from CHI. Hwa-I Publishing Co., Staff, illus. LC 90-60804. 28p. (gr. 3-6). Repr. of 1988 ed. 7.95x (ISBN 1-56162-062-9). Wonder Kids.

—Chinese Children's Stories, Vol. 63: To Speak or Not, The Dark Village. Ching, Emily, et al, eds. Wonder Kids Publications Staff, tr. from CHI. Hwa-I Publishing Co., Staff, illus. LC 90-60804. 28p. (gr. 3-6). Repr. of 1988 ed. 7.95x (ISBN 1-56162-063-7). Wonder Kids.

—Chinese Children's Stories, Vol. 64: Why Is the Sky So High?, Turning into Stone. Ching, Emily, et al, eds. Wonder Kids Publications Staff, tr. from CHI. Hwa-I Publishing Co., Staff, illus. LC 90-60804. 28p. (gr. 3-6). Repr. of 1988 ed. 7.95x (ISBN 1-56162-064-5). Wonder Kids.

—Chinese Children's Stories, Vol. 65: Lugging Mountains, What's a Life Span? Ching, Emily, et al, eds. Wonder Kids Publications Staff, tr. from CHI. Hwa-I Publishing Co., Staff, illus. LC 90-60804. 28p. (gr. 3-6). Repr. of 1988 ed. 7.95x (ISBN 1-56162-065-3). Wonder Kids.

—Chinese Children's Stories, Vol. 67: The After-Meal Bell, Passing the Three Gorges. Ching, Emily, et al, eds. Wonder Kids Publications Staff, tr. from CHI. Hwa-I Publishing Co., Staff, illus. LC 90-60805. 28p. (gr. 3-6). Repr. of 1988 ed. 7.95x (ISBN 1-56162-067-X). Wonder Kids.

—Chinese Children's Stories, Vol. 68: The Donkey-Riding Poet, The Backyard Song. Ching, Emily, et al, eds. Wonder Kids Publications Staff, tr. from CHI. Hwa-I Publishing Co., Staff, illus. LC 90-60805. 28p. (gr. 3-6). Repr. of 1988 ed. 7.95x (ISBN 1-56162-068-8). Wonder Kids.

—Chinese Children's Stories, Vol. 69: The Young Family, Tsuei's Beautiful Bride. Ching, Emily, et al, eds. Wonder Kids Publications Staff, tr. from CHI. Hwa-I Publishing Co., Staff, illus. LC 90-60805. 28p. (gr. 3-6). Repr. of 1988 ed. 7.95x (ISBN 1-56162-069-6). Wonder Kids.

—Chinese Children's Stories, Vol. 7: Dragon Eye & Cassia Circle, The Conceited Barber. Ching, Emily, et al, eds. Wonder Kids Publications Staff, tr. from CHI. Hwa-I Publishing Co., Staff, illus. LC 90-60792. 28p. (gr. 3-6). Repr. of 1988 ed. 7.95x (ISBN 1-56162-007-6). Wonder Kids.

—Chinese Children's Stories, Vol. 70: Ji's Jokes, The Scrooge. Ching, Emily, et al, eds. Wonder Kids Publications Staff, tr. from CHI. Hwa-I Publishing Co., Staff, illus. LC 90-60805. 28p. (gr. 3-6). Repr. of 1988 ed. 7.95x (ISBN 1-56162-070-X). Wonder Kids.

—Chinese Children's Stories, Vol. 72: The Lotus Child, The Ghost in the Basin. Ching, Emily, et al, eds. Wonder Kids Publications Staff, tr. from CHI. Hwa-I Publishing Co., Staff, illus. LC 90-60806. 28p. (gr. 3-6). Repr. of 1988 ed. 7.95x (ISBN 1-56162-072-6). Wonder Kids.

—Chinese Children's Stories, Vol. 73: Walking through Walls, Who Is the Real Lord Ji? Ching, Emily, et al, eds. Wonder Kids Publications Staff, tr. from CHI. Hwa-I Publishing Co., Staff, illus. LC 90-60806. 28p. (gr. 3-6). Repr. of 1988 ed. 7.95x (ISBN 1-56162-073-4). Wonder Kids.

—Chinese Children's Stories, Vol. 74: Chaos in the Heavenly Palace, Eating the Ginseng Fruit. Ching, Emily, et al, eds. Wonder Kids Publications Staff, tr. from CHI. Hwa-I Publishing Co., Staff, illus. LC 90-60806. 28p. (gr. 3-6). Repr. of 1988 ed. 7.95x (ISBN 1-56162-074-2). Wonder Kids.

—Chinese Children's Stories, Vol. 75: Tang's Strange Journey, Dwarfs & Giants. Ching, Emily, et al, eds. Wonder Kids Publications Staff, tr. from CHI. Hwa-I Publishing Co., Staff, illus. LC 90-60806. 28p. (gr. 3-6). Repr. of 1988 ed. 7.95x (ISBN 1-56162-075-0). Wonder Kids.

—Chinese Children's Stories, Vol. 77: Sir Guan's Big Red Face, Turning Cranes into Words. Ching, Emily, et al, eds. Wonder Kids Publications Staff, tr. from CHI. Hwa-I Publishing Co., Staff, illus. LC 90-60807. 28p. (gr. 3-6). Repr. of 1988 ed. 7.95x (ISBN 1-56162-077-7). Wonder Kids.

—Chinese Children's Stories, Vol. 78: Tang Buohu's Drawings, The General & the Water Tank. Ching, Emily, et al, eds. Wonder Kids Publications Staff, tr. from CHI. Hwa-I Publishing Co., Staff, illus. LC 90-60807. 28p. (gr. 3-6). Repr. of 1988 ed. 7.95x (ISBN 1-56162-078-5). Wonder Kids.

—Chinese Children's Stories, Vol. 79: Black-Faced Sir Bao, Doctor Hwa-Tuo. Ching, Emily, et al, eds. Wonder Kids Publications Staff, tr. from CHI. Hwa-I Publishing Co., Staff, illus. LC 90-60807. 28p. (gr. 3-6). Repr. of 1988 ed. 7.95x (ISBN 1-56162-079-3). Wonder Kids.

—Chinese Children's Stories, Vol. 8: The Millets Won't Go Home, The Immortal Palm. Ching, Emily, et al, eds. Wonder Kids Publications Staff, tr. from CHI. Hwa-I Publishing Co., Staff, illus. LC 90-60792. 28p. (gr. 3-6). Repr. of 1988 ed. 7.95x (ISBN 1-56162-008-4). Wonder Kids.

—Chinese Children's Stories, Vol. 80: The Dwarf Minister, The Fabulous Chimera's Gift. Ching, Emily, et al, eds. Wonder Kids Publications Staff, tr. from CHI. Hwa-I Publishing Co., Staff, illus. LC 90-60807. 28p. (gr. 3-6). Repr. of 1988 ed. 7.95x (ISBN 1-56162-080-7). Wonder Kids.

—Chinese Children's Stories, Vol. 82: The Fish Minister, The Hidden Sword. Ching, Emily, et al, eds. Wonder Kids Publications Staff, tr. from CHI. Hwa-I Publishing Co., Staff, illus. LC 90-60808. 28p. (gr. 3-6). Repr. of 1988 ed. 7.95x (ISBN 1-56162-082-3). Wonder Kids.

—Chinese Children's Stories, Vol. 83: The Revenge of Chao's Orphan, Tien's Wonderful Strategies. Ching, Emily, et al, eds. Wonder Kids Publications Staff, tr. from CHI. Hwa-I Publishing Co., Staff, illus. LC 90-60808. 28p. (gr. 3-6). Repr. of 1988 ed. 7.95x (ISBN 1-56162-083-1). Wonder Kids.

—Chinese Children's Stories, Vol. 84: Who Is the Real Liu Bong?, Kong Borrows the East Wind. Ching, Emily, et al, eds. Wonder Kids Publications Staff, tr. from CHI. Hwa-I Publishing Co., Staff, illus. LC 90-60808. 28p. (gr. 3-6). Repr. of 1988 ed. 7.95x (ISBN 1-56162-084-X). Wonder Kids.

—Chinese Children's Stories, Vol. 85: The Battle of the Fei River, The Princess' Engagement. Ching, Emily, et al, eds. Wonder Kids Publications Staff, tr. from CHI. Hwa-I Publishing Co., Staff, illus. LC 90-60808. 28p. (gr. 3-6). Repr. of 1988 ed. 7.95x (ISBN 1-56162-085-8). Wonder Kids.

—Chinese Children's Stories, Vol. 87: Fan Bridge & Escape Alley, The Stream of Flowers. Ching, Emily, et al, eds. Wonder Kids Publications Staff, tr. from CHI. Hwa-I Publishing Co., Staff, illus. LC 90-60809. 28p. (gr. 3-6). Repr. of 1988 ed. 7.95x (ISBN 1-56162-087-4). Wonder Kids.

—Chinese Children's Stories, Vol. 88: Five Stone Goats, Six-Foot Street. Ching, Emily, et al, eds. Wonder Kids Publications Staff, tr. from CHI. Hwa-I Publishing Co., Staff, illus. LC 90-60809. 28p. (gr. 3-6). Repr. of 1988 ed. 7.95x (ISBN 1-56162-088-2). Wonder Kids.

—Chinese Children's Stories, Vol. 89: Peach Blossom Cave, Mt. Lee. Ching, Emily, et al, eds. Wonder Kids Publications Staff, tr. from CHI. Hwa-I Publishing Co. Staff, illus. LC 90-60809. 28p. (gr. 3-6). Repr. of 1988 ed. 7.95x (ISBN 1-56162-089-0). Wonder Kids.

—Chinese Children's Stories, Vol. 9: The Story of Rice, The Cows & the Trumpet. Ching, Emily, et al, eds. Wonder Kids Publications Staff, tr. from CHI. Hwa-I Publishing Co., Staff, illus. LC 90-60792. 28p. (gr. 3-6). Repr. of 1988 ed. 7.95x (ISBN 1-56162-009-2). Wonder Kids.

—Chinese Children's Stories, Vol. 90: The Dragon Who Puts out Fires, The Golden Hairpin Well. Ching, Emily, et al, eds. Wonder Kids Publications Staff, tr. from CHI. Hwa-I Publishing Co., Staff, illus. LC 90-60809. 28p. (gr. 3-6). Repr. of 1988 ed. 7.95x (ISBN 1-56162-090-4). Wonder Kids.

—Chinese Children's Stories, Vol. 92: White-Rice Magic Cave, Sun-Moon Lake. Ching, Emily, et al, eds. Wonder Kids Publications Staff, tr. from CHI. Hwa-I Publishing Co., Staff, illus. LC 90-60810. 28p. (gr. 3-6). Repr. of 1988 ed. 7.95x (ISBN 1-56162-092-0). Wonder Kids.

—Chinese Children's Stories, Vol. 93: Mt. Anvil & the Sword Well, Two Waters. Ching, Emily, et al, eds. Wonder Kids Publications Staff, tr. from CHI. Hwa-I Publishing Co., Staff, illus. LC 90-60810. 28p. (gr. 3-6). Repr. of 1988 ed. 7.95x (ISBN 1-56162-093-9). Wonder Kids.

—Chinese Children's Stories, Vol. 94: Muddy Water Stream, Sister Lakes & Brother Trees. Ching, Emily, et al, eds. Wonder Kids Publications Staff, tr. from CHI. Hwa-I Publishing Co., Staff, illus. LC 90-60810. 28p. (gr. 3-6). Repr. of 1988 ed. 7.95x (ISBN 1-56162-094-7). Wonder Kids.

—Chinese Children's Stories, Vol. 95: Half-Shield Mountain, The Adopted Daughter Lake. Ching, Emily, et al, eds. Wonder Kids Publications Staff, tr. from CHI. Hwa-I Publishing Co., Staff, illus. LC 90-60810. 28p. (gr. 3-6). Repr. of 1988 ed. 7.95x (ISBN 1-56162-095-5). Wonder Kids.

—Chinese Children's Stories, Vol. 97: Tiger Aunty, Ah-Long & Ah-Hwa. Ching, Emily, et al, eds. Wonder Kids Publications Staff, tr. from CHI. Hwa-I Publishing Co., Staff, illus. LC 90-60811. 28p. (gr. 3-6). Repr. of 1988 ed. 7.95x (ISBN 1-56162-097-1). Wonder Kids.

—Chinese Children's Stories, Vol. 98: Ai-Yu Jello, Granny & the Fox. Ching, Emily, et al, eds. Wonder Kids Publications Staff, tr. from CHI. Hwa-I Publishing Co., Staff, illus. LC 90-60811. 28p. (gr. 3-6). Repr. of 1988 ed. 7.95x (ISBN 1-56162-098-X). Wonder Kids.

—Chinese Children's Stories, Vol. 99: The Underground People, Half-Street Lai. Ching, Emily, et al, eds. Wonder Kids Publications Staff, tr. from CHI. Hwa-I Publishing Co., Staff, illus. LC 90-60811. 28p. (gr. 3-6). Repr. of 1988 ed. 7.95x (ISBN 1-56162-099-8). Wonder Kids.

Ireson, Barbara, ed. Fighting in Break: And Other Stories. Helland, Susan, illus. 128p. (gr. 3-6). 1987. 10.95 (ISBN 0-571-14623-6). Faber & Faber.

Irving, Washington. The Legend of Sleepy Hollow. Van Nutt, Robert, adapted by. & illus. LC 88-33375. 32p. (ps up). 1989. 14.95 (ISBN 0-88708-088-X, Rabbit Ears); incl. cassette 19.95 (ISBN 0-88708-089-8). Picture Bk Studio.

—Legend of Sleepy Hollow & Other Stories. (gr. 6 up). 1964. pap. 2.75 (ISBN 0-8049-0050-7, CL-50). Airmont.

—Washington Irving's Tales of the Supernatural. Wagenknecht, Edward, ed. Alley, R. W., illus. LC 80-29313. 288p. (gr. 6 up). 1982. 17.95 (ISBN 0-916144-64-X). Stemmer Hse.

James, Henry. Daisy Miller & Other Stories. LC 84-29480. (gr. 9 up). 1968. pap. 1.75 (ISBN 0-8049-0178-3, CL-178). Airmont.

Jameson, Mack & Nist, Al. The Last Good-Bye & Other Stories. Roderman, Winifred H., ed. (Illus.). 64p. (Orig.). (gr. 7-12). 1981. pap. text ed. 3.95 (ISBN 0-915510-55-3); tchr's. manual avail. Janus Bks.

—Time to Change & Other Stories. Roderman, Winifred H., ed. (Illus.). (gr. 7-12). 1981. pap. text ed. 3.95 (ISBN 0-915510-56-1). Janus Bks.

Janger, Kathie, ed. Rainbow Collection, 1987: Stories & Poetry by Young People. Ishikawa, Yoko, illus. Johnson, Rafer, intro. by. (Illus.). 160p. (gr. 1-8). 1987. pap. text ed. 6.00 (ISBN 0-929889-02-9). Young Writers Contest Found.

—Rainbow Collection, 1988: Stories & Poetry by Young People. Turtiainen, Tuomas, illus. Valenti, Jack, intro. by. (Illus.). 160p. (gr. 1-8). 1988. pap. 6.00 (ISBN 0-929889-03-7). Young Writers Contest Found.

Janger, Kathie & Korenblit, Joan, eds. Rainbow Collection, 1985: Stories & Poetry by Young People. Allen, Steve, frwd. by. 160p. (gr. 1-8). 1985. pap. 6.00 (ISBN 0-929889-00-2). Young Writers Contest Found.

—Rainbow Collection, 1986: Stories & Poetry by Young People. Scott, Willard, frwd. by. 160p. (gr. 1-8). 1986. pap. 6.00 (ISBN 0-929889-01-0). Young Writers Contest Found.

Janssen, Lawrence H. Green Lake Tales & Trails. Janssen, Beverly B., illus. LC 84-71073. 96p. (ps-6). 1984. pap. 4.95 (ISBN 0-917575-00-8). Cedars WI.

Johnson, Ralph E. Children's Stories Two: Coloring Nature's Harmony. Johnson, Paul T., ed. Clark, Melissa & Johnson, Gloria, illus. Johnson, Paul. 100p. (Orig.). (gr. k-12). 1989. pap. write for info. (ISBN 0-9621929-0-2). J-p Press.

Jones, Michael P. Works in Progress, Vol. 1. (Illus.). 16p. 1984. pap. text ed. 1.60 (ISBN 0-89904-075-6). Crumb Elbow Pub.

Jones, Michael P., ed. Writing Works Catalogue: Wholesale Edition Vol. 1. (Illus.). 202p. 1984. pap. 5.00 (ISBN 0-89904-059-4); composition 6.00 (ISBN 0-89904-058-6). Crumb Elbow Pub.

Kennedy, Richard. Richard Kennedy: Collected Stories. Sewall, Marcia, illus. LC 86-45495. 416p. (gr. 2-6). 1987. 14.95 (ISBN 0-06-023255-2); PLB 14.89 (ISBN 0-06-023256-0). HarpC Child Bks.

Kipling, Rudyard. Just So Stories. (Illus.). (gr. 2-9). 1979. 3.98 (ISBN 0-517-26655-5). Outlet Bk Co.

—New Illustrated Just So Stories. Nicholas, illus. (gr. 1-7). 1952. 13.95 (ISBN 0-385-02129-1). Doubleday.

Kittelson, Pat & Connor, Brooke. Cedar Breaks for Kids. (Illus.). (gr. k-4). 1979. pap. 1.00 (ISBN 0-915630-14-1). Zion.

Konigsburg, E. L. Altogether, One at a Time. Haley, Gail E., et al, illus. LC 70-134814. 88p. (gr. 4-7). 1971. 13.95 (ISBN 0-689-20638-0, Atheneum Child Bk). Macmillan Child Grp.

Lenski, Lois. Lois Lenski's Big Big Book of Mr. Small. (Illus.). 300p. (ps-1). 1985. 5.98 (ISBN 0-517-46307-5). Outlet Bk Co.

Lester, Julius. The Knee-High Man & Other Tales. Pinto, Ralph, illus. LC 72-181785. 32p. (ps-3). 1985. pap. 3.95 (ISBN 0-8037-0234-5, 0383-120). Dial Bks Young.

Levy, Nathan. Stories to Stretch Minds, 4 vols. 24p. (gr. 2 up). 1981. Vol. I. 1.99 (ISBN 0-88092-000-9); Vol. II. 1.99 (ISBN 0-88092-001-7); Vol. III. 1.99 (ISBN 0-88092-005-X); Vol. IV. 1.99 (ISBN 0-88092-006-8). Trillium Pr.

Lewis, Shari. One Minute Stories of Brothers & Sisters. Oechsli, Kelly, illus. LC 87-20056. 48p. (ps-3). 1988. pap. 7.95 (ISBN 0-385-23425-2). Doubleday.

Lines, Kathleen, ed. The Faber Book of Magical Tales. Howard, Alan, illus. LC 85-4437. 176p. (Orig.). (gr. 5-9). 1985. pap. 7.95 (ISBN 0-571-13648-6). Faber & Faber.

London, Jack. Jack London in the High School Aegis. Sisson, James E., ed. Lttell, Katherine, pref. by. (Illus.). 125p. (Orig.). (gr. 7-12). 1980. pap. 5.95 (ISBN 0-932458-01-7). Star Rover.

—Short Stories. (gr. 9 up). 1969. pap. 2.50 (ISBN 0-8049-0198-8, CL-198). Airmont.

McLeish, Kenneth. Tales of the Mediterranean, 4 bks. Roussou, Maria, ed. Sharpe, Caroline, et al, illus. 56p. (Orig.). (gr. 4-7). 1986. Set. pap. text ed. 23.80 incl. teacher's notes (ISBN 1-55624-013-9). Wright Group.

McQueen, Lucinda, illus. Bedtime Stories. Anastasio, Dina, compiled by. (Illus.). (ps-2). 1987. 11.95 (ISBN 0-448-10551-9, G&D). Putnam Pub Group.

McQueen, Priscilla L. We Can Read: Story Pack-54 Little Stories. 1973. pap. 18.66 (ISBN 0-685-47089-X). McQueen.

—We Can Read: Story Pack-54 Little Stories. 1973. pap. 18.66 (ISBN 0-685-47089-X). McQueen.

Magic Flute & Other Children's Stories. (gr. 5 up). 1981. pap. 4.95 (ISBN 0-8351-0850-3). China Bks.

Magorian, James. Plucked Chickens. LC 80-68263. 32p. (gr. 4-6). 1981. 5.00 (ISBN 0-930674-04-9). Black Oak.

Mahy, Margaret. The Chewing-Gum Rescue & Other Stories. Ormerod, Jan, illus. 142p. (gr. 3-7). 1991. 12.95 (ISBN 0-87951-424-8). Overlook Pr.

—Door in the Air: And Other Stories. 1991. 13.95 (ISBN 0-385-30252-5). Delacorte.

—Nonstop Nonsense. Blake, Quentin, illus. (gr. 1 up). 1989. 12.95 (ISBN 0-689-50483-7, M K McElderry). Macmillan Child Grp.

Mark, Jan. Nothing to Be Afraid Of. LC 81-48064. 128p. (gr. 6 up). 1982. HarpC Child Bks.

Marks, Lis. Ghostly Towers. Barrett, Angela, illus. LC 86-6207. 16p. (gr. 2-6). 1986. 12.95 (ISBN 0-8037-0334-1). Dial Bks Young.

Marsh, Carole. The Drawers of Ocracoke. (Illus., Orig.). (ps-7). 1988. 19.95 (ISBN 1-55609-163-X); pap. 14.95 (ISBN 1-55609-236-9). Gallopade Pub Group.

—Island of the Calamari. (Illus., Orig.). (ps-7). 1988. 19.95 (ISBN 1-55609-172-9); pap. 14.95 (ISBN 0-317-66069-1). Gallopade Pub Group.

—Palm Fever. (Illus.). (gr. 4-12). 1988. 19.95 (ISBN 1-55609-185-0); pap. 14.95 (ISBN 1-55609-237-7). Gallopade Pub Group.

—Saturnalia. (Illus., Orig.). (gr. 4-12). 1988. 19.95 (ISBN 1-55609-187-7); pap. 14.95 (ISBN 1-55609-238-5). Gallopade Pub Group.

Marshall, James. Rats on the Roof: And Other Stories. Marshall, James, illus. LC 90-44084. 80p. (gr. 1-5). 1991. 12.95 (ISBN 0-8037-0834-3); lib. bdg. 12.89 (ISBN 0-8037-0835-1). Dial Bks Young.

Marten, Phyllis. Why Papa Went Away & Other Stories. 112p. (gr. 8 up). 1987. pap. 4.95 (ISBN 0-919797-45-8). Kindred Pr.

Martin, Eva. Tales of the Far North. Gal, Laszlo, illus. LC 85-46068. 124p. (ps up). 1987. 12.95 (ISBN 0-8037-0319-8). Dial Bks Young.

Miller, Teresa & Pellowski, Anne. Joining In: An Anthology of Audience Participation Stories & How to Tell Them. Livo, Norma J., ed. Simms, Laura, intro. by. 125p. (Orig.). 1988. pap. text ed. 11.95 (ISBN 0-938756-21-4). Yellow Moon.

Milne, A. A. A Gallery of Children: A Reproduction of the Milne Classic. Le Mair, Henriette W., illus. 72p. 1989. 15.95 (ISBN 0-399-22166-2, Philomel Bks). Putnam Pub Group.

Minor, Lee. Table in the Skies. LC 88-51386. 53p. (gr. k-3). 1989. 5.95 (ISBN 1-55523-197-7). Winston-Derek.

Mitchelhill, Barbara. Little Books, Nos. 7-12: White Level. Bottomley, Jane, et al, illus. 12p. (ps-1). 1986. Set. pap. text ed. 12.95 (ISBN 1-55624-060-0, WG0600). Wright Group.

Moffett, James & McElheny, Kenneth, eds. Points of View. 576p. (gr. 9-12). Date not set. pap. 4.95 (ISBN 0-451-62491-2, Ment). NAL-Dutton.

Monrad, Jean. How Many Kisses Goodnight: Just Right for 2's & 3's. Wilkin, Eloise, illus. LC 88-6453. 24p. (ps). 1986. 4.95 (ISBN 0-394-88253-9, Random Juv). Random.

Moore, Lilian & Lobel, Arnold. The Magic Spectacles & Other Easy to Read Stories. 80p. (Orig.). (gr. 6). 1985. pap. 2.25 (ISBN 0-553-15329-3). Bantam.

Mowry, Jess. Rats in the Trees: Stories. LC 89-27909. 160p. (Orig.). 1990. pap. 8.95 (ISBN 0-936784-81-4). J Daniel.

Muntean, Michaela. Bert & the Magic Lamp & Other Good-Night Stories. (Illus.). 24p. (ps-1). 1989. write for info. (ISBN 0-307-12073-2, Pub. by Golden Bks). Western Pub.

—Herry's New Shoes & Other Good-Night Stories. (Illus.). 24p. (ps-1). 1989. write for info. (ISBN 0-307-12061-9, Pub. by Golden Bks). Western Pub.

Munteau, Michaela. What's in Oscar's Trash Can? And Other Good-Night Stories. Cooke, Tom, illus. (ps-1). 1991. 3.25 (ISBN 0-307-12342-1, Golden Pr). Western Pub.

Myers, Ruth S. & Banfield, Beryle, eds. Embers: Stories for a Changing World. LC 82-73499. (Illus.). 175p. (gr. 3-6). 1983. pap. 8.95 (ISBN 0-930040-47-3); tchr's manual 18.95 (ISBN 0-930040-46-5). CIBC.

Oda, Stephanie. Quality Time Little Readers: Our Friends. 1991. 1.49 (ISBN 0-8317-7274-3). Smithmark.

—Quality Time Little Readers: Three Little Pigs. 1991. 1.49 (ISBN 0-8317-7276-X). Smithmark.

Offen, Hilda, illus. A Treasury of Bedtime Stories. Yeatman, Linda, compiled by. (Illus.). 160p. (ps-3). 1981. pap. 9.95 (ISBN 0-671-44463-8, Little Simon). S&S Trade.

O. Henry. Four Million & Other Stories. (gr. 8 up). 1964. pap. 1.25 (ISBN 0-8049-0025-6, CL-25). Airmont.

Pearce, Philippa. Who's Afraid? & Other Strange Stories. LC 86-14299. 160p. (gr. 5-9). 1987. 10.25 (ISBN 0-688-06895-2). Greenwillow.

Pelgrom, Els. Little Sophie & Lanky Flop. Pomerans, Arnold, tr. from DUT. Khing, Tjong, illus. LC 87-45752. 96p. (gr. 2-5). 1988. 11.95 (ISBN 0-374-34624-0). FS&G.

Pepper, Bob. The Care Bears' Book of Favorite Bedtime Stories. Cooke, Tom, illus. 48p. (ps-3). 1984. 5.95 (ISBN 0-910313-20-2). Parker Bros.

Perkins, Lee & Perkins, Jim. Healthier & Happier Children Through Bedtime Meditations & Stories, Bk. II. (gr. 3-8). 1983. pap. text ed. 9.95 incl. cassette (ISBN 0-87604-149-7). ARE Pr.

Philadelphia Schools Students. From the Young at Heart: A Student Anthology. Goodman, Sharon L., ed. Saahaddin, Anwar, et al, illus. 20p. (Orig.). (gr. 1-8). 1989. pap. write for info. (ISBN 0-935369-19-8). In Tradition Pub.

Poe, Edgar Allan. Edgar Allan Poe, Stories & Poems. (gr. 9 up). pap. 3.25 (ISBN 0-8049-0008-6, CL-8). Airmont.

—Ten Great Mysteries by Edgar Allan Poe. Conklin, Groff, ed. 218p. (gr. 7 up). 1968. pap. 2.25 (ISBN 0-590-08595-6, Schol Pap). Scholastic Inc.

Porte, Barbara A. Jesse's Ghost & Other Stories. LC 83-1451. 128p. (gr. 7 up). 1983. reinforced 10.25 (ISBN 0-688-02301-0). Greenwillow.

Potter, Beatrix. The Complete Tales of Beatrix Potter. 1989. 29.95 (ISBN 0-685-30574-0). Viking Penguin.

The Power of a Promise. 32p. (Orig.). (gr. 1-5). 1989. 12.95 (ISBN 0-89800-196-X); pap. 5.95 (ISBN 0-89800-197-8). Dharma Pub.

Proysen, Alf. Little Old Mrs. Pepperpot. (gr. 1-4). 1960. 12.95 (ISBN 0-8392-3021-4). Astor-Honor.

—Mrs. Pepperpot Again. Berg, Bjorn, illus. (gr. 1-4). 1961. 12.95 (ISBN 0-8392-3023-0). Astor-Honor.

Pyle, Howard. The Wonder Clock or, Four & Twenty Marvelous Tales, Being One for Each Hour of the Day. (Illus.). xiv, 319p. (gr. 3-6). pap. 7.95 (ISBN 0-486-21446-X). Dover.

The Rabbit in the Moon. 32p. (Orig.). (gr. 1-5). 1989. 12.95 (ISBN 0-89800-190-0); pap. 5.95 (ISBN 0-89800-191-9). Dharma Pub.

Ramos, Lindsey. Four Chinese Children's Stories. Troupe, Connie, illus. 14.95 (ISBN 0-9628563-0-4). Lttle Peop Pr. Little Fawn & Baby Swan - A Story of Helping; Pandy the Chinese Panda - A Story of Loving; The Foolish Little Monkey - A Story of Learning; The Village Goats - A Story of Cooperation. These charming stories, new to the USA, are authentic translations of revered Chinese Children's Stories. Four hard-bound volumes come in a sturdy & colorful case. Each is exquisitely illustrated with vivid color & fine detail that will attract young readers. FOUR CHINESE CHILDREN'S STORIES is the first set in an international series by Little People's Press that will present children's stories from many cultures & nations. "Children can experience the paradox of unity & diversity among peoples, & it will encourage a foundation for understanding throughout their lives" says the publisher. "To promote such a foundation is our goal at Little People's Press." Through these animal tales that children love, FOUR CHINESE CHILDREN'S STORIES lives up to that ideal in a fun & colorful way. *Publisher Provided Annotation.*

Razzi, Jim. Terror in the Mirror. LC 89-5230. 96p. (gr. 7 up). 1989. PLB 9.89 (ISBN 0-8167-1684-6); pap. text ed. 2.95 (ISBN 0-8167-1685-4). Troll Assocs.

Richardson, Arleta. More Stories from Grandma's Attic. LC 78-73125. (Illus.). (gr. 1-4). 1979. pap. 3.95 (ISBN 0-89191-131-6). Cook.

Rockwell, Anne. Three Sillies & Ten Other Stories. Rockwell, Anne, illus. LC 85-45404. 96p. (ps-3). 1986. pap. 8.95 flexi-bind (ISBN 0-06-443093-6, Trophy). HarpC Child Bks.

Rossen, Estelle R. Poems & Short Stories for Children's Delight, Illustrated. (Illus.). 112p. (Orig.). (gr. 3-6). 1991. pap. 6.95 (ISBN 0-8059-3159-7). Dorrance.

Rossner, Richard. The Whole Story: Short Stories for Pleasure & Language Improvement. (gr. 9-12). 1988. pap. text ed. 10.46 (ISBN 0-582-79109-X, 78326); cass. 14.96 (ISBN 0-582-01887-0, 78325). Longman.

Roy, Cal. Bubble, the Birds, & the Noise. Roy, Cal, illus. (gr. k-4). 1968. 8.95 (ISBN 0-8392-3069-9). Astor-Honor.

Sakade, Florence. Kintaro's Adventures & Other Stories. Hayashi, Yoshio, illus. (gr. 1-5). 1958. pap. 8.95 (ISBN 0-8048-0343-9). C E Tuttle.

—Little One-Inch & Other Japanese Children's Favorite Stories. (Illus.). (gr. 1-5). 1958. pap. 8.95 (ISBN 0-8048-0384-6). C E Tuttle.

—Peach Boy & Other Japanese Children's Favorite Stories. Kurosaki, Yoshisuke, illus. (gr. 1-5). 1958. pap. 8.95 (ISBN 0-8048-0469-9). C E Tuttle.

Sakade, Florence, ed. Urashima Taro & Other Japanese Children's Stories. (Illus.). (gr. 1-6). 1958. pap. 8.95 (ISBN 0-8048-0609-8). C E Tuttle.

Scarry, Richard. Richard Scarry's Best Story Book Ever. Scarry, Richard, illus. (gr. 1-5). 1968. write for info. (ISBN 0-307-16548-5, Golden Bks). Western Pub.

Schotzko, Philip. Simple Faith: Stories from Guatemala. Bertrand, Catherine, illus. LC 89-60585. 104p. (Orig.). 1989. pap. 4.95 (ISBN 1-55612-265-9). Sheed & Ward MO.

Schwartz, Alvin. All of Our Noses Are Here & Other Noodle Tales. Weinhaus, Karen A., illus. LC 84-48330. 64p. (gr. k-3). 1987. pap. 3.50 (ISBN 0-06-444108-3, Trophy). HarpC Child Bks.

—Gold & Silver, Silver & Gold: Tales of Hidden Treasure. Christiana, David, illus. 128p. (gr. 5 up). 1988. 13.95 (ISBN 0-374-32690-8). FS&G.

—More Scary Stories to Tell in the Dark. Gammell, Stephen, illus. LC 83-49494. 112p. (gr. 4 up). 1986. pap. 3.50 (ISBN 0-06-440177-4, Trophy). HarpC Child Bks.

Segel, Elizabeth. Short Takes: A Collection of Short Stories. Smith, Joseph A., illus. 160p. (gr. 9 up). 1986. 12.95 (ISBN 0-688-06092-7). Lothrop.

Sendak, Maurice. Nutshell Library. Incl. Alligators All Around; Chicken Soup with Rice; One Was Johnny; Pierre. LC 62-13315. (Illus.). (ps-3). 1962. Set. 10.95i (ISBN 0-06-025500-5). HarpC Child Bks.

Shannon, George. Stories to Solve: Folktales from Around the World. Sis, Peter, illus. LC 84-18656. 56p. (gr. 3-5). 1985. 12.95 (ISBN 0-688-04303-8); PLB 12.88 (ISBN 0-688-04304-6). Greenwillow.

Sharmat, Marjorie W. Get Rich Mitch! Lustig, Loretta, illus. LC 85-8799. 160p. (gr. 3-7). 1985. 13.95 (ISBN 0-688-05790-X). Morrow Jr Bks.

Shepherd, William. Balloons, 6 bks. Biro, Val, et al, illus. 16p. (gr. k-1). Set. pap. text ed. 19.40 (ISBN 1-55624-143-7, WG1437). Wright Group.

Shepherd, William, et al. Little Books, Nos. 1-6: Red Level. Sleight, Katy, et al, illus. 12p. (ps-1). 1986. Set. pap. text ed. 12.95 (ISBN 1-55624-061-9, WG0619). Wright Group.

Siek, Marguerite, retold by. More Favourite Stories from Vietnam. (gr. 7-12). 1978. pap. text ed. 2.50x (ISBN 0-686-60450-4, 00320). Heinemann Ed.

Sierra, Judy. The Flannel Board Storytelling Book. LC 87-6260. 204p. (gr. 3-8). 1987. 34.00 (ISBN 0-8242-0747-5). Wilson.

Sieruta, Peter D. Heartbeats & Other Stories. LC 88-21351. 224p. (gr. 7 up). 1989. 12.95 (ISBN 0-06-025848-9); PLB 13.89 (ISBN 0-06-025849-7). HarpC Child Bks.

Singer, Isaac Bashevis. Naftali the Storyteller & His Horse, Sus. Zemach, Margot, illus. LC 76-26917. 144p. (gr. 4 up). 1976. 13.95 (ISBN 0-374-35490-1). FS&G.

—Stories for Children. LC 84-13612. 338p. (gr. k up). 1984. 16.95 (ISBN 0-374-37266-7); ltd. ed. 8.95 (ISBN 0-374-37267-5); pap. 7.95 (ISBN 0-374-46489-8). FS&G.

—Zlateh the Goat & Other Stories. Sendak, Maurice, illus. LC 66-8114. (gr. 1-6). 1966. 15.95 (ISBN 0-06-025698-2). HarpC Child Bks.

—Zlateh the Goat & Other Stories. Shub, Elizabeth, tr. Sendak, Maurice, illus. LC 66-8114. 96p. (gr. 3-7). 1984. pap. 4.95 (ISBN 0-06-440147-2, Trophy). HarpC Child Bks.

Skaggs, Calvin, ed. The American Short Story, Vol. I. 400p. (gr. 7 up). 1979. pap. 5.95 (ISBN 0-440-30294-3, LE). Dell.

Sleepytime Tales. 1990. 2.98 (ISBN 0-8317-7256-5). Smithmark.
Smith, Janice L. The Kid Next Door & Other Headaches: More Stories about Adam Joshua. Gackenbach, Dick, illus. LC 83-47689. 160p. (gr. 1-4). 1986. pap. 2.95 (ISBN 0-06-440182-0, Trophy). HarpC Child Bks.
—The Show-&-Tell War: And Other Stories about Adam Joshua. Gackenbach, Dick, illus. LC 85-45842. 176p. (gr. 1-4). 1988. 11.95 (ISBN 0-06-025814-4); PLB 11. 89 (ISBN 0-06-025815-2). HarpC Child Bks.
Sohn, David A., ed. Ten Top Stories. Bd. with Flowers for Algernon. Keyes; So Much Unfairness of Things. Bryan; Backward Boy. Coghlan; Denton's Daughter. Lowenberg; Hoods I Have Known. Spatt; Planet of the Condemned. Murphy; Test. Thomas; See How They Run. Coxe; Polar Night. Burke; The Turtle. Vukelich. (Orig.). (gr. 6-12). pap. 2.95 (ISBN 0-553-25326-3). Bantam.
Sonnenfeld, Shlomo Z. Jerusalem Gems: Great Tales about Everyday People In Old Jerusalem. Dershowitz, Y., illus. 160p. 1987. 10.95 (ISBN 0-89906-839-1); pap. 7.95 (ISBN 0-89906-840-5). Mesorah Pubns.
Stangl, Jean. Paper Stories. LC 84-60238. (ps-3). 1984. pap. 9.95 (ISBN 0-8224-5402-5). Fearon Teach Aids.
Starr, Aloa. I Want to Know. Tyree, Michael, illus. (Orig.). (ps-6). 1990. pap. 7.00 (ISBN 0-929686-02-0). Temple Golden Pubns.
Stevens, Margaret M. Stepping Stones Three. Stevens, David, illus. 32p. (gr. 1-8). 1983. pap. 4.00 (ISBN 0-87516-518-4). DeVorss.
Stockton, Frank. Lady or the Tiger & Other Stories. Gennie, F. R., intro. by. (gr. 5 up). 1968. pap. 1.95 (ISBN 0-8049-0163-5, CL-163). Airmont.
Stones, Rosemary, compiled by. More to Life Than Mr. Right: Stories for Young Feminists. 144p. (gr. 8 up). 1989. 13.95 (ISBN 0-8050-1175-7). H Holt & Co.
Storr, Catherine. Cold Marble & Other Ghost Stories. LC 85-10319. 129p. (gr. 6-9). 1985. 13.95 (ISBN 0-571-13582-X). Faber & Faber.
Szekeres, Cyndy. Cyndy Szekeres' Favorite Two-Minute Stories. (Illus.). 36p. (ps-1). 1989. write for info. (ISBN 0-307-12187-9, Pub. by Golden Bks). Western Pub.
Ten First Little Golden Books. (ps). 1981. Set. write for info (ISBN 0-307-93614-7, Golden Bks). Western Pub.
Thomas, Piri. Down These Mean Streets. LC 78-3287. (gr. 7 up). 1967. pap. 5.95 (ISBN 0-685-02840-2). Knopf.
Thomas, Vernon. More Stories from the Arabian Nights. Bose, R. K., illus. 135p. (gr. 1 up). 1981. 7.50 (ISBN 0-89744-232-6, Pub. by Hemkunt India). Auromere.
Townsend, John R. Written for Children. 3rd, rev. ed. LC 87-28143. 384p. 1988. 18.95 (ISBN 0-397-32298-4, Lipp Jr Bks). HarpC Child Bks.
Trussell, Margaret E. Sierra Summers: Fireside Tales to Share with Young & Old. Van Kleeck, Cynthia, illus. Trussell, Margaret E., et al, photos by. Bechtol, Bruce, intro. by. LC 89-51208. (Illus.). 200p. (Orig.). (gr. 8-9). 1989. pap. 10.95 (ISBN 0-9624235-1-3). Talking Mntn.
Twain, Mark. The Celebrated Jumping Frog of Calaveras County. (CHI.). 32p. (gr. 6). 1990. 10.95s.p. (ISBN 0-88682-296-3); 15.65 (ISBN 0-685-28211-2). Creative Ed.
—Short Stories of Mark Twain. Franklin, B., intro. by. (gr. 8 up). 1968. pap. 3.95 (ISBN 0-8049-0171-6, CL-171). Airmont.
—The Signet Classic Book of Mark Twain's Short Stories. 688p. 1989. pap. 4.50 (ISBN 0-451-52220-6, Sig Classics). NAL-Dutton.
Two Thousand & Forty-One: Twelve Short Stories about the Future. 1991. 16.00 (ISBN 0-385-30445-5). Delacorte.
Upgren, H. Ted, Jr. Across the Wheatgrass: A Collection of Hearthside Stories about Uncommon People, Wildlife, Days Afield, & Things, Times & Places of Some Centennial Years. Calkins, Burdette & Bruner, Mike, illus. LC 88-50045. 211p. (Orig.). (gr. 8-12). 1988. 18.95 (ISBN 0-9620122-0-3); pap. 12.95 (ISBN 0-9620122-1-1). Windfeather Pr.
Von Munchhausen, Angelita. The Real Munchhausen: Baron of Bodenwerder. Carter, Harry, illus. 224p. (gr. 6 up). 1960. 10.00 (ISBN 0-8159-6701-2). Devin.
Vonsild, Fred. Tales from the "Ile" of Mulberry. 1989. 7.95 (ISBN 0-533-08213-7). Vantage.
Wagenheim, Kal, ed. Cuentos: An Anthology of Short Stories from Puerto Rico. LC 78-54399. (gr. 9-12). 1987. pap. 7.95 (ISBN 0-8052-0608-6). Schocken.
Wagner, Paul. Thirteen, Vol. 1: Short Stories. 228p. (Orig.). (gr. 9-12). 1991. pap. text ed. 3.95 (ISBN 0-9628653-0-3). USA Entrps.
Walt Disney Story Land. 1987. write for info. (ISBN 0-317-66556-1, Golden Bks). Western Pub.
Watson, Wendy. Tales for a Winter's Eve. LC 87-13467. (Illus.). 32p. (ps up). 1988. 10.95 (ISBN 0-374-37373-6); pap. 3.95 (ISBN 0-374-47419-2). FS&G.
Wells, H. G. This Misery of Boots. 48p. (ps-12). 1987. pap. text ed. 2.50 (ISBN 0-930997-01-8, W-01). East Bay Bks.
West, Colin. The Beginner's Book of Bad Behaviour. West, Colin, illus. 96p. (gr. 4-7). 1988. 13.95 (ISBN 0-09-172120-2, Pub. by Hutchinson UK). Trafalgar Sq.
Westall, Robert. Echoes of War. 96p. (gr. 7 up). 1991. 13. 95 (ISBN 0-374-31964-2). FS&G.
Willcox Smith, Jessie. A Child's Book of Stories. (gr. k-6). 1986. 8.98 (ISBN 0-685-16856-5, 618869). Outlet Bk Co.
Wise, Francis H. & Wise, Joyce M. Storybooks. (Illus.). 105p. (gr. k-1). 1979. pap. 7.50 (ISBN 0-685-05433-0). Wise Pub.
Wonder Kids Publications Group Staff (USA) & Hwa-I Publishing Co., Staff (Taiwan) Animal Tales: Chinese Children's Stories, Vols. 11-15. Ching, Emily, et al, eds. Wonder Kids Publication Staff, tr. from CHI. Hwa-I Publishing Co., Staff, illus. LC 90-60793. 28p. (gr. 3-6). 1991. Repr. of 1988 ed. Five vol. set, 28p. ea. bk. 39.75 (ISBN 1-56162-011-4). Wonder Kids.
—Chinese Sites: Chinese Children's Stories, Vols. 86-90. Ching, Emily, et al, eds. Wonder Kids Publications Staff, tr. from CHI. Hwa-I Publishing Co., Staff, illus. LC 90-60809. (gr. 3-6). 1991. Repr. of 1988 ed. Five vol. set, 28p. ea. bk. 39.75 (ISBN 1-56162-086-6, Lucky Tiger Pr). Wonder Kids.
—Fables: Chinese Children's Stories, Vols. 16-20. Ching, Emily & Ching, Ko-Shee, eds. Wonder Kids Publications Staff, tr. from CHI. Hwa-I Publishing Co., Staff, illus. LC 90-60794. (gr. 3-6). 1991. Repr. of 1988 ed. Five vol. set, 28p. ea. bk. 39.75 (ISBN 1-56162-016-5, Lucky Tiger Pr). Wonder Kids.
—Fairy Tales: Chinese Children's Stories, Vols. 46-50. Ching, Emily, et al, eds. Wonder Kids Publications Staff, tr. from CHI. Hwa-I Publishing Co., Staff, illus. LC 90-60801. (gr. 3-6). 1991. Repr. of 1988 ed. Five vol. set, 28p. ea. bk. 39.75 (ISBN 1-56162-046-7, Lucky Tiger Pr). Wonder Kids.
—Festivals: Chinese Children's Stories, Vols. 26-30. Ching, Emily, et al, eds. Wonder Kids Publications Staff, tr. from CHI. Hwa-I Publishing Co., Staff, illus. LC 90-60797. (gr. 3-6). 1991. Repr. of 1988 ed. Five vol. set, 28p. ea. bk. 39.75 (ISBN 1-56162-026-2, Lucky Tiger Pr). Wonder Kids.
—Filial Piety: Chinese Children's Stories, Vols. 51-55. Ching, Emily, et al, eds. Wonder Kids Publications Staff, tr. from CHI. Hwa-I Publishing Co., Staff, illus. LC 90-60802. (gr. 3-6). 1991. Repr. of 1988 ed. Five vol. set, 28p. ea. bk. 39.75 (ISBN 1-56162-051-3, Lucky Tiger Pr). Wonder Kids.

—Folklore: Chinese Children's Stories, Vols. 1-5. Ching, Emily, et al, eds. Wonder Kids Publications Staff, tr. from CHI. Hwa-I Publishing Co., Staff, illus. LC 90-60791. 28p. (gr. 3-6). 1991. Repr. of 1988 ed. Five vol. set, 28p. ea. bk. 39.75 (ISBN 1-56162-001-7); Set (100 vols.) 795.00 (ISBN 1-56162-120-X). Wonder Kids.
"The most comprehensive collection of children's stories about Chinese culture, customs, philosophy, values, history, literature..."--World Journal. Fashioned together in myths, legends, folktale, fairy tales, fables, & short stories, 200 stories for children are packed with action, magic, love & moral teachings. Recommended for ESL & ages 8-12 reading to promote multi-cultural education & global awareness. Following each short story, a "parental guide" presents supplemental information to further clarify moral messages & cultural meaning. 20 titles of subjects include: Folklore, Tales about Plants, Animal Tales, Fables, Idioms, Festivals, Tales about Food, Inventions, 12 Beasts & the Years, Fairy Tales, Filial Piety, Wonder Kids, Mythology, Literature, Popular Narratives, Heroes, Historical Accounts, Chinese Sites, & Taiwanese Sites. Please refer to the individual subject listing in (Children's) Books in Print for a description of each title of subject in the collection.
Publisher Provided Annotation.

—Heroes: Chinese Children's Stories, Vols. 76- 80. Ching, Emily, et al, eds. Wonder Kids Publication s Staff, tr. from CHI. Hwa-I Publishing Co., Staff, illus. LC 90-60807. (gr. 3-6). 1991. Repr. of 1988 ed. Five vol. set, 28p. ea. bk. 39.75 (ISBN 1-56162-076-9, Lucky Tiger Pr). Wonder Kids.
—Historical Accounts: Chinese Children's Stories, Vols. 81-85. Ching, Emily, et al, eds. Wonder Kids Publications Staff, tr. from CHI. Hwa-I Publishing Co., Staff, illus. LC 90-60808. (gr. 3-6). 1991. Repr. of 1988 ed. Five vol. set, 28p. ea. bk. 39.75 (ISBN 1-56162-081-5, Lucky Tiger Pr). Wonder Kids.
—Idioms: Chinese Children's Stories, Vols. 21- 25. Ching, Emily, et al, eds. Wonder Kids Publications Staff, tr. from CHI. Hwa-I Publishing Co., Staff, illus. LC 90-60796. (gr. 3-6). 1991. Repr. of 1988 ed. Five vol. set, 28p. ea. bk. 39.75 (ISBN 1-56162-021-1, Lucky Tiger Pr). Wonder Kids.
—Inventions: Chinese Children's Stories, Vols. 36-40. Ching, Emily, et al, eds. Wonder Kids Publications Staff, tr. from CHI. Hwa-I Publishing Co., Staff, illus. LC 90-60799. (gr. 3-6). 1991. Repr. of 1988 ed. Five vol. set, 28p. ea. bk. 39.75 (ISBN 1-56162-036-X, Lucky Tiger Pr). Wonder Kids.
—Literature: Chinese Children's Stories, Vols. 66-70. Ching, Emily, et al, eds. Wonder Kids Publications Staff, tr. from CHI. Hwa-I Publishing Co., Staff, illus. LC 90-60805. (gr. 3-6). 1991. Repr. of 1988 ed. Five vol. set, 28p. ea. bk. 39.75 (ISBN 1-56162-066-1, Lucky Tiger Pr). Wonder Kids.
—Mythology: Chinese Children's Stories, Vols. 61-65. Ching, Emily, et al, eds. Wonder Kids Publications Staff, tr. from CHI. Hwa-I Publishing Co., Staff, illus. LC 90-60804. (gr. 3-6). 1991. Repr. of 1988 ed. Five vol. set, 28p. ea. bk. 39.75 (ISBN 1-56162-061-0, Lucky Tiger Pr). Wonder Kids.
—Popular Narratives: Chinese Children's Stories, Vols. 71-75. Ching, Emily, et al, eds. Wonder Kids Publications Staff, tr. from CHI. Hwa-I Publishing Co., Staff, illus. LC 90-60806. (gr. 3-6). 1991. Repr. of 1988 ed. Five vol. set, 28p. ea. bk. 39.75 (ISBN 1-56162-071-8, Lucky Tiger Pr). Wonder Kids.
—Taiwanese Folklore: Chinese Children's Stories, Vols. 96-100. Ching, Emily, et al, eds. Wonder Kids Publication Staff, tr. from CHI. Hwa-I Publishing Co., Staff, illus. LC 90-60811. (gr. 3-6). 1991. Repr. of 1988 ed. Five vol. set, 28p. ea. bk. 39.75 (ISBN 1-56162-096-3, Lucky Tiger Pr). Wonder Kids.
—Taiwanese Sites: Chinese Children's Stories, Vols. 91-95. Ching, Emily, et al, eds. Wonder Kids Publications Staff, tr. from CHI. Hwa-I Publishing Co., Staff, illus. LC 90-60810. (gr. 3-6). 1991. Repr. of 1988 ed. Five vol. set, 28p. ea. bk. 39.75 (ISBN 1-56162-091-2, Lucky Tiger Pr). Wonder Kids.
—Tales about Food: Chinese Children's Stories, Vols. 31-35. Ching, Emily, et al, eds. Wonder Kids Publications Staff, tr. from CHI. Hwa-I Publishing Co., Staff, illus. LC 90-60798. (gr. 3-6). 1991. Repr. of 1988 ed. Five vol. set, 28p. ea. bk. 39.75 (ISBN 1-56162-031-9, Lucky Tiger Pr). Wonder Kids.
—Twelve Beasts & the Years: Chinese Children's Stories, Vols. 41-45. Ching, Emily, et al, eds. Wonder Kids Publications Staff, tr. from CHI. Hwa-I Publishing Co., Staff, illus. LC 90-60800. (gr. 3-6). 1991. Repr. of 1988 ed. Five vol. set, 28p. ea. bk. 39.75 (ISBN 1-56162-041-6, Lucky Tiger Pr). Wonder Kids.
—Wonder Kids: Chinese Children's Stories, Vols. 56-60. Ching, Emily, et al, eds. Wonder Kids Publications Staff, tr. from CHI. Hwa-I Publishing Co., Staff, illus. LC 90-60803. (gr. 3-6). 1991. Repr. of 1988 ed. Five vol. set, 28p. ea. bk. 39.75 (ISBN 1-56162-056-4, Lucky Tiger Pr). Wonder Kids.
Zolotow, Charlotte, ed. Early Sorrow: Ten Stories of Youth. LC 79-2669. 224p. (gr. 7 up). 1986. 12.95 (ISBN 0-06-026936-7); PLB 12.89 (ISBN 0-06-026937-5). HarpC Child Bks.

SHRUBS

Gattis, L. S., III. Shrubs for Pathfinders: A Basic Youth Enrichment Skill Honor Packet. (Illus.). 20p. (Orig.). (gr. 5 up). 1989. pap. 5.00 tchr's. ed. (ISBN 0-936241-41-1). Cheetah Pub.

SIBERIA

Anderson, Madelyn K. Siberia. (gr. 5-9). 1987. 13.95 (ISBN 0-396-08662-4, Putnam). Putnam Pub Group.
Hautzig, Esther. Endless Steppe: Growing up in Siberia. LC 68-13582. 243p. (gr. 7 up). 1968. 13.95 (ISBN 0-690-26371-6, Crowell Jr Bks). HarpC Child Bks.

SIDEREAL SYSTEM

see Stars

SIERRA LEONE

Milsome, John. Sierra Leone. (Illus.). (gr. 5 up). 1988. 14. 95 (ISBN 0-7910-0106-7). Chelsea Hse.

SIERRA NEVADA MOUNTAINS

Williams, George, III. Hot Springs of the Eastern Sierra. Dalton, Bill, ed. LC 87-16230. (Illus.). 72p. (Orig.). (gr. 8-12). 1988. text ed. 12.95 (ISBN 0-935174-24-9); pap. 5.95 (ISBN 0-935174-23-0). Tree by River.

SIERRA NEVADA MOUNTAINS–FICTION

Wood, Phyllis A. Pass Me a Pine Cone. LC 82-1870. 160p. (gr. 7-9). 1982. 11.95 (ISBN 0-664-32692-7, Westminster). Westminster John Knox.

SIGHT

see Vision

SIGN BOARDS

see Signs and Signboards

SIGN LANGUAGE

see Indians of North America–Sign Language

SIGNALS AND SIGNALING

see also Flags; Radio

Greene, Laura & Dicker, Eva B. Sign Language Talk. Solomon, Maury, ed. Caraway, Caren, illus. 96p. (gr. 5 up). 1989. PLB 10.90 (ISBN 0-531-10597-0). Watts.
Signaling. (Illus.). 32p. (gr. 6-12). 1974. pap. 1.85 (ISBN 0-8395-3237-7, 3237). BSA.

SIGNERS OF THE DECLARATION OF INDEPENDENCE

see U. S. Declaration of Independence

SIGNS (ADVERTISING)

see Signs and Signboards

SIGNS AND SIGNBOARDS
see also Posters
Finton, Esther. Bulletin Boards Are More Than Something to Look at. 64p. (gr. k-6). 1979. 6.95 (ISBN 0-916456-32-3, GA97). Good Apple.
Goor, Ron & Goor, Nancy. Signs. LC 83-47649. (Illus.). (ps-1). 1983. PLB 12.89 (ISBN 0-690-04355-4, Crowell Jr Bks). HarpC Child Bks.
Hoban, Tana. I Walk & Read. Hoban, Tana, illus. LC 83-14215. 32p. (ps-1). 1984. 14.95 (ISBN 0-688-02575-7); PLB 14.88 (ISBN 0-688-02576-5). Greenwillow.
SIGNS AND SYMBOLS
see also Ciphers; Cryptography; Heraldry; Signals and Signaling; Symbolism
Bartusch, Nancy. Sign Numbers. (Illus.). 54p. (Orig.). (ps-3). 1988. pap. 5.00 (ISBN 0-916708-17-9). Modern Signs.
Brown, Charlene & Davis, Carolyn. Poster Fun. (Illus.). 64p. (Orig.). 1988. pap. 5.95 (ISBN 0-929261-30-5, BA05). W Foster Pub.
Hefter, Richard. Watch Out! Hefter, Richard, illus. LC 83-2190. 32p. (ps-1). 1983. 5.95 (ISBN 0-911787-03-8). Optimum Res Inc.
Schneider, D. Douglas. Symbolically Speaking. Holbrook, Clifford & LaMothe, Becky, illus. Michael, ed. 85p. (ps up). 1987. pap. 5.95 (ISBN 0-939169-01-0). World Peace Univ.
SILK
see also Silkworms
Dineen, Jacqueline. Cotton & Silk. 32p. (gr. 4-8). 1988. lib. bdg. 12.95 (ISBN 0-89490-213-X). Enslow Pubs.
SILKWORMS
Coldrey, Jenny. The Silkworm Story. Oxford Scientific Films, photos by. LC 85-71250. (Illus.). 32p. (ps-3). 1985. 10.95 (ISBN 0-233-97553-5). Andre Deutsch.
Johnson, Sylvia A. Silkworms. Kishida, Isao, illus. LC 82-250. 48p. (gr. 4 up). 1982. PLB 12.95 (ISBN 0-8225-1478-8, First Ave Edns); pap. 5.95 (ISBN 0-8225-9557-5, First Ave Edns). Lerner Pubns.

Miller, Billie M. Soo Ling: The Story of the Silkworm. Guerra, Mauricio, illus. Luna, Rose Mary, tr. from ENG & SPA. (Illus.). 12p. 1991. 12.00 (ISBN 1-878742-01-9); pap. 6.00 (ISBN 1-878742-02-7). Kidship Assoc.
A touching short story told by the silkworm, Soo Ling, about her fascinating life cycle. Soo Ling describes herself at each stage of her growth from egg to larva, to pupa & finally to her adult stage. She shares her feelings & pride in the miracle of her existence. SPECIAL FEATURES: Bilingual text (English in black, Spanish in blue) Literature integrating science & social studies *Simple text in a large print *Perfect for read aloud *Vocabulary list included *Available in soft or HARD-BOUND cover (8 1/2 x 11) *Developed for the elementary level student. Children love to learn about silkworms! Ignite the spark of scientific inquiry. Integrate this bilingual literature with your science unit on silkworms.
Publisher Provided Annotation.

SILVER
see also Money
Cobb, Vicki. Feeding Yourself. Hafner, Marylin, illus. LC 88-14192. 32p. (gr. k-3). 1989. 11.95 (ISBN 0-397-32324-7, Lipp Jr Bks); PLB 11.89 (ISBN 0-397-32325-5, Lipp Jr Bks). HarpC Child Bks.
Rickard, G. Silver. (Illus.). 48p. (gr. 5 up). Date not set. PLB 15.93 (ISBN 0-86592-273-X). Rourke Corp.
SILVERSMITHING
see also Metalwork
SIMHAT TORAH
Simon, Norma. Simhat Torah. Gordon, Ayala, illus. (ps-k). 1960. bds. 4.50 lam. (ISBN 0-8381-0704-4). United Syn Bk.
SINGAPORE
Brown, Marion M. Singapore. LC 89-34280. 128p. (gr. 5-9). 1989. PLB 25.27 (ISBN 0-516-02715-8). Childrens.
Elder, Bruce. Take a Trip to Singapore. Payne, Tony, illus. LC 84-51808. 32p. (gr. k-3). 1985. PLB 7.99 (ISBN 0-531-04942-6). Watts.
Stein, R. Conrad. Fall of Singapore. LC 82-9416. (Illus.). (gr. 3-8). 1982. PLB 14.60 (ISBN 0-516-04796-5). Childrens.
Wee, Jessie. Singapore. (Illus.). (gr. 5 up). 1988. 14.95 (ISBN 0-222-00988-8). Chelsea Hse.
—We Live in Malaysia & Singapore. LC 84-73585. (Illus.). 60p. (gr. 1-6). 1985. 9.49 (ISBN 0-531-18007-7, Pub. by Bookwright Pr). Watts.
Wright, David K. Singapore. LC 89-43196. (Illus.). 64p. (gr. 5-6). 1991. PLB 12.95 (ISBN 0-8368-0255-1). Gareth Stevens Inc.
SINGERS
Bain, Geri & Leather, Michael. Picture Life of Bruce Springsteen. 48p. (gr. 1-6). 1986. PLB 7.99 (ISBN 0-531-10204-1). Watts.
Byars, Betsy C. The Glory Girl. (ps-3). 1985. pap. 3.95 (ISBN 0-14-031785-6, Puffin). Puffin Bks.
Danny & Donnie. (Illus.). 64p. (gr. 3-12). 1990. pap. 2.95 (ISBN 0-87449-981-X). Modern Pub NYC.
De Veaux, Alexis. Don't Explain (A Song of Billie Holiday) LC 78-19471. (Illus.). 160p. (gr. 7 up). 1980. PLB 12.89 (ISBN 0-06-021630-1). HarpC Child Bks.
Garza, Hedda. Joan Baez. (Illus.). 112p. (gr. 5 up). 1991. PLB 17.95 (ISBN 0-7910-1233-6). Chelsea Hse.
Gillianti, Simone. Rick Springfield. 1984. pap. 2.95 (ISBN 0-671-53104-2, Little Simon). S&S Trade.
Haskins, James. Diana Ross: Star Supreme. Spence, Jim, photos by. LC 84-21897. (Illus.). 64p. (gr. 2-6). 1985. pap. 10.95 (ISBN 0-670-80549-1). Viking Child Bks.
Haskins, James S. Diana Ross: Star Supreme. Spence, Jim, illus. 64p. (gr. 2-6). 1986. pap. 3.95 (ISBN 0-14-032096-2, Puffin). Puffin Bks.
—I'm Gonna Make You Love Me: The Story of Diana Ross. 176p. (gr. 7 up). 1982. pap. 2.25 (ISBN 0-440-94172-5, LFL). Dell.
—Lena Horne. (Illus.). (gr. 6 up). 1983. 10.95 (ISBN 0-698-20586-3, Coward). Putnam Pub Group.
Haskins, James S. & Stifle, J. M. Donna Summer: An Unauthorized Biography. (Illus.). 144p. (gr. 7 up). 1983. 14.95 (ISBN 0-316-35003-6, Joy St Bks). Little.
Jordan & Jon. (Illus.). 64p. (gr. 3-12). 1990. pap. 2.95 (ISBN 0-87449-980-1). Modern Pub NYC.
Koenig, Terry. Tina Turner. LC 86-8950. (Illus.). 32p. (gr. 4-5). PLB 9.95 (ISBN 0-89686-305-0, Crestwood Hse). Macmillan Child Grp.
Krishef, Robert K. Dolly Parton. LC 79-28247. (Illus.). 72p. (gr. 5 up). 1980. PLB 7.95 (ISBN 0-8225-1411-7). Lerner Pubns.
—Jimmie Rodgers. LC 77-90156. (Illus.). 64p. (gr. 5 up). 1978. PLB 7.95 (ISBN 0-8225-1404-4). Lerner Pubns.
SINGING–FICTION
Beall, Pamela C. & Nipp, Susan. Wee Sing. (ps-2). 1982. pap. 2.95 (ISBN 0-8431-0676-X); pap. 9.95 incl. cassette (ISBN 0-8431-0522-4). Price Stern.
Christian, Mary B. Singin' Somebody Else's Song. LC 88-12000. 192p. (gr. 7 up). 1988. 13.95 (ISBN 0-02-718500-1, Mcmillan Child Bk). Macmillan Child Grp.
De Gasztold, Carmen B. Creature's Choir. (FRE., Illus.). (gr. 3-8). 29.95 (ISBN 0-685-11121-0). French & Eur.
Grimm, Jacob & Grimm, Wilhelm K. Grimm's Fairy Tales. (SPA & FRE.). Span. ed. 8.95 (ISBN 0-685-23350-2); fr. ed 5.50 (ISBN 0-685-23351-0). French & Eur.
Kraus, Robert. Screamy Mimi. Knight, Hilary, illus. 48p. (gr. 1-3). 1987. pap. 7.95 (ISBN 0-671-44471-9). S&S Trade.
Louis, Louise. Twin Playlets for Children: Mr. Wishing Match & Community Sing, 2 bks. (gr. 4-11). 1979. Set. pap. 3.95 (ISBN 0-941242-09-9). Pen-Art.
McEvoy, Seth & Smith, Laure. Backstage Surprise. Ashby, Ruth, ed. 144p. (Orig.). (gr. 7 up). 1990. pap. 3.50 (ISBN 0-671-73170-X, Archway). PB.
—Block Party. Ashby, Ruth, ed. (Orig.). (gr. 5 up). 1991. pap. 3.50 (ISBN 0-671-73321-4, Archway). PB.
Martin, Marla. A Sweet Singer. (gr. 2-4). 1976. 2.50 (ISBN 0-686-15487-8). Rod & Staff.
Paterson, Katherine. Come Sing, Jimmy Jo. LC 84-21123. 208p. (gr. 5 up). 1985. 12.95 (ISBN 0-525-67167-6, Lodestar Bks). Dutton Child Bks.
SINGING GAMES
Chase, Richard. Singing Games & Playparty Games. Tolford, Joshua, illus. 63p. (gr. 1-4). 1949. pap. 2.50 (ISBN 0-486-21785-X). Dover.
Corbett, Pie. Playtime Treasury. 1990. 16.95 (ISBN 0-385-26448-8). Doubleday.
Hello Rhythm: Rhythm Activities, Songs & Games to Develop Skills in Young Children. (ps-3). 1977. pap. 6.95 (ISBN 0-939514-01-X); album 9.95 (ISBN 0-685-03380-5); cassette 9.95 (ISBN 0-685-03381-3). Miss Jackie.
Hello Sound: Music Songs & Games Using Sound As a Theme. (ps-3). 1979. pap. 6.95 (ISBN 0-939514-00-1). Miss Jackie.
Rae, Mary M., illus. The Farmer in the Dell: A Singing Game. 32p. (ps-1). 1990. pap. 3.95 (ISBN 0-14-050788-4, Puffin). Puffin Bks.
Twinn, Colin. Bunnykins Rhyming Games. (Illus.). 23p. (ps-1). 1989. 4.95 (ISBN 0-7232-3603-8). Warne.
SISTERHOODS
see Monasticism and Religious Orders for Women
SISTERS–FICTION
Adler, C. S. Split Sisters. (gr. 4-7). 1990. pap. 3.95 (ISBN 0-689-71369-X, Aladdin). Macmillan Child Grp.
Adorjan, Carol. I Can! Can You? rev. ed. Levine, Abby, ed. Nerlove, Miriam, illus. 24p. (ps). 1990. 10.95 (ISBN 0-8075-3491-9). A Whitman.
Alcott, Louisa May. Little Women. (Illus.). (gr. 6 up). pap. 2.95 (ISBN 0-8049-0106-6, CL-106). Airmont.
—Little Women. Magagna, Anna M. & Jambor, Louis, illus. (gr. 4-6). 1981. Illustrated Junior Library. pap. 9.95 (ISBN 0-448-11019-9, G&D); deluxe ed. 14.95 (ISBN 0-448-06019-1); Companion Library 3.95 (ISBN 0-448-05466-3). Putnam Pub Group.
—Little Women. 59.95 (ISBN 0-8490-0547-7). Gordon Pr.
—Little Women. Smith, Jessie W., illus. (gr. 7 up). 1968. 17.95 (ISBN 0-316-03095-3). Little.
—Little Women. 320p. (gr. 3-7). 1983. pap. 2.25 (ISBN 0-14-035008-X, Puffin). Puffin Bks.
—Little Women. 1963. 37.50 (ISBN 0-685-20188-0, 144-7). Saphrograph.
—Little Women. Barish, Wendy, ed. Cheng, Judith, illus. 576p. 1982. 15.95 (ISBN 0-671-44447-6, Little Simon). S&S Trade.
—Little Women. 1983. Repr. lib. bdg. 18.95x (ISBN 0-89966-408-3). Buccaneer Bks.
—Little Women. Bedall, Madelon, intro. by. 1981. pap. 6.00 (ISBN 0-685-06605-3, Modern Lib). Random.
—Little Women. Douglas, Ann, intro. by. 480p. (gr. 3 up). 1983. pap. 3.95 (ISBN 0-451-52341-5, Sig Classic). NAL-Dutton.
—Little Women. Edwards, Gunvor, illus. Gliberry, Lysbeth, retold by. (Illus.). 48p. (gr. 7-12). 1975. pap. text ed. 2.25x (ISBN 0-19-421804-X). Oxford U Pr.
—Little Women. LC 62-20197. (gr. 4 up). 1986. pap. 3.95 (ISBN 0-02-041240-1, Collier). Macmillan.
—Little Women. (gr. 2 up). 8.98 (ISBN 0-517-63489-9). Outlet Bk Co.
—Little Women. (Orig.). (gr. k-6). 1987. pap. 6.95 (ISBN 0-440-44768-2, Pub. by Yearling Classics). Dell.
—Little Women. 256p. (gr. 3-7). 1986. pap. 2.50 (ISBN 0-590-40498-9, Pub. by Apple Classics). Scholastic Inc.
—Little Women. James, Derek, illus. LC 87-45450. 512p. 1988. 18.95 (ISBN 0-394-56279-8). Knopf.
—Little Women. Showalter, Elaine, intro. by. 608p. 1989. pap. 5.95 (ISBN 0-14-039069-3, Penguin Classics). Viking Penguin.
—Little Women. 1989. Repr. of 1867 ed. lib. bdg. 79.00 (ISBN 0-685-27395-4). Reprint Servs.
—Little Women. Auerbach, Nina, afterword by. 480p. 1983. pap. 3.95 (ISBN 0-553-21275-3, Bantam Classics Spectra). Bantam.
—Little Women, 4 vols. large type ed. (gr. 7 up). Repr. of 1946 ed. Set. write for info. NAVH.
—Little Women. large type ed. 336p. 1987. 15.95 (ISBN 0-7089-8384-7, Charnwood). Ulverscroft.
—Little Women. 1986. pap. 2.95 (ISBN 0-590-43797-6). Scholastic Inc.
—Little Women. 1988. 2.98 (ISBN 0-671-09222-7). S&S Trade.
—Little Women. Smith, Jessie W., illus. 388p. (gr. 4 up). 1986. 12.95 (ISBN 0-681-40055-2). Longmeadow Pr.
—Little Women, Vol. 2: The Sisters Grow Up. Lindskoog, Kathryn, ed. (Illus.). (gr. 3-7). 1991. pap. 6.99 (ISBN 0-88070-463-2). Multnomah.
—Reader's Digest Best Loved Books for Young Readers: Little Women. Ogburn, Jackie, ed. English, Mark, illus. 176p. (gr. 4-12). 1989. 3.99 (ISBN 0-945260-25-3). Choice Pub NY.
Alexander, Martha. Nobody Asked Me If I Wanted a Baby Sister. Alexander, Martha, illus. (gr. k-2). 1977. pap. 3.95 (ISBN 0-8037-6410-3). Dial Bks Young.
Allen, Suzanne. Suddenly Sisters. (gr. 4 up). 1990. pap. 2.75 (ISBN 0-425-12217-4). Berkley Pub.

Angel, Ann. Real for Sure Sister. LC 87-29217. (Illus.). 72p. (gr. 3-6). 1988. 12.95 (ISBN 0-9609504-7-8). Perspect Indiana.
Youngsters will readily identify with Amanda, the oldest in a family of soon-to-be four children, all of whom were adopted. Only as they await the arrival of a new biracial baby sister (yuck! it's been nice to be the only girl!) does Amanda become aware of the adoption issues around her-the social worker, the judges & their power; the neighbors, perfect strangers & their odd comments--& begin to deal with her own feelings about being adopted & being part of a multiracial family as well as about sibling rivalry. Whimsical illustrations add fun to this chapter book. Other adoption related children's books from Perspectives Press include Jane Schnitter's WILLIAM IS MY BROTHER (family built by adoption), Janice Koch's OUR BABY: A BIRTH & ADOPTION STORY (sex education), Anne Brodzinsky's THE MULBERRY BIRD (a birthmother's viewpoint), Susan Gabel's WHERE THE SUN KISSES THE SEA (international placement), & Susan Gabel's FILLING IN THE BLANKS: A GUIDED LOOK AT GROWING UP ADOPTED (adolescence). Distributed by Ingram, Baker & Taylor or contact the publisher at (317)

872-3055.
Publisher Provided Annotation.

Anholt, Catherine. Aren't You Lucky! 1991. 13.95 (ISBN 0-316-04264-1). Little.

Bradford, Jan. Caroline Zucker & the Birthday Disaster. Ramsey, Marcy, illus. LC 90-11159. 96p. (gr. 2-5). 1990. lib. bdg. 9.89 (ISBN 0-8167-2021-5); pap. text ed. 2.95 (ISBN 0-8167-2022-3). Troll Assocs.

—Caroline Zucker Helps Out. Ramsey, Marcy, illus. LC 90-11156. 96p. (gr. 2-5). 1990. PLB 9.89 (ISBN 0-8167-2025-8); pap. text ed. 2.95 (ISBN 0-8167-2026-6). Troll Assocs.

Byars, Betsy. Golly Sisters Go West. LC 84-48474. (Illus.). 64p. (gr. k-3). 1989. pap. 3.50 (ISBN 0-06-444132-6, Trophy). HarpC Child Bks.

—Hooray for the Golly Sisters! Truesdell, Sue, illus. LC 89-48147. 64p. (gr. k-3). 1990. 11.95 (ISBN 0-06-020898-8); PLB 11.89 (ISBN 0-06-020899-6). HarpC Child Bks.

Dunrea, Olivier. Eppie M. Says... Dunrea, Olivier, illus. LC 89-3134. 32p. (ps-2). 1990. 12.95 (ISBN 0-02-733205-5, Mcmillan Child Bk). Macmillan Child Grp.

Galbraith, Kathryn O. Roommates. (ps-3). 1990. 12.95 (ISBN 0-689-50487-X, M K McElderry). Macmillan Child Grp.

Gerber, Merrill J. Handsome As Anything. 1990. 13.95 (ISBN 0-590-43019-X). Scholastic Inc.

Greenwald, Sheila. Rosy's Romance. Greenwald, Sheila, illus. 112p. (gr. 3-6). 1990. pap. 2.75 (ISBN 0-671-70292-0, Minstrel). PB.

Hallinan, P. K. We're Very Good Friends, My Sister & I. Hallinan, P. K., illus. 24p. (ps-3). 1990. 3.95 (ISBN 0-8249-8470-6). Ideals.

Hazel, Beth & Harste, Jerome. My Icky Picky Sister. (Illus.). 24p. (gr. k-2). 1984. incl. cassette 1.95 (ISBN 0-87406-127-X, 23-14389-7). Willowisp Pr.

Hines, Anna G. Jackie's Lunch Box. LC 90-39715. (Illus.). 24p. (ps up). 1991. 13.95 (ISBN 0-688-09693-X); PLB 13.88 (ISBN 0-688-09694-8). Greenwillow.

Holland, Isabelle. Journey Home. (gr. 4-7). 1990. 13.95 (ISBN 0-590-43110-2). Scholastic Inc.

Kehret, Peg. Sisters, Long Ago. Kelly, Kathleen M., illus. LC 89-38677. 160p. (gr. 5 up). 1990. 14.95 (ISBN 0-525-65021-0, Cobblehill Bks). Dutton Child Bks.

Little Women. (gr. 4 up). 1988. pap. 4.87 (ISBN 0-582-54162-X, 74269). Longman.

Little Women. Centennial ed. (Illus.). (gr. 3-7). 1968. 17.95. Little.

Little Women. (Illus.). (gr. 3-5). 3.50 (ISBN 0-7214-5005-9). Ladybird Bks.

Noll, Sally. That Bothered Kate. LC 90-38488. (Illus.). 32p. (ps up). 1991. 13.95 (ISBN 0-688-10095-3); PLB 13.88 (ISBN 0-688-10096-1). Greenwillow.

Tsutsui, Yoriko. Anna in Charge. Hayashi, Akiki, illus. 32p. (ps-3). 1991. pap. 3.95 (ISBN 0-14-050733-7, Puffin). Puffin Bks.

Widerberg, Siv. The Big Sister. Sjogren, Birgitta, tr. from SWE. Torudd, Cecilia, illus. 1989. 9.95 (ISBN 91-29-59186-4, Pub. by R&S Bks). FS&G.

Wood, Audrey. Three Sisters. Hoffman, Rosekrans, illus. LC 85-29392. 48p. (ps-3). 1989. 4.95 (ISBN 0-8037-0597-2). Dial Bks Young.

Wooley, Catherine. Cathy's Little Sister. 176p. (gr. 5 up). 1988. pap. 3.95 (ISBN 0-14-032552-2, Puffin). Puffin Bks.

SITTING BULL, DAKOTA CHIEF, ca. 1831-1890

Black, Sheila. Sitting Bull. Furstinger, Nancy, ed. (Illus.). 144p. (gr. 5-7). 1989. PLB 12.98 (ISBN 0-382-09572-3); pap. 7.95 (ISBN 0-382-09761-0). Silver Burdett Pr.

Fleischer, Jane. Sitting Bull, Warrior of the Sioux. new ed. LC 78-18047. (Illus.). 48p. (gr. 4-6). 1979. PLB 9.89 (ISBN 0-89375-154-5); pap. 2.95 (ISBN 0-89375-144-8). Troll Assocs.

Hook, John. Sitting Bull & the Plains Indians. (Illus.). 64p. (gr. 4-8). 1987. PLB 12.40 (ISBN 0-531-18102-2, Pub. by Bookwright Pr). Watts.

Smith, Kathie B. Sitting Bull. (Illus.). (gr. k-5). 1987. pap. 2.25 (ISBN 0-671-64027-5, Little Simon). S&S Trade.

Smith, Kathy B. Sitting Bull. Seward, James, illus. LC 86-33888. 24p. (gr. 4-6). 1989. PLB 7.98 (ISBN 0-671-64603-6); PLB 5.99s.p. Messner.

Stein, R. Conrad. The Story of Little Bighorn. LC 83-6594. (Illus.). 32p. (gr. 3-6). 1983. PLB 13.27 (ISBN 0-516-04663-2); pap. 3.95 (ISBN 0-516-44663-0). Childrens.

Wheeler, Jill. The Story of Sitting Bull. Deegan, Paul, ed. Dodson, Liz, illus. 32p. (gr. 4). 1989. PLB 11.95 (ISBN 0-939179-67-9). Abdo & Dghtrs.

SIX DAY WAR

see Israel-Arab War, 1967-

SIZE AND SHAPE

see also Mensuration

Allington, Richard L. Shapes. Ehlert, Lois, illus. LC 79-19852. 32p. (gr. k-3). 1985. PLB 15.33 (ISBN 0-8172-1277-9); pap. 9.27 (ISBN 0-8172-2487-4). Raintree Pubs.

Baby Piggy's Shapes. 1988. write for info. (ISBN 0-02-689137-9). Checkerboard Pr.

Barrett, Peter & Barrett, Susan. The Circle Sarah Drew. Barrett, Peter & Barrett, Susan, illus. Incl. The Line Sophie Drew. LC 76-174716 (ISBN 0-87592-029-2); The Square Ben Drew (ISBN 0-87592-049-7). LC 72-89449. (Illus.). 32p. (ps-2). 1973. 8.95 ea. (ISBN 0-87592-012-8). Scroll Pr.

Big & Little. (Illus.). (ps). 1992. cased 3.50 (ISBN 0-7214-5211-6). Ladybird Bks.

Brown, Margery W. Afro-Bets: Book of Shapes. Blair, Culverson, illus. 24p. (Orig.). (ps-1). 1991. pap. 3.95 (ISBN 0-940975-28-9). Just Us Bks.

Bryant-Mole, K. Shapes. (Illus.). 24p. (ps up). 1991. pap. 3.50 (ISBN 0-7460-0593-8, Usborne). EDC.

Buddle, Jacqueline. Fun with Sizes & Shapes. Davis, Annelies, illus. 32p. (gr. k). 1988. PLB 13.85 (ISBN 0-88625-162-1); pap. 2.50 (ISBN 0-88625-143-5). Durkin Hayes Pub.

Carle, Eric. My Very First Book of Shapes. reissued ed. Carle, Eric, illus. LC 72-83778. 10p. (ps-1). 1985. 4.95 (ISBN 0-694-00013-2, Crowell Jr Bks). HarpC Child Bks.

Carson, Patti & Dellosa, JAnet. Shapes: Circle, Triangle, Square, Rectangle, Diamond. Carson, Patti & Dellosa, Janet, illus. 32p. (ps-1). 1983. pap. 1.98 (ISBN 0-88724-006-2, CD-7007). Carson-Dellos.

Charles, Donald. Calico Cat Looks at Shapes. Charles, Donald, illus. LC 75-12947. 32p. (ps-3). 1975. PLB 14.60 (ISBN 0-516-03436-7). Childrens.

Church, Ellin B. What Fits? 64p. (gr. k-3). 1984. 6.95 (ISBN 0-912107-13-8). Monday Morning Bks.

Colors & Shapes. (Illus.). (ps). pap. 1.25 (ISBN 0-7214-9555-9). Ladybird Bks.

Dr. Seuss. Shape of Me & Other Stuff. Dr. Seuss, illus. (ps-1). 1973. 6.95 (ISBN 0-394-82687-6, Random Juv); lib. bdg. 7.99 (ISBN 0-394-92687-0). Random.

Emberley, Ed E. The Wing on a Flea: A Book about Shapes. Emberley, Ed E., illus. (ps-3). 1988. lib. bdg. 14.95 (ISBN 0-316-23600-4). Little.

Fisher, Leonard E. Look Around! A Book about Shapes. (ps-k). 1987. pap. 11.95 (ISBN 0-670-80869-5). Viking Child Bks.

Les Formes. (FRE., Illus.). 3.50 (ISBN 0-7214-0802-8). Ladybird Bks.

Gregorich, Barbara. Alike-Not Alike & Go-Togethers: Kindergarten. Hoffman, Joan, ed. Koontz, Robin M., illus. 32p. (gr. k). 1990. wkbk. 3.49 (ISBN 0-88743-176-3). Sch Zone Pub Co.

—Igual O Diferente: Same or Different. Hoffman, Joan, ed. Shepherd-Bartram, tr. from ENG. Pape, Richard, illus. (SPA.). 32p. (Orig.). (ps). 1987. wkbk. 1.99 (ISBN 0-938256-80-7). Sch Zone Pub Co.

Hoban, Tana. Is It Larger? Is It Smaller? LC 84-13719. (Illus.). 32p. (ps-1). 1985. 14.95 (ISBN 0-688-04027-6); PLB 14.88 (ISBN 0-688-04028-4). Greenwillow.

Kinghorn, Harriet & Morberg, Mary. Research Shapes: Animals. (Illus.). 64p. (gr. 2-5). 1989. 6.95 (ISBN 1-878279-02-5, MM1919). Monday Morning Bks.

Laithwaite, Eric. Shape: The Purpose of Forms. (Illus.). 32p. (gr. 4-9). 1986. PLB 11.90 (ISBN 0-531-10182-7). Watts.

McMillan, Bruce. Fire Engine Shapes. McMillan, Bruce, photos by. LC 87-38145. (Illus.). 32p. (ps-2). 1988. 12.95 (ISBN 0-688-07842-7); PLB 12.88 (ISBN 0-688-07843-5). Lothrop.

Moncure, Jane B. Hide-&-Seek Word Bird. Hohag, Linda S., illus. LC 81-18068. (ps-2). 1982. lib. bdg. 11.97 (ISBN 0-89565-218-8). Childs World.

Moss, David. Shapes. (ps). 1989. 4.99 (ISBN 0-517-69422-0). Outlet Bk Co.

My Book of Shapes & Colors. (ps-2). 3.95 (ISBN 0-7214-5148-9). Ladybird Bks.

Oliver, Stephen, photos by. My First Look at Shapes. LC 89-63087. (Illus.). 24p. (ps-k). 1990. 6.95 (ISBN 0-679-80534-6). McKay.

—My First Look at Sizes. LC 89-63086. (Illus.). 24p. (ps-k). 1990. 6.95 (ISBN 0-679-80532-X). McKay.

One, Two, Three Board Shape Book. (Illus.). (ps). 1985. bds. 1.69 (ISBN 0-517-46320-2). Outlet Bk Co.

Opposites, 6 bks. Incl. Bk. 1. Big & Little (ISBN 0-448-12580-3, G&D). PLB (ISBN 0-448-13376-8, G&D); Bk. 2. Front & Back (ISBN 0-448-12581-1, G&D). PLB (ISBN 0-448-13377-6, G&D); Bk. 3. Top & Bottom (ISBN 0-448-12582-X, G&D); Bk. 4. Old & New (ISBN 0-448-12583-8, G&D); Bk. 5. Fast & Slow (ISBN 0-448-12584-6, G&D). PLB (ISBN 0-448-13380-6); Bk. 6. Noisy & Quiet (ISBN 0-448-12585-4, G&D). PLB (ISBN 0-448-13381-4, G&D). (ps-3). 1.95 ea. (G&D); PLB 2.99 ea. Putnam Pub Group.

Percy, Graham. Circles. 16p. (ps). 1986. bds. 3.95 (ISBN 0-915391-15-5, Pub by Mad Hatter Bks). Slawson Comm.

—Rectangles. 16p. (ps). 1986. bds. 3.95 (ISBN 0-915391-18-X, Pub by Mad Hatter Bks). Slawson Comm.

—Squares. 16p. (ps). 1986. bds. 3.95 (ISBN 0-915391-16-3, Pub. by Mad Hatter Bks). Slawson Comm.

—Triangles. 16p. (ps). 1986. bds. 3.95 (ISBN 0-915391-17-1, Pub by Mad Hatter Bks). Slawson Comm.

Petty, Kate. What's That Shape? Kopper, Lisa, illus. 24p. (gr. k-3). 1987. lib. bdg. 7.79 (ISBN 0-531-10281-5). Watts.

—What's That Size? Kopper, Lisa, illus. 24p. (gr. k-3). 1987. lib. bdg. 7.79 (ISBN 0-317-53452-1). Watts.

Pragoff, Fiona. Shapes. (Illus.). 16p. (ps-k). 1989. 5.95 (ISBN 0-385-26408-9, Zephyr-BFYR). Doubleday.

Radlauer, Ed. Big Bears - Little Bears. Radlauer Productions Staff, illus. 32p. (ps-4). 1991. PLB 9.95 (ISBN 1-878363-34-4). Forest Hse.
Forest House, a "sole source", no jobber/wholesaler sales, school & library publishing company, introduces our new for spring/fall 1991 series. All Forest House titles, in reinforced library bindings, are full, four color art which enhance & excite young & new readers. Our books encourage children & young adults, "to turn the page". Ed Radlauer introduces his first series for Forest House this spring. The RADLAUER BIG/LITTLE READERS, all done with actual photographs & easy text, show different examples of the concept, "Big & Little". Using full color photographs of bears, cats, & different vehicles with wheels, these delightful stories, done for pre K-4, are ideal for literature based reading. BIG BEARS/LITTLE BEARS, BIG CATS/LITTLE CATS, & BIG WHEELS/LITTLE WHEELS are 32 pages, $9.95 each. Each book has a glossary & word list. Series price: $29.85.
Publisher Provided Annotation.

Ross, Shirley & McCord, Cindy. Shape Creatures. 64p. (ps-2). 1987. 6.95 (ISBN 0-912107-64-2). Monday Morning Bks.

Shapes. (Illus.). (ps). 1992. cased 3.50 (ISBN 0-7214-5209-4). Ladybird Bks.

Shapes & Colors. (Illus.). (ps-2). 1.95 (ISBN 0-7214-5184-5). Ladybird Bks.

Simon, Seymour. Little Giants. Carroll, Pamela, illus. LC 82-14139. 48p. (gr. k-5). 1983. PLB 14.88 (ISBN 0-688-01731-2). Morrow Jr Bks.

Smalley, Guy, illus. My Very Own Book of Sizes. 24p. (ps-2). 1989. 9.95 (ISBN 0-929793-04-8). Camex Bks Inc.

Srivastava, Jane J. Spaces, Shapes, & Sizes. Lustig, Loretta, illus. LC 78-22516. 48p. (gr. 1-3). 1980. 12.95i (ISBN 0-690-03961-1, Crowell Jr Bks). HarpC Child Bks.

Taulbee, Annette. Shapes & Colors. (Illus.). 24p. (ps-k). 1986. 3.98 (ISBN 0-86734-068-1, FS-3061). Schaffer Pubns.

Taylor, Barbara. Ready Set Go: Shapes. 1991. 4.98 (ISBN 0-8317-7358-8). Smithmark.

Things That Go Board Shape Book. (Illus.). (ps). 1985. bds. 1.69 (ISBN 0-517-46322-9). Outlet Bk Co.

Thomson, Ruth. All about Shapes. Ives, Penny, illus. LC 87-42587. 32p. (gr. 1-2). 1987. PLB 10.95 (ISBN 1-55532-314-6). Gareth Stevens Inc.

Van der Meer, Ron & Van der Meer, Atie. Fun with Shapes. (Illus.). 10p. (ps-1). 1990. 7.99 (ISBN 0-399-21787-8, Putnam). Putnam Pub Group.

Watson, C. Shapes. Higham, David, illus. 24p. (gr. k-2). 1983. 2.95 (ISBN 0-86020-759-5). EDC.

—Sizes. Higham, David, illus. 24p. (gr. k-2). 1983. 2.95 (ISBN 0-86020-760-9). EDC.

Wheeler, Sharon. Shapes. Richesson, Robin, illus. (ps). 1984. wkbk 1.95 (ISBN 0-916119-00-9). Creat Teach Pr.

Worth, Bonnie. Muppet Babies Shape Machine. 1988. write for info. (ISBN 0-02-689107-7). Checkerboard Pr.

Yenawine, Philip. Shapes. (Illus.). (gr. 2-5). 1991. 14.00 (ISBN 0-385-30255-X); PLB 14.99 (ISBN 0-385-30315-7). Delacorte.

SIZE AND SHAPE–FICTION

Allen, Constance. Grover's Book of Cute Things to Touch. (ps). 1990. write for info. (ISBN 0-307-12320-0, Golden Pr). Western Pub.

Big & Little. (Illus.). 14p. (ps). 1979. bds. 2.50 (ISBN 0-448-16271-7, G&D). Putnam Pub Group.

Friedman, Frieda. Dot for Short. 168p. 1981. Repr. PLB 10.95x (ISBN 0-89967-038-5). Harmony Raine.

Gordon, Sharon. Playground Fun. Karas, G. Brian, illus. LC 86-30854. 32p. (gr. k-2). 1987. lib. bdg. 7.06 (ISBN 0-8167-0990-4); pap. text ed. 1.95 (ISBN 0-8167-0991-2). Troll Assocs.

Hargreaves, Roger. Little Miss Tiny. Hargreaves, Roger, illus. 32p. (ps-k). 1981. pap. 1.25 (ISBN 0-8431-0892-4). Price Stern.

Jonas, Ann. Holes & Peeks. Jonas, Ann, illus. LC 83-14128. 24p. (ps-1). 1984. 14.95 (ISBN 0-688-02537-4); PLB 14.88 (ISBN 0-688-02538-2). Greenwillow.

Joyce, William. George Shrinks. miniature ed. Joyce, William, illus. LC 90-46285. 32p. (ps-2). 1991. 3.95 (ISBN 0-06-023299-4). HarpC Child Bks.

Levy, Elizabeth. The Runt. (Orig.). (gr. k-6). 1986. pap. 2.95 (ISBN 0-440-47538-4, YB). Dell.

McDaniel, Becky B. Katie Couldn't. Axeman, Lois, illus. LC 85-11666. 30p. (gr. 1-2). 1985. PLB 11.93 (ISBN 0-516-02069-2); pap. 2.95 (ISBN 0-516-42069-0). Childrens.

Moncure, Jane B. Magic Monsters Look for Shapes. Magnuson, Diana, illus. LC 78-21529. (ps-3). 1979. PLB 11.97 (ISBN 0-89565-057-6). Childs World.

Myers, Walter D. Hoops. 192p. (gr. 7 up). 1983. pap. 3.25 (ISBN 0-440-93884-8, LFL). Dell.
Shreve, Susan. Lucy Forever & Miss Rosetree, Shrinks. LC 86-29513. 144p. (gr. 3-6). 1987. 13.95 (ISBN 0-8050-0340-1). H Holt & Co.
Smith-Moore, J. J. Sally Small. Smith-Moore, J. J., illus. 32p. (ps-2). 1989. 10.95 (ISBN 0-8431-2360-5). Price Stern.
Weiss, Ellen. Oh Beans! Starring String Bean. Hall, Susan, illus. LC 88-4907. 32p. (gr. k-3). 1989. PLB 8.79 (ISBN 0-8167-1396-0); pap. text ed. 1.95 (ISBN 0-8167-1397-9). Troll Assocs.

SKATEBOARDS

Caitlin, Stephen. Skateboard Fun. LC 87-19179. (ps-1). 1987. pap. 7.06 (ISBN 0-8167-1233-6); pap. 1.95 (ISBN 0-8167-1234-4). Troll Assocs.
Cassorla, Albert. The Ultimate Skateboard Book. LC 88-42604. (Illus.). 128p. (Orig.). (gr. 6 up). 1988. PLB 19.80 (ISBN 0-89471-565-8); pap. 9.95 (ISBN 0-89471-564-X). Running Pr.
Dickmeyer, Lowell A. Skateboarding Is for Me. LC 78-54361. (Illus.). 48p. (gr. 2-5). 1978. PLB 8.95 (ISBN 0-8225-1081-2). Lerner Pubns.
Gould, Marilyn. Skateboarding. 48p. (gr. 3-4). 1991. PLB 11.95 (ISBN 1-56065-048-6). Capstone Pr.
Hart, Cynthia. Skateboard: A Mini-Poster Book. 32p. (gr. 7 up). 1988. pap. 3.95 (ISBN 0-590-41150-0). Scholastic Inc.
King, Ron. Rad Boards: Skateboarding, Snowboarding, Bodyboarding. (gr. 4-7). 1991. pap. 9.95 (ISBN 0-316-49355-4). Little.
Schmitz, Dorothy C. Skateboarding. LC 78-7048. (Illus.). 32p. (gr. 3-4). 1978. PLB 9.95 (ISBN 0-913940-91-7, Crestwood Hse). Macmillan Child Grp.
Wood, Tim. Skateboarding. Fairclough, Chris, photos by. (Illus.). 32p. (gr. k-4). 1989. PLB 10.40 (ISBN 0-531-10830-9). Watts.

SKATING

Aaseng, Nathan. Eric Heiden: Winner in Gold. LC 80-16982. (Illus.). 56p. (gr. 4-9). 1980. PLB 8.95 (ISBN 0-8225-0481-2). Lerner Pubns.
Bailey, Donna. Skating. LC 90-36525. (Illus.). 32p. (gr. 1-4). 1990. PLB 14.64 (ISBN 0-8114-2854-0). Steck-V.
Dickmeyer, Lowell A. & Rolens, Lin. Ice Skating Is for Me. Tkash, Daniel G. & Kreklow, Pete, photos by. LC 79-20465. (Illus.). 48p. (gr. 2-5). 1980. PLB 8.95 (ISBN 0-8225-1088-X). Lerner Pubns.
Hamill, Dorothy & Clairmont, Elva. Dorothy Hamill on & off the Ice. LC 83-6170. (Illus.). 192p. (gr. 8-12). 1983. lib. bdg. 10.99 (ISBN 0-394-95610-9). Knopf.
Haney, Lynn. Skaters: Profile of a Pair. Curtis, Bruce, photos by. LC 83-13655. (Illus.). (gr. 5 up). 1983. 10.95 (ISBN 0-399-21013-X, Putnam). Putnam Pub Group.
Irland, Nancy B. Silver Skates. 128p. (Orig.). 1987. pap. 2.99 (ISBN 0-8163-0678-8). Pacific Pr Pub Assn.
Krementz, Jill. A Very Young Skater. (gr. 3-6). 1986. pap. 6.95 (ISBN 0-440-49214-9). Dell.
MacLean, Norman. Ice Skating Basics. Gow, Bill, illus. LC 84-6933. 48p. (gr. 3-7). 1984. 9.95 (ISBN 0-13-448762-1). P-H.
Nentl, Jerolyn. Roller Skating. LC 80-10475. (Illus.). 36p. (gr. 3-5). 1980. lib. bdg. 9.95 (ISBN 0-89686-072-8, Crestwood Hse); pap. 3.95 o. p. (ISBN 0-685-01270-0). Macmillan Child Grp.
Penner, Fred. Rollerskating. Hicks, Barbara, illus. 32p. (Orig.). (gr. 2-6). 1990. pap. 5.95 (ISBN 0-920534-64-3, Pub. by Hyperion Pr Ltd CN). Sterling.
Skating. (Illus.). 64p. (gr. 6-12). 1983. pap. 1.85 (ISBN 0-8395-3250-4, 3250). BSA.
Sullivan, George. Better Roller Skating for Boys & Girls. (Illus.). 64p. (gr. 3-7). 1980. 9.95 (ISBN 0-396-07784-6, Putnam); pap. 2.95 (ISBN 0-396-08291-2, Putnam). Putnam Pub Group.
Trenary, Jill. Day I Skated for the Gold. 1991. pap. 5.95 (ISBN 0-671-73348-6). S&S Trade.
Winter, Ginny L. Skating Book. Winter, Ginny L., illus. (gr. k-3). 1963. 8.95 (ISBN 0-8392-3035-4). Astor-Honor.
Wood, Tim. Ice Skating. Fairclough, Chris, photos by. (Illus.). 32p. (gr. k-4). 1990. PLB 10.40 (ISBN 0-531-14051-2). Watts.

SKATING–FICTION

Dodge, Mary M. Hans Brinker. Baldridge, C. L., illus. (gr. 4-6). 1945-63. deluxe ed. 11.95 (ISBN 0-448-06011-6, G&D); Companion Lib. Ed. o.p. 2.95 (ISBN 0-448-05462-0). Putnam Pub Group.
—Hans Brinker. (gr. k-6). 1985. pap. 4.95 (ISBN 0-440-43446-7, Pub. by Yearling Classics). Dell.
—Hans Brinker. Betts, Louise, adapted by. Elwell, Peter, illus. LC 87-15472. 48p. (gr. 3-6). 1988. PLB 12.89 (ISBN 0-8167-1205-0); pap. text ed. 3.95 (ISBN 0-8167-1206-9). Troll Assocs.
—Hans Brinker or the Silver Skates. 320p. (Orig.). (gr. 4-6). 1988. pap. 2.95 (ISBN 0-590-41295-7, Apple Paperbacks). Scholastic Inc.
—Hans Brinker: The Silver Skates. LC 54-14472. (gr. 5 up). pap. 2.50 (ISBN 0-8049-0099-X, CL-99). Airmont.
Douglass, Barbara. Sizzle Wheels. LC 80-39750. (Illus.). 174p. (gr. 3-6). 1981. 9.95 (ISBN 0-664-32680-3, Westminster). Westminster John Knox.
Fenner, Carol. The Skates of Uncle Richard. Forberg, Ati, illus. LC 78-55910. (gr. 2-5). 1978. (Random Juv); lib. bdg. 7.99 (ISBN 0-394-93553-5). Random.
—The Skates of Uncle Richard. Forberg, Ati, illus. LC 78-55910. 48p. 1990. pap. 2.95 (ISBN 0-394-82605-1, Bullseye Bks). Knopf.
Johnson, Mildred. Wait, Skates! Dunnington, Tom, illus. LC 82-22228. 32p. (ps-2). 1983. PLB 11.93 (ISBN 0-516-02039-0); pap. 2.95 (ISBN 0-516-42039-9). Childrens.
Laird, Elizabeth. The Day the Ducks Went Skating. Reeder, Colin, illus. LC 90-25899. 32p. (ps up). 1991. 11.95 (ISBN 0-688-10246-8, Tambourine Bks); PLB 11.88 (ISBN 0-688-10247-6, Tambourine Bks). Morrow.
Lee, Mildred. Skating Rink. LC 69-13443. 128p. (gr. 6 up). 1979. 7.95 (ISBN 0-395-28912-2, Clarion). HM.
Levy, Elizabeth. Cold As Ice. LC 88-12898. 176p. (gr. 7 up). 1988. 12.95 (ISBN 0-688-06579-1). Morrow Jr Bks.
Peck, Robert N. Soup on Ice. (gr. k-6). 1988. pap. 2.75 (ISBN 0-440-40115-1, YB). Dell.
Peters, Sharon. Champ on Ice. Paterson, Diane, illus. LC 87-10908. 32p. (gr. k-2). 1988. PLB 10.89 (ISBN 0-8167-1093-7); pap. text ed. 2.95 (ISBN 0-8167-1094-5). Troll Assocs.
Radin, Ruth Y. A Winter Place. O'Kelley, Mattie L., illus. LC 82-15349. 32p. (gr. 3 up). 1982. 15.95 (ISBN 0-316-73218-4, Joy St Bks). Little.
Sawyer, Ruth. Roller Skates. Angelo, Valenti, illus. 192p. (gr. 4-7). 1969. pap. 1.50 (ISBN 0-440-47499-X, YB). Dell.
Schulz, Charles M. She's a Good Skate, Charlie Brown. Schulz, Charles M., illus. LC 80-20285. 48p. (gr. 3-5). 1981. lib. bdg. 5.99 (ISBN 0-394-94495-X); bds. 4.95 (ISBN 0-394-84495-5). Random.
Streatfeild, Noel. Skating Shoes. (Orig.). (gr. 5 up). 1982. pap. 2.75 (ISBN 0-440-47731-X, YB). Dell.

SKELETON

Bailey, Donna. All about Your Skeleton. LC 90-10114. (Illus.). 48p. (gr. 2-5). 1990. PLB 15.96 (ISBN 0-8114-2780-3). Steck-V.
Balestrino, Philip. Skeleton Inside You. Bolognese, Don, illus. LC 72-132290. (gr. k-3). 1971. (Crowell Jr Bks). HarpC Child Bks.
—The Skeleton Inside You. rev. ed. Kelley, True, illus. LC 88-23672. 32p. (gr. k-3). 1989. 13.95 (ISBN 0-690-04731-2, Crowell Jr Bks); PLB 13.89 (ISBN 0-690-04733-9). HarpC Child Bks.
—The Skeleton Inside You. rev. ed. Kelley, True, illus. LC 88-24600. 32p. (gr. k-3). 1989. pap. 4.50 (ISBN 0-06-445087-2, Trophy). HarpC Child Bks.
Broekel, Ray. Your Skeleton & Skin. LC 84-7746. (Illus.). 48p. (gr. k-4). 1984. lib. bdg. 14.60 (ISBN 0-516-01934-1); pap. 4.95 (ISBN 0-516-41934-X). Childrens.
Cumbaa, Stephen. The Kids' Bones Book & Skeleton. LC 90-50368. (Illus.). 64p. (Orig.). (gr. 1-7). 1991. pap. 14.95 (ISBN 0-89480-860-5, 1860). Workman Pub.
Parker, Steve. Skeleton. Dowell, Philip, photos by. LC 87-26314. (Illus.). 64p. (gr. 5 up). 1988. 15.00 (ISBN 0-394-89620-3); lib. bdg. 14.99 (ISBN 0-394-99620-8). Knopf.
—The Skeleton & Movement. rev. ed. (Illus.). 48p. (gr. 5 up). 1991. pap. 4.95 (ISBN 0-531-24606-X). Watts.
Skeleton & Movement. 48p. (gr. 5-8). 1988. PLB 12.98 (ISBN 0-382-09702-5); 9.74s.p. (ISBN 0-685-24610-8). Silver Burdett Pr.
Ward, Brian. Skeleton & Movement. (Illus.). 48p. (gr. 4 up). 1981. lib. bdg. 12.40 (ISBN 0-531-04291-X). Watts.

SKETCHING

see Drawing

SKIING

see Skis and Skiing

SKIING, WATER

see Water Skiing

SKIN

Bailey, Donna. All about Skin, Hair & Teeth. LC 90-10050. (Illus.). 48p. (gr. 2-5). 1990. PLB 15.96 (ISBN 0-8114-2783-8). Steck-V.
Broekel, Ray. Your Skeleton & Skin. LC 84-7746. (Illus.). 48p. (gr. k-4). 1984. lib. bdg. 14.60 (ISBN 0-516-01934-1); pap. 4.95 (ISBN 0-516-41934-X). Childrens.
Montagna, William. Human Skin. Head, J. J., ed. Ito, Joel, illus. LC 84-45831. 16p. (Orig.). (gr. 10 up). 1986. pap. text ed. 2.15 (ISBN 0-89278-159-9, 45-9759). Carolina Biological.
Novick, Nelson L. Skin Care for Teens. Solomon, Maury, ed. Green, Anne, illus. 144p. (gr. 7 up). 1988. PLB 12.90 (ISBN 0-531-10521-0). Watts.
Riedman, Sarah R. & Barish, Wendy. The Good Looks Skin Book. (Illus.). 144p. (gr. 10 up). 1983. 9.29 (ISBN 0-685-06727-0, Little Simon). S&S Trade.
Showers, Paul. Your Skin & Mine. Galdone, Paul, illus. LC 65-16185. 40p. (gr. k-3). 1965. (Crowell Jr Bks); pap. 3.95 crocodile paperback ser. o.p. (ISBN 0-690-00205-X, Crowell Jr Bks). HarpC Child Bks.
Skin. (Illus.). (gr. 5 up). lib. bdg. 14.00 (ISBN 0-86625-276-2). Rourke Corp.
Zizmor, Jonathan. The Doctor's Do-It-Yourself Guide to Clearer Skin. Stevenson, Dinah, ed. LC 79-3014. (gr. 7 up). 1980. 9.57i (ISBN 0-397-31877-4, Lipp Jr Bks). HarpC Child Bks.

SKIN, COLOR OF

see Color of Man

SKIN–DISEASES

Lamberg, Lynn. Skin Disorders. (Illus.). (gr. 6-12). 1990. 18.95 (ISBN 0-7910-0076-1). Chelsea Hse.
Silverstein, Alvin, et al. Overcoming Acne: The How & Why of Healthy Skin Care. Papa, Christopher M., pref. by. LC 89-13748. (Illus.). 112p. (gr. 7 up). 1990. 12.95 (ISBN 0-688-08344-7). Morrow Jr Bks.

SKIN DIVING

see also Underwater Exploration

Barrett, Norman. Scuba Diving. (Illus.). 32p. (gr. k-6). 1990. 11.40 (ISBN 0-531-10631-4). Watts.
Briggs, Carole S. Skin Diving Is for Me. Ayres, Carter M., illus. LC 80-27409. 48p. (gr. 2-5). 1981. PLB 8.95 (ISBN 0-8225-1132-0). Lerner Pubns.
—Sport Diving. LC 82-35. (Illus.). (gr. 4-9). 1982. PLB 9.95 (ISBN 0-8225-0503-7). Lerner Pubns.
Scuba Diving & Snorkeling. 48p. (gr. 3-4). 1989. PLB 10.95 (ISBN 0-685-26388-6). Capstone Pr.

SKIN DIVING–FICTION

Carrick, Carol. Dark & Full of Secrets. Carrick, Donald, illus. LC 83-21017. 32p. (ps-4). 1984. 12.95 (ISBN 0-89919-271-8, Clarion). HM.

SKIS AND SKIING

see also Water Skiing

Bailey, Donna. Skiing. LC 90-36125. (Illus.). 32p. (gr. 1-4). 1990. PLB 14.64 (ISBN 0-8114-2856-7). Steck-V.
Chappell, Annette J. Skiing Is for Me. LC 78-12411. (Illus.). 48p. (gr. 2-5). 1978. PLB 8.95 (ISBN 0-8225-1082-0). Lerner Pubns.
Claridge, M. Skiing. (Illus.). 64p. (gr. 6 up). 1987. PLB 12.96 (ISBN 0-88110-248-2); pap. 7.95 (ISBN 0-7460-0096-0). EDC.
Hahn, James & Hahn, Lynn. Killy! The Sports Career of Jean-Claude Killy. LC 81-5419. (Illus.). 48p. (gr. 3 up). 1981. PLB 9.95 (ISBN 0-89686-132-5, Crestwood Hse). Macmillan Child Grp.
Hall, Jackie. Skiing & Snow Sports. 1990. PLB 12.90 (ISBN 0-531-19075-7). Watts.
Hulbert, Elizabeth M. I Love to Ski. Hulbert, Elizabeth M., illus. LC 87-51331. 64p. (Orig.). (gr. 1-3). 1986. pap. 4.95 (ISBN 0-932433-25-1). Windswept Hse.
Krementz, Jill. A Very Young Skier. LC 89-28760. (Illus.). 48p. (gr. k up). 1990. 14.95 (ISBN 0-8037-0821-1); PLB 14.89 (ISBN 0-8037-0823-8). Dial Bks Young.
Marozzi, Alfred. Skiing Basics. Gow, Bill, illus. 48p. (gr. 3-7). 1984. pap. 4.95 (ISBN 0-13-812264-4). P-H.
Nentl, Jerolyn. Freestyle Skiing. LC 78-8032. (Illus.). 32p. (gr. 3-4). 1978. pap. 9.95 (ISBN 0-913940-90-9, Crestwood Hse). Macmillan Child Grp.
Skiing. (Illus.). 56p. (gr. 6-12). 1980. pap. 1.85 (ISBN 0-8395-3364-0, 3364). BSA.
Smith, Alias & Pelkowski, Robert. Skiing: Speedy Slopes & Fluffy Snow in Ski School. 32p. (ps-3). 1989. pap. 3.95 (ISBN 0-8120-4244-1). Barron.
Symons & Westcott, Alvin. Dips 'n' Doodles. LC 74-108726. (Illus.). 48p. (gr. 3-5). 1970. PLB 10.95 (ISBN 0-87783-011-8); pap. 3.94 deluxe ed. (ISBN 0-87783-090-8). Oddo.
Washington, Rosemary G. Cross-Country Skiing Is for Me. Wolfe, Robert L., illus. LC 82-7225. 48p. (gr. 2-5). 1982. PLB 8.95 (ISBN 0-8225-1126-6). Lerner Pubns.

SKIS AND SKIING–FICTION

Beskow, Elsa. Ollie's Ski Trip. Ernest Benn Ltd. Staff, tr. from SWE. Beskow, Elsa, illus. (ps-2). Repr. of 1960 ed. 14.95 (ISBN 0-86315-091-8, Pub. by Floris Bks UK). Gryphon Hse.
De Brunhoff, Laurent. Babar Fait Du Ski. (FRE.). (gr. 2-3). 4.95 (ISBN 0-685-11029-X). French & Eur.

SKITS

McGee, Cecil. Drama for Fun. LC 69-14368. (gr. k up). 1991. 10.95 (ISBN 0-8054-7505-2). Broadman.
Sheridan, Jeff. Nothing's Impossible: Stunts to Entertain & Amaze. Moore, Jim, photos by. LC 81-20780. (Illus.). 64p. (gr. 5 up). 1982. 12.95 (ISBN 0-688-01169-1). Lothrop.

SKULL

see Brain

SKUNKS

Green, Carl R. & Sanford, William R. The Striped Skunk. LC 87-6652. (Illus.). 48p. (gr. 5-6). 1987. PLB 10.95 (ISBN 0-89686-338-7, Crestwood Hse). Macmillan Child Grp.
Skunk. 1990. 2.95 (ISBN 0-8378-2053-7). Gibson.
Stone, Lynn. Skunks. (Illus.). 24p. (gr. k-5). 1990. lib. bdg. 11.93 (ISBN 0-86593-046-5); lib. bdg. 8.95s.p. (ISBN 0-685-36341-4). Rourke Corp.

SKUNKS–FICTION

Bailey, Ted. Skunks! Go to Bed! (ps-3). 1990. write for info. (ISBN 0-307-12108-9). Western Pub.
Goldfield, Maud D. Feemore, the Baby Skunk, Finds a Home. (ps-8). 1989. 6.95 (ISBN 0-533-08320-6). Vantage.
Hanson, Fred E. Norman. Hanson, Ann R., ed. & illus. LC 89-90961. 63p. (Orig.). (gr. 4-6). 1989. pap. 7.95 (ISBN 0-685-28895-1). Black Willow Pr.
—Norman. 2nd ed. Hanson, Ann R., illus. 64p. (gr. 4-6). pap. 7.95 (ISBN 0-685-39311-9). Black Willow Pr.
McMullen, Shawn A. It's What's Inside That Counts. Haley, Amanda, illus. 32p. (ps-2). 1991. pap. text ed. 3.99 (ISBN 0-87403-808-1, 24-03898). Standard Pub.
Phillips, Walt. Stinky Skink Stinks & Other Stories. Phillips, Wald, illus. 98p. 1990. 7.95 (ISBN 0-533-08623-X). Vantage.
Sharmat, Marjorie W. Bartholomew the Bossy. Chartier, Normand, illus. LC 83-17603. 32p. (ps-3). 1984. 11.95 (ISBN 0-02-782520-5, Mcmillan Child Bk). Macmillan Child Grp.

SKY DIVING
see Skydiving
SKYDIVING
Barrett, Norman. Skydiving. Franklin Watts Ltd., ed. (Illus.). 32p. (ps-9). 1988. 10.90 (ISBN 0-531-10352-8). Watts.
Benson, Rolf. Skydiving. LC 78-26246. (Illus.). 48p. (gr. 4-9). 1979. PLB 9.95 (ISBN 0-8225-0425-1). Lerner Pubns.
Nentl, Jerolyn. Skydiving. LC 78-8702. (Illus.). 32p. (gr. 3-4). 1978. PLB 9.95 (ISBN 0-913940-87-9, Crestwood Hse). Macmillan Child Grp.
SKYSCRAPERS
Gibbons, Gail. Up Goes the Skyscraper! Gibbons, Gail, illus. LC 85-16245. 32p. (gr. k-3). 1986. 13.95 (ISBN 0-02-736780-0, Four Winds). Macmillan Child Grp.
—Up Goes the Skyscraper! Gibbons, Gail, illus. LC 90-31777. 32p. (gr. k-3). 1990. pap. 4.95 (ISBN 0-689-71411-4, Aladdin). Macmillan Child Grp.
Giblin, James C. The Skyscraper Book. Kramer, Anthony, illus. Anderson, David, photos by. LC 81-43038. (Illus.). 96p. (gr. 3-6). 1981. (Crowell Jr Bks); PLB 12.89 (ISBN 0-690-04155-1, Crowell Jr Bks). HarpC Child Bks.
Ingoglia, Gina. The Big Book of Real Skyscrapers. LaPadula, Tom, illus. 48p. (gr. 1-4). 1989. PLB 7.95 (ISBN 0-448-19186-5, G&D). Putnam Pub Group.
Michael, Duncan. How Skyscrapers Are Made. (Illus.). 32p. (gr. 5-12). 1987. 12.95 (ISBN 0-8160-1692-5). Facts on File.
Ostler, Tim. Skyscrapers. Franklin Watts Ltd., ed. Shone, Rob, illus. 32p. (gr. 7-9). 1988. PLB 8.90 (ISBN 0-531-17074-8, Gloucester Pr). Watts.
Sauvain, Philip. Skyscrapers. Stefoff, Rebecca, ed. LC 90-40358. (Illus.). 48p. (gr. 4-7). 1990. PLB 17.26 (ISBN 0-944483-78-X). Garrett Ed Corp.
Wilcox, Charlotte. A Skyscraper Story. Boucher, Jerry, photos by. (Illus.). 48p. (ps-4). 1990. PLB 12.95 (ISBN 0-87614-392-3). Carolrhoda Bks.
SLATER, SAMUEL, 1768-1835
Simonds, Christopher. Samuel Slater's Mill & the Industrial Revolution. (Illus.). 64p. (gr. 5 up). 1990. lib. bdg. 16.98 (ISBN 0-382-09951-6); pap. 7.95 (ISBN 0-382-09947-8). Silver Burdett Pr.
SLAVE TRADE
Fox, Paula. The Slave Dancer. Eros, Keith, illus. LC 73-80642. 192p. (gr. 5-8). 1982. 13.95 (ISBN 0-02-735560-8, Bradbury Pr). Macmillan Child Grp.
Leas, Allan. Abolition of the Slave Trade. (Illus.). 72p. (gr. 7-10). 1989. 19.95 (ISBN 0-7134-5868-2, Pub. by Batsford England). Trafalgar Sq.
Meltzer, Milton. All Times, All Peoples: A World History of Slavery. Fisher, Leonard E., illus. LC 79-2810. 80p. (gr. 5-9). 1980. PLB 14.89 (ISBN 0-06-024187-X). HarpC Child Bks.
Sterne, Emma G. The Slave Ship. Lockhart, David, illus. 192p. (Orig.). (gr. 4-6). 1988. pap. 2.50 (ISBN 0-590-40621-3). Scholastic Inc.
SLAVERY–FICTION
Anderson, Paul L. Slave of Catiline. LC 57-9446. 255p. (gr. 7-11). 1930. 18.00 (ISBN 0-8196-0101-2). Biblo.
Clark, Margaret G. Freedom Crossing. 160p. (gr. 3-7). 1991. 2.95 (ISBN 0-590-44569-3). Scholastic Inc.
Collier, James L. & Collier, Christopher. Jump Ship to Freedom. LC 81-65492. 192p. (gr. 4-6). 1981. pap. 13.95 (ISBN 0-385-28484-5). Delacorte.
—Who Is Carrie? LC 83-23947. 192p. (gr. 4-6). 1984. 14.95 (ISBN 0-385-29295-3). Delacorte.
De Angeli, Marguerite. Thee, Hannah! (Illus.). 96p. (gr. 2-5). 1970. 15.95 (ISBN 0-385-07525-1, Zephyr-BFYR). Doubleday.
Endore, Guy. Babouk. rev. ed. Kincaid, Jamaica & Trouillot, Michel-Rolphintro. by. 352p. (gr. 9-12). Date not set. 28.00 (ISBN 0-85345-759-X); pap. 9.00 (ISBN 0-85345-745-X). Monthly Rev.
Hurmence, Belinda. A Girl Called Boy. 180p. (gr. 3-6). 1982. 13.95 (ISBN 0-395-31022-9, Clarion). HM.
Levy, Elizabeth. Running Out of Time. Mars, W. T., illus. LC 79-28064. 128p. (gr. 3-6). 1980. lib. bdg. 4.99 (ISBN 0-394-94422-4). Knopf.
Marie, D. Tears for Ashan. Childers, Norman, illus. LC 88-63766. 32p. (ps-3). 1989. 11.95 (ISBN 0-9621681-0-6). Creative Pr Works.
Miner, Jane C. Corey, No. 22. 192p. (Orig.). (gr. 5-10). 1987. pap. 2.50 (ISBN 0-590-40395-8, Sunfire). Scholastic Inc.
Monjo, F. N. Drinking Gourd. Brenner, Fred, illus. LC 68-10782. 64p. (gr. k-3). 1970. PLB 11.89 (ISBN 0-06-024330-9). HarpC Child Bks.
—The Drinking Gourd. Brenner, Fred, illus. LC 68-10782. 64p. (gr. k-3). 1983. pap. 3.50 (ISBN 0-06-444042-7, Trophy). HarpC Child Bks.
Smucker, Barbara. Runaway to Freedom. Lilly, Charles, illus. LC 77-11834. 160p. (gr. 4-8). 1979. pap. 2.95 (ISBN 0-06-440106-5, Trophy). HarpC Child Bks.
Sterne, Emma G. The Slave Ship. 1988. 2.75 (ISBN 0-590-44360-7). Scholastic Inc.
Stowe, Harriet Beecher. Uncle Tom's Cabin. Corrigan, R. A., intro. by. (gr. 9 up). pap. 3.50 (ISBN 0-8049-0143-0, CL-143). Airmont.
Twain, Mark. Pudd'nhead Wilson. Gemme, F. R., intro. by. (Illus.). (gr. 8 up). pap. 1.75 (ISBN 0-8049-0124-4, CL-124). Airmont.
SLAVERY IN THE U. S.
see also Abolitionists; Slave Trade; Underground Railroad
Davidson, Margaret. Frederick Douglass Fights for Freedom. 80p. (gr. 2-5). 1989. pap. 2.50 (ISBN 0-590-42218-9, Apple Paperbacks). Scholastic Inc.
Davis, Ossie. Escape to Freedom: A Play about Young Frederick Douglass. (gr. 4-7). 1990. pap. 3.95 (ISBN 0-14-034355-5, Puffin). Puffin Bks.
Evitts, William J. Captive Bodies, Free Spirits: The Story of Southern Slavery. LC 85-13922. (Illus.). 160p. (gr. 7 up). 1985. lib. bdg. 13.98 (ISBN 0-671-54094-7). Messner.
Ferris, Jeri. Go Free or Die: A Story about Harriet Tubman. Ritz, Karen, illus. 64p. (gr. 3-6). 1989. pap. 4.95 (ISBN 0-685-25638-3, First Ave Edns). Lerner Pubns.
Gaines, Edith M. Freedom Light: Underground Railroad Stories from Ripley, Ohio. Clay, Cliff, illus. (Orig.). (gr. 5-8). 1991. pap. 5.00 (ISBN 0-913678-20-1). New Day Pr.
Hamilton, Virginia. Anthony Burns: The Defeat & Triumph of a Fugitive Slave. LC 87-38063. 192p. (gr. 5 up). 1988. 11.95 (ISBN 0-394-88185-0); lib. bdg. 12.99 (ISBN 0-394-98185-5). Knopf.
Lester, Julius. This Strange New Feeling. 164p. (gr. 7 up). 1985. pap. 2.75 (ISBN 0-590-44047-0). Scholastic Inc.
—To Be a Slave. Feelings, Tom, illus. LC 68-28738. (gr. 7-12). 1968. 13.95 (ISBN 0-8037-8955-6). Dial Bks Young.
—To Be a Slave. Feeling, Tom, illus. 160p. (gr. 7 up). 1986. pap. 2.50 (ISBN 0-590-40682-5, Point); tchr's. guide 1.25. Scholastic Inc.
—To Be a Slave. 1986. pap. 2.75 (ISBN 0-590-42460-2). Scholastic Inc.
Marsh, Carole. Out of the Mouths of Slaves. (gr. 3-12). 1989. 19.95 (ISBN 1-55609-312-8); pap. 14.95 (ISBN 1-55609-311-X); computer disk 29.95 (ISBN 1-55609-313-6). Gallopade Pub Group.
Petry, Ann. Tituba of Salem Village. LC 64-20691. 254p. (gr. 7 up). 1988. PLB 14.89 (ISBN 0-690-04766-5, Crowell Jr Bks). HarpC Child Bks.
Rappaport, Doreen. Escape from Slavery: Five Journeys to Freedom. Lilly, Charles, illus. LC 90-38170. 128p. (gr. 4-7). 1991. 12.95 (ISBN 0-06-021631-X); PLB 12.89 (ISBN 0-06-021632-8). HarpC Child Bks.
Rivers, Larry. Some American History: Slavery: The Black Man & the Man. Childs, Charles, intro. by. LC 72-153088. 50p. (Orig.). 1971. pap. text ed. 8.95 (ISBN 0-318-42723-0, Dist. by U of TX Pr). Inst for the arts.
Yates, Elizabeth. Amos Fortune, Free Man. Unwin, Nora S., illus. (gr. 7 up). 1967. 13.95 (ISBN 0-525-25570-2, DCB). Dutton Child Bks.
SLAVS IN THE U. S
Roucek, Joseph S. Czechs & the Slovaks in America. LC 67-15685. (Illus.). 72p. (gr. 5 up). 1967. PLB 11.95 (ISBN 0-8225-0209-7); pap. 3.95 (ISBN 0-8225-1004-9). Lerner Pubns.
SLEEP
see also Dreams
Edelson, Edward. Sleep. (Illus.). (gr. 6-12). 1992. lib. bdg. 18.95 (ISBN 0-7910-0092-3). Chelsea Hse.
Goffstein, M. B. Sleepy People. rev. ed. LC 66-10723. (Illus.). (ps-2). 1979. 6.95 (ISBN 0-374-37030-3). FS&G.
Little People Big Book About Bedtime. 64p. (ps-1). 1989. write for info. (ISBN 0-8094-7454-9); PLB write for info. (ISBN 0-8094-7455-7). Time-Life.
Parker, Steve. Dreaming in the Night: How You Rest, Sleep & Dream. (Illus.). 32p. (gr. k-4). 1991. PLB 11.40 (ISBN 0-531-14099-7). Watts.
Richardson, Joy. What Happens When You Sleep? LC 86-3680. (Illus.). 32p. (gr. 2-3). 1986. 10.95 (ISBN 1-55532-111-9). Gareth Stevens Inc.
Showers, Paul. Sleep Is for Everyone. Watson, Wendy, illus. LC 72-83785. 40p. (ps-3). 1974. PLB 13.89 (ISBN 0-690-01118-0, Crowell Jr Bks). HarpC Child Bks.
Silverstein, Alvin & Silverstein, Virginia B. Sleep & Dreams. LC 73-13825. (Illus.). 160p. (gr. 7 up). 1974. PLB 12.89 (ISBN 0-397-31325-X, Lipp Jr Bks). HarpC Child Bks.
Ziefert, Harriet. My Getting-Ready-for-Bed Book. Smith, Mavis, illus. LC 89-62012. 12p. (ps-1). 1990. 13.95 (ISBN 0-694-00299-2). HarpC Child Bks.
SLEEP–FICTION
Adams, Pam, illus. There Were Ten in the Bed. 24p. (ps-2). 1979. 5.50 (ISBN 0-85953-095-7, Pub. by Childs's Play England). Childs Play.
Asher, Sandy. Princess Bee & the Royal Good-Night Story. Mathews, Judith, ed. Smith, Cat B., illus. 32p. (ps-1). 1989. 12.95 (ISBN 0-8075-6624-1). A Whitman.
Beckman, Kaj. Lisa Can't Sleep. Beckman, Per, illus. 28p. (ps). 1990. 7.95 (ISBN 91-29-59768-4, Pub. by R & S Bks). FS&G.
Boynton, Sandra. Good Night, Good Night. Boynton, Sandra, illus. LC 85-2098. 40p. (ps-1). 1985. 6.95 (ISBN 0-394-87285-1, Random Juv). Random.
Cazet, Denys. Mother Night. LC 88-36439. (Illus.). 32p. (ps-1). 1989. 14.95 (ISBN 0-531-05830-1); PLB 14.99 (ISBN 0-531-08430-2). Orchard Bks Watts.
Dickinson, Mary. Alex's Bed. Firmin, Charlotte, illus. (ps-1). 1980. 7.95 (ISBN 0-233-97207-2). Andre Deutsch.
Dragonwagon, Crescent. Half a Moon & One Whole Star. Pinkney, Jerry, illus. LC 89-18643. 32p. (gr. k-3). 1990. pap. 3.95 (ISBN 0-689-71415-7, Aladdin). Macmillan Child Grp.
Dr. Seuss. Dr. Seuss's Sleep Book. Dr. Seuss, illus. (gr. 3-7). 1962. 13.00 (ISBN 0-394-80091-5, Random Juv); lib. bdg. 13.99 (ISBN 0-394-90091-X). Random.
Ford, Hildegard. My Go to Bed Book. (Illus.). (ps). 1976. 6.95 (ISBN 0-8054-4151-4, 4241-51). Broadman.
Fox, Mem. Night Noises. 1989. 13.95 (ISBN 0-15-200543-9). HarbraceJ.
Gregorich, Barbara. Say Good Night. Hoffman, Joan, ed. Stasiak, Krystyna, illus. 16p. (Orig.). (gr. k-2). 1984. pap. 1.99 (ISBN 0-88743-010-4, 06010). Sch Zone Pub Co.
Howard, Jane R. When I'm Sleepy. Cherry, Lynne, illus. LC 84-25895. 24p. (ps-3). 1985. 12.95 (ISBN 0-525-44204-9, DCB). Dutton Child Bks.
Jam, Teddy. Night Cars. LC 88-37230. (Illus.). 32p. (ps-1). 1989. 13.95 (ISBN 0-531-05793-3); PLB 13.99 (ISBN 0-531-08393-4). Orchard Bks Watts.
Koide, Tan. May We Sleep Here Tonight? Koide, Yasuko, illus. LC 82-72247. 32p. (ps-3). 1983. 11.95 (ISBN 0-689-50261-3, M K McElderry). Macmillan Child Grp.
Locker, Thomas, adapted by. & illus. Rip Van Winkle. LC 87-24448. 32p. (ps up). 1988. 15.95 (ISBN 0-8037-0520-4); PLB 15.89 (ISBN 0-8037-0521-2). Dial Bks Young.
McDaniel, Lurlene. Now I Lay Me Down to Sleep. 1991. pap. 2.95 (ISBN 0-553-28897-0). Bantam.
Matthews, Morgan. Whoo's Too Tired? Kolding, Richard M., illus. LC 88-1285. 48p. (Orig.). (gr. 1-3). 1988. PLB 9.89 (ISBN 0-8167-1331-6); pap. text ed. 2.95 (ISBN 0-8167-1332-4). Troll Assocs.
Michaels, Ski. Wake up, Sam! Garry-McCord, Kathi, illus. LC 85-14115. 48p. (Orig.). (gr. 1-3). 1986. PLB 9.89 (ISBN 0-8167-0580-1); pap. text ed. 2.95 (ISBN 0-8167-0581-X). Troll Assocs.
Morris, Ann. Sleepy, Sleepy. Roffey, Maureen, illus. LC 85-45333. 16p. (ps). 1986. 3.50 (ISBN 0-694-00075-2). HarpC Child Bks.
Newfield, Marcia. Where Did You Put Your Sleep? Da Rif, Andrea, illus. LC 83-2785. 32p. (gr. k-4). 1983. 11.95 (ISBN 0-689-50286-9, M K McElderry). Macmillan Child Grp.
Osborne, Mary P. A Visit to Sleep's House. Mathis, Melissa B., illus. LC 88-536. 32p. (ps-2). 1989. 11.95 (ISBN 0-394-89958-X); lib. bdg. 12.99 (ISBN 0-394-99958-4). Knopf.
Rosenberg, Liz. Adelaide & the Night Train. Desimini, Lisa, illus. LC 88-39948. 32p. (ps-2). 1989. 13.95 (ISBN 0-06-025102-6); PLB 13.89 (ISBN 0-06-025103-4). HarpC Child Bks.
Ross, Anna. Naptime. Gorbaty, Norman, illus. LC 89-34545. 24p. (ps). 1990. 3.95 (ISBN 0-394-85828-X). Random.
Rubel, Nicole. Goldie's Nap. Rubel, Nicole, illus. LC 90-4401. 32p. (ps-2). 1991. 14.95 (ISBN 0-06-025106-9); PLB 14.89 (ISBN 0-06-025107-7). HarpC Child Bks.
Sage, James. To Sleep. Hutton, Warwick, illus. LC 89-36931. 32p. (ps-3). 1990. 12.95 (ISBN 0-689-50497-7, M K McElderry). Macmillan Child Grp.
Schuchman, Joan. Two Places to Sleep. LaMarche, Jim, illus. LC 79-88201. 32p. (gr. 1-4). 1979. PLB 7.95 (ISBN 0-87614-108-4). Carolrhoda Bks.
Sharmat, Marjorie W. Goodnight, Andrew, Goodnight, Craig. Chalmers, Mary, illus. LC 69-10205. 32p. (ps-3). 1969. PLB 11.89 (ISBN 0-06-025548-X). HarpC Child Bks.
Stevenson, James. We Can't Sleep. LC 81-20307. (Illus.). 32p. (gr. k-3). 1982. 13.95 (ISBN 0-688-01213-2); PLB 13.88 (ISBN 0-688-01214-0). Greenwillow.
Stevenson, Sucie. I Forgot. Stevenson, Sucie, illus. LC 87-22991. 32p. (ps-1). 1988. 11.95 (ISBN 0-531-05744-5); PLB 11.99 (ISBN 0-531-08344-6). Orchard Bks Watts.
Storr, Catherine, retold by. Rip Van Winkle. LC 83-26996. (Illus.). 32p. (gr. k-5). 1984. PLB 16.67 (ISBN 0-8172-2108-5); pap. 9.27 (ISBN 0-8172-2252-9); PLB 27.99 incl. cassette (ISBN 0-8172-2236-7); pap. 23.95 incl. cassette (ISBN 0-8172-2267-7); cassette only 14.00 (ISBN 0-685-09499-5). Raintree Pubs.
Taylor, Livingston & Taylor, Maggie. Pajamas. Bowers, Tim, illus. 32p. (ps-3). 1988. 13.95 (ISBN 0-15-200564-1, Gulliver Bks). HarBraceJ.
Twining, Edith. Sandman. (ps-4). 1991. pap. 12.95 (ISBN 0-385-41258-4). Doubleday.
Waber, Bernard. Ira Sleeps over. (gr. k-5). 1984. incl. cassette 19.95 (ISBN 0-941078-36-1); pap. 12.95 incl. cassette (ISBN 0-941078-34-5); incl. 4 bks., cassette, & guide 27.95 (ISBN 0-941078-35-3); filmstrip 22.95 (ISBN 0-941078-43-4). Live Oak Media.
Wells, Rosemary. Good Night, Fred. Wells, Rosemary, illus. LC 81-65849. 32p. (ps-3). 1981. PLB 8.44 (ISBN 0-8037-2992-8). Dial Bks Young.
Wilkin, Eloise, illus. My Goodnight Book. 14p. (ps-k). 1981. write for info. (ISBN 0-307-12258-1, Golden Bks.). Western Pub.
Wood, Audrey. The Napping House. Wood, Don, illus. LC 83-13035. 32p. (ps-3). 1984. 13.95 (ISBN 0-15-256708-9, HJ). HarBraceJ.
Ziefert, Harriet. Good Night, Jessie! Smith, Mavis, illus. LC 90-55147. 32p. (ps-1). 1990. 4.95 (ISBN 0-06-107403-9). HarpC Child Bks.
Zolotow, Charlotte. The Summer Night. Shecter, Ben, illus. LC 88-44522. 32p. (ps-3). 1991. 13.95 (ISBN 0-06-026916-2); PLB 13.89 (ISBN 0-06-026917-0). HarpC Child Bks.
SLEIGHT OF HAND
see Magic

SLOTHS–FICTION
Bond, Felicia. Poinsettia & Her Family. Bond, Felicia, illus. LC 81-43035. 32p. (ps-3). 1981. PLB 12.89 (ISBN 0-690-04145-4, Crowell Jr Bks). HarpC Child Bks.
SLOW LEARNING CHILDREN–FICTION
Byars, Betsy C. Summer of the Swans. CoConis, Ted, illus. (gr. 7 up). 1970. pap. 12.95 (ISBN 0-670-68190-3). Viking Child Bks.
SLUMBER SONGS
see Lullabies
SLUMS
see Housing
SMALL ARMS
see Firearms
SMALL BUSINESS
Ashmore, M. Catherine, et al. Risks & Rewards of Entrepreneurship. LC 87-21787. 128p. (Orig.). 1987. pap. text ed. 7.95 (ISBN 0-8219-0323-3, 25658); tchr's. resource guide 19.00 (ISBN 0-8219-0324-1, TRG-25803). EMC.
Riehm, Sarah L. The Teenage Entrepreneur's Guide: 50 Money-Making Business Ideas. 2nd ed. LC 87-1904. (Illus.). 250p. (Orig.). (gr. 7-12). 1990. pap. 10.95 (ISBN 0-685-38392-X, Dist. by Publishers Group). Surrey Bks.
SMELL
Allington, Richard L. & Krull, Kathleen. Smelling. Gatzke, Lee, illus. LC 79-27147. 32p. (gr. k-3). 1985. PLB 15.33 (ISBN 0-8172-1293-0); pap. 9.27 (ISBN 0-8172-2488-2). Raintree Pubs.
McPhee Gribble Editorial Staff. Smells: Things to Do with Them. Lancashire, David, illus. (gr. 2-7). 1978. pap. 2.95 (ISBN 0-14-049148-1, Puffin). Puffin Bks.
Moncure, Jane B. What Your Nose Knows! Axeman, Lois, illus. LC 82-9464. 32p. (ps-3). 1982. PLB 14.60 (ISBN 0-516-03255-0); pap. 3.95 (ISBN 0-516-43255-9). Childrens.
Parramon, J. M. & Puig, J. J. Smell. Rius, Maria, illus. 32p. (ps). 1985. pap. 4.95 ea. (ISBN 0-8120-3565-8). Span. ed (ISBN 0-8120-3607-7). Barron.
Pluckrose, Henry. Smelling. Fairclough, Chris, photos by. 32p. (gr. k-3). 1986. lib. bdg. 7.99 (ISBN 0-531-10172-X). Watts.
Smith, Kathie B. & Crenson, Victoria. Smelling. Storms, Robert S., illus. LC 87-5887. 24p. (gr. k-3). 1987. PLB 10.89 (ISBN 0-8167-1010-4); pap. text ed. 1.95 (ISBN 0-8167-1011-2). Troll Assocs.
SMITH, JOHN, 1580-1631
Foster, Genevieve. World of Captain John Smith. Foster, Genevieve, illus. LC 59-11853. (gr. 5-11). 1978. Repr. of 1959 ed. lib. bdg. 25.00 (ISBN 0-684-15726-8, Scribner). Macmillan.
SMITH, JOSEPH, 1805-1844
Merrell, Karen D. Joseph Smith. 24p. (ps-2). pap. 4.95 (ISBN 0-87747-561-X). Deseret Bk.
SMITHSONIAN INSTITUTION
Lucas, Daryl. Choice Adventures, No. 2: The Smithsonian Connection. (gr. 3-7). 1991. PLB 3.95 (ISBN 0-8423-5026-8). Tyndale.
Stein, R. Conrad. The Story of the Smithsonian Institution. Wahl, Richard, illus. LC 79-12902. 32p. (gr. 3-6). 1979. PLB 13.27 (ISBN 0-516-04635-7). Childrens.
Thomson, Peggy. Auks, Rocks & the Odd Dinosaur: Inside Stories from the Smithsonian's Museum of Natural History. LC 85-47744. (Illus.). 128p. (gr. 3-7). 1985. PLB 14.89 (ISBN 0-690-04492-5, Crowell Jr Bks). HarpC Child Bks.
SMOKING
see also Tobacco Habit
Berger, Gilda. Smoking Not Allowed: The Debate. (Illus.). 144p. (gr. 7-12). 1987. PLB 12.90 (ISBN 0-531-10420-6). Watts.
Condon, Judith. Smoking. (Illus.). 32p. (gr. 5-9). 1989. PLB 8.90 (ISBN 0-531-17174-4). Watts.
Gano, Lila. Smoking. LC 89-12650. (Illus.). 96p. (gr. 5-8). 1989. PLB 11.95 (ISBN 1-56006-103-0). Lucent Bks.
Keyishian, Elizabeth. Everything You Need to Know about Smoking. Rosen, Ruth, ed. (gr. 7-12). 1989. PLB 12.95 (ISBN 0-8239-1017-2). Rosen Group.
Marr, John S. A Breath of Air & a Breath of Smoke. Sweat, Lynn, illus. LC 70-161362. 48p. (gr. 3 up). 1970. 4.95 (ISBN 0-87131-038-4). M Evans.
Sanders, Pete. Why Do People Smoke? (Illus.). 32p. (gr. 2-5). 1989. PLB 10.40 (ISBN 0-531-17192-2). Watts.
Sonnett, Sherry. Smoking. rev. ed. Greenberg, Lorna, ed. (Illus.). 72p. (gr. 7 up). 1988. PLB 10.40 (ISBN 0-531-10489-3). Watts.
Stronck, David. Tobacco - The Real Story. Nelson, Mary & Clark, Kay, eds. Ransom, Robert D., illus. 30p. (gr. 5-8). 1987. pap. text ed. 2.95 (ISBN 0-941816-34-6). Network Pubns.
Szumski, Bonnie. Smoking: Distinguishing Between Fact & Opinion. (Illus.). 32p. (gr. 3-6). 1990. PLB 8.95 (ISBN 0-89908-642-X). Greenhaven.
Ward, Brian. Smoking & Health. LC 85-52043. (Illus.). 48p. (gr. 4-12). 1986. PLB 12.40 (ISBN 0-531-10180-0). Watts.
SMUGGLING
Kamstra, Jerry. Weed: Adventures of a Dope Smuggler. rev. ed. (Illus.). 352p. (gr. 12). pap. text ed. 10.00 (ISBN 0-9617715-0-X). Peer Amid Pr.
SMUGGLING–FICTION
Alderson, Sue A. Ida & the Wool Smugglers. Blades, Ann, illus. LC 87-15487. 32p. (gr. k-4). 1988. 12.95 (ISBN 0-689-50440-3, M K McElderry). Macmillan Child Grp.

Westcott, Alvin. Rockets & Crackers. LC 75-108729. (Illus.). 80p. (gr. 4 up). 1970. PLB 10.95 (ISBN 0-87783-033-9); pap. 3.94 deluxe ed. (ISBN 0-87783-105-X). Oddo.
SMUTS, JAN CHRISTIAAN, 1870-1950
Haney, John D. Jan Smuts. (Illus.). (gr. 5-12). 1989. 17.95 (ISBN 1-55546-852-7). Chelsea Hse.
SNAILS
Braithwaite, Althea. Snails. (ps-6). 1988. PLB 7.95 (ISBN 0-88462-192-8); pap. 2.95 (ISBN 0-88462-193-6). Dearborn Finan.
Buholzer, Theres. Life of the Snail. Simon, Noel, tr. from GER. (Illus.). 48p. (gr. 2-5). 1987. PLB 12.95 (ISBN 0-87614-246-3). Carolrhoda Bks.
Henwood, Chris. Snails & Slugs. FS-Ltd Staff, ed. Watts, Barrie, photos by. (Illus.). 32p. (gr. 1-3). 1988. PLB 10.40 (ISBN 0-531-10621-7). Watts.
Johnson, Sylvia A. Snails. Masuda, Modoki, illus. LC 82-10086. 48p. (gr. 4 up). 1982. PLB 12.95 (ISBN 0-8225-1475-3, First Ave Edns); pap. 5.95 (ISBN 0-8225-9544-3, First Ave Edns). Lerner Pubns.
Olesen, Jens. Snail. LC 86-10084. (Illus.). 25p. (gr. 2-5). 1986. 6.95 (ISBN 0-382-09304-6); PLB 9.96 (ISBN 0-382-09289-9); 9.98 (ISBN 0-685-19359-4); pap. 3.95 (ISBN 0-685-19360-8). Silver Burdett Pr.
SNAILS–FICTION
Bush, Don. Jack Snake. Carbonnean, Lana, illus. 48p. (gr. k up). 1985. 5.50x (ISBN 0-943978-01-7). Rolling Hills Pr.
Giganti, Paul, Jr. How Many Snails? LC 87-26281. (Illus.). 24p. (ps-1). 1988. 13.95 (ISBN 0-688-06369-1); lib. bdg. 13.88 (ISBN 0-688-06370-5). Greenwillow.
Greenberg, David. Slugs. Chase, Victoria, illus. LC 82-10017. 32p. (gr. k-5). 1983. 12.95 (ISBN 0-316-32658-5, Joy St Bks); pap. 4.95i (ISBN 0-316-32659-3, Joy St Bks). Little.
Himmelman, John. The Ups & Downs of Simpson Snail. Himmelman, John, illus. LC 89-30547. 47p. (gr. 1-3). 1989. 9.95 (ISBN 0-525-44542-0, DCB). Dutton Child Bks.
McAllister, Angela. Snail's Birthday Problem. Jenkin-Pearce, Susie, illus. 32p. (ps-3). 1989. pap. 11.95 (ISBN 0-670-82991-9). Viking Child Bks.
Oneal, Zibby. Turtle & Snail. Tomes, Margot, illus. LC 78-14826. (gr. k-2). 1979. 11.95i (ISBN 0-397-31829-4, Lipp Jr Bks). HarpC Child Bks.
Rockwell, Anne. The Story Snail. Rockwell, Anne, illus. LC 87-1097. 64p. (gr. 1-4). 1987. pap. 3.95 (ISBN 0-689-71164-6, Aladdin). Macmillan Child Grp.
Ryder, Joan. The Snail's Spell. Cherry, Lynn, illus. (gr. 3-8). 1988. pap. 3.95 (ISBN 0-14-050891-0, Puffin). Puffin Bks.
Stadler, John. Hooray for Snail! LC 83-46164. (Illus.). 32p. (ps-2). 1984. PLB 11.89 (ISBN 0-690-04413-5, Crowell Jr Bks). HarpC Child Bks.
—Snail Saves the Day. Stadler, John, illus. LC 85-47539. 32p. (ps-3). 1985. 11.95 (ISBN 0-690-04468-2, Crowell Jr Bks). HarpC Child Bks.
Stevenson, James. Fast Friends. LC 78-14828. (Illus.). 64p. (gr. 1-3). 1979. PLB 10.88 (ISBN 0-688-84197-X). Greenwillow.
SNAKES
Baker, Lucy. Snakes. (Illus.). 32p. (gr. 2-6). 1990. pap. 4.95 (ISBN 0-14-034434-9, Puffin). Puffin Bks.
Bargar & Johnson. Anacondas. (Illus.). 24p. (gr. 1-4). 1987. PLB 11.93 (ISBN 0-86592-249-7). Rourke Corp.
—Coral Snakes. (Illus.). 24p. (gr. 1-4). 1987. PLB 11.93 (ISBN 0-86592-246-2). Rourke Corp.
—King Snakes. (Illus.). 24p. (gr. 1-4). 1987. PLB 11.93 (ISBN 0-86592-248-9). Rourke Corp.
—Pythons. (Illus.). 24p. (gr. 1-4). 1987. PLB 11.66 (ISBN 0-86592-244-6). Rourke Corp.
—Rat Snakes. (Illus.). 24p. (gr. 1-4). 1987. PLB 11.93 (ISBN 0-86592-247-0). Rourke Corp.
—Tree Vipers. (Illus.). 24p. (gr. 1-4). 1987. PLB 11.93 (ISBN 0-86592-245-4). Rourke Corp.
Barger & Johnson. Boa Constrictors, Reading Level 2. (Illus.). 24p. (gr. k-5). Date not set. PLB 11.93 (ISBN 0-86592-959-9). Rourke Corp.
—Cobras, Reading Level 2. (Illus.). 24p. (gr. k-5). Date not set. PLB 11.94 (ISBN 0-86592-955-6). Rourke Corp.
—Copperheads, Reading Level 2. (Illus.). 24p. (gr. k-5). Date not set. PLB 11.94 (ISBN 0-86592-957-2). Rourke Corp.
—Cottonmouths, Reading Level 2. (Illus.). 24p. (gr. k-5). Date not set. PLB 11.94 (ISBN 0-86592-958-0). Rourke Corp.
—Mambas, Reading Level 2. (Illus.). 24p. (gr. k-5). Date not set. PLB 11.93 (ISBN 0-86592-960-2). Rourke Corp.
—Rattlesnake, Reading Level 2. (Illus.). 24p. (gr. k-5). Date not set. PLB 11.93 (ISBN 0-86592-956-4). Rourke Corp.
—Snake Discovery Library, 6 bks, Set I, Reading Level 2. (Illus.). 144p. (gr. k-5). Date not set. Set. PLB 71.60 (ISBN 0-86592-954-8). Rourke Corp.
Barrett, Norman. Poisonous Snakes. (Illus.). 32p. (gr. k-4). 1991. PLB 11.40 (ISBN 0-531-14153-5). Watts.
—Serpientes. (SPA., Illus.). 32p. (gr. k-4). 1990. PLB 11.40 (ISBN 0-531-07909-0). Watts.
Barrett, Norman S. Snakes. (Illus.). 32p. (gr. k-6). 1989. PLB 11.40 (ISBN 0-531-10701-9). Watts.
Bender, Lionel. Pythons & Boas. (Illus.). 32p. (gr. 4 up). 1991. pap. 3.95 (ISBN 0-531-17261-9). Watts.

—Pythons & Constrictors. Franklin Watts Ltd., ed. (Illus.). 32p. (gr. k-9). 1988. PLB 11.90 (ISBN 0-531-17076-4, Gloucester Pr). Watts.
Brenner, Barbara. A Snake-Lover's Diary. Brenner, Barbara, illus. LC 84-43136. 96p. (gr. 4-6). 1990. PLB 12.89 (ISBN 0-06-020697-7). HarpC Child Bks.
Broekel, Ray. Snakes. LC 81-38487. (Illus.). 48p. (gr. k-4). 1982. PLB 14.60 (ISBN 0-516-01649-0); pap. 4.95 (ISBN 0-516-41649-9). Childrens.
Chace, Earl G. Rattlesnakes. (Illus.). (gr. 2-5). 1984. 9.95 (ISBN 0-396-08453-2, Putnam). Putnam Pub Group.
Cole, Joanna. A Snake's Body. Wexler, Jerome, photos by. LC 81-9443. (Illus.). 48p. (gr. k-3). 1981. 12.95 (ISBN 0-688-00702-3); 12.88 (ISBN 0-688-00703-1, Morrow Jr Bks). Morrow Jr Bks.
Curtis, Neil. Discovering Snakes & Lizards. LC 85-72248. (Illus.). 48p. (gr. k-6). 1986. lib. bdg. 11.90 (ISBN 0-531-18048-4, Pub. by Bookwright Pr). Watts.
—Discovering Snakes & Wasps. 1990. pap. 4.95 (ISBN 0-531-18363-7). Watts.
Elting, Mary. Snakes & Other Reptiles. Santoro, Christopher, illus. (gr. 3-7). 1987. pap. 8.95 (ISBN 0-671-61835-0, Little Simon). S&S Trade.
Fine, Edith H. The Python & Anaconda. LC 88-5421. (Illus.). 48p. (gr. 5-6). 1988. PLB 10.95 (ISBN 0-89686-391-3, Crestwood Hse). Macmillan Child Grp.
Freedman, Russell. Rattlesnakes. Freedman, Russell, illus. LC 84-4602. 40p. (gr. 1-4). 1984. reinforced bdg. 12.95 (ISBN 0-8234-0536-2). Holiday.
Green, Carl R. & Sanford, William R. The Cobra. LC 85-14969. (Illus.). 48p. (gr. 5-6). 1986. PLB 10.95 (ISBN 0-89686-266-6, Crestwood Hse). Macmillan Child Grp.
Gross, Ruth B. Snakes. 2nd ed. LC 89-38254. (Illus.). 64p. (ps-3). 1990. Repr. of 1973 ed. 13.95 (ISBN 0-02-737022-4, Four Winds Press). Macmillan Child Grp.
—Snakes. 64p. (gr. 1-4). 1991. pap. 2.50 (ISBN 0-590-44090-X). Scholastic Inc.
Harrison, Virginia. The World of Snakes. Oxford Scientific Films Staff, photos by. LC 89-4634. (Illus.). 32p. (gr. 2-3). 1989. PLB 10.95 (ISBN 0-8368-0143-1). Gareth Stevens Inc.
Hess, Lilo. That Snake in the Grass. Hess, Lilo, photos by. LC 86-24826. (Illus.). 48p. (gr. 3-6). 1987. 12.95 (ISBN 0-684-18591-1, Scribners Young Read). Macmillan Child Grp.
Hoffman, Mary. Snake. LC 86-6774. (Illus.). 24p. (gr. k-5). 1986. PLB 13.32 (ISBN 0-8172-2398-3). Raintree Pubs.
—Snake: Animals in the Wild. (Illus.). 24p. (gr. 1-4). 1988. pap. 1.95 (ISBN 0-590-41234-5). Scholastic Inc.
Johnson, Sylvia A. Snakes. Masuda, Modoki, photos by. LC 87-7162. (Illus.). 48p. (gr. 4 up). 1986. PLB 12.95 (ISBN 0-8225-1484-2, First Ave Edns); pap. 5.95 (ISBN 0-8225-9503-6, First Ave Edns). Lerner Pubns.
Lauber, Patricia. Snakes Are Hunters. Keller, Holly, illus. LC 87-47695. 32p. (ps-3). 1988. 13.95 (ISBN 0-690-04628-6, Crowell Jr Bks); PLB 13.89 (ISBN 0-690-04630-8, Crowell Jr Bks). HarpC Child Bks.
Lavies, Bianca. Secretive Timber Rattlesnakes. (gr. 4-7). 1990. 13.95 (ISBN 0-525-44572-2, DCB). Dutton Child Bks.
Lindblom, Steven. Golden Book of Snakes & Other Reptiles. 1990. write for info. (ISBN 0-307-15852-7, Pub. by Golden Bks). Western Pub.
Linley, Mike. The Snake in the Grass. Oxford Scientific Films Staff, photos by. LC 89-4621. (Illus.). 32p. (gr. 4-6). 1989. PLB 10.95 (ISBN 0-8368-0118-0). Gareth Stevens Inc.
Mccarthy, Colin. First Sight: Poisonous Snakes. 1990. pap. 3.95 (ISBN 0-531-17260-0). Watts.
—Poisonous Snakes. (Illus.). 32p. (gr. 1-6). 1987. PLB 11.90 (ISBN 0-531-17053-5, Gloucester Pr). Watts.
McClung, Robert. Snakes: Their Place in the Sun. Dennis, David M., illus. 64p. (gr. 2-4). 1991. 14.95 (ISBN 0-8050-1718-6). H Holt & Co.
McGowen, Tom. Album of Snakes & Reptiles. Ruth, Rod, illus. 64p. (gr. 3-7). 1987. pap. 4.95 (ISBN 0-02-688503-4). Checkerboard Pr.
Morris, Dean. Snakes & Lizards. rev. ed. LC 87-16697. (Illus.). 48p. (gr. 2-6). 1987. PLB 17.32 (ISBN 0-8172-3212-5). Raintree Pubs.
Palmer, William M. Poisonous Snakes of North Carolina. (Illus.). 22p. (gr. 6-12). 1974. pap. 2.00 (ISBN 0-917134-00-1). NC Natl Sci.
Parsons, Alexandra. Amazing Snakes. Young, Jerry, photos by. LC 89-38944. (Illus.). 32p. (gr. 1-5). 1990. 6.95 (ISBN 0-679-80225-8); PLB 9.99 (ISBN 0-679-90225-2). McKay.
Petty, Kate. Snakes. Baker, Alan, illus. LC 84-51811. 32p. (gr. k-3). 1985. PLB 10.90 (ISBN 0-531-04901-9). Watts.
Roever, Joan M. Snake Secrets. Roever, Joan M., illus. LC 78-4318. (gr. 5 up). 1979. PLB 11.85 (ISBN 0-8027-6333-2). Walker & Co.
Sanford, William R. & Green, Carl R. The Boa Constrictor. LC 86-32868. (Illus.). 48p. (gr. 5-6). 1987. PLB 10.95 (ISBN 0-89686-320-4, Crestwood Hse). Macmillan Child Grp.
—The Rattlesnake. LC 83-20865. (Illus.). 48p. (gr. 5-6). 1984. PLB 10.95 (ISBN 0-89686-247-X, Crestwood Hse). Macmillan Child Grp.
Selsam, Millicent E. A First Look at Poisonous Snakes. 32p. (gr. 1-4). 1987. 11.95 (ISBN 0-8027-6681-1); PLB 12.85 (ISBN 0-8027-6683-8). Walker & Co.

Simon, Seymour. Poisonous Snakes. Downey, William R., illus. LC 85-24202. 80p. (gr. 3-7). 1984. 14.95 (ISBN 0-02-782850-6, Four Winds). Macmillan Child Grp.
Smith, Mavis. A Snake Mistake. Smith, Mavis, illus. LC 90-43152. 32p. (gr. k-3). 1991. PLB 11.89 (ISBN 0-06-026909-X); pap. 3.95 (ISBN 0-06-107426-8). HarpC Child Bks.
Snake Discovery Library, 6 bks, Set II, Reading Level 2. (Illus.). 144p. (gr. k-5). Date not set. Set. PLB 71.60 (ISBN 0-86592-243-8). Rourke Corp.
Snakes. (gr. 4-6). 1975. pap. 2.95 (ISBN 0-685-09281-X). Wonder.
Snakes of Arizona. (Illus.). 32p. (gr. 3 up). 1984. pap. 1.00 (ISBN 0-935810-17-X). Primer Pubs.
Spizzirri Publishing Co. Staff. Poisonous Snakes: Educational Coloring Book. Spizzirri, Linda, ed. (Illus.). 32p. (gr. 1-8). 1984. pap. 1.95 (ISBN 0-86545-054-4). Spizzirri.
Tropea, S. Snakes, A Photo-Fact Book. (Illus.). 24p. (Orig.). 1988. pap. 1.95 (ISBN 0-942025-15-6). Kidsbks.
Vrbova, Zuza. Snakes. McAulay, Robert, illus. 48p. 1990. PLB 9.95 (ISBN 0-86622-557-9, J-007). TFH Pubns.
Wildlife Education, Ltd. Staff. Snakes. Hoopes, Barbara & Oden, Dick, illus. 20p. (Orig.). (gr. 5 up). 1981. pap. 2.25 (ISBN 0-937934-05-4). Wildlife Educ.
Wimberly, Christine A. Poisonous Snakes of Alabama. DeJarnette, Tom, illus. 46p. (Orig.). (gr. 4-12). 1970. pap. 3.35 (ISBN 0-9605938-0-2). Explorer Bks.
Zim, Herbert S. Snakes. Irving, James G., illus. LC 49-10266. (gr. 3-7). 1949. PLB 12.88 (ISBN 0-688-31549-6). Morrow Jr Bks.

SNAKES–FICTION

Adams, Laurie & Coudert, Allison. Alice & the Boa Constrictor. McCully, Emily A., illus. LC 82-15769. 96p. (gr. 3-6). 1983. 9.95 (ISBN 0-395-33068-8). HM.
Allard, Harry. The Cactus Flower Bakery. Delaney, Ned, illus. LC 90-36565. 32p. (ps-3). 1991. 14.95 (ISBN 0-06-020046-4); PLB 14.89 (ISBN 0-06-020047-2). HarpC Child Bks.
Barrett, Judith. A Snake Is Totally Tail. Johnson, Lonni S., illus. LC 83-2657. 32p. (ps-1). 1983. 12.95 (ISBN 0-689-30979-1, Atheneum Child Bk). Macmillan Child Grp.
Charbonnet, Gabrielle. Snakes Are Nothing to Sneeze At. Carter, Abby, illus. 80p. (gr. 2-4). 1990. PLB 12.95 (ISBN 0-8050-1373-3). H Holt & Co.
Clifford, Eth. Harvey's Horrible Snake Disaster. LC 83-27299. 128p. (gr. 3-6). 1984. 13.95 (ISBN 0-395-35378-5, 5-83913). HM.
Cosgrove, Stephen. Kartusch. James, Robin, illus. (gr. k-4). 1978. pap. 2.95 (ISBN 0-8431-0568-2). Price Stern.
Davis, Burke. King Snake. (gr. 2-5). 1989. pap. 2.50 (ISBN 0-590-06734-6). Scholastic Inc.
Edler, Timothy J. Maurice the Snake & Gaston the Near-Sighted Turtle: Tim Edler's Tales from the Atchafalaya. (Illus.). 36p. (gr. k-8). 1977. pap. 6.00 (ISBN 0-931108-00-4). Little Cajun Bks.
Faulkner, Keith. The Snake's Mistake. Lambert, Jonathan, illus. 24p. (ps-3). 1989. 10.95 (ISBN 0-8431-2370-2). Price Stern.
Kahn, Jonathan. Patulous: The Prairie Rattlesnake. Thatch, Nancy R., ed. Kahn, Jonathan, illus. Melton, David, intro. by. (Illus.). 26p. (gr. k-4). 1991. PLB 12.95 (ISBN 0-933849-36-2). Landmark Edns.
Kudrna, C. Imbior. To Bathe a Boa. Kudrna, C. Imbiore., illus. 32p. (ps-4). 1986. PLB 12.95 (ISBN 0-87614-306-0); pap. 5.95 (ISBN 0-87614-490-3). Carolrhoda Bks.
Lauber, Patricia. Snakes Are Hunters. LC 87-47695. (Illus.). 32p. (ps-4). 1989. pap. 4.50 (ISBN 0-06-445091-0, Trophy). HarpC Child Bks.
Littke, Lael. The Day Snake Saved Time at Peanut Butter Pond. Britt, Stephanie M., illus. 36p. (ps-1). 1990. pap. 15.95 incl. audiocassette (ISBN 1-55999-122-4). LinguiSystems.
Noble, Trinka H. Jimmy's Boa & the Big Splash Birthday Bash. Kellog, Steven, illus. LC 88-10933. 32p. (ps-3). 1989. 13.95 (ISBN 0-8037-0539-5); PLB 13.89 (ISBN 0-8037-0540-9). Dial Bks Young.
—Jimmy's Boa Bounces Back. Kellog, Steven, illus. LC 83-14289. 32p. (ps-3). 1984. 13.95 (ISBN 0-8037-0049-0); PLB 13.89 (ISBN 0-8037-0050-4). Dial Bks Young.
—Jimmy's Boa Bounces Back. Kellogg, Steven, illus. LC 83-14289. 32p. (ps-3). 1987. pap. 4.95 (ISBN 0-8037-0228-0). Dial Bks Young.
Rodieck, Jorma. The Little Bitty Snake. Burnett, Yumiko M. & Contreras, Moyra, trs. LC 82-60393. (Illus.). 24p. (ps up). 1983. English-Japanese. pap. 4.95 (ISBN 0-940880-07-5); English-Spanish. pap. 4.95 (ISBN 0-940880-03-2); English-French. pap. 4.95 (ISBN 0-940880-05-9). Open Hand.
Waber, Bernard. The Snake: A Very Long Love Story. Waber, Bernard, illus. (ps-1). 1978. PLB 7.95 (ISBN 0-685-02310-9). HM.

SNORKELLING

see Skin Diving

SNOW

Bentley, W. A. & Humphreys, W. J. Snow Crystals. (Illus.). (gr. 5 up). 20.00 (ISBN 0-8446-1660-5). Peter Smith.
Branley, Franklyn M. Snow Is Falling. rev. ed. Keller, Holly, illus. LC 85-48256. 32p. (ps-3). 1986. 13.95 (ISBN 0-690-04547-6, Crowell Jr Bks); PLB 13.89 (ISBN 0-690-04548-4, Crowell Jr Bks). HarpC Child Bks.
Dolan, Edward F., Jr. Great Mysteries of the Ice & Snow. (Illus.). 128p. (gr. 9-12). 1985. 8.95 (ISBN 0-396-08642-X, Putnam). Putnam Pub Group.
Lampton, Christopher. Blizzard. (Illus.). 64p. (gr. 4-6). 1991. PLB 17.25 (ISBN 1-56294-029-5). Millbrook Pr.
McKie, Roy & Eastman, Philip D. Snow. LC 62-15114. (Illus.). 72p. (gr. 1-2). 1962. 6.95 (ISBN 0-394-80027-3); lib. bdg. 7.99 (ISBN 0-394-90027-8). Beginner.
Phillips, Louise S. The First Snowflake of Winter. LC 87-62210. (Illus.). 40p. (gr. k-4). pap. 6.95 (ISBN 0-932433-36-7). Windswept Hse.
Riehecky, Janet. Snow: When Will It Fall? Friedman, Joy, illus. LC 89-28084. 32p. (ps-2). 1990. lib. bdg. 11.97 (ISBN 0-89565-560-8). Childs World.
Steele, Philip. Snow: Causes & Effects. (Illus.). 32p. (gr. 5-8). 1991. PLB 11.90 (ISBN 0-531-10990-9). Watts.
Tresselt, Alvin. White Snow Bright Snow. Duvoisin, Roger, illus. LC 88-10018. (ps-3). 1988. pap. 3.95 (ISBN 0-688-08294-7, Mulberry). Morrow.
Williams, Terry T. & Major, Ted. The Secret Language of Snow. Dewey, Jennifer, illus. LC 83-19410. 144p. (gr. 3-7). 1984. 10.95 (ISBN 0-394-86574-X, Pant Bks Young). Pantheon.

SNOW–FICTION

Bauer, Caroline F., ed. Snowy Day: Stories & Poems. Tomes, Margot, illus. LC 85-45858. 80p. (gr. 2-5). 1986. PLB 11.89 (ISBN 0-685-12398-7, Lipp Jr Bks); PLB 12.89 (ISBN 0-397-32177-5). HarpC Child Bks.
Bodecker, N. M. Snowman Sniffles & Other Verse. Bodecker, N. M., illus. LC 82-13927. 80p. (gr. 4-7). 1983. 11.95 (ISBN 0-689-50263-X, M K McElderry). Macmillan Child Grp.
Briggs, Raymond. The Snowman. Briggs, Raymond, illus. LC 78-55904. 32p. (ps-3). 1978. 12.95 (ISBN 0-394-83973-0, Random Juv). Random.
—The Snowman. miniature ed. LC 90-60078. (Illus.). 32p. (ps-8). 1990. 4.95 (ISBN 0-679-80906-6). Random.
—The Snowman Board Books. Briggs, Raymond, illus. Incl. Building the Snowman (ISBN 0-316-10813-8); Dressing up. 1985. pap. 3.95 (ISBN 0-316-10814-6); Walking in the Air. 1985. pap. 3.95 (ISBN 0-316-10815-4); The Party (ISBN 0-316-10816-2). (Illus.). (ps-k). 1985. pap. 3.95 ea. Little.
—The Snowman Storybook. Briggs, Raymond, illus. LC 90-8029. 24p. (ps). 1990. 4.95 (ISBN 0-679-80840-X). Random.
Burningham, John. The Snow. LC 75-2492. (Illus.). (ps-1). 1975. PLB 11.89 (ISBN 0-690-00905-4, Crowell Jr Bks). HarpC Child Bks.
Burton, Virginia L. Katy & the Big Snow. (Illus.). (gr. k-3). 1973. reinforced bdg. 13.95 (ISBN 0-395-18155-0). HM.
Butterworth, Nick. One Snowy Night. (ps-3). 1990. 12.95 (ISBN 0-316-11918-0). Little.
Carlson, Nancy. Take Time to Relax. (ps-3). 1991. 13.95 (ISBN 0-670-83287-1). Viking Child Bks.
Coleridge, Sara. January Brings the Snow. Oliver, Jenni, illus. LC 85-23789. 32p. (ps-3). 1986. 10.95 (ISBN 0-8037-0313-9); PLB 10.89 (ISBN 0-8037-0314-7). Dial Bks Young.
—January Brings the Snow. Chartier, Normand, illus. (ps-3). 1987. 5.95 (ISBN 0-671-64152-2, Little Simon); pap. 2.25 (ISBN 0-671-72338-3). S&S Trade.
Corbalis, Judy. The Ice Cream Heroes. Parkins, David, illus. LC 89-8069. (gr. 4-7). 1989. 13.95 (ISBN 0-316-15648-5). Little.
Coutant, Helen. First Snow. Vo-Dinh, illus. LC 74-1187. 48p. (gr. 1-3). 1974. lib. bdg. 6.99 (ISBN 0-394-92831-8). Knopf.
Damon, Laura. Fun in the Snow. Paterson, Diane, illus. LC 87-10843. 32p. (gr. k-2). 1988. PLB 10.89 (ISBN 0-8167-1081-3); pap. text ed. 2.95 (ISBN 0-8167-1082-1). Troll Assocs.
Edwards, Amelia B. The Phantom Coach. Richardson, I. M., adapted by. Ashmead, Hal, illus. LC 81-19862. 32p. (gr. 5-10). 1982. PLB 10.79 (ISBN 0-89375-634-2); pap. text ed. 2.95 (ISBN 0-89375-635-0). Troll Assocs.
Firmin, Peter. Pinney in the Snow. Firmin, Peter, illus. 32p. (ps-3). 1986. pap. 4.95 (ISBN 0-670-80958-6). Viking Child Bks.
Goffstein, M. B. Our Snowman. LC 85-45836. (Illus.). 32p. (ps up). 1986. 12.95 (ISBN 0-06-022152-6); PLB 12.89 (ISBN 0-06-022153-4). HarpC Child Bks.
Gold. Frosty the Snow Man. 2.95 (ISBN 0-307-10321-8, Golden Pr). Western Pub.
Greene, Carol. Snow Joe. LC 82-9403. (Illus.). (ps-2). 1982. PLB 11.93 (ISBN 0-516-02035-8); pap. 2.95 (ISBN 0-516-42035-6). Childrens.
Hader, Berta & Hader, Elmer. The Big Snow. 2nd ed. Hader, Berta & Hader, Elmer, illus. LC 87-38488. 48p. (gr. k-4). 1988. pap. 4.95 (ISBN 0-689-71260-X, Aladdin). Macmillan Child Grp.
Hader, Elmer & Hader, Berta. The Big Snow. LC 48-10240. (Illus.). 48p. (gr. 1-3). 1972. 13.95 (ISBN 0-02-737910-8, Mcmillan Child Bk); pap. 4.95 (ISBN 0-02-043300-X). Macmillan Child Grp.
Harshman, Marc. Snow Company. (ps-3). 1990. 12.95 (ISBN 0-525-65029-6, Cobblehill Bks). Dutton Child Bks.
Hoff, Syd. When Will It Snow? Chalmers, Mary, illus. LC 64-16657. 32p. (gr. k-3). 1971. PLB 11.89 (ISBN 0-06-022554-8). HarpC Child Bks.
Horneck, Heribert. Tracks in the Snow. Young, Richard G., ed. Mangold, Paul, illus. LC 89-11890. 24p. (gr. 1-3). 1989. PLB 13.26 (ISBN 0-944483-53-4). Garrett Ed Corp.
Huddy, Delia. Snowman's Christmas. 1990. 13.95 (ISBN 0-385-30173-1). Delacorte.
Hudson, Jan. Sweetgrass. 1991. pap. 2.95 (ISBN 0-590-43486-1). Scholastic Inc.
Hutchins, H. Ben's Snow Song. (Illus.). 24p. (ps-8). 1987. 12.95 (ISBN 0-920303-91-9); pap. 4.95 (ISBN 0-920303-90-0). Firefly Bks Ltd.
—Norman's Snowball. (Illus.). 24p. (ps-8). 1989. 12.95 (ISBN 1-55037-053-7); pap. 4.95 (ISBN 1-55037-050-2). Firefly Bks Ltd.
Jenkins, Jerry B. Daniel & the Big Blizzard. (gr. 4-7). 1990. pap. 4.50 (ISBN 0-8024-0808-7). Moody.
Keats, Ezra J. Un Dia de Nieve. (SPA., Illus.). 32p. (ps-1). 1991. pap. 3.95 (ISBN 0-14-054363-5, Puffin). Puffin Bks.
—The Snowy Day. Keats, Ezra J., illus. LC 62-15441. 40p. (ps-1). 1962. pap. 11.95 (ISBN 0-670-65400-0). Viking Child Bks.
Kessler, Ethel & Kessler, Leonard. Stan the Hot Dog Man. Kessler, Leonard, illus. LC 89-34474. 64p. (gr. k-3). 1990. 10.95 (ISBN 0-06-023279-X); PLB 10.89 (ISBN 0-06-023280-3). HarpC Child Bks.
Krensky, Stephen. Snow & Ice. Hayes, John, illus. 48p. (Orig.). (gr. k-3). 1989. pap. 2.50 (ISBN 0-590-41449-6). Scholastic Inc.
Lobe, Mira. The Snowman Who Went for a Walk. Opgenoorth, Winifried, illus. LC 83-27298. 32p. (ps-2). 1984. 11.95 (ISBN 0-688-03865-4, Morrow Junior Books); PLB 11.88 (ISBN 0-688-03866-2). Morrow.
Loretan, Sylvia. Bob the Snowman. (ps-3). 1991. 13.95 (ISBN 0-670-83677-X). Viking Child Bks.
McArthur, Dalton R. The First Snowflake. Minson, Grant L., illus. 32p. (Orig.). (ps-4). Date not set. pap. 4.95xg (ISBN 0-9626111-0-7). McArthur UT.
McCraw, Louise H. As the Snow on the High Hills. 198p. (Orig.). 1979. pap. 3.25 (ISBN 0-89323-001-4, 771). Bible Memory.
McKie, Roy & Eastman, Philip D. Snow. LC 62-15114. (Illus.). 72p. (gr. 1-2). 1962. 6.95 (ISBN 0-394-80027-3); lib. bdg. 7.99 (ISBN 0-394-90027-8). Beginner.
Mayper, Monica. Oh Snow. Otani, June, illus. LC 90-42088. 32p. (ps-1). 1991. 14.95 (ISBN 0-06-024203-5); PLB 14.89 (ISBN 0-06-024204-3). HarpC Child Bks.
Mazer, Harry. Snow Bound. 144p. (gr. 5 up). 1975. pap. 3.25 (ISBN 0-440-96134-3, LFL). Dell.
Mendez, Phil. The Black Snowman. Byard, Carole, illus. 48p. 1991. pap. 3.95 (ISBN 0-590-44873-0, Blue Ribbon Bks). Scholastic Inc.
Miller, Ned. Emmett's Snowball. Guevara, Susan, illus. LC 89-77787. 40p. (ps-3). 1990. 14.95 (ISBN 0-8050-1394-6). H Holt & Co.
Moncure, Jane B. Biggest Snowball of All. Friedman, Joy, illus. LC 88-25600. 32p. (ps-2). 1989. lib. bdg. 11.97 (ISBN 0-89565-391-5); pap. 6.96 (ISBN 0-89565-517-9). Childs World.
Morgan, Allen. Sadie & the Snowman. Clark, Brenda, illus. 32p. (ps-2). 1987. pap. 2.25 (ISBN 0-590-40632-9). Scholastic Inc.
Prelutsky, Jack. It's Snowing! It's Snowing! Titherington, Jeanne, illus. LC 83-16583. 48p. (gr. 1-3). 1984. 12.95 (ISBN 0-688-01512-3); PLB 12.88 (ISBN 0-688-01513-1). Greenwillow.
Sachs, Marilyn. A Secret Friend. 128p. (gr. 3-7). 1987. pap. 2.50 (ISBN 0-590-40403-2, Apple Paperback). Scholastic Inc.
Sharmat, Marjorie W. Nate the Great & The Snowy Trail. Simont, Marc, illus. 48p. (gr. 6-9). 1982. pap. 6.99 (ISBN 0-698-30738-0, Coward). Putnam Pub Group.
Silk, Silvia. My Friendly Snowman. (Illus.). 53p. (Orig.). (gr. 1 up). pap. write for info. (ISBN 0-938861-04-2); cassette avail. (ISBN 0-938861-05-0). Jasmine Texts.
Stine, R. L. Snowman. 1991. pap. 2.95 (ISBN 0-590-43280-X). Scholastic Inc.
Sugarman, Joan. Snowflakes. Dewey, Jennifer, illus. 48p. (gr. 4-6). 1985. 13.95 (ISBN 0-316-82112-8). Little.
Tallarico, Tony, illus. Snow Boy & Snow Girl. 12p. (ps-1). Date not set. bds. 3.95 (ISBN 0-89828-404-X). Tuffy Bks.
Taylor, Mark. Henry the Explorer. Booth, Graham, illus. 48p. (ps-3). 1988. pap. 5.95 (ISBN 0-316-83384-3). Little.
Tibo, Gilles. Simon Et Les Flocons de Neige. (FRE.). 1988. 10.95 (ISBN 0-88776-219-0). Tundra Bks.
Tresselt, Alvin. White Snow, Bright Snow. Duvoisin, Roger, illus. (ps-3). 1989. 13.95 (ISBN 0-688-41161-4); PLB 13.88 (ISBN 0-688-51161-9). Lothrop.
Warrener. Bunnykins in the Snow. Hayward, Walter, illus. 24p. (ps-1). 1986. pap. 4.95 (ISBN 0-670-80568-8). Viking Child Bks.
Wise, Francis H. & Wise, Joyce M. Snowman. Wise, Joyce M., illus. (gr. 1). 1976. pap. 1.50 (ISBN 0-915766-37-X). Wise Pub.
Ziefert, Harriet. Max & Diana & the Snowy Day. Johnson, Lonnie S., illus. LC 86-45341. 32p. (ps-2). 1987. 3.95 (ISBN 0-694-00089-2). HarpC Child Bks.
—The Small Potatoes & the Snowball Fight. (Orig.). (gr. k-3). 1986. pap. 2.75 (ISBN 0-440-48115-5, YB). Dell.
—Snow Magic. Schumacher, Claire, illus. (ps-1). 1988. pap. 12.95 (ISBN 0-670-82423-2). Viking Child Bks.

Zolotow, Charlotte. Something Is Going to Happen. Stock, Catherine, illus. LC 87-26661. 32p. (ps-3). 1988. 13.95 (ISBN 0-06-027028-4); PLB 13.89 (ISBN 0-06-027029-2). HarpC Child Bks.

SOAP

Simon, Seymour. Soap Bubble Magic. Ormai, Stella, illus. LC 84-4432. 48p. (ps-3). 1985. PLB 13.88 (ISBN 0-688-02685-0). Lothrop.

SOAP BOX DERBIES–FICTION

Radlauer, Ed & Radlauer, Ruth. Soap Box Winners. LC 82-17867. (Illus.). 48p. (gr. 3 up). 1983. PLB 13.27 (ISBN 0-516-07816-X). Childrens.

SOARING FLIGHT

see Gliding and Soaring

SOCCER

Arnold, Caroline. Soccer: From Neighborhood Play to the World Cup. (Illus.). 64p. (gr. 5-8). 1991. PLB 11. 90 (ISBN 0-531-20037-X). Watts.

Bloom, Marc. Know Your Game: Soccer. (gr. 4-7). 1990. pap. 2.95 (ISBN 0-590-43315-6). Scholastic Inc.

Bryce, James, et al. Power Basics of Soccer. LC 84-22839. 112p. 1984. 5.95 (ISBN 0-13-688326-5, Busn). P-H.

Dewazien, Karl. Fundamental Soccer Goalkeeping. Lavery, Vincent J., ed. (Illus.). 128p. (Orig.). (gr. 6). 1986. pap. 7.95 (ISBN 0-9619139-1-6). F Feathers.

—Fundamental Soccer Practice. Lavery, Vincent J., ed. Garcia, Joseph G., illus. 128p. (Orig.). (gr. 6). 1985. pap. 7.95 (ISBN 0-9619139-0-8). F Feathers.

—**FUNdamental Soccer Series. Maher, Alan, ed. Garcia, Joe, illus. 128p. pap. write for info. (ISBN 0-9619139-4-0). F Feathers.**
FUNdamental Soccer Practice; A recent survey (Jan. 1990) of the National Soccer Coaches Association of America shows this bestselling guide to be the most popular of its kind in the USA today. Written by Karl Dewazien, California Youth Soccer Association, Inc. Director of Coaching, for youth coaches, the book shows how to develop, organize & run practice sessions. It has been translated & is currently used by youth coaches in the People's Republic of China. This is a delightfully illustrated volume of FUN soccer games & activities which can be easily implemented by anyone. FUNdamental Soccer-Goalkeeping; The "kick off" to becoming a successful goalkeeper, FUNdamental SOCCER-Goalkeeping Offers tips for youth coaches & players. Descriptive illustrations interspersed with down-to-earth instructions on technique development for this specialized position. Dr. Joseph Machnik, current U.S. National team goalkeeper coach said, I loved it!...It fulfills the needs of the very young goalkeepers & their coaches by emphasizing the positive aspects of the position & the enjoyment which comes through efforts to perform properly as a goalkeeper. FUNdamental SOCCER-Tactics; FUNdamental Soccer-Tactics was written to assist youth coaches in prior planning & organized practice, which will prevent poor game performance. The illustrations together with the written instructions simplify the teaching of tactics. FUNdamental action plans for successful attack & defense teaching are included in this 128 p. manual. FUNdamental SOCCER-Parents; This book is perhaps Dewazien's finest effort. Using a maximum number of clever illustrations & a minimum of words, the book covers the world of youth soccer from a parent's perspective. This book covers important parental roles as teacher, coach, administrator, referee & spectator. Included are safety & nutritional tips along with sections on laws & basics of the game.
Publisher Provided Annotation.

—Fundamental Soccer Tactics. Lavery, Vincent J., ed. (Illus.). 128p. (Orig.). (gr. 6). 1987. pap. 7.97 (ISBN 0-9619139-2-4). F Feathers.

Dolan, Edward F., Jr. Starting Soccer: A Handbook for Boys & Girls. Goldner, Jameson C., photos by. LC 76-3838. (Illus.). (gr. 4-8). 1976. 5.95 (ISBN 0-06-021682-4). HarpC Child Bks.

Gardner, James. Illustrated Soccer Dictionary for Young People. Ross, David, illus. 125p. (gr. 4 up). 1978. pap. 2.50 (ISBN 0-13-451146-8, Pub. by Treehouse). P-H.

Gemme, Leila B. El Futbol Es Nuestro Juego (Soccer Is Our Game) LC 79-13245. (SPA., Illus.). 32p. (gr. k-3). 1990. PLB 15.93 (ISBN 0-516-33615-0); pap. 3.95 (ISBN 0-516-53615-X). Childrens.

—Soccer Is Our Game. Caliger, Roberta, illus. LC 79-13245. 32p. (gr. k-3). 1979. PLB 15.93 (ISBN 0-516-03615-7); pap. 3.95 (ISBN 0-516-43615-5). Childrens.

Gutman, Bill. Go for It: Soccer. Brown, Ben, illus. 64p. (gr. 3-7). 1989. PLB 16.50 (ISBN 0-942545-90-7). Grey Castle.

—Modern Soccer Superstars. (Illus.). 128p. (gr. 9-12). 1979. 8.95 (ISBN 0-396-07731-5, Putnam). Putnam Pub Group.

Harris, Paul & Walsh, Adrian. You Can Control the Soccer Ball: World Champion Adrian Walsh's Little Book of Secrets. (Illus.). (gr. 2-6). 1977. pap. 3.95 (ISBN 0-916802-05-1). Soccer for Am.

Jackson, C. Paul. How to Play Better Soccer. Madden, Don, illus. LC 76-51450. (gr. 3-7). 1978. (Crowell Jr Bks); PLB 12.89 (ISBN 0-690-03828-3, Crowell Jr Bks). HarpC Child Bks.

Laitin, Ken & Laitin, Steve. Playing Soccer. Laitin, Lindy, illus. LC 79-63980. (gr. 2-7). 1979. pap. 7.95 (ISBN 0-916802-22-1). Soccer for Am.

Make the Team: Soccer. (gr. 3-7). 1990. 13.95 (ISBN 0-316-10751-4); pap. 5.95 (ISBN 0-316-10750-6). Little.

Morrison, Ian. Soccer Basics. (Illus.). 32p. (gr. 3-8). 1988. 2.95 (ISBN 0-87406-361-2, 53-17969-5). Willowisp Pr.

Rosenthal, Bert. Soccer. LC 82-19753. (Illus.). 48p. (gr. k-4). 1983. PLB 14.60 (ISBN 0-516-01658-X); pap. 4.95 (ISBN 0-516-41658-8). Childrens.

Rosenthal, Gary. Soccer: The Game & How to Play It. rev. ed. Bolle, Frank, illus. LC 72-129116. 256p. (gr. 3-9). 1978. PLB 14.95 (ISBN 0-87460-258-0). Lion Bks.

Sakurai, Jennifer. Rules of the Game: Soccer. 48p. 1990. pap. 3.95 (ISBN 0-8431-2431-8). Price Stern.

Soccerasaurus. 1989. pap. 1.50 (ISBN 0-590-42312-6). Scholastic Inc.

Sullivan, George. Better Soccer for Boys & Girls. (Illus.). 64p. (gr. 3-7). 1978. 10.99 (ISBN 0-399-61232-7, Putnam); (Putnam). Putnam Pub Group.

Woods, P. Soccer Skills. (Illus.). 48p. (gr. 6-10). 1987. PLB 11.96 (ISBN 0-88110-296-2); pap. 5.95 (ISBN 0-7460-0167-3). EDC.

The World Cup (Soccer) 32p. (gr. 4). 1990. 12.95 s.p. (ISBN 0-88682-320-X); 18.50 (ISBN 0-685-28235-X). Creative Ed.

Yannis, Alex. Soccer Basics. Gow, Bill, illus. Chinaglia, George, intro. by. (Illus.). 48p. (gr. 3-7). 1982. 9.95 (ISBN 0-13-815290-X). P-H.

SOCCER–FICTION

Avi. S.O.R. Losers. LC 84-11022. 112p. (gr. 5-7). 1984. 12.95 (ISBN 0-02-793410-1, Bradbury Pr). Macmillan Child Grp.

Berenstain, Stan & Berenstain, Janice. The Berenstain Bears' Soccer Star. LC 83-60055. (Illus.). 32p. (ps-2). 1983. pap. 1.25 (ISBN 0-394-85922-7). Random.

Christopher, Matt. Soccer Halfback. Johnson, Larry, illus. (gr. 4-6). 1985. 13.95 (ISBN 0-316-13946-7); pap. 3.95 (ISBN 0-316-13981-5). Little.

Dickmeyer, Lowell & Humphreys, Martha. A. J. Goes to Germany. Christiansen, Diane, illus. LC 83-7628. 96p. (gr. 5 up). 1983. PLB 8.95 (ISBN 0-87518-246-1, Dillon). Macmillan Child Grp.

—The Adams See Australia. Boddy, Joe, illus. LC 83-23194. 112p. (gr. 4 up). 1984. pap. 4.95 (ISBN 0-87518-257-7, Dillon). Macmillan Child Grp.

—The Eagles Fly to Scotland. Boddy, Joe, illus. LC 83-23192. 96p. (gr. 4 up). 1984. pap. 4.95 (ISBN 0-87518-256-9, Dillon). Macmillan Child Grp.

—Hana Discovers Japan. Boddy, Joe, illus. LC 83-23193. 112p. (gr. 4 up). 1984. pap. 4.95 (ISBN 0-87518-258-5, Dillon). Macmillan Child Grp.

—Lyndsey Sees the Midnight Sun. Christiansen, Diane, illus. LC 83-7816. 96p. (gr. 5 up). 1983. PLB 8.95 (ISBN 0-87518-251-8, Dillon). Macmillan Child Grp.

—Paul Meets the Masters. Christiansen, Diane, illus. LC 83-7582. 96p. (gr. 5 up). 1983. PLB 8.95 (ISBN 0-87518-250-X, Dillon). Macmillan Child Grp.

Dygard, Thomas J. Soccer Duel. 224p. (gr. 4 up). 1990. pap. 3.95 (ISBN 0-14-034116-1, Puffin). Puffin Bks.

Fraser, Sheila. I Can Play Soccer. Kopper, Lisa, illus. 24p. (ps-3). 1991. 5.95 (ISBN 0-8120-6225-6). Barron.

Glenn, Mel. Play-by-Play. LC 85-13990. 112p. (gr. 3-7). 1986. 12.95 (ISBN 0-89919-392-7, Pub. by Clarion). Ticknor & Fields.

Hallowell, Tommy. Shot from Midfield. 112p. (gr. 3 up). 1990. pap. 2.95 (ISBN 0-14-032912-9, Puffin). Puffin Bks.

—Shot from Midfield. (gr. 4-7). 1991. 12.95 (ISBN 0-670-83730-X). Viking Child Bks.

Hughes, Dean. Defense, Bk. 2. Lyall, Dennis, illus. LC 91-8281. 112p. (Orig.). (gr. 2-6). 1991. lib. bdg. 6.99 (ISBN 0-679-91543-5, Bullseye Bks); pap. 2.99 (ISBN 0-679-81543-0, Bullseye Bks). Knopf.

Jenkins, Jerry. The Weird Soccer Match. (Orig.). (gr. 9-12). 1986. pap. text ed. 3.95 (ISBN 0-8024-8237-6). Moody.

Kessler, Leonard. Old Turtle's Soccer Team. LC 87-14870. (Illus.). 48p. (gr. k-3). 1988. 11.95 (ISBN 0-688-07157-0); lib. bdg. 11.88 (ISBN 0-688-07158-9). Greenwillow.

—Old Turtle's Soccer Team. 1990. pap. 2.95 (ISBN 0-440-40285-9). Dell.

Marzollo, Jean. Soccer Sam. Sims, Blanche, illus. LC 86-47533. 48p. (gr. 1-3). 1987. lib. bdg. 6.99 (ISBN 0-394-98406-4, Random Juv); pap. 2.95 (ISBN 0-394-88406-X, Random Juv). Random.

Napoli, Donna J. Soccer Shock. Johnson, Meredith, illus. 128p. (gr. 4-7). 1991. 13.95 (ISBN 0-525-44827-6, DCB). Dutton Child Bks.

Roper, Gail. Seventh Grade Soccer Star. LC 88-9496. 132p. (gr. 3-7). 1988. pap. 4.49 (ISBN 1-55513-507-2, Chariot Bks). Cook.

Rowan, Barbara C. Does That Goal Count? Manning, Janet, illus. LC 89-61850. 23p. (Orig.). (gr. 4-7). 1989. pap. 4.50 (ISBN 0-9622863-1-1). Bristlecone Pubns.
Does That Goal Count?--an illustrated, short story for eight to twelve year olds, features the love of two young soccer players, Timmy & Mack, & how that love keeps them together, even when the rules of the game, the coach & other players try to break them apart. But don't blame the coach & the players--they've just never heard of a dog playing soccer. Mack, you see, is Timmy's pet sheltie, & the two have been playing with soccer balls since both were young pups. Does That Goal Count?, an off-beat story for children who love sports & animals, offers exciting descriptions of soccer for the young sports fans, but more importantly, it underscores the virtues of loyalty, love & understanding.
Publisher Provided Annotation.

Russman, Penny & Wright, Sheila. Changing Bodies, Changing Goals & Other Youth Soccer Stories. Woog, Dan, ed. Wright, Curt, photos by. LC 84-71345. (Illus.). 96p. (Orig.). (gr. 5-9). 1984. pap. 5.95 (ISBN 0-9613538-0-5). Ascot Pr.

Seabrooke, Brenda. Jerry on the Line. LC 90-1745. 128p. (gr. 3-5). 1990. 12.95 (ISBN 0-02-781432-7, Bradbury Pr). Macmillan Child Grp.

Solomon, Chuck. Our Soccer League. (Illus.). 40p. (ps-2). 1988. PLB 11.95 (ISBN 0-517-56956-6). Crown.

SOCIAL ADJUSTMENT

Lucas, Betty. For Children's Sake. 1989. 7.95 (ISBN 0-533-08080-0). Vantage.

Parkison, Ralph F. The Pea in the Pod, Bk. 3. Withrow, Marion O., ed. Bush, William, illus. 10p. (Orig.). (gr. 2-6). 1988. pap. text ed. 3.00 (ISBN 0-929949-02-1). Little Wood Bks.

SOCIAL CHANGE

Greene, Laura. Change: Getting to Know about Ebb & Flow. Mayo, Gretchen, illus. LC 80-81081. 32p. (gr. k-3). 1981. 16.95 (ISBN 0-87705-401-0). Human Sci Pr.

Middleton, Nick. Atlas of Social Issues. (Illus.). 64p. 1990. 16.95x (ISBN 0-8160-2024-8). Facts on File.

SOCIAL CONDITIONS

see also Economic Conditions; Labor and Laboring Classes; Social Problems

Middleton, Nick. Atlas of Social Issues. (Illus.). 64p. 1990. 16.95x (ISBN 0-8160-2024-8). Facts on File.

SOCIAL CONFLICT

Schmidt, Fran & Friedman, Alice. Creative Conflict Solving for Kids. 2nd., rev. ed. Cranford, Kay K., et al, illus. 80p. (gr. 4-9). 1985. pap. text ed. 19.95 incl. poster (ISBN 1-878227-00-9). GCAPEF.

—Peacemaking Skills for Little Kids. Le Shane, Phyllis, contrib. by. (Illus.). 76p. (Orig.). (gr. k-2). 1988. pap. text ed. 54.95 incl. poster, puppet, cassette (ISBN 1-878227-03-3). GCAPEF.

SOCIAL CUSTOMS

see Manners and Customs

SOCIAL EQUALITY

see Equality

SOCIAL HISTORY

see Social Conditions

SOCIAL HYGIENE

see Hygiene; Public Health

SOCIAL LIFE AND CUSTOMS

see Manners and Customs

SOCIAL PROBLEMS
see also Child Labor; Crime and Criminals; Discrimination; Divorce; Housing; Immigration and Emigration; Juvenile Delinquency; Public Health; Race Problems
Barden, Renardo. Gangs. (Illus.). 64p. (gr. 7 up). 1990. lib. bdg. 15.93 (ISBN 0-86593-073-2); lib. bdg. 11.95s.p. (ISBN 0-685-36324-4). Rourke Corp.
—Gun Control. (Illus.). 64p. (gr. 7 up). 1990. lib. bdg. 15.93 (ISBN 0-86593-072-4); lib. bdg. 11.95s.p. (ISBN 0-685-36325-2). Rourke Corp.
Crary, Elizabeth. I Can't Wait. Horosko, Marina M., illus. LC 82-6277. 32p. (Orig.). (ps-2). 1982. PLB 14.95 (ISBN 0-9602862-6-8); pap. 4.95 (ISBN 0-9602862-3-3). Parenting Pr.
—I Want It. Horosko, Marina M., illus. LC 82-2129. 32p. (Orig.). (ps-2). 1982. PLB 14.95 (ISBN 0-9602862-5-X); pap. 4.95 (ISBN 0-9602862-2-5). Parenting Pr.
—I Want to Play. Horosko, Marina M., illus. LC 82-3610. 32p. (Orig.). (ps-2). 1982. PLB 14.95 (ISBN 0-9602862-7-6); pap. 4.95 (ISBN 0-9602862-4-1). Parenting Pr.
Hyde, Margaret O. The Homeless: Profiling the Problem. LC 88-21195. 96p. (gr. 6 up). 1989. lib. bdg. 16.95 (ISBN 0-89490-159-1). Enslow Pubs.
Marx, Doug. Homeless. (Illus.). 64p. (gr. 7 up). 1990. lib. bdg. 15.93 (ISBN 0-86593-071-6); lib. bdg. 11.95s.p. (ISBN 0-685-36326-0). Rourke Corp.

SOCIAL PROBLEMS–FICTION
Bonham, Frank. Mystery of the Fat Cat. Smith, Alvin, illus. 160p. (gr. 5-9). 1971. pap. 1.25 (ISBN 0-440-46226-6, YB). Dell.
Hinton, Susie E. That Was Then, This Is Now. Siegel, Hal, illus. (gr. 7 up). 1971. pap. 12.95 (ISBN 0-670-69798-2). Viking Child Bks.
Staples, Suzanne F. Shabanu: Daughter of the Wind. LC 89-2714. (Illus.). 256p. (gr. 7 up). 1989. 13.95 (ISBN 0-394-84815-2); lib. bdg. 16.99 (ISBN 0-394-94815-7). Knopf.
Wagner, Jane. J. T. Parks, Gordon, photos by. (Illus.). 128p. (gr. 3-8). 1972. pap. 3.25 (ISBN 0-440-44275-3, YB). Dell.

SOCIAL PSYCHOLOGY
see also Attitude (Psychology); Human Relations; Psychology, Applied; Social Adjustment
Dale, Mitzi. Round the Bend. 1991. 15.00 (ISBN 0-385-30308-4). Doubleday.

SOCIAL REFORM
see Social Problems

SOCIAL SCIENCES
see also Economics; Political Science; Social Change; Sociology
Anderson, Marcie. Exploring Fifty States. 176p. (gr. 3-6). 1983. 7.95 (ISBN 0-87406-171-7); pap. 2.50 (ISBN 0-87406-114-8). Willowisp Pr.
Cobb, Vicki. This Place Is Cold. Lavallee, Barbara, illus. (gr. 2-4). 1989. 13.95 (ISBN 0-8027-6852-0); PLB 13.85 (ISBN 0-8027-6853-9). Walker & Co.
—This Place Is Dry. Lavallee, Barbara, illus. (gr. 2-4). 1989. 12.95 (ISBN 0-8027-6854-7); PLB 13.85 (ISBN 0-8027-6855-5). Walker & Co.
Forte, Imogene & MacKenzie, Joy. Kids' Stuff: Social Studies. 312p. (gr. 2-6). 1976. 12.95 (ISBN 0-913916-23-4, IP 23-4). Incentive Pubns.
Frinks, Donna. All about Me. (gr. k). 1989. text incl. activity program 160.00 (ISBN 0-318-41077-X). Southwinds Pr.
Gabet, Marcia. Fun with Social Studies. Gabet, Marcia, illus. 48p. (gr. k-3). 1985. wkbk. 5.95 (ISBN 1-55734-037-4). Tchr Create Mat.
Gakken Co. Ltd. Editors, ed. World We Live In. Time-Life Books Inc Editors, tr. 90p. (gr. k-3). 1989. write for info. (ISBN 0-8094-4885-8); PLB write for info. (ISBN 0-8094-4886-6). Time-Life.
Hargreaves, Margaret & Davis, Pat. At Home & School. (Illus.). (gr. 1). 1988. text incl. activity program 259.00 (ISBN 0-318-41078-8). Southwinds Pr.
—Extending My World. (gr. 3). 1988. text incl. activity program 259.00 (ISBN 0-318-41080-X). Southwinds Pr.
—My Neighborhood & Me. (gr. 2). 1988. text incl. activity program 259.00 (ISBN 0-318-41081-8). Southwinds Pr.
Issues for the Nineteen Nineties Series, 6 bks. (Illus.). (gr. 7-10). 1989. Set. PLB 77.88 (ISBN 0-671-94194-1). Messner.
McCumsey, Janet. Exploring the Future. Mohrmann, Gary, illus. 64p. (gr. 4-8). 1984. wkbk. 6.95 (ISBN 0-86653-183-1, GA 545). Good Apple.
Schwartz, L. Trivia Trackdown - Social Studies & Famous People. (gr. 4-6). 1985. 3.95 (ISBN 0-88160-120-9, LW 253). Learning Wks.
Spark Duplicating Masters: Social Studies, 2 Vols. (gr. k-4). 1978. Vol. 1, Gr. K-2. 8.95 (ISBN 0-89273-553-8); Vol. 2, Gr. 2-4. 8.95 (ISBN 0-89273-554-6). Educ Serv.
Spizman, Robyn. Bulletin Boards: For Social Studies & Current Events. Pesiri, Evelyn, illus. 48p. (gr. k-6). 1984. wkbk. 5.95 (ISBN 0-86653-252-8, GA 576). Good Apple.

SOCIAL SCIENCES–STUDY AND TEACHING
Cherryholmes, C. & Manson, G. Investigating Societies. (Illus.). (gr. 6). 1979. text ed. 28.04 (ISBN 0-07-011986-4). McGraw.
Geoffrion, Sondra. Power Study to up Your Grades in Social Studies. LC 88-61277. 60p. (gr. 11 up). 1989. pap. text ed. 3.95 (ISBN 0-88247-786-2). R & E Pubs.
Hegeman, Kathryn T. Our Community. Hegeman, Mark, et al, illus. (Orig.). (gr. k-3). 1982. tchr's manual 10.00 (ISBN 0-89824-034-4); wkbk. 4.99 (ISBN 0-89824-035-2). Trillium Pr.

SOCIAL SERVICE
see Social Work

SOCIAL SETTLEMENTS
see also Playgrounds;
also names of settlements, e.g. Hull House, Chicago; etc.

SOCIAL STUDIES
see Geography; Social Sciences

SOCIAL WELFARE
see Social Problems; Social Work

SOCIAL WORK
Campolo, Anthony. Ideas for Social Action. 160p. (gr. 9-12). 1985. pap. 8.95 (ISBN 0-310-45251-1, 11375P, Pub. by Youth Specialities). Zondervan.
Weiss, Ann E. Welfare: Helping Hand or Trap? LC 89-16843. (Illus.). 128p. 1990. lib. bdg. 17.95 (ISBN 0-89490-169-9). Enslow Pubs.

SOCIALISM
see also Communism; Individualism; Labor and Laboring Classes; Labor Unions; National Socialism

SOCIETY, PRIMITIVE
see also Indians of North America–Social Life and Customs; Man, Prehistoric

SOCIETY OF FRIENDS
see Friends, Society of

SOCIOLOGY
see also Cities and Towns; Civilization; Communism; Equality; Immigration and Emigration; Individualism; Labor and Laboring Classes; Population; Race Problems; Social Change; Social Conditions; Social Problems; Psychology
Beckelman, Laurie. The Homeless. LC 89-1432. (Illus.). 48p. (gr. 4 up). 1989. 10.95 (ISBN 0-89686-439-1, Crestwood Hse). Macmillan Child Grp.
Stull, Donald D., ed. On the Banks of the Grasshopper: Oral Traditions of the Kansas Kickapoo. Thomas, Fred, frwd. by. (Illus.). 82p. (Orig.). (gr. 7-12). 1984. pap. text ed. 7.95 (ISBN 0-317-13553-8). Kickapoo Tribal.
Trundle. People of the World. (gr. 4-9). 1978. (Usborne-Hayes); PLB 13.96 (ISBN 0-88110-116-8); pap. 6.95 (ISBN 0-86020-189-9). EDC.

SOCIOLOGY, RURAL
see also Country Life

SOCIOLOGY, URBAN
see also Cities and Towns; Urban Renewal

SOFTBALL
Berst, Barbara J. I Love Softball. LC 84-62470. (Illus.). 72p. (Orig.). (gr. 3-6). 1985. pap. 4.25 (ISBN 0-9614126-0-7). Natl Lilac Pub.
Gutman, Bill. Go for It: Softball. Brown, Ben, illus. 64p. (gr. 3-7). 1989. PLB 16.50 (ISBN 0-942545-91-5). Grey Castle.

SOFTBALL–FICTION
Martin, Ann M. Kristy & the Walking Disaster. 160p. (gr. 3-7). 1989. pap. 2.75 (ISBN 0-590-42004-6, Apple Paperbacks). Scholastic Inc.

SOIL CONSERVATION
see also Erosion
Soil & Water Conservation. (Illus.). 96p. (gr. 6-12). 1983. pap. 1.85 (ISBN 0-8395-3291-1, 3291). BSA.

SOIL EROSION
see Erosion

SOIL FERTILITY
see Soils

SOILS
see also Clay; Irrigation
also headings beginning with the word Soil
Bourgeois, Paulette. Amazing Dirt Book. 1990. pap. 6.68 (ISBN 0-201-55096-2). Addison-Wesley.
Catherall, Ed. Exploring Soil & Rocks. LC 90-10024. (Illus.). 48p. (gr. 3-7). 1990. PLB 18.60 (ISBN 0-8114-2595-9). Steck-V.
Jennings, Terry. Rocks & Soil. LC 88-22889. (Illus.). 32p. (gr. 3-6). 1989. PLB 14.60 (ISBN 0-516-08407-0); pap. 4.95 (ISBN 0-516-48407-9). Childrens.
Milne, Lorus J. & Milne, Margery. A Shovelful of Earth. LaFarge, Margaret, illus. LC 86-4735. 128p. (gr. 4-6). 1987. 12.95 (ISBN 0-8050-0028-3). H Holt & Co.
Petty, Kate. Earth. LC 90-31022. (Illus.). 32p. (gr. k-4). 1991. PLB 11.90 (ISBN 0-531-14098-9). Watts.
Stille, Darlene. Soil Erosion & Pollution. LC 89-25360. (Illus.). 48p. (gr. k-4). 1990. 14.60 (ISBN 0-516-01188-X); pap. 4.95 (ISBN 0-516-41188-8). Childrens.
Wyler, Rose. Science Fun with Mud & Dirt. Stewart, Pat, illus. LC 86-8388. 48p. (gr. 2-4). 1986. PLB 11.38 (ISBN 0-671-55569-3); PLB 8.54s.p.; pap. 4.95 (ISBN 0-671-62904-2); pap. 3.71s.p. Messner.

SOLAR ENERGY
Adams, Florence. Catch a Sunbeam: A Book of Solar Study & Experiments. Komoda, Kiyo, illus. LC 78-52820. (gr. 4-7). 1978. 10.95 (ISBN 0-15-215197-4, HJ). HarBraceJ.
Asimov, Isaac. How Did We Find Out about Solar Power? Wool, David, illus. 64p. (gr. 4-7). 1983. PLB 12.85 (ISBN 0-8027-6423-1). Walker & Co.
Brooke, Bob. Solar Energy. (Illus.). (gr. 5 up). 1992. PLB 19.95 (ISBN 0-7910-1590-4). Chelsea Hse.
Cross, Wilbur. Solar Energy. LC 84-23243. (Illus.). (gr. 5 up). 1984. lib. bdg. 21.27 (ISBN 0-516-00511-1). Childrens.
Crump, Donald J., ed. Exploring Your Solar System. (gr. 3-8). 1989. 6.95 (ISBN 0-685-24967-0); PLB 8.50 (ISBN 0-87044-703-3). Natl Geog.
Gadler, Steve & Adamson, Wendy. Sun Power: Facts About Solar Energy. LC 77-92290. (Illus.). 104p. (gr. 5 up). 1978. PLB 8.95 (ISBN 0-8225-0643-2). Lerner Pubns.
Gould, Alan. Hot Water & Warm Homes from Sunlight. Bergman, Lincoln & Fairwell, Kay, eds. Baker, Lisa H. & Byal, Chris, illus. Sneider, Cary I., photos by. 40p. (Orig.). (gr. 4-8). 1986. pap. 7.50 (ISBN 0-912511-24-9). Lawrence Science.
Hillerman, Anne. Done in the Sun: Solar Projects for Children. Yamashita, Mina, illus. LC 83-638. 48p. (Orig.). (gr. 3-5). 1983. pap. 6.95 (ISBN 0-86534-018-8). Sunstone Pr.
Kaufman, Allan. Exploring Solar Energy: Principles & Projects. LC 86-60262. (Illus.). 98p. (gr. 7-12). 1989. pap. 8.95 (ISBN 0-911168-60-5). Prakken.
McKee, Robin. Solar Power. LC 85-70599. (Illus.). 31p. (gr. 4-8). 1985. PLB 11.90 (ISBN 0-531-17006-3, Gloucester Pr). Watts.
Petersen, David. Solar Energy at Work. LC 84-23208. (Illus.). 48p. (gr. k-4). 1985. lib. bdg. 14.60 (ISBN 0-516-01942-2). Childrens.
Rickard, Graham. Solar Energy. (Illus.). 32p. (gr. 4-6). 1991. PLB 11.95 (ISBN 0-8368-0709-X). Gareth Stevens Inc.

SOLAR HEAT
see Solar Energy; Sun

SOLAR PHYSICS
see Sun

SOLAR POWER
see Solar Energy

SOLAR RADIATION
see also Solar Energy

SOLAR SYSTEM
Adams, Richard. Our Wonderful Solar System. Burns, Raymond, illus. LC 82-17413. 32p. (gr. 3-6). 1983. PLB 10.59 (ISBN 0-89375-872-8); pap. text ed. 2.95 (ISBN 0-89375-873-6). Troll Assocs.
Asimov, Isaac. What Is an Eclipse? (Illus.). 24p. (gr. 2-3). 1991. PLB 11.95 (ISBN 0-8368-0440-6). Gareth Stevens Inc.
Baker, D. Family of the Sun, Reading Level 3. (Illus.). 32p. (gr. 2-6). Date not set. PLB 13.20 (ISBN 0-86592-969-6). Rourke Corp.
Brandt, Keith. Planets & the Solar System. Veno, Joseph, illus. LC 84-2714. 32p. (gr. 3-6). 1985. PLB 9.49 (ISBN 0-8167-0300-0); pap. text ed. 2.95 (ISBN 0-8167-0301-9). Troll Assocs.
Branley, Franklyn M. Eclipse: Darkness in Daytime. rev. ed. Crews, Donald, illus. LC 87-47692. 32p. (ps-3). 1988. 13.95 (ISBN 0-690-04617-0, Crowell Jr Bks); PLB 12.89 (ISBN 0-690-04619-7, Crowell Jr Bks). HarpC Child Bks.
—Eclipse: Darkness in Daytime. rev. ed. Crews, Donald, illus. LC 87-45276. 32p. (ps-3). 1988. pap. 4.50 (ISBN 0-06-445081-3, Trophy). HarpC Child Bks.
—The Planets in Our Solar System. rev. ed. Madden, Don, illus. LC 86-45171. 32p. (ps-3). 1987. pap. 4.50 (ISBN 0-06-445064-3, Trophy). HarpC Child Bks.
—Saturn. Kessler, Leonard, illus. LC 81-43890. 64p. (gr. 3-6). 1983. (Crowell Jr Bks); PLB 12.89 (ISBN 0-690-04214-0, Crowell Jr Bks). HarpC Child Bks.
Brown, Peter L. Astronomy. LC 84-1654. (Illus.). 64p. (gr. 7 up). 15.95 (ISBN 0-87196-985-8). Facts on File.
Burack, Jonathan. A Trip to the Planets. (Illus.). 12p. (ps-3). incl. filmstrip, cass. 25.00 (ISBN 0-915291-90-8, 5154). Know Unltd.
Gallant, Roy. The Planets: Exploring the Solar System. rev. ed. LC 84-29725. (Illus.). 192p. (gr. 7 up). 1990. Repr. of 1982 ed. 15.95 (ISBN 0-02-735773-2, Four Winds). Macmillan Child Grp.
Lambert, David. The Solar System. 48p. (gr. 5 up). 1984. lib. bdg. 11.40 (ISBN 0-531-03803-3, A Bookwright Press Bk). Watts.
Lewellen, John. La Luna, el Sol, y las Estrellas. Kratky, Lada, tr. from ENG. LC 81-7749. (SPA., Illus.). 48p. (gr. k-4). 1984. lib. bdg. 14.60 (ISBN 0-516-31637-0); pap. 4.95 (ISBN 0-516-51637-X). Childrens.
Pfister, Marcus. Sun & Moon. Pfister, Marcus, illus. Lanning, Rosemary, tr. from GER. LC 89-43251. (Illus.). 32p. (gr. k-3). 1990. 13.95 (ISBN 1-55858-088-3). North-South Bks NYC.
Pomeroy, Johanna P. Content Area Reading Skills Solar System: Locating Details. (Illus.). (gr. 4). 1987. pap. text ed. 3.25 (ISBN 0-89525-858-7). Ed Activities.
Simon, Seymour. The Long View into Space. LC 78-11388. (Illus.). (gr. 2-4). 1987. 13.95 (ISBN 0-517-53659-5). Crown.
—Neptune. LC 90-13213. (Illus.). (gr. k up). 1991. 13.95 (ISBN 0-688-09631-X); PLB 13.88 (ISBN 0-688-09632-8, Morrow Jr Bks). Morrow Jr Bks.
The Solar System. (Illus.). 32p. (Orig.). (gr. 3-6). 1989. pap. 2.95 (ISBN 0-8431-2373-7). Price Stern.
Spangenburg, Ray & Moser, Diane. Exploring the Reaches of the Solar System. 1990. 22.95 (ISBN 0-8160-1850-2). Facts on File.
Whyman, Kathryn. Solar System. Nevett, Louise, illus. 32p. (gr. 1-6). 1987. PLB 11.90 (ISBN 0-531-17059-4, Gloucester). Watts.
Williams, Brenda & Williams, Brian. Sun, Stars & Planets. Bull, Peter, illus. LC 90-42979. 40p. (Orig.). (gr. 2-5). 1991. pap. 3.95 (ISBN 0-679-80862-0). Random.

SOLDIERS
Here are entered works dealing with members of the armed forces in general, including the Navy, Marine Corps, etc. as well as the Army.
see also Generals; Military Art and Science; Military Service–Vocational Guidance; Scouts and Scouting

also names of countries with the subdivision Army–Military Life, e.g. U. S. Army–Military life; etc.

Soldiers. (Illus.). (gr. 1-4). 3.50 (ISBN 0-7214-0388-3). Ladybird Bks.

SOLDIERS, DISABLED

see Physically Handicapped

SOLDIERS–FICTION

Adams, Pam, illus. Oh, Soldier! Soldier! 16p. (ps-2). 1978. 8.00 (ISBN 0-85953-093-0, Pub. by Child's Play England). Childs Play.

Brown, Marcia. Stone Soup. reissued ed. Brown, Marcia, illus. LC 86-10964. 48p. (ps-2). 1986. pap. 3.95 (ISBN 0-689-71103-4, Aladdin). Macmillan Child Grp.

Collington, Peter. The Angel & the Soldier Boy. Schulman, Janet, ed. Collington, Peter, illus. LC 86-20169. 32p. (ps-3). 1987. 9.95 (ISBN 0-394-88626-7); lib. bdg. 10.99 (ISBN 0-394-98626-1). Knopf.

—The Angel & the Soldier Boy. Collington, Peter, illus. LC 86-20169. 32p. (ps-2). 1988. pap. 4.95 (ISBN 0-394-81967-5). Knopf.

Greene, Bette. Summer of My German Soldier. 208p. (gr. 7-12). 1984. pap. 3.50 (ISBN 0-553-27247-0). Bantam.

—Summer of My German Soldier. 224p. (gr. 7 up). 1973. 14.95 (ISBN 0-8037-8321-3). Dial Bks Young.

—The Summer of My German Soldier. large type ed. 272p. 1989. Repr. of 1973 ed. PLB 15.95 (ISBN 1-55736-134-7, Crnrstn Bks). ABC-CLIO.

Johnston, Annie F. The Little Colonel: Maid of Honor. (gr. 5 up). 13.95 (ISBN 0-89201-034-7). Zenger Pub.

—The Little Colonel Stories: First Series. (gr. 5 up). 13.95 (ISBN 0-89201-070-3). Zenger Pub.

—The Little Colonel Stories: Second Series. (gr. 5 up). 15.95 (ISBN 0-89201-071-1). Zenger Pub.

—The Little Colonel's Chum: Mary Ware. (gr. 5 up). 13.95 (ISBN 0-89201-036-3). Zenger Pub.

—The Little Colonel's Hero. (gr. 5 up). 13.95 (ISBN 0-89201-037-1). Zenger Pub.

—The Little Colonel's Knight Comes Riding. (gr. 5 up). 13.95 (ISBN 0-89201-072-X). Zenger Pub.

Lerangis, Peter. The Sultan's Secret. (gr. 8 up). 1988. pap. 2.95 (ISBN 0-345-35099-5). Ballantine.

Nimmo, Jenny. The Chestnut Soldier. (gr. 4-7). 1991. 14.95 (ISBN 0-525-44656-7, DCB). Dutton Child Bks.

Ritchie, Jo-An. Jonie & Her Soldier. Wheeler, Gerald, ed. 128p. (Orig.). (gr. 8 up). 1985. pap. 5.50 (ISBN 0-8280-0249-5). Review & Herald.

Windrow, Martin & Hook, Richard. The Footsoldier. (Illus.). 80p. (ps-5). 1988. bds. 17.95 (ISBN 0-19-273147-5). Oxford U Pr.

—The Horse Soldier. (Illus.). 80p. (ps-5). 1988. bds. 17.95 (ISBN 0-19-273157-2). Oxford U Pr.

SOLDIERS–U. S.

Matthews, L. Soldiers. (Illus.). 32p. (gr. 3-8). Date not set. PLB 17.26 (ISBN 0-86625-365-3). Rourke Corp.

The World War II Soldier at Monte Cassino. 48p. (gr. 5-6). 1989. lib. bdg. 10.95 (ISBN 0-685-26160-3). Capstone Pr.

SOLDIERS IN ART

Forte, Nancy. Warrior in Art. LC 65-29039. (Illus.). (gr. 5 up). 1966. PLB 5.95 (ISBN 0-8225-0162-7). Lerner Pubns.

SOLDIERS' LIFE

see Soldiers

SOLID GEOMETRY

see Geometry

SOLOMON, KING OF ISRAEL

Frank, Penny. Solomon's Golden Temple. (Illus.). 24p. (ps-4). 1987. 3.95 (ISBN 0-85648-745-7). Lion USA.

Wise King Solomon. 1989. text ed. 3.95 cased (ISBN 0-7214-5261-2). Ladybird Bks.

SOMME, 2ND BATTLE OF THE, 1918

Tames, Richard. The First Day of the Somme. (Illus.). 64p. (gr. 7-11). 1990. 19.95 (ISBN 0-85219-829-9, Pub. by Batsford England). Trafalgar Sq.

SONG BOOKS

see Songbooks

SONGBOOKS

Baron, Phil. The Do-Along Songbook. Forse, Ken, ed. High, David, et al, illus. 26p. (ps). 1986. 9.95 (ISBN 0-934323-34-8); pre-programmed audio cass. tape incl. Alchemy Comms.

Barratt, C. Mother Goose Songbook. (gr. k up). 1986. 4.98 (ISBN 0-685-16882-4, 615754). Outlet Bk Co.

Bates, Kathy F. & Fahlman, Dorothy. If You're Happy & You Know It. 24p. (ps-3). 1989. pap. write for info. (ISBN 0-307-14033-4). Western Pub.

Beal, K. Big Book Package, 4 vols. (Illus.). 16p. (gr. 1-3). 1990. Set. pap. text ed. 80.25 (ISBN 0-201-52205-5). Addison-Wesley.

—Here It's Winter Big Book. (Illus.). 16p. (gr. 1-3). 1990. pap. text ed. 22.95 (ISBN 0-201-52203-9). Addison-Wesley.

—I Like You Big Book. (Illus.). 16p. (gr. 1-3). 1990. pap. text ed. 22.95 (ISBN 0-201-52204-7). Addison-Wesley.

—I Like You Little Book. (Illus.). 16p. (gr. 1-3). 1990. pap. text ed. 4.50 (ISBN 0-201-52209-8). Addison-Wesley.

—I Love My Family Big Book. (Illus.). 16p. (gr. 1-3). 1990. pap. text ed. 22.95 (ISBN 0-201-52202-0). Addison-Wesley.

—I Love My Family Little Book. (Illus.). 16p. (gr. 1-3). 1990. pap. text ed. 4.50 (ISBN 0-201-52207-1). Addison-Wesley.

—I Love My Family Little Books Four-Pack. (Illus.). 16p. (gr. 1-3). 1990. Set. pap. text ed. 12.95 (ISBN 0-201-52211-X). Addison-Wesley.

—It's Pink I Think Big Book. (Illus.). 16p. (gr. 1-3). 1990. pap. text ed. 22.95 (ISBN 0-201-52201-2). Addison-Wesley.

—It's Pink I Think Little Book. (Illus.). 16p. (gr. 1-3). 1990. pap. text ed. 4.50 (ISBN 0-201-52206-3). Addison-Wesley.

—It's Pink I Think Little Books Four-Pack. (Illus.). 16p. (gr. 1-3). 1990. Set. pap. text ed. 12.95 (ISBN 0-201-52210-1). Addison-Wesley.

—It's Winter Little Book. (Illus.). 16p. (gr. 1-3). 1990. pap. text ed. 4.50 (ISBN 0-201-52208-X). Addison-Wesley.

—It's Winter Little Books Four-Pack. (Illus.). 16p. (gr. 1-3). 1990. Set. pap. text ed. 12.95 (ISBN 0-201-52212-8). Addison-Wesley.

Beall, Pamela C. & Nipp, Susan. Wee Color Wee Sing America. (Illus.). 48p. (ps-2). 1988. pap. 1.95 (ISBN 0-8431-2277-3); pap. 9.95 incl. cass. & 6 pens (ISBN 0-8431-2299-4). Price Stern.

—Wee Sing for Christmas. (Illus.). 64p. (Orig.). (ps-2). 1984. incl. cass. 9.95 (ISBN 0-8431-1071-6); pap. 2.95 (ISBN 0-8431-1197-6). Price Stern.

The Best Country Songs Ever. 240p. (gr. 4-12). 1984. pap. 14.95 (ISBN 0-88188-428-6, HL00359135). H Leonard Pub Corp.

Biene, Susanna & Moneli, illus. Sing Through the Seasons: Ninety-Nine Songs for Children. Society of Brothers Staff, ed. LC 70-164916. 144p. (gr. k-6). 1972. 16.00 (ISBN 0-87486-006-7); cassette 7.00 (ISBN 0-87486-040-7). Plough.

Boy Scouts of America. Boy Scout Songbook. 128p. (gr. 6-12). 1970. pap. 1.50x (ISBN 0-8395-3224-5, 3224A). BSA.

Brady, Janeen. Standin' Tall Songbook, Vol. 2. 71p. (ps-6). 1988. pap. text ed. 6.95 (ISBN 0-944803-63-6). Brite Intl.

—Standin' Tall Songbook, Vol. 3. 72p. (ps-6). 1989. pap. text ed. 6.95 (ISBN 0-944803-64-4). Brite Intl.

Bryer, James. Reading Skills Songbook, Vol. 1: Read, Rapp, & Rock to the Skills of Reading. Evangelist, Gary, illus. 48p. (Orig.). (gr. 2-6). 1989. pap. 14.95 incl. audiocassette (ISBN 0-9622499-0-4). Soundbox Pubns.

Caggiano, Rosemary & Martinez, Larry. The Circus. 48p. (gr. k-6). 1978. pap. 10.95 (ISBN 0-86704-000-9). Clarus Music.

Cassidy, John & Cassidy, Nancy. Book of Kids Songs Two: Another Holler-along Handbook. M'Guinness, Jim, illus. 70p. (Orig.). 1989. pap. 10.95 incl. 48-min. stereo cassette (ISBN 0-932592-20-1). Klutz Pr.

Cinderella - Night Songs. (Illus.). 72p. (gr. 9-12). 1988. saddle-stitch 17.95 (ISBN 0-88188-766-8, HL00692375). H Leonard Pub Corp.

Cooper, Don. Dino-Songs. Boyd, Patti, illus. 32p. (ps-3). 1988. pap. 5.95 bk. & cassette pkg. (ISBN 0-394-89810-9, Random Juv). Random.

—Happy Birthday Songs & Games. Freeze, Marla, illus. Elkins, Stephen, contrib. by. (Illus.). 32p. (Orig.). (ps-3). 1988. pap. 5.95 bk. & cassette pkg. (ISBN 0-394-80826-6, Random Juv). Random.

Cooper, Don, read by. Songs of America. Fritz, Ron, illus. 32p. (ps-3). 1990. pap. 6.95 (ISBN 0-394-85225-7); cass. incl. Random.

Coopersmith, Harry, ed. More of the Songs We Sing. Oechsli, K., illus. (ENG & HEB.). 288p. (gr. 4-10). 1970. 9.50x (ISBN 0-8381-0217-4). United Syn Bk.

Cosgrove, Shaerie. A Country Song. McGlinn, Merry A., illus. 32p. (ps-3). 1988. pap. 4.95 incl. cassette (ISBN 0-8249-7274-0). Ideals.

—A Nursery Rhyme. McGlinn, Merry A., illus. 32p. (ps-3). 1988. pap. 4.95 incl. cassette (ISBN 0-8249-7276-7). Ideals.

—A Rainy Day. McGlinn, Merry A., illus. 32p. (ps-3). 1988. pap. 4.95 incl. cassette (ISBN 0-8249-7271-6). Ideals.

—A Silly Song. McGlinn, Merry A., illus. 32p. (ps-3). 1988. pap. 4.95 incl. cassette (ISBN 0-8249-7275-9). Ideals.

—A Sleepy Song. McGlinn, Merry A., illus. 32p. (ps-3). 1988. pap. 4.95 incl. cassette (ISBN 0-8249-7273-2). Ideals.

—Sunday Song. McGlinn, Merry A., illus. 32p. (ps-3). 1988. pap. 4.95 incl. cassette (ISBN 0-8249-7272-4). Ideals.

Fass, Bernie & Caggiano, Rosemary. Children Are People. 48p. (gr. 2-10). 1977. pap. 10.95 (ISBN 0-86704-003-3). Clarus Music.

—The Four Seasons. 48p. (gr. k-6). 1976. pap. 10.95 (ISBN 0-86704-001-7). Clarus Music.

—Happy Birthday Party Time. 48p. (gr. k-6). 1976. pap. 10.95 (ISBN 0-86704-002-5). Clarus Music.

—The Power Is You. 48p. (gr. 2-12). 1979. pap. 10.95 (ISBN 0-86704-005-X). Clarus Music.

—The Weather Company. 48p. (gr. k-8). 1978. pap. 10.95 (ISBN 0-86704-004-1). Clarus Music.

Fass, Bernie, et al. Old MacDonald Had a Farm. 32p. (gr. k-4). 1981. pap. 10.95 (ISBN 0-86704-007-6). Clarus Music.

Favorite Children's Songs. 48p. (ps-8). 1986. pap. 4.95 (ISBN 0-88188-495-2, 00240251). H Leonard Pub Corp.

Gallina, Michael & Gallina, Jill. Movin' Right along with Me. (gr. k-6). 1989. 14.95 (ISBN 0-931205-51-4). Jenson Pubns.

Garson, Eugenia, ed. The Laura Ingalls Wilder Songbook. LC 68-24327. (Illus.). 160p. (gr. 4 up). 1968. 18.95 (ISBN 0-06-021933-5); PLB 18.89 (ISBN 0-06-021934-3). HarpC Child Bks.

Gerson, Trina. Holiday Songs. Gerson, Ivan, illus. 84p. (ps-7). 1984. pap. text ed. write for info. (ISBN 0-9605878-2-9). Anirt Pr.

Girl Scouts of the U. S. A. Staff. Brownies' Own Songbook. Roos, Ann, et al. 48p. (gr. 1-3). 1968. pap. 3.50 (ISBN 0-88441-351-9, 23-130). Girl Scouts USA.

—Girl Scout Pocket Songbook: For Juniors, Cadettes, Seniors, & Leaders. 56p. (gr. 3 up). 1973. pap. 0.85 (ISBN 0-88441-306-3, 20-192). Girl Scouts USA.

Glazer, Tom. Mother Goose Songbook. 1990. 17.95 (ISBN 0-385-41474-9); pap. 12.95 (ISBN 0-385-24631-5). Doubleday.

—Tom Glazer's Christmas Songbook. Corrigan, Barbara, illus. 14.95 (ISBN 0-685-29548-6). Doubleday.

—Tom Glazer's Treasury of Songs for Children. O'Brien, John F., illus. LC 86-753397. 256p. (gr. k-6). 1988. pap. 14.95 (ISBN 0-385-23693-X, Zephyr-BFYR). Doubleday.

Goldstein, Rose B. Songs to Share. Schloss, E., illus. (HEB & ENG.). 64p. (ps-5). 2.95x (ISBN 0-8381-0720-6, 10-720). United Syn Bk.

Gutmann, Bessie P. Nursery Songs & Lullabies. (Illus.). 32p. 1990. 9.95x (ISBN 0-448-23457-2, G&D). Putnam Pub Group.

Hart, Jane, ed. Singing Bee! A Collection of Favorite Children's Songs. Lobel, Anita, illus. LC 82-15296. 160p. 1989. Repr. of 1982 ed. 17.95 (ISBN 0-688-41975-5). Lothrop.

Holland, Margaret. Willowisp Christmas Songbook. (Illus.). 24p. (gr. k-8). 1987. incl. cassette 6.95 (ISBN 0-87406-253-5). Willowisp Pr.

The Kids' Car Songbook. 64p. (gr. 1 up). 1988. pap. 4.95 (ISBN 0-89471-602-6). Running Pr.

The Kids' Car Songbook & Audiocassette. (ps up). 1988. 9.95 (ISBN 0-89471-603-4); pap. write for info. Running Pr.

Krull, Kathleen, selected by. Songs of Praise. De Paola, Tomie, illus. 32p. (ps up). 1989. 15.95 (ISBN 0-15-277108-5). HarBraceJ.

Lansky, Vicki. Vicki Lansky's Sing Along as You Ride Along Travel Songs. (ps-1). 1988. pap. 5.95 (ISBN 0-590-63233-7). Scholastic Inc.

Livingston, Myra C. Sea Songs. Fisher, Leonard E., illus. LC 85-16422. 32p. (gr. 1-4). 1986. reinforced bdg. 14.95 (ISBN 0-8234-0591-5). Holiday.

Masters, Brien, ed. The Waldorf Song Book. 1988. pap. 8.50 (ISBN 0-86315-059-4, 20243). Gryphon Hse.

Mattox, Cheryl W., ed. Shake It to the One That You Love the Best: Play Songs & Lullabies from Black Musical Traditions. Honeywood, Varnette P. & Joysmith, Brenda, illus. (Orig.). (ps-6). 1990. pap. 7.95 (ISBN 0-9623381-0-9). Warren-Mattox.

Metropolitan Museum of Art Staff. Go in & out the Window: An Illustrated Songbook for Children. Marks, Claude, commentary by. LC 87-752208. (Illus.). 144p. (gr. k up). 1987. 22.95 (ISBN 0-8050-0628-1, Co-Pub with Metropolitan Museum of Art). H Holt & Co.

Mochnick, Beth R. New Holiday Songs for Children: A Creative Approach. Davis, Barbara, ed. (Illus.). iv, 44p. 1988. pap. text ed. 14.95 (ISBN 0-916656-25-X). Mark Foster Mus.

Mussiett, Salomon R., ed. Cancionero para Preescolares. (SPA.). 54p. (ps). 1989. pap. 3.50 (ISBN 0-311-32226-3). Casa Bautista.

My Play a Tune Book: The Berenstain Bears' Family Favorites Sing a Song, Play Along. (gr. k-5). 1990. 15.95 (ISBN 0-938971-08-5). JTG Nashville.

Nelson, Esther L. The Great Rounds Songbook. Behr, Joyce, illus. LC 85-752326. 96p. (gr. 3 up). 1985. 10.95 (ISBN 0-8069-4718-7); pap. 9.95 (ISBN 0-8069-6234-8). Sterling.

Olshansky, Joanne. The Pizza Boogie Songbook. Colucci, Kristina & Boughton, Narda, illus. 33p. (Orig.). (gr. k-6). 1990. pap. 9.95 (ISBN 0-9626239-0-3). JHO Music.

Paris, Pat. This Old Man. (Illus.). 12p. (ps-1). 1989. text ed. 9.95 (ISBN 0-8120-6109-8). Barron.

Polisar, Barry L. Noises from under the Rug: The Barry Louis Polisar Songbook. Stewart, Michael, illus. 208p. (gr. k-6). 1985. 17.98 (ISBN 0-9615696-0-3); pap. 13.95 (ISBN 0-9615696-1-1). Rainbow Morn.

Raffi. The Raffi Everything Grows Songbook. (Illus.). 48p. (ps up). 1989. 13.95 (ISBN 0-517-57110-2). Crown.

Running Press Staff, ed. KIDZ Family Car Songbook & Audiocassette. (Illus.). 128p. (Orig.). (gr. 1 up). 1991. incl. audiocassette 9.95 (ISBN 0-89471-996-3). Running Pr.

Russell, Hannah. Songs about the Sky. rev. ed. Hendrickson, June, illus. 18p. 1988. pap. 4.50 (ISBN 0-9614089-2-8). Avitar Bks.

Samoa. (Illus.). Date not set. write for info. Songbird & Seabird.

Sing with Me Sing-along Take-along Library: Lullabies, Mother Goose, & Play-Along & Counting Songs, 3 bks. 72p. (ps-1). 1988. Set. pap. 9.95 bks. & cassette pkg. (ISBN 0-394-89966-0, Random Juv). Random.

Smollin, Michael, illus. Laugh-Along Songs. 32p. (Orig.). (ps-2). 1990. pap. 6.95 incl. cass. (ISBN 0-679-80305-X). Random.

Songs for Well Behaved Children. (gr. k-6). 1979. incls. cassette 9.95 (ISBN 0-9615696-6-2). Rainbow Morn.

Stevens, Jill. A Happy Life Songbook: Imagination Songs for Children. Boldway, John & Stevens, Jill, illus. Sacks, Jonathan, contrib. by. 63p. (Orig.). (ps-5). 1988. pap. 10.95 spiral bound (ISBN 1-877614-02-5). Two Wings.

—We Are Free! Songbook: Children's Songs of America. Boldway, John, illus. Sacks, Jonathan, contrib. by. (Illus.). 72p. (Orig.). (ps-5). 1989. pap. 10.95 spiral bound (ISBN 1-877614-04-1). Two Wings.

Stevens, Jill & Gaskill, Rebecca. Believing in Yourself: Songbook for Children. Boldway, John, illus. Sacks, Jonathan. (Illus.). 70p. (Orig.). (ps up). 1987. pap. 10. 95 spiral bound (ISBN 1-877614-00-9). Two Wings.

Walt Disney's Peter Pan. (Illus.). 32p. (gr. 4-12). 1985. 7.95 (ISBN 0-88188-414-6, HL 00360819). H Leonard Pub Corp.

Weissman, Jackie. All about Me: Picture Song by Miss Jackie. (Illus., Orig.). (ps-3). 1981. pap. 3.75 (ISBN 0-939514-04-4). Miss Jackie.

—Let's Be Friends: Picture Song by Miss Jackie. (Illus., Orig.). (ps-3). 1981. pap. 3.75 (ISBN 0-939514-03-6). Miss Jackie.

Winn, Marie, ed. The Fireside Book of Fun & Game Songs. Darrow, Whitney, Jr., illus. Miller, Allan, contrib. by. (Illus.). 224p. (gr. 1 up). 1974. 14.95 (ISBN 0-671-65213-3, Little Simon). S&S Trade.

Young, Roger & Caggiano, Rosemary. The Safari. 48p. (gr. k-8). 1979. pap. 10.95 (ISBN 0-86704-006-8). Clarus Music.

SONGS

see also Ballads; Carols; Folk Songs; Hymns; Lullabies; Music, Popular (Songs, Etc.); National Songs; Songbooks

Action Songs. (Illus.). (ps-k). 3.50 (ISBN 0-7214-1166-5). Ladybird Bks.

Allen, Linda & Snider, Chrystle L., eds. Washington Songs & Lore. Green, Donald A., illus. 200p. (gr. 1-12). 1988. pap. 15.95 (ISBN 0-9616441-3-3); Abridged ed., 72 pg. comb bdg. 8.95 (ISBN 0-9616441-4-1). Melior Dist.

Arnsteen, Katy K. Children's Songs: Hide 'n' Seek. 1990. 3.99 (ISBN 0-517-02569-8). Crown.

Bacon, M. Songs That Every Child Should Know. (ps-6). 59.95 (ISBN 0-8490-1086-1). Gordon Pr.

Beall, Pamela C. & Nipp, Susan. Wee Sing & Play. (Illus.). 64p. (Orig.). (ps-6). 1983. pap. 2.95 (ISBN 0-8431-0391-4); pap. 9.95 incl. cassette (ISBN 0-8431-0743-X). Price Stern.

—Wee Sing Around the Campfire. (Illus.). 64p. (ps-6). 1983. pap. 2.95 (ISBN 0-8431-0311-6); pap. 9.95 incl. cassette (ISBN 0-8431-0742-1). Price Stern.

Beall, Pamela C. & Nipp, Susan H. Wee Color Wee Sing. Klein, Nancy, illus. 48p. (ps-3). 1985. pap. 1.95 (ISBN 0-8431-1423-1). Price Stern.

—Wee Sing Silly Songs. (Illus.). 64p. (ps-6). 1983. pap. 2.95 (ISBN 0-8431-0310-8); pap. 9.95 incl. cass. (ISBN 0-8431-0741-3). Price Stern.

The Best Easy Listening Songs Ever. 336p. (gr. 5 up). 1986. 14.95 (ISBN 0-88188-431-6, HL 00359193). H Leonard Pub Corp.

Bleiler, E. F. Mother Goose Melodies. 128p. (ps up). 1985. pap. 2.95 (ISBN 0-486-22577-1). Dover.

Brady, Janeen. I Have a Song for You, Vol. 1: About People & Nature. rev. ed. (Illus.). (ps-4). Illus. by Linda Howard, 1986, 50pgs. pap. text ed. 6.95 activity bk. (ISBN 0-944803-02-4); Ed. by Ted Brady, Illus. by Phyllis & Warren Luch, 1979, 39pgs. songbook 6.95 (ISBN 0-944803-00-8); cassette 7.95 (ISBN 0-944803-01-6). Brite Intl.

—I Have a Song for You, Vol. 2: About Seasons & Holidays. (Illus., Orig.). (ps-4). Illus. by Linda Howard, 1987, 50pgs. pap. text ed. 6.95 activity bk. (ISBN 0-944803-05-9); Ed. by Ted Brady, Illus. by Phyllis & Warren Luch, 1979, 45 pgs. songbook 6.95 (ISBN 0-944803-03-2); cassette 7.95 (ISBN 0-944803-04-0). Brite Intl.

—I Have a Song for You, Vol. 3: About Animals. Howard, Linda, illus. 50p. (ps-4). 1988. pap. text ed. 6.95 activity bk. (ISBN 0-944803-08-3); Ed. by Ted Brady, Illus. by Phyllis & Warren Luch, 1979, 42pgs. songbook 6.95 (ISBN 0-944803-06-7); cassette 7.95 (ISBN 0-944803-07-5). Brite Intl.

—Standin' Tall Songbook, Vol. 1. 52p. (ps-6). 1987. pap. text ed. 6.95 (ISBN 0-944803-62-8). Brite Intl.

—Watch Me Sing, Vol. 1. Noyce, Robert, illus. 31p. (ps-2). 1977. pap. text ed. 5.95 songbk. (ISBN 0-944803-09-1); cassette 7.95 (ISBN 0-944803-10-5). Brite Intl.

—Watch Me Sing, Vol. 2. Twede, Evan & Nelson, Eloise, illus. 30p. (ps-2). 1986. pap. text ed. 5.95 songbk. (ISBN 0-944803-11-3); cassette 7.95 (ISBN 0-944803-12-1). Brite Intl.

Brimhall, John. Children's Songs for Piano. 96p. (Orig.). (gr. 1-6). 1985. pap. text ed. 7.95 (ISBN 0-8494-2264-7, 0496). Hansen Ed Mus.

—My Favorite Classics Level One. 120p. (Orig.). (gr. 3-6). pap. text ed. 10.95 (ISBN 0-8494-2180-2, 0114). Hansen Ed Mus.

Caldecott, Randolph. A Second Collection: Sing a Song for Sixpence, the Three Jovial Hunters. Caldecott, Randolph, illus. 64p. 1986. 4.95 (ISBN 0-7232-3433-7). Warne.

Carey, Karla. Julie & Jackie at Christmas-Time: The Play & Musical Play (with Music Book, Story-&-Song Cassette & Piano Cassette) Nolan, Dennis, illus. LC 88-12909. 39p. 1990. pap. 35.00 complete pkg. (ISBN 1-55768-151-1); pap. 25.00 book only (ISBN 1-55768-026-4); story-&-song or piano cass. 8.00 (ISBN 0-685-19710-7). LC Pub.

—Julie & Jackie at the Circus: The Play & Musical Play (with Music Book, Story-&-Song Cassette & Piano Cassette) Nolan, Dennis, illus. LC 88-12910. 44p. 1990. pap. 35.00 complete pkg. (ISBN 1-55768-152-X); pap. 25.00 book only (ISBN 1-55768-177-5); story-&-song or piano cass. 8.00 (ISBN 1-55768-027-2). LC Pub.

The talent behind the Julie & Jackie Children's Series: Karla Carey, well-known California author-composer. "Outstanding composer," said Frederick Jagel (former Metropolitan Opera & teacher in San Francisco). "Up-&-coming San Francisco composer's brilliant music brings inspiration in song" (Army of Stars coast-to-coast broadcast, USA & Canada). In speaking of another work, R. Frederick Henry (prominent artist & teacher in Berkeley, California) said, "These etudes, Poems for Piano, are a treasure belonging in the active repertoire of every pianist." Karla Carey now brings remarkable descriptive music & fascinating stories to each of these five children's books. Dennis Nolan, now-renowned award-winning illustrator, at an early age on his first professional assignment, provided the 71 charming colorful pictures in the five Julie & Jackie books - which will bring encouragement to all budding artists. The Series (" Christmastime," "Calendar," "Circus," "Journeying," "Ranch") brings fun while teaching. A child reads & listens to cassette, while watching colorful pictures & learning from storytellers & songs that bring the many characters to life. Each production includes: Children's Book, Music Book & Musical Play (complete instructions, explicit detail, laymen's terms, dialogue hints, directions, gestures, song-presentation, costuming, choreography, stage-settings, property, lighting) each book with cassette.
Publisher Provided Annotation.

—Julie & Jackie Go a'Journeying: The Play & Musical Play (with Music Book, Story-&-Song Cassette & Piano Cassette) Nolan, Dennis, illus. LC 88-9171. 73p. 1990. pap. 35.00 complete pkg. (ISBN 1-55768-153-8); pap. 25.00 book only (ISBN 1-55768-028-0); story-&-song or piano cass. 8.00 (ISBN 0-685-19711-5). LC Pub.

—Julie & Jackie on the Ranch: The Play & Musical Play (with Music Book, Story-&-Song Cassette & Piano Cassette) Nolan, Dennis, illus. LC 88-12911. 46p. 1990. pap. 35.00 complete pkg. (ISBN 1-55768-154-6); pap. 25.00 book only (ISBN 1-55768-029-9); story-&-song or piano cass. 8.00 (ISBN 0-685-19712-3). LC Pub.

Carle, Eric. I See a Song. Carle, Eric, illus. LC 72-9249. 32p. (ps-2). 1973. PLB 13.89 (ISBN 0-690-43307-7, Crowell Jr Bks). HarpC Child Bks.

Cassidy, Nancy & Cassidy, John. Book of Kid's Songs: A Holler along Handbook. M'Guinness, Jim, illus. 86p. (Orig.). 1986. pap. 10.95 incl. 48 min. stereo cassette (ISBN 0-932592-13-9). Klutz Pr.

Children at Sunrise Ranch, illus. Songs for the Joy of Living. 50p. (gr. 1-10). 1985. ring-bound 11.95 (ISBN 0-932869-01-7). Emissaries Divine.

Chroman, Eleanor. Songs That Children Sing. new ed. LC 79-93961. (Orig.). (gr. k-6). 1970. pap. 6.95 (ISBN 0-8256-0011-1, Oak). Music Sales.

Clarkson, Ginger. Stop, Look & Listen: Songs of Awareness for Young Children. (ps). 1986. pap. text ed. 4.95 (ISBN 0-8497-5924-2, WE8). KJOS.

Collier, Roberta, illus. Sing with Me Lullabies. (ps-1). 1987. Incl cassette. 5.95 (ISBN 0-394-88811-1, Random Juv). Random.

Cooper, Don. Spooky Tunes. Daniel, Frank, illus. 32p. (Orig.). (ps-3). 1990. pap. 6.95 incl. cassette (ISBN 0-679-80303-3). Random.

Cooper, Don, read by. Star Tunes. Fritz, Ronald, illus. 32p. (Orig.). (ps-3). 1991. pap. 6.95 incls. cassette (ISBN 0-679-81243-1). Random.

Cosgrove, Shaerie. More Sunday Songs. McGlinn, Merry A., illus. Cosgrove, Stephen, contrib. by. (Illus.). 32p. (ps-3). 1989. pap. 4.95 incl. 20 min. cassette (ISBN 0-8249-7344-5). Ideals.

Cross, David & Morse, Sarah. Easy As One Two Three: Fifty Dulcimer Tunes for Beginners. (Illus.). 32p. (Orig.). (gr. 1-6). 1985. pap. text ed. 2.25 (ISBN 0-9614939-4-1); tchr's. ed. 5.95 (ISBN 0-9614939-5-X). Backyard Music.

Delacre, Lulu, selected by. & illus. Las Navidades: Popular Christmas Songs from Latin America. Paz, Elena, contrib. by. (ps up). 1990. 12.95 (ISBN 0-590-43548-5). Scholastic Inc.

Delacre, Lulu, illus. Sing with Me Mother Goose. (ps-1). 1987. incl. cassette 5.95 (ISBN 0-394-88812-X, Random Juv). Random.

De La Mare, Walter. Songs of Childhood. 106p. (gr. 3 up). pap. 4.50 (ISBN 0-486-21972-0). Dover.

DiSilvestro, Frank. Sing Along with Me. Likht, Marina, illus. 52p. (gr. 8-10). 1985. pap. 7.95 (ISBN 0-934591-00-8). Songs & Stories.

Duke, Kate, illus. Tingalayo. (ps-2). 1988. 9.95 (ISBN 0-517-56926-4). Crown.

Ellis, John S., ed. My Play a Tune Book: All Time Disney Classics. (Illus.). 26p. (gr. k up). 1988. PLB 15. 95 (ISBN 0-938971-07-7). JTG Nashville.

Ellis, John S. & Leary, Mary B., eds. My Play a Tune Book: Twelve Favorite Children's Songs. Trebing, Tom, illus. 26p. (ps up). 1985. PLB 14.95 (ISBN 0-938971-00-X). JTG Nashville.

Ellis, Toni. My Play a Tune Book: Nintendo. Nintendo, illus. 26p. (ps-5). 1989. 15.95 (ISBN 0-938971-21-2). JTG Nashville.

Ellis, Toni, ed. My Play a Tune Book: American Songs. (Illus.). 26p. (gr. k up). 1988. PLB 15.95 (ISBN 0-938971-12-3). JTG Nashville.

Engvick, William, ed. Lullabies & Night Songs. Sendak, Maurice, illus. LC 65-22880. (ps-3). 1965. 25.95 (ISBN 0-06-021820-7). HarpC Child Bks.

Fass, Bernie & Caggiano, Rosemary. Children Are People. 48p. (gr. 2-10). 1977. pap. 10.95 (ISBN 0-86704-003-3). Clarus Music.

First Songs for Baby. (Illus.). (ps-k). 3.50 (ISBN 0-7214-1122-3). Ladybird Bks.

Gilbert, Yvonne. Baby's Book of Lullabies & Cradle Songs. LC 89-25898. (Illus.). 48p. (ps). 1990. 12.95 (ISBN 0-8037-0794-0); PLB 12.89 (ISBN 0-8037-0795-9). Dial Bks Young.

Glazer, Tom. Music for Ones & Twos: Songs & Games for the Very Young Child. Weinhaus, Karen T., illus. LC 82-45199. 96p. (ps). 1983. pap. 9.95 (ISBN 0-385-14252-8, Pub. by Zephyr-BFYR). Doubleday.

Glazer, Tom, ed. Tom Glazer's Treasury of Songs for Children. (Illus.). (gr. 1-6). 12.95 (ISBN 0-686-74302-4). J R Pubns.

Goodman, Ailene S. Abe Lincoln in Song & Story. LC 88-753827. (gr. 4-12). 1988. incl. cassette 11.98 (ISBN 0-9620704-0-8). A S Goodman.

ABE LINCOLN IN SONG & STORY - toe-tapping tunes, sparkling narrative! A must for music lovers & Civil War history buffs. Authentic Americana in life of 16th president. Fascinates Children. Entertaining, challenging, witty, & dignified. Highest quality. A marvelous gift for young & old. "Bargain...Storyteller Ailene Goodman captures Abe Lincoln in song & story... Biographical anecdotes...& ballads from the time of Lincoln's childhood, his presidency, & the Civil War. Teacher's guide included."--LEARNING 91. "Songs, poetry, & folksy tales...a unique look at Abraham Lincoln's life... An asset...in the classroom."--SCHOOL LIBRARY JOURNAL. "Puts a human touch to Lincoln's history."--BILLBOARD. "A happy marriage of traditional folk tunes...via songs, narration, quotations, & humor... Touching & funny..Thoughtfully composed."--BOOKLIST. "For elementary children as well as senior high school students,...can be used individually or as classroom listening for music & social studies enrichment." --CURRICULUM PRODUCTS NEWS. "Local educator recounts... ballads, history & anecdotes from Lincoln's life." "Try It!"--THE WASHINGTON POST. "If you liked the PBS series THE CIVIL WAR,... use the audiocassette tape ABE LINCOLN IN SONG & STORY... Songs, narration, readings from

primary sources, & touches of humor from the frontier & from Lincoln himself...paint a picture of a central figure in history...11-page teacher guide...gives background material & suggests questions/activities...Lower-cost, lower-tech...than TV series: uses songs & story to grab children's interest."--HISTORY MATTERS. *Publisher Provided Annotation.*

Greene, Carol. Columbus & Frankie the Cat. Dunnington, Tom, illus. LC 88-33067. 32p. (ps-2). 1989. PLB 14.60 (ISBN 0-516-03462-6); pap. 3.95 (ISBN 0-516-43462-4). Childrens.

—The Pilgrims Are Marching. Dunnington, Tom, illus. LC 88-20219. 32p. (ps-2). 1988. PLB 14.60 (ISBN 0-516-08234-5); pap. 3.95 (ISBN 0-516-48234-3). Childrens.

Haglund, Diane. Sing Along! (Illus.). 16p. (ps up). 1989. pap. write for info. (ISBN 0-307-14046-6). Western Pub.

Hawthorn, P. & Roberts, S. Easy Recorder Tunes. (Illus.). 64p. (gr. 2-6). 1990. lib. bdg. 13.96 (ISBN 0-88110-414-0, Usborne); pap. 7.95 (ISBN 0-7460-0457-5, Usborne). EDC.

Hoban, Russell. Egg Thoughts & Other Frances Songs. Hoban, Lillian, illus. LC 70-183162. 32p. (ps-3). 1972. 12.95 (ISBN 0-06-022331-6); PLB 12.89 (ISBN 0-06-022332-4). HarpC Child Bks.

Juengst, Sara C. Silver Ships-Green Fields. Pace, Anne, illus. 52p. (Orig.). (gr. 1-6). 1986. pap. 5.95 (ISBN 0-377-00161-9). Friendship Pr.

Kahn, Elithe A. Lani Goose Sings...for Hawaii's Children. Ruble, Allison, illus. (Orig.). (ps up). 1988. pap. 14.95 incl. audio cassette (ISBN 0-944264-03-4). Lani Goose Pubns.

Kolosick, Timothy & Kolosick, Helga. The Canons Austrian Children Sing. (Illus.). 32p. (Orig.). (gr. k-8). 1987. pap. text ed. 15.00 (ISBN 0-943121-00-0). AZU Music Pr.

Lancaster, Francine. Favorite Animal Songs. (gr. k up). 1985. Boxed Set incl. cassette. 16.95 (ISBN 0-930647-01-7). Lancaster Prodns.

Landes, William-Alan & Rizzo, Jeff. Rumpelstiltskin: Music & Lyrics. rev. ed. (gr. 3-12). 1985. pap. text ed. 15.00 (ISBN 0-88734-004-0). Players Pr.

Langstaff, John. Oh, A-Hunting We Will Go. Parker, Nancy W., illus. LC 74-76274. 32p. (ps-3). 1974. 14.95 (ISBN 0-689-50007-6, M K McElderry). Macmillan Child Grp.

Langstaff, Nancy & Langstaff, John. Sally Go Round the Moon & Other Revels Songs & Singing Games for Young Children. Pienkowski, Jan, illus. LC 86-90535. 127p. (ps-1). 1986. pap. 12.95 (ISBN 0-9618334-0-8). Revels Pubns.

Larrick, Nancy, ed. Songs from Mother Goose: With the Traditional Melody for Each. Spowart, Robin, illus. LC 88-754466. 80p. (ps up). 1989. 16.95 (ISBN 0-06-023713-9); PLB 16.89 (ISBN 0-06-023714-7). HarpC Child Bks.

Lewis, O. G. Good News. (Illus.). (gr. k-6). 1978. visualized song 2.99 (ISBN 3-90117-005-7). CEF Press.

Leyerle, Anne L. & Leyerle, William D. Song Anthology One. 3rd, rev. ed. LC 79-90829. 159p. (gr. 9 up). 1985. pap. 12.95 plastic comb (ISBN 0-9602296-3-9). Leyerle Pubns.

Leyerle, Anne L. & Leyerle, William D., eds. Song Anthology Two. 159p. (gr. 9 up). 1984. pap. 12.95 plastic comb. (ISBN 0-9602296-4-7). Leyerle Pubns.

Livingston, Myra C. Earth Songs. Fisher, Leonard E., illus. LC 86-341. 32p. (gr. 1-4). 1986. reinforced bdg. 14.95 (ISBN 0-8234-0615-6). Holiday.

—Space Songs. Fisher, Leonard E., illus. LC 87-19628. 32p. (gr. 1-4). 1988. reinforced bdg. 14.95 (ISBN 0-8234-0675-X). Holiday.

Lowry, Robert. Nothing but the Blood. (Illus.). (gr. k-6). illustrated song 2.99 (ISBN 3-90117-009-X). CEF Press.

McKernan, Llewellyn. More Songs of Gladness (Suppl.) (Illus.). 24p. (gr. k-4). 1987. pap. 1.39 (ISBN 0-570-09004-0, 59-1432). Concordia.

McKinney, Roberta, ed. Songs for Children of the World. 16p. (Orig.). (gr. 1-8). 1984. pap. 12.95 set of 10 (ISBN 0-87487-740-7, Suzuki Method). Summy-Birchard.

Magers, Pat, illus. Sing with Me Animal Songs. (ps-1). 1987. incl. cassette 5.95 (ISBN 0-394-88809-X, Random Juv). Random.

May, Dorothy. Dulcimer Songbag Study Guide. Kelly, Addie, illus. LC 82-670027. 36p. (Orig.). (gr. 3 up). 1981. pap. 1.95 (ISBN 0-941126-03-X). Meadowlark.

Mayfield, Larry. Jesus Is Caring for You. Behl, Deborah, illus. 20p. (gr. k-6). 1982. visualized song 5.99 (ISBN 3-90117-026-X). CEF Press.

Messenger, Jannat. Lullabies & Baby Songs. Messenger, Jannat, illus. LC 87-15590. 32p. (ps-k). 1988. 11.95 (ISBN 0-8037-0491-7). Dial Bks Young.

Miller, Reid. Hear a Story! Sing a Song! (Illus.). 16p. (ps up). 1989. pap. write for info. (ISBN 0-307-14045-8). Western Pub.

Milne, A. A. & Fraser-Simon, H. The Pooh Song Book. Shepard, E. H., illus. LC 61-1021. 154p. 1985. pap. 8.95 (ISBN 0-87923-557-8). Godine.

Mitchell, Donald & Biss, Roderick, eds. The Children's Songbook. Le Cain, Errol, illus. 95p. (gr. k up). 1984. pap. 7.95 (ISBN 0-571-10054-6). Faber & Faber.

Moss, Jeffrey & Axelrod, David. Songs of Sesame Street in Poems & Pictures. LC 83-3329. (Illus.). 48p. (ps-3). 1983. Random.

My Wonderful Lord Kit. (gr. k-6). 19.99 (ISBN 1-55976-107-5). CEF Press.

Nelson, Esther. World's Best Funny Songs. Behr, Joyce, illus. LC 87-753871. 128p. (gr. 1-8). 1989. pap. 4.95 (ISBN 0-8069-6893-1). Sterling.

Nelson, Esther L. The Funny Songbook. Behr, Joyce, illus. LC 84-89. 96p. (gr. k-5). 1984. 14.95 (ISBN 0-8069-4682-2); pap. 9.95 (ISBN 0-8069-4683-0). Sterling.

Nelson, Esther L., ed. The Fun-to-Sing Songbook. LC 86-752869. (Illus.). 96p. (Orig.). (gr. k-6). 1986. 14.95 (ISBN 0-8069-4760-8); PLB 16.79 (ISBN 0-8069-4761-6); pap. 10.95 (ISBN 0-8069-4762-4). Sterling.

One Thousand Two the Complete Children's Song Book: The Complete Children's Song Book. Date not set. incl. cass. 24.95 (ISBN 0-685-32067-7, Z019). Hansen Ed Mus.

Ong, Cristina, illus. Mother Goose's Melodies. (ps-2). 1987. incl. cassette 5.95 (ISBN 0-448-19087-7, G&D). Putnam Pub Group.

Osborne, Mary P., ed. The Calico Book of Bedtime Rhymes from Around the World. Lewis, T., illus. 64p. 1990. 14.95 (ISBN 0-8092-4300-8). Contemp Bks.

Page, Parker. Getting Along: A Set of Fun-Filled Stories, Songs, & Activities to Help Children Work & Play Together. Rose, Mitchell, illus. LC 88-71899. 64p. (Orig.). (ps-5). 1989. 14.95 (ISBN 0-929831-00-4). Childrens TV Resource.

Palmer, Hap. Baby Songs. Ryan, Susannah, illus. LC 89-753454. 64p. 1990. 13.95 (ISBN 0-517-57593-0). Crown.

Paton, Sandy & Paton, Caroline. I've Got a Song! A Collection of Songs for Youngsters. 2nd ed. Paton, Sandy & Paton, David, illus. 40p. (Orig.). (gr. k-4). 1989. pap. 10.98 (ISBN 0-938702-05-X). Folk-Legacy.

Pearce, Elvina T. Four O'Clock Tunes. Clark, Frances & Goss, Louise, eds. (gr. 2 up). 1986. pap. text ed. 3.50 (ISBN 0-913277-19-3). New Schl Mus Study.

Peek, Merle. Roll Over! A Counting Song. Peek, Merle, illus. 32p. (ps-2). 1981. 13.95 (ISBN 0-395-29438-X, Clarion). HM.

Perry, Frances B., ed. Let's Sing Together: Favorite Primary Songs of Members of the Church of Jesus Christ of Latter-day Saints. Heaston, Claudia, illus. 96p. (ps-6). 1981. 10.98 (ISBN 0-941518-00-0). Perry Enterprises.

—Let's Sing Together: Favorite Primary Songs. Heaston, Claudia, illus. 96p. (ps-6). 1984. hard cover music 12.98 (ISBN 0-941518-02-7). Perry Enterprises.

Play Songs. (Illus.). (ps-k). 3.50 (ISBN 0-7214-1167-3). Ladybird Bks.

Plotz, Helen. A Week of Lullabies. Russo, Marisabina, illus. LC 86-18458. 32p. (ps-3). 1988. 11.95 (ISBN 0-688-06652-6); lib. bdg. 11.88 (ISBN 0-688-06653-4). Greenwillow.

Poffenberger, Nancy. Instant Fun With Sacred Songs. 24p. (gr. k up). pap. 5.95 (ISBN 0-938293-27-3). Fun Pub OH.

Rae, Mary M., illus. The Farmer in the Dell: A Singing Game. 32p. (ps-1). 1990. pap. 3.95 (ISBN 0-14-050788-4, Puffin). Puffin Bks.

Reader's Digest Editors, ed. The Reader's Digest Children's Songbook. (Illus.). 252p. (ps up). 1985. lie-flat spiral bdg. 29.95 (ISBN 0-89577-214-0, Dist. by Random). RD Assn.

Reichmeier, Betty, illus. Sing with Me Play-along & Counting Songs. (ps-1). 1987. incl. cassette 5.95 (ISBN 0-394-88810-3, Random Juv). Random.

Reynolds, Malvina. Tweedles & Foodles for Young Noodles. Robbin, Jodi, illus. LC 73-80670. 42p. (gr. k-4). 1961. pap. 5.75 (ISBN 0-915620-08-1). Schroder Music.

Roes, Carol. Children's Songs from Hawaii. Stone, Lloyd, illus. LC 81-670132. (ps-3). 1973. PLB 31.95 (ISBN 0-930932-01-3, A875377). M Loke.

—Eight Children's Songs from Hawaii. Stone, Lloyd, illus. (gr. 3-4). 1958. pap. text ed. 5.50 (ISBN 0-930932-06-4, EP126127). M Loke.

Rohmer, Harriet, adapted by. Uncle Nacho's Hat (Elsombrero de Tio Nacho) Ada, Alma F. & Zubizarreta, Rosalma, trs. Reisberg, Veg, illus. (ENG & SPA.). 32p. (ps-5). 1989. 12.95 (ISBN 0-89239-043-3). Childrens Book Pr.

Ronnholm, Ursula O. Two Way Bilingual Songs for Elementary School. Archo, Mayra, illus. 41p. (gr. k-12). 1987. pap. text ed. 8.00 (ISBN 0-941911-06-3); cassettes incl. Two Way Bilingual.

Rosen, Gary & Shontz, Bill. Sing a Happy Song. Petach, Heidi, illus. 24p. (ps-1). 1990. pap. 9.95 incl. cassette (ISBN 0-679-80805-1). Random.

Roth, Kevin, read by. Dinosaurs & Dragons. Byrd, Robert, illus. 24p. (ps-1). 1991. pap. 9.95 incls. cassette (ISBN 0-679-81744-1). Random.

—Unbearable Bears. Hearn, Diane D., illus. 24p. (Orig.). (ps-1). 1991. pap. 9.95 incls. cassette (ISBN 0-679-81742-5). Random.

Royer, Katherine, ed. Nursery Songbook. (Illus.). 48p. (ps). 1957. pap. 2.95x (ISBN 0-8361-1278-4). Herald Pr.

Sackson, Eugenia. Jokes, Riddles & Silly Songs. (Illus.). 16p. (ps up). 1989. pap. write for info. (ISBN 0-307-14047-4). Western Pub.

Sharon, Lois & Sharon, Bram. Elephant Jam. Shaw, David, illus. LC 89-750476. 128p. 1989. 12.95 (ISBN 0-517-57377-6). Crown.

Siebert, Diane. Truck Song. Barton, Byron, illus. LC 83-46173. 32p. (ps-3). 1984. 13.95 (ISBN 0-690-04410-0, Crowell Jr Bks); PLB 13.89 (ISBN 0-690-04411-9). HarpC Child Bks.

Songs We Sing Around the Clock. Date not set. 3.50 (ISBN 0-685-31996-2, H480). Hansen Ed Mus.

Songs We Sing on the Bus. Date not set. 3.50 (ISBN 0-685-31995-4, G011). Hansen Ed Mus.

Staines, Bill. All God's Critters Got a Place in the Choir. Zemach, Margot, illus. 32p. (ps-2). 1989. 13.95 (ISBN 0-525-44469-6, DCB). Dutton Child Bks.

Steele, Mary Q. Anna's Summer Songs. Anderson, Lena, illus. LC 86-27109. (SWE.). 32p. (gr. k-3). 1988. 11.95 (ISBN 0-688-07180-5); lib. bdg. 11.88 (ISBN 0-688-07181-3). Greenwillow.

Stewart, Margaret A. The Best Book a Mother Ever Had. Imholte, Max, illus. 146p. (ps-3). 1985. pap. 12.95 spiral bdg. (ISBN 0-931047-00-5). KinderPr. AS SWEET AS APPLE PIE! A double-ringed spiral bound illustrated collection of all those traditional songs, fingerplays, games, & crafts for babies & young children which you may think you know, but discover you have forgotten over the years. Included with the collection is a "baby memories" section which provides a special memorabilia area for recording family data, baby "firsts", & children's pictures for up to four children. Throughout the book are black & white illustrations for your children to color or just enjoy with the songs. Over one hundred songs include such titles as "Here Comes Peter Cottontail", "Frosty the Snowman", "Rudolph the Red-nosed Reindeer", "Here Comes Santa Claus", & "This Land Is Your Land", in addition to traditional lullabies, nursery rhymes, holiday, Bible, patriotic & favorite childhood songs. Favorite games for parties, jumprope rhymes, & craft ideas, methods, & recipes round out this book to make it a must for every new mother, father, grandparent, or newborn to primary teacher & daycare operator. Recommended for all those who take delight in children from newborn through age eight. *Publisher Provided Annotation.*

Swinger, Marlys. Sing Through the Day: Ninety Songs for Younger Children. 3rd ed. Society of Brothers Staff, ed. Jeanie And Joanie And Judy, photos by. LC 68-9673. (Illus.). 144p. (gr. 5 up). 1968. 16.00 (ISBN 0-87486-005-9). Plough.

Teach Me Now 2. 80p. (ps). 4.95 (ISBN 1-55976-402-3); 6.99 (ISBN 0-685-30468-X). CEF Press.

Teacher & Cookman. The Family Car Songbook. LC 83-3195. 96p. (Orig.). (gr. 4-12). 1983. lib. bdg. 12.90 (ISBN 0-89471-213-6); pap. 4.95 (ISBN 0-89471-212-8). Running Pr.

Tucker, Kerry & Morgan, Hal, eds. The Kids' Bathtub Songbook. Marsh, Susan, illus. 10p. (Orig.). (ps-3). 1985. pap. 4.95 (ISBN 0-942820-14-2). Steam Pr MA.

Watch. (gr. k-6). illustrated song 4.50 (ISBN 3-90117-008-1). CEF Press.

Watson, Clyde. Father Fox's Feast of Songs. Watson, Wendy, illus. LC 83-2967. 32p. 1983. 10.95 (ISBN 0-399-20886-0, Philomel); pap. 5.95 (ISBN 0-399-20928-X). Putnam Pub Group.

Watson, Wendy. Wendy Watson's Frog Went A-Courting. Watson, Wendy, illus. LC 89-63022. 32p. (ps-2). 1990. 13.95 (ISBN 0-688-06539-2); lib. bdg. 13.88 (ISBN 0-688-06540-6). Lothrop.

Weissman, Jackie. Sniggles, Squirrels & Chicken Pox: Forty Original Songs with Activities for Early Childhood. 64p. (ps-5). 1984. pap. 8.95 (ISBN 0-939514-06-0); Vol. I. album 9.95 (ISBN 0-685-09111-2); cassette 9.95 (ISBN 0-685-09112-0); Vol. II. album 9.95 (ISBN 0-685-09113-9); cassette 9.95 (ISBN 0-685-09114-7). Miss Jackie.

Wilson, Valerie & Hull, Shirley, eds. Preschoolers Sing & Say. (ps). 1976. wire spiral bdg. 3.50 (ISBN 0-87227-045-9). Reg Baptist.

Winn, Marie & Miller, Allan. The Fireside Book of Children's Songs. Alcorn, John, illus. LC 65-17108. (gr. 3 up). 1966. 12.95 (ISBN 0-671-25820-6, Little Simon). S&S Trade.

Yolen, Jane. The Lullaby Songbook. Mikolaycak, Charles, illus. LC 85-752885. 32p. (ps up). 1986. 13.95 (ISBN 0-15-249903-2, HJ). HarBraceJ.

SONGS, NATIONAL

see National Songs

SONGS, POPULAR

see Music, Popular (Songs, etc.)

SOOTHSAYING

see Divination

SOPORIFICS

see Narcotics

SORCERY

see Occult Sciences; Witchcraft

SOUND

Ardley, Neil. Sound & Music. LC 83-51441. (Illus.). 32p. (gr. 4-8). 1984. PLB 11.90 (ISBN 0-531-03776-2). Watts.

—Sound Waves to Music: Projects with Sound. (Illus.). 32p. (gr. 5-8). 1990. PLB 11.90 (ISBN 0-531-17236-8). Watts.

Barrett, Sally. The Sound of the Week. 144p. (gr. k-4). 1980. 11.95 (ISBN 0-916456-63-3, GA 184). Good Apple.

Brandt, Keith. Sound. Sweat, Lynn, illus. LC 84-2632. 32p. (gr. 3-6). 1985. PLB 9.49 (ISBN 0-8167-0128-8); pap. text ed. 2.95 (ISBN 0-8167-0129-6). Troll Assocs.

Cash, Terry. Sound. Chen, Kuo K. & Bull, Peter, illus. 40p. (gr. 5-6). 1989. PLB 12.90 (ISBN 0-531-19064-1). Watts.

Gregorich, Barbara. Sound Starts. Hoffman, Joan, ed. Sandford, John, illus. 32p. (gr. k). 1988. tchr's. ed. 1.49 (ISBN 0-88743-156-9). Sch Zone Pub Co.

Kettelkamp, Larry. The Magic of Sound. Rev. ed. Kramer, Anthony, illus. LC 82-6510. 96p. (gr. 4-6). 1982. lib. bdg. 12.88 (ISBN 0-688-01493-3). Morrow Jr Bks.

Knight, David C. All about Sound. Johnson, Lewis, illus. LC 82-17387. 32p. (gr. 3-6). 1983. PLB 10.59 (ISBN 0-89375-878-7); pap. text ed. 2.95 (ISBN 0-89375-879-5). Troll Assocs.

Pomeroy, Johanna P. Content Area Reading Skills Sound & Hearing: Detecting Sequence. (Illus.). (gr. 4). 1987. pap. text ed. 3.25 (ISBN 0-89525-860-9). Ed Activities.

Sound. (Illus.). 56p. (gr. 7-12). 1990. 8.80 (ISBN 0-941008-88-6). Tops Learning.

Thomson, Ruth. All about Sounds. Rees, Mary, illus. LC 87-42589. 32p. (gr. 1-2). 1987. PLB 10.95 (ISBN 1-55532-313-8). Gareth Stevens Inc.

Walsh, Amanda. The Mysterious Hubbub. Walsh, Amanda, illus. 32p. (gr. 1-8). 1990. 13.95 (ISBN 0-395-53783-5). HM.

Wittner, Seth H. Sounds Around Us. Nusbaum, Linda, illus. 32p. (Orig.). (ps). 1988. Incl. audio-cassette. pap. 9.95 (ISBN 0-9619269-8-8). Sound World Record.

Wood, Robert W. Forty-Nine Easy Experiments with Acoustics. (Illus.). 224p. 1990. 16.95 (ISBN 0-8306-7392-X, 3392); pap. 9.95 (ISBN 0-8306-3392-8). TAB Bks.

SOUND–EXPERIMENTS

Gardner, Robert. Experimenting with Sound. (Illus.). 128p. (gr. 9-12). 1991. PLB 12.40 (ISBN 0-531-12503-3). Watts.

Taylor, Barbara. Sound & Music. (Illus.). 32p. (gr. 5-8). 1991. PLB 11.40 (ISBN 0-531-14185-3). Watts.

Ward, Alan. Experimenting with Sound. (Illus.). 48p. (gr. 2-7). 1991. PLB 12.95 (ISBN 0-7910-1511-4). Chelsea Hse.

SOUND–RECORDING AND REPRODUCING

Wicks, Keith. Sound & Recording. (Illus.). 64p. (gr. 7 up). 1982. PLB 10.90 (ISBN 0-531-09197-X). Watts.

SOUND EFFECTS

see Sounds

SOUND WAVES

Wood, Nicholas & Rye, Jennifer. Listen...What Do You Hear? Douglas, Julie, illus. LC 90-40136. 32p. (gr. k-3). 1990. lib. bdg. 10.89 (ISBN 0-8167-2120-3); pap. text ed. 2.95 (ISBN 0-8167-2121-1). Troll Assocs.

SOUNDS

Bennett, David. Bear Facts: Sounds. Kightley, Rosalinda, illus. (ps-k). 1989. 3.95 (ISBN 0-553-05494-5, Little Rooster). Bantam.

Dubov, Christine S. Ding Dong! & Other Sounds. Hathon, Elizabeth, photos by. LC 90-47301. (Illus.). 12p. (ps). 1991. bds. 3.95 (ISBN 0-688-10162-3, Tambourine Bks). Morrow.

—Knock! & Other Sounds. Hathon, Elizabeth, photos by. LC 90-47302. (Illus.). 12p. (ps). 1991. bds. 3.95 (ISBN 0-688-10161-5, Tambourine Bks). Morrow.

Gregorich, Barbara. Los Sonidos para Empezar: Beginning Sounds. Hoffman, Joan, ed. Shepherd-Bartram, tr. from ENG. Pape, Richard, illus. (SPA.). 32p. (Orig.). (ps). 1987. wkbk. 1.99 (ISBN 0-685-26762-8). Sch Zone Pub Co.

Hello Sound: Music Songs & Games Using Sound As a Theme. (ps-3). 1979. pap. 6.95 (ISBN 0-939514-00-1). Miss Jackie.

Jennings, Terry. Making Sounds. (Illus.). 24p. (gr. k-4). 1990. PLB 10.40 (ISBN 0-531-17212-0). Watts.

—Sounds. LC 88-36213. (Illus.). 32p. (gr. 3-6). 1989. PLB 14.60 (ISBN 0-516-08443-7); pap. 4.95 (ISBN 0-516-48443-5). Childrens.

Lieberman, Lillian. ABC Sounds. 64p. (gr. k-2). 1984. 6.95 (ISBN 0-912107-11-1). Monday Morning Bks.

McConnell, Em. Strange Sounds. Moser, Jeanie W., illus. (gr. k-3). Bk. & cassette 4.95 (ISBN 0-932715-09-5). Evans FL.

Oliver, Stephen, photos by. Noises. LC 90-8587. (Illus.). 24p. (ps-k). 1991. 6.95 (ISBN 0-679-81161-3). Random.

Ross, Katharine. The Little Quiet Book. Hirashima, Jean, illus. LC 88-62101. 28p. (ps). 1989. bds. 2.95 (ISBN 0-394-82899-2, Random Juv). Random.

Silvers, Vicki. Sing a Song of Sound. Ehlert, Lois, illus. LC 72-90695. 32p. (ps-2). 1973. 7.95 (ISBN 0-87592-046-2). Scroll Pr.

Spier, Peter. Crash! Bang! Boom! (ps-1). 1990. 5.95 (ISBN 0-385-26569-7). Doubleday.

SOUNDS–FICTION

Baylor, Byrd. The Other Way to Listen. Parnall, Peter, illus. LC 78-23430. 32p. (ps-3). 1978. 13.95 (ISBN 0-684-16017-X, Scribners Young Read). Macmillan Child Grp.

Fitzgerald, Rick. Helen & the Great Quiet. MacGregor, Marilyn, illus. LC 88-5095. 32p. (ps-2). 1989. 13.95 (ISBN 0-688-07723-4); PLB 13.88 (ISBN 0-688-07724-2, Morrow Jr Bks). Morrow Jr Bks.

Kline, Suzy W. SHHHH! Fay, Ann, ed. LC 84-26032. (Illus.). (ps). 1984. PLB 10.95 (ISBN 0-8075-7321-3). A Whitman.

Koch, Michelle. Hoot, Howl, Hiss. LC 90-38484. (Illus.). 24p. (ps up). 1991. 13.95 (ISBN 0-688-09651-4); PLB 13.88 (ISBN 0-688-09652-2). Greenwillow.

Shebar, Sharon. Night Monsters. Wasserman, Dan, ed. Reese, Bob, illus. (gr. k-1). 1979. PLB 7.95 (ISBN 0-89868-068-9); pap. 2.95 (ISBN 0-89868-079-4). ARO Pub.

SOUPS

Palmer, Michele. Zoup Soup. Gugler, Janine, illus. LC 78-66342. (ps-1). 1978. pap. 1.95 (ISBN 0-932306-00-4). Rocking Horse.

Peck, Robert N. Soup's Goat. (gr. k-6). 1989. pap. 2.95 (ISBN 0-440-40130-5, YB). Dell.

SOUTH, THE

see Southern States

SOUTH AFRICA

see Africa, South

SOUTH AFRICA, REPUBLIC OF

Feinberg, Brian. Nelson Mandela. (Illus.). 84p. (gr. 3-5). 1991. PLB 12.95 (ISBN 0-7910-1569-6). Chelsea Hse.

Griffiths, I. Crisis in South Africa. (Illus.). 80p. (gr. 7 up). Date not set. PLB 17.26 (ISBN 0-86592-035-4). Rourke Corp.

Harris, Sarah. Sharpeville. (gr. 7 up). 1989. 19.95 (ISBN 0-85219-767-5, Pub. by Batsford England). Trafalgar Sq.

Jacobsen, Karen. South Africa. LC 89-10044. 48p. (gr. k-4). 1989. PLB 14.60 (ISBN 0-516-01176-6); pap. 4.95 (ISBN 0-516-41176-4). Childrens.

Pascoe, Elaine. South Africa: Troubled Land. (Illus.). 128p. (gr. 7-12). 1987. PLB 12.90 (ISBN 0-531-10432-X). Watts.

Paton, Jonathan. The Land & People of South Africa. LC 89-2477. (Illus.). 304p. (gr. 6 up). 1990. 14.95 (ISBN 0-397-32361-1, Lipp Jr Bks); PLB 14.89 (ISBN 0-397-32362-X, Lipp Jr Bks). HarpC Child Bks.

SOUTH AFRICA, REPUBLIC OF–FICTION

Case, Dianne. Love, David. Andreasen, Dan, illus. 128p. (gr. 3-8). 1991. 14.95 (ISBN 0-525-67350-4, Lodestar Bks). Dutton Child Bks.

Lewin, Hugh. Jafta. Kopper, Lisa, illus. LC 82-12847. 24p. (ps-3). 1983. PLB 9.95 (ISBN 0-87614-207-2); pap. 3.95 (ISBN 0-87614-494-6). Carolrhoda Bks.

—Jafta. Kopper, Lisa, illus. 24p. (ps-3). 1989. pap. 3.95 (ISBN 0-685-24887-9, First Ave Edns). Lerner Pubns.

—Jafta & the Wedding. Kopper, Lisa, illus. LC 82-12836. 24p. (ps-3). 1983. PLB 9.95 (ISBN 0-87614-210-2); pap. 3.95 (ISBN 0-87614-497-0). Carolrhoda Bks.

—Jafta & the Wedding. Kopper, Lisa, illus. 24p. (ps-3). 1989. pap. 3.95 (ISBN 0-685-24884-4, First Ave Edns). Lerner Pubns.

—Jafta's Mother. Kopper, Lisa, illus. LC 82-12863. 24p. (ps-3). 1983. PLB 9.95 (ISBN 0-87614-208-0); pap. 3.95 (ISBN 0-87614-495-4). Carolrhoda Bks.

—Jafta's Mother. Kopper, Lisa, illus. 24p. (ps-3). 1989. pap. 3.95 (ISBN 0-685-24885-2, First Ave Edns). Lerner Pubns.

Naidoo, Beverley. Chain of Fire. Velesquez, Eric, illus. LC 89-27551. 256p. (gr. 6 up). 1990. 12.95 (ISBN 0-397-32426-X, Lipp Jr Bks); PLB 12.89 (ISBN 0-397-32427-8, Lipp Jr Bks). HarpC Child Bks.

Naidoo, Beverly. Journey to Jo'burg: A South African Story. Velasquez, Eric, illus. LC 85-45508. 96p. (gr. 4-7). 1986. 11.95 (ISBN 0-397-32168-6, Lipp Jr Bks); PLB 13.89 (ISBN 0-397-32169-4, Lipp Jr Bks). HarpC Child Bks.

Rochman, Hazel, ed. Somehow Tenderness Survives: Stories of Southern Africa. LC 88-916. 160p. (gr. 7 up). 1988. 12.95 (ISBN 0-06-025022-4); PLB 12.89 (ISBN 0-06-025023-2). HarpC Child Bks.

Sacks, Margaret. Beyond Safe Boundaries. LC 88-27311. 160p. (gr. 7 up). 1989. 13.95 (ISBN 0-525-67281-8, Lodestar Bks). Dutton Child Bks.

SOUTH AMERICA

Carter, William E. South America. rev. ed. (Illus.). 72p. (gr. 4 up). 1983. PLB 10.40 (ISBN 0-531-04531-5). Watts.

Georges, D. V. South America. LC 86-9584. (Illus.). 48p. (gr. k-4). 1986. PLB 14.60 (ISBN 0-516-01296-7); pap. 4.95 (ISBN 0-516-41296-5). Childrens.

Greene, Carol. Simon Bolivar: South American Liberator. LC 89-34663. (gr. 4 up). 1989. PLB 17.27 (ISBN 0-516-03267-4). Childrens.

Henry-Biabaud, Chantal. Living in South America. Bogard, Vicki, tr. from FRE. Dagan, Bernard, illus. LC 90-50773. 38p. (gr. k-5). 1991. 4.95 (ISBN 0-944589-28-6, 286). Young Discovery Lib.

Sabin, Francene. South America. Eitzen, Allan, illus. LC 84-8586. 32p. (gr. 3-6). 1985. PLB 9.49 (ISBN 0-8167-0292-6); pap. text ed. 2.95 (ISBN 0-8167-0293-4). Troll Assocs.

SOUTH AMERICA–DISCOVERY AND EXPLORATION

see America–Discovery and Exploration

SOUTH AMERICA–HISTORY

Simon Bolivar. (Illus.). 32p. (gr. 3-5). 1988. PLB 16.67 (ISBN 0-8172-2902-7); pap. 9.27 (ISBN 0-685-28500-6). Raintree Pubs.

SOUTH ATLANTIC STATES

see Atlantic States

SOUTH CAROLINA

Aylesworth, Thomas G. & Aylesworth, Virginia L. Lower Atlantic (North Carolina, South Carolina) (Illus.). 64p. (gr. 4-6). 1991. PLB 16.95 (ISBN 0-7910-1042-2). Chelsea Hse.

Carole Marsh South Carolina Books, 31 bks. Set. 638.45 (ISBN 0-7933-1315-5). Gallopade Pub Group.

Carpenter, Allan. South Carolina. LC 79-11453. (Illus.). 96p. (gr. 4 up). 1979. PLB 19.93 (ISBN 0-516-04140-1). Childrens.

Fradin, Dennis. South Carolina: In Words & Pictures. LC 79-22550. (Illus.). 48p. (gr. 2-5). 1980. PLB 15.93 (ISBN 0-516-03940-7). Childrens.

Gasque, Pratt. Rum Gully Tales from Tuck'em Inn. (Illus.). 148p. 1990. 15.95 (ISBN 0-87844-094-1); pap. 8.95 (ISBN 0-87844-095-X). Sandlapper Pub Co.

Hembree, Mike, et al. Journey Home. Todd, Sharon, ed. (Illus.). 208p. (gr. 8 up). 1988. text ed. 22.95 (ISBN 0-685-22594-1). GNP Pub.

Jones, Lewis P. South Carolina: One of the Fifty States. LC 85-1882. (Illus.). 720p. (gr. 8). 1985. text ed. 30.95x (ISBN 0-87844-062-3); tchr's. manual avail. (ISBN 0-87844-063-1). Sandlapper Pub Co.

Kent, Deborah. South Carolina. LC 89-858. 144p. (gr. 4 up). 1989. PLB 25.27 (ISBN 0-516-00486-7). Childrens.

Marsh, Carole. Avast, Ye Slobs! South Carolina Pirate Trivia. (Illus.). 1990. PLB 19.95 (ISBN 0-7933-1028-8); pap. 14.95 (ISBN 0-7933-1027-X); computer disk 29.95 (ISBN 0-7933-1029-6). Gallopade Pub Group.

—The Beast of the South Carolina Bed & Breakfast. (Illus.). 1990. PLB 19.95 (ISBN 0-7933-1995-1); pap. 14.95 (ISBN 0-7933-1996-X); computer disk 29.95 (ISBN 0-7933-1997-8). Gallopade Pub Group.

—The Hard-to-Believe-But-True! Book of South Carolina History, Mystery, Trivia, Legend, Lore, Humor & More. (Illus.). 1990. PLB 19.95 (ISBN 0-7933-1025-3); pap. 14.95 (ISBN 0-7933-1024-5); computer disk 29.95 (ISBN 0-7933-1026-1). Gallopade Pub Group.

—If My South Carolina Mama Ran the World! (Illus.). 1990. lib. bdg. 19.95 (ISBN 0-7933-2003-8); pap. 14.95 (ISBN 0-7933-2004-6); computer disk 29.95 (ISBN 0-7933-2005-4). Gallopade Pub Group.

—Let's Quilt South Carolina & Stuff It Topographically! (Illus.). 1990. PLB 19.95 (ISBN 0-7933-1987-0); pap. 14.95 (ISBN 1-55609-053-6); computer disk 29.95 (ISBN 0-7933-1988-9). Gallopade Pub Group.

—South Carolina & Other State Greats (Biographies) (Illus.). 1990. PLB 19.95 (ISBN 0-7933-2006-2); pap. 14.95 (ISBN 0-7933-2007-0); computer disk 29.95 (ISBN 0-7933-2008-9). Gallopade Pub Group.

—South Carolina Bandits, Bushwackers, Outlaws, Crooks, Devils, Ghosts, Desperadoes & Other Assorted & Sundry Characters! (Illus.). 1990. PLB 19.95 (ISBN 0-7933-1010-5); pap. 14.95 (ISBN 0-7933-1009-1); computer disk 29.95 (ISBN 0-7933-1011-3). Gallopade Pub Group.

—South Carolina Classic Christmas Trivia: Stories, Recipes, Activities, Legends, Lore & More! (Illus.). 1990. PLB 19.95 (ISBN 0-7933-1013-X); pap. 14.95 (ISBN 0-7933-1012-1); computer disk 29.95 (ISBN 0-7933-1014-8). Gallopade Pub Group.

—South Carolina Coastales. (Illus.). 1990. PLB 19.95 (ISBN 0-7933-2001-1); pap. 14.95 (ISBN 1-55609-115-X); computer disk 29.95 (ISBN 0-7933-2002-X). Gallopade Pub Group.

—The South Carolina Hot Air Balloon Mystery. (Illus.). (gr. 2-9). 1990. 19.95 (ISBN 0-7933-2678-8); pap. 14.95 (ISBN 0-7933-2679-6); computer disk 29.95 (ISBN 0-7933-2680-X). Gallopade Pub Group.

—South Carolina "Jography" A Fun Run Thru Our State! (Illus.). 1990. PLB 19.95 (ISBN 0-7933-1985-4); pap. 14.95 (ISBN 1-55609-049-8); computer disk 29.95 (ISBN 0-7933-1986-2). Gallopade Pub Group.

—South Carolina Jography: A Fun Run Through the Palmetto State. (Illus.). 50p. (Orig.). (gr. 3-9). 1986. pap. 14.95 (ISBN 0-935326-96-0). Gallopade Pub Group.

—South Carolina Kid's Cookbook: Recipes, How-to, History, Lore & More! (Illus.). 1990. PLB 19.95 (ISBN 0-7933-1022-9); pap. 14.95 (ISBN 0-7933-1021-0); computer disk 29.95 (ISBN 0-7933-1023-7). Gallopade Pub Group.

—South Carolina Quiz Bowl Crash Course! (Illus.). 1990. PLB 19.95 (ISBN 0-7933-1998-6); pap. 14.95 (ISBN 0-7933-1999-4); computer disk 29.95 (ISBN 0-7933-2000-3). Gallopade Pub Group.

—South Carolina School Trivia: An Amazing & Fascinating Look at Our State's Teachers, Schools & Students! (Illus.). 1990. PLB 19.95 (ISBN 0-7933-1019-9); pap. 14.95 (ISBN 0-7933-1018-0); computer disk 29.95 (ISBN 0-7933-1020-2). Gallopade Pub Group.

—South Carolina Silly Basketball Sportsmysteries, Vol. 1. (Illus.). 1990. PLB 19.95 (ISBN 0-7933-1016-4); pap. 14.95 (ISBN 0-7933-1015-6); computer disk 29.95 (ISBN 0-7933-1017-2). Gallopade Pub Group.

—South Carolina Silly Basketball Sportsmysteries, Vol. 2. (Illus.). 1990. PLB 19.95 (ISBN 0-7933-2009-7); pap. 14.95 (ISBN 0-7933-2010-0); computer disk 29.95 (ISBN 0-7933-2011-9). Gallopade Pub Group.

—South Carolina Silly Football Sportsmysteries, Vol. 1. (Illus.). 1990. PLB 19.95 (ISBN 0-7933-1989-7); pap. 14.95 (ISBN 0-7933-1990-0); computer disk 29.95 (ISBN 0-7933-1991-9). Gallopade Pub Group.

—South Carolina Silly Football Sportsmysteries, Vol. 2. (Illus.). 1990. PLB 19.95 (ISBN 0-7933-1992-7); pap. 14.95 (ISBN 0-7933-1993-5); computer disk 29.95 (ISBN 0-7933-1994-3). Gallopade Pub Group.

—South Carolina Silly Trivia! (Illus.). 1990. PLB 19.95 (ISBN 0-7933-1983-8); pap. 14.95; computer disk 29.95 (ISBN 0-7933-1984-6). Gallopade Pub Group.

—South Carolina's (Most Devastating!) Disasters & (Most Calamitous!) Catastrophies! (Illus.). 1990. PLB 19.95 (ISBN 0-7933-1007-5); pap. 14.95 (ISBN 0-7933-1006-7); computer disk 29.95 (ISBN 0-7933-1008-3). Gallopade Pub Group.

Turner Educational Services, Inc. Staff & Clark, James I. South Carolina. 48p. (gr. 3 up). 1986. PLB 17.32 (ISBN 0-86514-475-3); pap. text ed. 9.27 (ISBN 0-86514-550-4); cancelled Beta video (ISBN 0-86514-107-X); cancelled VHS video (ISBN 0-86514-182-7); cancelled 3/4" video (ISBN 0-86514-257-2); cancelled tchr's. study guide (ISBN 0-86514-332-3); cancelled student activity bk. (ISBN 0-86514-407-9); cancelled index. Raintree Pubs.

SOUTH CAROLINA–FICTION

Bodie, Idella. Ghost in the Capitol. Kovach, Gay H., illus. 116p. (gr. 5-9). 1986. pap. 6.95 (ISBN 0-87844-072-0). Sandlapper Pub Co.

SOUTH CAROLINA–HISTORY

Bagwell, Joyce B. Low Country Quake Tales. 88p. 1986. pap. 7.50 (ISBN 0-89308-593-6, SC 84). Southern Hist Pr.

Burney, Eugenia. The Story of Fort Sumter. LC 74-28435. (Illus.). 32p. (gr. 3-6). 1975. 13.27 (ISBN 0-516-04611-X). Childrens.

Harris, Hazel. The History of South Carolina in the Building of the Nation. (Illus.). 330p. (gr. 8). 1991. tchr's ed. 15.00 (ISBN 0-9628232-1-X). A G Furman.

Huff, Archie V., Jr. The History of South Carolina in the Building of the Nation. (Illus.). 528p. (gr. 8). 1991. text ed. 20.99 (ISBN 0-9628232-0-1). A G Furman.

SOUTH DAKOTA

Ames, Mary. Memories of the Pasque & Prairie. Wong, Vera M., illus. Thornley, Phyllis, intro. by. (Illus.). 79p. (gr. 9-12). 1987. 13.95 (ISBN 0-9619407-0-0). Country Messenger Inc.

Carole Marsh South Dakota Books, 31 bks. Set. 638.45 (ISBN 0-7933-1316-3). Gallopade Pub Group.

Carpenter, Allan. South Dakota. new ed. LC 78-3385. (Illus.). 96p. (gr. 4 up). 1978. PLB 19.93 (ISBN 0-516-04141-X). Childrens.

Fradin, Dennis. South Dakota: In Words & Pictures. Wahl, Richard, illus. LC 80-25349. 48p. (gr. 2-5). 1981. PLB 15.93 (ISBN 0-516-03941-5). Childrens.

Jensen, Delwin A. Fort Pierre-Deadwood Trail: Route to the Gold Fields of the Black Hills. (Illus.). 60p. (Orig.). (gr. 8-12). 1989. pap. text ed. 4.00 (ISBN 0-9624413-0-9). D A Jensen.

Marsh, Carole. Avast, Ye Slobs! South Dakota Pirate Trivia. (Illus.). 1990. PLB 19.95 (ISBN 0-7933-1052-0); pap. 14.95 (ISBN 0-7933-1051-2); computer disk 29.95 (ISBN 0-7933-1053-9). Gallopade Pub Group.

—The Beast of the South Dakota Bed & Breakfast. (Illus.). 1990. PLB 19.95 (ISBN 0-7933-2026-7); pap. 14.95 (ISBN 0-7933-2027-5); computer disk 29.95 (ISBN 0-7933-2028-3). Gallopade Pub Group.

—The Hard-to-Believe-But True! Book of South Dakota History, Mystery, Trivia, Legend, Lore, Humor & More. (Illus.). 1990. PLB 19.95 (ISBN 0-7933-1049-0); pap. 14.95 (ISBN 0-7933-1048-2); computer disk 29.95 (ISBN 0-7933-1050-4). Gallopade Pub Group.

—If My South Dakota Mama Ran the World! (Illus.). 1990. lib. bdg. 19.95 (ISBN 0-7933-2035-6); pap. 14.95 (ISBN 0-7933-2036-4); computer disk 29.95 (ISBN 0-7933-2037-2). Gallopade Pub Group.

—Let's Quilt South Dakota & Stuff It Topographically! (Illus.). 1990. lib. bdg. 19.95 (ISBN 0-7933-2018-6); pap. 14.95 (ISBN 1-55609-136-2); computer disk 29.95 (ISBN 0-7933-2019-4). Gallopade Pub Group.

—South Dakota & Other State Greats (Biographies) (Illus.). 1990. PLB 19.95 (ISBN 0-7933-2038-0); pap. 14.95 (ISBN 0-7933-2039-9); computer disk 29.95 (ISBN 0-7933-2040-2). Gallopade Pub Group.

—South Dakota Bandits, Bushwackers, Outlaws, Crooks, Devils, Ghosts, Desperadoes & Other Assorted & Sundry Characters! (Illus.). 1990. PLB 19.95 (ISBN 0-7933-1034-2); pap. 14.95 (ISBN 0-7933-1033-4); computer disk 29.95 (ISBN 0-7933-1035-0). Gallopade Pub Group.

—South Dakota Classic Christmas Trivia: Stories, Recipes, Activities, Legends, Lore & More! (Illus.). 1990. PLB 19.95 (ISBN 0-7933-1037-7); pap. 14.95 (ISBN 0-7933-1036-9); computer disk 29.95 (ISBN 0-7933-1038-5). Gallopade Pub Group.

—South Dakota Coastales. (Illus.). 1990. PLB 19.95 (ISBN 0-7933-2032-1); pap. 14.95 (ISBN 0-7933-2033-X); computer disk 29.95 (ISBN 0-7933-2034-8). Gallopade Pub Group.

—The South Dakota Hot Air Balloon Mystery. (Illus.). (gr. 2-9). 1990. 19.95 (ISBN 0-7933-2687-7); pap. 14.95 (ISBN 0-7933-2688-5); computer disk 29.95 (ISBN 0-7933-2689-3). Gallopade Pub Group.

—South Dakota "Jography" A Fun Run Thru Our State! (Illus.). 1990. PLB 19.95 (ISBN 0-7933-2015-1); pap. 14.95 (ISBN 0-7933-2016-X); computer disk 29.95 (ISBN 0-7933-2017-8). Gallopade Pub Group.

—South Dakota Kid's Cookbook: Recipes, How-to, History, Lore & More! (Illus.). 1990. PLB 19.95 (ISBN 0-7933-1046-6); pap. 14.95 (ISBN 0-7933-1045-8); computer disk 29.95 (ISBN 0-7933-1047-4). Gallopade Pub Group.

—South Dakota Quiz Bowl Crash Course! (Illus.). 1990. PLB 19.95 (ISBN 0-7933-2029-1); pap. 14.95 (ISBN 0-7933-2030-5); computer disk 29.95 (ISBN 0-7933-2031-3). Gallopade Pub Group.

—South Dakota School Trivia: An Amazing & Fascinating Look at Our State's Teachers, Schools & Students! (Illus.). 1990. PLB 19.95 (ISBN 0-7933-1043-1); pap. 14.95 (ISBN 0-7933-1042-3); computer disk 29.95 (ISBN 0-7933-1044-X). Gallopade Pub Group.

—South Dakota Silly Basketball Sportsmysteries, Vol. 1. (Illus.). 1990. PLB 19.95 (ISBN 0-7933-1040-7); pap. 14.95 (ISBN 0-7933-1039-3); computer disk 29.95 (ISBN 0-7933-1041-5). Gallopade Pub Group.

—South Dakota Silly Basketball Sportsmysteries, Vol. 2. (Illus.). 1990. PLB 19.95 (ISBN 0-7933-2041-0); pap. 14.95 (ISBN 0-7933-2042-9); computer disk 29.95 (ISBN 0-7933-2043-7). Gallopade Pub Group.

—South Dakota Silly Football Sportsmysteries, Vol. 1. (Illus.). 1990. PLB 19.95 (ISBN 0-7933-2020-8); pap. 14.95 (ISBN 0-7933-2021-6); computer disk 29.95 (ISBN 0-7933-2022-4). Gallopade Pub Group.

—South Dakota Silly Football Sportsmysteries, Vol. 2. (Illus.). 1990. PLB 19.95 (ISBN 0-7933-2023-2); pap. 14.95; computer disk 29.95 (ISBN 0-7933-2025-9). Gallopade Pub Group.

—South Dakota Silly Trvia! (Illus.). 1990. PLB 19.95 (ISBN 0-7933-2012-7); pap. 14.95 (ISBN 0-7933-2013-5); computer disk 29.95 (ISBN 0-7933-2014-3). Gallopade Pub Group.

—South Dakota's (Most Devastating!) Disasters & (Most Calamitous!) Catastrophies! (Illus.). 1990. PLB 19.95 (ISBN 0-7933-1031-8); pap. 14.95 (ISBN 0-7933-1030-X); computer disk 29.95 (ISBN 0-7933-1032-6). Gallopade Pub Group.

Turner Educational Services, Inc. Staff, et al. South Dakota. 48p. (gr. 3 up). 1986. PLB 17.32 (ISBN 0-86514-458-3); pap. text ed. 9.27 (ISBN 0-86514-533-4); cancelled Beta video (ISBN 0-86514-083-9); cancelled VHS video (ISBN 0-86514-158-4); cancelled 3/4" video (ISBN 0-86514-233-5); cancelled tchr's. study guide (ISBN 0-86514-308-0); cancelled student activity bk. (ISBN 0-86514-383-8); cancelled index. Raintree Pubs.

SOUTH DAKOTA–FICTION

Wilder, Laura I. Little Town on the Prairie. rev. ed. Williams, Garth, illus. LC 52-7531. 308p. (gr. 4-8). 1953. 14.95 (ISBN 0-06-026450-0); PLB 14.89 (ISBN 0-06-026451-9). HarpC Child Bks.

—The Long Winter. rev. ed. Williams, Garth, illus. LC 52-7530. 334p. (gr. 4-8). 1953. 14.95 (ISBN 0-06-026460-8); PLB 14.89 (ISBN 0-06-026461-6). HarpC Child Bks.

—These Happy Golden Years. rev. ed. Williams, Garth, illus. LC 52-7532. 289p. (gr. 5-9). 1961. 14.95 (ISBN 0-06-026480-2); PLB 14.89 (ISBN 0-06-026481-0). HarpC Child Bks.

SOUTH POLE

Mason, Theodore K. Two Against the Ice, Amundsen & Ellsworth. 1982. 13.95 (ISBN 0-396-08092-8, Putnam). Putnam Pub Group.

SOUTH SEA ISLANDS

see Islands of the Pacific

SOUTHEAST ASIA

see Asia, Southeastern

SOUTHERN STATES

Aylesworth, Thomas G. & Aylesworth, Virginia L. South Central (Louisiana, Arkansas, Missouri, Kansas, Oklahoma) (Illus.). 66p. (Orig.). (gr. 3 up). 1988. PLB 16.95 (ISBN 1-55546-561-7); pap. 6.95 (ISBN 0-7910-0542-9). Chelsea Hse.

—The South (Mississippi, Alabama, Florida) (Illus.). 64p. (gr. 4-6). 1991. PLB 16.95 (ISBN 0-7910-1044-9). Chelsea Hse.

Beeger, Gilda. The Southeast States. 96p. (gr. 4 up). 1984. lib. bdg. 10.40 (ISBN 0-531-04738-5). Watts.

Greenfield, Eloise & Little, Lessie J. Childtimes: A Three-Generation Memoir. Pinkney, Jerry, illus. LC 77-26581. 160p. (gr. 5 up). 1979. (Crowell Jr Bks); PLB 12.89 (ISBN 0-690-03875-5, Crowell Jr Bks). HarpC Child Bks.

Herda, D. J. Environmental America: The South Central States. (Illus.). 64p. (gr. 5-8). 1991. PLB 13.90 (ISBN 1-878841-09-2). Millbrook Pr.

—Environmental America: The Southeastern States. (Illus.). 64p. (gr. 5-8). 1991. PLB 13.90 (ISBN 1-878841-07-6). Millbrook Pr.

Hoey, Mary. Journey South: Discovering the Americas. (gr. 4-6). 1980. pap. 3.50 (ISBN 0-377-00099-X). Friendship Pr.

Touchstone, Samuel J. Jessie Jackson Touchstone Clan & Parallel Touchstones. LC 90-81215. (Illus.). 80p. (Orig.). (gr. 6-12). 1990. pap. text ed. 14.95 (ISBN 0-914917-06-4). Folk-Life.

Woods, Geraldine & Woods, Harold. The South Central States. 72p. (gr. 4up). 1984. lib. bdg. 10.40 (ISBN 0-531-04737-7). Watts.

SOUTHERN STATES–FICTION

Aylesworth, Thomas G. & Aylesworth, Virginia L. The Southeast (Kentucky, Tennessee, Georgia) (Illus.). 66p. (gr. 3 up). 1988. pap. 6.95 (ISBN 0-7910-0543-7). Chelsea Hse.

Harris, Joel C. Uncle Remus Stories. (gr. 5-6). 17.95 (ISBN 0-89190-311-9, Pub. by Am Repr). Amereon Ltd.

L'Engle, Madeleine. The Other Side of the Sun. 344p. 1971. 6.95 (ISBN 0-374-22805-1). FS&G.

Marshall, James. A Summer in the South. Marshall, James, illus. (gr. 1 up). 1977. 12.95 (ISBN 0-395-25840-5). HM.

Peck, Kay. Folsom Boy. LC 88-51030. 174p. 1989. pap. 6.95 (ISBN 1-55523-173-X). Winston-Derek.

Pyrnelle, Louise-Clarke. Diddie, Dumps & Tot. (Illus.). 117p. (gr. 4-8). 1963. 13.95 (ISBN 0-911116-17-6). Pelican.

Standish, Burt L. Frank Merriwell Down South. Rudman, Jack, ed. (gr. 9 up). 9.95 (ISBN 0-8373-9305-1); pap. 3.95 (ISBN 0-8373-9005-2). F Merriwell.

SOUTHWEST, NEW

Here are entered works on that part of the United States which corresponds roughly with the old Spanish province of New Mexico, including the present Arizona, New Mexico, southern Colorado, Utah, Nevada and California.

Anderson, Joan. Spanish Pioneers of the Southwest. Ancona, George, photos by. LC 88-16121. (Illus.). 64p. (gr. 3-6). 1989. 14.95 (ISBN 0-525-67264-8, Lodestar Bks). Dutton Child Bks.

Aylesworth, Thomas G. & Aylesworth, Virginia L. The Southwest (Texas, New Mexico, Colorado) (Illus.). 66p. 1988. lib. bdg. 16.95x (ISBN 1-55546-562-5). Chelsea Hse.

Herda, D. J. Environmental America: The Southwestern States. (Illus.). 64p. (gr. 5-8). 1991. PLB 13.90 (ISBN 1-878841-11-4). Millbrook Pr.

McCarty, John L. Maverick Town: The Story of Old Tascosa. Bugbee, Harold D., illus. Sonnichsen, C. L., frwd. by. LC 87-5946. (Illus.). 320p. (gr. 6-12). 1988. pap. 12.95 (ISBN 0-8061-2089-4). U of Okla Pr.

SOVEREIGNS

see Kings and Rulers

SOVIET UNION

Anderson, Madelyn K. Soviet Life: A View of the Peoples of the U. S. S. R. (Illus.). 128p. (gr. 7-12). 1989. PLB 11.90 (ISBN 0-531-10814-7). Watts.

Baker. Soviet Air Force. LC 88-12121. (Illus.). 48p. (gr. 3-8). Date not set. PLB 18.60 (ISBN 0-86625-331-9). Rourke Corp.

—Soviet Forces in Space. LC 88-14050. (Illus.). 48p. (gr. 3-8). Date not set. PLB 18.60 (ISBN 0-86625-335-1). Rourke Corp.

Boyette, William. Soviet Georgia. (Illus.). 96p. (gr. 5 up). 1988. lib. bdg. 14.95 (ISBN 1-55546-779-2). Chelsea Hse.

The Continuing Revolution. (Illus.). 48p. (gr. 3 up). 1989. PLB 17.32 (ISBN 0-8172-3357-1). Raintree Pubs.

Dolphin, Laurie. Georgia to Georgia: Making Friends in the U. S. S. R. McGee, E. Alan, illus. LC 90-47494. 40p. (gr. 2 up). 1991. 15.95 (ISBN 0-688-09896-7, Tambourine Bks); PLB 15.88 (ISBN 0-688-09897-5, Tambourine Bks). Morrow.

Fannon, Cecilia. Soviet Union. (Illus.). 64p. (gr. 7 up). 1990. lib. bdg. 15.93 (ISBN 0-86593-092-9); lib. bdg. 11.95s.p. (ISBN 0-685-36367-8). Rourke Corp.

Finney, Susan. The Soviet Union. 64p. (gr. 4-8). 1991. 6.95 (ISBN 0-86653-580-2). Good Apple.

Gantz, David. Let's Visit the Soviet Union. Gantz, David, illus. (gr. 1 up). 1989. pap. 4.95 (ISBN 0-671-67214-2). S&S Trade.

Geography of the Soviet Union. (Illus.). 48p. (gr. 3 up). 1989. PLB 17.32 (ISBN 0-8172-3353-9). Raintree Pubs.

Gillies, John. The Soviet Union: The World's Largest Country. LC 84-23024. (Illus.). 176p. (gr. 5 up). 1985. PLB 14.95 (ISBN 0-87518-290-9, Dillon). Macmillan Child Grp.

Jackson, W. A., ed. Soviet Union. rev. ed. LC 87-83270. (Illus.). 160p. (gr. 6 up). 1988. text ed. 16.95 (ISBN 0-934291-34-9); tchr's. guide 9.95 (ISBN 0-934291-35-7). Gateway Pr MI.

Jacobsen, Karen. The Soviet Union. LC 90-2177. (Illus.). 48p. (gr. k-4). 1990. PLB 14.60 (ISBN 0-516-01109-X); pap. 4.95 (ISBN 0-516-41109-8). Childrens.

James, Ian. Soviet Union. (Illus.). 32p. (gr. k-6). 1989. PLB 11.90 (ISBN 0-531-10762-0). Watts.

Keeler, Stephen. Passport to the Soviet Union. Franklin Watts Ltd., ed. (Illus.). 48p. (gr. 7 up). 1988. PLB 12.90 (ISBN 0-531-10495-8). Watts.
Lerner Publications, Department of Geography Staff, ed. Soviet Union in Pictures. (Illus.). 64p. (gr. 5 up). 1989. PLB 12.95 (ISBN 0-8225-1864-3). Lerner Pubns.
Lye, Keith. Take a Trip to Russia. LC 82-50062. (gr. 1-3). 1982. PLB 7.99 (ISBN 0-531-04472-6). Watts.
Miller. Soviet Navy. LC 88-11327. (Illus.). 48p. (gr. 3-8). 1988. PLB 18.60 (ISBN 0-86625-336-X). Rourke Corp.
—Soviet Rocket Forces. LC 88-11367. (Illus.). 48p. (gr. 3-8). 1988. PLB 18.60 (ISBN 0-86625-333-5). Rourke Corp.
—Soviet Submarines. (Illus.). 48p. (gr. 3-8). Date not set. PLB 18.60 (ISBN 0-86625-332-7). Rourke Corp.
Murphy, Claire R. Friendship Across Arctic Waters: Alaskan Cub Scouts Visit Their Soviet Neighbors. Mason, Charles, photos by. (Illus.). 48p. (gr. 3-8). 1991. 15.95 (ISBN 0-525-67348-2, Lodestar Bks). Dutton Child Bks.
Oparenko, Christine. Ukraine. (Illus.). (gr. 5 up). 1988. 14.95 (ISBN 0-7910-0177-6). Chelsea Hse.
Perovskaya, Olga. Wolf in Olga's Kitchen. Glagoleva, Fainna, tr. Culfogienis, Angie, illus. LC 69-12440. (gr. 4-8). 1969. 5.50 (ISBN 0-672-50590-8, Bobbs). Macmillan.
Portrait of the Soviet Union Series. (Illus.). (gr. 3 up). 1989. Set of 7 titles, 48 pp. ea. PLB 121.24 (ISBN 0-8172-3350-4). Raintree Pubs.
Resnick, Abraham. The Union of Soviet Socialist Republics. LC 84-7602. (Illus.). 128p. (gr. 5-9). 1984. lib. bdg. 25.27 (ISBN 0-516-02789-1). Childrens.
Riordan, James. Soviet Union: The Land & Its People. rev. ed. LC 86-11808. 48p. (gr. 5 up). 1986. PLB 15.96 (ISBN 0-382-09255-4); pap. 6.95 (ISBN 0-382-09461-1). Silver Burdett Pr.
Soviet Union. 1990. 29.98 (ISBN 0-7924-5167-8, Mallard Pr). BDD Promo Bk.
The Soviet Union, a Portrait. (Illus.). 48p. (gr. 3 up). 1989. PLB 17.32 (ISBN 0-8172-3351-2). Raintree Pubs.
Stewart, Gail B. The Soviet Union. LC 90-38408. (Illus.). 48p. (gr. 5-6). 1990. RSBE 10.95 (ISBN 0-89686-537-1, Crestwood Hse). Macmillan Child Grp.
Tolhurst, Marilyn. U. S. S. R. (Illus.). 48p. (gr. 4-8). 1988. PLB 14.98 (ISBN 0-382-09507-3). Silver Burdett Pr.
Wood. Soviet Army. (Illus.). 48p. (gr. 3-8). Date not set. PLB 18.60 (ISBN 0-86625-334-3). Rourke Corp.

SOVIET UNION–BIOGRAPHY

Caulkins, Janet. The Picture Life of Mikhail Gorbachev. LC 85-15023. (Illus.). 47p. (gr. 2-4). 1985. PLB 10.90 (ISBN 0-531-10085-5). Watts.
Kort, Michael. Mikhail Gorbachev. (Illus.). 160p. (gr. 9-12). 1990. PLB 13.90 (ISBN 0-531-10941-0). Watts.
Oleksy, Walter. Mikhail Gorbachev: A Leader for Soviet Change. LC 88-36960. (Illus.). 152p. (gr. 4 up). 1989. PLB 17.27 (ISBN 0-516-03265-8). Childrens.
Resnick, Abraham. Lenin: Founder of the Soviet Union. LC 87-13249. (Illus.). 152p. (gr. 4 up). 1987. PLB 17.27 (ISBN 0-516-03260-7). Childrens.
Selfridge, John W. Mikhail Gorbachev. (Illus.). 84p. (gr. 3-5). 1991. PLB 12.95 (ISBN 0-7910-1567-X). Chelsea Hse.
Sproyle, Anna. Mikhail Gorbachev: Revolutionary for Democracy. LC 90-10010. (Illus.). 64p. (gr. 5-6). 1991. PLB 12.95 (ISBN 0-8368-0401-5). Gareth Stevens Inc.
Sullivan, George. Mikhail Gorbachev. rev. ed. (Illus.). 128p. (gr. 7 up). 1990. lib. bdg. 13.98 (ISBN 0-671-72913-6); text ed. 7.95 (ISBN 0-671-72914-4). Messner.

SOVIET UNION–FICTION

Cole, Joanna. Bony-Legs. Zimmer, Dirk, illus. LC 85-5070. 48p. (ps-3). 1984. 12.95 (ISBN 0-02-722970-X, Four Winds). Macmillan Child Grp.
Dostoyevsky, Fyodor. Brothers Karamazov. Rudzik, O. H., intro. by. (gr. 11 up). pap. 3.95 (ISBN 0-8049-0128-7, CL-128). Airmont.
—Crime & Punishment. Canon, R. R., intro. by. (Illus.). (gr. 11 up). pap. 3.95 (ISBN 0-8049-0145-7, CL-145). Airmont.
Gogol, Nikolai V. Dead Souls. Girling, Z., intro. by. (gr. 11 up). pap. 1.75 (ISBN 0-8049-0122-8, CL-122). Airmont.
Gross, Sukey S. Passport to Russia. Backman, Aidel, illus. 158p. (gr. 5-8). 1989. 10.95 (ISBN 0-935063-59-5); pap. 7.95 (ISBN 0-935063-60-9). CIS Comm.
Holman, Felice. The Wild Children. LC 85-3541. 152p. (gr. 5-9). 1985. pap. 4.95 (ISBN 0-14-031930-1, Puffin). Puffin Bks.
Kasakov. Goluboe i Zelenoe. (gr. 7-12). 1972. pap. 5.95 (ISBN 0-88436-053-9, 65253). EMC.
Laskin. Spasibo za Vnimanie. (gr. 7-12). pap. 5.95 (ISBN 0-88436-052-0, 65251). EMC.
Pargment, Lila, adapted by. How the Moolah Was Taught a Lesson & Other Tales from Russia. Titiev, Estelle, adapted by. LC 75-9200. (Illus.). 56p. 1985. (Dial); PLB 5.47 (ISBN 0-8037-5746-8, Dial). Doubleday.
Posell, Elsa. Homecoming. 208p. (gr. 7 up). 1987. 14.95 (ISBN 0-15-235160-4, HJ). HarBraceJ.
Samstag, Nicholas. Kay Kay Comes Home. Shahn, Ben, illus. (gr. 5-7). 1962. 10.95 (ISBN 0-8392-3015-X). Astor-Honor.
Schloneger, Florence E. Sara's Trek. Quinn, Sidney, illus. 100p. (gr. 7 up). 1982. pap. 4.95 (ISBN 0-87303-071-0). Faith & Life.
Sherman, Josepha, adapted by. Vassilisa the Wise: A Tale of Medieval Russia. San Souci, Daniel, illus. LC 87-8563. 32p. (gr. 5-8). 1988. 14.95 (ISBN 0-15-293240-2). HarBraceJ.
Shulevitz, Uri. Soldier & Tsar in the Forest: A Russian Tale. Lourie, Richard, tr. from RUS. Shulevitz, Uri, illus. LC 72-188254. 32p. (ps-3). 1972. 14.95 (ISBN 0-374-37126-1). FS&G.
Singer, Isaac Bashevis. When Shlemiel Went to Warsaw & Other Stories. Zemach, Margot, illus. Shub, Elizabeth, tr. from YID. LC 68-30932. (Illus.). 128p. (gr. 4 up). 1969. 13.95 (ISBN 0-374-38316-2). FS&G.
Tompert, Ann. The Tzar's Bird. Rayevsky, Robert, illus. LC 89-31376. 32p. (gr. k-3). 1990. 14.95 (ISBN 0-02-789401-0, Mcmillan Child Bk). Macmillan Child Grp.
Turgenev, Ivan S. Fathers & Sons. Garnett, Constance, tr. Canon, R. R., intro. by. (gr. 11 up). pap. 1.95 (ISBN 0-8049-0129-5, CL-129). Airmont.
Zheleznikov, Vladimir. Scarecrow. Bouis, Antonina, tr. from RUS. LC 90-6698. 160p. (gr. 5 up). 1990. 12.95 (ISBN 0-397-32316-6, Lipp Jr Bks); PLB 12.89 (ISBN 0-397-32317-4, Lipp Jr Bks). HarpC Child Bks.

SOVIET UNION–HISTORY

Andrews, William G. The Land & People of the Soviet Union. LC 90-5746. (Illus.). 320p. (gr. 6 up). 1991. 17.95 (ISBN 0-06-020034-0); PLB 17.89 (ISBN 0-06-020035-9). HarpC Child Bks.
Culture in the Soviet Union. (Illus.). 48p. (gr. 3 up). 1989. PLB 17.32 (ISBN 0-8172-3355-5). Raintree Pubs.
Jones, Dianne. Old Russia. 47p. (gr. k-8). 1989. 16.95 (ISBN 0-913705-46-2, ZP17). Zephyr Pr AZ.
Peoples of the Soviet Union. (Illus.). 48p. (gr. 3 up). 1989. PLB 17.32 (ISBN 0-8172-3354-7). Raintree Pubs.
Resnick, Abraham. Russia: A History to 1917. LC 83-7369. (Illus.). 128p. (gr. 5-8). 1983. PLB 25.27 (ISBN 0-516-02785-9). Childrens.
Russia Under the Czars. (Illus.). 48p. (gr. 3 up). 1989. PLB 17.32 (ISBN 0-8172-3352-0). Raintree Pubs.
The Soviet Economy. (Illus.). 48p. (gr. 3 up). 1989. PLB 17.32 (ISBN 0-8172-3356-3). Raintree Pubs.

SOVIET UNION–HISTORY–FICTION

Krichevsky, David J. What Price Revolution. LC 76-18448. 175p. (gr. 9-12). 1976. 8.95 (ISBN 0-87881-052-8). Mojave Bks.
Turgenev, Ivan S. Fathers & Sons. (gr. 10 up). 1972. pap. 3.25 (ISBN 0-685-03980-3, RE). PB.

SOVIET UNION–HISTORY–1689-1800

Stanley, Diane. Peter the Great. Stanley, Diane, illus. LC 85-13060. 32p. (gr. k-3). 1986. 13.95 (ISBN 0-02-786790-0, Four Winds). Macmillan Child Grp.

SOVIET UNION–HISTORY–1917-

Campling, Elizabeth. U. S. S. R. Since Nineteen Forty-Five. (Illus.). 64p. (gr. 7-11). 1990. 19.95 (ISBN 0-7134-6063-6, Pub. by Batsford England). Trafalgar Sq.

SOVIET UNION–HISTORY–REVOLUTION, 1917-1921

Kindle, Pat & Finney, Susan. Russia to the Revolution. McKay, Ardis, illus. 64p. (gr. 4-8). 1987. pap. 6.95 (ISBN 0-86653-398-2, GA 1020). Good Apple.
Ross, Stewart. The Russian Revolution, Nineteen Fourteen to Nineteen Twenty-Four. (Illus.). 64p. (gr. 7-12). 1989. PLB 12.90 (ISBN 0-531-18221-5). Watts.

SOVIET UNION–HISTORY–1925-1953

Stein, R. Conrad. Siege of Leningrad. LC 82-17841. (Illus.). 48p. (gr. 4-8). 1983. PLB 14.60 (ISBN 0-516-04773-6). Childrens.

SOVIET UNION–POLITICS AND GOVERNMENT

Bradley, John. Soviet Union: Will Perestroika Work? LC 89-31649. (Illus.). 36p. (gr. 4-7). 1989. PLB 11.90 (ISBN 0-531-17170-1, Gloucester Pr). Watts.
Hawkes, Nigel. Glasnost & Perestroika. (Illus.). 48p. (gr. 5 up). 1990. lib. bdg. 18.00 (ISBN 0-86592-149-0); lib. bdg. 13.50s.p. (ISBN 0-685-36378-3). Rourke Corp.
Kort, Michael. Mikhail Gorbachev. (Illus.). 160p. (gr. 9-12). 1990. PLB 13.90 (ISBN 0-531-10941-0). Watts.
Perkovich, George. Thinking about the Soviet Union. (Illus.). 256p. (Orig.). 1989. pap. text ed. 25.00 (ISBN 0-942349-00-8). Eductrs Soc Respons.
Ross, Stewart. The U. S. S. R. under Stalin. (Illus.). 64p. (gr. 9-12). 1991. RLB 12.90 (ISBN 0-531-18409-9, Pub. by Boatwright Pr). Watts.
Sproyle, Anna. Mikhail Gorbachev: Revolutionary for Democracy. LC 90-10010. (Illus.). 64p. (gr. 5-6). 1991. PLB 12.95 (ISBN 0-8368-0401-5). Gareth Stevens Inc.
Trager, Oliver, ed. Gorbachev's Glasnost: Red Star Rising. 224p. 1989. 29.95x (ISBN 0-8160-2220-8). Facts on File.
Yost, Graham. The KGB. (Illus.). 160p. (gr. 8-12). 1989. 16.95x (ISBN 0-8160-1940-1). Facts on File.

SPACE, OUTER

see Outer Space

SPACE AND TIME

see also Relativity (Physics)

Ferguson, Kitty. Black Holes in Space-Time. (Illus.). 128p. (gr. 7-9). 1991. PLB 12.40 (ISBN 0-531-12524-6). Watts.

SPACE AND TIME–FICTION

Anderson, Margaret J. The Druid's Gift. LC 88-22028. 192p. 1989. 12.95 (ISBN 0-394-81936-5); lib. bdg. 13.99 (ISBN 0-394-91936-X). Knopf.
Banks, Lynne R. The Secret of the Indian. (gr. 5 up). 1989. pap. 14.95 (ISBN 0-385-26292-2). Doubleday.
Bellairs, John. The Trolley to Yesterday. LC 88-7113. (Illus.). 192p. (gr. 5 up). 1989. 13.95 (ISBN 0-8037-0581-6); PLB 13.89 (ISBN 0-8037-0582-4). Dial Bks Young.
Boston, Lucy. Treasure of Green Knowe. Deeter, Catherine & Boston, Peter, illus. 224p. (gr. 3-7). 1989. pap. 3.95 (ISBN 0-15-289982-0). HarBraceJ.
Cameron, Eleanor. Beyond Silence. LC 80-10350. (gr. 5-9). 1980. 9.95 (ISBN 0-525-26463-9, DCB). Dutton Child Bks.
—The Court of the Stone Children. 192p. (gr. 4 up). 1990. pap. 3.95 (ISBN 0-14-034289-3, Puffin). Puffin Bks.
Christopher, John. New Found Land. LC 82-18354. 160p. (gr. 5-9). 1983. 9.95 (ISBN 0-525-44049-6, DCB). Dutton Child Bks.
Cresswell, Helen. The Secret World of Polly Flint. Felts, Shirley, illus. LC 83-24861. 176p. (gr. 4-7). 1984. 13.95 (ISBN 0-02-725400-3, Mcmillan Child Bk). Macmillan Child Grp.
—Secret World of Polly Flint. Felts, Shirley, illus. 178p. (gr. 4-6). 1985. pap. 3.50 (ISBN 0-14-031542-X, Puffin). Puffin Bks.
De Vos, Janifer C. The Silver Glass. Davis, Deena, ed. Babbitt, Gwendolyn, illus. (Orig.). (gr. 3-7). 1991. pap. 5.99 (ISBN 0-88070-410-1). Multnomah.
Eager, Edward. The Time Garden. Bodecker, N. M., illus. (gr. 4-6). 17.50 (ISBN 0-8446-6233-X). Peter Smith.
—The Time Garden. Treherne, Katie T. & Bodecker, N. M., illus. 192p. (gr. 3-7). 1990. pap. 4.95 (ISBN 0-15-288193-X). HarBraceJ.
Foley, Bernice W. Spaceships of the Ancients. Hoffman, Lee, illus. LC 78-59116. (gr. 3-6). 1978. 6.95 (ISBN 0-915964-04-X). Veritie Pr.
Hamilton, Virginia. The Gathering. LC 80-12512. 192p. (gr. 7 up). 1980. 11.75 (ISBN 0-688-80269-9); PLB 11.88 (ISBN 0-688-84269-0). Greenwillow.
Jones, Diana W. The Homeward Bounders. LC 81-1905. 224p. (gr. 5 up). 1981. 11.75 (ISBN 0-688-00678-7). Greenwillow.
Jordan, Sherryl. Time of Darkness. (gr. 9-12). 1990. 10.95 (ISBN 0-590-43363-6). Scholastic Inc.
Levy, Elizabeth. Running Out of Magic with Houdini. Sims, Blanche & Rutherford, Jenny, illus. LC 80-28427. 128p. (gr. 3-6). 1981. lib. bdg. 4.99 (ISBN 0-394-94685-5); pap. 1.95 (ISBN 0-394-84685-0). Knopf.
—Running Out of Time. Mars, W. T., illus. LC 79-28064. 128p. (gr. 3-6). 1980. lib. bdg. 4.99 (ISBN 0-394-94422-4). Knopf.
Maestro, Betsy. Where Is My Friend? A Word Concept Book. Maestro, Giulio, illus. LC 75-15902. 32p. (ps-1). 1986. PLB 12.95 (ISBN 0-517-52436-8). Crown.
Odgers, Sally F. Drummond: The Search for Sarah. Jones, Carol, illus. LC 90-55198. 112p. (gr. 2-5). 1990. reinforced 16.95 (ISBN 0-8234-0851-5). Holiday.
Peck, Richard. Blossom Culp & the Sleep of Death. LC 85-16188. 224p. (gr. 4-6). 1986. pap. 14.95 (ISBN 0-385-29433-6). Delacorte.
—The Dreadful Future of Blossom Culp. 224p. (gr. 7-12). 1984. pap. 2.95 (ISBN 0-440-92162-7, LFL). Dell.
Pinkwater, Daniel. Borgel. LC 89-13421. 176p. (gr. 5 up). 1990. 12.95 (ISBN 0-02-774671-2, Mcmillan Child Bk). Macmillan Child Grp.
Rodda, Emily. Finders Keepers. LC 90-47850. (Illus.). (gr. 5 up). 1991. 13.95 (ISBN 0-688-10516-5). Greenwillow.
Sleator, William. The Green Futures of Tycho. LC 80-23020. (gr. 5-9). 1981. 14.95 (ISBN 0-525-31007-X, DCB). Dutton Child Bks.
Voigt, Cynthia. Building Blocks. LC 83-15853. 132p. (gr. 3-7). 1984. 12.95 (ISBN 0-689-31035-8, Atheneum Child Bk). Macmillan Child Grp.
Wandelmaier, Roy. Secret of the Old Museum. Smolinski, Dick, illus. LC 85-2533. 112p. (gr. 3-6). 1985. lib. bdg. 9.49 (ISBN 0-8167-0531-3); pap. text ed. 2.95 (ISBN 0-8167-0532-1). Troll Assocs.

SPACE EXPLORATION (ASTRONAUTICS)

see Outer Space–Exploration

SPACE FLIGHT

see also Interplanetary Voyages; Outer Space–Exploration

Baker, D. Danger on Apollo Thirteen. (Illus.). 32p. (gr. 4 up). Date not set. PLB 14.00 (ISBN 0-86592-871-1). Rourke Corp.
Berliner, Don. Distance Flights. (Illus.). 72p. (gr. 5 up). 1990. 15.95 (ISBN 0-8225-1589-X). Lerner Pubns.
Branley, Franklyn M. Is There Life in Outer Space? Maddem, Don, illus. LC 85-45057. 32p. (gr. k-3). 1986. pap. 4.50 (ISBN 0-06-445049-X, Trophy). HarpC Child Bks.
Cave, Ron & Cave, Joyce. What about-Space Shuttle? West, David, illus. LC 82-81167. 32p. (gr. k-3). 1982. PLB 10.90 (ISBN 0-531-03465-8). Watts.
Cross, Wilbur. Space Shuttle. LC 84-7702. (Illus.). 100p. (gr. 5-12). 1985. lib. bdg. 21.27 (ISBN 0-516-00513-8). Childrens.
Darling, David. Could You Ever Fly to the Stars? (Illus.). (gr. 4 up). 1990. 14.95 (ISBN 0-87518-446-4, Dillon). Macmillan Child Grp.
DeOld, Alan R. & Judge, Joseph W. Space Travel: A Technological Frontier. (Illus.). 144p. (Orig.). (gr. 7-12). 1990. pap. text ed. 12.95 (ISBN 0-87192-206-1). Davis Mass.
Embury, Barbara & Crouch, Tom D. The Dream Is Alive: A Flight of Discovery Aboard the Space Shuttle. LC 90-55194. (Illus.). 64p. (gr. 3-7). 1990. 14.95 (ISBN 0-06-021813-4); PLB 14.89 (ISBN 0-06-021814-2). HarpC Child Bks.
Fradin, Dennis. Moon Flights. LC 84-23154. (Illus.). 48p. (gr. k-4). 1985. PLB 14.60 (ISBN 0-516-01940-6). Childrens.

—The Voyager Space Probes. LC 84-23250. (Illus.). 48p. (gr. k-4). 1985. lib. bdg. 14.60 (ISBN 0-516-01944-9). Childrens.
Friskey, Margaret. Space Shuttles. LC 81-16648. (Illus.). 48p. (gr. k-4). 1982. PLB 14.60 (ISBN 0-516-01655-5); pap. 4.95 (ISBN 0-516-41655-3). Childrens.
Gatland, K. Spaceflight. 32p. (gr. 4-8). 1976. lib. bdg. 13.96 (ISBN 0-88110-436-1, Usborne); pap. 6.95 (ISBN 0-86020-049-3). EDC.
Graham, Ian. Space Shuttles. Hayward, Ron, illus. 32p. (gr. 5-6). 1989. PLB 11.90 (ISBN 0-531-17172-8). Watts.
Hansen, Rosanna & Bell, Robert. My First Book about Space. (ps-3). 1985. pap. 8.95 (ISBN 0-671-60262-4, Little Simon). S&S Trade.
Hawkes, Nigel. Space Shuttle. (Illus.). 32p. (gr. 7-9). 1990. 8.90 (ISBN 0-531-17139-6). Watts.
Lauber, Patricia. Seeing Earth from Space. LC 89-77523. (Illus.). 80p. (gr. 5 up). 1990. 19.95 (ISBN 0-531-05902-2); PLB 19.99 (ISBN 0-531-08502-3). Orchard Bks Watts.
McDonnell, Janet. Space Travel: Blast-Off Day. Collette, Rondi, illus. LC 89-23999. 32p. (ps-2). 1990. lib. bdg. 11.97 (ISBN 0-89565-556-X). Childs World.
McGowen, Tom. Album of Space Flight. Brubaker, Lee, illus. 64p. (gr. 3-7). write for info. (ISBN 0-528-82133-4). Checkerboard Pr.
Marko, Katherine M. Animals in Orbit: Monkeynauts & Other Pioneers in Space. (Illus.). 64p. (gr. 3-5). 1991. PLB 11.90 (ISBN 0-531-20003-5). Watts.
Smith, Howard E., Jr. Daring the Unknown: A History of N. A. S. A. LC 86-33617. (Illus.). 128p. (gr. 2-7). 1987. 16.95 (ISBN 0-15-200435-1, Gulliver Bks). HarBraceJ.
Sonneborn, Ruth A. The Star Wars Question & Answer Book of Space. (Illus.). (gr. k-3). 1979. (Random Juv). Random.
Space. (Illus.). 32p. (ps up). 1986. 2.95 (ISBN 0-8431-4285-5). Price Stern.
Space Exploration. (Illus.). 64p. (gr. 6-12). 1983. pap. 1.85 (ISBN 0-8395-3354-3, 3354). BSA.
Stewart, G. In Space. (Illus.). 32p. (gr. 3-8). 1989. lib. bdg. 13.26 (ISBN 0-86592-116-4). Rourke Corp.
Sullivan, George. The Day We Walked on the Moon: A Photo History of Space Exploration. (Illus.). (gr. 3-9). 1990. write for info. Scholastic Inc.
Taylor, L. B., Jr. Space: Battleground of the Future? Kline, M., ed. (Illus.). 128p. (gr. 7-12). 1988. PLB 12.90 (ISBN 0-531-10514-8). Watts.
Tobias, Russell R. America in Space: An Annotated Bibliography. 200p. 1991. PLB 40.00x (ISBN 0-89356-669-1, Magill Bks). Salem Pr.
Vogt, Gregory. Space Shuttles: Projects for Young Scientists. (Illus.). 128p. (gr. 9up). PLB 12.90 (ISBN 0-531-04669-9). Watts.

SPACE FLIGHT–FICTION

Alexander, Martha. Marty McGee's Space Lab, No Girls Allowed. (Illus.). 32p. (ps-2). 1983. pap. 3.25 (ISBN 0-8037-0018-0). Dial Bks Young.
Appleton, Victor. Tom Swift: The Alien Probe. 192p. (Orig.). (gr. 3-7). 1981. 8.95 (ISBN 0-671-42538-2, Little Simon); pap. 2.75 (ISBN 0-671-42578-1). S&S Trade.
—Tom Swift: The City in the Stars. 192p. (Orig.). (gr. 3-7). 1981. 8.95 (ISBN 0-671-41120-9, Little Simon); pap. 3.50 (ISBN 0-671-41115-2). S&S Trade.
—Tom Swift: The Rescue Mission. 192p. (gr. 3-7). 1981. 8.95 (ISBN 0-671-43370-9, Little Simon); pap. 2.50 (ISBN 0-671-43386-5). S&S Trade.
—Tom Swift: The Space Fortress. 192p. (gr. 3-7). 1981. 8.95 (ISBN 0-671-43369-5, Little Simon); pap. 3.95 (ISBN 0-671-43385-7). S&S Trade.
—Tom Swift: The War in Outer Space. 192p. (Orig.). (gr. 3-7). 1981. 8.95 (ISBN 0-671-42539-0, Little Simon); pap. 3.95 (ISBN 0-671-42579-X). S&S Trade.
Atkinson, Stuart. Journey into Space. Asimov, Isaac, intro. by. 80p. (gr. 5-7). 1988. pap. 14.95 (ISBN 0-670-82306-6). Viking Child Bks.
Blumberg, Rhoda. The First Travel Guide to the Moon: What to Pack, How to Go, & What to See When You Get There. Doty, Roy, illus. LC 84-28757. 96p. (gr. 3-7). 1984. Repr. of 1980 ed. 13.95 (ISBN 0-02-711680-8, Four Winds). Macmillan Child Grp.
Bowles, Charles. The Sometimes Invisible Spaceship. LC 87-71712. 113p. (Orig.). 1987. pap. 6.00 (ISBN 0-916383-25-3). Aegina Pr.
Brooks, Walter R. Freddy & the Men from Mars. Morrill, Leslie & Wiese, Kurt, illus. LC 86-40421. 256p. (gr. 3-7). 1987. pap. 3.95 (ISBN 0-394-88887-1). Knopf.
Cameron, Eleanor. Stowaway to the Mushroom Planet. Henneberger, Robert, illus. (gr. 3-7). 1956. 14.95 (ISBN 0-316-12534-2, Joy St Bks). Little.
—Stowaway to the Mushroom Planet. (gr. 3-7). 1988. pap. 4.95 (ISBN 0-316-12541-5). Little.
Greydanus, Rose. Trouble in Space. Page, Don, illus. LC 81-5114. 32p. (gr. k-2). 1981. PLB 10.89 (ISBN 0-89375-517-6); pap. text ed. 2.95 (ISBN 0-89375-518-4). Troll Assocs.
Hill, Douglas. The Moon Monster. Ford, Jeremy, illus. 42p. (gr. 2-4). 1989. 3.95 (ISBN 0-8120-6138-1). Barron.
Ionesco, Eugene. Conte..., 3: Contes Numero 3 (Pour Enfants de Moins de Trois Ans) (Illus.). 30p. 1976. 11.95 (ISBN 0-686-54191-X). French & Eur.
Jensen, Lillian. Mother Goose in the Space Age. Larson, Leonard, illus. (gr. 5-9). 1985. 7.95 (ISBN 0-933494-28-9). Earthwise Pubns.
Lawhead, Steve. Howard Had a Spaceship. (Illus.). 32p. (gr. k-3). 1986. 7.95 (ISBN 0-7459-1101-3). Lion USA.
Lawrence, Louise. Moonwind. LC 85-45507. 192p. (gr. 7 up). 1987. pap. 2.95 (ISBN 0-06-447037-7, Trophy). HarpC Child Bks.
MacDonald, Suse. Space Spinners. (ps-3). 1991. 13.95 (ISBN 0-8037-1008-9); PLB 13.89 (ISBN 0-8037-1009-7). Dial Bks Young.
Malone, P. Mae. The Reluctant Little Astronaut. (Illus.). 32p. (gr. 3). 1985. Repr. of 1967 ed. 4.00 (ISBN 0-685-10582-2). Exposition-Phoenix.
Marshall, Edward. Space Case. Marshall, James, illus. 40p. (gr. k-3). 1982. pap. 4.95 (ISBN 0-8037-8431-7). Dial Bks Young.
Marshall, James. Merry Christmas, Space Case. Marshall, James, illus. LC 85-1664. 32p. (ps-3). 1986. 11.95 (ISBN 0-8037-0215-9); PLB 11.89 (ISBN 0-8037-0216-7). Dial Bks Young.
Marzollo, Jean & Marzollo, Claudio. Jed & the Space Bandits. Sis, Peter, illus. LC 84-15616. 48p. (ps-3). 1987. 9.95 (ISBN 0-8037-0135-7); PLB 9.89 (ISBN 0-8037-0136-5). Dial Bks Young.
Moncure, Jane B. The Magic Moon Machine. Hohag, Linda, illus. LC 87-30959. 32p. (ps-2). 1987. PLB 11.97 (ISBN 0-89565-410-5); pap. 6.96 (ISBN 0-89565-438-5). Childs World.
Murdock, M. S. Armageddon off Vesta. LC 88-51716. (Illus.). 288p. (Orig.). 1989. pap. 3.95 (ISBN 0-88038-761-0). TSR Inc.
—Hammer of Mars. LC 88-51715. (Illus.). 288p. (Orig.). 1989. pap. 3.95 (ISBN 0-88038-751-3). TSR Inc.
—Rebellion 2456. LC 88-51714. 288p. (Orig.). 1989. pap. 3.95 (ISBN 0-88038-728-9). TSR Inc.
Nord, Barry M. The Spaceship Earth. Palmer, Norman D., illus. 64p. (Orig.). (gr. 6 up). pap. 9.95 (ISBN 0-935656-09-X). Chrome Yellow.
Oana, Katherine. Spacebear Lands on Earth. Baird, Tate, ed. Wallace, Dorathye, illus. LC 86-51210. 16p. (Orig.). (ps up). 1988. pap. 3.72 (ISBN 0-914127-26-8). Univ Class.
Phillips, Dave. Space Age Mazes. (gr. 2 up). 1988. pap. 2.95 (ISBN 0-486-25659-6). Dover.
Pinkwater, D. Manus. Fat Men from Space. Pinkwater, D. Manus, illus. 64p. (gr. 4-6). 1980. pap. 2.95 (ISBN 0-440-44542-6, YB). Dell.
Pollotta, Nick & Foglio, Phil. Illegal Aliens. Foglio, Phil, illus. LC 88-51727. 320p. (Orig.). 1989. pap. 3.95 (ISBN 0-88038-715-7). TSR Inc.

Raichert, Lane. D.C. Hopper, the First Starbunny. Raichert, Lane, illus. LC 91-23055. 32p. (gr. 2-6). 1991. 15.95 (ISBN 1-880009-81-1, DC-P1). Blue Zero Pub.
Why is D.C. Hopper, a respected doctor of applied carrotology, building a rocket in his garage? Why has he left his job just when everybody needs him the most? Why is he walking around his apartment in a color coordinated space suit? Has the poor rabbit gone harebrained? No one is sure. All they know is that D.C. is obsessed with the dream of visiting space. Hurled from the safety of his home planet, D.C. Hopper discovers that the rewards from following your dreams are far more than can be imagined. In warm color pencil illustrations, rich with detail & humor, Lane Raichert's first picture book shows that there is truly hope for the future. D.C. Hopper, The First Starbunny, is printed on 100 pound acid free paper with illustrations printed at a line resolution of 225 - a level usually reserved for limited art prints. Don't miss the stunning achievement of this important new author. Blue Zero Publishing Company, PO Box 10699, Burbank, CA, 91510. Call (818) 840-0918 or fax (818) 840-8503.
Publisher Provided Annotation.

Richelson, Geraldine, et al. Star Wars Movie Storybook Trilogy. LC 87-12684. (Illus.). 144p. (gr. 3-7). 1987. pap. 11.95 (ISBN 0-394-89327-1, Random Juv). Random.
Rodgers, G. Kryptic: The Little Space Guy. (Illus.). 32p. (gr. 2-6). 1989. 10.95 (ISBN 0-88625-246-6). Durkin Hayes Pub.
Rotsler, William & Barish, Wendy. Star Trek II: Biographies. 160p. (gr. 3-7). 1982. pap. 3.80 (ISBN 0-671-46391-8, Little Simon). S&S Trade.
—Star Trek II: Short Stories. LC 82-17558. 160p. (gr. 3-7). 1982. pap. 2.95 (ISBN 0-671-46390-X, Little Simon). S&S Trade.
Rubel, Nicole. Pirate Jupiter & the Moondogs. Rubel, Nicole, illus. LC 84-13815. 32p. (ps-3). 1985. 11.95 (ISBN 0-8037-0145-4); PLB 11.89 (ISBN 0-8037-0146-2). Dial Bks Young.
Rubinstein, Gillian. Space Demons. LC 87-27542. 240p. (gr. 5-9). 1988. 13.95 (ISBN 0-8037-0534-4). Dial Bks Young.
Rymer, Alta M. Oopletrump's Odyssey, Bk. 4. Rymer, Alta M., illus. LC 85-61861. 38p. (Orig.). (gr. 4-6). 1987. pap. text ed. 12.50 (ISBN 0-9600792-5-4). Rymer Bks.
Sargent, Pamela. Earthseed. LC 79-2666. 224p. (gr. 7 up). 1987. pap. 2.95 (ISBN 0-06-447045-8, Trophy). HarpC Child Bks.
Saunders, Susan. Runaway Spaceship. 64p. 1985. pap. 2.25 (ISBN 0-553-15463-X). Bantam.
Svaren, Jacqueline. Lojor's Letters: A Space-Age Story about a Boy & a Gnome & Learning Italic Handwriting. Kisvet, Fran, illus. Reynolds, Lloyd J., intro. by. LC 78-60185. (Illus.). 72p. (Orig.). (gr. 1 up). 1981. pap. 10.00 (ISBN 0-931474-04-3). TBW Bks.
Sweeney, Toni. Spacedog's Best Friend. Sweeney, Toni, illus. (Orig.). (gr. 5-12). 1989. pap. 6.95 (ISBN 0-933025-13-0). Blue Bird Pub.
Teague, Mark. Moog-Moog Space Barber. (gr. 4-7). 1990. 13.95 (ISBN 0-590-43332-6). Scholastic Inc.
Wells, H. G. First Men in the Moon. Lowndes, R. A., intro. by. (gr. 7 up). pap. 1.25 (ISBN 0-8049-0078-7, CL-78). Airmont.
Williams, Geoffrey & Regan, Dennis. Adventures in the Solar System. Svenson, Borje, illus. 64p. 1986. 9.95x (ISBN 0-8431-1552-1); incl. cass. 13.95x (ISBN 0-8431-1553-X). Price stern.
Yolen, Jane. Commander Toad & the Space Pirates. Degen, Bruce, illus. 64p. (gr. 1-4). 1987. 9.99 (ISBN 0-698-30749-6, Coward); pap. 5.95 (ISBN 0-698-20633-9, Coward). Putnam Pub Group.
Zebrowski, George. The Stars Will Speak. LC 85-42638. 224p. (gr. 7 up). 1987. pap. 2.95 (ISBN 0-06-447050-4, Trophy). HarpC Child Bks.

SPACE FLIGHT, MANNED

see Manned Space Flight

SPACE FLIGHT TO THE MOON

see also Apollo Project; Moon–Exploration

Sullivan, George. Day We Walked On the Moon. 1990. pap. 4.95 (ISBN 0-590-42760-1). Scholastic Inc.

SPACE MEDICINE

see also Manned Space Flight

Rambaut, Paul. Space Medicine. Head, J. J., ed. LC 84-45837. (Illus.). 16p. (Orig.). (gr. 10 up). 1985. pap. text ed. 2.15 (ISBN 0-89278-366-4, 45-9766). Carolina Biological.

SPACE PROBES

Couper, Heather & Henbest, Nigel. Spaceprobes & Satellites. (Illus.). 32p. (gr. 4-6). 1987. PLB 8.99 (ISBN 0-531-10360-9). Watts.

SPACE RESEARCH

see Outer Space–Exploration; Space Sciences

SPACE SCIENCES

see also Astronautics; Astronomy; Outer Space; Space Medicine

Cabellero, Jane A. Aerospace Projects for Young Children. rev. ed. (Illus.). 112p. (Orig.). (ps-3). 1987. pap. 14.95 (ISBN 0-89334-100-2). Humanics Ltd.
Fradin, Dennis. Spacelab. LC 84-12702. (Illus.). 48p. (gr. k-4). 1984. PLB 14.60 (ISBN 0-516-01930-9); pap. 4.95 (ISBN 0-516-41930-7). Childrens.
Gardner, Robert. Projects in Space Science. (Illus.). 136p. (gr. 4-8). 1989. PLB 11.98 (ISBN 0-671-63639-1); PLB 8.99s.p.; pap. 4.95 (ISBN 0-671-65993-6); pap. 3.71s.p. Messner.
Kerrod, Robin. See Inside a Space Station. rev. ed. Warwick Press, ed. 32p. (gr. 4-9). 1988. PLB 11.90 (ISBN 0-531-19031-5, Warwick). Watts.
Lampton, Christopher. Space Sciences. (Illus.). 96p. (gr. 4 up). 1983. PLB 10.40 (ISBN 0-531-04539-0). Watts.
McKay, David W. & Smith, Bruce G. Space Science Projects for Young Scientists. LC 86-7745. (Illus.). 128p. (gr. 7-12). 1986. PLB 12.90 (ISBN 0-531-10244-0). Watts.
Trefil, James S. Living in Space. LC 81-14532. 128p. (gr. 8 up). 1981. 12.95 (ISBN 0-684-17171-6, Scribner). Macmillan.
Vogt, Gregory. Space Laboratories. (Illus.). 32p. (gr. 4-6). 1989. PLB 11.90 (ISBN 0-531-10404-4). Watts.
—Space Stations. Sloan, Frank, ed. (Illus.). 32p. (gr. 7-9). 1990. PLB 11.90 (ISBN 0-531-10460-5). Watts.

SPACE SHIPS–PILOTS

see Astronauts

SPACE TELECOMMUNICATION

see Interstellar Communication

SPACE TRAVEL

see Interplanetary Voyages; Manned Space Flight; Space Flight

SPACE VEHICLES

see also Artificial Satellites; Space Probes

Abernathy, Susan. Space Machines. LaPadula, Tom, illus. (gr. 3-6). 1991. 8.50 (ISBN 0-307-17872-2, Golden Pr). Western Pub.
Apfel, Necia H. Space Station. (Illus.). 72p. (gr. 4-9). 1987. PLB 10.40 (ISBN 0-531-10394-3). Watts.
Barrett, Norman. The Picture World of Space Shuttles. (Illus.). 32p. (gr. k-4). 1990. PLB 11.40 (ISBN 0-531-14056-3). Watts.

—Spacecraft. LC 85-50160. (Illus.). 32p. (gr. k-6). 1986. lib. bdg. 10.90 (ISBN 0-531-10006-5). Watts.

Blocksma, Dewey & Blocksma, Mary. Space-Crafting: Invent Your Own Flying Spaceships. Seiden, Art, illus. LC 86-9422. 64p. (gr. 2-6). 1986. PLB 11.95 (ISBN 0-671-66300-3). S&S Trade.

Bolognese, Don. Drawing Spaceships & Other Spacecraft. (Illus.). 64p. (gr. 4-6). 1982. PLB 10.90 (ISBN 0-531-04470-X). Watts.

Branley, Franklyn M. From Sputnik to Space Shuttle: Into the New Space Age. LC 85-43186. (Illus.). 80p. (gr. 3-6). 1986. 12.95 (ISBN 0-690-04531-X, Crowell Jr Bks); PLB 12.89 (ISBN 0-690-04533-6, Crowell Jr Bks). HarpC Child Bks.

—Rockets & Satellites. rev. ed. Maestro, Giulio, illus. LC 86-47748. 32p. (ps-3). 1987. (Crowell Jr Bks); PLB 13.89 (ISBN 0-690-04593-X). HarpC Child Bks.

—Rockets & Satellites. rev. ed. Maestro, Giulio, illus. LC 86-27047. 32p. (ps-3). 1987. pap. 4.50 (ISBN 0-06-445061-9, Trophy). HarpC Child Bks.

Dwiggins, Don. Flying the Space Shuttles. (Illus.). 64p. (gr. 3-7). 1985. 11.95 (ISBN 0-396-08510-5, Putnam). Putnam Pub Group.

Fichter, George S. The Space Shuttle. (Illus.). 72p. (gr. 4 up). 1981. lib. bdg. 10.40 (ISBN 0-531-04354-1). Watts.

Fradin, Dennis B. Skylab. LC 83-23180. (Illus.). 48p. (gr. k-4). 1984. lib. bdg. 14.60 (ISBN 0-516-01727-6). Childrens.

Friskey, Margaret. Lanzaderas Espaciales. Kratky, Lada, tr. from ENG. LC 81-16648. (SPA., Illus.). 48p. (gr. k-4). 1984. lib. bdg. 14.60 (ISBN 0-516-31655-9); pap. 4.95 (ISBN 0-516-51655-8). Childrens.

Hamilton, Sue. Space Shuttle Challenger's Explosion. Hamilton, John, ed. (Illus.). 32p. (gr. 4). 1989. PLB 11.95 (ISBN 0-939179-40-7). Abdo & Dghtrs.

Hawkes, Nigel. Space Shuttle. LC 82-50855. (Illus.). 40p. (gr. 4 up). 1983. PLB 12.40 (ISBN 0-531-04583-8). Watts.

Italia, Bob. Voyagers One & Two. Walner, Rosemary, ed. (Illus.). 32p. (gr. 4). 1990. PLB 11.95 (ISBN 0-939179-96-2). Abdo & Dghtrs.

Jay, Michael. Space Shuttle. (Illus.). 32p. (gr. 2-4). 1984. lib. bdg. 7.99 (ISBN 0-531-04708-3). Watts.

Kerrod, Robin. Spacecraft. Full, Roger, et al, illus. LC 88-17655. 24p. (Orig.). (gr. 2-5). 1989. PLB 5.99 (ISBN 0-394-99989-4); pap. 2.95 (ISBN 0-394-89989-X). Random.

McCarter, James. The Space Shuttle Disaster. Caulkins, Janet, ed. (Illus.). 32p. (gr. 1-6). 1988. PLB 10.90 (ISBN 0-531-18164-2, Pub. by Bookwright Pr). Watts.

Moche, Dinah. The Big Book of Real Spacecraft. Guzzi, George, illus. 48p. (gr. 1-4). 1990. 7.95 (ISBN 0-448-19190-3, G&D). Putnam Pub Group.

Radlauer, Ruth & Young, Carolynn. Voyagers One & Two: Robots in Space. LC 86-29922. (Illus.). 48p. (gr. 4 up). 1987. PLB 15.93 (ISBN 0-516-07840-2). Childrens.

The Space Boat. (Illus.). (ps-2). 1990. 3.50 (ISBN 0-7214-1316-1); parent/tchr's. guide 3.95; Series 9011-3, No. 3. activity bk. 2.95 (ISBN 0-7214-3222-0). Ladybird Bks.

Spizzirri Publishing Co. Staff. Shuttle Craft: An Educational Coloring Book. Spizzirri, Linda, ed. (Illus.). 32p. (gr. 1-8). 1986. pap. 1.95 (ISBN 0-86545-077-3). Spizzirri.

—Space Craft: An Educational Coloring Book. Spizzirri, Linda, ed. Spizzirri, Peter M., illus. 32p. (gr. 1-8). 1981. pap. 1.95 (ISBN 0-86545-036-6). Spizzirri.

Taylor, L. B., Jr. Space Shuttle. LC 78-4777. (Illus.). 128p. (gr. 6 up). 1979. 12.95 (ISBN 0-690-03897-6, Crowell Jr Bks). HarpC Child Bks.

Vogt, Gregory. An Album of Modern Spaceships. (Illus.). 96p. (gr. 4 up). 1987. PLB 13.90 (ISBN 0-531-10397-8). Watts.

—The Space Shuttle. (Illus.). 112p. (gr. 4-6). 1991. PLB 19.25 (ISBN 1-56294-049-X). Millbrook Pr.

—Spaceships. (Illus.). 32p. (gr. 4-6). 1989. PLB 11.90 (ISBN 0-531-10405-2). Watts.

—Spaceships. (Illus.). 32p. (gr. 1). 1988. 11.90 (ISBN 0-318-37440-4). Watts.

SPACE VEHICLES–MODELS

Halpin, Myra J. The Enterprise & Beyond. Baloy, Rosemarie, ed. & illus. 127p. 1988. pap. text ed. 12.95 (ISBN 0-944620-00-0). M J Halpin.

SPAIN

Getting to Know Spain. 48p. 1989. 7.95 (ISBN 0-8442-7627-8, Passport Bks). Natl Textbk.

Howard, John. Spain. (Illus.). 48p. (gr. 5-10). 1988. PLB 16.98 (ISBN 0-382-09470-0); pap. 6.95 (ISBN 0-382-09477-8). Silver Burdett Pr.

James, Ian. Spain. (Illus.). 32p. (gr. k-6). 1989. PLB 11.90 (ISBN 0-531-10834-1). Watts.

Lye, Keith. Passport to Spain. (Illus.). 48p. (gr. 4-6). 1987. PLB 12.90 (ISBN 0-531-10402-8). Watts.

Miller, Arthur. Spain. (Illus.). 96p. (gr. 5 up). 1989. lib. bdg. 14.95 (ISBN 1-55546-795-4). Chelsea Hse.

Rutland, Jonathan. Take a Trip to Spain. LC 80-52718. (gr. 1-3). 1981. PLB 7.99 (ISBN 0-531-00991-2). Watts.

Tollhurst, Marilyn. Spain. (Illus.). 48p. (gr. 4-8). 1989. lib. bdg. 14.98 (ISBN 0-382-09821-8). Silver Burdett Pr.

SPAIN–FICTION

Baroja. Las Inquietudes de Shanti Andia. (gr. 7-12). 1973. pap. 5.95 (ISBN 0-88436-062-8, 70267). EMC.

Bunuel. Las Tres de la Madrugada. 1972. pap. 4.95 (ISBN 0-88436-061-X, 70265). EMC.

De Cervantes, Miguel. Don Quixote. (gr. 11 up). 1967. pap. 2.75 (ISBN 0-8049-0153-8, CL-153). Airmont.

Leaf, Munro. The Story of Ferdinand. Lawson, Robert, illus. LC 36-19452. (gr. k-3). 1936. pap. 11.95 (ISBN 0-670-67424-9). Viking Child Bks.

O'Dell, Scott. The Spanish Smile. (gr. 7 up). 1982. 12.95 (ISBN 0-395-32867-5). HM.

Reeves, James, retold by. Exploits of Don Quixote. Ardizzone, Edward, illus. LC 85-11170. (gr. 5 up). 1985. 12.95 (ISBN 0-87226-025-9, Bedrick Blackie); (Bedrick Blackie). P Bedrick Bks.

SPAIN–HISTORY

The Spanish Armada. (Illus.). (gr. 5 up). 3.50 (ISBN 0-7214-1093-6). Ladybird Bks.

SPAIN–HISTORY–FICTION

Cervantes. Don Quijote de la Mancha: Primer Parte. (gr. 7-12). pap. 5.95 (ISBN 0-88436-056-3, 70275). EMC.

Lehmann, Marcus. Family y Aguilar. Breuer, Jacob, adapted by. (gr. 7 up). 8.95 (ISBN 0-87306-122-5). Feldheim.

SPAIN–HISTORY–711-1516

McCaughrean, Geraldine. El Cid. Ambros, Victor G., illus. 128p. (gr. 5 up). 1989. 19.95 (ISBN 0-19-276077-7). Oxford U Pr.

SPAIN–HISTORY–CIVIL WAR, 1936-1939

Katz, William L. & Crawford, Marc. The Lincoln Brigade: A Picture History. LC 88-27522. (Illus.). 96p. (gr. 5 up). 1989. 14.95 (ISBN 0-689-31406-X, Atheneum Child Bk). Macmillan Child Grp.

SPANISH AMERICA

see Latin America

SPANISH-AMERICAN WAR, 1898

see U. S.–History–War of 1898

SPANISH LANGUAGE

Bouwman, Constance, et al. Beginning Spanish: A Teacher's Manual: Comprehension Based Activities for the Learnables, Book One. Baker, Syd, illus. 163p. (gr. 7 up). 1989. pap. text ed. 28.00 (ISBN 0-939990-78-4). Intl Linguistics.

Colvin, L. & Irving, N. Essential Spanish. (Illus.). 64p. 1990. lib. bdg. 12.96 (ISBN 0-88110-421-3); pap. 5.95 (ISBN 0-7460-0320-X). EDC.

Daizovi, Lonnie G. & Saxon, Ed. Spanish Alive, Level I. (SPA., Illus.). 177p. (Orig.). (ps-3). 1990. Repr. of 1986 ed. songbook & cassette 11.95 (ISBN 0-935301-50-X); tchr's. manual 18.95 (ISBN 0-935301-59-3). Vibrante Pr.

De Brunhoff, Laurent. Je Parle Espagnol avec Babar. (FRE., Illus.). (gr. 4-6). 15.95 (ISBN 0-685-11273-X). French & Eur.

Hazzan, Anne-Francoise. Let's Learn Spanish Coloring Book. (Illus.). 64p. (gr. 4 up). 1988. pap. 3.95 (ISBN 0-8442-7549-2, Passport Bks). Natl Textbk.

Kidship Associates Staff. Lluvia de Palabras. Kidship Associates Staff, illus. (SPA.). 109p. (gr. 1-3). 1988. pap. text ed. 2.00 (ISBN 1-878742-00-0). Kidship Assoc.

Mahoney, Judy & Cronan, Mary. Teach Me More Spanish. 20p. (ps-5). 1989. incl. cassette 13.95 (ISBN 0-934633-14-2). Teach Me.

Martinez, Eliseo R. & Martinez, Irma C. Spanish Readiness Skills, Vol. 1. (Illus.). 78p. (ps-3). 1986. wkbk. 8.75 (ISBN 1-878300-01-6). Childrens Work.

Pen Notes Staff. Learn to Print Spanish: (Aprendiendo a Escribir las Letras. (ps up). 1989. Bilingual instrns. 10.95 (ISBN 0-939564-17-3). Pen Notes.

Spanish in a Taco Shell. (ENG & SPA.). (gr. 2-8). Date not set. 8.95 (ISBN 0-935303-04-9). Victory Pub.

Wilkes, Angela. Spanish for Beginners. 48p. (ps-1). 1988. 7.95 (ISBN 0-8442-7628-6, Passport Bks). Natl Textbk.

Winitz, Harris. Basic Structures - Spanish, Bk. 1: A Textbook for the Learnables. Sagarna, Blanca, tr. Baker, Syd, illus. 106p. (gr. 7 up). 1990. pap. text ed. 42.00 incl. 4 cass. tapes. Intl Linguistics.

Wolfe, Gerard R. Spanish Study Aid. 1978. pap. 2.75 (ISBN 0-87738-033-3). Youth Ed.

SPANISH LANGUAGE–CONVERSATION AND PHRASE BOOKS

Berlitz. Berlitz Jr. Spanish. (ps-2). 1989. bds. 19.95 incl. cassette (ISBN 0-689-71317-7, Aladdin). Macmillan Child Grp.

Cosby, Bill, et al. Universal Spanish--Cambios: Descubriendo lo Mejor Que Hay en Ti. Callejas, Juan, et al, eds. Trevant, Pierre, tr. from ENG. Ordonez, Maria A. & Espada, Frank, illus. (SPA.). 181p. (Orig.). (gr. 6-8). 1988. pap. text ed. 6.85 (ISBN 0-933419-44-9). Quest Intl.

Finocchiaro, Mary, ed. Children's Living Spanish. (Illus.). 1987. manual 5.00 (ISBN 0-517-56335-5); manual, incl. cassette 20.00 (ISBN 0-517-56333-9); dictionary 5.00 (ISBN 0-517-56336-3). Crown.

Foster, Lorri & Gitchel, Sam. Hablemos Acerca del...S-E-X-O: Un Libro para Toda la Familia Acerca de la Pubertad. (SPA & ENG., Illus.). 90p. (gr. 4-8). 1985. pap. 4.95 (ISBN 0-9610122-1-8). Plan Par Ctrl CA.

Gregorich, Barbara. Los Colores. Hoffman, Joan, ed. Shepherd-Bartram, tr. from ENG. Pape, Richard, illus. (SPA.). 32p. (Orig.). (ps). 1987. wkbk. 1.99 (ISBN 0-938256-78-5). Sch Zone Pub Co.

Palmer, Helen. A Fish Out of Water in English & Spanish. Rivera, Carlos, tr. (Illus.). (gr. k-3). 1967. lib. bdg. 5.99 (ISBN 0-394-91598-4). Random.

Ronnholm, Ursula O. Aprende a Leer a Trave's de Musica, Juegos y Ritmos. rev. ed. Rabell, Edda, ed. & tr. Montero, Miguel, illus. (SPA.). 42p. (gr. k-2). 1989. pap. text ed. 20.00 incl. cass. (ISBN 0-941911-07-1). Two Way Bilingual.

Sagarna, Blanca. Medios de Transporte: Transportation - Spanish. Baker, Syd, illus. Winitz, Harris, intro. by. (SPA., Illus.). 50p. (gr. 7 up). 1989. pap. text ed. 20.00 incl. cassette (ISBN 0-939990-75-X). Intl Linguistics.

Saloom, Barbara B. Conversational Spanish: Quick & Easy. Cogger, Virginia & Ricardo-Gil, Jose, eds. Mrvlein, Mark, illus. 120p. (Orig.). 1988. pap. text ed. 12.95 (ISBN 0-9627755-0-9). B B Saloom.

Segal, Bertha E. Aprendemos el Espanol por Medio de Accion. (SPA.). 106p. (Orig.). (gr. 3-12). 1987. pap. text ed. 12.50 (ISBN 0-938395-12-2). B Segal.

Utley, Derek. Espana Viva. (SPA.). 224p. 1988. pap. text ed. 11.50 (ISBN 0-8219-0335-7, 70291); tchr's. guide 5.95 (ISBN 0-8219-0336-5, TG-70826); text-wkbk. 18.95 (ISBN 0-8219-0337-3, TXTWK-70662). EMC.

SPANISH LANGUAGE–DICTIONARIES

Bailey, Kenneth. Enciclopedia Juvenil Molino en Color, 5 vols. (SPA.). 510p. 1972. Set. leatherette 150.00 (ISBN 84-272-5900-X, S-22861). French & Eur.

Enciclopedia Tematica Juvenil: La Agricultura, los Arboles, la Arqueologia, las Aves, la Caramica, el Cuerpo Humano, la Fisica, los Insectos, los Minerales, los Animales Prehistoricos, el Transporte, la Vivienda, 12 vols. (SPA.). 624p. 1976. Set. leatherette 250.00 (ISBN 84-201-0188-5). French & Eur.

Langronet, Michel. Enciclopedia Juvenil Larousse, 8 vols. 4th ed. (SPA.). 1552p. 1978. Set. 495.00 (ISBN 84-7178-241-3, S-50479). French & Eur.

Passport Books Staff, ed. Let's Learn Spanish: Picture Dictionary. Goodman, Marlene, illus. 72p. Date not set. 9.95 (ISBN 0-8442-7558-1). Natl Textbk.

Sheheen, Dennis, illus. A Child's Picture English-Spanish Dictionary. LC 84-71801. (gr. k-2). 1984. 9.95 (ISBN 0-915361-11-6, 09407-3, Dist. by Watts). Adama Pubs Inc.

SPANISH LANGUAGE–DICTIONARIES–ENGLISH

Webster's Spanish-English - English-Spanish Dictionary. (ENG & SPA.). (gr. 4 up). 1988. pap. 3.95 (ISBN 0-318-37119-7). Scholastic Inc.

SPANISH LANGUAGE–GRAMMAR

Glenn, Eula M. The Direct Objects Pronouns Move to the Barrio. Phipps-Bazmore, Effie, ed. (Illus.). 50p. (gr. 3). 1989. pap. text ed. write for info. Eula Intl Pub.

—King Definite Articles. Phipps-Bazmore, Effie, ed. Wilson, James P., illus. 40p. (Orig.). (gr. 3). 1989. pap. text ed. write for info. Eula Intl Pub.

—King Definite Articles Meets His Bride. Phipps-Bazmore, Effie, ed. Wilson, James P., illus. 35p. (Orig.). (gr. 3). 1989. pap. text ed. write for info. Eula Intl Pub.

Hendirckson, James M. Spanish Grammar Flipper: A Guide to Correct Spanish Usage. 49p. (gr. 5 up). 1988. trade edition 5.95 (ISBN 1-878383-11-6). C Lee Pubns.

Rico, Armando B. School Adventures: Aventuras Escolares. 27p. (Orig.). 1989. pap. text ed. 4.95 (ISBN 1-879219-04-2). Veracruz Pubs.

Ronnholm, Ursula O. Mi Libro de Escritura. Montero, Miguel, illus. (SPA.). 74p. (gr. k-3). 1986. 4.00 (ISBN 0-941911-05-5). Two Way Bilingual.

Thomas, Keith A. The Idioms. Thomas, Keith A., illus. (SPA & ENG.). 44p. (gr. 3 up). pap. write for info. (ISBN 0-9617451-4-2). Cross Lengua Prod.

SPANISH LANGUAGE–READERS

Ada, Alma F. Manzano, Manzano! Kalthoff, Sandra C., illus. 24p. (Orig.). (gr. k-3). 1989. Six-Pack Set. pap. text ed. 25.50 (ISBN 0-917837-46-0). Hampton-Brown.

—Manzano, Manzano! (Big Book) Kalthoff, Sandra C., illus. (SPA.). 24p. (Orig.). (gr. k-3). 1989. pap. text ed. 24.95 (ISBN 0-917837-09-6). Hampton-Brown.

—El Oso Mas Elegante. Kalthoff, Sandra C., illus. 24p. (Orig.). (gr. k-3). 1989. Six-Pack Set. pap. text ed. 25.50 (ISBN 0-917837-43-6). Hampton-Brown.

—El Oso Mas Elegante (Big Book) Kalthoff, Sandra C., illus. (SPA.). 24p. (Orig.). (gr. k-3). 1989. pap. text ed. 24.95 (ISBN 0-917837-10-X). Hampton-Brown.

—Los Seis Deseos de la Jirafa (Big Book) Roy, Doug, illus. (SPA.). 16p. (Orig.). (gr. k-3). 1988. pap. text ed. 24.95 (ISBN 0-917837-02-9). Hampton-Brown.

—Una Semilla Nada Mas (Big Book) Remkiewicz, Frank, illus. (SPA.). 16p. (Orig.). (gr. k-3). 1990. pap. text ed. 28.95 (ISBN 0-917837-56-8). Hampton-Brown.

Amery, Heather. First Thousand Words in Spanish. Cartwrigh, Stephen, illus. 50p. (ps-7). 1979. 11.95 (ISBN 0-86020-277-1). EDC.

Behrens, June. El Libro de los Modales. LC 79-22377. (SPA., Illus.). 32p. (gr. k-3). 1987. PLB 14.60 (ISBN 0-516-38750-2); pap. 3.95 (ISBN 0-516-58750-1). Childrens.

Big Book - Tape Set. (ENG & SPA.). 16p. (Orig.). (gr. k-3). 1990. Set. pap. text ed. 176.50 incl. tchr's. ed. (ISBN 0-917837-61-4). Hampton-Brown.

Big Book Classroom Set. (ENG & SPA.). 32p. (Orig.). (gr. k-3). 1990. Set. pap. text ed. 87.50 incl. tchr's. guide (ISBN 0-917837-68-1). Hampton-Brown.

Big Book Set. (ENG & SPA., Illus.). 32p. (Orig.). (gr. k-3). 1988. Set. pap. 99.50 incl. tchr's. guide (ISBN 0-917837-50-9). Hampton-Brown.

Blocksma, Mary. Chirrinchinchina - Que Hay en la Tina? Martin, Sandra K., illus. LC 84-12139. (SPA.). 24p. (ps-2). 1988. PLB 12.33 (ISBN 0-516-31586-2); pap. 3.95 (ISBN 0-516-51586-1). Childrens.

Bonsall, Crosby N. Caso del Forastero Hambriento. Belpre, Pura, tr. Bonsall, Crosby N., illus. LC 69-14449. (SPA.). 64p. (gr. k-3). 1969. PLB 10.89 (ISBN 0-06-020574-1). HarpC Child Bks.

Classroom Set. (ENG & SPA.). 16p. (Orig.). (gr. k-3). 1990. Set. pap. text ed. 248.00 incl. tchr's guide (ISBN 0-917837-60-6). Hampton-Brown.
Classroom Set. (ENG & SPA.). 768p. (Orig.). (gr. k-3). 1990. pap. 143.00 incl. tchr's. guide, 27p. (ISBN 0-685-38986-3). Hampton-Brown.
Classroom Single-Copy Set. (ENG & SPA.). 32p. (Orig.). (gr. k-3). 1990. Set. pap. 39.50 incl. tchr's. guide (ISBN 0-917837-69-X). Hampton-Brown.
Content Area Connections (Single-Copy Set) (SPA.). 32p. (Orig.). (gr. k-3). 1990. Set. pap. text ed. 17.25 (ISBN 0-917837-67-3). Hampton-Brown.
Cuentitos Mios. (SPA.). 72p. (Orig.). (gr. k-3). 1988. pap. text ed. 6.50 (ISBN 0-917837-08-8). Hampton-Brown.
Cuentitos Mios. (SPA.). 65p. (Orig.). (gr. k-3). 1990. pap. text ed. 3.95 (ISBN 0-917837-58-4). Hampton-Brown.
Cuentitos Mios Twenty-Pack. (SPA., Illus.). 72p. (Orig.). (gr. k-3). 1988. Set. pap. text ed. 119.60 (ISBN 0-917837-51-7). Hampton-Brown.
Cuentitos Mios Twenty-Pack. (SPA.). 65p. (Orig.). (gr. k-3). 1990. Set. pap. text ed. 73.00 (ISBN 0-917837-65-7). Hampton-Brown.
Cumpiano, Ina. Pan, Pan, Gran Pan (Big Book) Murdocca, Sal, illus. (SPA.). 16p. (Orig.). (gr. k-3). 1990. pap. text ed. 28.95 (ISBN 0-917837-52-5). Hampton-Brown.
Dr. Seuss. The Cat in the Hat in English & Spanish. Dr. Seuss, illus. Rivera, Carlos, tr. LC 67-5819. (Illus.). 72p. (gr. 1-2). 1967. 6.95 (ISBN 0-394-81626-9); lib. bdg. 6.99 (ISBN 0-394-91626-3). Beginner.
Eastman, Patricia. A Veces las Cosas Cambian. Fleishman, Seymour, illus. LC 83-10090. (SPA.). 32p. (ps-2). 1988. PLB 11.93 (ISBN 0-516-32044-0); pap. 2.95 (ISBN 0-516-52044-X). Childrens.
Emberley, Rebecca. My House, Mi Casa: A Book in Two Languages. Emberley, Rebecca, illus. LC 89-12893. (ps-2). 1990. 14.95 (ISBN 0-316-23637-3). Little.
Four Paperback Classroom Set. (SPA.). 32p. (Orig.). (gr. k-3). 1990. Set. pap. text ed. 20.75 (ISBN 0-917837-74-6). Hampton-Brown.
Garcia, Maria. The Adventures of Connie & Diego. rev. ed. (ENG & SPA., Illus.). 32p. (gr. 2-9). 1987. 12.95 (ISBN 0-89239-028-X). Childrens Book Pr.
Jarvis-Sladky, Kay. Un Grabado de Goya: Reader 3. Bakke, Eric, illus. LC 81-7783. (SPA.). 40p. (Orig.). (gr. 7-12). 1982. pap. 2.50 (ISBN 0-88436-860-2, 70261). EMC.
—La Guitarra Misteriosa: Reader 1. Bakke, Eric, illus. LC 81-7785. (SPA.). 40p. (Orig.). (gr. 7-12). 1982. pap. 2.50 (ISBN 0-88436-858-0, 70259). EMC.
—El Penitente Elusivo: Reader 4. Bakke, Eric, illus. LC 81-7842. (SPA., Orig.). (gr. 7-12). 1982. pap. 2.50 (ISBN 0-88436-861-0, 70262). EMC.
—Secretos de Famalia: Reader 2. Bakke, Eric, illus. LC 81-7780. (SPA.). 40p. (Orig.). (gr. 7-12). 1982. pap. 2.50 (ISBN 0-88436-859-9, 70260). EMC.
Kessler, Leonard. Aqui Viene el Ponchado. Belpre, Pura, tr. Kessler, Leonard, illus. LC 69-14451. (SPA.). 64p. (gr. k-3). 1969. PLB 11.89 (ISBN 0-06-023154-8). HarpC Child Bks.
Kratky, Lada J. Chirrinchinchina. Kalthoff, Sandra C., illus. (SPA.). 24p. (Orig.). (gr. k-3). 1989. Six-Pack Set. pap. text ed. 25.50 (ISBN 0-917837-44-4). Hampton-Brown.
—Chirrinchinchina Que Hay en la Tina? Kalthoff, Sandra C., illus. (SPA.). 24p. (Orig.). (gr. k-3). 1989. pap. text ed. 24.95 (ISBN 0-917837-11-8). Hampton-Brown.
—Chirrinchinchina Que Hay en la Tina? Kalthoff, Sandra C., illus. (SPA.). 24p. (Orig.). (gr. k-3). 1989. pap. text ed. 10.25 small book (ISBN 0-917837-13-4). Hampton-Brown.
—El Chivo en la Huerta (Big Book) Remkiewicz, Frank, illus. (SPA.). 16p. (Orig.). (gr. k-3). 1988. pap. text ed. 24.95 (ISBN 0-917837-04-5). Hampton-Brown.
—La Gallinita, el Gallo y el Frijol (Big Book) Yerkes, Lane, illus. (SPA.). 24p. (Orig.). (gr. k-3). Date not set. pap. text ed. 28.95 (ISBN 0-917837-05-3). Hampton-Brown.
—Pequeno Coala. Kalthoff, Sandra C., illus. (SPA.). 24p. (Orig.). (gr. k-3). 1989. Six-Pack Set. pap. text ed. 25.50 (ISBN 0-917837-45-2). Hampton-Brown.
—Pequeno Coala Busca Casa. Kalthoff, Sandra C., illus. (SPA.). 24p. (Orig.). (gr. k-3). 1989. pap. text ed. 10.25 (ISBN 0-917837-14-2). Hampton-Brown.
—Pequeno Coala Busca Casa (Big Book) Kalthoff, Sandra C., illus. (SPA.). 24p. (Orig.). (gr. k-3). 1989. pap. text ed. 24.95 (ISBN 0-917837-12-6). Hampton-Brown.
—Pinta, Pinta, Gregorita (Big Book) Hockerman, Dennis, illus. (SPA.). 16p. (Orig.). (gr. k-3). 1990. pap. text ed. 28.95 (ISBN 0-917837-53-3). Hampton-Brown.
—Veo, Veo, Que Veo? (Big Book) Yerkes, Lane, illus. (SPA.). 16p. (Orig.). (gr. k-3). 1990. pap. text ed. 28.95 (ISBN 0-917837-57-6). Hampton-Brown.
Library-Bound Single Copy Set. (ENG & SPA.). 128p. (gr. k-3). 1990. PLB 59.00 incl. tchr's. guide, 27p. (ISBN 1-56334-002-X). Hampton-Brown.
Lionni, Leo. Pulgada a Pulgada. (SPA., Illus.). (gr. k-1). 1961. 10.95 (ISBN 0-8392-3030-3). Astor-Honor.
Lopez, N. C. King Pancho & the First Clock. Gutierrez, M., illus. LC 63-16396. 32p. (gr. 2-7). 1967. PLB 9.95 (ISBN 0-87783-020-7); pap. 3.94 deluxe ed. (ISBN 0-87783-098-3); cassette 7.94x (ISBN 0-685-03701-0). Oddo.
Lopez, Norbert. Cuento Del Rey Pancho y el Primer Reloj. LC 70-108730. (Illus.). 32p. (gr. 2-7). 1970. PLB 9.95 (ISBN 0-87783-010-X); pap. 3.94 deluxe ed. (ISBN 0-87783-104-1); cassette 7.94x (ISBN 0-685-03700-2). Oddo.
McKissack, Patricia & McKissack, Fredrick. Ada, la Desordenada: Messy Bessey. Hackney, Richard, illus. LC 87-15079. (SPA.). 32p. (ps-2). 1988. PLB 11.93 (ISBN 0-516-32083-1); pap. 2.95 (ISBN 0-516-52083-0). Childrens.
—Los Tres Chivitos. Dunnington, Tom, illus. LC 86-33450. (SPA.). 32p. (ps-2). 1988. PLB 11.93 (ISBN 0-516-32366-0); pap. 3.95 (ISBN 0-516-52366-X). Childrens.
Matthias, Catherine. Los Gatos Me Gustan Mas. Dunnington, Tom, illus. LC 83-7215. (SPA.). 32p. (ps-2). 1988. PLB 11.93 (ISBN 0-516-32041-6); pap. 2.95 (ISBN 0-516-52041-5). Childrens.
Moreno, Leslie B. Companeros: Activity Book in Spanish & English for Children. 144p. (gr. 7-11). 1983. pap. 5.95 (ISBN 0-917168-09-7). Executive Comm.
Neasi, Barbara J. Escuchame. Sharp, Gene, illus. LC 86-10665. (SPA.). 32p. (ps-2). 1988. PLB 11.93 (ISBN 0-516-32072-6); pap. 2.95 (ISBN 0-516-52072-5). Childrens.
—Igual Que Yo. Axeman, Lois, illus. LC 83-23154. (SPA.). 32p. (ps-2). 1988. PLB 11.93 (ISBN 0-516-32047-5); pap. 2.95 (ISBN 0-516-52047-4). Childrens.
Ozaeta, Pablo. Mis Primeros Cuentos. Frank, Marjorie & Lono, Luz P., eds. Sussman, Dee, illus. LC 75-16546. (gr. 4-8). 1975. pap. 4.95 student ed. (ISBN 0-8325-9642-6); teachers's ed. 7.95 (ISBN 0-8325-9641-8); program package (1 teacher's ed. & 10 student wkbks.) 49.95 (ISBN 0-8325-9640-X). Natl Textbk.
Padilla, Jaime & Taylor, Maurie. Easy Spanish Word Games. (SPA., Illus.). 64p. (gr. 4 up). 1983. pap. 4.95 (ISBN 0-8442-7242-6, Passport Bks.). Natl Textbk.
Paperback Single Copy Set, 4 bks. (ENG & SPA.). 128p. (Orig.). (gr. k-3). 1990. pap. 39.00 incl. tchr's. guide, 27p. Hampton-Brown.
Petrie, Catherine. A Pedro Perez le Gustan los Camiones. Warshaw, Jerry, illus. LC 81-17076. (SPA.). 32p. (ps-2). 1988. PLB 11.93 (ISBN 0-516-33525-1); pap. 2.95 (ISBN 0-516-53525-0). Childrens.
Ramboz, Ina W. Christmas Songs in Spanish. (SPA.). 32p. (gr. 6-9). 1983. pap. 4.95 (ISBN 0-8442-7097-0, 7097-0, Passport Bks.). Natl Textbk.
Rivera, Carlos & Eastman, P. D., trs. Are You My Mother? (SPA & ENG.). (gr. 2-4). 1967. 8.95 (ISBN 0-394-81596-3); lib. bdg. 6.99 (ISBN 0-394-91596-8). Random.
Seventy-Two Paperback Set. (SPA.). 32p. (Orig.). (gr. k-3). 1990. Set. pap. text ed. 198.00 (ISBN 0-917837-70-3). Hampton-Brown.
Single Copy Set (Library-Bound) (ENG & SPA.). 192p. (gr. k-3). 1990. PLB 75.00 incl. tchr's. guide, 25p. (ISBN 1-56334-003-8). Hampton-Brown.
Tallon, Robert, illus. ABCDEFGHIJKLMNOPQRSTUVWXYZ. LC 76-86987. (ENG & SPA.). 64p. (gr. k-2). 1969. PLB 14.95 (ISBN 0-87460-131-2). Lion Bks.
Twelve Library Bound Set. (SPA.). 32p. (Orig.). (gr. k-3). 1990. Set. PLB 119.40 (ISBN 0-917837-72-X). Hampton-Brown.
Twelve Paperback Set. (SPA.). 32p. (Orig.). (gr. k-3). 1990. Set. pap. text ed. 33.50 (ISBN 0-917837-71-1). Hampton-Brown.
Twenty-Four Paperback Classroom Set. (SPA.). 32p. (Orig.). (gr. k-3). 1990. Set. pap. text ed. 124.00 (ISBN 0-917837-73-8). Hampton-Brown.
Webber, Irma E. Esta Cosa Se Ve Asi. Urquidi, Maria, tr. Webber, Irma E., illus. LC 76-43571. (SPA.). (gr. k-3). 1978. pap. text ed. 6.88 perfect bound (ISBN 0-918970-23-7). Intl Gen Semantics.
Wilcoxon, Kathrane. Beginning Spanish Reading: Letters, Colors, Numbers. 79p. (Orig.). (gr. k-3). 1988. 8.00 (ISBN 1-878253-00-X). Fisher Wilcoxon.

SPANISH LITERATURE

Garcia, Yolanda. Espanol Divertido: Spanish Fun. LC 86-90286. (Illus.). (gr. 1-6). 1986. pap. 7.95 (ISBN 0-935303-00-6). Victory Pub.

SPANISH POETRY–COLLECTIONS

Del Rosario Marquez, Nieves. Raices y Alas (Poesias Para Ninos y Jovenes) Montes, Jesus, illus. LC 81-65415. (Orig.). (gr. 6). 1981. pap. 5.00 (ISBN 0-89729-289-8). Ediciones.

SPARRING

see Boxing

SPARROWS

Pohl, Kathleen. Sparrows. (Illus.). 32p. (gr. 3-7). 1986. PLB 16.67 (ISBN 0-8172-2719-9); pap. text ed. 9.27 (ISBN 0-8172-2737-7). Raintree Pubs.
Posner, Richard. Sparrows Flight. LC 88-14021. 256p. (gr. 7 up). 1988. 12.95 (ISBN 0-87131-544-0). M Evans.

SPARROWS–FICTION

Bauer, Fred & Reufenacht, Peter. Chilp. LC 72-89351. (Illus.). 24p. (gr. k-4). 1973. 7.95 (ISBN 0-87592-011-X). Scroll Pr.
Doney, Meryl. The Very Worried Sparrow. Geldart, William, illus. 32p. (ps-6). 1991. 11.95 (ISBN 0-7459-1919-7). Lion USA.

SPARTA–HISTORY–FICTION

Levy, Elizabeth. Running Out of Time. Mars, W. T., illus. LC 79-28064. 128p. (gr. 3-6). 1980. lib. bdg. 4.99 (ISBN 0-394-94422-4). Knopf.

SPASTIC PARALYSIS

see Cerebral Palsy

SPEAKING

see Debates and Debating; Public Speaking; Rhetoric; Voice

SPECIE

see Money

SPECIMENS, PRESERVATION OF

see Zoological Specimens–Collection and Preservation

SPECTACLES

see Eyeglasses

SPECTERS

see Apparitions; Ghosts

SPEECH

see also Language and Languages; Phonetics; Voice

Childs, Phyllis. Speak Up. 78p. (ps-k). 1985. wkbk. 6.50 (ISBN 0-931749-00-X). PJC Lrng Mtrls.
DeVaney, Janet S. Speech Stations: The One-Stop Speech Book. DeVaney, Janet S., illus. 205p. (ps-5). 1987. 19.95 (ISBN 0-937857-03-3). Speech Bin.
Littlefield, Kathy M. & Littlefield, Robert S. Speak Up! Stark, Steve, illus. 32p. (Orig.). (gr. 3-6). 1989. pap. text ed. 8.95 (ISBN 1-879340-00-3, K0101). Kidspeak.
—What Did You Say? Stark, Steve, illus. 32p. (Orig.). (gr. 3-6). 1989. pap. text ed. 8.95 (ISBN 1-879340-01-1, K0102). Kidspeak.
Minn, Loretta. Teach Speech. 64p. (gr. 3-7). 1982. 6.95 (ISBN 0-86653-058-4, GA 418). Good Apple.
Moncure, Jane B. My "e" Sound Box. Gohman, Vera, illus. LC 84-17021. 32p. (ps-2). 1984. 11.97 (ISBN 0-89565-297-8); pap. 6.96 (ISBN 0-89565-336-2). Childs World.
—My "I" Sound Box. Gohman, Vera K., illus. LC 84-17022. 32p. (ps-2). 1984. lib. bdg. 11.97 (ISBN 0-89565-298-6); pap. 6.96 (ISBN 0-89565-337-0). Childs World.
—My "o" Sound Box. Gohman, Vera, illus. LC 84-17023. 32p. (ps-2). 1984. lib. bdg. 11.97 (ISBN 0-89565-299-4); pap. 6.96 (ISBN 0-89565-338-9). Childs World.
Pinkney, Nathaniel, illus. Conversation Games: Vol. I-People Times. 87p. (Orig.). (ps-6). 1978. pap. 15.00 (ISBN 0-939632-17-9). ILM.
—Conversation Games: Vol. II-Experiences. 87p. (Orig.). (ps-6). 1978. pap. 15.00 (ISBN 0-939632-20-9). ILM.
Reville, Julie D. The Many Voices of Paws: A Book for Young Stutterers. Metayer, Phil, illus. 64p. (ps-3). 1989. 25.00 (ISBN 0-937857-11-4, 1568). Speech Bin.
Rosenbloom, Joseph. World's Toughest Tongue Twisters. Kendrick, Dennis, illus. LC 86-5983. 128p. (gr. 2-8). 1987. pap. 3.95 (ISBN 0-8069-6596-7). Sterling.
Showers, Paul. How You Talk. Galster, Robert, illus. LC 66-15766. 40p. (ps-3). 1967. PLB 13.89 (ISBN 0-690-42136-2, Crowell Jr Bks). HarpC Child Bks.
Silverstein, Alvin & Silverstein, Virginia. Wonders of Speech. LC 87-31370. (Illus.). 160p. (gr. 7 up). 1988. 12.95 (ISBN 0-688-06534-1). Morrow Jr Bks.
Suid, Murray. For the Love of Speaking & Listening. 112p. (gr. 2-6). 1983. 9.95 (ISBN 0-912107-03-0). Monday Morning Bks.

SPEECH, LIBERTY OF

see Free Speech

SPEECH THERAPY

Berger, Gilda. Speech & Language Disorders. LC 80-85052. (gr. 7 up). 1981. PLB 12.90 (ISBN 0-531-04263-4). Watts.

SPEECH THERAPY–FICTION

Hulme, Joy. The Other Side of the Door. LC 90-41020. 125p. (gr. 3-6). 1990. pap. 4.95 (ISBN 0-87579-412-2). Deseret Bk.
Lee, Mildred. Skating Rink. LC 69-13443. 128p. (gr. 6 up). 1979. 7.95 (ISBN 0-395-28912-2, Clarion). HM.

SPEED

Rutland, Jonathan. Built to Speed. Atkinson, Mike, illus. LC 87-4790. 24p. (gr. 2-5). 1987. lib. bdg. 5.99 (ISBN 0-394-99215-6, Random Juv); pap. 2.95 (ISBN 0-394-89215-1, Random Juv). Random.

SPELEOLOGY

see Caves

SPELLERS

Dougherty, Margaret M., et al, eds. Instant Spelling Dictionary. (gr. 9 up). 1967. 4.95 (ISBN 0-531-01697-8). Watts.
Gerver, Jane, ed. My First Book of Spelling. McCarthy, Kathleen, et al, illus. 32p. (gr. 1-3). 1986. wkbk. 3.95 (ISBN 0-394-88171-0). Random.

SPELLING

see names of languages with the subdivision Spelling, e.g. English Language–Spelling

SPIDERS

Back, Christine & Watts, Barrie. Spider's Web. LC 86-10017. (Illus.). 25p. (gr. 2-5). 1986. 6.95 (ISBN 0-382-09303-8); PLB 9.98 (ISBN 0-382-09288-0); pap. 3.95 (ISBN 0-382-24020-0). Silver Burdett Pr.
Barrett, Norman. Aranas. LC 88-51514. (SPA., Illus.). 32p. (gr. k-4). 1990. PLB 11.40 (ISBN 0-531-07901-5). Watts.
Barrett, Norman S. Spiders. (Illus.). 32p. (gr. k-6). 1989. PLB 11.40 (ISBN 0-531-10702-7). Watts.
Bender, Lionel. Spiders. Franklin Watts Ltd., ed. (Illus.). 32p. (gr. k-9). 1988. PLB 11.90 (ISBN 0-531-17077-2, Gloucester Pr). Watts.
Climo, Shirley. Someone Saw a Spider: Spider Facts & Folktales. LC 85-45340. (Illus.). 128p. (gr. 4-7). 1985. 12.95 (ISBN 0-690-04435-6, Crowell Jr Bks); PLB 13.89 (ISBN 0-690-04436-4, Crowell Jr Bks). HarpC Child Bks.
Craig, Janet. Amazing World of Spiders. Helmer, Jean, illus. LC 89-5005. 32p. (gr. 2-4). 1990. PLB 10.89 (ISBN 0-8167-1751-6); pap. text ed. 2.95 (ISBN 0-8167-1752-4). Troll Assocs.
Dallinger, Jane. Spiders. LC 80-27548. (Illus.). 48p. (gr. 4 up). 1981. PLB 12.95 (ISBN 0-8225-1456-7, First Ave Edns); pap. 5.95 (ISBN 0-8225-9534-6, First Ave Edns). Lerner Pubns.

Green, Carl R. & Sanford, William R. The Tarantulas. LC 87-22342. (Illus.). 48p. (gr. 5-6). 1987. PLB 10.95 (ISBN 0-89686-339-5, Crestwood Hse). Macmillan Child Grp.

Hawes, Judy. My Daddy Longlegs. LC 74-175107. (Illus.). 40p. (gr. k-3). 1972. PLB 13.89 (ISBN 0-690-56656-5, Crowell Jr Bks). HarpC Child Bks.

Hopf, Alice L. Spiders. Moreton, Ann, illus. LC 89-9716. 64p. (gr. 5 up). 1990. 13.95 (ISBN 0-525-65017-2, Cobblehill Bks). Dutton Child Bks.

Horton, et al. Amazing Fact Book of Spiders. (Illus.). 32p. 1987. 11.95 (ISBN 0-87191-850-1). Creative Ed.

Jennings, Terry. Spiders. Anstey, David, illus. LC 88-83614. 24p. (gr. 1-3). 1989. PLB 10.40 (ISBN 0-531-17176-0). Denison.

LaBonte, Gail. The Tarantula. (Illus.). 60p. (gr. 3 up). 1991. RSBE 12.95 (ISBN 0-87518-452-9, Dillon). Macmillan Child Grp.

Levi, Herbert W. & Levi, Lorna R. Spiders & Their Kin. rev. ed. Zim, Herbert S. & Fichter, George S., eds. Strekalovsky, Nicholas, illus. (gr. 9 up). 1969. pap. write for info. (ISBN 0-307-24021-5, Golden Pr). Western Pub.

Lovett, Sarah, text by. Extremely Weird Spiders. (Illus.). 48p. (gr. 3 up). 1991. 9.95 (ISBN 1-56261-007-4). John Muir.

Martin, L. Bird Eating Spiders. (Illus.). 24p. (gr. k-5). Date not set. PLB 11.93 (ISBN 0-86592-966-1). Rourke Corp.

—Black Widow Spiders. (Illus.). 24p. (gr. k-5). Date not set. PLB 11.93 (ISBN 0-86592-965-3). Rourke Corp.

—Fishing Spiders. (Illus.). 24p. (gr. k-5). Date not set. PLB 11.93 (ISBN 0-86592-964-5). Rourke Corp.

—Funnel Web Spiders. (Illus.). 24p. (gr. k-5). Date not set. PLB 11.93 (ISBN 0-86592-962-9). Rourke Corp.

—Tarantulas. (Illus.). 24p. (gr. k-5). Date not set. PLB 11.93 (ISBN 0-86592-967-X). Rourke Corp.

—Trapdoor Spiders. (Illus.). 24p. (gr. k-5). Date not set. PLB 11.93 (ISBN 0-86592-963-7). Rourke Corp.

Merrians, Deborah. I Can Read About Spiders. McKeown, Gloria, illus. LC 76-54576. (gr. 2-5). 1977. pap. 1.95 (ISBN 0-89375-043-3). Troll Assocs.

Morris, Dean. Spiders. rev. ed. LC 87-16695. (Illus.). 48p. (gr. 2-6). 1987. PLB 17.32 (ISBN 0-8172-3213-3). Raintree Pubs.

Nielsen, Nancy. Black Widow Spider. LC 89-28271. (Illus.). 48p. (gr. 5 up). 1990. 10.95 (ISBN 0-89686-513-4, Crestwood Hse). Macmillan Child Grp.

Parsons, Alexandra. Amazing Spiders. Young, Jerry, photos by. LC 89-38833. (Illus.). 32p. (gr. 1-5). 1990. 6.95 (ISBN 0-679-80226-6); PLB 9.99 (ISBN 0-679-90226-0). McKay.

Penny, Malcolm. Discovering Spiders. LC 85-62088. (Illus.). 64p. (gr. k-6). 1986. 19.95 (ISBN 0-531-18045-X, Pub. by Bookwright Pr). Watts.

Perry, Malcolm. Discovering Spiders. (Illus.). 48p. (gr. 2 up). 1990. pap. 4.95 (ISBN 0-531-18365-3). Watts.

Petty, Kate. Spiders. (Illus.). 32p. (gr. 1-6). 1990. PLB 10.90 (ISBN 0-531-10026-X); pap. 2.95 (ISBN 0-531-15157-3). Watts.

Podendorf, Illa. Spiders. LC 81-38444. (Illus.). 48p. (gr. k-4). 1982. PLB 14.60 (ISBN 0-516-01653-9); pap. 4.95 (ISBN 0-516-41653-7). Childrens.

Ryder, Joanne. The Spiders Dance. Blake, Robert, illus. LC 78-22495. 48p. (gr. 1-4). 1981. 8.95i (ISBN 0-06-025133-6). HarpC Child Bks.

Sarracino, William L., illus. Mother Spider & Her Little Ones. 16p. (Orig.). (ps-7). 1982. pap. 3.75 (ISBN 0-915347-11-3). Pueblo Acoma Pr.

Schnieper, Claudia. Amazing Spiders. Meier, Max, photos by. (Illus.). 48p. (gr. 2-5). 1989. 12.95 (ISBN 0-87614-342-7); pap. 6.95 (ISBN 0-87614-518-7). Carolrhoda Bks.

Story of the Spider. (Illus.). (gr. 4 up). 3.50 (ISBN 0-7214-0631-9). Ladybird Bks.

Wildlife Education, Ltd. Staff. Spiders. Stuart, Walter, et al, illus. 20p. (Orig.). (gr. 5 up). 1985. pap. 2.25 (ISBN 0-937934-39-9). Wildlife Educ.

The World in Your Backyard: And Other Stories of Insects & Spiders. (Illus.). 63p. (gr. 3-5). 1989. 10.95 (ISBN 0-88309-132-1). Zaner-Bloser.

SPIDERS–FICTION

Edwards, Nicholas. Arachnophobia. (gr. 4-7). 1990. pap. 2.95 (ISBN 0-590-44228-7). Scholastic Inc.

Fontenot, Mary A. Clovis Crawfish & the Spinning Spider. (Illus.). 32p. 1987. 11.95 (ISBN 0-88289-644-X). Pelican.

Graham, Margaret B. Be Nice to Spiders. Graham, Margaret B., illus. LC 67-17101. 32p. (gr. k-3). 1967. PLB 13.89 (ISBN 0-06-022073-2). HarpC Child Bks.

Keller, Beverly. A Garden of Love to Share. Paris, Pat & Posey, Pam, illus. 40p. (ps-3). 1984. 5.95 (ISBN 0-910313-49-0). Parker Bros.

Kraus, Robert. How Spider Saved Halloween. Kraus, Robert, illus. 32p. (ps-3). 1988. pap. 2.25 (ISBN 0-671-66889-7). S&S Trade.

—Spider's First Day at School. (Illus.). 32p. (Orig.). (ps-2). 1987. pap. 2.50 (ISBN 0-590-41091-1). Scholastic Inc.

—Spider's Hometown: A Story to Color. (Illus.). 32p. (ps-3). 1988. pap. 1.95 (ISBN 0-590-41792-4). Scholastic Inc.

Lane, Margaret. The Spider. Firth, Barbara, illus. LC 82-71354. 32p. (ps-4). 1982. 9.95 (ISBN 0-8037-8303-5, 0339-110). Dial Bks Young.

—The Spider. Firth, Barbara, illus. LC 82-71354. 32p. (ps-4). 1983. pap. 3.50 (ISBN 0-8037-8308-6, 0340-100). Dial Bks Young.

McDermott, Gerald, retold by. & illus. Anansi the Spider: A Tale from the Ashanti. LC 76-150028. 40p. (gr. k-2). 1972. reinforced bdg. 14.95 (ISBN 0-8050-0310-X); pap. 5.95 (ISBN 0-8050-0311-8). H Holt & Co.

MacDonald, Suse. Space Spinners. (ps-3). 1991. 13.95 (ISBN 0-8037-1008-9); PLB 13.89 (ISBN 0-8037-1009-7). Dial Bks Young.

McNulty, Faith. The Lady & the Spider. Marstall, Bob, illus. LC 85-5427. 48p. (gr. 1-4). 1986. 12.95i (ISBN 0-06-024191-8); PLB 12.89 (ISBN 0-06-024192-6). HarpC Child Bks.

Martin, C. L. G. Three Brave Women. Elwell, Peter, illus. LC 89-77770. 32p. (gr. k-3). 1991. RSBE 13.95 (ISBN 0-02-762445-5, Mcmillan Child Bk). Macmillan Child Grp.

Nimmo, Jenny. The Snow Spider. large type ed. 208p. (gr. 3-7). 1987. lib. bdg. 13.95x (ISBN 0-7451-0590-4, Pub. by Chivers Pr UK). G K Hall.

—The Snow Spider. 136p. (gr. 5-9). 1990. pap. 2.95 (ISBN 0-8167-2264-1). Troll Assocs.

Patent, Dorothy H. Spider Magic. LC 81-85088. (Illus.). 40p. (gr. 1-4). 1982. reinforced bdg. 12.95 (ISBN 0-8234-0438-2). Holiday.

Webster, Jean. Daddy-Long-Legs. 176p. (gr. 5-8). 1988. pap. 2.50 (ISBN 0-590-41517-4, Pub. by Apple Classics). Scholastic Inc.

White, E. B. Charlotte's Web. Williams, Garth, illus. LC 52-9760. (gr. 2-6). 1952. 10.95 (ISBN 0-06-026385-7); PLB 11.89 (ISBN 0-06-026386-5). HarpC Child Bks.

—Charlotte's Web. LC 52-9760. (Illus.). 1974. pap. 3.50 (ISBN 0-06-440055-7, Trophy). HarpC Child Bks.

—Charlotte's Web. (Illus.). 192p. (ps-8). 1990. Repr. lib. bdg. 21.95x (ISBN 0-89966-696-5). Buccaneer Bks.

—E. B. White Boxed Set. Incl. Charlotte's Web; The Trumpet of the Swan; Stuart Little. (Illus.). (gr. 3 up). 27.60i (ISBN 0-686-77171-0). HarpC Child Bks.

—E. B. White Boxed Set. Incl. Charlotte's Web; The Trumpet of the Swan; Stuart Little. (Illus.). (gr. 3 up). 1974. pap. 10.50 (ISBN 0-06-440061-1, Trophy). HarpC Child Bks.

—Tela Charlottae. Fox, Bernice, tr. Williams, Garth, illus. LC 90-55691. (LAT.). 256p. (gr. 2 up). 1991. 18.95 (ISBN 0-06-026401-2). HarpC Child Bks.

SPIES

see also Secret Service; World War, 1939-1945–Underground Movements

Aaseng, Nathan. Baseball's Worst Teams. (Illus.). 72p. (gr. 4 up). 1985. PLB 9.95 (ISBN 0-8225-1527-X). Lerner Pubns.

Levine, Ellen. Secret Missions: Four True Life Stories. (Illus.). 128p. (gr. 3-7). 1988. pap. 2.50 (ISBN 0-590-41183-7). Scholastic Inc.

Marrin, Albert. The Secret Armies: Spies, Counterspies, & Saboteurs in World War II. LC 85-7944. (Illus.). 192p. (gr. 5 up). 1985. 14.95 (ISBN 0-689-31165-6, Atheneum Child Bk). Macmillan Child Grp.

Reit, Seymour. Behind Rebel Lines: The Incredible Story of Emma Edmonds, Civil War Spy. 146p. (gr. 4-7). 1991. pap. 4.95 (ISBN 0-15-200424-6, HJ). HarBraceJ.

Silverstein, Herma. Spies among Us: The Truth about Modern Espionage. FS Staff, ed. (Illus.). 144p. (gr. 6-12). 1988. PLB 12.90 (ISBN 0-531-10600-4). Watts.

Travis, F. & Hindley, J. The KnowHow Book of Spycraft: Lots of Secret Codes, Tricks & Disguises. (Illus.). 32p. (gr. 3-6). 1977. pap. 5.95 (ISBN 0-86020-005-1). EDC.

SPIES–FICTION

Arthur, Robert, ed. Spies & More Spies. Lambert, Saul, illus. (gr. 7-11). 1972. lib. bdg. 5.39 (ISBN 0-394-91673-5, Random Juv). Random.

—Spies & More Spies. Lambert, Saul, illus. (gr. 7-11). 1972. lib. bdg. 5.39 (ISBN 0-394-91673-5, Random Juv). Random.

Fitzhugh, Louise. Harriet the Spy. Fitzhugh, Louise, illus. LC 64-19711. 224p. (gr. 4-7). 1964. 14.95 (ISBN 0-06-021910-6); PLB 14.89 (ISBN 0-06-021911-4). HarpC Child Bks.

—Harriet the Spy. Fitzhugh, Louise, illus. LC 64-19711. 304p. (gr. 3-7). 1990. pap. 3.95 (ISBN 0-06-440331-9, Trophy). HarpC Child Bks.

Follett, Ken. The Key to Rebecca. 352p. (gr. 9-12). 1981. pap. 4.95 (ISBN 0-451-15510-6, Sig). NAL-Dutton.

Furman, Abraham L., ed. Teen-Age Secret Agent Stories. (gr. 5-10). PLB 6.70 (ISBN 0-8313-0042-6). Lantern.

—Teen-Age Spy Stories. (gr. 6-10). 6.70 (ISBN 0-8313-0041-8); PLB 6.19. Lantern.

Gerson, Corinne. My Grandfather the Spy. 1990. 14.95 (ISBN 0-8027-6955-1). Walker & Co.

Griffin, Judith B. Phoebe the Spy. 48p. (gr. 3-6). 1989. pap. 2.75 (ISBN 0-590-42432-7). Scholastic Inc.

Haynes, Betsy. Spies on the Devils Belt. 1990. pap. 2.75 (ISBN 0-590-40567-5). Scholastic Inc.

Johnston, Norma. Return to Morocco. LC 88-6880. 176p. (gr. 7 up). 1988. 13.95 (ISBN 0-02-747712-6, Four Winds). Macmillan Child Grp.

Kraus, Robert. Boris Bad Enough. Aruego, Jose & Dewey, Ariane, illus. 32p. (ps-3). 1988. pap. 12.95 (ISBN 0-671-66894-3); pap. 5.95 (ISBN 0-671-66895-1). S&S Trade.

Lawson, Don & Barish, Wendy. The French Resistance. 192p. (gr. 3-7). 1984. (Little Simon); PLB 8.79 (ISBN 0-685-07808-6). S&S Trade.

Leibold, Jay. Spy for George Washington. 128p. (gr. 4). 1985. pap. 2.25 (ISBN 0-553-25497-9). Bantam.

Leppard, Lois G. Mandie & the Foreign Spies. 160p. (Orig.). (gr. 3-8). 1990. pap. 3.95 (ISBN 1-55661-147-1). Bethany Hse.

—Mandie & the Silent Catacombs. 160p. (gr. 3-8). 1990. 3.95 (ISBN 1-55661-148-X). Bethany Hse.

Lisle, Janet T. Sirens & Spies. LC 84-21518. 192p. (gr. 7 up). 1985. 13.95 (ISBN 0-02-759150-6, Bradbury Pr). Macmillan Child Grp.

Martini, Teri. Secret Is Out. (gr. 4-7). 1990. 14.95 (ISBN 0-316-54864-2, Joy St Bks). Little.

Myers, Walter D. The Nicholas Factor. 180p. (gr. 6 up). 1983. pap. 11.50 (ISBN 0-670-51055-6). Viking Child Bks.

Patent, Dorothy H. The Lives of Spiders. LC 80-14801. (Illus.). 128p. (gr. 5 up). 1980. 13.95 (ISBN 0-8234-0418-8). Holiday.

Schenkman, Richard, ed. The Illustrated James Bond, 007. McLusky, John, illus. 90p. (Orig.). (gr. 5 up). 1981. pap. 6.95 (ISBN 0-9605838-0-7). Bond Double-O Seven.

Sharmat, Marjorie W. Sly Spy: Olivia Sharp, Agent for Secrets. 1990. 12.95 (ISBN 0-385-29974-5). Doubleday.

—Spy in the Neighborhood. 1989. pap. 2.75 (ISBN 0-590-42633-8). Scholastic Inc.

Sobol, Donald J. Encyclopedia Brown's Book of Wacky Spies. Enik, Ted, illus. 112p. (gr. 4-6). 1984. pap. 2.25 (ISBN 0-553-15369-2, Skylark). Bantam.

—Secret Agents Four. Shortall, Leonard, illus. 144p. (gr. 3-7). 1988. pap. 2.50 (ISBN 0-590-40565-9). Scholastic Inc.

SPIRITS

see Apparitions; Ghosts; Witchcraft

SPIRITUAL LIFE

see also Christian Life; Faith

Auer, Jim. Ten Ways to Meet God: Spirituality for Teens. 64p. (gr. 7-12). 1989. pap. 1.95 (ISBN 0-89243-299-3). Liguori Pubns.

Brunton, Paul. Inspiration & the Overself: The Notebooks of Paul Brunton, Vol. 14. Cash, Paul & Smith, Timothy, eds. (Illus.). 256p. (gr. 7 up). 1988. 22.50 (ISBN 0-943914-40-X, Dist. by NBN); pap. 14.95 (ISBN 0-943914-41-8, Dist. by NBN). Larson Pubns.

Carrozzi, Craig J. Wedding of the Waters. LC 88-60526. (Illus.). 396p. (Orig.). 1988. pap. 10.95 (ISBN 0-9620286-0-6). Suthrn Trails Pub.

Case, Riley B. & Keysor, Charles W. We Believe: Jr. High. rev. ed. Heidinger, James V., II, et al, eds. Myers, Glenn, illus. 60p. (gr. 6-9). 1988. wkbk. 3.95 (ISBN 0-917851-20-X). Bristol Hse.

Crook, Carol. Spiritual Warfare Manual, Pt. I: Personal Preparation for Warfare. 54p. (Orig.). 1989. pap. text ed. 3.50x (ISBN 0-939399-15-6). Bks of Truth.

—Spiritual Warfare Manual, Pt. II: Preparation Knowledge. 95p. (Orig.). 1989. pap. text ed. 4.95x (ISBN 0-939399-16-4). Bks of Truth.

—Spiritual Warfare Manual, Pt. III: Actions of Combat. 112p. (Orig.). (gr. 9-12). 1989. pap. 5.25 (ISBN 0-939399-17-2). Bks of Truth.

Curtis, Donald. New Age Understanding. LC 72-92276. 144p. 1990. pap. 7.95 (ISBN 0-941992-23-3). Los Arboles Pub.

Hodgson, Joan. Hullo Sun. Ripper, Peter, illus. (ps-3). 1972. 6.95 (ISBN 0-85487-019-9). DeVorss.

Johnson, Tom. Heaven Is an Action, Not a Place. 32p. (Orig.). 1990. pap. 3.50 (ISBN 0-941992-22-5). Los Arboles Pub.

Jones, James A., III. Conversations with Children. Cook, Debbie, illus. LC 85-40201. 96p. (gr. 4-8). 1985. 8.95 (ISBN 0-938232-72-X). Winston-Derek.

Keith, Gretchen L. The Life to Come: Stories for Children about the Spiritual World. Cook, Richard J., illus. 89p. (Orig.). (gr. 3-7). 1990. pap. 5.00 (ISBN 0-945003-03-X). General Church.

Lehn, Cornelia. Peace Be with You. Neely, Keith R., illus. Regier, Harold R. & Schwartzentruber, Hubertintro. by. LC 80-70190. (Illus.). 126p. (gr. k-5). 1981. 12.95 (ISBN 0-87303-061-3). Faith & Life.

L'Engle, Madeleine. Trailing Clouds of Glory: Spiritual Values in Children's Books. Brooke, Avery, contrib. by. LC 84-29081. 144p. (gr. 5-9). 1985. 12.95 (ISBN 0-664-32721-4, Westminster). Westminster John Knox.

Lindstrom, Marilyn. The Voice from Inner Space: Answers Who Am I? Why Am I Here? Beckman, Jean, ed. LC 90-35087. 112p. (Orig.). 1990. pap. 7.95 (ISBN 0-941992-20-9). Los Arboles Pub.

MacKenthun, Carole & Dwyer, Paulinus. Gentleness. Filkins, Vanessa, illus. 48p. (gr. 2 up). 1987. pap. 6.95 (ISBN 0-86653-395-8, SS879). Good Apple.

Mitchell, Lorayne. And the Winner Is... A Book about Inner Beauty. Lee, Jeff, illus. 32p. (ps-4). 1987. PLB 12.95 (ISBN 0-943491-00-2). Valued Pubns.

Ray, Sandy. The Little Seed. Sytsma, Cheryle, ed. LC 90-63623. (Illus.). 30p. (Orig.). (gr. k-5). 1991. pap. write for info. (ISBN 1-879068-01-X). Ray-Ma Natsal.

—Sir Joshua, Himself. Sytsma, Cheryle, ed. LC 90-63622. (Illus.). 30p. (Orig.). (gr. k-5). 1991. pap. write for info. (ISBN 1-879068-02-8). Ray-Ma Natsal.

Richelieu, Frank E. Reincarnation: The Inheritance of a Soul. 32p. (Orig.). 1991. pap. 3.50 (ISBN 0-941992-25-X). Los Arboles Pub.

Roberts, Sharon L. Somebody Lives Inside: The Holy Spirit. (Illus.). 24p. (Orig.). (gr. k-4). 1986. pap. 3.95 saddlestitched (ISBN 0-570-08530-6, 56-1557). Concordia.

Spiritual Warfare Manual, 3 pts. 259p. 1989. Set. pap. text ed. 13.50 (ISBN 0-939399-14-8). Bks of Truth.

Sumrall, Lester. A Teenager Who Dared Obey God. 97p. (Orig.). 1985. pap. text ed. 1.95 (ISBN 0-937580-44-9). LeSEA Pub Co.

Taylor, Connie R. Before Birth, Beyond Death. 64p. (gr. 4-6). 1987. pap. 5.95 (ISBN 0-88290-315-2). Horizon Utah.

Vissell, Rami. Rami's Book: The Inner Life of a Child. Vissell, Rami, illus. Vissell, Barry, intro. by. LC 88-91345. (Illus.). 56p. 1989. 13.95 (ISBN 0-9612720-4-X, 104). Ramira Pub. Vividly describing the extraordinary inner world of a deeply sensitive eleven year old girl, RAMI'S BOOK has already opened the hearts of thousands of children & adults alike. With a child's simple & direct language, & refreshing full-color drawings, Rami offers a profound way of looking at life. She shares openly & without pretense about the lessons that come directly out of her own life experience, lessons we all need to learn, however old we are. Rami Vissell is the daughter of established authors, Joyce & Barry Vissell, well known nurse & medical doctor couple who wrote THE SACRED HEART, MODELS OF LOVE, & RISK TO BE HEALED. Gerald Jampolsky, M.D., celebrated author & child psychiatrist, says, "RAMI'S BOOK is like a breath of fresh air, teaching us about our innocence & the simplicity of loving ourselves & others." "We have been taught for a long time that the entrance to God's presence is through the eyes of the child. Rami flings wide that delicious door of perception. Thank you Rami!"--Rev. Stan Hampson, President, Association of Unity Churches. ISBN 0-9612720-4-X, $13. 95, Hardcover, Full color illustrations, 53 pp., Ramira Publishing, P.O. Box 1707, Aptos, CA 95001.
Publisher Provided Annotation.

Wenig, Laurin J. The Prophets: Showing Us the Way to Justice & Peace. (Illus.). 80p. (Orig.). (gr. 9-12). 1990. pap. text ed. 4.90 (ISBN 0-937997-16-1); tchr's. ed. 8.90 (ISBN 0-937997-17-X). Hi-Time Pub.

Woody, Sandra. Run So Fast. Sytsma, Cheryle, ed. LC 90-63615. (Illus.). 25p. (Orig.). (gr. k-5). 1991. pap. write for info. (ISBN 1-879068-05-2). Ray-Ma Natsal.

SPIRITUALS

Bryan, Ashley. All Night, All Day: A Child's First Book of African-American Spirituals. Bryan, Ashley, illus. LC 90-753145. 48p. (ps-4). 1991. SBE 14.95 (ISBN 0-689-31662-3, Atheneum Child Bk). Macmillan Child Grp.

Langstaff, John. What a Morning! The Christmas Story in Black Spirituals. Bryan, Ashley, illus. LC 87-750130. 32p. 1987. 13.95 (ISBN 0-689-50422-5, M K McElderry). Macmillan Child Grp.

SPLICING

see Knots and Splices

SPORTS

see also Amusements; Athletics; Coaching (Athletics); Games; Gymnastics; Olympic Games; Outdoor Life; Physical Education and Training; Rodeos; School Sports; Water Sports; Winter Sports

also names of sports, e.g. baseball; etc.

Aaseng, Nathan. Pro Sports' Greatest Rivalries. (Illus.). 80p. (gr. 4 up). 1985. PLB 9.95 (ISBN 0-8225-1530-X). Lerner Pubns.

Adoff, Arnold. Sports Pages. Kuzma, Steve, illus. LC 85-45169. 80p. (gr. 3 up). 1990. pap. 5.95 (ISBN 0-06-446098-3, Trophy). HarpC Child Bks.

Allen, Anne. Sports for the Handicapped. (gr. 6 up). 1981. lib. bdg. 10.85 reinforced (ISBN 0-8027-6437-1). Walker & Co.

Beard, Daniel C. American Boys Handy Book: What to Do & How to Do It. facs. ed. LC 66-15858. (Illus.). (gr. 4 up). 1966. 14.95 (ISBN 0-8048-0006-5). C E Tuttle.

Berger, Gilda. Violence & Sports. 1990. PLB 12.90 (ISBN 0-531-10907-0). Watts.

Braden, Vic & Phillips, Louis. Sportsathon Puzzles, Jokes, Facts & Games. Eberbach, Andrea, illus. (ps-k). 1986. pap. 4.95 (ISBN 0-14-032028-8, Puffin). Puffin Bks.

Childress, Valerie & Nelson, Jane. Drill Team Is for Me. LC 85-19737. (Illus.). 48p. (gr. 2-5). 1986. lib. bdg. 8.95 (ISBN 0-8225-1148-7). Lerner Pubns.

Cook, J. & Way, P. Windsurfing. (Illus.). (gr. 6 up). 1988. PLB 12.96 (ISBN 0-88110-314-4); pap. 7.95 (ISBN 0-7460-0195-9). EDC.

Curveballs: Wacky Facts to Bat Around. (gr. 3-7). 1990. pap. 3.95 (ISBN 0-316-75452-8). Little.

Dean, Anabel. Wind Sports. LC 82-13460. (Illus.). 170p. (gr. 5-9). 1982. 12.95 (ISBN 0-664-32696-X, Westminster). Westminster John Knox.

Deegan & Zadra, Dan. Track & Field: Building Strength. (Illus.). 1981. 13.95 (ISBN 0-89813-011-5); PLB 9. 75s.p. (ISBN 0-685-23232-8). Creative Ed.

—Track & Field: Running Faster. (Illus.). 1981. 15.35 (ISBN 0-89813-013-1); PLB 10.75s.p. (ISBN 0-685-23233-6). Creative Ed.

—Track & Field: Warming Up. (Illus.). 1981. 15.35 (ISBN 0-89813-014-X); PLB 10.75s.p. (ISBN 0-685-23234-4). Creative Ed.

D'Ham, Claude. Sport. 20p. (Orig.). (ps-2). 1975. pap. 2.00 (ISBN 0-85953-035-3, Pub. by Child's Play England). Childs Play.

Emberley, Michael. The Sports Equipment Book. Emberley, Michael, illus. 32p. (gr. 3 up). 1982. 12.95 (ISBN 0-316-23405-2). Little.

Frommer, Harvey. Sports Date Book. (Orig.). (gr. 5 up). 1981. pap. 2.50 (ISBN 0-448-17214-3, Pub. by Tempo). Ace Bks.

Gardner, Robert. Science & Sports. Rasof, Henry, ed. LC 88-14042. (Illus.). 112p. (gr. 7-12). 1988. PLB 12.40 (ISBN 0-531-10593-8). Watts.

Gay, Kathlyn. They Don't Wash Their Socks! 112p. 1991. pap. 2.95 (ISBN 0-380-71302-0, Camelot). Avon.

Grosshandler, Henry & Grosshandler, Janet. Everyone Wins at Tee Ball. Grosshandler, Henry & Grosshandler, Janet, illus. LC 89-7875. 32p. (gr. k-3). 1990. 12.95 (ISBN 0-525-65016-4, Cobblehill Bks). Dutton Child Bks.

Hamilton, Harley & Jones, Nancy K. Sport Signs. Incl. Signs & Printed Words, General Vocabulary. 64p. pap. 6.00 (ISBN 0-317-42767-9); Football. 48p. pap. 5.00 (ISBN 0-317-42768-7); Basketball. 48p. pap. 5.00 (ISBN 0-317-42769-5); Baseball-Softball. 48p. pap. 5.00 (ISBN 0-317-42770-9); Track & Field. 40p. pap. 4.00 (ISBN 0-317-42771-7); Volley Ball. 28p. pap. 3.00 (ISBN 0-317-42772-5). 1985. pap. 17.00 set (ISBN 0-317-42766-0). Modern Signs.

Hammond, Tim. Sports. King, Dave, photos by. LC 88-1573. (Illus.). 64p. (gr. 5 up). 1988. 13.95 (ISBN 0-394-89616-5); lib. bdg. 14.99 (ISBN 0-394-99616-X). Knopf.

Hang Gliding & Para-Sailing. 48p. (gr. 3-4). 1989. PLB 10.95 (ISBN 0-685-26393-2). Capstone Pr.

Highlights for Children Staff. Action Book of Sports. Highlights for Children Staff, illus. 32p. (gr. 3-8). 1988. pap. 2.95 (ISBN 0-87534-229-9). Highlights.

—Summer Games. Highlights for Children Staff, illus. 48p. (gr. 3-7). 1990. pap. 2.95 (ISBN 0-87534-352-X). Highlights.

Hinds, Bill. Buzz Beamer's Radical Sports. (gr. 4-7). 1990. pap. 3.95 (ISBN 0-316-36448-7). Little.

Hollander, Phyllis & Hollander, Zander. Amazing but True Sports Stories. (Illus.). 128p. (Orig.). (gr. 3 up). 1986. pap. 2.25 (ISBN 0-590-33377-1). Scholastic Inc.

—More Amazing but True Sport Stories. 144p. (Orig.). (gr. 3 up). 1990. pap. 2.75 (ISBN 0-590-43876-X). Scholastic Inc.

Hot Air Ballooning. 48p. (gr. 3-4). 1989. PLB 10.95 (ISBN 0-685-26392-4). Capstone Pr.

Hot Dogging & Snow Boarding. 48p. (gr. 3-4). 1989. PLB 10.95 (ISBN 0-685-26389-4). Capstone Pr.

Hot! Magazine. (Illus.). 40p. (gr. 3-6). 1989. 0.50 (ISBN 0-87406-402-3, 57-19044-1). Willowisp Pr.

Jennings, Jay. Comebacks. (Illus.). 64p. (gr. 5-7). 1991. PLB 14.98 (ISBN 0-382-24109-6); PLB 11.24s.p.; pap. 8.95 (ISBN 0-382-24115-0); pap. 6.71s.p. Silver Burdett Pr.

—Sports Triumphs Series, 4 vols. (Illus.). 256p. (gr. 5-7). 1991. Set. PLB 59.92 (ISBN 0-382-24104-5); Set. PLB 44.94s.p.; Set. pap. 35.80 (ISBN 0-382-24111-8); Set. pap. 26.85s.p. Silver Burdett Pr.

Kaplan, Andrew. Careers for Sports Fans. (Illus.). 64p. (gr. 7 up). 1991. PLB 12.90 (ISBN 1-56294-023-6). Millbrook Pr.

Kettelkamp, Larry. Modern Sports Science. LC 86-8754. (Illus.). 160p. (gr. 7 up). 1986. 12.95 (ISBN 0-688-05494-3). Morrow Jr Bks.

Knudson, Richard L. Rallying. LC 80-17863. (Illus.). 48p. (gr. 4-9). 1981. PLB 9.95 (ISBN 0-8225-0445-6). Lerner Pubns.

Langley, Andrew. Sports & Politics. (Illus.). 48p. (gr. 5 up). 1990. lib. bdg. 18.00 (ISBN 0-86592-117-2); lib. bdg. 13.50s.p. Rourke Corp.

Lerner, Mark. Racquetball Is for Me. Wolfe, Robert L., illus. LC 83-13611. 48p. (gr. 2-5). 1983. PLB 8.95 (ISBN 0-8225-1144-4). Lerner Pubns.

Lerner Publications, Department of Geography Staff, ed. Sri Lanka in Pictures. (Illus.). 64p. (gr. 5 up). 1988. 12.95 (ISBN 0-8225-1853-8). Lerner Pubns.

Let's Discover Sport & Entertainment. (Illus.). 80p. (gr. k-6). 1981. pap. text ed. 13.27 (ISBN 0-8172-1768-1). Raintree Pubs.

Liss, Howard. The Giant Book of More Strange but True Sports Stories. Mathieu, Joe, illus. LC 82-13236. 160p. (gr. 5-10). 1983. pap. 8.95 (ISBN 0-394-85633-3). Random.

—The Giant Book of Strange but True Sports Stories. Mathieu, Joe, illus. LC 76-8132. (gr. 5-9). 1976. 9.00 (ISBN 0-394-83287-6, Random Juv). Random.

Mohun, Janet. Drugs Steroids & Sports. FS-Aladdin Staff, ed. (Illus.). 64p. (gr. 6-12). 1988. PLB 11.90 (ISBN 0-531-10626-8). Watts.

Moran, Tom. Frisbee Disc Flying Is for Me. Moran, Tom, illus. LC 82-244. 48p. (gr. 2-5). 1982. PLB 8.95 (ISBN 0-8225-1137-1). Lerner Pubns.

Myers, Gail A. FunSports for Everyone. LC 84-21032. (Illus.). 160p. (gr. 5-9). 1985. 12.95 (ISBN 0-664-32720-6, Westminster). Westminster John Knox.

—A World of Sports for Girls. LC 81-10440. (Illus.). 160p. (gr. 5-9). 1981. 10.95 (ISBN 0-664-32683-8, Westminster). Westminster John Knox.

Nardo, Don. Drugs & Sports. LC 90-6686. (Illus.). 112p. (gr. 5-8). 1990. PLB 11.95 (ISBN 1-56006-112-X). Lucent Bks.

Nash, Bruce & Zullo, Allan. Freebies for Sports Fans. Doty, Roy, illus. 96p. (gr. 1 up). 1990. pap. 4.95 (ISBN 0-671-70339-0). S&S Trade.

—The Sports Hall of Shame: Young Fans Edition. MacDonald, Patricia, ed. 176p. 1990. pap. 2.75 (ISBN 0-671-69355-7, Archway). PB.

Nelson, Cordner. Careers in Pro Sports. Rosen, Ruth, ed. LC 89-37641. (Illus.). 143p. (gr. 7-12). 1990. PLB 12. 95 (ISBN 0-8239-1027-X). Rosen Group.

O'Sullivan, Carol. Drugs & Sports: Locating the Author's Main Idea. (Illus.). 32p. (gr. 3-6). 1990. PLB 8.95 (ISBN 0-89908-637-3). Greenhaven.

The Parents' Guide to Kids' Sports. (gr. 3-7). 1990. pap. 8.95 (ISBN 0-316-77471-5). Little.

Parietti, Jeff. One Hundred & One Wacky Sports Quotes. (gr. 4-7). 1991. pap. 1.95 (ISBN 0-590-44146-9). Scholastic Inc.

Photo Finishes: Great Last-Second Bottom-of-the-Ninth, Sudden-Death Victories. (gr. 3-7). 1990. 17.95 (ISBN 0-316-32023-4). Little.

Reisberg, Ken. Martial Arts. (Illus.). (gr. 4 up). 1979. s&l 10.40 (ISBN 0-531-04077-1). Watts.

Rollerskating & Rollerblading. 48p. (gr. 3-4). 1989. PLB 10.95 (ISBN 0-685-26390-8). Capstone Pr.

Rosenbloom, Joseph. Sports Riddles. Weissman, Sam Q., illus. LC 81-7232. 64p. (gr. 6 up). 1982. 8.95 (ISBN 0-15-277994-9, HJ). HarBraceJ.

Rowen, Larry. Beyond Winning: Group Centered Games & Sports. (gr. 2-6). 1990. pap. 7.95 (ISBN 0-8224-3380-X). Fearon Teach Aids.

Sail Racing. 48p. (gr. 3-4). 1989. PLB 10.95 (ISBN 0-685-26383-5). Capstone Pr.

Schneider, Tom. Everybody's a Winner: A Kid's Guide to New Sports & Fitness. (Illus.). (gr. 3 up). 1976. 14.95 (ISBN 0-316-77398-0, Brown Paper School); pap. 8.95 (ISBN 0-316-77399-9). Little.

Schulman, L. M. Random House Book of Sports Stories. (gr. 4-7). 1990. 15.95 (ISBN 0-394-82874-7). Random.

Schulman, L. M., ed. The Random House Book of Sports Stories. Allen, Thomas B., illus. LC 89-12834. 256p. (gr. 5 up). 1990. 16.99 (ISBN 0-394-92874-1); lib. bdg. 16.99 (ISBN 0-317-99916-8). Random.

Schwartz, Linda. Trivia Trackdown-Sports & Space. (Illus.). 32p. (gr. 4-6). 1986. 3.95 (ISBN 0-88160-138-1, LW257). Learning Wks.

Sheffer, H. R. The Last Meet. LC 80-28766. (Illus.). 48p. (gr. 3 up). 1980. PLB 9.95 (ISBN 0-89686-103-1, Crestwood Hse). Macmillan Child Grp.

Sobol, Donald J. Encyclopedia Brown's Book of Wacky Sports. Enik, Ted, illus. 128p. (Orig.). (gr. 3-7). 1984. pap. 2.50 (ISBN 0-553-15497-4, Skylark). Bantam.

The Special Olympics. 32p. (gr. 4). 1990. 12.95s.p. (ISBN 0-88682-311-0); 18.50 (ISBN 0-685-28226-0). Creative Ed.

Sports. (Illus.). 72p. (gr. 6-12). 1972. pap. 1.85 (ISBN 0-8395-3255-5, 3255). BSA.

Sports & Entertainment. (Illus.). 80p. (gr. k-6). 1986. pap. 13.27 (ISBN 0-8172-2590-0). Raintree Pubs.

Sports & Recreation, 11 vols. (Illus.). 96p. (gr. 3 up). 1987. Set. PLB 240.00 (ISBN 0-317-64441-6); pap. 13.27 (ISBN 0-8172-3061-0). Raintree Pubs.

The Sports Day. (Illus.). (ps-2). 1990. 3.50 (ISBN 0-7214-1322-6); parent/tchr's. guide 3.95. Ladybird Bks.

Three Hundred Sixty-Five Amazing Days in Sports. (gr. 3-7). 1990. pap. 10.95 (ISBN 0-316-78537-7). Little.

Trager, Oliver, ed. Sports in America: Paradise Lost? 224p. 1990. 29.95x (ISBN 0-8160-2412-X). Facts on File.

Ward, Carl. Field Hockey. (Illus.). 80p. (gr. 5 up). 1991. pap. 6.95 (ISBN 0-7063-6770-7, Pub. by Ward Lock UK). Sterling.

Winston, Lynn. Recreation & Sports: An Activity Guide. Garee, Betty, ed. LC 85-72420. 72p. (Orig.). (gr. 9-12). 1985. pap. 4.95 (ISBN 0-915708-18-3, #1770). Cheever Pub.

Zadra, Dan. The Secrets to Goal-Setting. (Illus.). 32p. (gr. 6 up). 1986. PLB 10.95s.p. (ISBN 0-88682-017-0); PLB 15.65. Creative Ed.

SPORTS–BIOGRAPHY

Aaseng, Nathan. Eric Heiden: Winner in Gold. LC 80-16982. (Illus.). 56p. (gr. 4-9). 1980. PLB 8.95 (ISBN 0-8225-0481-2). Lerner Pubns.

—Little Giants of Pro Sports. LC 80-12031. (Illus.). 64p. (gr. 4 up). 1983. PLB 7.95 (ISBN 0-8225-1059-6). Lerner Pubns.

—Record Breakers of Pro Sports. (Illus.). 80p. (gr. 4 up). 1987. PLB 9.95 (ISBN 0-8225-1533-4). Lerner Pubns.

Gutman, Bill. Pro Sports Champions. (Illus.). 144p. (Orig.). (gr. 5 up). 1990. pap. 2.75 (ISBN 0-671-69334-4, Archway). PB.

Hahn, James & Hahn, Lynn. Patty! The Sports Career of Patricia Berg. LC 80-28744. (Illus.). 48p. (gr. 3-5). 1981. PLB 9.95 (ISBN 0-89686-127-9, Crestwood Hse). Macmillan Child Grp.
Johnson, Ann D. The Value of Fairness: The Story of Nellie Bly. Pileggi, Stephen, illus. LC 77-13275. (gr. k-6). 1977. 9.95 (ISBN 0-916392-16-3, Pub. by Value Communications). Oak Tree Pubns.
The Lincoln Library of Sports Champions, 20 vols. (gr. 6-12). 1989. Set. 419.00. Ency Brit Ed.
Ogden, Dale. Hoosier Sports Heroes. Day, Richard, illus. 192p. 1990. 19.95 (ISBN 1-878208-01-2). Guild Pr In.
Paprocki, Ray. Sports Superstars. 40p. (gr. 4-8). 1989. pap. 3.50 (ISBN 0-87406-389-2). Willowisp Pr.
Smith, Simpson E. Bear Bryant: Football's Winning Coach. LC 83-40404. (Illus.). 128p. (gr. 7 up). 1984. 11.95 (ISBN 0-8027-6526-2). Walker & Co.

SPORTS–DICTIONARIES

Berger, Melvin. Sports. (Illus.). 96p. (gr. 4 up). 1983. PLB 10.40 (ISBN 0-531-04540-4). Watts.

SPORTS–FICTION

Bryant, Bonnie. Team Play. (gr. 4-7). 1991. pap. 2.95 (ISBN 0-553-15862-7). Bantam.
Cabral, Brian & Parolini, Stephen. Second String Champion. 108p. (Orig.). (gr. 9-12). 1990. pap. 7.95 (ISBN 1-55945-008-8, Teenage Bks). Group Pub.
Carrier, Roch. Un Champion. Cohen, Sheldon, illus. (FRE.). 24p. (gr. 3 up). 1991. 14.95 (ISBN 0-88776-250-6). Tundra Bks.
Christopher, Matt. Long Shot For Paul. (gr. 3-7). 1990. pap. 3.95 (ISBN 0-316-14244-1). Little.
—Red-Hot Hightops. Mock, Paul D., illus. 128p. (gr. 4-6). 1987. 13.95 (ISBN 0-316-14056-2). Little.
Collura, Mary-Ellen L. Winners. LC 86-6286. 136p. (gr. 6 up). 1986. 10.95 (ISBN 0-8037-0011-3). Dial Bks Young.
Cornell, Donald. Ice Told Tales. Rosoff, Barbara, tr. Cornell, Donald, illus. (ENG & FRE.). 58p. (Orig.). (ps-2). 1991. pap. 4.00 (ISBN 0-9620738-1-4). D Cornell.
Ellis, Lucy. Pink Parrots, No. 4: Fielder's Choice. (gr. 4-7). 1991. pap. 3.50 (ISBN 0-316-12447-8). Little.
Fitzhugh, Louise. Sport. 224p. (gr. k-6). 1990. pap. 3.50 (ISBN 0-440-48221-6, YB). Dell.
Fleischman, Sid. McBroom & the Great Race. Lorraine, Walter H., illus. 64p. (gr. 3-7). 1980. 13.95 (ISBN 0-316-28568-4, Joy St Bks). Little.
French, Michael. The Throwing Season. LC 79-53598. (gr. 9-12). 1980. 8.95 (ISBN 0-440-08600-0). Delacorte.
Gilligan, Shannon. The Search for Champ. Kramer, Anthony, illus. 50p. (gr. 4). 1983. pap. 2.25 (ISBN 0-553-15442-7). Bantam.
Golenbock, Peter. Teammates. Bacon, Paul, illus. (gr. 1-4). 1990. 5.95 (ISBN 0-15-284285-3, Gulliver Bks). HarBraceJ.
Gutman, Bill. Rookie Summer. (gr. 7-12). 1988. PLB 2.95 (ISBN 0-89872-300-0). Turman Pub.
Hafner, Everett. Sports Riddles. Hafner, Marylin, illus. 48p. (gr. 1-4). 1989. pap. 9.95 (ISBN 0-670-81968-9). Viking Child Bks.
Howker, Janni. Isaac Campion. LC 86-9843. 128p. (gr. 5 up). 1987. 10.25 (ISBN 0-688-06658-5). Greenwillow.
Hughes, Dean. Pressure Play. (Illus.). 96p. (gr. 2-4). 1990. lib. bdg. 6.99 (ISBN 0-679-90431-X, Bullseye Bks); pap. 2.95 (ISBN 0-679-80431-5, Bullseye Bks). Knopf.
—Winning Streak. (Illus.). 96p. (gr. 2-4). 1990. lib. bdg. 6.99 (ISBN 0-679-90428-X, Bullseye Bks); pap. 2.95 (ISBN 0-679-80428-5, Bullseye Bks). Knopf.
Jack B. Quick, Sports Detective: The Case of the Basketball Joker & Other Mysteries. (gr. 3-7). 1990. pap. 3.50 (ISBN 0-316-72910-8). Little.
Jack B. Quick, Sports Detective: The Case of the Missing Playbook & Other Mysteries. (gr. 3-7). 1990. pap. 3.50 (ISBN 0-316-72911-6). Little.
Jenkins, Jerry. The Angry Gymnast. (Orig.). (gr. 9-12). 1986. pap. text ed. 3.95 (ISBN 0-8024-8235-X). Moody.
Johnson, Annabel & Johnson, Edgar. Gamebuster. Marchesi, Stephen, illus. LC 90-1330. 192p. (gr. 7 up). 1990. 14.95 (ISBN 0-525-65033-4, Cobblehill Bks). Dutton Child Bks.
Kehret, Peg. The Winner. (gr. 7-12). 1988. PLB 2.95 (ISBN 0-89872-302-7). Turman Pub.
Kessler, Leonard. Big Mile Race. (gr. 4-7). 1991. pap. 2.95 (ISBN 0-440-40413-4). Dell.
—The Worst Team Ever. Kessler, Leonard, illus. LC 84-25883. 47p. (gr. 1-3). 1985. 10.25 (ISBN 0-688-04234-1); lib. bdg. 10.88 (ISBN 0-688-04235-X). Greenwillow.
—Worst Team Ever. (ps-3). 1991. pap. 2.95 (ISBN 0-440-40428-2). Dell.
Klass, David. Wrestling with Honor. 208p. (gr. 8-12). 1990. pap. 2.95 (ISBN 0-590-43187-0). Scholastic Inc.
Knudson, R. R. Rinehart Lifts. 88p. (gr. 4-7). 1982. pap. 1.95 (ISBN 0-380-57059-9, 57059-9, Camelot). Avon.
—Rinehart Shouts. LC 86-29540. 115p. (gr. 4 up). 1987. 10.95 (ISBN 0-374-36296-3). FS&G.
Levy, Elizabeth. Bad Break. 1989. pap. 2.75 (ISBN 0-590-42195-6). Scholastic Inc.
—The Captain of the Team. 1989. pap. 2.75 (ISBN 0-590-42820-9). Scholastic Inc.
—Crush on the Coach. 1990. pap. 2.75 (ISBN 0-590-42821-7). Scholastic Inc.
—The New Coach? 128p. (gr. 3-7). 1991. pap. 2.75 (ISBN 0-590-44695-9). Scholastic Inc.
—Nobody's Perfect. 128p. (gr. 3-7). 1988. pap. 2.50 (ISBN 0-318-36504-9). Scholastic Inc.
—The Trouble with Elizabeth. 1989. pap. 2.75 (ISBN 0-590-42194-8). Scholastic Inc.
—Tumbling Ghosts. 1989. pap. 2.75 (ISBN 0-590-42221-9). Scholastic Inc.
—The Tumbling Run, No. 3. 128p. (gr. 3-7). 1988. pap. 2.50 (ISBN 0-590-41564-6). Scholastic Inc.
Lipsyte, Robert. The Contender. LC 67-19623. 176p. (gr. 7 up). 1987. pap. 2.95 (ISBN 0-06-447039-3, Trophy). HarpC Child Bks.
McBrier, Page. The Kickball Crisis. 96p. 1989. pap. 2.50 (ISBN 0-380-75781-8, Camelot). Avon.
Mallett, Jerry & Bartch, Marian. On Your Mark...Get Set... Help! Smith, Mark D., illus. 55p. (gr. 2-5). 1986. PLB 7.05 (ISBN 0-8479-9931-9, 222340). Perma Bound.
Peet, Bill. Merle the High Flying Squirrel. Peet, Bill, illus. 30p. (gr. k-3). 1983. pap. 4.95 (ISBN 0-395-34923-0). HM.
Pellowski, Michael J. Karate Bear. Robison, Don, illus. 24p. (gr. k-3). 1987. 1.95 (ISBN 0-87406-250-0, 14-14716-4). Willowisp Pr.
Perkins, Thornton. Junior High Champs. Chappick, Joseph, illus. 49p. (Orig.). (gr. 6-9). 1989. pap. 3.00 (ISBN 0-9623407-0-7). NVEM.
Riddle, Tohby. Careful with That Ball, Eugene! LC 90-43015. (Illus.). 32p. (ps-1). 1991. 12.95 (ISBN 0-531-05917-0); PLB 12.99 (ISBN 0-531-08517-1). Orchard Bks Watts.
Schulz, Charles M. You're the Greatest, Charlie Brown. Schulz, Charles M., illus. LC 79-4622. (gr. 1 up). 1979. (Random Juv); lib. bdg. 5.99 (ISBN 0-394-94260-4). Random.
Sheffer, H. R. Partners on Wheels. LC 80-28428. (Illus.). 48p. (gr. 3 up). 1981. PLB 9.95 (ISBN 0-89686-105-8, Crestwood Hse). Macmillan Child Grp.
—Sarah Sells Soccer. LC 80-28622. (Illus.). 48p. (gr. 3 up). 1981. PLB 9.95 (ISBN 0-89686-100-7, Crestwood Hse). Macmillan Child Grp.
—Second-String Nobody. LC 80-28767. (Illus.). 48p. (gr. 3 up). 1981. PLB 9.95 (ISBN 0-89686-101-5, Crestwood Hse). Macmillan Child Grp.
—Street-Hockey Lady. LC 80-29531. (Illus.). 48p. (gr. 3 up). 1981. PLB 9.95 (ISBN 0-89686-102-3, Crestwood Hse). Macmillan Child Grp.
—Swim for Pride. LC 80-28774. (Illus.). 48p. (gr. 3 up). 1981. PLB 9.95 (ISBN 0-89686-104-X, Crestwood Hse). Macmillan Child Grp.
—Two at the Net. LC 80-28429. (Illus.). 48p. (gr. 3 up). 1981. PLB 9.95 (ISBN 0-89686-108-2, Crestwood Hse). Macmillan Child Grp.
—Weekend in the Dunes. LC 80-28624. (Illus.). 48p. (gr. 3 up). 1981. PLB 9.95 (ISBN 0-89686-109-0, Crestwood Hse). Macmillan Child Grp.
—Winner on the Court. LC 80-28451. (Illus.). 48p. (gr. 3 up). 1981. PLB 9.95 (ISBN 0-89686-107-4, Crestwood Hse). Macmillan Child Grp.
Sobol, Donald J. Encyclopedia Brown's Book of Wacky Sports. Enik, Ted, illus. LC 82-84250. 128p. (gr. 3-7). 1984. 11.95 (ISBN 0-688-03884-0). Morrow Jr Bks.
Sports Day. 22p. (ps-1). 1985. 1.98 (ISBN 0-517-42789-3). Outlet Bk Co.
Standish, Burt L. Frank Merriwell's Sports Afield. Rudman, Jack, ed. (gr. 9 up). Date not set. 9.95 (ISBN 0-8373-9310-8); pap. 3.95 (ISBN 0-8373-9010-9). F Merriwell.
Winthrop, Elizabeth. Sledding. Wilson, Sarah, illus. LC 89-1761. 32p. (ps-2). 1989. 12.95 (ISBN 0-06-026528-0); PLB 12.89 (ISBN 0-06-026566-3). HarpC Child Bks.

SPORTS–HISTORY

Aaseng, Nathan. Comeback Stars of Pro Sports. LC 83-737. (Illus.). 80p. (gr. 4up). 1983. PLB 7.95 (ISBN 0-8225-1327-7). Lerner Pubns.
—Supersubs of Pro Sports. LC 83-738. (Illus.). 80p. (gr. 4up). 1983. PLB 7.95 (ISBN 0-8225-1328-5). Lerner Pubns.
Benson, Michael. Dream Teams: the Best Teams of All Time. (gr. 4-7). 1991. 17.95 (ISBN 0-316-08993-1). Little.
David, Andrew & Moran, Tom. River Thrill Sports. LC 82-24966. (Illus.). 48p. (gr. 4-9). 1983. PLB 9.95 (ISBN 0-8225-0506-1). Lerner Pubns.
Great Sports Performances. 48p. (gr. 5-6). 1989. PLB 10.95 (ISBN 0-685-26336-3). Capstone Pr.
Gutman, Bill. Great Sports Upsets. (gr. 5 up). 1988. pap. 2.50 (ISBN 0-318-37403-X). PB.
Hollander, Phyllis. Sports Bloopers. 1985. pap. 2.95 (ISBN 0-590-43712-7). Scholastic Inc.
Hollander, Phyllis & Hollander, Zander. Sports Bloopers: Weird, Wacky & Unexpected Moments in Sports. (Illus.). 64p. (Orig.). (gr. 4 up). 1985. pap. 2.50 (ISBN 0-590-41947-1). Scholastic Inc.
Sperling, Anita. Sports Tracing Fun Book. (gr. 3-7). 1989. pap. 1.95 (ISBN 0-590-42492-0). Scholastic Inc.
Sporting News Staff. The Sporting News Dynasty-Sports Greatest Teams. (Illus.). (gr. 7-12). 1989. 19.95 (ISBN 0-89204-313-X). Sporting News.
Sullivan, George. Any Number Can Play. Caldwell, John, illus. LC 89-35501. 128p. (gr. 3-7). 1990. 13.95 (ISBN 0-690-04812-2, Crowell Jr Bks); PLB 13.89 (ISBN 0-690-04814-9, Crowell Jr Bks). HarpC Child Bks.

SPORTS–POETRY

Morrison, Lillian, ed. Sprints & Distances: Sports in Poetry & the Poetry in Sport. Ross, Clare & Ross, John, illus. LC 65-14906. 224p. (gr. 4-7). 1990. PLB 13.89 (ISBN 0-690-04840-8, Crowell Jr Bks). HarpC Child Bks.

SPRING

Allington, Richard L. & Krull, Kathleen. Spring. Rahn, Dee, illus. LC 80-25093. 32p. (gr. k-3). 1985. PLB 15.33 (ISBN 0-8172-1342-2); pap. 9.27 (ISBN 0-8172-2489-0). Raintree Pubs.
Anglund, Joan W. Spring Is a New Beginning. Anglund, Joan W., illus. LC 63-7892. (gr. k-3). 1963. 8.95 (ISBN 0-15-278161-7, HJ). HarBraceJ.
Barker, Cicely M. Flower Fairies of the Spring. Barker, Cicely M., illus. (ps up). 1991. 5.95 (ISBN 0-7232-3753-0). Warne.
Carson, Patti & Dellosa, Janet. Spring Fun Book. Carson, Patti & Dellosa, Janet, illus. 32p. (ps-2). 1984. pap. 1.59 (ISBN 0-88724-059-3, CD-8047). Carson-Dellos.
—Spring Preschool-K Practice. Carson, Patti & Dellosa, Janet, illus. 32p. (ps-k). 1984. pap. 1.98 (ISBN 0-88724-019-4, CD-8034). Carson-Dellos.
—Spring Primary Reading & Art Activities. Carson, Patti & Dellosa, Janet, illus. 32p. (gr. 1-3). 1984. pap. 1.98 (ISBN 0-88724-066-6, CD-8046). Carson-Dellos.
Davis, Nancy M., et al. Spring & May. Davis, Nancy M., illus. 46p. (Orig.). (ps-4). 1986. pap. 5.95 (ISBN 0-937103-11-X). DaNa Pubns.
Glover, Susanne & Grewe, Georgeann. A Splash of Spring. Grewe, Georgeann, illus. 128p. (gr. 2-5). 1987. pap. 9.95 (ISBN 0-86653-412-1). Good Apple.
Hirschi, Ron. Spring. (ps-3). 1990. 13.95 (ISBN 0-525-65037-7, Cobblehill Bks). Dutton Child Bks.
Kalman, Bobbie. We Celebrate Spring. (Illus.). 56p. (gr. 3-4). 1985. 15.95 (ISBN 0-86505-043-0); pap. 7.95 (ISBN 0-86505-053-8). Crabtree Pub Co.
Lambert, David. Spring. (Illus.). 48p. (gr. 4-6). 1987. lib. bdg. 12.90 (ISBN 0-531-18105-7, Pub. by Bookwright Pr). Watts.
McInnes, Celia. Projects for Spring & Holiday Activities. Young, Richard G., ed. Walker, Malcom, illus. LC 88-33514. 32p. (gr. 3-5). 1989. PLB 14.60 (ISBN 0-944483-40-2). Garrett Ed Corp.
Maniscalco, Joe. Old Barn: Springtime. Wheeler, Penny E., ed. 32p. (gr. 2-4). 1988. pap. 3.95 (ISBN 0-8280-0423-4). Review & Herald.
Markle, Sandra. Exploring Spring: A Season of Science Activities, Puzzlers & Games. LC 89-394. (Illus.). 128p. (gr. 3-7). 1990. SBE 13.95 (ISBN 0-689-31341-1, Atheneum Child Bk). Macmillan Child Grp.
Mason, John. Spring Weather. (Illus.). 32p. (gr. 1-5). 1991. PLB 11.90 (ISBN 0-531-18437-4, Pub. by Bookwright Pr). Watts.
Moncure, Jane B. Step into Spring: A New Season. Williams, Jenny, illus. LC 90-30375. 32p. (ps-2). 1990. lib. bdg. 11.97 (ISBN 0-89565-571-3). Childs World.
—Word Bird's Spring Words. Gohman, Vera, illus. LC 85-5902. 32p. (gr. k-2). 1985. lib. bdg. 11.97 (ISBN 0-89565-310-9); pap. 6.96 (ISBN 0-89565-425-3). Childs World.
Parramon, J. M., et al. La Primavera. (SPA.). (ps). 1986. pap. 4.95 (ISBN 0-8120-3648-4). Barron.
Rosen, Mike. Spring Festivals. (Illus.). 32p. (gr. 3-7). 1991. PLB 11.90 (ISBN 0-531-18384-X). Watts.
Santrey, Louis. Spring. Sabin, Francene, illus. LC 82-19381. 32p. (gr. 4-7). 1982. lib. bdg. 10.79 (ISBN 0-89375-909-0); pap. text ed. 2.95 (ISBN 0-89375-910-4). Troll Assocs.
Sibley, Kenneth E. A Spring Surprise. (Illus.). 19p. (Orig.). (gr. 7 up). 1989. pap. 6.95 (ISBN 0-9619934-1-3). K E Sibley.
Thomson, Ruth. Spring. 1990. PLB 11.90 (ISBN 0-531-14018-0). Watts.
Zimmermann, H. Werner. Alphonse Knows...The Colour of Spring. (Illus.). 24p. (ps-2). 1991. bds. 9.95 laminated (ISBN 0-19-540743-1). Oxford U Pr.

SPRING–FICTION

Barnes, Jill & Ishinabe, Fusako. Spring Snowman. Rubin, Caroline, ed. Japan Foreign Rights Centre Staff, tr. from JPN. Ishinabe, Fusako, illus. LC 90-37748. 32p. (gr. k-3). 1990. PLB 15.93 (ISBN 0-944483-83-6). Garrett Ed Corp.
Clifton, Lucille. The Boy Who Didn't Believe in Spring. Turkle, Brinton, illus. (gr. 3-4). 1973. 13.95 (ISBN 0-525-27145-7, DCB); pap. 1.95 (ISBN 0-525-45038-6, DCB). Dutton Child Bks.
—The Boy Who Didn't Believe in Spring. Turkle, Brinton, illus. LC 87-27145. 32p. (ps-3). 1988. pap. 3.95 (ISBN 0-525-44365-7, 0383-120, DCB). Dutton Child Bks.
Gordon, Sharon. First Day of Spring. Willis, Christine, illus. LC 81-2750. 32p. (gr. k-2). 1981. PLB 10.89 (ISBN 0-89375-531-1); pap. text ed. 2.95 (ISBN 0-89375-532-X). Troll Assocs.
Johnson, Crockett. Will Spring Be Early or Will Spring Be Late? Johnson, Crockett, illus. LC 59-9424. 48p. (gr. k-3). 1961. PLB 12.89 (ISBN 0-690-89423-6, Crowell Jr Bks). HarpC Child Bks.
—Will Spring Be Early? or Will Spring Be Late? Johnson, Crockett, illus. LC 59-9424. 48p. (gr. k-3). 1990. pap. 3.95 (ISBN 0-06-443224-6, Trophy). HarpC Child Bks.
Krensky, Stephen. Lionel in the Spring. LC 88-30885. 1990. 9.95 (ISBN 0-8037-0630-8); PLB 9.89 (ISBN 0-8037-0631-6). Dial Bks Young.
Kroll, Steven. I Love Spring. Shoemaker, Kathryn E., illus. LC 86-14844. 32p. (ps-1). 1987. reinforced bdg. 12.95 (ISBN 0-8234-0634-2). Holiday.
Miller, Moira. The Search for Spring. Deuchar, Ian, illus. LC 86-32898. 32p. (ps-3). 1988. 11.95 (ISBN 0-8037-0445-3). Dial Bks Young.

Minarik, Else H. It's Spring! Graham, Margaret B., illus. LC 87-37202. 24p. (ps up). 1989. 11.95 (ISBN 0-688-07619-X); PLB 11.88 (ISBN 0-688-07620-3). Greenwillow.
Moncure, Jane B. Spring Is Here! Hook, Frances, illus. LC 75-14202. (ps-2). 1975. 8.95 (ISBN 0-913778-11-7); cassette 13.95; walk chart 10.95 (ISBN 0-685-01065-1). Childs World.
Rockwell, Anne. First Comes Spring. LC 84-45331. (Illus.). 32p. (ps-1). 1985. 14.95 (ISBN 0-694-00106-6, Crowell Jr Bks); PLB 12.89 (ISBN 0-690-04455-0). HarpC Child Bks.
—First Comes Spring. Rockwell, Anne, illus. LC 84-45331. 32p. (ps-1). 1991. pap. 4.95 (ISBN 0-06-107412-8). HarpC Child Bks.
Smith, Viola B. Touch of Spring. Michel, Sandra S., ed. Keane, Marie, illus. (gr. k up). 1976. pap. 4.00 (ISBN 0-917178-02-5). Lenape Pub.
Tibo, Gilles. Simon Fete le Printemps. Tibo, Gilles, illus. (FRE.). (ps-4). 1990. 10.95 (ISBN 0-88776-248-4). Tundra Bks.
—Simon Welcomes Spring. Tibo, Gilles, illus. 24p. (ps-4). 1990. 10.95 (ISBN 0-88776-247-6). Tundra Bks.
Ziefert, Harriet. Let's Trade. LC 88-82401. (Illus.). 32p. (ps-3). 1989. pap. 8.95 (ISBN 0-670-82666-9). Viking Child Bks.

SQUANTO, WAMPANOAG INDIAN, d. 1622

Bulla, Clyde R. Squanto: Friend of the Pilgrims. (gr. 2-3). 1971. pap. 2.50 (ISBN 0-590-33937-0, Schol Pap). Scholastic Inc.
—Squanto, Friend of the Pilgrims. 112p. (gr. 2-5). 1985. pap. 2.50 (ISBN 0-590-40465-2). Scholastic Inc.
Jassem, Kate. Squanto, the Pilgrim Adventure. new ed. LC 78-18042. (Illus.). 48p. (gr. 4-6). 1979. PLB 9.89 (ISBN 0-89375-161-8); pap. 2.95 (ISBN 0-89375-151-0). Troll Assocs.
The Story of Squanto. 1990. pap. 2.95 (ISBN 0-440-40360-X, YB). Dell.
Zadra, Dan. Indians of America: Squanto. rev. ed. (gr. 2-4). 1987. PLB 11.50s.p. (ISBN 0-88682-161-4); 16.45 (ISBN 0-685-19789-1). Creative Ed.
Ziner, Feenie. Squanto. LC 88-13982. x, 158p. (gr. 7 up). 1988. 17.50 (ISBN 0-208-02218-X, Linnet); pap. 9.95 (ISBN 0-208-02274-0, Linnet). Shoe string.

SQUARE DANCING

Hammond, Mildred. Square Dancing Is for Me. Tabb, James C., illus. LC 82-17134. 48p. (gr. 2-5). 1983. PLB 8.95 (ISBN 0-8225-1138-X). Lerner Pubns.

SQUIRRELS

Bare, Colleen S. Busy, Busy Squirrels. Bare, Colleen S., photos by. LC 90-44219. (Illus.). 32p. (gr. 1-4). 1991. 12.95 (ISBN 0-525-65063-6, Cobblehill Bks). Dutton Child Bks.
—Tree Squirrels. (gr. 8-12). 1983. 10.95 (ISBN 0-396-08208-4, Putnam). Putnam Pub Group.
Coldrey, Jennifer. The Squirrel in the Trees. LC 85-30292. (Illus.). 32p. (gr. 4-6). 1986. 10.95 (ISBN 1-55532-062-7). Gareth Stevens Inc.
—The World of Squirrels. LC 85-30296. (Illus.). 32p. (gr. 2-3). 1987. 10.95 (ISBN 1-55532-065-1). Gareth Stevens Inc.
Dalmais. Squirrel, Reading Level 3-4. (Illus.). 28p. (gr. 2-5). Date not set. PLB 14.60 (ISBN 0-86592-857-6). Rourke Corp.
Komoto, Sachiko. Chessie's First Year. Komoto, Sachiko, illus. LC 90-46860. 64p. (gr. 1-3). 1991. PLB 12.95 (ISBN 0-685-35738-4). Gareth Stevens Inc.
Lane, Margaret. The Squirrel. Lilly, Kenneth, illus. LC 81-1229. 32p. (ps-4). 1981. 7.95 (ISBN 0-8037-8230-6). Dial Bks Young.
McConoughey, Jana. Squirrel. LC 83-2085. (Illus.). 48p. (gr. 5-6). 1983. lib. bdg. 10.95 (ISBN 0-89686-223-2, Crestwood Hse). Macmillan Child Grp.
Royston, Angela. Squirrel. Pledger, Maurice, illus. 24p. (gr. k-3). 1989. pap. 2.95 (ISBN 0-8249-8372-6). Ideals.
Squirrel. 1990. 2.95 (ISBN 0-8378-2057-X). Gibson.
Tabor, Roger. Survival: Could You Be a Squirrel? Brown, Derick, illus. 32p. (gr. 1-6). 1990. 10.95 (ISBN 0-8249-8413-7). Ideals.

SQUIRRELS–FICTION

Brennan, Gale. Earl the Squirrel. Flint, Russ, illus. 16p. (Orig.). (gr. k-6). 1981. pap. 1.25 (ISBN 0-685-02455-5). Brennan Bks.
Bussard, Paula J., et al. Snuggles' Great Adventure. Wigginton, Shirley, ed. Goodridge, Lawrence, illus. 30p. (gr. k-4). 1987. 1.39 (ISBN 0-87403-254-7, 3454). Standard Pub.
Cosgrove, Stephen. Squeakers. James, Robin, illus. 32p. (Orig.). (gr. 1-4). 1985. pap. 2.95 (ISBN 0-8431-1442-8). Price Stern.
Davies, Stanley C. Squiffy Squirrel. 1988. 5.95 (ISBN 0-533-07760-5). Vantage.
Downing, Johnette. A Squirrel Jumped Out of the Tree. Downing, Johnette, illus. (ps). 1990. pap. 2.50 (ISBN 0-938991-57-4). Colonial Pr AL.
Fowler, Richard. Squirrel's Tale. 24p. (ps-3). 1984. 9.95 (ISBN 0-88110-157-5). EDC.
Gordon, Sharon. Show & Tell. Kolding, Richard M., illus. LC 86-30855. 32p. (gr. k-2). 1987. PLB 7.06 (ISBN 0-8167-0994-7); pap. text ed. 1.95 (ISBN 0-8167-0995-5). Troll Assocs.

Hannah, Valerie. Cyril Squirrel & Sheryl: An Ecological Tale. Herrick, George H., ed. Meek, Barbara, illus. 46p. (Orig.). (gr. k-3). 1991. pap. 8.95 (ISBN 0-941281-78-7). V H Pub. With "Fun to Answer" questions & printed on recycled paper & Beatrix Potter-like illustrations, this lucid story is about a city squirrel who visits his country cousin Sheryl. When camping in the forest, Cyril only just avoids an ecological disater. "A wonderful reading & learning experience & a child's treasure."--Independent Small Press Review, Spring 1991. "Cyril & Sheryl squirrel share stories of the secrets & exciting places in which they live. This is an enchanting tale full of the quiet wisdom of the ages."--Book Reader, May 1991. "Join the adventures of Cyril, a squirrel who has never seen a tree, who lives an urban environment & skateboards for exercise...This delightful story is populated with many family squirrel members who have plenty to teach Cyril when he goes to the woods to visit his grandparents. Hannah has provided a learning experience for grade school children (k-3) in this timely ecological adventure."--Bloomsbury Review, May 1991.
Publisher Provided Annotation.

Kesey, Ken. Little Tricker the Squirrel Meets Big Double the Bear. Moser, Barry, illus. 1990. 14.95 (ISBN 0-670-81136-X). Viking Child Bks.
—The Little Trickler, The Squirrel. 1988. write for info. Viking Child Bks.
McCabe, Eugene. Cyril: Quest of an Orphaned Squirrel. 72p. (ps-8). 1987. 13.95 (ISBN 0-86278-116-7, Pub. by O'Brien Press Ltd Eire); pap. 7.95 (ISBN 0-86278-131-0, Pub. by O'Brien Press Ltd Eire). Dufour.
McMullen, Shawn A. Justin Ordinary Squirrel. Haley, Amanda, illus. 32p. (ps-2). 1991. pap. text ed. 3.99 (ISBN 0-87403-807-3, 24-03897). Standard Pub.
Miller, Edna. Scamper: A Gray Tree Squirrel. Miller, Edna, illus. 32p. (gr. k-3). 1991. PLB 14.95 (ISBN 0-945912-12-9). Pippin Pr.
Peet, Bill. Merle the High Flying Squirrel. Peet, Bill, illus. LC 73-18371. 32p. (gr. k-3). 1974. reinforced bdg. 13.95 (ISBN 0-395-18452-5). HM.
Peterson, Hans. Erik Has a Squirrel. Wikland, Ilon, illus. Hyatt, Christine, tr. (Illus.). 32p. (ps up). 1989. 12.95 (ISBN 9-12-959140-6, Pub. by R & S Bks). FS&G.
Potter, Beatrix. Meet Squirrel Nutkin. (Illus.). 12p. (ps). 1987. bds. 2.95 (ISBN 0-7232-3452-3). Warne.
—Tale of Squirrel Nutkin. (Illus.). (ps-2). 1973. 4.95 (ISBN 0-7232-0593-0); pap. 2.25 (ISBN 0-7232-6226-8). Warne.
—The Tale of Squirrel Nutkin. Atkinson, Allen, illus. 64p. 1984. pap. 2.25 (ISBN 0-553-15205-X). Bantam.
—The Tale of Squirrel Nutkin. (Illus.). 64p. (ps-3). 1986. 3.95 (ISBN 0-671-62926-3, Little Simon). S&S Trade.
—The Tale of Squirrel Nutkin. 1987. 5.95 (ISBN 0-7232-3461-2); pap. 2.25 (ISBN 0-7232-3486-8). Warne.
—The Tale of Squirrel Nutkin. Bond, Gary, read by. (Illus.). (ps-3). 1989. pap. 6.95 bk. & tape (ISBN 0-7232-3671-2). Warne.
—The Tale of Squirrel Nutkin. (Illus.). 60p. (gr. 1-5). 1972. pap. 1.75 (ISBN 0-486-22828-2). Dover.
—The Tale of Squirrel Nutkin. (Illus.). (ps-2). 3.95 (ISBN 0-7214-5045-8). Ladybird Bks.
—Tale of Squirrel Nutkin. (Illus.). (ps). 1991. pap. 1.99 (ISBN 0-7232-3766-2). Warne.
Sammy the Squirrel. (Illus.). (ps-1). 2.98 (ISBN 0-517-46987-1). Outlet Bk Co.
Shannon, George. The Surprise. Aruego, Jose & Dewey, Ariane, illus. LC 83-1434. 32p. (gr. k-3). 1983. 13.95 (ISBN 0-688-02313-4). Greenwillow.
Sharmat, Marjorie W. Attila the Angry. Hoban, Lillian, illus. LC 84-15860. 32p. (gr. k-3). 1985. reinforced bdg. 11.95 (ISBN 0-8234-0545-1). Holiday.
Sir. Squirrel Starts a Business. (Illus.). (ps-1). 1.98 (ISBN 0-517-45740-7). Outlet Bk Co.
Squirrels on the Move (EV, Unit 8. (gr. 2). 1991. 5-pack 21.25 (ISBN 0-88106-765-2). Charlesbridge Pub.
Wolkstein, Diane. Squirrel's Song. Hoban, Lillian, illus. LC 76-5483. (ps-2). 1976. Knopf.
Yep, Laurence. The Curse of the Squirrel. Zimmer, Dirk, illus. LC 87-4612. 64p. (gr. 2-4). 1987. lib. bdg. 6.99 (ISBN 0-394-98200-2, Random Juv); pap. 1.95 (ISBN 0-394-88200-8, Random Juv). Random.
Young, Miriam. Miss Suzy's Easter Surprise. Lobel, Arnold, illus. LC 80-16966. 48p. (ps-3). 1984. Repr. of 1972 ed. 12.95 (ISBN 0-02-793680-5, Four Winds). Macmillan Child Grp.
—Miss Suzy's Easter Surprise. LC 89-37842. (Illus.). 48p. (ps-3). 1990. pap. 4.95 (ISBN 0-689-71374-6, Aladdin). Macmillan Child Grp.

STABILIZATION IN INDUSTRY
see Economic Conditions

STAGE
see Acting; Actors and Actresses; Theater

STAGE SCENERY
see Theaters–Stage Setting and Scenery

STAGE SETTING
see Theaters–Stage Setting and Scenery

STAINED GLASS
see Glass Painting and Staining

STALIN, JOSEPH VISSARIONOVICH, 1879-1953

Caulkins, Janet. Joseph Stalin. (Illus.). 160p. (gr. 9-12). 1990. PLB 13.90 (ISBN 0-531-10945-3). Watts.
Italia, Bob. Joseph Stalin. Walner, Rosemary, ed. (Illus.). 32p. (gr. 4). 1990. PLB 11.95 (ISBN 0-939179-83-0). Abdo & Dghtrs.
Marrin, Albert. Stalin: Russia's Man of Steel. 256p. (gr. 7 up). 1988. pap. 14.95 (ISBN 0-670-82102-0). Viking Child Bks.
Ross, Stewart. The U. S. S. R. under Stalin. (Illus.). 64p. (gr. 9-12). 1991. RLB 12.90 (ISBN 0-531-18409-9, Pub. by Boatwright Pr). Watts.

STAMINA, PHYSICAL
see Physical Fitness

STAMPS, POSTAGE
see Postage Stamps

STANDARD OF VALUE
see Money

STANDARD TIME
see Time

STANLEY, SIR HENRY MORTON, 1841-1904

Clinton, Susan. Henry Stanley & David Livingstone. LC 90-2172. (Illus.). 128p. (gr. 3 up). 1990. PLB 25.27 (ISBN 0-516-03055-8). Childrens.

STANTON, ELIZABETH CADY, 1815-1902

Gleiter, Jan & Thompson, Kathleen. Elizabeth Cady Stanton. (Illus.). 32p. (Orig.). (gr. 2-5). 1988. PLB 16.67 (ISBN 0-8172-2677-X); pap. 9.27 (ISBN 0-8172-2681-8). Raintree Pubs.
Kendall, Martha E. Elizabeth Cady Stanton. Knight, Anne R., illus. LC 88-81556. 72p. (gr. 6-8). text ed. 10.95 (ISBN 0-945783-03-5); pap. 5.95 (ISBN 0-945783-02-7). Highland Pub Group.

STAR TREK (TELEVISION PROGRAM)

Cohen, Daniel & Cohen, Susan. Strange & Amazing Facts about Star Trek. (Illus.). (gr. 4 up). 1988. pap. 2.75 (ISBN 0-671-68173-7, Archway). PB.

STARFISHES

Hurd, Edith T. Starfish. Bloch, Lucienne, illus. LC 62-7742. 40p. (gr. k-2). 1962. PLB 13.89 (ISBN 0-690-77069-3, Crowell Jr Bks). HarpC Child Bks.

STARS
see also Astrology; Astronomy; Meteors; Planets; Solar System

Asimov, Isaac. The Birth & Death of Stars. LC 88-42892. (Illus.). 32p. (gr. 3-4). 1989. PLB 11.95 (ISBN 1-55532-367-7). Gareth Stevens Inc.
—Why Do Stars Twinkle? (Illus.). 24p. (gr. 2-3). 1991. PLB 11.95 (ISBN 0-8368-0437-6). Gareth Stevens Inc.
Bailey, Donna. Looking at the Stars. LC 90-40076. (Illus.). 48p. (gr. 2-5). 1990. PLB 15.96 (ISBN 0-8114-2522-3). Steck-V.
Baker, David. Flight to the Stars. (Illus.). 48p. (gr. 3-8). 1989. lib. bdg. 18.60 (ISBN 0-86592-373-6). Rourke Corp.
Barrett, Norman. The Picture World of Sun & Stars. (Illus.). 32p. (gr. k-4). 1990. PLB 11.40 (ISBN 0-531-14058-X). Watts.
—Sun & Stars. LC 85-50161. (Illus.). 32p. (gr. k-6). 1986. lib. bdg. 11.40 (ISBN 0-531-10007-3). Watts.
Berger, Melvin. Bright Stars, Red Giants & White Dwarfs. LC 82-23052. (Illus.). 64p. (gr. 5-9). 1983. 12.99 (ISBN 0-399-61209-2, Putnam). Putnam Pub Group.
Branley, Franklyn M. The Big Dipper. rev. ed. Coxe, Molly, illus. LC 90-33198. 32p. (ps-1). 1991. pap. 4.50 (ISBN 0-06-445100-3, Trophy). HarpC Child Bks.
—The Big Dipper. rev. ed. Coxe, Molly, illus. LC 90-31199. 32p. (ps-1). 1991. 13.95 (ISBN 0-06-020511-3); PLB 13.89 (ISBN 0-06-020512-1). HarpC Child Bks.
—The Sky Is Full of Stars. Bond, Felicia, illus. LC 81-43037. 40p. (gr. k-3). 1981. PLB 13.89 (ISBN 0-690-04123-3, Crowell Jr Bks). HarpC Child Bks.
Darling, David J. The Stars: From Birth to Black Hole. Swofford, Jeanette, illus. LC 84-23067. 64p. (gr. 4 up). 1985. PLB 10.95 (ISBN 0-87518-284-4, Dillon). Macmillan Child Grp.
Gallant, Roy A. The Constellations: How They Came to Be. rev. ed. LC 84-28755. (Illus.). 224p. (gr. 7 up). 1991. SBE 15.95 (ISBN 0-02-735776-7, Four Winds). Macmillan Child Grp.
—Private Lives of the Stars. LC 86-5338. (Illus.). 128p. (gr. 5 up). 1986. 13.95 (ISBN 0-02-737350-9, Mcmillan Child Bk). Macmillan Child Grp.
Hatchett, Clint. The Glow-in-the-Dark Night Sky Book. Marchesi, Stephen, illus. LC 87-61531. 24p. (gr. 3-7). 1988. 11.95 (ISBN 0-394-89113-9, Random Juv). Random.
Herbst, Judith. The Golden Book of Stars & Planets. LaPadula, Tom, illus. 48p. (gr. 3-7). 1988. write for info. (ISBN 0-307-15572-2). Western Pub.
Jefferies, Lawrence. All about Stars. Veno, Joseph, illus. LC 82-20027. 32p. (gr. 3-6). PLB 10.59 (ISBN 0-89375-888-4); pap. text ed. 2.95 (ISBN 0-89375-889-2). Troll Assocs.

Kerrod, Robin. Big Book of Stars & Planets. 1990. 5.98 (ISBN 0-8317-0861-1). Smithmark.

Lampton, Christopher. Stars & Planets: A Useful & Entertaining Tool to Guide Youngsters into the Twenty-First Century. Miller, Ron, illus. LC 87-13628. 48p. (gr. 1-7). 1988. PLB 11.99 (ISBN 0-385-23786-3); pap. 10.95 (ISBN 0-385-23785-5). Doubleday.

Maynard. Stars & Planets: Discovering the Secrets of the Sky at Night. (Illus.). 32p. (gr. 4-8). 1976. PLB 13.96 (ISBN 0-88110-313-6); pap. 6.95 (ISBN 0-86020-094-9). EDC.

Rey, H. A. Find the Constellations. rev. ed. (Illus.). 80p. (gr. 3-7). 1976. 14.95 (ISBN 0-395-24509-5). HM.

—Find the Constellations. rev. ed. Rey, H. A., illus. 72p. (gr. 3-7). 1976. pap. 7.95 (ISBN 0-395-24418-8, Sandpiper). HM.

—The Stars: A New Way to See Them. 3rd ed. (Illus.). (gr. 8 up). 1973. 16.95 (ISBN 0-395-08121-1). HM.

Sabin, Louis. Stars. Acosta, Andres, illus. LC 84-2605. 32p. (gr. 3-6). 1985. PLB 9.49 (ISBN 0-8167-0152-0); pap. text ed. 2.95 (ISBN 0-8167-0153-9). Troll Assocs.

Santrey, Laurence. Discovering the Stars. Watling, James, illus. LC 81-7489. 32p. (gr. 2-4). 1982. PLB 10.89 (ISBN 0-89375-568-0); pap. text ed. 2.95 (ISBN 0-89375-569-9); cassette 9.95 (ISBN 0-685-04946-9). Troll Assocs.

Simon, Seymour. Galaxies. LC 87-23967. (Illus.). (ps-3). 1988. 14.95 (ISBN 0-688-08002-2); PLB 14.88 (ISBN 0-688-08004-9, Morrow Jr Bks). Morrow Jr Bks.

—Stars. LC 85-32012. (Illus.). 32p. (ps-3). 1986. 14.95 (ISBN 0-688-05855-8); lib. bdg. 14.88 (ISBN 0-688-05856-6, Morrow Jr Bks); pap. 5.95 (ISBN 0-688-09237-3, Mulberry Bks). Morrow Jr Bks.

Sneider, Cary I. Earth, Moon, & Stars. Bergman, Lincoln & Fairwell, Kay, eds. Baker, Lisa H. & Bevilacqua, Carol, illus. Sneider, Cary I., photos by. 50p. (Orig.). (gr. 5-9). 1986. pap. 9.00 (ISBN 0-912511-18-4). Lawrence Science.

Wandelmaier, Roy. Stars. Trivas, Irene, illus. LC 84-8642. 32p. (gr. k-2). 1985. PLB 10.89 (ISBN 0-8167-0339-6); pap. text ed. 2.95 (ISBN 0-8167-0442-2). Troll Assocs.

West, Robin. Far Out: How to Create Your Own Star World. Wolfe, Bob, photos by. (Illus.). 72p. (gr. k-4). 1987. lib. bdg. 14.95 (ISBN 0-87614-279-X); pap. 5.95 (ISBN 0-87614-463-6). Carolrhoda Bks.

Zim, Herbert S. & Baker, Robert H. Stars. rev. ed. Irving, James G., illus. (gr. 6 up). 1985. pap. write for info. (ISBN 0-307-24493-8, Golden Pr). Western Pub.

STARS, FALLING

see Meteors

STARS–FICTION

Booht, David. Til All the Stars Have Fallen. (gr. 4-7). 1990. 14.95 (ISBN 0-670-83272-3). Viking Child Bks.

Edens, Cooper. The Starcleaner Reunion. Edens, Cooper, illus. LC 79-122663. 1979. pap. 8.95 (ISBN 0-914676-77-6). Green Tiger Pr.

Ekker, Ernst A. What Is Beyond the Hill? Heyduck-Huth, Hilde, illus. LC 85-45446. 28p. (ps-1). 1986. 8.95 (ISBN 0-397-32166-X, Lipp Jr Bks). HarpC Child Bks.

Ginolfi, Arthur. Tiny Star. (Illus.). 32p. 1989. 6.95 (ISBN 1-56288-134-5). Checkerboard Pr.

Hort, Lenny. How Many Stars in the Sky. Ransome, James, illus. 32p. (ps-3). 1991. 12.95 (ISBN 0-688-10103-8, Tambourine Bks); PLB 12.88 (ISBN 0-688-10104-6, Tambourine Bks). Morrow.

Ichikawa, Satomi. Nora's Stars. Ichikawa, Satomi, illus. 32p. (ps-3). 1989. 13.95 (ISBN 0-399-21616-2, Philomel Bks). Putnam Pub Group.

Lee, Jeanne M., retold by. & illus. The Legend of the Milky Way. LC 81-6906. 32p. (gr. k-3). 1982. 11.50 (ISBN 0-8050-0217-0). H Holt & Co.

Lurie, Alison. The Heavenly Zoo: Legends & Tales of the Stars. Beisner, Monika, illus. LC 79-21263. 64p. (ps-3). 1980. 12.95 (ISBN 0-374-32910-9). FS&G.

Morey, Walt. Sandy & the Rock Star. LC 78-12375. (gr. 4-7). 1979. 13.95 (ISBN 0-525-38785-4, DCB). Dutton Child Bks.

Needham, Michael O. Night of the Shooting Stars: Meteors, Meteoroids & Meteorites. Nichols, Susan, ed. Blanchette, David, illus. LC 86-63289. 48p. (gr. 2-5). pap. 6.95 (ISBN 0-9617056-3-9). Spiral Galaxy.

Ray, Deborah K. Stargazing Sky. Ray, Deborah K., illus. LC 90-36775. 32p. (ps-2). 1991. 13.95 (ISBN 0-517-57816-6); PLB 14.99 (ISBN 0-517-57838-7). Crown.

Saunders, Susan. Rent-a-Star. LC 87-33116. 105p. (Orig.). (gr. 3-5). 1989. lib. bdg. 5.99 (ISBN 0-394-99605-4); pap. 2.95 (ISBN 0-394-89605-X). Knopf.

Vautier, Ghislaine. The Way of the Stars. McLeish, Kenneth, adapted by. (Illus.). 1989. pap. 6.95 (ISBN 0-521-37913-X). Cambridge U Pr.

Widman, Christine. The Star Grazers. Spowart, Robin, illus. LC 87-29377. 32p. (ps-3). 1989. PLB 11.89 (ISBN 0-06-026473-X). HarpC Child Bks.

Wrightson, Patricia. The Nargun & the Stars. LC 86-10600. 184p. (gr. 7 up). 1986. 13.95 (ISBN 0-689-50403-9, M K McElderry). Macmillan Child Grp.

Zimelman, Nathan. The Star of Melvin. Dunrea, Olivier, illus. LC 86-171. 32p. (ps-2). 1987. 12.95 (ISBN 0-02-793750-X, Mcmillan Child Bk). Macmillan Child Grp.

STATE AND CHURCH

see Church and State

STATE CHURCH

see Church and State

STATE FLOWERS

Dowden, Anne O. State Flowers. Reissue. ed. Dowden, Anne O., illus. LC 78-41927. 96p. (gr. 5 up). 1978. PLB 13.89 (ISBN 0-690-03884-4, Crowell Jr Bks). HarpC Child Bks.

STATE GOVERNMENTS

see also Governors;

also names of states with the subdivision Politics and Government, e.g. New York (State)–Politics and government; etc.

Santrey, Laurence. State & Local Government. Dole, Bob, illus. LC 84-8440. 32p. (gr. 3-6). 1985. PLB 9.49 (ISBN 0-8167-0270-5); pap. text ed. 2.95 (ISBN 0-8167-0271-3). Troll Assocs.

Silvani, Harold. States & Capitals, 2 bks. Creative Teaching Assocs. Staff, illus. (gr. 3-6). 1975. Bks. A & B. write for info. set (ISBN 1-878669-12-5, 4348); wkbk. 6.95 ea. Bk. A, 28p (ISBN 1-878669-13-3, 4348). Bk. B, 53p (4395). Crea Tea Assocs.

STATESMEN

Beilenson, John. Sukarno. Schlsinger, Arthur M., intro. by. (Illus.). 112p. (gr. 5 up). 1990. 17.95 (ISBN 1-55546-853-5). Chelsea Hse.

Berry, Lynn. Wojciech Jaruzelski. (Illus.). (gr. 5 up). 1990. 17.95 (ISBN 1-55546-838-1). Chelsea Hse.

Butson, Thomas. Mikhail Gorbachev. Schlesinger, Arthur M., Jr., intro. by. (Illus.). 112p. (Orig.). (gr. 5 up). 1989. 17.95 (ISBN 1-55546-200-6); pap. 9.95 (ISBN 0-7910-0571-2). Chelsea Hse.

Caulkins, Janet. The Picture Life of Mikhail Gorbachev. LC 85-15023. (Illus.). 47p. (gr. 2-4). 1985. PLB 10.90 (ISBN 0-531-10085-5). Watts.

Cockcroft, James D. Mohammed Reza Pahlevi. Schlesinger, Arthur M., intro. by. (Illus.). 112p. (gr. 5 up). 1989. 17.95x (ISBN 1-55546-847-0). Chelsea Hse.

Condit, Erin. Francois & Jean-Claude Duvalier. Schlesinger, Arthur M., Jr., intro. by. (Illus.). 112p. (gr. 5 up). 1989. 17.95 (ISBN 1-55546-832-2). Chelsea Hse.

Eide, Lorraine. Robert Mugabe. Schlesinger, Arthur M., intro. by. (Illus.). 112p. (gr. 5 up). 1989. 17.95 (ISBN 1-55546-845-4). Chelsea Hse.

Fortier, E. H. Judas Maccabeus. Schlesinger, Arthur M., Jr., intro. by. (Illus.). 112p. (gr. 5 up). 1988. lib. bdg. 17.95 (ISBN 0-87754-539-1). Chelsea Hse.

Franklin, Benjamin. Autobiography of Benjamin Franklin. Bigoness, J. W., intro. by. LC 80-26312. (gr. 8 up). pap. 2.75 (ISBN 0-8049-0071-X, CL-71). Airmont.

Friese, Kai. Tenzin Gyatso. (Illus.). (gr. 5 up). 1990. 17.95 (ISBN 1-55546-836-5). Chelsea Hse.

Garza, Hedda. Salvador Allende. Schlesinger, Arthur M., Jr., intro. by. (Illus.). 112p. (gr. 5 up). 1989. 17.95 (ISBN 1-55546-824-1). Chelsea Hse.

Geelan, Agnes. The Dakota Maverick. (Illus.). 186p. (gr. 9-12). 1983. pap. 7.95 (ISBN 0-911007-03-2). Prairie Hse.

Ghose, Malini. Kim Il-Sung. (Illus.). (gr. 5-12). 1989. 17.95 (ISBN 1-55546-854-3). Chelsea Hse.

Gordon, Matthew. Hafez al-Assad. (Illus.). (gr. 5 up). 1989. 17.95 (ISBN 1-55546-827-6). Chelsea Hse.

Gordon, Matthew S. The Gemayels. Schlesinger, Arthur M., Jr., intro. by. (Illus.). 112p. (gr. 5 up). 1988. 17.95 (ISBN 1-55546-834-9). Chelsea Hse.

Haney, John. Clement Attlee. Schlesinger, Arthur M., Jr., intro. by. (Illus.). 112p. (gr. 5 up). 1988. lib. bdg. 17.95 (ISBN 0-87754-508-1). Chelsea Hse.

Haney, John D. Charles Stewart Parnell. (Illus.). (gr. 5 up). 1989. 17.95 (ISBN 1-55546-820-9). Chelsea Hse.

Hicks, Nancy. The Honorable Shirley Chisholm: Congresswoman from Brooklyn. (gr. 7 up). PLB 11.95 (ISBN 0-87460-259-9). Lion Bks.

Kaye, Tony. Lech Walesa. (Illus.). (gr. 5 up). 1989. 17.95 (ISBN 1-55546-856-X); pap. 9.95 (ISBN 0-7910-0689-1). Chelsea Hse.

Kellner, Douglas. Ernesto "Che" Guevara. Schlesinger, Arthur M., intro. by. (Illus.). 112p. (gr. 5 up). 1989. 17.95 (ISBN 1-55546-835-7). Chelsea Hse.

King, Perry. Pericles. Schlesinger, Arthur M., Jr., intro. by. (Illus.). 112p. (gr. 5 up). 1988. lib. bdg. 17.95 (ISBN 0-87754-547-2). Chelsea Hse.

Kittredge, Mary. Marc Antony. Schlesinger, Arthur M., Jr., intro. by. (Illus.). 112p. (gr. 5 up). 1988. lib. bdg. 17.95 (ISBN 0-87754-505-7). Chelsea Hse.

Kuckreja, Madhari. Prince Norodom Sihanouk. (Illus.). (gr. 5 up). 1990. 17.95 (ISBN 1-55546-851-9). Chelsea Hse.

Kurkowski, David C., ed. Current Leaders of Nations. LC 89-81456. (Illus.). 180p. (gr. 9-12). 1990. 3-ring binder 95.00 (ISBN 0-9624900-0-8). Current Leaders Pub.

Lewis, Gavin. Tomas Masaryk. (Illus.). (gr. 5 up). 1990. 17.95 (ISBN 1-55546-816-0). Chelsea Hse.

Lubetkin, Wendy. Deng Xiaoping. Schlesinger, Arthur M., Jr., intro. by. (Illus.). 112p. (gr. 5 up). 1988. 17.95 (ISBN 1-55546-830-6). Chelsea Hse.

MacNamara, Desmond. Eamon De Valera. Schlesinger, Arthur M., Jr. (Illus.). 112p. (gr. 5 up). 1988. lib. bdg. 17.95 (ISBN 0-87754-520-0). Chelsea Hse.

Matusky, Gregory & Hayes, John P., Jr. Hussein. (Illus.). 112p. (gr. 5 up). 1987. lib. bdg. 17.95 (ISBN 0-87754-533-2). Chelsea Hse.

Navazelskis, Ina. Alexander Dubcek. (Illus.). (gr. 5 up). 1991. 17.95 (ISBN 1-55546-831-4). Chelsea Hse.

Powers, Elizabeth. Nero. Schlesinger, Arthur M., Jr., intro. by. (Illus.). 112p. (gr. 5 up). 1988. lib. bdg. 17.95 (ISBN 0-87754-544-8). Chelsea Hse.

Ragan, John D. Emiliano Zapata. Schlesinger, Arthur M., intro. by. (Illus.). 112p. (gr. 5 up). 1989. 17.95 (ISBN 1-55546-823-3). Chelsea Hse.

Schlesinger, Arthur M., Jr., intro. by. World Leaders, 54 vols. (Illus.). 112p. (gr. 5 up). 1988. Set. text ed. 969.30x (ISBN 1-55546-857-8). Chelsea Hse.

Shearman, Deirdre. David Lloyd George. (Illus.). 112p. (gr. 5 up). 1988. lib. bdg. 17.95 (ISBN 0-87754-581-2). Chelsea Hse.

Slack, Gordy. Ferdinand Marcos. Schlesinger, Arthur M. (Illus.). 112p. (gr. 5 up). 1988. 17.95 (ISBN 1-55546-842-X). Chelsea Hse.

Solecki, John. Hosni Mubarak. (Illus.). (gr. 5 up). 1991. 17.95 (ISBN 1-55546-844-6). Chelsea Hse.

Stefoff, Rebecca. Faisal. (Illus.). 112p. (gr. 5 up). 1989. 17.95 (ISBN 1-55546-833-0). Chelsea Hse.

—Pol Pot. (Illus.). (gr. 5 up). 1990. 17.95 (ISBN 1-55546-848-9). Chelsea Hse.

Stockwell, John. Daniel Ortega. Schlesinger, Arthur M., Jr., intro. by. (Illus.). 112p. (gr. 5 up). 1991. 17.95 (ISBN 1-55546-846-2). Chelsea Hse.

Viola, Tom. Willy Brandt. Schlesinger, Arthur M., Jr., intro. by. (Illus.). 112p. (gr. 5 up). 1988. lib. bdg. 17.95 (ISBN 0-87754-512-X). Chelsea Hse.

Walworth, Nancy Z. Constantine. (Illus.). (gr. 5 up). 1990. 17.95 (ISBN 1-55546-805-5). Chelsea Hse.

STATISTICS

Kumbaraci, Turkan & Gardenier, George H. Branching Trees: Statistical Methods: Games & Songs. Gardenier, Turhan K., illus. LC 89-90944. 27p. (gr. 1-8). 1989. 30.00x (ISBN 0-685-29039-5, 0003). Teka Trends. BRANCHING TREES provides a unique approach to teaching math without fear by combining poetry, music, & 3-D games. It simplifies complicated concepts used by scientists & industrial engineers & presents them using media familiar to children. It's sub-components are: a) FUN WITH NUMBERS presents an overview of terms such as "matrix", "run", & "factor". b) BRANCHES makes children use the "factorial" design & introduces them to Latin Square. c) COMPUTER MODELS designs a "metamodel" equation & plots it in 3-D form. d) TIME traces changes over time & relates it to quality control concepts with examples in environmental monitoring. e) TWO-by-TWO provides templates for "stem & leaf" charts, an innovation in statistical presentation, & presents methods to compare two sets of data. Provides a bridge between mathematics & science by illustrating how to design experiments with minimal cost. Methods for reducing sample size are illustrated & several such statistical plans, usually taught at college level (or post graduate level) are incorporated. Orientation is through use of poetry, music, & dexterity-oriented 3-D games. Music theory knowledge is not essential, because notes are presented in text form. Teamwork is emphasized by presenting dexterity tasks for groups of 4. Central theme of the examples is a planting exercise which can be tried out at school or home. The series have been pilot-tested at grades 2-3. Class exercise component (which can be duplicated by teacher) is incorporated. *Publisher Provided Annotation.*

Srivastava, Jane J. Statistics. Reiss, John, illus. LC 72-7559. (gr. 1-5). 1973. PLB 12.89 (ISBN 0-690-77300-5, Crowell Jr Bks). HarpC Child Bks.

STATUE OF LIBERTY, NEW YORK

Behrens, June. Miss Liberty: First Lady of the World. LC 86-2320. (Illus.). 32p. (gr. 2-5). 1986. PLB 13.27 (ISBN 0-516-03295-X). Childrens.

Birenbaum, Barbara. Lady Liberty's Light. Birenbaum, Barbara, illus. LC 85-32061. 50p. (gr. 3-5). 1986. pap. 5.95 (ISBN 0-935343-11-3). Peartree.

Burchard, S. H. The Statue of Liberty: Birth to Rebirth. LC 85-5525. (Illus.). 192p. (gr. 9-12). 1985. 13.95 (ISBN 0-15-279969-9, Pub. by HJ). HarBraceJ.

Coerr, Eleanor. Lady with a Torch. De Mejo, Oscar, illus. LC 85-45262. 96p. (gr. 2-6). 1986. PLB 11.89; PLB 11.89 (ISBN 0-06-021347-7). HarpC Child Bks.
Fisher, Leonard E. The Statue of Liberty. Fisher, Leonard E., illus. LC 85-42878. 64p. (gr. 3-7). 1985. reinforced bdg. 13.95 (ISBN 0-8234-0586-9). Holiday.
Hargrove, Jim. Gateway to Freedom: The Story of the Statue of Liberty & Ellis Island. LC 86-14707. (Illus.). 112p. (gr. 5 up). 1986. PLB 22.60 (ISBN 0-516-03296-8). Childrens.
Haskins, Jim. The Statue of Liberty: America's Proud Lady. LC 85-18061. (Illus.). 48p. (gr. 4-8). 1986. lib. bdg. 10.95 (ISBN 0-8225-1706-X). Lerner Pubns.
Maestro, Betsy. The Story of the Statue of Liberty. Maestro, Giulio, illus. LC 85-11324. 40p. (ps-3). 1986. PLB 12.88 (ISBN 0-688-05774-8). Lothrop.
—The Story of the Statue of Liberty. LC 85-11324. (Illus.). (gr. 1 up). 1989. pap. 5.95 (ISBN 0-688-08746-9, Mulberry). Morrow.
Marsh, Carole. Will Somebody Hold This Thing a Minute? Statue of Liberty Silly Trivia Book. (Illus.). 60p. (Orig.). (gr. 3-12). 1986. 19.95 (ISBN 1-55609-192-3); pap. 14.95 (ISBN 0-935326-75-8). Gallopade Pub Group.
Mercer, Charles. Statue of Liberty. LC 78-21305. (Illus.). 96p. (gr. 5 up). 1979. 17.95 (ISBN 0-399-20670-1, Putnam). Putnam Pub Group.
Miller, Natalie. Story of the Statue of Liberty. Hawkinson, John & Hawkinson, Lucy, illus. LC 65-12216. 32p. (gr. 2-5). 1965. PLB 13.27 (ISBN 0-516-04637-3); pap. 3.95 (ISBN 0-516-44637-1). Childrens.
Shapiro, Mary J. How They Built the Statue of Liberty. Scarry, Huck, illus. LC 85-42720. 64p. (gr. 10 up). 1985. 9.95 (ISBN 0-394-86957-5, Random Juv); lib. bdg. 9.99 (ISBN 0-394-96957-X). Random.
—How They Built the Statue of Liberty. Scarry, Huck, illus. LC 85-42720. 64p. (gr. 10 up). 1985. 9.95 (ISBN 0-394-86957-5, Random Juv); lib. bdg. 9.99 (ISBN 0-394-96957-X). Random.
Wolf, D. M. A Bird's Eye View of the Statue of Liberty: As Seen by Lorenzo the Parrot. McDaniel, Jerry, illus. 32p. (gr. 3-4). 1988. pap. 4.95 (ISBN 0-9617057-2-8). Storyviews Pub.

STAUFFENBERG, BERTHOLD VON, 1907-1944

Forman, James. Code Name Valkyrie: Count Claus von Stauffenberg & the Plot to Kill Hitler. LC 72-12581. (Illus.). 256p. (gr. 9-12). 1973. PLB 21.95 (ISBN 0-87599-188-2). S G Phillips.

STEAM ENGINES

Moseley, Keith. Steam Locomotives. LC 88-63961. (Illus.). 14p. 1989. 17.95 (ISBN 0-531-05844-1). Orchard Bks Watts.
Siegel, Beatrice. The Steam Engine. LC 86-5616. (Illus.). 64p. (gr. 5 up). 1986. 10.95 (ISBN 0-8027-6655-2); PLB 10.85 (ISBN 0-8027-6656-0). Walker & Co.
Weitzman, David. Superpower: The Making of a Steam Locomotive. LC 86-46255. (Illus.). 1987. 24.95 (ISBN 0-87923-671-X). Godine.

STEAM-SHOVELS–FICTION

Burton, Virginia L. Mike Mulligan & His Steam Shovel. (Illus.). (gr. k-3). 1939. PLB 11.95 (ISBN 0-395-06681-6). HM.

STEAMBOATS

Braynard, Frank O. U. S. Steamships: A Picture Postcard History. Cronkite, Walter, intro. by. (Illus.). 144p. (Orig.). Date not set. pap. write for info. (ISBN 0-930256-20-4). Almar.
Chant, Chris. Steamships. Batchelor, John, illus. LC 88-28764. 63p. (gr. 3 up). 1989. PLB 16.95 (ISBN 0-685-35040-1). Marshall Cavendish.
Hartford, John. Steamboat in a Cornfield. LC 86-4154. (Illus.). (gr. 7 up). 1986. 10.95 (ISBN 0-517-56141-7). Crown.
McCall, Edith. Mississippi Steamboatman: The Story of Henry Miller Shreve. LC 85-13795. (Illus.). 115p. (gr. 5-8). 1986. 11.95 (ISBN 0-8027-6597-1). Walker & Co.
—Steamboats to the West. Borja, Robert, illus. LC 59-3665. 128p. (gr. 3-10). 1980. PLB 14.60 (ISBN 0-516-03368-9). Childrens.
Stein, R. Conrad. The Story of Mississippi Steamboats. Dunnington, Tom, illus. 32p. (gr. 3-6). 1987. PLB 13.27 (ISBN 0-516-04726-4); pap. 3.95 (ISBN 0-516-44726-2). Childrens.
Ward, Ralph T. Steamboats: A History of the Early Adventure. LC 72-9888. (gr. 3-6). 1973. 8.95 (ISBN 0-672-51785-X, Bobbs). Macmillan.

STEAMSHIPS

see Steamboats

STEEL

see also Iron;
also headings beginning with the word Steel

Lambert, M. Iron & Steel. (Illus.). 48p. (gr. 5 up). Date not set. PLB 15.93 (ISBN 0-86592-268-3). Rourke Corp.

STEEL INDUSTRY AND TRADE

see also Iron Industry and Trade

STEIN, GERTRUDE, 1874-1946

La Farge, Ann. Gertrude Stein. Horner, Matina, intro. by. (Illus.). 112p. (gr. 5 up). 1988. lib. bdg. 17.95 (ISBN 1-55546-678-8). Chelsea Hse.

STEVENSON, ROBERT LOUIS, 1850-1894

Willard, Nancy, et al. The Voyage of the Ludgate Hill: A Journey with Robert Louis Stevenson. Provensen, Martin & Provensen, Alice, illus. LC 86-19502. 32p. (gr. 5-8). 1987. 14.95 (ISBN 0-15-294464-8). HarBraceJ.

STOCK EXCHANGE

see also Investments; Stocks; Wall Street

King, Nadia. Inside Truths about the Stock Brokerage Business. Kriks, Bill, ed. 75p. (Orig.). Date not set. pap. text ed. 5.00 (ISBN 0-685-29786-1). Kings Inc.
Young, Robin. The Stock Market. (Illus.). 80p. (gr. 5 up). 1991. PLB 14.95 (ISBN 0-8225-1780-9). Lerner Pubns.

STOCK MARKET

see Stock Exchange

STOCK RAISING

see Livestock

STOCKS

see also Investments; Stock Exchange

Dunnan, Nancy. The Stock Market. (Illus.). 128p. (gr. 7-10). 1990. lib. bdg. 14.98 (ISBN 0-382-09914-1); pap. 7.95 (ISBN 0-382-24025-1). Silver Burdett Pr.

STONE

see also Masonry; Rocks

STONE AGE

see also Man, Prehistoric

Ask about Prehistoric Life. 64p. (gr. 4-5). 1987. PLB 18.25 (ISBN 0-8172-2879-9); pap. 13.27 (ISBN 0-8172-2891-8). Raintree Pubs.
Benton, Michael. Prehistoric World. (Illus.). 128p. (gr. 5-9). 1988. pap. 14.95 (ISBN 0-671-64492-0, Little Simon). S&S Trade.
Carrick, Carol. Patrick's Dinosaurs. Carrick, Donald, illus. LC 83-2049. 32p. (gr. k-3). 1983. 13.95 (ISBN 0-89919-189-4, Clarion). HM.
Craig, A. Prehistoric Facts: Records-Lists-Facts-Comparisons. (Illus.). 48p. (gr. 3-7). 1986. PLB 12.96 (ISBN 0-88110-228-8); pap. 5.95 (ISBN 0-86020-973-3). EDC.
Dunrea, Olivier. Skara Brae: The Story of a Prehistoric Village. Dunrea, Olivier, illus. LC 85-42882. 40p. (gr. 3-7). 1986. reinforced bdg. 12.95 (ISBN 0-8234-0583-4). Holiday.
Killingray, David. The Neolithic Revolution. Yapp, Malcolm, et al, eds. (Illus.). 32p. (gr. 6-11). 1980. pap. text ed. 2.95 (ISBN 0-685-24559-4). Greenhaven.
Let's Discover the Prehistoric World. LC 80-22949. (Illus.). 80p. (gr. k-9). 1981. pap. text ed. 13.27 (ISBN 0-8172-2582-X). Raintree Pubs.
Spizzirri Publishing Co. Staff. Prehistoric Birds: An Educational Coloring Book. Spizzirri, Linda, ed. Spizzirri, Peter M., illus. 32p. (gr. 1-8). 1981. pap. 1.95 (ISBN 0-86545-023-4). Spizzirri.
—Prehistoric Sea Life: An Educational Coloring Book. Spizzirri, Linda, ed. Kohn, Arnie, illus. 32p. (gr. 1-8). 1981. pap. 1.95 (ISBN 0-86545-020-X). Spizzirri.

STONE AGE–FICTION

Kipling, Rudyard. How the Alphabet Was Made. Cheese, Chloe, illus. LC 86-28881. 32p. (gr. 1-5). 1987. PLB 10.95 (ISBN 0-87226-136-0). P Bedrick Bks.
Little Treasury of Flintstones. 1989. 5.95 (ISBN 0-318-41671-9). Outlet Bk Co.

STONEHENGE

Abels, Harriette S. Stonehenge. LC 87-13638. (Illus.). 48p. (gr. 5-6). 1987. PLB 10.95 (ISBN 0-89686-346-8, Crestwood Hse). Macmillan Child Grp.
Lyon, Nancy. The Mystery of Stonehenge. LC 77-10044. (Illus.). 48p. (gr. 4 up). 1983. PLB 17.32 (ISBN 0-8172-1049-0); pap. 9.27 (ISBN 0-8172-2164-6). Raintree Pubs.
Roop, Peter & Roop, Connie. Stonehenge: Opposing Viewpoints. LC 89-37441. (Illus.). 112p. (gr. 3-10). 1989. PLB 13.95 (ISBN 0-89908-066-9). Greenhaven.

STONES, PRECIOUS

see Precious Stones

STONEWARE

see Pottery

STORIES

see also Anecdotes; Animals–Fiction; Ballet–Fiction; Bible Stories; Birds–Fiction; Christmas–Fiction; Fairy Tales; Horror Stories; Legends; Mystery and Detective Stories; Sea Stories; Short Stories; Storytelling; Trees–Fiction; Vocational Stories

Ackerman, Karen. Just Like Max. Schmidt, George, illus. LC 88-13214. 32p. (ps-3). 1990. 12.95 (ISBN 0-394-80176-8); lib. bdg. 13.99 (ISBN 0-394-90176-2). Knopf.
Adler, C. S. The Lump in the Middle. LC 88-35922. 160p. (gr. 4-8). 1989. 13.95 (ISBN 0-89919-869-4, Clarion Bks). HM.
Adoff, Arnold. The Cabbages Are Chasing the Rabbits. Stevens, Janet, illus. LC 85-893. 32p. (ps-3). 1985. 15.95 (ISBN 0-15-213875-7, HJ). HarBraceJ.
Aguiar, Elithe. Legends of Hawaii As Told By Lani Goose. Aguiar, Elithe & Sakamoto, Dean, illus. 20p. (gr. k up). 1986. pap. 8.95 incl. audio cassette (ISBN 0-944264-00-X). Lani Goose Pubns.
Ahlberg, Allan. Red Nose Readers. McNaughton, Colin, illus. Incl. Big Bad Pig. LC 84-27748. 1985; Fee Fi Fo Fum. LC 84-27745. 1985; Happy Worm. LC 84-27742. 1985; Help! LC 84-27739. 1985. 32p. (ps-2). 1985. (Random Juv). Random.
Aiken, Joan. The Last Slice of Rainbow: And Other Stories. Berenzy, Alix, illus. LC 87-45271. 160p. (gr. 3-7). 1990. pap. 3.50 (ISBN 0-06-440334-3, Trophy). HarpC Child Bks.
—A Touch of Chill. (gr. k up). 1989. pap. 3.25 (ISBN 0-440-20459-3, LFL). Dell.
Albright, Nancy T. Do Tell! Holiday Draw & Tell Stories. rev. & enlg. ed. (ps-4). 1989. pap. 5.00 (ISBN 0-913545-13-9). Moonlight FL.
Alexander, Lloyd. Time Cat. Sokol, Bill, illus. (gr. 4-7). 16.00 (ISBN 0-8446-6237-2). Peter Smith.
Allard, Harry. Miss Nelson Has a Field Day. Marshall, James, illus. LC 84-27791. 32p. (gr. k-3). 1985. 12.95 (ISBN 0-395-36690-9). HM.
Andersen, Hans Christian. It's Perfectly True. LC 87-7567. (Illus.). 32p. (ps-3). 1988. reinforced bdg. 13.95 (ISBN 0-8234-0672-5). Holiday.
Andrews, Jean F. The Flying Fingers Club. LC 88-19875. 104p. (gr. 3-5). 1988. pap. 4.95 (ISBN 0-930323-44-0, Kendall Green Pubns). Gallaudet Univ Pr.
Andrews, Wendy. Are We There Yet? LC 84-22716. 160p. (gr. 7 up). 1985. 11.95 (ISBN 0-448-47758-0, G&D). Putnam Pub Group.
Apple, Margot. Blanket. Apple, Margot, illus. 32p. (ps-3). 1990. 12.95 (ISBN 0-395-51522-X). HM.
Armstrong, Velma. The Banana Horse. Graves, Helen, ed. LC 85-51966. 104p. (gr. 3-6). 1986. pap. 6.95 (ISBN 0-938232-98-3). Winston-Derek.
Arroyo, Anita. El Grillo Grunon: Cuentos para Chicos y Grandes. Robain, Armando O., illus. LC 84-13199. (SPA.). 122p. (Orig.). (gr. 1-6). 1984. pap. 5.50 (ISBN 0-8477-3527-3). U of PR Pr.
Atwell, Lucy. Lucy Atwell's Goodnight Stories. (Illus.). (ps-1). 1985. 3.98 (ISBN 0-517-46903-0). Outlet Bk Co.
Aylesworth, Jim. Shenandoah Noah. Rounds, Glen, illus. LC 84-22554. 32p. (gr. k-2). 1985. 11.95 (ISBN 0-03-003749-2). H Holt & Co.
Baldner, Jean V. Pebbles in the Wind. Webster, Carroll, illus. 52p. (Orig.). (gr. 7 up). pap. 5.95 (ISBN 0-9615317-0-3). Baldner J V.
Barrett, Judith. Cloudy with a Chance of Meatballs. LC 87-29643. (Illus.). (ps-3). 1982. pap. 3.95 (ISBN 0-689-70749-5, Aladdin). Macmillan Child Grp.
Barth, Nancy & Wittenborn, Sally. On Halloween Night. Wittenborn, Sally, illus. 12p. (Orig.). (ps-1). 1987. pap. 4.95 (ISBN 0-942565-00-2). Country Schl Pubns.
Bashful Bard. Being Part of a Family. Bashful Bard, illus. LC 89-84968. 28p. (Orig.). (ps-1). 1989. pap. 2.99 (ISBN 1-877906-09-3). Kenney Pubns.
—Cricket Gets the Monster: Fears & Feelings. Bashful Bard, illus. LC 89-84969. 28p. (Orig.). (ps-1). pap. 2.99 (ISBN 1-877906-02-6). Kenney Pubns.
—Cricket Loses His Shadow. Bashful Bard, illus. LC 89-84963. 28p. (Orig.). (ps-1). 1989. pap. 2.99 (ISBN 1-877906-04-2). Kenney Pubns.
—A Dragon in Dew Drop Dell. Bashful Bard, illus. LC 89-84965. 28p. (Orig.). (ps-1). pap. 2.99 (ISBN 1-877906-05-0). Kenney Pubns.
—Having Fun Outdoors. Bashful Bard, illus. LC 89-84966. 28p. (Orig.). (ps-1). 1989. pap. 2.99 (ISBN 0-685-26942-6). Kenney Pubns.
—Things to Wonder About. Bashful Bard, illus. LC 89-84970. 28p. (Orig.). (ps-1). 1989. pap. 2.99 (ISBN 1-877906-08-5). Kenney Pubns.
Bauer, Caroline F., ed. Rainy Day: Stories & Poems. Chessare, Michele, illus. LC 85-45170. 96p. (gr. 2-5). 1986. 13.95 (ISBN 0-397-32104-X, Lipp Jr Bks); PLB 13.89 (ISBN 0-397-32105-8, Lipp Jr Bks). HarpC Child Bks.
Baum, L. Frank. The Surprising Adventures of the Magical Monarch of Mo & His People. (gr. 5-6). 17.95 (ISBN 0-88411-771-5, Pub. by Aeonian Pr). Amereon Ltd.
Beamer, Winona D. Talking Story with Nona Beamer: Stories of a Hawaiian Family. Kahalewai, Marilyn, illus. Hannahs, Neil J., afterword by. LC 83-70357. (Illus.). 80p. (gr. 2-6). 1984. 9.95 (ISBN 0-935848-20-7). Bess Pr.
Beckett, Sheilah, illus. Lullaby & Good Night Poems, Prayers, & Songs for Bedtime. 32p. (ps-2). 1987. 5.95 (ISBN 0-448-19092-3, G&D); cassette incl. Putnam Pub Group.
Bedtime Stories. (Illus.). (ps-5). 8.95 (ISBN 0-7214-7521-3). Ladybird Bks.
Belle, Barbara. Pixel Helps Pooper out of a Pickle. (Illus.). 24p. (Orig.). (gr. 1-5). pap. 3.25 (ISBN 0-935163-02-6). Pixel Prods Pubns.
Berleth, Richard. Samuel's Choice. Mathews, Judith, ed. Watling, James, illus. 40p. (gr. 3-6). 1990. PLB 13.95 (ISBN 0-8075-7218-7). A Whitman.
Best-Selling Apples, 4 vols. Incl. Nothing's Fair in Fifth Grade. DeClements, Barthe; Yours Till Niagara Falls, Abby. O'Connor, Jane; Tough-Luck Karen. Hurwitz, Johanna; Amy & Laura. Sachs, Marilyn. (gr. 4-6). 1985. Boxed Set. pap. 9.50 (ISBN 0-590-63049-0, Apple Paperbacks). Scholastic Inc.
Big Bird Says...A Game to Read & Play. Incl. Lerner, Sharon. Mathieu, Joe, illus. LC 85-1959. (ps up). 1985. lib. bdg. 6.99 (ISBN 0-394-97499-9); pap. 2.95 (ISBN 0-394-87499-4); So Sick. Ziefert, Harriet. Nicklaus, Carol, illus. LC 85-1957. 32p. (ps-1). 1985. lib. bdg. 6.99 (ISBN 0-394-97580-4); pap. 2.95 (ISBN 0-394-87580-X); Happy Birthday, Little Witch. Hautzig, Deborah. Brown, Marc, illus. 1985. lib. bdg. 6.99 (ISBN 0-394-97365-8); pap. 2.95 (ISBN 0-394-87365-3); Deputy Dan Gets His Man. Rosenbloom, Joseph. Raglin, Tim, illus. 48p. (gr. 2-3). 1985. lib. bdg. 6.99 (ISBN 0-394-97250-3); pap. 2.95 (ISBN 0-394-87250-9). (ps-1). 1985. pap. (Random Juv). Random.
The Big Pancake. (Illus.). (ps-4). 3.50 (ISBN 0-7214-5014-8). Ladybird Bks.
Bingham, et al. Challenges. 240p. (gr. 8 up). 1984. 14.95 (ISBN 0-685-09859-1, LW CHA). Learning Wks.
Blacker, Terence. Ms Wiz Spells Trouble. Goffe, Toni, illus. 64p. (gr. 3-6). 1990. pap. 2.95 (ISBN 0-8120-4420-7). Barron.

Blackwell, B. Believe It or Not Stories. 15p. (gr. 7-10). 1986. 15.00X (ISBN 0-7223-2003-5, Pub. by A H Stockwell England). State Mutual Bk.

Boegehold, Betty D. You Are Much Too Small-Bank Street. (ps-3). 1990. PLB 9.99 (ISBN 0-553-05895-9, Little Rooster); pap. 3.50 (ISBN 0-553-34925-2). Bantam.

Boesky, Amy. Planet Was, Vol. 1. (ps-3). 1990. 14.95 (ISBN 0-316-10084-6, Joy St Bks). Little.

Bond, Felicia. Poinsettia & Her Family. Bond, Felicia, illus. LC 81-43035. 32p. (ps-3). 1985. pap. 4.95i (ISBN 0-06-443076-6, Trophy). HarpC Child Bks.

Bond, Ruskin. Tales Told at Twilight. 166p. (gr. 4-6). 1970. 1.25 (ISBN 0-88253-394-0). Ind-US Inc.

Bourque, Nina. The Best Trade of All. Urbanovic, Jackie, illus. LC 83-7352. 32p. (gr. 3-6). 1984. PLB 27.99 incl. cassette (ISBN 0-8172-2280-4); cassette only 14.00 (ISBN 0-317-19659-6). Raintree Pubs.

Bowden, Joan. Pop up Just Ben. 1989. 4.95 (ISBN 0-671-67555-9). S&S Trade.

Bowkett, Stephen. Catch: And Other Stories. 128p. (gr. 6-10). 1990. 17.95 (ISBN 0-575-04399-7, Pub. by Gollancz England). Trafalgar Sq.

Boyle, Vere, illus. Beauty & the Beast. LC 87-24394. 32p. (ps up). 1988. 8.95 (ISBN 0-8120-5902-6). Barron.

Brott, Ardyth. Jeremy's Decision. Martchenko, Michael, illus. 32p. (ps-3). 1990. 12.95 (ISBN 0-916291-31-6). Kane-Miller Bk.

Brown, Irene B. Answer Me, Answer Me. LC 85-7452. 192p. (gr. 7 up). 1985. 13.95 (ISBN 0-689-31114-1, Atheneum Child Bk). Macmillan Child Grp.

Butler, Dorothy. Higgledy Piggledy Hobbledy Hoy. LC 89-77503. (Illus.). 30p. (ps up). 1991. 13.95 (ISBN 0-688-08660-8); PLB 13.88 (ISBN 0-688-08661-6). Greenwillow.

Byrd, Robert. Marcella Was Bored. Byrd, Robert, illus. LC 84-28674. 32p. (ps-2). 1985. 11.95 (ISBN 0-525-44156-5, DCB). Dutton Child Bks.

Caldecott, Randolph. A Third Caldecott Collection: The Queen of Hearts, The Farmer's Boy. Caldecott, Randolph, illus. 64p. 1986. 4.95 (ISBN 0-7232-3434-5). Warne.

Callenbach, Ernest & Leefeldt, Christine. Humphrey the Wayward Whale. Buell, Carl, illus. 24p. (Orig.). (gr. k-6). 1986. pap. 3.95 (ISBN 0-930588-23-1). Heyday Bks.

Cameron, Ann. More Stories Julian Tells. Strugnell, Ann, illus. LC 84-10095. 96p. (gr. k-3). 1989. pap. 2.99 (ISBN 0-394-82454-7). Knopf.

—The Stories Julian Tells. Strugnell, Ann, illus. LC 80-18023. 88p. (gr. k-3). 1989. pap. 2.95 (ISBN 0-394-82892-5). Knopf.

The Canterbury Tales. (gr. 4 up). 1988. pap. 4.87 (ISBN 0-582-54150-6, 74258). Longman.

Caple, Kathy. The Biggest Nose. Caple, Kathy, illus. LC 84-19745. 32p. (gr. k-3). 1988. 13.95 (ISBN 0-395-36894-4); pap. 5.95 (ISBN 0-395-47943-6). HM.

Carle, Eric. Do You Want to Be My Friend? 40p. (ps-2). 1988. PLB 3.95 (ISBN 0-399-21598-0, Philomel Bks). Putnam Pub Group.

Carlson, Lori M. & Ventura, Cynthia L., eds. Where Angels Glide at Dawn: New Stories from Latin America. Ortega, Jose, illus. LC 90-6697. 128p. (gr. 5 up). 1990. 13.95 (ISBN 0-397-32424-3, Lipp Jr Bks); PLB 13.89 (ISBN 0-397-32425-1, Lipp Jr Bks). HarpC Child Bks.

Carlstrom, Nancy W. Light: Stories of a Small Bright Kindness. (gr. 4-7). 1990. 15.95 (ISBN 0-316-12857-0). Little.

Carmi, Giora. Night, Farm. Carmi, Giora, illus. 24p. (ps). 1989. 11.95 (ISBN 0-8092-4352-0, Calico Bks). Contemp Bks.

Carter, Alden R. Wart, Son of Toad. 208p. (gr. 7 up). 1985. 12.95 (ISBN 0-448-47770-X, Putnam). Putnam Pub Group.

Castle, Caroline. The Hare & the Tortoise. Weevers, Peter, illus. LC 84-9569. 32p. (ps-3). 1985. 10.95 (ISBN 0-8037-0138-1). Dial Bks Young.

Chetwin, Grace. Box & Cox. Small, David, illus. LC 88-35337. 32p. (gr. k-3). 1990. 13.95 (ISBN 0-02-718314-9, Bradbury Pr). Macmillan Child Grp.

Chevalier, Christa. Spence Isn't Spence Anymore. Levine, Abby, ed. Chevalier, Christa, illus. 32p. (ps-1). 1985. 10.95 (ISBN 0-8075-7565-8). A Whitman.

A Child's Treasury of the Worthwhile. (gr. 3-11). 5.95 (ISBN 0-87741-007-0). Makepeace Colony.

Christian, Mary B. Go West, Swamp Monsters. Brown, Marc, illus. LC 84-12686. 48p. (ps-3). 1985. 8.95 (ISBN 0-8037-0091-1); PLB 8.89 (ISBN 0-8037-0144-6). Dial Bks Young.

Christopher, Matt. Supercharged Infield. Downing, Julie, illus. (gr. 4-6). 1985. 13.95 (ISBN 0-316-13983-1). Little.

Coffin, Carlyn. Noel & His Friends. (Illus.). 130p. (ps up). 1987. pap. 10.95 over boards (ISBN 0-931474-30-2). TBW Bks.

Cohen, Daniel. The UFOS Third Wave. LC 88-16558. 172p. (gr. 7 up). 1988. 12.95 (ISBN 0-87131-541-6). M Evans.

Cole, Babette. The Trouble with Grandad. Cole, Babette, illus. 32p. (ps-3). 1988. 13.95 (ISBN 0-399-21545-X, Putnam). Putnam Pub Group.

Collins, Ann M. The Great Sun Must Die. 96p. (Orig.). 1985. pap. 3.15 (ISBN 0-88120-731-4). SRA.

Connelly, Tony & Holley, Cindy. Holiday Stories. Champlin, John, ed. (Illus.). 38p. (gr. 3-6). 1982. pap. 8.95 (ISBN 0-938594-02-8). Spec Lit Pr.

Corcoran, Mark. Night, Storyland. Corcoran, Mark, illus. 24p. (ps). 1989. 11.95 (ISBN 0-8092-4351-2, Calico Bks). Contemp Bks.

Coren, Alan. Arthur the Kid. 80p. (gr. 4-6). 1984. pap. text ed. 2.25 (ISBN 0-553-15169-X, Skylark). Bantam.

Cornell, S. A. Little Eagle Learns to Fly. Jones, John, illus. LC 85-14086. 48p. (Orig.). (gr. 1-3). 1986. lib. bdg. 9.89 (ISBN 0-8167-0618-2); pap. text ed. 2.95 (ISBN 0-8167-0619-0). Troll Assocs.

Corrin, Sara & Corrin, Stephen, eds. Stories for Seven-Year-Olds & Other Young Readers. Hughes, Shirley, illus. 188p. (gr. 1-3). 1982. 12.95 (ISBN 0-571-05823-X); pap. 9.95 (ISBN 0-571-12910-2). Faber & Faber.

Cosgrove, Stephen. Crabby Gabby. James, Robin, illus. LC 85-14351. 32p. (Orig.). (gr. 1-4). 1985. pap. 2.95 (ISBN 0-8431-1441-X). Price Stern.

—Whimsie Storybooks. Reasoner, Charles, illus. Incl. Gimme. LC 85-1958. 1985; Tattletale. LC 85-42713. 1985; Gobble & Gulp. LC 85-42715. 1985; Cranky. LC 85-42712. 1985; Chatterbox. LC 85-42714. 1985; Giggle. LC 85-42716. 1985. 40p. (ps-3). 1985. (Random Juv). Random.

Cowley, Joy. Don't You Laugh at Me! McRae, Rodney, illus. 16p. (gr. k-2). 1989. pap. text ed. 23.00 (ISBN 1-55911-293-X). Wright Group.

—Don't You Laugh at Me, 6 bks. McRae, Rodney, illus. (gr. k-2). 1986. Set. pap. text ed. 19.80 (ISBN 1-55911-367-7). Wright Group.

—The Sunshine Series, 32 titles, Level 1, Sets A-D. rev. ed. Fuller, E., et al, illus. 32p. (ps-1). Set. pap. text ed. 49.20 Americanized version (ISBN 1-55624-126-7). Wright Group.

—The Sunshine Series, Level 1, Set A: Baby Gets Dressed; Huggles' Breakfast; Huggles Can Juggle; The Birthday Cake; Huggles Goes Away; Dinner; Down to Town & I Can Fly, 8 titles. rev. ed. Fuller, Elizabeth, et al, illus. 8p. (ps-1). pap. text ed. 12.30 Americanized version (ISBN 1-55624-069-4, WG0694). Wright Group.

—The Sunshine Series, Level 1, Set B: Snap!; Major Jump; My Puppy; Little Brother; The Long, Long Tail; What Is a Huggles?; Yuk Soup & Our Granny, 8 titles. rev. ed. Van der Voo, Jan, et al, illus. 8p. (ps-1). pap. text ed. 12.30 Americanized version (ISBN 1-55624-070-8, WG0708). Wright Group.

—The Sunshine Series, Level 1, Set C: I Love My Family; Our Street; My Home; Uncle Buncle's House; Big & Little; I Am a Bookworm; When Itchy Witchy Sneezes & Shoo, 8 titles. rev. ed. Allpress, Jill, et al, illus. 8p. (ps-1). pap. text ed. 12.30 (ISBN 1-55624-071-6, WP0716). Wright Group.

—The Sunshine Series, Level 1, Set D: The Race; Buzzing Flies; Ice Cream; I Can Jump; A Hug Is Warm; "Scat!" Said the Cat; Shark in a Sack & Up in a Tree, 8 titles. rev. ed. Fuller, Elizabeth, et al, illus. 8p. (ps-1). pap. text ed. 12.30 Americanized version (ISBN 1-55624-072-4, WP0724). Wright Group.

—The Sunshine Series, Level 1, Set E: Spider, Spider; Let's Have a Swim; Wake up, Mom!; Mr. Grump; I'm Bigger Than You!; Good for You; What Would You Like? & The Monkey Bridge, 8 bks. Stuart, Michelle, et al, illus. 128p. (gr. k-1). pap. text ed. 21.90 (ISBN 1-55624-085-6, WP0856). Wright Group.

—The Sunshine Series, Level 1, Set F: Bread; The Seed; The Wind Blows Strong; Goodbye Lucy; Aong Comes Jake; Come for a Swim; Don't You Laugh at Me! & Where Are You Going, Aja Rose, 8 bks. Biro, Val, et al, illus. 128p. (gr. k-1). pap. text ed. 21.90 (ISBN 1-55624-086-4, WP0864). Wright Group.

—The Sunshine Series, Level 1, Set G: Noise; Dad's Headache; The Terrible Tiger; One Thousand Currant Buns; Old Grizzly; My Boat; The Cooking Pot & Little Car, 8 bks. Webb, Philip, et al, illus. 128p. (gr. k-1). pap. text ed. 21.90 (ISBN 1-55624-087-2, WP0872). Wright Group.

—The Sunshine Series, Level 1, Set H: Red Socks & Yellow Socks; Ratty-Tatty; The Poor Sore Paw; Nowhere & Nothing; The Giant's Boy; Mr. Whisper; My Sloppy Tiger & The Tiny Woman's Coat, 8 bks. Price, Nick, et al, illus. 128p. (gr. k-1). pap. text ed. 21.90 (ISBN 1-55624-088-0, WP0880). Wright Group.

—The Sunshine Series, Level 1, Set I: When Dad Went to Playschool; Boggywooga; Letters for Mr. James; Mrs. Grindy's Shoes; Mishi-Na; Just This Once; Mom's Birthday & Quack, Quack, Quack, 8 bks. (Illus.). 128p. (Orig.). (gr. k-1). 1987. pap. text ed. 21.90 (ISBN 1-55624-089-9). Wright Group.

—The Sunshine Series, Level 1, Set J: My Sloppy Tiger Goes to School; Boring Old Bed; Space Race; Tess & Paddy; The Ha-Ha Powder; Mom's Diet; A Hundred Hugs & The Secret of Spooky House, 8 bks. (Illus.). 128p. (Orig.). (gr. k-1). 1987. pap. text ed. 21.90 (ISBN 1-55624-090-2). Wright Group.

Cowley, Joy & Le Sueur, Elaine. The Sunshine Series, Level 2: The Train Ride Story; The Giant Pumpkin; Road Robber; Soup; Soup Fit for a King & Little Red Hen, 6 bks. (Illus.). 96p. (Orig.). (gr. 1-2). 1988. Set. pap. text ed. 19.70 (ISBN 1-55624-073-2). Wright Group.

Cowley, Joy & Young, Christine. The Sunshine Series, Level 3: Silly Billys; The Person from Planet X; The Big Family; Christmas Dog; Where's My Snack & The Gingerbread Man, 6 bks. (Illus.). 96p. (Orig.). (gr. 1-2). 1988. Set. pap. text ed. 19.70 (ISBN 1-55624-074-0). Wright Group.

Cowley, Joy, et al. The Sunshine Series, Level 5: Morning Bath; Jojo & the Robot; Library Day; Cousin Kira; Shopping & The Noise Festival, 6 bks. (Illus.). 128p. (Orig.). (gr. 1-2). 1988. Set. pap. text ed. 23.50 (ISBN 1-55624-076-7). Wright Group.

Crabtree, Mary B. The Secret. 120p. (Orig.). 1985. pap. 3.15 (ISBN 0-88120-734-9). SRA.

—This Summer. 84p. (Orig.). 1985. pap. 3.15 (ISBN 0-88120-730-6). SRA.

Craig, Janet. Santa's Cookie Surprise. Loh, Carolyn, illus. LC 88-19997. 32p. (gr. k-2). 1988. lib. bdg. 7.06 (ISBN 0-8167-1538-6); pap. text ed. 1.95 (ISBN 0-8167-1539-4). Troll Assocs.

Creighton, Susan. Hugs from the Heart. Ewers, Joe, illus. 32p. (ps-3). 1985. pap. 0.99 (ISBN 0-87372-005-9). Parker Bros.

Cresswell, Helen. Time Out. Elwell, Peter, illus. LC 89-36798. 80p. (gr. 2-5). 1990. 12.95 (ISBN 0-02-725425-9, Mcmillan Child Bk). Macmillan Child Grp.

Cutting, Jillian. Sunshine Series, Set AA: Birthday Party; Building with Blocks; The Barbeque; Just Look at You!; Dressing Up; I Am...; Getting Dressed; Shopping & What's in This Egg, 9 bks. Van der Voo, Jan, illus. 72p. (gr. k-1). pap. text ed. 16.80 (ISBN 1-55911-042-2). Wright Group.

—Sunshine Series, Set CC: I Write; Faces; My Family; The Great, Enormous Hamburger; Books; Where's Tim?; The Storm; Look...& The Farm, 9 bks. Van der Voo, Jan, illus. 72p. (gr. k-1). pap. text ed. 16.80 (ISBN 1-55911-044-9). Wright Group.

Cutting, Jillian & DePree, Helen. Sunshine Series, Set BB: At School; I Like...; Our Grandad; Come On; Run; To School; Space Journey; Bubbles & My Shadow, 9 bks. Van der Voo, Jan, illus. 72p. (gr. k-1). pap. text ed. 16.80 (ISBN 1-55911-043-0). Wright Group.

Dahl, Roald. Roald Dahl Boxed Set: Includes; Charlie & the Chocolate Factory; Charlie & the Great Glass Elevator; the Big. (Illus.). (gr. 3-7). 1989. pap. 11.95 (ISBN 0-14-095040-0, Puffin). Puffin Bks.

Daly, Niki. Ben's Gingerbread Man. LC 85-3327. (Illus.). 24p. (ps-1). 1985. 4.95 (ISBN 0-670-80806-7). Viking Child Bks.

—Monsters Are Like That. LC 85-3328. (Illus.). 24p. (ps-1). 1985. pap. 4.95 (ISBN 0-670-80807-5). Viking Child Bks.

Daniel, Jennifer. Spin-a-Story, Twenty Thousand French Fries under the Sea & Other Crazy Classics. Brown, Jean, illus. 24p. (gr. 4-7). 1990. pap. 2.95 (ISBN 1-878890-01-8). Palisades Prodns.

Daniel, Kira. Backyard Tent. Burns, Ray, illus. LC 85-14068. 48p. (Orig.). (gr. 1-3). 1986. PLB 9.89 (ISBN 0-8167-0626-3); pap. text ed. 2.95 (ISBN 0-8167-0627-1). Troll Assocs.

—The Magic Kite. Getchell, Marianne S., illus. LC 85-14015. 48p. (Orig.). (gr. 1-3). 1986. PLB 9.89 (ISBN 0-8167-0614-X); pap. text ed. 2.95 (ISBN 0-8167-0615-8). Troll Assocs.

Danziger, Paula. Make Like a Tree & Leave. (gr. 4-7). 1990. 13.95 (ISBN 0-385-30151-0). Delacorte.

Davis, Emmett. Only in Dreams. Wheeler, Cindy, illus. LC 83-8627. 32p. (gr. 3-6). 1984. PLB 27.99 (ISBN 0-8172-2282-0); cassette 14.00 (ISBN 0-685-10545-8). Raintree Pubs.

Davis, Robert. Kimura. 224p. 1989. 18.95 (ISBN 0-8027-5736-7). Walker & Co.

Davoll, Barbara. The White Trail. Hockerman, Dennis, illus. 24p. 1988. 5.99 (ISBN 0-89693-404-7); cassette 8.99 (ISBN 0-89693-615-5). Victor Bks.

DeFelice, Cynthia C. Weasel. LC 89-37794. 128p. (gr. 5 up). 1990. 12.95 (ISBN 0-02-726457-2, Mcmillan Child Bk). Macmillan Child Grp.

Deitz, Lawrence. Jimmy Coon Story Book, No. 3. 37p. 1986. pap. 2.95 (ISBN 0-934750-85-8). Mntn Memories Bks.

—Jimmy Coon Story Book, No. 4. McCoy, Beverly, illus. 30p. 1986. pap. 2.95 (ISBN 0-934750-14-9). Mntn Memories Bks.

Disney, Walt, Productions Staff. Walt Disney's Story Land. (Illus.). 320p. (gr. 1-5). 1987. write for info. (ISBN 0-307-16547-7, Golden Bks). Western Pub.

—Words, Riddles, & Stories. LC 85-43074. 80p. 1985. pap. 5.95 (ISBN 0-553-05535-6). Bantam.

Dr. Seuss. And to Think That I Saw It on Mulberry Street. Dr. Seuss, illus. LC 88-38411. 32p. (ps-3). 1989. Repr. of 1937 ed. 9.95 (ISBN 0-394-84494-7); lib. bdg. 10.99 (ISBN 0-394-94494-1). Random.

Doherty, Berlie. Paddiwak & Cozy. O'Brien, Teresa, illus. LC 88-3599. 32p. (ps-2). 1989. 12.95 (ISBN 0-8037-0483-6). Dial Bks Young.

Edgar, Pamela & Matz, Dale. Adventures of Jason: Mythical Magical Journey into Self-Discovery. LC 85-9695. (Illus.). 64p. (Orig.). (gr. 1-5). 1985. pap. 7.95 (ISBN 0-941992-05-5). Los Arboles Pub.

Eller, Scott. Short Season. 144p. (Orig.). (gr. 4-6). 1985. pap. 2.25 (ISBN 0-590-33573-1, Apple Paperbacks). Scholastic Inc.

Ellis, Jana. Junior Weekend. LC 88-19988. 160p. (gr. 7 up). 1988. pap. text ed. 2.50 (ISBN 0-8167-1364-2). Troll Assocs.

Engel, Diana. Josephina, the Great Collector. Engel, Diana, illus. LC 87-20358. 32p. (ps-2). 1988. 12.95 (ISBN 0-688-07542-8); PLB 12.88 (ISBN 0-688-07543-6, Morrow Jr Bks). Morrow Jr Bks.

Erickson, Jon. Andersen Fairy Tales. Mogensen, Jan, illus. (gr. 2-4). 1987. Set. PLB 43.80 (ISBN 1-55532-419-3). Gareth Stevens Inc.

Ernst, Lisa C. Up to Ten & down Again. LC 84-21852. (Illus.). 40p. (ps). 1986. 13.95 (ISBN 0-688-04541-3); PLB 13.88 (ISBN 0-688-04542-1). Lothrop.
Erskine, Jim. Bedtime Story. Schweninger, Ann, illus. LC 81-3163. 32p. (ps-1). 1981. PLB 8.95 (ISBN 0-517-54540-3). Crown.
Evans, Olive. Secrets of the Forest. (gr. 3-12). 1985. pap. text ed. 6.00 (ISBN 0-88734-502-6). Players Pr.
Favorite Bedtime Stories. LC 64-17442. (ps-2). 1978. write for info. (ISBN 0-528-82217-9). Checkerboard Pr.
Favorite Pillowtime Tales. LC 62-15044. (ps-2). 1978. write for info. (ISBN 0-528-82218-7). Checkerboard Pr.
Fisher, Barbara & Spiegel, Richard, eds. In Search of a Song: Jefferson Market Library, Vol. 3. (Illus.). 64p. (Orig.). (gr. 1-6). 1982. pap. 2.00 (ISBN 0-934830-27-4). Ten Penny.
Five-Minute Bedtime Stories. (Illus.). (ps-1). 1985. 2.98 (ISBN 0-517-46988-X). Outlet Bk Co.
Five Sesame Street Golden Super Shape Books. (gr. 2-5). 1987. pap. write for info. (ISBN 0-307-15533-1, Pub. by Golden Bks). Western Pub.
Flax, Zena, ed. The Old Fashioned Children's Storybook. LC 82-80875. (Illus.). 64p. (gr. k up). 1982. 6.95 (ISBN 0-448-12537-4, G&D). Putnam Pub Group.
Fleischman, Paul. Coming-&-Going Men: Four Tales. Gaul, Randy, illus. LC 84-48336. 160p. (gr. 6 up). 1985. PLB 12.89 (ISBN 0-06-021884-3). HarpC Child Bks.
Fosburgh, Liza. Cruise Control. 224p. (gr. 7 up). 1988. 13.95 (ISBN 0-553-05491-0, Starfire). Bantam.
Fox, Mem. With Love, at Christmas. Lippincott, Gary, illus. (gr. 2 up). 1988. 12.95 (ISBN 0-687-45863-3). Abingdon.
Fox, Paula. Maurice's Room. Fetz, Ingrid, illus. LC 85-7200. 64p. (gr. 2-6). 1985. 13.95 (ISBN 0-02-735490-3, Mcmillan Child Bk). Macmillan Child Grp.
Freeman, Lydia. Corduroy's Party. McCue, Lisa, illus. LC 84-40476. 14p. (ps). 1985. pap. 3.95 (ISBN 0-670-80520-3). Viking Child Bks.
Friend, Janet. To Grow by Storybook Readers. Capezio, Betsy, illus. (gr. k-3). 1990. Set. pap. text ed. 44.95 (ISBN 0-910311-69-2). Huntington Hse.
Fuentes, Vilma M. Manggob & His Golden Top. Inis, Ninabeth R., illus. 48p. (Orig.). (gr. k-3). 1985. pap. 4.00 (ISBN 971-10-0218-3, Pub. by New Day Philippines). Cellar.
Fujikawa, Gyo, illus. Oh, What a Busy Day. 80p. (gr. k-3). 1976. 8.95 (ISBN 0-448-12511-0, G&D). Putnam Pub Group.
Furman, Abraham L., ed. Teen-Age Party Time Stories. (gr. 6-10). 1966. PLB 6.70 (ISBN 0-8313-0039-6). Lantern.
Gabhart, Ann. A Kindred Spirit. (gr. 6 up). 1987. pap. 2.25 (ISBN 0-373-98013-2). Harlequin Bks.
Gauz, Yaffa. From Head to Toe: A Book About You. (gr. 5-8). 1988. 11.95 (ISBN 0-87306-446-1). Feldheim.
Geiss, Tony, et al. The Sesame Street Bedtime Storybook. Cooke, Tom, et al, illus. LC 77-93774. (ps-2). 1978. 8.95 (ISBN 0-394-83843-2, Random Juv); lib. bdg. 7.99 (ISBN 0-394-93843-7). Random.
Giant Treasury of Beatrix Potter. (Illus.). (gr. k-6). 1985. 5.95 (ISBN 0-517-43121-1). Outlet Bk Co.
Gibbons, Gail. Check It Out: The Book about Libraries. Gibbons, Gail, illus. LC 85-5414. 32p. (ps-3). 1985. 12.95 (ISBN 0-15-216400-6, HJ). HarBraceJ.
Gill, Shelley R. Kiana's Iditarod. Cartwright, Shannon, illus. 52p. (Orig.). (gr. 2-6). 1984. pap. 8.95 (ISBN 0-934007-00-4). Paws Four Pub.
Gillham, Bill. What Happens Next? Siegieda, Jan, illus. LC 84-26293. 32p. (ps-k). 1985. 7.95 (ISBN 0-399-21255-8, Putnam). Putnam Pub Group.
Gilson, Jamie. Hello, My Name Is Scrambled Eggs. Wallner, John, illus. LC 84-10075. 160p. (gr. 4-6). 1985. 12.95 (ISBN 0-688-04095-0). Lothrop.
Ginsburg, Mirra. The Sun's Asleep Behind the Hill. Zelinsky, Paul O., illus. LC 81-6615. 32p. (ps-1). 1982. 12.95 (ISBN 0-688-00824-0); PLB 12.88 (ISBN 0-688-00825-9). Greenwillow.
Girst, Jack. Deer Rufus, You're a Bull. (Illus.). 32p. (gr. k-2). 1989. pap. 1.95 (ISBN 0-87403-632-1, 3971). Standard Pub.
Girst, Jack A. A Mighty Muddy Lesson. Girst, Jack A., illus. 32p. (gr. k-2). 1989. pap. 1.95 (ISBN 0-87403-631-3, 3974). Standard Pub.
—Renfro Would Rather Rest. Girst, Jack A., illus. 32p. (gr. k-2). 1989. pap. 1.95 (ISBN 0-87403-633-X, 3972). Standard Pub.
Goffin, Jeffrey. My Gun is Pink. (Illus.). 32p. (Orig.). (gr. 6 up). 1987. pap. 2.50 (ISBN 0-88680-280-6). I E Clark.
Gollehon, John. Pay the Line! 160p. 1987. pap. 3.95 (ISBN 0-399-51459-7, Perigee Bks). Putnam Pub Group.
Gondosch, Linda. Who Needs a Bratty Brother? Cogancheyy, Helen, illus. LC 85-6943. 112p. (gr. 4-6). 1985. 11.95 (ISBN 0-525-67170-6, Lodestar Bks). Dutton Child Bks.
Good Night, Sammy. (ps-k). Date not set. write for info. (ISBN 0-307-12238-7, Golden Pr). Western Pub.
Gorog, Judith. A Taste for Quiet: And Other Disquieting Tales. Titherington, Jeanne, illus. 124p. (gr. 4 up). 1982. 9.95 (ISBN 0-399-20922-0, Philomel). Putnam Pub Group.
Greenwald, Sheila. Mariah Delany's Author-of-the-Month-Club. (gr. 4-7). 1990. 13.95 (ISBN 0-316-32713-1, Joy St Bks). Little.
Grifalconi, Ann. Osa's Pride, Vol. 1. (Illus.). (ps-3). 1990. 14.95 (ISBN 0-316-32865-0, Joy St Bks). Little.
Grindley, Sally. Read to Me Treasury. 1990. 15.95 (ISBN 0-385-26677-4). Doubleday.
Hagman, Harlan L. A Seasonal Present & Other Stories. LC 88-34712. (Illus.). xiv, 341p. (gr. 9 up). 1989. 19.95 (ISBN 0-931600-08-1). Green Oak Pr.
Haiduck, Robert. Ten Tiny Tales, Bk. 1. 87p. (gr. 1-8). Date not set. write for info. (ISBN 0-9627661-0-0). Tiny Tales.
Hands & Feet. (Illus.). (gr. 5 up). lib. bdg. 14.00 (ISBN 0-86625-279-7). Rourke Corp.
Hardinge, Miriam. Long Ago Stories. Wheeler, Gerald, ed. 144p. (Orig.). (ps). 1987. pap. 6.95 (ISBN 0-8280-0351-3). Review & Herald.
Hardt, Elaine. Stories from Beyond the Double Rainbow. (Orig.). (gr. 1-8). 1982. pap. 10.50 (ISBN 0-932960-03-0). Thinking Caps.
Hargreaves, Roger. Little Miss Chatterbox. 32p. (ps-k). 1984. pap. 1.25 (ISBN 0-8431-1479-7). Price Stern.
—Little Miss Contrary. 32p. (ps-k). 1984. pap. 1.25 (ISBN 0-8431-1480-0). Price Stern.
—Little Miss Dotty. 32p. (ps-k). 1984. pap. 1.25 (ISBN 0-8431-1478-9). Price Stern.
—Little Miss Fickle. 32p. (ps-k). 1984. pap. 1.25 (ISBN 0-8431-1481-9). Price Stern.
—Little Miss Giggles. 32p. (ps-k). 1984. pap. 1.25 (ISBN 0-8431-1475-4). Price Stern.
—Little Miss Lucky. 32p. (ps-k). 1984. pap. 1.25 (ISBN 0-8431-1476-2). Price Stern.
—Little Miss Magic. 32p. 1982. pap. 1.25 (ISBN 0-8431-1483-5). Price Stern.
—Little Miss Star. 32p. (ps-k). 1984. pap. 1.25 (ISBN 0-8431-1482-7). Price Stern.
—Little Miss Twins. 32p. (ps-k). 1984. pap. 1.25 (ISBN 0-8431-1477-0). Price Stern.
Harriot, Ray. Stories for Around the Campfire. 2nd ed. (Illus.). 224p. (gr. 5-10). 1986. pap. 5.95 (ISBN 0-317-93072-9). Campfire Pub.
Hartley, Mary M. Mariposa: A Tough Texan in a Time Capsule. 64p. (gr. 4-7). 1986. 10.95 (ISBN 0-89015-544-5, Pub. by Panda Bks). Eakin Pr.
Harvey, Brett. Cassie's Journey: Going West in the 1860s. Ray, Deborah K., illus. LC 87-23599. 40p. (gr. 1-4). 1987. reinforced bdg. 12.95 (ISBN 0-8234-0684-9). Holiday.
Hathorn, Elizabeth. The Tram to Bondi Beach. Vivas, Julie, illus. 32p. (gr. 4-8). 1989. 12.95 (ISBN 0-916291-20-0). Kane-Miller Bk.
Havill, Juanita. Jamaica's Find. O'Brien, Anne S., illus. (ps-3). 1986. 13.95 (ISBN 0-395-39376-0). HM.
Hazen, Barbara S. The Gorilla Did It. LC 73-84828. (Illus.). (ps-1). 1978. pap. 3.95 (Aladdin). Macmillan.
Henkes, Kevin. Shhhh. LC 88-18771. (Illus.). 24p. (ps up). 1989. 11.95 (ISBN 0-688-07985-7); PLB 11.88 (ISBN 0-688-07986-5). Greenwillow.
Herigstad, Joni. I Was So Mad: Storybook for Young Children in Sign Language. Herigstad, Joni, illus. 50p. (Orig.). (ps-4). 1986. pap. 4.50 (ISBN 0-916708-16-0). Modern Signs.
Hezlep, William. Pharaoh's Dagger. (Orig.). (gr. 3-12). 1985. pap. text ed. 5.00 (ISBN 0-88734-404-6). Players Pr.
Hilliard, Susan. Day of the Fire Storm. Ostendorf, Ned, illus. 144p. (gr. 5-7). 1989. pap. 3.95 (ISBN 0-87403-583-X, 3983). Standard Pub.
Hitchcock, Alfred, ed. Alfred Hitchcock's Monster Museum. LC 81-13883. (Illus.). 224p. (gr. 5 up). 1982. pap. 3.95 (ISBN 0-394-84899-3). Random.
Hoobler, Thomas. The Revenge of Ho-Tai. 208p. (gr. 7 up). 1989. 15.95 (ISBN 0-8027-6870-9). Walker & Co.
Hopkins, Lila. Talking Turkey. 128p. (gr. 7-9). 1990. 12.90 (ISBN 0-531-10797-3). Watts.
Hughes, Ted. Tales of the Early World. (gr. 4-8). 1991. 13.95 (ISBN 0-374-37377-9). FS&G.
Illustrated Classics for Children. 1987. 5.98 (ISBN 0-671-08501-8). S&S Trade.
Izawa, Tadasu & Hijikata, Shigemi, illus. A Puppet Treasure Book of Nursery Tales. 94p. (ps-1). 1981. 5.95 (ISBN 0-448-12289-8, G&D). Putnam Pub Group.
Jackson, Kathryn. Golden Book of Three Hundred Sixty-Five Stories. Scarry, Richard, illus. 1955. write for info. (ISBN 0-307-15557-9, Golden Bks). Western Pub.
Jackson, Tim. The Case of: The Great Graffiti. Jackson, Tim, illus. 19p. (Orig.). (gr. 5-8). 1987. pap. 1.95 (ISBN 0-942675-04-5). Creative License.
Janger, Kathie, ed. Rainbow Collection, 1990: Stories & Poetry by Young People. Sarecky, Melody, illus. Bush, Barbara, frwd. by. (Illus.). 176p. 1990. pap. 6.00 (ISBN 0-929889-06-1). Young Writers Contest Found.
Jenkins, Gerald & Wild, Anne. The Gift Box Book. (Illus.). 32p. (gr. 3 up). 1985. pap. 6.95 (ISBN 0-906212-36-7). Parkwest Pubns.
Johnson, Lois W. Secrets of the Best Choice. Peck, Virginia, illus. LC 88-60475. 192p. (Orig.). 1988. pap. 4.95 (ISBN 0-89109-232-3). NavPress.
Johnson, Sue. The Little Green Monsters. Herigstad, Joni, illus. 36p. (ps-6). 1985. pap. 4.50 (ISBN 0-916708-15-2). Modern Signs.
Johnston, Norma. The Time of the Cranes. LC 89-39818. 176p. (gr. 7 up). 1990. 13.95 (ISBN 0-02-747713-4, Four Winds). Macmillan Child Grp.
Joly-Berbesson, Fanny. Marceau Bonappetit. Mathieu, Agnes, illus. 32p. (ps-3). 1989. PLB 9.95 (ISBN 0-87614-369-9). Carolrhoda Bks.
Jonas, Ann. Where Can It Be? Jonas, Ann, illus. LC 86-304. 32p. (ps-1). 1986. 14.95 (ISBN 0-688-05169-3); PLB 14.88 (ISBN 0-688-05246-0). Greenwillow.
Kavanaugh, Michelle. Emerald Explosion. LC 87-30196. 200p. (gr. 9-12). 1988. PLB 11.95 (ISBN 0-910923-46-9). Pineapple Pr.

Keckeis, M. B. The Black Rose. Steiner, Frank, et al, trs. Cassidy, Christoph, illus. (ENG, SPA, FRE & GER.). 256p. (gr. 3-9). 1991. 23.50 (ISBN 1-879870-54-1). Pro Lingua Pr.
This richly-illustrated storybook for children ages 5 through 12 is designed to promote both reading skills & learning of foreign languages. Each story is simultaneously presented in four different languages - English, French, German & Spanish. In this totally new approach to foreign-language learning, no longer is the text an incomprehensible maze of strange sounding words, but the mirrored image of a story well understood by the young reader. It is like a puzzle falling delightfully into place. Everyone is able to master foreign words or phrases in this easy, enjoyable way. And the story translations are meticulous. The five absorbing stories selected for this book bring back the art of storytelling, making it ideal even for listeners under age 5. Whether the storyline is about a puppet struggling to break free from its master or a little star in the heavens striving for fame, the dreams & hopes of these characters are similar to every child's & in the end we all learn from their quest. With its superb, woodcut-like illustrations, this heirloom-quality book makes a fine gift & is truly a collector's edition. It also is suitable for use in ESL classes.
Publisher Provided Annotation.

Kelleher, Victor. The Red King. Fogelman, Phyllis J., ed. LC 89-23745. (Illus.). 176p. (gr. 6 up). 1990. 14.95 (ISBN 0-8037-0758-4). Dial Bks Young.
Kerr, Rita. The Immortal Thirty-Two. 64p. (gr. 4-7). 1986. 7.95 (ISBN 0-89015-538-0, Pub. by Panda Bks). Eakin Pr.
Kingsley, Charles. The Water-Babies. (Illus.). 256p. 1987. Repr. PLB 22.95x (ISBN 0-89966-579-9). Buccaneer Bks.
Kipling, Rudyard. Tales from the Jungle Book. McKinley, Robin, adapted by. Smith, J. A., illus. LC 84-11724. 64p. (gr. k-3). 1985. (Random Juv); lib. bdg. 8.99 (ISBN 0-394-96940-5). Random.
Klass, Sheila S. Credit-Card Carole. 144p. 1989. pap. 2.95 (ISBN 0-553-27355-8, Starfire). Bantam.
Klimo, Kate, ed. The Tasha Tudor's Bedtime Book. LC 77-853. (Illus.). 48p. (gr. 1-7). 1978. 6.95 (ISBN 0-448-47217-1, G&D); PLB 5.99 (ISBN 0-448-13038-6). Putnam Pub Group.
Kohaine, Chayele. Operation C. H. E. S. E. D. & other Stories. Scheinberg, Shepsil, illus. 139p. (gr. 2-5). 1989. 10.95 (ISBN 0-935063-81-1); pap. text ed. 7.95 (ISBN 0-935063-82-X). CIS Comm.
Kohls, Tom. Green Cord. 31p. 1987. pap. 3.25 (ISBN 0-8163-0705-9). Pacific Pr Pub Assn.
Konigsburg, E. L. The Second Mrs. Giaconda. LC 75-6946. (Illus.). (gr. 5-9). 1978. pap. 4.95 (ISBN 0-689-70450-X, Aladdin). Macmillan Child Grp.
Korman, Gordon. No Coins, Please. 192p. (Orig.). (gr. 3-7). 1991. pap. 2.95 (ISBN 0-590-44208-2, Apple Paperbacks). Scholastic Inc.
Korman, Justine. Big Bird's New Nest & Other Good-Night Stories. Cooke, Tom, illus. (ps-1). 1989. write for info. (ISBN 0-307-12060-0, 12060). Western Pub.
Koulomzin, Sophie. Sbornik Detskij, Tysacha Let (988-1988) (RUS.). (gr. 2-4). 1985. write for info. RBR.
Krauss, Ruth. Somebody Else's Nut Tree & Other Tales from Children. Sendak, Maurice, illus. LC 89-28056. 43p. (ps-5). 1990. Repr. of 1958 ed. lib. bdg. 14.00 (ISBN 0-208-02264-3, Linnet). Shoe String.
Krupinsky, Jacquelyn S. Henry, the Hesitant Heron. Cutri, Anne C. & Cutri, Anne, illus. 32p. (Orig.). (gr. k-3). 1987. pap. 6.95 (ISBN 0-912123-02-8). Woodbury Pr.
Landes, William-Alan. Pyramus & Thisbe. rev. ed. LC 90-53083. (gr. 3 up). 1984. pap. text ed. 5.00 (ISBN 0-88734-103-9); pap. text ed. 6.00 (ISBN 0-685-09727-7). Players Pr.

Landes, William-Alan & Standish, Marilyn. The Wizard of Oz. rev. ed. LC 89-63872. (gr. 3-12). 1985. pap. text ed. 6.00 (ISBN 0-88734-105-5); tchr's. ed. 30.00 (ISBN 0-88734-011-3). Players Pr.

Larson, Greg. The Magic Garden & Other Stories. Muir, Michael, illus. LC 88-18879. 95p. (gr. 3-6). 1988. 7.95 (ISBN 0-87579-141-7). Deseret Bk.

Lawhead, Steve. Howard Had a Shrinking Machine. Lawhead, Steve, illus. 32p. (gr. k-3). 1988. 7.95 (ISBN 0-7459-1316-4). Lion USA.

Leeper, John H. The Brothers of the Sled & Other Faith-Building Stories. (Orig.). (gr. 6). 1985. pap. 4.95 (ISBN 0-8024-0622-X). Moody.

Lehner, Devony. Tinker's Journey Home. Maloney, P. Dennis, ed. Adamson, Charlotte, illus. 34p. (ps-6). 12.95 (ISBN 0-940305-00-3). P D Maloney.

Let's Take a Trip. 22p. (ps-1). 1985. 5.95 (ISBN 0-8431-1463-0). Price Stern.

Levoy, Myron. Witch of Fourth Street & Other Stories. LC 74-183174. (Illus.). 128p. (gr. 3-7). 1974. pap. 3.50 (ISBN 0-06-440059-X, Trophy). HarpC Child Bks.

Liebowitz, Janet Z. The Gumdrops. 1988. 5.95 (ISBN 0-533-07857-1). Vantage.

Lillington, Kenneth. The Real Live Dinosaur & Other Stories. Floyd, Gareth, illus. 96p. (gr. 3-7). 1990. bds. 10.95 laminated (ISBN 0-571-14144-7). Faber & Faber.

Lipson, Greta B. Tales with a Twist. 160p. (gr. 5-9). 1991. 11.95 (ISBN 0-86653-609-4, GA1328). Good Apple.

Littke, Lael. Shanny on Her Own. LC 85-8451. 160p. (gr. 7 up). 1985. 12.95 (ISBN 0-15-273531-3, HJ). HarBraceJ.

Little, Jean. Lost & Found. O'Young, Leoung, illus. LC 85-40836. 80p. (gr. 3-7). 1986. pap. 10.95 (ISBN 0-670-80835-0). Viking Child Bks.

Lobato, Arcadio. The Greatest Treasure. Lobato, Arcadio, illus. LC 89-3612. 28p. (ps up). 1989. 14.95 (ISBN 0-88708-093-6). Picture Bk Studio.

Lolling, Atsuko G. Aki & the Banner of Names: And Other Stories from Japan. (Orig.). (gr. 1-6). 1991. pap. 4.95 (ISBN 0-377-00218-6). Friendship Pr.
This book introduces young readers to children in Japan like Masaki, who watches anxiously as his once playful brother becomes frustrated by declining test marks; & Mariko who envies her friends' special celebration of a Shinto holiday. Young readers will be introduced to Japanese culture & society--they will recognize some familiar problems such as the pressure to do well in school & tensions within the family. A Teacher's Guide is also available.
Publisher Provided Annotation.

LoPresti, Joan. Calendar Capers: A Child's School Year in Celebration. Danner, Robert W., illus. LC 90-36812. 32p. (gr. k-3). 1990. lib. bdg. 12.95 (ISBN 0-8368-0428-7). Gareth Stevens Inc.

Luttrell, Ida. Ottie Slockett. Fogelman, Phyllis J., ed. Krause, Ute, illus. LC 88-30884. 40p. (ps-3). 1990. 9.95 (ISBN 0-8037-0709-6); PLB 9.89 (ISBN 0-8037-0711-8). Dial Bks Young.

McBrier, Page. Oliver & the Lucky Duck. Sims, Blanche, illus. LC 85-8417. 96p. (gr. 3-6). 1986. PLB 9.89 (ISBN 0-8167-0541-0); pap. text ed. 2.95 (ISBN 0-8167-0542-9). Troll Assocs.

—Oliver's Lucky Day. Sims, Blanche, illus. LC 85-8437. 96p. (gr. 3-6). 1986. lib. bdg. 9.89 (ISBN 0-8167-0537-2); pap. text ed. 2.95 (ISBN 0-8167-0538-0). Troll Assocs.

MacDonald, Amy. Rachel Fister's Blister. Priceman, Marjorie, illus. 32p. (ps-3). 1990. 13.95 (ISBN 0-395-52152-1). HM.

McDowell, Robert E. & Lavitt, Edward, eds. Third World Voices for Children. Isaac, Barbara K., illus. LC 71-169091. 156p. (gr. 5-9). 1971. 5.95 (ISBN 0-89388-020-5, Odarkai). Okpaku Communications.

McKinnon, Elizabeth S. & Warren, Jean, eds. Short-Short Stories: Simple Stories for Young Children Plus Seasonal Activities. Ekberg, Marion, illus. LC 86-51509. 80p. (Orig.). 1987. pap. 6.95 (ISBN 0-911019-13-8). Warren Pub Hse.

McPhail, David. Emma's Pet. McPhail, David, illus. LC 85-4414. 24p. (ps-k). 1985. 9.95 (ISBN 0-525-44210-3, DCB). Dutton Child Bks.

—Farm Morning. McPhail, David, illus. LC 84-19167. 32p. (ps-3). 1985. 15.95 (ISBN 0-15-227299-2, HJ). HarBraceJ.

McQueen, Priscilla L. We Can Read: Story Pack-54 Little Stories. 1973. pap. 18.66 (ISBN 0-685-47089-X). McQueen.

Maglione, Robin S. Alyndoria: Tales of Inner Magic. Wheeling, Darren, illus. 71p. (Orig.). (gr. k-12). 1986. pap. 12.00 (ISBN 0-910609-11-X). Gifted Educ Pr.

Mahy, Margaret. The Sunshine Series, Level 7: Muppy's Ball; The Garden Party; The Tree Doctor & Feeling Funny. rev. ed. McRae, Rodney, et al, illus. 24p. (gr. 3-4). pap. text ed. 16.24 Americanized version (ISBN 1-55624-078-3, WP0783). Wright Group.

Mahy, Margaret & Ciantar, George. The Sunshine Series, Level 11: The Mad Puppet; Iris La Bonga & the Helpful Taxi Driver; The Haunting of Miss Cardamon; The Girl Who Washed in Moonlight; Elliot & the Kelly Cats & Eating Out, 6 bks. (Illus.). 144p. (Orig.). (gr. 3-5). 1987. Set. pap. text ed. 23.50 (ISBN 1-55624-092-9). Wright Group.

—The Sunshine Series, Level 8: A Pet to the Vet; The King's Treasure; The New House Villain & The Funny Funny Clown Face. rev. ed. Webb, Philip, et al, illus. 24p. (gr. 4-5). pap. text ed. 16.24 Americanized version (ISBN 1-55624-079-1, WP0791). Wright Group.

—The Sunshine Series, Level 9: Tai Taylor Is Born; Grow up Sally-Sue; Trouble on the Bus; Shuttle-4; Mr. Rumfitt & The Terrible, Topsy-Turvy, Tissy-Tossy Tangle, 6 bks. rev. ed. (Illus.). 144p. (gr. 3-5). Set. pap. text ed. 23.50 (ISBN 1-55624-080-5). Wright Group.

Mahy, Margaret & McRae, Rodney. The Sunshine Series, Level 6: The Trouble with Heathrow; The Pop Group; Baby's Breakfast & The Man Who Enjoyed Grumbling. rev. ed. Beasley, Madeline, et al, illus. 24p. (gr. 2-4). pap. text ed. 16.24 Americanized version (ISBN 1-55624-077-5, WP0775). Wright Group.

Mark, Jan. Nothing to Be Afraid Of. LC 81-48064. 128p. (gr. 6 up). 1982. HarpC Child Bks.

Marron, Carol A. Someone Just Like Me. Wheeler, Cindy, illus. LC 83-8898. 32p. (gr. 3-6). 1984. PLB 27.99 (ISBN 0-8172-2283-9); cassette only 14.00 (ISBN 0-317-19667-7). Raintree Pubs.

Marshall, James. The Cut-Ups Cut Loose. (Illus.). 32p. (ps-3). 1987. pap. 12.95 (ISBN 0-670-80740-0). Viking Child Bks.

Martignoni, Margaret E., ed. & intro. by. Illustrated Treasury of Children's Literature. (Illus.). 512p. (gr. 5-8). 1955. 17.95 (ISBN 0-448-04101-4, G&D). Putnam Pub Group.

Matthews, Morgan. Icky, Sticky Gloop. Victor, Ymonne, illus. LC 85-14013. 48p. (Orig.). (gr. 1-3). 1986. lib. bdg. 9.89 (ISBN 0-8167-0616-6); pap. text ed. 2.95 (ISBN 0-8167-0617-4). Troll Assocs.

Mayer, Mercer. Little Critter's Bedtime Storybook. Mayer, Mercer, illus. LC 86-23419. 48p. (ps-1). 1987. write for info. (ISBN 0-307-15588-9, Pub. by Golden Bks). Western Pub.

Maynard, Joyce. Camp-Out. Bethel, Steve, illus. LC 85-5504. 32p. (ps-3). 1985. 12.95 (ISBN 0-15-214077-8, HJ). HarBraceJ.

Mazer, Anne. The Yellow Button. Pedersen, Judy, illus. LC 89-34921. 40p. (ps-2). 1990. 12.95 (ISBN 0-394-82935-2); PLB 13.99 (ISBN 0-394-92935-7). Knopf.

Michels, Tilde. Come Here, Little Hedgehog. Ball, Sara, illus. LC 88-16600. (gr. 2 up). 1988. 1.00 (ISBN 0-687-08876-3). Abingdon.

Mills, Claudia. Boardwalk with Hotel. LC 84-42976. 144p. (gr. 3-7). 1985. 12.95 (ISBN 0-02-767010-4, Mcmillan Child Bk). Macmillan Child Grp.

—Dynamite Dinah. LC 89-13300. 128p. (gr. 3-7). 1990. 12.95 (ISBN 0-02-767101-1, Mcmillan Child Bk). Macmillan Child Grp.

Mills, Jane L. & Johnson, Larry D. Arnie's Surprise. Hebert, Kim T., illus. LC 86-60363. 14p. (Orig.). (ps). 1986. pap. 4.00 (ISBN 0-938155-05-9); pap. 12.00 set of 3 bks. (ISBN 0-685-13523-3). Read A Bol.

Mills, Kathi. Life Can Be Tough. McIntosh, Guy, illus. 96p. (gr. 1-3). 1989. pap. 2.95 (ISBN 0-87403-603-8, 3941). Standard Pub.

Moncure, Jane B. Butterfly Express. Hohag, Linda, illus. LC 88-22944. 32p. (ps-2). 1989. PLB 11.97 (ISBN 0-89565-392-3); pap. 6.96 (ISBN 0-89565-516-0). Childs World.

—My "u" Sound Box. Peltier, Pam, illus. LC 84-17012. 32p. (ps-2). 1984. lib. bdg. 11.97 (ISBN 0-89565-300-1); pap. 6.96 (ISBN 0-89565-339-7). Childs World.

Morin, illus. Puss in Boots. 32p. (ps up). 1988. 8.95 (ISBN 0-8120-5901-8). Barron.

Mother. Tales of All Times. (Illus.). 138p. (gr. 3-8). 1983. pap. 3.00 (ISBN 0-89071-321-9, Pub. by Sri Aurobindo Ashram India). Aurobindo Assn.

Munro, Alice. Dance of the Happy Shades & Other Stories. 240p. 1985. pap. 6.95 (ISBN 0-14-006681-0, Penguin Bks). Viking Penguin.

Munsch, Robert. Thomas' Snowsuit. Martchenko, Michael, illus. 24p. (gr. k-3). 1985. 12.95 (ISBN 0-920303-32-3); pap. 4.95 (ISBN 0-920303-33-1). Firefly Bks Ltd.

My Bedtime Book. (Illus.). 8p. (ps). 1978. 2.50 (ISBN 0-448-46806-9, G&D); PLB 5.99 (ISBN 0-448-13362-8). Putnam Pub Group.

My Biggest Bedtime Book Ever. 1988. 8.98 (ISBN 0-671-07571-3). S&S Trade.

Myers, Bernice. Sidney Rella & the Glass Sneaker. Myers, Bernice, illus. LC 85-3044. 32p. (gr. k-3). 1985. 13.95 (ISBN 0-02-767790-7, Mcmillan Child Bk). Macmillan Child Grp.

Newman, Robert. The Case of the Baker Street Irregular. LC 77-15463. (gr. 3-7). 1984. pap. 4.95 (ISBN 0-689-70766-5, Aladdin). Macmillan Child Grp.

Norris, Carolyn. Jeans Christmas Stocking. Norris, Carolyn, illus. 24p. (Orig.). (ps-4). 1982. pap. 3.25 (ISBN 0-916708-10-1). Modern Signs.

Noyes, Beppie. Wigglesworth. Noyes, Beppie, illus. LC 85-62022. 74p. (gr. k-4). 1985. pap. 5.95 (ISBN 0-932433-08-1). Windswept Hse.

Oakley, Graham. The Church Cat Abroad. LC 73-76327. (Illus.). (gr. k-3). 1980. pap. 4.95 (ISBN 0-689-70472-0, Aladdin). Macmillan Child Grp.

Oechsli, Kelly. Home Sweet Home. Oechsli, Kelly, illus. LC 83-8607. 32p. (gr. k-3). 1984. PLB 27.99g (ISBN 0-8172-2281-2); cassette only 14.00 (ISBN 0-317-19660-X). Raintree Pubs.

O. Henry. The Last Leaf. rev. ed. (gr. 9-12). 1989. Repr. of 1906 ed. multi-media kit 35.00 (ISBN 0-685-31126-0). Balance Pub.

Once upon a Time. 64p. (ps-1). pap. 14.95 (ISBN 0-399-21369-4, Putnam); pap. 6.95 (ISBN 0-399-21370-8). Putnam Pub Group.

Orgel, Doris. Whiskers, Once & Always. Newsom, Carol, illus. 96p. (gr. 2-5). 1989. pap. 3.95 (ISBN 0-14-032038-5, Puffin). Puffin Bks.

Osborne, Mary P. Mo to the Rescue. Disalvo-Ryan, Dyanne, illus. LC 84-28796. 56p. (ps-3). 1985. 8.95 (ISBN 0-8037-0180-2); PLB 8.89 (ISBN 0-8037-0182-9). Dial Bks Young.

Parker, Nancy W. Poofy Loves Company. (Illus.). 32p. (ps-3). 1988. pap. 3.95 (ISBN 0-14-050855-4, Puffin). Puffin Bks.

Pascal, Francine. Love, Betrayal & Hold the Mayo! LC 84-20905. (gr. 6 up). 1985. pap. 11.95 (ISBN 0-670-80547-5). Viking Child Bks.

Pellowski, Michael J. Benny's Bad Day. Cushman, Doug, illus. LC 85-14016. 48p. (Orig.). (gr. 1-3). 1986. PLB 9.89 (ISBN 0-8167-0620-4); pap. text ed. 2.95 (ISBN 0-8167-0621-2). Troll Assocs.

Perrault, Charles & Kipling, Rudyard. Cinderella & How the Elephant Got Its Trunk. (Illus.). 48p. (gr. 1-4). 1985. 5.95 (ISBN 0-88110-252-0). EDC.

Pershall, Mary K. You Take the High Road. 1990. 14.95 (ISBN 0-8037-0700-2). Dial Bks Young.

Peterson, Carolyn S. Story Programs Activities for Older Children. Sterchele, Christina, illus. (Orig.). (gr. 3-6). 1987. 20.00 (ISBN 0-913545-11-2). Moonlight FL.

Phillips, Mildred & Zemach, Margot, illus. The Sign in Mendel's Window. LC 85-5049. 32p. (gr. k-3). 1985. 12.95 (ISBN 0-02-774600-3, Mcmillan Child Bk). Macmillan Child Grp.

Pirotta, Saviour. Solomon's Secret. 1989. 11.95 (ISBN 0-8037-0694-4). Dial Bks Young.

Polsky, Milton, et al. The King of Escapes. (Orig.). (gr. 3-12). 1985. pap. text ed. 6.00 (ISBN 0-88734-510-7). Players Pr.

Poppel, Hans & Bodden, Ilona. When the Moon Shines Brightly on the House. 24p. (ps). 1985. 5.95 (ISBN 0-8120-5669-8). Barron.

Poskanzer, Susan C. The Great Soap-Bubble Ride. Fiammenghi, Gioia, illus. LC 85-14022. 48p. (Orig.). (gr. 1-3). 1986. PLB 9.89 (ISBN 0-8167-0622-0); pap. text ed. 2.95 (ISBN 0-8167-0623-9). Troll Assocs.

Potter, Beatrix. The Tale of Peter Rabbit & Other Favorite Stories, 7 vols. 447p. (gr. 2 up). Boxed Set. pap. 12.25 (ISBN 0-486-23903-9). Dover.

Price, Rosalind. The Viking Bedtime Treasury. 1991. 14.95 (ISBN 0-670-83147-6). Viking Child Bks.

Pronzini, Bill, ed. More Wild Westerns. 192p. 1989. 19.95 (ISBN 0-8027-4097-9). Walker & Co.

Purdy, Carol. Iva Dunnit & the Big Wind. Kellogg, Steven, illus. LC 84-17441. 32p. (ps-3). 1985. 12.95 (ISBN 0-8037-0183-7); PLB 12.89 (ISBN 0-8037-0184-5). Dial Bks Young.

Quackenbush, Robert. Detective Mole & the Haunted Castle Mystery. LC 84-20141. (Illus.). 32p. (gr. k-3). 1985. lib. bdg. 12.88 (ISBN 0-688-04641-X). Lothrop.

Rabe, Berniece. Tall Enough to Own the World. LC 88-39139. 160p. (gr. 5-7). 1989. PLB 12.90 (ISBN 0-531-10681-0). Watts.

Reingold, Beverly, ed. Classics-A Child's Introduction to Treasure Island, Black Beauty, Adventures of Tom Sawyer & Robin Hood. Craft, Kinuko Y., illus. LC 77-76562. (gr. 2-7). 1977. 4.95 (ISBN 0-448-47232-5, G&D). Putnam Pub Group.

Reit, Seymour V., et al. When Small Is Tall: And Other Read-Together Tales. Munsinger, Lynn, illus. LC 83-9811. 32p. (ps-1). 1985. lib. bdg. 5.99 (ISBN 0-394-95836-5, Random Juv). Random.

Richard Scarry's Take-Along Library Staff. Richard Scarry's Take-Along Library. (Illus.). 32p. (gr. 3-6). 1986. pap. 11.50 boxed set (ISBN 0-394-88238-5, Random Juv). Random.

Richardson, Frederick, illus. Great Children's Stories: Classic Volland Edition. Hunt, Irene, intro. by. LC 72-83891. (Illus.). 160p. (ps-3). 1938. 12.95 (ISBN 1-56288-040-3). Checkerboard Pr.

Rockwell, Anne. The Three Bears & Fifteen Other Stories. LC 74-5381. (Illus.). 128p. (gr. k-5). 1975. 13.95 (ISBN 0-690-00597-0, Crowell Jr Bks); PLB 13.89 (ISBN 0-690-00598-9). HarpC Child Bks.

Rodda, Emily. Something Special. Young, Noela, illus. 80p. (gr. 2-4). 1989. 12.95 (ISBN 0-8050-1127-7). H Holt & Co.

Roland, Donna. Grandfather's Stories from Mexico. (gr. 1-3). 1986. pap. 4.50 (ISBN 0-941996-09-3). Open My World.

—Grandfather's Stories from the Philippines. (gr. 1-3). 1985. pap. 4.50x (ISBN 0-941996-07-7). Open My World.

—Grandfather's Stories from Vietnam. (gr. 1-3). 1985. pap. 4.50x (ISBN 0-941996-11-5). Open My World.

—More of Grandfather's Stories from the Philippines. (gr. 1-3). 1985. pap. 4.50x (ISBN 0-941996-08-5). Open My World.

—More of Grandfather's Stories from Vietnam. (gr. 1-3). 1985. pap. 4.50x (ISBN 0-941996-12-3). Open My World.

Ross, Tony. The Boy Who Cried Wolf. Ross, Tony, illus. LC 84-23273. 32p. (gr. k up). 1985. 10.95 (ISBN 0-8037-0193-4). Dial Bks Young.

Rudolph, Stormy. Many Horses (Sequel to Quest for Courage) (Illus.). (gr. 5-12). 1987. PLB 12.95 (ISBN 0-89992-412-3); pap. 6.95 (ISBN 0-89992-112-4). Coun India Ed.

Rylant, Cynthia. Every Living Thing. Schindler, Stephen D., illus. LC 85-7701. 96p. (gr. 5-7). 1985. 10.95 (ISBN 0-02-777200-4, Bradbury Pr). Macmillan Child Grp.

—Henry & Mudge in the Sparkle Days: The Fifth Book of Their Adventures. Stevenson, Sucie, illus. LC 86-23432. 48p. (gr. 1-3). 1988. 11.95 (ISBN 0-02-778005-8, Bradbury Pr). Macmillan Child Grp.

Rymer, Alta M. Hobart & Humbert Gruzzy. Rymer, Alta M., illus. LC 85-61860. 28p. (Orig.). (gr. 4-6). 1988. pap. 12.50 (ISBN 0-9600792-6-2). Rymer Bks.

Sanders, Scott R. Hear the Wind Blow: American Folk Songs Retold. Goembel, Ponder, illus. LC 85-4160. 224p. (gr. 6 up). 1985. 14.95 (ISBN 0-02-778140-2, Bradbury Pr). Macmillan Child Grp.

Sandford, John. The Gravity Company. Sanford, John, illus. (gr. 2 up). 1988. 1.50 (ISBN 0-687-15686-6). Abingdon.

Santos, Elsie S. The Frog in the Bog. Santos, Duarte, illus. 44p. (Orig.). (ps-2). 1986. pap. 3.95 (ISBN 0-914151-04-5). Shawme Ent.

Sattler, Helen R. Train Whistles. rev. ed. LC 84-11279. (Illus.). 32p. (ps-2). 1985. 13.00 (ISBN 0-688-03978-2). Lothrop.

Scarry, Richard. The Funniest Storybook Ever. (Illus.). (ps-2). 1972. 8.95 (ISBN 0-394-82432-6, Random Juv); lib. bdg. 6.99 (ISBN 0-394-92432-0). Random.

—Richard Scarry's Bedtime Stories. LC 86-484. (Illus.). 32p. (ps-1). 1990. pap. 5.95 incl. cassette (ISBN 0-679-80803-5). Random.

Schwartz, Alvin. All of Our Noses Are Here & Other Noodle Tales. Weinhaus, Karen A., illus. LC 84-48330. 64p. (gr. k-3). 1985. PLB 10.89 (ISBN 0-685-09667-X). HarpC Child Bks.

Schwartz, Betty, ed. The Old-Fashioned Storybook. Howell, Troy, illus. 144p. (gr. k-6). 1985. 12.95 (ISBN 0-685-10340-4, Little Simon). S&S Trade.

Sefton, Catherine. Island of the Strangers. LC 85-5437. 128p. (gr. 3-7). 1985. 12.95 (ISBN 0-15-239100-2, HJ). HarBraceJ.

Sendak, Maurice. Where the Wild Things Are. (Illus.). 1985. Includes doll - Wild Thing No. 2. 19.95 (ISBN 0-694-00096-5). HarpC Child Bks.

Service, Pamela F. Winter of Magic's Return. LC 85-7952. 224p. (gr. 4-8). 1985. 14.95 (ISBN 0-689-31130-3, Atheneum Child Bk). Macmillan Child Grp.

Sesame Street Story Land. LC 86-80134. (Illus.). 192p. (ps-k). 1986. write for info. (ISBN 0-307-16530-2, Pub. by Golden Bks). Western Pub.

Sesame Street Take-Along Library. (Illus.). 32p. (gr. 4-8). 1986. pap. 11.50 boxed set (ISBN 0-394-88405-1, Random Juv). Random.

Shanat, Marjorie W. Nate the Great & the Sticky Prize. Simont, Marc, illus. LC 84-15545. 48p. (gr. 4). 1985. lib. bdg. 9.99 (ISBN 0-698-30745-3, Coward). Putnam Pub Group.

Sharmat, Marjorie W. Mitchell Is Moving. Aruego, Jose & Dewey, Ariane, illus. LC 85-47782. 48p. (gr. 1-4). 1985. pap. 3.95 (ISBN 0-02-045260-8, Aladdin). Macmillan Child Grp.

Shearer, Marilyn J. Cinderella & the Glass Slipper: A Retelling. Edwards, Ron, illus. LC 90-60394. 16p. (ps-6). 1990. 19.95 (ISBN 0-685-33063-X); pap. 10.95 (ISBN 1-878389-02-5). L Ashley & Joshua.

Showell, Ellen H. Our Mountain. Carpenter, Nancy, illus. LC 90-2392. 80p. (gr. 2-6). 1991. SBE 12.95 (ISBN 0-02-782551-5, Bradbury Pr). Macmillan Child Grp.

Sieveking, Anthea. What's Inside? LC 89-11897. 1990. 9.95 (ISBN 0-8037-0719-3). Dial Bks Young.

Signer, Billie T. Cry of the Eagle. Bliss, Bob, illus. 190p. (Orig.). (gr. 5-8). 1990. pap. 4.95 (ISBN 0-8198-1455-5). Dghtrs St Paul.

—Shetland Summer. Bliss, Bob, illus. 125p. (Orig.). (gr. 5-8). 1990. pap. 3.95 (ISBN 0-8198-6884-1). Dghtrs St Paul.

Singer, George. Haltevene. Wentose, G., illus. 96p. (Orig.). (gr. 5-12). 1994. pap. 12.95 (ISBN 0-943920-65-5). Metamorphous Pr.

Sisson, Jo A. That Lonesome Prairie. 96p. (Orig.). 1985. pap. 3.15 (ISBN 0-88120-735-7). SRA.

Six Little Golden Book Classics. (gr. 3-7). 1987. pap. write for info. (ISBN 0-307-15531-5, Pub. by Golden Bks). Western Pub.

Slaby, Zdenck K. Book of Bedtime Stories. 1988. 6.98 (ISBN 0-671-08105-5). S&S Trade.

Small, David. Imogene's Antlers. Small, David, illus. LC 84-12085. 32p. (ps-2). 1988. PLB 12.95 (ISBN 0-517-55564-6); pap. 3.95 (ISBN 0-517-56242-1). Crown.

Smith, Carole. Who Burned the Hartley House? Levine, Abby, ed. Dickson, Glenn, illus. 128p. (gr. 3-9). 1985. 9.95 (ISBN 0-8075-8993-4). A Whitman.

Smith, Elizabeth S. Five First Ladies. (Illus.). 122p. (gr. 10 up). 1986. 12.95 (ISBN 0-8027-6640-4); lib. bdg. 14.85 (ISBN 0-8027-6641-2). Walker & Co.

Smith, Louisa & Smith, Glen, eds. The Not Like Any Other Children's Book, Book. Smith, Glen, illus. 40p. (Orig.). (gr. 2 up). 1982. pap. 8.95 (ISBN 0-9609230-0-4). Smith & Smith Pub.

Smith, Martha. Arabella the Itchy Witch. Graves, Helen, ed. Smith, Martha, illus. LC 85-40893. 86p. (gr. 3 up). 1986. 6.95 (ISBN 1-55523-007-5). Winston-Derek.

The Snow Goose & Other Stories. (gr. 4 up). 1988. pap. 4.50 (ISBN 0-582-54141-7, 74251). Longman.

Sorenson, Jane. Angels on Holiday. Smith, Kathleen L., illus. 144p. (gr. 3-6). 1989. 3.95 (ISBN 0-87403-562-7, 3962). Standard Pub.

—First Job. Smith, Kathleen L., illus. 144p. (gr. 3-6). 1989. 3.95 (ISBN 0-87403-561-9, 3961). Standard Pub.

—Left Behind. Smith, Kathleen L., illus. 144p. (gr. 3-6). 1989. 3.95 (ISBN 0-87403-564-3, 3964). Standard Pub.

—The New Me. Smith, Kathleen L., illus. 144p. (gr. 3-6). 1989. 3.95 (ISBN 0-87403-563-5, 3963). Standard Pub.

Stamper, J. B. More Tales for the Midnight Hour. 128p. (Orig.). (gr. 4-6). 1987. pap. 2.50 (ISBN 0-590-41184-5, Apple Paperbacks). Scholastic Inc.

Stevenson, Robert Louis. Treasure Island. (gr. 5-6). 17.95 (ISBN 0-89190-236-8, Pub. by Am Repr). Amereon Ltd.

Stine, Megan & Stine, H. William. Thriller Diller. 1989. lib. bdg. 6.99 (ISBN 0-394-92936-5). Random.

Stolz, Mary. Night of Ghosts & Hermits: Nocturnal Life on the Seashore. Gallagher, Susan, illus. LC 84-15665. 48p. (gr. 3-7). 1985. 12.95 (ISBN 0-15-257333-X, HJ). HarBraceJ.

Stories That Never Grow Old. (Illus.). 48p. (gr. 1-7). 1978. 5.95 (ISBN 0-448-42004-X, G&D). Putnam Pub Group.

Stover, Marjorie. When the Dolls Woke. Levine, Abby, ed. Loccisano, Karen, illus. 128p. (gr. 3-6). 1985. PLB 9.95 (ISBN 0-8075-8882-2). A Whitman.

Strichartz, Naomi. The Wise Woman. Moore, Ella, illus. 43p. (Orig.). (gr. 2-6). 1986. pap. 3.50 (ISBN 0-9618182-0-4). Cranehill Pr.

Sunanda. Stories & Plays for Children. 91p. (gr. 3-8). 1984. pap. 2.50 (ISBN 0-89071-329-4, Pub. by Sri Aurobindo Ashram India). Aurobindo Assn.

Swajeski, Donna M. The Revolution Machine. rev. ed. (gr. 3-12). 1985. pap. text ed. 6.00 (ISBN 0-88734-511-5). Players Pr.

Taylor, Judy. Dudley Bakes a Cake. Cross, Peter, illus. 32p. (gr. 1-4). 1988. 12.95 (ISBN 0-399-21450-X, Putnam). Putnam Pub Group.

Thomas, Earl. Unusual Events, 5 novels. (Illus.). 1986. Set, 48p. pap. 15.00 (ISBN 0-87879-530-8, High Noon Books). Acad Therapy.

Thomas, Marlo. Free to Be...You & Me. Hart, Carole, ed. 1987. pap. 9.95 (ISBN 0-07-062189-0). McGraw.

Thornton, Don, ed. & intro. by. Whiffle. (Illus.). 52p. (gr. 4-8). 1986. pap. write for info. (ISBN 0-933727-02-X). Cajun Pubs.

Thortnton, Terry & Thornton, Sandy. Report Card, 1987. (Illus.). 32p. (gr. 2-5). pap. 0.30 (ISBN 0-687-36140-0). Abingdon.

Three Bedtime Stories. (Illus.). (ps-1). 1985. 2.98 (ISBN 0-517-46989-8). Outlet Bk Co.

Three Hundred Sixty-Five Stories for Bedtime. (ps-1). 1985. 5.98 (ISBN 0-517-46715-1). Outlet Bk Co.

Tolstoy, Leo. The Lion & the Puppy. Sievert, Claus, illus. Riordan, James, tr. from RUS. LC 87-28653. (Illus.). 80p. (gr. 1 up). 1988. 15.95 (ISBN 0-8050-0735-0, Seaver Bks). H Holt & Co.

Tudor, Tasha, illus. Tasha Tudor's Bedtime Book. 48p. (ps-5). 1990. 10.95 (ISBN 0-448-09328-6, G&D). Putnam Pub Group.

Vail, Virginia. Good Sports. Bode, Daniel, illus. LC 89-31345. 128p. (gr. 4-6). 1990. lib. bdg. 9.89 (ISBN 0-8167-1629-3); pap. text ed. 2.95 (ISBN 0-8167-1630-7). Troll Assocs.

—Horse Play. Bode, Daniel, illus. LC 89-31347. 128p. (gr. 4-6). 1990. lib. bdg. 9.89 (ISBN 0-8167-1659-5); pap. text ed. 2.95 (ISBN 0-8167-1660-9). Troll Assocs.

Van Allen, Diane. Always Alvin. Reilly, Veronica, illus. (Orig.). (ps). 1984. pap. 3.95 (ISBN 0-939332-11-6). J Pohl Assocs.

Van Woerkom, Dorothy O. Old Devil Is Waiting: Three Folktales. Brett, Jan, illus. LC 85-919. 64p. (ps-3). 1985. (HJ). HarBraceJ.

Vesper, Joan. Joey Becomes a Boomer. De Faye, Monique, illus. LC 85-70354. 63p. (Orig.). (ps-5). 1985. pap. 5.95 (ISBN 0-9615007-0-0). Green Bough Pr.

Wallace, Barbara B. Peppermints in the Parlor. LC 80-12326. 198p. (gr. 4-6). 1985. pap. 3.95 (ISBN 0-689-71048-8, Aladdin). Macmillan Child Grp.

Walter, Mary W., illus. Story Books for We Can Read. Incl. Eel, Ail, Ole (ISBN 0-917186-03-6); Happenings (ISBN 0-917186-04-4); We Learn at Play (ISBN 0-917186-05-2); Things for All Seasons (ISBN 0-917186-06-0); Tales & Tails (ISBN 0-917186-07-9); Just Like Me (ISBN 0-917186-08-7); All Around Me (ISBN 0-917186-09-5); Bridging the Summer (ISBN 0-917186-10-9). 5.40 ea. McQueen.

Walter, Mildred P. Mariah Loves Rock. LC 88-2595. 128p. (gr. 3-7). 1988. 12.95 (ISBN 0-02-792511-0, Bradbury Pr). Macmillan Child Grp.

Warren, William E. The Graveyard: And Other Not-So-Scary Stories. Frascino, Ward, illus. 128p. 1984. 11.95 (ISBN 0-13-363623-2). P-H.

Watty, Piper. Gateway to Storyland. Eulalie, illus. 64p. (ps-2). 1985. 6.95 (ISBN 0-448-42006-6, G&D). Putnam Pub Group.

We Read More Stories. pap. 10.62 set (ISBN 0-917186-11-7); tchrs guide 4.72 (ISBN 0-917186-12-5). McQueen.

Weck, Thomas. Back-Back & the Lima Bear. Graves, Helen, ed. Taylor, Neil, illus. LC 85-51963. 64p. (gr. 1-6). 1986. 6.95 (ISBN 0-938232-97-5). Winston-Derek.

Weinberger, Jane. Kiltie, the Laird of Kiltarnen. 2nd ed. Cap, photos by. (Illus.). 44p. (ps-5). 1987. 5.95 (ISBN 0-932433-09-X). Windswept Hse.

—Lemon Drop. Berber, Richard, illus. LC 85-62023. 64p. (gr. 1-6). 1985. Repr. of 1953 ed. PLB 5.95 (ISBN 0-932433-10-3). Windswept Hse.

Weir, Alison. Peter, Good Night. Ray, Deborah K., illus. LC 88-23344. 24p. (ps-1). 1989. 11.95 (ISBN 0-525-44464-5, DCB). Dutton Child Bks.

Weiss, Ellen. Oh Beans! Starring Bean Sprout. Hall, Susan, illus. LC 88-19980. 32p. (gr. k-3). 1989. lib. bdg. 8.79 (ISBN 0-8167-1406-1); pap. text ed. 1.95 (ISBN 0-8167-1407-X). Troll Assocs.

—Oh Beans! Starring Boston Bean. Hall, Susan, illus. LC 88-19981. 32p. (gr. k-3). 1989. lib. bdg. 8.79 (ISBN 0-8167-1414-2); pap. text ed. 1.95 (ISBN 0-8167-1415-0). Troll Assocs.

—Oh Beans! Starring Green Bean. Hall, Susan, illus. LC 88-19970. 32p. (gr. k-3). 1989. lib. bdg. 8.79 (ISBN 0-8167-1398-7); pap. text ed. 1.95 (ISBN 0-8167-1399-5). Troll Assocs.

—Oh Beans! Starring Lima Bean. Hall, Susan, illus. LC 88-19969. 32p. (gr. k-3). 1989. lib. bdg. 8.79 (ISBN 0-8167-1394-4); pap. text ed. 1.95 (ISBN 0-8167-1395-2). Troll Assocs.

—Oh Beans! Starring Mean Bean. Hall, Susan, illus. LC 88-19982. 32p. (gr. k-3). 1989. lib. bdg. 8.79 (ISBN 0-8167-1400-2); pap. text ed. 1.95 (ISBN 0-8167-1401-0). Troll Assocs.

—Oh Beans! Starring Superbean. Hall, Susan, illus. LC 88-19979. 32p. (gr. k-3). 1989. lib. bdg. 8.79 (ISBN 0-8167-1416-9); pap. text ed. 1.95 (ISBN 0-8167-1417-7). Troll Assocs.

Wells, Christie. A Class Act. LC 88-16940. 128p. (gr. 5-8). 1989. lib. bdg. 9.89 (ISBN 0-8167-1500-9); pap. text ed. 2.95 (ISBN 0-8167-1501-7). Troll Assocs.

—Love Letters. LC 88-16938. 128p. (gr. 5-8). 1989. lib. bdg. 9.89 (ISBN 0-8167-1504-1); pap. text ed. 2.95 (ISBN 0-8167-1505-X). Troll Assocs.

—No More Promises. LC 88-16939. 128p. (gr. 5-8). 1989. lib. bdg. 9.89 (ISBN 0-8167-1502-5); pap. text ed. 2.95 (ISBN 0-8167-1503-3). Troll Assocs.

—Rival Roommates. LC 88-16954. 128p. (gr. 5-8). 1988. lib. bdg. 9.89 (ISBN 0-8167-1496-7); pap. text ed. 2.95 (ISBN 0-8167-1497-5). Troll Assocs.

—Secret Crush. LC 88-16941. 128p. (gr. 5-8). 1988. lib. bdg. 9.89 (ISBN 0-8167-1498-3); pap. text ed. 2.95 (ISBN 0-8167-1499-1). Troll Assocs.

Wells, Rosemary. Hazel's Amazing Mother. Wells, Rosemary, illus. LC 85-1447. 32p. (ps-2). 1985. 13.95 (ISBN 0-8037-0209-4); PLB 13.89 (ISBN 0-8037-0210-8). Dial Bks Young.

West, Cindy. Henry's Cat: The Funtime Book. Godfrey, Bob, illus. (gr. 1-5). 1987. pap. 2.25 (ISBN 0-671-63775-4, Little Simon). S&S Trade.

Weyland, Jack. Brenda at the Prom. LC 88-14880. viii, 113p. (gr. 7-12). 1988. 9.95 (ISBN 0-87579-150-6). Deseret Bk.

Wiggin, Kate D. The Birds' Christmas Carol. (Illus.). 66p. 1987. Repr. lib. bdg. 19.95x (ISBN 0-89966-580-2). Buccaneer Bks.

Wilder, Laura I. Little House Books, 9 vols. Williams, Garth, illus. Incl. Little House in the Big Woods. 1971. pap. 3.50 (ISBN 0-06-440001-8); Little House on the Prairie. 1971. pap. 3.50 (ISBN 0-06-440002-6); Farmer Boy. 1971. pap. 3.50 (ISBN 0-06-440003-4); On the Banks of Plum Creek. 1971. pap. 3.50 (ISBN 0-06-440004-2); By the Shores of Silver Lake. 1971. pap. 3.50 (ISBN 0-06-440005-0); The Long Winter. 1971. pap. 3.50 (ISBN 0-06-440006-9); Little Town on the Prairie. 1971. pap. 3.50 (ISBN 0-06-440007-7); These Happy Golden Years. 1971. pap. 3.50 (ISBN 0-06-440008-5); The First Four Years. 1972. pap. 2.95 (ISBN 0-06-440031-X). (gr. 3-7). 1973. Boxed set. pap. 29.95 (ISBN 0-06-440040-9, Trophy). HarpC Child Bks.

Willard, Nancy. Sailing to Cythera. McPhail, David, illus. LC 74-5602. 72p. (gr. 3-7). 1985. pap. 5.95 (ISBN 0-15-269961-9, VoyB). HarBraceJ.

Willig, Janet. Runway! 144p. 1989. pap. 4.95 (ISBN 0-87403-588-0, 3991). Standard Pub.

The Wizard of Oz: Music & Lyrics. rev. ed. (gr. 3-12). 1985. pap. text ed. 15.00 (ISBN 0-88734-010-5). Players Pr.

Wood, Audrey. King Bidgood's in the Bathtub. Wood, Don, illus. LC 85-5472. 32p. (ps-3). 1985. 14.95 (ISBN 0-15-242730-9, HJ). HarBraceJ.

Worcester, Donald. Lone Hunter & the Cheyennes. Pauley, Paige, illus. LC 85-4746. 78p. (gr. 4 up). 1985. Repr. of 1957 ed. 10.95 (ISBN 0-87565-018-X). Tex Christian.

Yates, Madeleine. Mommy Says It's Naptime. Flood, Maureen, illus. (gr. 2 up). 1988. casebound board bk. .50 (ISBN 0-687-27153-3). Abingdon.

—Mommy's Coming Back. Flood, Maureen, illus. (gr. 2 up). 1988. bds. 0.50 casebound (ISBN 0-687-27152-5). Abingdon.

Yeatman, Linda. My Favorite Goodnight Stories. 1987. pap. 9.95 (ISBN 0-671-63360-0). S&S Trade.
The Young King. (gr. 4 up). Date not set. pap. 4.87 (ISBN 0-582-54158-1, 74265). Longman.
Zdanys, Al P. BRI. Kelsey, Robin, illus. 24p. (Orig.). (gr. 3-5). 1989. pap. 6.95 (ISBN 0-685-26934-5). Appletree Bks.
Zdanys, Al P. & Beaulieu, Denise. Deliana. Palozny, Patricia, illus. 24p. (Orig.). 1989. pap. 6.95 (ISBN 0-685-26935-3). Appletree Bks.
Ziefert, Harriet. Say Good Night! Brown, Richard, illus. 32p. 1987. pap. 8.95 (ISBN 0-670-81722-8, Puffin); pap. 3.50 (ISBN 0-14-050747-7, Puffin). Puffin Bks.
Zimelman, Nathan. Lovely, Lovely Mehitchabel. Newman, Stephanie, illus. LC 90-30120. 80p. (Orig.). (gr. 2-4). 1990. pap. 6.95 (ISBN 0-943173-63-9). Harbinger AZ.
Zolotow, Charlotte, ed. An Overpraised Season. LC 73-5499. 204p. (gr. 7 up). 1973. PLB 12.89 (ISBN 0-06-026954-5). HarpC Child Bks.

STORKS

Fischer-Nagel, Andreas & Fischer-Nagel, Heiderose. Season of the White Stork. Fischer-Nagel, Andreas & Fischer-Nagel, Heiderose, illus. 48p. (gr. 2-5). 1986. lib. bdg. 12.95 (ISBN 0-87614-242-0). Carolrhoda Bks.

STORKS–FICTION

Bocheck in Poland. (gr. 2-8). 10.00 (ISBN 0-317-02772-7). Polanie.
Brown, Margaret W. Wheel on the Chimney. Gergely, Tibor, illus. LC 84-48379. 32p. (ps-3). 1954. 13.95 (ISBN 0-397-30288-6, Lipp Jr Bks); PLB 13.89 (ISBN 0-397-30296-7). HarpC Child Bks.
Carrick, Carol. The Washout. Carrick, Donald, illus. LC 78-8135. 32p. (gr. 1-4). 1979. 13.95 (ISBN 0-395-28781-2, Clarion). HM.
DeJong, Meindert. Wheel on the School. Sendak, Maurice, illus. LC 54-8945. 256p. (gr. 4-7). 1954. 14.95 (ISBN 0-06-021585-2); PLB 14.89 (ISBN 0-06-021586-0). HarpC Child Bks.
—Wheel on the School. LC 54-8945. (Illus.). (gr. 4-7). 1972. pap. 3.50 (ISBN 0-06-440021-2, Trophy). HarpC Child Bks.
Hort, Lenny. The Tale of the Caliph Stork. Henstra, Friso, photos by. LC 87-24511. (Illus.). 32p. (ps-3). 1989. 12.95 (ISBN 0-8037-0525-5); PLB 12.89 (ISBN 0-8037-0526-3). Dial Bks Young.
Pyle, Howard. King Stork. Hyman, Trina S., illus. (gr. k-3). 1986. pap. 6.95 (ISBN 0-316-72441-6). Little.

STORMS

see also Hurricanes; Meteorology; Rain and Rainfall; Snow; Thunderstorms; Tornadoes; Winds;
also other kinds of storms

Broekel, Ray. Storms. LC 81-15455. (Illus.). 48p. (gr. k-4). 1982. PLB 14.60 (ISBN 0-516-01654-7); pap. 4.95 (ISBN 0-516-41654-5). Childrens.
Deery, Ruth. Tornadoes & Hurricanes. Micallef, Mary, illus. 48p. (gr. 4-8). 1985. wkbk. 6.95 (ISBN 0-86653-318-4, GA 631). Good Apple.
Dineen, Jacqueline. Hurricanes & Typhoons. (Illus.). 32p. (gr. 5-8). 1991. PLB 11.90 (ISBN 0-531-17339-9, Gloucester Pr). Watts.
Gross, Virginia T. The Day It Rained Forever: A Story of the Johnstown Flood. Himler, Ronald, illus. 64p. (gr. 2-6). 1991. 11.95 (ISBN 0-670-83552-8). Viking Child Bks.
Knapp, Brian. Storm. LC 89-11536. (Illus.). 48p. (gr. 5-9). 1990. PLB 17.28 (ISBN 0-8114-2372-7). Steck-V.
Lee, Sally. Predicting Violent Storms. (Illus.). 144p. (gr. 7-12). 1989. PLB 12.90 (ISBN 0-531-10787-6). Watts.
Micallef, Mary. Storms & Blizzards. Micallef, Mary, illus. 48p. (gr. 4-8). 1985. wkbk. 6.95 (ISBN 0-86653-321-4, GA 683). Good Apple.
Oana. Bobby Bear & the Blizzard. LC 80-82950. (Illus.). 32p. (ps-1). 1981. PLB 9.95 (ISBN 0-87783-151-3). Oddo.
Simon, Seymour. Storms. LC 88-22045. (Illus.). 32p. (gr. k-3). 1989. 12.95 (ISBN 0-688-07413-8); PLB 12.88 (ISBN 0-688-07414-6, Morrow Jr Bks). Morrow Jr Bks.
Steele, Philip. Storms: Causes & Effects. (Illus.). 32p. (gr. 5-8). 1991. PLB 11.90 (ISBN 0-531-11026-5). Watts.
Storm. (Illus.). 176p. (gr. 7 up). 1982. 18.60 (ISBN 0-8094-4314-7); lib. bdg. 24.60 (ISBN 0-8094-4313-9). Time-Life.
Wood, Jenny. Storms: Nature's Fury. LC 90-55461. (Illus.). 32p. (gr. 3-4). 1990. PLB 11.95 (ISBN 0-8368-0471-6). Gareth Stevens Inc.

STORMS–FICTION

Carrick, Carol. Lost in the Storm. Carrick, Donald, illus. LC 74-1051. 32p. (ps-3). 1979. 12.95 (ISBN 0-395-28776-6, Clarion). HM.
Dann, Colin. In the Path of the Storm. 144p. 1990. 17.95 (ISBN 0-09-173858-X, Pub. by Hutchinson UK). Trafalgar Sq.
Jenkins, Jerry B. Daniel & the Big Blizzard. (gr. 4-7). 1990. pap. 4.50 (ISBN 0-8024-0808-7). Moody.
Parker, Mary. City Storm. (gr. 4-7). 1990. 12.95 (ISBN 0-590-42307-X). Scholastic Inc.
Peterson, John. The Littles & the Big Storm. Clark, Robert C., illus. (gr. 4-6). 1979. pap. 2.25 (ISBN 0-590-32010-6). Scholastic Inc.
Roop, Peter & Roop, Connie. Keep the Lights Burning, Abbie. Hanson, Peter E., illus. (gr. 2-4). 1989. incl. cass. 19.95 (ISBN 0-87499-135-8); pap. 12.95 incl. cass. (ISBN 0-87499-134-X); Set; incl. 4 bks., guide, & cass. pap. 27.95 (ISBN 0-87499-136-6). Live Oak Media.
Stolz, Mary. Storm in the Night. Cummings, Pat, illus. LC 85-45838. 32p. (gr. k-3). 1988. 13.95 (ISBN 0-06-025912-4); PLB 12.89 (ISBN 0-06-025913-2). HarpC Child Bks.
Zolotow, Charlotte. Hold My Hand. Reissue. ed. Di Grazia, Thomas, illus. LC 72-76506. 32p. (gr. k-3). 1972. 12.95 (ISBN 0-06-026951-0); PLB 12.89 (ISBN 0-06-026952-9). HarpC Child Bks.
—Storm Book. Graham, Margaret B., illus. LC 52-7880. (gr. k-3). 1952. PLB 13.89 (ISBN 0-06-027026-8). HarpC Child Bks.

STORYTELLING

Catron, Carol & Parks, Barbara. Super Story Telling. 239p. (ps). 1986. 15.95 (ISBN 0-513-01793-3). Denison.
Champlin, Connie & DeVasure, John. Storytelling with the Computer. (Illus.). 64p. (gr. k-6). 1986. pap. 24.95 (ISBN 0-938594-09-5); diskette incl. Spec Lit Pr.
Littlefield, Kathy M. & Littlefield, Robert S. Tell Me a Story! Stark, Steve, illus. 32p. (Orig.). (gr. 3-6). 1989. pap. text ed. 8.95 (ISBN 1-879340-02-X, K0103). Kidspeak.
Marshall, James. Three up a Tree. Marshall, James, illus. LC 86-2163. 48p. (ps-3). 1986. 9.95 (ISBN 0-8037-0328-7); PLB 9.89 (ISBN 0-685-13452-0). Dial Bks Young.
Suid, Murray. For the Love of Stories. 64p. (gr. 4-6). 1986. 6.95 (ISBN 0-912107-49-9). Monday Morning Bks.

STORYTELLING–COLLECTIONS

Child Study Association of America. Read-to-Me Storybook Staff. Lenski, Lois L., illus. LC 47-31488. (ps-1). 1947. 12.95i (ISBN 0-690-68832-6, Crowell Jr Bks). HarpC Child Bks.
Morton, Miriam, ed. A Harvest of Russian Children's Literature. Viguers, Ruth H., frwd. by. LC 67-21384. (Illus.). (ps up). 1967. 47.50x (ISBN 0-520-00886-3). U of Cal Pr.
Robinson, Matt. Gordon of Sesame Street Storybook. (Illus.). (gr. 7-9). 1972. (Random Juv); lib. bdg. 5.99 (ISBN 0-394-92406-1). Random.

STOVES–FICTION

Ginsburg, Mirra. The Magic Stove. Heller, Linda, illus. LC 82-12523. (gr. 2-4). 1983. 11.95 (ISBN 0-698-20566-9, Coward). Putnam Pub Group.

STOWE, HARRIET ELIZABETH (BEECHER), 1811-1896

Jakoubek, Robert. Harriet Beecher Stowe. Horner, Matina S., intro. by. (Illus.). 112p. (gr. 5 up). 1989. 17.95 (ISBN 1-55546-680-X). Chelsea Hse.

STRATEGIC MATERIALS

see Materials

STRATIGRAPHIC GEOLOGY

see Geology, Stratigraphic

STREET TRAFFIC

see Traffic Regulations

STREETS

see also Roads

STRINGED INSTRUMENTS

see also names of stringed instruments, e.g. Guitar; etc.

Flesch, Carl. The Art of Violin Playing, Bk. 1. rev. ed. Martens, Frederick H., tr. (Illus.). 188p. 1924. pap. 19.95 (ISBN 0-8258-0135-4, 01317). Fischer Inc NY.
—The Art of Violin Playing: Artistic Realization & Instruction, Book 2. Martens, Frederick H., tr. 237p. 1930. pap. 19.95 (ISBN 0-8258-0136-2, 0 2046). Fischer Inc NY.
Kimura, Hideo M. How to Pick & Strum the Ukulele, Bk. II. rev. ed. Kimura, Hideo M., illus. 44p. (gr. 7 up). 1988. pap. text ed. write for info. (ISBN 0-917822-18-8). Heedays.
Kreutzer, Rudolph. Forty-Two Studies for Violin. Singer, Edmund, ed. 73p. pap. 8.00 (ISBN 0-8258-0025-0). Fischer Inc NY.
May, Dorothy. Dulcimer a la Mode. LC 84-60272. (Illus.). 75p. 1983. pap. 7.95 (ISBN 0-941126-05-6). Meadowlark.
—Dulcimer Songbag: A Book for Beginners. (Illus.). 48p. (gr. 3 up). 1978. pap. 2.95 (ISBN 0-941126-00-5). Meadowlark.
Miller, Miamon. How to Play Romanian Folk Violin. Fraenkel, Eran, ed. (Illus.). 31p. (Orig.). 1990. pap. 19.95 (ISBN 0-9626468-0-6). Cocek Pr.
Sevcik, Otakar. School of Technic for Violin, Op. 1, Part 2. (FRE, GER & ENG.). 49p. 1900. pap. 8.00 (ISBN 0-8258-0035-8, L 283). Fischer Inc NY.
—School of Technic for Violin: Op. 1 Part 1. (GER, FRE & ENG.). (gr. 6-12). 1900. pap. 8.00 (ISBN 0-8258-0034-X, L 282). Fischer Inc NY.
Suzuki, Shinichi. Suzuki Cello School, Vol. 3: Piano Accompaniment. 32p. (gr. k-12). 1983. pap. text ed. 6.50 (ISBN 0-87487-265-0, Suzuki Method). Summy-Birchard.
Wohlfahrt, Franz. Easiest Elementary Method for Violin: Op. 38. 56p. 1894. pap. 7.00 (ISBN 0-8258-0053-6, L1061). Fischer Inc NY.

STRUCTURAL DRAFTING

see Mechanical Drawing

STUDENT ACTIVITIES

see also College and School Journalism; School Sports

Reum, Earl. The Spirit of Student Council. Bruce, C., ed. (gr. 7-9). 1981. pap. 6.00 (ISBN 0-88210-117-X). Natl Assn Principals.

STUDENT AID

see Scholarships, Fellowships, Etc.; Student Loan Funds

STUDENT GUIDANCE

see Vocational Guidance

STUDENT LIFE AND CUSTOMS

see Students

STUDENT LOAN FUNDS

see also Scholarships, Fellowships, Etc.

Sullivan, John W. & Luther, Barbara. Federal Student Aid: What to Do, When to Do It. Thompson, Kent, illus. Sullivan, John W., intro. by. (Illus.). 80p. (gr. 11 up). 1990. 29.95 (ISBN 0-9627866-0-8); PLB 29.95; pap. 29.95 (ISBN 0-685-38402-0); wkbk. 29.95 (ISBN 0-685-38403-9); videocass. tape 29.95 (ISBN 0-685-38404-7). Aiducation.

STUDENT MOVEMENT

see Youth Movement

STUDENT PROTESTS

see Youth Movement

STUDENT REVOLT

see Youth Movement

STUDENTS

Going to School. 1990. 2.99 (ISBN 0-517-69196-5). Outlet Bk Co.
Kalman, Bobbie. I Like School. (Illus.). 32p. (gr. k-2). 1985. 6.95 (ISBN 0-86505-064-3); pap. 5.95 (ISBN 0-86505-088-0). Crabtree Pub Co.
Klingel, Fitterer. School Safety. (Illus.). 32p. (ps up). 1986. 14.95; PLB 10.45 (ISBN 0-87191-737-8). Creative Ed.
Landau, Elaine. Teenagers Talk about School. Steltenpohl, Jane, ed. LC 88-23065. 120p. (gr. 7 up). 1989. pap. 5.95 (ISBN 0-671-68148-6); 12.98 (ISBN 0-671-64568-4). Messner.
LeNoir, Betty. Creative Student Assignment Sheets. Mohrmann, Gary, illus. 48p. (gr. 3-8). 1985. wkbk. 5.95 (ISBN 0-86653-322-2, GA 657). Good Apple.
Loeper, John J. Going to School in 1776. LC 72-86940. (Illus.). 112p. (gr. 4-7). 1973. 13.95 (ISBN 0-689-30089-1, Atheneum). Macmillan Child Grp.
Maher, Robert. Leadership: Self, School, Community. Bruce, C., ed. 96p. (Orig.). (gr. 9-12). 1988. pap. 9.00 (ISBN 0-88210-217-6). Natl Assn Student.
Page, Parker, et al. Getting Along Complete Kit. (gr. k-4). 1991. 99.95 (ISBN 0-88671-407-9). Am Guidance.
—Getting Along Student Activities: Level 1. (Orig.). (gr. k-1). Date not set. pap. 2.50 (ISBN 0-88671-409-5). Am Guidance.
—Getting Along Student Activities: Level 2. (Orig.). (gr. 2-4). Date not set. pap. 2.50 (ISBN 0-88671-410-9). Am Guidance.
Roehlkepartain, Jolene L. Surviving School Stress. 108p. (Orig.). (gr. 9-12). 1990. pap. 6.95 (ISBN 0-931529-95-6, Teenage Bks). Group Pub.
Rydberg, Denny. How to Survive College. 160p. (Orig.). 1988. pap. 8.95 (ISBN 0-310-35351-3). Zondervan.
Schweninger, Ann. Off to School. LC 86-26736. (Illus.). (ps-1). 1987. pap. 10.95 (ISBN 0-670-81447-4). Viking Child Bks.
Smith, Allan H., ed. How to Make School Fun. Trachsler, Don, illus. LC 84-90227. 200p. (Orig.). (gr. 6-12). 1984. pap. 10.00 (ISBN 0-931113-03-2). Success Publ.
Smith, Margaret D. Mississippi High School Students & the Law, Vol. II. LC 89-3745. 206p. (gr. 8-12). 1990. pap. 9.95 (ISBN 0-937552-36-4). Quail Ridge.

STUDENTS–EMPLOYMENT

Sullivan, Mick. Spare Time Cash: Every Student's Guide to Making Money on the Side. Moe, Mary, ed. 114p. (Orig.). (gr. 10 up). 1989. pap. 12.95 (ISBN 1-878330-00-4). Sullivan MT.

STUDENTS–FICTION

Alexander, Martha. Move over, Twerp. Alexander, Martha, illus. LC 80-21405. 32p. (ps-2). 1989. Repr. of 1981 ed. 11.95 (ISBN 0-8037-6139-2). Dial Bks Young.
Avi. Romeo & Juliet - Together (& Alive) at Last. 128p. 1988. pap. 2.95 (ISBN 0-380-70525-7, Camelot). Avon.
Balducci, Carolyn. Is There a Life after Graduation, Henry Birnbaum? (Illus.). (gr. 7 up). 1971. 7.95 (ISBN 0-395-12749-1). HM.
Barbato, Juli. From Bed to Bus. Schatell, Brian, illus. LC 84-20159. 32p. (ps-2). 1985. 12.95 (ISBN 0-02-708380-2, Macmillan Child Bk). Macmillan Child Grp.
Bingham, et al. Choices. 240p. (gr. 8 up). 1983. 14.95 (ISBN 0-685-09848-6, LW CHO). Learning Wks.
Blair, Alison. Back to School. (gr. 10 up). 1989. pap. 2.95 (ISBN 0-8041-0329-1). Ivy Books.
—Social Studies. (gr. 10 up). 1989. pap. 2.95 (ISBN 0-8041-0330-5). Ivy Books.
—Study Break. (gr. 10 up). 1988. pap. 2.95 (ISBN 0-8041-0327-5). Ivy Books.
Blume, Judy. Tales of a Fourth Grade Nothing. large type ed. Doty, Roy, illus. 174p. (gr. 2-6). 1987. Repr. of 1972 ed. lib. bdg. 14.95 (ISBN 1-55736-015-4). ABC-CLIO.
Bunting, Eve. Janet Hamm Needs a Date for the Dance. 112p. 1987. pap. 2.95 (ISBN 0-553-15537-7, Skylark). Bantam.
Catling, Patrick S. John Midas in Dreamtime. 96p. (gr. 3-7). 1987. pap. 2.75 (ISBN 0-553-15567-9, Skylark). Bantam.
Chase, Emily. Who's Got... 1989. pap. 2.50 (ISBN 0-590-42149-2). Scholastic Inc.
Cohen, Barbara. King of the Seventh Grade. LC 82-15247. (gr. 4 up). 1982. 13.95 (ISBN 0-688-01302-3). Lothrop.
Conford, Ellen. We Interrupt This Semester for an Important Bulletin. LC 79-9133. (Illus.). (gr. 5 up). 1979. 14.95 (ISBN 0-316-15309-5). Little.

Cooney, Linda A. Class of Eighty-Nine: Senior. 192p. (gr. 7up). 1988. pap. 2.50 (ISBN 0-318-36486-7). Scholastic Inc.
—Senior, No. 4. (gr. 7-12). 1988. pap. 2.50 (ISBN 0-590-41678-2). Scholastic Inc.
—Sophomore: Class of Eighty-Nine. 224p. (gr. 7 up). 1988. pap. 2.50 (ISBN 0-590-41675-8). Scholastic Inc.
Cooper, Ilene. Mean Streak. 160p. (gr. 4 up). 1991. 13.95 (ISBN 0-688-08431-1). Morrow Jr Bks.
—Queen of the Sixth Grade. LC 88-18859. 128p. (gr. 4-7). 1988. 12.95 (ISBN 0-688-07933-4). Morrow Jr Bks.
Davis, Melissa. Yearbook II: Best All-Round Couple. 208p. (gr. 7 up). 1988. pap. 2.50 (ISBN 0-590-41546-8, Point). Scholastic Inc.
DeClements, Barthe. The Fourth Grade Master Wizards. 144p. (gr. 3-7). 1988. pap. 12.95 (ISBN 0-670-82290-6). Viking Child Bks.
—Fourth Grade Wizards. large type ed. 144p. 1989. PLB 15.95 (ISBN 1-55736-111-8, Crnrstn Bks). ABC-CLIO.
—The Fourth Grade Wizards. 144p. (gr. 3 up). 1990. pap. 3.95 (ISBN 0-14-032760-6, Puffin). Puffin Bks.
—Sixth Grade Can Really Kill You. 160p. (gr. 4-7). pap. 2.50 (ISBN 0-590-40180-7, Apple Paperbacks). Scholastic Inc.
—Sixth Grade Can Really Kill You. large type ed. 163p. 1989. PLB 15.95 (ISBN 1-55736-108-8, Crnrstn Bks). ABC-CLIO.
—Sixth Grade Can Really Kill You. 1986. pap. 2.75 (ISBN 0-590-42883-7). Scholastic Inc.
Duncan, Lois. Killing Mr. Griffin. (gr. 7 up). 1978. 14.95 (ISBN 0-316-19549-9). Little.
Eggleston, Edward. The Hoosier Schoolboy. 1988. Repr. of 1883 ed. lib. bdg. 59.00x (ISBN 0-317-90247-4). Reprint Servs.
—The Schoolmaster's Stories for Boys & Girls. 1988. Repr. of 1874 ed. lib. bdg. 59.00x (ISBN 0-317-90227-X). Reprint Servs.
Erlbach, Arlene. Dropout Blues. (gr. 6 up). 1988. write for info. (ISBN 0-373-98020-5). S&S Trade.
Geller, Mark. My Life in the Seventh Grade. LC 85-45265. 128p. (gr. 5 up). 1988. pap. 3.50 (ISBN 0-06-440276-2, Trophy). HarpC Child Bks.
Gilden, Mel. Things That Go Bark in the Park. 96p. 1989. pap. 2.75 (ISBN 0-380-75786-9, Camelot). Avon.
—Yuckers. 96p. 1989. pap. 2.75 (ISBN 0-380-75787-7, Camelot). Avon.
Gormley, Beatrice. Paul's Volcano. 160p. 1988. pap. 2.50 (ISBN 0-380-70562-1, Camelot). Avon.
Great Homework Chase. 1990. 4.98 (ISBN 1-55521-687-0). Bk Sales Inc.
Gross, Alan. What If the Teacher Calls on Me? Venezia, Mike, illus. LC 79-18560. 32p. (ps-3). 1980. PLB 13.93 (ISBN 0-516-03671-8); pap. 3.95 (ISBN 0-516-43671-6). Childrens.
Harrell, Janice. Wild Times at West Mount High. (gr. 6-9). 1989. pap. 2.75 (ISBN 0-671-68570-8, Archway). PB.
Haynes, Betsy. The Great Boyfriend Trap. 160p. (gr. 4-7). 1987. pap. 2.75 (ISBN 0-553-15530-X, Skylark). Bantam.
—Seventh-Grade Rumors: The Fabulous Five, No. 1. (gr. 4-7). 1988. pap. 2.95 (ISBN 0-553-15625-X, Skylark). Bantam.
—The Trouble with Flirting. (gr. 4-7). 1988. pap. 2.75 (ISBN 0-553-15633-0, Skylark). Bantam.
Heyman, Anita. Final Grades. 192p. (gr. 7-11). 1983. (Putnam); pap. 3.95 (ISBN 0-396-08745-0, Putnam). Putnam Pub Group.
Hodgman, Ann. Galaxy High School. 96p. (gr. 2-6). 1987. pap. 2.50 (ISBN 0-553-15545-8, Skylark). Bantam.
Hurwitz, Johanna. Class Clown. Hamanaka, Sheila, illus. 112p. (gr. 2-5). 1988. pap. 2.75 (ISBN 0-590-41821-1). Scholastic Inc.
—Class President. Hamanaka, Sheila, illus. LC 89-28600. 96p. (gr. 2 up). 1990. 12.95 (ISBN 0-688-09114-8). Morrow Jr Bks.
Kauffman, M. K. The Right Moves. (gr. 7 up). pap. 2.25 (ISBN 0-317-62895-X). S&S Trade.
Kenyon, Kate. Starting the Eighth Grade. 176p. (Orig.). (gr. 7 up). 1988. pap. 2.50 (ISBN 0-590-41161-6). Scholastic Inc.
Kerr, M. E. Fell. LC 86-45776. 176p. (gr. 7 up). 1988. pap. 3.25 (ISBN 0-06-447031-8, Trophy). HarpC Child Bks.
Klein, Robin. Tearaways: Stories to Make You Think Twice. 144p. (gr. 5-9). 1991. 12.95 (ISBN 0-670-83212-X). Viking Child Bks.
Kline, Susan. Horrible Harry & the Green Slime. Remkiewicz, Frank, illus. 64p. (gr. 2-5). 1989. pap. 10.95 (ISBN 0-670-82468-2). Viking Child Bks.
Korman, Gordon. This Can't Be Happening at Macdonald Hall. 128p. (gr. 4-6). 1979. pap. 2.50 (ISBN 0-590-40534-9, Apple Paperbacks). Scholastic Inc.
Lewis, Shari. Lamb Chop in the Land of No Manners. (Illus.). 24p. 1989. pap. 3.50 (ISBN 0-685-23303-0) (ISBN 1-55802-290-2). Lynx Bks.
Lois, Susan. Reunion Affairs. (Orig.). 1988. pap. 3.95 (ISBN 0-440-20213-2). Dell.
McKenna, Colleen O. Fifth Grade: Here Comes Trouble. 128p. (gr. 3-7). 1991. pap. 2.95 (ISBN 0-590-41734-7, Apple Paperbacks). Scholastic Inc.
Martin, Thomas. Private High. 25p. (Orig.). (gr. 7 up). 1986. pap. 4.50 playscript (ISBN 0-87602-267-0). Anchorage.
New Seed Press Collective Staff. A Book about Us. (Illus.). (ps-5). 1977. 4.95 (ISBN 0-938678-04-3). New Seed.
O'Sullivan, Anna-Margaret. The Green Bank Year. LC 88-62114. 255p. 1989. pap. 6.95 (ISBN 1-55523-183-7). Winston-Derek.
Pascal, Francine. Against the Odds. large type ed. 151p. (gr. 5-8). 1989. Repr. of 1988 ed. PLB 10.50 (ISBN 1-55905-016-0, Dist. by Gareth Stevens); 9.50 (ISBN 1-55905-006-3, Dist. by Gareth Stevens). Grey Castle.
—Class Trip. (Orig.). (gr. 7 up). 1988. pap. 3.50 (ISBN 0-553-15588-1). Bantam.
—Decisions. (gr. 6 up). 1988. pap. 2.95 (ISBN 0-553-27278-0). Bantam.
—Double Jeopardy. 214p. (Orig.). (gr. 7-12). 1987. pap. 2.95 (ISBN 0-553-26905-4). Bantam.
—Double Love. large type ed. 186p. (gr. 5-8). 1989. Repr. of 1983 ed. PLB 10.50 (ISBN 1-55905-010-1, Dist. by Gareth Stevens); 9.50 (ISBN 1-55905-000-4). Grey Castle.
—Family Secrets. 160p. (Orig.). (gr. 7 up). 1988. pap. 2.95 (ISBN 0-553-27176-8). Bantam.
—Jealous Lies. 144p. (Orig.). (gr. 7-12). 1986. pap. 2.75 (ISBN 0-553-25816-8). Bantam.
—Keeping Secrets. 96p. (Orig.). 1987. pap. 2.50 (ISBN 0-553-15538-5, Skylark). Bantam.
—Ms. Quarterback. (gr. 9-12). 1990. pap. 2.95 (ISBN 0-553-28767-2). Bantam.
—Out of Place. (gr. 7 up). 1988. pap. 2.75 (ISBN 0-553-15628-4). Bantam.
—Out of Reach. large type ed. 151p. (gr. 5-8). 1989. Repr. of 1988 ed. PLB 10.50 (ISBN 1-55905-015-2, Dist. by Gareth Stevens); 9.50 (ISBN 1-55905-005-5). Grey Castle.
—Perfect Shot. 1989. pap. 2.95 (ISBN 0-553-27915-7). Bantam.
—Playing for Keeps. (gr. 7 up). 1988. pap. 2.95 (ISBN 0-553-27477-5). Bantam.
—Playing Hooky. (gr. 6 up). 1988. pap. 2.99 (ISBN 0-553-15606-3). Bantam.
—Playing with Fire. large type ed. 149p. (gr. 5-8). 1989. Repr. of 1983 ed. PLB 10.50 (ISBN 1-55905-002-0); PLB 10.50 (ISBN 0-685-26540-4, Dist. by Gareth Stevens). Grey Castle.
—Power Play. large type ed. 150p. (gr. 5-8). 1989. Repr. of 1983 ed. PLB 10.50 (ISBN 1-55905-013-6, Dist. by Gareth Stevens); 9.50 (ISBN 1-55905-003-9). Grey Castle.
—Promises. 160p. (Orig.). (gr. 7-12). 1985. pap. 2.75 (ISBN 0-553-26765-5). Bantam.
—Rags to Riches. 160p. (Orig.). (gr. 5 up). 1985. pap. 2.95 (ISBN 0-553-27431-7). Bantam.
—Second Chance. (ps-1). 1989. pap. 2.95 (ISBN 0-553-27771-5). Bantam.
—Second Chance. large type ed. 133p. (gr. 5-8). 1989. Repr. of 1989 ed. PLB 10.50 (ISBN 1-55905-018-7, Dist. by Gareth Stevens); 9.50 (ISBN 1-55905-008-X). Grey Castle.
—Secrets. large type ed. 118p. (gr. 5-8). 1989. Repr. of 1983 ed. PLB 10.50 (ISBN 1-55905-011-X, Dist. by Gareth Stevens); 9.50 (ISBN 1-55905-001-2). Grey Castle.
—Slam Book. 1988. pap. 3.95 (ISBN 0-553-05496-1). Bantam.
—Spring Fever: Spring Super Edition, No. 2. 240p. (Orig.). (gr. 7-12). 1987. pap. 2.95 (ISBN 0-553-26420-6). Bantam.
—Starring Jessica. (gr. 9-12). 1991. pap. 2.95 (ISBN 0-553-28796-6). Bantam.
—Sweet Valley High, No. 68. 1990. pap. 2.95 (ISBN 0-553-28618-8). Bantam.
—Teamwork. (ps-1). 1989. pap. 2.75 (ISBN 0-553-15681-0, SVT #27). Bantam.
—That Fatal Night. (gr. 7 up). 1989. pap. 2.95 (ISBN 0-553-28264-6). Bantam.
—Trouble at Home. 1990. pap. 2.95 (ISBN 0-553-28518-1). Bantam.
—Two-Boy Weekend. 1989. pap. 2.95 (ISBN 0-553-27856-8). Bantam.
—Two-Boy Weekend. large type ed. 150p. (gr. 5-8). 1989. Repr. of 1989 ed. PLB 10.50 (ISBN 1-55905-019-5, Dist. by Gareth Stevens); 9.50 (ISBN 1-55905-009-8). Grey Castle.
—White Lies. large type ed. 137p. (gr. 5-8). 1989. Repr. of 1989 ed. PLB 10.50 (ISBN 1-55905-017-9); 9.50 (ISBN 1-55905-007-1, Dist. by Gareth Stevens). Grey Castle.
—Who's to Blame. 1990. pap. 2.95 (ISBN 0-553-28555-6). Bantam.
Pascal, Francine, created by. Against the Odds. 160p. 1989. pap. 2.95 (ISBN 0-553-27650-6). Bantam.
—Alone in the Crowd. 160p. (Orig.). (gr. 7-12). 1986. pap. 2.75 (ISBN 0-553-26825-2). Bantam.
—Buried Treasure. (gr. 3-7). 1987. pap. 2.50 (ISBN 0-553-15533-4, Skylark). Bantam.
—Jumping to Conclusions. 112p. (Orig.). 1988. pap. 2.75 (ISBN 0-553-15635-7). Bantam.
—The New Jessica. 160p. (Orig.). (gr. 7-12). 1986. pap. 2.75 (ISBN 0-553-26113-4). Bantam.
—On the Edge. 160p. (gr. 7 up). 1987. pap. 2.95 (ISBN 0-553-27692-1). Bantam.
—Out of Reach. 160p. 1988. pap. 2.95 (ISBN 0-553-27596-8). Bantam.
—Secret Admirer. 160p. (gr. 7 up). 1987. pap. 2.95 (ISBN 0-553-27691-3). Bantam.
—Standing Out. 112p. 1989. pap. 2.75 (ISBN 0-553-15653-5). Bantam.
—Stretching the Truth. (gr. 3-7). 1987. pap. 2.95 (ISBN 0-553-15654-3, Skylark). Bantam.
—Sweet Valley High. 160p. (Orig.). 1989. pap. 2.95 (ISBN 0-553-27720-0). Bantam.
—Sweet Valley High Super Thriller, No. 3. 240p. (Orig.). 1988. pap. 3.50 (ISBN 0-553-27554-2). Bantam.
—Taking Charge. 112p. (Orig.). 1989. pap. 2.75 (ISBN 0-553-15669-1). Bantam.
—Taking Sides. 160p. (Orig.). (gr. 7-12). 1986. pap. 2.75 (ISBN 0-553-25886-9). Bantam.
Pasnak, William. Degrassi Junior High: Exit Stage Left. 128p. (Orig.). (gr. 5 up). 1987. pap. 2.50 (ISBN 0-590-41478-X). Scholastic Inc.
Perl, Lila. Dumb Like Me, Olivia Potts. LC 76-7986. 194p. (gr. 5 up). 1979. 12.95 (ISBN 0-395-28870-3, Clarion). HM.
Pike, Christopher. The Graduation. (Orig.). (gr. 9 up). 1989. pap. 2.95 (ISBN 0-671-70012-X, Archway). PB.
Ransom, Candice F. Going on Twelve. 176p. (gr. 6-8). 1988. pap. 2.50 (ISBN 0-590-40848-8). Scholastic Inc.
Roberts, Nadine. Terror in Oak Grove High. 128p. (Orig.). 1991. pap. 3.50 (ISBN 0-449-70382-7, Juniper). Fawcett.
Roos, Stephen. Confessions of a Wayward Preppie. (gr. k-12). 1987. pap. 2.75 (ISBN 0-440-91586-4, LFL). Dell.
Sachar, Louis. Sideways Stories from Wayside School. 128p. (gr. 2-6). 1990. Repr. of 1985 ed. PLB 12.99 (ISBN 0-679-90413-1). McKay.
Sansevere, Carol Q. Head of the Class. 144p. (Orig.). (gr. 5-9). 1989. pap. 2.95 (ISBN 1-55802-202-3). Lynx Bks.
—Lonely Heart. 160p. (Orig.). (gr. 5-7). Date not set. pap. 2.95 (ISBN 1-55802-204-X). Lynx Bks.
—New Girl in Town. 128p. (Orig.). (gr. 7 up). 1989. pap. 2.95 (ISBN 1-55802-200-7). Lynx Bks.
—Stolen Kisses. 144p. (Orig.). (gr. 5-9). 1989. pap. 2.95 (ISBN 1-55802-201-5). Lynx Bks.
Sarasin, Jennifer. Here to Stay. 176p. (gr. 6-10). 1988. pap. 2.50 (ISBN 0-590-41876-9). Scholastic Inc.
Schrfranz, Vivian. Overboard. (gr. 7-12). 1988. pap. 2.50 (ISBN 0-590-41875-0). Scholastic Inc.
Schwartz, Sheila. Bigger Is Better. (gr. 7 up). pap. 2.25 (ISBN 0-373-98009-4). S&S Trade.
Seniors. 1984. pap. write for info. Dell.
Spring Break. 160p. (Orig.). (gr. 7 up). 1989. pap. 2.95 (ISBN 1-55802-078-0). Lynx Bks.
Stine, Megan & Stine, H. William. Fifth Grade Flop. Henry, Paul, illus. LC 89-20624. 96p. (gr. 4-6). 1990. lib. bdg. 9.89 (ISBN 0-8167-1704-4); pap. text ed. 2.95 (ISBN 0-8167-1705-2). Troll Assocs.
Stone, Bruce. Been Clever Forever. LC 86-45774. 384p. (gr. 7 up). 1988. 14.95 (ISBN 0-06-025918-3); PLB 14.89 (ISBN 0-06-025919-1). HarpC Child Bks.
Suzanne, Jamie. Teacher's Pet. large type ed. Pascal, Francine, created by. 103p. (gr. 7-12). 1990. Repr. of 1986 ed. 9.95 (ISBN 1-55905-065-9). Grey Castle.
Thompson, Julian F. Simon Pure. 336p. (gr. 7 up). 1988. pap. 3.50 (ISBN 0-590-41823-8, Point). Scholastic Inc.
Tunis, John R. Schoolboy Johnson. LC 58-5728. 192p. (gr. 5 up). 1991. pap. 4.95 (ISBN 0-688-10150-X, Pub. by Beech Tree Bks). Morrow.
Wells, Rosemary. Timothy Goes to School. Wells, Rosemary, illus. LC 80-20785. 32p. (ps-2). 1981. 13.95 (ISBN 0-8037-8948-3); PLB 11.89 (ISBN 0-8037-8949-1). Dial Bks Young.
Wenk, Laurie P. Francine Pascal's Sweet Valley High Slam Book. (gr. 7 up). 1988. pap. 3.95 (ISBN 0-318-36514-6). Bantam.
Young, Ginevra M. I Got My Report Card Today. LC 89-51084. (Illus.). 44p. (gr. k-3). 1990. pap. 5.95 (ISBN 1-55523-254-X). Winston-Derek.

STUDY, METHOD OF

see also Self-Culture;
also subjects with the subdivision Study and Teaching, e.g. Art–Study and Teaching; etc.

Adams, Kathleen. Family Homework. (ps-1). 1989. pap. 5.95 (ISBN 0-8224-3052-5). Fearon Teach Aids.
American College Testing Program Staff. Study Power Leader's Guide. 99p. (Orig.). (gr. 7 up). 1987. tchr's. ed. 4.00 (ISBN 0-937734-63-2). Am Coll Testing.
—Study Power, Managing Time & Environment. 30p. (Orig.). (gr. 7 up). 1987. wkbk. 1.00 (ISBN 0-937734-65-9). Am Coll Testing.
—Study Power, Preparing for Tests. 14p. (Orig.). (gr. 7 up). 1987. wkbk. 1.00 (ISBN 0-937734-69-1). Am Coll Testing.
—Study Power, Reading Textbooks. 21p. (Orig.). (gr. 7 up). 1987. wkbk. 1.00 (ISBN 0-937734-66-7). Am Coll Testing.
—Study Power, Student Workbook Set. (Orig.). (gr. 7 up). 1987. wkbk. 5.00 (ISBN 0-937734-64-0). Am Coll Testing.
—Study Power, Taking Class Notes. 22p. (Orig.). (gr. 7 up). 1987. wkbk. 1.00 (ISBN 0-937734-67-5). Am Coll Testing.
—Study Power, Taking Tests. 13p. (Orig.). (gr. 7 up). 1987. wkbk. 1.00 (ISBN 0-937734-70-5). Am Coll Testing.
—Study Power, Using Resources. 14p. (Orig.). (gr. 7 up). 1987. wkbk. 1.00 (ISBN 0-937734-68-3). Am Coll Testing.
Bacon, Alvin. Bud's Easy Term Paper Typing Kit. 6th, rev. ed. (gr. 7-12). 1984. pap. text ed. write for info. (ISBN 0-9609436-2-5). Lawrence Hse.
Bank Street College of Education Staff. Barron's Book of Fun & Learning. 384p. (gr. k). 1987. pap. 19.95 (ISBN 0-8120-3822-3). Barron.

Baron, Alvin. Bud's Easy Term Paper Kit. 24p. (gr. 7-12). 1987. pap. text ed. write for info. (ISBN 0-9609436-3-3). Lawrence Hse.

Barrett, Susan L. It's All in Your Head: A Guide to Understanding Your Brain & Boosting Your Brain Power. LC 85-80631. (Illus.). 144p. (Orig.). (gr. 4-9). 1985. pap. 8.95 (ISBN 0-915793-03-2). Free Spirit Pub.

Bergreen, Gary. Coping with Study Strategies. rev. ed. (gr. 7-12). 1990. 12.95 (ISBN 0-8239-1140-3). Rosen Group.

Berry, Marilyn. Help Is on the Way for Reading Skills. (Illus.). 48p. (gr. 4-6). 1984. pap. 4.95 (ISBN 0-516-43232-X). Childrens.

—Help Is on the Way for Schoolwork. Barhtolomew, illus. 48p. (gr. 4-6). 1984. pap. 4.95 (ISBN 0-516-43233-8). Childrens.

Biener, Laurence, et al. How to Study Study Aid. 1978. pap. 2.50 (ISBN 0-317-64276-6). Youth Ed.

Carola, Robert. How Do I Know? Crawford, Mel, illus. 32p. (gr. 2-4). 1990. Repr. of 1988 ed. PLB 9.95 (ISBN 1-878363-12-3). Forest Hse.

Carson, Patti & Dellosa, Janet. Sporty Blank Reproducible Worksheets. Dellosa, Janet & Carson, Patti, illus. 96p. (gr. 1-6). pap. 6.95 (ISBN 0-88724-031-3, 0919). Carson-Dellos.

Churchill, E. Richard. Essays & Reports: What It Takes to Research, Write & Present an A-Plus Paper! (Illus.). 96p. (Orig.). 1989. pap. 4.95 (ISBN 0-89586-775-3). Price Stern.

—Tests: How to Study for, Take & Ace Any Test! (Illus.). 96p. (Orig.). 1989. pap. 4.95 (ISBN 0-89586-774-5). Price Stern.

Cohen, Elaine R. Spring Activity Book. Rittenour, Gary, illus. 32p. (gr. 4 up). 1984. pap. 1.98 (ISBN 0-88724-068-2, CD-8052). Carson-Dellos.

—Winter Activity Book. Rittenour, Gary, illus. 32p. (gr. 4-7). 1984. pap. 1.98 (ISBN 0-88724-064-X, CD-8044). Carson-Dellos.

Colligan, Louise. The A-Plus Guide to Taking Tests. 112p. (gr. 7 up). 1984. pap. 2.25 (ISBN 0-590-33318-6). Scholastic Inc.

—Scholastic's A-Plus Jr. Guide to Studying. 96p. (Orig.). (gr. 4-7). 1987. pap. 2.50 (ISBN 0-590-40590-X). Scholastic Inc.

—Scholastic's A-Plus Junior Guide to Taking Tests. 1990. pap. 2.50 (ISBN 0-590-43148-X). Scholastic Inc.

Communication & Learning Center Staff. One Hundred Twenty-Five Ways to Be a Better Student: A Program for Study Skills Success. 1987. spiral reproducible wkbk. 21.95 (ISBN 1-55999-063-5). LinguiSystems.

De Ponce, Blanca N. La Aventura de Estudiar: Programa para Desarrollar Destrezas de Estudio e Informacion en el nivel Elemental e Intermedio. Figueroa, Ivelisse, illus. (SPA.). 100p. (Orig.). (gr. 5-9). 1984. write for info. B Ponce.

Dickinson, Lavona & Watts, Ramona. Storytime Learning. (ps). 1989. pap. 13.95 (ISBN 0-8224-6277-X). Fearon Teach Aids.

Falkenberg, P. R. Fifteen Days to Study Power. 2nd ed. (Illus.). 378p. (Orig.). (gr. 7 up). 1985. pap. 12.95 (ISBN 0-939800-01-2). Greencrest.

Geoffrion, Sondra. Power Study to up Your Grades & Grade Point Average. LC 88-61283. 60p. (gr. 11 up). 1989. pap. 3.95 (ISBN 0-88247-787-0). R & E Pubs.

Gilbert, Sara. How to Take Tests. LC 83-7115. 160p. (gr. 5up). 1983. 11.95 (ISBN 0-688-02469-6); pap. 7.50 (ISBN 0-688-02470-X, Pub. by Beech Tree Bks). Morrow Jr Bks.

Hornnes, Esther & Magos, Eunice. Indoor Trips That Teach. Sussman, Ellen, intro. by. Burris, Priscilla, illus. 76p. (Orig.). (gr. k-6). 1988. pap. 7.95 (ISBN 0-933606-61-3). Monkey Sisters.

Kern, Roy & Smith, Richard. The Grade Booster Guide for Kids. Mattingly, Marshall T., ed. Nunn, Mike, illus. 50p. (Orig.). (gr. 5-8). 1987. pap. 7.95 (ISBN 0-944162-00-2). Hilton Thomas.

Kesselman-Turkel, Judi & Peterson, Franklynn. Study Smarts: How to Learn More in Less Time. 64p. 1981. pap. 4.95 (ISBN 0-8092-5852-8). Contemp Bks.

Lauderdale, Leslie. You Can Do It Guide to Great School Reports. (Illus.). 96p. (Orig.). (gr. 5-9). 1988. pap. 2.25 (ISBN 0-87406-350-7). Willowisp Pr.

Learning Forum Staff. Study Skills Set. (gr. 8-12). 1989. 130.00 (ISBN 0-945525-13-3). Supercamp.

McCutcheon, Randall J. Get off My Brain: A Survival Guide for Lazy Students. Wagner, Pete, illus. LC 84-82166. 120p. (gr. 9 up). 1985. pap. 8.95 (ISBN 0-915793-02-4). Free Spirit Pub.

McInerney, Claire. Tracking the Facts: How to Develop Research Skills. Pulver, Harry, illus. 64p. (gr. 4 up). 1990. PLB 9.95 (ISBN 0-8225-2426-0). Lerner Pubns.

McMillan, Dana. Language Boosters. 64p. (gr. 2-6). 1988. 6.95 (ISBN 0-912107-83-9, MM999). Monday Morning Bks.

McMillan, Dana & Martin, Sidney. More Brain Boosters. 64p. (gr. 2-6). 1988. 6.95 (ISBN 0-912107-81-2, MM997). Monday Morning Bks.

Mancuso, Robert A. Question the Direction: A Program for Teaching Careful Listening & the Questioning of Unclear Directions. (gr. 1-7). 1988. manual & reproducible wkbk. 29.95 (ISBN 1-55999-065-1). LinguiSystems.

Martin, Sidney & McMillan, Dana. Learning Ideas Through the Year. 112p. (gr. 2-6). 1989. 9.95 (ISBN 0-912107-91-X, MM1908). Monday Morning Bks.

Mayo, Patty, et al. Study Smart. Madsen, Kris, illus. 59p. (gr. 5-12). 1990. bd. game 39.00 (ISBN 0-930599-64-0). Thinking Pubns.

Moran, John, et al. Term Paper Study Aids. 1986. pap. 2.25 (ISBN 0-87738-025-2). Youth Ed.

Paterra, Mary E. Cambridge Stratford Study Skills Course, 20 Hour Edition. (Illus.). 196p. (gr. 6-8). 1986. tchr's. ed. 64.95 (ISBN 0-935637-03-6); wkbk. 12.95 (ISBN 0-935637-02-8); transparency set 60.00 (ISBN 0-935637-00-1); listening tape set 40.00 (ISBN 0-935637-01-X). Cambridge Strat.

Paterro, Mary E. Cambridge Stratford Study Skills Course, 30 Hour Edition. (Illus.). (gr. 9-11). 1986. tchr's. ed. 64.95 (ISBN 0-935637-07-9); wkbk. 12.95 (ISBN 0-935637-06-0); transparency set 120.00 (ISBN 0-935637-04-4); listening tape set 40.00 (ISBN 0-935637-05-2). Cambridge Strat.

Quackenbush, Ross & Gastineau, Jerrel. Homework? My Locker Ate It! An Effective Method for Parents to Help Their Student Study at Home & Improve in School. Thiesies, Darlene, illus. 143p. (Orig.). (gr. 6-12). 1988. pap. 19.95 (ISBN 0-9621701-0-0). CWP.

Schwartz, Linda. Study Skills Shortcake. 32p. (gr. 4-6). 1979. 3.95 (ISBN 0-88160-071-7, LW 804). Learning Wks.

Sedita, Joan. Landmark Study Skills Guide. LC 89-27870. (Orig.). (gr. 4-12). 1989. pap. text ed. 15.00 (ISBN 0-9624119-0-6). Landmark Found.

Shepherd, C. A., et al. The Sly Fox. (Orig.). (gr. 3-12). 1985. pap. text ed. 6.00 (ISBN 0-88734-503-4). Players Pr.

Simon, Jeffrey R. Are Your Grades Going Up? Kaplan, Carol, intro. by. (Illus.). 48p. (gr. 4-9). 1983. pap. 3.95 (ISBN 0-916343-00-6). J R Simon.

Tomasik, Kris. You Can Do It Guide to Better Grades. (Illus.). 128p. (Orig.). (gr. 5-9). 1988. pap. 1.95 (ISBN 0-87406-298-5). Willowisp Pr.

Ulrich, Cindy & Guild, Pat. No Sweat! How to Use Your Learning Style to Be a Better Student. Craig, Dorothy, ed. Hall, Mary A., illus. 52p. (gr. 8-12). 1986. wkbk. 5.95 (ISBN 0-317-92552-0). Teaching Advisory.

Wathen, Judy & Sussman, Ellen. Teach Me Everyday Skills. Burris, Priscilla, illus. 40p. (ps-k). 1989. pap. 4.95 (ISBN 0-933606-77-X); tchr's. guide avail. Monkey Sisters.

Zakalik, Leslie S. Study Skills Sorcery. 48p. (gr. 4-6). 1978. 5.95 (ISBN 0-88160-028-8, LW 213). Learning Wks.

STUYVESANT, PETER, 1592-1672

Crouse, Anna & Crouse, Russel. Peter Stuyvesant of Old New York. (gr. 4-6). 1963. Random.

Quackenbush, Robert. Old Silver Leg Takes Over: A Story of Peter Stuyvesant. Quackenbush, Robert, illus. 40p. (gr. 1-5). 1986. 10.95 (ISBN 0-13-633934-4). P-H.

STYLE, LITERARY

see also Criticism; Letter Writing; Literature–History and Criticism; Rhetoric

STYLE IN DRESS

see Costume; Fashion

SUBCONSCIOUS

see also Dreams; Hypnotism; Mind and Body; Psychoanalysis; Sleep; Thought Transference

SUBMARINE CABLES

see Cables, Submarine

SUBMARINE DIVING

see Skin Diving

SUBMARINE EXPLORATION

see Underwater Exploration

SUBMARINE GEOLOGY

Arnold, Caroline. A Walk on the Great Barrier Reef. (Illus.). 48p. (gr. 2-5). 1988. PLB 12.95 (ISBN 0-87614-285-4); pap. 6.95 (ISBN 0-87614-501-2). Carolrhoda Bks.

SUBMARINE TELEGRAPH

see Cables, Submarine

SUBMARINE WARFARE

see also Submarines

Stephen, R. J. Picture World of Submarines. 1990. PLB 11.40 (ISBN 0-531-14011-3). Watts.

SUBMARINES

Baker, David. Anti-Submarine Warfare. 48p. (gr. 3-8). 1989. lib. bdg. 18.60 (ISBN 0-86592-532-1). Rourke Corp.

Gibbons, Tony. Submarines. Gibbons, Tony, et al, illus. 48p. (gr. 5 up). 1987. PLB 9.95 (ISBN 0-8225-1383-8, First Ave Edns); pap. 4.95 (ISBN 0-8225-9542-7, First Ave Edns). Lerner Pubns.

Graham, Ian. Submarines. (Illus.). 32p. (gr. 5-6). 1989. PLB 11.90 (ISBN 0-531-17153-1). Watts.

Humble, Richard. U-Boat. 1990. PLB 11.90 (ISBN 0-531-14023-7). Watts.

Norman, C. J. Submarines. 32p. (gr. 3-6). 1989. pap. 3.95 (ISBN 0-531-15144-1). Watts.

Petersen, David. Submarines. LC 83-26253. (Illus.). 48p. (gr. k-4). 1984. lib. bdg. 14.60 (ISBN 0-516-01728-4). Childrens.

Price, Stern & Sloan Staff. Ships & Submarines. (Illus.). 32p. (gr. 7-12). 1987. pap. 2.95 (ISBN 0-8431-4289-8). Price Stern.

Rawlinson, J. Hunter-Killer Submarines. (Illus.). 48p. (gr. 3-8). 1989. lib. bdg. 18.60 (ISBN 0-86625-086-7). Rourke Corp.

Rutland, Jonathan. See Inside a Submarine. rev. ed. 1988. PLB 11.90 (ISBN 0-531-19032-3). Watts.

Submarines. (Illus.). 64p. (gr. 3-9). 1990. PLB 16.95 (ISBN 1-85435-116-8). Marshall Cavendish.

Weiss, Harvey. Submarines & Other Underwater Craft. Weiss, Harvey, illus. LC 89-37614. 64p. (gr. 3-7). 1990. 12.95 (ISBN 0-690-04759-2, Crowell Jr Bks); PLB 12.89 (ISBN 0-690-04761-4, Crowell Jr Bks). HarpC Child Bks.

White, D. Submarines. (Illus.). 48p. (gr. 3-8). Date not set. PLB 18.60 (ISBN 0-86592-452-X). Rourke Corp.

SUBMARINES–FICTION

Lawhead, Steve. Howard Had a Submarine. (Illus.). 32p. (gr. 1 up). 1987. pap. 7.95 (ISBN 0-7459-1179-X). Lion USA.

Roddy, Lee. Secret of the Sunken Sub. Kobobel, Janet, ed. 160p. (Orig.). (gr. 3-6). 1990. pap. 4.99 (ISBN 0-929608-63-1). Focus Family.

Verne, Jules. Reader's Digest Best Loved Books for Young Readers: Twenty Thousand Leagues under the Sea. Ogburn, Jackie, ed. Hildibrand, illus. 176p. (gr. 4-12). 1989. 3.99 (ISBN 0-945260-29-6). Choice Pub NY.

—Twenty Thousand Leagues under the Sea. (gr. 8 up). 1964. pap. 1.95 (ISBN 0-8049-0012-4, CL-12). Airmont.

—Twenty Thousand Leagues under the Sea. new ed. Binder, Otto, ed. Gamboa, Romy & Patricio, Ernie, illus. LC 73-75466. 64p. (Orig.). (gr. 5-10). 1973. pap. 2.95 (ISBN 0-88301-104-2); student activity bk. 1.25 (ISBN 0-88301-180-8). Pendulum Pr.

—Twenty Thousand Leagues under the Sea. Butz, Steve, illus. Nordlicht, Lillian, adapted by. LC 79-23887. 48p. (gr. 4 up). 1983. PLB 17.32 (ISBN 0-8172-1652-9); pap. 9.27 (ISBN 0-8172-2028-3). Raintree Pubs.

SUBURBAN HOMES

see Architecture, Domestic

SUBURBAN LIFE

Heide, Florence P. Time's Up! Hafner, Marylin, illus. LC 81-13240. 128p. (gr. 3-7). 1982. 12.95 (ISBN 0-8234-0441-2). Holiday.

SUBVERSIVE ACTIVITIES

see also Political Crimes and Offenses; Spies

SUBWAYS

Hovey, Tamara. Paris Underground. LC 90-7980. (Illus.). 96p. (gr. 5 up). 1991. 14.95 (ISBN 0-531-05931-6); PLB 14.99 (ISBN 0-531-08531-7). Orchard Bks Watts.

SUBWAYS–FICTION

Bahar, Mehrdad. Bastoor. new & rev. ed. Jabbari, Ahmad, ed. Alyeshmreni, Mansoor, tr. from PER. LC 83-60451. (Illus.). 32p. (Orig.). (gr. 1 up). 1983. pap. 4.95 (ISBN 0-939214-17-2). Mazda Pubs.

Benson, Kathleen. Joseph on the Subway Trains. McCully, Emily A., illus. LC 84-46022. 48p. (gr. k-2). 1981. 11.95i (ISBN 0-201-03996-6, Crowell Jr Bks). HarpC Child Bks.

Crifasi, Kathleen. Woodley Rides the Subway Train. LC 87-62212. 54p. (ps-4). 1987. pap. 6.95 (ISBN 0-932433-30-8). Windswept Hse.

Donovan, Donna. Countdown on the Metro. (Illus.). 14p. (gr. 3-7). 1988. incl. puzzle 9.95 (ISBN 0-922242-07-0). Lombard Mktg.

Gabhart, Ann. Wish Come True. 160p. (gr. 7 up). 1988. pap. 2.50 (ISBN 0-380-75653-6, Flare). Avon.

Holman, Felice. Slake's Limbo. LC 74-11675. 126p. (gr. 4-8). 1974. 12.95 (ISBN 0-684-13926-X, Scribners Young Read). Macmillan Child Grp.

—Slake's Limbo. LC 85-26795. 128p. (gr. 6 up). 1986. pap. 3.95 (ISBN 0-689-71066-6, Aladdin). Macmillan Child Grp.

SUCCESS

see also Business; Leadership

Aaseng, Nathan. Close Calls: From the Brink of Ruin to Business Success. (Illus.). 80p. (gr. 5 up). 1990. PLB 13.95 (ISBN 0-8225-0682-3). Lerner Pubns.

Alger, Horatio, Jr. Struggling Upward. 1971. Fasc. 6.95 (ISBN 0-87874-005-8, Nautilus). Galloway.

Bode, Janet. Beating the Odds: Stories of Unexpected Achievers. 160p. (gr. 9-12). 1991. 13.95 (ISBN 0-531-15230-8); PLB 13.90 (ISBN 0-531-10985-2). Watts.

Brooks, B. David & Paull, Robert C. How to Be Successful in Less Than Ten Minutes a Day. 180p. (gr. 7 up). 1984. tchr's. ed. 69.50 (ISBN 0-938308-11-4); wkbk. 69.95 (ISBN 0-685-20975-X). T Jefferson Ctr.

—How to Be Successful in Less Than Ten Minutes a Day: Supplement. 59p. (gr. 7-9). 1984. tchr's. ed. 24.95 (ISBN 0-938308-12-2). T Jefferson Ctr.

—How to Live the Good Life Seminars. 158p. (Orig.). (gr. 9 up). 1984. wkbk. 24.50 (ISBN 0-938308-10-6). T Jefferson Ctr.

Buhay, Debra. Black & White of Success. 30p. (gr. 12). Date not set. pap. 2.00 (ISBN 1-878056-01-8). D Hockenberry.

Conway, L. M. Goal Getters. 48p. (gr. 3-6). 1984. 5.95 (ISBN 0-88160-105-5, LW 245). Learning Wks.

DeVenzio, Richard. Smart Moves: How Young Adults Can Succeed in School, Sports, Career & Life. 300p. (gr. 6-12). 1989. pap. 12.95 (ISBN 0-87975-546-6). Prometheus Bks.

McDiarmid, T. Making Money. (Illus.). 48p. (gr. 2-6). 1988. pap. 4.95 (ISBN 0-88625-152-4). Durkin Hayes Pub.

Martin. Reaching Your Goal, 8 bks, Set I, Reading Level 2. (Illus.). 192p. (gr. 1-4). Date not set. Set. PLB 98.66 (ISBN 0-86592-166-0). Rourke Corp.

Mascola, et al. Reaching Your Goal, 8 bks, Set II, Reading Level 2. (Illus.). 192p. (gr. 1-4). Date not set. Set. PLB 98.66 (ISBN 0-86592-425-2). Rourke Corp.

Ormondroyd, Edward. Johnny Castleseed. Thewlis, Diana, illus. LC 85-8189. 32p. (gr. k-3). 1988. 12.95 (ISBN 0-395-38355-2); pap. 4.95 (ISBN 0-395-47947-9). HM.

Peet, Bill. The Luckiest One of All. Peet, Bill, illus. (gr. k-3). 1985. 13.95 (ISBN 0-395-31863-7); pap. 3.95 (ISBN 0-395-39593-3). HM.

Richardson, Joseph T. The Seven Keys to Success. 62p. (Orig.). (gr. 7-12). 1989. pap. 4.95 (ISBN 0-685-25963-3). Richardson Pubns.

Roets, Lois S. Understanding Success & Failure. 36p. (gr. 5 up). 1985. 8.00 (ISBN 0-911943-07-2). Leadership Pubs.

Rolliet, D. G. Your Name & Colors: Secret Keys to Your Beauty, Personality, & Success, the Rolliett Letter-Color Theory. Reanult, Michael & Wolf, Jeannie, eds. Sherwood, Ed, illus. LC 89-91991. 192p. (Orig.). 1990. pap. text ed. 12.95 (ISBN 0-9621693-0-7). Spectra Pubns Hse.

Rutkovsky, Paul. Get. Rutkovsky, Paul, illus. 72p. (Orig.). (gr. 9-12). 1987. pap. 8.95 (ISBN 0-317-57497-3). Visual Studies.

Schlachter, Rita. Good Luck, Bad Luck. Karas, G. Brian, illus. LC 85-14069. 48p. (Orig.). (gr. 1-3). 1986. PLB 9.89 (ISBN 0-8167-0572-0); pap. text ed. 2.95 (ISBN 0-8167-0573-9). Troll Assocs.

Schulman, Janet. The Great Big Dummy. Hoban, Lillian, illus. 32p. (gr. 1-3). 1961. pap. 2.50 (ISBN 0-440-43072-0, YB). Dell.

Seltzer, Joan. Go for It! 62p. (gr. 5-12). 1981. pap. 5.95 (ISBN 0-9607732-1-5); write for info. tchr's ed.; write for info. wkbk. Jory Pubns.

Symonds, Martha. Think Big. 76p. (gr. 4-6). 1977. 7.95 (ISBN 0-88160-024-5, LW 209). Learning Wks.

Terry, Jim & Terry, Mary. Soaring to the Top: The Success Manual for Young Adults. 300p. Date not set. pap. 8.95 (ISBN 0-931731-07-0). Jimar Prodns.

Youngs, Bettie B. & Tracy, Brian S. Achievement, Popularity, & Success: Getting What You Want from Life. 276p. (Orig.). (gr. 6-12). 1988. pap. 12.95 (ISBN 0-317-89982-1). Phoenix Educ Found.

SUFFRAGE
see also classes of people with the subdivision Suffrage, e.g. Women–Suffrage; etc.

SUGAR
Cobb, Vicki. Gobs of Goo. Schatell, Brain, illus. LC 82-48457. 40p. (gr. 1-3). 1983. 12.95 (ISBN 0-397-32021-3, Lipp Jr Bks); PLB 12.89 (ISBN 0-397-32022-1). HarpC Child Bks.

Dineen, Jacqueline. Sugar. 32p. (gr. 4-8). 1988. lib. bdg. 12.95 (ISBN 0-89490-223-7). Enslow Pubs.

Mitgutsch, Ali. From Beet to Sugar. LC 80-29603. (Illus.). 24p. (ps-3). 1981. PLB 6.95 (ISBN 0-87614-145-9). Carolrhoda Bks.

SUGIMOTO, ETSU (INAGAKI) 1874-1950
Sugimoto, Etsu I. Daughter of the Samurai. LC 66-15849. (gr. 9 up). 1966. pap. 13.95 (ISBN 0-8048-1655-7). C E Tuttle.

SUICIDE
Booher, Albert R. Adolescent Suicide. 11p. (gr. 5-9). 1988. pap. text ed. 5.95 (ISBN 0-685-28968-0). Madonna Edu Syst.

Crook, Marion. Teenagers Talk about Suicide. 128p. (gr. 7-12). 1988. pap. 9.95 (ISBN 1-55021-013-0, Pub. by NC Press Ltd). U of Toronto Pr.

—Teenagers Talk about Suicide. 2nd ed. (gr. 9-12). 1989. pap. 10.95 (ISBN 1-55021-052-1, Pub. by NC Press Ltd). Seven Hills Bk Dists.

Dolce, Laura. Suicide. (Illus.). (gr. 6-12). 1992. 18.95 (ISBN 0-7910-0053-2). Chelsea Hse.

Faulk, Tim. What Causes Our Teens to Take Their Lives? Dying to Live. 80p. (Orig.). (gr. 9 up). 1989. pap. text ed. 5.95 (ISBN 0-685-29873-6). T Faulk Ministries.

Flanders, Stephen A. Library in a Book: Suicide. 240p. (gr. 9-12). 1991. 22.95x (ISBN 0-8160-1909-6). Facts on File.

Francis, Dorothy B. Suicide, a Preventable Tragedy. LC 88-26856. 144p. (gr. 7 up). 1989. 13.95 (ISBN 0-525-67279-6, Lodestar Bks). Dutton Child Bks.

Gardner, Sandra & Rosenberg, Gary B. Teenage Suicide. rev. ed. (Illus.). 128p. (gr. 7 up). 1990. lib. bdg. 12.98 (ISBN 0-671-70200-9); pap. 5.95 (ISBN 0-671-70201-7). Messner.

Hyde, Margaret O. & Forsyth, Elizabeth H. Suicide. 3rd, updated ed. (Illus.). 144p. (gr. 9-12). 1991. PLB 13.90 (ISBN 0-531-11003-6). Watts.

Kolehmainen, Janet & Handwerk, Sandra. Teen Suicide: A Book for Friends, Family, & Classmates. 72p. (gr. 7 up). 1986. PLB 9.95 (ISBN 0-8225-0037-X, First Ave Edns); pap. 4.95 (ISBN 0-8225-9514-1, First Ave Edns). Lerner Pubns.

Langone, John. Dead End: A Book about Suicide. LC 85-25620. (gr. 6 up). 1986. 14.95 (ISBN 0-316-51432-2). Little.

Leder, Jane M. Dead Serious: A Book for Teenagers about Teenage Suicide. LC 86-25880. 160p. (gr. 7 up). 1987. 13.95 (ISBN 0-689-31262-8, Atheneum Child Bk). Macmillan Child Grp.

—Dead Serious: A Book for Teenagers about Teenage Suicide. 160p. (gr. 7 up). 1989. pap. 3.50 (ISBN 0-380-70661-X, Flare). Avon.

McGuire, Leslie. Suicide. (Illus.). 64p. (gr. 7 up). 1990. lib. bdg. 15.93 (ISBN 0-86593-069-4); lib. bdg. 11. 95s.p. Rourke Corp.

Madison, Arnold. Suicide & Young People. LC 77-13240. 144p. (gr. 6 up). 1981. 13.95 (ISBN 0-395-28913-0, Clarion); (Clarion). HM.

Miller, Michael. Dare to Live: A Guide to the Prevention & Understanding of Teenage Suicide & Depression. (gr. 7-12). 1989. pap. 9.95 (ISBN 0-941831-22-1). Beyond Words Pub.

Powell, Donalyn. A Reason to Live. 160p. (Orig.). (gr. 9 up). 1989. pap. 5.95 (ISBN 1-55661-076-9). Bethany Hse.

Roos, Stephen. You'll Miss Me When I'm Gone. LC 87-25961. 160p. (gr. 7 up). 1988. pap. 13.95 (ISBN 0-385-29633-9). Delacorte.

Rosenthal, Howard. Not with My Life I Don't: Preventing Your Suicide & That of Others. LC 88-70011. 232p. (gr. 9 up). 1988. pap. text ed. 17.95 (ISBN 0-915202-77-8). Accel Devel.

Schliefer, Jay. Everything You Need to Know about Teen Suicide. rev. ed. (Illus.). 64p. (gr. 7 up). 1990. 12.95 (ISBN 0-8239-1244-2). Rosen Group.

Smith, Judie. Coping with Suicide. rev. ed. LC 86-10076. 128p. (gr. 7-12). 1990. PLB 12.95 (ISBN 0-8239-1052-0). Rosen Group.

Stewart, Gail. Teen Suicide. LC 88-20281. (Illus.). 48p. (gr. 5-6). 1988. PLB 10.95 (ISBN 0-89686-413-8, Crestwood Hse). Macmillan Child Grp.

SUICIDE–FICTION
Arrick, Fran. Tunnel Vision. 176p. (gr. 7 up). 1981. pap. 3.25 (ISBN 0-440-98579-X, LE); tchr's. guide by Lou Stanek 0.50 (ISBN 0-685-01410-X). Dell.

Azaad, Meyer. The Tale of Ringy. Ghanoonparvar, Mohammad R. & Wilcox, Diane L., trs. from PER. Haqiqat, Nahid, illus. 24p. (Orig.). (gr. 3 up). 1983. pap. 4.95 (ISBN 0-686-43078-6). Mazda Pubs.

Bunting, Eve. Face at the Edge of the World. LC 85-2684. 192p. (gr. 7 up). 1988. 13.95 (ISBN 0-89919-399-4, Clarion); pap. 3.95 (ISBN 0-89919-800-7). Ticknor & Fields.

Calvert, Patricia. The Hour of the Wolf. LC 83-14184. 160p. (gr. 7 up). 1983. 12.95 (ISBN 0-684-17961-X, Scribners Young Read). Macmillan Child Grp.

—The Hour of the Wolf. LC 83-14184. 160p. (gr. 7 up). 1983. 12.95 (ISBN 0-684-17961-X, Scribners Young Read). Macmillan Child Grp.

Cannon, Bettie. A Bellsong for Sarah Raines. LC 87-4299. 192p. (gr. 7 up). 1987. 13.95 (ISBN 0-684-18839-2, Scribners Young Read). Macmillan Child Grp.

Faucher, Elizabeth. Surviving. 168p. (Orig.). (gr. 7 up). 1985. pap. 2.50 (ISBN 0-590-41068-7, Point); tchr's. guide 1.25. Scholastic Inc.

Gerson, Corrine. Passing Through. 208p. (gr. 8 up). 1980. pap. 1.50 (ISBN 0-440-96958-1, LFL). Dell.

Grant, Cynthia D. Phoenix Rising: Or, How to Survive Your Life. LC 88-7370. 160p. (gr. 6 up). 1989. 12.95 (ISBN 0-689-31458-2, Atheneum Child Bk). Macmillan Child Grp.

Irwin, Hadley. So Long at the Fair. LC 88-12813. 208p. (gr. 9 up). 1988. PLB 13.95 (ISBN 0-689-50454-3, M K McElderry). Macmillan Child Grp.

Nunes, Lygia B. My Friend the Painter. Pontiero, Giovanni, tr. from POR. 80p. (gr. 4-8). 1991. 13.95 (ISBN 0-15-256340-7). HarBraceJ.

Tapp, Kathy K. The Sacred Circle of the Hula Hoop. LC 88-27369. 208p. (gr. 6-9). 1989. 13.95 (ISBN 0-689-50461-6, M K McElderry). Macmillan Child Grp.

Zalben, Jane B. Maybe It Will Rain Tomorrow. LC 82-15677. 181p. (gr. 7 up). 1983. 12.95 (ISBN 0-374-34878-2). FS&G.

—Maybe It Will Rain Tomorrow. LC 82-15677. 181p. (gr. 7 up). 1983. 12.95 (ISBN 0-374-34878-2). FS&G.

SUKKOTH
Edelman, Lily. Sukkah & the Big Wind. Kessler, Leonard, illus. (gr. k-2). 1956. 5.95 (ISBN 0-8381-0716-8). United Syn Bk.

Simon, Norma. Our First Sukkah. Gordon, Ayala, illus. (ps-k). 1959. plastic cover 4.50 (ISBN 0-8381-0703-6). United Syn Bk.

SUMER
Florian, Douglas. A Summer Day. LC 87-8484. (Illus.). 24p. (ps-1). 1988. 11.95 (ISBN 0-688-07564-9); lib. bdg. 11.88 (ISBN 0-688-07565-7). Greenwillow.

Sussman, Ellen. Here Comes Summer! Cathleen, Mella, illus. 32p. (Orig.). (gr. 2-5). 1990. pap. text ed. 3.95 (ISBN 0-933606-84-2, MS-688). Monkey Sisters.

SUMER–FICTION
Good, Elaine. It's Summertime! LC 89-28895. (Illus.). 32p. (ps-1). 1990. 12.95 (ISBN 0-934672-68-7). Good Bks PA.

Hogg, Elizabeth. Gorgonzola Summer. 88p. (gr. 6-8). 1989. 16.95 (ISBN 0-09-173653-6, Pub. by Hutchinson UK). Trafalgar Sq.

SUMERIANS
Foster, Leila M. The Sumerians. (Illus.). 64p. (gr. 5-8). 1990. PLB 11.90 (ISBN 0-531-10874-0). Watts.

Odijk, Pamela. The Sumerians. (Illus.). 48p. (gr. 5-8). 1990. lib. bdg. 16.98 (ISBN 0-382-09892-7). Silver Burdett Pr.

SUMMER
Allington, Richard L. & Krull, Kathleen. Summer. Hockerman, Dennis, illus. LC 80-25097. 32p. (gr. k-3). 1985. PLB 15.33 (ISBN 0-8172-1341-4); pap. 9.27 (ISBN 0-8172-2491-2). Raintree Pubs.

Barker, Cicely M. Flower Fairies of the Summer. Barker, Cicely M., illus. (ps up). 1991. 5.95 (ISBN 0-7232-3754-9). Warne.

Blades, Ann. Summer. (Illus.). (ps-k). 1990. bds. 4.95 (ISBN 0-688-09231-4). Lothrop.

Hurwitz, Johanna. Hot & Cold Summer. 1985. pap. 2.75 (ISBN 0-590-42858-6). Scholastic Inc.

MacKenthun, Carole. Celebrate Summer. Grossman, Dan, illus. 144p. (gr. k-3). 1985. wkbk. 10.95 (ISBN 0-86653-265-X, SS 837). Good Apple.

Mason, John. Summer Weather. LC 90-41063. (Illus.). 32p. (gr. 1-4). 1991. PLB 11.90 (ISBN 0-531-18382-3, Pub. by Bookwright Pr). Watts.

Moncure, Jane B. Step into Summer: A New Season. McCallum, Jodie, illus. LC 90-30456. 32p. (ps-2). 1990. lib. bdg. 11.97 (ISBN 0-89565-572-1). Childs World.

Parramon, J. M., et al. El Verano. (SPA.). (ps). 1986. pap. 3.95 (ISBN 0-8120-3645-X). Barron.

Rosen, Mike. Summer Festivals. (Illus.). 32p. (gr. 3-7). 1991. PLB 11.90 (ISBN 0-531-18383-1). Watts.

Santrey, Louis. Summer. LC 82-19384. (Illus.). 32p. (gr. 4-7). 1982. lib. bdg. 10.79 (ISBN 0-89375-911-2); pap. text ed. 2.95 (ISBN 0-89375-912-0). Troll Assocs.

Thomson, Ruth. Summer. 1990. PLB 11.90 (ISBN 0-531-14019-9). Watts.

Ware, Cindy. Summer Options for Teenagers. 576p. (Orig.). (gr. 8-12). 1990. pap. 16.95 (ISBN 0-13-296443-0). Arco.

Webber, Helen. Summer Sun. Webber, Helen, illus. (gr. k-6). 1968. 8.95 (ISBN 0-8392-3056-7). Astor-Honor.

Webster, David. Summer. Steadman, Barbara, illus. 48p. (gr. 2-4). 1990. lib. bdg. 10.98 (ISBN 0-671-65859-X); pap. 4.95 (ISBN 0-671-65984-7). Messner.

SUMMER–FICTION
Asher. Summer Smith Begins. (gr. 7 up). 1987. pap. 2.50 (ISBN 0-553-25883-4). Bantam.

Ballard, Kimberly M. Light at Summer's End. 160p. (Orig.). (gr. 9-12). 1991. pap. 6.95 (ISBN 0-87788-503-6). Shaw Pubs.

Bobo, Carmen P. Sarah's Growing-up Summer. LC 88-62111. 52p. 1989. 5.95 (ISBN 1-55523-187-X). Winston-Derek.

Calhoun, Mary. Katie John. LC 60-5775. (Illus.). 128p. (gr. 3-6). 1972. pap. 3.50 (ISBN 0-06-440028-X, Trophy). HarpC Child Bks.

Cavanna, Betty. Paintbox Summer. 239p. 1981. Repr. PLB 16.95x (ISBN 0-89967-031-8). Harmony Raine.

Coville, Bruce. How I Survived My Summer Vacation. Newsom, Tom, illus. 96p. (Orig.). (gr. 3-5). 1988. pap. 2.75 (ISBN 0-671-68176-1, Minstrel Bks). PB.

Cusick, Richie T. The Lifeguard. 192p. (Orig.). (gr. 7 up). 1988. pap. 2.50 (ISBN 0-590-41549-2). Scholastic Inc.

Daly, Maureen. Seventeenth Summer. 288p. 1981. Repr. PLB 19.95x (ISBN 0-89967-029-6). Harmony Raine.

Davidson, Linda. Cool Breezes. (gr. 10 up). 1989. pap. 2.95 (ISBN 0-8041-0244-9). Ivy Books.

—On the Edge. (gr. 10 up). 1988. pap. 2.95 (ISBN 0-8041-0243-0). Ivy Books.

De Angeli, Marguerite. Copper-Toed Boots. LC 88-34417. (Illus.). 96p. (gr. 4 up). 1989. Repr. of 1938 ed. 14.95x (ISBN 0-8143-1922-X). Wayne St U Pr.

Duncan, Lois. I Know What You Did Last Summer. (gr. 7 up). 1986. pap. 2.95 (ISBN 0-671-63970-6, Archway). PB.

Easton, Patricia H. Summer's Chance. LC 87-17728. 160p. (gr. 12 up). 1988. 13.95 (ISBN 0-15-200591-9, Gulliver Bks). HarBraceJ.

Effinger, Marta. Bunker & Me: Summer Adventures of Best Friends, Vol. I. Lawrence & Penny, ed. Effinger, Michael, illus. Washington, Pat, intro. by. (Illus.). 30p. (gr. 3-5). 1990. 12.95xg (ISBN 0-929917-02-2). Magnolia PA.

Elliott, Suzanne. Summer's Quest. Parrish, William, illus. 144p. (gr. 7-9). 1987. pap. 3.95 (ISBN 0-87403-269-5, 2946). Standard Pub.

Eyerly, Jeannette. The Seeing Summer. LC 81-47440. (Illus.). 128p. (gr. 4-6). 1981. (Lipp Jr Bks). HarpC Child Bks.

Farjam, Farideh & Azaad, Meyer. Uncle Noruz (Uncle New Year) Jabbari, Ahmad, ed. & tr. from PER. Mesqali, Farshid, illus. LC 83-60450. 24p. (Orig.). (gr. k up). 1983. pap. 4.95 (ISBN 0-939214-14-8). Mazda Pubs.

Ferris, Jean. Invincible Summer. LC 87-7385. 176p. (gr. 9-12). 1987. 12.95 (ISBN 0-374-33642-3). FS&G.

Fowler, Susi G. When Summer Ends. Russo, Marisabina, illus. LC 87-14937. 32p. (ps up). 1989. 11.95 (ISBN 0-688-07605-X); PLB 11.88 (ISBN 0-688-07606-8). Greenwillow.

Fowler, Zinita. The Last Innocent Summer. LC 89-20417. 145p. (gr. 6-9). 1990. pap. 11.95 (ISBN 0-87565-045-7). Tex Christian. THE LAST INNOCENT SUMMER is a story about a small town with a swimming pool, the Ritz Theater, a city park, a town square & a J.C. Penney store. It's a story about slumber parties, small-town funerals, community picnics & local intrigues. It's also a story about honor & caring & the way we live. Skeeter, the ten-year-old narrator, tells about the murder of two little girls that rocked the small Texas town in which she lived, & of how her close-knit family's involvement in events beyond their

control changed their lives in that troubled summer of 1931. Skeeter learns some disturbing lessons: people can do bad things & then make them worse trying to keep from being found out; not all mothers love their children, nor all children love their mothers; it's hard to say "I love you" to those you love. "Fowler's deftly crafted story has depth & pace & a picture of a community that may remind some readers of Harper Lee's TO KILL A MOCKINGBIRD."--Bulletin of the Center for Children's Books, Univ. of Chicago. "The emotion of small town joys & sorrows & the prejudices of different groups as they struggle to coexist are brought together with good clear dialogue & colorful description to make (a) most enjoyable story."--VOYA. Chosen best Juvenile of 1991 by the Texas Institute of Letters. *Publisher Provided Annotation.*

Gauch, Patricia L. The Year the Summer Died. 160p. (gr. 7 up). 1985. 12.95 (ISBN 0-399-21114-4, Putnam). Putnam Pub Group.
Godden, Rumer. Greengage Summer. 206p. (gr. 7 up). 1986. pap. 3.95 (ISBN 0-14-031982-4, Puffin). Puffin Bks.
Godfrey, Martyn N. I Spent My Summer Vacation Kidnapped. (gr. 5-7). 1990. pap. 2.75 (ISBN 0-590-43418-7). Scholastic Inc.
Greene, Carol. The Jenny Summer. Eagle, Ellen, illus. LC 87-45283. 80p. (gr. 1-4). 1988. 11.95 (ISBN 0-06-022208-5); PLB 12.89 (ISBN 0-06-022209-3). HarpC Child Bks.
Gulley, Judie. Rodeo Summer. LC 84-9129. 192p. (gr. 5-9). 1984. 11.95 (ISBN 0-395-36174-5). HM.
Hahn, Mary D. The Jellyfish Season. LC 85-3759. 192p. (gr. 5-8). 1985. 13.95 (ISBN 0-89919-344-7, Clarion). Ticknor & Fields.
Hayward, Linda. Ernie & Bert's Summer Project. Nicklaus, Carol, illus. LC 90-60821. 32p. (Orig.). (ps-3). 1991. pap. 1.50 (ISBN 0-679-81051-X). Random.
Haywood, Carolyn. Betsy's Busy Summer. Haywood, Carolyn, illus. LC 56-7894. (gr. 3-7). 1956. PLB 13.88 (ISBN 0-688-31087-7, Morrow Junior Books). Morrow.
—Summer Fun. Durrell, Julie, illus. LC 85-25864. 128p. (gr. 1-4). 1986. 11.95 (ISBN 0-688-04958-3). Morrow Jr Bks.
—Summer Fun. (gr. 2-4). 1987. pap. 2.95 (ISBN 0-8167-1037-6). Troll Assocs.
Hunter, Mollie. The Mermaid Summer. LC 87-45984. 160p. (gr. 3-7). 1988. PLB 13.89 (ISBN 0-06-022628-5). HarpC Child Bks.
—The Mermaid Summer. LC 87-45984. 128p. (gr. 3-7). 1990. pap. 3.50 (ISBN 0-06-440344-0, Trophy). HarpC Child Bks.
Hurwitz, Johanna. Hot & Cold Summer. Owen, Gail, illus. LC 83-19336. 176p. (gr. 3-5). 1984. 12.95 (ISBN 0-688-02746-6). Morrow Jr Bks.
—The Hot & Cold Summer. Owens, Gail, illus. 176p. (gr. 4-6). 1985. pap. 2.50 (ISBN 0-590-33572-3, Apple Paperbacks). Scholastic Inc.
Komoda, Beverly. The Too Hot Day. Komoda, Beverly, illus. LC 90-1620. 32p. (ps-1). 1991. 14.95 (ISBN 0-06-021611-5); PLB 14.89 (ISBN 0-06-021612-3). HarpC Child Bks.
Lee, Robert C. Summer of the Green Star. LC 80-27427. 128p. (gr. 5-9). 1981. 10.95 (ISBN 0-664-32681-1, Westminster). Westminster John Knox.
Leonard, Marcia. Secret Summer. (gr. 3-7). 1990. 12.95 (ISBN 0-943021-04-9). Funchess Jones.
Lipsyte, Robert. The Summerboy. 160p. 1984. pap. 2.25 (ISBN 0-553-24130-3). Bantam.
McGraw, Eloise J. A Really Weird Summer. LC 90-31542. 224p. (gr. 7 up). 1990. pap. 3.95 (ISBN 0-02-044483-4, Collier Young Ad). Macmillan Child Grp.
Martin, Ann M. Bummer Summer. (gr. 4-7). 1990. pap. 2.95 (ISBN 0-590-43622-8). Scholastic Inc.
Moncure, Jane B. Word Bird's Summer Words. Miracle, Ric, illus. LC 85-5930. 32p. (gr. k-2). 1985. lib. bdg. 11.97 (ISBN 0-89565-311-7); pap. 6.96 (ISBN 0-89565-426-1). Childs World.
My Totally Awesome Summer Vacation. 64p. (Orig.). (gr. 1-4). 1992. pap. 6.95 (ISBN 0-8249-8510-9). Ideals.
Nicolai, D. Miles. The Summer the Flowers Had No Scent. 3rd ed. Poyser, Victoria, illus. 28p. (gr. 3-5). 1977. pap. 2.75 (ISBN 0-933992-19-X). Coffee Break.
O'Connor, Jane. Yours Till Niagara Falls, Abby. Apple, Margot, illus. 128p. (gr. 4-6). 1982. pap. 2.50 (ISBN 0-590-41119-5, Apple Paperbacks). Scholastic Inc.
O'Neal, Zibby. In Summer Light. 160p. (gr. 6 up). 1986. pap. 3.50 (ISBN 0-553-25940-7). Bantam.
Pare, R. Summer Days. (Illus.). 24p. (ps-8). 1988. 12.95 (ISBN 1-55037-043-X); pap. 4.95 (ISBN 1-55037-044-8). Firefly Bks Ltd.
Parr, Letitia. When Sea & Sky Are Blue. Watts, John, illus. LC 78-151272. 32p. (ps-3). 7.95 (ISBN 0-87592-059-4). Scroll Pr.
Perl, Lila. Fat Glenda's Summer Romance. LC 86-2653. 144p. (gr. 4-8). 1986. 12.95 (ISBN 0-89919-447-8, Pub. by Clarion). Ticknor & Fields.
—Telltale Summer of Tina C. 1984. pap. 2.50 (ISBN 0-590-41324-4). Scholastic Inc.
Petroski, Catherine. The Summer That Lasted Forever. 176p. (gr. 3-6). 1984. 11.95 (ISBN 0-395-35388-2). HM.
Prelutsky, Jack. What I Did Last Summer. Abolafia, Yossi, illus. LC 83-11561. 48p. (gr. 1-3). 1984. 13.95 (ISBN 0-688-01754-1). Greenwillow.
Quinn, Patrick. Matthew Pinkowski's Special Summer. Quinn, Patrick, illus. LC 91-10982. 150p. (Orig.). (gr. 5-8). 1991. pap. 5.95 (ISBN 0-930323-82-3, Pub. by K Green Pubns). Gallaudet Univ Pr.
Rodgers, Mary. Summer Switch. LC 79-2690. 192p. (gr. 5 up). 1982. 12.95 (ISBN 0-06-025058-5); PLB 12.89 (ISBN 0-06-025059-3). HarpC Child Bks.
Sachs, Marilyn. A Summer's Lease. LC 78-12486. 128p. (gr. 5-9). 1979. 13.95 (ISBN 0-525-40480-5, 0898-270, DCB). Dutton Child Bks.
Scariano, Margaret. Summer Strike-Out. Kratoville, Betty L., ed. Govig, Mathew, illus. 64p. (gr. 3-9). 1989. lib. bdg. 4.95 (ISBN 0-87879-617-7, High Noon Books). Acad Therapy.
Schwartz, Joel L. Upchuck Summer. Degen, Bruce, illus. LC 81-65838. 144p. (gr. 4-6). 1982. 10.95 (ISBN 0-385-29099-3); pap. 10.95 (ISBN 0-385-29100-0). Delacorte.
Shaw, Janet. Kirsten Saves the Day: A Summer Story. Thieme, Jeanne, ed. Graef, Renee, illus. 72p. (gr. 2-5). 1990. PLB 12.95 (ISBN 0-937295-91-4). Pleasant Co.
Slepian, Jan. The Alfred Summer. 128p. (gr. 7 up). 1982. (Apple Paperbacks); tchr's. guide 1.25 (ISBN 0-590-40983-2). Scholastic Inc.
Stucky, Naomi R. Sara's Summer. 144p. (Orig.). (gr. 6-12). 1990. pap. 5.95 (ISBN 0-8361-3534-2). Herald Pr.
Summer Job. 1990. 4.98 (ISBN 1-55521-688-9). Bk Sales Inc.
Thacker, Nola. Summer Stories. Low, William, illus. LC 87-45880. 160p. (gr. 3-7). 1988. 12.95 (ISBN 0-397-32287-9, Lipp Jr Bks); PLB 12.89 (ISBN 0-397-32288-7, Lipp Jr Bks). HarpC Child Bks.
—Summer Stories. Low, William, illus. (gr. 3-7). 1989. pap. 2.75 (ISBN 0-590-42191-3, Apple Paperbacks). Scholastic Inc.
Tomlinson, Theresa. Summer Witches. LC 90-38162. 96p. (gr. 2-7). 1991. SBE 11.95 (ISBN 0-02-789206-9, Mcmillan Child Bk). Macmillan Child Grp.
Tripp, Valerie. Molly Saves the Day: A Summer Story. Thieme, Jeanne, ed. Backes, Nick, illus. 72p. (gr. 2-5). 1990. PLB 12.95 (ISBN 0-937295-93-0). Pleasant Co.
Vandevenne, Jean. Some Summer! (Illus.). 178p. (Orig.). (gr. 4-6). 1987. pap. 4.95 (ISBN 0-89084-380-5). Bob Jones Univ Pr.
Weyn, Suzanne. The Makeover Summer. 128p. (gr. 7 up). 1988. pap. 2.95 (ISBN 0-380-75521-1, Flare). Avon.
Woodson, Jacqueline. Last Summer with Maizon. 1990. 13.95 (ISBN 0-385-30045-X). Doubleday.
Zable, Rona S. An Almost Perfect Summer. (gr. 7 up). 1989. pap. 2.95 (ISBN 0-553-27967-X, Starfire). Bantam.

SUMMER–POETRY
Moncure, Jane B. Summer Is Here! Hook, Frances, illus. LC 75-12945. (ps-2). 1975. 8.95 (ISBN 0-913778-12-5); cassette 13.95; walk chart 10.95. Childs World.

SUMMER HOMES
see Architecture, Domestic; Houses

SUN
see also Solar Energy; Solar System
Adams, Florence. Catch a Sunbeam: A Book of Solar Study & Experiments. Komoda, Kiyo, illus. LC 78-52820. (gr. 4-7). 1978. 10.95 (ISBN 0-15-215197-4, HJ). HarBraceJ.
Adams, Richard. Our Amazing Sun. Boyd, Patti, illus. LC 82-17419. 32p. (gr. 3-6). 1983. PLB 10.59 (ISBN 0-89375-890-6); pap. text ed. 2.95 (ISBN 0-89375-891-4). Troll Assocs.
Ardley, Neil. Sun & Light. 32p. (gr. k-3). 1983. PLB 11.90 (ISBN 0-531-04616-8). Watts.
Asimov, Isaac. How Did We Find Out about Sunshine. 64p. (gr. 5 up). 1987. 10.95 (ISBN 0-8027-6697-8); PLB 12.85 (ISBN 0-8027-6698-6). Walker & Co.
—The Sun. LC 87-42595. (Illus.). 32p. (gr. 3-4). 1988. PLB 11.95 (ISBN 1-55532-350-2). Gareth Stevens Inc.
Barrett, Norman. The Picture World of Sun & Stars. (Illus.). 32p. (gr. k-4). 1990. PLB 11.40 (ISBN 0-531-14058-X). Watts.
—Sun & Stars. LC 85-50161. (Illus.). 32p. (gr. k-6). 1986. lib. bdg. 11.40 (ISBN 0-531-10007-3). Watts.
Baylor, Byrd. The Way to Start a Day. Parnall, Peter, illus. LC 85-28802. 32p. (gr. 1-4). 1986. pap. 3.95 (ISBN 0-689-71054-2, Aladdin). Macmillan Child Grp.
Brandt, Keith. Sun. Sweat, Lynn, illus. LC 84-2715. 32p. (gr. 3-6). 1985. PLB 9.49 (ISBN 0-8167-0190-3); pap. text ed. 2.95 (ISBN 0-8167-0191-1). Troll Assocs.
Branley, Franklyn M. The Sun: Our Nearest Star. rev. ed. Madden, Don, illus. LC 87-47764. 32p. (ps-3). 1988. 13.95 (ISBN 0-690-04680-4, Crowell Jr Bks); PLB 13.89 (ISBN 0-690-04678-2). HarpC Child Bks.
—The Sun: Our Nearest Star. rev. ed. Madden, Don, illus. LC 87-45678. 32p. (ps-3). 1988. pap. 4.50 (ISBN 0-06-445073-2, Trophy). HarpC Child Bks.
—Sunshine Makes the Seasons. rev. ed. Maestro, Giulio, illus. LC 85-42750. 32p. (ps-3). 1988. incl. cassette 7.95 (ISBN 0-694-00203-8, Trophy); pap. 4.50 (ISBN 0-06-445019-8, Trophy). HarpC Child Bks.
Gibbons, Gail. Sun up, Sun Down. Gibbons, Gail, illus. LC 82-23420. 32p. (gr. 1-3). 1983. 13.95 (ISBN 0-15-282781-1, HJ). HarBraceJ.
Lampton, Christopher. The Sun. (Illus.). 72p. (gr. 4 up). 1982. PLB 10.40 (ISBN 0-531-04390-8). Watts.
Moncure, Jane B. The Sun: Our Daytime Star. Endres, Helen, illus. LC 89-24009. 32p. (ps-2). 1990. lib. bdg. 11.97 (ISBN 0-89565-551-9). Childs World.
Palazzo, Janet. Our Friend the Sun. Hall, Susan, illus. LC 81-11460. 32p. (gr. k-2). 1982. PLB 10.89 (ISBN 0-89375-650-4); pap. 2.95 (ISBN 0-89375-651-2). Troll Assocs.
Robson, Denny. The Sun. (Illus.). 32p. (gr. k-4). 1991. PLB 11.90 (ISBN 0-531-17336-4, Gloucester Pr). Watts.
Shedd, Edith S. & Shedd, Alan. Do It with the Sun. Higginbotham, David, illus. LC 82-81309. 208p. (Orig.). (gr. 6-9). 1982. pap. 12.95 (ISBN 0-9608358-0-6). Integ Energy.
Simon, Seymour. The Sun. LC 85-32018. (Illus.). 32p. (ps-3). 1986. 14.95 (ISBN 0-688-05857-4); lib. bdg. 14.88 (ISBN 0-688-05858-2, Morrow Jr Bks); pap. 5.95 (ISBN 0-688-09236-5, Mulberry Bks). Morrow Jr Bks.
Ziefert, Harriet. Good Morning Sun. 1988. pap. 3.95 (ISBN 0-670-81578-0). Viking Child Bks.

SUN–FICTION
Ashley, Bernard. A Break in the Sun. Keeping, Charles, illus. 186p. (gr. 6 up). 1980. 18.95 (ISBN 0-87599-230-7). S G Phillips.
Baron, Lindamichelle. The Sun Is On. rev. ed. Elam, Keith, illus. Dee, Ruby, intro. by. (Illus.). 48p. (gr. 1-6). 1982. pap. 5.95 (ISBN 0-940938-02-2). Harlin Jacque.
Farjam, Farideh. The Crystal Flower & the Sun. new & rev. ed. Jabbari, Ahmad, ed. & tr. from PER. Nojoomi, Nikzad, illus. LC 83-60453. 24p. (Orig.). (gr. k up). 1983. pap. 4.95 (ISBN 0-939214-16-4). Mazda Pubs.
Gerstein, Mordicai. The Sun's Day. LC 88-24738. (Illus.). 32p. (ps-1). 1989. 12.95 (ISBN 0-06-022404-5); PLB 12.89 (ISBN 0-06-022405-3). HarpC Child Bks.
Ginsburg, Mirra. Where Does the Sun Go at Night? Aruego, Jose & Dewey, Ariane, illus. LC 79-16151. 32p. (gr. k-3). 1980. 10.95 (ISBN 0-688-80245-1); PLB 10.88 (ISBN 0-688-84245-3). Greenwillow.
Greene, Carol. Shine, Sun! Sharp, Gene, illus. LC 82-19853. 32p. (ps-2). 1983. PLB 11.93 (ISBN 0-516-02038-2); pap. 2.95 (ISBN 0-516-42038-0). Childrens.
Hadley, Eric & Hadley, Tessa. Legends of the Sun & Moon. LC 82-17720. (Illus.). 32p. (gr. 3-7). 1989. 11.95 (ISBN 0-521-25227-X); pap. 7.95 (ISBN 0-521-37912-1). Cambridge U Pr.
Harrison, David. Wake up, Sun. Wilhelm, Hans, illus. LC 85-30053. 32p. (ps-1). 1986. lib. bdg. 6.99 (ISBN 0-394-98256-8, Random Juv); pap. 2.95 (ISBN 0-394-88256-3, Random Juv). Random.
Himler, Ronald. Wake up, Jeremiah. Himler, Ronald, illus. LC 77-25679. (ps-1). 1979. 8.95 (ISBN 0-06-022323-5). HarpC Child Bks.
Kandoian, Ellen. Under the Sun. (Illus.). (ps-3). 1990. 14.95 (ISBN 0-399-22025-9, Philomel Bks). Putnam Pub Group.
Likhanov, Albert. Shadows Across the Sun. Lourie, Richard, tr. from RUS. LC 80-8440. 128p. (gr. 7 up). 1983. HarpC Child Bks.
Wildsmith, Brian. What the Moon Saw. Wildsmith, Brian, illus. 32p. (ps-3). 1978. 14.95 (ISBN 0-19-279724-7); pap. 6.95 (ISBN 0-19-272157-7). Oxford U Pr.

SUN-DIALS
see Sundials

SUN GLASSES
see Eyeglasses

SUNDAY
see Sabbath

SUNDIALS
Jenkins, Gerald & Bear, Magdalen. Sun Dials & Time Dials: A Collection of Working Models to Cut & Glue Together. (Illus.). 40p. (gr. 6 up). 1988. pap. 11.95 (ISBN 0-906212-59-6, Tarquin). Parkwest Pubns.
Simon, Seymour. Shadow Magic. Ormai, Stella, illus. LC 84-4433. 48p. (ps-3). 1985. PLB 13.88 (ISBN 0-688-02682-6). Lothrop.

SUNKEN CITIES
see Cities and Towns, Ruined, Extinct, Etc.

SUNKEN TREASURE
see Buried Treasure

SUPERMARKETS–FICTION
Barkan, Joanne. Whiskerville Grocery. (Illus.). 12p. (ps-k). 1991. bds. 3.95 (ISBN 0-448-40091-X, G&D). Putnam Pub Group.
Grossman, Bill. Tommy at the Grocery Store. Chess, Victoria, illus. LC 88-35756. 32p. (ps-2). 1991. pap. 4.95 (ISBN 0-06-443266-1, Trophy). HarpC Child Bks.
Kent, Jack. Supermarket Magic. LC 78-55908. (ps-2). 1978. 3.95 (ISBN 0-394-83921-8, Random Juv). Random.
Rockwell, Anne & Rockwell, Harlow. The Supermarket. LC 79-11411. (Illus.). 24p. (ps-k). 1979. 12.95 (ISBN 0-02-777580-1, Mcmillan Child Bk). Macmillan Child Grp.
Witch Weed. 1991. pap. 14.00 (ISBN 0-385-30426-9). Doubleday.

SUPERNATURAL–FICTION

Bierhorst, John, ed. The Whistling Skeleton: American Indian Tales of the Supernatural. Parker, Robert A., illus. Grinnell, George B., compiled by. LC 81-69517. (Illus.). 128p. (gr. 3-7). 1984. 13.95 (ISBN 0-02-709770-6, Four Winds). Macmillan Child Grp.

Briggs, Katharine M. An Encyclopedia of Fairies: Hobgoblins, Brownies, Bogies, & Other Supernatural Creatures. LC 76-12939. (Illus.). (gr. 4 up). 1977. pap. 16.95 (ISBN 0-394-73467-X). Pantheon.

Brittain, Bill. Professor Popkin's Prodigious Polish: A Tale of Coven Tree. Glass, Andrew, illus. LC 89-78221. 160p. (gr. 3-7). 1990. 13.95 (ISBN 0-06-020726-4); PLB 13.89 (ISBN 0-06-020727-2). HarpC Child Bks.

Buffie, Margaret. Warnings. 1991. 12.95 (ISBN 0-590-43665-1, Scholastic Hardcover). Scholastic Inc.

Cameron, Eleanor. The Court of the Stone Children. 208p. (gr. 5 up). 1973. 13.95 (ISBN 0-525-28350-1, DCB). Dutton Child Bks.

Chittum, Ida. The Ghost Boy of el Toro. LC 78-1079. (gr. 4 up). 1978. 8.00 (ISBN 0-8309-0201-5). Ind Pr MO.

Denan, Corinne. Tales of Magic & Spells. Watling, James, illus. 48p. (gr. 3-6). 1980. PLB 9.89 (ISBN 0-89375-318-1); pap. text ed. 2.95 (ISBN 0-89375-317-3); cassette avail. Troll Assocs.

Feil, Hila. Blue Moon. LC 89-36915. 208p. (gr. 5-9). 1990. 13.95 (ISBN 0-689-31607-0, Atheneum Child Bk). Macmillan Child Grp.

Garden, Nancy. The Door Between. LC 87-8778. 192p. (gr. 5 up). 1987. 13.95 (ISBN 0-374-31833-6). FS&G.

—Watersmeet. LC 83-11512. 202p. (gr. 5 up). 1983. 13.95 (ISBN 0-374-38244-1). FS&G.

Hitchcock, Alfred, ed. Alfred Hitchcock's Supernatural Tales of Terror & Suspense. (Illus.). (gr. 5 up). 1983. (Random Juv); pap. 3.95 (ISBN 0-394-85622-8). Random.

Honeycutt, Natalie. Invisible Lissa. Rutherford, Jenny, illus. LC 84-20466. 192p. (gr. 4-6). 1985. 13.95 (ISBN 0-02-744360-4, Bradbury Pr). Macmillan Child Grp.

Katz, Welwyn W. False Face. LC 88-12847. 176p. (gr. 5-9). 1988. 13.95 (ISBN 0-689-50456-X, M K McElderry). Macmillan Child Grp.

Mahy, Margaret. The Changeover: A Supernatural Romance. LC 83-83446. 224p. (gr. 7 up). 1984. 14.95 (ISBN 0-689-50303-2, M K McElderry). Macmillan Child Grp.

Peck, Richard. Ghosts I Have Been. LC 77-9469. 224p. (gr. 7 up). 1977. pap. 13.95 (ISBN 0-670-33813-3). Viking Child Bks.

Pierce, Meredith A. The Darkangel. 256p. 1984. pap. 2.95 (ISBN 0-8125-4900-7, Dist. by Warner Pub. Services & Saint Martin's Press). Tor Bks.

Sobol, Donald J. The Amazing Power of Ashur Fine: A Fine Mystery. LC 86-12407. 144p. (gr. 5-9). 1986. 12.95 (ISBN 0-02-786270-4, Mcmillan Child Bk). Macmillan Child Grp.

Walker, Mary A. The Scathach & Maeve's Daughters. LC 90-141. 128p. (gr. 7 up). 1990. 12.95 (ISBN 0-689-31638-0, Atheneum Child Bk). Macmillan Child Grp.

Wrightson, Patricia. Balyet. 1990. pap. 3.95 (ISBN 0-14-034339-3, Puffin). Puffin Bks.

Yolen, Jane. The Faery Flag: Stories & Poems of Fantasy & the Supernatural. LC 88-34866. 128p. (gr. 5 up). 1989. 15.95 (ISBN 0-531-05838-7); PLB 15.99 (ISBN 0-531-08438-8). Orchard Bks Watts.

SUPERSTITION

see also Apparitions; Astrology; Divination; Dreams; Fairies; Folklore; Fortune Telling; Ghosts; Occult Sciences; Witchcraft

Ainsworth, Catherine H. Superstitions from Seven Towns of the United States. LC 43-7320. 64p. (ps-12). 1973. 4.00 (ISBN 0-933190-00-X). Clyde Pr.

Crosby, Nina E. & Marten, Elizabeth H. Don't Teach! Let Me Learn about World War II, Adventure, Dreams & Superstition. Rossi, Richard, illus. 72p. (Orig.). (gr. 3-10). 1984. 8.95 (ISBN 0-88047-044-5, 8411). DOK Pubs.

Lord, Suzanne. Superstitions. LC 89-70867. (Illus.). 48p. (gr. 5 up). 1990. 10.95 (ISBN 0-89686-512-6, Crestwood Hse). Macmillan Child Grp.

Perl, Lila & Weihs, Erika. Don't Sing Before Breakfast, Don't Sleep in the Moonlight: Everyday Superstitions & How They Began. LC 87-24295. (Illus.). 96p. (gr. 3-6). 1988. 13.95 (ISBN 0-89919-504-0, Pub. by Clarion). Ticknor & Fields.

Schwartz, Alvin. Cross Your Fingers, Spit in Your Hat: Superstitions & Other Beliefs. Rounds, Glen, illus. LC 73-21912. 128p. (gr. 4-6). 1990. PLB 12.89 (ISBN 0-397-32436-7, Lipp Jr Bks). HarpC Child Bks.

SURF

see Ocean Waves

SURFING

King, Ron. Rad Boards: Skateboarding, Snowboarding, Bodyboarding. (gr. 4-7). 1991. pap. 9.95 (ISBN 0-316-49355-4). Little.

Nentl, Jerolyn. Surfing. LC 78-8723. (Illus.). 32p. (gr. 3-4). 1978. PLB 9.95 (ISBN 0-913940-93-3, Crestwood Hse). Macmillan Child Grp.

Smith, Don. Surfing, the Big Wave. new ed. LC 75-21847. (Illus.). 32p. (gr. 5-10). 1976. PLB 10.79 (ISBN 0-89375-011-5); pap. 2.95 (ISBN 0-89375-027-1). Troll Assocs.

Wind Surfing. 48p. (gr. 3-4). 1989. PLB 10.95 (ISBN 0-685-26382-7). Capstone Pr.

SURFING–FICTION

Cavanna, Betty. The Surfer & the City Girl. LC 80-25901. 96p. (gr. 7-9). 1981. 8.95 (ISBN 0-664-32679-X, Westminster). Westminster John Knox.

Daniels, Lee. Capsized! 144p. (Orig.). (gr. 7-9). 1989. pap. 2.95 (ISBN 1-55802-069-1). Lynx Bks.

—Hidden Reef. 144p. (gr. 7-9). 1989. pap. 2.95 mass mrkt. (ISBN 1-55802-068-3). Lynx Bks.

—Storm Warnings. 144p. (Orig.). (gr. 7-9). 1988. pap. 2.95 (ISBN 1-55802-066-7). Lynx Bks.

—Wipeout. 160p. (Orig.). (gr. 7-9). 1988. pap. 2.95 (ISBN 1-55802-065-9). Lynx Bks.

Roddy, Lee. Mystery of the Wild Surfer. Kobobel, Janet, ed. 160p. (Orig.). (gr. 3-6). 1990. pap. 4.99 (ISBN 0-929608-64-X). Focus Family.

SURGERY

Facklam, Margery & Facklam, Howard. Spare Parts for People. (Illus.). 128p. (gr. 9-12). 1987. 15.95 (ISBN 0-15-277410-6, HJ). HarBraceJ.

SURINAM

Beatty, Noelle B. Suriname. (Illus.). 96p. (gr. 5 up). 1988. lib. bdg. 14.95 (ISBN 1-55546-196-4). Chelsea Hse.

SURVEYING

see also Geodesy

Surveying. (Illus.). 64p. (gr. 6-12). 1984. pap. 1.85 (ISBN 0-8395-3327-6, 3327). BSA.

SURVIVAL (AFTER AIRPLANE ACCIDENTS, SHIPWRECKS, ETC.)

see also Wilderness Survival

Bright, Michael. Killing for Luxury. Franklin Watts Ltd., ed. (Illus.). 32p. (gr. 7-9). 1988. PLB 8.99 (ISBN 0-531-17089-6, Gloucester Pr). Watts.

Coble, Cindy & Stoffel, Maureen. Survival Basics for Kids. (Illus.). 32p. pap. 3.00 (ISBN 0-913724-26-2). Emerg Response Inst.

East, Ben & Nentl, Jerolyn. Danger in the Air. Dahl, Jack, illus. LC 79-53774. 48p. (gr. 3 up). 1979. PLB 9.95 (ISBN 0-89686-047-7, Crestwood Hse); cass. 7.95 (ISBN 0-89686-481-2). Macmillan Child Grp.

—Desperate Search. Dahl, Jack, illus. LC 79-5186. 48p. (gr. 3 up). 1979. PLB 9.95 (ISBN 0-89686-043-4, Crestwood Hse); cass. 7.95 (ISBN 0-89686-479-0). Macmillan Child Grp.

—Mistaken Journey. Dahl, Jack, illus. LC 79-53775. 48p. (Orig.). (gr. 3 up). 1979. PLB 9.95 (ISBN 0-89686-046-9, Crestwood Hse); cass. 7.95 (ISBN 0-89686-480-4). Macmillan Child Grp.

—Trapped in Devil's Hole. Dahl, Jack, illus. LC 79-53773. 48p. (gr. 3 up). 1979. PLB 9.95 (ISBN 0-89686-048-5, Crestwood Hse); cass. 7.95 (ISBN 0-89686-482-0). Macmillan Child Grp.

Smith, L. Survival Skills. (Illus.). 48p. (gr. 6-10). 1987. PLB 11.96 (ISBN 0-88110-303-9); pap. 5.95 (ISBN 0-7460-0169-X). EDC.

SURVIVAL (AFTER AIRPLANE ACCIDENTS, SHIPWRECKS, ETC.)–FICTION

Cazzola, Gus. To Touch the Deer. LC 81-10452. 130p. (gr. 5-9). 1981. 9.95 (ISBN 0-664-32684-6, Westminster). Westminster John Knox.

Defoe, Daniel. Reader's Digest Best Loved Books for Young Readers: The Life & Strange Surprising Adventures of Robinson Crusoe. Ogburn, Jackie, ed. Foster, Robert, illus. 168p. (gr. 4-12). 1989. 3.99 (ISBN 0-945260-27-X). Choice Pub NY.

—Robinson Crusoe. (gr. 6 up). 1964. pap. 2.25 (ISBN 0-8049-0022-1, CL-22). Airmont.

—Robinson Crusoe. Dolch, Edward W., et al, eds. (gr. k-3). 1988. pap. 2.50 (ISBN 0-590-41841-6). Scholastic Inc.

—Robinson Crusoe. (gr. 3-6). 1981. 6.95 (ISBN 0-86020-554-1, Usborne-Hayes); PLB 11.96 (ISBN 0-88110-062-5); pap. 3.95 (ISBN 0-86020-553-3). EDC.

Fiore, Carmen A. The Snakeskin. Ferri, Penny J., illus. 112p. (gr. 3-7). 1991. 14.95 (ISBN 0-939219-07-7). Townhouse Pub.

Golding, William G. Lord of the Flies. Forster, E. M. (gr. 9 up). 1962. 16.95 (ISBN 0-698-10219-3, Coward). Putnam Pub Group.

Greene, Laura. Help: Getting to Know about Needing & Giving. Mayo, Gretchen, illus. LC 80-81082. 32p. (ps-3). 1981. 16.95 (ISBN 0-87705-402-9). Human Sci Pr.

Hallman, Ruth. Tough Is Not Enough. LC 81-11490. (Illus.). 112p. (gr. 7-10). 1981. 9.95 (ISBN 0-664-32686-2, Westminster). Westminster John Knox.

Harte, Bret. The Outcasts of Poker Flat. Nuemeier, Marty, illus. 48p. (gr. 6 up). 1980. PLB 10.95s.p. (ISBN 0-87191-768-8); PLB 15.65 (ISBN 0-685-01264-6). Creative Ed.

Houston, James. Frozen Fire: A Tale of Courage. Houston, James, illus. LC 77-6366. 160p. (gr. 7 up). 1977. 13.95 (ISBN 0-689-50083-1, M K McElderry). Macmillan Child Grp.

Mazer, Harry. The Island Keeper: A Tale of Courage & Survival. LC 80-39762. 192p. (gr. 7 up). 1981. pap. 11.95 (ISBN 0-385-28446-2). Delacorte.

—Snow Bound. 144p. (gr. 5 up). 1975. pap. 3.25 (ISBN 0-440-96134-3, LFL). Dell.

Moeri, Louise. Save Queen of Sheba. LC 80-23019. (gr. 4-7). 1981. 14.95 (ISBN 0-525-33202-2, DCB). Dutton Child Bks.

Morey, Walt. Canyon Winter. (gr. 4 up). 1972. 15.95 (ISBN 0-525-27410-3, DCB). Dutton Child Bks.

Paulsen, Gary. Hatchet. large type ed. 232p. 1989. Repr. of 1987 ed. PLB 15.95 (ISBN 1-55736-117-7, Crnrstn Bks). ABC-CLIO.

Phleger, Marjorie. Pilot Down, Presumed Dead. LC 63-16244. 224p. (gr. 5-9). 1975. pap. 3.95 (ISBN 0-06-440067-0, Trophy). HarpC Child Bks.

Robinson Crusoe. (gr. 4 up). 1988. pap. 4.87 (ISBN 0-582-54156-5, 74263). Longman.

Robinson Crusoe. (Illus.). (gr. 1). 3.50 (ISBN 0-7214-5123-3). Ladybird Bks.

Sutherland, Robert D. Sticklewort & Feverfew. LC 79-92898. (Illus.). 360p. (gr. 2 up). 1980. 16.00 (ISBN 0-936044-00-4); pap. 9.00 (ISBN 0-936044-01-2). Pikestaff Pr.

Taylor, Theodore. Cay. LC 69-15161. 160p. (gr. 6-9). 1987. pap. 13.95 (ISBN 0-385-07906-0). Doubleday.

Thompson, Julian F. A Question of Survival. 320p. (gr. 8 up). 1984. pap. 2.50 (ISBN 0-380-87775-9, 87775-9, Flare). Avon.

Treece, Henry. Further Adventures of Robinson Crusoe. Nickless, Will, illus. LC 58-9623. (gr. 7-11). 1958. 18.95 (ISBN 0-87599-116-5). S G Phillips.

Wyss, Johann. Swiss Family Robinson. (gr. 5 up). 1964. pap. 2.95 (ISBN 0-8049-0013-2, CL-13). Airmont.

—The Swiss Family Robinson. James, Raymond, ed. Beier, Ellen, illus. LC 89-33888. 48p. (gr. 3-6). 1990. lib. bdg. 12.89 (ISBN 0-8167-1875-X); pap. text ed. 3.95 (ISBN 0-8167-1876-8). Troll Assocs.

SUSPENSION BRIDGES

see Bridges

SWALLOWS–FICTION

Politi, Leo. Song of the Swallows. Politi, Leo, illus. 32p. (gr. k-3). 1987. pap. 4.95 (ISBN 0-689-71140-9, Aladdin). Macmillan Child Grp.

—Song of the Swallows. 1987. 13.95 (ISBN 0-684-18831-7, Scribners Young Read). Macmillan Child Grp.

SWAMPS

see Marshes

SWANS

Braithwaite, Althea. Swans. (ps-6). 1988. PLB 7.95 (ISBN 0-88462-194-4); pap. 2.95 (ISBN 0-88462-195-2). Dearborn Finan.

Coldrey, Jennifer. The Swan on the Lake. LC 86-5719. (Illus.). 32p. (gr. 4-6). 1987. 10.95 (ISBN 1-55532-066-X). Gareth Stevens Inc.

—The World of Swans. LC 86-5721. (Illus.). 32p. (gr. 2-3). 1987. 10.95 (ISBN 1-55532-070-8). Gareth Stevens Inc.

Featherly, Jay. Ko-hoh: The Call of the Trumpeter Swan. (Illus.). 48p. (gr. 2-5). 1986. lib. bdg. 12.95 (ISBN 0-87614-288-9). Carolrhoda Bks.

Hogan, Paula Z. The Black Swan. Hockerman, Dennis, illus. LC 78-27416. 32p. (gr. 1-4). 1979. PLB 16.67 (ISBN 0-8172-1254-X). Raintree Pubs.

—The Black Swan. LC 78-27416. (Illus.). 32p. (gr. 1-4). 1984. PLB 27.99 incl. cassette (ISBN 0-8172-2225-1); cassette 14.00 (ISBN 0-685-09514-2). Raintree Pubs.

Horton, Tom. Swanfall: Journey of the Tundra Swans. Harp, Dave, photos by. (Illus.). 48p. (gr. 1-3). 1991. 14.95 (ISBN 0-8027-8106-3); PLB 15.85. Walker & Co.

Rothaus, Jim. Ducks, Geese, & Swans. 24p. (gr. 3). 1988. 17.10 (ISBN 0-88682-224-6); PLB 11.95s.p. (ISBN 0-318-37905-8). Creative Ed.

Scott, Jack D. Swans. Sweet, Ozzie, photos by. (Illus.). 64p. (gr. 5 up). 1988. 13.95 (ISBN 0-399-21406-2, Putnam). Putnam Pub Group.

Selsam, Millicent E. & Hunt, Joyce. A First Look at Ducks, Geese & Swans. Springer, Harriet, illus. 32p. (gr. 1-4). 1990. 11.95 (ISBN 0-8027-6975-6); lib. bdg. 12.85 (ISBN 0-8027-6976-4). Walker & Co.

Smock, Jerri. The Swan: A Storybook for Adults & Other Children. Poppler, Susan, illus. 21p. (gr. 7 up). 1989. incl. cassette 13.95g (ISBN 0-944586-00-7). WIN Pub.

THE SWAN: A STORYBOOK FOR ADULTS & OTHER CHILDREN is a four color fairytale book with accompanying seven minute cassette. It is a teaching tool for therapists, school teachers & families to learn about commitment, separation & individuality. It is a metaphor of two swans on puddle pond who meet & fall in love. Thomas the Toad narrates the love story with other characters such as Bucky Beaver & the guppy fish sharing their thoughts & ideas about Crystal, the female swan & her love for the male swan, & for herself. In the back of the book are questions & activities for therapy groups, classes & families to work together on & to learn about each other & their own strengths in living their lives, separately & collectively. The illustrations are beautifully done & the tape recorded voices weave a magical story of symbols & meaningful messages.
Publisher Provided Annotation.

SWANS–FICTION

Andersen, Hans Christian. The Ugly Duckling. Ross, Katharine, adapted by. Oberdieck, Bernhard, illus. LC 90-34336. 24p. (Orig.). (ps-2). 1991. pap. 2.25 (ISBN 0-685-38460-8). Random.

—The Wild Swans. Jeffers, Susan, illus. Ehrlich, Amy, retold by. LC 81-65843. (Illus.). 40p. (gr. k up). 1981. 14.95 (ISBN 0-8037-9381-2); PLB 12.89 (ISBN 0-8037-9391-X). Dial Bks Young.

—The Wild Swans. (Illus.). 44p. (gr. 1-4). 1986. 7.95 (ISBN 0-8120-5711-2); Creative Character Building ed. 7.95 (ISBN 0-8120-5719-8). Barron.

—Wild Swans. Jeffers, Susan, illus. LC 81-65843. 40p. (gr. k up). 1987. pap. 4.95 (ISBN 0-8037-0451-8). Dial Bks Young.

Canfield, Jane W. Swan Cove. Polseno, Jo, illus. LC 77-11832. 32p. (ps-3). 1978. 7.64i (ISBN 0-06-020948-8). HarpC Child Bks.

Clement, Claude. Painter & the Wild Swans. LC 86-2154. (gr. k up). 1990. pap. 4.95 (ISBN 0-8037-0840-8). Dial Bks Young.

Lasky, Kathryn. Sea Swan. Stock, Catherine, illus. LC 88-1444. 32p. (gr. k-3). 1988. 13.95 (ISBN 0-02-751700-4, Mcmillan Child Bk). Macmillan Child Grp.

Wellington, Monica. Seasons of Swans. (ps). 1990. 12.95 (ISBN 0-525-44621-4, DCB). Dutton Child Bks.

White, E. B. E. B. White Boxed Set. Incl. Charlotte's Web; The Trumpet of the Swan; Stuart Little. (Illus.). (gr. 3 up). 27.60i (ISBN 0-686-77171-0). HarpC Child Bks.

—E. B. White Boxed Set. Incl. Charlotte's Web; The Trumpet of the Swan; Stuart Little. (Illus.). (gr. 3 up). 1974. pap. 10.50 (ISBN 0-06-440061-1, Trophy). HarpC Child Bks.

—Trumpet of the Swan. Frascino, Edward, illus. LC 72-112484. (gr. 3-6). 1970. 10.95 (ISBN 0-06-026397-0); PLB 11.89 (ISBN 0-06-026398-9). HarpC Child Bks.

—The Trumpet of the Swan. Frascino, Edward, illus. LC 72-112484. 222p. (gr. 3 up). 1973. pap. 3.50 (ISBN 0-06-440048-4, Trophy). HarpC Child Bks.

Willard, Barbara. A Flight of Swans. (gr. k up). 1989. pap. 3.25 (ISBN 0-440-20458-5, LFL). Dell.

SWEDEN

Keeler, Stephan & Fairclough, Chris. We Live in Sweden. (Illus.). 64p. (gr. k up). 1984. PLB 9.49 (ISBN 0-531-03833-5). Watts.

Lye, Keith. Take a Trip to Sweden. (Illus.). 32p. (gr. k-3). 1983. PLB 7.99 (ISBN 0-531-03760-6). Watts.

Zickgraf, Ralph. Sweden. (Illus.). 96p. (gr. 5 up). 1988. lib. bdg. 14.95 (ISBN 1-55546-797-0). Chelsea Hse.

SWEDEN–FICTION

Beskow, Elsa. Pelle's New Suit. Beskow, Elsa, illus. 16p. (ps-1). 1929. PLB 13.89 (ISBN 0-06-020496-6). HarpC Child Bks.

Lindgren, Astrid. Pippi Goes on Board. Glanzman, Louis S., illus. (gr. 4-6). 1957. pap. 12.95 (ISBN 0-670-55677-7). Viking Child Bks.

—Pippi in the South Seas. Bothmer, Gerry, tr. Glanzman, Louis S., illus. (gr. 4-6). 1959. pap. 11.95 (ISBN 0-670-55711-0). Viking Child Bks.

—Pippi Longstocking. Lamborn, Florence, tr. Glanzman, Louis S., illus. (gr. 4-6). 1950. pap. 11.95 (ISBN 0-670-55745-5). Viking Child Bks.

—The Tomten. Wiberg, Harald, illus. LC 61-10658. (gr. 1-3). 1979. 8.95 (ISBN 0-698-20147-7, Coward); (Coward); pap. 6.95 (ISBN 0-698-20487-5, Coward). Putnam Pub Group.

Nilsson, Ulf. If You Didn't Have Me. Eriksson, Eva, illus. Blecher, Lone T. & Blecher, George, trs. LC 86-21327. (Illus.). 128p. (gr. 2-5). 1987. 11.95 (ISBN 0-689-50406-3, M K McElderry). Macmillan Child Grp.

SWEDES IN THE U. S.

Hillbrand, Percie V. The Swedes in America. LC 66-10152. (Illus.). 84p. (gr. 5 up). 1966. PLB 11.95 (ISBN 0-8225-0201-1); pap. 3.95 (ISBN 0-8225-1023-5). Lerner Pubns.

McGill, Allyson. The Swedish Americans. Moynihan, Daniel P., intro. by. (Illus.). 112p. (gr. 5 up). 1988. lib. bdg. 17.95 (ISBN 1-55546-135-2). Chelsea Hse.

SWIMMING

see also Diving

Bailey, Donna. Swimming. LC 90-36527. (Illus.). 32p. (gr. 1-4). 1990. PLB 14.64 (ISBN 0-8114-2852-4). Steck-V.

Berridge, Celia. Going Swimming. Berridge, Celia, illus. LC 86-31591. 24p. (ps). 1987. 3.95 (ISBN 0-394-89165-1, Random Juv); lib. bdg. 7.99 (ISBN 0-394-99165-6). Random.

Carson, Charles. Make the Team: Swimming & Diving. (gr. 4-7). 1991. pap. 5.95 (ISBN 0-316-13028-1). Little.

Chiefari, Janet & Wightman, Nancy. Better Synchronized Swimming for Boys & Girls. (Illus.). 64p. (gr. 3-7). 1981. 9.95 (ISBN 0-396-07995-4, Putnam). Putnam Pub Group.

Fischel, E. Swimming & Diving Skills. (Illus.). 48p. (gr. 6-12). 1989. lib. bdg. 12.96 (ISBN 0-88110-395-0, Usborne); pap. 5.95 (ISBN 0-7460-0171-1). EDC.

Gutman, Bill. Go for It: Swimming. Brown, Ben, illus. 64p. (gr. 3-7). 1989. PLB 16.50 (ISBN 0-942545-89-3). Grey Castle.

Henning, Jean M. Six Days to Swim-Jeff Farrell: A Story of Olympic Courage. Daland, P., intro. by. LC 71-103031. (Illus.). (gr. 6-12). 1970. 3.50 (ISBN 0-911822-02-X). Swimming.

Kolbisen, Irene M. Froggie Kicks & Duck Dives: A Child's Primer for Beginning Swimming. Reiter, John, ed. Zmolek, Sandy D., illus. Graves, Steve, intro. by. (Illus.). (ps). 1990. 12.95 (ISBN 1-877863-02-5); pap. 8.95 (ISBN 0-685-26751-2). I Think I Can.

—Starfish Floats & Motorboats: A Child's Primer for Beginning Swimming. Reiter, John, ed. Zmolek, Sandy D., illus. Graves, Steve, intro. by. (Illus.). 20p. (ps). 1990. 12.95g (ISBN 1-877863-01-7); pap. 8.95g (ISBN 0-685-26750-4). I Think I Can.

—Wiggle-Butts & Up-Faces: A Child's Primer for Beginning Swimming. Reiter, John, ed. Zmolek, Sandy D., illus. Graves, Steve, intro. by. (Illus.). 32p. (ps). 1989. PLB 14.95 (ISBN 1-877863-00-9). I Think I Can.

Noble, Jim. Swimming. (Illus.). 32p. (gr. k-4). 1991. RLB 11.40 (ISBN 0-531-18466-8, Pub. by Boatwright Pr). Watts.

Orr, C. Rob & Tyler, Jane B. Swimming Basics. Gow, Bill, illus. 48p. 1984. pap. 4.95 (ISBN 0-13-879594-0). P-H.

Sanborn, Laura & Eberhardt, Lorraine. Swim Free. Jones, Shari, illus. 32p. (gr. 6-12). 1982. pap. 6.95x (ISBN 0-910715-00-9). Search Public.

Sullivan, George. Better Swimming for Boys & Girls. (Illus.). 64p. (gr. 3-7). 1982. 9.95 (ISBN 0-396-08071-5, Putnam); (Putnam). Putnam Pub Group.

Winter, Ginny L. Swimming Book. Winter, Ginny L., illus. (gr. k-3). 1964. 8.95 (ISBN 0-8392-3037-0). Astor-Honor.

YMCA of the U. S. A. Staff. Splash: YMCA Progressive Swimming. Barrett, Jerry, illus. (Orig.). (gr. 1-5). 1986. pap. text ed. 5.00x (ISBN 0-87322-058-7, LYMC4733). Human Kinetics.

SWIMMING–FICTION

Brown, M. K. Let's go Swimming with Mr. Sillypants. Brown, M. K., illus. (ps-1). 1986. PLB 9.95 (ISBN 0-517-56185-9). Crown.

Byars, Betsy. The Night Swimmers. Howell, Troy, illus. 144p. (gr. 5-9). 1983. pap. 3.25 (ISBN 0-440-45857-9, YB). Dell.

—Night Swimmers. large type ed. 1990. Repr. PLB 15.95 (ISBN 1-55736-177-0, Crnrstn Bks). ABC-CLIO.

Cousins, Lucy. Maisy Goes Swimming. (ps). 1990. 10.95 (ISBN 0-316-15834-8). Little.

Cowley, Joy. Let's Have a Swim. Van der Voo, Jan, illus. 16p. (gr. k-2). 1989. pap. text ed. 23.00 (ISBN 1-55911-289-1). Wright Group.

—Let's Have a Swim, 6 bks. Van der Voo, Jan, illus. 16p. (gr. k-2). 1986. Set. pap. text ed. 19.80 (ISBN 1-55911-359-6). Wright Group.

Crutcher, Chris. Stotan! LC 85-12712. 192p. (gr. 7 up). 1986. reinforced trade ed. 10.25 (ISBN 0-688-05715-2). Greenwillow.

Day, Alexandra. River Parade. (Illus.). 32p. (ps-2). 1990. pap. 12.95 (ISBN 0-670-82946-3). Viking Child Bks.

Fraser, Sheila. I Can Swim. Kopper, Lisa, illus. 24p. (ps-3). 1991. 5.95 (ISBN 0-8120-6226-4). Barron.

George, Lindsay B. William & Boomer. George, Lindsay B., illus. LC 86-9789. 24p. (ps-1). 1987. 12.95 (ISBN 0-688-06640-2); PLB 12.88 (ISBN 0-688-06641-0). Greenwillow.

Godfrey, Jan. Me at the Swimming Pool. (ps-3). 1989. pap. 1.95 (ISBN 0-7459-1734-8). Lion USA.

Jenkins, Jerry. The Strange Swimming Coach. (Orig.). (gr. 9-12). 1986. pap. text ed. 3.95 (ISBN 0-8024-8238-4). Moody.

Kessler, Leonard. Last One in Is a Rotten Egg. Kessler, Leonard, illus. LC 69-10209. 64p. (gr. k-3). 1969. PLB 11.89 (ISBN 0-06-023158-0). HarpC Child Bks.

—Last One in Is a Rotten Egg. Kessler, Leonard, illus. LC 69-10209. 64p. (gr. k-3). 1989. pap. 3.50 (ISBN 0-06-444118-0, Trophy). HarpC Child Bks.

Klein, Robin. Boss of the Pool. Geraghty, Paul, illus. (gr. 3-7). 1988. 11.95 (ISBN 0-317-69308-5). Viking Penguin.

Korman, Gordon. Go Jump in the Pool! 192p. (gr. 4-6). 1991. pap. 2.75 (ISBN 0-590-44209-0, Apple Paperbacks). Scholastic Inc.

Larsen, Rebecca. Slow As a Panda. LC 85-25431. 136p. (gr. 5 up). 1986. PLB 9.95 (ISBN 0-87518-327-1, Dillon). Macmillan Child Grp.

Makris, Kathryn. A Different Way. 192p. 1989. pap. 2.95 (ISBN 0-380-75728-1, Flare). Avon.

Miles, Betty. Sink or Swim. Soileau, Hodges, illus. LC 85-23134. 198p. (gr. 5-9). 1986. 11.95 (ISBN 0-394-85515-9). Knopf.

—Sink or Swim. 208p. (gr. 3-7). 1987. pap. 2.95 (ISBN 0-380-69913-3, Camelot). Avon.

Preston-Mauks, Susan. Synchronized Swimming Is For Me. Francetic, Karl D. & Sheehan-Burke, Julia, photos by. LC 82-17102. (Illus.). 48p. (gr. 2-5). 1983. PLB 8.95 (ISBN 0-8225-1139-8). Lerner Pubns.

Strub, Susanne. Lulu Goes Swimming. (ps). 1990. 8.95 (ISBN 0-670-83460-2). Viking Child Bks.

SWINE

see Hogs

SWING MUSIC

see Jazz Music

SWITZERLAND

Hintz, Martin. Switzerland. LC 86-9581. (Illus.). 128p. (gr. 5-9). 1986. PLB 25.27 (ISBN 0-516-02790-5). Childrens.

Jacobsen, Peter & Kristensen, Preben. A Family in Switzerland. LC 84-73578. 32p. (gr. 7-9). 1985. s&l 11.90 (ISBN 0-531-18002-6, Pub. by Bookwright Pr). Watts.

Lye, Keith. Take a Trip to Switzerland. 32p. (gr. k-7). 1984. lib. bdg. 7.99 (ISBN 0-531-04874-8). Watts.

Moore, James. Switzerland. (Illus.). (gr. 5 up). 1988. 14.95 (ISBN 0-222-00812-1). Chelsea Hse.

Schrepfer, Margaret. Switzerland: The Summit of Europe. LC 88-35913. (Illus.). 144p. (gr. 5 up). 1989. lib. bdg. 14.95 (ISBN 0-87518-405-7, Dillon). Macmillan Child Grp.

SWITZERLAND–FICTION

Heidi. (Illus.). (gr. 1). 3.50 (ISBN 0-7214-5169-1). Ladybird Bks.

Heidi. (Illus.). (gr. 3-5). 1990. 3.50 (ISBN 0-7214-1210-6). Ladybird Bks.

Spyri, Johanna. Heidi. LC 85-13292. (gr. 5 up). 1964. pap. 1.95 (ISBN 0-8049-0018-3, CL-18). Airmont.

—Heidi. LC 85-13292. (Illus.). (gr. 4-6). 1988. pap. 2.95 (ISBN 0-590-42046-1). Scholastic Inc.

—Heidi. LC 85-13292. 240p. (gr. 3-7). 1983. pap. 2.25 (ISBN 0-14-035002-0, Puffin). Puffin Bks.

SYMBIOSIS

see Botany–Ecology

SYMBOLISM

see also Christian Art and Symbolism; Heraldry

Barth, Edna. Lilies, Rabbits, & Painted Eggs: The Story of the Easter Symbols. Arndt, Ursula, illus. LC 74-79033. (gr. 3-6). 1979. 13.95 (ISBN 0-395-28844-4, Clarion); pap. 4.95 (ISBN 0-395-30550-0, Clarion). HM.

Fisher, Leonard E. Symbol Art: Thirteen Squares, Circles & Triangles from Around the World. Fisher, Leonard E., illus. LC 85-42805. 64p. (gr. 4-6). 1986. 14.95 (ISBN 0-02-735270-6, Four Winds). Macmillan Child Grp.

SYMBOLISM OF NUMBERS

Dodge, Ellin. Numerology for Children. Mackler, Carole B., ed. (Illus.). 48p. 1989. text ed. 12.95 (ISBN 0-317-94102-X). SSGI Pr.

SYNAGOGUES

Freeman, Grace & Sugarman, Joan. Inside the Synagogue. rev. ed. Mass, Ronald, photos by. (Illus.). 64p. (gr. 1-3). 1984. pap. 6.00 (ISBN 0-8074-0268-0, 301785). UAHC.

Levin, Meyer & Kurzband, Toby. Story of the Synagogue. LC 57-13093. (gr. 4-6). 1957. pap. 6.95x (ISBN 0-87441-006-1); activity bk. 3.50 (ISBN 0-87441-007-X). Behrman.

Rosenblum, Richard. The Old Synagogue. Rosenbloom, Roger, illus. 32p. (gr. k-3). 1989. 12.95 (ISBN 0-8276-0322-3). JPS Phila.

Weisser, M. My Synagogue. Rosenblum, R., illus. 25p. (gr. k-5). 1984. pap. text ed. 4.25 (ISBN 0-87441-386-9). Behrman.

SYNTHETIC PRODUCTS

see also Plastics

also names of snythetic products, e.g. Rubber, Artificial; etc.

SYRIA

Beaton, Margaret. Syria. LC 88-18697. (Illus.). 128p. (gr. 5-9). 1988. PLB 25.27 (ISBN 0-516-02708-5). Childrens.

Lerner Publications, Department of Geography Staff. Syria in Pictures. (Illus.). 64p. (gr. 5 up). 1990. lib. bdg. 12.95 (ISBN 0-8225-1867-8). Lerner Pubns.

Mulloy, Martin. Syria. (Illus.). (gr. 5 up). 1988. 14.95 (ISBN 0-7910-0095-8). Chelsea Hse.

Patterson, Charles. Hafez Al-Asad. (Illus.). 128p. (gr. 8 up). 1991. lib. bdg. 13.98 (ISBN 0-671-69468-5); pap. 7.95 (ISBN 0-671-69469-3). Messner.

SYSTEMS ENGINEERING

see also Bionics

T

T V

see Television

TABLE

Giblin, James C. From Hand to Mouth: Or, How We Invented Knives, Forks, Spoons, & Chopsticks, & the Table Manners To Go with Them. LC 86-29341. (Illus.). 96p. (gr. 3-7). 1987. 12.95 (ISBN 0-690-04660-X, Crowell Jr Bks); PLB 12.89 (ISBN 0-690-04662-6, Crowell Jr Bks). HarpC Child Bks.

TADPOLES

see Frogs

TAFT, WILLIAM HOWARD, PRESIDENT U. S. 1857-1930

Casey, Jane C. William Howard Taft. LC 88-8675. (Illus.). 100p. (gr. 3 up). 1989. PLB 17.27 (ISBN 0-516-01366-1). Childrens.

Falkof, Lucille. William H. Taft: Twenty-Seventh President of the United States. Young, Richard G., ed. LC 89-39947. (Illus.). 128p. (gr. 5-9). 1990. PLB 17.26 (ISBN 0-944483-56-9). Garrett Ed Corp.

TAHITI–FICTION

Fremantle, Anne. Island of Cats. Sapieha, Christine, illus. (gr. 1-4). 1964. 12.95 (ISBN 0-8392-3011-7). Astor-Honor.

TAILORING

Here are entered works on the cutting and making of men's, or men's and women's clothing. Works limited to the cutting and making of women's clothes are entered under Dressmaking.

see also Dressmaking

TAILORS–FICTION
Grimm, Jacob & Grimm, Wilhelm K. The Brave Little Tailor: A Classic Tale. Jose, Eduard, adapted by. Moncure, Jane B., tr. from SPA. Rovira, Francesc, illus. LC 88-35311. 32p. (gr. 1-4). 1988. PLB 10.95 (ISBN 0-89565-460-1). Childs World.
Littledale, Freya. Brave Little Tailor. 1990. pap. 2.50 (ISBN 0-590-42797-0). Scholastic Inc.
Potter, Beatrix. Tailor of Gloucester. (Illus.). (ps). 1991. pap. 1.99 (ISBN 0-7232-3767-0). Warne.
—The Tale of the Tailor of Gloucester. (Illus.). 64p. (ps-3). 1987. 3.95 (ISBN 0-671-63234-5, Little Simon). S&S Trade.
TAIWAN
see Formosa
TALES
see Fables; Fairy Tales; Folklore; Legends
TALKING
see Speech
TALL TALES
see American Wit and Humor; Folklore; Legends
TANKS (MILITARY SCIENCE)
Barrett, Norman. Tanques. (SPA., Illus.). 32p. (gr. k-4). 1991. PLB 11.40 (ISBN 0-531-07922-8). Watts.
Cave, Ron & Cave, Joyce. What about... Tanks. West, David, illus. 32p. (gr. k-3). 1983. PLB 10.90 (ISBN 0-531-03470-4). Watts.
Hogg, Ian. Tanks & Armored Vehicles. 48p. (gr. 6). 1984. PLB 12.90 (ISBN 0-531-04868-3). Watts.
Hogg, Ian V. Tanks. Sarson, Peter & Bryan, Tony, illus. LC 84-9650. 48p. (gr. 5 up). 1985. PLB 9.95 (ISBN 0-8225-1378-1, First Ave Edns); pap. 4.95 (ISBN 0-8225-9507-9, First Ave Edns). Lerner Pubns.
Jay, Michael. Tanks. (Illus.). 32p. (gr. k-3). 1987. PLB 7.99 (ISBN 0-531-10279-3). Watts.
Jefferis, David. Battle Kings: The History of Tanks. (Illus.). 32p. (gr. 5-8). 1991. PLB 11.90 (ISBN 0-531-14193-4). Watts.
Nicholaus, J. Main Battle Tanks. (Illus.). 48p. (gr. 3-8). 1989. lib. bdg. 18.60 (ISBN 0-86592-420-1). Rourke Corp.
Norman, C. J. Tanks. (Illus.). 32p. (gr. 2 up). 1991. pap. 3.95 (ISBN 0-531-15145-X). Watts.
Stephen, R. J. Picture World of Tanks. 1990. PLB 11.40 (ISBN 0-531-14012-1). Watts.
TANZANIA
Aardema, Verna. Bimwili & the Zimwi. Meddaugh, Susan, illus. LC 85-4449. 32p. (ps-3). 1985. 12.95 (ISBN 0-8037-0212-4); PLB 12.89 (ISBN 0-8037-0213-2). Dial Bks Young.
Department of Geography, Lerner Publications. Tanzania in Pictures. (Illus.). 64p. (gr. 5 up). 1988. PLB 12.95 (ISBN 0-8225-1838-4). Lerner Pubns.
McCulla, Patricia E. Tanzania. (Illus.). 96p. (gr. 5 up). 1989. lib. bdg. 14.95 (ISBN 1-55546-784-9). Chelsea Hse.
Margolies, Barbara A. Rehema's Journey: A Visit in Tanzania. (gr. 4-7). 1990. 13.95 (ISBN 0-590-42846-2). Scholastic Inc.
TAPESTRY
Denny, Norman & Filmer-Sankey, Josephine. The Bayeux Tapestry: The Norman Conquest 1066. (Illus.). 68p. (gr. 6 up). 1988. 14.95 (ISBN 0-318-33335-X). Parkwest Pubns.
TARBELL, IDA, 1857-1944
Paradis, Adrian A. Ida M. Tarbell: Pioneer Woman Journalist & Biographer. LC 85-16586. (Illus.). 120p. (gr. 5-8). 1985. PLB 17.27 (ISBN 0-516-03217-8). Childrens.
TARKENTON, FRAN, 1940
Hahn, James & Hahn, Lynn. Tark! The Sports Career of Francis Tarkenton. LC 80-28881. (Illus.). 48p. (gr. 3-5). 1981. PLB 8.95 (ISBN 0-89686-121-X, Crestwood Hse). Macmillan Child Grp.
TAVERNS
see Restaurants, Bars, etc.
TAXATION–U. S.
Larsen, Kent P. The Angry Taxpayer's Tax Book. 144p. (Orig.). 1989. pap. 14.95 (ISBN 0-685-27246-X). K P Larsen Inc.
Lubov, Andrea. Taxes & Government Spending. (Illus.). 88p. (gr. 5 up). 1990. 15.95 (ISBN 0-8225-1777-9). Lerner Pubns.
TAXIDERMY
see also Zoological Specimens–Collection and Preservation
TAYLOR, ZACHARY, PRESIDENT U.S. 1784-1850
Collins, David R. Zachary Taylor: Twelfth President of the United States. Young, Richard G., ed. LC 88-24539. (Illus.). (gr. 5-9). 1989. PLB 17.26 (ISBN 0-944483-17-8). Garrett Ed Corp.
TCHAIKOVSKY, PETER ILYICH, 1840-1893
Clark, Elizabeth. Tchaikovsky. Caulkins, Janet, ed. (Illus.). 32p. (gr. 1-6). 1988. PLB 11.90 (ISBN 0-531-18245-2, Pub. by Bookwright Pr). Watts.
Tames, Richard. Peter Ilyich Tchaikovsky. (Illus.). 32p. (gr. 5-8). 1991. PLB 11.90 (ISBN 0-531-14108-X). Watts.
TEA ROOMS
see Restaurants, Bars, etc.
TEACHERS
see also Educators; Teaching
Anderson, William T. A Wilder in the West: Eliza Jane's Story of a Lady Homesteader. (Illus.). 44p. (gr. 8 up). 1985. pap. 3.95 (ISBN 0-9610088-4-9). Anderson MI.
Beckman, Beatrice. I Can Be a Teacher. LC 84-23236. (Illus.). 32p. (gr. k-3). 1985. lib. bdg. 13.93 (ISBN 0-516-01843-4); pap. 3.95 (ISBN 0-516-41843-2). Childrens.
Bergreen, Gary. Coping with Difficult Teachers. Rosen, Roger, ed. LC 88-20107. (gr. 7 up). 1988. lib. bdg. 12.95 (ISBN 0-8239-0788-0). Rosen Group.
Braithwaite, E. R. To Sir, with Love. (gr. 9-12). 1973. pap. 2.95 (ISBN 0-515-09031-X). Jove Pubns.
Daniel, Kira. Teacher. Paterson, Diane, illus. LC 88-10041. 32p. (gr. k-2). 1988. PLB 10.89 (ISBN 0-8167-1430-4); pap. text ed. 2.50 (ISBN 0-8167-1431-2). Troll Assocs.
Johnson, Jean. Teachers: A to Z. (Illus.). (gr. 1-3). 1987. 11.95 (ISBN 0-8027-6676-5); PLB 12.85 (ISBN 0-8027-6677-3). Walker & Co.
Neimark, Anne E. A Deaf Child Listened: Thomas Gallaudet, Pioneer in American Education. LC 82-23942. 160p. (gr. 7up). 1983. 11.95 (ISBN 0-688-01719-3). Morrow Jr Bks.
Rich, Beverly. Louis Braille: Inventor of a Way to Read & Write That Has Helped Millions of Blind People Communicate with the World. LC 89-4275. (Illus.). 64p. (gr. 5-6). 1989. PLB 12.95 (ISBN 0-8368-0097-4). Gareth Stevens Inc.
TEACHERS–FICTION
Allard, Harry & Marshall, James. Miss Nelson Is Missing! Marshall, James, illus. (gr. k-3). 1985. reinforced bdg. 13.95 (ISBN 0-395-25296-2); pap. 3.95 (ISBN 0-395-40146-1). HM.
Arter, Jim. Gruel & Unusual Punishment. (gr. 3-7). 1991. 13.95 (ISBN 0-385-30298-3). Delacorte.
Brown, Marc. Arthur's Teacher Trouble. Brown, Marc, illus. 32p. (ps-3). 1989. 13.95 (ISBN 0-316-11244-5, Joy St Bks); pap. 4.95 (ISBN 0-316-11186-4, Joy St Bks). Little.
Chardiet, Bernice. Best Teacher in the World. (ps-3). 1990. 11.95 (ISBN 0-590-44108-6, Scholastic Hardcover). Scholastic Inc.
Cohen, Miriam. The New Teacher. (Illus.). 32p. (ps-k). 1974. pap. 3.95 (ISBN 0-02-042390-X, Aladdin Bks). Macmillan Child Grp.
Cooper, Ilene. The Winning of Miss Lynn Ryan. Magurn, Susan, illus. 128p. (gr. 3-7). 1989. pap. 3.95 (ISBN 0-14-032755-X, Puffin). Puffin Bks.
Coville, Bruce. My Teacher Is an Alien. (Orig.). (gr. 3-6). 1989. pap. 2.75 (ISBN 0-671-64748-2, Minstrel Bks). PB.
Cusick, Richie T. Teacher's Pet. 224p. (Orig.). (gr. 8-12). 1990. pap. 2.95 (ISBN 0-590-43114-5). Scholastic Inc.
Edwards, Sally. George Midgett's War. LC 85-1954. 144p. (gr. 5-7). 1985. 12.95 (ISBN 0-684-18315-3, Scribners Young Read). Macmillan Child Grp.
Feder, Paula K. Where Does the Teacher Live? Hoban, Lillian, illus. LC 78-13157. (gr. k-3). 1979. 12.95 (ISBN 0-525-42586-1, DCB). Dutton Child Bks.
Hallinan, P. K. My Teacher's My Friend. (Illus.). 24p. (ps-3). 1989. pap. 3.95 (ISBN 0-8249-8392-0). Ideals.
—My Teacher's My Friend. Hallinan, P. K., illus. LC 90-2153. 32p. (ps-3). 1990. PLB 13.27 (ISBN 0-516-09217-0). Childrens.
Hilton, James. Goodbye, Mr. Chips. (gr. 7 up). 1969. pap. 2.95 (ISBN 0-553-25613-0). Bantam.
Howe, James. The Day the Teacher Went Bananas. Hoban, Lillian, illus. LC 84-1536. 32p. (ps-2). 1987. 12.95 (ISBN 0-525-44107-7, DCB); pap. 3.95 (ISBN 0-525-44321-5, DCB). Dutton Child Bks.
Hurwitz, Johanna. Teacher's Pet. Hamamaka, Sheila, illus. LC 87-24003. 128p. (gr. 2-5). 1988. 12.95 (ISBN 0-688-07506-1). Morrow Jr Bks.
Legend of Sleepy Hollow. 1991. pap. 7.00 (ISBN 0-385-41929-5). Doubleday.
McKee, Craig & Holland, Margaret. The Teacher Who Could Not Count. Romney, Steve, illus. 24p. (ps-3). 1986. 1.95 (ISBN 0-685-40026-3, 12-07112-9). Willowisp Pr.
Mallett, Jerry & Bartch, Marian. Close the Curtains. Smith, Mark D., illus. 54p. (gr. 2-5). 1986. PLB 7.05 (ISBN 0-8479-9927-0, 056115). Perma Bound.
Nastick, Sharon. Mr. Radagast Makes an Unexpected Journey. Glasser, Judy, illus. LC 80-8107. 96p. (gr. 3-7). 1981. (Crowell Jr Bks). HarpC Child Bks.
Oppenheim, Joanne. Mrs. Peloki's Class Play. (Illus.). 32p. (ps-3). 1983. 10.95 (ISBN 0-396-08178-9, Putnam). Putnam Pub Group.
—Mrs. Peloki's Substitute. Zarins, Joyce A., illus. 32p. (ps-3). 1987. 12.95 (ISBN 0-396-08918-6, Putnam). Putnam Pub Group.
Parish, Peggy. Teach Us, Amelia Bedelia. Sweat, Lynn, illus. 64p. (gr. k-3). 1987. pap. 2.75 (ISBN 0-590-43345-8). Scholastic Inc.
Pascal, Francine. The Substitute Teacher. (gr. k-3). 1990. pap. 2.75 (ISBN 0-553-15760-4, Skylark). Bantam.
Richardson, Arleta. Eighteen & on Her Own. LC 85-29050. 173p. (gr. 4 up). 1986. pap. 3.95 (ISBN 0-89191-512-5). Cook.
Schick, Eleanor. Art Lessons. LC 86-243. (Illus.). 48p. (gr. k-3). 1987. 11.75 (ISBN 0-688-05120-0); lib. bdg. 11.88 (ISBN 0-688-05121-9). Greenwillow.
Slack, Thomas, ed. The Pleasing Instructor. Graham, Joanne, et al. 368p. 1973. Repr. of 1785 ed. 66.75 (ISBN 3-261-01008-8). P Lang Pubs.
Stretton, Barbara. The Truth of the Matter. LC 83-4305. 256p. (gr. 7-12). 1983. Knopf.
Thaler, Mike. Teacher from the Black Lagoon. 1989. pap. 2.50 (ISBN 0-590-41962-5). Scholastic Inc.
Weiss, Leatie. My Teacher Sleeps in School. 1986. pap. 13.95 (ISBN 0-670-81095-9). Viking Child Bks.
TEACHING
see also Child Study; Education; Kindergarten; Study, Method of
also subjects with the subdivision Study and Teaching, e.g. Science–Study and Teaching
Brisson, Lynn. Three-D Teaching Aids. (Illus.). 64p. (gr. k-6). 1989. pap. text ed. 6.95 (ISBN 0-86530-072-0, IP 166-2). Incentive Pubns.
Dickson, Sue. Complete Classroom Kit. rev. ed. Portadino, Norma, illus. 7968p. (gr. k-3). 1984. pap. 533.00 (ISBN 1-55574-000-6, KC 510). CBN Publishing.
Peterson, Sherrie. Help! for Substitutes. Schmid, Ross, illus. 80p. 1985. tchr's. wkbk. 5.95 (ISBN 0-86653-277-3, GA 642). Good Apple.
Rybak, Sharon. First-Year Teacher. 128p. (gr. k-6). 1991. 10.95 (ISBN 0-86653-620-5, GA1339). Good Apple.
—Good Apple Lesson Organizer. 128p. (gr. k-6). 1990. 19.95 (ISBN 0-86653-563-2, GA1149). Good Apple.
Stuart, Jesse. The Thread That Runs So True. 1977. lib. bdg. 30.00 (ISBN 0-684-15160-X, Scribner); pap. 8.95 (ISBN 0-684-71904-5, Scribner). Macmillan.
TEACHING–VOCATIONAL GUIDANCE
Shockley, Robert & Cutlip, Glen W. Careers in Teaching. rev. ed. 64p. (gr. 7-12). 1990. lib. bdg. 12.95 (ISBN 0-8239-1137-3). Rosen Group.
TEACHINGS OF JESUS
see Jesus Christ–Teachings
TEAROOMS
see Restaurants, Bars, etc.
TECHNOLOGY
see also Building; Engineering; Inventions; Machinery; Manufactures
Aaseng, Nathan. Better Mousetraps: Product Improvements That Led to Success. (Illus.). 80p. (gr. 5 up). 1989. PLB 13.95 (ISBN 0-8225-0680-7). Lerner Pubns.
Bender, David L. & Leone, Bruno, eds. Science & Technology Annual, 1989. 144p. (gr. 10 up). 1989. pap. text ed. 5.45 (ISBN 0-89908-552-0). Greenhaven.
Diamond, Bert. Technology You Can Build. (Illus.). 92p. (Orig.). 1990. pap. text ed. 12.95 (ISBN 0-87192-215-0). Davis Mass.
Fleisher, Paul & Keeler, Patricia. Looking Inside: Machines & Constructions. (Illus.). 40p. (gr. 2-7). 1991. RSBE 13.95 (ISBN 0-689-31483-3, Atheneum Child Bk). Macmillan Child Grp.
Folsom, Michael & Folsom, Marcia. The Macmillan Book of How Things Work. Hammann, Brad, illus. LC 86-23761. 80p. (gr. 3-7). 1987. 15.95 (ISBN 0-02-735360-5, Mcmillan Child Bk). Macmillan Child Grp.
—The Macmillan Book of How Things Work. Hammann, Brad, illus. 80p. (gr. 3-7). 1987. pap. 8.95 (ISBN 0-689-71139-5, Aladdin). Macmillan Child Grp.
Fuller, Melvin L. & Weisberg, Maggie. Student Inventors Lesson Plan. Christensen, Don, illus. 75p. (Orig.). (gr. 4-12). 1989. pap. 14.95x (ISBN 0-685-25993-5). M&M Assocs.
Hillman, Susan, et al. Future World. Smith, Guy, et al, illus. LC 89-42981. 48p. (gr. 4-5). 1989. PLB 11.95 (ISBN 0-8368-0135-0). Gareth Stevens Inc.
Iozzi, Louis A. & Bastardo, Peter J. Decisions for Today & Tomorrow. (gr. 9-12). 1990. tchr's. ed. 50.00 (ISBN 0-944584-22-5). Sopris.
Lee, Essie E. A Matter of Life & Technology. LC 86-18233. (Illus.). 128p. (gr. 5 up). 1986. lib. bdg. 12.98 (ISBN 0-671-49847-9). Messner.
Marsh, Richard S. Reading & Understanding Technical Information. (Illus.). (gr. 5). 1986. wkbk. 4.95 (ISBN 0-89525-758-0). Ed Activities.
Myring, L. & Graham, I. Information Revolution. Ashman, Iain, illus. 48p. (gr. 6 up). 1983. lib. bdg. 13.96 (ISBN 0-88110-153-2); pap. 6.95 (ISBN 0-86020-726-9). EDC.
Parker, Steve. The Random House Book of How Things Work. LC 90-9137. (Illus.). 160p. (Orig.). (gr. 3-7). 1991. PLB 19.99 (ISBN 0-679-90908-7); pap. 14.95 (ISBN 0-679-80908-2). Random.
Potter, T. & Guild, I. Robotics. Priddy, R., illus. 48p. (gr. 6 up). 1983. PLB 13.96 (ISBN 0-88110-152-4); pap. 6.95 (ISBN 0-86020-724-2). EDC.
Ross, Frank, Jr. Oracle Bones, Stars, & Wheelbarrows: Ancient Chinese Science & Technology. Goodman, Michael, illus. (gr. 7 up). 1982. 8.95 (ISBN 0-395-32083-6). HM.
Simon & Schuster Staff. How Things Work: A Guide to How Human-Made & Living Things Function. (Illus.). 128p. (gr. 3-7). 1988. pap. 7.95 (ISBN 0-671-67032-8). S&S Trade.
—Why Things Are: A Guide to Understanding the World Around Us. (Illus.). 128p. (gr. 3-7). 1988. pap. 7.95 (ISBN 0-671-67031-X). S&S Trade.
Technology. (Illus.). 112p. (gr. 4-9). Date not set. 19.95x (ISBN 1-85435-073-0). Marshall Cavendish.
Timms, Howard. Living in the Future. (ps-3). 1990. PLB 12.40 (ISBN 0-531-17224-4). Watts.
Why Things Are. (Illus.). (gr. 1 up). 1984. pap. 10.95 (ISBN 0-671-49897-5, Little Simon). S&S Trade.
TECHNOLOGY–FICTION
Discovery with Cap'n Bob & Matey: Voyages of Courage & Adventure. (Illus.). 32p. (gr. 1-4). 1991. 13.95 (ISBN 0-931595-08-8); pap. 7.95 (ISBN 0-931595-09-6). Seascape Enters.
MacGregor, Ellen & Pantell, Dora. Miss Pickerell Meets Mr. H. U. M. new ed. Greer, Charles, illus. 160p. (gr. 2-6). 1974. o.p. (ISBN 0-07-044577-X). McGraw.

Malone, Mary. Barbara Walters: T. V. Superstar. LC 89-16811. (Illus.). 128p. 1990. lib. bdg. 17.95 (ISBN 0-89490-287-3). Enslow Pubs.
Patterson, Lillie & Wright, Cornelia H. Oprah Winfrey: Talk Show Host & Actress. 128p. (gr. 6 up). 1990. 17.95 (ISBN 0-89490-289-X). Enslow Pubs.
St. Pierre, Stephanie. Story of Jim Henson. (gr. 4-7). 1991. pap. 2.95 (ISBN 0-440-40453-3). Dell.

TELEVISION PLAYS

Zadra, Dan. The Cosby Show. LC 86-23998. (gr. 4 up). 1986. PLB 9.75 (ISBN 0-88682-078-2); 13.95 (ISBN 0-685-17409-3). Creative Ed.
—M A S H. LC 86-24062. (gr. 4 up). 1986. PLB 9.75 (ISBN 0-88682-077-4); 13.95 (ISBN 0-685-17411-5). Creative Ed.

TELL, WILLIAM

Shane, Harold G. William Tell. Clark, William, ed. Winkler, Albert, illus. 16p. (gr. 3-5). pap. 29.95 6 bks. & 1 cass. (ISBN 0-89290-078-4, BC15-1); pap. 10.95 1 bk. & 1 cass. Soc for Visual.
William Tell. (Illus.). (gr. 1). 3.50 (ISBN 0-7214-5174-8). Ladybird Bks.

TEMPERATURE

see also Heat; Thermometers and Thermometry
Ardley, Neil. Hot & Cold. (Illus.). 32p. (gr. k-3). 1983. PLB 11.90 (ISBN 0-531-04614-1). Watts.
Llewellyn, Claire. First Look at Keeping Warm. LC 91-9423. (Illus.). 32p. (gr. 1-2). 1991. PLB 10.95 (ISBN 0-8368-0704-9). Gareth Stevens Inc.
Maestro, Betsy. Temperature & You. Maestro, Guilio, illus. 32p. (gr. k-3). 1990. 13.95 (ISBN 0-525-67271-0, Lodestar Bks). Dutton Child Bks.
Maury, Jean-Pierre. Heat & Cold. 80p. (gr. 8 up). 1989. pap. 4.95 (ISBN 0-8120-4211-5). Barron.

TEN COMMANDMENTS

De Graaf, Anne. The Two Greatest Commandments. (Illus.). 32p. 1989. 4.95 (ISBN 0-310-52760-0). Zondervan.
Haffey, Richard. H. R. Cornelius Learns about Love: A Commandments Book for Children. (Illus.). 20p. (Orig.). (gr. 2-5). 1985. pap. 2.95 (ISBN 0-89622-235-7). Twenty-Third.
Lovasik, Lawrence G. The Ten Commandments. (Illus.). (gr. 1-6). flexible bdg. 0.95 (ISBN 0-89942-287-X, 287). Catholic Bk Pub.
O'Connor, Francine & Boswell, Kathryn. ABC's of the Ten Commandments. (Illus.). 32p. (Orig.). (gr. 1-4). 1980. pap. 2.95 (ISBN 0-89243-125-3). Liguori Pubns.
Pingry, Patricia. The Story of Moses & the Ten Commandments. Britt, Stephanie, illus. (ps-k). 1990. pap. 3.95 (ISBN 0-8249-8418-8). Ideals.
The Ten Commandments. 1989. text ed. 3.95 cased (ISBN 0-7214-5262-0). Ladybird Bks.
Truitt, Gloria A. The Ten Commandments: Learning about God's Law. LC 56-1398. (gr. 1 up). 1983. pap. 3.95 (ISBN 0-570-08527-6). Concordia.

TENNESSEE

Cannon, Devereaux D., Jr. Flags of Tennessee. Tullier, Debra L., illus. 112p. (gr. 6-8). 1990. 13.95 (ISBN 0-88289-794-2). Pelican.
Carole Marsh Tennessee Books, 31 bks. Set. 638.45 (ISBN 0-7933-1317-1). Gallopade Pub Group.
Carpenter, Allan. Tennessee. LC 78-11522. (Illus.). 96p. (gr. 4 up). 1979. PLB 19.93 (ISBN 0-516-04142-8). Childrens.
Children's Museum of Oak Ridge, Tennessee Staff & Overholt, Jim, eds. Ridges & Valleys: A Mini-Encyclopedia of Anderson County, TN. 3rd ed. (Illus.). 126p. (Orig.). (gr. 5-12). 1990. pap. 5.50 (ISBN 0-9606832-5-9). Children's Mus.
Deegan, Paul. Nashville, Tennessee. LC 89-32913. (Illus.). 48p. (gr. 4-5). 1989. 12.95 (ISBN 0-89686-468-5, Crestwood Hse). Macmillan Child Grp.
Fradin, Dennis. Tennessee: In Words & Pictures. LC 79-19218. (Illus.). 48p. (gr. 2-5). 1980. PLB 15.93 (ISBN 0-516-03942-3); pap. 4.95 (ISBN 0-516-43942-1). Childrens.
Lynch, Amy. Nashville. (Illus.). 60p. (gr. 3 up). 1991. 12.95 (ISBN 0-87518-453-7, Dillon). Macmillan Child Grp.
Marsh, Carole. Avast, Ye Slobs! Tennessee Pirate Trivia. (Illus.). 1990. PLB 19.95 (ISBN 0-7933-1076-8); pap. 14.95 (ISBN 0-7933-1075-X); computer disk 29.95 (ISBN 0-7933-1077-6). Gallopade Pub Group.
—The Beast of the Tennessee Bed & Breakfast. (Illus.). 1990. PLB 19.95 (ISBN 0-7933-2056-9); pap. 14.95 (ISBN 0-7933-2057-7); computer disk 29.95 (ISBN 0-7933-2058-5). Gallopade Pub Group.
—The Hard-to-Believe-But-True! Book of Tennessee History, Mystery, Trivia, Legend, Lore, Humor & More. (Illus.). 1990. PLB 19.95 (ISBN 0-7933-1073-3); pap. 14.95 (ISBN 0-7933-1072-5); computer disk 29.95 (ISBN 0-7933-1074-1). Gallopade Pub Group.
—If My Tennessee Mama Ran the World! (Illus.). 1990. lib. bdg. 19.95 (ISBN 0-7933-2065-8); pap. 14.95 (ISBN 0-7933-2066-6); computer disk 29.95 (ISBN 0-7933-2067-4). Gallopade Pub Group.
—Let's Quilt Tennessee & Stuff It Topographically! (Illus.). 1990. PLB 19.95 (ISBN 0-7933-2048-8); pap. 14.95 (ISBN 1-55609-079-X); computer disk 29.95 (ISBN 0-7933-2049-6). Gallopade Pub Group.
—Tennessee & Other State Greats (Biographies) (Illus.). 1990. PLB 19.95 (ISBN 0-7933-1055-5); pap. 14.95 (ISBN 0-7933-1054-7); computer disk 29.95 (ISBN 0-7933-1056-3). Gallopade Pub Group.
—Tennessee Bandits, Bushwackers, Outlaws, Crooks, Devils, Ghosts, Desperadoes & Other Assorted & Sundry Characters! (Illus.). 1990. PLB 19.95 (ISBN 0-7933-1058-X); pap. 14.95 (ISBN 0-7933-1057-1); computer disk 29.95 (ISBN 0-7933-1059-8). Gallopade Pub Group.
—Tennessee Classic Christmas Trivia: Stories, Recipes, Activities, Legends, Lore & More! (Illus.). 1990. PLB 19.95 (ISBN 0-7933-1061-X); pap. 14.95 (ISBN 0-7933-1060-1); computer disk 29.95 (ISBN 0-7933-1062-8). Gallopade Pub Group.
—Tennessee Coastales. (Illus.). 1990. PLB 19.95 (ISBN 0-7933-2062-3); pap. 14.95 (ISBN 0-7933-2063-1); computer disk 29.95 (ISBN 0-7933-2064-X). Gallopade Pub Group.
—The Tennessee Hot Air Balloon Mystery. (Illus.). (gr. 2-9). 1990. 19.95 (ISBN 0-7933-2696-6); pap. 14.95 (ISBN 0-7933-2697-4); computer disk 29.95 (ISBN 0-7933-2698-2). Gallopade Pub Group.
—Tennessee "Jography" A Fun Run Thru Our State! (Illus.). 1990. PLB 19.95 (ISBN 0-7933-2046-1); pap. 14.95 (ISBN 1-55609-089-7); computer disk 29.95 (ISBN 0-7933-2047-X). Gallopade Pub Group.
—Tennessee Kid's Cookbook: Recipes, How-to, History, Lore & More! (Illus.). 1990. PLB 19.95 (ISBN 0-7933-1070-9); pap. 14.95 (ISBN 0-7933-1069-5); computer disk 29.95 (ISBN 0-7933-1071-7). Gallopade Pub Group.
—Tennessee Quiz Bowl Crash Course! (Illus.). 1990. PLB 19.95 (ISBN 0-7933-2059-3); pap. 14.95 (ISBN 0-7933-2060-7); computer disk 29.95 (ISBN 0-7933-2061-5). Gallopade Pub Group.
—Tennessee School Trivia: An Amazing & Fascinating Look at Our State's Teachers, Schools & Students! (Illus.). 1990. PLB 19.95 (ISBN 0-7933-1067-9); pap. 14.95 (ISBN 0-7933-1066-0); computer disk 29.95 (ISBN 0-7933-1068-7). Gallopade Pub Group.
—Tennessee Silly Basketball Sportsmysteries, Vol. 1. (Illus.). 1990. PLB 19.95 (ISBN 0-7933-1064-4); pap. 14.95 (ISBN 0-7933-1063-6); computer disk 29.95 (ISBN 0-7933-1065-2). Gallopade Pub Group.
—Tennessee Silly Basketball Sportsmysteries, Vol. 2. (Illus.). 1990. PLB 19.95 (ISBN 0-7933-2071-2); pap. 14.95 (ISBN 0-7933-2072-0); computer disk 29.95 (ISBN 0-7933-2073-9). Gallopade Pub Group.
—Tennessee Silly Football Sportsmysteries, Vol. 1. (Illus.). 1990. PLB 19.95 (ISBN 0-7933-2050-X); pap. 14.95 (ISBN 0-7933-2051-8); computer disk 29.95 (ISBN 0-7933-2052-6). Gallopade Pub Group.
—Tennessee Silly Football Sportsmysteries, Vol. 2. (Illus.). 1990. PLB 19.95 (ISBN 0-7933-2053-4); pap. 14.95 (ISBN 0-7933-2054-2); computer disk 29.95 (ISBN 0-7933-2055-0). Gallopade Pub Group.
—Tennessee Silly Trivia! (Illus.). 1990. PLB 19.95 (ISBN 0-7933-2044-5); pap. 14.95 (ISBN 1-55609-036-6); computer disk 29.95 (ISBN 0-7933-2045-3). Gallopade Pub Group.
—Tennessee's (Most Devastating!) Disasters & (Most Calamitous!) Catastrophies! (Illus.). 1990. PLB 19.95 (ISBN 0-7933-2068-2); pap. 14.95 (ISBN 0-7933-2069-0); computer disk 29.95 (ISBN 0-7933-2070-4). Gallopade Pub Group.
Turner Program Services, Inc. Staff & Clark, James I. Tennessee. 48p. (gr. 3 up). 1985. PLB 17.32 (ISBN 0-86514-444-3); pap. text ed. 9.27 (ISBN 0-86514-519-9); cancelled Beta video (ISBN 0-86514-069-3); cancelled VHS video (ISBN 0-86514-144-4); cancelled 3/4" video (ISBN 0-86514-219-X); cancelled tchr's. guide (ISBN 0-86514-294-7); cancelled student activity bk. (ISBN 0-86514-369-2); cancelled index. Raintree Pubs.

TENNESSEE–FICTION

Galbreath, Bob. Tennessee Red Berry Tales. Garrett, Deborah G., ed. 97p. (Orig.). (gr. 3 up). 1986. pap. 7.95 (ISBN 0-9616918-0-8). Whites Creek Pr.
Steele, William O. Winter Danger. Galdone, Paul, illus. LC 54-5157. (gr. 4-6). 1954. 6.75 (ISBN 0-685-02109-2, HJ). HarBraceJ.

TENNESSEE–HISTORY

Hirsch, Virginia R. Heart Country Tennessee: A Tribute to the Tennessee Songmaker. rev. ed. LC 85-82468. 80p. (gr. 5 up). 1986. pap. 5.00 (ISBN 0-9616334-0-9). Heart Ctry Pubns.
Phillips, Margaret I. Governors of Tennessee. LC 77-26845. (Illus.). 193p. (gr. 6-12). 1978. 14.95 (ISBN 0-88289-169-3). Pelican.

TENNIS

Bradlee, Dick. Instant Tennis. (Illus.). 124p. (gr. 7 up). 1962. 9.95 (ISBN 0-8159-5811-0). Devin.
Deegan & Zadra, Dan. Tennis: Serving & Returning. (Illus.). 1976. 15.35 (ISBN 0-87191-495-6); PLB 10.75s.p. (ISBN 0-685-23237-9). Creative Ed.
Ganeri, A. Tennis Skills. (Illus.). 48p. (gr. 6-12). Date not set. lib. bdg. 12.96 (ISBN 0-88110-396-9, Usborne); pap. 5.95 (ISBN 0-7460-0173-8). EDC.
Gutman, Bill. Go for It: Tennis. Brown, Ben, illus. 64p. (gr. 3-7). 1989. PLB 16.50 (ISBN 0-942545-88-5). Grey Castle.
LaMarche, Bob. Tennis Basics. Gow, Bill, illus. LC 82-21542. 48p. (gr. 3-7). 1983. 9.95 (ISBN 0-13-903237-1). P-H.
Singleton, Skip. The Junior Tennis Handbook. LC 90-21927. (Illus.). 176p. (Orig.). (gr. 5 up). 1991. pap. 12.95 (ISBN 1-55870-192-3, Shoe Tree Pr). Betterway Pubns.
Smith, Stan & Valentine, Tom. Inside Tennis. new ed. LC 73-20692. (Illus.). 96p. (gr. 5-8). 1974. pap. 5.95 (ISBN 0-8092-8886-9). Contemp Bks.
Sullivan, George. Better Tennis for Boys & Girls. (Illus.). 64p. (gr. 3-7). 1987. 10.99 (ISBN 0-399-61264-5, Putnam). Putnam Pub Group.
Whitney, Marceil. Teenie Tennis: A Love Game. 72p. (Orig.). (ps up). 1991. pap. write for info. (ISBN 0-9629089-0-8). ATS Pub.
Wimbledon. 32p. (gr. 4). 1990. 12.95s.p. (ISBN 0-88682-319-6) (ISBN 0-685-28234-1). Creative Ed.

TENNIS–BIOGRAPHY

Aaseng, Nathan. Winning Men of Tennis. LC 80-28598. (Illus.). 80p. (gr. 4 up). 1981. PLB 7.95 (ISBN 0-8225-1068-5). Lerner Pubns.
—Winning Women of Tennis. LC 81-6033. (Illus.). 80p. (gr. 4 up). 1981. PLB 7.95 (ISBN 0-8225-1067-7). Lerner Pubns.
Eliot, Chip. Ivan Lendl. LC 88-1829. (Illus.). 48p. (gr. 5-6). 1988. PLB 10.95 (ISBN 0-89686-380-8, Crestwood Hse). Macmillan Child Grp.
Leder, Jane M. Martina Navratilova. (Illus.). 48p. (gr. 5-6). 1985. PLB 10.95 (ISBN 0-89686-252-6, Crestwood Hse). Macmillan Child Grp.
Martina Navratilova. (gr. 2-6). 1989. pap. 3.50 (ISBN 0-14-033218-9, Puffin). Puffin Bks.
Monroe, Judy. Steffi Graf. LC 87-30115. (Illus.). 48p. (gr. 5-6). 1988. PLB 10.95 (ISBN 0-89686-368-9, Crestwood Hse). Macmillan Child Grp.
Steffi Graf. (gr. 3-7). 1990. pap. 4.95 (ISBN 0-316-36239-5). Little.

TENNIS–FICTION

Barbic, Ivo. Playing Tennis with Bouncy & Fuzzy. Blanc, Henry, illus. 96p. 1987. pap. 9.95 (ISBN 0-88289-654-7). Pelican.
Schulman, Janet. Jenny & The Tennis Nut. Hafner, Marilyn, illus. 64p. (gr. 1-4). 1981. pap. 2.50 (ISBN 0-440-44211-7, YB). Dell.
Steiner, Barbara. Love Match. 128p. (gr. 5-8). 1988. 1.00 (ISBN 0-87406-312-4, 31-16381-3). Willowisp Pr.
Tunis, John R. Champion's Choice. 1990. pap. 3.95 (ISBN 0-15-216074-4). HarbraceJ.
Wells, Rosemary. When No One Was Looking. LC 80-12964. 256p. (gr. 6 up). 1980. 14.95 (ISBN 0-8037-9855-5, 01451-440). Dial Bks Young.

TENPINS

see Bowling

TERMITES–FICTION

Sickles, William. Herman the Termite. (Illus.). (gr. 3-5). 1968. 10.95 (ISBN 0-8392-3066-4). Astor-Honor.

TERRARIUMS

Broekel, Ray. Aquariums & Terrariums. LC 82-4428. (gr. k-4). 1982. 14.60 (ISBN 0-516-01660-1). Childrens.

TERROR, REIGN OF

see France–History–Revolution, 1789-1799

TEST PILOTS

see Air Pilots; Airplanes–Testing

TESTS

see Educational Tests and Measurements

TEXAS

Adams, Carolyn. Stars over Texas. rev. ed. (Illus.). 128p. (gr. 1-6). 1983. 8.95 (ISBN 0-89015-411-2, Pub. by Panda Bks). Eakin Pr.
Aylesworth, Thomas G. & Aylesworth, Virginia L. The Southwest (Texas, New Mexico, Colorado) (Illus.). 64p. (gr. 3 up). 1992. PLB 16.95 (ISBN 0-7910-1048-1). Chelsea Hse.
Brown, Richard, illus. A Kid's Guide to Texas. 160p. (gr. 1 up). 1989. pap. 6.95 (ISBN 0-318-37141-3, Gulliver Bks). HarBraceJ.
Carole Marsh Texas Books, 31 bks. Set. 638.45 (ISBN 0-7933-1318-X). Gallopade Pub Group.
Carpenter, Allan. Texas. LC 78-18430. (Illus.). 96p. (gr. 4 up). 1979. PLB 19.93 (ISBN 0-516-04143-6). Childrens.
Cummings, Joe. Texas Handbook. (Illus.). 483p. (Orig.). 1990. pap. 11.95 (ISBN 0-918373-53-0). Moon Pubns CA.
Elliott, Tony. Texas Outdoors. Elliott, Tony, illus. (gr. 1-8). 1986. pap. 4.95 (ISBN 0-914565-24-9, 24-9). Capstan Pubns.
Fradin, Dennis. Texas: In Words & Pictures. Wahl, Richard, illus. LC 80-27497. 48p. (gr. 2-5). 1981. PLB 15.93 (ISBN 0-516-03943-1). Childrens.
Gillies, John. Senor Alcalde: A Biography of Henry Cisneros. LC 87-32456. (Illus.). 112p. (gr. 6 up). 1988. PLB 12.95 (ISBN 0-87518-374-3, Dillon). Macmillan Child Grp.
Gipson, Fred. The Trail-Driving Rooster. Lich, Glen, intro. by. (Illus.). 88p. (gr. 4-7). 1987. Repr. of 1955 ed. 8.95 (ISBN 0-89015-620-4, Pub. by Panda Bks). Eakin Pr.
Jones, Martha T. The Great Texas Scare: A Story of the Runaway Scrape. La Freniere, Annette, ed. LC 88-767. (Illus.). 96p. (gr. 3-7). 1988. lib. bdg. 10.95 (ISBN 0-937460-31-1). Hendrick-Long.
Kerr, Rita. Texas Rebel. Eakin, Edwin M., ed. Kerr, Rita, illus. 80p. (gr. 4-6). 1989. 9.95 (ISBN 0-89015-695-6, Pub. by Panda Bks). Eakin Pr.
Koch, Susan C. Colormore Travels - Ft. Worth, Texas: The Travel Guide for Kids. Koch, Susan C., illus. (Orig.). (gr. k-4). 1989. pap. 4.50 (ISBN 0-945600-02-X). Colormore Inc.
—Colormore Travels - San Antonio, Texas: The Travel Guide for Kids. Koch, Susan C., illus. 32p. (Orig.). (gr. k-4). 1990. pap. 4.50 (ISBN 0-945600-05-4). Colormore Inc.
Lewein, David A. The ABC's of Texas. Lewein, Mary J., ed. Delia, illus. 64p. 1989. pap. 4.95 (ISBN 0-685-29420-X). TX Pride Pubns.

McAlister, George A. A Time to Love...a Time to Die. Godfrey, Raymond, illus. 216p. (Orig.). (gr. 10). 1988. pap. 7.95 (ISBN 0-924307-01-3). Docutex Inc.

Marsh, Carole. Avast, Ye Slobs! Texas Pirate Trivia. (Illus.). 1990. PLB 19.95 (ISBN 0-7933-1100-4); pap. 14.95 (ISBN 0-7933-1099-7); computer disk 0-7933-1101-2 29.95. Gallopade Pub Group.

—The Beast of the Texas Bed & Breakfast. (Illus.). 1990. PLB 19.95 (ISBN 0-7933-2086-0); pap. 14.95 (ISBN 0-7933-2087-9); computer disk 29.95 (ISBN 0-7933-2088-7). Gallopade Pub Group.

—The Hard-to-Believe-But-True! Book of Texas History, Mystery, Trivia, Legend, Lore, Humor & More. (Illus.). 1990. PLB 19.95 (ISBN 0-7933-1097-0); pap. 14.95 (ISBN 0-7933-1096-2); computer disk 29.95 (ISBN 0-7933-1098-9). Gallopade Pub Group.

—If My Texas Mama Ran the World! (Illus.). 1990. PLB 19.95 (ISBN 0-7933-2094-1); pap. 14.95 (ISBN 0-7933-2095-X); computer disk 29.95 (ISBN 0-7933-2096-8). Gallopade Pub Group.

—Let's Quilt Texas & Stuff It Topographically! (Illus.). 1990. PLB 19.95 (ISBN 0-7933-2078-X); pap. 14.95 (ISBN 1-55609-077-3); computer disk 29.95 (ISBN 0-7933-2079-8). Gallopade Pub Group.

—Texas & Other State Greats (Biographies) (Illus.). 1990. PLB 19.95 (ISBN 0-7933-2097-6); pap. 14.95 (ISBN 0-7933-2098-4); computer disk 29.95 (ISBN 0-7933-2099-2). Gallopade Pub Group.

—Texas Bandits, Bushwackers, Outlaws, Crooks, Devils, Ghosts, Desperadoes & Other Assorted & Sundry Characters! (Illus.). 1990. PLB 19.95 (ISBN 0-7933-1082-2); pap. 14.95 (ISBN 0-7933-1081-4); computer disk 29.95 (ISBN 0-7933-1083-0). Gallopade Pub Group.

—Texas Classic Christmas Trivia: Stories, Recipes, Activities, Legends, Lore & More! (Illus.). 1990. PLB 19.95 (ISBN 0-7933-1085-7); pap. 14.95 (ISBN 0-7933-1084-9); computer disk 29.95 (ISBN 0-7933-1086-5). Gallopade Pub Group.

—Texas Coastales. (Illus.). 1990. PLB 19.95 (ISBN 0-7933-2092-5); pap. 14.95 (ISBN 1-55609-121-4); computer disk 29.95 (ISBN 0-7933-2093-3). Gallopade Pub Group.

—The Texas Hot Air Balloon Mystery. (Illus.). (gr. 2-9). 1990. 19.95 (ISBN 0-7933-2705-9); pap. 14.95 (ISBN 0-7933-2706-7); computer disk 29.95 (ISBN 0-7933-2707-5). Gallopade Pub Group.

—Texas "Jography" A Fun Run Thru Our State! (Illus.). 1990. PLB 19.95 (ISBN 0-7933-2076-3); pap. 14.95 (ISBN 1-55609-087-0); computer disk 29.95 (ISBN 0-7933-2077-1). Gallopade Pub Group.

—Texas Kid's Cookbook: Recipes, How-To, History, Lore & More! (Illus.). 1990. PLB 19.95 (ISBN 0-7933-1094-6); pap. 14.95 (ISBN 0-7933-1093-8); computer disk 29.95 (ISBN 0-7933-1095-4). Gallopade Pub Group.

—Texas Quiz Bowl Crash Course! (Illus.). 1990. PLB 19.95 (ISBN 0-7933-2089-5); pap. 14.95 (ISBN 0-7933-2090-9); computer disk 29.95 (ISBN 0-7933-2091-7). Gallopade Pub Group.

—Texas School Trivia: An Amazing & Fascinating Look at Our State's Teachers, Schools & Students! (Illus.). 1990. PLB 19.95 (ISBN 0-7933-1091-1); pap. 14.95 (ISBN 0-7933-1090-3); computer disk 29.95 (ISBN 0-7933-1092-X). Gallopade Pub Group.

—Texas Silly Basketball sportsmysteries, Vol. 1. (Illus.). 1990. PLB 19.95 (ISBN 0-7933-1088-1); pap. 14.95 (ISBN 0-7933-1087-3); computer disk 29.95 (ISBN 0-7933-1089-X). Gallopade Pub Group.

—Texas Silly Basketball Sportsmysteries, Vol. 2. (Illus.). 1990. PLB 19.95 (ISBN 0-7933-2100-X); pap. 14.95 (ISBN 0-7933-2101-8); computer disk 29.95 (ISBN 0-7933-2102-6). Gallopade Pub Group.

—Texas Silly Football Sportsmysteries, Vol. 1. (Illus.). 1990. PLB 19.95 (ISBN 0-7933-2080-1); pap. 14.95 (ISBN 0-7933-2081-X); computer disk 29.95 (ISBN 0-7933-2082-8). Gallopade Pub Group.

—Texas Silly Football Sportsmysteries, Vol. 2. (Illus.). 1990. PLB 19.95 (ISBN 0-7933-2083-6); pap. 14.95 (ISBN 0-7933-2084-4); computer disk 29.95 (ISBN 0-7933-2085-2). Gallopade Pub Group.

—Texas Silly Trivia! (Illus.). 1990. PLB 19.95 (ISBN 0-7933-2074-7); pap. 14.95 (ISBN 1-55609-081-1); computer disk 29.95 (ISBN 0-7933-2075-5). Gallopade Pub Group.

—Texas's (Most Devastating!) Disasters & (Most Calamitous!) Catastrophies! (Illus.). 1990. PLB 19.95 (ISBN 0-7933-1079-2); pap. 14.95 (ISBN 0-7933-1078-4); computer disk 29.95 (ISBN 0-7933-1080-6). Gallopade Pub Group.

Martinello, Marian & Field, William T., Jr. Who Are the Chinese Texans? Ricks, Thorn, illus. 84p. (Orig.). (gr. 5-8). 8.95 (ISBN 0-933164-36-X); pap. 5.95 (ISBN 0-933164-46-7). U of Tex Inst Tex Culture.

Michael, Linda. Big As Texas: The A to Z Tour of Texas Cities & Places. Lowdermilk, Karen, ed. Lewis, Patrick, illus. LC 87-36793. 64p. (gr. k-3). 1988. pap. 6.95 (ISBN 0-937460-34-6). Hendrick-Long.

Peifer, Charles, Jr. Houston. LC 88-20197. (Illus.). 60p. (gr. 3 up). 1988. PLB 12.95 (ISBN 0-87518-387-5, Dillon). Macmillan Child Grp.

Petrucelli. Henry Cisneros, Reading Level 2. (Illus.). 24p. (gr. 1-4). Date not set. PLB 12.33 (ISBN 0-86592-431-7). Rourke Corp.

Phillips, Betty L. & Phillips, Bryce, eds. Texas. (Illus.). 96p. (gr. 4-9). PLB 10.40 (ISBN 0-531-10395-1). Watts.

Reeve, Agnesa, compiled by. & intro. by. My Dear Mollie: Love Letters of a Texas Sheep Rancher. (Illus.). 192p. 1990. 17.95 (ISBN 0-937460-62-1). Hendrick-Long.

Stein, R. Conrad. Texas. LC 88-38400. (Illus.). 144p. (gr. 4 up). 1989. PLB 25.27 (ISBN 0-516-00489-1). Childrens.

Stewart, G. Houston. (Illus.). 48p. (gr. 5 up). 1989. lib. bdg. 14.60 (ISBN 0-86592-539-9). Rourke Corp.

Turner Program Services, Inc. Staff & Clark, James I. Texas. LC 85-9980. 48p. (gr. 3 up). 1985. PLB 17.32 (ISBN 0-86514-445-1); pap. text ed. 9.27 (ISBN 0-86514-520-2); cancelled Beta video (ISBN 0-86514-070-7); cancelled VHS video (ISBN 0-86514-145-2); cancelled 3/4" video (ISBN 0-86514-220-3); cancelled tchr's. guide (ISBN 0-86514-295-5); cancelled student activity bk. (ISBN 0-86514-370-6); cancelled index. Raintree Pubs.

Von Rosenberg, Marjorie. Max & Martha: Children from Germany in the Texas Hill Country. (Illus.). 48p. (gr. 4-7). 1986. 8.95 (ISBN 0-89015-539-9, Pub. by Panda Bks). Eakin Pr.

TEXAS–FICTION

Abernethy, Francis E. How the Critters Created Texas. Sargent, Ben, illus. LC 82-80440. 40p. (gr. 4-12). 1982. pap. 8.95 (ISBN 0-936650-01-X). E C Temple.

Alter, Judy. After Pa Was Shot. Shaw, Charles, illus. LC 89-12176. 192p. (Orig.). (gr. 4-9). 1991. pap. 5.95 (ISBN 0-936650-12-5). E C Temple.

Baylor, Byrd. The Best Town in the World. Himler, Ronald, illus. LC 86-3381. 32p. (gr. 1-3). 1986. pap. 3.95 (ISBN 0-689-71086-0, Aladdin). Macmillan Child Grp.

Cheadle, J. A. A Donkey's Life: A Story for Children. Thomas, Toni, illus. LC 80-123421. iii, 88p. (Orig.). (gr. 2-6). 1979. pap. 3.50 (ISBN 0-9604244-0-7). Heahstan Pr.
The story follows Don Quixotito, a donkey of principle, across the American continent, with stops in North Carolina, Mississippi, Texas, Colorado, & California. Six songs, chiefly regional, which the donkey hears along the way, are included. After being almost successfully captured by rustlers in Texas, he leaves, this song echoing in his ears: "I'm departin' from this state; the Rangers nearly cornered me..." "Once upon a time a book brought children love. It is a children's story about an adventuresome little donkey named Don Quixotito whose travels take him to many exciting places. I read the book at least ten times--in the bathtub, while eating breakfast, & while everyone else watched the New Year's Day parade on T.V."--Peggy Drapo in the Denton Record-Chronicle. "This charming little book is not only a delightful story of the adventures of a cunning little donkey. It can be a very pleasant lesson in geography for a grown person as well as a child. There is also a touch of the lore of Texas & Texans in his Travels."--Carl Warlaw, Texas writer.
Publisher Provided Annotation.

Cole, Barbara H. Texas Star. Minton, Barbara, illus. LC 88-25205. 32p. (ps-2). 1990. 14.95 (ISBN 0-531-05820-4); PLB 14.99 (ISBN 0-531-08420-5). Orchard Bks Watts.

Crowder, Dorothy. In the Land of the Wichitas: Stories about Burkburnett, Texas for the Young Reader. (Illus.). 48p. (Orig.). (gr. 3-4). 1986. pap. text ed. 7.50x (ISBN 0-317-91365-4). Dorthenia Pubs.

Evey, Ethel L. Stowaway to Texas. Darst, Shelia S., ed. 201p. (gr. 4-7). 1986. 9.95 (ISBN 0-89896-102-5, Post Oak Pr); pap. 6.95 (ISBN 0-89896-101-7, Post Oak Pr). Larksdale.

Fowler, Zinita. The Last Innocent Summer. LC 89-20417. 145p. (gr. 6-9). 1990. pap. 11.95 (ISBN 0-87565-045-7). Tex Christian.
THE LAST INNOCENT SUMMER is a story about a small town with a swimming pool, the Ritz Theater, a city park, a town square & a J.C. Penney store. It's a story about slumber parties, small-town funerals, community picnics & local intrigues. It's also a story about honor & caring & the way we live. Skeeter, the ten-year-old narrator, tells about the murder of two little girls that rocked the small Texas town in which she lived, & of how her close-knit family's involvement in events beyond their control changed their lives in that troubled summer of 1931. Skeeter learns some disturbing lessons: people can do bad things & then make them worse trying to keep from being found out; not all mothers love their children, nor all children love their mothers; it's hard to say "I love you" to those you love. "Fowler's deftly crafted story has depth & pace & a picture of a community that may remind some readers of Harper Lee's TO KILL A MOCKINGBIRD."--Bulletin of the Center for Children's Books, Univ. of Chicago. "The emotion of small town joys & sorrows & the prejudices of different groups as they struggle to coexist are brought together with good clear dialogue & colorful description to make (a) most enjoyable story."--VOYA. Chosen best Juvenile of 1991 by the Texas Institute of Letters.
Publisher Provided Annotation.

Gipson, Fred. Old Yeller. LC 56-8780. (Illus.). (gr. 7-9). 1956. 19.95i (ISBN 0-06-011545-9, HarpT). HarperCollins.

Harman, Betty & Meador, Nancy. Paco & the Lion of the North. Roberts, Melissa, ed. 112p. (gr. 4-7). 1987. 8.95 (ISBN 0-89015-598-4, Pub. by Panda Bks). Eakin Pr.

Hoff, Carol. Johnny Texas on the San Antonio Road. (Illus.). 191p. (gr. 4 up). Repr. of 1953 ed. 13.95 (ISBN 0-937460-15-X). Hendrick-Long.

Jakes, John. Susanna of the Alamo. (Illus.). 32p. (ps-3). 1990. pap. 4.95 (ISBN 0-15-200595-1, VoyB). HarBraceJ.

Kerr, Rita. Texas Cavalier: The Story of James Butler Bonham. Roberts, Melissa, ed. Kerr, Rita, illus. 64p. (gr. 4-7). 1989. 8.95 (ISBN 0-89015-714-6, Pub. by Panda Bks). Eakin Pr.

—Texas Footprints. (gr. 3-7). 1988. 8.95 (ISBN 0-89015-676-X, Pub. by Panda Bks). Eakin Pr.

Ketner, Mary G. Ganzy Remembers. Sparks, Barbara, illus. LC 89-78261. 32p. (ps-3). 1991. SBE 13.95 (ISBN 0-689-31610-0, Atheneum Child Bk). Macmillan Child Grp.

Michener, James A. The Eagle & the Raven. Shaw, Charles, illus. 220p. 1990. 19.95 (ISBN 0-938349-57-0); ltd. ed. 100.00 (ISBN 0-938349-58-9). State House Pr.

Paulsen, Gary. Canyons. 1990. 14.95 (ISBN 0-385-30153-7). Delacorte.

Roderus, Frank. Duster. Conoly, Walle, illus. LC 85-14759. 266p. (gr. 4 up). 1987. Repr. of 1977 ed. 14.95 (ISBN 0-87565-055-4). Tex Christian.

Sinclair, Dorothy T. Tales of the Texians. Milam, Harris, illus. LC 85-90411. 104p. (Orig.). (gr. 4-7). 1986. 12.95 (ISBN 0-9615311-0-X); pap. 7.95 (ISBN 0-9615311-1-8). Sinclair Ent.

Smith, Beatrice S. The Road to Galveston. LC 72-7657. (Illus.). 132p. (gr. 4 up). 1973. PLB 7.95 (ISBN 0-8225-0755-2). Lerner Pubns.

Tillie Comes to Texas. 1987. incl. cassette & bk. 15.95 (ISBN 0-937460-57-5); cassette tape 6.95 (ISBN 0-937460-56-7). Hendrick-Long.

Tolliver, Ruby C. Muddy Banks. LC 85-20851. (Illus.). 154p. (gr. 4up). 1987. 14.95 (ISBN 0-87565-062-7); pap. 6.95 (ISBN 0-87565-049-X). Tex Christian.

Williams, Jeanne. Tame the Wild Stallion. Conoly, Walle, illus. LC 84-16257. 182p. (gr. 4 up). 1985. 14.95 (ISBN 0-87565-002-3); pap. 8.95 (ISBN 0-87565-009-0). Tex Christian.

Wisler, G. Clifton. Piper's Ferry. 144p. (gr. 5-9). 1990. 14.95 (ISBN 0-525-67303-2, Lodestar Bks). Dutton Child Bks.

TEXAS–HISTORY

Baker, Charlotte. Trails North - Stories of Texas Yesterdays. Roberts, Melissa, ed. Gholson, Virginia, illus. 128p. (gr. 4-7). 1991. 10.95 (ISBN 0-89015-701-4). Eakin Pr.

Chariton, Wallace O. Rainy Days in Texas Funbook. 144p. (Orig.). 1990. pap. 9.95 (ISBN 1-55622-130-4). Wordware Pub.

Cox, Bertha M. True Tales of Texas. Hendrick, Lura A., illus. LC 87-12091. 292p. (gr. 3-8). 1987. Repr. of 1949 ed. PLB 11.95 (ISBN 0-937460-28-1). Hendrick Long.

Crawford, Ann F. New Life, New Land: Women in Early Texas. (Illus.). 48p. 1986. 9.95 (ISBN 0-89015-560-7, Pub. by Panda Bks). Eakin Pr.

Gurasich, Marj. Benito & the White Dove: A Story of Jose Antonio Navarro, Hero of Early Texas. (Illus.). 112p. (gr. 4-6). 1989. 9.95 (ISBN 0-89015-693-X, Pub. by Diamond Bks). Eakin Pr.

Hackney, Ann. The Epic Adventure...Texas. 2nd ed. Hodges, Carol, illus. Johnson, Lady Bird, intro. by. LC 85-24854. (Illus.). 64p. (gr. 4-7). 1985. text ed. 19.95 includes tape (ISBN 0-935077-11-1); pap. 12.95 includes tape (ISBN 0-935077-12-X); pap. 5.95 (ISBN 0-935077-07-3); tchr's guide 16.95 (ISBN 0-935077-10-3); cassette 7.95 (ISBN 0-935077-08-1). Hist Jefferson Found.

Henderson, Shelia & George, Bonnie S. The Littlest Aggie. Darr, S. C., ed. La Rue, Doug, et al, illus. Williams, Clayton, Jr., frwd. by. 56p. 1990. 18.95 (ISBN 0-9623171-2-8); coloring bk. 4.95 (ISBN 0-9623171-3-6). Littlest Bk.

Jackson, Sarah & Patterson, Mary Ann. A Child's History of Texas. Jackson, Sarah & Patterson, Mary Ann, illus. (gr. 1-6). 1972. 7.95 (ISBN 0-89015-056-7, Pub. by Panda Bks). Eakin Pr.

Kerr, Rita. Juan Seguin: A Hero of Texas. 54p. (gr. 4-6). 1985. 9.95 (ISBN 0-89015-502-X, Pub. by Panda Bks). Eakin Pr.

—Texas' First Lady: Margaret Lea Houston, Wife of the President. Eakin, Edwin M., ed. (Illus.). 64p. (gr. 4-7). 1987. 7.95 (ISBN 0-89015-615-8, Pub. by Panda Bks). Eakin Pr.

Lawson, Don. The United States in the Mexican War. McCullough, Robert, illus. LC 76-11022. 160p. (gr. 7 up). 1988. PLB 12.89 (ISBN 0-690-04723-1, Crowell Jr Bks). HarpC Child Bks.

McCall, Edith. Stalwart Men of Early Texas. Aronson, Lou, illus. LC 78-101296. 128p. (gr. 3-10). 1980. PLB 14.60 (ISBN 0-516-03371-9). Childrens.

Martin, Jack. Border Boss: Captain John R. Hughes, Texas Ranger. Stanush, Frank A, illus. Cox, Mike, intro. by. LC 89-48043. (Illus.). 252p. 1990. 21.95 (ISBN 0-938349-49-X); limited edition 60.00 (ISBN 0-938349-51-1); pap. 14.95 (ISBN 0-938349-50-3). State House Pr.

Martinello, Marian L. & Nesmith, Samuel P. With Domingo Leal in San Antonio, 1734. Institute of Texan Cultures Staff, ed. Lowther, Marilyn, illus. 78p. (Orig.). (gr. 5-8). 1980. pap. 6.95 (ISBN 0-933164-40-8). U of Tex Inst Tex Culture.

Milligan, Bryce. Battle of the Alamo: You Are There. Shaw, Charles, illus. 156p. (gr. 5-10). 1989. pap. 3.95 (ISBN 0-87719-156-5, Lone Star Bks). Gulf Pub.

—Comanche Captive: You Are There. Shaw, Charles, illus. 156p. (gr. 5 up). 1989. pap. 3.95 (ISBN 0-87719-157-3, Lone Star Bks). Gulf Pub.

Munson, Sammye. Our Tejano Heroes: Outstanding Mexican-Americans. Eakin, Edwin M., ed. (Illus.). 96p. (gr. 4-6). 1989. 9.95 (ISBN 0-89015-691-3, Pub. by Panda Bks). Eakin Pr.

Rogers, Mary B. & Smith, Sherry A. We Can Fly: Stories of Katherine Stinson & Other Gutsy Texas Women. LC 82-80441. (Illus.). 184p. (Orig.). (gr. 7up). 1983. 14.95 (ISBN 0-936650-02-8); pap. 12.95 (ISBN 0-936650-03-6). E C Temple.

Seale, Jan. Deaf Smith: The Eyes & Ears of the Texas Army. Seale, Carl, illus. 30p. (gr. k-3). 1987. pap. 2.95 (ISBN 0-936927-20-8). Knowing Pr.

—Dilue Rose: The Girl Who Saw Texas Independence. Seale, Carl, illus. 30p. (gr. k-3). 1986. pap. 2.95 (ISBN 0-936927-21-6). Knowing Pr.

—Juan Seguin: The Tejano Who Wouldn't Give Up. Seale, Carl, illus. 28p. (gr. k-3). 1987. pap. 2.95 (ISBN 0-936927-19-4). Knowing Pr.

—Kian Long: The Slave Girl Who Helped Start Texas. Seale, Carl, illus. 30p. (gr. k-3). 1987. pap. 2.95 (ISBN 0-936927-18-6). Knowing Pr.

—Madam Candelaria: The Nurse at the Alamo. Seale, Carl, illus. 27p. (gr. k-3). 1987. pap. 2.95 (ISBN 0-936927-16-X). Knowing Pr.

—William Goyens: The Texan Who Said No to Failure. Seale, Carl, illus. 29p. (gr. k-3). 1987. pap. 2.95 (ISBN 0-936927-17-8). Knowing Pr.

Stanush, Barbara E. Texans: The Story of Texan Cultures for Young People. Cosgrove, Jim, illus. LC 88-50983. 122p. (gr. 4-7). 1988. 19.95 (ISBN 0-86701-040-1). U of Tex Inst Tex Culture.

Stein, R. Conrad. The Story of the Lone Star Republic. LC 87-35467. (Illus.). 30p. (gr. 4-8). 1988. PLB 13.27 (ISBN 0-516-04735-3); pap. 3.95 (ISBN 0-516-33735-1). Childrens.

Stewart, Gail. Texans. (Illus.). 32p. (gr. 3-8). 1990. PLB 17.26 (ISBN 0-86625-408-0). Rourke Corp.

Teague, Wells. Theo, the Indian Fighter. Eakin, Edwin M., ed. (Illus.). 112p. (gr. 4-7). 1987. 8.95 (ISBN 0-89015-614-X, Pub. by Panda Bks). Eakin Pr.

Warren, Betsy. Let's Remember Texas, the Twenty-Eighth State. (Illus.). 36p. (gr. 3-7). 1984. pap. 4.50 (ISBN 0-937460-13-3). Hendrick-Long.

—Let's Remember When Texas Belonged to Spain. Warren, Betsy, illus. 32p. (gr. 3-7). 1982. pap. 4.50 (ISBN 0-937460-04-4). Hendrick-Long.

—Let's Remember When Texas Was a Republic. Warren, Betsy, illus. 32p. (gr. 3-7). 1983. pap. 4.50 (ISBN 0-937460-09-5). Hendrick-Long.

—The Story of Texas: A History Picture Book. Warren, Betsy, illus. 46p. (gr. 3 up). Date not set. pap. 3.50 (ISBN 0-9618660-1-2). Ranch Gate Bks.

—Texas in Historic Sites & Symbols. Warren, Betsy, illus. 28p. (gr. k-3). 1982. pap. 4.50 (ISBN 0-937460-05-2). Hendrick-Long.

—Twenty Texans, Historic Lives for Young Readers. LC 85-13926. (Illus.). 114p. (gr. 3-7). 1985. lib. bdg. 11.95 (ISBN 0-937460-17-6). Hendrick-Long.

TEXAS INSTRUMENTS COMPUTERS

Kemnitz, Thomas M. & Mass, Lynne. Kids Working with Computers: The Texas Instruments BASIC Manual. Schlendorf, Lori, illus. 48p. (gr. 4-7). 1983. pap. 4.99 (ISBN 0-89824-059-X). Trillium Pr.

TEXTILE FABRICS

see Textile Industry and Fabrics

TEXTILE INDUSTRY AND FABRICS

see also Cotton Manufacture and Trade; Tapestry; Weaving

also names of special textile fabrics, (e.g. Silk); and names of articles manufactured, e.g. Carpets

Blood, Charles L. & Link, Martin. The Goat in the Rug. Parker, Nancy W., illus. LC 80-17315. 40p. (ps-3). 1984. Repr. of 1976 ed. 14.95 (ISBN 0-02-710920-8, Four Winds). Macmillan Child Grp.

Boy Scouts of America. Textile. 64p. (gr. 6-12). 1972. pap. 1.85 (ISBN 0-8395-3344-6, 3344). BSA.

Cobb, Vicki. Fuzz Does It! Schatell, Brian, illus. LC 81-47758. (gr. 1-3). 1982. 12.95i (ISBN 0-397-31975-4, Pub. by Lipp Jr Bks); pap. 4.75i (ISBN 0-397-31977-0). HarpC Child Bks.

Lancaster, John. Fabric Art. LC 90-12281. (Illus.). 48p. (gr. 5-8). 1991. PLB 11.90 (ISBN 0-531-14102-0). Watts.

O'Reilly, Susie. Textiles. (Illus.). 48p. (gr. 5-8). 1991. RLB 12.40 (ISBN 0-531-18441-2, Pub. by Boatwright Pr). Watts.

Smith, Elizabeth S. Cloth: Inventions That Changed Our Lives. LC 84-25768. (Illus.). 60p. (gr. 4-7). 1985. 10.85 (ISBN 0-8027-6577-7). Walker & Co.

THAILAND

Goldfarb, Mace. Fighters, Refugees, Immigrants: A Story of the Hmong. LC 82-4370. (Illus.). 48p. (gr. 4 up). 1982. lib. bdg. 9.95 (ISBN 0-87614-197-1). Carolrhoda Bks.

Jacobsen, Karen. Thailand. LC 89-34413. 48p. (gr. k-4). 1989. PLB 14.60 (ISBN 0-516-01179-0); pap. 4.95 (ISBN 0-516-41179-9). Childrens.

Jacobsen, P. & Kristensen, P. A Family in Thailand. (Illus.). 32p. (gr. k-6). 1986. lib. bdg. 11.90 (ISBN 0-531-18038-7, Pub. by Bookwright Pr). Watts.

Landon, Margaret. Anna & the King of Siam. Ayer, M., illus. 1944. 16.95 (ISBN 0-381-98135-5, A05201); 16.45i (ISBN 0-685-02093-2). HarpC Child Bks.

Lerner Publications, Department of Geography Staff, ed. Thailand in Pictures. (Illus.). 64p. (gr. 5 up). 1989. PLB 12.95 (ISBN 0-8225-1866-X). Lerner Pubns.

McNair, Sylvia. Thailand. LC 86-29933. (Illus.). 128p. (gr. 5-9). 1987. PLB 23.93 (ISBN 0-516-02792-1). Childrens.

Orihara, Kei. Children of the World: Thailand. LC 88-21050. (Illus.). 64p. (gr. 5-6). 1988. PLB 12.95 (ISBN 1-55532-223-9). Gareth Stevens Inc.

Wilkins, Frances. Thailand. (Illus.). (gr. 5 up). 1988. 14.95 (ISBN 0-222-00982-9). Chelsea Hse.

THAILAND–BIOGRAPHY

Thomson, Ruth & Thomson, Neil. A Family in Thailand. (Illus.). 32p. (gr. 2-5). 1988. lib. bdg. 9.95 (ISBN 0-8225-1684-5). Lerner Pubns.

THAILAND–FICTION

Ho, Minfong. Rice without Rain. LC 86-33745. 236p. (gr. 7 up). 1990. 12.95 (ISBN 0-688-06355-1). Lothrop.

THANKSGIVING DAY

Aemmer, Gail. Thanksgiving Activity Book. Brokaw, David, illus. 32p. (gr. 3-6). 1982. pap. 1.98 (ISBN 0-88724-042-9, CD-8016). Carson-Dellos.

Anderson, J. I. I Can Read About the First Thanksgiving. McKeown, Gloria, illus. LC 76-54400. (gr. 2-5). 1977. pap. 1.95 (ISBN 0-89375-034-4). Troll Assocs.

Anderson, Joan. The First Thanksgiving Feast. Ancona, George, photos by. LC 84-58040. (Illus.). (gr. 3-6). 1989. pap. 5.95 (ISBN 0-395-51886-5, Clarion Bks). HM.

Bains, Rae. Pilgrims & Thanksgiving. Wenzel, David, illus. LC 84-2686. 32p. (gr. 3-6). 1985. PLB 9.49 (ISBN 0-8167-0222-5); pap. text ed. 2.95 (ISBN 0-8167-0223-3). Troll Assocs.

Baker, James W. Thanksgiving Magic. Overlie, George, illus. 48p. (gr. 2-5). 1989. 8.95 (ISBN 0-8225-2233-0). Lerner Pubns.

Baldwin, Margaret. Thanksgiving. (Illus.). 72p. (gr. 4 up). 1983. PLB 10.40 (ISBN 0-531-04532-3). Watts.

Barkin, Carol & James, Elizabeth. Happy Thanksgiving! Carmi, Giora, illus. LC 86-33734. 96p. (gr. 4-7). 1987. 12.95 (ISBN 0-688-06800-6); PLB 12.88 (ISBN 0-688-06801-4). Lothrop.

Barth, Edna. Turkeys, Pilgrims, & Indian Corn: The Story of the Thanksgiving Symbols. Arndt, Ursula, illus. LC 75-4703. 96p. (gr. 3-6). 1981. pap. 4.95 (ISBN 0-89919-039-1, Pub. by Clarion). Ticknor & Fields.

—Turkeys, Pilgrims, & Indian Corn: The Story of the Thanksgiving Symbols. Arndt, Ursula, illus. LC 75-4703. 96p. (gr. 3-6). 1979. 13.95 (ISBN 0-395-28846-0, Clarion). HM.

Bartlett, Robert M. Thanksgiving Day. Mars, W. T., illus. LC 65-16178. 40p. (gr. 1-3). 1965. PLB 12.89 (ISBN 0-690-81045-8, Crowell Jr Bks). HarpC Child Bks.

Behrens, June. Feast of Thanksgiving. Siberell, Anne, illus. LC 74-3113. 32p. (gr. k-4). 1974. PLB 15.93 (ISBN 0-516-08725-8, Golden Gate). Childrens.

Boynton, Alice B. Priscilla Alden & the Story of the First Thanksgiving. Brook, Bonnie, ed. Kiefer, Christa, illus. 32p. (gr. k-2). 1990. 5.95 (ISBN 0-671-69111-2); PLB 10.98 (ISBN 0-671-69105-8). Silver Pr.

Bunting, Eve. How Many Days to America? A Thanksgiving Story. Peck, Beth, illus. LC 88-2590. 32p. (gr. k-4). 1988. 14.95 (ISBN 0-89919-521-0, Pub. by Clarion). Ticknor & Fields.

Butler, Elvie. Celebrate Thanksgiving with Stickers. 1989. pap. 3.95 (ISBN 0-590-42505-6). Scholastic Inc.

Carson, Patti & Dellosa, Janet. Thanksgiving Reading & Activity Book. (Illus.). 32p. (gr. 1-3). 1983. pap. 1.98 (ISBN 0-88724-037-2, CD-8028). Carson-Dellos.

Celsi, Teresa N. Squanto & the First Thanksgiving. (Illus.). 32p. (gr. 1-4). 1989. PLB 13.32 (ISBN 0-8172-3511-6). Raintree Pubs.

Conaway, Judith. Happy Thanksgiving: Things to Make & Do. Barto, Renzo, illus. LC 85-16463. 48p. (gr. 1-5). 1986. PLB 11.89 (ISBN 0-8167-0668-9); pap. text ed. 2.95 (ISBN 0-8167-0669-7). Troll Assocs.

Cracchiolo, Rachelle & Smith, Mary D. Thanksgiving Activities. Crachiolo, Rachelle & Smith, Mary D., illus. 32p. (gr. 1-4). 1985. wkbk. 4.95 (ISBN 1-55734-012-9). Tchr Create Mat.

Dalgliesh, Alice. Thanksgiving Story. Sewell, Helen, illus. (gr. k-3). 1950. 9.95 (ISBN 0-684-12330-4, Scribners Young Read). Macmillan Child Grp.

Davis, Nancy M., et al. November & Thanksgiving. Davis, Nancy M., illus. 31p. (Orig.). (ps-2). 1986. pap. 4.95 (ISBN 0-937103-02-0). DaNa Pubns.

Dellosa, Janet & Carson, Patti. Thanksgiving Fun Book. Dellosa, Janet & Carson, Patti, illus. 32p. (ps-2). 1981. pap. 1.59 (ISBN 0-88724-052-6, CD-8007). Carson-Dellos.

—Thanksgiving Readiness Activities. (Illus.). 32p. (ps-k). 1983. pap. 1.98 (ISBN 0-88724-048-8, CD-8024). Carson-Dellos.

Duden, Jane. Thanksgiving. LC 89-25397. (Illus.). 48p. (gr. 5 up). 1990. 10.95 (ISBN 0-89686-503-7, Crestwood Hse). Macmillan Child Grp.

Fradin, Dennis B. Thanksgiving. LC 89-7680. (Illus.). 48p. (gr. 2-3). 1990. PLB 12.95 (ISBN 0-89490-236-9). Enslow Pubs.

Gibbons, Gail. Thanksgiving Day. Gibbons, Gail, illus. LC 83-175. 32p. (ps-3). 1983. reinforced bdg. 14.95 (ISBN 0-8234-0489-7); pap. 5.95 (ISBN 0-8234-0576-1). Holiday.

Hayward, Linda. The First Thanksgiving: A Step 2 Book - Grades 1-3. Watling, James, illus. LC 90-52517. 48p. (Orig.). (gr. k-3). 1990. lib. bdg. 6.99 (ISBN 0-679-90218-X); pap. 2.95 (ISBN 0-679-80218-5). Random.

Kessel, Joyce K. Squanto & the First Thanksgiving. Donze, Lisa, illus. LC 82-10313. 48p. (gr. k-4). 1983. PLB 9.95 (ISBN 0-87614-199-8); pap. 3.95 (ISBN 0-87614-452-0). Carolrhoda Bks.

Kinnealy, Janice. Let's Celebrate Thanksgiving: A Book of Drawing Fun. Kinnealy, Janice, illus. LC 87-61373. 32p. (gr. 2-6). 1988. PLB 10.65 (ISBN 0-8167-1131-3); pap. text ed. 1.95 (ISBN 0-8167-1132-1). Troll Assocs.

Ludwig, Nancy. Thanksgiving, Plays & Art Project Puppets. Fowler, Christopher, illus. 32p. (gr. k-3). 1983. pap. 1.98 (ISBN 0-88724-044-5, CD-8020). Carson-Dellos.

Moncure, Jane B. My First Thanksgiving Book. Connelly, Gwen, illus. LC 84-9433. 32p. (ps-2). 1984. PLB 14.60 (ISBN 0-516-02903-7); pap. 3.95 (ISBN 0-516-42903-5). Childrens.

—Our Thanksgiving Book. rev. ed. Gohman, Vera, illus. LC 85-29077. 32p. (ps-3). 1986. lib. bdg. 11.97 (ISBN 0-89565-340-0). Childs World.

Parker, Margot. What Is Thanksgiving Day? Bates, Matt, illus. LC 88-11112. 32p. (gr. 4-8). 1988. PLB 14.60 (ISBN 0-516-03783-8); pap. 4.95 (ISBN 0-516-43783-6). Childrens.

Penner, Lucille R. The Thanksgiving Book. Donnelly, Judy, ed. LC 84-518. (Illus.). (gr. 4 up). 1985. 14.95 (ISBN 0-8038-7228-3); lib. bdg. 14.95 (ISBN 0-8038-9291-8). Hastings.

Prelutsky, Jack. It's Thanksgiving. 1986. pap. 2.25 (ISBN 0-590-32836-0). Scholastic Inc.

Stevenson, James. Fried Feathers for Thanksgiving. Stevenson, James, illus. LC 86-3100. 32p. (gr. k-3). 1986. 13.95 (ISBN 0-688-06675-5); PLB 13.88 (ISBN 0-688-06676-3). Greenwillow.

Whitlock, Ralph. Thanksgiving & Harvest. (Illus.). 48p. (gr. 3-8). 1987. PLB 14.60 (ISBN 0-86592-976-9). Rourke Corp.

THANKSGIVING DAY–FICTION

Alcott, Louisa May. An Old-Fashioned Thanksgiving. Johnson, Holly, illus. LC 73-15698. 72p. (gr. 4-6). 1974. 12.95 (ISBN 0-397-31515-5, Lipp Jr Bks). HarpC Child Bks.

—An Old-Fashioned Thanksgiving. McCurdy, Michael, illus. LC 89-1908. 32p. (gr. 3-7). 1989. reinforced 14.95 (ISBN 0-8234-0772-1). Holiday.

Barth, Jeff. A Thanksgiving Story in Vermont - 1852. Mitchinson, Shelia, illus. 60p. (Orig.). (gr. 3-8). 1989. pap. write for info. (ISBN 0-9624067-0-8). Parable Pub.

Berenstain, Stan & Berenstain, Jan. The Berenstain Bears & the Prize Pumpkin. Berenstain, Stan & Berenstain, Jan, illus. LC 90-32865. 32p. (Orig.). (ps-1). 1990. lib. bdg. 5.99 (ISBN 0-679-90847-1); pap. 2.25 (ISBN 0-679-80847-7). Random.

Brown, Marc. Arthur's Thanksgiving. Brown, Marc, illus. LC 83-798. 32p. (gr. 1-3). 1984. 14.95 (ISBN 0-316-11060-4, Joy St Bks); pap. 4.95 (ISBN 0-316-11232-1). Little.

Bunting, Eve. How Many Days to America: A Thanksgiving Story. Bunting, Eve, illus. 32p. (ps-3). 1990. pap. 5.95 (ISBN 0-395-54777-6, Clarion Bks). HM.

Child, Lydia M. Over the River & Through the Wood. Turkle, Brinton, illus. LC 74-79700. 32p. (ps-3). 1974. 8.95 (ISBN 0-698-20301-1, Coward). Putnam Pub Group.

—Over the River & Through the Wood. Turkle, Brinton, illus. (gr. k-3). 1975. pap. 1.95 (ISBN 0-590-09937-X). Scholastic Inc.

—Over the River & Through the Wood. Turkle, Brinton, illus. 32p. (gr. k-3). 1987. pap. 3.95 (ISBN 0-590-41190-X, Blue Ribbons Bks). Scholastic Inc.

Cohen, Miriam. Don't Eat Too Much Turkey! Hoban, Lillian, illus. LC 86-25660. 32p. (gr. k-3). 1987. 13.95 (ISBN 0-688-07141-4); lib. bdg. 13.88 (ISBN 0-688-07142-2). Greenwillow.

Cuyler, Margery. Daisy's Crazy Thanksgiving. Kramer, Robin, illus. 32p. (gr. k-3). 1990. 14.95 (ISBN 0-8050-0559-5). H Holt & Co.

Dalgliesh, Alice. The Thanksgiving Story. Sewell, Helen, illus. 32p. (Orig.). (gr. k-3). 1985. pap. 4.95 (ISBN 0-689-71053-4, Aladdin). Macmillan Child Grp.

—The Thanksgiving Story. Sewell, Helen, illus. LC 88-4448. 32p. (gr. k-3). 1988. Repr. of 1954 ed. 13.95 (ISBN 0-684-18999-2, Scribners Young Read). Macmillan Child Grp.

Devlin, Wende & Devlin, Harry. Cranberry Thanksgiving. Devlin, Harry, illus. LC 80-17070. 48p. (ps-3). 1984. Repr. of 1971 ed. 13.95 (ISBN 0-02-729930-9, Four Winds). Macmillan Child Grp.

—Cranberry Thanksgiving. Devlin, Wende & Devlin, Harry, illus. LC 89-18642. 40p. (gr. k-3). 1990. pap. 3.95 (ISBN 0-689-71429-7, Aladdin). Macmillan Child Grp.

Gibbons, Gail. Thanksgiving Day. Gibbons, Gail, illus. (gr. k-3). 1984. incl. cassette 19.95 (ISBN 0-941078-63-9); pap. 12.95 incl. cassette (ISBN 0-941078-61-2); pap. 27.95 4 bks., cassette & guide (ISBN 0-941078-62-0); sound filmstrip 22.95 (ISBN 0-941078-60-4). Live Oak Media.

Glovach, Linda. The Little Witch's Thanksgiving Book. (Illus.). (gr. 1-4). 1981. pap. 2.50 (ISBN 0-13-538009-X, Pub. by Treehouse). P-H.

Hoban, Lillian. Silly Tilly's Thanksgiving Dinner. Hoban, Lillian, illus. LC 89-29287. 64p. (gr. k-3). 1990. 11.95 (ISBN 0-06-022422-3); PLB 11.89 (ISBN 0-06-022423-1). HarpC Child Bks.

Janice. Little Bear's Thanksgiving. Mariana, illus. LC 67-22593. 32p. (gr. k-3). 1967. PLB 12.88 (ISBN 0-688-51078-7). Lothrop.

Kessel, Joyce K. Squanto & the First Thanksgiving. Donze, Lisa, illus. LC 82-10313. 48p. (gr. k-4). 1983. PLB 9.95 (ISBN 0-87614-199-8); pap. 3.95 (ISBN 0-87614-452-0). Carolrhoda Bks.

Kroll, Steven. Oh, What a Thanksgiving! Schindler, S. D., illus. LC 88-1973. (gr. k-3). 1988. pap. 12.95 (ISBN 0-590-40613-2, Scholastic Hardcover). Scholastic Inc.

—Oh, What a Thanksgiving! (Illus.). 32p. 1991. pap. 3.95 (ISBN 0-590-44874-9, Blue Ribbon Bks). Scholastic Inc.

Leedy, Loreen. The Dragon Thanksgiving Feast: Things to Make & Do. Leedy, Loreen, illus. LC 90-55110. 32p. (gr. k-3). 1990. reinforced 14.95 (ISBN 0-8234-0828-0). Holiday.

Marilue. Bobby Bear's Thanksgiving. LC 77-83623. (Illus.). 32p. (ps-1). 1978. PLB 9.95 (ISBN 0-87783-143-2); cassette o.s.i. 7.94x (ISBN 0-87783-187-4). Oddo.

Markham, Marion M. The Thanksgiving Day Parade Mystery. Cassidy, Dianne, illus. 64p. 1990. pap. 2.95 (ISBN 0-380-70967-8, Camelot). Avon.

Nerlove, Miriam. Thanksgiving. Mathews, Judith, ed. Nerlove, Meriam, illus. 24p. (ps-1). 1990. PLB 10.95 (ISBN 0-8075-7818-5). A Whitman.

Nixon, Joan L. The Thanksgiving Mystery. Fay, Ann, ed. Cummins, Jim, illus. LC 79-27346. (gr. 1-3). 1980. PLB 8.95 (ISBN 0-8075-7820-7). A Whitman.

Pilkey, Dav. Twas the Night Before Thanksgiving. Pilkey, Dav, illus. LC 89-48941. 32p. (ps-2). 1990. 13.95 (ISBN 0-531-05905-7); PLB 13.99 (ISBN 0-531-08505-8). Orchard Bks Watts.

Pinkwater, Daniel M. The Hoboken Chicken Emergency. LC 76-41910. (Illus.). (gr. 3-7). 1984. 10.95 (ISBN 0-13-392514-5); pap. 4.95 (ISBN 0-13-392499-8). P-H.

Prelutsky, Jack. It's Thanksgiving. Hafner, Marilyn, illus. 48p. (gr. k-3). 1987. Bk.-Cassette prepack. pap. 5.95 (ISBN 0-590-63169-1); pap. 2.50 (ISBN 0-590-41571-9). Scholastic Inc.

Quackenbush, Robert. Sheriff Sally Gopher & the Thanksgiving Caper. Quackenbush, Robert, illus. LC 82-135. 32p. (gr. 1-3). 1982. PLB 13.88 (ISBN 0-688-01293-0). Lothrop.

Rock, Gail. The Thanksgiving Treasure. Gehm, Charles, illus. LC 74-163. 96p. (gr. 2 up). 1974. PLB 9.99 (ISBN 0-394-92834-2). Knopf.

—The Thanksgiving Treasure. (gr. 3-6). 1986. pap. 2.95 (ISBN 0-440-49117-7, YB). Dell.

Schulz, Charles M. A Charlie Brown Thanksgiving. (gr. 3 up). 1974. 4.95 (ISBN 0-394-83047-4, Random Juv). Random.

Spinelli, Eileen. Thanksgiving at the Tappletons' Cocca-Leffler, Maryann, illus. LC 84-40793. 32p. (gr. k-3). 1984. 11.95 (ISBN 0-201-15892-2, Lipp Jr Bks). HarpC Child Bks.

—Thanksgiving at the Tappletons' LC 84-40793. (Illus.). 32p. (gr. k-3). 1989. pap. 4.95 (ISBN 0-06-443204-1, Trophy). HarpC Child Bks.

Stock, Catherine. Thanksgiving Treat. Stock, Catherine, illus. LC 89-49528. 32p. (ps-1). 1990. 11.95 (ISBN 0-02-788402-3, Bradbury Pr). Macmillan Child Grp.

Tripp, Valerie. Squirrel's Thanksgiving Surprise. Martin, Sandra K., illus. LC 87-35518. 24p. (gr. k-2). 1988. PLB 12.33 (ISBN 0-516-01568-0); pap. 3.95 (ISBN 0-516-41568-9). Childrens.

Williams, Barbara. Chester Chipmunk's Thanksgiving. Chorao, Kay, illus. LC 77-20812. (gr. k-3). 1988. 11.95 (ISBN 0-525-27655-6, DCB); pap. 3.95 (ISBN 0-525-44429-7, DCB). Dutton Child Bks.

THEATER

see also Acting; Actors and Actresses; Ballet; Mysteries and Miracle Plays; Opera; Puppets and Puppet Plays; Shadow Pantomimes and Plays

Bishop, Conrad & Fuller, Elizabeth. Get Happy. 36p. (Orig.). (gr. 9-12). 1990. pap. 4.00 acting ed. (ISBN 0-9624511-0-X). WordWorkers.

Boy Scouts of America. Theater. 64p. (gr. 6-12). 1968. pap. 1.85 (ISBN 0-8395-3328-4, 3328). BSA.

Evans, C. Acting & Theater. (Illus.). 64p. (gr. 6 up). 1992. lib. bdg. 13.96 (ISBN 0-88110-505-8, Usborne); pap. 7.95 (ISBN 0-7460-0699-3). EDC.

Franck, Irene M. & Brownstone, David M. Performers & Players. (Illus.). 208p. (gr. 7 up). 1988. 17.95 (ISBN 0-8160-1448-5). Facts on File.

Haskins, James. Black Theater in America. LC 81-43874. (Illus.). 192p. (gr. 7 up). 1982. 12.95 (ISBN 0-690-04128-4, Crowell Jr Bks). HarpC Child Bks.

Haycock, Kate. Plays. Stefoff, Rebecca, ed. LC 90-13937. (Illus.). 32p. (gr. 4-8). 1991. PLB 17.26 (ISBN 0-944483-98-4). Garrett Ed Corp.

Looking at Theater. 48p. (gr. 4-8). 1990. 13.95 (ISBN 1-85435-103-6). Marshall Cavendish.

Morin, Alice. Newspaper Theatre. (gr. 1-8). 1989. pap. 6.95 (ISBN 0-8224-6349-0). Fearon Teach Aids.

Novelly, Maria C. Theatre Games for Young Performers. Pijanowski, Kathy & Zapel, Arthur L., eds. LC 85-60572. (Illus.). 160p. (Orig.). (gr. 6-10). 1985. pap. text ed. 8.95 (ISBN 0-916260-31-3, B-188). Meriwether Pub.

Ratliff, Gerald L. & Troth, Susan. Onstage, Producing Musical Theatre. (Illus.). 109p. (gr. 7-12). 1988. PLB 14.95 (ISBN 0-8239-0697-3). Rosen Group.

THEATER–FICTION

Ashley, Ellen. Summer Stock. 1991. pap. 3.50 (ISBN 0-449-14588-3, Pub. by Girls Only). Fawcett.

Auch, Mary J. Glass Slippers Give You Blisters. LC 88-45865. 176p. (gr. 3-7). 1989. 13.95 (ISBN 0-8234-0752-7). Holiday.

Barkan, Joanne. Whiskerville Theater. (Illus.). 12p. (ps-k). 1991. bds. 3.95 (ISBN 0-448-40084-7, G&D). Putnam Pub Group.

Ende, Michael. Ophelia's Shadow Theater. Hechelmann, Friedrich, illus. 32p. (gr. 1 up). 1989. 14.95 (ISBN 0-87951-371-3). Overlook Pr.

Giff, Patricia R. The Almost Awful Play. Natti, Susanna, illus. LC 84-17922. 32p. (ps-3). 1985. pap. 3.95 (ISBN 0-14-050530-X, Puffin). Puffin Bks.

Howe, James. Stage Fright: A Sebastian Barth Mystery. 160p. (gr. 3-7). 1986. 12.95 (ISBN 0-689-31160-5, Atheneum Child Bk). Macmillan.

Kingman, Lee. Break a Leg, Betsy, Maybe. 192p. (gr. 7 up). 1979. pap. 1.50 (ISBN 0-440-90794-2, LFL). Dell.

Lukas, Cynthia K. Center Stage Summer. 157p. (Orig.). (gr. 8-12). 1988. pap. 4.95 (ISBN 0-938961-02-0, Stamp Out Sheep Press). Sq One Pubs.

Streatfeild, Noel. Theater Shoes. 208p. (gr. k-6). 1983. pap. 2.95 (ISBN 0-440-48791-9, YB). Dell.

THEATER–HISTORY

Sitarz, Paula Gaj. The Curtain Rises, Vol. 1: Early Origins & Eastern Theater. LC 90-21953. (Illus.). 144p. (gr. 5-9). 1991. 14.95 (ISBN 1-55870-198-2, Shoe Tree Pr). Betterway Pubns.

THEATER–PRODUCTION AND DIRECTION

see also Amateur Theatricals

Baylor, Byrd. Moon Song. Himler, Ronald, illus. LC 81-18427. 24p. (gr. 3-6). 1982. 11.95 (ISBN 0-684-17463-4, Scribners Young Read). Macmillan Child Grp.

Garrett, Dan, ed. Masks & Faces. (Illus.). 96p. (Orig.). 1990. pap. 14.95 (ISBN 0-333-36056-7, McMillan Ed UK). Players Pr.

—Scapegoats. (Illus.). 96p. (Orig.). 1990. pap. 14.95 (ISBN 0-333-36055-9, McMillan Ed UK). Players Pr.

Kezer, Claude D. Principles of Stage Combat. (Illus.). 62p. 1983. pap. 12.50 (ISBN 0-88680-156-7). I E Clark.

Poulsson, Emilie. Finger Plays for Nursery & Kindergarten. Bridgman, L. T., illus. LC 74-165397. (ps-k). 1971. pap. 2.25 (ISBN 0-486-22588-7). Dover.

Rabe, Berniece. Rehearsal for the Bigtime. De Groat, Diane, illus. Sloan, Frank, ed. (Illus.). 144p. (gr. 7-9). 1988. 12.90 (ISBN 0-531-10504-0). Watts.

Thompson, Gregory. Step by Step Theatre. (gr. 1-4). 1989. pap. 9.95 (ISBN 0-8224-6348-2). Fearon Teach Aids.

THEATERS–STAGE SETTING AND SCENERY

Hodgman, Ann. A Day in the Life of a Theater Set Designer. Jann, Gayle, illus. LC 87-10951. 32p. (gr. 4-8). 1988. PLB 11.79 (ISBN 0-8167-1127-5); pap. text ed. 2.95 (ISBN 0-8167-1128-3). Troll Assocs.

Molyneux, Lynn & Gordner, Brad. Act It Out: Original Plays Plus Crafts for Costumes & Scenery. Marasco, Pam, illus. 192p. (gr. 2-6). 1986. spiral bdg. 12.95 (ISBN 0-685-29139-1). Trellis Bks Inc.

THEATRICAL COSTUME

see Costume

THEATRICAL MAKE-UP

see Make-Up, Theatrical

THEATRICAL SCENERY

see Theaters–Stage Setting and Scenery

THEATRICALS, AMATEUR

see Amateur Theatricals

THEOLOGY

see also Baptism; Christianity; Church; Ethics; Faith; God; Jesus Christ; Religion; Religion and Science; Spiritual Life; Worship

THEOLOGY, DEVOTIONAL

see Prayers

THEORETICAL CHEMISTRY

see Chemistry, Physical and Theoretical

THEORY OF NUMBERS

see Numbers Theory

THEORY OF SETS

see Set Theory

THERMODYNAMICS

see also Heat

Jacobs, Linda. Letting off Steam: The Story of Geothermal Energy. (Illus.). 48p. (gr. 3-6). 1989. lib. bdg. 12.95 (ISBN 0-87614-300-1); pap. 6.95 (ISBN 0-87614-510-1). Carolrhoda Bks.

Rickard, Graham. Geothermal Energy. (Illus.). 32p. (gr. 4-6). 1991. PLB 11.95 (ISBN 0-8368-0708-1). Gareth Stevens Inc.

THERMOMETERS AND THERMOMETRY

see also Temperature

Maestro, Betsy. Temperature & You. Maestro, Guilio, illus. 32p. (gr. k-3). 1990. 13.95 (ISBN 0-525-67271-0, Lodestar Bks). Dutton Child Bks.

THIEVES

see Robbers and Outlaws

THINKING

see Thought and Thinking

THOREAU, HENRY DAVID, 1817-1862

Burleigh, Robert. A Man Named Thoreau. Bloom, Lloyd, illus. LC 85-7947. 48p. (gr. 3 up). 1985. 12.95 (ISBN 0-689-31122-2, Atheneum Child Bk). Macmillan Child Grp.

Miller, Douglas. Henry David Thoreau. Scott, John A., ed. (Illus.). 144p. (gr. 6-10). 1991. lib. bdg. 16.95x (ISBN 0-8160-2478-2). Facts on File.

THOREAU, HENRY DAVID, 1817-1862–DRAMA

Lawrence, Jerome & Lee, Robert E. The Night Thoreau Spent in Jail. 128p. (gr. 8-12). 1983. pap. 3.95 (ISBN 0-553-27838-X). Bantam.

THOROUGHFARES

see Roads

THORPE, JAMES, 1888-1953

Fago, John N. & Farr, Naunerle C. Jim Thorpe - Althea Gibson. Redondo, Frank & Carrillo, Fred, illus. (gr. 4-12). 1979. pap. text ed. 2.95 (ISBN 0-88301-360-6); wkbk. 1.25 (ISBN 0-88301-384-3). Pendulum Pr.

Richards, Gregory. Jim Thorpe: World's Greatest Athlete. LC 84-14240. (Illus.). 112p. (gr. 4 up). 1984. lib. bdg. 17.27 (ISBN 0-516-03207-0). Childrens.

Rivinus, Edward F. Jim Thorpe. Viola, Herman, intro. by. (Illus.). 32p. (gr. 3-6). 1990. PLB 16.67 (ISBN 0-8172-3403-9). Raintree Pubs.

Santrey, Laurence. Jim Thorpe: Young Athlete. Ulrich, George, illus. LC 82-15982. 48p. (gr. 4-6). 1983. PLB 10.79 (ISBN 0-89375-845-0); pap. text ed. 2.95 (ISBN 0-89375-846-9). Troll Assocs.

Van Riper, Guernsey, Jr. Jim Thorpe: Olympic Champion. Morrow, Gray, illus. LC 86-3478. 192p. (gr. 2-6). 1986. pap. 3.95 (ISBN 0-02-042140-0, Aladdin). Macmillan Child Grp.

THOUGHT AND THINKING

see also Intellect; Logic; Perception; Reasoning

Allington, Richard L. & Krull, Kathleen. Thinking. Garcia, Tom, illus. LC 80-15390. 32p. (ps-2). 1985. PLB 15.33 (ISBN 0-8172-1319-8); pap. 9.27 (ISBN 0-8172-2494-7). Raintree Pubs.

Aten, Jerry. Prime Time Thinking Skills. Filkins, Vanessa, illus. 64p. (gr. 2-5). 1985. wkbk. 6.95 (ISBN 0-86653-276-5, GA 628). Good Apple.

Clements, Zacharie J. & Hawhes, Richard R. Mastermind: Excercises in Critical Thinking. (gr. 4-6). 1985. pap. 7.50 (ISBN 0-673-16653-8). Scott F.

Dirkes, M. Ann. Math Through Creative Thinking. Zilliox, Elaine, ed. (Illus.). 44p. (Orig.). (gr. 4-12). 1984. 5.95 (ISBN 0-88047-034-8, 7707). DOK Pubs.

Fein, Sylvia. First Drawing: Genesis of Visual Thinking. (Illus.). 160p. Date not set. 32.50; pap. 24.95. Exelrod Pr. Analyzes the structure of first drawings & the similarity between the drawings of children, primitives, & other artists in all times & societies to demonstrate their identical artistic logic & process in visual thinking. In print by Sylvia

Fein: HEIDI'S HORSE ISBN 0-917388-02-X. A chronologic record of one child's drawings between the ages of 2 & 16 demonstrates consistent obedience to laws of visual thinking. *Publisher Provided Annotation.*

Forte, Imogene. I'm Ready to Learn about Thinking Skills. (Illus.). 64p. (ps-1). 1986. pap. text ed. write for info. (ISBN 0-86530-117-4, IP 111-1). Incentive Pubns.
Juntune, Joyce E. Developing Creative Thinking. Dougherty, Edie, illus. 30p. (gr. k-4). 1984. pap. 5.00 (ISBN 0-912773-09-X). One Hund Twenty Creat.
—Developing Creative Thinking: Fun Book, No. 3. Dougherty, Edie, illus. (ps-5). 1985. pap. 6.00 (ISBN 0-912773-10-3). One Hund Twenty Creat.
Katz, Marjorie P. & Arbeiter, Jean S., eds. Pegs to Hang Ideas on: A Book of Quotations. LC 76-187739. 320p. (gr. 6 up). 1976. 12.95 (ISBN 0-87131-085-6). M Evans.
Metos, Thomas H. The Human Mind: How We Think & Learn. (Illus.). 128p. (gr. 9-12). 1990. PLB 12.40 (ISBN 0-531-10885-6). Watts.
Richardson, Joy. What Happens When You Think? LC 86-1934. (Illus.). 32p. (gr. 2-3). 1986. PLB 10.95 (ISBN 1-55532-113-5). Gareth Stevens Inc.
Stevens, Lawrence A. Thinking Tools. Radrigan, Roberto, illus. 73p. (Orig.). (gr. 5-10). 1984. pap. text ed. 6.50 (ISBN 0-89550-223-2). Stevens & Shea.
Taulbee, Annette. Kindergarten Thinking Skills. (Illus.). 24p. (ps-k). 1986. 3.98 (ISBN 0-86734-067-3, FS-3060). Schaffer Pubns.
Westcott, Alvin. Word Bending with Aunt Sarah. LC 68-56821. (Illus.). 48p. (gr. 2-3). 1968. PLB 9.95 (ISBN 0-87783-052-5); pap. 3.94 deluxe ed (ISBN 0-87783-118-1). Oddo.

THOUGHT TRANSFERENCE
see also Extrasensory Perception; Hypnotism
Insel, Eunice & Edson, Ann. Developing Critical Thinking, Bk. 2. (gr. 5-6). 1983. wkbk. 4.25 (ISBN 1-55737-652-2). Ed Activities.

THUNDERSTORMS
see also Lightning
Branley, Franklyn M. Flash, Crash, Rumble, & Roll. rev. ed. Emberley, Ed E. & Emberley, Barbara, illus. LC 84-45333. 32p. (ps-3). 1985. PLB 13.89 (ISBN 0-690-04425-9, Crowell Jr Bks). HarpC Child Bks.
Cutts, David. I Can Read About Thunder & Lightning. LC 78-66273. (Illus.). (gr. 2-6). 1979. pap. 1.95 (ISBN 0-89375-217-7). Troll Assocs.

Sanchez, Brenda L. Max Science & the Thunderstorm. Sanchez, J. A., ed. Beard, Derrick, illus. 26p. (gr. k-5). 1991. pap. 3.95 (ISBN 1-879350-02-5). Max Sci Pub.

THUNDERSTORMS–FICTION
Polacco, Patricia. Thunder Cake. (Illus.). 32p. (ps-3). 1990. 14.95 (ISBN 0-399-22231-6, Philomel Bks). Putnam Pub Group.

TIBET
Gerstein, Mordicai. The Mountains of Tibet. LC 85-45684. (Illus.). 32p. (gr. 2 up). 1989. pap. 4.95 (ISBN 0-06-443211-4, Trophy). HarpC Child Bks.

TIBET–FICTION
Gerstein, Mordicai. The Mountains of Tibet. LC 85-45684. (Illus.). 32p. (gr. 2 up). 1989. pap. 4.95 (ISBN 0-06-443211-4, Trophy). HarpC Child Bks.
Morpurgo, Michael. King of the Cloud Forest. (Illus.). 160p. (gr. 5-9). 1991. pap. 3.95 (ISBN 0-14-032586-7, Puffin). Puffin Bks.

TIDAL WAVES
see Ocean Waves

TIDES
Bowden, Joan. Why the Tides Ebb & Flow. Brown, Marc, illus. 48p. (gr. k-3). 1990. pap. 4.95 (ISBN 0-395-54952-3). HM.

TIDES–FICTION
Cole, Sheila. When the Tide Is Low. Wright-Frierson, Virginia, illus. LC 84-10023. 32p. (ps-1). 1985. 12.95 (ISBN 0-688-04066-7); PLB 12.88 (ISBN 0-688-04067-5). Lothrop.
Pullman, Philip. The Tiger in the Well. LC 89-26677. 320p. (gr. 7 up). 1990. 15.95 (ISBN 0-679-80214-2); lib. bdg. 16.99 (ISBN 0-679-90214-7). Knopf.

TIGERS
Ashby, Ruth. Jane Goodall's Animal World: Tigers. Goodall, Jane, intro. by. LC 89-38547. (Illus.). 32p. (gr. 3-7). 1990. 11.95 (ISBN 0-689-31474-4, Atheneum Child Bk). Macmillan Child Grp.
Bender, Lionel. Lions & Tigers. FS-Aladdin Staff, ed. (Illus.). 32p. (gr. 1-6). 1988. PLB 11.90 (ISBN 0-531-17101-9, Gloucester Pr). Watts.
Bright, Michael. Tiger. (Illus.). 32p. (gr. 5-6). 1989. PLB 11.90 (ISBN 0-531-17141-8). Watts.
Cajacob, Thomas & Burton, Teresa. Close to the Wild: Siberian Tigers in a Zoo. Cajacob, Thomas, photos by. (Illus.). 48p. (gr. 2-5). 1986. PLB 12.95 (ISBN 0-87614-227-7); pap. 6.95 (ISBN 0-87614-451-2). Carolrhoda Bks.
Crump, Donald J., ed. Lions & Tigers & Leopards: The Big Cats. (Illus.). (gr. k-4). 1990. Set. 13.95 (ISBN 0-87044-820-X); Set. PLB write for info. (ISBN 0-87044-825-0). Natl Geog.
Goodall, Jane. Jane Goodall's Animal World: Tigers. 32p. (gr. 3-7). 1990. pap. 3.95 (ISBN 0-689-71393-2, Aladdin). Macmillan Child Grp.
Green, Carl R. & Sanford, William R. The Bengal Tiger. LC 85-31411. (Illus.). 48p. (gr. 5-6). 1986. PLB 10.95 (ISBN 0-89686-270-4, Crestwood Hse). Macmillan Child Grp.
Hoffman, Mary. Tiger. LC 84-15120. (Illus.). 24p. (gr. k-5). 1984. PLB 13.32 (ISBN 0-8172-2405-X). Raintree Pubs.
Hogan, Paula Z. The Tiger. Nachreiner, Tom, illus. LC 79-13604. (gr. 1-4). 1979. PLB 16.67 (ISBN 0-8172-1506-9). Raintree Pubs.
—The Tiger. LC 79-13604. (Illus.). 32p. (gr. 1-4). 1981. PLB 27.99 incl. cassette (ISBN 0-8172-1841-6); cassette 14.00 (ISBN 0-685-09537-1). Raintree Pubs.
Hunt, Patricia. Tigers. (gr. 2-5). 1981. 8.95 (ISBN 0-396-07932-6, Putnam). Putnam Pub Group.
Lavine, Sigmund A. Wonders of Tigers. (gr. 3-7). 1987. 11.95 (ISBN 0-396-09153-9, Putnam). Putnam Pub Group.
Lewin, Ted. Tiger Trek. Lewin, Ted, illus. LC 89-12710. 40p. (gr. 1-5). 1990. 14.95 (ISBN 0-02-757381-8, Macmillan Child Bk). Macmillan Child Grp.
Martin, L. Tigers. (Illus.). 24p. (gr. k-5). Date not set. PLB 11.93 (ISBN 0-86592-995-5). Rourke Corp.
Petty, Kate. Tigers. Kline, M., ed. (Illus.). 24p. (gr. k-3). 1991. PLB 10.40 (ISBN 0-531-17284-8, Gloucester Pr). Watts.
Royston, Angela. The Tiger. Allen, Graham, illus. 24p. (Orig.). (ps-2). 1988. pap. 2.95 (ISBN 0-8249-8247-9). Ideals.
—The Tiger. JV-Warwick Press Staff, ed. (Illus.). 24p. (gr. 1-3). 1988. 7.79 (ISBN 0-531-19043-9, Warwick). Watts.
Saunier. Tiger, Reading Level 3-4. (Illus.). 28p. (gr. 2-5). Date not set. PLB 14.60 (ISBN 0-86592-866-5). Rourke Corp.
Stone, L. Tigers. (Illus.). 24p. (gr. k-5). 1989. lib. bdg. 11.93 (ISBN 0-86592-504-6). Rourke Corp.
The Tiger. (gr. 2-5). 1988. pap. 2.50 (ISBN 0-8167-1571-8). Troll Assocs.
Wexo, John B. Tigers. 24p. (gr. 4). 1989. 11.50s.p. (ISBN 0-88682-266-1); 16.45 (ISBN 0-685-28182-5). Creative Ed.
Wildlife Education, Ltd. Staff. Tigers. Orr, Richard, et al, illus. 20p. (Orig.). (gr. k-12). 1985. pap. 2.25 (ISBN 0-937934-35-6). Wildlife Educ.
Wood, Jenny. Tigers. (Illus.). 32p. (Orig.). (gr. 3-7). 1989. pap. 4.95 (ISBN 0-14-034172-2, Puffin). Puffin Bks.

TIGERS–FICTION
Bailey, Jill. Save the Tiger. LC 89-48770. (Illus.). 48p. (gr. 3-7). 1990. PLB 17.28 (ISBN 0-8114-2703-X). Steck-V.
Baker, Keith. Who is the Beast? Baker, Keith, illus. 32p. (ps-3). Date not set. pap. write for info. (ISBN 0-15-296059-7). HarBraceJ.
—Who Is the Beast? Baker, Keith, illus. LC 89-29365. (ps-1). 1990. 12.95 (ISBN 0-15-296057-0). HarBraceJ.
Bannerman, Helen. Story of Little Black Sambo. (Illus.). (gr. k-3). 1923. 9.95 (ISBN 0-397-30006-9, HarpT). HarperCollins.
Blaustein, Muriel. Play Ball, Zachary! Blaustein, Muriel, illus. LC 87-45274. 32p. (ps-2). 1988. 11.95 (ISBN 0-06-020543-1); PLB 11.89 (ISBN 0-06-020544-X). HarpC Child Bks.
Brooks, Gwendolyn. The Tiger Who Wore White Gloves: Or What You Are Your Are. LC 74-75589. 1974. pap. 6.95 (ISBN 0-88378-031-3). Third World.
Cowley, Joy. The Terrible Tiger, 6 bks. Francis, John, illus. 16p. (Orig.). (gr. k-2). 1987. Set. pap. text ed. 19.80 (ISBN 1-55624-737-0). Wright Group.
—The Terrible Tiger. Francis, John, illus. 16p. (Orig.). (gr. k-2). 1987. pap. text ed. 23.00 (ISBN 1-55624-160-7). Wright Group.
Dodds, Siobhan. Charles Tiger. Dodds, Siobhan, illus. (ps-3). 1988. 9.95 (ISBN 0-316-18817-4, Joy Street Bks). Little.
Dr. Seuss. I Can Lick Thirty Tigers Today! & Other Stories. Dr. Seuss, illus. LC 71-86940. 64p. (gr. k-3). 1980. pap. 3.95 (ISBN 0-394-84543-9, Random Juv). Random.
Harley, Rex. Mary's Tiger. Porter, Sue, illus. LC 89-49009. 32p. (ps-2). 1990. 13.95 (ISBN 0-685-35583-7, Gulliver Bks). HarBraceJ.
Hawkins, Colin & Hawkins, Jacqui. Terrible, Terrible Tiger. Hawkins, Colin & Hawkins, Jacqui, illus. LC 87-40675. 32p. (ps-3). 1988. bds. 5.95 (ISBN 1-55782-043-0). Warner Bks.
Hubbell, Patricia. The Tigers Brought Pink Lemonade. Chen, Ju-Hong, illus. LC 87-27800. 32p. 1988. 12.95 (ISBN 0-689-31417-5, Atheneum Child Bk). Macmillan Child Grp.
Kraus, Robert, et al. Leo the Late Bloomer Takes a Bath. Aruego, Jose & Dewey, Ariane, illus. 10p. (ps). 1981. vinyl 2.95 (ISBN 0-671-42554-4, Little Simon). S&S Trade.
Krauss, Robert. Leo the Late Bloomer. Aruego, Jose, illus. LC 80-12511. (ps). 1987. pap. 5.95 (ISBN 0-671-66271-6). S&S Trade.
Kurkul, Edward. Tiger in the Lake. Petie, Haris, illus. LC 68-11183. (gr. 1-3). 1968. write for info. (ISBN 0-8313-0076-0); PLB 6.70. Lantern.
LaFleur, Tom & Brennan, Gale. Tuffy the Tiger. Murtagh, Betty, illus. 16p. (gr. k-6). 1982. pap. 1.25 (ISBN 0-685-05557-4). Brennan Bks.
Lewis, Sharon. Tiger! Roberts, Linda, illus. 20p. (ps-4). 1990. 8.95 (ISBN 0-694-00296-8). HarpC Child Bks.
Oetting, Rae. Timmy Tiger & the Elephant. LC 73-108730. (Illus.). 32p. (ps-2). 1970. PLB 9.95 (ISBN 0-87783-041-X); pap. 3.94 deluxe ed (ISBN 0-87783-111-4); cassette 7.94x (ISBN 0-87783-277-3). Oddo.
—Timmy Tiger to the Rescue. LC 70-108733. (Illus.). 32p. (ps-4). 1970. PLB 9.95x (ISBN 0-87783-043-6); pap. 3.94x deluxe ed (ISBN 0-87783-112-2); cassette 7.94x (ISBN 0-87783-229-3). Oddo.
—Timmy Tiger's New Coat. LC 74-108734. (Illus.). 32p. (ps-2). 1970. PLB 9.95 (ISBN 0-87783-044-4); pap. 3.94 deluxe ed (ISBN 0-87783-113-0); cassette 7.94x (ISBN 0-87783-230-7). Oddo.
—Timmy Tiger's New Friend. LC 77-108732. (Illus.). (ps-2). 1970. PLB 9.95 (ISBN 0-87783-042-8); pap. 3.94 deluxe ed (ISBN 0-87783-114-9); cassette 7.94x (ISBN 0-87783-231-5). Oddo.
Root, Phyllis. Moon Tiger. Young, Ed, illus. LC 85-7572. 32p. (gr. k-3). 1988. pap. 3.95 (ISBN 0-8050-0803-9). H Holt & Co.
Smith, Jean B. The Tartan Tiger. (Illus., Orig.). (gr. 7 up). 1986. pap. 8.00 (ISBN 0-935827-00-5). Tartan Tiger.
Stockton, Frank R. The Lady or the Tiger. Carlson, Claudia & DeNieff, Jacqueline S., illus. Horowitz, Paul J., frwd. by. Bd. with The Discourager of Hesitancy. Repr. of 1885 ed. (Orig.). (gr. 1-8). pap. 4.95 (ISBN 0-934254-11-7). Claymont Comm.
Timmy Tiger Series, 6 vols. (Illus.). (ps-4). 1981. Set. PLB 59.70 (ISBN 0-87783-166-1); Set Of 4 Vols. pap. 15.76 deluxe ed (ISBN 0-87783-167-X); cassettes set (4) 31.76x (ISBN 0-87783-228-5). Oddo.
Xiong, Blia, ed. Nine-in-One Grr! Grr! Spagnoli, Cathy, as told by. (Illus.). 32p. (ps-5). 1989. 12.95 (ISBN 0-89239-048-4). Childrens Book Pr.
Zahradka, Miroslav. The Un-Terrible Tiger. Zahradka, Miroslav, illus. LC 78-155815. 32p. (ps-3). 7.95 (ISBN 0-87592-056-X). Scroll Pr.
Zolotow, Charlotte. A Tiger Called Thomas. rev. ed. Stock, Catherine, illus. LC 86-20878. 40p. (ps-3). 1988. 12.95 (ISBN 0-688-06696-8); PLB 12.88 (ISBN 0-688-06697-6). Lothrop.

TIMBER
see Forests and Forestry; Lumber and Lumbering; Trees; Wood

TIME
see also Calendars; Clocks and Watches
Anno, Mitsumasa. Anno's Sundial. Anno, Mitsumasa, illus. 30p. (gr. 4 up). 1987. 16.95 (ISBN 0-399-21374-0, Philomel Bks). Putnam Pub Group.
Baumann, Hans. What Time Is It Around the World? LC 75-24710. (Illus.). (gr. k-5). 1979. 6.95 (ISBN 0-87592-061-6). Scroll Pr.
Beckmann, Beverly. Time in God's World. Edler, Jules, illus. 24p. (gr. 2-5). 1985. 6.95 (ISBN 0-570-04128-7, 56-1539). Concordia.
Bennett, David. Day & Night. Kightley, Rosalinda, illus. 32p. (ps up). 1988. pap. 3.95 (ISBN 0-553-05479-1). Bantam.
Breiter, Herta S. Time & Clocks. rev. ed. LC 87-23229. (Illus.). 48p. (gr. 2-6). 1987. PLB 17.32 (ISBN 0-8172-3262-1); pap. 9.27 (ISBN 0-8172-3287-7). Raintree Pubs.
Buck, Peggy J. Tommy Learns about Time & Eternity. Lautermilch, John, illus. 68p. (Orig.). (gr. 1-3). 1980. pap. 3.95 (ISBN 0-89323-006-5, 023). Bible Memory.
Burns, Marilyn. This Book Is about Time. Weston, Martha, illus. LC 78-6614. (gr. 5 up). 1978. 14.95 (ISBN 0-316-11752-8); pap. 8.95 (ISBN 0-316-11750-1). Little.
Cassidy, John. The Time Book. (ps-8). 1991. wire-o bdg. incl. watch 10.95 (ISBN 1-878257-08-0). Klutz Pr.
Darling, David. Could You Ever Build a Time Machine? (Illus.). 60p. (gr. 5 up). 1991. 14.95 (ISBN 0-87518-456-1, Dillon). Macmillan Child Grp.
Firmin, Peter, illus. Day & Night. 16p. (ps-1). 1986. 2.95 (ISBN 0-86020-963-6). EDC.
—Then & Now. 16p. (ps-1). 1986. 2.95 (ISBN 0-86020-965-2). EDC.
Fortune, J. J. Revenge in the Silent Tomb. 160p. (Orig.). (gr. 7-12). 1984. pap. 2.25 (ISBN 0-440-97707-X, LFL). Dell.
Grey, Judith. What Time Is It? Hall, Susan, illus. LC 81-5113. 32p. (gr. k-2). 1981. PLB 10.89 (ISBN 0-89375-509-5); pap. text ed. 2.95 (ISBN 0-89375-510-9). Troll Assocs.
Jenkins, Gerald & Bear, Magdalen. Sun Dials & Time Dials: A Collection of Working Models to Cut & Glue Together. (Illus.). 40p. (gr. 6 up). 1988. pap. 11.95 (ISBN 0-906212-59-6, Tarquin). Parkwest Pubns.
Jennings, Terry. Time. FS-Aladdin Staff, ed. Anstey, David, illus. 28p. (gr. 1-3). 1988. PLB 10.40 (ISBN 0-531-17112-4, Gloucester Pr). Watts.
—Time. 1990. pap. 2.95 (ISBN 0-531-17504-9). Watts.
Johnson, Merideth. When I Learn to Tell Time. 1990. 3.98 (ISBN 0-8317-9374-0). Smithmark.
Joy, Margaret. Days, Weeks & Months. Renny, Juliet, illus. 112p. (gr. 3 up). 1984. 12.95 (ISBN 0-571-13171-9). Faber & Faber.
Kalman, Bobbie. Time & the Seasons. (Illus.). 32p. (gr. 2-3). 1986. 14.95 (ISBN 0-86505-072-4); pap. 6.95 (ISBN 0-86505-094-5). Crabtree Pub Co.
Knowles, Tizzie. Weekdays. Knowles, Tizzie, illus. 24p. (gr. k-2). 1990. pap. 1.95 (ISBN 1-878624-20-2). McClanahan Bk.

L'Engle, Madeleine. Madeleine L'Engle's Time Trilogy, 3 bks. Incl. A Wrinkle in Time; A Wind in the Door; A Swiftly Tilting Planet. 1986. pap. 9.30 boxed set (ISBN 0-440-95207-7, LE). Dell.
Livoni, Cathy. Element of Time. LC 82-48761. 192p. (gr. 7 up). 1983. 12.95 (ISBN 0-15-225369-6, HJ). HarBraceJ.
Moran, W. Dean. It's about Time: Teacher's Time Teaching Resource Book & Student Work Sheets. 1988. 127.00 (ISBN 0-317-93590-9). Time Teaching.
Morning, Noon & Night. (Illus.). 14p. (ps). 1979. bds. 2.25 (ISBN 0-448-16272-5, G&D). Putnam Pub Group.
Ockenga, Earl & Rucker, Walt. Telling Time. Dawson, Dave, illus. 16p. (gr. 1). 1990. pap. text ed. 1.25 (ISBN 1-56281-120-7, M120). Extra Eds.
Oliver, Stephen, photos by. Time. LC 90-8576. (Illus.). 24p. (ps-k). 1991. 6.95 (ISBN 0-679-81164-8). Random.
Pellowski, Michael J. Teddy on Time. Epstein, Len, illus. LC 85-14127. 48p. (Orig.). (gr. 1-3). 1986. PLB 9.89 (ISBN 0-8167-0582-8); pap. text ed. 2.95 (ISBN 0-8167-0583-6). Troll Assocs.
Pen Notes Staff. Learn to Tell Time. (gr. 1 up). 1982. 8.95 (ISBN 0-939564-02-5). Pen Notes.
Pluckrose, Henry. Time. Fairclough, Chris, photos by. Franklin Watts Ltd., ed. (Illus.). 32p. (ps-6). 1988. PLB 10.40 (ISBN 0-531-10452-4). Watts.
Rand McNally Staff. Children's Atlas of Earth Through Time. Fagan, Elizabeth, ed. (Illus.). 80p. 1990. 14.95 (ISBN 0-528-83415-0). Rand McNally.
Rockwell, Anne. Bear Child's Book of Hours. Rockwell, Anne, illus. LC 86-24245. 32p. (ps-1). 1991. pap. 4.95 (ISBN 0-06-107410-1). HarpC Child Bks.
Rothman, Joel. A Moment in Time. Leake, Don, illus. LC 72-90693. 32p. (ps-2). 1973. 7.95 (ISBN 0-87592-034-9). Scroll Pr.
Roy, Cal. Time Is Day. (Illus.). (gr. k-3). 1968. 9.95 (ISBN 0-8392-3065-6). Astor-Honor.
Shibles, Warren. Time: A Critical Analysis for Children. LC 77-93811. (gr. 4-12). 1978. pap. 6.50 (ISBN 0-912386-17-7). Language Pr.
Singer, Marilyn. Nine O'Clock Lullaby. Lessac, Frane, illus. LC 90-32116. 32p. (ps-3). 1991. 14.95 (ISBN 0-06-025647-8); PLB 14.89 (ISBN 0-06-025648-6). HarpC Child Bks.
Skutina, Vladimir. Nobody Has Time for Me. Klein, Zanvel, ed. Herrmann, Dagmar, tr. from CZE. Sacre, Marie-Jose, illus. LC 91-4457. 32p. (gr. k-3). 1991. 14. 95 (ISBN 0-922984-07-7). Wellington IL.
Stuart, Daryl. Quality Time Little Readers: Let's Tell the Time. 1991. 1.49 (ISBN 0-8317-7269-7). Smithmark.
Tallarico, Tony. What Time Is It? (Illus.). 12p. (gr. 3-8). 1982. pap. 3.50 (ISBN 0-89828-302-7). Tuffy Bks.
Taylor, Barbara. Ready Set Go: What Time Is It? 1991. 4.98 (ISBN 0-8317-7359-6). Smithmark.
Tell Me the Time. (ps-k). 3.95 (ISBN 0-7214-5054-7). Ladybird Bks.
Tell the Time Pack, No. 467. (Illus.). (ps-k). incl. wall chart & activity bk. 6.95 (ISBN 0-7214-5164-0). Ladybird Bks.
Telling the Time. (Illus.). (ps-2). 3.50 (ISBN 0-7214-0516-9). Ladybird Bks.
Telling the Time. (Illus.). (ps). 1992. cased 3.50 (ISBN 0-7214-5210-8). Ladybird Bks.
Warren, Jean. Movement Time. 80p. (gr. k-2). 1984. 7.95 (ISBN 0-912107-17-0). Monday Morning Bks.
Wing, Ralph. Just Do It! Time Management. Pangaea Press Staff, ed. 144p. (Orig.). (gr. 10 up). 1990. pap. text ed. 6.95 (ISBN 0-9625534-0-9, P100). Pangaea Pr.
Young, Woody. Clockwise, Vol. Two: Learn to Tell Time. White, Craig, illus. 48p. (Orig.). 1985. pap. text ed. 4.95 (ISBN 0-939513-02-1). Joy Pub SJC.
Ziner, Feenie & Thompson, Elizabeth. Time. LC 81-18080. (Illus.). 48p. (gr. k-4). 1982. PLB 14.60 (ISBN 0-516-01651-2). Childrens.

TIME–POETRY
Allington, Richard L. & Krull, Kathleen. Time. Miyake, Yoshi, illus. LC 82-10170. 32p. (gr. k-3). 1985. PLB 15.33 (ISBN 0-8172-1388-0); pap. 9.27 (ISBN 0-8172-2495-5). Raintree Pubs.
Gordon, Ruth, ed. Time Is the Longest Distance. LC 90-4947. 96p. (gr. 7 up). 1991. 13.95 (ISBN 0-06-022297-2); PLB 13.89 (ISBN 0-06-022424-X). HarpC Child Bks.
Pearson, Kit. A Handful of Time. 186p. (gr. 5-8). 1988. pap. 13.95 (ISBN 0-670-81532-2). Viking Child Bks.

TIMEX-SINCLAIR 1000 (COMPUTER)
Hurley, L. ZX-81 TS-1000: Programming for Young Programmers. (Illus.). 96p. (gr. 9up). 1983. pap. text ed. 9.95 (ISBN 0-07-031449-7, BYTE Bks). McGraw.

TIMEX-SINCLAIR COMPUTERS
see also Timex-Sinclair 1000 (Computer)
Kemnitz, Thomas M. & Mass, Lynne. Kids Working with Computers: The Timex-Sinclair BASIC Manual. Schlendorf, Lori, illus. 48p. (gr. 4-7). 1983. pap. 4.99 (ISBN 0-89824-058-1). Trillium Pr.

TITANIC (STEAMSHIP)
Ballard, Robert D. Exploring the Titanic. LC 88-6478. (Illus.). (gr. 3-7). 1988. 14.95 (ISBN 0-590-41953-6, Scholastic Hardcovers). Scholastic Inc.
—Exploring the Titanic. (gr. 4-7). 1991. pap. 5.95 (ISBN 0-590-41952-8). Scholastic Inc.
Donnelly, Judy. The Titanic: Lost...& Found. Kohler, Keith, illus. LC 86-20402. 48p. (gr. 1-3). 1987. lib. bdg. 6.99 (ISBN 0-394-98669-5, Random Juv); pap. 2.95 (ISBN 0-394-88669-0, Random Juv). Random.
Dudman, John. The Sinking of the Titanic. Caulkins, Janet, ed. (Illus.). 32p. (gr. k-6). 1988. PLB 10.90 (ISBN 0-531-18160-X, Pub. by Bookwright Pr). Watts.
Hamilton, Sue. R. M. S. Titanic's Sinking. Hamilton, John, ed. (Illus.). 32p. (gr. 4). 1989. PLB 11.95 (ISBN 0-939179-42-3). Abdo & Dghtrs.
Lord, Walter. Night to Remember. (gr. 6-12). 1983. pap. 4.50 (ISBN 0-553-27827-4). Bantam.
Rawlinson, J. Titanic. (Illus.). 32p. (gr. 4 up). Date not set. PLB 14.00 (ISBN 0-86592-873-8). Rourke Corp.
Sloan, Frank. Titanic. (Illus.). 96p. (gr. 4-9). 1987. PLB 10.40 (ISBN 0-531-10396-X). Watts.
Stacey, Thomas. The Titanic. LC 89-33553. (Illus.). 64p. (gr. 5-8). 1989. PLB 11.95 (ISBN 1-56006-006-9). Lucent Bks.

TITHES
Clawson, Jan. Let's Learn about Tithing. Pardew, Les, illus. 24p. (gr. k-6). 1988. pap. 3.50 (ISBN 0-88290-339-X). Horizon Utah.
Merrell, Karen D. Tithing. 22p. (ps-2). pap. 4.95 (ISBN 0-87747-560-1). Deseret Bk.

TOADS
see Frogs

TOADSTOOLS
see Mushrooms

TOBACCO HABIT
Booher, Albert R. Tobacco. 11p. (gr. 5-9). 1988. pap. text ed. 5.95 (ISBN 0-685-28976-1). Madonna Edu Syst.
Gunn, Jeffrey. Pen Pals, Vol. 10: Facts about Nicotine. Wolfe, Debra, illus. (Orig.). (gr. 3). 1990. pap. write for info. (ISBN 1-879146-10-X). Knowldg Pub.
Perry, Robert. Focus on Nicotine & Caffeine. (Illus.). 64p. (gr. 3-7). 1990. PLB 14.95 (ISBN 0-941477-99-1). TFC Bks MD.
Seixas, Judith S. Tobacco: What It Is, What It Does. Huffman, Tom, illus. LC 81-837. 56p. (gr. 1-3). 1981. 12.95 (ISBN 0-688-00769-4, Mulberry); (Mulberry). Morrow.

TOES
see Foot

TOILET
see Beauty, Personal

TOILET PREPARATIONS
see Cosmetics

TOKYO
Davis, James E. & Hawke, Sharryl D. Tokyo. (Illus.). 64p. (gr. 4-9). 1990. PLB 18.00 (ISBN 0-8172-3032-7). Raintree Pubs.

TOLERATION
see also Discrimination; Religious Liberty
Gay, Kathlyn. Bigotry. LC 88-30428. (Illus.). 144p. (gr. 6 up). 1989. PLB 18.95 (ISBN 0-89490-171-0). Enslow Pubs.

TONGUE
Keller, Charles. Tongue Twisters. Fritz, Ron, illus. (ps-4). 1989. pap. 13.95 (ISBN 0-671-67123-5); pap. 5.95 (ISBN 0-671-67975-9). S&S Trade.

TOOLS
see also Agricultural Machinery; Machine Tools; Machinery
Bracy, Norma N. The Tool Box. (Illus.). 35p. (gr. k-12). 1987. pap. text ed. 2.00 (ISBN 0-915783-04-5). Book Binder.
Brown, William F. & Brown, Mary G. Wood Works: Experiments with Common Wood & Tools. LC 83-15905. (Illus.). 128p. (gr. 3 up). 1984. 13.95 (ISBN 0-689-31033-1, Atheneum Child Bk). Macmillan Child Grp.
Gibbons, Gail. Tool Book. Gibbons, Gail, illus. LC 81-13386. 32p. (ps-3). 1982. reinforced bdg. 14.95 (ISBN 0-8234-0444-7); pap. 5.95 (ISBN 0-8234-0694-6). Holiday.
Miller, Margaret. Who Uses This? LC 89-30456. (Illus.). 40p. (ps). 1990. 12.95 (ISBN 0-688-08278-5); PLB 12. 88 (ISBN 0-688-08279-3). Greenwillow.
Rockwell, Anne. Toolbox. Rockwell, Harlow, illus. LC 72-119836. 24p. (ps-2). 1971. 12.95 (ISBN 0-02-777540-2, Mcmillan Child Bk). Macmillan Child Grp.
—Toolbox. LC 89-34818. 24p. (ps-1). 1990. pap. 3.95 (ISBN 0-689-71382-7, Aladdin). Macmillan Child Grp.

TOOLS–HISTORY

Kalman, Bobbie. Tools & Gadgets. 1991. 14.95 (ISBN 0-86505-508-4); pap. 7.95 (ISBN 0-86505-488-6). Crabtree Pub CO.
In the old days people had to rely on tools & their own muscle power to get a job done. In TOOLS & GADGETS your students will have the opportunity to learn about the tools used by farmers, woodworkers, metalworkers, millers, & printers. They will take a close look at the gadgets found in the home, general store, doctor's office, & farm, such as cherry pitters, apple peelers, mustache cups, clock jacks, & fleams. They will be introduced to the gadgets that fascinated children long ago & have the chance to identify some mystery gadgets. This book is an excellent tool to be used before & after visits to historic communities.
Publisher Provided Annotation.

TOPOGRAPHICAL DRAWING
see also Map Drawing

TORNADOES
see also Storms
Archer, Jules. Tornado! LC 90-45373. (Illus.). 48p. (gr. 5-6). 1991. RSBE 10.95 (ISBN 0-89686-594-0, Crestwood Hse). Macmillan Child Grp.
Branley, Franklyn M. Tornado Alert. Maestro, Giulio, illus. LC 87-29379. 32p. (ps-3). 1988. 13.95 (ISBN 0-690-04686-3, Crowell Jr Bks); PLB 13.89 (ISBN 0-690-04688-X). HarpC Child Bks.
—Tornado Alert. Maestro, Giulio, illus. LC 87-29379. 32p. (gr. k-4). 1990. pap. 4.50 (ISBN 0-06-445094-5, Trophy). HarpC Child Bks.
Farris, John. The Dust Bowl. LC 89-33557. (Illus.). 64p. (gr. 5-8). 1989. PLB 11.95 (ISBN 1-56006-005-0). Lucent Bks.
Fradin, Dennis. Disaster! Tornadoes. LC 81-12277. (Illus.). 64p. (gr. 3 up). 1982. PLB 17.27 (ISBN 0-516-00854-4). Childrens.
Jenison, Norma J. & Benjamin, Starr J. The Eyes of the Storm: Belmond, Iowa Recalls the 1966 Homecoming Day Tornado. LC 89-84423. (Illus.). 256p. (Orig.). 1989. pap. 8.95 (ISBN 0-9623288-0-4). T Lydia Pr.
Lampton, Christopher. Tornado. (Illus.). 64p. (gr. 4-6). 1991. PLB 17.25 (ISBN 1-56294-032-5). Millbrook Pr.

TORTOISES
see Turtles

TOTALITARIANISM
see also Communism; Dictators; National Socialism
Archer, Jules. Police State: Could It Happen Here? LC 76-58720. 192p. (gr. 7 up). 1977. HarpC Child Bks.

TOTEMS AND TOTEMISM
Batdorf, Carol. Totem Poles: An Ancient Art. Cheney, Tracy, illus. 24p. (Orig.). (gr. 1-6). 1990. pap. 4.95 (ISBN 0-88839-248-6). Hancock House.

TOUCANS–FICTION
McKee, David. Two Can Toucan. McKee, David, illus. 32p. (gr. k-3). 1987. 13.95 (ISBN 0-86264-094-6, Pub. by Anderson Pr UK). Trafalgar Sq.

TOUCH
Allington, Richard L. & Krull, Kathleen. Touching. Miyake, Yoshi, illus. LC 79-28393. 32p. (gr. k-3). 1985. PLB 15.33 (ISBN 0-8172-1294-9); pap. 9.27 (ISBN 0-8172-2496-3). Raintree Pubs.
Berry, Joy W. Teach Me about Touching. Dickey, Kate, ed. LC 85-45089. (Illus.). 36p. (ps). 1986. 4.98 (ISBN 0-685-10728-0). Grolier Inc.
Moncure, Jane B. The Touch Book. Axeman, Lois, illus. LC 82-4154. (ps-3). 1982. PLB 14.60 (ISBN 0-516-03254-2); pap. 3.95 (ISBN 0-516-43254-0). Childrens.
Parramon, J. M. & Puig, J. J. Touch. Rius, Maria, illus. 32p. (Orig.). (ps). 1985. pap. 4.95 (ISBN 0-8120-3567-4); Span. ed. pap. 4.95 (ISBN 0-8120-3609-3). Barron.
Pluckrose, Henry. Touching. Fairclough, Chris, photos by. 32p. (gr. k-3). 1986. lib. bdg. 7.99 (ISBN 0-531-10174-6). Watts.
Smith, Kathie B. & Crenson, Victoria. Touching. Storms, Robert S., illus. LC 87-5885. 24p. (gr. k-3). 1987. PLB 9.59 (ISBN 0-8167-1012-0); pap. text ed. 1.95 (ISBN 0-8167-1013-9). Troll Assocs.
Wood, Nicholas. Touch...What Do You Feel? Willey, Lynne, illus. LC 90-10925. 32p. (gr. k-3). 1990. PLB 10.89 (ISBN 0-8167-2126-2); pap. text ed. 2.95 (ISBN 0-8167-2127-0). Troll Assocs.

TOUCH–FICTION
Isadora, Rachel. I Touch. LC 90-48260. (Illus.). 24p. (ps up). 1991. bds. 6.95 (ISBN 0-688-10524-6). Greenwillow.
Jamieson, Rita. Felt Fun, Flannel Board Stories. Jamieson, Myles, illus. (ps-8). 1990. pap. text ed. 5.00 (ISBN 0-9622329-1-2). R Jamieson.
Peck, Richard. Close Enough to Touch. 144p. (gr. 7 up). 1982. pap. 2.95 (ISBN 0-440-91282-2, LFL). Dell.

TOULOUSE-LAUTREC MONFA, HENRI MARIE RAYMOND DE, 1864-1901
Raboff, Ernest. Henri de Toulouse-Lautrec. De Toulouse-Lautrec, Henri, illus. LC 87-16861. 32p. (gr. 1 up). 1988. Repr. of 1970 ed. 11.95 (ISBN 0-397-32229-1, Lipp Jr Bks). HarpC Child Bks.
—Henri de Toulouse-Lautrec. De Toulouse-Lautrec, Henri, illus. LC 87-17703. 32p. (gr. 1 up). 1988. pap. 5.95 (ISBN 0-06-446070-3, Trophy). HarpC Child Bks.
Spizzirri Publishing Co. Staff. Lautrec Posters: Educational Coloring Book. Spizzirr, Linda, ed. (Illus.). 32p. (gr. 1-8). 1983. pap. 1.95 (ISBN 0-86545-052-8). Spizzirri.

TOURIST TRADE
see also Travel
Fenten, Barbara & Fenten, D. X. Tourism & Hospitality: Careers Unlimited. LC 78-19108. (Illus.). 160p. (gr. 7 up). 1978. 8.95 (ISBN 0-664-32634-X, Westminster). Westminster John Knox.
Grant, Edgar. Exploring Careers in the Travel Industry. rev. ed. Rosen, Ruth, ed. (gr. 7-12). 1989. PLB 12.95 (ISBN 0-8239-0961-1). Rosen Group.

TOURIST TRADE–FICTION
Martin, Charles E. For Rent. Martin, Charles E., illus. LC 85-864. 32p. (gr. k-3). 1986. 11.75 (ISBN 0-688-05716-0); PLB 11.88 (ISBN 0-688-05717-9). Greenwillow.

TOUSSAINT LOUVERTURE, PIERRE DOMINIQUE, 1746?-1803

Hoobler, Dorothy & Hoobler, Thomas. Toussaint L'Ouverture. (Illus.). (gr. 5 up). 1990. 17.95 (ISBN 1-55546-818-7). Chelsea Hse.

TOWN OFFICERS

see Local Government

TOWNS

see Cities and Towns

TOXICOLOGY

see Poisons

TOYS

see also Dollhouses; Dolls

Amery, H. The KnowHow Book of Action Toys: Lots of Toys & Machines to Make & Work. (Illus.). 32p. (gr. 3-6). 1977. pap. 5.95 (ISBN 0-86020-021-3). EDC.

Baby's First Toys. 12p. (ps). 1978. 3.95 (ISBN 0-448-40865-1, G&D). Putnam Pub Group.

Baby's Things. 12p. (ps). 1978. 3.95 (ISBN 0-448-40866-X, G&D). Putnam Pub Group.

Blocksma, Dewey & Blocksma, Mary. Action Contraptions. Hulst, Sandra, illus. LC 87-2295. 64p. (gr. 2-6). 1987. PLB 10.95 (ISBN 0-671-66378-X). S&S Trade.

—Easy-to-Make Water Toys That Really Work. Seiden, Art, illus. LC 84-24913. 64p. (gr. 2-6). 1988. pap. 5.95 (ISBN 0-671-66259-7). S&S Trade.

Blocksma, Mary. Todos Mis Juquetes: (All My Toys Are on the Floor) Kalthoff, Sandra C., illus. LC 85-27000. (SPA.). 24p. (ps-2). 1989. PLB 12.33 (ISBN 0-516-31579-X); pap. 3.95 (ISBN 0-516-51579-9). Childrens.

Blocksma, Mary & Blocksma, Dewey. Action Contraptions: Easy-to-Make Toys That Really Move. Hulst, Sandra, illus. 64p. (gr. 3-5). 1988. 10.95 (ISBN 0-13-003352-9). Prentice Hall Pr.

Bourne, Miriam A. Let's Visit a Toy Factory. Plunkett, Micheal, illus. LC 87-3489. 32p. (gr. 2-4). 1988. PLB 10.79 (ISBN 0-8167-1159-3); pap. text ed. 2.95 (ISBN 0-8167-1160-7). Troll Assocs.

Boyd. Toys. 1985. 2.95 (ISBN 0-671-54751-8). S&S Trade.

Burns, Elizabeth. Hanky Panky: Traditional Handkerchief Toys. Burns, Elizabeth, illus. 24p. (ps-6). 1989. pap. 4.50 (ISBN 0-9624152-0-0). E Burns.

—Hanky Panky: Traditional Handkerchief Toys, Benefit Edition. X1986 ed. (Illus.). 24p. (ps-6). pap. 4.50 (ISBN 0-9624152-1-9). E Burns.

Churchill, E. Richard. Fast & Funny Paper Toys You Can Make. LC 89-32411. (Illus.). 128p. (gr. 7-12). 1989. 14.95 (ISBN 0-8069-5770-0). Sterling.

—Instant Paper Toys to Pop, Spin, Whirl & Fly. Kendrick, Dennis, illus. LC 85-26229. 112p. (gr. 1-8). 1987. pap. 7.95 (ISBN 0-8069-6278-X). Sterling.

—Paper Science Toys. LC 90-9891. (Illus.). 128p. (gr. 3-10). 1990. 14.95 (ISBN 0-8069-5834-0). Sterling.

—Paper Toys That Fly, Soar, Zoom & Whistle. Michaels, James, illus. LC 88-30311. 192p. (gr. 10-12). 1989. 14.95 (ISBN 0-8069-6840-0). Sterling.

Flick, Pauline. Discovering Toys & Toy Museums. 2nd ed. (Illus.). 72p. (Orig.). (gr. 6 up). 1977. pap. 3.00 (ISBN 0-913714-38-0). Legacy Bks.

Fowler, Virginie. Folk Toys Around the World & How to Make Them. 160p. 1984. 10.95 (ISBN 0-13-323148-8). P-H.

Hodgson, Harriet. Toyworks. Savage, Beth, illus. 64p. 1986. 6.95 (ISBN 0-912107-40-5, Dist. by Good Apple). Monday Morning Bks.

Hutchings, Margaret. Big Book of Stuffed Toy & Doll Making: Instructions & Full-Size Patterns for 45 Playthings. (Illus.). 256p. (gr. 7 up). 1983. pap. 8.95 (ISBN 0-486-24266-8). Dover.

Jaffke, Freya. Toymaking with Children. 1988. pap. 10.95 (ISBN 0-86315-069-1, 20244). Gryphon Hse.

Kurland, Alexandra. Teddies to the Rescue. Kenyon, Mark, illus. 56p. (gr. k-4). 1986. 11.95 (ISBN 0-938209-27-2). Bear Hollow Pr.

Lohf, Sabine. Building Your Own Toys. LC 89-22276. 64p. 1989. lib. bdg. 19.93 (ISBN 0-516-09251-0); pap. 8.95 (ISBN 0-516-49251-9). Childrens.

Lynn, Sara. Toys. Lynn, Sara, illus. 14p. (ps). 1986. bds. 2.95 (ISBN 0-689-71096-8, Aladdin). Macmillan Child Grp.

Matthiesen, Thomas, photos by. A Child's Book of Everyday Things. (Illus.). 72p. (ps-1). 1981. 3.95 (ISBN 0-448-41057-5, G&D). Putnam Pub Group.

Mitgutsch, Ali. From Idea to Toy. (Illus.). 24p. (ps-3). 1988. PLB 6.95 (ISBN 0-87614-352-4). Carolrhoda Bks.

Moore, Marsha. The Teddy Bear Book. (Illus.). 165p. (ps up). 1984. 24.95 (ISBN 0-916410-09-9). A D Bragdon.

My Toys. (Illus.). (ps-k). bds. 3.50 (ISBN 0-7214-9121-9). Ladybird Bks.

Picture Book of Toys. (Illus.). (ps). 3.50 (ISBN 0-7214-0750-1). Ladybird Bks.

Schael, Hannelore, et al. Toys Made of Clay. LC 89-22253. 64p. 1989. PLB 19.93 (ISBN 0-516-09256-1); pap. 8.95 (ISBN 0-516-49256-X). Childrens.

Sibbett, Ed., Jr. Easy-to-Make Articulated Wooden Toys: Patterns & Instructions for 18 Playthings That Move. (Illus.). 48p. 1983. pap. 2.95 (ISBN 0-486-24411-3). Dover.

Smalley, Guy, illus. My Very Own Book of Toys. 24p. (ps-2). 1989. 9.95 (ISBN 0-929793-03-X). Camex Bks Inc.

Sullivan, S. Adams. Bats, Butterflies, & Bugs, Vol. 1. (ps-3). 1990. 14.95 (ISBN 0-316-82185-3, Joy St Bks). Little.

Toys. (Illus.). 32p. (ps-8). pap. 29.50 (ISBN 0-87474-615-9). Smithsonian.

Toys & Games. (ARA., Illus.). (gr. 4-6). 3.50x (ISBN 0-86685-241-7). Intl Bk Ctr.

Wiencek, Henry. The World of Lego Toys. (Illus.). 176p. 1987. 29.95 (ISBN 0-8109-1790-4); pap. 17.95 (ISBN 0-8109-2362-9). Abrams.

TOYS–FICTION

Andersen, Hans Christian. The Steadfast Tin Soldier. Di Grazia, Thomas, adapted by. (Illus.). 32p. (gr. 1-4). 1981. 8.95 (ISBN 0-13-846295-X). P-H.

Banks, Lynne R. The Secret of the Indian. (gr. 5 up). 1989. pap. 14.95 (ISBN 0-385-26292-2). Doubleday.

Barkan, Joanne. Whiskerville Toy Shop. (Illus.). 12p. (ps-k). 1991. bds. 3.95 (ISBN 0-448-40089-8, G&D). Putnam Pub Group.

Barrett, John. The Day the Toys Came to Silver Dollar City. Ruth, Rod, illus. (gr. k-10). 1978. 1.99 (ISBN 0-686-22891-X). Silver Dollar.

Bawden, Juliet & Pask, Helen. Good Teddy. (Illus.). 12p. (ps). 1987. 2.95 (ISBN 0-8120-5833-X). Barron.

—My Teddy. (Illus.). 12p. (ps). 1987. 2.95 (ISBN 0-8120-5832-1). Barron.

—Poor Teddy. (Illus.). 12p. (ps). 1987. 2.95 (ISBN 0-8120-5834-8). Barron.

Bibee, John. The Toy Campaign. Turnbaugh, Paul, illus. LC 87-3261. 216p. (Orig.). (gr. 4 up). 1987. pap. 6.95 (ISBN 0-8308-1201-6). InterVarsity.

Billam, Rosemary. Fuzzy Rabbit. Julian-Ottie, Vanessa, illus. LC 83-17637. 32p. (ps-3). 1984. (Random Juv); pap. 2.25 (ISBN 0-394-86346-1). Random.

—Fuzzy Rabbit & the Little Brother Problem. Julian-Ottie, Vanessa, illus. LC 88-4363. 32p. (Orig.). (ps-3). 1988. (Random Juv); (Random Juv). Random.

—Fuzzy Rabbit in the Park. Julian-Ottie, Vanessa, illus. LC 85-10794. 32p. (ps-3). 1986. pap. 1.95 (ISBN 0-394-87863-9). Random.

Blocksma, Mary. Todos Mis Juguetes. Kratky, Lada C., tr. Kalthoff, Sandra C., illus. (SPA.). 24p. (ps-1). 1989. PLB 8.25. Childrens.

Blyton, Enid. The Night the Toys Came to Life. 1989. 4.98 (ISBN 0-8317-6396-5). Smithmark.

—The Night the Toys Had a Party. 1989. 4.98 (ISBN 0-8317-6397-3). Smithmark.

Braune, Anna & Sloane, Savilla. The Wonderful Toys. Hale, James G., illus. LC 89-77889. 128p. (gr. 2-5). 1990. 12.95 (ISBN 0-06-020618-7); PLB 12.89 (ISBN 0-06-020619-5). HarpC Child Bks.

Brown, Marc. Teddy Bear, Teddy Bear. (gr. 2 up). 1989. 5.95 (ISBN 0-525-44531-5, DCB). Dutton Child Bks.

Brown, Margaret W. David's Little Indian. Charlip, Remy, illus. 48p. (gr. 2-5). 1989. Repr. of 1954 ed. 10.95 (ISBN 0-929077-02-4, Hopscotch Bks); PLB 10.95 (ISBN 0-317-92547-4, Hopscotch Bks). Watermark Inc.

Collier, James L. The Teddy Bear Habit. (gr. 5-9). 15.50 (ISBN 0-8446-6191-0). Peter Smith.

Couture, Susan A. The Block Book. Mathers, Petra, illus. LC 89-34504. 32p. (ps-3). 1990. 12.95 (ISBN 0-06-020523-7); PLB 12.89 (ISBN 0-06-020524-5). HarpC Child Bks.

Darling, Abigail. Teddy Bear's Picnic Cookbook. (ps-3). 1991. 13.95 (ISBN 0-670-82947-1). Viking Child Bks.

Delamare, David, illus. Steadfast Tin Soldier. Ingram, John W., ed. Delamare, David, illus. LC 90-10927. 48p. (gr. 1-5). 1990. 5.95 (ISBN 0-88101-077-4). Unicorn Pub.

First Toy Tales, 12 vols. LC 88-37693. (Illus.). 384p. (gr. 1). 1989. Set. 102.00 (ISBN 1-85435-056-0). Marshall Cavendish.

Freeman, Don. Beady Bear. Freeman, Don, illus. LC 54-12295. 48p. (ps-1). 1954. 13.95 (ISBN 0-670-15056-8). Viking Child Bks.

—Corduroy. Freeman, Don, illus. LC 68-16068. 32p. 1968. pap. 11.95 (ISBN 0-670-24133-4). Viking Child Bks.

Freeman, Lydia. Corduroy's Toys. McCue, Lisa, illus. LC 84-40478. 24p. 1985. pap. 2.95 (ISBN 0-670-80522-X). Viking Child Bks.

Gackenbach, Dick. Poppy the Panda. Gackenbach, Dick, illus. LC 84-4952. 32p. (ps-3). 1984. 13.95 (ISBN 0-89919-276-9, Clarion). HM.

Galbraith, Kathryn. Laura Charlotte. Cooper, Floyd, illus. 32p. (ps-3). 1990. 14.95 (ISBN 0-399-21613-8, Philomel Bks). Putnam Pub Group.

Godden, Rumer. The Rocking Horse Secret. Smith, Juliet S., photos by. (gr. 3-7). 1988. pap. 3.95 (ISBN 0-317-69650-5, Puffin). Puffin Bks.

Green, Cecile. Tale of Theodore Bear. LC 68-56812. (Illus.). 32p. (gr. 1-2). 1968. PLB 9.95 (ISBN 0-87783-038-X). Oddo.

Gretz, Susanna. Teddy Bears Stay Indoors. Gretz, Susanna, illus. LC 86-19511. 32p. (gr. k-3). 1987. 13.95 (ISBN 0-02-738150-1, Four Winds). Macmillan Child Grp.

Gundersheimer, Karen. Shapes to Show. Gundersheimer, Karen, illus. LC 85-45409. 32p. (ps-1). 1986. 3.95 (ISBN 0-694-00067-1). HarpC Child Bks.

Halpern, C. The Homontash That Ran Away. Halpern, C., illus. (ps-4). 2.95 (ISBN 0-87306-995-1). Feldheim.

Harris, Robie H. I Hate Kisses. Paterson, Diane, illus. LC 79-18370. 40p. (ps-2). 1981. Knopf.

Hayward, Linda. The Runaway Christmas Toy: (Just Right for 3's & 4's) Schweninger, Ann, illus. LC 88-4522. 32p. (ps). 1988. (Random Juv); lib. bdg. 5.99 (ISBN 0-394-99693-3, Random Juv). Random.

Herman, Charlotte. Max Malone & the Great Cereal Rip-Off. Smith, Catherine, illus. 80p. (gr. 2-4). 1990. 12.95 (ISBN 0-8050-1069-6). H Holt & Co.

Heyward, Mary H. The Toy Box. Agee, Jon, illus. 16p. (ps-k). 1989. 7.95 (ISBN 0-525-44434-3, DCB). Dutton Child Bks.

Hindley, Judy. The Little Train. Kendall, Robert, illus. LC 89-35385. 32p. (ps-1). 1990. 13.95 (ISBN 0-531-05850-6); PLB 13.99 (ISBN 0-531-08450-7). Orchard Bks Watts.

Hissey, Jane. Old Bear. (Illus.). 32p. (ps-2). 1986. 14.95 (ISBN 0-399-21401-1, Philomel). Putnam Pub Group.

Hoban, Lillian. Arthur's Honey Bear. Hoban, Lillian, illus. LC 73-14325. 64p. (gr. k-3). 1974. 11.95 (ISBN 0-06-022369-3); PLB 11.89 (ISBN 0-06-022370-7). HarpC Child Bks.

Hoban, Russell. Mouse & His Child. Hoban, Lillian, illus. LC 67-19624. (gr. 1-5). 1967. PLB 13.89 (ISBN 0-685-02063-0). HarpC Child Bks.

Hollyn, Lynn. Lynn Hollyn's Christmas Toyland. Anazlone, Lori, illus. LC 84-5212. 40p. (ps-1). 1985. Knopf.

Homer. The Return of Odysseus. Richardson, I. M., adapted by. Frenck, Hal, illus. LC 83-14234. 32p. (gr. 4-8). 1984. lib. bdg. 11.79 (ISBN 0-8167-0015-X); pap. text ed. 2.95 (ISBN 0-8167-0016-8). Troll Assocs.

Hoopes, Lyn L. Wing-a-Ding, Vol. 1. (ps-4). 1990. 14.95 (ISBN 0-316-37237-4, Joy St Bks). Little.

Howe, Deborah & Howe, James. Teddy Bear's Scrapbook. Rose, David S., illus. LC 87-1096. 80p. (gr. 2-6). 1988. pap. 3.50 (ISBN 0-689-71168-9, Aladdin). Macmillan Child Grp.

Howe, James. Babes in Toyland. Atkinson, Allen, illus. 96p. (gr. k-3). 1988. pap. 9.95 (ISBN 0-15-200410-6, VoyB). HarBraceJ.

Jacobs, Flora G. The Toy Shop Mystery. (Illus.). 96p. 1960. 5.95 (ISBN 0-686-31595-2). Wash Dolls Hse.

Johansen, Hanna. Seven X Seven: Tales of a Sevensleeper. 1989. 12.95 (ISBN 0-525-44491-2, DCB). Dutton Child Bks.

Jonas, Ann. Now We Can Go. Jonas, Ann, illus. LC 85-12614. 24p. (ps-1). 1986. 11.75 (ISBN 0-688-04802-1); PLB 11.88 (ISBN 0-688-04803-X). Greenwillow.

Jungman, Ann. The Day Teddy Didn't Clean Up. Goffe, Toni, illus. 24p. (ps-k). 1989. 5.95 (ISBN 0-8120-6112-8). Barron.

—The Day Teddy Got Very Worried. Goffe, Toni, illus. 24p. (ps-k). 1989. 5.95 (ISBN 0-8120-6113-6). Barron.

—The Day Teddy Made New Friends. Goffe, Toni, illus. 24p. (ps-k). 1989. 5.95 (ISBN 0-8120-6114-4). Barron.

—The Day Teddy Wanted Grandpa to Notice Him. Goffe, Toni, illus. 24p. (ps-k). 1989. 5.95 (ISBN 0-8120-6115-2). Barron.

Kelley, True. Day-Care Teddy Bear: (Just Right for 3's & 4's) Kelley, True, illus. LC 88-43280. 32p. (ps). 1990. 4.95 (ISBN 0-394-84305-3); lib. bdg. 5.99 (ISBN 0-394-94305-8). Random.

Koci, Marta. Sarah's Bear. LC 86-30241. (Illus.). 28p. (ps). 1987. 14.95 (ISBN 0-88708-038-3). Picture Bk Studio.

Lawrence, D. H. The Rocking Horse Winner. 40p. (gr. 6 up). 1982. PLB 10.95s.p. (ISBN 0-87191-893-5); PLB 15.65 (ISBN 0-685-06208-2). Creative Ed.

LeRoque, Ellen E. A Tale of a Teddy Bear. Arcaris, Mary, illus. 28p. (Orig.). (ps-2). 1985. pap. 3.95 (ISBN 0-932967-03-5). Pacific Shoreline.

Leslie, Amanda. Hidden Toys. Leslie, Amanda, illus. LC 88-4096. 32p. (ps-1). 1989. 6.95 (ISBN 0-8037-0568-9). Dial Bks Young.

Levy, Elizabeth. Dracula Is a Pain in the Neck. Gerstein, Mordicai, illus. LC 82-47707. 80p. (gr. 2-6). 1983. 12.95 (ISBN 0-06-023822-4); PLB 12.89 (ISBN 0-06-023823-2). HarpC Child Bks.

Lionni, Leo. Alexander & the Wind-up Mouse. Lionni, Leo, illus. LC 74-2088. 32p. (ps-3). 1974. pap. 3.95 (ISBN 0-394-82911-5). Pantheon.

Lippert, Donald F. Mister B. Hedden, Randall, illus. 32p. (ps). Date not set. write for info. Pastel Pubns.

Lynn, Elizabeth A. The Silver Horse. Gomoll, Jeanne, illus. 128p. 1986. pap. 7.95 (ISBN 0-312-94406-3). Bluejay Bks.

Lyon, David. The Runaway Duck. LC 84-5677. (Illus.). 32p. (ps-1). 1985. PLB 14.95 (ISBN 0-688-04003-9); 14.88 (ISBN 0-688-04002-0). Lothrop.

McDonald, Mandi. Babes in Toyland. Lisi, Victoria & Lisi, Victoria, illus. 72p. (gr. 3-7). 1990. 11.95 (ISBN 0-88101-100-2). Unicorn Pub.

McPhail, David. Those Terrible Toy-Breakers. McPhail, David, illus. LC 80-10450. 48p. (ps-3). 1980. 5.95 (ISBN 0-8193-1019-0); PLB 5.95 (ISBN 0-8193-1020-4). Parents.

Maris, Ron. Are You There, Bear? LC 84-4180. (Illus.). 32p. (ps-1). 1985. 13.95 (ISBN 0-688-03997-9); PLB 13.88 (ISBN 0-688-03998-7). Greenwillow.

Milne, A. A. Le Meilleur des Ours. (FRE.). (gr. 3-8). 9.95 (ISBN 0-685-23403-7). French & Eur.

—Winnie l'Ourson. (FRE., Illus.). (gr. 3-8). 9.95 (ISBN 0-685-23402-9). French & Eur.

—World of Christopher Robin. (gr. 1-4). 1958. Boxed with "World of Pooh" 29.95 (ISBN 0-525-43348-1, Dutton); 13.95 (ISBN 0-525-43292-2). NAL-Dutton.

Modesitt, Jeanne. The Night Call. Spowart, Robin, illus. 32p. (ps-1). 1989. pap. 12.95 (ISBN 0-670-82500-X). Viking Child Bks.

Mogensen, Jan. Lost & Found Teddy. Mogensen, Jan, illus. LC 90-10077. 32p. (gr. 3-4). 1990. PLB 11.95 (ISBN 0-8368-0432-5). Gareth Stevens Inc.

Muir, Helen. Modge & Podge. Gluzberg, Margarita, illus. LC 88-7114. 32p. (ps-3). 1989. 10.95 (ISBN 0-8037-0584-0). Dial Bks Young.

N, Ebi. Tiny Bear's Christmas. 11th ed. LC 88-3590. 1989. 7.95 (ISBN 0-525-44426-2, DCB). Dutton Child Bks.

Nemetz, Rowena. Bo's Search for Love & Understanding. LC 86-10379. (Illus.). 48p. (Orig.). (gr. 1-6). 1986. pap. 5.95 (ISBN 0-941992-09-8). Los Arboles Pub.

O'Brien, Anne S. Where's My Truck? LC 85-5579. (Illus.). 14p. (gr. k). 1985. 3.95 (ISBN 0-03-005013-8). H Holt & Co.

Omar, N. Bradley. My Toy Box. 1980. 2.95 (ISBN 0-671-41343-0). S&S Trade.

Ormondroyd, Edward. Theodore's Rival. Larrecq, John M., illus. LC 76-156876. 40p. (ps-3). 1971. (Pub. by Parnassus); PLB 4.59 (ISBN 0-87466-001-7). HM.

Oxenbury, Helen. Tom & Pippo & the Washing Machine. Oxenbury, Helen, illus. LC 87-37431. 14p. (ps-k). 1988. bds. 5.95 (ISBN 0-689-71255-3, Aladdin). Macmillan Child Grp.

—Tom & Pippo Go for a Walk. Oxenbury, Helen, illus. LC 87-37432. 14p. (ps-k). 1988. bds. 5.95 (ISBN 0-689-71254-5, Aladdin). Macmillan Child Grp.

—Tom & Pippo Make a Mess. Oxenbury, Helen, illus. LC 87-37437. 14p. (ps-k). 1988. bds. 5.95 (ISBN 0-689-71253-7, Aladdin). Macmillan Child Grp.

—Tom & Pippo Read a Story. Oxenbury, Helen, illus. LC 87-37438. 14p. (ps-k). 1988. bds. 5.95 (ISBN 0-689-71252-9, Aladdin). Macmillan Child Grp.

Petersham, Maud & Petersham, Miska. The Box with Red Wheels. 32p. (ps-2). 1978. pap. 2.50 (ISBN 0-02-044760-4, Aladdin). Macmillan Child Grp.

Phillips, Joan. Lucky Bear. Miller, J. P., illus. LC 85-14467. 32p. (ps-1). 1986. lib. bdg. 6.99 (ISBN 0-394-97987-7, Random Juv); pap. 2.95 (ISBN 0-394-87987-2, Random Juv). Random.

Poskitt, Kjartan. The Mystery of the Magic Toy. Higham, David, illus. 24p. (gr. k up). 1989. 4.95 (ISBN 0-8249-8380-7). Ideals.

Price, Leo. Hoover Wants to Help. (Illus.). 35p. (Orig.). (gr. 2-3). 1988. pap. 1.95 (ISBN 0-8198-3313-4). Dghtrs St Paul.

Prince, Pamela. Secret World of Teddy Bears. Keenan, Elaine F., photos by. LC 83-27. (gr. k up). 1984. 9.95 (ISBN 0-517-55022-9, Harmony). Crown.

Randall, Ronne. Gingerbread Man. 1988. text ed. 3.95 cased (ISBN 0-7214-5102-0). Ladybird Bks.

Rowland, Della. A World of Toys. Fried, Janice, illus. 24p. 1990. 8.95 (ISBN 0-8092-4275-3, Calico Bks). Contemp Bks.

Rylands, Ljiljana. Teddy Bear's Friend. (ps-k). 1989. 9.95 (ISBN 0-525-44532-3, DCB). Dutton Child Bks.

Schreier, Joshua. Luigi's All-Night Parking Lot. (ps-3). 1990. 12.95 (ISBN 0-525-44626-5, DCB). Dutton Child Bks.

Seymour, Peter. The Magic Toyshop. Welply, Michael, illus. (gr. 3 up). 1988. pap. 14.95 (ISBN 0-671-66907-9). S&S Trade.

Shennan, Christopher. Toymaker's Dream. (gr. 6-8). 1983. pap. 2.95 (ISBN 0-87508-767-1). Chr Lit.

Sherrow, Victoria. Wilbur Waits. Watts, James, illus. LC 87-28978. 32p. (ps-3). 1990. 13.95 (ISBN 0-06-025483-1); PLB 13.89 (ISBN 0-06-025484-X). HarpC Child Bks.

Slier, Debby. Teddy Beddy Bear's Bedtime Adventure. Reichmeier, Betty, illus. LC 85-60215. 28p. (ps). 1985. bds. 2.95 (ISBN 0-394-87535-4, Random Juv). Random.

Stahl, Hilda. Teddy Jo & the Great Dive. 128p. (Orig.). (gr. 2-7). 1985. pap. 2.95 (ISBN 0-8423-6952-X). Tyndale.

—Teddy Jo & the Magic Quill. 128p. (Orig.). (gr. 2-7). 1985. pap. 2.95 (ISBN 0-8423-6953-8). Tyndale.

Stain, Dan. Teddy Bears' Halloween Party. (gr. 1-7). 1989. pap. 2.25 (ISBN 0-89954-962-4). Antioch Pub Co.

Stringham, Alene. Kids & Their Toys. Sussman, Ellen, ed. Burris, Priscilla, illus. 60p. (Orig.). (gr. 1). 1986. pap. text ed. 5.95 (ISBN 0-933606-44-3, 644). Monkey Sisters.

Vernon, Tannie. Adriana & the Magic Clockwork Train. LC 89-49368. (Illus.). 32p. 1990. 12.95 (ISBN 0-517-57823-9); PLB 13.99 (ISBN 0-517-57824-7). Crown.

Waber, Bernard. Ira Sleeps Over. Waber, Bernard, illus. 48p. (gr. k-3). 1975. pap. 4.95 (ISBN 0-395-20503-4, Sandpiper). HM.

Waddell, Martin. The Park in the Dark. Briley, D., ed. Firth, Barbara, illus. LC 88-9169. 32p. (ps-1). 1989. 11.95 (ISBN 0-688-08516-4); PLB 11.88 (ISBN 0-688-08517-2). Lothrop.

Wahl, Jan. The Toy Circus. Bowers, Tim, illus. LC 85-30186. 32p. (gr. k-3). 1986. 13.95 (ISBN 0-15-200609-5, Gulliver Bks). HarBraceJ.

Weinbach, Shaindel. Shimmee & the Taste-Me Tree. Backman, Aidel, illus. (ps-2). 2.95 (ISBN 0-87306-991-9). Feldheim.

Williams, Karen L. Galimoto. Stock, Catherine, illus. LC 89-2258. 32p. (gr. k-3). 1990. 13.95 (ISBN 0-688-08789-2); lib. bdg. 13.88 (ISBN 0-688-08790-6). Lothrop.

Williams, Margery. The Velveteen Rabbit. Hickman, Estella L., illus. 40p. (gr. 2-6). 1989. 2.95 (ISBN 0-87406-393-0, 16-18842-5). Willowisp Pr.

—The Velveteen Rabbit: Or How Toys Become Real. Plume, Ilse, illus. LC 86-33544. 32p. 1987. 10.95 (ISBN 0-15-293500-2). HarBraceJ.

Wolf, Jill. My Teddy Bear Loves... (gr. 1-7). 1989. pap. 2.25 (ISBN 0-89954-959-4). Antioch Pub Co.

Wolf, Jill & Moore, Clement C. Teddy Bears Night Before Christmas. Rudegeair, Jean, illus. 24p. (gr. 3-6). 1985. pap. 2.25 (ISBN 0-89954-330-8). Antioch Pub Co.

Worthington, Phoebe & Worthington, Selby. Teddy Bear Baker. LC 84-26454. (Illus.). 20p. (ps-1). 1985. pap. 2.95 (ISBN 0-14-050499-0, Puffin). Puffin Bks.

Ziefert, Harriet. Come out, Jessie! Smith, Mavis, illus. LC 90-41880. 32p. (ps-1). 1991. 4.95 (ISBN 0-06-107414-4). HarpC Child Bks.

—Goodnight, Everyone. Baruffi, Andrea, illus. LC 88-80666. (ps-3). 1988. 11.95 (ISBN 0-316-98756-5). Little.

—Hurry up, Jessie! Smith, Mavis, illus. LC 90-41508. 32p. (ps-1). 1991. 4.95 (ISBN 0-06-107415-2). HarpC Child Bks.

TRACK ATHLETICS

see also Walking

Aaseng, Nathan. Track's Magnificent Milers. LC 80-27404. (Illus.). (gr. 4 up). 1981. PLB 7.95 (ISBN 0-8225-1066-9). Lerner Pubns.

—Ultramarathons: The World's Most Punishing Races. (Illus.). 72p. (gr. 4 up). 1987. PLB 9.95 (ISBN 0-8225-1534-2). Lerner Pubns.

Connolly, Pat. Coaching Evelyn: Fast, Faster, Fastest Woman in the World. LC 90-4835. (Illus.). 224p. (gr. 7 up). 1991. 15.95 (ISBN 0-06-021282-9); PLB 15.89 (ISBN 0-06-021283-7). HarpC Child Bks.

Durkin, John F. & Newton, Joe. Running to the Top of the Mountain. Cudworth, Chris, illus. 350p. (Orig.). (gr. 9-12). 1988. pap. text ed. 24.95 (ISBN 0-9621313-0-X). J & J Win Edge.

Gutman, Bill. Go for It: Track & Field. Brown, Ben, illus. 64p. (gr. 3-7). 1989. PLB 16.50 (ISBN 0-942545-87-7). Grey Castle.

McMane, Fred. Track & Field Basics. Seiden, Art, illus. LC 82-21458. 48p. (gr. 3-7). 1983. 9.95 (ISBN 0-13-925966-X). P-H.

Neff, Fred. Running Is for Me. Reid, James E., illus. LC 79-16789. 48p. (gr. 2-5). 1980. PLB 8.95 (ISBN 0-8225-1093-6). Lerner Pubns.

Nentl, Jerolyn. Marathon Running. LC 79-27799. (Illus.). 32p. (gr. 3-5). 1980. lib. bdg. 9.95 (ISBN 0-89686-074-4, Crestwood Hse). Macmillan Child Grp.

Parker, Steve. Running a Race: How You Walk, Run & Jump. (Illus.). 32p. (gr. k-4). 1991. PLB 11.40 (ISBN 0-531-14096-2). Watts.

Peach, S. Running Skills. (Illus.). 48p. (gr. 6-10). 1988. PLB 12.96 (ISBN 0-88110-304-7); pap. 5.95 (ISBN 0-7460-0165-7). EDC.

Santos, Jim & Shannon, Ken. Sports Illustrated Track: Championship Field Events. 224p. (gr. 5 up). 1991. pap. 10.95 (ISBN 0-452-26273-9). NAL-Dutton.

Stanley, Jerry W. The Track & Field Training Diary: Your Personal Workout Record. (gr. 7-12). Date not set. plastic bdg. 7.95. Sports Diary Pub.

Sullivan, George. Better Track for Boys. (Illus.). 64p. (gr. 3-7). 1985. 9.95 (ISBN 0-396-08604-7, Putnam); pap. 3.50 (ISBN 0-396-08628-4, Putnam). Putnam Pub Group.

—Run, Run Fast. Madden, Don, illus. LC 78-22502. 64p. (gr. 4 up). 1980. 11.89 (ISBN 0-690-03969-7, Crowell Jr Bks). HarpC Child Bks.

Zeleznak, Shirley. Jogging. LC 79-27770. (Illus.). 32p. (gr. 4 up). 1980. lib. bdg. 9.95 (ISBN 0-89686-068-X, Crestwood Hse). Macmillan Child Grp.

TRACK ATHLETICS–BIOGRAPHY

Aaseng, Nathan. World-Class Marathoners. LC 81-13660. (Illus.). 80p. (gr. 4 up). 1982. PLB 7.95 (ISBN 0-8225-1325-0). Lerner Pubns.

Rosenthal, Bert. Carl Lewis: The Second Jesse Owens. LC 83-23984. (Illus.). 48p. (gr. 2-8). 1984. lib. bdg. 13.27 (ISBN 0-516-04336-6); pap. 3.95 (ISBN 0-516-44336-4). Childrens.

TRACK ATHLETICS–FICTION

Halecroft, David. Setting the Pace. (Illus.). 128p. (gr. 3-7). 1991. pap. 2.95 (ISBN 0-14-034547-7, Puffin). Puffin Bks.

Jenkins, Jerry. The Silent Track Star. (Orig.). (gr. 9-12). 1986. pap. text ed. 3.95 (ISBN 0-8024-8239-2). Moody.

Knudson, R. R. Frankestein's 10K. Glasser, Judy, illus. LC 85-40884. 144p. (gr. 3-7). 1986. pap. 10.95 (ISBN 0-670-80779-6). Viking Child Bks.

—Zanboomer. LC 77-11831. (Illus.). 192p. (gr. 7 up). 1978. PLB 12.89 (ISBN 0-06-023218-8). HarpC Child Bks.

Peters, Sharon. Listos, En Sus Marcas, Adelante! Trivas, Irene, illus. (SPA.). 32p. (gr. k-2). 1981. PLB 7.06 (ISBN 0-89375-550-8); pap. 1.95 (ISBN 0-685-04949-3). Troll Assocs.

Platt, Kin. Run for Your Life. 96p. (gr. 7 up). 1979. pap. 1.95 (ISBN 0-440-97557-3, LFL). Dell.

Skipper, David. Runners. LC 87-21028. 120p. (gr. 7 up). 1988. pap. 11.95 (ISBN 0-670-81994-8). Viking Child Bks.

Tunis, John R. Duke Decides. 1990. pap. 3.95 (ISBN 0-15-224308-9). HarbraceJ.

—Iron Duke. 1990. pap. 3.95 (ISBN 0-15-238987-3). HarbraceJ.

TRACKING AND TRAILING

Selsam, Millicent E. How to Be a Nature Detective. Keats, Ezra J., illus. LC 66-15947. 48p. (gr. 1-5). 1966. PLB 13.89 (ISBN 0-06-025301-0). HarpC Child Bks.

TRACTION ENGINES

see Tractors

TRACTORS

Murphy, Jim. Tractors: From Yesterday's Steam Wagons to Today's Turbo-charged Giants. LC 82-48777. (Illus.). 64p. (gr. 3-6). 1984. 11.95i (ISBN 0-397-32050-7, Lipp Jr Bks). HarpC Child Bks.

Stickland, Paul. Tractors. Stickland, Paul, illus. 16p. (ps-1). 1988. 3.95 (ISBN 0-8249-8258-4). Ideals.

Strickland, Paul. All about Tractors. LC 90-9817. (Illus.). 16p. (ps-2). 1990. PLB 9.95 (ISBN 0-8368-0423-6). Gareth Stevens Inc.

Thompson, Graham. Tractors. LC 86-5689. (Illus.). 24p. (gr. 1-2). 1986. PLB 10.95 (ISBN 1-55532-102-X). Gareth Stevens Inc.

TRACTORS–FICTION

Amery, H. The Runaway Tractor. (Illus.). 16p. (ps). 1989. 2.95 (ISBN 0-7460-0262-9, Usborne); lib. bdg. 7.96 (ISBN 0-88110-377-2, Usborne). EDC.

Baynton, Martin. Fifty & the Fox. LC 85-17137. (Illus.). 32p. (gr. k-3). 1986. bds. 5.95 (ISBN 0-517-56069-0). Crown.

Burton, Virginia L. Katy & the Big Snow. Burton, Virginia L., illus. 40p. (gr. k-3). 1974. pap. 4.95 (ISBN 0-395-18562-9, Sandpiper). HM.

Swan, Walter. The Little Green Tractor. Swan, Deloris, ed. Asch, Connie, illus. 16p. (Orig.). (gr. 2-4). 1989. pap. 1.50 (ISBN 0-927176-04-1). Swan Enterp.

TRADE FAIRS

see Fairs

TRADE ROUTES

Franck, Irene M. & Brownstone, David M. Around Africa & Asia by Sea. (Illus.). 128p. 1990. 17.95 (ISBN 0-8160-1875-8). Facts on File.

—The Northern World: Trade & Travel Routes Ser. (Illus.). 128p. 1990. 17.95 (ISBN 0-8160-1879-0). Facts on File.

Frank, Irene M. & Brownstone, David M. The European Overland Routes. (Illus.). 128p. 1990. 17.95 (ISBN 0-8160-1877-4). Facts on File.

—From Gibraltar to the Ganges. (Illus.). 128p. 1990. 17.95 (ISBN 0-8160-1876-6). Facts on File.

TRADE UNIONS

see Labor Unions

TRADE WASTE

see Waste Products

TRADITIONS

see Folklore; Legends; Superstition

TRAFFIC ACCIDENTS

Hjelmeland, Andy. Drinking & Driving. LC 89-25406. (Illus.). 48p. (gr. 4 up). 1990. 10.95 (ISBN 0-89686-496-0, Crestwood Hse). Macmillan Child Grp.

Park, Jae S. Now What? Auto Accident Claims Guide. 100p. (Orig.). Date not set. pap. text ed. 3.95 (ISBN 0-685-28055-1). Park Pub Co.

Traffic Safety. (Illus.). 64p. (gr. 6-12). 1975. pap. 1.85 (ISBN 0-8395-3391-8, 3391). BSA.

TRAFFIC ACCIDENTS–FICTION

Byars, Betsy C. The Glory Girl. (ps-3). 1985. pap. 3.95 (ISBN 0-14-031785-6, Puffin). Puffin Bks.

Colman, Hila. Suddenly. LC 86-28460. 160p. (gr. 7 up). 1987. 12.95 (ISBN 0-688-05865-5). Morrow Jr Bks.

Jordan, Hope D. Haunted Summer. LC 67-15713. (gr. 5 up). 1967. 11.95 (ISBN 0-688-41638-1). Lothrop.

Kropp, Paul. Death Ride. Ruhl, Greg, illus. LC 88-11460. 96p. (Orig.). (gr. 5 up). 1989. pap. 2.95 (ISBN 0-02-041793-4, Collier Young Ad). Macmillan Child Grp.

Richmond, Sandra. Wheels for Walking. (Illus.). 176p. (gr. 9-12). 1988. pap. 2.50 (ISBN 0-451-15235-2, Sig). NAL-Dutton.

TRAFFIC REGULATIONS

see also Traffic Accidents

Hoban, Tana. I Read Signs. Hoban, Tana, illus. LC 83-1482. 32p. (ps-1). 1983. 13.95 (ISBN 0-688-02317-7); PLB 13.88 (ISBN 0-688-02318-5). Greenwillow.

—I Read Symbols. Hoban, Tana, illus. LC 83-1481. 32p. (ps-1). 1983. 14.95 (ISBN 0-688-02331-2); PLB 14.88 (ISBN 0-688-02332-0). Greenwillow.

TRAGEDY

Barnet, Sylvan, et al, eds. Eight Great Tragedies. 448p. (gr. 9-12). Date not set. pap. 4.95 (ISBN 0-317-02717-4, Ment). NAL-Dutton.

TRAILING

see Tracking and Trailing

TRAINED NURSES

see Nurses and Nursing

TRAINING OF ANIMALS

see Animals–Training

TRAINING OF CHILDREN

see Children–Management

TRAINS, RAILROAD

see Railroads

TRAMPS–FICTION

Hamilton, Dorothy. Winter Caboose. Converse, James, illus. LC 83-10816. 104p. (Orig.). (gr. 4-8). 1983. pap. 3.95 (ISBN 0-8361-3341-2). Herald Pr.

TRANSATLANTIC FLIGHTS

see Aeronautics–Flights

TRANSCONTINENTAL JOURNEYS

see Overland Journeys to the Pacific

TRANSISTORS

Aten, Jerry. Prime Time Reading Skills. Filkins, Vanessa, illus. 64p. (gr. 2-5). 1984. wkbk 6.95 (ISBN 0-86653-185-8, GA 525). Good Apple.

TRANSPLANTATION OF ORGANS, TISSUES, ETC.

Beckelman, Laurie. Transplants. LC 90-33665. (Illus.). 48p. (gr. 5-6). 1990. RSBE 10.95 (ISBN 0-89686-572-X, Crestwood Hse). Macmillan Child Grp.

Lee, Sally. Donor Banks: Saving Lives with Organ & Tissue Transplants. Solomon, Maury, ed. LC 87-27304. (Illus.). 96p. (gr. 5 up). 1988. PLB 10.40 (ISBN 0-531-10475-3). Watts.
Leinwand, Gerald. Transplants: Today's Medical Miracles. LC 84-27101. 128p. (gr. 7 up). 1985. PLB 12.90 (ISBN 0-531-04930-2). Watts.
Nolen, William A. Spare Parts for the Human Body. (Illus.). (gr. 5-9). 1971. 3.95 (ISBN 0-685-04243-X). Random.

TRANSPORTATION

see also Aeronautics, Commercial; Automobiles; Bridges; Canals; Commerce; Harbors; Postal Service; Railroads; Roads; Steamboats; Subways; Trade Routes; Traffic Regulations; Trucks; Waterways

Autos, Ships, Trains & Planes. 32p. (ps). 1985. 3.95 (ISBN 0-394-87689-X). Random.
Baer, Edith. This Is the Way We Go to School. 40p. (ps-2). 1990. 13.95 (ISBN 0-590-43161-7). Scholastic Inc.
Barner, Bob. Elevator Escalator Book: A Transportation Fact Book. (ps-3). 1990. 12.95 (ISBN 0-385-26666-9); PLB 13.99 (ISBN 0-385-26667-7). Doubleday.
—Elevator Escalator Book: A Transportation Fact Book. (ps-3). 1990. 12.95 (ISBN 0-385-26666-9); PLB 13.99 (ISBN 0-385-26667-7). Doubleday.
Boyer, Edward. River & Canal. Boyer, Edward, illus. LC 85-21900. 48p. (gr. 5 up). 1986. reinforced bdg. 11.95 (ISBN 0-8234-0598-2). Holiday.
Brandt, Keith. Transportation. Schneider, Rex, illus. LC 84-2584. 32p. (gr. 3-6). 1985. PLB 9.49 (ISBN 0-8167-0172-5); pap. text ed. 2.95 (ISBN 0-8167-0173-3). Troll Assocs.
Brown, Richard. One Hundred Words about Transportation. Brown, Richard, illus. LC 86-22781. 32p. (ps). 1987. 5.95 (ISBN 0-15-200551-X, Gulliver Bks). HarBraceJ.
Brown, Richard, illus. One Hundred Words about Transportation. (ps-1). 1989. pap. 3.95 (ISBN 0-15-200555-2, Voy B). HarBraceJ.
Cain, Wilma W., ed. Story of Transportation. rev. ed. LC 87-81355. (Illus.). 128p. (gr. 4 up). 1988. 1-4 copies 14.95 ea. (ISBN 0-934291-24-1); 5 or more copies 11.95 (ISBN 0-317-91142-2). Gateway Pr MI.
Carson, Patti & Dellosa, Janet. Transportation Fun Book. Carson, Patti & Dellosa, Janet, illus. 32p. (ps-2). 1984. pap. 1.59 (ISBN 0-88724-022-4, CD-8037). Carson-Dellos.
Frith, Michael. Some of Us Walk, Some Fly, Some Swim. LC 73-158391. (Illus.). (gr. k-6). 1971. PLB 4.95 (ISBN 0-394-82325-7). Beginner.
Gakken Co. Ltd. Editors, ed. Wheels & Wings. Time-Life Books Inc. Editors, tr. (Illus.). 90p. (gr. k-3). 1988. 15.93 (ISBN 0-8094-4861-0); PLB 21.27 (ISBN 0-8094-4862-9). Time-Life.
Graham, Ian. Transportation. (Illus.). 48p. (gr. 7-9). 1990. 12.90 (ISBN 0-531-19511-2). Watts.
Harris, Jack C. Personal Watercraft. LC 88-18930. (Illus.). 48p. (gr. 5-6). 1988. PLB 10.95 (ISBN 0-89686-377-8, Crestwood Hse). Macmillan Child Grp.
Hilton, Suzanne. Faster Than a Horse: Moving West with Engine Power. LC 83-17022. (Illus.). 224p. (gr. 5-9). 1983. 14.95 (ISBN 0-664-32709-5, Westminster). Westminster John Knox.
Keaton, Phyllis H. Buggies. LC 88-5951. (Illus.). 48p. (gr. 5-6). 1988. PLB 10.95 (ISBN 0-89686-375-1, Crestwood Hse). Macmillan Child Grp.
Kinghorn, Harriet & Morberg, Mary. Research Shapes: Transportation. (Illus.). 64p. (gr. 2-5). 1989. 6.95 (ISBN 1-878279-03-3, MM1920). Monday Morning Bks.
Land Travel. (Illus.). 80p. (gr. k-6). 1986. pap. 13.27 (ISBN 0-8172-2592-7). Raintree Pubs.
Little, Karen E. Finding Out about Things on Wheels. (Illus.). 24p. (gr. 2-4). 1987. PLB 11.96 (ISBN 0-88110-294-6); pap. 3.95 (ISBN 0-7460-0090-1). EDC.
Little, Karen E. & Thomas, A. Wings, Wheels & Water: A First Book of Transport. (Illus.). 72p. (gr. 2-4). 1988. 10.95 (ISBN 0-7460-0106-1). EDC.
Little People Big Book about Things We Ride. 64p. (ps-1). 1989. write for info. (ISBN 0-8094-7462-X); PLB write for info. (ISBN 0-8094-7463-8). Time-Life.
Machines, Cars, Boats, & Airplanes. Date not set. 5.98 (ISBN 0-517-68232-X). Outlet Bk Co.
Mellet, Peter, et al. Transportation. Smith, Guy & Bull, Peter, illus. LC 89-11358. 48p. (gr. 4-5). 1989. PLB 11.95 (ISBN 0-8368-0134-2). Gareth Stevens Inc.
Moolman, Valerie. The Future World of Transportation. LC 84-10787. 112p. (gr. k-8). 1984. lib. bdg. 12.90 (ISBN 0-531-04882-9). Watts.
Norris, Ann. On the Go. 32p. 1990. 13.95 (ISBN 0-688-06336-5); PLB 13.88 (ISBN 0-688-06337-3). Lothrop.
Rutland, Jonathan. The Age of Steam. Atkinson, Mike, illus. LC 87-4788. 24p. (gr. 2-5). 1987. lib. bdg. 5.99 (ISBN 0-394-99216-4, Random Juv); pap. 2.95 (ISBN 0-394-89216-X, Random Juv). Random.
Sacher, Rainer. Know about Wood. Behrendt, Hans-Joachim, illus. (gr. 1-5). 1979. 3.95 (ISBN 0-905778-03-0). Academy Chi Pubs.
Sandak, Cass R. Tunnels. (Illus.). 32p. (gr. 2-4). 1984. lib. bdg. 10.90 (ISBN 0-531-04712-1). Watts.
Schwartz, Linda. Trivia Trackdown-Communication & Transportation. (Illus.). 32p. (gr. 4-6). 1986. 3.95 (ISBN 0-88160-139-X, LW258). Learning Wks.
Spizzirri Publishing Co. Staff. Transportation: Educational Coloring Book. Spizzirri, Linda, ed. Spizzirri, Peter M., illus. 32p. (gr. 1-8). 1981. pap. 1.95 (ISBN 0-86545-038-2). Spizzirri.
Stein, Barbara. Kids' World Almanac of Transportation: Rockets, Planes, Trains, Cars, Boars & Other Ways to Travel. 1991. 14.95 (ISBN 0-88687-491-2); pap. 6.95 (ISBN 0-88687-490-4). Pharos Bks NY.
Thompson, Graham. Wheels, 4 vols. Thompson, Graham, illus. 96p. (gr. 1-2). 1986. Set. PLB 43.80 (ISBN 1-55532-121-6). Gareth Stevens Inc.
Trains. (Illus.). (gr. k-1). 1972. bds. 2.50 (ISBN 0-448-02686-4, G&D). Putnam Pub Group.
Twinn, Michael, illus. Transport. 12p. (Orig.). (ps-2). 1977. 4.50 (ISBN 0-85953-006-X, Pub. by Child's Play England). Childs Play.
Weiner, Beth L., illus. The Pudgy Book of Here We Go. 16p. (gr. k). 1984. pap. 2.95 (ISBN 0-448-10208-0, G&D). Putnam Pub Group.
Williams, Brenda & Williams, Brian. Wings, Wheels & Sails. Bull, Peter, illus. LC 90-42977. 40p. (Orig.). (gr. 2-5). 1991. pap. 3.95 (ISBN 0-679-80863-9). Random.
Ziefert, Harriet. Baby Ben's Go-Go Book. (Illus.). (ps). 1984. 2.95 (ISBN 0-394-86820-X, Pub. by BYR). Random.

TRANSPORTATION–FICTION

Kingman, Lee. Head over Wheels. 224p. (gr. 7 up). 1981. pap. 1.75 (ISBN 0-440-93129-0, LE). Dell.
Lowry, Goodrich. Streetcar Man: Tom Lowry & the Twin City Rapid Transit Company. LC 79-2584. (Illus.). 178p. (gr. 7 up). 1979. 9.95 (ISBN 0-8225-0764-1). Lerner Pubns.
Stuart, Doris. All Aboard! Bracken, Carolyn, illus. LC 87-81766. 22p. (ps). 1988. write for info. (ISBN 0-307-12117-8, Pub. by Golden Bks). Western Pub.

TRANSPORTATION, HIGHWAY

see also Automobiles; Trucks

TRANSPORTATION–HISTORY

Pollard, Michael. From Cycle to Spaceship: The Story of Transport. (Illus.). 48p. (gr. 1-4). 1987. 12.95x (ISBN 0-8160-1779-4). Facts on File.
Unstead, R. J. Travel by Road Through the Ages. (Illus.). (gr. 7-10). 1967. 14.95 (ISBN 0-7136-1812-4). Dufour.

TRAPPING

see also Fur Trade; Hunting

Gilsvik, Bob. The Complete Book of Trapping. Gilsvik, David, illus. 172p. (gr. 7). Repr. of 1976 ed. 10.95 (ISBN 0-936622-29-6). A R Harding Pub.

TRAPPING–FICTION

Thomas, Jane R. Fox in a Trap. Howell, Troy, illus. LC 86-17412. 96p. (gr. 3-6). 1987. 13.95 (ISBN 0-89919-473-7, Pub. by Clarion). Ticknor & Fields.

TRAVEL

see also Automobiles–Touring; Tourist Trade; Voyages and Travels; Voyages around the World;
also names of countries, states, etc. with the subdivision Description and Travel, e.g. U. S.–Description and travel

Brown, Laurene K. & Brown, Marc. Dinosaurs Travel: A Guide for Families on the Go. Brown, Marc, illus. 32p. (ps-3). 1988. 13.95 (ISBN 0-316-11076-0). Little.
Button, Beth. Here-There, Far-Near. Sussman, Ellen, ed. Burris, Priscilla, illus. 56p. (Orig.). (ps-3). 1990. pap. text ed. 6.95 (ISBN 0-933606-81-8, MS-685). Monkey Sisters.
Cothran, Betty. Destinations, Detours & Diversions: A Guide to Family Outings & Good Times. (Illus.). 75p. (Orig.). 1989. pap. 4.99 (ISBN 0-9625229-0-2). Seaworthy Pubns.
Hest, Amy. Travel Tips from Harry: A Guide to Family Vacations in the Sun. Truesdell, Sue, illus. LC 88-39887. 64p. (gr. 2 up). 1989. 11.95 (ISBN 0-688-07972-5); PLB 11.88 (ISBN 0-688-09291-8, Morrow Jr Bks). Morrow Jr Bks.
Kalman, Bobbie. How We Travel. (Illus.). 32p. (gr. 2-3). 1986. 14.95 (ISBN 0-86505-076-7). Crabtree Pub Co.
Koch, Susan C. Dallas, Texas: The Travel Guide for Kids. Koch, Richard L., illus. 32p. (gr. k-4). 1992. pap. 4.50 (ISBN 0-945600-03-8). Colormore Inc.
McKissack, Patricia & McKissack, Fredrick. Big Bug Book of Places to Go. Bartholomew, illus. LC 87-61652. 24p. (Orig.). (gr. k-1). 1987. spiral bdg. 14.95 (ISBN 0-88335-765-8); pap. text ed. 4.95 (ISBN 0-88335-775-5). Milliken Pub Co.
Travel & Communications. (Illus.). 96p. (gr. 3-8). 1987. PLB 240.00 set (ISBN 0-317-62835-6); pap. 13.27 (ISBN 0-317-62836-4). Raintree Pubs.
Ward, Elaine. Roots & Wings. (Orig.). (gr. 1-6). 1983. pap. 3.95 (ISBN 0-377-00130-9). Friendship Pr.

TRAVEL–FICTION

Barry, Sebastian. Elsewhere. (gr. 1-12). 1985. 15.95 (ISBN 0-85105-903-1, Pub. by Colin Smythe Ltd Britain). Dufour.
Bauer, Caroline F. My Mom Travels a Lot. 48p. (ps-3). 1985. pap. 3.95 (ISBN 0-14-050545-8, Puffin). Puffin Bks.
Beatty, Patricia. Be Ever Hopeful, Hannalee. LC 88-21581. 208p. (gr. 5-9). 1988. 12.95 (ISBN 0-688-07502-9). Morrow.
Brown, Margaret W. Four Fur Feet. Charlip, Remy, illus. 48p. (gr. 1-3). 1989. Repr. of 1961 ed. 13.95 (ISBN 0-929077-03-2, Hopscotch Bks); PLB 12.95 (ISBN 0-317-92548-2, Hopscotch Bks). Watermark Inc.

Cheadle, J. A. A Donkey's Life: A Story for Children. Thomas, Toni, illus. LC 80-123421. iii, 88p. (Orig.). (gr. 2-6). 1979. pap. 3.50 (ISBN 0-9604244-0-7). Heahstan Pr.
The story follows Don Quixotito, a donkey of principle, across the American continent, with stops in North Carolina, Mississippi, Texas, Colorado, & California. Six songs, chiefly regional, which the donkey hears along the way, are included. After being almost successfully captured by rustlers in Texas, he leaves, this song echoing in his ears: "I'm departin' from this state; the Rangers nearly cornered me..." "Once upon a time a book brought children love. It is a children's story about an adventuresome little donkey named Don Quixotito whose travels take him to many exciting places. I read the book at least ten times--in the bathtub, while eating breakfast, & while everyone else watched the New Year's Day parade on T.V."--Peggy Drapo in the Denton Record-Chronicle. "This charming little book is not only a delightful story of the adventures of a cunning little donkey. It can be a very pleasant lesson in geography for a grown person as well as a child. There is also a touch of the lore of Texas & Texans in his Travels."--Carl Warlaw, Texas writer.
Publisher Provided Annotation.

Eisemann, Henry. Hump-Free Visits Vancouver Expo. Campbell, Jay, illus. (Orig.). (gr. k-6). 1986. pap. 6.95 (ISBN 0-938129-01-5). Emprise Pubns.
Fujikawa, Gyo. Here I Am. Fujikawa, Gyo, illus. 14p. (ps). 1981. 2.25 (ISBN 0-448-15082-4, G&D). Putnam Pub Group.
Gilson, Jamie. Four-B Goes Wild. Edwards, Linda S., illus. LC 83-948. 160p. (gr. 4-6). 1983. 12.95 (ISBN 0-688-02236-7). Lothrop.
Gomi, Taro. Coco Can't Wait. Gomi, Taro, illus. (ps-1). 1985. pap. 3.95 (ISBN 0-14-050522-9, Puffin). Puffin Bks.
Halpern-Gold, Julia & Adler, Robin W. Travel Tales: A Mobility Storybook. Binns, Brenda S., illus. LC 88-62588. 107p. (Orig.). (ps-3). 1988. pap. text ed. 20.00 (ISBN 0-922637-00-8). Most Mobil.
Jonas, Ann. Round Trip. Jonas, Ann, illus. LC 82-12026. 32p. (gr. k-3). 1983. 13.95 (ISBN 0-688-01772-X); PLB 13.88 (ISBN 0-688-01781-9). Greenwillow.
Juster, Norton. The Phantom Tollbooth. (gr. 5 up). 1961. 15.95 (ISBN 0-394-81500-9, Random Juv); pap. 3.95 (ISBN 0-394-82199-8). Random.
L'Engle, Madeleine. The Moon by Night. LC 63-9072. 224p. (gr. 7 up). 1963. 14.95 (ISBN 0-374-35049-3). FS&G.
Moncure, Jane B. Stop! Go! Word Bird. Hohag, Linda S., illus. LC 80-16273. 32p. (ps-2). 1981. PLB 11.97 (ISBN 0-89565-160-2). Childs World.
Raphael, Morris. How Do You Know When You're in Acadiana. Hebert, Carrie, illus. 32p. (Orig.). (gr. 5 up). 1984. pap. 3.95 (ISBN 0-9608866-3-X). M Raphael.
Rogers, Paul. Forget-Me-Not. Berridge, Celia, illus. LC 83-5969. 32p. (gr. k-1). 1984. pap. 8.95 (ISBN 0-670-32365-9). Viking Child Bks.
Rogers, Paul T. Forget-Me-Not. Berridge, Celia, illus. 32p. (ps-k). 1986. pap. 3.50 (Puffin). Puffin Bks.
Turner, Ethel. Walking to School. LC 88-22365. (Illus.). 32p. (ps-2). 1989. 12.95 (ISBN 0-531-05799-2); PLB 12.99 (ISBN 0-531-08399-3). Orchard Bks Watts.
Verne, Jules. Around the World in Eighty Days. 238p. (gr. 7 up). 1964. pap. 2.25 (ISBN 0-590-33938-9). Scholastic Inc.
Ziefert, Harriet. Trip Day. Brown, Richard, illus. (gr. 2-5). 1987. 7.95 (ISBN 0-316-98765-4). Little.

TRAVELERS

see also Explorers

TRAVELERS–FICTION

Alcock, Vivien. Travelers by Night. (gr. k-6). 1990. pap. 2.95 (ISBN 0-440-40292-1, YB). Dell.
Mark, Jan. Trouble Half-Way. Parkins, David, illus. LC 85-20028. 128p. (gr. 4-7). 1986. 12.95 (ISBN 0-689-31210-5, Atheneum Child Bk). Macmillan Child Grp.
Peck, Richard. Those Summer Girls I Never Met. 224p. (gr. 7 up). 1988. 14.95 (ISBN 0-440-50054-0). Delacorte.
Tallarico, Tony. Let's Take a Trip. Tallarico, Tony, illus. 12p. (gr. 3-8). 1982. pap. 3.95 (ISBN 0-89828-305-1). Tuffy Bks.

TRAVELS

see Overland Journeys to the Pacific; Scientific Expeditions; Voyages and Travels; Voyages around the World

TREASURE-TROVE

see Buried Treasure

TREE PLANTING

see also Trees

TREES
see also Forests and Forestry; Fruit Culture; Leaves; Lumber and Lumbering; Shrubs; Wood
American Forestry Association Staff. Trees Every Boy & Girl Should Know. 4th ed. (Illus.). 89p. 1977. pap. text ed. 4.50. Am Forestry.
Barker, Cicely M. Flower Fairies of the Trees. Barker, Cicely M., illus. (ps up). 1991. 5.95 (ISBN 0-7232-3760-3). Viking Child Bks.
Bash, Barbara. Tree of Life: The World of the African Baobab. (gr. 1-5). 1989. 14.95 (ISBN 0-316-08305-4, Sierra Club). Little.
Boulton, Carolyn. Trees. Newman, Colin, illus. LC 84-50016. 32p. (gr. 2-4). 1984. PLB 11.90 (ISBN 0-531-04635-4). Watts.
Braithwaite, Althea. Tree. (ps-6). 1988. PLB 7.95 (ISBN 0-88462-196-0); pap. 2.95 (ISBN 0-88462-197-9). Dearborn Finan.
Brandt, Keith. Discovering Trees. Nigoghossian, Christine W., illus. LC 81-7522. 32p. (gr. 2-4). 1982. PLB 10.89 (ISBN 0-89375-566-4); pap. text ed. 2.95 (ISBN 0-89375-567-2). Troll Assocs.
Brockman, C. Frank. Trees of North America. Zim, Herbert S. & Fichter, George S., eds. Merrilees, Rebecca, illus. (gr. 9 up). 1968. pap. write for info (ISBN 0-307-13658-2, Golden Pr). Western Pub.
Burnie, David. Tree. Chadwick, Peter, photos by. LC 88-1572. (Illus.). 64p. (gr. 5 up). 1988. 15.00 (ISBN 0-394-89617-3); lib. bdg. 14.99 (ISBN 0-394-99617-8). Knopf.
Cochrane, Jennifer. Trees of the Tropics. LC 90-10023. (Illus.). 48p. (gr. 5-9). 1990. PLB 18.60 (ISBN 0-8114-2731-5). Steck-V.
Dickinson, Jane. All about Trees. D'Adamo, Anthony, illus. LC 82-17382. 32p. (gr. 3-6). 1983. PLB 10.59 (ISBN 0-89375-892-2); pap. text ed. 2.95 (ISBN 0-89375-893-0). Troll Assocs.
Dowden, Anne O. The Blossom on the Bough: A Book of Trees. LC 74-6192. (Illus.). 80p. (gr. 5 up). 1988. PLB 14.89 (ISBN 0-690-04655-3, Crowell Jr Bks). HarpC Child Bks.
Florian, Douglas. Discovering Trees. Florian, Douglas, illus. LC 85-22143. 32p. (ps-3). 1986. 12.95 (ISBN 0-684-18566-0, Scribners Young Read). Macmillan Child Grp.
—Discovering Trees. LC 89-37817. 32p. (ps-2). 1990. pap. 3.95 (ISBN 0-689-71377-0, Aladdin). Macmillan Child Grp.
Flowers & Trees. (Illus.). 88p. (ps-3). 1989. 15.93 (ISBN 0-8094-4857-2); lib. bdg. 21.27 (ISBN 0-8094-4858-0). Time-Life.
Fowler, Allan. It Could Still Be a Tree. LC 90-2207. (Illus.). 32p. (ps-2). 1990. PLB 12.60 (ISBN 0-516-04905-4); pap. 30.60 big bk. (ISBN 0-516-49464-3). Childrens.
—It Could Still Be a Tree. (Illus.). 32p. (ps-2). 1990. 12.60 (ISBN 0-516-04904-6). Childrens.
Greenaway, Theresa. Woodland Trees. LC 90-37227. (Illus.). 48p. (gr. 5-9). 1990. PLB 18.60 (ISBN 0-8114-2732-3). Steck-V.
Harlow, Rosie & Morgan, Gareth. Trees & Leaves. Peperell, Liz, illus. 40p. (gr. 5-8). 1991. PLB 12.90 (ISBN 0-531-19126-5, Warwick). Watts.
Hester, Nigel. The Living Tree. (Illus.). 32p. (gr. 5-8). 1990. PLB 11.40 (ISBN 0-531-14007-5). Watts.
Hiscock, Bruce. The Big Tree. Hiscock, Bruce, illus. LC 89-18286. 32p. (gr. 1-5). 1991. RSBE 13.95 (ISBN 0-689-31598-8, Atheneum Child Bk). Macmillan Child Grp.
Jennings, Terry. Trees. LC 88-37552. (Illus.). 32p. (gr. 3-6). 1989. PLB 14.60 (ISBN 0-516-08444-5); pap. 4.95 (ISBN 0-516-48444-3). Childrens.
Killion, Bette. The Apartment House Tree. Szilagyi, Mary, illus. LC 88-35700. 32p. (ps-2). 1989. 12.95 (ISBN 0-06-023273-0); PLB 12.89 (ISBN 0-06-023274-9). HarpC Child Bks.
Kirkpatrick, Rena K. Look at Trees. rev. ed. Worth, Jo & Knight, Ann, illus. LC 84-26225. 32p. (gr. 2-4). 1985. PLB 15.99 (ISBN 0-8172-2359-2); pap. text ed. 9.27 (ISBN 0-8172-2384-3). Raintree Pubs.
Langley, Andrew. Trees. rev. ed. Franklin Watts Ltd., ed. (Illus.). 32p. (ps-6). 1988. PLB 10.90 (ISBN 0-531-10446-X). Watts.
Lavies, Bianca. Tree Trunk Traffic. Lavies, Bianca, photos by. (Illus.). 32p. (ps-2). 1989. 13.95 (ISBN 0-525-44495-5, DCB). Dutton Child Bks.
Lerner, Sharon. I Found a Leaf. Lerner, Sharon, illus. LC 64-25679. 40p. (gr. 3-6). 1964. PLB 6.95 (ISBN 0-8225-0251-8). Lerner Pubns.
Lyon, George-Ella. A B Cedar: An Alphabet of Trees. Parker, Tom, illus. LC 88-22797. 32p. (ps-1). 1989. 14.95 (ISBN 0-531-05795-X); PLB 14.99 (ISBN 0-531-08395-0). Orchard Bks Watts.
Nelson, Cora. Trees. (Illus.). 50p. (Orig.). (gr. 2-6). 1990. pap. 4.95 (ISBN 0-920534-43-0, Pub. by Hyperion Pr Ltd CN). Sterling.
Nelson, JoAnne. A Home in a Tree. Cogbill, Mary, illus. 16p. (Orig.). (gr. k-2). 1990. pap. 3.95 (ISBN 1-878624-11-3). McClanahan Bk.
Podendorf, Illa. Trees. LC 81-12313. (Illus.). 48p. (gr. k-4). 1982. PLB 14.60 (ISBN 0-516-01657-1); pap. 4.95 (ISBN 0-516-41657-X). Childrens.
Russell, Naomi. The Tree. Russell, Naomi, illus. LC 88-23698. 32p. (ps-1). 1989. 9.95 (ISBN 0-525-44468-8, DCB). Dutton Child Bks.
Schnieder, Bill. The Tree Giants. Dowden, D. D., illus. LC 88-80225. 32p. 1988. pap. 4.95 (ISBN 0-937959-40-5). Falcon Pr MT.
Selsam, Millicent E. Tree Flowers. Lerner, Carol, illus. LC 83-17353. 32p. (gr. 4 up). 1984. PLB 12.88 (ISBN 0-688-02769-5). Morrow.
Thompson. Trees. (gr. 2-5). 1980. (Usborne-Hayes); PLB 11.96 (ISBN 0-88110-071-4); pap. 3.95 (ISBN 0-86020-473-1). EDC.
Trees of Arizona. (Illus.). 32p. (gr. 1 up). 1984. pap. 1.00 (ISBN 0-935810-18-8). Primer Pubs.
Udry, Janice M. Tree Is Nice. Simont, Marc, illus. LC 56-5153. 32p. (ps-1). 1957. 11.95 (ISBN 0-06-026155-2); PLB 12.89 (ISBN 0-06-026156-0). HarpC Child Bks.
Warren, Elizabeth. I Can Read About Trees & Plants. LC 74-24991. (Illus.). (gr. 2-4). 1975. pap. 1.95 (ISBN 0-89375-069-7). Troll Assocs.
Zim, Herbert S. & Martin, Alexander C. Trees. Barlowe, Dorothea & Barlowe, Sy, illus. (gr. 6 up). 1952. pap. write for info. (ISBN 0-307-24056-8, Golden Pr). Western Pub.

TREES–FICTION
Andersen, Hans Christian. The Fir Tree. Burkert, Nancy E., illus. LC 73-121800. 48p. (ps up). 1986. pap. 5.95 (ISBN 0-06-443109-6, Trophy). HarpC Child Bks.
—The Fir Tree. Goode, Diane, adapted by. & illus. LC 82-62172. 32p. (ps up). 1988. pap. 1.25 (ISBN 0-394-81941-1, Random Juv). Random.
—The Fir Tree. Burkert, Nancy E., illus. LC 73-121800. 48p. (gr. 3-6). 1970. 13.95 (ISBN 0-06-020077-4); PLB 13.89 (ISBN 0-06-020078-2). HarpC Child Bks.
—Fir Tree. Britt, Stephanie, illus. 24p. (ps-3). 1989. pap. 2.95 (ISBN 0-8249-8389-0). Ideals.
Barnes, Jill & Sato, Wakiko. Granny, Let Me In. Rubin, Caroline, ed. Japan Foreign Rights Centre Staff, tr. from JPN. Sato, Wakiko, illus. LC 90-37752. 40p. (gr. k-3). 1990. PLB 14.60 (ISBN 0-944483-82-8). Garrett Ed Corp.
Barnes, Jill & Tsurmi, Masao. Giant Tree & the Boy. Rubin, Caroline, ed. Japan Foreign Rights Centre Staff, tr. from JPN. Suzuki, Mamoru, illus. LC 90-37751. 40p. (gr. k-4). 1990. PLB 14.60 (ISBN 0-944483-80-1). Garrett Ed Corp.
Benedek, Elek & Illyes, Gyula. The Tree That Reached the Sky. 64p. 1988. 13.95 (ISBN 963-13-2535-0, Pub. by Corvina Kiado HU). Intl Spec Bk.
Blocksma, Mary. Apple Tree! Apple Tree! Kalthoff, Sandra C., illus. LC 82-19852. 24p. (ps-2). 1983. PLB 12.33 (ISBN 0-516-01584-2); pap. 3.95 (ISBN 0-516-41584-0). Childrens.
Brodeur, J. D. Igdor Twig. 80p. 8.75 (ISBN 0-8062-3734-1). Carlton.
Brown, Margaret W. The Little Fir Tree. Cooney, Barbara, illus. LC 54-5534. 24p. (gr. k-3). 1979. PLB 12.89 (ISBN 0-690-04016-4, Crowell Jr Bks). HarpC Child Bks.
Cates, Joe W. The Crooked Tree. Cates, Joe W., illus. 48p. (Orig.). (gr. k-6). 1986. PLB 9.95 (ISBN 0-942403-02-9); pap. 6.00 (ISBN 0-942403-00-2). J Barnaby Dist.
Coats, Laura J. The Oak Tree. Coats, Laura J., illus. LC 86-18099. 32p. (ps-1). 1987. 13.95 (ISBN 0-02-719052-8, Mcmillan Child Bk). Macmillan Child Grp.
Dodd, Lynley. The Apple Tree. Dodd, Lynley, illus. LC 85-9774. 26p. (gr. 1-2). 1985. PLB 10.95 (ISBN 0-918831-08-3). Gareth Stevens Inc.
Donahue, Michael & Strawn, Susan. The Grandpa Tree. 24p. (gr. 1-3). 1988. pap. 4.95 (ISBN 0-911797-42-4). R Rinehart Inc.
Duncan, Shirley E. The Tree That Would Not Grow But Did. Reid, Nancy G., ed. Gibson, Judy, illus. Date not set. 12.95 (ISBN 1-878647-02-4). M E Duncan & Co.
Fleischman, Paul. The Birthday Tree. Sewall, Marcia, illus. LC 78-22155. (gr. k-3). 1979. PLB 12.89 (ISBN 0-06-021916-5). HarpC Child Bks.
—The Birthday Tree. Sewall, Marcia, illus. LC 78-22155. 32p. (gr. k-3). 1991. pap. 4.50 (ISBN 0-06-443246-7, Trophy). HarpC Child Bks.
Haynes, Richard T. The Thong Tree. Haynes, Richard T., illus. LC 90-70508. 64p. (gr. 3-7). 1990. 11.95 (ISBN 0-929146-02-6). Voyageur Pub.
Heller, Nicholas. The Tooth Tree. LC 90-39791. (Illus.). 24p. (ps up). 1991. 13.95 (ISBN 0-688-09392-2); PLB 13.88 (ISBN 0-688-09393-0). Greenwillow.
Holling, Holling C. Tree in the Trail. (Illus.). (gr. 4-6). 16.95 (ISBN 0-395-18228-X). HM.
Howe, James. How the Ewoks Saved the Trees: An Old Ewok Legend. Velez, Walter, illus. LC 83-13708. 48p. (gr. k-3). 1984. (Random Juv); lib. bdg. 6.99 (ISBN 0-394-96129-3). Random.
James, Christopher. Bump & the Trees. (Illus.). 24p. (ps-3). 1990. 7.50 (ISBN 0-88625-276-8). Durkin Hayes Pub.
Jones, Jo. Amanda's Tree. Vansant, Jo, illus. (gr. 3-6). 1977. pap. 3.50 (ISBN 0-9602266-0-5). Jo-Jo Pubns.
Lionni, Leo. The Alphabet Tree. Lionni, Leo, illus. LC 67-29149. 32p. (ps-2). 1990. pap. 3.95 (ISBN 0-679-80835-3, Dragonfly Bks). Knopf.
Lisle, Janet T. The Great Dimpole Oak. Gammell, Stephen, illus. LC 87-11092. 144p. (gr. 4-6). 1987. 11.95 (ISBN 0-531-05716-X); PLB 11.99 (ISBN 0-531-08316-0). Orchard Bks Watts.
Lloyd, David. Hello, Goodbye. Voce, Louise, illus. LC 87-17110. (ps-1). 1988. 12.95 (ISBN 0-688-07698-X); lib. bdg. 12.88 (ISBN 0-688-07699-8). Lothrop.
Luger, Harriet. The Elephant Tree. 112p. (gr. 7-11). 1986. pap. 2.25 (ISBN 0-440-92394-8, LFL). Dell.
McCord, David. Every Time I Climb a Tree. Simont, Marc, illus. LC 67-25611. 48p. (gr. k-3). 1985. pap. 4.95 (ISBN 0-316-55518-5). Little.
Mattingley, Christobel. The Miracle Tree. Yamaguchi, Marianne, illus. LC 86-4541. 32p. (gr. 3 up). 1986. 11.95 (ISBN 0-15-200530-7, Gulliver Bks). HarBraceJ.
Oppenheimer, Evelyn. Tilli Comes to Texas. Haverfield, Mary, illus. LC 86-3089. 40p. (gr. k-3). 1986. PLB 9.95 (ISBN 0-937460-21-4). Hendrick-Long.
Pike, Norman. The Peach Tree. DeWitt, Robin & DeWitt, Patricia, illus. 36p. (ps up). 1984. 10.95 (ISBN 0-88045-014-2). Stemmer Hse.
Polacco, Patricia. Uncle Vova's Tree. Polacco, Patricia, illus. 32p. (ps-3). 1989. 14.95 (ISBN 0-399-21617-0, Philomel Bks). Putnam Pub Group.
Poulet, Virginia. Blue Bug Finds a Friend. Maloney, Mary & Fleming, Stan, illus. LC 76-30369. 32p. (gr. k-3). 1977. PLB 14.60 (ISBN 0-516-03426-X). Childrens.
Roche, Luane. The Proud Tree. 64p. (gr. 2-6). pap. 1.95 (ISBN 0-89243-146-6). Liguori Pubns.
Romanova, Natalia. Once There Was a Tree. Spirin, Gennady, illus. LC 85-6730. (ps up). 1989. pap. 4.95 (ISBN 0-8037-0705-3). Dial Bks Young.
Ryder, Donald G. The Inside Story: Living & Learning Through Life's Storms. Mullen, Don, illus. LC 85-27780. 56p. (gr. 7 up). 1985. 14.95 (ISBN 0-935973-38-9). Ryder Pub Co.
Sato, Satoru. I Wish I Had a Big, Big Tree. Murakami, Tsutomu, illus. LC 88-8080. 40p. (ps-2). 1989. 10.95 (ISBN 0-688-07303-4); PLB 10.88 (ISBN 0-688-07304-2). Lothrop.
Smith, Agnes. The Bluegreen Tree. Sharkey, J. Thomas, illus. LC 76-50105. 180p. (Orig.). 1977. 9.00 (ISBN 0-87012-271-1). Westwind Pr.
Stryker, Sandy. Tonia the Tree. LC 88-16769. (Illus.). 32p. (gr. k-8). 1988. 13.95 (ISBN 0-911655-16-6). Advocacy Pr.
Turin, Adela & Selig, Syvie. Of Cannons & Caterpillars. (Illus.). 32p. (gr. 3-6). 1980. 4.95 (ISBN 0-904613-62-3). Writers & Readers.
Watkins, Willie L. Danny Pine & Patty Plum Tree. LC 88-51763. (Illus.). 40p. (Orig.). (gr. k-7). 1989. pap. 8.95 (ISBN 0-87516-595-8). DeVorss.
Winter, Ginny L. What's in My Tree. Winter, Ginny L., illus. (gr. k-1). 1962. 8.95 (ISBN 0-8392-3044-3). Astor-Honor.

TRIAL BY JURY
see Jury

TRIALS
see also Crime and Criminals
David, Andrew. Famous Military Trials. LC 79-17537. (Illus.). 120p. (gr. 5 up). 1980. PLB 9.95 (ISBN 0-8225-1428-1). Lerner Pubns.
—Famous Political Trials. LC 79-16923. (Illus.). 112p. (gr. 5 up). 1980. PLB 9.95 (ISBN 0-8225-1429-X). Lerner Pubns.
Gustafson, Anita. Guilty or Innocent. LC 85-7608. (Illus.). 160p. (gr. 2-9). 1985. 12.95 (ISBN 0-8050-0555-2). H Holt & Co.
Ogawa, Brian K., et al. To Tell the Truth. Wagstaff, Bob, illus. LC 88-51256. 40p. (gr. 4-6). 1988. text ed. write for info. (ISBN 0-9621260-0-4). VWAP.

TRIBES AND TRIBAL SYSTEMS
Marcus, Rebecca. Survivors of the Stone Age: Nine Tribes Today. (Illus.). 160p. (gr. 7 up). 1975. PLB 9.95 (ISBN 0-8038-6726-3). Hastings.

TRICKS
see also Card Tricks; Magic
Ames, Gerald & Wyler, Rose. Magic Secrets. Stubis, Talivaldis, illus. LC 67-4229. 64p. (gr. k-3). 1967. PLB 10.89 (ISBN 0-06-020069-3). HarpC Child Bks.
Baker, James W. Independence Day Magic. Overlie, George, illus. 48p. (gr. 2-5). 1989. 8.95 (ISBN 0-8225-2236-5). Lerner Pubns.
Barry, Sheila A. Tricks & Stunts to Fool Your Friends. LC 84-87. (Illus.). 128p. (gr. 4-6). 1984. pap. 3.95 (ISBN 0-8069-7856-2). Sterling.
Boy Scouts of America. Cub Scout Magic. (Illus.). 146p. (gr. 3-5). 1960. pap. 5.95x (ISBN 0-8395-3219-9, 3219). BSA.
Brandreth, Gyles. Pranks, Tricks & Practical Jokes: 100 Harmless Ways to Fool Your Friends. LC 79-65291. (Illus.). 128p. (gr. 3 up). 1986. pap. 3.95 (ISBN 0-8069-6376-X). Sterling.
Chuchill, E. Richard. Sneaky Tricks to Fool Your Friends. Behr, Joyce, illus. LC 86-14448. 128p. (gr. 6-12). 1987. pap. 3.95 (ISBN 0-8069-4808-6). Sterling.
Disney, Walt, Productions Staff. The Mickey Mouse Magic Book. LC 74-16420. (Illus.). 48p. (gr. 1-2). 1975. 5.95 (ISBN 0-394-82567-5, Random Juv); lib. bdg. 4.99 (ISBN 0-394-92567-X). Random.
Eldin, Peter. Trickster's Handbook. LC 89-32073. (Illus.). 96p. (gr. 10-12). 1989. 12.95 (ISBN 0-8069-5740-9). Sterling.
King, Colin. Amazing Book of Puzzles & Tricks. 1990. 3.50 (ISBN 0-517-69194-9). Outlet Bk Co.
Rigney, Francis J. A Beginner's Book of Magic. (Illus.). (gr. 6 up). 1963. 9.95 (ISBN 0-8159-5103-5). Devin.
Van Rensselaer, Alexander. Your Book of Magic. (gr. 9 up). 1968. 7.95 (ISBN 0-571-06939-8). Transatl Arts.

TRICYCLES
see Bicycles and Bicycling

TROJAN WAR
Coolidge, Olivia E. Trojan War. Sandoz, E., illus. (gr. 7-12). 1952. 14.95 (ISBN 0-395-06731-6). HM.
—Trojan War. 1990. pap. 4.95 (ISBN 0-395-56151-5). HM.
Evslin, Bernard. The Trojan War. 160p. (gr. 5 up). 1988. pap. 2.95 (ISBN 0-590-41626-X). Scholastic Inc.

Homer. Iliad. Lang, Andrew, tr. Budgey, N. F., intro. by. (gr. 9 up). pap. 2.95 (ISBN 0-8049-0115-5, CL-115). Airmont.
Stewart, Gail. The Trojan War: Opposing Viewpoints. LC 89-11616. (Illus.). 112p. (gr. 3-10). 1989. PLB 13.95 (ISBN 0-89908-065-0). Greenhaven.
—The Trojan War: Opposing Viewpoints. LC 89-11616. (Illus.). 112p. (gr. 3-10). 1989. PLB 13.95 (ISBN 0-89908-065-0). Greenhaven.
Storr, Catherine. The Trojan Horse. Codd, Mike, illus. LC 84-18292. 32p. (gr. 2-5). 1985. PLB 16.67 (ISBN 0-8172-2114-X); pap. 9.27 (ISBN 0-8172-2257-X). Raintree Pubs.

TROLLS
see Fairies

TROPICAL FISH
Braemer & Scheurmann. Tropical Fish. (gr. 4 up). 1983. pap. 4.95 (ISBN 0-8120-2686-1). Barron.
Broekel, Ray. Tropical Fish. LC 82-19738. (Illus.). 48p. (gr. k-4). 1983. PLB 14.60 (ISBN 0-516-01687-3); pap. 4.95 (ISBN 0-516-41687-1). Childrens.
Emmens, Cliff W. A Step-by-Step Book about Tropical Fish. (Illus.). 64p. (gr. 9-12). 1988. pap. 3.95 (ISBN 0-86622-471-8, SK-018). TFH Pubns.
Jameson, P. Tropical Fish. (Illus.). 32p. (gr. 2-5). 1989. lib. bdg. 14.00 (ISBN 0-86625-185-5). Rourke Corp.

TROPICS
Catchpole, Clive. Jungles. Finney, Denise, illus. LC 83-7796. 32p. (ps-4). 1985. pap. 4.95 (ISBN 0-8037-0036-9, 0481-140). Dial Bks Young.
Landau, Elaine. Tropical Rain Forests Around the World. (gr. 3-5). 1990. PLB 11.90 (ISBN 0-531-10896-1). Watts.
Planche, Bernard. Living on a Tropical Island. Matthews, Sarah, tr. from FRE. Broutin, Christian, illus. LC 87-34592. 38p. (gr. k-5). 1988. 4.95 (ISBN 0-944589-13-8, 138). Young Discovery Lib.
Rowland-Entwistle, Thoedore. Jungles & Rainforests. (Illus.). 48p. (gr. 5-8). 1987. PLB 14.98 (ISBN 0-382-09500-6). Silver Burdett Pr.

TROPICS–DISEASES AND HYGIENE
see also names of tropical diseases, e.g. Yellow Fever

TROUT
Cole, Joanna. A Fish Hatches. LC 78-13445. (Illus.). (gr. k-3). 1978. PLB 12.88 (ISBN 0-688-32153-4, Morrow Jr Bks). Morrow Jr Bks.

TROY–FICTION

Curtis, Dorris. Skammy: Prince of Troy. Curtis, Dorris, illus. 231p. (gr. 5-9). 1988. lib. bdg. 18.50 (ISBN 0-944436-04-8). Univ Central AR Pr.
Skammy: Prince of Troy
Recommended reading group: 10-15 years. It captures the imagination, & connects young readers to the origins of western values. Skammy: Prince of Troy is an exciting story of adventure & mighty deeds which will appeal to both the imagination & the intellect of young readers. But this book offers more than mere entertainment. It does what the deepest thinkers about literature have always said good books should do. It teaches as it entertains. It clarifies & enhances life. It struggles with great questions of life, death, & immortality. It offers models of human thought, behavior, & morality ranging from heroism, courage, integrity, & endurance to cowardice & treachery. Prince Skamandrios (Skammy to his family & friends) is initiated into the adult world of violence & intrigue early in life because the Greek armies are threatening the walls of his hometown of Troy & because he is the son of Hector, the heroic champion of the city....all of this against the backdrop of the war that defined patriotism & heroism, as well as waste & inhumanity, in the art & literature of western civilization.
Publisher Provided Annotation.

Green, Roger L. Tale of Troy. (Illus., Orig.). (gr. 5-7). 1974. pap. 3.95 (ISBN 0-14-030120-8, Puffin). Puffin Bks.

TRS-80 COMPUTERS
Kemnitz, Thomas M. & Mass, Lynne. Kids Working with Computers: TRS-80 BASIC Manual. Schlendorf, Lori, illus. 44p. (gr. 4-7). 1983. pap. 4.99 (ISBN 0-89824-050-6). Trillium Pr.
Kressen, David P. Teach Your Computer to Think in BASIC. Jacobs, Russell, ed. (Illus.). 88p. (gr. 5 up). 1983. pap. text ed. 7.50 (ISBN 0-918272-10-6). Jacobs.

TRUANCY (SCHOOLS)
see School Attendance

TRUCK DRIVERS
Behrens, June. I Can Be a Truck Driver. LC 84-23246. (Illus.). 32p. (gr. k-3). 1985. lib. bdg. 13.93 (ISBN 0-516-01848-5). Childrens.
—Puedo Ser Conductor de Camion. Kratky, Lada, tr. LC 85-31402. (SPA., Illus.). 32p. (gr. k-3). 1986. PLB 13.93 (ISBN 0-516-31848-9); pap. 3.95 (ISBN 0-516-51848-8). Childrens.
Bourne, Miriam A. A Day in the Life of a Cross-Country Trucker. Jann, Gayle, illus. LC 87-13582. 32p. (gr. 4-8). 1987. PLB 11.79 (ISBN 0-8167-1117-8); pap. text ed. 2.95 (ISBN 0-8167-1118-6). Troll Assocs.
Wolverton, Ruth & Wolverton, Mike. Trucks & Trucking. LC 82-6967. (Illus.). 72p. (gr. 4-8). 1982. PLB 10.40 (ISBN 0-531-04468-8). Watts.
Wurmfeld, Hope H. Trucker. Wurmfeld, Hope H., illus. LC 89-3296. 64p. (gr. 3 up). 1990. 14.95 (ISBN 0-02-793581-7, Mcmillan Child Bk). Macmillan Child Grp.

TRUCK FARMING
see Vegetable Gardening

TRUCKS
Barrett, Norman. Trucks. (Illus.). 32p. (gr. 2 up). 1991. pap. 3.95 (ISBN 0-531-15146-8). Watts.
Barton, Byron. Trucks. Barton, Byron, illus. LC 85-47901. 32p. (ps-k). 1986. 4.95 (ISBN 0-694-00062-0, Crowell Jr Bks); PLB 11.89 (ISBN 0-690-04530-1). HarpC Child Bks.
Broekel, Ray. Trucks. LC 82-17907. (Illus.). 48p. (gr. k-4). 1983. PLB 14.60 (ISBN 0-516-01688-1). Childrens.
Bushey, Jerry. Monster Trucks & Other Giant Machines on Wheels. LC 84-23160. (Illus.). 32p. (gr. k-4). 1985. PLB 12.95 (ISBN 0-87614-271-4); pap. 4.95 (ISBN 0-87614-491-1). Carolrhoda Bks.
Cave, J. Ronald. Trucks. Bishop, Denis, illus. 32p. (ps-3). 1982. PLB 10.90 (ISBN 0-531-04421-1). Watts.
Crews, Donald. Truck. LC 84-18137. (Illus.). 32p. (ps). 1985. pap. 3.95 (ISBN 0-14-050506-7, Puffin). Puffin Bks.
Dorin, Patrick C. Yesterday's Trucks. LC 81-20717. (Illus.). 48p. (gr. 4-9). 1982. PLB 9.95 (ISBN 0-8225-0502-9). Lerner Pubns.
Eighteen-Wheelers. 48p. (gr. 3-4). 1989. PLB 10.95 (ISBN 0-685-26372-X). Capstone Pr.
Four by Fours & Pickups. 48p. (gr. 3-4). 1989. PLB 10.95 (ISBN 0-685-26374-6). Capstone Pr.
Gibbons, Gail. Trucks. Gibbons, Gail, illus. LC 81-43039. 32p. (ps-2). 1981. (Crowell Jr Bks); PLB 13.89 (ISBN 0-690-04119-5). HarpC Child Bks.
Grimm, Rosemary. Truck & Tractor Pullers. LC 87-30592. (Illus.). 48p. (gr. 5-6). 1988. PLB 10.95 (ISBN 0-89686-358-1, Crestwood Hse). Macmillan Child Grp.
Hawksley, Gerald. Trucks. Hawksley, Gerald, illus. 10p. (gr. 2-4). 1990. bds. 4.95 (ISBN 1-878624-17-2). McClanahan Bk.
Herman, Gail. Make Way for Trucks: Big Machines on Wheels. Santoro, Christopher, illus. LC 89-34458. 32p. (ps-2). 1990. 9.95 (ISBN 0-679-80110-3); lib. bdg. 10.99 (ISBN 0-679-90110-8). Random.
Holder, Bill & Dunn, Harry. Monster Wheels. LC 89-26170. (Illus.). 32p. (gr. 3-8). 1990. 12.95 (ISBN 0-8069-5844-8). Sterling.
Holder, Bill & Farquhar, John. Monster Truck Action. (Illus.). 32p. (gr. 3-8). 1989. 1.00 (ISBN 0-87406-397-3, 52-18988-0). Willowisp Pr.
Jefferis, David & Lafferty, Peter. Giants of the Road: The History of the Truck. LC 90-31659. (Illus.). 32p. (gr. 5-8). 1991. PLB 11.90 (ISBN 0-531-14123-3). Watts.
McNaught, Harry. The Truck Book. LC 77-79851. (ps-2). 1978. (Random Juv); pap. 2.25 (ISBN 0-394-83703-7). Random.
—Trucks. McNaught, Harry, illus. LC 75-36463. 14p. (ps-1). 1976. Repr. of 1976 ed. bds. 3.95 (ISBN 0-394-83240-X). Random.
Magee, Doug. Trucks You Can Count On. (gr. 5-8). 1986. 11.95 (ISBN 0-396-08507-5, Putnam). Putnam Pub Group.
Marston, Hope I. Big Rigs. (Illus.). 64p. (gr. k-3). 1980. 11.95 (ISBN 0-396-07785-4, Putnam). Putnam Pub Group.
Olson, Norman. I Can Read About Trucks & Cars. LC 72-96957. (Illus.). (gr. 2-4). 1973. pap. 1.95 (ISBN 0-89375-055-7). Troll Assocs.
Potter, Tony. See How It Works: Trucks. Lawrie, Robin, illus. 28p. (ps-3). 1989. pap. 7.95 (ISBN 0-689-71301-0, Aladdin). Macmillan Child Grp.
Robbins, Ken. Trucks of Every Sort. Robbins, Ken, photos by. (Illus.). 48p. (gr. 2-4). 1988. lib. bdg. 9.95 (ISBN 0-517-54164-5); pap. 4.95 (ISBN 0-517-56640-0). Crown.
Rockwell, Anne. Trucks. Rockwell, Anne, illus. LC 84-1556. 24p. (ps-1). 1984. 11.95 (ISBN 0-525-44147-6, DCB). Dutton Child Bks.
—Trucks. Rockwell, Anne, illus. LC 84-1556. 24p. (ps-1). 1988. pap. 3.95 (ISBN 0-525-44432-7, DCB). Dutton Child Bks.
Scarry, Richard. Richard Scarry's Cars & Trucks & Things That Go. (Illus.). (ps-2). 1974. write for info. (ISBN 0-307-15785-7, Golden Bks). Western Pub.
Seymour, Peter. The Pop-Up Book of Big Trucks. Murphy, Chuck, illus. (ps-3). 1989. 10.95 (ISBN 0-316-78197-5). Little.
Singer, Alan, illus. Fast Rolling Work Trucks. (ps). 1984. 5.95 (ISBN 0-448-09877-6, G&D). Putnam Pub Group.
Stamper, Judith B. Truck Driver. Ulrich, George, illus. LC 88-10039. 32p. (gr. k-2). 1988. PLB 10.89 (ISBN 0-8167-1424-X); pap. text ed. 2.95 (ISBN 0-8167-1425-8). Troll Assocs.
Steele, Philip. Cars & Trucks. LC 90-41180. (Illus.). 32p. (gr. 5-6). 1991. SBE 9.95 (ISBN 0-89686-521-5, Crestwood Hse). Macmillan Child Grp.
Stephen, R. J. The Picture World of Trucks. (Illus.). 32p. (gr. k-4). 1989. PLB 11.40 (ISBN 0-531-10729-9). Watts.
Strickland, Paul. All about Trucks. LC 90-9819. (Illus.). 16p. (ps-2). 1990. PLB 9.95 (ISBN 0-8368-0421-X). Gareth Stevens Inc.
Thompson, Graham. Cars & Trucks. LC 86-5702. (Illus.). 24p. (gr. 1-2). 1986. PLB 10.95 (ISBN 1-55532-100-3). Gareth Stevens Inc.
Truck Transportation. (Illus.). 32p. (gr. 6-12). 1973. pap. 1.85 (ISBN 0-8395-3371-3, 3371). BSA.
Trucks. LC 90-49260. 24p. (ps-k). 1991. pap. 6.95 (ISBN 0-689-71405-X, Aladdin). Macmillan Child Grp.
Wolfe, Robert L. The Truck Book. Wolfe, Robert L., illus. LC 80-15683. 32p. (gr. k-4). 1980. PLB 9.95 (ISBN 0-87614-125-4). Carolrhoda Bks.

TRUCKS–FICTION
Borden, Louise. Neighborhood Trucker. 1990. 12.95 (ISBN 0-590-42584-6). Scholastic Inc.
Bushey, Jerry. Monster Trucks & Other Giant Machines on Wheels. LC 84-23160. (Illus.). 32p. (gr. k-4). 1985. PLB 12.95 (ISBN 0-87614-271-4); pap. 4.95 (ISBN 0-87614-491-1). Carolrhoda Bks.
Holder, Bill & Farguhar, John. Monster Truck Action. (Illus.). 32p. (Orig.). (gr. 3-8). 1989. pap. text ed. 2.50 (ISBN 0-87406-456-2). Willowisp Pr.
Horenstein, Henry. Sam Goes Trucking. (ps-3). 1990. pap. 4.95 (ISBN 0-395-54950-7). HM.
—Sams Goes Trucking. (Illus.). 32p. (gr. k-3). 1990. pap. 4.95. HM.
Lakin, Patricia. Jet Black Pickup Truck. Hoffman, Rosekrans, illus. LC 89-71010. 32p. (ps-1). 1990. 14.95 (ISBN 0-531-05885-9); PLB 14.99 (ISBN 0-531-08485-X). Orchard Bks Watts.
McPhail, David. Ed & Me. LC 86-3175. (ps-3). 1990. 13.95 (ISBN 0-15-224888-9, HJ). HarBraceJ.
Nasta, Cynthia V. Peter & His Pick-up Truck: A Southwestern Children's Tale. Zilka, Pat, illus. LC 89-80351. 24p. (ps-8). 1989. pap. 6.95 (ISBN 0-9622064-0-7). Little Buckaroo.
Petrie, Catherine. Joshua James Likes Trucks. Warshaw, Jerry, illus. LC 81-17076. 32p. (ps-2). 1982. PLB 11.93 (ISBN 0-516-03525-8); pap. text ed. 2.95 (ISBN 0-516-43525-6). Childrens.
Walker, Sloan & Vasey, Andrew. Supertrucks. LC 85-5379. (Illus.). 48p. (gr. 1-4). 1985. 12.95 (ISBN 0-8027-6586-6); PLB 12.85 (ISBN 0-8027-6606-4). Walker & Co.
Ziefert, Harriet. Wait for Us! Aitken, Amy, illus. LC 89-8380. 24p. (ps-1). 1989. pap. 2.25 (ISBN 0-394-82002-9, Random Juv). Random.

TRUMAN, HARRY S., PRESIDENT U. S. 1884-1972
Collins, David R. Harry S. Truman: People's President. Frame, Paul, illus. 80p. (gr. 2-6). 1991. Repr. PLB 12.95 (ISBN 0-7910-1421-5). Chelsea Hse.
—Harry S. Truman: 33rd President of the United States. Young, Richard G., ed. LC 87-32750. (Illus.). (gr. 5-9). 1988. PLB 17.26 (ISBN 0-944483-00-3). Garrett Ed Corp.
Farley, Karin C. Harry Truman: The Man from Independence. Steltenpohl, Jane, ed. (Illus.). 160p. (gr. 5-9). 1989. lib. bdg. 11.98 (ISBN 0-671-65853-0). Messner.
Greenberg, Morrie. The Buck Stops Here: A Biography of Harry Truman. LC 88-20264. (Illus.). 128p. (gr. 5 up). 1989. PLB 12.95 (ISBN 0-87518-394-8, Dillon). Macmillan Child Grp.
Harry S. Truman: Mini Play. (gr. 8 up). 1977. 6.50 (ISBN 0-89550-373-5). Stevens & Shea.
Leavell, Perry. Harry Truman. (Illus.). 112p. (gr. 5 up). 1988. lib. bdg. 17.95 (ISBN 0-87754-558-8). Chelsea Hse.
Libbey, Theodore W., Jr. Harry S. Truman. (Illus.). 100p. (gr. 3 up). 1987. PLB 17.27 (ISBN 0-516-01388-2). Childrens.
O'Neal, Michael. President Truman & the Atomic Bomb: Opposing Viewpoints. LC 90-35611. (Illus.). 112p. (gr. 3-8). 1990. PLB 13.95 (ISBN 0-89908-079-0). Greenhaven.

TRUMPET–FICTION
Barfield, Owen. The Silver Trumpet. Mead, Marjorie L., intro. by. LC 85-71803. (Illus.). 134p. (gr. 3-8). 1986. 12.95 (ISBN 0-917665-05-8); pap. 9.95 (ISBN 0-917665-06-6). Bookmakers Guild.

TRUST IN GOD
see Faith

TRUTH, SOJOURNER, 1797?-1883
Claflin, Edward B. Sojourner Truth & the Struggle for Freedom. LC 87-19325. (Illus.). 144p. (gr. 3-6). 1987. pap. 4.95 (ISBN 0-8120-3919-X). Barron.
Ferris, Jeri. Walking the Road to Freedom: A Story about Sojourner Truth. Hanson, Peter E., illus. 64p. (gr. 3-6). 1988. lib. bdg. 9.95 (ISBN 0-87614-318-4); pap. 4.95 (ISBN 0-87614-505-5). Carolrhoda Bks.

—Walking the Road to Freedom: A Story about Sojourner Truth. Hanson, Peter E., illus. 64p. (gr. 3-6). 1989. pap. 4.95 (ISBN 0-685-25646-4, First Ave Edns). Lerner Pubns.

Krass, Peter. Sojourner Truth. King, Coretta Scott, intro. by. (Illus.). 112p. (Orig.). (gr. 5 up). 1988. 17.95 (ISBN 1-55546-611-7); pap. 9.95 (ISBN 0-7910-0215-2). Chelsea Hse.

Obaba, Al-Imam. Sojourner Truth Great Nubian Quiz. (Illus.). 43p. (Orig.). 1989. pap. 3.95 (ISBN 0-916157-08-3). African Islam Miss Pubns.

Ortiz, Victoria. Sojourner Truth: A Self-Made Woman. LC 73-22290. (Illus.). 160p. (gr. 7 up). 1986. PLB 11.89 (ISBN 0-397-32134-1, Lipp Jr Bks). HarpC Child Bks.

Shumate, Jane. Sojourner Truth & the Voice of Freedom. (Illus.). 32p. (gr. 2-4). 1991. PLB 11.50 (ISBN 1-56294-041-4); pap. 3.95 (ISBN 1-878841-71-8). Millbrook Pr.

Taylor-Boyd, Susan. Sojourner Truth: The Courageous Former Slave Whose Eloquence Helped Promote Human Equality. LC 89-4345. (Illus.). 68p. (gr. 5-6). 1990. PLB 12.95 (ISBN 0-8368-0101-6). Gareth Stevens Inc.

—Sojourner Truth: The Courageous Former Slave Who Led Others to Freedom. Tolan, Mary, adapted by. LC 90-37992. (Illus.). 64p. (gr. 3-4). 1991. PLB 12.95 (ISBN 0-8368-0458-9). Gareth Stevens Inc.

TRUTHFULNESS AND FALSEHOOD

Elliott, Dan. Ernie's Little Lie. Mathieu, Joe, illus. LC 82-7574. 40p. (ps-3). 1983. lib. bdg. 6.99 (ISBN 0-394-95440-8); pap. 4.95 (ISBN 0-394-85440-3). Random.

Frost, Lesley. Really, Not Really. Remington, Barbara, illus. 64p. (ps-3). 1966. 10.00 (ISBN 0-8159-6702-0). Devin.

Hopper, Nancy J. The Truth or Dare Trap. (gr. 7 up). 1988. pap. 2.50 (ISBN 0-380-70269-X, Flare). Avon.

Price, Joan. Truth Is a Bright Star. LC 82-1345. 1982. pap. 8.95 (ISBN 0-89087-333-X). Celestial Arts.

Seidler, Tor. Terpin. LC 82-11734. 96p. (gr. 7 up). 1982. 9.95 (ISBN 0-374-37413-9). FS&G.

TUAREGS–FICTION

Kaufmann, Herbert. Adventure in the Desert. Karlin, Eugene, illus. (gr. 7 up). 1961. 10.95 (ISBN 0-8392-3000-1). Astor-Honor.

—Lost Sahara Trail. (gr. 7 up). 1962. 10.95 (ISBN 0-8392-3022-2). Astor-Honor.

TUBMAN, HARRIET, 1820-1913

Bains, Rae. Harriet Tubman: The Road to Freedom. LC 81-23145. (Illus.). 48p. (gr. 4-6). 1982. PLB 10.79 (ISBN 0-89375-760-8); pap. text ed. 2.95 (ISBN 0-89375-761-6). Troll Assocs.

Bentley, Judith. Harriet Tubman. (Illus.). 144p. (gr. 9-12). 1990. PLB 13.90 (ISBN 0-531-10948-8). Watts.

Bisson, Terry. Harriet Tubman. King, Coretta Scott, intro. by. (Illus.). 112p. (Orig.). (gr. 5 up). 1991. pap. 9.95 (ISBN 0-7910-0249-7). Chelsea Hse.

Carter, Polly. Harriet Tubman. Brook, Bonnie, ed. Pinkney, Brian, illus. 32p. (gr. k-2). 1990. 5.95 (ISBN 0-671-69115-5); PLB 10.98 (ISBN 0-671-69109-0). Silver Pr.

Ferris, Jeri. Go Free or Die: A Story about Harriet Tubman. Ritz, Karen, illus. 64p. (gr. 3-6). 1988. lib. bdg. 9.95 (ISBN 0-87614-317-6); pap. 4.95 (ISBN 0-87614-504-7). Carolrhoda Bks.

—Go Free or Die: A Story about Harriet Tubman. Ritz, Karen, illus. 64p. (gr. 3-6). 1989. pap. 4.95 (ISBN 0-685-25638-3, First Ave Edns). Lerner Pubns.

Harriet Tubman: Mini Play. (gr. 5 up). 1977. 6.50 (ISBN 0-89550-359-X). Stevens & Shea.

Harriet Tubman, No. 19: Yearling Biography. (Orig.). (gr. k-6). 1991. pap. 2.95 (ISBN 0-440-40400-2, Pub. by Yearling Classics). Dell.

Johnson, Ann D. The Value of Helping: The Story of Harriet Tubman. Pileggi, Steve, illus. LC 79-21652. (gr. k-6). 1979. 9.95 (ISBN 0-916392-41-4, Pub. by Value Communications). Oak Tree Pubns.

Klingel, Cindy. Women of America: Harriet Tubman. (gr. 2-4). 1987. PLB 11.50s.p. (ISBN 0-88682-166-5); PLB 16.45 (ISBN 0-318-32936-0). Creative Ed.

McClard, Megan. Harriet Tubman: Slavery & the Underground Railroad. (Illus.). 160p. (gr. 5 up). 1990. lib. bdg. 16.98 (ISBN 0-382-09938-9); pap. 8.95 (ISBN 0-382-24047-2). Silver Burdett Pr.

McGovern, Ann. Wanted Dead or Alive: The Story of Harriet Tubman. (gr. 4-6). 1977. pap. 1.95 (ISBN 0-590-40259-5). Scholastic Inc.

—Wanted Dead Or Alive: The True Story of Harriet Tubman. 64p. (gr. 2-4). 1991. 2.95 (ISBN 0-590-44212-0). Scholastic Inc.

Meyer, Linda D. Harriet Tubman: They Called Me Moses. Kerstetter, J., illus. LC 87-43308. 32p. (Orig.). (ps-4). 1988. lib. bdg. 15.95 (ISBN 0-943990-33-5); pap. 5.95 (ISBN 0-943990-32-7). Parenting Pr.

Obaba, Al-Imam. Harriet Tubman Great Nubian Quiz. (Illus.). 43p. (Orig.). 1989. pap. 3.95 (ISBN 0-916157-09-1). African Islam Miss Pubns.

Petry, Ann. Harriet Tubman: Conductor on the Underground Railway. LC 55-9215. 247p. (gr. 7-11). 1955. 14.95 (ISBN 0-690-37236-1, Crowell Jr Bks). HarpC Child Bks.

Sabin, Francene. Harriet Tubman. Frenck, Hal, illus. LC 84-2667. 32p. (gr. 3-6). 1985. PLB 9.49 (ISBN 0-8167-0158-X); pap. text ed. 2.95 (ISBN 0-8167-0159-8). Troll Assocs.

Smith, Kathie B. Harriet Tubman. Steltenpohl, Jane, ed. Seward, James, illus. 24p. (gr. 4-6). 1989. lib. bdg. 7.98 (ISBN 0-671-67513-3); PLB 5.99s.p. (ISBN 0-685-25427-5). Messner.

Smith, Kathie B. & Bradbury, Pamela Z. Harriet Tubman. (Illus.). (ps up). 1989. pap. 2.25 (ISBN 0-671-64026-7, Little Simon). S&S Trade.

Sterling, Dorothy. Freedom Train: The Story of Harriet Tubman. 192p. (gr. 4-6). 1987. pap. 2.50 (ISBN 0-590-40640-X); tchr's. guide 1.25 (ISBN 0-590-40988-3). Scholastic Inc.

—Freedom Train: The Story of Harriet Tubman. 192p. (gr. 4-8). 1987. pap. 2.95 (ISBN 0-590-43628-7). Scholastic Inc.

TUGBOATS–FICTION

Gramatky, Hardie. Little Toot. Gramatky, Hardie, illus. LC 78-4801. (gr. k-3). 1978. 8.95 (ISBN 0-399-20144-0, Putnam); 9.99 (ISBN 0-399-60422-7, Putnam); pap. 5.95 (ISBN 0-399-20649-3, Putnam). Putnam Pub Group.

TUNISIA

Dixon, Mary. Tunisia. (Illus.). (gr. 5 up). 1988. 14.95 (ISBN 1-55546-183-2). Chelsea Hse.

Fox, Mary V. Tunisia. LC 90-2199. (Illus.). 128p. (gr. 5-9). 1990. PLB 25.27 (ISBN 0-516-02724-7). Childrens.

Lerner Publications, Department of Geography Staff, ed. Tunisia in Pictures. (Illus.). 64p. (gr. 5 up). 1989. 12.95 (ISBN 0-8225-1844-9). Lerner Pubns.

TUNNELS

see also Excavation; Subways

Bender, Lionel. Eurotunnel. (Illus.). 32p. (gr. 5-8). 1990. PLB 8.90 (ISBN 0-531-17178-7). Watts.

Booth, Eugene. Under the Ground. LC 77-8037. (Illus.). (gr. k-3). 1977. PLB 13.32 (ISBN 0-8393-0110-3). Raintree Pubs.

Epstein, Samuel & Epstein, Beryl. Tunnels. (Illus.). 128p. (gr. 5 up). 1985. 14.95 (ISBN 0-316-24573-9). Little.

Gibbons, Gail. Tunnels. Gibbons, Gail, illus. LC 83-18589. 32p. (ps-3). 1984. reinforced bdg. 14.95 (ISBN 0-8234-0507-9); pap. 5.95 (ISBN 0-8234-0670-9). Holiday.

Sauvain, Philip. Tunnels. Stefoff, Rebecca, ed. LC 90-40248. (Illus.). 48p. (gr. 4-7). 1990. PLB 17.26 (ISBN 0-944483-79-8). Garrett Ed Corp.

TURKEY

Cole, Cathy. Turkey. (Illus.). (gr. 5 up). 1988. 14.95 (ISBN 0-222-01033-9). Chelsea Hse.

Department of Geography, Lerner Publications. Turkey in Pictures. (Illus.). 64p. (gr. 5 up). 1988. PLB 12.95 (ISBN 0-8225-1831-7). Lerner Pubns.

Kherdian, David. Road from Home: The Story of an Armenian Girl. LC 78-72511. 256p. (gr. 7 up). 1979. 13.95 (ISBN 0-688-80205-2); PLB 13.88 (ISBN 0-688-84205-4). Greenwillow.

Spencer, William. The Land & People of Turkey. LC 89-2421. (Illus.). 224p. (gr. 6 up). 1990. 14.95 (ISBN 0-397-32363-8, Lipp Jr Bks); PLB 14.89 (ISBN 0-397-32364-6, Lipp Jr Bks). HarpC Child Bks.

TURKEY–FICTION

Bruni, Mary-Ann S. Elif: Child of Turkey. (Illus.). 48p. (gr. k-8). 1988. 12.95 (ISBN 0-935857-13-3); pap. text ed. write for info. (ISBN 0-935857-14-1). Texart.

St. Pierre, Stephanie. Where's That Turkey Lurking? Book & Cookie Cutter Pack. 16p. (Orig.). (gr. k-3). 1990. pap. 3.95 (ISBN 0-590-68984-3). Scholastic Inc.

Wickstrom, Sylvie. Turkey On the Loose! 32p. (ps-3). 1990. 10.95 (ISBN 0-8037-0818-1); PLB 10.89 (ISBN 0-8037-0820-3). Dial Bks Young.

TURKEYS

Lavine, Sigmund A. & Scuro, Vincent. Wonders of Turkeys. 1984. 10.95 (ISBN 0-396-08333-1, Putnam). Putnam Pub Group.

Patent, Dorothy H. Wild Turkey, Tame Turkey. Munoz, William, illus. LC 89-613. 64p. (gr. 3-6). 1989. 14.95 (ISBN 0-89919-704-3, Clarion Bks). HM.

TURKEYS–FICTION

Cohen, Miriam. Don't Eat Too Much Turkey. (gr. k-6). 1988. pap. 2.95 (ISBN 0-440-40106-2, YB). Dell.

TURNER, NAT, 1800-1831

Bisson, Terry. Nat Turner. King, Coretta Scott, intro. by. (Illus.). 112p. (Orig.). (gr. 5 up). 1988. 17.95 (ISBN 1-55546-613-3); pap. 9.95 (ISBN 0-7910-0214-4). Chelsea Hse.

TURTLES

Addison-Wesley Staff. El Conejo la Tortuga - Big Book. (SPA., Illus.). 16p. (gr. k-3). 1989. pap. text ed. 31.75 (ISBN 0-201-19937-8). Addison-Wesley.

—El Conejo la Tortuga - Little Book. (SPA., Illus.). 16p. (gr. k-3). 1989. pap. text ed. 4.50 (ISBN 0-201-19709-X). Addison-Wesley.

—The Hare & the Tortoise Little Book. (Illus.). 16p. (gr. k-3). 1989. pap. text ed. 4.50 (ISBN 0-201-19365-5). Addison-Wesley.

Ancona, George. Turtle Watch. Ancona, George, photos by. LC 87-9316. (Illus.). 48p. (gr. 1-5). 1987. 14.95 (ISBN 0-02-700910-6, Mcmillan Child Bk). Macmillan Child Grp.

Craig, Janet. Turtles. Kelleher, Kathie, illus. LC 81-11448. 32p. (gr. k-2). 1982. PLB 10.89 (ISBN 0-89375-664-4); pap. 2.95 (ISBN 0-89375-665-2). Troll Assocs.

Cromie, William J. Steven & the Green Turtle. Eaton, Tom, illus. LC 77-85040. 64p. (gr. k-3). 1970. PLB 11.89 (ISBN 0-06-021374-4). HarpC Child Bks.

Fine, Edith H. The Turtle & Tortoise. LC 88-10852. (Illus.). 48p. (gr. 5-6). 1988. PLB 10.95 (ISBN 0-89686-392-1, Crestwood Hse). Macmillan Child Grp.

Glass, Marvin. Go Like a Turtle. Glass, Marvin, illus. 12p. (gr. 2-4). 1990. bds. 3.95 (ISBN 1-878624-04-0). McClanahan Bk.

Holling, Holling C. Minn of the Mississippi. (Illus.). (gr. 4-6). 1951. 16.95 (ISBN 0-395-17578-X). HM.

Martin, L. Turtles. (Illus.). 24p. (gr. k-5). 1989. lib. bdg. 11.93 (ISBN 0-86592-578-X). Rourke Corp.

Oda, Hidetomo. The Turtle. Pohl, Kathy, ed. LC 85-28234. (Illus.). 32p. (gr. 3-7). 1986. PLB 16.67 (ISBN 0-8172-2547-1); pap. text ed. 9.27 (ISBN 0-8172-2572-2). Raintree Pubs.

Propper. Turtle, Reading Level 3-4. (Illus.). 28p. (gr. 2-5). Date not set. PLB 14.60. Rourke Corp.

Serventy, Vincent. Turtle & Tortoise. LC 84-15881. (Illus.). 24p. (gr. k-5). 1985. PLB 13.32 (ISBN 0-8172-2403-3). Raintree Pubs.

—Turtle & Tortoise. Serventy, Vincent, et al, illus. 24p. (gr. 1-4). 1987. pap. 1.95 (ISBN 0-590-40228-5). Scholastic Inc.

Vrbova, Zuza. Turtles. McAulay, Robert, illus. 48p. 1990. PLB 9.95 (ISBN 0-86622-559-5, J-009). TFH Pubns.

TURTLES–FICTION

Blotnick, Elihu. Blue Turtle Moon Queen. Robinson, Barbara, illus. 120p. (gr. 6-12). Date not set. pap. 6.95 (ISBN 0-915090-20-1). Calif Street.

Bourgeois, Paulette. Hurry Up, Franklin. 1990. pap. 11.95 (ISBN 0-590-42620-6). Scholastic Inc.

Brown, Ryan, et al. Teenage Mutant Ninja Turtles, Vol. 1. Berger, Dan, et al, illus. 150p. 1990. pap. 9.95 (ISBN 1-879450-00-3). Tundra MA.

Castle, Caroline, retold by. Hare & the Tortoise. Weevers, Peter, illus. LC 84-9569. 32p. (ps-3). 1987. pap. 4.95 (ISBN 0-8037-0147-0). Dial Bks Young.

Cromie, William J. Steven & the Green Turtle. Eaton, Tom, illus. LC 77-85040. 64p. (gr. k-3). 1970. PLB 11.89 (ISBN 0-06-021374-4). HarpC Child Bks.

Dahl, Roald. Esio Trot. Blake, Quentin, illus. 1990. 14.95 (ISBN 0-670-83451-3). Viking Child Bks.

Danly, Maria. Lullaby River. Dysart, Richard, narrated by. Dysart, Maria, illus. 40p. (ps-2). 1989. book, cassette & doll 19.95 (ISBN 0-394-89647-5). Knopf.

Dodd, Lynley. Smallest Turtle. Dodd, Lynley, illus. LC 85-9771. 29p. (gr. 1-2). 1985. PLB 10.95 (ISBN 0-918831-07-5). Gareth Stevens Inc.

Dr. Seuss. Yertle the Turtle & Other Stories. Dr. Seuss, illus. (gr. k-3). 1958. 12.95 (ISBN 0-394-80087-7, Random Juv); PLB 13.99 (ISBN 0-394-90087-1). Random.

Eastman, Kevin & Laird, Peter. Teenage Mutant Ninja Turtles in Intergalactic Wrestling & Other Adventures. Eastman, Kevin & Laird, Peter, illus. 96p. (Orig.). (gr. 2-8). 1991. pap. 6.95 incls. cassette (ISBN 0-679-81747-6). Random.

Edler, Timothy J. Maurice the Snake & Gaston the Near-Sighted Turtle: Tim Edler's Tales from the Atchafalaya. (Illus.). 36p. (gr. k-8). 1977. pap. 6.00 (ISBN 0-931108-00-4). Little Cajun Bks.

Florian, Douglas. Turtle Day. Florian, Douglas, illus. LC 88-30321. 32p. (ps-2). 1989. 12.95 (ISBN 0-690-04743-6, Crowell Jr Bks); PLB 12.89 (ISBN 0-690-04745-2, Crowell Jr Bks). HarpC Child Bks.

Galdone, Paul. The Turtle & the Monkey. Galdone, Paul, illus. 32p. (ps-3). 1990. pap. 4.95 (ISBN 0-395-54425-4, Clarion Bks). HM.

George, William T. Box Turtle at Long Pond. George, Lindsay B., illus. LC 88-18787. 24p. (ps-1). 1989. 13.95 (ISBN 0-688-08184-3); PLB 13.88 (ISBN 0-688-08185-1). Greenwillow.

Goldsmith, Howard. Toto the Timid Turtle. LC 80-15096. (Illus.). 32p. (ps-3). 1980. 16.95 (ISBN 0-87705-525-4). Human Sci Pr.

Greene, Shelley. Teenage Mutant Ninja Turtles Totally Awesome Activity Book. Lawson, Jim & Burger, Dan, illus. 96p. (gr. 1-5). 1990. pap. 3.95 (ISBN 0-679-81108-7). Random.

Haas, Dorothy. Two Friends Too Many. (gr. 4-7). 1990. pap. 2.50 (ISBN 0-590-43557-4). Scholastic Inc.

Hadithi, Mwenye. Tricky Tortoise. Kennaway, Adrienne, illus. (ps-3). 1988. 14.95 (ISBN 0-316-33724-2). Little.

Herman, Crystal & Holm, Astrid. Teenage Mutant Ninja Turtles Mini-Storybooks & Cassette. Daste, Larry & Mateu, Franc, illus. 32p. (ps-3). 1990. pap. 5.95 incl. cassette (ISBN 0-679-80807-8). Random.

Hiller, B. B. M-TV. (gr. 4-7). 1991. pap. 3.50 (ISBN 0-440-40451-7). Dell.

—Teenage Mutant Ninja Turtles. 1990. pap. 2.95 (ISBN 0-440-40322-7). Dell.

Holm, Astrid. Teenage Mutant Ninja Turtles: School Daze. Mateu, Franc, illus. LC 90-61185. 32p. (Orig.). (ps-3). 1991. pap. 1.50 (ISBN 0-679-81169-9). Random.

Holm, Astrid, adapted by. Teenage Mutant Ninja Turtles: A Visit to Stump Asteroid. Herbert, S. I., illus. LC 90-61217. 32p. (Orig.). (ps-3). 1991. pap. 1.50 (ISBN 0-679-81170-2). Random.

Hudson, Eleanor. Teenage Mutant Ninja Turtles Pizza Party: A Step 1 Book - Preschool-Grade 1. Herbert, S. I., illus. LC 90-53243. 32p. (Orig.). (ps-1). 1991. PLB 6.99 (ISBN 0-679-91452-8); pap. 2.95 (ISBN 0-679-81452-3). Random.

Jeffrey, Graham. Thomas the Tortoise. (Illus.). 32p. (ps-2). 1988. 9.95 (ISBN 0-517-57043-2). Crown.

Johnson, Sylvia A. Penelope the Tortoise. Hammarberg, Dyan, tr. from FRE. LC 76-3411. (Illus.). 24p. (gr. k-4). 1976. PLB 6.95 (ISBN 0-87614-072-X). Carolrhoda Bks.

Katz, Bobbi. Teenage Mutant Ninja Turtles Don't Do Drugs! A Rap Song. Mones, Isidre, illus. LC 90-53244. 32p. (Orig.). (ps-3). 1991. PLB 5.99 (ISBN 0-679-91485-4); pap. 2.25 (ISBN 0-679-81485-X). Random.

Kessler, Leonard. Old Turtle's Winter Games. (gr. k-6). 1990. pap. 2.95 (ISBN 0-440-40261-1, YB). Dell.

Morris, Dave. Dinosaur Farm. (gr. 4-7). 1991. pap. 3.50 (ISBN 0-440-40491-6). Dell.

—Splinter to the Fore. (gr. 4-7). 1991. pap. 3.50 (ISBN 0-440-40492-4). Dell.

O'Donnell, Elizabeth L. I Can't Get My Turtle to Move. Chambliss, Maxie, illus. LC 88-22046. 32p. (ps-1). 1989. 11.95 (ISBN 0-688-07323-9); PLB 11.88 (ISBN 0-688-07324-7, Morrow Jr Bks). Morrow Jr Bks.

Oke, Janette. The Impatient Turtle. Peterson, Pete, ed. Mann, Brenda, illus. 110p. (Orig.). (gr. 3-6). 1986. pap. 4.95 (ISBN 0-934998-24-8). Bethel Pub.

Oneal, Zibby. Turtle & Snail. Tomes, Margot, illus. LC 78-14826. (gr. k-2). 1979. 11.95i (ISBN 0-397-31829-4, Lipp Jr Bks). HarpC Child Bks.

Plociak, Barbara J. Little Tommy's Turtle. 32p. (ps-1). 1990. 6.95 (ISBN 0-8062-3857-7). Carlton.

Reed, Louis. Smiley the Proud Turtle. Jones, Kathryn, illus. 64p. (Orig.). (gr. 1-4). 1986. pap. text ed. 8.25x (ISBN 0-910653-14-3, 81010). Archival Servs.

Roger, Alan. Blue Tortoise. Roger, Alan, illus. LC 90-9833. 16p. (ps-1). 1990. PLB 9.95 (ISBN 0-8368-0404-X). Gareth Stevens Inc.

Ross, Dave. Tiny Turtle's Thanksgiving. Ross, Dave, illus. LC 86-5412. 32p. (ps-k). 1986. 12.95 (ISBN 0-688-06440-X); lib. bdg. 12.88 (ISBN 0-688-06441-8, Morrow Jr Bks). Morrow Jr Bks.

Schlachter, Rita. Winter Fun. Swan, Susan, illus. LC 85-14008. 48p. (Orig.). (gr. 1-3). 1986. PLB 9.89 (ISBN 0-8167-0584-4); pap. text ed. 2.95 (ISBN 0-8167-0585-2). Troll Assocs.

Serventy, Vincent. Turtle & Tortoise. (Illus.). 24p. (gr. 1-4). 1987. pap. 2.50 (ISBN 0-590-42133-6). Scholastic Inc.

Stevenson, James. Fast Friends. LC 78-14828. (Illus.). 64p. (gr. 1-3). 1979. PLB 10.88 (ISBN 0-688-84197-X). Greenwillow.

Teenage Mutant Ninja Turtles, 5 vols. (gr. 4-7). 1990. pap. 14.75 boxed set (ISBN 0-440-36030-7). Dell.

Troughton, Joanna, retold by. Tortoise's Dream: An African Folk Tale. Troughton, Joannna, illus. LC 85-15065. 28p. (ps-2). 1986. 14.95 (ISBN 0-87226-039-9, Bedrick Blackie). P Bedrick Bks.

Williams, Barbara. Albert's Toothache. Chorao, Kay, illus. LC 74-4040. 32p. (ps-1). 1974. 11.95 (ISBN 0-525-25368-8, Dutton); pap. 3.95 (ISBN 0-525-45037-8). NAL-Dutton.

Ziefert, Harriet. Letters & Papers of Admiral the Honorable Samuel Barrington. Lobel, Arnold, illus. LC 86-45951. 14p. (ps). 1987. 3.50 (ISBN 0-694-00183-X). HarpC Child Bks.

TUSKEGEE NORMAL AND INDUSTRIAL INSTITUTE

Washington, Booker T. Up from Slavery. Andrews, C. A., intro. by. (gr. 5 up). pap. 2.50 (ISBN 0-8049-0157-0, CL-157). Airmont.

TUTANKHAMON, KING OF EGYPT, 1360 B.C.?

Aldred, Cyril. A Book of Tutankhmun. (Illus.). (gr. 5). 1978. pap. 2.50 (ISBN 0-88388-059-8). Bellerophon Bks.

—Tut-Ankh-Amun-& His Friends. (gr. 8). pap. 3.95 (ISBN 0-88388-043-1). Bellerophon Bk.

Donnelly, Judy. Tut's Mummy: Lost & Found. Watling, James, illus. LC 87-20790. (Orig.). (gr. 2-3). 1988. lib. bdg. 6.99 (ISBN 0-394-99189-3, Random Juv); pap. 2.95 (ISBN 0-394-89189-9). Random.

Reiff, Stephanie A. Secrets of Tut's Tomb & the Pyramids. LC 77-22770. (Illus.). (gr. 4 up). 1983. PLB 17.32 (ISBN 0-8172-1051-2); pap. 9.27 (ISBN 0-8172-2166-2). Raintree Pubs.

Smith, Tony, illus. The Treasures of Tutankhamen. 48p. (gr. 3-5). 1987. 5.95x (ISBN 0-86685-453-3). Intl Bk Ctr.

TWAIN, MARK

see Clemens, Samuel Langhorne, 1835-1910

TWENTIETH CENTURY

Campling, Elizabeth. Portrait of a Decade: 1900-1909. (Illus.). 72p. (gr. 7-11). 1990. 19.95 (ISBN 0-7134-5989-1, Pub. by Batsford England). Trafalgar Sq.

Duden, Jane & Stewart, Gail B. Nineteen Eighties. LC 90-46827. (Illus.). 48p. (gr. 5-6). 1991. RSBE 10.95 (ISBN 0-89686-599-1, Crestwood Hse). Macmillan Child Grp.

Fyson, Nance L. Portrait of a Decade: The 1950s. (Illus.). 72p. (gr. 7-11). 1990. 19.95 (ISBN 0-7134-6070-9, Pub. by Batsford England). Trafalgar Sq.

TWINS

Ingram, Jay. Amazing Investigations: Twins. Chan, Harvey, illus. (gr. 3 up). 1989. pap. 12.95 (ISBN 0-671-66263-5). S&S Trade.

Rosenberg, Maxine B. Being a Twin, Having a Twin. Ancona, George, illus. LC 84-17159. 48p. (gr. 1-4). 1985. 11.95 (ISBN 0-688-04328-3); lib. bdg. 11.88 (ISBN 0-688-04329-1). Lothrop.

TWINS–FICTION

Adler, David A. The Fourth Floor Twins & Disappearing Parrot Trick, No. 3. Trivas, Irene, illus. LC 85-40833. 64p. (gr. 2-5). 1986. pap. 10.95 (ISBN 0-670-80926-8). Viking Child Bks.

—The Fourth Floor Twins & the Fish, No. 1. Trivas, Irene, illus. LC 84-25713. 64p. 1985. pap. 10.95 (ISBN 0-670-80087-2). Viking Child Bks.

—The Fourth Floor Twins & the Fish Snitch Mystery. Trivas, Irene, illus. 64p. (gr. 1-4). 1986. pap. 3.95 (ISBN 0-14-032082-2, Puffin). Puffin Bks.

—Fourth Floor Twins & the Fortune Cookie Chase. LC 84-21924. 64p. 1985. pap. 10.95 (ISBN 0-670-80641-2). Viking Child Bks.

—The Fourth Floor Twins & the Fortune Cookie Chase. Trivas, Irene, illus. 64p. (gr. 1-4). 1986. pap. 3.95 (ISBN 0-14-032083-0, Puffin). Puffin Bks.

—The Fourth Floor Twins & the Sand Castle Contest. Trivas, Irene, illus. (gr. 2-5). 1988. 9.95 (ISBN 0-318-37432-3). Viking Child Bks.

—The Fourth Floor Twins & the Silver Ghost. Trivas, Irene, illus. 64p. (gr. 2-5). 1986. pap. 10.95 (ISBN 0-670-81236-6). Viking Child Bks.

—Fourth Floor Twins & the Skyscraper Parade. Trivas, Irene, illus. LC 86-28961. (gr. 2-5). 1987. pap. 10.95 (ISBN 0-670-81603-5). Viking Child Bks.

—Fourth Floor Twins & the Skyscraper Parade. 1988. pap. 3.95 (ISBN 0-14-032298-1, Puffin). Puffin Bks.

Bach, Alice. Grouchy Uncle Otto. Kellogg, Steven, illus. LC 76-24304. 48p. (gr. k-4). 1977. 8.89 (ISBN 0-06-020344-7). HarpC Child Bks.

Burgess, Barbara H. Oren Bell. 1991. 15.00 (ISBN 0-385-30325-4). Delacorte.

Cleary, Beverly. Mitch & Amy. Porter, George, illus. LC 67-10041. 224p. (gr. 3-7). 1967. 15.95 (ISBN 0-688-21688-9); PLB 15.88 (ISBN 0-688-31688-3, Morrow Jr Bks). Morrow Jr Bks.

Cohen, Barbara. The Long Way Home. 176p. 1990. 12.95 (ISBN 0-688-09674-3). Lothrop.

Cohen, Dan. The Case of the Long Lost Twin. Overlie, George, illus. LC 79-84357. 32p. (gr. 1-4). 1979. PLB 5.95 (ISBN 0-87614-094-0). Carolrhoda Bks.

Cross, Gillian. Twin & Super-Twin. Bradley, Maureen, illus. LC 90-55098. 176p. (gr. 3-7). 1990. 13.95 (ISBN 0-8234-0840-X). Holiday.

Curry, Jane L. What the Dickens! LC 90-26864. 160p. (gr. 4-7). 1991. 13.95 (ISBN 0-689-50524-8, M K McElderry). Macmillan Child Grp.

Davis, Natalie L. The Space Twin. Taylor, Neil, illus. 112p. (gr. 4-8). 1987. 7.95 (ISBN 1-55523-037-7). Winston-Derek.

DeClements, Barthe & Greimes, Christopher. Double Trouble. LC 86-28984. (gr. 7 up). 1987. pap. 12.95 (ISBN 0-670-81567-5). Viking Child Bks.

DeVries, Douglas. Matilda & the Twins. (Illus.). 32p. (Orig.). (ps-3). 1990. pap. text ed. 8.00 (ISBN 1-877721-02-6). Jade Ram Pub.

Gay, John. Red Dust on the Green Leaves. Owen, Harrison, illus. Bruner, Jerome, intro. by. LC 73-77698. (Illus.). (gr. 7-12). 1973. pap. 9.95 (ISBN 0-933662-54-8, 305). Intercult Pr.

Greydanus, Rose. Double Trouble. Rodegast, Roland, illus. LC 81-2358. 32p. (gr. k-2). 1981. PLB 10.89 (ISBN 0-89375-529-X); pap. 2.95 (ISBN 0-89375-530-3). Troll Assocs.

Hope, Laura L. Adventure in the Country. Gonzalez, Pepe, illus. 120p. (gr. 2-5). 1989. 5.95 (ISBN 0-448-09072-4, G&D). Putnam Pub Group.

—The Bobbsey Twins: Mystery of the Laughing Dinosaur. Barish, Wendy, ed. (Illus.). 128p. (gr. 8-12). 1983. 7.95 (ISBN 0-671-43586-8, Little Simon); pap. 3.50 (ISBN 0-671-43587-6). S&S Trade.

—The Bobbsey Twins of Lakeport. Gonzalez, Pepe, illus. 120p. (gr. 2-5). 1989. 5.95 (ISBN 0-448-09071-6, G&D). Putnam Pub Group.

—The Bobbsey Twins on the Sun-Moon Cruise. new ed. LC 74-10460. (Illus.). 196p. (gr. 1-4). 1975. 4.50 (ISBN 0-448-08068-0, G&D). Putnam Pub Group.

—The Bobbsey Twins: The Mystery of the Hindu Temple. Barish, Wendy, ed. (Illus.). 128p. (Orig.). (gr. 7-10). 1985. pap. 3.50 (ISBN 0-671-55499-9, Little Simon). S&S Trade.

—The Bobbsey Twins: The Scarecrow Mystery. Barish, Wendy, ed. Speirs, John, illus. 128p. (gr. 2-5). 1984. pap. 3.50 (ISBN 0-671-53238-3, Little Simon). S&S Trade.

—Double Trouble, No. 7. Speirs, John, illus. 128p. (gr. 7-10). 1983. 8.50 (ISBN 0-671-43584-1, Little Simon); pap. 3.50 (ISBN 0-671-43585-X). S&S Trade.

—Mystery at School. Gonzalez, Pepe, illus. 120p. (gr. 2-5). 1989. 5.95 (ISBN 0-448-09074-0, G&D). Putnam Pub Group.

—The Secret at the Seashore. Gonzalez, Pepe, illus. 120p. (gr. 2-5). 1989. 5.95 (ISBN 0-448-09073-2, G&D). Putnam Pub Group.

Hope, Laura Lee. Bobbsey Twins, 4 vols. (gr. 4-7). 1990. pap. 11.80 boxed (ISBN 0-671-96364-3). S&S Trade.

Klein, Alan. Carousel Horses. 1991. 6.95 (ISBN 0-533-09160-8). Vantage.

Lawrence, James. Binky Brothers, Detectives. Kessler, Leonard, illus. LC 68-10374. 64p. (gr. k-3). 1968. PLB 11.89 (ISBN 0-06-023759-7). HarpC Child Bks.

Leaf, Munro. The Story of Simpson & Sampson. Lawson, Robert, illus. LC 88-39014. 64p. (gr. 1-3). 1989. Repr. of 1941 ed. lib. bdg. 15.00 (ISBN 0-208-02244-9, Pub. by Linnet). Shoe String.

McKissack, Patricia. Who Is Who? LC 83-7361. (Illus.). 32p. (ps-2). 1983. PLB 11.93 (ISBN 0-516-02042-0); pap. 2.95 (ISBN 0-516-42042-9). Childrens.

Mills, Adam. Cold Chills. (gr. 4 up). 1989. pap. 2.95 (ISBN 0-345-35929-1). Ballantine.

Mulford, Philippa G. The World Is My Eggshell. LC 85-16198. (gr. 7 up). 1986. pap. 14.95 (ISBN 0-385-29432-8). Delacorte.

Neasi, Barbara. Just Like Me. Axeman, Lois, illus. LC 83-23154. 32p. (ps-2). 1984. lib. bdg. 11.93 (ISBN 0-516-02047-1); pap. 2.95 (ISBN 0-516-42047-X). Childrens.

Pascal, Francine. Amy Moves In. (gr. 4-7). 1991. pap. 2.95 (ISBN 0-553-15837-6). Bantam.

—April Fool! 1989. pap. 2.75 (ISBN 0-553-15688-8). Bantam.

—Center of Attention. 1988. pap. 2.50 (ISBN 0-553-15581-4, Skylark). Bantam.

—Elizabeth's First Kiss. (gr. 4-7). 1990. pap. 2.95 (ISBN 0-553-15835-X). Bantam.

—Holiday Mischief. 144p. 1988. pap. 2.95 (ISBN 0-553-15641-1, Skylark). Bantam.

—Jessica & the Brat Attack. 1989. pap. 2.75 (ISBN 0-553-15695-0). Bantam.

—Jessica's Secret. (gr. 4-7). 1990. pap. 2.95 (ISBN 0-553-15824-4). Bantam.

—Left Behind. 112p. (Orig.). 1988. pap. 2.99 (ISBN 0-553-15609-8, Skylark). Bantam.

—Lucky Takes the Reins. (gr. 4-7). 1991. pap. 2.95 (ISBN 0-553-15843-0). Bantam.

—The New Girl. 96p. (Orig.). (gr. 7-12). 1987. pap. 2.50 (ISBN 0-553-15475-3, Skylark). Bantam.

—The Twins & the Wild West. (gr. 3-6). 1990. pap. 2.75 (ISBN 0-553-15811-2). Bantam.

—The Twins Get Caught. (gr. 4 up). 1990. pap. 2.99 (ISBN 0-553-15810-4). Bantam.

—War Between the Twins. (gr. 4-7). 1990. pap. 2.99 (ISBN 0-553-15779-5). Bantam.

Pascal, Francine, created by. Tug of War. 112p. (Orig.). (gr. 7-12). 1987. pap. 2.75 (ISBN 0-553-15663-2, Skylark). Bantam.

Paterson, Katherine. Jacob Have I Loved. LC 80-668. 228p. (gr. 7 up). 1980. 12.95 (ISBN 0-690-04078-4, Crowell Jr Bks); PLB 12.89 (ISBN 0-690-04079-2, Crowell Jr Bks). HarpC Child Bks.

Reich, Ali. The Care Bear & the Terrible Twos. Bracken, Carolyn, illus. 32p. (gr. k-3). 1983. pap. 1.95 (ISBN 0-394-85918-9). Random.

Ross, Pat. M & M & the Bad News Babies. Hafner, Marylin, illus. LC 81-18714. 48p. (gr. 6-9). 1983. Knopf.

Sawicki, Norma J. The Little Red House. Goffe, Toni, illus. LC 88-2740. 24p. (ps). 1989. 9.95 (ISBN 0-688-07891-5); PLB 9.88 (ISBN 0-688-07892-3). Lothrop.

Silverberg, Robert. Project Pendulum. (gr. 8 up). 1987. 15.95 (ISBN 0-8027-6712-5). Walker & Co.

Stahl, Hilda. The Tyler Twins, No. 1: Surprise at Big Key Ranch. 128p. (gr. 4-7). 1990. pap. 3.95 (ISBN 0-8423-7631-3). Tyndale.

—The Tyler Twins, No. 3: Pet Show Panic. 144p. (gr. 4-7). 1990. pap. 3.95 (ISBN 0-8423-7633-X). Tyndale.

—The Tyler Twins, No. 5: Tree House Hideaway. 128p. (gr. 4-7). 1990. pap. 3.95 (ISBN 0-8423-7635-6). Tyndale.

Stanely, Carol. Twin Switch. 1989. pap. 2.50 (ISBN 0-590-41665-0). Scholastic Inc.

Stanley, Carol. Twin Switch. (gr. 3-7). 1989. pap. 2.50 (ISBN 0-318-41679-4, Apple Paperbacks). Scholastic Inc.

Steiber, Ellen. Eighth Grade Changes Everything. LC 90-2495. 128p. (gr. 6-9). 1991. lib. bdg. 9.89 (ISBN 0-8167-2390-7); pap. text ed. 2.95 (ISBN 0-8167-2391-5). Troll Assocs.

Steinberg, Donna. The Karma Dharma Twins. Gendrun, Lobsang, illus. 128p. (Orig.). 1989. pap. 9.95 (ISBN 1-55045-006-9). Eden Pr.

TYLER, JOHN, PRESIDENT U.S. 1790-1862

Falkof, Lucille. John Tyler: Tenth President of the United States. Young, Richard G., ed. LC 89-39951. (Illus.). 128p. (gr. 5-9). 1990. PLB 17.26 (ISBN 0-944483-60-7). Garrett Ed Corp.

Lillegard, Dee. John Tyler. LC 87-18202. (Illus.). 100p. (gr. 3 up). 1987. PLB 17.27 (ISBN 0-516-01393-9). Childrens.

TYPESETTING

see also Printing

TYPEWRITING

Andujar, Maria D. & Iglesias, Jose L. Mecanografia Al Dia. rev. ed. (gr. 10 up). 1977. pap. text ed. 3.50 (ISBN 0-88345-306-1, 18482). Prentice ESL.

Marsh, Carole. Typing in Ten Minutes: On Any Keyboard - At Any Age. (Illus.). (gr. k-12). 1983. 19. 95 (ISBN 1-55609-194-X); pap. 14.95 (ISBN 0-935326-12-X). Gallopade Pub Group.

Mountford, Christine. Kids Can Type Too! 32p. (gr. 3-7). 1987. pap. 6.95 (ISBN 0-8120-3780-4). Barron.

Switzer, Mary E. Typing Fun. 48p. (gr. 3-6). 1977. 5.95 (ISBN 0-88160-027-X, LW 212). Learning Wks.

TYPOGRAPHY

see Printing

U

U BOATS

see Submarines

U. F. O.

see Flying Saucers

U. N.

see United Nations

UGANDA

African Triumph. (gr. 3-7). 3.00 (ISBN 0-8198-0225-5); pap. 2.00 (ISBN 0-8198-0226-3). Dghtrs St Paul.

Lisicky, Paul. Uganda. (Illus.). 96p. (gr. 5 up). 1988. lib. bdg. 14.95 (ISBN 1-55546-189-1). Chelsea Hse.

ULYSSES
Evslin, Bernard. The Adventures of Ulysses. Hunter, William, illus. 192p. (gr. 7 up). 1985. pap. 2.50 (ISBN 0-590-33948-6, Point). Scholastic Inc.
—Adventures of Ulysses. 1989. pap. 2.75 (ISBN 0-590-42599-4). Scholastic Inc.
Homer. Odyssey. Rouse, William H., tr. (gr. 7 up). 1946. pap. 3.50 (ISBN 0-451-62805-5, Sig Classics). NAL-Dutton.
Webb & Amery. Ulysses. (gr. 3-6). 1981. (Usborne-Hayes); PLB 11.96 (ISBN 0-88110-058-7); pap. 3.95 (ISBN 0-86020-567-3). EDC.

UMBRELLAS AND PARASOLS–FICTION
Biro, Val. Miranda's Umbrella. Biro, Val, illus. LC 89-77038. 30p. (ps). 1990. 12.95 (ISBN 0-87226-429-7). P Bedrick Bks.
Drescher, Henrik. The Yellow Umbrella. LC 87-70157. (Illus.). 40p. (ps-2). 1987. 10.95 (ISBN 0-02-733240-3, Bradbury Pr). Macmillan Child Grp.
Mandy's Umbrella. 1989. 2.99 (ISBN 0-517-69121-3). Outlet Bk Co.
Pinkwater, Daniel. Roger's Umbrella. Marshall, James, illus. LC 81-2294. 32p. (gr. 1-3). 1982. 11.95 (ISBN 0-525-38555-X, DCB). Dutton Child Bks.
—Roger's Umbrella. Marshall, James, illus. LC 81-2294. 32p. (gr. 1-3). 1985. pap. 3.95 (ISBN 0-525-44223-5, DCB). Dutton Child Bks.
Smath, Jerry & Smath, Valerie. Mr. Digby's Bad Day. Smath, Jerry, illus. LC 88-29856. 40p. (ps-3). 1989. PLB 13.95 (ISBN 0-671-67802-7). S&S Trade.

UNDER WATER EXPLORATION
see Underwater Exploration
UNDERDEVELOPED AREAS–ECONOMIC ASSISTANCE
see Economic Assistance
UNDERGROUND MOVEMENTS (WORLD WAR, 1939-1945)
see World War, 1939-1945–Underground Movements
UNDERGROUND RAILROAD
see also Slavery in the U. S.
Cosner, Shaaron. The Underground Railroad. (Illus.). 128p. (gr. 9-12). 1991. PLB 12.40 (ISBN 0-531-12505-X). Watts.
Ferris, Jeri. Go Free or Die: A Story about Harriet Tubman. Ritz, Karen, illus. 64p. (gr. 3-6). 1989. pap. 4.95 (ISBN 0-685-25638-3, First Ave Edns). Lerner Pubns.
Levine, Ellen. If You Traveled on the Underground Railroad. Williams, Richard, illus. 64p. (Orig). (gr. 4-6). 1988. pap. 2.95 (ISBN 0-590-40556-X). Scholastic Inc.
Marcey, Sally. Choice Adventures, No. 3: The Underground Railroad. (gr. 3-7). 1991. PLB 3.95 (ISBN 0-8423-5027-6). Tyndale.
Petry, Ann. Harriet Tubman: Conductor on the Underground Railway. LC 55-9215. 247p. (gr. 7-11). 1955. 14.95 (ISBN 0-690-37236-1, Crowell Jr Bks). HarpC Child Bks.
Rappaport, Doreen. Escape from Slavery: Five Journeys to Freedom. Lilly, Charles, illus. LC 90-38170. 128p. (gr. 4-7). 1991. 12.95 (ISBN 0-06-021631-X); PLB 12.89 (ISBN 0-06-021632-8). HarpC Child Bks.
Stein, R. Conrad. The Story of the Underground Railroad. LC 82-3801. (Illus.). 32p. (gr. 3-6). 1981. PLB 13.27 (ISBN 0-516-04643-8); pap. 3.95 (ISBN 0-516-44643-6). Childrens.

UNDERGROUND RAILROAD–FICTION
Meltzer, Milton. Underground Man. 288p. (gr. 3-7). 1990. 14.95 (ISBN 0-15-200617-6, Gulliver Bks); pap. 4.95 (ISBN 0-15-292846-4). HarBraceJ.
Monjo, F. N. Drinking Gourd. Brenner, Fred, illus. LC 68-10782. 64p. (gr. k-3). 1970. PLB 11.89 (ISBN 0-06-024330-9). HarpC Child Bks.

UNDERGROUND RAILROADS
see Subways
UNDERSEA EXPLORATION
see Underwater Exploration
UNDERSEA TECHNOLOGY
see Oceanography
UNDERSTANDING
see Intellect; Knowledge, Theory of
UNDERWATER EXPLORATION
see also Marine Biology; Skin Diving
Conley, Andrea. Window on the Deep: The Adventures of Underwater Explorer Sylvia Earle. (Illus.). 40p. (gr. 5-8). 1991. 13.95 (ISBN 0-531-15232-4); PLB 13.90 (ISBN 0-531-11119-9). Watts.
Crump, Donald J., ed. Hidden Treasures of the Sea. 104p. (gr. 3-8). 1988. pap. 6.95 (ISBN 0-87044-658-4); PLB 8.50 (ISBN 0-87044-663-0). Natl Geog.
Ferrier, Lucy. Diving the Great Barrier Reef. new ed. LC 75-23411. (Illus.). 32p. (gr. 5-10). 1976. PLB 10.79 (ISBN 0-89375-005-0); pap. 2.95 (ISBN 0-89375-021-2). Troll Assocs.
Greenberg, Judith E. & Carey, Helen H. Under the Sea. Tachiera, Andrea, illus. 32p. (gr. 2-4). 1990. 16.67 (ISBN 0-8172-3755-0); PLB 11.95. Raintree Pubs.
Hackwell, W. John. Diving to the Past: Recovering Ancient Wrecks. Hackwell, W. John, illus. LC 87-233529. 64p. (gr. 3-7). 1988. 14.95 (ISBN 0-684-18918-6, Scribners Young Read). Macmillan Child Grp.
Hayward, T. Deep Sea Divers. (Illus.). 32p. (gr. 4 up). Date not set. PLB 14.00 (ISBN 0-86592-413-9). Rourke Corp.

Humphrey, Kathryn L. Shipwrecks: Terror & Treasure. (Illus.). 64p. (gr. 5-8). 1991. PLB 11.90 (ISBN 0-531-20031-0). Watts.
Jensen, Antony & Bolt, Stephen. Undersea Mission. LC 88-42907. (Illus.). 32p. (gr. 4-5). 1989. PLB 10.95 (ISBN 1-55532-918-7). Gareth Stevens Inc.
Johnson, Rebecca L. Diving into Darkness: A Submersible Explores the Sea. (Illus.). 64p. (gr. 5 up). 1989. 16.95 (ISBN 0-8225-1587-3). Lerner Pubns.
Lampton, Christopher F. Undersea Archaeology. Solomon, Maury, ed. (Illus.). 96p. (gr. 5 up). 1988. PLB 10.40 (ISBN 0-531-10492-3). Watts.
McGovern, Ann. Down Under, Down Under: Diving Adventures on the Great Barrier Reef. McGovern, Ann, et al, illus. LC 88-30530. 48p. (gr. 2-6). 1989. 14.95 (ISBN 0-02-765770-1, Mcmillan Child Bk). Macmillan Child Grp.
Mackie, D. Undersea. (Illus.). 32p. (gr. 4-9). 1987. pap. 4.95 (ISBN 0-88625-156-7). Durkin Hayes Pub.
Rogers, Daniel. Exploring the Sea. (Illus.). 32p. (gr. 5-8). 1991. RLB 11.90 (ISBN 0-531-18389-0, Pub. by Boatwright Pr). Watts.
Underwater Exploration. (Illus.). (gr. 5 up). 3.50 (ISBN 0-7214-0834-6). Ladybird Bks.

UNDERWATER GEOLOGY
see Submarine Geology
UNDERWATER SWIMMING
see Skin Diving
UNICORNS–FICTION
Alden, Laura. Learning about Unicorns. Stasiak, Krystyna, illus. LC 85-9926. 48p. (gr. 3-5). 1985. PLB 17.27 (ISBN 0-516-06539-4); pap. 4.95 (ISBN 0-516-46539-2). Childrens.
Anderson, J. K. Unicorns-Coloring Book. 1985. pap. 3.95 (ISBN 0-88388-086-5). Bellerophon Bks.
Brigandi, Pat. Animals! Animals! Animals! A Feely Sticker Fun Kit. Duell, Nancy, illus. 24p. (Orig). (gr. k-3). 1987. pap. 3.95 (ISBN 0-590-40550-0). Scholastic Inc.
Coville, Bruce. Unicorn Treasury: Stories, Poems and Unicorn Lore. (gr. 4-7). 1991. pap. 9.00 (ISBN 0-385-41930-9). Doubleday.
Coville, Bruce & Coville, Katherine. Sarah's Unicorn. LC 79-2408. (Illus.). 48p. (ps-2). 1979. PLB 11.89 (ISBN 0-685-02085-1, Lipp Jr Bks); PLB 12.89 (ISBN 0-397-31873-1). HarpC Child Bks.
Coville, Bruce, compiled by. The Unicorn Treasury: Stories, Poems & Unicorn Lore. Hildebrandt, Tim, illus. LC 86-32919. 176p. (gr. 3 up). 1988. pap. 14.95 (ISBN 0-385-24000-7). Doubleday.
Edler, Timothy J. Rhombus: The Cajun Unicorn. (Illus.). 40p. (gr. k up). 1984. pap. 10.00 (ISBN 0-931108-10-1). Little Cajun Bks.
Gibbs, Greg. Willowby's World of Unicorns "Activity Book" 14p. (Orig). (gr. 2-6). 1984. pap. 4.00x (ISBN 0-910349-03-7). Cloud Ten.
Giblin, James C. The Truth about Unicorns. McDermott, Michael, illus. LC 90-47233. 128p. (gr. 3-7). 1991. 14.95 (ISBN 0-06-022478-9); PLB 14.89 (ISBN 0-06-022479-7). HarpC Child Bks.
Goodman, Deborah L. The Magic of the Unicorn. 128p. (Orig). (gr. 4). 1985. pap. 2.25 (ISBN 0-553-25242-9). Bantam.
Holland, Margaret & McKee, Craig. The Unicorn Who Had No Horn. Starner-Altop, Tammy, illus. 32p. (gr. k-4). 1985. 1.95 (ISBN 0-87406-015-X, 26-09340-9); 2.95 (ISBN 0-685-40025-5, 23-12254-1). Willowisp Pr.
Jones, Shelagh. Save the Unicorns. Myler, Terry, illus. 140p. (gr. 4-7). 1989. 11.95 (ISBN 0-947962-48-4, Pub. by Childrens Pr). Irish Bks Media.
Lee, Tanith. Black Unicorn. Cooper, Heather, illus. 144p. (gr. 7 up). 1991. 14.95 (ISBN 0-689-31575-9, Atheneum Child Bk). Macmillan Child Grp.
L'Engle, Madeleine. The Young Unicorns. 224p. (gr. 8 up). 1989. pap. 3.50 (ISBN 0-440-99919-7, LFL). Dell.
Luenn, Nancy. Unicorn Crossing. 64p. (gr. 2-9). pap. 2.50 (ISBN 0-8167-1321-9). Troll Assocs.
Mayer, Marianna. The Unicorn & the Lake. Hague, Michael, illus. LC 82-71356. 32p. (gr. k up). 1982. 13.95 (ISBN 0-8037-9337-5); PLB 13.89 (ISBN 0-8037-9338-3). Dial Bks Young.
—Unicorn & the Lake. (ps-3). 1990. 16.95 (ISBN 0-8037-0844-0). Dial Bks Young.
Moeri, Louise. The Unicorn & the Plow. Goode, Diane, illus. 32p. (gr. 2 up). 1982. 11.95 (ISBN 0-525-45116-1, DCB). Dutton Child Bks.
Morgan & Me. (gr. 1-6). 1975. pap. 2.95 (ISBN 0-8431-0560-7). Price Stern.
Preussler, Otfried. The Tale of the Unicorn. Spirin, Gennady, illus. LC 88-7141. 32p. (ps-up). 1989. 12.95 (ISBN 0-8037-0583-2). Dial Bks Young.
Razzi, Jim. Fun with Unicorns. 48p. (gr. 1-3). 1987. pap. 1.95 (ISBN 0-590-40787-2). Scholastic Inc.
Seitz, Eileen. The Message of the White Unicorn. Seitz, Eileen, illus. LC 87-50260. 35p. (Orig). (gr. 3-5). 1987. pap. 8.95 (ISBN 1-55523-057-1). Winston-Derek.
Smith, Kathie B. Enchanted Unicorn. 1987. pap. 2.25 (ISBN 0-671-63239-6). S&S Trade.
Vrooman, Christine W. Willowby's World of Unicorns. Kane, Sandy & Ogden, Peggy, eds. Sidaras, Nanci, illus. 56p. (gr. 2-6). 1982. pap. 8.95 with stickers incl. (ISBN 0-685-06580-4). Cloud Ten.

UNIDENTIFIED FLYING OBJECTS
see Flying Saucers

Arvey, Michael. UFO's: Opposing Viewpoints. LC 89-11645. (Illus.). 111p. (gr. 6 up). 1989. PLB 13.95 (ISBN 0-89908-060-X). Greenhaven.

UNDERWRITING
see Insurance
UNIFORMS
York, Susannah. In Search of Unicorns. (Illus.). 126p. (gr. 2 up). 1986. Repr. of 1973 ed. 14.95 (ISBN 0-340-33426-6, Pub. by Hodder & Stoughton UK). Trafalgar Sq.
UNION OF SOUTH AFRICA
see Africa, South
UNION PACIFIC RAILROAD
Stein, R. Conrad. The Story of the Golden Spike. Dunnington, Tom, illus. LC 78-4042. 32p. (gr. 3-6). 1978. PLB 13.27 (ISBN 0-516-04621-7). Childrens.
UNIONS, LABOR
see Labor Unions
UNISON SPEAKING
see Choral Speaking
UNITARIANISM
Evans-Tiller, Jan. Around the Church, Around the Year: Unitarian Universalism for Children. Lewis, Kathryn, et al, eds. Conteh-Morgan, Jane, illus. 144p. (Orig). (gr. k-3). 1990. pap. text ed. 29.95 (ISBN 1-55896-174-7). Unitarian Univ.
UNITED KINGDOM
see Great Britain
UNITED NATIONS
Carroll, Raymond. The Future of the U. N. LC 85-7533. (Illus.). 122p. (gr. 7up). 1985. PLB 12.90 (ISBN 0-531-10062-6). Watts.
Edmonds, I. G. The United Nations. LC 73-13229. (gr. 6-10). 1974. 6.95 (ISBN 0-672-51749-3, Bobbs). Macmillan.
Greene, Carol. The United Nations. LC 83-10068. (Illus.). 48p. (gr. k-4). 1983. PLB 14.60 (ISBN 0-516-01710-1); pap. 4.95 (ISBN 0-516-41710-X). Childrens.
Ross, Stewart. United Nations. 1990. PLB 12.90 (ISBN 0-531-18295-9). Watts.
Smith, Nigel. United Nations Since 1945. 1990. PLB 12.90 (ISBN 0-531-18297-5). Watts.
Stein, R. Conrad. The Story of the United Nations. Canaday, Ralph, illus. LC 85-31356. 32p. (gr. 3-6). 1986. PLB 13.27 (ISBN 0-516-04698-5). Childrens.
Woods, Harold & Woods, Geraldine. The United Nations. LC 85-5338. 65p. (gr. 4-6). 1985. PLB 10.40 (ISBN 0-531-10048-0). Watts.
UNITED STATES
see also names of regions of the U. S. and groups of states e.g. Atlantic States; Middle West; Mississippi valley; Northwest, Old; Northwest, Pacific; Southern States; Southwest, New; Southwest, Old; The West
The American Dream, 6 bks. (Illus.). (gr. 7-10). 1990. Set, 144p. ea. lib. bdg. 83.88 (ISBN 0-382-09933-8). Silver Burdett Pr.
Aten, Jerry. America: From Sea to Shining Sea. 160p. (gr. 4 up). 1988. wkbk. 11.95 (ISBN 0-86653-434-2, GA1044). Good Apple.
—Challenge Across America. 96p. (gr. 4-8). 1990. 11.95 (ISBN 0-86653-556-X, GA1157). Good Apple.
—Fifty Nifty States. (Illus.). 320p. (gr. 4 up). 1990. 19.95 (ISBN 0-86653-532-2, GA1138). Good Apple.
Aylesworth, Thomas G. Kids' World Almanac of the United States. 288p. (gr. 3-7). 1990. 14.95 (ISBN 0-88687-479-3); pap. 6.95 (ISBN 0-88687-478-5). Pharos Bks NY.
Beck, Michael & Scott, Judy. Getting into Geography: The States & Flags Through Research & Activities. Beck, Michael, illus. 240p. (Orig). (gr. 4-6). 1990. pap. text ed. 20.00 (ISBN 0-927867-00-1). Skippingstone Pr.
Brandt, Sue R. Facts about the Fifty States. 2nd, rev. ed. Greenberg, Lorna, ed. (Illus.). 72p. (gr. 4-9). 1988. PLB 10.40 (ISBN 0-531-10476-1). Watts.
Caney, Steven. Steven Caney's Kids' America. LC 77-27465. (Illus.). 416p. (ps-9). 1978. pap. 13.95 (ISBN 0-911104-80-1, 114). Workman Pub.
Deegan, Paul. A Revolutionary Idea. Abbott, Phyllis, et al, eds. Wadsworth, Elaine, illus. 48p. (gr. 4). 1987. lib. bdg. 10.95 (ISBN 0-939179-20-2). Abdo & Dghtrs.
Getting to Know United States. (Illus.). 48p. 1990. 7.95 (ISBN 0-8442-0682-2, Passport Bks). Natl Textbk.
Gibson, Roxie C. Hey, God! What Is America? Gibson, James, illus. Harvey, Paul, intro. by. LC 81-71025. (Illus.). 52p. (gr. 3-5). 1982. 4.95 (ISBN 0-938232-05-3, 32795). Winston-Derek.
James, Ian. United States. 1990. PLB 11.90 (ISBN 0-531-14029-6). Watts.
Johnson, Mabel. One Land - One Nation. (Illus.). 64p. (gr. 7 up). 1987. pap. 3.95 (ISBN 0-9600838-6-3). M Johnson.

Lancaster, Derek. Picture America: States & Capitals. Lancaster, Derek, illus. Anderson, Stevens, ed. (Illus.). 136p. (gr. 5). 1991. pap. 4.95 (ISBN 1-880184-02-8). Compact Classics. PICTURE AMERICA, an illustrated educational product using mnemonic "picture associations", enables any age student to learn more about the United States. In particular, the learner is provided with familiar points of

reference ("mnemonic keys") that build natural bridges between states & their capitals. Remembering which capital goes with which state will never be a problem again. Additional details regarding each state (its history, geography, popular name, official flower & bird, demographics, major agricultural & manufacturing interests, etc.) are tied together using exciting descriptions, maps & memory key illustrations. PICTURE AMERICA also contains follow-up worksheets that quiz & prompt the student, further reinforcing what has been taught. This book is both an ideal coloring book & an instructional source for young & old. Families can learn together. PICTURE AMERICA is an entertaining way to learn; a "fun book" rather than a "text book". Most importantly, PICTURE AMERICA introduces students to a strategy for permanent recall they can make use of again & again. PICTURE AMERICA's vivid state associations won't fade after "the test" is over--they'll remain a life-time.

Publisher Provided Annotation.

Latta, Rich. State the Facts. 56p. 1990. pap. 2.95 (ISBN 0-8431-2821-6). Price Stern.

Polette, Nancy. The Research Book of the Fifty States. (Illus.). 32p. (gr. 4-7). 1984. pap. 4.95 (ISBN 0-913839-37-X). Bk Lures.

Ronan, Margaret. All about Our Fifty States. rev. ed. Meyerriecks, William & Ronan, Frank, illus. LC 78-16658. (gr. 5-9). 1978. 9.95 (ISBN 0-394-80244-6). Random.

Schloredt, Valerie. United States of America. rev. ed. LC 86-15565. (Illus.). 48p. (gr. 5 up). 1986. PLB 16.98 (ISBN 0-382-09257-0). Silver Burdett Pr.

Somerville, L. First Book of America. (Illus.). 32p. 1990. PLB 13.96 (ISBN 0-88110-440-X); pap. 6.95 (ISBN 0-7460-0338-2). EDC.

Zenfell, Martha E. U. S. A. LC 88-18561. (Illus.). 48p. (gr. 4-8). 1988. PLB 14.98 (ISBN 0-382-09515-4). Silver Burdett Pr.

U. S. AIR FORCE

Rhea, John. The Department of the Air Force. (Illus.). (gr. 5 up). 1990. 14.95 (ISBN 0-87754-834-X). Chelsea Hse.

U. S. AIR FORCE ACADEMY

Smallwood, William L. The Air Force Academy Candidate Book. (Illus.). 200p. (Orig.). (gr. 10-12). 1988. pap. write for info. Beacon Bks.

U. S.–ANTIQUITIES

see also Indians of North America–Antiquities

Wimberly, Christine A. Exploring Prehistoric Alabama Through Archaeology. Anderson, John & Meredith, Marianne, illus. LC 80-70833. 96p. (Orig.). (gr. 5-12). 1981. pap. 8.95 (ISBN 0-9605938-3-7); pap. text ed. 6.18 (ISBN 0-9605938-1-0); tchr's ed. 9.49 (ISBN 0-9605938-2-9). Explorer Bks.

U. S.–ARMED FORCES

see also official names of branches of the Armed Forces, e.g. U. S. Army; U. S. Navy

Nicholaus, John. The Army Library, 6 bks, Reading Level 5. (Illus.). 288p. (gr. 3-8). Date not set. Set. PLB 111.60 (ISBN 0-86592-417-1). Rourke Corp.

White, Carl P. Citizen Soldier: Opportunities in the Reserves. Rosen, Ruth, ed. (gr. 7-12). 1990. PLB 14.95 (ISBN 0-8239-1023-7). Rosen Group.

U. S.–ARTISTS

see Artists, American

U. S.–AUTHORS

see Authors, American

U. S.–BIOGRAPHY

Ashabranner, Brent. People Who Make a Difference. LC 89-34593. (Illus.). (gr. 5 up). 1989. 15.95 (ISBN 0-525-65009-1, Cobblehill Bks). Dutton Child Bks.

Barnes, Jeremy. Samuel Goldwyn. Furstinger, Nancy, ed. (Illus.). 128p. (gr. 7-10). 1989. PLB 13.98 (ISBN 0-382-09586-3). Silver Burdett Pr.

Beard, Annie E. Our Foreign-Born Citizens. 6th ed. LC 68-17083. 276p. (gr. 4 up). 1968. 14.95 (ISBN 0-690-60525-0, Crowell Jr Bks). HarpC Child Bks.

Boynton, LaVerne L. The Enchantment of Beaver Creek. Richards, Linda, illus. 248p. 1988. 12.95. Starlite Pub.

Collins, David. Johnny Appleseed. LC 84-60315. (gr. 3-6). 1985. pap. 6.95 (ISBN 0-88062-134-6). Mott Media.

Davidson, Margaret. The Story of Benjamin Franklin: Amazing American. (Orig.). (gr. k-6). 1988. pap. 2.95 (ISBN 0-440-40021-X, YB). Dell.

Eisenhower, Julie N. Special People. (Illus.). 208p. 1990. pap. text ed. 6.95 (ISBN 0-685-35364-8). Thomas Publications.

Favors, John & Favors, Kathryne. White Americans Who Cared Kit. 26p. (gr. 4 up). 1990. Repr. of 1978 ed. 299.95 (ISBN 1-878794-01-9). Jonka Enter.

Fowler, Mary J. & Fisher, Margaret, eds. Great Americans. rev. ed. LC 87-81352. (Illus.). 160p. (gr. 4 up). 1988. 1-4 copies 14.95 ea. (ISBN 0-934291-25-X); 5 or more copies 11.95 (ISBN 0-317-91143-0). Gateway Pr MI.

Frazier, Neta L. Stout-Hearted Seven. 174p. (gr. 4-6). 1984. pap. text ed. 4.95 (ISBN 0-914019-22-8). Pacif NW Natl Pks.

Glassman, Bruce. J. Paul Getty. Furstinger, Nancy, ed. (Illus.). 112p. (gr. 7-10). 1989. PLB 13.98 (ISBN 0-382-09584-7). Silver Burdett Pr.

Hale, Janet. The Conners of Conner Prairie. Baxter, Nancy N., ed. Day, Richard, illus. 120p. (gr. 4-6). 1989. 13.95 (ISBN 0-9617367-5-5). Guild Pr IN.

Hanify, MaryLou. For the Love of a Ranger. Stafford, Dorene & Jansen, GLen, illus. 92p. (gr. 7). 1980. pap. 2.95 (ISBN 0-939116-04-9). Frontier WA.

Henry, Sondra & Taitz, Emily. Everyone Wears His Name: A Biography of Levi Strauss. LC 87-32455. (Illus.). 112p. (gr. 5 up). 1990. PLB 12.95 (ISBN 0-87518-375-1, Dillon). Macmillan Child Grp.

Jacobs, William J. Great Lives: Human Rights. LC 89-37211. (Illus.). 288p. (gr. 4-6). 1990. 22.95 (ISBN 0-684-19036-2, Scribners Young Read). Macmillan Child Grp.

Johnson, Hilda S. A Child's Diary - the 1930's. Johnson, Hilda S., illus. LC 88-51304. 64p. (Orig.). (gr. 3-8). 1988. pap. 3.95 (ISBN 0-931563-02-X). Wishing Rm.

Kurland, Gerald. George Wallace: Southern Governor & Presidential Candidate. Rahmas, D. Steve, ed. 32p. (Orig.). (gr. 7-12). 1972. lib. bdg. 4.20 incl. catalog cards (ISBN 0-87157-529-9). SamHar Pr.

—John D. Rockefeller: Nineteenth Century Industrialist & Oil Baron. Rahmas, D. Steve, ed. 32p. (gr. 7-12). 1972. lib. bdg. 4.20 incl. catalog cards (ISBN 0-87157-535-3). SamHar Pr.

—Lyndon Baines Johnson: President Caught in an Ordeal of Power. Rahmas, D. Steve, ed. LC 76-190243. 32p. (Orig.). (gr. 7-12). 1972. lib. bdg. 4.20 incl. catalog cards (ISBN 0-87157-525-6); pap. 2.95 vinyl laminated covers (ISBN 0-87157-025-4). SamHar Pr.

—Spiro Agnew: Controversial Vice-President of the Nixon Administration. Rahmas, D. Steve, ed. LC 72-190234. 32p. (Orig.). (gr. 7-12). 1972. PLB 4.20 incl. catalog cards (ISBN 0-87157-516-7). SamHar Pr.

Levert, Suzanne. Doubleday Book of Famous Americans. LC 87-26215. (Illus.). (gr. 5 up). 1989. 15.95 (ISBN 0-385-23699-9). Doubleday.

Lewis, Shari. One-Minute Stories of Great Americans. (ps-3). 1990. 9.95 (ISBN 0-385-24448-7). Doubleday.

Ludwig, Charles. Susanna Wesley. LC 84-60314. 195p. (gr. 3-6). 1984. pap. 6.95 (ISBN 0-88062-110-9). Mott Media.

McGovern, Ann. The Secret Soldier: The Story of Deborah Sampson. (gr. 4-6). 1977. pap. 2.25 (ISBN 0-590-32176-5). Scholastic Inc.

Marsh, Carole. State Greats. (gr. 4-9). 1988. 19.95 (ISBN 1-55609-254-7); pap. 14.95 (ISBN 0-318-37389-0); computer disk 29.95 (ISBN 1-55609-341-1). Gallopade Pub Group.

Martin, Patricia S. Samantha Smith: Little Ambassador. (Illus.). 24p. (gr. 1-4). 1987. PLB 12.33 (ISBN 0-86592-173-3). Rourke Corp.

Mashburn, William H. A Mountain Summer. Gayheart, Willard, illus. LC 88-11782. 140p. (Orig.). (gr. 9-12). 1988. pap. 8.95 (ISBN 0-936015-14-4). Pocahontas Pr.

Mather, Melissa. Rough Road Home. LC 58-9537. 256p. 1988. pap. 9.95 (ISBN 0-8397-7237-8). Eriksson.

O'Brien, P. M. The Promoter: His Life & Times. (Illus.). 118p. (gr. 10-12). 1988. pap. 5.65 (ISBN 0-9620540-0-3). P M O'Brien.

Olson, Kenfield & Houghton, Cleo, eds. Collected Memoirs of Central School: Kirkland, Washington, 1890-1980. 67p. (Orig.). (gr. 9-12). 1982. pap. 5.00 (ISBN 0-685-28866-8). Marymoor Mus.

Raphael, Morris. Weeks Hall: The Master of the Shadows. LC 81-90439. (Illus.). 207p. (gr. 5-12). 1981. 14.95 (ISBN 0-9608866-1-3). M Raphael.

Roberts, Naurice. Andrew Young: Freedom Fighter. LC 83-7633. (Illus.). 32p. (gr. 2-5). 1983. PLB 13.27 (ISBN 0-516-03450-2); pap. 3.95 (ISBN 0-516-43450-0). Childrens.

Smith, Kathy B. The Great Americans Series, 9 vols. Seward, James, illus. 216p. (gr. 4-6). 1989. Set. PLB 71.82 (ISBN 0-671-93118-0); Set. PLB 53.91s.p. Messner.

Smith, Kathy B. & Bradbury, Pamela. Men of the Constitution. Seward, James, illus. 24p. (gr. 4-6). 1987. PLB 7.98 (ISBN 0-671-64604-4); PLB 5.99s.p. Messner.

Smith, Richard H. Spymaster's Odyssey: The Secret Service of Allen Dulles. (Illus.). cancelled (ISBN 0-698-10703-9, Coward). Putnam Pub Group.

Stuart, Jesse. To Teach, To Love. LeMaster, J. R., intro. by. 317p. (gr. 10 up). 1987. Repr. of 1970 ed. 20.00 (ISBN 0-945084-02-1). J Stuart Found.

Turk, Ruth. They Reached for the Stars. Tripp, Ned, illus. (gr. 5-9). 1990. pap. 11.95 (ISBN 0-933025-20-3). Blue Bird Pub.

Verheyden-Hilliard, Mary Ellen. American Women in Science Engineering. Biro, Scarlet & Rom, Holly M., illus. 32p. 1988. pap. 5.00 (ISBN 0-932469-19-1); 70.00 set. Equity Inst.

This illustrated, 15-book series presents contemporary African-American Indian, Asian-American, Hispanic, & Caucasian women who, in girlhood, overcame barriers of gender, race, language, & poverty to become scientists. Five of the books are about girls with physical disabilities who also went on to become scientists. "Inspiring group of biographies of women in science...Children in the lower grades with reading problems can use them for...biographical information."-- SCHOOL LIBRARY JOURNAL. "... useful to teachers who want to help girls become more positive towards mathematics & science... recommended."-- CURRICULUM REVIEW. "...smoothly written texts..."-- BOOKLIST. "...help children...see the connection...between determination to persevere in the face of disabilities & later 'payoff'...in a variety of very exciting careers."-- NEWSLETTER, Association of Black Women in Higher Education. "...warm, lively & true stories of young girls who went on to become successful scientists..."-- GIFTED CHILDREN MONTHLY. "...these books are so attractively produced that I can't imagine elementary classroom teaching without them."-- PERSPECTIVES, National Women Studies Association. Also avaiable are tie-in Teaching Guide $10.00 (ISBN 0-932469-19-3), & video: "You Can Be a Scientist Too!" $46.00 (ISBN 0-932469-11-6). "Well written & filmed... appealing...inspiring production."-- BOOKLIST.

Publisher Provided Annotation.

Whitfield, Vallie J. Heritage History. 2nd ed. Whitfield, Joanne, ed. LC 87-50112. (Illus.). 265p. (gr. 10 up). 1988. 25.00 (ISBN 0-930920-19-8). Whitfield Bks.

U. S.–BIOGRAPHY–DICTIONARIES

Byrne, Pamela R. & Kinnell, Susan K. People & Politics in North America: Summaries of Biographical Articles in History Journals. 185p. (gr. 9-12). 1988. pap. text ed. 18.00 (ISBN 0-87436-538-4). ABC Clio.

—People & Religion in North America: Summaries of Biographical Articles in History Journals. 168p. (gr. 9-12). 1988. pap. text ed. 18.00 (ISBN 0-87436-542-2). ABC Clio.

—People & the Arts in North America. 182p. (gr. 7-12). 1988. pap. text ed. 18.00 (ISBN 0-87436-541-4). ABC Clio.

—People in Business & Industry in North America: Summaries of Biographical Articles in History Journals. 118p. (gr. 9-12). 1988. pap. text ed. 18.00 (ISBN 0-87436-539-2). ABC Clio.

U. S.–CENSUS

Ashabranner, Melissa & Ashabranner, Brent. Counting America: The Story of the United States Census. (Illus.). 96p. (gr. 5-9). 1989. 14.95 (ISBN 0-399-21747-9, Putnam). Putnam Pub Group.

U. S. CENTRAL INTELLIGENCE AGENCY

Archer, Jules. Superspies: The Secret Side of Government. LC 77-72640. (gr. 7up). 1977. pap. 7.95 (ISBN 0-440-08136-X). Delacorte.

Yost, Graham. The CIA. (Illus.). 176p. 1989. 16.95x (ISBN 0-8160-1941-X). Facts on File.

U. S.–CHURCH HISTORY

Morrison, Ellen E. The Church That Keeps Memories Alive: The Story of Christ Church, Alexandria, Virginia. 2nd, rev. ed. LC 79-114253. (Illus.). 12p. (gr. 6). 1979. saddle-stitched 1.75 (ISBN 0-9622537-0-7). Morielle Pr.

U. S.–CIVILIZATION

American Cultures. (Illus.). 32p. (gr. 6-12). 1980. pap. 1.85 (ISBN 0-8395-3388-8, 3388). BSA.

Dudley, William & Szumski, Bonnie, eds. America's Future: Opposing Viewpoints. LC 89-25885. (Illus.). 312p. (gr. 10 up). 1990. lib. bdg. 15.95 (ISBN 0-89908-448-6); pap. text ed. 8.95 (ISBN 0-89908-423-0). Greenhaven.

Lye, Keith. Passport to United States. FS-Watts Staff, ed. (Illus.). 48p. (gr. 4-9). 1988. 12.90 (ISBN 0-531-10534-2). Watts.

Mayers, Florence C. ABC: National Museum of American History. (Illus.). 32p. 1989. 10.95 (ISBN 0-8109-1875-7). Abrams.

U. S. COAST GUARD

Bishop, Eleanor. Prints in the Sand: The U. S. Coast Guard Beach Patrol During WWII. LC 89-62184. (Illus.). 92p. (Orig.). (gr. 8-12). 1989. pap. 9.95 (ISBN 0-929521-22-6). Pictorial Hist.

Ferrell, Nancy W. The U. S. Coast Guard. (Illus.). 72p. (gr. 5 up). 1989. 16.95 (ISBN 0-8225-1431-1). Lerner Pubns.

Noble, Dennis L. & O'Brien, Mike. U. S. Life-Saving Service 1889-1915, U. S. Coast Guard Service 1915-1989. (Illus.). 24p. (Orig.). (gr. 8 up). 1989. pap. text ed. 2.00 (ISBN 0-935549-12-9). MI City Hist.

U. S.–COLONIES

see U. S.–Territories and Possessions

U. S. CONGRESS

Barba, Harry & Barba, Marian, eds. What's Cooking in Congress? LC 79-83777. (Illus.). 144p. (gr. 5 up). 1979. pap. 7.95 (ISBN 0-911906-15-0). Harian Creative Bks.

Bernstein, Richard & Agel, Jerome. The Congress. LC 88-21025. (gr. 7 up). 1989. 12.95 (ISBN 0-8027-6832-6); PLB 13.85 (ISBN 0-8027-6833-4). Walker & Co.

Crawford, Ann F. Sam Houston: American Hero. Roberts, Melissa, ed. Warren, Betsy, illus. 48p. (gr. 2-3). 1988. 10.95 (ISBN 0-89015-644-1, Pub. by Panda Bks). Eakin Pr.

Green, Carl & Sanford, William. Congress. (Illus.). 96p. (gr. 7 up). 1990. lib. bdg. 18.60 (ISBN 0-86593-083-X); lib. bdg. 13.95s.p. Rourke Corp.

Greene, Carol. Congress. LC 84-23243. (Illus.). 48p. (gr. k-4). 1985. lib. bdg. 14.60 (ISBN 0-516-01939-2); pap. 4.95 (ISBN 0-516-41939-0). Childrens.

Jakoubek, Robert. Adam Clayton Powell, Jr. King, Coretta Scott, intro. by. (Illus.). 112p. 1988. lib. bdg. 17.95x (ISBN 1-55546-606-0); pap. 9.95 (ISBN 0-7910-0213-6). Chelsea Hse.

Ragsdale, Bruce A. The House of Representatives. Schlesinger, Arthur, Jr., intro. by. (Illus.). 96p. (gr. 5 up). 1989. lib. bdg. 14.95 (ISBN 1-55546-112-3). Chelsea Hse.

Sabin, Louis. Congressperson. Dole, Bob, illus. LC 84-2651. 32p. (gr. 3-6). 1985. PLB 9.49 (ISBN 0-8167-0266-7); pap. text ed. 2.95 (ISBN 0-8167-0267-5). Troll Assocs.

Scheader, Catherine. Shirley Chisholm: Teacher & Congresswoman. LC 89-34451. (Illus.). 128p. 1990. lib. bdg. 17.95 (ISBN 0-89490-285-7). Enslow Pubs.

Stein, R. Conrad. The Story of the Powers of Congress. Neely, Keith, illus. LC 85-10943. 31p. (gr. 3-4). 1985. PLB 13.27 (ISBN 0-516-04695-0); pap. 3.95 (ISBN 0-516-44695-9). Childrens.

U. S. CONGRESS. SENATE

Ritchie, Donald A. The Senate. Schlesinger, Arthur M., Jr., intro. by. (Illus.). 96p. (gr. 5 up). 1988. lib. bdg. 14.95 (ISBN 1-55546-121-2). Chelsea Hse.

U. S. CONGRESS. SENATE–BIOGRAPHY

Gould, Alberta. First Lady of the Senate: A Life of Margaret Chase Smith, U. S. Senator. Weinberger, Jane, ed. LC 89-51315. (Illus.). 150p. (gr. 5-10). 1990. 15.95 (ISBN 0-932433-64-2). Windswept Hse.

U. S. CONGRESS. SENATE–FICTION

Buchwald, Art. The Bollo Caper: A Furry Tail for All Ages. Primavera, Elise, illus. (gr. 3 up). 1983. pap. 4.95 (ISBN 0-399-21003-2, Putnam). Putnam Pub Group.

U. S. CONSTITUTION

Abromowitz, Jack & Uva, Kenneth. The Constitution & the Government of the U. S. (gr. 7-12). 1987. pap. text ed. 3.50 (ISBN 0-89525-747-5). Ed Activities.

Batchelor, John E. States' Rights. (Illus.). 72p. (gr. 4-9). 1986. lib. bdg. 10.40 (ISBN 0-531-10112-6). Watts.

Colman, Warren. The Bill of Rights. LC 86-33437. (Illus.). 48p. (gr. k-4). 1987. PLB 14.60 (ISBN 0-516-01232-0); pap. 4.95 (ISBN 0-516-41232-9). Childrens.

—La Carta de Derechos: (The Bill of Rights) LC 86-33437. (SPA.). 48p. (gr. k-4). 1989. PLB 14.60 (ISBN 0-516-31232-4); pap. 4.95 (ISBN 0-516-51232-3). Childrens.

—La Constitucion: (The Constitution) LC 86-30968. (SPA.). 48p. (gr. k-4). 1989. PLB 14.60 (ISBN 0-516-31231-6); pap. 4.95 (ISBN 0-516-51231-5). Childrens.

—The Constitution. LC 86-30968. (Illus.). 48p. (gr. k-4). 1987. PLB 14.60 (ISBN 0-516-01231-2); pap. 4.95 (ISBN 0-516-41231-0). Childrens.

Commager, Henry S. Great Constitution. LC 61-7914. (gr. 6-10). 1961. write for info. (ISBN 0-672-50299-2). Macmillan.

Constitution of the United States. 1987. pap. 5.00 (ISBN 0-930061-20-9). Interspace Bks.
"I saw them go into the tavern for coffee & cold tea. Above the cobbled streets & shop signs, stars shone brightly. The fragrance of primroses, yellow & red as the finest watered silk, scented the air, 'I have sometimes almost wished,' Dr. Franklin was speaking, 'it had been my destiny to be born two or three centuries hence.' 'You think the country is that great?' Mr. Madison, the quiet one, my master spoke up..." Also: Child of the Lily Bed by a seven year old for seven year olds. ..$5.00. For High Schoolers & Beyond: The Miracle of Believing--How career goals & Dreams can come true with confidence & planning. $9.95. Historical Novels: LaFayette & Harriet...How a lad who couldn't dance with the Queen helped to save America; Glory of Wooden Walls...of Sir Francis Drake & Queen Elizabeth's England, the son of the Royal Clockmaker who went to sea. $14.95 each. Interspace Books, 4500 Chesapeake St., N.W., Washington, D.C. 20016.
Publisher Provided Annotation.

Fisher, Dorothy C. Our Independence & the Constitution. LC 87-4656. 192p. (gr. 5-9). 1987. lib. bdg. 8.99 (ISBN 0-394-90305-6, Random Juv); pap. 2.95 (ISBN 0-394-89175-9, Random Juv). Random.

Gamiello, Elvira. We the People, the Unites States Constitution Fun Book. (Illus.). 32p. (Orig.). 1987. pap. 1.50 (ISBN 0-942025-08-3). Kidsbks.

Glisan, Ellen M. U. S. Constitution Text. rev. ed. (Illus.). 41p. (gr. 7-12). 1989. pap. text ed. write for info. (ISBN 0-944791-92-1, SS505). Peekan Pubns.

Haener, Donald R. & Fry, Janice K. The Era & Our Constitution. rev. ed. Baruffa, Joanne & Tunis, Edwin, illus. (gr. 6 up). 1987. pap. text ed. 5.00 (ISBN 0-942661-02-8). Discovry Enterp.

Hoobler, Dorothy & Hoobler, Thomas. Your Right to Privacy. (Illus.). 72p. (gr. 4-9). 1986. lib. bdg. 10.40 (ISBN 0-531-10110-X). Watts.

Howes, Janice. A Classroom Presents the Constitution of the United States: A Story for Elementary School Children. Howes, Janice, illus. LC 87-50078. 35p. (Orig.). (gr. k-5). 1987. pap. 7.00 (ISBN 0-942431-00-6). Teachers Pub Hse.

Janosik, Robert J. The American Constitution: An Annotated Bibliography. 200p. 1991. PLB 40.00x (ISBN 0-89356-665-9, Magill Bks). Salem Pr.

Jenkins, George. Constitution. (Illus.). 96p. (gr. 7 up). 1990. lib. bdg. 18.60 (ISBN 0-86593-085-6); lib. bdg. 13.95s.p. Rourke Corp.

Kleeberg, Irene Cumming. Separation of Church & State. (Illus.). 72p. (gr. 4-9). 1986. lib. bdg. 10.40 (ISBN 0-531-10111-8). Watts.

Lindop, Edmund. Birth of the Constitution. LC 86-13380. (Illus.). 160p. (gr. 6-12). 1987. PLB 18.95 (ISBN 0-89490-135-4). Enslow Pubs.

Mabie, Margot. The Constitution: Reflection of a Changing Nation. LC 86-33502. (Illus.). 112p. (gr. 6 up). 1987. 12.95 (ISBN 0-8050-0335-5). H Holt & Co.

McGee, Dorothy H. Framers of the Constitution. (gr. 9-12). 1987. 13.95 (ISBN 0-396-09032-X, Putnam). Putnam Pub Group.

Morris, Richard B. The Constitution. rev. ed. Fisher, Leonard E., illus. 72p. (gr. 5-10). 1985. PLB 9.95 (ISBN 0-8225-1702-7). Lerner Pubns.

Post, Libby, ed. Through the Eyes of Children: Liberty & Justice for All. Wachtter, Sol, intros. by. (Illus.). 48p. (Orig.). 1989. pap. write for info. NY State Alliance.

Prolman, Marilyn. The Story of the Constitution. Glaubke, Robert, illus. LC 69-14680. 32p. (gr. 4-8). 1969. PLB 13.27 (ISBN 0-516-04605-5); pap. 3.95 (ISBN 0-516-44605-3). Childrens.

Richie, Donald A. U. S. Constitution. Schlesinger, Arthur M., Jr., intro. by. (Illus.). 112p. (gr. 5 up). 1989. 14.95 (ISBN 0-87754-894-3). Chelsea Hse.

Scesney, Gladys. It's Your Constitution! rev. ed. Enrees, Michael B., illus. 32p. (gr. 1-6). 1987. pap. 1.50 (ISBN 0-9618667-1-3). Scesney Pubns.

Sgroi, Peter. This Constitution. (Illus.). 72p. (gr. 4-9). 1986. PLB 10.40 (ISBN 0-531-10167-3). Watts.

Spier, Peter. We the People: The Constitution of the United States of America. (ps). 1991. pap. 8.00 (ISBN 0-385-41903-1). Doubleday.

—We the People: The Story of the U. S. Constitution. Spier, Peter, illus. LC 86-24205. 48p. (gr. k-3). 1987. PLB 13.95 (ISBN 0-385-23589-5). Doubleday.

The U. S. Constitution: Locating the Author's Main Idea. (Illus.). 32p. (gr. 3-6). 1990. PLB 8.95 (ISBN 0-89908-601-2). Greenhaven.

Wolf, D. M. We the People: Bits, Bytes & Highlights of the U. S. Constitution & Bill of Rights from Honey Bees Tye & Sy. McDaniel, Jerry, illus. 32p. (Orig.). (gr. 3-5). 1987. pap. 4.95 (ISBN 0-9617057-1-X). Storyviews Pub.

U. S. CONSTITUTION–AMENDMENTS

Stein, R. Conrad. The Story of the Nineteenth Amendment. LC 82-4419. (Illus.). (gr. 3-6). 1982. PLB 13.27 (ISBN 0-516-04639-X); pap. 3.95 (ISBN 0-516-44639-8). Childrens.

U. S. CONSTITUTIONAL CONVENTION, 1787

Commager, Henry S. Great Constitution. LC 61-7914. (gr. 6-10). 1961. write for info. (ISBN 0-672-50299-2). Macmillan.

Hauptly, Denis J. A Convention of Delegates: The Creation of the Constitution. LC 86-17260. (Illus.). 160p. (gr. 3-7). 1987. 13.95 (ISBN 0-689-31148-6, Atheneum Child Bk). Macmillan Child Grp.

McPhillips, Martin. The Constitutional Convention. LC 85-40169. (Illus.). 64p. (gr. 5 up). 1986. 16.98 (ISBN 0-382-06827-0); pap. 5.75 (ISBN 0-382-09435-2). Silver.

Prolman, Marilyn. The Story of the Constitution. Glaubke, Robert, illus. LC 69-14680. 32p. (gr. 4-8). 1969. PLB 13.27 (ISBN 0-516-04605-5); pap. 3.95 (ISBN 0-516-44605-3). Childrens.

U. S.–CONSTITUTIONAL HISTORY

Faber, Harold & Faber, Doris. We the People: The Story of the United States Constitution since 1787. LC 86-31404. 256p. (gr. 7 up). 1987. 14.95 (ISBN 0-684-18753-1, Scribners Young Read). Macmillan Child Grp.

Maestro, Betsy. A More Perfect Union: The Story of Our Constitution. Maestro, Giulio, illus. LC 87-4083. 48p. (gr. 1-5). 1987. 15.95 (ISBN 0-688-06839-1); PLB 15.88 (ISBN 0-688-06840-5). Lothrop.

Smith, Kathie B. Men of the Constitution. (gr. k-5). 1987. pap. 2.25 (ISBN 0-671-64028-3, Little Simon). S&S Trade.

U. S.–CONSTITUTIONAL LAW

Meltzer, Milton. The Bill of Rights: How We Got It & What It Means. LC 90-1537. 180p. (gr. 7 up). 1990. 14.95 (ISBN 0-690-04805-X, Crowell Jr Bks); PLB 14.89 (ISBN 0-690-04807-6, Crowell Jr Bks). HarpC Child Bks.

Shaver, James R. Understanding the U. S. Constitution. 1986. pap. 3.25 (ISBN 0-87738-023-6). Youth Ed.

U. S. DECLARATION OF INDEPENDENCE

Commager, Henry S. Great Declaration. (Illus.). (gr. 6-10). 1958. 6.95 (ISBN 0-672-50301-8, Bobbs). Macmillan.

Dalgliesh, Alice. Fourth of July Story. Nonnast, Marie, illus. LC 56-6138. 32p. (ps-3). 1972. 13.95 (ISBN 0-684-13164-1, Scribners Young Read); (Scribner). Macmillan Child Grp.

La Declaracion de Independencia: (The Declaration of Independence) LC 88-11870. (ENG & SPA.). 48p. (gr. k-4). 1989. PLB 14.60 (ISBN 0-516-31153-0); pap. 4.95 (ISBN 0-516-51153-X). Childrens.

Fradin, Dennis B. The Declaration of Independence. LC 88-11870. (Illus.). 48p. (gr. k-4). 1988. PLB 14.60 (ISBN 0-516-01153-7); pap. 4.95 (ISBN 0-516-41153-5). Childrens.

Phelan, Mary K. Fourth of July. Shimin, Symeon, illus. LC 65-25909. 40p. (gr. k-3). 1966. PLB 12.89 (ISBN 0-690-31415-9, Crowell Jr Bks). HarpC Child Bks.

Richards, Norman. The Story of the Declaration of Independence. LC 68-24379. (Illus.). 32p. (gr. 2-5). 1968. PLB 13.27 (ISBN 0-516-04606-3); pap. 3.95 (ISBN 0-516-44606-1). Childrens.

U. S. DEPARTMENT OF AGRICULTURE

Hurt, R. Douglas. The Department of Agriculture. Schlesinger, Arthur M., Jr., intro. by. (Illus.). 112p. (gr. 5 up). 1989. lib. bdg. 14.95 (ISBN 0-87754-833-1). Chelsea Hse.

U. S. DEPARTMENT OF COMMERCE

Griffin, Robert J., Jr. The Department of Commerce. (Illus.). (gr. 5 up). 1991. 14.95 (ISBN 0-87754-836-6). Chelsea Hse.

U. S. DEPARTMENT OF DEFENSE

Heinsohn, Beth & Cohen, Andrew. The Department of Defense. (Illus.). (gr. 5 up). 1990. 14.95 (ISBN 0-87754-837-4). Chelsea Hse.

U. S. DEPARTMENT OF HEALTH, EDUCATION, AND WELFARE

Broberg, Merle. Department of Health & Human Services. (Illus.). (gr. 5 up). 1989. lib. bdg. 14.95 (ISBN 0-87754-840-4). Chelsea Hse.

Sneigoski, Stephen J. Department of Education. Schlesinger, Arthur M., Jr., intro. by. (Illus.). (gr. 5 up). 1988. lib. bdg. 14.95 (ISBN 0-87754-838-2). Chelsea Hse.

U. S. DEPARTMENT OF JUSTICE

Dunn, Lynne. The Department of Justice. (Illus.). (gr. 5 up). 1990. 14.95 (ISBN 0-87754-843-9). Chelsea Hse.

U. S. DEPARTMENT OF STATE

Bartz, Carl. The Department of State. Schlesinger, Arthur M., Jr., intro. by. (Illus.). 96p. (gr. 5 up). 1989. lib. bdg. 14.95 (ISBN 0-87754-846-3). Chelsea Hse.

U. S. DEPARTMENT OF THE INTERIOR

Clement, Fred. Department of the Interior. Schlesinger, Arthur M., Jr., intro. by. (Illus.). 112p. (gr. 5 up). 1989. lib. bdg. 14.95 (ISBN 0-87754-842-0). Chelsea Hse.

U. S.–DESCRIPTION AND TRAVEL

Anderson, Joan. Joshua's Westward Journal. Ancona, George, illus. LC 87-5509. 48p. (gr. 2-5). 1987. 13.00 (ISBN 0-688-06680-1, Morrow Junior Books); lib. bdg. 12.88 (ISBN 0-688-06681-X, Morrow Junior Books). Morrow.

Anno, Mitsumasa, illus. Anno's U. S. A. (ps up). 1988. pap. 4.95 (ISBN 0-399-21595-6, Putnam). Putnam Pub Group.

Babbitt, James E., ed. Rainbow Trails: Adventures in Rainbow Bridge Country. Lancaster, John, intro. by. 120p. (Orig.). 1989. pap. 5.95 (ISBN 0-317-93359-0). Glen Canyon Nat Hist Assn.

Carpenter, Allan. Far-Flung America. new ed. LC 79-12505. (Illus.). 96p. (gr. 4 up). 1979. PLB 19.93 (ISBN 0-516-04152-5). Childrens.

Carratello, John & Carratello, Patty. United States Geography. Chellton, Anna, et al, illus. 48p. (gr. 3-6). 1989. wkbk. 5.95 (ISBN 1-55734-160-5). Tchr Create Mat.
Crump, Donald J., ed. Discover America. (Illus.). 336p. 1989. 24.95 (ISBN 0-87044-807-2); deluxe ed. 39.95 (ISBN 0-87044-805-6); lib. bdg. 39.95 incl. flag (ISBN 0-685-28301-1); lib. bdg. 26.95 (ISBN 0-685-28302-X). Natl Geog.
—Great American Journeys. (Illus.). 1989. 7.95 (ISBN 0-87044-669-X); lib. bdg. 9.50 (ISBN 0-87044-674-6). Natl Geog.
Duncan, Patsy G. Know America Activity & Coloring Book. 72p. (gr. 2-6). 1989. 2.95 (ISBN 0-925449-00-8). D&M Pubns.
—Know America Coloring & Activity Book. (Illus.). 64p. (Orig.). (gr. 1-6). 1988. pap. text ed. 2.95 (ISBN 0-685-25274-4). D&M Pubns.
Gantz, David. Let's Visit the United States. Gantz, David, illus. (gr. 1 up). 1989. pap. 4.95 (ISBN 0-671-67212-6). S&S Trade.
Herda, D. J. Environmental America: The Northeastern States. (Illus.). 64p. (gr. 5-8). 1991. PLB 13.90 (ISBN 1-878841-06-8). Millbrook Pr.
Koch, Susan C. Colormore Travels - San Antonio, Texas: The Travel Guide for Kids. Koch, Susan C., illus. 32p. (Orig.). (gr. k-4). 1990. pap. 4.50 (ISBN 0-945600-05-4). Colormore Inc.
Marsh, Carole. U. S. A. Jography: A Fun Run Thru the United States, Vol. II. (Illus.). 60p. (gr. k-12). 1989. PLB 19.95 (ISBN 1-55609-301-2); pap. 14.95 (ISBN 1-55609-300-4); computer disk 29.95 (ISBN 1-55609-302-0). Gallopade Pub Group.
Paltrowitz, Stuart & Paltrowitz, Donna. Content Area Reading Skills U. S. Geography: Cause & Effect. (Illus.). (gr. 4). 1987. pap. text ed. 3.25 (ISBN 0-89525-855-2). Ed Activities.
The Promise of America. (gr. 5-11). 5.95 (ISBN 0-87741-008-9). Makepeace Colony.
Stewart, Frances T. & Stewart, Charles P., III. Geography: The United States of America. Koss, Martin, Jr., illus. 12p. (gr. k up). 1990. pap. 9.95 (ISBN 0-694-00297-6). HarpC Child Bks.
Wright, Sarah B. Islands of the Northeastern United States & Eastern Canada. (Illus.). 224p. (Orig.). 1990. pap. text ed. 9.95 (ISBN 0-934601-99-2). Peachtree Pubs.

U. S.–DESCRIPTION AND TRAVEL–MAPS
see U. S.–Maps

U. S.–DISCOVERY AND EXPLORATION
see America–Discovery and Exploration

U. S.–ECONOMIC CONDITIONS
Bender, David L. & Leone, Bruno, eds. America's Economy Annual, 1989. 144p. (gr. 10 up). 1989. pap. text ed. 5.45 (ISBN 0-89908-550-4). Greenhaven.
Davis, Bertha. Crisis in Industry. (Illus.). 128p. (gr. 10-12). 1990. 12.90 (ISBN 0-531-10659-4). Watts.
O'Toole, Thomas. Economic History of the United States. (Illus.). 88p. (gr. 5 up). 1990. 15.95 (ISBN 0-8225-1776-0). Lerner Pubns.
Stein, R. Conrad. The Story of the Great Depression. Greene, Nathan, illus. LC 85-11039. 31p. (gr. 3-4). 1985. PLB 13.27 (ISBN 0-516-04694-2); pap. 3.95 (ISBN 0-516-44694-0). Childrens.

U. S.–ECONOMIC POLICY
Kronenwetter, Michael. Capitalism vs. Socialism: Economic Policies of the U. S. & the U. S. S. R. LC 85-22579. (Illus.). 103p. (gr. 7-12). 1986. PLB 12.90 (ISBN 0-531-10152-5). Watts.
Lunt, Steven. Free Enterprises in America. LC 85-10484. (Illus.). 104p. (gr. 5-8). 1985. PLB 12.90 (ISBN 0-531-10061-8). Watts.

U. S.–EXECUTIVE POWER
see Executive Power–U. S.

U. S.–EXPLORING EXPEDITIONS
Here are entered works on exploration within the U. S. and for explorations in other countries which are sponsored by the U. S. Works on early exploration in territory which became a part of the U. S. are entered under America–Discovery and Exploration.
see also names of expeditions, e.g. Lewis and Clark expedition

U. S. FEDERAL BUREAU OF INVESTIGATION
Archer, Jules. Superspies: The Secret Side of Government. LC 77-72640. (gr. 7up). 1977. pap. 7.95 (ISBN 0-440-08136-X). Delacorte.
Hargrove, Jim. The Story of the FBI. LC 87-36815. (Illus.). 32p. (gr. 3-6). 1988. PLB 13.27 (ISBN 0-516-04733-7); pap. 3.95 (ISBN 0-516-44733-5). Childrens.
Israel, Fred L. The Federal Bureau of Investigation. Schlesinger, Arthur M., Jr., intro. by. (Illus.). 96p. (gr. 5 up). 1986. lib. bdg. 14.95 (ISBN 0-87754-821-8). Chelsea Hse.
Smith, Carter. A Day in the Life of an FBI Agent-in-Training. Jantzen, Franz, illus. LC 90-11150. 32p. (gr. 4-8). 1991. PLB 11.79 (ISBN 0-8167-2210-2); pap. text ed. 2.95 (ISBN 0-8167-2211-0). Troll Assocs.

U. S.–FICTION
Carrol, Jed L. The Adventures of Buffalo Barney, Vol. 1: A Romp Through the Middle Atlantic States. Gillen, Charles, illus. 96p. (Orig.). (gr. 2-5). 1989. Incl. cass., maps, stickers. pap. 14.95 (ISBN 0-9624301-1-0). Explore Your World Pubns.
Robertson, Keith. Henry Reed's Journey. McCloskey, Robert, illus. LC 63-8522. (gr. 4-6). 1963. pap. 13.95 (ISBN 0-670-36854-7). Viking Child Bks.

U. S.–FOLKLORE
see Folklore–U. S.

U. S. FOOD AND DRUG ADMINISTRATION
Patrick, Bill. The Food & Drug Administration. Schlesinger, Arthur M., Jr., intro. by. (Illus.). 96p. (gr. 5 up). 1989. lib. bdg. 14.95 (ISBN 0-87754-822-6). Chelsea Hse.

U. S.–FOREIGN POLICY
see U. S.–Foreign Relations

U. S.–FOREIGN POPULATION
see also U. S.–Immigration and Emigration; Minorities; U. S.–Immigration and Emigration;
also Italians in the U. S.; and similar headings
Ashabranner, Brent. An Ancient Heritage: The Arab-American Minority. Conklin, Paul, illus. LC 90-30641. 160p. (gr. 3-7). 1991. 14.95 (ISBN 0-06-020048-0); PLB 14.89 (ISBN 0-06-020049-9). HarpC Child Bks.
Avakian, Arra S. The Armenians in America. LC 77-73739. (Illus.). 88p. (gr. 5 up). 1977. PLB 11.95 (ISBN 0-8225-0228-3); pap. 3.95 (ISBN 0-8225-1026-X). Lerner Pubns.
Cantor, David. The Baltic Americans. Moynihan, Daniel P., intro. by. (Illus.). 112p. (gr. 5 up). 1991. 17.95 (ISBN 0-87754-890-0). Chelsea Hse.
Diamond, Arthur. The Romanian Americans. Moynihan, Daniel P., intro. by. (Illus.). 112p. (gr. 5 up). 1988. lib. bdg. 17.95 (ISBN 0-87754-898-6). Chelsea Hse.
Dwyer, Christopher. The Dominican Americans. Moynihan, Daniel P., intro. by. (Illus.). 112p. (gr. 5 up). 1991. lib. bdg. 17.95 (ISBN 0-87754-872-2). Chelsea Hse.
Ford, Doug. The Pacific Islanders. Moynihan, Daniel P. (Illus.). 112p. (gr. 5 up). 1990. 17.95 (ISBN 0-87754-883-8). Chelsea Hse.
Gernand, Renee. The Cuban Americans. Moynihan, Daniel P., intro. by. (Illus.). 112p. (gr. 5 up). 1989. lib. bdg. 17.95 (ISBN 0-87754-869-2). Chelsea Hse.
Hyung-Chan Kim & Patterson, Wayne. The Koreans in America. LC 77-73741. (Illus.). 64p. (gr. 5 up). 1977. PLB 11.95 (ISBN 0-8225-0230-5). Lerner Pubns.
Ifkovic, Edward. The Yugoslavs in America. LC 77-73742. (Illus.). 104p. (gr. 5 up). 1977. PLB 11.95 (ISBN 0-8225-0231-3). Lerner Pubns.
Lehrer, Brian. The Korean Americans. Moynihan, Daniel P., intro. by. (Illus.). 112p. (gr. 5 up). 1988. lib. bdg. 17.95 (ISBN 0-87754-888-9). Chelsea Hse.
Lick, Sue. The Iberian Americans. Moynihan, Daniel P., intro. by. (Illus.). 112p. (gr. 5 up). 1990. 17.95 (ISBN 0-87754-896-X). Chelsea Hse.
MacMillan, Dianne & Freeman, Dorothy. My Best Friend Mee-Yung Kim: Meeting a Korean-American Family. Steltenpohl, Jane, ed. Marstall, Bob, illus. 48p. (gr. 3-5). 1989. lib. bdg. 9.98 (ISBN 0-671-65691-0). Messner.
Mussari, Mark. The Danish Americans. Moynihan, Daniel P., intro. by. (Illus.). 112p. (gr. 5 up). 1988. lib. bdg. 17.95 (ISBN 0-87754-871-4). Chelsea Hse.
Osborn, Kevin. The Ukrainian Americans. Moynihan, Daniel P., intro. by. (Illus.). 112p. (gr. 5 up). 1989. PLB 17.95 (ISBN 1-55546-138-7). Chelsea Hse.
Shapiro, Ellen. The Croatian Americans. Moynihan, Daniel P. 112p. (gr. 5 up). 1989. 17.95x (ISBN 0-87754-891-9). Chelsea Hse.
Stern, Jennifer. The Filipino Americans. Moynihan, Daniel P., intro. by. (Illus.). 112p. (gr. 5 up). 1990. lib. bdg. 17.95 (ISBN 0-87754-877-3). Chelsea Hse.
Stolarik, Mark. The Slovak Americans. Moynihan, Daniel P., intro. by. (Illus.). 112p. (gr. 5 up). 1988. lib. bdg. 17.95 (ISBN 1-55546-134-4). Chelsea Hse.
Vehiller, Nina. The Haitian Americans. Moynihan, Daniel P., intro. by. (Illus.). 112p. (gr. 5 up). 1991. lib. bdg. 17.95 (ISBN 0-87754-882-X). Chelsea Hse.

U. S.–FOREIGN RELATIONS
Arnoldt, Robert P. Insights: A Guide to the American Experience in Vietnam, 1940 to Present. rev. ed. Marx, Jacqueline A. & Carpenter, Robert S., eds. 100p. (Orig.). (gr. 9 up). 1989. pap. text ed. write for info. Visions Unlimited.
Bender, David L. & Leone, Bruno, eds. Foreign Policy Annual, 1989. 144p. (gr. 10 up). 1989. pap. text ed. 5.45 (ISBN 0-89908-547-4). Greenhaven.
—Soviet-American Debate Annual, 1989. 144p. (gr. 10 up). 1989. pap. text ed. 5.45 (ISBN 0-89908-548-2). Greenhaven.
Cooney, James A. Foreign Policy. rev. ed. 160p. (gr. 7 up). 1991. PLB 15.85 (ISBN 0-8027-8116-0); pap. 8.95 (ISBN 0-8027-7368-0). Walker & Co.
Dolan, Edward F. Panama & the United States. 1990. PLB 13.90 (ISBN 0-531-10911-9). Watts.
Fincher, E. B. Mexico & the United States: Their Linked Destinies. LC 82-45581. (Illus.). 224p. (gr. 7 up). 1983. 12.95 (ISBN 0-690-04310-4, Crowell Jr Bks); (Crowell Jr Bks). HarpC Child Bks.
Freeman, Charles. U. S. A. - U. S. S. R. The Superpowers. (Illus.). 72p. (gr. 7-10). 1990. 19.95 (ISBN 0-7134-6077-6, Pub. by Batsford UK). Trafalgar Sq.
Kuhn, Ferdinand. Commodore Perry & the Opening of Japan. (Illus.). (gr. 4-6). 1955. 2.95 (ISBN 0-394-80356-6). Random.
Lawson, Don. The Eagle & the Dragon: The History of U. S.-China Relations. LC 85-47531. (Illus.). 192p. (gr. 7 up). 1985. 12.95 (ISBN 0-690-04485-2, Crowell Jr Bks); (Crowell Jr Bks). HarpC Child Bks.
Pascoe, Elaine. Neighbors At Odds: U. S. Policy in Latin America. 1990. PLB 12.90 (ISBN 0-531-10903-8). Watts.
Salzman, Marian & O'Reilly, Ann. War & Peace in the Persian Gulf: What Teenagers Want to Know. LC 91-2569. 123p. (Orig.). (gr. 8 up). 1991. pap. 5.95 (ISBN 1-56079-135-7). Petersons Guides.
Tessendorf, K. C. Uncle Sam in Nicaragua: A History. LC 86-17340. 144p. (gr. 7 up). 1987. 13.95 (ISBN 0-689-31286-5, Atheneum Child Bk). Macmillan Child Grp.
Weiss, Ann E. Good Neighbors: The United States & Latin America. (gr. 7 up). 1985. 12.95 (ISBN 0-395-36316-0). HM.

U. S.–FURNITURE
see Furniture, American

U. S.–GOVERNMENT
see U. S.–Politics and Government

U. S.–HISTORIC HOUSES, ETC.
Richards, Norman. The Story of Monticello. Mitchell, Chuck, illus. LC 70-100699. 32p. (gr. 4-8). 1970. PLB 13.27 (ISBN 0-516-04627-6). Childrens.

U. S.–HISTORY
Abramowitz, Jack. Readings in American History, Bk. 2. (gr. 4-5). 1987. pap. text ed. 5.25 (ISBN 0-89525-862-5). Ed Activities.
Adams, James T. Album of American History, 3 vols. rev. ed. LC 74-91746. (gr. 5 up). 1981. Set. 290.00 (ISBN 0-684-16848-0, Scribner). Macmillan.
American Heritage Illustrated History of the United States, Vol. 1: The New World. LC 87-73399. (Illus.). 128p. (gr. 7-12). 1988. Repr. of 1963 ed. 3.49 (ISBN 0-945260-01-6). Choice Pub NY.
American Heritage Illustrated History of the United States, 18 vols. LC 87-73397. (gr. 7-12). 1988. Repr. of 1963 ed. Set. 63.00 (ISBN 0-945260-00-8). Choice Pub NY.
American Heritage: Illustrated History of the United States, 19 vols. rev. ed. 2432p. (gr. 6 up). 1990. Set. PLB 399.00 (ISBN 0-382-09878-1); Set. PLB 299.00s.p. (ISBN 0-685-37322-3). Silver Burdett Pr.
The American Way West. (Illus.). 128p. 1990. 17.95x (ISBN 0-8160-1880-4). Facts on File.
Arnold, Pauline & White, Percival. How We Named Our States. LC 65-24208. (Illus.). 192p. (gr. 5-9). 1965. 13.95 (ISBN 0-200-71911-4, 339010, Crowell Jr Bks). HarpC Child Bks.
Batherman, Muriel. Before Columbus. Batherman, Muriel, illus. 32p. (gr. k-3). 1990. pap. 4.95 (ISBN 0-395-54954-X). HM.
Boorstin, Daniel J. & Boorstin, Ruth F. The Landmark History of the American People. rev. ed. LC 87-9603. (Illus.). 448p. (gr. 4-9). 1987. Vol. 1: From Plymouth to Appomattox. lib. bdg. 11.99 (ISBN 0-394-99118-4, Random Juv); Vol. 2: From Appomattox to the Moon. lib. bdg. 11.99 (ISBN 0-394-99119-2); Set. pap. 16.95 slipcased (ISBN 0-394-89120-1). Random.
Bouvier, Leon F. Immigration. rev. ed. 160p. (gr. 7 up). 1991. PLB 15.85 (ISBN 0-8027-8115-2); pap. 8.95 (ISBN 0-8027-7367-2). Walker & Co.
Brownstone, David & Franck, Irene. Historic Places of Early America. (Illus.). 64p. (gr. 3-7). 1989. pap. 7.95 (ISBN 0-689-71234-0, Aladdin). Macmillan Child Grp.
Brownstone, David M. & Franck, Irene M. Historic Places of Early America. LC 88-27521. (Illus.). 64p. (gr. 3-7). 1989. 14.95 (ISBN 0-689-31439-6, Atheneum Child Bk). Macmillan Child Grp.
Burda, Margaret. Amazing States. Sodac, David, illus. 160p. (gr. 4-8). 1984. wkbk. 11.95 (ISBN 0-86653-205-6, GA 546). Good Apple.
Campling, Elizabeth. The Postwar World: The USA since 1945. (Illus.). 64p. (gr. 7-9). 1988. 19.95 (ISBN 0-7134-5756-2, Pub. by Batsford England). Trafalgar Sq.
Cobblestone Publishing, Inc. Staff. U. S. History Cartoons: For Young People 8-14. (Illus.). 36p. (gr. 4-8). 1987. pap. text ed. 4.95 (ISBN 0-942389-02-6). Cobblestone Pub.
—U. S. History Word Finds: For Young People 8-14. (Illus.). 36p. (gr. 4-8). 1987. pap. 4.95 (ISBN 0-9607638-9-9). Cobblestone Pub.
Faber, Doris & Faber, Harold. The Birth of a Nation: The Early Years of the United States. LC 88-30805. (Illus.). 208p. (gr. 7 up). 1989. 13.95 (ISBN 0-684-19007-9, Scribners Young Read). Macmillan Child Grp.
Fast, Suellen M. America's Daughters. Fast, Suellen M., photos by. 100p. (Orig.). (gr. k up). pap. 19.00 (ISBN 0-935281-13-4). Daughter Cult.
Fisher, Trevor. Portrait of a Decade: The Nineteen Sixties. (Illus.). 72p. (gr. 7-9). 1988. 19.95 (ISBN 0-7134-5603-5, Pub. by Batsford England). Trafalgar Sq.
Greenberg, Morrie. American Adventures: True Stories from America's Past, 1770-1870. Long, Laurel, illus. 95p. (Orig.). (gr. 4-9). 1991. pap. text ed. 9.95 (ISBN 0-9622652-1-7). Brooke-Richards.
Greene, A. C. The Last Captive. (Illus.). 185p. (gr. 6-9). 1972. 20.00 (ISBN 0-88426-004-6). Encino Pr.
Greene, Jacqueline D. Out of Many Waters. (gr. 5 up). 1988. 16.95 (ISBN 0-8027-6811-3). Walker & Co.
Kallen, Stuart. A Modern Nation. Walner, Rosemary, ed. (Illus.). 32p. (gr. 4). 1990. PLB 12.95 (ISBN 0-939179-91-1). Abdo & Dghtrs.
—A Nation Divided Eighteen Fifty to Nineteen Hundred. Walner, Rosemary, ed. (Illus.). 64p. (gr. 4). 1990. PLB 12.95 (ISBN 0-939179-90-3). Abdo & Dghtrs.
—A Nation United 1780-1850. Walner, Rosemary, ed. (Illus.). 64p. (gr. 4). 1990. lib. bdg. 12.95 (ISBN 0-939179-89-X). Abdo & Dghtrs.

—New Comers to America, Fourteen Hundred to Sixteen Fifty. Walner, Rosemary, ed. (Illus.). 64p. (gr. 4). 1990. PLB 12.95 (ISBN 0-939179-86-5). Abdo & Dghtrs.
—Road to Freedom, Seventeen Fifty to Seventeen Eighty-Three. Walner, Rosemary, ed. (Illus.). 64p. (gr. 4). 1990. PLB 12.95 (ISBN 0-939179-88-1). Abdo & Dghtrs.
Killingray, David. The American Frontier. Yapp, Malcolm, et al, eds. (Illus.). 32p. (gr. 6-11). 1980. pap. text ed. 2.95 (ISBN 0-89908-206-8). Greenhaven.
Kranich, Roger E. & Corcoran, Eileen L. Our United States. (Illus.). 256p. (gr. 4-5). 1989. Incl. tchr's. key, 314. pap. text ed. 7.95 (ISBN 0-88323-247-2, 311). Pendergrass Pub.
Kruger, Herbert O., et al. American History Study Aid. 1975. pap. 1.95 (ISBN 0-87738-043-0). Youth Ed.
Kyle, Louisa V. The Witch of Pungo. Dool, Jan, illus. 87p. (gr. 3). 1973. 12.95 (ISBN 0-927044-00-5). Four Oclock Farms.
Napp, John L. United States History, Bk. I: To 1877. (Illus.). 344p. (gr. 7-12). 1988. text ed. 18.49 (ISBN 0-86601-692-9); tchr's. ed. 11.99 (ISBN 0-86601-693-7); wkbk. 4.99 (ISBN 0-86601-694-5). Media Materials.
Paltrowitz, Stuart & Paltrowitz, Donna. Content Area Reading Skills-Competency U. S. History: Detecting Sequence. (Illus.). (gr. 4). 1987. pap. text ed. 3.25 (ISBN 0-89525-856-0). Ed Activities.
Roberts, Paul M. Review Text in United States History. 2nd ed. (gr. 7-9). 1989. pap. text ed. 13.33 (ISBN 0-87720-857-3). AMSCO Sch.
Ross, Wilma S. Fabulous Facts about the Fifty States. rev. ed. Cummings, Bill, illus. 224p. (gr. 2-5). 1986. pap. 2.50 (ISBN 0-590-33958-3). Scholastic Inc.
Smock, Raymond W., et al. The American History Slide Collection. 265p. (Orig.). (gr. 7 up). 1977. incl. 2100 slides 895.00 (ISBN 0-923805-06-0). Instruc Resc MD.
—Master Guide to the American History Slide Collection. 265p. (gr. 7 up). 1977. pap. text ed. 25.00 (ISBN 0-923805-00-1). Instruc Resc MD.
Weitzman, David. My Backyard History Book. Robertson, James, illus. 128p. (gr. 4 up). 1975. 14.95 (ISBN 0-316-92901-8); pap. 8.95 (ISBN 0-316-92902-6). Little.

U. S.–HISTORY–CHRONOLOGY

see Chronology, Historical

U. S.–HISTORY–DRAMA

The Big Four: Mini-Play. (gr. 5 up). 1978. 6.50 (ISBN 0-89550-324-7). Stevens & Shea.
The Flint Sit-Down Strike: Mini-Play. (gr. 5 up). 1978. 6.50 (ISBN 0-89550-320-4). Stevens & Shea.
The Haymarket Affair: Mini-Play. (gr. 5 up). 1978. 6.50 (ISBN 0-89550-323-9). Stevens & Shea.

U. S.–HISTORY, ECONOMIC

see U. S.–Economic Conditions

U. S.–HISTORY–FICTION

Arntson, Herbert E. Caravan to Oregon. LC 57-13207. (Illus.). (gr. 7-11). 1957. 8.95 (ISBN 0-8323-0164-7). Binford Mort.
Carter, Russell G. A Patriot Lad of Old Cape Cod. Pitz, Henry & Sousa, Joseph, illus. LC 75-5092. 224p. (gr. 6-8). 1975. 4.95 (ISBN 0-88492-007-0); pap. 1.95 (ISBN 0-88492-008-9). W S Sullwold.
Collier, James L. & Collier, Christopher. Who Is Carrie? LC 83-23947. 192p. (gr. 4-6). 1984. 14.95 (ISBN 0-385-29295-3). Delacorte.
Johnson, Mabel. Escape from Scrooby. (gr. 7 up). 1975. pap. 4.50 (ISBN 0-9600838-2-0). M Johnson.
Langton, Jane. The Fragile Flag. Blegvaad, Erik, illus. LC 83-49471. 224p. (gr. 3-7). 1984. 12.95 (ISBN 0-06-023698-1); PLB 12.89 (ISBN 0-06-023699-X). HarpC Child Bks.
Longmeyer, Carole M. The Lost Colony Storybook. Rhodes, Priscilla, illus. (gr. 4 up). 1983. pap. 14.95 (ISBN 0-935326-38-3). Gallopade Pub Group.
Ormondroyd, Edward. Castaways on Long Ago. 1983. pap. 2.25 (ISBN 0-553-15457-5). Bantam.
O'Sullivan, Anna-Margaret. The Green Bank Year. LC 88-62114. 255p. 1989. pap. 6.95 (ISBN 1-55523-183-7). Winston-Derek.
Pagnucci, Franco & Pagnucci, Susan. Paul Revere & Other Story Hours. (Illus.). 72p. (Orig.). (gr. k-6). 1988. pap. 7.95 (ISBN 0-929326-00-8). Bur Oak Pr Inc.
Spicer-Zerner, Jessie & Brooks, Andrea, illus. One Hundred Years Ago. 96p. 1983. boxed set 7.95 (ISBN 0-448-81691-1, G&D). Putnam Pub Group.
Tripp, Valerie. Molly's Boxed Set, 6 bks. (Illus.). 432p. (gr. 2-5). 1990. Boxed set. pap. 34.95 (ISBN 0-937295-78-7). Pleasant Co.

U. S.–HISTORY, NAVAL

David Farragut. (Illus.). 32p. (gr. 3-6). 1988. PLB 16.67 (ISBN 0-8172-2904-3). Raintree Pubs.
Sweetman, Jack. American Naval History: An Illustrated Chronology of the U. S. Navy & Marine Corps, 1775-Prese t. 2nd ed. (Illus.). 384p. (gr. 7-12). 1991. 36.95 (ISBN 1-55750-785-6). Naval Inst Pr.

U. S.–HISTORY, POLITICAL

see U. S.–Politics and Government

U. S.–HISTORY–SOURCES

Steck-Vaughn Company Staff. Voices from America's Past. LC 90-44955. (Illus.). 128p. (gr. 5-8). 1990. PLB 18.60 (ISBN 0-8114-2770-6). Steck-V.

U. S.–HISTORY–COLONIAL PERIOD

see also Pilgrim Fathers; U. S.–History–French and Indian War, 1755-1763

Alderman, Clifford L. Story of the Thirteen Colonies. Fisher, L. E., illus. (gr. 5-9). 1966. lib. bdg. 9.99 (ISBN 0-394-90415-X, Random Juv). Random.
American Heritage Illustrated History of the United States, Vol. 2: Colonial America. LC 87-73399. (Illus.). 128p. (gr. 7-12). 1988. Repr. of 1963 ed. 3.49 (ISBN 0-945260-02-4). Choice Pub NY.
Carter, Alden R. The American Revolution: Colonies in Revolt. Kline, M., ed. (Illus.). 96p. (gr. 6 up). 1988. PLB 10.40 (ISBN 0-531-10576-8). Watts.
Colonial American Merchant. (Illus.). (gr. 3-8). lib. bdg. 14.00 (ISBN 0-86592-139-3). Rourke Corp.
Fisher, Margaret & Fowler, Mary J., eds. Colonial America: English Colonies. rev. ed. LC 87-81353. (Illus.). 128p. (gr. 4 up). 1988. 1-4 copies 14.95 ea. (ISBN 0-934291-23-3); 5 or more copies 11.95 (ISBN 0-317-91141-4). Gateway Pr MI.
Fradin, Dennis B. The Thirteen Colonies. LC 88-11827. (Illus.). 48p. (gr. k-4). 1988. PLB 14.60 (ISBN 0-516-01157-X); pap. 4.95 (ISBN 0-516-41157-8). Childrens.
Henrich, Stephen & Henrich, Jean. Story Starters on Colonial-Revolutionary America. rev. ed. (Illus.). 80p. (gr. 4-12). 1988. write for info. wkbk. (HE 200). Henrich Enter.
Johnston, Lucile. Celebrations of a Nation: Early American Holidays. 3rd ed. (Illus.). 174p. (gr. 8-12). 1989. 10.95 (ISBN 0-9620343-0-4); pap. 6.95 (ISBN 0-9620343-1-2). Johnston Bicent Found.
Kallen, Stuart. Life in the Thirteen Colonies 1650-1750. Walner, Rosemary, ed. (Illus.). 64p. (gr. 4). 1990. PLB 12.95 (ISBN 0-939179-87-3). Abdo & Dghtrs.

Kalman, Bobbie. A Colonial Town. 1991. 14.95 (ISBN 0-86505-489-4); pap. 7.95 (ISBN 0-86505-509-2). Crabtree Pub Co.
In A COLONIAL TOWN young readers are introduced to a historic community. They will take a journey into history to a time when people grew their own food & made their own tools. They will travel down the wide cobblestone streets of Williamsburg & enjoy the slow, peaceful pace of the restored city. They will admire the grand estates of long ago & tour the special buildings of Virginia's old capitol. They will find out about the Palace in which the governor lived, the Capitol where laws were made, the Powder Magazine where weapons were kept, & the Gaol where prisoners waited for their punishment. They will meet the apothecary & learn about some of his questionable "cures" & find out how a post mill grinds grain.
Publisher Provided Annotation.

Longmeyer, Carole M. The Lost Colony Activity Book. Rhodes, Priscilla, illus. (Orig.). (gr. 3 up). 1983. pap. 14.95 (ISBN 0-935326-41-3). Gallopade Pub Group.
McGovern, Ann. If You Lived in Colonial Times. (Illus.). (gr. k-3). 1985. pap. 2.95 (ISBN 0-590-41948-X). Scholastic Inc.
Madison, Arnold. How the Colonists Lived. (gr. 7 up). 1980. 8.95 (ISBN 0-679-20685-X). McKay.
Perl, Lila. Slumps, Grunts, & Snickerdoodles: What Colonial America Ate & Why. Cuffari, Richard, illus. LC 75-4894. 128p. (gr. 6 up). 1979. 13.95 (ISBN 0-395-28923-8, Clarion). HM.
Richards, Norman. The Story of the Mayflower Compact. Wiskur, Darrell, illus. LC 67-22901. 32p. (gr. 2-5). 1967. PLB 13.27 (ISBN 0-516-04625-X); pap. 3.95 (ISBN 0-516-44625-8). Childrens.
Riley, Edward M. Starting America: The Story of Independence Hall. rev. ed. (Illus.). 64p. 1990. pap. text ed. 4.95 (ISBN 0-939631-23-7). Thomas Publications.
Scott, John A. Settlers on the Eastern Shore: 1607-1750. (Illus.). 160p. 1990. 16.95x (ISBN 0-8160-2327-1). Facts on File.
Smith, Carter, ed. Arts & Sciences: A Sourcebook on Colonial America. (Illus.). 96p. (gr. 5 up). 1991. PLB 14.90 (ISBN 1-56294-037-6); pap. write for info. (ISBN 1-878841-67-X). Millbrook Pr.
—Battles in a New Land: A Sourcebook on Colonial America. (Illus.). 96p. (gr. 5 up). 1991. PLB 14.90 (ISBN 1-56294-034-1); pap. write for info. (ISBN 1-878841-65-3). Millbrook Pr.
—Daily Life: A Sourcebook on Colonial America. (Illus.). 96p. (gr. 5 up). 1991. PLB 14.90 (ISBN 1-56294-038-4); pap. write for info. (ISBN 1-878841-68-8). Millbrook Pr.
—Governing & Teaching: A Sourcebook on Colonial America. (Illus.). 96p. (gr. 5 up). 1991. PLB 14.90 (ISBN 1-56294-036-8); pap. write for info. (ISBN 1-878841-66-1). Millbrook Pr.
Speare, Elizabeth G. The Witch of Blackbird Pond. 256p. (gr. k-6). 1972. pap. 3.50 (ISBN 0-440-49596-2, YB). Dell.
Tames, Richard. Planters, Pilgrims & Puritans. 64p. (gr. 6-8). 1987. 19.95 (ISBN 0-7134-5477-6, Pub. by Batsford England). Trafalgar Sq.
Tunis, Edwin. Colonial Living. Tunis, Edwin, illus. LC 75-29611. 160p. (gr. 7 up). 1976. 24.95 (ISBN 0-690-01063-X, Crowell Jr Bks). HarpC Child Bks.
—The Tavern at the Ferry. Tunis, Edwin, illus. LC 73-4488. 128p. (gr. 5 up). 1973. 24.95 (ISBN 0-690-00099-5, Crowell Jr Bks). HarpC Child Bks.
Warren, Betsy. The Thirteen Colonies: A History Picture Book. (Illus.). 32p. (Orig.). (gr. 3 up). pap. 3.50 (ISBN 0-9618660-3-9). Ranch Gate Bks.

U. S.–HISTORY–COLONIAL PERIOD–FICTION

Blackburn, Joyce. The Bloody Summer of Seventeen Forty-Two: A Colonial Boy's Journal. Graham, Critt, illus. 64p. (gr. 5-8). 1985. pap. 4.25 (ISBN 0-930803-00-0). Fort Frederica.
This book vividly details an account of a child's life in colonial Georgia. The journal recounts the life of a young Scottish boy named Johnny "Little Jack" McLeod in the weeks surrounding the decisive battle for English/Spanish control over Georgia. Johnny lived in Frederica Town, the fortified settlement & southern military headquarters for British North America. The British victory at Bloody Marsh on St. Simons Island ended Spain's claims to Georgian lands. Frederica Town is brought to life through vibrant accounts of the boy's observations of the soldiers, craftsmen & families living in this bustling 18th century military town. This journal sparks a child's imagination & appreciation of Georgia's rich heritage. The 63 page bound paperback book is written to a mid-elementary grade reader level. It is handsomely illustrated by Critt Graham. Author Joyce Blackburn is a noted biographer of James Oglethorpe, Georgia's founder, & other prize winning historical novels for young readers. The book retails for $4.25, plus shipping & handling & is available from the Fort Frederica Association, Rt. #9, Box 286-C, St. Simons Island, GA 31522. (912) 638-3639. A 40% discount is available to booksellers. Library or educator discounts are also available.
Publisher Provided Annotation.

Butters, Dorothy G. The Bells of Freedom. Wilde, Carol, illus. (gr. 4-8). 1984. 15.50 (ISBN 0-8446-6162-7). Peter Smith.
Dillon, Eilis. The Seekers. LC 85-43347. 144p. (gr. 5-9). 1986. 12.95 (ISBN 0-684-18595-4, Scribners Young Read). Macmillan Child Grp.
Knight, James E. Blue Feather's Vision, the Dawn of Colonial America. Guzzi, George, illus. LC 81-23082. 32p. (gr. 5-9). 1982. PLB 10.79 (ISBN 0-89375-722-5); pap. text ed. 2.95 (ISBN 0-89375-723-3). Troll Assocs.
—Journey to Monticello, Traveling in Colonial Times. Guzzi, George, illus. LC 81-23156. 32p. (gr. 5-9). 1982. PLB 10.79 (ISBN 0-89375-736-5); pap. text ed. 2.95 (ISBN 0-89375-737-3). Troll Assocs.
—Sailing to America, Colonists at Sea. Guzzi, George, illus. LC 81-23161. 32p. (gr. 5-9). 1982. PLB 10.79 (ISBN 0-89375-726-8); pap. text ed. 2.95 (ISBN 0-89375-727-6). Troll Assocs.
—Salem Days, Life in a Colonial Seaport. Wenzel, David, illus. LC 81-23076. 32p. (gr. 5-9). 1982. PLB 10.79 (ISBN 0-89375-732-2); pap. text ed. 2.95 (ISBN 0-89375-733-0). Troll Assocs.
—The Village, Life in Colonial Times. Palmer, Jan, illus. LC 81-23084. 32p. (gr. 5-9). 1982. PLB 10.79 (ISBN 0-89375-728-4); pap. text ed. 2.95 (ISBN 0-89375-729-2); cassette avail. Troll Assocs.
—The Winter at Valley Forge, Survival & Victory. Guzzi, George, illus. LC 81-23151. 32p. (gr. 5-9). 1982. PLB 10.79 (ISBN 0-89375-738-1); pap. text ed. 2.95 (ISBN 0-89375-739-X). Troll Assocs.
Richter, Conrad. Light in the Forest. (gr. 5-12). 1990. pap. 3.50 (ISBN 0-553-26878-3). Bantam.

Speare, Elizabeth G. The Witch of Blackbird Pond. large type ed. 280p. 1989. Repr. of 1958 ed. PLB 15.95 (ISBN 1-55736-138-X, Crnrstn Bks). ABC-CLIO.

U. S.–HISTORY–FRENCH AND INDIAN WAR, 1755-1763

Marrin, Albert. Struggle for a Continent: The French & Indian Wars, 1690-1760. LC 86-26508. (Illus.). 232p. (gr. 5 up). 1987. 14.95 (ISBN 0-689-31313-6, Atheneum Child Bk). Macmillan Child Grp.

Meltzer, Milton. The American Revolutionaries: A History in Their Own Words. LC 86-47846. (Illus.). 256p. (gr. 7 up). 1987. 13.95 (ISBN 0-690-04641-3, Crowell Jr Bks); PLB 13.89 (ISBN 0-690-04643-X, Crowell Jr Bks). HarpC Child Bks.

Morris, Richard B. The Indian Wars. rev. ed. Fisher, Leonard E., illus. 86p. (gr. 5-10). 1985. PLB 9.95 (ISBN 0-8225-1703-5). Lerner Pubns.

U. S.–HISTORY–FRENCH AND INDIAN WAR, 1755-1763–FICTION

Cooper, James Fenimore. Last of the Mohicans. (gr. 6 up). 1964. pap. 3.50 (ISBN 0-8049-0005-1, CL-5). Airmont.

The Last of the Mohicans. (Illus.). (gr. 3-5). 3.50. Ladybird Bks.

Mott, Michael. Master Entrick. (gr. 3-6). 1986. pap. 2.95 (ISBN 0-440-45818-8, YB). Dell.

Speare, Elizabeth G. Calico Captive. Mars, Witold T., illus. 288p. (gr. 7-9). 1957. 13.95 (ISBN 0-395-07112-7). HM.

U. S.–HISTORY–REVOLUTION

American Heritage Illustrated History of the United States, Vol. 3: The Revolution. LC 87-73399. (Illus.). 128p. (gr. 7-12). 1988. Repr. of 1963 ed. 3.49 (ISBN 0-945260-03-2). Choice Pub NY.

Bliven, Bruce, Jr. The American Revolution. LC 80-20813. (Illus.). 160p. (gr. 5-9). 1987. PLB 7.99 (ISBN 0-685-04220-0, Random Juv); pap. 2.95 (ISBN 0-685-04221-9). Random.

—American Revolution. (Illus.). (gr. 4-6). 1963. 2.95 (ISBN 0-394-80383-3, Random Juv); lib. bdg. 8.99 (ISBN 0-394-90383-8). Random.

Carter, Alden R. The American Revolution: At the Forge of Liberty. (Illus.). 96p. (gr. 6 up). 1988. PLB 10.40 (ISBN 0-531-10569-5). Watts.

—The American Revolution: The Darkest Hours. Kline, M., ed. (Illus.). 96p. (gr. 6 up). 1988. PLB 10.40 (ISBN 0-531-10578-4). Watts.

Collier, James L. & Collier, Christopher. My Brother Sam Is Dead. 240p. (gr. 7 up). 1985. pap. 2.50 (ISBN 0-590-33694-0, Point). Scholastic Inc.

Constitution of the United States. 1987. pap. 5.00 (ISBN 0-930061-20-9). Interspace Bks.
"I saw them go into the tavern for coffee & cold tea. Above the cobbled streets & shop signs, stars shone brightly. The fragrance of primroses, yellow & red as the finest watered silk, scented the air, 'I have sometimes almost wished,' Dr. Franklin was speaking, 'it had been my destiny to be born two or three centuries hence.' 'You think the country is that great?' Mr. Madison, the quiet one, my master spoke up..." Also: Child of the Lily Bed by a seven year old for seven year olds. ..$5.00. For High Schoolers & Beyond: The Miracle of Believing--How career goals & Dreams can come true with confidence & planning. $9.95. Historical Novels: LaFayette & Harriet...How a lad who couldn't dance with the Queen helped to save America; Glory of Wooden Walls...of Sir Francis Drake & Queen Elizabeth's England, the son of the Royal Clockmaker who went to sea. $14.95 each. Interspace Books, 4500 Chesapeake St., N.W., Washington, D.C. 20016.
Publisher Provided Annotation.

Davis, Burke. Black Heroes of the American Revolution. (gr. 4-7). 1991. pap. 4.95 (ISBN 0-15-208561-0, HJ). HarBraceJ.

De Pauw, Linda G. Founding Mothers: Women of America in the Revolutionary Era. (Illus.). 228p. (gr. 7 up). 1975. 13.95 (ISBN 0-395-21896-9). HM.

Evans, R. E. The War of American Independence. (Illus.). 48p. (gr. 7 up). 1976. pap. 5.95 (ISBN 0-521-20903-X). Cambridge U Pr.

Fritz, Jean. Can't You Make Them Behave, King George? De Paolo, Tomie, illus. 48p. (gr. 3-6). 1982. 9.95 (ISBN 0-698-20315-1, Coward); pap. 5.95 (ISBN 0-698-20542-1). Putnam Pub Group.

—What's the Big Idea, Ben Franklin? (Illus.). 48p. (gr. 2-6). 1982. 9.95 (ISBN 0-698-20365-8, Coward); pap. 5.95 (ISBN 0-698-20543-X, Coward). Putnam Pub Group.

Garrison, Webb. Great Stories of the American Revolution. LC 90-33127. (Illus.). 256p. (gr. 8 up). 1990. 16.95 (ISBN 1-55853-072-X). Rutledge Hill Pr.

Hartley, Al. Yankee Doodle Rides Again. Hartley, Al, illus. LC 88-27171. 48p. 1989. 9.95 (ISBN 0-88070-293-1). Multnomah.

Marrin, Albert. The War for Independence: The Story of the American Revolution. LC 87-13711. (Illus.). 288p. (gr. 5 up). 1988. 14.95 (ISBN 0-689-31390-X, Atheneum Child Bk). Macmillan Child Grp.

Meltzer, Milton. The American Revolutionaries: A History in Their Own Words. LC 86-47846. (Illus.). 256p. (gr. 7 up). 1987. 13.95 (ISBN 0-690-04641-3, Crowell Jr Bks); PLB 13.89 (ISBN 0-690-04643-X, Crowell Jr Bks). HarpC Child Bks.

Merrill, Arthur A. Revolutionary War: An Outline & Calendar. (Illus.). (gr. 7 up). 1976. pap. 2.00 (ISBN 0-911894-35-7). Analysis.

Morris, Richard B. The American Revolution. rev. ed. Fisher, Leonard E., illus. LC 85-12878. 72p. (gr. 5-10). 1985. PLB 9.95 (ISBN 0-8225-1701-9). Lerner Pubns.

Richards, Dorothy F. George Washington, a Talk with His Grandchildren. Nelson, John, illus. LC 78-8564. (gr. k-4). 1978. PLB 10.95 (ISBN 0-89565-034-7). Childs World.

Richards, Norman. The Story of Monticello. Mitchell, Chuck, illus. LC 70-100699. 32p. (gr. 4-8). 1970. PLB 13.27 (ISBN 0-516-04627-6). Childrens.

Sabin, Francene. American Revolution. Baxter, Robert, illus. LC 84-2582. 32p. (gr. 3-6). 1985. PLB 9.49 (ISBN 0-8167-0136-9); pap. text ed. 2.95 (ISBN 0-8167-0137-7). Troll Assocs.

Smith, Carter, ed. The Revolutionary War: A Sourcebook on Colonial America. (Illus.). 96p. (gr. 5 up). 1991. PLB 14.90 (ISBN 1-56294-039-2); pap. write for info. (ISBN 1-878841-69-6). Millbrook Pr.

U. S.–HISTORY–REVOLUTION–BIOGRAPHY

Clinton, Susan. The Story of the Green Mountain Boys. LC 87-17380. (Illus.). 32p. (gr. 3-6). 1987. PLB 13.27 (ISBN 0-516-04731-0); pap. 3.95 (ISBN 0-516-44731-9). Childrens.

Davis, Burke. Black Heroes of the American Revolution. LC 75-42218. (Illus.). 96p. (gr. 5 up). 1976. 14.95 (ISBN 0-15-208560-2, HJ). HarBraceJ.

Gleiter, Jan & Thompson, Kathleen. Molly Pitcher. Shaw, Charles, illus. 32p. (gr. 2-5). 1987. PLB 16.67 (ISBN 0-8172-2652-4); pap. 9.27 (ISBN 0-8172-2656-7). Raintree Pubs.

McGovern, Ann. The Secret Soldier: The Story of Deborah Sampson. 64p. (Orig.). (gr. 3-7). 1990. pap. 2.50 (ISBN 0-590-43052-1). Scholastic Inc.

Shelley, Mary V. Dr. Ed: The Story of General Edward Hand. Weatherlow, Regina, illus. LC 78-10331. 36p. (gr. 4-7). 1978. 5.75 (ISBN 0-915010-24-0). Sutter House.

Stevenson, Augusta. Molly Pitcher: Young Patriot. Garriott, Gene, illus. LC 86-10744. 192p. (gr. 2-6). 1986. pap. 3.95 (ISBN 0-02-042040-4, Aladdin). Macmillan Child Grp.

U. S.–HISTORY–REVOLUTION–CAMPAIGNS AND BATTLES

McPhillips, Martin. The Battle of Trenton. LC 84-40382. (Illus.). 64p. (gr. 5 up). 1989. PLB 16.98 (ISBN 0-382-06823-8); pap. 7.95 (ISBN 0-382-09900-1). Silver Burdett Pr.

Merrill, Arthur A. Battle of White Plains. (Illus.). (gr. 7 up). 1976. pap. 3.00 (ISBN 0-911894-27-6). Analysis.

Phelan, Mary K. The Story of the Boston Massacre. Eitzen, Allan, illus. LC 75-25961. 160p. (gr. 5-9). 1976. 13.95 (ISBN 0-690-00716-7, Crowell Jr Bks). HarpC Child Bks.

The Revolutionary War Soldier at Saratoga. 48p. (gr. 5-6). 1989. PLB 10.95 (ISBN 0-685-26357-6). Capstone Pr.

Stein, R. Conrad. The Story of Lexington & Concord. LC 82-23518. (Illus.). 32p. (gr. 3-6). 1983. PLB 13.27 (ISBN 0-516-04661-6); pap. 3.95 (ISBN 0-516-44661-4). Childrens.

—The Story of Valley Forge. Eads, Nancy, illus. LC 84-23203. 31p. (gr. 3-5). 1985. lib. bdg. 13.27 (ISBN 0-516-04681-0); pap. 3.95 (ISBN 0-516-44681-9). Childrens.

U. S.–HISTORY–REVOLUTION–DRAMA

Lonergan, Carroll V. Brave Boys of Old Fort Ticonderoga. LC 87-22144. (gr. 6 up). 1987. write for info., 192 p. (ISBN 0-932334-57-1, Empire State Bks); pap. 7.95, 144 p. (ISBN 1-55787-018-7, NY16028, Empire State Bks). Heart of the Lakes.

U. S.–HISTORY–REVOLUTION–FICTION

Benchley, Nathaniel. George the Drummer Boy. Bolognese, Don, illus. LC 76-18398. 64p. (gr. k-3). 1977. 11.95 (ISBN 0-06-020500-8); PLB 11.89 (ISBN 0-06-020501-6). HarpC Child Bks.

—Sam the Minuteman. Lobel, Arnold, illus. LC 68-10211. 64p. (gr. k-3). 1969. 11.95 (ISBN 0-06-020479-6); PLB 11.89 (ISBN 0-06-020480-X). HarpC Child Bks.

Brown, Drollene. Sybil Rides for Independence. Levine, Abby, ed. Apple, Margot, illus. 48p. (gr. 2-5). 1985. 10.50 (ISBN 0-8075-7684-0). A Whitman.

Clyne, Patricia E. The Corduroy Road. Cary, illus. (gr. 5-9). 1984. 15.25 (ISBN 0-8446-6163-5). Peter Smith.

Collier, James L. & Collier, Christopher. The Bloody Country. LC 84-28737. 192p. (gr. 7 up). 1984. 13.95 (ISBN 0-02-722960-2, Four Winds). Macmillan Child Grp.

—The Bloody Country. 180p. (gr. 9 up). 1985. pap. 2.75 (ISBN 0-590-43126-9). Scholastic Inc.

—My Brother Sam Is Dead. LC 84-28787. 224p. (gr. 7 up). 1984. 14.95 (ISBN 0-02-722980-7, Four Winds). Macmillan Child Grp.

—My Brother Sam Is Dead. 182p. (gr. 7 up). 1977. pap. 2.50 (ISBN 0-590-40737-6, Point); tchr's. guide 1.25 (ISBN 0-590-40666-3). Scholastic Inc.

—My Brother Sam Is Dead. 182p. (gr. 9 up). 1985. pap. 2.95 (ISBN 0-590-42792-X). Scholastic Inc.

Cover, Arthur B. American Revolutionary. Martishuis, Walter & Nino, Alex, illus. 144p. (gr. 7-12). 1985. pap. 2.50 (ISBN 0-553-26773-6). Bantam.

Forbes, Esther. Johnny Tremain. Ward, Lynd, illus. 272p. (gr. k-6). 1969. pap. 3.50 (ISBN 0-440-94250-0, YB). Dell.

—Johnny Tremain. Ward, Lynd, illus. (gr. 7-9). 1943. 13.95 (ISBN 0-395-06766-9). HM.

Ford, Paul L. Janice Meredith. Teitel, N. R., intro. by. (gr. 11 up). pap. 0.95 (ISBN 0-8049-0148-1, CL-148). Airmont.

Fritz, Jean. Early Thunder. Ward, Lynd, illus. LC 67-24217. (gr. 7-11). 1967. 9.95 (ISBN 0-698-20036-5, Coward). Putnam Pub Group.

Gauch, Patricia L. Aaron & the Green Mountain Boys. Tomes, Margot, illus. LC 87-60671. 64p. (gr. 1-4). 1988. (Shoe Tree Pr); pap. 5.95 (ISBN 1-55870-220-2, Shoe Tree Pr). Betterway Pubns.

—This Time, Tempe Wick? Tomes, Margot, intro. by. LC 74-79706. (Illus.). 48p. (gr. 2-6). 1974. 6.95 (ISBN 0-698-20300-3, Coward). Putnam Pub Group.

Jensen, Dorothea. Riddle of Penncroft Farm. 1989. 14.95 (ISBN 0-15-200574-9). HarbraceJ.

Johnston, Mary. To Have & to Hold. Gemme, F. R., intro. by. (gr. 8 up). pap. 1.95 (ISBN 0-8049-0160-0, CL-160). Airmont.

Lawson, Robert. Mr. Revere & I. Lawson, Robert, illus. 152p. (gr. 3-6). 1988. pap. 5.95 (ISBN 0-316-51729-1). Little.

Lee, Beverly. The Secret of Van Rink's Cellar. LC 79-52909. 180p. (gr. 4 up). 1979. 9.95 (ISBN 0-8225-0763-3). Lerner Pubns.

Marko, Katherine M. Away to Fundy Bay. LC 84-25680. (Illus.). 128p. (gr. 4 up). 1985. 11.95 (ISBN 0-8027-6576-9); PLB 12.85 (ISBN 0-8027-6594-7). Walker & Co.

Moore, Ruth N. Distant Thunder. 160p. (Orig.). (gr. 4-8). 1991. pap. 5.95 (ISBN 0-8361-3557-1). Herald Pr.

Odell, Scott. Sara Bishop. (gr. 7 up). 1988. pap. 2.95 (ISBN 0-590-44363-1). Scholastic Inc.

Reit, Seymour. Guns for General Washington: The Impossible Journey. Ross, Richard, illus. 144p. (gr. 3-7). 1990. 15.95 (ISBN 0-15-200466-1, Gulliver Bks). HarBraceJ.

Smith, Mary P. Boys & Girls of Seventy-Seven. 2nd ed. Silvester, Susan B., ed. Grunwald, C., illus. LC 86-30607. 333p. (gr. 5 up). 1987. Repr. of 1909 ed. 14.00 (ISBN 0-913993-08-5). Paideia MA.

Tharp, Louise H. Tory Hole. (Illus.). (gr. 4up). 1976. pap. 7.50 (ISBN 0-686-16261-7). DCA.

Walkington, Ethlyn. Betsy Ross, Little Rebel. 140p. (Orig.). (gr. 4-6). 1990. pap. 8.95 (ISBN 0-944350-13-5). Friends United.

U. S.–HISTORY–REVOLUTION–NAVAL OPERATIONS

Cook, Fred J. Privateers of Seventy Six. LC 75-30808. (Illus.). 192p. (gr. 10 up). 1976. 7.95 (ISBN 0-672-52127-X, Bobbs). Macmillan.

U. S.–HISTORY–1783-1809

see also Lewis and Clark Expedition; Louisiana Purchase; U. S.–Constitutional History

American Heritage Illustrated History of the United States, Vol. 4: A New Nation. LC 87-73399. (Illus.). 128p. (gr. 7-12). 1988. Repr. of 1963 ed. 3.49 (ISBN 0-945260-04-0). Choice Pub NY.

Morris, Richard B. The Founding of the Republic. rev. ed. Fisher, Richard B., illus. 72p. (gr. 5-10). 1985. PLB 9.95 (ISBN 0-8225-1704-3). Lerner Pubns.

Tames, Richard. The American West. (Illus.). 64p. (gr. 7-9). 1988. 19.95 (ISBN 0-7134-5731-7, Pub. by Batsford England). Trafalgar Sq.

U. S.–HISTORY–1783-1809–FICTION

Lomask, Milton. The Spirit of Seventeen Eighty-Seven: The Making of Our Constitution. LC 80-14654. 224p. (gr. 7 up). 1980. 10.95 (ISBN 0-374-37149-0). FS&G.

Opie, William. Shenandoah Spector. 120p. (Orig.). 1989. pap. write for info. Opie Pub.

U. S.–HISTORY–1783-1865–BIOGRAPHY

James, Bessie R. & James, Marquis. Six Feet Six. (gr. 7-9). 1931. 5.95 (ISBN 0-672-50499-5, Bobbs). Macmillan.

U. S.–HISTORY–WAR OF 1812

Bosco, Peter I. War of 1812. (Illus.). 128p. (gr. 7 up). 1991. PLB 21.95 (ISBN 1-56294-004-X). Millbrook Pr.

Marrin, Albert. Eighteen Twelve: The War Nobody Won. LC 84-21623. (Illus.). 190p. (gr. 5 up). 1985. 14.95 (ISBN 0-689-31075-7, Atheneum Child Bk). Macmillan Child Grp.

Morris, Richard B. The War of Eighteen Twelve. rev. ed. Fisher, Leonard E., illus. 72p. (gr. 5-10). 1985. PLB 9.95 (ISBN 0-8225-1705-1). Lerner Pubns.

Stein, R. Conrad. The Story of the Burning of Washington. Wahl, Richard, illus. LC 84-12124. 32p. (gr. 3-6). 1985. lib. bdg. 13.27 (ISBN 0-516-04678-0). Childrens.

U. S.–HISTORY–WAR OF 1812–CAMPAIGNS AND BATTLES

Coker, William S. John Forbes & Company & the War of 1812 in the Spanish Borderlands. Coling, Jerome F., illus. 37p. (gr. 7 up). 1979. pap. 2.50 (ISBN 0-933776-08-X). Perdido Bay.

The War of Eighteen Twelve Soldier at New Orleans. 48p. (gr. 5-6). 1989. PLB 10.95 (ISBN 0-685-26361-4). Capstone Pr.

U. S.–HISTORY–WAR OF 1812–FICTION

Mitchell, Barbara. Cornstalks & Cannonballs. Ritz, Karen, illus. LC 79-91304. (gr. k-4). 1980. PLB 9.95 (ISBN 0-87614-121-1). Carolrhoda Bks.

U. S.–HISTORY–WAR OF 1812–NAVAL OPERATIONS

Richards, Norman. Story of Old Ironsides. Dunnington, Tom, illus. LC 67-20099. 32p. (gr. 2-5). 1967. PLB 13.27 (ISBN 0-516-04628-4); pap. 3.95 (ISBN 0-516-44628-2). Childrens.

U. S.–HISTORY–1815-1861

American Heritage Illustrated History of the United States, Vol. 5: Young America. LC 87-73399. 128p. (gr. 7-12). 1988. Repr. of 1963 ed. 3.49 (ISBN 0-945260-05-9). Choice Pub NY.

American Heritage Illustrated History of the United States, Vol. 6: The Frontier. LC 87-73399. 128p. (gr. 7-12). 1988. Repr. of 1963 ed. 3.49 (ISBN 0-945260-06-7). Choice Pub NY.

American Heritage Illustrated History of the United States, Vol. 9: Winning the West. LC 87-73399. 128p. (gr. 7-12). 1988. Repr. of 1963 ed. 3.49 (ISBN 0-945260-09-1). Choice Pub NY.

Baker, Betty. Pig War. Lopshire, Robert, illus. LC 69-10212. 64p. (gr. k-3). 1969. PLB 11.89 (ISBN 0-06-020333-1). HarpC Child Bks.

Eades, Jo A. A New Salem Primer. (Illus.). 80p. (Orig.). (gr. 5-8). 1989. pap. text ed. 5.95 (ISBN 0-685-26274-X). J A Eades.

U. S.–HISTORY–WAR WITH MEXICO, 1845-1848

American Heritage Illustrated History of the United States, Vol. 7: The War with Mexico. LC 87-73399. 128p. (gr. 7-12). 1988. Repr. of 1963 ed. 3.49 (ISBN 0-945260-07-5). Choice Pub NY.

Lawson, Don. The United States in the Mexican War. McCullough, Robert, illus. LC 76-11022. 160p. (gr. 7 up). 1988. PLB 12.89 (ISBN 0-690-04723-1, Crowell Jr Bks). HarpC Child Bks.

U. S.–HISTORY–CIVIL WAR

see also Slavery in the U. S.

American Heritage Illustrated History of the United States, Vol. 8: The Civil War. LC 87-73399. 128p. (gr. 7-12). 1988. Repr. of 1963 ed. 3.49 (ISBN 0-945260-08-3). Choice Pub NY.

Burney, Eugenia. The Story of Fort Sumter. LC 74-28435. (Illus.). 32p. (gr. 3-6). 1975. 13.27 (ISBN 0-516-04611-X). Childrens.

Canon, Jill. Civil War Heroines. Archambault, Alan, illus. (Orig.). (gr. 7 up). 1989. pap. 3.95 (ISBN 0-88388-147-0). Bellerophon Bks.

Civil War. (gr. 4-6). pap. 2.95 (ISBN 0-8431-4251-0). Wonder.

The Civil War Soldier at Atlanta. 48p. (gr. 5-6). 1989. PLB 10.95 (ISBN 0-685-26356-8). Capstone Pr.

Coates, Earl J. & Thomas, Dean S. An Introduction to Civil War Small Arms. (Illus.). 96p. 1990. pap. text ed. 7.95 (ISBN 0-685-35363-X). Thomas Publications.

Colby, C. B. Civil War Weapons: Small Arms, & Artillery of the Blue & Gray. (Illus.). (gr. 4-7). 1962. PLB 6.99 (ISBN 0-698-30046-7, Coward). Putnam Pub Group.

Colver, Anne. Abraham Lincoln. Moyers, William, illus. 76p. (gr. 1-7). 1981. pap. 2.95 (ISBN 0-440-40001-5, YB). Dell.

DeLeon, Thomas C. Four Years in Rebel Capitals. LC 83-9280. (gr. 7 up). 1983. Kivar binding 26.60 (ISBN 0-8094-4462-3, Pub. by Time-Life). Silver Burdett Pr.

Durwood, Thomas A., et al. The History of the Civil War Series, 10 vols. (Illus.). 1600p. (gr. 5 up). 1990. Set. PLB 169.80 (ISBN 0-382-09935-4); Set. pap. 89.50 (ISBN 0-382-24044-8). Silver Burdett Pr.

Goodman, Ailene S. Abe Lincoln in Song & Story. LC 88-753827. (gr. 4-12). 1988. incl. cassette 11.98 (ISBN 0-9620704-0-8). A S Goodman.
ABE LINCOLN IN SONG & STORY - toe-tapping tunes, sparkling narrative! A must for music lovers & Civil War history buffs. Authentic Americana in life of 16th president. Fascinates Children. Entertaining, challenging, witty, & dignified. Highest quality. A marvelous gift for young & old. "Bargain...Storyteller Ailene Goodman captures Abe Lincoln in song & story... Biographical anecdotes...& ballads from the time of Lincoln's childhood, his presidency, & the Civil War. Teacher's guide included."--LEARNING 91. "Songs, poetry, & folksy tales...a unique look at Abraham Lincoln's life... An asset...in the classroom."--SCHOOL LIBRARY JOURNAL. "Puts a human touch to Lincoln's history."--BILLBOARD. "A happy marriage of traditional folk tunes...via songs, narration, quotations, & humor... Touching & funny..Thoughtfully composed."--BOOKLIST. "For elementary children as well as senior high school students,...can be used individually or as classroom listening for music & social studies enrichment." --CURRICULUM PRODUCTS NEWS. "Local educator recounts... ballads, history & anecdotes from Lincoln's life." "Try It!"--THE WASHINGTON POST. "If you liked the PBS series THE CIVIL WAR,... use the audiocassette tape ABE LINCOLN IN SONG & STORY... Songs, narration, readings from primary sources, & touches of humor from the frontier & from Lincoln himself...paint a picture of a central figure in history...11-page teacher guide...gives background material & suggests questions/activities...Lower-cost, lower-tech...than TV series: uses songs & story to grab children's interest."--HISTORY MATTERS.
Publisher Provided Annotation.

Henrich, Stephen & Henrich, Jean. Story Starters on the Civil War - Old West. rev. ed. Henrich, Jean, illus. 80p. (gr. 4-12). 1988. write for info. wkbk. (HE 300). Henrich Enter.

Hinsdale, Harriet. Confederate Gray: Traveller. (gr. 4 up). 1963. 9.95 (ISBN 0-87233-823-1). Bauhan.

Katz, William L. Breaking the Chains: African-American Slave Resistance. LC 89-36355. (Illus.). 208p. (gr. 5 up). 1990. 14.95 (ISBN 0-689-31493-0, Atheneum Child Bk). Macmillan Child Grp.

Kent, Zachary. The Story of the Surrender at Appomattox Court House. LC 87-22468. (Illus.). 32p. (gr. 3-6). 1987. PLB 13.27 (ISBN 0-516-04732-9); pap. 3.95 (ISBN 0-516-44732-7). Childrens.

McPherson, James M. Marching Toward Freedom: Blacks in the Civil War, 1861-1865. Scott, John A., ed. (Illus.). 128p. (gr. 7-12). 1990. 16.95 (ISBN 0-8160-2337-9). Facts on File.

Meltzer, Milton. Voices from the Civil War. (gr. 7 up). 1990. 13.95 (ISBN 0-685-34879-2). HarperCollins.

—Voices from the Civil War: A Documentary History of the Great American Conflict. LC 88-34067. (Illus.). 224p. (gr. 7 up). 1989. 14.95 (ISBN 0-690-04800-9, Crowell Jr Bks); PLB 13.89 (ISBN 0-690-04802-5, Crowell Jr Bks). HarpC Child Bks.

Miller, Howard. Abraham Lincoln's Flag: We Won't Give up a Star. Heiser, John, illus. 26p. (gr. 4-6). 1990. pap. text ed. 4.95 (ISBN 0-939631-19-9). Thomas Publications.

Murphy, Jim. The Boys' War: Confederate & Union Soldiers Talk about the Civil War. (Illus.). 128p. (gr. 4-9). 1990. 15.95 (ISBN 0-89919-893-7, Clarion Bks). HM.

Powell, Robert M. Recollections of a Texas Colonel at Gettysburg. Coco, Gregory A., ed. (Illus.). 62p. 1990. pap. text ed. 4.95 (ISBN 0-939631-26-1). Thomas Publications.

Ray, Delia. Behind the Blue & Gray: The Soldier's Life in the Civil War. (Illus.). 112p. (gr. 5-9). 1991. 15.95 (ISBN 0-525-67333-4, Lodestar Bks). Dutton Child Bks.

—A Nation Torn: The Story of How the Civil War Began. (Illus.). 128p. (gr. 5-9). 1990. 15.95 (ISBN 0-525-67308-3, Lodestar Bks). Dutton Child Bks.

Shorto, Russell. David Farragut & the Great Naval Blockade. (Illus.). 160p. (gr. 5 up). 1990. lib. bdg. 16.98 (ISBN 0-382-09941-9); pap. 8.95 (ISBN 0-382-24050-2). Silver Burdett Pr.

Smith, Gene. Lee & Grant. 448p. (gr. 9-12). 1985. pap. 11.95 (ISBN 0-452-01000-4, Mer). NAL-Dutton.

U. S.–HISTORY–CIVIL WAR–BIOGRAPHY

Baxter, Nancy N. Gallant Fourteenth: The Story of an Indiana Civil War Regiment. Niblack, John L., pref. by. 205p. 1986. 16.95 (ISBN 0-9617367-8-X). Guild Pr IN.

De Grummond, Lena & Delaune, Lynn. Jeb Stuart. LC 62-16298. (Illus.). 160p. (gr. 4-6). 1979. pap. 5.95 (ISBN 0-88289-247-9). Pelican.

Reit, Seymour. Behind Rebel Lines: The Incredible Story of Emma Edmonds, Civil War Spy. LC 87-28079. 144p. (gr. 8-12). 1988. 12.95 (ISBN 0-15-200416-5, Gulliver Bks). HarBraceJ.

—Behind Rebel Lines: The Incredible Story of Emma Edmonds, Civil War Spy. 146p. (gr. 4-7). 1991. pap. 4.95 (ISBN 0-15-200424-6, HJ). HarBraceJ.

U. S.–HISTORY–CIVIL WAR–CAMPAIGNS AND BATTLES

see also names of battles, e.g. Gettysburg, Battle of, 1863

Beller, Susan P. Cadets at War: The True Story of Teenage Heroism at the Battle of New Market. LC 90-21952. (Illus.). 96p. (gr. 3-7). 1991. 9.95 (ISBN 1-55870-196-6, Shoe Tree Pr). Betterway Pubns.

Brown, Herbert O. & Nitz, Dwight V. Fields of Glory: The Facts Book of the Battle of Gettysburg. (Illus.). 120p. 1990. pap. text ed. 5.95 (ISBN 0-685-35365-6). Thomas Publications.

Fritz, Jean. Stonewall. (Illus.). (gr. 3-7). 1979. 14.95 (ISBN 0-399-20698-1, Putnam). Putnam Pub Group.

Haselberger, Francis E. Yanks from the South! The First Land Campaign of the Civil War; Rich Mountain, West Virginia. Haselberger, Francis E., illus. LC 87-91999. 323p. (gr. 12). 1987. 22.00 (ISBN 0-9619953-0-0). Past Glories.

Kent, Zachary. The Story of John Brown's Raid on Harpers Ferry. LC 87-35714. (Illus.). 32p. (gr. 3-6). 1988. PLB 13.27 (ISBN 0-516-04734-5); pap. 3.95 (ISBN 0-516-44734-3). Childrens.

—The Story of the Battle of Bull Run. Catrow, David J., III, illus. LC 86-9642. 32p. (gr. 3-6). 1986. PLB 13.27 (ISBN 0-516-04703-5); pap. 3.95 (ISBN 0-516-44703-3). Childrens.

U. S.–HISTORY–CIVIL WAR–FICTION

Beachy, J. Wayne. A Bird of Peace Is Born in Petersburg. Hawkins, Beverly, illus. (Orig.). (gr. 5). 1981. pap. 2.50 (ISBN 0-9608084-0-X). B Hawkins Studio.

Beatty, Patricia. Be Ever Hopeful, Hannalee. LC 88-21581. 208p. (gr. 5-9). 1988. 12.95 (ISBN 0-688-07502-9). Morrow.

—Jayhawker. LC 91-17890. 192p. (gr. 5 up). 1991. 13.95 (ISBN 0-688-09850-9). Morrow Jr Bks.

Biros, Florence K. Dog Jack. Libb, Melva, ed. (Illus.). 192p. (Orig.). 1988. pap. 6.95 (ISBN 0-936369-22-1). Son-Rise Pubns.
DOG JACK, real-life mascot of the 102nd Regiment of the Pennsylvania Volunteers, finds his way into the hearts of young readers as they learn of his experiences during the Civil War as told by Florence W. Biros in the novel bearing his name. The actual historic events known about this canine hero are interwoven into this saga of love & adventure about Jed, a runaway slave boy, & his canine companion & friend. The story also shares of the allegiance of the men of the Niagara Volunteers toward their loyal mascot. DOG JACK, 192 page trade paper, is illustrated by a cover portrait by famed artist Ron DiCianni; the final pages are filled with a LIVING HISTORY GALLERY--actual photographs of the reenactment of the 125th Anniversary of the Battle of Gettysburg. DOG JACK, published by Son-Rise Publications, Route 3, Box 202, New Wilmington, PA 16142 retails for $7. 95. Son-Rise phone number: (412) 946-8334.
Publisher Provided Annotation.

Clapp, Patricia C. The Tamarack Tree. 256p. (Orig.). (gr. 5-9). 1988. pap. 3.95 (ISBN 0-14-032406-2, Puffin). Puffin Bks.

Climo, Shirley. A Month of Seven Days. LC 87-5259. 192p. (gr. 5 up). 1987. 12.95 (ISBN 0-690-04658-8, Crowell Jr Bks); PLB 12.89 (ISBN 0-690-04656-1, Crowell Jr Bks). HarpC Child Bks.

Crane, Stephen. Reader's Digest Best Loved Books for Young Readers: The Red Badge of Courage. Ogburn, Jackie, ed. Barnett, Isa, illus. 120p. (gr. 4-12). 1989. 3.99 (ISBN 0-945260-34-2). Choice Pub NY.

—Red Badge of Courage. (gr. 7 up). 1964. pap. 2.25 (ISBN 0-8049-0003-5, CL-3). Airmont.

—The Red Badge of Courage. Shapiro, Irwin, ed. Cruz, E. R., illus. LC 73-75464. 64p. (Orig.). (gr. 5-10). 1973. pap. 2.95 (ISBN 0-88301-101-8). Pendulum Pr.

—The Red Badge of Courage. Wright, Betty R., adapted by. Shaw, Charles, illus. LC 81-2611. 48p. (gr. 4 up). 1983. PLB 17.32 (ISBN 0-8172-1670-7); pap. 9.27 (ISBN 0-8172-2019-4). Raintree Pubs.

—Red Badge of Courage. 180p. (gr. 7-12). 1972. pap. 2.25 (ISBN 0-590-02117-6); tchr's. guide 1.25 (ISBN 0-590-40678-7). Scholastic Inc.

—The Red Badge of Courage & Other Stories. 224p. (gr. 9-12). Date not set. pap. 1.50 (ISBN 0-451-51592-7, Sig Classics). NAL-Dutton.

U. S. NAVY–BIOGRAPHY
Goffstein, M. B. Me & My Captain. Goffstein, M. B., illus. LC 74-6699. 32p. (ps up). 1974. 6.95 (ISBN 0-374-34901-0). FS&G.
Worcester, Donald E. John Paul Jones. (gr. 4-6). 1961. 4.36 (ISBN 0-395-01755-6, Piper). HM.

U. S.–PAINTERS
see Painters, American

U. S. PEACE CORPS
Ashabranner, Brent. The Times of My Life: A Memoir. (gr. 4-7). 1990. 14.95 (ISBN 0-525-65047-4, Cobblehill Bks). Dutton Child Bks.
Fitzgerald, Merni I. The Peace Corps Today. (gr. 3-7). 1986. 11.95 (ISBN 0-396-08511-3, Putnam). Putnam Pub Group.
Kent, Zachary. The Story of the Peace Corps. LC 90-2113. (Illus.). 32p. (gr. 3-6). 1990. PLB 13.27 (ISBN 0-516-04752-3); pap. 3.95 (ISBN 0-516-44752-1). Childrens.
Weitsman, Madeline. The Peace Corps. Schlesinger, Arthur M., Jr., intro. by. (Illus.). 112p. (gr. 5 up). 1989. 14.95 (ISBN 0-87754-832-3). Chelsea Hse.

U. S.–POLITICS AND GOVERNMENT
Acheson, Patricia. Our Federal Government. 1984. pap. 11.95 (ISBN 0-396-08312-9, Putnam). Putnam Pub Group.
Arrington, Karen. The Commission on Civil Rights. (Illus.). (gr. 5 up). 1992. 14.95 (ISBN 1-55546-127-1). Chelsea Hse.
Barnes-Svarney, Patricia. The National Science Foundation. Schlesinger, Arthur M., Jr., intro. by. (Illus.). 112p. (gr. 5 up). 1989. lib. bdg. 14.95 (ISBN 1-55546-117-4). Chelsea Hse.
Bernotas, Bob. Department of Housing & Urban Development. Schlesinger, Arthur M., Jr., intro. by. (Illus.). (gr. 5up). 1991. lib. bdg. 14.95 (ISBN 0-87754-841-2). Chelsea Hse.
Bernotas, Bob, Jr. The Federal Government: How it Works. (Illus.). (gr. 5 up). 1990. 14.95 (ISBN 0-87754-859-5). Chelsea Hse.
Bernstein, Richard & Agel, Jerome. The Presidency. LC 88-21026. (gr. 7 up). 1989. 12.95 (ISBN 0-8027-6829-6); PLB 13.85 (ISBN 0-8027-6831-8). Walker & Co.
Burkhardt, Robert. The Federal Aviation Administration. Schlesinger, Arthur M., Jr., intro. by. (Illus.). 112p. (gr. 5 up). 1989. lib. bdg. 14.95 (ISBN 1-55546-107-7). Chelsea Hse.
Clement, Fred. The Nuclear Regulatory Commission. (Illus.). (gr. 5 up). 1988. 14.95 (ISBN 1-55546-129-8). Chelsea Hse.
Coffey, William E. & Riddel, Frank S. American Government: The U. S. A. & West Virginia. Buckalew, Marshall, ed. Harvey, Eve S. & Harvey, Cliff, illus. 304p. (gr. 8). 1990. 25.00 (ISBN 0-914498-08-8). WV Hist Ed Found.
Crouch, Tom D. The National Aeronautics & Space Administration. (Illus.). (gr. 5 up). 1990. 14.95 (ISBN 1-55546-120-4). Chelsea Hse.
Dickson, Edward & Galan, Mark. The Immigration & Naturalization Service. (Illus.). (gr. 5 up). 1990. 14.95 (ISBN 1-55546-113-1). Chelsea Hse.
Doggett, Clinton L. Equal Employment Opportunities Commission. (Illus.). (gr. 5 up). 1990. lib. bdg. 14.95 (ISBN 1-55546-106-9). Chelsea Hse.
Dwyer, Christopher, Jr. The Small Business Administration. (Illus.). (gr. 5 up). 1991. 14.95 (ISBN 1-55546-122-0). Chelsea Hse.
Faber, Doris & Faber, Harold. Great Lives: American Government. LC 88-4968. (Illus.). 288p. (gr. 4-6). 1988. 22.95 (ISBN 0-684-18521-0, Scribners Young Read). Macmillan Child Grp.
Goode, Stephen. The New Federalism. (Illus.). 160p. (gr. 7 up). 1983. PLB 13.90 (ISBN 0-531-04501-3). Watts.
Green, Carl, et al. American Government, 4 bks. (Illus.). 384p. (gr. 7 up). 1990. Set. lib. bdg. 74.40 (ISBN 0-86593-082-1); Set. lib. bdg. 55.80s.p. Rourke Corp.
Griffiths, John. Cuban Missile Crisis. LC 86-20255. (Illus.). 77p. (gr. 7 up). 1987. 17.26 (ISBN 0-86592-028-1). Rourke Corp.
Hacker, Jeffrey H. Government Subsidy to Industry. (Illus.). 96p. (gr. 7 up). 1982. PLB 12.90 (ISBN 0-531-04487-4). Watts.
Highland, Jean. The Federal Communications Commission. (Illus.). (gr. 5 up). 1992. 14.95 (ISBN 1-55546-108-5). Chelsea Hse.
Hopson, Glover E. The Veteran's Administration. Schlesinger, Arthur M., Jr., intro. by. (Illus.). 96p. (gr. 5 up). 1988. lib. bdg. 14.95 (ISBN 1-55546-131-X). Chelsea Hse.
Koslow, Philip. The Securities & Exchange Commission. (Illus.). (gr. 5 up). 1990. 14.95 (ISBN 1-55546-119-0). Chelsea Hse.
Kownslar, Allan O. & Smart, Terry L. Civics: Citizens & Society. 2nd ed. (Illus.). 576p. (gr. 7-8). 1983. text ed. 31.88 (ISBN 0-07-035443-2). McGraw.
Law, Kevin J. The Environmental Protection Agency. Schlesinger, Arthur M., Jr., intro. by. (Illus.). 96p. (gr. 5 up). 1988. lib. bdg. 14.95 (ISBN 1-55546-105-0). Chelsea Hse.
Matusky, Gregory & Hayes, John P. The U. S. Secret Service. Schlesinger, Arthur M., Jr., intro. by. (Illus.). 96p. (gr. 5 up). 1988. lib. bdg. 14.95 (ISBN 1-55546-130-1). Chelsea Hse.
Meltzer, Milton. American Politics: How It Really Works. LC 88-26635. (Illus.). 192p. (gr. 7 up). 1989. 12.95 (ISBN 0-688-07494-4). Morrow Jr Bks.

Parker, Nancy W. The President's Cabinet & How It Grew. Parker, Nancy W., illus. LC 89-70851. 40p. (gr. 3-5). 1991. 14.95 (ISBN 0-06-021617-4); PLB 14.89 (ISBN 0-06-021618-2). HarpC Child Bks.
Raber, Thomas R. Election Night. (Illus.). 88p. (gr. 4 up). 1988. lib. bdg. 10.95 (ISBN 0-8225-1751-5). Lerner Pubns.
Rudysmith, Christina. National Archives & Record Administration. Schlesinger, Arthur M., Jr., intro. by. (Illus.). 112p. (gr. 5 up). 1989. 14.95 (ISBN 1-55546-073-9). Chelsea Hse.
Sawyer, Kem K. National Foundation on the Arts & Humanities. (Illus.). 112p. (gr. 5 up). 1989. lib. bdg. 14.95 (ISBN 1-55546-115-8). Chelsea Hse.
Simpson, Andrew L. The Library of Congress. (Illus.). (gr. 5 up) 1989. 14.95 (ISBN 1-55546-109-3). Chelsea Hse.
Stefoff, Rebecca. The Drug Enforcement Administration. (Illus.). (gr. 5 up) 1990. 14.95 (ISBN 0-87754-849-8). Chelsea Hse.
Stuart, Pamela B. The Federal Trade Commission. (Illus.). (gr. 5 up) 1991. 14.95 (ISBN 1-55546-114-X). Chelsea Hse.
Sullivan, George. How the White House Really Works. 1990. pap. 2.95 (ISBN 0-590-43403-9). Scholastic Inc.
Taylor, Gary. The Federal Reserve System. (Illus.). (gr. 5 up). 1989. 14.95 (ISBN 1-55546-136-0). Chelsea Hse.
Tuggle, Catherine & Weir, Gary. The Department of Energy. (Illus.). (gr. 5 up) 1990. 14.95 (ISBN 0-87754-839-0). Chelsea Hse.
Ulrich & Lefkowitz. Our Government in Action. (Illus.). 184p. (gr. 7 up). 1986. text ed. 12.95 (ISBN 0-88102-047-8); tchr's ed. 14.95 (ISBN 0-88102-048-6). Janus Bks.

U. S.–POSTAL SERVICE
see Postal Service

U. S.–RELIGION
Bach, Julie & Modl, Tom, eds. Religion in America: Opposing Viewpoints. LC 88-24359. (Illus.). 250p. (gr. 10 up). 1988. PLB 15.95 (ISBN 0-89908-437-0); pap. text ed. 8.95 (ISBN 0-89908-412-5). Greenhaven.
Lowry, James W. North America Is the Lord's. (gr. 5). 1980. 17.05x (ISBN 0-87813-916-8). Christian Light.

U. S.–RELIGIOUS HISTORY
see U. S.–Church History

U. S.–SOCIAL CONDITIONS
Bender, David L., ed. American Values: Opposing Viewpoints. LC 89-36526. (Illus.). 312p. (gr. 10 up). 1989. lib. bdg. 15.95 (ISBN 0-89908-436-2); pap. text ed. 8.95 (ISBN 0-89908-411-7). Greenhaven.
Gardner, Robert & Shortelle, Dennis. The Future & the Past. Steltenpohl, Jane, ed. (Illus.). 176p. (gr. 6-10). 1989. lib. bdg. 14.98 (ISBN 0-671-65742-6). Messner.
Haskins, James & Benson, Kathleen. The Sixties Reader. LC 85-40886. (Illus.). 256p. (gr. 7 up). 1988. pap. 13. 95 (ISBN 0-670-80674-9). Viking Child Bks.
Hays, Scott, et al. Troubled Society, 6 bks. (Illus.). 384p. (gr. 7 up). 1990. Set. lib. bdg. 95.60 (ISBN 0-86593-068-6); Set. lib. bdg. 71.70s.p. (ISBN 0-685-36321-X). Rourke Corp.
Johnson, Hilda S. A Child's Diary - the 1930's. Johnson, Hilda S., illus. LC 88-51304. 64p. (Orig.). (gr. 3-8). 1988. pap. 3.95 (ISBN 0-931563-02-X). Wishing Rm.
Wekesser, Carol, ed. America's Children: Opposing Viewpoints. LC 90-24085. (Illus.). 240p. (gr. 10 up). 1991. PLB 15.95 (ISBN 0-89908-486-9); pap. 8.95 (ISBN 0-89908-461-3). Greenhaven.

U. S.–SOCIAL LIFE AND CUSTOMS
Ainsworth, Catherine H. American Calendar Customs, Vol. I. LC 79-52827. 112p. (Illus.). (ps-12). 1979. pap. 10.00 (ISBN 0-933190-06-9). Clyde Pr.
Everyday Life. (Illus.). 88p. (ps-3). 1990. write for info. (ISBN 0-8094-4865-3); lib. bdg. write for info. (ISBN 0-8094-4866-1). Time-Life.
Loeper, John J. Going to School in 1876. LC 83-15669. (Illus.). 96p. (gr. 4-7). 1984. 12.95 (ISBN 0-689-31015-3, Atheneum). Macmillan Child Grp.
Mitchell, Barbara. Hush, Puppies. Wyman, Cherie R., illus. LC 82-4465. 48p. (gr. k-4). 1983. PLB 9.95 (ISBN 0-87614-201-3). Carolrhoda Bks.

U. S.–SOCIAL LIFE AND CUSTOMS–COLONIAL PERIOD
Bowen, Gary. My Village, Sturbridge. Bowen, Gary & Miller, Randy, illus. LC 77-10059. 64p. (ps up). 1977. 10.95 (ISBN 0-374-35110-4). FS&G.

Coon, Alma S. Amy, Ben, & Catalpa the Cat: A Fanciful Story of This & That. Owens, Gail, illus. 40p. (ps-2). 1990. 5.95 (ISBN 0-87935-079-2). Williamsburg.
In this beautifully illustrated, full-color alphabet storybook in verse, Amy, Ben, & Catalpa the Cat take children on a fun-filled day in eighteenth-century Williamsburg. The story, set in early autumn, opens at Amy & Ben's home, where Ben is harvesting pumpkins, Amy is baking apple pies, & playful Catalpa is constantly underfoot. But no sooner does the fifer pass by their window than they are off to the fair!

During their adventures in Williamsburg the heroes introduce young readers to George Washington & other eighteenth-century characters as well as to various colonial activities such as a fair, a ride in an oxcart, children's games, & a visit to Tarpley's Store. The inviting illustrations colorfully re-create authentic colonial clothing, architecture, agriculture, & animal husbandry. To order: Colonial Williamsburg Wholesale Sales, PO Box C, Williamsburg, VA 23187, (804) 220-7178.
Publisher Provided Annotation.

Kalman, Bobbie. Colonial Crafts. 1991. 14.95 (ISBN 0-86505-490-8); pap. 7.95 (ISBN 0-86505-510-6). Crabtree Pub CO.
In COLONIAL CRAFTS your young readers will take a journey into the 18th century & meet the craftspeople who created useful works of art with handmade tools. They will visit the workshops of the wheelwright, cooper, founder, peruker, shoemaker, milliner, gunsmith, & many more. They will find out how the artisans learned their trades through many years of apprenticeship. They will gain an appreciation for the goods made two hundred years ago that are still beautiful today. They will learn why the craftspeople were an essential part of the colonial community.
Publisher Provided Annotation.

— A Colonial Town. 1991. 14.95 (ISBN 0-86505-489-4); pap. 7.95 (ISBN 0-86505-509-2). Crabtree Pub Co.
In A COLONIAL TOWN young readers are introduced to a historic community. They will take a journey into history to a time when people grew their own food & made their own tools. They will travel down the wide cobblestone streets of Williamsburg & enjoy the slow, peaceful pace of the restored city. They will admire the grand estates of long ago & tour the special buildings of Virginia's old capitol. They will find out about the Palace in which the governor lived, the Capitol where laws were made, the Powder Magazine where weapons were kept, & the Gaol where prisoners waited for their punishment. They will meet the apothecary & learn about some of his questionable "cures" & find out how a post mill grinds grain.
Publisher Provided Annotation.

—The Gristmill. (Illus.). 32p. (gr. 3-4). 1990. lib. bdg. 14.95 (ISBN 0-86505-486-X); pap. 7.95 (ISBN 0-86505-506-8). Crabtree Pub Co.
THE GRISTMILL takes a step-by-step look at how a simple water-powered gristmill grinds grain. Detailed diagrams show how the waterwheel, gears, & millstones worked. The book also looks at the role of the miller in the community, the dangers of milling, & the parts of grain that make up wholewheat flour. THE GRISTMILL is part of THE HISTORIC COMMUNITIES SERIES, fun-to-read books that provides a wealth of information for young readers. The

series introduces children to the concept of earlier times in history & looks at community life. THE HISTORIC COMMUNITIES SERIES is beautifully designed, presenting information in two-page spreads through lively text, a multitude of color photographs, & detailed sketches. The books provide a close-up look at each topic, with step-by-step explanations of how tools & processes work. They are excellent for preparing young children for visits to historic sites & provide good follow-up material.
Publisher Provided Annotation.

—Home Crafts. (Illus.). 32p. (gr. 3-4). 1990. lib. bdg. 14.95 (ISBN 0-86505-485-1); pap. 7.95 (ISBN 0-86505-505-X). Crabtree Pub Co.
HOME CRAFTS is a colorful potpourri of the domestic industries carried out by settler men & mostly women. It explains how candles & soap were made, wool & flax were cleaned, spun, & woven, & looks at various needle crafts such as sewing quilts & stitching samplers. HOME CRAFTS also explores the transition of crafts from the home to workshop to factory. HOME CRAFTS is part of The Historic Communities Series, fun-to-read books that provide a wealth of information for young readers. The series introduces children to the concept of earlier times in history & looks at community life. The Historic Communities Series is beautifully designed, presenting information in two-page spreads through lively text, a multitude of color photographs, & detailed sketches. The books provide a close-up look at each topic, with step-by-step explanations of how tools & processes work. They are excellent for preparing young children for visits to historic sites & provide good follow-up material.
Publisher Provided Annotation.

—The Kitchen. (Illus.). 32p. (gr. 3-4). 1990. lib. bdg. 14.95 (ISBN 0-86505-484-3); pap. 7.95 (ISBN 0-86505-504-1). Crabtree Pub Co.
In THE KITCHEN, young readers enter a settler home. They take a close look at the early fireplace, the tools & utensils surrounding it, & the domestic chores that were carried out there such as baking bread & making butter. Comparing an early kitchen with a kitchen of today will allow children to realize the difficulties settlers had just getting food on their tables. Your young readers will gain an understanding of how the settlers made do in a world without refrigerators, toasters, & food processors. THE KITCHEN is part of The Historic Communities Series, fun-to-read books that provide a wealth of information for young readers. The series introduces children to the concept of earlier times in history & looks at community life. The Historic Communities Series is beautifully designed, presenting information in two-page spreads through lively text, a multitude of color photographs, &

detailed sketches. The books provide a close-up look at each topic, with step-by-step explanations of how tools & processes work. They are excellent for preparing young children for visits to historic sites & provide good follow-up material.
Publisher Provided Annotation.

—Tools & Gadgets. 1991. 14.95 (ISBN 0-86505-508-4); pap. 7.95 (ISBN 0-86505-488-6). Crabtree Pub CO.
In the old days people had to rely on tools & their own muscle power to get a job done. In TOOLS & GADGETS your students will have the opportunity to learn about the tools used by farmers, woodworkers, metalworkers, millers, & printers. They will take a close look at the gadgets found in the home, general store, doctor's office, & farm, such as cherry pitters, apple peelers, mustache cups, clock jacks, & fleams. They will be introduced to the gadgets that fascinated children long ago & have the chance to identify some mystery gadgets. This book is an excellent tool to be used before & after visits to historic communities.
Publisher Provided Annotation.

Sabin, Louis. Colonial Life in America. Frenck, Hal, illus. LC 84-2669. 32p. (gr. 3-6). 1985. PLB 9.49 (ISBN 0-8167-0138-5); pap. text ed. 2.95 (ISBN 0-8167-0139-3). Troll Assocs.

U. S.–SOLDIERS
see Soldiers–U. S.

U. S.–STATE GOVERNMENTS
see State Governments

U. S. SUPREME COURT
Bains, Rae. Supreme Court. Dole, Bob, illus. LC 84-2736. 32p. (gr. 3-6). 1985. PLB 9.49 (ISBN 0-8167-0272-1); pap. text ed. 2.95 (ISBN 0-8167-0273-X). Troll Assocs.
Fox, Mary V. Justice Sandra Day O'Connor. LC 82-8857. (Illus.). 96p. (gr. 5-11). 1983. PLB 16.95 (ISBN 0-89490-073-0). Enslow Pubs.
Gherman, Beverly. Sandra Day O'Connor. (gr. 4-7). 1991. 10.95 (ISBN 0-670-82756-8). Viking Child Bks.
Greene, Carol. The Supreme Court. LC 84-23230. (Illus.). 48p. (gr. k-4). 1985. lib. bdg. 14.60 (ISBN 0-516-01943-0). Childrens.
Lawson, Don. Landmark Supreme Court Cases. LC 86-19735. 128p. (gr. 6-12). 1987. lib. bdg. 17.95 (ISBN 0-89490-132-X). Enslow Pubs.
Macht, Norman L. Sandra Day O'Connor. (Illus.). (gr. 3-5). 1992. PLB 12.95 (ISBN 0-7910-1756-7). Chelsea Hse.
Rierden, Anne B. Reshaping the Supreme Court: New Justices, New Directions. Ribaroff, Margaret, ed. (Illus.). 128p. (gr. 7-12). 1988. PLB 12.90 (ISBN 0-531-10512-1). Watts.
Stein, R. Conrad. The Story of the Powers of the Supreme Court. LC 89-15885. 32p. (gr. 3-6). 1989. PLB 13.27 (ISBN 0-516-04721-3). Childrens.
Weiss, Ann E. The Supreme Court. LC 86-8929. 96p. (gr. 6-12). 1987. PLB 16.95 (ISBN 0-89490-131-1). Enslow Pubs.

U. S.–TAXATION
see Taxation–U. S.

U. S.–TERRITORIES AND POSSESSIONS
Dunnahoo, Terry. U. S. Territories Freely Associated States. Rakos, Jennie, ed. LC 88-16982. (Illus.). 96p. 1988. PLB 12.40 (ISBN 0-531-10605-5). Watts.

U. S. TREASURY DEPARTMENT
Walston, Mark. The Department of the Treasury. (Illus.). (gr. 5 up). 1989. 14.95 (ISBN 0-87754-848-X). Chelsea Hse.

U. S.–VICE-PRESIDENTS
see Vice-Presidents–U. S.

U. S.–WOMEN
see Women in the U. S.

U. S.–WORLD WAR, 1939-1945
see World War, 1939-1945–U. S.

UNIVERSAL HISTORY
see World History

UNIVERSE
Asimov, Isaac. How Did We Find Out about the Universe? Wool, David, illus. LC 82-42531. 64p. (gr. 5-8). 1983. PLB 12.85 (ISBN 0-8027-6477-0). Walker & Co.
—Isaac Asimov's Library of the Universe, 33 vols. Sachner, Mark, ed. (Illus.). 1056p. (gr. 3-4). Date not set. Set. lib. bdg. 394.35 (ISBN 1-55532-420-7). Gareth Stevens Inc.
Berger, Melvin. Quasars, Pulsars & Black Holes in Space. new ed. LC 76-50057. (Illus.). (gr. 3-6). 1977. PLB 6.99 (ISBN 0-399-61051-0). Putnam Pub Group.

Branley, Franklyn M. Mysteries of the Universe. Bensusen, Sally J., illus. LC 83-25302. 96p. (gr. 5-9). 1984. 10.95 (ISBN 0-525-66914-0, Lodestar Bks). Dutton Child Bks.
Ciupik, Larry. The Universe. rev. ed. LC 87-20805. (Illus.). 48p. (gr. 2-6). 1987. PLB 17.32 (ISBN 0-8172-3264-8); pap. 9.27 (ISBN 0-8172-3289-3). Raintree Pubs.
Couper, Heater & Murtagh, Terence. Heavens Above! (Illus.). 64p. (gr. 5 up) 1981. lib. bdg. 11.90 (ISBN 0-531-04287-1). Watts.
Darling, David J. The New Astronomy: An Ever-Changing Universe. Swofford, Jeanette, illus. LC 84-23083. 64p. (gr. 4 up). 1985. PLB 10.95 (ISBN 0-87518-288-7, Dillon). Macmillan Child Grp.
—The Universe: Past, Present & Future. Swofford, Jeanette, illus. LC 84-23068. 64p. (gr. 4 up). 1985. PLB 10.95 (ISBN 0-87518-286-0, Dillon). Macmillan Child Grp.
Gallant, Roy A. One Hundred & One Questions & Answers about the Universe. LC 84-7875. (Illus.). 96p. (gr. 1-5). 1984. 12.95 (ISBN 0-02-736750-9, Mcmillan Child Bk). Macmillan Child Grp.
Gallant, Roy A. & Sedeen, Magaret. National Geographic Picture Atlas of Our Universe. Collins, Michael, frwd. by. (Illus.). 276p. (gr. 6 up). 1980. lib. bdg. 18.95 (ISBN 0-87044-357-7). Natl Geog.
Jacobs, Francine. Cosmic Countdown: What Astronomers Have Learned about the Life of the Universe. Jastrow, Robert, frwd. by. LC 83-5535. (Illus.). 160p. (gr. 7 up). 1983. 9.95 (ISBN 0-87131-404-5). M Evans.
Jespersen, James & Fitz-Randolph, Jane. Looking at the Invisible Universe. Hiscock, Bruce, illus. LC 89-14998. 160p. (gr. 7 up). 1990. 13.95 (ISBN 0-689-31457-4, Atheneum Child Bk). Macmillan Child Grp.
Jugendhandbuch Naturwissen: Erde und Weltall, Vol. 4. (GER.). 128p. 1976. pap. 5.95 (ISBN 3-499-16206-7, M-7489, Pub. by Rowohlt). French & Eur.
Jugendhandbuch Naturwissen: Saeugetiere, Vol. 3. (GER.). 144p. 1976. pap. 5.95 (ISBN 0-686-56619-X, M-7488, Pub. by Rowohlt). French & Eur.
Lampton, Christopher. New Theories on the Birth of the Universe. (Illus.). 176p. (gr. 7-12). 1989. PLB 13.40 (ISBN 0-531-10782-5). Watts.
Muirden, James. The Universe. (Illus.). 128p. (gr. 5-9). 1988. pap. 14.95 (ISBN 0-671-64493-9, Little Simon). S&S Trade.
Myring. First Guide to the Universe. (gr. 2-5). 1982. 10.95 (ISBN 0-86020-611-4, Usborne-Hayes). EDC.
Rand McNally Staff. Children's Atlas of the Universe. (Illus.). (gr. 3-7). 1990. 14.95 (ISBN 0-528-83408-8). Rand McNally.
Scrunch the Universe. 48p. (gr. 4-5). 1989. PLB 10.95 (ISBN 0-685-26331-2). Capstone Pr.
Snyder, Al. How Our Universe Works. 150p. (Orig.). (gr. 3-7). 1978. pap. 6.95 (ISBN 0-686-27926-3). Snyder Inst Res.

UNIVERSITIES AND COLLEGES–FICTION
see also Schools–Fiction
Balducci, Carolyn. Is There a Life after Graduation, Henry Birnbaum? (Illus.). (gr. 7 up). 1971. 7.95 (ISBN 0-395-12749-1). HM.
Holman, Dianne K. Plenty to Do at MSU. (Illus.). 32p. (Orig.). 1989. pap. 5.95 (ISBN 0-9626188-0-2). Cupery Pr.
Langton, Jane. Paper Chains. LC 76-41520. (gr. 7 up). 1977. HarpC Child Bks.
Quin-Harkin, Janet. Campus Cousins. LC 88-91245. 186p. 1989. pap. 2.95 (ISBN 0-8041-0335-6). Ivy Books.
Schneider, Meg. I Wonder What College Is Like? Steltenpohl, Jane, ed. (Illus.). 160p. (gr. 7-9). 1989. lib. bdg. 13.98 (ISBN 0-671-65847-6); pap. 5.95 (ISBN 0-671-67815-9). Messner.
Standish, Burt L. Frank Merriwell's Schooldays. Rudman, Jack, ed. (gr. 9 up). 9.95 (ISBN 0-8373-9309-4); pap. 3.95 (ISBN 0-8373-9009-5). F Merriwell.
Tunis, John R. Iron Duke. 1990. pap. 3.95 (ISBN 0-15-238987-3). HarbraceJ.

UNIVERSITY OF NOTRE DAME
Deegan, Paul. University of Notre Dame. (Illus.). 48p. (gr. 4 up). 1988. lib. bdg. 11.95 (ISBN 0-939179-51-2). Abdo & Dghtrs.

UNMARRIED MOTHERS
Beauchamp, Andre. Teenage Mothers: Their Experience, Strength, & Hope. Fisher, Rosemarie, tr. from FRE. LC 90-38476. (Illus.). 80p. (Orig.). (gr. 7-12). 1990. pap. 8.95 (ISBN 0-89390-180-6). Resource Pubns.
McGuire, Paula. It Won't Happen to Me: Teenagers Talk about Pregnancy. LC 82-72754. 224p. (gr. 7 up). 1983. 14.95 (ISBN 0-385-29244-9); pap. 6.95 (ISBN 0-685-06445-X). Delacorte.
—It Won't Happen to Me: Teenagers Talk about Pregnancy. Ryan, George M., frwd. by. 1923. pap. 6.95 (ISBN 0-385-29201-5, Delta). Dell.

UNMARRIED MOTHERS–FICTION
Eyerly, Jeannette. Someone to Love Me. LC 86-45501. 160p. (gr. 7 up). 1987. PLB 11.89 (ISBN 0-397-32206-2, Lipp Jr Bks). HarpC Child Bks.
Hunt, Irene. William. LC 76-52455. (gr. 5 up). 1977. SBE 11.95 (ISBN 0-684-14902-8, Scribners Young Read). Macmillan Child Grp.
Minshull, Evelyn W. But I Thought You Really Loved Me. LC 76-14992. 150p. (gr. 7 up). 1976. 7.25 (ISBN 0-664-32600-5, Westminster). Westminster John Knox.
Woodson, Jacqueline. Dear One. (gr. 4-7). 1991. 14.00 (ISBN 0-385-30416-1). Delacorte.

UPPER ATMOSPHERE
see Atmosphere, Upper
URBAN RENEWAL
Anno, Mitsumasa, illus. Anno's Italy. 48p. (gr. 4 up). 1984. 10.95 (ISBN 0-399-20770-8, Philomel); pap. 5.95 (ISBN 0-399-21032-6, Philomel). Putnam Pub Group.
URUGUAY
Haverstock, Nathan A. Uruguay in Pictures. (Illus.). 64p. (gr. 5 up). 1987. PLB 12.95 (ISBN 0-8225-1823-6). Lerner Pubns.
Morrison, Marion. Uruguay. (Illus.). (gr. 5 up). 1988. 14.95 (ISBN 0-222-00953-5). Chelsea Hse.
USEFUL ARTS
see Technology
UTAH
Aylesworth, Thomas G. & Aylesworth, Virginia L. The West (Arizona, Nevada, Utah) (Illus.). 64p. (gr. 3 up). 1992. PLB 16.95 (ISBN 0-7910-1049-X). Chelsea Hse.
Ayres, Becky. Salt Lake City. (Illus.). 60p. (gr. 3 up). 1990. PLB 12.95 (ISBN 0-87518-436-7, Dillon). Macmillan Child Grp.
Carole Marsh Utah Books, 31 bks. Set. 638.45 (ISBN 0-7933-1319-8). Gallopade Pub Group.
Carpenter, Allan. Utah. new ed. LC 79-12433. (Illus.). 96p. (gr. 4 up). 1979. PLB 19.93 (ISBN 0-516-04144-4). Childrens.
Fradin, Dennis. Utah: In Words & Pictures. LC 80-15177. (Illus.). 48p. (gr. 2-5). 1980. PLB 15.93 (ISBN 0-516-03944-X). Childrens.
Hinton, Wayne K. Utah: Unusual Beginning to Unique Present. (Illus.). 192p. (gr. 7 up). 1988. 29.95 (ISBN 0-89781-247-6). Windsor Pubns Inc.
McCarthy, Betty. Utah. LC 89-35083. 144p. (gr. 4 up). 1989. PLB 25.27 (ISBN 0-516-00490-5). Childrens.
Marsh, Carole. Avast, Ye Slobs! Utah Pirate Trivia. (Illus.). 1990. PLB 19.95 (ISBN 0-7933-1124-1); pap. 14.95 (ISBN 0-7933-1123-3); computer disk 29.95 (ISBN 0-7933-1125-X). Gallopade Pub Group.
—The Beast of the Utah Bed & Breakfast. (Illus.). 1990. PLB 19.95 (ISBN 0-7933-2117-4); pap. 14.95 (ISBN 0-7933-2118-2); computer disk 29.95 (ISBN 0-7933-2119-0). Gallopade Pub Group.
—The Hard-to-Believe-But-True! Book of Utah History, Mystery, Trivia, Legend, Lore, Humor & More. (Illus.). 1990. PLB 19.95 (ISBN 0-7933-1121-7); pap. 14.95 (ISBN 0-7933-1120-9); computer disk 29.95 (ISBN 0-7933-1122-5). Gallopade Pub Group.
—If My Utah Mama Ran the World! (Illus.). 1990. PLB 19.95 (ISBN 0-7933-2126-3); pap. 14.95 (ISBN 0-7933-2127-1); computer disk 29.95 (ISBN 0-7933-2128-X). Gallopade Pub Group.
—Let's Quilt Utah & Stuff It Topographically! (Illus.). 1990. PLB 19.95 (ISBN 0-7933-2109-3); pap. 14.95 (ISBN 1-55609-129-X); computer disk 29.95 (ISBN 0-7933-2110-7). Gallopade Pub Group.
—Utah & Other State Greats (Biographies) (Illus.). 1990. PLB 19.95 (ISBN 0-7933-2129-8); pap. 14.95 (ISBN 0-7933-2130-1); computer disk 29.95 (ISBN 0-7933-2131-X). Gallopade Pub Group.
—Utah Bandits, Bushwackers, Outlaws, Crooks, Devils, Ghosts, Desperadoes & Other Assorted & Sundry Characters! (Illus.). 1990. PLB 19.95 (ISBN 0-7933-1106-3); pap. 14.95; computer disk 29.95 (ISBN 0-7933-1107-1). Gallopade Pub Group.
—Utah Classic Christmas Trivia: Stories, Recipes, Activities, Legends, Lore & More! (Illus.). 1990. PLB 19.95 (ISBN 0-7933-1109-8); pap. 14.95 (ISBN 0-7933-1108-X); computer disk 29.95 (ISBN 0-7933-1110-1). Gallopade Pub Group.
—Utah Coastales. (Illus.). 1990. PLB 19.95 (ISBN 0-7933-2123-9); pap. 14.95 (ISBN 0-7933-2124-7); computer disk 29.95. Gallopade Pub Group.
—The Utah Hot Air Balloon Mystery. (Illus.). (gr. 2-9). 1990. 19.95 (ISBN 0-7933-2714-8); pap. 14.95 (ISBN 0-7933-2715-6); computer disk 29.95 (ISBN 0-7933-2716-4). Gallopade Pub Group.
—Utah "Jography" A Fun Run Thru Our State! (Illus.). 1990. PLB 19.95 (ISBN 0-7933-2106-9); pap. 14.95 (ISBN 0-7933-2107-7); computer disk 29.95 (ISBN 0-7933-2108-5). Gallopade Pub Group.
—Utah Kid's Cookbook: Recipes, How-to, History, Lore & More! (Illus.). 1990. PLB 19.95 (ISBN 0-7933-1118-7); pap. 14.95 (ISBN 0-7933-1117-9); computer disk 29.95 (ISBN 0-7933-1119-5). Gallopade Pub Group.
—Utah Quiz Bowl Crash Course! (Illus.). 1990. PLB 19.95 (ISBN 0-7933-2120-4); pap. 14.95 (ISBN 0-7933-2121-2); computer disk 29.95 (ISBN 0-7933-2122-0). Gallopade Pub Group.
—Utah School Trivia: An Amazing & Fascinating Look at Our State's Teachers, Schools & Students! (Illus.). 1990. PLB 19.95 (ISBN 0-7933-1115-2); pap. 14.95 (ISBN 0-7933-1114-4); computer disk 29.95 (ISBN 0-7933-1116-0). Gallopade Pub Group.
—Utah Silly Basketball Sportsmysteries, Vol. 1. (Illus.). 1990. PLB 19.95 (ISBN 0-7933-1112-8); pap. 14.95 (ISBN 0-7933-1111-X); computer disk 29.95 (ISBN 0-7933-1113-6). Gallopade Pub Group.
—Utah Silly Basketball Sportsmysteries, Vol. 2. (Illus.). 1990. PLB 19.95 (ISBN 0-7933-2132-8); pap. 14.95 (ISBN 0-7933-2133-6); computer disk 29.95 (ISBN 0-7933-2134-4). Gallopade Pub Group.
—Utah Silly Football Sportsmysteries, Vol. 1. (Illus.). 1990. PLB 19.95 (ISBN 0-7933-2111-5); pap. 14.95 (ISBN 0-7933-2112-3); computer disk 29.95 (ISBN 0-7933-2113-1). Gallopade Pub Group.
—Utah Silly Football Sportsmysteries, Vol. 2. (Illus.). 1990. PLB 19.95 (ISBN 0-7933-2114-X); pap. 14.95 (ISBN 0-7933-2115-8); computer disk 29.95 (ISBN 0-7933-2116-6). Gallopade Pub Group.
—Utah Silly Trivia! (Illus.). 1990. PLB 19.95 (ISBN 0-7933-2103-4); pap. 14.95 (ISBN 0-7933-2104-2); computer disk 29.95 (ISBN 0-7933-2105-0). Gallopade Pub Group.
—Utah's (Most Devastating!) Disasters & (Most Calamitous!) Catastrophies! (Illus.). 1990. PLB 19.95 (ISBN 0-7933-1103-9); pap. 14.95 (ISBN 0-7933-1102-0) (ISBN 0-7933-1104-7). Gallopade Pub Group.
Pearson, Carol L. A Lasting Peace. LC 90-37361. 158p. (gr. 9-12). 1990. pap. 5.95 (ISBN 0-87579-302-9). Deseret Bk.
Turner Program Services, Inc. Staff & Clark, James I. Utah. 48p. (gr. 3 up). 1985. PLB 17.32 (ISBN 0-86514-446-X); pap. text ed. 9.27 (ISBN 0-86514-521-0); cancelled Beta video (ISBN 0-86514-071-5); cancelled VHS video (ISBN 0-86514-146-0); cancelled 3/4" video (ISBN 0-86514-221-1); cancelled tchr's. guide (ISBN 0-86514-296-3); cancelled student activity bk. (ISBN 0-86514-371-4); cancelled index. Raintree Pubs.
Westwood, Dick. Champin' at the Bit: An Autobiography. (Illus.). 161p. (Orig.). (gr. 6-12). 1986. pap. 10.00x (ISBN 0-9617118-1-7). Westwood Ent.
UTAH–FICTION
Fitzgerald, John D. The Great Brain. Mayer, Mercer, illus. LC 67-22252. (gr. 4-8). 1985. 12.95 (ISBN 0-8037-3074-8); PLB 11.89 (ISBN 0-8037-3076-4). Dial Bks Young.
—Me & My Little Brain. 144p. (gr. 4-7). 1972. 3.25 (ISBN 0-440-45533-2, YB). Dell.
—More Adventures of the Great Brain. Mayer, Mercer, illus. LC 73-85547. (gr. 4-8). 1985. 12.95 (ISBN 0-8037-5819-7, 01160-350); PLB 11.89 (ISBN 0-8037-5821-9). Dial Bks Young.
UTENSILS, KITCHEN
see Household Equipment and Supplies

V

VACATIONS–FICTION
Andrews, Wendy. Vacation Fever! 160p. (gr. 7 up). 1984. 10.95 (ISBN 0-399-21084-9, Putnam); pap. 2.25 (ISBN 0-399-21083-0, Putnam). Putnam Pub Group.
Avi. A Place Called Ugly. Adams, illus. LC 80-23326. 224p. (gr. 7-9). 1981. lib. bdg. 8.99 (ISBN 0-394-94755-X). Pantheon.
Brandenburg, Franz. A Fun Weekend. Brandenburg, Alexa, illus. LC 89-77502. 24p. (ps up). 1991. 13.95 (ISBN 0-688-09720-0); PLB 13.88 (ISBN 0-688-09721-9). Greenwillow.
Enright, Elizabeth. Gone-Away Lake. Dyer, Jane & Krush, Beth, illus. 240p. (gr. 3-7). 1990. pap. 4.95 (ISBN 0-15-231649-3). HarBraceJ.
—Return to Gone-Away. Dyer, Jane & Krush, Beth, illus. 192p. (gr. 3-7). 1990. pap. 4.95 (ISBN 0-15-266377-0). HarBraceJ.
Godfrey, Martyn N. I Spent My Summer Vacation Kidnapped. (gr. 5-7). 1990. pap. 2.75 (ISBN 0-590-43418-7). Scholastic Inc.
Harwood, Pearl A. Long Vacation for Mr. & Mrs. Bumba. Overlie, George, illus. LC 71-156359. 32p. (gr. k-3). 1971. PLB 4.95 (ISBN 0-8225-0121-X). Lerner Pubns.
Kahn, Peggy. The Popples' Vacation. Kolding, Richard M., illus. LC 86-62220. 32p. (ps-3). 1987. pap. 1.25 (ISBN 0-394-88758-1, Random Juv). Random.
Khalsa, Dayal K. My Family Vacation. Khalsa, Dayal K., illus. 24p. (gr. k-8). 1988. 14.95 (ISBN 0-88776-226-3). Tundra Bks.
Levy, Elizabeth. Something Queer on Vacation. Gerstein, Mordicai, illus. 48p. (gr. 1-4). 1982. pap. 2.75 (ISBN 0-440-47968-1, YB). Dell.
McPhail, David. Emma's Vacation. McPhail, David, illus. LC 86-24066. (ps-k). 1987. 7.95 (ISBN 0-525-44315-0, DCB). Dutton Child Bks.
My Totally Awesome Summer Vacation. 64p. (Orig.). (gr. 1-4). 1992. pap. 6.95 (ISBN 0-8249-8510-9). Ideals.
Nelson, Jackie & Halpern-Segal, Janice. My Trip. Schoonover, Annette, illus. 24p. (Orig.). (ps-3). 1989. pap. 6.95 (ISBN 0-685-29177-4). Take Along Pubns.
Nielsen, Shelly. Only Kidding, Victoria. 130p. (gr. 5-6). 1986. pap. 3.95 (ISBN 0-89191-474-9). Cook.
Perl, Lila. Telltale Summer of Tina C. 1984. pap. 2.50 (ISBN 0-590-41324-4). Scholastic Inc.
Ressner, Phillip. Dudley Pippin's Summer. Schecter, Ben, illus. LC 78-19831. 48p. (gr. 2-5). 1979. PLB 12.89 (ISBN 0-06-024888-2). HarpC Child Bks.
Roberts, Willo D. Nightmare. 192p. (gr. 5-9). 1989. 13.95 (ISBN 0-689-31551-1, Atheneum Child Bk). Macmillan Child Grp.
Rockwell, Anne. On Our Vacation. Rockwell, Anne, illus. 32p. (ps-1). 1989. 12.95 (ISBN 0-525-44487-4, DCB). Dutton Child Bks.
Skurzynski, Gloria. Dangerous Ground. LC 88-31394. 160p. (gr. 3-7). 1989. 12.95 (ISBN 0-02-782731-3, Bradbury Pr). Macmillan Child Grp.
Stevenson, James. When I Was Nine. Stevenson, James, illus. LC 85-9777. 32p. (gr. k-3). 1986. 12.95 (ISBN 0-688-05942-2); PLB 12.88 (ISBN 0-688-05943-0). Greenwillow.
Tolan, Stephanie S. The Great Skinner Getaway. LC 86-22874. 204p. (gr. 7 up). 1987. 13.95 (ISBN 0-02-789361-8, Four Winds). Macmillan Child Grp.
Towne, Mary. Steve the Sure. LC 90-584. 144p. (gr. 4-7). 1990. 12.95 (ISBN 0-689-31646-1, Atheneum Child Bk). Macmillan Child Grp.
Townsend, John R. Tom Tiddler's Ground. LC 85-45859. 176p. (gr. 3-6). 1986. PLB 11.89 (ISBN 0-397-32191-0, Lipp Jr Bks). HarpC Child Bks.
Wells, Carolyn. Marjorie's Vacation. 232p. 1981. Repr. PLB 16.95x (ISBN 0-89966-337-0). Buccaneer Bks.
—Marjorie's Vacation. 315p. 1980. Repr. PLB 12.95x (ISBN 0-89967-012-1). Harmony Raine.
VACCINATION
see also Immunity
VACUUM TUBES
see also Electronics
VALENTINE'S DAY
Barkin, Carol & James, Elizabeth. Happy Valentines Day. LC 87-35812. (Illus.). 96p. (gr. 4-7). 1988. 12.95 (ISBN 0-688-06796-4); PLB 12.88 (ISBN 0-688-06797-2). Lothrop.
Barth, Edna. Hearts, Cupids, & Red Roses: The Story of the Valentine Symbols. Arndt, Ursula, illus. LC 73-7128. 64p. (gr. 3-6). 1982. pap. 5.95 (ISBN 0-89919-036-7, Clarion). HM.
Bennett, Marian & Peltier, Pam. My First Valentine's Day Book. LC 84-21511. (Illus.). 32p. (ps-2). 1985. lib. bdg. 14.60 (ISBN 0-516-02906-1); pap. 3.95 (ISBN 0-516-42906-X). Childrens.
Brown, Fern G. Valentine's Day. (Illus.). 72p. (gr. 4 up). 1983. PLB 10.40 (ISBN 0-531-04533-1). Watts.
Bulla, Clyde R. St. Valentine's Day. Angelo, Valenti, illus. LC 65-11643. 40p. (gr. 1-3). 1965. PLB 12.89 (ISBN 0-690-71744-X, Crowell Jr Bks). HarpC Child Bks.
Carson, Patti & Dellosa, Janet. Valentine Day Fun Book. Carson, Patti & Dellosa, Janet, illus. 32p. (ps-1). 1982. pap. 1.59 (ISBN 0-88724-054-2, CD-8009). Carson-Dellos.
—Valentine-February Primary Reading & Art Activities. Carson, Patti & Dellosa, Janet, illus. 32p. (gr. 1-3). 1984. pap. 1.98 (ISBN 0-88724-026-7, CD-8041). Carson-Dellos.
—Valentine Preschool-K Practice. Carson, Patti & Dellosa, Janet, illus. 32p. (ps-k). 1984. pap. 1.98 (ISBN 0-88724-018-6, CD-8033). Carson-Dellos.
Corwin, Judith H. Valentine Fun. Corwin, Judith H., illus. LC 82-6047. 64p. (gr. 3 up). 1983. PLB 10.29 (ISBN 0-671-45945-7); PLB 7.71s.p.; pap. 5.95 (ISBN 0-671-49755-3); pap. 4.46s.p. Messner.
Davis, Nancy M., et al. February & Valentines. Davis, Nancy M., illus. 29p. (Orig.). (ps-2). 1986. pap. 4.95 (ISBN 0-937103-07-1). DaNa Pubns.
Dietz, Sarah S. & Brokaw, David. Valentine Activity Book. (Illus.). 32p. (gr. 4 up). 1984. pap. 1.98 (ISBN 0-88724-065-8, CD-8045). Carson-Dellos.
Folmer, A. P. Valentine Pop-up Cards to Make. (ps-3). 1991. pap. 3.95 (ISBN 0-590-44033-0). Scholastic Inc.
Fradin, Dennis B. Valentine's Day. LC 89-7682. (Illus.). 48p. (gr. 2-3). 1990. PLB 12.95 (ISBN 0-89490-237-7). Enslow Pubs.
Glovach, Linda. The Little Witch's Valentine Book. (Illus.). 48p. 1984. 9.95 (ISBN 0-13-538026-X). P-H.
Graham-Barber, Lynda. Mushy! The Complete Book of Valentine Words. Lewin, Betsy, illus. LC 90-33047. 128p. (gr. 4-10). 1991. 13.95 (ISBN 0-02-736941-2, Bradbury Pr). Macmillan Child Grp.
Kalman, Bobbie. We Celebrate Valentine's Day. (Illus.). 56p. (gr. 3-4). 1986. 15.95 (ISBN 0-86505-047-3); pap. 7.95 (ISBN 0-86505-057-0). Crabtree Pub Co.
Kent, Jack. Jack Kent's Valentine Sticker Book. 40p. (ps-3). 1987. pap. 2.50 (ISBN 0-590-32400-4). Scholastic Inc.
Kessel, Joyce K. Valentine's Day. Ritz, Karen, illus. 48p. (gr. k-4). 1988. pap. 3.95 (ISBN 0-685-25644-8, First Ave Edns). Lerner Pubns.
Moncure, Jane B. Our Valentine's Day Book. Rev. ed. McLean, Mina G., illus. LC 86-28387. 32p. (ps-3). 1987. PLB 11.97 (ISBN 0-89565-343-5). Childs World.
Prelutsky, Jack. It's Valentine's Day. Abolafia, Yossi, illus. 48p. (gr. k-3). 1985. pap. 2.50 (ISBN 0-590-40979-4). Scholastic Inc.
—It's Valentine's Day. Abolafia, Yossi, illus. 48p. (gr. k-3). 1988. pap. 5.95 bk & cassette (ISBN 0-590-63172-1). Scholastic Inc.
Sandak, Cass. Valentine's Day. (Illus.). 48p. (gr. 5 up). 1990. 10.95 (ISBN 0-89686-504-5, Crestwood Hse). Macmillan Child Grp.
Spivak, Darlene & Sterling, Mary E. Valentine's Day Activities. Wright, Theresa & Spence, Paula, illus. 48p. (gr. 1-4). 1989. wkbk. 5.95 (ISBN 1-55734-009-9). Tchr Create Mat.
Supraner, Robyn. Valentine's Day: Things to Make & Do. Barto, Renzo, illus. LC 80-23780. 48p. (gr. 1-5). 1981. PLB 11.89 (ISBN 0-89375-424-2); pap. 2.95 (ISBN 0-89375-425-0). Troll Assocs.
Thayer, Marjorie. The Valentine Box. Burgeson, Marjorie, illus. LC 76-46543. 32p. (gr. k-4). 1977. PLB 15.93 (ISBN 0-516-08746-0, Golden Gate). Childrens.
Tudor, Tasha. The Jenny Wren Book of Valentines. Tudor, Tasha, illus. Wren, Jenny, intro. by. LC 88-51832. (Illus.). 16p. (Orig.). (gr. k up). 1989. pap. 6.95 (ISBN 0-9621753-1-5). Jenny Wren Pr.

VALENTINE'S DAY–FICTION

Balian, Lorna. A Sweetheart for Valentine. rev. ed. Balian, Lorna, illus. LC 79-3957. 32p. (gr. k-3). 1987. 11.95 (ISBN 0-687-40771-0); PLB 5.95 (ISBN 0-685-00022-2). Abingdon.

Barth, Nancy & Wittenborn, Sally. But Will You Be My Valentine? (Illus., Orig.). (ps-k). 1987. pap. 4.95 (ISBN 0-942565-01-0). Country Schl Pubns.

Blos, Joan W. One Very Best Valentine's Day. 1990. pap. 8.95 (ISBN 0-671-64639-7, Wallaby). S&S Trade.

Bond, Felicia. Four Valentines in a Rainstorm. Bond, Felicia, illus. LC 82-45586. 32p. (ps-3). 1986. 4.95 (ISBN 0-694-00154-6, Crowell Jr Bks). HarpC Child Bks.

Carlson, Nancy. Louanne Pig in the Mysterious Valentine. (ps-3). 1987. pap. 3.95 (ISBN 0-14-050604-7, Puffin). Puffin Bks.

—The Mysterious Valentine. Carlson, Nancy, illus. LC 85-3757. 32p. (ps-3). 1985. PLB 9.95 (ISBN 0-87614-282-X). Carolrhoda Bks.

Cleaver, Vera & Cleaver, Bill. Queen of Hearts. LC 77-18252. 160p. (gr. 6 up). 1978. 13.95 (ISBN 0-397-31771-9, Lipp Jr Bks). HarpC Child Bks.

Cohen, Miriam. Bee My Valentine. Hoban, Lillian, illus. LC 77-21950. 32p. (gr. k-3). 1978. PLB 11.88 (ISBN 0-688-84129-5). Greenwillow.

—Bee My Valentine! Hoban, Lillian, illus. (gr. k-3). 1983. pap. 2.95 (ISBN 0-440-40507-6, YB). Dell.

Cuyler, Margery. Freckles & Willie: A Valentine's Day Story. Winborn, Marsha, illus. LC 85-8646. 32p. (gr. k-2). 1986. 12.95 (ISBN 0-03-003772-7). H Holt & Co.

—Freckles & Willie: A Valentine's Day Story. Winborn, Marsha, illus. LC 85-8646. 32p. (gr. k-2). 1989. pap. 4.95 (ISBN 0-8050-0949-3). H Holt & Co.

Devlin, Wende & Devlin, Harry. Cranberry Valentine. Devlin, Wende & Devlin, Harry, illus. LC 85-24047. 32p. (gr. k-3). 1986. 13.95 (ISBN 0-02-729200-2, Four Winds). Macmillan Child Grp.

—Cranberry Valentine. Devlin, Wende & Devlin, Harry, illus. 40p. (gr. k-3). 1992. pap. 3.95 (ISBN 0-689-71509-9, Aladdin). Macmillan Child Grp.

Gantz, David. Biggest Valentine. 1990. pap. 2.50 (ISBN 0-590-43329-6). Scholastic Inc.

Giff, Patricia R. The Valentine Star. Sims, Blanche, illus. 80p. (Orig.). (gr. k-6). 1985. pap. 2.75 (ISBN 0-440-49204-1, YB). Dell.

Greenwald, Sheila. Valentine Rosy. Greenwald, Sheila, illus. LC 84-9694. 89p. (gr. 4 up). 1984. 11.95 (ISBN 0-316-32708-5, Joy St Bks). Little.

Greydanus, Rose. Valentine's Day Grump. Page, Don, illus. LC 81-4712. 32p. (gr. k-2). 1981. PLB 10.89 (ISBN 0-89375-515-X); pap. text ed. 2.95 (ISBN 0-89375-516-8). Troll Assocs.

Haynes, Betsy. Melanie's Valentine. (gr. 4-7). 1991. pap. 2.95 (ISBN 0-553-15845-7). Bantam.

Haywood, Carolyn. A Valentine Fantasy. Ambrus, Victor G. & Ambrus, Victor G., illus. LC 75-23083. 32p. (gr. k-3). 1976. PLB 14.88 (ISBN 0-688-32055-4). Morrow.

Himmel, Roger J. Lollipop Dragon's Valentine Party. new ed. Manoni, Mary H., ed. Peters, Luther J. & Ross, Connie, illus. LC 70-739484. (gr. k-3). 1978. pap. text ed. 29.95 6 bks & 1 cass. (ISBN 0-89290-041-5); pap. text ed. 10.95 1 bk. & 1 cass. Soc for Visual.

Hoban, Lillian. Arthur's Great Big Valentine. Hoban, Lillian, illus. LC 88-21202. 64p. (gr. k-3). 1989. 11.95 (ISBN 0-06-022406-1); PLB 11.89 (ISBN 0-06-022407-X). HarpC Child Bks.

—Arthur's Great Big Valentine. Hoban, Lillian, illus. LC 88-21202. 64p. (gr. k-3). 1991. pap. 3.50 (ISBN 0-06-444149-0, Trophy). HarpC Child Bks.

Kelley, True. A Valentine for Fuzzboom. Kelley, True, illus. LC 80-24284. 24p. (gr. k-3). 1982. pap. 1.95 (ISBN 0-395-31888-2). HM.

Kessel, Joyce K. Valentine's Day. Ritz, Karen, illus. LC 81-3842. 48p. (gr. k-4). 1981. PLB 9.95 (ISBN 0-87614-166-1); pap. 3.95 (ISBN 0-87614-502-0). Carolrhoda Bks.

Kraus, Robert. How Spider Saved Valentine's Day. Kraus, Robert, illus. 32p. (Orig.). (ps-1). 1986. pap. 2.50 (ISBN 0-590-42514-5). Scholastic Inc.

Kunhardt, Edith. Danny's Mystery Valentine. LC 86-19400. 1987. 12.88 (ISBN 0-688-06854-5). Greenwillow.

—Danny's Mystery Valentine. (Illus.). 24p. (ps-1). 1987. 11.75 (ISBN 0-688-06853-7); PLB 11.88. Greenwillow.

Lexau, Joan M. Don't Be My Valentine. Hoff, Syd, illus. (gr. 1-4). 1990. incl. cass. 19.95 (ISBN 0-87499-150-1); pap. 12.95 incl. cass. (ISBN 0-87499-149-8); Set; incl. 4 bks., cass., & guide. pap. 27.95 (ISBN 0-685-38539-6). Live Oak Media.

Mariana. Miss Flora McFlimsey's Valentine. rev. ed. Mariana, illus. LC 86-15254. 40p. (gr. k-3). 1987. 9.95 (ISBN 0-688-04547-2). Lothrop.

Modell, Frank. One Zillion Valentines. LC 81-2215. (Illus.). 32p. (gr. k-3). 1981. 11.75 (ISBN 0-688-00565-9); PLB 11.88 (ISBN 0-688-00569-1). Greenwillow.

Mooser, Stephen. Crazy Mixed-up Valentines. (gr. k-6). 1990. pap. 2.75 (ISBN 0-440-40269-7, YB). Dell.

Prelutsky, Jack. It's Valentine's Day. Abolafia, Yossi, illus. LC 83-1449. 48p. (gr. 1-3). 1983. 14.95 (ISBN 0-688-02311-8); PLB 14.88 (ISBN 0-688-02312-6). Greenwillow.

Roos, Stephen. My Secret Admirer. Newsom, Carol, illus. LC 84-5010. 112p. (gr. 4-6). 1984. 14.95 (ISBN 0-385-29342-9); PLB 13.95 (ISBN 0-385-29343-7). Delacorte.

St. Pierre, Stephanie. Valentine Kittens. 1990. pap. 3.95 (ISBN 0-590-63481-X). Scholastic Inc.

Saunders, Susan. A Valentine for Patti. (gr. 4-7). 1991. pap. 2.75 (ISBN 0-590-43927-8). Scholastic Inc.

Schweninger, Ann. Valentine Friends. (Illus.). 32p. (ps-1). 1990. pap. 3.95 (ISBN 0-14-050662-4, Puffin). Puffin Bks.

Sharmat, Marjorie W. Best Valentine in the World. LC 81-13345. (Illus.). 32p. (gr. k-3). 1982. reinforced bdg. 13.95 (ISBN 0-8234-0440-4). Holiday.

Stevenson, James. Happy Valentine's Day, Emma! LC 87-13. (Illus.). 32p. (gr. k-3). 1987. 11.75 (ISBN 0-688-07357-3); lib. bdg. 11.88 (ISBN 0-688-07358-1). Greenwillow.

Stock, Catherine. Secret Valentine. Stock, Catherine, illus. LC 90-1916. 32p. (ps-1). 1991. SBE 11.95 (ISBN 0-02-788372-8, Bradbury Pr). Macmillan Child Grp.

Wittman, Sally. The Boy Who Hated Valentine's Day. Burstein, Chaya, illus. LC 85-45817. 32p. (gr. k-3). 1987. 11.95 (ISBN 0-06-026593-0). HarpC Child Bks.

VALLEY FORGE

Stein, R. Conrad. The Story of Valley Forge. Eads, Nancy, illus. LC 84-23203. 31p. (gr. 3-5). 1985. lib. bdg. 13.27 (ISBN 0-516-04681-0); pap. 3.95 (ISBN 0-516-44681-9). Childrens.

VAN BUREN, MARTIN, PRESIDENT U. S. 1782-1862

Ellis, Rafaela. Martin Van Buren: Eighth President of the United States. Young, Richard G., ed. LC 88-24535. (Illus.). (gr. 5-9). 1989. PLB 17.26 (ISBN 0-944483-12-7). Garrett Ed Corp.

Hargrove, James. Martin Van Buren. LC 87-16023. (Illus.). 100p. (gr. 3 up). 1987. PLB 17.27 (ISBN 0-516-01391-2). Childrens.

Welles, Ted. Van Buren, Wizard of O.K. & 8th U. S. A. President. Johnson, Mercy, ed. LC 87-60750. (Illus.). 96p. (Orig.). (gr. 6 up). 1987. July 30, 1987. lib. bdg. 12.00 (ISBN 0-915189-04-6); June 30, 1987. pap. 5.95 (ISBN 0-915189-05-4). Oceanus.

VANDALISM

see Crime and Criminals

VAN SWEARINGEN, MARMADUKE, 1752-1824?

Eckert, Allan W. Blue Jacket: War Chief of the Shawnees. LC 69-10656. (Illus.). (gr. 7 up). 1969. 14.95 (ISBN 0-316-20863-9). Little.

VASSALS

see Feudalism

VATICAN (CITY)

Conry, Kieran. The Vatican. (Illus.). (gr. 5 up). 1988. 14.95 (ISBN 0-222-01009-6). Chelsea Hse.

The Vatican. 48p. (gr. 4-5). 1989. PLB 10.95 (ISBN 0-685-26415-7). Capstone Pr.

VEGETABLE GARDENING

see also Vegetables

Fryer, Lee & Bradford, Leigh. A Child's Organic Garden. Albert, Eddie, frwd. by. 96p. 1989. 9.45 (ISBN 0-87491-963-0); pap. 9.95 (ISBN 0-685-28260-0). Acropolis.

Gardening. (Illus.). 64p. (gr. 6-12). 1982. pap. 1.85 (ISBN 0-8395-3240-7, 3240). BSA.

Watts, Barrie. Tomato. (Illus.). 25p. (ps-4). 1990. 6.95 (ISBN 0-685-35170-X); PLB 9.98 (ISBN 0-685-35171-8). Silver Burdett Pr.

VEGETABLE GARDENING–FICTION

Buria, Maria E. Billy the Bean. Siu, Emma, illus. 36p. (Orig.). (ps-k). 1989. pap. 5.95 (ISBN 1-878926-04-7). Colorful Lrngs.

Burningham, John. Avocado Baby. LC 81-43844. (Illus.). 32p. (ps-1). 1982. (Crowell Jr Bks). HarpC Child Bks.

Carlstrom, Nancy W. Moose in the Garden. Desimini, Lisa, illus. LC 89-29407. 32p. (ps-2). 1990. 13.95 (ISBN 0-06-021015-X); PLB 13.89 (ISBN 0-06-021014-1). HarpC Child Bks.

Poulet, Virginia. Blue Bug's Vegetable Garden. Charles, Donald, illus. LC 73-8896. 32p. (gr. k-3). 1973. PLB 14.60 (ISBN 0-516-03421-9). Childrens.

Taylor, Judy. Sophie & Jack Help Out. Gantner, Susan, illus. LC 83-13302. 32p. (gr. k-2). 1984. 8.95 (ISBN 0-399-21059-8, Philomel). Putnam Pub Group.

Westcott, Nadine B. The Giant Vegetable Garden. (Illus.). 32p. (ps-3). 1981. 14.95i (ISBN 0-316-93129-2, Pub. by Atlantic Monthly Pr); pap. 4.95 (ISBN 0-316-93130-6). Little.

VEGETABLE KINGDOM

see Botany; Plants

VEGETABLES

see also Vegetable Gardening; Vegetarianism

Cross, Gillian. Born of the Sun. LC 84-3740. (Illus.). 240p. (gr. 7 up). 1984. 11.95 (ISBN 0-8234-0528-1). Holiday.

Dineen, Jacqueline. Vegetables & Oils. 32p. (gr. 4-8). 1988. lib. bdg. 12.95 (ISBN 0-89490-224-5). Enslow Pubs.

Green, Harriet & Martin, Sue. Sprouts. 144p. (gr. 3-8). 1981. 10.95 (ISBN 0-86653-028-2, GA256). Good Apple.

Overbeck, Cynthia. The Vegetable Book. Lerner, Sharon, illus. LC 74-12746. 32p. (gr. k-3). 1975. PLB 6.95 (ISBN 0-8225-0297-6). Lerner Pubns.

Pohl, Kathleen. Potatoes. (Illus.). 32p. (gr. 3-7). 1986. PLB 16.67 (ISBN 0-8172-2723-7); pap. text ed. 9.27 (ISBN 0-8172-2741-5). Raintree Pubs.

Simmons, Paula. The Zucchini Cookbook. 3rd, rev. ed. Richardson, Ruth, illus. Guzzo, Louis, intro. by. LC 74-77037. (Illus.). 132p. 1983. pap. 6.95 (ISBN 0-914718-81-9). Pacific Search.

Sobol, Harriet L. A Book of Vegetables. Agre, Patricia A., photos by. (Illus.). 48p. (gr. k-3). 1984. 10.95 (ISBN 0-396-08450-8, Putnam). Putnam Pub Group.

Turner, Dorothy. Potatoes. Yates, John, illus. 32p. (gr. 1-4). 1989. PLB 9.95 (ISBN 0-87614-362-1). Carolrhoda Bks.

Wake, Susan. Vegetables. (Illus.). 32p. (gr. 1-4). 1990. PLB 9.95 (ISBN 0-87614-390-7). Carolrhoda Bks.

Wasserman, Debra & Stahler, Charles, eds. I Love Animals & Broccoli. Ransom, Ruth, intro. by. 48p. (Orig.). 1985. pap. 5.00 (ISBN 0-931411-01-7). Vegetarian Resc.

Watts, Barrie. Potato. LC 87-16702. (Illus.). 25p. (gr. 1-5). 1988. 6.95 (ISBN 0-382-09528-6); PLB 9.98 (ISBN 0-382-09527-8); pap. 3.95 (ISBN 0-382-24018-9). Silver Burdett Pr.

—Tomato. (Illus.). 25p. (gr. k-4). 1990. 6.95 (ISBN 0-382-24010-3); 5.21s.p.; PLB 9.98 (ISBN 0-382-24008-1); PLB 7.49s.p. Silver Burdett Pr.

Whitlatch, Issac. Me & My Veggies. Whitlatch, Issac, illus. LC 87-2920. 24p. (gr. 1-7). 1987. PLB 12.95 (ISBN 0-933849-16-8). Landmark Edns.

VEGETABLES–CANNING

see Canning and Preserving

VEGETABLES–MARKETING

see Farm Produce–Marketing

VEGETARIANISM

Salter, Charles A. The Vegetarian Teen. (Illus.). 112p. (gr. 7 up). 1991. PLB 13.90 (ISBN 1-56294-048-1). Millbrook Pr.

Singer, Marcia. Eating for a Fresh Start: A P.L.A.Y. Book. Rendal, Camille, illus. LC 90-91969. 64p. (Orig.). (gr. 1-7). 1990. pap. write for info. (ISBN 0-9622543-1-2). PLAY House.
A family guide to beginning vegetarianism & ecologically sound eating habits. Easy to follow help with sprouting, food combining, good digestion practices & yummy recipes. Features scientific definitions, charming illustrations, activities, "rap" style verse. Promotes physical, mental & emotional health. "Sorely needed as an educational tool."-- Malibu Action For Safe Food. "Helpful introduction to healthful, planet-healing cuisine."--Michael Klaper, M.D., EarthSave. "Balances sound nutritional principles with games & activities.--Marilyn Diamond, Fit For Life. "Helps children be more aware & healthy."--John Robbins, Diet For A New America. "I particularly like the drawings & simple recipes."--Kim Fella, Pres. Peace Child Foundation. "Pictures, recipes, poetry, hard facts for kids who like food."--Carolyn Rueben, LA Weekly "Excellent intro to healthy eating habits for any kid or parent."--Garbage Magazine. "On our reference list for school health coordinators."--Susan Lordi, LA County Office of Education. "Also creates awareness about animal rights, environmental concerns."--Vegetarian Society of So. CA. "Nice beginner's guide."--Gabriel Cousens, M.D., Spiritual Nutrition. "Promotes dieting practices uniquely."--Sandra French, LB Unified School District. "Magically creative teaching tool."--Kathy Arnos, Mother-to-Mother newsletter. *Publisher Provided Annotation.*

VEHICLES

Emergency Vehicles. 48p. (gr. 3-4). 1989. PLB 10.95 (ISBN 0-685-26373-8). Capstone Pr.

Go-Karts. 48p. (gr. 3-4). 1989. PLB 10.95 (ISBN 0-685-26375-4). Capstone Pr.

Lafferty, Peter & Jefferis, David. To the Rescue: The History of Emergency Vehicles. (Illus.). 32p. (gr. 5-8). 1990. PLB 11.90 (ISBN 0-531-14085-7). Watts.

Oliver, Stephen, photos by. Things That Go. LC 90-23562. (Illus.). 24p. (ps-k). 1991. 7.00 (ISBN 0-679-81804-9, Random Juv). Random.

RV's & Vans. 48p. (gr. 3-4). 1989. PLB 10.95 (ISBN 0-685-26379-7). Capstone Pr.

Stacy, Tom. Wings, Wheels & Sails. (Illus.). 40p. (gr. 4-5). 1991. PLB 11.40 (ISBN 0-531-19105-2). Watts.
Vehicles: Land, Sea, Air. 1991. pap. 3.95 (ISBN 0-7214-5322-8). Ladybird Bks.
Zokeisha. Let's Go for a Ride. Zokeisha, illus. 16p. (ps-k). 1982. 2.95 (ISBN 0-671-44896-X, Little Simon). S&S Trade.

VEHICLES, MILITARY

Maynard, Christopher. War Vehicles. LC 79-5063. (Illus.). 36p. (gr. 3-6). 1980. PLB 9.95 (ISBN 0-8225-1185-1). Lerner Pubns.
Military Vehicles. (Illus.). 64p. (gr. 3-9). 1990. PLB 16.95 (ISBN 1-85435-090-0). Marshall Cavendish.
Nicholaus, J. Tracked Vehicles. (Illus.). 48p. (gr. 3-8). 1989. lib. bdg. 18.60 (ISBN 0-86592-422-8). Rourke Corp.

VELAZQUEZ, DIEGO RODRIQUEZ DE SILVA Y, 1599-1660–FICTION

De Trevino, Elizabeth B. I, Juan De Pareja. LC 65-19330. 192p. (gr. 7 up). 1987. (Sunburst); pap. 3.50 (ISBN 0-374-43525-1, Sunburst). FS&G.

VELOCITY

see Speed

VENEREAL DISEASES

Felman, Yehudi M. Genital Herpes. Head, J. J., ed. Steffen, Ann T. & Whitely, Derek, illus. LC 84-71142. 16p. (Orig.). (gr. 10 up). 1987. pap. text ed. 2.15 (ISBN 0-89278-153-X, 45-9753). Carolina Biological.
Landau, Elaine. Sexually Transmitted Diseases. Heimlich, Hermelie, illus. Armstrong, Donald & Haundsfield, Hunterfrwd. by. LC 85-4349. (Illus.). 96p. (gr. 6-12). 1986. lib. bdg. 16.95 (ISBN 0-89490-115-X). Enslow Pubs.
Little, Marjorie. Sexually Transmitted Diseases. (Illus.). (gr. 6-12). 1991. 18.95 (ISBN 0-7910-0080-X). Chelsea Hse.
Nourse, Alan E. Herpes. LC 85-5152. 104p. (gr. 6up). 1985. PLB 11.90 (ISBN 0-531-10069-3). Watts.

VENEZUELA

Fox, Geoffrey. The Land & People of Venezuela. LC 90-20431. (Illus.). 208p. (gr. 6 up). 1991. 17.95 (ISBN 0-06-022476-2); PLB 17.89 (ISBN 0-06-022477-0). HarpC Child Bks.
Lerner Publications, Department of Geography Staff. Venezuela in Pictures. (Illus.). 64p. (gr. 5 up). 1987. PLB 12.95 (ISBN 0-8225-1824-4). Lerner Pubns.
Lye, Keith. Take a Trip to Venezuela. Franklin Watts Ltd., ed. (Illus.). 32p. (ps-9). 1988. PLB 7.99 (ISBN 0-531-10469-9). Watts.
Morrison, Marion. Venezuela. (Illus.). (gr. 5 up). 1988. 14.95 (ISBN 1-55546-174-3). Chelsea Hse.
—Venezuela. LC 88-30493. (Illus.). 128p. (gr. 5-9). 1989. PLB 25.27 (ISBN 0-516-02711-5). Childrens.

VENEZUELA–FICTION

Hudson, William H. Green Mansions. Teitel, N. R., intro. by. (gr. 8 up). pap. 1.95 (ISBN 0-8049-0087-6, CL-87). Airmont.

VENICE–HISTORY

Ventura, Piero. Venice: Birth of a City. Ventura, Piero, illus. 40p. (gr. 5 up). 1988. 13.95 (ISBN 0-399-21531-X, Putnam). Putnam Pub Group.

VENOM

see Poisons

VENTRILOQUISM

Kraus, Robert. Phil the Ventriloquist. LC 88-11. (Illus.). 32p. (ps up). 1989. 11.95 (ISBN 0-688-07987-3); PLB 11.88 (ISBN 0-688-07988-1). Greenwillow.

VENUS (PLANET)

Asimov, Isaac. Venus: A Shrouded Mystery. LC 89-43135. (Illus.). 32p. (gr. 3-4). 1990. PLB 12.95 (ISBN 1-55532-365-0). Gareth Stevens Inc.
Baker, David. Exploring Venus & Mercury. LC 88-33707. (Illus.). 48p. (gr. 4-6). 1989. PLB 18.60 (ISBN 0-86592-371-X). Rourke Corp.
Fradin, Dennis B. Venus. LC 88-39121. (Illus.). 48p. (gr. k-4). 1989. PLB 13.27 (ISBN 0-516-01168-5); pap. 4.95 (ISBN 0-516-41168-3). Childrens.
Schloss, Muriel. Venus. (Illus.). 64p. (gr. 3-5). 1991. PLB 11.90 (ISBN 0-531-20019-1). Watts.

VERDI, GIUSEPPE, 1813-1901

Tames, Richard. Verdi. (Illus.). 32p. 1991. PLB 11.90 (ISBN 0-531-14109-8). Watts.

VERMONT

Budbill, David. Snowshoe Trek to Otter River. (Illus.). 96p. (gr. 4-6). 1984. pap. 2.50 (ISBN 0-553-15469-9, Skylark). Bantam.
Carole Marsh Vermont Books, 31 bks. Set. 638.45 (ISBN 0-7933-1320-1). Gallopade Pub Group.
Carpenter, Allan. Vermont. new ed. LC 79-829. (Illus.). 96p. (gr. 4 up). 1979. PLB 19.93 (ISBN 0-516-04145-2). Childrens.
Cheney, Cora. Vermont, the State with the Storybook Past. rev. ed. MacLean, Robert, illus. Muller, H. N., III, intro. by. LC 86-60341. (Illus.). 272p. (gr. 5-9). 1986. pap. 14.95 (ISBN 0-933050-36-4). New Eng Pr VT.
Fradin, Dennis. Vermont: In Words & Pictures. LC 79-22069. (Illus.). 48p. (gr. 2-5). 1980. PLB 15.93 (ISBN 0-516-03946-6). Childrens.
Guyette, Elise. Vermont: A Cultural Patchwork. (Illus.). 144p. (Orig.). (gr. 4-8). 1986. pap. text ed. 9.85 (ISBN 0-9607638-5-6). Cobblestone Pub.
Kelley, Shirley. Little Settlers of Vermont. 1987. 7.95. Equity Pub NH.
Lasky, Kathryn. Sugaring Time. Knight, Christopher G., photos by. LC 86-3468. (Illus.). 64p. (gr. 3-7). 1986. pap. 4.95 (ISBN 0-689-71081-X, Aladdin). Macmillan Child Grp.
Marsh, Carole. Avast, Ye Slobs! Vermont Pirate Trivia. (Illus.). 1990. PLB 19.95 (ISBN 0-7933-1148-9); pap. 14.95; computer disk 29.95 (ISBN 0-7933-1149-7). Gallopade Pub Group.
—The Beast of the Vermont Bed & Breakfast. (Illus.). 1990. PLB 19.95 (ISBN 0-7933-2149-2); pap. 14.95 (ISBN 0-7933-2150-6); computer disk 29.95 (ISBN 0-7933-2151-4). Gallopade Pub Group.
—The Hard-to-Believe-But-True! Book of Vermont History, Mystery, Trivia, Legend, Lore, Humor & More. (Illus.). 1990. PLB 19.95 (ISBN 0-7933-1145-4); pap. 14.95 (ISBN 0-7933-1144-6) (ISBN 0-7933-1146-2). Gallopade Pub Group.
—If My Vermont Mama Ran the World! (Illus.). 1990. PLB 19.95 (ISBN 0-7933-2158-1); pap. 14.95 (ISBN 0-7933-2159-X); computer disk 29.95 (ISBN 0-7933-2160-3). Gallopade Pub Group.
—Let's Quilt Vermont & Stuff It Topographically! (Illus.). 1990. PLB 19.95 (ISBN 0-7933-2141-7); pap. 14.95 (ISBN 1-55609-066-8); computer disk 29.95 (ISBN 0-7933-2142-5). Gallopade Pub Group.
—Vermont & Other State Greats (Biographies) (Illus.). 1990. PLB 19.95 (ISBN 0-7933-2161-1); pap. 14.95 (ISBN 0-7933-2162-X); computer disk 29.95 (ISBN 0-7933-2163-8). Gallopade Pub Group.
—Vermont Bandits, Bushwackers, Outlaws, Crooks, Devils, Ghosts, Desperadoes & Other Assorted & Sundry Characters! (Illus.). 1990. PLB 19.95 (ISBN 0-7933-1130-6); pap. 14.95 (ISBN 0-7933-1129-2) (ISBN 0-7933-1131-4). Gallopade Pub Group.
—Vermont Classic Christmas Trivia: Stories, Recipes, Activities, Legends, Lore & More! (Illus.). 1990. PLB 19.95 (ISBN 0-7933-1133-0); pap. 14.95 (ISBN 0-7933-1132-2); computer disk 29.95 (ISBN 0-7933-1134-9). Gallopade Pub Group.
—Vermont Coastales. (Illus.). 1990. PLB 19.95 (ISBN 0-7933-2155-7); pap. 14.95 (ISBN 0-7933-2156-5); computer disk 29.95 (ISBN 0-7933-2157-3). Gallopade Pub Group.
—The Vermont Hot Air Balloon Mystery. (Illus.). (gr. 2-9). 1990. 19.95 (ISBN 0-7933-2723-7); pap. 14.95 (ISBN 0-7933-2724-5); computer disk 29.95 (ISBN 0-7933-2725-3). Gallopade Pub Group.
—Vermont "Jography" A Fun Run Thru Our State! (Illus.). 1990. PLB 19.95 (ISBN 0-7933-2138-7); pap. 14.95 (ISBN 0-7933-2139-5); computer disk 29.95 (ISBN 0-7933-2140-9). Gallopade Pub Group.
—Vermont Kid's Cookbook: Recipes, How-to, History, Lore & More! (Illus.). 1990. PLB 19.95 (ISBN 0-7933-1142-X); pap. 14.95; computer disk 29.95 (ISBN 0-7933-1143-8). Gallopade Pub Group.
—Vermont Quiz Bowl Crash Course! (Illus.). 1990. PLB 19.95 (ISBN 0-7933-2152-2); pap. 14.95 (ISBN 0-7933-2153-0); computer disk 29.95 (ISBN 0-7933-2154-9). Gallopade Pub Group.
—Vermont School Trivia: An Amazing & Fascinating Look at Our State's Teachers, Schools & Students! (Illus.). 1990. PLB 19.95 (ISBN 0-7933-1139-X); pap. 14.95 (ISBN 0-7933-1138-1); computer disk 29.95 (ISBN 0-7933-1140-3). Gallopade Pub Group.
—Vermont Silly Basketball Sportsmysteries, Vol. 1. (Illus.). 1990. PLB 19.95 (ISBN 0-7933-1136-5); pap. 14.95 (ISBN 0-7933-1135-7); computer disk 29.95 (ISBN 0-7933-1137-3). Gallopade Pub Group.
—Vermont Silly Basketball Sportsmysteries, Vol. 2. (Illus.). 1990. PLB 19.95 (ISBN 0-7933-2164-6); pap. 14.95 (ISBN 0-7933-2165-4); 29.95 (ISBN 0-7933-2166-2). Gallopade Pub Group.
—Vermont Silly Football Sportsmysteries, Vol. 1. (Illus.). 1990. PLB 19.95 (ISBN 0-7933-2143-3); pap. 14.95 (ISBN 0-7933-2144-1); computer disk 29.95 (ISBN 0-7933-2145-X). Gallopade Pub Group.
—Vermont Silly Football Sportsmysteries, Vol. 2. (Illus.). 1990. PLB 19.95; pap. 14.95 (ISBN 0-7933-2147-6); computer disk 29.95 (ISBN 0-7933-2148-4). Gallopade Pub Group.
—Vermont Silly Trivia! (Illus.). 1990. PLB 19.95 (ISBN 0-7933-2135-2); pap. 14.95 (ISBN 0-7933-2136-0); computer disk 29.95 (ISBN 0-7933-2137-9). Gallopade Pub Group.
—Vermont's (Most Devastating!) Disasters & (Most Calamitous!) Catastrophies! (Illus.). 1990. PLB 19.95 (ISBN 0-7933-1127-6); pap. 14.95 (ISBN 0-7933-1126-8); computer disk 29.95 (ISBN 0-7933-1128-4). Gallopade Pub Group.
Turner Educational Services, Inc. Staff & Clark, James I. Vermont. 48p. (gr. 3 up). 1986. PLB 17.32 (ISBN 0-86514-459-1); pap. text ed. 9.27 (ISBN 0-86514-534-2); cancelled Beta video (ISBN 0-86514-084-7); cancelled VHS video (ISBN 0-86514-159-2); cancelled 3/4" video (ISBN 0-86514-234-3); cancelled tchr's. study guide (ISBN 0-86514-309-9); cancelled student activity bk. (ISBN 0-86514-384-6); cancelled index. Raintree Pubs.

VERMONT–FICTION

Carty, Margaret F. Christmas in Vermont: Three Stories. Langley, Marilynn, illus. LC 83-62750. 48p. (Orig.). (gr. 5 up). 1983. pap. 2.95 (ISBN 0-933050-21-6). New Eng Pr VT.
Jackson, Edgar N. Green Mountain Hero. 192p. (gr. 6 up). 1988. pap. 9.95 (ISBN 0-933050-61-5). New Eng Pr VT.
Peck, Robert N. Justice Lion. 264p. (gr. 7 up). 1981. 13. 95 (ISBN 0-316-69658-7). Little.
—Trig. 64p. (gr. 4-6). 1979. pap. 1.25 (ISBN 0-440-49098-7, YB). Dell.
Stolz, Mary. Cider Days. LC 77-25652. (gr. 3-7). 1978. PLB 12.89 (ISBN 0-06-025838-1). HarpC Child Bks.
—Ferris Wheel. LC 76-41511. 144p. (gr. 4-7). 1977. PLB 12.89 (ISBN 0-06-025860-8). HarpC Child Bks.

VERNE, JULES, 1828-1905

Quackenbush, Robert. Who Said There's No Man on the Moon? A Story of Jules Verne. LC 84-22314. (Illus.). 40p. (gr. 2-6). 1986. PLB 11.95 (ISBN 0-671-66848-X). S&S Trade.

VERSIFICATION

see also Poetry

Simms, Susan R. Rhyme Time with the Rymons: Kitchen Magician. Dallgas-Frey, Paul, illus. 36p. (ps-3). 1990. pap. 15.95 incl. audiocassette (ISBN 1-55999-136-4). LinguiSystems.
—Rhyme Time with the Rymons: My Think 'n' Do Book. Basso, Bill, illus. 100p. (ps-3). 1990. pap. 10.95 spiral bdg., wkbk. (ISBN 1-55999-139-9). LinguiSystems.
—Rhyme Time with the Rymons: Squeeze for the Keys. Dallgas-Frey, Paul, illus. 36p. (ps-3). 1990. pap. 15.95 incl. audiocassette (ISBN 1-55999-138-0). LinguiSystems.
—Rhyme Time with the Rymons: Wakin' to the Bacon. Dallgas-Frey, Paul, illus. 36p. (ps-3). 1990. pap. 15.95 incl. audiocassette (ISBN 1-55999-137-2). LinguiSystems.

VERTEBRATES

see also Amphibians; Birds; Fishes; Mammals; Reptiles

Bone, Q. The Origin of Chordates. 2nd ed. Head, J. J., ed. LC 77-93433. (Illus.). 16p. (gr. 10 up). 1979. pap. 2.15 (ISBN 0-89278-218-8, 45-9618). Carolina Biological.
Selsam, Millicent E. & Hunt, Joyce. A First Look at Animals with Backbones. Springer, Harriet, illus. LC 78-4321. (gr. k-3). 1978. PLB 9.85 (ISBN 0-8027-6339-1). Walker & Co.

VESPUCCI, AMERIGO, 1451-1512

Fradin, Dennis B. Amerigo Vespucci. (Illus.). 64p. (gr. 5-8). 1991. PLB 11.90 (ISBN 0-531-20035-3). Watts.

VESSELS (SHIPS)

see Ships

VETERINARIANS

Bellville, Rod & Bellville, Cheryl W. Large Animal Veterinarians. LC 82-19750. (Illus.). 32p. (gr. k-4). 1983. PLB 9.95 (ISBN 0-87614-211-0). Carolrhoda Bks.
Greene, Carla. Animal Doctors: What Do They Do? Kessler, L., illus. LC 67-14065. 64p. (gr. k-3). 1967. PLB 11.89 (ISBN 0-06-022078-3). HarpC Child Bks.
Herriot, James. All Creatures Great & Small. (gr. 6 up). 1985. pap. 5.95 (ISBN 0-553-26812-0). Bantam.
Jaspersohn, William. A Day in the Life of a Veterinarian. (Illus.). (gr. 3-7). 1978. 15.95 (ISBN 0-316-45810-4). Little.
Paige, David. A Day in the Life of a Zoo Veterinarian. Mauney, Michael, illus. LC 84-6538. 32p. (gr. 4-8). 1985. PLB 11.79 (ISBN 0-8167-0095-8); pap. text ed. 2.95 (ISBN 0-8167-0096-6). Troll Assocs.
San Diego Zoo Doctor. 1991. pap. 14.95 (ISBN 0-671-73921-2). S&S Trade.
Steig, William. Doctor De Soto. LC 82-15701. (Illus.). 32p. (ps-3). 1982. 15.95 (ISBN 0-374-31803-4). FS&G.

VETERINARY MEDICINE

Holderness-Roddam, Jane. First Aid. Vincer, Carole, illus. 24p. (Orig.). (gr. 3 up). 1989. pap. 7.95 (ISBN 0-901366-98-6, Pub. by Threshold Bks). Half Halt Pr.
Imershein, Betsy. Animal Doctor. Imershein, Betsy, illus. LC 87-20266. 32p. (gr. 1-5). 1988. lib. bdg. 9.98 (ISBN 0-671-64183-2); pap. 4.95 (ISBN 0-671-65862-X). Messner.
Sobol, Harriet L. Pet Doctor. Agre, Patricia, photos by. (Illus.). 32p. (gr. 2-5). 1988. 13.95 (ISBN 0-399-21533-6). Putnam Pub Group.
Veterinary Science. (Illus.). 40p. (gr. 6-12). 1973. pap. 1.85 (ISBN 0-8395-3261-X, 3261). BSA.

VETERINARY MEDICINE–FICTION

Dodd, Lynley. Hairy Maclary's Rumpus at the Vet. Dodd, Lynley, illus. LC 89-43120. 28p. (gr. 1-2). 1989. PLB 10.95 (ISBN 0-8368-0126-1). Gareth Stevens Inc.
Lofting, Hugh. Dr. Dolittle's Caravan. (gr. k-6). 1988. pap. 3.50 (ISBN 0-440-40071-6). Dell.
—Dr. Dolittle's Circus. (gr. k-6). 1988. pap. 3.50 (ISBN 0-440-40058-9). Dell.
—Dr. Doolittle in the Moon. (gr. k-6). 1988. pap. 3.25 (ISBN 0-440-40113-5, YB). Dell.

VETERINARY MEDICINE–VOCATIONAL GUIDANCE

Duncan, Jane C. Careers in Veterinary Medicine. (Illus.). (gr. 7-12). 1988. lib. bdg. 12.95 (ISBN 0-8239-0804-6). Rosen Group.
Jeffers, Susan. The Rosen Photo Guide to a Career in Animal Care. (Illus.). (gr. 7-12). 1988. lib. bdg. 12.95 (ISBN 0-8239-0818-6). Rosen Group.
Lee, Mary P. Ms. Veterinarian. LC 74-14990. (Illus.). 138p. (gr. 7-12). 1976. 8.95 (ISBN 0-664-32594-7, Westminster). Westminster John Knox.
Miller, Louise. Careers for Animal Lovers: And Other Zoological Types. LC 90-50725. 160p. (Orig.). (gr. 7 up). 1991. pap. 8.95 (ISBN 0-8442-8125-5, VGM Career Horzns). Natl Textbk.
Stamper, Judith. What's It Like to Be a Veterinarian. Ramsey, Marcy D., illus. LC 89-34391. 32p. (gr. k-3). 1989. lib. bdg. 10.89 (ISBN 0-8167-1817-2); pap. text ed. 2.50 (ISBN 0-8167-1818-0). Troll Assocs.

VIADUCTS

see Bridges

VIANNEY, JEAN BAPTISTE, MARIE, SAINT, 1786-1859

Daughters of St. Paul. The Country Road Home. (gr. 3-7). 3.00 (ISBN 0-8198-0232-8); pap. 2.00 (ISBN 0-8198-1412-1). Dghtrs St Paul.

VIBRATION

see also Light

VICE

see Crime and Criminals

VICE-PRESIDENTS–U. S.

Dorman, Michael. Second Man: The Changing Role of the Vice Presidency. LC 67-19765. (gr. 7 up). 1968. pap. 6.95 (ISBN 0-440-07703-6). Delacorte.

Feerick, John D. & Feerick, Amalie P. The Vice-Presidents of the United States. (Illus.). (gr. 4-6). 1977. PLB 10.40 s&l (ISBN 0-531-02907-7). Watts.

Hoopes, Roy. The Changing Vice-Presidency. LC 79-8039. (Illus.). 192p. (gr. 5 up). 1981. (Crowell Jr Bks). HarpC Child Bks.

Lindop, Edmund. Presidents by Accident. (Illus.). 208p. (gr. 9-12). 1991. PLB 14.90 (ISBN 0-531-11059-1). Watts.

VIDEO GAMES

DeKeles, Jon C., ed. Video Game Quest: The Complete Guide to Home Game Systems, Video Games & Accessories. LC 90-80079. (Illus.). 256p. (Orig.). (gr. 3 up). 1990. pap. 14.95 (ISBN 0-9625057-2-2). DMS ID.

—Video Game Secrets: A Top Secret Guide to One Thousand Tips, Tricks & Codes. (Illus.). 176p. (Orig.). (gr. 6 up). 1990. pap. 9.95 (ISBN 0-9625057-3-0). DMS ID.

DeKeles, Jon C. & Wells, Jim, eds. Doc's One Minute Encyclopedia of Simplified Nintendo Game Instructions: Simple & Easy to Understand Instructions to 300 Games. 320p. (Orig.). (gr. 5 up). 1990. pap. 12.95 (ISBN 0-685-35597-7). DMS ID.

DeNure, Dennis. The Age of the Video Athlete. (Illus.). 1984. write for info. (ISBN 0-915659-00-X). Video Athlete.

Lampton, Christopher. Nintendo Action Games. (Illus.). 72p. (gr. 4-6). 1991. PLB 17.25 (ISBN 1-878841-26-2); pap. 3.95 (ISBN 1-878841-53-X). Millbrook Pr.

—Nintendo Role-Playing Games. (Illus.). 72p. (gr. 4-6). 1991. PLB 17.25 (ISBN 1-878841-25-4); pap. 3.95 (ISBN 1-878841-52-1). Millbrook Pr.

VIENNA–FICTION

Henry, Marguerite. White Stallion of Lipizza. Dennis, Wesley, illus. LC 64-17445. 112p. (gr. 3-8). write for info. (ISBN 0-02-743628-4, Mcmillan Child Bk). Macmillan Child Grp.

VIETNAM

Garland, Sherry. Vietnam: Rebuilding a Nation. (Illus.). (gr. 5 up). 1990. PLB 14.95 (ISBN 0-87518-422-7, Dillon). Macmillan Child Grp.

Hauptly, Denis J. In Vietnam. LC 85-7464. (Illus.). 224p. (gr. 5 up). 1985. 13.95 (ISBN 0-689-31079-X, Atheneum Child Bk). Macmillan Child Grp.

Mabie, Margot C. Vietnam There & Here. LC 84-20518. (Illus.). 176p. (gr. 4 up). 1985. 11.95 (ISBN 0-8050-0545-5). H Holt & Co.

Nhuong, Nuynh Quang. The Land I Lost: Adventures of a Boy in Vietnam. LC 80-8437. (Illus.). 128p. (gr. 4-7). 1990. 12.95 (ISBN 0-397-32447-2, Lipp Jr Bks); PLB 12.89 (ISBN 0-397-32448-0, Lipp Jr Bks). HarpC Child Bks.

Nurland, Patricia. Vietnam. Vu Viet Dung, photos by. LC 89-43178. (Illus.). 64p. (gr. 5-6). 1991. PLB 12.95 (ISBN 0-8368-0230-6). Gareth Stevens Inc.

Tran Khan Tuyet. Children of Viet-Nam. (gr. k-2). 1973. 2.50 (ISBN 0-686-10278-9). Asia Resource.

Wright, David K. Vietnam. LC 88-30486. (Illus.). 128p. (gr. 5-9). 1989. PLB 25.27 (ISBN 0-516-02712-3). Childrens.

VIETNAM–FICTION

Huynh Quang Nhuong. The Land I Lost. Vo-Dinh, Mai, illus. LC 80-8437. 128p. (gr. 4-7). 1986. pap. 3.50 (ISBN 0-06-440183-9, Trophy). HarpC Child Bks.

Miller, Marvin. You Be the Jury. 1990. pap. 2.50 (ISBN 0-590-43048-3). Scholastic Inc.

VIETNAM WAR, 1961-1975

see Vietnamese Conflict, 1961-1975

VIETNAMESE CONFLICT, 1961-1975

Arnoldt, Robert P. Insights: A Guide to the American Experience in Vietnam, 1940 to Present. rev. ed. Marx, Jacqueline A. & Carpenter, Robert S., eds. 100p. (Orig.). (gr. 9 up). 1989. pap. text ed. write for info. Visions Unlimited.

Donnelly, Judy. A Wall of Names: The Story of the Vietnam Veterans Memorial A Step 4 Book - Grades 2-4. Wenzel, Paul, illus. LC 90-30275. 48p. (Orig.). (gr. 2-4). 1991. PLB 6.99 (ISBN 0-679-90169-8); pap. 2.95 (ISBN 0-679-80169-3). Random.

Edwards, Richard. Vietnam War, Reading Level 8. LC 86-20295. (Illus.). 77p. (gr. 7 up). 1987. PLB 17.26 (ISBN 0-86592-031-1). Rourke Corp.

Fincher, E. B. The Vietnam War. (gr. 7 up). 1980. PLB 12.90 (ISBN 0-531-04112-3, C07). Watts.

Griffiths, John. The Last Day in Saigon. 64p. (gr. 6-8). 1987. 19.95 (ISBN 0-85219-671-7, Pub. by Batsford England). Trafalgar Sq.

Hoobler, Dorothy & Hoobler, Thomas. Vietnam: An Illustrated History. LC 89-71645. (Illus.). 208p. (gr. 5 up). 1990. 17.95 (ISBN 0-394-81943-8); PLB 18.99 (ISBN 0-394-91943-2). Knopf.

Kurland, Gerald. The My Lai Massacre. Rahmas, D. Steve, ed. 32p. (gr. 7-12). 1973. lib. bdg. 4.20 incl. catalog cards (ISBN 0-87157-708-9). SamHar Pr.

—The My Lai Massacre. Rahmas, D. Steve, ed. 32p. (gr. 7-12). 1973. lib. bdg. 4.20 incl. catalog cards (ISBN 0-87157-708-9). SamHar Pr.

Lawson, Don. An Album of the Vietnam War. LC 85-26624. (Illus.). 88p. (gr. 4-9). 1986. PLB 13.90 (ISBN 0-531-10139-8). Watts.

—The United States in the Vietnam War. LC 80-2460. (Illus.). 160p. (gr. 7 up). 1981. 12.95 (ISBN 0-690-04104-7, Crowell Jr Bks); PLB 12.89 (ISBN 0-690-04105-5). HarpC Child Bks.

—The War in Vietnam. (Illus.). 96p. (gr. 4 up). 1981. PLB 10.40 (ISBN 0-531-04331-2). Watts.

Lens, Sidney. Vietnam: A War on Two Fronts. (Illus.). (gr. 7 up). 1990. 15.95 (ISBN 0-525-67320-2, Lodestar). Dutton Child Bks.

Nickelson, Harry. Vietnam. LC 89-13100. (Illus.). 80p. (gr. 5-8). 1989. PLB 11.95 (ISBN 1-56006-110-3). Lucent Bks.

Simons, Frank D. You Don't Cry for Heroes. Ferrell, Robert, intro. by. 197p. (Orig.). (gr. 12 up). 1989. pap. 7.95 (ISBN 0-685-26939-6). CFFC POWs MIAs.

The Vietnam War. LC 87-18224. 768p. (gr. 6 up). 1988. PLB 199.95x (ISBN 0-86307-852-4). Marshall Cavendish.

The Vietnam War Soldier at Con Thien. 48p. (gr. 5-6). 1989. PLB 10.95 (ISBN 0-685-26360-6). Capstone Pr.

Warren, James A. Portrait of a Tragedy: America & the Vietnam War. Summers, Harry G., Jr., frwd. by. LC 88-39560. (Illus.). 208p. (gr. 5 up). 17.95 (ISBN 0-688-07454-5). Lothrop.

Wills, Charles. The Tet Offensive. (Illus.). 64p. (gr. 5 up). 1989. PLB 16.98 (ISBN 0-382-09849-8); pap. 7.95 (ISBN 0-382-09855-2). Silver Burdett Pr.

Wright, David K. The Story of the Vietnam Veterans Memorial. LC 89-713. (Illus.). 32p. (gr. 3-6). 1989. PLB 13.27 (ISBN 0-516-04745-0); pap. 3.95 (ISBN 0-516-44745-9). Childrens.

—War in Vietnam, Bks. I-IV. (Illus.). 144p. (gr. 4 up). 1989. PLB 85.27 (ISBN 0-516-02285-7). Book I, Eve of Battle. Book II, A Wider War. Book III, Vietnamization. Book IV, The Fall of Vietnam. Childrens.

VIETNAMESE CONFLICT, 1961-1975–FICTION

Ashabranner, Brent. Always to Remember: The Story of the Vietnam Veterans Memorial. Ashabranner, Jennifer, photos by. (Illus.). 40p. (gr. 6 up). 1988. 14.95 (ISBN 0-399-22031-3, Putnam). Putnam Pub Group.

Carn, John B. Vietnam Blues. (Orig.). (ps-12). 1988. pap. 3.25 (ISBN 0-318-36112-4). Holloway.

Hahn, Mary D. December Stillness. LC 88-2572. 192p. (gr. 5-9). 1988. 13.95 (ISBN 0-89919-758-2, Pub. by Clarion). Ticknor & Fields.

Jensen, Kathryn. Pocket Change. 176p. (gr. 7 up). 1989. 13.95 (ISBN 0-02-747731-2, Mcmillan Child Bk). Macmillan Child Grp.

—Pocket Change. 192p. (gr. 7 up). 1991. pap. 2.95 (ISBN 0-590-43419-5, Point). Scholastic Inc.

Jones, Adrienne. Long Time Passing. LC 90-4046. 256p. (gr. 7 up). 1990. 14.95 (ISBN 0-06-023055-X); PLB 14.89 (ISBN 0-06-023056-8). HarpC Child Bks.

Nelson, Theresa. And One for All. LC 88-22490. 192p. (gr. 6-8). 1989. 12.95 (ISBN 0-531-05804-2); PLB 12.99 (ISBN 0-531-08404-3). Orchard Bks Watts.

Paterson, Katherine. Park's Quest. 160p. (gr. 5 up). 1989. pap. 3.95 (ISBN 0-14-034262-1, Puffin). Puffin Bks.

Rostkowski, Margaret I. The Best of Friends. LC 88-33077. 192p. (gr. 7 up). 1989. 12.95 (ISBN 0-06-025104-2); PLB 12.89 (ISBN 0-06-025105-0). HarpC Child Bks.

Wolitzer, Meg. Caribou. 176p. (gr. 7-12). 1986. pap. 2.50 (ISBN 0-553-25560-6). Bantam.

VIEWS

Simon, Seymour. Hidden Worlds: Pictures of the Invisible. LC 83-5407. (Illus.). 48p. (gr. 3up). 1983. 13.95 (ISBN 0-688-02464-5); lib. bdg. 13.88 (ISBN 0-688-02465-3, Morrow Jr Bks). Morrow Jr Bks.

VIKING PROJECT

Vogt, Gregory. Viking & the Mars Landing. (Illus.). 112p. (gr. 4-6). 1991. PLB 19.25 (ISBN 1-878841-32-7); pap. 4.95 (ISBN 1-878841-38-6). Millbrook Pr.

VIKINGS

see Northmen

VILLAS

see Architecture, Domestic

VIOLINISTS, VIOLONCELLISTS, ETC.

Chan, Margie. The Eye 'N' Hand, Book One for Violin. (gr. 2). 1988. write for info. GIM-Ho.

—Music Concepts & Vocabulary for Violin, Bk. 1. 41p. (gr. 2 up). 1984. wkbk. 4.95 (ISBN 0-9615006-0-3). Gim-Ho.

—Music Concepts & Vocabulary for Violin, Bk. 2. 48p. (gr. 2 up). 1985. wkbk. 4.95 (ISBN 0-9615006-1-1). Gim Ho.

Clement, Claude. The Voice of the Wood. Clement, Frederic, photos by. LC 88-22892. (Illus.). 32p. (gr. k up). 1989. 14.95 (ISBN 0-8037-0635-9). Dial Bks Young.

Miller, Miamon. How to Play Romanian Folk Violin. Fraenkel, Eran, ed. (Illus.). 31p. (Orig.). 1990. pap. 19.95 (ISBN 0-9626468-0-6). Cocek Pr.

Preucil, Doris. Suzuki Viola School, Viola Part, Vol. 1. Suzuki, Shinichi, ed. 32p. (gr. k-12). 1981. pap. text ed. 6.50 (ISBN 0-87487-241-3). Summy-Birchard.

—Suzuki Viola School, Viola Part, Vol. 2. Suzuki, Shinichi, ed. 32p. (gr. k-12). 1982. pap. text ed. 6.50 (ISBN 0-87487-242-1). Summy-Birchard.

Preucil, Doris & Suzuki, Shinichi, eds. Suzuki Viola School, Vol. A. 64p. (gr. k-12). 1982. pap. text ed. 10.95 (ISBN 0-87487-245-6, Suzuki Method). Summy-Birchard.

Suzuki, Shinichi. Suzuki Cello School, Cello Part, Vol. 7. 24p. (gr. k-12). 1987. pap. text ed. 6.50 (ISBN 0-87487-360-6, Suzuki Method). Summy-Birchard.

—Suzuki Cello School, Vol. 7: Piano Accompaniments. 32p. (gr. k-12). 1987. pap. text ed. 6.50 (ISBN 0-87487-362-2, Suzuki Method). Summy-Birchard.

—Suzuki Viola School, Piano Accompaniments, Vol. 5. 52p. (gr. k-12). 1986. pap. text ed. 8.95 (ISBN 0-87487-250-2, Suzuki Method). Summy-Birchard.

VIOLONCELLISTS

see Violinists, Violoncellists, etc.

VIPERS

see Snakes

VIRGIN ISLANDS OF THE U. S.

Bailey, Katharine R. & Bourne, Gloria. U. S. Virgin Islands: Jewels of the Caribbean--St. Croix, St. Thomas, St. John. Henle, Fritz, photos by. LC 86-82891. (Illus.). 48p. (Orig.). (gr. 7-12). 1987. pap. 5.95 (ISBN 0-88714-012-2). KC Pubns.

Petersen, Arona. Food & Folklore of the Virgin Islands. 300p. (Orig.). (gr. 9-12). 1990. 20.00 (ISBN 0-9626577-0-0). A Petersen.

VIRGIN MARY

see Mary, Virgin

VIRGINIA

Ashabranner, Brent. A Grateful Nation: The Story of Arlington National Cemetery. (Illus.). 112p. 1990. 15.95 (ISBN 0-399-22188-3, Putnam). Putnam Pub Group.

Aylesworth, Thomas G. & Aylesworth, Virginia L. The Atlantic (Virginia, West Virginia, District of Columbia) (Illus.). 66p. (Orig.). 1990. lib. bdg. 16.95x (ISBN 1-55546-555-2); pap. 6.95 (ISBN 0-7910-0533-X). Chelsea Hse.

Carole Marsh Virginia Books, 31 bks. Set. 638.45 (ISBN 0-7933-1321-X). Gallopade Pub Group.

Carpenter, Allan. Virginia. LC 78-8002. (Illus.). 96p. (gr. 4 up). 1978. PLB 19.93 (ISBN 0-516-04146-0). Childrens.

Coffey, William E., et al. West Virginia Government. Buckalew, Marshall & Thoenen, Eugenia G., eds. (Illus.). 112p. (Orig.). (gr. 8). 1984. pap. 10.00 (ISBN 0-914498-05-3). WV Hist Ed Found.

Kyle, Louisa V. My Virginia Childhood. (Illus.). 45p. (gr. 3). 1976. write for info. Four Oclock Farms.

McNair, Sylvia. Virginia. LC 88-38203. (Illus.). 144p. (gr. 4 up). 1989. PLB 25.27 (ISBN 0-516-00492-1). Childrens.

Marsh, Carole. Avast, Ye Slobs! Virginia Pirate Trivia. (Illus.). 1990. PLB 19.95 (ISBN 0-7933-1172-1); pap. 14.95 (ISBN 0-7933-1171-3); computer disk 29.95 (ISBN 0-7933-1173-X). Gallopade Pub Group.

—The Beast of the Virginia Bed & Breakfast. (Illus.). 1990. PLB 19.95 (ISBN 0-7933-2179-4); pap. 14.95 (ISBN 0-7933-2180-8); computer disk 29.95 (ISBN 0-7933-2181-6). Gallopade Pub Group.

—The Hard-to-Believe-But-True! Book of Virginia History, Mystery, Trivia, Legend, Lore, Humor & More. (Illus.). 1990. PLB 19.95 (ISBN 0-7933-1169-1); pap. 14.95 (ISBN 0-7933-1168-3); computer disk 29.95 (ISBN 0-7933-1170-5). Gallopade Pub Group.

—If My Virginia Mama Ran the World! (Illus.). 1990. PLB 19.95 (ISBN 0-7933-2187-5); pap. 14.95 (ISBN 0-7933-2188-3); computer disk 29.95 (ISBN 0-7933-2189-1). Gallopade Pub Group.

—Let's Quilt Virginia & Stuff It Topographically! (Illus.). 1990. PLB 19.95 (ISBN 0-7933-2171-9); pap. 14.95 (ISBN 1-55609-051-X); computer disk 29.95 (ISBN 0-7933-2172-7). Gallopade Pub Group.

—Mariner's & More! Virginia People, Places & Things Everyone Should Know. (Illus.). (gr. 9-12). Date not set. PLB 19.95 (ISBN 0-7933-0000-2); pap. 14.95 (ISBN 0-7933-0001-0); computer disk 29.95 (ISBN 0-7933-0002-9). Gallopade Pub Group.

—Virginia & Other State Greats (Biographies) (Illus.). 1990. PLB 19.95 (ISBN 0-7933-2190-5); pap. 14.95 (ISBN 0-7933-2191-3); computer disk 29.95 (ISBN 0-7933-2192-1). Gallopade Pub Group.

—Virginia Bandits, Bushwackers, Outlaws, Crooks, Devils, Ghosts, Desperadoes & Other Assorted & Sundry Characters! (Illus.). 1990. PLB 19.95 (ISBN 0-7933-1154-3); pap. 14.95 (ISBN 0-7933-1153-5); computer disk 29.95 (ISBN 0-7933-1155-1). Gallopade Pub Group.

—Virginia Classic Christmas Trivia: Stories, Recipes, Activities, Legends, Lore & More. (Illus.). 1990. PLB 19.95 (ISBN 0-7933-1157-8); pap. 14.95 (ISBN 0-7933-1156-X); computer disk 29.95 (ISBN 0-7933-1158-6). Gallopade Pub Group.

—Virginia Coastales. (Illus.). 1990. PLB 19.95; pap. 14.95 (ISBN 1-55609-116-8); computer disk 29.95 (ISBN 0-7933-2186-7). Gallopade Pub Group.

—The Virginia Hot Air Balloon Mystery. (Illus.). (gr. 2-9). 1990. 19.95 (ISBN 0-7933-2732-6); pap. 14.95 (ISBN 0-7933-2733-4); computer disk 29.95 (ISBN 0-7933-2734-2). Gallopade Pub Group.

—Virginia Jography: A Fun Run Through the Old Dominion State. (Illus.). 50p. (Orig.). (gr. 3-12). 1986. pap. 14.95 (ISBN 0-935326-99-5). Gallopade Pub Group.

—Virginia "Jography" A Fun Run Thru Our State. (Illus.). 1990. PLB 19.95; pap. 14.95 (ISBN 1-55609-057-9); computer disk 29.95 (ISBN 0-7933-2170-0). Gallopade Pub Group.

—Virginia Kid's Cookbook: Recipes, How-to, History, Lore & More! (Illus.). 1990. PLB 19.95 (ISBN 0-7933-1166-7); pap. 14.95 (ISBN 0-7933-1165-9); computer disk 29.95 (ISBN 0-7933-1167-5). Gallopade Pub Group.

—Virginia Quiz Bowl Crash Courses! (Illus.). 1990. PLB 19.95 (ISBN 0-7933-2182-4); pap. 14.95 (ISBN 0-7933-2183-2); computer disk 29.95 (ISBN 0-7933-2184-0). Gallopade Pub Group.

—Virginia School Trivia: An Amazing & Fascinating Look at Our State's Teachers, Schools & Students! (Illus.). 1990. PLB 19.95 (ISBN 0-7933-1163-2); pap. 14.95 (ISBN 0-7933-1162-4); computer disk 29.95 (ISBN 0-7933-1164-0). Gallopade Pub Group.

—Virginia Silly Basketball Sportsmysteries, Vol. 1. (Illus.). 1990. PLB 19.95 (ISBN 0-7933-1160-8); pap. 14.95 (ISBN 0-7933-1159-4); computer disk 29.95 (ISBN 0-7933-1161-6). Gallopade Pub Group.

—Virginia Silly Basketball Sportsmysteries, Vol. 2. (Illus.). 1990. PLB 19.95 (ISBN 0-7933-2195-6); pap. 14.95 (ISBN 0-7933-2196-4); computer disk 29.95 (ISBN 0-7933-2197-2). Gallopade Pub Group.

—Virginia Silly Football Sportsmysteries, Vol. 1. (Illus.). 1990. PLB 19.95; pap. 14.95 (ISBN 0-7933-2174-3); computer disk 29.95 (ISBN 0-7933-2175-1). Gallopade Pub Group.

—Virginia Silly Football Sportsmysteries, Vol. 2. (Illus.). 1990. PLB 19.95 (ISBN 0-7933-2176-X); pap. 14.95 (ISBN 0-7933-2177-8); computer disk 29.95 (ISBN 0-7933-2178-6). Gallopade Pub Group.

—Virginia Silly Trivia. (Illus.). 60p. (Orig.). (gr. 3-12). 1986. pap. 14.95 (ISBN 0-935326-94-4). Gallopade Pub Group.

—Virginia Silly Trivia! (Illus.). 1990. PLB 19.95 (ISBN 0-7933-2167-0); pap. 14.95; computer disk 29.95 (ISBN 0-7933-2168-9). Gallopade Pub Group.

—Virginia's (Most Devastating!) Disasters & (Most Calamitous!) Catastrophies! (Illus.). 1990. PLB 19.95 (ISBN 0-7933-2193-X); pap. 14.95 (ISBN 0-7933-1150-0); computer disk 29.95 (ISBN 0-7933-2194-8). Gallopade Pub Group.

Sirvaitis, Karen. Virginia. (Illus.). 72p. (gr. 3-6). 1991. PLB 12.95 (ISBN 0-8225-2702-2). Lerner Pubns.

VIRGINIA–FICTION

Henry, Marguerite. Misty of Chincoteague. Dennis, Wesley, illus. LC 47-11404. 176p. (gr. 2-9). 1990. 12.95 (ISBN 0-02-743622-5, Mcmillan Child Bk); pap. 3.95 (ISBN 0-02-688759-2). Macmillan Child Grp.

—Stormy: Misty's Foal. Dennis, Wesley, illus. LC 63-13334. 224p. (gr. 2-9). 1987. 8.95 (ISBN 0-528-82083-4, Aladdin Bks); pap. 3.95 (ISBN 0-02-688762-2, Aladdin Bks). Macmillan Child Grp.

Perdue, Charles L., Jr., ed. Outwitting the Devil: Jack Tales from Wise County, Virginia. LC 87-71657. (Illus.). 129p. (Orig.). (gr. 9-12). 1987. 19.95 (ISBN 0-941270-43-2); pap. 9.95 (ISBN 0-941270-42-4). Ancient City Pr.

Reeder, Carolyn. Shades of Gray. 176p. (gr. 3-7). 1989. 12.95 (ISBN 0-02-775810-9, Mcmillan Child Bk). Macmillan Child Grp.

Sharpe, Susan. Waterman's Boy. LC 89-39332. 176p. (gr. 3-8). 1990. 12.95 (ISBN 0-02-782351-2, Bradbury Pr). Macmillan Child Grp.

VIRGINIA–HISTORY

Beachy, J. Wayne. Richmond Theater Fire, 1862. Hawkins, Beverly, illus. 24p. (Orig.). (gr. 5 up). 1987. pap. 3.00 (ISBN 0-9608084-3-4). B Hawkins Studio.

Brown, Kent, et al, eds. Virginia Country's Civil War Quarterly, Vol. XII. (Illus.). 80p. (gr. 8-12). 1988. pap. 4.95 (ISBN 0-939685-03-5). Country Pub Inc.

Fradin, Dennis. Virginia in Words & Pictures. LC 76-7387. (Illus.). 48p. (gr. 2-5). 1976. PLB 15.93 (ISBN 0-516-03945-8). Childrens.

Fradin, Dennis B. The Virginia Colony. LC 86-13639. (Illus.). 160p. (gr. 4 up). 1986. PLB 22.60 (ISBN 0-516-00387-9). Childrens.

Kent, Zachary. The Story of the Surrender at Yorktown. LC 89-33784. 32p. (gr. 3-6). 1989. PLB 13.27 (ISBN 0-516-04723-X); pap. 3.95 (ISBN 0-516-44723-8). Childrens.

Turner Program Services, Inc. Staff & Clark, James I. Virginia. 48p. (gr. 3 up). 1985. PLB 17.32 (ISBN 0-86514-447-8); pap. text ed. 9.27 (ISBN 0-86514-522-9); cancelled Beta video (ISBN 0-86514-072-3); cancelled VHS video (ISBN 0-86514-147-9); cancelled 3/4" video (ISBN 0-86514-222-X); cancelled tchr's. guide (ISBN 0-86514-297-1); cancelled student activity bk. (ISBN 0-86514-372-2); cancelled index. Raintree Pubs.

VIRUSES

Flint, S. Jane. Viruses. Head, J. J., ed. Imrick, Ann T., illus. LC 87-70987. 16p. (Orig.). (gr. 10 up). 1988. pap. text ed. 2.15 (ISBN 0-89278-094-0, 45-9794). Carolina Biological.

LeMaster, Leslie J. Bacteria & Viruses. LC 84-27414. (Illus.). 48p. (gr. k-4). 1985. lib. bdg. 14.60 (ISBN 0-516-01937-6). Childrens.

Nourse, Alan E. Viruses. rev. ed. (Illus.). 72p. (gr. 4 up). 1983. PLB 10.40 (ISBN 0-531-04534-X). Watts.

VISION

see also Blind; Eye; Optical Illusions

Allington, Richard L. & Krull, Kathleen. Looking. Bober, Bill, illus. LC 79-27083. 32p. (gr. k-3). 1985. PLB 15.33 (ISBN 0-8172-1290-6); pap. 9.27 (ISBN 0-8172-2481-5). Raintree Pubs.

Fleischman, Paul. Finzel the Farsighted. Sewall, Marcia, illus. LC 83-1416. 48p. (gr. 1-5). 1983. 11.95 (ISBN 0-525-44057-7, DCB). Dutton Child Bks.

Hobbs, Jack & Salome, Richard. The Visual Experience. (Illus.). 1990. text ed. 35.95 (ISBN 0-87192-226-6, 226-6). Davis Mass.

Legge, Gordon E. & Campbell, Fergus W. Vision of Color & Pattern. Head, J. J., ed. Steffen, Ann T., illus. LC 84-45835. 16p. (Orig.). (gr. 10 up). 1987. pap. text ed. 2.15 (ISBN 0-89278-365-6, 45-9765). Carolina Biological.

Moncure, Jane B. The Look Book. Axeman, Lois, illus. LC 82-4517. 32p. (ps-3). 1982. PLB 14.60 (ISBN 0-516-03251-8); pap. 3.95 (ISBN 0-516-43251-6). Childrens.

O'Connor, Katherine H. The Dot Book for Visual Perception Training. (Illus.). 27p. (gr. k-2). 1972. wkbk. .90 (ISBN 0-910812-08-X). Johnny Reads.

Parker, Steve. Eye & Seeing. 1989. PLB 12.90 (ISBN 0-531-10654-3). Watts.

—The Eye & Seeing. rev. ed. (Illus.). 48p. (gr. 5 up). 1991. pap. 4.95 (ISBN 0-531-24602-7). Watts.

Parramon, J. M. & Puig, J. J. Sight. Rius, Maria, illus. 32p. (Orig.). (ps). 1985. pap. 3.95 ea. (ISBN 0-8120-3564-X). Span. ed (ISBN 0-8120-3605-0). Barron.

Pluckrose, Henry. Seeing. Fairclough, Chris, photos by. (Illus.). 32p. (gr. k-3). 1986. lib. bdg. 7.99 (ISBN 0-531-10171-1). Watts.

Richardson, Joy. What Happens When You Look? LC 86-3677. (Illus.). 32p. (gr. 2-3). 1986. PLB 10.95 (ISBN 1-55532-109-7). Gareth Stevens Inc.

Samz, Jane. Vision. (Illus.). (gr. 6-12). 1990. 18.95 (ISBN 0-7910-0031-1). Chelsea Hse.

Showers, Paul. In the Night. Keats, Ezra J., illus. LC 61-6138. 40p. (gr. k-3). 1961. PLB 13.89 (ISBN 0-690-44621-7, Crowell Jr Bks). HarpC Child Bks.

Simon, Hilda. Sight & Seeing: A World of Light & Color. LC 82-3721. (Illus.). 96p. (gr. 8 up). 1983. PLB 12.95 (ISBN 0-399-20929-8, Philomel). Putnam Pub Group.

Smith, Kathie B. & Crenson, Victoria. Seeing. Storms, Robert S., illus. LC 87-5862. 24p. (gr. k-3). 1987. PLB 9.59 (ISBN 0-8167-1008-2); pap. text ed. 1.95 (ISBN 0-8167-1009-0). Troll Assocs.

Ziebel, Peter. Look Closer! Ziebel, Peter, illus. 32p. (gr. 1-3). 1989. 13.95 (ISBN 0-89919-815-5, Pub. by Clarion). Ticknor & Fields.

VISUAL INSTRUCTION

see Audio-Visual Education

VITAMINS

Asimov, Isaac. How Did We Find Out About Vitamins? Wool, David, illus. LC 73-92453. 64p. (gr. 5-8). 1974. PLB 11.85 (ISBN 0-8027-6184-4). Walker & Co.

Barber, Jacqueline. Vitamin C Testing. Bergman, Lincoln & Fairwell, Kay, eds. Bevilacqua, Carol, illus. Barber, Jacqueline & Hoyt, Richard, photos by. (Illus.). 48p. (Orig.). (gr. 4-8). 1988. pap. 6.50 (ISBN 0-912511-70-2). Lawrence Science.

Seixas, Judith S. Vitamins - What They Are, What They Do. Juffman, Tom, illus. LC 85-17761. 56p. (gr. 1-4). 1986. 12.95 (ISBN 0-688-06065-X); PLB 12.88 (ISBN 0-688-06066-8). Greenwillow.

VIVARIUMS

see Terrariums

VIVEKANANDA, SWAMI, 1863-1902

Ray, Irene R. & Gupta, Mallika C. Story of Vivekananda. Banerjee, Ramananda, illus. (gr. 4-7). 1971. pap. 1.95 (ISBN 0-87481-125-2). Vedanta Pr.

VOCABULARY

see also Words, New

Aemmer, Gail. Vocabulary Development. Rittenour, Gary, illus. 20p. (gr. 5-6). 1985. pap. 5.95 (ISBN 0-88724-123-9, CD-0551). Carson-Dellos.

—Vocabulary Development. Black, Rebecca, illus. 20p. (gr. 3-4). 1985. pap. 5.95 (ISBN 0-88724-122-0, CD-0550). Carson-Dellos.

—Vocabulary Development. Nemeroff, Patti, illus. 20p. (gr. 1-2). 1985. pap. 5.95 (ISBN 0-88724-120-4, CD-0548). Carson-Dellos.

Ahlberg, Janet & Ahlberg, Allan. The Baby's Catalogue. LC 82-9928. (Illus.). 32p. (gr. k up). 1983. 14.95i (ISBN 0-316-02037-0, Joy St Bks). Little.

Allington, Richard L. & Krull, Kathleen. Words. Cruz, Ray, illus. LC 82-9787. 32p. (gr. k-3). 1982. PLB 15.33 (ISBN 0-8172-1385-6); pap. 9.27 (ISBN 0-8172-2498-X). Raintree Pubs.

Amery, Heather & Cartwright, Stephen. The First Hundred Words. Cartwright, Stephen, illus. 32p. (ps up). 1988. PLB 11.96 (ISBN 0-88110-322-5); pap. 7.95 (ISBN 0-7460-0186-X). EDC.

Animals, Birds, Bees, & Flowers. Date not set. 5.98 (ISBN 0-517-68230-3). Outlet Bk Co.

Armstrong, B. Primary Awards Galore. (gr. k-3). 1985. 5.95 (ISBN 0-88160-121-7, LW 132). Learning Wks.

Asher, Sandy. Wild Words & How to Tame Them. Kendrick, Dennis, illus. 96p. (gr. 5 up). 1989. 13.95 (ISBN 0-8027-6887-3); PLB 14.85 (ISBN 0-8027-6888-1). Walker & Co.

Ashton, Christina. Words Can Tell: A Book about Our Language. LC 87-20333. (Illus.). 128p. (gr. 6-9). 1989. lib. bdg. 12.98 (ISBN 0-671-65223-0). Messner.

At Home. (gr. 2-6). 1986. 2.98 (ISBN 0-685-16876-X, 614952). Outlet Bk Co.

At School. (gr. 2-6). 1986. 2.98 (ISBN 0-685-16872-7, 614960). Outlet Bk Co.

Banchek, Linda. Snake In, Snake Out. Arnold, Elaine, illus. LC 78-51935. (ps-1). 1978. (Crowell Jr Bks). HarpC Child Bks.

Barrett, Mark, et al. The Word Test--Adolescent - Complete Kit: A Test of Expressive Vocabulary & Semantics. (gr. 7-12). 1989. complete kit 49.90 (ISBN 1-55999-096-1). LinguiSystems.

Blake, Robert. All Around the Town. Blake, Robert, illus. 48p. (ps-2). 1987. 15.93 (ISBN 0-516-08306-6). Childrens.

Bornstein, Scott. Vocabulary Mastery. Vincent, Ben, illus. 272p. (gr. 9-12). 1982. 22.50 (ISBN 0-9602610-1-X); pap. 14.95 (ISBN 0-9602610-2-8). Bornstein Memory.

Brandts, Lois. Word Wowzers. 48p. (gr. 4-8). 1982. 5.95 (ISBN 0-88160-043-1, LW 228). Learning Wks.

Burningham, John. Slam Bang. LC 83-23549. 24p. 1985. pap. 4.95 (ISBN 0-670-65076-5). Viking Child Bks.

—Sniff Shout. LC 83-23551. (Illus.). 24p. (ps). 1984. pap. 4.95 (ISBN 0-670-65349-7). Viking Child Bks.

—Wobble Pop. LC 83-23533. (Illus.). 24p. (ps). 1984. pap. 4.95 (ISBN 0-670-77713-7). Viking Child Bks.

Carle, Eric. My Very First Book of Words. Carle, Eric, illus. LC 72-83779. 10p. (ps-1). 1991. 4.95 (ISBN 0-694-00014-0, Crowell Jr Bks). HarpC Child Bks.

Chirinian, Helene. Camping Out. (Illus.). 48p. (Orig.). (gr. k-3). 1989. pap. 2.95 (ISBN 0-8431-2415-6). Price Stern.

—Future Park. (Illus.). 48p. (Orig.). (gr. k-3). 1989. pap. 2.95 (ISBN 0-8431-2416-4). Price Stern.

—Scavenger Hunt. (Illus.). 48p. (Orig.). (gr. k-3). 1989. pap. 2.95 (ISBN 0-8431-2414-8). Price Stern.

Daly, Kathleen N. The Macmillan Picture Wordbook. Wallner, John, illus. LC 82-6619. 80p. (ps-1). 1982. 7.95 (ISBN 0-02-725600-6). Macmillan.

Daniel, Becky. Word Thinker Sheets. 64p. (gr. 4-8). 1988. wkbk. 7.95 (ISBN 0-86653-394-X, GA1034). Good Apple.

Dellosa, Janet & Carson, Patti. The Color Words. Dellosa, Janet & Carson, Patti, illus. 32p. (ps-1). 1983. pap. 1.98 (ISBN 0-88724-001-1, CD-7002). Carson-Dellos.

Donatelli, Betty. Sounding Words with Roy & Joy. Donatelli, Betty, illus. 11p. (Orig.). (gr. k-2). 1984. pap. 1.00 (ISBN 0-912981-06-7). Hse Bon Giovanni.

Duncan, Leonard C. Greek Roots. Bigelow, Holly, illus. 82p. (Orig.). (gr. 6-12). 1982. pap. 10.00 (ISBN 0-941414-01-9). LCD.

Fearn, Leif. Geocabulary Cards. (gr. 3-9). 1978. card pack 8.40 (ISBN 0-940444-06-2). Kabyn.

Fry, Edward B. Dictionary Drills. 128p. (gr. 9 up). 1980. pap. text ed. 8.25 (ISBN 0-89061-206-4, 752). Jamestown Pubs.

Gantz, David. On the Move. Gantz, David, illus. 48p. (ps-2). 1987. 15.93 (ISBN 0-516-08307-4). Childrens.

—Race Around the World. Gantz, David, illus. 48p. (ps-2). 1987. 15.93 (ISBN 0-516-08308-2). Childrens.

Gill, Nancy. Vocabulary Boosters I. (gr. 3-6). 1985. pap. 6.95 (ISBN 0-8224-7280-5). Fearon Teach Aids.

—Vocabulary Boosters II. (gr. 3-6). 1985. pap. 6.95 (ISBN 0-8224-7281-3). Fearon Teach Aids.

Gregorich, B. Vocabulary Vampire. (gr. 7-12). 1982. 5.95 (ISBN 0-88160-083-0, LW 1001). Learning Wks.

Gregorich, Barbara. Word Wagon. Hoffman, Joan, ed. Alexander, Barbara, et al, illus. 32p. (Orig.). (ps-1). wkbk. 1.99 (ISBN 0-88743-129-1). Sch Zone Pub Co.

Hill, Eric. More Opposites. 20p. (Orig.). (ps-k). 1985. 4.95 (ISBN 0-8431-0921-1). Price Stern.

—Spot's Big Book of Words. (gr. 2 up). 1988. 9.95 (ISBN 0-399-21563-8, Putnam). Putnam Pub Group.

Hoban, Tana. Over, Under & Through. Hoban, Tana, illus. LC 86-20675. 32p. (ps-3). 1987. pap. 3.95 (ISBN 0-689-71111-5, Aladdin). Macmillan Child Grp.

Huisingh, Rosemary, et al. ACHIEV-Blue (Activities for Children Involving Everyday Vocabulary) (ps-5). 1989. complete pkg. 186.70 (ISBN 1-55999-002-3). LinguiSystems.

—ACHIEV-Blue Books (Activities for Children Involving Everyday Vocabulary) (ps-5). 1986. spiral manual 49.95 (ISBN 1-55999-004-X). LinguiSystems.

In the Country. (gr. 2-6). 1986. 2.98 (ISBN 0-685-16869-7, 614987). Outlet Bk Co.

Johnson, Odette & Johnson, Bruce H. Apples, Alligators, & Also Alphabets. (Illus.). 32p. (ps-1). 1991. 13.95 (ISBN 0-19-540757-1). Oxford U Pr.

Klawitter, P. Wordwise. (gr. 4-6). 1989. write for info. (ISBN 0-88160-186-1, LW 288). Learning Wks.

Krauss, Ruth. A Hole Is to Dig. Sendak, Maurice, illus. (gr. k-3). 1990. incl. cass. 19.95 (ISBN 0-87499-174-9); pap. 12.95 incl. cass. (ISBN 0-87499-173-0); Set; incl. 4 bks., cass., & guide. pap. 27.95 (ISBN 0-87499-175-7). Live Oak Media.

—Open House for Butterflies. reissued ed. Sendak, Maurice, illus. LC 60-5782. 48p. (ps-3). 1990. 10.95 (ISBN 0-06-023445-8); PLB 10.89 (ISBN 0-06-023446-6). HarpC Child Bks.

Lamport, Joan, et al. The WordShop Activity Book. Hefter, Richard, illus. (gr. 2-3). 1976. 0.95 (ISBN 0-89796-845-X, XTW 05). New Dimens Educ.

Levey, Judith, ed. The Macmillan Picture Wordbook. rev. ed. LC 90-6274. (Illus.). 64p. (ps-1). 1990. 8.95 (ISBN 0-02-754641-1, Mcmillan Child Bk). Macmillan Child Grp.

Levitt, Paul M., et al. The Weighty Word Book. Stevens, Janet, illus. 99p. (gr. 4-9). 1990. Repr. of 1985 ed. 17.95 (ISBN 0-9627979-0-1). Manuscripts.

Lieberman, Lillian. Vocabulary. 64p. (gr. 2-5). 1987. 6.95 (ISBN 0-912107-68-5). Monday Morning Bks.

—Word Structure. 64p. (gr. k-3). 1987. 6.95 (ISBN 0-912107-67-7). Monday Morning Bks.

LinguiSystems Staff. ACHIEV-Blue Sing-a-Longs Manual (Activities for Children Involving Everyday Vocabulary - Community & Special Events Vocabulary) 1989. 24.95 (ISBN 1-55999-007-4). LinguiSystems.

—ACHIEV-Red Sing-a-Longs Manual (Activities for Children Involving Everyday Vocabulary - Home & Family Vocabulary) (ps-3). 1989. 24.95 (ISBN 1-55999-006-6). LinguiSystems.

McNaught, Harry. Five Hundred Words to Grow on. LC 73-2442. (Illus.). (ps-1). 1973. pap. 2.25 (ISBN 0-394-82668-X). Random.

Maestro, Betsy. Taxi: A Book of City Words. Maestro, Giulio, illus. (ps-3). 1990. pap. 4.95 (ISBN 0-395-54811-X, Clarion Bks). HM.

Maker, Janet, et al. The Word Works. 76p. (gr. 4-8). 1979. 7.95 (ISBN 0-88160-030-X, LW 215). Learning Wks.

Miller, Margaret. My First Words: At My House. Miller, Margaret, illus. 16p. (ps). 1989. 3.95 (ISBN 0-694-00276-3, Crowell Jr Bks). HarpC Child Bks.

—My First Words: Me & My Clothes. Miller, Margaret, illus. 16p. (ps). 1989. 3.95 (ISBN 0-694-00272-0, Crowell Jr Bks). HarpC Child Bks.

—My First Words: Time to Eat. Miller, Margaret, illus. 16p. (ps). 1989. 3.95 (ISBN 0-694-00264-X, Crowell Jr Bks). HarpC Child Bks.

Moncure, Jane B. Word Bird Makes Words with Cat. Hohag, Linda, illus. LC 83-23948. 32p. (gr. k-2). 1984. PLB 11.97 (ISBN 0-89565-259-5). Childs World.

—Word Bird Makes Words with Dog. Gohman, Vera, illus. LC 83-23946. 32p. (gr. k-1). 1984. PLB 11.97 (ISBN 0-89565-263-3). Childs World.

—Word Bird Makes Words with Duck. Hohag, Linda, illus. LC 83-23943. 32p. (gr. k-2). 1984. PLB 11.97 (ISBN 0-89565-261-7). Childs World.

—Word Bird Makes Words with Hen. Hohag, Linda, illus. LC 83-23944. 32p. (gr. k-2). 1984. PLB 11.97 (ISBN 0-89565-260-9). Childs World.

—Word Bird's Fall Words. Miracle, Ric, illus. LC 85-5935. 32p. (gr. k-2). 1985. lib. bdg. 11.97 (ISBN 0-89565-308-7); pap. 6.96 (ISBN 0-89565-399-0). Childs World.

—Word Bird's Hats. Gohman, Vera, illus. LC 81-18065. (ps-2). 1982. lib. bdg. 11.97 (ISBN 0-89565-221-8). Childs World.

Monfried, Lucia. Baby's World. (ps). 1990. 13.95 (ISBN 0-525-44617-6, DCB). Dutton Child Bks.

Most, Bernard. There's an Ant in Anthony. Most, Bernard, illus. LC 79-23089. 32p. (gr. k-3). 1980. PLB 12.88 (ISBN 0-688-32226-3). Morrow Jr Bks.

My First Vocabulary. (Illus.). 32p. (ps). 1985. 3.95 (ISBN 0-394-87699-7). Random.

My First Words. (Illus.). 32p. (ps). 1985. 3.95 (ISBN 0-394-87685-7). Random.

Nicholls, Judith, ed. Wordspells. Barker, Alan, illus. (gr. 3-7). 1988. 12.95 (ISBN 0-571-14891-3). Faber & Faber.

Picture Word Book. (Illus.). (ps-k). 8.95 (ISBN 0-7214-7510-8). Ladybird Bks.

Pluckrose, Henry. Change It! Fairclough, Chris, photos by. (Illus.). 32p. (gr. k-4). 1990. PLB 10.40 (ISBN 0-531-14064-4). Watts.

—Store It! 1990. PLB 10.40 (ISBN 0-531-14021-0). Watts.

Salt, Jane. First Words: For Babies & Toddlers. Hawksley, Gerald, illus. LC 90-8037. 192p. (ps-k). 1991. 9.95 (ISBN 0-679-80831-0). Random.

—See & Say Picture Word Book. Pooley, Sarah, illus. LC 89-3624. 48p. (ps-2). 1989. 9.95 (ISBN 0-679-80099-9, Random Juv); PLB 12.99 (ISBN 0-679-90099-3). Random.

Sarnoff, Jane. Words: A Book about the Origins of Every Day Words & Phrases. Ruffins, Reynold, illus. LC 81-8943. 64p. (gr. 4-8). 1981. 12.95 (ISBN 0-684-16958-4, Scribners Young Read). Macmillan Child Grp.

Scarry, Huck. Things That Go. (ps-1). 1986. 3.98 (ISBN 0-685-16834-4, 616556). Outlet Bk Co.

—Things That Sail. (ps-1). 1986. 3.98 (ISBN 0-685-16828-X, 616564). Outlet Bk Co.

Scarry, Richard. Early Words. Scarry, Richard, illus. LC 75-36466. 14p. (ps-1). 1976. 3.95 (ISBN 0-394-83238-8, Random Juv). Random.

—Richard Scarry's Best Word Book Ever. Scarry, Richard, illus. (ps-3). 1963. write for info. (ISBN 0-307-15510-2, Golden Bks). Western Pub.

—Richard Scarry's Biggest Word Book Ever! Scarry, Richard, illus. 12p. (ps-1). 1985. bds. 29.95 (ISBN 0-394-87374-2, Random Juv). Random.

—Richard Scarry's Lowly Worm Word Book. Scarry, Richard, illus. LC 80-53103. 28p. (ps). 1981. pap. 2.95 board (ISBN 0-394-84728-8). Random.

Schaffer, Frank, Publications Staff. My First Words. (Illus.). 24p. (gr. 1-3). 1978. wkbk. 3.98 (ISBN 0-86734-005-3, FS 3006). Schaffer Pubns.

Schuster, E. H. Words Are Important Series. Incl. Level A (Blue) Bk. (gr. 5) (ISBN 0-8437-7985-3); Level B (Red) Bk. (gr. 6) (ISBN 0-8437-7991-8); Level C (Green) Bk. (gr. 7) (ISBN 0-8437-7980-2); Level D (Orange) Bk. (gr. 8) (ISBN 0-8437-7950-0); Level E (Purple) Bk. (gr. 9) (ISBN 0-8437-7955-1); Level F (Brown) Bk. (gr. 10) (ISBN 0-8437-7960-8); Level G (Pink) Bk. (gr. 11) (ISBN 0-8437-7965-9); Level H (Grey) Bk. (gr. 12) (ISBN 0-8437-7970-5). 1985. pap. 3.00 (ISBN 0-685-02045-2). Hammond Inc.

Schwartz, L. I Love Lists! 264p. (gr. 3-6). 1988. 19.95 (ISBN 0-88160-157-8, LW 275). Learning Wks.

—Preschool Teacher's Pet. 192p. (ps). 1989. 14.95 (ISBN 0-88160-185-3, LW 147). Learning Wks.

Schwartz, Linda. The Usage Sleuth. 24p. (gr. 4-7). 1978. 3.95 (ISBN 0-88160-055-5, LW 603). Learning Wks.

—The Word Bird. 48p. (gr. 4-7). 1976. 5.95 (ISBN 0-88160-018-0, LW 202). Learning Wks.

Scott, Foresman. Good Morning, Words! (ps). 1990. 8.95 (ISBN 0-06-017902-3, HarpT). HarperCollins.

Shaw, Marie-Jose. Jumbo Vocabulary Development Yearbook: Grade 3. 96p. (gr. 3). 1980. 18.00 (ISBN 0-8209-0052-4, JVDY 3). ESP.

Slawter, Anamary. Vocabulary Development. Brokaw, David, illus. 32p. (gr. 3-4). 1984. pap. 1.98 (ISBN 0-88724-073-9, CD-7016). Carson-Dellos.

Spot's Big Book of Words. (FRE & ENG., Illus.). 32p. (ps-k). 1990. 10.95 (ISBN 0-399-21826-2, Putnam). Putnam Pub Group.

Stanford, Gene. McGraw-Hill Vocabulary, Bk. 3. 2nd ed. (Illus.). 128p. 1981. pap. text ed. 6.80 (ISBN 0-07-060773-7). McGraw.

Steffens, J. & Carr, J. Action & Adventure. (gr. 7-12). 1983. 9.95 (ISBN 0-88160-101-2, LW 1007). Learning Wks.

Stern, Leonard & Price, Roger. Spooky Silly Mad Libs. (Illus.). 48p. (Orig.). 1989. pap. 2.95 (ISBN 0-8431-2758-9). Price Stern.

Supraner, Robyn. I Can Read About Homonyms. Snyder, Joel, illus. LC 76-54442. (gr. 2-5). 1977. pap. 1.95 (ISBN 0-89375-036-0). Troll Assocs.

—I Can Read About Synonyms & Antonyms. McKeown, Gloria, illus. LC 76-54441. (gr. 2-5). 1977. pap. 1.95 (ISBN 0-89375-035-2). Troll Assocs.

Sweat, Lynn. Vacation & Holiday Fun. Sweat, Lynn, illus. 48p. (ps-2). 1987. 15.93 (ISBN 0-516-08309-0). Childrens.

Terban, Marvin. Superdupers: Really Funny Real Words. Maestro, Giulio, illus. LC 88-38325. 63p. (gr. 4-8). 1989. 13.95 (ISBN 0-89919-804-X, Clarion Bks); pap. 4.95 (ISBN 0-395-51123-2, Clarion Bks). HM.

Tyler, J. & Stitt, S. Mealtime Words. (Illus.). 16p. (ps up). 1988. 2.95 (ISBN 0-7460-0221-1). EDC.

Tyler, Vicki. The A-Plus Guide to a Better Vocabulary. 144p. (Orig.). (gr. 7 up). 1986. pap. 2.25 (ISBN 0-590-33962-1). Scholastic Inc.

Urdang, Laurence. The Basic Book of Synonyms & Antonyms. rev. & enl. ed. 448p. (gr. 9-12). Date not set. pap. 3.95 (ISBN 0-451-14987-4, Sig). NAL-Dutton.

Vacations, Parties, People, & Places. Date not set. 5.98 (ISBN 0-517-68229-X). Outlet Bk Co.

Van Dermeer, Ron & Van Dermeer, Atie. I Can Learn Twenty-Five Words, Bk. 3. (Illus.). 12p. (ps-1). 1989. bds. 4.95 (ISBN 0-8431-2383-4). Price Stern.

Vaughn, Jim. Jumbo Vocabulary Development Yearbook: Grade 7. 96p. (gr. 7-9). 1981. 18.00 (ISBN 0-8209-0056-7, JVDY J). ESP.

Weiler, Susan K. Mini-Myths & Maxi-Words. 1986. pap. text ed. 13.32 (ISBN 0-88334-191-3, 76156). Longman.

Word Fun. (Illus.). 32p. (gr. 2-5). 1985. 3.95 (ISBN 0-394-87693-8). Random.

Word World. 48p. (gr. 5-6). 1989. PLB 10.95 (ISBN 0-685-26339-8). Capstone Pr.

Worth, Bonnie. Muppet Babies Word Book. 1988. write for info. (ISBN 0-02-689106-9). Checkerboard Pr.

Zachman, Linda, et al. ACHIEV-Blue Worksheets (Activities for Children Involving Everyday Vocabulary) 1989. spiral reproducible wkbk. 24.95 (ISBN 1-55999-009-0). LinguiSystems.

—ACHIEV-Red (Activities for Children Involving Everyday Vocabulary) Package. (ps-5). 1989. complete pkg. 186.70 (ISBN 1-55999-001-5). LinguiSystems.

—ACHIEV-Red Books (Activities for Children Involving Everyday Vocabulary) (ps-5). 1985. spiral manuals 49.95 (ISBN 1-55999-005-8). LinguiSystems.

—ACHIEV-Red Worksheets (Activities for Children Involving Everyday Vocabulary) 1989. spiral wkbk. 24.95 (ISBN 1-55999-008-2). LinguiSystems.

Zaslow, David. What's in a Word? Henson, Grace, illus. 80p. (gr. 4-8). 1983. wkbk. 7.95 (ISBN 0-86653-148-3, GA 476). Good Apple.

VOCAL CULTURE

see Voice

VOCATION, CHOICE OF

see Vocational Guidance

VOCATIONAL GUIDANCE

For general works only. Works on guidance in a specific vocation are entered under such headings as Law–Vocational Guidance.

see also Blind–Education; Counseling; Deaf–Education; Occupations; Professions

Aaseng, Nathan. Midstream Changes: People Who Started over & Made It Work. (Illus.). 80p. (gr. 5 up). 1990. PLB 13.95 (ISBN 0-8225-0681-5). Lerner Pubns.

Abrams, Kathleen S. Guide to Careers Without College. Rasof, Henry, ed. (Illus.). 112p. (gr. 7-12). 1988. PLB 11.90 (ISBN 0-531-10585-7). Watts.

Akinsheye, Dexter & Akinsheye, Dayo. I Want to Be... Akinwsheye, Dexter, illus. 56p. (gr. k-4). Date not set. pap. 7.00 (ISBN 1-877835-47-1); pap. text ed. 5.00 (ISBN 1-877835-48-X). TD Pub.

Alexander, Sue. Finding Your First Job. LC 79-26487. (Illus.). (gr. 9 up). 1980. 10.95 (ISBN 0-525-29725-1, DCB); (DCB). Dutton Child Bks.

Allman, Paul. Exploring Careers in Video. rev. ed. Rosen, Ruth, ed. (gr. 7-12). 1989. PLB 12.95 (ISBN 0-8239-1018-0). Rosen Group.

Anema, Durlynn. Don't Get Fired: Thirteen Ways to Hold Your Job. (Illus.). 64p. (gr. 7-12). 1978. pap. text ed. 4.55 (ISBN 0-915510-24-3). Janus Bks.

Barrett, Linda & Guengerich, Galen. Health Care. Culleton, P., ed. (Illus.). 96p. (gr. 6-12). 1991. PLB 13.40 (ISBN 0-531-11102-4). Watts.

—Personal Services. (Illus.). 96p. (gr. 6-12). 1991. PLB 13.40 (ISBN 0-531-11103-2). Watts.

—Sales & Distribution. (Illus.). 96p. (gr. 6-12). 1991. PLB 13.40 (ISBN 0-531-11105-9). Watts.

—Telecommunications. (Illus.). 96p. (gr. 6-12). 1991. PLB 13.40 (ISBN 0-531-11104-0). Watts.

Beckman, Beatrice. Puedo Ser Maestra: (I Can Be a Teacher) LC 84-23236. (SPA.). 32p. (gr. k-3). 1989. PLB 13.93 (ISBN 0-516-31843-8); pap. 3.95 (ISBN 0-516-51843-7). Childrens.

Behrens, June. Puedo Ser Enfermera: (I Can Be a Nurse) LC 85-29086. (SPA., Illus.). 32p. (ps-2). 1988. PLB 13.93 (ISBN 0-516-31893-4); pap. 3.95 (ISBN 0-516-51893-3). Childrens.

Bissonnette-Lamendella, Denise. Pathways: A Job Search Curriculum. 275p. (Orig.). 1987. student wkbk. 7.95 (ISBN 0-942071-05-0). M Wright & Assocs.

—Pathways: A Job Search Curriculum. rev. ed. 265p. 1987. Repr. of 1986 ed. tchr's. ed. 87.95 (ISBN 0-942071-02-6). M Wright & Assocs.

Brownley, Margaret. A Youths' Guide to Job Hunting. 28p. (Orig.). (gr. 8-12). 1988. pap. 3.95 (ISBN 0-945485-02-6). Comm Intervention.

Cannastra, Lyn & Raynor, Tom, eds. Career Sourcebook I: A Guide to Career Planning & Job Hunting. 2nd, rev. ed. (Illus.). 184p. (gr. 9-12). 1988. pap. text ed. 10.00 (ISBN 0-931032-25-3). Edison Electric.

Careers: A Beginning. Date not set. Repr. of 1981 ed. 3.50 (ISBN 1-55646-732-X, 019972); Set of 10 wkbks. 35.00 (ISBN 1-55646-733-8, 019977). Career Aids.

Christophersen, Susan & Farr, J. Michael. Career Preparation: Getting the Most from Training & Education. Croy, Greg, ed. Kreffel, Mike, illus. 64p. (gr. 9-12). 1990. pap. 6.95 (ISBN 0-942784-59-6, JWCP). Jist Works.

—Your Career: Thinking about Jobs & Careers. Croy, Greg, ed. Kreffel, Mike, illus. 64p. (gr. 9-12). 1990. pap. 6.95 (ISBN 0-942784-60-X, JWMC). Jist Works.

Como, Jay. Career Choice & Job Search. 96p. (Orig.). (gr. 9-12). 1986. wkbk. 5.95 (ISBN 0-936007-01-X, 3070); instr's. guide 3.95 (ISBN 0-936007-02-8, 3070). Meridian Educ.

Direct, R. F. Art Distribution Manual. (gr. 10). Date not set. pap. write for info. (ISBN 0-945661-03-7). PASE Pubns.

—Brochure Distribution Manual. rev. ed. (gr. 12). Date not set. pap. text ed. 45.00 (ISBN 0-945661-14-2). PASE Pubns.

—Handwriting Analysis for Pay. rev. ed. (gr. 12). Date not set. pap. text ed. 45.00 (ISBN 0-945661-13-4). PASE Pubns.

—Mailing Letters for Pay. rev. ed. (gr. 12). 1989. pap. text ed. 45.00 (ISBN 0-945661-12-6). PASE Pubns.

Dogin, Yvette. Teen-Agers at Work. 64p. (gr. 8 up). 1988. pap. text ed. 3.75 (ISBN 0-88323-244-8, 164); tchr's. key 1.25 (ISBN 0-318-33412-7, 277). Pendergrass Pub.

Dubrovin, Vivian. Guide to Alternative Education & Training. Rasof, Henry, ed. (Illus.). 112p. (gr. 7-12). 1988. PLB 11.90 (ISBN 0-531-10584-9). Watts.

Dunnan, Nancy. Entrepreneurship. (Illus.). 128p. (gr. 7-10). 1990. lib. bdg. 14.98 (ISBN 0-382-09916-8); pap. 7.95 (ISBN 0-382-24027-8). Silver Burdett Pr.

—Inside Track Library, 4 bks. (Illus.). (gr. 7-10). 1990. Set. lib. bdg. 59.92 (ISBN 0-382-09913-3); pap. 31.80 (ISBN 0-382-24024-3). Silver Burdett Pr.

Edwards, E. W. Exploring Careers Using Foreign Languages. rev. ed. Rosen, Ruth, ed. (gr. 7-12). 1990. PLB 12.95 (ISBN 0-8239-0968-9). Rosen Group.

Farr, J. Michael & Pavlicko, Marie. The JIST Job Search Course: A Young Person's Guide to Getting & Keeping a Good Job. Croy, Greg, ed. Kreffel, Mike, et al, illus. (gr. 7-12). 1990. pap. 6.95 121p. (ISBN 0-942784-34-0, JWYP); data minder, 22p. 1.00 (ISBN 0-942784-35-9). Jist Works.

—The JIST Job Search Course: A Young Person's Guide to Getting & Keeping a Good Job. Croy, Greg, ed. Kreffel, Mike, et al, illus. 138p. (gr. 7-12). 1990. pap. 12.95 instr's. guide (ISBN 0-942784-36-7, JWYPTM). Jist Works.

Gourley, Pamela R., ed. Careers to Think About: A Young Person's Guide to Future Job Opportunities. (Illus.). 315p. (Orig.). (gr. 5-9). 1987. PLB 12.95 (ISBN 0-943621-21-6). TechWest Pubns.

Handville, Elizabeth, ed. OCCU-FACTS: Facts on over 565 Occupations. 624p. (Orig.). (gr. 6 up). 1989. pap. text ed. 38.00 (ISBN 0-9623657-0-X). Careers Inc.

Heron, Jackie. Careers in Health & Fitness. rev. ed. Rosen, Ruth, ed. (Illus.). 160p. (gr. 7 up). 1990. 12.95 (ISBN 0-8239-1162-4). Rosen Group.

Hopke, William E. & Parramore, Barbara M. Children's Dictionary of Occupations. (Illus.). 112p. (gr. 3-8). 1987. pap. text ed. 12.95 (ISBN 0-936007-07-9, 3054). Meridian Educ.

How to Get a Job Study Aid. 1975. pap. 1.50 (ISBN 0-87738-049-X). Youth Ed.

How to Write a Book Report Study Aid. 1975. pap. 1.95 (ISBN 0-87738-031-7). Youth Ed.

Jew, Wing & Tong, Robert. The Janus Job Interview Kit. (gr. 7-12). 1976. 39.95 (ISBN 0-915510-06-5). Janus Bks.

Kaplan, Andrew. Careers for Outdoor Types. (Illus.). 64p. (gr. 7 up). 1991. PLB 12.90 (ISBN 1-56294-022-8). Millbrook Pr.

—Careers for Sports Fans. (Illus.). 64p. (gr. 7 up). 1991. PLB 12.90 (ISBN 1-56294-023-6). Millbrook Pr.

Kratoville, Betty L. You Are the Banker. Zwicky, Jill, illus. 80p. (gr. 4-12). 1989. wkbk. 8.50 (ISBN 0-87879-676-2, High Noon Books). Acad Therapy.

—You Are the School Counselor. Zwicky, Jill, illus. 80p. (Orig.). (gr. 4-12). 1989. wkbk. 8.50 (ISBN 0-87879-675-4, High Noon Books). Acad Therapy.

Lee, Rose P. A Real Job for You: An Employment Guide for Teens. Burke, Cynthia, illus. LC 85-1233. 128p. (gr. 9 up). 1985. pap. 7.95 (ISBN 0-932620-45-0). Betterway Pubns.

Lerner, Mark. Careers in Auto Racing. LC 80-12047. (Illus.). 36p. (gr. 2-5). 1980. PLB 7.95 (ISBN 0-8225-0343-3). Lerner Pubns.

Los Angeles Unified School District Staff. Getting a Job. (Illus.). 48p. (Orig.). (gr. 7-12). 1990. Set. 10 wkbks. & tchr's. guide 44.95 (ISBN 1-56119-095-0); wkbk. 4.95 (ISBN 1-56119-093-4); tchr's. guide 1.95 (ISBN 1-56119-094-2). Educ Pr MD.

—Starting Your New Job. (Illus.). 48p. (Orig.). (gr. 7-12). 1990. Set. 10 wkbks. & tchr's. guide 44.95 (ISBN 1-56119-098-5); wkbk. 4.95 (ISBN 1-56119-096-9); tchr's. guide 1.95 (ISBN 1-56119-097-7). Educ Pr MD.

McCombs, Barbara L. & Brannan, Linda. Help, Please! (Illus.). 32p. (Orig.). (gr. 7-12). 1990. Set. 10 wkbks. & tchr's. guide 44.95 (ISBN 1-56119-077-2); tchr's. guide 1.95 (ISBN 1-56119-038-1); software 39.95 (ISBN 1-56119-119-1). Educ Pr MD.

—How Does It Work? (Illus.). 32p. (Orig.). (gr. 7-12). 1990. Set. 10 wkbks. & tchr's. guide 44.95 (ISBN 1-56119-075-6); tchr's. guide 1.95 (ISBN 1-56119-034-9); software 39.95 (ISBN 1-56119-117-5). Educ Pr MD.

—How Should I Do It? (Illus.). 32p. (Orig.). (gr. 7-12). 1990. Set. 10 wkbks. & tchr's. guide 44.95 (ISBN 1-56119-069-1); tchr's. guide 1.95 (ISBN 1-56119-022-5); software 39.95 (ISBN 1-56119-111-6). Educ Pr MD.

—Keep Calm! (Illus.). 32p. (Orig.). (gr. 7-12). 1990. Set. 10 wkbks. & tchr's. guide 44.95 (ISBN 1-56119-070-5); tchr's. guide 1.95 (ISBN 1-56119-024-1); software 39.95 (ISBN 1-56119-112-4). Educ Pr MD.

—Late Work. (Illus.). 32p. (Orig.). (gr. 7-12). 1990. Set. 10 wkbks. & tchr's. guide 44.95 (ISBN 1-56119-065-9); tchr's. guide 1.95 (ISBN 1-56119-014-4); software 39.95 (ISBN 1-56119-107-8). Educ Pr MD.

—Leaving Early. (Illus.). 32p. (Orig.). (gr. 7-12). 1990. Set. 10 wkbks. & tchr's. guide 44.95 (ISBN 1-56119-078-0); tchr's. guide 1.95 (ISBN 1-56119-040-3); software 39.95 (ISBN 1-56119-120-5). Educ Pr MD.

—May I Try It? (Illus.). 32p. (Orig.). (gr. 7-12). 1990. Set. 10 wkbks. & tchr's. guide 44.95 (ISBN 1-56119-085-3); tchr's. guide 1.95 (ISBN 1-56119-054-3); software 39.95 (ISBN 1-56119-127-2). Educ Pr MD.

Males, Carolyn & Feigen, Roberta. Life after High School: A Career Planning Guide. LC 85-43383. 176p. (gr. 7 up). 1986. lib. bdg. 11.98 (ISBN 0-671-54664-3). Messner.

Martin, Phyllis. Job-Hunt Success Plan, High School Edition. rev. & abr. ed. Savage, Kent V., contrib. by. (Illus.). 118p. (gr. 11-12). 1989. pap. text ed. 8.50 (ISBN 0-685-31060-4). Ctr Career Dev.

Moffett, Carol G. & Strydesky, Rebecca. The Receiving-Checking-Marking-Stocking Clerk. 2nd ed. (Illus.). 160p. (gr. 10-12). 1979. text ed. 13.32 (ISBN 0-07-042667-8). McGraw.

Neufld, Rose. Exploring Nontraditional Jobs for Women. rev. ed. Rosen, Ruth, ed. (gr. 7-12). 1989. PLB 11.95 (ISBN 0-8239-0971-9). Rosen Group.

Ourth, John & Tamarri, Kathie T. Career Caravan. 64p. (gr. 4-8). 1979. 6.95 (ISBN 0-916456-52-8, GA121). Good Apple.

Parramore, Barbara & Hopke, William E. Career Exploration Activities Booklet: 25 Activities to Help Explore Occupations. 48p. (Orig.). (gr. 6 up). 1989. pap. text ed. 17.75 pkg. of 10 (ISBN 0-685-31414-6). Careers Inc.

Popular Careers. (gr. 4-7). 3.95 (ISBN 0-317-42454-8). Learning Well.

Primm, E. Russell, ed. Career Discovery Encyclopedia, 6 vols. LC 89-26000. (gr. 4-8). 1990. Set. 109.95 (ISBN 0-89434-106-5). Ferguson.

Rand, Kenneth J. Time Cards & Paychecks. (Illus.). 64p. (gr. 7-12). 1981. pap. 4.55 (ISBN 0-915510-50-2). Janus Bks.

Ressler, Ralph. A World of Choice: Careers & You - Student Workbook. LC 77-4182. (Illus.). (gr. 9-12). 1978. pap. 12.95 (ISBN 0-88280-050-7); tchr's guide 15.95 (ISBN 0-88280-051-5). ETC Pubns.

Richey, Jim. Job Application Language. (Illus.). 48p. (gr. 7-12). 1978. pap. text ed. 3.45 (ISBN 0-915510-22-7). Janus Bks.

Ryan, Joseph. U. S. Employment Opportunities. 300p. (gr. 12). looseleaf (includes quarterly updates) 184.00 (ISBN 0-937801-01-1). Wash Res Assocs.

Schauer, Donald D. Careers in Trucking. Rosen, R., ed. (Illus.). 144p. (gr. 7-12). 1987. PLB 12.95 (ISBN 0-8239-0748-1). Rosen Group.

Schulz, Marjorie R. Community Services. (Illus.). 96p. (gr. 9-12). 1990. PLB 13.40 (ISBN 0-531-10972-0). Watts.

—Hospitality & Recreation. (Illus.). 96p. (gr. 9-12). 1990. PLB 13.40 (ISBN 0-531-10973-9). Watts.

—Transportation. (Illus.). 96p. (gr. 9-12). 1990. PLB 13.40 (ISBN 0-531-10974-7). Watts.

—Travel & Tourism. (Illus.). 96p. (gr. 9-12). 1990. PLB 13.40 (ISBN 0-531-10975-5). Watts.

Shafe, James C. & Strickland, A. G. Career Direction: Facilitator's Guide. (Illus.). 100p. (gr. 11 up). 1987. tchr's. manual 25.00 (ISBN 0-685-26165-4). Sales & Mgmt Trg.

Shanahan, William F. College: Yes or No? The High School Student's Career Decision-Making Handbook. 2nd ed. LC 82-6775. 304p. (gr. 9 up). 1983. pap. 7.95 (ISBN 0-668-05590-1). Arco.

Swanson, Steve. Is There Life after High School? Making Decisions about Your Future. LC 90-15499. 112p. (Orig.). (gr. 9 up). 1991. pap. 4.95 (ISBN 0-8066-2500-7, 9-2500, Augsburg). Augsburg Fortress.

Tomchek, Ann. Puedo Ser Cocinero: (I Can Be a Chef) LC 85-11016. (SPA., Illus.). 32p. (ps-2). 1988. PLB 13.93 (ISBN 0-516-31886-1); pap. 3.95 (ISBN 0-516-51886-0). Childrens.

Unger, Harlow G. But What If I Don't Want to Go to College? A Guide to Successful Careers Through Alternative Education. 176p. (gr. 10-12). 1992. lib. bdg. 18.95x (ISBN 0-8160-2534-7). Facts on File.

U. S. Department of Labor Staff. Exploring Careers. rev. ed. JIST Staff, ed. (Illus.). 462p. (gr. 6-12). 1989. pap. 19.95 (ISBN 0-942784-27-8, JWEXP). Jist Works.

Wilkes, Donald L. & Hamilton-Wilkes, Viola. Teen Guide Job Search: Ten Easy Steps to Your Future. Carter, Carl, illus. 112p. (gr. 10-12). 1991. pap. 10.95 (ISBN 0-9628787-1-5). Jem Job Educ.

It is a guide to prepare teenagers for effective job hunting. The book includes: Identifying areas of interest; How to write a resume; Places to look for a job; What to wear when job hunting; How to prepare to be interviewed; How to complete employment applications; Explanation of government forms; Tips for keeping your job. The book also contains two vocabulary sections with common words used on employment applications & in interviews. An added bonus is the perforated Form I-9, W-4 form, & employment application. The Work Permit & request form is also shown. This manual is a helpful tool, not only to teenagers but to any audience seeking employment. It is the best, most thorough book on the subject. The contents are current & the illustrative examples enhance the context tremendously.

Publisher Provided Annotation.

VOCATIONAL STORIES

Furman, Abraham L., ed. Everygirls Career Stories. (Illus.). (gr. 6-10). PLB 6.70 (ISBN 0-8313-0049-3). Lantern.

Kraus, Robert. Owliver. Aruego, Jose & Dewey, Ariane, illus. LC 80-13664. 32p. (ps up). 1979. (Little Simon). S&S Trade.

VOCATIONS

see Professions

VOICE

see also Phonetics; Public Speaking; Speech; Ventriloquism

Allington, Richard L. Talking. Thrun, Rick, illus. Krull, Kathleen. LC 80-17021. (Illus.). 32p. (ps-2). 1985. pap. 9.27 (ISBN 0-8172-2492-0); PLB 15.33 (ISBN 0-685-10546-6). Raintree Pubs.

Richardson, Joy. What Happens When You Talk? LC 86-3681. (Illus.). 32p. (gr. 2-3). 1986. PLB 10.95 (ISBN 1-55532-112-7). Gareth Stevens Inc.

Showers, Paul. How You Talk. Galster, Robert, illus. LC 66-15766. 40p. (ps-3). 1967. PLB 13.89 (ISBN 0-690-42136-2, Crowell Jr Bks). HarpC Child Bks.

Wilbur, Richard. Loudmouse. D'Andrade, Diane, ed. Almquist, Don, illus. 32p. (ps-5). 1991. 12.95 (ISBN 0-15-249494-4). HarBraceJ.

VOICE CULTURE

see Voice

VOLCANOES

Arvetis, Chris & Palmer, Carole. What Is a Volcano? Buckley, James, illus. (ps-3). 1987. Repr. 3.95 (ISBN 0-528-82434-1). Checkerboard Pr.

Asimov, Isaac. How Did We Find Out about Volcanoes? Wool, David, illus. 64p. (gr. 4-7). 1981. PLB 12.85 (ISBN 0-8027-6412-6). Walker & Co.

—How did We Find Out about Volcanoes? 64p. (gr. 2-7). 1982. pap. 1.95 (ISBN 0-380-59626-1, 59626-1, Camelot). Avon.

Ask about Volcanoes. 64p. (gr. 4-5). 1987. PLB 18.25 (ISBN 0-8172-2878-0); pap. 13.27 (ISBN 0-8172-2890-X). Raintree Pubs.

Aylesworth, Thomas G. & Aylesworth, Virginia L. The Mount St. Helens Disaster: What We've Learned. 96p. (gr. 7 up). 1983. PLB 12.90 (ISBN 0-531-04488-2). Watts.

Barrett, Norman. Volcanes. (SPA., Illus.). 32p. (gr. k-4). 1990. PLB 11.40 (ISBN 0-531-07911-2). Watts.

—Volcanoes. (Illus.). 32p. (gr. 2 up). 1991. pap. 3.95 (ISBN 0-531-24618-3). Watts.

Bender, Lionel. Volcano. FS-Watts Staff, ed. (Illus.). 32p. (gr. 1-6). 1988. PLB 11.90 (ISBN 0-531-10553-9). Watts.

Branley, Franklyn M. Volcanoes. Simont, Marc, illus. LC 84-45344. 32p. (ps-3). 1985. 13.95 (ISBN 0-690-04451-8, Crowell Jr Bks); PLB 13.89 (ISBN 0-690-04431-3). HarpC Child Bks.

—Volcanoes. Simont, Marc, illus. LC 84-45344. 32p. (ps-3). 1986. pap. 4.50 (ISBN 0-06-445059-7, Trophy). HarpC Child Bks.

Challand, Helen J. Volcanoes. LC 82-17888. (Illus.). 48p. (gr. k-4). 1983. PLB 14.60 (ISBN 0-516-01690-3); pap. 4.95 (ISBN 0-516-41690-1). Childrens.

Curran, Eileen. Mountains & Volcanoes. Watling, James, illus. LC 84-8638. 32p. (gr. k-2). 1985. PLB 10.89 (ISBN 0-8167-0347-7); pap. text ed. 2.95 (ISBN 0-8167-0348-5). Troll Assocs.

Damon, Laura. Discovering Earthquakes & Volcanoes. Jones, John R., illus. LC 89-4974. 32p. (gr. 2-4). 1990. PLB 10.89 (ISBN 0-8167-1757-5); pap. text ed. 2.95 (ISBN 0-8167-1758-3). Troll Assocs.

Deery, Ruth. Earthquakes & Volcanoes. Miller-Ray, Sue E., illus. 48p. (gr. 4-8). 1985. wkbk. 6.95 (ISBN 0-86653-272-2, GA 630). Good Apple.

Dineen, Jacqueline. Volcanoes. (Illus.). 32p. (gr. 5-8). 1991. PLB 11.90 (ISBN 0-531-17338-0, Gloucester Pr). Watts.

Elting, Mary. Volcanoes & Earthquakes. Courtney, illus. 48p. (gr. 3-7). 1990. PLB 9.95 (ISBN 0-671-67217-7). S&S Trade.

Field, Nancy & Machlis, Sally. Discovering Northwest Volcanoes. rev. ed. Machlis, Sally, illus. 32p. (Orig.). (gr. 2-6). 1980. pap. 3.50 (ISBN 0-941042-03-0). Dog Eared Pubns.

Fradin, Dennis. Disaster! Volcanoes. LC 81-12294. (Illus.). 64p. (gr. 3 up). 1982. PLB 17.27 (ISBN 0-516-00851-X). Childrens.

Greenberg, Judith E. & Carey, Helen H. Volcanoes. Shaw, Charles, illus. 32p. (gr. 2-4). 1990. 16.67 (ISBN 0-8172-3756-9); PLB 11.99. Raintree Pubs.

Hamilton, Sue. Mount St. Helen's Eruption. Hamilton, John, ed. (Illus.). 32p. (gr. 4). 1989. PLB 11.95 (ISBN 0-939179-41-5). Abdo & Dghtrs.

Humphrey, Kathryn L. Pompeii: Nightmare at Midday. 1990. PLB 11.90 (ISBN 0-531-10895-3). Watts.

Knapp, Brian. Volcano. LC 89-11584. (Illus.). 48p. (gr. 5-9). 1990. PLB 17.28 (ISBN 0-8114-2373-5). Steck-V.

Knowledge Unlimited Staff. The Earth Exhales: The Story of Volcanoes. (Illus.). 28p. (gr. 7 up). 1983. incl. filmstrip, cass., guide 25.00 (ISBN 0-915291-02-9). Know Unltd.

Kunhardt, Edith. Pompeii...Buried Alive! Eagle, Michael, illus. LC 87-4512. 48p. (gr. 2-3). 1987. lib. bdg. 6.99 (ISBN 0-394-98866-3, Random Juv); pap. 2.95 (ISBN 0-394-88866-9, Random Juv). Random.

Lampton, Christopher. Volcano. (Illus.). 64p. (gr. 4-6). 1991. PLB 17.25 (ISBN 1-56294-028-7). Millbrook Pr.

Lauber, Patricia. Volcano: The Eruption & Healing of Mt. St. Helens. LC 85-22442. (Illus.). 64p. (gr. 3-5). 1986. 15.95 (ISBN 0-02-754500-8, Bradbury Pr). Macmillan Child Grp.

—Volcanoes & Earthquakes. 80p. (gr. 4-7). 1991. pap. 2.75 (ISBN 0-590-42592-7). Scholastic Inc.

Marcus, Elizabeth. All about Mountains & Volcanoes. Veno, Joseph, illus. LC 83-4834. 32p. (gr. 3-6). 1984. lib. bdg. 10.59 (ISBN 0-89375-969-4); pap. text ed. 2.95 (ISBN 0-89375-970-8). Troll Assocs.

Merrians, Deborah. I Can Read About Earthquakes & Volcanoes. LC 74-24966. (Illus.). (gr. 2-4). 1975. pap. 1.95 (ISBN 0-89375-067-0). Troll Assocs.

Michel, Francois & Larvor, Yves. The Restless Earth: The Secrets of Earthquakes, Volcanoes, & Continental Drift in Three-Dimensional Moving Pictures. (Illus.). (gr. 5 up). 1990. 15.95 (ISBN 0-670-83361-4). Viking Child Bks.

Place, Marian T. Mount St. Helens. (gr. 7-11). 1981. 10.95 (ISBN 0-396-07976-8, Putnam). Putnam Pub Group.

Radlauer, Ruth. Volcanoes. LC 80-24564. (Illus.). 48p. (gr. 3 up). 1981. PLB 15.93 (ISBN 0-516-07835-6, Elk Grove Bks); pap. 4.95 (ISBN 0-516-47835-4). Childrens.

Raintree Publishers Inc. Volcanoes. LC 87-27785. (Illus.). 64p. (Orig.). (gr. 5-9). 1988. PLB 19.99 (ISBN 0-8172-3081-5); pap. text ed. 11.93 (ISBN 0-8172-3098-X). Raintree Pubs.

Santrey, Laurence. Earthquakes & Volcanoes. Jones, John, illus. LC 84-2676. 32p. (gr. 3-6). 1985. PLB 9.49 (ISBN 0-8167-0212-8); pap. text ed. 2.95 (ISBN 0-8167-0213-6). Troll Assocs.

Simon, Seymour. Volcanoes. LC 87-33316. (Illus.). 32p. (gr. k-3). 1988. 12.95 (ISBN 0-688-07411-1); PLB 12.88 (ISBN 0-688-07412-X, Morrow Jr Bks). Morrow Jr Bks.

Sotnak, Lewann. Hawaii Volcanoes. LC 89-33550. (Illus.). 48p. (gr. 4-5). 1989. 12.95 (ISBN 0-89686-432-4, Crestwood Hse). Macmillan Child Grp.

Thomas, Margaret. Volcano! LC 90-45372. (Illus.). 48p. (gr. 5-6). 1991. RSBE 10.95 (ISBN 0-89686-595-9, Crestwood Hse). Macmillan Child Grp.

Vogt, Gregory. Predicting Volcanic Eruptions. (Illus.). 144p. (gr. 7-12). 1989. PLB 12.90 (ISBN 0-531-10786-8). Watts.

Whitfield, Phillip. Why Do Volcanoes Erupt? Questions about Our Unique Planet. 1990. 16.95 (ISBN 0-670-83385-1). Viking Child Bks.

Wood, Jenny. Volcanoes: Fire from Below. LC 90-55460. (Illus.). 32p. (gr. 3-4). 1990. PLB 11.95 (ISBN 0-8368-0472-4). Gareth Stevens Inc.

VOLCANOES–FICTION

Carpenter. The Solitary Volcano. write for info. HM.

Castaneda, Omar. Among the Volcanoes. 192p. (gr. 7 up). 1991. 14.95 (ISBN 0-525-67332-6, Lodestar Bks). Dutton Child Bks.

Drury, Roger. The Finches Fabulous Furnace. Blegvad, Erik, illus. (gr. 4-6). 1971. 13.95 (ISBN 0-316-19348-8). Little.

—Finches Fabulous Furnace. 1989. pap. 2.75 (ISBN 0-590-42448-3). Scholastic Inc.

Gormley, Beatrice. Paul's Volcano. Smith, Catherine B., illus. LC 86-27543. (gr. 4-6). 1987. 12.95 (ISBN 0-395-43079-8). HM.

McBarnet, Gill. Fountain of Fire. McBarnet, Gill, illus. 32p. (gr. k-2). 1987. 6.95 (ISBN 0-9615102-3-4). Ruwanga Trad.

VOLUNTARISM

Gilbert, Sara. Lend a Hand: The How, Where & Why of Volunteering. LC 87-32077. (gr. 5 up). 1988. 12.95 (ISBN 0-688-07247-X). Morrow Jr Bks.

Salzman, Marian & Reisgies, Teresa. One Hundred Fifty Ways Teens Can Make a Difference. 156p. (Orig.). 1991. pap. 7.95 (ISBN 1-56079-093-8). Petersons Guides.

VON BRAUN, WERNHER, 1912-

Lampton, Christopher. Wernher von Braun. Solomon, Maury, ed. (Illus.). 160p. (gr. 7 up). 1988. PLB 13.90 (ISBN 0-531-10606-3). Watts.

VOTING

see Elections

VOYAGERS

see Explorers

VOYAGES AND TRAVELS

The AAA Travel Activity Book: The Official AAA Fun Book for Kids. 144p. (gr. k-6). 1990. 4.95 (ISBN 0-916748-65-0). AAA.

Brown, Ann & Bold, Mary. Travel-Ogs: The Do-It-Yourself Survival Kit for Traveling with Parents, Siblings, & Dirty Socks. Small, Carol B., illus. 80p. (Orig.). (gr. 1-6). 1988. wkbk. 6.95 (ISBN 0-938267-06-X). Bold Prodns.

Crump, Donald J., ed. Beyond the Horizon: Adventures in Faraway Lands. (Illus.). 1992. 8.95 (ISBN 0-317-99620-7); lib. bdg. 9.50 (ISBN 0-317-99621-5). Natl Geog.

—Excursion to Enchantment. (Illus.). 1988. 7.95 (ISBN 0-87044-667-3); lib. bdg. 9.50 (ISBN 0-87044-672-X). Natl Geog.

—Exploring Your World. (Illus.). 1989. 29.95 (ISBN 0-87044-726-2); deluxe ed. 41.95 (ISBN 0-87044-728-9); lib. bdg. 34.95 (ISBN 0-87044-727-0). Natl Geog.

Going Places. (Illus.). 32p. (ps). 1985. 3.95 (ISBN 0-394-87690-3). Random.

Hansen, Judith. Seashells in My Pocket: A Child's Guide to Exploring the Atlantic Coast from Maine to North Carolina. Sabaka, Donna, illus. LC 88-14442. 144p. (gr. 1-12). 1988. pap. 8.95 (ISBN 0-910146-72-1). AMC Books.

Hogan, Paula. The Compass. LC 82-70439. (Illus.). 64p. (gr. 4-6). 1982. PLB 8.85 (ISBN 0-8027-6453-3). Walker & Co.

Kids' Trip Diary. 80p. (Orig.). 1988. pap. 5.95 (ISBN 0-943400-23-6). Marlor Pr.

Kids' U. S. Road Atlas. (gr. 4-7). 1991. pap. 3.95 (ISBN 0-528-80547-9). Rand McNally.

Marlor Editors. Kid's Vacation Diary: A Fun Diary & Vacation Book for Use While Traveling! Bree, Marlin, illus. 96p. (Orig.). (gr. 1-7). 1991. pap. 5.95 (ISBN 0-943400-56-2). Marlor Pr.

O'Dell, Scott. The Cruise of the Arctic Star. Bryant, Samuel, illus. 224p. (gr. 7-12). 1973. 13.95 (ISBN 0-395-16034-0). HM.

On Vacation. (gr. 4-7). 1991. pap. 1.95 (ISBN 0-528-80375-1). Rand McNally.

Polo, Marco. Travels of Marco Polo. (gr. 9 up). 1968. pap. 1.50 (ISBN 0-8049-0186-4, CL-186). Airmont.

Safari! LC 80-8799. (Illus.). 104p. (gr. 3-8). 1982. 6.95 (ISBN 0-87044-385-2); lib. bdg. 8.50 (ISBN 0-87044-390-9). Natl Geog.

Sanders, Pete. On the Road. (Illus.). 32p. (gr. 3-6). 1989. PLB 11.90 (ISBN 0-531-17149-3). Watts.

Stanish, Bob. Lessons from the Hearthstone Traveler. 136p. (gr. 3-12). 1988. wkbk. 10.95 (ISBN 0-86653-433-4, GA1043). Good Apple.

Sweetgall, Robert & Peleg, Dorith E. Road Scholars: The Story of Twenty-Eight Kids Who Decided to Take a Hike for Their Health. (Illus.). 64p. (Orig.). 1989. pap. 20.00 (ISBN 0-939041-07-3). Creative Walking.

Vowles, Andrew. My Travel Book. Williams, Harland & O'Halloran, Tim, illus. 32p. (gr. 1-5). 1985. pap. 2.95 (ISBN 0-88625-063-3). Durkin Hayes Pub.

Webster, Harriet. Going Places: The Young Traveler's Guide & Activity Book. Owens, Gail, illus. LC 90-1234. 112p. (gr. 3-7). 1991. pap. 5.95 (ISBN 0-689-71288-X, Aladdin). Macmillan Child Grp.

Wenzel, Dorothy. Ann Bancroft: On Top of the World. LC 89-11980. (Illus.). 64p. (gr. 3 up). 1989. PLB 10.95 (ISBN 0-87518-418-9, Dillon). Macmillan Child Grp.

VOYAGES AND TRAVELS–FICTION

Around the World in Eighty Days. (Illus.). (gr. 3-5). 3.50 (ISBN 0-7214-0721-8). Ladybird Bks.

Bond, Nancy. Another Shore. LC 87-3907. 320p. (gr. 7 up). 1988. PLB 15.95 (ISBN 0-689-50463-2, M K McElderry). Macmillan Child Grp.

Brisson, Pat. Kate Heads West. Brown, Rick, illus. LC 89-27590. 40p. (gr. 2-5). 1990. 12.95 (ISBN 0-02-714345-7, Bradbury Pr). Macmillan Child Grp.

—Magic Carpet. Schwartz, Amy, illus. LC 89-35993. 32p. (ps-3). 1991. RSBE 14.95 (ISBN 0-02-714340-6, Bradbury Pr). Macmillan Child Grp.

Carey, Karla. Julie & Jackie Go a'Journeying: The Narration & Music Book. Nolan, Dennis, illus. 76p. 1990. pap. 18.95 complete pkg. (ISBN 0-685-35755-4); pap. 9.95 (ISBN 1-55768-203-8); cassette 9.95 (ISBN 0-685-35756-2). LC Pub.

Carroll, Lewis. Alice's Adventures in Wonderland. Hitchner, Earle, adapted by. Billin-Frye, Paige, illus. LC 89-33889. 48p. (gr. 3-6). 1990. PLB 12.89 (ISBN 0-8167-1861-X); pap. text ed. 3.95 (ISBN 0-8167-1862-8). Troll Assocs.

Cooney, Barbara. Miss Rumphius. Cooney, Barbara, illus. LC 82-2837. 32p. (gr. k-3). 1982. pap. 14.95 (ISBN 0-670-47958-6). Viking Child Bks.

De Brunhoff, Jean. Le Voyage de Babar. (FRE & SPA., Illus.). bds. 15.95 (ISBN 0-685-11626-3). French & Eur.

Devi-Doolin, Daya. Dabney, Dormck & Wiggle's Slakadunan Adventure. Devi-Doolin, Daya & Joiner, Eddie, illus. 50p. (Orig.). (gr. 4-8). 1989. pap. text ed. 6.50 (ISBN 1-877945-02-1). Padaran Pubns.

Farber, Norma. As I Was Crossing Boston Common. Lobel, Arnold, illus. 32p. (ps-2). 1991. Repr. 14.95 (ISBN 0-525-25960-0, DCB). Dutton Child Bks.

Faulkner, Matt. The Amazing Voyage of Jackie Grace. Faulkner, Matt, illus. LC 86-31485. 32p. (gr. k-3). 1987. pap. 13.95 (ISBN 0-590-40713-9, Scholastic Hardcover). Scholastic Inc.

—The Amazing Voyage of Jackie Grace. Faulkner, Matt, illus. 1991. pap. 3.95 (ISBN 0-590-44860-9). Scholastic Inc.

Garland, Hamlin. Main-Travelled Roads. 1987. Repr. lib. bdg. 18.95x (ISBN 0-89966-555-1). Buccaneer Bks.

Gaskin, Carol. Caravan to China. (gr. 5 up). 1987. pap. 2.50 (ISBN 0-317-65091-2). Bantam.

Goldish, Meish. The Same But Different. (Illus.). 32p. (gr. 1-4). 1989. PLB 13.32 (ISBN 0-8172-3528-0). Raintree Pubs.

Gulliver's Travels. (Illus.). (gr. 3-5). 3.50 (ISBN 0-7214-0453-7). Ladybird Bks.

Gulliver's Travels. (Illus.). (ps-5). 8.95 (ISBN 0-7214-7524-8). Ladybird Bks.

Hunter, Mollie. The Wicked One: A Story of Suspense. LC 76-41515. 136p. (gr. 5-8). 1980. pap. 1.95 (ISBN 0-06-440117-0, Trophy). HarpC Child Bks.

Lasky, Kathryn. Beyond the Divide. LC 82-22867. 264p. (gr. 7 up). 1983. 14.95 (ISBN 0-02-751670-9, Mcmillan Child Bk). Macmillan Child Grp.

Lewin, Hugh. Jafta: The Journey. Kopper, Lisa, illus. LC 84-4326. 24p. (ps-3). 1984. PLB 9.95 (ISBN 0-87614-265-X). Carolrhoda Bks.

Marsh, Carole. Snowshoe & Earmuff Go North. (Illus.). (ps-4). 1989. 19.95 (ISBN 1-55609-646-1); pap. 14.95 (ISBN 1-55609-758-1). Gallopade Pub Group.

Martin, Ann M. Karen's Plane Trip. 144p. (gr. 2-4). 1991. pap. 2.95 (ISBN 0-590-44834-X). Scholastic Inc.

Massi, Jeri. The Myth of the Llama. Thompson, Del & Thompson, Dana, illus. 118p. (Orig.). (gr. 6). 1989. pap. 5.95 (ISBN 1-877778-00-1). Llama Bks.

Peterson, John. The Littles Take a Trip. Clark, Roberta C., illus. 96p. (gr. 4-6). 1972. pap. 2.25 (ISBN 0-590-40136-X). Scholastic Inc.

St. George, Judith. The Amazing Voyage of the New Orleans. Rounds, Glen, illus. LC 89-38453. 64p. (gr. 2-5). 1989. pap. 6.95 (ISBN 1-55870-136-2, Shoe Tree Pr). Betterway Pubns.

Sandin, Joan. The Long Way Westward. Sandin, Joan, illus. LC 89-2024. 64p. (gr. k-3). 1989. 11.95 (ISBN 0-06-025206-5); PLB 11.89 (ISBN 0-06-025207-3). HarpC Child Bks.

Sidney, Margaret. Five Little Peppers Abroad. 1987. Repr. lib. bdg. 21.95x (ISBN 0-89966-551-9). Buccaneer Bks.

Verne, Jules. Around the World in Eighty Days. (gr. 8 up). 1964. pap. 2.25 (ISBN 0-8049-0024-8, CL-24). Airmont.

—Around the World in Eighty Days. 253p. (gr. 5 up). 1964. pap. 2.95 (ISBN 0-440-90285-1, LFL). Dell.

—Around the World in Eighty Days. Moser, Barry, illus. LC 87-62829. 256p. (gr. 5 up). 1988. 19.95 (ISBN 0-688-07508-8); signed ltd. ed. 175.00 (ISBN 0-688-08257-2, Morrow Jr Bks). Morrow Jr Bks.

—Around the World in Eighty Days. 1990. pap. 2.75 (ISBN 0-590-43053-X). Scholastic Inc.

—Master of the World. Lowndes, R. A., intro. by. (gr. 7 up). pap. 1.25 (ISBN 0-8049-0073-6, CL-73). Airmont.

—Round the World in Eighty Days. (gr. 9-12). 1991. pap. text ed. 4.87 (ISBN 0-582-01817-X, 78331). Longman.

VOYAGES AROUND THE WORLD

see also Adventure and Adventurers; Aeronautics–Flights; Discoveries (In Geography); Explorers; Northwest Passage; Overland Journeys to the Pacific; Scientific Expeditions; Seafaring Life; Seamen; Shipwrecks; Travel; Voyages around the World

also names of countries, continents, etc. with the subdivision Description and Travel (e.g. U. S. –Description and Travel); also names of regions (e.g. Antarctic Regions)

Anno, Mitsumasa. Anno's Journey. 48p. (gr. 4 up). 1981. 14.95 (ISBN 0-399-20762-7, Philomel); pap. 7.95 (ISBN 0-399-20952-2, Philomel). Putnam Pub Group.

Asimov, Isaac. Ferdinand Magellan. LC 91-9207. (Illus.). 64p. (gr. 3-4). 1991. PLB 14.95 (ISBN 0-8368-0560-7). Gareth Stevens Inc.

Coote, Roger. First Voyage Around the World. (ps-3). 1990. PLB 11.40 (ISBN 0-531-18302-5). Watts.

Verne, Jules. Around the World in Eighty Days. new & abr. ed. Calhoun, D'Ann, ed. Redondo, Francisco, illus. (gr. 4-12). 1977. pap. text ed. 2.95 (ISBN 0-88301-261-8). Pendulum Pr.

VOYAGES TO THE MOON

see Space Flight to the Moon

VULTURES–FICTION

Byars, Betsy. The Blossoms Meet the Vulture Lady. (gr. k-6). 1987. pap. 2.75 (ISBN 0-440-40677-3, YB). Dell.

W

WAGNER, RICHARD, 1813-1883

Tames, Richard. Richard Wagner. (Illus.). 32p. (gr. 5-8). 1991. PLB 11.90 (ISBN 0-531-14178-0). Watts.

WALES

Davies, Kath. Wales. LC 90-10192. (Illus.). 96p. (gr. 6-11). 1990. PLB 18.60 (ISBN 0-8114-2437-5). Steck-V.

Haines, George. Wales. (Illus.). (gr. 5 up). 1988. 14.95 (ISBN 0-222-01029-0). Chelsea Hse.

Lye, Keith. Take a Trip to Wales. LC 86-50020. 32p. (gr. 1-6). 1986. PLB 7.99 (ISBN 0-531-10197-5). Watts.

Morris, Robert. Bare Ruined Choirs: The Fate of a Welsh Abbey. 52p. (gr. 11 up). 1987. pap. 7.95 (ISBN 0-85950-544-8, Pub. by S Thornes). Dufour.

Sutherland, Dorothy B. Wales. LC 86-29954. (Illus.). 128p. (gr. 5-9). 1987. PLB 25.27 (ISBN 0-516-02794-8). Childrens.

WALES–FICTION

Alexander, Lloyd. Castle of Llyr. 192p. (gr. k-6). 1969. pap. 3.50 (ISBN 0-440-41125-4, YB). Dell.

Bawden, Nina. Carrie's War. LC 72-13253. (gr. 4-7). 1973. PLB 13.89 (ISBN 0-397-31450-7, Lipp Jr Bks). HarpC Child Bks.

Bond, Nancy. A String in the Harp. LC 75-28181. 384p. (gr. 4-8). 1976. 14.95 (ISBN 0-689-50036-X, M K McElderry). Macmillan Child Grp.

Cameron, Eleanor. Time & Mr. Bass. Meise, Fred, illus. (gr. 4-6). 1967. 14.95 (ISBN 0-316-12536-9, Joy St Bks). Little.

Cronin, A. J. The Citadel. (gr. 7 up). 1983. 16.45 (ISBN 0-316-16158-6); pap. 8.95i (ISBN 0-316-16183-7). Little.

Kimmel, Margaret M. Magic in the Mist. Hyman, Trina S., illus. LC 74-18186. 32p. (gr. k-4). 1975. 13.95 (ISBN 0-689-50026-2, M K McElderry). Macmillan Child Grp.

Nimmo, Jenny. Orchard of the Crescent Moon. LC 88-36806. 176p. (gr. 5 up). 1989. 13.95 (ISBN 0-525-44438-6, DCB). Dutton Child Bks.

Thomas, Dylan. A Child's Christmas in Wales. Hyman, Trina S., illus. LC 85-766. 48p. (gr. 4-6). 1985. reinforced bdg. 14.95 (ISBN 0-8234-0565-6). Holiday.

WALKING

see also Hiking

Arnosky, Jim. Crinkleroot's Guide to Walking in Wild Places. Arnosky, Jim, illus. LC 89-38427. 32p. (ps-5). 1990. 13.95 (ISBN 0-02-705842-5, Bradbury Pr). Macmillan Child Grp.

Boy Scouts of America. Hiking. (Illus.). 36p. (gr. 6-12). 1991. pap. 1.85 (ISBN 0-8395-3380-2, 3380A). BSA.

Camping & Walking. (Illus.). 128p. (gr. 3 up). 1987. PLB 15.96 (ISBN 0-88110-287-3); pap. 9.95 (ISBN 0-7460-0129-0). EDC.

Girl Scouts of the U. S. A. Staff. Let's Take a Walk: An Activity Picture Book with Group Leader's Guide. (Illus.). (ps-3). 1975. pap. 0.75 (ISBN 0-88441-135-4, 19-992). Girl Scouts USA.

Kerber, Karen M. Walking Is Wild, Weird & Wacky. rev. ed. Thatch, Nan, ed. Melton, David, intro. by. LC 89-13547. (Illus.). 32p. (ps-2). 1989. lib. bdg. 12.95 (ISBN 0-933849-29-X). Landmark Edns.

Sweetgall, Rob. The Walking Wellness Student Workbook. Neeves, Robert, ed. (Illus.). 80p. (gr. 4-8). 1986. wkbk. 5.00 (ISBN 0-939041-00-6); tchr's. curriculum guidebk. 12.95 (ISBN 0-939041-01-4). Creative Walking.

Watanabe, Shigeo. I Can Take a Walk. Ohtomo, Yasuo, illus. 32p. (gr. k). 1985. 8.95 (ISBN 0-399-21044-X, Philomel); pap. 3.95 (ISBN 0-399-21043-1, Philomel). Putnam Pub Group.

WALL STREET

Flumiani, C. M. The Wall Street Manual for Teenagers. LC 72-89684. (Illus.). 80p. (gr. 7-12). 1973. 27.75 (ISBN 0-913314-24-2). Am Classical Coll Pr.

WALLACE, GEORGE, 1919-

Kurland, Gerald. George Wallace: Southern Governor & Presidential Candidate. Rahmas, D. Steve, ed. 32p. (Orig.). (gr. 7-12). 1972. lib. bdg. 4.20 incl. catalog cards (ISBN 0-87157-529-9). SamHar Pr.

WALRUSES

Green, Carl R. & Sanford, William R. The Walrus. LC 85-17509. (Illus.). 48p. (gr. 4-5). 1986. PLB 10.95 (ISBN 0-89686-273-9, Crestwood Hse). Macmillan Child Grp.

Palmer, S. Walruses. (Illus.). 24p. (gr. k-5). 1989. lib. bdg. 11.93 (ISBN 0-86592-358-2). Rourke Corp.

Schneider, Jeff. My Friend the Walrus: An Ocean Magic Book. Spoon, Wilfred, illus. LC 90-61581. 12p. (ps). 1991. 4.95g (ISBN 1-877779-11-3). Schneider Educational.

Sherrow, Victoria. Seals, Sea Lions, & Walruses. (Illus.). 64p. (gr. 5-8). 1991. PLB 11.90 (ISBN 0-531-20028-0). Watts.

WALRUSES–FICTION

Adoff, Arnold. Sports Pages. Kuzma, Steve, illus. LC 85-45169. 80p. (gr. 3-7). 1986. 13.95 (ISBN 0-397-32102-3, Lipp Jr Bks); PLB 13.89 (ISBN 0-397-32103-1, Lipp Jr Bks). HarpC Child Bks.

Bonsall, Crosby. What Spot? Bonsall, Crosby, illus. LC 63-8005. 64p. (gr. k-3). 1980. pap. 3.50 (ISBN 0-06-444027-3, Trophy). HarpC Child Bks.

Bonsall, Crosby N. What Spot? Bonsall, Crosby N., illus. LC 63-8005. 64p. (gr. k-3). 1963. PLB 11.89 (ISBN 0-06-020611-X). HarpC Child Bks.

Carroll, Lewis. The Walrus & the Carpenter. Zalben, Jane B., illus. LC 85-7591. 32p. (gr. 2-4). 1986. 13.95 (ISBN 0-8050-0071-2). H Holt & Co.

Hill, Lee. Wally, the Scholarly Walrus. 1990. 6.95 (ISBN 0-533-08401-6). Vantage.

Hoff, Syd. Walpole. LC 76-41514. (Illus.). 32p. (gr. k-3). 1977. HarpC Child Bks.

Phillips, Louis. How Do You Lift a Walrus with One Hand? Stevenson, James, illus. (gr. 3-7). 1988. pap. 10.95 (ISBN 0-670-82221-3). Viking Child Bks.

Riddell, Chris. When the Walrus Comes: The Screenplay. Riddell, Chris, illus. LC 89-31718. 1990. 13.95 (ISBN 0-385-29858-7). Doubleday.

WAR

see also Aeronautics, Military; Battles; Disarmament; International Law; Military Art and Science; Peace; Soldiers; Submarine Warfare

also names of wars, battles, etc., e.g. U. S.–History–Civil War; Gettysburg, Battle of, 1863

Hemming, Judith. Why Do Wars Happen? FS-Aladdin Staff, ed. (Illus.). 32p. (gr. 1-3). 1988. 10.40 (ISBN 0-531-17114-0, Gloucester). Watts.

Landau, Elaine. Chemical & Biological Warfare. 128p. (gr. 5-9). 1991. 14.95 (ISBN 0-525-67364-4, Lodestar Bks). Dutton Child Bks.

Mansfield, Sue & Hall, Mary B. Some Reasons for War: How Families, Myths & Warfare Are Connected. LC 87-47694. (Illus.). 224p. (gr. 7 up). 1988. 13.95 (ISBN 0-690-04664-2, Crowell Jr Bks); PLB 13.89 (ISBN 0-690-04666-9, Crowell Jr Bks). HarpC Child Bks.

Williams, Brian. War & Weapons. Berry, John, et al, illus. LC 86-26262. 24p. (gr. 2-5). 1987. lib. bdg. 5.99 (ISBN 0-394-98971-6, Random Juv); pap. 2.95 (ISBN 0-394-88971-1). Random.

WAR–FICTION

Anderson, Paul L. Swords in the North. LC 57-9448. 270p. (gr. 7-11). 1935. 18.00 (ISBN 0-8196-0103-9). Biblo.

Bach, Alice. Ragwars. (Orig.). (gr. k-6). 1987. pap. 2.95 (ISBN 0-440-47345-4, YB). Dell.

Baird, Thomas. Where Time Ends. LC 87-45864. 288p. (gr. 7 up). 1988. 13.95 (ISBN 0-06-020359-5); PLB 13.89 (ISBN 0-06-020360-9). HarpC Child Bks.

Beach, Lynn. Invisibility Island. (gr. 8 up). 1988. pap. 2.95 (ISBN 0-345-35097-9). Ballantine.

Cecil's Story. Catalanotto, Peter, illus. LC 90-7775. 32p. (gr. k-2). 1991. 14.95 (ISBN 0-531-05912-X); PLB 14.99 (ISBN 0-531-08512-0). Orchard Bks Watts.

Clapp, Patricia. The Tamarack Tree. LC 86-108. 224p. (gr. 7 up). 1986. 11.95 (ISBN 0-688-02852-7). Lothrop.

Corcoran, Barbara. The Private War of Lillian Adams. LC 88-27485. 176p. (gr. 3-7). 1989. 13.95 (ISBN 0-689-31443-4, Atheneum Child Bk). Macmillan Child Grp.

Eco, Umberto. The Bomb & the General. Weaver, William, tr. Carmi, Eugenio, illus. 40p. (gr. 5-7). 1989. 12.95 (ISBN 0-15-209700-7). HarBraceJ.

Falls, Gregory A. The Pushcart War. (Orig.). (gr. 4 up). 1985. pap. 4.50 (ISBN 0-87602-248-4). Anchorage.

Fitzhugh, Louise & Scoppettone, Sandra. Bang Bang You're Dead. LC 69-14440. (Illus.). 32p. (ps-3). 1969. PLB 12.89 (ISBN 0-06-021914-9). HarpC Child Bks.

Foreman, Michael. War & Peas. LC 74-10368. (Illus.). 32p. (ps-3). 1974. PLB 13.89 (ISBN 0-690-00629-2, Crowell Jr Bks). HarpC Child Bks.

Gross, Philip. The Song of Gail & Fludd. 208p. (gr. 3-6). 1991. 15.95 (ISBN 0-571-14374-1). Faber & Faber.

Horgan, Dorothy. The Edge of War. 80p. (gr. 6 up). 1988. 13.95 (ISBN 0-19-271574-7). Oxford U Pr.

Knox, Joann. The War Without Fighting - The Oil That Multiplied. 68p. (gr. 4-8). 1973. pap. 1.00 (ISBN 0-88243-772-0, 02-0772). Gospel Pub.

Lewis, C. S. Prince Caspian. Baynes, Pauline, illus. LC 51-12799. 192p. (gr. 4 up). 1988. 12.95 (ISBN 0-02-758580-8, Mcmillan Child Bk). Macmillan Child Grp.

Mazer, Harry. The War on Villa Street. 128p. (gr. 7 up). 1979. pap. 2.95 (ISBN 0-440-99062-9, LFL). Dell.

Moulton, Deborah. The First Battle of Morn. LC 87-37978. 192p. (gr. 6 up). 1988. 14.95 (ISBN 0-8037-0550-6). Dial Bks Young.

Perez, N. A. The Slopes of War. (Illus.). 224p. (gr. 7 up). 1990. 13.95 (ISBN 0-395-35642-3, 5-93140); pap. 4.95 (ISBN 0-395-54979-5). HM.

Phillips, Ann. The Peace Child. (Illus.). 160p. (gr. 5 up). 1988. 13.95 (ISBN 0-19-271560-7). Oxford U Pr.

Pilkey, Dav. World War Won. Pilkey, Dav, illus. LC 87-2711. 32p. (gr. 1 up). 1987. lib. bdg. 12.95 (ISBN 0-933849-22-2). Landmark Edns.

Smith, Janice L. The Show-&-Tell War: And Other Stories about Adam Joshua. Gackenbach, Dick, illus. LC 85-45842. 176p. (gr. 1-4). 1990. pap. 3.50 (ISBN 0-06-440312-2, J312, Trophy). HarpC Child Bks.

Steele, William O. Perilous Road. 1990. pap. 3.95 (ISBN 0-15-260647-5). HarbraceJ.

Stine, R. L. Jungle Raid. (gr. 8 up). 1988. pap. 2.95 (ISBN 0-318-32775-9). Ballantine.

Taylor, Theodore. The Battle off Midway Island. 144p. (Orig.). (gr. 7 up). 1985. pap. 3.95 (ISBN 0-380-78790-3, 78790-3, Flare). Avon.

Temperley, Alan. Murdo's War. 256p. (gr. 4-8). 1989. 17.95 (ISBN 0-86241-181-5, Pub. by Cnngt Pub Ltd). Trafalgar Sq.

Thompson, Julian F. The Taking of Mariasburg. 288p. (gr. 7 up). 1988. pap. 12.95 (ISBN 0-590-41247-7, Scholastic Hardcover). Scholastic Inc.

Westall, Robert. Echoes of War. 96p. (gr. 7 up). 1991. 13.95 (ISBN 0-374-31964-2). FS&G.

WAR CORRESPONDENTS

see Reporters and Reporting

WAR CRIPPLES

see Physically Handicapped

WAR OF 1812

see U. S.–History–War of 1812

WAR OF 1939-1945

see World War, 1939-1945

WAR OF SECESSION (U. S.)

see U. S.–History–Civil War

WAR OF THE AMERICAN REVOLUTION

see U. S.–History–Revolution

WAR SHIPS

see Warships

WARFARE, SUBMARINE

see Submarine Warfare

WARS

see Military History; Naval History

WARS OF THE ROSES, 1455-1485

see Great Britain–History–Wars of the Roses, 1455-1485

WARSAW–FICTION

Singer, Isaac Bashevis. A Day of Pleasure: Stories of a Boy Growing up in Warsaw. Vishniac, Roman, photos by. LC 70-95461. (Illus.). 160p. (gr. 3 up). 1986. write for info. (ISBN 0-374-41696-6, Sunburst). FS&G.

WARSHIPS

see also Aircraft Carriers; Submarines;

also names of countries with the subhead Navy (e.g. U. S. Navy)

Cave, Ron & Cave, Joyce. What about... War Ships. West, David, illus. 32p. (gr. k-3). 1983. PLB 10.90 (ISBN 0-531-03471-2). Watts.

Humble, Richard. World War One Battleship. (Illus.). 32p. (gr. 5-6). 1989. PLB 11.90 (ISBN 0-531-10739-6). Watts.

Norman, C. J. Buques de Guerra. LC 85-51458. (SPA., Illus.). 32p. (gr. k-4). 1991. PLB 11.40 (ISBN 0-531-07921-X). Watts.

—Warships. LC 85-51458. 32p. (gr. 1-6). 1989. PLB 11.40 (ISBN 0-531-10093-6); pap. 3.95 (ISBN 0-531-15147-6). Watts.

Rawlinson, J. Cruisers. (Illus.). 48p. (gr. 3-8). 1989. lib. bdg. 18.60 (ISBN 0-86625-085-9). Rourke Corp.

Stephen, R. J. Picture World of Warships. 1990. PLB 11.40 (ISBN 0-531-14013-X). Watts.

Walmer, M. Battleships. (Illus.). 48p. (gr. 3-8). 1989. lib. bdg. 18.60 (ISBN 0-86625-083-2). Rourke Corp.

—Destroyers. (Illus.). 48p. (gr. 3-8). 1989. lib. bdg. 18.60 (ISBN 0-86625-081-6). Rourke Corp.

WASHINGTON, BOOKER TALIAFERRO, 1859?-1915

Booker T. Washington. (Illus.). (gr. 2-5). 1989. 27.99 (ISBN 0-8172-2959-0). Raintree Pubs.

Booker T. Washington: Mini Play. (gr. 5 up). 1977. 6.50 (ISBN 0-89550-361-1). Stevens & Shea.

Gleiter, Jan & Thompson, Kathleen. Booker T. Washington. LC 87-26325. (Illus.). 32p. (Orig.). (gr. 2-5). 1987. PLB 16.67 (ISBN 0-8172-2663-X). Raintree Pubs.

Schroeder, Alan. Booker T. Washington. King, Coretta Scott, intro. by. (Illus.). 112p. (gr. 5 up). 1992. 17.95 (ISBN 1-55546-616-8). Chelsea Hse.

Washington, Booker T. Up from Slavery. Andrews, C. A., intro. by. (gr. 5 up). pap. 2.50 (ISBN 0-8049-0157-0, CL-157). Airmont.

WASHINGTON, GEORGE, PRESIDENT U. S. 1732-1799

Adler, David A. George Washington: Father of Our Country. Garrick, Jacqueline, illus. LC 88-4691. 48p. (gr. 1-4). 1988. reinforced bdg. 12.95 (ISBN 0-8234-0717-9). Holiday.

Boudreau, Allan & Bleimann, Alexander. George Washington in New York. Deutsch, David, ed. LC 87-91308. (Illus.). 275p. (Orig.). (gr. 9-12). 1989. 19.95 (ISBN 0-317-93022-2); pap. text ed. 8.95 (ISBN 0-317-93023-0). Amer Lodge Res.

Brandt, Keith. George Washington. Frenck, Hal, illus. LC 84-8624. 32p. (gr. 3-6). 1985. PLB 9.49 (ISBN 0-8167-0256-X); pap. text ed. 2.95 (ISBN 0-8167-0257-8). Troll Assocs.

Bulla, Clyde R. Washington's Birthday. Bolognese, Don, illus. LC 66-10504. 40p. (gr. 1-3). 1967. PLB 12.89 (ISBN 0-690-86796-4, Crowell Jr Bks). HarpC Child Bks.

Camp, Norma C. George Washington: Man of Courage & Prayer. Manderfield, Diane, illus. LC 76-3084. (gr. 3-6). 1977. pap. 6.95 (ISBN 0-915134-25-X). Mott Media.

Children of History, 6 vols. LC 89-585. (Illus.). 32p. (gr. 3-8). 1989. Set. 61.95 (ISBN 0-86307-922-9). Marshall Cavendish.

D'Aulaire, Ingri & D'Aulaire, Edgar P. George Washington. D'Aulaire, Ingri & D'Aulaire, Edgar P., illus. LC 36-27417. 64p. (gr. 1-4). 1936. pap. 13.95 (ISBN 0-385-07306-2). Doubleday.

—George Washington. LC 36-27417. (Illus.). 64p. (gr. 4-6). 1987. pap. 10.00 (ISBN 0-385-24107-0). Doubleday.

Falkof, Lucille. George Washington: First President of the United States. Young, Richard G., ed. LC 88-24564. (Illus.). (gr. 5-9). 1989. PLB 17.26 (ISBN 0-944483-19-4). Garrett Ed Corp.

Farr, Naunerle C. George Washington-Thomas Jefferson. Carrillo, Fred & Cruz, E. R., illus. (gr. 4-12). 1979. pap. text ed. 2.95 (ISBN 0-88301-355-X); wkbk. 1.25 (ISBN 0-88301-379-7). Pendulum Pr.

Fradin, Dennis B. Washington's Birthday. 48p. (gr. 2-5). 1990. 12.95 (ISBN 0-89490-235-0). Enslow Pubs.

George Washington. 1987. pap. 2.25 (ISBN 0-671-62981-6, Little Simon). S&S Trade.

Graff, Stewart. George Washington: Father of Freedom. (Illus.). 80p. (gr. 2-6). 1992. Repr. of 1964 ed. PLB 12.95 (ISBN 0-7910-1451-7). Chelsea Hse.

Gross, Ruth B. If You Grew up with George Washington. Kent, Jack, illus. 64p. (gr. 2-4). 1985. pap. 2.95 (ISBN 0-590-41950-1). Scholastic Inc.

Heilbroner, Joan. Meet George Washington. Mays, Victor, illus. (gr. 2-6). 1967. 4.95 (ISBN 0-394-80058-3, Random Juv); lib. bdg. 8.99 (ISBN 0-394-90058-8). Random.

Hellbroner, Joan. Meet George Washington. Marchesi, Stephen, illus. LC 88-19067. 72p. (gr. 2-4). 1989. PLB 6.99 (ISBN 0-394-91965-3); pap. 2.95 (ISBN 0-394-81965-9). Random.

Hilton, Suzanne. The World of Young George Washington. Bock, William S., illus. LC 86-13296. 112p. (gr. 5-9). 1987. 12.95 (ISBN 0-8027-6657-9); PLB 12.85 (ISBN 0-8027-6658-7). Walker & Co.

Hoobler, Dorothy & Hoobler, Thomas. George Washington. Brook, Bonnie, ed. Himler, Ronald, illus. 32p. (gr. k-2). Date not set. 5.95 (ISBN 0-671-69114-7); PLB 10.98 (ISBN 0-671-69108-2). Silver Pr.

Jacobs, William J. Washington. LC 90-8844. (Illus.). 48p. (gr. 4-6). 1991. SBE 12.95 (ISBN 0-684-19275-6, Scribners Young Read). Macmillan Child Grp.

Kent, Zachary. George Washington. LC 86-12896. (Illus.). 100p. (gr. 3 up). 1986. PLB 17.27 (ISBN 0-516-01381-5); pap. 6.95 (ISBN 0-516-41381-3). Childrens.

McGovern, Ann. If You Grew Up with George Washington. 64p. (gr. 2-4). 1985. 2.50 (ISBN 0-590-40688-4). Scholastic Inc.

McGowen, Tom. George Washington. (Illus.). 72p. (gr. 4-9). 1986. lib. bdg. 10.40 (ISBN 0-531-10108-8). Watts.

Meltzer, Milton. George Washington & the Birth of Our Nation. LC 86-9222. 176p. (gr. 7 up). 1986. PLB 13.90 (ISBN 0-531-10253-X). Watts.

Milton, Joyce. George Washington. (Orig.). (gr. k-6). 1988. pap. 2.95 (ISBN 0-440-40020-1, YB). Dell.

Moncure, Jane B. My First Presidents' Day Book. Halverson, Lydia, illus. LC 87-10309. 32p. (ps-2). 1987. PLB 14.60 (ISBN 0-516-02910-X); pap. 3.95 (ISBN 0-516-42910-8). Childrens.

Osborne, Mary P. George Washington: Leader of a New Nation. LC 90-42601. (Illus.). 96p. (gr. 4-7). 1991. 13.95 (ISBN 0-8037-0947-1); lib. bdg. 13.89 (ISBN 0-8037-0949-8). Dial Bks Young.

Richards, Dorothy F. George Washington, a Talk with His Grandchildren. Nelson, John, illus. LC 78-8564. (gr. k-4). 1978. PLB 10.95 (ISBN 0-89565-034-7). Childs World.

Roop, Peter & Roop, Connie. Buttons for General Washington. Hanson, Peter E., illus. LC 86-6120. 48p. (gr. k-4). 1986. lib. bdg. 9.95 (ISBN 0-87614-294-3); pap. 4.95 (ISBN 0-87614-476-8). Carolrhoda Bks.

Santrey, Laurence. George Washington: Young Leader. LC 81-23150. (Illus.). 48p. (gr. 4-6). 1982. PLB 10.79 (ISBN 0-89375-758-6); pap. text ed. 2.95 (ISBN 0-89375-759-4). Troll Assocs.

Siegel, Beatrice. George & Martha Washington at Home in New York. Aloise, Frank, illus. LC 88-24534. 80p. (gr. 4-7). 1989. 12.95 (ISBN 0-02-782721-6, Four Winds). Macmillan Child Grp.

Smith, Kathy B. George Washington. Seward, James, illus. 24p. (gr. 4-6). 1987. PLB 7.98 (ISBN 0-671-64147-6); PLB 5.99s.p. Messner.

Stevenson, Augusta. George Washington: Young Leader. Dreany, E. J., illus. LC 86-10914. 192p. (gr. 2-6). 1986. pap. 3.95 (ISBN 0-02-042150-8, Aladdin). Macmillan Child Grp.

WASHINGTON, GEORGE, PRESIDENT U. S. 1732-1799–FICTION

Fritz, Jean. George Washington's Breakfast. Galdone, Paul, illus. (gr. 2-6). 1984. PLB 5.99 (ISBN 0-698-30099-8, Coward); pap. 5.95 (ISBN 0-698-20616-9, Coward). Putnam Pub Group.

Johnston, Johanna. A Birthday for General Washington. Burgeson, Marjorie, illus. LC 75-38545. 32p. (gr. k-4). 1976. PLB 15.93 (ISBN 0-516-08881-5, Golden Gate). Childrens.

Marshall, James. George & Martha. (gr. 3 up). 1987. pap. 7.95 incl. cass. (ISBN 0-395-45739-4). HM.

Quackenbush, Robert. I Did It with My Hatchet: A Story of George Washington. Quackenbush, Robert, illus. 32p. (gr. 2-6). 1989. 13.95 (ISBN 0-945912-04-8). Pippin Pr.

WASHINGTON, MARTHA (DANDREGE) CUSTIS, 1731-1802

Anderson, LaVere. Martha Washington: First Lady of the Land. Cary, illus. 80p. (gr. 2-6). 1991. Repr. of 1973 ed. PLB 12.95 (ISBN 0-7910-1452-5). Chelsea Hse.

Wagoner, Jean B. Martha Washington: America's First First Lady. Goldstein, Leslie, illus. LC 86-10737. 192p. (gr. 2-6). 1986. pap. 3.95 (ISBN 0-02-042160-5, Aladdin). Macmillan Child Grp.

Waldrop, Ruth. Martha Washington. Hendrix, Hurston H., illus. LC 87-61391. 112p. (gr. 3-6). 1987. PLB 10.95 (ISBN 0-317-59028-6); pap. 6.95 (ISBN 0-317-59029-4). RuSk Inc.

WASHINGTON, D. C.

Aylesworth, Thomas G. & Aylesworth, Virginia L. The Atlantic (Virginia, West Virginia, District of Columbia) (Illus.). 66p. (Orig.). 1990. lib. bdg. 16.95x (ISBN 1-55546-555-2); pap. 6.95 (ISBN 0-7910-0533-X). Chelsea Hse.

Bluestone, Carol & Irwin, Susan. Washington, D. C. Guidebook for Kids. rev. ed. LC 87-50322. (Illus.). 64p. (gr. 3-9). 1987. pap. 5.95 (ISBN 0-9601022-2-1). Noodle Pr.

Carlson, Barbara. Our Nation's Capital City. (Illus.). 8p. (ps-3). 1988. incl. filmstrip 19.00 (ISBN 1-55933-003-1, 3187). Know Unltd.

Carol Marsh Washington D.C. Books, 31 bks. Set. 638.45 (ISBN 0-7933-1283-3). Gallopade Pub Group.

Carpenter, Allan. District of Columbia. new ed. LC 78-31683. (Illus.). 96p. (gr. 4 up). 1979. PLB 19.93 (ISBN 0-516-04151-7). Childrens.

Climo, Shirley. City! Washington, D. C. Ancona, George, illus. LC 90-1785. 64p. (gr. 3-7). 1991. SBE 15.95 (ISBN 0-02-719036-6, Mcmillan Child Bk). Macmillan Child Grp.

Davis, James E. & Hawke, Sharryl D. Washington, D. C. (Illus.). 64p. (gr. 4-9). 1990. PLB 18.00 (ISBN 0-8172-3026-2). Raintree Pubs.

Kent, Deborah. Washington, D. C. LC 90-35386. (Illus.). 144p. (gr. 4 up). 1990. PLB 25.27 (ISBN 0-516-00497-2). Childrens.

A Kid's Guide to Washington, D. C. (gr. 1 up). 1989. pap. 6.95 (ISBN 0-15-200459-9, Gulliver Bks). HarBraceJ.

Krementz, Jill. A Visit to Washington, D. C. Krementz, Jill, illus. LC 86-27973. 48p. (gr. 6 up). 1987. pap. 13.95 (ISBN 0-590-40582-9, Scholastic Hardcover). Scholastic Inc.

—A Visit to Washington, D.C. (gr. 1-3). 1989. pap. 3.95 (ISBN 0-590-40583-7). Scholastic Inc.

Loewen, N. Washington, D. C. (Illus.). (gr. 5 up). 1989. lib. bdg. 14.60 (ISBN 0-86592-544-5). Rourke Corp.

Lumley, Katherine W. District of Columbia: In Words & Pictures. Wahl, Richard, illus. LC 80-39645. 48p. (gr. 2-5). 1981. PLB 15.93 (ISBN 0-516-03951-2). Childrens.

McLean, Virginia O. In the Bag - Travel D. C. Robinson, Susan P., illus. 20p. (ps up). 1991. pap. 10.98 (ISBN 0-9606046-2-6). Redbird.

Marsh, Carole. Avast, Ye Slobs! Washington, D.C. (Illus.). (gr. 3-12). 1990. PLB 19.95 (ISBN 0-7933-0280-3); pap. 14.95 (ISBN 0-7933-0279-X); computer disk 29.95 (ISBN 0-7933-0281-1). Gallopade Pub Group.

—The Beast of the Washington, D.C. Bed & Breakfast. (Illus.). (gr. 3-12). 1990. PLB 19.95 (ISBN 0-7933-1468-2); pap. 14.95 (ISBN 0-7933-1469-0); computer disk 29.95 (ISBN 0-7933-1470-4). Gallopade Pub Group.

—The Hard-to-Believe-But-True! Book of Washington, D.C. History, Mystery, Trivia, Legend, Lore, Humor & More. (Illus.). (gr. 3-12). 1990. PLB 19.95; pap. 14.95 (ISBN 0-7933-0276-5); computer disk 29.95 (ISBN 0-7933-0278-1). Gallopade Pub Group.

—If My Washington, D.C. Mama Ran the World! (Illus.). (gr. 3-12). 1990. PLB 19.95 (ISBN 0-7933-1477-1); pap. 14.95 (ISBN 0-7933-1478-X); computer disk 29.95 (ISBN 0-7933-1479-8). Gallopade Pub Group.

—Let's Quilt Washington, D.C. & Stuff it Topographically! (Illus.). (gr. 3-12). 1990. PLB 19.95 (ISBN 1-55609-564-3); pap. 14.95; computer disk 29.95 (ISBN 0-7933-1461-5). Gallopade Pub Group.

—The Washington D. C. Hot Air Balloon Mystery. (Illus.). (gr. 2-9). 1990. 19.95 (ISBN 0-7933-2390-8); pap. 14.95 (ISBN 0-7933-2391-6); computer disk 29.95 (ISBN 0-7933-2392-4). Gallopade Pub Group.

—Washington, D.C. & Other State Greats (Biographies) (Illus.). (gr. 3-12). 1990. PLB 19.95 (ISBN 0-7933-1480-1); pap. 14.95 (ISBN 0-7933-1481-X); computer disk 29.95 (ISBN 0-7933-1482-8). Gallopade Pub Group.

—Washington, D.C. Bandits, Bushwackers, Outlaws, Crooks, Devils, Ghosts, Desperadoes & Other Assorted & Sundry Characters! (Illus.). (gr. 3-12). 1990. PLB 19.95 (ISBN 0-7933-0262-5); pap. 14.95 (ISBN 0-7933-0261-7); computer disk 29.95 (ISBN 0-7933-0263-3). Gallopade Pub Group.

—Washington, D.C. Classic Christmas Trivia: Stories, Recipes, Activities, Legends, Lore & More! (Illus.). (gr. 3-12). 1990. PLB 19.95 (ISBN 0-7933-0265-X); pap. 14.95 (ISBN 0-7933-0264-1); computer disk 29.95 (ISBN 0-7933-0266-8). Gallopade Pub Group.

—Washington, D.C. Coastales. (Illus.). (gr. 3-12). 1990. PLB 19.95 (ISBN 0-7933-1474-7); pap. 14.95 (ISBN 0-7933-1475-5); computer disk 29.95 (ISBN 0-7933-1476-3). Gallopade Pub Group.

—Washington, D.C. "Jography" A Fun Run Thru Our State! (Illus.). (gr. 3-12). 1990. PLB 19.95 (ISBN 1-55609-562-7); pap. 14.95 (ISBN 1-55609-561-9); computer disk 29.95 (ISBN 0-7933-1460-7). Gallopade Pub Group.

—Washington, D.C. Kid's Cookbook: Recipes, How-to, History, Lore & More! (Illus.). (gr. 3-12). 1990. PLB 19.95 (ISBN 0-7933-0274-9); pap. 14.95 (ISBN 0-7933-0273-0); computer disk 29.95 (ISBN 0-7933-0275-7). Gallopade Pub Group.

—Washington, D.C. Quiz Bowl Crash Course! (Illus.). (gr. 3-12). 1990. PLB 19.95 (ISBN 0-7933-1471-2); pap. 14.95 (ISBN 0-7933-1472-0); computer disk 29.95 (ISBN 0-7933-1473-9). Gallopade Pub Group.

—Washington, D.C. School Trivia: An Amazing & Fascinating Look at Our State's Teachers, Schools & Students! (Illus.). (gr. 3-12). 1990. PLB 19.95 (ISBN 0-7933-0271-4); pap. 14.95 (ISBN 0-7933-0270-6); computer disk 29.95 (ISBN 0-7933-0272-2). Gallopade Pub Group.

—Washington, D.C. Silly Basketball Sportsmysteries, Vol. 1. (Illus.). (gr. 3-12). 1990. PLB 19.95 (ISBN 0-7933-0268-4); pap. 14.95 (ISBN 0-7933-0267-6); computer disk 29.95 (ISBN 0-7933-0269-2). Gallopade Pub Group.

—Washington, D.C. Silly Basketball Sportsmysteries, Vol. 2. (Illus.). (gr. 3-12). 1990. PLB 19.95 (ISBN 0-7933-1483-6); pap. 14.95 (ISBN 0-7933-1484-4); computer disk 29.95 (ISBN 0-7933-1485-2). Gallopade Pub Group.

—Washington, D.C. Silly Football Sportsmysteries, Vol. 1. (Illus.). (gr. 3-12). 1990. PLB 19.95 (ISBN 0-7933-1462-3); pap. 14.95 (ISBN 0-7933-1463-1); computer disk 29.95 (ISBN 0-7933-1464-X). Gallopade Pub Group.

—Washington, D.C. Silly Football Sportsmysteries, Vol. 2. (Illus.). (gr. 3-12). 1990. PLB 19.95 (ISBN 0-7933-1465-8); pap. 14.95 (ISBN 0-7933-1466-6); computer disk 29.95 (ISBN 0-7933-1467-4). Gallopade Pub Group.

—Washington, D.C. Silly Trivia! (Illus.). (gr. 3-12). 1990. PLB 19.95 (ISBN 1-55609-560-0); pap. 14.95 (ISBN 1-55609-559-7); computer disk 29.95 (ISBN 0-7933-1459-3). Gallopade Pub Group.

—Washington, D.C.'s (Most Devastating!) Disasters & (Most Calamitous!) Catastrophies! (Illus.). (gr. 3-12). 1990. PLB 19.95 (ISBN 0-7933-0259-5); pap. 14.95 (ISBN 0-7933-0258-7); computer disk 29.95 (ISBN 0-7933-0260-9). Gallopade Pub Group.

Munro, Roxie. Inside Outside Book of Washington D.C. Munro, Roxie, illus. 48p. (ps up). 1987. 13.95 (ISBN 0-525-44298-7, DCB). Dutton Child Bks.

Pedersen, Anne. Kidding Around Washington, D. C. A Young Person's Guide to the City. Finnell, Jim, illus. 64p. (Orig.). (gr. 3 up). 1989. pap. 9.95 (ISBN 0-945465-25-4). John Muir.

Reef, Catherine. Washington, D. C. LC 89-12025. (Illus.). 60p. (gr. 3 up). 1989. PLB 12.95 (ISBN 0-87518-411-1, Dillon). Macmillan Child Grp.

Strickland, Alison. Washington, D. C. - Our Nation's Capital. (Illus.). 32p. (gr. 2-5). 1985. 2.25 (ISBN 0-87406-047-8, 50-08652-4). Willowisp Pr.

Tippet Shows Off Washington. 32p. (gr. 1-5). 1983. 6.95 (ISBN 0-686-47606-9). Outdoor Bks.

Turck, Mary. Washington, D. C. LC 89-7769. (Illus.). 48p. (gr. 4-5). 1989. 12.95 (ISBN 0-89686-470-7, Crestwood Hse). Macmillan Child Grp.

Turner Program Services, Inc. Staff, et al. Washington D. C. 48p. (gr. 4 up). 1986. PLB 15.99 (ISBN 0-86514-472-9); pap. text ed. 9.27 (ISBN 0-86514-547-4); cancelled Beta video (ISBN 0-86514-100-2); cancelled VHS video (ISBN 0-86514-175-4); cancelled 3/4" video (ISBN 0-86514-250-5); cancelled tchr's. study guide (ISBN 0-86514-325-0); cancelled student activity bk. (ISBN 0-86514-400-1); cancelled index. Raintree Pubs.

Westbrook, Charles L. The Talisman of the United States: The Mysterious Street Lines of Washington, D. C. (Illus.). 123p. (Orig.). (gr. 12). 1990. pap. 10.95x (ISBN 0-9626554-0-6). Westcom NC.

Weston, Marti & Decell, Florri. Washington! Adventure for Kids. 2nd ed. 64p. (gr. 1-9). 1990. pap. 6.95 (ISBN 0-918339-13-8). Vandamere.

WASHINGTON, D. C. CAPITOL

Prolman, Marilyn. The Story of the Capitol. Wiskur, Darrell, illus. LC 69-14681. 32p. (gr. 3-5). 1969. PLB 13.27 (ISBN 0-516-04604-7). Childrens.

WASHINGTON, D. C.–FICTION

Brady, Esther W. A Wish on Capitol Hill. (gr. 3 up). 1988. pap. 3.50 (ISBN 0-517-57253-2). Crown.

Cook, John M. Inside Four Ninety-Five. Haye, Caroline, ed. (Illus.). 128p. 1989. write for info. J M Cook Pub.

Hope, Laura L. Bobbsey Twins' Adventure in Washington. rev. ed. (gr. 1-4). 1963. 4.50 (ISBN 0-448-08012-5, G&D). Putnam Pub Group.

WASHINGTON, D. C.–HISTORY

Hoig, Stan. Capital for the Nation. (gr. 4-7). 1990. 15.95 (ISBN 0-525-65034-2, Cobblehill Bks). Dutton Child Bks.

Stein, R. Conrad. The Story of the Burning of Washington. Wahl, Richard, illus. LC 84-12124. 32p. (gr. 3-6). 1985. lib. bdg. 13.27 (ISBN 0-516-04678-0). Childrens.

WASHINGTON, D. C. WHITE HOUSE

St. George, Judith. The White House: Cornerstone of a Nation. (Illus.). 160p. (gr. 6-12). 1990. 15.95 (ISBN 0-399-22186-7, Putnam). Putnam Pub Group.

WASHINGTON (STATE)

Carol Marsh Washington Books, 31 bks. Set. 638.45 (ISBN 0-7933-1322-8). Gallopade Pub Group.

Carpenter, Allan. Washington. LC 79-13390. (Illus.). 96p. (gr. 4 up). 1979. PLB 19.93 (ISBN 0-516-04147-9). Childrens.

Cecotti, Loralie. Washington Wildlife. Hamer, Bonnie, illus. 24p. (Orig.). (gr. k-5). 1984. pap. text ed. 2.75 (ISBN 0-318-04105-7). Coffee Break.

Diamond, Lynnell & Mueller, Marge. Let's Discover the San Juan Islands. Diamond, Lynnell & Mueller, Marge, illus. 48p. (Orig.). 1989. pap. 4.95 (ISBN 0-89886-220-5). Mountaineers.

Field, Nancy & Machlis, Sally. Discovering Mount Rainier. Machlis, Sally, illus. 28p. (Orig.). (gr. 1-6). 1980. pap. 3.50 (ISBN 0-941042-02-2). Dog Eared Pubns.

Fradin, Dennis. Washington: In Words & Pictures. Wahl, Richard, illus. LC 80-14745. 48p. (gr. 2-5). 1980. PLB 15.93 (ISBN 0-516-03947-4). Childrens.

Johnston, Helen & Elvidge, Vivian, eds. Eastside Historic Coloring Book. Lippie, Joel & Lippie, Jane, illus. McClelland, John M., Jr. 32p. (Orig.). (gr. 1-4). 1985. pap. 2.00 (ISBN 0-685-28865-X). Marymoor Mus.

Johsnton, Helen & Johnston, Richard. Willowmoor: The Story of Marymoor Park. (Illus.). 48p. (Orig.). (gr. 9-12). 1976. pap. 2.50 (ISBN 0-685-28867-6). Marymoor Mus.

Lyons, Dianne J. Washington Handbook. 2nd ed. (Illus.). 400p. 1990. pap. 12.95 (ISBN 0-918373-58-1). Moon Pubns CA.

Marsh, Carole. Avast, Ye Slobs! Washington Pirate Trivia. (Illus.). 1990. PLB 19.95 (ISBN 0-7933-1196-9); pap. 14.95 (ISBN 0-7933-1195-0); computer disk 29.95 (ISBN 0-7933-1197-7). Gallopade Pub Group.

—The Beast of the Washington Bed & Breakfast. (Illus.). 1990. PLB 19.95 (ISBN 0-7933-2212-X); pap. 14.95 (ISBN 0-7933-2213-8); computer disk 29.95 (ISBN 0-7933-2214-6). Gallopade Pub Group.

—The Hard-to-Believe-But-True! Book of Washington History, Mystery, Trivia, Legend, Lore, Humor & More. (Illus.). 1990. PLB 19.95 (ISBN 0-7933-1193-4); pap. 14.95 (ISBN 0-7933-1192-6); computer disk 29.95 (ISBN 0-7933-1194-2). Gallopade Pub Group.

—If My Washington Mama Ran the World! (Illus.). 1990. PLB 19.95 (ISBN 0-7933-2221-9); pap. 14.95 (ISBN 0-7933-2222-7); computer disk 29.95 (ISBN 0-7933-2223-5). Gallopade Pub Group.

—Let's Quilt Washington & Stuff It Topographically! (Illus.). 1990. PLB 19.95 (ISBN 0-7933-2204-9); pap. 14.95 (ISBN 1-55609-133-8); computer disk 29.95 (ISBN 0-7933-2205-7). Gallopade Pub Group.

—Washington & Other State Greats (Biographies!) (Illus.). 1990. PLB 19.95 (ISBN 0-7933-2224-3); pap. 14.95 (ISBN 0-7933-2225-1); computer disk 29.95 (ISBN 0-7933-2226-X). Gallopade Pub Group.

—Washington Bandits, Bushwackers, Outlaws, Crooks, Devils, Ghosts, Desperadoes & Other Assorted & Sundry Characters! (Illus.). 1990. PLB 19.95 (ISBN 0-7933-1178-0); pap. 14.95 (ISBN 0-7933-1177-2); computer disk 29.95 (ISBN 0-7933-1179-9). Gallopade Pub Group.

—Washington Classic Christmas Trivia: Stories, Recipes, Activities, Legends, Lore & More! (Illus.). 1990. PLB 19.95 (ISBN 0-7933-1181-0); pap. 14.95 (ISBN 0-7933-1180-2); computer dik 29.95 (ISBN 0-7933-1182-9). Gallopade Pub Group.

—Washington Coastales. (Illus.). 1990. PLB 19.95 (ISBN 0-7933-2218-9); pap. 14.95 (ISBN 0-7933-2219-7); computer disk 29.95 (ISBN 0-7933-2220-0). Gallopade Pub Group.

—The Washington Hot Air Balloon Mystery. (Illus.). (gr. 2-9). 1990. 19.95 (ISBN 0-7933-2741-5); pap. 14.95 (ISBN 0-7933-2742-3); computer disk 29.95 (ISBN 0-7933-2743-1). Gallopade Pub Group.

—Washington "Jography" A Fun Run Thru Our State! (Illus.). 1990. PLB 19.95 (ISBN 0-7933-2201-4); pap. 14.95 (ISBN 0-7933-2202-2); computer disk 29.95 (ISBN 0-7933-2203-0). Gallopade Pub Group.

—Washington Kid's Cookbook: Recipes, How-to, History, Lore & More! (Illus.). 1990. PLB 19.95 (ISBN 0-7933-1190-X); pap. 14.95 (ISBN 0-7933-1189-6); computer disk 29.95 (ISBN 0-7933-1191-8). Gallopade Pub Group.

—Washington Quiz Bowl Crash Course! (Illus.). 1990. PLB 19.95 (ISBN 0-7933-2215-4); pap. 14.95 (ISBN 0-7933-2216-2); computer disk 29.95 (ISBN 0-7933-2217-0). Gallopade Pub Group.
—Washington School Trivia: An Amazing & Fascinating Look at Our State's Teachers, Schools & Students! (Illus.). 1990. PLB 19.95; pap. 14.95 (ISBN 0-7933-1186-1); computer disk 29.95 (ISBN 0-7933-1188-8). Gallopade Pub Group.
—Washington Silly Basketball Sportsmysteries, Vol. 1. (Illus.). 1990. PLB 19.95 (ISBN 0-7933-1184-5); pap. 14.95 (ISBN 0-7933-1183-7); computer disk 29.95 (ISBN 0-7933-1185-3). Gallopade Pub Group.
—Washington Silly Basketball Sportsmysteries, Vol. 2. (Illus.). 1990. PLB 19.95 (ISBN 0-7933-2227-8); pap. 14.95 (ISBN 0-7933-2228-6); computer disk 29.95 (ISBN 0-7933-2229-4). Gallopade Pub Group.
—Washington Silly Football Sportsmysteries, Vol. 1. (Illus.). 1990. PLB 19.95 (ISBN 0-7933-2206-5); pap. 14.95 (ISBN 0-7933-2207-3); computer disk 29.95 (ISBN 0-7933-2208-1). Gallopade Pub Group.
—Washington Silly Football Sportsmysteries, Vol. 2. (Illus.). 1990. PLB 19.95; pap. 14.95 (ISBN 0-7933-2210-3); computer disk 29.95 (ISBN 0-7933-2211-1). Gallopade Pub Group.
—Washington Silly Trivia! (Illus.). 1990. PLB 19.95 (ISBN 0-7933-2198-0); pap. 14.95 (ISBN 0-7933-2199-9); computer disk 29.95 (ISBN 0-7933-2200-6). Gallopade Pub Group.
—Washington's (Most Devastating!) Disasters & (Most Calamitous!) Catastrophies! (Illus.). 1990. PLB 19.95 (ISBN 0-7933-1175-6); pap. 14.95 (ISBN 0-7933-1174-8); computer disk 29.95 (ISBN 0-7933-1176-4). Gallopade Pub Group.
Olson, Joan & Olson, Gene. Washington Times & Trails. rev. ed. LC 75-83521. (Illus.). (gr. 7-12). 1983. pap. 8.97x (ISBN 0-913366-01-3). Windyridge.
Seablom, Seth H. Washington State Coloring Guide. (Illus.). 32p. (gr. 1-6). 1978. pap. 2.50 (ISBN 0-918800-03-X). Seablom.
Turner Educational Services, Inc. Staff & Clark, James I. Washington. 48p. (gr. 3 up). 1986. PLB 17.32 (ISBN 0-86514-470-2); cancelled Beta video (ISBN 0-86514-097-9); cancelled VHS video (ISBN 0-86514-172-X); cancelled 3/4" video (ISBN 0-317-47591-6); cancelled tchr's. study guide (ISBN 0-86514-322-6); cancelled student activity bk. (ISBN 0-86514-397-8); cancelled index. Raintree Pubs.
Way, Nancy. Our Town Redmond. Johnston, Helen, intro. by. (Illus.). (gr. 9-12). 1989. write for info. Marymoor Mus.
Yates, Richard. Our Evergreen State Government: State & Local Government in Washington. Smith-Danell, Paula, illus. 190p. 1989. 13.95 (ISBN 0-911927-10-7). Info Oregon.

WASHINGTON (STATE)–FICTION

Cecotti, Loralie. Seattle Center. Hamer, Bonnie, illus. 24p. (Orig.). (gr. 1-4). 1983. pap. 2.75 (ISBN 0-933992-30-0). Coffee Break.
Dumond, Val. Visiting Olympia. Ballman, Jean, illus. 24p. (Orig.). (gr. 1-4). 1983. pap. 2.75 (ISBN 0-933992-39-4). Coffee Break.
Helstrom, David C. My Tacoma Dome. Hamer, Bonnie, illus. 24p. (Orig.). (gr. 1-4). 1983. pap. 2.75 (ISBN 0-933992-29-7). Coffee Break.
—Visiting Mt. Rainier. Harder, Arvid & Hamer, Bonnie, illus. 28p. (Orig.). (gr. 1-4). 1984. pap. 2.75 (ISBN 0-933992-37-8). Coffee Break.
Luenn, Nancy, ed. A Horse's Tale: Ten Adventures in One Hundred Years. Megale, Marina & Schumacher, Sharon, illus. LC 88-61152. 96p. (Orig.). (gr. 2-6). 1988. lib. bdg. 15.95 (ISBN 0-943990-51-3); pap. 7.95 (ISBN 0-943990-50-5). Parenting Pr.
Parkhurst, Carole. Visiting Tacoma. Hamer, Bonnie, illus. 24p. (Orig.). (gr. 1-4). 1983. pap. 2.75 (ISBN 0-933992-38-6). Coffee Break.

WASPS

Curtis, Neil. Discovering Snakes & Wasps. 1990. pap. 4.95 (ISBN 0-531-18363-7). Watts.
Eastman, David. I Can Read About Bees & Wasps. LC 78-73773. (Illus.). (gr. 2-5). 1979. pap. 1.95 (ISBN 0-89375-203-7). Troll Assocs.
Lavies, Bianca. Wasps at Home. Lavies, Bianca, photos by. (Illus.). 32p. (gr. 4-7). 1991. 13.95 (ISBN 0-525-44704-0). Dutton Child Bks.
Ogawa, Hiroshi. The Potter Wasp. Pohl, Kathy, ed. (Illus.). 32p. (gr. 3-7). 1986. PLB 16.67 (ISBN 0-8172-2541-2); pap. text ed. 9.27 (ISBN 0-8172-2566-8). Raintree Pubs.
O'Toole, Christopher. Discovering Bees & Wasps. LC 85-72247. (Illus.). 48p. (gr. k-6). 1986. lib. bdg. 11.90 (ISBN 0-531-18047-6, Pub. by Bookwright Pr). Watts.
Otoole, Christopher. Discovering Bees And Wasps. 1990. pap. 4.95 (ISBN 0-531-18362-9). Watts.

WASTE DISPOSAL

see Refuse and Refuse Disposal; Sewage Disposal; Waste Products

WASTE PRODUCTS

see also Refuse and Refuse Disposal

Coltharpe, Barbara A. Mr. Rumples Recycles. Gullic, Bob, ed. Coltharpe, Barbara A., illus. 30p. (Orig.). (gr. 3-7). 1989. pap. 4.25x (ISBN 0-9622752-0-4). Hyacinth Hse.
Kronenwetter, Michael. Managing Toxic Wastes. Steltenpohl, Jane, ed. (Illus.). 126p. (gr. 7-10). 1989. lib. bdg. 12.98 (ISBN 0-671-69051-5). Messner.
Snodgrass, M. E. Environmental Awareness: Land Pollution. James, Jody, ed. Vista Three Design Staff, illus. LC 91-8303. 48p. (gr. 4 up). 1991. lib. bdg. 14.95 (ISBN 0-944280-29-3). BSP Pub Inc.
—Environmental Awareness: Solid Waste. James, Jody, ed. Vista Three Design Staff, illus. LC 90-20950. 48p. (gr. 4 up). 1991. PLB 14.95 (ISBN 0-944280-28-5). BSP Pub Inc.
—Environmental Awareness: Toxic Waste. James, Jody, ed. Vista Three Design Staff, illus. LC 91-7427. 48p. (gr. 4 up). 1991. lib. bdg. 14.95 (ISBN 0-944280-27-7). BSP Pub Inc.
Zipko, Stephen J. Toxic Threat: How Hazardous Substances Poison Our Lives. rev. ed. Steltenpohl, Jane, ed. (Illus.). 208p. (gr. 7 up). 1990. PLB 12.98 (ISBN 0-671-69330-1); pap. 5.95 (ISBN 0-671-69331-X). Messner.

WATCHES

see Clocks and Watches

WATER

see also Floods; Glaciers; Ice; Lakes; Ocean; Rain and Rainfall; Rivers; Snow

Ardley, Neil. The Science Book of Water. Van Doren, Liz, ed. (Illus.). 28p. (gr. 2-5). 1991. 9.95 (Gulliver Bks). HarBraceJ.
—Science Book of Water. (gr. 4-7). 1991. 9.95 (ISBN 0-15-200575-7). HarBraceJ.
—Working with Water. 32p. (gr. 4-6). 1983. PLB 11.90 (ISBN 0-531-04519-6). Watts.
Bains, Rae. Water. Garcia, T. R., illus. LC 84-2718. 32p. (gr. 3-6). 1985. PLB 9.49 (ISBN 0-8167-0194-6); pap. text ed. 2.95 (ISBN 0-8167-0195-4). Troll Assocs.
Barss, Karen J. Clean Water. (Illus.). (gr. 5 up). 1992. PLB 19.95 (ISBN 0-7910-1583-1). Chelsea Hse.
Cristini, Ermanno & Puricelli, Luigi. In the Pond. Cristini, Ermanno & Puricelli, Luigi, illus. LC 84-972. 28p. (ps up). 1985. 12.95 (ISBN 0-907234-43-7). Picture Bk Studio.
DeBruin, Jerry. Young Scientists Explore: The World of Water. Szerniak, Charlene, illus. 32p. (gr. 4 up). 1985. wkbk 4.95 (ISBN 0-86653-288-9, GA 656). Good Apple.
Dickinson, Jane. Wonders of Water. Schneider, Rex, illus. LC 82-17388. 32p. (gr. 3-6). 1983. PLB 10.59 (ISBN 0-89375-874-4); pap. text ed. 2.95 (ISBN 0-89375-875-2). Troll Assocs.
Dineen, Jacqueline. Water. 32p. (gr. 4-8). 1988. lib. bdg. 12.95 (ISBN 0-89490-225-3). Enslow Pubs.
Dorros, Arthur. Follow the Water from Brook to Ocean. Dorros, Arthur, illus. LC 90-1438. 32p. (gr. k-4). 1991. 13.95 (ISBN 0-06-021598-4); PLB 13.89 (ISBN 0-06-021599-2). HarpC Child Bks.
Edom, H. Science with Water. (Illus.). 24p. (gr. 1-4). 1991. lib. bdg. 11.96 (ISBN 0-88110-485-X, Usborne); pap. 3.95 (ISBN 0-7460-0604-7, Usborne). EDC.
Fine, Edith & Josephson, Judith. Water Wizard. 24p. (ps). 1982. 2.95 (ISBN 0-88160-093-8, LW 129). Learning Wks.
Gans, Roma. Water for Dinosaurs & You. LC 78-158691. (Illus.). (gr. k-3). 1973. PLB 11.89 (ISBN 0-690-87027-2, Crowell Jr Bks); pap. 4.95 (ISBN 0-690-00202-5, TYC-J). HarpC Child Bks.
Green, Ivah. Splash & Trickle. Connor, Bil, illus. (gr. 2-3). 1978. pap. 1.25 (ISBN 0-89508-062-1). Rainbow Bks.
Greene, Carol. Caring for Our Water. (Illus.). 32p. (gr. 1-4). 1991. PLB 12.95 (ISBN 0-89490-356-X). Enslow Pubs.
Hoff, Mary & Rodgers, Mary M. Our Endangered Planet: Groundwater. (Illus.). 64p. (gr. 4-6). 1991. PLB 15.95 (ISBN 0-8225-2500-3). Lerner Pubns.
—Our Endangered Planet: Rivers & Lakes. (Illus.). 64p. (gr. 4-6). 1991. PLB 15.95 (ISBN 0-8225-2501-1). Lerner Pubns.
Jennings, Terry. Water. LC 88-22871. (Illus.). 32p. (gr. 3-6). 1989. PLB 14.60 (ISBN 0-516-08410-0); pap. 4.95 (ISBN 0-516-48410-9). Childrens.
Johnston, Tom. Water, Water! Pooley, Sarah, illus. LC 87-42750. 32p. (gr. 4-6). 1988. PLB 10.95 (ISBN 1-55532-407-X). Gareth Stevens Inc.
Lewis. Water. (gr. 4-6). 1980. PLB 10.40 (ISBN 0-531-04176-X). Watts.
Parramon, J. M., et al. Water. 32p. (ps). 1985. pap. 3.95 (ISBN 0-8120-3599-2). Barron.
Peters, Lisa. Water's Way. Rand, Ted, illus. 32p. (ps-2). 1991. 14.95 (ISBN 1-55970-062-9). Arcade Pub Inc.
Pluckrose, Henry. Think about Floating & Sinking. Fairclough, Chris, photos by. (Illus.). (gr. k-3). 1987. PLB 7.99 (ISBN 0-531-10294-7). Watts.
Pollock, Penny. Water Is Wet. Beirne, Babara, photos by. LC 84-11466. (Illus.). 32p. (ps-2). 1985. 10.95 (ISBN 0-399-21180-2, Putnam). Putnam Pub Group.
Reidel, Marlene. From Ice to Rain. Reidel, Marlene, illus. 24p. (ps-3). 1981. PLB 6.95 (ISBN 0-87614-157-2). Carolrhoda Bks.
Schmid, Eleanore. The Water's Journey. Schmid, Eleanore, illus. LC 89-42872. 32p. (gr. k-3). 1990. 13.95 (ISBN 1-55858-013-1). North-South Bks NYC.
Seixas, Judith S. Water- What It Is, What It Does. Huffman, Tom, illus. LC 86-14926. 56p. (gr. 1-4). 1987. 12.95 (ISBN 0-688-06607-0); lib. bdg. 12.88 (ISBN 0-688-06608-9). Greenwillow.
Spar, J. Willy, a Story of Water. LC 68-56819. (Illus.). 32p. (gr. 2-3). 1968. PLB 9.95 (ISBN 0-87783-051-7); pap. 3.94 deluxe ed (ISBN 0-87783-117-3). Oddo.
Stangl, Jean. H20 Science. (gr. 3-6). 1990. pap. 8.95 (ISBN 0-8224-3604-3). Fearon Teach Aids.
Swallow, Su. Water. (Illus.). 32p. (gr. k-4). 1990. PLB 11.90 (ISBN 0-531-14061-X). Watts.
Taylor, Barbara. Water & Life. LC 90-32523. (Illus.). 32p. (gr. 5-8). 1991. PLB 11.40 (ISBN 0-531-14116-0). Watts.
—Water at Work. LC 90-32525. (Illus.). 32p. (gr. 5-8). 1991. PLB 11.40 (ISBN 0-531-14117-9). Watts.
Tesar, Jenny. Food & Water: Threats, Shortages & Solutions. Cayne, Bernard S., ed. (Illus.). 128p. (gr. 7-12). 1992. lib. bdg. 18.95x (ISBN 0-8160-2495-2). Facts on File.
Twist, Clint. Rain to Dams: Projects with Water. 1990. PLB 11.90 (ISBN 0-531-17199-X). Watts.
Walpole, Brenda. Water. (Illus.). 40p. (gr. 4-6). 1987. PLB 12.90 (ISBN 0-531-19025-0, Glouster Pr). Watts.
—Water. Stefoff, Rebecca, ed. Barber, Ed, photos by. LC 90-40381. (Illus.). 26p. (gr. 3-5). 1990. PLB 15.93 (ISBN 0-944483-72-0). Garrett Ed Corp.
Webb, Angela. Water. (Illus.). 32p. (gr. k-3). 1987. PLB 10.90 (ISBN 0-531-10372-2). Watts.
Wilkins, Mary-Jane. Air, Light & Water. Bull, Peter, illus. LC 90-42620. 40p. (Orig.). (gr. 2-5). 1991. pap. 3.95 (ISBN 0-679-80859-0). Random.

WATER–CONSERVATION

see Water Conservation

WATER–POLLUTION

see also Refuse and Refuse Disposal; Sewage Disposal; also Petroleum Pollution of Water and similar headings

Anderson, Madelyn K. Oil Spills. (Illus.). 64p. (gr. 5-8). 1990. PLB 11.90 (ISBN 0-531-10872-4). Watts.
Breiter, Herta S. Pollution. LC 87-23233. (Illus.). 48p. (Orig.). (gr. 2-6). 1987. PLB 17.32 (ISBN 0-8172-3259-1); pap. 9.27 (ISBN 0-8172-3284-2). Raintree Pubs.
Bright, Michael. Polluting the Oceans. (Illus.). 32p. (gr. k-4). 1991. PLB 11.40 (ISBN 0-531-17353-4, Gloucester Pr). Watts.
Brown, Joseph E. Oil Spills. (gr. 7-11). 1978. 8.95 (ISBN 0-396-07607-6, Putnam). Putnam Pub Group.
Carr, Terry. Spill! The Story of the Exxon Valdez. (Illus.). 64p. (gr. 5-8). 1991. 12.95 (ISBN 0-531-15217-0); PLB 12.90 (ISBN 0-531-10998-4). Watts.
Gay, Kathlyn. Water Pollution. (Illus.). 144p. (gr. 9-12). 1990. PLB 12.90 (ISBN 0-531-10949-6). Watts.
Greene, Jack. The Mudgrump. Florman, Lisa, illus. LC 80-68130. 56p. (Orig.). (gr. k-6). 1980. pap. text ed. 3.95 perfect binding (ISBN 0-9601258-3-3). Golden Owl Pub.
Hamilton, Sue. Exxon Valdez Oil Spill. Hamilton, John, ed. (Illus.). 32p. (gr. 4). 1990. PLB 11.95 (ISBN 0-939179-84-9). Abdo & Dghtrs.
Kiefer, Irene. Poisoned Land: The Problems of Hazardous Waste. LC 80-22120. (Illus.). 96p. (gr. 6-9). 1981. 13.95 (ISBN 0-689-30837-X, Atheneum Child Bk). Macmillan Child Grp.
O'Neill, Mary. Water Squeeze. Bindon, John, illus. LC 89-77456. 32p. (gr. 3-6). 1989. PLB 12.89 (ISBN 0-8167-2080-0); pap. text ed. 3.95 (ISBN 0-8167-2081-9). Troll Assocs.
Phillips, Anne W. The Ocean. LC 90-36296. (Illus.). 48p. (gr. 5-6). 1990. RSBE 10.95 (ISBN 0-89686-541-X, Crestwood Hse). Macmillan Child Grp.
Rothman, Joel. Once There Was a Stream. Roberts, Bruce, photos by. LC 72-90692. (Illus.). 32p. (gr. k-4). 1973. 8.95 (ISBN 0-87592-038-1). Scroll Pr.
Snodgrass, M. E. Environmental Awareness: Water Pollution. James, Jody, ed. Vista Three Design Staff, illus. LC 90-20949. 48p. (gr. 4 up). 1991. PLB 14.95 (ISBN 0-944280-26-9). BSP Pub Inc.
Woods, Geraldine & Woods, Harold. Pollution. LC 84-20982. (Illus.). 72p. (gr. 4 up). 1985. PLB 10.40 (ISBN 0-531-04916-7). Watts.

WATER ANIMALS

see Fresh-Water Animals; Marine Animals

WATER BIRDS

see also names of water birds, e.g. Penguins

Dewey, Jennifer O. The Wandering Albatross. Dewey, Jennifer O., illus. LC 88-31419. 48p. (gr. 3-6). 1989. 15.95 (ISBN 0-316-18209-5). Little.
Kerrod, Robin. Birds: Water Birds. Bailey, Jill, contrib. by. (Illus.). 1989. 17.95x (ISBN 0-8160-1962-2). Facts on File.

WATER CONSERVATION

see also Water Supply

Bailey, Donna. What We Can Do about Wasting Water. (Illus.). 32p. (gr. k-4). 1991. PLB 11.40 (ISBN 0-531-11019-2). Watts.
Green, Ivah. Splash & Trickle. LC 68-56818. (Illus.). 32p. (gr. 2-3). 1968. PLB 9.95 (ISBN 0-87783-037-1); pap. 3.94 deluxe ed. (ISBN 0-87783-109-2); cassette o.s.i. 7.94x (ISBN 0-87783-226-9). Oddo.
Greene, Carol. Caring for Our Water. (Illus.). 32p. (gr. 1-4). 1991. PLB 12.95 (ISBN 0-89490-356-X). Enslow Pubs.
Kourik, Robert. Gray Water Use in the Landscape: How to Use Gray Water to Save Your Landscape During Droughts. Schmidt, Heidi, illus. Hill, Amie, ed. (Illus.). 28p. (Orig.). 1988. pap. text ed. 6.00 (ISBN 0-9615848-1-5). Metamorphic Pr.
Soil & Water Conservation. (Illus.). 96p. (gr. 6-12). 1983. pap. 1.85 (ISBN 0-8395-3291-1, 3291). BSA.

WATER FOWL

see Water Birds

WATER PLANTS

see Marine Plants

WATER POLLUTION

see Water–Pollution

WATER POWER
Bailey, Donna. Energy from Wind & Water. LC 90-39388. (Illus.). 48p. (gr. 2-5). 1990. PLB 15.96 (ISBN 0-8114-2519-3). Steck-V.
Rickard, Graham. Water Energy. (Illus.). 32p. (gr. 4-6). 1991. PLB 11.95 (ISBN 0-8368-0710-3). Gareth Stevens Inc.

WATER RESOURCES DEVELOPMENT
see also Irrigation; Water Power; Water Supply

WATER SKIING
Benzel, David. Psyching for Slalom: An Illustrated Guide to the Mind & Muscle of the Complete Skier. Robertson, Jo, ed. (Illus.). 127p. (Orig.). 1989. pap. 15.95 (ISBN 0-944406-05-X). World Pub FL.
Briggs, Carole S. Waterskiing Is for Me. (Illus.). 48p. (gr. 2-5). 1986. lib. bdg. 8.95 (ISBN 0-8225-1140-1). Lerner Pubns.
Finn, Tony. Waterskiboarding - An Illustrated Guide to Learning & Mastering the Sport. Robertson, Jo, ed. LC 88-50675. (Illus.). 113p. (Orig.). 1988. pap. 14.95 (ISBN 0-944406-04-1). World Pub FL.
Kjellander, Mike. Power Slalom - Twenty-Eight Breakthrough Concepts for Mastering the Sport. Robertson, Jo, ed. (Illus.). 100p. (Orig.). 1989. pap. 14.95 (ISBN 0-944406-06-8). World Pub FL.
Klarich, Tony. Hot Dog Slalom Skiing: An Illustrated Guide to over Thirty Amazing Maneuvers. Robertson, Jo, ed. (Illus.). 128p. (Orig.). (gr. 7 up). 1988. pap. 11.95 (ISBN 0-944406-02-5). World Pub FL.
McMillan, Kent. Hydroslide Kneeboarding: An Illustrated Guide to Learning & Mastering the Sport. Robertson, Jo, ed. LC 88-50672. (Illus.). 166p. (Orig.). 1988. pap. 12.95 (ISBN 0-944406-03-3). World Pub FL.
Scarpa, Ron & Dorner, Terrence. Barefoot Water Skiing: An Illustrated Guide to Learning & Mastering the Sport. Robertson, Jo, ed. (Illus.). 176p. (Orig.). (gr. 7 up). 1988. pap. 11.95 (ISBN 0-944406-01-7). World Pub FL.
Water Skiing & Kneeboarding. 48p. (gr. 3-4). 1989. PLB 10.95 (ISBN 0-685-26385-1). Capstone Pr.
Waterskiing. (Illus.). 48p. (gr. 6-12). 1984. pap. 1.85 (ISBN 0-8395-3357-8, 3357). BSA.

WATER SPORTS
see also Boats and Boating; Canoes and Canoeing; Diving; Fishing; Rowing; Sailing; Skin Diving; Swimming
Barrett, Norman. Windsurfing. Franklin Watts Ltd., ed. (Illus.). 32p. (ps-9). 1988. 10.90 (ISBN 0-531-10354-4). Watts.
Chlad, Dorothy. In the Water...On the Water. Halverson, Lydia, illus. LC 88-12065. 32p. (ps-2). 1988. PLB 14.60 (ISBN 0-516-01974-0); pap. 3.95 (ISBN 0-516-41974-9). Childrens.
Wallace, Don. Water Sports Basics. Petronella, Michael, illus. LC 84-22294. 48p. (gr. 3-7). 1985. 9.95 (ISBN 0-13-945957-X). P-H.
Waterski Magazine Staff. Boating Watersports: The Ultimate Get Started Guide to Towing Fun. Robertson, Jo, ed. LC 89-52016. (Illus.). 100p. 1990. pap. 15.95 (ISBN 0-944406-07-6). World Pub FL.

WATER SPORTS–SAFETY MEASURES
Berenstain, Stan & Berenstain, Janice. Bears' Vacation. Berenstain, Stan & Berenstain, Janice, illus. LC 68-28460. 72p. (gr. k-3). 1968. 6.95 (ISBN 0-394-80052-4); lib. bdg. 7.99 (ISBN 0-394-90052-9). Beginner.
Sanders, Pete. Near Water. (Illus.). 32p. (gr. k-6). 1989. PLB 11.90 (ISBN 0-531-17181-7). Watts.

WATER SUPPLY
see also Dams; Irrigation; Water–Pollution; Water Conservation
Branley, Franklyn M. Water for the World. Kelley, True, illus. LC 81-43321. 96p. (gr. 5 up). 1982. 12.95 (ISBN 0-690-04172-1, Crowell Jr Bks). HarpC Child Bks.
Dolan, Edward F. Drought: The Past, Present, & Future Enemy. (gr. 4-7). 1990. PLB 13.40 (ISBN 0-531-10900-3). Watts.
Pringle, Laurence. Water: The Next Great Resource Battle. LC 81-23694. (Illus.). 144p. (gr. 6 up). 1982. 13.95 (ISBN 0-02-775400-6, Mcmillan Child Bk). Macmillan Child Grp.

WATERGATE AFFAIR, 1972-
Feinberg, Barbara S. Watergate: Scandal in the White House. (Illus.). 144p. (gr. 9-12). 1990. PLB 12.90 (ISBN 0-531-10963-1). Watts.
Hargrove, Jim. The Story of Watergate. LC 88-11881. (Illus.). 32p. (gr. 3-6). 1988. PLB 13.27 (ISBN 0-516-04741-8); pap. 3.95 (ISBN 0-516-44741-6). Childrens.
Kilian, Pamela. What Was Watergate. 1990. 15.95 (ISBN 0-312-04446-1). St Martin.

WATERWAYS
see also Canals; Rivers
McCall, Edith. Pioneers on Early Waterways. Rogers, Carl, illus. LC 61-10104. 128p. (gr. 3-10). 1980. PLB 14.60 (ISBN 0-516-03357-3). Childrens.

WATER WORKS
see Water Supply

WAVES
see also Light; Ocean Waves; Radiation

WEAPONS
see Arms and Armor; Firearms

WEASELS–FICTION
Cosgrove, Stephen E. Gossamer. Edelson, Wendy, illus. 32p. (ps-3). 1990. lib. bdg. 12.96 (ISBN 0-89565-662-0). Childs World.
Montgomery, Rutherford G. Pekan the Shadow. Nenninger, Jerome D., illus. LC 78-84779. (gr. 8-12). 1970. 3.95 (ISBN 0-87004-132-0). Caxton.

WEATHER
see also Climate; Meteorology; Rain and Rainfall; Snow; Storms; Weather Control; Winds
Adler, David. World of Weather. Burns, Raymond, illus. LC 82-17398. 32p. (gr. 3-6). 1983. PLB 10.59 (ISBN 0-89375-870-1); pap. text ed. 2.95 (ISBN 0-89375-871-X). Troll Assocs.
Arvetis, Chris & Palmer, Carole. Why Does It Thunder & Lightning? LC 85-60559. 32p. (ps-3). 1985. write for info. (ISBN 0-528-82671-9). Checkerboard Pr.
Branley, Franklyn M. It's Raining Cats & Dogs: All Kinds of Weather & Why We Have It. Kelley, True, illus. LC 86-27546. 128p. (gr. 3-8). 1987. 12.95 (ISBN 0-395-33070-X). HM.
Breiter, Herta S. Weather. rev. ed. LC 87-23226. (Illus.). 48p. (gr. 2-6). 1987. PLB 17.32 (ISBN 0-8172-3265-6); pap. 9.27 (ISBN 0-8172-3290-7). Raintree Pubs.
Catherall, Ed. Exploring Weather. LC 90-10025. (Illus.). 48p. (gr. 3-7). 1990. PLB 18.60 (ISBN 0-8114-2596-7). Steck-V.
Cosgrove, Brian. Weather. Shone, Karl & Percival, Keith, photos by. LC 90-4887. (Illus.). 64p. (gr. 5 up). 1991. 15.00 (ISBN 0-679-80784-5); PLB 15.99 (ISBN 0-679-90784-X). Knopf.
DeBruin, Jerry. Young Scientists Explore: The Weather. Czerniak, Jerry, illus. 32p. (gr. 4 up). 1983. wkbk. 4.95 (ISBN 0-86653-129-7, GA 456). Good Apple.
D'Ham, Claude, illus. The Weather. (Orig.). (ps-2). 1975. pap. 2.00 (ISBN 0-85953-037-X, Pub. by Child's Play England). Childs Play.
Fass, Bernie & Caggiano, Rosemary. The Weather Company. 48p. (gr. k-8). 1978. pap. 10.95 (ISBN 0-86704-004-1). Clarus Music.
Flint, David. Weather & Climate: Projects with Geography. (Illus.). 32p. (gr. 5-8). 1991. PLB 11.90 (ISBN 0-531-17321-6, Gloucester Pr). Watts.
Ford, Adam. Weather Watch. LC 81-637. (Illus.). 48p. (gr. 3-7). 1982. 11.95 (ISBN 0-688-00959-X). Lothrop.
Gakken Co. Ltd. Staff, ed. Wind & Weather. Time-Life Books Inc. Editors, tr. (Illus.). 90p. (gr. k-3). 1989. 15.93 (ISBN 0-8094-4829-7); PLB 21.27 (ISBN 0-8094-4830-0). Time-Life.
Ganeri, A. Weather Facts: Records-Lists-Facts-Comparisons. (Illus.). 48p. (gr. 3-7). 1987. PLB 12.96 (ISBN 0-88110-241-5); pap. 5.95 (ISBN 0-86020-975-X). EDC.
Gibbons, Gail. Weather Words & What They Mean. Gibbons, Gail, illus. LC 89-39515. 32p. (ps-3). 1990. 14.95g (ISBN 0-8234-0805-1). Holiday.
Glass, Marvin. All Kinds of Weather. Glass, Marvin, illus. 12p. (gr. 2-4). 1990. bds. 3.95 (ISBN 1-878624-01-6). McClanahan Bk.
Hefter, Richard. The Stickybear Book of Weather. Hefter, Richard, illus. LC 83-2191. 32p. (ps-1). 1983. 5.95 (ISBN 0-911787-01-1). Optimum Res Inc.
Jennings, Terry. Weather. Franklin Watts Ltd., ed. Anstey, David, illus. 28p. (gr. k-3). 1990. PLB 10.40 (ISBN 0-531-17088-8, Gloucester Pr); pap. 2.95 (ISBN 0-531-17505-7). Watts.
Kirkpatrick, Rena K. Look at Weather. rev. ed. Lewin, Janetta, illus. LC 84-26251. 32p. (gr. 2-4). 1985. PLB 15.99 (ISBN 0-8172-2360-6); pap. text ed. 9.27 (ISBN 0-8172-2385-1). Raintree Pubs.
Kohler, Pierre. Weather. (gr. 6 up). 1988. 4.95 (ISBN 0-8120-3833-9). Barron.
Lambert, David & Hardy, Ralph. Weather & Its Work. (Illus.). 64p. (gr. 7 up). 1985. 15.95 (ISBN 0-87196-987-4). Facts on File.
Linke, Siegfreid. Know about Weather. (Illus.). 28p. (gr. 1-5). 1979. 3.95 (ISBN 0-905778-06-5). Academy Chi Pubs.
Lye, Keith. The Earth. (Illus.). 64p. (gr. 4-6). 1991. PLB 13.90 (ISBN 1-56294-025-2). Millbrook Pr.
McMillan, Bruce. The Weather Sky. (Illus.). 40p. (gr. 5 up). 1991. 16.95 (ISBN 0-374-38261-1). FS&G.
McVey, Vicki. Sierra Club Book of Weatherwisdom. (gr. 4-7). 1991. 15.95 (ISBN 0-316-56341-2). Little.
Mandell, Muriel. Simple Weather Experiments with Everyday Materials. LC 90-37915. (Illus.). 128p. (gr. 4-10). 1990. 12.95 (ISBN 0-8069-7296-3). Sterling.
Markle, Sandra. Weather, Electricity, Environmental Investigations. 112p. (gr. 4-6). 1982. 9.95 (ISBN 0-88160-082-2, LW 902). Learning Wks.
Mason, John. Autumn Weather. LC 90-34585. (Illus.). 32p. (gr. 1-5). 1991. PLB 11.90 (ISBN 0-531-18357-2, Pub. by Bookwright Pr). Watts.
—Winter Weather. LC 90-828. (Illus.). 32p. (gr. 1-5). 1991. PLB 11.90 (ISBN 0-531-18358-0, Pub. by Bookwright Pr). Watts.
Owl's Weather Book. 1989. bds. 1.98 (ISBN 0-8317-0347-4). Smithmark.
Parramon, J. M., et al. El Agua. (SPA.). 32p. (ps). 1985. pap. 4.95 (ISBN 0-8120-3621-2). Barron.
—The Four Elements, 4 Bks. (ps). 1985. boxed set 23.95 (ISBN 0-8120-7367-3). Barron.
Pollard, Michael. Air, Water, Weather. (Illus.). 48p. (gr. 1-4). 1987. 12.95x (ISBN 0-8160-1781-6). Facts on File.
Pomeroy, Johanna P. Content Area Reading Skills Weather: Cause & Effect. (Illus.). (gr. 3). 1989. pap. text ed. 3.25 (ISBN 1-55737-689-1). Ed Activities.
Raintree Publishers Inc. Weather. LC 87-28715. (Illus.). 64p. (Orig.). (gr. 5-9). 1988. lib. bdg. 19.99 (ISBN 0-8172-3079-3); pap. 11.93 (ISBN 0-8172-3096-3). Raintree Pubs.
Rogers, Paul. What Will the Weather Be Like Today? LC 88-32736. (Illus.). (ps up). 1990. 13.95 (ISBN 0-688-08950-X); lib. bdg. 13.88 (ISBN 0-688-08951-8). Greenwillow.
Ruckman, Ivy. Night of the Twisters. LC 83-46168. 160p. (gr. 3-6). 1984. 13.95i (ISBN 0-690-04408-9, Crowell Jr Bks); PLB 13.89 (ISBN 0-690-04409-7, Crowell Jr Bks). HarpC Child Bks.
Sabin, Louis. Weather. Veno, Joseph, illus. LC 84-2706. 32p. (gr. 3-6). 1985. PLB 9.49 (ISBN 0-8167-0200-4); pap. text ed. 2.95 (ISBN 0-8167-0201-2). Troll Assocs.
Seymour, Peter. How the Weather Works. Springer, Sally, illus. (gr. 2-5). 1985. 8.95 (ISBN 0-02-782110-2, Mcmillan Child Bk). Macmillan Child Grp.
Simon, Seymour. Weather & Climate. (gr. 4-6). 1969. lib. bdg. 4.99 (ISBN 0-394-90804-X). Random.
Supraner, Robyn. I Can Read About Weather. LC 74-24992. (Illus.). (gr. 2-4). 1975. pap. 1.95 (ISBN 0-89375-070-0). Troll Assocs.
Tannenbaum, Beulah. Making & Using Your Own Weather Station. 1989. PLB 12.40 (ISBN 0-531-10675-6). Watts.
Taylor, Barbara. Wind & Weather. (Illus.). 32p. (gr. 5-8). 1991. PLB 11.40 (ISBN 0-531-14184-5). Watts.
Tester, Sylvia R. Magic Monsters Learn about Weather. Bowman, Patricia, illus. LC 79-24826. (gr. k-3). 1980. PLB 11.97 (ISBN 0-89565-120-3). Childs World.
Weather. 64p. (gr. 6-12). 1963. pap. 1.85 (ISBN 0-8395-3274-1, 3274). BSA.
Weather. (Illus.). (gr. 3-5). 3.50 (ISBN 0-7214-0825-7). Ladybird Bks.
Weather & Climate. LC 90-24089. (Illus.). 64p. (gr. 4-6). 1991. PLB 12.95 (ISBN 0-8368-0062-1). Gareth Stevens Inc.
Webster, Vera. Experimentos Atmosfericos. Kratky, Lada, tr. LC 85-31425. (SPA., Illus.). 48p. (gr. k-4). 1986. PLB 14.60 (ISBN 0-516-31662-1); pap. 4.95 (ISBN 0-516-51662-0). Childrens.
—Weather Experiments. LC 81-17062. (Illus.). 48p. (gr. k-4). 1982. PLB 14.60 (ISBN 0-516-01662-8); pap. 4.95 (ISBN 0-516-41662-6). Childrens.
Wilson, Francis. The Weather Pop-Up Book. Jacobs, Philip, illus. Wilgrass, Paul, contrib. by. (Illus.). (gr. 5 up). 1987. pap. 12.95 (ISBN 0-671-63699-5, Little Simon). S&S Trade.
Winitz, Harris. Weather. Baker, Syd, illus. 50p. (gr. 7 up). 1986. pap. text ed. 8.00 (ISBN 0-939990-47-4); incl. cassette tape 17.00 (ISBN 0-939990-74-1). Intl Linguistics.

WEATHER–FICTION
Arnold, Jeanne G. The Little Cloud That Couldn't: An Environmental Story for Children. Beattie, Linda D., illus. LC 90-62422. 76p. (Orig.). (gr. 3-7). 1990. pap. 4.95 (ISBN 0-9620887-1-4). Media Serv Unltd.
Barrett, Judith. Cloudy with a Chance of Meatballs. Barrett, Ron, illus. LC 78-2945. 32p. (ps-3). 1978. 13.95 (ISBN 0-689-30647-4, Atheneum Child Bk). Macmillan Child Grp.
Bellairs, John. The Dark Secret of Weatherend. Gorey, Edward, illus. 208p. (gr. 5 up). 1984. 13.95 (ISBN 0-8037-0072-5); PLB 13.89 (ISBN 0-8037-0074-1). Dial Bks Young.
Blotnick, Elihu. The Fog Line. Robinson, Barbara J., illus. 72p. (gr. 6 up). Date not set. pap. 5.95 (ISBN 0-915090-12-0). Calif Street.
Brittain, Bill. Dr. Dredd's Wagon of Wonders. Glass, Andrew, illus. LC 86-45775. 192p. (gr. 3-7). 1989. pap. 3.50 (ISBN 0-06-440289-4, Trophy). HarpC Child Bks.
Humphries, Gillinan & Thatcher, Francis. Sam Cat: A Story about Weather. LC 84-26297. (Illus.). 32p. (ps-3). 1984. lib. bdg. 15.93 (ISBN 0-516-08944-7). Childrens.
Lambert, David. Weather. (Illus.). 32p. (gr. k-3). 1983. PLB 7.99 (ISBN 0-531-04621-4). Watts.
Superlove. Sunstar: Sun of Superlove. LC 80-53694. (Illus.). 200p. (Orig.). (gr. 7 up). 1980. pap. 7.00 (ISBN 0-9602334-1-5); 20.00 (ISBN 0-685-04821-7). Superlove.

WEATHER CONTROL
DeWitt, Lynda. What Will the Weather Be? Croll, Carolyn, illus. LC 90-1446. 32p. (gr. k-4). 1991. 13.95 (ISBN 0-06-021596-8); PLB 13.89 (ISBN 0-06-021597-6). HarpC Child Bks.

WEATHER FORECASTING
Gibbons, Gail. Weather Forecasting. Gibbons, Gail, illus. LC 86-7602. 32p. (gr. k-3). 1987. 13.95 (ISBN 0-02-737250-2, Four Winds). Macmillan Child Grp.
Lampton, Christopher. Blizzard. (Illus.). 64p. (gr. 4-6). 1991. PLB 17.25 (ISBN 1-56294-029-5). Millbrook Pr.
McVey, Vicki. Sierra Club Book of Weatherwisdom. (gr. 4-7). 1991. 15.95 (ISBN 0-316-56341-2). Little.
Martin, Claire. I Can Be a Weather Forecaster. LC 86-31763. (Illus.). 32p. (gr. k-3). 1987. PLB 13.93 (ISBN 0-516-01908-2); pap. 3.95 (ISBN 0-516-41908-0). Childrens.
Palazzo, Janet. What Makes the Weather. Harvey, Paul, illus. LC 81-11383. 32p. (gr. k-2). 1982. PLB 10.89 (ISBN 0-89375-654-7); pap. 2.95 (ISBN 0-89375-655-5). Troll Assocs.
Ramsey, Dan. Weather Forecasting: A Young Meteorologist's Guide. (Illus.). 144p. 1990. 19.95 (ISBN 0-8306-8338-0, 3338); pap. 10.95 (ISBN 0-8306-3338-3). TAB Bks.
Steele, Philip. Frost: Causes & Effects. (Illus.). 32p. (gr. 5-8). 1991. PLB 11.90 (ISBN 0-531-11025-7). Watts.
—Heatwave: Causes & Effects. (Illus.). 32p. (gr. 5-8). 1991. PLB 11.90 (ISBN 0-531-11023-0). Watts.

—Wind: Causes & Effects. (Illus.). 32p. (gr. 5-8). 1991. PLB 11.90 (ISBN 0-531-11024-9). Watts.

WEAVING

see also Basket Making; Textile Industry and Fabrics also names of woven articles, e.g. Carpets

Harvey, Virginia. Split-Ply Twining. LC 75-4651. (Illus.). 44p. (gr. 7 up). 1976. pap. 7.95 (ISBN 0-916658-32-5). Shuttle Craft.

WEBSTER, DANIEL, 1782-1852

Allen, Robert. Daniel Webster: Defender of the Union. (Illus.). (gr. 3-6). 1989. pap. 6.95 (ISBN 0-88062-156-7). Mott Media.

WEBSTER, DANIEL, 1782-1852–FICTION

Gibbons, Ted. Daniel Webster & the Blacksmith's Fee. 8p. (Orig.). 1988. pap. 1.95 stiched with dustcover (ISBN 0-929985-03-6). Sonos.

WEBSTER, NOAH, 1758-1843

Collins, David. Noah Webster: Master of Words. (Illus.). (gr. 3-6). 1989. pap. 6.95 (ISBN 0-88062-158-3). Mott Media.

Ferris, Jeri. What Do You Mean? A Story about Noah Webster. Michaels, Steve, illus. 56p. (gr. 3-6). 1988. PLB 9.95 (ISBN 0-87614-330-3). Carolrhoda Bks.

WEDDINGS

see Etiquette; Marriage; Marriage Customs and Rites

WEEDS

Collins, Pat L. Tumble, Tumble, Tumbleweed. Fay, Ann, ed. LC 81-23968. (Illus.). 32p. (gr. 1-3). 1982. PLB 11.50 (ISBN 0-8075-8122-4). A Whitman.

Martin, Alexander C. Weeds. Zallinger, Jean, illus. 160p. (gr. 7 up). 1973. pap. write for info. (ISBN 0-307-24353-2, Golden Pr). Western Pub.

Podendorf, Illa. Weeds & Wild Flowers. LC 81-7737. (Illus.). 48p. (gr. k-4). 1981. PLB 14.60 (ISBN 0-516-01661-X). Childrens.

WEIGHT CONTROL

see also Diet; Exercise

Coyle, Neva & Chapian, Marie. Slimming down & Growing Up. LC 85-15028. 160p. (Orig.). (gr. 4-7). 1985. pap. 5.95 (ISBN 0-87123-833-0). Bethany Hse.

Jones, Lucile. Tony's Tummy. Van Dolson, Bobbie J., ed. 32p. (gr. k up). 1981. pap. 3.95 (ISBN 0-8280-0039-5). Review & Herald.

Kane, June K. Coping with Diet Fads. Rosen, Ruth, ed. (gr. 7-12). 1990. PLB 12.95 (ISBN 0-8239-1005-9). Rosen Group.

Landau, Elaine. Weight: A Teenage Concern. 160p. (gr. 7 up). 1991. 14.95 (ISBN 0-525-67335-0, Lodestar Bks). Dutton Child Bks.

Philips, Barbara. Don't Call Me Fatso. Cogancherry, Helen, illus. Okun, Barbara, intro. by. LC 85-24341. (Illus.). 32p. (gr. k-6). 1980. PLB 16.67 (ISBN 0-8172-1350-3). Raintree Pubs.

Sachs, Marilyn. The Fat Girl. 176p. (gr. 6 up). 1984. 13.95 (ISBN 0-525-44076-3, DCB). Dutton Child Bks.

Silverstein, Alvin, et al. So You Think You're Fat? LC 90-40761. 224p. (gr. 7 up). 1991. 13.95 (ISBN 0-06-021641-7); PLB 13.89 (ISBN 0-06-021642-5). HarpC Child Bks.

WEIGHT CONTROL–FICTION

Bottner, Barbara. Dumb Old Casey Is a Fat Tree. LC 78-19474. (Illus.). 48p. (gr. 1-4). 1979. 11.89 (ISBN 0-06-020616-0). HarpC Child Bks.

DeClements, Barthe. Nothing's Fair in Fifth Grade. 144p. (gr. 3 up). 1990. pap. 2.95 (ISBN 0-14-034443-8, Puffin). Puffin Bks.

Greenberg, Jan. The Pig-Out Blues. LC 82-2552. 121p. (gr. 7 up). 1982. 11.95 (ISBN 0-374-35937-7). FS&G.

Hargreaves, Roger. Little Miss Plump. Hargreaves, Roger, illus. 32p. (ps-k). 1981. pap. 1.25 (ISBN 0-8431-0895-9). Price Stern.

Holland, Isabelle. Dinah & the Green Fat Kingdom. 192p. (gr. 5 up). 1986. pap. 1.75 (ISBN 0-440-91918-5, LE). Dell.

Lipsyte, Robert. One Fat Summer. LC 76-49746. (gr. 7 up). 1977. PLB 13.89 (ISBN 0-06-023896-8). HarpC Child Bks.

Perl, Lila. Hey, Remember Fat Glenda? 192p. (gr. 3-6). 1981. 13.95 (ISBN 0-395-31023-7, Clarion). HM.

—Hey, Remember Fat Glenda? 192p. (gr. 5-7). 1988. pap. 2.50 (ISBN 0-671-64856-X, Archway). PB.

Ruckman, Ivy. The Hunger Scream. LC 83-6522. 200p. (gr. 6 up). 1983. 14.95 (ISBN 0-8027-6514-9). Walker & Co.

Williams, Barbara. Tell the Truth, Marly Dee. 128p. (gr. 4-6). 1982. 9.95 (ISBN 0-525-44020-8, DCB). Dutton Child Bks.

WEIGHTS AND MEASURES

see also Mensuration; Metric System

Bendick, Jeanne. How Much & How Many. (Illus.). 160p. (gr. 7-9). 1990. 13.90 (ISBN 0-531-10679-9). Watts.

Eagles, Douglas A. Your Weight. (Illus.). 72p. (gr. 4 up). 1982. PLB 10.40 (ISBN 0-531-04395-9). Watts.

Taylor, Barbara. Weight & Balance. (Illus.). 32p. (gr. 5-8). 1990. PLB 11.40 (ISBN 0-531-14082-2). Watts.

Weighing. (Illus.). 56p. (gr. 7-12). 1990. 8.80 (ISBN 0-941008-75-4). Tops Learning.

WELDING–VOCATIONAL GUIDANCE

Lillegard, Dee & Stoker, Wayne. I Can Be a Welder. LC 85-28995. (Illus.). 32p. (gr. k-3). 1986. PLB 13.93 (ISBN 0-516-01895-7). Childrens.

WELFARE STATE

see Economic Policy

WELFARE WORK

see Social Work

WELLS, HERBERT GEORGE, 1866-1946

Martin, C. H. G. Wells. (Illus.). 112p. (gr. 7 up). 1989. lib. bdg. 18.60 (ISBN 0-86592-297-7). Rourke Corp.

WELLS

see also Petroleum; Water Supply

WELLS–FICTION

Silverman, Maida. Magic Well. LC 89-5980. (Illus.). (gr. 2-4). 1989. pap. 13.95 (ISBN 0-671-67885-X). S&S Trade.

WESLEY, JOHN, 1703-1791

McNeer, May & Ward, Lynd. John Wesley. (gr. 4-9). 1957. pap. 3.95 (ISBN 0-687-20430-5). Abingdon.

Vickers, John. John Wesley. (gr. 2-7). 1977. 3.50 (ISBN 0-7214-0466-9). Chr Lit.

WEST, THE

see also Pacific States

Aylesworth, Thomas G. & Aylesworth, Virginia L. The West (Arizona, Nevada, Utah) (Illus.). 66p. (Orig.). 1988. lib. bdg. 16.95x (ISBN 1-55546-563-3). Chelsea Hse.

Bleeker, Sonia. The Sioux Indians: Hunters & Warriors of the Plains. Sasaki, Kisa N., illus. (gr. 3-6). 1962. PLB 11.88 (ISBN 0-688-31457-0). Morrow Jr Bks.

Courtault, Martine. Going West: Cowboys & Pioneers. Bogard, Vicki, tr. from FRE. Grant, Donald, illus. LC 89-5365. 38p. (gr. k-5). 1989. 4.95 (ISBN 0-944589-21-9, 021). Young Discovery Lib.

D'Apice, R. Gamblers. (Illus.). 32p. (gr. 3-8). 1990. PLB 17.26 (ISBN 0-86625-371-8); PLB 12.95s.p. (ISBN 0-685-34711-7). Rourke Corp.

Freedman, Russell. Children of the Wild West. (Illus.). (gr. 4-7). 1990. pap. 5.95 (ISBN 0-395-54785-7, Clarion Bks). HM.

Lake, A. L. Women of the West. (Illus.). 32p. (gr. 3-8). 1990. PLB 17.26 (ISBN 0-86625-373-4). Rourke Corp.

McCall, Edith. Steamboats to the West. Borja, Robert, illus. LC 59-3665. 128p. (gr. 3-10). 1980. PLB 14.60 (ISBN 0-516-03368-9). Childrens.

Shapley, R. Boomtowns. (Illus.). 32p. (gr. 3-8). 1990. lib. bdg. 17.26 (ISBN 0-86625-370-X). Rourke Corp.

Stein, R. Conrad. The Story of the Lewis & Clark Expedition. Aronson, Lou, illus. LC 78-4648. 32p. (gr. 3-6). 1978. PLB 13.27 (ISBN 0-516-04620-9); pap. 3.95 (ISBN 0-516-44620-7). Childrens.

Taylor, L. B., Jr. & Taylor, C. The Rocky Mountain States. (gr. 4 up). lib. bdg. 10.40 (ISBN 0-531-04735-0). Watts.

Time-Life Books Editors. The Old West. (Illus.). 432p. (gr. 7 up). 1990. PLB 43.95 (ISBN 0-671-73158-0); PLB 32.97s.p. (ISBN 0-685-37314-2); 39.95 (ISBN 0-13-631151-2). Silver Burdett Pr.

Twain, Mark. Roughing It. Girling, Z. N., intro. by. (Illus.). (gr. 8 up). pap. 2.95 (ISBN 0-8049-0134-1, CL-134). Airmont.

Upton, H. Cattle Ranchers. (Illus.). 32p. (gr. 3-8). 1990. lib. bdg. 17.26 (ISBN 0-86625-372-6). Rourke Corp.

—Trailblazers. (Illus.). 32p. (gr. 3-8). 1990. lib. bdg. 17.26 (ISBN 0-86625-369-6). Rourke Corp.

Williams, Lucy. The American West. (Illus.). 24p. (gr. k-4). 1991. RLB 10.40 (ISBN 0-531-18387-4, Pub. by Boatwright Pr). Watts.

WEST, THE–FICTION

Adler, David A. Wild Pill Hickok & Other Old West Riddles. Rounds, Glen, illus. LC 88-6480. 64p. (gr. 1-4). 1988. reinforced bdg. 10.95 (ISBN 0-8234-0718-7). Holiday.

Arntson, Herbert E. Caravan to Oregon. LC 57-13207. (Illus.). (gr. 7-11). 1957. 8.95 (ISBN 0-8323-0164-7). Binford Mort.

Bird, E. J. The Blizzard of Eighteen Ninety-Six. Bird, E. J., illus. 72p. (gr. 2-6). 1990. PLB 9.95 (ISBN 0-87614-651-5). Carolrhoda Bks.

Bower, B. M. Cabin Fever. 290p. 1981. Repr. of 1918 ed. PLB 16.35x (ISBN 0-89966-017-7). Buccaneer Bks.

—Flying U Ranch. 280p. 1981. Repr. PLB 16.95x (ISBN 0-89966-018-5). Buccaneer Bks.

Brisson, Pat. Kate Heads West. Brown, Rick, illus. LC 89-27590. 40p. (gr. 2-5). 1990. 12.95 (ISBN 0-02-714345-7, Bradbury Pr). Macmillan Child Grp.

Brown, Dee. Cavalry Scout. (gr. 7 up). 1989. pap. 2.95 (ISBN 0-440-20227-2). Dell.

—Yellow Horse. 1989. pap. 2.95 (ISBN 0-440-20246-9). Dell.

Brown, Towana J. Scottie. Brown, Becky E., illus. LC 88-93029. 150p. (Orig.). (gr. 5-6). 1989. pap. 3.50 (ISBN 0-9622060-1-6). T J Brown.

Byars, Betsy. Hooray for the Golly Sisters! Truesdell, Sue, illus. LC 89-48147. 64p. (gr. k-3). 1990. 11.95 (ISBN 0-06-020898-8); PLB 11.89 (ISBN 0-06-020899-6). HarpC Child Bks.

Ellison, Douglas W. David Lant: The Vanished Outlaw. 232p. (Orig.). 1988. pap. text ed. write for info. (ISBN 0-929918-01-0). Midstates Pub.

Fritz, Jean. Make Way for Sam Houston. Primavera, Elise, illus. LC 85-25601. 109p. (gr. 4-6). 1986. 12.95 (ISBN 0-399-21303-1, Putnam); pap. 5.95 (ISBN 0-399-21304-X). Putnam Pub Group.

Garland, Hamlin. The Long Trail. 1988. Repr. of 1907 ed. lib. bdg. 59.00x (ISBN 0-317-90307-1). Reprint Servs.

Gerrard, Roy. Rosie & the Rustlers. (ps up). 1989. 12.95 (ISBN 0-374-36345-5); pap. 4.95 (ISBN 0-374-46339-5). FS&G.

Giruad, Jean & Charlier, Jean-Michel. The Man with the Silver Star. (Illus.). 48p. pap. 4.95 (ISBN 2-205-06578-5). Dargaud Pub.

Greer, Gery & Ruddick, Bob. Max & Me & the Wild West. LC 87-12066. 144p. (gr. 4-6). 1988. 12.95 (ISBN 0-15-253136-X). HarBraceJ.

—Max & Me & the Wild West. 144p. (gr. 3-7). 1989. pap. 2.95 (ISBN 0-06-440305-X, Trophy). HarpC Child Bks.

Guthrie, Alfred B., Jr. The Big Sky. LC 85-4717. 384p. (gr. 6 up). 1984. pap. 4.95 (ISBN 0-553-26683-7). Bantam.

Hancock, Sibyl. Old Blue. Ingraham, Erick, illus. 48p. (gr. 1-4). 1980. PLB 6.99 (ISBN 0-399-61141-X, Putnam). Putnam Pub Group.

Hope, Laura L. Bobbsey Twins Visit to the Great West. rev. ed. (gr. 1-4). 1966. 4.50 (ISBN 0-448-08013-3, G&D). Putnam Pub Group.

Keller, Charles. Ohm on the Range. Cummings, Art, illus. 48p. (gr. 3-7). 1985. pap. 4.95 (ISBN 0-13-633546-2). P-H.

Kimmel, Eric A. Charlie Drives the Stage. Rounds, Glen, illus. LC 88-24558. 32p. (gr. k-3). 1989. reinforced bdg. 13.95 (ISBN 0-8234-0738-1). Holiday.

Koertge, Ron. The Arizona Kid. (gr. 9 up). 1988. 14.95 (ISBN 0-316-50101-8, Joy Street Bks). Little.

Ladd, Justin. Abilene Book XI: Hellion. 1989. pap. 2.95 (ISBN 0-671-68153-2, POCKET BOOKS). S&S Trade.

McCall, Edith. Message from the Mountains. Nankin, Fran, ed. LC 85-3142. (Illus.). 122p. (gr. 6-9). 1985. 11.95 (ISBN 0-8027-6582-3). Walker & Co.

McHugh, Elisabet. Wiggie Wins the West. (gr. 4-7). 1991. pap. 3.25 (ISBN 0-440-40457-6). Dell.

Moeri, Louise. Save Queen of Sheba. LC 80-23019. (gr. 4-7). 1981. 14.95 (ISBN 0-525-33202-2, DCB). Dutton Child Bks.

Mullin, Penn. High-Five Series: Whale Summer, Spirits of the Canyon & Trail to Danger, 3 bks. (Orig.). (gr. 7 up). 1991. Set, 64p. ea. pap. text ed. 12.50 ea. (ISBN 0-87879-913-3, High Noon Books). Acad Therapy.

The High Five Series is a set of 3 high interest (for ages 12-16)/low level (3rd grade readability) novels for youngsters who enjoy outdoor adventures based on real-life settings. Each short novel describes a vivid "close call" that rivets & holds the reader's attention. The central characters (brothers Mark & Jason Conway) are capable youngsters who use their heads in the crises that occur. Their reactions are neither too heroic nor unbelievable, & the real life facts included in each story add a ring of authenticity. Spirits of the Canyon: The world of Navajo secrets & legends about ancient spirits unfolds as the brothers explore Canyon de Chelly in the Southwest. Trail to Danger: The trail to Sky Lake leads to danger for Mark & Jason & a group of youngsters venturing into the mountains for a weekend backpacking trip. Whale Summer: A summer job at Sea Center holds excitement & surprises as Mark & Jason learn what goes on behind the scenes at the killer whale show. Each softcover novel is 64 pages & features 5 pen & ink illustrations & a 4-color cover. *Publisher Provided Annotation.*

Myers, John M. Silverlock, Bk. 5. LC 83-1039. 544p. (Orig.). (gr. 3-5). 1984. pap. 4.95 (ISBN 0-441-76674-9). Ace Bks.

Peck, Robert N. Soup in the Saddle. (gr. k-6). 1988. pap. 3.25 (ISBN 0-440-40032-5, YB). Dell.

Reese, Bob. Calico Jack & the Desert Critters. LC 83-7550. (Illus.). 32p. (ps-2). 1983. PLB 11.93 (ISBN 0-516-02321-7); pap. 3.95 (ISBN 0-516-42321-5). Childrens.

Saban, Vera. Test of the Tenderfoot. Elliot, Tony, illus. LC 89-9729. 147p. (gr. 5-8). 1989. 7.95 (ISBN 0-914565-35-4). Capstan Pubns.

Modern-day fiction, set in the West. Two young teen-aged boys experience an adventure in the western mountains that helps them see more clearly their own strengths & weaknesses & to face the realities of their lives. Lanny Curtis, a boy from the East, has entered Junior High School in a small

western town. He is eager to make friends but, small for his age & very near-sighted, he lacks self-confidence. When Steven Harper invites him to spend the weekend at his ranch home, Lanny is pleased & excited, for he is a lover of nature. Since the Harper ranch is at the foot of the mountains, Lanny hopes to have the opportunity to visit those high places. Steve, aggressive & often boastful, makes that visit possible. Their trip into those mountains becomes a frightening experience, one that is a test of each boy's strength & wisdom. This story, a TimberTrails Book, has adventure & suspense & will be enjoyed by Junior High School Students. The illustrations by Tony Elliot, an authority on Western settings, add interest to the book. To order this book & for additional information on other TimberTrails Books, call (307) 568-2604.
Publisher Provided Annotation.

Sewall, Marcia. Riding That Strawberry Roan. LC 84-21904. (Illus.). 32p. (ps-2). 1985. pap. 9.95 (ISBN 0-670-80623-4). Viking Child Bks.
Sharmat, Marjorie W. Gila Monsters Meet You at Airport. LC 89-38398. (Illus.). 32p. 1990. pap. 3.95 (ISBN 0-689-71383-5, Aladdin). Macmillan Child Grp.
—Gila Monsters Meet You at the Airport. Barton, Byron, illus. LC 80-12264. 32p. (gr. k-3). 1980. 13.95 (ISBN 0-02-782450-0, Mcmillan Child Bk). Macmillan Child Grp.
Shub, Elizabeth. The White Stallion. Isadora, Rachel, illus. LC 81-20308. 56p. (gr. 1-3). 1982. 13.95 (ISBN 0-688-01210-8); PLB 13.88 (ISBN 0-688-01211-6). Greenwillow.
Sonberg, Lynn. Wild Horse Country. 64p. (gr. 2-4). 1984. pap. 2.25 (ISBN 0-553-15489-3, Skylark). Bantam.
Stahl, Hilda. Sadie Rose & the Outlaw Rustlers. LC 89-50331. 128p. (gr. 4-7). 1989. pap. 4.95 (ISBN 0-89107-528-3, Crossway Bks). Good News.
Weinberg, Larry, adapted by. The Legend of the Lone Ranger Storybook. (Illus.). (gr. 4-7). 1981. lib. bdg. 6.99 (ISBN 0-394-94683-9). Random.
Wu, William F. Hong on the Range. Hale, Phil & Anderson, Darrel, illus. LC 88-29329. 224p. (gr. 7 up). 1989. 17.95 (ISBN 0-8027-6862-8). Walker & Co.
Yosemite Yarns-Stagecoach Stories. (gr. 7 up). pap. 2.00 (ISBN 0-915266-04-0). Awani Pr.

WEST, THE–HISTORY

Bartlett, Richard & Keller, Clair. Freedom's Trail. LC 78-53884. (Illus.). (gr. 8). 1979. text ed. 43.96 (ISBN 0-395-26197-X). HM.
Collins, James L. Lawmen of the Old West. (ps-3). 1990. PLB 11.90 (ISBN 0-531-10893-7). Watts.
Levine, Ellen. If You Traveled West in a Covered Wagon. Shaw, Charles, illus. 80p. (Orig.). (gr. 2-5). 1986. pap. 2.50 (ISBN 0-590-40153-X). Scholastic Inc.
Miller, Robert. Cowboys. Leonard, Richard, illus. 104p. (gr. 4-7). 1991. PLB 13.98 (ISBN 0-382-24079-0); PLB 8.99s.p.; pap. 7.95 (ISBN 0-382-24084-7); pap. 5.21s.p. Silver Burdett Pr.
Shapley, R., et al. Wild West in American History, 14 bks, Set 2. (Illus.). 448p. (gr. 3-8). 1990. Set. lib. bdg. 241.73 (ISBN 0-86625-367-X); Set. lib. bdg. 181.30s.p. (ISBN 0-685-36328-7). Rourke Corp.
Stein, R. Conrad. The Story of the Homestead Act. Koenig, Cathy, illus. LC 78-4839. 32p. (gr. 3-6). 1978. PLB 13.27 (ISBN 0-516-04616-0). Childrens.
Stewart, Gail. Rivermen. (Illus.). 32p. (gr. 3-8). 1990. PLB 17.26 (ISBN 0-86625-409-9). Rourke Corp.
—Scouts. (Illus.). 32p. (gr. 3-8). 1990. PLB 17.26 (ISBN 0-86625-404-8). Rourke Corp.
—Trappers & Traders. (Illus.). 32p. (gr. 3-8). 1990. PLB 17.26 (ISBN 0-86625-401-3). Rourke Corp.
Wilder, Laura I. West from Home: Letters of Laura Ingalls Wilder, San Francisco 1915. MacBride, Roger L., ed. LC 73-14342. (Illus.). 176p. (gr. 7 up). 1976. pap. 3.50 (ISBN 0-06-440081-6, Trophy). HarpC Child Bks.

WEST GERMANY

see Germany (Federal Republic)

WEST INDIES

Brothers, Don. West Indies. (Illus.). 96p. (gr. 5 up). 1989. lib. bdg. 14.95 (ISBN 1-55546-793-8). Chelsea Hse.
Lye, Keith. Take a Trip to the West Indies. 32p. (gr. 1-4). 1984. lib. bdg. 7.99 (ISBN 0-531-03762-2). Watts.

WEST VIRGINIA

Aylesworth, Thomas G. & Aylesworth, Virginia L. The Atlantic (Virginia, West Virginia, District of Columbia) (Illus.). 66p. (Orig.). 1990. lib. bdg. 16.95x (ISBN 1-55546-555-2); pap. 6.95 (ISBN 0-7910-0533-X). Chelsea Hse.
Carole Marsh West Virginia Books, 31 bks. Set. 638.45 (ISBN 0-7933-1323-6). Gallopade Pub Group.
Carpenter, Allan. West Virginia. new ed. LC 79-12900. (Illus.). 96p. (gr. 4 up). 1979. PLB 19.93 (ISBN 0-516-04148-7). Childrens.
Doherty, William T. West Virginia: Our Land - Our People. Buckalew, Marshall, ed. Harvey, Eve S. & Harvey, Cliff, illus. 320p. (gr. 8). 1990. 25.00 (ISBN 0-914498-07-X); punched for 3-ring binder tchr's. manual 25.00 (ISBN 0-914498-10-X). WV Hist Ed Found.
Doherty, William T. & Conley, Phil. West Virginia History. (Illus.). 494p. (gr. 8). 1974. 10.25 (ISBN 0-914498-00-2). WV Hist Ed Found.
Fradin, Dennis. West Virginia: In Words & Pictures. Wahl, Richard, illus. LC 80-12133. 48p. (gr. 2-5). 1980. PLB 15.93 (ISBN 0-516-03949-0). Childrens.
Marsh, Carole. Avast, Ye Slobs! West Virginia Pirate Trivia. (Illus.). 1990. PLB 19.95 (ISBN 0-7933-1220-5); pap. 14.95 (ISBN 0-7933-1219-1); computer disk 29.95 (ISBN 0-7933-1221-3). Gallopade Pub Group.
—The Beast of the West Virginia Bed & Breakfast. (Illus.). 1990. PLB 19.95 (ISBN 0-7933-2244-8); pap. 14.95 (ISBN 0-7933-2245-6); computer disk 29.95 (ISBN 0-7933-2246-4). Gallopade Pub Group.
—The Hard-to-Believe-But-True! Book of West Virginia History, Mystery, Trivia, Legend, Lore, Humor & More. (Illus.). 1990. PLB 19.95 (ISBN 0-7933-1217-5); pap. 14.95 (ISBN 0-7933-1216-7); computer disk 29.95 (ISBN 0-7933-1218-3). Gallopade Pub Group.
—If My West Virginia Mama Ran the World! (Illus.). 1990. PLB 19.95 (ISBN 0-7933-2253-7); pap. 14.95 (ISBN 0-7933-2254-5); computer disk 29.95 (ISBN 0-7933-2255-3). Gallopade Pub Group.
—Let's Quilt West Virginia & Stuff It Topographically! (Illus.). 1990. PLB 19.95 (ISBN 0-7933-2236-7); pap. 14.95 (ISBN 1-55609-052-8); computer disk 29.95 (ISBN 0-7933-2237-5). Gallopade Pub Group.
—West Virginia & Other State Greats (Biographies) (Illus.). 1990. PLB 19.95 (ISBN 0-7933-2256-1); pap. 14.95 (ISBN 0-7933-2257-X); computer disk 29.95 (ISBN 0-7933-2258-8). Gallopade Pub Group.
—West Virginia Bandits, Bushwackers, Outlaws, Crooks, Devils, Ghosts, Desperadoes & Other Assorted & Sundry Characters! (Illus.). 1990. PLB 19.95 (ISBN 0-7933-1202-7); pap. 14.95 (ISBN 0-7933-1201-9); computer disk 29.95 (ISBN 0-7933-1203-5). Gallopade Pub Group.
—West Virginia Classic Christmas Trivia: Stories, Recipies, Activities, Legends, Lore & More! (Illus.). 1990. PLB 19.95 (ISBN 0-7933-1205-1); pap. 14.95 (ISBN 0-7933-1204-3); computer disk 29.95 (ISBN 0-7933-1206-X). Gallopade Pub Group.
—West Virginia Coastales. (Illus.). 1990. PLB 19.95 (ISBN 0-7933-2250-2); pap. 14.95 (ISBN 0-7933-2251-0); computer disk 29.95 (ISBN 0-7933-2252-9). Gallopade Pub Group.
—The West Virginia Hot Air Balloon Mystery. (Illus.). (gr. 2-9). 1990. 19.95 (ISBN 0-7933-2750-4); pap. 14.95 (ISBN 0-7933-2751-2); computer disk 29.95 (ISBN 0-7933-2752-0). Gallopade Pub Group.
—West Virginia "Jography" A Fun Run Thru Our State! (Illus.). 1990. PLB 19.95 (ISBN 0-7933-2233-2); pap. 14.95 (ISBN 0-7933-2234-0); computer disk 29.95 (ISBN 0-7933-2235-9). Gallopade Pub Group.
—West Virginia Kid's Cookbook: Recipes, How-to, History, Lore & More! (Illus.). 1990. PLB 19.95 (ISBN 0-7933-1214-0); pap. 14.95 (ISBN 0-7933-1213-2); computer disk 29.95 (ISBN 0-7933-1215-9). Gallopade Pub Group.
—West Virginia Quiz Bowl Crash Course! (Illus.). 1990. PLB 19.95 (ISBN 0-7933-2247-2); pap. 14.95 (ISBN 0-7933-2248-0); computer disk 29.95 (ISBN 0-7933-2249-9). Gallopade Pub Group.
—West Virginia School Trivia: An Amazing & Fascinating Look at Our State's Teachers, Schools & Students! (Illus.). 1990. PLB 19.95 (ISBN 0-7933-1211-6); pap. 14.95 (ISBN 0-7933-1210-8); computer disk 29.95 (ISBN 0-7933-1212-4). Gallopade Pub Group.
—West Virginia Silly Basketball Sportsmysteries, Vol. 1. (Illus.). 1990. PLB 19.95 (ISBN 0-7933-1208-6); pap. 14.95 (ISBN 0-7933-1207-8); computer disk 29.95 (ISBN 0-7933-1209-4). Gallopade Pub Group.
—West Virginia Silly Basketball Sportsmysteries, Vol. 2. (Illus.). 1990. PLB 19.95 (ISBN 0-7933-2259-6); pap. 14.95 (ISBN 0-7933-2260-X); computer disk 29.95 (ISBN 0-7933-2261-8). Gallopade Pub Group.
—West Virginia Silly Football Sportsmysteries, Vol. 1. (Illus.). 1990. PLB 19.95 (ISBN 0-7933-2238-3); pap. 14.95 (ISBN 0-7933-2239-1); computer disk 29.95 (ISBN 0-7933-2240-5). Gallopade Pub Group.
—West Virginia Silly Football Sportsmysteries, Vol. 2. (Illus.). 1990. PLB 19.95 (ISBN 0-7933-2241-3); pap. 14.95 (ISBN 0-7933-2242-1); computer disk 29.95. Gallopade Pub Group.
—West Virginia Silly Trivia! (Illus.). 1990. PLB 19.95 (ISBN 0-7933-2230-8); pap. 14.95 (ISBN 0-7933-2231-6); computer disk 29.95 (ISBN 0-7933-2232-4). Gallopade Pub Group.
—West Virginia's (Most Devastating!) Disasters & (Most Calamitous!) Catastrophies! (Illus.). 1990. PLB 19.95 (ISBN 0-7933-1199-3); pap. 14.95 (ISBN 0-7933-1198-5); computer disc 29.95 (ISBN 0-7933-1200-0). Gallopade Pub Group.
Stein, R. Conrad. West Virginia. LC 90-33848. (Illus.). 144p. (gr. 4 up). 1990. PLB 25.27 (ISBN 0-516-00494-8). Childrens.
Thompson, Kathleen. West Virginia. LC 87-26483. 48p. (gr. 3 up). 1988. 17.32 (ISBN 0-86514-476-1); cancelled tchr's. study guide (ISBN 0-86514-616-0); cancelled Beta video (ISBN 0-86514-109-6); cancelled VHS video (ISBN 0-317-67108-1); cancelled 3/4" video (ISBN 0-86514-259-9). Raintree Pubs.
Waura, Grace. The First Families of West Virginia. Waura, Grace M., illus. LC 90-70666. 70p. (Orig.). (gr. 3-6). 1991. pap. 6.00 (ISBN 1-56002-007-5). Aegina Pr.
Williams, Tony L. West Virginia: Our State. Buckalew, Marshall, ed. Harvey, Eve S. & Harvey, Cliff, illus. 288p. (gr. 4). 1990. 20.00 (ISBN 0-914498-09-6); punched for 3-ring binder tchr's. manual 25.00 (ISBN 0-685-25544-1). WV Hist Ed Found.

WHALES

Albert, Burton. Sharks & Whales. Ford, Pamela, illus. LC 78-66936. (gr. 1-6). 1979. 5.95 (ISBN 0-448-48990-2, G&D); PLB 5.29 (ISBN 0-448-13620-1). Putnam Pub Group.
—Sharks & Whales. Johnson, Pamela, illus. 48p. (gr. 2-5). 1989. 7.95 (ISBN 0-448-09077-5, G&D). Putnam Pub Group.
Anderson, J. I. I Can Read About Whales & Dolphins. LC 72-96955. (Illus.). (gr. 2-4). 1973. pap. 1.95 (ISBN 0-89375-052-2). Troll Assocs.
Barrett, Norman. Ballenas. (SPA., Illus.). 32p. (gr. k-4). 1990. PLB 11.40 (ISBN 0-531-07903-1). Watts.
Barrett, Norman S. Whales. (Illus.). 32p. (gr. k-6). 1989. PLB 11.40 (ISBN 0-531-10703-5). Watts.
Barstow, Robbins. Grandiosas Criaturas del Mar: Una Introduccion al Mundo de las Ballenas y Otros Cetaceos. Accent, Inc. Staff, tr. from ENG. Sineti, Donald, illus. (SPA.). 46p. (Orig.). (gr. 7-12). 1988. pap. 5.00 (ISBN 0-9618858-2-3). Cetacean Society.
—Meet the Great Ones: An Introduction to Whales & Other Cetaceans. Sineti, Donald, illus. LC 87-70553. 46p. (Orig.). (gr. 7-12). 1987. pap. 5.95 (ISBN 0-9618858-1-5). Cetacean Society.
Behrens, June. Whales of the World. LC 87-8046. (Illus.). 48p. (gr. 1-4). 1987. PLB 14.60 (ISBN 0-516-08877-7); pap. 4.95 (ISBN 0-516-48877-5). Childrens.
—Whalewatch! Olguin, John, illus. LC 78-7338. (gr. 1-4). 1978. PLB 13.27 (ISBN 0-516-08873-4, Golden Gate); pap. 3.95 (ISBN 0-516-48873-2). Childrens.
Bender, Lionel. Whales. Franklin Watts Ltd., ed. (Illus.). 32p. (gr. k-9). 1988. PLB 11.90 (ISBN 0-531-17078-0, Gloucester Pr). Watts.
Berger, Gilda. Whales. Bonaforte, Lisa, illus. LC 86-16500. 48p. (gr. k-3). 1987. 11.99 (ISBN 0-685-18308-4); PLB 10.95 (ISBN 0-685-18309-2). Doubleday.
—Whales. (gr. 4-7). 1987. 10.95 (ISBN 0-385-23420-1). Doubleday.
Braithwaite, Althea. Whales. (ps-6). 1988. PLB 7.95 (ISBN 0-318-37640-7); pap. 2.95 (ISBN 0-318-37641-5). Dearborn Finan.
Bright, Michael. Humpback Whale. (ps-3). 1990. PLB 11.90 (ISBN 0-531-17216-3). Watts.
—Saving the Whale. (Illus.). 32p. (gr. 4-9). 1987. PLB 11.90 (ISBN 0-531-17061-6, Gloucester Pr). Watts.
Brittain, Mary Ann. A Whale Called Trouble. (Illus.). 24p. (gr. 1-12). 1985. pap. 1.50 (ISBN 0-917134-08-7). NC Natl Sci.
Bunting, Eve. The Sea World Book of Whales. LC 85-16409. (Illus.). 96p. (gr. 4-6). 1987. 14.95 (ISBN 0-15-271948-2, HJ); pap. 9.95 (ISBN 0-15-271953-9). HarBraceJ.
Craig, Janet. Discovering Whales & Dolphins. Johnson, Pamela, illus. LC 89-5004. 32p. (gr. 2-4). 1990. PLB 10.89 (ISBN 0-8167-1759-1); pap. text ed. 2.95 (ISBN 0-8167-1760-5). Troll Assocs.
Crump, Donald J., ed. Whales, Bk. 2. (Illus.). (ps-3). 1990. Set. 21.95 (ISBN 0-87044-810-2). Natl Geog.
Dow, Lesley. Whales. 72p. (gr. 3-10). 1990. 17.95 (ISBN 0-8160-2271-2). Facts on File.
Eisemann, Henry. Hump-Free Heads for Hawaii. Campbell, Jay, illus. 24p. (Orig.). (gr. k-6). 1989. pap. 6.95 (ISBN 0-938129-02-3). Emprise Pubns.
Gambell, Ray. How They Live: Whales. (ps up). 1990. PLB 3.98 (ISBN 0-7924-5146-5, Mallard Pr). BDD Promo Bk.
Gardner, Robert. The Whale Watchers' Guide. Sineti, Don, illus. LC 83-17425. 170p. (gr. 7 up). 1984. lib. bdg. 10.98 (ISBN 0-671-45811-6); pap. 5.95 (ISBN 0-671-49807-X). Messner.
Ginsberg, Daniel. Whales & Dolphins: An Educational Coloring Book. Ginsberg, Daniel, illus. 32p. (Orig.). (gr. 1-4). 1989. pap. 1.99 (ISBN 0-9623284-0-5). Ginsberg Pubns.

Gohier, Francois. Humpback Whales. Leon, Vicki, ed. (Illus.). 40p. (Orig.). (gr. 5 up). 1990. pap. 7.95 (ISBN 0-918303-26-5). Blake Pub.
In 30 photographs & 6,000 words of text, Gohier gives a detailed & accurate portrait of the humpback whale, perhaps the most beloved & recognizable of the great whales. Homely to look at, humpbacks wing

through the sea & leap above it with acrobatic grace. These long-distance singers may possess the most haunting voice in the animal kingdom, capable of reaching other whales across miles of ocean floor. This engrossing book, written in simple terms by a man who has followed the humpbacks for many years, contains a wealth of recent data on the whales. Social behavior, play, courtship, birth, male aggression, & numerous feeding techniques are talked about & depicted in oversized photos. Excerpts from humpback whale song are shown in easy-to-understand sonograms. The text further elaborates on what is known about humpback singing. Like other Blake nature titles, the type of both text & captions are very generously sized, making the books especially attractive to youngsters & to adults who have difficulty with standard type. A favorite with whale-watchers & report-writers too.
Publisher Provided Annotation.

—A Pod of Gray Whales. (Illus.). 40p. (Orig.). (ps-12). 1987. pap. 5.95 (ISBN 0-918303-14-1). Blake Pub.
Graham, Ada & Graham, Frank. Whale Watch. Tyler, D. D., illus. LC 77-20531. (gr. 5 up). 1978. 7.95 (ISBN 0-440-09505-0); pap. 6.46 (ISBN 0-440-09506-9). Delacorte.
Green, Carl R. & Sanford, William R. The Humpback Whale. LC 85-9645. (Illus.). 48p. (gr. 5-6). 1985. 10.95 (ISBN 0-89686-274-7, Crestwood Hse). Macmillan Child Grp.
Greenberg, Judith E. & Carey, Helen H. Whales. Fujiwara, Kim, illus. 32p. (gr. 2-4). 1990. PLB 16.67 (ISBN 0-8172-3757-7). Raintree Pubs.
Harris, Susan. Whales. (gr. 2-4). PLB 10.90 (ISBN 0-531-00444-9). Watts.
Himmelman, John. Ibis: A True Whale Story. 1990. 12.95 (ISBN 0-590-42848-9). Scholastic Inc.
Hogan, Paula Z. The Whale. Ruth, Rod, illus. LC 79-13379. 32p. (gr. 1-4). 1979. PLB 16.67 (ISBN 0-8172-1500-X). Raintree Pubs.
—The Whale. LC 79-13379. (Illus.). 32p. (gr. 1-4). 1981. PLB 27.99 incl. cassette (ISBN 0-8172-1847-5). Raintree Pubs.

Hoyt, Eric. Meeting the Whales: The Equinox Guide to Giants of the Deep. Folkens, Pieter, illus. 72p. 1991. lib. bdg. 17.95 (ISBN 0-921820-25-9); pap. 9.95 (ISBN 0-921820-23-2). Camden Hse Pub.
In the deep, dark canyons of the sea live the largest animals on Earth: the heart of the blue whale is the size of a sports car, the eye of a right whale is the size of a grapefruit, & the "wing span" of a humpback's flippers can reach 12 meters. In MEETING THE WHALES, author Erich Hoyt pieces together the life histories of the enigmatic giants that swim the waters of the northern hemisphere. Hoyt has spent years working with these mammals, & his fascination & empathy for them is evident in the fifth book in Camden House's science series for children. Bringing us face-to-face both with these intriguing creatures & with the scientists who study them, Hoyt leads us through the underwater world of whales, investigating their unique communication skills & feeding & mating behaviors, their remarkable migrations & their astounding acrobatics. Beautifully illustrated by whale specialist Pieter Folkens & the work of the world's best wildlife photographers, MEETING THE WHALES is a unique contribution to the study of this increasingly rare

animal.
Publisher Provided Annotation.

Kalman, Bobbie. Arctic Whales & Whaling. (Illus.). 56p. (gr. 3-4). 1988. 15.95 (ISBN 0-86505-146-1); pap. 7.95 (ISBN 0-86505-156-9). Crabtree Pub Co.
Knapp, Toni. The Six Bridges of Humphrey the Whale. Brown, Craig M., illus. LC 89-8417. 48p. (gr. 5 up). 1989. 15.95 (ISBN 1-882092-01-5). Rockrimmon Pr.
Lauber, Patricia. Great Whales: The Gentle Giants. Folkens, Pieter, illus. 64p. (gr. 2-4). 1991. 14.95 (ISBN 0-8050-1717-8). H Holt & Co.
McCoy, J. J. The Plight of the Whales. (Illus.). 144p. (gr. 7-12). 1989. PLB 12.90 (ISBN 0-531-10778-7). Watts.
McGowen, Tom. Album of Whales. Ruth, Rod, illus. 64p. (gr. 4-7). 1980. write for info. (ISBN 0-528-82287-X). Checkerboard Pr.
—Album of Whales. Ruth, Rod, illus. 64p. (gr. 3-7). 1987. pap. 4.95 (ISBN 0-02-688505-0). Checkerboard Pr.
Mallory, Kenneth & Conley, Andrea. Rescue of the Stranded Whales. Prescott, John H., intro. by. (gr. 3 up). 1989. pap. 14.95 (ISBN 0-671-67122-7). S&S Trade.
Martin, L. Whales. (Illus.). 24p. (gr. k-5). Date not set. PLB 11.93 (ISBN 0-86592-988-2). Rourke Corp.
Mell, Jan. Atlantic Gray Whale. LC 89-7868. (Illus.). 48p. (gr. 4-5). 1989. 10.95 (ISBN 0-89686-458-8, Crestwood Hse). Macmillan Child Grp.
Miller, Suzanne S. Whales & Sharks. Klimo, Kate, ed. Bonforte, Lisa, illus. 48p. 1982. pap. 8.95 (ISBN 0-671-45148-0, Little Simon). S&S Trade.
Milton, Joyce. Whales: The Gentle Giants. Langford, Alton, illus. LC 88-15616. 48p. (Orig.). (gr. k-3). 1989. lib. bdg. 6.99 (ISBN 0-394-99809-X); pap. 2.95 (ISBN 0-394-89809-5). Random.
Palmer, S. Blue Whales. (Illus.). 24p. (gr. k-5). Date not set. PLB 11.93 (ISBN 0-86592-480-5). Rourke Corp.
—Fin Whales. (Illus.). 24p. (gr. k-5). Date not set. PLB 11.93 (ISBN 0-86592-479-1). Rourke Corp.
—Gray Whales. (Illus.). 24p. (gr. k-5). Date not set. PLB 11.93 (ISBN 0-86592-477-5). Rourke Corp.
—Humpback Whales. (Illus.). 24p. (gr. k-5). Date not set. PLB 11.93 (ISBN 0-86592-478-3). Rourke Corp.
—Killer Whales. (Illus.). 24p. (gr. k-5). Date not set. PLB 11.93 (ISBN 0-86592-481-3). Rourke Corp.
—Narwhals. (Illus.). 24p. (gr. k-5). Date not set. PLB 11.93 (ISBN 0-86592-476-7). Rourke Corp.
Papastavrou, Vassili. Whales & Dolphins. (Illus.). 32p. (gr. k-4). 1991. RLB 11.90 (ISBN 0-531-18394-7, Pub. by Boatwright Pr). Watts.
Patent, Dorothy H. All about Whales. LC 86-27126. (Illus.). 48p. (gr. 1-4). 1987. reinforced bdg. 12.95 (ISBN 0-8234-0640-3). Holiday.
—Humpback Whales. Ferrari, Mark J. & Glockner-Ferrari, Deborah A., illus. LC 89-2026. 32p. (gr. k-3). 1989. reinforced 14.95 (ISBN 0-8234-0779-9). Holiday.
—Whales: Giants of the Deep. Patent, Dorothy H., illus. LC 84-729. 96p. (gr. 3-7). 1984. reinforced 14.95 (ISBN 0-8234-0530-3). Holiday.
Royston, Angela. Whale. Channel, Jim, illus. 24p. (gr. k-3). 1989. pap. 2.95 (ISBN 0-8249-8373-4). Ideals.
Sabin, Francene. Whales & Dolphins. Johnson, Pamela, illus. LC 84-2709. 32p. (gr. 3-6). 1985. PLB 9.49 (ISBN 0-8167-0286-1); pap. text ed. 2.95 (ISBN 0-8167-0287-X). Troll Assocs.
Selsam, Millicent E. & Hunt, Joyce. A First Look at Whales. (gr. k-3). 1980. PLB 12.85 (ISBN 0-8027-6388-X). Walker & Co.
Serventy, Vincent. Whale & Dolphin. LC 84-15118. (Illus.). 24p. (gr. k-5). 1985. PLB 13.32 (ISBN 0-8172-2401-7). Raintree Pubs.
—Whale & Dolphin. Serventy, Vincent, illus. 24p. (gr. k-3). 1986. pap. 1.95 (ISBN 0-590-40227-7). Scholastic Inc.
Simon, Seymour. Killer Whales. LC 77-20187. (Illus.). 96p. (gr. k-3). 1978. 12.95 (ISBN 0-397-31784-0, Lipp Jr Bks). HarpC Child Bks.
—Whales. LC 87-45285. (Illus.). 40p. (gr. k-3). 1989. 15.95 (ISBN 0-690-04756-8, Crowell Jr Bks); PLB 14.89 (ISBN 0-690-04758-4, Crowell Jr Bks). HarpC Child Bks.
—Whales. (Illus.). (ps-3). 1990. 14.95 (ISBN 0-685-34878-4). HarperCollins.
Smyth, Karen. Crystal: The Story of a Real Baby Whale. Cuneo, Norma, illus. LC 85-52440. 96p. (gr. 2 up). 1986. 12.95 (ISBN 0-89272-223-1). Down East.
Spizzirri Publishing Co. Staff. Dot-to-Dot Whales: An Educational Activity-Coloring Book. Spizzirri, Linda, ed. (Illus.). 32p. (gr. 1-8). 1986. pap. 0.99 (ISBN 0-86545-079-X). Spizzirri.
Stone, Lynn M. The Killer Whale. LC 86-32884. (Illus.). 48p. (gr. 5-6). 1987. PLB 10.95 (ISBN 0-89686-323-9, Crestwood Hse). Macmillan Child Grp.
Strachan, Elizabeth. A Closer Look at Whales & Dolphins. rev ed. LC 85-80643. 32p. (gr. 4-7). 1986. lib. bdg. 5.99 (ISBN 0-531-17015-2, Gloucester Pr). Watts.
Wax, Wendy & Rowland, Della. Ten Things I Know about Whales. Payne, Thomas, illus. 24p. 1990. 6.95 (ISBN 0-8092-4303-2, Calico Bks). Contemp Bks.
Wexo, John B. Whales. 24p. (gr. 4). 1989. 11.95s.p. (ISBN 0-88682-272-6); 17.10 (ISBN 0-685-28188-4). Creative Ed.
Whale Museum Staff. Gentle Giants of the Sea. 2nd ed. 214p. (gr. k-6). pap. 15.95 (ISBN 0-933331-25-8). Whale Museum.

Whittell, Giles. The Story of the Three Whales. Benson, Patrick, illus. LC 88-35630. 29p. (gr. 2-4). 1988. PLB 10.95 (ISBN 0-8368-0092-3). Gareth Stevens Inc.
Whyte, Malcolm. Whales. (gr. 2 up). pap. 3.95 (ISBN 0-685-25407-0). Troubador Pr.
Wilson, Lynn. Baby Whale. (Illus.). 32p. (ps-2). 1991. PLB 6.99 (ISBN 0-448-40073-1, G&D); pap. 1.95 (ISBN 0-448-40072-3, G&D). Putnam Pub Group.
Young, Jim. When the Whale Came to My Town. Bernstein, Dan, photos by. LC 74-159. (Illus.). 48p. (gr. 3 up). 1974. Knopf.

WHALES–FICTION

Allen, Joseph. Mikey Goes Whale Watching. Trout, M. D., ed. Woodaman, W., illus. 50p. (Orig.). (gr. 1-5). 1986. PLB 13.50 (ISBN 0-917071-05-0); pap. 8.95 (ISBN 0-917071-04-2). Ocean Allen Pub.
Bailey, Jill. Project Whale. Green, John, illus. LC 90-45159. 48p. (gr. 3-7). 1991. PLB 17.28 (ISBN 0-8114-2707-2). Steck-V.
Benchley, Nathaniel. Kilroy & the Gull. Schoenherr, John, illus. LC 76-24309. (gr. 4-6). 1978. pap. 3.50 (ISBN 0-06-440090-5, Trophy). HarpC Child Bks.
Boschini, Henny & Boschini, Luciano. Chasing Whales off Norway. LC 72-90690. (Illus.). 32p. (gr. k-4). 1973. 7.95 (ISBN 0-87592-010-1). Scroll Pr.
Chbosky, Stacy. Who Owns the Sun? Chbosky, Stacy, illus. LC 88-12694. 26p. (gr. 3-12). 1988. lib. bdg. 12.95 (ISBN 0-933849-14-1). Landmark Edns.
Coleridge, Ann. Stranded. 1989. 13.95 (ISBN 0-385-29825-0). Doubleday.

Cosgrove, Stephen. Harmony. Casad, Michael, illus. LC 89-83842. 72p. (gr. 7 up). 1991. 24.95 (ISBN 1-55868-008-X). Gr Arts Ctr Pub.
For the past several years, the national news media has reflected man's fascination with one of the most spiritual of all creatures - the whale. More & more people have followed the news stories with a sense of awe & wonder. The story, as sung by the whales, is narrated by Harmony & accented by characters such as Rhapsody, his mother; Symphony, the leader of the pod; & Cacophony, the mad bull. Through the eyes of Harmony, we view a panoramic picture relating the history of a pod of whales from the beginning of time to their ultimate beached destruction. Interwoven is the story of man & his senseless obsession with traditions, which could lead ultimately to his own destruction. Meant for the entire family, this novel is one of the first of its kind to include original color illustrations. HARMONY, the first in the trilogy, "Song of the Sea," concerns itself with man's relationship to nature. Michael Casad's 25 years of experience encompass everything from commissions by various foreign countries & portraits of famous personalities, to a 70' x 23' mural.
Publisher Provided Annotation.

Elsemann, Henry. Hump-Free: The Wrong Way Whale. (Illus., Orig.). (gr. k-6). 1985. pap. 6.95 (ISBN 0-938129-00-7). Emprise Pubns.
Evans-Smith, Deborah. The Whale's Tale. Evans, Valeria, illus. LC 85-51791. 25p. (gr. 2-6). 1986. 8.95 (ISBN 0-917507-02-9). Sea Fog Pr.
Fisher, R. L. The Prince of Whales. Satter, Denise, illus. 160p. (gr. 3 up). 1987. pap. 2.50 (ISBN 0-8125-6635-1). Tor Bks.
Heus, John & Robinson, Tom. The Tale of Humphrey the Humpback Whale. Brost, Victoria, illus. 32p. (Orig.). (ps-3). 1985. pap. 6.95 (ISBN 0-9616109-0-5). Brost Heus.
Hunt, Robert. Baleena the Blue Whale. LC 72-736440. (Illus.). (gr. 2-5). 1978. 6 bks. & 1 cass. 29.95 (ISBN 0-89290-025-3); 1 bk. & 1 cass. 10.95 (ISBN 0-685-04627-3). Soc for Visual.
Johnston, Tony. Whale Song. Young, Ed, illus. 32p. (ps-3). 1987. 12.95 (ISBN 0-399-21402-X, Putnam). Putnam Pub Group.
Kipling, Rudyard. How the Whale Got His Throat: Just So Stories. Langley, Jonathan, illus. LC 87-29226. 24p. (ps-3). 1988. 5.95 (ISBN 0-399-21552-2, Philomel Bks). Putnam Pub Group.
LaGrange, Lynn M. Winnie, the Humpback Whale & Her Second Tale. Wilcox, Kelly K., illus. 40p. (ps-3). 1990. lib. bdg. 10.95 (ISBN 1-878790-01-3). Fables CO.

—Winnie, the Humpback Whale & Her Second Tale. Wilcox, Kelly K., illus. 38p. (ps-3). 1990. pap. 6.95 (ISBN 1-878790-04-8). Fables CO.
Lay, Artie K. & Runnels, Gayle S. Amigo, the Friendly Gray Whale. LC 91-65227. (Illus.). 140p. (gr. 2-6). 1991. incl. audiocassette 24.95 (ISBN 0-9628626-0-6). Blubber Budd.
Lewis, Paul O. Davy's Dream. (Illus.). 64p. (ps-6). 1988. 14.95 (ISBN 0-941831-32-9); pap. 9.95 (ISBN 0-941831-28-0). Beyond Words Pub.
Lewis, Sharon. Orca! The Killer Whale. Roberts, Linda, illus. 20p. (ps-4). 1990. 8.95 (ISBN 0-694-00295-X). HarpC Child Bks.
McBarnet, Gill. The Whale Who Wanted to Be Small. McBarnet, Gill, illus. 32p. (gr. k-2). 1985. 6.95 (ISBN 0-9615102-0-X). Ruwanga Trad.
—A Whale's Tale. McBarnet, Gill, illus. 32p. (ps-2). Date not set. 6.95 (ISBN 0-9615102-4-2). Ruwanga Trad.
McCloskey, Robert. Burt Dow: Deep-Water Man. McCloskey, Robert, illus. LC 68-364. 64p. (gr. 4-6). 1963. pap. 15.95 (ISBN 0-670-19748-3). Viking Child Bks.
McClung, Robert M. Thor, the Last of the Sperm Whales. Hines, Bob, illus. LC 87-26090. 64p. (gr. 3-7). 1988. Repr. of 1971 ed. PLB 14.50 (ISBN 0-208-02186-8, Linnet). Shoe String.
Melville, Herman. Moby Dick. (gr. 11 up). 1964. pap. 3.95 (ISBN 0-8049-0033-7, CL-33). Airmont.
—Moby Dick. Daniels, Patricia, adapted by. LC 81-15386. (Illus.). 48p. (gr. 4 up). 1983. PLB 17.32 (ISBN 0-8172-1679-0); pap. 9.27 (ISBN 0-8172-2016-X). Raintree Pubs.
—Moby Dick. Selden, Bernice, adapted by. Gianni, Gary, illus. LC 87-16788. 48p. (gr. 3-6). 1988. PLB 12.89 (ISBN 0-8167-1207-7); pap. text ed. 3.95 (ISBN 0-8167-1208-5). Troll Assocs.
Moby Dick. (gr. 4 up). 1988. Incl. 26 cards. 22.00 (ISBN 0-8172-2186-7). Raintree Pubs.
Morpurgo, Michael. Why the Whales Came. (gr. 5-7). 1990. pap. 10.95 (ISBN 0-590-42911-6). Scholastic Inc.

Mullin, Penn. High-Five Series: Whale Summer, Spirits of the Canyon & Trail to Danger, 3 bks. (Orig.). (gr. 7 up). 1991. Set, 64p. ea. pap. text ed. 12.50 ea. (ISBN 0-87879-913-3, High Noon Books). Acad Therapy.
The High Five Series is a set of 3 high interest (for ages 12-16)/low level (3rd grade readability) novels for youngsters who enjoy outdoor adventures based on real-life settings. Each short novel describes a vivid "close call" that rivets & holds the reader's attention. The central characters (brothers Mark & Jason Conway) are capable youngsters who use their heads in the crises that occur. Their reactions are neither too heroic nor unbelievable, & the real life facts included in each story add a ring of authenticity. Spirits of the Canyon: The world of Navajo secrets & legends about ancient spirits unfolds as the brothers explore Canyon de Chelly in the Southwest. Trail to Danger: The trail to Sky Lake leads to danger for Mark & Jason & a group of youngsters venturing into the mountains for a weekend backpacking trip. Whale Summer: A summer job at Sea Center holds excitement & surprises as Mark & Jason learn what goes on behind the scenes at the killer whale show. Each softcover novel is 64 pages & features 5 pen & ink illustrations & a 4-color cover.
Publisher Provided Annotation.

Reese, Bob. Dale the Whale. LC 82-23588. (Illus.). 24p. (ps-2). 1983. PLB 11.27 (ISBN 0-516-02313-6); pap. 2.95 (ISBN 0-516-42313-4). Childrens.
Roy, Ronald. A Thousand Pails of Water. Mai, Vo-Dinh, illus. LC 78-3275. (gr. 1-3). 1978. Knopf.
Spinelli, Jerry. Night of the Whale. (gr. k-12). 1988. pap. 3.50 (ISBN 0-440-20071-7, LFL). Dell.
Starbuck, Deborah. Manny's Whale. O'Connor, Barbara, illus. LC 85-7674. 40p. (gr. 1-3). 1986. PLB 10.95 (ISBN 0-87518-299-2, Dillon). Macmillan Child Grp.
Steig, William. Amos & Boris. Steig, William, illus. LC 72-165403. 32p. (ps-3). 1971. 16.95 (ISBN 0-374-30278-2). FS&G.
Steiner, Barbara. Whale Brother. Mayo, Gretchen W., illus. (ps-3). 1988. 12.95 (ISBN 0-8027-6804-0); PLB 13.85 (ISBN 0-8027-6805-9). Walker & Co.
Strange, Florence. Rock-a-Bye Whale. LC 77-83196. (Illus.). (gr. k-4). 1977. 11.95 (ISBN 0-931644-00-3). Manzanita Pr.
Thrush, Robin A., ed. The Gray Whales Are Missing. De Groat, Diane, illus. LC 87-17822. 144p. (gr. 3-6). 1987. 14.95 (ISBN 0-15-200455-6, Gulliver Bks). HarBraceJ.
Vollmer, Dennis. Joshua Disobeys. Vollmer, Dennis, illus. LC 88-9464. 26p. (gr. k-3). 1988. lib. bdg. 12.95 (ISBN 0-933849-12-5). Landmark Edns.
Watanabe, Yuichi. Wally the Whale Who Loved Balloons. Ooka, D. T., tr. from JPN. Watanabe, Yuichi, illus. 32p. (ps-4). 1982. 11.95 (ISBN 0-89346-150-4). Heian Intl.
Ziefert, Harriet. Henry's Wrong Turn, Vol. 1. 1989. 13.95 (ISBN 0-316-98778-6). Little.

WHALING

Graham, Ada & Graham, Frank. Whale Watch. Tyler, D. D., illus. LC 77-20531. (gr. 5 up). 1978. 7.95 (ISBN 0-440-09505-0); pap. 6.46 (ISBN 0-440-09506-9). Delacorte.
Kalman, Bobbie. Arctic Whales & Whaling. (Illus.). 56p. (gr. 3-4). 1988. 15.95 (ISBN 0-86505-146-1); pap. 7.95 (ISBN 0-86505-156-9). Crabtree Pub Co.
Stein, R. Conrad. The Story of the New England Whalers. LC 81-18107. (Illus.). (gr. 3-6). 1982. PLB 13.27 (ISBN 0-516-04634-9); pap. text ed. 3.95 (ISBN 0-516-44634-7). Childrens.

WHALING–FICTION

Melville, Herman. Billy Budd. (gr. 9 up). 1982. pap. 2.50 (ISBN 0-685-03979-X, RE). PB.
—Moby Dick. new ed. Shapiro, Irwin, ed. Nino, Alex, illus. LC 73-75458. 64p. (Orig.). (gr. 5-10). 1973. pap. 2.95 (ISBN 0-88301-099-2). Pendulum Pr.
—Moby Dick. Kirn, Elaine, adapted by. (Illus.). 62p. (gr. 7 up). 1987. pap. text ed. write for info. (ISBN 0-13-586272-8, 20381). Prentice ESL.
Sohl, Marcia & Dackerman, Gerald. Moby Dick Student Activity Book. Nino, Alex, illus. (gr. 4-10). 1976. pap. 1.25 (ISBN 0-88301-181-6). Pendulum Pr.
Tokuda, Wendy & Hall, Richard. Humphrey: The Lost Whale. Wakiyama, Hanako, illus. 32p. (gr. k-4). 1986. 11.95 (ISBN 0-89346-270-5). Heian Intl.

WHARTON, EDITH NEWBOLD (JONES), 1862-1937

Leach, William. Edith Wharton. Horner, Matina, intro. by. (Illus.). 112p. (gr. 5 up). 1988. lib. bdg. 17.95 (ISBN 1-55546-682-6). Chelsea Hse.

WHEAT

Johnson, Sylvia A. Wheat. Suzuki, Masaharu, illus. 48p. (gr. 4 up). 1990. PLB 14.95 (ISBN 0-8225-1490-7). Lerner Pubns.
Mitgutsch, Ali. From Grain to Bread. Mitgutsch, Ali, illus. LC 80-28592. 24p. (ps-3). 1981. PLB 6.95 (ISBN 0-87614-155-6). Carolrhoda Bks.
Patent, Dorothy H. Wheat: The Golden Harvest. Munoz, William, photos by. (Illus.). (ps-8). 1987. 12.95 (ISBN 0-396-08781-7, Putnam). Putnam Pub Group.

WHEATLEY, PHILLIS, 1753?-1784

Richmond, Merle. Phyllis Wheatley. Horner, Matina, intro. by. (Illus.). 112p. (Orig.). (gr. 5 up). 1989. 17.95 (ISBN 1-55546-683-4); pap. 9.95 (ISBN 0-7910-0218-7). Chelsea Hse.
Sherrow, Victoria. Phillis Wheatley. (Illus.). (gr. 3-5). 1992. PLB 12.95 (ISBN 0-7910-1753-2). Chelsea Hse.

WHEELS

Barton, Byron. Wheels. Barton, Byron, illus. LC 78-20541. 32p. (ps-3). 1979. PLB 12.89 (ISBN 0-690-03952-2, Crowell Jr Bks). HarpC Child Bks.
Fitzpatrick, Julie. Wheels. (Illus.). 32p. (gr. 3-5). 1988. PLB 9.96 (ISBN 0-382-09534-0). Silver Burdett Pr.
My First Book: Wonderful Wheels. 1991. 2.98 (ISBN 0-8317-3254-7). Smithmark.
Seymour, Peter. How Things Are Made. (Illus.). 8p. (gr. k-3). 1988. 6.95 (ISBN 0-525-67242-7, Lodestar Bks). Dutton Child Bks.
Strickland, Paul & Flint, Russ. Wheels at Work & Play, 6 vols. (Illus.). 16p. (ps-2). 1990. Set. PLB 59.70 (ISBN 0-8368-0461-9). Gareth Stevens Inc.
Taylor, Barbara. Ready Set Go: Wheels. 1991. 4.98 (ISBN 0-8317-7360-X). Smithmark.
Taylor, Henry T. Know Your Wheels. Bylenok, Marsha, contrib. by. Greenough, Jackie & Taylor, Pamela, illus. 51p. (gr. 4-6). 1981. pap. write for info. (ISBN 0-938956-00-0). H T Taylor.
Tunis, Edwin. Wheels: A Pictorial History. Tunis, Edwin, illus. LC 76-25809. 96p. (gr. 6 up). 1977. 24.95 (ISBN 0-690-01282-9, Crowell Jr Bks). HarpC Child Bks.

WHITMAN, NARCISSA (PRENTISS), 1808-1847

Sabin, Louis. Narcissa Whitman: Brave Pioneer. LC 81-23066. (Illus.). 48p. (gr. 4-6). 1982. PLB 10.79 (ISBN 0-89375-762-4); pap. text ed. 2.95 (ISBN 0-89375-763-2). Troll Assocs.

WHITNEY, ELI, 1765-1825

Alter, Judith. Eli Whitney. (Illus.). 64p. (gr. 5-8). 1990. PLB 11.90 (ISBN 0-531-10875-9). Watts.
Latham, Jean L. Eli Whitney: Great Inventor. Cary, illus. 80p. (gr. 2-6). 1991. Repr. of 1963 ed. PLB 12.95 (ISBN 0-7910-1453-3). Chelsea Hse.

WHITTINGTON, RICHARD, 1358?-1423

Garry-McCord, Kathleen, illus. Dick Whittington. LC 80-28171. 32p. (gr. k-4). 1981. PLB 9.79 (ISBN 0-89375-482-X); pap. text ed. 1.95 (ISBN 0-89375-483-8). Troll Assocs.

WHITTLING

see Wood Carving

WILD ANIMALS

see Animals

WILD BOAR

Nicholson, Darrell. Wild Boars. Blacklock, Craig, photos by. (Illus.). 48p. (gr. 2-5). 1987. PLB 12.95 (ISBN 0-87614-308-7). Carolrhoda Bks.

WILD FLOWERS

Fichter, George S. Wildflowers of North America. Barlowe, Dot, illus. LC 81-17760. 96p. (gr. 2 up). 1982. pap. 5.95 (ISBN 0-394-84770-9). Random.
Gales, Donald M. Handbook of Wildflowers, Weeds, Wildlife & Weather of the South Bay & Palos Verdes (California) 3rd, rev. ed. 240p. (gr. 8 up). 1988. pap. 12.00 (ISBN 0-317-89904-X). D M Gales.
Grimmer. ABCs of Texas Wildflowers. (Illus.). 42p. (gr. 2-5). 1988. 9.95 (ISBN 0-89015-358-2, Pub. by Panda Bks). Eakin Pr.
Keleher, Gloria. Wildflowers. (Illus.). 40p. (Orig.). (gr. 2-6). 1990. pap. 4.95 (ISBN 0-920534-32-5, Pub. by Hyperion Pr Ltd CN). Sterling.
Kinucan, Edith S. & Brons, Penney R. Wild Wildflowers of the West. (Illus.). 135p. (Orig.). (gr. 7 up). pap. 8.95 (ISBN 0-9615444-0-6). Kinucan & Brons.
Kipping, John. North American Wildflowers. Saijo, Gomper, illus. 32p. 1974. pap. 4.50 (ISBN 0-8431-1717-6). Price Stern.
Landau, Elaine. Wildflowers Around the World. (Illus.). 64p. (gr. 3-5). 1991. PLB 11.90 (ISBN 0-531-20005-1). Watts.
McMillan, Bruce. Counting Wildflowers. LC 85-16607. (Illus.). 32p. (ps-1). 1986. 13.95 (ISBN 0-688-02859-4); PLB 13.88 (ISBN 0-688-02860-8). Lothrop.
Magley, Beverly. California Wildflowers. Dowden, D. D., illus. LC 88-83883. 32p. (Orig.). (gr. 3-6). 1989. pap. 4.95 (ISBN 0-937959-58-8). Falcon Pr MT.
Podendorf, Illa. Weeds & Wild Flowers. LC 81-7737. (Illus.). 48p. (gr. k-4). 1981. PLB 14.60 (ISBN 0-516-01661-X). Childrens.

WILD FOWL

see Water Birds

WILD LIFE–CONSERVATION

see Wildlife–Conservation

Schlein, Miriam. Project Panda Watch. Shetterly, Robert, illus. LC 84-2914. 96p. (gr. 4 up). 1984. 12.95 (ISBN 0-689-31071-4, Atheneum Child Bk). Macmillan Child Grp.
Stone, Lynn M. Endangered Animals. LC 83-26323. (Illus.). 48p. (gr. k-4). 1984. lib. bdg. 14.60 (ISBN 0-516-01724-1); pap. 4.95 (ISBN 0-516-41724-X). Childrens.

WILDLIFE–CONSERVATION

see also Forests and Forestry; Game Preserves; National Parks and Reserves

Adrian, Mary. American Prairie Chicken. Vaughan-Jackson, Genevieve, illus. LC 68-21353. (gr. 2-6). 1968. 5.95g (ISBN 0-8038-0316-8). Hastings.
Ancona, George. Turtle Watch. Ancona, George, photos by. LC 87-9316. (Illus.). 48p. (gr. 1-5). 1987. 14.95 (ISBN 0-02-700910-6, Mcmillan Child Bk). Macmillan Child Grp.
Banks, M. Endangered Wildlife. (Illus.). 48p. (gr. 5 up). Date not set. PLB 18.00 (ISBN 0-86592-284-5). Rourke Corp.
Barton, Miles. Vanishing Species. (Illus.). 40p. (gr. 5-8). 1991. PLB 11.90 (ISBN 0-531-17306-2, Gloucester Pr). Watts.
Braithwaite, Althea. Leopards. (ps-6). 1988. PLB 7.95 (ISBN 0-88462-172-3); pap. 2.95 (ISBN 0-88462-173-1). Dearborn Finan.
Brown, Vinson & Lawrence, George. Californian Wildlife Region. 3rd, rev. ed. (Illus.). 224p. (gr. 4 up). 15.95 (ISBN 0-87961-200-2); pap. 8.95 (ISBN 0-87961-201-0). Naturegraph.
Brown, Vinson & Livezey, Robert. The Sierra Nevadan Wildlife Region. 3rd, rev. ed. (Illus.). 192p. (gr. 4 up). 1962. 14.95 (ISBN 0-911010-03-3); pap. 7.95 (ISBN 0-911010-02-5). Naturegraph.
Brown, Vinson, et al. Wildlife of the Intermountain West. (Illus.). 144p. (gr. 4 up). 1968. 13.95 (ISBN 0-911010-15-7); pap. 6.95 (ISBN 0-911010-14-9). Naturegraph.
Clark, Margaret G. The Vanishing Manatee. LC 89-38676. (Illus.). 64p. (gr. 4 up). 1990. 13.95 (ISBN 0-525-65024-5, Cobblestone Bks). Dutton Child Bks.
Clifford, Eth. The Wild One. Stewart, Arvis, illus. LC 74-8899. 208p. (gr. 5-9). 1974. 5.95 (ISBN 0-395-19491-1). HM.
Cook, David. Ocean Life. Cook, David, illus. LC 84-12065. 32p. (gr. 3-7). 1985. bds. 5.95 (ISBN 0-517-55429-1). Crown.
Crump, Donald J., ed. Hidden Worlds of Wildlife. (Illus.). 1990. 8.95 (ISBN 0-87044-791-2). Natl Geog.
Curtis, Patricia. All Wild Creatures Welcome: The Story of a Wildlife Rehabilitation Center. Cupp, David, illus. LC 84-28756. 160p. (gr. 5-9). 1985. 13.95 (ISBN 0-525-67164-1, Lodestar Bks). Dutton Child Bks.
Duden, Jane. Ferret. LC 89-28268. (Illus.). 48p. (gr. 5 up). 1990. 10.95 (ISBN 0-89686-517-7, Crestwood Hse). Macmillan Child Grp.
Dunmire, Marj. Wildlife of Cactus & Canyon Country. Dunmire, Marj, illus. 48p. (gr. 2-6). 1988. pap. 3.95 (ISBN 0-942559-05-3). Pegasus Graphics.
Find the Mistakes Science: Wonders of the Wild. 48p. 1990. pap. 2.95 (ISBN 0-8431-2815-1). Price Stern.
Fishbein, Sy. Yellowstone Country: The Enduring Wonder. Crump, Donald J., ed. (Illus.). 1989. 7.95 (ISBN 0-318-42772-9); lib. bdg. 9.50 (ISBN 0-87044-713-0). Natl Geog.
Ford, Barbara. Wildlife Rescue. Tucker, Kathleen, ed. Ross, Steve, illus. LC 87-6133. 47p. (gr. 3-7). 1987. PLB 10.50 (ISBN 0-8075-9099-1). A Whitman.

Gray, Ian. Birds of Prey. LC 90-33768. (Illus.). 32p. (gr. 2-4). 1991. PLB 11.90 (ISBN 0-531-18367-X). Watts.
Green, I. Conservation from A to Z. LC 66-11443. (Illus.). 64p. (gr. 4 up). 1968. PLB 10.95 (ISBN 0-87783-009-6); pap. 3.94 deluxe ed. (ISBN 0-87783-088-6). Oddo.
Greene, Carol. Caring for Our Animals. (Illus.). 32p. (gr. 1-4). 1991. PLB 12.95 (ISBN 0-89490-352-7). Enslow Pubs.
Hare, Tony. Vanishing Habitats. (Illus.). 32p. (gr. k-4). 1991. PLB 11.40 (ISBN 0-531-17350-X, Gloucester Pr). Watts.
Harrison, Virginia. Arctic Wolves in Danger. Mech, L. David, photos by. (Illus.). 32p. (gr. 2-3). 1991. PLB 11.95 (ISBN 0-8368-0148-2). Gareth Stevens Inc.
Head, W. S. The California Chaparral: An Elfin Forest. LC 75-24239. 96p. (gr. 4 up). 1972. 13.95 (ISBN 0-87961-003-4); pap. 6.95 (ISBN 0-87961-002-6). Naturegraph.
—The California Chaparral: An Elfin Forest. LC 75-24239. 96p. (gr. 4 up). 1972. 13.95 (ISBN 0-87961-003-4); pap. 6.95 (ISBN 0-87961-002-6). Naturegraph.
Irvine, Georgeanne. Protecting Endangered Species at the San Diego Zoo. (Illus.). 48p. (gr. 3-7). 1990. PLB 14.95 (ISBN 0-671-68776-X). S&S Trade.
Johnson, Louise. Malunda. DuRose, Edward, illus. LC 81-15441. 48p. (gr. k-4). 1982. PLB 9.95 (ISBN 0-87614-177-7). Carolrhoda Bks.
Lazo, Caroline E. Endangered Species. LC 90-35494. (Illus.). 48p. (gr. 5-6). 1990. RSBE 10.95 (ISBN 0-89686-545-2, Crestwood Hse). Macmillan Child Grp.
Martin, L. Rhinoceros. (Illus.). 24p. (gr. k-5). Date not set. PLB 11.93 (ISBN 0-86592-997-1). Rourke Corp.
Mayfield, Sue. I Carried You on Eagles' Wings. LC 90-28554. 128p. (gr. 6 up). 1991. text ed. 12.95 (ISBN 0-688-10597-1). Lothrop.
North American Wildlife Color & Story Album. pap. 3.95. Price Stern.
Our World in Danger. (Illus.). (gr. k-3). 3.95 (ISBN 0-7214-5217-5). Ladybird Bks.
Penny, Malcolm. Bears. LC 90-35063. (Illus.). 32p. (gr. 2-4). 1991. PLB 11.90 (ISBN 0-531-18368-8, Pub. by Bookwright Pr). Watts.
—Protecting Wildlife. LC 90-9925. (Illus.). 48p. (gr. 4-9). 1990. PLB 18.60 (ISBN 0-8114-2389-1). Steck-V.
Pringle, Laurence. Living Treasure: Saving Earth's Threatened Biodiversity. 64p. (gr. 3 up). 1991. 12.95 (ISBN 0-688-07709-9); PLB 12.88 (ISBN 0-688-07710-2, Morrow Jr Bks). Morrow Jr Bks.
Rand McNally Staff. Children's Atlas of World Wildlife. Fagan, Elizabeth, ed. Willis, Jan, illus. 96p. (gr. 3-7). 1990. 14.95 (ISBN 0-528-83409-6). Rand McNally.
Ritchie, Rita. Mountain Gorillas in Danger. Nichols, Michael, photos by. LC 91-10831. (Illus.). 32p. (gr. 2-3). 1991. PLB 11.95 (ISBN 0-8368-0447-3). Gareth Stevens Inc.
Robinson, Howard F., ed. Ranger Rick's Answer Book. Fretz, Frank, et al, illus. LC 81-81734. 96p. (gr. 2-7). 1988. Repr. of 1981 ed. 14.95 (ISBN 0-912186-40-2, 19901). Natl Wildlife.
Sibbald, Jean H. The Manatee. LC 89-26048. (Illus.). 60p. (gr. 3 up). 1990. 12.95 (ISBN 0-87518-429-4, Dillon); PLB 12.95 (ISBN 0-685-31389-1). Macmillan Child Grp.
Smith, Ronald. Sea Otter Rescue, the Aftermath of an Oil Spill. (gr. 4-7). 1990. 13.95 (ISBN 0-525-65041-5, Cobblehill Bks). Dutton Child Bks.
Springstubb, Tricia. Which Way to the Wilderness. (gr. 4-7). 1984. 14.95 (ISBN 0-316-80787-7). Little.
Stuart, Gene S. Wildlife Alert. LC 79-1792. (Illus.). 104p. (gr. 3-8). 1980. 6.95 (ISBN 0-87044-318-6); PLB 8.50 (ISBN 0-87044-323-2). Natl Geog.
Wilkes. Jungles. (gr. 4-6). 1980. (Usborne-Hayes); PLB 11.96 (ISBN 0-88110-078-1); pap. 3.95 (ISBN 0-86020-466-9). EDC.
—Wild Places. (gr. 4-6). 1980. 11.95 (ISBN 0-86020-472-3, Usborne-Hayes). EDC.
Yocom, Charles & Dasmann, Raymond. Pacific Coastal Wildlife Region. rev. ed. (Illus.). 120p. (gr. 4 up). 1965. 13.95 (ISBN 0-911010-05-X); pap. 6.95 (ISBN 0-911010-04-1). Naturegraph.

WILD LIFE–CONSERVATION–FICTION

Bailey, Jill. Operation Elephant. Green, John, illus. LC 90-46056. 48p. (gr. 3-7). 1991. PLB 17.28 (ISBN 0-8114-2706-4). Steck-V.
George, Jean C. Who Really Killed Cock Robin? An Ecological Mystery. LC 90-38659. 176p. (gr. 3-7). 1991. 14.95 (ISBN 0-06-021980-7); PLB 14.89 (ISBN 0-06-021981-5). HarpC Child Bks.
Montgomery, Rutherford G. Pekan the Shadow. Nenninger, Jerome D., illus. LC 78-84779. (gr. 8-12). 1970. 3.95 (ISBN 0-87004-132-0). Caxton.
Schlein, Miriam. The Year of the Panda. Mak, Kam, illus. LC 89-71307. 96p. (gr. 3-7). 1990. 12.95 (ISBN 0-690-04864-5, Crowell Jr Bks); PLB 12.89 (ISBN 0-690-04866-1, Crowell Jr Bks). HarpC Child Bks.
Springstubb, Tricia. Which Way to the Nearest Wilderness? (gr. k-6). 1987. pap. 2.75 (ISBN 0-440-49554-7, YB). Dell.

WILDERNESS SURVIVAL

Dixon, Franklin W. & Link, Sheila. Hardy Boys Handbook: Seven Stories of Survival. (Illus.). 144p. (gr. 3-7). 1980. PLB 8.95 (ISBN 0-671-95705-8, Little Simon); pap. 3.95 (ISBN 0-671-95602-7). S&S Trade.
Goodchild, Peter. The Spark in the Stone: Skills & Projects from the Native American Tradition. LC 90-27324. (Illus.). 144p. (Orig.). (gr. 5 up). 1991. pap. 11.95 (ISBN 1-55652-102-2). Chicago Review.
McClung, Robert M. The True Adventures of Grizzly Adams. LC 85-8886. (Illus.). 208p. (gr. 5 up). 1985. 11.95 (ISBN 0-688-05794-2). Morrow Jr Bks.
Whitefeather, Willy. Willy Whitefeather's Outdoor Survival Handbook for Kids. Whitefeather, Willy, illus. LC 89-26929. 80p. (Orig.). (gr. 3 up). 1990. pap. 6.95 (ISBN 0-943173-47-7). Harbinger AZ.
Wilderness Challenge. LC 79-3241. (Illus.). 104p. (gr. 3-8). 1980. 6.95 (ISBN 0-87044-333-X); PLB 8.50 (ISBN 0-87044-338-0). Natl Geog.
Wilderness Survival. (Illus.). 48p. (gr. 6-12). 1984. pap. 1.85 (ISBN 0-8395-3265-2, 3265). BSA.

WILDERNESS SURVIVAL–FICTION

Dygard, Thomas J. Wilderness Peril. LC 84-25577. 208p. (gr. 7 up). 1985. 12.95 (ISBN 0-688-04146-9). Morrow Jr Bks.
London, Jack. White Fang. LC 85-4297000001. 272p. (gr. 4-6). 1985. pap. 2.95 (ISBN 0-14-035045-4, Puffin). Puffin Bks.
Mathieson, David. Trial by Wilderness. 1990. pap. 3.95 (ISBN 0-395-56456-5). HM.
Paulsen, Gary. River. 1991. 15.00 (ISBN 0-385-30388-2). Doubleday.
Swiss Family Robinson. (Illus.). (gr. 3-5). 3.50 (ISBN 0-7214-0598-3). Ladybird Bks.

WILLIAM 1ST, KING OF ENGLAND, 1027-1087

May, Robin. William the Conqueror & the Normans. Wood, Gerry, illus. 64p. (gr. 7-9). 1985. 12.40 (ISBN 0-531-18010-7, Pub. by Bookwright Pr). Watts.

WILLIAMSBURG, VIRGINIA

Anderson, Joan. A Williamsburg Household. Ancona, George, photos by. LC 87-33803. 48p. (gr. 3-6). 1988. 15.95 (ISBN 0-89919-516-4, Pub. by Clarion). Ticknor & Fields.
Anderson, Joan W. Williamsburg Household. (gr. 4-7). 1990. pap. 5.95 (ISBN 0-395-54791-1, Clarion Bks). HM.
Bethell, Jean & Axtell, Susan. A Colonial Williamsburg Activities Book: Fun Things to Do for Children 4 & Up. Wallner, Susan, illus. 40p. (ps). 1984. pap. 2.95 (ISBN 0-87935-068-7). Williamsburg.
Fortunato, Pat. A Colonial Williamsburg Activities Book: Fun Activities for Young Visitors. Wallner, John, illus. 48p. (Orig.). (gr. 1-4). 1982. pap. 2.95 (ISBN 0-87935-062-8). Williamsburg.
Wooten, Vernon. The Colonial Williamsburg Coloring Book. (Illus.). 36p. (Orig.). (gr. 1). 1979. pap. 1.50 (ISBN 0-87935-052-0). Williamsburg.

WILLIAMSBURG, VIRGINIA–FICTION

Cavanna, Betty. Two's Company. Smith, Edward J., illus. 190p. (gr. 5-9). 1951. 6.95 (ISBN 0-664-32080-5, Westminster). Westminster John Knox.

Coon, Alma S. Amy, Ben, & Catalpa the Cat: A Fanciful Story of This & That. Owens, Gail, illus. 40p. (ps-2). 1990. 5.95 (ISBN 0-87935-079-2). Williamsburg.
In this beautifully illustrated, full-color alphabet storybook in verse, Amy, Ben, & Catalpa the Cat take children on a fun-filled day in eighteenth-century Williamsburg. The story, set in early autumn, opens at Amy & Ben's home, where Ben is harvesting pumpkins, Amy is baking apple pies, & playful Catalpa is constantly underfoot. But no sooner does the fifer pass by their window than they are off to the fair! During their adventures in Williamsburg the heroes introduce young readers to George Washington & other eighteenth-century characters as well as to various colonial activities such as a fair, a ride in an oxcart, children's games, & a visit to Tarpley's Store. The inviting illustrations colorfully re-create authentic colonial clothing, architecture, agriculture, & animal husbandry. To order: Colonial Williamsburg Wholesale Sales, PO Box C, Williamsburg, VA 23187, (804) 220-7178.
Publisher Provided Annotation.

WILLIAMSBURG, VIRGINIA–HISTORY

Colonial Williamsburg Foundation Staff. The Apprentice. (Illus.). 38p. (Orig.). (gr. 5-7). 1984. pap. 2.50 (ISBN 0-87935-103-9). Williamsburg.

WILSON, WOODROW, PRESIDENT U. S. 1856-1924

Collins, David R. Woodrow Wilson: Twenty-Eighth President of the United States. Young, Richard G., ed. LC 88-24563. (gr. 5-9). 1989. PLB 17.26 (ISBN 0-944483-18-6). Garrett Ed Corp.
Osinski, Alice. Woodrow Wilson. LC 88-8678. (Illus.). 100p. (gr. 3 up). 1989. PLB 17.27 (ISBN 0-516-01367-X). Childrens.
Vexler, Robert I. Woodrow Wilson, 1856-1924: Chronology, Documents, Bibliographical Aids. LC 78-83747. 123p. (gr. 9 up). 1969. PLB 10.00 (ISBN 0-379-12061-5). Oceana.
Woodrow Wilson: Mini-Play. (gr. 8 up). 1978. 6.50 (ISBN 0-89550-315-8). Stevens & Shea.

WIND

see Winds

WIND INSTRUMENTS

see also Bands (Music)

Arban, Jean B. Complete Conservatory Method for Trumpet (Cornet) or E-Flat Alto, B-Flat Tenor, Baritone, Euphonium & B-Flat Bass in Treble Clef. Goldman, Edwin F. & Smith, Walter M., eds. 350p. (Orig.). 1936. pap. 21.95 (ISBN 0-8258-0010-2, 021). Fischer Inc NY.
Bunting, Janet. My First Recorder Book. (Illus.). 32p. (gr. 2-6). 1989. Incl. recorder. pap. 12.95 (ISBN 0-8120-7618-4). Barron.
Klose, Hyacinthe. Celebrated Method for the Clarinet: Complete Edition. Bellison, Simeon, ed. 293p. (Orig.). 1946. pap. 16.95 (ISBN 0-8258-0051-X, 0304). Fischer Inc NY.
Let's Play Recorder Pack. (Illus., Orig.). 1988. pap. 12.95 (ISBN 0-88188-849-4, HL 00710008). H Leonard Pub Corp.
Poffenberg, Nancy & Bane, Rosemary. Instant Recorder Package 2. Shaffer, Jim, illus. 32p. (Orig.). (gr. 3-6). 1989. pap. write for info. incl. recorder (ISBN 0-938293-17-6). Fun Pub OH.
Wagner, Ernst F. Foundation to Flute Playing: An Elementary Method. rev. ed. 120p. (Orig.). 1918. pap. 12.95 (ISBN 0-8258-0054-4, 0223). Fischer Inc NY.

WINDMILLS

Rickard, Graham. Wind Energy. (Illus.). 32p. (gr. 4-6). 1991. PLB 11.95 (ISBN 0-8368-0711-1). Gareth Stevens Inc.

WINDOW GARDENING

see also House Plants

WINDOWS, STAINED GLASS

see Glass Painting and Staining

WINDS

see also Hurricanes; Storms; Tornadoes

Bailey, Donna. Energy from Wind & Water. LC 90-39388. (Illus.). 48p. (gr. 2-5). 1990. PLB 15.96 (ISBN 0-8114-2519-3). Steck-V.
Cross, Mike. Wind Power. LC 85-70600. (Illus.). 31p. (gr. 4-8). 1985. PLB 11.90 (ISBN 0-531-17007-1, Gloucester Pr). Watts.
Dorros, Arthur. Feel the Wind. Dorros, Arthur, illus. LC 88-18961. 32p. (ps-3). 1989. 13.95 (ISBN 0-690-04739-8, Crowell Jr Bks); PLB 13.89 (ISBN 0-690-04741-X, Crowell Jr Bks). HarpC Child Bks.
Lafferty, Peter. Wind to Flight: Projects with the Wind. (Illus.). 32p. (gr. 5-6). 1989. PLB 11.90 (ISBN 0-531-17166-3). Watts.
McDonnell, Janet. Wind: What Can It Do? Connelly, Gwen, illus. LC 89-24011. 32p. (ps-2). 1990. lib. bdg. 11.97 (ISBN 0-89565-555-1). Childs World.
Pendergraft, Patricia. Hear the Wind Blow. 1989. pap. 2.75 (ISBN 0-590-42273-1). Scholastic Inc.
Santrey, Laurence. What Makes the Wind? Dodson, Bert, illus. LC 81-5486. 32p. (gr. 2-4). 1982. PLB 10.89 (ISBN 0-89375-584-2); pap. text ed. 2.95 (ISBN 0-89375-585-0); cassette avail. Troll Assocs.
Smith, Norman F. Wind Power. (gr. 3-7). 1981. PLB 6.99 (ISBN 0-698-30732-1, Coward). Putnam Pub Group.
Steele, Philip. Wind: Causes & Effects. (Illus.). 32p. (gr. 5-8). 1991. PLB 11.90 (ISBN 0-531-11024-9). Watts.
Taylor, Barbara. Wind & Weather. (Illus.). 32p. (gr. 5-8). 1991. PLB 11.40 (ISBN 0-531-14184-5). Watts.

WINDS–FICTION

Boyd, Patricia R. The Furry Wind. Spring, Grace J., illus. 28p. (gr. 2-3). 1982. pap. 2.25 (ISBN 0-9603840-4-9). Andrew Mtn Pr.
Fleischman, Sid. McBroom & the Big Wind. Lorraine, Walter H., illus. 48p. (gr. 3 up). 1982. (Pub. by Atlantic Monthly Pr); pap. 3.95 (ISBN 0-316-28544-7). Little.
Greene, Carol. Please, Wind? LC 82-4548. (Illus.). (ps-2). 1982. PLB 11.93 (ISBN 0-516-02033-1); pap. 2.95 (ISBN 0-516-42033-X). Childrens.
Hutchins, Pat. The Wind Blew. LC 73-11691. (Illus.). 32p. (ps-2). 1974. 13.95 (ISBN 0-02-745910-1, Mcmillan Child Bk). Macmillan Child Grp.
—The Wind Blew. Hutchins, Pat, illus. 32p. (ps-1). 1986. pap. 3.95 (ISBN 0-14-050236-X, Puffin). Puffin Bks.
McKay, Louise & McKay, George. Marny's Ride with the Wind. Smetana, Margaret, illus. (gr. k-3). 1979. 6.95 (ISBN 0-934986-00-2). New Harbinger.
Martin, Jacqueline B. Bizzy Bones & Uncle Ezra. Ormai, Stella, illus. LC 83-25618. 32p. (ps-2). 1984. PLB 12.88 (ISBN 0-688-03782-8). Lothrop.
Townsend, Tom. Queen of the Wind. Roberts, Melissa, ed. (Illus.). 144p. (gr. 8-10). 1989. 12.95 (ISBN 0-89015-715-4, Pub. by Panda Bks). Eakin Pr.
Widman, Christine. Housekeeper of the Wind. Desimini, Lisa, illus. LC 88-10979. 32p. (ps-3). 1990. 15.95 (ISBN 0-06-026467-5); PLB 15.89 (ISBN 0-06-026468-3). HarpC Child Bks.

WINTER

Allington, Richard L. & Krull, Kathleen. Winter. Wallner, John, illus. LC 80-25115. 32p. (gr. k-3). 1985. PLB 15.33 (ISBN 0-8172-1340-6); pap. 9.27 (ISBN 0-8172-2497-1). Raintree Pubs.
Bauman, Toni & Zinkgraf, June. Winter Wonders. 240p. (gr. k-6). 1978. 14.95 (ISBN 0-916456-29-3, GA89). Good Apple.

Carson, Patti & Dellosa, Janet. Winter Preschool-K Practice. Carson, Patti & Dellosa, Janet, illus. 32p. (ps-k). 1984. pap. 1.98 (ISBN 0-88724-016-X, CD-8031). Carson-Dellos.

—Winter Primary Reading & Art Activities. Carson, Patti & Dellosa, Janet, illus. 32p. (gr. 1-3). 1984. pap. 1.98 (ISBN 0-88724-023-2, CD-8038). Carson-Dellos.

Craig, Janet. Here Comes Winter. Karas, G. Brian, illus. LC 87-13738. 32p. (gr. k-2). 1988. PLB 7.06 (ISBN 0-8167-1225-5); pap. text ed. 1.95 (ISBN 0-8167-1226-3). Troll Assocs.

Davis, Nancy M., et al. Winter. Davis, Nancy M., illus. 29p. (ps-2). 1986. pap. 4.95 (ISBN 0-937103-05-5). DaNa Pubns.

Dellosa, Janet & Carson, Patti. Winter Fun Book. Dellosa, Janet & Carson, Patti, illus. 32p. (ps-2). 1984. pap. 1.59 (ISBN 0-88724-060-7, CD-8048). Carson-Dellos.

Freedman, Russell. When Winter Comes. Johnson, Pamela, illus. LC 80-22831. (gr. 1-3). 1981. 10.95 (ISBN 0-525-42583-7, DCB). Dutton Child Bks.

Glover, Suzanne & Grewe, Georgeann. A Splash of Winter. Grewe, Georgeann, illus. 128p. (gr. 2-5). 1987. pap. 9.95 (ISBN 0-86653-411-3). Good Apple.

Hartwig, Judy. Celebrate Winter. Filkins, Vanessa, illus. 144p. (gr. k-3). 1985. wkbk. 10.95 (ISBN 0-86653-266-8, SS 839). Good Apple.

Hirschi, Ron. Winter. (ps-3). 1990. 13.95 (ISBN 0-525-65026-1, Cobblehill Bks). Dutton Child Bks.

Kalman, Bobbie. We Celebrate Winter. (Illus.). 56p. (gr. 3-4). 1986. 15.95 (ISBN 0-86505-046-5); pap. 7.95 (ISBN 0-86505-056-2). Crabtree Pub Co.

Linam, Gail. God's Winter Gifts. (Illus.). (ps) 1991. pap. 3.75 (ISBN 0-8054-4158-1, 4142-58). Broadman.

McInnes, Celia. Projects for Winter & Holiday Activities. Young, Richard G., ed. Yates, John, illus. LC 88-33515. 32p. (gr. 3-5). 1989. PLB 14.60 (ISBN 0-944483-41-0). Garrett Ed Corp.

Markle, Sandra. Exploring Winter. Markle, Sandra, illus. LC 84-3049. 160p. (gr. 4-6). 1984. 14.95 (ISBN 0-689-31065-X, Atheneum Child Bk). Macmillan Child Grp.

Moncure, Jane B. Step into Winter: A New Season. Hohag, Linda, illus. LC 90-30636. 32p. (ps-2). 1990. lib. bdg. 11.97 (ISBN 0-89565-574-8). Childs World.

—Word Bird's Winter Words. Gohman, Vera, illus. LC 85-5942. 32p. (gr. k-2). 1985. lib. bdg. 11.97 (ISBN 0-89565-309-5); pap. 6.96 (ISBN 0-89565-427-X). Childs World.

Santrey, Louis. Winter. Sabin, Francene, illus. LC 82-19353. 32p. (gr. 4-7). 1982. lib. bdg. 10.79 (ISBN 0-89375-907-4); pap. text ed. 2.95 (ISBN 0-89375-908-2). Troll Assocs.

Thomson, Ruth. Winter. (Illus.). 32p. (gr. k-4). 1989. PLB 11.90 (ISBN 0-531-10733-7). Watts.

Webster, David. Winter. Steltenpohl, Jane, ed. Steadman, Barbara, illus. 48p. (gr. 2-4). 1989. lib. bdg. 10.98 (ISBN 0-671-65861-1); pap. 4.95 (ISBN 0-671-65986-3). Messner.

Webster, Harriet. Winter Book. Trivas, Irene, illus. LC 88-1662. 128p. (Orig.). (gr. 3-7). 1988. pap. 4.95 (ISBN 0-689-71235-9, Aladdin). Macmillan Child Grp.

—Winter Book. Trivas, Irene, illus. LC 88-4371. 128p. (gr. 3-7). 1988. 12.95 (ISBN 0-684-18891-0, Scribners Young Read). Macmillan Child Grp.

Whitlock, Ralph. Winter. (Illus.). 48p. (gr. 1-6). 1987. lib. bdg. 12.90 (ISBN 0-531-18141-3, Pub. by Bookwright Pr). Watts.

WINTER–FICTION

Andersen, Hans Christian. The Snow Queen. Philip, Neil, tr. from DAN. Holmes, Sally, illus. LC 89-45289. 64p. 1989. 14.95 (ISBN 0-688-09047-8); PLB 14.88 (ISBN 0-688-09048-6). Lothrop.

Blades, Ann. Winter. Blades, Ann, illus. (ps-k). 1990. bds. 4.95 (ISBN 0-688-09233-0). Lothrop.

Briggs, Raymond. The Snowman, No. 8612-4. (Illus.). (ps-4). 1990. 3.50 (ISBN 0-7214-1109-6). Ladybird Bks.

Cartwright, Ann. The Winter Hedgehog. Cartwright, Reg, illus. LC 90-5593. 32p. (ps-3). 1990. 12.95 (ISBN 0-02-717775-0, Mcmillan Child Bk). Macmillan Child Grp.

Coleridge, Sara. January Brings the Snow. 1989. pap. 4.95 (ISBN 0-8037-0704-5, Dial). Doubleday.

Craft, Ruth. The Winter Bear. Blegvad, Erik, illus. LC 74-18178. 32p. (ps-3). 1975. 13.95 (ISBN 0-689-50017-3, M K McElderry). Macmillan Child Grp.

Delton, Judy. Walk on a Snowy Night. Rosner, Ruth, illus. LC 81-48660. 32p. (gr. k-3). 1982. 9.57 (ISBN 0-685-05506-X). HarpC Child Bks.

Elliot, Suzanne. Winter's Gift. (Illus.). 160p. 1987. pap. 4.99 (ISBN 0-87403-270-9, 2947). Standard Pub.

Hasler, Eveline. Winter Magic. Lemieux, Michele, illus. LC 85-2944. (ps-3). 1985. lib. bdg. 12.88 (ISBN 0-688-05258-4). Morrow Jr Bks.

Haywood, Carolyn. Betsy's Winterhouse. Haywood, Carolyn, illus. LC 55-8453. 192p. (gr. 3-7). 1955. PLB 13.88 (ISBN 0-688-31090-7, Morrow Junior Books). Morrow.

Hol, Coby. Lisa & the Snowman. Hol, Coby, illus. LC 89-42614. 32p. (gr. k-3). 1989. 13.95 (ISBN 1-55858-022-0). North-South Bks NYC.

Hurwitz, Johanna. The Cold & Hot Winter. (gr. 3-7). 1989. pap. 2.75 (ISBN 0-590-42619-2, Apple Paperbacks). Scholastic Inc.

Josefowitz, Natasha. A Hundred Scoops of Ice Cream: Tiny Tales. Mietzelfeld, Mary, illus. 64p. (gr. 1 up). 1988. bds. 7.95x (ISBN 0-312-01444-9). St Martin.

Landis, Mary M. Ice Slide Winter: Merry Brook Farm Story. (gr. 5 up). 1981. 8.25 (ISBN 0-686-30772-0). Rod & Staff.

Lawson, Robert. The Tough Winter. Lawson, Robert, illus. (gr. 3-7). 1979. pap. 3.95 (ISBN 0-14-031215-3, Puffin). Puffin Bks.

Lewis, Rob. Henrietta's First Winter. (Illus.). 32p. (ps-3). 1990. 11.95 (ISBN 0-374-32951-6). FS&G.

Moncure, Jane B. Winter Is Here! Hook, Frances, illus. LC 75-14201. (ps-2). 1975. 8.95 (ISBN 0-913778-10-9); cassette 13.95 (ISBN 0-685-01068-6); walk chart 10.95. Childs World.

Morey, Walt. Canyon Winter. (gr. 4 up). 1972. 15.95 (ISBN 0-525-27410-3, DCB). Dutton Child Bks.

Morgan, Ellen. Another Winter's Tale. 179p. (gr. 5-8). 1989. 17.95 (ISBN 0-434-95166-8, Pub. by W Heinemann Ltd). Trafalgar Sq.

Parnall, Peter. Winter Barn. Parnall, Peter, illus. LC 86-23898. 32p. (gr. k-3). 1986. 13.95 (ISBN 0-02-770170-0, Mcmillan Child Bk). Macmillan Child Grp.

Paulsen, Gary. Winter Room. (gr. 4-7). 1991. pap. 3.50 (ISBN 0-440-40454-1). Dell.

Peters, Sharon. Here Comes Jack Frost. Connor, Eulala, illus. LC 81-4093. 32p. (gr. k-2). 1981. PLB 10.89 (ISBN 0-89375-513-3); pap. text ed. 2.95 (ISBN 0-89375-514-1). Troll Assocs.

Ransome, Arthur. Winter Holiday. LC 87-46246. (gr. 4-6). 1989. pap. 10.95 (ISBN 0-87923-661-2). Godine.

St. John, Patricia. Treasures of the Snow. (gr. 5-8). 1950. pap. 4.50 (ISBN 0-8024-0008-6). Moody.

Shaw, Janet. Changes for Kirsten: A Winter Story. Thieme, Jeanne, ed. Graef, Renee, illus. 72p. (gr. 2-5). 1990. PLB 12.95 (ISBN 0-937295-94-9). Pleasant Co.

Stevenson, James. Brrr! LC 89-34615. (Illus.). 32p. (ps up). 1991. 13.95 (ISBN 0-688-09210-1); PLB 13.88 (ISBN 0-688-09211-X). Greenwillow.

Todhunter, Jean M. Cipher in the Snow. 2nd ed. 6p. (gr. 8-12). 1988. pap. 1.95 stiched with dustcover (ISBN 0-929985-07-9). Sonos.

Tripp, Valerie. Changes for Molly: A Winter Story. Thieme, Jeanne, ed. Backes, Nick, illus. 72p. (gr. 2-5). 1990. PLB 12.95 (ISBN 0-937295-96-5). Pleasant Co.

—Changes for Samantha: A Winter Story. Thieme, Jeanne, ed. Grace, Robert & Niles, Nancy, illus. 72p. (gr. 2-5). 1990. PLB 12.95 (ISBN 0-937295-95-7). Pleasant Co.

Watson, Wendy. Has Winter Come? Watson, Wendy, illus. (gr. 1-4). 1981. 3.95 (ISBN 0-399-20799-6, Philomel). Putnam Pub Group.

Welber, Robert. Winter Picnic. Ray, Deborah, illus. LC 77-77418. (gr. 7 up). 1970. lib. bdg. 5.99 (ISBN 0-394-90444-3). Pantheon.

Ziefert, Harriet. Please Let It Snow. LC 88-82399. (Illus.). 32p. (ps-3). 1989. pap. 8.95 (ISBN 0-670-82665-0). Viking Child Bks.

WINTER–POETRY

Prelutsky, Jack. It's Snowing! It's Snowing! Titherington, Jeanne, illus. LC 83-16583. 48p. (gr. 1-3). 1984. 12.95 (ISBN 0-688-01512-3); PLB 12.88 (ISBN 0-688-01513-1). Greenwillow.

WINTER SPORTS
see also Hockey; Skating; Skis and Skiing
Barrett, Norman. Snow Sports. Franklin Watts Ltd., ed. (Illus.). 32p. (ps-9). 1989. 10.90 (ISBN 0-531-10353-6). Watts.

Galde, Dorothy A. Avalanche! LC 86-6212. 144p. (gr. 4-7). 1986. pap. 3.95 (ISBN 0-89191-253-3). Cook.

Hall, Jackie. Skiing & Snow Sports. 1990. PLB 12.90 (ISBN 0-531-19075-7). Watts.

Popp, Dennis. Ice Racing. LC 72-5421. (Illus.). 48p. (gr. 4-9). 1973. PLB 9.95 (ISBN 0-8225-0403-0). Lerner Pubns.

The Winter Olympics. 32p. (gr. 4). 1990. 12.95s.p. (ISBN 0-88682-317-X); 18.50 (ISBN 0-685-28232-5). Creative Ed.

WIRELESS
see Radio
WISCONSIN
Aylesworth, Thomas G. & Aylesworth, Virginia L. Western Great Lakes (Illinois, Iowa, Wisconsin, Minnesota) (Illus.). 64p. (gr. 3 up). 1992. PLB 16.95 (ISBN 0-7910-1046-5). Chelsea Hse.

Bratvold, Gretchen. Wisconsin. (Illus.). 72p. (gr. 3-6). 1991. PLB 12.95 (ISBN 0-8225-2700-6). Lerner Pubns.

Calhoun, Sharon C. & English, Billy J. The Wisconsin Story. 202p. (gr. 4). 1987. 12.95 (ISBN 0-9619484-0-X, TXU-299476); 49.95 (ISBN 0-318-23764-4). Apple Corps Pubs.

Carole Marsh Wisconsin Books, 31 bks. Set. 638.45 (ISBN 0-7933-1324-4). Gallopade Pub Group.

Carpenter, Allan. Wisconsin. new ed. LC 77-13666. (Illus.). 96p. (gr. 4 up). 1978. PLB 19.93 (ISBN 0-516-04149-5). Childrens.

Fradin, Dennis. Wisconsin: In Words & Pictures. Ulm, Robert, illus. LC 77-5330. 48p. (gr. 2-5). 1977. PLB 15.93 (ISBN 0-516-03948-2). Childrens.

Goc, Michael. Land Rich Enough: An Illustrated History of Oshkosh & Winnebago County. (Illus.). 128p. (gr. 7 up). 1988. 27.95 (ISBN 0-89781-253-0). Windsor Pubns Inc.

Hall, Betty L. Wisconsin Survival. rev. ed. 160p. (gr. 10-12). 1986. pap. text ed. 5.84 (ISBN 0-936159-01-4). Westwood Pr.

Marsh, Carole. Avast, Ye Slobs! Wisconsin Pirate Trivia. (Illus.). 1990. PLB 19.95 (ISBN 0-7933-1244-2); pap. 14.95 (ISBN 0-7933-1243-4); computer disk 29.95 (ISBN 0-7933-1245-0). Gallopade Pub Group.

—The Beast of the Wisconsin Bed & Breakfast. (Illus.). 1990. PLB 19.95 (ISBN 0-7933-2276-6); pap. 14.95 (ISBN 0-7933-2277-4); computer disk 29.95 (ISBN 0-7933-2278-2). Gallopade Pub Group.

—The Hard-to-Believe-But-True! Book of Wisconsin History, Mystery, Trivia, Legend, Lore, Humor & More. (Illus.). 1990. PLB 19.95 (ISBN 0-7933-1241-8); pap. 14.95 (ISBN 0-7933-1240-X); computer disk 29.95 (ISBN 0-7933-1242-6). Gallopade Pub Group.

—If My Wisconsin Mama Ran the World! (Illus.). 1990. PLB 19.95 (ISBN 0-7933-2285-5); pap. 14.95 (ISBN 0-7933-2286-3); computer disk 29.95 (ISBN 0-7933-2287-1). Gallopade Pub Group.

—Let's Quilt Wisconsin & Stuff It Topographically! (Illus.). 1990. PLB 19.95 (ISBN 0-7933-2268-5); pap. 14.95 (ISBN 1-55609-098-6); computer disk 29.95 (ISBN 0-7933-2269-3). Gallopade Pub Group.

—Wisconsin & Other State Greats (Biographies) (Illus.). 1990. PLB 19.95 (ISBN 0-7933-2288-X); pap. 14.95 (ISBN 0-7933-2289-8); computer Disk 29.95 (ISBN 0-7933-2290-1). Gallopade Pub Group.

—Wisconsin Bandits, Bushwackers, Outlaws, Crooks, Devils, Ghosts, Desperadoes & Other Assorted & Sundry Characters! (Illus.). 1990. PLB 19.95 (ISBN 0-7933-1226-4); pap. 14.95 (ISBN 0-7933-1225-6); computer disk 29.95 (ISBN 0-7933-1227-2). Gallopade Pub Group.

—Wisconsin Classic Christmas Trivia: Stories, Recipes, Activities, Legends, Lore & More. (Illus.). 1990. PLB 19.95 (ISBN 0-7933-1229-9); pap. 14.95 (ISBN 0-7933-1228-0); computer disk 29.95 (ISBN 0-7933-1230-2). Gallopade Pub Group.

—Wisconsin Coastales. (Illus.). 1990. 19.95 (ISBN 0-7933-2282-0); pap. 14.95 (ISBN 0-7933-2283-9); computer disk 29.95 (ISBN 0-7933-2284-7). Gallopade Pub Group.

—The Wisconsin Hot Air Balloon Mystery. (Illus.). (gr. 2-9). 1990. 19.95 (ISBN 0-7933-2759-8); pap. 14.95 (ISBN 0-7933-2760-1); computer disk 29.95 (ISBN 0-7933-2761-X). Gallopade Pub Group.

—Wisconsin "Jography" A Fun Run Thru Our State! (Illus.). 1990. PLB 19.95 (ISBN 0-7933-2265-0); pap. 14.95 (ISBN 0-7933-2266-9); computer disk 29.95 (ISBN 0-7933-2267-7). Gallopade Pub Group.

—Wisconsin Kid's Cookbook: Recipes, How-To, History, Lore & More! (Illus.). 1990. PLB 19.95 (ISBN 0-7933-1238-8); pap. 14.95 (ISBN 0-7933-1237-X); computer disk 29.95 (ISBN 0-7933-1239-6). Gallopade Pub Group.

—Wisconsin Quiz Bowl Crash Course! (Illus.). 1990. PLB 19.95 (ISBN 0-7933-2279-0); pap. 14.95 (ISBN 0-7933-2280-4); computer disk 29.95 (ISBN 0-7933-2281-2). Gallopade Pub Group.

—Wisconsin School Trivia: An Amazing & Fascinating Look at Our State's Teachers, Schools & Students! (Illus.). 1990. PLB 19.95 (ISBN 0-7933-1235-3); pap. 14.95 (ISBN 0-7933-1234-5); computer disk 29.95 (ISBN 0-7933-1236-1). Gallopade Pub Group.

—Wisconsin Silly Basketball Sportsmysteries, Vol. 1. (Illus.). 1990. PLB 19.95 (ISBN 0-7933-1232-9); pap. 14.95 (ISBN 0-7933-1231-0); computer disk 29.95 (ISBN 0-7933-1233-7). Gallopade Pub Group.

—Wisconsin Silly Basketball Sportsmysteries, Vol. 2. (Illus.). 1990. PLB 19.95 (ISBN 0-7933-2291-X); pap. 14.95 (ISBN 0-7933-2292-8); computer disk 29.95 (ISBN 0-7933-2293-6). Gallopade Pub Group.

—Wisconsin Silly Football Sportsmysteries, Vol. 1. (Illus.). 1990. PLB 19.95 (ISBN 0-7933-2270-7); pap. 14.95 (ISBN 0-7933-2271-5); computer disk 29.95 (ISBN 0-7933-2272-3). Gallopade Pub Group.

—Wisconsin Silly Football Sportsmysteries, Vol. 2. (Illus.). 1990. PLB 19.95 (ISBN 0-7933-2273-1); pap. 14.95 (ISBN 0-7933-2274-X); computer disk 29.95 (ISBN 0-7933-2275-8). Gallopade Pub Group.

—Wisconsin Silly Trivia! (Illus.). 1990. PLB 19.95 (ISBN 0-7933-2262-6); pap. 14.95 (ISBN 0-7933-2263-4); computer disk 29.95 (ISBN 0-7933-2264-2). Gallopade Pub Group.

—Wisconsin's (Most Devastating!) Disasters & (Most Calamitous!) Catastrophies! (Illus.). 1990. PLB 19.95 (ISBN 0-7933-1223-X); pap. 14.95 (ISBN 0-7933-1222-1); computer disk 29.95 (ISBN 0-7933-1224-8). Gallopade Pub Group.

Stein, R. Conrad. Wisconsin. LC 87-9376. (Illus.). 144p. (gr. 4 up). 1987. PLB 25.27 (ISBN 0-516-00495-6). Childrens.

Turner Program Services, Inc. Staff & Clark, James I. Wisconsin. 48p. (gr. 3 up). 1985. PLB 17.32 (ISBN 0-86514-448-6); pap. text ed. 9.27 (ISBN 0-86514-523-7); cancelled Beta video (ISBN 0-86514-073-1); cancelled VHS video (ISBN 0-86514-148-7); cancelled 3/4" video (ISBN 0-86514-223-8); cancelled tchr's. guide (ISBN 0-86514-298-X); cancelled student activity bk.; cancelled index. Raintree Pubs.

WISCONSIN–FICTION
Enright, Elizabeth. Thimble Summer. Enright, Elizabeth, illus. LC 38-27586. 134p. (gr. 4-6). 1938. 15.95 (ISBN 0-8050-0306-1). H Holt & Co.

Hall, Lynn. Flyaway. LC 87-12824. 128p. (gr. 7 up). 1987. 12.95 (ISBN 0-684-18888-0, Scribners Young Read). Macmillan Child Grp.

Pellowski, Anne. Winding Valley Farm: Annie's Story. Watson, Wendy, illus. 192p. 1982. 9.95 (ISBN 0-399-20863-1, Philomel). Putnam Pub Group.

Wilder, Laura I. Little House in the Big Woods. rev. ed. Williams, Garth, illus. LC 52-7525. (gr. 1-6). 1953. 14. 95i (ISBN 0-06-026430-6); PLB 14.89 (ISBN 0-06-026431-4). HarpC Child Bks.

WIT AND HUMOR

see also Anecdotes; Comedy; Epigrams; Nonsense Verses
also American Wit and Humor; English Wit and Humor

Ahlberg, Allan. Funnybones. Ahlberg, Janet, illus. LC 79-24872. 32p. (gr. k-3). 1981. 12.88 (ISBN 0-688-80238-9); PLB 11.88 (ISBN 0-688-84238-0). Greenwillow.

Ahlberg, Janet & Ahlberg, Allan. The Old Joke Book. (Illus.). (gr. 2-5). 1987. pap. 3.95 (ISBN 0-14-050596-2, Puffin). Puffin Bks.

Alden, Laura, compiled by. Dinosaur Jokes. Magnuson, Diana, illus. LC 88-17489. 48p. (gr. 1-5). 1988. lib. bdg. 13.27 (ISBN 0-516-01865-5); pap. 3.95 (ISBN 0-516-41865-3). Childrens.

Allard, Harry & Marshall, James. The Stupids Die. (Illus.). (gr. k-3). 1981. 13.95 (ISBN 0-395-30347-8); pap. 3.95 (ISBN 0-395-38364-1). HM.

Alpern, Lynne & Blumenfeld, Esther. In-Laws, Out-Laws & Other Theories of Relativity. Warlick, Cal, illus. 128p. (Orig.). 1990. pap. 6.95 (ISBN 0-934601-94-1). Peachtree Pubs.

Amery & Adair. Jokes & Tricks. (gr. 4-6). 1977. pap. 5.95 (ISBN 0-86020-034-5, Usborne-Hayes). EDC.

Batchelor, C. Fun, Magic & Jokes. (Illus.). 32p. (gr. 2-6). 1985. pap. 4.95 (ISBN 0-88625-072-2). Durkin Hayes Pub.

Baum, L. Frank. The Woggle-Bug Book. LC 78-6887. (gr. 1-6). 1978. Repr. of 1905 ed. 35.00x (ISBN 0-8201-1308-5). Schol Facsimiles.

Berger, Melvin. One Hundred & One Wacky Science Jokes. 1989. pap. 1.95 (ISBN 0-590-42388-6). Scholastic Inc.

—One Hundred One President Jokes. 1990. pap. 1.95 (ISBN 0-590-43166-8). Scholastic Inc.

Bernstein, Joanne E. & Cohen, Paul. Dizzy Doctor Riddles. Tucker, Kathy, ed. Whiting, Carl, illus. LC 89-35392. 32p. (gr. 2-4). 1989. 8.95 (ISBN 0-8075-1648-1). A Whitman.

—Out to Pasture! Jokes about Cows. Hanson, Joan, illus. 32p. (gr. 1-4). 1988. PLB 8.95 (ISBN 0-8225-0998-9). Lerner Pubns.

—Why Didn't the Dinosaur Cross the Road? And Other Prehistoric Riddles. Tucker, Kathy, ed. Whiting, Carl, illus. 32p. (gr. 1-5). 1990. 8.95 (ISBN 0-8075-9077-0). A Whitman.

Black, Sonia. Laugh-A-Minute Joke Book. (gr. 4up). 1989. pap. 1.95 (ISBN 0-590-42154-9). Scholastic Inc.

—One Hundred One Outer Space Jokes. 1990. pap. 1.95 (ISBN 0-590-42972-8). Scholastic Inc.

Blake, Robert, ed. One Hundred & One Elephant Jokes. (Illus., Orig.). (gr. 6-9). pap. 1.95 (ISBN 0-590-41062-8). Scholastic Inc.

Bleedorn, Berenice & McKelvey, Sara. Humor: Lessons in Laughter for Learning & Living. Rossi, Richard, illus. Torrance, E. Paul, intro. by. (Illus.). 28p. (Orig.). (gr. 3-12). 1984. 5.50 (ISBN 0-88047-042-9, 8407). DOK Pubs.

Blume, Judy. Superfudge. 176p. (gr. 2-6). 1981. pap. 3.50 (ISBN 0-440-48433-2, YB). Dell.

Bolton, Martha. T. V. Jokes & Riddles. (Illus.). 96p. (gr. 3-10). 1991. 12.95 (ISBN 0-8069-7244-0). Sterling.

Bonham, Frank. Durango Street. (gr. 7 up). 1967. 15.95 (ISBN 0-525-28950-X, DCB). Dutton Child Bks.

Bonham, Tal D. The Treasury of Clean Jokes for Children. (Orig.). (gr. 1-6). 1987. pap. 3.95 (ISBN 0-8054-5721-6). Broadman.

Brandeth, Gyles. The Emergency Joke Kit. Brown, Judy, illus. (Orig.). (ps-3). 1988. pap. 3.95 (ISBN 0-14-095322-1, Puffin). Puffin Bks.

Brandreth, Gyles. The Super Joke Book. Barrenger, Nick, illus. LC 83-397. 128p. (gr. 3 up). 1985. 12.95 (ISBN 0-8069-6200-3); pap. 3.95 (ISBN 0-8069-4672-5). Sterling.

Brill, Michael E. Bamboozled. (Orig.). (gr. 6 up). 1985. pap. 4.50 (ISBN 0-87602-240-9). Anchorage.

Brown, Marc. Spooky Riddles. LC 83-6051. (Illus.). 48p. (gr. k-3). 1983. 6.95 (ISBN 0-394-86093-4); PLB 7.99 (ISBN 0-394-96093-9). Beginner.

Brown, Mik. Joke Book. Warwick Press, ed. Brown, Mik, illus. 32p. (gr. k-6). 1988. 8.90 (ISBN 0-318-32458-X, Warwick). Watts.

Browne, Dik. Hagar the Horrible: Pillage Idiot, No. 11. 128p. (Orig.). 1986. pap. 1.95 (ISBN 0-8125-6788-9, Dist. by Warner Pub Services & Saint Martin's Press). Tor Bks.

Burgess, Gelett. Goop Tales. (Illus.). (gr. 4-8). 16.00 (ISBN 0-8446-4717-9). Peter Smith.

Burns, Diane & Burns, Clint. Hail to the Chief! Jokes about the Presidents. Hanson, Joan, illus. 32p. (gr. 1-4). 1989. 7.95 (ISBN 0-8225-0971-7, First Ave Edns); pap. 2.95 (ISBN 0-8225-9561-3, First Ave Edns). Lerner Pubns.

Burns, Diane L. Elephants Never Forget! A Book of Elephant Jokes. (Illus.). 32p. (gr. 1-4). 1987. pap. 2.95 (ISBN 0-8225-9518-4, First Ave Edns). Lerner Pubns.

—Snakes Alive! Jokes about Snakes. Hanson, Joan, illus. (gr. 1-4). 1988. PLB 7.95 (ISBN 0-8225-0996-2, First Ave Edns); pap. 2.95 (ISBN 0-8225-9543-5, First Ave Edns). Lerner Pubns.

Calmenson, Stephanie. One Hundred & One Silly Summertime Jokes. 1989. pap. 1.95 (ISBN 0-318-41672-7). Scholastic Inc.

—One Hundred One Silly Summertime Jokes. 1989. pap. 1.95 (ISBN 0-590-42556-0). Scholastic Inc.

Carkett, David. Quiver River. LC 90-24095. 224p. (gr. 7 up). 1991. 14.95 (ISBN 0-06-022453-3); PLB 14.89 (ISBN 0-06-022454-1). HarpC Child Bks.

Cerf, Bennett A. Bennett Cerf's Book of Laughs. LC 59-13387. (Illus.). 72p. (gr. 1-2). 1959. 6.95 (ISBN 0-394-80011-7); lib. bdg. 7.99 (ISBN 0-394-90011-1). Beginner.

Chmielewski, Gary. Animal Jokes. Clark, Ron G., illus. LC 86-17684. (gr. 2-3). 1986. 12.66 (ISBN 0-86592-687-5). Rourke Corp.

—Knock Knocks. Clark, Ron G., illus. LC 86-17780. (gr. 2-3). 1986. 12.66 (ISBN 0-86592-684-0). Rourke Corp.

—Sports Jokes. Clark, Ron G., illus. (gr. 2-3). 1986. 12.66 (ISBN 0-685-23106-2). Rourke Corp.

Corbett, Scott. Jokes to Tell to Your Worst Enemy. Gusman, Annie, illus. LC 83-16564. 80p. (gr. 2-6). 1984. 10.95 (ISBN 0-525-44082-8, DCB). Dutton Child Bks.

Corrin, Sara & Corrin, Sara, eds. A Time to Laugh: Funny Stories for Children. (Illus.). 142p. (ps). 1991. pap. 3.95 (ISBN 0-571-15499-9). Faber & Faber.

Cricket Magazine Editors & Leonard, Marcia. Cricket's Jokes, Riddles & Other Stuff. LC 77-3164. (Illus.). (gr. 1-6). 1977. 4.95 (ISBN 0-394-83545-X); lib. bdg. 3.99 (ISBN 0-394-93545-4). Random.

Dahl, Roald & Tannen, Mary. The Twits. Burgoyne, John, illus. LC 80-18410. (ps-5). 1981. 12.00 (ISBN 0-394-84599-4); lib. bdg. 12.99 (ISBN 0-394-94599-9). Knopf.

Danby, Mary. The Awful Joke Book. LC 89-33119. (Illus.). 96p. (Orig.). (gr. 4-9). 1990. 12.95 (ISBN 0-8069-5748-4); PLB 15.69 (ISBN 0-8069-5749-2); pap. 3.95 (ISBN 0-8069-7200-9). Sterling.

Davis, Mac. Great Sports Humor. McKie, Roy & Spilka, Arnold, illus. 128p. (gr. 3-7). 1982. pap. 4.95 (ISBN 0-448-12327-4, G&D). Putnam Pub Group.

Dinosaur Jokes & Riddles Book. (Illus.). (gr. k-9). 1988. pap. 1.50 (ISBN 0-318-36482-4). Scholastic Inc.

Dodds, Dayle A. Wheel Away! Hurd, Thacher, illus. LC 87-27091. 32p. (ps-1). 1989. 12.95 (ISBN 0-06-021688-3); PLB 13.89 (ISBN 0-06-021689-1). HarpC Child Bks.

Dr. Seuss. Bartholomew & the Oobleck. Dr. Seuss, illus. (gr. k-3). 1949. 10.95 (ISBN 0-394-80075-3, Random Juv); lib. bdg. 11.99 (ISBN 0-394-90075-8); pap. 3.95 (ISBN 0-394-84539-0). Random.

—King's Stilts. Dr. Seuss, illus. (gr. k-3). 1939. 9.95 (ISBN 0-394-80082-6, Random Juv); lib. bdg. 8.99 (ISBN 0-394-90082-0). Random.

Eckstein, Joan & Gleit, Joyce. The Best Joke Book for Kids, No. 1. Behr, J., illus. 48p. (gr. 7-12). 1977. pap. 2.50 (ISBN 0-380-01734-2, Camelot). Avon.

—The Best Joke Book for Kids, No. 2. Kohl, Joe, illus. 64p. (gr. 3 up). 1987. pap. 2.50 (ISBN 0-380-75209-3, Camelot). Avon.

Edens, Cooper. If You're Afraid of the Dark, Remember the Night Rainbow. Edens, Cooper, illus. LC 80-105693. 1981. 11.95 (ISBN 0-914676-26-1, Star & Elephant Bks.). Green Tiger Pr.

Eisenberg, Lisa & Hall, Katy. One Hundred & One Bug Jokes. Orehek, Don, illus. 96p. (ps up). pap. 1.95 (ISBN 0-590-33247-3). Scholastic Inc.

—One Hundred One Ghost Jokes. Orehek, Don, illus. (ps up). 1988. pap. 1.95 (ISBN 0-590-41811-4). Scholastic Inc.

Eldin, Peter. Amazing Pranks & Blunders. Blundell, Kim, illus. LC 88-10192. 128p. (gr. 2-8). 1989. pap. 3.95 (ISBN 0-8069-6938-5). Sterling.

Epaminondas. (Illus.). 24p. (ps-k). 1989. 1.29 (ISBN 0-02-898240-1). Checkerboard Pr.

Ertmer, David J. Laughing All the Way. (gr. 1-7). 1988. pap. 13.95 (ISBN 1-55999-051-1). LinguiSystems.

Fitzgerald, John D. Me & My Little Brain. Mayer, Mercer, illus. LC 71-153732. (gr. 4-7). 1985. 12.95 (ISBN 0-8037-5531-7); PLB 11.89 (ISBN 0-8037-5532-5). Dial Bks Young.

Gackenbach, Dick. Supposes. Gackenbach, Dick, illus. (ps up). 1989. 12.95 (ISBN 0-15-200594-3, Gulliver Bks). HarBraceJ.

Gamiello, Elvira. Silly Jokes & Riddles. (Illus.). 96p. (Orig.). 1988. pap. 1.95 (ISBN 0-942025-32-6). Kidsbks.

Gedye, Jane. Dinner's Ready! A Pig's Book of Table Manners. 1989. 9.95 (ISBN 0-385-26083-0); PLB 10. 99 (ISBN 0-385-26084-9). Doubleday.

George, Barbara. The Popples' Book of Jokes & Riddles. Henry, Barb, illus. LC 86-62222. 32p. (ps-3). 1987. pap. 1.25 (ISBN 0-394-88757-3, Random Juv). Random.

Geronimi, Clyde. Chips Quips. Geronimi, Clyde, illus. LC 83-72694. 55p. (gr. 4 up). 1983. pap. 3.95 (ISBN 0-939126-09-5). Back Bay.

Gounaud, Karen J. A Very Mice Joke Book. Munsinger, Lynn, illus. (gr. 2-5). 1981. pap. 12.95 (ISBN 0-395-30445-8); pap. 4.95 (ISBN 0-395-30442-3). HM.

Graham, Carolyn. The Electric Elephant & Other Stories. (Illus., Orig.). (gr. 7-12). 1982. pap. text ed. 6.50x (ISBN 0-19-503229-2). Oxford U Pr.

Hall, Kathy. One Hundred One Cat & Dog Jokes. 1990. pap. 1.95 (ISBN 0-590-43336-9). Scholastic Inc.

Hall, Katy & Eisenberg, Lisa. One Hundred One School Jokes. Orehek, Don, illus. 96p. (gr. 4-7). 1987. pap. 1.95 (ISBN 0-590-41182-9). Scholastic Inc.

Hall, Lynn. Dagmar Schultz & the Green-Eyed Monster. LC 90-43524. 80p. (gr. 5-8). 1991. SBE 11.95 (ISBN 0-684-19254-3, Scribners Young Read). Macmillan Child Grp.

Halligan, Terry. Funny Skits & Sketches. Behr, Joyce, illus. LC 87-6442. 128p. (gr. 2-8). 1987. 12.95 (ISBN 0-8069-6444-8). Sterling.

Hample, Stoo. Stoo Hample's Silly Joke Book. LC 78-50431. (Illus.). (gr. 1-6). 1978. pap. 5.47 (ISBN 0-440-08160-2); pap. 2.50 (ISBN 0-440-08154-8). Delacorte.

Hannan, Peter. The Battle of Sillyville. Hannan, Peter, illus. LC 90-4544. 32p. (Orig.). (ps-2). 1991. PLB 8.99 (ISBN 0-679-90286-4); pap. 3.95 (ISBN 0-679-80286-X). Knopf.

—Escape from Camp Wannabarf. Hannan, Peter, illus. LC 90-33203. 32p. (Orig.). (ps-2). 1991. PLB 8.99 (ISBN 0-679-90287-2); pap. 3.95 (ISBN 0-679-80287-8). Knopf.

—School after Dark. Hannan, Peter, illus. LC 90-33407. 32p. (Orig.). (ps-2). 1991. PLB 8.99 (ISBN 0-679-90288-0); pap. 3.95 (ISBN 0-679-80288-6). Knopf.

—Sillyville or Bust. Hannan, Peter, illus. LC 89-35342. 32p. (Orig.). (ps-2). 1991. PLB 8.99 (ISBN 0-679-90285-6); pap. 3.95 (ISBN 0-679-80285-1). Knopf.

Hargreaves, Roger. Mr. Funny. (Illus.). 32p. (ps-3). 1982. pap. 1.25 (ISBN 0-8431-0878-9). Price Stern.

Hartman, Victoria G. The Silly Joke Book. Orehek, Don, illus. 96p. (gr. 4-6). 1987. pap. 1.95 (ISBN 0-590-33846-3). Scholastic Inc.

Hayes, Frederick & Hayes, Jean. The Chile Pot. 1988. 6.95 (ISBN 0-925605-00-X). Pinto Pub.
THE CHILE POT portrays the humorous efforts of one courageous pinto bean who avoids becoming just another bean in the "big pot of chile." With the often reluctant help of his sidekick, Chapulin, he manages to escape the long spoon of the frustrated old lady, & so, happily, rides off on the grasshopper, Chapulin, into the sunset, singing his song, THE FRIJOLE ROAD. THE CHILE POT is our first effort in this new series THE ADVENTURES OF PINTO BEAN & CHAPULIN. Our second book entitled THE CAT THAT COULDNT MEOW will be published in middle September. It is a hilarious story of how Greta, the cat, finds her meow & also her great love. Our Christmas book, SANTA'S MYSTERIOUS PRESENT will be ready for the holidays. This heart-warming story features Pinto Bean & Chapulin & the mountain with two mouths. Each book has an accompanying cassette that tells the story & songs that children will love. Each of the above books may be purchased from the PINTO PUBLISHING COMPANY at 3610 Calle del Monte, NE, Albuquerque, NM 87110. THE CHILE POT price is $6.95. Postage will be paid by the PINTO PUBLISHING COMPANY with sales coming from this listing.
Publisher Provided Annotation.

Hemp, Kevin. Just Hogweed. Hemp, Kevin, illus. 128p. (Orig.). (gr. 9-12). 1988. pap. 4.95 (ISBN 0-9622059-0-7, VA-U-105-990). Wise Guys Pub.

Hirsch, Phil. One Hundred & One Hamburger Jokes. 96p. (gr. 4-7). 1986. pap. 1.95 (ISBN 0-590-40374-5). Scholastic Inc.

Hirsch, Phil & Hirsch, Hope. One Hundred & One Pet Jokes. Eaton, Tom, illus. 96p. (Orig.). (gr. 3-7). 1981. pap. 1.95 (ISBN 0-590-30380-5, Schol Pap). Scholastic Inc.

Hirsh, Phil. One Hundred One Fast Funny Food Jokes. Orehek, Don, illus. 96p. (Orig.). (gr. 4-6). 1987. pap. 1.95 (ISBN 0-590-32421-7). Scholastic Inc.

Hoff, Syd. Syd Hoff's Animal Jokes. Hoff, Syd, illus. LC 84-48353. 48p. (gr. k-3). 1986. 7.95 (ISBN 0-694-00145-7, Lipp Jr Bks); PLB 12.89 (ISBN 0-397-32117-1). HarpC Child Bks.

Hoye, David. The Official Dinosaur Joke Book: How Do You Get a One-Armed Stegosaurus out of a Tree? McEntee, Steve, illus. 20p. (Orig.). (gr. 1). 1989. plastic 2.95 (ISBN 0-317-94122-4). Kidzco Pub.

Ingoldsby, Pat. Zany Tales. (ps-8). Date not set. pap. 7.95 (ISBN 0-86278-151-5, Pub. by O'Brien Press Ltd Eire). Dufour.

Jackson, Ellen. Ants Can't Dance. Remkiewicz, Frank, illus. LC 90-5942. 32p. (gr. k-3). 1991. RSBE 12.95 (ISBN 0-02-747661-8, Mcmillan Child Bk). Macmillan Child Grp.

Johnson, Crockett. Who's Upside Down? LC 89-28059. (Illus.). 32p. (ps-3). 1990. Repr. of 1952 ed. lib. bdg. 14.00 (ISBN 0-208-02276-7, Pub. by Linnet). Shoe String.

Johnston, Tony. Odd Jobs & Friends. De Paola, Tomie, illus. 48p. 1982. lib. bdg. 6.99 (ISBN 0-399-61204-1, Putnam). Putnam Pub Group.

Johnstone, Michael. One Thousand What's What Jokes for Kids. (gr. k up). 1987. pap. 3.95 (ISBN 0-345-34654-8). Ballantine.

Jokes & Riddles. 96p. (gr. 2-5). 1988. pap. 2.95 (ISBN 0-8431-2275-7). Price Stern.

Keller, Charles. Alexander the Grape: Fruit & Vegetable Jokes. Filling, Gregory, illus. 48p. (gr. 2-6). 1985. 10. 95 (ISBN 0-13-021410-8); pap. 4.95 (ISBN 0-13-020918-X). P-H.

—Astronuts: Space Jokes & Riddles. Cummings, Art, illus. LC 84-18204. 64p. (gr. 3-7). 1990. PLB 11.95 (ISBN 0-671-66290-2). S&S Trade.

—Ballpoint Bananas & Other Jokes for Kids. Barrios, David, illus. LC 72-7338. 96p. (gr. 3-7). 1976. PLB 5.95 (ISBN 0-671-66965-6). S&S Trade.

—Belly Laughs! Food Jokes & Riddles. Fritz, Ron, illus. LC 89-28201. 32p. (gr. k-3). 1990. PLB 13.95 (ISBN 0-671-70068-5); pap. 5.95 (ISBN 0-671-70069-3). S&S Trade.

—Colossal Fossils: Dinosaur Jokes. Kessler, Leonard, illus. LC 86-22656. 64p. (gr. 4-7). 1987. PLB 11.95 (ISBN 0-671-66532-4). S&S Trade.

—Giggle Puss: Pet Jokes for Kids. Coker, Paul, Jr., illus. LC 76-44837. (gr. 3-7). 1977. (Pub. by Treehouse); pap. 3.95 (ISBN 0-13-356303-0). P-H.

—Grime Doesn't Pay: Law & Order Jokes. Kent, Jack, illus. 64p. 1984. 9.95 (ISBN 0-13-365503-2). P-H.

—Oh, Brother: And Other Family Jokes. Frascino, Edward, illus. 48p. (gr. 2-6). 1982. 8.95 (ISBN 0-13-633305-2). P-H.

—Ohm on the Range: Robot & Computer Jokes. Cumings, Art, illus. 48p. (gr. 3-7). 1982. 8.95 (ISBN 0-13-633552-7). P-H.

—What's up, Doc? Doctor & Dentist Jokes. Kessler, Leonard, illus. LC 84-6821. 64p. (gr. 3-7). 1984. 9.95 (ISBN 0-13-954967-6). P-H.

Keller, Charles, compiled by. Going Bananas: Jokes for Kids. Wilson, Roger B., illus. (gr. 2-5). 1977. 8.95 (ISBN 0-13-357772-4, Pub. by Treehouse); pap. 3.95 (ISBN 0-13-357780-5). P-H.

—More Ballpoint Bananas. Shortall, Leonard, illus. LC 77-5356. (gr. 1-3). 1980. 7.95 (ISBN 0-13-600767-8, Pub. by Treehouse). P-H.

Keller, Charles, ed. Remember the a la Mode! Riddles & Puns. Lorenz, Lee, illus. LC 83-13832. 64p. (gr. 3-5). 1983. 10.95 (ISBN 0-13-773358-5). P-H.

Keller, Charles, compiled by. Daffynitions. Fitzgerald, F. A., illus. LC 75-34280. (gr. 3 up). 1978. (Pub. by Treehouse); pap. 3.95 (ISBN 0-13-196576-X). P-H.

Kessler, Leonard. Old Turtle's Riddle & Joke Book. (gr. k-6). 1990. pap. 2.95 (ISBN 0-440-40268-9, YB). Dell.

Kidd, Ronald. Sizzle & Splat. LC 83-9022. 160p. (gr. 7 up). 1983. 12.95 (ISBN 0-525-66917-5, Lodestar Bks). Dutton Child Bks.

Kilgarriff, Michael. Oh No! Not Another One Thousand Jokes for Kids. (gr. k up). 1987. pap. 3.95 (ISBN 0-345-34035-3). Ballantine.

—One Thousand Jokes for Kids of All Ages. (gr. k up). 1986. pap. 3.95 (ISBN 0-345-33480-9); pap. write for info. (ISBN 0-345-00654-2). Ballantine.

—One Thousand More Jokes for Kids. (gr. k up). 1987. pap. 3.95 (ISBN 0-345-34034-5). Ballantine.

King, Colin. Amazing Book of Jokes. 1990. 3.99 (ISBN 0-517-69192-2). Outlet Bk Co.

Kline, Rufus. Watch Out for These Weirdos. Carlson, Nancy, illus. 32p. (ps-3). 1990. pap. 12.95 (ISBN 0-670-82376-7). Viking Penguin.

Kushner, Maureen. Funny Answers to Foolish Questions. Kendrick, Dennis, illus. LC 87-9926. 128p. (gr. 2-6). 1987. 12.95 (ISBN 0-8069-6442-1); PLB 15.69 (ISBN 0-8069-6443-X). Sterling.

—Funny Answers to Foolish Questions. Kendrick, Dennis, illus. LC 87-9926. 128p. (gr. 3-10). 1988. pap. 3.95 (ISBN 0-8069-3756-4). Sterling.

Kushner, Maureen & Hoffman, Sanford. Great All-Time Excuse Book. LC 89-49403. (Illus.). 96p. 1990. 12.95 (ISBN 0-8069-6964-4). Sterling.

Lake, Charles. Swine Lake. Filling, Gregory, illus. 48p. (gr. 3-7). 1985. 9.95 (ISBN 0-13-879743-9). P-H.

Lattimore, Deborah N. Lady with the Ship on Her Head. 1990. 14.95 (ISBN 0-15-243525-5). HarbraceJ.

LeSieg, Theo. I Wish That I Had Duck Feet. McKie, Roy, illus. 64p. (ps-1). 1988. pap. 5.95 bk. & cassette pkg. (ISBN 0-394-89777-3, Random Juv). Random.

—Ten Apples up on Top. McKie, Roy, illus. 64p. (ps-1). 1988. pap. 5.95 Bk. & Cassette pkg. (ISBN 0-394-89769-2, Random Juv). Random.

Le Sieg, Theodore. Please Try to Remember the First of Octember. Cumings, Arthur, illus. LC 77-4504. 48p. (gr. 1-4). 1977. lib. bdg. 7.99 (ISBN 0-394-93563-2). Beginner.

Levy, Elizabeth. Dracula Is a Pain in the Neck. Gerstein, Mordicai, illus. LC 82-47707. 80p. (gr. 2-5). 1984. pap. 3.50 (ISBN 0-06-440146-4, Trophy). HarpC Child Bks.

Levy, Elizabeth, adapted by. Fat Albert & the Cosby Kids: Take Two, They're Small. (gr. 2 up). pap. 1.95 (ISBN 0-686-74491-8, YB). Dell.

Lincoln, Abraham. Wisdom & Wit. (gr. 8 up). 6.95 (ISBN 0-88088-359-6). Peter Pauper.

Lindgren, Barbro. Sam's Bath. Eriksson, Eva, illus. LC 83-724. 32p. (ps-k). 1983. 6.95 (ISBN 0-688-02362-2). Morrow Jr Bks.

Little People Big Book about Silly Things. 64p. (ps-1). 1990. write for info. (ISBN 0-8094-7520-0); PLB write for info. (ISBN 0-8094-7521-9). Time-Life.

Lorenz, Lee. Driving Me Crazy: Fun on Wheels Jokes. Lorenz, Lee, illus. 40p. (gr. 2-5). 1989. 11.95 (ISBN 0-945912-05-6). Pippin Pr.

McCloskey, Robert. Homer Price. (Illus.). (gr. 3-7). 1976. pap. 3.95 (ISBN 0-14-030927-6, Puffin). Puffin Bks.

Mack, Stan. Where's My Cheese? Mack, Stan, illus. LC 76-3443. (ps-1). 1977. Pantheon.

Markowitz, Endel. Kid-Ish Yiddish. Klein, Debby, illus. 90p. (gr. 8-10). 1982. 8.95g (ISBN 0-686-97548-0). Haymark.

Marsh, Carole. Life Isn't Fair: Murphy's Laws for Kids. (Illus.). (gr. 4-12). 1983. 14.95 (ISBN 0-935326-08-1). Gallopade Pub Group.

Mazer, Norma F. Mrs. Fish, Ape & Me, the Dump Queen. 144p. (Orig.). (gr. 4 up). 1981. pap. 2.95 (ISBN 0-380-69153-1, Flare). Avon.

Miller, Madge. OPQRS, Etc. (Orig.). (gr. 4 up). 1984. pap. 4.50 (ISBN 0-87602-246-8). Anchorage.

Mulford, Philippa G. If It's Not Funny, Why Am I Laughing. LC 82-70321. 144p. (gr. 7 up). 1982. pap. 10.95 (ISBN 0-385-28441-1). Delacorte.

My Big Little Golden Book of Knock-Knocks & Other Jokes. (gr. k-9). 1988. pap. 1.39 (ISBN 0-318-36474-3). Scholastic Inc.

Nelson, Jeffrey. Monster Jokes & Riddles Book. (Illus.). 24p. (gr. 3 up). 1988. pap. 1.95 (ISBN 0-02-689069-0). Checkerboard Pr.

—Space Jokes & Riddles Book. (Illus.). 24p. (gr. 3 up). 1988. pap. 1.95 (ISBN 0-02-689071-2). Checkerboard Pr.

—Spooky Jokes & Riddles Books. (Illus.). 24p. (gr. 3 up). 1988. pap. 1.95 (ISBN 0-02-689070-4). Checkerboard Pr.

Palacios, Argentina. Peanut Butter, Apple Butter, Cinnamon Toast: Food Riddles for You to Guess. Mahan, Ben, illus. 24p. (ps-2). 1990. PLB 12.33 (ISBN 0-8172-3584-1); PLB 9.25 (ISBN 0-685-33580-1). Raintree Pubs.

Palin, Michael. The Mirrorstone. Lee, Alan, illus. (gr. 5 up). 14.95 (ISBN 0-317-52859-9). Knopf.

Pansini, Anna, ed. Great Riddles, Giggles & Jokes. Loh, Carolyn, illus. LC 89-5200. 48p. (gr. 2-6). 1990. PLB 8.59 (ISBN 0-8167-1915-2); pap. text ed. 2.50 (ISBN 0-8167-1916-0). Troll Assocs.

Parish, Peggy. Come Back, Amelia Bedelia. Tripp, Wallace, illus. LC 73-121799. 64p. (ps-3). 1971. 11.95 (ISBN 0-06-024667-7); PLB 11.89 (ISBN 0-06-024668-5). HarpC Child Bks.

Perret, Gene. Funny Comebacks to Rude Remarks. LC 90-37815. (Illus.). 96p. (gr. 3-9). 1990. pap. 3.95 (ISBN 0-8069-7240-8). Sterling.

—Super Funny School Jokes. (Illus.). 96p. (gr. 2-10). 1991. 12.95 (ISBN 0-8069-8294-2). Sterling.

Peterson, Scott K. Face the Music! Jokes about Music. Hanson, Joan, illus. 32p. (gr. 1-4). 1988. PLB 8.95 (ISBN 0-8225-0995-4). Lerner Pubns.

—What's Your Name? Jokes about Names. Hanson, Joan, illus. 32p. (gr. 1-4). 1987. PLB 7.95 (ISBN 0-8225-0994-6, First Ave Edns); pap. 2.95 (ISBN 0-8225-9520-6, First Ave Edns). Lerner Pubns.

Phillips, Bob. The Best of the Good Clean Jokes. LC 89-32386. 192p. (gr. 5 up). 1989. pap. 4.50 (ISBN 0-89081-769-3). Harvest Hse.

—World's Greatest Collection of Daffy Definitions & Riddles. 160p. (Orig.). (gr. 4 up). 1989. pap. 3.99 (ISBN 0-89081-700-6). Harvest Hse.

Phillips, Louis. Going Ape: Jokes from the Jungle. Shein, Bob, illus. 64p. (gr. 2 up). 1990. pap. 3.95 (ISBN 0-14-032263-9, Puffin). Puffin Bks.

—Haunted House Jokes. Marshall, James, illus. 64p. (gr. 2-5). 1988. pap. 3.95 (ISBN 0-14-032062-8, Puffin). Puffin Bks.

—How Do You Get a Horse Out of the Bathtub? Profound Answers to Preposterous Questions. Stevenson, James, illus. (gr. 4-6). 1983. pap. 4.95 (ISBN 0-14-031618-3, Puffin Bks). Puffin Bks.

—How Do You Lift a Walrus with One Hand? More Profound Answers to Preposterous Questions. Stevenson, James, illus. 80p. (gr. 3-6). 1989. pap. 3.95 (ISBN 0-14-032709-6, Puffin). Puffin Bks.

—Louis Phillip's Loose Leaf: The Wackiest School Notebook Yet. Farris, Joseph, illus. LC 89-28025. 48p. (gr. 5 up). 1990. 11.95 (ISBN 0-689-31437-X, Atheneum Child Bk). Macmillan Child Grp.

—Way Out! Jokes from Outer Space. Dubanevich, Arlene, illus. LC 89-14700. 58p. (gr. 4-8). 1989. pap. 10.95 (ISBN 0-670-82755-X). Viking Child Bks.

Pollack, Pamela, compiled by. The Random House Book of Humor for Children. Zelinsky, Paul O., illus. LC 86-31478. 320p. (gr. 2-6). 1988. 15.95 (ISBN 0-394-88049-8); lib. bdg. 16.99 (ISBN 0-394-98049-2). Random.

Popkin, Arlene. My April Fool Book. (Illus.). (ps-1). 1974. PLB 6.89x (ISBN 0-914844-04-0). J Alden.

Powell, Leroy. Out of My Head. Warlick, Cal, illus. LC 89-28418. 240p. 1990. 15.95 (ISBN 0-934601-95-X). Peachtree Pubs.

Pulver, Robin & R.W. Mrs. Toggle's Zipper. LC 88-37251. (Illus.). 32p. (ps-2). 1990. 12.95 (ISBN 0-02-775451-0, Four Winds Press). Macmillan Child Grp.

Quackenbush, Robert. It's Raining Cats & Dogs: Cat & Dog Jokes. Quackenbush, Robert, illus. 40p. (gr. 2-6). 1988. 11.95 (ISBN 0-945912-01-3). Pippin Pr.

—Quick, Annie, Give Me a Catchy Line! Quackenbush, Robert, illus. 32p. (gr. 3-7). 1983. 10.95 (ISBN 0-13-749762-8). P-H.

Ridley, Philip. Dakota of the White Flats. LC 90-5158. 144p. (gr. 5 up). 1991. 12.95 (ISBN 0-679-81168-0); PLB 13.99 (ISBN 0-679-91168-5). Knopf.

Rogers, Fred. If We Were All the Same. Sustendal, Pat, illus. LC 86-31598. 32p. (ps-1). 1987. lib. bdg. 5.99 (ISBN 0-394-98778-0, Random Juv); (Random Juv). Random.

Roop, Peter & Roop, Connie. Going Buggy! Jokes about Insects. (Illus.). 32p. (gr. 1-4). 1986. PLB 7.95 (ISBN 0-8225-0988-1, First Ave Edns); pap. 2.95 (ISBN 0-8225-9530-3, First Ave Edns). Lerner Pubns.

—Let's Celebrate! Jokes about Holidays. (Illus.). 32p. (gr. 1-4). 1986. PLB 7.95 (ISBN 0-8225-0989-X, First Ave Edns); pap. 2.95 (ISBN 0-8225-9529-X, First Ave Edns). Lerner Pubns.

—Stick Out Your Tongue! Jokes about Doctors & Patients. (Illus.). 32p. (gr. 1-4). 1986. PLB 7.95 (ISBN 0-8225-0990-3, First Ave Edns); pap. 2.95 (ISBN 0-8225-9546-X, First Ave Edns). Lerner Pubns.

Rose, Anne. The Triumphs of Fuzzy Fogtop. De Paola, Tomie, illus. LC 78-72204. (gr. k-3). 1979. PLB 8.44 (ISBN 0-8037-8647-6). Dial Bks Young.

Rosenbloom, Joseph. Doctor Knock-Knock's Official Knock-Knock Dictionary. Behr, Joyce, illus. LC 76-19796. 128p. (gr. 3 up). 1980. 12.95 (ISBN 0-8069-4536-2); pap. 3.95 (ISBN 0-8069-8936-X). Sterling.

—Funniest Haunted House Book Ever! Wilhelm, Hans, illus. LC 89-38605. 24p. (gr. 1-7). 1989. 12.95 (ISBN 0-8069-6818-4); PLB 15.69 (ISBN 0-8069-6819-2). Sterling.

—The Funniest Knock-Knock Book Ever! Wilhelm, Hans, illus. LC 86-5989. 24p. (gr. k-3). 1987. 12.95 (ISBN 0-8069-4758-6); PLB 15.69 (ISBN 0-8069-4759-4). Sterling.

—Funny Insults & Snappy Put-Downs. Behr, Joyce, illus. LC 82-50547. 128p. (gr. 4 up). 1982. pap. 3.95 (ISBN 0-8069-7644-6). Sterling.

—Get Well Quick Jokes & Riddles. LC 89-34019. (Illus.). 96p. (gr. 2-8). 1989. 12.95 (ISBN 0-8069-5752-2); PLB 15.69 (ISBN 0-8069-5753-0). Sterling.

—Gigantic Joke Book. Behr, Joyce, illus. LC 77-93310. 256p. (gr. 4-6). 1981. pap. 5.95 (ISBN 0-8069-7514-8); 16.95 (ISBN 0-8069-4590-7); PLB 19.99 (ISBN 0-8069-4591-5). Sterling.

—Giggles, Gags & Groaners. Hoffman, Sanford, illus. LC 86-30052. 128p. (gr. 2 up). 1987. 12.95 (ISBN 0-8069-6446-4); PLB 15.69 (ISBN 0-8069-6447-2). Sterling.

—Giggles, Gags & Groaners. LC 86-30052. (Illus.). 128p. (gr. 2-8). 1988. pap. 3.95 (ISBN 0-8069-6536-3). Sterling.

—Laughs, Hoots & Giggles: Riddles, Jokes, Knock-Knocks & Put-Downs. Behr, Joyce & Hoffman, Sanford, illus. 480p. (gr. 2 up). 1987. pap. 9.95 (ISBN 0-8069-6492-8). Sterling.

—Monster Madness: Riddles, Jokes, & Fun. Behr, Joyce, illus. LC 80-52339. 128p. (gr. 2 up). 1980. pap. 3.95 (ISBN 0-8069-7562-8). Sterling.

—Nutty Knock Knocks! Hoffman, Sandy, illus. LC 85-27626. 128p. (Orig.). (gr. 2 up). 1986. pap. 3.95 (ISBN 0-8069-6304-2). Sterling.

—Perfect Put-Downs & Instant Insults. LC 88-11710. (Illus.). 128p. (gr. 2-8). 1989. pap. 3.95 (ISBN 0-8069-6940-7). Sterling.

—School's Out: Great Vacation Riddles & Jokes. LC 88-31868. (Illus.). 96p. 1989. 12.95 (ISBN 0-8069-6942-3); lib. bdg. 15.69 (ISBN 0-8069-6943-1). Sterling.

—Six Hundred Ninety-Six School Jokes & Riddles. Kendrick, Dennis, illus. 128p. (gr. 2 up). 1987. pap. 3.95 (ISBN 0-8069-6392-1). Sterling.

—Spooky Riddles & Jokes. Hoffman, Sanford, illus. LC 87-17972. 128p. (gr. 2-8). 1988. pap. 3.95 (ISBN 0-8069-6736-6). Sterling.

—Super Sick Jokes & Riddles. Hoffman, Sanford, illus. 96p. (Orig.). (gr. 2-9). 1990. pap. 3.95 (ISBN 0-8069-7458-3). Sterling.

—Wacky Insults & Terrible Jokes. Hoffman, Sandy, illus. (gr. 3 up). 1985. pap. 3.95 (ISBN 0-8069-7992-5). Sterling.

—World's Best Sports Riddles & Jokes. Hoffman, Sanford, illus. LC 87-30434. 128p. (gr. 3-9). 1989. pap. 3.95 (ISBN 0-8069-6848-6). Sterling.

Ross, Dave. How to Prevent Monster Attacks. LC 83-26536. (Illus.). 64p. (gr. 4 up). 1984. 7.00 (ISBN 0-688-03790-9). Morrow Jr Bks.

Rothman, Joel. The Antcyclopedia. Freshman, Shelley, illus. 4.95 (ISBN 0-685-86236-4). Pubns Devl Co TX.

Rovin, Jeff. Five Hundred Hilarious Jokes for Kids. 144p. (Orig.). 1990. pap. 2.99 (ISBN 0-451-16549-7, Sig). NAL-Dutton.

—Five Hundred More Hilarious Jokes for Kids. 1990. pap. 2.95 (ISBN 0-451-16727-9, Sig). NAL-Dutton.

Rudner, Barry. Nonsense. Fahsbender, Thomas, illus. (gr. k-6). 1990. write for info. (ISBN 0-925928-04-6). Tiny Thought.
Sackson, Eugenia. Jokes, Riddles & Silly Songs. (Illus.). 16p. (ps up). 1989. pap. write for info. (ISBN 0-307-14047-4). Western Pub.
Schmeltz, Susan A. Oh, So Silly! Cocca, Maryann, illus. LC 83-23754. 48p. (ps-3). 1984. 5.95 (ISBN 0-8193-1122-7). Parents.
Schultz, Sam. One Hundred & One Animal Jokes. Hanson, Joan, illus. LC 81-20955. 48p. (gr. 1-4). 1982. PLB 8.95 (ISBN 0-8225-0978-4). Lerner Pubns.
—One Hundred & One Family Jokes. Hanson, Joan, illus. LC 81-20861. 48p. (gr. 1-4). 1982. PLB 8.95 (ISBN 0-8225-0981-4). Lerner Pubns.
—One Hundred & One Knock-Knock Jokes. Hanson, Joan, illus. LC 81-20954. 48p. (gr. 1-4). 1982. PLB 8.95 (ISBN 0-8225-0976-8). Lerner Pubns.
—One Hundred & One Monster Jokes. Hanson, Joan, illus. LC 81-20953. 48p. (gr. 1-4). 1982. PLB 8.95 (ISBN 0-8225-0977-6). Lerner Pubns.
—One Hundred & One School Jokes. Hanson, Joan, illus. LC 81-20912. 48p. (gr. 1-4). 1982. PLB 8.95 (ISBN 0-8225-0979-2). Lerner Pubns.
—One Hundred & One Sports Jokes. Hanson, Joan, illus. LC 81-20913. 48p. (gr. 1-4). 1982. PLB 8.95 (ISBN 0-8225-0980-6). Lerner Pubns.
Schulz, Charles M. A Boy Named Charlie Brown. LC 79-80346. 142p. (gr. 5 up). 1969. 7.95 (ISBN 0-03-081861-3). H Holt & Co.
—Snoopy & His Sopwith Camel. LC 78-91065. (Illus.). 64p. (gr. 5 up). 1969. 2.95 (ISBN 0-03-083177-6). H Holt & Co.
—Snoopy & the Red Baron. LC 66-22569. (Illus.). 64p. (gr. 5 up). 1966. 2.95 (ISBN 0-03-060560-1). H Holt & Co.
Shannon, J. Michael. Still More Jokes. Magnuson, Diana, illus. LC 85-27971. 48p. (gr. 3-6). 1986. lib. bdg. 13.27 (ISBN 0-516-01867-1); pap. 3.95 (ISBN 0-516-41867-X). Childrens.
Shere, Irene & Friedman, Sharon. Cat's out of the Bag: Jokes about Cats. Hanson, Joan, illus. 32p. (gr. 1-4). 1986. 8.95 (ISBN 0-8225-0986-5); pap. 2.95 (ISBN 0-8225-9527-3). Lerner Pubns.
—Grin & Bear It! Jokes about Teddy Bears. (Illus.). 32p. (gr. 1-4). 1986. lib. bdg. 8.95 (ISBN 0-8225-0985-7). Lerner Pubns.
—In the Doghouse! Jokes about Dogs. (Illus.). 32p. (gr. 1-4). 1986. lib. bdg. 7.95 (ISBN 0-8225-0987-3, First Ave Edns); pap. 2.95 (ISBN 0-8225-9528-1, First Ave Edns). Lerner Pubns.
Silverstein, Shel. Giraffe & a Half. Silverstein, Shel, illus. LC 64-19709. 48p. (gr. k-3). 1964. 12.95 (ISBN 0-06-025655-9); PLB 12.89 (ISBN 0-06-025656-7). HarpC Child Bks.
Skolsky, Mindy W. The Whistling Teakettle & Other Stories about Hannah. LC 76-21395. (Illus.). (gr. 2-5). 1977. 10.89 (ISBN 0-06-025688-5). HarpC Child Bks.
Smart Alex's Spooky Jokes for Kids, No. 6. 224p. 1990. pap. 3.95 (ISBN 0-345-35528-8). Ballantine.
Smith, Robert K. Jelly Belly. Jones, Bob, illus. LC 80-23898. 160p. (gr. 4-6). 1981. pap. 13.95 (ISBN 0-385-28477-2). Delacorte.
Steig, William. CDB! LC 80-12376. (Illus.). 48p. (gr. 1-4). 1987. pap. 3.95 (ISBN 0-671-66689-4). S&S Trade.
Stine, Bob. One Hundred & One Silly Monster Jokes. Taylor, B. K., illus. 96p. (Orig.). (gr. 4-7). 1986. pap. 1.95 (ISBN 0-590-33889-7). Scholastic Inc.
—One Hundred & One Wacky Kid Jokes. Orehek, Don, illus. 96p. 1988. pap. 1.95 (ISBN 0-590-41399-6). Scholastic Inc.
—One Hundred One More Monster Jokes. 96p. (Orig.). (gr. 4-7). 1990. pap. 1.95 (ISBN 0-590-43171-4). Scholastic Inc.
—One Hundred One School Cafeteria Jokes. 96p. (Orig.). (gr. 3-7). 1990. pap. 1.95 (ISBN 0-590-43759-3). Scholastic Inc.
Stolzenberg, Mark. How to Be Really Funny. LC 87-28077. (Illus.). 128p. (gr. 2-10). 1989. pap. 4.95 (ISBN 0-8069-6887-7). Sterling.
Stupid Jokes for Kids. 224p. (ps-8). 1991. pap. 3.95 (ISBN 0-345-37062-7). Ballantine.
Suire, Diane, compiled by. Monster Jokes. Hunter, Llyn, illus. LC 88-17487. 48p. (gr. 1-5). 1988. PLB 13.27 (ISBN 0-516-01866-3); pap. 3.95 (ISBN 0-516-41866-1). Childrens.
Taylor, Theodore. The Trouble with Tuck. 120p. (gr. 5 up). 1983. pap. 3.50 (ISBN 0-380-62711-6, 60023-4, Camelot). Avon.
Terban, Marvin. Guppies in Tuxedos: Funny Eponyms. Maestro, Giulio, illus. LC 87-32630. 64p. (gr. 4-7). 1988. 12.95 (ISBN 0-89919-509-1, Pub. by Clarion); pap. 4.95 (ISBN 0-89919-770-1, Pub. by Clarion). Ticknor & Fields.
Tompert, Ann. Nothing Sticks Like a Shadow. Munsinger, Lynn, illus. LC 83-18554. 32p. (gr. k-3). 1988. 12.95 (ISBN 0-395-35391-2, 5-97100); pap. 4.95 (ISBN 0-395-47950-9). HM.
Walton, Rick & Walton, Ann. Can You Match This? Jokes about Unlikely Pairs. Hanson, Joan, illus. 32p. (gr. 1-4). 1989. 8.95 (ISBN 0-8225-0973-3). Lerner Pubns.
—Can You Match This? Jokes about Unlikely Pairs. Hanson, Joan, illus. 36p. pap. 2.95 (ISBN 0-8225-9565-6). Lerner Pubns.
—Dumb Clucks! Jokes about Chickens. Hanson, Joan, illus. 32p. (gr. 1-4). 1987. PLB 7.95 (ISBN 0-8225-0991-1). Lerner Pubns.
—Fossil Follies! Jokes about Dinosaurs. Hanson, Joan, illus. 32p. (gr. 1-4). 1989. 7.95 (ISBN 0-8225-0974-1, First Ave Edns); pap. 2.95 (ISBN 0-8225-9560-5, First Ave Edns). Lerner Pubns.
—Kiss a Frog! Jokes about Fairy Tales, Knights, & Dragons. Hanson, Joan, illus. 32p. (gr. 1-4). 1989. 8.95 (ISBN 0-8225-0970-9). Lerner Pubns.
—Kiss a Frog! Jokes about Fairy Tales, Knights, & Dragons. Hanson, Joan, illus. 40p. (gr. 1-4). pap. 2.96g (ISBN 0-8225-9566-4). Lerner Pubns.
—Something's Fishy! Jokes about Sea Creatures. (Illus.). 32p. (gr. 1-4). 1987. PLB 7.95 (ISBN 0-8225-0993-8, First Ave Edns); pap. 2.95 (ISBN 0-8225-9519-2, First Ave Edns). Lerner Pubns.
—What a Ham! Jokes about Pigs. Hanson, Joan, illus. 32p. (gr. 1-4). 1989. 8.95 (ISBN 0-8225-0972-5). Lerner Pubns.
—What a Ham! Jokes about Pigs. Hanson, Joan, illus. 40p. (gr. 1-4). pap. 2.95 (ISBN 0-8225-9567-2). Lerner Pubns.
—What's Your Name, Again? More Jokes about Names. Hanson, Joan, illus. 32p. (gr. 1-4). 1988. PLB 7.95 (ISBN 0-8225-0997-0, First Ave Edns); pap. 2.95 (ISBN 0-8225-9553-2, First Ave Edns). Lerner Pubns.
Ward Lock, Ltd. Staff. One Thousand Knock Knock Jokes for Kids. (gr. k up). 1986. pap. 4.95 (ISBN 0-345-33481-7). Ballantine.
Wildsmith, Brian. Python's Party. (Illus.). 32p. (ps-1). 1987. 11.95 (ISBN 0-19-279705-0). Oxford U Pr.
Williams, Barbara. The Crazy Gang Next Door. LC 90-1350. 160p. (gr. 3-7). 1990. 13.95 (ISBN 0-690-04868-8, Crowell Jr Bks); PLB 13.89 (ISBN 0-690-04870-X, Crowell Jr Bks). HarpC Child Bks.
Yamamoto, Neil. Super Silly School Jokes & Riddles. (gr. 4-7). 1991. pap. 1.95 (ISBN 0-8125-9375-8). Tor Bks.
Young, Frederica & Kohl, Marguerite. Jokes for Children. Patterson, Bob, illus. 128p. (gr. 2 up). 1983. pap. 4.95 (ISBN 0-374-43832-3, Noonday). Hill & Wang.
—More Jokes for Children. Patterson, Bob, illus. (gr. 2-5). 1984. pap. 4.95 (ISBN 0-374-45360-8, Sunburst). FS&G.
Zadra, Dan. How to Beat the Jitters. (Illus.). 32p. (gr. 6 up). 1986. PLB 10.95s.p. (ISBN 0-88682-018-9); 15. 65. Creative Ed.
Zeigler, Judy. My First Book of Jokes & Riddles: How Do You Raise a Rhino. 1991. 4.98 (ISBN 0-8317-6298-5). Smithmark.
—My First Book of Jokes and Riddles: Quick Call Me a Taxi. 1991. 4.98 (ISBN 0-8317-6296-9). Smithmark.
—My First Book of Jokes & Riddles: Why Do Elephant's Wear Purple Suspenders? 1991. 4.98 (ISBN 0-8317-6297-7). Smithmark.
—My First Book of Jokes & Riddles: Waiter, Do You Serve Lobster? 1991. 4.98 (ISBN 0-8317-6299-3). Smithmark.
Ziegler, Sandra K. Jokes & More Jokes. Magnuson, Diana, illus. LC 82-19742. 48p. (gr. 1-5). 1983. PLB 13.27 (ISBN 0-516-01871-X); pap. 3.95 (ISBN 0-516-41871-8). Childrens.

WIT AND HUMOR, PICTORIAL

Anderson, Brad. Marmaduke: Sitting Pretty. 128p. (gr. 9). 1986. pap. 1.95 (ISBN 0-8125-7350-1, Dist. by Warner Pub Services & St. Martin's Press). Tor Bks.
Berg, Dave. Dave Berg Looks at Living. (Illus.). 192p. (Orig.). 1980. pap. 1.75 (ISBN 0-446-94400-9). Warner Bks.
—Dave Berg Looks at People. (Illus.). 192p. (Orig.). 1978. pap. 1.50 (ISBN 0-446-88901-6). Warner Bks.
—Dave Berg Looks at Things. (Illus.). 192p. 1985. pap. 2.50 (ISBN 0-446-32827-8). Warner Bks.
Bierce, Ambrose. Children's Illustrated Devils Dictionary. (gr. k up). 1991. pap. 3.95 (ISBN 0-425-12523-8). Berkley Pub.
Bird, Malcolm. The Witch's Handbook. Bird, Malcolm, illus. LC 88-911. 96p. (ps up). 1988. bds. 7.95 (ISBN 0-689-71237-5, Aladdin). Macmillan Child Grp.
Grindley, Sally. Dirty Denis. Dowling, Paul, illus. LC 88-40454. 32p. (ps-3). 1989. pap. 10.95 (ISBN 0-670-82686-3). Viking Child Bks.
Hall, Katy. Garfield: Big Fat Book of Jokes & Riddles. Fentz, Mike, illus. LC 84-62725. 96p. (gr. 6-10). 1985. pap. 5.95 (ISBN 0-394-87414-5, Random Juv). Random.
Hamm, Jack. Cartooning the Head & Figure. (Illus., Orig.). (gr. 9 up). 1967. pap. 6.95 (ISBN 0-399-50803-1, G&D). Putnam Pub Group.
Hendra, Judith, ed. The Illustrated Treasury of Humor for Children. (Illus.). 256p. (gr. k-3). 1980. 10.95 (ISBN 0-448-16429-9, G&D). Putnam Pub Group.
Jacobs, Frank. Mad's Talking Stamps. (Illus.). 192p. (Orig.). 1981. pap. 1.75 (ISBN 0-446-94439-4). Warner Bks.
Martin, Don. Mad's Don Martin Carries on. (Illus.). 1983. pap. 1.95 (ISBN 0-446-30451-4). Warner Bks.
Raving Mad. (Illus.). 192p. 1980. pap. 1.75 (ISBN 0-446-94382-7). Warner Bks.
Sesame Street Staff. Sesame Street Storybook. (Illus.). (ps-4). 1971. 5.95 (ISBN 0-394-82332-X, Random Juv); lib. bdg. 5.99 (ISBN 0-394-92332-4). Random.
Son of Mad. (Illus.). 192p. 1981. pap. 1.75 (ISBN 0-446-94386-X). Warner Bks.
The Token Mad. (Illus.). 192p. (Orig.). 1980. pap. 1.75 (ISBN 0-446-94389-4). Warner Bks.

WITCHCRAFT

see also Occult Sciences

Bird, Malcolm. The Witch's Handbook. Bird, Malcolm, illus. LC 88-911. 96p. (ps up). 1988. bds. 7.95 (ISBN 0-689-71237-5, Aladdin). Macmillan Child Grp.
Brown, Marc. Witches Four. Brown, Marc, illus. LC 79-5263. 48p. (ps-3). 1980. 5.95 (ISBN 0-8193-1013-1); PLB 5.95 (ISBN 0-8193-1014-X). Parents.
Cartwright & Rawson. Wizards. (gr. k-4). 1980. 6.95 (ISBN 0-86020-381-6, Usborne-Hayes); pap. 3.95 (ISBN 0-86020-380-8). EDC.
Cohen, Daniel. Curses, Hexes, & Spells. LC 74-6425. (Illus.). 128p. (gr. 6 up). 1974. (Lipp Jr Bks); pap. 2.50 (ISBN 0-397-31494-9). HarpC Child Bks.
Gawr, Rhuddlwm. The Triads: The Wisdom of the Welsh Witches. Gawr, Rhuddlwm, illus. LC 85-73755. 140p. (Orig.). 1989. 14.95 (ISBN 0-931760-45-3, CP 10123); pap. 10.95 (ISBN 0-931760-23-2). Camelot GA.
—The Way: The Discovery of the Grail of Immortality. Gawr, Rhuddlwm, et al, illus. LC 85-73759. (Orig.). 1987. 18.95 (ISBN 0-931760-50-X, CP 10128); pap. 15.95 (ISBN 0-931760-28-3). Camelot GA.
Glovach, Linda. The Little Witch's Summertime Book. (Illus.). 48p. (gr. 1-4). 1986. 10.95 (ISBN 0-13-538018-9). P-H.
Harrison, Michael. Scolding Tongues: The Persecution of Witches. 52p. (gr. 1 up). 1987. pap. 7.95 (ISBN 0-685-19631-3, Pub. by S Thornes). Dufour.
Jackson, Shirley. Witchcraft of Salem Village. (Illus.). (gr. 4-6). 1963. lib. bdg. 8.99 (ISBN 0-394-90369-2, Random Juv). Random.
Kent, Zachary. The Story of the Salem Witch Trials. Canaday, Ralph, illus. LC 86-9632. 32p. (gr. 3-6). 1986. PLB 13.27 (ISBN 0-516-04704-3); pap. 3.95 (ISBN 0-516-44704-1). Childrens.
Krensky, Stephen. Witch Hunt: It Happened in Salem Village. Watling, James, illus. LC 88-42865. 48p. (Orig.). (gr. 2-4). 1989. PLB 6.99 (ISBN 0-394-91923-8); pap. 2.95 (ISBN 0-394-81923-3). Random.
Low, Alice. Witches' Holiday. Walton, Tony, illus. (gr. k-3). 1971. lib. bdg. 5.99 (ISBN 0-394-92165-8). Pantheon.
Naylor-Reynolds, Phyllis. Witch Water. (gr. k-6). 1988. pap. 3.25 (ISBN 0-440-40038-4, YB). Dell.
O'Connell, Margaret. The Magic Cauldron: Witchcraft for Good & Evil. LC 75-26757. (Illus.). 256p. (gr. 9-12). 1975. 27.95 (ISBN 0-87599-187-4). S G Phillips.
Rawson & Carlwright. Witches. (gr. k-4). 1979. 6.95 (ISBN 0-86020-341-7, Usborne-Hayes). EDC.
Scot, Reginald. Discoverie of Witchcraft. 1989. pap. 7.95 (ISBN 0-486-26030-5). Dover.
Starkey, Marion L. The Visionary Girls: Witchcraft in Salem Village. (gr. 7 up). 1973. 15.95 (ISBN 0-316-81087-8). Little.

WITCHCRAFT–FICTION

Adams, Adrienne. Woggle of Witches. Adams, Adrienne, illus. LC 70-161536. 32p. (ps-3). 1971. 13.95 (ISBN 0-684-12506-4, Scribners Young Read). Macmillan Child Grp.
—A Woggle of Witches. Adams, Adrienne, illus. LC 87-18703. 32p. (Orig.). (ps-1). 1985. pap. 4.95 (ISBN 0-689-71050-X, Aladdin). Macmillan Child Grp.
Adler, David A. I Know I'm a Witch. Stevenson, Sucie, illus. LC 86-33508. 32p. (gr. k-3). 1990. pap. 4.95 (ISBN 0-8050-1480-2). H Holt & Co.
Alexander, Lloyd. Black Cauldron. 192p. (gr. k-6). 1980. pap. 3.50 (ISBN 0-440-40649-8, YB). Dell.
Alexander, Sue. More Witch, Goblin & Ghost Stories. Winter, Jeanette, illus. LC 78-3280. (gr. 1-4). 1978. 6.95 (ISBN 0-394-83933-1); lib. bdg. 7.99 (ISBN 0-394-93933-6). Pantheon.
—Witch, Goblin & Ghost in the Haunted Woods. Winter, Jeanette, illus. LC 80-20863. 72p. (gr. 1-4). 1981. 6.95 (ISBN 0-394-84443-2); lib. bdg. 7.99 (ISBN 0-394-94443-7). Pantheon.
Auch, Mary J. The Witching of Ben Wagner. LC 87-14999. 192p. (gr. 3-7). 1987. 12.95 (ISBN 0-395-44522-1). HM.
Barnes, Megan. Be Careful What You Wish For, No. 2. (gr. 7-12). 1988. pap. 2.50 (ISBN 0-590-41297-3). Scholastic Inc.
—Gone with the Witch. 160p. (gr. 5-9). 1989. pap. 2.50 (ISBN 0-590-41298-1). Scholastic Inc.
—Lucky Thirteen, No. 1. (gr. 7-12). 1988. pap. 2.50 (ISBN 0-590-41296-5). Scholastic Inc.
—Teen Witch: Witch Switch, No. 4. 1989. pap. 2.50 (ISBN 0-590-41299-X). Scholastic Inc.
Battles, Edith. The Witch in Room Six. LC 86-45785. 144p. (gr. 3-7). 1987. 11.95 (ISBN 0-06-020412-5); PLB 12.89 (ISBN 0-06-020413-3). HarpC Child Bks.
—The Witch in Room Six. LC 86-45785. 160p. (gr. 3-7). 1989. pap. 3.50 (ISBN 0-06-440204-5, Trophy). HarpC Child Bks.
Bawden, Nina. The Witch's Daughter. large type ed. 288p. (gr. 3 up). 1988. lib. bdg. 16.95x (ISBN 0-7451-0654-4, Pub. by Chivers Pr UK). G K Hall.
Bellairs, John. The Lamp from the Warlock's Tomb. (gr. 4-8). 1989. pap. 3.50 (ISBN 0-553-15697-7, Skylark). Bantam.
—The Letter, the Witch, & the Ring. Egielski, Richard, illus. LC 75-28968. (gr. 4-7). 1976. 13.95 (ISBN 0-8037-4740-3). Dial Bks Young.
Bennett, Anna E. Little Witch. Stone, Helen, illus. LC 52-1374. (gr. 3-5). 1953. PLB 12.89 (ISBN 0-397-30261-4, Lipp Jr Bks). HarpC Child Bks.
—Little Witch. Stone, Helen, illus. LC 52-13721. 128p. (gr. 3-5). 1981. pap. 3.50 (ISBN 0-06-440119-7, Trophy). HarpC Child Bks.
Borisoff, Norman. Bewitched & Bewildered: A Spooky Love Story. 112p. (Orig.). (gr. 7-11). 1982. pap. 1.75 (ISBN 0-440-90905-8, LFL). Dell.

Bridges, Laurie & Alexander, Paul. Swamp Witch, No. 6. 160p. (Orig.). (gr. 7-12). 1987. pap. 2.50 (ISBN 0-553-26792-2). Bantam.
Bridwell, Norman. The Witch Grows Up. (Illus.). 32p. (Orig.). (gr. k-3). 1987. pap. 1.95 (ISBN 0-590-40559-4). Scholastic Inc.
—The Witch Next Door. Bridwell, Norman, illus. 32p. (gr. k-3). 1986. pap. 2.50 (ISBN 0-590-40433-4). Scholastic Inc.
—The Witch's Christmas. Bridwell, Norman, illus. (gr. k-3). 1972. pap. 1.50 (ISBN 0-590-09216-2). Scholastic Inc.
—The Witch's Christmas. Bridwell, Norman, illus. 32p. (gr. k-3). 1986. pap. 1.95 (ISBN 0-590-40434-2). Scholastic Inc.
—The Witch's Vacation. Bridwell, Norman, illus. 32p. (Orig.). (gr. k-3). 1987. pap. 2.50 (ISBN 0-590-40558-6). Scholastic Inc.
Briggs, K. M. Kate Crackernuts. LC 79-9229. (Illus.). 224p. (gr. 7 up). 1980. 13.50 (ISBN 0-688-80240-0). Greenwillow.
Calhoun, Mary. The Witch of Hissing Hill. McCaffery, Janet, illus. LC 64-15475. (gr. k-3). 1964. PLB 13.88 (ISBN 0-688-31762-6). Morrow.
—The Witch Who Lost Her Shadow. Nobel, Trinka H., illus. (gr. k-3). 1979. 9.57i (ISBN 0-06-020946-1). HarpC Child Bks.
Calif, Ruth. The Over-the-Hill Witch. Holub, Joan, illus. 144p. (gr. 5). 1990. 10.95 (ISBN 0-88289-754-3). Pelican.
Carlson, Nancy. Witch Lady. Carlson, Nancy, illus. LC 85-3756. 32p. (ps-3). 1985. PLB 9.95 (ISBN 0-87614-283-8). Carolrhoda Bks.
Carlson, Natalie S. Spooky & the Bad Luck Raven. Glass, Andrew, illus. LC 87-15471. (ps-1). 1988. 12.95 (ISBN 0-688-07650-5); lib. bdg. 12.88 (ISBN 0-688-07651-3). Lothrop.
Cheatham, Ann. The Witch of Lagg. (Orig.). (gr. k-12). 1987. pap. 2.50 (ISBN 0-440-99412-8, LFL). Dell.
Chew, Ruth. No Such Thing As a Witch. Chew, Ruth, illus. LC 79-18153. (gr. 2 up). 1980. 8.95 (ISBN 0-8038-5073-5). Hastings.
—No Such Thing As a Witch. Chew, Ruth, illus. (gr. 4-6). 1972. pap. 2.25 (ISBN 0-590-09261-8). Scholastic Inc.
—No Such Thing As a Witch. (gr. 4-7). 1990. pap. 2.50 (ISBN 0-590-44053-5). Scholastic Inc.
—Wednesday Witch. 1989. pap. 2.50 (ISBN 0-590-42761-X). Scholastic Inc.
—The Witch & the Ring. (gr. 2-4). 1989. pap. 2.50 (ISBN 0-590-42056-9, Apple Paperbacks). Scholastic Inc.
Christelow, Eileen. Glenda Feathers Cast a Spell. Christelow, Eileen, illus. 32p. (ps-3). 1990. 13.95 (ISBN 0-395-51122-4). HM.
—Jerome & the Witchcraft Kids. Christelow, Eileen, illus. LC 88-2597. 32p. (gr. k-3). 1988. 13.95 (ISBN 0-89919-742-6, Pub. by Clarion). Ticknor & Fields.
—Jerome & the Witchcraft Kids. Christelow, Eileen, illus. 32p. (ps-3). 1990. pap. 4.95 (ISBN 0-395-54428-9, Clarion Bks). HM.
Cole, Babette. The Trouble with Mom. Cole, Babette, illus. 32p. (gr. 5-8). 1984. 12.95 (ISBN 0-698-20624-X, Coward); pap. 5.95 (Coward). Putnam Pub Group.
Cole, Hannah. Pantomime Witch. Aldridge, D. S., illus. 32p. (gr. k up). 1990. 12.95 (ISBN 0-8249-8462-5). Ideals.
Cole, Jeanna. Bony-Legs. Zimmer, Dirk, illus. 48p. (gr. k-3). 1986. pap. 2.95 (ISBN 0-590-33222-8, Hello Reader). Scholastic Inc.
Cole, Joanna. Bony-Legs. Zimmer, Dirk, illus. 48p. (ps-2). 1986. pap. 2.95 (ISBN 0-590-40516-0). Scholastic Inc.
Coombs, Patricia. Dorrie & the Blue Witch. Coombs, Patricia, illus. 48p. (gr. k-6). 1980. pap. 1.50 (ISBN 0-440-42210-8, YB). Dell.
—Dorrie & the Museum Case. LC 84-27812. (Illus.). 48p. (gr. 1-5). 1986. 11.95 (ISBN 0-688-04278-3); PLB 11.88 (ISBN 0-688-04279-1). Lothrop.
—Dorrie & the Pin Witch. Coombs, Patricia, illus. LC 88-12697. 32p. (gr. 1-4). 1989. 12.95 (ISBN 0-688-08055-3); PLB 12.88 (ISBN 0-688-08056-1). Lothrop.
—Dorrie & the Witches' Camp. Coombs, Patricia, illus. LC 82-9986. 48p. (gr. 1-5). 1983. PLB 12.88 (ISBN 0-688-01508-5). Lothrop.
—Dorrie & the Wizard's Spell. Coombs, Patricia, illus. LC 68-27601. 48p. (gr. 1-5). 1968. PLB 12.88 (ISBN 0-688-51083-3). Lothrop.
Corbett, Scott. Witch Hunt. 144p. (gr. 5 up). 1985. 14.95 (ISBN 0-316-15750-3, Joy St Bks). Little.
Cowley, Joy. When Itchy Witchy Sneezes. Hodder, Wendy, illus. 8p. (gr. k-2). 1989. pap. text ed. 15.00 (ISBN 1-55911-281-6). Wright Group.
—When Itchy Witchy Sneezes, 6 bks. Hodder, Wendy, illus. 8p. (gr. k-2). 1986. Set. pap. text ed. 12.60 (ISBN 1-55911-349-9). Wright Group.
Curry, Jane L. The Great Flood Mystery. LC 85-1322. 180p. (gr. 3-6). 1985. 13.95 (ISBN 0-689-50306-7, M K McElderry). Macmillan Child Grp.
Dahl, Roald. Magic Finger. Pene DuBois, William, illus. LC 66-18657. 46p. (gr. 3-6). 1966. 13.95 (ISBN 0-06-021381-7); PLB 13.89 (ISBN 0-06-021382-5). HarpC Child Bks.
—The Witches. Blake, Quentin, photos by. LC 83-14195. (Illus.). 202p. (gr. 1 up). 1983. 15.95 (ISBN 0-374-38457-6); limited ed. 35.00 (ISBN 0-374-38458-4). FS&G.
—The Witches. Blake, Quentin, illus. LC 85-519. 200p. (gr. 3-7). 1985. pap. 3.95 (ISBN 0-14-031730-9, Penguin Bks). Viking Penguin.
DaLage, Ida. Beware! Beware! A Witch Won't Share. (Illus.). 48p. (gr. k-4). 1991. Repr. of 1972 ed. PLB 12.95 (ISBN 0-7910-1473-8). Chelsea Hse.
—The Farmer & the Witch. Miret, Gil, illus. 48p. (gr. k-4). 1991. Repr. of 1966 ed. PLB 12.95 (ISBN 0-7910-1474-6). Chelsea Hse.
Degen, Bruce. The Little Witch & the Riddle. Degen, Bruce, illus. LC 78-19475. 64p. (gr. k-3). 1988. pap. 3.50 (ISBN 0-06-444125-3, Trophy). HarpC Child Bks.
De Gerez, Toni. Louhi, Witch of North Farm. Cooney, Barbara, illus. LC 84-21600. 32p. (ps-3). 1986. pap. 13.95 (ISBN 0-670-80556-4). Viking Child Bks.
DeLage, Ida. The Old Witch & Her Magic Basket. Sloan, Ellen, illus. 48p. (gr. k-4). 1991. Repr. of 1978 ed. PLB 12.95 (ISBN 0-7910-1475-4). Chelsea Hse.
—The Old Witch & the Crows. Smith, Marianne, illus. 48p. (gr. k-4). 1991. Repr. of 1983 ed. PLB 12.95 (ISBN 0-7910-1476-2). Chelsea Hse.
—The Old Witch & the Dragon. Unada, illus. 48p. (gr. k-4). 1991. Repr. of 1979 ed. PLB 12.95 (ISBN 0-7910-1477-0). Chelsea Hse.
—The Old Witch & the Ghost Parade. Taylor, Jody, illus. 48p. (gr. k-4). 1991. Repr. of 1978 ed. PLB 12.95 (ISBN 0-7910-1478-9). Chelsea Hse.
—The Old Witch & the Snores. Miret, Gil, illus. 48p. (gr. k-4). 1991. Repr. of 1970 ed. PLB 12.95 (ISBN 0-7910-1479-7). Chelsea Hse.
—The Old Witch & the Wizard. Korach, Mimi, illus. 48p. (gr. k-4). 1991. Repr. of 1974 ed. PLB 12.95 (ISBN 0-7910-1480-0). Chelsea Hse.
—The Old Witch Finds a New House. Paris, Pat, illus. 48p. (gr. k-4). 1991. Repr. of 1979 ed. PLB 12.95 (ISBN 0-7910-1481-9). Chelsea Hse.
—The Old Witch Gets a Surprise. Sloan, Ellen, illus. 48p. (gr. k-4). 1991. Repr. of 1981 ed. PLB 12.95 (ISBN 0-7910-1482-7). Chelsea Hse.
—The Old Witch Goes to the Ball. Nebel, Gustave E., illus. 48p. (gr. k-4). 1991. Repr. of 1969 ed. PLB 12.95 (ISBN 0-7910-1483-5). Chelsea Hse.
De Lage, Ida. The Old Witch's Party. Korach, Mimi, illus. 48p. (gr. k-4). 1991. Repr. of 1976 ed. PLB 12.95 (ISBN 0-7910-1484-3). Chelsea Hse.
DeLage, Ida. Weeny Witch. Oechsli, Kelli, illus. 48p. (gr. k-4). 1991. Repr. of 1966 ed. PLB 12.95 (ISBN 0-7910-1485-1). Chelsea Hse.
—What Does a Witch Need? Schroeder, Ted, illus. 48p. (gr. k-4). 1991. Repr. of 1971 ed. PLB 12.95 (ISBN 0-7910-1486-X). Chelsea Hse.
—The Witchy Broom. Peaver, Walt, illus. 48p. (gr. k-4). 1991. Repr. of 1969 ed. PLB 12.95 (ISBN 0-7910-1487-8). Chelsea Hse.
Denan, Corinne. Witch Tales. new ed. LC 79-66328. (Illus.). 48p. (gr. 3-6). 1980. lib. bdg. 9.89 (ISBN 0-89375-324-6); pap. 2.95 (ISBN 0-89375-323-8). Troll Assocs.
—Wizard Tales. new ed. LC 79-66331. (Illus.). 48p. (gr. 3-6). 1980. lib. bdg. 9.89 (ISBN 0-89375-330-0); pap. 2.95 (ISBN 0-89375-329-7). Troll Assocs.
Douglis, Marjie. Matrix Witch. LC 86-11590. 288p. (gr. 7 up). 1988. PLB 12.95 (ISBN 0-317-64814-4, Dillon). Macmillan Child Grp.
Duane, Diane. Deep Wizardry. (gr. k-12). 1988. pap. 3.25 (ISBN 0-440-20070-9, LFL). Dell.
Duncan, Lois. Summer of Fear. 252p. (gr. 7-12). 1976. 14.95 (ISBN 0-316-19548-0). Little.
Embry, Margaret. The Blue-Nosed Witch. Rose, Carl, illus. 48p. (gr. 2-5). 1984. pap. 2.75 (ISBN 0-553-15435-4). Bantam.
Estes, Eleanor. The Witch Family. Hewitt, Kathryn & Ardizzone, Edward, illus. 192p. (gr. 3-7). 1990. pap. 4.95 (ISBN 0-15-298572-7). HarBraceJ.
Fitzgerald, Bridget. Winkie, the Cross-Eyed Witch. LC 71-189878. (Illus.). (gr. 1-2). 1973. 2.50 (ISBN 0-87884-020-6). Unicorn Ent.
Frances, Marian. Witch on a Motorcycle. new ed. (Illus.). (gr. 3-4). 1972. pap. 1.95 (ISBN 0-89375-047-6). Troll Assocs.
Freeman, Don. Space Witch. (Illus.). (gr. k-3). 1979. pap. 4.95 (ISBN 0-14-050346-3, Puffin). Puffin Bks.
—Tilly Witch. (ps-k). 1978. pap. 3.95 (ISBN 0-14-050262-9, Puffin). Puffin Bks.
—Tilly Witch. Freeman, Don, illus. (gr. k-3). 1969. pap. 13.95 (ISBN 0-670-71303-1). Viking Child Bks.
Furlong, Monica. Juniper. LC 90-39800. 192p. (gr. 5-9). 1991. 12.95 (ISBN 0-394-83220-5); lib. bdg. 13.99 (ISBN 0-394-93220-X). Knopf.
—Wise Child. LC 87-3063. 192p. (gr. 5 up). 1987. lib. bdg. 12.99 (ISBN 0-394-99105-2). Knopf.
—Wise Child. LC 87-3063. 240p. (gr. 5 up). 1989. pap. 2.95 (ISBN 0-394-82598-5, Borzoi Sprinters). Knopf.
Gilmore, Kate. Enter Three Witches. 216p. (gr. 5-9). 1990. 13.95 (ISBN 0-395-50213-6). HM.
Godden, Rumer. Mr. McFadden's Hallowe'en. 128p. (gr. 4-6). 1975. pap. 10.95 (ISBN 0-670-49271-X). Viking Child Bks.
Gondosch, Linda. The Witches of Hopper Street. Coganchery, Helen, illus. LC 85-25401. 128p. (gr. 4-6). 1986. 12.95 (ISBN 0-525-67178-1, Lodestar Bks). Dutton Child Bks.
Griffiths, Helen. The Mysterious Appearance of Agnes. Ambrus, Victor, illus. LC 74-21793. 160p. (gr. 7 up). 1975. 12.95 (ISBN 0-8234-0267-3). Holiday.
Grimm, Jacob & Grimm, Wilhelm K. Jorinda & Joringel. Cutts, David, ed. Rickman, David, illus. LC 87-10937. 32p. (gr. k-4). 1988. PLB 9.79 (ISBN 0-8167-1065-1); pap. text ed. 1.95 (ISBN 0-8167-1066-X). Troll Assocs.
Guthrie, Donna. The Witch Has an Itch. Arnsteen, Katy K., illus. 24p. (ps-1). 1990. pap. 2.25 (ISBN 0-671-70346-3). S&S Trade.
—The Witch Who Lives down the Hall. Schwartz, Amy, illus. LC 85-887. 32p. (ps-3). 1985. 12.95 (ISBN 0-15-298610-3, Pub. by HJ). HarBraceJ.
Hader, Bertha. Hansel & Gretel. 1990. 3.98 (ISBN 0-8317-4268-2). Smithmark.
Hahn, Mary D. The Time of the Witch. 160p. (gr. 4-8). 1982. 12.95 (ISBN 0-89919-115-0, Clarion). HM.
Hall, Lynn. Dagmar Schultz & the Powers of Darkness. LC 88-30806. 80p. (gr. 5-8). 1989. 11.95 (ISBN 0-684-19037-0, Scribners Young Read). Macmillan Child Grp.
Harler, Anne. The Witch Switch. Doty, Bob, illus. 64p. (Orig.). (gr. k-2). 1987. pap. 1.95 (ISBN 0-87406-245-4). Willowisp Pr.
Hautzig, Deborah. Little Witch's Big Night. Brown, Marc, illus. LC 84-3309. 48p. (ps-2). 1984. PLB 6.99 (ISBN 0-394-96587-6, Pub. by BYR); pap. 2.95 (ISBN 0-394-86587-1). Random.
—Little Witch's Big Night. Graham, Alastair, illus. 48p. (gr. 1-3). 1986. pap. 5.95 book & cassette (ISBN 0-394-88334-9, Random Juv). Random.
Haynes, Betsy. The Witches of Wakeman. (gr. 4-7). 1990. pap. 2.75 (ISBN 0-553-15830-9). Bantam.
Henry, Terry H. The Witch Who Couldn't. O'Toole, Tom, illus. 96p. (gr. 5). 1988. 10.95 (ISBN 0-947962-39-5, Pub. by Anvil Bks Ltd Ireland). Irish Bks Media.
Himmelman, John. Amanda & the Witch Switch. Himmelman, John, illus. LC 84-19515. 32p. (ps). 1985. pap. 9.95 (ISBN 0-670-11531-2). Viking Child Bks.
Hughes, Frieda. Getting Rid of Aunt Edna. Levine, Edward, illus. LC 85-45255. 80p. (gr. 3-7). 1986. PLB 11.89 (ISBN 0-06-022637-4). HarpC Child Bks.
Hunt, Robert. The Accident & Derring-Do. McKissick, Vernon, illus. LC 76-730163. (gr. 3-5). 1978. pap. 29.95 6 bks. & 1 cass. (ISBN 0-89290-024-5); pap. 10.95 1 bk., 1 cass. (ISBN 0-685-04623-0). Soc for Visual.
—Bossy, Boring Maurice the Beast. McKissick, Vernon, illus. LC 76-730161. (gr. 3-5). 1978. pap. 29.95 6 bks. & 1 cass. (ISBN 0-89290-022-9); pap. 10.95 1 bk. & 1 cass. (ISBN 0-685-04630-3). Soc for Visual.
—The Glut's Peanut Butter Pie. McKissick, Vernon, illus. LC 76-730160. (gr. 3-5). 1978. pap. 29.95 6 bks. & 1 cass. (ISBN 0-89290-021-0); pap. 10.95 1 bk. & 1 cass. (ISBN 0-685-04645-1). Soc for Visual.
—The Lake Murkwood Monster. McKissick, Vernon, illus. LC 76-730159. (gr. 3-5). 1978. pap. 29.95 6 bks. & 1 cass. (ISBN 0-89290-020-2); pap. 10.95 1 bk. & 1 cass. (ISBN 0-685-04657-5). Soc for Visual.
—Lucifer & Bully Balderdash. McKissick, Vernon, illus. LC 76-730158. (gr. 3-5). 1978. pap. 29.95 6 bks. & 1 cass. (ISBN 0-89290-019-9); pap. 10.95 1 bk. & 1 cass. Soc for Visual.
—The Magic Words. McKissick, Vernon, illus. LC 76-730162. (gr. 3-5). 1978. pap. 29.95 6 bks. & 1 cass. (ISBN 0-89290-023-7); pap. 10.95 1 bk. & 1 cass. Soc for Visual.
Hutchins, Pat. Which Witch Is Which? LC 88-18781. (Illus.). 24p. (ps up). 1989. 14.95 (ISBN 0-688-06357-8); PLB 14.88 (ISBN 0-688-06358-6). Greenwillow.
Jackson, Steve & Livingstone, Ian. The Warlock of Firetop Mountain. (gr. 5 up). 1983. pap. 1.95 (ISBN 0-440-99381-4, LFL). Dell.
Jasner, W. K. Which Is the Witch? Chess, Victoria, illus. LC 78-11757. (gr. 2-4). 1979. Pantheon.
Johnson, Norma T. The Witch House. 144p. (Orig.). 1990. pap. 2.95 (ISBN 0-380-75789-3, Camelot). Avon.
Johnston, Tony. The Witch's Hat. Tomes, Margot, illus. LC 84-9948. 32p. (ps-3). 1984. 9.95 (ISBN 0-399-21010-5, Putnam). Putnam Pub Group.
Jones, Diane W. Witch Week. LC 82-6074. 224p. (gr. 5-9). 1982. reinforced bdg. 11.75 (ISBN 0-688-01534-4). Greenwillow.
Karlin, Nurit. The Tooth Witch. Karlin, Nurit, illus. LC 84-48495. 32p. (ps-2). 1985. 11.95 (ISBN 0-397-32119-8, Lipp Jr Bks); PLB 11.89 (ISBN 0-397-32120-1). HarpC Child Bks.
Katz, Welwyn W. Witchery Hill. (gr. k up). 1990. pap. 3.50 (ISBN 0-440-20637-5, LFL). Dell.
Keller, Charles. Little Witch Presents a Monster Joke Book. Glovach, Linda, illus. 40p. (ps-4). 1983. pap. 4.95 (ISBN 0-13-537811-7, Pub. by Treehouse). P-H.
Key, Alexander. Escape to Witch Mountain. Wisdom, Leon, Jr., illus. LC 68-11206. 172p. (gr. 5-10). 1968. 10.95 (ISBN 0-664-32417-7, Westminster). Westminster John Knox.
Kimmel, Margaret M. Magic in the Mist. Hyman, Trina S., illus. LC 74-18186. 32p. (gr. k-4). 1975. 13.95 (ISBN 0-689-50026-2, M K McElderry). Macmillan Child Grp.
Konigsburg, E. L. Jennifer, Hecate, Macbeth, William McKinley & Me, Elizabeth. Konigsburg, E. L., illus. LC 67-10458. 128p. (gr. 3-5). 1971. 12.95 (ISBN 0-689-30007-7, Atheneum Child Bk). Macmillan Child Grp.

WOLVES–FICTION

Aiken, Joan. The Wolves of Willoughby Chase. 176p. (gr. k-6). 1987. pap. 3.50 (ISBN 0-440-49603-9, YB). Dell.

—The Wolves of Willoughby Chase. Marriott, Pat, illus. LC 63-18034. 168p. (gr. 4-6). 1989. pap. 13.95 (ISBN 0-385-03594-2). Doubleday.

Barkan, Joanne. Whiskerville School. Schmidt, Karen L., illus. 12p. (ps-k). 1990. bds. 3.50 (ISBN 0-448-19465-1, G&D). Putnam Pub Group.

Bradman, Tony. Who's Afraid of the Big Bad Wolf? Chamberlain, Margaret, illus. LC 89-134. (ps). 1989. 11.95 (Aladdin). Macmillan.

Bykov, Vasilii. Pack of Wolves. Solotaroff, Lynn, tr. from RUS. LC 80-2456. 192p. (gr. 7 up). 1981. (Crowell Jr Bks). HarpC Child Bks.

Cuyler, Margery. Weird Wolf. Zimmer, Dirk, illus. 80p. (gr. 2-4). 1989. 12.95 (ISBN 0-8050-0835-7). H Holt & Co.

De Marolles, Chantal. The Lonely Wolf. Schmid, Eleonore, illus. LC 86-2511. 32p. (gr. k-3). 1986. 13.95 (ISBN 1-55858-073-5). North-South Bks NYC.

Dinardo, Jeffrey. The Wolf Who Cried Boy. Dinardo, Jeffrey, illus. 32p. (ps-2). 1989. 8.95 (ISBN 0-448-09314-6, G&D). Putnam Pub Group.

George, Jean C. The Wounded Wolf. Schoenherr, John, illus. LC 76-58711. (ps-3). 1978. PLB 13.89 (ISBN 0-06-021950-5). HarpC Child Bks.

Grimm, Jacob & Grimm, Wilhelm K. Little Red Riding Hood. Schmidt, Karen, illus. 32p. (Orig.). (gr. k-2). 1986. pap. 2.50 (ISBN 0-590-41881-5). Scholastic Inc.

Hasting, S. Peter & The Wolf. Hastings, Selina, retold by. Cartwright, Reg, illus. LC 86-27004. 32p. (gr. k-2). 1987. 12.95 (ISBN 0-8050-0408-4). H Holt & Co.

Helakisa, Kaarina. The Journey of Pietari & His Wolf. Rollerson, Michael, tr. from SWE. Tikka, Saara, illus. LC 84-80571. 72p. (gr. 7-12). 1984. 14.95 (ISBN 0-88138-043-1). Green Tiger Pr.

Horowitz, Lynn R. The Good Bad Wolf. Urbahn, Clara, illus. LC 89-63141. 26p. (Orig.). (ps-1). 1989. pap. 7.95 spiral bdg. (ISBN 0-938678-12-4). New Seed.

Huebel, Russ. The Big Bad Wolf in Texas. Espinosa, Tony, illus. 48p. (Orig.). 1983. pap. 6.25 (ISBN 0-9611604-2-X). C Del Grullo.

Kasza, Keiko. The Wolf's Chicken Stew. Kasza, Keiko, illus. (gr. k-3). 1987. 12.95 (ISBN 0-399-21400-3, Putnam). Putnam Pub Group.

LaFleur, Tom & Brennan, Gale. Woolly the Wolf. Bond, Bruce, illus. 16p. (Orig.). (gr. k-6). 1981. pap. 1.25 (ISBN 0-685-02459-8). Brennan Bks.

London, Jack. White Fang. (gr. 7 up). 1972. pap. 2.50 (ISBN 0-590-40523-3, Apple Classics). Scholastic Inc.

—White Fang. 256p. (gr. 6 up). 1986. pap. 2.75 (ISBN 0-590-42591-9). Scholastic Inc.

Loring, Honey & Harris, John. The Big Good Wolf. Deutsch, Nicholas, illus. 28p. (ps-6). 1990. pap. text ed. 2.75 (ISBN 0-9626566-0-7). Gone Dogs.

McCleery, William. Wolf Story. Chappell, Warren, illus. LC 87-25977. 82p. (gr. 1-6). 1988. Repr. of 1947 ed. PLB 15.00 (ISBN 0-208-02191-4, Linnet). Shoe String.

McGuire, Barry & White, Logan. In the Midst of Wolves. LC 90-80612. 224p. (Orig.). 1990. pap. 8.95 (ISBN 0-89107-572-0, Crossway Bks). Good News.

Morey, Walt. Kavik, the Wolf Dog. 192p. (gr. 4-7). 1989. pap. 2.95 (ISBN 0-590-44113-2). Scholastic Inc.

Nickl, Peter. The Story of the Kind Wolf. Wilkon, Jozef, illus. LC 87-42923. 32p. (gr. k-3). 1988. 12.95 (ISBN 1-55858-066-2); pap. 4.95 (ISBN 1-55858-058-1). North-South Bks NYC.

North, Sterling. The Wolfling. 256p. (gr. 3-7). 1980. pap. 2.25 (ISBN 0-590-30254-X). Scholastic Inc.

—The Wolfling. 256p. (gr. 4-6). pap. 2.50 (ISBN 0-590-41868-8). Scholastic Inc.

Oetting, R. Quetico Wolf. LC 71-190274. (Illus.). 48p. (gr. 4 up). 1972. PLB 9.95 (ISBN 0-87783-059-2); pap. 3.94 deluxe ed. (ISBN 0-87783-103-3). Oddo.

Porter, Sue. Little Wolf & the Giant. (ps-1). 1990. pap. 13.95 (ISBN 0-671-70363-3). S&S Trade.

Prokofiev, Sergei. Peter & the Wolf. Muller, Jorg, illus. LC 86-7462. 24p. (ps-6). 1986. Set. 15.95 (ISBN 0-394-88417-5); bk. & cassette 21.95 (ISBN 0-394-88418-3). Knopf.

—Peter & the Wolf. Carlson, Maria, tr. Mikolayack, Charles, illus. 32p. (ps-3). 1986. pap. 3.95 (ISBN 0-14-050633-0, Puffin). Puffin Bks.

—Peter & the Wolf. Crampton, Patricia, tr. Palecek, Josef, illus. LC 87-13915. (ps up). 1987. 13.95 (ISBN 0-88708-049-9). Picture Bk Studio.

—Peter & the Wolf. Voigt, Erna, illus. LC 79-92902. 32p. 1987. 14.95 (ISBN 0-87923-331-1). Godine.

—Peter & the Wolf Pop-up-Book. Cooney, Barbara, illus. (gr. k-12). 1986. pap. 16.95 (ISBN 0-670-80849-0). Viking Child Bks.

Richmond, Gary. Prodigal Wolf. 1990. write for info. (ISBN 0-8499-0746-2). Word Bks.

Sharmat, Marjorie W. Walter the Wolf. LC 74-26659. (Illus.). 32p. (gr. k-3). 1989. pap. 5.95 (ISBN 0-8234-0778-0). Holiday.

Shura, Mary F. Mister Wolf & Me. (gr. 3-7). Date not set. 8.95 (ISBN 0-396-07666-1, Putnam). Putnam Pub Group.

Spanjian, Beth. Baby Wolf. (ps-1). 1990. write for info. (ISBN 0-307-12598-X). Western Pub.

White Fang. 224p. 1989. pap. 2.50 (ISBN 0-8125-0512-3). Tor Bks.

Wisler, G. Clifton. Winter of the Wolf. LC 80-21851. (gr. 6 up). 1981. 10.95 (ISBN 0-525-66716-4, Lodestar Bks). Dutton Child Bks.

—The Wolf's Tooth. LC 87-543. 128p. (gr. 5-9). 1987. 12.95 (ISBN 0-525-67197-8, Lodestar Bks). Dutton Child Bks.

The Wolf & the Seven Little Kids. (Illus.). (ps-4). 3.50 (ISBN 0-7214-5011-3). Ladybird Bks.

Zdanys, Al P. Luke: The Canadian Timberwolf. (Illus., Orig.). 1989. pap. 6.95 (ISBN 0-685-29652-0). Appletree Bks.

Zoline, Pamela. Annika & the Wolves. Zoline, Pamela, illus. LC 84-28529. 26p. (gr. 4 up). 1985. 12.95 (ISBN 0-915124-91-2). Coffee Hse.

WOMEN

see also Girls; Mothers

Aten, Jerry. Women in History. Hyndman, Kathryn, illus. 144p. (gr. 4 up). 1986. wkbk. 11.95 (ISBN 0-86653-344-3, GA 692). Good Apple.

Epstein, Vivian S. History of Women for Children. Epstein, Vivian S., illus. 32p. (ps-5). 1984. 12.95 (ISBN 0-9601002-4-5); pap. 5.95 (ISBN 0-9601002-3-7). V S Epstein.

Harris, Sarah. Finding out About: Women in Twentieth Century Britain. (Illus.). 48p. (gr. 7-10). 1989. 19.95 (ISBN 0-7134-5661-2, Pub. by Batsford England). Trafalgar Sq.

Ingraham, Gloria D. & Ingraham, Leonard W. An Album of America Women: Their Changing Role. (Illus.). 96p. (gr. 4 up). 1987. PLB 13.90 (ISBN 0-531-10317-X). Watts.

Knudson, R. R. Martina Navratilova: Tennis Power. Angelini, George, illus. LC 85-40832. 64p. (gr. 2-6). 1986. pap. 10.95 (ISBN 0-670-80665-X). Viking Child Bks.

Mitchell, Joyce. Other Choices for Becoming a Woman. (gr. 7 up). 1975. pap. 6.00 (ISBN 0-912786-34-5). Know Inc.

Phelps, Ethel J., ed. Tatterhood & Other Tales. Baldwin-Ford, Pamela, illus. Phelps, Ethel, intro. by. LC 78-9352. (Illus.). 192p. (Orig.). (gr. 1 up). 1978. o. p. 11.95 (ISBN 0-912670-49-5); pap. 8.95 (ISBN 0-912670-50-9). Feminist Pr.

WOMEN–BIOGRAPHY

Archer, James. Breaking Barriers: The Feminist Movement. 1991. 14.95 (ISBN 0-670-83104-2). Viking Child Bks.

Aten, Jerry. Outstanding Women. Hierstein, Judy, illus. 64p. (gr. k-4). 1987. pap. 6.95 (ISBN 0-86653-413-X, GA1008). Good Apple.

Benavidez, Barbara. My School Years: Kindergarten Through Graduation. (Illus.). (gr. 5-12). 24.95 (ISBN 0-9619463-0-X). Barmarle Pubns.

Blau, Justine. Betty Friedan. Horner, Matina, intro. by. (Illus.). 112p. (gr. 5 up). 1991. lib. bdg. 17.95 (ISBN 1-55546-653-2). Chelsea Hse.

Byrne, Pamela R. & Kinnell, Susan. Women in North America: Summaries of Biographical Articles in History Journals. 146p. (gr. 9-12). 1988. pap. text ed. 18.00 (ISBN 0-87436-537-6). ABC Clio.

Cain, Michael. Louise Nevelson. Horner, Matina S., intro. by. (Illus.). 112p. (gr. 5 up). 1989. 17.95 (ISBN 1-55546-671-0). Chelsea Hse.

Daffron, Carolyn. Gloria Steinem. Horner, Matina, intro. by. (Illus.). 112p. (gr. 5 up). 1988. lib. bdg. 17.95 (ISBN 1-55546-679-6). Chelsea Hse.

Dengler, Sandy. Fanny Crosby: Writer of Eight Thousand Songs. (Orig.). (gr. 6). 1985. pap. 3.95 (ISBN 0-8024-2529-1). Moody.

De Pauw, Linda G. Founding Mothers: Women of America in the Revolutionary Era. (Illus.). 228p. (gr. 7 up). 1975. 13.95 (ISBN 0-395-21896-9). HM.

Doherty, Katherine M. & Doherty, Craig A. Benazir Bhutto. (Illus.). 144p. (gr. 9-12). 1990. PLB 13.90 (ISBN 0-531-10936-4). Watts.

Faber, Doris. Margaret Thatcher: Britain's Iron Lady. Masheris, Robert, illus. LC 85-40442. 57p. (gr. 3-6). 1985. pap. 10.95 (ISBN 0-670-80785-0). Viking Child Bks.

Giff, Patricia R. Mother Teresa: Sister to the Poor. Lewin, Ted, illus. (gr. 2-6). 1987. pap. 3.95 (ISBN 0-14-032225-6, Puffin). Puffin Bks.

Gray, Charlotte. Mother Teresa: Her Mission to Serve God by Caring for the Poor. Sherwood, Rhoda, ed. LC 88-2226. (Illus.). 68p. (gr. 5-6). 1988. PLB 12.95 (ISBN 1-55532-816-4). Gareth Stevens Inc.

Gurasich, Marjorie A. Red Wagons & White Canvas: Mollie Bailey, Circus Queen of the Southwest. Roberts, Melissa, ed. Hill, Francis, illus. 88p. (gr. 4-7). 1988. 8.95 (ISBN 0-89015-646-8, Pub. by Panda Bks). Eakin Pr.

Hamilton, Leni. Clara Barton. Horner, Matina, intro. by. (Illus.). 112p. (gr. 5 up). 1988. lib. bdg. 17.95 (ISBN 1-55546-641-9). Chelsea Hse.

Harrison, Pat. Jeanne Kirkpatrick. Horner, Matina, intro. by. (Illus.). 112p. (gr. 5 up). 1991. lib. bdg. 17.95 (ISBN 1-55546-663-X). Chelsea Hse.

Haskins, James. Shirley Temple Black: Actress to Ambassador. Ruff, Donna, illus. 64p. (gr. 2-7). 1988. pap. 10.95 (ISBN 0-670-81957-3). Viking Child Bks.

—Winnie Mandela: Life of Struggle. (Illus.). 192p. (gr. 6 up). 1988. 14.95 (ISBN 0-399-21515-8, Putnam). Putnam Pub Group.

Hazel Brannon Smith: Mini-Play. (gr. 6 up). 1978. 6.50 (ISBN 0-89550-304-2). Stevens & Shea.

Heard, Regie & Langenhahn, Bonnie. Regie's Love: A Daughter of Former Slaves Recalls. 2nd, rev. ed. Glueck, illus. Bonjean, Marilyn, frwd. by. LC 87-61795. (Illus.). 168p. (gr. 8 up). 1989. pap. 9.95 (ISBN 0-9618212-1-3). McCormick & Schilling.

Henry, Sondra & Taitz, Emily. One Woman's Power: A Biography of Gloria Steinem. Steinem, Gloria, afterword by. LC 86-11631. (Illus.). 128p. (gr. 6 up). 1987. PLB 12.95 (ISBN 0-87518-346-8, Dillon). Macmillan Child Grp.

Higgins, Ardis O. Portraits of Courageous Women. (Illus.). (gr. 5-8). 1978. pap. text ed. 4.00x (ISBN 0-912256-12-5). Halls of Ivy.

Hovde, Jane. Jane Addams. 144p. (gr. 5 up). 1989. 16.95 (ISBN 0-8160-1547-3). Facts on File.

Howe, James. Carol Burnett: The Sound of Laughter. Masheris, Robert, illus. 64p. (gr. 2-6). 1988. pap. 3.95 (ISBN 0-14-032075-X, Puffin). Puffin Bks.

IlgenFritz, Elizabeth. Anne Hutchinson. Horner, Matina, intro. by. (Illus.). 112p. (gr. 5 up). 1991. lib. bdg. 17.95 (ISBN 1-55546-660-5). Chelsea Hse.

James, Cary. Julia Morgan. Horner, Matina S., intro. by. (Illus.). 112p. (gr. 5 up). 1990. 17.95 (ISBN 1-55546-669-9). Chelsea Hse.

James, R. S. Mozambique. (Illus.). 104p. (gr. 5 up). 1988. lib. bdg. 14.95 (ISBN 1-55546-194-8). Chelsea Hse.

Johnson, Ann D. The Value of Friendship: The Story of Jane Addams. Pileggi, Steve, illus. LC 79-21643. (gr. k-6). 1979. 9.95 (ISBN 0-916392-45-7, Pub. by Value Communications). Oak Tree Pubns.

Jones, Constance. Karen Horney. Horner, Matina S., intro. by. (Illus.). 112p. (gr. 5 up). 1989. 17.95 (ISBN 1-55546-659-1). Chelsea Hse.

Kent, Charlotte. Barbara McClintock. Horner, Matina, intro. by. (Illus.). 112p. (gr. 5 up). 1991. lib. bdg. 17.95 (ISBN 1-55546-666-4). Chelsea Hse.

Klever, Anita. Women in Television. LC 75-22352. (Illus.). 142p. (gr. 9-11). 1975. 5.95 (ISBN 0-664-32579-3, Westminster). Westminster John Knox.

Kliment, Bud. Billie Holiday. King, Coretta Scott, intro. by. (Illus.). 112p. (gr. 5 up). 1990. lib. bdg. 17.95 (ISBN 1-55546-592-7). Chelsea Hse.

Knudson, R. R. Julie Brown: Racing Against the World. Pinkney, J. Brian, illus. (gr. 2-6). 1988. pap. 10.95 (ISBN 0-670-81487-3). Viking Child Bks.

—Martina Navratilova: Tennis Power. Angelini, George, illus. LC 85-40832. 64p. (gr. 2-6). 1986. pap. 10.95 (ISBN 0-670-80665-X). Viking Child Bks.

Laura Ingalls Wilder. (gr. 2-6). 1988. pap. 3.95 (ISBN 0-14-032074-1, Puffin). Puffin Bks.

Lefer, Diane. Emma Lazarus. Horner, Matina, intro. by. (Illus.). 112p. (gr. 5 up). 1988. lib. bdg. 17.95 (ISBN 1-55546-664-8). Chelsea Hse.

Madison, Curt & Yarber, Yvonne Y. Josephine Roberts - A Biography: Tanana. 64p. (Orig.). (gr. 6-8). 1983. pap. 6.95 (ISBN 0-910871-02-7). Spirit Mount Pr.

Martina Navratilova. (gr. 2-6). 1989. pap. 3.50 (ISBN 0-14-033218-9, Puffin). Puffin Bks.

Meltzer, Milton. Dorothea Lange: Life Through the Camera. Diamond, Donna, illus. Lange, Dorothea, photos by. 64p. (gr. 2-6). 1986. pap. 3.95 (ISBN 0-14-032105-5, Puffin). Puffin Bks.

—Tongue of Flame: The Story of Lydia Maria Child. LC 65-15228. 224p. (gr. 5 up). 1990. PLB 13.89 (ISBN 0-690-04903-X, Crowell Jr Bks). HarpC Child Bks.

—Winnie Mandela: The Soul of South Africa. Marchesi, Stephen, illus. LC 86-5531. 64p. (gr. 2-6). 1986. pap. 10.95 (ISBN 0-670-81249-8). Viking Child Bks.

Morrison, Ellen E. Lady of Legend: The Mystery of the Female Stranger of Gadsby's Tavern. 2nd, rev. ed. LC 87-460803. (Illus.). 16p. (gr. 6). 1986. saddle-stitched 1.75 (ISBN 0-9622537-2-3). Morielle Pr.

Murrow, Liza K. Lolly Cochran: Veterinarian. Schwarz, Marsha, photos by. LC 88-51682. (Illus.). 64p. (Orig.). (gr. 4-8). 1989. pap. text ed. 6.95 (ISBN 0-9621820-0-1). Teachers Lab.

—Susan Humphris: Geologist. Woods Hole Oceanographic Institution Staff, photos by. LC 88-51681. (Illus.). 64p. (Orig.). (gr. 4-8). 1989. pap. text ed. 6.95 (ISBN 0-9621820-1-X). Teachers Lab.

Paolucci, Bridget. Beverly Sills: Opera Singer. Horner, Matina S., intro. by. LC 89-17324. (Illus.). 112p. (gr. 5 up). 1990. 17.95 (ISBN 1-55546-677-X). Chelsea Hse.

Peavy, Linda & Smith, Ursula. Dreams into Deeds: Nine Women Who Dared. LC 85-40295. 160p. (gr. 6-9). 1985. 13.95 (ISBN 0-684-18484-2, Scribners Young Read). Macmillan Child Grp.

—Women Who Changed Things. LC 82-21612. (Illus.). 208p. (gr. 5 up). 1983. 14.95 (ISBN 0-684-17849-4, Scribners Young Read). Macmillan Child Grp.

Popson, Martha. That We Might Have Life. LC 80-2080. 128p. (gr. 6 up). 1981. pap. 2.75 (ISBN 0-385-17438-1, Im). Doubleday.

Roberts, Naurice. Barbara Jordan: The Great Lady from Texas. LC 83-23169. (Illus.). 32p. (gr. 2-5). 1984. lib. bdg. 13.27 (ISBN 0-516-03511-8); pap. 3.95 (ISBN 0-516-43511-6). Childrens.

Selden, Bernice. The Story of Annie Sullivan, Helen Keller's Teacher. (Orig.). (gr. k-6). 1987. pap. 2.95 (ISBN 0-440-48285-2, YB). Dell.

Shinn, Florence S. The Writings of Florence Scovel Shinn. 368p. (Orig.). 1988. pap. 12.95 sewn bdg. (ISBN 0-87516-610-5). DeVorss.

Shklar, Judith. Montesquieu. 144p. (gr. 5up). 1987. 24.95 (ISBN 0-19-287649-X); pap. 6.95 (ISBN 0-19-287648-1). Oxford U Pr.

Shrady, Maria. The Mother Teresa Story. Shrady, Frederick, illus. 48p. (gr. 5-8). 1987. pap. 3.95 (ISBN 0-8091-6567-8). Paulist Pr.

Siegel, Mary-Ellen K. Her Way: A Guide to Biographies of Women for Young People. 2nd ed. LC 83-22375. xxii, 418p. (gr. 6-9). 1984. pap. 10.00 (ISBN 0-8389-0462-9). ALA.

Silvani, Harold. Famous People - Women. Cruz, Harry H., illus. 52p. (gr. 4-8). 1975. wkbk. 6.95 (ISBN 1-878669-22-2, 4345). Crea Tea Assocs.

Storr, Catherine, as told by. Ruth's Story. (Illus.). 32p. (gr. k-4). 1985. PLB 14.65 (ISBN 0-8172-2043-7). Raintree Pubs.

Towns, Saundra. Lillian Hellman. Horner, Matina S., intro. by. (Illus.). 112p. (gr. 5 up). 1990. 17.95 (ISBN 1-55546-657-5). Chelsea Hse.

Verheyden-Hilliard, Mary Ellen. American Women in Science Engineering. Biro, Scarlet & Rom, Holly M., illus. 32p. 1988. pap. 5.00 (ISBN 0-932469-19-1); 70.00 set. Equity Inst.
This illustrated, 15-book series presents contemporary African-American Indian, Asian-American, Hispanic, & Caucasian women who, in girlhood, overcame barriers of gender, race, language, & poverty to become scientists. Five of the books are about girls with physical disabilities who also went on to become scientists. "Inspiring group of biographies of women in science...Children in the lower grades with reading problems can use them for...biographical information."-- SCHOOL LIBRARY JOURNAL. "... useful to teachers who want to help girls become more positive towards mathematics & science... recommended."-- CURRICULUM REVIEW. "...smoothly written texts..."-- BOOKLIST. "...help children...see the connection...between determination to persevere in the face of disabilities & later 'payoff'...in a variety of very exciting careers."-- NEWSLETTER, Association of Black Women in Higher Education. "...warm, lively & true stories of young girls who went on to become successful scientists..."-- GIFTED CHILDREN MONTHLY. "...these books are so attractively produced that I can't imagine elementary classroom teaching without them."-- PERSPECTIVES, National Women Studies Association. Also avaiable are tie-in Teaching Guide $10.00 (ISBN 0-932469-19-3), & video: "You Can Be a Scientist Too!" $46.00 (ISBN 0-932469-11-6). "Well written & filmed... appealing...inspiring production."-- BOOKLIST.
Publisher Provided Annotation.

Watson, D. Jeanene. Teresa of Calcutta. LC 84-60313. (gr. 3-6). 1984. pap. 6.95 (ISBN 0-88062-012-9). Mott Media.

Wenzel, Dorothy. Ann Bancroft: On Top of the World. LC 89-11980. (Illus.). 64p. (gr. 3 up). 1989. PLB 10.95 (ISBN 0-87518-418-9, Dillon). Macmillan Child Grp.

Wolitzer, Hilma. Introducing Shirley Braverman. LC 75-25872. 160p. (gr. 3 up). 1975. 9.95 (ISBN 0-374-33646-6). FS&G.

Wyllie, Stephen. There Was an Old Woman. Roffey, Maurenn, illus. LC 85-42639. 24p. (ps-3). 1985. 7.95 (ISBN 0-694-00050-7). HarpC Child Bks.

WOMEN–CLOTHING
see Clothing and Dress

WOMEN–DRESS
see Clothing and Dress; Costume

WOMEN–EMPLOYMENT

Berger, Gilda. Women, Work & Wages. LC 85-15379. (Illus.). 128p. (gr. 7-12). 1986. PLB 12.90 (ISBN 0-531-10074-X). Watts.

English, Betty L. Women at Their Work. English, Betty L., illus. LC 76-42924. 48p. (gr. k-4). 1988. pap. 4.95 (ISBN 0-8037-0496-8). Dial Bks Young.

Fenten, D. X. Ms. Attorney. LC 74-4492. (Illus.). 160p. (gr. 9 up). 1974. 7.50 (ISBN 0-664-32552-1, Westminster). Westminster John Knox.

Fox, Mary V. Women Astronauts: Aboard the Space Shuttle. rev. ed. LC 87-10814. (Illus.). 144p. (gr. 7 up). 1987. lib. bdg. 13.98 (ISBN 0-671-64840-3); pap. 5.95 (ISBN 0-671-64841-1). Messner.

Lee, Mary P. Ms. Veterinarian. LC 74-14990. (Illus.). 138p. (gr. 7-12). 1976. 8.95 (ISBN 0-664-32594-7, Westminster). Westminster John Knox.

Macdonald, Fiona. Working for Equality. MacDonald, Ed, ed. (Illus.). 48p. (gr. 4 up). 1988. PLB 11.90 (ISBN 0-531-19500-7, Hampstead Pr). Watts.

Mayfield, Susan. Timeline: Women & Power. (Illus.). 64p. (gr. 7-9). 1989. 19.95 (ISBN 0-85219-768-3, Pub. by Batsford England). Trafalgar Sq.

Neufld, Rose. Exploring Nontraditional Jobs for Women. rev. ed. Rosen, Ruth, ed. (gr. 7-12). 1989. PLB 11.95 (ISBN 0-8239-0971-9). Rosen Group.

Seed, Suzanne. Saturday's Child. Seed, Suzanne, illus. LC 72-12599. (gr. 6-12). 1973. PLB 8.95 (ISBN 0-87955-803-2); pap. 6.95 (ISBN 0-87955-203-4). O'Hara.

Sproule, Anna. Solidarity. MacDonald, Ed, ed. (Illus.). 48p. (gr. 4 up). 1988. PLB 11.90 (ISBN 0-531-19503-1, Hampstead Pr). Watts.

Steffens, Bradley. Working Mothers: Understanding Words in Context. (Illus.). 32p. (gr. 3-6). 1990. PLB 8.95 (ISBN 0-89908-644-6). Greenhaven.

Williams, Barbara. Breakthrough: Women in Archaeology. LC 80-7687. (Illus.). 174p. 1981. 9.95 (ISBN 0-8027-6406-1). Walker & Co.

WOMEN–EMPLOYMENT–FICTION

Furman, Abraham L., ed. Everygirls Career Stories. (Illus.). (gr. 6-10). PLB 6.70 (ISBN 0-8313-0049-3). Lantern.

Maury, Inez. My Mother the Mail Carrier - Mi Mama la Cartera. Alemany, Norah, tr. McCrady, Lady, illus. LC 76-14275. (ENG & SPA.). 32p. (Orig.). (gr. k-4). 1976. 7.95 (ISBN 0-935312-23-4). Feminist Pr.

WOMEN–ENFRANCHISEMENT
see Women–Suffrage

WOMEN–FICTION

Adams, Pam, illus. There Was an Old Lady Who Swallowed a Fly. 16p. (ps-2). 1973. pap. 5.00 (ISBN 0-85953-018-3, Pub. by Child's Play England). Childs Play.

Alcott, Louisa May. Good Wives. 320p. (gr. 3-7). 1983. pap. 2.25 (ISBN 0-14-035009-8, Puffin). Puffin Bks.

Alexander, Sue. World Famous Muriel. (gr. k-6). 1988. pap. 2.50 (ISBN 0-440-49610-1, YB). Dell.

Asch, Frank. Pearl's Promise. 160p. (gr. 1-4). 1984. pap. 2.95 (ISBN 0-440-46863-9, YB). Dell.

Blake, Quentin. Mrs. Armitage on Wheels. Blake, Quentin, illus. LC 87-3335. 32p. (gr. k-3). 1988. 10.95 (ISBN 0-394-89498-7); lib. bdg. 11.99 (ISBN 0-394-99498-1). Knopf.

Bowden, Joan. Why the Tides Ebb & Flow. (gr. k-3). 1979. 14.95 (ISBN 0-395-28378-7). HM.

Byars, Betsy. The Blossoms Meet the Vulture Lady. Rogers, Jacqueline, illus. LC 86-4429. 160p. (gr. 4-6). 1986. pap. 13.95 (ISBN 0-385-29485-9). Delacorte.

Cahill, Susan, ed. Women & Fiction: Short Stories by & About Women. (gr. 7 up). 1975. pap. 4.50 (ISBN 0-451-62411-4, ME2263, Ment). NAL-Dutton.

Cameron, Eleanor. The Private Worlds of Julia Redfern. LC 87-30695. 224p. (gr. 6 up). 1988. 13.95 (ISBN 0-525-44394-0, 01354-410, DCB). Dutton Child Bks.

Constant, Alberta W. Does Anyone Care about Lou Emma Miller? LC 78-4774. 256p. (gr. 5-8). 1979. (Crowell Jr Bks); PLB 12.89 (ISBN 0-690-03890-9, Crowell Jr Bks). HarpC Child Bks.

Cooney, Caroline B. New Year's Eve. 224p. (Orig.). (gr. 9 up). 1991. pap. 2.95 (ISBN 0-590-44627-4). Scholastic Inc.

Cooper, Ilene. The Winning of Miss Lynn Ryan. Magurn, Susan, illus. LC 87-15233. 128p. (gr. 3-6). 1987. 11.95 (ISBN 0-688-07231-3). Morrow Jr Bks.

Cosgrove, Stephen. The Kind & Gentle Ladies. Steelhammer, Ilona, illus. 24p. (gr. k-2). 1990. PLB 10.95 (ISBN 1-878363-20-4). Forest Hse.

—Lady Lonely. Steelhammer, Ilona, illus. 24p. (gr. k-2). 1990. PLB 10.95 (ISBN 1-878363-21-2). Forest Hse.

—Lady Rose. 32p. 1990. pap. 2.95 (ISBN 0-8431-2837-2). Price Stern.

Deaver, Julie R. Say Goodnight, Gracie. LC 87-45278. 224p. (gr. 7 up). 1988. 12.95 (ISBN 0-06-021418-X); PLB 12.89 (ISBN 0-06-021419-8). HarpC Child Bks.

Derby, Pat. Visiting Miss Pierce. LC 86-7559. 144p. (gr. 6 up). 1986. 11.95 (ISBN 0-374-38162-3). FS&G.

—Visiting Miss Pierce. 144p. (gr. 3 up). 1989. pap. 3.50 (ISBN 0-374-48156-3, Sunburst). FS&G.

Dexter, Catherine. Gerties's Green Thumb. (gr. 4-7). 1988. pap. 2.75 (ISBN 0-440-40018-X, YB). Dell.

Dillon, Barbara. Mrs. Tooey & the Terrible Toxic Tar. LC 87-45985. 96p. (gr. 3-7). 1988. 10.95 (ISBN 0-397-32276-3, Lipp Jr Bks); PLB 10.89 (ISBN 0-397-32277-1, Lipp Jr Bks). HarpC Child Bks.

Donnelly, Elfie. A Package for Miss Marshwater. Krause, Ute, illus. (gr. 2-5). 1987. 9.95 (ISBN 0-8037-0453-4); PLB 9.89 (ISBN 0-8037-0454-2). Dial Bks Young.

Fine, Anne. Alias Madame Doubtfire. (gr. 5 up). 1990. pap. 3.50 (ISBN 0-553-28189-5, Starfire). Bantam.

Fischer, Maureen. Little Mary. Haley, Patrick & Haley, Irene, eds. LC 85-82197. 106p. (gr. 7-12). 1986. 14.00 (ISBN 0-9605738-3-6); pap. 6.00 (ISBN 0-9605738-4-4). East Eagle.

Fosburgh, Liza. Bella Arabella. Stock, Catherine, illus. LC 85-42809. 128p. (gr. 4-7). 1986. 12.95 (ISBN 0-02-735430-X, Four Winds). Macmillan Child Grp.

Gabhart, Ann. The Gifting. (gr. 6 up). 1987. 2.25 (ISBN 0-373-98008-6). S&S Trade.

Garfield, Leon. The Strange Affair of Adelaide Harris. (gr. k-6). 1988. pap. 3.25 (ISBN 0-440-40057-0, YB). Dell.

Greenberg, Jan. Bye, Bye, Miss American Pie. LC 85-47590. 150p. (gr. 7 up). 1985. 11.95 (ISBN 0-374-31012-2). FS&G.

Hackman, Martha. The Old Woman of Trora. Cesari, Aura, illus. 12p. (Orig.). (gr. 7-9). 1982. pap. 2.50 (ISBN 0-914676-70-9). Green Tiger Pr.

Hale, Lucretia. The Lady Who Put Salt in Her Coffee. Schwartz, Amy, adapted by. & illus. (ps-3). 1989. 13.95 (ISBN 0-15-243475-5). HarBraceJ.

Hedlund, Irene. Mighty Mountain & the Three Strong Women. (Illus.). 32p. (gr. 2-5). 1990. 14.95 (ISBN 0-912078-86-3). Volcano Pr.

Holmes, Barbara W. Charlotte Cheetham: Master of Disaster. Himmelman, John, illus. LC 85-42617. 128p. (gr. 4-6). 1985. 12.95 (ISBN 0-06-022587-4); PLB 12.89 (ISBN 0-06-022588-2). HarpC Child Bks.

—Charlotte the Starlet. Himmelman, John, illus. LC 87-11938. 128p. (gr. 4-6). 1988. 12.95 (ISBN 0-06-022589-0); PLB 12.89 (ISBN 0-06-022608-0). HarpC Child Bks.

Hoover, H. M. The Dawn Palace: The Story of Medea. LC 87-30602. 256p. (gr. 7 up). 1988. 15.95 (ISBN 0-525-44388-6, 01549-460, DCB). Dutton Child Bks.

Irwin, Hadley. The Lilith Summer. LC 78-24379. 126p. (gr. 4-8). 1979. 8.95 (ISBN 0-912670-52-5). Feminist Pr.

Isherwood, Shirley. A Surprise for Mrs. Pinkerton-Trunks. (Illus.). 96p. (gr. k-2). 1986. 12.95 (ISBN 0-09-160380-3, Pub. by Hutchinson UK). Trafalgar Sq.

Jacobs, Anita. Where Has Deedie Wooster Been All These Years? LC 81-65493. 224p. (Orig.). (gr. 7 up). 1981. pap. 9.95 (ISBN 0-385-29133-7). Delacorte.

Knight, Ginny, et al. A Sampler of Women. LC 83-82097. 60p. (Orig.). (gr. 9-12). 1984. pap. text ed. 6.50 (ISBN 0-940248-18-2). Guild Pr.

Konigsburg, E. L. From the Mixed-Up Files of Mrs. Basil E. Frankweiler. 208p. (gr. 5 up). 1973. pap. 3.25 (ISBN 0-440-93180-0, LFL). Dell.

Kroll, Steven. Newsman Ned & the Broken Rules. Brunkus, Denise, illus. 32p. (Orig.). (ps-1). 1989. pap. 2.95 (ISBN 0-590-41368-6). Scholastic Inc.

Leslie-Melville, Betty. Daisy Rothschild: The Giraffe That Lives with Me. LC 86-29070. (Illus.). 48p. (gr. 2-5). 1987. PLB 13.99 (ISBN 0-385-23896-7); pap. 12.95 (ISBN 0-385-23895-9). Doubleday.

Livingstone, Ian & Jackson, Steve. Trial of Champions. (Orig.). (gr. k-12). 1987. pap. 2.50 (ISBN 0-440-98689-3, LFL). Dell.

McCurdy, Michael. Hannah's Farm: Seasons on an Early American Homestead. McCurdy, Michael, illus. LC 87-29631. 32p. (gr. 1-4). 1988. reinforced bdg. 12.95 (ISBN 0-8234-0700-4). Holiday.

MacLachlan, Patricia. The Facts & Fictions of Minna Pratt. LC 85-45388. 144p. (gr. 3-7). 1988. 11.95 (ISBN 0-06-024114-4); PLB 11.89 (ISBN 0-06-024117-9). HarpC Child Bks.

Mahy, Margaret. The Birthday Burglar & A Very Wicked Headmistress. LC 87-46288. 1988. 12.95 (ISBN 0-87923-720-1). Godine.

Martinez, Alejandro C. Iguana Woman. (Illus.). 32p. (gr. k-5). 1991. 13.95 (ISBN 0-89239-101-4). Childrens Book Pr.

Montgomery, L. M. Anne of Green Gables. 384p. (gr. 4-7). 1989. pap. 2.95 (ISBN 0-590-42243-X, Pub. by Apple Classics). Scholastic Inc.

Nelson, Peter. Sylvia Smith-Smith. (gr. 6 up). 1987. 2.25 (ISBN 0-373-98007-8). S&S Trade.

Okimoto, Jean D. Jason's Women. (gr. k-12). 1988. pap. 2.95 (ISBN 0-440-20000-8). Dell.

Parish, Peggy. Thank You, Amelia Bedelia. Siebel, Fritz, illus. LC 64-11835. 32p. (gr. k-3). 1983. pap. 3.50 (ISBN 0-06-443037-5, Trophy). HarpC Child Bks.

Perl, Lila. Annabelle Starr, E.S.P. LC 83-2068. 160p. (gr. 4-7). 1983. 11.95 (ISBN 0-89919-187-8, Clarion). HM.

Pierce, Tamora. The Woman Who Rides Like a Man. LC 85-20054. 256p. (gr. 6 up). 1990. pap. 3.50 (ISBN 0-679-80112-X). McKay.

Proysen, Alf. Little Old Mrs. Pepperpot. large type ed. (Illus.). 140p. (gr. 3-8). 1989. Repr. of 1959 ed. PLB 14.95 (ISBN 1-85089-964-9, Pub. by Clio Pr England). ABC-CLIO.

Ricchiuti, Paul B. Ellen: Trial & Triumph on the American Frontier. LC 76-44051. 160p. (gr. 6 up). 1988. pap. 7.95 (ISBN 0-945460-03-1). Upward Way.

Richardson, Arleta. At Home in North Branch. LC 88-9529. (gr. 3-7). 1988. pap. 3.95 (ISBN 1-55513-312-6, Chariot Bks). Cook.

Riordan, James. The Woman in the Moon & Other Tales of Forgotten Heroines. Barrett, Angela, illus. LC 84-20050. 96p. (ps up). 1985. 12.95 (ISBN 0-8037-0194-2); PLB 11.89 (ISBN 0-8037-0196-9). Dial Bks Young.

Springstubb, Tricia. Eunice Gottlieb & the Unwhitewashed Truth about Life. LC 86-23459. 208p. (gr. 4-6). 1987. pap. 14.95 (ISBN 0-385-29552-9). Delacorte.

Stoeke, Janet M. Minerva Louise. Stoeke, Janet M., illus. LC 87-24458. 24p. (ps-1). 1988. 10.95 (ISBN 0-525-44374-6, 01063-320, DCB). Dutton Child Bks.

Turin, Adela & Bosnia, Nella. Arthur & Clementine. (Illus.). 32p. (gr. 3-6). 1980. 6.95 (ISBN 0-904613-19-4). Writers & Readers.

Usher, Alice. The Sunny Hours. Kniffke, Sophie, illus. LC 83-82780. 40p. (Orig.). (ps-2). 1983. pap. 8.95 (ISBN 0-88138-018-0). Green Tiger Pr.

Warren, Cathy. Roxanne Bookman: Live at Five! LC 88-964. 128p. (gr. 3-7). 1988. 12.95 (ISBN 0-02-792492-0, Bradbury Pr). Macmillan Child Grp.

Wolitzer, Hilma. Introducing Shirley Braverman. (gr. 8 up). 1987. pap. 3.50 (ISBN 0-374-43597-9). FS&G.

Wright, Betty R. The Summer of Mrs. MacGregor. LC 86-45388. 160p. (gr. 3-7). 1986. 14.95 (ISBN 0-8234-0628-8). Holiday.

—The Summer of Mrs. MacGregor. 176p. (gr. 6-8). 1988. pap. 2.50 (ISBN 0-590-41052-0, Apple Paperbacks). Scholastic Inc.

WOMEN—OCCUPATIONS
see Women–Employment

WOMEN—SUFFRAGE
Oneal, Zibby. A Long Way to Go. Dooling, Michael, illus. 64p. (gr. 2-6). 1990. pap. 11.95 (ISBN 0-670-82532-8). Viking Child Bks.

Smith, Betsy C. Women Win the Vote. (Illus.). 64p. (gr. 5 up). 1989. PLB 16.98 (ISBN 0-382-09837-4); pap. 7.95 (ISBN 0-382-09854-4). Silver Burdett Pr.

WOMEN AS AIR PILOTS
see Women in Aeronautics

WOMEN AS ARTISTS
Brown, Betty A. & Raven, Arlene. Exposures, Women & Their Art. Love, Kenna, photos by. Comini, Alessandra, intro. by. (Illus.). 128p. (gr. 9 up). 1989. 39.95 (ISBN 0-939165-10-4); ltd. ed. 100.00 (ISBN 0-939165-13-9); pap. 29.95 (ISBN 0-939165-11-2). NewSage Press.

Sills, Leslie. Inspirations: Stories about Women Artists. Fay, Ann, ed. (Illus.). 56p. (gr. 2-8). 1989. PLB 16.95 (ISBN 0-8075-3649-0). A Whitman.

WOMEN AS AUTHORS
Rosenblatt, Aaron. Virginia Woolf for Beginners. Rosenblatt, Naomi, illus. (Orig.). (gr. 11 up). 1987. pap. 7.95 (ISBN 0-86316-133-2). Writers & Readers.

Smith, Lucinda I. Women Who Write: From the Past & the Present to the Future. Steltenpohl, Jane, ed. (Illus.). 192p. (gr. 7 up). 1989. lib. bdg. 14.98 (ISBN 0-671-65668-6); pap. 9.95 (ISBN 0-671-65669-4). Messner.

Weidt, Maryann N. Presenting Judy Blume. 168p. (gr. 9-12). 1989. lib. bdg. 19.95x (ISBN 0-8057-8208-7, Twayne). G K Hall.

WOMEN AS PHYSICIANS
Baker, Rachel. The First Woman Doctor. Copeland, Evelyn, illus. 192p. (gr. 4-6). 1987. pap. 2.50 (ISBN 0-590-40933-6). Scholastic Inc.

Bryan, Jenny. Health & Science. MacDonald, Ed, ed. (Illus.). 48p. (gr. 4 up). 1988. PLB 11.90 (ISBN 0-531-19501-5, Hampstead Pr). Watts.

Seide, Diane. Physician Power: New Vistas for Women in Medicine. LC 88-38020. 112p. (gr. 7 up). 1989. 14.95 (ISBN 0-525-67276-1, Lodestar Bks). Dutton Child Bks.

Steelsmith, Shari. Elizabeth Blackwell: The Story of the First Woman Doctor. Kerstetter, Judy, illus. LC 86-62434. 32p. (Orig.). (ps-4). 1987. lib. bdg. 15.95 (ISBN 0-943990-31-9); pap. 5.95 (ISBN 0-943990-30-0). Parenting Pr.

Wilson, Barbara K. Path Through the Woods. Stewart, Charles, illus. (gr. 7 up). 1958. 18.95 (ISBN 0-685-40040-9). S G Phillips.

WOMEN AS SCIENTISTS
Billings, Charlene W. Grace Hopper: Navy Admiral & Computer Pioneer. LC 89-1523. (Illus.). 128p. (gr. 7-12). 1989. PLB 17.95 (ISBN 0-89490-194-X). Enslow Pubs.

Scientist & Planner, Ru Chih Cheo Huang. 32p. (Orig.). (gr. 1-4). 1985. pap. 4.50 (ISBN 0-932469-03-5). Equity Inst.

Verheyden-Hilliard, Mary E. Engineer from the Comanche Nation, Nancy Wallace. Menzel, Marian, illus. LC 84-25935. 32p. (Orig.). (gr. 1-4). 1985. pap. 4.50 (ISBN 0-932469-10-8). Equity Inst.

—Mathematician & Administrator, Shirley Mathis McBay. Biro, Scarlet, illus. LC 84-25983. 32p. (Orig.). (gr. 1-4). 1985. pap. 4.50 (ISBN 0-932469-04-3). Equity Inst.

—Scientist & Administrator, Antoinette Rodez Schiesler. Menzel, Marian, illus. LC 84-25978. 32p. (Orig.). (gr. 1-4). 1985. pap. 4.50 (ISBN 0-932469-08-6). Equity Inst.

—Scientist & Astronaut, Sally Ride. Menzel, Marian, illus. LC 84-25940. 32p. (Orig.). (gr. 1-4). 1985. pap. 4.50 (ISBN 0-932469-07-8). Equity Inst.

—Scientist & Governor, Dixy Lee Ray. Menzel, Marian, illus. LC 84-25986. 32p. (Orig.). (gr. 1-4). 1985. pap. 4.50 (ISBN 0-932469-06-X). Equity Inst.

—Scientist & Puzzle Solver, Constance Tom Noguchi. Menzel, Mary, illus. LC 84-25924. 32p. (Orig.). (gr. 1-4). 1985. pap. 4.50 (ISBN 0-932469-05-1). Equity Inst.

—Scientist from Puerto Rico, Maria Cordero Hardy. Biro, Scarlet, illus. LC 84-25979. 32p. (Orig.). (gr. 1-4). 1985. pap. 4.50 (ISBN 0-932469-02-7). Equity Inst.

—Scientist from the Santa Clara Pueblo, Agnes Naranjo Stroud-Lee. Menzel, Marian, illus. LC 84-25959. 32p. (Orig.). (gr. 1-4). 1985. pap. 4.50 (ISBN 0-932469-09-4). Equity Inst.

—Scientist with Determination, Elma Gonzalez. Menzel, Marian, illus. LC 84-25981. 32p. (Orig.). (gr. 1-4). 1985. pap. 4.50 (ISBN 0-932469-01-9). Equity Inst.

Verheyden-Hilliard, Mary Ellen. American Women in Science Engineering. Biro, Scarlet & Rom, Holly M., illus. 32p. 1988. pap. 5.00 (ISBN 0-932469-19-1); 70.00 set. Equity Inst.

This illustrated, 15-book series presents

contemporary African-American Indian, Asian-American, Hispanic, & Caucasian women who, in girlhood, overcame barriers of gender, race, language, & poverty to become scientists. Five of the books are about girls with physical disabilities who also went on to become scientists. "Inspiring group of biographies of women in science...Children in the lower grades with reading problems can use them for...biographical information."-- SCHOOL LIBRARY JOURNAL. "...useful to teachers who want to help girls become more positive towards mathematics & science... recommended."-- CURRICULUM REVIEW. "...smoothly written texts..."-- BOOKLIST. "...help children...see the connection...between determination to persevere in the face of disabilities & later 'payoff'...in a variety of very exciting careers."-- NEWSLETTER, Association of Black Women in Higher Education. "...warm, lively & true stories of young girls who went on to become successful scientists..."-- GIFTED CHILDREN MONTHLY. "...these books are so attractively produced that I can't imagine elementary classroom teaching without them."-- PERSPECTIVES, National Women Studies Association. Also avaiable are tie-in Teaching Guide $10.00 (ISBN 0-932469-19-3), & video: "You Can Be a Scientist Too!" $46.00 (ISBN 0-932469-11-6). "Well written & filmed... appealing...inspiring production."-- BOOKLIST.
Publisher Provided Annotation.

WOMEN IN AERONAUTICS
Chadwick, Roxane. Anne Morrow Lindbergh: Pilot & Poet. (Illus.). 56p. (gr. 4 up). 1987. PLB 9.95 (ISBN 0-8225-0488-X); pap. 4.95 (ISBN 0-8225-9516-8). Lerner Pubns.

WOMEN IN INDUSTRY
see Women–Employment

WOMEN IN POLITICS
Chua-Eoan, Howard. Corazon Aquino. (Illus.). 112p. (gr. 5 up). 1988. 17.95x (ISBN 1-55546-825-X). Chelsea Hse.

Faber, Doris. Margaret Thatcher: Britain's Iron Lady. Masheris, Robert, illus. LC 85-40442. 57p. (gr. 3-6). 1985. pap. 10.95 (ISBN 0-670-80785-0). Viking Child Bks.

Gherman, Beverly. Sandra Day O'Connor. (gr. 4-7). 1991. 10.95 (ISBN 0-670-82756-8). Viking Child Bks.

Hughes, Libby. Madam Prime Minister: A Biography of Margaret Thatcher. (Illus.). 128p. (gr. 5 up). 1989. PLB 12.95 (ISBN 0-87518-410-3, Dillon). Macmillan Child Grp.

Whitney, Sharon & Raynor, Tom. Women in Politics. 144p. (gr. 7-12). 1986. PLB 12.40 (ISBN 0-531-10243-2). Watts.

WOMEN IN SPORTS
Buck, Ray. Tiffany Chin: A Dream on Ice. LC 86-9577. (Illus.). 48p. (gr. 2-8). 1986. PLB 13.27 (ISBN 0-516-04361-7); pap. 3.95 (ISBN 0-516-44361-5). Childrens.

Duden, Jane. Shirley Muldowney. LC 87-25570. (Illus.). 48p. (gr. 5-6). 1988. PLB 10.95 (ISBN 0-89686-369-7, Crestwood Hse). Macmillan Child Grp.

Monroe, Judy. Steffi Graf. LC 87-30115. (Illus.). 48p. (gr. 5-6). 1988. PLB 10.95 (ISBN 0-89686-368-9, Crestwood Hse). Macmillan Child Grp.

Rosenthal, Bert. Lynette Woodard: The First Female Globetrotter. LC 86-9662. (Illus.). 48p. (gr. 2-8). 1986. PLB 13.27 (ISBN 0-516-04360-9); pap. 3.95 (ISBN 0-516-44360-7). Childrens.

WOMEN IN THE BIBLE
Alex, Marlee. Esther. (Illus.). 32p. (gr. 3-6). 1987. 7.95 (ISBN 0-8028-5016-2). Eerdmans.

—Mary. 32p. (gr. 3-6). 1987. 7.95 (ISBN 0-8028-5018-9). Eerdmans.

—Ruth. (Illus.). 32p. (gr. 3-6). 1987. 7.95 (ISBN 0-8028-5017-0). Eerdmans.

Buckingham, Betty Jo, ed. Women at the Well: Expressions of Faith, Life & Worship Drawn from Our Own Wisdom. Carachel, Maria E., tr. LC 87-6224. (Orig.). (gr. 12). 1987. 7.95 (ISBN 0-9618243-0-1). Ch Brethren Womens Caucus.

Daniel, Rebecca. Women of the Bible. 48p. (ps-6). 1989. 6.95 (ISBN 0-86653-495-4, SS856). Good Apple.

Latham, Judy. Women in the Bible: Helpful Friends. Karch, Paul, illus. (gr. 1-6). 1979. 5.95 (ISBN 0-8054-4248-0, 4242-48). Broadman.

Sabin, Francene. Women Who Win. 160p. (gr. 5 up). 1977. pap. 1.50 (ISBN 0-440-99643-0, LFL). Dell.

Vos Wezeman, Phyllis & Wiessner, Colleen A. Gleanings from Ruth. 25p. (Orig.). (gr. 1-6). 1988. pap. 5.95 (ISBN 0-940764-61-4). Ed Ministries.

WOMEN IN THE U. S.
see also Presidents–U. S.–Wives
De Pauw, Linda G. Founding Mothers: Women of America in the Revolutionary Era. (Illus.). 228p. (gr. 7 up). 1975. 13.95 (ISBN 0-395-21896-9). HM.

Johnston, Johanna. They Led the Way: Fourteen American Women. 1987. 2.95 (ISBN 0-590-44431-X). Scholastic Inc.

Patteson, Nelda. Clara Driscoll: Savior of the Alamo: Her Life Story Presented Through the Clothes She Wore. (Illus.). 32p. (gr. 4-7). 1991. pap. write for info (ISBN 0-9629001-0-9). Smiley Originals.

This is a children's biography with a difference. On each narrative page B&W photographs & costume sketches in color combine to introduce the elegant, dynamic Mrs. Driscoll. 2 figures with 18 costumes march across color plates representing CLARA DRISCOLL's accomplishments as preservationist, playwright, New York socialite, politician, ambassador's wife, banker, cattlewoman, & philanthropist. At the time of her death in 1945, Time Magazine dubbed her an "empress." Her empires were several: cattle, oil, finance, politics, & philanthropy. Her extraordinary life becomes a costume history from the 1890's to the mid-1940's. Written & illustrated by an artist teacher, CLARA DRISCOLL puts upper elementary & middle school children in touch with greatness. "This book could be used for a book report by students in the fourth through seventh grades," said Nancy Ellis, District-Teacher-of-the-Year, Nixon-Smiley CISD.
Publisher Provided Annotation.

Rappaport, Doreen, ed. American Women: Their Lives in Their Words. LC 89-77621. (Illus.). 336p. (gr. 7 up). 1990. 16.95 (ISBN 0-690-04819-X, Crowell Jr Bks); PLB 16.89 (ISBN 0-690-04817-3, Crowell Jr Bks). HarpC Child Bks.

Scott, Elaine, ed. The Times & Triumphs of American Woman. (Illus.). 79p. (gr. 4-9). 1986. pap. text ed. 8.00 book only (ISBN 0-9610622-1-5). Natl Wmns Hall Fame.

Whiteley, Opal. Opal: The Journal of an Understanding Heart. Boulton, Jane, adapted by. LC 84-2418. (Illus.). 190p. (gr. 4 up). 1984. Repr. of 1976 ed. 14.95 (ISBN 0-935382-52-6). Tioga Pub Co.

WOMEN IN THE U. S.–BIOGRAPHY
Huber, Peter. Sandra Day O'Connor. (Illus.). 112p. (gr. 5 up). 1990. 17.95 (ISBN 1-55546-672-9). Chelsea Hse.

Johnston, Johana. They Led the Way: Fourteen American Women. Hollinger, Deanne, illus. 128p. (Orig.). (gr. 4-6). 1987. pap. 2.50 (ISBN 0-590-41342-2). Scholastic Inc.

Meltzer, Milton. Betty Friedan: A Voice for Women's Rights. Marchesi, Stephen, illus. LC 85-40441. 57p. (gr. 5 up). 1985. 10.95 (ISBN 0-670-80796-6). Viking Child Bks.

Sabin, Francene. Women Who Win. LC 74-20835. (Illus.). 192p. (gr. 7 up). 1975. Random.

Shuker, Nancy. Elizabeth Arden. Furstinger, Nancy, ed. (Illus.). 140p. (gr. 7-10). 1989. PLB 13.98 (ISBN 0-382-09587-1). Silver Burdett Pr.

WOMEN'S CLOTHING
see Clothing and Dress

WOMEN'S RIGHTS
Hanmer, Trudy J. Taking a Stand Against Sexism & Sex Discrimination. (Illus.). 144p. (gr. 9-12). 1990. PLB 13.40 (ISBN 0-531-10962-3). Watts.

Hoff, Mark. Gloria Steinem: The Women's Movement. (Illus.). 96p. (gr. 7 up). 1991. PLB 19.95 (ISBN 1-878841-19-X). Millbrook Pr.

WOMEN'S RIGHTS–FICTION
Miles, Betty. The Real Me. 124p. (gr. 4-7). 1978. pap. 2.75 (ISBN 0-380-00347-3, Camelot). Avon.

Oneal, Zibby. A Long Way to Go. Dooling, Michael, illus. 64p. (gr. 2-6). 1990. pap. 11.95 (ISBN 0-670-82532-8). Viking Child Bks.

WOOD
see also Forests and Forestry; Lumber and Lumbering; Woodwork;
also kinds of wood, e.g. Oak
Behrendt, Hans-Joachim. Know about Transport. Sacher, Rainer, illus. 22p. (gr. 1-5). 1979. 3.95 (ISBN 0-905778-02-2). Academy Chi Pubs.
Brown, William F. & Brown, Mary G. Wood Works: Experiments with Common Wood & Tools. LC 83-15905. (Illus.). 128p. (gr. 3 up). 1984. 13.95 (ISBN 0-689-31033-1, Atheneum Child Bk). Macmillan Child Grp.
Dineen, Jacqueline. Wood & Paper. 32p. (gr. 4-8). 1988. lib. bdg. 12.95 (ISBN 0-89490-226-1). Enslow Pubs.
WOOD BLOCK PRINTING
see Wood Engraving
WOOD CARVING
Barber, Joel. Wild Fowl Decoys. 2nd ed. Barber, Joel, illus. 151p. (gr. 10 up). Repr. of 1934 ed. 39.95 (ISBN 0-685-37775-X). Derrydale Pr.
Bruggen, Bill & Wade, Tom. Carve Your Own Carousel Horse. LC 89-85082. (Illus.). 96p. (Orig.). 1989. pap. 14.95 (ISBN 0-929758-04-8). Beeman Jorgensen.
LaBranche, Bud. Woodcarving the Female Head. (Illus.). 60p. (gr. 8 up). 1986. pap. 8.95 (ISBN 0-88625-137-0). Durkin Hayes Pub.
Wood Carving. (Illus.). 48p. (gr. 6-12). 1966. pap. 1.85 (ISBN 0-8395-3315-2, 3315). BSA.
WOOD ENGRAVING
Grafton, Carol B., ed. Victorian Spot Illustrations, Alphabets & Ornaments from Porret's Type Catalog. (Illus.). 96p. (gr. 5 up). 1982. pap. 5.95 (ISBN 0-486-24271-4). Dover.
Werley, Judith G., ed. The Artist.., & the Legend: A Visit to China Is Remembered & the Legends Unfold... Domjan, Evelyn A., compiled by. Domjan, Joseph, illus. LC 74-81927. (gr. 7 up). 1974. 25.00 (ISBN 0-933652-09-7). Domjan Studio.
WOOD WIND INSTRUMENTS
see Wind Instruments
WOODCUTS
see Wood Engraving
WOODPECKERS
Haley, Patrick. The Woodpecker & the Oak Tree. Kool, Jonna, illus. LC 82-82991. 64p. (gr. 3-4). 1982. 9.00 (ISBN 0-9605738-2-8). East Eagle.
Pembleton, Seliesa. The Pileated Woodpecker. LC 88-20220. (Illus.). 60p. (gr. 3 up). 1989. PLB 12.95 (ISBN 0-87518-392-1, Dillon). Macmillan Child Grp.
WOODS
see Forests and Forestry
WOODWORK
see also Carpentry; Furniture; Wood Carving
Boy Scouts of America. Woodwork. (Illus.). 48p. (gr. 6-12). 1970. pap. 1.85 (ISBN 0-8395-3316-0, 3316). BSA.
Buchanan, George. The Children's Book of Woodwork. (Illus.). 64p. (gr. 3-6). 1990. 24.95 (ISBN 0-7134-6122-5, Pub. by Batsford England). Trafalgar Sq.
Carrick, Graham. Wood. (Illus.). 32p. (gr. 2-6). 1990. lib. bdg. 13.26 (ISBN 0-86592-484-8); lib. bdg. 9.95s.p. (ISBN 0-685-36306-6). Rourke Corp.
Lawler. Woodwork. (gr. 4-9). 1980. pap. 2.95 (ISBN 0-86020-309-3). EDC.
Rose, Walter. The Village Carpenter. LC 88-3. (Illus.). 146p. (gr. 10 up). 1988. pap. 9.95 (ISBN 0-941533-18-2). New Amsterdam Bks.
WOOL
Dineen, Jacqueline. Wool. 32p. (gr. 4-8). 1988. lib. bdg. 12.95 (ISBN 0-89490-227-X). Enslow Pubs.
Dixon, Annabelle. Wool. Stefoff, Rebecca, ed. Barber, Ed, photos by. LC 90-40366. (Illus.). 26p. (gr. 3-5). 1990. PLB 15.93 (ISBN 0-944483-73-9). Garrett Ed Corp.
Edwards, E. Dean. The American Pioneer. (Illus.). 36p. (Orig.). (gr. 1 up). 1988. pap. 2.95. E D Edwards.
Jobin, Claire. All about Wool. Matthews, Sarah, tr. from FRE. Felix, Monique, illus. LC 87-31751. 38p. (gr. k-5). 1988. 4.95 (ISBN 0-944589-18-9, 189). Young Discovery Lib.
Mitgutsch, Ali. From Sheep to Scarf. Mitgutsch, Ali, illus. LC 80-29557. 24p. (ps-3). 1981. PLB 6.95 (ISBN 0-87614-164-5). Carolrhoda Bks.
Paladino, Catherine. Spring Fleece: A Day of Sheepshearing. (ps-3). 1990. 14.95 (ISBN 0-316-68890-8, Joy St Bks). Little.
Patterson, Geoffrey. Story of Wool. (Illus.). 32p. (gr. k-5). 1988. 10.95 (ISBN 0-233-97923-9). Andre Deutsch.
Wool & String. (ARA., Illus.). (gr. 4-6). 3.50x (ISBN 0-86685-244-1). Intl Bk Ctr.
WORD GAMES
Baker & Boyington. Down East Puzzles & Word Games. Hassett, John, illus. 80p. (Orig.). 1989. pap. 3.95 (ISBN 0-89272-272-X). Down East.
Bank Street College of Education Editors. Let's Play Word Games. (gr. 1-2). 1986. pap. 3.95 (ISBN 0-8120-3628-X). Barron.
Bank Street College of Education Staff. Let's Make Word Games. (gr. 1-2). 1986. pap. 3.95 (ISBN 0-8120-3629-8). Barron.
Brandreth, Gyles. Biggest Tongue Twister Book in the World. Chin, Alex, illus. LC 78-7784. 123p. (gr. 4 up). 1980. 12.95 (ISBN 0-8069-4594-X); PLB 15.69 (ISBN 0-8069-4595-8); pap. 3.95 (ISBN 0-8069-8972-6). Sterling.
Burgess, Allan. From Twisted Ear to Reverent Tear. Heston, Claudia, illus. 96p. (gr. 7-12). 1983. 5.98 (ISBN 0-941518-25-6). Perry Enterprises.
Charlip, Remy. Arm in Arm. Charlip, Remy, illus. LC 80-18081. 48p. (gr. 1-5). 1985. Repr. of 1969 ed. 12.95 (ISBN 0-02-718090-5, Four Winds). Macmillan Child Grp.
Conway, Lorraine. Science Graphs & Word Games. 48p. (gr. 5 up). 1981. 6.95 (ISBN 0-86653-029-0, GA 257). Good Apple.
Crosswords & Word Games Activity Books. (Illus.). 48p. (gr. 1-4). 1988. pap. 2.95 (ISBN 0-8431-2270-6). Price Stern.
Dunning, Mary & Dunning, David. Good Apple & Wonderful Word Games. 144p. (gr. 3-7). 1981. 10.95 (ISBN 0-86653-053-3, GA 254). Good Apple.
Espy, Willard R. A Children's Almanac of Words at Play. LC 82-7593. (Illus.). (gr. 3-9). 1988. 15.95 (ISBN 0-517-54660-4, C N Potter); pap. 10.95 (ISBN 0-517-54666-3). Crown.
Gackenbach, Dick, adapted by. & illus. Timid Timothy's Tongue Twisters. LC 85-30531. 32p. (ps-3). 1986. reinforced bdg. 13.95 (ISBN 0-8234-0610-5); pap. 5.95 (ISBN 0-8234-0711-X). Holiday.
Gameillo, Elvira. Kids Word Find Puzzles. (Illus.). 64p. (Orig.). (gr. 4-6). 1988. pap. 1.95 (ISBN 0-942025-43-1). Kidsbks.
Gamiello, Elvira. A-Maze-Ing Chiller Word Search Puzzles. (Illus., Orig.). (gr. 4-6). 1987. pap. 1.95 (ISBN 0-942025-05-9). Kidsbks.
—Crossword Crack-Up Puzzles. (Illus., Orig.). (gr. 4-6). 1987. pap. 1.95 (ISBN 0-942025-04-0). Kidsbks.
—Fun to Find Word Search Puzzles. (Illus., Orig.). (gr. 4-6). 1988. pap. 1.95 (ISBN 0-942025-37-7). Kidsbks.
—Scary Search a Word Puzzles. (Illus., Orig.). (gr. 4-6). 1988. pap. 1.95 (ISBN 0-942025-39-3). Kidsbks.
—Vacation Puzzle & Fun Book. (Illus., Orig.). (gr. 4-6). 1989. pap. 1.95 (ISBN 0-942025-63-6). Kidsbks.
—Wacky Word Search Puzzles. (Illus., Orig.). (gr. 4-6). 1987. pap. 1.95 (ISBN 0-942025-03-2). Kidsbks.
—Weird & Wacky Word Search Puzzles. (Illus., Orig.). (gr. 4-6). 1988. pap. 1.95 (ISBN 0-942025-42-3). Kidsbks.
—Word Find Puzzles for Kids. (Illus.). 64p. (Orig.). 1988. pap. 1.95 (ISBN 0-942025-38-5). Kidsbks.
Maestro, Betsy & Maestro, Giulio. Harriet Reads Signs & More Signs: A Word Concept Book. (Illus.). 32p. (ps-1). 1986. Crown.
Maleska, Eugene T. Children's Word Games & Crossword Puzzles, Vol. 2. (gr. 2-4). 1988. pap. 5.95 (ISBN 0-8129-1692-1, Times Bks). Random.
Maleska, Eugene T., ed. Children's Word Games & Crossword Puzzles, Vol. 1. LC 86-888. 80p. (gr. 1-3). 1986. pap. 5.95 (ISBN 0-8129-1243-8, Times Bks). Random.
—Children's Word Games & Puzzles. 2nd ed. LC 86-886. 80p. (gr. 3 up). 1986. pap. 5.95 (ISBN 0-8129-1308-6, Times Bks). Random.
Provensen, Alice & Provensen, Martin. Play on Words. (ps-2). 1972. (Random Juv). Random.
Schwartz, Alvin. Tomfoolery: Trickery & Foolery with Words. Rounds, Glen, illus. LC 72-12900. 128p. (gr. 4 up). 1973. 12.95 (ISBN 0-685-02088-6, Lipp Jr Bks). HarpC Child Bks.
—Tomfoolery: Trickery & Foolery with Words. Rounds, Glen, illus. LC 72-12900. 128p. (gr. 4-6). 1990. PLB 12.89 (ISBN 0-397-32437-5, Lipp Jr Bks). HarpC Child Bks.
Thiesen, Charles & King, Deanna. Wordplay. rev. ed. (Illus.). (gr. 3-8). 1987. pap. 5.95 (ISBN 0-88166-058-2, Dist. by Simon & Schuster). Meadowbrook.
Van der Meer, Ron & Van der Meer, Atie. I Can Learn Twenty-Five Words, Bk. 1. 12p. 1989. 4.95 (ISBN 0-8431-2381-8). Price Stern.
—I Can Learn Twenty-Five Words, Bk. 2. 12p. 1989. 4.95 (ISBN 0-8431-2382-6). Price Stern.
Warren, Jean. Language Games. 80p. (gr. k-2). 1983. 7.95 (ISBN 0-912107-05-7). Monday Morning Bks.
Wetterau, Bruce. Word Games. 352p. (gr. 9-12). 1990. 16.95 (ISBN 0-13-947334-3, Pub. by Websters New World); pap. 9.95 (ISBN 0-685-31180-5). Prentice Hall Pr.
Word Fun. 14p. (ps). 1979. bds. 2.25 (ISBN 0-448-16274-1, G&D). Putnam Pub Group.
WORD GAMES–FICTION
Fadiman, Clifton. Wally the Wordworm. Atherton, Lisa, illus. LC 83-9181. (gr. 3 up). 1984. 12.95 (ISBN 0-88045-038-X); cassette & bk. 21.90 (ISBN 0-88045-101-7); cassette only 8.95 (ISBN 0-88045-098-3). Stemmer Hse.
Parish, Peggy. Good Work, Amelia Bedelia. Sweat, Lynn, illus. LC 75-20360. 56p. (gr. 1-4). 1976. 12.95 (ISBN 0-688-80022-X); PLB 12.88 (ISBN 0-688-84022-1). Greenwillow.
Raskin, Ellen. The Mysterious Disappearance of Leon (I Mean Noel) (gr. 4-7). 1977. 14.95 (ISBN 0-525-35540-5, DCB); (DCB). Dutton Child Bks.
WORD PROCESSING
Dudley, Art. Word Processing Basics: An Introduction for Young People. Petronella, Michael, illus. LC 84-22315. 48p. (gr. 4-9). 1985. 9.95 (ISBN 0-13-963513-0). P-H.
Feeman, Maryellen & Feeman, Jeff. Computer Terms-Word Processing. Rittenour, Gary & Fowler, Christopher, illus. 32p. (gr. 2 up). 1984. pap. 1.98 (ISBN 0-88724-102-6, CD9045). Carson-Dellos.
Luft, Ira S. The Student's Guide to Word Processing with WordStar. 90p. (gr. 10 up). 1988. pap. 7.95 (ISBN 0-318-23581-1). Automatic Manuals.
Reide, Anne M. Coach's Clipboards. (Illus.). 306p. (Orig.). (gr. 5-8). 1986. 10.95 (ISBN 0-931983-02-9, BCLTXT-3). Basic Comp Lit.
Spencer, Jean. Careers in Word Processing & Desktop Publishing. Rosen, Ruth, ed. (gr. 7-12). 1989. PLB 12.95 (ISBN 0-8239-0967-0). Rosen Group.
WORDS
see Vocabulary
WORDS, NEW
Briggs, Noreen V. Bugaboo Words. (Illus.). 160p. (gr. 3 up). 1989. 25.00 (ISBN 0-937857-13-0, 1570). Speech Bin.
Lester, Alison. Bibs & Boots. (Illus.). 16p. (ps-k). 1989. 3.50 (ISBN 0-670-81988-3). Viking Child Bks.
—Crashing & Splashing. (Illus.). 16p. (ps-k). 1989. pap. 3.50 (ISBN 0-670-81989-1). Viking Child Bks.
Lewis, Shari. Baby Lamb Chop Loves Words. Beylon, Cathy, illus. 48p. (ps-k). 1991. 9.95 (ISBN 0-679-81722-0). Random.
Moncure, Jane B. Word Bird's School Words. Hohag, Linda, illus. LC 89-7179. 32p. (ps-2). 1989. PLB 11.97 (ISBN 0-89565-510-1); pap. 6.96 (ISBN 0-89565-537-3). Childs World.
My First Book of Words. (ps-2). bds. 2.50 (ISBN 0-448-02678-3, G&D). Putnam Pub Group.
Scott, Foresman. Good Morning, Words! (ps). 1990. 8.95 (ISBN 0-06-017902-3, HarpT). HarperCollins.
Woodhull, Angela V. Easy Words: An Easy Way to Learn New Words. Eddy, Hal, et al, illus. 150p. (gr. 8 up). 1988. pap. 5.95. Woodhull Pubns.
WORK
see also Labor and Laboring Classes
Belliston, Larry & Hanks, Kurt. Extra Cash for Kids. 1989. pap. 9.95 (ISBN 0-943497-70-1). Wolgemuth & Hyatt.
Brady, Janeen. Standin' Tall Work. Wilson, Grant & Galloway, Neil, illus. 22p. (Orig.). (ps-6). 1981. pap. text ed. 1.50 activity bk. (ISBN 0-944803-41-5); cassette & bk. 8.95 (ISBN 0-944803-42-3). Brite Intl.
Brown, Richard. One Hundred Words about Working. LC 87-8368. (Illus.). 32p. (gr. 3-5). 1988. 6.95 (ISBN 0-15-200553-6, Gulliver Bks). HarBraceJ.
Brown, Richard, illus. One Hundred Words about Working. (ps-1). 1989. pap. 3.95 (ISBN 0-15-200557-9, Voy B). HarBraceJ.
Kalman, Bobbie. People at Work. (Illus.). 32p. (gr. 2-3). 1986. 14.95 (ISBN 0-86505-068-6); pap. 6.95 (ISBN 0-86505-090-2). Crabtree Pub Co.
Los Angeles Unified School District Staff. Working with Others. (Illus.). 48p. (Orig.). (gr. 7-12). 1990. Set. 10 wkbks. & tchr's. guide 44.95 (ISBN 1-56119-092-6); wkbk. 4.95 (ISBN 1-56119-090-X); tchr's. guide 1.95 (ISBN 1-56119-091-8). Educ Pr MD.
—You & Your Attitude. (Illus.). 48p. (Orig.). (gr. 7-12). 1990. Set. 10 wkbks. & tchr's. guide 44.95 (ISBN 1-56119-089-6); wkbk. 4.95 (ISBN 1-56119-087-X); tchr's. guide 1.95 (ISBN 1-56119-088-8). Educ Pr MD.
McCombs, Barbara L. & Brannan, Linda. Adjusting to a New Boss. (Illus.). 32p. (Orig.). (gr. 7-12). 1990. Set. 10 wkbks. & tchr's. guide 44.95 (ISBN 1-56119-071-3); tchr's. guide 1.95 (ISBN 1-56119-026-8); software 39.95 (ISBN 1-56119-113-2). Educ Pr MD.
—Neatness Counts. (Illus.). 32p. (Orig.). (gr. 7-12). 1990. Set. 10 wkbks. & tchr's. guide 44.95 (ISBN 1-56119-081-0); tchr's. guide 1.95 (ISBN 1-56119-046-2); software 39.95 (ISBN 1-56119-123-X). Educ Pr MD.
—Notice & Think. (Illus.). 32p. (Orig.). (gr. 7-12). 1990. Set. 10 wkbks. & tchr's. guide 44.95 (ISBN 1-56119-059-4); tchr's. guide 1.95 (ISBN 1-56119-002-0); software 39.95 (ISBN 1-56119-101-9). Educ Pr MD.
—Respect for Property. (Illus.). 32p. (Orig.). (gr. 7-12). 1990. Set. 10 wkbks. & tchr's. guide 44.95 (ISBN 1-56119-072-1); tchr's. guide 1.95 (ISBN 1-56119-028-4); software 39.95 (ISBN 1-56119-114-0). Educ Pr MD.
—Say. (Illus.). 32p. (Orig.). (gr. 7-12). 1990. Set. 10 wkbks. & tchr's. guide 44.95 (ISBN 1-56119-060-8); tchr's. guide 1.95 (ISBN 1-56119-004-7); software 39.95 (ISBN 1-56119-102-7). Educ Pr MD.
—Taking Breaks. (Illus.). 32p. (Orig.). (gr. 7-12). 1990. Set. 10 wkbks. & tchr's. guide 44.95 (ISBN 1-56119-079-9); tchr's. guide 1.95 (ISBN 1-56119-042-X); software 39.95 (ISBN 1-56119-121-3). Educ Pr MD.
—Too Much Talking. (Illus.). 32p. (Orig.). (gr. 7-12). 1990. Set. 10 wkbks. & tchr's. guide 44.95 (ISBN 1-56119-064-0); tchr's. guide 1.95 (ISBN 1-56119-012-8); software 39.95 (ISBN 1-56119-106-X). Educ Pr MD.
—What Should I Do? (Illus.). 32p. (Orig.). (gr. 7-12). 1990. Set. 10 wkbks. & tchr's. guide 44.95 (ISBN 1-56119-074-8); tchr's. guide 1.95 (ISBN 1-56119-032-2); software 39.95 (ISBN 1-56119-116-7). Educ Pr MD.
—What's Next? (Illus.). 32p. (Orig.). (gr. 7-12). 1990. Set. 10 wkbks. & tchr's. guide 44.95 (ISBN 1-56119-068-3); tchr's. guide 1.95 (ISBN 1-56119-020-9); software 39.95 (ISBN 1-56119-110-8). Educ Pr MD.
—What's the Proper Way? (Illus.). 32p. (Orig.). (gr. 7-12). 1990. Set. 10 wkbks. & tchr's. guide 44.95 (ISBN 1-56119-067-5); tchr's. guide 1.95 (ISBN 1-56119-018-7); software 39.95 (ISBN 1-56119-109-4). Educ Pr MD.
—Which Tools to Use? (Illus.). 32p. (Orig.). (gr. 7-12). 1990. Set. 10 wkbks. & tchr's. guide 44.95 (ISBN 1-56119-083-7); tchr's. guide 1.95 (ISBN 1-56119-050-0); software 39.95 (ISBN 1-56119-125-6). Educ Pr MD.

—Which Way Is Right? (Illus.). 32p. (Orig.). (gr. 7-12). 1990. Set. 10 wkbks. & tchr's. guide 44.95 (ISBN 1-56119-084-5); tchr's. guide 1.95 (ISBN 1-56119-052-7); software 39.95 (ISBN 1-56119-126-4). Educ Pr MD.

—Who Can Help? (Illus.). 32p. (Orig.). (gr. 7-12). 1990. Set. 10 wkbks. & tchr's. guide 44.95 (ISBN 1-56119-076-4); tchr's. guide 1.95 (ISBN 1-56119-036-5); software 39.95 (ISBN 1-56119-118-3). Educ Pr MD.

—Will You Do Me a Favor? (Illus.). 32p. (Orig.). (gr. 7-12). 1990. Set. 10 wkbks. & tchr's. guide 44.95 (ISBN 1-56119-066-7); tchr's. guide 1.95 (ISBN 1-56119-016-0); software 39.95 (ISBN 1-56119-108-6). Educ Pr MD.

—Working Too Slowly. (Illus.). 32p. (Orig.). (gr. 7-12). 1990. Set. 10 wkbks. & tchr's. guide 44.95 (ISBN 1-56119-062-4); tchr's. guide 1.95 (ISBN 1-56119-008-X); software 39.95 (ISBN 1-56119-104-3). Educ Pr MD.

Perham, Molly. People at Work. LC 86-2014. (Illus.). 32p. (gr. 2 up). 1986. PLB 10.95 (ISBN 0-87518-333-6, Dillon). Macmillan Child Grp.

Rosen, Mike. The World of Work. LC 89-11327. (Illus.). 64p. (gr. 4-6). 1990. PLB 12.95 (ISBN 0-8368-0009-5). Gareth Stevens Inc.

Schliefer, Jay. The Work Ethic. (gr. 7-12). 1991. PLB 12.95 (ISBN 0-8239-1227-2). Rosen Group.

WORK–FICTION

Bridwell, Norman. Clifford Gets a Job. Bridwell, Norman, illus. (gr. k-3). 1972. pap. 1.50 o. p. (ISBN 0-590-01575-3). Scholastic Inc.

Goodall, John S. Paddy Under Water. Goodall, John S., illus. LC 83-71901. 32p. 1984. 12.95 (ISBN 0-689-50297-4, M K McElderry). Macmillan Child Grp.

Haas, Jessie. Working Trot. LC 83-1696. 160p. (gr. 5-9). 1983. reinforced 10.25 (ISBN 0-688-02384-3). Greenwillow.

Himmel, Roger J. Working Together. Manoni, Mary H., ed. Peters, Luther J. & Ross, Connie, illus. (gr. k-3). 1978. 6 bks. & 1 cass. 29.95 (ISBN 0-89290-044-X); 1 bk. & 1 cass. 10.95. Soc for Visual.

Hoban, Julia. Buzby. Himmelman, John, illus. LC 89-29408. 64p. (gr. k-3). 1990. 11.95 (ISBN 0-06-022399-5); PLB 11.89 (ISBN 0-06-022398-7). HarpC Child Bks.

Matthews, Morgan. Whoo's Too Tired? Kolding, Richard M., illus. LC 88-1285. 48p. (Orig.). (gr. 1-3). 1988. PLB 9.89 (ISBN 0-8167-1331-6); pap. text ed. 2.95 (ISBN 0-8167-1332-4). Troll Assocs.

Paterson, Katherine. Lyddie. 240p. (gr. 5-9). 1991. 14.95 (ISBN 0-525-67338-5, Lodestar Bks). Dutton Child Bks.

Scariano, Margaret & Cunningham, Marilyn. Nine to Five Series. (Illus.). 1985. Set, 48p. ea. pap. 15.00 ea. (ISBN 0-87879-502-2, High Noon Books). Acad Therapy.
The 9-5 Series is a set of 5 high interest (for ages 11-15)/low level (3rd grade readability) novels which feature teenagers embarking on their first summer job. Pre-teens & teenagers will easily identify with the central characters & will enjoy sharing in their triumphs over first job insecurities, unwarranted accusations, & other dilemmas. The Secret Solution: Can Jim Jackson keep his cool when, hired as a house painter, he is blamed for thievery although perfectly innocent? A Nugget of Gold: Lucy takes a summer job at the animal shelter. Can she stop her favorite dog from being sold to a laboratory by its new owner? The Set-Up: Is it Jake's good friend or someone else who is vandalizing cars at the auto shop? Box Girl: Why was it so difficult for Patty Walker to get her first job at the supermarket & how did she handle the difficulties encountered as a boxgirl? A New Leaf: Soon after taking a job in the local nursery, Troy is faced with a decision when he discovers illegal plants growing in the greenhouse. Each softcover novel is 48 pages & features 5 pen & ink illustrations & a 2-color cover.
Publisher Provided Annotation.

Strasser, Todd. Workin' for Peanuts. 208p. (Orig.). (gr. 7-12). 1984. pap. 2.95 (ISBN 0-440-99682-1, LFL). Dell.

Summer Job. 1990. 4.98 (ISBN 1-55521-688-9). Bk Sales Inc.

Watkins, Dawn L. Very Like a Star. Thompson, Dana, illus. 30p. (Orig.). (ps). 1990. pap. 4.95 (ISBN 0-89084-533-6). Bob Jones Univ Pr.

WORKING CLASSES
see Labor and Laboring Classes

WORKING GIRLS
see Child Labor

WORKINGMEN'S DWELLINGS
see Housing

WORLD
see Earth

WORLD ECONOMICS
see Economic Conditions; Economic Policy

WORLD HISTORY
see also Geography; History, Ancient; History, Modern

Arnold & Tease. Datelines of World History. (Illus.). 96p. (gr. 5up). PLB 13.90 (ISBN 0-531-09212-7). Watts.

Children's Atlas of World History. (Illus.). 96p. (gr. 4-8). 1989. 12.95 (ISBN 0-528-83349-9). Rand McNally.

Chisholm, J. World History Dates: All the Facts You Need to Know at a Glance. (Illus.). 128p. (gr. 6 up). 1987. PLB 16.96 (ISBN 0-88110-232-6); pap. 11.95 (ISBN 0-86020-954-7). EDC.

Foster, Genevieve. World of Captain John Smith. Foster, Genevieve, illus. LC 59-11853. (gr. 5-11). 1978. Repr. of 1959 ed. lib. bdg. 25.00 (ISBN 0-684-15726-8, Scribner). Macmillan.

Hicks, Clifford. The Peter Potts Book of World Records. Howell, Kathleen C., illus. (gr. 3-7). 1987. 13.95 (ISBN 0-8050-0409-2). H Holt & Co.

History Encyclopedia. (Illus.). 144p. (gr. 4 up). 1989. Repr. 14.95 (ISBN 0-02-689201-4). Checkerboard Pr.

History of the World. (Illus.). (gr. 4 up). 1988. Set of 6 titles, 80 pp. ea. PLB 124.02 (ISBN 0-8172-3300-8). Raintree Pubs.

Holsinger, Donald C., et al. Master Guide to the World History Slide Collection. rev. ed. 312p. (gr. 7 up). 1989. pap. text ed. 40.00 (ISBN 0-923805-07-9). Instruc Resc MD.

—The World History Slide Collection: Non-European History. (gr. 7 up). 1988. incl. 2100 slides 995.00 (ISBN 0-923805-08-7). Instruc Resc MD.

Kalman, Bobbie. Life Through the Ages. (Illus.). 32p. (gr. 2-3). 1986. 14.95 (ISBN 0-86505-075-9). Crabtree Pub Co.

Killingray, David & Yapp, Malcolm. The Enlightenment. (Illus.). 32p. (gr. 6-11). 1980. pap. text ed. 2.95 (ISBN 0-89908-225-4). Greenhaven.

Leeds, Chris. Peace & War: A First Sourcebook. (Illus.). 212p. 1988. pap. 15.95 (ISBN 0-85950-526-X, Pub. by S Thornes). Dufour.

Magill, Frank N., ed. Great Lives from History, 5 vols. 2500p. (gr. 9-12). 1989. Set. lib. bdg. 350.00x (ISBN 0-89356-551-2). Salem Pr.

Millard. Book of World History. (Illus.). 195p. (gr. 3-9). 1986. 19.95 (ISBN 0-86020-959-8). EDC.

—Exploration & Discovery. (gr. 4-9). 1979. (Usborne-Hayes); PLB 13.96 (ISBN 0-88110-111-7); pap. 6.95 (ISBN 0-86020-261-5). EDC.

—Warriors & Seafarers. (gr. 4-9). 1977. (Usborne-Hayes); PLB 13.96 (ISBN 0-88110-108-7); pap. 6.95 (ISBN 0-86020-140-6). EDC.

Murphy, Paul C. What's Happened since Seventeen Seventy-Six. (Illus.). 208p. (gr. 6 up). 1988. pap. 6.95 (ISBN 0-8431-2276-5). Price Stern.

Perry, Marvin. Man's Unfinished Journey: A World History. 2nd ed. LC 79-84595. (Illus.). (gr. 10-12). 1980. text ed. 43.96 (ISBN 0-395-27563-6); instr's. guide & key 23.48 (ISBN 0-395-27557-1); activities bk. 10.48 (ISBN 0-395-27562-8); Activities bk. instr's. annot. ed. 13.12 (ISBN 0-395-27558-X). HM.

Rao, B. V. Concise Book of World History. (Illus.). xvi, 295p. (gr. 7 up). 1988. text ed. 27.95x (ISBN 81-207-0808-3, Pub. by Sterling Pubs India). Apt Bks.

Reese, Lyn. Spindle Stories: World History Units for the Middle Grades, Bk. 1. Dougherty, Mary A. & Wilkinson, Jean B., eds. Gorell, Nancy, illus. 90p. (gr. 5-9). 1990. pap. text ed. 15.00g (ISBN 0-9625880-0-8). Women World CRP.

Time-Life Books Editors. This Fabulous Century, 8 vols. (gr. 8 up). kivar 23.96 ea. (Pub. by Time-Life). Silver Burdett Pr.

Vanags. Empires & Barbarians. (gr. 4-9). 1979. (Usborne-Hayes); PLB 13.96 (ISBN 0-88110-109-5); pap. 6.95 (ISBN 0-86020-142-2). EDC.

Van Loon, Hendrik W. The Story of Mankind: The Classic History of All Ages for All Ages, Updated in a New Version for the 1980's. (Illus.). (gr. 7 up). 1985. 19.95 (ISBN 0-685-07959-7). Liveright.

WORLD POLITICS
see also International Relations; World War, 1939-1945 also names of countries with the subdivisions Foreign Relations and Politics and Government, e.g. U. S. –Foreign Relations; U. S.–Politics and Government

Anno, Mitsumasa. In Shadowland. Anno, Mitsumasa, illus. LC 87-20362. 32p. (ps-2). 1988. PLB 14.99 (ISBN 0-531-08341-1). Orchard Bks Watts.

Coker, Christopher. Terrorism & Civil Strife. Chabluh, Stefor, photos by. LC 87-50225. (Illus.). 64p. (gr. 4 up). 1987. PLB 10.29 (ISBN 0-531-10385-4). Watts.

Foster, Leila M. The Story of the Cold War. LC 90-2175. (Illus.). 32p. (gr. 3-6). 1990. PLB 13.27 (ISBN 0-516-04750-7); pap. 3.95 (ISBN 0-516-44750-5). Childrens.

Heater, Derek. The Cold War. LC 88-7546. (Illus.). 63p. (gr. 7 up). 1989. PLB 12.90 (ISBN 0-531-18275-4, Pub. by Bookwright Pr). Watts.

Killoran, James, et al. The Key to Understanding Global Studies: A Regents-RCT Review Book. Zimmer, Ronald, illus. LC 89-92425. 362p. (Orig.). (gr. 9-10). 1990. pap. text ed. 5.95 (ISBN 0-9624723-0-1). Jarrett Pub.

Kurkowski, David C., ed. Current Leaders of Nations. LC 89-81456. (Illus.). 180p. (gr. 9-12). 1990. 3-ring binder 95.00 (ISBN 0-9624900-0-8). Current Leaders Pub.

WORLD SERIES (BASEBALL)

Aaseng, Nathan. Memorable World Series Moments. LC 81-13725. (Illus.). 80p. (gr. 4 up). 1982. PLB 7.95 (ISBN 0-8225-1073-1). Lerner Pubns.

Brenner, Richard J. The World Series: The Great Contests. (Illus.). 88p. (gr. 5 up). 1989. PLB 10.95 (ISBN 0-8225-1502-4). Lerner Pubns.

Gergen, Joe. World Series Heroes & Goats: The Men Who Made History in America's October Classics. LC 82-611. (Illus.). 160p. (gr. 5-9). 1982. pap. 1.95 (ISBN 0-394-85018-1). Random.

Gutman, Bill. World Series Classics. (gr. 5 up). 1973. lib. bdg. 3.69 (ISBN 0-394-92467-3, Random Juv). Random.

WORLD WAR, 1914-1918

Bosco, Peter. World War I. Bowman, John, ed. (Illus.). 128p. (gr. 9-12). 1991. 17.95x (ISBN 0-8160-2460-X). Facts on File.

Huggett, Renee. Growing up in the First World War. (Illus.). 72p. (gr. 7-12). 1985. 19.95 (ISBN 0-7134-4773-7, Pub. by Batsford England). Trafalgar Sq.

Jantzen, Steven L. Hooray for Peace, Hurrah for War: The United States During World War I. Scott, John A., ed. (Illus.). 160p. 1990. 17.95x (ISBN 0-8160-2453-7). Facts on File.

Ross, Stewart. War in the Trenches: World War One. (Illus.). 64p. (gr. 7-10). 1991. PLB 12.90 (ISBN 0-531-18434-X). Watts.

WORLD WAR, 1914-1918–AERIAL OPERATIONS

Blanco, Richard L. The Luftwaffe in World War II. LC 86-23514. (Illus.). 224p. (gr. 7 up). 1987. lib. bdg. 10.29 (ISBN 0-671-50232-8). Messner.

Maynard, Christopher & Jefferis, David. The Aces: Pilots & Planes of World War I. (Illus.). 32p. (gr. 1-3). 1987. PLB 11.90 (ISBN 0-531-10367-6). Watts.

—Air Battles: Air Combat in World War II. (Illus.). 32p. (gr. 1-6). 1987. PLB 11.90 (ISBN 0-531-10368-4). Watts.

WORLD WAR, 1914-1918–BIOGRAPHY

Roth-Hano, Renee. Touch Wood: A Girlhood Occupied In France. 304p. (gr. 5 up). 1989. pap. 4.95 (ISBN 0-14-034085-8, Puffin). Puffin Bks.

WORLD WAR, 1914-1918–CAMPAIGNS AND BATTLES

The World War I Soldier at Chateau Thierry. 48p. (gr. 5-6). 1989. PLB 10.95 (ISBN 0-685-26394-0). Capstone Pr.

WORLD WAR, 1914-1918–CAUSES

Gilfond, Henry. Black Hand at Sarajevo: Prologue to a World War. LC 74-17690. 176p. (gr. 7 up). 1975. pap. 6.95 (ISBN 0-672-52070-2, Bobbs). Macmillan.

Ross, Stewart. The Origins of World War I. LC 88-24269. (Illus.). 63p. (gr. 7 up). 1989. PLB 12.90 (ISBN 0-531-18260-6, Pub. by Bookwright Pr). Watts.

WORLD WAR, 1914-1918–FICTION

Dank, Milton. Khaki Wings. LC 80-65832. 160p. (gr. 8-12). 1980. pap. 8.95 (ISBN 0-385-28523-X). Delacorte.

Kudlinski, Kathleen. Hero over Here. Dodson, Bert, illus. 64p. (gr. 2-6). 1990. pap. 11.95 (ISBN 0-670-83050-X). Viking Child Bks.

WORLD WAR, 1939-1945

Aaron, Chester. Alex, Who Won His War. 144p. (gr. 5 up). 1991. 17.95 (ISBN 0-8027-8098-9). Walker & Co.

Black, Wallace B. & Blashfield, Jean F. America Prepares for War. LC 90-46581. (Illus.). 48p. (gr. 5-6). 1991. RSBE 11.95 (ISBN 0-89686-554-1, Crestwood Hse). Macmillan Child Grp.

—Blitzkrieg. LC 90-46580. (Illus.). 48p. (gr. 5-6). 1991. RSBE 11.95 (ISBN 0-89686-552-5, Crestwood Hse). Macmillan Child Grp.

Davis, Daniel S. Behind Barbed Wire: The Imprisonment of Japanese Americans During World War II. (Illus.). (gr. 7 up). 1982. 15.95 (ISBN 0-525-26320-9, DCB). Dutton Child Bks.

Friedman, Ina R. The Other Victims: First-Person Stories of Non-Jews Persecuted by the Nazis. 224p. (gr. 5-9). 1990. 14.95 (ISBN 0-395-50212-8). HM.

Fyson, Nance L. Growing up in the Second World War. (Illus.). 72p. (gr. 6 up). 1981. 19.95 (ISBN 0-7134-3574-7, Pub. by Batsford England). Trafalgar Sq.

Harris, Sarah. How & Why: The Second World War. (Illus.). 64p. (gr. 7-10). 1989. 19.95 (ISBN 0-85219-805-1, Pub. by Batsford England). Trafalgar Sq.

Hills, C. A. The Second World War. (Illus.). 72p. (gr. 7-12). 1985. 19.95 (ISBN 0-7134-4531-9, Pub. by Batsford England). Trafalgar Sq.

Hoobler, Dorothy & Hoobler, Thomas. An Album of World War II. LC 77-5090. (Illus.). (gr. 5 up). 1977. PLB 13.90 s&l (ISBN 0-531-02911-5). Watts.

Landau, Elaine. Nazi War Criminals. (Illus.). 128p. (gr. 9-12). 1990. 11.95 (ISBN 0-531-15181-6); PLB 12.40 (ISBN 0-531-10957-7). Watts.

Leckie, Robert. Story of World War II. (Illus.). (gr. 5-9). 1964. lib. bdg. 13.99 (ISBN 0-394-90295-5, Random Juv). Random.

Longman Twentieth Century History Series: Global War. 1990. pap. text ed. 10.92 (ISBN 0-582-34348-8, 78448). Longman.

Marrin, Albert. The Yanks Are Coming: The United States in the First World War. LC 86-3585. (Illus.). 256p. (gr. 5 up). 1986. 15.95 (ISBN 0-689-31209-1, Atheneum Child Bk). Macmillan Child Grp.

Maruki, Toshi. Hiroshima No Pika. Maruki, Toshi, illus. LC 82-15365. 48p. (gr. 7 up). 1982. 14.95 (ISBN 0-688-01297-3). Lothrop.

Messenger, Charles. The Second World War. LC 86-62905. (Illus.). 64p. (gr. 4-12). 1987. lib. bdg. 10.29 (ISBN 0-531-10321-8). Watts.

Patent, Gregory. Shanghai Passage. Lewin, Ted, illus. 128p. (gr. 5-9). 1990. 13.95 (ISBN 0-89919-743-4, Clarion Bks). HM.

Snyder, Louis L. World War II. (Illus.). 96p. (gr. 4 up). 1981. lib. bdg. 10.40 (ISBN 0-531-04333-9). Watts.

Stein, R. Conrad. Home Front. LC 86-11730. (Illus.). 48p. (gr. 4-8). 1986. PLB 14.60 (ISBN 0-516-04769-8). Childrens.

Third September Nineteen Thirty-Nine. (Illus.). 64p. (gr. 7-9). 1988. 19.95 (ISBN 0-85219-757-8, Pub. by Batsford England). Trafalgar Sq.

Tregaskis, Richard. Guadalcanal Diary. LC 83-17662. (Illus.). 176p. (gr. 5-9). 1984. pap. 4.95 (ISBN 0-394-86268-6, Random Juv). Random.

WORLD WAR, 1939-1945-AERIAL OPERATIONS

Spate, Wolfgang. Top Secret Bird: The Luftwaffe's ME-163 Comet. Machat, Mike, illus. LC 88-90967. 276p. (Orig.). (gr. 8-12). 1989. pap. text ed. 11.95 (ISBN 0-929521-08-0). Pictorial Hist.

WORLD WAR, 1939-1945-BATTLES
see World War, 1939-1945-Campaigns and Battles

WORLD WAR, 1939-1945-BIOGRAPHY

Grant, Neil. Heroes of World War Two. LC 90-9468. (Illus.). 48p. (gr. 4-8). 1990. PLB 18.60 (ISBN 0-8114-2754-4). Steck-V.

Sweeney, James B. Army Leaders of World War II. (Illus.). 72p. (gr. 4-8). 1984. lib. bdg. 10.40 (ISBN 0-531-04820-9). Watts.

Tames, Richard. Anne Frank. (Illus.). 32p. (gr. 5 up). 1991. pap. 3.95 (ISBN 0-531-24608-6). Watts.

WORLD WAR, 1939-1945-CAMPAIGNS AND BATTLES

Bliven, Bruce, Jr. From Casablanca to Berlin. (gr. 5-9). 1965. (Random Juv). Random.

—The Story of D-Day. LC 81-483. (Illus.). 160p. (gr. 5-9). 1981. PLB 7.99 (ISBN 0-685-04244-8, Random Juv); pap. 2.95 (ISBN 0-394-84886-1). Random.

—Story of D-Day: June 6, 1944. (Illus.). (gr. 6-8). 1963. (Random Juv); lib. bdg. 8.99 (ISBN 0-394-90362-5). Random.

Carter, Hodding. The Commandos of World War II. LC 80-21142. (Illus.). 160p. (gr. 5-9). 1981. 3.95 (ISBN 0-394-84735-0, Random Juv). Random.

McGowen, Tom. Midway & Guadalcanal. LC 84-10398. (Illus.). 104p. (gr. 7-12). 1984. PLB 12.90 (ISBN 0-531-04866-7). Watts.

Shapiro, William E. Pearl Harbor. LC 84-7324. (Illus.). 103p. (gr. 7-12). 1984. PLB 12.90 (ISBN 0-531-04865-9). Watts.

Skipper, G. C. Battle of the Coral Sea. LC 80-25088. (Illus.). 48p. (gr. 3 up). 1981. PLB 14.60 (ISBN 0-516-04787-6). Childrens.

—D-Day. LC 81-7645. (Illus.). 48p. (gr. 3-8). 1982. PLB 14.60 (ISBN 0-516-04791-4). Childrens.

—Invasion of Sicily. LC 80-27781. (Illus.). 48p. (gr. 3-8). 1981. PLB 14.60 (ISBN 0-516-04792-2). Childrens.

Stein, Conrad R. Road to Rome. LC 82-17853. (Illus.). 48p. (gr. 4-7). 1984. pap. 14.60 (ISBN 0-516-04772-8). Childrens.

Stein, R. Conrad. Dunkirk. LC 82-4595. (Illus.). (gr. 3-8). 1982. PLB 14.60 (ISBN 0-516-04795-7). Childrens.

—The Story of D-Day. Dunnington, Tom, illus. LC 77-5089. 32p. (gr. 3-5). 1977. PLB 13.27 (ISBN 0-516-04609-8); pap. 3.95 (ISBN 0-516-44609-6). Childrens.

Westerfeld, Scott. The Berlin Airlift. (Illus.). 64p. (gr. 5 up). 1989. PLB 16.98 (ISBN 0-382-09833-1); pap. 7.95 (ISBN 0-382-09852-8). Silver Burdett Pr.

WORLD WAR, 1939-1945-CAUSES

Nicholson, Michael & Winner, David. Raoul Wallenberg: The Swedish Diplomat Who Saved 100,000 Jews from the Nazi Holocaust Before Mysteriously Disappearing. Sherwood, Rhoda, ed. LC 88-2078. (Illus.). 68p. (gr. 5-6). 1989. PLB 12.95 (ISBN 1-55532-820-2). Gareth Stevens Inc.

WORLD WAR, 1939-1945-CHILDREN

Allen, Eleanor. Wartime Children, Nineteen Thirty-Nine to Nineteen Forty-Five. (Illus.). 64p. (gr. 6 up). 1978. 14.95 (ISBN 0-7136-1503-6). Dufour.

Tajiri, Vincent, ed. Through Innocent Eyes: Teen-agers' Impressions of WW2 Internment Camp Life. Kurushima, Eddie & Nakayama, Mike, illus. Ichioka, Yuji, intros. by. 120p. (Orig.). 1990. 49.50 (ISBN 0-9624450-0-2); pap. 29.50 (ISBN 0-9624450-1-0); audio tape 15.00 (ISBN 1-878385-00-3). Keiro Services.

In 1942, some 120,000 Japanese Americans, without benefit of due process, were removed from their homes & confined to stark internment centers in desolate areas of the United States. Of the Japanese Americans interned, 30,000 were school age children. For the first time, the writing & artwork of these young people have been compiled into a single volume to bring us their voices & visions. In this return to a historical time of racial stereotyping & hatred; war hysteria & paranoia, one finds the voices surprisingly restrained. There is little anger here--no bitterness or despair. Here are pages that are key to the young-vibrant with optimism & hope. Ray Franchi, a teacher at Poston (one of the ten internment camps) & Paul Takeda, a Red Cross worker compiled the original scrapbook of sketches & writings so that other school-aged children could become familiar with the plight of the Japanese Americans during the war. However, the scrapbook remained submerged until 45 years later. Keiro Services, a non-profit organization providing long-term care to the Japanese American elderly decided to make the collection available to increase awareness & education among the general public. Edited by Vincent Tajiri, the book contains the illustrations & sketches of fifty children along with contributing works by other known authors of the camp experience. Also included is a brief interview with the schoolteacher, Franchi. The audio version of Through Innocent Eyes was produced by Family Media with an introduction by George Takei (of Star Trek fame).
Publisher Provided Annotation.

WORLD WAR, 1939-1945-EUROPE

Adler, David. We Remember the Holocaust. LC 87-21139. (Illus.). 144p. (gr. 6-9). 1989. 16.95 (ISBN 0-8050-0434-3). H Holt & Co.

Baklanov, Grigory. Forever Nineteen. Bouis, Antonina W., tr. from RUS. LC 88-26622. 176p. (gr. 7 up). 1989. 13.95 (ISBN 0-397-32296-8, Lipp Jr Bks); PLB 13.89 (ISBN 0-397-32297-6, Lipp Jr Bks). HarpC Child Bks.

WORLD WAR, 1939-1945-FICTION

Anderson, Margaret J. Searching for Shona. LC 77-17056. 160p. (gr. 4-7). 1989. pap. 2.95 (ISBN 0-394-82587-X, Bullseye Bks). Knopf.

Arnothy, Christine. I Am Fifteen--& I Don't Want to Die. 128p. (gr. 7 up). 1986. pap. 2.50 (ISBN 0-590-40322-2, Point). Scholastic Inc.

Bishop, Claire H. Twenty & Ten. Pene du Bois, William, illus. (gr. 5-9). 1984. 16.50 (ISBN 0-8446-6168-6). Peter Smith.

Bograd, Larry. Los Alamos Light. LC 83-11638. 168p. (gr. 7 up). 1983. 12.95 (ISBN 0-374-34656-9). FS&G.

Chaikin, Miriam. Friends Forever. Egielski, Richard, illus. LC 86-45777. 128p. (gr. 3-6). 1988. 11.95 (ISBN 0-06-021203-9); PLB 11.89 (ISBN 0-06-021204-7). HarpC Child Bks.

Chang, Margaret & Chang, Raymond. In the Eye of War. (gr. 5-9). 1990. 13.95 (ISBN 0-689-50503-5, M K McElderry). Macmillan Child Grp.

Cooper, Susan. Dawn of Fear. Gill, Margery, illus. LC 71-115755. (gr. 3-7). 1988. 14.95 (ISBN 0-15-266201-4, HJ). HarBraceJ.

—Dawn of Fear. Gill, Margery, illus. 224p. (gr. 5 up). 1989. pap. 3.95 (ISBN 0-689-71327-4, Aladdin). Macmillan Child Grp.

DeJong, Meindert. House of Sixty Fathers. Sendak, Maurice, illus. LC 56-8148. 192p. (gr. 5-8). 1956. PLB 13.89 (ISBN 0-06-021481-3). HarpC Child Bks.

Ferry, Charles. One More Time. LC 84-20507. 171p. (gr. 7 up). 1985. 11.95 (ISBN 0-395-36692-5). HM.

—Raspberry One. LC 82-25476. 224p. (gr. 7 up). 1983. 11.95 (ISBN 0-395-34069-1). HM.

Frank, Rudolf. No Hero for the Kaiser. Crampton, Patricia, tr. from GER. Steffans, Klaus, illus. 224p. (gr. 7 up). 1986. Repr. of 1931 ed. 13.00 (ISBN 0-688-06093-5). Lothrop.

Glassman, Judy. The Morning Glory War. (gr. 4-7). 1990. 13.95 (ISBN 0-525-44637-0, DCB). Dutton Child Bks.

Greene, Bette. Summer of My German Soldier. 208p. (gr. 7-12). 1984. pap. 3.50 (ISBN 0-553-27247-0). Bantam.

—Summer of My German Soldier. 224p. (gr. 7 up). 1973. 14.95 (ISBN 0-8037-8321-3). Dial Bks Young.

—The Summer of My German Soldier. large type ed. 272p. 1989. Repr. of 1973 ed. PLB 15.95 (ISBN 1-55736-134-7, Crnrstn Bks). ABC-CLIO.

Kerr, Judith. When Hitler Stole Pink Rabbit. Kerr, Judith, illus. (gr. 6 up). 1972. 8.95 (ISBN 0-698-20182-5, Coward). Putnam Pub Group.

Laird, Christa. Shadow of the Wall. LC 89-34469. (gr. 7 up). 1990. 12.95 (ISBN 0-688-09336-1). Greenwillow.

Lingard, Joan. Tug of War. 208p. (gr. 7 up). 1990. 14.95 (ISBN 0-525-67306-7, Lodestar Bks). Dutton Child Bks.

Lowry, Lois. Autumn Street. 160p. (gr. 5 up). 1980. 13.95 (ISBN 0-395-27812-0). HM.

McSwigan, Marie. Snow Treasure. (Illus.). (gr. 6-9). pap. 2.50 (ISBN 0-590-41148-9). Scholastic Inc.

Mazer, Harry. The Last Mission. 192p. (gr. 7 up). 1981. pap. 3.25 (ISBN 0-440-94797-9, LE). Dell.

Mellecker, Judith. Randolph's Dream. Parker, Robert A., illus. LC 90-40612. 48p. 1991. 14.95 (ISBN 0-679-81115-X); lib. bdg. 15.99 (ISBN 0-679-91115-4). Knopf.

Nanus, Susan & Kornblatt, Marc. Mission to World War Two. 144p. (Orig.). (gr. 4 up). 1986. pap. 2.25 (ISBN 0-553-25431-6). Bantam.

Paton-Walsh, Jill. Fireweed. LC 73-109554. 144p. (gr. 6 up). 1970. 14.95 (ISBN 0-374-32310-0, Sunburst). FS&G.

Poynter, Margaret. A Time Too Swift. LC 89-30896. 192p. (gr. 5 up). 1990. 13.95 (ISBN 0-689-31146-X, Atheneum Child Bk). Macmillan Child Grp.

Reiss, Johanna. The Journey Back. LC 76-12615. 224p. (gr. 7 up). 1987. pap. 2.95 (ISBN 0-06-447042-3, Trophy). HarpC Child Bks.

—The Upstairs Room. LC 77-187940. 208p. (gr. 7 up). 1990. pap. 3.50 (ISBN 0-06-440370-X, Trophy). HarpC Child Bks.

Roseman, Kenneth. Escape from the Holocaust. 192p. (Orig.). (gr. 4-6). 1985. pap. 6.95 (ISBN 0-8074-0307-5, 140070). UAHC.

Serraillier, Ian. Escape from Warsaw. 218p. (gr. 7-9). 1972. pap. 2.50 (ISBN 0-590-41176-4). Scholastic Inc.

—Silver Sword. Hodges, C. Walter, illus. LC 59-6556. (gr. 7-9). 1959. 22.95 (ISBN 0-87599-104-1). S G Phillips.

Todd, Leonard. The Best Kept Secret of the War. LC 83-18756. 176p. (gr. 4-7). 1984. Knopf.

Watkins, Yoko K. So Far from the Bamboo Grove. Fritz, Jean, intro. by. LC 85-15939. 192p. (gr. 6 up). 1986. 12.95 (ISBN 0-688-06110-9). Lothrop.

Westall, Robert. The Machine Gunners. LC 76-13630. 186p. (gr. 5-9). 1976. PLB 11.88 (ISBN 0-688-84055-8). Greenwillow.

—The Machine Gunners. LC 76-13630. 192p. (gr. 5 up). 1990. pap. 3.50 (ISBN 0-679-80130-8). McKay.

Yee, Chiang. Men of the Burma Road. (Illus.). (gr. 4-6). 8.50 (ISBN 0-685-20604-1). Transatl Arts.

WORLD WAR, 1939-1945-GERMANY

Blanco, Richard L. The Luftwaffe in World War II. LC 86-23514. (Illus.). 224p. (gr. 7 up). 1987. lib. bdg. 10.29 (ISBN 0-671-50232-8). Messner.

Ossowski, Leonie. Star Without a Sky. LC 84-21834. 216p. (gr. 5 up). 1985. 12.95 (ISBN 0-8225-0771-4). Lerner Pubns.

WORLD WAR, 1939-1945-GREAT BRITAIN

Rawcliffe, Michael. Britain at War 1939-45. (Illus.). 72p. (gr. 7-11). 1991. 19.95 (ISBN 0-7134-6354-6, Pub. by Batsford UK). Trafalgar Sq.

WORLD WAR, 1939-1945-GUERRILLAS
see World War, 1939-1945-Underground Movements

WORLD WAR, 1939-1945-HOSPITALS
see World War, 1939-1945-Medical and Sanitary Affairs

WORLD WAR, 1939-1945-JAPAN

Skipper, G. C. Pearl Harbor. LC 83-6569. (Illus.). 48p. (gr. 4-8). 1983. PLB 14.60 (ISBN 0-516-04774-4). Childrens.

WORLD WAR, 1939-1945-JEWS

Finkelstein, Norman. Remember Not to Forget: A Memory of the Holocaust. Hokanson, Lars & Hokanson, Lois, illus. LC 84-17315. 32p. (gr. 1-3). 1985. PLB 10.90 (ISBN 0-531-04892-6). Watts.

Frank, Anne. Anne Frank: The Diary of a Young Girl. rev. ed. Mooyaart, B. M., tr. Roosevelt, Eleanor, intro. by. LC 52-6355. 312p. (gr. 7 up). 1967. 21.95 (ISBN 0-385-04019-9). Doubleday.

Neimark, Anne E. One Man's Valor: Leo Baeck & the Holocaust. LC 85-27366. (Illus.). 128p. (gr. 5-9). 1986. 14.95 (ISBN 0-525-67175-7, Lodestar Bks). Dutton Child Bks.

Nicholson, Michael & Winner, David. Raoul Wallenberg: The Swedish Diplomat Who Saved 100,000 Jews from the Nazi Holocaust Before Mysteriously Disappearing. Sherwood, Rhoda, ed. LC 88-2078. (Illus.). 68p. (gr. 5-6). 1989. PLB 12.95 (ISBN 1-55532-820-2). Gareth Stevens Inc.

Reiss, Johanna. The Upstairs Room. LC 77-187940. 196p. (gr. 7 up). 1987. 12.95 (ISBN 0-690-85127-8, Crowell Jr Bks); PLB 12.89 (ISBN 0-690-04702-9, Crowell Jr Bks). HarpC Child Bks.

WORLD WAR, 1939-1945-MEDICAL AND SANITARY AFFAIRS

Lewis, Linda. Two Young Two Go for Boys: A Combat Surgeon in World War II. (gr. 9-12). 1988. pap. 2.50 (ISBN 0-671-66576-6). S&S Trade.

WORLD WAR, 1939-1945-NAVAL OPERATIONS

Blassingame, Wyatt. The U. S. Frogmen of World War II. (gr. 5-9). 1964. Random.

Forester, C. S. The Last Nine Days of the Bismarck. (gr. 7 up). 1959. 14.45 (ISBN 0-685-03074-1). Little.

Sloan, Frank. Bismarck! (Illus.). 64p. (gr. 3-5). 1991. PLB 11.90 (ISBN 0-531-20002-7). Watts.

Taylor, Theodore. Battle in the Arctic Seas: The Story of Convoy PQ17. Parker, Robert A., illus. LC 75-33655. 156p. (gr. 5 up). 1976. 12.95 (ISBN 0-690-01084-2, Crowell Jr Bks). HarpC Child Bks.

WORLD WAR, 1939-1945–PACIFIC OCEAN

Ferry, Charles. Raspberry One. LC 82-25476. 224p. (gr. 7 up). 1983. 11.95 (ISBN 0-395-34069-1). HM.

Marrin, Albert. Victory in the Pacific. LC 82-6707. (Illus.). 224p. (gr. 6 up). 1983. 14.95 (ISBN 0-689-30948-1, Atheneum Child Bk). Macmillan Child Grp.

WORLD WAR, 1939-1945–PERSONAL NARRATIVES

Butterworth, Emma M. As the Waltz Was Ending. LC 82-70402. 192p. (gr. 7 up). 1984. 13.95 (ISBN 0-02-716190-0, Four Winds). Macmillan Child Grp.

—As the Waltz Was Ending. 262p. (gr. 7 up). 1991. pap. 2.95 (ISBN 0-590-44440-9, Point); tchr's. guide 1.25 (ISBN 0-590-40665-5). Scholastic Inc.

Reiss, Johanna. The Upstairs Room. LC 77-187940. 196p. (gr. 7 up). 1987. 12.95 (ISBN 0-690-85127-8, Crowell Jr Bks); PLB 12.89 (ISBN 0-690-04702-9, Crowell Jr Bks). HarpC Child Bks.

Tajiri, Vincent, ed. Through Innocent Eyes: Teen-agers' Impressions of WW2 Internment Camp Life. Kurushima, Eddie & Nakayama, Mike, illus. Ichioka, Yuji, intros. by. 120p. (Orig.). 1990. 49.50 (ISBN 0-9624450-0-2); pap. 29.50 (ISBN 0-9624450-1-0); audio tape 15.00 (ISBN 1-878385-00-3). Keiro Services.

In 1942, some 120,000 Japanese Americans, without benefit of due process, were removed from their homes & confined to stark internment centers in desolate areas of the United States. Of the Japanese Americans interned, 30,000 were school age children. For the first time, the writing & artwork of these young people have been compiled into a single volume to bring us their voices & visions. In this return to a historical time of racial stereotyping & hatred; war hysteria & paranoia, one finds the voices surprisingly restrained. There is little anger here--no bitterness or despair. Here are pages that are key to the young-vibrant with optimism & hope. Ray Franchi, a teacher at Poston (one of the ten internment camps) & Paul Takeda, a Red Cross worker compiled the original scrapbook of sketches & writings so that other school-aged children could become familiar with the plight of the Japanese Americans during the war. However, the scrapbook remained submerged until 45 years later. Keiro Services, a non-profit organization providing long-term care to the Japanese American elderly decided to make the collection available to increase awareness & education among the general public. Edited by Vincent Tajiri, the book contains the illustrations & sketches of fifty children along with contributing works by other known authors of the camp experience. Also included is a brief interview with the schoolteacher, Franchi. The audio version of Through Innocent Eyes was produced by Family Media with an introduction by George Takei (of Star Trek fame).
Publisher Provided Annotation.

WORLD WAR, 1939-1945–POLAND

Skipper, G. C. Invasion of Poland. LC 83-7634. 48p. (gr. 4-8). 1983. PLB 14.60 (ISBN 0-516-04775-2). Childrens.

WORLD WAR, 1939-1945–PRISONERS AND PRISONS

Nicholson, Michael & Winner, David. Raoul Wallenberg. (Illus.). (gr. 5-6). 1990. pap. 7.95 (ISBN 0-8192-1525-2). Morehouse Pub.

Sullivan, George. Great Escapes of World War II. 128p. (gr. 3-7). 1988. pap. 2.50 (ISBN 0-590-41024-5). Scholastic Inc.

WORLD WAR, 1939-1945–SANITARY AFFAIRS

see World War, 1939-1945–Medical and Sanitary Affairs

WORLD WAR, 1939-1945–SECRET SERVICE

Rogers, James T. The Secret War: Espionage in World War Two. (Illus.). 128p. (gr. 7-10). 1991. lib. bdg. 16.95x (ISBN 0-8160-2395-6). Facts on File.

WORLD WAR, 1939-1945–SOVIET UNION

Baklanov, Grigory. Forever Nineteen. Bouis, Antonina W., tr. from RUS. LC 88-26622. 176p. (gr. 7 up). 1989. 13.95 (ISBN 0-397-32296-8, Lipp Jr Bks); PLB 13.89 (ISBN 0-397-32297-6, Lipp Jr Bks). HarpC Child Bks.

WORLD WAR, 1939-1945–UNDERGROUND MOVEMENTS

Atkinson, Linda. In Kindling Flame: The Story of Hannah Senesh 1921-1944. LC 83-24392. 224p. (gr. 9 up). 1985. 14.95 (ISBN 0-688-02714-8). Lothrop.

Goldston, Robert. Sinister Touches: The Secret War Against Hitler. LC 81-65853. 176p. (gr. 7 up). 1982. 11.95 (ISBN 0-8037-7903-8, 01160-350). Dial Bks Young.

Stein, R. Conrad. Resistance Movements. LC 82-9399. (Illus.). (gr. 3-8). 1982. PLB 14.60 (ISBN 0-516-04798-1). Childrens.

WORLD WAR, 1939-1945–U. S.

Cross, Robin. Roosevelt: And the Americans at War. (Illus.). 64p. (gr. 5-8). 1990. PLB 11.90 (ISBN 0-531-17254-6). Watts.

Devaney, John. Nineteen Forty-One: America Goes to War. 192p. (gr. 12 up). 1991. 16.95 (ISBN 0-8027-6979-9); lib. bdg. 17.85 (ISBN 0-8027-6980-2). Walker & Co.

—Nineteen Forty-Two: America Fights the Tide. 192p. (gr. 12 up). 1991. 17.95 (ISBN 0-8027-6997-7); lib. bdg. 18.85 (ISBN 0-8027-6998-5). Walker & Co.

Dolan, Edward F. America in World War Two: 1942. (Illus.). 72p. (gr. 4-6). 1991. PLB 17.95 (ISBN 1-56294-007-4); pap. 5.95 (ISBN 1-878841-82-3). Millbrook Pr.

Skipper, G. C. Pearl Harbor. LC 83-6569. (Illus.). 48p. (gr. 4-8). 1983. PLB 14.60 (ISBN 0-516-04774-4). Childrens.

Weatherford, Doris. American Women & World War Two. (Illus.). 352p. 1990. 29.95x (ISBN 0-8160-2038-8). Facts on File.

WORLD'S FAIRS

see Exhibitions; Fairs

WORMS

Coldrey, Jennifer. Discovering Worms. LC 85-62087. (Illus.). 64p. (gr. k-6). 1986. lib. bdg. 11.90 (ISBN 0-531-18046-8). Watts.

—Discovering Worms. (Illus.). 48p. (gr. 2 up). 1990. pap. 4.95 (ISBN 0-531-18366-1). Watts.

Halton, Cheryl M. Those Amazing Leeches. LC 88-35908. (Illus.). 112p. (gr. 4 up). 1989. lib. bdg. 12.95 (ISBN 0-87518-408-1, Dillon). Macmillan Child Grp.

Sroda, George. No Angle Left Unturned: Facts About Nightcrawlers. Hughes, Janet, illus. 111p. (gr. 10 up). 1975. pap. 4.95 (ISBN 0-9604486-0-8). G Sroda.

WORMS–FICTION

Brown, Lynn. Ms. Worm. 3rd ed. Walker, Granville, Jr., ed. Jackson, Gregory A., illus. (Orig.). (ps-6). 1982. pap. 2.95x (ISBN 0-9608466-0-3). Fun Reading.

Deary, Terry. The Lambton Worm. Firmin, Charlotte, illus. LC 82-1327. 88p. (gr. 2-6). 1982. lib. bdg. 8.95 (ISBN 0-87614-196-3). Carolrhoda Bks.

Demi. Where Is Willie Worm? Demi, illus. LC 80-53680. 24p. (ps-1). 1981. 3.95 (ISBN 0-394-84759-8). Random.

Giff, Patricia R. The Winter Worm Business. Morrill, Leslie, illus. 144p. (gr. k-6). 1983. pap. 2.95 (ISBN 0-440-49259-9, YB). Dell.

Hargreaves, Roger. Count Worm. Hargreaves, Roger, illus. LC 81-15820. 32p. (ps-1). 1982. 3.95 (ISBN 0-448-12318-5, G&D). Putnam Pub Group.

Hunt, Rod. Worm Plans a Great Escape. Gordon, Mike, illus. 32p. (ps-2). 1987. 5.95 (ISBN 0-09-167230-9, Pub. by Hutchinson UK). Trafalgar Sq.

Magellan, Mauro. Home at Last. Magellan, Mauro, illus. LC 89-19994. 32p. 1989. 12.95 (ISBN 0-89334-119-3). Humanics Ltd.

Reese, Bob. Crab Apple. Wasserman, Dan, ed. Reese, Bob, illus. (gr. k-1). 1979. PLB 7.95 (ISBN 0-89868-072-7); pap. 2.95 (ISBN 0-89868-083-2). ARO Pub.

Scarry, Richard. Richard Scarry's Lowly Worm Storybook. Scarry, Richard, illus. LC 77-79842. 32p. (Orig.). (ps-1). 1989. pap. 2.25 (ISBN 0-394-88270-9). Random.

Sroda, George. Life Story of TV Star & Celebrity Herman the Worm. Hughes, Janet, illus. 189p. (gr. k-7). 1979. 4.95 (ISBN 0-9604486-2-4); pap. 3.95 (ISBN 0-685-01814-8). G Sroda.

Stevenson, James. National Worm Day. LC 88-34915. (Illus.). 40p. (gr. k up). 1990. 12.95 (ISBN 0-688-08771-X); lib. bdg. 12.88 (ISBN 0-688-08772-8). Greenwillow.

Torudd, Astrid. A Worm's Tale. Jonasson, Dianne, tr. from SWE. Torudd, Cecilia, illus. 28p. (ps up). 1988. 12.95 (ISBN 9-12-959068-X, R & S Bks). FS&G.

Van Laan, Nancy. The Big Fat Worm. Russo, Marisabina, illus. LC 86-20158. 32p. (ps-2). 1987. 11.95 (ISBN 0-394-88763-8). Knopf.

Ziefert, Harriet. Worm Day. Brown, Richard, illus. (gr. 2-4). 1987. 7.95 (ISBN 0-316-98767-0). Little.

WORSHIP

see also Prayer

Abraham, Ken. Hot Trax: Devotions for Girls. 160p. (Orig.). (gr. 9-12). 1987. pap. text ed. 6.95 (ISBN 0-8007-5241-4). Revell.

—Hot Trax: Devotions for Guys. 160p. (Orig.). (gr. 9-12). pap. 6.95 (ISBN 0-8007-5242-2). Revell.

Bacher, June M. When Hearts Awaken. 192p. 1988. pap. 5.99 (ISBN 0-89081-610-7). Harvest Hse.

Brooks, Bruce. The Moves Make the Man. LC 83-49476. 320p. (gr. 7 up). 1984. 14.95 (ISBN 0-06-020679-9); PLB 14.89 (ISBN 0-06-020698-5). HarpC Child Bks.

Call, Betty & Souther, Shelia. Children Can Worship, Bk. 3. (Orig.). (gr. 1-3). 1983. pap. text ed. 10.95 (ISBN 0-87148-178-2). Pathway Pr.

Draper, Edythe. Cool: How a Kid Should Live. (gr. 3-5). 1974. kivar 8.95 (ISBN 0-8423-0435-5). Tyndale.

Finley, Tom. The World Is Not Enough. Parrish, Annette, ed. LC 86-22049. 239p. (Orig.). (gr. 7-12). 1986. pap. 5.95 (ISBN 0-8307-1151-1, S183329). Regal.

Groth, Lynn. Reaching Tender Hearts, Vol. 1. Grunze, Richard, ed. May, Lawrence & Steele, Loren, illus. 157p. (ps-k). 1987. pap. 7.95 (ISBN 0-938272-42-X). WELS Board.

Johnson, Philip E. Celebrating the Seasons with Children. LC 84-14791. 112p. (Orig.). (ps-3). 1984. pap. 7.95 (ISBN 0-8298-0723-3). Pilgrim NY.

Moffatt, Marjorie. Children's Word Liturgies, Vol. 3. (Illus.). 112p. 1988. pap. 9.95 (ISBN 0-8146-1539-2). Liturgical Pr.

Oyer, Sharron, et al. Seekers in Sneakers: A Children's Devotional, Vol. 1. 128p. (Orig.). (gr. 2-5). 1988. pap. 5.99 (ISBN 0-89081-611-5). Harvest Hse.

Rathert, Donna & Prahlow, Lois. Time for Church. 24p. (gr. 2-5). 1985. pap. 2.95 (ISBN 0-570-04129-5, 56-1540). Concordia.

Rosser, Hershel. Worship-A Close Encounter of the Best Kind. (Illus.). 32p. (gr. 9-12). 1983. 1.50 (ISBN 0-88243-825-5, 02-0825); leader's guide 3.95 (ISBN 0-88243-845-X, 02-0845). Gospel Pub.

Taylor, Kenneth. Devotions for the Children's Hour. 2nd ed. (gr. 1-8). 1987. pap. 6.95 (ISBN 0-8024-2226-8). Moody.

—Stories for the Children's Hour. 2nd ed. (gr. 1-8). 1987. pap. 6.95 (ISBN 0-8024-2227-6). Moody.

Tirabassi, Becky. Live It! A Daily Devotional for Students. 192p. 1990. pap. 7.95 (ISBN 0-685-38929-4, Youth Bks). Zondervan.

Trzeciak, Cathi. Worship: Our Gift to God. (Illus.). 24p. (gr. k-4). 1986. pap. 3.95 saddlestitched (ISBN 0-570-08531-4, 56-1558). Concordia.

Tullis, Dawn. Teach Us to Pray. 2.25 (ISBN 0-686-13717-5). Crusade Pubs.

Van Pelt, Nancy L. The Compleat Tween. Coffen, Richard W., ed. 96p. (Orig.). (gr. 5 up). 1986. pap. 7.50 (ISBN 0-8280-0288-6). Review & Herald.

Watts, Dorothy E. Stepping Stones. Woolsey, Raymond, ed. 384p. (gr. 1 up). 1987. text ed. 9.50 (ISBN 0-8280-0384-X). Review & Herald.

WOUNDED, FIRST AID TO

see First Aid

WRECKS

see Shipwrecks

WRENS–FICTION

Ravilious, Robin. Two in a Pocket. (ps-3). 1991. 14.95 (ISBN 0-316-73449-7). Little.

WRESTLING

see also Judo

Cohen, Daniel & Cohen, Susan. Wrestling Superstars. (Illus.). (gr. 4 up). 1986. pap. 2.50 (ISBN 0-671-62853-4, Archway). PB.

Fox, Ron. Wrestling Basics. Schoolcraft, Robert, illus. LC 85-25595. 48p. (gr. 3-7). 1986. PLB 11.95 (ISBN 0-671-66289-9). S&S Trade.

Gutman, Bill. Go for It: Wrestling. Brown, Ben, illus. 64p. (gr. 3-7). 1989. PLB 16.50 (ISBN 0-942545-94-X). Grey Castle.

—Strange & Amazing Wrestling Stories. (Illus.). (gr. 4 up). 1986. pap. 2.50 (ISBN 0-671-61134-8, Archway). PB.

Janoff, Barry. Hulk Hogan: Eye of the Tiger. LC 85-28047. (Illus.). 48p. (gr. 2-8). 1986. pap. 3.95 (ISBN 0-516-44356-9). Childrens.

Sullivan, George. Better Wrestling for Boys. (Illus.). 64p. (gr. 8-12). 1986. 10.99 (ISBN 0-399-61237-8, Putnam). Putnam Pub Group.

Thomas, Art. Wrestling Is for Me. Thomas, Art, photos by. LC 79-1487. (Illus.). 48p. (gr. 2-5). 1979. PLB 8.95 (ISBN 0-8225-1085-5). Lerner Pubns.

Zadra, Dan. Andre the Giant. LC 86-72532. (gr. 4 up). 1986. lib. bdg. 9.75 (ISBN 0-88682-089-8). Creative Ed.

—Hulk Hogan. LC 86-72533. (gr. 4 up). 1986. lib. bdg. 9.75 (ISBN 0-88682-087-1); 13.95 (ISBN 0-685-17883-8). Creative Ed.

WRESTLING–FICTION

Christopher, Matt. Takedown. Sanfilippo, Margaret, illus. (gr. 3-7). 1990. 13.95 (ISBN 0-316-13930-0). Little.

WRIGHT, FRANK LLOYD, 1869-1959

Murphy, Wendy. Frank Lloyd Wright. (Illus.). 128p. (gr. 7-9). 1990. 14.95 (ISBN 0-382-24033-2); lib. bdg. 17.98 (ISBN 0-382-09905-2). Silver Burdett Pr.

WRIGHT, ORVILLE, 1871-1948

Johnson, Spencer. The Value of Patience: The Story of the Wright Brothers. 2nd ed. Pileggi, Steven, illus. LC 76-55022. (gr. k-6). 1976. 9.95 (ISBN 0-916392-08-2, Pub. by Value Communications). Oak Tree Pubns.

Kaufman, Mervyn D. The Wright Brothers: Kings of the Air. (Illus.). 80p. (gr. 2-6). 1992. Repr. of 1964 ed. PLB 12.95 (ISBN 0-7910-1428-2). Chelsea Hse.

Marquardt, Max. Wilbur, Orville & the Flying Machine. (Illus.). 32p. (gr. 1-4). 1989. PLB 13.32 (ISBN 0-8172-3530-2). Raintree Pubs.

Reynolds, Quentin. The Wright Brothers. LC 50-11766. (Illus.). 160p. (gr. 5-9). 1981. pap. 3.95 (ISBN 0-394-84700-8). Random.

—Wright Brothers. (Illus.). (gr. 4-6). 1963. lib. bdg. 8.99 (ISBN 0-394-90310-2, Random Juv). Random.

Sobol, Donald J. The Wright Brothers at Kitty Hawk. Blickenstaff, Wayne, illus. 128p. (gr. 3-7). 1987. pap. 2.50 (ISBN 0-590-40488-1). Scholastic Inc.

—The Wright Brothers at Kitty Hawk. 128p. (Orig.). (gr. 3-7). 1987. pap. 2.75 (ISBN 0-590-42904-3). Scholastic Inc.

Stevenson, Augusta. Wilbur & Orville Wright: Young Fliers. Doremus, Robert, illus. LC 86-10747. 192p. (gr. 2-6). 1986. pap. 3.95 (ISBN 0-02-042170-2, Aladdin). Macmillan Child Grp.

Tames, Richard. The Wright Brothers. (Illus.). 32p. (gr. 5-8). 1990. PLB 11.90 (ISBN 0-531-14002-4). Watts.

Taylor, Richard, L. First Flight: The Story of the Wright Brothers. (ps-3). 1990. PLB 11.90 (ISBN 0-531-10891-0). Watts.

The Wright Brothers. (ARA., Illus.). (gr. 5-12). 3.50x (ISBN 0-86685-245-X). Intl Bk Ctr.

WRIGHT, WILBUR, 1867-1912

Johnson, Spencer. The Value of Patience: The Story of the Wright Brothers. 2nd ed. Pileggi, Steven, illus. LC 76-55022. (gr. k-6). 1976. 9.95 (ISBN 0-916392-08-2, Pub. by Value Communications). Oak Tree Pubns.

Kaufman, Mervyn D. The Wright Brothers: Kings of the Air. (Illus.). 80p. (gr. 2-6). 1992. Repr. of 1964 ed. PLB 12.95 (ISBN 0-7910-1428-2). Chelsea Hse.

Marquardt, Max. Wilbur, Orville & the Flying Machine. (Illus.). 32p. (gr. 1-4). 1989. PLB 13.32 (ISBN 0-8172-3530-2). Raintree Pubs.

Reynolds, Quentin. The Wright Brothers. LC 50-11766. (Illus.). 160p. (gr. 5-9). 1981. pap. 3.95 (ISBN 0-394-84700-8). Random.

—Wright Brothers. (Illus.). (gr. 4-6). 1963. lib. bdg. 8.99 (ISBN 0-394-90310-2, Random Juv). Random.

Sabin, Louis. Wilbur & Orville Wright: The Flight to Adventure. Lawn, John, illus. LC 82-15879. 48p. (gr. 4-6). 1983. PLB 10.79 (ISBN 0-89375-851-5); pap. text ed. 2.95 (ISBN 0-89375-852-3). Troll Assocs.

Sobol, Donald J. The Wright Brothers at Kitty Hawk. Blickenstaff, Wayne, illus. 128p. (gr. 3-7). 1987. pap. 2.50 (ISBN 0-590-40488-1). Scholastic Inc.

—The Wright Brothers at Kitty Hawk. 128p. (Orig.). (gr. 3-7). 1987. pap. 2.75 (ISBN 0-590-42904-3). Scholastic Inc.

Stevenson, Augusta. Wilbur & Orville Wright: Young Fliers. Doremus, Robert, illus. LC 86-10747. 192p. (gr. 2-6). 1986. pap. 3.95 (ISBN 0-02-042170-2, Aladdin). Macmillan Child Grp.

Tames, Richard. The Wright Brothers. (Illus.). 32p. (gr. 5-8). 1990. PLB 11.90 (ISBN 0-531-14002-4). Watts.

Taylor, Richard, L. First Flight: The Story of the Wright Brothers. (ps-3). 1990. PLB 11.90 (ISBN 0-531-10891-0). Watts.

The Wright Brothers. (ARA., Illus.). (gr. 5-12). 3.50x (ISBN 0-86685-245-X). Intl Bk Ctr.

WRITERS

see Authors

WRITING

see also Alphabet; Ciphers; Cryptography; Hieroglyphics; Picture Writing; Typewriting

Allington, Richard L. & Krull, Kathleen. Writing. Miyake, Yoshi, illus. LC 80-15334. 32p. (ps-2). 1985. PLB 15.33 (ISBN 0-8172-1321-X); pap. 9.27 (ISBN 0-8172-2499-8). Raintree Pubs.

Aten, Jerry. Prime Time Writing Skills. Filkins, Vanessa, illus. 64p. (gr. 2-5). 1984. wkbk 6.95 (ISBN 0-86653-191-2, GA 526). Good Apple.

Baron, Nancy. Getting Started in Calligraphy. Baron, Nancy, illus. LC 78-66311. (gr. 7 up). 1979. spiral bdg. 9.95 (ISBN 0-8069-8840-1). Sterling.

Benjamin, Carol L. Writing for Kids. Benjamin, Carol L., illus. LC 85-47542. 80p. (gr. 3-7). 1985. PLB 11.89 (ISBN 0-690-04490-9, Crowell Jr Bks). HarpC Child Bks.

Bostick, William A. Calligraphy for Kids. (Illus.). 32p. (Orig.). (gr. 3-12). 1991. wkbk. 9.95 (ISBN 0-9606630-1-0). La Stampa Calligrafica.

A fun way for youngsters to learn calligraphy as well as beautiful & legible handwriting. Unfortunately, these skills aren't usually acquired in schools today. Before printing, sample pages were tested on sixth & seventh graders. The students' enthusiastic participation & delightful testimonials such as, "I think your book is great!" &, "If I saw it in a bookstore I would buy it," encouraged us to proceed. The budding calligrapher goes over the author's large Chancery quotation for

each letter & then repeats the calligraphy on his own, both large & at normal handwriting size. Cartoon 'live letters' liven each page & students are encouraged to draw their own. The cover reproduces Chancery & six other alphabets for kids to explore. It opens up the whole wonderful world of calligraphy to a youngster. But, of course, adults can also learn from it: the age range is 6 to 96! Book dealers & stores selling educational material for children tell us that there is nothing like "Calligraphy for Kids" on the market today. It's unique! *Publisher Provided Annotation.*

Carson, Patti & Dellosa, Janet. Capital & Lower Case Letters. (Illus.). 32p. (ps-1). 1983. pap. 1.98 (ISBN 0-88724-004-6, CD-7005). Carson-Dellos.

Carter, Patricia. Illuminated Calligraphy: Borders & Letters. (Illus.). 64p. (Orig.). pap. 14.95 (ISBN 0-85532-642-5, Pub. by Search Pr UK). A Schwartz & Co.

Cobb, Vicki. Writing It Down. Hafner, Marylin, illus. LC 88-14191. 32p. (gr. k-3). 1989. 11.95 (ISBN 0-397-32326-3, Lipp Jr Bks); PLB 11.89 (ISBN 0-397-32327-1, Lipp Jr Bks). HarpC Child Bks.

Copperplate Calligraphy Kit. (gr. 7 up). 1988. Boxed set. incl. script bklt., ink, pen holder, pen nibs, 100% rag paper, reusable template guides 17.95 (ISBN 0-939564-11-4). Pen Notes.

Davenport, May, ed. Courage: An Anthology of Short Stories, Articles & Poems. Kline, Gail, illus. LC 79-26261. (Orig.). (gr. 6-9). 1979. pap. text ed. 3.50x (ISBN 0-9603118-3-1). Davenport.

Engelmann, Siegfried & Silbert, Jerome. Expressive Writing, No. 2. (Orig.). (gr. 4 up). 1985. tchr's ed., 210 p 55.00, (ISBN 0-574-41850-4); student wkbk. (pkg. of 5), 182 pgs. 28.50, (ISBN 0-574-51852-5). SRA.

Evans, C. Calligraphy. (Illus.). 48p. (gr. 6 up). 1990. lib. bdg. 13.96 (ISBN 0-88110-432-9, Usborne); pap. 6.95 (ISBN 0-7460-0426-5). EDC.

Fellows, Marian & Parkhurst, Christine. Script Ease: Manuscript of Calligraphy. Gaus, Helen, illus. 61p. (gr. 2-6). 1982. pap. text ed. 9.95 (ISBN 0-317-62675-2). Kino Pubns.

Fisher, Jean & Reynolds, Patti, eds. Manuscript Writing. Remkiewicz, Frank, illus. 36p. (gr. 1). 1984. write for info. wkbk. (ISBN 0-307-23554-8, Golden Bks). Western Pub.

Get Ready to Write. 32p. (ps-k). 1986. write for info. (ISBN 0-307-05163-3, Pub. by Golden Bks). Western Pub.

Grislis, Peter. The Calligraphy Book. 64p. (gr. 4 up). 1990. pap. 5.95 (ISBN 0-590-42546-3). Scholastic Inc.

Hackwell, W. John. Signs, Letters, Words: Archaeology Discovers Writing. Hackwell, W. John, illus. LC 86-26237. 72p. (gr. 7 up). 1987. 13.95 (ISBN 0-684-18807-4, Scribners Young Read). Macmillan Child Grp.

Hoffman, Joan. Manuscript Writing. (Illus.). 32p. (gr. k-2). 1981. wkbk. 1.99 (ISBN 0-938256-01-7). Sch Zone Pub Co.

Knight, Tanis & Lewin, Larry. Tap the Deck. Hrebic, Herbert J., ed. Boehm, Terrie W., illus. (Orig.). (gr. 5-6). 1985. text ed. 9.10 (ISBN 0-933282-18-4); pap. text ed. 6.00 (ISBN 0-933282-17-6). Stack the Deck.

Kravitz, Alvin & Dramer, Dan. Skillbooster Series Level C. Incl. Building Wordpower. 1978. pap. text ed. 3.04 (ISBN 0-8136-1203-9); Increasing Comprehension. 1978. pap. text ed. 3.04 (ISBN 0-8136-1210-1); Organizing Information. 1978. pap. text ed. 3.04 (ISBN 0-8136-1224-1); Using References. 1978. pap. text ed. 3.04 (ISBN 0-8136-1231-4); Working with Facts & Details. 1978. pap. text ed. 1.92 (ISBN 0-87895-343-4). 48p. (gr. 3). Modern Curr.

Lieberman, Lillian, et al. Ready & Write. 64p. (gr. k-2). 1986. 6.95 (ISBN 0-912107-54-5). Monday Morning Bks.

Lincoln, Wanda. Write Through the Year. 112p. (gr. 2-6). 1989. 9.95 (ISBN 0-912107-90-1, MM1907). Monday Morning Bks.

O'Connor, Katherine H. My First Writing Book: Manuscript Writing. rev ed. (Illus.). 57p. (gr. k-2). 1972. wkbk 1.50 (ISBN 0-910812-07-1). Johnny Reads.

Pen Notes Staff. Italic Calligraphy Kit. (gr. 3 up). 1979. incl. chisel tip market, italic bklet. instrns., parchment paper, plastic reusable template guidelines 9.95 (ISBN 0-939564-10-6). Pen Notes.

Reading, Writing & Arithmetic: Grade 2. 160p. 1973. pap. 1.95 (ISBN 0-448-02912-X, G&D). Putnam Pub Group.

Robinson, Lafayette. Penmanship from A to Z. Robinson, Lafayette, illus. 72p. (gr. 3-4). 1988. wkbk. 7.95 (ISBN 0-317-91299-2). Educ Graphics.

Rothstein, Evelyn. Easy Writer Student Worksheets, 6 levels. Gess, Diane, ed. Schwartzfarb, Marilyn, illus. (Each level 35p.). (gr. 1-8). 1988. 14.95 ea. Level A Gr. 1-2 (ISBN 0-9606172-5-6). Level B Gr. 2-3 (ISBN 0-9606172-1-3). Level C Gr. 3-5 (ISBN 0-9606172-2-1). Level D Gr. 4-6 (ISBN 0-9606172-3-X). Level E Gr. 5-7 (ISBN 0-9606172-4-8). Level F Gr. 6-8 (ISBN 0-9606172-6-4). ERA-CCR.

Schaffer, Frank, Publications Staff. Getting Ready for Writing. (Illus.). 24p. (ps-k). 1980. wkbk. 3.98 (ISBN 0-86734-016-9, FS 3029). Schaffer Pubns.

—Handwriting with Harvey Hippo. (Illus.). 24p. (gr. 2-4). 1978. wkbk. 3.98 (ISBN 0-86734-009-6, FS 3010). Schaffer Pubns.

Schwartz, Linda. Handwriting Hamburger. Armstrong, Bev, illus. 32p. (gr. 3-6). 1979. wkbk. 3.95 (ISBN 0-88160-073-3, LW 806). Learning Wks.

—Handwriting Hot Dog. Armstrong, Bev, illus. 32p. (gr. k-3). 1979. wkbk. 3.95 (ISBN 0-88160-078-4, LW 811). Learning Wks.

Seward, Bernard. Writing American English. Olsen, Roger E., ed. (Illus.). 90p. (gr. 3-12). 1982. pap. text ed. 4.95 (ISBN 0-88084-023-4). Alemany Pr.

Slawter, Linda. Handwriting Practice. Slawter, Linda, illus. 32p. (gr. 2-3). 1984. pap. 1.98 (ISBN 0-88724-070-4, CD-7013). Carson-Dellos.

—Printing Practice. Slawter, Linda, illus. 32p. (ps-k). 1984. pap. 1.98 (ISBN 0-88724-071-2, CD-7014). Carson-Dellos.

Spellman, Linda. Castles, Codes, Calligraphy. 112p. (gr. 4-6). 1984. 9.95 (ISBN 0-88160-103-9, LW 904). Learning Wks.

Suid, Murray. Writing Hangups. 64p. (gr. 2-6). 1988. 6.95 (ISBN 0-912107-73-1, MM980). Monday Morning Bks.

Sweeney, Kathy, et al. Writing. 64p. (gr. 2-4). 1985. 6.95 (ISBN 0-912107-39-1). Monday Morning Bks.

Warburton, Lois. The Beginning of Writing. LC 90-6010. (Illus.). 112p. (gr. 5-8). 1990. PLB 11.95 (ISBN 1-56006-113-8). Lucent Bks.

Warren, Tana, ed. Ape Book. (Illus.). 64p. (gr. 2-3). 1983. 2.95 (ISBN 0-88037-024-6). Am Teaching.

—Bear Book. (Illus.). 64p. (gr. 2-3). 1983. 2.95 (ISBN 0-88037-023-8). Am Teaching.

—Elephant Book. (Illus.). 64p. (gr. k-1). 1983. 2.95 (ISBN 0-88037-021-1). Am Teaching.

—Tiger Book. 64p. (gr. 1-2). 1983. 2.95 (ISBN 0-88037-022-X). Am Teaching.

Wool, John D. & Bohn, Raymond J. Learning about Writing: (Cursive) 56p. (gr. 1 up). 1988. pap. text ed. 3.75 (ISBN 0-88323-234-0, 150). Pendergrass Pub.

WRITING (AUTHORSHIP)

see Authorship; Journalism

WYOMING

Carole Marsh Wyoming Books, 31 bks. Set. 638.45 (ISBN 0-7933-1325-2). Gallopade Pub Group.

Carpenter, Allan. Wyoming. new ed. LC 78-32135. (Illus.). 96p. (gr. 4 up). 1979. PLB 19.93 (ISBN 0-516-04150-9). Childrens.

Elliott, Tony. This Is Wyoming. Elliott, Tony, illus. LC 89-469. (gr. 3-6). 1989. pap. 3.95 (ISBN 0-914565-39-7, 39-7). Capstan Pubns.

Fradin, Dennis. Wyoming: In Words & Pictures. LC 79-26511. (Illus.). 48p. (gr. 2-5). 1980. PLB 15.93 (ISBN 0-516-03950-4). Childrens.

Marsh, Carole. Avast, Ye Slobs! Wyoming Pirate Trivia. (Illus.). 1990. PLB 19.95 (ISBN 0-7933-1268-X); pap. 14.95 (ISBN 0-7933-1267-1); computer disk 29.95 (ISBN 0-7933-1269-8). Gallopade Pub Group.

—The Beast of the Wyoming Bed & Breakfast. (Illus.). 1990. PLB 19.95 (ISBN 0-7933-2300-2); pap. 14.95 (ISBN 0-7933-2301-0); computer disk 29.95 (ISBN 0-7933-2302-9). Gallopade Pub Group.

—The Hard-to-Believe-But-True! Book of Wyoming History, Mystery, Trivia, Legend, Lore, Humor & More. (Illus.). 1990. PLB 19.95 (ISBN 0-7933-1265-5); pap. 14.95 (ISBN 0-7933-1264-7); computer disk 29.95 (ISBN 0-7933-1266-3). Gallopade Pub Group.

—If My Wyoming Mama Ran the World. (Illus.). 1990. PLB 19.95 (ISBN 0-7933-2309-6); pap. 14.95 (ISBN 0-7933-2310-X); computer disk 29.95 (ISBN 0-7933-2311-8). Gallopade Pub Group.

—Let's Quilt Wyoming & Stuff Topographically! (Illus.). 1990. PLB 19.95 (ISBN 1-55609-290-3); pap. 14.95 (ISBN 1-55609-134-6); computer disk 29.95 (ISBN 1-55609-291-1). Gallopade Pub Group.

—Wyoming & Other State Greats (Biographies) (Illus.). 1990. PLB 19.95 (ISBN 0-7933-2312-6); pap. 14.95 (ISBN 0-7933-2313-4); computer disk 29.95 (ISBN 0-7933-2314-2). Gallopade Pub Group.

—Wyoming Bandits, Bushwackers, Outlaws, Crooks, Devils, Ghosts, Desperadoes & Other Assorted & Sundry Characters! (Illus.). 1990. PLB 19.95 (ISBN 0-7933-1250-7); pap. 14.95 (ISBN 0-7933-1249-3); computer disk 29.95 (ISBN 0-7933-1251-5). Gallopade Pub Group.

—Wyoming Classic Christmas Trivia: Stories, Recipes, Activities, Legends, Lore & More! (Illus.). 1990. PLB 19.95 (ISBN 0-7933-1253-1); pap. 14.95 (ISBN 0-7933-1252-3); computer disk 29.95 (ISBN 0-7933-1254-X). Gallopade Pub Group.

—Wyoming Coastales. (Illus.). 1990. PLB 19.95 (ISBN 0-7933-2306-1); pap. 14.95 (ISBN 0-7933-2307-X); computer disk 29.95 (ISBN 0-7933-2308-8). Gallopade Pub Group.

—Wyoming "Jography" A Fun Run Thru Our State! (Illus.). (gr. 3-12). 1990. PLB 19.95 (ISBN 1-55609-295-4); pap. 14.95 (ISBN 1-55609-296-2); computer disk 29.95 (ISBN 1-55609-297-0). Gallopade Pub Group.

—Wyoming Kid's Cookbook: Recipes, How-To, History, Lore & More. (Illus.). 1990. PLB 19.95 (ISBN 0-7933-1262-0); pap. 14.95 (ISBN 0-7933-1261-2); 29.95 (ISBN 0-7933-1263-9). Gallopade Pub Group.

—Wyoming Quiz Bowl Crash Course! (Illus.). 1990. PLB 19.95 (ISBN 0-7933-2303-7); pap. 14.95 (ISBN 0-7933-2304-5); computer disk 29.95 (ISBN 0-7933-2305-3). Gallopade Pub Group.

—Wyoming School Trivia: An Amazing & Fascinating Look at Our State's Teachers, Schools & Students! (Illus.). 1990. PLB 19.95 (ISBN 0-7933-1259-0); pap. 14.95 (ISBN 0-7933-1258-2); computer disk 29.95 (ISBN 0-7933-1260-4). Gallopade Pub Group.

—Wyoming Silly Basketball Sportsmysteries, Vol. 1. (Illus.). 1990. PLB 19.95 (ISBN 0-7933-1256-6); pap. 14.95 (ISBN 0-7933-1255-8); computer disk 29.95 (ISBN 0-7933-1257-4). Gallopade Pub Group.

—Wyoming Silly Basketball Sportsmysteries, Vol. 2. (Illus.). 1990. PLB 19.95 (ISBN 0-7933-2315-0); pap. 14.95 (ISBN 0-7933-2316-9); computer disk 29.95 (ISBN 0-7933-2317-7). Gallopade Pub Group.

—Wyoming Silly Football Sportsmysteries, Vol. 1. (Illus.). 1990. PLB 19.95 (ISBN 0-7933-2294-4); pap. 14.95 (ISBN 0-7933-2295-2); computer disk 29.95 (ISBN 0-7933-2296-0). Gallopade Pub Group.

—Wyoming Silly Football Sportsmysteries, Vol. 2. (Illus.). 1990. PLB 19.95 (ISBN 0-7933-2297-9); pap. 14.95 (ISBN 0-7933-2298-7); computer disk 29.95 (ISBN 0-7933-2299-5). Gallopade Pub Group.

—Wyoming Silly Trivia. (Illus.). (gr. 3-12). 1990. PLB 19.95 (ISBN 1-55609-292-X); pap. 14.95 (ISBN 1-55609-293-8); computer disk 29.95 (ISBN 1-55609-294-6). Gallopade Pub Group.

—Wyoming's (Most Devastating!) Disasters & (Most Calamitous!) Catastrophies! (Illus.). 1990. PLB 19.95 (ISBN 0-7933-1247-7); pap. 14.95 (ISBN 0-7933-1246-9); computer disk 29.95 (ISBN 0-7933-1248-5). Gallopade Pub Group.

Pitcher, Don. Wyoming Handbook. (Illus.). 475p. (Orig.). 1991. pap. 12.95 (ISBN 0-918373-54-9). Moon Pubns CA.

Thompson, Kathleen. Wyoming. LC 87-16442. 48p. (gr. 3 up). 1987. 17.32 (ISBN 0-86514-460-5); cancelled tchr's. study guide (ISBN 0-86514-618-7); cancelled Beta video (ISBN 0-86514-085-5); cancelled VHS video (ISBN 0-86514-160-6); cancelled 3/4" video (ISBN 0-86514-235-1). Raintree Pubs.

WYOMING–FICTION

Collier, James L. & Collier, Christopher. The Bloody Country. 180p. (gr. 7 up). 1985. pap. 2.50 (ISBN 0-590-40948-4, Point); tchr's. ed 1.25 (ISBN 0-685-10090-1). Scholastic Inc.

Hayden, Jan & Kistler, Mary. Has Anyone Seen Allie? 144p. (gr. 5 up). 1991. 13.95 (ISBN 0-525-65057-1, Cobblehill Bks). Dutton Child Bks.

O'Hara, Mary. Thunderhead. 320p. (gr. 5-9). 1967. pap. 1.75 (ISBN 0-440-98875-6, LFL). Dell.

Saban, Vera. Johnny Egan of the Paintrock. Saban, Sonja, illus. LC 85-30958. 130p. (Orig.). (gr. 4-8). 1986. pap. 7.95x (ISBN 0-914565-13-3). Capstan Pubns.
Ten-year-old Johnny lives on a cattle ranch in the Big Horn Basin of Wyoming, where he is joined by his 14-year-old cousin. They live the life of typical boys: with the same joys & sadness, hopes & fears that youngsters are familiar with today. There is adventure & some mystery. There are problems & there are some decisions to be made. Young people reading this book will readily identify with all the situations & be inspired & encouraged with the working out of the lives of these two boys. The family travels in a horse-drawn wagon, but there are such things as automobiles & telephones, too. It's an interesting era for the reader to become acquainted with, & particularly in this part of America, one of our newest frontiers. The illustrations by Sonja Bernard, from suggestions by fourth-grade readers of the manuscript, add even more interest to the book. To order this book & for additional information on other TimberTrails Books, call (307) 568-2604.
Publisher Provided Annotation.

Schaefer, Jack. Shane. McCormick, J., illus. (gr. 7 up). 1954. 13.95 (ISBN 0-395-07090-2). HM.

Wister, Owen. Virginian. (gr. 8 up). 1964. pap. 2.95 (ISBN 0-8049-0046-9, CL-46). Airmont.

Y

YACHTS AND YACHTING

see also Sailing

YEARBOOKS

see also Almanacs; Calendars

Metropolitan Museum of Art Staff. Baby's First Year Calendar. Franc-Nohain, Marie M., illus. 24p. 1984. pap. 9.95 (ISBN 0-684-18258-0, Scribners Young Read). Macmillan Child Grp.

YELLOWSTONE NATIONAL PARK

Ekey, Robert. Fire! in Yellowstone. Mayer, Larry, illus. LC 89-43156. 32p. (gr. 2-4). 1989. lib. bdg. 10.95 (ISBN 0-8368-0226-8). Gareth Stevens Inc.

Marron, Carol. Yellowstone. LC 88-18643. (Illus.). (gr. 4-8). 1989. PLB 12.95 (ISBN 0-89686-405-7, Crestwood Hse). Macmillan Child Grp.

Patent, Dorothy H. Yellowstone Fires: Flames & Rebirth. Munoz, William, et al, illus. LC 89-24544. 40p. (gr. 3-7). 1990. reinforced bdg. 14.95 (ISBN 0-8234-0807-8). Holiday.

Radlauer, Ruth S. Yellowstone National Park. updated ed. Zillmer, Rolf, photos by. LC 75-2159. (Illus.). 48p. (gr. 3-12). 1975. PLB 17.27 (ISBN 0-516-07487-3). Childrens.

Staub, Frank. Yellowstone Park. Staub, Frank, illus. LC 89-34371. 32p. (gr. 3-6). 1990. lib. bdg. 10.79 (ISBN 0-8167-1737-0); pap. text ed. 2.95 (ISBN 0-8167-1738-9). Troll Assocs.

Tufts, Lorraine S. Secrets in Yellowstone & Grand Teton National Parks. 2nd ed. Koteff, Ellen & Holmes, Tracey, eds. 88p. (gr. 4 up). 1990. 29.95 (ISBN 0-9620255-2-6); pap. 19.95 (ISBN 0-9620255-1-8). Natl Photo Collections.

Vogel, Carole & Goldiner, Kathryn. The Great Yellowstone Fire. (Illus.). (gr. 2-6). 1990. write for info. Sierra.

Vogel, Carole G. Great Yellowstone Fire, Vol. 1. 1990. 14.95 (ISBN 0-316-90522-4). Little.

Vogt, Gregory. Forests on Fire: The Fight to Save Our Trees. (Illus.). 144p. (gr. 9-12). 1990. PLB 12.90 (ISBN 0-531-10940-2). Watts.

Whittlesey, Lee H. Yellowstone Place Names. Haynes, F. Jay, illus. Manns, Timothy R., intro. by. LC 88-21610. (Illus.). xiii, 179p. (Orig.). (gr. 8 up). 1988. pap. 11.95 (ISBN 0-917298-15-2); unabr. microfiche 8.95. MT Hist Soc.

YETI

Christian, Mary B. Bigfoot. LC 87-9024. (Illus.). 48p. (gr. 5-6). 1986. PLB 10.95 (ISBN 0-89686-341-7, Crestwood Hse). Macmillan Child Grp.

YOGA

Cheki-Haney, Erene & Richards, Ruth. Yoga for Children. LC 73-1758. 1973. 7.50 (ISBN 0-672-51801-5, Bobbs). Macmillan.

Hari Dass, Baba. A Child's Garden of Yoga. Thomas, Steven N., photos by. Ault, Karuna, ed. LC 80-80299. (Illus.). 108p. (ps-7). 1980. pap. 6.95 (ISBN 0-918100-02-X). Sri Rama.

Satsvarupa dasa Goswami. The Life Story of His Divine Grace A. C. Bhaktivedanta Swami Prabhupada. Ellwood, Robert S., pref. by. 32p. (gr. 4-7). 1984. saddlestitch 3.50 (ISBN 0-89647-019-9). Bala Bks.

Terkel, Susan N. Yoga Is for Me. Klein, Arthur, illus. LC 81-18623. 48p. (gr. 2-5). 1982. PLB 8.95 (ISBN 0-8225-1098-7). Lerner Pubns.

Yogaville Children. Hatha Yoga for Kids - By Kids. Satchidananda, Sri S., intro. by. (Illus.). 112p. (Orig.). (gr. 1-8). 1990. spiral bdg. 13.95g (ISBN 0-932040-36-5). Integral Yoga Pubns.

YOM KIPPUR

Chaikin, Miriam. Sound the Shofar: The Story & Meaning of Rosh HaShanah & Yom Kippur. Weihs, Erika, illus. LC 86-2651. 96p. (gr. 3-7). 1986. 13.95 (ISBN 0-89919-373-0, Pub. by Clarion); pap. 5.95 (ISBN 0-89919-427-3, Pub. by Clarion). Ticknor & Fields.

Friedman, Audrey M. & Zwerin, Raymond. High Holy Day Do It Yourself Dictionary. Ruten, Marlene L., illus. 32p. (gr. k-3). 1983. pap. 5.00 (ISBN 0-8074-0162-5, 101100). UAHC.

Saypol, Judyth R. & Wikler, Madeline. My Very Own Yom Kippur Book. (Illus.). 32p. (gr. k-6). 1978. pap. 2.95 (ISBN 0-930494-05-9). Kar Ben.

Simon, Norma. Yom Kippur. Gordon, Ayala, illus. (ps-k). 1959. plastic cover 4.50 (ISBN 0-8381-0702-8). United Syn Bk.

YOSEMITE NATIONAL PARK

Arrigo, Mary & Hargreaves, Connie. When I Visit Yosemite. Nishimura, Chris, illus. 43p. (Orig.). (ps). pap. 2.95 (ISBN 0-318-21253-6). Arrigo CA.

Cazin, Lorraine J. Yosemite. LC 88-20236. (Illus.). 48p. (gr. 4-5). 1988. 12.95 (ISBN 0-89686-407-3, Crestwood Hse). Macmillan Child Grp.

Crump, Donald J., ed. Yosemite: An American Treasure. (Illus.). 1990. 8.95 (ISBN 0-87044-789-0); lib. bdg. 9.50 (ISBN 0-87044-794-7). Natl Geog.

Radlauer, Ruth S. Yosemite National Park. updated ed. Zillmer, Rolf, photos by. LC 75-2160. (Illus.). 48p. (gr. 3 up). 1975. PLB 17.27 (ISBN 0-516-07486-5). Childrens.

Ross, Michael E. Yosemite Fun Book. 48p. (gr. 3-8). 1987. pap. 2.95 (ISBN 0-939666-45-6). Yosemite Assn.

YOUNG ADULTS

see Youth

YOUTH

see also Adolescence; Boys; Dropouts; Girls

Bergin, Feryl J. You...& Being a Teenager. Bergin, James E., illus. 112p. 4.95 (ISBN 0-936955-00-7). Eminent Pubns.

Brown, Maggie W. Making Decisions. Proof Positive-Farrowlyne Associates, Inc. Staff, illus. 61p. (Orig.). 1990. pap. text ed. 2.80 (ISBN 0-88489-200-X); tchr's ed. 6.00 (ISBN 0-88489-201-8). St Mary's.

Campbell, Stan. Nobody Like Me. 96p. (gr. 7-9). 1986. pap. 2.50 student bk. (ISBN 0-89693-515-9); tchr's. ed. 12.99 (ISBN 0-89693-188-9). Victor Bks.

Clayton-Felt, Josh. To Be Seventeen In Israel: Through the Eyes of an American Teenager. LC 86-24723. (Illus.). 96p. (gr. 7-12). 1987. lib. bdg. 12.90 (ISBN 0-531-10249-1). Watts.

Coping: All the Right Choices, 6 vols. (gr. 7-12). 1990. Set. lib. bdg. 77.70. Rosen Group.

Cosby, Bill, et al. You Are Somebody Special. 2nd ed. Shedd, Charlie W., ed. 205p. (gr. 9-12). 1989. Repr. of 1978 ed. text ed. 10.95 (ISBN 0-933419-50-3). Quest Intl.

Duckworth, John. The School Zone. 96p. (gr. 7-9). 1986. pap. 2.50 student bk. (ISBN 0-89693-558-2); tchr's. ed. 12.99 (ISBN 0-89693-198-6). Victor Bks.

Eagan, Andrea B. Why Am I So Miserable If These Are the Best Years of My Life? (gr. 7 up). 1979. pap. 2.50 (ISBN 0-380-46136-6, 60134-6, Flare). Avon.

Galbraith, Judy. The Gifted Kids Survival Guide (for ages 11-18) LC 84-80997. (Illus.). 144p. (Orig.). (gr. 5-12). 1983. pap. 8.95 (ISBN 0-915793-01-6). Free Spirit Pub.

Glenard East Echo Staff & Spanogle, Howard, eds. Voices of Hope: Teenagers Themselves, Pt. III. (Illus.). (gr. 7 up). 1988. 16.95 (ISBN 1-55774-012-7, Dist. by Watts). Adama Pubs Inc.

Hanff, Helene. Movers & Shakers: Young Activists of the Sixties. LC 77-110432. (Illus.). (gr. 10 up). 1970. 23.95 (ISBN 0-87599-166-1). S G Phillips.

Kaiser, Eldor. Your Journey into the Future. 108p. (Orig.). (gr. 9-12). 1990. pap. 6.95 (ISBN 0-931529-97-2, Teenage Bks). Group Pub.

Klagsbrun, Francine. Too Young to Die: Youth & Suicide. (gr. 7 up). 1976. 14.95 (ISBN 0-395-24752-7). HM.

Larsen, Sandy. For Real People Only. 96p. (gr. 7-9). 1986. pap. 2.50 student bk. (ISBN 0-89693-516-7); tchr's. ed. 12.99 (ISBN 0-89693-513-2). Victor Bks.

Maddox, Robert L. & Maddox, Linda C. Get off My Back. (Orig.). (gr. 7 up). 1987. pap. 5.95 (ISBN 0-8054-5344-X). Broadman.

Mitchell, Joyce S. Free to Choose: Decision Making for Young Men. LC 76-5589. (gr. 7 up). 1976. 8.95 (ISBN 0-440-02723-3). Delacorte.

Nutt, Grady. Being Me. LC 71-145984. (gr. 7 up). 1971. pap. 3.95 (ISBN 0-8054-6909-5, 4269-09). Broadman.

Peale, Norman Vincent, ed. Youth Prints. LC 88-16786. 128p. (Orig.). 1988. pap. 7.95 (ISBN 0-8066-2380-2, 10-7499, Augsburg). Augsburg Fortress.

Peterson, Lois C. The ABC's of Being a Teenager. LC 87-36464. (Orig.). (gr. 7-9). 1988. pap. 4.95 (ISBN 0-8054-4705-9). Broadman.

Rice, Wayne. Great Ideas for Small Youth Groups. 256p. (Orig.). (gr. 7-12). 1986. pap. 9.95 (ISBN 0-310-34891-9, 10823P). Zondervan.

Ristow, Kate S. & Comeaux, Maureen N. Harvest: A Faithful Approach to Life Issues for Junior High People. Titra, Stephen, illus. 167p. (gr. 6-8). 1984. pap. 24.50 (ISBN 0-940634-20-1). Puissance Pubns.

Rosengren, John. Life Is Just a Party: Portrait of Teenage Partier. Poll Communication Staff, illus. 128p. (gr. 8-12). 1990. pap. 6.95 (ISBN 0-925190-05-5). Deaconess Pr.

Shivers, Frank R. Heavy Stuff: Clear & Common-Sense Insight into Problems Youth Face. Hill, Junior, intro. by. (Illus., Orig.). (gr. 7-12). 1991. pap. 8.95 (ISBN 1-878127-00-4). F Shivers Evangelistic.

Stefoff, Rebecca. Adolescence. (Illus.). (gr. 6-12). 1990. 18.95 (ISBN 0-7910-0033-8). Chelsea Hse.

Who's Who in America's Youth Staff. Who's Who in America's Youth. (gr. k up). 1990. 85.00 (ISBN 0-9624408-1-7). Gen Res Amer.

Woodruff, Marian. Kiss Me, Creep. 192p. (gr. 7-12). 1984. pap. 2.25 (ISBN 0-553-24150-8). Bantam.

Youngs, Bettie B. Goal Setting Skills for Young People. 64p. (gr. 5-12). 1989. pap. 10.00 (ISBN 0-940221-04-7); tchr's. ed. 10.00 (ISBN 0-685-27131-5); wkbk. 10.00 (ISBN 0-685-27132-3); lab manual 10.00 (ISBN 0-685-27133-1). Lrng Tools-Bilicki Pubns.

Youngs, Bettie B. & Tracy, Brian S. Achievement, Happiness, Popularity & Success: A Self-Esteem Book for Young People. Baldwin, Cathy, ed. LC 88-90808. 169p. (Orig.). (gr. 5-12). 1989. pap. 12.95 (ISBN 0-929354-00-1). Phoenix Educ Found.

Zindel, Paul. My Darling, My Hamburger. LC 70-85025. 176p. (gr. 7 up). 1969. PLB 12.89 (ISBN 0-06-026824-7). HarpC Child Bks.

YOUTH–FICTION

Block, Francesca L. Weetzie Bat. LC 88-6214. 96p. (gr. 7 up). 1991. pap. 3.50 (ISBN 0-06-447068-7, Trophy). HarpC Child Bks.

Bunting, E. Jumping the Nail. 1991. 15.95 (ISBN 0-15-241357-X, HJ). HarBraceJ.

Conford, Ellen. If This Is Love, I'll Take Spaghetti. LC 82-84251. 176p. (gr. 7 up). 1984. 13.95 (ISBN 0-02-724250-1, Four Winds). Macmillan Child Grp.

Cooney, Caroline B. Last Dance. 256p. (Orig.). (gr. 7 up). 1987. pap. 2.50 (ISBN 0-590-40935-2, Point). Scholastic Inc.

Cormier, Robert. The Chocolate War. LC 73-15109. 272p. (gr. 7-9). 1974. 18.95 (ISBN 0-394-82805-4). Pantheon.

Crutcher, Chris. Running Loose. LC 82-20935. 160p. (gr. 10 up). 1983. reinforced bdg. 13.95 (ISBN 0-688-02002-X). Greenwillow.

Dagon, Janet. Missing: Carrie Phillips, Age 15. 125p. (Orig.). (gr. 5-8). 1989. pap. text ed. 2.95 (ISBN 0-87406-421-X). Willowisp Pr.

Daley, Maureen. Seventeenth Summer. (gr. 7-11). 1942. 10.95 (ISBN 0-396-02322-3, Putnam). Putnam Pub Group.

Davidson, Alan. The Bewitching of Alison Allbright. 164p. (gr. 5-9). 1989. 12.95 (ISBN 0-670-82015-6). Viking Child Bks.

Edwards, Sally. George Midgett's War. LC 85-1954. 144p. (gr. 5-7). 1985. 12.95 (ISBN 0-684-18315-3, Scribners Young Read). Macmillan Child Grp.

First, Julia. The Absolute, Ultimate End. LC 85-9030. 156p. (gr. 7-9). 1985. PLB 12.90 (ISBN 0-531-10075-8). Watts.

Gelb, Alan. Live From New York. 208p. 1991. pap. 2.95 (ISBN 0-380-75745-1, Flare). Avon.

Gunn, Robin J. A Whisper & a Wish: Sometimes One Quiet Word Changes Everything. Kobobel, Janet, ed. 176p. (Orig.). (gr. 1 up). 1989. pap. 4.99 (ISBN 0-929608-29-1). Focus Family.

Hall, Lynn. If Winter Comes. LC 85-43348. 128p. (gr. 7 up). 1986. 12.95 (ISBN 0-684-18575-X, Scribners Young Read). Macmillan Child Grp.

—Where Have All the Tigers Gone? LC 88-28835. 144p. (gr. 7 up). 1989. 12.95 (ISBN 0-684-19003-6, Scribners Young Read). Macmillan Child Grp.

Harper, Elaine. Homecoming. 157p. 1986. 1.95 (ISBN 0-373-06181-1). Silhouette.

Haven, Susan. Is It Them or Is It Me? 176p. 1990. 14.95 (ISBN 0-399-21916-1, Putnam). Putnam Pub Group.

Hedayat, Sadegh & Batmanglij, N. The Patient Stone. Batmanglij, M. & Batmanglij, N., trs. from PER. Franta, illus. LC 86-33301. 32p. (gr. 4 up). 1987. 18.50 (ISBN 0-934211-02-7). Mage Pubs Inc.

Hiller, B. B. & Kamen, Robert M. The Karate Kid II. (Illus.). 144p. (Orig.). (gr. 4 up). 1986. pap. 2.50 (ISBN 0-590-40292-7, Point). Scholastic Inc.

Hinton, S. E. The Outsiders. 160p. (gr. k up). 1968. pap. 3.50 (ISBN 0-440-96769-4, LFL). Dell.

—The Outsiders. (gr. 7 up). 15.00 (ISBN 0-8446-6372-7). Peter Smith.

Jones, McClure. No Boys? 192p. (Orig.). (gr. 7 up). 1984. pap. 2.25 (ISBN 0-590-33485-9, Wildfire). Scholastic Inc.

Korman, Gordon. Gordon Korman Boxed Set. (gr. 4-6). 1985. pap. 7.80 (ISBN 0-590-11154-X). Scholastic Inc.

Kurland, Morton L. Our Sacred Honor. Rosen, R., ed. 196p. (gr. 7-12). 1987. PLB 12.95 (ISBN 0-8239-0692-2). Rosen Group.

L'Engle, Madeleine. Camilla. 288p. (gr. 7 up). 1982. pap. 3.50 (ISBN 0-440-91171-0, LFL). Dell.

McGill, Joyce. Here We Go Again. 155p. 1986. 1.95 (ISBN 0-373-06184-6). Silhouette.

Marigold Beach. 155p. 1986. 1.95 (ISBN 0-373-06183-8). Silhouette.

Martin, Ann M. Boy Crazy Stacey. (gr. 4-7). 1987. pap. 2.95 (ISBN 0-590-43509-4). Scholastic Inc.

—With You & Without You. 192p. (gr. 7 up). 1987. pap. 2.50 (ISBN 0-590-40589-6, Apple Paperbacks). Scholastic Inc.

Miller-Lachmann, Lyn. Hiding Places. 206p. (Orig.). (gr. 9-12). 1987. pap. 4.95 (ISBN 0-938961-00-4, Stamp Out Sheep Pr). Sq One Pubs.

Nelson, Theresa M. For the Love of Casey. Mattingly, Jennie, ed. LC 87-50991. 230p. (Orig.). (gr. 7 up). 1987. pap. 8.95 (ISBN 1-55523-083-0). Winston-Derek.

Newton, Suzanne. A Place Between. LC 86-5520. 176p. (gr. 5-9). 1986. pap. 12.95 (ISBN 0-670-80778-8). Viking Child Bks.

Pfeffer, Susan B. Meg at Sixteen. 1990. 13.95 (ISBN 0-553-05854-1). Bantam.

Randall, Carrie. Dear Diary, No. 2: The Party. 1989. pap. 2.75 (ISBN 0-590-42477-7). Scholastic Inc.

Ransom, Candice F. Fourteen & Holding. 176p. (Orig.). (gr. 7 up). 1987. pap. 2.50 (ISBN 0-590-40501-2, Apple Paperbacks). Scholastic Inc.

Rowan, Barbara. Denial of Rights. Powell, Michelle, illus. LC 90-84008. 153p. (Orig.). (gr. 8 up). 1991. pap. 8.00 (ISBN 0-9622863-4-6). Bristlecone Pubns.

Fifteen-year-old Lindsey Crawford spent two months at Springhill Home, a small, short-term community institution for teenage girls who suffer emotional & behavioral problems. Lindsey hated it. "The kids in here are totally dinged out," she said. "There's a bunch of freaks in this place." So Lindsey ran away. Upon Lindsey's return, Janet Wayne, a counselor, seeks to uncover the emotional trauma she is sure Lindsey is suffering. However, Lindsey's case manager, Rhonda Newhy, wants her committed to a correctional institution instead. Only one week remains to uncover the real reasons behind Lindsey's inappropriate behavior. Has Lindsey been abused or is she a delinquent? She has never revealed her past to anyone. What happened during the three weeks that Lindsey was on the run which finally prompts her to reveal her secrets to Janet? Although DENIAL OF RIGHTS is fiction, the events & many of the conversations were taken from actual accounts of teenagers who were confined to a mental health facility. The author spent a year with the teenagers doing research for her master's thesis. DENIAL OF RIGHTS was born of the pain & suffering of those young people.

Publisher Provided Annotation.

Service, Pamela F. Vision Quest. LC 88-27486. 160p. (gr. 3-7). 1989. 12.95 (ISBN 0-689-31498-1, Atheneum Child Bk). Macmillan Child Grp.

Sorenson, Jody. Waiting. 176p. (Orig.). (gr. 7 up). 1986. pap. 2.25 (ISBN 0-590-40047-9). Scholastic Inc.

Tamar, Erika. Good-Bye, Glamour Girl. LC 83-49493. 224p. (gr. 5 up). 1984. (Lipp Jr Bks); PLB 12.89 (ISBN 0-397-32088-4, Lipp Jr Bks). HarpC Child Bks.

Thompson, Julian F. A Band of Angels. 304p. (gr. 7 up). 1986. pap. 12.95 (ISBN 0-590-33780-7, Scholastic Hardcover). Scholastic Inc.

—A Band of Angels. 304p. (gr. 7 up). 1987. pap. 2.50 (ISBN 0-590-40545-4, Point). Scholastic Inc.

Thornton, Jane F. Electric High: Breakaway, No. 1. 160p. (Orig.). 1984. pap. 2.25 (ISBN 0-446-32365-9). Warner Bks.

Wunsch, Josephine. The Perfect Ten. 156p. 1986. 1.95 (ISBN 0-373-06182-X). Silhouette.

Zindel, Paul. Harry & Hortense at Hormone High. LC 82-47697. 160p. (gr. 7 up). 1984. 12.95 (ISBN 0-06-026864-6); PLB 12.89 (ISBN 0-06-026869-7). HarpC Child Bks.

—I Never Loved Your Mind. 144p. (gr. 9 up). 1984. pap. 2.95 (ISBN 0-553-27323-X). Bantam.

—I Never Loved Your Mind. LC 73-105476. 192p. (gr. 7 up). 1970. PLB 12.89 (ISBN 0-06-026822-0). HarpC Child Bks.

YOUTH MOVEMENT

Costello, Gwen. Stations of the Cross for Teenagers. (Illus.). 32p. 1988. pap. 1.95 (ISBN 0-89622-386-8). Twenty-Third.

Sawyer, Kieran. The Risk of Faith: And Other Youth Ministry Activities. LC 87-72826. 168p. (Orig.). (gr. 9-12). 1988. spiral bdg. 9.95 (ISBN 0-87793-372-3). Ave Maria.

Ward, Elaine. Getting to Know You. 20p. (Orig.). (gr. 7-12). 1987. pap. 5.75 (ISBN 0-940754-49-5). Ed Ministries.

YUGOSLAVIA

Greene, Carol. Yugoslavia. LC 83-21049. (Illus.). 128p. (gr. 5-9). 1984. lib. bdg. 25.27 (ISBN 0-516-02791-3). Childrens.

Popescu, Julian. Yugoslavia. (Illus.). (gr. 5 up). 1988. 14.95 (ISBN 0-222-01026-6). Chelsea Hse.

YUKON–FICTION

London, Jack. To Build a Fire. Neumeier, Marty, illus. 48p. (gr. 6 up). 1980. PLB 10.45s.p. (ISBN 0-87191-769-6); PLB 14.95 (ISBN 0-685-01246-8). Creative Ed.

YUKON RIVER

Sturgis, Kent. Four Generations on the Yukon. (Illus.). 80p. (Orig.). (gr. 9-12). 1988. pap. 15.95 (ISBN 0-945397-01-1). Epicenter Pr.

Tjepkema, Edith R. Yukon Paradise. 126p. (Orig.). (gr. 8-12). 1990. pap. 4.50 (ISBN 0-9620280-2-9). Northland Pr.

YUKON TERRITORY–POETRY

Service, Robert. The Shooting of Dan McGrew. Harrison, Ted, illus. LC 88-6124. (gr. 3 up). 1988. 14.95 (ISBN 0-87923-748-1). Godine.

Z

ZACCHAEUS (BIBLICAL CHARACTER)

Higby, Roy C. A Man from the Past. 2nd ed. Lux, Don, illus. McLoughlin, William G., intro. by. (Illus.). (gr. 5-12). pap. 4.25 (ISBN 0-914692-02-X). Big Moose.

Lashbrook, Marilyn. Out on a Limb: The Story of Zacchaeus. LC 88-63782. (Illus.). 32p. (ps). 1989. 5.95 (ISBN 0-86606-436-2, 868). Roper Pr.

Stirrup Associates, Inc. Staff. My Jesus Pocketbook of the Big Little Person: The Story of Zacchaeus. Phillips, Cheryl M. & Harvey, Bonnie C., eds. Fulton, Ginger A., illus. LC 84-50917. 32p. (ps). 1984. pap. 0.69 (ISBN 0-937420-13-1). Stirrup Assoc.

ZAHARIAS, MILDRED BABE (DIDRIKSON) 1913-1956

Hahn, James & Hahn, Lynn. Zaharias: The Sports Career of Mildred Didrickson Zaharias. LC 80-28383. (Illus.). 48p. (Orig.). (gr. 3-5). 1981. PLB 9.95 (ISBN 0-89686-122-8, Crestwood Hse). Macmillan Child Grp.

Lynn, Elizabeth. Babe Didrickson Zaharias. Horner, Matina. (Illus.). 112p. (gr. 5 up). 1989. lib. bdg. 17.95 (ISBN 1-55546-684-2). Chelsea Hse.

ZAMBIA

Rogers, Barbara R. Zambia. Rogers, Stillman, photos by. LC 89-43178. (Illus.). 64p. (gr. 5-6). 1991. PLB 12.95 (ISBN 0-8368-0257-8). Gareth Stevens Inc.

ZEBRAS

Arnold, Caroline. Zebra. Hewett, Richard, illus. LC 87-1503. 48p. (gr. 2-5). 1987. 13.95 (ISBN 0-688-07067-1); lib. bdg. 13.88 (ISBN 0-688-07068-X, Morrow Jr Bks). Morrow Jr Bks.

Green, Carl R. & Sanford, William R. The Zebra. LC 88-1831. (Illus.). 48p. (gr. 5-6). 1988. PLB 10.95 (ISBN 0-89686-388-3, Crestwood Hse). Macmillan Child Grp.

Hoffman, Mary. Zebra. LC 84-24793. (Illus.). 24p. (gr. k-5). 1985. PLB 13.32 (ISBN 0-8172-2414-9). Raintree Pubs.

Saunier, Nadine. The Zebra. Geneste, Marcelle, illus. 20p. (ps up). 1989. 5.95 (ISBN 0-8120-5980-8). Barron.

Stone, Lynn. Zebras. (Illus.). 24p. (gr. k-5). 1990. lib. bdg. 11.93 (ISBN 0-86593-048-1); lib. bdg. 8.95s.p. (ISBN 0-685-36349-X). Rourke Corp.

Vouillemin. Zebra, Reading Level 3-4. (Illus.). 28p. (gr. 2-5). Date not set. PLB 14.60 (ISBN 0-86592-858-4). Rourke Corp.

ZEBRAS–FICTION

Dr. Seuss. On Beyond Zebra! Dr. Seuss, illus. LC 55-9321. 64p. (gr. k-3). 1980. pap. 3.95 (ISBN 0-394-84541-2, XBYR). Random.

Hadithi, Mwenye. Greedy Zebra. 1984 ed. Kennaway, Adrienne, illus. (ps-3). 1984. 14.95 (ISBN 0-316-33721-8). Little.

Henkes, Kevin. The Zebra Wall. LC 87-18454. 160p. (gr. 3 up). 1988. 10.95 (ISBN 0-688-07568-1). Greenwillow.

Herman, Erwin & Herman, Agnes. The Yanov Torah. Kahn, Katherine J., illus. LC 85-5269. 48p. (gr. 5 up). 1985. 10.95 (ISBN 0-930494-45-8); pap. 5.95 (ISBN 0-930494-46-6). Kar Ben.

Oana, Katherine. Zippy Zebra. Baird, Tate, ed. Butrick, Lyn M., illus. LC 88-51853. 16p. (Orig.). (ps). 1989. pap. 4.52 (ISBN 0-914127-11-X). Univ Class.

Van Curen, Barbara. When the Zebras Came for Lunch. Manierre, Betsy, illus. 64p. (ps-2). 1989. pap. text ed. 5.95 (ISBN 0-922510-01-6). Lucky Bks.

ZEPPELINS

see Airships

ZOOLOGICAL GARDENS

Altman, Joyce & Goldberg, Sue. Dear Bronx Zoo. Falk, Douglas, frwd. by. LC 89-28226. (Illus.). 160p. (gr. 3 up). 1990. 13.95 (ISBN 0-02-700640-9, Mcmillan Child Bk). Macmillan Child Grp.

Amos, Janine. Let's Go to a Safari Park. Rignell, John, illus. LC 89-17337. 32p. (gr. 1-3). 1990. PLB 9.95 (ISBN 1-85435-243-1). Marshall Cavendish.

Anderson, Madelyn K. New Zoos. (Illus.). 72p. 1987. lib. bdg. 10.40 (ISBN 0-531-10309-9). Watts.

Baby Zoo Animals. (Illus.). 32p. (ps-1). 1986. pap. 1.25 (ISBN 0-8431-1521-1). Price Stern.

Baby Zoo Animals. (Illus.). (ps). pap. 1.25 (ISBN 0-7214-9545-1). Ladybird Bks.

Barton, Miles. Zoos & Game Reserves. Franklin Watts Ltd., ed. (Illus.). 32p. (gr. 7-9). 1988. PLB 8.99 (ISBN 0-531-17090-X, Pub. by Gloucester Pr). Watts.

Better Homes & Gardens Editors. At the Zoo. (Illus.). 32p. 1989. 4.95 (ISBN 0-696-01891-8). Meredith Bks.

Bishop, Roma. At the Zoo: Match It Up. 1989. 3.99 (ISBN 0-517-68251-6). Outlet Bk Co.

Booth, Eugene. At the Zoo. LC 77-7627. (Illus.). (gr. k-3). 1977. PLB 13.32 (ISBN 0-8393-0107-3). Raintree Pubs.

Bornstein, Harry. Mealtime at the Zoo. Hrivnak, Suzette & Hrivnak, James R., illus. 48p. (ps-2). 1973. pap. 5.95 (ISBN 0-913580-11-2). Gallaudet Univ Pr.

Brennan, John & Keaney, Leonie. Zoo Day. (Illus.). 32p. (ps-2). 1989. PLB 9.95 (ISBN 0-87614-358-3). Carolrhoda Bks.

Butterworth, Nick & Inkpen, Mick. I Wonder at the Zoo. 14p. (ps). 1987. pap. 1.95 (ISBN 0-310-55411-X, 19041P). Zondervan.

Carle, Eric. One, Two, Three to the Zoo. LC 68-26967. (Illus.). (ps-2). 1989. 13.95 (ISBN 0-399-61172-X, Philomel); pap. 5.95 (ISBN 0-399-20847-X). Putnam Pub Group.

Curtis, Patricia. Animals & the New Zoos. (Illus.). 96p. (gr. 3-8). 1991. 15.95 (ISBN 0-525-67347-4, Lodestar Bks). Dutton Child Bks.

Gerstenfeld, Sheldon L. Zoo Clues: Making the Most of Your Visit to the Zoo. Doty, Eldon C., illus. 128p. (gr. 2-5). 1991. 13.95 (ISBN 0-670-82362-7). Viking Child Bks.

Gibbons, Gail. Zoo. Gibbons, Gail, illus. LC 87-582. 32p. (ps-3). 1987. 13.95 (ISBN 0-690-04631-6, Crowell Jr Bks); PLB 13.89 (ISBN 0-690-04633-2). HarpC Child Bks.

—Zoo. Gibbons, Gail, illus. LC 87-582. 32p (ps-3). 1991. pap. 4.95 (ISBN 0-06-446096-7, Trophy). HarpC Child Bks.

Hawksley, Gerald. Zoo. Hawksley, Gerald, illus. 10p. (gr. 2-4). 1990. bds. 4.95 (ISBN 1-878624-19-9). McClanahan Bk.

Irvine, Georgeanne. Let's Visit a Super Zoo. Fuller, Tim W., illus. LC 89-34370. 32p. (gr. 2-4). 1990. lib. bdg. 10.79 (ISBN 0-8167-1745-1); pap. text ed. 2.95 (ISBN 0-8167-1746-X). Troll Assocs.

—Raising Gordy Gorilla at the San Diego Zoo. (Illus.). 48p. (gr. 3-7). 1990. PLB 14.95 (ISBN 0-671-68775-1). S&S Trade.

Jacobson, Karen. Zoos. LC 82-9545. (Illus.). (gr. k-4). 1982. PLB 14.60 (ISBN 0-516-01664-4); pap. 4.95 (ISBN 0-516-41664-2). Childrens.

Machotka, Hana. What Do You Do at a Petting Zoo? Machotka, Hana, photos by. LC 89-34478. (Illus.). 32p. (gr. k up). 1990. 13.95 (ISBN 0-688-08737-X); PLB 13.88 (ISBN 0-688-08738-8, Morrow Jr Bks). Morrow Jr Bks.

My Book of Baby Zoo Animals. (ps-2). 3.95 (ISBN 0-7214-5149-7). Ladybird Bks.

Oana, Katherine. Zoo Fun Book. Clapsadle, Joan, illus. 32p. (ps-2). 1984. pap. 1.59 (ISBN 0-88724-063-1, CD-8054). Carson-Dellos.

Ormerod, Jan. When We Went to the Zoo. (ps-3) 1991. 13.95 (ISBN 0-688-09878-9). Lothrop.

Parramon, J. M. Mi Primera Vista al Zoo. 1990. pap. 4.95 (ISBN 0-8120-4402-9). Barron.

—My First Visit to the Zoo. Sales, G., illus. 32p. (ps). 1990. pap. 4.95 (ISBN 0-8120-4302-2). Barron.

Pienkowski, Jan. Zoo. Pienkowski, Jan, illus. 32p. (ps-1). 1985. 11.95 (ISBN 0-434-95652-X, Pub. by W Heinemann Ltd). Trafalgar Sq.

Rinard, Judith E. Zoos Without Cages. LC 79-3243. (Illus.). 104p. (gr. 3-8). 1981. 6.95 (ISBN 0-87044-335-6); PLB 8.50 (ISBN 0-87044-340-2). Natl Geog.

Tester, Sylvia R. A Visit to the Zoo. Pilot Productions Staff, et al, photos by. LC 84-12697. (Illus.). 32p. (gr. k-3). 1987. PLB 14.60 (ISBN 0-516-01494-3); pap. 3.95 (ISBN 0-516-41494-1). Childrens.

Thomson, Peggy. Keepers & Creatures at the National Zoo. Conklin, Paul S., photos by. LC 87-47697. (Illus.). 208p. (gr. 3-7). 1988. 12.95 (ISBN 0-690-04710-X, Crowell Jr Bks); PLB 13.89 (ISBN 0-690-04712-6, Crowell Jr Bks). HarpC Child Bks.

Unwin, Pippa. Great Zoo Hunt! (ps-3). 1990. 13.99 (ISBN 0-385-41107-3). Doubleday.

Wexo, John B. Big Cats. 24p. 1989. 11.95s.p. (ISBN 0-88682-264-5); 17.10 (ISBN 0-685-28180-9). Creative Ed.

The Zoo. (Illus.). (ps-2). 1990. 3.50 (ISBN 0-7214-1175-4). Ladybird Bks.

Zoo Animals. 32p. (Orig.). (ps-1). 1984. pap. 1.25 (ISBN 0-8431-1515-7). Price Stern.

ZOOLOGICAL GARDENS–FICTION

Ashabranner, Brent. I'm in the Zoo, Too. Stevens, Janet, illus. LC 88-32662. (gr. k-4). 1989. 12.95 (ISBN 0-525-65002-4, Cobblestone Bks). Dutton Child Bks.

Ashwill, Beverly. Charley the Fearless Zoo Keeper. Ashwill, Betty J., illus. LC 90-83311. 20p. (ps-3). 1990. pap. 3.98 (ISBN 0-941381-07-2). BJO Enterprises.

—The Invisible Dawn. Ashwill, Betty J., illus. LC 90-83310. 24p. (ps-5). 1990. pap. 3.98 (ISBN 0-685-37787-3). BJO Enterprises.

Brandenberg, Franz. Leo & Emily's Zoo. Abolafia, Yossi, illus. LC 87-17907. 32p. (ps-1). 1988. 11.95 (ISBN 0-688-07457-X); lib. bdg. 11.88 (ISBN 0-688-07458-8). Greenwillow.

Calmenson, Stephanie. Where Will the Animals Stay? Appleby, Ellen, illus. LC 83-13479. 48p. (ps-3). 1984. 5.95 (ISBN 0-8193-1119-7). Parents.

Carr, Jan. Things to Do in Zoobilee Zoo. Hudson, Carol, illus. 32p. (ps-3). 1988. pap. 1.95 (ISBN 0-590-42116-6). Scholastic Inc.

Cohen, Daniel & Cohen, Susan. Zoo Superstars. (Illus., Orig.). (gr. 4-6). 1989. pap. 2.75 (ISBN 0-671-66709-2, Minstrel Bks). PB.

Disney, Walt. Staff. Shoe at the Zoo. (ps). 1991. 3.95 (ISBN 1-56282-031-1). W Disney Pub.

Durrell, Gerald. Keeper. West, Keith, illus. 32p. (gr. 1-4). 1991. 13.95 (ISBN 1-55970-122-6). Arcade Pub Inc.

Dvorah-Leah. Lost in the Zoo on Erev Shabbat. rev. ed. (ps-1). 1987. 8.95 (ISBN 0-685-18057-3); pap. 6.95 (ISBN 0-685-18058-1). Judaica Pr.

Ford, Sharon. Come & See the Zoo. 32p. 1989. 6.95 (ISBN 0-8062-3555-1). Carlton.

Gire, Ken. Harmony's Hullabaloo at the Zoo: A Story about Dealing with Fears. Kobobel, Janet, ed. Dickenson, John & Payne, Bob, illus. LC 87-81590. 32p. (gr. 1-3). 1988. 5.99 (ISBN 0-929608-09-7). Focus Family.

Godfrey, Jan. Me at the Zoo. (ps-3). 1989. pap. 1.95 (ISBN 0-7459-1735-6). Lion USA.

Graham, Margaret B. Be Nice to Spiders. Graham, Margaret B., illus. LC 67-17101. 32p. (gr. k-3). 1967. PLB 13.89 (ISBN 0-06-022073-2). HarpC Child Bks.

Guild, Anne V. Mickey Mouse in Let's Go...to the Zoo! Scholefield, Ron, et al, illus. 26p. (ps up). 1987. pap. 14.95 (ISBN 1-55578-802-5). Worlds Wonder.

Howe, James. Morgan's Zoo. Morrill, Leslie, illus. LC 84-6325. 192p. (gr. 3-6). 1984. 13.95 (ISBN 0-689-31046-3, Atheneum Child Bk). Macmillan Child Grp.

—Morgan's Zoo. (Illus.). 192p. (gr. 3-7). 1986. pap. 3.50 (ISBN 0-380-69994-X, Camelot). Avon.

Hurd, Edith T. Stop Stop. Hurd, Clement, illus. LC 61-12095. 64p. (gr. k-3). 1961. PLB 11.89 (ISBN 0-06-022746-X). HarpC Child Bks.

Kent, Jack. The Biggest Shadow in the Zoo. Kent, Jack, illus. LC 80-25517. 48p. (ps-3). 1981. 5.95 (ISBN 0-8193-1047-6); PLB 5.95 (ISBN 0-8193-1048-4). Parents.

Leah, Devora. Lost Erev Shabbos in the Zoo. rev. ed. Forst, Siegmund, illus. 30p. (gr. k-3). 1986. 8.95 (ISBN 0-685-18123-5); pap. 6.95 (ISBN 0-685-18124-3). Judaica Pr.

Leeka, Melinda. Andy Goes to the Zoo. LC 89-51092. 44p. (gr. k-3). 1990. 5.95 (ISBN 1-55523-247-7). Winston-Derek.

Lippert, Donald F. Polly Popcan. Hedden, Randall, illus. 32p. (ps). Date not set. write for info. Pastel Pubns.

Lobel, Arnold. Holiday for Mister Muster. Lobel, Arnold, illus. LC 63-15323. 32p. (gr. k-3). 1963. PLB 12.89 (ISBN 0-06-023956-5). HarpC Child Bks.

—Zoo for Mister Muster. LC 62-7313. (Illus.). 32p. (ps-3). 1962. PLB 12.89 (ISBN 0-06-023991-3). HarpC Child Bks.

Maiboroda, Tanya. Zoo. (Illus.). 48p. (gr. 4-7). 1987. pap. 2.95 (ISBN 0-8431-1879-2). Price Stern.

Palazzo-Craig, Janet. Who's Who at the Zoo! Burns, Ray, illus. LC 85-14123. 48p. (Orig.). (gr. 1-3). 1986. PLB 9.89 (ISBN 0-8167-0658-1); pap. text ed. 2.95 (ISBN 0-8167-0659-X). Troll Assocs.

Ray, Deborah. Sunday Morning We Went to the Zoo. Ray, Deborah, illus. LC 80-7915. 32p. (ps-2). 1981. 8.95 (ISBN 0-06-024841-6). HarpC Child Bks.

Redhead, Janet S. The Muddledy Fuddledy Mixed-up Day. LC 90-10073. (Illus.). 16p. (gr. 1-4). 1990. PLB 14.64 (ISBN 0-8114-2691-2). Steck-V.

Rey, Margaret & Shalleck, Allan J. Curious George Visits the Zoo. 1988. pap. 6.95 incl. cass. (ISBN 0-395-48876-1). HM.

Richmond, Gary. A Scary Night at the Zoo. 1990. write for info. (ISBN 0-8499-0742-X). Word Bks.

Taylor, Theodore. Sniper. LC 89-7415. 227p. (gr. 5-9). 1989. 14.95 (ISBN 0-15-276420-8). HarBraceJ.

Thomas, Mary A. Jump with Jeremy: What Hoosiers Do on the Way to the Zoo. Hodge, Ellen & Poore, Luz, eds. Still, James & Escabar, URias, trs. from ENG. Graham-Rice, Kathy, illus. (SPA.). 47p. (Orig.). Date not set. pap. 9.95 (ISBN 0-944326-00-5). Childrens Corner.

Wilhelm, Hans. Waldo at the Zoo. 12p. 1989. 3.25 (ISBN 0-8378-1882-6). Gibson.

Winder, Jack. Who's New at the Zoo. Wasserman, Dan, ed. Reese, Bob, illus. (gr. k-1). 1979. PLB 7.95 (ISBN 0-89868-074-3); pap. 2.95 (ISBN 0-89868-085-9). Aro Pub.

Ziefert, Harriet. Zoo Parade! Taback, Simms, illus. 16p. (ps-1). 1990. 4.95 (ISBN 0-06-107404-7). HarpC Child Bks.

ZOOLOGICAL SPECIMENS–COLLECTION AND PRESERVATION

Harden, Cleo. How to Preserve Animal & Other Specimens in Clear Plastic. Harden, David G., illus. 64p. (gr. 4 up). 1963. 11.95 (ISBN 0-911010-47-5); pap. 4.95 (ISBN 0-911010-46-7). Naturegraph.

ZOOLOGY

see also Anatomy, Comparative; Animals; Embryology; Evolution; Fossils; Natural History
also names of divisions, classes, etc. of the animal kingdom (e.g. Invertebrates; Vertebrates; birds; Mammals; etc.)

Adams, Pam, illus. The Zoo. 24p. (ps-2). 1974. 4.50 (ISBN 0-85953-032-9, Pub. by Child's Play England). Childs Play.

Billout, Guy. Squid & Spider: A Look at the Animal Kingdom. Billout, Guy, illus. 32p. (Orig.). (gr. 6 up). 1982. 10.95 (ISBN 0-13-839928-X). P-H.

Chicago Zoological Society Staff, ed. Brookfield Zoo Connections: A Program to Enhance Classroom Studies. (Orig.). (gr. k-8). 1986. pap. text ed. 30.00 (ISBN 0-913934-03-8). Chicago Zoo.

Cooper, Gail. Inside Animals. Cooper, Gail, illus. LC 87-4526. 64p. (gr. 4-8). 1987. Repr. PLB 9.95 (ISBN 0-915391-23-6, Pub. by Mad Hatter Bks). Slawson Comm.

Gelman, Rita G. Dawn to Dusk in the Galapagos, Vol. 1. 1991. 16.95 (ISBN 0-316-30739-4). Little.

Howell, Judd, intro. by. Wildlife California. (Illus.). 64p. (ps-7). Date not set. text ed. 9.95 (ISBN 0-87701-886-3). Chronicle Bks.

Hughey, Pat. Scavengers & Decomposers: The Clean Up Crew. Hiscock, Bruce, illus. LC 83-17474. 64p. (gr. 4-6). 1984. 13.95 (ISBN 0-689-31032-3, Atheneum Child Bk). Macmillan Child Grp.

Nature Encyclopedia. (Illus.). 144p. 1989. Repr. 14.95 (ISBN 0-02-689203-0). Checkerboard Pr.

Ricciuti, Edward R. They Work with Wildlife: Jobs for People Who Want to Work with Animals. LC 80-7918. 160p. (gr. 7 up). 1983. 12.95 (ISBN 0-06-025003-8); PLB 12.89 (ISBN 0-06-025004-6). HarpC Child Bks.

Rose, Kenneth J. Classification of the Animal Kingdom. (gr. 7 up). 1980. 8.95 (ISBN 0-679-20508-X). McKay.

Smith, Dan & Whyte, Malcolm. Zoo Action Set, No. 2. (Illus.). 24p. 1990. pap. 5.95 (ISBN 0-8431-2831-3). Price Stern.

Stamper, Judith B. Zoo Worker. Garry-McCord, Kathleen, illus. LC 88-10046. 32p. (gr. k-2). 1988. PLB 10.89 (ISBN 0-8167-1440-1); pap. text ed. 2.50 (ISBN 0-8167-1441-X). Troll Assocs.

Venino, Suzanne. Amazing Animal Groups. Crump, Donald J., ed. LC 81-47743. 32p. (ps-3). 1981. lib. bdg. 12.95 library binding set (ISBN 0-87044-402-6); 10.95 set (ISBN 0-87044-407-7). Natl Geog.

Zokeisha. Zoo Animals. Zokeisha, illus. 16p. (ps). 1982. board 2.95 (ISBN 0-671-44895-1, Little Simon). S&S Trade.

Zoology. (Illus.). (gr. 3-5). 3.50 (ISBN 0-7214-0779-X). Ladybird Bks.

ZOOLOGY–ANATOMY
see Anatomy, Comparative

ZOOLOGY, ECONOMIC
see also Domestic Animals; Insects, Injurious and Beneficial

ZOOLOGY–GEOGRAPHIC DISTRIBUTION
see Geographical Distribution of Animals and Plants

ZOOLOGY OF THE BIBLE
see Bible–Natural History

ZOOS
see Zoological Gardens

ZULULAND–HISTORY

Stanley, Diane & Vennema, Peter. Shaka, King of the Zulus. Stanley, Stanley, illus. LC 87-27376. 40p. (gr. 1-4). 1988. 14.95 (ISBN 0-688-07342-5); PLB 14.88 (ISBN 0-688-07343-3, Morrow Jr Bks). Morrow Jr Bks.

ZULUS

Mckenna, Nancy D. A Zulu Family. (Illus.). 32p. (gr. 2-5). 1986. PLB 9.95 (ISBN 0-8225-1666-7). Lerner Pubns.

Ngubane, Harriet. Zulus of Southern Africa. (Illus.). 48p. (gr. 4-8). 1987. PLB 15.33 (ISBN 0-86625-261-4). Rourke Corp.

KEY TO
PUBLISHERS' AND DISTRIBUTORS'
ABBREVIATIONS

The following is a list of abbreviations for publishers' and distributors' names used in the book listings in this edition of **Subject Guide to Children's Books in Print 1991-1992.**

The entries in this list contain: Publisher's or distributor's abbreviation, followed by its full name, ISBN prefix, editorial address, telephone number, toll-free telephone number and SAN (Standard Address Number). Ordering and/or distributor name and address are listed if they differ from the editorial address. Abbreviations used to identify publishers' imprints are followed by the full name of the imprint. See the example listed below:

> **Modern Curr,** *(Modern Curriculum Pr., Inc.;*
> *0-87895; 0-8136),* Div. of Simon & Schuster, Inc.,
> 13900 Prospect Rd., Cleveland, OH 44136 (SAN 206-6572)
> Tel 216-238-2222; Toll free: 800-321-3106.

Book entries found in the main indexes of this work which include the term "Pub. by" should be ordered from the distributor, not the publisher. For example, the title listed below should be ordered from Kluwer Academic.

> **Reichardt, W.** Acoustics Dictionary. Date not set.
> lib. bdg. 28.50 (ISBN 90-247-2707-3, Pub. by
> Martinus Nijhoff Netherlands). Kluwer
> Academic.

A Armadillo Assocs, *(Arnie Armadillo & Assocs.; 1-879465),* 3532 Park Hill Dr., Fort Worth, TX 76109 Tel 817-923-7573.

A C Grasmick, *(Grasmick, Alta C.; 0-9621909),* 815 S. Ash St., North Platte, NE 69101 Tel 308-532-9546.

A Chalabian, *(Chalabian, Antranig; 0-9622741),* 17264 Melrose, Southfield, MI 48075 Tel 313-569-0676.

A Class Act, *(Class Act, A; 0-9620953),* 169 N. Baldwin Ave., Sierra Madre, CA 91024 (SAN 250-2712) Tel 818-355-7802.

A D Bragdon, *(Bragdon, Allen D., Pubs., Inc.; 0-916410),* Tupelo Rd., South Yarmouth, MA 02664 (SAN 208-5623) Tel 508-398-4440; Toll free: 800-334-1946; Dist. by: Talman Co., 150 Fifth Ave., New York, NY 10011 (SAN 200-5204) Tel 212-620-3182; Toll free: 800-537-8894; Dist. by: Antioch Publishing Co., 888 Dayton St., Yellow Springs, OH 45387 (SAN 654-7214) Tel 513-767-7379; Toll free: 800-543-2397. *Imprints:* BTime Classics (Bedtime Classics Library).

A E Ryter
See P Hunt

A G Furman, *(Furman, Alester G., Pub.; 0-9628232),* P.O. Box 4738, Greenville, SC 29608; 301 N. Main St., Daniel Bldg., Greenville, SC 29601 Tel 803-242-1213.

A M Huntington Art, *(Huntington, Archer M., Art Gallery; 0-935213),* Univ. of Texas at Austin, 23rd & San Jacinto, Austin, TX 78712-1205 (SAN 695-7730) Tel 512-471-7324.

A N Palmer, *(Palmer, A. N., Co., The; 0-914268; 0-913941),* 846 E. Algonquin, Schaumburg, IL 60173 (SAN 202-1374) Tel 312-894-4300; Toll free: 800-323-9563.

A Petersen, *(Petersen, Arona; 0-9626577),* 2855 W. Commercial Blvd., No. 446, Fort Lauderdale, FL 33309 Tel 305-486-5483.

A Plus Lrn, *(A Plus Learning, Inc.; 0-9624827),* P.O. Box 318, West Groton, MA 01472; 156 Pepperell Rd., West Groton, MA 01472 Tel 508-448-5440.

A R Black, *(Black, Auguste R.; 0-9628010),* 4016 Shelby Ave., SE, Huntsville, AL 35801 Tel 205-534-4006.

A R C Pub, *(ARC Publishing Co.; 0-917187),* P.O. Box 1138, Glendale, CA 91209 (SAN 655-8704) Tel 818-244-0113; Dist. by: DeVorss & Co., P.O. Box 550, 1046 Princeton Dr., Marina del Rey, CA 90292 (SAN 168-9886) Tel 213-870-7478; Toll free: 800-843-5743; 800-331-4719 (in California).

A R Harding Pub, *(Harding, A. R., Publishing Co.; 0-936622),* 2878 E. Main St., Columbus, OH 43209 (SAN 206-4936) Tel 614-231-9585.

A S Goodman, *(Goodman, Ailene S.; 0-9620704),* 3304 Rittenhouse St., NW, Washington, DC 20015 (SAN 249-5945) Tel 202-686-1722.

A Schiller, *(Schillerhaus; 0-9618682),* P.O. Box 2356, Cottonwood, AZ 86326 (SAN 696-7264) Tel 602-634-2455.

A Schwartz & Co, *(Schwartz, Arthur, & Co.),* P.O. Box 434, New York, NY 10028 (SAN 630-0464) Tel 212-794-9012; Toll free: 800-345-6665 (orders only).

A Sutton Pub, *(Sutton, Alan, Publishing, Inc.; 0-86299),* P.O. Box 848, Wolfeboro Falls, NH 03896-0848 Tel 603-522-3338.

A T Weinberg, *(Weinberg, Alyce T.; 0-9604552),* Box 16, Braddock Heights, MD 21714 (SAN 215-1928).

A Todd, *(Todd, Armor; 0-9623537),* 143M Seminary Dr., Mill Valley, CA 94941 Tel 415-381-2704; Dist. by: Terry Youmans & Assocs., 1669 Hollenbeck Ave., No. 135, Sunnyvale, CA 94087-5402 (SAN 630-3714).

A Whitman, *(Whitman, Albert, & Co.; 0-8075),* 6340 Oakton St., Morton Grove, IL 60053 (SAN 201-2049) Tel 708-581-0033; Toll free: 800-255-7675.

AAA, *(American Automobile Assn.; 0-916748; 1-56251),* 1000 AAA Dr., Heathrow, FL 32746-5063 (SAN 208-5194) Tel 407-444-7615; Dist. by: Macmillan Publishing Co., Front & Brown Sts., Riverside, NJ 08075 (SAN 202-5582) Tel 609-461-6500; Toll free: 800-257-5755.

Abaca Bks, *(Abaca Bks.; 0-933759),* 10 Clinton Pl., Normal, IL 61761 (SAN 692-6967) Tel 309-454-7141.

ABBE Pubs Assn, *(ABBE Pubs. Assn. of Washington, D.C.; 0-941864; 0-88164; 1-55914),* 4111 Gallows Rd., Virginia Div., Annandale, VA 22003 (SAN 239-1430) Tel 703-750-0255; Georgetown 3724, 1215 31st St., NW, Washington, DC 20007 (SAN 668-9450).

Abbey, *(Abbey Pr. Printing & Publishing; 0-87029),* Hwy. 545, Saint Meinrad, IN 47577 (SAN 201-2057) Tel 812-357-8011.

ABC Child Bks, *(ABC Children's Bks., Inc.; 0-926986),* 1274 49th St., No. 177, Brooklyn, NY 11219 Tel 718-435-3606.

ABC-CLIO, *(ABC-CLIO, Inc.; 0-87436; 1-85109; 0-903450),* P.O. Box 1911, Santa Barbara, CA 93116-1911; Toll free: 800-422-2546; 130 Cremona Dr., Santa Barbara, CA 93117 (SAN 301-5467) Tel 805-968-1911. *Imprints:* Crnrstn Bks (Cornerstone Books).

Abdo & Dghtrs, *(Abdo & Daughters; 0-939179; 1-56239),* P.O. Box 36036, Minneapolis, MN 55435 (SAN 662-9164); 6535 Cecilia Cir., Edina, MN 55439 (SAN 662-9172) Tel 612-944-5522; Dist. by: Rockbottom Bks., Pentagon Towers, P.O. Box 36036, Minneapolis, MN 55435 (SAN 108-4402) Tel 612-944-5522.

Abel II Pub, *(Abel 2 Publishing Co.; 0-9624398),* P.O. Box 15486, San Diego, CA 92115-0486; 4235 Altadena Ave., No. 4, San Diego, CA 92115 Tel 619-284-3366.

Abigail Pubns, *(Abigail Pubns.; 0-9628148),* 26281 Carrington Blvd., Perrysburg, OH 43551-9546 Tel 419-874-1551.

Abingdon, *(Abingdon Pr.; 0-687),* Div. of United Methodist Publishing Hse., P.O. Box 801, 201 Eighth Ave., S., Nashville, TN 37202 (SAN 201-0054) Tel 615-749-6290; Toll free: 800-251-3320; 341 Great Cir. Dr., Nashville, TN 37228 (SAN 699-9956).

Ablaze Pub, *(Ablaze Publishing; 0-9624370),* Div. of Ablaze Productions, Inc., P.O. Box 956236, Duluth, GA 30136; 2554 Davenport Rd., Duluth, GA 30136 Tel 404-476-0744.

Able Pub, *(Able Publishing; 1-878787),* 3463 State St., Suite 219, Santa Barbara, CA 93105 (SAN 297-2883) Tel 805-967-8015; Shipping & Receiving: 20 S. Salsipuedes, Santa Barbara, CA 93103 (SAN 297-2891).

ABP Abstracts, *(ABP Abstracts; 0-944992),* Rte. 1, Box 158C, Rocky Mount, NC 27803 (SAN 245-9469) Tel 919-469-2264.

Abrams, *(Abrams, Harry N., Inc.; 0-8109),* Subs. of Times Mirror Co., 100 Fifth Ave., New York, NY 10011 (SAN 200-2434) Tel 212-206-7715; Toll free: 800-345-1359.

Abscond Pubs, *(Abscond Pubs.; 0-944215),* P.O. Box 3112, Florence, AL 35630 (SAN 242-9888) Tel 205-760-0415.

Acad Sportfolio, *(Academic Sportfolio, Inc.; 0-924086),* 211 First Ave., Port Jefferson, NY 11777 (SAN 252-1288) Tel 516-331-9355; Toll free: 800-331-9355.

Acad Therapy, *(Academic Therapy Pubns., Inc.; 0-87879),* 20 Commercial Blvd., Novato, CA 94949-6191 (SAN 201-2111) Tel 415-883-3314; Toll free: 800-422-7249 (outside California). *Imprints:* High Noon Books (High Noon Books).

Academic Packs Co, *(Academic Packs Co.; 0-9619655)*, 5700 Lincoln Ave., Lanham, MD 20706 (SAN 245-9523) Tel 301-794-6031.

Academy Chi Pubs, *(Academy Chicago Pubs., Ltd.; 0-915864; 0-89733)*, 213 W. Institute Pl., Chicago, IL 60610-3125 (SAN 213-2001) Tel 312-751-7302; Toll free: 800-248-7323 (Orders, outside Illinois).

Acadia Pub Co, *(Acadia Publishing Co.; 0-934745)*, Div. of World Three, Inc., P.O. Box 170, Bar Harbor, ME 04609 (SAN 694-1648) Tel 207-288-9025; Toll free: 800-735-9025. Do not confuse with Acadia Publishing Co., Church Point, LA.

Acadiana Pr, *(Acadiana Pr., The; 0-937614)*, P.O. Box 42290, USL, Lafayette, LA 70504 (SAN 215-6156) Tel 318-662-3468.

Accel Devel, *(Accelerated Development, Inc.; 0-915202; 1-55959)*, 3400 Kilgore Ave., Muncie, IN 47304 (SAN 210-3346) Tel 317-284-7511; Toll free: 800-222-1166.

Accent Bks, *(Accent Bks.; 0-916406; 0-89636)*, Div. of Accent Pubns., P.O. Box 15337, Lakewood Sta., Denver, CO 80215 (SAN 208-5097); Toll free: 800-525-5550; 12100 W. Sixth Ave., Denver, CO 80215 (SAN 208-5100) Tel 303-988-5300.

Accent Pub NJ, *(Accent Publishing; 1-879267)*, 350 Sparta Ave., Bldg. "A", Sparta, NJ 07871 Tel 201-729-1151. Do not confuse with Accent Pubns., Scituate, MA.

Ace Bks, *(Ace Bks.; 0-441)*, Div. of Berkley Publishing Group, 200 Madison Ave., New York, NY 10016 (SAN 665-6404) Tel 212-951-8800; Toll free: 800-223-0510; Dist. by: Warner Pub. Services, 810 Seventh Ave., New York, NY 10019 (SAN 200-5522) Tel 212-397-8676; Dist. by: Berkley Publishing Group, 200 Madison Ave., New York, NY 10016 (SAN 201-3991) Tel 212-951-8966; Toll free: 800-631-8571.

Ace Pub Prodns, *(Ace Publishing/Productions; 0-9629317)*, 10335 Branigan Way, P.O. Box 70087, Riverside, CA 92505 Tel 714-351-0436.

ACEI, *(Association for Childhood Education International; 0-87173)*, 11141 Georgia Ave., Suite 200, Wheaton, MD 20902 (SAN 201-2200) Tel 301-942-2443; Toll free: 800-423-3563.

ACETO Bookmen, *(ACETO Bookmen; 0-9607906; 1-878545)*, 5721 Antietam Dr., Sarasota, FL 34231 (SAN 237-9252) Tel 813-924-9170.

Acid Rain Found, *(Acid Rain Foundation, Inc., The; 0-935577)*, 1410 Varsity Rd., Raleigh, NC 27606 (SAN 695-9946).

Acropolis, *(Acropolis Bks.; 0-87491)*, 13950 Park Ctr. Rd., Herndon, VA 22071-3222 (SAN 201-2227) Tel 804-689-2452; Toll free: 800-451-7771; 800-621-5199 (in Washington, DC).

Across the Road, *(Across the Road Publishing Co.; 0-9629949)*, P.O. Box 740293, Houston, TX 77274; 9450 Woodfair, No. 1405, Houston, TX 77274 Tel 713-779-8429.

Active Parenting, *(Active Parenting Pubs.; 0-9618020; 1-880283)*, 810 Franklin Ct., Suite B, Marietta, GA 30067-9085 (SAN 666-301X); Toll free: 800-825-0060.

Activities Learning, *(Activities for Learning; 0-9609636)*, Rte. 4, Box 34, Hutchinson, MN 55350 (SAN 283-2445) Tel 612-587-9146.

Activity Resources, *(Activity Resources Co., Inc.; 0-918932)*, P.O. Box 4875, 20655 Hathaway Ave., Hayward, CA 94541 (SAN 209-0201) Tel 415-782-1300; Dist. by: Cuisenaire Co. of America, 12 Church St., New Rochelle, NY 10805 (SAN 201-7806) Tel 914-235-0900; Dist. by: Dale Seymour Pubns., P.O. Box 10888, Palo Alto, CA 94303 (SAN 200-9781) Tel 415-324-2800; Toll free: 800-872-1100; 800-222-0766 (in California); Dist. by: DELTA Education, Inc., Factory St., Bldg. 4, Nashua, NH 03060 (SAN 630-1711) Tel 603-889-8899.

Adage Pubns, *(Adage Pubns.; 1-879889)*, P.O. Box 2377, Coeur d'Alene, ID 83814-1917; Toll free: 800-745-3170; 9975 Hillview Dr., Hayden, ID 83835 Tel 208-762-3177.

Adam Pub Co, *(Adam Publishing Co.; 0-9614209)*, Subs. of Adam Art Assocs., 412 Lyncrest Rd., Reading, PA 19607-1302 (SAN 686-9378) Tel 215-775-2739; Dist. by: Berkshire News, Inc., Third Ave. & Cherry St., West Reading, PA 19602 (SAN 169-7668) Tel 215-376-2851; Toll free: 800-223-0510. Do not confuse with Adam Publishing in Fullerton, CA.

Adama Pubs Inc, *(Adama Pubs., Inc.; 0-915361; 1-55774)*, P.O. Box 1202, Bellmore, NY 11710-0485 (SAN 291-0640); Toll free: 800-672-6672.

ADAPT Pub Co, *(A.D.A.P.T. Publishing Co.; 1-877709)*, P.O. Box 141381, Austin, TX 78714; 300 E. Huntland Dr., No. 105, Austin, TX 78752 Tel 512-451-2232.

Addison-Wesley, *(Addison-Wesley Publishing Co., Inc.; 0-201)*, Rte. 128, Reading, MA 01867 (SAN 200-2000) Tel 617-944-3700; Toll free: 800-447-221-2

Additions Pr, *(Additions Pr.; 0-9623940)*, 20370 Town Center Ln., Suite 155, Cupertino, CA 95014 Tel 408-446-4400; Dist. by: Publishes Services, P.O. Box 2510, Novato, CA 94948 (SAN 201-3037) Tel 415-883-3530; Toll free: 800-365-3453.

ADK Mtn Club, *(Adirondack Mountain Club, Inc.; 0-935272)*, R.R. 3, Box 3055, Lake George, NY 12845 (SAN 204-7691) Tel 518-668-4447.

ADL, *(Anti-Defamation League of B'nai B'rith; 0-88464)*, 823 United Nations Plaza, New York, NY 10017 (SAN 204-7616) Tel 212-490-2525.

Adon Bks, *(Adon Bks.; 0-9622942)*, 7 Donington Dr., Greenville, SC 29615 Tel 803-268-3236.

Adona Pub, *(Adona Publishing; 0-9622364)*, 11978 Woodside Ave., Lakeside, CA 92040 Tel 619-561-1787.

Adonis Pr, *(Adonis Pr.; 0-932776)*, Hawthorne Valley, Ghent, NY 12075 (SAN 218-463X); Orders to: Christy Barnes, R.D. Box 373, Hillsdale, NY 12529 (SAN 661-9320) Tel 518-325-7182.

Adonis Studio, *(Adonis Studio; 0-914827)*, P.O. Box 6626, Cleveland, OH 44101 (SAN 289-0461) Tel 216-226-1058.

Advan Learning, *(Advanced Learning Products; 0-916881)*, 10615 Cullman Ave., Whittier, CA 90603 (SAN 654-519X) Tel 213-947-8138.

Advance Cal Tech, *(Advance Cal Tech, Inc.; 0-943759)*, 5656 N. Rosemead Blvd., Temple City, CA 91780 (SAN 242-2603) Tel 818-285-0370.

Advantage Video, *(Advantage Video; 0-9622594)*, P.O. Box 6462, Omaha, NE 68106; Toll free: 800-776-8585; 5623 Pierce, Omaha, NE 68106 Tel 402-330-8211. Do not confuse with Advantage Video, Costa Mesa, CA.

Advent II
See Advent Times

Advent NY, *(Advent Bks., Inc.; 0-89891)*, 141 E. 44th St., Suite 511, New York, NY 10017 (SAN 170-1878) Tel 212-697-0887.

Advent Times, *(Advent Times, Inc.; 0-9627415)*, P.O. Box 9065, Springfield, IL 62791; 97 Andover Dr., Springfield, IL 62704 Tel 217-698-9548.

Adventure Pr, *(Adventure Pr.; 0-940589)*, 650 Alvarado Rd., Berkeley, CA 94705 (SAN 664-9904) Tel 415-849-9415. Do not confuse with Adventure Pr., also in Berkeley, CA.

Adventure VA, *(Adventure Publishing; 0-9620606)*, 1510 White Oak Ct., Martinsville, VA 24112 (SAN 249-1788) Tel 703-638-8979.

Advocacy Pr, *(Advocacy Pr.; 0-911655)*, Div. of Girls Inc., of Greater Santa Barbara, P.O. Box 4426, Santa Barbara, CA 93140 (SAN 263-9114) Tel 805-962-2728; Dist. by: Ingram Bk. Co., 1125 Heilquanker Blvd., La Vergne, TN 37086 (SAN 169-7978) Tel 615-793-5000; Toll free: 800-937-8000 (orders only); Dist. by: Bookpeople, 2929 Fifth St., Berkeley, CA 94710 (SAN 168-9517) Tel 415-549-3030; Toll free: 800-999-4650; Dist. by: Gordon's Bks., Inc., 2323 Delgany St., Denver, CO 80216 (SAN 169-0531) Tel 303-296-1830; Toll free: 800-525-6979 (West of the Mississippi) Tel 415-549-3030.

Aegean Park Pr, *(Aegean Park Pr.; 0-89412)*, P.O. Box 2837, Laguna Hills, CA 92654-0837 (SAN 210-0231) Tel 714-586-8811.

Aegina Pr, *(Aegina Pr., Inc.; 0-916383; 1-56002)*, 59 Oak Ln., Spring Valley, Huntington, WV 25704 (SAN 665-469X) Tel 304-429-7204. *Imprints:* Univ Edtns (University Editions).

Aeolus Bks, *(Aeolus Bks.; 0-9621448)*, P.O. Box 3, Irvington, VA 22480 (SAN 251-3870); Edgewood Ln., Irvington, VA 22480 (SAN 251-3889) Tel 804-438-5602.

AEON-Hierophant, *(AEON-Hierophant Communications, Inc.; 0-9606110)*, P.O. Box 46155, Los Angeles, CA 90046 (SAN 216-7816) Tel 213-876-1729.

Aerial Photo, *(Aerial Photography Services, Inc.; 0-936672)*, 2511 S. Tryon St., Charlotte, NC 28203 (SAN 214-2791) Tel 704-333-5143.

Aero Products, *(Aero Products Research, Inc.; 0-912682)*, 11201 Hindry Ave., Los Angeles, CA 90045 (SAN 205-5996) Tel 213-641-7242.

Aerodrome Pr, *(Aerodrome Pr.; 0-935092)*, P.O. Box 44, Story City, IA 50248 (SAN 213-4519) Tel 515-733-2589.

AFCOM Pub, *(AFCOM Publishing; 0-939339)*, P.O. Box H, Harbor City, CA 90710-0330 (SAN 662-4685); 27147 Eastvale Rd., Rolling Hills, CA 90274 (SAN 662-4693) Tel 213-377-4951.

Affect Skill, *(Affective Skill Development for Adolescents; 0-924609)*, 5930 S. 58th St., Suite N, Lincoln, NE 68156 Tel 402-423-1623.

Africa World, *(Africa World Pr.; 0-86543)*, P.O. Box 1892, Trenton, NJ 08607 (SAN 692-3925); 15 Industry Ct., Trenton, NJ 08638 (SAN 242-0309) Tel 609-771-1666; Dist. by: Inbook Distribution Co., P.O. Box 120470, East Haven, CT 06512 (SAN 630-5547) Tel 203-467-5434; Toll free: 800-253-3605.

African Islam Miss Pubns, *(African Islamic Mission Pubns.; 0-916157; 1-56505)*, Subs. of A.I.M. Graphics, 1390 Bedford Ave., Brooklyn, NY 11216 (SAN 294-6645) Tel 718-638-4588.

Afro-Am, *(Afro-Am Publishing Co., Inc.; 0-910030)*, Div. of Afro-Am Inc., 819 S. Wabash Ave., Rm. 610, Chicago, IL 60605 (SAN 201-2332) Tel 312-922-1147.

Afsaneh Pub, *(Afsaneh Publishing Co.; 1-877789)*, 3449 Three Springs Dr., Westlake Village, CA 91361 Tel 818-991-4151.

Afton Pub, *(Afton Publishing; 0-89359)*, P.O. Box 1399, Andover, NJ 07821-1399 (SAN 692-2570) Tel 201-579-2442.

AFUA Ent, *(AFUA Enterprises, Inc.; 0-918088)*, P.O. Box 9026, General Lafayette Sta., Jersey City, NJ 07304 (SAN 210-1599) Tel 201-451-0599.

Agatha Pub Co, *(Agatha Publishing Co.; 0-9620893)*, 83 Michael Rd., Stamford, CT 06903 (SAN 250-2526) Tel 203-329-1790.

Agee Pub, *(Agee Pubs., Inc.; 0-935265)*, P.O. Box 526, Athens, GA 30603 (SAN 695-7498); 454 Milledge Hts., Athens, GA 30606 (SAN 696-7035) Tel 404-548-5269.

Aid-U Pub, *(Aid-U Publishing Co.; 0-940370)*, P.O. Box 47226, Oak Park, MI 48237 (SAN 217-149X) Tel 313-569-8288.

Aiducation, *(Aiducation, Inc.; 0-9627866)*, 635 Park Meadow Rd., Suite 109, Westerville, OH 43081 Tel 614-794-2203; Toll free: 800-345-3308.

Aiki Works, *(Aiki Works, Inc.; 1-877803)*, P.O. Box 251, Victor, NY 14564; 538 Wintergreen Gr, Victor, NY 14564 Tel 716-924-7302.

Ainslie's, *(Ainslie's; 0-9618445)*, P.O. Box 7656, Menlo Park, CA 94026-7656 (SAN 667-9730); 1735 E. Bayshore Rd., Suite 30A, Redwood City, CA 94063 (SAN 667-9749) Tel 415-368-9865.

AIRE, *(Alternatives in Religious Education, Inc.; 0-86705)*, 3945 S. Oneida St., Denver, CO 80237 (SAN 216-6534) Tel 303-363-7779; Toll free: 800-346-7779.

Airmont, *(Airmont Publishing Co., Inc.; 0-8049)*, 401 Lafayette St., New York, NY 10003 (SAN 206-8710) Tel 212-598-0222; Toll free: 800-223-5251 (outside New York).

Ajuna Unlimited, *(Ajuna Unlimited; 0-9626254)*, P.O. Box 12454, Palm Oesert, CA 92255 Tel 619-320-3788.

Akiba Pr, *(Akiba Pr.; 0-934764),* Box 13086, Oakland, CA 94661 (SAN 212-0666) Tel 415-339-1283.

Al-Anon, *(Al-Anon Family Group Headquarters; 0-910034),* 1372 Broadway, 7th Flr., New York, NY 10018-6106 (SAN 201-2391) Tel 212-302-7240; P.O. Box 862 Midtown Sta., New York, NY 10018-0862 (SAN 662-7110).

Al Fresco, *(Al Fresco Enterprise; 0-9612596),* 1200 Liberty Ln., Pueblo, CO 81001 (SAN 211-5832) Tel 719-545-9524.

ALA, *(American Library Assn.; 0-8389),* 50 E. Huron St., Chicago, IL 60611 (SAN 201-0062) Tel 312-280-2424; Toll free: 800-545-2433.

Alacran Pr Inc, *(Alacran Pr., Inc.; 0-9621380),* 16308 Relindo Ct., Rancho Bernardo, CA 92128 (SAN 251-1320) Tel 619-673-9176.

Aladdin *Imprint of* **Macmillan Child Grp**

Aladdin Pub, *(Aladdin Publishing; 0-944677),* P.O. Box 364, Palmer, AK 99645 (SAN 245-1840); 650 N. Second, Palmer, AK 99645 (SAN 245-1859) Tel 907-892-7638; Dist. by: Alaska News Agency, Inc., 325 W. Potter Dr., Book Dept., Anchorage, AK 99502 (SAN 168-9274) Tel 907-563-3251; Dist. by: Fairbanks News Agency, 307 Ladd Ave., Fairbanks, AK 99701 (SAN 168-9282) Tel 907-456-5355.

Alahow-To-Parent, *(Alahow-To-Parent; 0-9624955),* P.O. Box 5047, Arcata, CA 95521; 1031 Hallen Dr., Apt. B, Arcata, CA 95521 Tel 707-822-2383.

Alaska Hist, *(Alaska Historical Commission; 0-943712),* Div. of State of Alaska, P.O. Box 107001, Anchorage, AK 99510-7001 (SAN 240-9933) Tel 907-762-2622; Dist. by: Alaska Historical Soc., Box 100299, Anchorage, AK 99510 (SAN 630-1533) Tel 907-276-1596.

Alaska Native, *(Alaska Native Language Ctr.; 0-933769; 1-55500),* Univ. of Alaska, P.O. Box 900111, Fairbanks, AK 99775-0120 (SAN 692-9796) Tel 907-474-6586.

Alaska Northwest, *(Alaska Northwest Bks.; 0-88240),* P.O. Box 3007, Bothell, WA 98041-3007 (SAN 201-2383); Toll free: 800-331-3510; 22026 20th Ave., SE, Bothell, WA 98021 Tel 206-487-6100.

Alaskan Viewpoint, *(Alaskan Viewpoint; 0-924663),* HCR 64, Box 453, Seward, AK 99664 (SAN 251-4095); Mile 19.5 Seward Hwy., Seward, AK 99664 Tel 907-288-3168.

Alchemy Comms, *(Alchemy Communications Group, Ltd.; 0-934323),* Div. of Alchemy II, Inc., 9311 Eton Ave., Chatsworth, CA 91311 (SAN 693-5990) Tel 818-700-8300; Dist. by: Worlds of Wonder, 4209 Technology Dr., Fremont, CA 94538 (SAN 630-1851) Tel 415-659-4300.

Alden P & M Corp, *(Alden Production & Marketing Corp.; 0-923059),* 4742 N. 24th St., Suite 340, Phoenix, AZ 85016 (SAN 251-5881) Tel 602-956-8830.

Alegra Hse Pubs, *(Alegra Hse. Pubs.; 0-933879),* Affil. of Kaya Bks., P.O. Box 1443B, Warren, OH 44482 (SAN 692-7858) Tel 216-372-2951; Dist. by: Bookpeople, 2929 Fifth St., Berkeley, CA 94710 (SAN 168-9517) Tel 415-549-3030; Toll free: 800-999-4650; Dist. by: Distributors, The, 702 S. Michigan, South Bend, ID 46618 (SAN 169-2488) Tel 219-232-8500; Toll free: 800-348-5200; Dist. by: Baker & Taylor Bks., Midwestern Div., 501 S. Gladiolus St., Momence, IL 60954 (SAN 169-2100) Tel 815-472-2444; Toll free: 800-435-5111; 800-892-1892 (Illinois); Dist. by: Pacific Pipeline, Inc., 19215 66th Ave., S., Kent, WA 98032 (SAN 208-2128) Tel 206-872-5523; Toll free: 800-562-4647 (in Washington); 800-426-4727 (in northern California, Nevada, Idaho, Oregon, Montana); Dist. by: Quality Bks., Inc., 918 Sherwood Dr., Lake Bluff, IL 60044-2204 (SAN 169-2127) Tel 708-295-2010; Toll free: 800-323-4241 (Libraries only); Dist. by: Baker & Taylor Bks., Southern Div., Mt. Olive Rd., Commerce, GA 30529 (SAN 169-1503) Tel 404-335-5000; Toll free: 800-241-6004; 800-282-6850 (in Georgia); Dist. by: Baker & Taylor Bks., Eastern Div., 50 Kirby Ave., Somerville, NJ 08876 (SAN 169-4901) Tel 201-722-8000; Toll free: 800-435-1845; 800-352-4833 (in New Jersey); Dist. by: Baker & Taylor Bks., Western Div., 380 Edison Way, Reno, NV 89564 (SAN 169-4464) Tel 702-786-6700; Toll free: 800-648-3450.

Alemany Pr, *(Alemany Pr., Inc.; 0-88084),* Div. of Prentice Hall Regents, Sylvan Ave., Rte. 9W, PHR Bldg., PHR Dept., Englewood Cliffs, NJ 07632 (SAN 240-1312); Toll free: 800-227-2375.

Alexander Graham, *(Bell, Alexander Graham, Assn. for the Deaf; 0-88200),* 3417 Volta Pl., NW, Washington, DC 20007 (SAN 203-6924) Tel 202-337-5220.

Alfred Pub, *(Alfred Publishing Co.; 0-88284),* 16380 Roscoe Blvd., Suite 200, Box 10003, Van Nuys, CA 91406-1215 (SAN 201-243X) Tel 818-891-5999; Toll free: 800-292-6122; 800-821-6083 (in California).

Algonquin Bks, *(Algonquin Bks. of Chapel Hill; 0-912697; 1-56512),* Div. of Workman Publishing Co., P.O. Box 2225, Chapel Hill, NC 27515 (SAN 282-7506); 307 W. Weaver St., Carrboro, NC 27510 (SAN 662-2011) Tel 919-967-0108; Dist. by: Workman Publishing Co., 708 Broadway, New York, NY 10003 (SAN 203-2821) Tel 212-254-5900; Toll free: 800-722-7202.

Alien Bks, *(Alien Bks.; 0-9622190),* 3815 Eastern Ave., N., No. 2, Seattle, WA 98103. Moved, left no forwarding address.

All Ireland Inc, *(All-Ireland Heritage, Inc.; 0-9621544),* Div. of D. R. H. Assocs., Pubs., Inc., P.O. Box 7, Dunn Loring, VA 22027 (SAN 251-5946); 2255 Cedar Ln., Vienna, VA 22180 (SAN 251-5954) Tel 703-560-4496.

ALL Ventura Pub, *(ALL Ventura Publishing Services; 0-9626133),* P.O. Box 5190, Pacific Grove, CA 93950; 71 Glen Lake Dr., Pacific Grove, CA 93950 Tel 408-375-1876.

Allgnc Advntg, *(Allegiance Advantage, Inc.; 0-9627801),* 555 W. 57th St., Suite 1323, New York, NY 10019 Tel 212-582-6344.

Almar, *(Almar Pr.; 0-930256),* 4105 Marietta Dr., Vestal, NY 13850 (SAN 210-5713).

Alpen & Jeffries, *(Alpen & Jeffries Pubs.; 1-879692),* 110 Brighton Way, Clayton, MO 63105-3602 Tel 314-863-0529.

Alpha & Omega, *(Alpha Omega; 0-941734),* 1026 E. Garden Ave., Coeur d'Alene, ID 83814 (SAN 239-1503) Tel 208-664-2954. Do not confuse with Alpha Omega, New York, NY.

Alpha Beto Music, *(Alpha-Beto Music; 0-9616528),* 152 Sabine, Portland, TX 78374 (SAN 659-4107) Tel 512-643-6309.

Alpha Iota, *(Alpha Iota of Pi Lambda Theta Pubns.; 0-914522),* 2260 N. Orange Grove Ave., Pomona, CA 91767 (SAN 206-3204) Tel 714-626-5065.

Alpine Pubns, *(Alpine Pubns.; 0-931866),* P.O. Box 7027 (Orders), Loveland, CO 80537 Tel 303-667-2017; Toll free: 800-777-7257; Dist. by: Baker & Taylor Bks., Eastern Div., 50 Kirby Ave., Somerville, NJ 08876-0734 (SAN 169-4901) Tel 201-722-8000; Toll free: 800-526-3825; Dist. by: Baker & Taylor Bks., Midwestern Div., 501 S. Gladiolus St., Momence, IL 60954-2444 (SAN 169-2100) Tel 815-472-2444; Toll free: 800-435-5111; 800-892-1892 (in Illinois); Dist. by: Baker & Taylor Bks., Southern Div., Mt. Olive Rd., Commerce, GA 30599-9988 (SAN 169-1503) Tel 303-296-1830; Toll free: 800-241-6004; 800-282-6854 (in Georgia); Dist. by: Baker & Taylor Bks., Western Div., 380 Edison Way, Reno, NV 89564 (SAN 169-4464) Tel 702-786-6700; Toll free: 800-648-3540; 800-524-2486 (in Canada); Dist. by: Gordon's Bks., Inc., 2323 Delgany St., Denver, CO 80216 (SAN 169-0531) Tel 303-296-1830; Toll free: 800-525-6979.

Alta Bk Co Pubs, *(Alta Bk. Co., Pubs.; 1-878598),* 16 Adrian Ct., Burlingame, CA 94010 (SAN 200-4674) Tel 415-692-2002; Toll free: 800-526-0505.

Altair Pr, *(Altair Pr.; 0-934768),* 264 McMillan Rd., Grosse Pointe Farms, MI 48236 (SAN 209-1585) Tel 313-881-9588.

Alyson Pubns, *(Alyson Pubns., Inc.; 0-932870; 1-55583),* 40 Plympton St., Boston, MA 02118 (SAN 213-6546) Tel 617-542-5679; Dist. by: Inbook Distribution Co., P.O. Box 120470, East Haven, CT 06512 (SAN 630-5547) Tel 203-467-5434; Toll free: 800-253-3605.

Am Assn Diabetes Ed, *(American Assn. of Diabetes Educators),* 500 N. Michigan Ave., Suite 1400, Chicago, IL 60611 (SAN 224-3091) Tel 312-661-1700.

Am Assn U, *(American Assn. of University Women; 0-9611476),* 2401 Virginia Ave., NW, Washington, DC 20037 (SAN 291-8617) Tel 202-785-7700; Toll free: 800-424-9717.

Am Assn Voc Materials, *(American Assn. for Vocational Instructional Materials; 0-914452; 0-89606),* 745 Gaines School Rd., Athens, GA 30605 (SAN 225-8811) Tel 404-543-7557; Toll free: 800-228-4689.

Am Atheist, *(American Atheist Pr., Inc.; 0-911826; 0-910309),* P.O. Box 140195, Austin, TX 78714-0195 (SAN 206-7188); 7215 Cameron Rd., Austin, TX 78752 Tel 512-458-1244.

Am Classic Ent, *(American Classic Enterprises, Inc.; 1-880210),* 4742 N. Western Ave., Chicago, IL 60625 Tel 312-561-9191; Dist. by: Baker & Taylor Bks., Midwestern Div., 501 S. Gladiola St., Momence, IL 60954-2444 (SAN 169-2100) Tel 815-472-2444; Toll free: 800-435-5111; 800-892-1892 (in Illinois).

Am Classical Coll Pr, *(American Classical College Pr.; 0-913314; 0-89266),* P.O. Box 4526, Albuquerque, NM 87196 (SAN 201-2618) Tel 505-296-2320.

Am Coll Testing, *(American College Testing Program; 0-937734; 1-56009),* 2201 N. Dodge St., Iowa City, IA 52243 (SAN 204-8027) Tel 319-337-1410; P.O Box 168, Iowa City, IA 52243 (SAN 696-5075).

Am Diabetes, *(American Diabetes Assn.; 0-945448),* 1660 Duke St., Alexandria, VA 22314 (SAN 224-3105) Tel 703-549-1500.

Am Faculty Pr, *(American Faculty Pr., Inc.; 0-912834),* 44 Lake Shore Dr., Rockaway, NJ 07866 (SAN 201-2650) Tel 201-627-2727.

Am Forestry, *(American Forestry Assn.; 0-935050),* Bk. Editorial Dept., P.O. Box 2000, Washington, DC 20013 (SAN 204-8175) Tel 202-667-3300.

Am Geog Pub
See Am Wrld Geog

Am Guidance, *(American Guidance Service, Inc.; 0-913476; 0-88671),* Publishers' Bldg., Circle Pines, MN 55014-1796 (SAN 201-694X) Tel 612-786-4343; Toll free: 800-328-2560.

Am Hist Soc Ger, *(American Historical Society of Germans from Russia; 0-914222),* 631 D St., Lincoln, NE 68502 (SAN 204-7543) Tel 402-474-3363.

Am Map, *(American Map Corp.; 0-8416),* Subs. of Langenscheidt Pubs., Inc., 46-35 54th Rd., Flushing, NY 11378 (SAN 202-4624) Tel 718-784-0055; Toll free: 800-432-6277; Dist. by: Hagstrom Map Co., Inc., 46-35 54th Rd., Flushing, NY 11378 (SAN 203-543X).

Am Printing Hse, *(American Printing Hse. for the Blind),* 1839 Frankfort Ave., Box 6085, Louisville, KY 40206-0085 (SAN 203-5235) Tel 502-895-2405.

Am Psychiatric, *(American Psychiatric Pr., Inc.; 0-89042; 0-88048),* Subs. of American Psychiatric Assn., 1400 K St., NW, Suite 1101, Washington, DC 20005 (SAN 293-2288) Tel 202-682-6262; Toll free: 800-368-5777. Publishing arm of the American Psychiatric Assn.

Am Psychol, *(American Psychological Assn.; 0-912704; 1-55798),* 1200 17th St., NW, Washington, DC 20036 (SAN 202-4705) Tel 202-955-7600; Orders to: P.O. Box 2710, Hyattsville, MD 20784 (SAN 685-3137) Tel 703-247-7705.

Am Standard, *(American Standard Text Corp.; 0-944452),* 235 Park Ave. S., 8th Flr., New York, NY 10003 (SAN 243-6256) Tel 212-254-8840.

Am Teaching, *(American Teaching Aids; 0-88037),* P.O. Box 1406, Covina, CA 91722 (SAN 238-9398). Moved, left no forwarding address.

Am Trust Pubns, *(American Trust Pubns.; 0-89259),* 10900 W. Washington St., Indianapolis, IN 46231 (SAN 664-6158) Tel 317-839-9278.

Am Univ Artforms, *(American Universal Artforms Corp.; 0-913632),* 6208 Quail Hollow, Austin, TX 78750 (SAN 202-4772) Tel 512-345-6235.

Am Wrld Geog, *(American World Geographic Publishing; 0-938314; 1-56037),* Box 5630, Helena, MT 59604 (SAN 220-0732); Toll free: 800-654-1105; 800-821-3874 (in Montana); 3020 Bozeman, Helena, MT 59601 Tel 406-443-2842; Dist. by: National Bk. Network, 4720A Boston Way, Lanham, MD 20706-4310 (SAN 630-0065) Tel 301-459-8696; Toll free: 800-462-6420.

AMC Books, *(Appalachian Mountain Club Bks.; 0-910146; 1-878239),* 5 Joy St., Boston, MA 02108 (SAN 203-4808) Tel 617-523-0636; Dist. by: Talman Co., Inc., 150 Fifth Ave., New York, NY 10011 (SAN 200-5204) Tel 212-620-3182; Toll free: 800-537-8894.

Amaknak Pr, *(Amaknak Pr.; 0-9626090),* 13505 SE River Rd., Portland, OR 97222 Tel 503-652-3072.

Amer Assn Teach German, *(American Assn. of Teachers of German; 0-942017),* 523 Bldg., Suite 201, Rte. 38, Cherry Hill, NJ 08034 (SAN 688-8577) Tel 609-663-5264.

Amer Classical, *(American Classical League, The; 0-939507),* Miami Univ., Oxford, OH 45056 (SAN 225-8358) Tel 513-529-7741.

Amer Dist Serv, *(American Distribution Services, Inc.; 1-878667),* 3400 Dundee Rd., Northbrook, IL 60062 (SAN 630-561X) Tel 708-498-5010.

Amer Edit Servs, *(American Editorial Services, Inc.; 1-879019),* 241 Olde Post Rd., Niceville, FL 32578 Tel 904-897-5289; Toll free: 800-243-3066.

Amer Educ Pub, *(American Education Publishing, Inc.; 1-56189),* 3790 E. Fifth Ave., Columbus, OH 43219 Tel 614-235-2000; Toll free: 800-542-7833.

Amer Etiquette Inst, *(American Etiquette Institute; 1-879322),* P.O. Box 700508, San Jose, CA 95170; Toll free: 800-748-6299; 1643 Edmonton Ave., Sunnyvale, CA 94087 Tel 408-996-9901.

Amer Intl Pr, *(American International Pr., Inc.; 0-9623476),* 419 Park Ave., S., New York, NY 10016 Tel 212-213-6699.

Amer Lodge Res, *(American Lodge of Research; 0-925658),* 71 W. 23rd St., New York, NY 10010 Tel 212-741-4505.

Amer Scholastic, *(American Scholastic Pr. Assn.; 1-878314),* P.O. Box 4400, College Point, NY 11356; 120-15A Riviera Ct., College Point, NY 11356 Tel 212-673-9030.

Amereon Ltd, *(Amereon, Ltd.; 0-88411; 0-89190; 0-8488),* P.O. Box 1200, Mattituck, NY 11952 (SAN 201-2413) Tel 516-298-5100.

American Studies Pr, *(American Studies Pr., Inc.; 0-934996),* 13511 Palmwood Ln., Tampa, FL 33624-4416 (SAN 213-2788) Tel 813-961-7200.

Amethyst Aura, *(Amethyst Aura; 0-944944),* P.O. Box 800842, Dallas, TX 75380 (SAN 245-789X); 9927 Silver Creek Rd., Dallas, TX 75243 (SAN 245-7903) Tel 214-699-8015.

Amethyst Bks, *(Amethyst Bks.; 0-944256),* P.O. Box 895, Woodstock, NY 12498 (SAN 243-0657) Tel 212-724-7988; Dist. by: Talman Co., 150 Fifth Ave., Rm. 630, New York, NY 10011 (SAN 200-5204) Tel 212-620-3182; Toll free: 800-537-8894 (orders only).

Amhara Corp, *(Amhara Corp.; 0-917450),* 6990 S. 1700 E., Salt Lake City, UT 84121 (SAN 208-063X).

AMI Pr, *(AMI Pr.; 0-911988; 1-56036),* Div. of Our Lady of Fatima, U.S.A., Inc., Box 976, Mountain View Rd., Washington, NJ 07882-0976 (SAN 213-6791) Tel 908-689-1700.

Amigo Pr, *(Amigo Pr.; 0-935098),* 620 Lombardi Ln., Laguna Beach, CA 92652 (SAN 213-2796) Tel 714-497-4022.

Ammie Enter, *(Ammie Enterprises; 0-932825),* P.O. Box 2132, Vista, CA 92083 (SAN 691-3008) Tel 619-758-4561.

Amnos Pubns, *(Amnos Pubns.; 0-9623721),* c/o Holy Apostle Greek Orthodox Church, 2501 S. Wolf Rd., Westchester, IL 60153 Tel 312-562-2744.

Amoke Omoleye Pub, *(Omoleye, Amoke, Publishing; 0-9625699),* P.O. Box A3662, Chicago, IL 60690; 1048-50 W. Foster Ave., Apt. 3C, Chicago, IL 60640 Tel 312-918-2020.

AMSCO Sch, *(AMSCO School Pubns., Inc.; 0-87720),* 315 Hudson St., 5th Fl., New York, NY 10013-1085 (SAN 201-1751) Tel 212-675-7000.

An Awareness, *(Awareness Production, An; 0-9625787),* P.O. Box 19178, Oakland, CA 94619; 2217 42nd Ave., Oakland, CA 94619 Tel 415-533-0795.

Ana Pubns, *(Ana Pubns.; 0-9618941),* 4427 Westover Place, NW, Washington, DC 20016-5556 (SAN 242-4533) Tel 202-362-5330.

Analysis, *(Analysis Pr.; 0-911894),* Subs. of Merrill Analysis, Inc., 3300 Darby Rd., No. 3325, Haverford, PA 19041 (SAN 210-9549) Tel 215-642-2011.

Ananse Pr, *(Ananse Pr.; 0-9605670),* P.O. Box 22565, Seattle, WA 98122 (SAN 216-3292); 1504 32nd Ave. S., Seattle, WA 98144 (SAN 241-6123) Tel 206-325-8205.

Anatomical Chart, *(Anatomical Chart Co.; 0-9603730),* 8221 N. Kimbell, Skokie, IL 60076 (SAN 223-5315) Tel 312-764-7171; Toll free: 800-621-7500.

Anchor Pr Imprint of Doubleday

Anchorage, *(Anchorage Pr.; 0-87602),* P.O. Box 8067, New Orleans, LA 70182 (SAN 203-4727) Tel 504-283-8868.

Ancient City Pr, *(Ancient City Pr.; 0-941270),* P.O. Box 5401, Santa Fe, NM 87502 (SAN 164-5552) Tel 505-982-8195.

Anderson Bks, *(Anderson Bks.; 0-9602128),* P.O. Box 1751, Naples, FL 33939 (SAN 209-5238) Tel 813-262-5592.

Anderson MI, *(Anderson Pubns.; 0-9610088),* Box 423, Davison, MI 48423 (SAN 267-5633) Tel 313-667-2012. Do not confuse with Anderson Pubns., Berkeley, CA.

Anderson Pr, *(Anderson Pr.; 0-942479),* 706 W. Davis, Ann Arbor, MI 48103-4855 (SAN 667-3600) Tel 313-994-6182.

Anderson Pub Co, *(Anderson Publishing Co.; 0-87084),* P.O. Box 1576, Cincinnati, OH 45201-1576 (SAN 208-2799); Toll free: 800-543-0883; 2035 Reading Rd., Cincinnati, OH 45202-1416 (SAN 661-9436) Tel 513-421-4142. Do not confuse with Anderson Publishing Co., Burley, ID.

Anderson World, *(Anderson World, Inc.; 0-89037),* 1400 N. Shoreline Blvd., P.O. Box 7211, Mountain View, CA 94043 (SAN 281-2754) Tel 415-965-8552; Toll free: 800-227-8318; Orders to: P.O. Box 366, Mountain View, CA 94042 (SAN 281-2762).

Andover Junction, *(Andover Junction Pubns.; 0-944119),* P.O. Box 1160, Andover, NJ 07821 (SAN 242-8040).

Andre Deutsch, *(Deutsch, Andre; 0-233),* c/o Penguin U. S. A., P.O. Box 120, Bergenfield, NJ 07621 (SAN 206-8087) Tel 201-387-0600; Toll free: 800-526-0275; Dist. by: E.P. Dutton, 2 Park Ave., New York, NY 10016 (SAN 201-0070) Tel 212-725-1818.

Andres & Co, *(Andre's & Co.; 0-936264),* 289 Varick St., Jersey City, NJ 07302 (SAN 214-0977).

Andrew Mtn Pr, *(Andrew Mountain Pr.; 0-9603840; 0-916897),* P.O. Box 14353, Hartford, CT 06114 (SAN 658-0130).

Andrews & McMeel, *(Andrews & McMeel; 0-8362),* Affil. of Universal Press Syndicate, 4900 Main St., Kansas City, MO 64112 (SAN 202-540X) Tel 816-932-6700; Toll free: 800-826-4216.

Animal Cracker, *(Animal Cracker Pr.),* 14032 Hilltop Dr., NE, Bemidji, MN 56601 (SAN 210-9123) Tel 218-586-3464.

Anirt Pr, *(Anirt Pr.; 0-9605878),* P.O. Box 979, Lawndale, CA 90260 (SAN 216-6550); 15707 Eastwood Ave., Lawndale, CA 90260 (SAN 241-6166) Tel 213-678-9753.

Anna Pub, *(Anna Publishing, Inc.; 0-89305),* P.O. Box 218, 8 S. Bluford Ave., Ocoee, FL 32761 (SAN 281-2789) Tel 407-656-6998.

Anne M Eccles, *(Eccles, Anne M.; 0-9618555),* 413 S. Uvalda Cir., Aurora, CO 80012 (SAN 668-0631) Tel 303-364-4589.

Annette Capps, *(Capps, Annette, Ministries; 0-9618975),* P.O. Box 10, Broken Arrow, OK 74013 (SAN 242-4738) Tel 918-251-2309.

Ansata Pubns, *(Ansata Pubns.; 0-9625644),* Rte. 2, Box 312A, Mena, AR 71953 Tel 501-394-5288.

Ansayre Pr, *(Ansayre Pr.; 0-937369),* 284 Huron Ave., Cambridge, MA 02138 (SAN 659-0071) Tel 617-547-0339.

Anschell Pub Co, *(Anschell Publishing Co.; 0-926060),* 2809 1/2 Mt. Rainier Dr., S., Seattle, WA 98144 Tel 206-723-5414; Dist. by: Pacific Pipeline, Inc., 19215 66th Ave., S., Kent, WA 98032 (SAN 208-2128) Tel 206-872-5523; Toll free: 800-426-4727 (in Oregon, Idaho, Montana, Nevada, & northern California); 800-562-4617 (in Washington); 800-444-7323.

Antarctic Pr, *(Antarctic Pr.; 0-930655),* P.O. Box 7134, Bellevue, WA 98008 (SAN 684-2631) Tel 206-885-6853; Dist. by: Pacific Pipeline, Inc., 19215 66th Ave. S., Kent, WA 98032 (SAN 208-2128) Tel 206-872-5523; Toll free: 800-426-4727 (in Northern California, Montana, Idaho, Nevada, Oregon); 800-562-4647 (in Washington).

Anthro Co, *(The Anthro Co.; 1-878464),* P. O. Box 661765, Sacramento, CA 95866-1765 Tel 916-971-1675.

Anthroposophic, *(Anthroposophic Pr., Inc.; 0-910142; 0-88010),* R.R. 4, Box 94A1, Hudson, NY 12534 (SAN 201-1824) Tel 518-851-2054; Dist. by: Bookpeople, 2929 Fifth St., Berkeley, CA 94710 (SAN 168-9517) Tel 415-549-3030; Toll free: 800-999-4650; Dist. by: Great Tradition, 750 Adrian Way, Suite 111, San Rafael, CA 94903 (SAN 200-5743) Tel 415-492-9382; Toll free: 800-275-2606; Dist. by: Inland Bk. Co., 140 Commerce St., East Haven, CT 06512 (SAN 200-4151) Tel 203-467-4257; Toll free: 800-243-0138; Dist. by: Samuel Weiser, Inc., P.O. Box 612, York Beach, ME 03910 (SAN 202-9588) Tel 207-363-4393; Toll free: 800-423-7087 (orders only); Dist. by: DeVorss & Co., P.O. Box 550, Marina del Rey, CA 90294-0550 (SAN 168-9886) Tel 213-870-7478; Toll free: 800-843-5743 (for bookstore orders only); 800-331-4719 (in California, for bookstore orders only).

Antioch Pub Co, *(Antioch Publishing Co.; 0-89954; 0-7824),* 888 Dayton St., Yellow Springs, OH 45387 (SAN 654-7214) Tel 513-767-7379; Toll free: 800-543-2397.

Antioch Publishes, *(Antioch Publishes The Word; 0-932345),* 1535 Ritchie Hwy., Arnold, MD 21012 (SAN 687-3537) Tel 301-757-5000; Dist. by: Pentecostal Publishing Hse., 8855 Dunn Rd., Hazelwood, MO 63042 (SAN 219-3817) Tel 314-837-7300.

Antique Pubns, *(Antique Pubns.; 0-915410),* Div. of Richardson Printing Corp., P.O. Box 553, Marietta, OH 45750 (SAN 216-3306); Toll free: 800-533-3433; 800-282-9771 (in Ohio).

Anton Enter, *(Anton Enterprises, Inc.; 0-9629701),* 36892 FoxGlen, Farmington Hills, MI 48331 Tel 313-788-2735.

Antroll Pub, *(Antroll Publishing Co.; 1-877656),* P.O. Box 239, College Park, MD 20740; 102 F Ames Rd., Silver Spring, MD 20903 Tel 301-434-4204.

Anyone Can Read Bks, *(Anyone Can Read Bks.; 0-914275),* Star Rte., P.O. Box 826, Lytle Creek, CA 92358 (SAN 286-6889) Tel 714-880-2332.

Anyones Pub, *(Anyone's Publishing Co.; 0-9623308),* 1130 E. Grab Creek Rd., Dickson, TN 37055 Tel 615-446-7557.

Apala Prodns, *(Apala Productions; 0-9627363),* P.O. Box 29371, Washington, DC 20017 (SAN 297-3073) Tel 202-529-6898.

Apex Creat, *(Apex Creative; 1-879253),* P.O. Box 1327, Durham, NC 27702; Toll free: 800-827-3901; 5 Geneva Ct., Durham, NC 27713 Tel 919-544-0660.

APIX Intl, *(APIX International; 1-877618),* Div. of Worzalla Publishing, 3535 Jefferson St., Stevens Point, WI 54481 Tel 715-344-9600; Toll free: 800-442-2463 (outside Wisconsin).

Appalach Consortium, *(Appalachian Consortium Pr.; 0-913239),* Div. of Appalachian Consortium, Inc., Appalachian State Univ., University Hall, Boone, NC 28608 (SAN 285-8150) Tel 704-262-2064.

Applause Inc, *(Applause, Inc.; 0-929632),* 6101 Variel Ave., Woodland Hills, CA 91365 (SAN 250-1716) Tel 818-992-6000; c/o Flavia, P.O. Box 42229, Santa Barbara, CA 93140 Tel 805-564-6905.

Applause Theatre Bk Pubs, *(Applause Theatre Bk. Pubs.; 0-936839; 1-55783),* 211 W. 71st St., New York, NY 10023 (SAN 658-3245) Tel 212-595-4735; Orders to: Ingram Pubs Service, P.O. Box 7001, LaVergne, TN 37086-7001 (SAN 248-4056); Toll free: 800-937-5557.

Apple Corps Pubs, *(Apple Corps Pubs.; 0-9619484),* P.O. Box 800030, Bethany, OK 73008 (SAN 245-0453); 1600 Sunset Ln., Oklahoma City, OK 73127 (SAN 245-0461) Tel 405-787-8191.

Apple Isl Bks, *(Apple Island Bks.; 0-934313),* Box 276, Shapleigh, ME 04076 (SAN 693-5338) Tel 207-324-9453.

Apple Paperbacks *Imprint of Scholastic Inc*

Apple Pie Pub Co, *(Apple Pie Publishing Co.; 0-911149),* 7521 E. Costilla Ave., Englewood, CO 80112 (SAN 267-6052) Tel 303-770-1784.

Apple Pub Wisc, *(Apple Publishing Co.; 0-937891),* Subs. of Educational Assessment Service, Inc., W. 6050 Apple Rd., Watertown, WI 53094 (SAN 659-4123) Tel 414-261-1118. Do not confuse with Apple Publishing Co., New York, NY.

Apple Valley, *(Apple Valley Publishing Co., Inc.; 1-880108),* 15431 Hornbrook Rd., Box 178, Hornbrook, CA 96044 Tel 916-842-7012.

Appletree Bks, *(Appletree Bks.; 1-877893),* 34 Elm Ridge Terr., Newington, CT 06111 Tel 203-666-6735.

Applewood, *(Applewood Bks.; 0-918222; 1-55709),* P.O. Box 365, Bedford, MA 01730-0365 (SAN 210-3419); Dist. by: Globe Pequot Pr., Box Q, Chester, CT 06412 (SAN 201-9892) Tel 203-526-9571; Toll free: 800-243-0495; 800-962-0973 (in Connecticut).

Apt Bks, *(Apt Bks., Inc.; 0-86590),* 141 E. 44th St., Suite 511, New York, NY 10017 (SAN 215-7209) Tel 212-697-0887.

Arcade Pub Inc, *(Arcade Publishing, Inc.; 1-55970),* Div. of Little, Brown & Co., 141 Fifth Ave., New York, NY 10010 (SAN 252-2012) Tel 212-475-2633; Toll free: 800-343-9204.

Arcadia Corp, *(Arcadia Corp.; 0-9614745),* P.O. Box 534, Franklin, NH 03235 (SAN 692-9206) Tel 603-934-6186.

Archival Servs, *(Archival Services, Inc.; 0-910653),* 3900 Roy Rd., No. 28, Shreveport, LA 71107 (SAN 270-1774) Tel 318-929-7776; P.O. Box 112, Blanchard, LA 71009 (SAN 662-0108).

Archives Pr, *(Archives Pr., The; 0-918501),* 334 State St., No. 536, Los Altos, CA 94022 (SAN 657-3207) Tel 415-941-8982; Toll free: 800-338-4454.

Archway *Imprint of PB*

Arco, *(Arco Publishing, Inc.; 0-668),* Div. of Prentice Hall Pr., Simon & Schuster, Inc., 15 Columbus Cir., New York, NY 10023 (SAN 201-0003) Tel 212-373-8931; Toll free: 800-223-2336 (accounts only); Dist. by: Prentice Hall Pr., 200 Old Tappan Rd., Old Tappan, NJ 07675 (SAN 215-3939) Tel 201-767-5937. No longer produces software. *Imprints:* Monarch Pr (Monarch Press).

Arcus Pub, *(Arcus Publishing Co.; 0-916955),* P.O. Box 228, Sonoma, CA 95476 (SAN 655-5667) Tel 707-996-9529.

ARE Pr, *(A.R.E. Pr.; 0-87604),* 215 67th St. & Atlantic Ave., Virginia Beach, VA 23451 (SAN 201-1484) Tel 804-428-3588; Toll free: 800-368-2727; P.O. Box 595, Virginia Beach, VA 23451 (SAN 692-8234).

Argee Pubs, *(Argee Pubs.),* 4453 Manitou, Okemos, MI 48864 (SAN 247-7858) Tel 517-349-1254.

Argonauts OTMI, *(Argonauts, O.T.M.I.; 0-9621990),* 1616 NW 67th St., Seattle, WA 98166 Tel 209-278-2105.

Argos Pub Co, *(Argos Publishing Co.; 0-915509),* Subs. of Aaron E. Freeman, Inc., 1156 Sidonia Ct., Leucadia, CA 92024 (SAN 291-0764) Tel 619-436-4271.

Ariana Prods, *(Ariana Productions; 0-916549),* P.O. Box 18627, Cleveland, OH 44118 (SAN 295-5350) Tel 216-283-5563.

Ariel Vamp Pr, *(Ariel Vamp Pr.; 0-9618752),* P.O. Box 3496, Berkeley, CA 94703 (SAN 668-7016) Tel 415-654-4849.

Arion Pr, *(Arion Pr.; 0-910457),* 460 Bryant St., San Francisco, CA 94107 (SAN 203-1361) Tel 415-777-9651.

Arlie Enter, *(Arlie Enterprises; 1-880175),* P.O. Box 360933, Strongsville, OH 44136 (SAN 297-4665); 17035 Raccoon Trail, Strongsville, OH 44136 (SAN 297-4673) Tel 216-238-9397.

Arlington Pr, *(Arlington Pr.; 0-9629992),* 1021 Arlington Blvd., No. 723, Arlington, VA 22209 Tel 703-522-7238.

Armstrong Assocs, *(Armstrong Assocs.; 0-925390),* P.O. Box 20174, Village of Oak Creek, AZ 86341; 240 Arrowhead Dr., Village of Oak Creek, AZ 86341 Tel 602-284-1557.

ARO Pub, *(ARO Publishing Co.; 0-89868),* Box 193, 398 S. 1100 W., Provo, UT 84601 (SAN 212-6370) Tel 801-377-8218; Toll free: 800-338-7317. *Imprints:* Read Res (Reading Research).

Aronson, *(Aronson, Jason, Inc.; 0-87668),* 230 Livingston St., Northvale, NJ 07647 (SAN 201-0127) Tel 201-767-4093; Orders to: 1205 O'Neill Hwy., Dunmore, PA 18512 (SAN 665-6536) Tel 717-342-1449; Toll free: 800-782-0015. Do not confuse with J. H. Aronson, Highmount, NY.

Arpel Gra CO *Imprint of R Rinehart Inc*

Arrants & Assoc, *(Arrants & Assoc.; 0-943704),* 16576 SE 19th St., Bellevue, WA 98008 (SAN 238-3675) Tel 206-644-1664.

Arraster Pub, *(Arrastar Publishing Co.; 0-9622596),* P.O. Box 916, Everett, WA 98206; Toll free: 800-245-0970 (Washington only); 2621 Grand, Everett, WA 98201 Tel 206-339-3637.

Arrays-Continent, *(Arrays, Inc./Continental Software; 0-88688),* 6711 Valjean Ave., Van Nuys, CA 91406 (SAN 265-0398) Tel 818-994-1899.

Arrigo CA, *(Arrigo, Hargreaves, Nishimura),* 21561 Balerma, Mission Viejo, CA 92692-1045 (SAN 663-4680) Tel 714-661-2751.

Arrow Press, *(Arrow Pr.; 0-940319),* P.O. Box 899, Pollock Pines, CA 95726 (SAN 664-323X) Tel 916-644-2341. Do not confuse with Arrow Pr., San Francisco, CA.

Arrowhead Pub, *(Arrowhead Publishing; 0-9623819),* 3643 Corral Canyon, Bonita, CA 92002 Tel 619-479-3331.

Art After Five, *(Art After Five; 0-9628710),* 1507 Marseille Pl., Dallas, TX 75204 Tel 214-826-0541.

Art & Earth, *(Art & Earth, Inc.; 0-926246),* 65 S. Main St., Payson, UT 84651 Tel 801-465-4633.

Art & Entertainment, *(Art & Entertainment Information of the United States; 0-9623944),* P.O. Box 1909, Los Angeles, CA 90078-1909 Tel 213-255-2537.

Art & Ref, *(Art & Reference Hse.; 0-910156),* 2453 W. Five Mile Pkwy., Dallas, TX 75233 (SAN 203-4921).

Art Ltd, *(Art, Ltd.; 0-9627043),* No. 8 Henderson Pl., New York, NY 10028 Tel 212-734-6165.

Art Room Pubns, *(Art Room Pubns.; 0-9620766),* 200 S. Rogers, Waxahachie, TX 75165 (SAN 249-7646) Tel 214-923-0744.

Arte Publico, *(Arte Publico Pr.; 0-934770; 1-55885),* Div. of Univ. of Houston, Univ. of Houston, 4800 Calhoun, Houston, TX 77204 (SAN 213-4594) Tel 713-749-4768.

Artisan IL, *(Artisan; 0-9621575),* 2221 Blacksmith Dr., Wheaton, IL 60187 (SAN 251-8287) Tel 708-690-8975.

Artist Profile Pub, *(Artist Profile Publishing; 1-878431),* 397 N. 14th St., Las Vegas, NV 89101 Tel 702-598-4393.

Artistic Endeavors, *(Artistic Endeavors; 0-9604500),* 114 Oakmoore Ct., Bel Air, MD 21014 (SAN 207-5733) Tel 301-836-7008.

Artists Registry, *(Artists Registry, Inc.; 0-9623079),* P.O. Box 8833, Wichita, KS 67208 Tel 316-267-1643.

Arts & Comns NY, *(Arts & Communications Network, Inc.; 0-9627366),* P.O. Box 435, Rosendale, NY 12472; 501 Mossy Brook Rd., Highfalls, NY 12440 Tel 914-687-0767.

Arts Factory, *(Arts Factory; 0-9615873),* 23604 49th Pl., W., Mountlake Terrace, WA 98043 (SAN 696-6802) Tel 206-778-7857; P.O. Box 55547, Seattle, WA 98155 (SAN 696-9836); Dist. by: Pacific Pipeline, Inc., 19215 66th. Ave., S., Kent, WA 98032 (SAN 208-2128) Tel 206-872-5523; Toll free: 800-562-4647 (in Washington); 800-426-4727 (in northern California, Nevada, Idaho, Montana, Oregon); Dist. by: Green Tiger Pr., Inc., 200 Old Tappan Rd., Old Tappan, NJ 07675-7005 (SAN 219-4775) Tel 619-744-7575; Toll free: 800-424-2443 (except California).

Arts Pubns, *(Arts Pubns.; 0-9607458; 1-878079),* 80 Piedmont Ct., Larkspur, CA 94939 (SAN 238-003X) Tel 415-924-2633; Dist. by: Educational Bk. Distributors, P.O. Box 551, San Mateo, CA 94401 (SAN 158-2259) Tel 415-344-8458.

ArtsAmerica, *(ArtsAmerica, Inc.; 0-942475),* 12 Havemeyer Pl., Greenwich, CT 06830 (SAN 667-1039) Tel 203-869-4693.

Arundel Pr, *(Arundel Pr.; 0-923980),* 11349 Santa Monica Blvd., Los Angeles, CA 90025 (SAN 252-175X) Tel 213-477-1640.

Aschley Pr, *(Aschley Pr., The; 0-940900),* 2898 Kingsley Rd., Cleveland, OH 44122 (SAN 223-1735) Tel 216-752-3535.

Ascot Pr, *(Ascot Pr.; 0-9613538),* 40 Mountain View Rd., Glastonbury, CT 06033 (SAN 669-7194) Tel 203-633-6911.

Ashley Bks, *(Ashley Bks., Inc.; 0-87949),* 4600 W. Commercial Blvd., Fort Lauderdale, FL 33319 (SAN 201-1409) Tel 305-739-2221; Orders to: P.O. Box 490659, Fort Lauderdale, FL 33349-0650 (SAN 201-1417).

Asia Resource, *(Asia Resource Ctr.; 0-9604518),* P.O. Box 15275, Washington, DC 20003 (SAN 207-7647) Tel 202-547-1114.

Askeladd Pr, *(Askeladd Pr.; 0-9619327),* Hwy. 74 N. & First St., W., Saint Charles, MN 55972 (SAN 243-7589) Tel 507-932-4099.

ASP PA, *(ASP; 1-878109),* P.O. Box 81270, Pittsburgh, PA 15217 Tel 412-422-4134.

Aspen Prods, *(Aspen Productions; 0-913635),* 7501 Monogram Dr., Sacramento, CA 95842 (SAN 286-0384) Tel 916-338-0212; P.O. Box 41289, Sacramento, CA 95841 (SAN 241-9203).

Assist Lea Bellingham, *(Assistance League of Bellingham; 0-9623545),* 6816 Buide Meridian, Lynden, WA 98264 Tel 206-398-1050.

Assn Family Living, *(Association for the Study of Family Living, The; 0-9602670),* P.O. Box 130, Brooklyn, NY 11208 (SAN 212-8772) Tel 718-647-7406.

Assoc Bk, *(Associated Booksellers; 0-87497),* Div. of Queue, Inc., 338 Commerce Dr., Fairfield, CT 06430 (SAN 203-5014) Tel 203-333-7268; Toll free: 800-232-2224.

Astor Bks, *(Astor Bks.; 0-943351),* 4 Deerwood Ln., Woodbury, CT 06798 (SAN 668-5439) Tel 203-263-4286. Do not confuse with Astor Bks., New York, NY.

Astor-Honor, *(Astor-Honor, Inc.; 0-8392),* 48 E. 43rd St., New York, NY 10017 (SAN 203-5022) Tel 212-687-6190.

Astor Pubns, *(Astor Pubns.; 0-9619757),* P.O. Box 840, Astor, FL 32002 (SAN 246-5434); 56411 Branch Rd., Astor, FL 32002 (SAN 246-5442) Tel 904-759-3369.

Atheneum *Imprint of* **Macmillan**

Atheneum Child Bk *Imprint of* **Macmillan Child Grp**

Athletic Inst, *(Athletic Institute; 0-87670),* 200 Castlewood Dr., North Palm Beach, FL 33408 (SAN 203-5065) Tel 407-842-3600; Toll free: 800-933-3335.

Athletics Cong, *(Athletics Congress/U.S.A.; 0-939256),* P.O. Box 120, Indianapolis, IN 46206 (SAN 220-164X) Tel 317-261-0500.

Atlan Formularies, *(Atlan Formularies),* P.O. Box 327, Harrison, AR 72601 (SAN 250-9156) Tel 501-743-2700.

Atlan States MFC, *(Atlantic States Marine Fisheries Commission; 0-9630072),* 1400 Sixteenth St. NW, Suite 310, Washington, DC 20036 Tel 202-387-5330.

Atlantic Monthly, *(Atlantic Monthly Pr.; 0-87113),* Affil. of Navarre Atlantic Co., 19 Union Sq. W., 11th Flr., New York, NY 10003 (SAN 226-4587) Tel 212-645-4462.

Atomic Bks, *(Atomic Bks.; 0-945474),* P.O. Box 505-A, Montpelier, VT 05602 (SAN 247-1701) Tel 802-223-1010.

Atomium Bks, *(Atomium Bks., Inc.; 1-56182),* 1013 Centre Rd., Suite 300, Wilmington, DE 19805 Tel 302-998-0592.

Aton Pr, *(Aton Pr.; 0-9626580),* P.O. Box 1723, Grafton, VA 23692-1723; 407 Wormley Creek Dr., Yorktown, VA 23692 Tel 804-898-6083.

Atrium Pubns, *(Atrium Pubns.; 0-942941),* P.O. Box 816, Middlebury, VT 05753 (SAN 667-9412) Tel 802-388-0922; Dist. by: New Leaf Distributing Co., 5425 Tulane Dr., SW, Atlanta, GA 30336-2323 (SAN 169-1449) Tel 404-691-6996; Toll free: 800-326-2665; Dist. by: Baker & Taylor Bks., Eastern Div., 50 Kirby Ave., Somerville, NJ 08876-0734 (SAN 169-4901) Tel 201-722-8000; Toll free: 800-435-1845; 800-352-4833 (in New Jersey); Dist. by: Book Hse., Inc., The, 208 W. Chicago St., Jonesville, MI 49250-0125 (SAN 169-3859) Tel 517-849-2117; Toll free: 800-248-1146; Dist. by: Brodart Co., 500 Arch St., Williamsport, PA 17705 (SAN 169-7684) Tel 717-326-2461; Toll free: 800-233-8467; Dist. by: Coutts Library Service, Inc., 736 Cayuga St., Lewiston, NY 14092 (SAN 169-5401) Tel 716-754-8145; Dist. by: DeVorss & Co., P.O. Box 550, Marina Del Rey, CA 90294-0550 (SAN 168-9886) Tel 213-870-7478; Toll free: 800-843-5743; 800-331-4719 (in California) bookstores only; Dist. by: Inland Bk. Co., 140 Commerce St., East Haven, CT 06512 (SAN 200-4151) Tel 203-467-4257; Toll free: 800-243-0138; Dist. by: Ingram Book Co., 1125 Heil Quaker Blvd., La Vergne, TN 37086-1986 (SAN 169-4243) Tel 615-793-5000; Toll free: 800-876-0186.

ATS Pub, *(ATS Publishing Co.; 0-9629089),* Div. of Teenie Tennis, P.O. Box 2285, Redmond, WA 98073-2285; 16219 NE 95th Ct., Redmond, WA 98052 Tel 206-881-1446.

Augsburg *Imprint of* **Augsburg Fortress**

Augsburg Fortress, *(Augsburg Fortress Pubs.; 0-8066; 0-8006),* Subs. of Publishing Hse. of The Evangelical Lutheran Church in America, 426 S. Fifth St., Box 1209, Minneapolis, MN 55440 (SAN 169-4081) Tel 612-330-3300; Toll free: 800-328-4648; Orders to: 57 E. Main St., Columbus, OH 43215 Tel 614-221-7411; Toll free: 800-848-2738; 800-282-7414 (in Ohio); Orders to: 5210 N. Lamar, P.O. Box 49337, Austin, TX 78765 Tel 512-459-1112; Toll free: 800-531-5461; 800-252-9739 (in Texas); Orders to: 2900 Queen Ln., Philadelphia, PA 19129 Tel 215-848-6800; Toll free: 800-367-8737. *Imprints:* Augsburg (Augsburg); Fortress Pr (Fortress Press).

August Hse, *(August Hse.; 0-935304; 0-87483),* P.O. Box 3223, Little Rock, AR 72203-3223 (SAN 223-7288) Tel 501-372-5450; Toll free: 800-284-8784.

August Pubns, *(August Pubns.; 0-9613902),* P.O. Box 3315, Newport, RI 02840-3315 (SAN 686-290X).

Aurelon, *(Aurelon Tales; 0-912388),* Div. of Aurelon Bedford Corp., R.F.D. No. 3, 177 Sarles St., Mt. Kisco, NY 10549 (SAN 203-509X) Tel 914-241-3786.

Aurobindo Assn, *(Sri Aurobindo Assn., Inc.; 0-89071),* 2550 Ninth St., Suite 206, Berkeley, CA 94710 (SAN 169-5541) Tel 415-848-1841.

Auromere, *(Auromere, Inc.; 0-89744),* 1291 Weber St., Pomona, CA 91768 (SAN 169-0043) Tel 714-629-8255; Toll free: 800-243-0138; Dist. by: Bookpeople, 2929 Fifth St., Berkeley, CA 94710 (SAN 168-9517) Tel 415-549-3030; Toll free: 800-999-4650; Dist. by: DeVorss & Co., P.O. Box 550, Marina del Rey, CA 90292 (SAN 168-9886) Tel 213-870-7478; Toll free: 800-843-5743; 800-331-4719 (in California); Dist. by: New Leaf Distributing Co., 5425 Tulane Dr., SW, Atlanta, GA 30336-2323 (SAN 169-1449) Tel 404-691-6996; Toll free: 800-326-2665; Dist. by: Samuel Weiser, Inc., P.O. Box 612, York Beach, ME 03910 (SAN 202-9588) Tel 207-363-4393; Toll free: 800-423-7087 (orders only); Dist. by: Inland Bk. Co., 140 Commerce St., East Haven, CT 06512 (SAN 200-4151) Tel 203-467-4257; Toll free: 800-677-3232; Dist. by: Distributors, The, 702 S. Michigan, South Bend, IN 46618 (SAN 169-2488) Tel 219-232-8500; Toll free: 800-348-5200; Dist. by: Starlite Distributors, P.O. Box 6750, Auburn, CA 05604-6750 (SAN 200-7789) Tel 916-888-8002; Toll free: 800-234-7827 (orders only).

Australian Book
See Terra Nova

Auto Bk, *(Auto Bk. Pr.; 0-910390),* P.O. Bin 711, San Marcos, CA 92069-0711 (SAN 201-1263) Tel 619-744-3582.

Automatic Manuals, *(Automatic Manuals),* P.O. Box 15315, Gainesville, FL 32604 (SAN 245-5986) Tel 904-374-8703.

Avalon Hill, *(Avalon Hill Pubs.; 0-911605; 1-56038),* Div. of Avalon Hill Game Co., 4517 Harford Rd., Baltimore, MD 21214 (SAN 204-4633) Tel 301-254-5300; Toll free: 800-638-9292; Dist. by: Ingram Bk. Co., 1125 Heilquaker Blvd., La Vergne, TN 37086 (SAN 169-7978) Tel 615-793-5000; Toll free: 800-937-8000.

Ave Maria, *(Ave Maria Pr.; 0-87793),* Campus of Notre Dame, Notre Dame, IN 46556 (SAN 201-1255) Tel 219-287-2831; Toll free: 800-282-1865.

Avis & Ward, *(Avis & Ward Nutrition Assocs., Inc.; 0-9628683),* 200 Professional Dr., West Monroe, LA 71291 Tel 318-323-7949; Dist. by: Wimmer Bros., 4210 B. F. Goodrich Blvd., Memphis, TN 38118 (SAN 630-5369) Tel 901-362-8900.

Avitar Bks, *(Avitar Bks.; 0-9614089),* P.O. Box 222073, Carmel, CA 93922 (SAN 685-9968) Tel 408-625-1666.

Avon, *(Avon Bks.; 0-380),* Div. of Hearst Corp., 1350 Ave. of the Americas, 2nd Fl., New York, NY 10019 (SAN 201-4009) Tel 212-261-6851; Toll free: 800-238-0658; Dist. by: Hearst Corp., International Circulation Div., 250 W. 55th St., 12th Flr., New York, NY 10019 (SAN 169-5800); Toll free: 800-223-0288; Orders to: P.O. Box 767, Dresden, TN 38225 (SAN 241-628X); Toll free: 800-223-0690. *Imprints:* Bard (Avon Bard Books); Camelot (Avon Camelot Books); Discus (Avon Discus Books); Flare (Avon Flare Books).

Avosett Bks, *(Avosett Bks.; 0-9625824),* 3413 45th Ave., W., Seattle, WA 98199 Tel 206-282-3777.

AVSTAR Pub, *(AVSTAR Publishing Corp.; 0-9623653; 1-878827),* P.O. Box 537, Lebanon, NJ 08833; 34C Burlinghoff Ln., Lebanon, NJ 08833 Tel 908-236-6210.

Awani Pr, *(Awani Pr.; 0-915266),* P.O. Box 881, Fredericksburg, TX 78624 (SAN 206-4626) Tel 512-997-5514.

AWE Pub, *(AWE Publishing Co.; 0-9626253),* Rte. 2, Comanche, TX 76442 Tel 512-656-3385.

Axelrod Pub, *(Axelrod Publishing of Tampa Bay; 0-936417),* 1304 De Soto Ave., No. 308, Tampa, FL 33606 (SAN 698-1658) Tel 813-251-5269; P.O. Box 14248, Tampa, FL 33690 (SAN 698-2611); Dist. by: Quality Bks., Inc., 918 Sherwood Dr., Lake Bluff, IL 60044-2204 (SAN 169-2127) Tel 708-295-2010; Toll free: 800-323-4241 (Libraries only); Dist. by: Baker & Taylor Bks., Eastern Div., 50 Kirby Ave., Somerville, NJ 08876 (SAN 169-4901) Tel 201-722-8000; Toll free: 800-435-1845; 800-352-4833 (in New Jersey); Dist. by: Baker & Taylor Bks., Midwestern Div., 501 S. Gladiolus St., Momence, IL 60954 (SAN 169-2100) Tel 815-472-2444; Toll free: 800-435-5111; 800-892-1892 (in Illinois); Dist. by: Baker & Taylor Bks., Southern Div., Mt. Olive Rd., Commerce, GA 30529 (SAN 169-1503) Tel 404-335-5000; Toll free: 800-241-6004; 800-282-6850 (in Georgia); Dist. by: Baker & Taylor Bks., Western Div., 380 Edison Way, Reno, NV 89564 (SAN 169-4464) Tel 702-786-6700; Toll free: 800-648-3540; Dist. by: Brodart Co., 500 Arch St., Williamsport, PA 17705 (SAN 169-7684) Tel 717-326-2461; Toll free: 800-233-8467.

Axiom Info Res, *(Axiom Information Resources; 0-943213),* P.O. Box 8015, Ann Arbor, MI 48107 (SAN 668-3088) Tel 313-761-4842.

Ayer Co Pubs, *(Ayer Co. Pubs., Inc.; 0-88143),* P.O. Box 958, Salem, NH 03079 (SAN 211-6936) Tel 603-669-5933.

AZ Hist Foun, *(Arizona Historical Foundation; 0-910152),* Hayden Memorial Library, Arizona State Univ., Tempe, AZ 85287 (SAN 201-7040) Tel 602-966-8331.

Azalar Pub, *(Azalar Publishing; 0-9624831),* P.O. Box 812, HCR30, Sedona, AZ 86336; 1706 Willow Dr., Cornville, AZ 86325 Tel 602-282-2321.

AZU Music Pr, *(Arizona Univ. Music Pr.; 0-943121),* Univ. of Arizona, Schl. of Music, Tucson, AZ 85721 (SAN 668-0933) Tel 602-621-5942.

B A Scott, *(Scott, Beverly A., Pub.),* P.O. Box 114, Chandler, AZ 85224 (SAN 207-6101) Tel 602-963-5787.

B & D Pub, *(B & D Publishing; 0-9613328),* 1915 Solano St., Suite B, Corning, CA 96021 (SAN 289-5854) Tel 916-824-1410.

B & R Samizdat, *(B & R Samizdat Express; 0-915232),* P.O. Box 161, West Roxbury, MA 02132 (SAN 207-1037) Tel 617-469-2269.

B B Saloom, *(Saloom, Barbara B.; 0-9627755),* 18 Hollow Tree Rd., Boxford, MA 01921 Tel 508-887-2581.

B B Stabell, *(Stabell, Brenda B.; 0-9610872),* 10827 Overbrook, Houston, TX 77042 (SAN 264-407X).

B B Williams, *(Williams, Bradley B.; 0-9620486),* 104B Simpson St., Greenville, SC 29605 (SAN 248-8531) Tel 803-269-3336.

B Bk Pub Co, *(B. Bk. Publishing Co.; 0-9625337),* P.O. Box 858, Stratford, CT 06497; 200 Glendale Rd., Stratford, CT 06497 Tel 203-261-7236.

B Brae, *(Bonnie Brae Pubns.; 0-944453),* Div. of DRG, Inc., 12 Pickens Ln., Weaverville, NC 28787 (SAN 243-6221) Tel 704-645-5293.

B Bumpers Inc, *(B. Bumpers, Inc.; 0-9621691),* 10309 Smokey Point Blvd., Suite B, Marysville, WA 98270 (SAN 251-8589) Tel 206-659-5528.

B C Pub Inc, *(B.C. Publishing, Inc.; 0-926521),* Rte. 3, Box 734, Broken Arrow, OK 74014; 26520 E. 57th St., Broken Arrow, OK 74014 Tel 918-357-3285.

B Crocker, *(Crocker, Betty),* Div. of Prentice Hall Pr., Simon & Schuster, Inc., 15 Columbus Cir., New York, NY 10023 Tel 212-373-8741.

B Cutlip, *(Cutlip, Burdette),* Box 215, Blackwoods, WV 26621 (SAN 668-3800) Tel 304-765-5828.

B Dolphin Pub, *(Blue Dolphin Publishing, Inc.; 0-931892),* P.O. Box 1908, Nevada City, CA 95959 (SAN 223-2480); 13386 N. Bloomfield Rd., Nevada City, CA 95959 (SAN 696-009X) Tel 916-265-6923; Orders to: 12380 Nevada City Hwy., Grass Valley, CA 95945 (SAN 169-4901); Dist. by: Baker & Taylor Bks., Eastern Div., 6 Kirby Ave., Somerville, NJ 08876 (SAN 169-4901) Tel 201-526-8000; Toll free: 800-333-7755; Dist. by: Distributors, The, 702 S. Michigan, South Bend, IN 46618 (SAN 169-2488) Tel 219-232-8500; Toll free: 800-348-5200 (outside IN); Dist. by: Bookpeople, 2929 Fifth St., Berkeley, CA 94710 (SAN 168-9517) Tel 415-549-3030; Toll free: 800-999-4650; Dist. by: New Leaf Distributing Co., 5425 Tulane Dr., SW, Atlanta, GA 30336-2323 (SAN 169-1449) Tel 404-691-6996; Toll free: 800-326-2665; Dist. by: Quality Bks., 918 Sherwood Dr., Lake Bluff, IL 60044-2204 (SAN 169-2127) Tel 708-295-2010; Toll free: 800-323-4241 (Libraries only); Dist. by: Moving Bks., 948 S. Doris St., Seattle, WA 98108 (SAN 159-0685) Tel 206-762-1750; Toll free: 800-777-6683; Dist. by: Ingram Bk. Co., 1125 Heilquaker Blvd., La Vergne, TN 37086 (SAN 169-7978) Tel 615-793-5000; Toll free: 800-525-6979 (west of the Mississippi); Dist. by: Inland Bk. Co., 140 Commerce St., East Haven, CT 06512 (SAN 200-4151) Tel 203-467-4257; Toll free: 800-937-8000 (orders only).

B G Keogh, *(Keogh, Brian G.; 0-9625072),* P.O. Box 0334, Baldwin, NY 11510; 2363 S. Grand Ave., No. 23-B3, Baldwin, NY 11510 Tel 516-868-1699.

B Hawkins Studio, *(Hawkins, Beverly, Studio & Gallery; 0-9608084),* 20104 Halloway Ave., Matoaca, VA 23803 (SAN 240-1495) Tel 804-861-9403; Orders to: 2557E S. Crater Rd., Petersburg, VA 23803 (SAN 665-7087).

B Hegne, *(Hegne, Barbara; 0-9623847),* 130 Onyx St., Eagle Point, OR 97524 Tel 503-826-9725.

B K Cho, *(Cho, Byung Kon; 0-9625199),* 2960 Allied Dr., Green Bay, WI 54304 Tel 414-336-0551.

B L Winch, *(Winch, B. L., & Assocs.; 0-935266),* 45 Hitching Post Dr., Bldg. 2, Rolling Hills Estates, CA 90274-4297 (SAN 247-2716) Tel 213-547-1240.

B Leahy, *(Leahy, Barbara; 0-9610312),* 15 Mission Rd., Sedona, AZ 86336 (SAN 264-1720) Tel 602-282-3518.

B Melger, *(Melger, Boyd; 0-9622463),* 3030 Bradshaw Dr., San Jose, CA 95148 Tel 408-270-3816.

B Ponce, *(Ponce, Blanca; 0-9622493),* 453 Jose B. Acevedo, Rio Piedras, PR 00923 Tel 809-763-7993.

B Scherer, *(Scherer, Bonnie; 0-9622421),* 1021 Alderson, Billings, MT 59102 Tel 406-245-7289.

B Scott Bks, *(Scott, Bob, Bks.; 0-9621201),* P.O. Box 3462, San Clemente, CA 92672 (SAN 250-6866); 201 Calle Dorado, San Clemente, CA 92672 (SAN 250-6874) Tel 714-492-8781.

B Segal, *(Segal, Berty, Inc.; 0-938395),* 1749 Eucalyptus St., Brea, CA 92621 (SAN 630-0553) Tel 714-529-5359.

B Sheldon, *(Sheldon, Bill, Pub.; 0-9616668),* 5478 Mary Jo Way, San Jose, CA 95124 (SAN 659-9079) Tel 408-264-2728.

B Williams, *(Williams, Bill; 0-9622114),* 1055 Linda St., Ashland, OR 97520 Tel 503-482-9842.

B Winston, *(Winston, Barbara; 0-9622810),* 19774 Cheyenne, Detroit, MI 48235 Tel 313-863-8832; Dist. by: School Hse., 19363 Livernois, Detroit, MI 48221 (SAN 630-3498) Tel 313-342-1261.

Babe Co, *(Babe Co.; 0-9620258),* P.O. Box 48381, Washington, DC 20002 (SAN 248-3203); 1005 F St., NE, Washington, DC 20002 (SAN 248-3211) Tel 202-543-5605.

Back Bay, *(Back Bay Bks., Inc.; 0-939126),* P.O. Box 1396, Newport Beach, CA 92663 (SAN 216-1060) Tel 714-645-4900.

Back to Bible, *(Back to the Bible Broadcast; 0-8474),* Box 82808, Lincoln, NE 68501 (SAN 211-6901); Toll free: 800-728-2425; 301 S. 12th St., Lincoln, NE 68508 Tel 402-474-4567.

Backroads, *(Backroads; 0-933294),* Box 14, Kelly, WY 83011 (SAN 213-831X) Tel 307-733-7730. Do not confuse with Backroads, Corte Madera, CA.

Backwards & Backwards, *(Backwards & Backwards Pr.; 0-910253),* 7561 Pearl Rd., Cleveland, OH 44130 (SAN 241-4724) Tel 216-243-5335.

Backyard Music, *(Backyard Music; 0-9614939),* P.O. Box 9047, New Haven, CT 06532 (SAN 693-6776) Tel 203-469-5756.

Backyard Scientist, *(Backyard Scientist/Jane Hoffman; 0-9618663),* P.O. Box 16966, Irvine, CA 92713 (SAN 219-1725); 14652 Beach Ave., Irvine, CA 92714 (SAN 667-4461) Tel 714-551-2392.

Baggeboda Pr, *(Baggeboda Pr.; 0-932591),* 107 N. Pine St., Little Rock, AR 72205 (SAN 687-505X) Tel 501-664-8183.

Baggiani-Tewell, *(Baggiani-Tewell Educational Materials; 0-934329),* 4 Spring Hill Ct., Chevy Chase, MD 20815 (SAN 693-6024) Tel 301-656-3353.

Baha'i, *(Baha'i Publishing Trust; 0-87743),* 415 Linden Ave., Wilmette, IL 60091 (SAN 213-7496) Tel 708-251-1854; Toll free: 800-999-9019.

Bainbridge Pr, *(Bainbridge Pr.; 1-877851),* 3500 First Interstate Ctr., 999 Third Ave., Seattle, WA 98104-4038 Tel 206-223-4600.

Bakebks & Cookbks, *(Bakebooks & Cookbooks, Inc.; 0-9606686),* P.O. Box 92185, Milwaukee, WI 53202 (SAN 219-7111) Tel 414-461-9813.

Baker Bk, *(Baker Bk. Hse.; 0-8010),* P.O. Box 6287, Grand Rapids, MI 49516-6287 (SAN 201-4041) Tel 616-676-9185; Toll free: 800-877-2665.

Baker Seaforth, *(Baker Seaforth Pubns.; 0-9623980),* HC 72, Box 43, Clinton, AR 72031 Tel 501-745-4035.

Bala Bks, *(Bala Bks.; 0-89647),* P.O. Box 311, Old Westbury, NY 11568 (SAN 284-9747) Tel 516-334-0909; Orders to: Bala Bks., 12520 Kirkham Court, Suite 7, Poway, CA 92064 Tel 619-679-9080.

Balaena Bks, *(Balaena Bks., Inc.; 0-9624094),* P.O. Box 1633, New Smyrna Beach, FL 32170; 4444 Sea Mist Dr., New Smyrna Beach, FL 32170 Tel 904-427-8798.

Balance Pub, *(Balance Publishing Co.; 1-878298),* 1346 S. Quality Ave., Sanger, CA 93657 Tel 209-875-4828; Dist. by: Entry Publishing, Inc., 27 W. 96th St., New York, NY 10025 (SAN 238-9754) Tel 212-662-9703.

Baldner J V, *(Baldner, Jean V.; 0-9615317),* 19203 N. 29th Ave., Phoenix, AZ 85027 (SAN 694-6526) Tel 602-582-0312.

Ballantine, *(Ballantine Bks., Inc.; 0-345),* Div. of Random Hse., Inc., 201 E. 50th St., New York, NY 10022 (SAN 214-1175) Tel 212-572-2620; Toll free: 800-726-0600 (customer service); 800-733-3000 (orders); Orders to: 400 Hahn Rd., Westminster, MD 21157 (SAN 214-1183) Tel 301-848-1900. *Imprints:* Del Rey (Del Rey Books).

Ballyhoo Bks, *(Ballyhoo Bks.; 0-936335),* P.O. Box 534, Shoreham, NY 11786 (SAN 697-8487); 1 Sylvan Dr., Wading River, NY 11792 (SAN 698-2239) Tel 516-929-8148.

BAN Pub Boston, *(BAN Publishing Co.; 0-983357),* 6 Rollins Pl., Boston, MA 02114 (SAN 698-178X) Tel 617-227-1332.

Bang A Drum, *(Bang A Drum Enterprises; 1-878130),* Div. of KMC Ideas, Inc., 815 Yale Ave., Terrace Park, OH 45174 Tel 513-248-0277.

Bank St Pr, *(Bank Street Pr., The; 0-935505),* 24 Bank St., New York, NY 10014 (SAN 696-0634) Tel 212-255-0692.

Banksiana, *(Banksiana Publishing Co.; 0-9627867),* 611 22 3/4 St., P.O. Box 804, Chetek, WI 54728 Tel 715-924-4668.

Banmar Inc, *(Banmar Inc.; 0-9614989),* 4239 Monroe St., Toledo, OH 43606 (SAN 693-7594) Tel 419-473-2940.

Banner of Truth, *(Banner of Truth, The; 0-85151),* P.O. Box 621, Carlisle, PA 17013 (SAN 112-1553) Tel 717-249-5747.

Bantam, *(Bantam Bks., Inc.; 0-553),* Div. of Bantam Doubleday Dell, 666 Fifth Ave., New York, NY 10103 (SAN 201-3975) Tel 212-765-6500; Toll free: 800-223-6834; Orders to: 414 E. Golf Rd., Des Plaines, IL 60016 (SAN 201-3983). *Imprints:* Bantam Classics (Bantam Classics); Falcon (Bantam Falcon); Little Rooster (Little Rooster); Loveswept (Loveswept); Skylark (Skylark); Spectra (Spectra); Starfire (Starfire); Sweet Dreams (Sweet Dreams).

Bantam Classics Imprint of **Bantam**

Banyan Bks, *(Banyan Bks.; 0-916224),* P.O. Box 431160, Miami, FL 33243 (SAN 208-340X) Tel 305-665-6011.

Baptist Pub Hse, *(Baptist Publishing Hse.; 0-89114),* Div. of Baptist Missionary Assn. of America, 1319 Magnolia St., Texarkana, TX 75501-4493 (SAN 183-6544) Tel 903-793-6531; Toll free: 800-333-1442.

Barbour & Co, *(Barbour & Co., Inc.; 0-916441; 1-55748),* Affil. of Book Bargains, Inc., 164 Mill St., P.O. Box 1219, Westwood, NJ 07675 (SAN 295-7094) Tel 201-664-0577; Toll free: 800-221-2648; Dist. by: Spring Arbor Distributors, 10885 Textile Rd., Belleville, MI 48111 (SAN 158-9016) Tel 313-481-0900; Toll free: 800-395-9955; Dist. by: Ingram Bk. Co., 1125 Heilquaker Blvd., La Vergne, TN 37086 (SAN 169-7978) Tel 615-793-5000; Toll free: 800-937-8000 (orders only); Dist. by: Baker & Taylor Bks., Eastern Div., 50 Kirby Ave., Somerville, NJ 08876 (SAN 169-4901) Tel 201-722-8000; Toll free: 800-435-1845; 800-352-4833 (in New Jersey); Dist. by: Riverside/World, 3040 Charlevoix Dr., Grand Rapids, MI 49546 (SAN 169-2666) Tel 616-940-2086; Toll free: 800-247-5111; Dist. by: Living Bks., Inc., 12155 Magnolia Ave., Bldg. 11-B, Riverside, CA 92503 (SAN 169-006X) Tel 714-354-7330; Toll free: 800-854-4746; 800-922-0047 (in California); Dist. by: Cicero Bible Pr., 1901 Airport Rd., Harrison, AR 72601 (SAN 170-3692) Tel 501-741-3400; Toll free: 800-643-9780.

Barclay Pr, *(Barclay Pr.; 0-913342),* Div. of Northwest Yearly Meeting of Friends Church, 600 E. Third St., Newberg, OR 97132 (SAN 201-7520) Tel 503-538-7345; Toll free: 800-962-4014.

Bard Imprint of **Avon**

Bard Hall Pr, *(Bard Hall Pr.; 0-916491),* 32 Nickerbocker at Oak, Tenafly, NJ 07670 (SAN 295-2459) Tel 201-567-7629; Dist. by: Persea Bks., Inc., 60 Madison Ave., New York, NY 10010 (SAN 212-8233) Tel 212-779-7668.

Barksdale Foun, *(Barksdale Foundation; 0-918588),* P.O. Box 187, Idyllwild, CA 92349 (SAN 210-1718) Tel 714-659-4676.

Barlenmir, *(Barlenmir Hse. Pubs.; 0-87929),* 413 City Island Ave., Bronx, NY 10464 (SAN 164-6044) Tel 212-885-2120.

Barmarle Pubns, *(Barmarle Pubns.; 0-9619463),* 735 Nardo Rd., Encinitas, CA 92024 (SAN 245-0070) Tel 619-753-6950.

Barnaby Bks, *(Barnaby Bks.; 0-940350),* 3290 Pacific Heights Rd., Honolulu, HI 96813 (SAN 217-5010) Tel 808-524-1490; Dist. by: Pacific Trade Group, 94-527 Puahi St., Waipahu, HI 96797 (SAN 169-1635) Tel 808-671-6735.

Barnwood Pr, *(Barnwood Pr. Cooperative; 0-935306),* 600 E. Washington, Muncie, IN 47305 (SAN 223-7245) Tel 317-288-0145.

Barrier & Kennedy, *(Barrier & Kennedy, ESL; 0-911743),* P.O. Box 58273, Raleigh, NC 27658 (SAN 276-9689) Tel 919-847-1477.

Barrington Hse, *(Barrington Hse. Publishing Co.; 0-935323),* 1119 Lorne Way, Sunnyvale, CA 94087 (SAN 695-7501) Tel 408-241-8422.

Barron, *(Barron's Educational Series, Inc.; 0-8120),* P.O. Box 8040, 250 Wireless Blvd., Hauppauge, NY 11788 (SAN 201-453X) Tel 516-434-3311; Toll free: 800-645-3476; 800-257-5729 (in New York).

Basic Comp Lit, *(Basic Computer Literacy, Inc.; 0-931983),* 370 N. Locust, Manteno, IL 60950 (SAN 686-0931) Tel 815-468-8178.

Basil Blackwell, *(Blackwell, Basil, Inc.; 0-631; 0-85520; 0-423; 0-900186; 0-904679; 0-7456; 0-233; 1-55786),* Subs. of Basil Blackwell, Ltd. (UK), 3 Cambridge Ctr., Cambridge, MA 02142 (SAN 680-5035) Tel 617-225-0430; Toll free: 800-638-3030; Dist. by: American International Distribution Corp., 64 Depot Rd., Colchester, VT 05446 (SAN 630-2238) Tel 802-878-0315; Toll free: 800-445-6638 (outside Canada & Vermont).

Basin Pub, *(Basin Publishing Co.; 0-940591),* 168 Weyford Terr., Garden City, NY 11530 (SAN 208-4562) Tel 516-741-0668.

Bassett & Brush, *(Bassett & Brush; 0-9605548),* W. 4108 Francis Ave., Spokane, WA 99205 (SAN 216-3349).

Batboy Pr, *(Batboy Pr.; 0-9629307),* 3 Beaver Pond Ct., New Freedom, PA 17349 Tel 717-993-3162.

Battelle, *(Battelle Pr.; 0-935470),* Div. of Battelle Memorial Institute, 505 King Ave., Columbus, OH 43201-2693 (SAN 213-4640) Tel 614-424-6393; Toll free: 800-451-3543.

Battledore Ltd, *(Battledore, Ltd.; 0-9627110),* P.O. Box 2288, Kingston, NY 12401; 77 W. Chestnut St., Kingston, NY 12401 Tel 914-339-6944.

Bauhan, *(Bauhan, William L., Inc.; 0-87233),* P.O. Box 443, Dublin, NH 03444-0443 (SAN 204-384X) Tel 603-563-8020.

Bayberry Pr, *(Bayberry Pr.; 0-916326),* 21 Little Fox Ln., Westport, CT 06880 (SAN 222-562X) Tel 203-226-5187. Do not confuse with Bayberry Pr., Port Washington, NY.

BaySailor Bks, *(BaySailor Bks.; 0-9618461),* P.O. Box 116, Royal Oak, MD 21662 (SAN 667-920X).

BCI-Bk Cook Inc, *(B.C.I./Bk. Cook, Inc.; 0-927008),* 3400 Trindle Rd., Camp Hill, PA 17011 Tel 717-737-9998; Dist. by: Hearst Corp., International Circulation Div., 250 W. 55th St., 12th Flr., New York, NY 10019 (SAN 169-5800) Tel 212-649-4474; Toll free: 800-223-0288.

BCM Pubn, *(BCM Pubn.; 0-86508),* 237 Fairfield Ave., Upper Darby, PA 19082 (SAN 211-7762) Tel 215-352-7177.

BCS Educ Aids, *(BCS Educational Aids, Inc.; 0-938416),* P.O. Box 100, Bothell, WA 98041 (SAN 239-9326) Tel 206-485-4110.

BDB Unlimited, *(BDB, Unlimited; 0-925022),* 2031 Rockhaven Dr., Decatur, GA 30032 Tel 404-458-3922.

BDD Promo Bk, *(BDD Promotional Bk. Co., Inc.; 0-7924),* Div. of Bantam Doubleday Dell, 666 Fifth Ave., 16th Flr., New York, NY 10103 (SAN 251-0650) Tel 212-765-6500; Toll free: 800-223-6834; Orders to: 1905 S. Prospect Rd., Des Plaines, IL 60018 (SAN 251-2874) Tel 708-803-1170; Toll free: 800-635-0256. *Imprints:* Mallard Pr (Mallard Press).

Bding Better People, *(Building Better People, Inc.; 0-9624760),* P.O. Box 2088, Newport Beach, CA 92663; 809 Promontory Dr., W., Newport Beach, CA 92660 Tel 503-673-3942.

Beachcomber Pr, *(Beachcomber Pr.; 0-9614628),* Box 500, Belgrade Rd., Oakland, ME 04963 (SAN 691-8891) Tel 207-465-7197; Dist. by: Magazines Inc., 1135 Hammond St., Bangor, ME 04401 (SAN 169-3034) Tel 207-942-8237; Toll free: 800-432-7993 (Maine only); Dist. by: Portland News Co., 270 Western Ave., P.O. Box 1728, South Portland, ME 04104 (SAN 169-3093) Tel 207-774-2633. Do not confuse with Beachcomber Pr. in Escondido, CA.

Beacon Bks, *(Beacon Bks.; 0-929311),* P.O. Box 555, Litchfield Park, AZ 85340 (SAN 248-9821); 220 Cardeno, Litchfield Park, AZ 85340 (SAN 248-983X) Tel 602-977-2380.

Beacon Hill, *(Beacon Hill Pr. of Kansas City; 0-8341),* Subs. of Nazarene Publishing Hse., P.O. Box 419527, Kansas City, MO 64141 (SAN 241-6328) Tel 816-931-1900.

Beacon Pr, *(Beacon Pr.; 0-8070),* 25 Beacon St., Boston, MA 02108 (SAN 201-4483) Tel 617-742-2110; Dist. by: Farrar, Straus & Giroux, Inc., 19 Union Sq., W., New York, NY 10003 (SAN 206-782X) Tel 212-741-6900; Toll free: 800-631-8571 (Rush orders).

Bead-Craft, *(Bead-Craft; 0-9613503),* 1549 Ashland Ave., Saint Paul, MN 55104 (SAN 657-2510) Tel 612-645-1216; Orders to: P.O. Box 4563, Saint Paul, MN 55104 (SAN 241-9629).

Bear Flag Bks, *(Bear Flag Bks.; 0-939919),* Subs. of Padre Productions, P.O. Box 840, Arroyo Grande, CA 93421-0840 Tel 805-473-1947. Do not confuse with Bear Flag Books, San Francisco, CA.

Bear Hollow Pr, *(Bear Hollow Pr.; 0-938209),* Subs. of Shuttle Hill Herb Shop, Inc., 110 Salisbury Rd., Delmar, NY 12054 (SAN 659-459X) Tel 518-439-9065.

Bear Paw Bks, *(Bear Paw Bks.; 0-9629760),* Div. of Bear Paw Quilts, 2289 Sunrise Point Rd., Las Cruces, NM 88001 Tel 505-522-1893.

Bear Tracks Pub, *(Bear Tracks Publishing Co.; 0-9617624),* 389 Greenfield Rd., Memphis, TN 38117 (SAN 664-9858) Tel 901-767-5160.

Bear Wallow Pub, *(Bear Wallow Publishing Co., The; 0-936376),* P.O. Box 370, Union, OR 97883 (SAN 223-3916) Tel 503-562-5687.

Beaufort Bks NY, *(Beaufort Bks., Pubs.; 0-8253),* 226 W. 26th St., New York, NY 10001 (SAN 215-2304). Out-of-Business.

Beautiful Am, *(Beautiful America Publishing Co.; 0-915796; 0-89802),* P.O. Box 646, Wilsonville, OR 97070 (SAN 251-2548); Toll free: 800-874-1233; 9725 SW Commerce Cir., Wilsonville, OR 97070 (SAN 211-4623) Tel 503-682-0173.

Beaver Valley, *(Beaver Valley Pubns.; 0-9622014),* Box 1015, 290th St., Glenwood City, WI 54013 Tel 715-772-4600.

Beavers, *(Beavers; 0-910208),* HCR 70, Box 537, La Porte, MN 56461 (SAN 202-389X) Tel 218-224-218270, .

Bedrick Blackie *Imprint of* **P Bedrick Bks**

Beeby Champ, *(Beeby-Champ Publishing; 0-944697),* P.O. Box 1714, Stillwater, OK 74076 (SAN 244-5700); 2911 N. Crescent Dr., Stillwater, OK 74075 (SAN 244-5719) Tel 405-624-2662.

Beechwood, *(Beechwood Bks.; 0-912221),* 720 Wehapa Cir., Leeds, AL 35094 (SAN 265-0797) Tel 205-699-6935.

Beeman Jorgensen, *(Beeman Jorgensen, Inc.; 0-929758),* 7510 Allisonville Rd., Indianapolis, IN 46250 (SAN 250-1279) Tel 317-841-7677.

Beginner, *(Beginner Bks.; 0-394),* Div. of Random Hse., Inc., 201 E. 50th St., New York, NY 10022 (SAN 202-3288) Tel 212-751-2600; Orders to: 400 Hahn Rd., Westminster, MD 21157 (SAN 202-3296) Tel 301-848-1900; Toll free: 800-733-3000 (orders).

Behavior Products, *(Behavior Products; 0-9621191),* 413 S. Vick Ln., Anaheim, CA 92804 (SAN 250-7471) Tel 714-826-5711.

Behrman, *(Behrman Hse., Inc.; 0-87441),* 235 Watchung Ave., West Orange, NJ 07052 (SAN 201-4459) Tel 201-669-0447; Toll free: 800-221-2755.

Bell Bks NY *Imprint of* **Boyds Mills Pr**

Bell Ent, *(Bell Enterprises, Inc.; 0-918340),* P.O. Box 9054, Pine Bluff, AR 71611 (SAN 209-1895) Tel 501-247-1922.

Bellerophon Bks, *(Bellerophon Bks.; 0-88388),* 36 Anacapa St., Santa Barbara, CA 93101 (SAN 202-392X) Tel 805-965-7034.

Bellwether UT, *(Bellwether Pubns.; 1-877822),* P.O. Box 280, Hyde Park, UT 84318; 12 W. 100 N., Hyde Park, UT 84318 Tel 801-563-6489.

Belnice Bks, *(Belnice Bks.; 0-941274),* 337 Eighth St., Manhattan Beach, CA 91711 (SAN 239-4103) Tel 213-379-5405.

Benmir Bks, *(Benmir Bks.; 0-917883),* 1529 Cypress St., Suite 105, Walnut Creek, CA 94596 (SAN 656-9641) Tel 415-933-5356.

Bennet Creek, *(Bennet Creek Publishing Co.; 0-9618450),* P.O. Box 6401, Cheyenne, WY 82003 (SAN 667-8890); 9211 Campstool Rd., Cheyenne, WY 82007 (SAN 667-8904) Tel 307-778-7675.

Bennett Il, *(Bennett Publishing Co.),* Div. of Macmillan Publishing Co., Inc., 866 Third Ave., New York, NY 10022 (SAN 201-4440).

Benson, *(Benson, W. S., & Co., Inc.; 0-87443),* P.O. Box 1866, Austin, TX 78767 (SAN 202-3989) Tel 512-476-5050.

Bentley, *(Bentley, Robert, Inc., Pubs.; 0-8376),* 1000 Massachusetts Ave., Cambridge, MA 02138 (SAN 213-9839) Tel 617-547-4170; Toll free: 800-423-4595.

Bentwerth Pr, *(Bentwerth Pr.; 1-878342),* P.O. Box 10321, Reno, NV 89510-0321 (SAN 297-2174); 13109 S. Virginia, No. 24, Reno, NV 89511 Tel 702-852-2129.

Bergh Pub, *(Bergh Publishing, Inc.; 0-930267),* 276 Fifth Ave., Suite 715, New York, NY 10001 (SAN 670-8633) Tel 212-686-8551.

Berkley Pub, *(Berkley Publishing Group; 0-425; 0-515),* 200 Madison Ave., New York, NY 10016 (SAN 201-3991) Tel 212-951-8966; Toll free: 800-631-8571; Dist. by: Warner Pub. Services, 810 Seventh Ave., New York, NY 10019 (SAN 200-5522) Tel 212-397-8676.

Berkshire Hse, *(Berkshire Hse. Pubs.; 0-936399),* P.O. Box 297, Stockbridge, MA 01262 (SAN 698-1666) Tel 413-298-3636; Dist. by: Publishers Group West, 4065 Hollis St., Emeryville, CA 94608 (SAN 202-8522) Tel 415-658-3453; Toll free: 800-365-3453.

Berry Bks, *(Berry Bks.; 0-9614746),* 114 Woodpecker Ln., Whispering Pines, NC 28327 (SAN 692-9214).

Berry Good Child Bks, *(Berry Good Children's Bks.; 0-9616555),* RR 2, P.O. Box 823, Lot 342, Coconut Creek, FL 33067 (SAN 659-4220); 6800 NW 39th Ave., Coconut Creek, FL 33067 (SAN 659-4239).

Bess Pr, *(Bess Pr., Inc.; 0-935848; 1-880188),* P.O. Box 22388, Honolulu, HI 96823 (SAN 239-4111); 2955 Dole St., Honolulu, HI 96816 (SAN 661-9584) Tel 808-734-7159.

Best Pubs Inc, *(Best Pubs., Inc.; 0-929281),* 6912 NW 46th St., Miami, FL 33166 (SAN 248-8469) Tel 305-592-7693.

Best Sllrs TX, *(Best Sellers Publishing, Inc.; 0-945362),* 11515 Sunnyside Dr., Baytown, TX 77520 (SAN 246-8387) Tel 713-576-5131.

Bet-Ken Prods, *(Bet-Ken Productions; 0-9603698),* 4363 Cherry Ave., San Jose, CA 95118 (SAN 213-683X) Tel 408-267-3425.

Beth Chana, *(Beth Chana Schl.; 0-9618441),* 620 Bedford Ave., Brooklyn, NY 11211 (SAN 667-6650) Tel 718-522-7422.

Bethany Hse, *(Bethany Hse. Pubs.; 0-87123; 1-55661),* Div. of Bethany Fellowship, Inc., 6820 Auto Club Rd., Minneapolis, MN 55438 (SAN 201-4416) Tel 612-829-2500; Toll free: 800-328-6109.

Bethel Pub, *(Bethel Publishing Co.; 0-934998),* Div. of Missionary Church, Inc., 1819 S. Main St., Elkhart, IN 46516 (SAN 201-7555) Tel 219-293-8585; Toll free: 800-348-7657.

Better Baby, *(Better Baby Pr., The; 0-936676; 0-944349),* Div. of Institutes for the Achievement of Human Potential, 8801 Stenton Ave., Philadelphia, PA 19118-2319 (SAN 215-7314) Tel 215-233-2050.

Betterway Pubns, *(Betterway Pubns., Inc.; 0-932620; 1-55870),* P.O. Box 219, Crozet, VA 22932 (SAN 215-2975) Tel 804-823-5661; Toll free: 800-522-2782 (orders). *Imprints:* Shoe Tree Pr (Shoe Tree Press).

Beyond Words Pub, *(Beyond Words Publishing, Inc.; 0-941831),* 13950 NW Pumpkin Ridge Rd., Hillsboro, OR 97123 (SAN 666-4210) Tel 503-647-5109; Toll free: 800-284-9673.

Bhaktivedanta, *(Bhaktivedanta Bk. Trust; 0-912776; 0-89213),* 3764 Watseka Ave., Los Angeles, CA 90034 (SAN 203-8560) Tel 213-559-4455.

BH&G
See Meredith Bks

BHF Memories, *(BHF Memories Unltd.; 0-9614108),* 3470 Rolling View Ct., White Bear Lake, MN 55110 (SAN 685-2998) Tel 612-770-1922.

Bible Memory, *(Bible Memory Assn., Inc.; 0-89323),* P.O. Box 12000, Ringgold, LA 71068 (SAN 214-1019).

Bible-Speak, *(Bible-Speak Enterprises; 0-911423),* 1940 Mount Vernon Ct., No. 4, Mountain View, CA 94040 (SAN 268-2931) Tel 415-965-9020.

Bible Temple, *(Bible Temple Publishing; 0-914936),* 7545 NE Glisan St., Portland, OR 97213-6396 (SAN 206-1953) Tel 503-253-9020; Toll free: 800-777-6057.

Biblio NY, *(Biblio Pr., the Jewish Women's Pub.; 0-9602036; 0-930395),* 1140 Broadway, Rm. 1507, New York, NY 10001 (SAN 217-0892) Tel 212-684-1257; Dist. by: Bookslinger, 2402 University Ave., Suite 507, Saint Paul, MN 55114 (SAN 169-4154); Toll free: 800-397-2613; Dist. by: Bookpeople, 2929 Fifth St., Berkeley, CA 94710 (SAN 168-9517) Tel 415-549-3030; Toll free: 800-999-4650; Dist. by: Inland Bk. Co., 140 Commerce St., East Haven, CT 06512 (SAN 200-4151) Tel 203-467-4257; Toll free: 800-243-0138; Dist. by: New Leaf Distributing Co., 5425 Tulane Dr, SW, Atlanta, GA 30336-2323 (SAN 169-1449) Tel 404-691-6996; Toll free: 800-326-2665.

Biblo, *(Biblo & Tannen Booksellers & Pubs., Inc.; 0-8196),* P.O. Box 302, Cheshire, CT 06410 (SAN 202-4071) Tel 203-272-2308.

Bibulophile Pr, *(Bibulophile Pr.; 0-911153),* P.O. Box 399, Bantam, CT 06750-0399 (SAN 268-2990) Tel 203-567-5543.

Bicent Era, *(Bicentennial Era Enterprises; 0-9605734),* P.O. Box 1148, Scappoose, OR 97056 (SAN 216-2245) Tel 503-684-3937.

Bicycle Books, *(Bicycle Bks., Inc.; 0-933201),* P.O. Box 2038, Mill Valley, CA 94941 (SAN 692-2600); Toll free: 800-468-8233; 32 Glen Dr., Mill Valley, CA 94941 (SAN 244-8335) Tel 415-381-0172; Dist. by: Bookpeople, 2929 Fifth Ave., Berkeley, CA 94710 (SAN 168-9517) Tel 415-549-3030; Toll free: 800-999-4650; Dist. by: Talman Co., 150 Fifth Ave., Rm. 630, New York, NY 10011 (SAN 250-5204) Tel 212-620-3182; Toll free: 800-537-8894; Dist. by: Pacific Pipeline, Inc., 19215 66th Ave., S., Kent, WA 98032-1171 (SAN 208-2128) Tel 206-872-5523; Toll free: 800-426-4727; Dist. by: Quality Books, Inc., 918 Sherwood Dr., Lake Bluff, IL 60044-2204 (SAN 169-2127) Tel 708-295-2010; Toll free: 800-323-4241; Dist. by: Alpenbooks, P.O. Box 761, Snohomish, WA 98290 (SAN 113-5309) Tel 206-568-4181.

Big Bend, *(Big Bend Natural History Assn., Inc.; 0-912001),* Affil. of National Park Service, Box 68, Big Bend National Park, TX 79834 (SAN 268-3075) Tel 915-477-2236.

Big Moose, *(Big Moose Pr.; 0-914692),* P.O. Box 180, Big Moose, NY 13331 (SAN 206-3336) Tel 315-357-2821.

Bilingual Ed Serv, *(Bilingual Educational Services, Inc.; 0-86624),* 2514 S. Grand Ave., Los Angeles, CA 90007 (SAN 218-4680) Tel 213-749-6213.

Bilingual Lang Mat, *(Bilingual Language Materials; 0-9624096),* 4912 River Ave., Newport Beach, CA 92663 Tel 714-642-3325.

Bilingue Pubns, *(Bilingue Pubns.; 0-933196),* P.O. Drawer H, Las Cruces, NM 88004 (SAN 223-6389) Tel 505-526-1557.

Binford Mort, *(Binford & Mort Publishing; 0-8323),* 1202 NW 17th Ave., Portland, OR 97209 (SAN 201-4386) Tel 503-221-0866.

Binney & Smith, *(Binney & Smith, Inc.; 0-86696),* P.O. Box 431, Easton, PA 18042 (SAN 216-5899).

Biostration, *(Biostration; 0-9626301),* P.O. Box 399, Wellington, CO 80549; 3714 Grant Ave., Wellington, CO 80549 Tel 303-568-3557.

Birch Bark Pr, *(Birch Bark Pr.; 0-945860),* 34190 Lodge Rd., Tollhouse, CA 93667 (SAN 248-188X) Tel 209-855-6227.

Birch Ln Pr *Imprint of Carol Pub Group*

Birmingham Hist Soc, *(Birmingham Historical Society; 0-943994),* 1 Sloss Quarters, Birmingham, AL 35222-1243 (SAN 240-1347).

Birmingham Mktg, *(Birmingham Marketing; 0-945772),* 5628 Hummingbird Ln., Clarkston, MI 48346 (SAN 247-9001) Tel 313-625-2262.

BJO Enterprises, *(BJO's Enterprises; 0-941381),* 837 Archie St., Eugene, OR 97402 (SAN 667-1276).

Bk Lures, *(Book Lures, Inc.; 0-913839; 1-879287),* P.O. Box 9450, O'Fallon, MO 63366 (SAN 286-7273); Toll free: 800-444-9450; 203 San Jose Ct., O'Fallon, MO 63366 Tel 314-272-4242.

BK Pubns, *(BK Pubns., Inc.; 0-9618890),* 7060 E. Calle del Sol, Tucson, AZ 85710 (SAN 242-4304) Tel 602-747-9352.

Bk Sales Inc, *(Book Sales, Inc.; 0-89009; 1-55521),* 110 Enterprise Ave., Secaucus, NJ 07094-1995 (SAN 169-488X) Tel 201-864-6341; Toll free: 800-526-7257; 276 Fifth Ave., New York, NY 10001.

Bks By Brooks, *(Books by Brooks; 0-9616207),* P.O. Box 22865, Denton, TX 76204 (SAN 658-3288) Tel 817-898-2166.

Bks by Kellogg, *(Books by Kellogg; 0-9603972),* P.O. Box 487, Annandale, VA 22003 (SAN 214-0454) Tel 703-256-2483.

Bks Demand UMI, *(Books on Demand; 0-8357),* Div. of University Microfilms International, 300 N. Zeeb Rd., Ann Arbor, MI 48106-1346 (SAN 212-2464) Tel 313-761-4700; Toll free: 800-521-0600. On-demand reprints of out-of-print books reproduced by xerography & bound in paper covers (cloth covers are available for 6.00 additional). Imprint of University Microfilms International.

Bks from the Christ Sci Monitor *Imprint of Chr Science*

Bks of Truth, *(Books of Truth; 0-939399),* P.O. Box 178, Bath, OH 44210-0178 (SAN 663-1304); 1742 Orchard Dr., Akron, OH 44333-1853 (SAN 663-1312) Tel 216-666-3852.

Black Belt Commns, *(Black Belt Communications Group; 0-9622815),* P.O. Box 551, Montgomery, AL 36101; 2750 Boultier, Montgomery, AL 36106 Tel 205-265-6753.

Black Birch Bks, *(Black Birch Bks.; 0-929545),* 12 Lockhaven Ct., Bedminster, NJ 07921 (SAN 249-6690) Tel 201-234-9309.

Black Classic, *(Black Classic Pr.; 0-933121),* P.O. Box 13414, Baltimore, MD 21203 (SAN 219-5836) Tel 301-602-0980.

Black Oak, *(Black Oak Pr.; 0-930674),* Box 4663, University Pl. Sta., Lincoln, NE 68504 (SAN 212-7261).

Black Star Pub, *(Black Star Publishing Co.; 0-9605426),* 116 E. 27th St., 11th Flr., New York, NY 10016 (SAN 204-4153) Tel 212-679-3288.

Black Tie Pr, *(Black Tie Pr.; 0-941749),* P.O. Box 440004, Houston, TX 77244-0004 (SAN 666-4156) Tel 713-789-5119.

Black Willow, *(Black Willow Poetry; 0-910047),* 401 Independence Dr., Sunrise Towamencin Township, Harleysville, PA 19438 (SAN 240-9682) Tel 215-368-0163. Out of business.

Blackberry ME, *(Blackberry: Salted in the Shell; 0-942396),* R.R. 1, Box 228, Nobleboro, ME 04555 (SAN 207-7949) Tel 207-729-5083. Do not confuse with Blackberry Bks., Ridgefield, CT.

Blackwater Pub Co, *(Blackwater Publishing Co., Inc.; 0-910341),* 530 Allison Ave., SW, Roanoke, VA 24016 (SAN 241-2756) Tel 703-362-4810.

Blair, *(Blair, John F., Pub.; 0-910244; 0-89587),* 1406 Plaza Dr., Winston-Salem, NC 27103 (SAN 201-4319) Tel 919-768-1374; Toll free: 800-222-9796.

Blake Pub, *(Blake Publishing, Inc.; 0-918303),* 2222 Beebee St., San Luis Obispo, CA 93401 (SAN 657-2618) Tel 805-543-7314; Toll free: 800-727-8558; Dist. by: Bookpeople, 2929 Fifth St., Berkeley, CA 94710 (SAN 168-9517) Tel 415-549-3030; Toll free: 800-999-4650; Dist. by: Pacific Pipeline, Inc., 19215 66th Ave., S., Kent, WA 98032 (SAN 208-2128) Tel 206-872-5523; Toll free: 800-444-7323 (US & Canada); Dist. by: Quality Bks., Inc., 918 Sherwood Dr., Lake Bluff, IL 60044-2204 (SAN 169-2127) Tel 708-295-2010; Toll free: 800-323-4241 (Libraries only).

Bleak Beauty Bks, *(Bleak Beauty Bks.; 0-9620992),* R.D. 1, Box 150, Barclay Rd., Clintondale, NY 12515 (SAN 250-6211) Tel 914-883-6077; Dist. by: Light Impressions Corp., 439 Monroe Ave., Rochester, NY 14607 (SAN 169-619X) Tel 716-271-8960; Toll free: 800-820-6216; Dist. by: Inland Bk. Co., 140 Commerce St., East Haven, CT 06512 (SAN 200-4151) Tel 203-467-4257; Toll free: 800-243-0138; Dist. by: Photo Eye, P.O. Box 1504, Austin, TX 78767 (SAN 630-3935) Tel 512-480-8409.

Blip Prods, *(Blip Productions; 0-936917),* P.O. Box 33146, Minneapolis, MN 55433 (SAN 658-3253) Tel 612-427-1004.

Bloch, *(Bloch Publishing Co.; 0-8197),* 37 W. 26th St., New York, NY 10010 (SAN 214-204X) Tel 212-532-3977.

Block, *(Block Pubs.; 0-916864),* P.O. Box 1802, Palm Springs, CA 92263 (SAN 208-5577) Tel 619-327-0321.

Blubber Budd, *(Blubber Buddies, Inc.; 0-9628626),* 1600 Marigold, McAllen, TX 78501 Tel 512-682-2755.

Blue Bird Pub, *(Blue Bird Publishing; 0-933025; 0-9615578),* 1713 E. Broadway, No. 306, Tempe, AZ 85282 (SAN 200-5603) Tel 602-968-4088; Toll free: 800-654-1993 (Orders only).

Blue Dmond Pub, *(Blue Diamond Publishing Co.; 0-9627307),* 8635 W. Sahara Ave., Suite 554, Las Vegas, NV 89117 (SAN 297-3499) Tel 702-255-8345.

Blue Dog Prodns, *(Blue Dog Productions, Inc.; 0-9627367),* 3302 Norman Ave., Baltimore, MD 21213-1025.

Blue Flame Pr, *(Blue Flame Pr.; 0-9621558),* 35-45 79th St., Apt. 3J, Flushing, NY 11372 (SAN 251-589X) Tel 718-335-5491.

Blue Her IL, *(Blue Heron Bks.; 0-9629064),* 1550 N. Damen, Chicago, IL 60622 Tel 312-276-6875.

Blue Heron OR, *(Blue Heron Publishing, Inc.; 0-936085),* 24450 NW Hansen Rd., Hillsboro, OR 97124 (SAN 696-6446) Tel 503-621-3911; Dist. by: Consortium Bk. Sales & Distribution, 287 E. Sixth St., Suite 365, Saint Paul, MN 55101 (SAN 200-6049) Tel 612-221-9035; Toll free: 800-283-3572.

Blue Heron WA, *(Blue Heron Pr.; 0-935317),* P.O. Box 5182, Bellingham, WA 98227 (SAN 695-7536); 4324 Gooding Ave., Bellingham, WA 98226 (SAN 662-3565) Tel 206-671-1155; Dist. by: Pacific Pipeline, Inc., 19215 66th Ave., S., Kent, WA 98032 (SAN 208-2128) Tel 206-872-5523; Toll free: 800-562-4617 (in Washington); 800-426-4727 (in northern California, Nevada, Idaho, Montana, Oregon). Do not confuse with other companies with the same name in Thibodaux, LA, Grand Rapids, MI.

Blue Jeans Pr, *(Blue Jeans Pr.; 0-934961),* Div. of Legal Education Ltd., 707 E. Jefferson St., Charlottesville, VA 22901 (SAN 695-0515) Tel 804-293-7360; Toll free: 800-662-9673.

Blue Mtn Pr CO, *(Blue Mountain Pr., Inc.; 0-88396),* P.O. Box 1007, Boulder, CO 80306 (SAN 169-0477) Tel 303-449-0536; Orders to: P.O. Box 4549, Boulder, CO 80306 (SAN 241-6379); Toll free: 800-525-0642.

Blue Norther, *(Blue Norther Pubns.; 0-9623081),* 123 N. El Camino Real, Suite F312, Encinitas, CA 92024 (SAN 200-3821) Tel 619-753-4680.

Blue Ribbon Bks *Imprint of Scholastic Inc*

Blue Water Pub, *(Blue Water Publishing; 0-926524),* P.O. Box 230893, Tigard, OR 97224; 14954 SW 109th Ave., Tigard, OR 97224 Tel 503-684-9749.

Blue Zero Pub, *(Blue Zero Publishing Co.; 1-880009),* Div. of RIM, Inc., P.O. Box 10699, Burbank, CA 91510; 334 S. California St., Burbank, CA 91505 Tel 818-840-0918.

Bluebird Pr CA, *(Bluebird Pr.; 0-934003),* P.O. Box 1000, Felicity, CA 92283 (SAN 692-669X) Tel 619-572-0100.

Bluechip Pubs, *(Bluechip Pubs.; 0-930251),* 2606 Third Ave., Seattle, WA 98121 (SAN 670-8595).

Bluejay Bks, *(Bluejay Bks.),* 26 Douglas Rd., Chappaqua, NY 10514-3105 (SAN 293-0188); Dist. by: St. Martin's Pr., Inc., 175 Fifth Ave., New York, NY 10010 (SAN 200-2132) Tel 212-674-5151; Toll free: 800-325-5525. Do not confuse with Bluejay Pr., Kokomo, IN.

Blyden Pr, *(Blyden, Edward W., Pr., Inc.; 0-914110),* P.O. Box 621, Manhattanville Sta., New York, NY 10027 (SAN 206-4804) Tel 212-222-3797.

Board Jewish Educ, *(Board of Jewish Education of Greater New York; 0-88384),* 426 W. 58th St., New York, NY 10019 (SAN 213-0165) Tel 212-245-8200.

Boars Head, *(Boar's Head Pr.; 0-932114),* 5890 Bluff Rd., Saint Louis, MO 63129 (SAN 211-1489) Tel 314-846-2694.

Bob Bks, *(Bob Bk. Pubns.; 0-9612104),* P.O. Box 633, West Linn, OR 97068 (SAN 685-3781) Tel 503-657-1883.

Bob Jones Univ Pr, *(Jones, Bob, Univ. Pr.; 0-89084),* Bob Jones Univ., Greenville, SC 29614 (SAN 223-7512) Tel 803-242-5100; Toll free: 800-845-5731.

Bobbi Ent, *(Bobbi Enterprises; 0-9603200),* 4433 Larner St., The Colony, TX 75056 (SAN 213-2885) Tel 218-735-8364.

Bobbs *Imprint of* **Macmillan**

Bold Prodns, *(Bold Productions; 0-938267),* P.O. Box 152281, Arlington, TX 76015 (SAN 659-8684); 3110 Fox Hill Dr., Arlington, TX 76015 (SAN 659-8692) Tel 817-468-9924.

Bond Double-O Seven, *(James Bond 007 Fan Club, The; 0-9605838),* P.O. Box 414, Bronxville, NY 10708 (SAN 216-5902) Tel 914-961-3440.

Bonjour Books, *(Bonjour Bks.; 0-915785),* 6221 Carlson Dr., New Orleans, LA 70122 (SAN 293-9096) Tel 504-282-4660; Orders to: P.O. Box 24327, New Orleans, LA 70184 (SAN 244-8246).

Bonus Books, *(Bonus Bks., Inc.; 0-933893; 0-929387),* Div. of Teach'em, Inc., 160 E. Illinois St., Chicago, IL 60611 (SAN 630-0804) Tel 312-467-0580; Toll free: 800-225-3775.

Book Binder, *(Book Binder; 0-915783),* 1560 Tamarack Ave., Atwater, CA 95301 (SAN 293-907X) Tel 209-358-2058.

Book-Lab, *(Book-Lab; 0-87594),* P.O. Box 7316, 500 74th St., North Bergen, NJ 07047-1016 Tel 201-861-6763; Toll free: 800-634-4081.

Book Peddlers, *(Book Peddlers; The; 0-916773),* 18326 Minnetonka Blvd., Deephaven, MN 55391 (SAN 653-9548) Tel 612-475-3527; Toll free: 800-255-3379; Dist. by: Publishers Group West, 4065 Hollis St., Emeryville, CA 94608 (SAN 202-8522) Tel 415-658-3453; Toll free: 800-365-3453.

Book Pub Co, *(Book Publishing Co.; 0-913990),* P.O. Box 99, Summertown, TN 38483 (SAN 202-439X) Tel 615-964-3571. Do not confuse with Book Publishing Co., Seattle, WA.

Bookling Pubs, *(Bookling Pubs., The; 0-910717),* 54 Flat Swamp Rd., Newtown, CT 06470 (SAN 268-4047) Tel 203-426-3021.

Bookmakers Guild, *(Bookmakers Guild, Inc.; 0-917665),* Subs. of Dakota Graphics, Inc., 9655 W. Colfax Ave., Lakewood, CO 80215 (SAN 657-1255) Tel 303-235-0203; Dist. by: Baker & Taylor Bks., Eastern Div., 50 Kirby Ave., Somerville, NJ 08876 (SAN 169-4901) Tel 201-722-8000; Toll free: 800-526-3825; 800-352-4833 (in New Jersey); Dist. by: Gordon's Bks., Inc., 2323 Delgany St., Denver, CO 80216 (SAN 169-0531) Tel 303-296-1830; Toll free: 800-525-6979 (west of the Mississippi); Dist. by: Blackwell North America (library sales only), 1001 Fries Mill Rd., Blackwood, NJ 08012 (SAN 169-4596) Tel 609-629-0700; Toll free: 800-257-7341; Dist. by: Ingram Bk. Co., 1125 Heilquaker Blvd., La Vergne, TN 37086 (SAN 169-7978) Tel 615-793-5000; Toll free: 800-937-8000 (orders only); Dist. by: EBSCO Industries, Inc., P.O. Box 1943, Birmingham, AL 35201-1943 (SAN 201-3584) Tel 205-991-6600; Dist. by: Golden-Lee Bk. Distributors, Inc., 1000 Dean St., Brooklyn, NY 11238 (SAN 169-5126) Tel 718-857-6333; Toll free: 800-473-7475; Dist. by: Bookazine Co., Inc., 303 W. Tenth St., New York, NY 10014 (SAN 169-5665) Tel 212-675-8877; Toll free: 800-221-8112.

Books Wonder, *(Books of Wonder; 0-929605),* 132 Seventh Ave., New York, NY 10011 (SAN 249-9916) Tel 212-989-3270.

Bookstore Pr, *(Bookstore Pr.; 0-912846),* Patterson's Wheeltrack, Freeport, ME 04032 (SAN 201-4211) Tel 207-865-6495.

Boone-Thomas, *(Boone-Thomas Enterprises; 0-9611780),* P.O. Box 1093, College Park, MD 20740 (SAN 285-2225); 13122 Serpentine Way, Silver Spring, MD 20904 (SAN 285-2233) Tel 301-384-6393.

Boosey & Hawkes, *(Boosey & Hawkes, Inc.; 0-913932),* Printed Music Div., 52 Cooper Sq., 10th Flr., New York, NY 10003 (SAN 213-6805) Tel 212-979-1090; Toll free: 800-645-9582.

Borden, *(Borden Publishing Co.; 0-87505),* 2623 San Fernando Rd., Los Angeles, CA 90065 (SAN 201-419X) Tel 213-223-4267.

Borderlands Pr, *(Borderlands Pr.; 0-9621792),* 400 Gulf Breeze Pkwy., Suite 202, Gulf Breeze, FL 32561 (SAN 252-239X) Tel 904-932-0501. Do not confuse with Borderlands Pr. in Baltimore, MD.

Borenson & Assocs, *(Borenson & Assocs.; 0-9618105),* P.O. Box 450, Dublin, PA 18917 (SAN 666-4261); 126 Middle Rd., Suite E15, Dublin, PA 18917 (SAN 666-427X) Tel 215-249-3212.

Borgo Pr, *(Borgo Pr.; 0-89370; 0-8095),* P.O. Box 2845, San Bernardino, CA 92406-2845 (SAN 208-9459) Tel 714-884-5813.

Bornstein Memory, *(Bornstein Memory Training Schls.; 0-9602610),* 11693 San Vicente Blvd., West Los Angeles, CA 90049 (SAN 213-0181) Tel 213-478-2056.

Borzoi Sprinters *Imprint of* **Knopf**

Bosck Pub Hse, *(Bosck Publishing Hse.; 0-9629887),* P.O. Box 2311, Los Angeles, CA 90051-0311; 1322 W. 60th St., Los Angeles, CA 90044 Tel 213-750-3413.

Bowker, *(Bowker, R. R.; 0-8352),* Div. of Reed Publishing U.S.A., 121 Chanlon Rd., New Providence, NJ 07974 (SAN 214-1191) Tel 908-464-6800; Toll free: 800-521-8110; 800-537-8416 (in Canada); 800-431-1713 subscriptions to: Publishers Weekly, School Library Journal, Library Journal (in Ohio: 614-383-3141); 800-257-7894 subscriptions to: Library Hotline, Reviews-on-Cards (in New Jersey: 609-786-1160); 800-999-8500.

Box Four Twenty-Four, *(Box 424 Pr.; 0-9614506),* Box 424, Pacific Grove, CA 93950 (SAN 691-7364) Tel 408-649-8215.

Boxwood, *(Boxwood Pr.; 0-910286; 0-940168),* 183 Ocean View Blvd., Pacific Grove, CA 93950 (SAN 201-4149) Tel 408-375-9110.

Boyce-Pubns, *(Boyce Pubns.; 0-918823),* 1023 Oxford, Clovis, CA 93612 (SAN 669-652X) Tel 209-299-8495.

Boyds Mills Pr, *(Boyds Mills Pr.; 1-878093; 1-56397),* 910 Church St., Honesdale, PA 18431 Tel 717-253-1164; Dist. by: St. Martin's Pr., Inc., 175 Fifth Ave., New York, NY 10010 (SAN 200-2132) Tel 212-674-5151; Toll free: 800-325-5525. *Imprints:* Bell Bks NY (Bell Books); Caroline Hse (Caroline House); Wordsong (Wordsong).

Boylen, *(Boylen; 0-9624099),* 337 Willoway Dr., Bolingbrook, IL 60439 Tel 312-972-0514.

Boynton Cook Pubs, *(Boynton Cook Pubs., Inc.; 0-86709),* Subs. of Heinemann Educational Bks., Inc., 361 Hanover St., Portsmouth, NH 03801 (SAN 216-6186) Tel 603-431-7894.

Bradbury Pr *Imprint of* **Macmillan Child Grp**

Bradley Mann, *(Bradley-Mann Pubs.; 0-9627882),* 5657 W. Folley St., Chandler, AZ 85226 Tel 819-684-8554.

Bradley Pubns, *(Bradley Pubns.; 0-89748),* Subs. of RBR Communications, Inc., 201 W 70th St., No. 40E, New York, NY 10023 (SAN 696-2912) Tel 212-724-6635; Dist. by: Warner Brothers Pubns., Inc., 265 Secaucus Rd., Secaucus, NJ 07094 (SAN 203-0586) Tel 201-348-0700; Toll free: 800-638-0005 (orders only).

Brady Bks, *(Brady Bks.; 0-87618; 0-87619; 0-89303; 0-913486),* Div. of Prentice Hall Pr., Simon & Schuster, Inc., 15 Columbus Cir., New York, NY 10023 (SAN 200-2175) Tel 212-373-8093; Toll free: 800-223-2336 (established accounts only); Dist. by: Prentice Hall Pr., 200 Old Tappan Rd., Old Tappan, NJ 07675 (SAN 215-3939) Tel 201-767-5937.

Brainworks Inc, *(Brainworks, Inc.; 0-944662),* 1918 Walnut Plaza, Carrollton, TX 75006 (SAN 244-5085) Tel 214-220-0444.

Branden Pub Co, *(Branden Publishing Co.; 0-8283),* Box 843, Brookline Village, Boston, MA 02147 (SAN 201-4106) Tel 617-734-2045.

Brandt Bks, *(Brandt Bks.; 0-9616327),* 1134 Willits Dr., Corona, CA 91720 (SAN 659-0454) Tel 714-735-6167.

Brandylane, *(Brandylane Pubs.; 0-9627635),* P.O. Box 43, Lively, VA 22507 Tel 804-435-6900; Toll free: 800-553-6922.

BRAT Pubns, *(B.R.A.T. Pubns.; 0-9623607),* P.O. Box 660, Little Elm, TX 75068; Hwy. 720, Little Elm, TX 75068 Tel 214-292-3424.

Braziller, *(Braziller, George, Inc.; 0-8076),* 60 Madison Ave., Suite 1001, New York, NY 10010 (SAN 201-9310) Tel 212-889-0909.

Bread for the World, *(Bread for the World Institute on Hunger & Development; 0-9628058),* 802 Rhode Island Ave., NE, Washington, DC 20018 (SAN 226-0182) Tel 202-269-0200.

Breadworks, *(Breadworks; 0-9627665),* R.R. 1, Box 238A, Canaan, NH 03741; Choate Rd., Canaan, NH 03741 Tel 603-632-9171.

Breitenbush Bks, *(Breitenbush Bks., Inc.; 0-932576),* P.O. Box 82157, Portland, OR 97282 (SAN 219-7707) Tel 503-230-1900.

Brennan Bks, *(Brennan Bks., Inc.; 0-89270),* 8419 Stickney Ave., Milwaukee, WI 53226-2808 (SAN 208-5674) Tel 414-786-4092.

Brenner Info Group, *(Brenner Information Group; 0-929535),* Div. of Brenner Microcomputing, Inc., 9282 Samantha Ct., San Diego, CA 92129 (SAN 249-6496) Tel 619-693-0355.

Brethren, *(Brethren Pr.; 0-87178),* Div. of Church of the Brethren, 1451 Dundee Ave., Elgin, IL 60120 (SAN 201-9329) Tel 312-742-5100; Toll free: 800-323-8039. Do not confuse with Brethren Publishing Co., Ashland, Ohio.

Brght Ideas CA, *(Bright Ideas Productions; 0-9627863),* Div. of LMN Productions, 30879 Thousand Oaks Blvd., No. 161, Westlake Village, CA 91362 Tel 818-707-7127.

Bridge Troll Pr, *(Bridge Troll Pr.; 0-9618225),* P.O. Box 12655, Northgate Sta., San Rafael, CA 94903 (SAN 666-9069); 60 Mount Lassen Dr., San Rafael, CA 94903 (SAN 666-9077) Tel 415-479-5808.

Brigham, *(Brigham Young Univ. Pr.; 0-8425),* 205 UPB, Provo, UT 84602 (SAN 201-9337) Tel 801-378-2809.

Bright Baby, *(Bright Baby Bks.; 0-930681),* 101 Star Ln., Whitethorn, CA 95489 (SAN 676-9608) Tel 707-986-7693.

Bright Bks, *(Bright Bks.; 0-9605968),* P.O. Box 428, Akron, IN 46910 (SAN 216-7204) Tel 219-893-4113. Do not confuse with companies of the same name in Elverson, PA, Austin, TX.

Bright Bks TX, *(Bright Bks.; 1-880092),* 8200 Neely Dr., No. 230, Austin, TX 78759 Tel 512-499-4164. Do not confuse with companies of the same name in Akron, IN, Elverson, PA.

Bright Ring, *(Bright Ring Publishing; 0-935607),* P.O. Box 5768-B, Bellingham, WA 98227 (SAN 696-0537); 1900 N. Shore Dr., Bellingham, WA 98226 (SAN 665-8989) Tel 206-734-1601; Dist. by: Pacific Pipeline, Inc., 19215 66th Ave., S., Kent, WA 98032 (SAN 208-2128) Tel 206-872-5523; Toll free: 800-426-4727 (in northern California, Oregon, Nevada, Montana, Idaho); 800-562-4647 (in Washington); Dist. by: Gryphon Hse., Inc., P.O. Box 275, Mount Rainier, MD 20712 (SAN 169-3190) Tel 301-779-6200; Toll free: 800-638-0928; Dist. by: Gordon's Bks., Inc., 2323 Delgany St., Denver, CO 80216 (SAN 169-0531) Tel 303-296-1830; Toll free: 800-525-6979 (West of Mississippi).

Brighton & Lloyd, *(Brighton & Lloyd; 0-922434),* P.O. Box 2903, Costa Mesa, CA 92628 (SAN 251-3072); 1875 Wren Cir., Costa Mesa, CA 92626 (SAN 251-3080) Tel 714-540-6466.

Bristlecone Pubns, *(Bristlecone Pubns.; 0-9622863),* 2405 Whirlaway, No. 1B, Las Vegas, NV 89108 Tel 702-648-4710.

Bristol Bks
See Bristol Hse

Bristol Hse, *(Bristol Hse., Ltd.; 0-917851),* 2201 Regency Rd., Suite 301, Lexington, KY 40503 (SAN 225-4638) Tel 606-276-4583; Toll free: 800-451-7323.

Bristol Pub Ent CA, *(Bristol Publishing Enterprises, Inc.; 0-911954; 1-55867),* P.O. Box 1737, San Leandro, CA 94577 (SAN 202-9197); Toll free: 800-346-4889; 14692 Wicks Blvd., San Leandro, CA 94577 (SAN 248-3874) Tel 415-895-4461.

Brite Intl, *(Brite International; 0-944803),* P.O. Box 9191, Salt Lake City, UT 84109 (SAN 244-948X); 2595 E. 33rd S., Salt Lake City, UT 84109 (SAN 244-9498) Tel 801-487-5891.

Brite Music Inc
See Brite Intl

British Amer Pub, *(British American Publishing, Ltd.; 0-945167),* 19B British American Blvd., Latham, NY 12110 (SAN 246-3008) Tel 518-786-6000; Dist. by: Simon & Schuster Trade, 1230 Ave. of the Americas, New York, NY 10020.

Broadblade Pr, *(Broadblade Pr.; 0-9614640; 0-9620249),* 11314 Miller Rd., Swartz Creek, MI 48473 (SAN 691-9227) Tel 313-635-3156; Dist. by: Baker & Taylor Bks., Midwestern Div., 501 S. Gladiolus St., Momence, IL 60954 (SAN 169-2100) Tel 815-472-2444; Toll free: 800-435-5111; 800-892-1892 (in Illinois); Dist. by: Hillsdale Educational Pubs., Inc., 39 North St., Box 245, Hillsdale, MI 49242 (SAN 159-8759) Tel 517-437-3179.

Broadman, *(Broadman Pr.; 0-8054),* Div. of Sunday School Board of the Southern Baptist Convention, 127 Ninth Ave., N., Mail Stop 137, Nashville, TN 37234 (SAN 201-937X) Tel 615-251-3641; Toll free: 800-251-3225.

Broadside Pr, *(Broadside Pr.; 0-910296; 0-940713),* P.O. Box 04257, Detroit, MI 48204 (SAN 201-9388); 4734 Sturtevant, Detroit, MI 48204 (SAN 664-6190) Tel 313-934-1231.

Broken Rifle Pr, *(Broken Rifle Pr.; 0-9620024),* P.O. Box 749, Trenton, NJ 08607 (SAN 247-4557) Tel 201-549-0631; Dist. by: Quality Bks., Inc., 918 Sherwood Dr., Lake Bluff, IL 60044-2204 (SAN 169-2127) Tel 708-295-2010; Toll free: 800-323-4241; Dist. by: Inland Bk. Co., 140 Commerce St., East Haven, CT 06512 (SAN 200-4151) Tel 203-467-4257; Toll free: 800-243-0138; Dist. by: Baker & Taylor Bks, Midwestern Div., 501 S. Gladiolus St., Momence, IL 60954-2444 (SAN 169-2100) Tel 815-472-2444; Toll free: 800-435-5111; Dist. by: Distributors, The, 702 S. Michigan, South Bend, IN 46618 (SAN 169-2488) Tel 219-232-8500; Toll free: 800-348-5200 (except Indiana).

Brooke-Richards, *(Brooke-Richards Pr.; 0-9622652),* 9420 Reseda Blvd., Suite 511, Northridge, CA 91324 Tel 818-893-8126.

Brost Heus, *(Brost-Heus; 0-9616109),* 98 Main St., Tiburon, CA 94920 (SAN 699-7392).

Brotherstone Pubs, *(Brotherstone Pubs.; 1-878925),* 1203 Lennoxshire Dr., Elgin, IL 60123 Tel 708-697-1371.

Brown Bk, *(Brown Bk. Co.; 0-910294),* P.O. Box 69-3883, Miami, FL 33269 (SAN 202-4276).

Brownlow Pub Co, *(Brownlow Publishing Co., Inc.; 0-915720; 1-877719),* 6309 Airport Freeway, Fort Worth, TX 76117 (SAN 207-5105) Tel 817-831-3831; Toll free: 800-433-7610.

Brunner-Mazel, *(Brunner/Mazel Pubs.; 0-87630),* 19 Union Sq., W., New York, NY 10003 (SAN 164-9167) Tel 212-924-3344.

Brunswick Pub, *(Brunswick Publishing Corp.; 0-931494; 1-55618),* Rte. 1, Box 1A1, Lawrenceville, VA 23868 (SAN 211-6332) Tel 804-848-3865.

Bryn Ffyliaid, *(Bryn Ffyliaid Pubns.; 0-9611114),* 300 Lake Marina Ave., No. 16BW, New Orleans, LA 70124 (SAN 283-2720) Tel 504-486-7036.

BSA, *(Boy Scouts of America; 0-8395),* P.O. Box 152079, 1325 W. Walnut Hill Ln., Irving, TX 75015-2079 (SAN 284-9798) Tel 214-580-2273; Orders to: National Distribution Ctr., 2109 Westinghouse Blvd., P.O. Box 7143, Charlotte, NC 28241-7143 (SAN 284-9801) Tel 704-588-4260.

BSP Pub Inc, *(Bancroft-Sage Publishing, Inc.; 0-944280),* 601 Elkcam Cir., Suite C7, Box 355, Marco, FL 33969 (SAN 243-0398) Tel 813-642-5600; Toll free: 800-942-1745.

BTime Classics *Imprint of* **A D Bragdon**

Buccaneer Bks, *(Buccaneer Bks.; 0-89966),* P.O. Box 168, Cutchogue, NY 11935 (SAN 209-1542). Do not confuse with Buccaneer Books, Laguna Beach, CA.

Buck Pub, *(Buck Publishing Co.; 0-934530),* 2409 Vestavia Dr., Birmingham, AL 35216 (SAN 213-0203) Tel 205-979-2296.

Buckingham Mint
See Derrydale Pr

Buddhist Text, *(Buddhist Text Translation Society; 0-917512),* Affil. of Dharma Realm Buddhist Assocs., City of Ten Thousand Buddhas, 2001 Talmage Rd., Talmage, CA 95481-0217 (SAN 281-3556) Tel 707-462-0939.

Bulfinch Pr *Imprint of* **Little**
Bullseye Bks *Imprint of* **Knopf**
Bur Oak Pr Inc, *(Bur Oak Pr., Inc.; 0-929326),* 8717 Mockingbird Rd., S., Platteville, WI 53818 (SAN 249-0463) Tel 608-348-8662.

Burdett CA, *(Burdett Design Studios; 0-932946),* 15192 Goldenwest Cir., Westminster, CA 92683 (SAN 295-1045) Tel 714-897-6177; Toll free: 800-634-6048.

Burgess Pub, *(Burgess Publishing, Inc.; 1-879470),* P.O. Box 520, Broken Arrow, OK 74011 Tel 918-455-6537; Toll free: 800-388-5437; Dist. by: Harrison Hse., Inc., P.O. Box 35035, Tulsa, OK 74153 (SAN 208-676X) Tel 918-582-2126; Toll free: 800-888-4126.

Burnshire Hse, *(Burnshire Hse. Pubns.; 1-880310),* P.O. Box 612434, South Lake Tahoe, CA 96512-2434; 1909 Cathedral Ct., South Lake Tahoe, CA 96512 Tel 916-544-6725.

Burton-Towner, *(Burton-Towner Publishing; 0-9623981),* 21007 Lull St., Canoga Park, CA 91304 Tel 818-999-1861.

Busn *Imprint of* **P-H**
Busn Resc Network, *(Business Resource Network, Inc.; 0-9619860),* P.O. Box 64, Elka Park, NY 12427 (SAN 246-7232); Green Hill Rd., Elka Park, NY 12427 (SAN 246-7240) Tel 718-263-4143.

Buttercup Bks, *(Buttercup Bks.; 0-9614997),* P.O. Box 1272, Casa Grande, AZ 85222 (SAN 693-9503) Tel 602-836-7831.

Butterfly Bear, *(Butterfly & Bear Pr.; 0-9629645),* 1818 Fourth Ave., W., Seattle, WA 98119 Tel 206-284-1691.

BYLS Pr, *(BYLS Pr.; 0-934402),* 6617 N. Mozart, Chicago, IL 60645 (SAN 212-7253) Tel 312-743-4241.

BYTE Bks *Imprint of* **McGraw**
C A M Co, *(C.A.M. Co. Pubs.; 0-942752),* P.O. Box 1773, Arvada, CO 80001-1773 (SAN 281-3645) Tel 303-421-6851; Dist. by: Distributors, The, 702 S. Michigan, South Bend, IN 46618 (SAN 169-2488) Tel 219-232-8500; Toll free: 800-348-5200; Dist. by: Baker & Taylor Bks., Midwestern Div., 501 S. Gladiolus St., Momence, IL 60954 (SAN 169-2100) Tel 815-472-2444; Toll free: 800-435-51111; 800-892-1892 (in Illinois); Dist. by: Baker & Taylor Bks., Southern Div., Mt. Olive Rd., Commerce, GA 30529 (SAN 169-1503) Tel 404-335-5000; Toll free: 800-241-6004; 800-282-6850 (in Georgia); Dist. by: Baker & Taylor Bks., Western Div., 380 Edison Way, Reno, NV 89564 (SAN 169-4464) Tel 702-786-6700; Toll free: 800-648-3540; Dist. by: Baker & Taylor Bks., Eastern Div., 50 Kirby Ave., Somerville, NJ 08876 (SAN 169-4901) Tel 201-722-8000; Toll free: 800-435-1845; 800-352-4833 (in New Jersey); Dist. by: Midwest Library Service, 11443 St. Charles Rock Rd., Bridgeton, MO 63044-9986 (SAN 169-4243) Tel 314-739-3100.

C & T Pub, *(C & T Publishing; 0-914881),* 5021 Blum Rd., No. 1, Martinez, CA 94553 (SAN 289-0720) Tel 415-370-9600; Toll free: 800-284-1114.

C C Partin, *(Partin, Charlotte Corry; 0-9619816),* 530 Yuma Ct., Sumter, SC 29150 (SAN 246-1242) Tel 803-469-4010.

C Chapman, *(Chapman, Carl; 0-9621529),* 205 Lancaster Ave., Chattanooga, TN 37415 (SAN 251-5067) Tel 615-877-6296.

C Coats Bestsellers, *(Coats', Carolyn, Bestsellers; 1-878722),* P.O. Box 560532, Orlando, FL 32856; 1336 Windsong Rd., Orlando, FL 32809 Tel 407-855-0780.

C D Pierce, *(Pierce, Catherine Doris; 0-9621397),* 1920 Barbara Dr., Palo Alto, CA 94303 (SAN 251-1738) Tel 415-322-5728.

C Del Grullo, *(Cayo del Grullo Pr.; 0-9611604),* c/o Texas A & I Univ., History Dept., Kingsville, TX 78363 (SAN 284-9313) Tel 512-595-3603.

C E Ludy, *(Ludy, Claude Edward; 0-9625164),* 4893 Century Dr., Saginaw, MI 48603; Orders to: Ed's Starlite Bks., P.O. Box 1585, Saginaw, MI 48605.

C E Tuttle, *(Tuttle, Charles E., Co., Inc.; 0-8048),* 77 Central St., Boston, MA 02109 (SAN 213-2621) Tel 617-338-9390; Toll free: 800-526-2778; Orders to: P.O. Box 410, 28 S. Main St., Rutland, VT 05702-0410 Tel 802-773-8930.

C F Fort, *(Fort, Chloe Friarson; 0-9626343),* 615 Belle Meade Blvd. A, No. 118, Nashville, TN 37205-3849 Tel 615-352-3613.

C-Four Res, *(C-4 Resources; 0-914527),* 313 N. Mattis Ave., No. 201, Champaign, IL 61821-2403 (SAN 289-1565) Tel 217-395-6242.

C Garcia, *(Garcia, Conrad; 0-9621124),* 1880 Lafayette Ave., 20F, Bronx, NY 10473 (SAN 250-6610) Tel 212-589-6095.

C H Fairfax, *(Fairfax, C. H., Co., Inc.; 0-935132),* P.O. Box 502, Columbia, MD 21045 (SAN 221-170X) Tel 301-730-2397.

C H Kerr, *(Kerr, Charles H., Publishing Co.; 0-88286),* 1740 W. Greenleaf Ave., Chicago, IL 60626 (SAN 207-7043) Tel 312-465-7774.

C J Brown, *(Brown, Cathy J.; 0-9614796),* Dist. by: Creative Expressions, P.O. Box 456, Colchester, VT 05446 (SAN 200-5816).

C K Himeda, *(Himeda, C. K.; 0-9621721),* 4204 Kilauea Ave., Honolulu, HI 96816 (SAN 252-0575) Tel 808-732-2681.

C Kaczmarek, *(Kaczmarek, Constant; 0-9626041),* 29747 Briarton, Farmington Hills, MI 48331 Tel 313-661-0253.

C Leachman, *(Leachman, Clara; 0-9618517),* 253 Congress St., Milford, MA 01757 (SAN 667-9927) Tel 508-473-3706.

C Lee Pubns, *(Christopher Lee Pubns., Inc.; 1-878383),* P.O. Box 6202, South Bend, IN 46660; Toll free: 800-822-6202; 15055 Cleveland Rd., Granger, IN 46530 Tel 219-277-3100.

C Mack Pub, *(Mack, Casey, Publishing Co.; 0-9620167),* 9542 E. Valley Ranch Pkwy., No. 1062, Irving, TX 75063 (SAN 247-865X) Tel 214-506-0900.

C Mooney, *(Mooney, Chuck, III; 0-9630239),* 3442 Dryden, Fort Worth, TX 76109 Tel 817-926-4274.

C N Potter Bks *Imprint of* **Crown**
C Salway Pr, *(Salway, C.; 0-9624887),* P.O. Box 4115, Menlo Park, CA 94026 Tel 415-368-7882; 83 Robleda Dr., Atherton, CA 94027 Tel 415-368-1983; Dist. by: Bookpeople, 2929 Fifth St., Berkeley, CA 94710 (SAN 168-9517) Tel 415-549-3030; Toll free: 800-999-4650; Dist. by: Pacific Pipeline, Inc., 19215 66th Ave., S., Kent, WA 98032 (SAN 208-2128) Tel 206-872-5523; Toll free: 800-426-4727 (in Oregon, Idaho, Montana, Nevada, & northern California); 800-562-4617 (in Washington); Dist. by: Baker & Taylor Bks., Eastern Div., 50 Kirby Ave., Somerville, NJ 08876-0734 (SAN 169-4901) Tel 201-435-5111; Toll free: 800-526-3825; Dist. by: Baker & Taylor Bks., Midwestern Div., 501 Gladiolus St., Momence, IL 60954-2444 (SAN 169-2100) Tel 815-472-2444; Toll free: 800-435-5111; Dist. by: Baker & Taylor Bks., Southern Div., Mount Olive Rd., Commerce, GA 30599-9988 (SAN 169-1503) Tel 404-335-5000; Toll free: 800-241-6004; Dist. by: Baker & Taylor Bks., Western Div., 380 Edison Way, Reno, NV 89564 (SAN 169-4464) Tel 702-786-6700; Toll free: 800-648-3540; 800-892-1892 (in Illinois); 800-282-6854 (in Georgia); Dist. by: Ingram Bk. Co., 1125 Heil Quaker Blvd., La Vergne, TN 37086-1986 (SAN 169-7978) Tel 615-793-5000; Toll free: 800-937-8000; Dist. by: Brodar & Co., 500 Arch St., Williamsport, PA 17705 (SAN 169-7684) Tel 717-326-2461; Toll free: 800-233-8467; Dist. by: Sunbelt Pubns., P.O. Box 191126, San Diego, CA 92119 (SAN 242-0198) Tel 619-448-0884; Toll free: 800-626-6579.

C Shore Pr, *(Shore, C., Pr.; 0-9612136),* P.O. Box 14008, Bradenton, FL 34280 (SAN 286-8733) Tel 813-792-4535.

C Weisfish, *(Weisfish, Chaya; 0-9630241),* 18 Yale Dr., Monsey, NY 10952 Tel 914-426-3785.

C Zolotow Bks *Imprint of* **HarpC Child Bks**
CA HPA, *(California Heritage Publishing Assocs.; 0-9623233),* 156 Del Norte Way, San Luis Obispo, CA 93405 Tel 805-541-4989.

CA Rocketry, *(California Rocketry; 0-912468),* Div. of U.S. Rockets, P.O. Box 1242, Claremont, CA 91711 (SAN 204-692X) Tel 714-621-0962; Toll free: 800-266-3111.

Caballero Pr, *(Caballero Pr.; 0-9601346),* 1936 Caballero Way, Las Vegas, NV 89109 (SAN 210-6825) Tel 702-735-3406.

Cajun Pubs, *(Cajun Pubs.; 0-933727),* Rte. 4, Box 88, New Iberia, LA 70560 (SAN 692-4948) Tel 318-363-6653; Toll free: 800-551-3076.

Cal Aero Pr, *(California Aero Pr.; 0-914379),* P.O. Box 1365, Carlsbad, CA 92008 (SAN 289-5943) Tel 619-729-6002.

Calico Bks *Imprint of* **Contemp Bks**

Calico Paws, *(Calico Paws Publishing; 0-944104),* P.O. Box 2364, Menlo Park, CA 94026-2364 (SAN 242-8016); 83 Alejandra Ave., Atherton, CA 94025 (SAN 242-8024) Tel 415-323-9616.

Calif Poets Schls, *(California Poets in the Schools; 0-939927),* 2845 24th St., San Francisco, CA 94110 (SAN 663-8325) Tel 415-695-7988.

Calif Street, *(California Street; 0-915090),* P.O. Box 1, Canyon, CA 94516 (SAN 207-673X). Moved, left no forwarding address.

Calif Video, *(California Video Institute; 1-880211),* P.O. Box 7043, Mission Hills, CA 91346; 6804 Baird Ave., No. 7, Reseda, CA 91335 Tel 818-881-8736; Dist. by: Carolina Biological Supply Co., Pubns Dept., 2700 York Rd., Burlington, NC 27215 (SAN 249-2784) Tel 919-584-0381; Toll free: 800-334-5551.

Calif Weekly, *(California Weekly Explorer, Inc.; 0-936778),* 285 E. Main St., Suite 3, Tustin, CA 92680 (SAN 217-0914) Tel 714-730-5991.

Calligrafree, *(Calligrafree-The Calligraphy Co.; 0-942032),* P.O. Box 98, Brookville, OH 45309 (SAN 240-9496) Tel 513-833-5677; Dist. by: Hunt Manufacturing Co., 230 S. Broad St., Philadelphia, PA 19102 (SAN 630-1703) Tel 215-732-7700; Toll free: 800-524-0916 (in Pennsylvania).

Cambdgport Pr, *(Cambridgeport Pr.; 0-944348),* 15 Chalk St., Cambridge, MA 02139 (SAN 243-4466) Tel 617-497-4437.

Cambridge Bk, *(Cambridge Bk. Co.; 0-8428),* Div. of Simon & Schuster, Inc., Sylvan Rd., Rte. 9W, Englewood Cliffs, NJ 07632 (SAN 169-5703) Tel 201-592-2000; Toll free: 800-221-4764.

Cambridge Strat, *(Cambridge Stratford, Ltd.; 0-935637),* 8560 Main St., Harris Hill Sq., Williamsville, NY 14221-7435 (SAN 696-2173) Tel 716-626-9044.

Cambridge U Pr, *(Cambridge Univ. Pr.; 0-521),* 40 W. 20th St., New York, NY 10011 (SAN 200-206X) Tel 212-924-3900; Toll free: 800-221-4512; Orders to: 110 Midland Ave., Port Chester, NY 10573 (SAN 281-3769) Tel 914-937-9600; Toll free: 800-227-0247 (New York only): 800-872-7423 (outside New York).

Camden Hse Pub, *(Camden Hse. Publishing, Inc.; 0-944475),* P.O. Box 1004, Ferry Rd., Charlotte, VT 05445 (SAN 243-6043) Tel 802-425-3961; Toll free: 800-344-3350.

Camelot *Imprint of* **Avon**

Camelot GA, *(Camelot Pr., Ltd.; 0-931760),* P.O. Box 674884, Marietta, GA 30067 (SAN 243-0665) Tel 404-423-9585; Dist. by: New Leaf Distributing Co., 5425 Tulane Dr., SW, Atlanta, GA 30336-2323 (SAN 169-1449) Tel 404-691-6996; Toll free: 800-326-2665; Dist. by: Bookpeople, 2929 Fifth St., Berkeley, CA 94710 (SAN 168-9517) Tel 415-549-3030; Toll free: 800-999-4650; Dist. by: Inland Bk. Co., 140 Commerce St., East Haven, CT 06512 (SAN 200-4151) Tel 203-467-4257; Toll free: 800-243-0138; Dist. by: Distributors, The, 702 S. Michigan, South Bend, IN 46618 (SAN 169-2488) Tel 219-232-8500; Toll free: 800-348-5200 (except Indiana); Dist. by: Great Tradition, 750 Adrian Way, Suite 111, San Rafael, CA 94903 Tel 415-492-9382; Toll free: 800-333-7755.

Camelot Pub, *(Camelot Publishing Co.; 0-89218),* P.O. Box 1357, Ormond Beach, FL 32175-1357 (SAN 202-5035) Tel 904-672-5672.

Camex Bks Inc, *(Camex Bks., Inc.; 0-929793),* 535 Fifth Ave., New York, NY 10017 (SAN 250-5274) Tel 212-682-8400.

Campfire Pub, *(Campfire Publishing Co.; 0-9617653),* 226 Easton, S., Laurel, MD 20724 (SAN 664-8932) Tel 301-498-4807.

Campus Life *Imprint of* **Zondervan**

Candlewick Pr, *(Candlewick Pr.; 1-56402),* Div. of Walker Books, London, England, 2067 Massachusetts Ave., Cambridge, MA 02140 Tel 617-661-3330.

Candy Apple Pub, *(Candy Apple Publishing Co.; 0-9616464),* P.O. Box 48421, St. Petersburg, FL 33743-8421 (SAN 659-3178); 6575 Bonnie Bay Cir. N., Pinellas Park, FL 33565 (SAN 659-3186) Tel 813-544-0355.

Canyon AZ, *(Canyon Publishing; 0-9624909),* Div. of Color Pro Printing & Graphics, Inc., 215 Coffee Pot Dr., Suite A, Sedona, AZ 86336 Tel 602-282-1886. Do not confuse with Canyon Publishing Co., Canoga Park, CA.

Canyon Country Pubns, *(Canyon Country Pubns.; 0-9614586; 0-925685),* P.O. Box 963, Moab, UT 84532 (SAN 630-1673); 23 La Sal Dr., Moab, UT 84532 Tel 801-259-6700.

Capital Enter, *(Capital Enterprises),* P.O. Box 716, West Springfield, MA 01090-0716 Tel 413-739-8231.

Capra Pr, *(Capra Pr.; 0-88496; 0-912264),* P.O. Box 2068, Santa Barbara, CA 93120 (SAN 201-9620) Tel 805-966-4590; Dist. by: Consortium Bk. Sales & Distribution, 287 E. Sixth St., Suite 365, Saint Paul, MN 55101 (SAN 200-6049) Tel 612-221-9035; Toll free: 800-283-3572.

Capstan Pubns, *(Capstan Pubns.; 0-914565),* P.O. Box 306, Basin, WY 82410 (SAN 289-162X) Tel 307-568-2604.

Capstone Pr, *(Capstone Press, Inc.; 1-56065),* P.O. Box 669, Mankato, MN 56001 Tel 507-625-2746.

Capstone Pub, *(Capstone Publishing, Inc.; 1-880450),* P.O. Box 1586, Bellingham, WA 98227; 215 W. Holly, Suite H-23, Bellingham, WA 98225 Tel 206-733-4703; Dist. by: Bookpeople, 2929 Fifth St., Berkeley, CA 94710 (SAN 168-9517) Tel 415-549-3030; Toll free: 800-999-4650.

Carabis, *(Carabis, Anne J.; 0-9605802),* 25 Nelson Ave., Latham, NY 12110 (SAN 216-5600) Tel 518-783-9807.

Cardamom, *(Cardamom Pr.; 0-9611118),* P.O. Box 275, Richmond, ME 04357 (SAN 283-2836) Tel 207-666-5645.

Cardot Entpr Inc, *(Cardot Enterprises; 0-9607516),* 214 Avenida Barbera, Sonoma, CA 95476 (SAN 238-6283).

Career Aids, *(Career Aids; 1-55646),* Div. of Opportunities for Learning, Inc., P.O. Box 8103, 941 Hickory Ln., Mansfield, OH 44901-8103 (SAN 219-3159) Tel 419-589-2010.

Career Pr Inc, *(Career Pr., Inc.; 0-934829; 1-56414),* 180 Fifth Ave., Hawthorne, NJ 07507 (SAN 694-3640) Tel 201-427-0229; Toll free: 800-227-3371.

Careers Inc, *(Careers, Inc.; 0-9623657),* P.O. Box 135, Largo, FL 34649; Toll free: 800-726-0441; 1211 Tenth St., SW, Largo, FL 34640 Tel 813-584-7333.

Careys Pub Co, *(Carey's Publishing Co.; 0-9617859; 0-9619313),* 6865 Tom King Bayou Rd., Gulf Breeze, FL 32561 (SAN 665-4436) Tel 904-939-1227.

Caribbean Rsch Ctr, *(Caribbean Research Ctr.; 1-878433),* 1150 Carroll St., Brooklyn, NY 11225 Tel 718-270-6422.

Caring Tree, *(Caring Tree Pubns.; 0-9618740),* 1459 Indiana Ave., South Pasadena, CA 91030 (SAN 668-7687) Tel 213-256-2987.

Carlisle Pr, *(Carlisle Pr.; 0-9627369),* P.O. Box 747, Mechanicsburg, PA 17055 Tel 717-697-1642.

Carlsons, *(Carlsons'; 0-944996),* P.O. Box 364, Lindsborg, KS 67456 (SAN 245-9485); 114 S. Main, Lindsborg, KS 67456 (SAN 245-9493) Tel 913-227-3360.

Carlton, *(Carlton Pr., Inc.; 0-8062),* 11 W. 32nd St., New York, NY 10001 (SAN 201-9655) Tel 212-714-0300; Dist. by: Confide, Personal Counseling Services, Inc., Box 56, Tappan, NY 10983 Tel 914-359-8860.

Carnegie Mus, *(Carnegie Museum of Natural History; 0-911239),* Div. of Carnegie Institute, ; Orders to: Pubns. Sec., 4400 Forbes Ave., Pittsburgh, PA 15213 (SAN 268-6686) Tel 412-622-3284.

Carol Mendel, *(Mendel, Carol; 0-9607696; 0-935179),* P.O. Box 6022, San Diego, CA 92106 (SAN 219-3329) Tel 619-226-1406.

Carol Paperbacks *Imprint of* **Carol Pub Group**

Carol Pub Group, *(Carol Publishing Group; 0-8184),* 600 Madison Ave., 11th Flr., New York, NY 10022 (SAN 201-1131) Tel 212-486-2200; Orders to: 120 Enterprise Ave., Secaucus, NJ 07094 (SAN 630-4524) Tel 201-866-8159. *Imprints:* Birch Ln Pr (Birch Lane Press); Carol Paperbacks (Carol Paperbacks); Citadel Pr (Citadel Press).

Carolina Acad Pr, *(Carolina Academic Pr.; 0-89089),* 700 Kent St., Durham, NC 27701 (SAN 210-7848) Tel 919-489-7486.

Carolina Biological, *(Carolina Biological Supply Co., Pubns. Dept.; 0-89278),* 2700 York Rd., Burlington, NC 27215 (SAN 249-2784) Tel 919-584-0381; Toll free: 800-334-5551.

Carolina Cnslts Network, *(Carolina Consultants Network - Publishing Div.; 0-9627795),* P.O. Box 374, Rock Hill, SC 29731; Toll free: 800-553-0958; 3425 Homestead Rd., Suite 100, Rock Hill, SC 29730 Tel 803-327-5488.

Caroline Hse *Imprint of* **Boyds Mills Pr**

Carolrhoda Bks, *(Carolrhoda Bks., Inc.; 0-87614),* 241 First Ave., N., Minneapolis, MN 55401 (SAN 201-9671) Tel 612-332-3344; Toll free: 800-328-4929.

Carriage Hse Studio Pubns, *(Carriage Hse. Studio Pubns.; 0-9624342),* P.O. Box 712, Ferndale, CA 95536; 847 Van Ness Ave., Ferndale, CA 95536 Tel 707-786-4042.

Carroll CA, *(Carroll Publishing Co.; 0-8449),* P.O. Box 1200, Palo Alto, CA 94302 (SAN 220-018X) Tel 415-424-1400; Orders to: P.O. Box 1200, Palo Alto, CA 94302 (SAN 220-0198). Do not confuse with Carroll Publishing Co., Washington, DC.

Carson-Dellos, *(Carson-Dellosa Publishing Co., Inc.; 0-88724),* P.O. Box 35665, Greensboro, NC 27425-5665 (SAN 287-5896) Tel 919-632-0084; Toll free: 800-321-0943; Orders to: P.O. Drawer 16327, Greensboro, NC 27416 (SAN 665-8296).

Carson Ent, *(Carson Enterprises, Inc.; 0-941620),* Drawer 71, Deming, NM 88031 (SAN 239-1716) Tel 505-546-3252.

Carson Pr, *(Carson Pr.; 0-934360),* 733 W. Carson St., Torrance, CA 90502 (SAN 213-2958) Tel 213-328-3180.

Carvin Pub, *(Carvin Publishing, Inc.; 0-9616390),* P.O. Box 850200, New Orleans, LA 70185-0200 (SAN 659-0888); 57 Neron Pl., New Orleans, LA 70118 (SAN 659-0896) Tel 504-866-4351.

Casa Bautista, *(Casa Bautista de Publicaciones; 0-311),* Div. of Southern Baptist Convention, P.O. Box 4255, 7000 Alabama St., El Paso, TX 79914 (SAN 220-0139) Tel 915-566-9656. *Imprints:* Edit Mundo (Editorial Mundo Hispano).

Castle Bks, *(Castle Bks., Inc.; 0-916693),* P.O. Box 17262, Memphis, TN 38187 (SAN 204-4005); 1445 Tuscany Way, Germantown, TN 38138-1823 (SAN 658-2575) Tel 901-754-4160.

Castlemarsh, *(Castlemarsh Pubns.; 0-942250),* P.O. Box 60728, Savannah, GA 31420 (SAN 240-8708) Tel 912-352-3273.

Cat-Tales Pr, *(Cat-Tales Pr.; 0-917107),* 51 Seventh Ave., Brooklyn, NY 11217 (SAN 655-6132) Tel 718-230-0724.

Catalina Creations, *(Catalina Creations; 0-9621316),* Div. of Kingett Art Service, P.O. Box 1211, Avalon, CA 90704 (SAN 251-0669) Tel 213-510-0660.

Catalpa Pr, *(Catalpa Pr.; 0-9619943),* P.O. Box 7468, Auburn, CA 95604 (SAN 246-9189) Tel 916-268-9534.

Catalyst Pr, *(Catalyst Pr.; 0-9623897),* P.O. Box 6181, Newport News, VA 23606; 9 Briar Patch Pl., Newport News, VA 23606 Tel 804-596-1031. Do not confuse with companies with the same name in Berkeley, CA, Kentfield, CA.

Cath Authors, *(Catholic Authors Pr.; 0-910334),* 1201 S. Kirkwood Rd., Kirkwood, MO 63122 (SAN 203-6274) Tel 314-965-4801.

Cathedral Shop, *(Cathedral Shop, The; 0-915075),* Cathedral of St. John the Divine, 112th St. at Amsterdam Ave., New York, NY 10025 (SAN 289-7792) Tel 212-222-7448.

Catholic Bk Pub, *(Catholic Bk. Publishing Co.; 0-89942),* 257 W. 17th St., New York, NY 10011 (SAN 204-3432) Tel 212-243-4515.

Caxton, *(Caxton Printers, Ltd.; 0-87004),* 312 Main St., Caldwell, ID 83605 (SAN 201-9698) Tel 208-459-7421.

Cay-Bel, *(Cay-Bel Publishing Co.; 0-941216),* 272 Center St., Bangor, ME 04401 (SAN 238-9215) Tel 207-941-2367.

CBH Pub, *(CBH Publishing, Inc.; 0-9604538),* P.O. Box 11738, Chicago, IL 60611 (SAN 216-2288) Tel 312-642-2990; Dist. by: Chicago Review Pr., 814 N. Franklin St., Chicago, IL 60610 (SAN 213-5744) Tel 312-337-0747.

CBHL Inc, *(Council on Botanical & Horticultural Libraries, Inc.; 0-9621791),* Univ. of Oregon, Knight Library, Eugene, OR 97403-1299 (SAN 252-2500) Tel 503-686-3078.

CBN Publishing, *(CBN Publishing; 1-55574),* CBN Ctr., WOSC 336, Virginia Beach, VA 23463 (SAN 699-9484) Tel 804-424-7777.

CBP, *(CBP Pr.; 0-8272),* Div. of Christian Board of Pubn., P.O. Box 179, Saint Louis, MO 63166 (SAN 201-4408) Tel 314-231-8500; Toll free: 800-366-3383; Dist. by: Abingdon Pr., 201 Eighth Ave., S., Box 801, Nashville, TN 37202 (SAN 201-0054) Tel 615-749-6290; Toll free: 800-251-3320.

CBridge Pubns, *(C'Bridge Pubns.; 0-9621018),* 5230 Pennridge Ln., Dallas, TX 75241 (SAN 250-6955) Tel 214-371-8935.

CCC Pubns, *(CCC Pubns.; 0-918259),* 20306 Tau Pl., Chatsworth, CA 91311 (SAN 669-666X) Tel 818-407-1661.

CCPr *Imprint of Macmillan*

CDA Commns, *(C.D.A. Communications, Inc.; 0-9626438),* P.O. Box 423, Severna Park, MD 21146-0423; 12500 Fletchertown Rd., General Service Office, Bowie, MD 20720 Tel 301-464-2995.

Cedar Glade Pr, *(Cedar Glade Pr.),* P.O. Box 1664, Jefferson City, MO 65102 (SAN 250-1031) Tel 314-635-8771.

Cedars WI, *(Cedars Pr., The; 0-917575),* N. 5597 County Hwy. T, Green Lake, WI 54941 (SAN 657-1301) Tel 414-294-6754.

CEF Inc, *(Children's Express Foundation, Inc.; 0-9621641),* 245 Seventh Ave., New York, NY 10001 (SAN 251-6993) Tel 212-620-0098.

CEF Press, *(Child Evangelism Fellowship Pr.; 1-55976),* Hwy., Warrenton, MO 63383 (SAN 211-7789) Tel 314-456-4321; Toll free: 800-748-7710; Dist. by: Spring Arbor Distributors, 10885 Textile Rd., Belleville, MI 48111 (SAN 158-9016) Tel 313-481-0900; Toll free: 800-395-9955; Dist. by: Child Evangelism Fellowship, P.O. Box 222, Parramatta, .

Ceise Corp, *(Ceise Corp.; 0-9623985),* P.O. Box 8, Hillsboro, OR 97123-0008; Toll free: 800-888-5268; HCR 61, 77-21, Banks, OR 97106 Tel 503-649-7631.

Celestial Arts, *(Celestial Arts Publishing Co.; 0-912310; 0-89087),* Subs. of Ten Speed Pr., P.O. Box 7327, Berkeley, CA 94707 (SAN 159-8333) Tel 415-524-1801; Toll free: 800-841-2665.

Celia Totus Enter, *(Celia Totus Enterprises, Inc.; 0-931363; 1-56041),* 1192 LaRue Rd., P.O. Box 192, Toppenish, WA 98948 (SAN 682-5567) Tel 509-865-2480.

Cellar, *(Cellar Bk. Shop),* 18090 Wyoming, Detroit, MI 48221 (SAN 213-4330) Tel 313-861-1776.

Centering Corp, *(Centering Corp.; 1-56123),* P.O. Box 3367, Omaha, NE 68103; 4902 Happy Hollow, Omaha, NE 68104 Tel 402-553-1200.

Centerstream Pub, *(Centerstream Publishing; 0-931759),* P.O. Box 5450, Fullerton, CA 92635 (SAN 683-8022) Tel 714-779-9390.

Central Agency, *(Central Agency for Jewish Education; 0-930029),* Affil. of Greater Miami Jewish Federation, 4200 Biscayne Blvd., Miami, FL 33137 (SAN 669-747X) Tel 305-576-4030.

Central Conf, *(Central Conference of American Rabbis; 0-916694; 0-88123),* 192 Lexington Ave., New York, NY 10016 (SAN 204-3262) Tel 212-684-4990.

CES Compu-Tech, *(CES/Compu-Tech, Inc.; 0-917531; 1-56177),* 155 Hempstead Tpke., West Hempstead, NY 11552 (SAN 669-6708) Tel 516-565-5110; Toll free: 800-443-8061.

CES Industries, *(CES Industries, Inc.; 0-86711),* 130 Central Ave., Farmingdale, NY 11735 (SAN 237-9864) Tel 516-293-1420.

Cetacean Society, *(Cetacean Society International; 0-9618858),* 190 Stillwold Dr., Wethersfield, CT 06109 (SAN 242-3952) Tel 203-563-6444.

CFFC POWs MIAs, *(Civil Fact Finding Commission for POWs/MIAs in Southeast Asia; 0-9623659),* Rte. 3, Box 96, Rochester, IN 46975 Tel 219-223-4971.

Ch Brethren Womens Caucus, *(Church of the Brethren, Women's Caucus; 0-9618243),* Rte. 1, Box 215, Mount Solon, VA 22843 (SAN 666-9042) Tel 703-350-2922.

Challenge Pr, *(Challenge Pr.; 0-89421),* Div. of Economic Research Ctr., Inc., 3955 Denlinger Rd., Dayton, OH 45426-2329 (SAN 210-0509).

Championship Bks & Vid Prodns, *(Championship Bks. & Video Productions; 0-932741; 1-56404),* P.O. Box 1166, ISU Sta., Ames, IA 50010 (SAN 656-1217); 400 Main St., Ames, IA 50010 Tel 515-232-3687.

Chandler White, *(Chandler/White Publishing Co.; 1-877804),* 30 E. Huron St., Suite 4402, Chicago, IL 60611 Tel 312-280-9451; Dist. by: Advanced Knowledge, 1840 Columbia Dr., Suite B, Decatur, GA 30032 (SAN 630-365X) Tel 404-289-0204.

Chaosium, *(Chaosium Inc.; 0-933635),* 950A 56th St., Oakland, CA 94608 (SAN 692-6460) Tel 415-547-7681.

Char Ed Inst, *(Character Education Institute; 0-913413),* Dimension II Bldg., 8918 Tesoro, Suite 220, San Antonio, TX 78217 (SAN 236-154X) Tel 512-829-1727; Toll free: 800-284-0499.

Char-L, *(Char-L Video Intensive Phonics, Inc.; 0-9605654; 1-880137),* 570 S. Church St., Apt. 2E, Decatur, IL 62522 (SAN 238-7751) Tel 217-422-0077.

Character Builders, *(Character Builders for Kids!; 0-9615279),* 4313 Hargrave St., Orlando, FL 32803 (SAN 694-4604) Tel 407-898-3622; Dist. by: Baker & Taylor Bks., Eastern Div., 50 Kirby Ave., Somerville, NJ 08876-0734 (SAN 169-4901) Tel 201-722-8000; Toll free: 800-526-3825; Dist. by: Baker & Taylor Bks., Midwestern Div., 501 S. Gladiolus St., Momence, IL 60954-2444 (SAN 169-2100) Tel 815-472-2444; Toll free: 800-435-5111; 800-892-1892 (in Illinois); Dist. by: Baker & Taylor Bks., Southern Div., Mt. Olive Rd., Commerce, GA 30599-9988 (SAN 169-1503) Tel 303-296-1830; Toll free: 800-241-6004; 800-282-6854 (in Georgia); Dist. by: Baker & Taylor Bks., Western Div., 380 Edison Way, Reno, NV 89564 (SAN 169-4464) Tel 702-786-6700; Toll free: 800-648-3540; 800-524-2486 (in Canada); Dist. by: Ingram Bk. Co., 1125 Heil Quaker Blvd., La Vergne, TN 37086-1986 (SAN 169-7978) Tel 615-793-5000; Toll free: 800-937-8000; Dist. by: Spring Arbor Distributors, 10885 Textile Rd., Belleville, MI 48111 (SAN 158-9016) Tel 313-481-0900; Toll free: 800-521-3690.

Character Res, *(Character Research Pr.; 0-915744),* 266 State St., Schenectady, NY 12305 (SAN 209-1240) Tel 518-370-0025.

Charcoal St Pr, *(Charcoal Street Pr.; 0-9624296),* 22531 Honnold Dr., Saugus, CA 91350 Tel 213-312-2394.

Charill Pubs, *(Charill Pubs.; 0-9620182),* P.O. Box 150124, Saint Louis, MO 63110 (SAN 247-9133); 4468 San Francisco Ave., Saint Louis, MO 63115 (SAN 247-9141) Tel 314-382-4998.

Chariot Bks *Imprint of Cook*

Charles A Lemoine, *(Lemoine, Charles A.; 0-941327),* 11311 Plank Rd., Baton Rouge, LA 70811 (SAN 666-4342) Tel 504-775-3056.

Charles River Bks, *(Charles River Bks.; 0-89182),* 1 Thompson Sq., P.O. Box 65, Boston, MA 02129 (SAN 209-2530) Tel 617-259-8857.

Charlesbridge Pub, *(Charlesbridge Publishing; 0-935508; 0-88106),* 85 Main St., Watertown, MA 02172 (SAN 240-5474) Tel 617-926-0329; Toll free: 800-225-3214.

Charming World, *(Charming World Pubns.; 0-9622564),* Div. of Marcella's Handicrafts, 320 Mesa Rd., Santa Monica, CA 90402 Tel 213-454-3623.

Charnwood *Imprint of Ulverscroft*

Chartwell, *(Chartwell Hse., Inc.; 0-910354),* P.O. Box 166, Bowling Green Sta., New York, NY 10004 (SAN 203-6398).

Chateau Thierry, *(Chateau Thierry Pr.; 0-935046),* Div. of Joan Thiry Enterprises, Ltd., 2100 W. Estes, Chicago, IL 60645 (SAN 281-4056) Tel 312-262-2234.

Chatham Pr, *(Chatham Pr., Inc.; 0-85699),* P.O. Box A, Old Greenwich, CT 06870 (SAN 201-9795) Tel 203-531-7807.

Chatham River Pr *Imprint of Outlet Bk Co*

Chatterbox Pr, *(Chatterbox Pr.; 0-943129),* P.O. Box 7933 F.D.R. Sta., New York, NY 10150-2411 (SAN 668-1417) Tel 212-702-9729; 248 94th St., Brooklyn, NY 11209 (SAN 668-1425) Tel 718-745-1809; Dist. by: Gryphon Hse., Inc., P.O. Box 275, Mount Rainier, MD 20712 (SAN 169-3190) Tel 301-779-6200; Toll free: 800-638-0928.

CHB Goodyear Comm, *(Childrens Hospital of Buffalo, Josephine Goodyear Committee; 0-9616699),* 219 Bryant St., Buffalo, NY 14222 (SAN 661-227X) Tel 716-634-7778.

Cheap St, *(Cheap Street; 0-941826),* Rte. 2, Box 293, New Castle, VA 24127 (SAN 239-1783) Tel 703-864-6288.

Checkerboard Pr, *(Checkerboard Pr., Inc.; 1-56288),* 30 Vesey St., New York, NY 10007 Tel 212-571-6300.

Cheers, *(Cheers; 0-9617744),* 253 Alberta Dr., Atlanta, GA 30305 (SAN 664-6859) Tel 404-233-4897.

Cheertime USA, *(Cheertime U.S.A.; 0-9614174),* P.O. Box 2844, Edmond, OK 73083 (SAN 686-6204) Tel 405-341-0853; Orders to: P.O. Box 2844, Edmond, OK 73083 (SAN 665-8636).

Cheeruppet, *(Cheeruppet World, Inc.; 0-914201),* 2264 Calle Iglesia, Mesa, AZ 85202 (SAN 287-6000) Tel 602-839-3319; Orders to: 2405 E. Southern Ave., Sta., Tempe, AZ 85282 (SAN 287-6019) Tel 602-831-6088.

Cheetah Pub, *(Cheetah Publishing, Inc.; 0-936241),* 275 N. Forest Lake Dr., Altamonte Springs, FL 32714 (SAN 697-0443) Tel 407-862-2726.

Cheever Pub, *(Cheever Publishing, Inc.; 0-915708),* P.O. Box 700, Bloomington, IL 61702 (SAN 207-9410) Tel 309-378-2961.

Chelsea Hse, *(Chelsea Hse. Pubs.; 0-87754; 1-55546; 0-7910),* Div. of Main Line Bk. Co., 95 Madison Ave., New York, NY 10016 (SAN 206-7609) Tel 212-683-4400; Toll free: 800-848-2665.

Chenier Educ Enter, *(Chenier Educational Enterprises, Inc.; 0-9626061),* P.O. Box 265, Wells, MI 49894; 5727 Second Ave., N., Wells, MI 49894 Tel 906-786-8088.

Cherokee, *(Cherokee Publishing Co.; 0-87797),* Div. of Larlin Corp., P.O. Box 1730, Marietta, GA 30061 (SAN 650-0404) Tel 404-424-6210.

Cherokee Comn, *(Cherokee Communication; 0-9628630),* Div. of Cherokee Boys Club, Inc., P.O. Box 507, Cherokee, NC 28719; 4 Acquoni Rd., Cherokee, NC 28719 Tel 704-497-5510.

Cherokee Pubns, *(Cherokee Pubns.; 0-935741),* P.O. Box 256, Cherokee, NC 28719 (SAN 696-2785) Tel 704-497-2202.

Cherry Lane, *(Cherry Lane Bks.; 0-89524),* Div. of Cherry Lane Music Co., Inc., 10 Midland Ave., Port Chester, NY 10573 (SAN 219-0788) Tel 914-937-8601; P.O. Box 430, Port Chester, NY 10573; Dist. by: Alfred Publishing Co., Inc., 16380 Roscoe Blvd., Suite 200, Van Nuys, CA 91406-1215 Tel 818-891-5999; Toll free: 800-292-6122; 800-821-6083 (in California).

Cherubim, *(Cherubim; 0-938574),* P.O. Box 75, Fort Tilden, NY 11695 (SAN 215-8523).

Chicago Review, *(Chicago Review Pr., Inc.; 0-914090; 0-914091; 1-55652),* 814 N. Franklin St., Chicago, IL 60610 (SAN 213-5744) Tel 312-337-0747.

Chicago Zoo, *(Chicago Zoological Society; 0-913934),* 3300 Golf Rd., Brookfield, IL 60513 (SAN 663-4672) Tel 312-485-0263.

Chick Pubns, *(Chick Pubns.; 0-937958),* P.O. Box 662, Chino, CA 91708-0662 (SAN 211-7770) Tel 714-987-0771.

Child Alphabet, *(Children's Alphabet; 0-940047),* 3228 Castle Rock Rd., Oklahoma City, OK 73120 (SAN 664-0540) Tel 405-755-3290.

Child Media Inst
See Family Media

Child Teens Dir, *(Children's & Teens' Directory; 0-9623899),* Div. of Johnson-Anderson Publishing Co., 12335 Santa Monica Blvd., No. 144, Los Angeles, CA 90025 Tel 213-473-8833.

Child Time Pubs, *(Child Time Pubs.; 0-929934),* 16000 W. Nine Mile Rd., Suite 512, Southfield, MI 48075 (SAN 250-7757) Tel 313-559-8446.

Child Ventures, *(Children's Ventures, Inc.; 0-9615985),* P.O. Box 3000, Grants Pass, OR 97526 (SAN 698-1569) Tel 503-479-2929; Dist. by: Pacific Pipeline, Inc., 19215 66th Ave., S., Kent, WA 98032 (SAN 208-2128) Tel 206-872-5523; Toll free: 800-426-4727 (in northern California, Montana, Idaho, Nevada, Montana); 800-562-4647 (in Washington).

Childbirth Graphics, *(Childbirth Graphics, Ltd.; 0-943114),* P.O. Box 20540, Rochester, NY 14602-0540 (SAN 240-3587) Tel 716-272-9230.

Children First, *(Children First Pr.; 0-9603696),* Box 8008, Ann Arbor, MI 48107 (SAN 212-4904) Tel 313-668-8056.

Children Learn Ctr, *(Children's Learning Ctr., Inc.; 0-917206),* 4660 E. 62nd St., Indianapolis, IN 46220 (SAN 208-5933) Tel 317-251-6241.

Childrens, *(Children's Pr.; 0-516),* Div. of Grolier, Inc., 5440 N. Cumberland Ave., Chicago, IL 60656 (SAN 201-9264) Tel 312-693-0800; Toll free: 800-621-1115. *Imprints:* Elk Grove Bks (Elk Grove Books); Golden Gate (Golden Gate).

Childrens Art, *(Children's Art Foundation, Inc.; 0-89409),* Box 83, Santa Cruz, CA 95063 (SAN 210-0533) Tel 408-426-5557; Toll free: 800-447-4569.

Childrens Book Pr, *(Children's Bk. Pr.; 0-89239),* 1461 Ninth Ave., San Francisco, CA 94122 (SAN 210-7864) Tel 415-664-8500; Marketing: 1339 61st St., Emeryville, CA 94608 (SAN 250-3271) Tel 415-655-3395; Dist. by: Talman Co., 150 Fifth Ave., Rm. 514, New York, NY 10011 (SAN 200-5204) Tel 212-620-3182; Dist. by: Raintree Pubs., Inc., 310 W. Wisconsin Ave., Mezzanine Level, Milwaukee, WI 53203 (SAN 207-9607) Tel 414-273-0873; Toll free: 800-558-7264.

Childrens Corner, *(Children's Corner Pr.; 0-944326),* 6125 Mooresville Rd., Indianapolis, IN 46241 (SAN 243-5276) Tel 317-856-5565.

Children's Mus, *(Children's Museum of Oak Ridge; 0-9606832),* P.O. Box 3066, Oak Ridge, TN 37830 (SAN 219-7227) Tel 615-482-1074.

Childrens Reading Inst, *(Children's Reading Institute; 0-923223),* Div. of GMH Marketing, Houston Dr., Durham, CT 06422 (SAN 251-7442) Tel 203-349-1014.

Childrens TV Resource, *(Children's Television Resource & Education Ctr.; 0-929831),* 330 Townsend St., 234, San Francisco, CA 94107 (SAN 250-636X) Tel 415-243-9943; Dist. by: JTG of Nashville, 1024C 18th Ave., S., Nashville, TN 37212 (SAN 630-3323) Tel 615-329-3036; Toll free: 800-222-2584.

Childrens Work, *(Children's Work; 1-878300),* 1307 S. 1100 E., Salt Lake City, UT 84105 Tel 801-467-6024; Dist. by: Educational Bk. Distributors, P.O. Box 551, San Mateo, CA 94401 (SAN 158-2259) Tel 415-344-8458.

Childs Gift
See Someday Baby

Childs Min Bk Co, *(Childs Miniature Bk. Co.; 1-878582),* P.O. Box 5878, Westport Sta., Kansas City, MO 64111; 4320 Wornall Rd., No. 452, Kansas City, MO 64111 Tel 816-531-2325.

Childs Play, *(Child's Play-International; 0-85953),* 137 E. 25th St., 9th Flr., New York, NY 10010 (SAN 216-2121) Tel 212-685-0838.

Childs Play
See PJC Lrng Mtrls

Childs World, *(Child's World, Inc.; 0-89565; 0-913778),* 123 S. Broad St., Mankato, MN 56001 (SAN 211-0032) Tel 507-345-6806; Toll free: 800-445-6209; Dist. by: Encyclopaedia Brittanica Education Corp., 310 S. Michigan, Chicago, IL 60604 (SAN 201-3851) Tel 312-347-7900; Toll free: 800-554-9862.

Chimurenga, *(Chimurenga; 0-9624153),* 2121 Seventh St., No. 212, Berkeley, CA 94710 Tel 408-287-9228.

China Bks, *(China Bks. & Periodicals, Inc.; 0-8351),* 2929 24th St., San Francisco, CA 94110 (SAN 145-0557) Tel 415-282-2994.

Chitra Pubns, *(Chitra Pubns.; 0-9622565),* P.O. Box 437, New Milford, PA 18834; 301 Church St., New Milford, PA 18834 Tel 717-465-3306.

Chocho Bks, *(Chocho Bks.; 0-922273),* 11929 Caminito Corriente, San Diego, CA 92128 (SAN 251-3196) Tel 619-487-8213.

Choice Pub NY, *(Choice Publishing, Inc.; 0-945260),* Affil. of Choice Concepts, Inc., 53 Watermill Ln., Great Neck, NY 11021 (SAN 246-2729) Tel 516-487-3060. Do not confuse with companies with the same name in Santa Monica, CA, Fullerton, CA, Nashville, TN.

Chosen Bks *Imprint of* Revell

Chowder Pr, *(Chowder Pr.; 0-9614546),* 13 Schuyler Dr., Saratoga Springs, NY 12866 (SAN 691-7984) Tel 518-587-2808.

Chr Classics, *(Christian Classics, Inc.; 0-87061),* P.O. Box 30, Westminster, MD 21158 (SAN 163-2949) Tel 301-848-3065; Toll free: 800-888-3065.

Chr Lit, *(Christian Literature Crusade, Inc.; 0-87508),* P.O. Box 1449, Fort Washington, PA 19034-8449 (SAN 169-7358) Tel 215-542-1240; Toll free: 800-659-1240.

Chr Pubns, *(Christian Pubns., Inc.; 0-87509),* 3825 Hartzdale Dr., Camp Hill, PA 17011 (SAN 202-1617) Tel 717-761-7044; Toll free: 800-233-4443.

Chr Science, *(Christian Science Publishing Society; 0-87510),* P.O. Box 1875, Boston, MA 02117 (SAN 203-6541) Tel 617-450-2000; Toll free: 800-225-7090; Orders to: P.O. Box 78643, Indianapolis, IN 46278 (SAN 203-655X); Toll free: 800-448-2466; Dist. by: National Bk. Network, 4720A Boston Way, Lanham, MD 20706-4310 (SAN 630-0065) Tel 301-459-8696; Toll free: 800-462-6420. *Imprints:* Bks from the Christ Sci Monitor (Books from the Christian Science Monitor).

Christian Center, *(Christian Ctr. of Christos Wisdom; 0-944517),* P.O. Box 14825, Long Beach, CA 90803-1380 (SAN 243-0320) Tel 213-434-2976.

Christian Light, *(Christian Light Pubns., Inc.; 0-87813),* P.O. Box 1126, Harrisonburg, VA 22801 (SAN 206-7315) Tel 703-434-0768.

Christian Pub, *(Christian Publishing Services, Inc.; 0-88144),* Subs. of Harrison Hse. Pubs., P.O. Box 55388, Tulsa, OK 74155-1388 (SAN 260-0285) Tel 918-584-5535.

Christianica, *(Christianica Ctr.; 0-911346),* 1807 Prairie St., Glenview, IL 60025 (SAN 204-739X) Tel 708-657-3818.

Christmans, *(Christmans; 0-9625413),* P.O. Box 510, Pittsburg, KS 66762; Rte. 1, P.O. Box 172A, Oronogo, MO 64855 Tel 417-842-3322.

Chrome Yellow, *(Chrome Yellow Private Pr./Nords Studio; 0-935656),* 200 Central Ave., Crescent City, FL 32112 (SAN 200-7614) Tel 904-698-1009; Toll free: 800-247-6657.

Chron Guide, *(Chronicle Guidance Pubns., Inc.; 0-912578; 1-55631),* P.O. Box 1190, Moravia, NY 13118-1190 (SAN 202-1641) Tel 315-497-0330; Toll free: 800-622-7284.

Chronicle Bks, *(Chronicle Bks.; 0-87701; 0-8118),* Div. of Chronicle Publishing Co., 275 Fifth St., San Francisco, CA 94103 (SAN 202-165X) Tel 415-777-7240; Toll free: 800-722-6657 (orders only).

Chrstn Life Workshops, *(Christian Life Workshops; 0-923463),* P.O. Box 2250, Gresham, OR 97030-0642 (SAN 251-656X) Tel 503-667-3942.

CIBC, *(Council on Interracial Bks. for Children, Inc.; 0-930040),* 1841 Broadway, Rm. 500, New York, NY 10023 (SAN 110-6643) Tel 212-757-5339.

Cinc Hist Soc, *(Cincinnati Historical Society, The; 0-911497),* Eden Park, Cincinnati, OH 45202 (SAN 263-9718) Tel 513-241-4622.

Cinco Puntos, *(Cinco Puntos Pr.; 0-938317),* 2709 Louisville, El Paso, TX 79930 (SAN 661-0080) Tel 915-566-9072.

Cinemed
See CNS Prods

Circuit Pubns, *(Circuit Pubns.; 0-923573),* P.O. Box 1201, Marblehead, MA 01945 (SAN 251-7736); 7545 Graves Rd., Cincinnati, OH 45243 (SAN 251-7744) Tel 513-561-5413.

Circuit Writer, *(Circuit Writer; 0-9617971),* 4107 Canterbury Way, Temple Hills, MD 20748 (SAN 666-2447) Tel 301-423-4356.

CIRI Found, *(CIRI Foundation, The; 0-938227),* P.O. Box 93330, Anchorage, AK 99509-3330 (SAN 666-6213); 2525 C St., Suite 507, Anchorage, AK 99503 (SAN 667-593X) Tel 907-274-8638.

CIS Comm, *(CIS Communications, Inc.; 0-935063; 1-56062),* 180 Park Avenue, Lakewood, NJ 08701 (SAN 694-5953) Tel 201-367-7858.

Citadel Pr *Imprint of* **Carol Pub Group**

CITE, *(Center for International Training & Education; 0-938960),* 777 United Nations Plaza, Suite 9A, New York, NY 10017 (SAN 217-0957) Tel 212-953-6920.

Civan Inc, *(Civan, Inc.; 0-9621700),* 100 Butterville Rd., New Paltz, NY 12561 (SAN 251-8619) Tel 914-255-0696.

Claitors, *(Claitors Publishing Div.; 0-87511),* 3165 S. Acadian at Interstate 10, Box 3333, Baton Rouge, LA 70821 (SAN 206-8346) Tel 504-344-0476.

Claremount Pr, *(Claremount Pr.),* Box 177, Cooper Sta., New York, NY 10003 (SAN 219-466X).

Clarion Bks *Imprint of* **HM**

Clarion Pr, *(Clarion Pr.; 0-923296),* 8551 Towson Blvd., No. H, Miamisburg, OH 45342-3714 (SAN 252-1911) Tel 513-866-4996.

Clark City Pr, *(Clark City Pr.; 0-944439),* P.O. Box 1358, Livingston, MT 59047 (SAN 243-699X); Toll free: 800-835-0814; 109 W. Callender, Livingston, MT 59047 (SAN 243-7007) Tel 406-222-7412; Dist. by: Consortium Bk. Sales & Distribution, 287 E. Sixth St., Suite 365, Saint Paul, MN 55101 (SAN 200-6049) Tel 612-221-9035; Toll free: 800-283-3572.

Clark Davis, *(Davis, Clark, Publishing Co.; 0-945938),* 12551 Carrington Hill Dr., Gaithersburg, MD 20878-2240 (SAN 248-1596) Tel 301-926-4588.

Clark Pub, *(Clark Publishing Co.; 0-931054),* Dist. by: Caxton Printers, Ltd., 312 Main St., Caldwell, ID 83605 (SAN 201-9698) Tel 208-459-7421; Toll free: 800-657-6465 (in Idaho).

Clarus Music, *(Clarus Music, Ltd.; 0-86704),* 340 Bellevue Ave., Yonkers, NY 10703 (SAN 216-6615) Tel 914-591-7715.

Claycomb Pr, *(Claycomb Pr., Inc.; 0-933905),* P.O. Box 70822, Chevy Chase, MD 20813-0822 (SAN 692-7521) Tel 301-656-1057.

Claymont Comm, *(Claymont Communications; 0-934254),* Box 112, Charles Town, WV 25414 (SAN 211-7010) Tel 304-725-1523.

Clementine Pub Co, *(Clementine Publishing Co.; 0-9623987),* Old Rte. 23B, P.O. Box 237, Leeds, NY 12451 Tel 212-864-6191.

Clemons Hartley, *(Clemons/Hartley; 0-9623084),* P.O. Box 1177, Philomath, OR 97370; 3339 Chintimini, Corvallis, OR 97333. Moved, left no forwarding address.

Clerc Bks *Imprint of* **Gallaudet Univ Pr**

Cleve Mus Nat Hist, *(Cleveland Museum of Natural History; 1-878600),* Wade Oval, Cleveland, OH 44106 Tel 216-231-4600.

Cliffs, *(Cliffs Notes, Inc.; 0-8220),* P.O. Box 80728, Lincoln, NE 68501 (SAN 202-1706); Toll free: 800-228-4078; 4851 S. 16th St., Lincoln, NE 68512 Tel 402-423-5050.

Clipboard, *(Clipboard Pubns.; 0-9606084),* 18 Observatory Ct., Pullman, WA 99163 (SAN 216-8006) Tel 509-633-1546.

Cloud Ten, *(Cloud 10 Creations, Inc.; 0-910349),* 805 Circuit Ct., Virginia Beach, VA 23454 (SAN 241-2896); Dist. by: Trillium Press, P.O. Box 209, Monroe, NY 10950 (SAN 212-4637) Tel 914-783-2999.

Clyde Pr, *(Clyde Pr.; 0-933190),* 373 Lincoln Pkwy., Buffalo, NY 14216 (SAN 213-8395) Tel 716-875-4713; 174 Depew Ave., Buffalo, NY 14214 (SAN 241-662X) Tel 716-834-1254.

CMark Pr, *(CMark Pr.; 0-9621308),* 211 N. Scrivener, Lake Elsinore, CA 92330 (SAN 251-0561) Tel 714-674-4785.

CMSP Projects, *(CMSP Projects; 0-942851),* School of Engineering, 51 Astor Pl., New York, NY 10003 (SAN 667-6731) Tel 212-228-0950.

CMU Clarke Hist Lib, *(Central Michigan Univ., Clarke Historical Library; 0-916699),* Central Michigan Univ., Park Bldg., No. 409, Mount Pleasant, MI 48859 (SAN 218-6799) Tel 517-774-3352.

CNS Prods, *(CNS Productions; 0-926544),* P.O. Box 96, Ashland, OR 97520-1962; Toll free: 800-888-0617; 130 Third St., Ashland, OR 97520 Tel 503-488-2805.

Cnsltnts Unlimited, *(Consultant's Unlimited; 0-9621505),* 88 Winwood Dr., R.F.D. Box 164, Center Barnstead, NH 03225 (SAN 251-4540) Tel 603-776-6937; Dist. by: Vantage Pr., Inc. (for ISBN 0-533-07464-9), 516 W. 34th St., New York, NY 10001 (SAN 206-8893) Tel 212-736-1767.

Coach Hse
See Dramatic Pub

Cobblehill Bks *Imprint of Dutton Child Bks*

Cobblestone Pub, *(Cobblestone Publishing, Inc.; 0-9607638; 0-942389),* 30 Grove St., Peterborough, NH 03458 (SAN 237-9937) Tel 603-924-7209.

Cocek Pr, *(Cocek Pr.; 0-9626468),* 2546 Kansas, No. 206, Santa Monica, CA 90404 Tel 213-829-9073.

Coffee Break, *(Coffee Break Pr.; 0-933992),* P.O. Box 103, Burley, WA 98322 (SAN 212-341X) Tel 206-851-4074.

Coffee Hse, *(Coffee Hse. Pr./Toothpaste Pr.; 0-915124; 0-918273),* 27 N. Fourth St., Minneapolis, MN 55401 (SAN 206-3883) Tel 612-338-0125; Dist. by: Consortium Bk. Sales & Distribution, 287 E. Sixth St., Suite 365, Saint Paul, MN 55101 (SAN 200-6049) Tel 612-221-9035; Toll free: 800-283-3572.

Cole Enter, *(Cole Enterprises; 1-878514),* 2195 E. River Rd., Suite 103, Tucson, AZ 85718-6586.

Coll Acceptance, *(College Acceptance; 0-9615165),* 2 Clover Ln., Randolph, NJ 07869 (SAN 694-3624) Tel 201-895-3390.

Collaborare Pub, *(Collaborare Publishing; 0-931881),* 354 Front, Upper Sandusky, OH 43351 (SAN 686-0486) Tel 419-294-3207; Dist. by: Gallopade: Carole Marsh Bks., General Delivery, Bath, NC 27808 (SAN 213-8441) Tel 919-923-4291.

Collaborative Learn, *(Collaborative Learning Systems; 0-910817),* Rte. 3, P.O. Box 1650, San Antonio, TX 78218 (SAN 269-0721) Tel 512-651-9100.

Collector Bks, *(Collector Bks.; 0-89145),* Div. of Schroeder Publishing Co., Inc., 5801 Kentucky Dam Rd., Paducah, KY 42001 (SAN 157-5368) Tel 502-898-6211; Toll free: 800-626-5420; P.O. Box 3009, Paducah, KY 42001 (SAN 200-7479).

College Pr Pub, *(College Pr. Publishing Co., Inc.; 0-89900),* Box 1132, 205 N. Main, Joplin, MO 64802 (SAN 211-9951) Tel 417-623-6280; Toll free: 800-289-3300.

Collier *Imprint of Macmillan*

Collier Young Ad *Imprint of Macmillan Child Grp*

Collins Assocs, *(Collins Assocs.; 0-9623393),* 170 E. 116th St., Suite 300, New York, NY 10029 Tel 212-996-6700.

Colonial Pr AL, *(Colonial Pr.; 0-938991),* 1237 Stevens Rd., Bessemer, AL 35023 (SAN 662-6599) Tel 205-428-2146.

Color Me Well, *(Color Me Well Pubns.; 1-878083),* P.O. Box 16321, Plantation, FL 33318 (SAN 297-2956); 6081 SW 14th St., Plantation, FL 33317 Tel 305-748-5535.

Colorful Lrngs, *(Colorful Learnings/Maria Elena Buria; 1-878926),* 7860 Imperial Hwy., Suite E162, Downey, CA 90242; 10440 Paramount Blvd., Apt. A102, Downey, CA 90241 Tel 213-927-8721.

Colormore Inc, *(Colormore, Inc.; 0-945600),* P.O. Box 111249, Carrollton, TX 75011-1249 (SAN 247-4530); 1024 N. Cypress, Wichita, KS 67206 (SAN 247-4549).

Colorsong Prodns, *(Colorsong Productions, Inc.; 0-9623234),* 2685 Valleyview Ln., NE, Saint Paul, MN 55112 Tel 612-780-3557.

Columbia Sacramento, *(Columbia Pubs.; 0-9622514),* 709 Columbia Dr., Suite 1200, Sacramento, CA 95864 Tel 916-973-0145. Do not confuse with Columbia Pubs., Cardiff, CA.

Columbia U Pr, *(Columbia Univ. Pr.; 0-231),* 562 W. 113th St., New York, NY 10025 (SAN 212-2472) Tel 212-316-7100; Orders to: 136 S. Broadway, Irvington-on-Hudson, NY 10533 (SAN 212-2480) Tel 914-591-9111.

Columbine *Imprint of Fawcett*

COMAL Users, *(COMAL Users Group, U.S.A., Ltd.; 0-928411),* 5501 Groveland Terrace, Madison, WI 53716-3251 (SAN 669-5256) Tel 608-222-4432.

COMAP Inc, *(COMAP, Inc.; 0-912843),* 60 Lowell St., Arlington, MA 02174 (SAN 282-9991) Tel 617-641-2600.

Comedy Writ, *(Comedy Writings & Co.; 0-9609224),* 2034 Grace Ave., Los Angeles, CA 90068 (SAN 240-9771).

Comico Comic Co, *(Comico The Comic Co.; 0-938965),* 1547 DeKalb St., Norristown, PA 19401 (SAN 661-6836) Tel 215-277-4305.

Comm & Learning, *(Communication & Learning Innovators, Ltd.; 0-932361),* 2727 29th St., NW, No. 201, Washington, DC 20008-5503 (SAN 687-3723) Tel 301-627-2488.

Comm Intervention, *(Community Intervention, Inc.; 0-9613416; 0-945485),* 529 S. Seventh St., Suite 570, Minneapolis, MN 55415 (SAN 656-9706) Tel 612-332-6537; Toll free: 800-328-0417.

Communication Skill, *(Communication Skill Builders; 0-88450),* 3830 E. Bellevue, P.O. Box 42050, Tucson, AZ 85733 (SAN 201-7768) Tel 602-323-7500.

Compact Bks, *(Compact Bks.; 0-936320),* 2131 Hollywood Blvd., Suite 204, Hollywood, FL 33020 (SAN 215-0670) Tel 305-925-5242.

Compact Classics, *(Compact Classics, Inc.; 1-880184),* 3855 S. 500 W., Suite A, Salt Lake City, UT 84115 Tel 801-268-9777; Toll free: 800-676-9777.

COMPAS, *(COMPAS; 0-927663),* 308 Landmark Ctr., 75 W. Fifth, Saint Paul, MN 55102 Tel 612-292-3249.

CompCare, *(CompCare Pubs.; 0-89638),* Div. of Comprehensive Care, Inc., 2415 Annapolis Ln., Minneapolis, MN 55441 (SAN 630-3153) Tel 612-559-4800; Toll free: 800-328-3330.

Comprehen Health Educ, *(Comprehensive Health Education Foundation; 0-935529),* 22323 Pacific Hwy., S., Seattle, WA 98198 (SAN 696-3668) Tel 206-824-2907; Toll free: 800-323-2433.

Comptr Pub Enterprises, *(Computer Publishing Enterprises; 0-945776),* P.O. Box 23478, San Diego, CA 92193 (SAN 247-9087); Toll free: 800-544-5541.

Compu-Aid, *(Compu-Aid Computer Consultants; 0-9624107),* 2859 Glacier, Saginaw, MI 48603 Tel 517-799-0243.

Compute Pubns, *(Compute Pubns. International, Ltd.; 0-87455; 0-942386),* 324 W. Wendover Ave., Greensboro, NC 27408 (SAN 202-1552) Tel 919-275-9809; Dist. by: Chilton Bk. Co., 201 King of Prussia Rd., Radnor, PA 19089-0230 (SAN 202-1552) Tel 215-964-4000; Toll free: 800-695-1214.

Computer Assis, *(Computer Assisted Library Information Co., Inc.; 0-916625),* P.O. Box 15916, Saint Louis, MO 63114 (SAN 296-4856) Tel 314-863-8028; Toll free: 800-762-9466.

Computer Lit Pr, *(Computer Literacy Pr.; 0-941681),* 353 E. Tenth St., Suite C624, Gilroy, CA 95021-2373 (SAN 666-3133) Tel 408-848-1483.

Computer Pub, *(Computer Publishing, Inc.; 0-928564),* 5900 Cassandra Smith Rd., Hixson, TN 37343 (SAN 670-9117) Tel 615-842-4600.

Comstock Bon, *(Comstock Bonanza Pr.; 0-933994),* 18919 William Quirk Memorial Dr., Grass Valley, CA 95945 (SAN 223-694X) Tel 916-273-6220.

Concept Spelling, *(Concept Spelling, Inc.; 0-935276),* P.O. Box 7200, Costa Mesa, CA 92626 (SAN 213-909X) Tel 714-770-0811.

Concepts N Pub, *(Concepts 'N' Publishing; 1-879940),* P.O. Box 51185, Pacific Grove, CA 93950; 582 Lighthouse Ave., Suite 7, Pacific Grove, CA 93950 Tel 408-899-8852. Do not confuse with Concepts Publishing in Waitsfield, VT.

Concern, *(Concern, Inc.; 0-937345),* 1794 Columbia Rd., NW, Washington, DC 20016 (SAN 225-1728) Tel 202-328-8160.

Conch Mag, *(Conch Magazine, Ltd. Pubs.; 0-914970),* Div. of Conch Communications Co., P.O. Box 777, Buffalo, NY 14213 (SAN 206-4855) Tel 716-885-3686.

Concordia, *(Concordia Publishing Hse.; 0-570),* Subs. of Lutheran Church Missouri Synod, 3558 S. Jefferson Ave., Saint Louis, MO 63118 (SAN 202-1781) Tel 314-268-1000; Toll free: 800-325-3040; 800-325-3040.

Condor Pubns Inc, *(Condor Pubns., Inc.; 0-929853),* P.O. Box 88366, Carol Stream, IL 60188-0366 (SAN 250-5215); 137 Pebblecreek Trail, Carol Stream, IL 60188-0366 (SAN 250-5223) Tel 708-690-9819.

Congdon & Weed, *(Congdon & Weed; 0-86553),* 180 N. Michigan Ave., Chicago, IL 60601-7401 (SAN 214-3585) Tel 312-782-9181; Toll free: 800-221-7945; Dist. by: Contemporary Bks., Inc., 180 N. Michigan Ave., Chicago, IL 60601 (SAN 202-5493) Tel 312-782-9181.

Construct Educ, *(Constructive Educational Concepts, Inc.; 0-934734),* 213 Duncaster Rd., Box 667, Bloomfield, CT 06002 (SAN 215-7446).

Consulting Psychol, *(Consulting Psychologists Pr., Inc.; 0-917592; 0-89106),* 3803 E. Bayshore Rd., Palo Alto, CA 94303 (SAN 201-7849) Tel 415-969-8901; Toll free: 800-624-1765.

Consumer Reports, *(Consumer Reports Bks.; 0-89043),* Div. of Consumers Union of U.S., Inc., 101 Truman Ave., Yonkers, NY 10703 (SAN 224-1048) Tel 914-378-2000.

Contemp Bks, *(Contemporary Bks., Inc.; 0-8092),* 180 N. Michigan Ave., Chicago, IL 60601 (SAN 202-5493) Tel 312-782-9181. *Imprints:* Calico Bks (Calico Books).

Continuum, *(Continuum Publishing Co.; 0-8264),* 370 Lexington Ave., New York, NY 10017 (SAN 213-8220) Tel 212-532-3650; Dist. by: Publisher Resources, Inc., 1224 Heil Quaker Blvd., P.O. Box 7001, La Vergne, TN 37086-7001 (SAN 630-5431) Tel 615-793-5090.

Cook, *(Cook, David C., Publishing Co.; 0-89191; 0-912692; 1-55513; 0-7814),* 850 N. Grove Ave., Elgin, IL 60120 (SAN 206-0981) Tel 708-741-2400; Toll free: 800-323-7543; 800-533-2201. *Imprints:* Chariot Bks (Chariot Books).

Copperfield Pr, *(Copperfield Pr.; 0-933857),* 1103 Saint Williams Ave., Round Rock, TX 78681-6460 (SAN 692-7351) Tel 512-255-7191.

Corita Comm, *(Corita Communications, Inc.; 0-933016),* 1301 N. Kenter Ave., Los Angeles, CA 90049 (SAN 212-2723) Tel 213-559-2375; Orders to: P.O. Box 49368, Los Angeles, CA 90049 (SAN 666-6531).

Cornerstone Pr, *(Cornerstone Pr.; 0-918476),* P.O. Box 388, Arnold, MO 63010-0388 (SAN 210-0584) Tel 314-296-9662. Do not confuse with companies with the same name in Chicago, IL, Pearland, TX, Edison, NJ.

Cornucop Pub, *(Carolina Cornucopia Educational Publishing Co.; 0-935911),* 5610 Laurel Crest Dr., Durham, NC 27712 (SAN 696-7213) Tel 919-471-1873; Dist. by: Nancy Roberts' Collection, 3600 Chevington Rd., Charlotte, NC 28211 (SAN 200-5786) Tel 704-364-4608.

Corona Pub, *(Corona Publishing, Co.; 0-931722),* 1037 S. Alamo, San Antonio, TX 78210 (SAN 211-8491) Tel 512-227-1771; Toll free: 800-759-8120; Dist. by: Taylor Publishing Co., 1550 W. Mockingbird Ln., Dallas, TX 78235 (SAN 202-7631) Tel 214-637-2800; Toll free: 800-677-2800, Ext. 589.

Corpuscles Intergalactica, *(Corpuscles Intergalactica; 0-9620961),* 40 Johnson Heights, Waterville, ME 04901 (SAN 250-202X) Tel 207-873-6486.

Cosmic Color Bks, *(Cosmic Coloring Bks.; 0-9622288),* 23 Tahoe Dr., Kalispell, MT 59901 Tel 406-752-5338.

Cosmic Concepts Pr, *(Cosmic Concepts Pr.; 0-9620507),* 2531 Dover Ln., Saint Joseph, MI 49085 (SAN 248-6431) Tel 616-428-2792.

Cosmic Hse NM, *(Cosmic Hse.; 0-932492),* P.O. Box 10515, Alameda, NM 87184 (SAN 211-9331) Tel 505-821-3147.

Cottage Bks, (Cottage Bks.; 0-911253), Subs. of Sam Yette Enterprises, P.O. Box 2071, Silver Spring, MD 20902 (SAN 285-0044); 1801A Duke Dr., Silver Spring, MD 20902 (SAN 241-6719) Tel 301-649-5123. Do not confuse with Cottage Bks., Oakland, CA.

Cottage Pr MA, (Cottage Pr., The; 1-882063), P.O. Box 135, Lincoln Center, MA 01773 (SAN 248-3319); 27 Lincoln Rd., Lincoln Center, MA 01773 (SAN 248-3327) Tel 617-259-8771.

Cottage Pub Co, (Cottage Publishing Co.; 0-915479), 200 Lafayette Ave., Hawthorne, NJ 07506 (SAN 291-1299) Tel 201-427-2830.

Cottage Wordsmiths, (Cottage Wordsmiths; 0-9624155), P.O. Box 81006, Pittsburgh, PA 15217; 6732 Reynolds St., Pittsburgh, PA 15206 Tel 412-661-7054.

Cottontail Creations, (Cottontail Creations, Inc.; 0-9624767), P.O. Box 11453, Charlotte, NC 28209; 320 Meacham, Charlotte, NC 28203 Tel 704-342-0750.

Cottonwood KS, (Cottonwood Pr.; 1-878434), P.O. Box J, Kansas Union, Univ. of Kansas, Lawrence, KS 66045 Tel 913-864-3777. Do not confuse with companies with the same name in Boulder, CO, Fort Collins,CO, Novato, CA.

Cottonwood Pr, (Cottonwood Pr.; 1-877673), 305 W. Magnolia, Suite 398, Fort Collins, CO 80521 Tel 303-493-1286. Do not confuse with companies with same name in Boulder, CO, Novato, CA, Lawrence, KS.

Coun India Ed, (Council for Indian Education; 0-89992), 517 Rimrock Rd., Billings, MT 59102 (SAN 252-2117) Tel 406-252-7451; Orders to: Box 31215, Billings, MT 59107 (SAN 689-836X) Tel 406-259-9153.

Coun Oak Bks, (Council Oak Bks.; 0-933031), 1408 S. St. Louis, Tulsa, OK 74120 (SAN 689-5522) Tel 918-587-6454; Orders to: Council Oak Distribution, 313 E. Rogers, Skiatook, OK 74070; Toll free: 800-247-8850 (orders only).

Country Messenger Inc, (Country Messenger, Inc.; 0-9619407), P.O. Box 207, Marine on Saint Croix, MN 55047 (SAN 244-5638); 16022 Oakhill Rd., N., Marine on Saint Croix, MN 55047 (SAN 244-5646) Tel 612-433-3845.

Country Pub Inc, (Country Pubs., Inc., The; 0-9610772; 0-939685), P.O. Box 798, Berryville, VA 22611 (SAN 265-1130) Tel 703-955-1298; Toll free: 800-247-6253; Dist. by: Kable News Co., Inc., 11 W. 42nd St., New York, NY 10036 (SAN 169-5835) Tel 212-768-1000; Toll free: 800-223-6640.

Country Schl Pubns, (Country School Pubns.; 0-942565), 6373 N. Eighth, Fresno, CA 93710 (SAN 667-2027) Tel 209-435-8845.

Countryman, (Countryman Pr., Inc.; 0-914378; 0-88150), P.O. Box 175, Woodstock, VT 05091-0175 (SAN 206-4901) Tel 802-457-1049.

Courage Bks Imprint of Running Pr

Cove Pr CA, (Cove Pr.; 0-9620065), 567 San Antonio Ave., San Diego, CA 92106 (SAN 247-526X) Tel 619-222-4666. Do not confuse with Cove Pr., Austin, TX.

Cove View, (Cove View Pr.; 0-931896), 375 Tudor St., Ashland, OR 97520 (SAN 220-0422).

Covenant Pubs, (Covenant Pub.; 1-879420), P.O. Box 26361, Philadelphia, PA 19141; 1931 Mather Way, Elkins Park, PA 19117 Tel 215-887-5108.

Coward Imprint of Putnam Pub Group

Cowley Pubns, (Cowley Pubns.; 0-936384; 1-56101), Div. of Society of St. John the Evangelist, 28 Temple Pl., Boston, MA 02111 (SAN 213-9987) Tel 617-423-2427; Toll free: 800-225-1534.

CPA Old Lyme, (Career Planning Assocs.; 0-922898), Div. of Madison Productions, 4 Davis Rd., W., Old Lyme, CT 06371 (SAN 251-5024) Tel 203-434-1456; Toll free: 800-243-1171.

CPI Pub, (CPI Publishing, Inc.), 145 E. 49th St., New York, NY 10017 (SAN 218-6896) Tel 212-753-3800; Dist. by: Modern Curriculum Press, 13900 Prospect Rd., Cleveland, OH 44136 (SAN 206-6572) Tel 216-238-2222; Toll free: 800-321-3106.

Crabtree Pub Co, (Crabtree Publishing Co.; 0-86505), 350 Fifth Ave., Suite 3308, New York, NY 10118 (SAN 251-4796) Tel 212-496-5040; Toll free: 800-387-7650. Do not confuse with Crabtree Publishing, Federal Way, WA.

Crains Muscle, (Crain's Muscle World; 0-929994), P.O. Box 1322, Shawnee, OK 74802-1322 (SAN 251-1223); 1510 N. Kickapoo, Shawnee, OK 74801 (SAN 251-1231) Tel 405-275-3689.

Cranberry Origs, (Cranberry Originals Pr.; 0-9622784), P.O. Box 25, Port Edwards, WI 54469; 1631 Fourth St., Port Edwards, WI 54469 Tel 715-887-3755; Dist. by: Baker & Taylor Bks., Midwestern Div., 501 S. Gladiolus St., Momence, IL 60954 (SAN 169-2100) Tel 815-472-2444; Toll free: 800-435-5111; 800-892-1892 (in Illinois).

Cranbrook Pub, (Cranbrook Publishing; 0-9604690), 2302 Windemere, Flint, MI 48503 (SAN 215-7470) Tel 313-338-6403.

Crane Pub Co, (Crane Publishing Co.; 0-89075), 1909 Yardley Rd., Yardley, PA 19067-3206 (SAN 207-1053) Tel 215-295-2843.

Cranehill Pr, (Cranehill Pr.; 0-9618182), 708 Comfort Rd., Spencer, NY 14883 (SAN 666-7538) Tel 607-277-3058.

Cranky Nell Bk Imprint of Kane-Miller Bk

Crayons Pubns, (Crayons Pubns.; 0-927024), P.O. Box 322, Milford, MA 01757 Tel 508-478-4400.

CRC Pubns, (CRC Pubns.; 0-933140; 0-930265; 1-56212), 2850 Kalamazoo Ave., SE, Grand Rapids, MI 49560 (SAN 212-727X) Tel 616-246-0752; Toll free: 800-333-8300.

Crea Tea Assocs, (Creative Teaching Assocs.; 1-878669), Div. of Master Creative Teaching Assocs., P.O. Box 7766, Fresno, CA 93747; 5629 E. Westover, Fresno, CA 93747 Tel 209-291-6626.

Creare Pubns, (Creare Pubns.; 0-943901), P.O. Box 1660, San Juan Capistrano, CA 92693 (SAN 242-2123); 32561 Carreterra, San Juan Capistrano, CA 92675 (SAN 242-2131) Tel 714-496-4093.

Creat Concern, (Creative Concern Pubns.; 0-917117), 12066 Suellen Cir., West Palm Beach, FL 33414 (SAN 655-6221) Tel 407-793-5854; Orders to: 3208 Mayaguana Ln., Lantana, FL 33462 (SAN 665-8431) Tel 407-433-5735.

Creat Lrng Consultants, (Creative Learning Consultants; 0-9623835; 1-880505), 1610 Brook Lynn Dr., Beavercreek, OH 45432 Tel 513-427-0530; Toll free: 800-729-5137.

Creat Res NC, (Creative Resources, Inc.; 0-937306), 3548 Round Oak Rd., Charlotte, NC 28210 (SAN 200-2779) Tel 704-554-8357.

Creat Teach Pr, (Creative Teaching Pr., Inc.; 0-916119), 10701 Holder St., Cypress, CA 90630 (SAN 294-9180) Tel 714-995-7888; Toll free: 800-444-4287.

Create Learn, (Creative Learning Assn., Inc.; 0-88193), R.R. 4, Box 330, Charleston, IL 61920 (SAN 669-4101) Tel 217-345-1010.

Creative Arts Bk, (Creative Arts Bk. Co.; 0-88739; 0-916870), 833 Bancroft Way, Berkeley, CA 94710 (SAN 208-4880) Tel 415-848-4777.

Creative Changes, (Creative Changes; 0-9621898), 368 S. 850, W., Orem, UT 84058 Tel 801-226-5533; Dist. by: Publishers Bk. Sales, Inc., P.O. Box 27734, Salt Lake City, UT 84127-0734 (SAN 200-8688) Tel 801-972-6338.

Creative Dimensions, (Creative Dimensions; 0-939985), 518 Highland Dr., Bellingham, WA 98225 (SAN 663-8872) Tel 206-733-5024; Orders to: P.O. Box 1393, Bellingham, WA 98227 (SAN 242-1445).

Creative Ed, (Creative Education, Inc.; 0-87191; 0-88682), 123 S. Broad St., P.O. Box 227, Mankato, MN 56001 (SAN 202-201X) Tel 507-388-6273; Toll free: 800-445-6209; Dist. by: Encyclopaedia Britannica, Inc., 310 S. Michigan Ave., Chicago, IL 60604-9839 (SAN 204-1464) Tel 312-347-7959; Toll free: 800-554-9862.

Creative Enterprise, (Creative Enterprise; 0-9623041), P.O. Box 830, New York, NY 10018; 475 E. 94th St., Brooklyn, NY 11212 Tel 718-346-1028.

Creative Learning, (Creative Learning Pr., Inc.; 0-936386), P.O. Box 50392, Saint Louis, MO 63105 (SAN 214-2368); Orders to: P.O. Box 320, Mansfield Center, CT 06250 Tel 203-423-8120.

Creative License, (Creative License Studio; 0-942675), 5861 N. Winthrop Ave., Chicago, IL 60660 (SAN 667-3805) Tel 312-784-5809.

Creative Pr Works, (Creative Press Works; 0-9621681), P.O. Box 280556, Memphis, TN 38128 (SAN 251-8708); 3966 S. Lakewood Dr., Memphis, TN 38128 (SAN 251-8716) Tel 901-382-8246.

Creative Storytime, (Creative Storytime Pr.; 0-934876), P.O. Box 572, Minneapolis, MN 55458 (SAN 211-6634) Tel 612-926-9740.

Creative Texas, (Creative Publishing Co.; 0-932702), P.O. Box 9292, College Station, TX 77842 (SAN 209-3499) Tel 409-775-6047.

Creative Therapeutics, (Creative Therapeutics; 0-933812), 155 County Rd., P.O. Box R, Cresskill, NJ 07626-0317 (SAN 212-6508) Tel 201-567-7295; Toll free: 800-544-6162.

Creative Walking, (Creative Walking, Inc.; 0-939041), 8230 Forsyth Blvd., Suite 209, Clayton, MO 63105 (SAN 662-6521) Tel 314-721-3600.

Creole Connect, (Creole Connection; 0-9630075), 27400 Tampa Ave., Suite 304, Hayward, CA 94544 Tel 415-782-3717.

Crest Imprint of Fawcett

Crestwood Hse Imprint of Macmillan Child Grp

CRIC Prod, (CRIC Productions, Inc.; 0-935357), Box 1214, Kingshill, Saint Croix, VI 00850 (SAN 696-4141) Tel 809-778-2043.

Cricket Power, (Cricket Power Records & Tapes; 0-9614998), 826 Wilton Rd., Greenville, NH 03048-1010 (SAN 693-9473) Tel 603-878-2587; P.O. Box 1010, .

Cricketfield Pr, (Cricketfield Pr.; 0-9614281), 3 High St., Camden, ME 04843 (SAN 687-4401) Tel 207-236-3083.

Critical Book, (Critical Thinking Bk. Co.; 0-935475), 110 Sarah Dr., Mill Valley, CA 94941 (SAN 696-415X) Tel 415-383-8805.

Crizmac, (Crizmac; 0-945666), 1641 N. Bentley, Tucson, AZ 85716 (SAN 667-1101) Tel 602-326-2373.

Crnrstn Bks Imprint of ABC-CLIO

Crocodile Bks Imprint of Interlink Pub

Cromlech Bks, (Cromlech Bks., Inc.; 0-9618059), Nobska Rd., Box 145, Woods Hole, MA 02543 (SAN 666-1025) Tel 508-540-1185.

Cross Lengua Prod, (Cross-Lengua Productions; 0-9617451), P.O. Box 144781, Miami, FL 33114-4781 (SAN 664-0613) Tel 305-386-9469.

Crossing Pr, (Crossing Pr., The; 0-912278; 0-89594), P.O. Box 1048, Freedom, CA 95019 (SAN 202-2060); Toll free: 800-777-1048; 97 Hangar Way, Watsonville, CA 95076 Tel 408-722-0711.

Crossroad NY, (Crossroad Publishing Co.; 0-8245), 370 Lexington Ave., New York, NY 10017 (SAN 287-0118) Tel 212-532-3650; Dist. by: Publisher Resources, Inc., 1224 Heil Quaker Blvd., P.O. Box 7001, La Vergne, TN 37086-7001 (SAN 630-5431); Toll free: 800-937-5557.

Crossway Bks Imprint of Good News

Crowell Jr Bks Imprint of HarpC Child Bks

Crown, (Crown Pubs., Inc.; 0-517), Div. of Random Hse., Inc., 201 E. 50th St., New York, NY 10022 (SAN 200-2639) Tel 212-572-2600; Toll free: 800-726-0600 (customer service only). Imprints: C N Potter Bks (Potter, Clarkson N., Books); Harmony (Harmony Books).

Crumb Elbow Pub, (Crumb Elbow Publishing; 0-89904), P.O. Box 294, Rhododendron, OR 97049 (SAN 679-128X) Tel 503-622-4798.

Crusade Pubs, (Crusade Pubns), 11326 Ranchito St., El Monte, CA 91732 (SAN 203-8595).

Crystal, (Crystal Productions; 0-924509; 1-56290), 1812 Johns Dr., P.O. Box 2159, Glenview, IL 60025 (SAN 653-2489) Tel 708-657-8144; Toll free: 800-255-8629.

Crystal Clarity, (Crystal Clarity, Pubs.; 0-916124; 1-878265), 14618 Tyler Foote Rd., Nevada City, CA 95959 (SAN 201-1778) Tel 916-292-3485; Toll free: 800-424-1055; Dist. by: Bookpeople, 2929 Fifth St., Berkeley, CA 94710 (SAN 168-9517) Tel 415-549-3030; Toll free: 800-999-4650.

Crystal Press, *(Crystal Pr., Inc.; 0-9623321),* c/o Crib Diaper Service, 5273 Hanson Ct., Crystal, MN 55429 Tel 612-533-1616. Do not confuse with Crystal Pr. Inc., Ukiah, CA.

Crystal Pubs, *(Crystal Pubs.; 0-934687),* 1900 E. Tropicana Ave., No. 56, Las Vegas, NV 89119 (SAN 694-1443) Tel 702-736-1665; Dist. by: Baker & Taylor Bks., Eastern Div., 50 Kirby Ave., Somerville, NJ 08876 (SAN 169-4901) Tel 201-722-8000; Toll free: 800-435-1845; 800-352-4833 (in New Jersey); Dist. by: Quality Bks., Inc., 918 Sherwood Dr., Lake Bluff, IL 60044-2204 (SAN 169-2127) Tel 708-295-2010; Toll free: 800-323-4241 (Libraries only); Dist. by: Brodart Co., 500 Arch St., Williamsport, PA 17705 (SAN 169-7684) Tel 717-326-2461; Toll free: 800-233-8467; Dist. by: Key Bk. Service, Inc., 425 Asylum St., Bridgeport, CT 06610 (SAN 169-0671) Tel 203-334-2165; Toll free: 800-243-2790.

Crystal TX, *(Crystal Pr.; 0-9625832),* Div. of The Room, Inc., 2235 Brentwood, Houston, TX 77019 Tel 713-524-6574. Do not confuse with companies with the same name in Flint, MI, Crystal River, FL.

CSI Pub, *(Common Sense Information Publishing; 0-9621230),* P.O. Box 218, Evanston, WY 82930 (SAN 250-782X) Tel 801-774-9683.

CSS of Ohio, *(CSS of Ohio; 0-89536; 1-55673),* 628 S. Main St., Lima, OH 45804 (SAN 207-0707) Tel 419-227-1818; Toll free: 800-537-1030.

Ctr Appl Res, *(Center for Applied Research in Education, The; 0-87628),* Subs. of Prentice Hall, Inc., Englewood Cliffs, NJ 07632 (SAN 206-6424) Tel 201-592-2481; Orders to: P.O. Box 430, West Nyack, NY 10994 (SAN 241-6492) Tel 201-767-5937.

Ctr Career Dev, *(Ctr. for Career Development, Inc.; 1-878472),* 7745 Reinhold Dr., Cincinnati, OH 45237 Tel 513-821-7477.

Ctr Env Educ, *(Center for Environmental Education; 0-9615294),* 1725 DeSales St., NW, Suite 500, Washington, DC 20036 (SAN 694-566X) Tel 202-429-5609.

Ctr Learning, *(Center for Learning, The; 1-56077),* 21590 Center Ridge Rd., Rocky River, OH 44116 (SAN 248-2029) Tel 216-331-1404; Dist. by: William C Brown Pubs. (Social studies & English titles only), 2460 Kerper Blvd., Dubuque, IA 52001 (SAN 203-2864) Tel 319-588-1451; Toll free: 800-922-7696; Orders to: Center for Learning, The (Religion & Novel/Drama titles only), P.O. Box 910, Villa Maria, PA 16155; Toll free: 800-767-9090.

Ctr Marine Cnsrv, *(Center for Marine Conservation; 1-879269),* 1725 Desales St. NW, No. 500, Washington, DC 20036 Tel 202-429-5609.

Ctr Sacred Healing, *(Ctr. for Sacred Healing Arts Publishing Co.; 0-936901),* 1329 W. 37th Dr., Los Angeles, CA 90007 (SAN 658-5558) Tel 213-733-1272.

Ctr Sci Public, *(Center for Science in the Public Interest; 0-89329),* 1875 Connecticut Ave. NW, No. 300, Washington, DC 20009-5728 (SAN 207-6543) Tel 202-332-9110.

Ctr Social Studies, *(Center for Social Studies Education; 0-945919),* 3857 Willow Ave., Pittsburgh, PA 15234 (SAN 248-0573) Tel 412-341-1967.

Ctr Stage Prodns, *(Center Stage Productions Corp.; 1-56213),* 1289 Bartlein Ct., Menasha, WI 54952 Tel 414-738-9692; Toll free: 800-553-4058.

Ctr Sutton Movement, *(Ctr. for Sutton Movement Writing, Inc., The; 0-914336),* P.O. Box 7344, Newport Beach, CA 92658-7344 (SAN 203-154X) Tel 714-644-8342.

Cttnwd Graphics, *(Cottonwood Graphics, Inc.; 0-9626999),* P.O. Box 848, Whitefish, MT 59937-0484; Toll free: 800-937-6343.

Cuchullain Pubns, *(Cuchullain Pubns.; 0-9614659),* 1 Rose Marie's Alley, Fort Wayne, IN 46802 (SAN 249-0781) Tel 219-423-9602.

CUE Pubns, *(CUE Pubns.; 0-9629647),* Div. of Creations Unlimited Enterprises, 13223 Black Mountain Rd., No. 384, San Diego, CA 92129 Tel 619-538-0204.

Cuisenaire, *(Cuisenaire Co. of America, Inc.; 0-914040; 0-938587),* 12 Church St., New Rochelle, NY 10805 (SAN 201-7806) Tel 914-235-0900.

Culpepper Pr, *(Culpepper Pr.; 0-929636),* 2901 Fourth St., SE, Minneapolis, MN 55414 (SAN 249-7719) Tel 612-378-2116.

Cumberland Pr, *(Cumberland Pr.; 0-87027),* P.O. Box 1082, Portland, ME 04104-1082 (SAN 203-2090) Tel 207-865-6045.

Cupery Pr, *(Cupery Pr.; 0-9626188),* 4819 Ardmore, Okemos, MI 48864 Tel 517-349-2533.

Curbstone, *(Curbstone Pr.; 0-915306),* 321 Jackson St., Willimantic, CT 06226 (SAN 209-4282) Tel 203-423-9190; Dist. by: InBook Distribution Co., P.O. Box 120470, 140 Commerce St., East Haven, CT 06512 (SAN 630-5547) Tel 203-467-5434; Toll free: 800-253-3605.

Current Inc, *(Current, Inc.; 0-944943),* Div. of Primerica Corp., P.O. Box 2559, Colorado Springs, CO 80901 (SAN 246-0378); 1005 E. Woodmen Rd., Colorado Springs, CO 80920 (SAN 246-0386) Tel 719-594-4100.

Current Leaders Pub, *(Current Leaders Publishing Co., Inc.; 0-9624900),* 815 Scott Way, Lansdale, PA 19446 Tel 215-584-8944; Toll free: 800-826-8574.

Custom Curriculum, *(Custom Curriculum Concepts; 0-9611480),* 1600 N-1-35E, Suite 112, Carrollton, TX 75006 (SAN 285-2373) Tel 214-466-0104.

Custom Hse, *(Custom Hse. Pr.; 0-940560),* 2900 Newark Rd., P.O. Box 2369, Zanesville, OH 43701 (SAN 216-3632).

CWP, *(Counseling & Workshop Professionals; 0-9621701),* 965 Ewald, SE, Salem, OR 97302 (SAN 251-8635) Tel 503-588-1010.

Cygnet Pr, *(Cygnet Pr.; 0-9623611),* 1033 Humble, Suite 1000, El Paso, TX 79915 Tel 915-779-6057.

CZM Pr, *(CZM Pr.; 1-878461),* Div. of CZM Assocs., Inc., 48 West St., Suite 104, Annapolis, MD 21401 Tel 301-263-2121.

D A Curtis, *(Curtis, Donald A.; 0-9610284),* 904 W. Main St., East Palestine, OH 44413 (SAN 263-9971) Tel 216-426-4389.

D A Jensen, *(Jensen, Delwin A.; 0-9624413),* 814 N. Grand, Pierre, SD 57501 Tel 605-224-5438.

D Adamson, *(Adamson, Douglas),* New Boston Rd., Box 173, Sanbornton, NH 03269 (SAN 208-1288) Tel 603-934-5333; Orders to: Douglas Adamson, P.O. Box 41, First New Hamshire Bank Bldg., Franklin, NH 03235 (SAN 661-9304) Tel 603-934-6226.

D & M Lena, *(Lena, Dan & Marie; 0-9617032),* P.O. Box 160, Chicago, IL 60635 (SAN 662-8745); 2506 N. Newcastle, Chicago, IL 60635 (SAN 662-8753) Tel 312-745-1025.

D C Comics, *(DC Comics, Inc.; 0-930289; 1-56389),* Div. of Time-Warner, Inc., 1325 Ave. of the Americas, New York, NY 10019 Tel 212-484-2800.

D C Raemsch, *(Raemsch, Dorothy C.; 0-9605398),* HCR Box 890, West Oneonta, NY 13861 (SAN 214-4530) Tel 607-432-4836.

D Cohen Mathman, *(Cohen, Don, The Mathman; 0-9621674),* 809 Stratford Dr., Champaign, IL 61821-4140 (SAN 251-866X) Tel 217-356-4555.

D Cornell, *(Cornell, Donald; 0-9620738),* P.O. Box 2160, R.D. 2, Rte. 196, Fort Ann, NY 12827 (SAN 249-9924) Tel 518-632-5391.

D E Donel, *(Donel, D. E., Co.; 0-913657),* P.O. Box 376, Loma Linda, CA 92354 (SAN 286-0929) Tel 714-796-5598.

D Garlits, *(Garlits, Don, Inc.; 0-9626565),* 13700 SW 16th Ave., Ocala, FL 32676 Tel 904-245-8661.

D Greenbaum, *(Greenbaum, David J.; 0-9621833),* 259-02 Pembroke Ave., Great Neck, NY 11020 Tel 516-484-4402.

D Hockenberry, *(Hockenberry, Debra; 1-878056),* 2030 Whitehall Ave., Allentown, PA 18104 Tel 215-437-2198.

D I Fine, *(Fine, Donald I., Inc.; 0-917657; 1-55611),* 19 W. 21st St., New York, NY 10010 (SAN 656-9749) Tel 212-727-3270; Dist. by: Penguin USA, P O Box 120, Bergenfield, NJ 07621-0120 (SAN 282-5074) Tel 201-387-0600; Toll free: 800-526-0275.

D K McCullough, *(McCullough, Duane K.; 0-9621605),* 31 Snapper Ave., Key Largo, FL 33037 (SAN 252-0494) Tel 305-451-0907.

D L Taylor, *(Taylor, Dorothy Loring; 0-9610640),* R. R. 2, Box 152, Virginia, IL 62691 (SAN 265-3567) Tel 217-458-2506.

D M Gales, *(Gales, Donald Moore; 0-9620623),* 19 N. Middleridge Ln., Rolling Hills, CA 90274 (SAN 249-4760) Tel 213-541-3030.

D Miller Fndtn, *(Miller, D., Foundation; 0-9622172),* 3040 Post Oak Blvd., Suite 1630, Houston, TX 77056-6512 Tel 713-961-3255.

DADA Pubns, *(DADA Pubns.; 0-9621598),* 2308 Sussex Ave., Modesto, CA 95351 (SAN 252-1725) Tel 209-572-2440.

Dagaz Pr, *(Dagaz Pr., Ltd.; 0-9623783),* 4202 Ashwoody Trail, Atlanta, GA 30319 Tel 404-458-5678.

Daily Hampshire, *(Daily Hampshire Gazette; 0-9618052),* 115 Conz St., Northampton, MA 01060 (SAN 666-2900) Tel 413-584-5000.

Damon Pub, *(Damon Publishing; 0-9617788),* 741 E. Montana, Saint Paul, MN 55106 (SAN 664-7480) Tel 612-776-7600.

DaNa Pubns, *(DaNa Pubns.; 0-937103),* 1050 Austin Ave., Idaho Falls, ID 83404 (SAN 658-568X) Tel 208-523-7237.

Dance Data, *(Dance Data; 0-9626651),* P.O. Box 5733, Kingwood, TX 77325-5733; 3706 Villa Pines, Kingwood, TX 77339 Tel 713-548-8708.

Dance Horizons Imprint of **Princeton Bk Co**

Dance Notation, *(Dance Notation Bureau, Inc.; 0-932582),* 31-33 W. 21st St., Third Flr., New York, NY 10010 (SAN 212-3452) Tel 212-807-7899; Dist. by: Princeton Bk. Co., P.O. Box 57, Pennington, NJ 08534 (SAN 630-1568) Tel 609-737-8177; Toll free: 800-326-7149.

Danceway Bks, *(Danceways Bks.; 0-937180),* 393 West End Ave., 14F, New York, NY 10024 (SAN 219-4724) Tel 212-799-2860; Dist. by: Variety Arts, Inc., 305 Riverside Dr., Suite 4A, New York, NY 10025 (SAN 200-691X); Toll free: 800-221-2154.

D&C Cape Verdeans, *(Documentation & Computerization of the Cape Verdeans; 0-9627637),* 176 Court St., New Bedford, MA 02740 Tel 508-996-3411.

D&M Pubns, *(D & M Pubns.; 0-925449),* P.O. Box 2409, Anthony, TX 79821; 1205 Antonio, Anthony, TX 79821 Tel 915-886-5250.

Dandy Lion, *(Dandy Lion Pubns.; 0-931724),* P.O. Box 190, San Luis Obispo, CA 93406 (SAN 211-5565) Tel 805-543-3332; Toll free: 800-776-8032.

Daneco Pubns, *(Daneco Pubns.; 0-910519),* 3451 18th Ave., S., Minneapolis, MN 55407 (SAN 260-180X) Tel 612-724-6285.

Darby Dinosaur, *(Darby The Dinosaur Enterprises, Inc.; 0-9623481),* 115 Curley Dr., Orchard Park, NY 14127 Tel 716-662-3752.

Dargaud Pub, *(Dargaud Publishing International, Ltd.; 0-917201),* c/o Bernstein Assocs., 555 Madison Ave., New York, NY 10022-3301 (SAN 655-8100) Tel 203-661-0707.

Daring Bks, *(Daring Bks.; 0-938936; 1-878302),* Div. of Daring Publishing Group, Inc., 913 Tuscarawas St., W., Canton, OH 44702 (SAN 216-0293) Tel 216-454-7519; Toll free: 800-445-6321; Orders to: P.O. Box 20050, Canton, OH 44701 (SAN 685-3242).

Dasan Prodns, *(Dasan Productions, Inc.; 0-9627806),* 4201 Hunt Club Ln., Westlake Village, CA 91361 Tel 818-597-8380; Toll free: 800-348-4401.

Daughter Cult, *(Daughter Culture Pubns.; 0-935281),* 1840 41st Ave., Suite 102-301, Capitola, CA 95010 (SAN 695-7447) Tel 408-476-0199.

Davar MD
See **Educ Pr MD**

Davenport, *(Davenport, May, Pubs.; 0-9603118; 0-943864),* 26313 Purissima Rd., Los Altos Hills, CA 94022 (SAN 212-467X) Tel 415-948-6499.

Davis Mass, *(Davis Pubns., Inc.; 0-87192),* 50 Portland St., Worcester, MA 01608 (SAN 201-3002) Tel 508-754-7201; Toll free: 800-533-2847. Do not confuse with Davis Pubns. Inc., New York, NY.

723

DAW Bks, *(DAW Bks.; 0-87997; 0-88677; 0-8099),* 375 Hudson St., New York, NY 10014-3658 (SAN 665-6846) Tel 212-366-2096; Dist. by: Penguin USA, 120 Woodbine St., Bergenfield, NJ 07621 (SAN 206-8087) Tel 201-387-0600; Toll free: 800-526-0275.

Dawah Pubns, *(Da'wah Pubns.; 1-878534),* P.O. Box 717, Dannemora, NY 12929; Cook St., Dannemora, NY 12929 Tel 518-492-7880.

Dayhiking Pr, *(Dayhiking Pr.; 0-9629536),* 3101 Bluffview Dr., Garland, TX 75043 Tel 214-303-0058.

Daystar Comm, *(Daystar Communications; 0-930037),* P.O. Box 748, Millville, NJ 08332 (SAN 669-7798) Tel 609-327-1231.

DB Inc CA, *(Discovery Bks., Inc.; 0-925258),* P.O. Box 410, Lagunitas, CA 94938 (SAN 200-318X); 7282 Sir Francis Drake Blvd., Lagunitas, CA 94938 Tel 415-488-9256.

DCA, *(Darien Community Assn., Inc.),* Orders to: Tory Hole, 274 Middlesex Rd., Darien, CT 06820 (SAN 208-4902) Tel 203-655-9050.

DCB *Imprint of* **Dutton Child Bks**

DCI Publishing, *(Diabetes Ctr., Inc., Publishing; 0-937721),* Div. of Diabetes Ctrs., Inc., 13911 Ridgedale Dr., Minnetonka, MN 55343 (SAN 659-252X) Tel 612-541-0239; Toll free: 800-444-5951; 800-848-2793 (Orders only); Orders to: P.O. Box 47945, Minneapolis, MN 55447 (SAN 665-9225).

Deaconess Pr, *(Deaconess Pr.; 0-925190),* 2312 S. Sixth St., Minneapolis, MN 55454 Tel 612-337-4311; Toll free: 800-544-8207.

DeadBase, *(DeadBase; 1-877657),* P.O. Box 499, Hanover, NH 03755.

Dearborn Finan, *(Dearborn Financial Publishing, Inc.; 0-88462; 0-7931),* 520 N. Dearborn, Chicago, IL 60610 (SAN 201-3622) Tel 312-836-4400.

Dearborn Trade, *(Dearborn Trade),* 520 N. Dearborn St., Chicago, IL 60610-4354 (SAN 211-2280) Tel 312-836-4400.

Dearh Pub, *(Dearh Publishing Co.; 0-944769),* Div. of Prison Bible Fellowship, Inc., P.O. Box 12005, Las Vegas, NV 89112-0005 (SAN 245-1727); 2175 Sunnyslope St., Las Vegas, NV 89119 (SAN 245-1735) Tel 702-736-7283.

DEC Special Stuff, *(DEC Special Stuff, Inc.; 0-9619653),* 65 Cadillac Sq., No. 233, Detroit, MI 48226 (SAN 245-9981) Tel 313-397-1624.

Deem Corp, *(Deem Corp., The; 0-918822),* 5860 W. Sioux Dr., Sedalia, CO 80135 (SAN 210-4113).

Deep Riv Pr, *(Deep River Pr.; 0-9626803),* 1871 S. 155 Cir., Omaha, NE 68144 Tel 402-334-5863.

Deer Creek NY, *(Deer Creek Publishing Co.; 0-9621599),* P.O. Box 83, Pulaski, NY 13142 (SAN 252-192X); 8358 Hinman Rd., Pulaski, NY 13142 (SAN 252-1938) Tel 315-298-4681.

Deer Creek Pr, *(Deer Creek Pr.; 0-9613596),* Div. of California Schl. of Design, 516 Olive St, Sausalito, CA 94965 (SAN 669-6732) Tel 415-332-1990.

Definition, *(Definition Pr.; 0-910492),* Subs. of Eli Siegel-Martha Baird Foundation, 141 Greene St., New York, NY 10012 (SAN 201-310X) Tel 212-777-4490.

Del Rey *Imprint of* **Ballantine**

Delacorte, *(Delacorte Pr.; 0-87459),* Div. of Bantam Doubleday Dell, 666 5th Ave., New York, NY 10103 (SAN 201-0097) Tel 212-765-6500; Toll free: 800-221-4676. *Imprints:* E Friede (Friede, Eleanor); Sey Lawr (Lawrence, Seymour).

Delafield Pr, *(Delafield Pr.; 0-916872),* P.O. Box 335, Suttons Bay, MI 49682 (SAN 208-3817) Tel 616-271-3826.

Delcon, *(Delcon Corp.; 0-934856),* 7797 Harlan Rd., Eddyville, OR 97343 (SAN 213-4853) Tel 503-875-4381.

Dell, *(Dell Publishing Co., Inc.; 0-440),* Div. of Bantam Doubleday Dell, 666 Fifth Ave., New York, NY 10103 (SAN 201-0097) Tel 212-765-6500; Toll free: 800-223-6834. *Imprints:* Dell Trade Pbks (Dell Trade Paperbacks); Delta (Delta Books); LE (Laurel Editions); LFL (Laurel Leaf Library); YB (Yearling Books).

Dell Trade Pbks *Imprint of* **Dell**

Delmar, *(Delmar Pubs., Inc.; 0-8273; 0-916032),* Div. of International Thomson Educational Publishing, Inc., 2 Computer Dr., W., Albany, NY 12205 (SAN 206-7544) Tel 518-459-1150; Toll free: 800-347-7707; P.O. Box 15-015, Albany, NY 12212-5015 (SAN 658-0440).

Delos Pubns, *(Delos Pubns.; 1-878473),* 726 Paris Way, Placentia, CA 92670 Tel 714-528-8900.

Delta *Imprint of* **Dell**

Denham Pub, *(Denham Publishing Co.; 0-9630135),* Div. of Smith Educational Enterprises, Inc., P.O. Box 11890, Lexington, KY 40578-1890; 2647 Regency Rd., Lexington, KY 40578 Tel 606-278-8841.

Denison, *(Denison, T. S., & Co., Inc.; 0-513),* 9601 Newton Ave. S., Minneapolis, MN 55431 (SAN 201-3142) Tel 612-888-1460; Toll free: 800-328-3831. Do not confuse with Dennison Pubns.

Dennis-Landman, *(Dennis-Landman Pubs.; 0-930422),* 1150 18th St., Santa Monica, CA 90403 (SAN 210-9352) Tel 213-453-4643.

Denver Busn Media, *(Denver Business Media Sales, Inc.; 0-932439),* Subs. of American City Business Journals, 2401 15th St., Suite 350, Denver, CO 80202 (SAN 686-7405) Tel 303-433-0033.

Derrydale Pr, *(Derrydale Pr.; 1-56416),* Div. of Buckingham Mint, Inc., P.O. Box 411, Lyon, MS 38645 (SAN 630-009X); Toll free: 800-443-6753; 226 Sunflower Ave., Clarksdale, MS 38614 Tel 601-624-5514. Do not confuse with Derrydale Pr., an imprint of Outlet Bk. Co.

Deseret Bk, *(Deseret Bk. Co.; 0-87747; 0-87579),* Div. of Deseret Management Corp., P.O. Box 30178, Salt Lake City, UT 84130 (SAN 150-763X) Tel 801-534-1515; Toll free: 800-453-3876.

Desert Bks, *(Desert Bks.; 0-9628227),* Div. of Leo J. Du Lac Construction Co., P.O. Box 3301, Hesperia, CA 92345; 12031 1/4 Regentview Ave., Downey, CA 90241 Tel 619-244-1074.

Desert Botanical, *(Desert Botanical Garden; 0-9605656),* Affil. of American Assn. of Botanical Gardens & Arboreta, 1201 N. Galvin Pkwy., Phoenix, AZ 85008 (SAN 212-9000) Tel 602-941-1225.

Desert Star Intl, *(Desert Star International; 1-879212),* P.O. Box 1850, Sparks, NV 89432-1850; 830 Glen Vista Dr., Sparks, NV 89434 Tel 702-356-7779.

Design Matters Inc, *(Design Matters, Inc.; 0-922656),* 138 Crofton, San Antonio, TX 78210 (SAN 251-3803) Tel 512-225-5606.

Detroit Black, *(Detroit Black Writers' Guild; 0-9613078),* 5601 W. Warren, Detroit, MI 48210 (SAN 294-7315) Tel 313-898-7629.

Develop Solutions, *(Developmental Solutions, Inc.; 0-9629205),* 1125 E. Baseline Rd., Suite 2-24, Mesa, AZ 85210 Tel 602-831-0301.

Devin, *(Devin-Adair Pubs., Inc.; 0-8159),* 6 N. Water St., Greenwich, CT 06830 (SAN 112-062X) Tel 203-531-7755.

Devon Pub, *(Devon Publishing Co., Inc., The; 0-941402),* 2700 Virginia Ave., NW, Washington, DC 20037 (SAN 238-9703) Tel 202-337-5197; Dist. by: Baker & Taylor Bks., Eastern Div., 50 Kirby Ave., Somerville, NJ 08876 (SAN 169-4901) Tel 201-722-8000; Toll free: 800-435-1845; 800-352-4833 (in New Jersey).

DeVorss, *(DeVorss & Co.; 0-87516),* P.O. Box 550, Marina del Rey, CA 90294-0550 (SAN 168-9886); Toll free: 800-843-5743 (for bookstore orders only); 800-331-4719 (in California, for bookstore orders only); 1046 Princeton Dr., Marina del Rey, CA 90292 Tel 213-870-7478.

DEW Educational, *(DEW Educational Consultants; 0-9623123),* P.O. Box 691001, Stockton, CA 95269-1001; 2546 W. Hammer Ln., Stockton, CA 95269 Tel 209-951-6601.

Dghtrs St Paul, *(Daughters of St. Paul; 0-8198),* 50 St. Paul's Ave., Boston, MA 02130 (SAN 203-8900) Tel 617-522-8911; Toll free: 800-876-4463 (orders).

Dharma Pub, *(Dharma Publishing; 0-913546; 0-89800),* 2425 Hillside Ave., Berkeley, CA 94704 (SAN 201-2723) Tel 415-548-5407; Toll free: 800-873-4276.

di Capua Bks *Imprint of* **FS&G**

Diablo, *(Diablo Pr., Inc.; 0-87297),* P.O. Box 7042, Berkeley, CA 94707 (SAN 201-3223) Tel 415-653-5310; Toll free: 800-445-6638 (Orders only); Orders to: 64 Depot Rd., Colchester, VT 05446 (SAN 248-3807).

Diablo Bks, *(Diablo Bks.; 0-9607520),* 1317 Cayonwood Ct., No. 1, Walnut Creek, CA 94595 (SAN 238-6232) Tel 415-939-8644.

Dial *Imprint of* **Doubleday**

Dial Bks Young, *(Dial Bks. for Young Readers; 0-8037),* Div. of Penguin USA, 375 Hudson St., New York, NY 10014-3657 (SAN 264-0058) Tel 212-366-2000; Orders to: Penguin USA, P.O. Box 120, Bergenfield, NJ 07261 (SAN 200-6758) Tel 201-387-0600.

Dial Easy to Read *Imprint of* **Puffin Bks**

Dial Pied Piper *Imprint of* **Puffin Bks**

Diamond Farm Bk, *(Diamond Farm Bk. Pubs.; 0-9506932),* Div. of Diamond Enterprises, P.O. Box 537, Alexandria Bay, NY 13607 (SAN 674-9054).

Dictation Disc, *(Dictation Disc Co.; 0-936862; 1-56243),* 14 E. 38th St., New York, NY 10016 (SAN 223-5234) Tel 212-683-9028; Toll free: 800-528-3897.

Didymus Pub, *(Didymus Publishing; 0-9626442),* P.O. Box 845, Galveston, TX 77553-0845; 6928 Schlitz Ln., Hitchcock, TX 77563 Tel 409-935-9613.

Dillon *Imprint of* **Macmillan Child Grp**

Dillon-Liederbach, *(Dillon/Liederbach, Inc.; 0-913228),* 4953 Stonington Rd., Winston-Salem, NC 27103 (SAN 201-3274) Tel 919-768-7014.

Disc Enter Ltd, *(Discovery Enterprises, Ltd.; 1-878668),* 134 Middle St., Suite 210, Lowell, MA 01852 (SAN 297-2611) Tel 508-459-1720; Toll free: 800-729-1720; Dist. by: Baker & Taylor Bks., Eastern Div., 50 Kirby Ave., Somerville, NJ 08876 (SAN 169-4901) Tel 201-722-8000; Toll free: 800-435-1845; Dist. by: Ingram Bk. Co., 1125 Heil Quaker Blvd., La Vergne, TN 37086-1986 (SAN 169-7978) Tel 615-793-5000; Toll free: 800-937-8000; Dist. by: Brodart Co., 500 Arch St., Williamsport, PA 17705 (SAN 169-7684) Tel 717-326-2461; Toll free: 800-223-8467; Dist. by: Gordon's Bks., Inc., 2323 Delgany St., Denver, CO 80216 (SAN 169-0531) Tel 303-296-1830; Toll free: 800-525-6979 (west of the Mississippi). Do not confuse with Discovery Enterprises Erie, PA.

Discovery Comics, *(Discovery Comics; 1-878181),* P.O. Box 726, Glenside, PA 19038; 233 Elm Ave., Glenside, PA 19038 Tel 215-887-3633.

Discovery GA, *(Discovery Pr., Inc.; 0-944770),* P.O. Box 670471, Marietta, GA 30066 (SAN 245-4564); 2619 Sandy Plains Rd., Marietta, GA 30066 (SAN 245-4572) Tel 404-926-2365. Do not confuse with Discovery Pr. Inc., Smithtown, NY.

Discovery Pr, *(Discovery Pr.; 0-9614261),* P.O. Box 12241, Portland, OR 97212 (SAN 687-1240) Tel 503-282-9372; Dist. by: Pacific Pipeline, Inc., 19215 66th Ave., S., Kent, WA 98032 (SAN 208-2128) Tel 206-872-5523; Toll free: 800-562-4647 (in Washington); 800-426-4727 (in Oregon, Idaho, Montana, Nevada, northern California); Dist. by: Far West Bk. Service, 3515 NE Hassalo, Portland, OR 97232 (SAN 107-6760) Tel 503-234-7664. Do not confuse with companies with the same name in Mission Viejo, CA, Flushing, NY, Sedona, AZ, Minneapolis, MN.

Discovry Enterp, *(Discovery Enterprises; 0-942661),* 931 Arbuckle Rd., Erie, PA 16509 (SAN 667-3759) Tel 814-825-9543; Dist. by: Brodart Co., 500 Arch St., Williamsport, PA 17705 (SAN 169-7684) Tel 717-326-2461; Toll free: 800-233-8467.

Discus *Imprint of* **Avon**

Disney Movie Bks *Imprint of* **WD Pub**

Disney Pr *Imprint of* **W Disney Pub**

Displays for Schs, *(Displays for Schls.; Inc.; 0-9600962),* P.O. Box 163, Gainesville, FL 32602 (SAN 157-9711) Tel 904-373-2030.

Diversity Pubs, *(Diversity Pubs.; 0-9629269),* 121 Allied St., Manchester, NH 03109 Tel 603-668-7016.

Divry, *(Divry, D. C., Inc.; 0-910516),* 148 W. 24th St., New York, NY 10011 (SAN 201-3320) Tel 212-255-2153.

DM Pub, *(D. M. Publishing Co.; 0-938419),* P.O. Box 5064, Sioux City, IA 51102 (SAN 661-0730); 901 N. St. Mary's, Sioux City, IA 51102 (SAN 661-0749) Tel 712-258-3133.

DMS ID, *(DMS; 0-9625057),* 4595 E. Highland Dr., Post Falls, ID 83854 Tel 208-773-7605; Dist. by: Publishers Distribution Service, 121 E. Front St., No. 203, Traverse City, MI 49684 (SAN 630-5717) Tel 616-929-0733; Toll free: 800-345-0096 (orders only).

Doane Info Servs, *(Doane Information Services; 0-932250; 0-924340),* Div. of Doane Agricultural Services, 8800 Queen Ave., S., Bloomington, MN 55431 (SAN 207-2149) Tel 612-921-6342; Toll free: 800-422-2434.

Docutex Inc, *(Docutex, Inc.; 0-924307),* 8918 Tesoro Dr., No. 106, San Antonio, TX 78217 Tel 512-824-8004.

Dodson Assocs, *(Dodson Assocs.; 0-9620550),* 613 Lincoln, Pueblo, CO 81004 (SAN 249-0552) Tel 719-545-3876.

Dog Eared Pubns, *(Dog-Eared Pubns.; 0-941042),* P.O. Box 863, Middleton, WI 53562 (SAN 281-6059) Tel 608-831-1410; Dist. by: Pacific Pipeline, Inc., 19215 66th Ave., S., Kent, WA 98032 (SAN 208-2128) Tel 206-872-5523; Toll free: 800-426-4727 (in northern California, Montana, Oregon, Nevada, Idaho); 800-562-4647 (in Washington); Dist. by: Bookpeople, 2929 Fifth St., Berkeley, CA 94710 (SAN 168-9517) Tel 415-549-3030; Toll free: 800-999-4650; Dist. by: Common Ground Distributors, Inc., 3829B Plyers Mill Rd., Kensington, MD 20895 (SAN 113-8006) Tel 301-946-4157; Toll free: 800-654-0626.

Dogwood NC, *(Dogwood Pr.; 0-9627049),* 4102 Dogwood Dr., Greensboro, NC 27410 Tel 919-299-3447. Do not confuse with Dogwood Pr., Stone Mountain, GA.

DOK Pubs, *(DOK Pubs.; 0-914634),* Div. of United Educational Services, Inc., Box 1099, Buffalo, NY 14224 (SAN 201-3347) Tel 716-668-7691; Toll free: 800-458-7900.

Dolan Pr, *(Dolan Pr.; 0-9622868),* 1645 Gales Ct., Forest Grove, OR 97116 Tel 503-232-8844.

Doll Works, *(Doll Works, The; 0-940070),* P.O. Box 15456, Newport Beach, CA 92659-5456 (SAN 220-214X)

Dolp Imprint of **Doubleday**

Domjan Studio, *(Domjan Studio; 0-933652),* West Lake Rd., Tuxedo Park, NY 10987 (SAN 293-2512) Tel 914-351-4596.

Don Bosco Multimedia, *(Don Bosco Multimedia; 0-89944; 1-55986),* Div. of Salesian Society, Inc., 475 North Ave., Box T, New Rochelle, NY 10802 (SAN 213-2613) Tel 914-576-0122; Toll free: 800-342-5850. Imprints: Patron (Patron Books).

Donna Dee Bks, *(Donna Dee Bks.; 0-9624299),* Box 18234, Tucson, AZ 85731-8234 Tel 602-298-6667.

Donning Co, *(Donning Co. Pubs.; 0-915442; 0-89865),* Subs. of Walsworth Publishing Co., 184 Business Park Dr., No. 106, Virginia Beach, VA 23462-6533 (SAN 211-6316) Tel 804-497-1789; Toll free: 800-446-8572; Warehouse: 801 S. Missouri Ave., Marceline, MO 64658 (SAN 661-9940); Dist. by: Schiffer Publishing, Ltd., 1649 Morstein Rd., West Chester, PA 19380 (SAN 208-8428) Tel 215-696-1001. Imprints: Starblaze (Starblaze).

DonSyl Pubns, *(DonSyl Pubns.; 0-9626263),* 4807 Fernwood Ct., Fairfield, CA 94533; 4807 Fernwood Ct., Fairfield, CA 94585 Tel 707-864-0522.

Doral Pub, *(Doral Publishing; 0-944875),* P.O. Box 596, Wilsonville, OR 97070 (SAN 245-4637) Tel 503-694-5707; Toll free: 800-876-5197.

Dorchester Pub Co, *(Dorchester Publishing Co., Inc.; 0-8439),* 276 Fifth Ave., New York, NY 10001 (SAN 264-0090) Tel 212-725-8811; Dist. by: Hearst Corp., International Circulation Div., 250 W. 55th St., 12th Flr., New York, NY 10019 (SAN 169-5800); Toll free: 800-223-0288.

Doris Demou, *(Demou, Doris Beck; 0-9604794),* 2013 Big Oak Dr., Burnsville, MN 55337 (SAN 209-1798) Tel 612-890-3579.

Doris Pubns, *(Doris Pubns.; 0-933865),* P.O. Box 1576, Louisville, KY 40201 (SAN 692-7033) Tel 502-774-3297.

Dorling Kindersley, *(Dorling Kindersley, Inc.; 1-879431; 1-56458),* 232 Madison Ave., Suite 1206, New York, NY 10016 Tel 212-684-0404.

Dorrance, *(Dorrance Publishing Co., Inc.; 0-8059),* 643 Smithfield St., Pittsburgh, PA 15222 (SAN 201-3363) Tel 412-288-1354.

Dorset Pr, *(Dorset Pr.; 0-88029),* Div. of Marboro Bks., 120 Fifth Ave., New York, NY 10011 Tel 212-924-8395.

Dorthenia Pubs, *(Dorthenia Pubs.; 0-9621196),* 1003 Janlee, Burkburnett, TX 76354 (SAN 250-7625) Tel 817-569-1129.

DOT Garnet, *(DOT Garnet; 0-9625620),* 2520 Barclay Ave., Union City, CA 94587-1701 Tel 415-487-7880; Dist. by: Talman Co., 150 Fifth Ave., Rm. 630, New York, NY 10011 (SAN 200-5204) Tel 212-620-3182; Toll free: 800-537-8894 (orders only).

Dot Pub
See DOT Garnet

Dots Pubns, *(Dots Pubns.; 0-9605204),* 1434 Redwood, Oxnard, CA 93033 (SAN 215-7535) Tel 805-483-1795.

Double B Pubns, *(Double B Pubns.; 0-929526),* 4113 N. Longview, Phoenix, AZ 85014 (SAN 249-6615) Tel 602-274-6821.

Double M Pr, *(Double M Pr.; 0-916634),* 16455 Tuba St., Sepulveda, CA 91343 (SAN 213-9510) Tel 818-360-3166.

Double M Pub, *(Double M Publishing Co.; 0-913392),* 21645 Nadia Dr., Joliet, IL 60436 (SAN 285-872X) Tel 815-741-0576; Dist. by: Baker & Taylor Bks., Midwestern Div., 501 S. Gladiolus St., Momence, IL 60954 (SAN 169-2100) Tel 815-472-2444; Toll free: 800-435-5111; 800-892-1892 (in Illinois).

Double Talk, *(Double Talk; 0-9615839),* P.O. Box 412, Amelia, OH 45102 (SAN 697-0575) Tel 513-753-7117.

Doubleday, *(Doubleday & Co., Inc.; 0-385),* Div. of Bantam Doubleday Dell, 666 Fifth Ave., New York, NY 10103 (SAN 201-0089) Tel 212-765-6500; Toll free: 800-223-6834; Orders to: Doubleday Consumer Services, P.O. Box 5071, Des Plaines, IL 60017-5071 (SAN 281-6083). Imprints: Anchor Pr (Anchor Press); Dial (Dial Press); Dolp (Dolphin Books); Galilee (Galilee); Zephyr (Zephyr).

Dove Pr TX, *(Dove Pr.; 1-879667),* P.O. Box 15128, San Antonio, TX 78212 Tel 512-637-0361.

Dover, *(Dover Pubns., Inc.; 0-486),* 180 Varick St., New York, NY 10014 Tel 212-255-3755; Toll free: 800-223-3130; Orders to: 31 E. Second St., Mineola, NY 11501 (SAN 201-338X) Tel 516-294-7000.

Down East, *(Down East Bks.; 0-89272),* Div. of Down East Enterprises, Inc., P.O. Box 679, Camden, ME 04843 (SAN 208-6301) Tel 207-594-9544.

Dragon Studio, *(Dragon Studio; 0-9620672),* 18 Lake Rd., Ridgefield, CT 06877 (SAN 249-5457) Tel 203-438-8668.

Dragon Tale, *(Dragon Tale Pr.; 0-9622905),* Div. of Ruth Sawyer Memorial Foundation, P.O. Box 86255, Madeira Beach, FL 33738; 5247 81st St., N., No. 24, Saint Petersburg, FL 33709 Tel 813-545-4323.

Dragonfly Bks Imprint of **Knopf**

Dramaline Pubns, *(Dramaline Pubns.; 0-9611792; 0-940669),* 10470 Riverside Dr., Suite 201, Toluca Lake, CA 91602 (SAN 285-239X) Tel 818-985-9148.

Dramatic Pub, *(Dramatic Publishing Co., Inc.; 0-88020),* Div. of Coach Hse. Pr., Inc., 311 Washington St., Woodstock, IL 80098 (SAN 201-7709) Tel 815-338-7170; Toll free: 800-448-7469.

Dream Tree Pr, *(Dream Tree Pr.; 0-9628216),* 3836 Thornwood Dr., Sacramento, CA 95218 Tel 916-488-4194.

Dream Weaver, *(Dream Weaver Bks.; 0-9621392),* 2609 Glen Oaks, Norman, OK 73071 (SAN 251-236X) Tel 405-366-7971.

Drollery Pr, *(Drollery Pr.; 0-940920),* 1615 Encinal Ave., Alameda, CA 94501 (SAN 223-1808) Tel 415-521-4087; Dist. by: Publishers Group West, 4065 Hollis St., Emeryville, CA 94608 (SAN 202-8522) Tel 415-658-3453; Toll free: 800-365-3453.

Druid Pr, *(Druid Pr.; 0-945301),* 2724 Shades Crest Rd., Birmingham, AL 35216 (SAN 246-6198) Tel 205-967-6580.

Drum Assocs, *(Drum Assocs.; 0-9611024),* Affil. of John Scherer & Assocs., W. 201 Sumner, Spokane, WA 99204 (SAN 277-674X) Tel 509-747-1029.

Dry Canyon Pr, *(Dry Canyon Pr.; 0-929796),* 914 River Heights Blvd., Logan, UT 84321 (SAN 250-5010) Tel 801-753-1021.

Dufour, *(Dufour Editions, Inc.; 0-8023),* Box 449, Chester Springs, PA 19425-0449 (SAN 201-341X) Tel 215-458-5005.

Duke Pub Co, *(Duke Publishing Co.; 0-9613727),* P.O. Box 22031, San Francisco, CA 94122 (SAN 677-5187) Tel 415-759-5136.

Duna Studios, *(Duna Studios, Inc.; 0-942928),* P.O. Box 24051, Minneapolis, MN 55424 (SAN 240-1428) Tel 612-926-5201.

Dunery Pr, *(Dunery Pr.; 0-944771),* P.O. Box 116, Harbert, MI 49115-0116 (SAN 245-453X) Tel 616-469-1278.

Dunwoody Pr, *(Dunwoody Pr.; 0-931745),* Div. of MRM, Language Research Ctr., Inc., P.O. Box 400, Kensington, MD 20895-0400 (SAN 683-5309) Tel 301-946-7006; 3910 Knowles Ave., Kensington, MD 20895 (SAN 664-6352) Tel 301-864-1411.

Durkin Hayes Pub, *(Durkin Hayes Publishing Ltd.; 0-88646; 0-88625),* 1 Colomba Dr., Niagara Falls, NY 14305 Tel 716-298-5150; Toll free: 800-962-5200. Canadian address: 3312 Mainway, Burlington, ON, CN L7M 1A7, 416-335-0393.

Dutton Child Bks, *(Dutton Children's Bks.; 0-525),* Div. of Penguin USA, 375 Hudson St., New York, NY 10014-3657 Tel 212-366-2000. Imprints: Cobblehill Bks (Cobblehill Books); DCB (Dutton Children's Books); Lodestar Bks (Lodestar Books); Unicorn Pbks (Dutton Unicorn Paperbacks).

Dutton-Truman Talley Imprint of **NAL-Dutton**

Dutton Unicorn Imprint of **Puffin Bks**

DVNH Assn, *(Death Valley Natural History Assn.; 1-878900),* Box 188, Death Valley, CA 92328 Tel 619-786-2331.

E Burns, *(Burns, Elizabeth; 0-9624152),* 7351 Mesa Dr., Aptos, CA 95003 Tel 408-688-1293.

E C Temple, *(Temple, Ellen C., Publishing, Inc.; 0-936650),* 5030 Champions Dr., Suite 100, Lufkin, TX 75901 (SAN 215-1162) Tel 409-639-4707; Dist. by: Taylor Publishing Co., 1550 W. Mockingbird Ln., Dallas, TX 75235 (SAN 202-7631) Tel 214-637-2800; Toll free: 800-677-2800.

E Cauper, *(Cauper, Eunice; 0-9617551),* 300 Lynn Shore Dr., Lynn, MA 01902 (SAN 664-4449) Tel 617-599-3041.

E D Edwards, *(Edwards, E. Dean; 0-9615120),* 126 Marshall St., Litchfield, MI 49252 (SAN 694-1664).

E E Stevens Pub, *(Stevens, Edward E., Pub.; 0-9621311),* 122 Seaward Ave., Bradford, PA 16701 (SAN 251-0413) Tel 814-368-6578.

E Friede Imprint of **Delacorte**

E G Johnson, *(Johnson, Esther; 0-9629143),* 1310 W. Woodhills Rd., Minneapolis, MN 55426 Tel 612-545-6413.

E J Wareing, *(Wareing, Eleanor J.; 0-9629175),* Box 156, Fifty Lakes, MN 56448; Shamrock Ln., Fire No. 1495, Fifty Lakes, MN 56448 Tel 218-763-3548.

E Mellen, *(Mellen, Edwin, Pr., The; 0-88946),* P.O. Box 450, Lewiston, NY 14092 (SAN 207-110X) Tel 716-754-8566; Toll free: 800-933-4867; 800-753-2788 (orders only); 240 Portage Rd., Lewiston, NY 14092 (SAN 658-1218) Tel 716-754-2795.

E ORourke, *(O'Rourke, Everett V.; 0-9621369),* 500 N St., Apt. 708, Sacramento, CA 95825 (SAN 251-1487) Tel 916-447-7531.

E P Press, *(E.P. Pr., Inc.),* P.O. Box 1172, Gastonia, NC 28052 (SAN 297-1771).

E Petrochilos, *(Petrochilos, Elizabeth; 0-9629730),* 3397 E. Fairmont, Fresno, CA 93726 Tel 209-225-2734.

E T Church, *(Church, Elmer Tuttle),* P.O. Box 42, Yukon, WV 24899 (SAN 665-2352).

E-W Pub Co, *(East/West Publishing Co.; 0-934788),* 838 Grant Ave., Suite 302, San Francisco, CA 94108 (SAN 215-8574) Tel 415-781-3194.

E Wynn Vogel, *(Vogel, E. Wynn, Co.; 0-912392),* Div. of Copy-Write Artograph Co., 1865 77th St., Brooklyn, NY 11214-1233 (SAN 203-588X) Tel 718-236-1459.

E Zolna Inc, *(Zolna, Edward, Inc.; 0-945975),* P.O. Box 1278, Roslyn, PA 19001 (SAN 248-2657); 2612 Belmont Ave., Roslyn, PA 19001 (SAN 248-2665) Tel 215-887-2851.

Eagle Gate UT, *(Eagle Gate Pubs.; 0-9628778),* P.O. Box 17, Logan, UT 84321 (SAN 297-3804); USU Aggie Village, No. 11K, Logan, UT 84321 Tel 801-750-6355.

Eagle Mktg Corp, *(Eagle Marketing Corp.; 0-911712),* Subs. of Eagle Systems International, 5600 N. University Ave., Provo, UT 84604 (SAN 204-3130) Tel 801-225-9000.

Eagles View, *(Eagles View Publishing; 0-943604),* Subs. of Westwind, Inc., 6756 N. Fork Rd., Liberty, UT 84310 (SAN 240-6330) Tel 801-745-0905; Toll free: 800-547-3364 (orders only); 168 W. 12th St., Ogden, UT 84404 Tel 801-393-4555; Dist. by: Quality Bks., Inc., 918 Sherwood Dr., Lake Bluff, IL 60044-2204 (SAN 169-2127) Tel 708-295-2010; Toll free: 800-323-4241 (Libraries only); Dist. by: Pacific Pipeline, Inc., 19215 66th Ave., S., Kent, WA 98032 (SAN 208-2128) Tel 206-872-5523; Toll free: 800-444-7323 (US & Canada); Dist. by: Gordon's Bk., Inc., 2323 Delgany St., Denver, CO 80216 (SAN 169-0531) Tel 303-296-1830; Toll free: 800-525-6979 (West of the Mississippi); Dist. by: Baker & Taylor Bks., Eastern Div., 50 Kirby Ave., Somerville, NJ 08876-0734 (SAN 169-4901) Tel 201-722-8000; Toll free: 800-526-3825.

Eagleye Bks Intl, *(Eagleye Bks. International; 0-924025),* P.O. Box 4550, Walnut Creek, CA 94596 (SAN 252-2020); 4159 Walnut Blvd., Walnut Creek, CA 94596 (SAN 252-2039) Tel 415-944-1999.

Eakin Pr, *(Eakin Pr.; 0-89015),* P.O. Drawer 90159, Austin, TX 78709-0159 (SAN 207-3633) Tel 512-288-1771; Dist. by: C.C. Publishing, P.O. Box 452114, Garland, TX 75045-2114 Tel 214-330-4845.

Earlham College Pr, *(Earlham College Pr.; 0-9619977; 1-879117),* Earlham College, Box 28, Richmond, IN 47374 (SAN 247-3496); Toll free: 800-327-5426; National Rd., W., Richmond, IN 47374 (SAN 247-350X) Tel 317-983-1323.

Early Childhood, *(Early Child Consultants; 0-9624257),* 15121 Regent Dr., Orland Park, IL 60462 Tel 708-403-5869.

Early Educators, *(Early Educators Pr.; 0-9604390),* P.O. Box 1177, Lake Alfred, FL 33850 (SAN 216-2407) Tel 813-956-1569; Dist. by: Gryphon Hse., Inc., P.O. Box 275, Mount Rainier, MD 20712 (SAN 169-3190) Tel 301-779-6200; Toll free: 800-638-0928.

Earthbooks Inc, *(Earthbooks, Inc.; 1-877731),* 7000 N. Broadway, Bldg. 1, Suite 103, Denver, CO 80221 Tel 303-429-1126; Toll free: 800-423-0395.

Earthwise Pubns, *(Earthwise Pubns.; 0-933494),* P.O. Box 680-536, Miami, FL 33168 (SAN 223-7407) Tel 305-688-8558.

East Bay Bks, *(East Bay Bks.; 0-930997),* P.O. Box 1165, Stauton, VA 24401-1395 (SAN 678-8939).

East Eagle, *(East Eagle Pr.; 0-9605738; 1-880531),* Affil. of Patrick Haley Co., P.O. Box 812, Huron, SD 57350 (SAN 216-3705); 766 Utah Ave. SE, Huron, SD 57350 Tel 605-352-5875.

EastWest Pr, *(EastWest Pr.; 0-9606090),* P.O. Box 4204, Minneapolis, MN 55414 (SAN 216-809X) Tel 612-379-2049.

Eclectical, *(Eclectical Publishing Co., Inc.; 0-912447),* P.O. Box 7326, New Orleans, LA 70186 (SAN 265-346X) Tel 504-246-5413.

ECS Lrn Systs, *(ECS Learning Systems, Inc.; 0-944459),* P.O. Box 791437, San Antonio, TX 78279 (SAN 243-6159); Toll free: 800-688-3224; 2340 W.R. Larson Rd., San Antonio, TX 78261 (SAN 243-6167) Tel 512-438-4262.

Ed Activities, *(Educational Activities, Inc.; 0-914296; 0-89525; 1-55737; 0-7925),* 1937 Grand Ave., Baldwin, NY 11510 (SAN 207-4400) Tel 516-223-4666; Toll free: 800-645-3739; Orders to: P.O. Box 392, Freeport, NY 11520.

Ed Francaises, *(Editions Francaises de Louisiane/Louisiana French Editions, Inc.; 0-935085),* P.O. Box 1344, Jennings, LA 70546 (SAN 695-0779) Tel 318-824-7380; 302 E. Nezpique St., Jennings, LA 70546 (SAN 695-0787).

Ed Lncln-Mrt, *(Editorial Lincoln-Marti; 0-9628780),* Div. of Lincoln-Marti Schools, 904 SW 23rd Ave., Miami, FL 33135 Tel 305-643-4888.

Ed Media Corp, *(Educational Media Corp.; 0-932796),* 4256 Central Ave., NE, Minneapolis, MN 55421-2920 (SAN 212-4203) Tel 612-781-0088; Orders to: P.O. Box 21311, Minneapolis, MN 55421 (SAN 665-6919) Tel 612-781-0088.

Ed Ministries, *(Educational Ministries, Inc.; 0-940754; 1-877871),* 2861-C Saturn St., Brea, CA 92621 (SAN 219-7316) Tel 714-961-0622; Toll free: 800-221-0910.

Ed Pub Serv, *(Educators Publishing Service, Inc.; 0-8388),* 75 Moulton St., Cambridge, MA 02138 (SAN 201-8225) Tel 617-547-6706; Toll free: 800-225-5750.

Ed Res Pub Co, *(Educational Resources Publishing Co.; 0-9629207),* P.O. Box 151139, San Diego, CA 92175; 9481 Tropico Dr., La Mesa, CA 91941.

Ed Skills Dallas, *(Educational Skills; 0-9604058),* 9636 Hollow Way, Dallas, TX 75220 (SAN 221-6086) Tel 214-363-7043.

Ed Solutions, *(Educational Solutions, Inc.; 0-87825),* 95 University Pl., New York, NY 10003-4555 (SAN 205-6186) Tel 212-674-2988.

Ed Sys Pub, *(Education System Pub.; 0-915676; 0-916011),* 38395 Trifone Rd., Sage, CA 92343-9693 (SAN 241-7820) Tel 714-652-3822; Orders to: P.O. Box 536, Hemet, CA 92343.

Ed-U Pr, *(Ed-U Pr., Inc.; 0-934978),* 7174 Mott Rd., Fayetteville, NY 13066 (SAN 221-1866) Tel 315-637-9524.

EDC, *(EDC Publishing; 0-88110),* Div. of Educational Development Corp., 10302 E. 55th Pl., Tulsa, OK 74146 (SAN 107-5322) Tel 918-622-4522; Toll free: 800-331-4418; P.O. Box 470663, Tulsa, OK 74147 (SAN 658-0505); P.O. Box 702253, Tulsa, OK 74170 (SAN 658-0513). *Imprints:* Usborne (Usborne).

Eden Pr, *(Eden Pr.; 0-920792; 0-88831; 1-55045),* Dist. by: Univ. of Toronto Pr., 340 Nagel Dr., Cheektowaga, NY 14225 (SAN 214-2651) Tel 716-852-0342.

Eden Press, *(Eden Pr./Art Reproductions; 0-939373),* P.O. Box 745, Corona del Mar, CA 92625 (SAN 687-6455) Tel 714-760-0985.

Edgewater, *(Edgewater Bk. Distributors; 0-937424),* P.O. Box 40238, Cleveland, OH 44140 (SAN 215-3033) Tel 216-835-3108.

Ediciones, *(Ediciones Universal; 0-89729),* 3090 SW Eighth St., Miami, FL 33135 (SAN 207-2203) Tel 305-642-3355; P.O. Box 450353, Shenandoah Sta., Miami, FL 33145 (SAN 658-0548).

Ediciones Huracan, *(Ediciones Huracan, Inc.; 0-940238; 0-929157),* Avenida Gonzalez 1002, Rio Piedras, PR 00925 (SAN 217-5134) Tel 809-763-7407.

Edison Electric, *(Edison Electric Institute; 0-931032),* 1111 19th St., NW, Washington, DC 20036 (SAN 224-7119) Tel 202-778-6400.

Edit Caribe, *(Editorial Caribe; 0-89922),* 3934 SW Eighth St., Suite 303, Miami, FL 33134 (SAN 215-1421) Tel 305-445-0564; 4237A NW 37th Ct., Miami, FL 33134 (SAN 658-0556).

Edit Concepts, *(Editorial Concepts, Inc.; 0-939193),* 11980 SW 46th St., Miami, FL 33175 (SAN 662-8958) Tel 305-871-6400; Dist. by: Spanish Periodical & Bk. Sales, 10100 NW 25th St., Miami, FL 33172 (SAN 200-7576); Dist. by: Agencia de Publicaciones de Puerto Rico, GPO Box 4903, San Juan, PR 00936 (SAN 169-9296); Dist. by: Southeast Periodicals, P.O. Box 340008, Coral Gables, FL 33134 (SAN 238-6909) Tel 305-856-5011.

Edit Mundo *Imprint of* **Casa Bautista**

Edit Plaza Mayor, *(Editorial Plaza Mayor, Inc.; 1-56328),* Edificio La Electronica, Ofc. 218, Carr. No. 1, KM 14.5, Rio Piedras, PR 00927 Tel 809-764-0455.

Edit Roche, *(Editorial Roche; 0-939081),* P.O. Box 3583, Hato Rey, PR 00919 (SAN 662-9083); Urb. Del Carmen 2, No. 19, Juana Diaz, PR 00665 (SAN 662-9091) Tel 809-837-2468.

Editorial Amer, *(Editorial America, S. A.; 0-944499; 1-56259),* 6355 NW 36th St., Virginia Gardens, FL 33166 (SAN 243-7384) Tel 305-871-6400; Dist. by: Spanish Periodical Bk. Sales, 10100 NW 25th St., Miami, FL 33172 (SAN 200-7576).

Editorial Unilit, *(Editorial Unilit; 0-945792; 1-56063),* Div. of Spanish Hse., Inc., 1360 NW 88th Ave., Miami, FL 33172 (SAN 247-5979) Tel 305-592-6136; Toll free: 800-327-4067.

Edlo Bks, *(Edlo Bks.; 0-9613007),* P.O. Box 259, RD 1, Marlton, NJ 08053 (SAN 292-482X) Tel 609-424-1305.

Educ Assess Pub, *(Educational Assessment Publishing Co.; 0-942277; 1-56269),* 1731 Kettner Blvd.,, San Diego, CA 92101 (SAN 666-9662) Tel 619-232-4248; Dist. by: School Bk. Pr., 1731 Kettner Blvd., San Diego, CA 92101 (SAN 630-5059) Tel 619-696-7747; Toll free: 800-888-5111.

Educ Dev Ctr, *(Education Development Ctr., Inc.; 0-89292),* 55 Chapel St., Newton, MA 02160 (SAN 207-821X) Tel 617-969-7100; Toll free: 800-225-4276.

Educ Excell Via, *(Educational Excellence Via Video; 0-9630443),* P.O. Box 10231, Rochester, NY 14609; 25 Berry St., Rochester, NY 14609 Tel 716-482-3114.

Educ Graphics, *(Education Graphics; 0-9621081),* 302 Clinton Ave., Brooklyn, NY 11205 (SAN 250-4243) Tel 718-638-6096.

Educ Ideas, *(Educational Ideas, Inc.; 1-878371),* 195 Exton Ct., Gahanna, OH 43230 Tel 614-478-3171.

Educ Insights, *(Educational Insights, Inc.; 0-88679),* 19560 S. Rancho Way, Dominguez Hills, CA 90220 (SAN 283-8745) Tel 213-637-2131; Toll free: 800-933-3277.

Educ Materials, *(Educational Materials Co.; 0-937117),* 10 Swett Rd., Windham, ME 04062 (SAN 658-5175).

Educ Pr MD, *(Educational Pr.; 1-56119),* P.O. Box 32382, Baltimore, MD 21208-8382; 6 Autumn Wind Ct., Reisterstown, MD 21136 Tel 301-561-5912.

Educ Racism & Apart, *(Educators Against Racism & Apartheid; 1-878537),* 164-04 Goethals Ave., Jamaica, NY 11432 Tel 201-836-6644.

Educ Serv, *(Educational Service, Inc.; 0-89273),* 6200 Eidson Rd., Saint Joseph, MI 49085 (SAN 206-9423); Toll free: 800-253-0763; 6190 Eidson Rd., Saint Joseph, MI 49085 (SAN 658-0564).

Educ Serv Pr, *(Educational Services Pr.; 0-914911),* 99 Bank St., Suite 2F, New York, NY 10014 (SAN 289-1212); Dist. by: Baker & Taylor Bks., Western Div., 380 Edison Way, Reno, NV 89564 (SAN 169-4464) Tel 702-786-6700; Toll free: 800-648-3540; Dist. by: Blackwell North America (library sales only), 1001 Fries Mill Rd., Blackwood, NJ 08012 (SAN 169-4596) Tel 609-629-0700; Toll free: 800-257-7341; Dist. by: Baker & Taylor Bks., Eastern Div., 50 Kirby Ave., Somerville, NJ 08876 (SAN 169-4901) Tel 201-722-8000; Toll free: 800-435-1845; 800-352-4833 (in New Jersey); Dist. by: Baker & Taylor Bks., Midwestern Div., 501 S. Gladiolus St., Momence, IL 60954 (SAN 169-2100) Tel 815-472-2444; Toll free: 800-435-5111; 800-892-1892 (in Illinois); Dist. by: Baker & Taylor Bks., Southern Div., Mt. Olive Rd., Commerce, GA 30599 (SAN 169-1503) Tel 404-335-5000; Toll free: 800-241-6004; 800-282-6850 (in Georgia).

Educare Pr, *(Educare Pr.; 0-944638),* P.O. Box 31511, Seattle, WA 98103 (SAN 244-5913); 9753 First Ave., NW, Seattle, WA 98117 Tel 206-781-2665.

Education Serv, *(Education Services; 0-936394),* P.O. Box 5281, Atlanta, GA 30307 (SAN 221-1920).

Educators Against Apartheid *See* **Educ Racism & Apart**

Eductrs Soc Respons, *(Educators for Social Responsibility; 0-942349),* 23 Garden St., Cambridge, MA 02138 (SAN 667-0903) Tel 617-492-1764.

Eduplay, *(Eduplay; 0-935609),* Div. of EPI Corp., 9707 Shelbyville Rd., Louisville, KY 40223 (SAN 696-3552) Tel 502-426-2242.

Edwards Music Pub, *(Edwards Music Publishing; 0-9624770),* 8890 N. 56th St., Temple Terrace, FL 33617 Tel 813-988-1419.

EEBART, *(EEBART; 0-9614991),* Box 127, Leaf River, IL 61047 (SAN 693-7632) Tel 815-738-2237; Dist. by: Hee Haw Bk. Service, 2901 N. Elm, Denton, TX 76201 (SAN 630-012X) Tel 817-382-6845.

Eerdmans, *(Eerdmans, William B., Publishing Co.; 0-8028),* 255 Jefferson Ave., SE, Grand Rapids, MI 49503 (SAN 220-0058) Tel 616-459-4591; Toll free: 800-253-7521.

EFC Pub, *(EFC Publishing; 0-9618324),* P.O. Box 522, Livermore, CA 94550 (SAN 667-3228); 977 Redondo Way, Livermore, CA 94550 (SAN 667-3236) Tel 415-447-3206.

Effect Pub, *(Effect Publishing, Inc.; 0-911971),* 501 Fifth Ave., Suite 1612, New York, NY 10017 (SAN 264-665X) Tel 212-557-1321; 50 Eastbourne Dr., Chestnut Ridge, NY 10977 (SAN 665-8180) Tel 914-356-6626.

Eko Pubns, *(Eko Pubns.),* P.O. Box 5492, Philadelphia, PA 19143 (SAN 201-4599).

ELF Assocs, *(ELF Assocs., Ltd.; 0-927256),* P.O. Box 3485, Mankato, MN 56001; 30 Hilltop Ln., Apt. 108, Mankato, MN 56001 Tel 507-625-7925.

Elfin Cove Pr, *(Elfin Cove Pr.; 0-944958),* P.O. Box 924, Redmond, WA 98052 (SAN 245-8578) Tel 206-868-4547.

Elijah-John, *(Elijah-John Pubns.; 0-9614311),* 103 Russell, Apt. 6, Saline, MI 48176 (SAN 687-5106) Tel 313-429-1809; Orders to: P.O. Box 271, Saline, MI 48176 (SAN 242-0155).

Elins Laboratories, *(Elins Laboratories; 0-9620526),* P.O. Box 90, West Chester, PA 19381 (SAN 249-0536); 149 Chandler Dr., West Chester, PA 19381 (SAN 249-0544) Tel 215-696-4022.

Elizabeth Pr, *(Elizabeth Pr.),* 103 Van Etten Blvd., New Rochelle, NY 10804 (SAN 201-3789).

Elk Grove Bks *Imprint of* **Childrens**

Ellicott Pr, *(Ellicott Pr.; 0-9623903),* 4550 N. Park Ave., Suite T206, Chevy Chase, MD 20815 Tel 301-652-2020.

Ellis Family Mus, *(Ellis Family Music Co., Inc.; 1-879542),* 30 Samana Dr., Miami, FL 33133 Tel 305-858-8189.

Elmer Bair, *(Bair's, Elmer, Story Publishing; 0-9618269),* P.O. Box 176, Carbondale, CO 81623 (SAN 667-0237); 116 S. Eighth St., Carbondale, CO 81623 (SAN 667-0245) Tel 303-963-2954.

ELRAMCO Enter, *(Elramco Enterprises, Inc.; 0-930355),* 257 Osborne Rd., Albany, NY 12211 (SAN 670-7629) Tel 518-458-9095.

EMC, *(EMC Publishing; 0-88436; 0-912022; 0-8219),* Div. of EMC Corp., 300 York Ave., Saint Paul, MN 55101 (SAN 201-3800) Tel 612-771-1555; Toll free: 800-328-1452.

Embassy Hall Edns, *(Embassy Hall Editions; 0-940945),* 1630 University Ave., Suite 42, Berkeley, CA 94703 (SAN 665-133X) Tel 415-486-0187.

Emerg Response Inst, *(Emergency Response Institute, Inc.; 0-913724),* 4537 Foxhall Dr., NE, Olympia, WA 98506 (SAN 204-6490) Tel 206-491-7785.

Emerson, *(Emerson Bks., Inc.; 0-87523),* 121 N. Hampton Dr., White Plains, NY 10603 (SAN 201-3819) Tel 914-761-2643.

Emijo Pubns, *(Emijo Pubns.; 0-9618303),* P.O. Box 971, Brookline, MA 02146 (SAN 667-1888) Tel 617-738-5533.

Eminent Pubns, *(Eminent Pubns. Enterprises; 0-936955),* P.O. Box 1026, Jeffersonville, IN 47131 (SAN 658-6589) Tel 812-282-8338.

Emissaries Divine, *(Emissaries of Divine Light; 0-932869),* 5569 N. County Rd. 29, Loveland, CO 80538 (SAN 688-9875) Tel 303-667-4675; Dist. by: Foundation Hse. Pubns., Inc., 4817 N. Country Rd. 29, Loveland, CO 80537 (SAN 630-0634) Tel 303-669-2166.

Emmaus Ministries, *(Emmaus Ministries; 0-945778),* 25 Parallel St., Norwalk, CT 06850 (SAN 247-8641) Tel 203-846-6892.

Emmett, *(Emmett Publishing Co.; 0-934682),* 2861 Burnham Blvd., Minneapolis, MN 55416 (SAN 210-556X) Tel 612-377-3887.

Empire Pub Srvs, *(Empire Publishing Service),* P.O. Box 1344, Studio City, CA 91614-0344 (SAN 630-5687) Tel 818-784-8918.

Empire State Bks *Imprint of* **Heart of the Lakes**

Emprise Pubns, *(Emprise Pubns.; 0-938129),* 1000 S. Main St., Suite 591, Salinas, CA 93901 (SAN 661-2423) Tel 408-422-0415.

En Passant NY, *(En Passant Publishing Co.; 0-9627638),* P.O. Box 1632, Buffalo, NY 14215; 2 Courtland Ave., Buffalo, NY 14215 Tel 716-893-2034.

Enchant Pub Oregon, *(Enchantments Publishing of Oregon; 0-9618185),* Rte. 1, Box 28H, Enterprise, OR 97828 (SAN 667-0121); 501 Evans Ln., Enterprise, OR 97828 (SAN 667-013X) Tel 503-426-3965.

Enchanted Rain Pr, *(Enchanted Rainforest Pr.; 0-9629895),* 1801 N. Commonwealth Ave., Los Angeles, CA 90027 Tel 213-663-3405.

Encino Pr, *(Encino Pr.; 0-88426),* 510 Baylor St., Austin, TX 78703 (SAN 201-3843) Tel 512-476-6821.

Ency Brit Ed, *(Encyclopaedia Britannica Educational Corp.; 0-87827; 0-8347; 0-7826),* Subs. of Encyclopaedia Britannica, Inc., 310 S. Michigan Ave., Chicago, IL 60604 (SAN 201-3851) Tel 312-347-7900; Toll free: 800-554-9862.

Ency Brit Inc, *(Encyclopaedia Britannica, Inc.; 0-85229),* 310 S. Michigan Ave., Chicago, IL 60604-9839 (SAN 204-1464) Tel 312-347-7959; Toll free: 800-554-9862.

Enfield Pubs, *(Enfield Pubs.; 0-9618241),* P.O. Box 3145, Enfield, CT 06082 (SAN 666-9433); 181 Oldefield Farms, Enfield, CT 06082 (SAN 666-9441) Tel 203-741-0771.

English Enterprises, *(English Enterprises, Inc.; 1-878931),* 692 W. Hurst, Bushnell, IL 61422-2244 Tel 309-772-3501.

Enrich, *(Enrich; 0-933358; 0-86582),* Div. of Price Stern Sloan, Inc., 360 N. La Cienega Blvd., Los Angeles, CA 90048 (SAN 213-2168) Tel 213-657-6100; Toll free: 800-421-0892.

Enrich Enter, *(Enrichment Enterprises; 0-9609612),* 1424 Hacienda Pl., Pomona, CA 91768 (SAN 264-0260) Tel 714-622-4887.

Enslow Pubs, *(Enslow Pubs., Inc.; 0-89490),* Bloy St. & Ramsey Ave., Box 777, Hillside, NJ 07205 (SAN 213-7518) Tel 908-964-4116.

Ent & Educ Found, *(Enterprise & Education Foundation; 0-943447),* 200 The Express House, Station Sq., Pittsburgh, PA 15219 (SAN 668-4432) Tel 412-471-1504.

Enteracom Inc, *(Enteracom, Inc.; 0-936509),* 5070 Parkside Ave., Suite 1420, Philadelphia, PA 19131 (SAN 697-8282) Tel 215-877-9409.

Enterprise Del, *(Enterprise Publishing, Inc.; 0-913864; 0-942103),* 725 N. Market St., Wilmington, DE 19801 (SAN 201-3932) Tel 302-654-0110; Toll free: 800-533-2665.

Enterprise Educ, *(Enterprise for Education, Inc.; 0-934653; 0-928609),* 1320-A Santa Monica Mall, Suite 202, Santa Monica, CA 90401 (SAN 694-0730) Tel 213-394-9864.

Entertainment Factory, *(Entertainment Factory, The; 0-936086),* P.O. Box 407, Cave Creek, AZ 85331 (SAN 214-0098) Tel 602-488-2510.

EntroCon, *(EntroCon; 0-942153),* 20123 60th Ave., NE, Seattle, WA 98155 (SAN 666-8992) Tel 206-483-2440.

Entropy Conserv
See EntroCon

Entrtnmnt Enter, *(Entertainment Enterprises; 0-9619056),* P.O. Box 781341, Los Angeles, CA 90016 (SAN 243-1092) Tel 213-281-7689.

Entry Pub, *(Entry Publishing, Inc.; 0-941342),* 27 W. 96th St., New York, NY 10025 (SAN 238-9754) Tel 212-662-9703.

Envelope Bks *Imprint of* **Green Tiger Pr**

Envision Pub, *(Envision Publishing Co.; 0-9624201),* P.O. Box 1089, Portland, OR 97207-1089; 1934 NE Portland Blvd., Portland, OR 97211 Tel 503-287-8011.

Epicenter Pr, *(Epicenter Pr., Inc.; 0-945397),* 18821 64th, NE, Seattle, WA 98155 (SAN 246-9405) Tel 206-485-6822; Dist. by: Pacific Pipeline, Inc., 19215 66th Ave., S., Kent, WA 98032 (SAN 208-2128) Tel 206-872-5523; Toll free: 800-426-4727 (in Oregon, Idaho, Montana, Nevada, northern California); 800-562-4647 (in Washington).

EPM Pubns, *(EPM Pubns.; 0-914440; 0-939009),* 1003 Turkey Run Rd., McLean, VA 22101 (SAN 206-7498) Tel 703-442-7810; Orders to: P.O. Box 490, McLean, VA 22101 (SAN 206-7501).

Equal Just Con, *(Equal Justice Consultants & Educational Products; 0-930413),* P.O. Box 5582, Eugene, OR 97405 (SAN 682-0492) Tel 503-343-6761.

Equal Partners, *(Equal Partners; 0-929577),* 11348 Connecticut Ave., Kensington, MD 20895 (SAN 249-7816) Tel 301-933-1489; Dist. by: Ed-U Pr., Inc., P.O. Box 583, Fayettville, NY 13066 (SAN 221-1866) Tel 315-637-9524; Dist. by: Kids Rights, 3700 Progress Blvd., Mount Dora, FL 32757 (SAN 248-0891) Tel 904-483-1100; Toll free: 800-892-5437; Dist. by: Child Welfare League of America, 440 First St., NW, Washington, DC 20001 (SAN 201-9876) Tel 202-638-2952.

Equilla Enterprises, *(Equilla Enterprises; 0-9624771),* P.O. Box 160244, Cupertino, CA 95016; 190 Adler, No. 1, Campbell, CA 95008 Tel 408-866-8600.

Equity Inst, *(Equity Institute; 0-932469),* P.O. Box 30245, Bethesda, MD 20814 (SAN 687-4215) Tel 301-654-2904.

Equity Pub NH, *(Equity Publishing Corp.; 0-87454),* Div. of Butterworth Legal Pubs., R.R. No. 1, Box 3, Orford, NH 03777; Main St., Orford, NH 03777 (SAN 204-1383) Tel 603-353-4351.

ERA-CCR, *(ERA/CCR Corp.; 0-913935),* P.O. Box 650, Nyack, NY 10960 (SAN 217-5622) Tel 914-358-6806; Toll free: 800-845-8402.

ERIC Clear, *(ERIC Clearinghouse on Information Resources; 0-937597),* Syracuse Univ., 30 Huntington Hall, Syracuse, NY 13244-2340 (SAN 672-8189) Tel 315-443-3640.

Ericson Bks, *(Ericson Bks.; 0-911317),* 1614 Redbud St., Nacogdoches, TX 75961 (SAN 263-0923) Tel 409-564-3625.

Erie Art Mus, *(Erie Art Museum; 0-9616623),* 411 State St., Erie, PA 16501 (SAN 661-2458) Tel 814-459-5477.

Eriksson, *(Eriksson, Paul S., Pub.; 0-8397),* 208 Battell Bldg., Middlebury, VT 05753 (SAN 201-6702) Tel 802-388-7303; Dist. by: Independent Publishers Group, 814 N. Franklin, Chicago, IL 60610 (SAN 202-0769) Tel 312-337-0747.

ERN Inc, *(Educational Resources Network, Inc.; 0-9623161),* 18 Marshall St., Norwalk, CT 06854 Tel 203-866-9973.

ESP, *(ESP, Inc.; 0-8209),* 7163 123rd Cir., N., Largo, FL 34643 (SAN 241-497X); Toll free: 800-643-0280. Do not confuse with E S P Inc., Houstan, TX.

Essai Seay Pubns, *(Essai Seay Publishing Co.; 0-9607958),* P.O. Box 55, East Saint Louis, IL 62202 (SAN 240-0715) Tel 618-271-7890.

Estella Graphics, *(Estella Graphics; 0-9608502),* R.R. 3 Box 369, Montrose, PA 18801 (SAN 240-5539) Tel 717-278-4504.

ETC Pubns, *(ETC Pubns.; 0-88280),* 700 E. Vereda del Sur, Palm Springs, CA 92262 (SAN 201-4637) Tel 619-325-5352.

Eternal Wrd TV, *(Eternal Word Television Network, Inc.; 1-55794),* 5817 Old Leeds Rd., Birmingham, AL 35210 (SAN 242-5440) Tel 205-956-9537.

Ethnic Role Model, *(Ethnic Role Model Productions; 0-945779),* P.O. Box 3474, Teaneck, NJ 07666 (SAN 247-8668); Teaneck, NJ 07666 (SAN 247-8676) Tel 201-836-5892.

Eula Intl Pub, *(Eula International Publishing Co.; 1-877860),* Div. of Exciting Unique Learning Alternatives, Intl., 13353 Kilbourne, Detroit, MI 48213 Tel 313-526-3503.

Eva Hruska, *(Hruska, Eva J. Cummings; 0-9614616),* Rte. 2, Schuyler, NE 68661 (SAN 691-6805) Tel 402-352-3645.

Evang Sisterhood Mary, *(Evangelical Sisterhood of Mary),* 9849 N. 40th St., Phoenix, AZ 85028 (SAN 211-8335) Tel 602-996-4040.

Evans FL, *(Evans Pubns.; 0-932715),* Subs. of Eva-Tone, Inc., 4801 Ulmerton Rd., Clearwater, FL 34622 (SAN 687-7419) Tel 813-572-7000. Do not confuse with Evans Pubns., Inola, OK.

Evans Pubns, *(Evans Pubns.; 0-934188),* P.O. Box 999, Inola, OK 74036 (SAN 212-9019) Tel 918-543-8786. Do not confuse with Evans Pubns., Clearwater, FL.

Everett Cos Pub, *(Everett Cos., Publishing Div.; 0-944419),* Div. of Everett's Bindery, Inc., P.O. Box 5376, Bossier City, LA 71171-5376 (SAN 243-7104); Toll free: 800-423-7033; 813 Whittington St., Bossier City, LA 71171-5376 (SAN 243-7112) Tel 318-742-6240.

Everett Pub
See Everett Cos Pub

Evergreen, *(Evergreen Pr., Inc.; 0-914510),* 3380 Vincent Rd., Pleasant Hill, CA 94523 (SAN 206-3638) Tel 415-933-9700.

Everyday Bks, *(Everyday Bks.; 0-942465),* 750 S. Clinton St. No. 5A, Denver, CO 80231 (SAN 667-0660) Tel 303-360-6655.

Excalibur Publishing, *(Excalibur Publishing; 0-9627226),* 434 Avenue of the Americas, Suite 790, New York, NY 10011 Tel 212-777-1790; Toll free: 800-345-6665.

Excel Pub, *(Excel Publishing, Inc.; 0-943449),* 5131 St. Helena Way, Napa, CA 94558-1332 (SAN 668-4440) Tel 707-257-3217.

Executive Comm, *(Executive Communications; 0-917168),* 919 Third Ave., New York, NY 10022 (SAN 208-3043) Tel 212-421-3713.

Exelrod Pr, *(Exelrod Pr.; 0-917388),* P.O. Box 2303, Pleasant Hill, CA 94523 (SAN 208-1555) Tel 510-934-3357.

Exer Fun Pub, *(Exer Fun Publishing; 0-924860),* 3089C Clairemont Dr., Suite 130, San Diego, CA 92117 Tel 619-268-0684.

Experiment Pr, *(Experiment Pr., The; 0-936141),* Div. of Experiment in International Living, Kipling Rd., Brattleboro, VT 05301 (SAN 696-7388) Tel 802-257-7751.

Explore Your World Pubns, *(Explore Your World Pubns., Inc.; 0-9624301),* 65 Charter Oaks, Williamsville, NY 14221 Tel 716-689-4736.

Explorer Bks, *(Explorer Bks.; 0-9605938),* 513 LeGrand, Rte. 6, Panama City Beach, FL 32413 (SAN 216-6240) Tel 904-234-1378.

Exposition-Phoenix, *(Exposition-Phoenix Pr., Inc.; 0-682),* 6721 NW 16th Terr., Fort Lauderdale, FL 33309-1515 (SAN 207-0642) Tel 305-358-7533.

Expressway Pubs, *(Expressway Pubs.; 0-9618466),* 1 Wilshire Dr., Syosset, NY 11791 (SAN 667-9463) Tel 516-364-8076.

Extension Div, *(Univ. of Missouri, Extension Div.; 0-933842),* Univ. of Missouri, Agricultural Editor's Office, 1-98 Agricultural Bldg., Columbia, MO 65211 (SAN 679-1638) Tel 314-882-8237; Orders to: Extension Pubns., Univ. of Missouri, 115 S. Fifth St., Columbia, MO 65211 (SAN 688-427X) Tel 314-882-7216.

Extra Eds, *(Extra Editions, Inc.; 1-56281),* P.O. Box 38, Urbana, IL 61801-0038; Toll free: 800-423-9872; 803 Stratford Dr., Champaign, IL 61821 Tel 217-355-9872.

Extra NY, *(Extra; 0-9627292),* P.O. Box 1255, Great Neck, NY 11027 Tel 718-224-0302.

Eyrie Pr, *(Eyrie Pr.; 0-9619465),* 3429 Johnson Ferry Rd., Roswell, GA 30075 (SAN 245-016X) Tel 404-641-9013.

EZ Nature, *(E Z Nature Bks.; 0-945092),* P.O. Box 4206, San Luis Obispo, CA 93403-4206 (SAN 200-9846); 1405 Fourth St., Los Osos, CA 93402 (SAN 244-8548) Tel 805-528-5292.

Ezra Pub Inc, *(Ezra Publishing, Inc.; 0-9621696),* 23019 Timberline Rd., Southfield, MI 48034 (SAN 251-8570) Tel 313-354-4120.

F A Pub, *(F & A Publishing; 0-9618730),* P.O. Box 1065, Hobe Sound, FL 33455 (SAN 668-6877) Tel 407-546-5529.

F & F Pub, *(F & F Publishing Co.; 0-9616875),* 50 Shady Glen Rd., Memphis, TN 38119 (SAN 661-3748) Tel 901-685-9915.

F Feathers, *(Feathers, Fred, Publishing Co.; 0-9619139),* 2904 Fine Ave., Clovis, CA 93612 (SAN 243-4075) Tel 209-291-5798.

F J Strauss, *(Strauss, F. J., Co., Inc.; 0-945987),* 3900 West Side Ave., North Bergen, NJ 07047 (SAN 248-1162) Tel 201-864-0100.

F M Swan, *(Swan, Frances M.; 0-9602126),* 11533 Old St. Charles Rd., Bridgeton, MO 63044 (SAN 212-3835).

F Merriwell, *(Merriwell, Frank, Inc.; 0-8373),* Subs. of National Learning Corp., 212 Michael Dr., Syosset, NY 11791 (SAN 209-259X) Tel 516-921-8888; Toll free: 800-645-6337.

F One Servs, *(F1 Services; 0-9629328),* 1950 Stemmons Freeway, Suite 5037N, Dallas, TX 75207 Tel 214-746-3646.

F Shivers Evangelistic, *(Shivers, Frank, Evangelistic Assn.; 1-878127),* P.O. Box 9991, Columbia, SC 29290; 2005 Congress Rd., Hopkins, SC 29061 Tel 803-776-3570.

F T Allum, *(Allum, Faith T.; 0-9613349),* 1104 Larke Ave., Rogers City, MI 49779 (SAN 655-8739) Tel 517-734-4517.

Faber & Faber, *(Faber & Faber, Inc.; 0-571; 0-905209),* Affil. of Faber & Faber, Ltd., London, 50 Cross St., Winchester, MA 01890 (SAN 218-7256) Tel 617-721-1427; Dist. by: American International Distribution Corp., 64 Depot Rd., Colchester, VT 05446 (SAN 630-2238) Tel 802-878-0315; Toll free: 800-445-6638.

Fables CO, *(Fables, Inc.; 1-878790),* P.O. Box 1219, Littleton, CO 80160; Toll free: 800-782-8072; 8167 S. Marshall St., Littleton, CO 80123 Tel 303-971-0814.

Facts on File, *(Facts on File, Inc.; 0-87196; 0-8160),* Subs. of Commerce Clearing Hse., 460 Park Ave., S., New York, NY 10016 (SAN 201-4696) Tel 212-683-2244; Toll free: 800-322-8755.

FAFCTPC, *(1st Aid for Children & Teens Publishing Co.; 0-9622812),* 211 Trysail Ct., Foster City, CA 94404 Tel 415-574-7179.

Faith & Fellowship Pr, *(Faith & Fellowship Pr.; 0-943167),* 704 W. Vernon Ave., Box 655, Fergus Falls, MN 56537-0655 (SAN 668-2065) Tel 218-736-7357.

Faith & Life, *(Faith & Life Pr.; 0-87303),* 718 Main St., Newton, KS 67114-0347 (SAN 201-4726) Tel 316-283-5100; Box 347, Newton, KS 67114-0347 (SAN 658-0637).

Faith Min & Pubns, *(Faith Ministries & Pubns.; 1-878725),* P.O. Box 1156, Warsaw, IN 46581 (SAN 297-3529) Tel 219-799-5813.

Faith Pub Hse, *(Faith Publishing Hse.),* P.O. Box 518, Guthrie, OK 73044 (SAN 204-1243); 920 W. Mansur, Guthrie, OK 73044 (SAN 658-0645) Tel 405-282-1479.

Falcon *Imprint of* **Bantam**

Falcon Pr MT, *(Falcon Pr. Publishing Co., Inc.; 0-934318; 0-937959; 1-56044),* P.O. Box 1718, Helena, MT 59624 (SAN 221-1726); Toll free: 800-582-2665; 48 N. Last Chance Gulch, Helena, MT 59601 (SAN 658-0653) Tel 406-442-6597; Orders to: P.O. Box 1718, Helena, MT 59624 (SAN 281-7047); Dist. by: Bookpeople, 2929 Fifth St., Berkeley, CA 94710 (SAN 168-9517) Tel 415-549-3030; Toll free: 800-999-4650; Dist. by: Inland Bk. Co., 140 Commerce St., East Haven, CT 06512 (SAN 200-4151) Tel 203-467-4257; Toll free: 800-4151; Dist. by: Pacific Pipeline, Inc., 19215 66th Ave., S., Kent, WA 98032 (SAN 208-2128) Tel 206-872-5523; Toll free: 800-426-4727 (in Oregon, Idaho, Montana, Nevada, & northern California); Dist. by: Baker & Taylor Bks., Eastern Div., 50 Kirby Ave., Somerville, NJ 08876-0734 (SAN 169-4901) Tel 201-435-5111; Toll free: 800-526-3825; Dist. by: Baker & Taylor Bks., Midwestern Div., 501 S. Gladiolus St., Momence, IL 60954-2444 (SAN 169-2100) Tel 815-472-2444; Toll free: 800-435-5111; Dist. by: Baker & Taylor Bks., Southern Div., Mount Olive Rd., Commerce, GA 30599-9988 (SAN 169-1503) Tel 404-335-5000; Toll free: 800-241-6004; Dist. by: Baker & Taylor Bks., Western Div., 380 Edison Way, Reno, NV 89564 (SAN 169-4464) Tel 702-786-6700; Toll free: 800-648-3540; Dist. by: Bookmen, Inc., 525 N. Third St., Minneapolis, MN 55401 (SAN 169-409X) Tel 612-341-3333; Toll free: 800-328-8411; Dist. by: Ingram Bk. Co., 1125 Heil Quaker Blvd., La Vergne, TN 37086-1986 (SAN 169-7978) Tel 615-793-5000; Toll free: 800-876-0186.

Fam Life Ed, *(Family Life Education Assocs.; 0-9628687),* P.O. Box 7466, Richmond, VA 23221; 4319 Fauquier Ave., Richmond, VA 23227 Tel 804-264-5929.

Fam Skills, *(Family Skills, Inc.; 0-934275),* Dist. by: Southeastern Printing Co., 3601 SE Dixie Hwy., Stuart, FL 34995 (SAN 200-9420) Tel 407-287-2141; Toll free: 800-228-1583.

Family Herit, *(Family Heritage Publishing Co.; 0-9615453),* 8275 Louisiana St., Merrillville, IN 46410 (SAN 695-7692) Tel 219-924-4124; Dist. by: Pratik Pubns., P.O. Box 11133, Merrillville, IN 46411 (SAN 200-7878).

Family Life, *(Family Life Publishing; 0-9619566),* P.O. Box 2010, Dennis, MA 02638 (SAN 244-9188); 900 Town Plaza, Rte. 134, Dennis, MA 02638 (SAN 244-9196) Tel 508-385-9109.

Family Media, *(Family Media, Inc.; 1-877773),* P.O. Box 19865, Birmingham, AL 35219; 2208 Manassas Dr., Birmingham, AL 35213 Tel 205-956-3003.

Family Relat, *(Family Relations Foundation; 0-9614218),* P.O. Box 462, Sebastopol, CA 95473 (SAN 687-1097) Tel 707-823-0876; Dist. by: Bookpeople, 2929 Fifth St., Berkeley, CA 94710 (SAN 168-9517) Tel 415-549-3030; Toll free: 800-999-4650.

Far Away Fam Playhse, *(Far Away Family Playhouse; 0-9627228),* P.O. Box 27-6304, Boca Raton, FL 33427-6304; 1074 NW 13th St., No. 257C, Boca Raton, FL 33486 Tel 407-392-8226.

Far Eastern Res, *(Far Eastern Research & Pubns. Ctr.; 0-912580),* P.O. Box 15151, Washington, DC 20003 (SAN 205-5759); Orders to: HY-FERPC, 10204 Bessmer Ln., Fairfax, VA 22032 (SAN 665-6943).

Fawcett, *(Fawcett Bk. Group; 0-449),* Div. of Ballantine Bks., Inc., 201 E. 50th St., New York, NY 10022 (SAN 201-4572) Tel 212-751-2600; Toll free: 800-733-3000. *Imprints:* Columbine (Columbine); Crest (Crest Books); GM (Gold Medal Books); Juniper (Juniper).

Fearon Teach Aids, *(Fearon Teacher Aids; 0-8224),* 1204 Buchanan, P.O. Box 280, Carthage, IL 62321 (SAN 212-775X) Tel 217-357-3900; Toll free: 800-242-7272.

Feldheim, *(Feldheim, Philipp, Inc.; 0-87306),* 200 Airport Executive Pk., Spring Valley, NY 10977 (SAN 106-6307) Tel 914-356-2282; Toll free: 800-237-7149.

Fell
See Lifetime

Fellowship Pr PA, *(Fellowship Pr.; 0-914390; 0-87728),* 5820 Overbrook Ave., Philadelphia, PA 19131 (SAN 201-6117) Tel 215-879-8604.

Feminist Pr, *(Feminist Pr. at the City Univ. of New York; 0-912670; 0-935312; 1-55861),* 311 E. 94th St., New York, NY 10128 (SAN 213-6813) Tel 212-360-5790; Dist. by: Talman Co., 150 Fifth Ave., Rm. 630, New York, NY 10011 (SAN 200-5204) Tel 212-620-3182; Toll free: 800-537-8894; Dist. by: Bookpeople, 2929 Fifth St., Berkeley, CA 94710 (SAN 168-9517) Tel 415-549-3030; Toll free: 800-999-4650.

Fen Winnie, *(Fen Winnie Ink; 0-9614438),* P.O. Box 13658, San Luis Obispo, CA 93406 (SAN 689-1586) Tel 805-927-3979.

Fenton Valley Pr, *(Fenton Valley Pr.; 0-9615149),* 657 Chaffeeville Rd., Storrs, CT 06268 (SAN 694-3683) Tel 203-429-0710; Dist. by: DeVorss & Co., P.O. Box 550, 1046 Princeton Dr., Marina del Rey, CA 90292 (SAN 168-9886) Tel 213-870-7478; Toll free: 800-843-5743; 800-331-4719 (in California); Dist. by: Inland Bk. Co., 140 Commerce St., East Haven, CT 06512 (SAN 200-4151) Tel 203-467-4257; Toll free: 800-243-0138; Dist. by: New Leaf Distributing Co., 5425 Tulane Dr., SW, Atlanta, GA 30336-2323 (SAN 169-1449) Tel 404-691-6996; Toll free: 800-326-2665; Dist. by: Baker & Taylor Bks., Eastern Div., 50 Kirby Ave., Somerville, NJ 08876 (SAN 169-4901) Tel 201-722-8000; Toll free: 800-435-1845; 800-352-4833 (in New Jersey).

Fenwick Pr, *(Fenwick Pr.; 0-9628981),* 2024 Southwood Rd., Jackson, MS 39211 Tel 601-366-0868.

Ferguson, *(Ferguson, J. G., Publishing Co.; 0-89434),* 200 W. Monroe, Suite 250, Chicago, IL 60606 (SAN 207-1363) Tel 312-580-5480.

Ferguson-Florissant, *(Ferguson-Florissant Schl. District/Early Education; 0-939418),* 1005 Waterford Dr., Florissant, MO 63033 (SAN 216-5740) Tel 314-831-8809.

Ferncreek Pub, *(Ferncreek Publishing; 0-9625737),* 3409 Fern Ridge Dr., E., Conyers, GA 30208 Tel 404-922-7915.

Fgn Lang Young Child, *(Foreign Language for Young Children; 0-937531),* 21 Lake Ave., Newton Centre, MA 02159 (SAN 658-8522) Tel 617-332-2427; Orders to: P.O. Box 336, Newton Highlands, MA 02161.

Fiesta Bks Inc, *(Fiesta Bks., Inc.; 0-943169),* P.O. Box 51234, Phoenix, AZ 85076 (SAN 668-1042) Tel 602-759-4555.

Fiesta City, *(Fiesta City Pubs.; 0-940076),* P.O. Box 5861, Santa Barbara, CA 93150-5861 (SAN 217-071X).

Fiesta Pub, *(Fiesta Publishing Corp.; 0-88473),* 6443 NW 82nd Ave., Miami, FL 33166-2735 (SAN 201-8470) Tel 305-592-0171.

FIG Ltd, *(F.I.G., Ltd.; 0-9601452),* P.O. Box 23, Northbrook, IL 60065 (SAN 211-8971).

Finney Co, *(Finney Co.; 0-912486),* 3943 Meadowbrook Rd., Minneapolis, MN 55426 (SAN 206-412X) Tel 612-938-9330.

Fins Pubns, *(Fins Pubns.; 0-9615221),* Box 13005, Roseville, MN 55113 (SAN 695-1511) Tel 612-483-8187; Toll free: 800-328-8411.

Firefly Bks Ltd, *(Firefly Bks., Ltd.; 0-920668),* P.O. Box 1325, Ellicott Sta., Buffalo, NY 14205; Toll free: 800-387-5085. Canadian address: 250 Sparks Ave., Willowdale, ON M2H 2S4.

Fireplug CA, *(Fireplug Pr.; 0-9626950),* P.O. Box 283, San Mateo, CA 94402; 422 Georgetown Ave., San Mateo, CA 94402 Tel 415-347-3359.

Fireside *Imprint of* **S&S Trade**

Firestein Bks, *(Firestein Bks.; 0-9602498),* P.O. Box 370643, El Paso, TX 79937-0643 (SAN 212-940X) Tel 915-594-2966.

Fireweed, *(Fireweed Pr.; 0-912683),* P.O. Box 6011, Falls Church, VA 22046 (SAN 277-6839) Tel 703-560-0810. Do not confuse with Fireweed Pr., Fairbanks, AK.

First Ave Edns *Imprint of* **Lerner Pubns**

First Pub IL, *(First Publishing, Inc.; 0-915419; 1-56520),* 435 N. LaSalle, Suite 204, Chicago, IL 60610 (SAN 291-1558) Tel 312-670-6770. Do not confuse with First Publishing, Inc., Birmingham, AL.

Fischer Inc NY, *(Fischer, Carl, Inc.; 0-8258),* 62 Cooper Sq., New York, NY 10003 (SAN 107-4245) Tel 212-772-0900; Toll free: 800-847-4260.

Fisher Wilcoxon, *(Fisher Wilcoxon; 1-878253),* 18602 Rhine Pl., Cerritos, CA 90701 Tel 213-920-9902.

Fithian Pr, *(Fithian Pr.; 0-931832; 1-56474),* Div. of Daniel & Daniel Pubs., Inc., P.O. Box 1525, Santa Barbara, CA 93102 (SAN 211-6103); Toll free: 800-662-8351; 21 W. Canon Perdido St., Suite 217, Santa Barbara, CA 93102 (SAN 250-0124) Tel 805-962-1780.

Five Star AZ, *(5 Star Pubns.; 0-9619853; 1-877749),* P.O. Box 3142, Scottsdale, AZ 85271-3142 (SAN 246-7429) Tel 602-941-0770; Toll free: 800-545-7827; Dist. by: Baker & Taylor Bks., Western Div., 380 Edison Way, Reno, NV 89564 (SAN 169-4464) Tel 702-786-6700; Dist. by: Distributors, The, 702 S. Michigan, South Bend, IN 46618 (SAN 169-2488) Tel 219-232-8500; Toll free: 800-348-5200 (except Indiana); Dist. by: Quality Bks., Inc., 918 Sherwood Dr., Lake Bluff, IL 60044-2204 (SAN 169-2127) Tel 708-295-2010; Toll free: 800-323-4241 (Libraries only); Dist. by: Merle Distributing Co., 27222 Plymouth Rd., Detroit, MI 48239 (SAN 169-3778); Toll free: 800-233-9380 (orders). Do not confuse with Five Star Pubns., Port Townsend, WA.

FJH Music Co Inc, *(FJH Music Co., Inc.; 0-929666),* 20432 NE 16th Pl., North Miami Beach, FL 33179 (SAN 249-8685) Tel 305-651-5466.

Flame Intl, *(Flame International, Inc.; 0-933184),* P.O. Box 961, Great Barrington, MA 01230-0961 (SAN 215-3114).

Flare *Imprint of* **Avon**

FlipTrack, *(FlipTrack Learning Systems; 0-917792),* Div. of Mosaic Media, Inc., 999 N. Main, Suite 200, Glen Ellyn, IL 60137 (SAN 286-9136) Tel 708-790-1117; Toll free: 800-424-8668.

Florida Classics, *(Florida Classics Library; 0-912451),* P.O. Drawer 1657, Port Salerno, FL 34992-1657 (SAN 265-2404) Tel 407-546-9380.

Flourtown Pub, *(Flourtown Publishing Co.; 0-9603376),* P.O. Box 148, Flourtown, PA 19031 (SAN 207-6381).

Flower Pr, *(Flower Pr.; 0-942256),* Subs. of Flowerfield Enterprises, 10332 Shaver Rd., Kalamazoo, MI 49002 (SAN 217-7358) Tel 616-327-0108.

Flying Diamond Bks, *(Flying Diamond Bks.; 0-918532),* Rte. 2, Box 612, Hettinger, ND 58639 (SAN 209-5580) Tel 701-567-2646.

Focus Family, *(Focus on the Family Publishing; 0-929608; 1-56179),* 801 Corporate Ctr. Dr., Pomona, CA 91768 (SAN 250-0949) Tel 714-620-8500; Dist. by: Word, Inc., P.O. Box 218, Waco, TX 76702 (SAN 203-283X) Tel 817-772-7650; Dist. by: Tyndale Hse. Pubs., P.O. Box 80, Wheaton, IL 60189 (SAN 206-7749) Tel 312-668-8300; Toll free: 800-323-9400.

Focus Quality, *(Focus Quality Games Corp.; 0-915236),* P.O. Box 114, Blythebourne Sta., Brooklyn, NY 11219 (SAN 207-1266).

Fodor *Imprint of* **McKay**

Folk-Legacy, *(Folk-Legacy Records, Inc.; 0-938702),* Sharon Mountain Rd., Sharon, CT 06069 (SAN 207-3390) Tel 203-364-5661.

Folk-Life, *(Folk-Life Bks.; 0-914917),* P.O. Box 128, Princeton, LA 71067 (SAN 289-1336); 3330 Hwy 80E, Haughton, LA 71037 (SAN 289-1344) Tel 318-949-3915.

Follett Pr, *(Follett Pr.; 0-695; 0-401),* 1000 W. Washington Blvd., Chicago, IL 60607 (SAN 169-1783) Tel 312-666-4300.

Footstool Pubns, *(Footstool Pubns.; 1-877818),* P.O. Box 161021, Memphis, TN 38186; 2625 Kate Bond Rd., Memphis, TN 38134 Tel 901-382-1918.

Forest Hse, *(Forest Hse. Publishing Co., Inc.; 1-878363),* P.O. Box 738, Lake Forest, IL 60045 Tel 708-295-8287.

Fort Frederica, *(Fort Frederica Assn., Inc.; 0-930803),* Rte. 9, Box 286-C, St. Simons Island, GA 31522 (SAN 677-6299) Tel 912-638-3639.

Fortress Pr *Imprint of* **Augsburg Fortress**

Fortson Pubs, *(Fortson Pubs.; 0-9623092),* 5208 Broad St., Pittsburgh, PA 15224 Tel 412-362-8218.

Forward March, *(Forward March, Inc.; 0-9620467),* 831 Sweeny, Unit G, Redwood City, CA 94063 (SAN 248-8426) Tel 415-366-0708; Dist. by: Ingram Bk. Co., 1125 Heilquake Blvd., La Vergne, TN 37086 (SAN 169-7978) Tel 615-793-5000; Toll free: 800-937-8000; Dist. by: Publishers Group West, 4065 Hollis St., Emeryville, CA 94608 (SAN 202-8522) Tel 415-658-3453; Toll free: 800-365-3453; Dist. by: Baker & Taylor Bks., Western Div., 380 Edison Way, Reno, NV 89564 (SAN 169-4464) Tel 702-786-6700.

Forword MN, *(Forword; 0-9623937),* P.O. Box 533, Crookston, MN 56716-0533; 335 Summit Ave., Crookston, MN 56716 Tel 218-281-1595.

Foto Fantasi Pr, *(Foto Fantasi Pr.; 0-9619414),* P.O. Box 40477, Grand Junction, CO 81504 (SAN 244-5018); 2937 View Dr., Grand Junction, CO 81504 (SAN 244-5026) Tel 303-245-4799.

Foun Bks, *(Foundation Bks., Inc.; 0-934988),* P.O. Box 29229, Lincoln, NE 68529 (SAN 201-6567) Tel 402-466-4988.

Fountain Light Pr, *(Fountain of Light Pr.; 0-9625059),* P.O. Box 751, Belton, TX 76513; Rte. 4, P.O. Box 4759D, Belton, TX 76513 Tel 817-939-3268.

Four OClock Farms, *(Four O'Clock Farms Publishing Co.; 0-927044),* 1422 N. Woodhouse Rd., Virginia Beach, VA 23454 Tel 804-481-0596.

Four Winds *Imprint of* **Macmillan Child Grp**

Four Zoas Night Ltd, *(Four Zoas Night Hse., Ltd.; 0-939622),* P.O. Box 111, Ashvelot Village, NH 03441 (SAN 216-6267) Tel 603-239-6830.

Foxhound Ent, *(Foxhound Enterprises; 0-940502),* 6577 Sand Wedge Ct., Alexandria, VA 22312 (SAN 223-1034) Tel 703-750-3439; Dist. by: Mary E. Repass, P.O. Box 68, Louisa, KY 41230 (SAN 223-1042).

Franciscan Comns, *(Franciscan Communications; 1-55944),* 1229 S. Santee St., Los Angeles, CA 90015 Tel 213-746-2916; Toll free: 800-421-8510.

Franciscan Herald, *(Franciscan Herald Pr.; 0-8199),* Subs. of Sacred Heart Province of Order of Friars Minor, 1434 W. 51st St., Chicago, IL 60609 (SAN 201-6621) Tel 312-254-4462.

Franklin Pr WA, *(Franklin, Charles, Pr., The; 0-932091; 0-9603516),* 7821 175th St., SW, Edmonds, WA 98020 (SAN 692-9001) Tel 206-774-6979.

Frantasy Wkshp, *(Frantasy Workshop; 0-9612696),* 1400 W. Cross St., Lakewood, NJ 08701 (SAN 289-193X) Tel 201-363-3988.

Fred Pr, *(Fred Pr.; 0-937393),* 59 Suydam St., New Brunswick, NJ 08901 (SAN 658-8573) Tel 201-878-7976; Orders to: 1178 Castleton Rd., Cleveland Heights, OH 44121 (SAN 662-4189).

Free & Easy Pubns, *(Free & Easy Pubns.; 0-916391),* P.O. Box 53248, Philadelphia, PA 19105 (SAN 295-7019) Tel 215-430-8367.

Free Spirit Pub, *(Free Spirit Publishing, Inc.; 0-915793),* 400 First Ave. N., Suite 616, Minneapolis, MN 55401 (SAN 293-9584) Tel 612-338-2068; Toll free: 800-735-7323.

Freedom Lights Pr, *(Freedom Lights Pr.; 0-945985),* P.O. Box 87, Chimney Rock, CO 81127 (SAN 248-1820); 146 Cortez Ct., Pagosa Springs, CO 81157 (SAN 248-1839) Tel 303-731-5508.

Freedom Rel Found, *(Freedom from Religion Foundation; 1-877733),* P.O. Box 750, Madison, WI 53701 (SAN 276-9484); 30 W. Mifflin, Suite 801, Madison, WI 53703 Tel 608-256-5800.

Freeland Pubns, *(Freeland Pubns.; 0-936868),* P.O. Box 18941, Philadelphia, PA 19119 (SAN 215-3130) Tel 215-226-2507.

Freels Fndtn, *(Freels Foundation; 0-9622526),* 655 Beach St., Suite 400, San Francisco, CA 94109 Tel 415-928-0550.

Freestone Pub Co, *(Freestone Publishing Co.; 0-913512),* Box 398, Monroe, UT 84754 (SAN 206-4154) Tel 801-527-3738; Dist. by: Bookpeople, 2929 Fifth St., Berkeley, CA 94710 (SAN 168-9517) Tel 415-549-3030; Toll free: 800-999-4650.

Freline, *(Freline, Inc.; 0-913853),* P.O. Box 889, 32 East Ave., Hagerstown, MD 21740 (SAN 286-7508) Tel 301-797-9689.

French & Eur, *(French & European Pubns., Inc.; 0-8288),* 115 Fifth Ave., New York, NY 10003 (SAN 206-8109) Tel 212-673-7400.

Friends Natl Zoo, *(Friends of the National Zoo; 0-9622062),* National Zoological Pk., Washington, DC 20008 Tel 202-673-4993.

Friends United, *(Friends United Pr.; 0-913408; 0-944350),* 101 Quaker Hill Dr., Richmond, IN 47374 (SAN 201-5803) Tel 317-962-7573; Toll free: 800-537-8838.

Friendship Pr, *(Friendship Pr.; 0-377),* Subs. of National Council of the Churches of Christ USA, 475 Riverside Dr., Rm. 860, New York, NY 10115 (SAN 201-5773) Tel 212-870-2586; Orders to: P.O. Box 37844, Cincinnati, OH 45222-0844 (SAN 201-5781) Tel 513-948-8733.

Friou Music, *(Friou Music; 0-9628120),* 470 W. California Ave., Glendale, CA 91203-2107 Tel 818-500-7786.

Fritz & Angel, *(Fritz & Angel Publishing, Inc.; 0-9629140),* 617A Don Felix St., Santa Fe, NM 87501 Tel 505-988-7465.

Froggy Bywater, *(Froggy Bywater Pr.; 0-9627621),* P.O. Box 7920, Fresno, CA 93747; 244 S. Minnewawa, Fresno, CA 93727 Tel 209-251-0243.

Front Row, *(Front Row Experience; 0-915256),* 540 Discovery Bay Blvd., Byron, CA 94514 (SAN 207-1274) Tel 415-634-5710.

Frontier Pr Co, *(Frontier Pr. Co.; 0-912168),* P.O. Box 1098, Columbus, OH 43216 (SAN 205-5953) Tel 614-864-3737.

Frontier WA, *(Frontier Publishing; 0-939116),* P.O. Box 441, Seaside, OR 97138 (SAN 110-9669) Tel 503-738-8489.

FS&G, *(Farrar, Straus & Giroux, Inc.; 0-374),* 19 Union Sq., W., New York, NY 10003 (SAN 206-782X) Tel 212-741-6900; Toll free: 800-631-8571. *Imprints:* di Capua Bks (di Capua, Michael, Books); Sunburst (Sunburst Books).

Fulcrum Inc
See Fulcrum Pub

Fulcrum Pub, *(Fulcrum Publishing; 1-55591),* 350 Indiana St., Suite 350, Golden, CO 80401 (SAN 200-2825) Tel 303-277-1623; Toll free: 800-992-2908.

Full Court VA, *(Full Court Pr., Inc.; 0-913767),* Box 8059, Roanoke, VA 24014 (SAN 285-2527) Tel 703-345-5440.

Fun Bk Enter, *(Fun Bk. Enterprises; 0-937511),* P.O. Box 50397, Atlanta, GA 30302-0397 (SAN 658-8492); 1980 Overton Trail, Stone Mountain, GA 30088 (SAN 658-8506) Tel 404-987-2178.

Fun Pub AZ, *(Fun Publishing Co.; 0-918858),* P.O. Box 2049, Scottsdale, AZ 85252 (SAN 210-4261) Tel 602-946-2093. Do not confuse with Fun Publishing Co., Cincinnati, OH.

Fun Pub OH, *(Fun Publishing Co.; 0-938293),* 5860 Miami Rd., Cincinnati, OH 45243 (SAN 661-1761) Tel 513-272-3672. Do not confuse with Fun Publishing Co., Scottsdale, AZ.

Fun Reading, *(Fun Reading Co.; 0-9608466),* 2409 Glenwood Rd., Brooklyn, NY 11210 (SAN 240-6055) Tel 718-453-5582.

Funchess Jones, *(Funchess-Jones Publishing; 0-943021),* P.O. Box 221578, Carmel, CA 93922-1578 (SAN 667-9072) Tel 408-626-0933.

Fund Feminist Majority, *(Fund for the Feminist Majority; 1-882037),* 8105 W. Third St., Los Angeles, CA 90048 (SAN 248-8183) Tel 213-938-0560.

Fundation, *(Fundation, The; 0-930451),* 1404 Briarwood Rd. NE, Atlanta, GA 30319 (SAN 670-946X) Tel 404-321-1376.

Funny Farm Pr, *(Funny Farm Pr.; 0-9621234),* P.O. Box 8882, Amarillo, TX 79114-8882 (SAN 250-7838); 6408 Drexel Rd., Amarillo, TX 79109 (SAN 250-7846) Tel 806-355-6376.

FVN Corp, *(FVN Corp.; 0-915687),* 1660 Dyerville Loop Rd., Redcrest, CA 95569 (SAN 292-496X) Tel 707-946-2206.

G A Johnson Pub, *(Johnson, Georgia A., Publishing Co.; 0-9626450),* P.O. Box 4796, East Lansing, MI 48826; 2608 Darien Dr., Lansing, MI 48912 Tel 517-372-9642; Dist. by: Partner's Bk. Distributing, Inc., 720 E. Shiawassee St., Lansing, MI 48912 (SAN 630-4559) Tel 517-485-0366; Toll free: 800-336-3137; Dist. by: Quality Bks., Inc., 918 Sherwood Dr., Lake Bluff, IL 60044-2204 (SAN 169-2127) Tel 708-295-2010; Toll free: 800-323-4241 (Libraries only); Dist. by: Baker & Taylor Bks., Midwestern Div., 501 S. Gladiolus St., Momence, IL 60954 (SAN 169-2100) Tel 815-472-2444; Toll free: 800-435-5111; 800-892-1892 (in Illinois); Dist. by: Baker & Taylor Bks., Southern Div., Mt. Olive Rd., Commerce, GA 30599 (SAN 169-1503) Tel 404-335-5000; Toll free: 800-241-6004; 800-282-6850 (in Georgia).

G Beale Pr, *(Beale, Guthrie, Pr.; 0-937781),* 7508 42nd Ave., NE, Seattle, WA 98115 (SAN 659-2279) Tel 206-525-6596.

G E Radke, *(Radke, George E.; 0-9607994),* 41 Harvard Rd., Havertown, PA 19083 (SAN 238-8308) Tel 215-446-0786.

G F Johnson, *(Johnson, George F.; 0-9623010),* 3419 Sixth St., Lewiston, ID 83501 Tel 208-743-6636.

G Foreman, *(Foreman, Gloria, Publishing Co.; 0-915198),* P.O. Box 123, Westville, OK 74965 (SAN 203-4263) Tel 918-723-5925.

G Gannett, *(Gannett Bks.; 0-930096; 0-929906),* Subs. of Guy Gannett Publishing Co., Inc., P.O. Box 1460B, Portland, ME 04101 (SAN 210-7295) Tel 207-775-5811; Toll free: 800-442-6036.

G Jacobson, *(Jacobson, Gloria; 0-9618399),* 912 Third St., Box 803, New Glarus, WI 53574 (SAN 667-738X) Tel 608-527-5150.

G K Hall, *(Hall, G. K., & Co.; 0-8161),* Div. of Macmillan Publishing Co., Inc., 70 Lincoln St., Boston, MA 02111 (SAN 206-8427) Tel 617-423-3990; Toll free: 800-343-2806. *Imprints:* Large Print Bks (Large Print Books); Lythway Large Print (Lythway Large Print); Twayne (Twayne Publishers).

G Konopka, *(Konopka, Gisela; 0-9621328),* 3809 Sheridan Ave., S., Minneapolis, MN 55410 (SAN 250-9687) Tel 612-926-8949.

G L Lowe, *(Lowe, George L., Pubs.; 0-9621263),* 401 E. 32nd St., Chicago, IL 60616 (SAN 217-1155) Tel 312-842-1084.

G Markim, *(Markim, Greg, Pubs.; 0-938251),* P.O. Box 183, Appleton, WI 54912 (SAN 661-3659); 1916 N. Drew St., Appleton, WI 54911 (SAN 661-3667) Tel 414-734-9678.

G P Pub, *(G.P./Publishing, Inc.; 0-917473),* 4140 S. Lapeer Rd., Pontiac, MI 48057 (SAN 656-0644) Tel 313-373-2500.

G Peterson, *(Peterson, George; 0-9621320),* 7 Chapman Rd., Marlborough, CT 06447 (SAN 250-9822) Tel 203-295-0121.

G R Schoepfer, *(Schoepfer, G. R.; 0-931436),* 786 Hudson Pkwy., Whiting, NJ 08759 (SAN 211-1659) Tel 201-849-0689.

G Ronald Pub, *(Ronald, George, Pub., Ltd.; 0-85398),* P.O. Box 447, Saint Louis, MO 63166 (SAN 679-1859).

G Schnatz Pubns, *(Schnatz, G, Pubns.; 0-9614145),* 192 Woodside Ave., Lodi, NJ 07644 (SAN 686-2276) Tel 201-471-2624.

G Sroda, *(Sroda, George; 0-9604486),* P.O. Box 97, Amherst Junction, WI 54407 (SAN 210-8607) Tel 715-824-3868.

G Talley, *(Talley, Gene; 0-9622222),* 1509 Harts Mill Rd., Atlanta, GA 30319 Tel 404-651-2350.

G Whittell Mem, *(Whittell, George, Memorial Pr.; 0-910781),* 3722 South Ave., Youngstown, OH 44502 (SAN 260-2776) Tel 216-783-0645.

Gale, *(Gale Research, Inc.; 0-8103),* Subs. of Thomson Corp., The, 835 Penobscot Bldg., Detroit, MI 48226-4094 (SAN 213-4373) Tel 313-961-2242; Toll free: 800-877-4253.

Galeria, *(Galerija; 0-9617756),* 4317 S. Wisconsin Ave., Stickney, IL 60402 (SAN 664-6999) Tel 708-749-2843.

Galilee *Imprint of* **Doubleday**

Galileo, *(Galileo Pr.; 0-913123),* 7215 York Rd., Baltimore, MD 21212-1530 (SAN 240-6543); Dist. by: Pathway Bk. Service, Lowe-Village, Gilsum, NH 03448 (SAN 110-6430) Tel 603-357-0236; Toll free: 800-345-6665.

Galison, *(Galison Bks.; 0-939456; 0-929648; 1-56155),* 36 W. 44th St., New York, NY 10036 (SAN 216-3888) Tel 212-354-8840.

Gallaudet Univ Pr, *(Gallaudet Univ. Pr.; 0-913580; 0-930323; 1-56368),* 800 Florida Ave., NE, Washington, DC 20002-3695 (SAN 205-261X) Tel 202-651-5488; Toll free: 800-451-1073. *Imprints:* Clerc Bks (Clerc Books).

Gallery Arts, *(Gallery Arts Pr.; 0-9608592),* P.O. Box 88, Rye, NY 10580 (SAN 238-2881).

Gallery Bks *Imprint of* **Smithmark**

Gallopade Pub Group, *(Gallopade: Publishing Group; 0-935326; 1-55609; 0-7933),* 235 E. Ponce de Leon Ave., Suite 100, Decatur, GA 30030 (SAN 213-8441) Tel 404-370-0420.

Galloway, *(Galloway Pubns.; 0-87874),* 2940 NW Circle Blvd., Corvallis, OR 97330-3999 (SAN 201-5854) Tel 503-754-7464.

Game Designers, *(Game Designers' Workshop; 0-943580; 1-55878),* 203 North St., Normal, IL 61761 (SAN 240-656X) Tel 309-452-3632.

Gamin Pr, *(Gamin Pr.; 0-9621714),* 302 Front St., New Haven, CT 06513 (SAN 252-0508) Tel 203-789-8072.

G&D *Imprint of* **Putnam Pub Group**

Gannam-Kubat, *(Gannam/Kubat Pubs.; 0-945201),* 2632 Saturn St., Brea, CA 92621 (SAN 246-7046) Tel 714-528-8683.

Garden Way Pub *Imprint of* **Storey Comm Inc**

Gardner Pub, *(Gardner Publishing, Inc.; 0-9617183),* 150 Marine St., Bronx, NY 10464 (SAN 663-2661) Tel 212-885-1036.

Gareth Stevens Inc, *(Stevens, Gareth, Inc.; 0-918831; 1-55532; 0-8368),* River Ctr. Bldg., 1555 N. River Center Dr., Suite 201, Milwaukee, WI 53212 (SAN 696-1592) Tel 414-225-0333; Toll free: 800-341-3569.

Garrett Ed Corp, *(Garrett Educational Corp.; 0-944483; 1-56074),* P.O. Box 1588, Ada, OK 74820 (SAN 169-6955); Toll free: 800-654-9366; 130 E. 13th St., Ada, OK 74820 (SAN 243-2722) Tel 405-332-6884.

Gateway Pr MI, *(Gateway Pr., Inc.; 0-934291; 0-88296),* P.O. Box 6013, Grand Rapids, MI 49516 (SAN 693-2592); Toll free: 800-346-8614. Do not confuse with Gateway Pr. Inc., Baltimore, MD.

Gaus, *(Gaus, Theo, Ltd.; 0-912444),* P.O. Box 1168, Brooklyn, NY 11202 (SAN 203-4174) Tel 718-625-4651.

Gazelle Prodns, *(Gazelle Productions; 0-945222),* 2108 104th SE, Bellevue, WA 98004 (SAN 246-2141) Tel 206-454-3307.

Gazelle Pubns, *(Gazelle Pubns.; 0-930192),* 5580 Stanley Dr., Auburn, CA 95603 (SAN 209-5610) Tel 916-878-1223.

GBS CA, *(GBS Pubns.; 0-913855),* 1969 Benecia Ave., Los Angeles, CA 90025 (SAN 287-7473) Tel 213-552-3460.

GCAPEF, *(Grace Contrino Abrams Peace Education Foundation; 1-878227),* 3550 Biscayne Blvd., Suite 400, Miami, FL 33137 Tel 305-576-5075.

GCNHA, *(Grand Canyon Natural History Assn.; 0-938216),* P.O. Box 399, Grand Canyon, AZ 86023 (SAN 215-7675) Tel 602-638-2481.

GDA Pubns, *(G.D.A. Pubns.; 0-938640),* P.O. Box 30119, Lafayette, LA 70503 (SAN 215-2452).

Geckostufs, *(Geckostufs, Inc.; 0-9621280),* P.O. Box 27244, Honolulu, HI 96827 (SAN 250-9326); 3123A Paty Dr., Honolulu, HI 96822 (SAN 250-9334) Tel 808-988-7664.

Gee Tee Bee, *(Gee Tee Bee; 0-917232),* 11901 Sunset Blvd., No. 102, Los Angeles, CA 90049 (SAN 206-9652) Tel 213-476-2622.

GEF White, *(White, Glenn E. F.; 0-9611926),* 101 Buckingham St., Meriden, CT 06450 (SAN 286-1011) Tel 203-235-7462.

Gen Res Amer, *(General Research of America, Inc.; 0-9624408),* 4988 N. University Dr., Suite 118, Lauderhill, FL 33321 Tel 305-741-8700; Toll free: 800-388-8858.

General Church, *(General Church of the New Jerusalem; 0-945003),* 1100 Papermill Rd., Box 278, Bryn Athyn, PA 19009 (SAN 245-7512) Tel 215-947-2317.

Genesis Inc, *(Genesis, Inc.; 0-9615457),* P.O. Box 42403, Pittsburgh, PA 15203 (SAN 696-3978) Tel 412-761-5505.

Genesis Pub PA, *(Genesis Publishing Co.; 0-940967),* P.O. Box 228, Malvern, PA 19355 (SAN 664-7812); 20 Line Rd., Malvern, PA 19355 (SAN 664-7820) Tel 215-648-0876. Do not confuse with Genesis Publishing, Bedford, MA.

Geneva Pr *Imprint of* **Westminster John Knox**

Gentian Servs, *(Gentian Services; 0-9628016),* P.O. Box 2140, Olympic Valley, CA 95730; 1690 Trapper McNutt Trail, Alpine Meadows, CA 95730 Tel 916-581-3625.

George Fox Pr, *(Fox, George, Pr.; 0-943701),* P.O. Box 44, Newberg, OR 97132 (SAN 668-7172); 600 E. Third, Newberg, OR 91732 (SAN 668-7180) Tel 503-538-7959.

Geoscience Pr, *(Geoscience Pr.; 0-945005),* 12629 N. Tatum Blvd., Suite 201, Phoenix, AZ 85032 (SAN 245-7571) Tel 602-953-2330.

Geron-X, *(Geron-X, Inc.; 0-87672),* P.O. Box 1108, Los Altos, CA 94023-1108 (SAN 201-5994) Tel 415-493-0871.

Geste Pub, *(Geste Publishing Co.; 0-925360),* 3366 Wichita Falls Ave., Simi Valley, CA 93063 Tel 805-527-2680.

GFHR, *(Good Fairies of Hullen Ridge, Inc.; 0-922597),* 509 Williams Blvd., Kenner, LA 70062 (SAN 250-9164) Tel 504-464-1410.

Ghost Town, *(Ghost Town Pubns.; 0-933818),* P.O. Drawer 5998, Carmel, CA 93921 (SAN 209-4401) Tel 408-624-9058.

Gibbs Smith Pub, *(Smith, Gibbs, Pub.; 0-87905),* P.O. Box 667, Layton, UT 84041 (SAN 201-9906) Tel 801-544-9800; Toll free: 800-421-8714. *Imprints:* Peregrine Smith (Peregrine Smith Books).

Gibson, *(Gibson, C. R., Co.; 0-8378; 0-937970),* 32 Knight St., Norwalk, CT 06856 (SAN 201-5765) Tel 203-847-4543; Toll free: 800-243-6004; Orders to: C. R. Gibson, Distribution Ctr., Beacon Falls, CT 06403 (SAN 665-7028) Tel 203-888-0573.

Gifted Educ Pr, *(Gifted Education Pr.),* 10201 Yuma Ct., P. O. Box 1586, Manassas, VA 22110 (SAN 694-132X) Tel 703-369-5017.

Gim-Ho, *(Gim-Ho Enterprises; 0-9615006; 0-929763),* 5781 Calaveras Cir., La Palma, CA 90623 (SAN 692-3038) Tel 714-521-4108.

Ginkgo Hut, *(Ginkgo Hut; 0-936620),* 13 Augusta Dr., Lincroft, NJ 07738 (SAN 215-3157) Tel 201-530-9572.

Ginsberg Pubns, *(Ginsberg Pubns; 0-9623284),* 2978 Loma Pl., Boulder, CO 80301 Tel 303-447-1198.

Girl Scouts USA, *(Girl Scouts of the USA; 0-88441),* 830 Third Ave., New York, NY 10022 (SAN 203-4611) Tel 212-940-7500.

Glacier Pub, *(Glacier Publishing Co.; 0-9617382),* 15795 Glacier Hwy., Juneau, AK 99801 (SAN 664-0966) Tel 907-789-7246.

Gladstone Pub, *(Gladstone Publishing, Ltd.; 0-944599),* Div. of Another Rainbow Publishing, Inc., P.O. Box 2079, Prescott, AZ 86302 (SAN 244-6197); 212 S. Montezuma, Prescott, AZ 86303 (SAN 244-6200) Tel 602-776-1300.

Gldn West Bks, *(Golden West Bks.; 0-87095),* P.O. Box 80250, San Marino, CA 91118-8250 (SAN 203-5057) Tel 213-283-3446.

Glen Abbey Bks, *(Glen Abbey Bks., Inc.; 0-934125),* 735 N. Northlake Way, Suite 100, Seattle, WA 98103 (SAN 244-8351) Tel 206-548-9360; Toll free: 800-782-2239; Dist. by: CompCare Pubs., 2415 Annapolis Ln., Minneapolis, MN 55441 (SAN 630-3153) Tel 612-559-4800; Toll free: 800-328-3330.

Glen Canyon Nat Hist Assn, *(Glen Canyon Natural History Assn.; 0-9622233),* Div. of National Park Service, P.O. Box 581, Page, AZ 86040 Tel 602-645-2471.

Glenwood Pubns, *(Glenwood Pubns.; 0-9626662),* 540 Glenwood Ln., East Meadow, NY 11554 (SAN 297-3952) Tel 516-536-7846.

Glide Word, *(Glide Word Pr.; 0-9622574),* 330 Ellis St., San Francisco, CA 94102 Tel 415-433-2070; Dist. by: Publishers Group West, 4065 Hollis, Emeryville, CA 94608 (SAN 202-8522) Tel 415-658-3453; Toll free: 800-365-3453.

Globe Pequot, *(Globe Pequot Pr.; 0-87106; 1-56440; 0-88742),* Box Q, Chester, CT 06412 (SAN 201-9892) Tel 203-526-9571; Toll free: 800-243-0495; 800-962-0973 (in Connecticut).

Glory Ministries, *(Glory Ministries; 0-923105),* P.O. Box 560919, Charlotte, NC 28256 (SAN 251-6152); 701Q Atando Ave., Charlotte, NC 28206 (SAN 251-6160) Tel 704-342-0576.

Gloucester Pr *Imprint of* **Watts**

Glove Compart Bks, *(Glove Compartment Bks.; 0-9618806),* P.O. Box 1602, Portsmouth, NH 03802 (SAN 242-6412); 7 Jennie Ln., Eliot, ME 03903 (SAN 242-6420) Tel 207-439-0789.

Glover Pr, *(Glover Pr.; 0-944782),* 500 County Ave., Secaucus, NJ 07094 (SAN 245-4904) Tel 201-867-5840; Toll free: 800-541-7248.

GM *Imprint of* **Fawcett**

GME Pub Co, *(GME Publishing Co.; 0-9617665),* 12973 Fiddle Creek Ln., Saint Louis, MO 63131 (SAN 664-9408) Tel 314-965-1261.

GNP Pub, *(GNP Publishing; 0-9620923),* Div. of Greenville News Piedmont Co., P.O. Box 1688, Greenville, SC 29602 (SAN 250-1503); 305 S. Main St., Greenville, SC 29601 (SAN 250-1511) Tel 803-298-4279.

Gnu Wine Pr, *(Gnu Wine Pr.; 0-9623588),* 201 Central Ave., E., Saint Michael, MN 55376 Tel 612-497-4383.

Go Jolly Pubns, *(Go Jolly Pubns.; 0-9629587),* 3260 Jewel Lake Rd., Sagle, ID 83860 Tel 208-265-4662.

Goal Ent, *(Goal Enterprises & Assocs.; 0-9612350),* 6354 N. 11th, Fresno, CA 93710 (SAN 297-1755).

Godine, *(Godine, David R., Pub., Inc.; 0-87923),* 300 Massachusetts Ave., Horticultural Hall, Boston, MA 02115 (SAN 213-4381) Tel 617-536-0761. *Imprints:* Nonpareil Bks (Nonpareil Books).

Golden Gate *Imprint of* **Childrens**

Golden Owl Pub, *(Golden Owl Pubs.; 0-9601258),* 182 Chestnut Rd., Lexington Park, MD 20653 (SAN 210-4288) Tel 301-863-9253.

Golden Pr *Imprint of* **Western Pub**

Goldn Eagle OR, *(Golden Eagle Publishing; 0-9629539),* P.O. Box 1181, Pendleton, OR 97801-0150; 2700 SW Goodwin Ave., No. 33, Pendleton, OR 97801 Tel 503-276-8673. Do not confuse with Golden Eagle Publishing Co. in Aurora, CO.

Gondwana Bks, *(Gondwana Bks.; 0-931926),* Div. of Alta Napa Pr., 1969 Mora Ave., Calistoga, CA 94515 (SAN 212-0208) Tel 707-942-4444.

Gone Dogs, *(Gone To The Dogs; 0-9626566),* R.R. 1, Box 958, Putney, VT 05346; Rte. S & Sandhill Rd., Putney, VT 05346 Tel 802-387-5673.

Gong Prods, *(Gong Productions),* 3525 Diamond Ave., Suite 104, Oakland, CA 94602 (SAN 289-1581) Tel 415-482-2164.

Good Apple, *(Good Apple; 0-916456; 0-86653; 1-56417),* Div. of Simon & Schuster, Inc., P.O. Box 299, Carthage, IL 62321-0299 (SAN 208-6646); Toll free: 800-435-7234; 1204 Buchanan St., Carthage, IL 62321 Tel 217-357-3981.

Good Bks PA, *(Good Bks.; 0-934672; 1-56148),* Subs. of Good Enterprises, Ltd., Main St., Intercourse, PA 17534 (SAN 693-9597) Tel 717-768-7171; Toll free: 800-762-7171; Dist. by: Baker & Taylor Bks., Southern Div., Mt. Olive Rd., Commerce, GA 30599 (SAN 169-1503) Tel 404-335-5000; Toll free: 800-241-6004; 800-282-6850 (in Georgia); Dist. by: Baker & Taylor Bks., Midwestern Div., 501 S. Gladiolus St., Momence, IL 60954 (SAN 169-2100) Tel 815-472-2444; Toll free: 800-435-5111; 800-892-1892 (in Illinois); Dist. by: Inland Bk. Co., 140 Commerce St., East Haven, CT 06512 (SAN 200-4151) Tel 202-467-4257; Toll free: 800-243-0138; Dist. by: Baker & Taylor Bks., Eastern Div., 50 Kirby Ave., Somerville, NJ 08876 (SAN 169-4901) Tel 201-722-8000; Toll free: 800-435-1845; 800-352-4833 (in New Jersey); Dist. by: Baker & Taylor Bks., Western Div., 380 Edison Way, Reno, NV 89564 (SAN 169-4464) Tel 702-786-6700; Toll free: 800-648-3540; Dist. by: Bookpeople, 2929 Fifth St., Berkeley, CA 94710 (SAN 168-9517) Tel 415-549-3030; Toll free: 800-999-4650; Dist. by: Distributors, The, 702 S. Michigan, South Bend, IN 46618 (SAN 169-2488) Tel 219-232-8500; Toll free: 800-348-5200 (except Indiana); Dist. by: Golden-Lee Bk. Distributors, Inc., 1000 Dean St., Brooklyn, NY 11238 (SAN 169-5126) Tel 718-857-6333; Toll free: 800-473-7475; Dist. by: Gordon's Bks., 2323 Delgany St., Denver, CO 80216 (SAN 169-0531) Tel 303-296-1830; Toll free: 800-525-6979 (west of Mississippi); 800-332-6351 (in Colorado); Dist. by: Ingram Bk. Co., 1125 Heilquaker Blvd., La Vergne, TN 37086 (SAN 169-7978) Tel 615-793-5000; Toll free: 800-937-8100.

Good Idea Kids, *(Good Idea Kids; 0-9621908),* 407 Wekva Springs Rd., No. 213, Longwood, FL 32779 Tel 407-682-2287.

Good News, *(Good News Pubs.; 0-89107),* 1300 Crescent St., Wheaton, IL 60187 (SAN 211-7991) Tel 708-682-4300; Toll free: 800-323-3890 (sales only). Do not confuse with Good News Bks., an imprint of Forum for Scriptural Christianity, Wilmore, KY. *Imprints:* Crossway Bks (Crossway Books).

Good News Min, *(Good News Ministries; 0-9629559),* 17 Landslide Ct., Palmyra, VA 22963 Tel 804-589-5239; Dist. by: Whitaker Hse., 580 Pittsburgh St., Springdale, PA 15144 (SAN 203-2104) Tel 412-274-4440; Toll free: 800-444-4484.

Good Sign, *(Good Sign Pubs.; 0-937730),* 457 Ruthven Ave., Palo Alto, CA 94301 (SAN 215-6482).

Goodale Pub, *(Goodale Publishing; 0-9609662),* 1903 Kenwood Pkwy., Minneapolis, MN 55405 (SAN 262-0294) Tel 612-377-5783.

Goodfellow, *(Goodfellow Catalog Pr., Inc.; 0-936016),* P.O. Box 4520, Berkeley, CA 94704 (SAN 206-4499) Tel 415-845-2062.

Goodheart, *(Goodheart-Willcox Co.; 0-87006),* 123 W. Taft Dr., South Holland, IL 60473-2089 (SAN 203-4387) Tel 708-333-7200; Toll free: 800-323-0440.

Gopher, *(Gopher Graphics; 0-936511),* RD 2, Box 323, Greene, NY 13778 (SAN 697-8649) Tel 607-656-4531.

Gordon & Breach, *(Gordon & Breach Science Pubs., Inc.; 0-677),* P.O. Box 786, Cooper Sta., New York, NY 10276 (SAN 201-6370) Tel 212-206-8900.

Gordon Pr, *(Gordon Pr. Pubs.; 0-87968; 0-8490),* P.O. Box 459, Bowling Green Sta., New York, NY 10004 (SAN 201-6362) Tel 718-624-8419.

Gospel Pub, *(Gospel Publishing Hse.; 0-88243),* Div. of General Council of the Assemblies of God, 1445 Boonville Ave., Springfield, MO 65802 (SAN 206-8826) Tel 417-831-8000; Toll free: 800-641-4310.

Gower Pub Co, *(Gower Publishing Co. a; 0-566; 0-939207),* Old Post Rd., Brookfield, VT 05036 (SAN 262-0308) Tel 802-276-3162.

Gr Arts Ctr Pub, *(Graphic Arts Ctr. Publishing Co.; 0-912856; 0-932575; 1-55868),* P.O. Box 10306, Portland, OR 97210 (SAN 201-6338) Tel 503-226-2402; Toll free: 800-452-3032.

Grace Dangberg, *(Dangberg, Grace, Foundation, Inc.; 0-913205),* 304 W. Fifth St., Carson City, NV 89703-4699 (SAN 283-0493) Tel 702-882-4466.

Graham Bks, *(Graham Bks.; 0-9619521),* 1400 Niagara, Claremont, CA 91711 (SAN 244-9285) Tel 714-621-2621.

Grammatical Sci, *(Grammatical Sciences),* 1236 Jackson St., Santa Clara, CA 95050 (SAN 203-4433).

Grand Hotel, *(Grand Hotel; 0-9627301),* Mackinac Island, MI 49757 Tel 906-847-3331.

Grandview, *(Grandview Publishing Co.; 1-880114),* Box 2863, Jackson, WY 83001-2863; Toll free: 800-525-7344; 1170 Grand View Dr., Jackson, WY 83001 Tel 307-733-4593.

Graphic Learning, *(Graphic Learning; 0-943068; 0-87746),* Div. of Abrams & Co. Pubs., Inc., 61 Mattatuck Heights, Waterbury, CT 06705 (SAN 240-3803) Tel 203-756-6562; Toll free: 800-874-0029.

Graphitti Designs, *(Graphitti Designs; 0-936211),* 1140 N. Kraemer Blvd., Unit B, Anaheim, CA 92806-1919 (SAN 697-1105) Tel 714-632-3356.

Grayson Bernard Pubs, *(Grayson Bernard Pubs.; 0-9628556),* 223 S. Pete Ellis Dr., Suite 12, Bloomington, IN 47408 Tel 812-331-8182.

Great Activities Pub Co, *(Great Activities Publishing Co.; 0-945872),* 2838 Stuart Dr., Durham, NC 27707 (SAN 248-0018) Tel 919-489-5990.

Great Impressions, *(Great Impressions; 0-925263),* Div. of Great Arts Pr., Inc., P.O. Box 65270, Tucson, AZ 85740-2270; 55 W. Adams, No. 210, Tucson, AZ 85705. Moved, left no forwarding address.

Great Northwest, *(Great Northwest Publishing & Distributing Co., Inc.; 0-937708),* P.O. Box 212383, Anchorage, AK 99521-2383 (SAN 219-9890).

Great Ocean, *(Great Ocean Pubs.; 0-915556),* 1823 N. Lincoln St., Arlington, VA 22207 (SAN 207-527X) Tel 703-525-0909.

Greater Portland, *(Greater Portland Landmarks, Inc.; 0-9600612; 0-939761),* 165 State St., Portland, ME 04101 (SAN 203-4484) Tel 207-774-5561.

Green & White Pub, *(Green & White Publishing Co.; 0-9624777),* P.O. Box 778, Sturgis, MI 49094-0778 Tel 517-783-4923.

Green Bough Pr, *(Green Bough Pr.; 0-9615007),* 3156 W. Laurelhurst Dr., NE, Seattle, WA 98105 (SAN 693-9333) Tel 206-523-0022.

Green Hill, *(Green Hill Pubs.; 0-916054; 0-89803; 0-915463),* 722 Columbus St., Ottawa, IL 61350 (SAN 281-7578) Tel 815-434-7905; Toll free: 800-426-1357; Dist. by: Kampmann & Co., Inc., 226 W. 26th St., New York, NY 10001 (SAN 202-5191) Tel 212-727-0190; Toll free: 800-462-6420 (orders).

Green Leaf CA, *(Green Leaf Pr.; 0-938462),* P.O. Box 6880, Alhambra, CA 91802 (SAN 239-3646) Tel 213-222-7480; 20 W. Commonwealth Ave., Alhambra, CA 91801 (SAN 239-3654) Tel 213-222-7480.

Green Oak Pr, *(Green Oak Pr.; 0-931600),*
9339 Spicer Rd., Brighton, MI 48116
(SAN 211-9544) Tel 313-449-4802.

Green Tiger *Imprint of* **S&S Trade**

Green Tiger Pr, *(Green Tiger Pr.; 0-88138;*
0-914676), 200 Old Tappan Rd., Old
Tappan, NJ 07675-7005 (SAN 219-4775);
Toll free: 800-424-2443. *Imprints:* Envelope
Bks (Envelope Books); Star & Elephant Bks
(Star & Elephant Books).

Green Timber, *(Green Timber Pubns.; 0-944443),*
Div. of Tirik Productions, P.O. Box 3884,
Portland, ME 04104 (SAN 243-5543); 24
Allen Ave. Extension, Falmouth, ME 04105
(SAN 243-5551) Tel 207-797-4180.

Greenbeck, *(Greenbeck; 0-9613079),* 31 Cypress
Tree Ln., Irvine, CA 92715-2211
(SAN 294-8133) Tel 714-988-9513.

Greenberg Pub Co, *(Greenberg Publishing Co.,*
Inc.; 0-89778), 7566 Main St., Sykesville,
MD 21784 (SAN 211-9552)
Tel 301-795-7447.

Greencrest, *(Greencrest Pr., Inc.; 0-939800),*
P.O. Box 7745, Winston-Salem, NC 27109
(SAN 216-8979) Tel 919-722-6463.

Greenhaven, *(Greenhaven Pr., Inc.; 0-912616;*
0-89908; 1-56510), P.O. Box 289009, San
Diego, CA 92198-0009 (SAN 201-6214)
Tel 619-485-7424; Toll free: 800-231-5163.

Greenhouse Pub, *(Greenhouse Publishing Co.;*
0-9616844), P.O. Box 525, Marshall, VA
22115 (SAN 661-1729) Tel 703-364-1959.

Greenlf Pubns, *(Greenleaf Pubns.; 0-9608812),*
P.O. Box 50357, Pasadena, CA 91105
(SAN 238-2938).

Greenpl Bks, *(Greenplace Bks.; 0-932881),* 3015
Woodsdale, Lincoln, NE 68502
(SAN 689-0024) Tel 402-421-3172.

Greenwich Hse *Imprint of* **Outlet Bk Co**

Greenwillow, *(Greenwillow Bks.; 0-688),* Div. of
William Morrow & Co., Inc., 1350 Avenue of
the Americas, New York, NY 10019
(SAN 202-5760) Tel 212-261-6500; Orders
to: William Morrow & Co., Inc., 39 Plymouth
St., P.O. Box 1219, Fairfield, NJ 07007
(SAN 202-5779); Toll free: 800-843-9389.

Grey Castle, *(Grey Castle Pr.; 0-942545;*
1-55905), Pocket Knife Sq., Lakeville, CT
06039 (SAN 667-383X) Tel 203-435-2518.

Grey Gull Pubns, *(Grey Gull Pubns.;*
0-9614592), HC 61 Box 069, Damariscotta,
ME 04543 (SAN 691-778X)
Tel 207-563-1625.

Grin A Bit, *(Grin Bit; 0-9620112),* 230 Windy
Ln., Rockwall, TX 75087 (SAN 247-7289)
Tel 214-771-2700.

Grnleaf Pubs, *(Greenleaf Pubs.; 0-929634),*
Depot St., Schenevus, NY 12155
(SAN 249-759X) Tel 607-638-5400; Dist.
by: Publishers Group West, 4065 Hollis St.,
Emeryville, CA 94608 (SAN 202-8522)
Tel 415-658-3453; Toll free: 800-365-3453.

Grolier Inc, *(Grolier, Inc.; 0-7172),* Sherman
Tpke., Danbury, CT 06801 (SAN 205-3195)
Tel 203-797-3500.

Grosvenor USA, *(Grosvenor U.S.A.; 0-901269;*
1-85239), Affil. of Grosvenor Bks., London,
UK, 3735 Cherry Ave., NE, Salem, OR
97303 (SAN 663-1606) Tel 503-393-2172.

Group Bks *Imprint of* **Group Pub**

Group M Probelications, *(Group M*
Probelications; 0-9623400), P.O. Box 49031,
No. 162, Los Angeles, CA 90049
(SAN 248-949X) Tel 213-476-5331.

Group Pub, *(Group Publishing, Inc.; 0-936664;*
0-931529; 1-55945), P.O. Box 481,
Loveland, CO 80539 (SAN 214-4689); Toll
free: 800-747-6060 (orders only); 2890 N.
Monroe Ave., Loveland, CO 80538
(SAN 662-1376) Tel 303-669-3836.
Imprints: Group Bks (Group Books);
Teenage Bks (Teenage Books).

Grove Educ Tech, *(Grove Educational*
Technologies; 0-936735), P.O. Box 405,
Lake Grove, NY 11755 (SAN 699-9840);
27 Hy Pl., Lake Grove, NY 11755
(SAN 699-9859) Tel 516-588-5948.

Grove Weidenfeld, *(Grove/Weidenfeld; 0-8021;*
1-55584), Div. of Wheatland Corp., 841
Broadway, 4th Flr., New York, NY
10003-4793 (SAN 201-4890)
Tel 212-614-7850.

Growth Unltd, *(Growth Unlimited, Inc.;*
0-9601334; 0-916927), 31 East Ave., S.,
Battle Creek, MI 49017 (SAN 210-8976)
Tel 616-965-2229.

Gryphon Hse, *(Gryphon Hse., Inc.; 0-87659),*
P.O. Box 275, Mount Rainier, MD 20712
(SAN 169-3190) Tel 301-779-6200; Toll
free: 800-638-0928.

Guavaberry Bks, *(Guavaberry Bks.; 0-9625560),*
944 Montgomery Ave., Suite 157, Narberth,
PA 19072 Tel 215-664-6336.

Guild Bks, *(Guild Bks., Catholic Polls, Inc.;*
0-912080), 86 Riverside Dr., New York, NY
10024 (SAN 203-4646) Tel 212-799-2600.

Guild Pr, *(Guild Pr.; 0-940248),* P.O. Box
22583, Robbinsdale, MN 55422
(SAN 220-3340) Tel 612-566-1842. Do not
confuse with companies with the same name
in Los Angeles, CA, New York, NY.

Guild Pr IN, *(Guild Pr. of Indiana; 0-9617367;*
1-878208), 6000 Sunset Ln., Indianapolis,
IN 46208 (SAN 663-7965)
Tel 317-253-0097.

Guild Psy, *(Guild for Psychological Studies*
Publishing Hse.; 0-917479), 2230 Divisadero
St., San Francisco, CA 94115
(SAN 656-0687) Tel 415-931-0668.

Gulf Pub, *(Gulf Publishing Co.; 0-87201),* P.O.
Box 2608, Houston, TX 77252
(SAN 201-6125) Tel 713-529-4301; Toll
free: 800-231-6275 (except Alaska & Hawaii);
800-392-4390 (in Texas).

Gulliver Bks *Imprint of* **HarBraceJ**

Gumbs & Thomas, *(Gumbs & Thomas Pubs.;*
0-936073), 2067 Broadway, Suite 41, New
York, NY 10023 (SAN 697-0877)
Tel 212-870-0969.

Gurze Bks, *(Gurze Bks.; 0-936077),* P.O. Box
2238, Carlsbad, CA 92008 (SAN 697-0818);
3420 Woodland Way, Carlsbad, CA 92018
(SAN 697-0826) Tel 619-434-7533; Dist.
by: Publishers Group West, 4065 Hollis St.,
Emeryville, CA 94608 (SAN 202-8522)
Tel 415-658-3453; Toll free: 800-365-3453;
Dist. by: Quality Bks., Inc., 918 Sherwood
Dr., Lake Bluff, IL 60044-2204
(SAN 169-2127) Tel 708-295-2010; Toll
free: 800-323-4241 (Libraries only).

Guzzy Pr, *(Guzzy Pr.; 0-9620999),* 1725
Underwood Ave., Wauwatosa, WI 53213
(SAN 250-4766) Tel 414-774-6278.

H & H Pub, *(H & H Publishing Co., Inc.;*
0-943202), 1231 Kapp Dr., Clearwater, FL
34625-2116 (SAN 240-5350)
Tel 813-442-7760; Toll free: 800-366-4079.

H C Gibbens, *(Gibbens, Harry C.; 0-9624921),*
11327 Louise Ave., Lynnewood, CA 90262
Tel 213-637-1929.

H Carwell, *(Carwell, Hattie; 0-9621372),* 4622
Meldon Ave., Oakland, CA 94619
(SAN 251-1762) Tel 415-536-9084.

H Christiansen, *(Christiansen, Helen;*
0-9621419), 46881 State Hwy. 116, Walsh,
CO 81090 (SAN 251-3110)
Tel 719-498-4231.

H H Kapelman, *(Kapelman, Helen H.;*
0-9621807), 575 Bronx River Rd., Apt 6H,
Yonkers, NY 10704 Tel 914-237-3599.

H Holt & Co, *(Holt, Henry, & Co.; 0-8050),* 115
W. 18th St., New York, NY 10011
(SAN 200-6472) Tel 212-886-9200; Toll
free: 800-488-5233. Former trade-book arm
of Holt, Rinehart & Winston. Acquired in
1985 by Verlagsgruppe Georg von
Holtzbrinck, from CBS.

H J Kramer Inc, *(Kramer, H. J., Inc.; 0-915811),*
P.O. Box 1082, Tiburon, CA 94920
(SAN 294-0833) Tel 415-435-5367; Dist.
by: New Leaf Distributing Co., 5425 Tulane
Dr., SW, Atlanta, GA 30336-2323
(SAN 169-1449) Tel 404-691-6996; Toll
free: 800-326-2665; Dist. by: Publishers
Group West, 4065 Hollis St., Emeryville, CA
94608 (SAN 202-8522) Tel 415-658-3453;
Toll free: 800-365-3453; Dist. by:
Bookpeople, 2929 Fifth St., Berkeley, CA
94710 (SAN 168-9517) Tel 415-549-3030;
Toll free: 800-999-4650; Dist. by: Inland Bk.
Co., 140 Commerce St., East Haven, CT
06512 (SAN 200-4151) Tel 203-467-4257;
Toll free: 800-243-0138.

H L Crist, *(Crist, Harold L.; 0-9621743),* P.O.
Box 7, Arbovale, WV 24915
(SAN 252-144X) Tel 304-456-4399.

H L Levin, *(Levin, Hugh Lauter, Assocs.;*
0-88363), 2507 Post Rd., Southport, CT
06490 (SAN 201-6109) Tel 203-254-7733;
Dist. by: Macmillan Publishing Co., Inc.,
Front & Brown Sts., Riverside, NJ 08370
(SAN 202-5582) Tel 609-461-6500; Toll
free: 800-257-5755.

H L Norskog, *(Norskog, Howard L.; 0-9625171),*
P.O. Box 55, Saint Anthony, ID 83445; 348
W. Main, Saint Anthony, ID 83445
Tel 208-624-7622.

H Leonard Pub Corp, *(Leonard, Hal, Publishing*
Corp.; 0-9607350; 0-88188; 0-7935), 7777
W. Bluemound Rd., P.O. Box 13819,
Milwaukee, WI 53213 (SAN 239-250X)
Tel 414-774-3630; Toll free: 800-422-2521.

H T Taylor, *(Taylor, Henry T.; 0-938956),* P.O.
Box 111, Eggertville, NY 14226
(SAN 264-5149) Tel 716-833-2964.

Habersham, *(Habersham; 0-944784),* 635 Gravio
St., Suite 1020, New Orleans, LA 70130
(SAN 245-4939) Tel 504-525-6390.

Hachai Pubns, *(Hachai Pubns., Inc.; 0-922613),*
705 Foster Ave., Brooklyn, NY 11230
(SAN 251-3749) Tel 718-692-3900.

Hairston & Hicks, *(Hairston & Hicks Pubs.;*
0-944890), 500 Yorkshire St., No. 12,
Salem, VA 24153 (SAN 245-4246)
Tel 703-389-4314.

Haker Books, *(Haker Bks.; 0-9609964),* 2707
First Ave., N, Great Falls, MT 59401
(SAN 262-0359) Tel 406-454-1487.

Halbur, *(Halbur Publishing; 0-9603520),* P.O.
Box 11354, Santa Rosa, CA 95406
(SAN 212-9469) Tel 707-544-7537.

Half Halt Pr, *(Half Halt Pr.; 0-939481),* 6416
Burkittsville Rd., Middletown, MD 21769
(SAN 663-270X) Tel 301-371-9110.

Hall Pr, *(Hall Pr.; 0-932218),* P.O. Box 5375,
San Bernardino, CA 92412
(SAN 211-7061); 17227 Hall Ranch Rd., San
Bernardino, CA 92407 (SAN 665-7060)
Tel 714-887-3466.

Halldin Pub, *(Halldin, A. G., Publishing Co.;*
0-935648), P.O. Box 667, Indiana, PA
15701 (SAN 208-208X) Tel 412-463-8450;
Toll free: 800-227-0667; 800-233-0667 (in
Pennsylvania).

Hallelujah Pr, *(Hallelujah Pr. Publishing Co.;*
0-9621235), P.O. Box 496, Gilbert, AZ
85234-0496 (SAN 250-8389); 137 E. Elliott
Rd., Gilbert, AZ 85234 (SAN 250-8397)
Tel 602-821-2287.

Halls of Ivy, *(Halls of Ivy Pr.; 0-912256),* 3445
Leora Ave., Simi Valley, CA 93063
(SAN 204-0204) Tel 805-527-0525.

Halo Bks, *(Halo Bks.; 0-9622874; 1-879904),*
P.O. Box 2529, San Francisco, CA 94126
(SAN 200-3147); 534 Pacific Ave., San
Francisco, CA 94133 Tel 415-981-5144.

Hamiltons, *(Hamilton's; 0-9608598),* 155 W.
Main, P.O. Box 932, Bedford, VA 24523
(SAN 264-0759) Tel 703-586-5592.

Hammond Dalby Music, *(Hammond Dalby*
Music; 0-9624262), 120 Ridge Rd., Nashua,
NH 03062 Tel 603-886-1088; Dist. by:
Musicart West, P.O. Box 1900, Orem, UT
84059-1900 (SAN 110-1250)
Tel 801-225-0851; Toll free: 800-950-1900;
Dist. by: Sounds of Zion, 5180 S. 300, W.,
Unit U, Murray, UT 84107
(SAN 200-7525) Tel 801-225-1991.

Hammond Inc, *(Hammond, Inc.; 0-8437),* 515
Valley St., Maplewood, NJ 07040
(SAN 202-2702) Tel 201-763-6000; Toll
free: 800-526-4953.

Hampshire Pr, *(Hampshire Pr.),* 900 Main St.,
Wilmington, MA 01887 (SAN 296-127X);
Dist. by: Henrietta Howard-Moineau, R.F.D.
1, Box 274, Lancaster, NH 03584
(SAN 296-1288).

Hampstead Pr *Imprint of* **Watts**

Hampton-Brown, *(Hampton-Brown Co.;*
0-917837; 1-56334), 26385 Carmel Rancho
Blvd., Suite 200, Carmel, CA 93923
(SAN 657-145X) Tel 408-625-3666.

Hancock House, *(Hancock Hse. Pubs., Ltd.;*
0-88839), 1431 Harrison Ave., Blaine, WA
98230 (SAN 665-7079).

Hands on Pubns, *(Hands on Pubns.; 0-931178),*
451 Silvera Ave., Long Beach, CA 90803
(SAN 213-9286) Tel 213-596-4738.

Hang Gliding, *(Hang Gliding Pr.; 0-938282),*
Box 22552, San Diego, CA 92122
(SAN 215-6520) Tel 619-452-1768.

Hannibal Bks, *(Hannibal Bks.; 0-929292),* 921
Center, Suite A, Hannibal, MO 63401
(SAN 249-0560) Tel 314-221-2462.

Hansen Ed Mus, *(Hansen, Charles, Educational*
Music & Bks., Inc.; 0-8494), 1860 West
Ave., Miami Beach, FL 33139
(SAN 205-0609) Tel 305-532-5461; Dist.
by: Hansen Hse., 1824 West Ave., Miami
Beach, FL 33139 (SAN 200-7908)
Tel 305-532-5461; Toll free: 800-327-8202.

Happibook Pr, *(Happibook Pr.; 0-937395),* P.O. Box 218, Montgomery, NY 12549-0218 (SAN 658-9561); E. Kaisertown Rd., Montgomery, NY 12549 (SAN 658-957X) Tel 914-457-9328.

Happy Music Pub, *(Happy Music Publishing; 0-9624162),* P.O. Box 1666, Mesa, AZ 85211; 326 E. Pierce St., Tempe, AZ 85281 Tel 602-946-4795.

Happy Rainbow, *(Happy Rainbow Pr.; 0-9629039),* Div. of Beldons Co., P.O. Box 701, Somerville, NJ 08876; 244 Hedgerow Rd., Bridgewater, NJ 08807 Tel 201-526-7154.

Happy Thoughts & Rainbow, *(Happy Thoughts & Rainbow Co., The; 0-9608686),* Rte. 2, P.O. Box 419, Aurora, MN 55705 (SAN 238-2954) Tel 218-229-3451.

Har-Row
See HarperCollins

Harbinger AZ, *(Harbinger Hse., Inc.; 0-943173),* 2802 N. Alvernon Way, Tucson, AZ 85712-1502 (SAN 668-3029) Tel 602-326-9595; Toll free: 800-447-9945.

Harbor City Pubns, *(Harbor City Pubns.; 0-9629414),* 2458 Pineapple Ave., No. 3, Melbourne, FL 32935 Tel 407-254-0464.

HarBraceJ, *(Harcourt Brace Jovanovich, Inc.; 0-15),* 1250 Sixth Ave., San Diego, CA 92101 (SAN 200-2736) Tel 619-231-6616; Toll free: 800-346-8648; 800-543-1918; 800-237-2665; Harcourt Brace Jovanovich Bldg., Orlando, FL 32887 (SAN 200-2299) Tel 407-345-2000; 555 Academic Ct., San Antonio, TX 78204 (SAN 200-2833) Tel 512-299-1061; 1627 Woodland Ave., Austin, TX 78741 (SAN 200-2841) Tel 512-440-5700; Trade Dept. Customer Service, 465 S. Lincoln Dr., Troy, MO 63379 (SAN 200-285X) Tel 314-528-8110; P.O. Box 819077, Dallas, TX 75381-9077 (SAN 200-2868) Tel 214-245-1118; 7555 Caldwell Ave., Chicago, IL 60648 (SAN 200-2914) Tel 312-647-8822; 8551 Esters Blvd., Irving, TX 75063 (SAN 200-3406). *Imprints:* Gulliver Bks (Gulliver Bks); Harv (Harvest Books); HJ (HarBraceJ Juvenile Books); J Yolen Bks (Yolen, Jane, Books); VoyB (Voyager Books).

Hard Hatted Women, *(Hard Hatted Women; 0-9627833),* P.O. Box 93384, Cleveland, OH 44101; 4209 Lorain Ave., Cleveland, OH 44113 Tel 216-961-4449.

Harian Creative Bks, *(Harian Creative Bks.; 0-911906),* Subs. of Harian Creative Assocs., 47 Hyde Blvd., Ballston Spa, NY 12020 (SAN 204-0255) Tel 518-885-7397.

Harimander Pub, *(Harimander Publishing, Inc.; 0-9624783),* 9616 Kirkside Dr., Los Angeles, CA 90035 Tel 213-204-6459.

Harlequin Bks, *(Harlequin Bks.; 0-373),* 300 E. 42nd St., 6th Flr., New York, NY 10017 Tel 212-682-6080; Dist. by: Pocket Books, 1230 Ave. of the Americas, New York, NY 10020 (SAN 202-5922) Tel 212-698-7406; Toll free: 800-223-2336 (orders).

Harlin Jacque, *(Harlin Jacque Pubns.; 0-940938),* 250 Fulton Ave., Suite 507, Hempstead, NY 11550 (SAN 281-7659) Tel 516-489-8564; Orders to: 71 N. Franklin St., Suite 207, Hempstead, NY 11550 (SAN 281-7667) Tel 516-489-0120.

Harlo Pr, *(Harlo Pr.; 0-8187),* 50 Victor Ave., Detroit, MI 48203 (SAN 202-2745) Tel 313-883-3600.

Harmony *Imprint of* **Crown**

Harmony Raine, *(Harmony Raine & Co.; 0-89967),* Div. of Buccaneer Bks., Inc., Box 133, Greenport, NY 11944 (SAN 262-0367) Tel 516-734-5650; Dist. by: Buccaneer Bks., Inc,, P.O. Box 168, Cutchogue, NY 11935 (SAN 209-1542).

Harner Pubns, *(Harner Pubns.; 1-877842),* 62 Ridge Rd., Prescott, AZ 86303 Tel 602-776-1202.

Harp PBks *Imprint of* **HarperCollins**

HarpC Child Bks, *(HarperCollins Children's Bks.; 0-06),* Div. of HarperCollins Pubs., Inc., 10 E. 53rd St., New York, NY 10022 (SAN 200-2086) Tel 212-207-7000; Dist. by: HarperCollins, Keystone Industrial Pk., Scranton, PA 18512 (SAN 215-3742) Tel 717-343-4761; Toll free: 800-242-7737; 800-982-4377 (in Pennsylvania). *Imprints:* C Zolotow Bks (Zolotow, Charlotte, Books); Crowell Jr Bks (T Y Crowell Junior Books); Lipp Jr Bks (Lippincott Children Books); Trophy (Trophy).

Harper Pr
See Harpers Voice

Harper Ref *Imprint of* **HarperCollins**

Harper SF, *(Harper San Francisco; 0-00; 0-06; 0-85924; 0-86683),* Div. of HarperCollins Pubs., Inc., Icehouse 1-401, 151 Union St., San Francisco, CA 94111 (SAN 215-3734) Tel 415-477-4400; Dist. by: HarperCollins, Keystone Industrial Pk., Scranton, PA 18512 (SAN 215-3742) Tel 717-343-4761; Toll free: 800-242-7737; 800-982-4377 (in Pennsylvania).

HarperCollins, *(HarperCollins Pubs., Inc.; 0-06; 0-694),* Subs. of News Corp., Ltd., 10 E. 53rd St., New York, NY 10022 (SAN 200-2086) Tel 212-207-7000; Toll free: 800-331-3761; 800-242-7737; 800-328-3443 (Customer service); Icehouse One-401, 151 Union St., San Francisco, CA 94111 (SAN 215-3734) Tel 415-477-4400; Orders to: Keystone Industrial Pk., Scranton, PA 18512 (SAN 215-3742) Tel 717-343-4761; Toll free: 800-242-7737; 800-982-4377 (in Pennsylvania). *Imprints:* Harp PBks (HarperCollins Paperback Books); Harper Ref (Harper Reference); HarpT (Harper Trade Books); PL (HarperPerennial); Torch (Torchbooks).

Harpers Voice, *(Harper's Voice; 0-929932),* 1605 Huge Oaks, Houston, TX 77055 (SAN 250-8737) Tel 713-827-1611.

HarpJ
See HarpC Child Bks

HarpR
See Harper SF

HarpT *Imprint of* **HarperCollins**

Harraps *Imprint of* **P-H**

Harris Academy, *(Harris Academy; 0-911181),* 2402 S. Newberry Ct., Denver, CO 80222 (SAN 264-0856) Tel 303-692-0478; Dist. by: Publishers Group West, 4065 Hollis St., Emeryville, CA 94608 (SAN 202-8522) Tel 415-658-3453; Toll free: 800-365-3453.

Harris & Co, *(Harris, H. E., & Co., Inc.; 0-937458),* 170 West Rd., P.O. Box 7087, Portsmouth, NH 03801 (SAN 202-1137) Tel 603-433-0400; Toll free: 800-635-6004.

Harrison Hse, *(Harrison Hse., Inc.; 0-89274),* P.O. Box 35035, Tulsa, OK 74153 (SAN 208-676X) Tel 918-582-2126; Toll free: 800-888-4126.

Hartley Hse, *(Hartley Hse.; 0-937518),* P.O. Box 1352, Hartford, CT 06143 (SAN 220-0570) Tel 203-525-2376.

Harv *Imprint of* **HarBraceJ**

Harvard Common Pr, *(Harvard Common Pr.; 0-916782; 1-55832),* 535 Albany St., Boston, MA 02118 (SAN 208-6778) Tel 617-423-5803; Dist. by: National Bk. Network, 4720A Boston Way, Lanham, MD 20706 (SAN 630-0065) Tel 301-459-8696; Toll free: 800-462-6420.

Harvest Hse, *(Harvest Hse. Pubs., Inc.; 0-89081; 1-56507),* 1075 Arrowsmith, Eugene, OR 97402 (SAN 207-4745) Tel 503-343-0123; Toll free: 800-547-8979.

Harvest IL, *(Harvest Pubns.; 0-935797),* Div. of Baptist General Conference, 2002 S. Arlington Heights Rd., Arlington Heights, IL 60005 (SAN 696-8023) Tel 708-228-0200; Toll free: 800-323-4215. Do not confuse with companies with the same name in Berkeley, CA, Knoxville, TN.

Haskett Spec, *(Haskett Specialties; 0-9609724),* 26 E. Harrison St., Mooresville, IN 46158 (SAN 270-6946) Tel 317-831-1668.

Hastings, *(Hastings Hse. Pubs.; 0-8038),* 141 Halstead Ave., Mamaroneck, NY 10543 Tel 914-835-4005.

Havet Pr, *(Havet Pr.; 0-9622528),* P.O. Box 722, Kirkland, WA 98083; 597 14th Ave., W., Kirkland, WA 98083 Tel 206-822-8654.

Hawaiian Isl Concepts, *(Hawaiian Island Concepts; 1-878498),* P.O. Box 6280, Kahului, HI 96732 (SAN 200-366X); 1826 Wili Pa Loop, Wailuku, HI 96793 Tel 808-572-2606.

Hawaiian Resources, *(Hawaiian Resources Co., Ltd.; 0-9627294),* 94-527 Puahi St., Waipahu, HI 96797 (SAN 200-4984) Tel 808-671-6735; Dist. by: Pacific Trade Group, 94-527 Puahi St., Waipahu, HI 96797 (SAN 169-1635) Tel 808-671-6735.

Hawaiian Serv, *(Hawaiian Service, Inc.; 0-930492),* P.O. Box 2835, Honolulu, HI 96803 (SAN 205-0463) Tel 808-841-0134.

Hawkes Pub Inc, *(Hawkes Publishing Inc.; 0-89036),* Box 15711, Salt Lake City, UT 84115 (SAN 205-6232) Tel 801-262-5555.

Hawthorne Pr, *(Hawthorne Pr.; 0-9620154),* P.O. Box 3910, Redding, CA 96049 (SAN 247-7521); 1256 Hawthorne Ave., Redding, CA 96002 (SAN 247-753X) Tel 916-222-4644.

Hawthorne Pubs, *(Hawthorne Pubs.; 0-929842),* Box 135, Wheeling, IL 60090 (SAN 250-4596); 8 Norbert Dr., Hawthorne Woods, IL 60047 (SAN 250-460X) Tel 312-438-6443.

Haymark, *(Haymark Pubns.; 0-933910),* P.O. Box 243, Fredericksburg, VA 22401 (SAN 213-2508) Tel 703-373-5780.

Haypenny Pr, *(Haypenny Pr.; 0-929885),* 211 New St., West Paterson, NJ 07424 (SAN 250-9571) Tel 201-881-9249.

Hazar NY, *(HAZAR; 0-9624922),* 2685 University Ave., Apt. 34E, Bronx, NY 10468 Tel 212-796-4406.

Hazelden, *(Hazelden Foundation; 0-89486),* Box 176, Center City, MN 55012 (SAN 209-4010) Tel 612-349-4200; Toll free: 800-328-9000.

HB Pubns, *(HB Pubns.; 0-940882),* Div. of Haunted Bookshop, 214 St. Francis St., Mobile, AL 36602 (SAN 223-1344) Tel 205-432-6606.

Headline Bks, *(Headline Bks.; 0-929915),* P.O. Box 52, Terra Alta, WV 26764 (SAN 250-8540); 402 E. State Ave., Terra Alta, WV 26764 (SAN 250-8559) Tel 304-789-2601.

Heahstan Pr, *(Heahstan Pr., The; 0-9604244),* P.O. Box 954, Denton, TX 76202 (SAN 214-3127).

Health Comm, *(Health Communications, Inc.; 0-932194; 1-55874),* 3201 SW 15th St., Deerfield Beach, FL 33442 (SAN 212-100X) Tel 305-360-0909; Toll free: 800-851-9100.

Hear & Learn Pubns, *(Hear & Learn Pubns.; 1-879459),* 14516 NE 24th Ave., Vancouver, WA 98686 Tel 206-573-3057.

Heard Mus, *(Heard Museum, The; 0-934351),* 22 E. Monte Vista Rd., Phoenix, AZ 85004 (SAN 279-0327) Tel 602-252-8840.

Heart Ctry Pubns, *(Heart Country Pubns.; 0-9616334),* Rte. 1, Box 196-B, Big Sandy, TN 38221 (SAN 658-960X) Tel 901-584-2038.

Heart of the Lakes, *(Heart of the Lakes Publishing; 0-932334; 1-55787),* 2989 Lodi Rd., P.O. Box 299, Interlaken, NY 14847-0299 (SAN 213-0769) Tel 607-532-4997. *Imprints:* Empire State Bks (Empire State Books).

Hearthstn Inn, *(Hearthstone Inn; 0-9616308),* 506 N. Cascade, Colorado Springs, CO 80903 (SAN 658-7283) Tel 719-473-4413.

Heartprint Pr, *(Heartprint Pr.; 0-942411),* P.O. Box 814421, Dallas, TX 75381-4421 (SAN 667-0539) Tel 817-354-4848.

Heartstone Pr, *(Heartstone Pr.; 0-945799),* 2302 Broadlawn Dr., Houston, TX 77058 (SAN 247-7432) Tel 713-488-1919.

Heartwise Pr, *(Heartwise Pr.; 0-9626348),* 4892 Saginaw Cir., Pleasanton, CA 94566 Tel 415-462-3367.

Hebrew Pub, *(Hebrew Publishing Co.; 0-88482),* P.O. Box 157, Rockaway Beach, NY 11693 (SAN 201-5404) Tel 718-945-3000.

Heedays, *(Heeday's Pubns.; 0-917822),* 94-12 Kipaa Pl., Waipahu, HI 96797 (SAN 209-5653) Tel 808-671-1422; Dist. by: Pacific Trade Group, 94-527 Puahi St., Waipahu, HI 96797 (SAN 169-1635) Tel 808-671-6735.

Heian Intl, *(Heian International Publishing, Inc.; 0-89346),* P.O. Box 1013, Union City, CA 94587 (SAN 213-2036) Tel 415-471-8440.

Heinemann Ed, *(Heinemann Educational Bks., Inc.; 0-435),* Subs. of Reed Publishing U.S.A., 361 Hanover St., Portsmouth, NH 03801-3959 (SAN 210-5829) Tel 603-431-7894.

Heinle & Heinle, *(Heinle & Heinle Pubs., Inc.; 0-8384),* Subs. of Wadsworth, Inc., 20 Park Plaza, Boston, MA 02116 (SAN 216-0730) Tel 617-451-1940; Toll free: 800-237-0053.

Heldreth Pub, *(Heldreth Publishing; 0-941595),* P.O. Box 430, Grafton, WV 26354 (SAN 666-0002); Heldreth Apt. Bldg., Rte. 3, Grafton, WV 26354 (SAN 666-0010) Tel 304-265-1357.

Hello Reader *Imprint of* **Scholastic Inc**

Henart Bks, *(Henart Bks.; 0-938059),* 4711 NW 24th Ct., Lauderdale Lakes, FL 33313 (SAN 661-1885) Tel 305-485-4286; Dist. by: Banyan Bks., P.O. Box 431160, Miami, FL 33243 (SAN 208-340X) Tel 305-665-6011.

Henchanted Bks, *(Henchanted Bks.; 0-9615756),* P.O. Box H, Calpella, CA 95418 (SAN 696-4648) Tel 707-485-7551.

Hendrick-Long, *(Hendrick-Long Publishing Co.; 0-937460),* 4811 W. Lovers Ln., Dallas, TX 75209 (SAN 281-7748) Tel 214-358-4677; Toll free: 800-544-3770; P.O. Box 25123, Dallas, TX 75225 (SAN 281-7756).

Henrich Enter, *(Henrich Enterprises; 0-926473),* 235 Windward Way, Niceville, FL 32578.

Herald Hse, *(Herald Hse.; 0-8309),* P.O. Box HH, Independence, MO 64055 (SAN 111-7556) Tel 816-252-5010; Toll free: 800-767-8181.

Herald Pr, *(Herald Pr.; 0-8361),* Div. of Mennonite Publishing Hse., Inc., 616 Walnut Ave., Scottdale, PA 15683 (SAN 202-2915) Tel 412-887-8500; Toll free: 800-245-7894.

Herb Studies, *(Herbal Studies Course; 0-9620838; 1-879687),* 219 Carl St., San Francisco, CA 94117-3804 (SAN 249-8480) Tel 415-564-6337.

Heres Life, *(Here's Life Pubs., Inc.; 0-89840; 0-86605; 0-918956),* Subs. of Campus Crusade for Christ, International, P.O. Box 1576, San Bernardino, CA 92402-1576 (SAN 212-4254) Tel 714-886-7981; Toll free: 800-950-4457 (orders); 800-950-1457 (customer service).

Herit Print Co, *(Heritage Printing Co.; 0-929537),* P.O. Box 792, Farmington, ME 04938 (SAN 249-6100); Porter Hill, Farmington, ME 04938 (SAN 249-6119) Tel 207-778-3581.

Herit Pub NC, *(Heritage Publishing Co.; 0-936013),* 207 Kimrod Ln., Charlotte, NC 28270 (SAN 696-818X) Tel 704-867-0247. Do not confuse with companies of the same name in North Little Rock, AR, Uniontown, PA, Baton Rouge, LA, Stockton, CA.

Herit Pubs AZ, *(Heritage Pubs., Inc.; 0-929690),* 2700 Blvd., Suite 300-200, Flagstaff, AZ 86001-7124 (SAN 249-9460) Tel 602-526-1129.

Heritage Bk, *(Heritage Bks., Inc.; 0-917890; 1-55613),* 1540E Pointer Ridge Pl., Bowie, MD 20716 (SAN 209-3367) Tel 301-390-7708.

Heritage Books, *(Heritage Bks.),* 5176 E. Country Club Rd., Salina, KS 67401 (SAN 212-0410) Tel 913-827-7861. Do not confuse with Heritage Bks., Rupert, ID.

Heritage West, *(Heritage West Bks.; 0-9623048),* 306 Regent Ct., Stockton, CA 95204 Tel 209-464-8818.

Heritage WI, *(Heritage Pr.; 0-9620823),* Rte. 1, Box 880B, Stoddard, WI 54658 (SAN 249-8529) Tel 608-457-2734. Do not confuse with Heritage Pr., Baltimore, MD.

Hermenejildo Pr, *(Hermenejildo Pr.; 0-9624264),* H-SU, Box 667, Abilene, TX 79698; 2200 Hickory St., Abilene, TX 79698 Tel 915-670-1303.

Hermon, *(Sepher-Hermon Pr., Inc.; 0-87203),* 1265 46th St., Brooklyn, NY 11219 (SAN 169-5959) Tel 718-972-9010.

Heyday Bks, *(Heyday Bks.; 0-930588),* P.O. Box 9145, Berkeley, CA 94709 (SAN 207-2351) Tel 415-549-3564; Toll free: 800-454-3564.

Hi-Hopes Pub, *(Hi-Hopes Publishing; 0-945203),* P.O. Box 31142, Washington, DC 20030-1142 (SAN 246-6694); 2902 Blooming Ct., Fort Washington, MD 20744 (SAN 246-6708) Tel 202-678-8511.

Hi Plains Pr, *(High Plains Pr.; 0-931271),* P.O. Box 123, 539 Cassa Rd, Glendo, WY 82213 (SAN 681-9907) Tel 307-735-4370.

Hi-Time Pub, *(Hi-Time Publishing Corp.; 0-937997),* P.O. Box 13337, Milwaukee, WI 53213-0337 (SAN 661-2520); Toll free: 800-558-2292; 12040F W. Feerick St., Wauwatosa, WI 53222-2136 (SAN 661-2539) Tel 414-466-2420.

Hickory Ridge Pr, *(Hickory Ridge Pr.; 0-9624607),* 8675 Ridgemont Dr., Pineville, LA 71360 Tel 318-640-4283.

Hiddigeigei, *(Hiddigeigei Bks.; 0-915560),* 120 E. Sunset Pl., Dekalb, IL 60115 (SAN 207-981X) Tel 815-756-9908.

High Noon Books *Imprint of* **Acad Therapy**

Highland Pr, *(Highland Pr.; 0-910722),* Rte. 3, Box 3125, Boerne, TX 78006 (SAN 204-0522). Do not confuse with companies of the same name in Sacramento, CA, Wilsonville, OR.

Highland Pub, *(Highland Publishing; 0-9615009),* 5226 Green Farms Rd., Edina, MN 55436 (SAN 694-0307) Tel 612-933-5797; Orders to: 9000 Tenth Ave. N., Golden Valley, MN 55472 (SAN 243-2854) Tel 612-788-2444.

Highlander, *(Highlander Research & Education Ctr.; 0-9602226),* Rte. 3 Box 370, New Market, TN 37820 (SAN 212-6664).

Highlights, *(Highlights for Children; 0-87534),* P.O. Box 269, Columbus, OH 43216-0269 (SAN 281-7810) Tel 614-486-0631; 803 Church St., Honesdale, PA 18431 (SAN 281-7802) Tel 717-253-1080.

Hill & Wang, *(Hill & Wang, Inc.; 0-8090),* Div. of Farrar, Straus & Giroux, Inc., 19 Union Sq., W., New York, NY 10003 (SAN 201-9299) Tel 212-741-6900; Toll free: 800-638-3030; Toll free: 800-242-7737.

Hill School, *(Hill Schl.; 0-942573),* E. High St., Pottstown, PA 19464 (SAN 667-2779) Tel 215-326-1000.

Hillsdale Educ, *(Hillsdale Educational Pubs., Inc.; 0-910726),* 39 North St., Box 245, Hillsdale, MI 49242 (SAN 159-8759) Tel 517-437-3179.

Hilltop Pub Co, *(Hilltop Publishing Co.; 0-912133),* P.O. Box 654, Sonoma, CA 95476 (SAN 264-6706) Tel 707-938-8110; Dist. by: Bookpeople, 2929 Fifth St., Berkeley, CA 94710 (SAN 168-9517) Tel 415-549-3030; Toll free: 800-999-4650.

Hilton Thomas, *(Hilton Thomas Pubs., Inc.; 0-944162),* 2035 Northside Dr., Atlanta, GA 30305 (SAN 243-1378) Tel 404-390-9546.

Himalayan Pubs, *(Himalayan Pubs.; 0-89389),* Div. of Himalayan International Institute of Yoga Science & Philosophy, RR 1, Box 400, Honesdale, PA 18431 (SAN 207-5067) Tel 717-253-5551; Toll free: 800-444-5772.

Hinterland Pubs, *(Hinterland Pubs.; 0-9622088),* 220 Norham Dr., Cary, NC 27513 Tel 919-481-3650.

Hippocrene Bks, *(Hippocrene Bks., Inc.; 0-87052; 0-88254; 0-7818),* 171 Madison Ave., New York, NY 10016 (SAN 213-2060) Tel 718-454-2366.

Hispanic Bk Dist, *(Hispanic Bks. Distributors & Pubs., Inc.; 0-938243),* 1665 W. Grant Rd., Tucson, AZ 85745 (SAN 200-9110) Tel 602-882-9484.

Hist Jefferson Found, *(Historic Jefferson Foundation; 0-935077),* Drawer 2049, Marshall, TX 75671 (SAN 695-0914) Tel 214-938-3390; Orders to: P.O. Box 1088, Hughes Springs, TX 75656 (SAN 662-3425) Tel 214-639-2012.

Hist Tales, *(Historical Tales Ink; 0-938404),* 158 Westerly Rd., Plymouth, MA 02360 (SAN 215-7748).

Historical Soc MI, *(Historical Society of Michigan; 0-9614344; 1-880311),* 2117 Washtenaw Ave., Ann Arbor, MI 48104 (SAN 687-8008) Tel 313-769-1828.

HJ *Imprint of* **HarBraceJ**

Hlth Educ Consults, *(Health Education Consultants; 0-9622034),* 1284 Manor Pk., Lakewood, OH 44107 Tel 216-521-1766.

Hlth Pub SF, *(Health Publishing Co.; 0-931421),* Div. of Northern California Medical Services, Inc., P.O. Box 3805, San Francisco, CA 94119 (SAN 683-5422) Tel 415-750-6165; 3700 California St., OPR-714, San Francisco, CA 94119 (SAN 658-2699) Tel 415-387-8700. Do not confuse with Health Publishing Co., Chula Vista, CA.

HM, *(Houghton Mifflin Co.; 0-395; 0-87466),* 1 Beacon St., Boston, MA 02108 (SAN 200-2388) Tel 617-725-5000; Toll free: 800-225-3362; 215 Park Ave., S., New York, NY 10003 (SAN 282-4043) Tel 212-420-5800; Orders to: Wayside Rd., Burlington, MA 01803 (SAN 215-3793) Tel 617-272-1500; Toll free: 800-225-3362. *Imprints:* Clarion Bks (Clarion Books); RivEd (Riverside Editions); Sandpiper (Sandpiper Paperbacks).

Holderby & Bierce, *(Holderby & Bierce; 0-916761),* 1332 42nd Ave., Rock Island, IL 61201 (SAN 654-3979) Tel 309-788-8200.

Holiday, *(Holiday Hse., Inc.; 0-8234),* 425 Madison Ave., New York, NY 10017 (SAN 202-3008) Tel 212-688-0085.

Holiday Time, *(Holiday Time; 1-879756),* 134 W. 26th St., Rm. 1103, New York, NY 10001 Tel 212-620-0933.

Holistic Learning, *(Holistic Learning; 0-9626864),* 911 S. Eighth St., Worland, WY 82401 Tel 307-347-3675.

Holland Hse Pr, *(Holland Hse. Pr.; 0-913042),* Box 42, Northville, MI 48167 (SAN 204-0611) Tel 313-273-0223.

Hollow Spring Pr, *(Hollow Spring Pr.; 0-936198),* RD 1, Chester, MA 01011 (SAN 213-8468).

Holloway, *(Holloway Hse. Publishing Co.; 0-87067),* 8060 Melrose Ave., Los Angeles, CA 90046 (SAN 206-8451) Tel 213-653-8060; Dist. by: All America Distributors Corp., 8431 Melrose Pl., Los Angeles, CA 90069 (SAN 168-972X) Tel 213-651-2650.

Hollybridge Pubns, *(Hollybridge Pubns.; 0-9617668),* P.O. Box 1707, Midlothian, VA 23113 (SAN 664-3884); 2914 Wood Bridge Crossing Dr., Midlothian, VA 23113 (SAN 664-645X) Tel 805-744-6503.

Hollym Intl, *(Hollym International Corp.; 0-930878),* 18 Donald Pl., Elizabeth, NJ 07208 (SAN 211-0172) Tel 908-353-1655.

Holt Assocs, *(Holt Assocs.; 0-913677),* 2269 Massachusetts Ave., Cambridge, MA 02140 (SAN 286-1119) Tel 617-864-3100.

Holy Apostles Convent, *(Holy Apostles Convent Pubns.; 0-944359),* P.O. Box 3118, Buena Vista, CO 81211 (SAN 243-3184) Tel 719-395-8898.

Holy Cow, *(Holy Cow! Pr.; 0-930100),* P.O. Box 3170, Mt. Royal Sta., Duluth, MN 55803 (SAN 685-3315) Tel 218-724-1653.

Holy Cross Orthodox, *(Holy Cross Orthodox Pr.; 0-917651),* 50 Goddard Ave., Brookline, MA 02146 (SAN 208-6840) Tel 617-731-3500.

Holy Trinity, *(Holy Trinity Monastery; 0-88465),* Jordanville, NY 13361 (SAN 207-3501) Tel 315-858-0940.

Home Mission, *(Home Mission Board of the Southern Baptist Convention; 0-937170),* 1350 Spring St., NW, Atlanta, GA 30367 (SAN 207-5318) Tel 404-873-4041.

Homeland Pubns, *(Homeland Pubns.; 0-939445),* 1808 Capri Ln., Seabrook, TX 77586 (SAN 663-3587) Tel 713-474-4730.

Homestead WY, *(Homestead Publishing; 0-943972),* Box 193, Moose, WY 83012 (SAN 241-029X) Tel 307-733-6926.

Honey Bear Bks *Imprint of* **Modern Pub NYC**

Honeycomb Pr, *(Honeycomb Pr.; 0-9612244),* Div. of Independent Inactive, 6633 N. Eighth St., Philadelphia, PA 19126 (SAN 287-7295) Tel 215-548-8453.

Honeysuckle, *(Honeysuckle Imprint; 0-9621455),* P.O. Box 793, Huntsville, AL 35804 (SAN 251-3773) Tel 205-539-5651.

Honor Bks OK, *(Honor Bks.; 1-56292),* P.O. Box 55388, Tulsa, OK 74155; Toll free: 800-678-2126; 1029 N. Utica, Tulsa, OK 74110 Tel 918-585-5033. Do not confuse with Honor Bks., Rapid City, SD.

Honor Pub, *(Honor Publishing Co.; 0-9616996),* P.O. Box 932, Greenwood, MS 38930 (SAN 693-0913); 802 W. President, Greenwood, MS 38930 (SAN 662-3123) Tel 601-453-6230.

Hooked Games, *(Hooked on Games; 0-9623096),* P.O. Box 6217, Springvale, AR 72766-6217; 2103B Ashlee Dr., Springvale, AR 72764 Tel 501-750-2193.

Hope Pr CA, *(Hope Pr.; 1-878267),* Box 188, Duarte, CA 91009-0188 (SAN 200-3244); 59 Crestview Ct., Duarte, CA 91010 Tel 818-303-0644. Do not confuse with Hope Pr., Washington, DC.

Hope Pub Hse, *(Hope Publishing Hse.; 0-932727),* Affil. of Southern California Ecumenical Council, P.O. Box 60008, Pasadena, CA 91116 (SAN 688-4849) Tel 818-792-6123; Toll free: 800-326-2671 (orders only); Dist. by: Spring Arbor Distributors, 10885 Textile Rd., Belleville, MI 48111 (SAN 158-9016) Tel 313-481-0900; Toll free: 800-395-9955; Dist. by: Ingram Bk. Co., 1125 Heil Quaker Blvd., La Vergne, TN 37086-1986 (SAN 169-7978) Tel 615-793-5000; Toll free: 800-937-8000.

HoppyTalk Prodns, *(HoppyTalk Productions; 0-9626309),* P.O. Box 15968, North Hollywood, CA 91615-5968; 4521 Colfax Ave., No. 106, North Hollywood, CA 91602 Tel 818-761-3560.

Horizon Utah, *(Horizon Pubs. & Distributors, Inc.; 0-88290),* P.O. Box 490, 50 S. 500 W., Bountiful, UT 84011-0490 (SAN 159-4885) Tel 801-295-9451; Toll free: 800-453-0812.

Hot Riffs, *(Hot Riffs; 0-9620045),* 898 Urbano Dr., San Francisco, CA 94127 (SAN 247-5111) Tel 415-585-4170.

Hot Water Pubs, *(Hot Water Publishing Co.; 0-941904),* P.O. Box 771283, Eagle River, AK 99577 (SAN 239-2283) Tel 907-272-8644.

House Nia, *(House of Nia; 0-9623205),* 4014 Calmoor St., National City, CA 92050 Tel 619-479-4425.

HP Books *Imprint of* **Price Stern**

HPL Pub, *(H.P.L. Publishing; 0-944131),* P.O. Box 305, Kelseyville, CA 95451 (SAN 242-9365); 3780 Main St., Kelseyville, CA 95451 (SAN 242-9373) Tel 707-279-4386.

HR&W, *(Holt, Rinehart & Winston, Inc.; 0-03; 0-8175),* Div. of Harcourt Brace Jovanovich, Inc., 301 Commerce St., Suite 3700, Fort Worth, TX 76102 (SAN 297-4711) Tel 817-334-7500; Toll free: 800-447-9479; Orders to: 6277 Sea Harbor Dr., Orlando, FL 32887 (SAN 250-0086); Toll free: 800-782-4479.

Hse Bon Giovanni, *(House of Bon Giovanni; 0-912981),* 129 W. Neshannock Ave., New Wilmington, PA 16142 (SAN 283-0442) Tel 412-946-3501.

Hubbard Sci, *(Hubbard Scientific; 0-8331),* Div. of Spectrum Industries, P.O. Box 104, 1946 Raymond Dr., Northbrook, IL 60065-9976 (SAN 202-3121) Tel 708-272-7810; Toll free: 800-323-8368.

Huber-Copeland Pub, *(Huber/Copeland Publishing; 0-934293),* P.O. Box 665, Mattoon, IL 61938 (SAN 693-2657) Tel 317-872-4472.

Hudson Hills, *(Hudson Hills Pr., Inc.; 0-933920),* 230 Fifth Ave., Suite 1308, New York, NY 10001-7704 (SAN 213-0815) Tel 212-889-3090; Dist. by: Rizzoli International Pubns., Inc., 300 Park Ave., S., New York, NY 10010 (SAN 111-9192) Tel 212-387-3400.

Hulogosi Inc, *(Hulogosi Communications, Inc.; 0-938493),* P.O. Box 1188, Eugene, OR 97440 (SAN 661-4132) Tel 503-343-0606.

Human Kinetics, *(Human Kinetics Pubs.; 0-931250; 0-87322),* P.O. Box 5076, Champaign, IL 61825-5076 (SAN 211-7088); Toll free: 800-747-4457; 1607 N. Market St., Champaign, IL 61820 (SAN 658-0866) Tel 217-351-5076. *Imprints:* YMCA USA (Y M C A of the U. S. A.).

Human Res Ctr, *(Human Resources Ctr.),* Rehabilitation Research Library, Albertson, NY 11507 (SAN 227-0323) Tel 516-747-5400.

Human Res Dev Pr, *(Human Resource Development Pr.; 0-914234; 0-87425),* 22 Amherst Rd., Amherst, MA 01002 (SAN 201-9213) Tel 413-253-3488; Toll free: 800-822-2801.

Human Sci Pr, *(Human Sciences Pr., Inc.; 0-87705; 0-89885),* Subs. of Plenum Publishing Corp., 233 Spring St., New York, NY 10013-1578 (SAN 200-2159) Tel 212-620-8000; Toll free: 800-221-9369.

Human Servs Inst, *(Human Services Institute, Inc.; 0-943519),* 4301 32nd St., W., No. C8, Bradenton, FL 34205 (SAN 668-5749) Tel 813-746-7088; Toll free: 800-828-9474; Orders to: P.O. Box 14610, Bradenton, FL 34280-4610 (SAN 247-0314).

Humanics Ltd, *(Humanics, Ltd.; 0-89334),* P.O. Box 7447, Atlanta, GA 30309 (SAN 208-3833); Toll free: 800-874-8844; 1482 Mecaslin St., NW, Atlanta, GA 30309 (SAN 658-0882) Tel 404-874-2176. Do not confuse with Humanics in Encino, CA.

Hunt & Peck Pub, *(Hunt & Peck Publishing; 0-9624583),* 585 Woodbine Dr., Suite 200, Terre Haute, IN 47803 Tel 812-877-9371.

Hunt Hse Pub, *(Hunt Hse. Publishing, Inc.; 0-9623524),* 3704 Meadowbank, Austin, TX 78703 Tel 512-453-1368; Toll free: 800-825-2356.

Hunter Hse, *(Hunter Hse., Inc.; 0-89793),* Box 847, Claremont, CA 91711 (SAN 281-7969) Tel 714-624-2277; Orders to: Publisher's Services, Box 2510, Novato, CA 94948 (SAN 281-7977) Tel 415-883-3530; Dist. by: Publishers Group West, 4065 Hollis St., Emeryville, CA 94608 (SAN 202-8522) Tel 415-658-3453; Toll free: 800-365-3453; Dist. by: Bookpeople, 2929 Fifth St., Berkeley, CA 94710 (SAN 168-9517) Tel 415-549-3030; Toll free: 800-999-4650; Dist. by: Inland Bk. Co., 140 Commerce St., East Haven, CT 06512 (SAN 200-4151) Tel 203-467-4257; Toll free: 800-243-0138; Dist. by: New Leaf Distributing Co., 5425 Tulane Dr., SW, Atlanta, GA 30336-2323 (SAN 169-1449) Tel 404-691-6996; Toll free: 800-326-2665; Dist. by: Quality Bks., Inc., 918 Sherwood Dr., Lake Bluff, IL 60044-2204 (SAN 169-2127) Tel 708-295-2010; Toll free: 800-323-4241 (libraries only).

Hunter Textbks, *(Hunter Textbooks, Inc.; 0-88725),* 823 Reynolda Rd., Winston-Salem, NC 27104 (SAN 209-567X) Tel 919-725-0608.

Huntington Hse, *(Huntington Hse. Pubs.; 0-910311; 1-56384),* P.O. Box 53788, Lafayette, LA 70508 (SAN 241-5208); Toll free: 800-749-4009; 104 Row 2, Suite A1 & A2, Lafayette, LA 70505 Tel 318-237-7049.

HVHA, *(Happy Valley Healing Arts; 0-9628511),* 2014 Pine Cliff Rd., State College, PA 16801 Tel 814-234-4428.

Hyacinth Hse, *(Hyacinth Hse., Ltd.; 0-9622752),* P.O. Box 14603, Baton Rouge, LA 70898; 8500 Bluebonnet Ave., Baton Rouge, LA 70814 Tel 504-767-6717.

Hyperion Child *Imprint of* **W Disney Pub**

I Can, *(I Can; 1-877594),* P.O. Box 20953, Saint Petersburg, FL 33742; 10587 55th Ave., N., Semi00le, FL 33542 Tel 813-345-2224.

I D I C P, *(Inka Dinka Ink Childrens Pr.; 0-939700),* Div. of HeBo, Inc., 4741 Guerley Rd., Cincinnati, OH 45238 (SAN 293-2814) Tel 513-471-0825; Dist. by: Baker & Taylor Bks., Midwestern Div., 501 S. Gladiolus St., Momence, IL 60954 (SAN 169-2100) Tel 815-472-2444; Toll free: 800-435-5111; 800-892-1892 (in Illinois); Dist. by: Baker & Taylor Bks., Southern Div., Mt. Olive Rd., Commerce, GA 30529 (SAN 169-1503) Tel 404-335-5000; Toll free: 800-241-6004; 800-282-6850 (in Georgia); Dist. by: Baker & Taylor Bks., Eastern Div., 50 Kirby Ave., Somerville, NJ 08876 (SAN 169-4901) Tel 201-722-8000; Toll free: 800-435-1845; 800-352-4833 (in New Jersey).

I E Clark, *(Clark, I. E., Inc.; 0-88680),* St. Johns Rd., Schulenburg, TX 78956 (SAN 282-7433) Tel 409-743-3232; Orders to: P.O. Box 246, Schulenburg, TX 78956 (SAN 662-2003).

I Like Me Pub, *(I Like Me Publishing Co., The; 0-9608516),* 300 N. State St., Chicago, IL 60610 (SAN 240-6772) Tel 312-464-9130.

I-Med Pr, *(I-Med Pr., The; 0-933131),* 306 N. West El Norte Pkwy., Escondido, CA 92026 (SAN 689-7606) Tel 619-737-0343; Dist. by: Baker & Taylor Bks., Southern Div., Mount Olive Rd., Commerce, GA 30599-9988 (SAN 169-1503) Tel 404-335-5000; Toll free: 800-241-6004; Dist. by: Baker & Taylor Bks., Western Div., 380 Edison Way, Reno, NV 89564 (SAN 169-4464) Tel 702-786-6700; Toll free: 800-648-3540; Dist. by: Baker & Taylor Bks., Eastern Div., 50 Kirby Ave., Somerville, NJ 08876-0734 (SAN 169-4901) Tel 201-435-5111; Toll free: 800-526-3825; Dist. by: Baker & Taylor Bks., Midwestern Div., 501 S. Gladiolus St., Momence, IL 60954-2444 (SAN 169-2100) Tel 815-472-2444; Toll free: 800-435-5111; Dist. by: Pacific Pipeline, Inc., 19215 66th Ave., S., Kent, WA 98032 (SAN 208-2128) Tel 206-872-5523; Toll free: 800-426-4727 (in Oregon, Idaho, Montana, Nevada, & northern California); 800-562-4617 (in Washington).

I Think I Can, *(I Think I Can, Publishing; 1-877863),* Div. of La Petite Baleen, Inc., 775 Main St., Half Moon Bay, CA 94019 Tel 415-342-9181.

IASB Enviro, *(International Academy at Santa Barbara, Environmental Studies Institute; 0-9610590),* 800 Garden St., Suite D, Santa Barbara, CA 93101-1552 (SAN 271-1850) Tel 805-965-5010.

IBD Ltd, *(i.b.d., Ltd.; 0-88431),* 24 Hudson St., Kinderhook, NY 12106 Tel 518-758-1411; Toll free: 800-343-3531.

IBS Intl, *(I. B. S. International; 0-89564),* 3144 Dove St., San Diego, CA 92103 (SAN 210-3001) Tel 619-298-5061.

Ide Hse, *(Ide Hse., Inc.; 0-86663),* 4631 Harvey Dr., Mesquite, TX 75150-1609 (SAN 216-146X) Tel 214-686-5332.

Ideals, *(Ideals Publishing Corp.; 0-89542; 0-8249),* 565 Marriott Dr., Suite 800, Nashville, TN 97210; Toll free: 800-336-6438 (Customer service); Orders to: P.O. Box 140300, Nashville, TN 37214-0300 Tel 615-885-8270; Toll free: 800-327-5113; Dist. by: Fleming H. Revell (CBA Mkt. only), 120 White Plains Rd., Tarrytown, NY 10591.

Ignatius Pr, *(Ignatius Pr.; 0-89870),* Div. of Guadalupe Assocs., Inc., 2515 McAllister St., San Francisco, CA 94118 (SAN 214-3887) Tel 415-387-2324; Orders to: 15 Oakland Ave., Harrison, NY 10528 Tel 914-835-4216; Toll free: 800-537-0390 (credit card orders).

Ill St Museum, *(Illinois State Museum Society; 0-89792),* Spring & Edwards, Springfield, IL 62706 (SAN 201-5137) Tel 217-782-7386.

Illini Pubns, *(Illini Pubns.; 0-9622667),* P.O. Box 944, Champaign, IL 61824-0944 Tel 217-352-9083.

Illum Arts, *(Illumination Arts, Inc.; 0-935699),* P.O. Box 1586, Bellingham, WA 98227 (SAN 696-2599) Tel 206-733-4703.

ILM, *(Interdependent Learning Model; 0-939632),* Fordham Univ. at Lincoln Ctr., 113 W. 60th St., Rm. 1003, New York, NY 10023 (SAN 216-6305) Tel 212-841-5282.

Image NY, *(Image Publishing of New York; 0-9627508),* 2083 Hempstead Tpke., Suite 150, East Meadow, NY 11554 Tel 516-794-1074.

Image Pubns, *(Image Pubns.; 0-942772),* 6409 Appalachian Way, P.O. Box 5016, Madison, WI 53705 (SAN 238-8499) Tel 608-233-5033.

Image West, *(Image West Pr.; 0-918966),* P.O. Box 5511, Eugene, OR 97405 (SAN 210-4407) Tel 503-342-3797.

Imagery Pubns, *(Imagery Pubns.; 0-9624721),* P.O. Box 1339, Albany, OR 97321; 1197 NE Century Dr., No. 23, Albany, OR 97321 Tel 503-928-7093.

Imagination Dust, *(Imagination Dust Publishing; 0-9611072),* P.O. Box 5415, Scottsdale, AZ 85261 (SAN 282-8839) Tel 602-391-0205.

Impact Bks MO, *(Impact Bks., Inc.; 0-89228),* 137 W. Jefferson, Kirkwood, MO 63122 (SAN 214-0330) Tel 314-822-3309.

Impact Pubs Cal, *(Impact Pubs., Inc.; 0-915166),* P.O. Box 1094, San Luis Obispo, CA 93406 (SAN 202-6864) Tel 805-543-5911.

Impresora Sahuaro, *(Impresora Sahuaro),* 7575 Sendero De Juana, Tucson, AZ 85718 (SAN 218-7760) Tel 602-297-3089.

Impressive Pubns, *(Impressive Pubns.; 0-9622327),* 6145 Larry Way, North Highlands, CA 95660 Tel 916-344-3308.

In Between, *(In Between Bks.; 0-935430),* Affil. of Plain View Pr., Box T, Sausalito, CA 94966 (SAN 213-6236) Tel 415-383-8447.

In Educ, *(IN Education, Inc.; 0-918433),* 2000 Valley Forge Cir., Suite 624, King of Prussia, PA 19406 (SAN 657-6206) Tel 215-783-5939.

In Sight Pr NM, *(In Sight Pr.; 0-942524),* 535 Cordova Rd., Suite 228, Santa Fe, NM 87501 (SAN 238-1680) Tel 505-471-7511.

In-Time Pubns, *(In-Time Pubns.; 0-944397),* Div. of JEP Enterprises, P.O. Box 9541, New Haven, CT 06535 (SAN 243-5578) Tel 203-288-4850.

In Tradition Pub, *(In the Tradition Publishing Co.; 0-935369),* P.O. Box 58142, Philadelphia, PA 19102-8142 (SAN 696-267X) Tel 215-438-0379.

InBook, *(InBook Distribution Co.),* P.O. Box 120470, East Haven, CT 06512 (SAN 630-5547) Tel 203-467-5434; Toll free: 800-253-3605.

Incentive Pubns, *(Incentive Pubns., Inc.; 0-913916; 0-86530),* 3835 Cleghorn Ave., Nashville, TN 37215 (SAN 203-8005) Tel 615-385-2934; Toll free: 800-421-2830.

Ind Pr MO, *(Independence Pr.; 0-8309),* Div. of Herald Hse., P.O. Box HH, 3225 S. Noland Rd., Independence, MO 64055 (SAN 202-6902) Tel 816-252-5010; Toll free: 800-821-7550.

Ind U Pr, *(Indiana Univ. Pr.; 0-253),* 601 N. Morton St., Bloomington, IN 47404-3797 (SAN 202-5647) Tel 812-855-4203.

Ind-US Inc, *(Ind-U.S., Inc.; 0-86578),* Box 56, East Glastonbury, CT 06025 (SAN 213-5809) Tel 203-633-0045.

Indian Trail, *(Indian Trail Pr.; 0-9629284),* P.O. Box 55, Salado, TX 76571; 1113 Indian Trail, Salado, TX 76571 Tel 817-947-9205.

Indiv Educ Syst, *(Individualized Education Systems; 0-938911),* P.O. Box 5136, Fresno, CA 93755 (SAN 661-8405); 134 Poppy Ln., Clovis, CA 93612 (SAN 661-8413) Tel 209-299-4639.

Indp Pubs, *(Independence Pubs., Inc.; 0-945740),* P.O. Box 29905, Atlanta, GA 30359 (SAN 247-7114); 1840B Briarcliff Cir., Atlanta, GA 30329 (SAN 247-7122) Tel 404-636-7092.

Infini Educ, *(Infini Educational Supplies; 0-929916),* Div. of Infini, Inc., 244 Mercury Cir., Pomona, CA 91768 (SAN 250-9784) Tel 818-967-6667.

Info All Bk, *(Info-All Bk. Co.; 0-9617218),* 5 Old Well Ln., Dallas, PA 18612 (SAN 663-4087) Tel 717-288-9375.

Info Oregon, *(Information Pr., The; 0-911927),* P.O. Box 1422, Eugene, OR 97440 (SAN 264-1127) Tel 503-689-0188.

Info Plus TX, *(Information Plus; 0-936474; 1-878623),* Div. of Information Aids, Inc., 2812 Exchange St., Wylie, TX 75098 (SAN 220-2557) Tel 214-442-0167. Do not confuse with companies with the same name in Loomis, CA, Warren, NJ.

Info Res Cons, *(Information Resource Consultants; 0-931821; 1-55804),* 11920 Hargrove, Saint Louis, MO 63131 (SAN 685-2874) Tel 314-822-7072.

Inkstone Books, *(Inkstone Bks.; 0-9604542),* P.O. Box 22172, Carmel, CA 93922 (SAN 262-043X); 22 Ridge Ave., Mill Valley, CA 94941 (SAN 241-7286) Tel 415-389-6335.

Innovative Educ Pub, *(Innovative Education Publishing Co.; 0-915925),* P.O. Box 5066, Milford, CT 06460 (SAN 287-2927); 73 Morningside Dr., Milford, CT 06460 (SAN 650-8154) Tel 203-874-6046.

Innovative Learn, *(Innovative Learning Designs; 0-931303),* 7811 SE 27th, Suite 104, Mercer Island, WA 98040 (SAN 685-2106) Tel 206-232-2697.

Innovative Lrn, *(Innovative Learning Strategies; 0-9616224),* 570 Pennsylvania Ave., San Francisco, CA 94107 (SAN 658-5507) Tel 415-647-1672; Dist. by: Berty Segal, Inc., 1749 Eucalptus St., Brea, CA 92621 (SAN 630-0553) Tel 714-529-5359.

Inquisitors Pub, *(Inquisitors Publishing Co.; 0-923889),* P.O. Box 10, North Aurora, IL 60542 (SAN 251-8376); 122 Juniper Dr., North Aurora, IL 60542 (SAN 251-8384) Tel 708-801-0607; Dist. by: Baker & Taylor Bks., Midwestern Div., 501 S. Gladiolus St., Momence, IL 60954-2444 (SAN 169-2100) Tel 815-472-2444; Toll free: 800-435-5111; 800-892-1892 (in Illinois); Dist. by: Ingram Bk. Co., 1125 Heil Quaker Blvd., La Vergne, TN 37086-1986 (SAN 169-7978) Tel 615-793-5000; Toll free: 800-937-8000; Dist. by: Quality Bks., 918 Sherwood Dr., Lake Bluff, IL 60044-2204 (SAN 169-2127) Tel 708-295-2010; Toll free: 800-323-4241 (Libraries only).

Insiders Guide, *(Insiders' Guides, Inc.; 0-912367),* P.O. Box 2057, Manteo, NC 27954 (SAN 265-0940) Tel 919-473-6100.

Insight Data, *(Insight Data; 0-945876),* P.O. Box 15225, Jacksonville, FL 32239 (SAN 248-1626) Tel 904-743-8628.

Insight Pub, *(Insight Publishing; 0-940735),* 2101 Wilshire Blvd., Santa Monica, CA 90403 (SAN 667-4259) Tel 213-829-9816. Do not confuse with Insight Publishing in Royal Oak, MI.

Inspir Univ, *(Inspiration Univ.; 0-945793),* P.O. Box 234, Sierraville, CA 96126 (SAN 247-5634); 1 Campbell Hot Springs Rd., Sierraville, CA 96126-0234 (SAN 247-5642) Tel 916-893-8643; Orders to: Box 5320, Chico, CA 95927.

Inst Advncmnt Philos Child, *(Institute for the Advancement of Philosophy for Children; 0-916834),* Montclair State College, Upper Montclair, NJ 07043 (SAN 281-7144) Tel 201-893-4279.

Inst Basic Youth, *(Institute in Basic Youth Conflicts; 0-916888),* P.O. Box 1, Oak Brook, IL 60522-3001 (SAN 208-6972) Tel 312-323-9800.

Inst Creation *Imprint of Master Bks*

Inst Fam Blind Child, *(Institute for Families of Blind Children; 0-9630118),* 1300 N. Vermont Ave., Suite 909, Los Angeles, CA 90027 Tel 213-669-4649.

Inst Food & Develop, *(Institute for Food & Development Policy; 0-935028),* 145 Ninth St., San Francisco, CA 94103 (SAN 213-327X) Tel 415-864-8555.

Inst for the arts, *(Rice Univ., Institute for the Arts Catalogues; 0-914412),* Menil Foundation, 1511 Branard, Houston, TX 77006 (SAN 218-933X) Tel 713-525-9400.

Inst Karmic, *(Institute of Karmic Guidance; 0-924944),* P.O. Box 73025, Washington, DC 20056; 1015 Quebec Pl., NW, Washington, DC 20010 Tel 202-547-1203.

Inst Rational-Emotive, *(Institute for Rational-Emotive Therapy; 0-917476),* 45 E. 65th St., New York, NY 10021 (SAN 210-3079) Tel 212-535-0822.

Inst Subs Abuse Res, *(Institute for Substance Abuse Research; 0-935847),* Subs. of Security Consultant Services, Inc., 2501 27th Ave., Suite F-6, Vero Beach, FL 32960 (SAN 699-7759) Tel 407-569-3121; Orders to: P.O. Box 6837, Vero Beach, FL 32961-6837 (SAN 662-4065).

Inst Womens Policy Rsch, *(Institute for Women's Policy Research; 1-878428),* 1400 20th St. NW, No. 104, Washington, DC 20036 Tel 202-785-5100.

Institute Government, *(Institute of Government; 1-56011),* c/o Univ. of North Carolina-Chapel Hill, Knapp Bldg. 3330, Chapel Hill, NC 27599-3330 (SAN 204-8752) Tel 919-966-4119.

Instr Res Co, *(Instructional Resources Co.; 1-879478),* 1013 E. Dimond Blvd., No. 188, Anchorage, AK 99515 Tel 907-345-6689.

Instruc Resc MD, *(Instructional Resources Corp.; 0-923805),* 1819 Bay Ridge Ave., Suite 160, Annapolis, MD 21403 (SAN 251-7922) Tel 301-263-0025; Toll free: 800-922-1711.

Integ Energy, *(Integrated Energy Systems; 0-9608358),* Div. of Edith Shedd & Assocs., Inc., Rte. 2, Box 61A1, Monroe, GA 30655 (SAN 240-6802) Tel 404-267-3534.

Integral Yoga Pubns, *(Integral Yoga Pubns.; 0-932040),* Satchidananda Ashram-Yogaville, Rte. 1, Box 172, Buckingham, VA 23921 (SAN 285-0338) Tel 804-969-1049.

Inter-Am Tropical, *(Inter-American Tropical Tuna Commission; 0-9603078),* C/O Scripps Institute of Oceanography, La Jolla, CA 92093 (SAN 241-7294) Tel 619-546-7100.

Inter Dev Res Assn, *(Intercultural Development Research Assn.; 1-878550),* 5835 Callaghan Rd., Suite 350, San Antonio, TX 78228 Tel 512-684-8180.

Inter Print Pubs, *(Interstate Printers & Pubs., Inc.; 0-8134),* P.O. Box 50, Danville, IL 61834-0050 (SAN 206-6548) Tel 217-446-0500; Toll free: 800-843-4774.

Inter Skills Pr, *(Interactive Skills Pr.; 0-9618132),* 25B Broun Pl., Bronx, NY 10475 (SAN 666-3575) Tel 212-379-2007.

Interbk Inc, *(Interbook, Inc.; 0-913456; 0-89192),* 131 Varick St., 2nd Flr., New York, NY 10013 (SAN 202-7070) Tel 212-691-7248.

Intercult Pr, *(Intercultural Pr., Inc.; 0-933662; 1-877864),* P.O. Box 700, Yarmouth, ME 04096 (SAN 212-6699) Tel 207-846-5168.

Interlink Pub, *(Interlink Publishing Group, Inc.; 0-940793),* 99 Seventh Ave., Brooklyn, NY 11215 (SAN 664-8908) Tel 718-797-4292. *Imprints:* Crocodile Bks (Crocodile Bks.).

Interspace Bks, *(Interspace Bks.; 0-930061),* 4500 Chesapeake St., NW, Washington, DC 20016 (SAN 669-8913) Tel 202-363-9082.

Interurban, *(Interurban Pr.; 0-916374; 1-56342),* P.O. Box 6444, Glendale, CA 91225-0444 (SAN 207-9593) Tel 818-240-9130.

Intervale Pub Co, *(Intervale Publishing Co., Inc.; 0-932400),* R.R. 1, Box 288, Center Sandwich, NH 03227 (SAN 211-9633) Tel 603-284-7726.

InterVarsity, *(InterVarsity Pr.; 0-87784; 0-8308),* Div. of InterVarsity Christian Fellowship of the USA, P.O. Box 1400, 5206 Main St., Downers Grove, IL 60515 (SAN 202-7089) Tel 708-964-5700; Toll free: 800-843-7225; 800-873-0143 (electronic ordering).

Intl Bible Soc, *(International Bible Society; 1-56320),* 1820 Jet Stream Dr., Colorado Springs, CO 80921 Tel 719-488-9200; Toll free: 800-524-1588.

Intl Bk Ctr, *(International Bk. Ctr.; 0-917062; 0-86685),* 2007 Laurel Dr., P.O. Box 295, Troy, MI 48099 (SAN 169-4014) Tel 313-879-8436.

Intl Gamester, *(International Gamester, Ltd.; 0-9627003),* P.O. Box 2116, Ann Arbor, MI 48106; 912 N. Main St., Ann Arbor, MT 48106 Tel 313-662-2720.

Intl Gen Semantics, *(International Society for General Semantics; 0-918970),* P.O. Box 2469, San Francisco, CA 94126 (SAN 203-8161) Tel 415-543-1747.

Intl Info NY, *(International Information Publishing, Inc.; 1-879696),* 432 Park Ave. S., Rm. 1201, New York, NY 10016 Tel 212-213-6200.

Intl Learn Syst, *(International Learning Systems, Inc.),* 1715 Connecticut Ave., NW, Washington, DC 20009 (SAN 209-1615) Tel 202-223-5358.

Intl Linguistics, *(International Linguistics Corp.; 0-939990),* 3505 E. Red Bridge Rd., Kansas City, MO 64137 (SAN 220-2573) Tel 816-765-8855; Toll free: 800-237-1830.

Intl Marriage, *(International Marriage Encounter, Inc.; 0-936098),* 955 Lake Dr., Saint Paul, MN 55120 (SAN 215-6830).

Intl Reading, *(International Reading Assn.; 0-87207),* 800 Barksdale Rd., P.O. Box 8139, Newark, DE 19714-8139 (SAN 203-8218) Tel 302-731-1600.

Intl Society Tech Educ, *(International Society for Technology in Education; 0-924667; 1-56484),* Univ. of Oregon, 1787 Agate St., Eugene, OR 97403 (SAN 296-7693) Tel 503-346-4414.

Intl Spec Bk, *(International Specialized Bk. Services; 0-89955),* 5602 NE Hassalo St., Portland, OR 97213-3640 (SAN 169-7129) Tel 503-287-3093; Toll free: 800-547-7734.

Ion Books, *(Ion Bks., Inc.; 0-938507),* P.O. Box 111327, Memphis, TN 38111-1327 (SAN 661-3330) Tel 901-323-8858; Dist. by: Small Pr. Distribution, Inc., 1814 San Pablo Ave., Berkeley, CA 94702 (SAN 204-5826) Tel 415-549-3336; Dist. by: Baker & Taylor Bks., Midwestern Div., 501 S. Gladiolus St., Momence, IL 60954 (SAN 169-2100) Tel 815-472-2444; Toll free: 800-435-5111; 800-892-1892 (in illinois).

Iowa St U Pr, *(Iowa State Univ. Pr.; 0-8138),* 2121 S. State Ave., Ames, IA 50010 (SAN 202-7194) Tel 515-292-0140.

Iran Bks, *(Iran Bks.; 0-936347),* 8014 Old Georgetown Rd., Bethesda, MD 20814 (SAN 696-866X) Tel 301-986-0079.

Irish Bks Media, *(Irish Bks. & Media, Inc.; 0-937702),* Franklin Business Ctr., 1433 Franklin Ave., E., Minneapolis, MN 55404-2135 (SAN 111-8870) Tel 612-871-3505; Toll free: 800-229-3505.

Iron Bks, *(Iron Bks.; 0-9625740),* P.O. Box 2307, Venice, CA 90294 Tel 213-823-1366.

Iron Crown Ent Inc, *(Iron Crown Enterprises, Inc.; 0-915795; 1-55806),* P.O. Box 1605, Charlottesville, VA 22902 (SAN 294-0272) Tel 804-295-3918; Toll free: 800-325-0479; 108 Fifth St., SE, 3rd Flr., Charlottesville, VA 22901 (SAN 693-5109) Tel 804-295-3917; Dist. by: Berkley Publishing Group, 200 Madison Ave., New York, NY 10016 (SAN 201-3991) Tel 212-951-8966; Toll free: 800-223-0510.

Irresistible, *(Irresistible Bks.),* P.O. Box 1059, Angleton, TX 77515 (SAN 283-3816).

Irvington, *(Irvington Pubs.; 0-89197; 0-8290; 0-8422; 0-512),* 195 McGregor St., Manchester, NH 03103 (SAN 207-2408) Tel 603-669-5933.

Isabels, *(Isabel's; 0-9629612),* 17 S. High St., Suite 800, Columbus, OH 43215 Tel 614-224-0700.

ISC Pr, *(International Self-Counsel Pr.; 0-88908),* Subs. of International Self-Counsel Pr., Ltd., 1704 N. State St., Bellingham, WA 98225 (SAN 240-9925) Tel 206-676-4530; Toll free: 800-663-3007.

ISHA Enterprises, *(ISHA Enterprises; 0-936981),* 5503 E. Beck Ln., Scottsdale, AZ 85254 (SAN 658-7895) Tel 602-482-1346.

Isis NY, *(Isis),* County Rte. 9, P.O. Box 357, Chatham, NY 12037 Tel 518-392-4526; Dist. by: Mercedes Bk. Distributors Corp., 60 Imlay St., Brooklyn, NY 11231 (SAN 169-5150) Tel 718-522-7110.

Island Heritage, *(Island Heritage; 0-89610; 0-931548),* 99880 Iwaena St., Honolulu, HI 96701-3202 (SAN 211-1403).

Island-Metro Pubns, *(Island-Metro Pubns., Inc.; 0-9619832),* 1 Dupont St., Plainview, NY 11803 (SAN 246-1056) Tel 516-349-8282.

Island Pr Pubs, *(Island Pr. Pubs.; 0-87208),* 175 Bahia Via, Fort Myers Beach, FL 33931 (SAN 202-7216) Tel 813-463-9482.

Isld Conser Effort, *(Island Conservation Effort; 0-9629613),* 2 Wagon Wheel Rd., Sherman, CT 06784 Tel 203-355-3022.

It Takes Two, *(It Takes Two, Inc.; 0-942865),* 704 N. Main St., Le Sueur, MN 56058 (SAN 667-8386) Tel 612-665-6271; Toll free: 800-331-9843.

ITA Pubns, *(ITA Pubns.; 0-933935),* P.O. Box 1599, Willits, CA 95490 (SAN 693-062X) Tel 707-459-6100. Do not confuse with ITA Pubns., Grand Blanc, MI.

ITS Pub, *(Is That Sew? Publishing; 0-9622968),* P.O. Box 68, Mill Valley, CA 94942; 232 Miller Ave., Mill Valley, CA 94942 Tel 415-383-4417.

Ivory Pal, *(Ivory Palaces Music Publishing Co., Inc.; 0-943644),* 3141 Spottswood Ave., Memphis, TN 38111 (SAN 238-3020) Tel 901-323-3509.

Ivy Books, *(Ivy Bks.; 0-8041),* Div. of Ballantine Bks., Inc., 201 E. 50th St., New York, NY 10022 (SAN 661-7832) Tel 212-572-2573; Toll free: 800-733-3000 (orders); 800-726-0600 (customer svc./credit).

Ivystone, *(Ivystone Pubns.; 0-935604),* 247 Alabama St., Saint Simons Island, GA 31522 (SAN 215-3211).

J A Eades, *(Eades, Jo Ann; 0-9623325),* P.O. Box 432, Jacksonville, IL 62651; 1320 Maple, Jacksonville, IL 62650 Tel 217-245-1608.

J Alden, *(Alden, Jay, Pubs.; 0-914844),* P.O. Box 1295, 546 S. Hofgaarden St., La Puente, CA 91749 (SAN 204-7780) Tel 818-968-6424.

J & G Ferguson, *(Ferguson, Jane, & Gary; 0-9624846),* P.O. Box 1490, Red Lodge, MT 59068; 11 S. Broadway, Red Lodge, MT 59068 Tel 406-446-2388; Dist. by: GCBA, P.O. Box 292, Grand Canyon, AZ 86023 (SAN 295-8074) Tel 602-638-2597.

J & J Pub IL, *(J & J Publishing, Inc.; 0-929509),* P.O. Box 142, Frankfort, IL 60423 (SAN 249-5503); 314 Nebraska, Frankfort, IL 60423 (SAN 249-5511). Moved, left no forwarding address.

J & J Win Edge, *(J & J Winning Edge Pr., Inc.; 0-9621313),* 25 E. Irving Park Rd., Roselle, IL 60172 (SAN 251-0456) Tel 312-529-6634.

J & S Pub, *(J&S Publishing; 1-877969),* 1832 Adams St., Prescott, AZ 86301 Tel 602-445-0487.

J B Baily, *(Baily, Jane B.; 0-9626642),* 60 Davidson Rd., West Chester, PA 19382 Tel 215-793-1861.

J B Barnes, *(Barnes, Joyce B.; 0-9628493),* Rte. 3, Box 54, Bay City, TX 77414 Tel 409-244-1573.

J B Pal, *(Pal, J. B., & Co., Inc.; 0-916836),* 904 W. Castlewood Terr., Chicago, IL 60640 (SAN 208-0567) Tel 312-271-0123.

J Barnaby Dist, *(Barnaby, J., Distributors; 0-942403),* 1709 Hawthorne Ln., Plano, TX 75074 (SAN 667-0512) Tel 214-423-2411.

J Boulden, *(Boulden, Jim; 1-878076),* P.O. Box 9358, Santa Rosa, CA 95405; 821 Vaughn Ct., Santa Rosa, CA 95409 Tel 707-538-3797.

J Chernak, *(Chernak, Judy, Productions; 0-944633),* 3114 Hatton Rd., Pikesville, MD 21208 (SAN 244-5859) Tel 301-484-7088.

J Chesterfield Bks, *(Chesterfield, J., Bks.; 0-9620909),* 65 Holland Ave., Suite 2B, Staten Island, NY 10303 (SAN 250-2836) Tel 718-273-3551.

J Daniel, *(Daniel, John, & Co., Pubs.; 0-936784; 1-880284),* Div. of Daniel & Daniel Pubs., Inc., P.O. Box 21922, Santa Barbara, CA 93121 (SAN 215-1995); Toll free: 800-662-8351; 21 E. Canon Perdido, Santa Barbara, CA 93101 Tel 805-962-1780; Dist. by: National Bk. Network, 4720A Boston Way, Lanham, MD 20706-4310 (SAN 630-0065) Tel 301-459-8696; Toll free: 800-462-6420.

J Duco, *(Duco, Joyce; 0-9612896),* BNA Corporate Ctr., Bldg. 200, Suite 207, Nashville, TN 37217 (SAN 291-140X) Tel 615-366-0455; Dist. by: DeVorss & Co., P.O. Box 550, 1046 Princeton Dr., Marina del Rey, CA 90294 (SAN 168-9886) Tel 213-870-7478; Toll free: 800-843-5743; 800-331-4719 (in California); Dist. by: Spring Arbor Distributors, 10885 Textile Rd., Belleville, MI 48111 (SAN 158-9016) Tel 313-481-0900; Toll free: 800-395-9955; Dist. by: Ingram Bk. Co., 1125 Heilquaker Blvd., La Vergne, TN 37086 (SAN 169-7978) Tel 615-793-5000; Toll free: 800-937-8000 (orders only).

J E Stewart, *(Stewart, J. E.; 1-877866),* 18518 Kenlake Pl., NE, Seattle, WA 98155 Tel 206-486-4510.

J Franklin, *(Franklin, J., Pub.; 0-9616736),* P.O. Box 14057, Tulsa, OK 74159 (SAN 661-4302); Toll free: 800-234-9384; 4123 S. Victor Ct., Tulsa, OK 74105 (SAN 661-4310) Tel 918-747-9858.

J Gile Comm, *(Gile, John, Communications; 0-910941),* 1710 N. Main St., Rockford, IL 61103 (SAN 270-5109) Tel 815-968-6601.

J Herzberg, *(Herzberg, Jack, Pub.; 0-943077),* 1740 Kings Row, Reno, NV 89503 (SAN 668-016X) Tel 702-747-5254.

J Jons LA, *(Jons, John; 0-9623099),* 213 Surrey Dr., La Place, LA 70068 Tel 504-652-7412.

J L Estes, *(Estes, James L.; 0-9628634),* c/o The Writer's Service (Agent), 816 Pierremont Rd., Shreveport, LA 71106 Tel 318-869-3587.

J L Kum, *(Kum, J. L., Inc.; 0-9626817),* 3814 Moraga St., San Francisco, CA 94122 Tel 415-665-5741.

J L Shubert, *(Shubert, Joseph L.; 0-9627015),* Rte. 27, P.O. Box 188, Kingfield, ME 04947 Tel 207-628-4626.

J Laster Pub Co, *(Laster, Jim, Publishing Co.; 0-9612780),* P.O. Box 50512, Nashville, TN 37205 (SAN 289-7474) Tel 615-356-5318.

J Leslie Enter, *(Leslie, J., Enterprises; 0-9629445),* P.O. Box 14233, Cleveland, OH 44114; 1170 Piermont Rd., South Euclid, OH 44121 Tel 216-291-1782.

J Liebowitz, *(Liebowitz, Jay, & Assocs.; 0-9623252),* 966 Farm Haven Dr., Rockville, MD 20852 Tel 301-231-8040; Dist. by: Great Tradition, 11270 Clayton Creek Rd., Lower Lake, CA 95457 (SAN 200-5743) Tel 707-995-3906; Toll free: 800-275-2606.

J Lynn Pub, *(J-Lynn Publishing; 1-877797),* P.O. Box 163, Grantsboro, NC 28529 Tel 919-745-3030.

J M Cook Pub, *(Cook, John M., Publishing Co.; 0-9622602),* P.O. Box 22171, Baltimore, MD 21202; 2530 Edgecomb Cir., N., Apt. 1, Baltimore, MD 21215 Tel 301-362-2899.

J M Herren, *(Herren, Janet M.; 0-9613025),* 4750 Crystal Springs Dr., Bainbridge Island, WA 98110 (SAN 293-9967) Tel 206-842-3484; Dist. by: Pacific Pipeline, Inc., 19215 66th Ave., S., Kent, WA 98032 (SAN 208-2128) Tel 206-872-5523; Toll free: 800-562-4647 (in Washington); 800-426-4727 (in northern California, Oregon, Montana, Idaho, Nevada).

J McBurney, *(McBurney, Jim; 0-9629471),* 890 S. Wolfe Rd., Sunnyvale, CA 94086 Tel 408-733-9479.

J Muckle, *(Muckle, Jim; 0-9620445),* 7021 Fellers Ln., Sebastopol, CA 95472 (SAN 248-6296) Tel 707-829-9109.

J N Townsend, *(Townsend, J. N., Publishing; 0-9617426; 1-880158),* 12 Greenleaf Dr., Exeter, NH 03833 (SAN 630-303X) Tel 603-778-9883; Toll free: 800-333-9883 (Orders only).

J-p Press, *(J.-p. Pr.; 0-9621929),* P.O. Box 48, Ellenville, NY 12428; 53 Market St., Ellenville, NY 12428 Tel 914-647-7016.

J Pohl Assocs, *(Pohl, J., Assocs.; 0-939332),* 1706 Berkwood Dr., Pittsburgh, PA 15243 (SAN 220-181X) Tel 412-279-5000.

J R Berry, *(Berry, John R., Evangelistic Assn.; 0-9616900),* P.O. Box 8252, Philadelphia, PA 19101 (SAN 661-4949); 605 S. 60th St., Philadelphia, PA 19143 (SAN 661-4957) Tel 215-747-0606.

J R Pubns, *(J.R. Pubns.; 0-913952),* 170 NE 33rd St., Fort Lauderdale, FL 33334 (SAN 202-7283) Tel 305-563-1844.

J R Simon, *(Simon, Jeffrey R., Publishing Co.; 0-916343),* P.O. Box 13390, Pittsburgh, PA 15243 (SAN 295-9801) Tel 412-279-6525.

J Sears, *(Sears, Jeanne; 0-9621086),* 32087 Hamilton Ct., No. 204A, Solon, OH 44139 (SAN 250-491X) Tel 216-349-2794.

J Sisson, *(Sisson, Joan; 0-9622498),* 2750 Marina Ave., Livermore, CA 94550 Tel 415-443-5524.

J Stuart Found, *(Stuart, Jesse, Foundation, The; 0-945084),* P.O. Box 391, Ashland, KY 41114 (SAN 245-8837); 1212 Bath Ave., Ashland, KY 41101 (SAN 245-8845) Tel 606-329-5233.

J Vernon, *(Vernon, Judy; 0-9617776),* P.O. Box 5384, NWJC, Senatobia, MS 38668 (SAN 664-8061); Thompson St., Apt. A8, Senatobia, MS 38668 (SAN 664-807X) Tel 601-562-6270.

J Vesty Co, *(Vesty, John, Co.; 0-9626876),* Bennett Rd., Indian Lake, NY 12842 Tel 518-648-5742.

J Yolen Bks Imprint of HarBraceJ

JAARS Inc, *(Jungle Aviation & Radio Service (JAARS); 0-9615959; 1-878606),* Affil. of Summer Institute of Linguistics, Box 248, JAARS Rd., Waxhaw, NC 28173 (SAN 697-2896) Tel 704-843-6055; Dist. by: Wycliffe Bible Translators, P.O. Box 2727, Huntington Beach, CA 92647 (SAN 211-5484) Tel 714-969-4600.

Jackson Pub, *(Jackson Publishing; 0-9623915),* 631 N. 400 W., Salt Lake City, UT 84103 Tel 801-521-2411. Do not confuse with Jackson Publishing, Clarkston, MI.

Jacobs, *(Jacobs Publishing Co.; 0-918272),* 3334 E. Indian School Rd., Suite C, Phoenix, AZ 85018 (SAN 209-4525) Tel 602-954-6581.

JACP Inc, *(JACP, Inc.; 0-934609),* 414 E. Third Ave., San Mateo, CA 94401 (SAN 693-8841) Tel 415-343-9408; Orders to: P.O. Box 367, San Mateo, CA 94401 (SAN 662-3271).

Jacqueline Enter, *(Jacqueline Enterprises, Inc.; 0-932446),* 9725 E. Hampden Ave., No. 203, Denver, CO 80231 (SAN 221-0487) Tel 303-779-8278.

Jade Ram Pub, *(Jade Ram Publishing; 1-877721),* P.O. Box 202163, Anchorage, AK 99520-2163; 3000 E. 16th, Anchorage, AK 99520 Tel 907-272-8432.

Jalmar Pr, *(Jalmar Pr.; 0-915190; 1-880396),* Subs. of B. L. Winch & Assocs., 45 Hitching Post Dr., Bldg. 2, Rolling Hills Estates, CA 90274 (SAN 113-3640) Tel 213-547-1240; Toll free: 800-662-9662; Dist. by: Slawson Communications, Inc., 165 Vallecitos de Oro, San Marcos, CA 92069 (SAN 200-6901) Tel 619-744-2299; Toll free: 800-752-9766 (orders only).

Jamestown Pubs, *(Jamestown Pubs., Inc.; 0-89061),* P.O. Box 9168, Providence, RI 02940 (SAN 201-5196) Tel 401-351-1915; Toll free: 800-872-7323.

Jan Prods, *(January Productions, Inc.; 0-934898; 0-87386),* P.O. Box 66, 210 Sixth Ave., Hawthorne, NJ 07507 (SAN 222-822X) Tel 201-423-4666; Toll free: 800-451-7450.

Janson Pubns, *(Janson Pubns.; 0-939765),* 222 Richmond St., Providence, RI 02903 (SAN 663-7663) Tel 401-272-0009.

Janus Bks, *(Janus Bk. Pubs., Inc.; 0-88102; 0-915510; 0-88084),* Div. of S&S Higher Education Publishing Group, 500 Harbor Blvd., Belmont, CA 94002-4021 (SAN 208-0478) Tel 415-592-7810; Toll free: 800-227-2375.

Japan Pubns USA, *(Japan Pubns. (U.S.A.), Inc.; 0-87040),* 45 Hawthorn Pl., Briarcliff Manor, NY 10510 (SAN 680-0513); Dist. by: Kodansha International U. S. A., Ltd., 114 Fifth Ave., New York, NY 10011 (SAN 201-0526) Tel 212-727-6460; Toll free: 800-638-3030.

Jarrett Pub, *(Jarrett Publishing Co.; 0-9624723),* 833 Riley Dr., Suite 96, Albany, CA 94706 Tel 415-527-4523.

Jasmine Texts, *(Jasmine Texts; 0-938861),* 1641 Third Ave., Suite 8BE, New York, NY 10128 (SAN 661-7328) Tel 212-348-8487.

Jason & Nordic Pubs, *(Jason & Nordic Pubs.; 0-944727),* P.O. Box 441, Hollidaysburg, PA 16648 (SAN 244-9374).

Jay & Assocs, *(Jay & Assocs., Pubs.; 0-939422),* P.O. Box 2222, Brevard, NC 28712-2222 (SAN 281-837X) Tel 704-885-2062.

JED, *(JED & Assocs.; 0-9602200),* P.O. Box 7143 RC, Toledo, OH 43615 (SAN 212-3622) Tel 419-885-2932.

Jelm Mtn, *(Jelm Mountain Pubns.; 0-936204),* 209 Park St., Laramie, WY 82070 (SAN 216-1419) Tel 307-721-5058.

JEM Job Educ, *(JEM/Job Educational Materials; 0-9628787),* 1230 E. Main St., Alhambra, CA 91801 Tel 818-308-7642.

Jen Chen Buddhism, *(Jen Chen Buddhism Ctr.; 1-56369),* P.O. Box 4643, West Covina, CA 91791-4643; 418 S. Azusa Ave., West Covina, CA 91791 Tel 818-917-1899.

Jenny Wren Pr, *(Jenny Wren Pr., The; 0-9621753),* P.O. Box 505, Mooresville, IN 46158 (SAN 252-2071); 5 Daniel St., Mooresville, IN 46158 (SAN 252-208X).

Jenson Pubns, *(Jenson Pubns., Inc.; 0-931205),* P.O. Box 13819, Milwaukee, WI 53213-0819 (SAN 679-9914) Tel 414-774-3630.

Jesus Bks, *(Jesus Bks.; 0-932588),* 1565 Madison St., Oakland, CA 94612 (SAN 212-1034) Tel 415-763-4324.

JHO Music, *(JHO Music; 0-9626239),* 11 Marshall Terr., Wayland, MA 01778 Tel 508-358-5213.

Jilcoe, *(Jilcoe; 0-9624976),* Div. of Hempe Manufacturing Co., Inc., 2750 S. 163rd St., New Berlin, WI 53151 Tel 414-784-2710.

Jimar Prodns, *(Jimar Productions; 0-931731),* 2 Corporate Ctr., Suite 100, Springfield, MO 65804 (SAN 667-7908) Tel 417-694-2454.

Jist Works, *(Jist Works, Inc.; 0-942784; 1-56370),* 720 N. Park Ave., Indianapolis, IN 46202-3431 (SAN 240-2351) Tel 317-264-3720; Toll free: 800-648-5478.

JJJ Pubs, *(JJJ Pubs.; 0-941951),* P.O. Box 196, Paola, KS 66071 (SAN 666-7708); R.R. 3, Box 121, Paola, KS 66071 (SAN 666-7716) Tel 913-294-4133.

JK Pub, *(JK Publishing; 0-945878),* P.O. Box 994, Kings Park, NY 11754 (SAN 248-1642); 48 Janet Pl., Valley Stream, NY 11581 (SAN 248-1650) Tel 516-544-2424.

JM Pub, *(JM Publishing; 0-923133),* 701 Orange Ln., Laguna Vista, TX 78578 (SAN 251-5997) Tel 512-943-6857.

JML Enter MD, *(JML Enterprises, Inc.; 0-938464),* P.O Box 488, Bel Air, MD 21014 (SAN 238-5279) Tel 301-879-8552.

Jo-Jo Pubns, *(Jo-Jo Pubns.; 0-9602266),* 208 N. Sparrow Rd., Chesapeake, VA 23325 (SAN 212-5153) Tel 804-420-8614.

Job Data, *(Job Data, Inc.; 0-918443),* 105 W. Madison, Suite 1708, Chicago, IL 60602 (SAN 657-6303) Tel 312-263-2542.

John Muir, *(Muir, John, Pubns.; 0-912528; 0-945465; 1-56261),* P.O. Box 613, Santa Fe, NM 87504-0613 (SAN 203-9079) Tel 505-982-4078; Toll free: 800-888-7504; Dist. by: W. W. Norton & Co., Inc., 500 Fifth Ave., New York, NY 10110 (SAN 202-5795) Tel 212-354-5500; Toll free: 800-223-2584.

Johnny Reads, *(Johnny Reads, Inc.; 0-910812),* 2221 Calexico Way, S., Saint Petersburg, FL 33712 (SAN 201-0283) Tel 813-867-7647.

Johnson Bks, *(Johnson Bks.; 0-933472; 1-55566),* Div. of Johnson Publishing Co., 1880 S. 57th Ct., Boulder, CO 80301 (SAN 201-0313) Tel 303-443-1576; Toll free: 800-662-2665.

Johnson Chi, *(Johnson Publishing Co., Inc.; 0-87485),* 820 S. Michigan Ave., Chicago, IL 60605 (SAN 201-0305) Tel 312-322-9248. Do not confuse with Johnson Publishing Co. Inc., Loveland, CO.

Johnson Repr, *(Johnson Reprint Corp.; 0-384),* Subs. of Harcourt Brace Jovanovich, Inc., 111 Fifth Ave., New York, NY 10003 (SAN 285-0362) Tel 212-614-3150.

Johnston Bicent Found, *(Johnston Bicentennial Foundation; 0-9620343),* 1701 Governors Dr., SE, Huntsville, AL 35801 (SAN 248-1987) Tel 205-534-8252.

Jonah Pr, *(Jonah Pr.; 0-929422),* P.O. Box 5473, Sherman Oaks, CA 91413 (SAN 249-4000) Tel 818-986-1809.

Jonathan David, *(Jonathan David Pubs., Inc.; 0-8246),* 68-22 Eliot Ave., Middle Village, NY 11379 (SAN 169-5274) Tel 718-456-8611.

Jonka Enter, *(Jonka Enterprises; 1-878794),* P.O. Box 13661, Sacramento, CA 95853; 875 Turnstone Dr., Sacramento, CA 95834 Tel 916-929-0631.

Jordan Valley, *(Jordan Valley Heritage Hse.; 0-939810),* 43592 Hwy. 226, Stayton, OR 97383 (SAN 216-7425) Tel 503-859-3144.

Jordane Pub, *(Jordane Publishing; 0-9621221),* Rte. 2, Box 1291, Wild Rose, WI 54984 (SAN 250-8605) Tel 414-622-3976.

Jory Pubns, *(Jory Pubns.; 0-9607732),* 12535 Sunview Dr., Creve Coeur, MO 63146 (SAN 238-0935) Tel 314-434-0066.

Journeys Together, *(Journeys Together; 0-9619040),* P.O. Box 1254, La Mesa, CA 92044 Tel 619-441-8104.

Jove Pubns, *(Jove Pubns., Inc.; 0-515),* Div. of Berkley Publishing Group, 200 Madison Ave., New York, NY 10016 (SAN 215-8817) Tel 212-951-8800; Toll free: 800-631-8571; Dist. by: Warner Pub. Services, 810 Seventh Ave., New York, NY 10019 (SAN 200-5522) Tel 212-397-8676.

Joy-Co, *(Joy-Co Pr.; 0-9605984),* 2636 Burgener Blvd., San Diego, CA 92110 (SAN 216-7433) Tel 619-276-9760.

Joy Deliverance, *(Joy of Deliverance Co.; 0-9620133),* P.O. Box 2913, Ann Arbor, MI 48106 (SAN 247-6568); 35725 Bibbins, Romulus, MI 48174 (SAN 247-6576) Tel 313-941-4246.

Joy Pub SJC, *(Joy Publishing; 0-939513),* Div. of California Clock Co., P.O. Box 827, San Juan Capistrano, CA 92675 (SAN 663-3544) Tel 714-545-4321; Toll free: 800-783-6265.

Joy St Bks *Imprint of* **Little**

Joyce Media, *(Joyce Media, Inc.; 0-917002),* P.O. Box 57, Acton, CA 93510 (SAN 208-7197) Tel 805-269-1169.

JPS Phila, *(Jewish Pubn. Society; 0-8276),* 1930 Chestnut St., Philadelphia, PA 19103 (SAN 201-0240) Tel 215-564-5925; Toll free: 800-234-3151.

JRBB Pubs, *(JRBB Pubs.; 0-9627951),* 900 Leonard Dr., Rock Hill, MO 63119 Tel 314-962-4391.

JSP Pub, *(JSP Publishing; 0-9622328),* 9879 Zig Zag Rd., Cincinnati, OH 45242 Tel 513-791-4096.

JTG Nashville, *(JTG of Nashville; 0-938971),* 1024C 18th Ave., S., Nashville, TN 37212 (SAN 630-3323) Tel 615-329-3036; Toll free: 800-222-2584.

JTM Pr, *(JTM Pr.; 0-9625679),* 6076 E. Geddes Cir., Englewood, CO 80112 Tel 303-741-5814.

Judaica Pr, *(Judaica Pr., Inc.; 0-910818),* 123 Ditmas Ave., Brooklyn, NY 11230 (SAN 204-9856) Tel 718-972-6200.

Judson, *(Judson Pr.; 0-8170),* Div. of American Baptist Churches, U.S.A., P.O. Box 851, Valley Forge, PA 19482-0851 (SAN 201-0348) Tel 215-768-2117; Toll free: 800-331-1053.

Jugglebug, *(Jugglebug; 0-9615521),* 7506 J Olympic View Dr., Edmonds, WA 98026 (SAN 696-2882) Tel 206-774-2127.

Juniper *Imprint of* **Fawcett**

Juniper Pr WI, *(Juniper Pr.; 1-55780),* 1310 Shorewood Dr., La Crosse, WI 54601 (SAN 207-8570) Tel 608-788-0096. Do not confuse with companies of the same name in Bangor, ME, Long Island City, NY, Albuquerque, NM.

Juniper Ridge, *(Juniper Ridge Pr.; 0-916289),* P.O. Box 338, Ashland, OR 97520 (SAN 295-8899) Tel 503-482-9585; Toll free: 800-869-7342.

Just Pub Hse, *(Just Publishing Hse.; 0-9618532),* 131 Winslow Ct., Melbourne, FL 32935 (SAN 668-0976) Tel 407-259-8213.

Just Us Bks, *(Just Us Bks., Inc.; 0-940975),* 301 Main St., Suite 22-24, Orange, NJ 07050 (SAN 664-7413) Tel 201-676-4345; Toll free: 800-866-7701.

K A Pubns, *(K.A. Pubns.; 0-9623442),* Div. of Keto Assocs., Inc., P.O. Box 278, Blackwood, NJ 08012 Tel 609-783-4573.

K Bachrach Co, *(Bachrach, K., Co., Inc.; 1-878530),* 342 Taft Rd., River Edge, NJ 07661 Tel 201-343-3974.

K E Sibley, *(Sibley, Kenneth E.; 0-9619934),* 32 Mishawaka Dr., Rochester, IL 62563 (SAN 247-0926) Tel 217-498-9439.

K Flores Min, *(Flores, Kathy, Ministries; 0-9626862),* P.O. Box 673, Sun City, CA 92381; 31245 Oak Valley Rd., Homeland, CA 92348 Tel 714-926-4256.

K Jensen, *(Jensen, Kent; 0-9621024),* c/o Abbie Ramirez, Los Angeles Mission College, Special Education Office, 1212 San Fernando Rd., San Fernando, CA 91340 (SAN 250-6858) Tel 818-365-8271.

K K Aharon, *(Kollel Kedushas Aharon; 0-9629684),* 33 Lincoln Ave., New Square, NY 10977 Tel 914-354-6275.

K K Pub Co, *(Kaye's & Knight Publishing Co.; 0-9612140),* P.O. Box 2065, 503 Broadway, Fargo, ND 58107 (SAN 287-2765) Tel 701-237-4525.

K P Larsen Inc, *(Larsen, Kent P., Inc.; 0-9623798),* 30252 Pacific Island Dr., No. 198, Laguna Niguel, CA 92677 Tel 714-495-2838.

K Q Assocs, *(K-Q Assocs., Inc.; 0-941988),* P.O. Box 2132, Cedar Rapids, IA 52406 (SAN 238-4655).

KABEL Pubs, *(Kabel Pubs.; 0-930329),* 11225 Huntover Dr., Rockville, MD 20852 (SAN 670-8323) Tel 301-468-6463.

Kabyn, *(Kabyn Bks.; 0-940444),* 10135 Hermosa Way, La Mesa, CA 92041 (SAN 159-1002) Tel 619-447-8865.

KAC, *(KAC, Inc.; 0-9622353),* 3425 S. 94th Ave., Omaha, NE 68124 Tel 402-393-8537.

Kalimat, *(Kalimat Pr.; 0-933770),* 1600 Sawtelle Blvd., Suite 34, Los Angeles, CA 90025 (SAN 213-7666) Tel 213-479-5668.

Kalmbach, *(Kalmbach Publishing Co.; 0-89024; 0-913135),* P.O. Box 1612, Waukesha, WI 53187 (SAN 201-0399) Tel 414-796-0126; Toll free: 800-558-1544 (except Wisconsin & Canada).

Kalnoky Pr, *(Kalnoky Pr.; 0-9619982),* 108 Florida G Rd., Keasbey, NJ 08832 (SAN 248-8078) Tel 201-826-4006.

Kane-Miller Bk, *(Kane/Miller Bk. Pubs.; 0-916291),* P.O. Box 529, Brooklyn, NY 11231 (SAN 295-8945) Tel 718-624-5120; Orders to: P.O. Box 529, Brooklyn, NY 11231 (SAN 685-3897) Tel 718-624-5120. *Imprints:* Cranky Nell Bk (Cranky Nell Book, A).

Kaplan Pr, *(Kaplan Pr., Inc.; 0-88076),* P.O. Box 609, Lewisville, NC 27023 (SAN 239-9407) Tel 919-766-7374.

Kar Ben, *(Kar-Ben Copies, Inc.; 0-930494; 0-929371),* 6800 Tildenwood Ln., Rockville, MD 20852 (SAN 210-7511) Tel 301-984-8733; Toll free: 800-452-7236.

Karwyn Ent, *(Karwyn Enterprises; 0-939938),* 17227 17th Ave., W., Lynnwood, WA 98036 (SAN 289-0143) Tel 206-743-0722.

Kauai Museum, *(Kauai Museum Assn., Ltd.; 0-940948),* Box 248, Lihue, HI 96766 (SAN 213-1013); 4428 Rice St., Lihue, HI 96766 (SAN 685-3412) Tel 808-245-6931.

Kay Productions, *(Kay Productions; 0-929201),* P.O. Box 1728, Sonoma, CA 95476 (SAN 248-6156); 124 E. Napa St., Sonoma, CA 95476 (SAN 248-6164) Tel 707-935-1666.

Kaylor Christ Co, *(Kaylor, Christopher, Co.; 0-916039),* P.O. Box 737, Huntsville, AL 35804 (SAN 294-8524); 110 King Ave., Huntsville, AL 35801 (SAN 294-8532) Tel 205-534-3029.

Kazi Pubns, *(Kazi Pubns.; 0-935782; 0-933511),* 3023 W. Belmont Ave., Chicago, IL 60618 (SAN 162-3397) Tel 312-267-7001.

KC Enterprise *See* Wonder Kids

KC Pubns, *(KC Pubns.; 0-916122; 0-88714),* P.O. Box 14447, Las Vegas, NV 89114 (SAN 201-0364); Toll free: 800-626-9673; 2901 Industrial Rd., Las Vegas, NV 89109 (SAN 658-103X) Tel 702-731-3123.

Keepsake Bks *See* Sonos

Keiro Services, *(Keiro Services; 0-9624450),* 325 S. Boyle Ave., Los Angeles, CA 90033 Tel 213-263-1007.

Kelby Pub, *(Kelby Publishing; 0-937555),* P.O. Box 369, Los Lunas, NM 87031 (SAN 658-9022) Tel 505-299-7719.

Kelly Bear Bks, *(Kelly Bear Bks.; 0-9621054),* Rte. 3, Box 99, Sturkie Rd., Lafayette, AL 36862 (SAN 250-5746) Tel 205-749-3346.

Kemtec Educ, *(Kemtec Educational Corp.; 1-877960),* 9889 Crescent Park Rd., West Chester, OH 45069 Tel 513-777-3535; Toll free: 800-733-0266.

Kendall-Hunt, *(Kendall/Hunt Publishing Co.; 0-8403),* Subs. of Wm. C. Brown Co., Pubs., 2460 Kerper Blvd., Dubuque, IA 52001 (SAN 203-9184) Tel 319-588-1451; Toll free: 800-338-5578.

Kennebec River, *(Kennebec River Pr., Inc.; 0-933858),* 36 Old Mill Rd., Falmouth, ME 04105-1637 (SAN 221-458X) Tel 207-781-3002.

Kenney Pubns, *(Kenney Pubns.; 1-877906),* 1310A SW 14th, Topeka, KS 66604 Tel 913-233-1062.

Kenyon, *(Kenyon Pubns.; 0-934286),* 361 Pin Oak Ln., Westbury, NY 11590 (SAN 201-5072) Tel 516-333-3236; Dist. by: Hal Leonard Publishing Corp., 7777 W. Bluemound Rd., P.O. Box 13819, Milwaukee, WI 53213 (SAN 239-250X) Tel 414-774-3630; Toll free: 800-642-6692.

Kern Historical, *(Kern County Historical Society; 0-943500),* P.O. Box 141, Bakersfield, CA 93302 (SAN 240-6969) Tel 805-322-4962.

Kesend Pub Ltd, *(Kesend, Michael, Publishing, Ltd.; 0-935576),* 1025 Fifth Ave., New York, NY 10028 (SAN 213-6902) Tel 212-249-5150.

Kettle Country Pr, *(Kettle Country Pr.; 0-924563),* P.O. Box 532, Fond du Lac, WI 54936-0532; 552 Newport Ave., Fond du Lac, WI 54935 Tel 414-922-5900.

Key Curr Pr, *(Key Curriculum Pr.; 0-913684; 1-55953),* P.O. Box 2304, Berkeley, CA 94702 (SAN 202-6538); Toll free: 800-338-7638; 2512 Martin Luther King Way, Berkeley, CA 94704 (SAN 250-331X) Tel 415-548-2304.

Key of David, *(Key of David Pubns.; 0-943374),* Presentation BVM Rectory, 204 Haverford Rd., Wynnewood, PA 19096 (SAN 239-4480) Tel 215-896-1970.

Keystone PA, *(Keystone Pr.; 0-940701),* Box 6163, Bradenton, FL 34281 (SAN 665-2433); 6515 Mass. St., Bradenton, FL 34207 Tel 813-753-5179.

Kickapoo Tribal, *(Kickapoo Tribal Pr.; 0-931045),* P.O. Box 106, Powhattan, KS 66527 (SAN 678-8998) Tel 913-474-3550.

Kiddyhawk Pub, *(Kiddyhawk Publishing; 0-941889),* P.O. Box 234, Plymouth, MI 48170 (SAN 666-3664) Tel 616-271-4287.

Kids Ink Pr, *(Kids Ink Pr.; 0-923999),* 46716 Crawford St., Suite 4, Fremont, CA 94539. Moved, left no forwarding address.

Kids Intl Inc, *(Kids International, Inc.; 0-943593),* 5401 S. Sheridan Rd., No. 204, Tulsa, OK 74145 (SAN 668-6486) Tel 918-665-1085.

Kids Kitchen, *(Kids In The Kitchen, Inc.; 0-9629589),* 5999 Dry Ridge Rd., Cincinnati, OH 45252 Tel 513-741-7775.

Kids Matter, *(Kids Matter, Inc.; 0-89411),* 692 Elkader St., Ashland, OR 97520 (SAN 209-3561) Tel 503-482-5805; Orders to: P. O. Box 3460, Ashland, OR 97520 (SAN 169-7978); Dist. by: Ingram Bk. Co., 1125 Heilquaker Blvd., La Vergne, TN 37086 (SAN 169-7978) Tel 615-793-5000; Toll free: 800-937-8000 (orders only).

Kids Talk CT, *(Kids Talk Communications, Inc.; 1-877819),* P.O. Box 481, Old Lyme, CT 06371; Toll free: 800-543-8256; 5 Osprey Rd., Old Lyme, CT 06371 Tel 203-434-8772.

Kidsbks, *(Kidsbooks, Inc.; 0-942025; 1-56156),* 7004 N. California Ave., Chicago, IL 60645 (SAN 666-3729) Tel 312-262-5565.

Kidship Assoc, *(Kidship Assocs.; 1-878742),* P.O. Box 1348, South Gate, CA 90280; 4508 Firestone Blvd., South Gate, CA 90280 Tel 213-569-3349.

Kidsmart, *(Kidsmart; 0-936985),* 3276 Hawksmoor Pl., Cordova, TN 38018 (SAN 658-5647) Tel 901-372-7550; Dist. by: Margie Poe, 2276 Hawksmoor Pl., Cordova, TN 38018 (SAN 630-0952).

Kidspeak, *(Kidspeak; 1-879340),* P.O. Box 1028, Moorhead, MN 56561-1028; 2212 S. 17th St., Moorhead, MN 56560 Tel 218-233-4427.

Kidsrights, *(Kidsrights; 1-55864),* 3700 Progress Blvd., Mount Dora, FL 32757 (SAN 248-0891) Tel 904-483-1100.

Kidzco Pub, *(Kidzco Publishing Co.; 1-877776),* Rocky Canyon Rd., Creston, CA 93432 Tel 805-238-9142.

Kilroy Pr, *(Kilroy Pr.; 0-9621001),* P.O. Box 16551, Chapel Hill, NC 27516 (SAN 250-4804) Tel 919-967-7601.

Kimbo Educ, *(Kimbo Educational; 0-937124; 1-56346),* Div. of United Sound Arts, Inc., P.O. Box 477, Long Branch, NJ 07740 (SAN 630-1592); Toll free: 800-631-2187; 10 N. Third Ave., Long Branch, NJ 07740 Tel 908-229-4949.

Kinder Read, *(Kinder Read; 0-934361),* P.O. Box 18, Ingomar, PA 15127 (SAN 693-4552); 1547 King Albert Dr., Pittsburgh, PA 15237 (SAN 662-3247) Tel 412-366-9761.

Kinderpr, *(Kinderpress; 0-931047),* 2240 135th Pl., SE, Bellevue, WA 98005 (SAN 678-9005) Tel 206-643-2695; P.O. Box 5761, Bellevue, WA 98006 (SAN 662-2534); Dist. by: Pacific Pipeline, Inc., 19215 66th Ave., S., Kent, WA 98032 (SAN 208-2128) Tel 206-872-5523; Toll free: 800-562-4617 (in Washington); 800-426-4727 (in northern California, Nevada, Idaho, Oregon, Montana); 800-444-7323 (in California).

Kindle Bks, *(Kindle Bks.; 0-9624790),* 639 1/2 29th Rd., Grand Junction, CO 81506 Tel 303-245-8290.

Kindred Pr, *(Kindred Pr.; 0-9606436),* Orders to: 315 S. Lincoln St., Hillsboro, KS 67063 (SAN 202-2915) Tel 316-947-3151.

King Fisher Pr, *(King Fisher Pr.; 0-9612972),* 5115 E. Virginia, Phoenix, AZ 85008 (SAN 292-5567) Tel 602-840-2342.

King ME, *(King, Helen B.; 0-9615366),* 11 Pierce St., Orono, ME 04473 (SAN 695-2240) Tel 207-866-3309.

Kings Inc, *(Kings, Inc.; 0-9624924),* 3715 Balboa St., San Francisco, CA 94121-2605; 223A Monterey Blvd., San Francisco, CA 94131 Tel 415-387-4737.

Kingshead Corp, *(Kingshead Corp.; 1-55941),* 600 Sylvan Way, Apt. 3FL, Englewood Cliffs, NJ 07632 (SAN 250-9938) Tel 201-894-0011; Toll free: 800-223-0309.

Kingston Ellis, *(Kingston Ellis Pr.; 0-914425),* 1014 Freemason St., Knoxville, TN 37917 (SAN 291-820X) Tel 615-687-8467.

Kinloch Bks, *(Kinloch Bks.; 0-929639),* P.O. Box 32400, Washington, DC 20007 (SAN 249-7964); 2801 New Mexico Ave., No. 1120, Washington, DC 20007 (SAN 249-7972) Tel 202-337-2845.

Kinnickinnic Pr, *(Kinnickinnic Pr.; 0-9615065),* 1101 W. Division St., River Falls, WI 54022 (SAN 694-1397) Tel 715-425-6897.

Kino Pubns, *(Kino Pubns.; 0-9607366),* 6625 N. First Ave., Tucson, AZ 85718 (SAN 238-2547) Tel 602-297-7278; Dist. by: Trillium Pr., P.O. Box 209, Monroe, NY 10950 (SAN 212-4637) Tel 914-783-2999.

Kinucan & Brons, *(Kinucan & Brons, Pubs.; 0-9615444),* P.O. Box 87, Clark Fork, ID 83811 (SAN 695-7234) Tel 208-266-1452.

Kipling Pr, *(Kipling Pr.; 0-943718),* 496 LaGuardia Pl., No. 332, New York, NY 10012 (SAN 241-015X) Tel 212-969-8925.

Kitwardo Pubs, *(Kitwardo Pubs., Inc.; 0-932641),* P.O. Box 12275, Jacksonville, FL 32209 (SAN 687-8091) Tel 904-768-6796.

Kiyoko & Co, *(Kiyoko & Co.; 0-9623210),* P.O. Box 277, Pescadero, CA 94060; 51 Eden West Rd., Pescadero, CA 94060 Tel 415-879-0061; Dist. by: Bookpeople, 2929 Fifth St., Berkeley, CA 94710 (SAN 168-9517) Tel 415-549-3030; Toll free: 800-999-4650.

Kjos, *(Kjos, Neil A., Music Co.; 0-910842; 0-8497),* 4380 Jutland Dr., San Diego, CA 92117-0894 (SAN 201-0488) Tel 619-270-9800; Toll free: 800-854-1592.

Klar-Iden Pub, *(Klar-Iden Publishing; 0-9629795),* 6963 Douglas Blvd., P.O. Box 115, Granite Bay, CA 95661 Tel 415-856-1059.

Klutz Pr, *(Klutz Pr.; 0-932592; 1-878257),* 2121 Staunton Ct., Palo Alto, CA 94306 (SAN 212-7539) Tel 415-857-0888.

Knees Pbk, *(Knees Paperback Publishing Co.; 0-9600978),* 4115 Marshall St., Dallas, TX 75210 (SAN 208-760X) Tel 214-428-4160; P.O. Box 26098, Dallas, TX 75226 (SAN 241-743X).

Knickerbocker, *(Knickerbocker Publishing Co.; 0-911635),* P.O. Box 113, 10 Summit Ave., Fiskdale, MA 01518 (SAN 264-1569) Tel 508-347-2039.

Knopf, *(Knopf, Alfred A., Inc.; 0-394),* Subs. of Random Hse., Inc., 201 E. 50th St., New York, NY 10022 (SAN 202-5825) Tel 212-572-2103; Toll free: 800-733-3000; Orders to: 400 Hahn Rd., Westminster, MD 21157 (SAN 202-5833) Tel 301-848-1900; Toll free: 800-733-3000 (orders). *Imprints:* Borzoi Sprinters (Borzoi Sprinters); Bullseye Bks (Bullseye Books); Dragonfly Bks (Dragonfly Books).

Know Inc, *(Know, Inc.; 0-912786),* P.O. Box 86031, Pittsburgh, PA 15221 (SAN 201-050X) Tel 412-241-4844.

Know Unltd, *(Knowledge Unlimited; 0-915291; 1-55933),* P.O. Box 52, Madison, WI 53701 (SAN 290-0017); 2800 Laura Ln., Middleton, WI 53562 (SAN 290-0025) Tel 608-836-6660. Do not confuse with companies of the same name in Buffalo Grove, IL, Pleasant Grove, UT.

Knowing Pr, *(Knowing Pr., The; 0-936927),* 400 Sycamore, McAllen, TX 78501 (SAN 658-361X) Tel 512-686-4033.

Knowldg Pub, *(Knowledge Publishing Co.; 1-879146),* 915 Welton Rd., Baxter, MN 56401 Tel 218-828-4341.

Koala Pub Co, *(Koala Publishing Co.; 1-877995),* 15445 SE Stephens Ct., Portland, OR 97233 Tel 503-254-7445.

Koalaroo Enter, *(Koalaroo Enterprises; 0-9621386),* 15445 Ventura Blvd., Suite 271, Sherman Oaks, CA 91413 (SAN 251-091X).

Kodansha, *(Kodansha America, Inc.; 0-87011),* Subs. of Kodansha, Ltd. (Japan), 114 Fifth Ave., 18th Fl., New York, NY 10011 (SAN 201-0526) Tel 212-727-6460; Toll free: 800-631-8571; Dist. by: Farrar, Straus & Giroux, Inc., 19 Union Sq. W., New York, NY 10003 (SAN 206-782X) Tel 212-741-6900; Toll free: 800-631-8571.

Kolowalu Bk Imprint of **UH Pr**

Korn Kompany, *(Korn Kompany; 0-939827),* P.O. Box 7414, Menlo Park, CA 94026 (SAN 663-835X) Tel 415-965-3524.

Kosciuszko, *(Kosciuszko Foundation; 0-917004),* 15 E. 65th St., New York, NY 10021 (SAN 208-7251) Tel 212-734-2130.

Kreysa, *(Kreysa, Francis John; 0-9611398),* 12520 Needle Dr., Clarksburg, MD 20871 (SAN 285-3752) Tel 301-349-5001.

Kripalu Pubns, *(Kripalu Pubns.; 0-940258),* Div. of Kripalu Ctr. for Yoga & Health, Rte. 183, Box 793, Lenox, MA 01240 (SAN 217-5320) Tel 413-637-3280; Dist. by: New Leaf Distributing Co., 5425 Tulane Dr., SW, Atlanta, GA 30336-2323 (SAN 169-1449) Tel 404-691-6996; Toll free: 800-326-2665.

Krishna Pr, *(Krishna Pr.),* Div. of Gordon Pr., P.O. Box 459, Bowling Green Sta., New York, NY 10004 (SAN 202-6570).

Ktav, *(Ktav Publishing Hse.; 0-87068; 0-88125),* Box 6249, Hoboken, NJ 07030 (SAN 201-0038); 900 Jefferson St., Hoboken, NJ 07030 (SAN 200-8866) Tel 201-963-9524.

Kudzu, *(Kudzu & Co.; 0-9615015),* Box 415, Walls, MS 38680 (SAN 693-823X) Tel 601-781-0267.

Kuehn Radtke, *(Kuehn Radtke Pubns. & Productions; 0-916639),* 13-3541 Maile St., Pahoa, HI 96778 (SAN 296-6409). Moved, left no forwarding address.

Kusel, *(Kusel, George; 0-9604476),* 600 Lakevue Dr., Willow Grove, PA 19090 (SAN 215-7837).

Kyo-Sa Pub, *(Kyo-Sa Publishing; 0-9622792),* 202 Olive Mill Rd., Santa Barbara, CA 93108 Tel 805-969-4521.

L & M Bks, *(L & M Bks.; 0-914237),* 18387 Hwy. 18, Apple Valley, CA 92307 (SAN 287-525X) Tel 619-242-8102.

L Ashley & Joshua, *(Lauren Ashley & Joshua Storybooks & Publishing, Inc.; 1-878389),* 279 S. Beverly Dr., Suite 24A, Beverly Hills, CA 90212; Toll free: 800-247-8679.

L Eide, *(Eide, Lucille; 0-9610668),* 3966 Wilshire Blvd., Apt. 205, Los Angeles, CA 90010 (SAN 264-7370); Dist. by: Arcturus Bk. Service, P.O. Box 831383, Stone Mountain, GA 30083-0023 (SAN 200-9293).

L F Lewis, *(Lewis, Lois F.; 0-9620136),* 515 E. Main St., Ravenna, OH 44266 (SAN 247-6592) Tel 216-297-1525.

L Hill Bks, *(Hill, Lawrence, Bks.; 0-88208),* Subs. of Chicago Review Pr., 230 Park Pl., Suite 6A, Brooklyn, NY 11238 Tel 718-857-1015; Toll free: 800-888-4741 (Orders only); Dist. by: Independent Pubs. Group, 814 N. Franklin St., Chicago, IL 60610 (SAN 202-0769) Tel 312-337-0747.

L-L Resrch, *(L/L Research; 0-945007),* 1504 Hobbs Park Rd., Louisville, KY 40223 (SAN 245-775X) Tel 502-245-6495.

L L Wegrzecki, *(Wegrzecki, Lester L.; 0-9620774),* 28551 San Marino Dr., Southfield, MI 48034 (SAN 249-7840) Tel 313-355-3542.

L LaMac Productions, *(Liz LaMac Productions, Inc.; 0-927278),* P.O. Box 25265, Nashville, TN 37202-5265 Tel 615-254-9003.

L Lambert, *(Lambert, Lee; 0-9621630),* P.O. Box 25212, Tamarac, FL 33320 (SAN 251-6934); 5540 NW 61st Pl., Tamarac, FL 33319 (SAN 251-6942) Tel 305-476-1100.

L P Pohl, *(Pohl, Linda Perelman; 0-9625453),* 69 Forestview Ct., Williamsville, NY 14221 Tel 716-688-3838; Dist. by: Empire State News Co., 2800 Walden Ave., Cheektowaga, NY 14225-4772 (SAN 169-5177) Tel 716-681-1100.

L Ross Pubns, *(Lucia Ross Pubns.; 1-879599),* Div. of Paige, Ross & Wood, P.O. Box 1524, South Pasadena, CA 91031-1524; 1015 Adelaine Ave., South Pasadena, CA 91030 Tel 818-441-3650.

L Shouse, *(Shouse, Lucille, & Kay Scott; 0-9620819),* 10895 Hwy. 2, Leavenworth, WA 98826 (SAN 249-8308) Tel 509-548-7883.

L T Litho & Printing See L T Pub

L T Pub, *(L.T. Publishing; 1-879480),* 16811 Noyes Ave., Irvine, CA 92714 Tel 714-863-1340.

La Stampa Calligrafica, *(La Stampa Calligrafica; 0-9606630),* P.O. Box 209, Franklin, MI 48025 (SAN 281-8582) Tel 313-646-5176; Dist. by: Bookpeople, 2929 Fifth St., Berkeley, CA 94710 (SAN 168-9517) Tel 415-549-3030; Toll free: 800-999-4650; Dist. by: Inland Bk. Co., 140 Commerce St., East Haven, CT 06512 (SAN 200-4151) Tel 203-467-4257; Toll free: 800-243-0138.

Lacret Pub, *(Lacret Publishing Co.; 0-943144),* 601 12th St., P.O. Box 8231, Union City, NJ 07087 (SAN 240-3927) Tel 201-866-5257.

LAD Redondo Beach, *(L.A.D. Publishing; 0-9620053),* P.O. Box 7000-176, Redondo Beach, CA 90277 (SAN 247-4174); 217 Ave. F, Redondo Beach, CA 90277 (SAN 247-4182) Tel 213-543-4736.

Ladybird Bks, *(Ladybird Bks., Inc.),* 49 Omni Cir., Auburn, ME 04210 (SAN 107-7864) Tel 207-783-6329; Toll free: 800-523-9247; P.O. Box 1690, Auburn, ME 04211.

Laffing Cow, *(Laffing Cow Pr.; 1-879894),* P.O. Box 3106, 1400 E. College Dr., Cheyenne, WY 82003 Tel 307-637-4533; Toll free: 800-722-6932.

LAM Co, *(Look at Me Co.; 0-945405),* P.O. Box 135, Wheeling, IL 60090 (SAN 246-9499); 8 Norbert Dr., Hawthorn Woods, IL 60047 (SAN 246-9502) Tel 312-438-6443; Dist. by: Kimbo Educational, P.O. Box 477D, Long Branch, NJ 07740 (SAN 630-1592) Tel 201-229-4949; Toll free: 800-631-2187.

Lambgel Family, *(Lambgel Family, Inc.; 1-877765),* P.O. Box 1674, Ada, OK 74820; 231 N. Turner, Ada, OK 74820 Tel 405-463-0948.

Lancaster Prodns, *(Lancaster Productions; 0-930647),* 6221 B Hollis St., Emeryville, CA 94608 (SAN 676-2840) Tel 415-652-3228; Orders to: P.O. Box 7820, Berkeley, CA 94707 (SAN 241-9807); Dist. by: Talman Co., 150 Fifth Ave., Rm. 630, New York, NY 10011 (SAN 200-5204) Tel 212-620-3182; Toll free: 800-537-8894 (orders only).

Landfall Pr, *(Landfall Pr., Inc.; 0-913428),* 5171 Chapin St., Dayton, OH 45429 (SAN 202-6627) Tel 513-298-9123. Do not confuse with Landfall Pr. Inc., Chicago, IL.

Landmark Edns, *(Landmark Editions, Inc.; 0-933849),* P.O. Box 4469, 1402 Kansas Ave., Kansas City, MO 64127 (SAN 692-6916) Tel 816-241-4919.

Landmark Found, *(Landmark Foundation; 0-9624119),* Hale St., Prides Crossing, MA 01965 Tel 508-927-4440.

Landmark ID, *(Landmark Publishing; 0-9624209),* P.O. Box 776, Pocatello, ID 83204; 1738 E. Terry, Pocatello, ID 83201 Tel 208-233-0075.

Lang Pubns, *(Lang Pubns.; 0-942242),* 490 N. 31st St., Suite 100, Billings, MT 59101 (SAN 238-4337); Dist. by: World Bible Pubs., Inc., P.O. Box 370, Iowa Falls, IA 50126 (SAN 215-2797); Toll free: 800-247-5111; Dist. by: Riverside/World, 3040 Charlevoix Dr., Grand Rapids, MI 49546 (SAN 169-2666) Tel 616-940-2086; Toll free: 800-247-5111.

Langenscheidt, *(Langenscheidt Pubs., Inc.; 0-88729; 3-468),* Subs. of Langenscheidt KG, 46-35 54th Rd., Maspeth, NY 11378 (SAN 276-9441) Tel 718-784-0055; Toll free: 800-432-6277.

Langtry Pubns, *(Langtry Pubns.; 0-915369),* 7838 Burnet Ave., Van Nuys, CA 91405-1051 (SAN 291-2473) Tel 818-781-9144.

Language Lrn Assocs, *(Language for Learning Assocs.; 0-9628238),* 194 Brookfield Ave., Paramus, NJ 07652 Tel 201-845-7850.

Language Pr, *(Language Pr.; 0-912386),* P.O. Box 342, Whitewater, WI 53190 (SAN 201-0674) Tel 414-473-8822.

Lani Goose Pubns, *(Lani Goose Pubns., Inc.; 0-944264),* 583 Kamoku St., Suite 3803, Honolulu, HI 96826 (SAN 243-5101) Tel 808-947-7330; Dist. by: Pacific Trade Group, 94-527 Puahi St., Waipahu, HI 96797 (SAN 169-1635) Tel 808-671-6735.

Lantern, *(Lantern Pr., Inc., Pubs.; 0-8313),* 354 Hussey Rd., Mount Vernon, NY 10552 (SAN 201-0682) Tel 212-838-7821.

Lantern Bks, *(Lantern Bks., Inc.; 0-945161),* 88-43 75th St., Jamaica, NY 11421 (SAN 245-923X) Tel 718-296-3981; Dist. by: Amereon, Ltd., P.O. Box 1200, Mattituck, NY 11952 (SAN 201-2413) Tel 516-298-5100; Toll free: 800-367-9692 (except New York). Do not confuse with Lantern Books, Farwell, MN.

Large Print Bks *Imprint* of **G K Hall**

Larksdale, *(Larksdale; 0-89896),* P.O. Box 70456, Houston, TX 77270-0456 (SAN 220-0643); Toll free: 800-321-0065; 8700 Long Point, Houston, TX 77055 Tel 713-461-7200. *Imprints:* Post Oak Pr (Post Oak Press).

Larkspur, *(Larkspur Pubns.; 0-939942),* P.O. Box 211, Bowmansville, NY 14026 (SAN 216-8286) Tel 716-337-2758.

Larson Pubns, *(Larson Pubns.; 0-943914),* 4936 Rte. 414, Burdett, NY 14818 (SAN 241-130X) Tel 607-546-9342; Dist. by: National Book Network, 4720A Boston Way, Lanham, MD 20706 (SAN 630-0065) Tel 301-459-8696; Toll free: 800-462-6420 (orders); Dist. by: Samuel Weiser, Inc., P.O. Box 612, York Beach, ME 03910 (SAN 202-9588) Tel 207-363-4393; Toll free: 800-423-7087 (orders only); Dist. by: New Leaf Distributing Co., 5425 Tulane Dr., SW, Atlanta, GA 30336-2323 (SAN 169-1449) Tel 404-691-6996; Toll free: 800-326-2665; Dist. by: Bookpeople, 2929 Fifth St., Berkeley, CA 94710 (SAN 168-9517) Tel 415-549-3030; Toll free: 800-999-4650; Dist. by: Moving Bks., P.O. Box 20037, Seattle, WA 98102 (SAN 159-0685) Tel 206-325-9077; Toll free: 800-777-6683; Dist. by: Gordon's Books, Inc., 2323 Delgany St., Denver, CO 80216 (SAN 169-0531) Tel 303-296-1830; Toll free: 800-525-6979 (west of the Mississippi); Dist. by: Inland Book Co., 140 Commerce St., East Haven, CT 06512 (SAN 200-4151) Tel 203-467-4257; Toll free: 800-243-0138; Dist. by: Baker & Taylor Bks., Eastern Div., 50 Kirby Ave., Somerville, NJ 08876 (SAN 169-4901) Tel 201-722-8000; Toll free: 800-0435-1845; 800-352-4833 (in New Jersey); Dist. by: The Great Tradition, 11270 Clayton Creek Rd., Lower Lake, CA 95457 (SAN 200-5743) Tel 707-995-3906; Toll free: 800-275-2606. Do not confuse with Larson Pubns., Joliet, IL.

Lasertech, *(Lasertech, Bk. Publishing Div.; 0-943155),* 18627 Brookhurst St., Suite 191, Fountain Valley, CA 92708 (SAN 667-1284) Tel 714-843-0517.

Lat Am Lit Rev Pr, *(Latin American Literary Review Pr.; 0-935480),* 2300 Palmer St., Pittsburgh, PA 15218 (SAN 215-2142) Tel 412-351-1477; Dist. by: Bookslinger, 2402 University Ave., Suite 507, Saint Paul, MN 55114 (SAN 169-4154); Toll free: 800-397-2613; Dist. by: Small Pr. Distribution, Inc., 1814 San Pablo Ave., Berkeley, CA 94702 (SAN 204-5826) Tel 415-549-3336; Dist. by: Book Hse., Inc., 208 E. Chicago St., Jonesville, MI 49250-0125 (SAN 169-3859) Tel 517-849-2117; Toll free: 800-248-1146; Dist. by: Inland Bk. Co., 140 Commerce St., East Haven, CT 06512 (SAN 200-4151) Tel 203-467-4257; Toll free: 800-243-0138.

Laughing Fox, *(Laughing Fox Legends; 0-9625214),* 4213 W. Culver, Phoenix, AZ 85009. Moved, left no forwarding address.

Laughs Unltd, *(Laughs Unlimited, Inc.; 0-9624792),* 1124 Firehouse Alley, Sacramento, CA 95814 Tel 916-446-8128; Dist. by: Publishers Group West, 4065 Hollis St., Emeryville, CA 94608 (SAN 202-8522) Tel 415-658-3453; Toll free: 800-365-3453.

Launch Pr, *(Launch Pr.; 0-9613205; 1-877872),* P.O. Box 5629, Rockville, MD 20855 (SAN 295-0154); 2827 Concord Blvd., Concord, CA 94519 Tel 301-869-0442; Dist. by: Bookpeople, 2929 Fifth St., Berkeley, CA 94710 (SAN 168-9517) Tel 415-549-3030; Toll free: 800-999-4650; Dist. by: Inland Bk. Co., 140 Commerce St., East Haven, CT 06512 (SAN 200-4151) Tel 203-457-4257; Toll free: 800-243-0138; Dist. by: Pacific Pipeline, 19215 66th Ave., S., Kent, WA 98032 (SAN 208-2128) Tel 206-872-5523; Toll free: 800-426-4727 (in Oregon, Montana, Nevada, & northern California); 800-562-4617 (in Washington); Dist. by: Baker & Taylor Bks., Western Div., 380 Edison Way, Reno, NV 89564 (SAN 169-4464) Tel 702-786-6700; Toll free: 800-648-3540.

Laurelwood Pr, *(Laurelwood Pr.; 0-9624210),* P.O. Box 518, Cloverdale, CA 95425; 31669 Pine Mountain Rd., Cloverdale, CA 95425 Tel 707-894-2987.

Lauri Inc, *(Lauri, Inc.; 0-937763),* P.O. Box F, Phillips-Avon, ME 04966 (SAN 659-2597); Avon Valley Rd., Phillips-Avon, ME 04966 (SAN 659-2600) Tel 207-639-2000.

Lavender Pr, *(Lavender Pr.; 0-9622719),* P.O. Box 45542, Westlake, OH 44145-0542; 27505 Seneca Dr., Westlake, OH 44145 Tel 216-871-5616. Do not confuse with Lavender Press, Norwalk, CT.

Lavinia Pub, *(Lavinia Publishing; 0-9619625),* P.O. Box 085222, Racine, WI 53408 (SAN 245-9043).

Lawco, *(Lawco, Ltd.; 0-945071),* Affil. of Moneytree Publishing, P.O. Box 2009, Manteca, CA 95336 (SAN 245-7628); 1212 W. Center, No. 6, Manteca, CA 95336 (SAN 245-7636) Tel 209-239-6006.

Lawrence Hse, *(Lawrence Hse.; 0-9609436),* 718 Sherwood St., North Woodmere, NY 11581 (SAN 260-0935) Tel 516-791-5725.

Lawrence Science, *(Univ. of California, Berkeley, Lawrence Hall of Science; 0-924886; 0-912511),* Univ. of California, Berkeley, CA 94720 (SAN 271-9754) Tel 415-642-1016.

LC Pub, *(LC Publishing Co.; 1-55768),* 89 Lane Ct., Oakland, CA 94611 Tel 415-658-3444.

LCD, *(L.C.D. Pub.; 0-941414),* 663 Calle Miramar, Redondo Beach, CA 90277 (SAN 239-0035) Tel 213-375-6336.

LE *Imprint of* **Dell**

Leadership Pub, *(Leadership Pub., Inc.; 0-911943),* 4030 39th Pl., Des Moines, IA 50310-2801 (SAN 264-1712) Tel 515-278-4765; Orders to: P.O. Box 8358, Des Moines, IA 50301-8358 (SAN 251-2599); Dist. by: Dale Seymour Pubns., P.O. Box 10888, Palo Alto, CA 94303 (SAN 200-9781) Tel 415-324-2800; Toll free: 800-872-1100; 800-222-0766 (in California); Dist. by: Educational Impressions, 210 Sixth Ave., P.O. Box 77, Hawthorne, NJ 07507 (SAN 274-4899) Tel 201-423-4666; Toll free: 800-451-7450; Dist. by: Creative Learning Pr., Inc., P.O. Box 50392, Saint Louis, MO 63105 (SAN 214-2368); Dist. by: Zephyr Pr., P.O. Box 13448, Tucson, AZ 85732-3448 (SAN 270-6830) Tel 602-322-5090.

Learn Concepts OH, *(Learning Concepts, Inc.; 0-934902),* 7622 Palmerston Dr., Mentor, OH 44060 (SAN 213-411X) Tel 216-255-1107.

Learn Inc, *(Learn, Inc.; 0-913286; 1-55678),* 113 Gaither Dr., Mount Laurel, NJ 08054-9987 (SAN 205-6801) Tel 609-234-6100; Toll free: 800-729-7323.

Learn Tools, *(Learning Tools Co.; 0-938017),* P.O. Box 657, Berkeley Springs, WV 25411 (SAN 692-7297); 714 Rockwell St., Berkeley Springs, WV 25422 Tel 304-258-1304.

Learning Expo, *(Learning Expo; 0-9625907),* 4000 Middlefield Rd., Palo Alto, CA 94303 Tel 415-858-2006.

Learning KY, *(Learning Hse., The; 0-939991),* P.O. Box 5176, Louisville, KY 40205 (SAN 664-1040); 1548 Cherokee Rd., Louisville, KY 40205 (SAN 664-1059) Tel 502-459-7975.

Learning Pubns, *(Learning Pubns., Inc.; 0-918452; 1-55691),* 5351 Gulf Dr., Holmes Beach, FL 34218 (SAN 208-1695) Tel 813-778-6651; Orders to: P.O. Box 1338, Holmes Beach, FL 34218-1338 (SAN 688-3990) Tel 813-778-6651; Toll free: 800-222-1525.

Learning Well, *(Learning Well; 0-917109; 0-936850; 1-55596),* 200 S. Service Rd., Roslyn Heights, NY 11577 (SAN 240-7027) Tel 516-621-1540; Toll free: 800-645-6564.

Learning Wks, *(Learning Works, Inc., The; 0-88160),* P.O. Box 6187, Santa Barbara, CA 93160 (SAN 272-0078) Tel 805-964-4220; Toll free: 800-235-5767.

Lectorum Pubns, *(Lectorum Pubns., Inc.; 0-9625162; 1-880507),* 137 W. 14th St., New York, NY 10011 (SAN 169-586X) Tel 212-929-2833; Toll free: 800-345-5946.

Legacy Bks, *(Legacy Bks.; 0-913714),* Box 494, Hatboro, PA 19040 (SAN 202-2389); 12 Meetinghouse Rd., Hatboro, PA 19040 (SAN 658-1129) Tel 215-675-6762.

Legacy Hse, *(Legacy Hse., Inc.; 0-9608008),* Box 786, Orofino, ID 83544 (SAN 238-0684) Tel 208-476-5632.

Lego Dacta, *(Lego Dacta; 0-914831),* 555 Taylor Rd., Enfield, CT 06082 (SAN 245-3460) Tel 203-749-2291; Toll free: 800-527-8339.

Lego Systs
See **Lego Dacta**

Lemonade Kids, *(Lemonade Kids, Inc.; 0-9625075),* 301 Almeria Ave., No. 330, Coral Gables, FL 33134 Tel 305-445-8869; Toll free: 800-852-4544; Dist. by: Business Kids, 301 Almeria Ave., Suite 330, Coral Gables, FL 33134 (SAN 630-4273) Tel 305-445-8869; Toll free: 800-852-4544.

Lenape Pub, *(Lenape Publishing, Ltd.; 0-917178),* 3 Lanark Dr., Wilmington, DE 19803 (SAN 208-7324) Tel 302-479-0251.

Leonardo Pr, *(Leonardo Pr.; 0-914051),* P.O. Box 1326, Camden, ME 04843 (SAN 287-542X) Tel 207-236-8649.

Leonardos Work, *(Leonardo's Workshop; 1-879777),* P.O. Box 11115, Saint Paul, MN 55111; 7620 16th Ave., S., Richfield, MN 55423 Tel 612-869-0001.

Lerner Pubns, *(Lerner Pubns. Co.; 0-8225),* 241 First Ave., N., Minneapolis, MN 55401 (SAN 201-0828) Tel 612-332-3344; Toll free: 800-328-4929. *Imprints:* First Ave Edns (First Avenue Editions).

LeSEA Pub Co, *(LeSEA Publishing Co.; 0-937580),* Div. of Lester Sumrall Evangelistic Assn., Inc., P.O. Box 12, South Bend, IN 46624; 530 E. Ireland Rd., South Bend, IN 46614 Tel 219-291-3292.

Levi Strauss, *(Strauss, Levi, & Co.; 0-9617460),* 1155 Battery St., San Francisco, CA 94111 (SAN 664-1253) Tel 415-544-6000.

Levite Apache, *(Levite of Apache Publishing; 0-9618634; 0-927562),* 1005 N. Flood, Suite 107, Norman, OK 73069 (SAN 668-3983) Tel 405-366-6442.

Lex Pr, *(Lex Pr.; 1-878653),* P.O. Box 859, Los Gatos, CA 95030; 131 Hillbrook Dr., Los Gatos, CA 95032 Tel 408-358-2453.

Lexikos, *(Lexikos Publishing; 0-938530),* P.O. Box 296, Lagunitas, CA 94938 (SAN 219-8517) Tel 415-488-0401.

Lexington-Fayette, *(Lexington-Fayette County Historic Commission; 0-912839),* Div. of Lexington-Fayette Urban County Government, 253 Market St., Lexington, KY 40508 (SAN 277-6936) Tel 606-255-8312.

Leyerle Pubns, *(Leyerle Pubns.; 0-9602296; 1-878617),* 28 Stanley St., Mount Morris, NY 14510 (SAN 211-5700) Tel 716-658-2193; Orders to: P.O. Box 384, Geneseo, NY 14454 (SAN 211-5719).

LFL *Imprint of* **Dell**

Li-Sem Enter, *(Li-Sem Enterprises, Inc.; 0-929909),* 490 El Camino Real, Suite 215, Belmont, CA 94002 (SAN 250-7285) Tel 415-592-4901; Toll free: 800-331-4120.

Liberty Pub, *(Liberty Publishing Co., Inc.; 0-89709),* 440 S. Federal Hwy., Suite 202, Deerfield Beach, FL 33441 (SAN 211-030X) Tel 305-360-9000.

Libr Commns Servs, *(Library Communications Services; 0-941237),* 13 Norwood St., Albany, NY 12203 (SAN 665-3685) Tel 518-438-0617.

Libs Unl, *(Libraries Unlimited, Inc.; 0-87287; 1-56308),* P.O. Box 3988, Englewood, CO 80155-3988 (SAN 202-6767) Tel 303-770-1220; Toll free: 800-237-6124.

Libthelit, *(Libthelit Bks.; 1-879721),* P.O. Box 11905, Baltimore, MD 21207-0905; 24 Armitage Ct., Baltimore, MD 21207 Tel 301-597-8386.

Lichtner, *(Lichtner, Schomer; 0-941074),* 2626A N. Maryland Ave., Milwaukee, WI 53211 (SAN 223-1891) Tel 414-962-7519.

Life Pubs Intl, *(Life Pubs. International; 0-8297; 0-943258),* 3333 SW 15th St., Deerfield, FL 33442-8134 (SAN 213-5817) Tel 305-570-8765.

LifeCom, *(LifeCom; 0-9615722),* 1248 N. 13th Ave., Saint Cloud, MN 56303 (SAN 696-2572) Tel 612-252-9866; P.O. Box 1832, Saint Cloud, MN 56302 (SAN 242-0724).

Lifetime, *(LIFETIME Bks., Inc.; 0-8119),* 2131 Hollywood Blvd., Suite 204, Hollywood, FL 33020 (SAN 208-2365) Tel 305-925-5242; Toll free: 800-771-3355. Do not confuse with Lifetime Books, Inc. in Portland, OR.

Lifetime Pr, *(Lifetime Pr.; 0-931571),* Subs. of Royal Publishing, 137 Campbell Ave., Roanoke, VA 24011 (SAN 686-1636) Tel 703-982-1444.

Lifeworks, *(Lifeworks; 0-9630453),* 85 East Ave., Norwalk, CT 06851 Tel 203-857-0135.

Light & Life, *(Light & Life Pr.; 0-89367),* P.O. Box 535002, Indianapolis, IN 46253-5002 (SAN 206-8419) Tel 317-244-3660; Toll free: 800-348-2513.

Light & Living, *(Light for Living Pubns.; 0-9627630),* 1050 Sunlight Ct., Madison, GA 30650-9370 Tel 404-342-2544.

Light&Life Pub Co MN, *(Light & Life Publishing Co.; 0-937032),* 4836 Park Glen Rd., Minneapolis, MN 55416 (SAN 213-8565) Tel 612-925-3888.

Lighthse Bks MA, *(Lighthouse Bks.; 0-945692),* P.O. Box 1201, West Chatham, MA 02669 (SAN 247-7092); 15 Barcliff Ave. Extension, West Chatham, MA 02669 (SAN 247-7106) Tel 617-945-2216. Do not confuse with Lighthouse Bks., Harrisburg, PA.

Lightyear, *(Lightyear Pr., Inc.; 0-89968),* P.O. Box 507, Laurel, NY 11948 (SAN 213-1102); Dist. by: Buccaneer Bks., P.O. Box 168, Cutchogue, NY 11935 (SAN 209-1542).

Liguori Pubns, *(Liguori Pubns.; 0-89243),* 1 Liguori Dr., Liguori, MO 63057 (SAN 202-6783) Tel 314-464-2500; Toll free: 800-325-9521 (Orders).

Lil Daisy Bks, *(L'il Daisy Bks.; 0-9621283),* 3419 Sterne St., San Diego, CA 92106 (SAN 250-9393) Tel 619-222-1886.

Lil Push Pub, *(Little Push Publishing Co.; 0-924005),* 3036 Larkin Rd., Pebble Beach, CA 93953 (SAN 252-0672). Moved, left no forwarding address.

Lil Red Hen OK, *(Little Red Hen; 0-9621669),* 412 Claremont Dr., Norman, OK 73069 (SAN 251-8457) Tel 405-329-0415.

Lilium Pr, *(Lilium Pr.; 0-9624794),* P.O. Box 21, Western Springs, IL 60558; 4050 Howard Ave., Western Springs, IL 60558 Tel 312-246-2102.

Limberlost Pr, *(Limberlost Pr.; 0-931659),* P.O. Box 1113, HC 33, Boise, ID 83706-9702 (SAN 683-7212) Tel 208-344-2120.

Linden Pubns, *(Linden Pubns.; 0-89642),* 1750 N. Sycamore, No. 305, Hollywood, CA 90028 (SAN 206-7218).

Lindsay Pubns, *(Lindsay Pubns., Inc.; 0-917914; 1-55918),* P.O. Box 12, Bradley, IL 60915 (SAN 209-9462) Tel 815-468-3668.

Line Drive, *(Line Drive Publishing),* 113 Pleasant St., Hanover, MA 02339 (SAN 663-4575) Tel 617-878-5035.

LinguiSystems, *(LinguiSystems, Inc.; 1-55999),* 3100 Fourth Ave., P.O. Box 747, East Moline, IL 61244 Tel 309-755-2300; Toll free: 800-776-4332.

Linking Ed Med, *(Linking Education & Medicine, Inc.; 0-9629417),* P.O. Box 357, Burtonsville, MD 20866-9357; 7818 Chapel Cove Dr., Laurel, MD 20707 Tel 301-384-9229.

Linmore Pub, *(Linmore Publishing, Inc.; 0-916591),* 409 E. South St., Barrington, IL 60010 (SAN 296-4503) Tel 312-382-7606; Orders to: P.O. Box 1545, Palatine, IL 60078 (SAN 662-2291) Tel 815-223-7499.

Lintel, *(Lintel; 0-931642),* P.O. Box 8609, Roanoke, VA 24014 (SAN 213-6325) Tel 703-982-2265.

Lion Bks, *(Lion Bks.; 0-87460),* 210 Nelson Rd., Suite B, Scarsdale, NY 10583 (SAN 241-7529) Tel 914-725-2280.

Lion House Pr, *(Lion Hse. Pr.; 0-914107),* P.O. Box 791, Canby, OR 97013 (SAN 287-5101) Tel 503-263-6688.

Lion USA, *(Lion Publishing Corp.; 0-7459; 0-85648),* Subs. of Lion Publishing, PLC, UK, 1705 Hubbard Ave., Batavia, IL 60510 (SAN 663-611X) Tel 708-879-0707; Toll free: 800-447-5466.

Lions Head Pr, *(Lions Head Pr.; 0-934661),* P.O. Box 5202, Klamath Falls, OR 97601 (SAN 694-0447) Tel 503-883-2101.

Lip Smackers, *(Lip Smackers, Inc.; 0-9629459),* P.O. Box 5385, Culver City, CA 90231-5385; 5870 Green Valley Cir., Suite 202, Culver City, CA 90231 Tel 213-641-0578.

Lipp Jr Bks *Imprint of* **HarpC Child Bks**

Lippincott, *(Lippincott, J. B., Co.; 0-397; 0-89313),* Subs. of Wolters Kluwer U.S. Corp., 227 E. Washington Sq., Philadelphia, PA 19106-3780 (SAN 201-0933); Toll free: 800-441-4526; 800-982-4377 (in Pennsylvania).

Listen USA, *(Listen U.S.A.),* 323 Railroad Ave., Greenwich, CT 06830 (SAN 695-4839) Tel 203-661-0101.

Lit Pubns, *(Literary Pubns.; 0-9617819),* Div. of Caswell Corp., 34 Oak Bluff, Avon, CT 06001 (SAN 665-3197) Tel 203-677-8944.

Lith Scouts, *(Lithuanian Scouts Assn., Inc.; 0-9611488),* 5620 S. Claremont Ave, Chicago, IL 60636 (SAN 285-3485) Tel 312-434-4545.

Little, *(Little, Brown & Co.; 0-316; 0-8212),* Div. of Time Warner Publishing, 34 Beacon St., Boston, MA 02108 (SAN 200-2205) Tel 617-227-0730; Toll free: 800-343-9204; Orders to: 200 West St., Waltham, MA 02254 (SAN 281-8892); Toll free: 800-343-9204. *Imprints:* Bulfinch Pr (Bulfinch Press); Joy St Bks (Joy Street Books).

Little Buckaroo, *(Little Buckaroo Pr.; 0-9622064),* P.O. Box 3016, West Sedona, AZ 86340; 365 Concord Dr., Sedona, AZ 86336 Tel 602-282-6278.

Little Cajun Bks, *(Little Cajun Bks.; 0-931108),* Subs. of Edler Bks., Box 777, Loreauville, LA 70552 (SAN 212-5250) Tel 318-229-8455.

Little Feat, *(Little Feat; 0-940112),* P.O. Box R, Mastic Beach, NY 11951 (SAN 217-0760) Tel 516-281-5661.

Little Gnome, *(Little Gnome Delights; 0-9615584),* Div. of Artmarx, Inc., P.O. Box 22582, Denver, CO 80222 (SAN 696-0499) Tel 303-758-7905.

Little Great Whale, *(Little Great Whale Productions; 0-9624929),* 305 SW 95th Pl., Miami, FL 33174 Tel 305-221-9339.
Little Prodns, *(Little Productions; 0-922112),* 6751 N. Blackstone Ave., No. 214, Fresno, CA 93710 (SAN 251-1541) Tel 209-435-7166.
Little Rooster *Imprint of Bantam*
Little Simon *Imprint of S&S Trade*
Little Spirit, *(Little Spirit Co., Inc.; 0-9619482),* P.O. Box 680252, Orlando, FL 32808 (SAN 244-9269) Tel 407-294-7201.
Little Spruce, *(Little Spruce Productions; 0-9630107),* 2232 River Rd., Caledonia, NY 14423 Tel 716-226-3392.
Little Wood Bks, *(Little Wooden Bks.; 0-929949),* 1890 Rd. 24, SW, Mattawa, WA 99344 (SAN 250-7943) Tel 509-932-4729.
Littlebee, *(Littlebee Pr.; 0-940674),* 445 Ford Ave., Fords, NJ 08863-1203 (SAN 239-4510) Tel 201-867-2595.
Littlepage, *(Littlepage Co.; 1-878872),* P.O. Box 2059, Palm City, FL 34990.
Littlest Bk, *(Littlest Bk. Co.; 0-9623171),* 6800 Falcata Cove, Austin, TX 78750 Tel 512-343-0040.
Liturgical Pr, *(Liturgical Pr., The; 0-8146),* Div. of Order of St. Benedict, Inc., St. John's Abbey, Collegeville, MN 56321 (SAN 202-2494) Tel 612-363-2213.
Liturgy Tr Pubns, *(Liturgy Training Pubns.; 0-930467; 0-929650),* 1800 N. Hermitage Ave., Chicago, IL 60622-1101 (SAN 670-9052) Tel 312-486-8970; Toll free: 800-933-1800.
Live Oak Media, *(Live Oak Media; 0-941078; 0-87499),* P.O. Box 34, Ancramdale, NY 12503 (SAN 217-3921); Overmountain Rd, Ancramdale, NY 12503 (SAN 669-1498) Tel 518-329-6300.
Liveright, *(Liveright Publishing Corp.; 0-87140),* Subs. of W. W. Norton Co., Inc., 500 Fifth Ave., New York, NY 10110 (SAN 201-0976) Tel 212-354-5500; Toll free: 800-233-4830.
Living Flame Pr, *(Living Flame Pr.; 0-914544),* 325 Rabro Dr., Hauppauge, NY 11788 (SAN 202-6805) Tel 516-348-5252.
Living Planet Pr, *(Living Planet Pr.; 0-9626072; 1-879326),* 558 Rose Ave., Venice, CA 90291 Tel 213-396-0188; Dist. by: Publishers Group West, 4065 Hollis St., Emeryville, CA 94608 (SAN 202-8522) Tel 415-658-3453; Toll free: 800-365-3453.
Living Skills, *(Living Skills Pr.; 0-941510),* P.O. Box 83, Sebastopol, CA 95473 (SAN 239-1082) Tel 707-823-5104; Dist. by: Institute of Living Skills, P.O. Box 1461, Fallbrook, CA 92028 (SAN 239-1090) Tel 619-728-6437; Dist. by: Grolier Enterprises, Sherman Tpke., Danbury, CT 06816 (SAN 203-283X) Tel 203-797-3500; Dist. by: Word, Inc., 4800 W. Waco Dr., Waco, TX 76710 (SAN 665-7311) Tel 817-772-7650.
Lkng Glass Pubns, *(Looking Glass Pubns.; 0-936485),* 1735 Willard St., NW, Suite 5, Washington, DC 20009 (SAN 698-0988) Tel 202-462-3080. Do not confuse with Looking Glass Pubns., Quincy, IL.
Llama Bks, *(Llama Bks.; 1-877778),* 821 Lenhardt Rd., Easley, SC 29640 Tel 803-859-8060.
Llewellyn Pubns, *(Llewellyn Pubns.; 0-87542),* Div. of Llewellyn Worldwide, Ltd., P.O. Box 64383, Saint Paul, MN 55164 (SAN 201-100X) Tel 612-291-1970; Toll free: 800-843-6666.
LLU Pr, *(Loma Linda Univ. Pr.; 0-944450),* School of Religion, Riverside, CA 92515 (SAN 243-5489) Tel 714-785-2256.
LMI TX, *(Leadership Management, Inc.; 0-924121),* 45-67 Lake Shore Dr., Waco, TX 76710 (SAN 252-1261) Tel 817-776-2060.
LMR Prodns, *(LMR Productions; 0-9629541),* Rte. 3, Box 3706, Saint James, MO 65559 Tel 314-265-7047.
LNR Pubns, *(LNR Pubns.; 0-9627894),* P.O. Box 3305, Windsor Locks, CT 06096; 440 North St., Windsor Locks, CT 06096 Tel 203-627-6553.
Lodestar Bks *Imprint of Dutton Child Bks*
Loizeaux, *(Loizeaux Brothers, Inc.; 0-87213),* P.O. Box 277, Neptune, NJ 07754-0277 (SAN 202-6848); Toll free: 800-526-2796; 1238 Corlies Ave., Neptune, NJ 07753 (SAN 699-5411) Tel 908-774-8144.

Lola Library, *(Lola Library Collection; 0-930825),* 10348 La Canada Way, Sunland, CA 91040 (SAN 677-6108) Tel 818-352-0402.
Lollipop Power, *(Lollipop Power Bks.; 0-914996),* Div. of Carolina Wren Pr., P.O. Box 277, Carrboro, NC 27510 (SAN 206-9733) Tel 919-560-2738.
Lombard Mktg, *(Lombard Marketing; 0-922242),* 45 Wintonbury Ave., Bloomfield, CT 06002 (SAN 251-2041) Tel 203-286-4222; Toll free: 800-874-6556.
Long Acre Pub, *(Long Acre Publishing; 1-879564),* P.O. Box 292, Mount Vernon, OH 43050; 212 Sychar Rd., Mount Vernon, OH 43050 Tel 614-397-1408.
Longanecker, *(Longanecker Bks.; 0-9601126),* P.O. Box 127, Brewster, WA 98812 (SAN 210-2323) Tel 509-689-2441.
Longman, *(Longman Publishing Group; 0-582; 0-8013),* Div. of Addison-Wesley Publishing Co., 95 Church St., White Plains, NY 10601-1566 (SAN 202-6856) Tel 914-993-5000.
Longman Finan
See Dearborn Finan
Longman Trade
See Dearborn Trade
Longmeadow Pr, *(Longmeadow Pr.),* P.O. Box 10218, 201 High Ridge Rd., Stamford, CT 06904 (SAN 200-9579) Tel 203-352-2110.
Longwood Pr, *(Longwood Pr.; 0-89341),* Stoneham Rd., Wakefield, NH 03872-0757 Tel 603-522-3338. Do not confuse with Longwood Pr. in Brookline, MA.
Look & See, *(Look & See Pubns.; 1-877827),* P.O. Box 64216, Tucson, AZ 85740-1216 Tel 602-529-2857.
Loonfeather, *(Loonfeather Pr.; 0-926147),* 426 Bemidji Ave., Bemidji, MN 56601 Tel 218-751-4869.
Lorien Hse, *(Lorien Hse.; 0-934852),* P.O. Box 1112, Black Mountain, NC 28711 (SAN 209-2999) Tel 704-669-6211.
Los Angeles, *(Los Angeles Children's Museum; 0-914953),* 310 N. Main St., Los Angeles, CA 90012 (SAN 289-310X) Tel 213-687-8801.
Los Arboles Pub, *(Los Arboles; 0-941992),* 820 Calle de Arboles, Redondo Beach, CA 90277 (SAN 238-020X) Tel 213-375-0759; Orders to: P.O. Box 7000-54, Redondo Beach, CA 90277 (SAN 662-0752).
Lothrop, *(Lothrop, Lee & Shepard Bks.; 0-688),* Div. of William Morrow & Co., Inc., 1350 Avenue of the Americas, New York, NY 10019 (SAN 201-1034) Tel 212-261-6500; Toll free: 800-843-9389; Orders to: William Morrow & Co., Inc., 39 Plymouth St., P.O. Box 1219, Fairfield, NJ 07007 (SAN 202-5779) Tel 201-227-7200; Toll free: 800-843-9389.
Lotus, *(Lotus Pr., Inc.; 0-916418),* P.O. Box 21607, Detroit, MI 48221 (SAN 213-8867) Tel 313-861-1280.
Lotus Light, *(Lotus Light Pubns.; 0-941524),* P.O. Box 2, Wilmot, WI 53192 (SAN 239-1120) Tel 414-862-2395.
Louvin Pub, *(Louvin Publishing Co.),* 37 Crescent Rd., Poughkeepsie, NY 12601 (SAN 217-2496).
Love From Sea, *(Love From the Sea; 1-878291),* P.O. Box 711236, Santee, CA 92072-1236; 8729 Graves Ave., Santee, CA 92072 Tel 619-258-2017.
Love Pub Co, *(Love Publishing Co.; 0-89108),* 1777 S. Bellaire St., Denver, CO 80222 (SAN 205-2482) Tel 303-757-2579.
Love Song Mess Assn, *(Love Song to the Messiah Assn., Inc.; 0-915775),* 2030 NW 49th Ave., Fort Lauderdale, FL 33313 (SAN 293-8871) Tel 305-733-0656; Dist. by: Starburst Pubs. (selected titles only), P.O. Box 4123, Lancaster, PA 17604 (SAN 158-9016) Tel 717-569-5558; Toll free: 800-441-1456.
Loveswept *Imprint of Bantam*
Lowell Museum, *(Lowell Museum Corp.; 0-942472),* P.O. Box 8415, Lowell, MA 01853 (SAN 239-9423) Tel 508-459-1066.
Lowell Pr, *(Lowell Pr., The; 0-913504; 0-932845),* 115 E. 31st St., Box 411877, Kansas City, MO 64141-1877 (SAN 207-0774) Tel 816-753-4545; Toll free: 800-736-7660.
Lowry Hse, *(Lowry Hse.; 0-9629591),* P.O. Box 1014, Eugene, OR 97440-1014 Tel 503-683-3778.

Loyola, *(Loyola Univ. Pr.; 0-8294),* 3441 N. Ashland Ave., Chicago, IL 60657 (SAN 211-6537) Tel 312-281-1818; Toll free: 800-621-1008.
Lrn Links, *(Learning Links; 0-88122),* 2300 Marcus Ave., New Hyde Park, NY 11042 (SAN 241-3302) Tel 516-437-9071.
Lrng Tools-Bilicki Pubns, *(Learning Tools/Bilicki Pubns.; 0-940221),* P.O. Box 2588, Del Mar, CA 92014 (SAN 664-1733) Tel 619-481-6360.
Lttle Peop Pr, *(Little People's Pr.; 0-9628563),* Div. of Thomas Ramos & Co., 290 Nichols Dr., Santa Cruz, CA 95060 Tel 408-429-9506. Do not confuse with Little People's Productions in Warsaw, IN.
Lubin Pr, *(Lubin Pr.; 0-9612396),* 396 N. Cleveland, Memphis, TN 38104 (SAN 289-4114) Tel 901-278-0561.
Lubrecht & Cramer, *(Lubrecht & Cramer, Ltd.; 0-934454; 0-945345),* R.D. 1, Box 244, 38 County Rd. 48, Forestburgh, NY 12777 (SAN 214-1256); Rte. 42, Forestburgh Rd., Forestburgh, NY 12777 Tel 914-794-8539.
Lucas Comns, *(Lucas Communications Group, Inc.; 0-9616276),* 90 Dayton Ave., Passaic, NJ 07055 (SAN 658-6201) Tel 201-471-5980.
Luce, *(Luce, Robert B., Inc.; 0-88331),* 195 McGregor St., Manchester, NH 03102 Tel 603-623-5949; c/o Integrated Distribution, 195 McGregor St., Manchester, NH 03102 Tel 603-669-5933.
Lucent Bks, *(Lucent Bks.; 1-56006),* P.O. Box 289011, San Diego, CA 92198-0011; Toll free: 800-231-5163; 10907 Technology Pl., San Diego, CA 92127 Tel 619-485-7424; Dist. by: Greenhaven Pr., 10907 Technology Pl., San Diego, CA 92127 (SAN 201-6214) Tel 619-485-7424.
Lucky Bks, *(Lucky Bks.; 0-922510),* P.O. Box 1415, Winchester, VA 22601 (SAN 251-348X); 3358 Jones Rd., Winchester, VA 22601 (SAN 251-3498) Tel 703-662-3424.
Lucky Star *Imprint of Scholastic Inc*
Lucky Tiger Pr *Imprint of Wonder Kids*
Lucy & Co, *(Lucy & Co.; 0-910079),* 7711 Lake Ballinger Way, NE, Edmonds, WA 98020 (SAN 241-3116) Tel 206-623-9426.
LUISA Prods, *(LUISA Productions; 0-939584),* P.O. Box 6836-AB, Santa Barbara, CA 93160 (SAN 216-4108).
Lumanett Pr, *(Lumanett Pr.; 0-9620137),* 7083 E. Ohio Dr., Denver, CO 80224 (SAN 247-6614) Tel 303-320-6022.
Luna Bisonte, *(Luna Bisonte Prods; 0-935350),* 137 Leland Ave., Columbus, OH 43214 (SAN 209-8326) Tel 614-846-4126.
Luth & Assocs, *(Luth & Assocs.; 0-9626153),* 5829 Tittabawassee Rd., Saginaw, MI 48604 Tel 517-792-9776.
Lutheran Braille, *(Lutheran Braille Workers, Inc., Sight-Saving Div.),* 495 Ninth Ave., San Francisco, CA 94118 (SAN 208-2969) Tel 415-221-7500.
LWV Houston Ed Fund, *(League of Women Voters Houston Education Fund; 0-939903),* 5373 W. Alabama, Suite 500, Houston, TX 77056 (SAN 663-9240) Tel 713-552-1776.
LWV WA, *(League of Women Voters of Washington, The; 1-878170),* 1411 Fourth Ave., No. 803, Seattle, WA 98101-2216 Tel 206-622-8961.
Lynn's Bookshelf, *(Lynn's Bookshelf; 0-9618608),* P.O. Box 2224, Boise, ID 83701 (SAN 667-1314); 4015 Taft, Boise, ID 83703 Tel 208-336-7629.
Lynx Bks, *(Lynx Bks.; 1-55802),* Div. of Lynx Communications, Inc., 137 Fifth Ave., 9th Flr., New York, NY 10010-7103 (SAN 242-7168); Toll free: 800-232-5969 (outside of New York).
Lyons & Burford, *(Lyons & Burford, Pubs., Inc.; 0-941130; 1-55821),* 31 W. 21st St., New York, NY 10010 (SAN 208-1881) Tel 212-620-9580.
Lythway Large Print *Imprint of G K Hall*
M A Salant, *(Salant, Michael Alan; 0-9609288),* 2412 19th St., NW, Apt. 9, Washington, DC 20009-1552 (SAN 260-129X) Tel 202-332-2368; Orders to: P.O. Box 33421, Farragut Sta., Washington, DC 20033-0421 (SAN 200-2760).
M A Thomas, *(Thomas, M. Angele; 0-9619293),* 2055 Royal Fern Ct., Reston, VA 22091 (SAN 243-8224) Tel 703-860-1508.

M & D Made Easy, *(M&D Made Easy;*
0-9627585), 11601 E. 186th St., Artesia, CA
90701 Tel 213-865-5553.

M & H Enter, *(M & H Enterprises; 0-936997),*
P.O. Box 276374, Sacramento, CA 95827
(SAN 658-3180); 9230 Elmgrove Ct.,
Sacramento, CA 95826 (SAN 658-3199)
Tel 916-366-1053.

M & W Pub Co, *(McDonald & Woodward*
Publishing Co., The; 0-939923), P.O. Box
10308, Blacksburg, VA 24062-0308
(SAN 663-6977) Tel 703-951-9465.

M B Pub, *(M B Publishing; 0-932543),* P.O.
Box 12, Hugo, OK 74743 (SAN 687-4827)
Tel 405-326-2677.

M Bitker, *(Bitker, Marian; 0-9628150),* 3061 W.
Pincushion, Tucson, AZ 85746
Tel 602-883-6841.

M Burns Educ Assocs, *(Burns, Marilyn,*
Education Assocs.; 0-941355), 150 Gate 5
Rd., Suite 101, Sausalito, CA 94965
(SAN 665-5424) Tel 415-332-4181; Dist.
by: Cuisenaire Co. of America, Inc., 12
Church St., Box D, New Rochelle, NY
10802 (SAN 201-7806) Tel 914-235-0900.

M C Cook, *(Cook, Malcolm C.)* P.O. Box
26482, Birmingham, AL 35226
Tel 205-979-6689.

M C Mosley, *(Mosley, Marilyn C.; 0-9614850),*
P.O. Box 1883, 13117 Burma Rd., SW,
Vashon, WA 98070 (SAN 693-0972)
Tel 206-567-4751.

M Camphouse, *(Camphouse, Marylyn, Pub.;*
0-9623948), 1653 Hollingsworth Dr.,
Mountain View, CA 94040
Tel 415-968-1644.

M Craft, *(Craft, Mary; 0-9624842),* 1147
Presidio Blvd., Pacific Grove, CA 93950
Tel 408-372-2239.

M D E A, *(MDEA Pr.; 0-9614629),* 79
Knollwood Dr., Newport News, VA 23602
(SAN 691-8948) Tel 804-877-1172.

M E Buria
See Colorful Lrngs

M E Duncan & Co, *(Duncan, M.E., Co.;*
1-878647), P.O. Box 1137, Edgewood, MD
21040; 705 Mallard, Edgewood, MD 21040
Tel 301-538-5579.

M E Sharpe, *(Sharpe, M. E., Inc.; 0-87332;*
1-56324), 80 Business Pk. Dr., Armonk, NY
10504 (SAN 202-7100) Tel 914-273-1800;
Toll free: 800-541-6563.

M Evans, *(Evans, M., & Co., Inc.; 0-87131),* 216
E. 49th St., New York, NY 10017
(SAN 203-4050) Tel 212-688-2810; Dist.
by: National Bk. Network, 4720 Boston Way,
Lanham, MD 20706 (SAN 630-0065)
Tel 301-459-8696; Toll free: 800-462-6420.

M Foote, *(Foote, Margaret; 0-9630411),* 1725
N. Garfield, Loveland, CO 80538
Tel 303-667-4636.

M G Ricketts, *(Ricketts, Marijane G.;*
0-9618223), 10203 Clearbrook Pl.,
Kensington, MD 20895 (SAN 666-8097)
Tel 301-564-0852.

M Hyman Assocs, *(Hyman, Mark, Assocs., Inc.;*
0-9621141), 5070 Parkside Ave., No. 1122,
Philadelphia, PA 19131 (SAN 250-6823)
Tel 215-473-0050; Dist. by: Winston-Derek
Pubs., Inc., P.O. Box 90883, Nashville, TN
37209-0883 (SAN 112-6113)
Tel 615-321-0535; Toll free: 800-826-1888.

M J Halpin, *(Halpin, Myra J.; 0-944620),* 120
East St., Fuquay-Varina, NC 27526
(SAN 244-4879) Tel 919-552-7213.

M J P Barry, *(Barry, M. J. P.; 0-9617009),* 323
W. Harvard Ave., Anchorage, AK 99501
(SAN 662-9148) Tel 907-272-0668.

M Johnson, *(Johnson, Mabel, Quality*
Paperbacks; 0-9600838), P.O. Box 7, Boring,
OR 97009 (SAN 206-1015)
Tel 503-663-3428.

M K Look, *(Look, Margaret K.; 0-9616922),*
P.O. Box 1173, Powell, WY 82435
(SAN 661-5074); 940 Shoshone Dr., Powell,
WY 82435 (SAN 661-5082)
Tel 307-754-4656; Dist. by: Central
Wholesale, Inc., 143 S. 25th St., Pittsburgh,
PA 15203 (SAN 666-7082)
Tel 412-488-2800; Toll free: 800-245-6262.

M K McElderry *Imprint of* **Macmillan Child**
Grp

M L Appell, *(Appell, Morey L., Human*
Relations Foundation, The; 0-943501), P.O.
Box 4181, Greenwich, CT 06830
(SAN 668-5110); 145 Old Church Rd.,
Greenwich, CT 06830 (SAN 668-5129)
Tel 203-661-7891.

M Loke, *(Mele Loke Publishing Co.; 0-930932),*
P.O. Box 240024, Honolulu, HI 96824-0024
(SAN 211-1330) Tel 808-734-8611; Dist.
by: Pacific Trade Group, 94-527 Puahi St.,
Waipahu, HI 96797 (SAN 169-1635)
Tel 808-671-6735.

M Lynch, *(Lynch, Marietta, & Patricia Perry;*
0-9610962), 240 Atlantic Rd., Gloucester,
MA 01930 (SAN 265-2722)
Tel 508-283-6322.

M M Fain, *(Fain, Max M.; 0-9618960),* 880
Briarcliff Terr., NE, No. 3, Atlanta, GA
30306 (SAN 242-8091).

M McMillion Pub, *(McMillion, Mac, Publishing*
Co.; 0-9619399), P.O. Box 7, Nettie, WV
26681 (SAN 244-5352) Tel 304-846-2397.

M Moon, *(Moon, Marjorie; 0-9620834),* 3476
N. Shepard Ave., Milwaukee, WI 53211
(SAN 249-8596) Tel 414-962-5036.

M Press CA, *(M Pr.; 0-9619004),* 4605 Fairway
Dr., Soquel, CA 95073 (SAN 242-8792)
Tel 408-476-1475. Do not confuse with M
Pr., Washington, DC.

M R K, *(M-R-K Publishing; 0-9601292),* Div. of
Meisterfeld & Assocs., 448 Seavey Ln.,
Petaluma, CA 94952 (SAN 210-461X)
Tel 707-763-0056.

M R Stone Minst, *(Stone, Maggie Ruth,*
Ministries; 0-9627059), 76 Tusculum Rd.,
Antioch, TN 37013 Tel 615-255-1928.

M Raphael, *(Raphael, Morris, Bks.; 0-9608866),*
1404 Bayou Side Dr., New Iberia, LA 70560
(SAN 241-0737) Tel 318-369-3220.

M Taliaferro
See F A Pub

M Valladares, *(Valladares, Margaret; 1-879588),*
P.O. Box 141681, Coral Gables, FL 33114;
9126 SW 203 Terrace, Miami, FL 33189
Tel 305-235-9384.

M Wetherbee, *(Wetherbee, Martha, Bks.;*
0-9609384), Star Rte. 35, Sanbornton, NH
03269 (SAN 260-2709) Tel 603-286-8927.

M Wright & Assocs, *(Wright, Milt, & Assocs.;*
0-942071), 17624 Romar St., Northridge,
CA 91325 (SAN 666-735X)
Tel 818-349-0858.

M Wyatt, *(Wyatt, Margaret; 0-9616117),* 1127
St. Mary, Casper, WY 82601
(SAN 699-721X) Tel 307-237-7531.

M-Z Info, *(M-Z Information; 0-937559),* P.O.
Box 2129, Wilton, NY 12866
(SAN 658-8999); 6 Timberlane Dr.,
Gansevoort, NY 12831 (SAN 248-4064).

MAC Pub, *(MAC Publishing; 0-910223),* Div. of
Claudia, Inc., 5005 E. 39th Ave., Denver,
CO 80207 (SAN 241-4031)
Tel 303-331-0148.

Macalester, *(Macalester Park Publishing Co.;*
0-910924), 1571 Grand Ave., Saint Paul,
MN 55105 (SAN 110-8077)
Tel 612-698-8877.

McArthur UT, *(McArthur Publishing;*
0-9626111), 911 W. 180th S., Orem, UT
84058 Tel 801-226-3625. Do not confuse
with McArthur Publisher, Alexandria, LA.

McClanahan Bk, *(McClanahan Bk. Co., Inc.;*
1-878624; 1-56293), 23 W. 26th St., New
York, NY 10010 Tel 212-725-1515.

McCormack Co, *(McCormack Co.; 0-942459),*
455 Arrowhead Trail, Knoxville, TN 37919
(SAN 667-0601) Tel 615-525-8667.

McCormick & Schilling, *(McCormick &*
Schilling; 0-9618212), P.O. Box 722,
Menomonee Falls, WI 53051
(SAN 666-9328); N82 W15855 Valley View
Dr., Menomonee Falls, WI 53051
(SAN 666-9336) Tel 414-255-7706.

McDougal-Littell, *(McDougal, Littell & Co.;*
0-86609; 0-88343; 0-8123), P.O. Box 1667,
Evanston, IL 60204 (SAN 202-2532)
Tel 708-869-2300; Toll free: 800-225-3809.

McFarland & Co, *(McFarland & Co., Inc., Pubs.;*
0-89950), Box 611, Jefferson, NC 28640
(SAN 215-093X) Tel 919-246-4460.

McGraw, *(McGraw-Hill Publishing Co.; 0-07;*
0-390), Div. of McGraw-Hill, Inc., 1221
Ave. of the Americas, New York, NY 10020
(SAN 200-2248) Tel 212-512-3825; Toll
free: 800-262-4729 (retail); 800-338-3987
(college); 800-722-4726 (consumer); Orders
to: Princeton Rd., Hightstown, NJ 08520
(SAN 200-254X) Tel 609-426-5254; Orders
to: 13311 Monterrey Ave., Blue Ridge,
Summit, PA 17294-0850 (SAN 200-2558);
Toll free: 800-822-8138. *Imprints:* BYTE
Bks (BYTE Books).

Machon Historia, *(Machon Historia; 0-9618174),*
1835 E. 14th St., Brooklyn, NY 11229
(SAN 666-8070) Tel 718-645-8416.

McKay, *(McKay, David, Co., Inc.; 0-679),* Subs.
of Random Hse., Inc., 201 E. 50th St., MD
4-6, New York, NY 10022
(SAN 200-240X) Tel 212-751-2600; Orders
to: Random Hse., Inc., 400 Hahn Rd.,
Westminster, MD 21157 (SAN 202-5515)
Tel 301-848-1900; Toll free: 800-733-3000
(orders only). *Imprints:* Fodor (Fodor's
Travel Guides).

Mackinac Island, *(Mackinac Island State Park*
Commission; 0-911872), P.O. Box 370,
Mackinac Island, MI 49757
(SAN 202-5981) Tel 906-847-3328.

McKinzie Pub, *(McKinzie Publishing Co.;*
0-86626), 11000 Wilshire Blvd., P.O. Box
241777, Los Angeles, CA 90024
(SAN 216-2644) Tel 213-934-7685.

MacManiman, *(MacManiman, Inc.; 0-9611998),*
3023 362nd, SE, Fall City, WA 98024
(SAN 212-0216) Tel 206-222-5587.

Macmillan, *(Macmillan Publishing Co., Inc.;*
0-02), Div. of Maxwell Communication
Corp., 866 Third Ave., New York, NY
10022 (SAN 202-5574) Tel 212-702-2000;
Toll free: 800-257-5755; Orders to: Front &
Brown Sts., Riverside, NJ 08075
(SAN 202-5582) Tel 609-461-6500.
Imprints: Atheneum (Atheneum); Bobbs
(Bobbs Merrill Company); Collier (Collier
Books); CCPr (Crowell-Collier Press); Merrill
Pub Co (Merrill Publishing Company);
Scribner (Scribner's, Charles, Sons).

Mcmillan Child Bk *Imprint of* **Macmillan Child**
Grp

Macmillan Child Grp, *(Macmillan Children's Bk.*
Group; 0-02), Div. of Macmillan Publishing
Co., Inc., 866 3rd. Ave., New York, NY
10022 Tel 212-702-3598. *Imprints:*
Aladdin (Aladdin); Atheneum Child Bk
(Atheneum Children's Book); Bradbury Pr
(Bradbury Press); Collier Young Ad (Collier
Book for Young Adults); Crestwood Hse
(Crestwood House, Incorporated); Dillon
(Dillon Press, Incorporated); Four Winds
(Four Winds Press); M K McElderry
(McElderry, Margaret K., Books); Mcmillan
Child Bk (Macmillan Children's Books);
Scribners Young Read (Scribner Books for
Young Readers).

MacPherson Pub, *(MacPherson Publishing Co.;*
0-9614849), 907 Comstock Ave., Syracuse,
NY 13210 (SAN 693-1065)
Tel 315-475-0339.

McQueen, *(McQueen Publishing Co.; 0-917186),*
P.O. Box 198, Tiskilwa, IL 61368
(SAN 203-9516) Tel 815-646-4591.

Macra-Tack Inc, *(Macra-Tack, Inc.; 0-9611536),*
P.O. Box 326, Stevensville, MT 59870
(SAN 285-3248) Tel 406-777-5408; Dist.
by: Johnson Bks., 1880 S. 57th St., Boulder,
CO 80301 (SAN 201-0313)
Tel 303-443-1576.

McVie Pub, *(McVie Publishing Co.; 0-917487),*
17630 15th Pl., W., Lynnwood, WA 98037
(SAN 656-0733) Tel 206-743-3706.

Madison Aves, *(Madison Avenues; 0-942553),*
5061 E. 98th Ave., Anchorage, AK 99516
(SAN 667-4089) Tel 907-346-3150.

Madison Park Pr, *(Madison Park Pr.; 0-942178),*
3816 E. Madison St., Seattle, WA 98112
(SAN 238-7867).

Madonna Edu Syst, *(Madonna Educational*
Systems, Inc.; 1-56104), 1901 Ulmerton Rd.
E., No. 318, Largo, FL 34641-3708
Tel 813-587-7010; Toll free: 800-553-7766.

Mage Pubs Inc, *(Mage Pubs., Inc.; 0-934211),* 1032 29th St., NW, Washington, DC 20007 (SAN 693-0476) Tel 202-342-1642; Toll free: 800-962-0922 (orders only); Dist. by: Baker & Taylor Bks., Eastern Div., 50 Kirby Ave, Somerville, NJ 08876 (SAN 169-4901) Tel 201-722-8000; Toll free: 800-435-1845; 800-352-4833 (in New Jersey); Dist. by: Baker & Taylor Bks., Western Div., 380 Edison Way, Reno, NV 89564 (SAN 169-4464) Tel 702-786-6700; Toll free: 800-648-3540; Dist. by: Baker & Taylor Bks., Southern Div., Mt. Olive Rd., Commerce, GA 30529 (SAN 169-1503) Tel 404-335-5000; Toll free: 800-241-6004; 800-282-6850 (in Georgia); Dist. by: Baker & Taylor Bks., Midwestern Div., 501 S. Gladiolus St., Momence, IL 60954 (SAN 169-2100) Tel 815-472-2444; Toll free: 800-435-5111; 800-892-1892 (in Illinois); Dist. by: New Leaf Distributing Co., 5425 Tulane Dr., SW, Atlanta, GA 30336-2323 (SAN 169-1449) Tel 404-691-6996; Dist. by: Blackwell North America, 6024 SW Jean Rd., Bldg. G, Lake Oswego, OR 97035 (SAN 169-7048) Tel 503-684-1140; Toll free: 800-547-0700 (in Oregon); Dist. by: Interlink Publishing Group, Inc., 99 Seventh Ave., Brooklyn, NY 11215 (SAN 664-8908) Tel 718-783-6067.

Magic Fishes Pr, *(Magic Fishes Pr.; 0-942255),* P.O. Box 3243, Lihue, HI 96766 (SAN 666-9190); 2846 Makau St., Lihue, HI 96766 (SAN 666-9204) Tel 808-245-5257.

Magic Lantrn, *(Magic Lantern Pubns.; 0-9619250),* 200 Midlake, Suite C, Knoxville, TN 37918 (SAN 243-8658) Tel 615-688-1303.

Magic Ltd, *(Magic Limited-Lloyd E. Jones; 0-915926),* P.O. Box 3186, San Leandro, CA 94578 (SAN 208-7480) Tel 415-352-1854; 4064 39th Ave., Oakland, CA 94619 (SAN 208-7499) Tel 415-531-5490.

Magical Rainbow, *(Magical Rainbow Pubns.; 0-911281),* P.O. Box 717, Ojai, CA 93023 (SAN 272-1775).

Magill Bks *Imprint of* **Salem Pr**

Magination Pr, *(Magination Pr.; 0-945354),* Div. of Brunner/Mazel, Inc., 19 Union Sq., W., 8th Flr., New York, NY 10003 (SAN 246-6511) Tel 212-924-3344.

Magnolia PA, *(Magnolia Pr.; 0-929917),* P.O. Box 6101, Pittsburgh, PA 15212 (SAN 250-9717); 36 Foster Sq., Pittsburgh, PA 15212 (SAN 250-9725) Tel 412-321-5041. Do not confuse with Magnolia Pr., Gainesville, GA.

Magnolia Pr, *(Magnolia Pr.; 0-916369),* P.O. Box 2921, Gainesville, GA 30503 (SAN 295-6233) Tel 404-531-0644. Do not confuse with Magnolia Pr., Pittsburgh, PA.

Magnum Pr, *(Magnum Pr.; 0-9623698),* 2223 W. Eighth St., Stillwater, OK 74074 Tel 405-377-0950.

Magpie AL, *(Magpie Publishing; 0-9624870),* 2041 St. Charles Ave., Montgomery, AL 36107 Tel 205-263-0158.

Magpie Pubns, *(Magpie Pubns.; 0-936480),* P.O. Box 636, Alamo, CA 94507 (SAN 221-4091) Tel 415-838-9287.

Mah-Tov Pubns, *(Mah-Tov Pubns.; 0-917274),* 1680 45th St., Brooklyn, NY 11204 (SAN 208-7502) Tel 718-871-5337.

Mailbox, *(Mailbox Club Bks.; 0-9603752; 1-879224),* 404 Eager Rd., Valdosta, GA 31602 (SAN 281-9686) Tel 912-244-6812.

Maimes, *(Maimes, S. L.; 0-917246),* 59 Franklin St., Rochester, NH 03867 (SAN 208-1830) Tel 603-332-8889.

Main St Pub, *(Main Street Publishing, Inc.; 0-935399),* 2022 E. Edgewood, Shorewood, WI 53211 (SAN 696-3129) Tel 414-964-5757.

Maine Heritage, *(Maine Heritage Bks.; 0-9629543),* P.O. Box 1462, Scarborough, ME 04070-1462 Tel 207-772-3813.

Maitland Enter, *(Maitland Enterprises; 0-936759),* 8118 N. 28th Ave., Phoenix, AZ 85051 (SAN 699-8437) Tel 602-995-4365.

Maji Bks, *(Maji Bks.; 0-9615163),* 18 Ivest Dr., East Falmouth, MA 02536 (SAN 694-3047) Tel 508-564-5242.

Makepeace Colony, *(Makepeace Colony Pr., The; 0-87741),* P.O. Box 111, Stevens Point, WI 54481 (SAN 203-9575) Tel 715-344-2636.

Malibu Graphics, *(Malibu Graphics, Inc.; 0-944735; 1-56398),* 1355 Lawrence Dr., No. 212, Newbury Park, CA 91320 (SAN 244-9668) Tel 805-499-3015.

Malki Mus Pr, *(Malki Museum Pr.; 0-939046),* Div. of Malki Museum Inc., 11-795 Fields Rd., Banning, CA 92220 (SAN 281-9724) Tel 714-849-7289.

Mallard Pr *Imprint of* **BDD Promo Bk**

Man Mtn Pub, *(Man Mountain Publishing; 0-943981),* 1810 W. Cortland, Chicago, IL 60622 (SAN 242-665X) Tel 312-486-4381; Dist. by: Baker & Taylor Bks., Eastern Div., 50 Kirby Ave., Somerville, NJ 08876 (SAN 169-4901) Tel 201-722-8000; Toll free: 800-435-1845; 800-352-4833 (in New Jersey).

Man-Root, *(Man-Root),* P.O. Box 762, Boyes Hot Springs, CA 95416 (SAN 207-8635); Dist. by: Small Pr. Distribution, Inc., 1814 San Pablo Ave., Berkeley, CA 94702 (SAN 204-5826) Tel 415-549-3336; Dist. by: Bookslinger, Inc., 2402 University Ave., Suite 507, Saint Paul, MN 55114 (SAN 169-4154); Toll free: 800-397-2613.

M&J Mick Schol, *(M & J Mick Scholastic Publishing; 1-878885),* P.O. Box 2138, Fairborn, OH 45324; 250 E. Doris Dr., Fairborn, OH 45324 Tel 513-878-0237.

M&M Assocs, *(M&M Assocs.; 1-877782),* P.O. Box 748, Chehalis, WA 98532.

Mango Entrps, *(Mango Enterprises, Inc.; 0-9627586),* 836 "M" St., Suite 105, Anchorage, AK 99501 Tel 907-277-2886.

Manuscript Pr, *(Manuscript Pr.; 0-936414),* Box 336, Mountain Home, TN 37684 (SAN 214-3224) Tel 615-926-7495. Do not confuse with Manuscript Pr., Nashville, TN.

Manuscripts, *(Manuscripts, Ltd.; 0-9627979),* P.O. Box 12030, 2590 Baseline, Boulder, CO 80303; 1610 Hillside Rd., Boulder, CO 80302 Tel 303-442-3596.

Manzanita Canyon, *(Manzanita Canyon Pr.; 0-9622057),* P.O. Box 2271, Redlands, CA 92373; 11485 Acropolis Dr., Yucaipa, CA 92399 Tel 714-797-7054.

Manzanita Pr, *(Manzanita Pr.; 0-931644),* 4777 Hillsborough Dr., Petaluma, CA 94954 (SAN 211-0342) Tel 707-778-8081. Do not confuse with Manzanita Pr., Three Rivers, CA.

Mapakam Inc, *(Mapakam, Inc.; 0-9623773),* P.O. Box 587, Nixa, MO 65714; Rte. 2, Box 166W, Nixa, MO 65714 Tel 417-725-5582.

Maral Ent, *(Maral Enterprises; 0-9629968),* P.O. Box 361, New York, NY 10028; 455 E. 86th St., No. 24AB, New York, NY 10028 Tel 212-348-7080.

Marcroft Prods, *(Marcroft Productions; 0-935849),* P.O. Box 16405, Salt Lake City, UT 84116-0405 (SAN 695-9776) Tel 801-596-3127.

Marginal Med, *(Marginal Media; 0-942788),* P.O. Box 241, Fredonia, NY 14063 (SAN 240-2475); 292 Water St., Fredonia, NY 14063 (SAN 241-7650) Tel 716-679-0462.

Mari, *(Mari, Inc.; 0-926706; 1-56096),* P.O. Box 92404, Pasadena, CA 91109 (SAN 134-6792); 630 Orange Grove Ave., South Pasadena, CA 91030 (SAN 134-6784) Tel 818-441-2087.

Mariah Pr, *(Mariah Pr.; 0-945436),* 865 Ahwahnee Dr., Millbrae, CA 94030 (SAN 247-137X) Tel 415-697-4682.

Marianas Red Pub, *(Marianas Red Publishing Co.; 0-9624930),* P.O. Box 22482 GMF, Barrigada, GU 96921-2482; 100 Sr. Ecurita Dr., Yona, GU 96914.

Marine Endeavors, *(Marine Endeavors Pr.; 0-935181),* P.O. Box 4423, Berkeley, CA 94705 (SAN 695-4677) Tel 415-531-3887; Dist. by: Bookpeople, 2929 Fifth St., Berkeley, CA 94710 (SAN 168-9517) Tel 415-549-3030; Toll free: 800-999-4650.

Marine Mammal Fund, *(Marine Mammal Fund; 0-9617803),* Ft. Mason Ctr., Bldg. E, San Francisco, CA 94123 (SAN 664-6603) Tel 415-775-4636; Dist. by: Hawaiian Resources, 1123 Kapahulu Ave., Honolulu, HI 96816 (SAN 200-4984) Tel 808-737-8726.

Mariposa Print Pub, *(Mariposa Printing & Publishing, Inc.; 0-933553),* 922 Baca St., Santa Fe, NM 87501 (SAN 691-8743) Tel 505-988-5582.

Mark Excell Pub, *(Mark of Excellence Publishing Co.; 0-933415),* 4620 Northridge Dr., Los Angeles, CA 90043 (SAN 691-5019) Tel 213-294-2136.

Mark Foster Mus, *(Foster, Mark, Music Co.; 0-916656),* P.O. Box 4012, Champaign, IL 61824-4012 (SAN 208-2861) Tel 217-398-2760; Toll free: 800-359-1386.

MarKel Pr, *(MarKel Pr.; 0-9621406),* P.O. Box 134, Springfield, OR 97477 (SAN 251-1886) Tel 503-726-6541; 94854 Kelso Ln., Marcola, OR 97454 (SAN 251-1894) Tel 503-933-2831.

Marketcom, *(Marketcom, Inc.; 0-943409),* 550 Rudder Rd., Fenton, MO 63026 (SAN 668-5838) Tel 314-343-8000; Toll free: 800-325-3884; Dist. by: Troll Assocs., 100 Corporate Dr., Mahwah, NJ 07430 (SAN 200-4895) Tel 201-529-4000; Toll free: 800-526-5289; Dist. by: Scholastic, Inc., 730 Broadway, New York, NY 10003 (SAN 202-5442) Tel 212-505-3000; Toll free: 800-392-2179; Dist. by: Great American Bk. Fairs, 150 Hope St., Longwood, FL 32750 (SAN 200-5077) Tel 407-831-9977; Dist. by: Field Pubns., 245 Long Hill Rd., Middletown, CT 06457 (SAN 207-060X) Tel 203-638-2400; Dist. by: California Schl. Bk. Fairs, 1221 N. Lakeview Ave., Anaheim, CA 92807-1898 (SAN 200-5093) Tel 714-970-2700.

Markins Enter, *(Markins Enterprises; 0-937729),* 2039 SE 45th Ave., Portland, OR 97215 (SAN 659-3224) Tel 503-235-1036.

Marlin Pub, *(Marlin Publishing; 1-878474),* 1138 16th St., Suite 4, Santa Monica, CA 90403 Tel 213-393-2276.

MarLor Pr, *(MarLor Pr.; 0-943400),* 4304 Brigadoon Dr., Saint Paul, MN 55126 (SAN 240-7140) Tel 612-484-4600; Dist. by: Contemporary Bks., Inc., 180 N. Michigan Ave., Chicago, IL 60601 (SAN 202-5493) Tel 312-782-9181.

Marshall Cavendish, *(Cavendish, Marshall, Corp.; 0-85685; 0-86307),* Subs. of Marshall Cavendish, Ltd., 2415 Jerusalem Ave., North Bellmore, NY 11710 (SAN 238-437X) Tel 516-826-4200; Toll free: 800-821-9881.

Marshall Regnl Arts, *(Marshall Regional Arts Council; 1-879703),* P.O. Box C, Marshall, TX 75671; 2501 E. End Blvd., S., Marshall, TX 75670 Tel 903-935-4484.

Marshfilm, *(Marshfilm Enterprises, Inc.; 0-925159; 1-55942),* P.O. Box 8082, Shawnee Mission, KS 66208 (SAN 656-3228); Toll free: 800-821-3303; Orders to: 5903 Main St., Kansas City, MO 64113 Tel 816-523-1059.

Martin Press, *(Martin Pr.; 0-9617044),* P.O. Box 2109, San Anselmo, CA 94960 (SAN 662-8702); 63 Durham Rd., San Anselmo, CA 94960 (SAN 662-8710) Tel 415-454-7985; Dist. by: Bookpeople, 2929 Fifth St., Berkeley, CA 94710 (SAN 168-9517) Tel 415-549-3030; Toll free: 800-999-4650; Dist. by: Publishers Group West, 4065 Hollis St., Emeryville, CA 94608 (SAN 202-8522) Tel 415-658-3453; Toll free: 800-365-3453. Do not confuse with companies with the same name in Los Angeles, CA, Torrance, CA.

Mary Ann Johnson, *(Johnson, Mary Ann; 0-9621465),* Rte. 1, Box 1400, Rocky Mount, VA 24151 (SAN 251-4664) Tel 703-483-4360.

Mary Bee Creat, *(Mary Bee Creations; 1-879414),* 24 E. 25th Ave., San Mateo, CA 94403 Tel 415-571-7979.

Mary Janes Cookbook, *(Mary Jane's Cookbook; 0-9620670),* P.O. Box 70593, Marietta, GA 30067 (SAN 249-4647); 2526 Sunny Ln., SE, Marietta, GA 30067 (SAN 249-4655) Tel 404-565-3646.

Marymoor Mus, *(Marymoor Museum; 0-9624587),* P.O. Box 162, Redmond, WA 98073; 6046 W. Lake Sammamish Pkwy., NE, Redmond, WA 98073 Tel 206-885-3684.

MAS Pr, *(MAS-Pr.; 0-9607984),* P.O. Box 57374, Washington, DC 20037 (SAN 238-5392) Tel 202-659-9580; 1129 New Hampshire Ave., NW, No. 610, Washington, DC 20037 (SAN 241-7685) Tel 202-331-1218; Dist. by: Borden Publishing Co., 1855 W. Main St., Alhambra, CA 91801 (SAN 201-419X) Tel 818-283-5031; Dist. by: Unique Bks., 4200 Grove Ave., Gurnee, IL 60031 (SAN 630-0472) Tel 312-623-9171; Toll free: 800-533-5446.

Master Bks, *(Master Bks.; 0-89051),* Subs. of Creation-Life Pubs., Inc., P.O. Box 1606, El Cajon, CA 92022 (SAN 205-6119) Tel 619-448-1121; Toll free: 800-999-3777. *Imprints:* Inst Creation (Institute for Creation Research).

Master-Player Lib, *(Master-Player Library; 1-877873),* Div. of William Grant Still Music, P.O. Box 3044, Flagstaff, AZ 86003; 22 S. San Francisco St., Suite 422, Flagstaff, AZ 86003 Tel 602-526-9355.

Masterminds Pubns, *(Masterminds Pubns.; 1-877890),* P.O. Box 670882, Marietta, GA 30066; 1229 Overton Dr., Lawrenceville, GA 30244 Tel 404-973-8590.

Masters Pubns, *(Masters Pubns.; 0-89808),* 215 Hillcrest Rd., Berkeley, CA 94705 (SAN 226-2959) Tel 415-540-1928.

Material Dev, *(Material Development Ctr.; 0-916671),* Div. of Stout Vocational Rehabilitation Institute, Stout Vocational Rehabilitation Institute, Univ. of Wisconsin-Stout, Menomonie, WI 54751 (SAN 297-1917) Tel 715-232-1342.

Math Hse, *(Math Hse.; 0-917792),* Div. of Mosaic Media, Inc., 999 Main, Glen Ellyn, IL 60137 (SAN 209-2956) Tel 708-790-1117; Toll free: 800-222-3547.

Mathematical, *(Mathematical Concepts; 0-9623593),* 85 First St., Keyport, NJ 07735-1503 Tel 201-739-3951.

Mathom, *(Mathom Pr. Enterprises; 0-930000),* P.O. Box 362, Oswego, NY 13126 (SAN 285-0508) Tel 315-343-4851.

Maureen Points, *(Maureen Points),* 2905 Van Ness Ave., No. 101, San Francisco, CA 94109 (SAN 211-3236).

Maverick Bks, *(Maverick Bks.; 0-9608612; 0-916941),* Box 549, Perryton, TX 79070 (SAN 240-7183) Tel 806-435-7611.

Max Sci Pub, *(Max Science Publishing Co.; 1-879350),* P.O. Box 12143, Research Triangle Park, NC 27709-2143; 1322 Seaton Rd., Durham, NC 27713 Tel 919-544-5144.

Maxrom Pr, *(Maxrom Pr., Inc.; 0-930339),* 11 E. Fayette St., Baltimore, MD 21202 (SAN 670-6800) Tel 301-539-2370.

Mayfield Printing, *(Mayfield Printing & Office Equipment, Pubs.; 0-910513),* 810 Keyser, Natchitoches, LA 71457 (SAN 260-1028) Tel 318-357-0058.

Mazda Pubs, *(Mazda Pubs.; 0-939214),* P.O. Box 2603, Costa Mesa, CA 92626 (SAN 285-0524); 2991 Grace Ln., Costa Mesa, CA 92626 (SAN 658-120X) Tel 714-751-5252.

Maznaim, *(Moznaim Publishing Corp.; 0-940118),* 4304 12th Ave., Brooklyn, NY 11219 (SAN 214-4123) Tel 718-438-7680.

MD Hist Pr, *(Maryland Historical Pr.; 0-917882),* 9205 Tuckerman St., Lanham, MD 20706 (SAN 202-6147) Tel 301-577-5308.

Mdsn Pub Assocs, *(Madison Publishing Assocs.; 0-933813),* 20 Exchange Pl., New York, NY 10005 (SAN 692-8927) Tel 212-425-3466. Do not confuse with Madison Publishing Co., Huntsville, AL.

Me Two Pubns, *(Me Two Pubns.; 0-9623800),* 606 Yale Ave., N., Seattle, WA 98109 Tel 206-623-9426; Toll free: 800-638-9622.

Meadora Pub, *(Meadora Publishing; 0-9627956),* P.O. Box 4212, Cerritos, CA 90703-4212; 13351 Ridgecrest, Cerritos, CA 90701 Tel 213-865-0682.

Meadowbrook, *(Meadowbrook, Pr.; 0-915658; 0-88166),* 18318 Minnetonka Blvd., Deephaven, MN 55391 (SAN 207-3404) Tel 612-473-5400; Toll free: 800-338-2232; Dist. by: Simon & Schuster Trade, 1230 Ave. of the Americas, New York, NY 10020.

Meadowlark, *(Meadowlark Pr.; 0-941126),* P.O. Box 8172, Prairie Village, KS 66208 (SAN 238-8979) Tel 913-341-9031. Do not confuse with Meadowlark Pr., Laramie, WY.

Meckler Corp, *(Meckler Corp.; 0-930466; 0-88736; 0-913672),* 11 Ferry Ln., W., Westport, CT 06880 (SAN 211-0334) Tel 203-226-6967.

Medfd Pr, *(Medford Pr.; 0-9606824),* P.O. Box 416, Williamsburg, VA 23187 (SAN 209-1984) Tel 804-253-1393.

Media Basics, *(Media Basics, Inc.; 0-87438; 0-925202),* 1200 Post Rd., Guilford, CT 06437 (SAN 656-2175) Tel 203-458-2505; Toll free: 800-542-2505.

Media Materials, *(Media Materials, Inc.; 0-912974; 0-89539; 0-86601; 0-7916),* Div. of Queue, Inc., Holobird Industrial Pk., 1821 Portland Ave., Baltimore, MD 21211 (SAN 206-9989) Tel 203-335-0908; Toll free: 800-232-2224.

Media Prods & Mktg
See Media Pub

Media Pub, *(Media Publishing; 0-939644),* Div. of Westport Pubs., 2440 "O" St., Suite 202, Lincoln, NE 68510-1125 (SAN 216-6372) Tel 402-474-2676; Toll free: 800-627-9919.

Media Serv Unltd, *(Media Services Unlimited; 0-9620887),* P.O. Box 335, Saint Helena Island, SC 29920-0335 (SAN 250-0477).

Mediaor Co, *(Mediaor Co.; 0-942206),* Box 631, Prineville, OR 97754 (SAN 238-7859).

Medlicott Pr, *(Medlicott Pr.; 0-9625261),* Carriage House, 2496 E St., San Diego, CA 92102 Tel 619-236-7937; Dist. by: Green Tiger Pr., 200 Old Tappan Rd., Old Tappan, NJ 07675-7005 (SAN 219-4775) Tel 619-744-7575; Toll free: 800-424-2443.

Medtext, *(Medtext; 0-9629279),* 15W560 89th St., Hinsdale, IL 60521 Tel 708-325-3278.

Mee Enterp, *(Mee Enterprises Publishing Co.; 0-9618854),* P.O. Box 6992, Beverly Hills, CA 90212-6992 (SAN 242-5254); 3596 Centinela Ave., No. 201, Los Angeles, CA 90066 (SAN 242-5262) Tel 213-397-7176.

Megakinetics, *(Megakinetics - Climbing to Success; 1-56495),* P.O. Box 915649, Longwood, FL 32779; Toll free: 800-238-0909; 210 Crown Point Cir., No. 200, Longwood, FL 32779 Tel 407-682-6466.

Megans Wld, *(Megan's World; 0-9610150),* 1820 Skyline Dr., P.O. Box 3399, Fullerton, CA 92634 (SAN 272-3239) Tel 714-871-1369.

Melior Dist, *(Melior Distributors; 0-9616441; 0-929766),* S. 45 Girard, Spokane, WA 99212 (SAN 658-9154) Tel 509-924-1925; Toll free: 800-733-9696.

Melior Pubns
See Melior Dist

Melius Pub, *(Melius Publishing, Inc.; 0-9610130; 0-937603),* Div. of Video Resources, Inc., P.O. Box 925, Aberdeen, SD 57402-0925 (SAN 262-7477); Toll free: 800-882-5171; 202 S. Main, Citizen Bldg., Suite 524, Aberdeen, SD 57401 (SAN 658-1900) Tel 605-226-0488; Dist. by: Publishers Group West, 4065 Hollis, Emeryville, CA 94608 (SAN 202-8522) Tel 415-658-3453; Toll free: 800-365-3453.

Memories In Print, *(Memories In Print; 0-9625397),* P.O. Box 788, Issaquah, WA 98027; 245 SW Clark St., No. F3, Issaquah, WA 98027 Tel 206-392-5446.

Memory Ln Bks, *(Memory Lane Bks.; 0-9618951),* 14 Noon Dr., E., North Vernon, IN 47265 (SAN 242-9403) Tel 812-346-6985.

Mensch Makers Pr, *(Mensch Makers Pr.; 0-9619880),* 1588 Northrop, Saint Paul, MN 55108 (SAN 246-9138) Tel 612-644-8533.

Ment *Imprint of* **NAL-Dutton**

Mer *Imprint of* **NAL-Dutton**

Merc Pr NY, *(Mercury Pr.; 0-936132; 0-929979),* Fellowship Community, 241 Hungry Hollow Rd., Spring Valley, NY 10977 (SAN 221-3923) Tel 914-425-9357.

Mercedes Ministries, *(Mercedes Ministries; 0-926044),* 123 Kings Way, Lexington, SC 29072-8816 Tel 301-551-9173.

Meredith Bks, *(Meredith Bks.; 0-696),* 1716 Locust St., Des Moines, IA 50309-3023 (SAN 202-4055); Toll free: 800-678-8091.

Meridian Educ, *(Meridian Education Corp.; 0-936007; 1-877844; 1-56191),* 236 E. Front St., Bloomington, IL 61701 (SAN 696-6012) Tel 309-827-5455; Toll free: 800-727-5507.

Meridional Pubns, *(Meridional Pubns.; 0-939710),* 7101 Winding Way, Wake Forest, NC 27587 (SAN 216-7484) Tel 919-556-2940.

Meriwether Pub, *(Meriwether Publishing, Ltd.; 0-916260),* Box 7710, Colorado Springs, CO 80933 (SAN 208-4716); Toll free: 800-937-5297; 885 Elkton Dr., Colorado Springs, CO 80907 (SAN 658-2877) Tel 719-594-4422.

Merriam-Eddy, *(Merriam-Eddy Co., Inc.; 0-914562),* P.O. Box 25, South Waterford, ME 04081 (SAN 202-6252).

Merriam-Webster Inc, *(Merriam-Webster, Inc.; 0-87779),* Subs. of Encyclopaedia Britannica, Inc., P.O. Box 281, Springfield, MA 01102 (SAN 202-6244); Toll free: 800-828-1880; 47 Federal St., Springfield, MA 01102 (SAN 658-1226) Tel 413-734-3134.

Merrill Ct Pr, *(Merrill Court Pr.; 0-9627239),* P.O. Box 85785, Seattle, WA 98145 Tel 206-325-5785.

Merrill Pub Co *Imprint of* **Macmillan**

Merry Bears, *(Merry Bears; 0-933103),* 22835 NE 51st St., Redmond, WA 98053 (SAN 689-5778) Tel 206-868-8061.

Merry Thoughts, *(Merry Thoughts; 0-88230),* 380 Adams St., Bedford Hills, NY 10507 (SAN 169-5061) Tel 914-241-0447.

Merryant Pubs, *(Merryant Pubs.; 1-877599),* 7615 SW 257th St., Vashon, WA 98070 Tel 206-463-3879.

Merrybooks VA, *(Merrybooks; 0-9615407),* 1214 Rugby Rd., Charlottesville, VA 22903 (SAN 695-5053) Tel 804-979-3658; Dist. by: Publishers Group West, 4065 Hollis St., Emeryville, CA 94608 (SAN 202-8522) Tel 415-658-3453; Toll free: 800-365-3453.

Mesorah Pubns, *(Mesorah Pubns., Ltd.; 0-89906),* 4401 Second Av., Brooklyn, NY 11232 (SAN 213-1269) Tel 718-921-9000; Toll free: 800-637-6724.

Messianic Jewish, *(Messianic Jewish Perspective; 0-9616148),* Div. of Jews for Jesus, 60 Haight St., San Francisco, CA 94102-5895 (SAN 699-8240) Tel 415-864-2600.

Messner, *(Messner, Julian; 0-671),* Div. of Silver Burdett Pr., Simon & Schuster, Inc., 190 Sylvan Ave., Englewood Cliffs, NJ 07632 (SAN 202-6260) Tel 201-592-2646; Dist. by: Prentice Hall Pr., 200 Old Tappan Rd., Old Tappan, NJ 07675 (SAN 215-3939) Tel 201-767-5937; Toll free: 800-843-3464.

Metagnosis, *(Metagnosis Pubns.; 1-879203),* P.O. Box 2777, Estes Park, CO 80517; 1726 Devils Gulch Rd., Estes Park, CO 80517 Tel 303-586-5940. Do not confuse with New Dawn Pr., Mesa, AZ.

Metamorphic Pr, *(Metamorphic Pr.; 0-9615848),* P.O. Box 1841, Santa Rosa, CA 95402 (SAN 696-6489) Tel 707-874-2606.

Metamorphous Pr, *(Metamorphous Pr., Inc.; 0-943920; 1-55552),* P.O. Box 10616, Portland, OR 97210-0616 (SAN 110-8786); Toll free: 800-937-7771 (orders only); 1136 NW Hoyt, Portland, OR 97209 Tel 503-228-4972.

MH & Pr, *(MH & Pr.; 0-9622211),* 209 Underwood St., NW, Washington, DC 20012 Tel 202-829-0452.

MI City Hist, *(Michigan City Historical Society, Inc.; 0-935549),* P.O. Box 512, Michigan City, IN 46360 (SAN 696-2335) Tel 219-872-6133.

MI Dept Hist, *(Michigan Dept. of State, Bureau of History; 0-935719),* 717 W. Allegan, Lansing, MI 48918 (SAN 695-9415) Tel 517-373-3703.

Micah Pubns, *(Micah Pubns.; 2-916288),* 255 Humphrey St., Marblehead, MA 01945 (SAN 209-1577) Tel 617-631-7601.

Michigan Mus, *(Univ. of Michigan, Museum of Art, Alumni Memorial Hall; 0-912303),* 525 S. State St., Ann Arbor, MI 48109 (SAN 280-9028) Tel 313-764-0395.

Micro Text Pubns, *(Micro Text Pubns., Inc.; 0-942412),* 1 Lincoln Plaza, Suite 27C, New York, NY 10023 (SAN 238-1753) Tel 212-877-8539.

Micronesian, *(Micronesian Productions; 0-930839),* P.O. Box 6608, Tammuning, GU 96911 (SAN 677-6906).

Mid Atlantic, *(Middle Atlantic Pr.; 0-912608),* P.O. Box 945, Wilmington, DE 19899 (SAN 202-6341); Toll free: 800-441-7025; 848 Church St., Wilmington, DE 19899 (SAN 667-4534).

Mid-Peninsula Lib, *(Mid-Peninsula Library Cooperative; 0-933249),* 424 Stephenson Ave., Iron Mountain, MI 49801-3455 (SAN 692-3836) Tel 906-774-3005.

MidCoast Comns, *(MidCoast Communications; 0-910025),* Subs. of MidCoast Pubns., 65 Aberdeen Pl., Suite 200, Saint Louis, MO 63105-2274 (SAN 285-0613) Tel 314-727-3748; Dist. by: Baker & Taylor Bks., Western Div., 380 Edison Way, Reno, NV 89564 (SAN 169-4464) Tel 702-786-6700; Toll free: 800-648-3540; Dist. by: Baker & Taylor Bks., Eastern Div., 50 Kirby Ave., Somerville, NJ 08876 (SAN 169-4464) Tel 201-722-8000; Toll free: 800-435-1845; Dist. by: Baker & Taylor Bks., Midwestern Div., 501 S. Gladiolus St., Momence, IL 60954 (SAN 169-2100) Tel 815-472-2444; Toll free: 800-435-5111; 800-892-1892 (in Illinois).

MidCoast Pubns
See MidCoast Comns

Middleburg Pr, *(Middleburg Pr., The; 0-931940),* Box 166, Orange City, IA 51041 (SAN 212-9183).

Midstates Pub, *(Midstates Publishing; 0-929918),* 1216 S. Main, Aberdeen, SD 57401 (SAN 250-9741) Tel 605-225-5287.

Midwest Heritage, *(Midwest Heritage Publishing Co.; 0-934582),* 108 Pearl St., Iowa City, IA 52245-4435 (SAN 213-1161) Tel 319-337-3149.

Miles River, *(Miles River Pr.; 0-917917),* 1009 Duke St., Alexandria, VA 22314 (SAN 657-0550) Tel 703-683-1500.

Mill Creek Ent, *(Mill Creek Enterprises; 0-940273),* P.O. Box 153, Arena, WI 53503 (SAN 664-2322); 905 Pine, Arena, WI 53503 (SAN 664-2330) Tel 608-753-2343.

Millbrook Pr, *(Millbrook Pr., Inc.; 1-878841; 1-56294),* 2 Old New Milford Rd., Brookfield, CT 06804 Tel 203-740-2220; 18 W. 55th St., New York, NY 10019. Do not confuse with Millbrook Pr., Fresno, CA.

Millenial Pr, *(Millenial Pr.; 0-910613),* 108 N. State St., Orem, UT 84057 (SAN 260-227X) Tel 801-226-1274.

Miller Bks, *(Miller Bks.; 0-912472),* 2908 W. Valley Blvd., Alhambra, CA 91803 (SAN 203-9931) Tel 818-284-7607.

Miller Ent, *(Miller Enterprises; 0-89566),* P.O. Box 395, Boulder Creek, CA 95006 (SAN 210-6426) Tel 408-338-9633. Do not confuse with Miller Enterprises, Athens, OH.

Miller Family Pubns, *(Miller Family Pubns.; 0-945145),* P.O. Box 812, John's Island, SC 29457 (SAN 246-1552) Tel 803-762-1585.

Miller OH, *(Miller Enterprises; 0-9607658),* P.O. Box 353, Athens, OH 45701 (SAN 241-5631). Do not confuse with Miller Enterprises, Boulder Creek, CA.

Millers River Pub Co, *(Millers River Publishing Co.; 0-912395),* Box 159, Athol, MA 01331 (SAN 265-3605) Tel 508-249-7612; Dist. by: Inland Bk. Co., 140 Commerce St., East Haven, CT 06512 (SAN 200-4151) Tel 203-467-4257; Toll free: 800-243-0138.

Milliken Pub Co, *(Milliken Publishing Co.; 0-88335; 1-55863),* 1100 Research Blvd., Saint Louis, MO 63132-0579 (SAN 205-8405) Tel 314-991-4220; Toll free: 800-643-0008.

Miils Pub Co, *(Mills Publishing Co.; 0-935356),* King Sta., P.O. Box 6158, Santa Ana, CA 92706 (SAN 272-4464) Tel 714-541-5750. Do not confuse with Mills Publishing Co., Halstead, KS.

Millsmont Pub, *(Millsmont Publishing; 0-9623257),* 1465 W. Tuolumne Rd., Turlock, CA 95380 Tel 209-632-1607.

Milrob Pr, *(Milrob Pr.; 0-9625221),* 3350 Lakeshore Dr., Muskegon, MI 49441 Tel 616-755-3427.

Mina Pr, *(Mina Pr. Publishing, Inc.; 0-942610),* P.O. Box 854, Sebastopol, CA 95473 (SAN 238-5430) Tel 707-829-0854.

Mind Pubns, *(Mind Pubns.; 0-9628382),* P.O. Box 4254, Cleveland, TN 37320-4254; 3250 Blueberry Hill Pl., Cleveland, TN 37312 Tel 615-479-5747.

MindMatters, *(MindMatters; 0-9622879),* P.O. Box 16557, Minneapolis, MN 55416; 4409 Washburn Ave., Minneapolis, MN 55410 Tel 612-925-4090.

Mink Ministries, *(Mink, Len, Ministries; 0-9620866),* P.O. Box 41184, Cincinnati, OH 45241 (SAN 249-9908) Tel 513-777-0949; Toll free: 800-426-5766.

Minn Hist, *(Minnesota Historical Society Pr.; 0-87351),* 690 Cedar St., Saint Paul, MN 55101 (SAN 202-6384) Tel 612-296-2264; Toll free: 800-647-7827; Orders to: 690 Cedar St., Saint Paul, MN 55101 (SAN 202-6392) Tel 612-297-3243; Toll free: 800-647-7827.

Minn Med Found, *(Minnesota Medical Foundation, Inc.; 0-940210),* Univ. of Minnesota, P.O. Box 73 Mayo Bldg., 420 Delaware St., SE, Minneapolis, MN 55455 (SAN 217-541X) Tel 612-373-7933.

Minstrel Bks *Imprint of* **PB**

MIP Pub, *(MIP Publishing; 0-9617204),* P.O. Box 50632, Montecito, CA 93150 (SAN 663-2815) Tel 805-969-4504.

Mirage Bks, *(Mirage Bks.; 0-939137),* Subs. of Dephi-Pacific, P.O. Box 1213, Agana Facilty, Agana, GU 96910 (SAN 662-6327).

Miramonte Pr, *(Miramonte Pr.; 0-9624932),* P.O. Box 390328, Mountain View, CA 94039 (SAN 200-514X); 2124 Rock St., Suite 3, Mountain View, CA 94043 Tel 415-967-6547; Dist. by: Children's Small Pr. Collection, 719 N. Fourth Ave., Ann Arbor, MI 48104 (SAN 630-4133) Tel 313-668-8056; Toll free: 800-221-8056 (Orders only).

Miss Jackie, *(Miss Jackie Music Co.; 0-939514),* 10001 El Monte, Overland Park, KS 66207 (SAN 216-4191) Tel 913-381-3672.

Mississippi Archives, *(Mississippi Dept. of Archives & History; 0-938896),* Div. of State of Mississippi, P.O. Box 571, Jackson, MS 39205 (SAN 279-618X) Tel 601-359-6850; Dist. by: Univ. Pr. of Mississippi, 3825 Ridgewood Rd., Jackson, MS 39211 (SAN 203-1914) Tel 601-982-6205; Dist. by: Old Capitol Sales Shop, P.O. Box 571, Jackson, MS 39205-0571 (SAN 630-1436) Tel 601-359-6920.

Misty Hill Pr, *(Misty Hill Pr.; 0-930079),* 5024 Turner Rd., Sebastopol, CA 95472 (SAN 670-0942) Tel 707-823-7437; Dist. by: Bookpeople, 2929 Fifth St., Berkeley, CA 94710 (SAN 168-9517) Tel 415-549-3030; Toll free: 800-999-4650; Dist. by: Baker & Taylor Bks., Midwestern Div., 501 S. Gladiolus St., Momence, IL 60954 (SAN 169-2100) Tel 815-472-2444; Toll free: 800-435-5111; 800-892-1892 (in Illinois).

MIT Pr, *(MIT Pr.; 0-262),* 55 Hayward St., Cambridge, MA 02142 (SAN 202-6414) Tel 617-253-2884; Toll free: 800-356-0343 (orders). Do not confuse with Massachusetts Institute of Technology in Cambridge, MA.

Mitchell Pub, *(Mitchell Publishing, Inc.; 0-938188),* Div. of Random Hse., Inc., 55 Penny Ln., No. 103, Watsonville, CA 95076 (SAN 215-7896) Tel 408-724-0195; Toll free: 800-435-2665; Dist. by: Random Hse., Inc., 400 Hahn Rd., Westminster, MD 21157 (SAN 202-5515) Tel 301-848-1900; Toll free: 800-733-3000 (orders). Do not confuse with Mitchell Publishing in Spokane, WA.

MLE, *(MLE, Inc.; 0-929548),* Div. of Mark Long Enterprises, Inc., 1614 NE Third Ct., Fort Lauderdale, FL 33301 (SAN 249-597X) Tel 305-767-4687.

MMB Music, *(MMB Music, Inc.; 0-918812),* 10370 Page Industrial Blvd., Saint Louis, MO 63132 (SAN 210-4601) Tel 314-427-5660; Toll free: 800-543-3771.

MMI Pr, *(Mountain Missionary Pr.; 0-912145),* Div. of Mountain Missionary Institute, Inc., Aldworth Rd., P.O. Box 279, Harrisville, NH 03450 (SAN 264-7664) Tel 603-827-3361; Toll free: 800-367-1888.

MMI Pubns, *(MMI Pubns., Inc.; 0-9627714),* 9 Elm St., Natick, MA 01760-4401.

MN DPPD Inc, *(MN Design Productions-Publishing Div., Inc.; 0-9623254),* P.O. Box 1099, Murray Hill Sta., New York, NY 10156-0604 Tel 201-679-5639.

MN Humanities, *(Minnesota Humanities Commission; 0-9629298),* 26 E. Exchange St., Lower Level S., Saint Paul, MN 55101 Tel 612-224-5739.

MNP Star, *(MNP Star Enterprises; 0-938880),* P.O. Box 1552, Cupertino, CA 95015-1552 (SAN 215-9708).

Mntn Memories Bks, *(Mountain Memories Bks.; 0-938985),* 216 Sutherland Dr., South Charleston, WV 25303 (SAN 200-4852) Tel 304-744-5772.

Mntn Rainbow *Imprint of* **Rainbow NC**

Mocha Pub, *(Mocha Publishing Co.; 0-9626403),* 8475 SW Morgan Dr., Beaverton, OR 97005 Tel 503-643-7591.

Mockngbrd Square, *(Mockingbird Square; 0-9626541),* P.O. Box 3, Wilmington, MA 01887; 3 Ring Ave., Wilmington, MA 01887 Tel 508-658-2843.

MoDel Pubs, *(MoDel Pubs.; 0-9618650),* P.O. Box 645, Byron, CA 94514 (SAN 668-3878); 4991 Cabrillo Point, Byron, CA 94514 (SAN 668-3886) Tel 415-634-5382.

Modern Curr, *(Modern Curriculum Pr., Inc.; 0-87895; 0-8136),* Div. of Simon & Schuster, Inc., 13900 Prospect Rd., Cleveland, OH 44136 (SAN 206-6572) Tel 216-238-2222; Toll free: 800-321-3106.

Modern Lib *Imprint of* **Random**

Modern Pub NYC, *(Modern Publishing; 0-87449; 1-56144),* Div. of Unisystems, Inc., 155 E. 55th St., New York, NY 10022 Tel 212-826-0850. *Imprints:* Honey Bear Bks (Honey Bear Books).

Modern Signs, *(Modern Signs Pr., Inc.; 0-916708),* 10443 Los Alamitos Blvd., Los Alamitos, CA 90720 (SAN 282-0048) Tel 213-596-8548; Orders to: P.O. Box 1181, Los Alamitos, CA 90720 (SAN 282-0056) Tel 213-493-4168.

Mojave Bks, *(Mojave Bks.; 0-87881),* 7118 Canby Ave., No. C, Reseda, CA 91335-4391 (SAN 202-6430).

MOL Bks, *(MOL Bks.; 0-9622406),* P.O. Box 3085, Ashland, OR 97520; 4400 Shale City Rd., Ashland, OR 97520 Tel 503-482-5323.

Monarch Pr *Imprint of* **Arco**

Monarch Toy, *(Monarch Toy Co., Ltd.; 0-939871),* 4517 Harford Rd., Baltimore, MD 21214 (SAN 663-9593) Tel 301-254-9200.

Monday Morning Bks, *(Monday Morning Bks., Inc.; 0-912107; 1-878279),* 1111 Greenwood Ave., Palo Alto, CA 94301 (SAN 264-7656) Tel 415-327-3374; Dist. by: Good Apple, Inc., P.O. Box 299, Carthage, IL 62321-0299 (SAN 208-6646) Tel 217-357-3981; Toll free: 800-435-7234.

Monkey Sisters, *(Monkey Sisters, Inc., The; 0-933606),* 22971 Via Cruz, Laguna Niguel, CA 92677 (SAN 212-7660) Tel 714-859-5014; Toll free: 800-445-3892.

Monroe County Lib, *(Monroe County Library System; 0-940696),* 3700 S. Custer Rd., Monroe, MI 48161 (SAN 213-5396) Tel 313-241-5277.

Monroe Pr, *(Monroe Pr.; 0-936781),* 16107 Gledhill St., Sepulveda, CA 91343-2918 (SAN 699-9883) Tel 818-891-6464; Dist. by: New Concepts Bks. & Tape Distributors, 9722 Pine Lake, Box 55068, Houston, TX 77055 (SAN 114-2682) Tel 713-465-7736; Toll free: 800-842-4807; Dist. by: Quality Bks., Inc., 918 Sherwood Dr., Lake Bluff, IL 60044-2204 (SAN 169-2127) Tel 708-295-2010; Toll free: 800-323-4241 (Libraries only); Dist. by: Publishers Group West, 4065 Hollis St., Emeryville, CA 94608 (SAN 202-8522) Tel 415-658-3453; Toll free: 800-365-3453; Dist. by: New Leaf Distributing Co., 5425 Tulane Dr., SW, Atlanta, GA 30336-2323 (SAN 169-1449) Tel 404-691-6996; Toll free: 800-326-2665.

Montevista Pr, *(Montevista Pr.; 0-931551),* 5041 Meridian Rd., Bellingham, WA 98226 (SAN 682-191X) Tel 206-734-4279; Dist. by: Pacific Pipeline, Inc., 19215 66th Ave., S., Kent, WA 98032 (SAN 208-2128) Tel 206-872-5523; Toll free: 800-562-4647 (in Washington); 800-426-4727 (in northern California, Montana, Idaho, Nevada, Oregon); Dist. by: Baker & Taylor Bks., Eastern Div., 50 Kirby Ave., Somerville, NJ 08876 (SAN 169-4901) Tel 201-722-8000; Dist. by: Baker & Taylor Bks., Western Div., 380 Edison Way, Reno, NV 89564 (SAN 169-4464) Tel 702-786-6700; Toll free: 800-435-1845; 800-352-4833 (in New Jersey); Dist. by: Alaska News Agency, Inc., Book Dept., 325 W. Potter Dr., Anchorage, AK 99502 (SAN 168-9274) Tel 907-563-3251; Toll free: 800-648-3540.

Monthly Rev, *(Monthly Review Pr.; 0-85345),* Div. of Monthly Review Foundation, Inc., 122 W. 27th St., New York, NY 10001 (SAN 202-6481) Tel 212-691-2555.

Moody, *(Moody Pr.; 0-8024),* Div. of Moody Bible Institute, 820 N. LaSalle Dr., Chicago, IL 60610 (SAN 202-5604) Tel 312-329-2108; Toll free: 800-678-8812.

Moon Pubns CA, *(Moon Pubns., Inc.; 0-9603322; 0-918373),* 722 Wall St., Chico, CA 95928 (SAN 221-7406); Toll free: 800-345-5473; Dist. by: Publishers Group West, 4065 Hollis St., Emeryville, CA 94608 (SAN 202-8522) Tel 415-658-3453; Toll free: 800-365-3453; Dist. by: Quality Bks., Inc., 918 Sherwood Dr., Lake Bluff, IL 60044-2204 (SAN 169-2127) Tel 708-295-2010; Toll free: 800-323-4241 (Libraries only).

Moonbeam Magic Pub, *(Moonbeam Magic Publishing; 0-9623215),* P.O. Box 62194, Honolulu, HI 96839; 2623 Halelena Pl., Honolulu, HI 96822 Tel 808-946-6424.

Moonbeam Pubns, *(Moonbeam Pubns., Inc.; 0-931013; 1-56271),* 18530 Mack Ave., Grosse Pointe, MI 48236 (SAN 159-0308) Tel 313-884-5255; Toll free: 800-343-9789.

Moonlight FL, *(Moonlight Pr.; 0-913545),* 3407 Crystal Lake Dr., Orlando, FL 32806 (SAN 293-3063) Tel 407-857-1113. Do not confuse with companies of the same name in Menomonie, WI, Arlington Heights, IL, Westminster, CA, Troy, NY.

Moons Creat Prods, *(Moon's Creative Products; 0-922694),* Div. of Eraser Products Co., Inc., P.O. Box 1788, Lewisburg, TN 37091 (SAN 251-611X); 305 First Ave., N., Lewisburg, TN 37091 (SAN 251-6128) Tel 615-359-6613.

Moose Schl Records, *(Moose Schl. Records; 1-877942),* P.O. Box 960, Topanga, CA 90290; 1424 Old Topanga Canyon Rd., Topanga, CA 90290 Tel 213-455-2318.

Mor-Mac, *(Mor-Mac Publishing Co.; 0-912178),* P.O. Box 985, Daytona Beach, FL 32015 (SAN 204-0042) Tel 904-255-4427.

Moran Pub Corp, *(Moran Publishing Corp.; 0-86518),* 5425 Florida Blvd., P.O. Box 66538, Baton Rouge, LA 70896 (SAN 214-0616) Tel 504-923-2550; Dist. by: Aviation Bk. Co., 1640 Victory Blvd., Glendale, CA 91201-2999 (SAN 120-1530) Tel 213-240-1771; Toll free: 800-423-2708; 800-542-6657 (in California).

More than Card, *(More than a Card, Inc.; 0-922589),* 4334 Earhart Blvd., New Orleans, LA 70125 (SAN 251-3331) Tel 504-822-7594; Toll free: 800-635-9672.

Morehouse Pub, *(Morehouse Publishing Co.; 0-8192),* 871 Ethan Allen Highway, Suite 204, Ridgefield, CT 06877 (SAN 202-6511) Tel 203-431-3927; Orders to: P.O. Box 1321, Harrisburg, PA 17105 Tel 717-541-8130; Toll free: 800-877-0012.

Morgan Virginia Pub, *(Morgan Virginia Publishing Co.; 0-945237),* 8566 Prest St., Detroit, MI 48228 (SAN 246-6805) Tel 313-584-9071.

Morielle Pr, *(Morielle Pr.; 0-9622537),* P.O. Box 10612, Alexandria, VA 22310-0612; 4214 Shannon Hill Rd., Alexandria, VA 22310.

Morning Glory, *(Morning Glory Pr., Inc.; 0-930934),* 6595 San Haroldo Way, Buena Park, CA 90620-3748 (SAN 211-2558) Tel 714-828-1998.

Morrow, *(Morrow, William, & Co., Inc.; 0-688),* Subs. of Hearst Corp., 1350 Avenue of the Americas, New York, NY 10019 (SAN 202-5760) Tel 212-261-6500; Toll free: 800-843-9389; 800-237-0657 (customer service); Orders to: Wilmor Warehouse, P.O. Box 1219, 39 Plymouth St., Fairfield, NJ 07007 (SAN 202-5779) Tel 201-227-7200. *Imprints:* Mulberry (Mulberry Books); Quill (Quill Paperbacks); Tambourine Bks (Tambourine Books).

Morrow Jr Bks, *(Morrow Junior Bks.; 0-688),* Div. of William Morrow & Co., Inc., 1350 Avenue of the Americas, New York, NY 10019 (SAN 202-5760) Tel 212-261-6691.

Morse Pr, *(Morse Pr., Inc.; 0-933350),* Div. of Cone-Heiden, 3441 Thorndyke Ave., W., Seattle, WA 98119 (SAN 211-8165) Tel 206-282-9988; Orders to: P.O. Box 24947, Seattle, WA 98124 (SAN 665-7427).

Most Mobil, *(Mostly Mobility; 0-922637),* R.D. 1, Box 1448A, Bethel, PA 19507 (SAN 251-3706); Rte. 183, Bethel, PA 19507 (SAN 251-3714) Tel 717-933-5681.

Mother Courage, *(Mother Courage Pr.; 0-941300),* 1667 Douglas Ave., Racine, WI 53404 (SAN 239-4618) Tel 414-637-2227.

Motorbooks Intl, *(Motorbooks International, Pubs. & Wholesalers, Inc.; 0-87938),* 729 Prospect Ave., Osceola, WI 54020 (SAN 169-9164) Tel 715-294-3345; Toll free: 800-458-0454; Orders to: Box 2, Osceola, WI 54020 (SAN 699-5462).

Mott Media, *(Mott Media; 0-915134; 0-88062),* 1000 E. Huron, Milford, MI 48042 (SAN 207-1460) Tel 313-685-8773.

Mount Falcon, *(Mount Falcon Publishing; 0-9624060),* 3240 Edmund Blvd., Minneapolis, MN 55406 Tel 612-722-1092.

Mountain Pr, *(Mountain Pr. Publishing Co., Inc.; 0-87842),* P.O. Box 2399, Missoula, MT 59806 (SAN 202-8832); Toll free: 800-234-5308; 2016 Strand, Missoula, MT 59801 (SAN 662-0868) Tel 406-728-1900.

Mountaineers, *(Mountaineers Bks., The; 0-916890; 0-89886),* Div. of Mountaineers, 1011 SW Klickitat Way, No. 107, Seattle, WA 98134-1162 (SAN 212-8756) Tel 206-223-6303; Toll free: 800-553-4453.

Moyer Bell Limited, *(Moyer Bell, Ltd.; 0-918825; 1-55921),* Colonial Hill, RFD 1, Mount Kisco, NY 10549 (SAN 630-1762) Tel 914-666-0084; Toll free: 800-759-4100 (charge orders only); Dist. by: Rizzoli International Pubns., Inc., 300 Park Ave. S., 5th Flr., New York, NY 10010 (SAN 111-9192) Tel 212-387-3400; Toll free: 800-433-1238 (outside New York, orders only).

MS Pub, *(Mustard Seed Publishing; 0-9623349),* P.O. Box 3544, Huntington Beach, CA 92605-3544; 16652 Tiber Ln., Huntington Beach, CA 92647 Tel 714-842-3963.

MstrWorks Pub, *(MasterWorks Publishing, Inc.; 0-9619326),* P.O. Box 1677, Norman, OK 73070 (SAN 243-8836); 15205 Edna Rd., Oklahoma City, OK 73165 (SAN 243-8844) Tel 405-799-6306.

MT Hist Soc, *(Montana Historical Society Pr.; 0-917298),* 225 N. Roberts St., Helena, MT 59620 (SAN 208-7693) Tel 406-444-2890.

MTH Soc Inc, *(Mountain Top Historical Society, Inc.; 0-9624216),* P.O. Box 263, Haines Falls, NY 12436; Twilight Park-T2, Haines Falls, NY 12436 Tel 518-589-6191.

Mtn St Pr, *(Mountain State Pr.; 0-941092),* c/o Univ. of Charleston, 2300 MacCorkle Ave., SE, Charleston, WV 25304 (SAN 276-4156) Tel 304-727-2798.

Mu Alpha Theta, *(Mu Alpha Theta, National High Schl. Mathematics Club; 0-940790),* 601 Elm Ave., Rm. 423, Norman, OK 73019 (SAN 204-0077) Tel 405-325-4489.

Muffin Enter, *(Muffin Enterprises; 0-9621949),* P.O. Box 614, Howland, ME 04448 Tel 207-732-3749.

Mulberry Imprint **of Morrow**

Multnomah, *(Multnomah Pr.; 0-930014; 0-88070),* Affil. of Multnomah Schl. of the Bible, 10209 SE Division St., Portland, OR 97266 (SAN 210-4679) Tel 503-257-0526; Toll free: 800-547-5890; Dist. by: Spring Arbor Distributors, 10885 Textile Rd., Belleville, MI 48111 (SAN 158-9016) Tel 313-481-0900; Toll free: 800-395-9955; Dist. by: Riverside/World, 3040 Charlevoix Dr., Grand Rapids, MI 49546 (SAN 169-2666) Tel 616-940-2086; Toll free: 800-247-5111.

Murdoch Bks, *(Murdoch Bks.; 1-878767),* P.O. Box 390, Nazareth, PA 18064-0390; Green & Prospects Sts., Nazareth, PA 18064-0390 Tel 215-258-5665.

Murrays Leprechaun Bks, *(Murray's Leprechaun Bks.; 1-879313),* 200 Capps Rd., Hendersonville, NC 28792-9504.

Mus Am Ind
See Natl Mus Am Ind

Mus Art Carnegie, *(Carnegie Museum of Art, The; 0-88039),* 4400 Forbes Ave., Pittsburgh, PA 15213 (SAN 239-1171) Tel 412-622-3223.

Mus Fed Ink, *(Muse Federation Ink; 0-9614084),* P.O. Box 642 St. Albans Sta., Jamaica, NY 11412 (SAN 686-0044) Tel 718-723-9880.

Mus Fine Arts Boston, *(Museum of Fine Arts, Boston; 0-87846),* 465 Huntington Ave., Boston, MA 02115 (SAN 202-2230) Tel 617-267-9300.

Museum NM Pr, *(Museum of New Mexico Pr.; 0-89013),* P.O. Box 2087, Santa Fe, NM 87504 (SAN 202-2575) Tel 505-827-6454.

Music Educ Pubns, *(Music Education Pubns.; 0-943988),* P.O. Box 3402, Fullerton, CA 92634 (SAN 241-5674) Tel 714-525-1397.

Music Inst CA, *(Music Institute of California; 0-9624062),* P.O. Box 3535, Vista, CA 92083; 1868 College Blvd., No. 226, Oceanside, CA 92056 Tel 619-724-2897.

Musical Idiot, *(Musical Idiot Pr.; 0-918321),* R.R. 3, Box 3400, Middlesex, VT 05602-9233 (SAN 657-2839) Tel 802-223-1544; Dist. by: Publishers Group West, 4065 Hollis St., Emeryville, CA 94608 (SAN 202-8522) Tel 415-658-3453; Toll free: 800-365-3453.

Musical Munchkins, *(Musical Munchkins, Inc.; 0-944333),* P.O. Box 356, Pound Ridge, NY 10576 (SAN 243-4490) Tel 914-764-8568.

Mustang Pub, *(Mustang Publishing; 0-914457),* P.O. Box 3004, Memphis, TN 38173 (SAN 289-6702) Tel 901-521-1406; Dist. by: National Bk. Network, 4720 Boston Way, Lanham, MD 20706 (SAN 630-0065) Tel 301-459-8696; Toll free: 800-462-6420.

My Picture Bks, *(My Picture Bks.; 0-9621427),* 5143 Nadine St., Orlando, FL 32807 (SAN 251-3439) Tel 407-275-6545.

MYLAC Pub Co, *(MYLAC Publishing Co.; 0-9624309),* 5636 W. Hanover, Dallas, TX 75209 Tel 214-358-0886.

MyndSeye, *(MyndSeye, Inc.; 0-9629093),* P.O. Box 171, The Plains, VA 22171; Corner of Main & Bragg Sts., The Plains, VA 22171 Tel 703-253-5486.

Mystic Garden, *(Mystic Garden; 0-922848),* P.O. Box 51, Crestone, CO 81131-0051 (SAN 251-432X) Tel 719-256-4137.

Mystic Jhamom, *(Mystic Jhamom Pubs.; 0-933961),* 1650 Rocky Pl., Arroyo Grande, CA 93420 (SAN 693-0689) Tel 805-922-8802; P.O. Box 904, Santa Maria, CA 93456 (SAN 694-972X).

N A Hardegrove, *(Hardegrove, Nelle A.; 0-9619227),* 120 Holder Rd., Baltimore, OH 43105 (SAN 243-5454) Tel 614-862-4473.

N & N Pub Co, *(N&N Publishing Co., Inc.; 0-9606036),* 18 Montgomery St., Middletown, NY 10940 (SAN 216-4221) Tel 914-342-1677; Orders to: 44 Wisner Ave., Middletown, NY 10940 (SAN 662-0884) Tel 914-342-1677.

N Dak Inst, *(North Dakota Institute for Regional Studies; 0-911042),* State Univ. Sta., Fargo, ND 58105 (SAN 203-1574) Tel 701-237-8655.

N Geller Pub, *(Geller, Norman, Pubs.; 0-915753),* P.O. Box 3217, Auburn, ME 04210 (SAN 293-9681) Tel 207-783-2400.

N Howard, *(Howard, Neva; 0-9622666),* 6943 S. Euclid Ave., Chicago, IL 60649 Tel 312-769-5280.

N Klas, *(Klas, Nell; 0-9628560),* 5685 Shadow Ridge Dr., Castro Valley, CA 94552 Tel 415-537-7706.

N McNutt Assocs, *(McNutt, Nan, & Assocs.; 0-9614534),* P.O. Box 295, Petersburg, AK 99833 (SAN 692-3453) Tel 907-772-4809; Dist. by: Pacific Pipeline, Inc., 19215 66th Ave., S., Kent, WA 98032 (SAN 208-2128) Tel 206-872-5523; Toll free: 800-562-4647 (in Washington); 800-426-4727 (in Nevada, Montana, Idaho, northern California, Oregon).

N Point Pr, *(North Point Pr.; 0-86547),* 1563 Solano Ave., Suite 353, Berkeley, CA 94707-2116 (SAN 220-133X) Tel 415-704-8046; Dist. by: Farrar, Straus & Giroux, Inc., 19 Union Sq., W., New York, NY 10003 (SAN 206-782X) Tel 212-741-6900; Toll free: 800-242-7737.

NAAHE
See NAHEE

Nags Head Art, *(Nags Head Art; 0-9616344; 1-878405),* P.O. Box 88, Nags Head, NC 27959 (SAN 200-9145); 7734 Virginia Dare Trail, Nags Head, NC 27959 (SAN 658-8107) Tel 919-441-7480.

NAHEE, *(National Assn. for Humane & Environmental Education; 0-941246),* Div. of Humane Society of the U.S., P.O. Box 362, East Haddam, CT 06423 (SAN 285-0680) Tel 203-434-8666.

NAL-Dutton, *(NAL/Dutton),* Div. of Penguin USA, 375 Hudson St., New York, NY 10014-3657 Tel 212-366-2000. *Imprints:* Dutton-Truman Talley (Dutton/Truman Talley); Ment (Mentor); Mer (Meridian Books); Onyx (Onyx); Plume (Plume Books); Sig (Signet Books); Sig Classics (Signet Classics); Sig Vista (Signet Vista).

NAPSAC Reprods, *(NAPSAC Reproductions; 0-934426),* Rte. 1, Box 646, Marble Hill, MO 63764 (SAN 222-4607) Tel 314-238-4273.

NAR Prodns, *(NAR Productions; 0-89780),* P.O. Box 233, Barryville, NY 12719 (SAN 212-3878) Tel 914-557-8713.

Natl AIDS Prevent, *(National AIDS Prevention Institute; 0-944373),* P.O. Box 2500, Culpeper, VA 22701 (SAN 243-3893); 205 S. East St., Culpeper, VA 22701 (SAN 243-3907) Tel 703-825-4040.

Natl Archives & Records, *(National Archives & Records Administration; 0-911333),* Pubns. Div., 601 Penn Ave., NW, NEPF, Washington, DC 20408 (SAN 210-363X) Tel 202-724-0099. Official records of the federal government on microfilm; facsimiles & reproductions of important historical documents, census records from 1790 to 1910 on microfilm. Catalog of National Archives Microfilm Publications, Black Studies, Indian Studies, immigration, & genealogical records. Catalogs of Federal Population Census, 1790 to 1910. Books & guides on the preservation & use of federal records.

Natl Assn Deaf, *(National Assn. of the Deaf; 0-913072),* 814 Thayer Ave., Silver Spring, MD 20910 (SAN 159-4974) Tel 301-587-1788.

Natl Assn Principals, *(National Assn. of Secondary Schl. Principals; 0-88210),* 1904 Association Dr., Reston, VA 22091 (SAN 676-8776) Tel 703-860-0200.

Natl Assn Student, *(National Assn. of Student Councils; 0-88210),* Div. of National Assn. of Secondary School Principals, 1904 Association Dr., Reston, VA 22091 (SAN 260-3888) Tel 703-860-0200; Orders to: NASSP, P.O. Box 3250, Reston, VA 22090 (SAN 665-7451) Tel 703-860-0200.

Natl BIE Pub, *(National B.I.E. Publishing Agency; 0-925783),* P.O. Box 923, Casselberry, FL 32707-0923; 211 Shore Rd., Winter Springs, FL 32708 Tel 407-327-3779.

Natl Book, *(National Bk. Co.; 0-89420),* Div. of Educational Research Assocs., P.O. Box 8795, Portland, OR 97207-8795 (SAN 212-4661) Tel 503-228-6345.

Natl Ctr Constitutional, *(National Ctr. for Constitutional Studies; 0-88080),* 5288 S. 320 West, Salt Lake City, UT 84107 (SAN 237-7055) Tel 801-261-1776; Toll free: 800-388-4512; Orders to: P.O. Box 30776, Salt Lake City, UT 84130 (SAN 693-9570).

Natl Dairy Coun, *(National Dairy Council; 1-55647),* 6300 N. River Rd., Rosemont, IL 60018-4233 (SAN 224-702X) Tel 312-696-1020.

Natl Fire Serv Support Systs, *(National Fire Service Support Systems, Inc.; 0-9626076),* 919 Westfall Rd., Rochester, NY 14618 Tel 716-442-0370.

Natl Flag Foun, *(National Flag Foundation),* Flag Plaza, Pittsburgh, PA 15219 (SAN 225-3097) Tel 412-261-1776.

Natl Gardening Assn, *(National Gardening Assn., Inc., The; 0-915873),* 180 Flynn Ave., Burlington, VT 05401 (SAN 294-0086) Tel 802-863-1308.

Natl Geog, *(National Geographic Society; 0-87044; 0-7922),* 1145 17th St., NW, Washington, DC 20036 (SAN 202-8956) Tel 202-857-7000; Toll free: 800-638-4077; Orders to: P.O. Box 1640, Washington, DC 20013-9861 Tel 301-921-1200.

Natl Lilac Pub, *(National Lilac Publishing Co.; 0-9614126),* 295 Sharpe Rd., Anacortes-Fidalgo Island, WA 98221 (SAN 686-4716).

Natl Live Stock, *(National Live Stock & Meat Board; 0-88700),* 444 N. Michigan Ave., Chicago, IL 60611 (SAN 273-6276) Tel 312-467-5520.

Natl Marfan Foun, *(National Marfan Foundation, The; 0-918335),* 382 Main St., Port Washington, NY 11050 (SAN 657-2855) Tel 516-883-8712.

Natl Mat Dev, *(National Materials Development Ctr. for French; 0-911409),* Orders to: Univ. of New Hampshire, Dept. of Cultural Affairs, 20 Park St., Concord, NH 03301-6303 Tel 603-862-2429.

Natl Mus Am Ind, *(National Museum of the American Indian; 0-934490),* 3753 Broadway at 155th St., New York, NY 10032-1596 (SAN 204-0085) Tel 212-283-2420.

Natl Paperback, *(National Paperback Bks., Inc.; 0-89826),* Orders to: 3102 Schaad Rd., Knoxville, TN 37921 (SAN 211-5344) Tel 615-947-3575.

Natl Photo Collections, *(National Photographic Collections; 0-9620255),* 390F Golfview Rd., North Palm Beach, FL 33408 (SAN 248-0204) Tel 407-626-3233.

Natl Pr Inc, *(National Pr., Inc.; 0-915765),* 7200 Wisconsin Ave., Suite 212, Bethesda, MD 20814 (SAN 293-8839) Tel 301-657-1616; Toll free: 800-275-8888.

Natl Res Unltd, *(Natural Resources Unlimited, Inc.; 0-912475),* 3531 Roesner Dr., Markham, IL 60426 (SAN 265-2846) Tel 708-331-7964.

Natl School, *(National Schl. Services; 0-932957),* 632 S. Wheeling Rd., Wheeling, IL 60090 (SAN 689-9986) Tel 312-541-2768.

Natl Textbk, *(National Textbook Co.; 0-8442; 0-8325; 0-88499),* Div. of NTC Publishing Group, 4255 W. Touhy Ave., Lincolnwood, IL 60646-1975 (SAN 169-2208) Tel 708-679-5500; Toll free: 800-323-4900 (orders). *Imprints:* Passport Bks (Passport Books); VGM Career Horzns (V G M Career Horizons).

Natl Wildlife, *(National Wildlife Federation; 0-912186; 0-945051),* 8925 Leesburg Pike, Vienna, VA 22184 (SAN 202-8980) Tel 703-790-4000.

Natl Wmns Hall Fame, *(National Women's Hall of Fame; 0-9610622),* 76 Falls St. P.O. Box 335, Seneca Falls, NY 13148 (SAN 223-9299) Tel 315-568-8060.

Natl Writ Pr, *(National Writers Pr., The; 0-88100),* Div. of National Writers Club, Subs. of Association Headquarters, Inc., 1450 S. Havana, Suite 620, Aurora, CO 80012 (SAN 240-320X) Tel 303-751-7844.

Naturegraph, *(Naturegraph Pubs., Inc.; 0-911010; 0-87961),* P.O. Box 1075, Happy Camp, CA 96039 (SAN 202-8999) Tel 916-493-5353.

Nauset Marsh, *(Nauset Marsh Pr.; 0-9618300),* Rte. 6, P.O. Box 1076, N. Eastham, MA 02651 (SAN 667-3309); Tomahawk Trail, Eastham, MA 02642 (SAN 667-3317) Tel 508-255-9090.

Navajo Curr
See Rough Rock Pr

Naval Inst Pr, *(Naval Institute Pr.; 0-87021; 1-55750),* U. S. Naval Institute, Preble Hall, 118 Maryland Ave., Annapolis, MD 21402-5035 (SAN 202-9006) Tel 301-268-6110; Orders to: U. S. Naval Institute Operations Ctr., Customer Service, 2062 Generals Hwy., Annapolis, MD 21401 (SAN 662-0930) Tel 301-224-3378; Toll free: 800-233-8764.

NAVH, *(National Assn. for Visually Handicapped; 0-89064),* 3201 Balboa St., San Francisco, CA 94121 (SAN 202-0971) Tel 415-221-8755; 22 W. 21st St., 6th Flr., New York, NY 10010 (SAN 669-1870) Tel 212-889-3141.

NavPress, *(Navpress, A Ministry of The Navigators; 0-89109),* P.O. Box 35001, Colorado Springs, CO 80935 (SAN 211-5352) Tel 719-548-9222; Toll free: 800-366-7788.

NC Archives, *(North Carolina Div. of Archives & History; 0-86526),* Historical Pubns. Section, 109 E. Jones St., Raleigh, NC 27601-2807 (SAN 203-7246) Tel 919-733-7442.

NC Learn Inst Fitness, *(North Carolina Learning Institute for Fitness & Education; 0-9620900),* P.O. Box 10245, Greensboro, NC 27404 (SAN 250-0906) Tel 919-292-6999.

NC Natl Sci, *(North Carolina State Museum of Natural Sciences; 0-917134),* Div. of North Carolina Dept. of Agriculture, P.O. Box 27647, Raleigh, NC 27611 (SAN 662-0973); 102 N. Salisbury St., Raleigh, NC 27603 (SAN 208-788X) Tel 919-733-7450.

NC Yrly Pubns Bd, *(North Carolina Yearly Meeting Pubns. Board; 0-942727),* 5506 W. Friendly, Greensboro, NC 27410 (SAN 667-7193) Tel 919-292-6957.

NCAT, *(National Ctr. for Appropriate Technology; 1-55579),* Box 3838, Butte, MT 59702 (SAN 260-342X) Tel 406-494-4572.

NCMA, *(North Carolina Museum of Art; 0-88259),* 2110 Blue Ridge Blvd., Raleigh, NC 27607 (SAN 202-9030) Tel 919-833-1935.

NCTE, *(National Council of Teachers of English; 0-8141),* 1111 Kenyon Rd., Urbana, IL 61801 (SAN 202-9049) Tel 217-328-3870.

NCTM, *(National Council of Teachers of Mathematics; 0-87353),* 1906 Association Dr., Reston, VA 22091 (SAN 202-9057) Tel 703-620-9840.

NE Library Commission, *(Nebraska Library Commission; 0-9624668),* 1420 P St., Lincoln, NE 68508 Tel 402-471-2045; Toll free: 800-742-7691.

NE U Pr, *(Northeastern Univ. Pr.; 0-930350; 1-55553),* 360 Huntington Ave., 272 Huntington Plaza, Boston, MA 02115 (SAN 205-3764) Tel 617-437-5480; Orders to: P.O. Box 6525, Ithaca, NY 14851 (SAN 282-0668) Tel 607-277-2211.

Neahtawanta Pr, *(Neahtawanta Pr.; 0-943806),* 161 E. Front St., Suite 200, Traverse City, MI 49684 (SAN 239-3689) Tel 616-946-0044; Dist. by: Baker & Taylor Bks., Midwestern Div., 501 S. Gladiolus St., Momence, IL 60954 (SAN 169-2100) Tel 815-472-2444; Toll free: 800-435-5111; 800-892-1892 (in Illinois).

NECA, *(Network of Educators' on Central America; 1-878554),* P.O. Box 43509, Washington, DC 20010-9509 Tel 202-429-0137.

Nel-Mar Pub, *(Nel-Mar Publishing; 0-9615760; 1-877740),* HC2, Box 267C, Canyon Lake, TX 78133-2705 (SAN 695-8699) Tel 512-935-2420.

Nelson, *(Nelson, Thomas, Pubs.; 0-8407),* P.O. Box 141000, Nelson Pl. at Elm Hill Pike, Nashville, TN 37214-1000 (SAN 209-3820) Tel 615-889-9000; Toll free: 800-251-4000.

Network Pubns, *(Network Pubns.; 0-941816; 1-56071),* Div. of ETR Assocs., Inc., P.O. Box 1830, Santa Cruz, CA 95061-1830 (SAN 216-2881); 4 Carbonero Way, Scotts Valley, CA 95066 Tel 408-438-4060.

Neuse Pr, *(Neuse Pr.; 0-9613763),* P.O. Box 71, New Bern, NC 28560 (SAN 683-2938) Tel 919-637-4267.

New Age CT, *(New Age Bks. & Games; 1-878064),* P.O. Box 58, Somers, CT 06071; 48 S. Road, Somers, CT 06071 Tel 203-763-2606.

New Amsterdam Bks, *(New Amsterdam Bks.; 0-941533; 1-56131),* 171 Madison Ave., New York, NY 10016 (SAN 630-1886) Tel 212-685-6159.

New Boundary Design, *(New Boundary Designs, Inc.; 0-913703),* 1453 Park Rd., Chanhassen, MN 55317 (SAN 286-0899) Tel 612-474-9525; Toll free: 800-999-5858.

New Connect Pub, *(New Connection Publishing; 0-923766),* Div. of New Connection Programs, Inc., 6222 Bury Dr., Eden Prairie, MN 55344 (SAN 251-7965) Tel 612-934-0234.

New Dawn Pr CO
See Metagnosis

New Day Pr, *(New Day Pr.; 0-913678),* c/o Karamu Hse., 2355 E. 89th St., Cleveland, OH 44106 (SAN 279-2664) Tel 216-795-7070.

New Dimens Educ, *(New Dimensions in Education; 0-89796; 0-914876; 0-8073),* 61 Mattatuck Heights Rd., No. 7, Waterbury, CT 06705-3832 (SAN 207-7078) Tel 914-592-8143; Toll free: 800-227-9120.

New Dir Pr, *(New Directions Pr.; 0-9609616),* 80 Eighth Ave., New York, NY 10011 (SAN 260-2326) Tel 212-255-0230.

New Directions, *(New Directions Publishing Corp.; 0-8112),* 80 Eighth Ave., New York, NY 10011 (SAN 202-9081) Tel 212-255-0230; Dist. by: W. W. Norton & Co., Inc., 500 Fifth Ave., New York, NY 10110 (SAN 202-5795) Tel 212-354-5500; Toll free: 800-223-2588.

New Eng Pr VT, *(New England Pr., Inc., The; 0-933050),* P.O. Box 575, Shelburne, VT 05482 (SAN 213-6376) Tel 802-863-2520.

New Eng Pub MA, *(New England Publishing Co.; 0-914265),* 728 Hampden St., Holyoke, MA 01040 (SAN 287-5837) Tel 413-533-4231.

New Falcon Pubns, *(New Falcon Pubns.; 1-56184),* 7025 E. First Ave., No. 5, Scottsdale, AZ 85251 Tel 602-246-3546.

New Harbinger, *(New Harbinger Pubns.; 0-934986; 1-879237),* 5674 Shattuck Ave., Oakland, CA 94609 (SAN 205-0587) Tel 415-652-0215; Toll free: 800-748-6273; Dist. by: Publishers Group West, 4065 Hollis St., Emeryville, CA 94608 (SAN 202-8522) Tel 415-658-3453; Toll free: 800-365-3453; Dist. by: Bookpeople, 2929 Fifth St., Berkeley, CA 94710 (SAN 168-9517) Tel 415-549-3030; Toll free: 800-999-4650.

New Hope *Imprint of* **Womans Mission Union**

New Hrzns Pub, *(New Horizons Bk. Publishing Co.; 0-932279),* P. O. Box 10904, Marina del Rey, CA 90295 (SAN 686-547X) Tel 213-827-4940.

New Impres UT, *(New Impressions; 0-9626244),* P.O. Box 510026, Salt Lake City, UT 84151-0026; 328 West 200 S., Suite 100, Salt Lake City, UT 84101 Tel 801-359-5446. Do not confuse with New Impressions, Lancaster, NH.

New Leaf, *(New Leaf Pr.; 0-89221),* P.O. Box 311, Green Forest, AR 72638 (SAN 207-9518) Tel 501-438-5288; Toll free: 800-643-9535. Do not confuse with New Leaf Pr., Pacific Grove, CA.

New Leaf Dist, *(New Leaf Distributing Co.; 0-9627209),* Div. of Al-Wali Corp., 5425 Tulane Dr., SW, Atlanta, GA 30336-2323 (SAN 169-1449) Tel 404-691-6996; Toll free: 800-326-2665.

New Mexico Mag, *(New Mexico Magazine; 0-937206),* 1100 St. Francis Dr., Joseph M. Montoya Bldg., Santa Fe, NM 87503 (SAN 677-072X) Tel 505-827-0220.

New Plays Inc, *(New Plays, Inc.; 0-932720),* Box 5074, Charlottesville, VA 22905 (SAN 220-9411) Tel 804-979-2777.

New Readers, *(New Readers Pr.; 0-88336; 1-56420),* Div. of Laubach Literacy International, Box 131, Syracuse, NY 13210 (SAN 202-1064); Toll free: 800-448-8878; 1320 Jamesville Ave., Syracuse, NY 13210 Tel 315-422-9121.

New Schl Mus Study, *(New Schl. for Music Study Pr.; 0-913277),* P.O. Box 407, Princeton, NJ 08542 (SAN 285-8266) Tel 609-921-2900.

New Seed, *(New Seed Pr.; 0-938678),* P.O. Box 9488, Berkeley, CA 94709 (SAN 282-0501) Tel 415-540-7576; Dist. by: Bookpeople, 2929 Fifth St., Berkeley, CA 94710 (SAN 168-9517) Tel 415-549-3030; Toll free: 800-999-4650; Dist. by: Bookslinger, 2402 University Ave., Suite 507, Saint Paul, MN 55114 (SAN 169-4154); Toll free: 800-397-2613; Dist. by: Childrens Small Pr. Collection, 719 N. Fourth Ave., Ann Arbor, MI 48104 (SAN 200-514X) Tel 313-668-8056; Toll free: 800-221-8056; Dist. by: Inland Bk. Co., 140 Commerce St., East Haven, CT 06512 (SAN 200-4151) Tel 203-467-4257; Toll free: 800-243-0138; Dist. by: Kidsrights, 401 S. Highland, Box 851, Mount Dora, FL 32757 (SAN 248-0891) Tel 904-483-1100; Dist. by: New Leaf Distributing, The, 5424 Tulane Dr., SW, Atlanta, GA 30336 (SAN 169-1449) Tel 404-691-6996; Toll free: 800-326-2665.

New Soc Pubs, *(New Society Pubs.; 0-86571),* Div. of New Society Education Foundation, Inc., 4527 Springfield Ave., Philadelphia, PA 19143 (SAN 213-540X) Tel 215-382-6543; P.O. Box 582, Santa Cruz, CA 95061 (SAN 244-805X) Tel 408-458-1191.

New Wrinkle, *(New Wrinkle Pr.; 0-944314),* P.O. Box 20737, Milwaukee, WI 53220 (SAN 243-492X); 3700 S. 43rd St., Milwaukee, WI 53200 (SAN 243-4938) Tel 414-327-0761; Dist. by: Ideals Publishing Co., P.O. Box 141000, Nashville, TN 37214-1000 (SAN 213-4403) Tel 615-889-9000; Toll free: 800-558-0740.

Newhouse Pr, *(Newhouse Pr.; 0-918050),* 146 N. Rampart Blvd., Los Angeles, CA 90026 (SAN 209-2689) Tel 213-383-1089; Orders to: P.O. Box 76145, Los Angeles, CA 90076 (SAN 209-2697).

Newington, *(Newington Pr.; 1-878137),* 2 Old New Milford Rd., Brookfield, CT 06804 Tel 203-740-2220.

Newmarket, *(Newmarket Pr.; 0-937858; 1-55704),* Div. of Newmarket Publishing & Communications, 18 E. 48th St., New York, NY 10017 (SAN 217-2585) Tel 212-832-3575; Toll free: 800-669-3903; Dist. by: Random Hse., Inc., 400 Hahn Rd., Westminster, MD 21157 (SAN 202-5515) Tel 301-848-1900; Dist. by: Random Hse., Inc., Random Hse. Publicity, (11-6), 201 E. 50th St., 31st Flr., New York, NY 10022 (SAN 202-5507) Tel 212-751-2600; Toll free: 800-733-3000 (orders).

News & Observer, *(News & Observer, The; 0-935400),* P.O. Box 191, Raleigh, NC 27602 (SAN 222-6189); 215 S. McDowell St., Raleigh, NC 27602 Tel 919-829-4699.

NewSage Press, *(NewSage Pr.; 0-939165),* P.O. Box 41029, Pasadena, CA 91114 (SAN 662-8370) Tel 818-795-0266.

Niagara Cnty Hist Soc, *(Niagara County Historical Society, Inc.; 1-878233),* 215 Niagara St., Lockport, NY 14094 Tel 716-665-2251.

Nickel Pr, *(Nickel Pr.; 1-879424),* Div. of J.R. Jacobs & Associates, 10585 N. Meridian St., Suite 220, Indianapolis, IN 46290 Tel 317-844-9400.

NightinGale Res, *(NightinGale Resources; 0-911389),* P.O. Box 322, Cold Spring, NY 10516 (SAN 274-1016) Tel 914-753-5383; 6 Chestnut St., Cold Spring, NY 10516 (SAN 248-3866); Dist. by: Baker & Taylor Co., Eastern Div., 652 E. Main, Box 6920, Bridgewater, NJ 08807-0920 (SAN 200-9080) Tel 201-218-0400; Dist. by: Inland Bk. Co., 140 Commerce St., East Haven, CT 06512 (SAN 200-4151) Tel 203-467-4257; Toll free: 800-243-0138; Dist. by: Information Dynamics, 111 Claybrook Dr., Silver Spring, MD 20902 (SAN 630-222X) Tel 301-593-8650; Dist. by: Blackwell North America (library sales only), 1001 Fries Mill Rd., Blackwood, NJ 08012 (SAN 169-4596) Tel 609-629-0700; Toll free: 800-257-7341; Dist. by: Midwest Library Serv., 11443 St. Charles Rock Rd., Bridgeton, MO 63044 (SAN 169-4243) Tel 314-739-3100; Dist. by: Pacific Pipeline, Inc., 19215 66th Ave., S., Kent, WA 98032-1171 (SAN 208-2128) Tel 206-872-5523; Toll free: 800-444-7323; Dist. by: L-S Distributors, 480 Ninth St., San Francisco, CA 94103 (SAN 169-0213) Tel 415-861-6300.

Nightsun MD, *(Nightsun Bks.; 0-945073),* 520 Greene St., Cumberland, MD 21502 (SAN 245-9337) Tel 301-722-2127.

Nighty-Nite, *(Nighty-Nite Pr.; 1-880219),* P.O. Box 34656, North Kansas City, MO 64116; 1232 E. 23rd Ave., North Kansas City, MO 64116 Tel 816-842-9210.

Niota Pr, *(Niota Pr.; 0-9614973),* 1633 Pullan Ave., Cincinnati, OH 45223 (SAN 693-5567) Tel 513-542-4645.

NL Assoc Inc, *(Levy, Nathan, Assocs., Inc.; 0-9608240),* P.O. Box 1199, Hightstown, NJ 08520 (SAN 240-3951) Tel 201-329-6981.

NL Assocs, *(NL Assocs., Inc.; 1-878347),* P.O. Box 1199, Hightstown, NJ 08520; 3 Marilyn Ct., Lawrenceville, NJ 08648 Tel 201-329-6981.

NM Pub Co, *(New Mexico Publishing Co.; 0-9622468),* P.O. Box 1272, Santa Fe, NM 87504 Tel 505-473-9854. Do not confuse with Univ. of New Mexico Pr.

Noahs Ark, *(Noah's Ark Publishing Co.; 0-9619082),* 8323 SW Freeway, Suite 250, Houston, TX 77074 (SAN 243-1165) Tel 713-771-7143.

Nocaine, *(Nocaine; 0-9626964),* P.O. Box 5273, Chatsworth, CA 91313; 21606 Devonshire St., Chatsworth, CA 91313 Tel 805-259-6089.

Noles Pub, *(Noles Publishing Co.; 0-9624731),* P.O. Box 38, Buffalo, NY 14209; 780 Maryvale Dr., Cheektowaga, NY 14225 Tel 716-634-0888; Dist. by: Johnhill Advertising, Inc., 210 Cornwall Ave., Buffalo, NY 14215 (SAN 630-4079) Tel 716-892-0005.

Non Fiction Pubns, *(Non-Fiction Pubns. Corp.; 0-913279),* P.O. Box 129, Island Park, NY 11558 (SAN 285-9106) Tel 516-431-2933.

Nonpareil Bks *Imprint of* **Godine**

Noodle Pr, *(Noodle Pr.; 0-9601022),* P.O. Box 42542, Washington, DC 20015 (SAN 208-7871) Tel 202-363-5078.

North Atlantic, *(North Atlantic Bks.; 0-938190; 0-913028; 1-55643),* Div. of Society of the Study of Native Arts & Science, 2800 Woolsey St., Berkeley, CA 94705 (SAN 203-1655) Tel 415-652-5309.

North Light Bks, *(North Light Bks.; 0-89134),* Div. of F & W Pubns., Inc., 1507 Dana Ave., Cincinnati, OH 45207 (SAN 287-0274) Tel 513-531-2222; Toll free: 800-289-0963.

North River, *(North River Pr., Inc.; 0-88427),* P.O. Box 309, Croton-on-Hudson, NY 10520 (SAN 202-1048) Tel 914-941-7175.

North Scale Co, *(North Scale Institute Publishing Co.; 0-916299),* P.O. Box 27555, San Francisco, CA 94127 (SAN 295-7418); 2205 Taraval St., San Francisco, CA 94116 (SAN 295-7426) Tel 415-759-9491.

North-South Bks NYC, *(North-South Bks.; 1-55858),* Subs. of Nord-Sud Verlag (SZ), ; Orders to: 1133 Broadway, Suite 1016, New York, NY 10010 (SAN 251-2459) Tel 212-463-9736; Toll free: 800-282-8257.

North Star, *(North Star Pr. of St. Cloud; 0-87839),* P.O. Box 451, Saint Cloud, MN 56302-0451 (SAN 203-7491) Tel 612-253-1636.

Northcross Hse, *(Northcross Hse.; 0-9617256),* 9662 Roanoke Rd., Elliston, VA 24087 (SAN 663-5725) Tel 703-268-5005.

Northland
See Northland AZ

Northland AZ, *(Northland Publishing; 0-87358),* Div. of Justin Industries, P.O. Box N, Flagstaff, AZ 86002 (SAN 202-9251) Tel 602-774-5251; Toll free: 800-346-3257. Do not confuse with Northland Publishing, Menomonie, WI.

Northland Pr, *(Northland Pr.; 0-9620280),* P.O. Box 62, Boon, MI 49618-0062 (SAN 248-5818); 4198 S. 27th Rd., Cadillac, MI 49601-9641 (SAN 248-5826) Tel 616-775-4095. Do not confuse with companies with the same name in Winona, MN, Flagstaff, AZ.

Northwest Pub, *(Northwestern Publishing Hse.; 0-8100),* 1250 N. 113th St., Milwaukee, WI 53226-0975 (SAN 206-7943) Tel 414-475-6600; P.O. Box 26975, Milwaukee, WI 53226-0975 (SAN 665-7494).

Northwind Pr, *(Northwind Pr.; 0-945887),* Div. of OZ Enterprises, Inc., P.O. Box 637, 800 Thompson Rd., Sandpoint, ID 83864 (SAN 247-8447) Tel 208-263-7756.

Northword, *(NorthWord Pr., Inc.; 0-942802; 1-55971),* P.O. Box 1360, Minocqua, W 54548 (SAN 240-4842) Tel 715-356-9800; Toll free: 800-336-5666 (orders only); Dist. by: Bookmen, Inc., 525 N. Third St., Minneapolis, MN 55401 (SAN 169-409X) Tel 612-341-3333; Toll free: 800-328-8411; Dist. by: Portland News Co., 270 Western Ave., P.O. Box 1728, South Portland, ME 04104 (SAN 169-3093) Tel 207-774-2633; Dist. by: Baker & Taylor Bks., Eastern Div., 50 Kirby Ave., Somerville, NJ 08876 (SAN 169-4901) Tel 201-722-8000; Toll free: 800-435-1845; 800-352-4833 (in New Jersey); Dist. by: Baker & Taylor Bks., Western Div., 380 Edison Way, Reno, NV 89564 (SAN 169-4464) Tel 702-786-6700; Toll free: 800-648-3540; Dist. by: Baker & Taylor Bks., Midwestern Div., 501 S. Gladiolus St., Momence, IL 60954 (SAN 169-2100) Tel 815-472-2444; Toll free: 800-435-5111; 800-892-1892 (in Illinois); Dist. by: Baker & Taylor Bks., Southern Div., Mt. Olive Rd., Commerce, GA 30529 (SAN 169-1503) Tel 404-335-5000; Toll free: 800-241-6004; 800-282-6850 (in Georgia); Dist. by: Ingram Bk. Co., 1125 Heilquaker Blvd., La Vergne, TN 37086 (SAN 169-7978) Tel 615-793-5000; Toll free: 800-937-8000 (orders only).

Norton, *(Norton, W. W., & Co., Inc.; 0-393),* 500 Fifth Ave., New York, NY 10110 (SAN 202-5795) Tel 212-354-5500; Toll free: 800-223-2584; 800-233-4830 (orders). *Imprints:* NortonC (Norton College Division).

NortonC *Imprint of* **Norton**

Norwich Bulletin, *(Norwich Bulletin; 0-9621270),* 66 Franklin St., Norwich, CT 06360 (SAN 250-7935) Tel 203-887-9211.

Nova Media, *(Nova Media, Inc.; 0-9618567),* P.O. Box 414, Big Rapids, MI 49307 (SAN 668-0372) Tel 616-796-0144; 1724 N. State, Big Rapids, MI 49307 (SAN 668-0380).

Novelty Bks, *(Novelty Bks.; 0-9623353),* P.O. Box 2482, Norman, OK 73070-2482; 1722 NE 19th St., Oklahoma City, OK 73111 Tel 405-495-4607.

Noviysvet, *(Noviysvet; 1-878860),* Div. of H.O.A.S.C.A.N.I.M., Inc., 877 Montgomery St., Brooklyn, NY 11213 Tel 212-509-1378.

Now Comns, *(Now Communications Co.; 0-940175),* P.O. Box 5668, Austin, TX 78763 (SAN 664-3019); 2511 Hartford Rd., Austin, TX 78703 (SAN 664-3027) Tel 512-478-7109.

Ntrl Science Indus, *(Natural Science Industries, Ltd.; 1-878501),* 50-01 Rockaway Beach Blvd., Far Rockaway, NY 11691 Tel 718-945-5400.

NuBaby AL, *(NuBaby, Inc.; 0-9626614),* P.O. Box 030132, Tuscaloosa, AL 35403; 6309 Eastbrook Dr., Tuscaloosa, AL 35405 Tel 205-556-1011.

Nugget Pub, *(Nugget Publishing Co.; 0-9622684),* P.O. Box 60004, San Diego, CA 92166; 2240 Shelter Island Dr., San Diego, CA 92166 Tel 619-226-4028.

Nugget Truth Minist, *(Nugget of Truth Ministries, Inc.; 0-942847),* P.O. Box 33110, Tulsa, OK 74153 (SAN 667-7711); 3429 E. 56th Pl., Tulsa, OK 74135 (SAN 667-772X) Tel 918-747-9803; Dist. by: Spring Arbor Distributors, 10885 Textile Rd., Belleville, MI 48111 (SAN 158-9016) Tel 313-481-0900; Toll free: 800-395-9955; Dist. by: Riverside/World, 3040 Charlevoix Dr., Grand Rapids, MI 49546 (SAN 169-2666) Tel 616-940-2086; Toll free: 800-247-5111.

Numismatic Fine Arts, *(Numismatic Fine Arts International, Inc.),* Member of Association internationale des Numismatistes professionels, 10100 Santa Monica Blvd., 6th Flr., Los Angeles, CA 90067 (SAN 205-9029) Tel 213-278-1535; P.O. Box 378, Beverly Hills, CA 90212 (SAN 241-8029) Tel 213-282-7502.

Nutrition Encounter, *(Nutrition Encounter, Inc.; 0-944501),* P.O. Box 2736, Novato, CA 94948 (SAN 243-685X) Tel 415-883-5154.

Nutshell Enterprises, *(Nutshell Enterprises, Ltd.; 0-930723),* 3327 Charles St., Fallston, MD 20147 (SAN 677-6043) Tel 301-557-7583.

Nutshell Pub, *(Nutshell Publishing Co.; 0-942385),* 7095 Hollywood Blvd., No. 104, Hollywood, CA 90028 (SAN 666-9832) Tel 213-653-5928.

NVEM, *(New Visions Educational Materials; 0-9623407),* 4329 Second Ave., Los Angeles, CA 90008 Tel 213-294-2451.

NW Family Srvs, *(Northwest Family Services; 1-880220),* 4805 NE Glisan St., Portland, OR 97213 Tel 503-230-6377.

NW Island, *(Northwest Island Pubs.; 0-9629778),* 444 Guemes Island Rd., Anacortes, WA 98221 Tel 206-293-3721.

NW Monarch Pr, *(Northwest Monarch Pr.; 0-9626870),* P.O. Box 409, Hub Sta., Bronx, NY 10455; 2223 Homer Ave., Bronx, NY 10473 Tel 212-585-6340.

NY State Alliance, *(New York State Alliance for Arts Education; 0-9624123),* Empire State Plaza, Cultural Education Ctr., Rm. 9B38, Albany, NY 12230 Tel 518-473-0823.

NYC Law Dept, *(New York City Law Dept.; 0-9619599),* 100 Church St., New York, NY 10007 (SAN 245-9639) Tel 212-556-3300; Dist. by: City Bks., 1 Center St., Rm. 2223, New York, NY 10007 (SAN 630-1401) Tel 212-669-8245.

NYC Pub Co, *(New York City Publishing Co.; 0-9614772),* 37 W. 37th St., 4th Flr., New York, NY 10018 (SAN 696-0758) Tel 212-944-7480.

Nystrom, *(Nystrom; 0-88463; 0-7825),* Div. of Herff Jones, 3333 N. Elston Ave., Chicago, IL 60618 (SAN 203-5529) Tel 312-463-1144; Toll free: 800-621-8086. Do not confuse with Nystrom Publishing, Inc., Maple Grove, MN.

O E Wilson, *(Wilson, Olga E.; 0-9623513),* P.O. Box 16185, Plantation, FL 33318; 5420 NW 12th Ct., Lauderhill, FL 33313 Tel 305-791-1951.

Oak Creek Pr, *(Oak Creek Pr.; 0-9627589),* P.O. Box 498, Dripping Springs, TX 78620; 1007 Oak Springs Dr., Dripping Springs, TX 78620 Tel 512-858-4401; Dist. by: State Hse. Pr., P.O. Drawer 15247, Austin, TX 78761 (SAN 660-9651) Tel 512-454-1959.

Oak Knoll, *(Oak Knoll Bks.; 0-938768),* 414 Delaware St., New Castle, DE 19720 (SAN 216-2776) Tel 302-328-7232.

Oak Pr, *(Oak Pr.; 0-9615242),* 904 Broadway Ave., Wausau, WI 54401 (SAN 695-1643) Tel 715-842-7369.

Oak Tree Pubns, *(Oak Tree Pubns., Inc.; 0-916392; 0-86679),* Div. of Vizcom, Inc., P.O. Box 119, Stamford, CT 06904-0119 (SAN 211-4828) Tel 203-322-8977; Toll free: 800-626-1170. *Imprints:* Value Comm (Value Communications).

Observational, *(Observational Research Pubns. Co.; 0-942884),* 2961 Industrial Rd., No. 440, Las Vegas, NV 89109 (SAN 240-2629) Tel 805-496-3136.

Ocean Allen Pub, *(Ocean Allen Publishing; 0-917071),* 13130 Sundance Ave., San Diego, CA 92129 (SAN 655-2382) Tel 619-484-5401; Rte. 4, Box 369, Spokane, WA 99204 (SAN 691-4276) Tel 509-466-7095.

Ocean East, *(Ocean East Publishing, Inc.; 0-9607028),* 1655 71st Ct., Vero Beach, FL 32966 (SAN 239-0159) Tel 407-567-9899.

Oceana, *(Oceana Pubns., Inc.; 0-379),* 75 Main St., Dobbs Ferry, NY 10522 (SAN 202-5744) Tel 914-693-8100.

Oceana Educ Comm, *(Oceana Educational Communications; 0-89976),* Div. of Oceana Pubns., Inc., 75 Main St., Dobbs Ferry, NY 10522 (SAN 221-9425) Tel 914-693-8100.

Oceanus, *(Oceanus Institute, Inc.; 0-915189),* Learning Pl., Manset, ME 04656 (SAN 289-7784) Tel 207-244-5015; Dist. by: Door Hse., HCR33-145, Manset, ME 04656 (SAN 200-9064) Tel 207-244-5015.

Ocelot Pr, *(Ocelot Pr.; 0-912434),* P.O. Box 504, Claremont, CA 91711 (SAN 203-7602) Tel 714-621-2200.

Octameron Assocs, *(Octameron Assocs.; 0-917760; 0-945981),* 1900 Mount Vernon Ave., Alexandria, VA 22301-1302 (SAN 282-0714) Tel 703-836-5480; Dist. by: Dearborn Trade, 520 N. Dearborn St., Chicago, IL 60610 (SAN 211-2280) Tel 312-836-0466; Toll free: 800-621-9621 Ext. 270 (in Illinois).

Oddo, *(Oddo Publishing, Inc.; 0-87783),* Storybook Acres, Box 68, Fayetteville, GA 30214 (SAN 282-0757) Tel 404-461-7627.

Offset Hse, *(Offset Hse.),* P.O. Box 329, Essex, VT 05401-0329 (SAN 698-1496) Tel 802-878-4440; Dist. by: Creative Expressions, P.O. Box 456, Colchester, VT 05446 (SAN 200-5816).

Ohana Pr, *(Ohana Pr.; 0-9627275),* Div. of Loge International Corp., 2931 Poni Moi Rd., Honolulu, HI 96815 Tel 808-922-3716.

O'Hara, *(O'Hara, J. Philip, Inc., Pubs.; 0-87955),* Subs. of Scroll Pr., Inc., ; c/o Scroll Pr., Inc., 2858 Valerie Ct., Merrick, NY 11566 (SAN 202-5868) Tel 516-379-4283. Do not confuse with Betsy O'Hara, San Francisco, CA.

Ohio St U Pr, *(Ohio State Univ. Pr.; 0-8142),* 1070 Carmack Rd., Rm. 180 Pressey Hall, Columbus, OH 43210-1002 (SAN 202-8158) Tel 614-292-6930.

Ohio U Pr, *(Ohio Univ. Pr.; 0-8214),* Scott Quadrangle, Athens, OH 45701 (SAN 282-0773) Tel 614-593-1155; Orders to: C.U.P. Services, Box 6525, Ithaca, NY 14851 (SAN 244-8068) Tel 607-277-2211; Toll free: 800-666-2211.

Okpaku Communications, *(Okpaku Communications Corp.; 0-89388),* Div. of Third Pr. Review of Bks. Co., 222 Forest Ave., New Rochelle, NY 10804 (SAN 202-5701) Tel 914-632-2355.

Old Amer Pr, *(Old American Pr.; 0-9622541),* 506 Joe Carrol St., Tahlequah, OK 74464 Tel 918-456-4849.

Old Fort Niagara Assn, *(Old Fort Niagara Assn., Inc.; 0-941967),* P.O. Box 169, Youngstown, NY 14174 (SAN 666-7783); Ft. Niagara State Pk., Youngstown, NY 14174 (SAN 666-7791) Tel 716-745-7611.

Old Harbor Pr, *(Old Harbor Pr.; 0-9615529),* P.O. Box 97, Sitka, AK 99835 (SAN 695-880X) Tel 907-747-3584.

Old Saltbox Pub Hse, *(Old Saltbox Publishing Hse., Inc.; 0-9626162),* 40 Felt St., Salem, MA 01970 (SAN 630-4583) Tel 508-741-3458.

Old Violin, *(Old Violin-Art Publishing; 0-918554),* Affil. of Hobby, Box 500, 225 S. Cooke St., Helena, MT 59624 (SAN 209-9756) Tel 406-442-8963.

Oliver-Nelson, *(Oliver-Nelson; 0-8407),* Div. of Thomas Nelson Pubs., Nelson Pl. at Elm Hill Pike, Nashville, TN 37214 (SAN 689-1470) Tel 615-889-9000; Toll free: 800-251-4000.

Olympic Pub, *(Olympic Publishing, Inc.; 0-940828),* 7450 Oak Bay, Port Ludlow, WA 98365 (SAN 219-6417) Tel 206-437-2277.

Olympus Pub Co, *(Olympus Publishing Co.; 0-913420),* 1670 E. 13th, S., Salt Lake City, UT 84105 (SAN 202-8204) Tel 801-583-3666.

OMF Bks, *(OMF Bks.; 0-85363),* Div. of Overseas Missionary Fellowship, P.O. Box 101208, Denver, CO 80210-1208 (SAN 211-8351); Toll free: 800-422-5330; 10 W. Dry Creek Cir., Littleton, CO 80122.

Omni Hawthorne, *(Omni Pubns.; 0-88418),* 13801 S. Inglewood Ave., P.O. Box 216, Hawthorne, CA 90251 (SAN 202-1315) Tel 213-772-3920.

Omniun, *(Omniun; 0-944204),* P.O. Box 5020, Kukuihaele, HI 96727 (SAN 243-1912); Main Government Rd., Waipio Valley, HI 96727 (SAN 243-1920) Tel 808-775-0207.

One Hund Twenty Creat, *(120 Creative Corner; 0-912773),* 4175 Lovell Rd., Box 18, Circle Pines, MN 55014 (SAN 283-1252) Tel 612-784-8375.

One Percent, *(One Percent Publishing; 0-935442),* 2888 Bluff St., Suite 143, Boulder, CO 80301 (SAN 216-1702).

One Ten Records, *(One Ten Records; 0-9605778),* 110 Chambers St., New York, NY 10007 (SAN 216-5066) Tel 212-964-2296.

O'Neill Pr, *(O'Neill Pr.; 0-930970),* 305 Great Neck Rd., Waterford, CT 06385 (SAN 212-1239).

Online Pr, *(Online Pr., Inc.; 1-879399),* 14320 NE 21st St., Suite 18, Bellevue, WA 98007 Tel 206-641-3434; Dist. by: Publisher's Group West, 4065 Hollis, Emeryville, CA 94608 (SAN 202-8522) Tel 415-658-3453; Toll free: 800-365-3453.

OnTrack Inc, *(OnTrack, Inc.; 0-927971),* 560 S. State, Suite B2, Orem, UT 84058 Tel 801-225-2136.

Onyx *Imprint of NAL-Dutton*

OP Inc, *(Organization Plus, Inc.; 0-9623354),* 8203 Gwinett Rd., Richmond, VA 23286-4335 Tel 804-741-4284.

OPC, *(Our Publishing Co., Inc.; 0-9603632),* 38764 N. Gratton Rd., Lake Villa, IL 60046 (SAN 213-7852) Tel 708-356-5944.

Open Books, *(Open Bks.; 0-931416),* 1631 Grant St., Berkeley, CA 94703 (SAN 211-7517).

Open Hand, *(Open Hand Publishing, Inc.; 0-940880),* P.O. Box 22048, Seattle, WA 98122 (SAN 219-6174) Tel 206-323-3868; Dist. by: Talman Co., 150 Fifth Ave., New York, NY 10011 (SAN 200-5204) Tel 212-620-3182; Toll free: 800-537-8894 (orders only).

Open My World, *(Open My World Publishing; 0-941996),* P.O. Box 15011, San Diego, CA 92175 (SAN 238-602X) Tel 619-588-5389; Dist. by: Educational Activities, Inc., 1937 Grand Ave., Baldwin, NY 11510 (SAN 207-4400) Tel 516-223-4666; Toll free: 800-645-3739; Dist. by: Perma Bound Bks., 617 E. Vandalia Rd., Jacksonville, IL 62650 (SAN 169-202X) Tel 217-243-5451; Toll free: 800-637-6581.

Opening Doors, *(Opening Doors Bks.; 1-877829),* 14 School St., Bristol, VT 05443 Tel 802-897-7022.

Opie Pub, *(Opie Publishing; 0-9623964),* 15 Cedar St., Binghampton, NY 13905 Tel 607-722-8844.

Opportunities Learn, *(Opportunities for Learning, Inc.; 0-86703),* P.O. Box 8103, Mansfield, OH 44901 (SAN 216-6895); 941 Hickory Ln., Mansfield, OH 44901 Tel 419-589-1760.

Optext, *(Optext; 0-9611266),* Div. of Optext Design Typography, 405 N. Wabash, Chicago, IL 60611-3517 (SAN 282-9843) Tel 312-321-1211; Dist. by: Bookpeople, 2929 Fifth St., Berkeley, CA 94710 (SAN 168-9517) Tel 415-549-3030; Toll free: 800-999-4650; Dist. by: New Leaf Distributing Co., 5425 Tulane Dr., SW, Atlanta, GA 30336-2323 (SAN 169-1449) Tel 404-691-6996; Toll free: 800-326-2665; Dist. by: Distributors, The, 702 S. Michigan, South Bend, IN 46618 (SAN 169-2488) Tel 219-232-8500; Toll free: 800-348-5200; Dist. by: DeVorss & Co., P.O. Box 550, Marina del Rey, CA 90294 (SAN 168-9886) Tel 213-870-7478; Toll free: 800-843-5743 (bookstores only); 800-331-4719 (in California); Dist. by: Children's Small Pr. Collection, 719 N. Fourth Ave., Ann Arbor, MI 48104 (SAN 200-514X) Tel 313-668-8056; Dist. by: Island Pacific Northwest, P.O. Box 999, Eastsound, WA 98245 (SAN 630-4281) Tel 206-376-5005; Toll free: 800-828-2006.

Optimalearning, *(Optimalearning Co.; 1-878245),* 88 Belvedere St., Suite D, San Rafael, CA 94901 Tel 415-459-4474; Toll free: 800-672-1717.

Optimum Res Inc, *(Optimum Resource, Inc.; 0-911787; 1-55913),* 10 Station Pl., Norfolk, CT 06058 (SAN 264-2743) Tel 203-542-5558; Toll free: 800-327-1473.

OR Students Writing, *(Oregon Students Writing & Art Foundation; 0-9616058),* P.O. Box 2100, Portland, OR 97208-2100 (SAN 698-0546) Tel 503-280-6333; 1826 SE 54th Ave., Portland, OR 97206 (SAN 698-2468) Tel 503-232-7737.

Orchard Bks Watts, *(Orchard Bks.; 0-531),* 387 Park Ave., S., New York, NY 10016 (SAN 243-2595) Tel 212-686-7070; Toll free: 800-672-6672.

Orchard Hse MA, *(Orchard Hse., Inc.; 0-933510; 1-878172),* 112 Balls Hill Rd., Concord, MA 01742 (SAN 285-0796) Tel 508-369-0467; Toll free: 800-423-1303.

Oregon Hist, *(Oregon Historical Society Pr.; 0-87595),* 1230 SW Park Ave., Portland, OR 97205-2483 (SAN 202-8301) Tel 503-222-1741.

Oregon Info, *(Oregon Information; 0-9630050),* P.O. Box 3211, Portland, OR 97208 Tel 503-624-9469.

Oriel Pr, *(Oriel Pr.; 0-938628),* 2020 SW Kanan, Portland, OR 97201 (SAN 282-0870) Tel 503-245-6696; Dist. by: Childrens Small Pr. Collection, The, 719 N. Fourth Ave., Ann Arbor, MI 48104 (SAN 200-514X) Tel 313-668-8056; Toll free: 800-221-8056.

Origami Intl, *(Origami International, Ltd.; 1-879610),* 1071 Fairfield Ave., Suite 57, Eugene, OR 97402 Tel 503-688-3956.

Origin Syst, *(Origin Systems, Inc.; 0-929373),* 110 Wild Basin Rd., No. 230, Austin, TX 78746 (SAN 655-7457) Tel 512-328-5490; Toll free: 800-999-4939.

Orinda Art Coun, *(Orinda Art Council; 0-9613069),* P.O. Box 121, Orinda, CA 94563 (SAN 294-6408) Tel 415-254-6744.

Oryx Pr, *(Oryx Pr.; 0-912700; 0-89774),* 4041 N. Central, Suite 700, Phoenix, AZ 85012-3330 (SAN 220-0201) Tel 602-265-2651; Toll free: 800-279-6799.

Other Eye, *(Other Eye Exercises; 0-926178),* P.O. Box 617, Kirkland, WA 98083; 12242 NE 70th, Kirkland, WA 98033 Tel 206-822-9156.

Our Child Pr, *(Our Child Pr.; 0-9611872),* 800 Maple Glen Ln., Wayne, PA 19087 (SAN 682-272X) Tel 215-964-0606.

Our Sunday Visitor, *(Our Sunday Visitor, Publishing Div.; 0-87973),* 200 Noll Plaza, Huntington, IN 46750 (SAN 202-8344) Tel 219-356-8400; Toll free: 800-348-2440.

Outdoor Bks, *(Outdoor Bks., Nature Series, Inc.; 0-942806),* 3813 Fenchurch Rd., Baltimore, MD 21218 (SAN 238-8561) Tel 301-243-1179.

Outdoor Pict, *(Outdoor Pictures; 0-911080),* P.O. Box 277, Anacortes, WA 98221 (SAN 203-7815) Tel 206-679-4837.

Outlaw MT, *(Outlaw Bks.; 0-945960),* P.O. Box 4466, Bozeman, MT 59772 (SAN 250-2151); 512 N. Fifth, Bozeman, MT 59772 (SAN 250-216X) Tel 406-586-7248.

Outlet Bk Co, *(Outlet Bk. Co.; 0-87000; 0-517),* Affil. of Crown Publishing Co., Inc., 225 Park Ave., S., New York, NY 10003 (SAN 200-2620) Tel 212-254-1600; Toll free: 800-526-4264; 800-726-0600 (customer service); Orders to: Random House, Inc., 400 Hahn Rd., Westminster, MD 21157 (SAN 202-5507) Tel 301-848-1900; Toll free: 800-733-3000. Promotional books of all kinds; remainders, reprints, imports, original publications. *Imprints:* Chatham River Pr (Chatham River Press); Greenwich Hse (Greenwich House).

Outrider Pr, *(Outrider Pr.; 0-9621039),* 1004 E. Steger Rd., Suite C3, Crete, IL 60417-1362 (SAN 250-4057) Tel 708-672-6630.

Overcomer Pr, *(Overcomer Pr., Inc.; 0-942504),* Editorial Vencedor, 310 W. Main St., P.O. Box 248, Owosso, MI 48867 (SAN 238-1834) Tel 517-725-7888.

Overlook Pr, *(Overlook Pr.; 0-87951),* 149 Wooster St., 4th Flr., New York, NY 10012 (SAN 202-8360) Tel 212-477-7162; Orders to: R.R. 1, Box 496, Woodstock, NY 12498 (SAN 663-6527); Dist. by: Viking Penguin, Inc., 40 W. 23rd St., New York, NY 10010 (SAN 200-2442) Tel 212-337-5200; Toll free: 800-631-3577.

Owl Pub CA, *(Owl Publishing; 0-9626686),* 1450 Harbor Island Dr., San Diego, CA 92101 Tel 619-491-1665.

Ox Bow, *(Ox Bow Pr.; 0-918024),* P.O. Box 4045, Woodbridge, CT 06525 (SAN 210-2501) Tel 203-387-5900.

Oxford U Pr, *(Oxford Univ. Pr., Inc.; 0-19; 0-917000; 0-904147; 0-947946; 1-85221),* 200 Madison Ave., New York, NY 10016 (SAN 202-5884) Tel 212-679-7300; Toll free: 800-334-4249; Orders to: 2001 Evans Rd., Cary, NC 27513 (SAN 202-5892) Tel 919-677-0977; Toll free: 800-451-7556.

Oxmoor Hse, *(Oxmoor Hse., Inc.; 0-8487),* Div. of Southern Progress Corp., P.O. Box 2262, Birmingham, AL 35201 (SAN 205-3462) Tel 205-877-6249; Toll free: 800-633-4712; Dist. by: Little, Brown & Co., 34 Beacon St., Boston, MA 02108 (SAN 200-2205) Tel 617-227-0730; Toll free: 800-343-9204.

Oyster River Pr, *(Oyster River Pr.; 0-9617481),* 20 Riverview Rd., Durham, NH 03824 (SAN 664-2128) Tel 603-868-5006.

P A Bell Enterps, *(Bell, P. A., Enterprises; 0-9621056),* 4201 Palmetto Way, San Diego, CA 92103 (SAN 250-586X) Tel 619-291-1636.

P Andersen, *(Andersen, Paul; 0-9604720),* P.O. Box 2184, Laguna Hills, CA 92654 (SAN 215-1286).

P Bedrick Bks, *(Bedrick, Peter, Bks.; 0-911745; 0-87226),* 2112 Broadway, Rm. 318, New York, NY 10023 (SAN 263-9335) Tel 212-496-0751; Dist. by: Publishers Group West, 4065 Hollis St., Emeryville, CA 94608 (SAN 202-8522) Tel 415-658-3453; Toll free: 800-365-3453. *Imprints:* Bedrick Blackie (Bedrick/Blackie).

P D Maloney, *(Maloney, P. Dennis; 0-940305),* 405 W. 36th St., Suite 200, Anchorage, AK 99503 (SAN 664-242X) Tel 907-561-4603.

P E Randall Pub, *(Randall, Peter E.; 0-914339),* Nobles Island Market St., P.O. Box 4726, Portsmouth, NH 03801 (SAN 223-0496) Tel 603-431-5667.

P Erickson, *(Erickson, Phoebe; 0-9613390),* P.O. Box 46, Hartland, VT 05048 (SAN 657-1077) Tel 802-436-2788.

P F Skolout, *(Skolout, Patricia Farris; 0-9625712),* 3122 Spring Meadow Dr., Colorado Springs, CO 80906 Tel 719-576-0318.

P Goodrich, *(Goodrich/Patricia; 0-9625348),* P.O. Box 190, Richlandtown, PA 18955 Tel 215-538-0268.

P-H, *(Prentice Hall; 0-13),* Div. of Simon & Schuster, Inc., 15 Columbus Cir., New York, NY 10023 (SAN 200-2175) Tel 212-373-8500; Toll free: 800-922-0579; Dist. by: Prentice Hall Pr., 200 Old Tappan Rd., Old Tappan, NJ 07675 (SAN 215-3939) Tel 201-767-5937. *Imprints:* Busn (Business & Professional Division); Harraps (Harrap's); Parker Publishing Co (Parker Publishing Company); Reston (Reston).

P Hunt, *(Hunt, Paul),* P.O. Box 10907, Burbank, CA 91510 (SAN 281-3777) Tel 818-845-0460.

P J Neuberger, *(Neuberger, Phyllis J.; 0-9610050),* 5855 Sheridan Rd., Chicago, IL 60660 (SAN 262-9607) Tel 312-334-7744; c/o Ten Plus, Inc., Thomas Graphics, Inc., 547 S. Clark St., Chicago, IL 60605 (SAN 262-9615) Tel 312-922-1301.

P Lang Pubs, *(Lang, Peter, Publishing, Inc.; 0-8204),* Subs. of Verlag Peter Lang AG (SZ), 62 W. 45th St., 4th Flr., New York, NY 10036-4202 (SAN 241-5534) Tel 212-302-6740; 140 Second St., Suite 604, San Francisco, CA 94105 (SAN 241-7456) Tel 415-979-0305.

P M O'Brien, *(O'Brien, P. M.; 0-9620540),* 7213 Edgewater Ct., Eau Claire, WI 54703 (SAN 248-8973) Tel 715-832-4440.

P T Ryan, *(Ryan, Perry T.; 0-9625504),* Atty. at Law, Rte. 3, Breckwood, Hardinsburg, KY 40143 Tel 502-756-2330.

PA Coun Churches, *(Pennsylvania Council of Churches; 0-9618164),* 900 S. Arlington Ave., Rm. 100, Harrisburg, PA 17109-5089 (SAN 666-7341) Tel 717-545-4761.

Pacif NW Natl Pks, *(Pacific Northwest National Parks & Forests Assn.; 0-914019),* 83 S. King St., Suite 212, Seattle, WA 98104 (SAN 286-8504) Tel 206-553-7958.

Pacific Bks, *(Pacific Bks., Pubs.; 0-87015),* P.O. Box 558, Palo Alto, CA 94302-0558 (SAN 202-8468) Tel 415-965-1980.

Pacific Pr Pub Assn, *(Pacific Pr. Publishing Assn.; 0-8163),* P.O. Box 7000, Boise, ID 83707-1000 (SAN 202-8409) Tel 208-465-2500; Toll free: 800-447-7377.

Pacific Sci Ctr, *(Pacific Science Ctr.; 0-935051),* 200 Second Ave., N, Seattle, WA 98109 (SAN 694-5244) Tel 206-443-2001.

Pacific Search, *(Pacific Search Pr.; 0-914718; 0-931397),* P.O. Box 18000, Florence, OR 97439 (SAN 202-8476) Tel 206-385-6082.

Pacific Shoreline, *(Pacific Shoreline Pr.; 0-932967),* P.O. Box 217, Temple City, CA 91780 (SAN 689-9897) Tel 818-287-4767.

Padakami Pr, *(Padakami Pr.; 0-9628914),* 23 Dana St., Forty-Fort, Kingston, PA 18704 Tel 717-287-5441.

Padaran Pubns, *(Padaran Pubns.; 1-877945),* P.O. Box 6417, Deltona, FL 32728 Tel 407-321-9610.

Padre Pio Pubs, *(Padre Pio Pubs.; 0-9615916),* P.O. Box 468, Patagonia, AZ 85624 (SAN 696-8864) Tel 602-394-2018; 223 Duquesne Ave., Patagonia, AZ 85624 (SAN 696-8872).

Padre Prods, *(Padre Productions; 0-914598),* P.O. Box 840, Arroyo Grande, CA 93420 (SAN 202-8484) Tel 805-473-1947; Dist. by: BookLink Distributors, P.O. Box 840, 1715 Bee Canyon Rd., Grande, CA 93420 Tel 805-473-1947.

Paganiniana Pubns, *(Paganiniana Pubns., Inc.; 0-87666),* Div. of T.F.H. Pubns., Inc., P.O. Box 427, Neptune, NJ 07753 (SAN 209-309X) Tel 908-988-8400; Toll free: 800-631-2188.

Paideia MA, *(Paideia Pubns.; 0-913993),* P.O. Box 343, Ashfield, MA 01330 (SAN 287-7511) Tel 413-628-3838; P.O. Box 1096, Northampton, MA 01061 (SAN 241-9319) Tel 413-586-5153.

Paisley Bks, *(Paisley Bks.; 0-926611),* 510 N. Tenth St., Belen, NM 87002 Tel 505-864-7236.

Paisley Pub, *(Paisley Publishing; 0-922127),* P.O. Box 201853, Anchorage, AK 99520-1853 (SAN 251-0847) Tel 907-346-2789; Dist. by: Pacific Pipeline, Inc. (West Coast only), 19215 66th Ave., S., Kent, WA 98032 (SAN 208-2128) Tel 206-872-5523; Toll free: 800-444-7323 (orders); 800-562-4617 (in Washington); 800-426-4727 (in northern California, Idaho, Nevada, Montana, Oregon); Dist. by: Alaska News Agency, Inc. (in Alaska), 325 W. Potter Dr., Book Dept., Anchorage, AK 99502 (SAN 168-9274) Tel 907-563-3251. Do not confuse with Paisley Publishing, San Antonio, TX.

Pajari Pr, *(Pajari Pr.; 0-9624315),* 11104 Snow Heights Blvd., NE, Albuquerque, NM 87112 Tel 505-299-7733.

PAL Pr, *(P.A.L. Pr.; 0-938034),* P.O. Box 487, San Anselmo, CA 94960 (SAN 220-0791) Tel 415-453-8547.

Palace Pub, *(Palace Publishing; 0-932215),* R.D. 1, Box 320, Moundsville, WV 26041 (SAN 686-5763) Tel 304-843-1600; Toll free: 800-322-7262; Dist. by: Baker & Taylor Bks., Midwestern Div., 501 S. Gladiolus St., Momence, IL 60954 (SAN 169-2100) Tel 815-472-2444; Toll free: 800-435-5111; 800-892-1892 (in Illinois); Dist. by: Great Tradition, 750 Adrian Way, Suite 111, San Rafael, CA 94903 (SAN 200-5743) Tel 415-492-9382; Toll free: 800-275-2606; Dist. by: New Leaf Distributing Co., 5425 Tulane Dr., SW, Atlanta, GA 30336-2323 (SAN 169-1449) Tel 404-691-6996; Toll free: 800-326-2665.

Palisades Prodns, *(Palisades Productions, Inc.; 1-878890),* 29 Chesapeake Ave., Lake Hiawatha, NJ 07034 Tel 201-825-8805.

Palladium Bks, *(Palladium Bks., Inc.; 0-916211),* 5926 Lonyo Ave., Detroit, MI 48210 (SAN 294-9504) Tel 313-843-1275.

Palm Pub, *(Palm Publishing Co.; 0-9623503),* P.O. Box 362, Boca Raton, FL 33429; NE Second St., Boca Raton, FL 33429 Tel 407-338-0058. Do not confuse with Palm Publishing Co., Laguna Hills, CA.

Palm Springs Pub, *(Palm Springs Publishing; 0-914445),* 1380 Tamarisk Rd., Palm Springs, CA 92262 (SAN 289-663X) Tel 619-323-9968.

Palm Tree Ent, *(Palm Tree Enterprises; 0-9618755),* 1514 Roosevelt Ave., Landover, MD 20785 (SAN 668-761X) Tel 301-322-5510.

Palos Verdes, *(Palos Verdes Bk. Co.; 0-936848),* Div. of Morgan Pr., P.O. Box 456, Lomita, CA 90717 (SAN 218-4532).

Pan-Am Publishing Co, *(Pan-American Publishing Co.; 0-932906),* P.O. Box 1505, Las Vegas, NM 87701 (SAN 212-5366).

Pando Pubns, *(Pando Pubns.; 0-944705),* 540 Longleaf Dr., Roswell, GA 30075 (SAN 244-9048) Tel 404-587-3363.

Pandora's Treasures, *(Pandora's Treasures; 0-9605236),* 1609 Eastover Terr., Boise, ID 83706 (SAN 282-1036) Tel 208-342-4002.

Pangaea Pr, *(Pangaea Pr.; 0-9625534),* Div. of Pangaea Group, Inc., 483 S. Kirkwood Rd., Suite 183, Saint Louis, MO 63122 Tel 314-821-3871.

Panpipes Pr, *(Panpipes Pr.; 1-882046),* P.O. Box 25226, Los Angeles, CA 90025-0226 (SAN 248-2185) Tel 213-207-0832.

Pantheon, *(Pantheon Bks.; 0-394),* Div. of Random Hse., Inc., 201 E. 50th St., New York, NY 10022 (SAN 202-862X) Tel 212-872-8238; Toll free: 800-638-6460; Orders to: Random Hse., Inc., 400 Hahn Rd., Westminster, MD 21157 (SAN 202-5515) Tel 301-848-1900; Toll free: 800-733-3000 (orders).

Paper Bag, *(Paper Bag Players; 0-9606662),* 50 Riverside Dr., New York, NY 10024 (SAN 212-9566); Orders to: Walter Baker Co., 100 Chauncey St., Boston, MA 02111 (SAN 662-1074); Orders to: Eeyore Bookstore, 82nd & Madison Ave., New York, NY 10028 (SAN 662-1082).

Paper Memories, *(Paper Memories; 0-9626165),* P.O. Box 234, Glen Echo, MD 20812; 5308 Portsmouth Rd., Bethesda, MD 20816 Tel 301-229-6834.

Paper Press, *(Paper Pr.; 0-9618419),* 2852 San Antonio Dr., Walnut Creek, CA 94598 (SAN 667-6367) Tel 415-943-1232.

Paper Tiger Pap, *(Paper Tiger Paperbacks, Inc.; 0-933334),* 1512 NW Seventh Pl., Gainesville, FL 32603 (SAN 212-5374) Tel 904-371-7771; Dist. by: Hippocrene Bks., Inc., 171 Madison Ave., New York, NY 10016 (SAN 213-2060) Tel 212-685-4371.

Papillon Pr, *(Papillon Pr.; 0-9608826),* 1232 Vallecito Rd., Carpinteria, CA 93013 (SAN 213-1447) Tel 805-684-5038. Do not confuse with Papillon Pr., Saint Helena, CA.

Papyrus Pubs, *(Papyrus Pubs.; 0-943698),* P.O. Box 466, Yonkers, NY 10704 (SAN 238-079X) Tel 914-664-0840.

PAR Inc, *(P.A.R., Inc.; 0-913310; 0-89702),* Subs. of Abbott Park Assocs., Inc., 272 W. Exchange St., Providence, RI 02903 (SAN 203-0209) Tel 401-331-0130; Toll free: 800-556-7277.

Parable Pr, *(Parable Pr.; 0-917250),* 136 Gray St., Amherst, MA 01002 (SAN 208-4449) Tel 413-253-5634.

Parable Pub, *(Parable Publishing Hse.; 0-9624067),* R.D. 1, Box 1281, Charlotte, VT 05445; Mount Philo Rd., Charlotte, VT 05445 Tel 802-425-2155.

Parabola Bks, *(Parabola Bks.; 0-930407),* 656 Broadway, New York, NY 10012-2317 (SAN 219-5763) Tel 212-505-6200; Dist. by: New Leaf Distributing Co., 5425 Tulane Dr., SW, Atlanta, GA 30336 (SAN 169-1449) Tel 404-691-6996; Toll free: 800-326-2665; Dist. by: Bookpeople, 2929 Fifth St., Berkeley, CA 94710 (SAN 168-9517) Tel 415-549-3030; Toll free: 800-999-4650; Dist. by: Consortium Book Sales & Distribution, 287 E. Sixth St., Suite 365, Saint Paul, MN 55101 (SAN 200-6049) Tel 612-221-9035; Toll free: 800-283-3572; Dist. by: Inland Book Co., 140 Commerce St., East Haven, CT 06512 (SAN 200-4151) Tel 203-467-4257; Toll free: 800-243-0138.

Parabola Mag
See Parabola Bks

Paraclete MI, *(Paraclete Pr.; 0-9621150),* P.O. Box 624, Pentwater, MI 49449 (SAN 250-8907); 9458 N. Montgomery Blvd., Pentwater, MI 49449 (SAN 250-8915) Tel 616-869-8401. Do not confuse with Paraclete Pr., Orleans, MA.

Paradise Cay Pubns, *(Paradise Cay Pubns.; 0-939837),* 1001 Bridgeway, No. 405, Sausalito, CA 94965 (SAN 663-690X) Tel 415-381-4509.

Paradise NJ, *(Paradise Publishing; 0-9628933),* R. R. 1, Box 424, Highland Lakes, NJ 07422; Sheppard Ln., Highland Lakes, NJ 07422 Tel 201-764-6139.

Paradon Pub Co, *(Paradon Publishing Co.; 0-936750),* 2920 Dean Pkwy., Minneapolis, MN 55416 (SAN 222-1977) Tel 612-929-0303.

Parapan, *(Parapan; 0-9622764),* 1209 Parkwood Dr., Fort Collins, CO 80525 Tel 303-482-9303.

Parchment Pr, *(Parchment Pr.; 0-88428),* 1136 Lipscomb Dr., Nashville, TN 37204 (SAN 202-8670) Tel 615-292-6335; Toll free: 800-727-6335. Do not confuse with Parchment Pr., Washington, DC.

Parent-Child Pr, *(Parent-Child Pr.; 0-9601016; 0-939195),* P.O. Box 767, Altoona, PA 16603 (SAN 208-4333); 4201 Second Ave., Altoona, PA 16602 (SAN 662-7331) Tel 814-946-5213.

Parenting Pr, *(Parenting Pr.; 0-9602862; 0-943990),* P.O. Box 75267, Seattle, WA 98125 (SAN 215-6938); Toll free: 800-992-6657; 11065 Fifth Ave. NE, No. F, Seattle, WA 98125 (SAN 699-5500) Tel 206-364-2900.

Parents, *(Parents Magazine Pr.; 0-8193),* Div. of Gruner & Jahr, USA, Publishing, 685 Third Ave., New York, NY 10017 (SAN 202-8697) Tel 212-878-8700; Dist. by: Putnam Publishing Group, The, 200 Madison Ave., New York, NY 10016 (SAN 202-5531) Tel 212-951-8400; Toll free: 800-631-8571.

Park Pub Co, *(Park Publishing Co.; 0-9624004),* 8283 N. Hayden Rd., No. 130, Scottsdale, AZ 85258-2455 Tel 602-948-4232.

Parker Bros, *(Parker Brothers Publishing; 0-910313; 0-87372; 0-926088),* Div. of Parker Brothers, 50 Dunham Rd., Beverly, MA 01915 (SAN 241-4260) Tel 508-927-7600; Toll free: 800-225-0540.

Parker Dstb, *(Parker Distributing; 1-878406),* 11844 N. Delbert, Parker, CO 80134 Tel 303-841-2607.

Parker Publishing Co *Imprint of P-H*

Parkside Pub, *(Parkside Publishing Corp.; 0-942421),* Subs. of Parkside Medical Services, 205 W. Touhy Ave., Park Ridge, IL 60068 (SAN 667-0318) Tel 708-698-8586; Toll free: 800-221-6364; Dist. by: Inland Book Co., Inc., 254 Bradley St., East Haven, CT 06512 (SAN 200-4151) Tel 203-467-4257; Dist. by: New Leaf Distributing Co., 5425 Tulane Dr. S.W., Atlanta, GA 30336-2323 (SAN 169-1449) Tel 404-691-6996; Dist. by: Moving Bks., Inc., P.O. Box 20037, Seattle, WA 98102 (SAN 159-0685) Tel 206-762-1894; Toll free: 800-777-6683.

Parkwest Pubns, *(Parkwest Pubns., Inc.; 0-88186),* 238 W. 72nd St., New York, NY 10023 (SAN 264-6846) Tel 212-877-1040. *Imprints:* Tarquin (Tarquin).

Parmly Lib, *(Parmly Billings Library; 0-9613224),* 510 N. Broadway, Billings, MT 59101 (SAN 295-1347) Tel 406-657-8294.

Parnassus Imprints, *(Parnassus Imprints; 0-940160),* Box 335, Orleans, MA 02653 (SAN 217-0809); 21 Canal Rd., Orleans, MA 02653 (SAN 658-1366) Tel 508-255-2932.

Parnell Pub, *(Parnell Publishing; 0-940649),* P.O. Box 16432, Phoenix, AZ 85011 (SAN 664-8509); Toll free: 800-545-2778; 1034 E. Whitton, Phoenix, AZ 85014 (SAN 664-8517) Tel 602-279-2358.

Partnership Foundation, *(Partnership Foundation, The; 0-934538),* C/O Capon Springs & Farms, Capon Springs, WV 26823 (SAN 220-9918).

Pascal Pubs, *(Pascal Pubs.; 0-938836),* 21 Sunnyside Ave., Wellesley, MA 02181 (SAN 215-3319).

PASE Pubns, *(PASE Pubns.; 0-945661),* Div. of Ace Publishing, 161 S. Lincolnway, North Aurora, IL 60542 (SAN 247-3518) Tel 312-844-9600.

Passport Bks *Imprint of Natl Textbk*

Past Glories, *(Past Glories; 0-9619953),* 625 Orpington Rd., Baltimore, MD 21229-2128 (SAN 247-1647) Tel 202-394-4440.

Pastel Pubns, *(Pastel Pubns.; 0-925737),* 3202 E. Presidio Rd., Phoenix, AZ 85032; 3131 E. Thunderbird Rd., No. 8-123, Phoenix, AZ 80532 Tel 602-971-9058.

Patch As Patch, *(Patch As Patch Can; 0-9601896),* P.O. Box 843, Port Washington, NY 11050 (SAN 239-8575); 85 Highland Rd., Glen Cove, NY 11542 (SAN 241-8169) Tel 516-671-7342.

Pathway Bk Serv, *(Pathway Bk. Service),* Div. of MLES, Inc., Lowe-Village, Gilsum, NH 03448 (SAN 110-6430) Tel 603-357-0236; Toll free: 800-345-6665.

Pathway Pr, *(Pathway Pr.; 0-87148),* Div. of Church of God Publishing Hse., 1080 Montgomery Ave., Cleveland, TN 37311 (SAN 202-8727) Tel 615-476-4512; Toll free: 800-251-7216; 800-523-4849 (in Tennessee); 800-821-4179 (in Tennessee, trade only); 800-553-8506; Orders to: P.O. Box 2250, Cleveland, TN 37320-2250 (SAN 665-7567). Do not confuse with companies of the same name in Birmingham, AL, San Rafael, CA.

Pathwys Pr CA, *(Pathways Pr.; 0-9605022),* P.O. Box 60196-A, Palo Alto, CA 94306 (SAN 283-4367) Tel 415-961-7794; Dist. by: Bookpeople, 2929 Fifth St., Berkeley, CA 94710 (SAN 168-9517) Tel 415-549-3030; Toll free: 800-999-4650; Dist. by: New Leaf Distributing Co., 5425 Tulane Dr., SW, Atlanta, GA 30336-2323 (SAN 169-1449) Tel 404-691-6996; Toll free: 800-326-2665. Do not confuse with Pathways Pr., El Cajon, CA.

Patio Pubns, *(Patio Pubns.; 0-9696040),* 850 Woodhollow Ln., Buffalo Grove, IL 60090 (SAN 216-9223) Tel 312-259-8500.

Patrice Pr, *(Patrice Pr.; 0-935284; 1-880397),* 1701 S. Eighth St., Saint Louis, MO 63104 (SAN 203-1019) Tel 314-436-3242; Toll free: 800-367-9242 (in Missouri & USA).

Patricks Pr, *(Patrick's Pr.; 0-9609412; 0-944322),* P.O. Box 5189, Columbus, GA 31906 (SAN 274-466X); Toll free: 800-654-1052; 2210 Wynnton Rd., Suite 109, Columbus, GA 31906 (SAN 243-2773) Tel 404-322-1584; Dist. by: Educational Impressions, 210 Sixth Ave., P.O. Box 77, Hawthorne, NJ 07507 (SAN 274-4899) Tel 201-423-4666; Toll free: 800-451-7450; Dist. by: American Econo-Clad Service, P.O. Box 1777, Topeka, KS 66608 (SAN 169-2763) Tel 913-233-4252.

Patron *Imprint of* **Don Bosco Multimedia**

Paula Di Ed, *(Paula Di Educational Enterprises, Inc.; 0-9613130; 0-936543),* 181-21 Aberdeen Rd., Jamaica, NY 11432-1424 (SAN 294-6467) Tel 718-969-3320.

Paulist Pr, *(Paulist Pr.; 0-8091),* 997 MacArthur Blvd., Mahwah, NJ 07430 (SAN 202-5159) Tel 201-825-7300.

Paupieres Pub, *(Paupieres Publishing Co.; 0-944064),* 111 John St., Houma, LA 70360 (SAN 242-8334) Tel 504-876-9223.

Pawnee Pub, *(Pawnee Publishing Co., Inc.; 0-913688),* P.O. Box 630, Higginsville, MO 64037 (SAN 207-4036) Tel 816-394-2424.

Paws Four Pub, *(Paws IV Publishing; 0-934007),* P.O. Box 2364, Homer, AK 99603 (SAN 692-7890) Tel 907-235-7697.

PAZ Pub, *(PAZ Publishing; 0-942253),* Div. of PAZ Percussion, P.O. Box 2481, North Canton, OH 44720 (SAN 666-8100); 623 S. Main St., North Canton, OH 44720-0481 (SAN 666-8119) Tel 216-499-3701.

Pazific Queen, *(Pazific Queen Communications; 0-9629255),* 6195 Oak Crest Way, Los Angeles, CA 90042 Tel 213-259-8918.

PB, *(Pocket Bks.; 0-671),* Div. of Simon & Schuster, Inc., 1230 Ave. of the Americas, New York, NY 10020 (SAN 202-5922) Tel 212-698-7000; Toll free: 800-223-2336 (orders); 800-223-2348 (customer service); Dist. by: Prentice Hall Pr., 200 Old Tappan Rd., Old Tappan, NJ 07675 (SAN 215-3939) Tel 201-767-5937. *Imprints:* Archway (Archway Paperbacks); Minstrel Bks (Minstrel Books); WSP (Washington Square Press).

Peabody Harvard, *(Peabody Museum of Archaeology & Ethnology, Harvard Univ., Pubns. Dept.; 0-87365),* 11 Divinity Ave., Cambridge, MA 02138 (SAN 203-1426) Tel 617-495-3938; Dist. by: Harvard Univ. Pr., 79 Garden St., Cambridge, MA 02138 (SAN 200-2043) Tel 617-495-2600.

Peace Grows, *(Peace Grows, Inc.; 0-9619819),* 475 W. Market St., Akron, OH 44303 (SAN 693-0204) Tel 216-864-5442.

Peaceable Pub, *(Peaceable Pr.; 0-936001),* 4664 N. Rob's Ln., Bloomington, IN 47408 (SAN 696-6241) Tel 812-336-8396.

Peachtree Pubs, *(Peachtree Pubs., Ltd.; 0-931948; 0-934601; 1-56145),* 494 Armour Cir., NE, Atlanta, GA 30324 (SAN 212-1999) Tel 404-876-8761; Toll free: 800-241-0113.

Pearce Evetts, *(Pearce-Evetts Publishing; 0-936823),* 624 Ridgeview Dr., Pittsburgh, PA 15228-1706 (SAN 699-9271) Tel 412-344-5451; Toll free: 800-842-9571.

Peartree, *(Peartree; 0-935343),* P.O. Box 14533, Clearwater, FL 34629 (SAN 169-0981) Tel 813-531-4973; Dist. by: Baker & Taylor Bks., Southern Div., Mt. Olive Rd., Commerce, GA 30599 (SAN 169-1503) Tel 404-335-5000; Toll free: 800-241-6004; 800-282-6850 (in Georgia); Dist. by: Baker & Taylor Bks., Midwestern Div., 501 S. Gladiolus St., Momence, IL 60954 (SAN 169-2100) Tel 815-472-2444; Toll free: 800-435-5111; 800-892-1892 (in Illinois); Dist. by: Southern Bk. Service, 3625 E. Tenth Ct., Hialeah, FL 33013 (SAN 169-0981) Tel 305-836-4140; Toll free: 800-432-3356; Dist. by: Learning Plant, The, P.O. Box 17233, West Palm Beach, FL 33416 (SAN 630-4001) Tel 305-686-9456; Dist. by: Book Wholesalers, 3759 NW 16th St., Bay 10, Lauderhill, FL 33311 (SAN 200-8750) Tel 305-792-1988; Toll free: 800-330-9303 (in Florida).

Pecan Tree Pr, *(Pecan Tree Pr.; 0-938169),* P.O. Box 3824, Bryan, TX 77805 (SAN 659-7203) Tel 409-774-0124.

Pedlar Pr, *(Pedlar Pr.),* 53 Whittemore Rd., Sturbridge, MA 01566 (SAN 244-6839); Dist. by: Legacy Bks., P.O. Box 494, Hatboro, PA 19040 (SAN 202-2389) Tel 215-675-6762.

Peekan Pubns, *(Peekan Pubns., Inc.; 0-944791; 0-922996),* P.O. Box 513, Freeport, IL 61032 (SAN 245-4998); Toll free: 800-747-7731; 118 N. Powell, Freeport, IL 61032 (SAN 245-5005) Tel 815-235-9130.

Peel Prod, *(Peel Productions; 0-939217),* P.O. Box 185, Molalla, OR 97038-0185 (SAN 662-6726) Tel 503-829-6849.

Peer Amid Pr, *(Peer Amid Pr.; 0-9617715),* 545 Wisconsin, San Francisco, CA 94107 (SAN 665-1658) Tel 415-821-3652.

Peg Hoenack, *(Peg Hoenack's MusicWorks; 0-913500),* 8409 Seven Locks Rd., Bethesda, MD 20817 Tel 308-365-1818.

Pegasus Bks, *(Pegasus Bks., Ltd.; 0-929624),* 678 Massachusetts Ave., Boston, MA 02118-1820 (SAN 249-8820).

Pegasus Graphics, *(Pegasus Graphics; 0-942559),* 1352 Marys Lake Rd., Moraine Rte., Estes Park, CO 80517 (SAN 667-2698) Tel 303-586-3757.

Pelican, *(Pelican Publishing Co., Inc.; 0-911116; 0-88289; 1-56554),* 1101 Monroe St., Gretna, LA 70053 (SAN 212-0623) Tel 504-368-1175; Toll free: 800-843-1724; 800-843-4558 (in Louisiana); P.O. Box 189, Gretna, LA 70053 (SAN 658-1374).

Pelican Bks *Imprint of* **Viking Penguin**

Pelona Pr, *(Pelona Pr.; 0-9623455),* P.O. Box 1882, Joplin, MO 64802; 6642 Main St., Kansas City, MO 64113 Tel 816-523-8472; Dist. by: Sax Arts & Crafts, P.O. Box 51710, New Berlin, WI 53151 (SAN 630-3676) Tel 414-784-6880; Toll free: 800-558-6696.

Pen-Art, *(Pen-Art Pubs.; 0-941242),* 402 Fairview Ave., Westwood, NJ 07675 (SAN 211-3287) Tel 201-664-8412; Dist. by: New York Poetry Forum, Inc, 3035 Cherry St., No. 40, Hoquiam, WA 98550-3007 (SAN 200-8092).

Pen-Dec, *(Pen-Dec Pr.; 0-915199),* 3922 Monte Carlo, SE, Kentwood, MI 49508 (SAN 289-792X) Tel 616-942-0056.

Pen Notes, *(Pen Notes, Inc.; 0-939564),* 134 Westside Ave., Freeport, NY 11520 (SAN 107-3621) Tel 516-868-5753.

Pendergrass Pub, *(Pendergrass Publishing Co., Inc.; 0-88323),* P.O. Box 66, Phoenix, NY 13135 (SAN 203-0861) Tel 315-695-7261.

Pendulum Pr, *(Pendulum Pr., Inc.; 0-88301),* Academic Bldg., Saw Mill Rd., West Haven, CT 06516 (SAN 202-8808) Tel 203-933-2551.

Penguin Bks *Imprint of* **Viking Penguin**

Peniel Pubns, *(Peniel Pubns.; 0-945818),* 6135 Jones Rd., College Park, GA 30349 (SAN 247-9656) Tel 404-969-5871.

Peninsula WA, *(Peninsula Publishing, Inc.; 0-918146),* P.O. Box 412, Port Angeles, WA 98362 (SAN 210-1300) Tel 206-457-7550; Dist. by: Pacific Pipeline, Inc., 19215 66th Ave., S., Kent, WA 98032 (SAN 208-2128) Tel 206-872-5523; Toll free: 800-426-4727 (in Oregon, Idaho, Montana, Nevada, northern California); 800-562-4647 (in Washington).

Pennington, *(Pennington Trading Post; 0-911120),* c/o Eunice Pennington, Fremont, MO 63941 (SAN 204-9392).

Penns Valley, *(Penns Valley Pubs.; 0-931992),* Div. of PVP, Inc., 4104 York, Harrisburg, PA 17111 (SAN 202-1455) Tel 717-232-5844.

PennWell Bks, *(PennWell Bks.; 0-87814),* Div. of PennWell Publishing Co., 1421 S. Sheridan St., Tulsa, OK 74112 (SAN 282-1559) Tel 918-835-3161; Toll free: 800-752-9764 (orders only); Orders to: P.O. Box 21288, Tulsa, OK 74121 (SAN 282-1567) Tel 918-831-9421.

Penny Lane Pubns, *(Penny Lane Pubns., Inc.; 0-911211),* P.O. Box 425, Lenox Hill Sta., New York, NY 10021 (SAN 274-4961) Tel 212-570-2970.

Pennypress, *(Pennypress, Inc.; 0-937604),* 1100 23rd Ave., E., Seattle, WA 98112 (SAN 215-6954) Tel 206-325-1419.

Penrod-Hiawatha, *(Penrod/Hiawatha Co.; 0-942618),* 10116 M-140, Berrien Center, MI 49102 (SAN 238-5546) Tel 616-461-6993.

Penstemon Pr, *(Penstemon Pr.; 0-9613938),* 1218 18th Ave., Apt. 4, San Francisco, CA 94122 (SAN 679-176X) Tel 415-661-9314. Do not confuse with Penstemon Pr., Berkeley, CA.

Penworthy Pub, *(Penworthy Publishing Co.; 0-87617),* 219 N. Milwaukee St., Milwaukee, WI 53202 (SAN 630-2300) Tel 414-272-4889.

Perception Pubns, *(Perception Pubns.; 0-940406),* 1814 W. Seldon Ln., Phoenix, AZ 85021 (SAN 265-3931) Tel 602-997-2292.

Perdido Bay, *(Perdido Bay Pr., The; 0-933776),* 13082 Rosirito Pl., Pensacola, FL 32506 (SAN 215-1693) Tel 904-456-0517.

Peregrine Smith *Imprint of* **Gibbs Smith Pub**

Pergamon, *(Pergamon Pr., Inc.; 0-08),* Subs. of Maxwell Communications Corp., Maxwell Hse., Fairview Pk., Elmsford, NY 10523 (SAN 213-9022) Tel 914-592-7700; Orders to: Pergamon Pr., Front & Brown Sts., Riverside, NJ 08075-1197 Tel 609-461-6500; Toll free: 800-257-5755.

Perigee Bks *Imprint of* **Putnam Pub Group**

Perish Pr, *(Perish Pr.; 0-934038),* P.O. Box 75, Mystic, CT 06355 (SAN 212-789X) Tel 203-536-2304.

Periwinkle MA, *(Periwinkle Pr.; 0-9621650),* P.O. Box 354, White Horse Beach, MA 02381 (SAN 251-7523); 102 Cary Rd., White Horse Beach, MA 02381 (SAN 251-7531) Tel 508-224-6427; Dist. by: Krikorian Miller Assocs., Inc., 59 Middlesex Tpke., Bedford, MA 01730 (SAN 630-3137) Tel 617-275-6236. Do not confuse with companies with the same name in Woodland Hills, CA, Snohomish, WA.

Perk-Lo Pk Prodns, *(Perk-Lo Park Productions; 0-9626570),* P.O. Box 489, Redway, CA 95560; 145 D Rd., Garberville, CA 95440 Tel 707-923-9288.

Perma Bound, *(Perma-Bound Bks.; 0-8479; 0-8000; 0-7804),* Div. of Hertzberg-New Method, Inc., 617 E. Vandalia Rd., Jacksonville, IL 62650 (SAN 169-202X) Tel 217-243-5451; Toll free: 800-637-6581.

Permanent Pr, *(Permanent Pr., The; 0-932966; 1-877946),* Affil. of Second Chance Pr., R.D. 2, Noyac Rd., Sag Harbor, NY 11963 (SAN 212-2995) Tel 516-725-1101.

Perry Enterprises, *(Perry Enterprises; 0-941518),* P.O. Box 677, 856 N. Sage Dr., Pleasant Grove, UT 84062 (SAN 171-0281) Tel 801-226-1002.

Personal Prods, *(Personal Products Group, Inc.; 0-9629597),* 17510 Indiana St., Detroit, MI 48221 Tel 313-864-3407.

Perspect Indiana, *(Perspectives Pr.; 0-9609504; 0-944934),* P.O. Box 90318, Indianapolis, IN 46290-0318 (SAN 262-5059) Tel 317-872-3055.

Peter Pauper, *(Peter Pauper Pr., Inc.; 0-88088),* 202 Mamaroneck Ave., White Plains, NY 10601 (SAN 204-9449) Tel 914-681-0144; Toll free: 800-833-2311 (orders only). Do not confuse with Pauper Pr. Inc., Two Rivers, WI.

Peter Smith, *(Smith, Peter, Pub., Inc.; 0-8446),* 6 Lexington Ave., Magnolia, MA 01930 (SAN 206-8885) Tel 508-525-3562.

Petersons Guides, *(Peterson's Guides, Inc.; 0-87866; 1-56079),* P.O. Box 2123, Princeton, NJ 08543-2123 (SAN 200-2167); Toll free: 800-338-3282; 202 Carnegie Ctr., Princeton, NJ 08543 Tel 609-243-9111.

Petit Appetit, *(Petit Appetit; 0-9616883),* 9215 Ensley Ln., Leawood, KS 66206 (SAN 661-6496) Tel 913-383-3610; Dist. by: Baker & Taylor Bks., Midwestern Div., 501 S. Gladiolus St., Momence, IL 60954 (SAN 169-2100) Tel 815-472-2444; Toll free: 800-435-5111; 800-892-1892 (in Illinois).

Petra Pub Co, *(Petra Publishing Co.; 1-880015),* 938 E. Swan Creek Rd., Suite 301, Fort Washington, MD 20744 Tel 301-292-1534.

Petrified Forest Mus Assn, *(Petrified Forest Museum Assn.; 0-945695),* Park Rd., P.O. Box 277, Petrified Forest National Pk., AZ 86028 (SAN 247-7726) Tel 602-524-6228.

Petroglyph, *(Petroglyph Pr., Ltd.; 0-912180),* 201 Kinoole St., Hilo, HI 96720 (SAN 204-9457) Tel 808-935-6006; Dist. by: Pacific Trade Group, 94-527 Puahi St., Waupahu, HI 96797 (SAN 169-1635) Tel 808-671-6735.

PH-Enterp, *(PH Enterprises; 0-9629564),* 222 W. Fifth Ave., Collegeville, PA 19426 Tel 215-489-3451.

Phaidon Universe
See Universe

Phantom Pubns, *(Phantom Pubns., Inc.; 0-9625372),* 3657 Country Club Rd., Endwell, NY 13760 Tel 607-785-1726.

Pharmaco-Video Pubns, *(Pharmaco-Video Pubns.; 1-879278),* 117 E. Louisa St., No. 110, Seattle, WA 98102-3203 Tel 206-328-6466.

Pharos Bks NY, *(Pharos Bks.; 0-911818; 0-88687),* Div. of Scripps Howard, 200 Park Ave., New York, NY 10166 (SAN 211-7703) Tel 212-692-3830; Dist. by: St. Martin's Pr., Inc., 175 Fifth Ave., New York, NY 10010 (SAN 200-2132) Tel 212-674-5151; Toll free: 800-325-5525; Dist. by: World Almanac Education Div., 1278 W. Ninth St., Cleveland, OH 44113 (SAN 630-0294) Tel 216-621-7300; Toll free: 800-521-6600. *Imprints:* Sparkler Bks (Sparkler Books); World Almanac (World Almanac).

Phi Delta Kappa, *(Phi Delta Kappa Educational Foundation; 0-87367),* Eighth & Union, Box 789, Bloomington, IN 47402 (SAN 289-1859) Tel 812-339-1156.

Philmar Pub, *(Philmar Pubs.; 0-88100),* P.O. Box 402, Diablo, CA 94528 (SAN 262-0596) Tel 415-837-3490.

Philomel Bks *Imprint of* **Putnam Pub Group**

Philos Pub, *(Philosophical Publishing Co.; 0-932785),* RD 3, Clymeir Rd., Quakertown, PA 18951 (SAN 295-8430) Tel 215-536-5168.

Phoenix Educ Found, *(Phoenix Educational Foundation; 0-929354),* 462 Stevens Ave., No. 202, Solana Beach, CA 92075 (SAN 249-0919) Tel 619-481-2977.

Phoenix Pub, *(Phoenix Publishing; 0-914016; 0-914659),* Main St., Sugar Hill, NH 03585 (SAN 691-4209) Tel 603-823-8531. Do not confuse with companies with the same name in Redmond, WA, Newark, NJ.

Phunn Pubs, *(Phunn Pubs.; 0-931762),* P.O. Box 70, Elsah, IL 62028-0070 (SAN 212-128X) Tel 618-374-2551.

Pi Pr, *(Pi Pr., Inc.; 0-931420),* Box 23371, Honolulu, HI 96822 (SAN 669-2400); 3169-A Alika Ave., Honolulu, HI 96817 Tel 808-595-3426.

Piccadilly TX, *(Piccadilly Pr.; 0-9630147),* P.O. Box 50515, Austin, TX 78763; 4007 Sinclair Ave., Austin, TX 78756 Tel 512-453-2051.

Pickwick Pubs, *(Pickwick Pubs., Ltd.; 1-877830),* 177 Webster St., Suite A384, Monterey, CA 93940 Tel 408-375-1075.

Pictorial Hist, *(Pictorial Histories Publishing Co.; 0-933126; 0-929521),* 713 S. Third, W., Missoula, MT 59801 (SAN 212-4351) Tel 406-549-8488.

Pictorial Legends, *(Pictorial Legends; 0-939031),* Subs. of Event Co., 435 Holland Ave., Los Angeles, CA 90042 (SAN 662-8486) Tel 213-254-4416; Dist. by: Publishers Group West, 4065 Hollis St., Emeryville, CA 94608 (SAN 202-8522) Tel 415-658-3453; Toll free: 800-365-3453; Dist. by: Pacific Trade Group, 94-527 Puahi St., Waipahu, HI 96797 (SAN 169-1635) Tel 808-671-6735; Dist. by: Ingram Pr., 611 Fifth St. SE, Cedar Rapids, IA 52401-2158 (SAN 263-1709) Tel 319-366-5335.

Picture Bk Studio, *(Picture Bk. Studio, Ltd.; 0-88708; 0-907234),* 10 Central St., Saxonville, MA 01701 (SAN 293-8227) Tel 508-788-0911; Toll free: 800-462-1252. *Imprints:* Rabbit Ears (Rabbit Ears Storybook Classics).

Picture Me Bks, *(Picture Me Bks.; 1-878338),* 734 Mentor Rd., Akron, OH 44303 Tel 216-836-1236.

Picture This Bks, *(Picture This! Bks.; 0-9624673),* 5 Harvard Dr., Fort Mitchell, KY 41017 Tel 606-331-0547.

Pikestaff Pr, *(Pikestaff Pr., The; 0-936044),* Div. of Pikestaff Pubns., Inc., P.O. Box 127, Normal, IL 61761 (SAN 213-8654) Tel 309-452-4831.

Pilgrim NY, *(Pilgrim Pr., The United Church Pr.; 0-8298),* Div. of United Church Board for Homeland Ministries, 700 Prospect Ave., E., Cleveland, OH 44115-1100 (SAN 212-601X) Tel 212-736-3700; Dist. by: Publishers Distribution Ctr., P.O. Box C831, Rutherford, NJ 07070 (SAN 200-5018) Tel 201-939-6064; Toll free: 800-654-5129.

Pinata Pubns, *(Pinata Pubns.; 0-934925),* 427 Grand Ave., Oakland, CA 94610 (SAN 694-6062) Tel 415-893-6682.

Pine Isl Pr, *(Pine Island Pr.; 0-9620092),* 69 Pine Island Lake, Westhampton, MA 01027 (SAN 247-5510) Tel 413-527-5172.

Pine Tree NY, *(Pine Tree Pr.; 0-9629159),* 1904A N. George St., Rome, NY 13440 Tel 315-337-3314; Dist. by: North Country Bks., Inc., 18 Irving Pl., Utica, NY 13501 (SAN 110-828X) Tel 315-735-4877. Do not confuse with Pine Tree Pr. in Laguna Niguel, CA.

Pineapple MI, *(Pineapple Pr.; 1-878526),* P.O. Box 1531, East Lansing, MI 48826 Tel 517-332-1140. Do not confuse with Pineapple Pr., Inc., Sarasota, FL.

Pineapple Pr, *(Pineapple Pr., Inc.; 0-910923; 1-56164),* P.O. Drawer 16008, Southside Sta., Sarasota, FL 34239 (SAN 285-0850) Tel 813-952-1085. Do not confuse with Pineapple Pr., East Lansing, MI.

Pineapple Pubns, *(Pineapple Pubns.; 0-929249),* 24 Bridge St., Newport, RI 02840 (SAN 248-9864) Tel 401-847-0859.

Pink Inc, *(Pink, Inc.; 0-9622585),* P.O. Box 866, Atlantic Beach, FL 32233-0866 Tel 904-285-9276.

Pinto Pub, *(Pinto Publishing Co.; 0-925605),* 3610 Calle del Monte, NE, Albuquerque, NM 87110 Tel 505-268-1302.

Pioneer Farm, *(Pioneer Farm; 0-9614899),* Ohop Valley Rd., Eatonville, WA 98328 (SAN 693-2738) Tel 206-832-6923.

Piper, *(Piper Publishing; 0-87832),* Box 1, Blue Earth, MN 56013 (SAN 202-005X) Tel 507-526-5448.

Pippin Bks, *(Pippin Bks., Inc.; 0-9624993),* 8919 Old Pine Rd., Boca Raton, FL 33433 Tel 407-487-4508.

Pippin Pr, *(Pippin Pr.; 0-945912),* Gracie Sta., Box 92, 229 E. 85th St., New York, NY 10028 (SAN 247-8366) Tel 212-288-4920.

Pisces Pr CA, *(Pisces Pr., Inc.; 0-9623802),* P.O. Box 9352, Rancho Santa Fe, CA 92067; 6510 Monte Fuego, Rancho Santa Fe, CA 92067 Tel 619-755-0156. Do not confuse with companies with the same name in Lubbock, TX, Sun City, AZ.

Pisces Pr TX, *(Pisces Pr.; 0-938328),* 3209 26th St., Lubbock, TX 79410 (SAN 215-7993) Tel 806-799-4939. Do not confuse with Pisces Pr., Sun City, AZ.

Pittenbruach Pr, *(Pittenbruach Pr.; 0-938875),* P.O. Box 553, Northampton, MA 01061 (SAN 662-6688); 15 Walnut, Northampton, MA 01060 (SAN 662-6696).

Pittman Pub, *(Pittman Pub.; 0-9615382),* Rte. 1, Box 255, Aulander, NC 27805 (SAN 695-4456) Tel 919-332-2511.

Pixel Prods Pubns, *(Pixel Products & Pubns.; 0-935163),* R.D. 2, Box C110, Lock Haven, PA 17745 (SAN 695-3557) Tel 717-748-7064.

PJC Lrng Mtrls, *(PJC-Learning Materials; 0-931749),* 5080 Timberway Trail, Clarkston, MI 48346 (SAN 683-5120) Tel 313-620-2736.

PL *Imprint of* **HarperCollins**

Place in the Woods, *(Place in the Woods; 0-932991),* 3900 Glenwood Ave., Golden Valley, MN 55422-5302 (SAN 689-058X) Tel 612-374-2120; Dist. by: Bacon Pamphlet Service, Inc., Box 228B, Hand Hollow Rd., East Chatham, NY 12060 (SAN 200-5573) Tel 518-794-7722; Orders to: LTO Enterprises, 6036 N. Tenth Way, Phoenix, AZ 85014 (SAN 662-1805) Tel 602-265-7765; Dist. by: Midwest Library Service, 11443 St. Charles Rock Rd., Bridgeton, MO 63044-9986 (SAN 169-4243) Tel 314-739-3100; Dist. by: BookFare, 5609-2A Fishers Ln., Rockville, MD 20852 (SAN 135-292X).

Plan Par Ctrl CA, *(Planned Parenthood of Central California; 0-9610122),* 255 N. Fulton Ave., Fresno, CA 93701 (SAN 274-6662) Tel 209-486-2647.

Plan Parent, *(Planned Parenthood Federation of America, Inc.; 0-934586),* 810 Seventh Ave., New York, NY 10019 (SAN 205-1281) Tel 212-541-7800.

PLAN Pubs, *(PLAN Pubs.; 0-9625085),* R.R. 1, P.O. Box 88, Rushville, NE 69360 Tel 308-327-2064.

Plan Success, *(Plan for Success; 0-9628095),* 7720 Carroll Ave., No. 2, Takoma Park, MD 20912 Tel 301-270-2605.

Planet Playmates, *(Planet Playmates Co., Inc.; 0-9624497),* 8235 Mackall Rd., Saint Leonard, MD 20685 Tel 301-586-2043.

Planetary Pubns, *(Planetary Pubns.; 1-879052),* P.O. Box 66, Boulder Creek, CA 95006; Toll free: 800-372-3100; 14795 W. Park Ave., Boulder Creek, CA 95006 Tel 408-338-2161.

Platt & Munk Pubs *Imprint of* **Putnam Pub Group**

Platypus Bks, *(Platypus Bks., Ltd.; 0-930905),* 1315 Angelina, College Station, TX 77840-4854 (SAN 679-1727); Dist. by: Writers & Bks., 740 University Ave., Rochester, NY 14607 (SAN 156-9678) Tel 716-473-2590.

PLAY House, *(P.L.A.Y. Hse.; 0-9622543),* 4376 Stewart Ave., Los Angeles, CA 90066.

Play Schs, *(Play Schls. Assn.; 0-936426),* 9 E. 38th St., New York, NY 10016 (SAN 202-0076) Tel 212-725-6540.

Player Pr, *(Player Pr.; 0-9623966),* 139-22 Caney Ln., Rosedale, NY 11422 Tel 718-528-3285.

Players Pr, *(Players Pr., Inc.; 0-88734),* P. O Box 1132, Studio City, CA 91614 (SAN 239-0213) Tel 818-789-4980.

Playland Bks *Imprint of* **Putnam Pub Group**

Plays, *(Plays, Inc.; 0-8238),* 120 Boylston St., Boston, MA 02116 (SAN 202-0084) Tel 617-423-3157.

Playspaces
See Childs Play

Pleasant Co, *(Pleasant Co.; 0-937295; 1-56247),* 8400 Fairway Pl., Middleton, WI 53562 Tel 608-836-4848; Orders to: P.O. Box 998, Middleton, WI 53562-0998; Toll free: 800-233-0264.

Plenum Pr *Imprint of* **Plenum Pub**

Plenum Pub, *(Plenum Publishing Corp.; 0-306),* 233 Spring St., New York, NY 10013-1578 (SAN 201-9248) Tel 212-620-8000; Toll free: 800-221-9369. *Imprints:* Plenum Pr (Plenum Press).

Plough, *(Plough Publishing Hse., The; 0-87486),* Subs. of Hutterian Brethren Service Committee, Spring Valley Rte. 381 N., Farmington, PA 15437-9506 (SAN 202-0092) Tel 412-329-1100.

Plum Apple Pub, *(Plum Apple Publishing; 0-9616794),* 1401 Tower Rd., Winnetka, IL 60093 (SAN 659-9400) Tel 312-446-2079.

Plume *Imprint of* **NAL-Dutton**

Plus One Pub, *(Plus One Publishing, Inc.; 0-934822),* 625 N. Mansfield Ave., Hollywood, CA 90036 (SAN 213-1404) Tel 213-936-1783.

Plutonium Pr, *(Plutonium Pr.; 0-929611),* P.O. Box 61564, Phoenix, AZ 85082 (SAN 249-9673) Tel 602-956-9382.

Pnnywhstlrs Pr, *(Pennywhistler's Pr.; 0-9623456),* P.O. Box 2473, New York, NY 10108; 467 W. 46th St., New York, NY 10036 Tel 212-247-3231. Do not confuse with Pennywhistle Pr., Malibu, CA.

Pocahontas Pr, *(Pocahontas Pr., Inc.; 0-936015),* 2805 Wellesley Ct., Blacksburg, VA 24060-4126 (SAN 630-124X) Tel 703-951-0467; Dist. by: Baker & Taylor Bks., Western Div., 380 Edison Way, Reno, NV 89564 (SAN 169-4464) Tel 702-786-6700; Toll free: 800-348-5200; Dist. by: Baker & Taylor Bks., Eastern Div., 50 Kirby Ave., Somerville, NJ 08876 (SAN 169-4901) Tel 201-722-8000; Toll free: 800-435-1845; 800-352-4833 (in New Jersey); Dist. by: Baker & Taylor Bks., Midwestern Div., 501 S. Gladiolus St., Momence, IL 60954 (SAN 169-2100) Tel 815-472-2444; Toll free: 800-435-5111; 800-892-1892 (in Illinois); Dist. by: Midwest Library Service, 11443 St. Charles Rock Rd., Bridgeton, MO 63044-2789 (SAN 169-4243) Tel 314-739-3100; Dist. by: Yankee Bk. Peddler, Inc., Maple St., Contoocook, NH 03229 (SAN 169-4510) Tel 603-746-3102; Toll free: 800-258-3774; Dist. by: Coutts Library Service, Inc., 736 Cayuga St., Lewiston, NY 14092 (SAN 169-5401) Tel 716-754-8145; Dist. by: Blackwell North America, Inc., 1001 Fries Mill Rd., Blackwood, NJ 08012 (SAN 169-4596) Tel 609-629-0700; Toll free: 800-257-7341; 800-547-6426 (in Oregon); Dist. by: Praxis Pubns., Inc., P.O. Box 9869, Madison, WI 53715 (SAN 695-9989) Tel 608-244-5633; Dist. by: Independent Pubs. Marketing, 6824 Oaklawn Ave., Edina, MN 55435 (SAN 630-5725) Tel 612-920-9044; Toll free: 800-669-9044.

Pocumtuck Valley Mem, *(Pocumtuck Valley Memorial Assn.; 0-9612876),* Memorial Hall Museum, Deerfield, MA 01342 (SAN 211-2663) Tel 413-774-7476.

Poetry Unltd, *(Poetry Unlimited; 0-9614337),* 11709 Pawnee Dr., SW, Tacoma, WA 98499 (SAN 687-8326) Tel 206-588-7451.

Point *Imprint of* **Scholastic Inc**

Point Publications, *(Point Pubns.; 0-9620888),* P.O. Box 145, Point Lookout, NY 11569 (SAN 250-0434); 59 Cedarhurst Ave., Point Lookout, NY 11569 (SAN 250-0442) Tel 516-889-3526. Do not confuse with companies with the same name in Oakland, CA, Wayzata, MN.

Point View Pr, *(Point of View Pr.; 0-9624129),* P.O. Box 751, Forestville, CA 95436; 303 Burton Ave., Rohnert Park, CA 94928 Tel 707-664-0477.

Polanie, *(Polanie Publishing Co.; 0-911154),* 643 Madison St., NE, Minneapolis, MN 55413 (SAN 204-9031) Tel 612-379-9134.

Polaris AZ, *(Polaris Pr.; 0-9622985),* 1281 W. Elko St., Tucson, AZ 85704 Tel 602-887-7637. Do not confuse with other companies with the same name in Los Gatos, CA, Tigard, OR.

Polaris Pr, *(Polaris Pr.; 0-930504),* 16540 Camellia Terr., Los Gatos, CA 95030 (SAN 204-904X).

Polestar, *(Polestar Pubns.; 0-942044),* 620 S. Minnesota Ave., Sioux Falls, SD 57104 (SAN 239-474X) Tel 605-338-2888.

Pollyanna Prodns, *(Pollyanna Productions; 0-945842),* 4700 Poplar St., P.O. Box 3222, Terre Haute, IN 47803 (SAN 247-8285) Tel 812-877-3286.

Popcorn Pubs, *(Popcorn Pubs.; 0-930506),* P.O. Box 1308, Pittsfield, MA 01202 (SAN 211-044X) Tel 413-443-5601.

Porch Swing, *(Porch Swing Pr., Inc.; 0-9606550),* P.O. Box 15014, Nashville, TN 37215 (SAN 219-8118).

Porcupine Enter, *(Porcupine Enterprises; 0-9621976),* 106 Woodside Rd., Sudbury, MA 01776 Tel 508-443-7199.

Portals Pr, *(Portals Pr.; 0-916620),* P.O. Box 1048, Tuscaloosa, AL 35403 (SAN 208-8126) Tel 205-758-1874.

Portfolio Pub, *(Portfolio Publishing Co., Inc.; 0-943255),* P.O. Box 7802, The Woodlands, TX 77387 (SAN 668-3576); 142 Golden Shadow Cir., The Woodlands, TX 77381 (SAN 668-3584) Tel 713-363-3577.

Post Oak Pr *Imprint of* **Larksdale**

Potes Poets, *(Potes & Poets Pr., Inc.; 0-937013),* 181 Edgemont Ave., Elmwood, CT 06110 (SAN 658-6759) Tel 203-233-2023; Dist. by: Segue Foundation, 300 Bowery, New York, NY 10012 (SAN 200-8823) Tel 212-353-0555; Dist. by: Small Pr. Distribution, Inc., 1814 San Pablo Ave., Berkeley, CA 94702 (SAN 204-5826) Tel 415-549-3336; Dist. by: Sun & Moon Pr., P.O. Box 481170, Los Angeles, CA 90048 (SAN 216-3063) Tel 213-653-6711.

Pound Sterling Pub, *(Pound Sterling Publishing; 0-943991),* 462 Poenisch Dr., Corpus Christi, TX 78412 (SAN 242-2743) Tel 512-991-4660.

Power Bks *Imprint of* **Revell**

Pr MacDonald & Reinecke, *(Press of MacDonald & Reinecke, The; 1-877947),* Subs. of Padre Productions, P.O. Box 840, Arroyo Grande, CA 93421 Tel 805-473-1947.

Pr Pacifica, *(Press Pacifica, Ltd.; 0-916630),* P.O. Box 47, Kailua, HI 96734 (SAN 249-292X) Tel 808-261-6594; Dist. by: Pacific Trade Group, 94-527 Puahi St., Waipahu, HI 96797 (SAN 169-1635) Tel 808-671-6735.

Prac Psych Pr, *(Practical Psychology Pr.; 0-944227),* P.O. Box 535, Portland, OR 97207 (SAN 243-1793) Tel 503-289-3295.

Prairie Family Pubs, *(Prairie Family Pubs.; 0-944793),* HCR, Box 78, Bowdle, SD 57428 (SAN 245-3967); County Rd. 3, Bowdle, SD 57428 (SAN 245-3975) Tel 605-285-6337.

Prairie Hse, *(Prairie Hse., Inc.; 0-911007),* P.O. Box 9199, Fargo, ND 58106 (SAN 262-9844) Tel 701-235-0210; Toll free: 800-866-2665.

Prairie Lark, *(Prairie Lark Pr.; 0-918533),* P.O. Box 699, Springfield, IL 62705 (SAN 657-7113) Tel 618-234-2415.

Prairie Plains Res Inst, *(Prairie/Plains Resource Institute; 0-945614),* 1307 L St., Aurora, NE 68818 (SAN 247-3933) Tel 402-694-5535.

Prairie Shark Pr, *(Prairie Shark Pr.; 0-9621151),* P.O. Box 545, Derby, KS 67037 (SAN 250-829X); 1612 Brendonwood Rd., Derby, KS 67037 (SAN 250-8303) Tel 316-269-3477.

Prakken, *(Prakken Pubns., Inc.; 0-911168),* 416 Longshore Dr., Ann Arbor, MI 48107 (SAN 204-9112) Tel 313-769-1211; Toll free: 800-530-9673 (orders).

Prayer Bk, *(Prayer Bk. Pr., Inc.; 0-87677),* Subs. of Media Judaica, Inc., 304 E. 49th St., New York, NY 10017 (SAN 282-1788) Tel 212-319-6666; Orders to: Media Judaica, Inc., 1363 Fairfield Ave., Bridgeport, CT 06605 (SAN 207-0022) Tel 203-384-2284.

Precious Res, *(Precious Resources; 0-937836),* 620 Summer, Weston, MO 64098 (SAN 213-3512) Tel 816-386-5867.

Premier Personalized, *(Premier Personalized Publishing, Inc.; 1-879680),* 670 International Pkwy., No. 120, Richardson, TX 75081 Tel 214-231-3598.

Prentice ESL, *(Prentice Hall, ESL Dept.; 0-88345),* Rte. 9W, Englewood Cliffs, NJ 07632 (SAN 200-2175) Tel 201-592-2000; Toll free: 800-922-0579.

Prentice Hall Pr, *(Prentice Hall Pr.; 0-13),* Div. of Simon & Schuster, Inc., 15 Columbus Cir., New York, NY 10023 (SAN 205-2725); Toll free: 800-223-2348; Orders to: 200 Old Tappan Rd., Old Tappan, NJ 07675 (SAN 215-3939) Tel 201-767-5937. *Imprints:* Websters New Wrld (Webster's New World Dictionary).

Pres Soc Asheville, *(Preservation Society of Asheville & Buncombe County, Inc.; 0-937481),* P.O. Box 2806, Asheville, NC 28802 (SAN 659-0365) Tel 704-254-2343.

Presby & Reformed, *(Presbyterian & Reformed Publishing Co.; 0-87552),* P.O. Box 817, Phillipsburg, NJ 08865 (SAN 205-3918); Toll free: 800-631-0094; Marble Hill Rd., Phillipsburg, NJ 08865 (SAN 658-1463) Tel 908-454-0505. Do not confuse with Presbyterian Renewal Pubns., Oklahoma City, OK.

Preservation Pr, *(Preservation Pr., The; 0-89133),* Div. of National Trust for Historic Preservation, 1785 Massachusetts Ave., NW, Washington, DC 20036 (SAN 209-3146) Tel 202-673-4058.

Press N Amer, *(Press North America; 0-938271),* 835 Lakechime Dr., Sunnyvale, CA 94089 (SAN 659-8285) Tel 408-734-1680.

Pressed Duck, *(Pressed Duck Publishing; 0-9628888),* 2956 Red Hawk Way, Sacramento, CA 95833-1605 Tel 916-920-0741.

Pretty Penny Pr, *(Pretty Penny Pr., Inc.; 0-938509),* 12851 Evanston St., Los Angeles, CA 90049-3712 (SAN 661-0226) Tel 213-476-7843.

Price Pub SC, *(Price Publishing Co.; 0-9626318),* 801 Brooks Rd., Mauldin, SC 29662 Tel 803-458-8484. Do not confuse with Price Publishing Co., Gardena, CA.

Price Stern, *(Price Stern Sloan, Inc.; 0-8431),* 11150 Olympic Blvd., Suite 650, Los Angeles, CA 90064 (SAN 202-0246) Tel 213-477-4118; Toll free: 800-421-0892; 1900 Sacramento St., Los Angeles, CA 90021 (SAN 658-148X). *Imprints:* HP Books (H P Books).

Prima Design, *(Prima Design, Inc.; 0-9621029),* R.R. 1, Box 38, Ossipee, NH 03864 (SAN 250-6475) Tel 603-539-5033; 501 Ferncroft Dr., Danvers, MA 01923 (SAN 250-6483) Tel 508-777-3187.

Primary Progs, *(Primary Programs; 0-9612060),* 15 Elrond Dr., Pittsburgh, PA 15235 (SAN 286-8555) Tel 412-824-6116.

Primate Pub, *(Primate Publishing; 0-9615289),* 1710 Baker St., San Francisco, CA 94115 (SAN 694-4191) Tel 415-563-5160.

Primer Pubs, *(Primer Pubs.; 0-935810),* 5738 N. Central, Phoenix, AZ 85012 (SAN 220-0864); Dist. by: Many Feathers Bks. & Maps, 2626 W. Indian School Rd., Phoenix, AZ 85017 (SAN 158-8877) Tel 602-266-1043.

Princess Pub, *(Princess Publishing; 0-943367),* P.O. Box 386, Beaverton, OR 97075 (SAN 668-4718); 10127 SW Trapper Terr., Beaverton, OR 97005 (SAN 668-4726) Tel 503-646-1234.

Princeton Bk Co, *(Princeton Bk. Co.; 0-916622; 0-87127),* P.O. Box 57, Pennington, NJ 08534 (SAN 630-1568); Toll free: 800-326-7149; 12 W. Delaware Ave., Pennington, NJ 08534 (SAN 244-8076) Tel 609-737-8177. *Imprints:* Dance Horizons (Dance Horizons).

Princeton U Pr, *(Princeton Univ. Pr.; 0-691),* 41 William St., Princeton, NJ 08540 (SAN 202-0254) Tel 609-258-4900; Toll free: 800-777-4726 (orders); Orders to: 3175 Princeton Pike, Lawrenceville, NJ 08648 (SAN 662-1171) Tel 609-896-1344.

Prinit Pr, *(Prinit Pr.; 0-932970),* Box 65, Dublin, IN 47335 (SAN 212-680X) Tel 317-478-4885.

Printek, *(Printek; 0-938042),* 6989 Oxford St., Minneapolis, MN 55426 (SAN 215-7012).

Printemps Bks, *(Printemps Bks.; 0-9621844),* P.O. Box 746, Wilmette, IL 60091; 1920 Washington Ave., Wilmette, IL 60091 Tel 312-251-5418.

Prism Leisure, *(Prism Leisure Corp.; 1-877832),* Div. of Prism Leisure Corp., Public Ltd. Corp., 10475 Perry Hwy., Suite G103, Wexford, PA 15090 Tel 412-935-5066.

Prisma Pr, *(Prisma Pr.; 0-942647),* P.O. Box 1203, Coeur d'Alene, ID 83814 (SAN 667-1772); 1111 E. Lakeshore Dr., Coeur d'Alene, ID 83814 (SAN 667-1780) Tel 208-667-9205; Dist. by: New Leaf Distributing, 5425 Tulane Dr., SW, Atlanta, GA 30336-2323 (SAN 169-1449) Tel 404-691-6996; Toll free: 800-326-2665; Dist. by: Samuel Weiser, Inc., P.O. Box 612, York Beach, ME 03910 (SAN 202-9588) Tel 207-363-4393; Toll free: 800-423-7087 (orders only); Dist. by: DeVorss & Co., P.O. Box 550, 1046 Princeton Dr., Marina del Rey, CA 90292 (SAN 168-9886) Tel 213-870-7478; Toll free: 800-843-5743; 800-331-4719 (in California).

Pritchett & Hull, *(Pritchett & Hull Assocs., Inc.; 0-939838),* 3440 Oakcliff Rd., NE, Suite 110, Atlanta, GA 30340 (SAN 216-9258) Tel 404-451-0602; Toll free: 800-241-4925.

Pro-Am Music, *(Pro/Am Music Resources, Inc.; 0-912483),* 63 Prospect St., White Plains, NY 10606 (SAN 265-1874) Tel 914-948-7436.

Pro Ed, *(Pro-Ed; 0-936104; 0-89079),* 8700 Shoal Creek Blvd., Austin, TX 78758-6897 (SAN 222-1349) Tel 512-451-3246.

Pro Golfers, *(Professional Golfers Assn. of America; 0-9614856),* 100 Ave. of the Champions, Palm Beach Gardens, FL 33410 (SAN 224-5655) Tel 407-626-3600.

Pro Lingua, *(Pro Lingua Assocs., Inc.; 0-86647),* 15 Elm St., Brattleboro, VT 05301 (SAN 216-0579) Tel 802-257-7779; Toll free: 800-366-4775.

Pro Lingua Pr, *(Pro Lingua Pr.; 1-879870),* Div. of European American R.E. Inv., Inc., P.O. Box 24368, Los Angeles, CA 90024; 1117 Roscomare Rd., Los Angeles, CA 90077 Tel 213-472-8396.

Pro Pub Inc, *(Pro Publishing, Inc.; 1-877833),* P.O. Box 350335, Fort Lauderdale, FL 33335; 408 SE 11th Ct., Fort Lauderdale, FL 33316 Tel 305-463-1912.

Prod Concept, *(Product Concept, Inc.; 0-927106),* 3334 Adobe Ct., Colorado Springs, CO 80907-5461 Tel 719-632-1089.

Prod Info Analysis, *(Product Information & Analysis; 0-9621865),* P.O. Box 76127, Saint Paul, MN 55175; 7601 Carillon Plaza E., Woodbury, MN 55125 Tel 612-731-9789.

Prof Reading Serv, *(Professional Reading Services, Inc.; 0-9614374),* P.O. Box 7281, Roanoke, VA 24019 (SAN 688-5985) Tel 703-563-0634.

Proficiency Pr, *(Proficiency Pr. Co., Inc.; 1-879279),* 18 Lucille Ave., Elmont, NY 11003 Tel 516-354-0669.

Prog Bapt Pub, *(Progressive Baptist Publishing Hse.; 0-89191),* Div. of David C. Cook Publishing Co., 850 N. Grove Ave., Elgin, IL 60120 (SAN 277-7010).

Programs Educ, *(Programs for Education, Inc.; 0-935493),* RRB167, Rosemont, NJ 08556 (SAN 695-9962) Tel 609-397-2214.

Promethean Arts, *(Promethean Arts; 0-942624),* P.O. Box 2619, Toledo, OH 43606 (SAN 238-5627) Tel 419-536-4257.

Prometheus Bks, *(Prometheus Bks.; 0-87975),* 700 E. Amherst St., Buffalo, NY 14215 (SAN 202-0289) Tel 716-837-2475; Toll free: 800-421-0351.

Proof Pr, *(Proof Pr.; 0-935070),* P.O. Box 1256, Berkeley, CA 94701 (SAN 209-8687) Tel 415-521-8741; Dist. by: Social Studies School Services, 10200 Jefferson Blvd., P.O. Box 802, Culver City, CA 90232-0802 (SAN 168-9592) Tel 213-839-2436; Toll free: 800-421-4246; Dist. by: National Women's History Project, 7738 Bell Rd., Windsor, CA 95492 (SAN 200-8920) Tel 707-838-6000.

Prophecy Pubns, *(Prophecy Pubns.; 0-941241),* P.O. Box 7000, Oklahoma City, OK 73153 (SAN 665-5319) Tel 405-634-1234; Toll free: 800-245-5577.

Proscenium, *(Proscenium Pr.; 0-912262),* P.O. Box 361, Newark, DE 19715 (SAN 203-0950) Tel 302-764-8477.

Prosperity & Profits, *(Prosperity & Profits Unlimited, Distribution Services),* Box 570213, Houston, TX 77257-0213 (SAN 200-4682).

Proteus LA, *(Proteus; 0-9620541),* Div. of St. George Assocs., Inc., 7715 Sunset Blvd., Suite 218, Los Angeles, CA 90046 (SAN 248-8760) Tel 213-850-3214; Toll free: 800-662-7768.

Prow Bks-Franciscan, *(Prow Bks./Franciscan Marytown Pr.; 0-913382),* 1600 W. Park Ave., Libertyville, IL 60048 (SAN 205-1060) Tel 708-367-7800.

Pruett, *(Pruett Publishing Co.; 0-87108),* 2928 Pearl St., Boulder, CO 80301 (SAN 205-4035) Tel 303-449-4919; Toll free: 800-247-8224.

PS Assocs Croton, *(Policy Studies Assocs.; 0-936826),* P.O. Box 337, Croton-on-Hudson, NY 10520 (SAN 214-4417) Tel 914-271-2039.

PS Enterprises, *(PS Enterprises; 0-9617764),* 1765 Cranberry Ln., NE, No. 226, Warren, OH 44483-3644 (SAN 664-7073) Tel 216-372-5255; Orders to: P.O. Box 8802, Warren, OH 44484-0802 (SAN 250-3549).

Psychegenics, *(Psychegenics Pr.; 0-931865),* Subs. of MCM Inc., P.O. Box 332, Gaithersburg, MD 20884-0332 (SAN 686-0567) Tel 301-948-1122.

Pt Orchard Spec, *(Port Orchard Specialties; 0-9616198),* 7775 SE Blakeview Dr., Port Orchard, WA 98366 (SAN 699-9581) Tel 206-871-5535.

Pub Div JCS, *(Publishing Div. of JCS; 0-932411),* 3998 W. Akron Rd., Akron, MI 48701 (SAN 687-4053) Tel 517-691-5484.

Pub Mark, *(Publishers Mark, The; 0-9614636),* P.O. Box 6939, Incline Village, NV 89450 (SAN 691-9154) Tel 702-831-5139; Dist. by: Baker & Taylor Bks., Western Div., 380 Edison Way, Reno, NV 89564 (SAN 169-4464) Tel 702-786-6700; Toll free: 800-648-3540; Dist. by: Baker & Taylor Bks., Midwestern Div., 501 S. Gladiolus St., Momence, IL 60954 (SAN 169-2100) Tel 815-472-2444; Toll free: 800-435-5111; 800-892-1892 (in Illinois); Dist. by: Baker & Taylor Bks., Eastern Div., 50 Kirby Ave., Somerville, NJ 08876 (SAN 169-4901) Tel 201-722-8000; Toll free: 800-435-1845; 800-352-4833 (in New Jersey).

Pub Service, *(Publishers Services; 0-937602),* P.O. Box 2510, Novato, CA 94948 (SAN 201-3037) Tel 415-883-3530; 11A Commercial Blvd., Novato, CA 94947 (SAN 200-7223) Tel 415-883-3530.

Publicaciones Nuevos, *(Publicaciones Nuevos Horizontes; 0-9624458),* P.O. Box 3727, Huntington Park, CA 90255; 7800 State St., Huntington Park, CA 90255 Tel 213-750-2155.

Pubns Devl Co, *(Publications Development Co.; 0-936431),* P.O. Box 1075, Crockett, TX 75835 (SAN 211-0490); Hwy. 287 N., Crockett, TX 75835 (SAN 699-5543) Tel 409-544-5137.

Pubns Intl Ltd, *(Publications International, Ltd.; 0-88176; 1-56173),* 7373 N. Cicero Ave., Lincolnwood, IL 60646 (SAN 263-9823) Tel 312-676-3470; Dist. by: Crown Pubs., Inc., 225 Park Ave., S, New York, NY 10003 (SAN 200-2639) Tel 212-254-1600; Toll free: 800-526-4264; Dist. by: NAL Penguin, Inc., 1633 Broadway, New York, NY 10019 (SAN 206-8079) Tel 212-397-8000.

Puckerbrush, *(Puckerbrush Pr.; 0-913006),* 76 Main St., Orono, ME 04473 (SAN 202-0327) Tel 207-866-4868; Univ. of Maine, English Dept., Orono, ME 04469 (SAN 241-8304) Tel 207-581-3832; Dist. by: Inland Bk. Co., 140 Commerce St., East Haven, CT 06512 (SAN 200-4151) Tel 203-467-4257; Toll free: 800-243-0138; Dist. by: Maine Writers & Pubs. Alliance, 19D Mason St., Brunswick, ME 04011 (SAN 224-2303) Tel 207-729-6333.

Pueblo Acoma Pr, *(Pueblo of Acoma Pr.; 0-915347),* P.O. Box 449, Acomita, NM 87034 (SAN 290-0386) Tel 505-552-9833.

Puffin *Imprint of* **Puffin Bks**

Puffin Bks, *(Puffin Bks.; 0-14),* Div. of Penguin USA, 375 Hudson St., New York, NY 10014-3657 Tel 212-366-2000. *Imprints:* Dial Easy to Read (Dial Easy to Read); Dial Pied Piper (Dial Pied Piper); Dutton Unicorn (Dutton Unicorn); Puffin (Puffin).

Puissance Pubns, *(Puissance Pubns., Inc.; 0-940634),* P.O. Box 1268, Wheeling, IL 60090 (SAN 218-5229) Tel 708-202-0242.

Pulse Pubns, *(Pulse Pubns.; 0-9628850),* Div. of Biological Therapy Institute, Hospital Dr., Franklin, TN 37064 Tel 615-790-7535.

Pumpkin Patch Pubs, *(Pumpkin Patch Pubs.; 0-9628321),* 718 Ott St., Harrisonburg, VA 22801 Tel 703-434-8385.

Pumpkin Pr Pub Hse, *(Pumpkin Pr. Publishing Hse.; 0-939973),* P.O. Box 139, Shasta, CA 96087 (SAN 665-2387) Tel 916-244-6251.

Punches Prodns, *(Punches Productions; 0-929883),* P.O. Box 601477, South Lake Tahoe, CA 95702 (SAN 250-6513) Tel 916-544-7981; Toll free: 800-833-8778.

Purcell Prods, *(Purcell Productions, Inc.; 0-9610742),* 484 W. 43rd St., 23M, New York, NY 10036 (SAN 264-780X) Tel 212-279-0795.

Purple Turtle Bks, *(Purple Turtle Bks.; 0-943925),* Div. of Scott Publishing, Inc., 400 Dayton, Suite B, Edmonds, WA 98020 (SAN 242-2425) Tel 206-775-8777; Toll free: 800-888-7853.

Purple Turtle Pub
See Purple Turtle Bks

Pussywillow Pub, *(Pussywillow Publishing Hse.; 0-934739),* 500 E. Encinas Ave., P.O. Box 1806, Gilbert, AZ 85234 (SAN 694-1702) Tel 602-892-1316; Dist. by: Baker & Taylor Bks., Eastern Div., 50 Kirby Ave., Somerville, NJ 08876 (SAN 169-4901) Tel 201-722-8000; Toll free: 800-435-1845; 800-352-4833 (in New Jersey); Dist. by: Baker & Taylor Bks., Western Div., 380 Edison Way, Reno, NV 89564 (SAN 169-4464) Tel 702-786-6700; Toll free: 800-648-3540; Dist. by: New Leaf Distributing Co., 5425 Tulane Dr., SW, Atlanta, GA 30336-2323 (SAN 169-1449) Tel 404-691-6996; Toll free: 800-326-2665; Dist. by: Many Feathers Bks. & Maps, 2626 W. Indian School Rd., Phoenix, AZ 85017 (SAN 158-8877) Tel 602-266-1043; Dist. by: Canyonlands Pubs., 4999 E. Empire, Unit A, Flagstaff, AZ 86004 (SAN 114-3824) Tel 602-527-0730; Toll free: 800-283-1983.

Putnam *Imprint of* **Putnam Pub Group**

Putnam Pub Group, *(Putnam Publishing Group, The; 0-399; 0-698),* 200 Madison Ave., New York, NY 10016 (SAN 202-5531) Tel 212-951-8400; Toll free: 800-631-8571. *Imprints:* Coward (Coward-McCann); G&D (Grossett & Dunlap, Incorporated); Perigee Bks (Perigee Books); Philomel Bks (Philomel Books); Platt & Munk Pubs (Platt & Munk Publishers); Playland Bks (Playland Books); Putnam (Putnam's, G. P., Sons); Sandcastle Bks (Sandcastle Books); Tuffy (Tuffy).

Pyramid TX, *(Pyramid Publishing Co.; 0-9629102),* 3323 Rushwood Ln., Sugar Land, TX 77479 Tel 713-265-1816. Do not confuse with Pyramid Publishing Co. in San Diego, CA.

Quail Ridge, *(Quail Ridge Pr., Inc.; 0-937552),* P.O. Box 123, Brandon, MS 39043 (SAN 214-2201) Tel 601-825-2063; Toll free: 800-343-1583; Dist. by: Dot Gibson Pubns., 161 Knight Ave. Cir., Waycross, GA 31501 (SAN 200-9676) Tel 912-285-2848; Dist. by: Southwest Cookbook Distributors, Inc., 1901 South Shore Dr., Bonham, TX 75418 (SAN 200-4925) Tel 214-583-8898; Dist. by: Ingram Bk. Co., 1125 Heilquaker Blvd., La Vergne, TN 37086 (SAN 169-7978) Tel 615-793-5000; Toll free: 800-937-8000 (orders only); Dist. by: Forest Sales, 2616 Spain St., New Orleans, LA 70117 (SAN 157-5511) Tel 504-947-2106; Toll free: 800-277-2106.

Qual-Tech, *(Qual-Tech Publishing; 1-880354),* 14 Miller St., Norwich, NY 13815 Tel 607-334-4576.

Quali-Type, *(Quali-Type, Inc.; 0-929443),* 4047 First St., Suite 201, Livermore, CA 94550 (SAN 249-4256) Tel 415-447-6121.

Quality MO, *(Quality Bks. of Kansas City, Missouri; 0-9606586),* P.O. Box 8487, Kansas City, MO 64114 (SAN 219-0923) Tel 913-383-2160.

Quality Pubns, *(Quality Pubns.; 0-89137),* Div. of Quality Printing Co., Inc., P.O. Box 1060, Abilene, TX 79604 (SAN 203-0071) Tel 915-677-6262; Toll free: 800-359-7708.

Quest Intl, *(Quest International, Inc.; 0-933419; 1-56095),* P.O. Box 566, Granville, OH 43023-0566 (SAN 691-506X); Toll free: 800-288-6401; 537 Jones Rd., Granville, OH 43023 Tel 614-587-2800.

Questar Pubs, *(Questar Pubs., Inc.; 0-945564),* P.O. Box 1720, Sisters, OR 97759 (SAN 247-123X); Toll free: 800-933-7526; 305 W. Adams St., Sisters, OR 97759 Tel 503-549-1144; Dist. by: Spring Arbor Distributors, 10885 Textile Rd., Belleville, MI 48111 (SAN 158-9016) Tel 313-481-0900; Toll free: 800-395-5599.

Quill *Imprint of* **Morrow**

Quilt Digest Pr, *(Quilt Digest Pr., The; 0-913327),* P.O. Box 1331, Gualala, CA 95445 (SAN 293-4531) Tel 707-884-4100; Dist. by: Publishers Group West, 4065 Hollis St., Emeryville, CA 94608 (SAN 202-8522) Tel 415-658-3453; Toll free: 800-365-3453.

Quin Tel Prodns, *(Quin-Tel Productions, Inc.; 0-9618349),* 35 Wendt Ave., Larchmont, NY 10538 (SAN 667-2744) Tel 914-834-0797.

Quintilone Ent, *(Quintilone Enterprises; 0-9616980),* 29 Merrimac St., Buffalo, NY 14214 (SAN 661-7433) Tel 716-836-0945.

Quixote Pr IA, *(Quixote Pr.; 1-878488),* 604 Ave. F, Fort Madison, IA 52627 Tel 319-372-4383. Do not confuse with Quixote Pr., Houston TX.

R & D Bks, *(R&D Bks.; 0-9623504),* 1031 Holbrook Rd., Newnan, GA 30263 Tel 404-251-1212.

R & E Pubs, *(R & E Pubs.; 0-88247),* P.O. Box 2008, Saratoga, CA 95070-2008 (SAN 293-3195) Tel 408-866-6303.

R & S Books, *(R & S Bks.; 0-929297),* 7142 Rutgers Ave., Westminster, CA 92683 (SAN 249-0889) Tel 714-893-6100. Do not confuse with R & S Bks., an imprint of Farrar, Straus & Giroux.

R B Phillips Pub, *(Phillips, Robert B., Pub.; 0-9620577),* 175 Slagle Rd., Bakersville, NC 28705 (SAN 249-1400) Tel 704-688-4850.

R Bane Ltd, *(Bane, Robert, Ltd.; 0-9622646),* 8025 Melrose Ave., Los Angeles, CA 90046 Tel 213-205-0555; Toll free: 800-325-2765.

R C Law & Co, *(Law, R. C., & Co., Inc.; 0-939925),* 579 S. State College Blvd., Fullerton, CA 92631 (SAN 200-609X) Tel 714-871-0940; Toll free: 800-777-5292.

R E Moen, *(Moen, R. E.; 0-9614819),* 3152 S. 27th St., La Crosse, WI 54601 (SAN 693-0794) Tel 608-788-8753.

R E Todd, *(Todd, Richard E.; 0-9605324),* 8055 N. Marion Dr., Clovis, CA 93612 (SAN 215-9805).

R Finkelstein, *(Finkelstein, Ruth; 0-9628157),* 216 Private Way, Lakewood, NJ 08701 Tel 201-367-1673.

R H Barnes, *(Barnes, Robert H.; 0-930480),* P.O. Box 418, Grayland, WA 98547 (SAN 210-3532) Tel 206-267-3601.

R H Pub, *(Renaissance Hse. Pubs.; 0-939650; 1-55838),* P.O. Box 177A, Frederick, CO 80530 (SAN 169-0574); Toll free: 800-521-9221 (orders); 541 Oak St., Frederick, CO 80530 (SAN 658-1404) Tel 303-833-2030.

R Hall, *(Hall, Rachel; 0-9624855),* 6721 Samuel Ct., Anchorage, AK 99516 Tel 907-345-3245.

R Jamieson, *(Jamieson, Rita; 0-9622329),* 5308 River Ave., Newport Beach, CA 92663 Tel 714-645-6570.

R K Garrity, *(Garrity, Robert K.; 0-9628375),* 537 Los Vientos Dr., Newbury Park, CA 91320 Tel 805-498-2410.

R-Kids Pub, *(R-Kids Publishing Co.; 1-878392),* P.O. Box 05796, Milwaukee, WI 53205 (SAN 200-3473); 1453 N. 50th Pl., Milwaukee, WI 53208 Tel 414-453-4852.

R L Breeding
See Thriftecon

R L Merriam, *(Merriam, Robert L.; 0-918507),* Newhall Rd., Conway, MA 01341 (SAN 163-4070) Tel 413-369-4052.

R M Campbell, *(Campbell, Robert M.; 0-9613542),* P.O. Box 7906, Ann Arbor, MI 48107 (SAN 670-1752) Tel 313-737-8980.

R M Wingate, *(Wingate, Rosalee Martin; 0-9625391),* 2105 Teakwood Dr., Austin, TX 78758 Tel 512-454-7420.

R R Dahlstedt, *(Dahlstedt, Richard R., The Attic; 0-9621827),* 2613 Bay Ave., Beach Haven, NJ 08008 Tel 609-492-1064.

R Rinehart Inc, *(Rinehart, Roberts, Inc., Pubs.; 0-911779; 1-879373),* P.O. Box 666, Niwot, CO 80544 (SAN 264-3510) Tel 303-652-2921. *Imprints:* Arpel Gra CO (Arpel Graphics).

R S Kelley, *(Kelley, Rosemary Sue; 0-9616905),* P.O. Box 505, HCR 69, School St., Friendship, ME 04547 (SAN 661-5171) Tel 207-832-4206.

R S Lapp, *(Lapp, Rhoda Snader; 0-9624350),* 33 Reifsnyder Rd., Lititz, PA 17543 Tel 717-627-0173.

R S Rauch, *(Rauch, Robert S.; 0-9624076),* 91 Cherry St., Milford, CT 06460 Tel 203-874-5577.

R Shackelford, *(Shackelford, Robert, Pub.; 0-9616308),* P.O. Box 101, Delaware, OH 43015 (SAN 667-3007); 174 Kensington Dr., Delaware, OH 43015 (SAN 667-3015) Tel 614-363-8964.

R Talsorian, *(Talsorian, R., Games, Inc.; 0-937279),* P.O. Box 7356, Berkeley, CA 94707-0356 (SAN 658-6600) Tel 415-549-1373.

R W Robinson, *(Robinson, Ronald W., Corp.; 0-9622692),* P.O. Box 2703, Petersburg, VA 23804 Tel 804-862-9144.

R Wagner Pub, *(Wagner, Roger, Publishing, Inc.; 0-927796),* 1050 Pioneer Way, Suite P, El Cajon, CA 92020 (SAN 653-5178) Tel 619-442-0522; Toll free: 800-421-6526.

R Wornall, *(Wornall, Ruthie; 0-9624467),* 9800 W. 104th St., Overland Park, KS 66212 Tel 913-888-1530; Dist. by: Cookbook Collection, Inc., 2500 E. 195th St., Belton, MO 64012 (SAN 200-6359) Tel 816-322-2122.

Rabbit Ears *Imprint of* **Picture Bk Studio**

Rabeth Pub Co, *(Rabeth Publishing Co.; 0-9626735),* P.O. Box 171, Kirksville, MO 63501; 201 S. Cottage Grove, Kirksville, MO 63501.

Raconteurs, *(Raconteurs, Inc.; 0-9621758),* 4661 Lake Club Cir., Oconomowoc, WI 53066 (SAN 252-080X) Tel 414-567-4009.

Radiant LA, *(Radiant Publishing Co., The; 0-944512),* P.O. Box 796, Thibodaux, LA 70302 (SAN 243-7554); 112 Juniper St., Thibodaux, LA 70302 (SAN 243-7562) Tel 504-446-0591.

Rae Pub, *(Rae Publishing; 0-9626052),* 13210 NE 199th St., Battle Ground, WA 98604 Tel 206-687-3767.

RAEYC, *(Rochester Assn. for the Education of Young Children; 0-9613271),* 246 Archer Rd., Churchville, NY 14428 (SAN 297-035X) Tel 716-624-3775.

Railhead Pubns, *(Railhead Pubns.; 0-912113),* P.O. Box 6579, Canton, OH 44706 (SAN 264-7826) Tel 216-454-5551.

Rainbow Bend, *(Rainbow Bend Storytelling; 0-9624224),* 7 Kevin Dr., East Windsor, CT 06088 Tel 203-627-8330.

Rainbow Bks, *(Rainbow Bks., Inc.; 0-89508),* 725 Dell Rd., Carlstadt, NJ 07072 (SAN 209-9918) Tel 201-935-3369. Do not confuse with Rainbow Bks., Inc., New York, NY.

Rainbow Cat Pubs, *(Rainbow Cat Pubs.; 0-929986),* 266 Patterson Dr., Myrtle Beach, SC 29572 (SAN 250-9245) Tel 803-272-7194; Dist. by: New Leaf Distributing Co. (for title, The Rainbow Child), 5425 Tulane Dr., SW, Atlanta, GA 30336 (SAN 169-1449) Tel 404-691-6996; Toll free: 800-326-2665; Dist. by: DeVorss & Co. (for title, Questions to ask a Cat), P.O. Box 550, Marina del Rey, CA 90294-0550 (SAN 168-9886) Tel 213-870-7478; Toll free: 800-843-5743 (bookstore orders only); 800-331-4719 (in California, bookstores only).

Rainbow Morn, *(Rainbow Morning Music Alternatives; 0-9615696),* 2121 Fairland Rd., Silver Spring, MD 20904 (SAN 218-2963) Tel 301-384-9207; Dist. by: Talman Co., 150 Fifth Ave., Rm. 630, New York, NY 10011 (SAN 200-5204) Tel 212-620-3182; Toll free: 800-537-8894; Dist. by: Baker & Taylor Bks., Eastern Div., 50 Kirby Ave., Somerville, NJ 08876-0734 (SAN 169-4901) Tel 201-722-8000; Toll free: 800-526-3825; Dist. by: Baker & Taylor Bks., Midwestern Div., 501 S. Gladiolus St., Momence, IL 60954-2444 (SAN 169-2100) Tel 815-472-2444; Toll free: 800-435-5111; 800-892-1892 (in Illinois); Dist. by: Baker & Taylor Bks., Southern Div., Mt. Olive Rd., Commerce, GA 30599-9988 (SAN 169-1503) Tel 303-296-1830; Toll free: 800-241-6004; 800-282-6854 (in Georgia); Dist. by: Baker & Taylor Bks., Western Div., 380 Edison Way, Reno, NV 89564 (SAN 169-4464) Tel 702-786-6700; Toll free: 800-648-3540; 800-524-2486 (in Canada).

Rainbow NC, *(Rainbow Connection; 1-878321),* 477 Hannah Branch Rd., Burnsville, NC 28714 Tel 704-675-5909; Dist. by: Compassion Bk. Service, 479 Hannah Branch Rd., Burnsville, NC 28714-9582 (SAN 200-9277) Tel 704-675-9670; Dist. by: Inland Bk. Co., 140 Commerce St., East Haven, CT 06512 (SAN 200-4151) Tel 203-467-4257; Toll free: 800-243-0138; Dist. by: New Leaf Distributing Co., 5425 Tulane Dr., SW, Atlanta, GA 30336 (SAN 169-1449) Tel 404-691-6996; Toll free: 800-326-2665. *Imprints:* Mntn Rainbow (Mountain Rainbow Publications).

Rainbow Pr NY, *(Rainbow Pr.; 0-943156),* 222 Edwards Dr., Fayetteville, NY 13066 (SAN 240-4354); Dist. by: Baker & Taylor Bks., Eastern Div., 50 Kirby Ave., Somerville, NJ 08876 (SAN 169-4901) Tel 201-722-8000; Toll free: 800-435-1845; 800-352-4833 (in New Jersey). Do not confuse with Rainbow Pr., Clackamas, OR.

Rainbow Rhapsody, *(Rainbow Rhapsody; 0-9625920),* 793 Garner Dr., Lander, WY 82520 Tel 307-332-7298.

Raintree Pubs, *(Raintree Pubs., Inc.; 0-8172; 0-8393),* Div. of Raintree I Limited Partnership, 310 W. Wisconsin Ave., Mezzanine Level, Milwaukee, WI 53203 (SAN 207-9607) Tel 414-273-0873; Toll free: 800-558-7264.

Raitport Co, *(Raitport Co.; 0-944182),* 1580 41st St., Brooklyn, NY 11218 (SAN 242-7826) Tel 718-435-5027.

Ralls Cnty Bk, *(Ralls County Bk. Co.; 0-9617769),* P.O. Box 375, New London, MO 63459 (SAN 664-7138) Tel 314-985-8211.

Rallysport Video Prodns, *(Rallysport Video Productions; 0-926727),* P.O. Box 29809, Los Angeles, CA 90029; 1755 N. Kenmore Ave., No. 8, Los Angeles, CA 90027 Tel 213-661-4278.

Ralmar Enter, *(Ralmar Enterprises; 0-941977),* 1340 W. 30th St., Los Angeles, CA 90007 (SAN 666-7503) Tel 213-734-3312.

RAM Res Pub, *(RAM Research Publishing Co.; 0-943329),* P.O. Box 1916, Frederick, MD 21701 (SAN 668-4262); Toll free: 800-344-7714; 1809 Pinecroft Ct., Frederick, MD 21701 (SAN 668-4270) Tel 301-695-4660.

Ramira Pub, *(Ramira Publishing; 0-9612720),* P.O. Box 1707, Aptos, CA 95001 (SAN 289-8128) Tel 408-429-9311; Dist. by: Bookpeople, 2929 Fifth St., Berkeley, CA 94710 (SAN 168-9517) Tel 415-549-3030; Toll free: 800-999-4650; Dist. by: New Leaf Distributing Co., 5425 Tulane Dr., SW, Atlanta, GA 30336-2323 (SAN 169-1449) Tel 404-691-6996; Toll free: 800-326-2665; Dist. by: DeVorss & Co., P.O. Box 550, 1046 Princeton Dr., Marina del Rey, CA 90292 (SAN 168-9886) Tel 213-870-7478; Toll free: 800-843-5743; 800-331-4719 (in California); Dist. by: Omega Pr., R.D. 1, Box 1030E, Lebanon Springs, NY 12117 (SAN 214-1493) Tel 518-794-8181; Toll free: 800-443-7107 (orders only); Dist. by: Moving Bks., Inc., P.O. Box 20037, Seattle, WA 98102 (SAN 159-0685) Tel 206-762-1750; Toll free: 800-777-7683; Dist. by: Baker & Taylor Bks. Western Div., 380 Edison Way, Reno, NV 89564 (SAN 169-4464) Tel 702-786-6700.

Rams Horn Bks, *(Rams Horn Bks.; 1-879911),* Rams Horn Mountain, Box 20622, Estes Park, CO 80511; 1460 Front Nine Dr., Unit D, Fort Collins, CO 80525 Tel 303-223-6981.

Ranch Gate Bks, *(Ranch Gate Bks.; 0-9618660),* 2409 Dormarion, Austin, TX 78703 (SAN 668-4033) Tel 512-476-2185; Dist. by: Hendrick-Long Publishing Co., 4811 W. Lovers Ln., Dallas, TX 75209 (SAN 281-7748) Tel 214-358-4677.

Ranch House Pr, *(Ranch Hse. Pr.; 1-878438),* Rte. 2, Box 296, Pagosa Springs, CO 81147 (SAN 240-1126) Tel 303-264-2647.

Rand McNally, *(Rand McNally & Co.; 0-528),* P.O. Box 7600, Chicago, IL 60680 (SAN 203-3917) Tel 312-673-9100.

Randall Hse, *(Randall Hse. Pubns.; 0-89265),* 114 Bush Rd., P.O. Box 17306, Nashville, TN 37217 (SAN 207-5040) Tel 615-361-1221; Toll free: 800-251-5762; 800-624-6538 (in Tennessee).

Randelle Pubns, *(Randelle Pubns.; 0-910445),* 1527 First Ave., Charleston, WV 25312 (SAN 260-1222) Tel 304-344-4494.

R&M Pub Co, *(R&M Publishing Co.; 0-936026),* P.O. Box 1276, Holly Hill, SC 29059 (SAN 213-6392) Tel 804-732-4094.

757

Random, *(Random Hse., Inc.; 0-394; 0-676; 0-375),* Random Hse. Publicity, (11-6), 201 E. 50th St., 31st Flr., New York, NY 10022 (SAN 202-5507) Tel 212-751-2600; Toll free: 800-733-3000 (orders); 800-726-0600 (credit, inquiries, customer service); Orders to: 400 Hahn Rd., Westminster, MD 21157 (SAN 202-5515) Tel 301-848-1900. *Imprints:* Modern Lib (Modern Library); Random Ref (Random House Reference); Times Bks (Times Books); Vin (Vintage).

Random Ref *Imprint of* **Random**

RAPCOM Enter, *(RAPCOM Enterprises),* 2109 Wilkinson Pl., Alexandria, VA 22306 (SAN 689-0563).

Rape Abuse Crisis, *(Rape & Abuse Crisis Ctr. of Fargo Moorhead; 0-914633),* P.O. Box 2984, Fargo, ND 58108 (SAN 289-5684) Tel 701-293-7273; Toll free: 800-627-3675.

Rape Crisis Ctr, *(Rape Crisis Ctr.),* P.O. Box 21005, Washington, DC 20009 (SAN 225-9680).

Rapids Christian, *(Rapids Christian Pr., Inc.; 0-915374),* P.O. Box 487, 5630 Schroeder Dr., Wisconsin Rapids, WI 54495 (SAN 205-0986) Tel 715-423-4670.

Raspberry IL, *(Raspberry Pr., Ltd.; 0-929568),* P.O. Box 1, Dixon, IL 61021 (SAN 250-2194); 1989 Grand Detour Rd., Dixon, IL 61021 (SAN 250-2208) Tel 815-288-4910.

Raspberry Rec, *(Raspberry Recordings; 0-934721),* Div. of Raconteur Records, P.O. Box 11247 Dr., Capitol Sta., Columbia, SC 29211 (SAN 694-1605) Tel 803-254-5466; Dist. by: Baker & Taylor Bks., Midwestern Div., 501 S. Gladiolus St., Momence, IL 60954 (SAN 169-2100) Tel 815-472-2444; Toll free: 800-435-5111; 800-892-1892 (in Illinois); Dist. by: Sabayt Pubns., 5441 S. Kenwood Ave., Chicago, IL 60615 (SAN 630-2432) Tel 312-667-2227.

Ray-Foster, *(Ray/Foster Pubs.; 0-9612346),* P.O. Box 4044, McCall, ID 83638 (SAN 289-2294) Tel 208-634-5054.

Ray-Ma Natsal, *(Ray-Ma Natsal Publishing; 1-879068),* Rte. 3, Box 128, Greenbrier, AR 72058 Tel 501-679-3206.

Raynel, *(Raynel; 0-9623068),* P.O. Box 833, Sequim, WA 98382; 124B Secor Rd., Sequim, WA 98382 Tel 206-683-7340.

RBR, *(RBR (Religious Bks. for Russia); 0-934927),* P.O. Box 522, Glen Cove, NY 11542-0522 (SAN 695-0167) Tel 516-676-3268; Dist. by: MCA Pr., 575 Scarsdale Rd., Crestwood, NY 10707 (SAN 200-5514) Tel 914-478-2151.

RCC-Berkshires Pr, *(Rape Crisis Ctr. of the Berkshires Pr.; 0-9618618),* 18 Charles St., Pittsfield, MA 01201 (SAN 668-3436) Tel 413-442-6708.

RD Assn, *(Reader's Digest Assn., Inc.; 0-89577),* 260 Madison Ave., New York, NY 10016 (SAN 240-9720) Tel 212-850-7007; Orders to: Customer Service, Reader's Digest Rd., Pleasantville, NY 10570 (SAN 282-2091); Toll free: 800-431-1246; Dist. by: Random Hse., Inc., 400 Hahn Rd., Westminster, MD 21157 (SAN 202-5515); Toll free: 800-733-3000 (orders).

Read A Bol, *(Read-A-Bol Group, The; 0-938155),* 301 Village Run, E., Encinitas, CA 92024 (SAN 659-8994) Tel 619-753-0663; Orders to: 199 N. El Camino Real F-137, Encinitas, CA 92024 (SAN 242-1135).

Read Me Pub, *(Read Me Publishing Co.; 0-9602842),* 514 Anneslie Rd., Baltimore, MD 21212 (SAN 222-2248).

Read Res *Imprint of* **ARO Pub**

Reading Inc, *(Reading, Inc.; 0-943867),* 603 12th St., Oregon City, OR 97045 (SAN 242-3871) Tel 503-655-4192; Toll free: 800-523-3391.

Reading Matters, *(Reading Matters, Inc.; 0-9614780),* P.O. Box 300309, Denver, CO 80203 (SAN 692-6827) Tel 303-757-3506; Dist. by: Bookpeople, 2929 Fifth St., Berkeley, CA 94710 (SAN 168-9517) Tel 415-549-3030; Toll free: 800-999-4650.

Ready Work, *(Ready Work; 0-9617529),* 6 Dogwood Dr., Old Farm Estates, Waynesville, MO 65583 (SAN 664-3493) Tel 314-774-2494.

Rebecca Hse, *(Rebecca Hse.; 0-945522),* 1550 California St., Suite 330, San Francisco, CA 94109 (SAN 247-1361) Tel 415-752-1453; Toll free: 800-321-1912.

Recorded Pubns, *(Recorded Pubns. Laboratories, Inc.; 1-879755),* 1100 State St., Camden, NJ 08105 Tel 609-963-3000; Toll free: 800-235-2679.

Recovery SD, *(Recovery Pubns.; 0-941405),* 1201 Knoxville St., San Diego, CA 92110 (SAN 665-5882) Tel 619-275-1350; Toll free: 800-873-8384 (orders only). Do not confuse with Recovery Pubns., Amarillo, TX.

Red Baron Pub Co, *(Red Baron Publishing Co.; 0-9622242),* 1175 Lockhaven Dr., NE, Salem, OR 97303 Tel 503-393-3570.

Red Branch Pr, *(Red Branch Pr.; 1-878941),* 170 Augusta Ave., Staten Island, NY 10312 Tel 718-967-3728.

Red Bus Pub, *(Red Bus Publishing; 0-945286),* P.O. Box 151, Hurst, IL 62949 (SAN 246-0599); 200 W. Pulley, Hurst, IL 62949 (SAN 246-0602) Tel 618-987-2006.

Red Crane Bks, *(Red Crane Bks.; 1-878610),* Div. of O'Shaughnessy, Mafchir & Mayans, Inc., 826 Camino Del Monte Rey, Santa Fe, NM 87501 Tel 505-988-7070.

Red Earth OK, *(Red Earth Bks.; 0-9619712),* 1200 Caddell, Norman, OK 73069 (SAN 246-1218) Tel 405-360-2730.

Red Hen Pr, *(Red Hen Pr.; 0-931093),* P.O. Box 3774, Santa Barbara, CA 93130 (SAN 678-9420) Tel 805-682-1278; P.O. Box 419, Summerland, CA 93067 Tel 805-969-7058; Dist. by: Children's Small Pr. Collection, 719 N. Fourth Ave., Ann Arbor, MI 48104 (SAN 200-514X) Tel 313-668-8056; Toll free: 800-221-8056.

Red Rose Studio, *(Red Rose Studio; 0-932514),* 358 Flintlock Dr., Willow Street, PA 17584 (SAN 212-162X) Tel 717-464-3873.

Redbird, *(Redbird Pr., Inc.; 0-9606046),* 3838 Poplar Ave., Memphis, TN 38111 (SAN 216-9304) Tel 901-323-2233; Orders to: P.O. Box 11441, Memphis, TN 38111 (SAN 665-7656); Dist. by: Publishers Group West, 4065 Hollis St., Emeryville, CA 94608 (SAN 202-8522) Tel 415-658-3453; Toll free: 800-365-3453.

Redleaf Pr, *(Redleaf Pr.; 0-934140),* Div. of Resources for Child Caring, Inc., 450 Syndicate, Suite 5, Saint Paul, MN 55104 (SAN 212-8691) Tel 612-641-0305; Toll free: 800-423-8309; Dist. by: Gryphon Hse., Inc., P.O. Box 275, Mount Rainier, MD 20712 (SAN 169-3190) Tel 301-779-6200; Toll free: 800-638-0928.

Redwood Seed, *(Redwood City Seed Co.; 0-933421),* P.O. Box 361, Redwood City, CA 94064 (SAN 691-5078) Tel 415-325-7333.

Ref Desk Bks, *(Reference Desk Bks.; 0-9625749),* 655 Morro Bay Blvd., Suite 146, Morro Bay, CA 93442 Tel 805-772-8806.

Refhouse Pubns, *(Refhouse Pubns.; 0-9627108),* 4356 College View Way, Carmichael, CA 95608 Tel 916-488-4114.

Reg Baptist, *(Regular Baptist Pr.; 0-87227),* Div. of General Assn. of Regular Baptist Churches, 1300 N. Meacham Rd., Schaumburg, IL 60173-4888 (SAN 205-2229) Tel 708-843-1600; Toll free: 800-727-4440.

Regal, *(Regal Bks.; 0-8307),* Div. of Gospel Light Pubns., 2300 Knoll Dr., Ventura, CA 93003 (SAN 658-1528) Tel 805-644-9721; Toll free: 800-235-3415 (USA & California); 800-446-7735.

Regent Pr, *(Regent Pr.; 0-916147),* 6020A Adeline, Oakland, CA 94608 (SAN 294-9717) Tel 415-547-7602.

Regina Pr, *(Regina Pr., Malhame & Co.; 0-88271),* 145 Sherwood Ave., Farmingdale, NY 11735 (SAN 203-0853) Tel 516-694-8600.

Regmar Pub, *(Regmar Publishing Co., Inc.; 0-914338),* P.O. Box 11358, Memphis, TN 38111 (SAN 203-2015) Tel 901-323-7442.

Reid Ent, *(Ace Reid Enterprises; 0-917207),* P.O. Box 868, Kerrville, TX 78029-0868 (SAN 656-089X) Tel 512-257-7446.

Reiman Assocs, *(Reiman Assocs.; 0-89821),* 5400 S. 60th St., Greendale, WI 53129 (SAN 208-4368) Tel 414-423-0100; Orders to: Country Store, P.O. Box 572, Milwaukee, WI 53201 (SAN 208-4376); Toll free: 800-558-1013; 800-248-6065 (in Wisconsin).

Rekalb Pr, *(Rekalb Pr.; 0-9604614),* 6203 Jane Ln., Columbus, GA 31909 (SAN 282-2415) Tel 404-561-3497.

Religious Soc Friends, *(Philadelphia Yearly Meeting, Religious Society of Friends, Pubns.; 0-941308),* 1515 Cherry St., Philadelphia, PA 19102 (SAN 239-3778) Tel 215-241-7225.

Remco Wrldserv Bks, *(Remco Worldservice Bks.; 0-924359),* 850 Maple Ave., Ardsley, PA 19038 (SAN 252-2357) Tel 215-886-5512.

Rendezvous Pubns, *(Rendezvous Pubns.; 0-938447),* P.O. Box 4269, Tequesta, FL 33469-4269 (SAN 660-9929) Tel 407-744-6149.

Renfro Studios, *(Renfro, Nancy, Studios; 0-931044),* P.O. Box 164226, Austin, TX 78716 (SAN 211-9730) Tel 512-327-9588; Toll free: 800-933-5512.

Reprint Servs, *(Reprint Services Corp.; 0-932051; 0-7812),* 3972 Barranca Pkwy., Suite J412, Irvine, CA 92714 (SAN 686-2640) Tel 714-699-5731.

Resc World Hlth, *(Resources for World Health, Inc.; 0-939508),* P.O. Box 42721, Tucson, AZ 85733 (SAN 216-4183); Dist. by: Bookpeople, 2929 Fifth St., Berkeley, CA 94710 (SAN 168-9517) Tel 415-549-3030; Toll free: 800-999-4650.

Resource Pubns, *(Resource Pubns., Inc.; 0-89390),* 160 E. Virginia St., No. 290, San Jose, CA 95112-5848 (SAN 209-3081) Tel 408-286-8505; Toll free: 800-736-7600. Do not confuse with Resource Pubns., Inc., Provo, UT.

Resources Children, *(Resources for Children in Hospitals; 0-9608150),* P.O. Box 10, Belmont, MA 02178 (SAN 240-2734) Tel 617-492-6220.

Respect Inc, *(Respect, Inc.; 0-945745),* P.O. Box 349, Bradley, IL 60915 (SAN 247-6509); 231 E. Broadway, Hoover Bldg., Bradley, IL 60915 (SAN 247-6517) Tel 815-932-8389.

Reston *Imprint of* **P-H**

Revell, *(Revell, Fleming H., Co.; 0-8007),* Subs. of Guideposts Assocs., 120 White Plains Rd., Tarrytown, NY 10591 (SAN 203-3801) Tel 914-332-8500; Toll free: 800-631-1970. *Imprints:* Chosen Bks (Chosen Books); Power Bks (Power Books).

Revels Pubns, *(Revels Pubns.; 0-9618334),* Div. of Revels, Inc., 1 Kendall Sq., Bldg. 600, Cambridge, MA 02139 (SAN 667-1950) Tel 617-621-0505.

Review & Herald, *(Review & Herald Publishing Assn.; 0-8280),* 55 W. Oak Ridge Dr., Hagerstown, MD 21740 (SAN 203-3798) Tel 301-791-7000; Toll free: 800-771-9098.

Revivals & Missions, *(Revivals & Missions, Inc.; 0-9626490),* 1298 SOM Ctr. Rd., Mayfield Heights, OH 44124.

Reymont, *(Reymont Assocs.; 0-918734),* P.O. Box 114, New York, NY 10276-0114 (SAN 204-6857) Tel 212-473-8031; P.O. Box 114, Cooper Sta., New York, NY 10276 Tel 212-473-8031.

Rhinos Pr, *(Rhino's Pr., The; 0-937382),* P.O. Box 3520, Laguna Hills, CA 92654 (SAN 214-4565) Tel 714-997-3217; Toll free: 800-872-3274.

RHS Ent, *(RHS Enterprises; 0-914503),* P.O. Box 5779, Garden Grove, CA 92645 (SAN 289-6699); 11368 Matinicus Ct., Cypress, CA 90630 (SAN 241-936X) Tel 714-892-9012.

Rhyme & Reason, *(Rhyme & Reason Publishing Co.; 0-9623411),* P.O. Box 25944, Honolulu, HI 96825; 7243 Pulehu St., Honolulu, HI 96825 Tel 808-548-6485.

Ricara Features, *(Ricara Features; 0-911737),* P.O. Box 664, Sanborn, NY 14132 (SAN 264-3472) Tel 916-444-7890.

Richardson Pubns, *(Richardson Pubns.; 0-9623222),* 2660 Chili Ave., Suite 12-19, Rochester, NY 14624 Tel 716-325-6120.

Richelieu Court, *(Richelieu Court Pubns., Inc.;
0-911519),* 8 Leesome Ln., Altamont, NY
12009 (SAN 264-3480) Tel 518-861-7209;
Dist. by: Baker & Taylor Bks., Eastern Div.,
50 Kirby Ave., Somerville, NJ 08876
(SAN 169-4901) Tel 201-722-8000; Toll
free: 800-435-1845; 800-352-4833 (in New
Jersey); Dist. by: Spring Arbor Distributors,
10885 Textile Rd., Belleville, MI 48111
(SAN 158-9016) Tel 313-481-0900; Toll
free: 800-395-9955; Dist. by: Ingram Bk. Co.,
1125 Heilquaker Blvd., La Vergne, TN 37086
(SAN 169-7978) Tel 615-793-5000; Toll
free: 800-937-8000 (orders only); Dist. by:
Baker & Taylor Bks., Midwestern Div., 501
S. Gladiolus St., Momence, IL 60954-2444
(SAN 169-2100) Tel 815-472-2444; Toll
free: 800-435-5111; 800-892-1892 (in
Illinois); Dist. by: Baker & Taylor Bks.,
Western Div., 380 Edison Way, Reno, NV
89564 (SAN 169-4464) Tel 702-786-6700;
Toll free: 800-648-3540; 800-524-2486 (in
Canada); Dist. by: Baker & Taylor Bks.,
Southern Div., Mt. Olive Rd., Commerce,
GA 30599-9988 (SAN 169-1503)
Tel 303-296-1830; Toll free: 800-241-6004;
800-282-6854 (in Georgia).

Richmar Prodns, *(Richmar Productions;
0-9624225),* 601 NE Eighth St., No. A,
Grants Pass, OR 97526-2106
Tel 503-479-3594.

Richmond Saddlery, *(Richmond Saddlery Pr.;
0-9628937),* Div. of Richmond Camera
Shop, Inc., P.O. Box 27461, Richmond, VA
23261; 215 W. Broad, Richmond, VA 23220
Tel 804-649-1079.

Ridge Enter, *(Ridge Enterprises, Ltd.;
0-9628323),* P.O. Box 69041, Pleasant
Ridge, MI 48069; 52 Cambridge, Pleasant
Ridge, MI 48069 Tel 313-399-1719.

Riegel Pub, *(Riegel Publishing; 0-944871),* P.O.
Box 3241, San Clemente, CA 92674
(SAN 245-3916) Tel 714-582-7562.

Right Brain, *(Right Brain Publishing; 0-935295),*
7812 NW Hampton Rd., Kansas City, MO
64152 (SAN 695-9350) Tel 816-587-8687.

Right to Life, *(Right to Life League of Southern
California; 0-9613809),* 1616 W. Ninth St.,
Suite 220, Los Angeles, CA 90015
(SAN 219-8142) Tel 213-380-8750.

RivEd *Imprint of* **HM**

River-Light Pub, *(River-Light Publishing Co.,
Inc.; 0-925039),* P.O. Box 3283, Pasco, WA
99302; 824 Maitland Ave., Pasco, WA 99301
Tel 509-545-8240.

Riverside FL, *(Riverside Bks.; 1-879710),* P.O.
Box 2184, Ormond Beach, FL 32175; 710
Riverside Dr., Ormond Beach, FL 32176
Tel 904-672-4386. Do not confuse with
Riverside Bks. in New York, NY.

Riverstone Pr, *(Riverstone Pr.; 0-9617206),* 795
River Heights Dr., Meridian, ID 83642
(SAN 663-2548) Tel 208-888-6290. Do not
confuse with Riverstone Pr., Chicago, IL.

Riviana Foods, *(Riviana Foods, Inc.; 0-9629736),*
P.O. Box 2636, Houston, TX 77252; 2777
Allen Pkwy., Suite 1500, Houston, TX 77019
Tel 713-529-3251.

Roanoke Park, *(Roanoke Park Pr.; 0-9622496),*
4539 132nd Ave., SE, Bellevue, WA 98006
Tel 206-643-8204.

Rob Briggs, *(Briggs, Robert, Assocs.; 0-9609850;
0-931191),* 400 Second St., No. 108, Lake
Oswego, OR 97034 (SAN 268-4632)
Tel 503-635-0435; Orders to: Publishers
Services, P.O. Box 2510, Novato, CA 94948
(SAN 200-7223) Tel 415-883-3140.

Robbinspring, *(Robbinspring Pubns.; 0-9630060),*
3037 Fawn Ln., Jackson, MI 49201
Tel 517-784-6621.

Robinson Pr, *(Robinson Pr., Inc.; 0-913730),*
1137 Riverside Dr., Fort Collins, CO 80524
(SAN 205-2369) Tel 303-482-5393; Toll
free: 800-747-5395 (orders only).

Rochester Folk Art, *(Rochester Folk Art Guild),*
Rte. 1, Box 10, Middlesex, NY 14507
(SAN 210-9492) Tel 716-554-3539.

Rochester Pub Lib Dist, *(Rochester Public
Library District; 0-9621759),* P.O. Box 617,
Rochester, IL 62563 (SAN 252-0753);
Rochester Sta., No 2, Rochester, IL 62563
(SAN 252-0761) Tel 217-498-8454.

Rockdale Ridge, *(Rockdale Ridge Pr.;
0-9602338),* 8501 Ridge Rd., Cincinnati,
OH 45236 (SAN 212-4459)
Tel 513-891-9900; Dist. by: Baker & Taylor
Bks., Midwestern Div., 501 S. Gladiolus St.,
Momence, IL 60954-1799 (SAN 169-2100)
Tel 815-472-2444; Toll free: 800-435-5111;
800-892-1892 (in Illinois); Dist. by: Dot
Gibson Pubns., P.O. Box 117, Waycross, GA
31502-0117 (SAN 200-4143)
Tel 912-285-2848; Dist. by: Cookbook
Collection, Inc., 2500 E. 195th St., Belton,
MO 64012 (SAN 630-4893)
Tel 816-322-2122.

Rocking Horse, *(Rocking Horse Pr.; 0-932306),*
32 Ellise Rd., Storrs, CT 06268
(SAN 212-4467) Tel 203-429-1474.

Rockmasters Intl, *(Rockmasters International
Network; 1-878476),* 5736 Shenandoah
Ave., Norfolk, VA 23509 Tel 804-623-5565;
Orders to: 317 Granby St., Norfolk, VA
23516.

Rockrimmon Pr, *(Rockrimmon Pr., Inc., The;
1-882092),* 110 Enterprise, Colorado
Springs, CO 80918 (SAN 248-5001)
Tel 719-594-6337.

Rocky Mntn Child, *(Rocky Mountain Children's
Pr., Inc.; 0-940611),* 1520 Shaw Mountain
Rd., Boise, ID 83712 (SAN 664-7065)
Tel 208-336-3858.

Rocky River Pubs, *(Rocky River Pubs.;
0-944576),* P.O. Box 1679, Shepherdstown,
WV 25443 (SAN 243-9409)
Tel 304-876-2711.

Rod & Staff, *(Rod & Staff Pubs., Inc.),* Hwy.
172, Crockett, KY 41413 (SAN 206-7633)
Tel 606-522-4348.

Rodney, *(Rodney Pubns., Inc.; 0-913830),* 10201
Grosvenor Pl., No. 1122, Rockville, MD
20852 (SAN 204-6954) Tel 301-493-6334.

Rodor & Co, *(Rodor & Co.; 0-9619944),* 28221
Lomo Dr., Rancho Palos Verdes, CA 90274
(SAN 246-9642) Tel 213-541-4559.

RoKarn Pubns, *(RoKarn Pubns.; 0-9625502),*
P.O. Box 195, Nokesville, VA 22123; Toll
free: 800-869-0563; 8534 Stonewall Rd.,
Manassas, VA 22110 Tel 703-330-8249.

Rolling Hills Pr, *(Rolling Hills Pr.; 0-943978),*
40 Pilgrim Pk., San Rafael, CA 94903
(SAN 282-2601) Tel 415-499-8135; Dist.
by: Bookpeople, 2929 Fifth St., Berkeley, CA
94710 (SAN 168-9517) Tel 415-549-3030;
Toll free: 800-999-4650.

Roman IL, *(Roman, Inc.; 0-937739),* 555
Lawrence Ave., Roselle, IL 60172
(SAN 659-2899) Tel 312-529-3000.

Romar Bks, *(Romar Bks.; 0-945265),* 18002
15th, NE, Seattle, WA 98133
(SAN 246-1935) Tel 206-368-8157.

Ron Denzer, *(Denzer, Ron, Publishing;
0-9616331),* P.O. Box 631, Crescent City,
CA 95531 (SAN 659-1566)
Tel 707-464-3278.

Rondy Pubns, *(Rondy Pubns.; 0-9616638),* 6704
Cheyenne Trail, Edina, MN 55435
(SAN 659-6800) Tel 612-941-2292.

Ronmar Ent, *(Ronmar Enterprises; 0-9619988),*
46 Nicholas Dr., Albany, NY 12205
(SAN 247-2996) Tel 518-869-3263.

Ronnie Two Pub, *(Ronnie II Publishing Co.;
1-878439),* 53 Longview Dr., R.R. 7,
Springfield, IL 62707 Tel 217-498-9619.

Roper Pr, *(Roper Pr., Inc.; 0-86606),* 4737A
Gretna, Dallas, TX 75207
Tel 214-630-4808.

Rose Pub, *(Rose Publishing Co., Inc.; 0-914546),*
2723 Foxcroft Rd., Suite 208, Little Rock,
AR 72207 (SAN 203-3739)
Tel 501-227-8104. Do not confuse with other
companies with the same name in Keystone
Heights, FL, Grand Rapids, MI, Alameda,
CA, Tucson, AZ, Flagtown, NJ.

Rosedale Pr, *(Rosedale Pr.; 0-9626413),* Div of
BBE Assocs., Ltd., 4401 N. Classen Blvd.,
Suite 500, Oklahoma City, OK 73118
Tel 405-557-1039.

Rosedown Plantation, *(Rosedown Plantation &
Gardens; 0-929317),* P.O. Box 1816, Saint
Francisville, LA 70775 (SAN 248-9856)
Tel 504-635-3332.

Rosemary Corp, *(Rosemary Corp., The;
0-9621952),* 1653 Robert St., New Orleans,
LA 70115 Tel 504-895-4247; Dist. by:
Music in Motion, 783 N. Grove, No. 108,
Richardson, TX 75081 (SAN 630-3528)
Tel 214-231-0403; Dist. by: MMB Music,
Inc,, 10370 Page Industrial Blvd., Saint
Louis, MO 63132 (SAN 210-4601)
Tel 314-427-5660.

Rosen Group, *(Rosen Publishing Group, Inc.,
The; 0-8239),* 29 E. 21st St., New York, NY
10010 (SAN 203-3720) Tel 212-777-3017;
Toll free: 800-237-9932 (outside New York).

Rosholt Hse, *(Rosholt Hse.; 0-910417),* Box
104, Rosholt, WI 54473 (SAN 260-1249)
Tel 715-677-4722.

Rosicrucian, *(Rosicrucian Fellowship, The;
0-911274),* P.O. Box 713, 2222 Mission
Ave., Oceanside, CA 92049-0713
(SAN 203-0756) Tel 619-757-6600.

Rossel Bks, *(Rossel Bks.; 0-940646),* Div. of
Seymour Rossel Co., Inc., 4815 Westgrove
Dr., No. 2505, Dallas, TX 75248
(SAN 213-6414) Tel 214-713-8001; Dist.
by: Behrman Hse., Inc., 235 Watchung Ave.,
West Orange, NJ 07052 (SAN 201-4459)
Tel 201-669-0447; Toll free: 800-221-2755.

Roth Pub Inc, *(Roth Publishing, Inc.; 0-89609;
0-8486),* 185 Great Neck Rd., Great Neck,
NY 11021 (SAN 210-9735)
Tel 516-466-3676; Orders to: P.O. Box 406,
Great Neck, NY 11022 (SAN 241-7073);
Toll free: 800-327-0295.

Rough Rock Pr, *(Rough Rock Pr.; 0-936008),*
Rough Rock Demonstration Schl., Box 217,
Chinle, AZ 86503 (SAN 203-1604)
Tel 602-728-3311; Toll free: 800-833-7553.

Roundtable Pub, *(Roundtable Publishing;
0-915677),* 29169 Heathercliff Rd., No. 215,
Malibu, CA 90265 (SAN 237-9260)
Tel 213-457-8433; Toll free: 800-222-5322.

Rourke Corp, *(Rourke Corp.; 0-86593),* P.O.
Box 3328, Vero Beach, FL 32964
(SAN 673-3069); 226 Egret, Vero Beach, FL
32963 (SAN 249-3136) Tel 407-465-4575.

Roush Bks, *(Roush Bks.; 0-934044),* 7423
Arizona Ave., Los Angeles, CA 90045
(SAN 219-2705).

Routledge Chapman & Hall, *(Routledge,
Chapman & Hall, Inc.; 0-416; 0-7100),* Subs.
of International Thomson Organization, Inc.,
29 W. 35th St., New York, NY 10001-2291
(SAN 213-196X) Tel 212-244-3336.

Rovey Res Per Arts, *(Rovey Research in
Performing Arts; 0-9627847),* P.O. Box 638,
Scottsdale, AZ 85252-0638; 7764 E. Rovey
Ave., Scottsdale, AZ 85253
Tel 602-948-5850.

Rowan Tree, *(Rowan Tree Pr., Ltd.; 0-937672),*
124 Chestnut St., Boston, MA 02108
(SAN 214-4638) Tel 617-523-7627; Dist.
by: Inland Bk. Co., 140 Commerce St., East
Haven, CT 06512 (SAN 200-4151)
Tel 203-467-4257; Toll free: 800-243-0138;
Dist. by: Small Pr. Distribution, Inc., 1814
San Pablo Ave., Berkeley, CA 94702
(SAN 204-5826) Tel 415-549-3336; Dist.
by: Bookslinger, 2402 University Ave., Suite
507, Saint Paul, MN 55114
(SAN 169-4154); Toll free: 800-397-2613.

Royalty Pub, *(Royalty Publishing Co.;
0-910487),* P.O. Box 2016, Manassas, VA
22110 (SAN 260-1265) Tel 703-368-9878;
Dist. by: Spring Arbor Distributors, 10885
Textile Rd., Belleville, MI 48111
(SAN 158-9016) Tel 313-481-0900; Toll
free: 800-395-9955; Dist. by: Whitaker Hse.,
580 Pittsburgh St., Springdale, PA 15144
(SAN 203-2104) Tel 412-274-4440; Toll
free: 800-444-4484.

Rubbers Bros Comics, *(Rubbers Brothers
Comics, The; 1-880058),* P.O. Box 431,
Wilbraham, MA 01095; 131 Johnson St.,
Springfield, MA 01108 Tel 413-734-1057.

Rubes Pubns, *(Rubes Pubns.; 0-943384;
0-941364),* 14447 Titus St., Panorama City,
CA 91402 (SAN 240-7647)
Tel 818-782-0800.

Ruggs Recommend, *(Rugg's Recommendation;
0-9608934),* 5749 Colonial Oaks Blvd.,
Sarasota, FL 34232 (SAN 237-9694)
Tel 813-378-4324.

Running Pr, *(Running Pr. Bk. Pubs.; 0-89471;
1-56138),* 125 S. 22nd St., Philadelphia, PA
19103 (SAN 204-5702) Tel 215-567-5080;
Toll free: 800-345-5359 (orders only).
Imprints: Courage Bks (Courage Books).

Running Water, *(Running Water Pr.; 0-9623363),* P.O. Box 2024, Hollywood, CA 90078; 2062 N. Vine St., Hollywood, CA 90068 Tel 213-467-1447.

RuSK Inc, *(RuSK, Inc.; 0-9616894),* Univ. of Alabama, P.O. Box 2504, Tuscaloosa, AL 35486 (SAN 661-5910) Tel 205-345-4720.

Rutgers U Pr, *(Rutgers Univ. Pr.; 0-8135),* 109 Church St., New Brunswick, NJ 08901 (SAN 203-364X) Tel 201-932-7764; Toll free: 800-446-9323 (orders); Orders to: R.U.P. Distribution Ctr., P.O. Box 4869, Baltimore, MD 21211 (SAN 662-1325) Tel 301-338-6947.

Rutledge Hill Pr, *(Rutledge Hill Pr.; 0-934395; 1-55853),* 513 Third Ave., S., Nashville, TN 37210 (SAN 693-8116) Tel 615-244-2700; Toll free: 800-234-4234.

Ruwanga Trad, *(Ruwanga Trading; 0-9615102),* P.O. Box 1027, Puunene, HI 96784 (SAN 694-2776) Tel 808-877-4737; Dist. by: Pacific Trade Group, 94-527 Pauhi St., Waipahu, HI 96797 (SAN 169-1635) Tel 808-671-6735.

RWS Bks, *(RWS Bks.; 0-939400),* 4296 Mulholland St., Salt Lake City, UT 84124 (SAN 220-1593) Tel 801-272-7835.

Ryder Pub Co, *(Ryder Publishing Co.; 0-935973),* 528 Rock Creek Way, Pleasant Hill, CA 94523-4728 (SAN 696-5822).

Rymer Bks, *(Rymer Bks.; 0-9600792; 0-934723),* P.O. Box 104, Tollhouse, CA 93667 (SAN 207-1010) Tel 209-298-0761.

S & M Basinger, *(Basinger, Sherry & Michelle; 0-9620945),* P.O. Box 1054, Clackamas, OR 97015 (SAN 250-1228); 11313 SE Lenore, Clackamas, OR 97015 (SAN 250-1236) Tel 503-698-2294.

S C Toof, *(Toof, S. C., & Co.; 0-942249),* 670 S. Cooper St., P.O. Box 14607, Memphis, TN 38114 (SAN 289-5498) Tel 901-278-2200; Toll free: 800-826-5355; 800-367-8012 (in Tennessee).

S G Phillips, *(Phillips, S. G., Inc.; 0-87599),* P.O. Box 83, Chatham, NY 12037 (SAN 293-3152) Tel 518-392-3068; Orders to: 11 Brookside Ave., Chatham, NY 12037 (SAN 293-3160) Tel 518-392-6300.

S Heiderscheit, *(Heiderscheit, Sara; 0-9620385),* 519 N. Seventh St., Osage, IA 50461 (SAN 249-3780) Tel 515-732-5619.

S I NJOKU, *(Njoku, Scholastica Ibari; 0-9617833),* P.O. Box 11557, Portland, OR 97211 (SAN 665-0724); 307 NE Holland, Portland, OR 97211 Tel 503-285-8160.

S Ill U Pr, *(Southern Illinois Univ. Pr.; 0-8093),* Div. of Southern Illinois Univ., P.O. Box 3697, Carbondale, IL 62902-3697 (SAN 203-3623) Tel 618-453-2281.

S Ink WA, *(Storytellers Ink; 0-9623072),* P.O. Box 33398, Seattle, WA 98133-0398 Tel 206-365-8265.

S J Durst, *(Durst, Sanford J.; 0-915262; 0-942666),* 29-28 41st Ave., Long Island City, NY 11101 (SAN 211-6987) Tel 718-706-0303.

S J F Co, *(SJF Co.; 0-9614185),* 1471 Treasure Ln., Santa Ana, CA 92705 (SAN 676-9411) Tel 714-669-8034.

S J Nash Pub, *(Nash, Steven J., Publishing; 1-878995),* P.O. Box 2115, Highland Park, IL 60035 Tel 708-433-6731; Toll free: 800-843-8545; Dist. by: Baker & Taylor Bks., Eastern Div., 50 Kirby Ave., Somerville, NJ 08876-0734 (SAN 169-4901) Tel 201-722-8000; Toll free: 800-526-3825; Dist. by: Baker & Taylor Bks., Midwestern Div., 501 S. Gladiolus St., Momence, IL 60954-2444 (SAN 169-2100) Tel 815-472-2444; Toll free: 800-435-5111; 800-892-1892 (in Illinois); Dist. by: Baker & Taylor Bks., Southern Div., Mt. Olive Rd., Commerce, GA 30599-9988 (SAN 169-1503) Tel 303-296-1830; Toll free: 800-241-6004; 800-282-6854 (in Georgia); Dist. by: Baker & Taylor Bks., Western Div., 380 Edison Way, Reno, NV 89564 (SAN 169-4464) Tel 702-786-6700; Toll free: 800-648-3540; 800-524-2486 (in Canada); Dist. by: Ingram Bk. Co., 1125 Heil Quaker Blvd., La Vergne, TN 37086-1986 (SAN 169-7978) Tel 615-793-5000; Toll free: 800-937-8000; Dist. by: DeVorss & Co., P.O. Box 550, 1046 Princeton Dr., Marina del Rey, CA 90294 (SAN 168-9886) Tel 213-870-7478; Toll free: 800-843-5743; 800-331-4719 (in California); Dist. by: Bookpeople, 2929 Fifth St., Berkeley, CA 94710 (SAN 168-9517) Tel 415-549-3030; Toll free: 800-999-4650; Dist. by: Spring Arbor Distributors, 10885 Textile Rd., Belleville, MI 48111 (SAN 158-9016) Tel 313-481-0900; Toll free: 800-395-9955; Dist. by: Moving Bks., Inc., P.O. Box 20037, Seattle, WA 98102 (SAN 159-0685) Tel 206-762-1892; Toll free: 800-777-6683; Dist. by: New Leaf Distributing Co., 5425 Tulane Dr., SW, Atlanta, GA 30336-6996 (SAN 169-1449) Tel 404-691-6996; Toll free: 800-326-2665.

S Michaels Pub, *(Michaels, Scott, Publishing Co.; 0-9622535),* 815 N. Lincoln St., Burbank, CA 91506 Tel 818-848-4880.

S Powell, *(Powell, Shirley; 0-9628995),* 146 Cedar St., Rockland, ME 04841 Tel 207-594-4730.

S R Severs, *(Severs, Susan Reist; 0-9618501),* 1288 Barclay Dr., Lancaster, PA 17601 (SAN 668-3304) Tel 717-392-6430.

S Stafford, *(Stafford, Shirley; 0-9607580),* 4231 Casa de Machado, La Mesa, CA 92041 (SAN 239-9806).

S Varney, *(Varney, Sharon; 0-9617579),* Rte. 1, Box 181A, Camden-on-Gauley, WV 26208 (SAN 664-5011) Tel 304-226-5358; Cranberry Ridge Rd., State Rte. 48, Camden-on-Gauley, WV 26208 (SAN 664-502X).

S Yonay, *(Yonay, Shahar; 0-9616783; 0-927580),* 126 Dover St., Brooklyn, NY 11235 (SAN 661-0544) Tel 718-615-0027.

Sabal Pub, *(Sabal Publishing, Inc.; 0-927149),* 2456 Bond Ave., Clearwater, FL 34619 Tel 813-762-2221.

Saban Pub, *(Saban Publishing; 1-879551),* Div. of Saban Entertainment, Inc., 4000 W. Alameda Ave., Burbank, CA 91505 Tel 818-972-4800; Dist. by: Video Treasures, 1767 Morris Ave., Union, NJ 07083 (SAN 630-5512) Tel 201-964-5604; Toll free: 800-237-8843.

Sacred Mntn Pr
See Anthro Co

Sadlier, *(Sadlier, William H., Inc.; 0-8215),* 11 Park Pl., New York, NY 10007 (SAN 204-0948) Tel 212-227-2120; Toll free: 800-221-5175.

Saeta, *(Saeta Ediciones; 0-917049),* P.O. Box 440156, Miami, FL 33144-0156 (SAN 655-2226); 7642 SW 96 Ct., Miami, FL 33173 Tel 305-596-4097.

Safari Museum Pr, *(Safari Museum Pr.),* 16 S. Grant Ave., Chanute, KS 66720 (SAN 110-8840) Tel 314-431-2730.

Safari Pr, *(Safari Pr.; 0-940143),* Div. of Woodbine Publishing Co., 15621 Chemical Ln., Suite B, Huntington Beach, CA 92649 (SAN 663-0723) Tel 714-894-9080; Toll free: 800-451-4788 (orders only).

Sailors Fantasies Pub, *(Sailors Fantasies Publishing; 0-9621212),* P.O. Box 1323, Scottsdale, AZ 85251 (SAN 251-0308); 7433 E. Thomas Rd., Scottsdale, AZ 85251 (SAN 251-0316) Tel 602-946-2125.

Sakura Press, *(Sakura Pr.; 0-936845),* 36787 Sakura Ln., Pleasant Hill, OR 97455 (SAN 658-3350) Tel 503-747-5817.

Sala Enterp, *(Sala Enterprises; 0-9622340),* P.O. Box 76122, Los Angeles, CA 90076; 1308 S. Rimpau Blvd., Los Angeles, CA 90019 Tel 213-859-4602.

Salem Pr, *(Salem Pr., Inc.; 0-89356),* P.O. Box 1097, Englewood Cliffs, NJ 07632 (SAN 208-838X) Tel 201-871-3700; Toll free: 800-221-1592; 150 S. Los Robles Ave., Pasadena, CA 91011 (SAN 241-841X) Tel 818-584-0106. *Imprints:* Magill Bks (Magill Books).

Sales & Mgmt Trg, *(Sales & Management Training of Atlanta, Inc.; 1-877846),* 3273 Shallowford Rd., Atlanta, GA 30341 Tel 404-455-1345; Toll free: 800-367-3523.

Salinas Salinas & Matthews, *(Salinas, Salinas & Matthews; 0-942673),* P.O. Box 376, Montebello, CA 90640 (SAN 667-2876); 145 E. Fifth St., Montebello, CA 90640 (SAN 667-2884) Tel 818-286-9648.

Salmon Falls Pub, *(Salmon Falls Publishing; 0-9620429),* P.O. Box 171, Buhl, ID 83316 (SAN 248-7152); R.R. 3, Buhl, ID 83316 (SAN 248-7160) Tel 208-543-6002.

Salvation Army, *(Salvation Army; 0-89216),* 120 W. 14th St., New York, NY 10011 (SAN 237-2649) Tel 212-337-7200.

Samara Pubns, *(Samara Pubns.; 0-935513),* 15505 SE Arista Dr., Milwaukie, OR 97267 (SAN 695-8923) Tel 503-659-1067; Dist. by: Blanchard's, P.O. Box 855, Clackamas, OR 97015 (SAN 112-1715) Tel 503-657-9838; Toll free: 800-547-9755, Ext. 15 (orders).

SamHar Pr, *(SamHar Pr.; 0-85157),* Div. of Story Hse. Corp., Bindery Ln., Charlotteville, NY 12036 (SAN 203-3585) Tel 607-397-8725; Toll free: 800-847-2105 (orders only).

San Marco Bk, *(San Marco Bookstore; 0-935259),* 1971 San Marco Blvd., Jacksonville, FL 32207 (SAN 693-3734) Tel 904-396-7597.

Sand & Silk, *(Sand & Silk; 0-9617284),* P.O. Box 846, Banning, CA 92220 (SAN 663-5210); P.O. Box 5194, San Bernardino, CA 92412-5194 (SAN 249-3268) Tel 714-849-9244.

Sandcastle Bks Imprint of **Putnam Pub Group**

Sandlapper Pub Co, *(Sandlapper Publishing Co., Inc.; 0-87844),* P.O. Box 730, Orangeburg, SC 29116 (SAN 203-2678) Tel 803-531-1658.

Sandollar Pr, *(Sandollar Pr.),* Div. of Sandollar Enterprises, P.O. Box 4157, Santa Barbara, CA 93140-4157 (SAN 202-9952) Tel 805-963-7077.

Sandpiper Imprint of **HM**

Sandpiper OR, *(Sandpiper Pr.; 0-9603748),* P.O. Box 286, Brookings, OR 97415 (SAN 213-5582) Tel 503-469-5588. Do not confuse with companies with the same name in Solana Beach, CA, Saint Clair Shores, MI.

S&S BYR Imprint of **S&S Trade**

S&S Trade, *(Simon & Schuster Trade; 0-671),* Div. of Simon & Schuster, Inc., 1230 Ave. of the Americas, New York, NY 10020 Tel 212-698-7000. *Imprints:* Fireside (Fireside Paperbacks); Green Tiger (Green Tiger Press); Little Simon (Little Simon); S&S BYR (Simon & Schuster Books for Young Readers); Touchstone Bks (Touchstone Books).

Sanford Hse Pr, *(Sanford Hse. Pr.; 0-9618645),* Hat Shop Hill, Bridgewater, CT 06752 (SAN 668-4238) Tel 203-354-9035.

Sant Bani Ash, *(Sant Bani Ashram, Inc.; 0-89214),* Franklin, NH 03235 (SAN 209-5114) Tel 603-934-5640.

Santabear Bks, *(Santabear Bks.; 0-9619204),* 700 On the Mall, Minneapolis, MN 55402 (SAN 244-6820) Tel 612-375-3489.

Santillana, *(Santillana Publishing Co.; 0-88272; 1-56014),* 901 W. Walnut St., Bldg. A, Compton, CA 90220 (SAN 205-1133) Tel 201-767-6961; Toll free: 800-245-8584; 800-526-0107; 6 Industrial Pkwy., Northvale, NJ 07647.

Saphrograph, *(Saphrograph Corp.; 0-87557),* 4910 Ft. Hamilton Pkwy., Brooklyn, NY 11219 (SAN 110-4128) Tel 718-331-1233.

Sasquatch Bks, *(Sasquatch Bks.; 0-912365),* Div. of Sasquatch Publishing Co., Sales: 1931 Second Ave., Seattle, WA 98101 (SAN 289-0208) Tel 206-441-5555; Dist. by: Pacific Pipeline, Inc., 19215 66th Ave., S., Kent, WA 98032 (SAN 208-2128) Tel 206-872-5523; Toll free: 800-562-4647 (in Washington); 800-426-4727 (in northern California, Montana, Nevada, Oregon, Idaho); Dist. by: Ingram Bk. Co., 1125 Heilquaker Blvd., La Vergne, TN 37086 (SAN 169-7978) Tel 615-793-5000; Toll free: 800-937-8000 (orders only); Dist. by: Baker & Taylor Bks., Western Div., 380 Edison Way, Reno, NV 89564 (SAN 169-4464) Tel 702-786-6700; Dist. by: Gordon's Bks., Inc., 2323 Delgany St., Denver, CO 80216 (SAN 169-0531) Tel 303-296-1830; Toll free: 800-525-6979 (west of the Mississippi); Dist. by: Bookpeople, 2929 Fifth St., Berkeley, CA 94710 (SAN 168-9517) Tel 415-549-3030; Toll free: 800-999-4650.

Saundras Story Bks, *(Saundra's Story Bks., Inc.; 1-879209),* 14742 Beach Blvd., Suite 461, La Habra, CA 90631 Tel 213-690-4767.

Savant Pub, *(Savant Publishing Co.; 0-940527),* P.O. Box 27058, Milwaukee, WI 53227 (SAN 664-5259); W222 N2872 Timberwood Ct., Waukesha, WI 53186 (SAN 664-5267) Tel 414-549-3306.

Sawan Kirpal Pubns, *(Sawan Kirpal Pubns.; 0-918224),* 4653 Windward Ct., No. 20, Lisle, IL 60532 (SAN 211-0571) Tel 708-778-0222; Orders to: Rte. 1, Box 24, Bowling Green, VA 22427 (SAN 211-058X) Tel 804-633-5789.

SBS Pub, *(SBS Publishing, Inc.; 0-89961),* 50 Railroad Ave., Closter, NJ 07624 (SAN 213-3695) Tel 201-767-9450; Toll free: 800-631-2564.

Scarecrow, *(Scarecrow Pr., Inc.; 0-8108),* Div. of Grolier Educational Corp., 52 Liberty St., Box 4167, Metuchen, NJ 08840 (SAN 203-2651) Tel 201-548-8600; Toll free: 800-537-7107.

Scarf Pr, *(Scarf Pr.; 0-934386),* 58 E. 83rd St., New York, NY 10028 (SAN 212-9698) Tel 212-744-3901.

Scepter Pubs, *(Scepter Pubs.; 0-933932),* 481 Main St., New Rochelle, NY 10801 (SAN 207-2858) Tel 914-636-3377.

Scesney Pubns, *(Scesney Pubns., Inc.; 0-9618667),* 11 Edgemoor Rd., Timonium, MD 21093 (SAN 668-4068) Tel 301-252-2509.

Sch Zone Pub Co, *(School Zone Publishing Co.; 0-938256; 0-88743),* 1819 Industrial Dr., P.O. Box 777, Grand Haven, MI 49417 (SAN 289-8314) Tel 616-846-5030; Toll free: 800-253-0564.

Schaffer Pubns, *(Schaffer, Frank, Pubns., Inc.; 0-86734),* 23740 Hathorne Blvd., Torrance, CA 90505 (SAN 217-5827) Tel 213-378-1133; Toll free: 800-421-5565.

Schiffer, *(Schiffer Publishing, Ltd.; 0-916838; 0-88740),* 1469 Morstein Rd., West Chester, PA 19380 (SAN 208-8428) Tel 215-696-1001.

Schiller Inst, *(Schiller Institute, Inc.; 0-9621095),* P.O. Box 66082, Washington, DC 20035 (SAN 250-4944); 1430 K St. NW, Suite 901, Washington, DC 20005 (SAN 250-4952) Tel 202-628-0272.

Schirmer Bks, *(Schirmer Bks.; 0-911320),* Div. of Macmillan Publishing Co., Inc., 866 Third Ave., New York, NY 10022 (SAN 222-9544) Tel 212-702-4283; Dist. by: Macmillan Publishing Co., Inc., Front & Brown Sts., Riverside, NJ 08370 (SAN 202-5582) Tel 609-461-6500; Toll free: 800-257-5755.

Schneider Educational, *(Schneider Educational Products; 1-877779),* 2880 Green St., San Francisco, CA 94123 Tel 415-567-4455.

Schocken, *(Schocken Bks., Inc.; 0-8052),* Div. of Random Hse., Inc., 201 E. 50th St., New York, NY 10022 (SAN 213-7585) Tel 212-872-8238; Orders to: Random House, Inc., 400 Hahn Rd., Westminster, MD 21157 (SAN 202-5515) Tel 301-848-1900; Toll free: 800-733-3000 (orders).

Schoenhof, *(Schoenhof's Foreign Bks., Inc.; 0-87774),* Subs. of Editions Gallimard, 76A Mt. Auburn St., Cambridge, MA 02138 (SAN 212-0062) Tel 617-547-8855.

Schol Facsimiles, *(Scholars' Facsimiles & Reprints; 0-8201),* P.O. Box 344, Delmar, NY 12054 (SAN 203-2627) Tel 518-439-5978.

Scholar Pub Co, *(Scholar Publishing Co.; 0-9624016),* P.O. Box 850165, New Orleans, LA 70185 Tel 504-486-2294.

Scholastic Hardcover Imprint of **Scholastic Inc**

Scholastic Inc, *(Scholastic, Inc.; 0-590; 0-439),* Subs. of SI Holdings, Inc., 730 Broadway, New York, NY 10003 (SAN 202-5442) Tel 212-505-3000; Toll free: 800-392-2179; Orders to: P.O. Box 7502, 2931 E. McCarty St., Jefferson City, MO 65102 (SAN 202-5450); Toll free: 800-325-6149 (orders only). *Imprints:* Apple Paperbacks (Apple Paperbacks); Blue Ribbon Bks (Blue Ribbon Books); Hello Reader (Hello Reader); Lucky Star (Lucky Star); Point (Point); Scholastic Hardcover (Scholastic Hardcover); Sunfire (Sunfire); Vagabond (Vagabond); Wildfire (Wildfire Press).

Scholium Intl, *(Scholium International, Inc.; 0-87936),* 99 Seaview Blvd., Port Washington, NY 11050-4610 (SAN 169-5282) Tel 516-484-3290.

Schroder Music, *(Schroder Music Co.; 0-915620),* 1450-6th St., Berkeley, CA 94710 (SAN 207-3935) Tel 415-524-5804; Dist. by: Children's Small Pr. Collection, 719 N. Fourth Ave., Ann Arbor, MI 48104 (SAN 200-514X) Tel 313-668-8056; Toll free: 800-221-8056.

Schumacher Pubns
See **Zenith City**

Sci of Mind, *(Science of Mind Communications; 0-917849; 0-911336),* Div. of United Church of Religious Science, P.O. Box 75127, Los Angeles, CA 90075 (SAN 203-2570) Tel 213-388-2181; Toll free: 800-247-6463; Dist. by: DeVorss & Co., P.O. Box 550, 1046 Princeton Dr., Marina del Rey, CA 90294 (SAN 168-9886) Tel 213-870-7478; Toll free: 800-843-5743; 800-331-4719 (in California); Dist. by: New Leaf Distributing Co., 5425 Tulane Dr., SW, Atlanta, GA 30336-2323 (SAN 169-1449) Tel 404-691-6996; Toll free: 800-326-2665.

Sci Pubs, *(Scientific Pubs., Inc.; 0-945417),* P.O. Box 15718, Gainesville, FL 32601 (SAN 247-0098); 738 NE Seventh Ave., Gainesville, FL 32604 (SAN 247-0101) Tel 904-373-5630.

Science Man Pr, *(Science Man Pr.; 0-936046),* Div. of TSM Marketing, Inc., 4738 N. Harlem Ave., Harwood Heights, IL 60656 (SAN 213-7968) Tel 708-867-4441.

SCOAL Pr, *(SCOAL Pr.; 0-933556),* 53 Pondview Cir., Brockton, MA 02401 (SAN 213-3717) Tel 508-587-4275.

Scott F, *(Scott, Foresman & Co.; 0-673),* Subs. of HarperCollins Pubs., Inc., 1900 E. Lake Ave., Glenview, IL 60025 (SAN 200-2140) Tel 708-729-3000.

Scribblers Pub, *(Scribblers Publishing; 0-924649),* Div. of G.E.T., Inc., 14205 Cashel Forest Dr., Houston, TX 77069 Tel 713-440-5698.

Scribner Imprint of **Macmillan**

Scribners Young Read Imprint of **Macmillan Child Grp**

Scriptorium Pr, *(Scriptorium Pr., The; 0-931485),* 71 S. Main St., Alfred, NY 14802 (SAN 683-1354) Tel 607-587-9371.

Scroll Pr, *(Scroll Pr., Inc.; 0-87592),* 2858 Valerie Ct., Merrick, NY 11566 (SAN 206-796X) Tel 516-379-4283.

Sea Fog Pr, *(Sea Fog Pr., Inc.; 0-917507),* P.O. Box 210056, San Francisco, CA 94121-0056 (SAN 656-1012) Tel 415-221-8527.

Sea Island, *(Sea Island Information Group; 1-877610),* 11210 Cherry Hill Rd., No. 102, Beltsville, MD 20705 Tel 301-937-2494.

Sea Rock Pr, *(Sea Rock Pr.; 0-9630091),* P.O. Box 58, Elk, CA 95432; 5951 S. Highway 1, Elk, CA 95432 Tel 707-877-3204.

Sea Urchin, *(Sea Urchin Pr.; 0-9605208),* P.O. Box 10503, Oakland, CA 94610-0503 (SAN 215-8086).

Seabird
See **Stagecoach Rd Pr**

Seablom, *(Seablom Design Bks.; 0-918800),* 2106 Second Ave., N., Seattle, WA 98109 (SAN 210-4962) Tel 206-285-2308.

Seabright, *(Seabright; 0-9613824),* 712 Ott St., Harrisonburg, VA 22801 (SAN 679-9973) Tel 703-434-8553; Rte. 1, Box 135, Nags Head, NC 27959 (SAN 248-3998); Dist. by: Storie/McOwen Pubs., Inc., P.O. Box 308, Manteo, NC 27954 (SAN 265-0940) Tel 919-473-1225; Toll free: 800-832-773; 800-443-5879 (in North Carolina).

Seagull Pub Co, *(Seagull Publishing Co.; 0-9612698),* 2915 Stanford Ave., Suite 7, Marina del Rey, CA 90291 (SAN 295-0235).

Seal Pr Feminist, *(Seal Pr.-Feminist; 0-931188; 1-878067),* 3131 Western Ave., No. 410, Seattle, WA 98121-1028 (SAN 215-3416) Tel 206-283-7844; Dist. by: Bookslinger, 2402 University Ave., Suite 507, Saint Paul, MN 55114 (SAN 169-4151); Toll free: 800-397-2613; Dist. by: Inland Bk. Co., 140 Commerce St., East Haven, CT 06512 (SAN 200-4151) Tel 203-467-4257; Toll free: 800-243-0138; Dist. by: Pacific Pipeline, Inc., 19215 66th Ave., S., Kent, WA 98032 (SAN 208-2128) Tel 206-872-5523; Toll free: 800-562-4617 (in Washington); 800-426-4727 (in northern California, Nevada, Idaho, Oregon, Montana); Dist. by: Bookpeople, 2929 Fifth St., Berkeley, CA 94710 (SAN 168-9517) Tel 415-549-3030; Toll free: 800-999-4650; Dist. by: Consortium Bk. Sales, 287 E. Sixth St., Suite 365, Saint Paul, MN 55101 (SAN 200-6049) Tel 612-221-9035; Toll free: 800-283-3572.

Seanglim Bit, *(Bit, Seanglim; 0-9628625),* 5210 Gordon Ave., El Cerrito, CA 94530 Tel 415-233-4682.

Search Public, *(Search Pubns.; 0-910715),* Div. of Sanborn Education Research, Inc., 2000 Old Stage Rd., Florissant, CO 80816 (SAN 262-0766) Tel 303-748-3341.

Seascape Enters, *(Seascape Enterprises; 0-931595),* P.O. Box 176, Colonial Heights, VA 23834 (SAN 682-4765) Tel 804-526-7119; Dist. by: Talman Co., 150 Fifth Ave., New York, NY 10011 (SAN 200-5204) Tel 212-620-3182; Toll free: 800-537-8894; Dist. by: C Plath North American Division of Litton Systems, Inc., 222 Severn Ave., Annapolis, MD 21403 (SAN 301-263-6700.

Seaver Bks, *(Seaver Bks.; 0-394; 0-8050),* c/o Arcade Publishing, Inc., 141 Fifth Ave., New York, NY 10010 Tel 212-475-2633.

SeaWard Graph, *(SeaWard Graphics; 0-9628939),* 13 Narrows Rd., Narragansett, RI 02882 (SAN 297-4274) Tel 401-783-1817; Toll free: 800-366-1817.

Seaworthy Pubns, *(Seaworthy Pubns.; 0-9625229),* 5914 Stuart Dr., Flowery Branch, GA 30542 Tel 404-967-4319.

Selena Pr, *(Selena Pr.; 0-938451),* 1010 Southwood Dr., Fargo, ND 58103 (SAN 660-9880) Tel 701-235-2890.

Self-Taught Pubs, *(Self-Taught Pubs.; 0-9624077),* 1041 Monterey Ct., University Park, IL 60466 Tel 312-534-0859.

Sells Pub, *(Sells Publishing Co.; 0-926739),* 3053 E. Flora Pl., Denver, CO 80210 Tel 303-691-0473.

Sengstack Grp
See **Summy-Birchard**

Sennet & Sarnoff, *(Sennet & Sarnoff Learning Systems, Inc.; 1-879871),* 20 E. 49th, New York, NY 10017 Tel 212-308-5926.

Sentinel Bks, *(Sentinel Bks.; 0-941263),* Subs. of Tribune Co., 633 N. Orange Ave., Orlando, FL 32801 (SAN 665-5297) Tel 407-420-5588; Toll free: 800-347-6868.

Setubandh Pubns, *(Setubandh Pubns.; 0-9623674),* 1 Lawson Ln., Great Neck, NY 11023 Tel 516-482-6938.

Seven Arrows, *(Seven Arrows; 0-9622341),* 1497 Stratton Pl., Mount Pleasant, SC 29464 Tel 803-884-2816.

Seven Locks Pr, *(Seven Locks Pr.; 0-932020),* P.O. Box 27, Cabin John, MD 20818 (SAN 211-9781); Toll free: 800-537-9359; 7307 MacArthur Blvd., Bethesda, MD 20816 (SAN 658-1587) Tel 301-320-2130; Dist. by: Independent Pubs. Group, 814 N. Franklin, Chicago, IL 60610 (SAN 202-0769) Tel 312-337-0747.

Seventh-Wing Pubns, *(Seventh-Wing Pubns.; 0-944208),* 515 E. Washington St., Colorado Springs, CO 80907 (SAN 243-0428) Tel 719-471-2932.

Sevgo Pr, *(Sevgo Pr.; 0-943487),* Div. of Sevgo, Inc., 1955 22nd St., Northport, AL 35476 (SAN 668-4998) Tel 205-339-1888.

Sey Lawr *Imprint of* **Delacorte**

Seymour Pubns, *(Seymour, Dale, Pubns.; 0-86651),* P.O. Box 10888, Palo Alto, CA 94303-0879 (SAN 200-9781); Toll free: 800-872-1100; 800-222-0766 (in California); 1100 Hamilton Ct., Menlo Park, CA 94025 (SAN 216-0110) Tel 415-324-2800.

SF Study Ctr, *(San Francisco Study Ctr.; 0-936434),* P.O. Box 5646, San Francisco, CA 94101 (SAN 214-4654) Tel 415-626-1650.

SG Prodns, *(SG Productions; 0-9621071),* P.O. Box 432, 508 Fourth St., Dayton, OR 97114 (SAN 250-6262) Tel 503-864-2987.

SGC Biomedical, *(SGC Biomedical Engineering; 0-925395),* P.O. Box 2414, Garden Grove, CA 92642-2414 Tel 714-534-5479.

SH Ltd Pubs, *(SH Ltd., Pubs.; 0-9621376),* 1225 E. Ft. Union Blvd., Suite 200, Midvale, UT 84047 (SAN 251-1118) Tel 801-566-5644.

Shade Tree NV, *(Shade Tree Bks.; 0-9617609),* 1200 Nelson Ct., Boulder City, NV 89005 (SAN 664-8614) Tel 702-293-2177.

Shaker Her Soc, *(Shaker Heritage Society),* Albany Shaker Rd., Albany, NY 12211 (SAN 289-0410) Tel 518-456-7890.

Shakespere VT, *(Shakespeare-For-Today Trust; 0-9628103; 1-880026),* P.O. Box 66, Whiting, VT 05778-0066; Rte. 30, Whiting, VT 05778 Tel 802-623-6651.

Shalom, *(Shalom, P., Pubns., Inc.; 0-87559),* 5409 18th Ave., Brooklyn, NY 11204 (SAN 204-5893) Tel 718-256-1954. Do not confuse with companies with the same name in Victor, MT, Hazelwood, MO, Loveland, CO.

Shambhala Pubns, *(Shambhala Pubns., Inc.; 0-87773; 0-394),* Horticultural Hall, 300 Massachusetts Ave., Boston, MA 02115 (SAN 203-2481) Tel 617-424-0030; Dist. by: Random Hse., Inc., 400 Hahn Rd., Westminster, MD 21157 (SAN 202-5515) Tel 301-848-1900; Toll free: 800-733-3000 (orders).

Shamrock Pr, *(Shamrock Pr. & Publishing Co.; 0-910583),* P.O. Box 7256, Alexandria, VA 22307 (SAN 260-2636) Tel 703-683-3114.

Shapeless Enterprises, *(Shapeless Enterprises; 0-9623368),* P.O. Box 297, Harbor City, CA 90710 Tel 213-539-0313.

Shapolsky Pubs, *(Shapolsky Pubs., Inc.; 0-933503; 0-944007; 1-56171),* 136 W. 22nd St., New York, NY 10011 (SAN 200-8068) Tel 212-633-2022; Dist. by: Carol Publishing Group, 120 Enterprise Ave., Secaucus, NJ 07094 (SAN 630-4524) Tel 201-866-8159; Dist. by: Bookazine Co., Inc., 303 W. Tenth St., New York, NY 10014 (SAN 169-5665) Tel 212-675-8877; Toll free: 800-221-8112; Dist. by: Pacific Pipeline, 19215 66th Ave., S., Kent, WA 98032-1171 (SAN 208-2128) Tel 206-872-5523; Toll free: 800-562-4647 (in Washington); 800-426-4727 (in northern California, Idaho, Oregon, Montana, Neveda); 800-444-7323 (orders only); Dist. by: Golden-Lee Bk. Distributors, Inc., 1000 Dean St., Brooklyn, NY 11238 (SAN 169-5126) Tel 718-857-6333; Toll free: 800-473-7475; Dist. by: Ingram Bk. Co., 1125 Heilquaker Blvd,, La Vergne, TN 37086 (SAN 169-7978) Tel 615-793-5000; Toll free: 800-937-8000 (orders only); Dist. by: Baker & Taylor Bks., Midwestern Div., 501 S, Gladiola St., Momence, IL 60954 (SAN 169-2100) Tel 815-472-2444; Toll free: 800-435-5111; 800-892-1892 (in Illinois); Dist. by: Baker & Taylor Bks., Southern Div., Mount Olive Rd., Commerce, GA 30599 (SAN 169-1503) Tel 404-335-5000; Toll free: 800-241-6004; 800-282-6850 (in Georgia); Dist. by: Baker & Taylor Bks., Eastern Div., 50 Kirby Ave., Sommerville, NJ 08876 (SAN 169-4901) Tel 201-722-8000; Toll free: 800-526-3811; Dist. by: Baker & Taylor Bks., Western Div., 380 Edison Way, Reno, NV 89564 (SAN 169-4464) Tel 702-786-6700; Toll free: 800-648-3540; Dist. by: Brodart Co., 500 Arch St., Williamsport, PA 17705 (SAN 169-7684) Tel 717-326-2462; Toll free: 800-233-8467.

Shared Learning, *(Shared Learning, Inc.; 1-877667),* 975 Walnut, Suite 253, Cary, NC 27511 Tel 919-467-4602.

Sharp & Dunn, *(Sharp & Dunnigan, Pubns., Inc.; 0-918495),* 165 Piper Ave., Chico, CA 95926 (SAN 657-3029) Tel 916-891-6602; Toll free: 800-327-1149; Dist. by: Baker & Taylor Bks., Eastern Div., 50 Kirby Ave., Somerville, NJ 08876 (SAN 169-4901) Tel 201-722-8000; Toll free: 800-435-1845; 800-352-4833 (in New Jersey); Dist. by: Ingram Bk. Co., 1125 Heilquaker Blvd., La Vergne, TN 37086 (SAN 169-7978) Tel 615-793-5000; Toll free: 800-937-8000 (orders only).

Shasta San Rafael, *(Shasta Pubns.; 0-941611),* Div. of Shasta Enterprises, P.O. Box 12456, San Rafael, CA 94913 (SAN 666-1750) Tel 415-479-4491. Do not confuse with Shasta Pubns., Cincinnati, OH.

Shaw & Co, *(Shaw & Co.; 0-944900),* 18 S. Mill, Glastonbury, CT 06073 (SAN 245-6745) Tel 203-275-5000.

Shaw Pubs, *(Shaw, Harold, Pubs.; 0-87788),* P.O. Box 567, 388 Gundersen Dr., Wheaton, IL 60189 (SAN 203-2473) Tel 708-665-6793; Toll free: 800-742-9782. Do not confuse with (Melvin) Shaw Publishing, LaBelle, FL.

Shawme Ent, *(Shawme Enterprises; 0-914151),* 36 Rte. 6A, R.F.D. 1, Sandwich, MA 02563 (SAN 287-556X) Tel 508-888-2519.

Shearer Pub, *(Shearer Publishing; 0-940672),* 406 Post Oak Rd., Fredericksburg, TX 78624 (SAN 218-5989) Tel 512-997-6529; Toll free: 800-458-3808.

Sheba Bks Intl, *(Sheba Bks. International; 1-878950),* 220 W. 71st St., New York, NY 10023 (SAN 297-2336).

Sheed & Ward MO, *(Sheed & Ward; 0-934134; 1-55612),* Div. of National Catholic Reporter Publishing Co., Inc., P.O. Box 419492, Kansas City, MO 64141-6492 (SAN 207-7396); Toll free: 800-444-8910; 800-333-7373 (orders); 115 E. Armour Blvd., Kansas City, MO 64111 (SAN 658-1269) Tel 816-531-0538.

Sheffield WI, *(Sheffield Publishing Co.; 0-917974; 0-88133; 1-879215),* Subs. of Waveland Pr., Inc., P.O. Box 359, Salem, WI 53168 (SAN 658-4519); 9009 Antioch Rd., Salem, WI 53168 (SAN 658-4527) Tel 414-843-2281.

Sheffield Wisc
See **Sheffield WI**

Shelby Hse, *(Shelby Hse.; 0-942179),* Affil. of St. Lukes Pr., 1407 Union Ave., Suite 401, Memphis, TN 38104 (SAN 666-8895) Tel 901-357-5441; Toll free: 800-524-5554.

Shengold, *(Shengold Pubs., Inc.; 0-88400),* 18 W. 45th St., New York, NY 10036 (SAN 203-2465) Tel 212-944-2555.

Shepherd Minst, *(Shepherd Ministries; 0-923417),* 2845 W. Airport Freeway, Suite 137, Irving, TX 75062 (SAN 252-0893) Tel 214-570-7599.

Sheriar Pr, *(Sheriar Pr., Inc.; 0-913078),* 3005 Hwy. 17 Bypass N., Myrtle Beach, SC 29577 (SAN 203-2457) Tel 803-448-1107.

Sheridan, *(Sheridan Hse., Inc.; 0-911378; 0-924486),* 145 Palisade St., Dobbs Ferry, NY 10522 (SAN 204-5915) Tel 914-693-2410.

Shining IL, *(Shining Star Pubns.),* Div. of Good Apple, Inc., P.O. Box 299, Carthage, IL 62321-0299 Tel 217-357-3981; Toll free: 800-435-7234.

Shirk-Heath, *(Shirk-Heath, Sandra J.; 0-9615104),* 1935 42nd St., NW, Rochester, MN 55901 (SAN 694-2784) Tel 507-289-0711.

Shirlee, *(Shirlee Pubns.; 0-9613476),* P.O. Box 22122, Carmel, CA 93922 (SAN 657-3789) Tel 408-646-0600.

Shoe String, *(Shoe String Pr., Inc.; 0-208),* P.O. Box 4327, Hamden, CT 06514 (SAN 213-2079); 925 Sherman Ave., Hamden, CT 06514 (SAN 696-9410) Tel 203-248-6307.

Shoe Tree Pr *Imprint of* **Betterway Pubns**

Shorey, *(Shorey Bk. Store; 0-8466),* 1411 First Ave., No. 200, Seattle, WA 98101 (SAN 204-5958) Tel 206-624-0221.

Shulsinger Sales, *(Shulsinger Sales, Inc.; 0-914080),* 50 Washington St., Brooklyn, NY 11201 (SAN 205-9851) Tel 718-852-0401.

Shuttle Craft, *(Shuttle Craft Bks., Inc.; 0-916658),* P.O. Box 550, Coupeville, WA 98239 (SAN 208-1148) Tel 206-678-4648.

Sierra, *(Sierra Club Bks.; 0-87156),* 100 Bush St., 13th Flr., San Francisco, CA 94104 (SAN 203-2406) Tel 415-291-1600; Dist. by: Random Hse., Inc., 400 Hahn Rd., Westminster, MD 21157 (SAN 202-5515) Tel 301-848-1900; Toll free: 800-733-3000 (orders).

Sierra Oaks Pub, *(Sierra Oaks Publishing Co.; 0-940113),* 1370 Sierra Oaks Ct., Newcastle, CA 95658-9791 (SAN 664-063X) Tel 916-663-1474.

Sig *Imprint of* **NAL-Dutton**

Sig Classics *Imprint of* **NAL-Dutton**

Sig Vista *Imprint of* **NAL-Dutton**

Sight & Sound, *(Sight & Sound International, Inc.; 0-88704),* 3200 S. 166th St., P.O. Box 27, New Berlin, WI 53151 (SAN 283-4065) Tel 414-784-5850.

Sights Prods, *(Sights Productions; 0-9629978),* 15130 Black Ankle Rd., Mount Airy, MD 21771 Tel 301-795-4582.

Signal Media, *(Signal Media Corp., K-Lite 94 Radio; 0-916677),* 14951 Dallas Pkwy., Suite 1030, Dallas, TX 75240 (SAN 659-6789) Tel 214-458-8400.

Signal Research Inc, *(Signal Research, Inc.; 0-929307),* P.O. Box 29364, Greensboro, NC 27429 (SAN 248-8698); 300A S. Westgate Dr., Greensboro, NC 27407 (SAN 248-8701) Tel 919-299-9902.

Silbert Bress, *(Silbert & Bress Pubns.; 0-89544),* P.O. Box 68, Mahopac, NY 10541 (SAN 210-5020) Tel 914-628-7910.

Silhouette, *(Silhouette),* 300 E. 42nd St., New York, NY 10017 Tel 212-698-7450; Dist. by: Pocket Books, 1230 Ave. of the Americas, New York, NY 10020 (SAN 202-5922) Tel 212-698-7406; Toll free: 800-223-2336 (orders).

Silicon Pr, *(Silicon Pr.; 0-9615336; 0-929306),* 25 Beverly Rd., Summit, NJ 07901 (SAN 695-1538) Tel 908-273-8919.

Silver, *(Silver, Burdett & Ginn, Inc.; 0-382; 0-663),* Div. of Simon & Schuster, Inc., 250 James St., Morristown, NJ 07960 (SAN 204-5982) Tel 201-285-8135; Toll free: 800-631-8081; 108 Wilmot Rd., Deerfield, IL 60015 (SAN 111-6517) Tel 312-945-1240; 1925 Century Blvd., NE, Suite 14, Atlanta, GA 30345 (SAN 111-6509) Tel 404-321-7455; 3814 West St., Mariemont Executive Bldg., Cincinnati, OH 45227 (SAN 111-6495) Tel 513-272-2200; 641 W. Mockingbird, Dallas, TX 75247 (SAN 108-0458) Tel 214-631-5185; 255 Constitution Dr., Menlo Park, CA 94025 (SAN 111-6525) Tel 415-326-4351.

Silver Burdett Pr, *(Silver Burdett Pr.; 0-382),* Subs. of Simon & Schuster, Inc., 190 Sylvan Ave., Englewood Cliffs, NJ 07632 (SAN 243-2617) Tel 201-592-2646; Toll free: 800-624-4843; Orders to: P.O. Box 1226, Westwood, NJ 07675-1226 (SAN 243-2625); Toll free: 800-843-3464.

Silver Dollar, *(Silver Dollar City, Inc.),* Silver Dollar City, MO 65616 (SAN 210-3699) Tel 417-388-2611.

Silver Forest Pub, *(Silver Forest Publishing; 0-929684),* P.O. Box 3520, Evergreen, CO 80439-3520 (SAN 250-1783); 30596 Bryant Dr., Evergreen, CO 80439 (SAN 297-357X) Tel 303-674-5755.

Silver Pr, *(Silver Pr.; 0-671),* Subs. of Silver Burdett Pr., Simon & Schuster, Inc., 190 Sylvan Ave., Englewood Cliffs, NJ 07632 Tel 201-592-2646; Orders to: P.O. Box 1226, Westwood, NJ 07675-1226; Toll free: 800-843-3464.

Silver Prescrip Pr, *(Silver Prescription Pr., Inc.; 0-945214),* 524 Camino del Monte Sol, Santa Fe, NM 87501 (SAN 246-2303) Tel 505-983-3868.

Silver Pubns, *(Silver Pubns.; 0-9624811),* 5215 W. Clearwater, Suite 10725B, Kennewick, WA 99336 Tel 509-783-3337.

Silver Rim Pr, *(Silver Rim Pr.; 1-878611),* 2759 Park Lake Dr., Boulder, CO 80301 Tel 303-666-4290.

Silver Sea, *(Silver Sea Pr.; 0-916005),* 820 Pacific Coast Hwy., Suite 103, Hermosa Beach, CA 90254 (SAN 294-6610) Tel 213-379-8959.

Silver Seal Bks, *(Silver Seal Bks.; 0-910867),* P.O. Box 106, Fox Island, WA 98333 (SAN 264-3871).

Simplicity Pr, *(Simplicity Pr.; 0-929225),* 1064 Ardmore, Redlands, CA 92374 (SAN 248-7179) Tel 714-792-0276.

Simpson NJ, *(Simpson Publishing Co.; 0-9622508),* P.O. Box 220, Boonton, NJ 07005; 338 W. Main St., Boonton, NJ 07005 Tel 201-334-7400. Do not confuse with Simpson Publishing Co., Kirksville, MO.

Simpson Pub, *(Simpson Publishing Co.),* 1115 S. Franklin St., Kirksville, MO 63501 (SAN 202-9928) Tel 816-665-7251. Do not confuse with Simpson Publishing Co., Boonton, NJ.

Sinclair Ent, *(Sinclair, Dorothy, Enterprises; 0-9615311),* P.O. Box 782, Bellaire, TX 77401-0782 (SAN 694-5996) Tel 713-664-9809.

Sing Out Corp, *(Sing Out Corp.; 0-9626704),* P.O. Box 5253, Bethlehem, PA 18015; 125 E. Third St., Bethlehem, PA 18015 Tel 215-399-0684; Dist. by: Independent Pubs. Group, 814 N. Franklin, Chicago, IL 60610 (SAN 202-0769) Tel 312-337-0747.

Singing Rock, *(Singing Rock Pr.; 0-9629395),* 5901 Bell Cir., Minnetonka, MN 55345 Tel 612-934-6458.

Sirius Leag, *(Sirius League, The; 0-9610762),* P.O. Box 40507, Albuquerque, NM 87196 (SAN 264-6366) Tel 505-262-0720.

Six Pr, *(6 Pr.; 0-943310),* 11889 Dogwood Ave., Fountain Valley, CA 92708 (SAN 240-7752) Tel 714-839-1857.

Sizzy Bks, *(Sizzy Bks.; 0-945590),* P.O. Box 401, Los Alamos, NM 87544 (SAN 247-0934); 382 Catherine Ave., Los Alamos, NM 87544 (SAN 247-0942) Tel 505-672-3416.

Skandisk, *(Skandisk, Inc.; 0-9615394),* 3424 19th Ave. S., Minneapolis, MN 55407 (SAN 695-4405) Tel 612-724-6561.

Skeetoonies, *(Skeetoonies; 0-9622109),* S. 37 W. 26867 Holiday Hill Rd., Waukesha, WI 53188 Tel 414-549-1843.

SkippingStone Pr, *(SkippingStone Pr., Inc.; 0-927867),* P.O. Box 22105, Denver, CO 80222 Tel 303-733-9307; Dist. by: Empire Publishing Service, P.O. Box 1344, Studio City, CA 91614-0344 (SAN 630-5687) Tel 818-784-8918.

Skribent, *(Skribent Pr.; 0-9609374),* 9700 SW Lakeside Dr., Tigard, OR 97223 (SAN 283-2542) Tel 503-620-0471; Dist. by: Quality Bks., Inc., 918 Sherwood Dr., Lake Bluff, IL 60044-2204 (SAN 169-2127) Tel 708-295-2010; Toll free: 800-323-4241 (Libraries only).

Skylark *Imprint of* **Bantam**

Skylight, *(Skylight Pr., Inc.; 0-910423),* 100 E. Glenside Ave., Glenside, PA 19038 (SAN 240-9070) Tel 215-886-7333.

Skyspec Pub, *(Skyspec Publishing; 0-9627534),* P.O. Box 75171, Cincinnati, OH 45275; Toll free: 800-521-8226; 5878 Rabbit Hash Rd., Union, KY 41091 Tel 606-586-7454.

Slack Inc, *(Slack, Inc.; 0-913590; 0-943432; 1-55642),* 6900 Grove Rd., Thorofare, NJ 08086-9447 (SAN 201-8632) Tel 609-848-1000; Toll free: 800-257-8290.

Slawson Comm, *(Slawson Communications, Inc.; 0-915391; 0-932238),* 165 Vallecitos de Oro, San Marcos, CA 92069-1436 (SAN 200-6901) Tel 619-744-2299; Toll free: 800-752-9766.

Sloan Manry Pubs, *(Sloan/Manry Pubs.; 0-9622316),* 16809 Holbrook, Shaker Heights, OH 44120 Tel 216-752-1717.

Small Busn Pr, *(Small Business Pr., Inc.; 0-942221),* 7515 Greenville, LB 534, Suite 510, Dallas, TX 75231 (SAN 666-8763) Tel 214-739-0058. Do not confuse with Small Business Pubs., Inc., Hyannis, MA.

Small Hands Pr, *(Small Hands Pr.; 0-9619208),* 3337 N. Miller Rd., Suite 105, Scottsdale, AZ 85251 (SAN 243-5519) Tel 602-994-9773.

Smartworm Corp, *(Smartworm Corp.; 1-877820),* P.O. Box 1176, Newnan, GA 30264; Toll free: 800-477-7627 (outside Georgia); 339 Millard Farmers Blvd., Newnan, GA 30263 Tel 404-254-1094.

Smarty Pants, *(Smarty Pants; 1-55886),* 15104 Detroit Ave., Suite 2, Lakewood, OH 44107 (SAN 249-0110) Tel 216-221-5300; Dist. by: Macmillian, Inc., Front & Brown Sts., Riverside, NJ 08370 (SAN 202-5582) Tel 609-461-6500; Toll free: 800-257-5755.

SME Pr, *(SME Pr.; 0-945026),* P.O. Box 777, Sanibel, FL 33957 (SAN 245-6249); 3516 W. Gulf Dr., Sanibel, FL 33957 (SAN 245-6257) Tel 813-472-2465. Do not confuse with Society of Manufacturing Engineers (SME), Dearborn, MI.

Smiley Originals, *(Smiley Originals; 0-9629001),* P.O. Box 099, Smiley, TX 78159-0099 (SAN 297-4045); Anglin St., Smiley, TX 78159 Tel 512-587-6113.

Smith & Smith Pub, *(Smith & Smith Publishing Co.; 0-9609230),* 119 N. Fourth St., Suite 411, Minneapolis, MN 55401 (SAN 241-4570) Tel 612-338-8235.

Smith Pubs
See Smithmark

Smithmark, *(Smithmark Pubs., Inc.; 0-8317),* 112 Madison Ave., New York, NY 10016 (SAN 216-3241) Tel 212-532-6600; Toll free: 800-645-9990; 800-932-0070 (in New Jersey); 80 Distribution Blvd., Edison, NJ 08817 (SAN 658-1625) Tel 201-287-3550. *Imprints:* Gallery Bks (Gallery Books).

Smithsonian, *(Smithsonian Institution Pr.; 0-87474; 1-56098),* 470 L'Enfant Plaza, Suite 7100, Washington, DC 20560 (SAN 206-8044) Tel 202-287-3738; Orders to: TAB Bks., Inc., Dept. 900, Blue Ridge Summit, PA 17294-0900 (SAN 202-568X) Tel 717-794-2148; Toll free: 800-782-4612.

SMU Press, *(Southern Methodist Univ. Pr.; 0-87074),* P.O. Box 415, Dallas, TX 75275 (SAN 203-3615); 6410 Airline Dr., Dallas, TX 75205 (SAN 658-1641) Tel 214-739-5959; Dist. by: Texas A & M Univ. Pr., Drawer C, College Station, TX 77843 (SAN 207-5237); Toll free: 800-826-8911.

SNB Pub, *(SNB Publishing; 0-932909),* 4343 Shallowford Rd., No. B-3A, Mariettalle, GA 30062-5005 (SAN 688-9093).

Snow Lion, *(Snow Lion Pubns., Inc.; 0-937938; 1-55939),* P.O. Box 6483, Ithaca, NY 14851 (SAN 281-7292); Toll free: 800-950-0313; 110 N. Geneva St., Ithaca, NY 14850 (SAN 250-328X) Tel 607-273-8506; Dist. by: Bookpeople, 2929 Fifth St., Berkeley, CA 94710 (SAN 168-9517) Tel 415-549-3030; Toll free: 800-999-4650; Dist. by: Inland Bk. Co., 140 Commerce St., East Haven, CT 06512 (SAN 200-4151) Tel 203-467-4257; Toll free: 800-243-0138; Dist. by: Samuel Weiser, Inc., P.O. Box 612, York Beach, ME 03910 (SAN 202-9588) Tel 207-363-4393; Toll free: 800-423-7087; Dist. by: Great Tradition, 11270 Clayton Creek Rd., Lower Lake, CA 95457 (SAN 200-5743) Tel 707-995-3906; Toll free: 800-275-2606; Dist. by: New Leaf Distributing Co., 5425 Tulane Dr., SW, Atlanta, GA 30336-2323 (SAN 169-1449) Tel 404-691-6996; Toll free: 800-326-2665; Dist. by: Moving Bks., Inc., P.O. Box 20037, Seattle, WA 98102 (SAN 159-0685) Tel 206-325-9077; Toll free: 800-777-6683; Dist. by: S.C.B. Distributors, P.O. Box 5446, Carson, CA 90749-5446 (SAN 630-4818) Tel 213-631-6090; Toll free: 800-729-6423.

Snyder Inst Res, *(Snyder Institute of Research; 0-940714),* 508 N. Pacific Coast Hwy., Redondo Beach, CA 90277 (SAN 204-9694) Tel 213-372-4469.

Sobriety Pr, *(Sobriety Pr.; 0-939847),* 159 Lincoln Ave., Box 201, Washington, NJ 07882 (SAN 664-0532) Tel 201-689-6476.

Soc for Visual, *(Society for Visual Education, Inc.; 0-89290; 1-56357),* 1345 W. Diversey Pkwy., Chicago, IL 60614-1299 (SAN 208-3930) Tel 312-525-1500; Toll free: 800-829-1900.

Soc Issues, *(Social Issues Resources Series, Inc.; 0-89777),* P.O. Box 2348, Boca Raton, FL 33427-2348 (SAN 222-8920) Tel 407-994-0079; Toll free: 800-232-7477.

Soccer for Am, *(Soccer for Americans; 0-916802),* P.O. Box 836, Manhattan Beach, CA 90266 (SAN 208-3787) Tel 213-372-9000. Do not confuse with Sport-Shelf.

Solar Studio, *(Solar Studio, The; 0-932320),* 178 Cowles Rd., Woodbury, CT 06798 (SAN 222-8823) Tel 203-263-3147.

Solipaz Pub Co, *(Solipaz Publishing Co.; 0-913999),* P.O. Box 366, Lodi, CA 95241 (SAN 286-8814) Tel 209-368-1595.

Soma Pr, *(Soma Pr.; 0-932510),* P.O. Box 416, Yellow Springs, OH 45387 (SAN 222-8858) Tel 513-767-1573.

Someday Baby, *(Someday Baby, Inc.; 0-927945),* Div. of Child's Gift of Lullabyes, 1508 16th Ave., S., Nashville, TN 37212 Tel 615-385-0022.

Son-Rise Pubns, *(Son-Rise Pubns. & Distribution Co.; 0-936369),* Rte. 3, Box 202, New Wilmington, PA 16142 (SAN 698-0031) Tel 412-946-8334; Dist. by: Spring Arbor Distributors, 10885 Textile Rd., Belleville, MI 48111 (SAN 158-9016) Tel 313-481-0900; Toll free: 800-395-9955; Dist. by: Whitaker Hse., 580 Pittsburgh St., Springdale, PA 15144 (SAN 203-2104) Tel 412-274-4440; Toll free: 800-444-4484.

Soncino Pr, *(Soncino Pr.),* 123 Ditmas Ave., Brooklyn, NY 11218 (SAN 681-2740) Tel 718-972-6200.

Sonflower Bks *Imprint of* **SP Pubns**

Songbird & Seabird, *(Songbird & Seabird Bks.; 0-925398),* P.O. Box 1569, Aptos, CA 95003; 921 Duane, Sunnyvale, CA 94086 Tel 408-684-0194.

Songs & Co, *(Songs & Co.; 0-9624135),* 601 Van Ness Ave., Suite E3125, San Francisco, CA 94102 Tel 415-564-2400.

Songs & Stories, *(Songs & Stories Children Love; 0-934591),* 4243 Carpenter Ave., Bronx, NY 10466 (SAN 694-0609) Tel 212-325-5587.

Songs Sottongs, *(Songs of Sottongs; 0-9624136),* 709 Parsons Ln., Signal Mountain, TN 37377 Tel 615-886-2208.

Sonos, *(Sonos Publishing, Inc.; 0-929985; 1-56509),* 1386 W. Center, Orem, UT 84057 (SAN 250-9210) Tel 801-224-5330.

Sopris, *(Sopris West, Inc.; 0-944584),* 1140 Boston Ave., Longmont, CO 80501 (SAN 243-945X) Tel 303-651-2829.

Sound Ent, *(Sound Enterprises Publishing Co.; 0-935565),* 970 Cornwallis Dr., West Chester, PA 19380 (SAN 696-1886) Tel 215-431-4512; Dist. by: Baker & Taylor Bks., Eastern Div., 50 Kirby Ave., Somerville, NJ 08876 (SAN 169-4901) Tel 201-722-8000; Toll free: 800-435-1845; 800-352-4833 (in New Jersey); Dist. by: Baker & Taylor Bks., Southern Div., Mt. Olive Rd., Commerce, GA 30529 (SAN 169-1503) Tel 404-335-5000; Toll free: 800-241-6004; 800-282-6850 (in Georgia); Dist. by: Baker & Taylor Bks., Midwestern Div., 501 S. Gladiolus St., Momence, IL 60954 (SAN 169-2100) Tel 815-472-2444; Toll free: 800-435-5111; 800-892-1892 (in Illinois); Dist. by: Baker & Taylor Bks., Western Div., 380 Edison Way, Reno, NV 89564 (SAN 169-4464) Tel 702-786-6700; Toll free: 800-648-3540.

Sound Pub WA, *(Sound Publishing; 0-9629860),* P.O. Box 7192, Tacoma, WA 98407; 4203 Olympic Blvd., W., Tacoma, WA 98466 Tel 206-565-6568. Do not confuse with companies of the same name in Denver, CO, Great Neck, NY.

Sound World Record, *(Sound World Recordings; 0-9619269),* 1200 S. Brand Blvd., Suite 11, Glendale, CA 91204 (SAN 243-6124) Tel 818-953-7381; 1041 "A" Linden Ave., Glendale, CA 91202 (SAN 243-6132).

Soundboard Bks, *(Soundboard Bks.; 1-878636),* 1016 E. El Camino Real, No. 124, Sunnyvale, CA 94087-3759 Tel 408-738-1705.

Soundbox Pubns, *(Soundbox Pubns.; 0-9622499),* 5541 Lakeside Dr., Bldg. 1, Unit 206, Margate, FL 33063 Tel 305-979-3112.

Soundprints, *(Soundprints Corp.; 0-924483),* Div. of TMC Corp., P.O. Box 679, 165 Water St., Norwalk, CT 06856 Tel 203-838-6009; Toll free: 800-228-7839.

Sounds Kansas, *(Sounds of Kansas; 0-9615597),* Rte. 1, Box 176, Inman, KS 67546 (SAN 696-1657) Tel 316-585-2389.

Southern Hist Pr, *(Southern Historical Pr., Inc.; 0-89308),* P.O. Box 1267, Greenville, SC 29602-1267 (SAN 208-8657); 275 W. Broad St., Greenville, SC 29601 Tel 803-233-2346.

Southern Rose Prodns, *(Southern Rose Productions; 0-929560),* Rte. 3, Box 272D, Ripley, MS 38663 (SAN 249-6968) Tel 601-837-1125.

Southwinds Pr, *(Southwinds Pr.; 0-931581),* P.O. Box 13421, Tallahassee, FL 32317 (SAN 683-1338) Tel 904-385-1383.

SP Pubns, *(Scripture Pr. Pubs., Inc.; 0-88207; 0-89693),* 1825 College Ave., Wheaton, IL 60187 (SAN 222-9471) Tel 708-668-6000; Toll free: 800-323-9409. *Imprints:* Sonflower Bks (Sonflower Books).

Spacone Pub, *(Spacone Publishing Co.; 0-944712),* 5350 W. Evans Dr., Glendale, AZ 85306 (SAN 244-8882) Tel 602-978-2677.

Sparhawk, *(Sparhawk Bks., Inc.; 0-9605776),* Div. of Pawprints, Inc., Pierce Crossing Rd., Jaffrey, NH 03452 (SAN 216-5538) Tel 603-532-9337; Toll free: 800-633-2900; Orders to: Box 2, Jaffrey, NH 03452 (SAN 699-5608) Tel 603-532-7091.

Sparkler Bks *Imprint of* **Pharos Bks NY**

Sparky Star Pr, *(Sparky Star Pr.; 0-9621616),* P.O. Box 216, Bellevue, WA 98009 (SAN 252-1202); 3233 76th, NE, Bellevue, WA 98004 (SAN 252-1210) Tel 206-454-2272.

Sparrow Pr CA *See* Sparrow TN

Sparrow TN, *(Sparrow Corp., The; 0-917143),* P.O. Box 5010, Brentwood, TN 37024-5010 (SAN 655-8844); 101 Winners Cir., Brentwood, TN 37024 Tel 615-371-6800.

Spec Creations, *(Special Creations; 1-878329),* P.O. Box 17248, Indianapolis, IN 46217; 8413 Garni Ct., Indianapolis, IN 46227 Tel 317-882-9832.

Spec Lit Pr, *(Special Literature Pr.; 0-938594),* P.O. Box 20522, Bacon Sta., Indianapolis, IN 46220 (SAN 215-8175) Tel 317-257-4467; Toll free: 800-777-5165.

Special Touch, *(Special Touch, Inc., Publishing; 0-945232),* P.O. Box 427, Springfield, KY 40069-0427; 124 E. Main St., Springfield, KY 40069 Tel 606-336-7749.

Specialty Bks Intl, *(Specialty Bks., International; 0-89445),* P.O. Box 1785, Ann Arbor, MI 48106 (SAN 210-2714) Tel 517-456-4764.

Spect Ln Pr, *(Spectacle Lane Pr., Inc.; 0-930753),* 106 Spectacle Lane, Wilton, CT 06897 Tel 203-762-3786.

Spectra *Imprint of* **Bantam**

SPECTRA Inc, *(SPECTRA, Inc., Pubs.; 1-877936),* Div. of SPECTRA, Inc., P.O. Box 13591, New Orleans, LA 70185-3591; Toll free: 800-359-8152; 701 Jefferson Ave., Metairie, LA 70001 Tel 504-831-4440.

Spectra Pubns Hse, *(Spectra Pubns. Hse.; 0-9621693),* P.O. Box 21, Crockett, CA 94525 (SAN 251-785X); 2158 Vista del Rio, Crockett, CA 94525 (SAN 251-7868) Tel 415-787-2282.

Speech Bin, *(Speech Bin, The; 0-937857),* 1766 20th Ave., Vero Beach, FL 32960 (SAN 630-1657) Tel 407-770-0007.

Speller, *(Speller, Robert, & Sons, Pubs., Inc.; 0-8315),* P.O. Box 411, Madison Sq. Sta., New York, NY 10159 (SAN 203-2295) Tel 212-473-0333; Orders to: P.O. Box 461, Times Sq. Sta., New York, NY 10108 (SAN 203-2309).

Spencer Muse Art, *(Spencer Museum of Art; 0-913689),* Affil. of Univ. of Kansas, Univ. of Kansas, Lawrence, KS 66045 (SAN 111-347X) Tel 913-864-4710.

Spencers Intl, *(Spencer's International Enterprises; 0-937771),* P.O. Box 43822, Los Angeles, CA 90043 (SAN 659-333X) Tel 213-937-3099; Toll free: 800-752-5909; Dist. by: Baker & Taylor Bks., Eastern Div., 50 Kirby Ave., Somerville, NJ 08876 (SAN 169-4901) Tel 201-722-8000; Toll free: 800-435-1845; 800-352-4833 (in New Jersey); Dist. by: Ingram Bk. Co., 1125 Heilquaker Blvd., La Vergne, TN 37086 (SAN 169-7978) Tel 615-793-5000; Toll free: 800-937-8000 (orders only).

Spheric Hse, *(Spheric Hse.; 0-935984),* 4633 E. Broadway, Suite 108, Tucson, AZ 85711 (SAN 222-0032).

SPI Pub, *(SPI Publishing; 0-9624280),* Div. of Security Photo, Inc., 44211 Village Ct., Canton, MI 48187 Tel 313-455-1910.

Spice Pr, *(Spice Pr.; 0-9623300),* 1555P S. Havana, No. 324, Aurora, CO 80012 Tel 303-751-0910.

Spiral Galaxy, *(Spiral Galaxy Publishing; 0-9617056),* P.O. Box 235, Kingston, MA 02364 (SAN 662-9245); 7 Surrey Ln., Kingston, MA 02364 (SAN 662-9253) Tel 617-585-8965.

Spirit Mount Pr, *(Spirit Mountain Pr.; 0-910871),* P.O. Box 1214, Fairbanks, AK 99707 (SAN 283-9156).

Spiritseeker, *(Spiritseeker Publishing, Inc.; 0-9630419),* P.O. Box 2441, Fargo, ND 58108-2441; 518 NP Ave., Suite 306, Fargo, ND 58102 Tel 701-232-5966.

Spizzirri, *(Spizzirri Publishing Co., Inc.; 0-86545),* P.O. Box 9397, Rapid City, SD 57709 (SAN 215-2851); Toll free: 800-325-9819.

Spoken English Pubns, *(Spoken English Pubns.; 0-929350),* 210 W. 21st St., New York, NY 10011 (SAN 249-0927) Tel 212-989-2719.

Spooner & Thomson, *(Spooner & Thomson Bks.),* 2 Tinkham Ln., Lakeville, MA 02347 (SAN 667-1330).

Sporting News, *(Sporting News Publishing Co.; 0-89204),* Subs. of Times Mirror Co., P.O. Box 56, Saint Louis, MO 63166 (SAN 203-2260); 1212 N. Lindbergh Blvd., Saint Louis, MO 63132 (SAN 699-5616) Tel 314-993-7734; Orders to: P.O. Box 44, Saint Louis, MO 63166 (SAN 662-1481).

Sports Diary Pub, *(Sports Diary Publishing Co.; 0-929861),* P.O. Box 1141, Norman, OK 73070 (SAN 250-734X); 3003 River Oaks Dr., No. 148, Norman, OK 73072 (SAN 250-7358) Tel 405-360-4180.

Sports Focus Pub, *(Sports Focus Publishing; 0-9622039),* 1023 Hook Ave., Pleasant Hill, CA 94523 Tel 415-937-4059; Toll free: 800-431-2700.

Sports Plan Consult, *(Sports Planning Consultants; 0-9620914),* 7620 Northfield Ln., Manlius, NY 13104 (SAN 250-0353) Tel 315-682-7334.

Spring Creek Pubns, *(Spring Creek Pubns.; 0-945184),* P.O. Box 243, Rose Hill, KS 67133 (SAN 246-6309); 5810 S. Webb, Derby, KS 67037 (SAN 246-6317) Tel 316-788-2182.

Sproing, *(Sproing Bks.; 0-916176),* 10612 Altman St., Tampa, FL 33612 (SAN 206-3816).

Sq One Pubs, *(Square One Pubs., Inc.; 0-938961),* 6 Birch Hill Rd., Ballston Lake, NY 12019 (SAN 661-7271) Tel 508-877-4946.

Squared Away, *(Squared Away Farm; 0-9624179),* Rte. 3, Box 311, Tallahassee, FL 32308 Tel 904-893-0693.

SRA, *(Science Research Assocs.; 0-574; 0-88120),* Div. of Macmillan/McGraw-Hill School Publishing Co., 155 N. Wacker Dr., Chicago, IL 60606 (SAN 295-3498) Tel 312-984-7000; Toll free: 800-621-0476.

Sri Rama, *(Sri Rama Publishing; 0-918100),* 161 Robles Dr., Santa Cruz, CA 95060 (SAN 282-3578) Tel 408-426-5098; Orders to: P.O. Box 2550, Santa Cruz, CA 95063 (SAN 282-3586).

SSGI Pr, *(SSGI Pr.; 1-877768),* Div. of Sedona Spectrum Group International, P.O. Box 2091, Sedona, AZ 86336; Toll free: 800-552-3356; 50 Wild Horse Mesa, Sedona, AZ 86336 Tel 602-284-9229.

St Johann Pr, *(St. Johann Pr.; 1-878282),* 315 Schraalenburgh Rd., Haworth, NJ 07641 Tel 201-387-1529.

St Lukes Pr, *(St. Luke's Pr.; 0-918518),* Div. of The Wimmer Companies, 4210 B. F. Goodrich Blvd., Memphis, TN 38118 Tel 901-362-8900; Toll free: 800-727-1034.

St Martin, *(St. Martin's Pr.; 0-312; 0-9603648),* Subs. of Macmillan Publishing Co., Inc., 175 Fifth Ave., New York, NY 10010 (SAN 200-2132) Tel 212-674-5151; Toll free: 800-525-5525.

St Mary's, *(St. Mary's Pr.; 0-88489),* Subs. of Christian Brothers of Minnesota, 702 Terrace Heights, Winona, MN 55987-1320 (SAN 203-073X) Tel 507-457-7900; Toll free: 800-533-8095.

St Nectarios, *(St. Nectarios Pr.; 0-913026),* 10300 Ashworth Ave., N., Seattle, WA 98133-9410 (SAN 203-3542) Tel 206-522-4471.

ST Two, *(ST2; 0-943542),* 203 Si Town Rd., Castle Rock, WA 98611 (SAN 238-3810) Tel 206-636-2645.

St Ursula, *(St. Ursula Academy; 0-9607918),* 1339 E. McMillan St., Cincinnati, OH 45206 (SAN 238-5767) Tel 513-961-4877.

Staccato Prodns, *(Staccato Productions, Inc.; 1-879783),* P.O. Box 995, Cedar Grove, NJ 07009; 160 Myrtle Ave., Cedar Grove, NJ 07009 Tel 201-857-0059.

Stack the Deck, *(Stack the Deck, Inc.; 0-933282),* 9126 Sandpiper Ct., Orland Park, IL 60462 (SAN 212-5668) Tel 312-349-8345.

Stadium Bks, *(Stadium Bks.; 0-9625132; 1-879458),* 11 Ferry Lane, W., Westport, CT 06880 Tel 203-226-6967.

Stafford Lowery, *(Stafford Lowery Pr.; 0-943153),* P.O. Box 62177, Washington, DC 20029-2177 (SAN 668-1182); 2003 Bunker Hill Rd., NE, Washington, DC 20011 (SAN 668-1190) Tel 202-398-5006.

Stagecoach Rd Pr, *(Stagecoach Road Pr.; 0-933499),* P.O. Box 33, Ashland, OR 97520 (SAN 691-8859); 202 Oak Lawn, Ashland, OR 97520 Tel 503-482-4417.

Standard Ed, *(Standard Educational Corp.; 0-87392),* 200 W. Monroe, Chicago, IL 60606 (SAN 204-6326) Tel 312-346-7440.

Standard Pub, *(Standard Publishing Co.; 0-87239; 0-87403),* Div. of Standex International, 8121 Hamilton Ave., Cincinnati, OH 45231 (SAN 110-5515) Tel 513-931-4050; Toll free: 800-543-1301.

Standards & Trg, *(Standards & Training, Inc.; 0-9627536),* 3225 Brookhaven Club Dr., Dallas, TX 75234 Tel 214-247-7731.

Star & Elephant Bks *Imprint of* **Green Tiger Pr**

Star Bks Inc, *(Star Bks., Inc.; 0-915541),* 408 Pearson St., Wilson, NC 27893 (SAN 291-4468) Tel 919-237-1591; Toll free: 800-476-1591.

Star City Pubns, *(Star City Pubns.; 0-9615937),* 1735 S. 20th St., Lincoln, NE 68502 (SAN 696-8244) Tel 402-477-5025; Orders to: P.O. Box 2914, Lincoln, NE 68502 (SAN 662-3883).

Star Dust Bks, *(Star Dust Bks.; 0-9621782),* 15 Lenox Rd., Kensington, CA 94707 Tel 415-526-5844.

Star Light Pr, *(Star Light Pr.; 1-879817),* 1811 S. First St., Austin, TX 78704-4299 Tel 512-441-0157.

Star Pubns MO, *(Star Pubns.; 0-932356),* 1211 W. 60th Terr., Kansas City, MO 64113 (SAN 212-4564) Tel 816-523-8228. Do not confuse with Star Pubns., Orange Park, FL.

Star Rover, *(Star Rover Hse. at Jack London Heritage Hse.; 0-932458),* 1914 Foothill Blvd., Oakland, CA 94606 (SAN 212-4572) Tel 415-532-8408; Orders to: Lexikos, P.O. Box 296, Lagunitas, CA 94938 Tel 415-488-0401.

Starblaze *Imprint of* **Donning Co**

Starboard Cove, *(Starboard Cove Publishing; 0-9622221),* HCR 70, Box 442, Bucks Harbor, ME 04618; Starboard Cove Rd., Bucks Harbor, ME 04618 Tel 207-255-4426.

Starbright, *(Starbright Bks.; 0-9606248),* 1611 E. Dow Rd., Freeland, WA 98249 (SAN 282-3632) Tel 206-321-6138.

Stardom, *(Stardom Co., Ltd.; 1-880171),* 6939 W. Glenbrook Rd., Milwaukee, WI 53223 Tel 414-357-7807; Toll free: 800-368-2276.

Starfire *Imprint of* **Bantam**

Starlite Pub, *(Starlite Publishing Co.; 0-9621359),* 9289 Village Glen Dr., No. 116, San Diego, CA 92123 (SAN 251-1339) Tel 619-277-0863.

Starmakers, *(Starmakers; 0-9619773),* P.O. Box 161212, Atlanta, GA 30321 (SAN 246-5566); 3900 Crown Rd., Atlanta, GA 30354 (SAN 246-5574). Moved, left no forwarding address.

Starset Pub, *(Starset Publishing; 0-9622770),* P.O. Box 1146, Northbrook, IL 60065-1146; 6150-52 N. Hoyne Ave., Chicago, IL 60659 Tel 312-338-3747.

Start Smart Bks, *(Start Smart Bks.; 1-878396),* P.O. Box 3446, Bradlee Shopping Ctr., Alexandria, VA 22313; 12 W. Cedar St., Alexandria, VA 22301 Tel 703-683-3278.

Starword Bks, *(Starword Bks., Inc.; 0-945710),* P.O. Box 280267, Lakewood, CO 80228 (SAN 247-3119); 833 Marion St., Denver, CO 80218 (SAN 247-3127) Tel 303-832-2587.

State House Pr, *(State Hse. Pr.; 0-938349; 1-880510),* P.O. Drawer 15247, Austin, TX 78761 (SAN 660-9651); Toll free: 800-421-3378; 8906 Wall St., Suite 702, Austin, TX 78754 (SAN 660-966X).

State U NY Pr, *(State Univ. of New York Pr.; 0-87395; 0-88706; 0-7914),* State Univ. Plaza, Albany, NY 12246-0001 (SAN 658-1730) Tel 518-472-5000; Toll free: 800-662-211; Orders to: P.O. Box 6525, Ithaca, NY 14851 (SAN 203-3496) Tel 607-277-2211; Toll free: 800-666-2211.

Statesman Exam, *(Statesman-Examiner, Inc.; 0-940151),* 220 S. Main, Box 271, Colville, WA 99114 (SAN 664-2691) Tel 509-684-4567.

Statford CA, *(Statford Publishing, Inc.; 0-913087),* 1259 El Camino Real, Suite 1500, Menlo Park, CA 94025 (SAN 283-4197) Tel 415-854-9355.

Steam Pr MA, *(Steam Pr.; 0-942820),* 154 N. Fair St., Guilford, CT 06437-2444 (SAN 238-8642); Dist. by: National Bk. Network, 4720A Boston Way, Lanham, MD 20706 (SAN 630-0065) Tel 301-459-8696; Toll free: 800-462-6420.

Steck-V, *(Steck-Vaughn Co.; 0-8114),* Subs. of National Education Corp., P.O. Box 26015, Austin, TX 78755 (SAN 203-347X); Toll free: 800-531-5015; 3520 Executive Center Dr., Travis Bldg., Suite 300, Austin, TX 78731 (SAN 699-5632) Tel 512-343-8227; 3301 Steck Ave., Austin, TX 78758 (SAN 658-1757); 11 Prospect St., Library Div., Madison, NJ 07940 Tel 201-514-1525.

Steele Hollow, *(Steele Hollow Pr.; 0-9624282),* R.R. 1, Box 144C, Hunns Lake, Stanfordville, NY 12581 Tel 914-868-7316.

Stemmer Hse, *(Stemmer Hse. Pubs., Inc.; 0-916144; 0-88045),* 2627 Caves Rd., Owings Mills, MD 21117 (SAN 207-9623) Tel 301-363-3690.

Steppingstone Ent, *(Steppingstone Enterprises, Inc.; 0-939728),* 2108 S. University Dr., Park Place Plaza, Suite 103, Fargo, ND 58103 (SAN 216-7646) Tel 701-237-4742.

Sterling, *(Sterling Publishing Co., Inc.; 0-8069),* 387 Park Ave., S., New York, NY 10016-8810 (SAN 211-6324) Tel 212-532-7160; Toll free: 800-367-9692; Warehouse: Bldg. 2C, Terminal Way, Avenel, NJ 07001-2216 (SAN 658-1773) Tel 201-396-3111.

Stern & Stern, *(Stern & Stern Publishing Co.; 1-879417),* 9104 Falcon Creek Cir., Elk Grove, CA 95624 Tel 916-685-2618.

Stevens & Shea, *(Stevens & Shea Pubs.; 0-89550),* P.O. Box 794, Stockton, CA 95201 (SAN 206-3670) Tel 209-465-1880.

Stew & Rice, *(Stew & Rice Productions; 0-9629842),* 339 Kauila St., Hilo, HI 96720 Tel 808-969-7069.

Stewart Tabori & Chang, *(Stewart, Tabori & Chang, Inc.; 0-941434; 1-55670),* 575 Broadway, New York, NY 10012 (SAN 293-4000) Tel 212-941-2929; Dist. by: Workman Publishing Co., Inc., 708 Broadway, New York, NY 10003 (SAN 203-2821) Tel 212-254-5900; Toll free: 800-722-7202; Dist. by: Random Hse., Inc., 400 Hahn Rd., Westminster, MD 21157 (SAN 202-5515) Tel 301-848-1900; Toll free: 800-733-3000 (orders).

Sthrn Cal Perf, *(Southern California Performance Products, Inc.; 1-879748),* 12915 Telegraph Rd., Suite D, Santa Fe Springs, CA 90670 Tel 213-698-8641.

Stiff Lip, *(Stiff Lip Productions; 0-9623469),* 898 Cedar Ave., Sunnyvale, CA 94086 Tel 408-245-6960.

Still Waters, *(Still Waters Pr.; 1-877801),* 112 W. Duerer St., Galloway Township, NJ 08201 Tel 609-652-1790. Do not confuse with Still Waters Pr. in Pomfret Center, CT.

Stillpoint, *(Stillpoint Publishing; 0-913299),* Div. of Stillpoint International, Inc., P.O. Box 640, Walpole, NH 03608 (SAN 285-8630) Tel 603-756-9281; Toll free: 800-847-4014 (credit card orders only); Orders to: Penguin U.S.A., 100 Fabrite Rd., Newbern, TN 38059-1334 (SAN 200-3023) Tel 901-627-2521; Toll free: 800-526-0275.

Stilwell Studio, *(Stilwell Studio, The; 0-9605862),* P.O. Box 50, Carmel, CA 93921 (SAN 220-1895) Tel 408-624-0340.

Stipes, *(Stipes Publishing Co.; 0-87563),* P.O. Box 526, 10-12 Chester St., Champaign, IL 61820 (SAN 206-8664) Tel 217-356-8391.

Stirrup Assoc, *(Stirrup Assocs., Inc.; 0-937420),* Div. of David C. Cook Publishing Co., 850 N. Grove Ave., Elgin, IL 60120 (SAN 215-1863) Tel 312-741-2400.

STL Intl, *(STL International, Inc.; 0-936215),* P.O. Box 35918, Tulsa, OK 74153-0918 (SAN 696-8783) Tel 918-250-1488; Dist. by: International Cassette Corp., P.O. Box 1928, Greenville, TX 75401 (SAN 200-5824).

Stoneback Pub, *(Stoneback, Jean, Publishing Co.; 0-931440),* 588 Franklin St., Alburtis, PA 18011 (SAN 222-8440) Tel 215-966-3991.

Stonehaven Pubs, *(Stonehaven Pubs.; 0-937775),* Box 367, Lena, IL 61048 (SAN 659-347X); 602 Oak St., Lena, IL 61048 (SAN 659-3488) Tel 815-369-2823. Do not confuse with Stonehaven Pubs., Fort Worth, TX.

Stoneway Ltd, *(Stoneway, Ltd.; 0-934593; 1-55923),* P.O. Box 548, Southeastern, PA 19399 (SAN 693-8817) Tel 215-337-9600; Toll free: 800-237-7558.

Stopher, *(Stopher, Inc.; 0-9628204),* P.O. Box 65172, Baltimore, MD 21209; 6930 Ten Timbers Ln., Baltimore, MD 21209 Tel 301-486-8858.

Storey Comm Inc, *(Storey Communications, Inc.; 0-88266),* Schoolhouse Rd., Pownal, VT 05261 (SAN 203-4158) Tel 802-823-5811; Toll free: 800-827-8673; Dist. by: HarperCollins, Keystone Industrial Pk., Scranton, PA 18512 (SAN 215-3742) Tel 717-343-4761; Toll free: 800-242-7737; 800-982-4377 (in Pennsylvania). *Imprints:* Garden Way Pub (Garden Way Publishing).

Story Hse Corp, *(Story Hse. Corp.; 0-87157),* Bindery Ln., Charlotteville, NY 12036 (SAN 169-5193) Tel 607-397-8725; Toll free: 800-847-2105; 800-428-1008 (in New York).

Storypole, *(Storypole Pr.; 0-9609940),* 11015 Bingham Ave., E., Tacoma, WA 98446 (SAN 275-8199) Tel 206-531-2032.

Storytime Ink, *(Storytime Ink International; 0-9628769),* P.O. Box 470505, Broadview Heights, OH 44147 Tel 216-838-4881.

Storyviews Pubs, *(Storyviews Publishing Co.; 0-9617057),* 44 Oak St., Shrewsbury, MA 01545 (SAN 662-8354) Tel 508-845-5881; Dist. by: Bookazine Co., Inc., 303 W. Tenth St., New York, NY 10014 (SAN 169-5665) Tel 212-675-8877; Toll free: 800-221-8112; Dist. by: Baker & Taylor Bks., Eastern Div., 50 Kirby Ave., Somerville, NJ 08876 (SAN 169-4901) Tel 201-722-8000; Toll free: 800-526-3825.

Stravon, *(Stravon Educational Pr.; 0-87396),* Subs. of Stravon Pubs., Inc., 845 Third Ave., New York, NY 10022 (SAN 202-7402) Tel 212-371-2880.

Strawberry Hill, *(Strawberry Hill Pr.; 0-89407),* 3848 SE Division St., Portland, OR 97202 (SAN 238-8103) Tel 503-235-5989.

Strode, *(Strode Pubs.; 0-87397),* Div. of Circle Bk. Service, P.O. Box 626, Tomball, TX 77375 (SAN 202-7429) Tel 713-255-6824; Toll free: 800-227-1591.

Strytllr Co, *(Storyteller Co.; 0-9622500),* P.O. Box 543, Tarrytown, NY 10591; 42 Riverview Ave., Tarrytown, NY 10591 Tel 914-631-1990.

Student Sccss, *(Student Success Consultants, Inc.; 0-9621214),* 2911 Eighth Ave., W., Bradenton, FL 34205 (SAN 251-0340) Tel 813-748-4237.

Stuttman, *(Stuttman, H. S., Inc.; 0-87475),* 333 Post Rd., W., Westport, CT 06889 (SAN 202-7453) Tel 203-226-7841; Dist. by: Marshall Cavendish Corp, 2415 Jerusalem Ave., North Bellmore, NY 11710 (SAN 238-437X) Tel 516-826-4200; Toll free: 800-821-9881.

Styx Enter, *(Styx Enterprises; 1-882121),* P.O. Box 2587, Eugene, OR 97402 (SAN 248-4560); 3991 Royal, Eugene, OR 97402 (SAN 248-4579).

Success Publ, *(Success Publishing; 0-931113),* Div. of Success Group, 2812 Bayonne Dr., Palm Beach Gardens, FL 33410 (SAN 678-9501) Tel 407-626-4643.

Sugar Marbel Pr, *(Sugar Marbel Pr.; 0-9608320),* 1547 Shenandoah Ave., Cincinnati, OH 45237 (SAN 240-1002) Tel 513-761-8000.

Sugar Plum Pr, *(Sugar Plum Pr.; 0-9629632),* 1739 St. Andrews Cir., Blacksburg, VA 24060 (SAN 662-388) Tel 703-951-3721.

Sugar Sign Pr, *(Sugar Sign Pr.; 0-939849),* 1407 Fairmont St., Greensboro, NC 27403 (SAN 664-0524) Tel 919-273-9838.

Sullivan MT, *(Sullivan & Assocs.; 1-878330),* 113 E. Wyoming, Kalispell, MT 59901 Tel 406-257-9021.

Summa Pub, *(Summa Publishing Co.; 0-932423),* 240 Lombard St., Suite 206, Thousand Oaks, CA 91360 (SAN 687-4096) Tel 805-524-2944.

Summers Pub, *(Summers Publishing; 0-916109),* Div. of Central Missouri Medical Services, 529 E High St., No. A, Jefferson City, MO 65101-3216 (SAN 294-9083) Tel 314-634-2925; Dist. by: Cowley Distributing Agency, 732 Heisinger Rd., Jefferson City, MO 65101 (SAN 169-426X) Tel 314-636-6511; Toll free: 800-636-6511.

Summit TX, *(Summit Publishing; 0-9626219; 1-56530),* Div. of Summit Group, 1227 W. Magnolia, Suite 500, Fort Worth, TX 76104 Tel 817-921-3346; Toll free: 800-875-3346. Do not confuse with Summit Publishing, Los Angeles, CA.

Summit Univ, *(Summit Univ. Pr.; 0-916766; 0-922729),* Box A, Livingston, MT 59047-1390 (SAN 208-4120); Toll free: 800-323-5228 (orders only); 710 E. Gallatin, Livingston, MT 59047-1390 Tel 406-222-8300.

Summy-Birchard, *(Summy-Birchard, Inc.; 0-87487),* 265 Secaucus Rd., Secaucus, NJ 07096-2037 (SAN 202-7461) Tel 201-348-0700. *Imprints:* Suzuki Method (Suzuki Method International).

Sun Pr FL, *(Sun Pr. of Florida; 0-937039),* 35 Trotters Cir., Kissimmee, FL 32743 (SAN 658-702X) Tel 305-933-1586.

Sun Star Pubns, *(Sun Star Pubns.; 0-937787),* 3104 E. Camelback Rd., Box 519, Phoenix, AZ 85016 (SAN 659-3550) Tel 602-948-4346.

Sunburst, *(Sunburst; 0-9609618),* 1322 Coral Dr., W., Tacoma, WA 98446-5832 (SAN 275-8571) Tel 206-565-2041.

Sunburst *Imprint of FS&G*

Sundance Pubs, *(Sundance Pubs. & Distributors; 0-940146),* Newtown Rd., Littleton, MA 01460 (SAN 169-3484) Tel 508-486-9201; Toll free: 800-456-5584.

Sunfire *Imprint of Scholastic Inc*

Sunflower Hill, *(Sunflower Hill; 0-9623184),* R.D. No. 4, Box 9F, Addison, NY 14801 Tel 607-359-3354.

Sunlakes Pub, *(Sunlakes Publishing Co.; 0-9615884),* 4153 Bayard Rd., South Euclid, OH 44121 (SAN 696-7663) Tel 216-951-9100.

Sunlight Prodns, *(Sunlight Productions; 0-945086),* P.O. Box 1300, Sedona, AZ 86336 (SAN 245-8470); 390 Jordan Rd., No. 1, Sedona, AZ 86336 (SAN 245-8489) Tel 602-282-2877; Dist. by: Bookpeople, 2929 Fifth St., Berkeley, CA 94710 (SAN 168-9517) Tel 415-549-3030; Toll free: 800-999-4650; 800-624-4466 (in California); Dist. by: New Leaf Distributing Co., 5425 Tulane Dr., SW, Atlanta, GA 30336-2323 (SAN 169-1449) Tel 404-691-6996; Toll free: 800-326-2665; Dist. by: Moving Bks., Inc., P.O. Box 20037, Seattle, WA 98122 (SAN 159-0685) Tel 206-325-9077; Dist. by: Baker & Taylor Bks., Western Div., 380 Edison Way, Reno, NV 89546 (SAN 169-4464) Tel 702-786-6700; Toll free: 800-648-3540.

Sunrise Bks, *(Sunrise Bks.; 0-940652),* 1707 "E" St., Eureka, CA 95501 (SAN 665-7893) Tel 707-442-4004.

Sunrise Pub NY, *(Sunrise Publishing Co., Inc.; 0-934401),* P.O. Box 408, New York, NY 10019 (SAN 693-4269) Tel 212-541-7143; Orders to: Sunrise Pub., 170 NE 33rd St., Ft. Lauderdale, FL 33334 (SAN 662-3220) Tel 305-563-1844.

Sunset Mktg, *(Sunset Marketing; 0-9620446),* P.O. Box 944, Summerland Key, FL 33042 (SAN 248-630X) Tel 305-745-2671.

Sunset Prods, *(Sunset Products; 0-939755),* 157 Santa Ana Ave., Long Beach, CA 90803 Tel 213-433-0697.

Sunshine Music, *(Sunshine Music Co.; 0-9620648),* P.O. Box 1203, Ephrata, WA 98823 (SAN 249-4779); 368 Third Ave., SE, Ephrata, WA 98823 (SAN 249-4787) Tel 509-754-5836.

Sunstone Pr, *(Sunstone Pr., The; 0-913270; 0-86534),* Subs. of Sunstone Corp., P.O. Box 2321, Santa Fe, NM 87504-2321 (SAN 214-2090) Tel 505-988-4418; Toll free: 800-243-5644 (orders only).

Sunstone Pubns, *(Sunstone Pubns.; 0-913319),* Div. of Sunstone, Inc., R.D. 4, Box 700A, Cooperstown, NY 13326 (SAN 283-4227) Tel 607-547-8207.

Super Santa Prodns, *(Super Santa Productions; 1-882052),* P.O. Box 6545, San Rafael, CA 94903 (SAN 248-3424) Tel 415-472-0653.

Supercamp, *(Supercamp; 0-945525),* 1725 S. Hill St., Oceanside, CA 92054 (SAN 247-1108) Tel 619-722-0072.

Superlove, *(Superlove; 0-9602334),* 2128 Watauga Ave., Orlando, FL 32812 (SAN 211-982X) Tel 407-894-1773; 4245 Ladoga Ave., Lakewood, CA 90713 Tel 213-429-6447.

Supplemental Learning, *(Supplemental Learning Co.; 1-878910),* P.O. Box 35067, Houston, TX 77235-5067; 12212 Bob White Dr., Houston, TX 77035 Tel 713-723-4300.

Surge Pub, *(Surge Publishing Co., The; 0-9620420),* 2045 Menominee Dr., Oshkosh, WI 54901 (SAN 248-6792) Tel 414-233-4218.

Surrey Bks, *(Surrey Bks.; 0-9609516; 0-940625),* 230 E. Ohio, Suite 120, Chicago, IL 60611 (SAN 275-8857) Tel 312-751-7330; Toll free: 800-326-4430; Dist. by: Publishers Group West, 4065 Hollis St., Emeryville, CA 94608 (SAN 202-8522) Tel 415-658-3453; Toll free: 800-365-3453.

Susan Hunter, *(Hunter, Susan, Publishing; 0-932419),* 15 Maddox Dr., NE, Atlanta, GA 30309 (SAN 200-8653) Tel 404-874-5473.

Suthrn Trails Pub, *(Southern Trails Publishing Co.; 0-9620286),* 529 Brussels St., San Francisco, CA 94134 (SAN 248-2703) Tel 415-467-7038.

Sutter House, *(Sutter Hse.; 0-915010),* P.O. Box 212, Lititz, PA 17543 (SAN 207-1207) Tel 717-626-0800.

Sutton Pubns, *(Sutton Pubns.; 0-9617199),* 14252 Culver Dr., Suite A644, Irvine, CA 92714 (SAN 663-2610) Tel 714-838-6067.

Suttons Bay Pubns, *(Suttons Bay Pubns.; 0-9621466),* Box 361, Suttons Bay, MI 49682 (SAN 251-4222) Tel 616-271-6821.

Suzuki Method *Imprint of Summy-Birchard*

SW Pks Mnmts, *(Southwest Parks & Monuments Assn.; 0-911408; 1-877856),* 221 N. Court Ave., Tucson, AZ 85701 (SAN 202-750X) Tel 602-622-1999; Orders to: 157 W. Cedar St., P.O. Box 2173, Globe, AZ 85502 (SAN 241-8541) Tel 602-425-8184.

Swamp Pr, *(Swamp Pr.; 0-934714),* 323 Pelham Rd., Amherst, MA 01002 (SAN 218-0901).

Swan Books, *(Swan Bks.; 0-934048),* P.O. Box 2498, Fair Oaks, CA 95628 (SAN 212-7016) Tel 916-961-8778.

Swan Enterp, *(Swan Enterprises; 0-927176),* P.O. Box 4309, Bisbee, AZ 85603-4309 Tel 602-366-5466.

Swan Pub, *(Swan Publishing Co.; 0-943629),* P.O. Box 580242, Houston, TX 77258 (SAN 668-6974) Tel 713-388-2547.

Swan Sea Music, *(Swan Sea Music; 0-9623226),* 1293 Russwood Rd., Memphis, TN 38122 Tel 901-682-1768.

SwanMark Bks, *(SwanMark Bks.; 1-878200),* P.O. Box 2056, Valdez, AK 99686; 5405 Chalet Dr., Valdez, AK 99686 Tel 907-835-4385.

Swanson, *(Swanson Publishing Co.; 0-911466),* P.O. Box 334, Moline, IL 61265 (SAN 204-6520); 824 20th Ave., Moline, IL 61265 (SAN 241-8630) Tel 309-762-0464.

Swarovski Amer Ltd, *(Swarovski America Ltd.; 0-9626365),* 2 Slater Rd., Cranston, RI 02920 Tel 401-463-3000; Toll free: 800-556-6478.

Sweet Dreams *Imprint of Bantam*

Sweet Koala Pr, *(Sweet Koala Pr.; 0-9617889),* 613L Villa Rd., Springfield, OH 45503 (SAN 665-4975) Tel 513-399-3701.

Swimming, *(Swimming World; 0-911822),* Subs. of Sports Pubns., Inc., 116 W. Hazel, Inglewood, CA 90302-2905 (SAN 204-6539) Tel 213-674-2120.

SYF Enter, *(SYF Enterprises; 0-9621556),* 990 Wimbleton, Medina, OH 44256 (SAN 251-5709) Tel 216-722-7808.

Sylvan Pubns, *(Sylvan Pubns.; 0-9606678),* 42185 Baintree Cir., Northville, MI 48167 (SAN 219-6433) Tel 313-349-4827.

Symbiosis Bks, *(Symbiosis Bks.; 0-9615903),* 8 Midhill Dr., Mill Valley, CA 94941 (SAN 696-8457) Tel 415-383-7722; Dist. by: American Teaching Aids, P.O. Box 1406, Covina, CA 91722 (SAN 238-9398) Tel 818-967-4128; Dist. by: Unique Crafters Co., P.O. Box 2972, 844 Kingsland Ave., Saint Louis, MO 63130 (SAN 630-0510) Tel 314-721-1241.

Synaxis Pr, *(Synaxis Pr.; 0-911523),* P.O. Box 689, Lynden, WA 98264 (SAN 685-4338).

Syndistar, *(Syndistar, Inc.; 1-56230),* 125 Mallard St., Suite A, Saint Rose, LA 70087 Tel 504-468-1100; Toll free: 800-841-9532.

Synergistic Pr, *(Synergistic Pr., Inc.; 0-912184),* 3965 Sacramento St., San Francisco, CA 94118 (SAN 205-4116) Tel 415-387-8180.

Synergy Pubns, *(Synergy Pubns.),* 1017 Wilda Dr., Westminster, MD 21157 (SAN 667-7894) Tel 301-876-5616.

Syracuse U Pr, *(Syracuse Univ. Pr.; 0-8156),* 1600 Jamesville Ave., Syracuse, NY 13210-5160 (SAN 206-9776) Tel 315-443-2597; Toll free: 800-365-8929 (Orders only).

Systems Co, *(Systems Co.; 0-937041; 1-56216),* P.O. Box 876, Graham, WA 98338-0876 (SAN 699-7880) Tel 206-847-5775; 25407 67th Ave., Ct. E, Graham, WA 98338 Tel 206-847-5775.

T Assicurato, *(Assicurato, Thomas; 0-9621591),* 2026 Yates Ave., Bronx, NY 10461 (SAN 251-7612) Tel 212-823-7672.

T B J Pubns, *(TBJ Pubns.; 0-935855),* Div. of Teddy Bear Craftworks, 10 Brookfield Rd., Methuen, MA 01844 (SAN 695-8907) Tel 508-686-3145.

T Baize, *(Baize, Timothy; 0-9625193),* 2305 Glenn Ave., Evansville, IN 47711 Tel 812-473-1955; Dist. by: Baker & Taylor Bks., Midwestern Div., 501 S. Gladiolus St., Momence, IL 60954 (SAN 169-2100) Tel 815-472-2444; Toll free: 800-435-5111; 800-892-1892 (in Illinois); Dist. by: Distributors, The, 702 S. Michigan, South Bend, IN 46618 (SAN 169-2488) Tel 219-232-8500; Toll free: 800-348-5200 (except Indiana).

T C Deleon, *(DeLeon, T. C., Pr.; 0-944284),* 957 Augusta St., Mobile, AL 36604 (SAN 243-0487) Tel 205-433-6717.

T C Wilson, *(Wilson, Terry C.; 0-9623886),* 1569 Collins Rd., Colorado Springs, CO 80920 Tel 719-548-0317.

T Faulk Ministries, *(Faulk, Tim, Ministries; 0-9625026),* P.O. Box 1189, Woodbury, CT 06798; 3 Lower Commons, Woodbury, CT 06798 Tel 203-263-0924.

T J Brown, *(Brown, Towana J.; 0-9622060),* Rte. 8, Box 684, Cullman, AL 35055 Tel 205-796-2095.

T Jefferson Ctr, *(Jefferson, Thomas, Ctr.; 0-938308),* 202 S. Lake Ave., No. 240, Pasadena, CA 91101 (SAN 239-670X) Tel 818-792-8130.

T Jefferson Res Ctr
See T Jefferson Ctr

T L Campbell, *(Campbell, Tammie Lang; 0-9623947),* 1219 Kingscreek Trail, Missouri City, TX 77459 Tel 713-499-7966.

T Lydia Pr, *(Lydia, T., Pr.; 0-9623288),* 7561 Upper 17th St., N., Oakdale, MN 55119 Tel 612-731-9698.

T Mack Glamour, *(Teri Mack Glamour; 0-9623808),* 166 Derby Woods Dr., Lynn Haven, FL 32444 Tel 904-265-3690.

T Sawyer Bks, *(Tom Sawyer Bks.; 0-937573),* 2801 New Mexico Ave., NW, Penthouse No. 4, Washington, DC 20007 (SAN 659-1442) Tel 202-965-5686.

T Scott Pub, *(Scott, Tim, Publishing Co.; 1-877784),* 96 Saint James Ave., P.O. Box 91079, Springfield, MA 01139-1079 Tel 413-739-0904.

TAB-Aero *Imprint of TAB Bks*

TAB Bks, *(TAB Bks.; 0-8306),* Div. of McGraw-Hill, Inc., P.O. Box 40, Blue Ridge Summit, PA 17294-0850 (SAN 202-568X) Tel 717-794-2191; Toll free: 800-822-8138; 800-233-1128. *Imprints:* TAB-Aero (T A B-Aero).

Tabor Pub, *(Tabor Publishing; 0-913592; 0-89505; 1-55924; 0-7829),* Div. of DLM, Inc., One DLM Pk., Allen, TX 75002 Tel 212-248-6300; Toll free: 800-527-4747; Orders to: P.O. Box 7000, Allen, TX 75002 (SAN 241-6212) Tel 214-248-6300; Toll free: 800-527-4748.

Tabor Sarah Bks, *(Tabor Sarah Bks.; 0-935079),* 2419 Jefferson Ave., Berkeley, CA 94703 (SAN 695-0353) Tel 415-843-2779.

TACM Inc, *(T.A.C.M., Inc.; 0-929946),* Subs. of Center for Creative Change, 52136 Lilac Rd., South Bend, IN 46628 (SAN 250-801X) Tel 219-272-9128.

TadAlex Bks, *(TadAleX Bks.; 0-929301),* 10834 Dixon Dr., S., Seattle, WA 98178 (SAN 249-0064) Tel 206-772-2059.

Tadpole, *(Tadpole; 0-9615253),* 6030 Autumn Arbor, Houston, TX 77092 (SAN 695-0965) Tel 713-681-8377.

Tahoe Tourist, *(Tahoe Tourist Promotions; 0-9626792),* P.O. Box 986, Kings Beach, CA 95719; 8612 N. Lake Blvd., Kings Beach, CA 95719 Tel 916-546-3303; Dist. by: Sierra News Co., 21 Locust St., Reno, NV 89520 (SAN 169-4472) Tel 702-329-1714.

Tahrike Tarsile Quran, *(Tahrike Tarsile Quran, Inc.; 0-940368; 1-879402),* P.O. Box 1115, Flushing, NY 11373 (SAN 217-1341); 80-10 51st Ave., Flushing, NY 11373 (SAN 658-1870) Tel 718-779-6505.

Take Along Pubns, *(Take Along Pubns.; 0-9624141),* P.O. Box 612146, South Lake Tahoe, CA 95761; 764 Lassen, South Lake Tahoe, CA 95761 Tel 916-544-3506.

Tale Weaver, *(Tale Weaver; 0-942139),* 1115 N. Larrabee St., Suite 304, West Hollywood, CA 90069 (SAN 666-7570) Tel 213-652-1992.

Talent-Ed, *(Talent-Ed; 0-935003),* P.O. Box 40204, Fort Wayne, IN 46804-0204 (SAN 694-6577) Tel 219-436-6035.

Taliaferro IN, *(Taliaferro Publishing Co.; 0-9626633),* P.O. Box 2891, Gary, IN 46403; 8644 Lakewood Ave., Gary, IN 46403 Tel 219-938-2236.

Talking Mntn, *(Talking Mountain Publishing Co.; 0-9624235),* P.O. Box 621, Bodega Bay, CA 94923 (SAN 200-3619); 1856 Whaleship Rd., Bodega Bay, CA 94923 Tel 707-875-2106.

Tallstone Pub, *(Tallstone Publishing; 0-936191),* 10 Vine Ave., Sharon, PA 16146 (SAN 696-7604) Tel 412-347-5857.

TAM Assoc, *(TAM Assocs.; 0-913005),* 911 Chicago, Oak Park, IL 60302 (SAN 283-4235) Tel 312-848-6760.

Tambourine Bks *Imprint of Morrow*

Tamerac Pub, *(Tamerac Publishing Co.; 0-9621292),* 510 Marsh Creek Rd., Gettysburg, PA 17325 (SAN 250-9466) Tel 717-334-1823.

TAN Bks Pubs, *(TAN Bks. & Pubs., Inc.; 0-89555),* 2135 N. Central Ave., Rockford, IL 61103 (SAN 282-390X) Tel 815-962-2662; Orders to: P.O. Box 424, Rockford, IL 61105 (SAN 282-3918).

Tangram Pr, *(Tangram Pr.; 0-940352),* P.O. Box 2249, Cranbury, TX 76048 (SAN 217-5797) Tel 817-579-1777.

Taplinger, *(Taplinger Publishing Co., Inc.; 0-8008),* P.O. Box 1324, New York, NY 10185; Orders to: Parkwest Pubns., Inc., 451 Communipaw Ave., Jersey City, NJ 07304 (SAN 264-6846) Tel 201-432-3257.

TAPPI, *(Technical Assn. of the Pulp & Paper Industry; 0-89852),* P.O. Box 105113, Atlanta, GA 30348-5113 (SAN 676-5629); Toll free: 800-332-8686; 800-446-9431 (in Canada); 15 Technology Pkwy., Atlanta, GA 30392 (SAN 241-8681) Tel 404-446-1400.

Tara Educ Servs, *(Tara Educational Services; 0-929404),* 65 Cretin Ave., N., Saint Paul, MN 55104 (SAN 249-4329) Tel 612-645-0625; Dist. by: Inland Bk. Co., 140 Commerce St., East Haven, CT 06512 (SAN 200-4151) Tel 203-467-4257; Toll free: 800-243-0138.

Targum Pr, *(Targum Pr., Inc.; 0-944070),* 22700 W. Eleven Mile Rd., Southfield, MI 48034 (SAN 242-8997) Tel 313-355-2266; Dist. by: Philipp Feldheim, Inc., 200 Airport Executive Pk., Spring Valley, NY 10977 (SAN 106-6307) Tel 914-356-2282; Toll free: 800-237-7149.

Tari Bk Pubs, *(Tari Bk. Pubs.; 0-9604258),* 146 E. 34th St., Eugene, OR 97405 (SAN 214-1523).

Tarquin *Imprint of Parkwest Pubns*

Tartan Tiger, *(Tartan Tiger; 0-935827),* 2320 144th SE, Bellevue, WA 98007 (SAN 696-6535) Tel 206-747-7655.

Tator Enterprises, *(Tator Enterprises, Inc.; 0-9624285),* 4701 Ninth Ave., N., Saint Petersburg, FL 33713 Tel 813-323-7596.

Taunton, *(Taunton Pr., Inc.; 0-918804; 0-942391; 1-56158),* 63 S. Main St., Box 5506, Newtown, CT 06470-5506 (SAN 210-5144) Tel 203-426-8171; Toll free: 800-243-7252 (orders); Dist. by: W. W. Norton & Co., Inc., 500 Fifth Ave., New York, NY 10110 (SAN 202-5795) Tel 212-354-5500; Toll free: 800-223-4830.

Taylor Prodns, *(Taylor Productions, Ltd.; 0-929093),* 250 W. 24th St., New York, NY 10011 (SAN 248-4536) Tel 212-425-3466; Dist. by: Talman Co., 150 Fifth Ave., New York, NY 10011 (SAN 200-5204) Tel 212-620-3182; Toll free: 800-557-8894.

TBW Bks, *(TBW Bks.; 0-931474),* P.O Box 2038, RFD 5, Brunswick, ME 04011 (SAN 224-2303).

TCA PA, *(Train Collectors Assn.; 0-917896),* P.O. Box 248, Strasburg, PA 17579.

TCA Pub, *(TCA Publishing; 0-9626932),* 8426 C. Summerdale, San Diego, CA 92126 Tel 619-549-8620.

Tches Pr, *(Teachers Pr.; 0-9627538),* P.O. Box 14391, Austin, TX 78761; 3308 Pennsylvania Ave., Austin, TX 78721 Tel 512-926-2874.

Tchr Create Mat, *(Teacher Created Materials, Inc.; 1-55734),* 6421 Industry Way, Westminster, CA 92683-3608 (SAN 665-5270) Tel 714-891-7895; Toll free: 800-662-4321.

Tchr Tested-Child, *(Teacher Tested-Child Satisfying; 0-915505),* 1726 W. Montecito Way, San Diego, CA 92103 (SAN 242-4514) Tel 619-298-6439.

Tchrs & Writers Coll, *(Teachers & Writers Collaborative; 0-915924),* 5 Union Sq. W., New York, NY 10003 (SAN 206-3859) Tel 212-691-6590.

Tchrs Coll, *(Columbia Univ., Teachers College, Teachers College Pr.; 0-8077),* 1234 Amsterdam Ave., New York, NY 10027 (SAN 282-3985) Tel 212-678-3929; Orders to: P.O. Box 2032, Colchester, VT 05449 (SAN 248-3904); Toll free: 800-445-6638.

TD Pub, *(Three Dimensional Publishing; 1-877835),* 1015 Stirling Rd., Silver Spring, MD 20901 Tel 301-593-3284; Toll free: 800-673-8210 (USA/Canada).

Teach Me, *(Teach Me Tapes, Inc.; 0-934633),* 10500 Bren Rd., E., Minneapolis, MN 55343 (SAN 693-9309) Tel 612-933-8086; Toll free: 800-365-3453; Dist. by: Publishers Group West, 4065 Hollis St., Emeryville, CA 94608 (SAN 202-8522) Tel 415-658-3453; Toll free: 800-456-4656.

Teachers Lab, *(Teachers Laboratory, Inc., The; 0-9621820),* P.O. Box 6480, Brattleboro, VT 05301; 104 Canal St., Brattleboro, VT 05301 Tel 802-254-3457.

Teachers Pub Hse, *(Teachers Publishing Hse.; 0-942431),* P.O. Box 9358, Canton, OH 44711 (SAN 667-0326) Tel 216-784-3181.

Teaching Advisory, *(Teaching Advisory, The; 0-9621619),* P.O. Box 99131, Seattle, WA 98199 (SAN 252-1032); 2632 40th Ave., W., Seattle, WA 98199 Tel 206-282-3420.

Teal Pr, *(Teal Pr.; 0-913793),* P.O. Box 4098, Santa Fe, NM 87502-4098 (SAN 286-2042) Tel 505-989-7861.

TechWest Pubns, *(TechWest Pubns.; 0-943621),* 560 S. Hartz Ave., Suite 447, Danville, CA 94526 (SAN 668-6885) Tel 415-838-2670.

Tee Loftin, *(Tee Loftin Pubs., Inc.; 0-934812),* 3100 R St., NW, Washington, DC 20007 (SAN 215-9635) Tel 202-338-6049.

Teen Round-Up, *(Teen Round-Up, Inc.; 0-9614268),* Rte. 1, Box 226A, Duncan, OK 73533 (SAN 687-1534) Tel 405-255-5207.

Teenage Bks Imprint of **Group Pub**

Teka Trends, *(Teka Trends, Inc.; 1-878356),* 1000 Salt Meadow Ln., McLean, VA 22101 Tel 703-356-7572.

Teknek, *(Teknek; 0-930363),* 23048 Park Privado, Calabasas, CA 91302 (SAN 670-7793) Tel 818-347-4138.

Telcraft Imprint of **Tell Pubns OH**

Telesis CA, *(Telesis II of California, Inc.; 1-56117),* 3180 University Ave., San Diego, CA 92104 Tel 619-280-1828; Toll free: 800-542-2966.

Tell Pubns OH, *(Tell Pubns.; 1-878893),* 3800 Mogadore Industrial Pkwy., Mogadore, OH 44260 Tel 216-628-2772. *Imprints:* Telcraft (Telcraft).

Temple Golden Pubns, *(Temple Golden Pubns.; 0-929686),* P.O. Box 10501, Sedona, AZ 86336 (SAN 250-1872); 305 Mountain Shadow Dr., Sedona, AZ 86336 (SAN 250-1880) Tel 602-282-6864.

Templeton, *(Templeton, Larry D.; 0-9608914),* 320 W. Algre Dr., Litchfield Park, AZ 85340 (SAN 241-1571) Tel 602-935-4346.

Tempus Pr, *(Tempus Pr.; 0-9620456),* P.O. Box 235, Tell City, IN 47586 (SAN 248-4609); 104 Geneva Dr., Tell City, IN 47586 (SAN 248-4617) Tel 812-547-8144.

Ten Penny, *(Ten Penny Players, Inc.; 0-934830),* 393 St. Paul's Ave., Staten Island, NY 10304-2127 (SAN 213-8743) Tel 718-442-7429; Dist. by: Waterways Project, 393 St. Paul's Ave., Staten Island, NY 10304-2127 (SAN 219-5402) Tel 718-442-7429.

Ten Pubns, *(10 Pubns., Inc.; 0-925237),* Subs. of Southwest Visuals, Inc., 6925 Fifth Ave., Suite E, Scottsdale, AZ 85251 Tel 602-951-2974.

Ten Speed Pr, *(Ten Speed Pr.; 0-913668; 0-89815),* P.O. Box 7123, Berkeley, CA 94707 (SAN 202-7674) Tel 510-845-8414; Toll free: 800-841-2665.

Tenderfoot Pr, *(Tenderfoot Pr.; 0-9615397),* P.O. Box 533, Narberth, PA 19072 (SAN 695-4669) Tel 215-667-4769.

Tern Pubns, *(Tern Pubns.; 0-9618945),* P.O. Box 28, Cape Porpoise, ME 04014 (SAN 242-4622); Winter Harbor Rd., Cape Porpoise, ME 04014 (SAN 242-4630) Tel 207-967-5673.

Terra Nova, *(Terra Nova Pr.; 0-944176),* 1309 Redwood Ln., Davis, CA 95616 (SAN 242-8741) Tel 916-753-1519.

Teruko Inc, *(Teruko, Inc.; 0-938789),* P.O. Box 1116, La Mirada, CA 90637-1116 (SAN 662-5657); 2254 Rosecrans Ave., Fullerton, CA 92633 (SAN 662-5665) Tel 714-773-5437.

Tesseract SD, *(Tesseract Pubns.; 1-877649),* 3001 W. 57th St., Sioux Falls, SD 57106-2652 Tel 605-361-6942.

Test Taking Advan, *(Test Taking Advantage Co.; 0-9627360),* 17 Via Capistrano, Tiburon, CA 94920 Tel 415-435-2186.

Teton Bkshop, *(Teton Bookshop Publishing Co.; 0-933160),* Box 1903, Jackson, WY 83001 (SAN 213-1781) Tel 307-733-9220.

Tex A&M Univ Pr, *(Texas A & M Univ. Pr.; 0-89096),* Drawer C, College Station, TX 77843 (SAN 207-5237); Toll free: 800-826-8911 (orders); Lewis St., University Campus, John Lindsey Bldg., College Station, TX 77843 (SAN 658-1919) Tel 409-845-1436.

Tex Christian, *(Texas Christian Univ. Pr.; 0-912646; 0-87565),* Box 30783, Fort Worth, TX 76129 (SAN 202-7690) Tel 817-921-7822; Dist. by: Texas A & M Univ. Pr., Drawer C, College Station, TX 77843 (SAN 207-5237); Toll free: 800-826-8911.

Tex Tech Univ Pr, *(Texas Tech Univ. Pr.; 0-89672),* Affil. of Texas Tech Univ., Texas Tech Univ., Lubbock, TX 79409-1037 (SAN 218-5989) Tel 806-742-0158; Toll free: 800-832-4042.

Texart, *(TexArt Services, Inc.; 0-935857),* P.O. Box 15440, San Antonio, TX 78212-8640 (SAN 696-0022) Tel 512-826-2889.

Textile Bridge, *(Textile Bridge Pr.; 0-938838),* Div. of Moody Street Irregulars, Inc., P.O. Box 157, Clarence Center, NY 14032 (SAN 216-0676) Tel 716-741-3393.

TFC Bks MD, *(21st Century Bks., Inc.; 0-941477),* 38 S. Market St., Frederick, MD 21701 (SAN 666-0827) Tel 301-698-0210. Do not confuse with Twenty-First Century Bks., Inc., Lafayette, LA.

TFFACC, *(Foundation for a Christian Civilization, Inc., The; 1-877905),* 1 Guard Hill Rd., Bedford, NY 10506 Tel 914-241-7015.

TFH Pubns, *(TFH Pubns., Inc.; 0-87666; 0-86622; 0-7938),* 1 TFH Plaza, Union & Third Aves., Neptune City, NJ 07753 (SAN 202-7720) Tel 201-988-8400; Toll free: 800-631-2188; Box 427, Neptune, NJ 07753 (SAN 658-1862).

TGNW Pr, *(T.G.N.W.; 0-9619560),* 2429 E. Aloha, Seattle, WA 98112 (SAN 245-4742) Tel 206-328-9656.

Thames Hudson, *(Thames & Hudson; 0-500),* 500 Fifth Ave., New York, NY 10110 (SAN 667-4577) Tel 212-354-3763; Dist. by: W. W. Norton & Co., Inc., 500 Fifth Ave., New York, NY 10110 (SAN 202-5795) Tel 212-354-5500; Toll free: 800-233-4830.

Theos U Pr, *(Theosophical Univ. Pr.; 0-911500; 1-55700),* P.O. Bin C, Pasadena, CA 91109 (SAN 205-4299) Tel 818-798-3378.

Think Shop, *(Think Shop, Inc.; 0-937871),* 13110 Constitution Ave. NE, No. 404, Albuquerque, NM 87112-6151 (SAN 659-5944).

Thinking Caps, *(Thinking Caps, Inc.; 0-9610876),* P.O. Box 7239, Phoenix, AZ 85011 (SAN 239-4960) Tel 602-956-1515.

Thinking Kids Pr, *(Thinking Kids' Pr.; 0-939707),* P.O. Box 3112, South Pasadena, CA 91030-6112 (SAN 663-5172) Tel 818-282-7339.

Thinking Pubns, *(Thinking Pubns.; 0-9610370; 0-930599),* Div. of McKinley Co., Inc., 1731 Westgate Rd., Box 163, Eau Claire, WI 54702-0163 (SAN 264-4320) Tel 715-832-2488; Toll free: 800-225-4769; 800-362-4769 (in U.S. and Canada).

Third World, *(3rd World Pr.; 0-88378),* 7524 S. Cottage Grove, Box 730, Chicago, IL 60619 (SAN 202-778X) Tel 312-651-0700.

Thomas Geale, *(Geale, Thomas, Pubns., Inc.; 0-912781),* P.O. Box 370540, Montara, CA 94037 (SAN 283-3735) Tel 415-728-5219.

Thomas More, *(More, Thomas, Pr.; 0-88347),* Subs. of Thomas More Assn., 205 W. Monroe St., 6th Flr., Chicago, IL 60606 (SAN 203-0675) Tel 312-609-8880; Toll free: 800-835-8965.

Thomas Publications, *(Thomas Pubns.; 0-939631),* 202 S. Stratton St., Gettysburg, PA 17325 (SAN 663-7213) Tel 717-334-1921. Do not confuse with companies with the same name in Austin, TX, La Crescenta, CA.

Thomasson-Grant, *(Thomasson-Grant, Inc.; 0-934738),* 1 Morton Dr., Charlottesville, VA 22901 (SAN 239-3948) Tel 804-977-1780; Toll free: 800-999-1780.

Thompson, *(Thompson Pubns.; 0-933479),* 2555 N. 19th St., Milwaukee, WI 53206 (SAN 691-8972) Tel 414-264-9241.

Thompson Pr, *(Thompson Pr.; 0-931947),* P.O. Box 263, Conway, NH 03818 (SAN 685-9399) Tel 603-447-5569.

Thompson's, *(Thompson's),* P.O. Box 550, Albertville, AL 35950 (SAN 207-4656) Tel 205-878-2021.

Thorndike Pr, *(Thorndike Pr.; 0-89621; 1-56054),* P.O. Box 159, Thorndike, ME 04986 (SAN 212-2375); Toll free: 800-223-6121; Depot Street, Unity, ME 04988 Tel 207-948-2962; Orders to: Macmillan Pub. Co., Inc., 100 Front St., Riverside, NJ 08075 (SAN 202-5582) Tel 609-461-6500.

Thorne Enterprises, *(Thorne Enterprises; 0-9628329),* 149 Gambel Ln., Sedona, AZ 86336 Tel 602-282-7508.

Thornsbury Bailey Brown, *(Thornsbury Bailey & Brown; 0-945253),* P.O. Box 5169, Arlington, VA 22205 (SAN 246-2192); 1110 N. Rockingham St., Arlington, VA 22205 (SAN 246-2206) Tel 703-532-2210.

Thorsons SF, *(Thorsons),* Div. of Harper San Francisco, 601 Icehouse 1-401, 151 Union St., San Francisco, CA 94111 Tel 415-477-4400.

Thoth MO, *(Thoth Publishing Co.; 0-9628067),* P.O. Box 11027, Springfield, MO 65808; 963 S. Delaware, Springfield, MO 65802 Tel 417-862-5520. Do not confuse with Thoth Publishing Co., West Hartford, CT.

Thought Wave Pr, *(Thought Wave Pr.; 0-922073),* P.O. Box 504, Hunt Valley, MD 21030 (SAN 251-1088); 71 Burkshire Rd., Baltimore, MD 21204 (SAN 251-1096) Tel 301-823-2123.

Three Continents, *(3 Continents Pr.; 0-89410; 0-914478),* 1901 Pennsylvania Ave., NW, Suite 407, Washington, DC 20006 (SAN 212-0070) Tel 202-223-2554.

Three Cs Ent, *(Three C's Enterprises; 1-880121),* 4330 Barranca Pkwy., No. 101-353, Irvine, CA 92714; 61 Claret, Irvine, CA 92714 Tel 714-669-1339.

Three-D Zone, *(3-D Zone, The; 0-925300),* 333 N. Hobart Pl., Los Angeles, CA 90004 Tel 213-662-3831.

Three E Co, *(3-E Co., Inc.; 0-9623752),* Div. of Eads Co., Inc., P.O. Box 1525, Marietta, GA 30061; 1775 Kimberly Dr., Marietta, GA 30060 Tel 404-422-1085.

Three Elves Pr, *(Three Elves Pr.; 1-878070),* 350 Eighth Ave., Suite 8, Tierra Verde, FL 33715 Tel 813-867-3784.

Three Riv Ctr, *(3 Rivers Ctr.; 0-9615677),* 3327 W. Pryor Ave., Visalia, CA 93277 (SAN 696-1622) Tel 209-732-3759.

Three River Ctr
See **Three Riv Ctr**

Three Star Ent, *(3 Star Enterprises; 0-912507),* 9709 Raymond Dr., Belleville, IL 62223 (SAN 265-2293) Tel 618-397-1155.

Three-Stones Pubns, *(3-Stones Pubns., Ltd.; 0-933673),* P.O. Box 69143, Seattle, WA 98168 (SAN 692-5421) Tel 206-431-0195; Orders to: P.O. Box 24831, Seattle, WA 98124 (SAN 244-8343) Tel 206-242-5174.

Thriftecon, *(Thriftecon Publications; 1-880258),* 3328 Cunningham Rd., Knoxville, TN 37918 Tel 615-922-8411.

Thum Print, *(Thum Printing; 0-932920),* 116 W. Pierce St., Elburn, IL 60119 (SAN 212-3150).

Thunder & Ink, *(Thunder & Ink; 0-9623227),* P.O. Box 7014, Evanston, IL 60201; 2307 Central St., No. 2-South, Evanston, IL 60201 Tel 708-492-1823.

Thunder River, *(Thunder River Pr.; 0-9604274),* P.O. Box 10935, Aspen, CO 81611 (SAN 214-4786).

Thunderbird Bks, *(Thunderbird Bks.; 0-9622361),* 5358 E. Fairmount, Tucson, AZ 85712 Tel 602-327-1265.

Thy Word, *(Thy Word Creations; 1-879099),* Rte. 76, Box 28, Glenville, WV 26351 Tel 304-462-7912.

Ticknor & Fields, *(Ticknor & Fields; 0-89919),* Affil. of Houghton Mifflin Co., 215 Park Ave., S., New York, NY 10003 (SAN 282-4043) Tel 212-420-5800; Toll free: 800-225-3362; Dist. by: Houghton Mifflin Co., Wayside Rd., Burlington, MA 01803 (SAN 215-3793) Tel 617-272-1500.

Tidal Pr, *(Tidal Pr.; 0-930954),* P.O. Box 160, Cranberry Isles, ME 04625 (SAN 211-3783) Tel 207-244-3090; 129 Mount Vernon St., Boston, MA 02108 Tel 617-523-7995. Do not confuse with Tidal Pr., San Diego, CA.

Tidewater, *(Tidewater Pubns.; 0-87033),* Div. of Cornell Maritime Pr., Inc., P.O. Box 456, Centreville, MD 21617 (SAN 202-0459) Tel 301-758-1075; Toll free: 800-638-7641.

Tiffany Pub, *(Tiffany Publishing Co.; 0-9616079),* 98 Puritan Ave., Worcester, MA 01604 (SAN 698-1321) Tel 508-756-1911.

Tiger Pub, *(Tiger Pubns., Inc.; 0-9611318),* 32 Friendship Ct., Red Bank, NJ 07701 (SAN 283-3506) Tel 908-747-9042.

Tigertail Ent, *(Tigertail Enterprises; 0-938921),* P.O. Box 1914, Santa Monica, CA 90402 (SAN 661-6690) Tel 805-683-2938.

Tilbury Hse, *(Tilbury Hse. Pubs.; 0-937966; 0-88448),* 132 Water St., Gardiner, ME 04345 Tel 207-582-1899; Dist. by: Consortium Bk. Sales & Distribution, 287 E. Sixth St., Suite 365, Saint Paul, MN 55101 (SAN 200-6049) Tel 612-221-9035; Toll free: 800-283-3572.

Timberline Pr, *(Timberline Pr.; 0-9608284),* Box 70071, Eugene, OR 97401 (SAN 240-4559) Tel 503-345-1771. Do not confuse with Timberline Pr., Fulton, MO.

Time Grow Co, *(Time to Grow Co.; 0-9623115),* 5174 Emerald Dr., Mound, MN 55364 Tel 612-472-6170.

Time-Life, *(Time Life, Inc.; 0-8094),* Div. of Time Warner Publishing, 777 Duke St., Alexandria, VA 22314 (SAN 202-7836) Tel 703-838-7000; Toll free: 800-621-7026; 4200 N. Industrial Blvd., Indianapolis, IN 46254 (SAN 658-1951); Orders to: Silver Burdett Co. (Library & School Orders), 250 James St., Morristown, NJ 07960 (SAN 204-5982) Tel 201-285-7700.

Time Teaching, *(Time Teaching Systems, Inc.; 0-9622487),* 10 Park Ave., Apt. 14D, New York, NY 10016 Tel 212-683-7398.

Timeless Sales, *(Timeless Tales; 0-9624183),* 404 W. Sumac Ct., Louisville, CO 80027 Tel 303-666-5440.

Times Bks *Imprint of Random*

Tin Man Pr, *(Tin Man Pr.; 0-936110),* Box 219, Stanwood, WA 98292 (SAN 222-0156) Tel 206-387-0459.

Tiny Tales, *(Tiny Tales; 0-9627661),* P.O. Box 12212, Wilmington, DE 19850.

Tiny Thought, *(Tiny Thought Pr.; 0-925928),* 1427 S. Jackson St., Louisville, KY 40217 Tel 502-637-6870; Toll free: 800-456-3208.

Tinys Self Help Bks, *(Tiny's Self Help Bks. for Children; 0-9616549),* 174 Main St., Apt. 401W, Bangor, ME 04401 (SAN 659-5421) Tel 207-947-2239; Orders to: Mr. Paperback Bk. Stores, 133 Hammond St., Bangor, ME 04401 (SAN 662-4294) Tel 207-942-8237; Dist. by: Magazines, Inc., 1135 Hammond St., Bangor, ME 04401 (SAN 169-3034) Tel 207-942-8237; Toll free: 800-432-7993 (Maine only).

Tioga Pub Co, *(Tioga Publishing Co.; 0-935382),* 150 Coquito Way, Portola Valley, CA 94028 (SAN 669-280X) Tel 415-854-2445; Orders to: P.O. Box 50490, Palo Alto, CA 94303 Tel 415-965-4081; Dist. by: Publishers Group West, 4065 Hollis St., Emeryville, CA 94608 (SAN 202-8522) Tel 415-658-3453; Toll free: 800-365-3453.

Tipi Pr, *(Tipi Pr.; 1-877976),* Saint Joseph's Indian School, Chamberlain, SD 57326 Tel 605-734-3300.

TK Pubs, *(T. K. Pubs.; 0-9614023),* P.O. Box 779, Cocoa, FL 32923-0779 (SAN 683-6232) Tel 407-636-1952.

TLC Bks, *(TLC Bks.; 0-9617081),* P.O. Box 1391, Mishawaka, IN 46544 (SAN 662-6165); 416 N. Byrkit St., Mishawaka, IN 46544 (SAN 662-6173) Tel 219-259-1775.

TLT, *(TLT Pubns.; 0-943314),* 202 S. Fifth St., Goshen, IN 46526 (SAN 240-7841) Tel 616-361-8013.

TMC CT, *(TMC, Inc.; 0-9627537),* 20 S. Lakeshore Dr., Brookfield, CT 06804 Tel 203-775-5167.

Toad Hse Bks, *(Toad Hse. Bks.; 1-878467),* 1703 Victor Ave., Redding, CA 96003-4027.

Toadwood Pubs, *(Toadwood Pubs.; 0-9610878),* R.R. 6, Box 63, Edwardsville, IL 62025 (SAN 282-5775) Tel 618-656-0531; Dist. by: Shar Products, Inc., P.O. Box 1411, Ann Arbor, MI 48106 (SAN 251-1673) Tel 313-665-7711; Toll free: 800-528-3430.

Tomato Enter, *(Tomato Enterprises; 0-9617357),* P.O. Box 2805, Fairfield, CA 94533 (SAN 664-0427) Tel 707-426-3970.

Tonnis, *(Tonnis Productions, Inc.; 0-917057),* P.O. Box 311, Harleysville, PA 19438 (SAN 655-1319) Tel 215-256-9633.

Top Mtn Pub, *(Top of the Mountain Publishing; 0-914295; 1-56087),* 11701 Belcher Rd. S., No. 123, Largo, FL 34643-5117 (SAN 287-590X) Tel 813-530-0110; Dist. by: Quality Bks., Inc., 918 Sherwood Dr., Lake Bluff, IL 60044-2204 (SAN 169-2127) Tel 708-295-2010; Toll free: 800-323-4241 (Libraries only); Dist. by: New Leaf Distributing Co., 5425 Tulane Dr., SW, Atlanta, GA 30336-2323 (SAN 169-1449) Tel 404-691-6996; Toll free: 800-326-2665; Dist. by: Baker & Taylor Bks., Southern Div., Mt. Olive Rd., Commerce, GA 30599 (SAN 169-1503) Tel 702-786-6700; Dist. by: The Distributors, 702 S. Michigan, South Bend, IN 46618 (SAN 212-0364) Tel 219-232-8500.

Topgallant, *(Topgallant Publishing Co., Ltd.; 0-914916),* 3180 Pacific Heights Rd., Honolulu, HI 96813 (SAN 209-4932) Tel 808-524-0884.

Tops Learning, *(Tops Learning Systems; 0-941008),* 10970 S. Mulino Rd., Canby, OR 97013 (SAN 217-4456) Tel 503-266-8550.

Tor Bks, *(Tor Bks.; 0-8125),* Div. of Tom Doherty Assocs., Inc., 49 W. 24th St., New York, NY 10010 (SAN 239-3956) Tel 212-741-3100; Dist. by: St. Martin's Pr., Inc., 175 Fifth Ave., New York, NY 10010 (SAN 200-2132) Tel 212-674-5151; Toll free: 800-325-5525; Dist. by: Warner Pub. Services, 810 Seventh Ave., New York, NY 10019 (SAN 200-5522) Tel 212-397-8676.

Torah Aura, *(Torah Aura Productions; 0-933873),* 4423 Fruitland Ave., Los Angeles, CA 90058 (SAN 692-7025) Tel 213-585-7312; Toll free: 800-238-6724.

Torah Umesorah, *(Torah Umesorah Pubns.; 0-914131; 1-878895),* 5723 18th Ave., Brooklyn, NY 11204 (SAN 218-9992) Tel 718-259-1223.

Torch *Imprint of HarperCollins*

Torrence Pubns, *(Torrence Pubns.; 0-914281),* P.O. Box 2715, Santa Barbara, CA 93120 (SAN 287-5667) Tel 805-682-6821; Dist. by: Sunbelt Pubns., P.O. Box 191126, San Diego, CA 92119 (SAN 242-0198) Tel 619-697-4811; Dist. by: L-S Distributors, 480 Ninth St., San Francisco, CA 94103 (SAN 169-0213) Tel 415-861-6300; Dist. by: E Z Nature Bks., P.O. Box 4206, San Luis Obispo, CA 93403-4206 (SAN 200-9846) Tel 805-595-7346.

Tory Corner Editions, *(Tory Corner Editions; 1-878452),* P.O. Box 8100, Glen Ridge, NJ 07028 Tel 201-669-8367.

Total Lrn, *(Total Learning Commitment; 0-9617737),* 7513 34th Ave. W., Bradenton, FL 33529 (SAN 664-7855) Tel 813-792-5839.

Total Pub, *(Total Publishing; 0-914997),* 657 W. Milford Ave., Unit 19, Glendale, CA 91203 (SAN 289-453X). Moved, left no forwarding address.

Touch & See Educ, *(Touch & See Educational Resources; 1-879218),* P.O. Box 794, 2921 Via La Selva, Palos Verdes Estates, CA 90274 Tel 213-375-0016.

Touchstone Bks *Imprint of S&S Trade*

Tourmaline Pub, *(Tourmaline Publishing; 0-941099),* 1056 Vassar Dr., Napa, CA 94558 (SAN 665-0937) Tel 707-224-5969.

Tower Hill Pr, *(Tower Hill Pr.; 0-941668),* P.O. Box 1132, Doylestown, PA 18901 (SAN 239-3298); 4030G Skyron Dr., Doylestown, PA 18901 Tel 215-345-1338.

Townhouse Pub, *(Townhouse Publishing; 0-939219),* 301 N. Harrison St., Bldg. B, Suite 115, Princeton, NJ 08540 (SAN 662-6254) Tel 609-585-5539. Do not confuse with Townhouse Publishing Corp. in Orlando, FL.

Toy Works Pr, *(Toy Works Pr.; 0-938715),* Div. of Toy Works, 902 Broadway, Penthouse, New York, NY 10010 (SAN 661-6216) Tel 212-982-2269.

Toys 'n Things
See Redleaf Pr

TP Assocs, *(TP Assocs./TP Pr.; 0-913939),* P.O. Box 3226, Newport Beach, CA 92663 (SAN 286-8962); 22181 Wood Island Ln., Huntington Beach, CA 92646 (SAN 286-8970) Tel 714-963-4482.

Traditions Pr, *(Traditions Pr.; 0-937745),* P.O. Box 1296, Lexington, SC 29072 (SAN 659-364X); Rte. 6, Box 261, Shirway Rd., Lexington, SC 29072 (SAN 659-3658) Tel 803-359-0045.

Trafalgar Sq, *(Trafalgar Square),* P.O. Box 257, North Pomfret, VT 05053 (SAN 213-8859); Toll free: 800-423-4525; Howe Hill Rd., North Pomfret, VT 05053 Tel 802-457-1911.

Trafalgar Sq-David & Charles
See Trafalgar Sq

Trailblazer Bks, *(Trailblazer Bks.; 0-9626025),* 13030 Cannon City Blvd., Northfield, MN 55057 Tel 507-645-4242.

Trails West Pub, *(Trails West Publishing; 0-939729),* P.O. Box 8619, Santa Fe, NM 87504-8619 (SAN 663-7809) Tel 505-982-8058.

Transatl Arts, *(Transatlantic Arts, Inc.; 0-693),* P.O. Box 6086, Albuquerque, NM 87197 (SAN 202-7968) Tel 505-898-2289. Do not confuse with Trans-Atlantic Pubns., Inc., Philadelphia, PA.

Transitions, *(Transitions),* P.O. Box 478, Peoria, AZ 85345 (SAN 287-282X) Tel 602-972-7504. Do not confuse with Transitions, Minnetonka, MN.

Treadle Pr, *(Treadle Pr.; 0-935143),* Div. of Binding & Printing Co., Box D, Sheperdstown, WV 25443 (SAN 695-2070) Tel 304-876-2557.

Treas Chest Ent, *(Treasure Chest Enterprises, Inc.; 0-939161),* 1710 Carrie Hills Ln., La Habra Heights, CA 90631 (SAN 662-9385) Tel 213-694-4486; 16914 Harvard Blvd., Gardena, CA 90247 (SAN 242-133X) Tel 213-324-1448.

Treasure Chest, *(Treasure Chest Pubns.; 0-918080),* 1802 W. Grant Rd., Suite 101, Tucson, AZ 85745 (SAN 209-3243) Tel 602-623-9558; Toll free: 800-627-0048; Orders to: P.O. Box 5250, Tucson, AZ 85703 (SAN 209-3251); Dist. by: Gordon's Bks., Inc., 2323 Delgany St., Denver, CO 80216 (SAN 169-0531) Tel 303-296-1830; Toll free: 800-525-6979 (west of the Mississippi).

Tree by River, *(Tree by the River Publishing/Music Business Bks.; 0-935174),* P.O. Box 935, Dayton, NV 89403 (SAN 213-389X) Tel 702-246-5409; Dist. by: Baker & Taylor Bks., Eastern Div., 50 Kirby Ave., Somerville, NJ 08876 (SAN 169-4901) Tel 201-722-8000; Toll free: 800-435-1845; 800-352-4833 (in New Jersey); Dist. by: Baker & Taylor Bks., Midwestern Div., 501 S. Gladiolus St., Comence, IL 60954 (SAN 169-2100) Tel 815-472-2444; Toll free: 800-435-5111; 800-892-1892 (in Illinois); Dist. by: Baker & Taylor Bks., Southern Div., Mt. Olive Rd., Commerce, GA 30529 (SAN 169-1503) Tel 404-335-5000; Toll free: 800-241-6004; 800-282-6850 (in Georgia); Dist. by: Baker & Taylor Bks., Western Div., 380 Edison Way, Reno, NV 89564 (SAN 169-4464) Tel 702-786-6700; Toll free: 800-648-3540; Dist. by: Quality Bks., Inc., 918 Sherwood Dr., Lake Bluff, IL 60044-2204 (SAN 169-2127) Tel 708-295-2010; Toll free: 800-323-4241 (Libraries only).

Tree City Pr, *(Tree City Pr.; 0-9619365),* P.O. Box 66, Sylvania, OH 43560 (SAN 243-9174); 7633 Gillcrest Rd., Sylvania, OH 43560 (SAN 243-9182) Tel 419-882-4862.

Treehaus Comns, *(Treehaus Communications, Inc.; 0-929496),* P.O. Box 249, Loveland, OH 45140 (SAN 249-5325); 906 W. Loveland Ave., Loveland, OH 45140 (SAN 249-5333) Tel 513-683-5716.

Treehouse, *(Treehouse Enterprises; 0-935571),* P.O. Box 7134, Jupiter, FL 33468-7134 (SAN 696-2025) Tel 407-575-0547; Dist. by: New Leaf Distributing Co., 5425 Tulane Dr., SW, Atlanta, GA 30336-2323 (SAN 169-1449) Tel 404-691-6996; Toll free: 800-326-2665. Do not confuse with either Tree House Pr., of Shelter Island, NY or Treehouse Pr., of Chagrin Falls, OH.

Trellis Bks Inc, *(Trellis Bks., Inc.; 1-878236),* 3705 Timberline, Canandaigua, NY 14424 Tel 716-396-3141; Toll free: 800-344-0559; Dist. by: Fahy-Williams Publishing, Inc., P.O. Box 1080, 171 Reed St., Geneva, NY 14456 (SAN 630-3889) Tel 315-789-0458.

Tremaine Graph & Pub, *(Tremaine Graphic & Publishing; 0-939860),* 2727 Front St., Klamath Falls, OR 97601 (SAN 216-9398) Tel 503-884-4193.

TRI Pubns, *(TRI Pubns.; 0-943693),* Div. of TRI, P.O. Box 89338, Honolulu, HI 96830-9338 (SAN 668-6818); 330 Saratoga, Honolulu, HI 96815 (SAN 668-6826) Tel 808-734-5047.

Triad Pub FL, *(Triad Publishing Co., Inc.; 0-9600472; 0-937404),* Div. of Triad Communications, Inc., 1110 NW Eighth Ave., Gainesville, FL 32601 (SAN 205-4574) Tel 904-373-5800; Toll free: 800-525-6902.

Trifecta Charley, *(Trifecta Charley, Ltd.),* P.O. Box 281, Niceville, FL 32578 (SAN 659-2120).

Trillium Pr, *(Trillium Pr.; 0-89824),* First Ave., Unionville, NY 10988 (SAN 212-4637) Tel 914-726-4444. Do not confuse with Trillium Pr. in San Antonio, TX.

Trinas Pr, *(Dr. Trina's Pr.; 0-9615840),* P.O. Box 4777, Laguna Beach, CA 92651 (SAN 697-0109) Tel 714-497-5071.

Trinity Comns, *(Trinity Communications; 0-937495),* P.O. Box 3610, Manassas, VA 22110 (SAN 659-0675); Toll free: 800-247-9079; 9380 C1 Forestwood Ln., Manassas, VA 22110 (SAN 659-0683) Tel 703-369-2429.

Triumph Pub, *(Triumph Publishing Co.; 0-917182),* P.O. Box 292, Altadena, CA 91001 (SAN 207-3927).

Troll Assocs, *(Troll Assocs.; 0-89375; 0-8167),* Subs. of Educational Reading Services, 100 Corporate Dr., Mahwah, NJ 07430 (SAN 169-4758) Tel 201-529-4000; Toll free: 800-526-5289.

Trophy *Imprint of HarpC Child Bks*

Trotwood Press, *(Trotwood Pr.; 0-9627061),* P.O. Box 1043, Larkspur, CA 94939; 17 Skylark Dr., No. 43, Larkspur, CA 94939 Tel 415-924-2389.

Troubador Pr, *(Troubador Pr.; 0-912300; 0-89844),* 11150 Olympic Blvd., Suite 650, Los Angeles, CA 90064 (SAN 285-0931).

Trout Creek, *(Trout Creek Pr.; 0-916155),* 5976 Billings Rd., Parkdale, OR 97041 (SAN 294-9881) Tel 503-352-6494.

True Heitz, *(Tru Heitz-Thelma Yes Pr.),* 1400 McAndrew Rd., Ojai, CA 93023 (SAN 262-1029).

Trust Hidden Villa, *(Trust for Hidden Villa, The),* 26870 Moody Rd., Los Altos Hills, CA 94022 (SAN 661-4566) Tel 415-948-4690.

TSG Ent Pubns
See TSG Pub Found

TSG Pub Found, *(T.S.G. Publishing Foundation; 0-929874),* P.O. Box 4273, West Hills, CA 91308 (SAN 250-6718); 7658 Quimby Ave., West Hills, CA 91304 (SAN 250-6726) Tel 818-888-7850.

TSM Books, *(TSM Bks., Inc.; 0-941316),* 535 Broad Hollow Rd., Suite A-11, Melville, NY 11747 (SAN 239-040X) Tel 516-420-0961.

TSR Inc, *(TSR, Inc.; 0-935696; 0-88038; 1-56076),* P.O. Box 756, Lake Geneva, WI 53147 (SAN 222-0091); Toll free: 800-372-4667; 201 Sheridan Springs, Lake Geneva, WI 53147 Tel 414-248-3625; Dist. by: Random Hse., Inc., 400 Hahn Rd., Westminster, MD 21157 (SAN 202-5515) Tel 301-848-1900; Toll free: 800-733-3000 (orders); Toll free: 800-492-0782 (in Maryland).

Tuffy *Imprint of Putnam Pub Group*

Tuffy Bks, *(Tuffy Bks.; 0-89828),* 200 Madison Ave., New York, NY 10016 (SAN 213-3903) Tel 212-951-8400.

Tumbleweed Pub Co, *(Tumbleweed Publishing Co.; 0-9612160),* 3112 Van Ave., Eugene, OR 97401 (SAN 289-5102) Tel 503-345-7770.

Tundra Bks, *(Tundra Bks. of Northern New York; 0-912766; 0-88776),* Affil. of Tundra Bks. (Canada), P.O. Box 1030, Plattsburgh, NY 12901 (SAN 202-8085) Tel 514-932-5434; Dist. by: Univ. of Toronto Pr., 340 Nagel Dr., Buffalo, NY 14225 (SAN 214-2651) Tel 416-667-7791.

Tundra MA, *(Tundra Publishing; 1-879450),* 320 Riverside Dr., Northampton, MA 01060 Tel 413-586-9525.

Turman Pub, *(Turman Publishing Co.; 0-89872),* 1319 Dexter Ave., N., Suite 30, Seattle, WA 98109 (SAN 222-4372) Tel 206-282-6900.

Turn the Page, *(Turn-the-Page Pr., Inc.; 0-931540; 0-931793),* 203 Baldwin Ave., Roseville, CA 95678 (SAN 281-3629) Tel 916-444-7933.

Turner Pub KY, *(Turner Publishing Co.; 0-938021; 1-56311),* P.O. Box 3101, Paducah, KY 42002-3101 (SAN 659-803X); 412 Broadway, Paducah, KY 42002 Tel 502-443-0121. Do not confuse with companies with the same name in Houston, TX, Eastchester, NY, Atlanta, GA.

Turtle Prints, *(Turtle Prints; 0-9622052),* P.O. Box 273, Nevada City, CA 95959; 17750 Rock Creek Rd., Nevada City, CA 95959 Tel 916-265-6586.

Tusky Enterprises, *(Tusky Enterprises; 1-879100),* 1733 Hutchinson Ln., Silver Spring, MD 20906 Tel 202-726-9225.

Tutorial Press, *(Tutorial Pr., Inc., The; 0-912329),* 711A Encino Pl., NE, Albuquerque, NM 87102 (SAN 265-1467) Tel 505-296-8636.

Twayne *Imprint of G K Hall*

Twenty-Third, *(23rd Pubns.; 0-89622),* P.O. Box 180, Mystic, CT 06355 (SAN 210-9204); Toll free: 800-321-0411; 185 Willow St., Mystic, CT 06355 (SAN 658-2052) Tel 203-536-2611.

Two Ems, *(2 Ems, Inc.; 0-936652),* 786 Boston Post Rd., Madison, CT 06443 (SAN 222-1853) Tel 203-245-8211.

Two Saints Pub, *(2 Saints Publishing; 0-9625782),* P.O. Box 2197, Kalispell, MT 59901; 615 Mennonite Church Rd., Kalispell, MT 59901 Tel 406-756-1959.

Two Way Bilingual, *(2 Way Bilingual, Inc.; 0-941911),* Jaime Drew 782, Urb. Los Maestros, Rio Piedras, PR 00923 (SAN 666-0169).

Two Wings, *(2 Wings Publishing; 1-877614),* 1635 S. Rancho Santa Fe, San Marcos, CA 92069 Tel 619-471-1418.

TX Pride Pubns, *(Texas Pride Pubns.; 0-9624742),* 2420 Colcord Ave., Waco, TX 76707 Tel 817-754-8930.

TX Wesleyan Coll, *(Texas Wesleyan College; 0-924303),* P.O. Box 50010, Fort Worth, TX 76105; 1201 Wesleyan St., Fort Worth, TX 76105 Tel 817-531-4440.

Tyke Corp, *(Tyke Corp.; 0-924067),* 2750 W. 35th St., Chicago, IL 60632-1640 (SAN 252-0850) Tel 312-927-5599; Toll free: 800-533-8953.

Tyndale, *(Tyndale Hse. Pubs.; 0-8423),* P.O. Box 80, Wheaton, IL 60189 (SAN 206-7749) Tel 708-668-8300.

Typographeum, *(Typographeum Bookshop, The; 0-930126),* The Stone Cottage, Bennington Rd., Francestown, NH 03043 (SAN 211-3031).

U Assocs, *(U Assocs., Inc.; 0-9615393),* 1160 N. Federal Hwy., Suite 721, Fort Lauderdale, FL 33304 (SAN 695-3530) Tel 305-763-5991.

U Force Dynamics, *(Universal Force Dynamics; 0-9622627),* 410 Delaware, Leavenworth, KS 66048 Tel 913-682-6518.

U Iowa IPA, *(Univ. of Iowa, Institute of Public Affairs),* N310 Oakdale Hall, Iowa City, IA 52242 (SAN 262-1231) Tel 319-335-4520.

U M H & C, *(Univ. of Minnesota Hospital & Clinic, Patient Education; 0-937423),* Box 603, Harvard St. at East River Rd., Minneapolis, MN 55455 (SAN 659-0934) Tel 612-626-6356.

U-Music, *(U-Music, Inc.; 0-938925),* 389 Marin Ave., Mill Valley, CA 94941 (SAN 661-7956) Tel 415-381-8865; Dist. by: Bookpeople, 2929 Fifth St., Berkeley, CA 94710 (SAN 168-9517) Tel 415-549-3030; Toll free: 800-999-4650; Dist. by: New Leaf Distributing Co., 5425 Tulane Dr., SW, Atlanta, GA 30336-2323 (SAN 169-1449) Tel 404-691-6996; Toll free: 800-326-2665; Dist. by: Inland Bk. Co., 140 Commerce St., East Haven, CT 06512 (SAN 200-4151) Tel 203-467-4257; Toll free: 800-243-0138.

U NDak Pres, *(Univ. of North Dakota, Office of the President; 0-9608700; 1-880400),* Box 8143, University Sta., Grand Forks, ND 58202 (SAN 238-4043); Twamley Hall, Rm. 411, Grand Forks, ND 58202 Tel 701-777-2731.

U of Ala Pr, *(Univ. of Alabama Pr.; 0-8173),* Box 870380, Tuscaloosa, AL 35487-0380 (SAN 202-5272) Tel 205-348-5182.

U of Ariz Pr, *(Univ. of Arizona Pr.; 0-8165),* 1230 N. Park, No. 102, Tucson, AZ 85719 (SAN 205-468X) Tel 602-621-1441; Toll free: 800-426-3797 (orders only).

U of Ark Pr, *(Univ. of Arkansas Pr.; 0-938626; 1-55728),* Univ. of Arkansas Press, 201 Ozark St., Fayetteville, AR 72701 (SAN 239-3972) Tel 501-575-3246; Toll free: 800-525-1823.

U of AZ Ed Mat, *(Univ. of Arizona, Arizona Educational Materials Ctr.; 0-940870),* College of Education, P.O. Box 601, Tucson, AZ 85721 (SAN 219-6514) Tel 602-621-3724.

U of Cal Intl St, *(Univ. of California, Institute of International Studies; 0-87725),* 215 Moses Hall, Berkeley, CA 94720 (SAN 203-3038) Tel 415-642-4065.

U of Cal Pr, *(Univ. of California Pr.; 0-520),* 2120 Berkeley Way, Berkeley, CA 94720 (SAN 203-3046) Tel 415-642-4247; Toll free: 800-822-6657. Canadian users/subscribers: do not confuse U of Cal Pr, Berkeley, CA, with the Univ. of Calgary Pr., Calgary, AB, Canada.

U of Chicago Pr, *(Univ. of Chicago Pr.; 0-226),* Div. of Univ. of Chicago, 5801 Ellis Ave., 4th Flr., Chicago, IL 60637 (SAN 202-5280) Tel 312-702-7700; Toll free: 800-621-2736; Orders to: 11030 S. Langley Ave., Chicago, IL 60628 (SAN 202-5299) Tel 312-568-1550; Toll free: 800-621-2736.

U of Denver Teach, *(Univ. of Denver, Ctr. for Teaching, International Relations Pubns.; 0-943804),* Univ. of Denver, GSIS, Denver, CO 80208 (SAN 241-0877) Tel 303-871-2400.

U of Ga Pr, *(Univ. of Georgia Pr.; 0-8203),* Terrell Hall, Athens, GA 30602 (SAN 203-3054) Tel 404-542-2830.

U of Idaho Pr, *(Univ. of Idaho Pr.; 0-89301),* 16 Brink Hall, Moscow, ID 83843 (SAN 208-905X) Tel 208-885-5939.

U of KS Mus Nat Hist, *(Univ. of Kansas, Museum of Natural History; 0-89338),* 602 Dyche Hall, Lawrence, KS 66045-2454 (SAN 206-0957) Tel 913-864-4540.

U of Mich Pr, *(Univ. of Michigan Pr.; 0-472),* P.O. Box 1104, Ann Arbor, MI 48106 (SAN 282-4884) Tel 313-764-4388.

U of Mo Pr, *(Univ. of Missouri Pr.; 0-8262),* 2910 LeMone Blvd., Columbia, MO 65201 (SAN 203-3143) Tel 314-882-0180; Toll free: 800-828-1894 (orders only).

U of Nebr Pr, *(Univ. of Nebraska Pr.; 0-8032),* 901 N. 17th St.Room 327, Lincoln, NE 68588-0520 (SAN 202-5337) Tel 402-472-3581; Toll free: 800-755-1105.

U of NM Pr, *(Univ. of New Mexico Pr.; 0-8263),* 1720 Lomas Blvd., NE, Albuquerque, NM 87131-1591 (SAN 213-9588) Tel 505-277-2346; Toll free: 800-622-8667 (FAX orders only). Do not confuse with University of New Mexico, Native American Studies, Albuquerque, NM.

U of Okla Pr, *(Univ. of Oklahoma Pr.; 0-8061),* 1005 Asp Ave., Norman, OK 73019-0445 (SAN 203-3194) Tel 405-325-5111; Toll free: 800-627-7377; Orders to: P.O. Box 787, Norman, OK 73070-0787 (SAN 203-3194) Tel 405-325-2000.

U of Pittsburgh Pr, *(Univ. of Pittsburgh Pr.; 0-8229),* 127 N. Bellefield Ave., Pittsburgh, PA 15260 (SAN 203-3216) Tel 412-624-4111; Dist. by: Cornell Univ. Pr., Box 6525, Ithaca, NY 14850 (SAN 202-1862) Tel 607-277-2211; Toll free: 800-666-2211.

U of PR Pr, *(Univ. of Puerto Rico Pr.; 0-8477),* Subs. of Univ. of Puerto Rico, P.O. Box 23322, Univ. of Puerto Rico Sta., Rio Piedras, PR 00931-3322 (SAN 208-1245) Tel 809-250-0550.

U of Tenn Pr, *(Univ. of Tennessee Pr.; 0-87049),* Div. of Univ. of Tennessee & Member of Assn. of American Univ. Presses, 293 Communications Bldg., Knoxville, TN 37996-0325 (SAN 212-9930) Tel 615-974-3321; Orders to: Chicago Distribution Center, 11030 S. Langley, Chicago, IL 60628 (SAN 662-1740) Tel 607-277-2211; Toll free: 800-666-2211 (orders only); Toll free: 800-521-8412 (Credit only).

U of Tex Inst Tex Culture, *(Univ. of Texas Institute of Texan Cultures at San Antonio; 0-933164; 0-86701),* P.O. Box 1226, San Antonio, TX 78294-1226 (SAN 213-8778) Tel 512-226-7651; Toll free: 800-776-7651.

U of Tex Pr, *(Univ. of Texas Pr.; 0-292),* P.O. Box 7819, Austin, TX 78713-7819 (SAN 212-9876) Tel 512-471-7233; Toll free: 800-252-3206.

U of Toronto Pr, *(Univ. of Toronto Pr.; 0-8020),* 340 Nagel Dr., Cheektowaga, NY 14225 (SAN 214-2651) Tel 716-683-4547.

U of Wis Pr, *(Univ. of Wisconsin Pr.; 0-299),* Orders to: 114 N. Murray St., Madison, WI 53715-1199 (SAN 203-3259) Tel 608-262-8782.

U Pr of Miss, *(University Pr. of Mississippi; 0-87805),* 3825 Ridgewood Rd., Jackson, MS 39211 (SAN 203-1914) Tel 601-982-6205.

U Pr of New Eng, *(University Pr. of New England; 0-87451),* 17 1/2 Lebanon St., Hanover, NH 03755 (SAN 203-3283) Tel 603-646-3340; Toll free: 800-421-1561 (orders).

U Presses Fla, *(University Presses of Florida; 0-8130),* 15 NW 15th St., Gainesville, FL 32611 (SAN 207-9275) Tel 904-392-1351.

U TX Inst Lat Am Stud, *(Univ. of Texas at Austin, Institute of Latin American Studies; 0-86728),* Sid Richardson Hall 1-310, Austin, TX 78712 (SAN 220-3103) Tel 512-471-5551.

UAHC, *(UAHC Pr.; 0-8074),* 838 Fifth Ave., New York, NY 10021 (SAN 203-3291) Tel 212-249-0100.

UBH Pubns, *(UBH Pubns., Ltd.; 0-9628330),* 1390 S. Honey Way, Denver, CO 80224 Tel 303-691-2877.

UCPANB, *(United Cerebral Palsy Assn. of the North Bay; 0-9616891),* 959 Transport Way, No. A1, Petaluma, CA 94952 (SAN 661-6453) Tel 707-765-6770; Toll free: 800-441-2711. Do not confuse with United Cerebral Palsy Assns., Inc., New York, NY.

UFO Photo, *(UFO Photo Archives; 0-9608558; 0-934269),* P.O. Box 17206, Tucson, AZ 85710 (SAN 240-7949) Tel 602-296-6753.

UH Pr, *(Univ. of Hawaii Pr., The; 0-8248),* 2840 Kolowalu St., Honolulu, HI 96822 (SAN 202-5353) Tel 808-956-8255; 99-1422 Koaha Pl., Aiea, HI 96701 (SAN 658-215X). *Imprints:* Kolowalu Bk (Kolowalu Book).

Ultramarine Pub, *(Ultramarine Publishing Co., Inc.; 0-89366),* P.O. Box 303, Hastings-on-Hudson, NY 10706 (SAN 208-8762) Tel 914-478-2522.

Ulverscroft, *(Ulverscroft Large Print Bks., Ltd.; 0-7089),* 279 Boston St., Guilford, CT 06437 (SAN 208-3035) Tel 203-453-2080; Toll free: 800-955-9659. Headquarters: The Green, Bradgate Rd., Anstey, Leicester LE7 7FU, England. *Imprints:* Charnwood (Charnwood Library Series).

Ulysses Pr, *(Ulysses Pr.; 0-915233),* P.O. Box 3440, Berkeley, CA 94703-3440 (SAN 289-8764); 3286 Adeline St., Suite 1, Berkeley, CA 94703 (SAN 289-8772) Tel 415-601-8301; Dist. by: Publishers Group West, 4065 Hollis St., Emeryville, CA 94608 (SAN 202-8522) Tel 415-658-3453; Toll free: 800-365-3453.

UM Ctr NENAS, *(Univ. of Michigan, Ctr. for Near Eastern & North African Studies; 0-932098),* 144 Lane Hall, Ann Arbor, MI 48109-1290 (SAN 211-7150) Tel 313-764-8523; Orders to: Univ. of Michigan Language Laboratory, 2018 ML Bldg., Ann Arbor, MI 48109-1275 (SAN 653-483X) Tel 313-764-0424; Dist. by: Univ. of Michigan Pr., Pubns. Distribution Ctr., 839 Greene St., Ann Arbor, MI 48106 (SAN 282-4884) Tel 313-764-4394; Dist. by: Cambridge Univ. Pr., 510 North Ave., New Rochelle, NY 10801 (SAN 169-4014) Tel 914-235-0300; Toll free: 800-872-7423 (Orders only); Dist. by: International Bk. Ctr., 2007 Laurel Dr., P.O. Box 295, Troy, MI 48099 (SAN 208-7022) Tel 313-879-8436. Do not confuse with Univ. of Michigan, Dept. of Near Eastern Studies.

UN, *(United Nations; 0-680),* 2 United Nations Plaza, Sales Section, Publishing Div., Rm. DC2-853, New York, NY 10017 (SAN 206-6718) Tel 212-963-8302; Toll free: 800-553-3210 (Bookshop).

Underwood-Miller, *(Underwood/Miller; 0-934438; 0-88733),* Orders to: 708 Westover Dr., Lancaster, PA 17601 (SAN 666-6779) Tel 717-285-2255.

Unicorn Ent, *(Unicorn Enterprises; 0-87884),* 1620 Collinsdale Ave., Cincinnati, OH 45230 (SAN 206-6696).

Unicorn Game Pubns, *(Unicorn Game Pubns.; 0-9628003),* Box 4284, Fresno, CA 93728; 1340 N. Linden, Suite 10, Fresno, CA 93728 Tel 209-233-0237.

Unicorn Pbks *Imprint of* **Dutton Child Bks**

Unicorn Pub, *(Unicorn Publishing Hse., Inc., The; 0-88101),* 120 American Way, Morris Plains, NJ 07950 (SAN 240-4567) Tel 201-292-6863.

Union Hosp Found, *(Union Hospital Foundation; 0-9621620),* 695 Chestnut St., Union, NJ 07083 (SAN 252-1067) Tel 201-687-1900.

Unitarian Univ, *(Unitarian Universalist Assn.; 0-933840; 1-55896),* 25 Beacon St., Boston, MA 02108-2800 (SAN 225-4840) Tel 617-742-2100.

United Ed, *(United Educators, Inc.; 0-87566),* 900 Armour Dr., Lake Bluff, IL 60044 (SAN 204-8795) Tel 708-234-3700.

United Pr, *(United Pr., Inc.; 0-932972),* P.O. Box 4064, Sarasota, FL 33578 (SAN 212-6931); Dist. by: Nutri Bks. Corp., P.O. Box 5793, Denver, CO 80217 (SAN 169-054X) Tel 303-778-8383; Toll free: 800-279-2048 (orders only); Dist. by: Bookpeople, 2929 Fifth St., Berkeley, CA 94710 (SAN 168-9517) Tel 415-549-3030; Toll free: 800-999-4650.

United Pub Co, *(United Publishing Co.; 0-937323),* 11 Elm Pl., Albany, NY 12203 (SAN 658-8077) Tel 518-456-1321.

United Soc Shakers, *(United Society of Shakers; 0-915836),* Sabbathday Lake, Poland Spring, ME 04274 (SAN 158-619X) Tel 207-926-4597.

United Syn Bk, *(United Synagogue of America Bk. Service; 0-8381),* Subs. of United Synagogue of America, 155 Fifth Ave., New York, NY 10010 (SAN 203-0551) Tel 212-533-7800.

Unity School, *(Unity Schl. of Christianity; 0-87159),* Unity Village, MO 64065 (SAN 204-8817) Tel 816-524-3550.

Univ Central AR Pr, *(Univ. of Central Arkansas Pr.; 0-9615143; 0-944436),* P.O. Box 4933, Conway, AR 72032 (SAN 694-2083) Tel 501-450-5150.

Univ Class, *(University Classics, Ltd., Pubs.; 0-914127),* 1 Bryan Rd., Briarwood, Athens, OH 45701 (SAN 287-5934) Tel 614-592-4543.

Univ Edtns *Imprint of* **Aegina Pr**

Universe, *(Universe Publishing, Inc.; 0-87663; 1-55550),* Div. of Rizzoli International Pubns., Inc., 300 Park Ave. S., 5th Flr., New York, NY 10010 (SAN 202-537X) Tel 212-387-3400; Dist. by: St. Martin's Pr., Inc., 175 Fifth Ave., New York, NY 10010 (SAN 200-2132) Tel 212-674-5151; Toll free: 800-325-5525.

University MT, *(University Pr.; 0-9624819),* 302 Crestline, Missoula, MT 59803 Tel 406-243-6840. Do not confuse with companies with the same name in San Francisco, CA, Edina, MN.

UNTX Pr, *(Univ. of North Texas Pr.; 0-929398),* P.O. Box 13856, Denton, TX 76203 (SAN 249-4280); Chestnut Hall, Suite 1, Denton, TX 76203 (SAN 249-4299) Tel 817-565-2142.

Upper Room, *(Upper Room, The; 0-8358; 0-941478),* 1908 Grand Ave., P.O. Box 189, Nashville, TN 37202 (SAN 203-3364) Tel 615-340-7243; Dist. by: Abingdon Pr., 201 Eighth Ave., S., Nashville, TN 37202 (SAN 201-0054) Tel 615-749-6290; Toll free: 800-251-3320.

Upper Strata, *(Upper Strata Ink, Inc.; 0-9616589),* P.O. Box 250, Bernalillo, NM 87004 (SAN 659-8064); 500 Beehive Ln., Bernalillo, NM 87004 (SAN 659-8072) Tel 505-867-5812.

Upstart Eagle Pr, *(Upstart Eagle Pr.; 0-929778),* P.O. Box 159, Orono, ME 04473 (SAN 250-0833); 35 Forest Ave., Orono, ME 04473 (SAN 250-0841) Tel 207-866-4088.

Upton Sons, *(Upton & Sons; 0-912783),* 917 Hillcrest St., El Segundo, CA 90245 (SAN 160-5216) Tel 213-322-7202.

Upward Way, *(Upward Way, The; 0-945460),* P.O. Box 369, Pleasant View, TN 37146 (SAN 247-0551) Tel 615-746-4234; Toll free: 800-367-2665 (orders only).

Urban Res Pr, *(Urban Research Pr., Inc.; 0-941484),* 840 E. 87th St., Chicago, IL 60619 (SAN 239-0515) Tel 312-994-7200; Toll free: 800-626-6661.

Ursa Major Corp, *(URSA Major Corp.; 0-9625388),* P.O. Box 3368, Ashland, OR 97520; Toll free: 800-999-3433; 695 Mistletoe Rd., No. 2, Ashland, OR 97520 Tel 503-482-1322.

US Catholic, *(U. S. Catholic Conference; 1-55586),* Affil. of National Conference of Catholic Bishops, Pubns. Services, 3211 Fourth St., NE, Washington, DC 20017-1194 (SAN 207-5350) Tel 202-541-3090; Toll free: 800-235-8722.

USA Entrps, *(USA Enterprises, Inc.; 0-9628653),* 415 S. Sixth St., Suite 200, Las Vegas, NV 89101 Tel 702-385-0855.

Usborne *Imprint of* **EDC**

Useful Lrn, *(Useful Learning; 1-878712),* 711 Meadowlane Ct., Mount Vernon, IA 52314 Tel 319-335-5304; Toll free: 800-862-3855.

USGPO, *(U. S. Government Printing Office; 0-16),* USGPO Stop SSMR, Washington, DC 20402 (SAN 206-152X); Orders to: Superintendent of Documents, Washington, DC 20402-9325 (SAN 658-0785) Tel 202-783-3238.

USPS, *(U. S. Postal Service, Philatelic Marketing Div.; 0-9604756; 1-877707),* 475 L'Enfant Plaza, Washington, DC 20260-6755 (SAN 219-8304) Tel 202-268-2350.

V B Wood, *(Wood, Vivian Bee; 0-9621567),* 7370-142 Parkview Ct., Santee, CA 92071 (SAN 251-5725) Tel 619-562-0253.

V H Pub, *(VHW Publishing; 0-9610912; 0-941281),* 930 Via Fruteria, Santa Barbara, CA 93110 (SAN 265-153X) Tel 805-687-4087.

V Lockman, *(Lockman, Vic; 0-936175),* P.O. Box 1916, Ramona, CA 92065 (SAN 697-2063); Toll free: 800-648-6095.

V M H Cain, *(Cain, V. M. Helen; 0-9624837),* P.O. Box 091224, Columbus, OH 43209 Tel 614-236-2617.

V S Epstein, *(Epstein, Vivian Sheldon; 0-9601002),* 212 S. Dexter St., Denver, CO 80222 (SAN 208-6425) Tel 303-322-7450.

V S Morris, *(Morris, Victoria S., Bks.; 0-914318),* P.O. Box 1068, Alameda, CA 94501-0109 (SAN 202-2125) Tel 415-652-2013.

V Sharp, *(Sharp, Vera; 0-9616987),* 204C Edgewater Towers, 17530 Sunset Blvd., Pacific Palisades, CA 90272 (SAN 658-8360) Tel 213-454-2111.

V W Hensley, *(Hensley, Virgil W., Inc.; 1-56322),* 6116 E. 32nd St., Tulsa, OK 74135 Tel 918-664-8520; Toll free: 800-288-8520.

V W Snyder, *(Snyder, Vern W.; 0-926366),* 3660 Walnut Blvd., No. 90, Brentwood, CA 94513 Tel 415-634-1117.

Vade Denver, *(Vade Mecum Pr.; 0-945847),* 5200 DTC Pkwy., No. 260, Englewood, CO 80111-2715 (SAN 247-7939) Tel 303-935-6703. Do not confuse with Vade Mecum Pr., Sterling, VA.

Vagabond *Imprint of Scholastic Inc*

Vail Pub, *(Vail Publishing; 0-9607872),* 8285 SW Brookridge, Portland, OR 97225 (SAN 240-0766) Tel 503-292-9964.

Valkyrie Pub Hse, *(Valkyrie Publishing Hse.; 0-912760; 0-934616; 0-912589),* 8245 26th Ave., N, Saint Petersburg, FL 33710 (SAN 203-1671) Tel 813-345-8864.

Value Comm *Imprint of Oak Tree Pubns*

Valued Pubns, *(Valued Pubns.; 0-943491),* P.O. Box 1982, Placentia, CA 92670 (SAN 668-5269); 2419 Navajo, Placentia, CA 92670 (SAN 668-5277) Tel 714-524-9237.

Van Buren Cty Hist Soc, *(Van Buren County Historical Society; 0-9621012),* P.O. Box 452, Hartford, MI 49057 (SAN 250-9105); 58471 Red Arrow Hwy., Hartford, MI 49057 (SAN 250-9113) Tel 616-674-8914.

Vandamere, *(Vandamere Pr.; 0-918339),* Subs. of AB Assocs., P.O. Box 5243, Arlington, VA 22205 (SAN 657-3088) Tel 703-525-5488.

Vanderbilt U Pr, *(Vanderbilt Univ. Pr.; 0-8265),* Div. of Vanderbilt Univ., 1211 18th Ave., S., Nashville, TN 37212 (SAN 202-9308) Tel 615-322-3585.

Vantage, *(Vantage Pr., Inc.; 0-533),* 516 W. 34th St., New York, NY 10001 (SAN 206-8893) Tel 212-736-1767; Toll free: 800-882-3273.

Vashon Pt Prod, *(Vashon Point Productions; 0-9616103),* Rte. 1, P.O. Box 432, Vashon, WA 98070 (SAN 659-5642) Tel 206-567-4829.

Vedanta Pr, *(Vedanta Pr.; 0-87481),* Div. of Vedanta Society, 1946 Vedanta Pl., Hollywood, CA 90068-3996 (SAN 202-9340) Tel 213-465-7114.

Vegetarian Resc, *(Vegetarians Resource Group, The; 0-931411),* P.O. Box 1463, Baltimore, MD 21203 (SAN 630-172X) Tel 301-366-8343; Dist. by: New Leaf Distributing Co., 5425 Tulane Dr., SW, Atlanta, GA 30336-2323 (SAN 169-1449) Tel 404-691-6996; Toll free: 800-326-2665; Dist. by: Inland Bk. Co., 140 Commerce St., East Haven, CT 06512 (SAN 200-4151) Tel 203-467-4257; Toll free: 800-243-0138.

Veracruz Pubs, *(Veracruz Pubs.; 1-879219),* P.O. Box 5262, Tucson, AZ 85703; 1531 N. Hualpai, Tucson, AZ 85745 Tel 602-628-1135.

Verbal Images Pr, *(Verbal Images Pr.; 0-9625136),* 19 Fox Hill Dr., Fairport, NY 14450 Tel 716-377-3807.

Veritie Pr, *(Veritie Pr.; 0-915964),* P.O. Box 222, Novelty, OH 44072 (SAN 207-6977) Tel 216-338-3374.

Vernier Soft, *(Vernier Software; 0-918731),* 2920 SW 89th St., Portland, OR 97225 (SAN 293-1753) Tel 503-297-5317.

Versailles, *(Versailles, Elizabeth Starr; 0-9606002),* 42 Nash Hill Rd., Williamsburg, MA 01096 (SAN 203-0330) Tel 413-268-7576.

Very Idea, *(Very Idea, The; 0-9615130),* Brambly Hedge Cottage, HCR 31, Box 39, Jasper, AR 72641 (SAN 694-1869) Tel 501-446-5849.

Vestal, *(Vestal Pr., Ltd.; 0-911572; 1-879511),* 320 N. Jensen Rd., P.O. Box 97, Vestal, NY 13851-0097 (SAN 205-4825) Tel 607-797-4872.

VF&AL Pub Inc, *(VF & AL Publishing, Inc.; 1-877724),* P.O. Box 11872, Shorewood, WI 53211; 3574 N. 11th St., Milwaukee, WI 53206 Tel 414-265-1042.

VGM Career Horzns *Imprint of Natl Textbk*

Vibrante Pr, *(Vibrante Pr.; 0-935301),* 2430 Juan Tabo, NE, Suite 110, Albuquerque, NM 87112 (SAN 696-2351) Tel 505-298-4793.

Victor Bks, *(Victor Bks.; 0-88207; 0-89693; 1-56476),* Div. of Scripture Pr. Pubns., Inc., 1825 Wheaton Ave., Wheaton, IL 60187 (SAN 207-7310) Tel 708-668-6000; Toll free: 800-323-9409.

Victory Press, *(Victory Pr.; 0-9620765; 1-878217),* 543 Lighthouse Ave., Monterey, CA 93940 (SAN 249-700X) Tel 408-883-1725; Dist. by: Distributors, The, 702 S. Michigan, South Bend, IN 46618 (SAN 169-2488) Tel 219-232-8500; Toll free: 800-348-5200 (except Indiana); Dist. by: Bookpeople, 2929 Fifth St., Berkeley, CA 94710 (SAN 168-9517) Tel 415-549-3030; Toll free: 800-999-4650; Dist. by: Inland Bk. Co., 140 Commerce St., East Haven, CT 06512 (SAN 200-4151) Tel 203-467-4257; Toll free: 800-243-0138; Dist. by: New Leaf Distributing Co., 5424 Tulane Dr., SW, Atlanta, GA 30336 (SAN 169-1449) Tel 404-691-6996; Toll free: 800-326-2665; Dist. by: Great Tradition, 11270 Clayton Creek Rd., Lower Lake, CA 95457 (SAN 200-5743) Tel 707-995-3906; Toll free: 800-275-2606.

Victory Pub, *(Victory Publishing; 0-935303),* 3504 Oak Dr., Menlo Park, CA 94025 (SAN 696-2408) Tel 415-323-1650.

Video Athlete, *(Video Athlete Corp.; 0-915659),* Div. of Dennis DeNure Enterprises, P.O. Box 281, Madison, WI 53701-0281 (SAN 287-2358) Tel 608-257-2697.

Viking *Imprint of Viking Penguin*

Viking Child Bks, *(Viking Children's Bks.; 0-670),* Div. of Penguin USA, 375 Hudson St., New York, NY 10014-3657 Tel 212-366-2000.

Viking Penguin, *(Viking Penguin; 0-670; 0-14),* Div. of Penguin USA, 375 Hudson St., New York, NY 10014-3657 (SAN 200-2442) Tel 212-366-2000; Toll free: 800-631-3577; Orders to: P.O. Box 120, Bergenfield, NJ 07621-0120 (SAN 282-5074) Tel 201-387-0600; Toll free: 800-526-0275; Orders to: 100 Fabright Rd., Newbern, TN 38059-1334 (SAN 200-3023) *Imprints:* Pelican Bks (Pelican Books); Penguin Bks (Penguin Books); Viking (Viking).

Vilate Pub, *(Vilate Publishing; 0-9623144),* B13, 65 Verde Valley School Rd., Sedona, AZ 86336 Tel 602-284-1613.

Vimach Assocs, *(Vimach Assocs.; 0-917949),* 5865 Cummington Ct., Columbus, OH 43213 (SAN 657-0283) Tel 614-755-9597.

Vin *Imprint of Random*

Vincent Marzilli, *(Marzilli, Vincent; 0-9617809),* R.F.D. No. 5, Box 240-C, Bangor, ME 04401 Tel 207-990-0704.

Visions Unlimited, *(Visions Unlimited; 0-9622776),* Div. of Jackie Marx Enterprises, Inc., 899 Village Quarter Rd., Dundee, IL 60118 Tel 312-426-6733.

Vistas, *(Vistas, Inc.; 1-879827),* 809 N. 800 E., Logan, UT 84321 Tel 801-755-0210.

Visual Evangels, *(Visual Evangels Publishing Co.; 0-915398),* 1401 Ohio St., Michigan City, IN 46360 (SAN 212-002X) Tel 219-874-3902.

Visual Studies, *(Visual Studies Workshop; 0-89822),* 31 Prince St., Rochester, NY 14607 (SAN 218-1606).

Vital Edits, *(Vital Editions; 0-9629982),* P.O. Box 637, New York, NY 10008 Tel 718-857-4434.

Viz Commns Inc, *(Viz Communications, Inc.; 0-929279),* Subs. of Shogakukan, Inc., P.O. Box 77010, San Francisco, CA 94107 (SAN 248-8604) Tel 415-546-7073.

VJR Passports, *(V.J.R. Passports; 0-9625515),* 1945 Northwestern Ave., Madison, WI 53704 Tel 608-249-7167.

Voc-Offers, *(Voc-Offers; 0-918995),* P.O. Box 700252, San Jose, CA 95170-0252 (SAN 669-8247) Tel 408-255-6579.

Volcano Pr, *(Volcano Pr., Inc.; 0-912078),* P.O. Box 270, Volcano, CA 95689 (SAN 220-0015) Tel 209-296-3445.

Vous Etes Tres Belle, *(Vous Etes Tres Belle, Inc.; 0-9619641),* 2205 Tonga Dr., Fort Washington, MD 20744 (SAN 245-8233) Tel 301-292-9144.

Voyager BH, *(Voyager Pr.; 0-943513),* 421 Shirley Pl., Beverly Hills, CA 90212 (SAN 668-4564) Tel 213-277-2386. Do not confuse with Voyager Pr., Los Angeles, CA.

Voyageur Pr, *(Voyageur Pr.; 0-89658),* 123 N. Second St., Stillwater, MN 55082 (SAN 287-2668) Tel 612-430-2210; Toll free: 800-888-9653.

Voyageur Pub, *(Voyageur Publishing Co., Inc.; 0-929146),* P.O. Box 150127, Nashville, TN 37215 (SAN 248-6709); 4506 Beacon Dr., Nashville, TN 37215 (SAN 248-6717) Tel 615-665-2636.

VoyB *Imprint of HarBraceJ*

VWAP, *(Victim Witness Assistance Program; 0-9621260),* 200 S. High St., Wailuku, HI 96793 (SAN 250-913X) Tel 808-243-7777.

Vyoupoint, *(Vyoupoint; 0-9618083),* P.O. Box 13860, San Luis Obispo, CA 93406 (SAN 666-0657) Tel 805-543-6892.

W Dean Editions, *(Dean, Wayne, Editions; 0-9616161),* 3217 Petunia Ct., San Diego, CA 92117 (SAN 699-8364) Tel 619-272-6075; Dist. by: Dale Seymour Pubns., P.O. Box 10888, Palo Alto, CA 94303 (SAN 200-9781) Tel 415-324-2800; Toll free: 800-872-1100; 800-222-0766 (in California).

W Disney Pub, *(Walt Disney Publishing Group, Inc.; 1-56282),* 114 5th Ave., New York, NY 10011 Tel 212-633-4418; Dist. by: Little, Brown & Co., 200 W. St., Waltham, MA 02254 Tel 617-890-0250; Toll free: 800-343-9204. *Imprints:* Disney Pr (Disney Press); Hyperion Child (Hyperion Books for Children).

W F Cox, *(Cox, Willis F.; 0-9610758),* Box 47, James Store, VA 23080 (SAN 264-7060) Tel 804-693-4533.

W Foster Pub, *(Foster, Walter, Publishing, Inc.; 0-929261; 1-56010),* 430 W. Sixth St., Tustin, CA 92680-9990 (SAN 249-051X) Tel 714-544-7510; Toll free: 800-426-0099.

W H Freeman, *(Freeman, W. H., & Co.; 0-7167),* Subs. of Scientific American, Inc., 41 Madison Ave., E. 26th, 35th Flr., New York, NY 10010 (SAN 290-6864) Tel 212-576-9400; Orders to: 4419 W. 1980, S., Salt Lake City, UT 84104 (SAN 290-6872) Tel 801-973-4660.

W J Fantasy, *(W.J. Fantasy, Inc.; 1-56021),* 181 Regents Pk., Westport, CT 06880 Tel 203-254-8137; Toll free: 800-222-7529.

W Keast, *(Keast, Winifred; 0-9613847),* 740 Memorial Dr., Winthrop, ME 04364 (SAN 655-4326) Tel 207-377-8087.

W M Farmer, *(Farmer, Wesley M.; 0-937772),* 3591 Ruffin Rd., No. 226, San Diego, CA 92116 (SAN 215-6431); Dist. by: Sunbelt Pubns., P.O. Box 191126, San Diego, CA 92119 (SAN 242-0198) Tel 619-697-4811.

W P Allen, *(Allen, W. P., & Co., Inc.; 0-916777),* P.O. Box 702, Portland, OR 97207 (SAN 654-2921) Tel 503-538-2311.

W Ruth Co, *(Ruth, William, & Co.; 0-9627697),* 2404 Owens Rd., Oxon Hill, MD 20745 Tel 301-899-3434.

W S Nelson & Co, *(Nelson, Waldemar S., & Co., Inc.; 0-9619160),* 1200 St. Charles Ave., New Orleans, LA 70130 (SAN 243-3435) Tel 504-523-5281.

W S Sullwold, *(Sullwold, William S., Publishing; 0-88492),* 18 Pearl St., Taunton, MA 02780 (SAN 203-1744) Tel 508-823-0924.

Wadsworth Pub, *(Wadsworth Publishing Co.; 0-534),* Div. of Wadsworth, Inc., 10 Davis Dr., Belmont, CA 94002 (SAN 200-2213) Tel 415-595-2350; Toll free: 800-354-9706; Orders to: Wadsworth, Inc., Distribution Ctr., 7625 Empire Dr., Florence, KY 41042-2978 (SAN 200-2663) Tel 606-525-2230; Toll free: 800-354-9706. Requests for college catalogs, desk copies, review copies, supplementary materials & instructional aids to: Distribution Ctr., Florence, KY address; 800-243-0563. Requests for software & software information to Sales Office, Belmont, CA address; 800-876-2350. Requests for general information & professional reference catalogs, information for retailers & wholesalers to: Corporate Mktg., Belmont, CA address; 800-831-6996.

Wafer Mache, *(Wafer Mache Pubns., Inc.; 0-935009),* 16 Elmgate Rd., Marlton, NJ 08053 (SAN 695-2143) Tel 609-983-5360.

Wahr, *(Wahr, George, Publishing Co.; 0-911586),* 304 1/2 S. State St., Ann Arbor, MI 48104 (SAN 205-5015) Tel 313-668-6097.

Walker & Co, *(Walker & Co.; 0-8027),* Div. of Walker Publishing Co., Inc., 720 Fifth Ave., New York, NY 10019 (SAN 202-5213) Tel 212-265-3632; Toll free: 800-289-25537 (orders).

Walker Educ, *(Walker Educational Bk. Corp.; 0-8027),* Affil. of Walker & Co., 720 Fifth Ave., New York, NY 10019 (SAN 206-1899) Tel 212-265-3632.

Walker Pubns, *(Walker Pubns.; 0-9615182),* P.O. Box 17924, Irvine, CA 92713 (SAN 694-3462).

Wall To Wall, *(Wall To Wall Pubns.; 0-9626427),* 825 West End Ave., New York, NY 10025 Tel 212-662-9764.

Wallbuilders, *(Wallbuilders, Inc.; 0-925279),* P.O. Box 397, Aledo, TX 76008; 950 Chapman Ct., Aledo, TX 76008 Tel 817-441-6044.

Ward Hill Pr, *(Ward Hill Pr.; 0-9623380),* 40 Willis Ave., Staten Island, NY 10301 (SAN 200-3139) Tel 718-816-9449.

Warne, *(Warne, Frederick, & Co.; 0-7232),* Div. of Penguin USA, 375 Hudson St., New York, NY 10014-3657 (SAN 212-9884) Tel 212-366-2000; Dist. by: Penguin USA, P.O. Box 120, Bergenfield, NJ 07621-0120 (SAN 282-5074) Tel 201-387-0600; Toll free: 800-526-0275.

Warner Bks, *(Warner Bks., Inc.; 0-446),* Div. of Time Warner Publishing, 666 Fifth Ave.9th Floor, New York, NY 10103 (SAN 282-5368) Tel 212-484-3165; Dist. by: Little, Brown & Co., 200 West St., Waltham, MA 02254 (SAN 281-8892); Toll free: 800-343-9204.

Warner Pr, *(Warner Pr. Pubs.; 0-87162),* 1200 E. Fifth St., Anderson, IN 46012 (SAN 111-8110) Tel 317-644-7721; Toll free: 800-428-6427; 800-428-6409 (orders only); Orders to: P.O. Box 2499, Anderson, IN 46018 (SAN 691-4241).

Warren-Mattox, *(Warren-Mattox Productions; 0-9623381),* 4009 Minuet Cir., El Sobrante, CA 94803 Tel 415-223-7089; Dist. by: Lancaster Productions, P.O. Box 7820, Berkeley, CA 94707 (SAN 241-9807) Tel 415-549-7110.

Warren Pub Hse, *(Warren Publishing Hse., Inc.; 0-911019),* 11625G Airport Rd., Everett, WA 98204 (SAN 667-4585) Tel 206-353-3100; Toll free: 800-334-4769.

Warwick *Imprint of* **Watts**

Wash Dolls Hse, *(Washington Dolls' Hse. & Toy Museum),* 5236 44th St., NW, Washington, DC 20015 (SAN 217-2747) Tel 202-363-6400.

Wash Res Assocs, *(Washington Research Assocs.; 0-937801),* 1660 S. Albion St., Suite 309, Denver, CO 80222 (SAN 659-378X) Tel 303-756-9038.

Wash Writers Pub, *(Washington Writers' Publishing Hse.; 0-931846),* P.O. Box 15271, Washington, DC 20003 (SAN 211-9250) Tel 202-543-1905.

Water St Missouri, *(Water Street Pubs.; 0-9616799),* 6125 Marwinette Ave., Saint Louis, MO 63116 (SAN 661-0382) Tel 314-351-2427.

Waterfront Bks, *(Waterfront Bks.; 0-914525),* 98 Brookes Ave., Burlington, VT 05401 (SAN 289-6923) Tel 802-658-7477; Toll free: 800-639-6063; Dist. by: Talman Co., 150 Fifth Ave., Rm. 630, New York, NY 10011 (SAN 200-5204) Tel 212-620-3182; Toll free: 800-537-8894 (orders only); Dist. by: Publishers Group West, 4065 Hollis St., Emeryville, CA 94608 (SAN 202-8522) Tel 415-658-3452; Toll free: 800-365-3453; Dist. by: Quality Bks., Inc., 918 Sherwood Dr., Lake Bluff, IL 60044-2204 (SAN 169-2127) Tel 708-295-2010; Toll free: 800-323-4241 (libraries only); Dist. by: Children's Small Pr. Collection, 719 N. Fourth Ave., Ann Arbor, MI 48104 (SAN 200-514X) Tel 313-668-8056; Toll free: 800-221-8056; Dist. by: Bookpeople, 2929 Fifth St., Berkeley, CA 94710 (SAN 168-9517) Tel 415-549-3030; Toll free: 800-999-4650; Dist. by: Baker & Taylor Bks., Eastern Div., 50 Kirby Ave., Somerville, NJ 08876-0734 (SAN 169-4901) Tel 201-722-8000; Toll free: 800-526-3825; Dist. by: Baker & Taylor Bks., Midwestern Div., 501 S. Gladiolus St., Momence, IL 60954-2444 (SAN 169-2100) Tel 815-472-2444; Toll free: 800-435-5111; 800-892-1892 (in Illinois); Dist. by: Baker & Taylor Bks., Southern Div., Mt. Olive Rd., Commerce, GA 30599-9988 (SAN 169-1503) Tel 303-296-1830; Toll free: 800-241-6004; 800-282-6854 (in Georgia); Dist. by: Baker & Taylor Bks., Western Div., 380 Edison Way, Reno, NV 89564 (SAN 169-4464) Tel 702-786-6700; Toll free: 800-648-3540; 800-524-2486 (in Canada).

Waterlinc Prodns, *(Waterlinc Productions; 0-929592),* 74 Trinity Turn, Willingboro, NJ 08046 (SAN 249-7034) Tel 609-871-5359.

WaterMark Inc, *(WaterMark, Inc.; 0-929077),* 3250 Independence Dr., Homewood, AL 35209 (SAN 248-2010) Tel 205-879-6379; Toll free: 800-676-6371.

Watermark MD, *(Watermark Pr.; 1-56167),* P.O. Box 217, Owings Mills, MD 21117; 5E Gwinns Mill Ct., Owings Mills, MD 21117 Tel 301-356-2000. Do not confuse with Watermark Pr., Wichita, KS.

Waterston Product, *(Waterston Productions, Inc.; 0-9628129; 1-880452),* 115 NW Oregon Ave., Bend, OR 97701 Tel 503-385-7025.

Waterworks Pub, *(Waterworks Publishing Co.; 0-9620034),* P.O. Box 264, Eureka Springs, AR 72632 (SAN 247-5294); 61 Kingshighway, Eureka Springs, AR 72632 (SAN 247-5308) Tel 501-253-9755; Dist. by: New Leaf Distributing Co., 5425 Tulane Dr., SW, Atlanta, GA 30336-2323 (SAN 169-1449) Tel 404-691-6996; Toll free: 800-326-2665; Dist. by: Bookpeople, 2929 Fifth St., Berkeley, CA 94710 (SAN 168-9517) Tel 415-549-3030; Toll free: 800-999-4650.

Watson-Guptill, *(Watson-Guptill Pubns., Inc.; 0-8230; 0-8174; 0-87165),* Div. of Billboard Pubns., Inc., 1 Astor Plaza, 1515 Broadway, New York, NY 10036 (SAN 282-5384) Tel 908-536-5129; Toll free: 800-451-1741 (Orders & Customer Service); Orders to: 1695 Oak St., Lakewood, NJ 08701 (SAN 282-5392) Tel 201-363-5679.

Watts, *(Watts, Franklin, Inc.; 0-531),* Subs. of Grolier, Inc., 387 Park Ave., S.4th Flr., New York, NY 10016 (SAN 285-1156) Tel 212-686-7070; Toll free: 800-672-6672 (customer Service); 800-433-3411. *Imprints:* Gloucester Pr (Gloucester Press); Hampstead Pr (Hampstead Press); Warwick (Warwick Press).

Wayne St U Pr, *(Wayne State Univ. Pr.; 0-8143),* Leonard N. Simons Bldg., 5959 Woodward Ave., Detroit, MI 48202 (SAN 202-5221) Tel 313-577-4600.

Wayside Pub, *(Wayside Publishing; 1-877653),* 129 Commonwealth Ave., Concord, MA 01742 Tel 508-369-2519.

WBGM CA
  See W Disney Pub

WD Pub, *(WD Publishing; 1-56115),* Subs. of Walt Disney Co., Inc., 500 S. Buena Vista, Burbank, CA 91521 Tel 818-560-1475. *Imprints:* Disney Movie Bks (Disney Movie Books).

Weaselsleeves Pr, *(Weaselsleeves Pr.; 1-878460),* P.O. Box 8187, Santa Fe, NM 87504; Las Dos Subdivision, Lot 27, Santa Fe, NM 87504 Tel 505-988-3871.

Weatherhill, *(Weatherhill, Inc.; 0-8348),* 420 Madison Ave., 15th Flr., New York, NY 10017 (SAN 202-9529) Tel 212-223-3008; Dist. by: Weatherhill Distribution, Inc., 300 Long Beach Blvd., Stratford, CT 06497-7116 Tel 203-377-6150; Toll free: 800-437-7840.

Weber Systems, *(Weber Systems, Inc.; 0-938862; 0-9604892; 0-929704),* 8437 Mayfield Rd., No. 102, Chesterland, OH 44026 (SAN 240-8201) Tel 216-729-2858.

Websters New Wrld *Imprint of* **Prentice Hall Pr**

Wee-Chee-Taw, *(Wee-Chee-Taw Publishing; 0-9622632),* 4450 Phillips Dr., Wichita Falls, TX 76308 Tel 817-692-3791.

Wee Pr, *(Wee Pr.; 0-9625005),* 800 S. 38th St., Terre Haute, IN 47803 Tel 812-234-6033.

Wee Smile, *(Wee Smile Bks.; 0-9605444),* P.O. Box 1329, Sparks, NV 89431 (SAN 215-983X) Tel 702-356-0216.

Weider Health, *(Weider Health & Fitness; 0-945797),* 21100 Erwin St., Woodland Hills, CA 91367 (SAN 247-5588) Tel 818-715-0635.

Weinberg, *(Weinberg, Michael Aron; 0-9601014),* P.O. Box 27957, Los Angeles, CA 90027 (SAN 208-2314); 4408 Russell St., No. 3, Los Angeles, CA 90027 (SAN 241-8924) Tel 213-669-0158.

Weiss Pub, *(Weiss Publishing Co., Inc.; 0-916720),* 5309 W. Grace St., Richmond, VA 23226 (SAN 208-4775) Tel 804-282-4641.

Wellington IL, *(Wellington Publishing, Inc.; 0-922984),* P.O. Box 14877, Chicago, IL 60614-0877 (SAN 251-7795); 360 W. Wellington Ave., Chicago, IL 60657 (SAN 251-7809) Tel 312-472-4820.

WELS Board, *(WELS Board for Parish Education; 0-938272),* 2929 N. Mayfair Rd., Milwaukee, WI 53222 (SAN 216-3160) Tel 414-771-9357.

Wenkart, *(Wenkart, Henri; 0-911612),* 40 Central Park S., Suite 6D, New York, NY 10019 (SAN 206-300X) Tel 212-751-9223.

Wesley Inst, *(Wesley Institute, Inc.; 0-9614501),* 243 Johnston Rd., Pittsburgh, PA 15241 (SAN 689-9625) Tel 412-831-9390; Orders to: P.O. Box 113445, Pittsburgh, PA 15241 (SAN 662-2879).

West Pub, *(West Publishing Co., College & Schl. Div.; 0-8299; 0-314),* P.O. Box 64526, 50 W. Kellogg Blvd., Saint Paul, MN 55164-0526 (SAN 202-9618) Tel 612-228-2778; Toll free: 800-328-2209 (Customer Service); College & School Div., P.O. Box 64779, 58 W. Kellogg Blvd., Saint Paul, MN 55164-9424 (SAN 241-8932) Tel 612-668-3600.

West Side Pubns, *(West Side Pubns.; 1-877924),* 140 W. 102nd St., New York, NY 10025 Tel 212-865-3522.

West Village, *(West Village Publishing Co.; 0-933308),* 2904 E. Vanowen Ave., Orange, CA 92667 (SAN 213-1870) Tel 714-633-1420.

Westcom NC, *(Westcom Pr.; 0-9626554),* 715 Washington St., Ayden, NC 28513 Tel 919-355-0902; Toll free: 800-422-8591.

Western Guideways, *(Western Guideways, Ltd.; 0-931788),* P.O. Box 15532, Lakewood, CO 80215 (SAN 210-6264) Tel 303-237-0583.

Western Pub, *(Western Publishing Co., Inc.; 0-307),* Subs. of Western Publishing Group, Inc., 850 Third Ave., New York, NY 10022 (SAN 202-523X) Tel 212-753-8500; 1220 Mound Ave., Racine, WI 53404 (SAN 669-2982) Tel 414-633-2431; Orders to: Dept. M, P.O. Box 700, Racine, WI 53401; Toll free: 800-235-3089; Dist. by: Children's Pr., 1224 W. Van Buren St., Chicago, IL 60607 (SAN 201-9264) Tel 312-666-4200; Toll free: 800-621-1115. Do not confuse with Western Pubs., Lake Worth, FL. *Imprints:* Golden Pr (Golden Press).

Western Slope Pubns, *(Western Slope Pubns.; 0-944523),* P.O. Box 55332-BW, Grand Junction, CO 81505-5332 (SAN 242-9624) Tel 303-241-9426.

Westminster *Imprint of* **Westminster John Knox**

Westminster John Knox, *(Westminster/John Knox Pr.; 0-664; 0-8042),* 100 Witherspoon St., Louisville, KY 40202-1396 (SAN 202-9669) Tel 502-569-5043; Toll free: 800-523-1631 (orders). *Imprints:* Geneva Pr (Geneva Press); Westminster (Westminster Press).

Westport Pubs, *(Westport Pubs., Inc.; 0-9611286; 0-933701),* 4050 Pennsylvania, Suite 310, Kansas City, MO 64111 (SAN 283-3492) Tel 816-756-1490; Toll free: 800-347-2665.

WestSea Pub, *(WestSea Publishing Co., Inc.; 0-937820),* 149D Allen Blvd., Farmingdale, NY 11735 (SAN 215-7144) Tel 516-420-1110.

Westwind Pr, *(Westwind Pr.; 0-9602342),* Rte. 1, Box 208, Farmington, WV 26571 (SAN 215-7152).

Westwood Ent, *(Westwood Enterprises; 0-9617118),* 5302 N. 79th Pl., Scottsdale, AZ 85253 (SAN 662-8028) Tel 602-994-8244.

Westwood Pr, *(Westwood Pr., Inc.; 0-936159),* 251 Park Ave. S., New York, NY 10010 (SAN 696-7183) Tel 212-420-8008.

Whale Museum, *(Whale Museum/Moclips Cetological Society, The; 0-933331),* 62 First St., N., Box 945, Friday Harbor, WA 98250 (SAN 692-2864) Tel 206-378-4710; Dist. by: Pacific Pipeline, Inc., 19215 66th Ave., S., Kent, WA 98032 (SAN 208-2128) Tel 206-872-5523; Toll free: 800-426-4727 (in Oregon, Idaho, Montana, Nevada, northern California); 800-562-4647 (in Washington); Dist. by: Bookpeople, 2929 Fifth St., Berkeley, CA 94710 (SAN 168-9517) Tel 415-549-3030; Toll free: 800-999-4650.

Whatcom Cty Opp, *(Whatcom County Opportunity Council; 0-934671),* Div. of Coalition for Child Advocacy, P.O. Box 159, 314 E. Holly St., Bellingham, WA 98227 (SAN 694-0781) Tel 206-734-5121.

Wheat'N Flower, *(Wheat'N Flower Designs; 0-9613993),* P.O. Box 2433, Springfield, IL 62705 (SAN 683-129X) Tel 217-546-5096.

Whirlwind Pr, *(Whirlwind Pr.; 0-922827),* P.O. Box 109, Camden, NJ 08101 (SAN 251-4281); 805 Corinthian St., Philadelphia, PA 19103 (SAN 251-429X) Tel 215-925-9914.

Whistle Pr, *(Whistle Pr.; 0-9624893),* P.O. Box 762, Durham, NH 03824; Durham Professional Ctr., Mast Rd. & Spinney Ln., Durham, NH 03824. Moved, left no forwarding address.

Whit Prodns, *(Whit Productions, Inc.; 0-9624744),* P.O. Box 1397, Murray, KY 40175; 1204 College Cts., Murray, KY 40175 Tel 502-759-9448.

White & Spencer, *(White, Laurie A., & Steven L. Spencer; 0-9612024),* 4340 Tamarac Trail, Harbor Springs, MI 49740 (SAN 287-7791) Tel 616-347-6701.

White Feather & Co, *(White Feather & Co. Publishing; 0-9625641),* P.O. Box 354, Solomons, MD 20688 Tel 703-758-8964; Toll free: 800-444-2583.

White G E F
See GEF White

White Lilac Pr, *(White Lilac Pr.; 0-929571),* P.O. Box 2556, Providence, RI 02906 (SAN 250-0361); 20 Lorimer Ave., Providence, RI 02906 (SAN 250-037X) Tel 401-273-6678.

White Mane Pub, *(White Mane Publishing Co., Inc.; 0-942597),* P.O. Box 152, Shippensburg, PA 17257 (SAN 667-1926); 63 W. Burd St., Shippensburg, PA 17257 (SAN 667-1934) Tel 717-532-2237.

White Oak Pr, *(White Oak Pr.; 0-935069),* P.O. Box 188, Reeds Springs, MO 65737 (SAN 694-695X) Tel 417-272-3507. Do not confuse with White Oak Pr., imprint of Candeur Manuscripts, Spring Valley, NY.

White Pine MI
See Pineapple MI

White Rose Pr, *(White Rose Pr.; 0-940561),* 65 Monroe Ave., Memphis, TN 38103 (SAN 664-7545) Tel 901-525-1836.

White Wing Pub, *(White Wing Publishing Hse. & Pr.; 0-934942),* P.O. Box 3000, Cleveland, TN 37311 (SAN 203-2198) Tel 615-476-8536; Toll free: 800-221-5027.

White Wolf, *(White Wolf; 0-9627790; 1-56504),* 4153 Indian Manor Dr., Stone Mountain, GA 30083 Tel 404-292-1819.

Whitehall Pr, *(Whitehall Pr.-Budget Pubns.; 0-916565),* Whitehall, Rte. 1, Box 603, Sandersville, GA 31082 (SAN 295-5512) Tel 912-552-7455.

Whitehorse, *(Whitehorse; 0-937591),* 4154 Ticonderoga Way, Boise, ID 83706 (SAN 659-1299) Tel 208-336-8650; Orders to: P.O. Box 6125, Boise, ID 83707 (SAN 242-1062).

Whites Creek Pr, *(Whites Creek Pr.; 0-9616918),* P.O. Box 266, Whites Creek, TN 37189 (SAN 661-5430); 4772 Lickton Pike, Whites Creek, TN 37189 (SAN 661-5449) Tel 615-876-2622.

Whitfield Bks, *(Whitfield Bks.; 0-930920),* 1841 Pleasant Hill Rd., Pleasant Hill, CA 94523 (SAN 210-6280) Tel 415-938-6759.

Wholeness Intl, *(Wholeness International Network (W.I.N.); 1-877616),* 4309 Overland, Culver City, CA 90230 Tel 213-840-2211.

Whsprng Coyote Pr, *(Whispering Coyote Pr.; 1-879085),* P.O. Box 2159, Halesite, NY 11743-2159; 54 Bay Crest, Huntington Bay, NY 11743 Tel 516-424-5566.

Wibat Pubns, *(Wibat Pubns.; 0-935996),* P.O. Box 60, Forestville, CA 95436 (SAN 214-1698).

Wide-A-Wake Bks
See Wide-Awake Bks

Wide-Awake Bks, *(Wide-Awake Bks.; 0-9623473),* P.O. Box 659, El Cerrito, CA 94530 Tel 415-235-5516; Toll free: 800-468-2239.

Wiener Pub Inc, *(Wiener, Markus, Publishing, Inc.; 0-910129; 1-55876),* 114 Jefferson Rd., Princeton, NJ 08540 (SAN 282-5465) Tel 609-921-1141; Orders to: 225 W. 34th St., Suite 1105, New York, NY 10001 (SAN 630-3463) Tel 212-947-6100.

Wieser & Wieser, *(Wieser & Wieser, Inc.; 0-914373),* 118 E. 25th St., New York, NY 10010 (SAN 289-6958) Tel 212-260-0860.

Wild Bore Bks, *(Wild Bore Bks.; 0-942379),* P.O. Box 25, Banks, OR 97106 (SAN 666-9050) Tel 503-324-7041.

Wild Foods Co, *(Wild Foods Co., Inc.; 0-936699),* c/o Wild Food Co., 3531 W. Glendale Ave., Suite 369, Phoenix, AZ 85051 (SAN 248-4048) Tel 602-930-1067; Dist. by: Baker & Taylor Bks., Midwestern Div., 501 S. Gladiolus St., Momence, IL 60954 (SAN 169-2100) Tel 815-472-2444; Toll free: 800-435-5111; 800-892-1892 (in Illinois); Dist. by: New Leaf Distributing Co., 5425 Tulane Dr., SW, Atlanta, GA 30336-2323 (SAN 169-1449) Tel 404-691-6996; Toll free: 800-326-2665.

Wild Horses, *(Wild Horses Publishing Co.; 0-9601088; 0-937148),* 12310 Concepcion Rd., Los Altos Hills, CA 94022 (SAN 211-8289) Tel 415-941-3396.

Wild Meadows, *(Wild Meadows Publishing; 1-879318),* P.O. Box 12634, Jackson, MS 39236-2634; 3168 Alameda Dr., Box A, Jackson, MS 39212 Tel 601-372-8131.

Wilderness Adventure Bks, *(Wilderness Adventure Bks.; 0-9611596; 0-923568),* 320 Garden Ln., P.O. Box 968, Fowlerville, MI 48836 (SAN 110-8883) Tel 517-223-9581; Toll free: 800-852-8652; Dist. by: Baker & Taylor Bks., 652 E. Main St., Bridgewater, NJ 08807 (SAN 169-5606) Tel 908-218-0400; Dist. by: Gordon's Bks., Inc., 2323 Delgany St., Denver, CO 80216 (SAN 169-0531) Tel 303-296-1830; Toll free: 800-525-6979 (west of the Mississip); Dist. by: Ingram Bk. Co., 7315 Innovation Blvd., Fort Wayne, IN 46818-1371 (SAN 630-4788); Toll free: 800-937-8000; Dist. by: Pacific Pipeline, Inc., 19215 66th Ave., S., Kent, WA 98032 (SAN 208-2128) Tel 206-872-5523; Toll free: 800-444-7323 (US & Canada).

Wilderness Hse, *(Wilderness Hse.; 0-931798),* 11129 Caves Hwy., Cave Junction, OR 97523 (SAN 208-0907) Tel 503-592-2106.

Wildfire *Imprint of* **Scholastic Inc**

Wildflower, *(Wildflower Pr.; 0-938370),* 3901 Bedford Ave., Oceanside, CA 92056-3388 (SAN 215-8280).

Wildlife Educ, *(Wildlife Education, Ltd.; 0-937934),* 3590 Kettner Blvd., San Diego, CA 92101-1139 (SAN 215-8299) Tel 619-299-5034; Toll free: 800-477-5034.

Wiley, *(Wiley, John, & Sons, Inc.; 0-471; 0-8260),* 605 Third Ave., New York, NY 10158-0012 (SAN 200-2272) Tel 212-850-6000; Orders to: John Wiley & Sons, Inc., Eastern Distribution Ctr., 1 Wiley Dr., Somerset, NJ 08873-1272 Tel 908-469-4400.

Willard Pr, *(Willard Pr.; 0-9615349),* P.O. Box 1254, Summit, NJ 07901 (SAN 695-099X) Tel 609-497-0062.

Williams SC, *(Williams Assocs., Inc.; 0-9612296; 0-944514),* P.O. Box 1849, Orangeburg, SC 29115 (SAN 263-2365); 1215 Perry Dr., Orangeburg, SC 29115 (SAN 243-2803) Tel 803-531-1662.

Williamsburg, *(Colonial Williamsburg Foundation; 0-910412; 0-87935),* P.O. Box 1776, Williamsburg, VA 23187-1776 (SAN 128-4630) Tel 804-220-7340.

Williamson Pub Co, *(Williamson Publishing Co.; 0-913589),* Church Hill Rd., P.O. Box 185, Charlotte, VT 05445 (SAN 285-3884) Tel 802-425-2102; Toll free: 800-234-8791.

Willow Creek Pr, *(Willow Creek Pr., Inc.; 0-932558),* P.O. Box 1360, Minocqua, WI 54548 (SAN 211-2825) Tel 715-356-9800; Toll free: 800-336-5666 (orders only).

Willow Pr, *(Willow Pr.; 0-9617159),* 19630 166th Ave., NE, Woodinville, WA 98072 (SAN 663-253X) Tel 206-483-9198. Do not confuse with Willow Pr., Littleton, CO.

Willow Run UT, *(Willow Run Pr.; 0-9621033),* P.O. Box 524, Ephraim, UT 84627 (SAN 250-6491); 45 E. 100th, N., Apt. 5, Box 1-6, Ephraim, UT 84627 (SAN 250-6505) Tel 801-283-4556.

Willow Tree NY, *(Willow Tree Pr.; 0-9606960),* P.O. Box 249, Monsey, NY 10952 (SAN 217-4588) Tel 914-354-9139.

Willowisp Pr, *(Willowisp Pr., Inc.; 0-87406),* 10100 SBF Dr., Pinellas Park, FL 34666 (SAN 687-4592) Tel 813-578-7600; Toll free: 800-726-8090.

Wilson, *(Wilson, H. W.; 0-8242),* 950 University Ave., Bronx, NY 10452 (SAN 203-2961) Tel 212-588-8400; Toll free: 800-367-6770.

Wilson Investment, *(Wilson Investment, Inc.; 0-9627193),* 114 Chaussee Blvd., Summerville, SC 29483 Tel 803-875-1396.

Wilson Oregon, *(Wilson, Marie M.; 0-9615259),* 3595 Belmont Dr., Hood River, OR 97031 (SAN 695-1597) Tel 503-386-4026. Do not confuse with companies with similar names, particularly H. W. Wilson, Bronx, NY. Please use ISBN to determine correct publisher.

Wimmer Bros, *(Wimmer Brothers; 0-918544; 0-939114),* Div. of The Wimmer Companies, 4210 B. F. Goodrich Blvd., Memphis, TN 38118 (SAN 630-5369) Tel 901-362-8900; Toll free: 800-727-1034.

WIN Pub, *(WIN Publishing; 0-944586),* Subs. of WIN Systems, Inc., 1652 W. Texas St., Suite 105, Fairfield, CA 94533 (SAN 243-9522) Tel 916-447-7885.

Winbush Pub, *(Winbush Publishing Co.; 1-880234),* 16821 Muirland St., Detroit, MI 48221 Tel 313-861-6590.

Windfeather Pr, *(Windfeather Pr.; 0-9620122),* P.O. Box 7397, Bismarck, ND 58502 (SAN 247-7246); 1203 N. 27th St., Bismarck, ND 58501 (SAN 247-7254) Tel 701-258-5047.

Windom Bks, *(Windom Bks.; 1-879244),* Div. of Windom, Inc., P.O. Box 6444, Santa Fe, NM 87502; 2442 Cerrillos Rd., Suite 152, Santa Fe, NM 87501 Tel 505-983-3800.

Window World NY, *(Window to the World, Inc.; 0-922049),* P.O. Box 308, Schroon Lake, NY 12870 (SAN 251-1029) Tel 518-532-7322.

Windsor Medallion, *(Windsor Medallion Publishing Co.; 0-9626293),* P.O. Box 223756, Carmel, CA 93922; 27612 Shulte Rd., Carmel Valley, CA 93922 Tel 408-624-5655.

Windsor Pub CA
See Windsor Medallion

Windsor Pubns Inc, *(Windsor Pubns., Inc.; 0-89781),* 9121 Oakdale Ave., P.O. Box 2500, Chatsworth, CA 91313 (SAN 265-3699) Tel 818-700-0200; Toll free: 800-678-2574.

Windswept Hse, *(Windswept Hse. Pubs.; 0-932433),* P.O. Box 159, Mount Desert, ME 04660 (SAN 687-4363) Tel 207-244-7149; Dist. by: Koen Bk. Distributors, 10 Twosome Dr., P.O. Box 600, Moorestown, NJ 08057 (SAN 169-4642) Tel 609-235-4444; Toll free: 800-257-8481; Dist. by: Children's Small Pr. Collection, 719 N. Fourth Ave., Ann Arbor, MI 48104 (SAN 200-514X) Tel 313-668-8056; Toll free: 800-221-8056 (orders only).

Windward Bks, *(Windward Bks.; 0-929155),* P.O. Box 142, Lincoln, MA 01773 (SAN 248-5710) Tel 617-259-0423.

Windward Pub, *(Windward Publishing, Inc.; 0-89317),* 105 NE 25th St., P.O. Box 371005, Miami, FL 33137 (SAN 208-3663) Tel 305-576-6232; Toll free: 800-330-6232 (in Florida).

Windyridge, *(Windyridge Pr.; 0-913366),* P.O. Box 327, Medford, OR 97501 (SAN 206-3948) Tel 503-773-5740; Orders to: Northwest Textbook Depository, P.O. Box 5608, Portland, OR 97228 (SAN 206-3956).

Wings MA, *(Wings Pr.; 0-9629756),* 15 Arnold Ave., Northampton, MA 01060 Tel 413-586-1473. Do not confuse with companies of the same name in Union, ME, Houston, TX.

Winstead Pr, *(Winstead Pr., Ltd.; 0-940787),* 202 Slice Dr., Stamford, CT 06907 (SAN 664-6913) Tel 203-322-4941.

Winston-Derek, *(Winston-Derek Pubs., Inc.; 0-938232; 1-55523),* P.O. Box 90883, Nashville, TN 37209 (SAN 112-6113) Tel 615-321-0535; Toll free: 800-826-1888; Dist. by: Baker & Taylor Bks., Midwestern Div., 501 S. Gladiolus St., Momence, IL 60954 (SAN 169-2100) Tel 815-472-2444; Toll free: 800-435-5111; 800-892-1892 (in Illinois).

Winters Pubns, *(Winters' Pubns.; 0-935011),* P.O. Box 156, North Adams, MI 49262 (SAN 695-1929) Tel 517-287-5712.

Wisdom Intl, *(Wisdom International; 1-56394),* 1939 Westridge Dr., Dallax, TX 75038 Tel 214-518-1833; Dist. by: Harrison Hse., Inc., P.O. Box 35035, Tulsa, OK 74153 (SAN 208-676X) Tel 918-582-2126; Toll free: 800-888-4126.

Wisdom MA, *(Wisdom Pubns.; 0-86171),* 361 Newbury St., Boston, MA 02115 (SAN 246-022X) Tel 617-536-3358; Toll free: 800-272-4050 (Orders only).

Wise Guys Pub, *(Wise Guys Publishing; 0-9622059),* 9680 Millville Way, Millville, CA 96062 Tel 916-342-2366.

Wise Pub, *(Wise Publishing Co.; 0-915766),* 5625 Wilhelmina Ave., Woodland Hills, CA 91367 (SAN 203-1876) Tel 818-883-7527; Orders to: 199 Thousand Oaks Blvd., No. 105, Thousand Oaks, CA 91360 (SAN 666-6868) Tel 805-495-5404.

Wise Works Inc, *(Wise Works, Inc.; 0-9621228),* 973 Corbin Ct., Westerville, OH 43081 (SAN 251-0324) Tel 614-898-1997.

Wishing Rm, *(Wishing Room, Inc., The; 0-931563),* P.O. Box 337, Mechanicsville, VA 23111 (SAN 682-207X) Tel 804-746-0375.

Wisla Pubs, *(Wisla Pubs.; 0-9614274),* 1404 Twisted Oak Ln., Baton Rouge, LA 70810 (SAN 687-4169) Tel 504-766-6036; Orders to: P.O. Box 65042, Baton Rouge, LA 70896-5042 (SAN 662-2763).

With Kids Mind Pubns, *(With Kids in Mind Pubns.; 0-929790),* P.O. Box 46, Bishop, CA 93514 (SAN 250-4421); 417 Wildrose Ln., Bishop, CA 93514 (SAN 250-443X) Tel 619-873-4773.

WLC Enterprises, *(W.L.C. Enterprises; 0-9623230),* P.O. Box 7819, Birmingham, AL 35228; 3232 Hemlock Ave., SW, Birmingham, AL 35221 Tel 205-923-9175.

Wm C Brown, *(Brown, William C., Pubs.; 0-697),* 2460 Kerper Blvd., Dubuque, IA 52001 (SAN 203-2864) Tel 319-588-1451; Toll free: 800-338-5578.

WOFPPM, *(Word of Faith & Power, Prison Ministry; 0-925306),* P.O. Box 2732, Los Angeles, CA 90051; 10410 Ruthelen St., Los Angeles, CA 90047 Tel 213-779-9411.

Wolgemuth & Hyatt, *(Wolgemuth & Hyatt, Pubs., Inc.; 0-943497; 1-56121),* 1749 Mallory Ln., Suite 110, Brentwood, TN 37027 (SAN 668-4939) Tel 615-371-1210.

Wolverine Gallery, *(Wolverine Gallery; 0-941875),* P.O. Box 572, Greybull, WY 82426 (SAN 666-1203); 449 Seventh Ave., S, Greybull, WY 82426 (SAN 666-1211) Tel 307-765-2603.

Woman Warrior Heart, *(Woman Warrior of the Heart Corp.; 0-9622031),* 16 Graceland Dr., San Rafael, CA 94901-1922 Tel 415-664-8829.

Woman Warrior Pr
See Woman Warrior Heart

Womans Mission Union, *(Woman's Missionary Union; 0-936625; 1-56309),* P.O. Box 830010, Birmingham, AL 35283-0010 (SAN 699-7015); Hwy. 280, 100 Missionary Ridge, Birmingham, AL 35243-5235 (SAN 699-7023) Tel 205-991-8100.
Imprints: New Hope (New Hope).

Womansource, *(Womansource; 1-877747),* 625 Heather Dr., Dayton, OH 45001 Tel 513-278-3000.

Women World CRP, *(Women in the World Curriculum Resource Project; 0-9625880),* 1030 Spruce St., Berkeley, CA 94707 Tel 415-524-0304; Dist. by: Social Studies School Service, P.O. Box 802, Culver City, CA 90232-0802 (SAN 168-9592) Tel 213-839-2436; Toll free: 800-421-4246; Dist. by: National Women's History Project, 7738 Bell Rd., Windsor, CA 95492 (SAN 200-8920) Tel 707-526-5974.

Wonder, *(Wonder-Treasure Bks., Inc.; 0-448),* Div. of Price Stern Sloan, Inc., 360 N. La Cienega Blvd., Los Angeles, CA 90048 (SAN 205-5457) Tel 213-657-6100; Toll free: 800-421-0892; 800-227-8801 (In California).

Wonder Kids, *(Wonder Kids Pubns.; 1-56162),* Div. of KC Enterprise, P.O. Box 3485, Cerritos, CA 90703; Toll free: 800-937-1688; 1145 S. Hacienda Blvd., No. 106, Hacienda Heights, CA 91745 Tel 818-964-6228.
Imprints: Lucky Tiger Pr (Lucky Tiger Pr.).

Wonder Works Studio, *(Wonder Works Studio; 0-942953),* Skunk Hollow Rd., R.F.D. 3, Box 412J, Jericho, VT 05465 (SAN 667-9560) Tel 802-899-5496.

Woodbine House, *(Woodbine Hse.; 0-933149),* 5615 Fishers Ln., Rockville, MD 20852 (SAN 630-4052) Tel 301-468-8800; Toll free: 800-843-7323.

Woodbury Pr, *(Woodbury Pr.; 0-912123),* Whippoorwill Rd., P.O. Box 700, R.F.D No. 1, Litchfield, ME 04350 (SAN 264-6463) Tel 207-268-4604; Dist. by: Portland News Co., 270 Western Ave., P.O. Box 1728, South Portland, ME 04106 (SAN 169-3093) Tel 207-774-2633; Dist. by: Maine Writers & Pubs. Alliance, 19D Mason St., Brunswick, ME 04011 (SAN 224-2303) Tel 207-729-6333. Do not confuse with Woodbury Pr., in Lowville, NY.

Woodcock Pr, *(Woodcock Pr.; 0-941674),* P.O. Box 4744, Santa Rosa, CA 95402 (SAN 239-3514) Tel 707-542-6326.

Woodhull Pubns, *(Woodhull Pubns.; 0-9621296),* P.O. Box 14423, Gainesville, FL 32604-2423 (SAN 251-0731); 5800 SW 20th Ave., Gainesville, FL 32607 (SAN 251-074X) Tel 904-332-7746.

Woodland, *(Woodland Publishing Co., Inc.; 0-934104),* Box 85, Wayzata, MN 55391 (SAN 213-1900) Tel 612-473-2725.

Woodland Pr, *(Woodland Pr.; 0-9620502),* 99 Woodland Cir., Minneapolis, MN 55424 (SAN 249-0935) Tel 612-926-2665. Do not confuse with Woodland Pr., Moscow, ID.

Woodmere Press, *(Woodmere Pr.; 0-942493),* P.O. Box 20190, Park West Finance Sta., New York, NY 10025-1511 (SAN 678-3058) Tel 212-678-7839.

Woods Hole Hist, *(Woods Hole Historical Collection; 0-9611374),* P.O. Box 185, Woods Hole, MA 02543 (SAN 283-1791) Tel 508-548-7270.

Woodside Pr ID, *(Woodside Pr.; 0-938191),* P.O. Box 1935, Sun Valley, ID 83353 (SAN 659-7181); 1018 Baldy View Dr., Hailey, ID 83333 (SAN 659-719X) Tel 208-788-2306. Do not confuse with Woodside Pr., Mountain View, CA.

Woodsong Graph, *(Woodsong Graphics, Inc.; 0-912667),* P.O. Box 238, New Hope, PA 18938-0238 (SAN 282-8235) Tel 215-794-8321.

Word Aflame, *(Word Aflame Pr.; 0-912315; 0-932581),* Subs. of Pentecostal Publishing Hse., 8855 Dunn Rd., Hazelwood, MO 63042 (SAN 212-0046) Tel 314-837-7300.

Word Among Us, *(Word Among Us Pr.; 0-932085),* P.O. Box 369, Gaithersburg, MD 20877 (SAN 686-4651) Tel 301-977-2500; Toll free: 800-638-8539; Dist. by: Spring Arbor Distributors, 10885 Textile Rd., Belleville, MI 48111 (SAN 158-9016) Tel 313-481-0900; Toll free: 800-395-9955; Dist. by: Charismatic Renewal Services, 237 N. Michigan St., South Bend, IN 46601 (SAN 268-8492) Tel 219-234-6021.

Word & Image Pr, *(Word & Image Pr.; 0-9623759),* 436 Deer Lake Dr., Nashville, TN 37221-2107 Tel 615-662-1117.

Word Bks, *(Word, Inc.; 0-87680; 0-8499),* Subs. of Capital Cities/ABC, Inc., 5221 N. O'Connor Blvd., Suite 1000, Irving, TX 75039 (SAN 203-283X) Tel 214-556-1900; Orders to: P.O. Box 2518, Waco, TX 76702; Toll free: 800-299-9673.

Word Blossoms, *(Word Blossoms; 0-9626557),* P.O. Box 66812, Baton Rouge, LA 70896; 3318 Covention St., Baton Rouge, LA 70806 Tel 504-344-7042.

Word Dist Intl, *(Word Distributors International; 1-877902),* P.O. Box 371, McKeesport, PA 15134; 904 Huey St., No. 2, McKeesport, PA 15132 Tel 412-673-9673.

Word for Today, *(Word for Today, The; 0-936728),* P.O. Box 8000, Costa Mesa, CA 92628 (SAN 110-8379); 2230 Anne St., Santa Ana, CA 92628 (SAN 214-2260) Tel 714-979-0706; Dist. by: Living Bks., Inc., 12155 Magnolia Ave., Bldg. 11-B, Riverside, CA 92503 (SAN 169-006X) Tel 714-354-7330; Toll free: 800-854-4746; 800-922-0047 (in California).

Word Process, *(Word Process, The/Yorona Pr.; 0-945937),* P.O. Box 5699, Santa Fe, NM 87502 (SAN 247-9540) Tel 505-988-3465.

Words & Muse Prodns, *(Words & Muse Productions; 0-9626294),* P.O. Box 2123, Davis, CA 95617-2123; 2737 Cumberland Pl., Davis, CA 95616 Tel 916-756-4064.

Words Pub CO, *(Words Publishing; 0-9625802),* P.O. Box 107, Firestone, CO 80520; 342 Berwick, Firestone, CO 80520 Tel 303-833-4053. Do not confuse with Words Publishing, San Francisco, CA.

Wordsong *Imprint of* **Boyds Mills Pr**

Wordsworth KS, *(Wordsworth; 0-945530),* 702 NE 24th St., Newton, KS 67114 (SAN 247-0640) Tel 316-283-6708.

Wordware Pub, *(Wordware Publishing, Inc.; 0-915381; 1-55622),* 1506 Capital Ave., Suite 101, Plano, TX 75074 (SAN 291-4786) Tel 214-423-0090; Toll free: 800-229-4949.

WordWorkers, *(WordWorkers Pr.; 0-9624511),* Affil. of Small Theatre, P.O. Box 1363, Lancaster, PA 17603; 20 E. James St., Lancaster, PA 17602 Tel 717-299-1380.

Work Study Assn, *(Work Study Assn., Inc.; 0-9626729),* 3140 Maple Ave., Walworth, NY 14568 Tel 315-597-2348.

Working Father, *(Working Father; 0-9623787),* P.O. Box 867, Hudson, MA 01749; 5 Utica Dr., Hudson, MA 01749 Tel 508-562-1420.

Workman Pub, *(Workman Publishing Co., Inc.; 0-911104; 0-89480; 1-56305),* 708 Broadway, New York, NY 10003 (SAN 203-2821) Tel 212-254-5900; Toll free: 800-722-7202.

Workshop Pubns, *(Workshop Pubns.; 0-939223),* P.O. Box 120, Acme, MI 49610 (SAN 662-667X) Tel 616-946-3712.

World Almanac *Imprint of* **Pharos Bks NY**

World Bible, *(World Bible Pubs., Inc.; 0-529),* Subs. of Riverside/World, 3040 Charlevoix Dr., Grand Rapids, MI 49546 (SAN 215-2789) Tel 616-940-2086; Orders to: Riverside/World, 3040 Charlevoix Dr., Grand Rapids, MI 49546 (SAN 169-2666); Toll free: 800-247-5111.

World Bk, *(World Bk., Inc.; 0-7166),* A Scott Fetzer Co., 525 W. Monroe, 20th Flr., Chicago, IL 60661 (SAN 201-4815) Tel 312-258-3700; Toll free: 800-621-8202.

World Bk SW, *(World Bk., Inc., Software Dept.; 0-7166),* Merchandise Mart Plaza, 5th Flr., Mail Sta. 13, Chicago, IL 60654 (SAN 693-4617); Toll free: 800-323-6366.

World Eagle, *(World Eagle, Inc.; 0-9608014; 0-930141),* 64 Washburn Ave., Wellesley, MA 02181 (SAN 239-9555) Tel 617-235-1415; Toll free: 800-634-3805.

World Peace Univ, *(World Peace Univ.; 0-939169),* P.O. Box 10869, Eugene, OR 97440 (SAN 662-8567) Tel 503-741-1794.

World Pub FL, *(World Pubns.; 0-944406),* P.O. Box 2456, Winter Park, FL 32790 (SAN 243-5942); 809 S. Orlando Ave., Suite H, Winter Park, FL 32789 (SAN 243-5950) Tel 407-628-4802. Do not confuse with companies with the same name in Kingwood, TX, Tampa, FL.

World Relations Pr, *(World Relations Pr.; 0-9615032),* P.O. Box 67 E 33, Century City, CA 90067 (SAN 693-787X) Tel 213-657-0246.

World Shaker, *(World of Shaker, The; 0-944178),* P.O. Box 1645, Holland, MI 49422-1645 (SAN 242-7788); 807 Central Ave., Holland, MI 49423 (SAN 242-7796) Tel 616-396-4588.

World Wide Pubs, *(World Wide Pubns.; 0-89066),* 1303 Hennepin Ave., Minneapolis, MN 55403 (SAN 159-9941) Tel 612-338-0500; Toll free: 800-328-2027.

Worlds Wonder, *(Worlds of Wonder; 1-55578),* 4209 Technology Dr., Fremont, CA 94538 (SAN 630-1851) Tel 415-659-4300.

Worldwide Sports, *(Worldwide Sports, Inc.; 0-9624325),* P.O. Box 382, Smithville, MO 64089; Rte. 1, Box 262, Tillman Rd., Smithville, MO 64089 Tel 816-532-4880.

Wounded Coot, *(Wounded Coot Greetings; 0-935583),* 13670 Valley View Rd., No. 222, Eden Prairie, MN 55344 (SAN 695-796X) Tel 612-934-8680.

Wright Group, *(Wright Group, The; 0-940156; 1-55624; 1-55911; 0-7802),* Div. of Thomas C. Wright, Inc., 19201 120th Ave., NE, Bothell, WA 98011-9512 (SAN 201-9884) Tel 206-486-8011; Toll free: 800-523-2371; 800-345-6073.

Wright Monday Pr, *(Wright/Monday Pr.; 0-9617597),* 214 James Thurber Ct., Falls Church, VA 22046 (SAN 664-8657) Tel 703-548-4930.

Write Place, *(Write Place, The; 0-945767),* 354 E. 1650 S., Bountiful, UT 84010 (SAN 247-7890) Tel 801-295-8982.

Write Source, *(Write Source, The; 0-9605312; 0-939045),* P.O. Box J, Burlington, WI 53105 (SAN 215-2959) Tel 414-763-8258; Toll free: 800-445-8613.

Writers & Readers, *(Writers & Readers Publishing, Inc.; 0-904613; 0-906386; 0-906495; 0-86316),* 625 Broadway, Suite 903, New York, NY 10012 (SAN 665-813X) Tel 212-982-3158; Dist. by: Publishers Group West, 4065 Hollis St., Emeryville, CA 94608 (SAN 202-8522) Tel 415-658-3453; Toll free: 800-365-3453.

Writers Pub Serv, *(Writers Publishing Service Co.; 0-910303),* 1512 Western Ave., Seattle, WA 98101 (SAN 276-8666) Tel 206-284-9954.

WSP *Imprint of PB*

WV Hist Ed Found, *(West Virginia Historical Education Foundation, Inc.; 0-914498),* P.O. Box 1187, Charleston, WV 25324 (SAN 204-1685) Tel 304-342-0855; Dist. by: James & Law Co., The, P.O. Box 2468, Clarksburg, WV 26302-2468 (SAN 169-894X) Tel 304-624-7401.

WW Pr, *(Weston Woods Pr.; 0-927370),* Div. of Weston Woods Studios, Inc., 389 New Town Tpke., Weston Woods, Weston, CT 06883 Tel 203-226-3355; Toll free: 800-243-5020.

Wyrick & Co, *(Wyrick & Co.; 0-941711),* P.O. Box 89, Charleston, SC 29402 (SAN 666-2412); Toll free: 800-227-5898; 12 Exchange St., Charleston, SC 29401 (SAN 666-2420) Tel 803-722-0881.

Xiquan Pub Hse, *(Xiquan Publishing Hse.; 1-879585),* P.O. Box 42561, Phoenix, AZ 85080 (SAN 297-5092); 510 E. Townley Ave., Phoenix, AZ 85015 Tel 602-436-3862.

XYZ Group, *(XYZ Group, Inc.; 1-879332),* P.O. Box 51499, New Berlin, WI 53151-0499; Toll

free: 800-541-2205; 2885 S. James Dr., New Berlin, WI 53151 Tel 414-821-0320.

Y-Knot, *(Y-Knot, Inc.; 0-9618803),* 13420 Riker Rd., Chelsea, MI 48118 (SAN 668-7415) Tel 313-426-5840; Dist. by: Baker & Taylor Bks., Midwestern Div., 501 S. Gladiolus St., Momence, IL 60954 (SAN 169-2100) Tel 815-472-2444; Toll free: 800-435-5111; 800-892-1892 (in Illinois).

Yale U Pr, *(Yale Univ. Pr.; 0-300),* 302 Temple St., New Haven, CT 06511 (SAN 203-2740) Tel 203-432-0960; Orders to: 92A Yale Sta., New Haven, CT 06520 (SAN 203-2759) Tel 203-432-0940.

Yangs Martial Arts, *(Yang's Martial Arts Assn.; 0-940871),* 38-54 Hyde Pk. Ave., Jamaica Plain, MA 02130 (SAN 665-2077) Tel 617-524-8892.

Yankee Bks, *(Yankee Bks.; 0-911658; 0-89909),* P.O. Box 1248, Camden, ME 04843 (SAN 200-8343); 62 Bay View, Camden, ME 04843 Tel 207-236-0933.

Yankee Peddler, *(Yankee Peddler Bk. Co.; 0-911660),* Drawer O, Southampton, NY 11968 (SAN 205-5570) Tel 516-283-1612.

Yankton Sioux Tribe, *(Yankton Sioux Tribe, Elderly Board; 0-9621936),* P.O. Box 248, Marty, SD 57361 Tel 605-744-2850; Dist. by: Dakota West Bks., P.O. Box 9324, Rapid City, SD 57701 (SAN 630-351X) Tel 605-348-1075.

Yarrow Pr, *(Yarrow Pr.; 1-878274),* 225 Lafayette St., New York, NY 10012 Tel 212-941-1275; Dist. by: Publishers Group West, 4065 Hollis St., Emeryville, CA 94608 (SAN 202-8522) Tel 415-658-3453; Toll free: 800-365-3453.

YB *Imprint of Dell*

YCP Pubns, *(Y.C.P. Pubns., Inc.; 1-878756),* P.O. Box 931766, Los Angeles, CA 90093 (SAN 297-4355); 5820 Wilshire Blvd., Suite 503, Los Angeles, CA 90036 Tel 213-857-8683.

Ye Galleon, *(Ye Galleon Pr.; 0-87770),* P.O. Box 287, Fairfield, WA 99012 (SAN 205-5597) Tel 509-283-2422; Toll free: 800-621-1504 (Orders only).

Yellow Brick Rd, *(Yellow Brick Road Pubs., Inc.; 0-9630101),* 2140 Waterby St., Westlake Village, CA 91361 Tel 818-889-5594.

Yellow Hook Pr, *(Yellow Hook Pr.; 0-9622705),* Div. of International Weather Corp., 719 Bay Ridge Ave., Brooklyn, NY 11220 Tel 718-748-8066.

Yellow Moon, *(Yellow Moon Pr.; 0-938756),* P. O. Box 1316, Cambridge, MA 02238 (SAN 216-4809) Tel 617-776-2230.

Yellow Pr MN, *(Yellowstone Pr.; 0-9626225),* 24020 Yellowstone Trail, Shorewood, MN 55331 Tel 612-944-2519; Dist. by: Booksales/Marketing, Inc., 407 E. 100th St., Bloomington, MN 55420-5031 (SAN 630-4575). Do not confuse with Yellowstone Pr., Livingston, MT.

YMCA USA *Imprint of Human Kinetics*

Yng Peoples Pr, *(Young People's Pr.; 0-9606964),* Box 1005, Avon, CT 06001 (SAN 239-4022) Tel 203-677-6409.

Yoknapatawpha, *(Yoknapatawpha Pr.; 0-916242),* Box 248, Oxford, MS 38655 (SAN 213-7593) Tel 601-234-0909.

York Hse, *(York Hse.; 0-9615809),* 148 York Ave., Kensington, CA 94708 (SAN 276-9468) Tel 415-525-7167.

Yosemite Assn, *(Yosemite Assn.; 0-939666),* Box 545, Yosemite National Pk., CA 95389 (SAN 225-2201) Tel 209-379-2648; Orders to: P.O. Box 230, El Portal, CA 95318 (SAN 662-197X).

Young Creations, *(Young Creations, Inc.; 0-9618437),* 15245 Minnetonka Blvd., Minnetonka, MN 55345 (SAN 667-8211) Tel 612-933-1147.

Young Discovery Lib, *(Young Discovery Library; 0-944589),* P.O. Box 229, Ossining, NY 10562 (SAN 243-9530); Toll free: 800-343-7854; 217 Main St., Ossining, NY 10562 (SAN 243-9549) Tel 914-945-0600.

Young Life Pub, *(Young Life Pub.; 0-945705),*

612 North B, Livingston, MT 59047 (SAN 247-7572) Tel 406-222-3284.

Young Sparrow Pr, *(Young Sparrow Pr., The; 0-9621500),* P.O. Box 265, Worcester, PA 19490-0265 (SAN 251-8856); 1116 Keats Ct., Lansdale, PA 19446 Tel 215-361-7139.

Young Writers Contest Found, *(Young Writer's Contest Foundation; 0-929889),* P.O. Box 6092, McLean, VA 22101 (SAN 250-975X); 1502 Mintwood Dr., McLean, VA 22101 (SAN 250-9768) Tel 703-893-6097.

Youth Bks *Imprint of Zondervan*

Youth Ed, *(Youth Education Systems, Inc.; 0-87738),* Box 223, Scarborough Sta., Scarborough, NY 10510 (SAN 205-5635) Tel 914-762-2200; Orders to: Rte. 100, Millwood, NY 10562 (SAN 241-9009).

Yuletide Intl, *(Yuletide International; 0-911049),* 9665 Malad St., Boise, ID 83709 (SAN 264-5181) Tel 208-322-1260.

YWCO, *(Young Women's Christian Organization; 0-9608282),* 201 St. Charles St., Baton Rouge, LA 70802 (SAN 240-4613).

Z M Johnson, *(Johnson, Zenobia M.; 0-9617411),* 1319 S. Genois St., New Orleans, LA 70125 (SAN 663-9739) Tel 504-488-1514.

Zaner-Bloser, *(Zaner-Bloser, Inc.; 0-88309; 0-88085),* Subs. of Highlights for Children, P.O. Box 16764, Columbus, OH 43216-6764 (SAN 282-5678); 2200 W. Fifth Ave., Columbus, OH 43215 Tel 614-486-0221.

Zebra, *(Zebra Bks.; 0-89083; 0-8217),* Div. of Kensington Publishing Corp., 475 Park Ave., S., New York, NY 10016 (SAN 207-9860) Tel 212-889-2299; Toll free: 800-221-2647; Dist. by: Pocket Books (wholesale only), 1230 Ave. of the Americas, New York, NY 10020 (SAN 202-5922) Tel 212-698-7406; Toll free: 800-223-2336 (orders).

Zenagraf, *(Zenagraf; 0-9627254),* 7 Lois Ct., Ann Arbor, MI 48103 Tel 313-662-3770.

Zenger Pub, *(Zenger Publishing Co., Inc.; 0-89201),* P.O. Box 42026, Washington, DC 20015 (SAN 208-0427) Tel 301-881-1470.

Zenith City, *(Zenith City Pubns.; 0-917378),* 28 Holly Ln., Zenith Terr., Proctor, MN 55810 (SAN 208-8436) Tel 218-624-7728.

Zenon Pub, *(Zenon Publishing; 0-9628006),* 24503 128th Ave., E., Graham, WA 98338 Tel 206-893-5588.

Zephyr *Imprint of Doubleday*

Zephyr Pr AZ, *(Zephyr Pr.; 0-913705; 0-912777),* P.O. Box 13448, Tucson, AZ 85732-3448 (SAN 270-6830) Tel 602-322-5090.

Zeppelin, *(Zeppelin Publishing Co.; 0-915628),* P.O. Box 7543, Fort Lauderdale, FL 33338-7543 (SAN 204-6776).

Zinks Career Guide, *(Zinks International Career Guidance; 0-939469),* P.O. Box 585, Dearborn, MI 48121-0585 (SAN 663-334X).

Zion, *(Zion Natural History Assn.; 0-915630),* Zion National Pk., Springdale, UT 84767 (SAN 205-9959) Tel 801-772-3256.

Zoland Bks, *(Zoland Bks., Inc.; 0-944072),* P.O. Box 2766, Cambridge, MA 02238 (SAN 242-8571) Tel 617-864-6252; Dist. by: Independent Literary Pubs. Assn., P.O. Box 816, Oak Park, IL 60303 (SAN 630-1665) Tel 708-848-6333; Toll free: 800-242-4572.

Zondervan, *(Zondervan Publishing Corp.; 0-310),* Div. of HarperCollins Pubs., Inc., 1415 Lake Dr., SE, Grand Rapids, MI 49506 (SAN 203-2694) Tel 616-698-6900; Toll free: 800-727-1309 (orders & customer service). *Imprints:* Campus Life (Campus Life); Youth Bks (Youth Books).

Zoo-phonics, *(Zoo-phonics, Inc.; 0-9617342),* P.O. Box 1219, Groveland, CA 95321 (SAN 663-8589); 20060 Upper Skyridge, Groveland, CA 95321 (SAN 663-8597) Tel 209-962-7634.

Zorba Pr, *(Zorba Pr.; 0-927379),* Alexander Lake, P.O. Box 666, Dayville, CT 06241 (SAN 200-3740); 12 Arrowhead Ln., Dayville, CT 06241 Tel 203-774-4651.